State Alpha Code Table

Code	State	Code	State	Code	State
AL	Alabama	LA	Louisiana	OK	Oklahoma
AK	Alaska	ME	Maine	OR	Oregon
AZ	Arizona	MD	Maryland	PA	Pennsylvania
AR	Arkansas	MA	Massachusetts	PR	Puerto Rico
CA	California	MI	Michigan	RI	Rhode Island
CO	Colorado	MN	Minnesota	SC	South Carolina
CT	Connecticut	MS	Mississippi	SD	South Dakota
DE	Delaware	MO	Missouri	TN	Tennessee
DC	District of Columbia	MT	Montana	TX	Texas
FL	Florida	NE	Nebraska	UT	Utah
GA	Georgia	NV	Nevada	VT	Vermont
HI	Hawaii	NH	New Hampshire	VA	Virginia
ID	Idaho	NJ	New Jersey	WA	Washington
IL	Illinois	NM	New Mexico	WV	West Virginia
IN	Indiana	NY	New York	WI	Wisconsin
IA	Iowa	NC	North Carolina	WY	Wyoming
KS	Kansas	ND	North Dakota		
KY	Kentucky	OH	Ohio		

Time Zones and Abbreviations

Abbr.	Name	Standard Meridian	Hours from Greenwich Mean Time Standard	Daylight (War)
A	Atlantic	60°	4:00	3:00
E	Eastern	75°	5:00	4:00
C	Central	90°	6:00	5:00
M	Mountain	105°	7:00	6:00
P	Pacific	120°	8:00	7:00
Y	Yukon	135°	9:00	8:00
AH	Alaska-Hawaii	150°	10:00	9:00
H	Hawaiian	157°30′	10:30	9:30
B	Bering	165°	11:00	10:00

Abbr.	Time Type
S	Standard
D	Daylight
W	War

The American Atlas

Expanded Fifth Edition

U.S. Longitudes & Latitudes
Time Changes and Time Zones

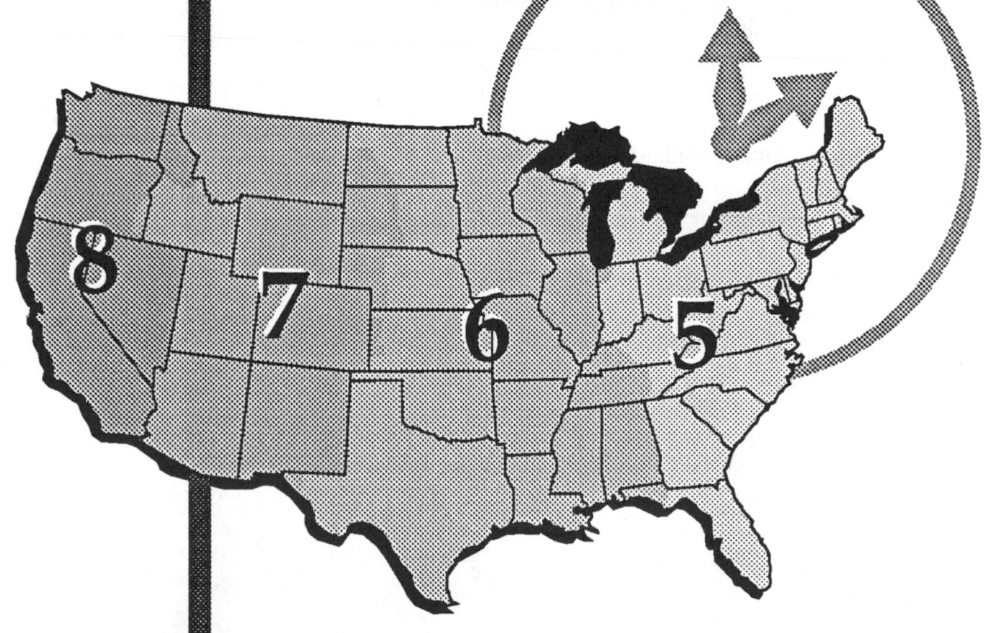

Compiled and Programmed by

Thomas G. Shanks

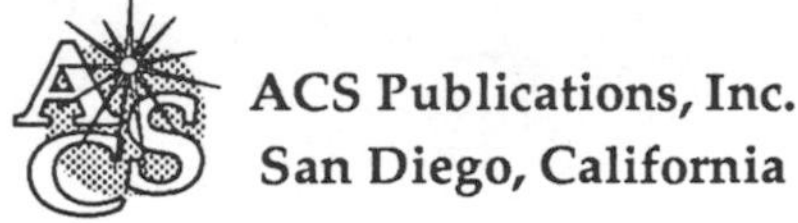

ACS Publications, Inc.
San Diego, California

First Edition published 1978. Fourth Edition 1987. Fifth Edition 1990.

International Standard Book Number 0-935127-13-5

Printed in the United States of America

Published by ACS Publications, Inc.
P.O. Box 34487
San Diego, CA 92103-0802

First printing, July, 1978

Fifth printing, March, 1990

PREFACE
TO THE FOURTH EDITION

The information contained in this book was originally assembled as an on-line data base for an astrological calculation service, for, as a group, astrologers are most concerned with precision in geographical place coordinates and the history of time changes. As the data accumulated from a variety of sources, the desirability of making the information available to the public in the form of a book became apparent. *The American Atlas*, first printed in 1978, is the result of this effort.

The original place names and geographical coordinates came from four main sources. Although much time was spent in integrating and condensing the information, no individual or computer procedures could edit and resolve all conflicts and redundant information.

The major early sources for time changes were the pioneering works of Doris Chase Doane's *Time Changes in the U.S.A.* and Curran & Taylor's *World Daylight Saving Time*. To this base were added the results of primary research, as well as the contributions of individuals who researched the history of time changes at local libraries using newspaper microfilm collections. The time change information will continue to be refined in future editions.

More than a year has been spent preparing this fourth edition, which contains many significant improvements in the time change tables. New results of primary research and further individual contributions have been integrated into the tables, making them substantially different and more correct than previous editions. In particular a collection of *The Official Guide of the Railways...of the United States...*published by the National Railway Publication Co., dating from 1931 has been obtained, and the wealth of time change information it contains has enriched this edition. Further, a more general effort has been made to show small towns near larger ones as following the time changes of the larger neighbor. Though this will be incorrect in a few cases, the general rule is usually correct.

Critics have raised the issue of early observance of sundial time vs. local mean time and have suggested a more gradual adoption of standard time at the close of the 19th century. These issues have been tabled for attention in a subsequent edition.

Thomas Shanks
October, 1987

PREFACE
TO THE FIFTH EDITION

The 5th edition of the *American Atlas* has been expanded by the incorporation of new geographical coordinates from the 'Geographic Names Information System' of the *United States Geological Survey*. By merging in locations not given in the previous edition of the *American Atlas* the number of entries has increased from 105,015 to 152,713, an increase of 44%. In addition, the accuracy of the new sources has permitted coordinates to be given to the nearest second in a majority of cases. The time change information has not changed appreciably from the previous edition.

Thomas Shanks
San Diego, CA
March, 1990

ACKNOWLEDGMENTS

Major contributions have been made by the following published materials and journals: Doris Chase Doane, *Time Changes in the U.S.A.*; Curran and Taylor, *World Daylight Saving Time*; documents published by the Interstate Commerce Commission; National Railway Publication Co., *The Official Guide of the Railways ... of the United States...; The Mercury Hour; AFA Bulletin*; and *Astro Psychological Problems*.

Individuals making major contributions include: Mark Pottenger, Mary Brandes, Don Borkowski, Eugene Seger, Wayne Lee Holt, Mary Frances Wood and Arthur Blackwell.

Significant material was also provided by: Dorothy Pierce, John Adkins, Lillian Celic, Edith Custer, Gary Duncan, Lynne Burmyn, Liz Anderson, and Susan Aiu.

Contents

Preface iii

Acknowledgments iv

How to Use this Book vii

How to Calculate Sidereal Time viii

Solar-Sidereal Time Correction ix

The American Atlas 1

SUBMITTING CORRECTIONS

Additions or corrections to the material presented in the *Atlas* are requested. We ask that copies of printed documentation be submitted supporting the suggested change. Submit such material to:

The American Atlas
ACS Publications, Inc.
P O Box 16430
San Diego, CA 92116-0430

How To Use This Book

Turn to the state desired. For each state there are time tables, a list of counties with each county numbered, and a list of cities and towns. Any comments are noted before a state's time tables. Cities are arranged alphabetically with city name, county number, time table number, latitude, longitude and longitude time equivalent (hours, minutes and seconds from Greenwich), in that order.

LATITUDE AND LONGITUDE
Find the target city. If there is more than one with the same name, check the county. For cities with no county shown, none was given in the sources used in compiling this reference. Once you have found your city, the latitude, longitude and time equivalent of the longitude can be read right from that line.

TIME CHANGE TABLES
The Time Tables have a single entry for each change of time zone or time type. That entry is effective until the next time change, whether the period is one day or thirty-five years.

The first letter gives the time zone (two letters for Alaska-Hawaii); see the Table of Time Zones and Abbreviations. The next letter gives the time type: D for Daylight, S for Standard, W for War (which has the same effect as Daylight). The last letter is T for time. An entry of EST spells out Eastern Standard Time, CDT is Central Daylight Time, MWT is Mountain War Time, and so on. LMT is the abbreviation for Local Mean Time.

The appropriate time table for each location is designated in the column preceding the latitude. Find the time table number for your target city and then locate the time table with that number in the 'Time Tables' section for that state. (If there is only one time table for the whole state, then no time table number is given after the city and county number.) Scan down the column of dates to the date you want. The last date entry before the target date and time gives the time zone and standard/daylight time observance in effect at the target date and time.

The following example shows that clocks in a certain part of Delaware were set ahead to Eastern War Time at 2:00 AM on March 31, 1918, and were set back to Eastern Standard time at 2:00 AM on October 27, 1918. Any birth that took place between those times would have been recorded in EWT.

DE #11

Before 11/18/1883		**LMT**
11/18/1883	**12:00**	**EST**
3/31/1918	**02:00**	**EWT**
10/27/1918	**02:00**	**EST**

Some time tables give a reference to another table in the same state instead of a time change. Refer to the second table for time changes if your date is in the period before the next entry in the first table.

US TABLES
Most time tables end with "US#x". This is a reference to one of the US Time Tables at the front of the book, which give the more common time observance shifts without reference to zone as well as the daylight time shifts to the year 2000, assuming continued use of the Uniform Time Act. The time type from the US table is combined with the last time zone specified in the state table.

If the last entry in a state table is not a reference to a US Table but indicates a regular time shift, then there has been no change since that date; the time zone and observance last listed continue to be in effect. For example, the last Arizona entry is:

10/29/1967 02:00 MST

meaning that Arizona has been on Mountain Standard Time continuously since 2:00 AM October 29, 1967.

Table I

How To Calculate Sidereal Time

	Example 1	**Example 2**	**Example**
	May 11, 1931 1:30 PM New York City	November 11, 1931 6:15 PM Honolulu, HI	May 11, 1931 12:15 AM San Francisco, CA
1) Convert the time of birth to the 24-hour clock.	13:30	18:15	00:1
2) Find the time zone and daylight/standard time observance from *The American Atlas* and then use the table of **Time Zones and Abbreviations** to convert to Universal Time (UT).	EDT 4:00 17:30	HST 10:30 28:45	PST 8:0 8:1
3) Reduce to less than 24 hours and add 1 day to obtain the Greenwich birth date, if necessary. Greenwich birth date is used to enter the ephemeris to obtain the sidereal time as in step 5 below.	17:30 *May 11, 1931*	−24:00 4:45 *Nov. 12, 1931*	8:1 *May 11, 193*
4) Use the UT of birth and Table II to determine the solar/sidereal time correction (acceleration).	00:02:52 17:32:52	00:00:47 4:45:47	00:01:2 8:16:2
5) Find the midnight sidereal time for birthdate from *The American Ephemeris* or other reference and add to the birthtime UT.	15:11:16 32:44:08	3:20:39 8:06:26	15:11:1 23:27:3
6) Subtract the longitude time equivalent obtained from *The American Atlas* to get the sidereal time of birth.	−4:55:48 27:48:20	−10:31:28 −2:25:02	−8:09:4 15:17:5
7) Add or subtract 24 hours, if necessary, to put sidereal time in the range between 0 to 24 hours.	−24:00:00 3:48:20	+24:00:00 21:34:58	15:17:5

Table II

Solar-Sidereal Time Correction (Acceleration)

MIN	0h	1h	2h	3h	4h	5h	6h	7h	8h	9h	10h	11h	12h	13h	14h	15h	16h	17h	18h	19h	20h	21h	22h	23h	MIN
	m s	m s	m s	m s	m s	m s	m s	m s	m s	m s	m s	m s	m s	m s	m s	m s	m s	m s	m s	m s	m s	m s	m s	m s	
0	0 0	0 10	0 20	0 30	0 39	0 49	0 59	1 9	1 19	1 29	1 39	1 48	1 58	2 8	2 18	2 28	2 38	2 48	2 57	3 7	3 17	3 27	3 37	3 47	0
1	0 0	0 10	0 20	0 30	0 40	0 49	0 59	1 9	1 19	1 29	1 39	1 49	1 58	2 8	2 18	2 28	2 38	2 48	2 58	3 7	3 17	3 27	3 37	3 47	1
2	0 0	0 10	0 20	0 30	0 40	0 50	0 59	1 9	1 19	1 29	1 39	1 49	1 59	2 8	2 18	2 28	2 38	2 48	2 58	3 8	3 17	3 27	3 37	3 47	2
3	0 0	0 10	0 20	0 30	0 40	0 50	0 60	1 9	1 19	1 29	1 39	1 49	1 59	2 9	2 18	2 28	2 38	2 48	2 58	3 8	3 18	3 27	3 37	3 47	3
4	0 1	0 11	0 20	0 30	0 40	0 50	0 60	1 10	1 20	1 29	1 39	1 49	1 59	2 9	2 19	2 29	2 38	2 48	2 58	3 8	3 18	3 28	3 37	3 47	4
5	0 1	0 11	0 21	0 30	0 40	0 50	0 60	1 10	1 20	1 30	1 39	1 49	1 59	2 9	2 19	2 29	2 39	2 48	2 58	3 8	3 18	3 28	3 38	3 48	5
6	0 1	0 11	0 21	0 31	0 40	0 50	1 0	1 10	1 20	1 30	1 40	1 49	1 59	2 9	2 19	2 29	2 39	2 49	2 58	3 8	3 18	3 28	3 38	3 48	6
7	0 1	0 11	0 21	0 31	0 41	0 50	1 0	1 10	1 20	1 30	1 40	1 50	1 59	2 9	2 19	2 29	2 39	2 49	2 59	3 8	3 18	3 28	3 38	3 48	7
8	0 1	0 11	0 21	0 31	0 41	0 51	1 0	1 10	1 20	1 30	1 40	1 50	1 60	2 9	2 19	2 29	2 39	2 49	2 59	3 9	3 18	3 28	3 38	3 48	8
9	0 1	0 11	0 21	0 31	0 41	0 51	1 1	1 10	1 20	1 30	1 40	1 50	1 60	2 10	2 19	2 29	2 39	2 49	2 59	3 9	3 19	3 28	3 38	3 48	9
10	0 2	0 11	0 21	0 31	0 41	0 51	1 1	1 11	1 20	1 30	1 40	1 50	1 60	2 10	2 20	2 29	2 39	2 49	2 59	3 9	3 19	3 29	3 38	3 48	10
11	0 2	0 12	0 22	0 31	0 41	0 51	1 1	1 11	1 21	1 31	1 40	1 50	2 0	2 10	2 20	2 30	2 40	2 49	2 59	3 9	3 19	3 29	3 39	3 49	11
12	0 2	0 12	0 22	0 32	0 41	0 51	1 1	1 11	1 21	1 31	1 41	1 50	2 0	2 10	2 20	2 30	2 40	2 50	2 59	3 9	3 19	3 29	3 39	3 49	12
13	0 2	0 12	0 22	0 32	0 42	0 51	1 1	1 11	1 21	1 31	1 41	1 51	2 0	2 10	2 20	2 30	2 40	2 50	2 60	3 9	3 19	3 29	3 39	3 49	13
14	0 2	0 12	0 22	0 32	0 42	0 52	1 1	1 11	1 21	1 31	1 41	1 51	2 1	2 10	2 20	2 30	2 40	2 50	2 60	3 10	3 19	3 29	3 39	3 49	14
15	0 2	0 12	0 22	0 32	0 42	0 52	1 2	1 11	1 21	1 31	1 41	1 51	2 1	2 11	2 20	2 30	2 40	2 50	2 60	3 10	3 20	3 29	3 39	3 49	15
16	0 3	0 12	0 22	0 32	0 42	0 52	1 2	1 12	1 21	1 31	1 41	1 51	2 1	2 11	2 21	2 30	2 40	2 50	3 0	3 10	3 20	3 30	3 39	3 49	16
17	0 3	0 13	0 23	0 32	0 42	0 52	1 2	1 12	1 22	1 32	1 41	1 51	2 1	2 11	2 21	2 31	2 40	2 50	3 0	3 10	3 20	3 30	3 40	3 49	17
18	0 3	0 13	0 23	0 33	0 42	0 52	1 2	1 12	1 22	1 32	1 42	1 51	2 1	2 11	2 21	2 31	2 41	2 51	3 0	3 10	3 20	3 30	3 40	3 50	18
19	0 3	0 13	0 23	0 33	0 43	0 52	1 2	1 12	1 22	1 32	1 42	1 52	2 1	2 11	2 21	2 31	2 41	2 51	3 1	3 10	3 20	3 30	3 40	3 50	19
20	0 3	0 13	0 23	0 33	0 43	0 53	1 2	1 12	1 22	1 32	1 42	1 52	2 2	2 11	2 21	2 31	2 41	2 51	3 1	3 11	3 20	3 30	3 40	3 50	20
21	0 3	0 13	0 23	0 33	0 43	0 53	1 3	1 12	1 22	1 32	1 42	1 52	2 2	2 12	2 21	2 31	2 41	2 51	3 1	3 11	3 21	3 30	3 40	3 50	21
22	0 4	0 13	0 23	0 33	0 43	0 53	1 3	1 13	1 22	1 32	1 42	1 52	2 2	2 12	2 22	2 31	2 41	2 51	3 1	3 11	3 21	3 31	3 40	3 50	22
23	0 4	0 14	0 23	0 33	0 43	0 53	1 3	1 13	1 23	1 32	1 42	1 52	2 2	2 12	2 22	2 32	2 41	2 51	3 1	3 11	3 21	3 31	3 41	3 50	23
24	0 4	0 14	0 24	0 34	0 43	0 53	1 3	1 13	1 23	1 33	1 43	1 52	2 2	2 12	2 22	2 32	2 42	2 52	3 1	3 11	3 21	3 31	3 41	3 51	24
25	0 4	0 14	0 24	0 34	0 44	0 53	1 3	1 13	1 23	1 33	1 43	1 53	2 2	2 12	2 22	2 32	2 42	2 52	3 2	3 11	3 21	3 31	3 41	3 51	25
26	0 4	0 14	0 24	0 34	0 44	0 54	1 3	1 13	1 23	1 33	1 43	1 53	2 3	2 12	2 22	2 32	2 42	2 52	3 2	3 12	3 21	3 31	3 41	3 51	26
27	0 4	0 14	0 24	0 34	0 44	0 54	1 4	1 13	1 23	1 33	1 43	1 53	2 3	2 13	2 22	2 32	2 42	2 52	3 2	3 12	3 22	3 31	3 41	3 51	27
28	0 5	0 14	0 24	0 34	0 44	0 54	1 4	1 14	1 23	1 33	1 43	1 53	2 3	2 13	2 23	2 32	2 42	2 52	3 2	3 12	3 22	3 32	3 41	3 51	28
29	0 5	0 15	0 24	0 34	0 44	0 54	1 4	1 14	1 24	1 33	1 43	1 53	2 3	2 13	2 23	2 33	2 42	2 52	3 2	3 12	3 22	3 32	3 42	3 51	29
30	0 5	0 15	0 25	0 34	0 44	0 54	1 4	1 14	1 24	1 34	1 43	1 53	2 3	2 13	2 23	2 33	2 43	2 52	3 2	3 12	3 22	3 32	3 42	3 52	30
31	0 5	0 15	0 25	0 35	0 45	0 54	1 4	1 14	1 24	1 34	1 44	1 54	2 3	2 13	2 23	2 33	2 43	2 53	3 3	3 12	3 22	3 32	3 42	3 52	31
32	0 5	0 15	0 25	0 35	0 45	0 55	1 4	1 14	1 24	1 34	1 44	1 54	2 4	2 13	2 23	2 33	2 43	2 53	3 3	3 13	3 22	3 32	3 42	3 52	32
33	0 5	0 15	0 25	0 35	0 45	0 55	1 5	1 14	1 24	1 34	1 44	1 54	2 4	2 14	2 23	2 33	2 43	2 53	3 3	3 13	3 23	3 32	3 42	3 52	33
34	0 6	0 15	0 25	0 35	0 45	0 55	1 5	1 15	1 24	1 34	1 44	1 54	2 4	2 14	2 24	2 33	2 43	2 53	3 3	3 13	3 23	3 33	3 42	3 52	34
35	0 6	0 16	0 25	0 35	0 45	0 55	1 5	1 15	1 25	1 34	1 44	1 54	2 4	2 14	2 24	2 34	2 43	2 53	3 3	3 13	3 23	3 33	3 43	3 52	35
36	0 6	0 16	0 26	0 35	0 45	0 55	1 5	1 15	1 25	1 35	1 44	1 54	2 4	2 14	2 24	2 34	2 44	2 53	3 3	3 13	3 23	3 33	3 43	3 53	36
37	0 6	0 16	0 26	0 36	0 46	0 55	1 5	1 15	1 25	1 35	1 45	1 54	2 4	2 14	2 24	2 34	2 44	2 54	3 3	3 13	3 23	3 33	3 43	3 53	37
38	0 6	0 16	0 26	0 36	0 46	0 56	1 5	1 15	1 25	1 35	1 45	1 55	2 5	2 14	2 24	2 34	2 44	2 54	3 4	3 14	3 23	3 33	3 43	3 53	38
39	0 6	0 16	0 26	0 36	0 46	0 56	1 6	1 15	1 25	1 35	1 45	1 55	2 5	2 15	2 24	2 34	2 44	2 54	3 4	3 14	3 24	3 33	3 43	3 53	39
40	0 7	0 16	0 26	0 36	0 46	0 56	1 6	1 16	1 25	1 35	1 45	1 55	2 5	2 15	2 25	2 34	2 44	2 54	3 4	3 14	3 24	3 34	3 43	3 53	40
41	0 7	0 17	0 26	0 36	0 46	0 56	1 6	1 16	1 26	1 35	1 45	1 55	2 5	2 15	2 25	2 35	2 44	2 54	3 4	3 14	3 24	3 34	3 44	3 53	41
42	0 7	0 17	0 27	0 36	0 46	0 56	1 6	1 16	1 26	1 36	1 45	1 55	2 5	2 15	2 25	2 35	2 45	2 54	3 4	3 14	3 24	3 34	3 44	3 54	42
43	0 7	0 17	0 27	0 37	0 46	0 56	1 6	1 16	1 26	1 36	1 46	1 55	2 5	2 15	2 25	2 35	2 45	2 55	3 4	3 14	3 24	3 34	3 44	3 54	43
44	0 7	0 17	0 27	0 37	0 47	0 57	1 6	1 16	1 26	1 36	1 46	1 56	2 6	2 15	2 25	2 35	2 45	2 55	3 5	3 15	3 24	3 34	3 44	3 54	44
45	0 7	0 17	0 27	0 37	0 47	0 57	1 7	1 16	1 26	1 36	1 46	1 56	2 6	2 16	2 25	2 35	2 45	2 55	3 5	3 15	3 25	3 34	3 44	3 54	45
46	0 8	0 17	0 27	0 37	0 47	0 57	1 7	1 17	1 26	1 36	1 46	1 56	2 6	2 16	2 26	2 35	2 45	2 55	3 5	3 15	3 25	3 35	3 44	3 54	46
47	0 8	0 18	0 27	0 37	0 47	0 57	1 7	1 17	1 27	1 36	1 46	1 56	2 6	2 16	2 26	2 36	2 45	2 55	3 5	3 15	3 25	3 35	3 45	3 54	47
48	0 8	0 18	0 28	0 37	0 47	0 57	1 7	1 17	1 27	1 37	1 46	1 56	2 6	2 16	2 26	2 36	2 46	2 55	3 5	3 15	3 25	3 35	3 45	3 55	48
49	0 8	0 18	0 28	0 38	0 47	0 57	1 7	1 17	1 27	1 37	1 47	1 56	2 6	2 16	2 26	2 36	2 46	2 56	3 5	3 15	3 25	3 35	3 45	3 55	49
50	0 8	0 18	0 28	0 38	0 48	0 57	1 7	1 17	1 27	1 37	1 47	1 57	2 6	2 16	2 26	2 36	2 46	2 56	3 6	3 15	3 25	3 35	3 45	3 55	50
51	0 8	0 18	0 28	0 38	0 48	0 58	1 8	1 17	1 27	1 37	1 47	1 57	2 7	2 17	2 26	2 36	2 46	2 56	3 6	3 16	3 26	3 35	3 45	3 55	51
52	0 9	0 18	0 28	0 38	0 48	0 58	1 8	1 18	1 27	1 37	1 47	1 57	2 7	2 17	2 27	2 36	2 46	2 56	3 6	3 16	3 26	3 36	3 45	3 55	52
53	0 9	0 19	0 28	0 38	0 48	0 58	1 8	1 18	1 28	1 37	1 47	1 57	2 7	2 17	2 27	2 37	2 46	2 56	3 6	3 16	3 26	3 36	3 46	3 55	53
54	0 9	0 19	0 29	0 38	0 48	0 58	1 8	1 18	1 28	1 38	1 47	1 57	2 7	2 17	2 27	2 37	2 47	2 56	3 6	3 16	3 26	3 36	3 46	3 56	54
55	0 9	0 19	0 29	0 39	0 48	0 58	1 8	1 18	1 28	1 38	1 48	1 57	2 7	2 17	2 27	2 37	2 47	2 57	3 6	3 16	3 26	3 36	3 46	3 56	55
56	0 9	0 19	0 29	0 39	0 49	0 58	1 8	1 18	1 28	1 38	1 48	1 58	2 7	2 17	2 27	2 37	2 47	2 57	3 7	3 16	3 26	3 36	3 46	3 56	56
57	0 9	0 19	0 29	0 39	0 49	0 59	1 9	1 18	1 28	1 38	1 48	1 58	2 8	2 17	2 27	2 37	2 47	2 57	3 7	3 17	3 26	3 36	3 46	3 56	57
58	0 10	0 19	0 29	0 39	0 49	0 59	1 9	1 19	1 28	1 38	1 48	1 58	2 8	2 18	2 28	2 37	2 47	2 57	3 7	3 17	3 27	3 37	3 46	3 56	58
59	0 10	0 20	0 29	0 39	0 49	0 59	1 9	1 19	1 29	1 38	1 48	1 58	2 8	2 18	2 28	2 38	2 47	2 57	3 7	3 17	3 27	3 37	3 47	3 56	59
60	0 10	0 20	0 30	0 39	0 49	0 59	1 9	1 19	1 29	1 39	1 48	1 58	2 8	2 18	2 28	2 38	2 48	2 57	3 7	3 17	3 27	3 37	3 47	3 57	60

TIME TABLES

AL # 1
Before 11/18/1883 LMT
11/18/1883 12:00 CST
3/31/1918 02:00 CWT
10/27/1918 02:00 CST
3/30/1919 02:00 CWT
10/26/1919 02:00 CST
7/21/1941 00:01 CDT
10/01/1941 00:01 CST
2/09/1942 02:00 CWT
9/30/1945 02:00 CST
4/30/1967 02:00 US#1

AL # 2
Before 11/18/1883 LMT
11/18/1883 12:00 CST
3/31/1918 02:00 CWT
10/27/1918 02:00 CST
3/30/1919 02:00 CWT
10/26/1919 02:00 CST
7/21/1941 00:01 CDT
10/01/1941 00:01 CST
2/09/1942 02:00 CWT
9/30/1945 02:00 CST
4/27/1958 02:00 CDT
10/25/1958 02:00 CST
4/26/1959 02:00 CDT
9/27/1959 02:00 CST
4/24/1960 02:00 CDT
9/25/1960 02:00 CST
4/30/1967 02:00 US#1

AL # 3
Before 11/18/1883 LMT
11/18/1883 12:00 CST
3/31/1918 02:00 CWT
10/27/1918 02:00 CST
3/30/1919 02:00 CWT
10/26/1919 02:00 CST
7/21/1941 00:01 CDT
10/01/1941 00:01 CST
2/09/1942 02:00 CWT
9/30/1945 02:00 CST
4/27/1958 00:01 CDT
10/25/1958 00:01 CST
4/30/1967 02:00 US#1

AL # 4
Before 11/18/1883 LMT
11/18/1883 12:00 CST
3/31/1918 02:00 CWT
10/27/1918 02:00 CST
3/30/1919 02:00 CWT
10/26/1919 02:00 CST
5/18/1935 00:01 CDT
9/02/1935 00:01 CST
4/28/1940 02:00 CDT
9/29/1940 02:00 CST
7/21/1941 00:01 CDT
10/01/1941 00:01 CST
2/09/1942 02:00 CWT
9/30/1945 02:00 CST
4/30/1967 02:00 US#1

AL # 5
Before 11/18/1883 LMT
11/18/1883 12:00 CST
3/31/1918 02:00 CWT
10/27/1918 02:00 CST
3/30/1919 02:00 CWT
10/26/1919 02:00 CST
7/21/1941 00:01 CDT
10/01/1941 00:01 CST
2/09/1942 02:00 CWT
9/30/1945 02:00 CST
4/24/1966 02:00 US#1

AL # 6
Before 11/18/1883 LMT
11/18/1883 12:00 CST
3/31/1918 02:00 CWT
10/27/1918 02:00 CST
3/30/1919 02:00 CWT
10/26/1919 02:00 CST
4/28/1940 02:00 CDT
9/29/1940 02:00 CST
7/21/1941 00:01 CDT
10/01/1941 00:01 CST
2/09/1942 02:00 CWT
9/30/1945 02:00 CST
4/30/1967 02:00 US#1

AL # 7
Before 1/01/1903 LMT
1/01/1903 12:00 CST
3/31/1918 02:00 CWT
10/27/1918 02:00 CST
3/30/1919 02:00 CWT
10/26/1919 02:00 CST
3/23/1941 12:00 EST
2/09/1942 02:00 EWT
2/14/1943 02:00 CWT
9/30/1945 02:00 EST
4/30/1967 02:00 US#1

COUNTIES

1 Autauga
2 Baldwin
3 Barbour
4 Bibb
5 Blount
6 Bullock
7 Butler
8 Calhoun
9 Chambers
10 Cherokee
11 Chilton
12 Choctaw
13 Clarke
14 Clay
15 Cleburne
16 Coffee
17 Colbert
18 Conecuh
19 Coosa
20 Covington
21 Crenshaw
22 Cullman
23 Dale
24 Dallas
25 De Kalb
26 Elmore
27 Escambia
28 Etowah
29 Fayette
30 Franklin
31 Geneva
32 Greene
33 Hale
34 Henry
35 Houston
36 Jackson
37 Jefferson
38 Lamar
39 Lauderdale
40 Lawrence
41 Lee
42 Limestone
43 Lowndes
44 Macon
45 Madison
46 Marengo
47 Marion
48 Marshall
49 Mobile
50 Monroe
51 Montgomery
52 Morgan
53 Perry
54 Pickens
55 Pike
56 Randolph
57 Russell
58 St Clair
59 Shelby
60 Sumter
61 Talladega
62 Tallapoosa
63 Tuscaloosa
64 Walker
65 Washington
66 Wilcox
67 Winston

Abanda 9	1	33N06'03	85W31'47	5:42:07
Abbeville 34	1	31N34'18	85W15'02	5:41:00
Abbot Springs 59	1	33N21'39	86W28'54	5:45:56
Abel 15	1	33N32'55	85W42'45	5:42:51
Abercrombie 4	1	32N57	87W08	5:48:32
Aberfoil 6	1	32N04'13	85W41'16	5:42:45
Abernant 63	1	33N17'25	87W11'53	5:48:48
Abernathy 15	1	33N39'02	85W24'27	5:41:38
Acipcoville 37	6	33N33'22	86W50'35	5:47:22
Ackerville 66	1	32N01'46	87W03'59	5:48:16
Acmar 58	1	33N37'17	86W29'46	5:45:59
Active 4	1	32N52'04	86W58'37	5:47:54
Acton 37	6	33N25'36	86W44'07	5:46:56
Ada 51	1	32N06'19	86W16'35	5:45:06
Adair Ford 45	2	34N40'15	86W25'52	5:45:43
Adams 11	1	32N44'22	86W49'58	5:47:20
Adamsburg 25	1	34N23'56	85W40'20	5:42:41
Adams Crossroads 10	1	34N04'39	85W29'16	5:41:57
Adamsville 37	1	33N36'03	86W57'22	5:47:49
Addison 67	1	34N12'08	87W10'53	5:48:44
Aden 59	1	33N09'31	86W59'48	5:47:59
Adger 37	1	33N23	87W06	5:48:24
Adkin Hill 26	1	32N36'32	86W18'40	5:45:15
Adler 53	1	32N41	87W13	5:48:52
Adville 5	1	33N53'02	86W38'41	5:46:35
Agricola 62	1	32N46'06	85W44'19	5:42:57
Ai 15	1	33N38	85W35	5:42:20
Aimwell 46	1	32N07'17	87W54'22	5:51:37
Airport Highlands 37	6	33N35'06	86W44'30	5:46:58
Akinsville 3	1	31N38'08	85W36'40	5:42:27
Akka 49	1	30N46'38	88W01'23	5:52:06
Akron 33	1	32N52'35	87W44'33	5:50:58
Alabama City 28	6	34N01'20	86W02'44	5:44:11
Alabama Fork 42	1	34N51'05	86W58'26	5:47:54
Alabama Port 49	1	30N21'46	88W06'53	5:52:28
Alabama Shores 17	1	34N47'47	87W33'09	5:50:13
Alabaster 59	1	33N14'39	86W48'59	5:47:16
Alaga 35	1	31N07'34	85W04'21	5:40:17
Alberta 66	1	32N13'55	87W24'36	5:49:38
Alberta City 63	6	33N12	87W32	5:50:08
Alberton 16	1	31N16'40	86W07'33	5:44:30
Albertville 48	1	34N16'03	86W12'32	5:44:50
Alden 37	1	33N38'20	86W57'55	5:47:52
Alder Springs 48	1	34N20'35	86W12'57	5:44:52
Aldrich 59	1	33N06'27	86W53'28	5:47:34
Aldridge 64	1	33N42'25	87W14'31	5:48:58
Aldridge Grove 40	1	34N25'23	87W14'26	5:48:58
Alexander City 62	1	32N56'38	85W57'14	5:43:49
Alexander Heights 39	1	34N50'50	87W40'51	5:50:43
Alexandria 8	1	33N46'26	85W53'08	5:43:33
Alexis 10	1	34N10'44	85W30'44	5:42:03
Alfalfa 46	1	32N30'37	87W45'52	5:51:03
Aliceville 54	1	33N07'46	88W09'05	5:52:36
Allen 13	1	31N36	87W44	5:50:56
Allens Crossroads 48	1	34N25'40	86W32'31	5:46:10
Allenton 66	1	31N55'50	87W01'25	5:48:06
Allenville 33	1	32N29'27	87W39'39	5:50:39
Allenville 49	1	30N42'10	88W04'44	5:52:19
Allgood 5	1	33N54'43	86W30'34	5:46:02
Alliance 44	1	32N28'51	85W33'44	5:42:15
Allison 32	1	32N47'12	87W58'33	5:51:54
Allison 36	1	34N52'40	85W57'34	5:43:50
Allison Mills 61	1	33N23'23	86W06'54	5:44:28
Allsboro 17	1	34N41'39	88W06'37	5:52:26
Allsop 8	1	33N56'28	85W42'59	5:42:52
Alma 13	1	31N27'50	87W45'14	5:51:01
Almeria 6	1	32N01'35	85W51'02	5:43:24
Almond 56	1	33N08'47	85W37'18	5:42:29
Almont 59	1	33N06'52	86W52'45	5:47:31
Alpha Springs 11	1	33N23'72	86W25'28	5:45:42
Alpine 61	1	33N20'55	86W14'19	5:44:57
Alta 29	1	33N40'15	87W31'54	5:50:08
Altadena Valley 37	6	33N28	86W45	5:47:00
Altamont Park 37	6	33N30'34	86W45'56	5:47:04
Alton 37	1	33N34'45	86W38'15	5:46:33
Altoona 28	1	34N01'34	86W19'34	5:45:18
America 64	1	33N44'16	87W15'09	5:49:01
Andalusia 20	1	31N18	86W29	5:45:56
Anderson 28	6	34N04'16	85W55'17	5:43:41
Anderson 39	1	34N55'42	87W15'59	5:49:04
Andrews Chapel 52	1	34N25	87W05	5:48:20
Angel 8	1	33N50'07	85W50'13	5:43:21
Anita 59	1	33N10'27	86W58'49	5:47:55
Anne Manie 66	1	32N03'10	87W34'15	5:50:17
Anniston 8	6	33N39'35	85W49'54	5:43:20
Ansley 55	1	31N53'10	86W06'57	5:44:28
Antioch 8	1	33N36	86W01	5:44:04
Antioch 10	1	34N13'50	85W38'17	5:42:33
Antioch 20	1	31N23'08	86W22'59	5:45:32
Antioch 39	1	34N53'35	87W28'24	5:49:54
Antioch 55	1	31N45'32	85W53'21	5:43:33
Apple Grove 52	1	34N23'55	86W36'37	5:46:26
Appleton 27	1	31N13'15	87W07'17	5:48:29
Aqua Vista 39	1	34N49'49	87W29'07	5:49:56
Aquilla 12	1	31N42'44	88W24'50	5:53:39
Arab 48	1	34N19'05	86W29'45	5:45:59
Ararat 12	1	31N58'05	88W08'48	5:52:35
Arbacoochee 15	1	33N34'34	85W31'02	5:42:04
Arcola 33	1	32N33'25	87W46'03	5:51:04
Ardell 22	1	33N59'43	87W05'55	5:48:24
Ardilla 35	1	31N10'32	85W21'37	5:41:26
Ardmore 42	1	34N59'31	86W50'49	5:47:23
Ardmore Highway 45	2	34N43	86W38	5:46:32
Argo 37	1	33N40'54	86W31'50	5:46:07
Argo 64	1	33N48'05	87W07'01	5:48:28
Argo Heights 64	1	33N46	87W11	5:48:44
Arguta 23	1	31N34'09	85W35'43	5:42:23
Ariton 23	1	31N36'00	85W43'08	5:42:53
Arkadelphia 22	1	33N54'18	86W57'45	5:47:51
Arkdell 39	1	34N57'35	87W25'47	5:49:43
Arkwright 59	1	33N22'17	86W24'09	5:45:37
Arley 67	1	34N04'44	87W12'44	5:48:51
Arley Landing 67	1	34N02'39	87W15'57	5:49:04
Arlington 66	1	32N03'25	87W35'19	5:50:21
Armstead 5	1	33N52'55	86W31'29	5:46:06
Armstrong 44	1	32N14'22	85W39'28	5:42:38
Arona 25	1	34N13'18	86W04'55	5:44:20
Arrowhead 51	4	32N23	86W15	5:45:00
Asahel 66	1	31N52'04	87W25'15	5:49:41
Asberry 8	1	33N53'40	85W44'41	5:42:59
Asbury 23	1	31N30'42	85W32'43	5:42:11
Asbury 48	1	34N16	86W12	5:44:48
Ashbank 67	1	34N00'37	87W29'15	5:49:57
Ashby 4	1	33N01'15	86W55'10	5:47:41
Ashford 35	1	31N10'58	85W14'11	5:40:57
Ashland 14	1	33N16'25	85W50'10	5:43:21
Ashridge 67	1	34N14'05	87W28'07	5:49:52
Ashville 58	1	33N50'13	86W15'16	5:45:01
Askea Grove 48	1	34N17'07	86W27'34	5:45:50
Aspel 36	1	34N37'15	86W09'56	5:44:40
Athens 42	1	34N48'10	86W58'18	5:47:53
Atkinson 13	1	31N57'55	87W41'11	5:50:45
Atmore 27	1	31N01'25	87W29'38	5:49:59
Attalla 28	1	34N01'18	86W05'19	5:44:21
Atwood 30	1	34N21'38	87W59'42	5:51:59
Aubrey 41	5	32N40'01	85W27'09	5:41:49
Auburn 41	5	32N36'35	85W28'51	5:41:55
Augustin 53	1	32N30'22	87W06'28	5:48:26
Aurora 28	1	34N07'00	86W11'33	5:44:46
Aurora Springs 17	1	34N46	87W58	5:51:52
Austinville 52	3	34N34'29	87W00'31	5:48:02
Autaugaville 1	1	32N26'02	86W39'17	5:46:37
Ava 56	1	33N20'35	85W28'41	5:41:55
Avalon Park 37	1	33N25'50	86W59'25	5:47:58
Avant 7	1	31N37'17	86W42'05	5:46:48
Avery 36	1	34N53	85W50	5:43:20
Avoca 40	1	34N30	87W44	5:50:56
Avon 35	1	31N11'21	85W17'10	5:41:09
Avondale 37	6	33N31'18	86W46'41	5:47:07
Avondale Village 58	1	33N35'35	86W16'34	5:45:06
Avon Park 37	6	33N32'46	86W46'17	5:47:05
Awin 66	1	31N50'16	86W56'56	5:47:48
Axis 49	1	30N55'47	88W01'38	5:52:07
Axle 50	1	31N35'44	87W19'47	5:49:19
Ayres 37	1	33N43'53	86W33'49	5:46:15
Babbie 20	1	31N16'46	86W19'32	5:45:18
Backers Landing 50	1	31N48'30	87W27'28	5:49:50
Bacon Level 56	1	33N07'43	85W17'27	5:41:10
Bagley 37	1	33N45'20	87W00'06	5:48:00
Bailey Cove Estates 45	2	34N39'54	86W32'39	5:46:11
Bailey Crossroads 31	1	31N11'27	85W35'38	5:42:23
Baileys Landing 13	1	31N40'52	88W04'54	5:52:20
Baileys Landing 50	1	31N24'53	87W35'36	5:50:22
Bailey Springs 39	1	34N53'44	87W34'17	5:50:17
Baileyton 22	1	34N15'44	86W36'46	5:46:27
Baileytown 22	1	34N09'49	86W39'35	5:46:38
Baileytown 36	1	34N51'32	86W10'10	5:44:41
Baker Hill 3	1	31N46'52	85W18'08	5:41:13
Bald Hill 31	1	31N09'49	85W38'08	5:42:33
Baldwin 22	1	34N11'21	86W55'01	5:47:40
Baldwin Farms 44	1	32N17	85W51	5:43:24
Balkum 34	1	31N25'03	85W13'39	5:40:55
Ballfield Landing 13	1	31N36'45	88W04'29	5:52:18
Ball Flat 10	1	34N01'04	85W44'02	5:42:56
Ballplay 28	6	34N03'31	85W48'29	5:43:14
Baltic 55	1	31N39'06	86W00'15	5:44:01
Baltimore Hill 45	2	34N50'12	86W32'32	5:46:10
Bamford 59	1	33N16'33	86W55'55	5:47:44
Bangor 5	1	33N58'28	86W45'24	5:47:02
Bankhead 25	1	34N33'37	85W33'11	5:42:13
Bankhead 64	1	33N46'36	87W18'04	5:49:12
Banks 55	1	31N48'54	85W50'35	5:43:22
Bankston 29	1	33N40'17	87W40'17	5:50:41
Barachias 51	1	32N17'58	86W11'47	5:44:47
Barber 35	1	31N14'03	85W14'08	5:40:57
Barclay 61	1	33N25'09	86W10'01	5:44:40
Barefield Crossroads 23	1	31N33'06	85W27'09	5:41:49
Barfield 14	1	33N21'40	85W42'57	5:42:52
Barlow 65	1	31N38	88W20	5:53:20
Barlow Bend 13	1	31N27'16	87W38'05	5:50:32
Barlow Landing 2	1	30N57'26	87W52'21	5:51:29
Barnes 23	1	31N32'33	85W40'28	5:42:42
Barnes 34	1	31N28'04	85W07'08	5:40:29
Barnesville 47	1	34N08	87W59	5:51:56
Barnesville 62	1	32N42'20	85W48'57	5:43:16
Barnett Chapel 67	1	34N09'43	87W17'58	5:49:12
Barnett Crossroads 27	1	31N13'16	87W18'16	5:49:13

Barney 64 1 33N42'58 87W09'31 5:48:38
Barneys Lower Landing 46
1 31N59'32 88W04'32 5:52:18
Barnisdale Forest 37
1 33N35'24 86W40'43 5:46:43
Barnwell 2 1 30N25'29 87W52'46 5:51:31
Barrett 35 1 31N11'31 85W25'15 5:41:41
Barrett Crossroads 56
1 33N11'43 85W17'38 5:41:11
Barrytown 12 1 31N50'14 88W15'10 5:53:01
Barton 17 1 34N44'19 87W53'28 5:51:34
Bartonville 37 6 33N34'29 86W46'50 5:47:07
Basham 52 1 34N30'53 87W01'05 5:48:04
Bashi 13 1 31N58'16 87W51'41 5:51:27
Bashi 65 1 31N39'34 88W14'05 5:52:56
Basin 16 1 31N20'29 86W07'51 5:44:31
Basnesville 47 1 34N08'23 88W04'40 5:52:19
Bass 36 1 34N55'55 85W54'47 5:43:39
Bassetts Creek 65
1 31N27'52 88W01'56 5:52:08
Batesville 3 1 32N00'32 85W18'40 5:41:15
Bath Springs 28 1 34N06'42 85W53'23 5:43:34
Battelle 25 1 34N38'58 85W33'55 5:42:16
Battens Crossroads 16
1 31N15'39 85W53'24 5:43:34
Battery Hill 36 1 34N57'10 85W42'30 5:42:50
Battleground 22 1 34N18'16 86W59'47 5:47:59
Battles Wharf 2 1 30N29'39 87W55'40 5:51:43
Baxters 3 1 31N45'27 85W34'52 5:42:19
Bayleys Corner 49
1 30N27'53 88W06'52 5:52:27
Bay Minette 2 1 30N52'58 87W46'23 5:51:06
Bayou La Batre 49
1 30N24'11 88W14'54 5:53:00
Bayside 52 3 34N33'23 86W58'03 5:47:52
Bay Springs 10 1 34N10'33 85W42'56 5:42:52
Bay View 37 1 33N33'31 86W58'25 5:47:54
Bazemore 29 1 33N53'40 87W42'00 5:50:48
Beamon 23 1 31N31'08 85W35'10 5:42:21
Bean Rock 48 1 34N24 86W27 5:45:48
Beans Crossroads 6
1 31N59'57 85W51'13 5:43:25
Beans Mill 41 5 32N41'49 85W16'03 5:41:04
Bear Creek 47 1 34N16'29 87W42'02 5:50:48
Beards Mill 54 1 33N21'56 88W07'11 5:52:29
Beasley 54 1 33N12'43 88W06'00 5:52:24
Beasons Mill 15 1 33N38 85W35 5:42:20
Beatrice 50 1 31N44'00 87W12'17 5:48:49
Beaty Crossroads 25
1 34N41'44 85W40'10 5:42:41
Beaverton 38 1 33N55'52 88W01'13 5:52:05
Beaver Town 54 1 33N11'40 88W11'53 5:52:48
Beck 20 1 31N15'22 86W35'05 5:46:20
Beda 20 1 31N03'03 86W34'58 5:46:20
Beechwood 43 1 32N07'33 86W39'22 5:46:37
Beehive 41 5 32N33'13 85W34'41 5:42:19
Bel Air 37 6 33N35'06 86W43'17 5:46:53
Bel Air 49 1 30N40 88W06 5:52:24
Belchers 4 1 33N06'34 87W12'32 5:48:50
Belforest 2 1 30N36'13 87W51'09 5:51:25
Belfountain 2 1 30N37 87W20 5:49:20
Belgreen 30 1 34N28'29 87W51'59 5:51:28
Belk 29 1 33N38'51 87W55'53 5:51:44
Belknap 24 1 32N12'22 87W00'50 5:48:03
Bell 54 1 33N20'20 87W57'38 5:51:51
Bellamy 60 1 32N26'56 88W08'01 5:52:32
Belle Ellen 4 1 33N07'28 87W03'26 5:48:14
Bellefontaine 49
1 30N29'36 88W06'13 5:52:25
Bellefonte 36 1 34N42'40 85W56'43 5:43:47
Belle Haven 37 6 33N27'39 86W53'19 5:47:33
Bellemeade 39 1 34N50'52 87W35'42 5:50:23
Belle Mina 42 1 34N39'24 86W52'45 5:47:31
Belleville 18 1 31N25'47 87W06'33 5:48:26
Bellevue 24 1 32N26'15 87W22'49 5:49:31
Bellevue 28 6 34N02'04 86W01'19 5:44:05
Bell Factory 45 2 34N49'26 86W28'26 5:45:54
Bell Mills 15 1 33N36'59 85W28'29 5:41:54
Bells Crossroads 3
1 31N53'43 85W31'25 5:42:06
Bells Crossroads 23
1 31N31'21 85W27'03 5:41:48
Bell Springs 52 1 34N19'02 86W54'55 5:47:40
Belltown 15 1 33N36'12 85W36'24 5:42:26
Bellview 36 1 34N32'42 85W56'01 5:43:44
Bellview 66 1 31N50'37 87W21'22 5:49:25
Bellwood 31 1 31N10'23 85W47'36 5:43:10
Bellwood 37 1 33N28 86W56 5:47:44
Belmont 60 1 32N33'31 87W56'33 5:51:46
Beloit 24 1 32N21'15 87W08'55 5:48:36
Beltona 37 1 33N47'54 86W50'55 5:47:24
Belview Heights 17
1 34N42'54 87W41'30 5:50:46
Belwood 37 1 33N28'05 86W54'42 5:47:39
Bemiston 61 1 33N24'36 86W07'15 5:44:29
Bendale 37 6 33N33'43 86W46'52 5:47:07
Benevola 54 1 33N06'33 87W57'54 5:51:52
Benoit 64 1 33N45'14 87W09'26 5:48:38
Bentley Hills 37
6 33N30'48 86W44'40 5:46:59
Bentleyville 19 1 32N57'22 86W15'37 5:45:02
Benton 43 1 32N18'24 86W49'04 5:47:16
Ben Vines Gap 37
1 33N33 86W59 5:47:56
Berkley 45 2 34N38'23 86W25'45 5:45:43
Berkley Hills 37
1 33N37'02 86W41'49 5:46:47
Berlin 22 1 34N10'53 86W44'32 5:46:58
Berlin 24 1 32N15'33 87W00'30 5:48:02
Bermuda 18 1 31N29'14 87W11'18 5:48:45
Berney Points 37
6 33N29'11 86W51'45 5:47:27
Berneys 61 1 33N20'37 86W08'58 5:44:36
Berry 29 1 33N39'35 87W36'00 5:50:24
Berry Springs 10
1 34N25'46 85W30'31 5:42:02
Bertha 23 1 31N32'28 85W25'41 5:41:43
Berwick 14 1 33N16'32 85W40'10 5:42:41
Bessemer 37 1 33N24'06 86W57'16 5:47:49
Bessemer Gardens 37
1 33N25'27 86W58'42 5:47:55
Bessemer Homestead 37
1 33N24'13 86W56'20 5:47:45
Bessemer Junction 37
1 33N25'29 86W58'09 5:47:53
Bessie 11 1 32N56'39 86W49'57 5:47:20
Bessie 37 1 33N38'59 87W01'59 5:48:08
Bessie Junction 37
1 33N38'13 87W02'11 5:48:09
Bethany 63 1 33N15 87W41 5:50:44
Bethel 3 1 31N37'41 85W40'55 5:42:44
Bethel 18 1 31N42'02 86W54'51 5:47:39
Bethel 22 1 34N11'40 86W58'58 5:47:56
Bethel 42 1 34N55'59 86W49'11 5:47:17
Bethel Grove 1 1 32N37'40 86W51'00 5:47:24
Bethlehem 51 1 32N03'12 86W20'37 5:45:22
Betts Lower Landing 13
1 31N12'27 87W50'59 5:51:24
Beulah 20 1 31N13'44 86W13'57 5:44:56
Beulah 32 1 32N54 87W47 5:51:08
Beulah 41 5 32N42'40 85W10'56 5:40:44
Beulah Land 42 1 34N41'19 87W00'05 5:48:00
Bevelle 62 1 32N59 85W52 5:43:28
Beverly Station 37
6 33N29'02 86W51'12 5:47:25
Bexar 47 1 34N11'27 88W08'50 5:52:35
Bibb Mill 4 1 32N56'50 86W54'37 5:47:38
Bibbville 4 1 33N11'36 87W10'35 5:48:42
Biddle Crossroads 25
1 34N39'29 85W41'37 5:42:46
Bigbee 65 1 31N36'50 88W09'59 5:52:40
Big Creek 35 1 31N04'06 85W26'02 5:41:44
Big Oak 39 1 34N51'03 87W27'12 5:49:49
Big Ridge 64 1 33N44'41 87W14'12 5:48:57
Big Springs 4 1 33N13 87W09 5:48:36
Big Springs 56 1 33N16'57 85W18'23 5:41:14
Billingsley 1 1 32N39'34 86W43'04 5:46:52
Billy Goat Hill 10
1 34N11'39 85W41'42 5:42:47
Bingham 17 1 34N38'47 87W29'51 5:49:59
Birdeye 32 1 32N36'47 87W49'45 5:51:19
Birdine 32 1 32N39 87W53 5:51:32
Birdsong 22 1 34N14'42 86W38'48 5:46:35
Birmingham 37 6 33N31'14 86W48'09 5:47:13
Biscayne Highlands 37
1 33N35'07 86W41'36 5:46:46
Bishop 17 1 34N39'56 88W06'50 5:52:27
Biven 37 6 33N34 86W52 5:47:28
Black 31 1 31N00'33 85W44'40 5:42:59
Blackankle 36 1 34N44'42 86W01'17 5:44:05
Black Bottom 22 1 33N56'53 86W51'36 5:47:26
Blackburn 39 1 34N55'51 87W38'46 5:50:35
Blackburn 42 1 34N47'30 87W03'16 5:48:13
Black Creek 37 6 33N36'51 86W46'52 5:47:07
Black Diamond 37
1 33N20'41 87W05'12 5:48:21
Blackman 9 5 32N52'05 85W31'36 5:42:06
Black Pond 67 1 34N03'35 87W21'06 5:49:24
Black Rock 21 1 31N44 86W19 5:45:16
Blacksher 2 1 31N12'38 87W44'18 5:50:57
Blackwood 34 1 31N23'14 85W24'30 5:41:38
Bladon Springs 12
1 31N43'50 88W11'51 5:52:47
Bladon Springs Landing 12
1 31N45'46 88W09'25 5:52:38
Blairs 20 1 31N15'50 86W13'24 5:44:54
Blakeley 2 1 30N44'31 87W55'27 5:51:42
Blalock 24 1 32N18'33 87W23'01 5:49:32
Blanche 10 1 34N21'48 85W36'36 5:42:26
Blands Landing 41
5 32N40'53 85W08'21 5:40:33
Blanton 41 5 32N44'04 85W08'02 5:40:32
Bleecker 41 7 32N34'56 85W09'51 5:40:39
Blockton Junc 4 1 33N12'32 87W08'36 5:48:34
Blossburg 37 1 33N37'50 86W56'48 5:47:47
Bloucher Ford 45
2 34N52'31 86W28'32 5:45:54
Blount Landing 65
1 31N38'10 88W05'14 5:52:21
Blount Springs 5
1 33N55'52 86W47'39 5:47:11
Blountsville 5 1 34N04'53 86W35'28 5:46:22
Blow Gourd 5 1 33N56'48 86W35'09 5:46:21
Blue Creek 37 1 33N22'15 87W04'34 5:48:18
Blue Creek Junction 37
1 33N24'45 86W57'57 5:47:52
Blue Ford Landing 49
1 31N09'49 87W58'24 5:51:54
Blue Mountain 8 6 33N41'04 85W50'34 5:43:22
Blue Pond 10 1 34N14'13 85W43'13 5:42:53
Blue Ridge Estates 37
6 33N25 86W48 5:47:12
Blues Old Stand 6
1 31N59'05 85W43'01 5:42:52
Blue Spring (P O) 45
2 34N46'08 86W35'55 5:46:24
Blue Springs 3 1 31N39'49 85W30'24 5:42:02
Blue Springs 5 1 34N07'35 86W32'34 5:46:10
Blue Springs 19 1 33N04'24 86W28'41 5:45:55
Blue Springs 20 1 31N12'32 86W18'47 5:45:15
Bluff 29 1 33N49'14 87W54'23 5:51:38
Bluff City 52 1 34N32'44 86W46'53 5:47:08
Bluff Park 37 1 33N24'05 86W51'22 5:47:25
Bluffport 60 1 32N35'38 88W06'56 5:52:28
Bluff Springs 14
1 33N09'48 85W49'39 5:43:19
Bluff Springs 16
1 31N34'15 86W04'02 5:44:16
Bluffton 10 1 34N00'25 85W26'24 5:41:46
Boar Tush 67 1 34N11'28 87W37'19 5:50:29
Boaz 48 1 34N12'02 86W09'59 5:44:40
Boaz Corner 61 1 33N16'24 86W18'05 5:45:12
Bobo 29 1 33N52'38 87W49'21 5:51:17
Bobo 45 2 34N57'44 86W43'31 5:46:54
Bogue Chitto 24 1 32N21'56 87W18'13 5:49:13
Bogueloosa 12 1 31N59'15 88W19'57 5:53:20
Bohannon Ford 25
1 34N26'45 85W51'40 5:43:27
Boiling Spring 8
6 33N36'53 85W47'34 5:43:10
Boiling Springs 8
1 33N44'11 86W02'32 5:44:10
Boldo 64 1 33N51'14 87W10'58 5:48:44
Boley Springs 29
1 33N38'35 87W30'36 5:50:02
Boligee 32 1 32N45'21 88W01'44 5:52:07
Bolinger 12 1 31N46'42 88W19'52 5:53:19
Bolivar 36 1 34N54'48 85W46'30 5:43:06
Bolling 7 1 31N43'31 86W42'21 5:46:49
Bomar 10 1 34N06'31 85W34'49 5:42:19
Bon Acre Landing 57
7 32N17'11 84W55'29 5:39:42
Bon Air 37 1 33N26'40 86W55'58 5:47:44
Bon Air 61 1 33N15'49 86W20'08 5:45:21
Bonita 1 1 32N32'40 86W49'42 5:47:19
Bonneville 42 1 34N50'47 86W56'09 5:47:45
Bonnie Doone 42 1 34N46'27 86W57'51 5:47:51
Bonny Brook 8 1 33N46'54 85W45'41 5:43:03
Bon Secour 2 1 30N18'55 87W43'46 5:50:55
Booker Heights 37
1 33N32'33 87W00'26 5:48:02
Bookers Mill 18 1 31N31'36 87W36'56 5:48:08
Booneville 27 1 31N12'03 87W36'11 5:50:25
Booth 1 1 32N30'01 86W34'19 5:46:17
Booth Ford 59 1 33N11'07 87W00'07 5:48:00
Boot Hill 3 1 31N52'33 85W38'33 5:42:34
Boothton 59 1 33N10'47 86W59'26 5:47:58
Boozer Heights 8
6 33N40 85W50 5:43:20
Borden Springs 15
1 33N55'47 85W28'13 5:41:53
Borden Wheeler Springs 15
1 33N54'49 85W27'57 5:41:52
Boromville 44 1 32N18'23 85W26'30 5:41:46
Boston 20 1 31N28'04 85W28'55 5:45:56
Boston 47 1 34N01 87W46 5:51:04
Boswell 6 1 31N48 85W56 5:43:44
Bosworth 9 5 33N01'22 85W33'41 5:42:15
Bowden Grove 14 1 33N20'21 85W50'37 5:43:22
Bowles 18 1 31N34'24 86W58'37 5:47:54
Bowman Crossroads 36
1 34N36'08 85W51'23 5:43:26
Boyd 60 1 32N37'10 88W18'15 5:53:13
Boyd Crossing 63
1 33N05 87W14 5:48:56
Boyds 9 5 32N49'02 85W24'17 5:41:37
Boykin 20 1 31N30'36 86W34'24 5:46:18
Boykin 27 1 31N08'45 86W52'28 5:47:30
Boykin 66 1 32N04'40 87W16'53 5:49:08
Boyles Highlands 37
6 33N34'03 86W46'28 5:47:06
Boylston 51 4 32N25'42 86W16'46 5:45:07
Boys Ranch 24 1 32N05 87W00 5:48:00
Bradford 19 1 32N59'41 86W05'06 5:44:20
Bradford (Dixiana P O) 37
1 33N45'07 86W42'14 5:46:49
Bradley 27 1 31N02'00 86W43'32 5:46:54
Bradley Landing 57
7 32N19'48 85W00'27 5:40:02
Bradleyton 21 1 31N54'06 86W14'32 5:44:58
Bradleytown 64 1 33N42'00 87W14'57 5:49:00
Braggs 43 1 32N03'01 86W47'44 5:47:11
Braggsville 58 1 33N35'57 86W30'26 5:46:02
Braggville 32 1 32N40'56 87W59'50 5:51:59
Branchville 58 1 33N39'31 86W25'57 5:45:44
Brandontown 45 2 34N44'58 86W38'04 5:46:32
Brannon Springs 28
1 33N47 86W01 5:44:04
Brannon Stand 35
1 31N14'24 85W28'51 5:41:55
Brantley 21 1 31N34'56 86W15'26 5:45:02
Brantley 24 1 32N25'44 86W56'48 5:47:47
Brantley Crossing 18
1 31N29'47 87W07'09 5:48:29
Brantleyville 59
1 33N12'57 86W52'30 5:47:30
Braodwells Mill 8
1 33N48'16 85W47'38 5:43:11
Brasfield Landing 60
1 32N37'15 87W52'49 5:51:31
Brassell 51 1 32N23'58 86W02'25 5:44:10
Brassell Bottom 51
1 32N23'56 86W11'05 5:44:44
Bremen 22 1 33N59'40 86W58'12 5:47:53
Brent 4 1 32N56'14 87W09'53 5:48:40
Brentwood Hills 37
6 33N25 86W48 5:47:12
Brewersville 60 1 32N30'59 88W05'31 5:52:22
Brewton 27 1 31N06'18 87W04'20 5:48:17
Briar Hill 55 1 31N57'32 86W07'48 5:44:31
Brice 28 6 34N05'40 85W58'19 5:43:53
Brick 17 1 34N45 87W41 5:50:44
Brickhouse Ford 40
1 34N42'45 87W18'55 5:49:16
Brickyard Junction 37
1 33N24'35 86W56'32 5:47:46
Brides Hill 40 1 34N40'13 87W14'39 5:48:59
Bridgehead 2 1 30N40'04 87W54'40 5:51:39
Bridgeport 36 1 34N56'51 85W42'52 5:42:51
Bridgeport Landing 66
1 32N02'26 87W16'28 5:49:06
Bridgeville 54 1 33N06'17 88W08'31 5:52:34
Bridlewood Forest Estates 37
1 33N37'48 86W41'43 5:46:47
Brierfield 4 1 33N02'20 86W54'32 5:47:38
Brighton 37 1 33N26'03 86W56'50 5:47:47
Bright Star 5 1 34N09'37 86W25'49 5:45:43
Brilliant 47 1 34N01'31 87W45'30 5:51:02
Brisco Store 36 1 34N53 85W50 5:43:20
Bristow 10 1 34N11'45 85W46'40 5:43:07
Broach Mill 44 1 32N32'55 85W45'24 5:43:02
Broadmoor 37 1 33N26 86W57 5:47:48
Bromley 2 1 30N44'19 87W52'03 5:51:28
Brompton 58 1 33N34'55 86W28'10 5:45:53
Brookhurst 37 6 33N35'21 86W41'37 5:46:46
Brookhurst 45 2 34N46'59 86W36'18 5:46:25
Brookland 16 1 31N13 86W10 5:44:40
Brooklane Place 37
1 33N26'14 86W58'55 5:47:56
Brooklyn 16 1 31N18'46 86W10'16 5:44:41
Brooklyn 18 1 31N15'45 86W46'16 5:47:05
Brooklyn 22 1 34N13'33 86W36'55 5:46:28
Brooks 20 1 31N28'54 86W41'06 5:46:44
Brooks Acres 39 1 34N50'05 87W30'19 5:50:01
Brooks Crossroads 25
1 34N35'47 85W47'04 5:43:08
Brookside 37 1 33N38'16 86W55'00 5:47:40
Brookside 47 1 34N00'03 87W44'43 5:50:59
Brooksville 5 1 34N09'43 86W28'32 5:45:54

Brooksville 52 1 34N30'03 86W51'18 5:47:25
Brookwood 63 1 33N15'20 87W19'15 5:49:17
Brookwood Forest 42 1 34N47'44 86W55'50 5:47:43
Brookwood Village Mall 37 6 33N27 86W49 5:47:16
Broomtown 10 1 34N21'38 85W31'18 5:42:05
Broughton 56 1 33N10'57 85W26'30 5:41:46
Browns 24 1 32N26'12 87W21'58 5:49:28
Brownsboro 45 2 34N44'57 86W26'35 5:45:46
Browns Corner 45 2 34N55'58 86W42'49 5:46:51
Browns Crossroad 23 1 31N24'58 85W31'39 5:42:07
Browns Crossroad 34 1 31N25'39 85W12'03 5:40:48
Browns Landing 2 1 30N30'40 87W26'56 5:49:48
Brownstown 60 1 32N36'07 87W55'52 5:51:43
Brownsville 14 1 33N07'33 86W02'50 5:44:11
Browntown 36 1 34N36'10 85W49'50 5:43:19
Browntown 64 6 33N35'28 87W20'26 5:49:22
Brownville 18 1 31N28'06 86W54'02 5:47:36
Brownville 37 1 33N26'27 86W54'43 5:47:39
Brownville 63 6 33N23'33 87W45'12 5:51:01
Bruceville 6 1 32N05'52 85W50'54 5:43:24
Brundidge 55 1 31N43'12 85W48'58 5:43:16
Brunnet Heights 37 6 33N35 86W46 5:47:04
Brushy Creek 7 1 31N40'06 86W40'14 5:46:41
Brushy Pond 22 1 34N01'43 87W00'27 5:48:02
Bryan 64 1 33N41'58 87W02'52 5:48:11
Bryant 36 1 34N56'37 85W37'56 5:42:32
Bryant Landing 2 1 30N25'16 87W54'37 5:51:38
Bryants Landing 35 1 31N06'28 85W02'12 5:40:09
Buchanan Peninsula 17 1 34N46 87W58 5:51:52
Buck Ford 48 1 34N31'07 86W19'43 5:45:19
Buckhorn 45 2 34N52'03 86W27'20 5:45:49
Buckhorn 55 1 31N48'12 85W45'38 5:43:03
Bucks 49 1 31N00'37 88W01'27 5:52:06
Bucks Mill 45 2 34N59'26 86W31'21 5:46:05
Bucksnort 48 1 34N30'11 86W18'14 5:45:13
Bucksville 63 1 33N16'42 87W05'08 5:48:21
Buckville 62 1 32N31'15 85W51'49 5:43:27
Buena Vista 50 1 31N47'35 87W14'55 5:49:00
Buena Vista Highlands 37 6 33N27'45 86W48'31 5:47:14
Buffalo 9 5 32N56'46 85W24'07 5:41:36
Buggs Chapel 45 2 34N35 86W28 5:45:52
Buhl 63 1 33N15'25 87W45'10 5:51:01
Bulgers 62 1 32N49'07 85W58'05 5:43:52
Bull City 63 1 33N24'59 87W15'30 5:49:02
Bullock 21 1 31N32'26 86W10'43 5:44:43
Burbank 65 1 31N13'04 88W23'26 5:53:34
Burchfield 63 1 33N20'41 87W17'55 5:49:12
Burgess 10 1 34N25'48 85W33'05 5:42:12
Burgreen Corners 42 1 34N41 86W41 5:46:44
Burgreen Gin 42 1 34N43'44 86W47'47 5:47:11
Burks Gardens 63 6 33N12 87W32 5:50:08
Burkville 43 1 32N19'41 86W32'13 5:46:09
Burl 66 1 31N50 87W06 5:48:24
Burlington 26 1 32N34'49 85W56'20 5:43:45
Burningtree Estates 52 1 34N31'07 86W56'19 5:47:45
Burningtree Mountain 52 3 34N31'05 86W55'17 5:47:41
Burns 8 1 33N50'18 85W36'24 5:42:26
Burns Crossroad 8 1 33N37'12 85W56'30 5:43:46
Burnstown 17 1 34N38'35 88W07'08 5:52:29
Burnsville 24 1 32N28'28 86W53'30 5:47:34
Burnt Corn 18 1 31N33'12 87W09'37 5:48:38
Burntout 30 1 34N27'03 88W01'22 5:52:05
Burnwell 64 1 33N42'28 87W05'15 5:48:21
Burrows 45 2 34N34'04 86W32'27 5:46:10
Burrows Crossroads 64 1 33N54'46 87W09'36 5:48:38
Bush 8 6 33N43'49 85W52'43 5:43:31
Bush 37 1 33N26'54 86W58'59 5:47:56
Bushy Creek 7 1 31N38 86W44 5:46:56
Bushy Pond 22 1 33N54 86W58 5:47:52
Butler 12 1 32N05'22 88W13'19 5:52:53
Butler Mill 45 2 34N34'47 86W18'07 5:45:12
Butler Springs 7 1 31N48'07 86W51'58 5:47:28
Butts Mill 26 1 32N33'40 85W57'46 5:43:51
Buttston 62 1 32N56'47 85W38'18 5:42:33
Buyck 26 1 32N42'16 86W15'25 5:45:02
Buzbee Landing 2 1 30N42'08 87W53'52 5:51:35
Bynum 8 1 33N36'47 85W57'40 5:43:51
Caddo 40 1 34N34'09 87W08'24 5:48:34
Caffee Junction 63 1 33N14'43 87W08'16 5:48:33
Cahaba 24 1 32N19'00 87W06'05 5:48:24
Cahaba Crest 37 1 33N37'48 86W35'56 5:46:24
Cahaba Heights 37 6 33N27'50 86W43'55 5:46:56
Cahaba Hills 37 1 33N32'20 86W34'27 5:46:18
Cahaba Mall 37 6 33N28 86W45 5:47:00
Cahaba River Estates 59 1 33N21'17 86W49'34 5:47:18
Cain Landing 52 1 34N33'00 86W48'05 5:47:12
Cairo 42 1 34N52'14 87W08'40 5:48:35
Calcis 59 1 33N25'35 86W25'54 5:45:44
Caldwell 58 1 33N48'44 86W21'52 5:45:27
Calebee 44 1 32N23'07 85W53'04 5:43:32
Caledonia 66 1 31N53'25 87W05'15 5:48:21
Calera 59 1 33N06'10 86W45'13 5:47:01
Calhoun 43 1 32N03'00 86W32'42 5:46:11
Calumer 64 1 33N47'41 87W17'13 5:49:09
Calvary 46 1 32N13'31 87W47'35 5:51:10
Calvert 49 1 31N09'18 88W00'36 5:52:02
Camden 66 1 31N59'27 87W17'26 5:49:10
Camelot 45 2 34N37'37 86W31'53 5:46:08
Cameron 64 1 33N47'45 87W16'18 5:49:05
Cameronsville 36 1 34N52'14 85W44'44 5:42:59
Campbell 11 1 32N53'33 86W50'48 5:47:23
Campbell 13 1 31N55'24 87W58'52 5:51:55
Campbell Mill 48 1 34N29'35 86W14'39 5:44:59
Campbells Crossroads 14 1 33N22'12 85W52'36 5:43:30
Campbells Landing 13 1 31N57'39 88W04'08 5:52:17
Campbell Springs 14 1 33N22'12 85W52'04 5:43:28
Campbellville 64 1 33N50'11 87W03'19 5:48:13
Camp Hill 62 1 32N48'01 85W39'13 5:42:37
Camp Horne 59 6 33N25'01 86W44'08 5:46:57
Camp Oliver 37 1 33N46 87W20 5:49:20
Canaan 51 1 32N12'17 86W18'13 5:45:13
Canoe 27 1 31N01'34 87W24'43 5:49:39
Cantelous 51 1 32N19'24 86W27'21 5:45:49
Canton Bend 66 1 32N00 87W18 5:49:12
Canty 51 1 32N09'48 86W04'59 5:44:20
Capell 66 1 32N00 87W18 5:49:12
Capital Heights 51 4 32N23 86W16 5:45:04
Capps 34 1 31N29'49 85W18'43 5:41:15
Capshaw 42 1 34N46'23 86W47'34 5:47:10
Carara 61 1 33N23'59 86W02'09 5:44:09
Carbon Hill 64 1 33N53'30 87W31'34 5:50:06
Cardiff 37 1 33N38'44 86W56'01 5:47:44
Card Switch 36 1 34N52'22 85W51'20 5:43:25
Carey 42 1 34N52'35 86W56'03 5:47:44
Carleys 66 1 32N16'01 87W29'29 5:49:58
Carlisle 28 1 34N07'44 86W07'13 5:44:29
Carlowville 24 1 32N05'13 87W02'03 5:48:08
Carlton 13 1 31N20'35 87W50'44 5:51:23
Carmen 21 1 31N37'56 86W11'21 5:44:45
Carney 2 1 30N55'38 87W43'09 5:50:53
Carns 36 1 34N48'33 85W58'27 5:43:54
Carolina 20 1 31N14'26 86W31'40 5:46:07
Carolyn 51 4 32N21 86W17 5:45:08
Carpenter 2 1 30N51'25 87W51'58 5:51:28
Carpenter 65 1 31N32'29 88W14'11 5:52:57
Carriger 42 1 34N48 86W58 5:47:52
Carr Mill 14 1 33N12'19 85W56'38 5:43:47
Carroll Crossroads 30 1 34N22'00 87W35'01 5:50:20
Carrollton 54 1 33N16 88W06 5:52:24
Carrville 62 1 32N32'59 85W52'12 5:43:29
Carson 65 1 31N28'20 87W56'29 5:51:46
Carter Grove 45 2 34N56'52 86W41'45 5:46:47
Carters Hill 51 1 32N11'34 86W07'02 5:44:28
Cartwright 42 1 34N52'20 87W03'53 5:48:16
Carver Court 44 1 32N25 85W42 5:42:48
Casemore 33 1 32N34'49 87W41'02 5:50:44
Casey 24 1 32N23 87W00 5:48:00
Castleberry 18 1 31N17'56 87W01'21 5:48:05
Caswell 2 1 30N17'37 87W32'22 5:50:09
Catalpa 55 1 31N52'46 85W49'59 5:43:20
Catherine 66 1 32N11'04 87W28'10 5:49:53
Catherwood Park 37 1 33N32 86W57 5:47:48
Catoma 51 4 32N22 86W20 5:45:20
Cavalry Hill 45 2 34N44'26 86W36'40 5:46:27
Cave Spring 36 1 34N54'29 85W57'38 5:43:51
Cave Spring 45 2 34N35 86W28 5:45:52
Cave Springs 17 1 34N44 87W42 5:50:48
Cave Springs 28 6 34N04'42 86W03'54 5:44:16
Cecil 51 1 32N18'09 86W00'31 5:44:02
Cedar Bluff 10 1 34N13'12 85W36'28 5:42:26
Cedar Cove 63 1 33N10'29 87W19'19 5:49:17
Cedar Fork 13 1 31N39 87W42 5:50:48
Cedar Grove 2 1 30N14'40 87W50'21 5:51:21
Cedar Grove 20 1 31N21'06 86W19'44 5:45:19
Cedar Grove 36 1 34N50'00 85W52'22 5:43:29
Cedar Grove 39 1 34N51'24 87W12'53 5:48:52
Cedar Hill 29 1 33N41'14 87W52'20 5:51:29
Cedar Hill 42 1 34N58'37 86W49'12 5:47:17
Cedar Hills Estates 17 1 34N42'20 87W45'11 5:51:01
Cedar Lake 52 3 34N33'16 86W58'25 5:47:54
Cedar Plains 52 1 34N21'54 86W59'47 5:47:59
Cedar Point 45 2 34N35'58 86W20'25 5:45:22
Cedar Springs 5 1 33N51'50 86W39'16 5:46:37
Cedar Springs 8 1 33N49'12 85W50'06 5:43:20
Cedarville 33 1 32N36'45 87W40'10 5:50:41
Cedrum 64 1 33N51'05 87W26'48 5:49:47
Centenary 21 1 31N46'43 86W22'03 5:45:28
Center 67 1 34N15'52 87W35'16 5:50:21
Center Community 22 1 34N02'17 86W48'39 5:47:15
Centercrest 37 1 33N39'26 86W40'23 5:46:42
Center Dale 52 1 34N19'16 86W43'23 5:46:54
Center Grove 52 1 34N23'02 86W38'19 5:46:33
Center Hill 11 1 32N58'20 86W46'18 5:47:05
Center Hill 22 1 34N05'22 86W43'29 5:46:54
Center Hill 39 1 34N57'20 87W26'54 5:49:48
Center Hill 42 1 34N51'27 86W47'43 5:47:11
Center Point 13 1 31N47'18 88W01'48 5:52:07
Center Point 37 1 33N38'44 86W41'01 5:46:44
Center Point Gardens 37 1 33N38'17 86W40'58 5:46:44
Center Ridge 21 1 31N48'57 86W24'45 5:45:39
Center Springs 5 1 33N49 86W44 5:46:56
Center Star 39 1 34N51'41 87W27'20 5:49:49
Centerville 18 1 31N26 86W56 5:47:44
Centerville 22 1 34N16'34 86W55'46 5:47:43
Centerwood Estates 37 1 33N38'41 86W40'09 5:46:41
Central 22 1 34N13'29 87W00'33 5:48:02
Central 26 1 32N40'56 86W05'51 5:44:23
Central 36 1 34N39'58 85W47'26 5:43:10
Central City 16 1 31N14'35 85W53'06 5:43:32
Central Crossroads 36 1 34N38 85W45 5:43:00
Central Heights 39 1 34N53'40 87W47'27 5:51:10
Central Highlands 37 1 33N33'15 86W42'58 5:46:52
Central Mills 24 1 32N17'10 87W26'27 5:49:46
Central Park Highlands 37 6 33N29'24 86W52'55 5:47:32
Centre 10 1 34N09'07 85W40'44 5:42:43
Centreville 4 1 32N56'40 87W08'19 5:48:33
Ceramic 57 7 32N28 85W01 5:40:04
Chalkville 37 1 33N39'11 86W38'52 5:46:35
Chalybeate Springs 40 1 34N33'54 87W13'36 5:48:54
Chambers 63 1 33N14'30 87W09'29 5:48:38
Chambers Springs 14 1 33N17'31 86W02'26 5:44:10
Chamblees Mill 5 1 34N03'42 86W40'10 5:46:41
Champion 5 1 33N56'08 86W26'44 5:45:47
Chance 13 1 31N44'55 87W31'55 5:50:08
Chancellor 31 1 31N10'53 85W52'38 5:43:31
Chancellor Crossroads 59 1 33N17'47 86W23'59 5:45:36
Chances Crossroad 22 1 34N10'27 87W03'31 5:48:14
Chandler Springs 61 1 33N19'50 85W59'54 5:44:00
Chapel Hill 9 5 32N59'40 85W25'59 5:41:44
Chapel Hill 12 1 32N14'23 88W11'19 5:52:45
Chapel Hill 37 6 33N23'55 86W47'52 5:47:11
Chapel Hill 64 1 33N49'02 87W12'37 5:48:50
Chapel Hill 65 1 31N41'36 88W26'25 5:53:46
Chapman 7 1 31N40'16 86W42'44 5:46:51
Chapman Heights 45 2 34N45'13 86W34'08 5:46:17
Chase 45 2 34N47'00 86W32'48 5:46:11
Chastang 49 1 31N02'15 88W01'24 5:52:06
Chatom 65 1 31N27'54 88W15'16 5:53:01
Chavies 25 1 34N28'22 85W48'49 5:43:15
Chehaw 44 1 32N28'48 85W43'08 5:42:53
Chelsea 45 2 34N41'26 86W36'36 5:46:26
Chelsea 59 1 33N20'24 86W37'49 5:46:31
Chepultepec 5 1 33N54'14 86W29'41 5:45:59
Cherokee 17 1 34N45'25 87W58'22 5:51:53
Cherokee Bluffs 62 1 32N40'55 85W54'23 5:43:38
Cherokee Forest 37 6 33N28'07 86W45'58 5:47:04
Cherokee Village 21 1 31N43'46 86W20'13 5:45:21
Cherry Grove 42 1 34N54'50 87W12'10 5:48:49
Cherrytree 45 2 34N38'44 86W26'40 5:45:47
Chesson 44 1 32N17'37 85W55'28 5:43:42
Chestang 65 1 31N09'42 88W06'52 5:52:27
Chesterfield 10 1 34N26'48 85W31'26 5:42:06
Chestnut 50 1 31N48'27 87W13'56 5:48:56
Chestnut Grove 16 1 31N35'49 85W54'49 5:43:39
Chetopa 37 1 33N40'44 86W58'05 5:47:52
Chewacla 41 5 32N37'12 85W20'14 5:41:21
Chickasaw 49 1 30N45'49 88W04'29 5:52:18
Chickasaw Terrace 49 1 30N44 88W05 5:52:20
Chigger Hill 25 1 34N23'51 86W00'59 5:44:04
Childersburg 61 1 33N16'41 86W21'18 5:45:25
Chilton 13 1 31N46'55 87W50'39 5:51:23
China 18 1 31N31'24 87W01'04 5:48:04
China Grove 55 1 32N01'46 85W56'41 5:43:47
Chinn 37 1 33N22'19 87W02'53 5:48:12
Chinnabee 61 1 33N27'46 85W58'01 5:43:52
Chisholm 51 4 32N25'02 86W17'08 5:45:09
Choccolocco 8 1 33N39'33 85W42'13 5:42:49
Choctaw Bluff 13 1 31N23'19 87W47'20 5:51:09
Choctaw City 12 1 32N12'32 88W05'39 5:52:23
Choctow Corner 13 1 31N55 87W45 5:51:00
Chosea Springs 8 6 33N40 85W50 5:43:20
Christiana 56 1 33N22'38 85W38'25 5:42:34
Christmas Landing 13 1 31N42'41 88W05'26 5:52:22
Chrysler 50 1 31N18'18 87W42'04 5:50:48
Chulafinnee 15 1 33N32'43 85W38'56 5:42:36
Chulavista 58 1 33N35'44 86W22'00 5:45:28
Chunchula 49 1 30N55'18 88W12'02 5:52:48
Chunnenuggee 6 1 32N09'23 85W38'37 5:42:34
Church Hill 62 1 32N44 85W37 5:42:28
Circlewood 63 6 33N12 87W32 5:50:08
Citico 28 6 34N04'57 85W55'53 5:43:44
Citronelle 49 1 31N05'26 88W13'41 5:52:55
Clackville 9 5 33N05'20 85W27'03 5:41:48
Claiborne 50 1 31N32'24 87W30'56 5:50:04
Claiborne Landing 50 1 31N33'00 87W30'50 5:50:03
Clairmont Springs 14 1 33N21'01 85W55'49 5:43:43
Clanton 11 1 32N50'19 86W37'46 5:46:31
Clarence 5 1 34N05'01 86W25'42 5:45:43
Clark Crossroads 35 1 31N11'43 85W28'33 5:41:54
Clarkdale 45 2 34N48'26 86W46'22 5:47:05
Clarke 64 1 33N54'52 87W34'36 5:50:18
Clarksville 13 1 31N43'44 87W53'35 5:51:34
Clarksville Landing 45 2 34N29'15 86W30'18 5:46:01
Claud 26 1 32N34'44 86W04'14 5:44:17
Clay 37 1 33N42'09 86W35'59 5:46:24
Clay City 2 1 30N29'08 87W48'24 5:51:14
Clayhatchee 23 1 31N14'08 85W43'22 5:42:53
Clayhill 46 1 32N00'59 87W45'02 5:51:00
Claysville 48 1 34N24'28 86W16'19 5:45:05
Clayton 3 1 31N52'41 85W26'59 5:41:48
Clear Springs 5 1 33N51'48 86W33'51 5:46:15
Clearview 20 1 31N27'02 86W26'52 5:45:47
Clearview 21 1 31N57 86W19 5:45:16
Cleburne 15 1 33N38'53 85W37'47 5:42:31
Clemons Crossroad 52 1 34N28'30 86W53'46 5:47:35
Cleveland 5 1 33N59'27 86W34'39 5:46:19
Cleveland 29 1 33N41'22 87W38'59 5:50:36
Cleveland Crossroads 14 1 33N06'47 85W59'15 5:43:57
Cleveland Mills 53 1 32N42'15 87W11'56 5:48:48
Cliff Haven 17 1 34N46'38 87W40'23 5:50:42
Clift Acres 45 2 34N42'11 86W44'16 5:46:57
Clinton 32 1 32N54'49 87W59'33 5:51:58
Clintonville 16 1 31N24'25 85W53'39 5:43:35
Clio 3 1 31N42'31 85W36'38 5:42:27
Clopton 23 1 31N36'30 85W25'48 5:41:43

Cloverdale 37 6 33N36'09 86W42'56 5:46:52
Cloverdale 39 1 34N56'19 87W46'17 5:51:05
Cloverdale 63 6 33N14'02 87W38'06 5:50:32
Cloverdale Heights 39 1 34N52'11 87W41'31 5:50:46
Clover Hill 43 1 31N59'52 86W42'06 5:46:48
Cloverland 51 4 32N20 86W19 5:45:16
Clowers Crossroads 16 1 31N35'29 85W53'36 5:43:34
Clubview Heights 28 6 33N58'41 86W00'57 5:44:04
Cluttsville 45 2 34N49'50 86W44'57 5:47:00
Coal Bluff 66 1 31N56'42 87W26'18 5:49:45
Coalburg 37 6 33N35'37 86W51'26 5:47:26
Coal City 58 1 33N39'38 86W15'48 5:45:03
Coaldale 37 1 33N49'36 86W47'27 5:47:10
Coal Fire 54 1 33N24'14 88W05'05 5:52:20
Coaling 63 1 33N09'32 87W20'27 5:49:22
Coalmont 59 1 33N15'17 86W52'59 5:47:32
Coal Valley 64 1 33N44'24 87W25'05 5:49:40
Coates 34 1 31N43'35 85W09'00 5:40:36
Coatopa 60 1 32N29'06 88W04'10 5:52:17
Cobb City 28 1 33N55'00 85W54'45 5:43:39
Cobbs Ford 26 4 32N27 86W19 5:45:16
Cobbs Landing Access Point 66 1 32N04'01 87W24'05 5:49:36
Cobb Town 8 6 33N38'34 85W52'03 5:43:28
Cochrane 54 1 33N03'55 88W15'04 5:53:00
Cochran Landing 66 1 32N02'50 87W15'41 5:49:03
Coden 49 1 30N22'58 88W14'18 5:52:57
Cody 38 1 33N41 87W50 5:51:20
Coffee Springs 31 1 31N09'52 85W54'34 5:43:38
Coffeeville 13 1 31N45'28 88W05'23 5:52:22
Coffeeville Landing 13 1 31N45'23 88W06'06 5:52:24
Cohassett 18 1 31N23'41 86W41'36 5:46:46
Coker 63 1 33N14'45 87W41'16 5:50:45
Colbert 57 7 32N16'57 85W14'12 5:40:57
Colbert Heights 17 1 34N39'39 87W41'40 5:50:47
Cold Spring (Bremen P O) 22 1 33N58'54 87W02'00 5:48:08
Cold Spring 26 1 32N36'32 86W22'05 5:45:28
Cold Springs 22 1 33N54 86W58 5:47:52
Cold Springs 26 1 32N37 86W24 5:45:36
Coldwater 8 1 33N35'10 85W55'06 5:43:40
Coldwater 15 1 33N44 85W26 5:41:44
Coldwater 20 1 31N26'05 86W25'24 5:45:42
Coleanor 4 1 33N05'44 87W02'09 5:48:09
Coleman 53 1 32N36'02 87W28'41 5:49:55
Cole Spring 52 1 34N21'14 86W49'58 5:47:20
Collbran 25 1 34N22'33 85W46'43 5:43:07
Collins 37 1 33N26'47 86W57'52 5:47:51
Collins Chapel 11 1 32N56'33 86W40'50 5:46:43
Collinsville 25 1 34N15'50 85W51'38 5:43:27
Collirene 43 1 32N10'33 86W49'25 5:47:18
Coloma 10 1 34N09 85W41 5:42:44
Colonial Heights 17 1 34N42'52 87W41'02 5:50:44
Colony 63 6 33N14 87W36 5:50:24
Columbia 35 1 31N17'33 85W06'42 5:40:27
Columbiana 59 1 33N10'41 86W36'26 5:46:26
Columbus 37 1 33N45'29 86W45'12 5:47:01
Columbus City 48 1 34N27'38 86W14'00 5:44:56
Colwell 8 1 33N52'45 85W55'09 5:43:41
Comer 3 1 32N01'58 85W23'00 5:41:32
Commerce 18 1 31N40'54 86W58'02 5:47:52
Compton Landing 46 1 32N07'44 88W02'25 5:52:10
Concord 5 1 33N59 86W35 5:46:20
Concord 37 1 33N28'03 87W01'52 5:48:07
Congo 10 1 34N18'39 85W39'03 5:42:36
Conifer 26 1 32N31 85W53 5:43:32
Consul 46 1 32N15'51 87W32'24 5:50:10
Contwell 12 1 31N42'29 88W25'43 5:53:43
Cooks 51 1 32N24'41 86W08'48 5:44:35
Cooks Crossroads 18 1 31N34'05 86W58'35 5:47:54
Cooks Springs 58 1 33N35'24 86W23'40 5:45:35
Cooley Crossroads 14 1 33N10'06 85W42'21 5:42:49
Cool Springs 58 1 33N47'48 86W19'45 5:45:19
Coon Creek 64 1 33N49'52 87W01'42 5:48:07
Cooper 11 1 32N46'30 86W32'44 5:46:11
Coopers Mill 36 1 34N56'53 85W47'58 5:43:12
Coosa Court 61 1 33N16'45 86W20'44 5:45:23
Coosada 26 1 32N30 86W20 5:45:20
Coosa Pines 61 1 33N19'39 86W21'33 5:45:26
Coosa River 26 1 32N38'52 86W22'11 5:45:29
Copeland 65 1 31N33'36 88W25'09 5:53:41
Copeland Bridge 25 1 34N17'48 85W53'07 5:43:32
Copeland School 42 1 34N50'07 86W49'53 5:47:20
Copper Springs 58 1 33N40'25 86W26'27 5:45:46
Coppinville 16 1 31N18'33 85W48'52 5:43:15
Corbinville 48 1 34N16'59 86W11'15 5:44:45
Corcoran 55 1 31N49'53 85W56'59 5:43:48
Cordova 64 1 33N45'35 87W11'00 5:48:44
Corinth 6 1 31N54'13 85W45'16 5:43:01
Corinth 22 1 34N18'16 87W04'24 5:48:18
Corinth 56 1 33N10'06 85W33'27 5:42:14
Corinth 64 1 33N47'06 87W12'12 5:48:49
Corner 37 1 33N48'01 86W56'32 5:47:46
Cornerstone 6 1 32N09'21 85W50'32 5:43:22
Cornhouse 56 1 33N13'21 85W27'21 5:41:49
Cornwall Furnace 10 1 34N14'26 85W35'14 5:42:21
Corona 64 1 33N42'30 87W28'10 5:49:53
Cortelyou 65 1 31N25'24 88W00'30 5:52:02
Cotaco 52 1 34N28 86W48 5:47:12
Cottage Grove 19 1 32N51'20 86W07'21 5:44:29
Cottage Hill 37 1 33N28'55 86W58'42 5:47:55
Cottage Hill 49 1 30N39'00 88W08'46 5:52:35
Cotton 26 1 32N40'52 86W01'04 5:44:04
Cottondale 63 1 33N11'22 87W27'06 5:49:48
Cotton Hill 3 1 31N50'04 85W16'50 5:41:07
Cottonton 57 7 32N08'48 85W04'26 5:40:18
Cottontown 17 1 34N39'19 87W28'52 5:49:55
Cotton Valley 44 1 32N17'34 85W41'32 5:42:46
Cottonville 48 1 34N27'12 86W20'08 5:45:21
Cottonwood 35 1 31N02'55 85W18'18 5:41:13
Council Bluff 25 1 34N35'12 85W40'24 5:42:42
Country Club Acres 42 1 34N45'18 86W57'19 5:47:49
Country Club Estates 49 1 30N41'01 88W08'57 5:52:36
Country Club Highlands 37 6 33N25 86W48 5:47:12
Country Club Village 49 1 30N41'39 88W09'53 5:52:40
Country Estates 37 1 33N38'04 86W40'00 5:46:40
County Line 5 1 33N49'17 86W43'07 5:46:52
County Line 20 1 31N13 86W10 5:44:40
County Line 22 1 34N17'57 86W41'53 5:46:48
Courtland 40 1 34N40'08 87W18'34 5:49:14
Covin 38 1 33N41'24 87W53'21 5:51:33
Cowarts 35 1 31N12'00 85W18'17 5:41:13
Cowpens 62 1 33N02'07 85W49'22 5:43:17
Cox 4 1 32N51'17 86W53'00 5:47:32
Cox Beach 49 1 30N51'07 88W02'24 5:52:10
Coxey 42 1 34N48'07 87W10'42 5:48:43
Coxheath 46 1 32N05'16 87W54'37 5:51:38
Coxs Landing 13 1 31N49'56 88W10'01 5:52:40
Coy 66 1 31N53'41 87W27'46 5:49:51
Cragford 14 1 33N15'03 85W40'21 5:42:41
Craig 24 1 32N22 86W59 5:47:56
Craig Air Force Base 24 1 32N23 87W00 5:48:00
Crane Hill 22 1 34N05'38 87W03'47 5:48:15
Crawford 57 7 32N27'24 85W11'23 5:40:46
Crawford Fork 32 1 32N49'04 88W03'15 5:52:13
Creek Ford 48 1 34N34'11 86W19'55 5:45:20
Creek Stand 44 1 32N17'40 85W28'39 5:41:55
Creel 64 1 33N48'47 86W59'40 5:47:59
Creola 49 1 30N53'30 88W02'23 5:52:10
Crescent Heights 37 1 33N26'19 86W54'57 5:47:40
Crestline 37 6 33N29 86W46 5:47:04
Crestline Gardens 37 1 33N31'15 86W43'22 5:46:53
Crestline Heights 37 6 33N30'24 86W45'10 5:47:01
Crestline Park 37 6 33N30'49 86W44'02 5:46:56
Crestview Gardens 58 1 33N35'39 86W16'09 5:45:05
Crestview Hills 37 6 33N31'24 86W44'02 5:46:56
Creswell 59 1 33N19'45 86W22'59 5:45:32
Crews 38 1 33N54'47 88W04'50 5:52:19
Crewsville 19 1 32N56'36 86W08'12 5:44:33
Crichton 49 1 30N42'22 88W06'22 5:52:25
Crockard Junction 37 1 33N32'08 86W59'07 5:47:56
Crocker Junction 37 1 33N40'03 86W54'38 5:47:39
Cromwell 12 1 32N13'43 88W16'28 5:53:06
Crooked Oak 17 1 34N35'06 87W47'58 5:51:12
Cropwell 58 1 33N33'08 86W16'09 5:45:05
Crosby 35 1 31N02'19 85W05'11 5:40:21
Cross Key 42 1 34N52'16 87W01'06 5:48:04
Cross Keys 44 1 32N20'01 85W53'36 5:43:34
Crossroad 36 1 34N30'20 86W03'01 5:44:12
Crossroads 2 1 30N50'05 87W51'40 5:51:27
Cross Roads 13 1 31N37 88W01 5:52:04
Crossroads 48 1 34N19'19 86W19'54 5:45:20
Crosston 37 1 33N43'42 86W43'54 5:46:56
Crossville 25 1 34N17'15 85W59'39 5:43:59
Crossville 38 1 33N44'38 88W00'08 5:52:01
Crowtown 52 3 34N32'40 86W55'14 5:47:41
Crudup 28 6 34N06'07 86W00'36 5:44:02
Crumley Chapel 37 6 33N34'14 86W54'46 5:47:39
Crumptonia 24 1 32N12'49 87W17'22 5:49:09
Cuba 60 1 32N25'41 88W22'35 5:53:30
Culebra 9 5 32N49'00 85W32'07 5:42:08
Cullman 22 1 34N10'29 86W50'37 5:47:22
Cullomburg 12 1 31N42'49 88W17'49 5:53:11
Culpeper 66 1 31N53'13 87W34'39 5:50:19
Cumbee Mill 9 5 33N04'07 85W18'51 5:41:15
Cumberland Junction 36 1 34N56'35 85W46'04 5:43:04
Cunningham 13 1 31N54'01 88W04'34 5:52:18
Cunningham 54 1 33N10'26 88W06'27 5:52:26
Cunningham Landing 13 1 31N54'43 88W05'05 5:52:20
Curry 55 1 31N56'28 86W02'39 5:44:11
Curry 61 1 33N29'11 86W01'02 5:44:04
Curry 64 1 33N57'13 87W12'52 5:48:51
Currys 51 1 32N01'06 86W04'51 5:44:19
Currytown 23 1 31N19 85W29 5:41:56
Curtis 16 1 31N23'51 86W09'25 5:44:38
Curtis Crossroads 67 1 34N04'38 87W21'24 5:49:26
Curtiston 28 6 34N00'04 86W07'17 5:44:29
Cusseta 9 5 32N47'05 85W18'21 5:41:13
Cypress 32 1 32N56'52 87W40'01 5:50:40
Cypress Heights 39 1 34N49'22 87W42'55 5:50:52
Cyril 12 1 32N10'41 88W25'20 5:53:41
Dadeville 62 1 32N49'52 85W45'49 5:43:03
Daisey City 37 1 33N37'01 86W55'18 5:47:41
Daisy 7 1 31N53'56 86W29'05 5:45:56
Daisy 28 6 34N04'03 85W57'27 5:43:50
Dale Ferry Landing 50 1 31N28'49 87W33'49 5:50:15
Daleville 23 1 31N18'36 85W42'47 5:42:51
Dallas 5 1 33N50'58 86W39'38 5:46:39
Dallas 45 2 34N44'38 86W34'36 5:46:18
Damascus 16 1 31N19'13 86W00'16 5:44:01
Damascus 27 1 31N10'22 86W51'25 5:47:26
Dancy 54 1 33N00'40 88W17'34 5:53:10
Danielsville 21 1 31N55'14 86W24'23 5:45:38
Danleys Crossroads 16 1 31N25'08 86W10'04 5:44:40
Danville 37 6 33N35'32 86W46'12 5:47:05
Danville 52 1 34N24'52 87W05'15 5:48:21
Danway 9 5 32N45'30 85W22'38 5:41:31
Danzey 34 1 31N28'02 85W17'26 5:41:10
Daphne 2 1 30N36'12 87W54'13 5:51:37
Dargin 59 1 33N09'08 86W45'32 5:47:02
Darling Landing 2 1 30N26'35 87W54'48 5:51:39
Darlington 66 1 31N58'39 87W07'50 5:48:31
Darrah 33 1 32N51'20 87W47'18 5:51:09
Darwin Downs 45 2 34N44'42 86W33'47 5:46:15
Dauphin Island 49 1 30N15'19 88W06'35 5:52:26
Davis Crossroads 51 1 32N08'08 86W10'33 5:44:42
Davis Hills 45 2 34N45'56 86W36'43 5:46:27
Davis Landing 13 1 31N14'23 87W50'43 5:51:23
Daviston 62 1 33N03'10 85W38'23 5:42:34
Davistown 36 1 34N32'30 86W01'11 5:44:05
Davisville 44 1 32N19'39 85W40'11 5:42:41
Dawes 49 1 30N36'27 88W15'19 5:53:01
Dawson 25 1 34N18'14 85W55'34 5:43:42
Dayton 46 1 32N21'03 87W38'31 5:50:34
Deans 18 1 31N39'36 86W56'20 5:47:45
Deans Landing 60 1 32N23'18 88W02'44 5:52:11
DeArmanville 8 1 33N37'35 85W45'05 5:43:00
Deas 12 1 32N13'45 88W05'50 5:52:23
Deason Hill 64 1 33N46 87W11 5:48:44
Deatsville 26 1 32N36'29 86W23'45 5:45:35
Deavers Town 5 1 33N55'23 86W35'15 5:46:21
Deavertown 5 1 33N59 86W35 5:46:20
Decatur 52 3 34N36'21 86W59'00 5:47:56
Decatur Junction 42 3 34N37'36 86W58'15 5:47:53
Deerhurst 59 1 33N16'59 86W45'49 5:47:03
Deer Park 65 1 31N13'00 88W19'02 5:53:16
DeFoor 67 1 34N13'14 87W34'04 5:50:16
Delchamps 49 1 30N24'02 88W08'56 5:52:36
Dells Vista Shores 39 1 34N45'43 87W16'29 5:49:06
Delma 54 1 33N23'10 88W11'04 5:52:44
Delmar 67 1 34N10'12 87W36'21 5:50:25
Delta 14 1 33N26'24 85W41'26 5:42:46
Demopolis 46 1 32N31'03 87W50'11 5:51:21
Dempsey 30 1 34N29'03 87W56'59 5:51:48
Denson 9 5 32N55'57 85W18'07 5:41:12
Denver 62 1 32N59'38 85W36'24 5:42:26
Deposit 45 2 34N51'08 86W27'29 5:45:50
Derby 60 1 32N21'44 88W10'28 5:52:42
Derder Landing 60 1 32N37'50 87W55'51 5:51:43
Detroit 38 1 34N01'41 88W10'12 5:52:41
Devenport 51 1 32N03'56 86W24'23 5:45:38
Dewey 10 1 34N19'34 85W30'28 5:42:02
Dexter 26 1 32N38'21 86W08'59 5:44:36
Diamond 48 1 34N18'08 86W23'47 5:45:35
Dickert 56 1 33N07'54 85W28'23 5:41:54
Dickinson (Dickenson Station 13 1 31N45'48 87W42'38 5:50:51
Dill 23 1 31N30'39 85W39'13 5:42:37
Dillard 23 1 31N31'03 85W41'42 5:42:47
Dillburg 54 1 33N11'37 88W06'05 5:52:24
Dilworth 64 1 33N48'08 87W03'13 5:48:13
Dime 30 1 31N55 87W59 5:51:56
Dingler 56 1 33N19'52 85W37'51 5:42:31
Dixiana 37 1 33N44 86W42 5:46:48
Dixie 11 1 32N43'23 86W54'21 5:47:37
Dixie 27 1 31N09 86W44 5:46:56
Dixieland 57 7 32N28 85W01 5:40:04
Dixie Springs 64 1 33N42'49 87W22'15 5:49:29
Dixon Corner 49 1 30N27'07 88W14'31 5:52:58
Dixon Shop 10 1 34N08'24 85W45'33 5:43:02
Dixons Mills 46 1 32N03'29 87W47'15 5:51:09
Dixonville 27 1 31N00'01 87W02'10 5:48:09
Docena 37 1 33N33'34 86W55'52 5:47:43
Dock 7 1 31N50 86W38 5:46:32
Docray 63 1 33N13'25 87W09'56 5:48:40
Dog 25 1 34N24 85W41 5:42:44
Dog Town 25 1 34N21'10 85W44'13 5:42:57
Dogtown 64 1 33N56'53 87W34'00 5:50:16
Dogwood 25 1 34N27 85W43 5:42:52
Dogwood 59 1 33N09'04 86W52'23 5:47:30
Dolcito 37 6 33N35 86W46 5:47:04
Doliska 64 1 33N42'42 87W06'04 5:48:24
D'Olive 2 1 30N52'13 87W47'45 5:51:11
Dollar 19 1 32N52'43 86W25'27 5:45:42
Dolomite 37 1 33N27'46 86W57'41 5:47:51
Dolonar 37 1 33N23'20 86W59'29 5:47:58
Dolonar Junction 37 1 33N25'35 86W58'17 5:47:53
Donaldson Mill 67 1 34N15'03 87W37'33 5:50:30
Dora 64 1 33N43'43 87W05'25 5:48:22
Dora Junction 64 1 33N45'39 87W03'41 5:48:15
Doster 3 1 31N38'51 85W40'26 5:42:42
Dosterville 1 1 32N26'18 86W26'59 5:45:48
Dothan 35 1 31N13'23 85W23'26 5:41:34
Double Bridges 34 1 31N33 85W15 5:41:00
Double Bridges 48 1 34N13'56 86W07'25 5:44:30
Doublehead 9 5 33N05'39 85W23'39 5:41:35
Double Springs 67 1 34N08'47 87W24'08 5:49:37
Douglas 25 1 34N25'37 85W43'43 5:42:55
Douglas 48 1 34N10'25 86W19'25 5:45:18
Douglasville 2 1 30N51'57 87W47'08 5:51:09
Douglasville 37 6 33N33'15 86W47'54 5:47:12
Dove 60 1 32N29'29 88W23'29 5:53:34
Dovertown 64 1 33N44'16 87W09'13 5:48:37
Dowdle 63 1 33N10'51 87W12'36 5:48:50
Downing 51 1 32N10 86W00 5:44:00
Downs 44 1 32N15'53 85W47'03 5:43:08
Dozier 21 1 31N29'31 86W21'54 5:45:28
Drewry 50 1 31N29'10 87W15'11 5:49:01
Drifton 64 1 33N40'53 87W13'58 5:48:56

Dripping Springs 22
1 34N14'32 87W00'16 5:48:01
Drummond 64 1 33N46'58 87W01'07 5:48:04
Dry Forks 66 1 31N54'05 87W22'00 5:49:28
Dry Valley 61 1 33N35'00 86W05'27 5:44:22
Dublin 51 1 32N01'55 86W09'33 5:44:38
Duck Springs 28 1 34N08'45 85W59'57 5:44:00
Dudley 63 1 33N09'39 87W18'00 5:49:12
Dudleyville 62 1 32N54'54 85W36'00 5:42:24
Dug Hill 45 2 34N42'48 86W29'16 5:45:57
Duke 8 1 33N51'02 85W54'09 5:43:37
Duketon 30 1 34N21'54 87W49'56 5:51:20
Dulin 47 1 33N55 87W48 5:51:12
Dunavant 59 1 33N29'36 86W32'39 5:46:11
Dunbar 65 1 31N40'41 88W20'46 5:53:23
Duncan 37 6 33N27'25 86W52'58 5:47:32
Duncan Crossroads 36
1 34N32'40 85W54'52 5:43:39
Duncanville 63 1 33N03'42 87W26'32 5:49:46
Dundee 31 1 31N07'13 85W40'18 5:42:41
Dunn 55 1 31N50'42 85W53'46 5:43:35
Dunns 20 1 31N25'55 86W28'11 5:45:53
Dupree 35 1 31N07'42 85W14'02 5:40:56
Dupree 41 5 32N28'06 85W22'04 5:41:28
Dutton 36 1 34N36'39 85W55'01 5:43:40
Duvall 20 1 31N16'34 86W14'31 5:44:58
Dwight 65 1 31N09'06 88W15'31 5:53:02
Dyas 2 1 30N57'44 87W40'34 5:50:42
Dyers Crossroads 22
1 34N14'57 86W49'14 5:47:17
Dykes Crossroad 23
1 31N36'00 85W33'40 5:42:15
Eady City 9 5 32N49'41 85W10'30 5:40:42
Eagle 67 1 34N08'48 87W10'56 5:48:44
Earlytown 31 1 31N07'42 86W07'46 5:44:31
Easley 5 1 33N57'33 86W32'33 5:46:10
Eastaboga 8 1 33N36'21 86W01'17 5:44:05
East Birmingham 37
6 33N32'39 86W46'55 5:47:08
East Brewton 27 1 31N05'35 87W03'46 5:48:15
East Brighton 37
1 33N26'13 86W57'06 5:47:48
Eastbrook 51 4 32N23 86W15 5:45:00
East Brookwood 63
1 33N16'39 87W17'25 5:49:10
East Chapman 7 1 31N39'56 86W41'48 5:46:47
Eastern Valley 37
1 33N21'34 86W58'07 5:47:52
East Escambia 27
1 31N06 86W55 5:47:40
East Florence 39
1 34N48'34 87W38'58 5:50:36
East Gadsden 28 1 34N00'09 85W58'07 5:43:52
East Hampton 42 1 34N47'34 86W55'55 5:47:44
East Haven 37 1 33N37'23 86W41'02 5:46:44
East Irondale 37
1 33N31'50 86W41'20 5:46:45
East Jasper 64 1 33N50 87W14 5:48:56
East Killen 39 1 34N51'41 87W31'32 5:50:06
East Lake 37 6 33N34'00 86W43'30 5:46:54
East Mill 14 1 33N07'49 86W03'10 5:44:13
Easton 62 1 32N54'33 85W41'48 5:42:47
East Point 22 1 34N10'59 86W47'37 5:47:10
East Port Landing 33
1 32N44'55 87W48'19 5:51:13
East Royles 37 6 33N34'00 86W47'04 5:47:08
East Saginaw 59 1 33N17'07 86W39'27 5:46:38
East Side 63 6 33N12 87W32 5:50:08
East Tallassee 62
1 32N32 85W53 5:43:32
East Thomas 37 6 33N31'10 86W50'17 5:47:21
East Thomas Gardens 37
6 33N31'47 86W51'55 5:47:28
Eastwood 5 1 33N56'27 86W27'26 5:45:50
Eastwood 37 6 33N32'53 86W45'41 5:47:03
Ebenezer 22 1 34N14 86W52 5:47:28
Echo 23 1 31N28'32 85W27'57 5:41:52
Echola 63 1 33N20'41 87W47'22 5:51:09
Echols Crossroads 52
1 34N31'36 86W47'21 5:47:09
Echols Hill 45 2 34N43'53 86W34'31 5:46:18
Eclectic 26 1 32N38'07 86W02'04 5:44:08
Eddy 48 1 34N21'19 86W30'34 5:46:02
Eden 58 1 33N35'31 86W18'37 5:45:14
Edgefield 3 1 31N43'00 85W22'20 5:41:29
Edgefield 36 1 34N54'14 85W48'30 5:43:14
Edgemont 37 6 33N27'56 86W49'21 5:47:17
Edgemont Park 37
6 33N27'11 86W49'57 5:47:20
Edgemoor Estates 37
6 33N27'25 86W49'56 5:47:20
Edgewater 37 1 33N31'36 86W57'28 5:47:50
Edgewater Junction 37
1 33N31'51 86W57'32 5:47:50
Edgewood 37 6 33N28'03 86W48'39 5:47:15
Edmonton Heights 45
2 34N46'39 86W33'59 5:46:16
Edna 12 1 32N17'12 88W04'27 5:52:18
Edsons 43 1 32N19'05 86W46'31 5:47:06
Edwardsville 15 1 33N42'26 85W30'33 5:42:02
Edwin 34 1 31N39'55 85W22'31 5:41:30
Egypt 28 1 34N04'25 86W09'21 5:44:37
Egypt 48 1 34N20'39 86W32'02 5:46:08
Egypt Ford 40 1 34N44'14 87W20'24 5:49:22
Eight Mile 49 1 30N45'48 88W07'37 5:52:30
Eiler 12 1 31N57'45 88W25'25 5:53:42
Elamville 3 1 31N40'03 85W39'23 5:42:38
Elba 16 1 31N24'52 86W04'04 5:44:16
Elberta 2 1 30N24'51 87W35'52 5:50:23
Eldridge 64 1 33N55'22 87W37'02 5:50:28
Eleanor 24 1 32N20'24 87W19'09 5:49:17
Elgin 39 1 34N50'55 87W23'28 5:49:34
Eliska 50 1 31N21'09 87W40'59 5:50:44
Elkmont 42 1 34N55'44 86W58'26 5:47:54
Elko 45 2 34N42'33 86W40'16 5:46:41
Elkwood 45 1 34N58'39 86W43'25 5:46:54
Ellards 53 1 32N48'53 87W15'39 5:49:03
Elliotsville 59 1 33N12 86W47 5:47:08
Elliott Crossroads 25
1 34N36'46 85W46'07 5:43:04
Ellis 24 1 32N08'10 87W14'07 5:48:56
Ellis Crossroads 43
1 31N58'41 86W27'05 5:45:48
Ellison Crossroads 5
1 34N02'43 86W20'07 5:45:20
Ellisville 2 1 30N37 87W45 5:51:00
Ellisville 10 1 34N03'53 85W36'36 5:42:26
Ellisville 65 1 31N32'43 88W12'48 5:52:51
Elm Bluff 24 1 32N09'10 87W04'19 5:48:17
Elmore 26 1 32N32'19 86W18'54 5:45:16
Elon 45 2 34N32'34 86W28'08 5:45:53
Elrath 10 1 34N08'17 85W44'35 5:42:58
Elrod 63 1 33N15'22 87W47'32 5:51:10
Elsanor 2 1 30N32'42 87W35'01 5:50:20
Elsmeade 51 4 32N20 86W16 5:45:04
Elting 39 1 34N49 87W40 5:50:40
Elvira 59 1 33N19'24 86W51'57 5:47:28
Elyton 37 6 33N30'05 86W50'27 5:47:22
Emauhee 61 1 33N13'13 86W11'34 5:44:46
Emco-Listerhill Junction 17
1 34N42'49 87W35'36 5:50:22
Emelle 60 1 32N43'45 88W18'52 5:53:15
Emerald Shores 39
1 34N51'29 87W34'09 5:50:17
Emory 12 1 31N48'38 88W27'27 5:53:50
Empire 64 1 33N48'30 87W00'38 5:48:03
Englewood 63 6 33N06'42 87W33'35 5:50:14
English Village 37
6 33N29'39 86W46'56 5:47:08
English Village 45
2 34N37'35 86W34'11 5:46:17
Enoe 64 1 33N40'40 87W23'19 5:49:33
Enon 6 1 32N09'19 85W29'48 5:41:59
Enon 22 1 34N18'11 86W47'04 5:47:08
Enon 35 1 31N12'56 85W16'37 5:41:06
Enon 55 1 31N49'32 85W42'23 5:42:50
Ensley 37 6 33N30'34 86W53'10 5:47:33
Ensley Junction 37
1 33N29'36 86W55'05 5:47:40
Enterprise 11 1 32N44'05 86W37'05 5:46:28
Enterprise 16 1 31N18'54 85W51'19 5:43:25
Eoda 20 1 31N22'28 86W19'09 5:45:17
Eoline 4 1 32N59'42 87W13'56 5:48:56
Epes 60 1 32N41'25 88W07'34 5:52:30
Equality 62 1 32N45'43 86W06'07 5:44:24
Erin 14 1 33N21'45 85W54'31 5:43:38
Erratta 59 1 33N18'01 86W22'20 5:45:29
Escatawpa 65 1 31N17'22 88W23'14 5:53:33
Estelle 66 1 31N58'09 87W12'09 5:48:49
Estes Crossroads 10
1 33N59'45 85W42'36 5:42:50
Estillfork 36 1 34N54'36 86W10'14 5:44:41
Estothel 20 1 31N14'40 86W11'54 5:44:48
Ethel 55 1 31N49 85W51 5:43:24
Ethelsville 54 1 33N24'56 88W13'00 5:52:52
Euclid Estates 37
6 33N30'38 86W44'43 5:46:59
Eufaula 3 1 31N53'28 85W08'44 5:40:35
Eulaton 8 1 33N38'44 85W54'45 5:43:39
Eunola 31 1 31N02'23 85W50'51 5:43:23
Eureka 36 1 34N54'00 85W53'01 5:43:32
Eureka Landing 50
1 31N24'08 87W41'51 5:50:47
Eutaw 32 1 32N50'26 87W53'15 5:51:33
Eva 52 1 34N19'56 86W45'32 5:47:02
Evansboro 12 1 31N53'01 88W28'05 5:53:52
Evansville 33 1 32N50'17 87W45'09 5:51:01
Everglade 62 1 32N59'52 85W39'19 5:42:37
Evergreen 1 1 32N33'08 86W45'28 5:47:02
Evergreen 18 1 31N26'00 86W57'25 5:47:50
Ewell 23 1 31N25'17 85W34'29 5:42:18
Ewing 10 1 34N12'09 85W45'52 5:43:03
Ewing 28 1 33N59'26 85W54'21 5:43:37
Ewing Farms 27 1 31N04'57 87W35'15 5:50:21
Excel 50 1 31N25'40 87W20'29 5:49:22
Exmoor 46 1 32N03'23 87W52'27 5:51:30
Exum 37 1 33N30'10 86W56'00 5:47:44
Ezra 37 1 33N26'45 87W08'35 5:48:34
Fabius 36 1 34N48'39 85W46'39 5:43:07
Fackler 36 1 34N47'33 85W54'36 5:43:38
Fadette 31 1 31N02'40 85W32'15 5:42:09
Failetown 13 1 31N55'40 88W00'59 5:52:04
Fairdale 4 1 32N55'52 87W08'46 5:48:35
Fairfax 9 5 32N47'46 85W11'02 5:40:44
Fairfield 20 1 31N15'06 86W38'44 5:46:35
Fairfield 37 1 33N33'46 86W47'53 5:47:12
Fairfield 40 1 34N28'27 87W11'35 5:48:46
Fairfield Highlands 37
1 33N27'12 86W56'33 5:47:46
Fairfield Village 37
1 33N28'31 86W54'45 5:47:39
Fairford 65 1 31N10'05 88W03'51 5:52:15
Fairhope 2 1 30N31'22 87W54'12 5:51:37
Fairmount 42 1 34N48'11 86W52'37 5:47:30
Fairnelson 18 1 31N33'49 87W04'36 5:48:18
Fair Oaks 60 1 32N56'22 88W15'06 5:53:00
Fairview 5 1 33N57'28 86W33'44 5:46:15
Fairview 11 1 32N46'28 86W43'17 5:46:53
Fairview 16 1 31N14'17 86W02'40 5:44:11
Fairview 18 1 31N25'09 87W00'19 5:48:01
Fairview 22 1 34N15'19 86W41'17 5:46:45
Fairview 25 1 34N20'18 85W55'35 5:43:42
Fairview 30 1 34N33'39 87W43'44 5:50:55
Fair View 36 1 34N37'36 85W47'25 5:43:10
Fairview 42 1 34N48'11 86W49'57 5:47:20
Fairview 45 2 34N58'33 86W28'25 5:45:54
Fairview 47 1 34N15'07 87W47'23 5:51:10
Fairview 52 3 34N34'53 86W58'21 5:47:53
Fairview 54 1 33N22'43 87W53'08 5:51:33
Fairview 58 1 33N44'33 86W12'27 5:44:50
Fairview 64 1 33N36'10 87W20'59 5:49:24
Fairview 67 1 34N08'27 87W21'26 5:49:26
Fairview West 22
1 34N01'59 86W47'44 5:47:11
Falakto 11 1 32N48'17 86W35'39 5:46:23
Falco 20 1 31N02'56 86W37'06 5:46:28
Falkner 26 1 32N41'43 86W03'01 5:44:12
Falkville 52 1 34N22'06 86W54'31 5:47:38
Falliston 59 1 33N17'22 86W51'36 5:47:26
Falls City 67 1 34N01'27 87W16'58 5:49:08
Falls Junction 37
1 33N30'12 86W55'24 5:47:42
Fannie 27 1 31N00 87W15 5:49:00
Fannings Crossing 45
2 34N53'02 86W26'34 5:45:46
Farill 10 1 34N14'46 85W29'36 5:41:58
Farley 45 2 34N35'43 86W33'44 5:46:15
Farmers Landing 34
1 31N34'29 85W03'30 5:40:14
Farmersville 43 1 32N04'41 86W53'31 5:47:34
Farmville 41 5 32N38 85W23 5:41:32
Farnell 49 1 30N38'36 88W06'12 5:52:25
Fatama 66 1 31N53'56 87W14'08 5:48:57
Faulkner Ford 5 1 34N00'04 86W29'25 5:45:58
Faunsdale 46 1 32N27'35 87W35'38 5:50:23
Faustinas 49 1 30N26'01 88W06'20 5:52:25
Fayette 29 1 33N41'04 87W49'51 5:51:19
Fayetteville 61 1 33N08'44 86W24'21 5:45:37
Fays 26 1 32N28'50 86W24'36 5:45:38
Ferguson Crossroad 58
1 33N56'51 86W17'55 5:45:12
Fernbank 38 1 33N34'45 88W08'30 5:52:34
Fernland 49 1 30N28'59 88W17'35 5:53:10
Fernwood Estates 37
1 33N37'34 86W40'44 5:46:43
Ferry Shores 39 1 34N46'33 87W18'24 5:49:14
Fieldstown 37 1 33N38'31 86W51'21 5:47:25
Finchburg 50 1 31N38'33 87W30'39 5:50:03
Finley 9 5 33N03'34 85W16'59 5:41:08
Finley Crossing 13
1 31N57'42 87W41'09 5:50:45
Fisher Crossroads 25
1 34N28'01 85W38'55 5:42:36
Fishermans Resort 40
1 34N47'03 87W23'38 5:49:35
Fishhead 14 1 33N26 85W41 5:42:44
Fishpond 19 1 32N52'04 86W01'24 5:44:06
Fish Pond 40 1 34N38'33 87W08'26 5:48:34
Fishtrap 61 1 33N29'25 86W14'26 5:44:58
Fishtrap Ford 45
2 34N32'58 86W18'45 5:45:15
Fisk 45 2 34N57'41 86W34'24 5:46:18
Fitzpatrick 6 1 32N12'59 85W53'20 5:43:33
Five Forks 25 1 34N22'11 86W04'33 5:44:18
Five Points 5 1 34N01'11 86W33'02 5:46:12
Five Points 9 5 33N01'05 85W21'01 5:41:24
Five Points 15 1 33N35'02 85W40'49 5:42:43
Five Points 20 1 31N26'26 86W18'12 5:45:13
Five Points 23 1 31N18'06 85W37'31 5:42:30
Five Points 24 1 32N14'55 87W14'08 5:48:57
Five Points 26 4 32N29'22 86W21'06 5:45:24
Five Points 32 1 32N43'55 87W59'45 5:51:59
Five Points 35 1 31N01'55 85W24'40 5:41:39
Five Points 40 1 34N28'28 87W09'27 5:48:38
Five Points 45 2 34N44'19 86W34'37 5:46:18
Five Points 48 1 34N26'50 86W10'38 5:44:43
Five Points 61 1 33N11'36 86W16'28 5:45:06
Five Points 64 1 33N53'18 87W17'00 5:49:08
Five Points East 37
1 33N31'52 86W42'31 5:46:50
Five Points South 37
6 33N30'02 86W48'00 5:47:12
Flanders 25 1 34N12'26 85W54'10 5:43:37
Flat Creek 37 1 33N38'39 87W05'33 5:48:22
Flat Rock 14 1 33N18 85W45 5:43:00
Flat Rock 36 1 34N46'11 85W41'40 5:42:47
Flat Rock 40 1 34N32'12 87W29'07 5:49:56
Flat Top 37 1 33N39'56 87W01'25 5:48:06
Flatwood 46 1 32N08'57 87W31'23 5:50:06
Flatwood 51 4 32N27'01 86W15'40 5:45:03
Flatwood 64 1 33N56'42 87W30'12 5:50:01
Flatwoods 43 1 31N58'43 86W25'51 5:45:43
Fleetwood 63 1 33N14'21 87W24'16 5:49:37
Fleming Hills 45
2 34N39'41 86W34'58 5:46:20
Fleming Meadows 45
2 34N40'58 86W34'19 5:46:17
Flemington Heights 45
2 34N40'09 86W33'34 5:46:14
Fleta 51 1 32N06'34 86W21'08 5:45:25
Flint City 52 1 34N31'23 86W58'13 5:47:53
Flint Hill 37 1 33N21'18 87W00'23 5:48:02
Flippo Ford 36 1 34N43'38 86W14'52 5:44:59
Flomaton 27 1 31N00'00 87W15'39 5:49:03
Florala 20 1 31N00'18 86W19'41 5:45:19
Floral Crest 36 1 34N52'25 85W35'25 5:42:22
Florence 39 1 34N47'59 87W40'38 5:50:43
Florette 52 1 34N24'59 86W42'11 5:46:49
Flournoys 57 7 32N22'11 85W00'28 5:40:02
Flower Hill 40 1 34N40'49 87W09'22 5:48:37
Floyd 26 1 32N36'00 86W01'02 5:44:04
Flynn Gin Landing 13
1 31N25'39 87W35'09 5:50:21
Foley 2 1 30N24'23 87W41'01 5:50:44
Folsom 53 1 32N40'57 87W24'21 5:49:37
Folsom 56 1 33N25 85W30 5:42:00
Foots Landing 2 1 30N24'20 87W53'56 5:51:36
Ford City 17 1 34N47'09 87W31'43 5:50:07
Fordyce 9 5 32N56'59 85W35'08 5:42:21
Forest 54 1 33N25 88W13 5:52:52
Forest Acres 37 1 33N37'32 86W41'23 5:46:46
Forest Brook Estates 37
6 33N25 86W48 5:47:12
Forestdale 37 1 33N34'12 86W53'47 5:47:35
Forester 1 1 32N26'13 86W35'53 5:46:24
Forester Chapel 56
1 33N07 85W34 5:42:16
Forest Hill 49 1 30N42'53 88W09'12 5:52:37
Forest Hills 8 6 33N40 85W50 5:43:20
Forest Hills 37 1 33N28'13 86W55'30 5:47:42
Forest Hills 39 1 34N51'10 87W40'58 5:50:44
Forest Hills 61 1 33N17'45 86W20'10 5:45:21
Forest Home 7 1 31N51'44 86W50'34 5:47:22
Forest Park 37 6 33N30'54 86W45'59 5:47:04
Forest Park 49 1 30N37'43 88W05'20 5:52:21
Forkland 32 1 32N38'53 87W53'00 5:51:32
Forkville 67 1 34N16'09 87W33'05 5:50:12
Forney 10 1 34N05'10 85W27'43 5:41:51
Fort Benning 57 7 32N26 84W57 5:39:48
Fort Dale 7 1 31N53'29 86W39'27 5:46:38
Fort Davis 44 1 32N14'35 85W42'35 5:42:50
Fort Deposit 43 1 31N59'04 86W34'43 5:46:19
Fort Gaines 49 1 30N14'55 88W04'30 5:52:18
Fort McClellan 8
1 33N43 85W47 5:43:08
Fort McDermott 2
1 30N40'14 87W55'02 5:51:40
Fort Mitchell 57
7 32N20'29 85W01'18 5:40:05

Fort Morgan 2 1 30N13'42 88w01'23 5:52:06
Fort Payne 25 1 34N26'39 85w43'11 5:42:53
Fort Rucker 23 5 31N20 85w43 5:42:52
Fort Stoddard 49 1 31N05'59 87w58'45 5:51:55
Foshee 27 1 31N07'00 87w13'35 5:48:54
Fosheeton 62 1 32N59'52 85w49'37 5:43:18
Foster Crossroad 56 1 33N25'21 85w33'19 5:42:13
Foster Crossroads 9 5 32N59'37 85w31'05 5:42:04
Foster Landing 50 1 31N43'07 87w30'24 5:50:02
Fosters 63 1 33N05'41 87w41'09 5:50:45
Fosters Mill 17 1 34N46'02 87w25'05 5:49:40
Fostoria 43 1 32N05'11 86w49'48 5:47:19
Fountain 50 1 31N35'40 87w24'32 5:49:38
Fountain Heights 37 6 33N31'45 86w49'35 5:47:18
Fourmile 59 1 33N14'55 86w33'11 5:46:13
Four Point 65 1 31N18'04 88w21'52 5:53:27
Fowler 18 1 31N35'21 87w05'50 5:48:23
Fowler 32 1 32N43'44 88w03'43 5:52:15
Fowlers Crossroads 29 1 33N48'04 87w39'48 5:50:39
Fowler Spring 5 1 34N02'02 86w35'14 5:46:21
Fowl River 49 1 30N27'44 88w10'08 5:52:41
Fox 63 6 33N12 87w32 5:50:08
Frances Heights 37 6 33N36'47 86w50'12 5:47:21
Francis 8 1 33N46'29 86w02'01 5:44:08
Francisco 36 1 34N59'14 86w14'57 5:45:00
Francis Mill 8 1 33N47 86w01 5:44:04
Frankfort 30 1 34N33'48 87w50'32 5:51:22
Franklin 44 1 32N28'42 85w48'09 5:43:13
Franklin 50 1 31N42'52 87w24'41 5:49:39
Franklin Ford 25 1 34N29'34 85w47'45 5:43:11
Franklin Gardens 37 6 33N33'30 86w50'07 5:47:20
Frankville 65 1 31N38'47 88w08'51 5:52:35
Fredonia 9 5 32N59'23 85w17'19 5:41:09
Freeman Acres 40 1 34N46'58 87w20'46 5:49:23
Freemanville 27 1 31N04'18 87w31'15 5:50:05
Fremont 1 1 32N32'43 86w53'41 5:47:35
French Mill 42 1 34N46'00 86w52'40 5:47:31
Fresco 16 1 31N43 85w49 5:43:16
Fridays Crossing 5 1 34N03'35 86w26'02 5:45:44
Friendship 20 1 31N24'12 86w12'24 5:44:50
Friendship 26 1 32N32'13 85w58'29 5:43:54
Friendship 48 1 34N22'16 86w27'15 5:45:49
Friendship 51 1 32N00'22 86w09'23 5:44:38
Frisco 16 1 31N35'43 85w51'56 5:43:28
Frisco City 50 1 31N26'00 87w24'05 5:49:36
Frisco Quarters 64 1 33N49'27 87w16'11 5:49:05
Frog Eye 62 1 33N01'57 85w35'39 5:42:23
Frog Mountain 10 1 34N01'21 85w34'27 5:42:18
Frost 4 1 32N57 87w08 5:48:32
Fruitdale 65 1 31N20'33 88w24'28 5:53:38
Fruithurst 15 1 33N43'51 85w26'02 5:41:44
Fuller Crossroad 56 1 33N23'23 85w36'55 5:42:28
Fullers Crossroads 21 1 31N49'04 86w18'40 5:45:15
Fullerton 10 1 34N17'46 85w29'36 5:41:58
Fulton 13 1 31N47'18 87w43'38 5:50:55
Fulton Bridge 47 1 34N05'18 88w00'44 5:52:03
Fultondale 37 6 33N36'17 86w47'38 5:47:11
Fulton Road 49 1 30N38 88w05 5:52:20
Fulton Springs 37 6 33N37'06 86w48'06 5:47:12
Furman 66 1 32N00'24 86w58'01 5:47:52
Fyffe 25 1 34N26'48 85w54'15 5:43:37
Gadsden 28 6 34N00'51 86w00'24 5:44:02
Gainer 31 1 31N04'59 86w06'25 5:44:26
Gainestown 13 1 31N26'43 87w41'36 5:50:46
Gainestown Landing 13 1 31N24'20 87w41'53 5:50:48
Gainesville 60 1 32N49'15 88w09'32 5:52:38
Gaino 3 1 31N50'28 85w20'39 5:41:23
Gallant 28 1 33N59'55 86w14'43 5:44:59
Gallion 33 1 32N29'48 87w42'58 5:50:52
Galloway Landing 49 1 30N36'38 88w23'28 5:53:34
Gallups Crossroads 59 1 33N20'57 86w27'39 5:45:51
Gamble 64 1 33N52'46 87w20'04 5:49:20
Gandys Cove 52 1 34N22 86w54 5:47:36
Gann Crossroad 25 1 34N43'34 85w37'00 5:42:28
Gantt 20 1 31N24'24 86w29'03 5:45:56
Gantts Junction 61 1 33N10'05 86w17'53 5:45:12
Gantts Quarry 61 1 33N08 86w18 5:45:12
Gap of the Mountain 11 1 32N54'40 86w36'27 5:46:26
Garden 54 1 33N09'24 88w11'00 5:52:44
Garden City 22 1 34N00'52 86w44'49 5:46:59
Gardendale 37 1 33N39'36 86w48'46 5:47:15
Garden Highlands 37 6 33N28 86w52 5:47:28
Gardiners Gin 64 1 33N48'53 87w12'07 5:48:48
Garland 7 1 31N33'23 86w49'24 5:47:18
Garmon Crossroads 3 1 31N56'22 85w33'12 5:42:13
Garnersville 21 1 31N52'34 86w16'22 5:45:05
Garnsey 4 1 33N07'55 87w00'30 5:48:02
Garnsey Number 2 4 1 33N09'25 86w59'20 5:47:57
Garretts Crossroads 35 1 31N02'45 85w26'20 5:41:45
Garth 36 1 34N43'31 86w18'11 5:45:13
Gary Springs 4 1 32N58'03 87w05'17 5:48:21
Garywood 37 1 33N27'35 86w57'50 5:47:51
Gasque 2 1 30N15'11 87w49'11 5:51:17
Gaston 60 1 32N21'03 88w13'25 5:52:54
Gastonburg 66 1 32N12'26 87w26'15 5:49:45
Gate City 37 1 33N32'52 86w43'36 5:46:54
Gateswood 2 1 30N43'15 87w34'51 5:50:19
Gave Spring 17 1 34N43'45 87w36'15 5:50:25
Gaylesville 10 1 34N16'06 85w33'25 5:42:14
Gayosa 64 1 33N42'56 87w19'32 5:49:18
Geiger 60 1 32N52'05 88w18'18 5:53:13
Genery 37 1 33N18'31 86w54'14 5:47:37
Geneva 31 1 31N01'58 85w51'50 5:43:27
Gentilly Forest 37 6 33N27 86w47 5:47:08
Georgetown 2 1 31N17'47 87w44'08 5:50:57
Georgetown 17 1 34N50'08 87w56'46 5:51:47
Georgetown 36 1 34N41'53 85w53'32 5:43:34
Georgetown 49 1 30N53'18 88w16'13 5:53:05
Georgia 52 1 34N27'12 86w55'41 5:47:43
Georgiana 7 1 31N38'13 86w44'31 5:46:58
Gerald 23 1 31N19'25 85w45'26 5:43:02
Geraldine 25 1 34N21'05 86w00'03 5:44:00
German Crossing 67 1 34N03'09 87w33'57 5:50:16
German Ford 65 1 31N23'08 87w59'50 5:51:59
Germania 37 6 33N28'39 86w52'21 5:47:29
Gibson 51 1 32N05'36 86w09'22 5:44:37
Gibson Crossroads 25 1 34N27'44 85w57'10 5:43:49
Gibsonville 14 1 33N11'37 85w46'55 5:43:08
Gilbert 58 1 33N54'53 86w13'55 5:44:56
Gilbert Crossroads 25 1 34N21'43 85w56'08 5:43:45
Gilbertown 12 1 31N52'37 88w19'17 5:53:17
Gilbertsboro 42 1 34N59 87w09 5:48:36
Giles 4 1 33N13'53 87w09'03 5:48:36
Gilliam Springs 48 1 34N19 86w30 5:46:00
Gilmore 37 1 33N30'59 87w08'48 5:48:35
Gilmore Quarters 33 1 32N37'52 87w46'46 5:51:07
Gipsy 42 1 34N53'37 87w04'57 5:48:20
Girard 57 7 32N28 85w01 5:40:04
Glades 14 1 33N12'40 85w59'23 5:43:58
Gladstone 45 2 34N52'21 86w38'35 5:46:34
Gladys Landing 32 1 32N47'04 88w03'59 5:52:16
Glasgow 7 1 31N45'47 86w31'40 5:46:07
Glasgow 37 1 33N36'38 86w57'10 5:47:49
Glasgow Corner 30 1 34N26'13 87w52'03 5:51:28
Glass 9 5 32N47'06 85w10'26 5:40:42
Gleandean 41 5 32N36 85w27 5:41:48
Glen Allen 47 1 33N54'54 87w44'30 5:50:58
Glen Carbon 59 1 33N12'15 86w57'30 5:47:50
Glen City 58 1 33N34'39 86w17'03 5:45:08
Glencoe 28 1 33N57'25 85w55'57 5:43:44
Glencoe 37 6 33N30'14 86w44'30 5:46:58
Glendale 37 6 33N36'17 86w48'17 5:47:13
Glen Hills 37 1 33N22'41 86w58'39 5:47:55
Glen Mary 67 1 34N07'27 87w37'25 5:50:30
Glen Oaks 37 1 33N27'22 86w56'12 5:47:45
Glenview 37 1 33N28'41 86w53'39 5:47:35
Glenville 57 7 32N07'43 85w10'37 5:40:42
Glenwood 21 1 31N39'52 86w10'17 5:44:41
Glover 13 1 31N56'13 87w50'24 5:51:22
Gnatville 10 1 33N59'43 85w40'34 5:42:42
Gobblers Crossing 64 1 33N45'03 87w13'05 5:48:52
Goddard 47 1 34N14'46 87w42'13 5:50:49
Godwin Estates 37 1 33N38'36 86w39'17 5:46:37
Gold Branch 19 1 32N59'39 86w23'15 5:45:33
Golddust 44 1 32N33'49 85w46'52 5:43:07
Golden Springs 8 6 33N38'37 85w47'09 5:43:09
Gold Hill 41 5 32N43'18 85w30'28 5:42:02
Gold Mine 47 1 34N02'21 87w44'37 5:50:58
Gold Ridge 22 1 34N15'35 86w45'12 5:47:01
Gold Ridge 41 5 32N44 85w37 5:42:28
Gold Ridge 56 1 33N29'22 85w23'08 5:41:33
Goldville 62 1 33N05'01 85w47'02 5:43:08
Gonce 36 1 34N59'14 85w57'16 5:43:49
Good Hope 22 1 34N06'57 86w51'49 5:47:27
Good Hope 26 1 32N34'24 86w00'48 5:44:03
Goodman 16 1 31N16'46 85w59'37 5:43:58
Goodson 4 1 32N56 87w10 5:48:40
Good Springs 30 1 34N32'30 87w41'49 5:50:47
Good Springs 42 1 34N56'50 87w11'39 5:48:47
Goodsprings 64 1 33N40'08 87w13'54 5:48:56
Goodwater 19 1 33N03'56 86w03'12 5:44:13
Goodway 50 1 31N20'12 87w25'33 5:49:42
Goodwins Mill 58 1 33N49'13 86w23'07 5:45:32
Goodwyn 44 1 32N26'16 85w56'02 5:43:44
Goose Pond Crossroads 36 1 34N39 86w01 5:44:04
Gordo 54 1 33N19'12 87w54'10 5:51:37
Gordon 35 1 31N08'28 85w05'48 5:40:23
Gordon Heights 37 1 33N25'42 86w55'31 5:47:42
Gordon Landing 35 1 31N08'51 85w04'12 5:40:17
Gordonsville 43 1 32N09'46 86w43'57 5:46:56
Gorgas 64 1 33N38'57 87w12'29 5:48:50
Gosa 32 1 32N50'46 87w51'42 5:51:27
Goshen 55 1 31N43'22 86w07'06 5:44:28
Gosport 13 1 31N34'57 87w35'01 5:50:20
Gosport Landing 13 1 31N32'48 87w34'43 5:50:19
Gourdsville 42 1 34N59'22 87w05'25 5:48:22
Graball 34 1 31N35'11 85w16'33 5:41:06
Grace 7 1 31N36'43 86w52'50 5:47:31
Grady 51 1 31N59'41 86w12'04 5:44:48
Graham 56 1 33N27'27 85w19'15 5:41:17
Grand Bay 49 1 30N28'34 88w20'32 5:53:22
Grandberry Crossroads 34 1 31N21'15 85w13'43 5:40:55
Grandview 22 1 34N07'39 86w54'22 5:47:37
Grangeburg 35 1 31N00'28 85w12'42 5:40:51
Grant 48 1 34N31'43 86w15'12 5:45:01
Grantley 15 1 33N51'14 85w32'46 5:42:11
Grants Mill 37 1 33N30'28 86w38'59 5:46:36
Granttown 61 1 33N32 85w57 5:43:48
Grasmere 61 1 33N23'49 86w19'58 5:45:20
Grasselli 37 1 33N26'55 86w54'34 5:47:38
Grassland 10 1 34N17'54 85w35'18 5:42:21
Grassy 39 1 34N58'17 87w17'59 5:49:12
Grassy 48 1 34N21'15 86w26'12 5:45:45
Gravel Hill 30 1 34N29'07 87w44'31 5:50:58
Gravelly Springs 39 1 34N53'09 87w54'29 5:51:38
Gravleeton 64 1 33N46 87w03 5:48:12
Gray Hill 4 1 33N12'58 87w03'28 5:48:14
Graymont 37 6 33N30'50 86w49'59 5:47:20
Grays Chapel 36 1 34N55 86w10 5:44:40
Grayson 67 1 34N16'49 87w19'10 5:49:17
Graystone 5 1 33N55'34 86w30'30 5:46:02
Graysville 37 1 33N37'14 86w58'17 5:47:53
Grayton 8 1 33N48'00 85w58'02 5:43:52
Greeley 63 1 33N20 87w01 5:48:04
Green Acres 35 1 31N13'13 85w28'32 5:41:54
Green Acres 37 1 33N28'19 86w53'46 5:47:35
Greenbrier 39 1 34N49'57 87w38'51 5:50:35
Greenbrier 42 1 34N40'15 86w50'37 5:47:22
Green Chapel 25 1 34N27 85w54 5:43:36
Greenfield 45 2 34N49'40 86w24'44 5:45:39
Green Hill 39 1 34N58'23 87w30'44 5:50:03
Green Lantern 51 4 32N20 86w16 5:45:04
Greenleas Heights 37 6 33N34'20 86w49'55 5:47:20
Green Pond 4 1 33N13'30 87w07'35 5:48:30
Greensboro 33 1 32N42'16 87w35'45 5:50:23
Greens Chapel 5 1 33N59 86w35 5:46:20
Greensport 58 1 33N43 86w24 5:45:36
Green Street 18 1 31N34'37 87w07'51 5:48:31
Green Valley 28 6 33N57 86w01 5:44:04
Green Valley 37 6 33N27 86w47 5:47:08
Greenview Estate 37 6 33N25 86w48 5:47:12
Greenville 7 1 31N49'46 86w37'04 5:46:28
Greenwood 13 1 31N46'46 87w45'36 5:51:02
Greenwood 37 1 33N19'33 86w56'10 5:47:45
Greenwood 44 1 32N25 85w42 5:42:48
Greenwycke Village 45 2 34N42'12 86w33'02 5:46:12
Griffen Mill 41 7 32N31'33 85w15'59 5:41:04
Griffin Addition 52 3 34N35'16 87w01'19 5:48:05
Grimes 23 1 31N18'16 85w26'53 5:41:48
Grimes 63 1 33N10'03 87w23'28 5:49:34
Grove Hill 13 1 31N42'31 87w46'38 5:51:07
Grove Oak 25 1 34N26'17 86w03'09 5:44:13
Grove Park 37 6 33N28'44 86w48'09 5:47:13
Grove Park 61 1 33N16'18 86w21'44 5:45:27
Grover 10 1 34N24'44 85w30'42 5:42:03
Guard 57 7 32N27'23 85w00'16 5:40:01
Guerryton 6 1 32N13'15 85w30'05 5:42:00
Guest 25 1 34N25'27 85w52'24 5:43:30
Guin 47 1 33N57'56 87w54'53 5:51:40
Guinea 32 1 32N56'37 87w39'04 5:50:36
Guinn Cross Roads 30 1 34N29'12 87w55'27 5:51:42
Gulfcrest 49 1 31N01 88w14 5:52:56
Gulf Highlands 2 1 30N13'52 87w52'47 5:51:31
Gulf Shores 2 1 30N14'45 87w42'03 5:50:48
Gum Pond 52 1 34N20 86w46 5:47:04
Gum Spring 52 1 34N26'10 86w49'07 5:47:16
Gum Springs 5 1 34N02'55 86w39'50 5:46:39
Gunter Air Force Base 51 4 32N24 86w17 5:45:08
Guntersville 48 1 34N21'29 86w17'41 5:45:11
Gunthertown 14 1 33N22'26 85w57'09 5:43:49
Gurley 45 2 34N42'06 86w22'33 5:45:30
Gurnee 59 1 33N11'22 86w58'07 5:47:52
Gurnee Junction 59 1 33N11'53 86w57'51 5:47:51
Guthery Crossroads 22 1 34N06'56 87w00'39 5:48:03
Gu-Win 47 1 33N57'39 87w52'50 5:51:31
Hackleburg 47 1 34N16'38 87w49'43 5:51:19
Hackneyville 62 1 33N03'37 85w55'59 5:43:44
Hacoda 31 1 31N04'29 86w09'59 5:44:40
Haden 45 2 34N41'21 86w30'17 5:46:01
Hagler 63 1 33N02'02 87w20'24 5:49:22
Halawaka 41 7 32N39'52 85w10'17 5:40:41
Haleburg 34 1 31N24'23 85w08'14 5:40:33
Hales (Newala P O) 59 1 33N05'44 86w48'24 5:47:14
Haleys 47 1 34N14 87w37 5:50:28
Haleyville 67 1 34N13'35 87w37'17 5:50:29
Half Acre 46 1 32N11'40 87w54'44 5:51:39
Half Chance 46 1 32N17'59 87w43'40 5:50:55
Hall Creek 60 1 32N30'57 87w57'04 5:51:48
Halls Crossroads 50 1 31N24'08 87w19'53 5:49:20
Halltown 30 1 34N27'11 88w03'41 5:52:15
Halsell 12 1 32N17'02 88w16'38 5:53:07
Halso Mill 7 1 31N42'47 86w31'14 5:46:05
Hamburg 53 1 32N31'40 87w17'11 5:49:09
Hamilton 47 1 34N08'32 87w59'19 5:51:57
Hamilton Crossroads 55 1 31N38'37 85w48'30 5:43:14
Hammac 27 1 31N07'20 87w13'23 5:48:54
Hammondville 25 1 34N34'54 85w37'36 5:42:30
Hamner 60 1 32N44'36 88w16'09 5:53:05
Hampden 46 1 32N04'53 87w37'44 5:50:31
Hampton 62 1 32N57'31 85w36'43 5:42:27
Hanceville 22 1 34N03'38 86w46'03 5:47:04
Hancock Crossroads 36 1 34N32'05 85w59'37 5:43:58
Hannah 42 1 34N47'16 86w57'17 5:47:49
Hannon 44 1 32N14'21 85w31'34 5:42:06
Hanover 19 1 33N00'17 86w12'09 5:44:49
Happy Hill 65 1 31N10'53 88w03'06 5:52:12
Hardaway 44 1 32N17'11 85w50'56 5:43:24
Hardwick 58 1 33N41'18 86w21'09 5:45:25
Hardwickburg 34 1 31N29'55 85w09'03 5:40:36
Hardy 59 1 33N15'49 86w48'39 5:47:15
Harkins Crossroads 14 1 33N13'52 85w52'02 5:43:28
Harkness Crossroads 5 1 33N54'51 86w43'22 5:46:53
Harlem Heights 37 1 33N27'37 86w58'50 5:47:55
Harmon 4 1 33N01'55 87w16'24 5:49:06

Harmon Crossroads 56 1 33N12'09 85w28'49 5:41:55
Harmony 20 1 31N21'26 85w22'30 5:45:30
Harmony 40 1 34N29 87w17 5:49:08
Harmony 48 1 34N16 86w12 5:44:48
Harper Hill 33 1 32N51'24 87w36'45 5:50:27
Harpers Store 18 1 31N35'38 87w08'05 5:48:32
Harpersville 59 1 33N20'38 86w26'17 5:45:45
Harrell 24 1 32N26'35 87w12'56 5:48:52
Harriman Park 37 6 33N33'59 86w47'36 5:47:10
Harris 36 1 34N53'14 85w51'34 5:43:26
Harrisburg 4 1 32N52'33 87w13'28 5:48:54
Harrisburg 58 1 33N35'32 86w17'22 5:45:09
Harrisville 28 1 34N04 86w21 5:45:24
Hartford 31 1 31N06'08 85w41'49 5:42:47
Hartselle 52 1 34N26'36 86w56'07 5:47:44
Harvest 45 2 34N51'20 86w45'03 5:47:00
Hatchechubbee 57 7 32N16'14 85w16'33 5:41:06
Hatchet 19 1 33N01'00 86w06'18 5:44:25
Hatters 49 1 30N54'12 88w03'03 5:52:12
Hatton 40 1 34N33'46 87w24'55 5:49:40
Havana 33 1 32N53'42 87w37'13 5:50:29
Hawk 56 1 33N26'04 85w22'07 5:41:28
Hawkins Ford 38 1 33N57'27 88w04'39 5:52:19
Hawkinsville 3 1 32N02'03 85w13'40 5:40:55
Hawthorn 65 1 31N19'59 88w05'18 5:52:21
Hayden 5 1 33N53'33 86w45'28 5:47:02
Hayes 34 1 31N30'10 85w04'22 5:40:17
Hayes Crossing 64 1 33N41'54 87w26'19 5:49:45
Hayes Highland 37 6 33N34'40 86w49'52 5:47:19
Haynes 1 1 32N37'32 86w40'23 5:46:42
Haynes Crossing 36 1 34N52'56 85w48'57 5:43:16
Haynes Crossroad 14 1 33N26'16 85w43'55 5:42:56
Hayneville 43 1 32N11'02 86w34'49 5:46:19
Hays Ford 38 1 33N59'36 88w03'09 5:52:13
Haysland Estates 45 2 34N39'13 86w34'40 5:46:19
Hays Mill 42 1 34N52'48 86w58'11 5:47:53
Haywood 56 1 33N18'13 85w23'19 5:41:33
Hazel Green 45 2 34N55'56 86w34'19 5:46:17
Hazen 24 1 32N20'24 87w12'14 5:48:49
Headland 34 1 31N21'04 85w20'32 5:41:22
Healing Springs 65 1 31N37'56 88w20'12 5:53:21
Heath 20 1 31N21'38 86w28'11 5:45:53
Hebron 4 1 33N10'02 87w04'02 5:48:16
Hebron 48 1 34N29'07 86w22'49 5:45:31
Hector 6 1 32N06'44 85w54'32 5:43:38
Heflin 15 1 33N38'56 85w35'15 5:42:21
Heiberger 53 1 32N45'29 87w17'12 5:49:09
Helena 59 1 33N17'46 86w50'37 5:47:22
Helicon 21 1 31N54'48 86w12'43 5:44:51
Helicon 67 1 34N07'34 87w08'18 5:48:33
Hellum Ford 48 1 34N36'25 86w19'53 5:45:20
Henagar 25 1 34N38'06 85w46'02 5:43:04
Henderson 52 1 34N29'06 86w49'52 5:47:19
Henderson 55 1 31N39'59 86w04'24 5:44:18
Hendrick Mill 5 1 33N52'33 86w34'08 5:46:17
Hendrix 5 1 34N02'17 86w27'12 5:45:49
Henryville 48 1 34N25'28 86w15'44 5:45:03
Henson Springs 38 1 34N01'09 88w03'51 5:52:15
Hephzibah 55 1 31N45'55 86w00'47 5:44:03
Hepzibah 61 1 33N26'49 86w13'54 5:44:56
Herbert 18 1 31N50'09 86w48'19 5:47:13
Heron Bay 49 1 30N21'16 88w07'49 5:52:31
Hester Heights 30 1 34N32'35 87w42'32 5:50:50
Hestle 66 1 31N55'46 87w37'41 5:50:31
Hickory 54 1 33N09'46 88w03'47 5:52:15
Hickory Flat 9 1 33N09 85w22 5:41:28
Hickory Grove 37 1 33N20'30 86w59'59 5:48:00
Hickory Grove 40 1 34N25'49 87w26'40 5:49:47
Hickory Hills 39 1 34N49'51 87w39'01 5:50:36
Hickory Hills 52 3 34N32'55 86w55'30 5:47:42
Hicks 8 6 33N34'51 85w46'39 5:43:07
Hicks Hill 43 1 32N14'20 86w44'56 5:47:00
Hideaway Hills 39 1 34N51'21 87w33'41 5:50:15
Higdon 25 1 34N50'44 85w36'59 5:42:28
High Bluff 31 1 31N09'23 85w43'53 5:42:56
Highfalls 31 1 31N05'54 85w48'00 5:43:12
Highland 11 1 32N47'35 86w40'24 5:46:42
Highland 14 1 33N21'20 85w49'32 5:43:18
Highland Home 21 1 31N57'12 86w18'50 5:45:15
Highland Lake 5 1 33N53 86w25 5:45:40
High Level 64 1 33N39'56 87w12'46 5:48:51
Highmound 5 1 34N08'38 86w22'44 5:45:31
Highnote 31 1 30N59'45 85w41'33 5:42:46
High Pine 14 1 33N15'12 85w54'23 5:43:38
High Point 25 1 34N34'17 85w43'42 5:42:55
High Point 48 1 34N14'32 86w16'43 5:45:07
High Ridge 6 1 32N03'45 85w53'42 5:43:35
High Rock 5 1 33N57'34 86w41'26 5:46:46
Hightogy 38 1 33N41'42 88w05'41 5:52:23
Hightower 15 1 33N31'54 85w23'44 5:41:35
Hillandale 45 2 34N43'54 86w36'56 5:46:28
Hillcrest 53 1 32N27'05 87w28'29 5:49:54
Hilliard 64 1 33N48'52 87w22'35 5:49:30
Hillman 37 1 33N26'42 86w54'29 5:47:38
Hillman Gardens 37 1 33N26'52 86w54'11 5:47:37
Hillman Park 37 1 33N26'41 86w54'02 5:47:36
Hillsboro 40 1 34N38'21 87w11'30 5:48:46
Hillsboro 45 2 34N56'20 86w25'24 5:45:42
Hillsdale 59 1 33N08'43 86w36'18 5:46:25
Hillsdale 64 1 33N52'06 87w15'59 5:49:04
Hilltop 37 1 33N26 86w57 5:47:48
Hill Top 46 1 32N15'34 87w54'01 5:51:36
Hillview 37 6 33N34'32 86w53'03 5:47:32
Hillwood 19 1 32N55'31 86w21'41 5:45:27
Hines 39 1 34N57'35 87w38'37 5:50:34
Hines Landing 32 1 32N32'50 87w50'41 5:51:23
Hinton 12 1 32N05'31 88w26'32 5:53:46
Hirsch 57 7 32N10'18 85w07'19 5:40:29
Hissop 19 1 32N53'32 86w09'12 5:44:37
Hixon 50 1 31N34'22 87w25'34 5:49:42
Hixon 60 1 32N32'44 88w13'29 5:52:54
Hobbie Farm 51 1 32N11'38 86w14'41 5:44:59
Hobbs Island 45 2 34N38 86w34 5:46:16
Hobdy 3 1 31N48'54 85w31'54 5:42:08
Hobgood 17 1 34N42'51 87w38'05 5:50:32
Hoboken 3 1 31N54'42 85w08'56 5:40:36
Hoboken 46 1 32N01'33 87w52'37 5:51:30
Hobson 37 1 33N30'35 86w55'48 5:47:43
Hobson City 8 6 33N37'17 85w50'39 5:43:23
Hodge 36 1 34N37'10 85w56'58 5:43:48
Hodges 30 1 34N19'37 87w55'35 5:51:42
Hodges Store 52 1 34N25 87w05 5:48:20
Hodgesville 35 1 31N04'57 85w22'23 5:41:30
Hodgewood 12 1 31N56'14 88w18'08 5:53:13
Hogglesville 33 1 32N51'15 87w29'30 5:49:58
Hog Jaw 48 1 34N19'56 86w33'37 5:46:14
Hokes Bluff 28 1 33N59'53 85w51'59 5:43:28
Holiday Gardens 37 1 33N31'19 86w42'38 5:46:51
Holiday Park Estates 37 1 33N39'11 86w40'11 5:46:41
Holland Gin 42 1 34N57'48 86w53'14 5:47:33
Holley Crossroads 8 1 33N48'05 85w41'01 5:42:44
Hollins 14 1 33N07'03 86w08'40 5:44:35
Hollis Crossroads 15 1 33N31'25 85w38'14 5:42:33
Holloway 39 1 34N53'25 87w32'19 5:50:09
Holly Grove 64 1 33N50'19 87w25'21 5:49:41
Holly Pond 22 1 34N10'27 86w36'59 5:46:28
Holly Springs 5 1 33N49'28 86w28'42 5:45:55
Hollytree 36 1 34N48'10 86w14'59 5:45:00
Hollywood 36 1 34N43'27 85w58'21 5:43:53
Hollywood 37 6 33N28'22 86w46'59 5:47:08
Holman 63 1 33N16'47 87w49'24 5:51:18
Holman Crossroads 19 1 33N06'15 86w11'33 5:44:46
Holt 63 6 33N14'02 87w29'04 5:49:56
Holtville 26 1 32N38'10 86w19'36 5:45:18
Holy Trinity 57 7 32N13'20 85w00'19 5:40:01
Homewood 37 6 33N28'18 86w48'03 5:47:12
Homewood 50 1 31N22'10 87w35'58 5:50:24
Honoraville 21 1 31N51'02 86w24'22 5:45:37
Hoods Crossroads 5 1 33N59'18 86w25'13 5:45:41
Hooks 57 7 32N11'30 85w13'57 5:40:56
Hooks Crossroads 6 1 32N03'05 85w51'10 5:43:25
Hooper City 37 6 33N33'19 86w50'28 5:47:22
Hoover 37 6 33N24'19 86w48'41 5:47:15
Hoover 45 2 34N51'19 86w44'08 5:46:57
Hopeful 61 1 33N29'38 85w54'45 5:43:39
Hope Hull 51 1 32N16'11 86w21'26 5:45:26
Hopewell 5 1 34N15'22 86w28'05 5:45:52
Hopewell 10 1 34N12'04 85w43'46 5:42:55
Hopewell 15 1 33N37'55 85w22'58 5:41:32
Hopewell 25 1 34N22'28 86w02'51 5:44:11
Hopewell 37 1 33N21'38 86w56'19 5:47:45
Hopewell 41 7 32N31'30 85w18'09 5:41:13
Hopper 28 1 34N03'19 86w15'05 5:45:00
Hornady 44 1 32N27'54 85w51'55 5:43:28
Horn Hill 20 1 31N14'44 86w19'00 5:45:16
Horton 25 1 34N23'04 85w50'47 5:43:23
Horton 48 1 34N12'03 86w17'49 5:45:11
Hortons Mill 5 1 33N55 86w27 5:45:48
Hotamville 46 1 31N59'32 87w56'24 5:51:46
Houston 67 1 34N08'29 87w15'29 5:49:02
Houstontown 39 1 34N49'38 87w26'06 5:49:44
Houstonville 2 1 30N30'06 87w54'01 5:51:36
Howard 29 1 33N51'15 87w34'03 5:50:16
Howard Landing 50 1 31N27'21 87w33'57 5:50:16
Howe 3 1 32N01'06 85w09'51 5:40:39
Howells 20 1 31N03'08 86w12'33 5:44:50
Howells Crossroads 10 1 34N10'41 85w32'44 5:42:11
Howelton 28 1 34N03'21 86w11'01 5:44:44
Howton 63 1 33N15'32 87w20'25 5:49:22
Hubbard 11 1 32N53'56 86w49'05 5:47:16
Hubbard Landing 2 1 31N03'45 87w52'14 5:51:29
Hubertville 29 1 33N49'40 87w44'24 5:50:58
Huckaville 20 1 31N04'46 86w24'58 5:45:40
Hudson Gardens 37 1 33N25'38 86w56'09 5:47:45
Hudson Grove 37 1 33N25'52 86w55'51 5:47:43
Hudson Settlement 64 1 33N53'07 87w17'57 5:49:12
Hueytown 37 1 33N27'04 86w59'48 5:47:59
Hueytown Crest 37 1 33N27'40 86w59'49 5:47:59
Huffman 37 1 33N35'57 86w41'35 5:46:46
Huffman Gardens 37 1 33N36'14 86w40'30 5:46:42
Hughes Mill 25 1 34N25'08 85w47'02 5:43:08
Hugley 57 7 32N25'55 85w14'46 5:40:59
Hugo 46 1 32N16'00 87w41'20 5:50:45
Huguley 9 5 32N50'04 85w13'47 5:40:55
Hulaco 52 1 34N18'44 86w35'55 5:46:24
Hull 63 6 33N03'13 87w34'18 5:50:17
Hull 64 1 33N46'27 87w03'32 5:48:14
Humpton 48 1 34N32'51 86w18'18 5:45:13
Hunter 51 4 32N23'44 86w23'44 5:45:35
Huntsville 45 2 34N43'49 86w35'10 5:46:21
Huntsville Park 45 2 34N42'16 86w37'08 5:46:29
Hurley 10 1 34N16'30 85w37'23 5:42:30
Hurricane 2 1 30N50'27 87w54'07 5:51:36
Hurtsboro 57 7 32N14'30 85w24'59 5:41:40
Hustleville 48 1 34N18'42 86w10'03 5:44:40
Hustontown 39 1 34N52 87w32 5:50:08
Huxford 27 1 31N13'12 87w27'43 5:49:51
Hyatt 48 1 34N14'03 86w20'35 5:45:22
Hybart 50 1 31N49'35 87w22'55 5:49:32
Hycutt 32 1 32N42'24 87w59'43 5:51:59
Hyde Park 37 6 33N28'40 86w52'48 5:47:31
Hytop 36 1 34N54'58 86w05'17 5:44:21
Idaho 14 1 33N16 85w50 5:43:20
Ider 25 1 34N42'51 85w40'51 5:42:43
Independence 1 1 32N31'23 86w42'05 5:46:48
Indian Creek 6 1 31N57 85w42 5:42:48
Indian Hill 61 1 33N17'51 86w21'10 5:45:25
Indian Springs 12 1 32N15'08 88w06'03 5:52:24
Indian Springs 39 1 34N49'34 87w36'07 5:50:24
Indland Junction 5 1 33N50'57 86w33'55 5:46:16
Industrial City 37 1 33N26'38 86w58'55 5:47:56
Industry 7 1 31N36'15 86w36'46 5:46:27
Ingate 4 1 32N58'06 87w12'57 5:48:52
Inglenook 37 6 33N33'56 86w46'43 5:47:07
Ingle Terrace 37 6 33N33'55 86w46'33 5:47:06
Ingram 33 1 32N52'12 87w32'31 5:50:10
Ingram Ford 39 1 34N54'19 87w15'57 5:49:04
Ingram Wells 8 1 33N46'45 85w58'46 5:43:55
Inland 5 1 33N55 86w27 5:45:48
Inmanfield 67 1 34N14'42 87w11'18 5:48:45
Ino 16 1 31N16'16 86w05'41 5:44:23
Institute 66 1 32N00 87w00 5:48:00
Interburan Heights 37 1 33N28 86w56 5:47:44
Intercourse 60 1 32N24'58 88w14'25 5:52:58
Interurban Heights 37 1 33N28'53 86w54'51 5:47:39
Inverness 6 1 32N00'53 85w44'46 5:42:59
Ireland Hill 47 1 34N14 87w37 5:50:28
Ironaton 61 1 33N25'36 85w58'16 5:43:53
Iron City 8 6 33N40'04 85w39'51 5:42:39
Irondale 37 1 33N32'17 86w42'26 5:46:50
Irvington 42 1 34N38'23 86w55'45 5:47:43
Irvington 49 1 30N30'24 88w14'02 5:52:56
Isabella 11 1 32N49'42 86w47'12 5:47:09
Isbell 30 1 34N27'19 87w45'14 5:51:01
Ishkooda 37 1 33N27'35 86w51'41 5:47:27
Island Landing 2 1 31N03'08 87w51'54 5:51:28
Isney 12 1 31N46'56 88w27'20 5:53:49
Ivalee 28 6 34N02'04 86w08'43 5:44:35
Ivanhoe 37 1 33N28'59 86w53'41 5:47:35
Ivy Creek 21 1 31N42'25 86w21'55 5:45:28
Jachin 12 1 32N13'47 88w10'06 5:52:40
Jack 16 1 31N34'26 86w00'01 5:44:00
Jackson 12 1 31N55 88w19 5:53:16
Jackson 13 1 31N30'32 87w53'40 5:51:35
Jacksonburg 39 1 34N53'27 87w39'49 5:50:39
Jackson Heights 49 1 30N40'13 88w09'29 5:52:38
Jackson Oak 2 1 30N37'21 87w54'43 5:51:39
Jackson Quarters 32 1 32N38'41 87w51'06 5:51:24
Jacksons Gap 62 1 32N53'10 85w48'42 5:43:15
Jackson Spur 12 1 31N57'24 88w18'54 5:53:16
Jacksonville 8 1 33N48'49 85w45'41 5:43:03
Jack Springs 27 1 31N10 87w32 5:50:08
Jagger 64 1 33N59 87w29 5:49:56
Jamback 6 1 31N54'36 85w39'55 5:42:40
James 41 5 32N38'41 85w34'23 5:42:18
Jamestown 10 1 34N23'52 85w34'39 5:42:19
Jamesville 41 5 32N42'46 85w37'16 5:42:29
Janes Mill 18 1 31N16'41 87w09'12 5:48:37
Jarrett 9 5 32N48 85w11 5:40:44
Jasper 64 1 33N49'52 87w16'39 5:49:07
Java 16 1 31N33'28 85w50'38 5:43:23
Jeddo 50 1 31N19'56 87w30'51 5:50:03
Jeff 45 2 34N49'22 86w42'49 5:46:51
Jefferson 46 1 32N23'12 87w53'53 5:51:36
Jefferson Hills 37 6 33N34'20 86w46'24 5:47:06
Jefferson Park 37 1 33N32'30 86w38'40 5:46:35
Jemison 11 1 32N57'35 86w44'48 5:46:59
Jena 32 1 33N07'50 87w50'49 5:51:23
Jenifer 61 1 33N32'57 85w56'11 5:43:45
Jenkins 8 1 33N47'58 85w40'12 5:42:41
Jenkins Crossroads 6 1 32N01'34 85w46'28 5:43:06
Jericho 36 1 34N58'39 86w04'45 5:44:19
Jericho 53 1 32N46'26 87w16'31 5:49:06
Jernigan 57 7 32N07'34 85w04'20 5:40:17
Jerusalem 40 1 34N42'18 87w13'37 5:48:54
Jerusalem Heights 63 6 33N12 87w32 5:50:08
Jester 41 5 32N42'12 85w08'37 5:40:34
Jet 37 1 33N40'04 86w55'55 5:47:44
Joe Wheeler Dam 40 1 34N41 87w24 5:49:36
Joffre 1 1 32N33'46 86w38'21 5:46:33
Johnny Ford 64 1 33N49'58 87w23'08 5:49:33
Johns 37 1 33N21'42 87w06'35 5:48:26
Johnson Crossroads 39 1 34N57'39 87w45'06 5:51:00
Johnson Landing 52 1 34N32'54 86w39'37 5:46:38
Johnsons Crossing 22 1 34N05'20 86w47'48 5:47:11
Johnsons Mill 48 1 34N17'00 86w27'01 5:45:48
Johnsonville 18 1 31N26 86w56 5:47:44
Jones 1 1 32N35'02 86w53'51 5:47:35
Jonesboro 2 1 30N36 87w54 5:51:36
Jonesboro 30 1 34N30 87w44 5:50:56
Jonesboro 37 1 33N22'55 86w57'43 5:47:51
Jones Chapel 22 1 34N12'37 87w03'07 5:48:12
Jones Crossroads 35 1 31N12'38 85w29'05 5:41:56
Jones Crossroads 42 1 34N43'05 87w00'06 5:48:00
Jones Mill 9 5 32N45'02 85w33'34 5:42:14
Jones Valley 37 6 33N27'54 86w52'44 5:47:31
Jones Valley Estates 45 2 34N41'00 86w33'28 5:46:14
Jonesville 55 1 31N53'35 85w54'15 5:43:37
Joppa 22 1 34N17'52 86w33'22 5:46:13
Joquin 21 1 31N47'11 86w09'51 5:44:39
Jordan 26 1 32N42'19 86w00'08 5:44:01
Jordan 65 1 31N29'37 88w11'40 5:52:47

Jordans Mill 30 1 34N27'37 88W00'10 5:52:01
Josephine 2 1 30N19'35 87W31'52 5:50:07
Joseph Springs 8
6 33N41'43 85W40'25 5:42:42
Josie 55 1 31N52'11 85W43'08 5:42:53
Joy 5 1 34N02'00 86W37'00 5:46:28
Judson 9 5 32N50'09 85W35'10 5:42:21
Jumbo 11 1 32N58'02 86W35'26 5:46:22
Kalona 11 1 32N58'50 86W46'09 5:47:05
Kansas 64 1 33N54'06 87W33'07 5:50:12
Kaolin 25 1 34N37'39 85W34'54 5:42:20
Kaolin 57 7 32N26'39 85W00'37 5:40:02
Kaulton 63 6 33N12 87W32 5:50:08
Keego 27 1 31N03'38 87W07'39 5:48:31
Keener 28 6 34N09'22 85W57'04 5:43:48
Keith 25 1 34N40'42 85W41'32 5:42:46
Keith 50 1 31N40'38 87W21'41 5:49:27
Kellar Quarry Landing 17
1 34N44'04 87W45'29 5:51:02
Kellerman 63 1 33N20'26 87W18'17 5:49:13
Kelly 23 1 31N19'25 85W39'19 5:42:37
Kellys Crossroads 19
1 32N50'14 86W20'04 5:45:20
Kellys Crossroads 31
1 31N04'10 85W45'06 5:43:00
Kelly Springs 35
1 31N16'33 85W27'20 5:41:49
Kellyton 19 1 32N58'47 86W02'01 5:44:08
Kendale Gardens 39
1 34N49 87W40 5:50:40
Kendall Crossroads 9
5 32N50'12 85W30'26 5:42:02
Kennedy 38 1 33N35'13 87W59'04 5:51:56
Kent 26 1 32N37'08 85W56'55 5:43:48
Kent 55 1 31N57'09 86W10'29 5:44:42
Kentuck 61 1 33N31'51 85W49'50 5:43:19
Kenwood 37 6 33N25 86W48 5:47:12
Kershaw 64 1 33N45'35 87W06'33 5:48:26
Ketona 37 6 33N36'19 86W45'55 5:47:04
Kewahatchie 59 1 33N07'12 86W32'37 5:46:10
Key 10 1 34N06'09 85W32'04 5:42:08
Keyno 19 1 32N56'13 86W06'33 5:44:26
Keysburg 28 1 33N56'42 85W55'05 5:43:40
Keys Mill 45 2 34N56'12 86W31'26 5:46:06
Keystone 59 1 33N16'04 86W48'35 5:47:14
Keyton 16 1 31N16'57 85W49'32 5:43:18
Keytons 35 1 31N06'32 85W22'14 5:41:29
Kilby 51 4 32N24'34 86W15'56 5:45:04
Kilgore 37 1 33N40'46 87W01'50 5:48:07
Killen 39 1 34N51'46 87W32'15 5:50:09
Killian Mill 25 1 34N23'14 85W48'07 5:43:12
Killough Springs 37
1 33N36'47 86W42'23 5:46:50
Kilpatrick 25 1 34N16'05 86W04'35 5:44:18
Kimberly 37 1 33N46'24 86W48'50 5:47:15
Kimbrell 63 1 33N16'34 87W04'02 5:48:16
Kimbrough 66 1 32N02'00 87W33'55 5:50:16
Kimbrough Crossroads 39
1 34N49'36 87W45'48 5:51:03
Kincheon 11 1 32N45'25 86W42'07 5:46:48
Kingdom Crossroads 59
1 33N09'39 86W33'18 5:46:13
Kings Landing 24
1 32N15'21 87W04'55 5:48:20
Kings Log Landing 50
1 31N48'28 87W27'42 5:49:51
Kings Mill 64 1 33N44'04 87W21'33 5:49:26
Kingston 37 6 33N32'17 86W46'09 5:47:05
Kingsway Terrace 37
6 33N33'45 86W44'39 5:46:59
Kingtown 39 1 34N54'19 87W22'59 5:49:32
Kingville 38 1 33N40'03 88W02'26 5:52:10
Kinsey 35 1 31N17'56 85W20'40 5:41:23
Kinston 16 1 31N12'57 86W10'16 5:44:41
Kinterbish 60 1 32N19'57 88W18'46 5:53:15
Kiowa 5 1 33N47'57 86W40'02 5:46:40
Kirbytown 48 1 34N30'17 86W07'43 5:44:31
Kirk 54 1 33N14'29 87W53'15 5:51:33
Kirkland 27 1 31N11'18 87W01'50 5:48:07
Kirklands Crossroads 34
1 31N24'09 85W24'52 5:41:39
Kirkpatrick Landing 32
1 32N37'08 87W51'16 5:51:25
Kirks Grove 10 1 34N11'25 85W27'25 5:41:50
Klein 59 1 33N17'01 86W26'59 5:45:48
Klondike 63 1 33N15'52 87W18'08 5:49:13
Knightens Crossroads 8
1 33N57'23 85W42'52 5:42:51
Knoxville 32 1 32N59'32 87W47'26 5:51:10
Koenton 65 1 31N38'24 88W15'34 5:53:02
Kowaliga 26 1 32N44'24 85W58'09 5:43:53
Kowaliga Beach 26
1 32N59 85W52 5:43:28
Krafton 49 1 30N44 88W05 5:52:20
Kushla 49 1 30N48'56 88W09'29 5:52:38
Kyles 36 1 34N47'41 86W00'31 5:44:02
Kymulga 61 1 33N20'02 86W17'56 5:45:12
Labuco 37 1 33N36'34 87W05'21 5:48:21
Laceys Chapel 37
1 33N22'22 86W55'15 5:47:41
Laceys Spring 52
1 34N32'03 86W36'15 5:46:25
Lacon 52 1 34N20'05 86W54'12 5:47:37
Ladiga 8 1 33N56'56 85W34'52 5:42:19
Ladonia 57 7 32N28'05 85W04'45 5:40:19
Lafayette 9 5 32N53'59 85W24'04 5:41:36
Lake Bend Landing 33
1 32N38'00 87W48'45 5:51:15
Lake Coves 39 1 34N50'45 87W34'09 5:50:17
Lake Drive Estates 37
6 33N26'56 86W48'27 5:47:14
Lake Forest 2 1 30N36 87W54 5:51:36
Lake Highlands 37
6 33N34'22 86W43'51 5:46:55
Lake Howard 25 1 34N30'25 85W36'42 5:42:27
Lake Shore Estates 37
6 33N27'32 86W48'22 5:47:13
Lakeside Acres 39
1 34N52'20 87W33'34 5:50:14
Lakeside Highlands 39
1 34N48'41 87W37'07 5:50:28
Lakeview 17 1 34N47'22 87W37'00 5:50:28
Lakeview 25 1 34N23'27 85W58'42 5:43:55
Lakeview 40 1 34N42'09 87W09'14 5:48:37
Lakeview 48 1 34N19'49 86W19'20 5:45:17
Lakeview Estates 37
6 33N27'09 86W48'11 5:47:13
Lakeview Highlands 17
1 34N47'14 87W36'12 5:50:25
Lakeview Park 37
6 33N27'06 86W48'58 5:47:16
Lakewood 25 1 34N30'54 85W40'11 5:42:41
Lakewood 37 1 33N33'28 86W42'48 5:46:51
Lakewood 42 1 34N49'04 86W58'58 5:47:56
Lakewood 45 2 34N46'46 86W35'16 5:46:21
Lakewood Estate 37
1 33N22'53 86W58'35 5:47:54
Lakewood Hills 37
6 33N26'39 86W48'39 5:47:15
Lamar 56 1 33N23'48 85W23'43 5:41:35
Lamison 66 1 32N07'16 87W34'00 5:50:16
Land 12 1 32N01'43 88W19'42 5:53:19
Landersville 40 1 34N28'08 87W24'03 5:49:36
Lands Crossroads 25
1 34N28'47 85W51'24 5:43:26
Lane Springs 17 1 34N50'03 87W58'51 5:51:55
Lanett 9 5 32N52'07 85W11'26 5:40:46
Laneville 33 1 32N31'21 87W35'47 5:50:23
Laney 8 1 33N51'23 85W54'20 5:43:37
Langdale 9 5 32N49'13 85W10'20 5:40:41
Langston 36 1 34N32'20 86W04'28 5:44:18
Langston Ford 59
1 33N19'46 86W50'32 5:47:22
Langtown 40 1 34N40 87W19 5:49:16
Laniers 61 1 33N22'53 86W19'39 5:45:19
Lapine 51 1 31N57'56 86W17'04 5:45:08
La Place 44 1 32N22'42 85W51'46 5:43:27
Lardent 8 6 33N40 85W50 5:43:20
Larkin 36 1 34N54'34 86W12'55 5:44:52
Larkinsville 36 1 34N41'27 86W07'29 5:44:30
Larkwood 37 1 33N39'13 86W41'47 5:46:47
Lasca 46 1 32N00'59 87W57'30 5:51:50
Latham 2 1 31N05'05 87W50'03 5:51:20
Lathamville 25 1 34N16'24 86W02'00 5:44:08
Lathrop 54 1 33N22'15 87W59'32 5:51:58
Lato 57 7 32N19'27 85W06'08 5:40:25
Lattiwood 48 1 34N16'22 86W17'03 5:45:08
Lauderdale Beach 39
1 34N51'48 87W34'08 5:50:17
Laurel Shanty Landing 65
1 31N13'47 87W59'21 5:51:57
Laurendine 49 1 30N29'52 88W10'12 5:52:41
Lavaca 12 1 32N08'25 88W04'48 5:52:19
Lawley 4 1 32N51'34 86W57'05 5:47:48
Lawley 59 1 33N30'04 86W26'51 5:45:47
Lawngate 42 1 34N43'33 87W05'35 5:48:22
Lawrence 10 1 34N13'56 85W31'52 5:42:07
Lawrence Cove 52
1 34N20 86W46 5:47:04
Lawrence Mill 29
1 33N41 87W50 5:51:20
Lawrenceville 34
1 31N39'27 85W16'09 5:41:05
Lawson 42 1 34N43'30 87W04'22 5:48:17
Lawson Ford 25 1 34N24'16 85W54'52 5:43:39
Lawsontown 37 1 33N20'02 87W05'55 5:48:24
Lay Springs 28 1 34N10'06 85W51'24 5:43:26
Leatherwood 8 6 33N43'02 85W52'36 5:43:30
Lebanon 15 1 33N40'52 85W22'29 5:41:30
Lebanon 25 1 34N21'57 85W48'57 5:43:16
Lecta 15 1 33N35'18 85W25'58 5:41:44
Ledbetters 61 1 33N17'27 86W11'17 5:44:45
Lee Crossroads 56
1 33N11'59 85W16'25 5:41:06
Leeds 37 1 33N32'53 86W32'40 5:46:11
Leeds Mineral Well 37
1 33N33 86W32 5:46:08
Leesburg 10 1 34N10'47 85W45'41 5:43:03
Leesdale 52 1 34N23'23 86W54'42 5:47:39
Leggett Landing 50
1 31N43'39 87W28'58 5:49:56
Leggtown 42 1 34N57'21 87W03'56 5:48:16
Le Grand 51 1 32N09'44 86W16'07 5:45:04
Lehigh 5 1 33N52 86W41 5:46:44
Leighton 17 1 34N42'03 87W31'44 5:50:07
Lenlock 8 6 33N40 85W50 5:43:20
Lennon Hill 40 1 34N44'22 87W24'58 5:49:40
Lenoir Landing 12
1 31N51'25 88W09'31 5:52:38
Lenox 18 1 31N20'11 87W11'08 5:48:45
Lentzville 42 1 34N50'39 87W08'27 5:48:34
Leon 21 1 31N33'27 86W23'34 5:45:34
Leonard 10 1 34N12'27 85W49'49 5:43:19
Leroy 65 1 31N30'16 87W59'05 5:51:56
Leslie 11 1 32N40 86W55 5:47:40
Lester 42 1 34N59'26 87W09'12 5:48:37
Letcher 36 1 34N45'07 86W09'44 5:44:39
Letchers 8 6 33N39'43 85W51'22 5:43:25
Letohatchee 43 1 32N07'46 86W29'09 5:45:57
Letson Settlement 40
1 34N34'36 87W17'30 5:49:10
Level Plains Crossroads 23
1 31N17'58 85W46'41 5:43:07
Levelroad 56 1 33N07 85W34 5:42:16
Levert 53 1 32N45'33 87W14'29 5:48:58
Lewis 23 1 31N24'35 85W28'03 5:41:52
Lewisburg 37 6 33N34'57 86W48'20 5:47:13
Lewiston 32 1 33N02'27 88W01'13 5:52:05
Lexington 39 1 34N58'09 87W22'16 5:49:29
Leydens Mill 8 1 33N48'07 85W50'17 5:43:21
Liberty 5 1 34N06'28 86W30'57 5:46:04
Liberty 7 1 31N49'32 86W42'05 5:46:48
Liberty 25 1 34N12'31 86W02'44 5:44:11
Liberty City 62 1 32N34'52 85W44'57 5:43:00
Liberty Crossroads 9
5 32N48'06 85W24'48 5:41:39
Liberty Highlands 37
1 33N33'50 86W39'17 5:46:37
Liberty Hill 15 1 33N50'55 85W34'22 5:42:17
Liberty Hill 30 1 34N20'51 87W45'54 5:51:04
Liberty Hill 36 1 34N49'40 85W42'52 5:42:51
Libertyville 20 1 31N14'29 86W27'41 5:45:51
Lightwood 26 1 32N42'42 86W23'21 5:45:33
Ligon Springs 17
1 34N35'25 87W42'58 5:50:52
Lilita 60 1 32N29'01 88W07'42 5:52:31
Lillian 2 1 30N24'46 87W26'13 5:49:45
Lily Flagg 45 2 34N39'05 86W34'00 5:46:16
Lime 56 1 33N09'31 85W15'36 5:41:02
Lime Kiln 17 1 34N45'54 88W02'21 5:52:09
Lime Rock 17 1 34N36'19 87W44'46 5:50:59
Lime Sink 3 1 31N46'58 85W23'53 5:41:36
Limestone 50 1 31N31 87W20 5:49:20
Lim Rock 36 1 34N40'20 86W11'18 5:44:45
Lincoln 45 2 34N44'44 86W35'15 5:46:21
Lincoln 61 1 33N36'47 86W07'06 5:44:28
Lincoln Park 63 6 33N12 87W32 5:50:08
Lincoya Estates 37
6 33N27 86W47 5:47:08
Lindbergh 37 1 33N36 86W58 5:47:52
Linden 46 1 32N18'22 87W47'53 5:51:12
Lindsey 3 1 31N45'29 85W28'10 5:41:53
Lindseys Crossing 59
1 33N13'49 86W55'38 5:47:43
Lineville 14 1 33N18'38 85W45'16 5:43:01
Linn Crossing 37
1 33N40'38 86W57'59 5:47:52
Linton 37 1 33N50'00 86W48'05 5:47:12
Linwood 55 1 31N55'36 85W51'51 5:43:27
Lipscomb 37 1 33N25'32 86W55'36 5:47:42
Lisman 12 1 32N10'07 88W16'57 5:53:08
Listerhill 17 1 34N45'27 87W34'56 5:50:20
Little Nashville 36
1 34N45'10 86W13'52 5:44:55
Little New York 48
1 34N23'16 86W11'09 5:44:45
Little Oak 55 1 31N43'51 86W03'14 5:44:13
Little River 2 1 31N18 87W44 5:50:56
Little River 10 1 34N16'53 85W40'24 5:42:42
Little Rock 27 1 31N06'52 87W23'20 5:49:33
Little Shawmut 9
5 32N50'48 85W12'36 5:40:50
Little Shoal 37 1 33N30'03 87W14'55 5:49:00
Little Texas 44 1 32N26'34 85W34'06 5:42:16
Littleton 28 6 34N04'01 86W07'59 5:44:32
Littleton 37 1 33N41'19 86W59'53 5:48:00
Littleville 17 1 34N35'26 87W40'37 5:50:42
Littleville 67 1 34N15'05 87W34'30 5:50:18
Little Walker 12
1 32N09'01 88W10'40 5:52:43
Little Warrior 5
1 33N54'27 86W35'54 5:46:24
Live Oak 21 1 31N48'30 86W14'51 5:44:59
Live Oak Landing 2
1 30N42'45 87W52'45 5:51:31
Liveoak Landing 49
1 30N50'13 88W01'03 5:52:04
Liverpool 44 1 32N22'00 85W46'42 5:43:07
Livingston 60 1 32N35'03 88W11'14 5:52:45
Lizzieville 32 1 32N47'15 88W01'44 5:52:07
Lloyds 49 1 30N37'03 88W07'41 5:52:31
Loachapoka 41 5 32N36'15 85W35'36 5:42:22
Loango 20 1 31N19'46 86W38'56 5:46:36
Locke Crossroads 42
1 34N56'08 86W57'06 5:47:48
Lock Five 33 1 32N34'59 87W44'12 5:50:57
Lockhart 20 1 31N00'37 86W20'59 5:45:24
Lock Six 39 1 34N50'54 87W32'11 5:50:09
Lock Three 39 1 34N48'42 87W24'38 5:49:39
Locust Fork 5 1 33N54'27 86W36'55 5:46:28
Loflin 57 7 32N11'49 85W02'06 5:40:08
Logan 22 1 34N08'17 87W00'23 5:48:02
Logan 43 1 31N59'09 86W29'26 5:45:58
Logton 55 1 31N57'10 85W54'52 5:43:39
Lois Spring 54 1 33N13'50 88W05'38 5:52:23
Lola City 37 1 33N34'22 86W36'04 5:46:24
Lomax 11 1 32N52'44 86W39'39 5:46:39
London 18 1 31N17'51 87W05'16 5:48:21
London 51 1 32N16'23 86W03'01 5:44:12
London 58 1 33N33 86W16 5:45:04
Long Island 36 1 34N58'25 85W40'16 5:42:41
Longleaf Estates 52
3 34N32'40 86W59'47 5:47:59
Longview 22 1 34N15'02 86W53'10 5:47:33
Longview 59 1 33N12'01 86W46'54 5:47:08
Longwood 45 2 34N43'08 86W34'53 5:46:20
Lookout Mountain 28
1 34N07 85W47 5:43:08
Loop 10 1 34N13 85W36 5:42:24
Loop 49 1 30N40 88W06 5:52:24
Loper 65 1 31N34'53 88W18'00 5:53:12
Loree 18 1 31N29'14 87W05'24 5:48:22
Loretto 22 1 34N04'07 86W54'58 5:47:40
Lorton 64 1 33N45'19 87W03'44 5:48:15
Lottie 27 1 31N07'44 87W37'20 5:50:29
Lou 12 1 31N55'08 88W12'40 5:52:51
Louina 56 1 33N07'28 85W33'08 5:42:13
Louisville 3 1 31N47'00 85W33'21 5:42:13
Love Hill 35 1 31N06'57 85W16'26 5:41:06
Lovelace Crossroads 39
1 34N51'39 87W45'24 5:51:02
Loveless 25 1 34N19'04 85W45'44 5:43:03
Loveless Park 37
1 33N19'28 86W58'56 5:47:56
Lovick 37 1 33N33'32 86W36'50 5:46:27
Lower Hall Landing 2
1 30N49'09 87W54'55 5:51:40
Lower Peach Tree 66
1 31N50'26 87W32'43 5:50:11
Lowery 31 1 31N10'02 86W08'34 5:44:34
Lowerytown 4 1 33N06'43 87W09'06 5:48:36
Lowetown 37 1 33N18'31 87W04'31 5:48:18
Low Gap 58 1 33N40 86W25 5:45:40
Lowndesboro 43 1 32N16'30 86W36'41 5:46:27
Lowrimores Crossroads 8
1 33N46'04 85W56'11 5:43:45
Lowry Mill 16 1 31N32'19 85W58'56 5:43:56
Loxley 2 1 30N37'05 87W45'11 5:51:01
Loyola Villa 2 1 30N30'02 87W55'28 5:51:42
Lucille 4 1 33N05'18 87W08'51 5:48:35
Lucy 35 1 31N01'12 85W02'28 5:40:10
Lugo 3 1 31N57'56 85W12'54 5:40:52
Luke 28 6 34N03'01 85W53'58 5:43:36
Lukes Landing 60
1 32N40'16 88W03'33 5:52:14
Lum 43 1 32N03'57 86W39'03 5:46:36
Lumbull 47 1 34N15'11 87W43'53 5:50:56
Luttrell 25 1 34N26'25 85W56'05 5:43:44
Luverne 21 1 31N42'59 86W15'50 5:45:03

Lydia 25 1 34N25'59 85w51'03 5:43:24
Lyeffion 18 1 31N32'33 86w59'10 5:47:57
Lyle 19 1 32N53'19 86w20'07 5:45:20
Lynn 67 1 34N02'49 87w32'59 5:50:12
Lynn Acres 37 1 33N37'11 86w42'24 5:46:50
Lynn Crossing 37
1 33N36 86w58 5:47:52
Lynndale 51 4 32N19'25 86w15'57 5:45:04
Lynn Haven 63 6 33N12 87w32 5:50:08
Lynns Park 64 1 33N48'22 87w08'38 5:48:35
Lynntown 52 1 34N25'50 86w42'19 5:46:49
Lytle 31 1 31N04'32 85w57'09 5:43:49
Mabson 23 1 31N28'05 85w33'47 5:42:15
Macedonia 15 1 33N34'38 85w22'15 5:41:29
Macedonia 36 1 34N31'12 86w00'01 5:44:00
Macedonia 43 1 31N59'33 86w48'14 5:47:13
Macedonia 51 1 32N17'40 86w13'18 5:44:53
Macedonia 64 1 33N50 87w17 5:49:08
Mackey 10 1 34N10'18 85w47'24 5:43:10
Mackies 49 1 30N49'58 88w04'05 5:52:16
MacMillan 66 1 31N58'22 87w31'21 5:50:05
Macon 8 1 33N47 86w01 5:44:04
Madison 37 1 33N26'39 86w56'21 5:47:45
Madison 45 2 34N41'57 86w44'54 5:47:00
Madison 51 4 32N25'25 86w13'55 5:44:54
Madison Crossroads 45
2 34N54'12 86w42'51 5:46:51
Madrid 35 1 31N02'08 85w23'36 5:41:34
Magazine 49 1 30N44'03 88w03'09 5:52:13
Magnolia 46 1 32N08'08 87w40'05 5:50:40
Magnolia Beach 2
1 30N30'56 87w55'03 5:51:40
Magnolia Courts 37
1 33N36'13 86w42'09 5:46:49
Magnolia Shores 21
1 31N55'57 86w17'39 5:45:11
Magnolia Springs 2
1 30N23'58 87w46'34 5:51:06
Magnolia Terminal 46
1 32N04 87w35 5:50:20
Mahan Crossroads 25
1 34N34'24 85w46'31 5:43:06
Mahlep 8 6 33N44'41 85w52'52 5:43:31
Majestic 37 1 33N44'58 86w45'38 5:47:03
Malbis 2 1 30N39'20 87w51'07 5:51:24
Malcolm 65 1 31N11'28 88w00'27 5:52:02
Malone 17 1 34N43'20 88w06'12 5:52:25
Malone 56 1 33N11'55 85w35'03 5:42:20
Malta 27 1 31N01'29 87w27'17 5:49:49
Malvern 31 1 31N08'21 85w31'09 5:42:05
Mamie 51 1 32N11'11 86w02'26 5:44:10
Manack 43 1 32N19'42 86w30'40 5:46:03
Manchester 48 1 34N24'40 86w20'54 5:45:24
Manchester 64 1 33N54'23 87w18'05 5:49:12
Manila 13 1 31N30'30 87w43'23 5:50:54
Manila 24 1 32N26'54 86w55'16 5:47:41
Manistee 50 1 31N26'27 87w29'40 5:49:59
Manley Crossroads 45
2 34N41 86w41 5:46:44
Mann 49 1 30N35'35 88w08'38 5:52:35
Manningham 7 1 31N53'09 86w44'47 5:46:59
Mansion View 39 1 34N51'44 87w43'43 5:50:55
Mantua 32 1 33N03'13 87w55'44 5:51:43
Maple Ford 48 1 34N33'48 86w18'39 5:45:15
Maple Forks 22 1 34N12'45 87w01'28 5:48:06
Maple Grove 10 1 34N07'13 85w46'10 5:43:05
Maple Hill 45 1 34N59 86w51 5:47:24
Maplesville 11 1 32N47'18 86w52'18 5:47:29
Maplewood 37 1 33N32'20 86w33'10 5:46:13
Maplewood 45 2 34N41'53 86w45'30 5:47:02
Marble City Heights 61
1 33N10 86w19 5:45:16
Marble Valley 19
1 33N02'38 86w27'07 5:45:48
Marbury 11 1 32N42'04 86w28'16 5:45:53
Marcoot 9 5 32N57'28 85w29'21 5:41:57
Marengo 46 1 32N03'25 87w48'51 5:51:15
Margaret 58 1 33N41'10 86w28'30 5:45:54
Margerum 17 1 34N46'01 88w04'06 5:52:16
Marietta 64 1 33N42'02 87w23'38 5:49:35
Marigold 64 1 33N56'17 87w18'54 5:49:16
Marion 53 1 32N37'56 87w19'09 5:49:17
Marion Junction 24
1 32N26'14 87w14'20 5:48:57
Markeeta 58 1 33N34'48 86w32'21 5:46:09
Marks Village 37
1 33N32'38 86w43'29 5:46:54
Markton 28 1 33N52'48 86w00'36 5:44:02
Marl 31 1 31N05'25 85w58'48 5:43:55
Marley Mill 23 1 31N29'34 85w41'45 5:42:47
Marlow 2 1 30N27'27 87w47'57 5:51:12
Marshall 24 1 32N26'03 87w19'30 5:49:18
Marshall 48 1 34N14'34 86w08'41 5:44:35
Marshall Space Flight Center 45
2 34N44 86w36 5:46:24
Marshall Upper Landing 13
1 31N39'45 87w34'01 5:50:16
Mars Hill 11 1 32N57'12 86w49'48 5:47:19
Mars Hill 39 1 34N51'06 87w39'39 5:50:39
Martin 24 1 32N18'46 87w18'22 5:49:13
Martins 37 1 33N29'15 86w53'32 5:47:34
Martins Mill 61 1 33N38'05 86w04'06 5:44:16
Martintown 36 1 34N44'37 85w55'14 5:43:41
Martintown 67 1 34N17'27 87w35'08 5:50:21
Martinville 27 1 31N05'32 87w28'50 5:49:55
Martling 48 1 34N22'02 86w10'03 5:44:40
Marvel 4 1 33N08'48 87w00'11 5:48:01
Marvyn 41 5 32N26'20 85w21'51 5:41:27
Mary 62 1 32N45'20 85w41'19 5:42:45
Marylee 64 1 33N58'45 87w11'30 5:48:46
Maryville 28 6 34N05'46 86w05'26 5:44:22
Masena 4 1 33N09'42 87w02'37 5:48:10
Mashville 7 1 31N48'11 86w32'28 5:46:10
Mason City 37 6 33N28'05 86w50'59 5:47:24
Massey 52 1 34N22'13 87w01'20 5:48:05
Masseyline 37 1 33N47'30 86w41'10 5:46:45
Massillon 24 1 32N26'16 87w17'45 5:49:11
Masterson Mill 40
1 34N32'19 87w17'00 5:49:08
Mattawana 5 1 33N55'22 86w29'25 5:45:58
Matthews 51 1 32N15'55 86w00'14 5:44:01
Maud 4 1 32N52'47 86w58'54 5:47:56
Maud 17 1 34N38'35 88w06'35 5:52:26
Mauvilla 49 1 30N50'12 88w11'04 5:52:44
Maxine 37 1 33N34'40 87w08'56 5:48:36
Maxwell 63 6 33N04'45 87w33'20 5:50:13
Maxwell Air Force Base 51
4 32N22 86w18 5:45:12
Maxwellborn 8 1 33N52'51 85w43'01 5:42:52
Mayes Crossroad 28
1 34N01'06 85w50'06 5:43:20
Mayfair 37 6 33N28'18 86w47'36 5:47:10
Mayfair 45 2 34N42'43 86w35'11 5:46:21
Maylene 59 1 33N12'12 86w51'42 5:47:27
Maynard Cove 36 1 34N47'12 86w04'38 5:44:19
Mays Crossroads 13
1 31N36'13 87w59'15 5:51:57
Maysville 45 2 34N46'11 86w25'49 5:45:43
Maytown 37 1 33N32'09 86w59'50 5:47:59
McAding 61 1 33N33'40 85w49'52 5:43:19
McAdory 37 1 33N23'13 87w00'55 5:48:04
McBrydes 66 1 31N59'32 87w01'17 5:48:05
McCainville 60 1 32N39'10 88w12'53 5:52:52
McCaleb Mill 45 2 34N49'17 86w29'04 5:45:56
McCalla 37 1 33N20'55 87w00'51 5:48:03
McCartys Landing 12
1 31N57'04 88w07'18 5:52:29
McClure 32 1 32N50'47 87w50'32 5:51:22
McClure Town 55 1 31N50'40 85w57'40 5:43:51
McCollum 64 1 33N49'04 87w19'31 5:49:18
McCombs 37 1 33N33'48 86w37'02 5:46:28
McCord Crossroads 10
1 34N06'59 85w27'35 5:41:50
McCosh Mill 9 5 33N06'28 85w14'09 5:40:57
McCrary 54 1 33N27'52 88w16'56 5:53:08
McCrory Village 63
6 33N14 87w36 5:50:24
McCulley 4 1 33N08'21 87w05'21 5:48:21
McCulley Hill 4 1 33N07 87w07 5:48:28
McCulloh 41 5 32N42'23 85w08'59 5:40:36
McCullough 27 1 31N10'00 87w31'35 5:50:06
McCullum 64 1 33N50 87w17 5:49:08
McDade 51 1 32N18'56 86w02'47 5:44:11
McDonald Chapel 37
1 33N31'18 86w56'01 5:47:44
McDonald Lower Landing 2
1 31N13'47 87w50'08 5:51:21
McDowell 60 1 32N31'24 87w55'19 5:51:41
McElderry 61 1 33N29'11 85w57'49 5:43:51
McEntyre 13 1 31N48'30 87w57'56 5:51:52
McFarland 63 6 33N12 87w32 5:50:08
McFrey Crossroads 10
1 33N58'34 85w34'30 5:42:18
McGee Town 39 1 34N51'05 87w44'53 5:51:00
McGehees 51 1 32N16'11 86w22'29 5:45:30
McGhee 10 1 34N10'04 85w43'57 5:42:56
McGhees Bend 10 1 34N09 85w41 5:42:44
McGinty 9 5 32N46'38 85w09'08 5:40:37
McGuire Ford 4 1 33N03'46 86w59'44 5:47:59
McIntosh 65 1 31N15'58 88w01'53 5:52:08
McKenzie 7 1 31N32'32 86w42'54 5:46:52
McKestes 25 1 34N23'51 85w53'41 5:43:35
McKinley 46 1 32N17'54 87w32'25 5:50:10
McLarty 5 1 34N10'36 86w24'07 5:45:36
McLendon 57 7 32N09'17 85w05'40 5:40:23
McMullen 54 1 33N08 88w10 5:52:40
McPherson Landing 63
6 33N04'34 87w35'19 5:50:21
McRae 20 1 31N03'31 86w15'41 5:45:03
McRitchie Mill 9
5 32N37'09 85w37'57 5:42:32
McShan 54 1 33N22'51 88w08'30 5:52:34
McVay 13 1 31N36'24 87w53'44 5:51:35
McVille 48 1 34N17'10 86w07'40 5:44:31
McWilliams 66 1 31N49'51 87w05'38 5:48:23
Meadow Hills 45 2 34N47'35 86w34'51 5:46:19
Meadowood 48 1 34N21'49 86w30'37 5:46:02
Meadows Crossroads 41
7 32N31'13 85w15'16 5:41:01
Meadows Mill 41 7 32N31'45 85w15'17 5:41:01
Meadville 51 1 32N04'04 86w08'38 5:44:35
Meadwood Heights 37
6 33N34'32 86w45'07 5:47:00
Mechanicsville 41
7 32N40'00 85w08'49 5:40:35
Media 37 1 33N40'10 87w02'45 5:48:11
Meeksville 55 1 31N55'04 86w00'20 5:44:01
Megargel 50 1 31N22'47 87w25'42 5:49:43
Mehaffey 65 1 31N37'03 88w23'55 5:53:36
Mehama 40 1 34N30 87w44 5:50:56
Mellow Valley 14
1 33N11'09 85w44'53 5:43:00
Melrose 8 1 33N45'32 85w53'24 5:43:34
Melrose 18 1 31N20'56 86w44'13 5:46:57
Melrose 54 1 33N23'34 88w07'04 5:52:28
Melton 33 1 32N44'24 87w41'00 5:50:44
Meltonsville 48 1 34N26'06 86w11'24 5:44:46
Melville 67 1 34N05 87w13 5:48:52
Melvin 12 1 31N55'49 88w27'32 5:53:50
Memphis 54 1 33N08'11 88w17'51 5:53:11
Mentone 25 1 34N34'46 85w35'26 5:42:22
Mercury 45 2 34N47'09 86w32'10 5:46:09
Meridianville 45
2 34N51'05 86w34'20 5:46:17
Merrellton 8 1 33N51'48 85w44'31 5:42:58
Merrill Mill 21 1 31N35'35 86w24'09 5:45:37
Merritts Crossroads 35
1 31N05'13 85w29'06 5:41:56
Merriwether 32 1 32N37'33 87w51'09 5:51:25
Merry 51 1 32N20'48 86w05'40 5:44:23
Mertz 4 1 32N54'19 87w22'31 5:49:30
Mertz 49 1 30N39'45 88w05'18 5:52:21
Mexboro 50 1 31N29'37 87w22'28 5:49:30
Mexia 50 1 31N30'25 87w23'18 5:49:33
Mexia Crossing 50
1 31N29'18 87w22'17 5:49:29
Micaville 15 1 33N29'48 85w32'28 5:42:10
Middle Brooks Crossroads 41
5 32N41'38 85w36'09 5:42:25
Middleton 8 1 33N46'11 85w59'05 5:43:56
Midfield 37 1 33N27'41 86w54'32 5:47:38
Midland City 23 1 31N19'08 85w29'38 5:41:59
Midway 6 1 32N04'37 85w31'20 5:42:05
Midway 7 1 31N48'48 86w27'49 5:45:51
Midway 11 1 32N43'31 86w29'02 5:45:56
Midway 13 1 31N53'08 87w47'20 5:51:09
Midway 14 1 33N07'49 86w05'47 5:44:23
Midway 17 1 34N44'23 87w26'30 5:49:46
Midway 50 1 31N43'08 87w02'57 5:48:12
Midway 66 1 32N05'03 87w24'18 5:49:37
Midway Plaza 41 5 32N38 85w23 5:41:32
Miflin 2 1 30N22'13 87w36'39 5:50:27
Mignon 61 1 33N11 86w18 5:45:12
Miles 37 1 33N28 86w56 5:47:44
Military Bridge Landing 2
1 30N42'00 87w54'09 5:51:37
Milk Springs 17 1 34N40'33 87w42'47 5:50:51
Millbrook 26 1 32N28'47 86w21'43 5:45:27
Miller 32 1 32N42'45 88w04'43 5:52:19
Miller 34 1 31N26'26 85w09'14 5:40:37
Miller 46 1 32N09'23 87w47'08 5:51:09
Millers Ferry 66
1 32N06 87w22 5:49:28
Millers Ford 3 1 31N47'20 85w26'13 5:41:45
Millerville 14 1 33N11'29 85w55'33 5:43:42
Million Dollar Lake Estates 63
1 33N16'24 87w08'46 5:48:35
Millport 38 1 33N33'48 88w04'53 5:52:20
Millry 65 1 31N38'02 88w18'48 5:53:15
Milltown 9 5 33N03'16 85w29'05 5:41:56
Mill Village 48 1 34N20'17 86w18'52 5:45:15
Millville 60 1 32N31'37 88w20'09 5:53:21
Milner 56 1 33N24'08 85w32'38 5:42:11
Milstead 44 1 32N26'33 85w53'51 5:43:35
Milton 1 1 32N33'31 86w48'26 5:47:14
Mincoka 11 1 33N02'55 86w45'34 5:47:02
Mineola 50 1 31N16'46 87w38'02 5:50:32
Mineral Springs 11
1 32N57'06 86w38'43 5:46:35
Mineral Springs 37
6 33N37'34 86w52'43 5:47:31
Minooka 11 1 33N06 86w45 5:47:00
Minor 37 1 33N32'14 86w56'26 5:47:46
Minor Terrace 61
1 33N16'16 86w20'53 5:45:24
Minter 24 1 32N04'40 86w59'37 5:47:58
Mint Spring 45 2 34N57'06 86w28'05 5:45:52
Minvale 25 1 34N27'33 85w42'42 5:42:51
Mitchell 6 1 32N14'46 85w56'16 5:43:45
Mitchell Crossroads 41
5 32N32'19 85w24'48 5:41:39
Mitchelltown 39 1 34N52'54 87w25'44 5:49:43
Mitylene 51 1 32N22'58 86w10'27 5:44:42
Mixonville 18 1 31N42'17 86w56'55 5:47:48
Mobile 49 1 30N41'39 88w02'35 5:52:10
Mobile Junction 37
1 33N22'05 86w58'36 5:47:54
Moffat 4 1 33N03'11 87w10'59 5:48:44
Moffet 49 1 30N51'15 88w23'51 5:53:35
Moffits Mill 41 7 32N30'36 85w11'07 5:40:44
Molder 45 2 34N42 86w22 5:45:28
Mollie 12 1 32N14'29 88w16'18 5:53:05
Molloy 38 1 33N54 88w08 5:52:32
Mon Louis 49 1 30N26'25 88w06'21 5:52:25
Monmouth 37 1 33N44'08 86w44'52 5:46:59
Monroeton 50 1 31N32'17 87w16'41 5:49:07
Monroeville 50 1 31N31'40 87w19'29 5:49:18
Monrovia 45 2 34N47'11 86w42'50 5:46:51
Montague 36 1 34N58'10 85w48'02 5:43:12
Monterey 7 1 31N54'12 86w52'55 5:47:32
Monterey Heights 41
7 32N30'43 85w05'27 5:40:22
Monte-Sano 37 1 33N28'49 86w54'10 5:47:37
Montevallo 59 1 33N06'02 86w51'51 5:47:27
Monte Vista 28 6 34N02'11 86w00'16 5:44:01
Montgomery 51 4 32N22'00 86w18'00 5:45:12
Montgomery Hill Landing 2
1 31N10'53 87w51'15 5:51:25
Monticello 55 1 31N49'31 85w46'43 5:43:07
Montrose 2 1 30N33'56 87w54'06 5:51:36
Moody 58 1 33N35'27 86w29'27 5:45:58
Moody Ford 39 1 34N53'35 87w15'23 5:49:02
Moodys Crossroads 21
1 31N44'05 86w23'41 5:45:35
Moontown 45 2 34N44'00 86w27'25 5:45:50
Moore Corner 37 1 33N31'10 86w39'25 5:46:38
Moorefield 9 5 32N49'30 85w26'39 5:41:47
Moores Bridge 54
1 33N26'55 87w47'37 5:51:10
Moores Crossroads 25
1 34N24'59 85w57'09 5:43:49
Moores Crossroads 56
1 33N09'13 85w18'46 5:41:15
Moores Mill 45 2 34N50'38 86w31'06 5:46:04
Moores Valley 46
1 32N03'39 87w37'48 5:50:31
Mooresville 42 1 34N37'42 86w52'49 5:47:31
Moore Town 60 1 32N33'03 88w06'25 5:52:26
Moragne 28 6 34N01'46 86w06'40 5:44:27
Moreland 67 1 34N14'28 87w18'02 5:49:12
Morgan 37 1 33N20'01 86w55'00 5:47:40
Morgan City 52 1 34N28'19 86w34'11 5:46:17
Morgans Crossroads 28
6 33N57'26 86w02'22 5:44:09
Morgan Springs 53
1 32N44'43 87w24'57 5:49:40
Moriah 19 1 32N56'01 86w20'45 5:45:23
Morningside 37 1 33N37'46 86w39'57 5:46:40
Morris 37 1 33N44'53 86w48'31 5:47:14
Morris Chapel 40
1 34N32 87w11 5:48:44
Morris Crossroads 42
1 34N55'44 86w59'20 5:47:57
Morris Mill 36 1 34N38'52 85w51'28 5:43:26
Morrison Crossroad 56
1 33N25'35 85w29'36 5:41:58
Morrisville 8 1 33N43'36 85w57'26 5:43:50
Morrows Grove 32
1 33N03'12 87w59'41 5:51:59
Morvin 13 1 31N59'08 87w59'36 5:51:58
Moscow 38 1 33N52'11 88w06'10 5:52:25
Moscow 46 1 32N26'16 87w59'46 5:51:59
Moshat 10 1 34N07'07 85w37'20 5:42:29
Mossboro 59 1 33N15'03 86w53'54 5:47:36
Mossy Grove 55 1 31N45'16 85w57'36 5:43:50
Mostellers 59 1 33N06'23 86w30'31 5:46:02
Motley 14 1 33N07'01 85w39'32 5:42:38
Motts 41 7 32N34'20 85w08'19 5:40:33
Moulton 40 1 34N28'52 87w17'36 5:49:10

Moulton Heights 52 3 34N35'50 87w00'52 5:48:03
Moundville 33 1 32N59'51 87w37'48 5:50:31
Mountainboro 28 1 34N08'49 86w07'50 5:44:31
Mountain Brook 37 6 33N30'03 86w45'08 5:47:01
Mountain Brook 45 2 34N43'30 86w32'52 5:46:11
Mountain Brook Village 37 6 33N29'01 86w46'26 5:47:06
Mountain Chest 48 1 34N21 86w19 5:45:16
Mountain Creek 11 1 32N42'38 86w28'44 5:45:55
Mountaindale 37 6 33N30'44 86w43'57 5:46:56
Mountain Grove 5 1 34N05'19 86w37'02 5:46:28
Mountain Home 40 1 34N40 87w19 5:49:16
Mountain Park 37 6 33N33'54 86w46'17 5:47:05
Mountain Star 30 1 34N32'29 87w39'13 5:50:37
Mountain View 48 1 34N18'18 86w17'53 5:45:12
Mountain Woods Park 37 6 33N27 86w47 5:47:08
Mount Andrew 3 1 31N58'16 85w31'29 5:42:06
Mount Andrew 44 1 32N20'40 85w44'10 5:42:57
Mount Carmel 36 1 34N56'11 85w46'33 5:43:06
Mount Carmel 45 2 34N47'57 86w29'51 5:45:59
Mount Carmel 48 1 34N23'21 86w22'09 5:45:29
Mount Carmel 51 1 32N03'39 86w21'55 5:45:28
Mount Hebron 32 1 32N52'26 88w04'47 5:52:19
Mount Hebron 48 1 34N08'32 86w17'22 5:45:09
Mount Herman Valley 33 1 32N47 87w31 5:50:04
Mount Hester 17 1 34N43'42 88w00'43 5:52:03
Mount Hope 40 1 34N27'30 87w28'54 5:49:56
Mount Hope 64 1 33N46'09 87w14'28 5:48:58
Mount Ida 21 1 31N35 86w15 5:45:00
Mount Jefferson 41 5 32N42'34 85w22'21 5:41:29
Mount Lebanon 45 2 34N51'52 86w36'26 5:46:26
Mount Meigs 51 1 32N21'45 86w06'07 5:44:24
Mount Moriah 40 1 34N32'39 87w19'28 5:49:18
Mount Nebo 24 1 32N17'23 87w03'09 5:48:13
Mount Olive 5 1 33N54'58 86w42'57 5:46:52
Mount Olive 7 1 31N34'42 86w50'53 5:47:24
Mount Olive 19 1 33N04'10 86w08'06 5:44:32
Mount Olive 25 1 34N50'52 85w37'24 5:42:30
Mount Olive 37 1 33N40'15 86w51'22 5:47:25
Mount Olive 48 1 34N27'25 86w33'24 5:46:14
Mount Pinson 37 1 33N43 86w40 5:46:40
Mount Pleasant 15 1 33N44'27 85w30'31 5:42:02
Mount Pleasant 16 1 31N19 85w49 5:43:16
Mount Pleasant 50 1 31N20'00 87w41'45 5:50:47
Mount Pleasant Landing 50 1 31N20'57 87w43'16 5:50:53
Mount Rozell 42 1 34N56'06 87w08'25 5:48:34
Mount Sharon 61 1 33N12'37 86w24'39 5:45:39
Mount Sinai 1 1 32N32'57 86w32'42 5:46:11
Mount Star 30 1 34N30 87w44 5:50:56
Mount Sterling 12 1 32N05'37 88w09'47 5:52:39
Mount Tabor 52 1 34N26'26 86w52'00 5:47:28
Mount Union 18 1 31N26 86w56 5:47:44
Mount Vernon 22 1 34N14 86w52 5:47:28
Mount Vernon 25 1 34N17'33 85w47'16 5:43:09
Mount Vernon 38 1 33N44'03 87w54'37 5:51:38
Mount Vernon 49 1 31N05'06 88w00'48 5:52:03
Mount View 22 1 34N15'17 86w47'05 5:47:08
Mount Willing 43 1 32N03'36 86w42'05 5:46:48
Mount Zion 22 1 34N06'45 87w06'19 5:48:25
Mount Zion 51 1 32N03 86w13 5:44:52
Movico 49 1 31N03'52 88w01'32 5:52:06
Muck City 40 1 34N28'57 87w21'17 5:49:25
Mud Creek 10 1 34N05 85w31 5:42:04
Mud Creek 36 1 34N43 85w58 5:43:52
Mud Creek 37 1 33N23 87w06 5:48:24
Mud Landing 2 1 30N55'28 87w52'33 5:51:30
Mulberry 1 1 32N27'34 86w46'35 5:47:06
Mulberry 11 1 32N40'15 86w43'03 5:46:52
Mulberry 21 1 31N35'41 86w26'01 5:45:44
Mulga 37 1 33N32'59 86w58'27 5:47:54
Mulga Mine 37 1 33N33'22 86w59'37 5:47:58
Mullins Flat 45 2 34N39 86w41 5:46:44
Munford 61 1 33N31'47 85w57'03 5:43:48
Munk City 40 1 34N29 87w17 5:49:08
Murphree Place 42 1 34N41'55 86w57'25 5:47:50
Murphy 39 1 34N55 88w04 5:52:16
Murphy Cross Roads 39 1 34N58'55 87w53'53 5:51:36
Murphy Ford 5 1 34N00'26 86w28'53 5:45:56
Murrays Chapel 58 1 33N46 86w29 5:45:56
Murrycross 28 1 34N07'14 85w51'31 5:43:26
Muscadine 15 1 33N44'04 85w23'10 5:41:33
Muscle Shoals 17 1 34N44'41 87w40'03 5:50:40
Muscoda 37 1 33N22'46 86w56'23 5:47:46
Mynot 17 1 34N38'44 88w03'02 5:52:12
Myrtlewood 46 1 32N15'01 87w56'59 5:51:48
Nadawah 50 1 31N48'51 87w10'20 5:48:41
Naftel 51 1 32N00'34 86w17'21 5:45:09
Naheola 12 1 32N13'39 88w01'44 5:52:07
Nanafalia 46 1 32N06'46 87w59'17 5:51:57
Nances Creek 8 1 33N51'28 85w39'25 5:42:38
Napier 23 1 31N15 85w26 5:41:44
Napier Field 23 1 31N18'55 85w27'15 5:41:49
Napoleon 56 1 33N19'26 85w21'33 5:41:26
Nat 36 1 34N38 86w16 5:45:04
Natchez 50 1 31N43'39 87w15'38 5:49:03
Nathan 67 1 34N05 87w13 5:48:52
Natis 67 1 34N02'31 87w25'45 5:49:43
Natural Bridge 67 1 34N05'36 87w36'07 5:50:24
Nauvoo 64 1 33N59'22 87w29'20 5:49:57
Navco 49 1 30N37'46 88w06'19 5:52:25
Nave 53 1 32N29'09 87w16'01 5:49:04
Nebo 45 2 34N33'18 86w20'15 5:45:21
Nectar 5 1 33N57'35 86w38'22 5:46:33
Needham 12 1 31N59'16 88w20'12 5:53:21
Needmore 14 1 33N28'02 85w42'05 5:42:48
Needmore 40 1 34N27'49 87w28'54 5:49:56
Needmore 48 1 34N11'30 86w14'39 5:44:59
Needmore 55 1 31N54'07 85w56'27 5:43:46
Needmore 67 1 34N14'50 87w34'47 5:50:19
Neel 52 1 34N27'56 87w03'40 5:48:15
Neely 49 1 30N43'55 88w06'01 5:52:24
Neenah 66 1 31N54'52 87w10'41 5:48:43
Neighbors Mill 48 1 34N23'19 86w25'29 5:45:42
Nellie 66 1 31N54'05 87w22'58 5:49:32
Nelson 9 5 32N48'42 85w14'41 5:40:59
Nelson 59 1 33N12'55 86w34'52 5:46:19
Nelson Heights 37 6 33N36'08 86w42'41 5:46:51
Nelson Landing 2 1 31N05'08 87w51'49 5:51:27
Neman 26 1 32N34'47 85w59'03 5:43:56
Nenemoosha 49 1 30N48'35 88w00'17 5:52:01
Neshota 49 1 30N38'21 88w05'21 5:52:21
Nesmith 22 1 34N10'32 87w06'33 5:48:26
Ne Smith 40 1 34N35'46 87w25'42 5:49:43
Nettleboro 13 1 31N47'56 87w37'20 5:50:29
Newala 59 1 33N13'17 86w48'31 5:47:14
Newbern 33 1 32N35'35 87w31'58 5:50:08
Newberry Crossroads 10 1 34N09'46 85w34'20 5:42:17
New Bingham 26 1 32N28'09 86w09'43 5:44:39
New Brashier Chapel 48 1 34N16 86w12 5:44:48
New Brockton 16 1 31N23'08 85w55'46 5:43:43
Newburg 30 1 34N28'49 87w34'33 5:50:18
Newby 16 1 31N33'20 86w07'54 5:44:32
New Canaan 22 1 34N16'56 86w29'40 5:45:59
New Castle 37 1 33N38'56 86w46'07 5:47:04
New Center 52 1 34N27 86w57 5:47:48
New Convert 11 1 32N49'11 86w50'14 5:47:21
New Dora 64 1 33N44 87w07 5:48:28
Newell 56 1 33N25'59 85w26'01 5:41:44
New Georgia 67 1 34N14'14 87w09'44 5:48:39
New Harmony 9 5 32N46'48 85w31'48 5:42:07
New Harmony 22 1 34N14'33 86w32'00 5:46:08
New Haven 45 2 34N38'00 86w45'41 5:47:03
New Hill 37 1 33N25'06 86w55'19 5:47:41
New Home 25 1 34N36'08 85w41'57 5:42:48
New Hope 16 1 31N33'10 85w52'04 5:43:28
New Hope 21 1 31N32'25 86w20'31 5:45:22
New Hope 22 1 34N12'18 86w38'28 5:46:34
New Hope 36 1 34N35'05 86w06'25 5:44:26
New Hope 42 1 34N35'23 86w49'01 5:47:16
New Hope 45 2 34N32'13 86w23'40 5:45:35
New Hope 47 1 33N58'50 87w49'06 5:51:16
New Hope 56 1 33N19'35 85w25'21 5:41:41
New Hope 59 6 33N21'33 86w44'14 5:46:57
New Hopewell 15 1 33N38 85w35 5:42:20
New Lexington 63 1 33N33'44 87w39'27 5:50:38
New London 58 1 33N28'54 86w21'34 5:45:26
New Market 45 2 34N54'36 86w25'40 5:45:43
New Moon 10 1 34N23'35 85w31'13 5:42:05
New Mount Hebron 32 1 32N51'25 88w06'04 5:52:24
New Prospect 1 1 32N43 86w29 5:45:56
New Prospect 33 1 32N50'23 87w44'11 5:50:57
New Sharon 45 2 34N56'50 86w38'30 5:46:34
New Site 62 1 33N02'14 85w46'27 5:43:06
Newsome 25 1 34N32 85w49 5:43:16
Newton 23 1 31N20'06 85w36'19 5:42:25
Newton 35 1 31N09'45 85w23'44 5:41:35
Newton Springs 35 1 31N15 85w26 5:41:44
Newtonville 29 1 33N32'43 87w48'05 5:51:12
Newtown 30 1 34N30 87w44 5:50:56
New Town 36 1 34N52'24 85w49'03 5:43:16
Newville 34 1 31N25'18 85w20'16 5:41:21
New West Greene 32 1 32N55'26 88w08'06 5:52:32
Nichburg 18 1 31N28'46 87w08'12 5:48:33
Nichols Landing 13 1 31N45'46 88w06'45 5:52:27
Nicholsville 46 1 32N00'29 87w54'07 5:51:36
Nitrate City 17 1 34N45'26 87w33'35 5:50:14
Nix 30 1 34N21'05 87w47'03 5:51:08
Nixburg 62 1 32N49'40 86w06'40 5:44:27
Nix Mill 30 1 34N20'50 87w48'25 5:51:14
Nixon Chapel 48 1 34N12'14 86w23'05 5:45:32
Noah 10 1 34N07'56 85w33'31 5:42:14
Nokomis 27 1 31N00'36 87w33'53 5:50:16
Nolandale 45 2 34N41 86w41 5:46:44
Nolan Hills 45 2 34N42'35 86w43'27 5:46:54
Norala Junction 17 1 34N43'10 87w39'34 5:50:38
Normal 45 2 34N47'20 86w34'19 5:46:17
Norman 53 1 32N33'24 87w17'53 5:49:12
Norris Junction 37 1 33N32'59 86w40'24 5:46:42
North Alabama Junction 63 1 33N16'56 87w17'09 5:49:09
North Arab 48 1 34N20'35 86w30'16 5:46:01
North Athens 42 1 34N48 86w58 5:47:52
North Auburn 41 5 32N39'17 85w27'04 5:41:48
North Birmingham 37 6 33N33'13 86w49'08 5:47:17
North Carrollton 37 1 33N24 87w02 5:48:08
North Dadeville 62 1 32N51'27 85w46'22 5:43:05
North Daye Hill 45 2 34N51'23 86w43'27 5:46:54
North Elmore 26 4 32N33'23 86w19'09 5:45:17
North Florence 39 1 34N49'06 87w40'50 5:50:43
North Highlands 37 1 33N25'23 86w59'21 5:47:57
North Johns 37 1 33N22'02 87w06'13 5:48:25
North Lake Park 37 6 33N35'46 86w44'49 5:46:59
North Mobile 49 1 30N45'41 88w05'29 5:52:22
Northport 63 6 33N13'44 87w34'38 5:50:19
North River 29 1 33N50 87w42 5:50:48
North Selma 24 1 32N23 87w00 5:48:00
Northside 28 6 34N02'04 85w58'37 5:43:54
Northside 35 1 31N15 85w26 5:41:44
Northside Acres 45 2 34N48'42 86w39'17 5:46:37
North Smithfield Estates 37 6 33N34 86w52 5:47:28
North Vinemont 22 1 34N16'45 86w51'20 5:47:25
North Walter 22 1 34N07'53 86w40'55 5:46:44
Northwood Hills 39 1 34N51'18 87w41'45 5:50:47
Norton 28 6 34N02'35 86w06'42 5:44:27
Norton 45 2 34N33'12 86w32'21 5:46:09
Norwood 37 6 33N32'02 86w47'57 5:47:12
Notasulga 44 5 32N33'38 85w40'21 5:42:41
Nottingham 61 1 33N21'44 86w13'22 5:44:53
Nuckols 57 7 32N20'17 85w03'17 5:40:13
Nunnally Ford 59 1 33N18'45 86w52'02 5:47:28
Nymph 18 1 31N26 86w56 5:47:44
Nyota 5 1 33N51'00 86w44'43 5:46:59
Oak 2 1 30N19'04 87w42'23 5:50:50
Oakahalla 64 1 33N42'54 87w04'34 5:48:18
Oak Bowery 9 5 32N45'02 85w26'11 5:41:45
Oakchia 12 1 32N17'54 88w00'38 5:52:03
Oak Crossing 37 1 33N31'33 86w32'46 5:46:11
Oakdale 28 6 34N05'35 85w57'18 5:43:49
Oakdale 42 1 34N49'15 86w54'43 5:47:39
Oakdale Acres 42 1 34N48'59 86w54'35 5:47:38
Oak Grove 1 1 32N37'20 86w32'44 5:46:11
Oak Grove 11 1 32N59'27 86w45'32 5:47:02
Oak Grove 25 1 34N39'26 85w37'46 5:42:31
Oak Grove 33 1 32N32'46 87w40'39 5:50:43
Oak Grove 37 1 33N27'17 87w09'13 5:48:37
Oak Grove 40 1 34N33'28 87w27'04 5:49:48
Oak Grove 42 1 34N55'07 86w51'21 5:47:25
Oak Grove 45 2 34N30'52 86w26'17 5:45:45
Oak Grove 49 1 30N51'25 88w10'55 5:52:44
Oak Grove 61 1 33N11'30 86w17'58 5:45:12
Oak Grove Estates 37 6 33N27'32 86w49'37 5:47:18
Oak Hill 25 1 34N18'57 86w01'46 5:44:07
Oakhill 66 1 31N55'15 87w04'58 5:48:20
Oak Hills 37 1 33N29'24 86w54'08 5:47:37
Oakhurst 37 6 33N33'21 86w50'12 5:47:21
Oakland 9 5 33N00'49 85w14'20 5:40:57
Oakland 39 1 34N50'30 87w47'56 5:51:12
Oakland 42 1 34N49'39 87w05'07 5:48:20
Oak Lawn 37 6 33N34'53 86w45'10 5:47:01
Oak Level 15 1 33N50'58 85w28'41 5:41:55
Oakley 4 1 32N59'28 86w54'08 5:47:37
Oakman 64 1 33N42'48 87w23'19 5:49:33
Oakmulgee 53 1 32N47'47 87w02'38 5:48:11
Oak Park 37 6 33N34'32 86w46'09 5:47:05
Oak Park 45 2 34N44'56 86w33'09 5:46:13
Oak Ridge 52 1 34N28'41 86w59'42 5:47:59
Oak Ridge 58 1 33N36'03 86w16'46 5:45:07
Oak Ridge Park 37 6 33N32'22 86w44'24 5:46:58
Oak Village 33 1 32N53'51 87w45'53 5:51:04
Oakville 37 1 33N34'28 86w41'53 5:46:48
Oakville 40 1 34N26'43 87w09'44 5:48:39
Oakwood 37 1 33N23'26 86w57'52 5:47:51
Oakwood 45 2 34N44'46 86w36'32 5:46:26
Oakwood College 45 2 34N43 86w35 5:46:20
Oakworth 52 3 34N35'25 86w59'23 5:47:58
Oaky Grove 34 1 31N25 85w20 5:41:20
Oaky Streak 7 1 31N34'41 86w33'13 5:46:13
Oateston 3 1 31N45'43 85w22'28 5:41:30
Ocampo 11 1 33N01'53 86w45'49 5:47:03
Oceola 10 1 34N09'54 85w29'13 5:41:57
Octagon 46 1 32N12'15 87w45'19 5:51:01
Odena 61 1 33N12'39 86w16'43 5:45:07
Oden Ridge 52 1 34N22'26 86w45'44 5:47:03
Odenville 58 1 33N40'38 86w23'48 5:45:35
Odom 7 1 31N32'16 86w47'10 5:47:09
Ofelia 56 1 33N19'06 85w36'49 5:42:27
Ohatchee 8 1 33N47'00 86w00'09 5:44:01
Oil Well Landing 65 1 31N35'21 88w03'58 5:52:16
Okatuppa 12 1 31N56'41 88w23'46 5:53:35
Old Atkinson Crossing 9 5 32N57'48 85w14'06 5:40:56
Old Bethel 17 1 34N34'52 87w31'25 5:50:06
Old Bingham 26 1 32N26'30 86w07'49 5:44:31
Old Blevins Mill 25 1 34N44'23 85w37'56 5:42:32
Old Bluffport 60 1 32N35'32 88w03'25 5:52:14
Old Burleson 30 1 34N24'39 88w02'12 5:52:09
Old Coloma 10 1 34N01'50 85w37'06 5:42:28
Old Davistown 8 6 33N40 85w50 5:43:20
Old Davisville 8 6 33N38'55 85w39'21 5:42:37
Old Eastaboga 61 1 33N35'11 86w01'18 5:44:05
Old Fabius 36 1 34N49'44 85w46'38 5:43:07
Oldfield 61 1 33N12'10 86w13'05 5:44:52
Old Fort Stoddard Mount Vern 49 1 31N05'21 87w58'43 5:51:55
Old Harmony 28 6 33N56'19 86w03'43 5:44:15
Old Island Landing 2 1 31N07'02 87w51'39 5:51:27
Old Jonesboro 37 1 33N23'35 86w59'04 5:47:56
Old Kingston 1 1 32N34'25 86w36'03 5:46:24
Old Maylene 59 1 33N11'39 86w51'41 5:47:27
Old Monrovia 45 2 34N46'11 86w42'23 5:46:50
Old Nauvoo 30 1 34N27'00 87w55'38 5:51:43
Old Samuel 12 1 31N52'20 88w18'22 5:53:13
Old Spring Hill 46 1 32N26'15 87w46'25 5:51:06
Old Texas 50 1 31N53 87w00 5:48:00
Old Town 18 1 31N26 86w56 5:47:44
Old Town 24 1 32N14'20 86w52'22 5:47:29
Oleander 48 1 34N24'50 86w31'41 5:46:07
Oliver 39 1 34N48'39 87w15'01 5:49:00

Ollie 50 1 31N28'17 87W20'32 5:49:22
Olmsted 63 1 33N11 87W27 5:49:48
Olney 54 1 33N08'28 88W02'19 5:52:09
Olustee 55 1 31N53 86W07 5:44:28
Omaha 56 1 33N18'09 85W18'37 5:41:14
Omega 6 1 31N58'33 85W47'06 5:43:08
O'Neal 42 1 34N51'05 87W02'30 5:48:10
Oneonta 5 1 33N56'53 86W28'22 5:45:53
Onycha 20 1 31N12'50 86W17'00 5:45:08
Opelika 41 5 32N38'43 85W22'42 5:41:31
Ophir 25 1 34N21'36 85W56'44 5:43:47
Opine 13 1 31N54'17 87W56'02 5:51:44
Opine 20 1 31N19'39 86W17'14 5:45:09
Opp 20 1 31N16'57 86W15'20 5:45:01
Orange Beach 2 1 30N17'39 87W34'25 5:50:18
Orchard 49 1 30N43'10 88W12'26 5:52:50
Orion 55 1 31N57'31 86W00'20 5:44:01
Orrville 24 1 32N18'22 87W14'44 5:48:59
Orrville 42 1 34N40'02 86W58'37 5:47:54
Osage Woodyard Landing 13 1 31N51'28 88W08'54 5:52:36
Osaka 27 1 31N03'49 87W13'26 5:48:54
Osanippa 9 5 32N45'40 85W09'04 5:40:36
Osborn 53 1 32N41'01 87W08'35 5:48:34
Osco 3 1 31N52'37 85W14'09 5:40:57
Oswichee 57 7 32N16'46 85W00'14 5:40:01
Otho 34 1 31N41'22 85W07'47 5:40:31
Ottery 8 1 33N47'57 86W02'14 5:44:09
Our Town 62 1 32N49'41 85W57'43 5:43:51
Overbrook 61 1 33N07 86W12 5:44:48
Overton 37 6 33N30'16 86W41'23 5:46:46
Owassa 18 1 31N29'35 86W55'54 5:47:44
Owens 28 1 34N07'46 85W51'01 5:43:24
Owens Cross Roads 45 2 34N35'17 86W27'32 5:45:50
Owenton 37 6 33N30'53 86W51'20 5:47:25
Oxanna 8 6 33N38'57 85W50'16 5:43:21
Oxford 8 6 33N36'51 85W50'06 5:43:20
Oxford Lake 8 6 33N40 85W50 5:43:20
Ox Level 6 1 32N01'47 85W37'43 5:42:31
Oxmoor 37 6 33N25'58 86W51'34 5:47:26
Ozan 59 1 33N06'21 86W42'56 5:46:52
Ozark 23 1 31N27'32 85W38'26 5:42:34
Packards Bend 50 1 31N46'33 87W29'22 5:49:57
Painter 25 1 34N18'46 86W04'39 5:44:19
Paint Rock 36 1 34N39'38 86W19'44 5:45:19
Palestine 15 1 33N56'29 85W27'01 5:41:48
Palmerdale (Palmers Station) 37 1 33N44'19 86W38'46 5:46:35
Palmers Crossroads 50 1 31N17'59 87W32'55 5:50:12
Palmetto 54 1 33N29'02 87W58'40 5:51:55
Palmetto Beach 2 1 30N14'51 87W50'23 5:51:22
Palmyra 43 1 31N59'51 86W45'09 5:47:01
Palos 37 1 33N38'44 87W02'42 5:48:11
Panhandle 53 1 32N41'10 87W01'33 5:48:06
Panola 21 1 31N58'17 86W23'20 5:45:33
Panola 60 1 32N57'02 88W16'08 5:53:05
Pansey 35 1 31N09'14 85W10'32 5:40:42
Paradise Points 17 1 34N47'57 87W32'59 5:50:12
Paradise Shores 40 1 34N43'19 87W07'49 5:48:31
Paragon 12 1 31N52'34 88W22'28 5:53:30
Paramount 59 1 33N18'48 86W49'44 5:47:19
Paran 56 1 33N12'25 85W15'20 5:41:01
Park City 2 1 30N38'35 87W54'44 5:51:39
Park Courts 37 6 33N28'39 86W53'11 5:47:33
Parkdale 19 1 33N05'52 86W06'44 5:44:27
Parker 42 1 34N42'52 86W48'55 5:47:16
Parker 60 1 32N38'19 88W10'04 5:52:40
Parker Heights 37 6 33N33'22 86W45'05 5:47:00
Parkers Crossroads 41 5 32N33'42 85W20'41 5:41:23
Parker Springs 27 1 31N03'17 86W48'35 5:47:14
Park Hill 58 1 33N35'47 86W17'10 5:45:09
Parkland 64 1 33N50 87W17 5:49:08
Park Place 37 6 33N33'26 86W49'18 5:47:17
Parkway Estates 45 2 34N39'32 86W34'27 5:46:18
Parkwood 37 1 33N21'44 86W52'46 5:47:31
Parnell 11 1 32N41'41 86W54'53 5:47:40
Parrish 64 1 33N43'50 87W17'04 5:49:08
Parsons 58 1 33N37'40 86W30'01 5:46:00
Partridge Crossroads 37 1 33N45'42 86W56'08 5:47:45
Pasqua 59 1 33N08'27 86W45'10 5:47:01
Pate 1 1 32N28'57 86W30'21 5:46:01
Patsburg 21 1 31N47'11 86W13'42 5:44:55
Pattersontown 63 1 33N18'23 87W13'21 5:48:53
Patton 64 1 33N42'02 87W27'17 5:49:49
Patton Chapel 37 6 33N23'39 86W47'53 5:47:12
Paul 18 1 31N19'12 86W44'38 5:46:59
Pauls Hill 37 1 33N24'44 86W55'47 5:47:43
Pawnee 37 6 33N35 86W46 5:47:04
Pawnee Heights 37 6 33N37'43 86W44'45 5:46:59
Paynesville 60 1 32N36'48 88W20'48 5:53:23
Peace 1 1 32N24'31 86W46'16 5:47:05
Peaceburg 8 6 33N44'22 85W54'38 5:43:39
Peachburg 6 1 32N09'49 85W37'27 5:42:30
Peacock 13 1 31N45'26 87W46'29 5:51:06
Pearce 35 1 31N15'31 85W13'34 5:40:54
Pearces Mills 47 1 34N07'15 87W50'12 5:51:21
Pea Ridge 27 1 31N06'57 87W05'52 5:48:23
Pea Ridge 29 1 33N44'00 87W34'12 5:50:17
Pea Ridge 47 1 34N03'50 87W52'01 5:51:28
Pea Ridge 59 1 33N09 87W00 5:48:00
Pea Ridge Crossroads 25 1 34N38'18 85W42'53 5:42:52
Pearson 63 1 33N01'29 87W19'06 5:49:16
Peaveys Landing Boat Ramp 65 1 31N36'21 88W04'54 5:52:20
Peavy 56 1 33N08'35 85W27'15 5:41:49
Pebble 67 1 34N17'11 87W32'47 5:50:11
Pebble Hill 66 1 31N56'20 87W20'36 5:49:22
Peeks Corner 25 1 34N23'35 85W52'23 5:43:30
Peeks Hill 8 1 33N47 86W01 5:44:04
Peets Corner 42 1 34N43'49 86W52'39 5:47:31
Pelham 12 1 32N16'46 88W07'12 5:52:29
Pelham 59 1 33N17'08 86W48'36 5:47:14
Pelham Heights 8 6 33N43'56 85W48'06 5:43:12
Pell City 58 1 33N35'10 86W17'10 5:45:09
Pendley 64 1 33N43'59 87W30'43 5:50:03
Penfield Heights 37 6 33N35'39 86W43'47 5:46:55
Penn 52 1 34N21'22 87W05'00 5:48:20
Pennington 12 1 32N12'25 88W03'22 5:52:13
Pennsylvania 49 1 30N52'23 88W02'51 5:52:11
Penton 9 5 33N00'23 85W27'56 5:41:52
Pentonville 19 1 32N48'56 86W13'40 5:44:55
Pepperell 41 5 32N38'07 85W25'14 5:41:41
Pera 31 1 31N08'07 86W05'31 5:44:22
Perdido 2 1 31N00'27 87W37'38 5:50:31
Perdido Beach 2 1 30N20'26 87W30'18 5:50:01
Perdue Hill 50 1 31N30'50 87W29'36 5:49:58
Perkins Landing 2 1 30N50'28 87W54'11 5:51:37
Perote 6 1 31N56'51 85W42'19 5:42:49
Perrys Mill 51 1 32N17'28 86W09'30 5:44:38
Perry Store 16 1 31N16'48 86W09'26 5:44:38
Perryville 53 1 32N37'00 87W06'51 5:48:27
Perryville 62 1 33N01'16 85W48'05 5:43:12
Persimmon Grove 42 1 34N51'56 87W03'10 5:48:13
Persimmon Grove 60 1 32N19'05 88W04'38 5:52:19
Persons 57 7 32N11'10 85W15'33 5:41:02
Peterman 35 1 31N11'59 85W28'45 5:41:55
Peterman 50 1 31N35'04 87W15'34 5:49:02
Peterson 63 1 33N13'57 87W25'25 5:49:42
Petersville 39 1 34N51'19 87W41'30 5:50:46
Petes Crossroads 37 1 33N45'02 87W00'05 5:48:00
Petey 42 1 34N48 86W58 5:47:52
Petrey 21 1 31N50'55 86W12'28 5:44:50
Petronia 43 1 32N15'57 86W47'19 5:47:09
Pettusville 42 1 34N58'18 86W56'46 5:47:47
Peytonia Points 17 1 34N48'22 87W33'19 5:50:13
Phalin 63 1 33N04 87W27 5:49:48
Phelan 22 1 34N07'59 86W49'02 5:47:16
Phenix City 57 7 32N28'15 85W00'03 5:40:00
Philadelphia 35 1 31N09'39 85W06'27 5:40:26
Phil Campbell 30 1 34N21'03 87W42'23 5:50:50
Phillips Crossroads 23 1 31N37'00 85W36'25 5:42:26
Phillips Estates 37 1 33N20'51 86W55'48 5:47:43
Phillipsville 2 1 30N53'46 87W38'08 5:50:33
Phipps 33 1 32N55'46 87W30'10 5:50:01
Phoenixville 37 1 33N27'21 86W53'39 5:47:35
Pickens Ferry 54 1 33N13'41 88W17'27 5:53:10
Pickens Landing 13 1 31N58'55 88W03'58 5:52:16
Pickensville 54 1 33N13'38 88W15'59 5:53:04
Pickering 24 1 32N34 86W55 5:47:40
Pickett 6 1 31N58'40 85W37'34 5:42:30
Piedmont 8 1 33N55'28 85W36'41 5:42:27
Piedmont 45 2 34N42'02 86W34'37 5:46:18
Piedmont Heights 9 5 32N59'28 85W12'35 5:40:50
Piedmont Springs 8 1 33N54'01 85W40'16 5:42:41
Pierce 49 1 30N44 88W28 5:53:52
Pigeon Creek 7 1 31N39'27 86W30'26 5:46:02
Pigeye 47 1 34N17'52 87W55'27 5:51:42
Pike Road 51 1 32N17'03 86W06'11 5:44:25
Pikeville 36 1 34N44'37 86W02'19 5:44:09
Pikeville 47 1 34N02'17 87W57'04 5:51:48
Pilgrims Rest 28 6 33N57 86W01 5:44:04
Pinchona 2 1 30N55'23 87W43'27 5:50:54
Pinckard 23 1 31N18'41 85W33'11 5:42:13
Pinder Hill 36 1 34N51'22 85W49'15 5:43:17
Pine Apple 66 1 31N52'21 86W59'28 5:47:58
Pine Beach 2 1 30N16 87W41 5:50:44
Pinebelt 24 1 32N10'11 87W10'43 5:48:43
Pine Bluff Landing 65 1 31N13'38 87W58'53 5:51:56
Pine Crest 37 1 33N22'18 86W59'13 5:47:57
Pine Dale 42 1 34N57'44 86W49'39 5:47:19
Pinedale 51 4 32N17'42 86W14'19 5:44:57
Pinedale Acres 39 1 34N51'55 87W28'09 5:49:53
Pinedale Acres 42 1 34N47'37 86W59'35 5:47:58
Pinedale Shores 58 1 33N50'18 86W18'51 5:45:15
Pine Flat 11 1 32N39'15 86W25'52 5:45:43
Pine Grove 2 1 30N50'00 87W44'28 5:50:58
Pine Grove 6 1 32N02'09 85W35'20 5:42:21
Pine Grove 10 1 34N01'59 85W42'28 5:42:50
Pine Grove 41 5 32N42'58 85W15'07 5:41:00
Pine Grove 49 1 30N42'47 88W07'52 5:52:31
Pine Grove 62 1 32N46'11 85W42'18 5:42:49
Pine Haven Shores 39 1 34N51'25 87W21'36 5:49:26
Pine Hill 56 1 33N28'01 85W24'40 5:41:39
Pine Hill 66 1 31N58'46 87W35'17 5:50:21
Pine Lake Village 48 1 34N20'13 86W32'22 5:46:09
Pine Level 1 1 32N35'01 86W27'56 5:45:52
Pine Level 16 1 31N28'32 86W11'11 5:44:45
Pine Level 51 1 32N04'04 86W03'35 5:44:14
Pine Mountain 5 1 33N49 86W36 5:46:24
Pineola 49 1 31N03'26 88W06'42 5:52:27
Pine Orchard 50 1 31N38'26 87W08'11 5:48:33
Pine Springs 38 1 33N56'34 88W09'08 5:52:37
Pine Tuckey 56 1 33N28'21 85W32'21 5:42:09
Pineview 37 1 33N32'15 86W40'54 5:46:44
Pineville 50 1 31N44'33 87W10'38 5:48:43
Pinewood Terrace 61 1 33N17'15 86W21'32 5:45:26
Piney 10 1 34N09'07 85W37'35 5:42:30
Piney Bend 30 1 34N27'15 87W59'24 5:51:58
Piney Chapel 42 1 34N51'18 86W56'01 5:47:44
Piney Grove 31 1 31N10'07 86W03'03 5:44:12
Piney Grove 40 1 34N18'50 87W06'53 5:48:28
Piney Grove 47 1 34N05'09 87W44'51 5:50:59
Piney Woods 15 1 33N49'17 85W26'02 5:41:44
Pin Hook 46 1 32N21'27 87W52'18 5:51:29
Pinkney City 37 6 33N37'38 86W56'05 5:47:44
Pinkneyville 14 1 33N06'24 85W57'33 5:43:50
Pinnell 62 1 32N45'21 85W39'19 5:42:37
Pinson (Mt Pinson Station) 37 1 33N41'20 86W41'00 5:46:44
Pintlalla 51 1 32N10'32 86W22'03 5:45:28
Pioneer 54 1 33N09'59 87W53'06 5:51:32
Piper 4 1 33N05'22 87W02'29 5:48:10
Pisgah 36 1 34N40'51 85W50'52 5:43:23
Pisgah 42 1 34N54 86W44 5:46:56
Pisgah 51 1 31N59'48 86W07'06 5:44:28
Pittsview 57 7 32N11'17 85W09'48 5:40:39
Plainview 15 1 33N39'55 85W23'36 5:41:34
Plainview 23 1 31N22'02 85W36'47 5:42:27
Plainview 25 1 34N28'59 85W49'14 5:43:17
Plain View 37 6 33N34'28 86W46'17 5:47:05
Plano 10 1 34N06'51 85W43'39 5:42:55
Plant City 9 5 32N51'11 85W11'27 5:40:46
Plantersville 24 1 32N39'24 86W55'28 5:47:42
Plantersville 61 1 33N22'11 86W14'09 5:44:57
Plateau 49 1 30N44'10 88W03'50 5:52:15
Pleasant Gap 10 1 33N59'15 85W31'12 5:42:05
Pleasant Grove 11 1 32N55'18 86W47'41 5:47:11
Pleasant Grove 30 1 34N34'17 87W55'05 5:51:40
Pleasant Grove 36 1 34N43'57 86W12'51 5:44:51
Pleasant Grove 37 1 33N29'27 86W58'13 5:47:53
Pleasant Grove 48 1 34N16'08 86W20'19 5:45:21
Pleasant Grove 54 1 33N08'25 87W55'29 5:51:42
Pleasant Grove 58 1 33N31'16 86W24'33 5:45:38
Pleasant Grove Estates 37 1 33N29'24 86W57'33 5:47:50
Pleasant Hill 3 1 31N44'41 85W14'01 5:40:56
Pleasant Hill 12 1 31N55'48 88W12'52 5:52:51
Pleasant Hill 24 1 32N09'55 86W54'43 5:47:39
Pleasant Hill 25 1 34N26'24 85W50'02 5:43:20
Pleasant Hill 27 1 31N03'47 87W29'28 5:49:58
Pleasant Hill 36 1 34N33'49 86W07'59 5:44:32
Pleasant Hill 37 1 33N19'51 86W59'46 5:47:59
Pleasant Hill 44 1 32N27'30 85W36'57 5:42:28
Pleasant Hill 67 1 34N13'08 87W26'35 5:49:46
Pleasant Home 20 1 31N17 86W27 5:45:48
Pleasant Plains 35 1 31N18'15 85W13'47 5:40:55
Pleasant Ridge 30 1 34N30'20 87W41'20 5:50:45
Pleasant Ridge 32 1 33N00'51 88W05'01 5:52:20
Pleasant Ridge 47 1 34N10'18 87W59'26 5:51:58
Pleasant Ridge 55 1 31N39'52 86W03'16 5:44:13
Pleasant Site 30 1 34N32'31 88W03'55 5:52:16
Pleasant Valley 58 1 33N36'47 86W15'13 5:45:01
Pleasant View 22 1 34N14'05 86W45'56 5:47:04
Pletcher 11 1 32N42'10 86W47'06 5:47:08
Plevna 45 2 34N57'42 86W25'00 5:45:40
Poarch 27 1 31N07'02 87W31'46 5:50:07
Pocahontas 64 1 33N52'22 87W28'59 5:49:56
Pogo 30 1 34N33'26 88W06'50 5:52:27
Point Clear 2 1 30N28'26 87W55'09 5:51:41
Polk 24 1 32N16'20 86W53'19 5:47:33
Pollard 27 1 31N01'37 87W10'25 5:48:42
Pollards Bend 10 1 34N11 85W46 5:43:04
Ponders 62 1 32N42'37 85W46'27 5:43:06
Pondville 4 1 32N54'18 87W18'40 5:49:15
Pool 40 1 34N25 87W05 5:48:20
Pooles Crossroad 56 1 33N06'59 85W27'32 5:41:50
Pools Crossroads 11 1 32N44'55 86W43'10 5:46:53
Pope 10 1 34N03'31 85W38'12 5:42:33
Pope 25 1 34N29'56 85W53'10 5:43:33
Pope 46 1 32N03'46 87W37'28 5:50:30
Poplar Creek 40 1 34N43'53 87W08'30 5:48:34
Poplar Point 40 1 34N43'42 87W08'15 5:48:33
Poplar Ridge 48 1 34N35'14 86W21'53 5:45:28
Poplar Springs 48 1 34N24'52 86W08'13 5:44:33
Poplar Springs 67 1 34N01'57 87W23'46 5:49:35
Poplar Springs Branch 39 1 34N47'49 87W15'20 5:49:01
Port Birmingham 37 1 33N33'59 87W06'24 5:48:26
Porter 37 1 33N37'23 87W03'17 5:48:13
Porter Square 35 1 31N15 85W26 5:41:44
Portersville 25 1 34N19'16 85W49'15 5:43:17
Portland 24 1 32N09'16 87W10'07 5:48:40
Posey Mill 30 1 34N19'27 87W34'55 5:50:20
Poseys Crossroads 1 1 32N34'24 86W33'07 5:46:12
Poseys Crossroads 11 1 32N56'12 86W49'59 5:47:20
Postoak 6 1 32N00'03 85W49'12 5:43:17

Potash 56 1 33N16'38 85w21'09 5:41:25
Potter 24 1 32N25'52 87w06'29 5:48:26
Powderly 37 6 33N28'06 86w52'17 5:47:29
Powderly Hills 37 6 33N27'52 86w51'50 5:47:27
Powell 25 1 34N17'11 85w44'58 5:43:00
Powell Crossroads 25 1 34N32'02 85w53'19 5:43:33
Powellville 64 1 33N54'30 87w05'58 5:48:24
Powers 33 1 32N57'56 87w39'21 5:50:37
Powes Landing 12 1 31N48'57 88w10'54 5:52:44
Powhatan 37 1 33N35'26 87w06'31 5:48:26
Powledge 41 7 32N37'37 85w09'16 5:40:37
Praco 37 1 33N36'49 87w06'45 5:48:27
Prairie 66 1 32N09'14 87w26'24 5:49:46
Prairie Bluff 66 1 32N08'03 87w24'13 5:49:37
Prairieville 33 1 32N30'36 87w41'40 5:50:47
Pratt City 37 6 33N32'24 86w52'08 5:47:29
Prattmont 1 1 32N28 86w27 5:45:48
Pratts 3 1 31N49'51 85w30'35 5:42:02
Prattville 1 1 32N27'50 86w27'35 5:45:50
Prattville Junction 26 4 32N28'02 86w20'34 5:45:22
Prescott 58 1 33N34'06 86w26'45 5:45:47
Preston 48 1 34N31'33 86w10'21 5:44:41
Prestwick 65 1 31N27'10 87w57'58 5:51:52
Prices 8 1 33N53'25 85w41'45 5:42:47
Priceville 52 3 34N31'30 86w53'41 5:47:35
Prichard 49 1 30N44'19 88w04'44 5:52:19
Pride 17 1 34N44 87w42 5:50:48
Pride Landing 17 1 34N43'58 87w49'02 5:51:16
Primitive Ridge 4 1 33N06'01 87w07'34 5:48:30
Prince Crossroads 41 7 32N31'14 85w13'18 5:40:53
Princeton 36 1 34N50'36 86w14'35 5:44:58
Proctor 42 1 34N42'51 87w03'24 5:48:14
Pronto 55 1 31N45'26 85w49'03 5:43:16
Prospect 64 1 33N55'57 87w26'45 5:49:47
Providence 7 1 31N43'19 86w49'22 5:47:17
Providence 22 1 34N16'21 86w48'44 5:47:15
Providence 46 1 32N30 87w43 5:50:52
Providence 64 1 33N43'19 87w20'02 5:49:20
Prudence 57 7 32N11 85w10 5:40:40
Pruitton 39 1 34N59'25 87w36'34 5:50:26
Pull Tight 47 1 34N01'16 87w47'05 5:51:08
Pumpkin Center 25 1 34N26'07 85w38'07 5:42:32
Pumpkin Center 52 1 34N28'03 87w05'12 5:48:21
Pumpkin Center 64 1 33N38'22 87w09'16 5:48:37
Pushmataha 12 1 32N11'36 88w21'12 5:53:25
Putnam 46 1 32N01'21 88w01'53 5:52:08
Pyriton 14 1 33N21'47 85w50'02 5:43:20
Queenstown 37 1 33N35'17 86w37'16 5:46:29
Quinns Landing 12 1 31N56'14 88w07'00 5:52:28
Quinsey 19 1 32N56'58 86w27'52 5:45:51
Quintard Mall 8 6 33N40 85w50 5:43:20
Quinton 64 1 33N40'19 87w04'00 5:48:16
Quintown 64 1 33N38'11 87w05'30 5:48:22
Rabb 18 1 31N26 86w56 5:47:44
Rabbittown 8 1 33N49'11 85w38'34 5:42:34
Rabbit Town 48 1 34N16'47 86w15'30 5:45:02
Rabbittown 67 1 34N15'50 87w29'44 5:49:59
Rabun 2 1 31N01'36 87w43'30 5:50:54
Radford 53 1 32N35'21 87w12'00 5:48:48
Ragland 58 1 33N44'40 86w09'21 5:44:37
Rahatchie 61 1 33N16 86w21 5:45:24
Raimund 37 1 33N22'04 86w57'41 5:47:51
Rainbow 45 2 34N45'09 86w44'11 5:46:57
Rainbow City 28 6 33N57'17 86w02'31 5:44:10
Rainbow Mountain Heights 45 2 34N44'52 86w42'52 5:46:51
Rainsville 25 1 34N29'39 85w50'52 5:43:23
Raleigh 54 1 33N12 87w58 5:51:52
Ralph 63 1 33N02'31 87w46'08 5:51:05
Ramah 18 1 31N36'44 87w08'15 5:48:33
Ramer 51 1 32N03'01 86w13'17 5:44:53
Ramsey 28 6 33N59'32 86w08'57 5:44:36
Ranburne 15 1 33N31'22 85w20'41 5:41:23
Randolph 4 1 32N53'58 86w54'39 5:47:39
Range (Deer Range Station) 18 1 31N18'45 87w14'08 5:48:57
Rash 36 1 34N52'26 85w53'42 5:43:35
Rawls 20 1 31N27'11 86w28'52 5:45:55
Ray 19 1 32N53'14 86w02'16 5:44:09
Rayburn 48 1 34N20'56 86w16'03 5:45:04
Rays Crossroads 14 1 33N15'02 85w53'46 5:43:35
Reads Mill 8 1 33N52'23 85w54'06 5:43:36
Ready Crossing 45 2 34N55'58 86w43'45 5:46:55
Red Bank 40 1 34N46'02 87w22'12 5:49:29
Red Bay 30 1 34N26'23 88w08'27 5:52:34
Reddock Springs 7 1 31N50 86w38 5:46:32
Red Eagle 4 1 33N05'04 87w07'56 5:48:32
Red Gap Junction 37 1 33N32 86w42 5:46:48
Red Hill 5 1 33N43 87w00 5:48:00
Red Hill 26 1 32N41'06 85w56'35 5:43:46
Red Hill 48 1 34N15'21 86w25'27 5:45:42
Redland Heights 9 5 32N49 85w10 5:40:40
Red Level 9 1 33N05'23 85w28'40 5:41:55
Red Level 20 1 31N24'25 86w36'44 5:46:27
Red Level 51 1 32N08'03 86w13'24 5:44:54
Redmont Park 37 6 33N30'11 86w46'31 5:47:06
Red Ore 37 1 33N26 86w57 5:47:48
Red Rock 17 1 34N41'52 87w51'50 5:51:27
Red Springs 12 1 32N01'47 88w16'16 5:53:05
Red Star 64 1 33N42'45 87w07'17 5:48:29
Redstone Arsenal 45 2 34N44 86w36 5:46:24
Redstone Park 45 2 34N35'50 86w33'59 5:46:16
Redtown 2 1 31N08'16 87w37'57 5:50:32
Red Wine 37 1 33N37'04 86w57'38 5:47:51

Reece City 28 6 34N04'20 86w02'00 5:44:08
Reedtown 30 1 34N29'48 87w44'30 5:50:58
Reeltown 62 1 32N36'13 85w48'19 5:43:13
Reform 54 1 33N22'42 88w00'55 5:52:04
Regent Forest 37 6 33N25 86w48 5:47:12
Rehobeth 35 1 31N07'22 85w27'10 5:41:49
Rehoboth 66 1 32N11'44 87w22'53 5:49:32
Reid 42 1 34N44'57 87w02'19 5:48:09
Reid Settlement 65 1 31N14'45 88w05'56 5:52:24
Rembert 46 1 32N13'04 87w52'11 5:51:29
Remlap 5 1 33N49'00 86w36'03 5:46:24
Rendalia 61 1 33N19'03 86w09'26 5:44:38
Renfroe 61 1 33N25'52 86w12'06 5:44:48
Reno 63 1 33N20 87w01 5:48:04
Renson 50 1 31N33'14 87w17'02 5:49:08
Repton 18 1 31N24'32 87w14'21 5:48:57
Republic 37 6 33N36'04 86w53'27 5:47:34
Reynolds 40 1 34N37'59 87w10'22 5:48:41
Reynolds Mill 61 1 33N21'19 86w12'57 5:44:52
Rhoades 16 1 31N15'45 86w09'43 5:44:39
Rhodes 7 1 31N34'41 86w41'30 5:46:46
Rhodesville 39 1 34N52'20 87w52'14 5:51:29
Rice 37 1 33N22'24 86w58'29 5:47:54
Rice 48 1 34N19'06 86w32'01 5:46:08
Rice Creek Landing 2 1 31N00'55 87w52'48 5:51:31
Richards Crossroads 3 1 31N44'13 85w15'52 5:41:03
Richardson 10 1 34N12'02 85w44'33 5:42:58
Richburg 16 1 31N23'48 85w57'39 5:43:51
Richland 55 1 31N43'58 85w43'40 5:42:55
Richmond 24 1 32N06'50 87w03'18 5:48:13
Richmond Hills 17 1 34N43'40 87w43'01 5:50:52
Richville 19 1 32N48'54 86w19'06 5:45:16
Rickey 63 1 33N15'08 87w07'43 5:48:31
Riddle 26 1 32N39'17 86w14'55 5:45:00
Rideout Village 45 2 34N45'02 86w40'08 5:46:41
Riderville 11 1 32N40'38 86w55'53 5:47:44
Riderwood 12 1 32N07'43 88w19'40 5:53:19
Ridge 32 1 33N00'29 88w08'55 5:52:36
Ridge Grove 41 5 32N39'28 85w31'05 5:42:04
Ridgeville 7 1 31N52 86w50 5:47:20
Ridgeville 28 6 34N01 86w04 5:44:16
Ridgway Mill 42 1 34N56'07 87w11'32 5:48:46
Rigdom 40 1 34N38'46 87w21'44 5:49:27
Riley 50 1 31N43'34 87w07'34 5:48:30
Ringgold 10 1 34N20'02 85w32'52 5:42:11
Ripley 42 1 34N45'43 87w07'15 5:48:29
Riverbend 4 1 33N07 87w07 5:48:28
River Bend 22 1 34N02'21 86w42'49 5:46:51
River Bend 33 1 32N39 87w39 5:50:36
Riverdale 25 1 34N33'36 85w34'51 5:42:19
River Falls 20 1 31N21'10 86w32'21 5:46:09
Rivermont 17 1 34N44'08 87w43'28 5:50:54
River Park 2 1 30N27'02 87w48'43 5:51:15
River Park 25 1 34N30'19 85w36'37 5:42:26
River Ridge 50 1 31N42'49 87w18'47 5:49:15
Riverside 5 1 34N04'03 86w29'36 5:45:58
Riverside 22 1 34N05'41 86w40'04 5:46:40
Riverside 28 6 33N56'23 86w01'25 5:44:06
Riverside 58 1 33N36'22 86w12'16 5:44:49
Riverton 17 1 34N52'50 88w04'36 5:52:18
River View 9 5 32N47'20 85w08'42 5:40:35
Riverview 27 1 31N05 87w04 5:48:16
Riverview 63 6 33N13'11 87w31'42 5:50:07
Roanoke 56 1 33N09'04 85w22'20 5:41:29
Roanoke Junction 41 5 32N40'46 85w22'12 5:41:29
Roba 44 1 32N14'38 85w35'39 5:42:23
Robbins Crossroads 37 1 33N44'04 86w59'44 5:47:59
Roberson Beach 39 1 34N45'55 87w17'12 5:49:09
Roberta 59 1 33N05'45 86w48'25 5:47:14
Roberts 27 1 31N04'54 86w53'20 5:47:33
Roberts Crossroads 23 1 31N36'03 85w31'44 5:42:07
Robertsdale 2 1 30N33'13 87w42'43 5:50:51
Robertsville 64 1 34N52 85w23 5:41:32
Robinson Crossroads 21 1 31N44'08 86w22'32 5:45:30
Robinson Crossroads 51 1 32N09'05 86w13'48 5:44:55
Robinsons 43 1 32N19'48 86w33'33 5:46:14
Robinson Springs 26 4 32N30'42 86w22'36 5:45:30
Robinsonville 27 1 31N03'40 87w26'18 5:49:45
Robinwood 37 6 33N36'54 86w44'56 5:47:00
Robjohn 12 1 32N12'50 88w07'38 5:52:31
Rock City 36 1 34N31'57 85w57'01 5:43:48
Rock City 47 1 33N59'04 87w42'31 5:50:50
Rock Creek 17 1 34N35'48 87w55'00 5:51:40
Rock Creek 67 1 34N11'42 87w23'22 5:49:33
Rockdale 37 1 33N20'46 86w58'41 5:47:55
Rocket 45 2 34N41 86w40 5:46:40
Rock Fence 9 5 33N02'10 85w26'19 5:41:45
Rockford 19 1 32N53'22 86w13'11 5:44:53
Rock Hill 27 1 31N06'59 86w59'57 5:48:00
Rock House 36 1 34N35 85w59 5:43:56
Rockhouse Landing 42 1 34N33'45 86w50'45 5:47:23
Rockledge 28 1 34N05'21 86w06'46 5:44:27
Rock Mills 56 1 33N09'35 85w17'15 5:41:09
Rock Run 10 1 34N01'40 85w29'43 5:41:59
Rock Spring 28 1 33N56'12 85w54'38 5:43:39
Rock Springs 5 1 34N10'05 86w32'12 5:46:09
Rock Springs 12 1 32N04'42 88w21'59 5:53:28
Rock Springs 13 1 31N57'00 88w04'52 5:52:19
Rock Stand 56 1 33N09 85w22 5:41:28
Rockville 13 1 31N25'12 87w50'33 5:51:22
Rockwest 66 1 31N59'59 87w22'18 5:49:29
Rockwood 30 1 34N27'18 87w47'05 5:51:08
Rocky Ford 32 1 32N42'21 87w50'30 5:51:22
Rocky Head 23 1 31N34'05 85w46'07 5:43:04
Rocky Hill 40 1 34N40'46 87w20'40 5:49:23
Rocky Hollow 64 1 33N46'53 87w05'05 5:48:20
Rocky Mount 11 1 32N59'27 86w43'01 5:46:52

Rocky Point 52 1 34N31'42 86w48'21 5:47:13
Rocky Ridge 37 6 33N25'01 86w46'23 5:47:06
Rocky Ridge 48 1 34N35'45 86w16'30 5:45:06
Rocky Springs 36 1 34N57'28 85w45'12 5:43:01
Rodentown 25 1 34N14'04 86w01'01 5:44:04
Rodgers 25 1 34N39'19 85w36'02 5:42:24
Roebuck 37 1 33N34'53 86w42'11 5:46:49
Roebuck 59 1 33N16'38 86w52'21 5:47:29
Roebuck Crest Estates 37 1 33N35'47 86w42'06 5:46:48
Roebuck Forest 37 1 33N34'59 86w40'53 5:46:44
Roebuck Gardens 37 1 33N36'37 86w41'54 5:46:48
Roebuck Park 37 1 33N36'19 86w41'42 5:46:47
Roebuck Plaza 37 1 33N35'15 86w39'36 5:46:38
Roebuck Springs 37 1 33N34'37 86w42'13 5:46:49
Roebuck Terrace 37 6 33N34'48 86w43'21 5:46:53
Roe Landing 32 1 32N36'16 87w50'23 5:51:22
Roeton 16 1 31N35'51 85w50'05 5:43:20
Rogers 25 1 34N20'29 86w05'29 5:44:22
Rogersville 39 1 34N49'32 87w17'41 5:49:11
Rolling Hills 52 3 34N33'46 86w55'14 5:47:41
Rollins 9 5 32N56'46 85w25'31 5:41:42
Romar Beach 2 1 30N15'38 87w37'20 5:50:29
Rome 20 1 31N08'30 86w40'08 5:46:41
Romulus 63 1 33N08'51 87w45'07 5:51:00
Roosevelt 37 1 33N26'22 86w55'59 5:47:44
Roosevelt Cairo Village 37 1 33N26'46 86w55'06 5:47:40
Roper 37 1 33N36'23 86w34'49 5:46:19
Rosa 5 1 33N59'26 86w30'48 5:46:03
Rosalie 36 1 34N41'59 85w46'07 5:43:04
Roseboro 45 2 34N59'03 86w24'09 5:45:37
Rosebud 66 1 31N56'28 87w08'13 5:48:33
Rosedale 37 6 33N29'01 86w47'39 5:47:11
Rosedale 63 6 33N12 87w32 5:50:08
Rose Hill 20 1 31N26'57 86w20'22 5:45:21
Rose Hill 37 1 33N32'56 86w39'51 5:46:39
Roselle 14 1 33N11'08 86w02'59 5:44:12
Rosemary 33 1 32N38'52 87w34'30 5:50:18
Rosemont 32 1 32N40'16 87w54'29 5:51:38
Rosemont 37 6 33N27'28 86w53'06 5:47:32
Rose Park 39 1 34N51'37 87w40'19 5:50:41
Rosinton 2 1 30N37'06 87w41'37 5:50:46
Ross Ford 14 1 33N06'40 86w03'46 5:44:15
Rossland City 29 1 33N40'47 87w46'53 5:51:08
Roundhill 13 1 31N53'33 87w42'42 5:50:51
Round Mountain 10 1 34N12'56 85w41'02 5:42:44
Rowells Crossroads 41 5 32N41'10 85w34'38 5:42:19
Roxana 9 5 32N41'13 85w40'09 5:42:41
Roxana 51 1 32N10'59 86w16'18 5:45:05
Royal 5 1 34N04'19 86w30'08 5:46:01
Roy Ford 59 1 33N19'29 86w50'52 5:47:23
Ruffner 37 1 33N32'58 86w42'17 5:46:49
Rural 13 1 31N51'51 87w44'19 5:50:57
Russell 29 1 33N50 87w50 5:51:20
Russell 49 1 31N07 88w14 5:52:56
Russell Heights 37 1 33N33'12 86w33'37 5:46:14
Russell Mill 62 1 32N59 85w52 5:43:28
Russell Village 52 3 34N33'44 86w59'28 5:47:58
Russellville 30 1 34N30'28 87w43'43 5:50:55
Rutan 65 1 31N26'22 88w11'22 5:52:45
Ruth 48 1 34N21'51 86w33'24 5:46:14
Rutherford 57 7 32N11'20 85w19'05 5:41:16
Rutledge 21 1 31N43'49 86w18'35 5:45:14
Rutledge 37 1 33N28 86w55 5:47:40
Rutledge Heights 45 2 34N44'47 86w38'29 5:46:34
Rutledge Springs 37 1 33N27'40 86w56'51 5:47:47
Rutthven 66 1 31N51'12 87w01'47 5:48:07
Ryan 59 1 33N10'04 86w52'00 5:47:28
Ryan Crossroads 52 1 34N20'31 86w36'37 5:46:26
Ryland 45 2 34N46'11 86w28'51 5:45:55
Saco 55 1 31N57'18 85w49'15 5:43:17
Safford 24 1 32N17'16 87w22'17 5:49:29
Saginaw 59 1 33N12'58 86w47'31 5:47:10
Sahama Village 63 6 33N12 87w32 5:50:08
Saint Bernard 22 1 34N10 86w49 5:47:16
Saint Clair 43 1 32N19'24 86w37'00 5:46:28
Saint Clair Springs 58 1 33N45'47 86w24'11 5:45:37
Saint Clair Store 45 2 34N50'12 86w24'44 5:45:39
Saint Elmo 49 1 30N30'12 88w15'15 5:53:01
Saint Florian 39 1 34N52'24 87w37'24 5:50:30
Saint Ives 61 1 33N25'48 86w15'01 5:45:00
Saints Crossroads 30 1 34N32'56 87w35'20 5:50:21
Saint Stephens 65 1 31N32'25 88w03'19 5:52:13
Saks 8 6 33N41'55 85w50'23 5:43:22
Salco 49 1 30N58'03 88w02'07 5:52:08
Salem 24 1 32N21'01 87w15'44 5:49:03
Salem 29 1 33N40'41 87w29'53 5:50:00
Salem 41 7 32N35'48 85w14'19 5:40:57
Salem 42 1 34N56'20 87w06'53 5:48:28
Salem Corner 42 1 34N42'03 86w52'42 5:47:31
Salitpa 13 1 31N37'46 88w01'12 5:52:05
Salt Well 46 1 32N27'25 87w55'52 5:51:43
Samantha 63 1 33N25'20 87w36'19 5:50:25
Samford University 37 6 33N27 86w49 5:47:16
Samoset 64 1 33N44'11 87w07'39 5:48:31
Samson 31 1 31N06'46 86w02'46 5:44:11
Samuels Chapel 28 1 34N04 86w21 5:45:24
Sanders Hill 55 1 31N42'19 86w02'11 5:44:09

Sandfield 55 1 31N54'21 85W48'28 5:43:14
Sandfort 57 7 32N20'17 85W13'24 5:40:54
Sand Landing 49 1 30N55'25 87W57'54 5:51:52
Sand Mountain 4 1 32N51'17 86W54'45 5:47:39
Sand Rock 10 1 34N14'34 85W46'07 5:43:04
Sand Springs 42 1 34N55 86W51 5:47:24
Sandtown 63 1 33N35'24 87W29'31 5:49:58
Sandusky 37 6 33N32'59 86W54'01 5:47:36
Sandy Creek 9 5 32N48 85W39 5:42:36
Sandy Point 3 1 31N47'31 85W16'12 5:41:05
Sandy Ridge 43 1 32N01'28 86W27'07 5:45:48
Sandy Springs 10
1 34N04'23 85W29'56 5:42:00
Sanford 20 1 31N17'53 86W23'21 5:45:33
Sanford Springs 10
1 34N01'05 85W34'24 5:42:18
Sanie 58 1 33N39'37 86W28'44 5:45:55
San Souci Beach 49
1 30N23'19 88W15'30 5:53:02
Santuck 26 1 32N37'58 86W07'47 5:44:31
Sapps 54 1 33N13'15 88W10'09 5:52:41
Saragossa 64 1 33N53'56 87W23'57 5:49:36
Saraland 49 1 30N49'14 88W04'14 5:52:17
Saratoga 48 1 34N15'10 86W11'34 5:44:46
Sardine 27 1 31N00 87W15 5:49:00
Sardis 6 1 32N05'20 85W45'46 5:43:03
Sardis 21 1 31N54'10 86W18'57 5:45:16
Sardis 24 1 32N17'15 86W59'09 5:47:57
Sardis 64 1 33N47'48 87W08'56 5:48:36
Sardis City 28 1 34N10'27 86W07'22 5:44:29
Sardis Springs 42
1 34N50'11 86W53'07 5:47:32
Satsuma 49 1 30N51'11 88W03'22 5:52:13
Saucer 7 1 31N52 86W50 5:47:20
Savannah Ford 39
1 34N59'18 87W35'04 5:50:20
Saville 21 1 31N52'38 86W19'52 5:45:19
Sawyerville 33 1 32N45'06 87W43'46 5:50:55
Sayre 37 1 33N42'44 86W58'28 5:47:54
Sayreton 37 6 33N33'42 86W49'47 5:47:19
Scant City 48 1 34N21'44 86W25'25 5:45:42
Scarce Grease 42
1 34N58'14 87W07'57 5:48:32
Scenic Heights 28
6 34N03'16 86W02'02 5:44:08
Schenks 8 1 33N49 85W54 5:43:36
Schley 19 1 32N47'35 86W22'12 5:45:29
Schmits Mill 61 1 33N37 86W07 5:44:28
Schultys Landing 13
1 31N56'21 88W06'04 5:52:24
Schuster 66 1 31N51'50 87W02'49 5:48:11
Scotland 50 1 31N40'00 87W16'23 5:49:06
Scott City 37 1 33N32'49 86W34'47 5:46:19
Scott Ford 30 1 34N22'15 87W55'10 5:51:41
Scottland 6 1 32N01'35 85W42'23 5:42:50
Scottrock 59 1 33N15'04 86W49'24 5:47:18
Scottsboro 36 1 34N40'20 86W02'03 5:44:08
Scottsboro Crossroads 34
1 31N41'57 85W12'43 5:40:51
Scrange 2 1 31N10 87W32 5:50:08
Scranton 31 1 31N11'34 85W50'31 5:43:22
Scratch Ankle 50
1 31N39'45 87W26'15 5:49:45
Scratch Hill 60 1 32N26'41 88W15'52 5:53:03
Screamer 34 1 31N39'41 85W12'24 5:40:50
Scrougeout 28 6 34N10'51 85W52'09 5:43:29
Scruggs Landing 13
1 31N53'47 88W07'50 5:52:31
Scyrene 13 1 31N45'20 87W38'52 5:50:35
Seaboard 65 1 31N19'16 88W11'19 5:52:45
Seacliff 2 1 30N32'42 87W54'10 5:51:37
Seale 57 7 32N17'50 85W10'08 5:40:41
Sealy Springs 35
1 31N02'12 85W18'32 5:41:14
Searcy 7 1 31N54'55 86W36'19 5:46:25
Searight 21 1 31N28'15 86W23'36 5:45:34
Searles 63 1 33N19'27 87W19'18 5:49:17
Section 36 1 34N34'44 85W59'12 5:43:57
Seddon 58 1 33N35'32 86W13'39 5:44:55
Sedgefield 6 1 32N11'01 85W42'17 5:42:49
Sedgefield 24 1 32N14'22 87W21'41 5:49:27
Segco 64 1 33N44 87W17 5:49:08
Self Creek 37 1 33N46'55 86W45'02 5:47:00
Selfville 5 1 33N49'49 86W40'05 5:46:40
Sellers 51 1 32N03'22 86W18'11 5:45:13
Sellers Landing 13
1 31N51'48 88W08'27 5:52:34
Sellersville 31 1 31N07'47 86W00'15 5:44:01
Selma 24 1 32N24'26 87W01'16 5:48:05
Selma Mall 24 1 32N23 87W00 5:48:00
Selmont 24 1 32N23'42 87W00'30 5:48:02
Seloca 37 1 33N47'55 86W49'16 5:47:17
Seman 26 1 32N43'57 86W06'44 5:44:27
Seminole 2 1 30N30'54 87W28'26 5:49:54
Semmes 49 1 30N46'41 88W15'33 5:53:02
Serange 2 1 31N13'04 87W38'21 5:50:33
Service 12 1 31N44 88W12 5:52:48
Sessions 62 1 32N55'48 85W44'48 5:42:59
Seven Hills 49 1 30N39'14 88W18'11 5:53:13
Seven Pines 30 1 34N28'26 88W04'07 5:52:16
Sewell 56 1 33N23'23 85W18'23 5:41:14
Seymour 4 1 33N06'52 87W01'30 5:48:06
Shacklesville 7 1 31N38 86W44 5:46:56
Shades Cliff 37 6 33N25'52 86W49'37 5:47:18
Shades Creek 37 6 33N27 86W49 5:47:16
Shades Crest Estates 37
6 33N25 86W48 5:47:12
Shady Brook 37 1 33N21'59 86W58'13 5:47:53
Shady Grove 14 1 33N10'08 86W00'22 5:44:01
Shady Grove 16 1 31N31'26 86W02'16 5:44:09
Shady Grove 30 1 34N21 87W42 5:50:48
Shady Grove 37 1 33N35'35 87W00'12 5:48:01
Shady Grove 55 1 31N54'34 86W09'45 5:44:39
Shady Grove 65 1 31N37'51 88W23'29 5:53:34
Shady Lane 45 2 34N45'23 86W37'14 5:46:29
Shadywood 37 1 33N34'38 86W41'30 5:46:46
Shanghai 42 1 34N51'00 87W05'06 5:48:20
Shannon 37 1 33N24'19 86W52'19 5:47:29
Sharps Mill 39 1 34N54'29 87W42'20 5:50:49
Shaw 54 1 33N30'23 88W05'39 5:52:23
Shawmut 9 5 32N50'25 85W11'00 5:40:44
Shawnee 66 1 32N00 87W18 5:49:12
Sheffield 17 1 34N45'54 87W41'55 5:50:48

Shelby 59 1 33N06'37 86W35'03 5:46:20
Shelby Shores 59
1 33N07'42 86W27'57 5:45:52
Shelby Springs 59
1 33N08'06 86W41'12 5:46:45
Shell 7 1 31N36'04 86W39'13 5:46:37
Shellhorn 55 1 31N52'33 86W04'47 5:44:19
Shell Landing 2 1 30N54'38 87W52'17 5:51:29
Shepherd Hill 51
1 32N11'08 86W03'59 5:44:16
Sherman Heights 8
6 33N43'59 85W47'53 5:43:12
Sherman Heights 37
6 33N31'17 86W54'19 5:47:37
Sherwood Forest 39
1 34N50'37 87W40'54 5:50:44
Sherwood Park 45
2 34N43'11 86W39'45 5:46:39
Shiloh 9 5 33N01'15 85W32'12 5:42:09
Shiloh 25 1 34N27'45 85W52'47 5:43:31
Shiloh 46 1 32N07'38 87W44'07 5:50:56
Shiloh 55 1 31N46'52 85W44'39 5:42:59
Shinebone 14 1 33N18 85W45 5:43:00
Shingle 30 1 34N21 87W42 5:50:48
Shirleys Crossroads 21
1 31N42'53 86W09'54 5:44:40
Shoals Acres 39 1 34N52'07 87W33'10 5:50:13
Shopton 6 1 32N07'01 85W56'32 5:43:46
Short Creek 37 1 33N33'04 87W06'05 5:48:24
Shorter 44 1 32N23'41 85W55'01 5:43:40
Shorterville 34 1 31N34'12 85W06'05 5:40:24
Shortleaf 46 1 32N30'42 87W51'20 5:51:25
Shottsville 47 1 34N15'39 88W07'38 5:52:31
Shotwell 41 7 32N35'03 85W11'01 5:40:44
Shrader 36 1 34N42'54 85W44'03 5:42:56
Shreve 18 1 31N30'34 86W42'25 5:46:50
Sibert 49 1 30N44'40 88W03'36 5:52:14
Sico 61 1 33N10 86W19 5:45:16
Siddonsville 46 1 32N25'05 87W36'48 5:50:27
Sidney 48 1 34N16'44 86W21'57 5:45:28
Sidney 49 1 31N07 88W14 5:52:56
Sigma 35 1 31N16'55 85W11'50 5:40:47
Sigsbee 25 1 34N20'29 85W42'36 5:42:50
Sikes 9 5 32N53'19 85W33'31 5:42:14
Sikesville 14 1 33N07'35 85W40'29 5:42:42
Silas 12 1 31N45'55 88W19'45 5:53:19
Siloam 60 1 32N25'22 88W16'03 5:53:04
Siluria 59 1 63N13'45 86W49'30 5:47:18
Silver Cross 65 1 31N40'51 88W10'27 5:52:42
Silverhill 2 1 30N32'43 87W45'06 5:51:00
Silver Landing 2
1 31N13'58 87W50'52 5:51:23
Silver Run 61 1 33N33'54 85W54'29 5:43:38
Simcoe 22 1 34N13'27 86W44'04 5:46:56
Simmons Crossroads 62
1 32N40'02 85W43'21 5:42:53
Simmsville 59 1 33N19'28 86W42'32 5:46:50
Simpson 62 1 33N04'18 85W43'19 5:42:53
Simsville 6 1 32N06'16 85W52'15 5:43:29
Sipsey 64 1 33N49'29 87W05'10 5:48:21
Sixmile 4 1 33N00'28 87W00'20 5:48:01
Six Mile 52 1 34N25'26 86W45'23 5:47:02
Six Way 52 1 34N31'28 86W52'58 5:47:32
Sizemore Landing 2
1 30N51'49 87W53'44 5:51:35
Skaggs Corner 25
1 34N41'47 85W41'26 5:42:46
Skeggs Crossroads 14
1 33N06'55 86W06'46 5:44:27
Skinem 45 2 34N57'27 86W31'07 5:46:04
Skinnerton 18 1 31N40'11 87W03'54 5:48:16
Skipperville 23 1 31N33'27 85W32'44 5:42:11
Skirum 25 1 34N19'25 85W58'02 5:43:52
Sky Ball 5 1 34N01'19 86W38'10 5:46:33
Skyhaven Estates 28
1 34N09'06 86W08'59 5:44:36
Skyline 36 1 34N39 86W01 5:44:04
Skyline Acres 45
2 34N42'55 86W42'24 5:46:50
Skyline Estates 37
6 33N25 86W48 5:47:12
Sky Ranch 37 6 33N25 86W48 5:47:12
Skyview 37 1 33N23'17 86W58'33 5:47:54
Slackland 10 6 34N08'48 85W49'48 5:43:19
Slater 12 1 31N59'36 88W06'00 5:52:24
Slaughter Landing 45
1 34N35'14 86W41'59 5:46:48
Slaughters 62 1 32N49'31 85W40'21 5:42:41
Sledge 60 1 32N41'58 88W18'36 5:53:14
Slick Ford 67 1 34N05'14 87W16'05 5:49:04
Slickrock Ford 30
1 34N31'37 87W54'47 5:51:39
Slidocco Springs 61
1 33N27'20 86W08'17 5:44:33
Sloan 5 1 33N50'51 86W57'21 5:47:49
Slocomb 31 1 31N06'29 85W35'40 5:42:23
Sloss 64 1 33N45'07 87W04'42 5:48:19
Smithfield 37 6 33N30'30 86W50'31 5:47:22
Smith Hill 4 1 33N07'20 87W06'07 5:48:24
Smith Institute 28
1 34N11'06 86W03'02 5:44:12
Smithport 49 1 30N27'33 88W06'54 5:52:28
Smiths 41 7 32N32 85W06 5:40:24
Smiths Ford 4 1 33N02'46 87W11'56 5:48:48
Smiths Mill 61 1 33N33'36 86W07'12 5:44:29
Smithson 37 1 33N18'35 86W57'09 5:47:49
Smithsonia 39 1 34N47'39 87W52'45 5:51:31
Smiths Station 41
7 32N32'24 85W05'55 5:40:24
Smithtown 49 1 30N51'39 88W12'31 5:52:50
Smuteye 6 1 31N58'40 85W39'01 5:42:36
Smyer 13 1 31N53'36 88W01'44 5:52:07
Smyrna 35 1 31N14'06 85W19'32 5:41:18
Snead 5 1 34N07'10 86W23'44 5:45:35
Snead Crossroads 5
1 34N07'10 86W23'44 5:45:35
Snells Crossroads 23
1 31N31'32 85W26'10 5:41:45
Snoddy 32 1 33N02'19 87W52'32 5:51:30
Snowdoun 51 1 32N14'29 86W17'47 5:45:11
Snow Hill 23 1 31N27'33 85W28'50 5:41:55
Snow Hill 66 1 32N00'16 87W00'26 5:48:02
Snowtown 37 1 33N39'47 87W02'18 5:48:09

Socapatoy 19 1 32N59'11 86W04'02 5:44:16
Social Town 21 1 31N42'42 86W10'55 5:44:44
Society Hill 44 1 32N25'35 85W26'43 5:41:47
Soleo 19 1 33N00'49 86W02'07 5:44:08
Somerville 52 1 34N28'23 86W47'55 5:47:12
Sonoma 28 1 34N04'30 85W54'10 5:43:37
South 20 1 31N24 86W37 5:46:28
South Calera 59 1 33N04'28 86W44'58 5:47:00
Southern Junction 35
1 31N01'45 85W28'12 5:41:53
South Gadsden 28
6 34N00'06 86W02'43 5:44:11
South Gate Mall 17
1 34N45 87W41 5:50:44
South Guntersville 48
1 34N21 86W19 5:45:16
South Haleyville 47
1 34N12'40 87W38'06 5:50:32
South Highlands 37
6 33N34'11 86W42'47 5:46:51
South Hill 25 1 34N24'37 86W02'18 5:44:09
South Holt 63 6 33N12 87W32 5:50:08
South Lowell 64 1 33N54'36 87W16'10 5:49:05
Southmont 51 4 32N19'22 86W17'57 5:45:12
South Orchard 49
1 30N27'53 88W09'02 5:52:36
South Sheffield 17
1 34N44'32 87W42'13 5:50:49
Southside 28 1 33N55'28 86W01'21 5:44:05
Southtown 48 1 34N21'00 86W18'35 5:45:14
Southwood 37 6 33N28'11 86W46'57 5:47:08
Souwilpa 12 1 31N49'12 88W19'45 5:53:19
Spain Ford 67 1 34N02'11 87W22'42 5:49:31
Spanish Fort 2 1 30N40 87W54 5:51:36
Spaulding 37 6 33N28'07 86W50'33 5:47:22
Speake 40 1 34N24'57 87W10'03 5:48:40
Spears 31 1 31N08'41 85W59'08 5:43:57
Speed 19 1 32N46'29 86W13'55 5:44:56
Speeds Water Mill 54
1 33N20 87W54 5:51:36
Speigner 26 1 32N35'02 86W20'41 5:45:23
Spencer Store 42
1 34N54'57 87W02'29 5:48:10
Spocari 46 1 32N31'04 87W48'49 5:51:15
Sprague 51 1 32N07'58 86W16'12 5:45:05
Springbrook 63 6 33N12 87W32 5:50:08
Springdale 37 6 33N36'03 86W45'59 5:47:04
Springfield 13 1 31N50'01 87W45'43 5:51:03
Springfield 39 1 34N53'17 87W23'17 5:49:33
Springfield 56 1 33N12'43 85W19'02 5:41:16
Spring Garden 10
1 33N58'22 85W33'14 5:42:13
Spring Hill 3 1 32N04'45 85W20'13 5:41:21
Spring Hill 7 1 31N52'21 86W37'27 5:46:18
Spring Hill 12 1 31N56'49 88W08'14 5:52:33
Springhill 14 1 33N18'37 85W55'19 5:43:41
Spring Hill 22 1 34N11'40 86W57'23 5:47:50
Spring Hill 27 1 31N06'28 87W02'07 5:48:08
Spring Hill 49 1 30N41'54 88W08'20 5:52:33
Spring Hill 55 1 31N41'27 85W57'38 5:43:51
Spring Hill 64 1 33N58'39 87W33'29 5:50:14
Spring Lake Estates 37
1 33N37'08 86W40'26 5:46:42
Springs Junction 59
1 33N06'42 86W41'10 5:46:45
Spring Valley 17
1 34N39'24 87W37'00 5:50:28
Spring Villa 41 5 32N35'18 85W18'41 5:41:15
Springville 58 1 33N46'30 86W28'18 5:45:53
Springville Lake Estates 58
1 33N47'29 86W30'58 5:46:04
Sprott 53 1 32N40'36 87W13'17 5:48:53
Spruce Pine 30 1 34N23'31 87W43'35 5:50:54
Stafford 54 1 33N26'48 88W14'42 5:52:59
Stamp 25 1 34N35'16 85W43'34 5:42:54
Standard 60 1 32N24'50 88W17'32 5:53:10
Standard 64 1 33N44'09 87W16'14 5:49:05
Standing Rock 9 5 33N04'47 85W15'11 5:41:01
Stanley 20 1 31N12'03 86W26'52 5:45:47
Stanley Crossroads 27
1 31N08'04 87W20'25 5:49:22
Stansel 54 1 33N19'10 88W02'44 5:52:11
Stanton 11 1 32N44'08 86W53'59 5:47:36
Stapler Ford 48 1 34N31'07 86W20'57 5:45:24
Stapleton 2 1 30N44'33 87W47'36 5:51:10
Star Hill 3 1 31N54'45 85W37'54 5:42:32
Starlington 7 1 31N40'29 86W49'31 5:47:18
Staryeacre Ford 37
1 33N25'39 87W04'52 5:48:19
State Line 35 1 30N57 85W24 5:41:36
State Line 45 2 34N59'26 86W34'17 5:46:17
Statesville 1 1 32N28'10 86W49'50 5:47:19
Steam Mill Landing 2
1 30N45'17 87W54'59 5:51:40
Stedman 20 1 31N04'16 86W18'13 5:45:13
Steele 58 1 33N56'23 86W12'06 5:44:48
Steele Crossing 45
2 34N58'41 86W24'38 5:45:39
Steelwood 2 1 30N42'56 87W47'05 5:51:08
Steenson Hollow 17
1 34N47'09 87W36'41 5:50:27
Steiner 51 4 32N21'01 86W15'39 5:45:03
Stemley 61 1 33N31'06 86W13'21 5:44:53
Stems 59 1 33N07'52 86W45'20 5:47:01
Stephenson Crossing 64
1 33N41'55 87W24'58 5:49:40
Steppville 22 1 34N04 86W46 5:47:04
Sterrett 59 1 33N26'55 86W28'48 5:45:55
Stevenson 36 1 34N52'07 85W50'22 5:43:21
Stewart 33 1 32N54'40 87W42'22 5:50:49
Stewarts 58 1 33N37'07 86W18'57 5:45:16
Stewarts Crossroads 58
1 33N32'26 86W27'27 5:45:50
Stewartville 19 1 33N04'45 86W14'40 5:44:59
Stills Crossroads 55
1 31N59'50 85W53'35 5:43:34
Stinson 47 1 34N01'15 87W54'28 5:51:38
Stockdale 61 1 33N25'22 86W01'38 5:44:07
Stockton 2 1 30N59'37 87W51'29 5:51:26
Stokeley 20 1 31N17 86W27 5:45:48
Stokes 63 1 33N08'07 87W30'18 5:50:01
Stonewall 24 1 32N33'53 87W02'18 5:48:09
Stonewall 41 5 32N42'23 85W28'39 5:41:55

Stoney Point 1 1 32n35'27 86w25'56 5:45:44
Stotesville 4 1 33n07 87w07 5:48:28
Stough 29 1 33n41'44 87w44'40 5:50:59
Straight Mountain 5
1 33n55 86w27 5:45:48
Strata 51 1 32n02'04 86w17'39 5:45:11
Straughn 20 1 31n23'17 86w25'05 5:45:40
Straven 59 1 33n13'10 86w53'23 5:47:34
Strawberry 5 1 34n14'57 86w29'42 5:45:59
Strickland Crossroads 19
1 33n03'46 86w23'10 5:45:33
Stringer 52 1 34n26'08 86w45'23 5:47:02
Stroud 9 5 33n03'17 85w19'51 5:41:19
Stroups Crossroads 52
1 34n25 87w05 5:48:20
Studdards Crossroads 29
1 33n48'30 87w35'15 5:50:21
Sturdivant 62 1 32n54'39 85w51'07 5:43:24
Sturkie 9 5 32n47'52 85w28'08 5:41:53
Sublett Mill 45 2 34n41'56 86w25'07 5:45:40
Sueann 37 1 33n46'13 86w40'13 5:46:41
Sugar Creek 5 1 33n56'20 86w40'48 5:46:43
Suggsville 13 1 31n35'22 87w41'35 5:50:46
Sulligent 38 1 33n54'06 88w08'04 5:52:32
Sullivan Crossroads 39
1 34n54'01 87w48'03 5:51:12
Sulphur Spring 61
1 33n06'56 86w26'37 5:45:46
Sulphur Springs 8
1 33n41'39 86w03'20 5:44:13
Sulphur Springs 22
1 34n03'51 87w01'59 5:48:08
Sulphur Springs 25
1 34n41'51 85w34'49 5:42:19
Sulphur Springs 36
1 34n47'47 85w44'31 5:42:58
Sulphur Springs 45
2 34n55'03 86w30'21 5:46:01
Sumiton 64 1 33n45'20 87w03'00 5:48:12
Summer Bluff 36 1 34n57'33 85w46'02 5:43:04
Summerdale 2 1 30n29'15 87w41'59 5:50:48
Summerfield 24 1 32n31'14 87w02'30 5:48:10
Summerville 49 1 30n44'43 88w04'36 5:52:18
Summit 5 1 34n12'16 86w29'39 5:45:59
Summit Farm 37 1 33n18'04 86w59'00 5:47:56
Sumter 37 1 33n21'12 87w07'40 5:48:31
Sumterville 60 1 32n42'42 88w14'20 5:52:57
Sunflower 65 1 31n22'56 88w00'30 5:52:02
Sunlight 64 1 33n55'37 87w12'37 5:48:50
Sunny Cove 49 1 30n29'02 88w06'03 5:52:24
Sunny Home 47 1 34n05'03 87w41'57 5:50:48
Sunnyside Landing 52
1 34n34'33 86w43'33 5:46:54
Sunny South 66 1 31n57'53 87w38'24 5:50:34
Sunset Acres 48 1 34n19'09 86w30'50 5:46:03
Sunset Cove 45 2 34n38'40 86w31'43 5:46:07
Sunset Mill Village 24
1 32n23 87w00 5:48:00
Sun Valley 37 1 33n38'39 86w41'56 5:46:48
Superior 59 1 33n12'38 86w55'49 5:47:43
Surginer 46 1 32n03'19 87w42'33 5:50:50
Suspension 6 1 32n11'47 85w35'17 5:42:21
Suttell Ford 25 1 34n27'33 85w50'48 5:43:23
Suttle 53 1 32n32'10 87w10'47 5:48:43
Swagg 56 1 33n22'28 85w32'53 5:42:12
Swaim 36 1 34n52'10 86w11'54 5:44:48
Swancott 45 1 34n35'50 86w47'19 5:47:09
Swearengin 48 1 34n33'48 86w11'25 5:44:46
Sweet Water 46 1 32n05'50 87w52'03 5:51:28
Swift Ford 45 2 34n33'28 86w28'05 5:45:52
Swink 24 1 32n08'15 86w59'43 5:47:59
Sycamore 61 1 33n15'04 86w12'09 5:44:49
Sylacauga 61 1 33n10'23 86w15'06 5:45:00
Sylvan Grove 23 1 31n21'13 85w27'56 5:41:52
Sylvania 25 1 34n33'44 85w48'45 5:43:15
Sylvan Springs 37
1 33n30'56 87w00'54 5:48:04
Tabernacle 16 1 31n27'04 85w52'17 5:43:29
Tabernacle 35 1 31n10'54 85w28'06 5:41:52
Tabor 28 6 34n09'05 85w55'05 5:43:40
Tacoa 59 1 33n18'07 86w51'15 5:47:25
Tacon 49 1 30n41'16 88w06'17 5:52:25
Taft 10 1 34n20'32 85w37'38 5:42:31
Taits Gap 5 1 33n57'53 86w23'58 5:45:36
Talladega 61 1 33n26'09 86w06'21 5:44:25
Talladega Springs 61
1 33n07'17 86w26'36 5:45:46
Tallahatta Springs 13
1 31n54'34 87w52'36 5:51:30
Tallapoosa City 62
1 32n32 85w53 5:43:32
Tallassee 26 1 32n32'09 85w53'36 5:43:34
Tallaweka 26 1 32n31 85w53 5:43:32
Talucah 45 1 34n33'22 86w42'03 5:46:48
Tanner 42 1 34n43'53 86w58'14 5:47:53
Tanner Crossroads 42
1 34n43'52 86w57'18 5:47:49
Tanner Heights 52
1 34n25'20 86w55'53 5:47:44
Tanner Williams 49
1 30n43'26 88w22'12 5:53:29
Tanyard 6 1 31n53'19 85w42'15 5:42:49
Tanyard 58 1 33n38'08 86w19'29 5:45:18
Tarentum 55 1 31n38'21 85w52'44 5:43:31
Tarpley 37 6 33n26'41 86w53'27 5:47:34
Tarrant 37 6 33n35'00 86w46'22 5:47:05
Tarrant City 37 6 33n35'00 86w46'22 5:47:05
Tarrant Heights 37
6 33n35'44 86w45'25 5:47:02
Tarsus 8 1 33n38'11 85w54'40 5:43:39
Tasso 24 1 32n13'02 87w11'48 5:48:47
Tattlersville 13
1 31n42'45 88w03'23 5:52:14
Tayloe 53 1 32n26'53 87w26'17 5:49:45
Taylor 35 1 31n09'53 85w28'06 5:41:52
Taylor 51 1 31n58'31 86w14'00 5:44:56
Taylor Ford 25 1 34n35'12 85w33'55 5:42:16
Taylors Crossroads 56
1 33n13'33 85w21'38 5:41:27
Taylorville 63 6 33n08'36 87w32'50 5:50:11
Teals Crossroads 3
1 31n38'27 85w34'07 5:42:16

Teasleys Mill 51
1 32n09'15 86w06'41 5:44:27
Tecumseh 10 1 33n59'56 85w25'27 5:41:42
Tecumseh Furnace 10
1 33n58'51 85w25'29 5:41:42
Teddy 27 1 31n05 87w04 5:48:16
Tenant 56 1 33n16 85w27 5:41:48
Ten Broeck 25 1 34n25'04 85w59'13 5:43:57
Tennala 10 1 34n05'52 85w40'28 5:42:42
Tennant 56 1 33n16'05 85w27'25 5:41:50
Tennille 55 1 31n37'23 85w46'07 5:43:04
Tensaw 2 1 31n09'24 87w47'57 5:51:12
Terese 3 1 31n48'17 85w09'50 5:40:39
Terry Crossroads 35
1 31n06'23 85w17'11 5:41:09
Terry Heights 40
1 34n39'44 87w17'14 5:49:09
Terry Heights 45
2 34n43'57 86w36'15 5:46:25
Terrytown 40 1 34n37'29 87w20'39 5:49:23
Texas 47 1 33n55'47 87w40'43 5:50:43
Texasville 3 1 31n42'54 85w25'28 5:41:42
Thach 42 1 34n55'11 86w53'34 5:47:34
Thaddeus 62 1 32n34 85w39 5:42:36
Tharptown 30 1 34n31'20 87w37'43 5:50:31
Theba 21 1 31n33'20 86w18'13 5:45:13
The Bottle 41 5 32n40'34 85w29'11 5:41:57
The Cedars 39 1 34n50'08 87w39'34 5:50:38
The Highlands 28
6 34n02'56 86w01'07 5:44:04
The Highlands 45
2 34n45'24 86w38'02 5:46:32
Theodore 49 1 30n32'51 88w10'31 5:52:42
The Ridge 50 1 31n31 87w20 5:49:20
Thomas 37 6 33n31'57 86w51'25 5:47:26
Thomas Acres 37 1 33n22'46 86w58'51 5:47:55
Thomas Crossroad 55
1 31n46'35 86w07'43 5:44:31
Thomas Hill 61 1 33n10 86w19 5:45:16
Thomas Place 52 1 34n19'12 86w59'35 5:47:58
Thomaston 46 1 32n15'59 87w37'31 5:50:30
Thomasville 13 1 31n54'48 87w44'09 5:50:57
Thompson 6 1 32n11'06 85w49'05 5:43:16
Thorin 51 1 32n12'16 86w17'02 5:45:08
Thornhill 32 1 32n41'17 87w55'56 5:51:44
Thorn Hill 47 1 34n14 87w37 5:50:28
Thornton 39 1 34n46'15 87w18'12 5:49:13
Thornton 62 1 32n42'07 85w44'53 5:43:00
Thornton Springs 12
1 31n54'07 88w12'58 5:52:52
Thorntontown 39 1 34n50'22 87w21'20 5:49:25
Thorsby 11 1 32n54'56 86w42'57 5:46:52
Thrasher Crossroads 22
1 34n16'44 86w28'53 5:45:56
Three Forks 45 2 34n49'25 86w28'54 5:45:56
Three Forks 63 1 33n33'12 87w19'59 5:49:20
Three Notch 6 1 32n06'22 85w34'45 5:42:19
Three Notches 49
1 30n36 88w10 5:52:40
Threet 39 1 34n57'02 87w49'44 5:51:19
Thurston 31 1 31n00'53 85w46'55 5:43:08
Tibbie 65 1 31n21'43 88w14'55 5:53:00
Tilden 24 1 32n03'57 87w08'35 5:48:34
Till 7 1 31n38 86w44 5:46:56
Tiller Crossroads 9
5 32n59'23 85w34'20 5:42:17
Tillery Crossroad 41
5 32n41'37 85w11'46 5:40:47
Tillmans Corner 49
1 30n35'24 88w10'15 5:52:41
Tinela 50 1 31n48'30 87w23'50 5:49:35
Tishabee 32 1 32n38'15 87w59'55 5:52:00
Titus 26 1 32n42'44 86w19'06 5:45:16
Toadvine 37 1 33n26 86w57 5:47:48
Toddtown 13 1 31n37'07 87w52'36 5:51:30
Tohopeka 62 1 32n57'20 85w45'38 5:43:03
Toinette 65 1 31n20'22 88w00'30 5:52:02
Tompkinsville 12
1 32n12'11 88w01'13 5:52:05
Toney 45 2 34n53'53 86w44'01 5:46:56
Toonersville 39 1 34n51'47 87w20'16 5:49:21
Topton 65 1 31n17'10 88w09'00 5:52:36
Toulminville 49 1 30n43'07 88w05'27 5:52:22
Town Creek 40 1 34n40'52 87w24'22 5:49:37
Townley 64 1 33n49'44 87w25'54 5:49:44
Townsend Crossroads 25
1 34n38'58 85w39'47 5:42:39
Toxey 12 1 31n54'46 88w18'34 5:53:14
Trace Ford 40 1 34n31'49 87w21'24 5:49:26
Trade 22 1 34n03'58 87w05'26 5:48:22
Trafford 37 1 33n49'05 86w44'34 5:46:58
Trammel Crossroads 9
5 32n58'16 85w32'07 5:42:08
Travelers Rest 19
1 32n49'10 86w19'50 5:45:19
Travis Bridge 18
1 31n26 86w56 5:47:44
Tredegar 8 1 33n51'09 85w46'25 5:43:06
Trenton 36 1 34n44'41 86w15'06 5:45:00
Triana 45 2 34n35'10 86w44'00 5:46:56
Triana Landing 45
2 34n34'49 86w43'51 5:46:55
Trickem 15 1 33n33'22 85w24'40 5:41:39
Trickem 43 1 32n16'24 86w44'49 5:46:59
Trimble 22 1 34n05'36 86w56'55 5:47:48
Trinity 8 6 33n35'22 85w52'08 5:43:29
Trinity 52 1 34n36'24 87w05'18 5:48:21
Trio 4 1 32n54'44 87w01'29 5:48:06
Trotwood Park 37
6 33n33'56 86w44'08 5:46:57
Troy 55 1 31n48'31 85w58'12 5:43:53
Truett 62 1 33n05'49 85w35'43 5:42:23
Trussville 37 1 33n37'11 86w36'32 5:46:26
Tuckabatchie 26 1 32n31 85w53 5:43:32
Tuckahoe Heights 28
6 34n04'11 86w01'13 5:44:05
Tucker 47 1 33n58'15 87w46'25 5:51:06
Tucker Crossroads 10
1 34n08'06 85w34'19 5:42:17
Tuckersburg 9 5 32n45'34 85w22'03 5:41:28
Tullis 3 1 31n53'14 85w11'16 5:40:45
Tulse 59 1 33n14'42 86w54'10 5:47:37
Tumbleton 34 1 31n24'23 85w15'24 5:41:02

Tunnel Springs 50
1 31n38'33 87w14'24 5:48:58
Tupelo 36 1 34n45'03 86w04'40 5:44:19
Turkestan 50 1 31n46'36 87w09'18 5:48:37
Turkey Branch 2 1 30n25'18 87w50'11 5:51:21
Turkeytown 28 1 34n05'35 85w53'54 5:43:36
Turnbough Town 58
1 33n40'28 86w28'11 5:45:53
Turnbull 50 1 31n42'53 87w07'55 5:48:32
Turner 59 1 33n14'41 86w57'20 5:47:49
Turner 61 1 33n32'10 86w02'38 5:44:11
Turner Crossroads 16
1 31n18'44 85w58'27 5:43:54
Turney Crossroads 52
1 34n26'47 86w47'02 5:47:08
Tuscahoma Landing 12
1 32n03'29 88w06'54 5:52:28
Tuscaloosa 63 6 33n12'35 87w34'09 5:50:17
Tuscumbia 17 1 34n43'52 87w42'09 5:50:49
Tuskegee 44 1 32n25'26 85w41'30 5:42:46
Tuskegee Institute 44
1 32n25 85w42 5:42:48
Twilley Town 64 1 33n39'45 87w05'13 5:48:21
Twin 47 1 33n57 87w53 5:51:32
Twinsprings 3 1 31n53 85w09 5:40:36
Tyler 24 1 32n20'21 86w52'47 5:47:31
Tyler Crossroads 3
1 31n42'11 85w31'36 5:42:06
Tyler Ford 19 1 32n54'43 86w17'01 5:45:08
Tyson 43 1 32n11'12 86w26'22 5:45:45
Tysonville 44 1 32n24'01 85w59'55 5:44:00
Uchee 57 7 32n21'02 85w21'53 5:41:28
Uhland 57 7 32n25'34 85w17'12 5:41:09
Underwood 39 1 34n52'16 87w42'03 5:50:48
Underwood 59 1 33n05 86w51 5:47:24
Underwood Crossroads 17
1 34n45'23 87w31'45 5:50:07
Uniform 65 1 31n20'57 88w14'04 5:52:56
Union 14 1 33n26'44 85w46'17 5:43:05
Union 28 1 34n09'31 86w12'03 5:44:48
Union 32 1 32n59'17 87w54'54 5:51:40
Union 34 1 31n31'13 85w11'29 5:40:46
Union 52 1 34n27'24 86w44'17 5:46:57
Union 62 1 32n41'55 85w50'50 5:43:23
Union Academy 16
1 31n19 85w49 5:43:16
Union Chapel 64 1 33n49'00 87w10'40 5:48:43
Union Church 49 1 30n33'55 88w20'38 5:53:23
Union Grove 11 1 32n58'57 86w40'51 5:46:43
Union Grove 22 1 34n12'10 86w34'00 5:46:16
Union Grove 37 1 33n35'52 86w58'36 5:47:54
Union Grove 45 2 34n55'42 86w28'57 5:45:56
Union Grove 48 1 34n24'06 86w26'57 5:45:48
Union Hill 9 5 33n00'10 85w31'22 5:42:05
Union Hill 15 1 33n32'25 85w23'22 5:41:33
Union Hill 22 1 34n17'59 86w30'43 5:46:03
Union Hill 42 1 34n58'38 87w12'02 5:48:48
Union Hill 52 1 34n28'25 86w37'19 5:46:29
Union Springs 6 1 32n08'39 85w42'54 5:42:52
Uniontown 53 1 32n26'58 87w30'51 5:50:03
Unity 19 1 33n00'19 86w21'33 5:45:26
Unity 63 6 33n12 87w32 5:50:08
Universal Heights 63
6 33n12 87w32 5:50:08
Upper Coalburg 37
6 33n36'44 86w51'03 5:47:24
Upper Gordon Landing 35
1 31n09'58 85w06'12 5:40:25
Upper Green Hill 39
1 34n59'05 87w30'24 5:50:02
Upper Hall Landing 2
1 30n52'28 87w53'33 5:51:34
Upshaw 67 1 34n16'53 87w09'21 5:48:37
Upton 28 6 34n04'26 85w56'46 5:43:47
Uptown 37 1 33n26 86w57 5:47:48
Uriah 50 1 31n18'18 87w30'08 5:50:01
Vaiden 53 1 32n31'11 87w22'16 5:49:29
Valdosta 17 1 34n42'59 87w43'25 5:50:54
Valhalla 37 1 33n26'57 86w55'36 5:47:42
Valhermoso Springs 52
1 34n30'04 86w41'09 5:46:45
Vallegrande 24 1 32n23 87w00 5:48:00
Valley Creek 37 1 33n23'15 87w04'20 5:48:17
Valley Creek Junction 24
1 32n34'06 86w56'56 5:47:48
Valley Head 25 1 34n34'08 85w36'54 5:42:28
Valley of Shiloh 20
1 31n24'57 86w28'00 5:45:52
Valley View 52 1 34n28'02 86w56'26 5:47:46
Vance 63 1 33n10'27 87w14'01 5:48:56
Vanderbilt 37 6 33n32'59 86w47'13 5:47:09
Vandiver 59 1 33n28'14 86w30'48 5:46:03
Vangale 46 1 32n04'17 87w49'51 5:51:19
Vanlandingham Mill 31
1 31n02'36 85w45'32 5:43:02
Varnons 59 1 33n09'58 86w45'43 5:47:03
Vashti 13 1 31n42'11 87w38'17 5:50:33
Vaughn 2 1 31n01'47 87w51'40 5:51:27
Vaughn Corners 45
2 34n46'19 86w42'51 5:46:51
Verbena 11 1 32n44'59 86w30'41 5:46:03
Vernledge 21 1 31n46'16 86w17'34 5:45:10
Vernon 38 1 33n45'25 88w06'32 5:52:26
Vernontown 4 1 33n03'23 87w11'38 5:48:47
Vestavia Hills 37
1 33n26'55 86w47'16 5:47:09
Vesthaven 37 6 33n27 86w47 5:47:08
Veterans Hospital 63
6 33n12 87w32 5:50:08
Veto 42 1 34n59'40 86w59'20 5:47:57
Vick 4 1 32n56'27 87w05'00 5:48:20
Victoria 16 1 31n31'47 85w56'18 5:43:45
Vida 1 1 32n36'36 86w40'28 5:46:42
Vida Junction 1 1 32n34'26 86w40'56 5:46:44
Vidette 21 1 31n43'58 86w11'42 5:44:47
Vienna 54 1 33n01'07 88w11'31 5:52:46
Viewpoint 25 1 34n18 85w56 5:43:44
Vigo 8 1 33n55'05 85w33'29 5:42:14
Village Creek 37
6 33n33'13 86w48'30 5:47:14
Village Creek Junction 37
6 33n31'43 86w53'31 5:47:34
Village No 1 17 1 34n44'24 87w43'04 5:50:52

Village Springs 37
1 33N45'30 86W38'19 5:46:33
Villula 57 7 32N15'57 85W09'53 5:40:40
Vilula 53 1 32N32'59 87W16'14 5:49:05
Vina 30 1 34N22'35 88W03'31 5:52:14
Vincent 59 1 33N23'04 86W24'43 5:45:39
Vinegar Bend 65 1 31N15'49 88W20'41 5:53:23
Vine Hill 1 1 32N36'44 86W54'08 5:47:37
Vineland 46 1 32N02'08 87W39'34 5:50:38
Vineland Park 37
1 33N26'23 86W59'41 5:47:59
Vinemont 22 1 34N14'30 86W51'58 5:47:28
Vines Mill 37 1 33N29'35 87W09'52 5:48:39
Vinnette 8 1 33N37'34 85W55'08 5:43:41
Virginia 37 1 33N24'32 87W03'02 5:48:12
Virginia Shores 17
1 34N47'37 87W32'48 5:50:11
Vocation 50 1 31N01 87W30 5:50:00
Volanta 2 1 30N32'01 87W54'06 5:51:36
Vredenburgh 50 1 31N49'42 87W19'18 5:49:17
Vulcan 37 1 33N41'44 86W58'25 5:47:54
Vulcan City 37 6 33N33'30 86W47'48 5:47:11
Waco 30 1 34N28'55 87W39'14 5:50:37
Wacoochee Valley 41
7 32N37'46 85W08'18 5:40:33
Wadley 56 1 33N07'17 85W33'59 5:42:16
Wadsworth 1 1 32N23'51 86W31'42 5:46:07
Wadsworth 11 1 32N40'29 86W27'03 5:45:48
Wagar 65 1 31N26'30 87W59'37 5:51:58
Wagarville 65 1 31N26'10 88W01'42 5:52:07
Wahl 27 1 31N00'18 87W13'17 5:48:53
Wahouma 37 6 33N33'10 86W44'07 5:46:56
Wainwright 50 1 31N38'56 87W29'13 5:49:57
Walco 61 1 33N10 86W19 5:45:16
Wald 7 1 31N45'28 86W39'56 5:46:40
Walden Quarters 32
1 32N44'49 87W51'45 5:51:27
Waldo 61 1 33N22'49 86W01'37 5:44:06
Walker Chapel 37
6 33N36'24 86W49'21 5:47:17
Walker Mill Ford 36
1 34N43'29 86W16'27 5:45:06
Walkers Corner 22
1 34N10'41 86W44'33 5:46:58
Walker Springs 13
1 31N32'26 87W47'28 5:51:10
Walkerton 58 1 33N35'06 86W17'47 5:45:11
Wallace 27 1 31N12'34 87W13'06 5:48:52
Walley 65 1 31N11'04 88W25'30 5:53:42
Wallsboro 26 1 32N35'12 86W12'33 5:44:50
Wallstown 5 1 33N53'54 86W42'02 5:46:48
Wall Street 42 1 34N41 86W41 5:46:44
Walnut Grove 28 1 34N03'56 86W18'23 5:45:14
Walnut Grove 37 1 33N27'23 86W55'22 5:47:41
Walnut Hill 62 1 32N42'36 85W47'08 5:43:09
Walnut Park 28 6 34N00'52 86W03'33 5:44:14
Walter 22 1 34N07'07 86W40'37 5:46:42
Wannville 36 1 34N46'39 85W52'40 5:43:31
Ward 60 1 32N21'43 88W16'41 5:53:07
Wards Mill 9 5 32N58'17 85W20'38 5:41:23
Ware 26 1 32N27'23 86W03'03 5:44:12
Ware 37 6 33N26'08 86W53'09 5:47:33
Warley 49 1 30N49'41 88W21'56 5:53:28
Warrenton 48 1 34N21'24 86W21'34 5:45:26
Warrior 37 1 33N48'51 86W48'34 5:47:14
Warriorstand 44 1 32N18'42 85W33'12 5:42:13
Warsaw 60 1 32N56'15 88W12'11 5:52:49
Washington Heights 37
6 33N33'55 86W49'36 5:47:18
Washington Hill 1
1 32N24'29 86W28'04 5:45:52
Waterford 23 1 31N21'09 85W36'05 5:42:24
Waterloo 39 1 34N55'05 88W03'51 5:52:15
Waterloo Springs 10
1 34N19'20 85W35'18 5:42:21
Water Valley 12 1 31N53'38 88W23'35 5:53:34
Watkins 59 1 33N20'11 86W41'39 5:46:47
Watson 10 1 34N19'41 85W34'26 5:42:18
Watson 37 1 33N38'01 86W52'46 5:47:31
Watsonville 66 1 31N52'03 87W09'54 5:48:40
Watts Crossroads 14
1 33N22'21 85W46'23 5:43:06
Watts Mill 14 1 33N18 85W45 5:43:00
Wattsville 58 1 33N40'53 86W16'47 5:45:07
Waugh 51 4 32N21'54 86W02'42 5:44:11
Waverly 9 5 32N44'07 85W34'45 5:42:19
Wawbeek 27 1 31N01'40 87W21'39 5:49:27
Wayne 46 1 32N06'20 87W48'03 5:51:12
Weatherly Heights 45
2 34N38'12 86W33'10 5:46:13
Weathers 14 1 33N20'05 85W57'45 5:43:51
Weaver 8 1 33N45'07 85W48'41 5:43:15
Webb 35 1 31N15'37 85W16'24 5:41:06
Webb Addition 36
1 34N40'15 86W01'19 5:44:05
Webbs Landing 46
1 32N31'06 87W50'32 5:51:22
Webster Chapel 8
6 33N57 86W01 5:44:04
Wedgeworth 33 1 32N48'29 87W45'45 5:51:03
Wedowee 56 1 33N18'32 85W29'05 5:41:56
Weed Crossroad 21
1 31N31'07 86W13'23 5:44:54
Weeden Heights 39
1 34N49'16 87W38'17 5:50:33
Weeks 31 1 31N09'02 86W06'59 5:44:28
Weems 37 1 33N33'21 86W39'46 5:46:39
Wegra 64 1 33N38'03 87W06'15 5:48:25
Wehadkee 56 1 33N13'57 85W17'17 5:41:09
Welch 9 5 33N05'17 85W20'22 5:41:21
Welka 27 1 31N00'48 87W12'03 5:48:48
Weller 37 1 33N20'06 87W08'50 5:48:35
Wellington 8 1 33N49'21 85W53'34 5:43:34
Wells Ford 36 1 34N42'26 86W18'22 5:45:13
Welona 19 1 32N46'20 86W20'10 5:45:21
Welti 22 1 34N08'21 86W44'20 5:46:57
Wende 57 7 32N15'27 85W20'22 5:41:21
Wenonah 37 6 33N26'22 86W53'46 5:47:35
Weogufka 19 1 33N00'59 86W18'44 5:45:15
Weoka 26 1 32N43'03 86W11'03 5:44:44
Weoka Mills 26 1 32N40'54 86W18'02 5:45:12
Wesoda 22 1 34N06'40 86W47'58 5:47:12
Wessington 11 1 33N00'09 86W46'40 5:47:07
West 45 2 34N44 86W36 5:46:24
West Alexandria 8
1 33N46 85W53 5:43:32
West Anniston 8 6 33N40 85W50 5:43:20
West Bend 13 1 31N49'27 88W07'56 5:52:32
West Blocton 4 1 33N07'05 87W07'30 5:48:30
Westbrook 24 1 32N19'24 87W20'00 5:49:20
West Butler 12 1 32N04'07 88W20'07 5:53:20
West Corona 64 1 33N42'31 87W29'54 5:50:00
West Decatur 52 3 34N36'15 86W59'44 5:47:59
West End 8 1 33N40 85W55 5:43:40
West End 37 6 33N29'25 86W51'57 5:47:28
West End Anniston 8
6 33N40 85W50 5:43:20
West Ensley 37 1 33N31'43 86W55'33 5:47:42
Western Hills 49
1 30N42 88W10 5:52:40
Western Hills Estates 45
2 34N48'41 86W44'44 5:46:59
Western Hills Mall 37
1 33N28 86W55 5:47:40
West Fairfield 37
1 33N27'15 86W56'52 5:47:47
Westfield 37 1 33N29'04 86W56'26 5:47:46
West Greene 32 1 32N55'25 88W05'07 5:52:20
West Highlands 37
1 33N26 86W57 5:47:48
West Hill 49 1 30N41'24 88W10'51 5:52:43
West Huntsville 45
2 34N42'52 86W36'11 5:46:25
West Jasper 64 1 33N48 87W20 5:49:20
West Jefferson 37
1 33N38'57 87W04'07 5:48:16
West Lake Highlands 37
1 33N23'48 86W58'17 5:47:53
Westlawn 45 2 34N43'11 86W37'39 5:46:31
West Monroeville 50
1 31N30'56 87W21'13 5:49:25
Weston 47 1 34N09'35 88W01'55 5:52:08
Westover 59 1 33N20'58 86W32'09 5:46:09
West Point 22 1 34N14'19 86W57'33 5:47:50
West Point 52 1 34N27'06 86W38'44 5:46:35
West Pratt 64 1 33N44 87W07 5:48:28
West Sayre 37 1 33N42'50 86W59'15 5:47:57
West Selmont 24 1 32N23'28 87W01'02 5:48:04
West Side 37 1 33N26 86W57 5:47:48
West Side 51 4 32N22 86W20 5:45:20
West Wellington 8
1 33N49'29 85W54'36 5:43:38
Westwood 37 6 33N35'10 86W55'31 5:47:42
Wetumpka 26 1 32N32'37 86W12'43 5:44:51
Whatley 13 1 31N39'02 87W42'18 5:50:49
Whatley Cross Road 47
5 32N29'51 85W22'29 5:41:30
Wheat 22 1 34N06 87W04 5:48:16
Wheeler 40 1 34N39'09 87W14'59 5:49:00
Wheeler Dam Village 40
1 34N47'36 87W22'41 5:49:31
Wheelerville 49 1 30N41'24 88W11'30 5:52:46
Wheeling Crossroad 37
1 33N24'34 86W55'12 5:47:41
Whistler 49 1 30N45'23 88W06'11 5:52:25
White City 1 1 32N38'54 86W35'58 5:46:24
White City 22 1 34N05'34 86W46'28 5:47:06
White Crossroads 56
1 33N11'44 85W20'36 5:41:22
White Hall 43 1 32N19'37 86W42'43 5:46:51
Whitehead 39 1 34N53'17 87W19'38 5:49:19
Whitehouse 47 1 34N07'17 87W43'56 5:50:56
Whitehouse Forks 2
1 30N48'28 87W48'51 5:51:15
White House Springs 17
1 34N38'54 87W41'38 5:50:47
White Oak 3 1 31N54'01 85W20'21 5:41:21
Whiteoak 17 1 34N39'11 87W31'43 5:50:07
White Oak 30 1 34N32'51 87W59'40 5:51:59
White Oak 34 1 31N46'06 85W09'09 5:40:37
White Oak 48 1 34N14'25 86W14'40 5:44:59
White Plains 8 6 33N44'50 85W41'21 5:42:45
White Plains 9 5 32N59'32 85W23'57 5:41:36
Whites Bluff 24 1 32N19 87W17 5:49:08
Whitesboro 28 1 34N09'48 86W04'10 5:44:17
Whitesburg 45 2 34N34'35 86W33'49 5:46:15
Whitesburg Estates 45
2 34N38'00 86W34'37 5:46:18
Whites Chapel 58
1 33N36 86W32 5:46:08
Whites Gap 8 1 33N46'42 85W44'22 5:42:57
Whiteside 42 3 34N38 86W57 5:47:48
Whitesides Mill 8
6 33N44'18 85W39'29 5:42:38
White Signboard Crossroad 56
1 33N14'59 85W23'03 5:41:32
Whitesville 48 1 34N10'18 86W14'34 5:44:58
Whitewater 1 1 32N27'50 86W38'08 5:46:33
Whitfield 60 1 32N21'55 88W05'25 5:52:22
Whitney 58 1 33N52'04 86W17'29 5:45:10
Whitney Junction 58
1 33N52'29 86W17'58 5:45:12
Whiton 25 1 34N21'20 86W04'43 5:44:19
Whitsitt 33 1 32N36'03 87W35'32 5:50:22
Whitson 63 6 33N34'07 87W24'28 5:49:38
Whorton 10 1 34N07'50 85W30'24 5:42:02
Wicksburg 35 1 31N12'29 85W37'21 5:42:29
Wiggins 20 1 31N18'57 86W19'43 5:45:19
Wigginsville 42 1 34N47'58 86W54'45 5:47:39
Wiginton 47 1 34N17'12 87W52'33 5:51:30
Wilburn 22 1 33N57'06 87W02'03 5:48:08
Wilcox 18 1 31N30'30 86W52'35 5:47:30
Wildcat Landing 12
1 31N57'54 88W05'31 5:52:22
Wildwood 56 1 33N26'36 85W34'48 5:42:19
Wiley 51 4 32N17'42 86W18'35 5:45:14
Wiley 63 1 33N31'58 87W27'48 5:49:51
Wilhites 52 1 34N18'36 86W53'34 5:47:34
Wilkes 37 1 33N27'17 86W55'48 5:47:43
Wilkinstown 16 1 31N36'29 85W59'53 5:44:00
Williams 28 6 33N54'19 86W06'37 5:44:26
Williams 35 1 31N18'20 85W09'50 5:40:39
Williams 60 1 32N27'00 88W18'21 5:53:13
Williamstown 64 1 33N42'12 87W18'07 5:49:12
Willowbrook 45 2 34N39'24 86W32'13 5:46:09
Willowbrook Estates 45
2 34N39'29 86W32'51 5:46:11
Willow Springs 26
1 32N28'05 86W11'23 5:44:46
Wills Crossroads 34
1 31N33'22 85W10'47 5:40:43
Wills Valley 25 1 34N28'40 85W42'51 5:42:51
Wilmer 49 1 30N49'23 88W21'41 5:53:27
Wilson Bend 67 1 34N00'54 87W07'46 5:48:31
Wilsonia 28 1 34N05'59 85W54'15 5:43:37
Wilson Lake Shores 17
1 34N48'11 87W34'44 5:50:19
Wilson Quarters 35
1 31N09'35 85W20'40 5:41:23
Wilsonville 59 1 33N14'03 86W29'01 5:45:56
Wilton 59 1 33N04'43 86W52'54 5:47:32
Wimberly 12 1 31N55 88W19 5:53:16
Wimbly 12 1 31N54'54 88W14'54 5:53:00
Winburn 59 1 33N30'29 86W32'49 5:46:11
Windham Springs 63
1 33N29'29 87W29'55 5:50:00
Windsor Highlands 37
6 33N28'06 86W47'38 5:47:11
Winetka 37 1 33N26'13 86W54'41 5:47:39
Winfield 47 1 33N55'44 87W49'02 5:51:16
Wing 20 1 31N01'39 86W36'38 5:46:27
Wingard 55 1 31N49'59 86W08'55 5:44:36
Wininger 36 1 34N44'34 86W09'34 5:44:38
Winn 13 1 31N39'06 87W55'02 5:51:40
Winn Crossroads 52
1 34N20'16 86W36'59 5:46:28
Winninger 36 1 34N38 86W16 5:45:04
Winslow 1 1 32N30'58 86W46'12 5:47:05
Winterboro 61 1 33N19'17 86W11'49 5:44:47
Winton 52 1 34N30'42 86W45'03 5:47:00
Wolf Creek 58 1 33N31'45 86W22'55 5:45:32
Wolf Springs 40 1 34N35'42 87W28'22 5:49:53
Wolftown 52 1 34N30'49 87W06'22 5:48:25
Womack Hill 12 1 31N51'11 88W11'19 5:52:45
Woodaire Estates 37
1 33N39'28 86W40'56 5:46:44
Woodall Place 48
1 34N33'03 86W15'27 5:45:02
Woodbluff 13 1 31N55 87W59 5:51:56
Woodcrest 37 6 33N35'43 86W42'55 5:46:52
Woodfin Mill 42 1 34N57'45 86W55'09 5:47:41
Woodford 60 1 32N30'14 88W00'23 5:52:02
Woodland 39 1 34N45'02 87W49'22 5:51:17
Woodland 44 1 32N31'47 85W46'22 5:43:05
Woodland 56 1 33N22'27 85W23'59 5:41:36
Woodland Mills 52
1 34N28'27 86W41'41 5:46:47
Woodlawn 37 6 33N32'26 86W45'06 5:47:00
Woodlawn Heights 30
1 34N31'51 87W43'27 5:50:54
Woodlawn Heights 37
6 33N32'00 86W44'50 5:46:59
Woodmeadow 37 6 33N25 86W48 5:47:12
Woodmont 37 1 33N26'55 86W59'35 5:47:58
Woods Bluff 13 1 31N56'08 88W03'42 5:52:15
Woodstock 4 1 33N12'24 87W09'00 5:48:36
Woodville 36 1 34N37'40 86W16'28 5:45:06
Woodward 37 1 33N26'07 86W57'29 5:47:50
Woodward Junction 37
1 33N25'18 86W56'02 5:47:44
Woolfolk 61 1 33N25'02 85W59'54 5:44:00
Wren 40 1 34N26'03 87W17'37 5:49:10
Wright 39 1 34N54'31 87W59'24 5:51:58
Wright Crossroads 41
5 32N31'58 85W28'12 5:41:53
Wyatt 64 1 33N41'56 87W04'42 5:48:19
Wylam 37 1 33N30'21 86W55'31 5:47:42
Wylaunee 3 1 31N59'58 85W05'41 5:40:23
Wynnville 5 1 34N04'51 86W23'37 5:45:34
Yampertown 47 1 34N00'19 87W51'23 5:51:26
Yantley 12 1 32N14'45 88W22'46 5:53:31
Yarbo 65 1 31N32'37 88W16'40 5:53:07
Yarbrough 41 5 32N42'57 85W11'57 5:40:48
Yelling Settlement 2
1 30N37'19 87W50'11 5:51:21
Yellow Bluff 66 1 31N58'03 87W28'05 5:49:52
Yellow Creek Falls 10
1 34N13 85W36 5:42:24
Yellowleaf 59 1 33N15 86W30 5:46:00
Yellow Pine 65 1 31N24'20 88W25'47 5:53:43
Yerkwood 64 1 33N41'16 87W04'48 5:48:19
Yolande 63 1 33N18'24 87W11'29 5:48:46
York 60 1 32N29'10 88W17'47 5:53:11
Yorks Mill 25 1 34N44'41 85W40'25 5:42:42
Younds Landing 62
1 32N49'18 85W51'15 5:43:25
Youngblood 55 1 31N50'42 86W04'10 5:44:17
Youngs Chapel 28
6 33N57 86W01 5:44:04
Youngtown 40 1 34N25'00 87W23'27 5:49:34
Yucca 36 1 34N47'57 85W48'24 5:43:14
Yupon 2 1 30N24'31 87W49'01 5:51:16
Zana 62 1 33N01'37 85W42'46 5:42:51
Zimco 13 1 31N42'10 87W52'41 5:51:31
Zimmerman 53 1 32N36'56 87W22'57 5:49:32
Zion 54 1 33N25'16 87W52'39 5:51:31
Zion City 37 6 33N34'55 86W43'48 5:46:55
Zion Heights 37 6 33N33'27 86W50'03 5:47:20
Zip City 39 1 34N57'17 87W40'12 5:50:41
Zoar 16 1 31N31'53 86W06'25 5:44:26
Zubers 61 1 33N13'55 86W18'03 5:45:12

TIME TABLES

AK # 1
Before 8/20/1900 LMT
8/20/1900 12:00 YST
2/09/1942 02:00 YWT
9/30/1945 02:00 YST
4/27/1969 02:00 YDT
10/26/1969 02:00 YST
4/26/1970 02:00 YDT
10/25/1970 02:00 YST
4/25/1971 02:00 YDT
10/31/1971 02:00 YST
4/30/1972 02:00 YDT
10/29/1972 02:00 YST
4/29/1973 02:00 YDT
10/28/1973 02:00 YST
1/06/1974 02:00 YDT
10/27/1974 02:00 YST
2/23/1975 02:00 YDT
10/26/1975 02:00 YST
4/25/1976 02:00 YDT
10/31/1976 02:00 YST
4/24/1977 02:00 YDT
10/30/1977 02:00 YST
4/30/1978 02:00 YDT
10/29/1978 02:00 YST
4/29/1979 02:00 YDT
10/28/1979 02:00 YST
4/27/1980 02:00 YDT
10/26/1980 02:00 YST
4/26/1981 02:00 YDT
10/25/1981 02:00 YST
4/25/1982 02:00 YDT
10/31/1982 02:00 YST
4/24/1983 02:00 YDT
10/30/1983 02:00 YST
4/29/1984 02:00 US#1
....

AK # 2
Before 8/20/1900 LMT
8/20/1900 12:00 BST
2/09/1942 02:00 BWT
9/30/1945 02:00 BST
9/22/1968 02:00 AHST
4/27/1969 02:00 AHDT
10/26/1969 02:00 AHST
4/26/1970 02:00 AHDT
10/25/1970 02:00 AHST
4/25/1971 02:00 AHDT
10/31/1971 02:00 AHST
4/30/1972 02:00 AHDT
10/29/1972 02:00 AHST
4/29/1973 02:00 AHDT
10/28/1973 02:00 AHST
1/06/1974 02:00 AHDT
10/27/1974 02:00 AHST
2/23/1975 02:00 AHDT
10/26/1975 02:00 AHST
4/25/1976 02:00 AHDT
10/31/1976 02:00 AHST
4/24/1977 02:00 AHDT
10/30/1977 02:00 AHST
4/30/1978 02:00 AHDT
10/29/1978 02:00 AHST
4/29/1979 02:00 AHDT
10/28/1979 02:00 AHST
4/27/1980 02:00 AHDT
10/26/1980 02:00 AHST
4/26/1981 02:00 AHDT
10/25/1981 02:00 AHST
4/25/1982 02:00 AHDT
10/31/1982 02:00 AHST
4/24/1983 02:00 AHDT
10/30/1983 02:00 YST
4/29/1984 02:00 US#1
....

AK # 3
Before 8/20/1900 LMT
8/20/1900 12:00 BST
2/09/1942 02:00 BWT
9/30/1945 02:00 BST
10/27/1968 02:00 AHST
4/27/1969 02:00 AHDT
10/26/1969 02:00 AHST
4/26/1970 02:00 AHDT
10/25/1970 02:00 AHST
4/25/1971 02:00 AHDT
10/31/1971 02:00 AHST
4/30/1972 02:00 AHDT
10/29/1972 02:00 AHST
4/29/1973 02:00 AHDT
10/28/1973 02:00 AHST
1/06/1974 02:00 AHDT
10/27/1974 02:00 AHST
2/23/1975 02:00 AHDT
10/26/1975 02:00 AHST
4/25/1976 02:00 AHDT
10/31/1976 02:00 AHST
4/24/1977 02:00 AHDT
10/30/1977 02:00 AHST
4/30/1978 02:00 AHDT
10/29/1978 02:00 AHST
4/29/1979 02:00 AHDT
10/28/1979 02:00 AHST
4/27/1980 02:00 AHDT
10/26/1980 02:00 AHST
4/26/1981 02:00 AHDT
10/25/1981 02:00 AHST
4/25/1982 02:00 AHDT
10/31/1982 02:00 AHST
4/24/1983 02:00 AHDT
10/30/1983 02:00 YST
4/29/1984 02:00 US#1
....

AK # 4
Before 8/20/1900 LMT
8/20/1900 12:00 PST
2/09/1942 02:00 PWT
9/30/1945 02:00 PST
4/27/1969 02:00 PDT
10/26/1969 02:00 PST
4/26/1970 02:00 PDT
10/25/1970 02:00 PST
4/25/1971 02:00 PDT
10/31/1971 02:00 PST
4/30/1972 02:00 PDT
10/29/1972 02:00 PST
4/29/1973 02:00 PDT
10/28/1973 02:00 PST
1/06/1974 02:00 PDT
10/27/1974 02:00 PST
2/23/1975 02:00 PDT
10/26/1975 02:00 PST
4/25/1976 02:00 PDT
10/31/1976 02:00 PST
4/24/1977 02:00 PDT
10/30/1977 02:00 PST
4/30/1978 02:00 PDT
10/29/1978 02:00 PST
4/29/1979 02:00 PDT
10/28/1979 02:00 PST
4/27/1980 02:00 PDT
10/26/1980 02:00 PST
4/26/1981 02:00 PDT
10/25/1981 02:00 PST
4/25/1982 02:00 PDT
10/31/1982 02:00 PST
4/24/1983 02:00 PDT
10/30/1983 02:00 YST
4/29/1984 02:00 US#1
....

AK # 5
Before 8/20/1900 LMT
8/20/1900 12:00 AHST
2/09/1942 02:00 AHWT
9/30/1945 02:00 AHST
4/27/1969 02:00 AHDT
10/26/1969 02:00 AHST
4/26/1970 02:00 AHDT
10/25/1970 02:00 AHST
4/25/1971 02:00 AHDT
10/31/1971 02:00 AHST
4/30/1972 02:00 AHDT
10/29/1972 02:00 AHST
4/29/1973 02:00 AHDT
10/28/1973 02:00 AHST
1/06/1974 02:00 AHDT
10/27/1974 02:00 AHST
2/23/1975 02:00 AHDT
10/26/1975 02:00 AHST
4/25/1976 02:00 AHDT
10/31/1976 02:00 AHST
4/24/1977 02:00 AHDT
10/30/1977 02:00 AHST
4/30/1978 02:00 AHDT
10/29/1978 02:00 AHST
4/29/1979 02:00 AHDT
10/28/1979 02:00 AHST
4/27/1980 02:00 AHDT
10/26/1980 02:00 AHST
4/26/1981 02:00 AHDT
10/25/1981 02:00 AHST
4/25/1982 02:00 AHDT
10/31/1982 02:00 AHST
4/24/1983 02:00 AHDT
10/30/1983 02:00 YST
4/29/1984 02:00 US#1
....

AK # 6
Before 8/20/1900 LMT
8/20/1900 12:00 BST
2/09/1942 02:00 BWT
9/30/1945 02:00 BST
4/27/1969 02:00 BDT
10/26/1969 02:00 BST
4/26/1970 02:00 BDT
10/25/1970 02:00 BST
4/25/1971 02:00 BDT
10/31/1971 02:00 BST
4/30/1972 02:00 BDT
10/29/1972 02:00 BST
4/29/1973 02:00 BDT
10/28/1973 02:00 BST
1/06/1974 02:00 BDT
10/27/1974 02:00 BST
2/23/1975 02:00 BDT
10/26/1975 02:00 BST
4/25/1976 02:00 BDT
10/31/1976 02:00 BST
4/24/1977 02:00 BDT
10/30/1977 02:00 BST
4/30/1978 02:00 BDT
10/29/1978 02:00 BST
4/29/1979 02:00 BDT
10/28/1979 02:00 BST
4/27/1980 02:00 BDT
10/26/1980 02:00 BST
4/26/1981 02:00 BDT
10/25/1981 02:00 BST
4/25/1982 02:00 BDT
10/31/1982 02:00 BST
4/24/1983 02:00 BDT
10/30/1983 02:00 YST
4/29/1984 02:00 US#1
....

AK # 7
Before 8/20/1900 LMT
8/20/1900 12:00 BST
2/09/1942 02:00 BWT
9/30/1945 02:00 BST
4/27/1969 02:00 BDT
10/26/1969 02:00 BST
4/26/1970 02:00 BDT
10/25/1970 02:00 BST
4/25/1971 02:00 BDT
10/31/1971 02:00 BST
4/30/1972 02:00 BDT
10/29/1972 02:00 BST
4/29/1973 02:00 BDT
10/28/1973 02:00 BST
1/06/1974 02:00 BDT
10/27/1974 02:00 BST
2/23/1975 02:00 BDT
10/26/1975 02:00 BST
4/25/1976 02:00 BDT
10/31/1976 02:00 BST
4/24/1977 02:00 BDT
10/30/1977 02:00 BST
4/30/1978 02:00 BDT
10/29/1978 02:00 BST
4/29/1979 02:00 BDT
10/28/1979 02:00 BST
4/27/1980 02:00 BDT
10/26/1980 02:00 BST
4/26/1981 02:00 BDT
10/25/1981 02:00 BST
4/25/1982 02:00 BDT
10/31/1982 02:00 BST
4/24/1983 02:00 BDT
10/30/1983 02:00 AHST
4/29/1984 02:00 US#1

COUNTIES

1 Aleutian Islands
2 Aleutians East
3 Anchorage
4 Bethel
5 Bristol Bay
6 Dillingham
7 Fairbanks North Star
8 Haines
9 Juneau
10 Kenai Peninsula
11 Ketchikan Gateway
12 Kodiak Island
13 Lake and Peninsula
14 Matanuska-Susitna
15 Nome
16 North Slope
17 Northwest Arctic
18 Pr of Wales-O Ketchikan
19 Sitka
20 Skagway-Yakutat-Angoon
21 Southeast Fairbanks
22 Valdez-Cordova
23 Wade Hampton
24 Wrangell-Petersburg
25 Yukon-Koyukuk

Ac 4 2 61N00 159w57 10:39:48
Adak 1 7 51N52'48 176w39'29 11:46:38
Adak Naval Station 1
7 51N52 176w39 11:46:36
Afognak 12 5 58N00'28 152w46'05 10:11:04
Akhiok 12 5 56N56'44 154w10'13 10:16:41
Akiachak 4 3 60N54'34 161w25'53 10:45:44
Akiak 4 3 60N54'44 161w12'50 10:44:51
Akolmiut 4 6 60N54 162w30 10:50:00
Akutan 1 6 54N08 165w46 11:03:04
Alakanuk 23 6 62N41'20 164w36'55 10:58:28
Alatna 25 5 66N34 152w39 10:10:36
Aleknagik 6 2 59N16'23 158w37'04 10:34:28
Aleknagik Mission 6
2 59N17 158w36 10:34:24
Aleksashkina 12
5 57N46'48 152w21'19 10:09:25
Aleutian Islands 1
7 52N07 176w36 11:46:24
Alexander 14 5 61N25 150w36 10:02:24
Alitak 12 5 57N21 153w10 10:12:40
Allakaket 25 5 66N33'56 152w38'44 10:10:35
Alyeska 3 5 60N57'39 149w06'39 9:56:27
Ambler 17 2 67N05'10 157w51'05 10:31:24
Anaktuvuk Pass 16
5 68N08'36 151w44'09 10:06:57
Anchorage 3 5 61N13'05 149w54'01 9:59:36
Anchor Point 10
5 59N46'36 151w49'53 10:07:20
Anderson 25 5 64N20'39 149w11'13 9:56:45
Andreafsky 23 6 62N03 163w10 10:52:40
Angoon 20 4 57N30'12 134w35'02 8:58:20
Aniak 4 2 61N34'42 159w31'20 10:38:05
Annette 18 4 55N04 131w33 8:46:12
Anvik 25 2 62N39'22 160w12'24 10:40:50
Arctic Village 25
5 68N07'37 145w32'16 9:42:09
Artesian Village 3
5 61N13'39 149w46'53 9:59:08
Atka 1 7 52N12 174w12 11:36:48
Atmautluak 4 6 60N49 162w43 10:50:52
Atqasuk 16 5 70N28'10 157w23'45 10:29:35
Auke Bay 9 4 58N23'00 134w39'35 8:58:38
Aurora 7 5 64N51'25 147w45'31 9:51:02
Aurora Lodge 7
5 64N28'14 146w56'19 9:47:45
Baranof 19 4 57N05'22 134w49'59 8:59:20
Barrow 16 5 71N17'26 156w47'19 10:27:09
Bartlett Cove 20
4 58N25 135w44 9:02:56
Basher 3 5 61N10 149w41 9:58:44
Beaver 25 5 66N21'34 147w23'47 9:49:35
Belkofski 2 6 55N05 162w02 10:48:08
Bell Island Hot Springs 18
4 55N55'54 131w33'55 8:46:16
Bethel 4 3 60N47'32 161w45'21 10:47:01
Bettles 25 5 66N54'25 151w40'59 10:06:44
Big Delta 21 5 64N09'09 145w50'32 9:43:22
Big Lake 17 5 67N30 149w27 9:57:48
Bill Moores 23
6 62N56'59 163w46'44 10:55:07
Biorka 1 6 53N50 166w13 11:04:52
Birch Creek 16
5 69N00 147w22 9:49:28
Birch Lake 21 5 64N51 147w47 9:51:08
Birchwood 3 5 61N24'19 149w28'08 9:57:53
Bjerremark 7 5 64N51 147w47 9:51:08
Bluff 7 5 64N42'54 147w10'33 9:48:42
Bluff 15 6 64N34'22 163w45'15 10:55:01
Bonibrook 3 5 61N11'59 149w46'27 9:59:06
Border 21 5 63N07 143w22 9:33:28
Boswell Bay 22
5 60N33 145w45 9:43:00
Boundary 21 5 64N04 141w06 9:24:24
Boyd 7 5 64N51 147w47 9:51:08
Brevig Mission 15
6 65N20'05 166w29'21 11:05:57
Broadmoor 7 5 64N49'26 147w52'33 9:51:30
Broadmoor Acres 7
5 64N51 147w47 9:51:08
Broad Pass 14 5 63N14 149w16 9:57:04
Browerville 16
5 71N17'53 156w46'12 10:27:05
Buckland 17 3 65N58'47 161w07'23 10:44:30
Butte 14 5 61N33 149w03 9:56:12
Campbell 3 5 61N10'19 149w53'39 9:59:35
Campbell 18 4 55N22 132w43 8:50:52
Candle 17 3 65N54'48 161w55'28 10:47:42
Cannery 20 4 57N47'07 135w05'47 9:00:23
Cantwell 25 5 63N23'30 148w57'03 9:55:48
Cape Fanshaw 20
4 57N13 133w30 8:54:00
Cape Lisburne 16
6 68N52 166w05 11:04:20
Cape Newenham Air Force Sta 4
3 59N01 161w49 10:47:16
Cape Nome 15 6 64N27'50 164w57'34 10:59:50
Cape Pole 18 4 55N57'54 133w47'36 8:55:10
Cape Romanzof 23
6 60N49 162w43 10:50:52
Cape Sarichef Radio Relay 1
6 53N53 166w32 11:06:08
Cape Yakataga 22
5 60N04 142w26 9:29:44
Carlanna 11 4 55N24 132w08 8:48:32
Caro 25 5 67N10'03 148w01'11 9:52:05
Central 25 5 65N34'21 144w48'11 9:39:13
Chakaktolik 23
6 61N46'06 163w37'20 10:54:29
Chalkyitsik 25
5 66N39'16 143w43'20 9:34:53
Chandalar 25 5 67N30'19 148w29'37 9:53:58
Chaniliut 23 6 63N02 163w25 10:53:40
Charcoal Point 11
4 55N24 132w08 8:48:32
Chase 14 5 62N28 150w07 10:00:28
Chatanika 7 5 65N06'44 147w28'38 9:49:55
Chatham 19 4 57N30'55 134w56'37 8:59:46
Chefornak 4 6 60N13 164w12 10:56:48
Chena Hot Springs 7
5 65N03'11 146w03'20 9:44:13
Chenega 22 5 60N16'53 148w04'34 9:52:18
Chernofski 1 6 53N25 167w33 11:10:12
Chevak 23 6 61N31'40 165w35'11 11:02:21
Chickaloon 14 5 61N47'48 148w27'46 9:53:51
Chicken 21 5 64N04'24 141w56'10 9:27:45
Chignik 13 2 56N17'43 158w24'08 10:33:37
Chignik Lagoon 13
2 56N20 158w29 10:33:56
Chignik Lake 13
2 56N14 158w47 10:35:08
Chisana 21 5 62N04 142w03 9:28:12
Chistochina 22
5 62N33'54 144w39'53 9:38:40
Chitina 22 5 61N30'57 144w26'13 9:37:45
Christian 25 5 67N21'36 145w11'46 9:40:47
Chuathbaluk 4 2 61N34 159w16 10:37:04
Chugiak 3 5 61N23'20 149w28'55 9:57:56
Circle 25 5 65N49'32 144w03'38 9:36:15
Circle Hot Springs 25
5 65N29'00 144w38'03 9:38:32
Clam Gulch 10 5 60N13'52 151w23'37 10:05:34
Clarks Point 6
2 58N50'39 158w33'03 10:34:12
Clear 25 5 64N25 149w15 9:57:00
Clear Creek Park 7
5 64N49'07 147w33'57 9:50:16
Clearwater Ranch 21
5 63N47 145w14 9:40:56
Clover Pass 11
4 55N25 131w48 8:47:12
Coal Creek 21 5 65N19 143w09 9:32:36
Cohoe 10 5 60N22'07 151w18'23 10:05:14
Cold Bay 2 6 55N11'09 162w43'16 10:50:53
College 7 5 64N51'25 147w48'10 9:51:13
Colorado 14 5 63N09'46 149w26'09 9:57:45
Colville River 16
5 71N18 156w47 10:27:08
Cooper Landing 10
5 60N29'24 149w50'03 9:59:20

Copper Center 22
5 61N57'18 145W18'19 9:41:13
Cordova 22 5 60N32'34 145W45'27 9:43:02
Cottonwood 14 5 61N34 149W43 9:58:52
Council 15 6 64N53'42 163W40'35 10:54:42
Crab Bay 22 5 60N03'58 148W00'29 9:52:02
Craig 18 4 55N28'35 133W08'54 8:52:36
Crooked Creek 4
2 61N52'12 158W06'39 10:32:27
Crooked Creek 21
5 64N56 141W40 9:26:40
Crystal Fall 22
5 60N29'09 145W43'45 9:42:55
Curry 14 5 62N36'53 150W00'43 10:00:03
Curry's Corner 7
5 64N51 147W47 9:51:08
Dairy 11 4 55N18'25 131W33'59 8:46:16
Davidsons Landing 15
6 65N14'31 165W16'18 11:01:05
Deadhorse 16 5 70N11 148W29 9:53:56
DeBarr Vista 3
5 61N12'44 149W45'11 9:59:01
Deering 17 6 66N04'32 162W43'02 10:50:52
Delta Junction 21
5 64N02'16 145W43'56 9:42:56
Denali 14 5 63N11 147W28 9:49:52
Dennis Manor 7
5 64N49'45 147W32'23 9:50:10
Derby Tract 7 5 64N51 147W47 9:51:08
Dillingham 6 2 59N02'23 158W27'27 10:33:50
Dime Landing 15
3 65N07'12 161W09'35 10:44:38
Diomede 15 6 65N47 169W00 11:16:00
Discovery 25 2 62N27'09 157W56'02 10:31:44
Dobson Landing 9
4 58N29'26 134W47'03 8:59:08
Dogpatch 7 5 64N53'44 147W48'23 9:51:14
Donnelly 21 5 63N41 145W53 9:43:32
Dot Lake 21 5 63N40 144W04 9:36:16
Douglas 9 4 58N16'32 134W23'33 8:57:34
Duncan Canal 24
4 56N48 132W58 8:51:52
Dutch Harbor 1
6 53N53 166W32 11:06:08
Eagle 21 5 64N47'17 141W12'00 9:24:48
Eagle River 3 5 61N19'17 149W34'04 9:58:16
Eagle Village 21
5 64N46'50 141W06'49 9:24:27
Edna Bay 18 4 55N56'56 133W39'44 8:54:39
Eek 4 6 60N13'08 162W01'28 10:48:06
Egavik 15 2 64N02'25 160W55'21 10:43:41
Egegik 13 5 58N12'56 157W22'33 10:29:30
Eielson 7 5 64N38 147W06 9:48:24
Eielson Air Force Base 7
5 64N38 147W06 9:48:24
Eklutna 3 5 61N27'29 149W21'44 9:57:27
Ekuk 6 2 58N49 158W34 10:34:16
Ekwok 6 5 59N20'59 157W28'31 10:29:54
Elephant Point 17
3 66N15'35 161W20'46 10:45:23
Elfin Cove 20 4 58N11'40 136W20'36 9:05:22
Elim 15 6 64N37'03 162W15'38 10:49:03
Ellamar 22 5 60N53'44 146W41'51 9:46:47
Elmendorf 3 5 61N15 149W49 9:59:16
Elmendorf Air Force Base 3
5 61N17 149W49 9:59:16
Elmendorf Reservation 3
5 61N15 149W49 9:59:16
Emanguk 23 6 62N45 164W30 10:58:00
Emmonak 23 6 62N46'40 164W31'23 10:58:06
English Bay 10
5 59N22 151W55 10:07:40
Entrance Island 20
4 57N25 133W27 8:53:48
Eska 14 5 61N44'16 148W54'31 9:55:38
Espenberg 15 6 66N35'34 163W57'53 10:55:52
Ester 7 5 64N51 148W01 9:52:04
Eureka 14 5 61N36 149W20 9:57:20
Eureka 25 5 65N00 150W38 10:02:32
Eureka Roadhouse 22
5 61N56 147W10 9:48:40
Evansville 25 5 66N55'22 151W30'29 10:06:02
Excursion Inlet 20
4 58N25 135W27 9:01:48
Eyak 22 5 60N32 145W36 9:42:24
Eyak River Cabins 22
5 60N33 145W45 9:43:00
Fairbanks 7 5 64N50'16 147W42'59 9:50:52
Fairbanks North Star 7
5 64N48 148W21 9:53:24
Fairhaven 9 4 58N22'41 134W42'13 8:58:49
Falls 10 5 60N25'12 149W22'13 9:57:29
False Pass 1 6 54N51 163W25 10:53:40
Farewell 25 5 63N06 154W44 10:18:56
Farewell Lake Lodge 25
5 62N31 153W54 10:15:36
Federal 7 5 64N51 147W47 9:51:08
Fink Creek 17 6 65N53'44 163W01'07 10:52:04
Fire Lake 3 5 61N21 149W32 9:58:08
Fish Village 13
5 59N56'50 154W51'30 10:19:26
Fish Village 23
6 62N31'16 163W50'36 10:55:22
Flat 25 2 62N27'13 158W00'27 10:32:02
Fort Greely 21
5 64N00 145W44 9:42:56
Fort Richardson 3
5 61N15'16 149W41'18 9:58:45
Fortuna Ledge 23
6 61N53 162W05 10:48:20
Fort Wainwright 7
5 64N50 147W38 9:50:32
Fortymile Roadhouse 21
5 63N47 145W14 9:40:56
Fort Yukon 25 5 66N33'53 145W16'26 9:41:06
Fox 7 5 64N57'29 147W37'06 9:50:28
Fritz Cove 9 4 58N22 134W39 8:58:36
Fritz Creek 10
5 59N42 151W21 10:05:24
Funter 20 4 58N15 134W51 8:59:24
Funter Bay 20 4 58N21 134W33 8:58:12
Gakona 22 5 62N18'07 145W18'07 9:41:12

Gakona Junction 22
5 62N17'19 145W21'05 9:41:24
Galena 25 5 64N44'00 156W55'39 10:27:43
Gambell 15 7 63N46'47 171W44'28 11:26:58
Ganes Creek 25
5 62N56 156W04 10:24:16
Garner 25 5 63N50 148W59 9:55:56
Geist 7 5 64N51 147W47 9:51:08
Gilpatricks 10
5 60N36'05 149W32'15 9:58:09
Girdwood 3 5 60N56'33 149W09'59 9:56:40
Glenallen 22 5 62N06'33 145W32'47 9:42:11
Glen Alps 3 5 61N06 149W42 9:58:48
Goat Creek 14 5 61N25 149W26 9:57:44
Goddard 19 4 56N50'07 135W22'22 9:01:29
Gold Creek 14 5 62N46 149W41 9:58:44
Golovin (Cheenik) 15
6 64N32'36 163W01'45 10:52:07
Goodnews 4 3 59N07'07 161W35'19 10:46:21
Goodnews Mining Camp 4
3 58N55'34 161W43'48 10:46:55
Gost Creek 25 2 62N12'38 159W47'09 10:39:09
Graehl 7 5 64N51 147W44 9:50:56
Granite Mountain 17
6 64N57 165W49 11:03:16
Grayling 25 2 62N57 160W03 10:40:12
Gulkana 22 5 62N16'17 145W22'56 9:41:32
Gulkana Airport 22
5 62N12 145W28 9:41:52
Gustavus 20 4 58N24'48 135W44'13 9:02:57
Hadley 18 4 55N32'05 132W17'12 8:49:09
Haines 8 4 59N14'09 135W26'42 9:01:47
Halibut Cove 10
5 59N35 151W14 10:04:56
Hallersville 13
5 59N02'33 156W50'22 10:27:21
Hamilton 23 6 62N53'46 163W53'39 10:55:35
Hamilton Acres 7
5 64N50'49 147W40'14 9:50:41
Happy Valley 10
5 59N47 151W50 10:07:20
Harding Lake 7
5 64N51 147W47 9:51:08
Hawk Inlet 20 4 58N21 134W33 8:58:12
Haycock 15 3 65N12'35 161W09'56 10:44:40
Healy 25 5 63N51'28 148W57'59 9:55:52
Herendeen Bay 2
2 55N50 160W50 10:43:20
Herring Cove 11
4 55N20 131W31 8:46:04
Highland Park 7
5 64N45'25 147W21'38 9:49:27
Hogatza 25 5 66N13 155W41 10:22:44
Holikachuk 25 2 62N54'35 159W31'03 10:38:04
Hollis 11 4 55N24 132W08 8:48:32
Holy Cross 25 2 62N11'58 159W46'17 10:39:05
Homer 10 5 59N38'33 151W32'54 10:06:12
Homesite Park 3
5 61N13'09 149W44'28 9:58:58
Hood Bay 20 4 57N22'57 134W23'55 8:57:36
Hoonah 20 4 58N06'36 135W26'37 9:01:46
Hooper Bay 23 6 61N31'52 166W05'48 11:04:23
Hope 10 5 60N55'13 149W38'25 9:58:34
Houston 14 5 61N38'01 149W50'28 9:59:22
Hughes 25 5 66N02'56 154W15'20 10:17:01
Huslia 25 5 65N41'55 156W23'59 10:25:36
Hydaburg 18 4 55N12'29 132W49'36 8:51:18
Hyder 18 4 55N55'01 130W01'29 8:40:06
Igiugig 13 5 59N19'40 155W53'41 10:23:35
Igloo 15 6 65N08'52 165W03'48 11:00:15
Ikatan 1 6 54N45 163W19 10:53:16
Iliamna 13 5 59N45 154W55 10:19:40
Indian River 25
5 66N34 152W39 10:10:36
Ingregamiut 4 2 61N57'00 160W34'00 10:42:16
Ingrihak 23 6 61N45'22 162W00'05 10:48:00
Iniskin 10 5 59N44'49 153W14'15 10:12:57
Island Homes 7
5 64N51 147W47 9:51:08
Ivanof Bay 13 2 55N54 159W29 10:37:56
Jennie M Fairbanks 7
5 64N51 147W47 9:51:08
Joe Ward Camp 25
5 66N52 143W42 9:34:48
Johnston 7 5 64N51 147W47 9:51:08
Jonesville 14 5 61N43'50 148W56'05 9:55:44
Juneau 9 4 58N18'07 134W25'11 8:57:41
Kachemak 10 5 59N40'12 151W26'03 10:05:44
Kaguyak 12 5 56N52 153W46 10:15:04
Kake 24 4 56N58'33 133W56'50 8:55:47
Kakhonak 13 5 59N26 154W51 10:19:24
Kako Landing 23
3 61N51'14 161W20'47 10:45:23
Kaktovik 16 5 70N07'55 143W37'26 9:34:30
Kalakaket Creek Radio Relay 25
5 64N44 156W56 10:27:44
Kalifonsky 10 5 60N25'06 151W17'24 10:05:10
Kalskag 4 2 61N32'14 160W18'19 10:41:13
Kaltag 25 2 64N19'38 158W43'19 10:34:53
Kamishak 13 5 59N07'30 154W15'00 10:17:00
Karluk 12 5 57N34'19 154W27'20 10:17:49
Kasaan 18 4 55N32'20 132W24'03 8:49:36
Kashega 1 6 53N28 167W10 11:08:40
Kashegelok 25 5 61N42 157W10 10:28:40
Kasigluk 4 6 60N53'44 162W31'14 10:50:05
Kasilof 10 5 60N20'15 151W16'28 10:05:06
Katalla 22 5 60N11'50 144W31'06 9:38:04
Kenai 10 5 60N33'16 151W15'30 10:05:02
Kenai Lake 10 5 60N29 149W50 9:59:20
Kenai Packers Cannery 10
5 60N33 151W16 10:05:04
Kennicott 22 5 61N29'11 142W53'11 9:31:33
Ketchikan 11 4 55N20'32 131W38'46 8:46:35
Ketchikan Gateway 11
4 55N33 131W28 8:45:52
Kiana 17 2 66N58'30 160W25'22 10:41:41
King Cove 2 6 55N03 162W19 10:49:16
Kingegan 15 6 65N36'33 168W05'15 11:12:21
King Salmon 5 5 58N41'18 156W39'41 10:26:39
Kipnuk 4 6 59N56'20 164W02'29 10:56:10
Kivalina 17 6 67N43'37 164W32'00 10:58:08
Kiwalik 17 3 66N01'22 161W50'31 10:47:22
Klawock 18 4 55N33'08 133W05'45 8:52:23

Klery Creek 17
2 67N10'46 160W24'11 10:41:37
Klikitarik 15 6 63N28'10 161W28'16 10:45:53
Klukwan 8 4 59N23'57 135W53'38 9:03:35
Knik 14 5 61N27'28 149W43'44 9:58:55
Knudson Cove 11
4 55N24 132W08 8:48:32
Kobuk 17 5 66N54'26 156W52'52 10:27:31
Kodiak 12 5 57N47'24 152W24'26 10:09:38
Kodiak Island 12
5 57N54 153W03 10:12:12
Kodiak Naval Station 12
5 57N45 152W29 10:09:56
Koggiung 13 5 58N52'01 157W00'27 10:28:02
Kokhanok 13 5 59N38 154W53 10:19:32
Kokrines 25 5 64N56'16 154W41'31 10:18:46
Koliganek 6 5 59N43'43 157W17'04 10:29:08
Kongiganak 4 6 59N52 163W02 10:52:08
Kotlik 23 6 63N02'03 163W33'12 10:54:13
Kotzebue 17 6 66N53'54 162W35'48 10:50:23
Koyuk 15 3 64N55'55 161W09'25 10:44:38
Koyukuk 25 2 64N52'49 157W42'03 10:30:48
Kupreanof 24 4 56N48 132W58 8:51:52
Kuskokwim 4 5 62N12 156W49 10:27:16
Kustatan 10 5 61N04 151W08 10:04:32
Kwethluk 4 3 60N48'44 161W26'09 10:45:45
Kwigillingok 4
6 59N51'52 163W08'03 10:52:32
Kwiguk 23 6 62N46 164W30 10:58:00
Kwinhagak 4 3 59N44'56 161W54'57 10:47:40
Lake Minchumina 25
5 63N52'58 152W18'44 10:09:15
Lakeview 10 5 60N21'18 149W21'20 9:57:25
Larsen Bay 12 5 57N32'24 153W58'43 10:15:55
Lawing 10 5 60N24'08 149W21'52 9:57:27
Lemeta 7 5 64N51'35 147W43'56 9:50:56
Lemon Creek 9 4 58N21 134W29 8:57:56
Lena Cove 9 4 58N24 134W46 8:59:04
Levelock 13 5 59N06'54 156W51'24 10:27:26
Lignite 25 5 63N55 149W01 9:56:04
Lime Village 4
5 61N21'23 155W26'08 10:21:45
Livengood 25 5 65N31'28 148W32'41 9:54:11
Long 25 5 64N24'13 155W29'50 10:21:59
Long Island 14
5 61N33 149W52 9:59:28
Loring 11 4 55N36'09 131W38'10 8:46:33
Lost River 20 1 59N33 139W44 9:18:56
Lower Kalskag 4
2 61N30'44 160W21'29 10:41:26
Lower Mendenhall Valley 9
4 58N22 134W35 8:58:20
Lower Tonsina 22
5 61N39'18 144W39'31 9:38:38
Mack 7 5 64N51 147W47 9:51:08
Manley Hot Springs 25
5 65N00'04 150W38'02 10:02:32
Manokotak 6 2 58N59 159W03 10:36:12
Marshall 23 6 61N52'40 162W04'52 10:48:19
Marvel Creek 4
2 61N34 159W24 10:37:36
Marys Igloo 15
6 65N09 165W04 11:00:16
Matanuska 14 5 61N33 149W14 9:56:56
May Creek 22 5 61N21 142W42 9:30:48
McCarthy 22 5 61N26'00 142W55'18 9:31:41
McCord 12 5 57N09 153W12 10:12:48
McGrath 25 5 62N57'23 155W35'45 10:22:23
McKinley Acres 7
5 64N51 147W47 9:51:08
McKinley Park 25
5 63N44 148W55 9:55:40
Meakerville 22
5 60N33 145W44 9:42:56
Medfra 25 5 63N06'24 154W42'51 10:18:51
Mekoryuk 4 6 60N23'17 166W11'06 11:04:44
Mellicks Trading Post 4
5 61N41'04 157W10'41 10:28:43
Mendeltna Lodge 14
5 61N36 149W20 9:57:20
Mendenhall Flats 9
4 58N22 134W38 8:58:32
Mendenhaven 9 4 58N23'31 134W34'01 8:58:16
Mentasta Lake 22
5 62N55 143W45 9:35:00
Meshik 13 2 56N54'45 158W40'55 10:34:44
Metlakatla 18 4 55N07'45 131W34'20 8:46:17
Meyers Chuck 18
4 55N44'27 132W15'23 8:49:02
Miller House 25
5 65N32 145W13 9:40:52
Minto 25 5 64N53 149W11 9:56:44
Montana 14 5 62N05 150W04 10:00:16
Moore Creek 25
5 62N36'02 157W08'31 10:28:34
Moose Creek 7 5 64N42'36 147W08'37 9:48:34
Moose Creek 14
5 61N41 149W02 9:56:08
Moose Pass 10 5 60N29 149W22 9:57:28
Morzhovoi 2 6 54N55 163W18 10:53:12
Moses Point Fishing Village 15
6 64N41'52 162W01'41 10:48:07
Mountain Point 11
4 55N17'40 131W31'57 8:46:08
Mountain View 3
5 61N13'35 149W48'15 9:59:13
Mountain Village 23
6 62N05 163W43 10:54:52
Mount Edgecombe 19
4 57N03'04 135W21'16 9:01:25
Mud Bay 11 4 55N25'15 131W46'05 8:47:04
Mumtrak 4 3 59N07 161W35 10:46:20
Musk Ox 7 5 64N54'01 147W49'21 9:51:17
Muskwa Village 10
5 60N24'12 149W21'33 9:57:26
Nabesna 22 5 62N22'19 143W00'31 9:32:02
Naknek 5 5 58N43'42 157W00'50 10:28:03
Nancy 14 5 61N45 150W03 10:00:12
Napaimiut 4 2 61N32'24 158W40'27 10:34:42
Napakiak 4 3 60N41'48 161W57'07 10:47:48
Napaskiak 4 3 60N42'29 161W45'58 10:47:04
Naptowne 10 5 60N31'39 150W43'30 10:02:54
Nash Harbor 4 6 60N12'20 166W56'18 11:07:45

Navy Town 1 7 52N50'27 173w10'32 11:32:42
Nelson Lagoon 2 2 55N55 161w00 10:44:00
Nelsonville 6 2 59N00'24 158w32'01 10:34:08
Nenana 25 5 64N33'50 149w05'35 9:56:22
Newhalen 13 5 59N43'12 154w53'50 10:19:35
New Igloo 15 6 65N07'39 165w10'06 11:00:40
New Knockhock 23 6 62N07'39 164w53'18 10:59:33
New Stuyahok 6 5 59N27'10 157w18'43 10:29:15
Newtok 4 6 60N56'34 164w37'46 10:58:31
Nightmute 4 6 60N28'46 164w43'26 10:58:54
Nikishka 10 5 60N33 151w16 10:05:04
Nikolai 25 5 63N00'48 154w22'30 10:17:30
Nikolski 1 6 52N56'17 168w52'04 11:15:28
Nilak 23 6 62N32 164w52 10:59:28
Ninilchik 10 5 60N03'05 151w40'08 10:06:41
Noatak 17 6 67N34'16 162w57'55 10:51:52
Nolan 17 5 67N29 150w14 10:00:56
Nome 15 6 64N30'04 165w24'23 11:01:38
Nondalton 13 5 59N58'25 154w50'45 10:19:23
Noorvik 17 3 66N50'18 161w01'58 10:44:08
North Douglas 9 4 58N19 134w28 8:57:52
North Kenai 10 5 60N33 151w16 10:05:04
North Pole 7 5 64N45'04 147w20'58 9:49:24
Northway 21 5 62N57'42 141w56'14 9:27:45
Northway Indian Village 21 5 62N58'56 141w57'06 9:27:48
Nulato 25 2 64N43'10 158w06'11 10:32:25
Nunachuak 6 5 59N35'48 157w03'30 10:28:14
Nunachuk 4 6 60N56'17 162w34'58 10:50:20
Nunaka Valley 3 5 61N12 149w46 9:59:04
Nunapitchuk 4 6 60N53'49 162w27'34 10:49:50
Nunapitsinchak 4 3 60N47'44 161w22'32 10:45:30
Nushagak 6 2 58N56'53 158w29'32 10:33:58
Nyac 4 2 61N00'15 159w56'26 10:39:46
Odiak Slough 22 5 60N33 145w45 9:43:00
Ohogamiut 23 6 61N34'04 161w51'49 10:47:27
Old Andreafski 23 6 62N03 163w14 10:52:56
Old Harbor 12 5 57N12'10 153w18'14 10:13:13
Old Minto 25 5 64N53'14 149w10'49 9:56:43
Old Valdez 22 5 61N06'57 146w15'59 9:45:04
Olnes 7 5 65N05 147w40 9:50:40
Ophir 25 5 63N08'41 156w31'10 10:26:05
Orca 22 5 60N40 145w43 9:42:52
Oscarville 4 3 60N44 161w46 10:47:04
Otter 25 2 62N28 158w13 10:32:52
Outer Ketchikan 18 4 55N05 131w32 8:46:08
Ouzinki 12 5 57N56 152w30 10:10:00
Paimiut 4 2 61N57'51 160w13'55 10:40:56
Palmer 14 5 61N35'59 149w06'46 9:56:27
Paradise 25 2 62N25 160w03 10:40:12
Paradise Hill 25 2 62N12 159w46 10:39:04
Pauloff Harbor 1 6 54N28 162w42 10:50:48
Paxson 22 5 63N02 145w30 9:42:00
Pederson Point 5 5 58N44 157w01 10:28:04
Pedro Bay 13 5 59N47 154w07 10:16:28
Pelican 20 4 57N57'39 136w13'39 9:04:55
Peninsula Point 11 4 55N23 131w44 8:46:56
Pennock Island 11 4 55N20 131w38 8:46:32
Perkinsville 15 6 64N33'02 165w24'54 11:01:40
Perryville 13 2 55N55 159w09 10:36:36
Petersburg 24 4 56N48'45 132w57'20 8:51:49
Peters Creek 3 5 61N24'40 149w26'44 9:57:47
Pile Bay Village 13 5 59N47 153w53 10:15:32
Pilgrim Springs 15 6 65N05'37 164w55'26 10:59:42
Pilot Point 13 2 57N33'51 157w34'45 10:30:19
Pilot Station 23 6 61N56'20 162w52'30 10:51:30
Pitkas Point 23 6 62N01'58 163w17'16 10:53:09
Platinum 4 3 59N00'47 161w48'59 10:47:16
Point Baker 18 4 56N21'10 133w37'16 8:54:29
Point Barrow 16 5 71N17'26 156w47'19 10:27:09
Point Hope 16 6 68N20'52 166w48'29 11:07:14
Point Lay 16 6 69N45'27 163w03'04 10:52:12
Point Retreat 20 4 58N21 134w33 8:58:12
Point Whiteshed 22 5 60N33 145w45 9:43:00
Popof Island 1 2 55N20'23 160w29'50 10:41:59
Portage 3 5 60N50 148w59 9:55:56
Portage Creek 6 2 59N24 158w38 10:34:32
Port Alexander 19 4 56N14'59 134w38'40 8:58:35
Port Alsworth 13 5 60N12'09 154w18'46 10:17:15
Port Ashton 22 5 60N03'27 148w03'08 9:52:13
Port Chilkoot 8 4 59N13'44 135w26'16 9:01:45
Port Clarence 15 6 65N15'44 166w50'45 11:07:23
Port Graham 10 5 59N21'05 151w49'47 10:07:19
Port Heiden 13 2 56N55 158w41 10:34:44
Port Higgins 11 4 55N27 131w49 8:47:16
Port Lions 12 5 57N52'03 152w52'56 10:11:32
Port Moller 2 2 56N00 160w35 10:42:20
Port Nellie Juan 22 5 60N33 148w10 9:52:40
Port Safety 15 6 64N27'06 164w49'32 10:59:18
Port Wakefield 12 5 58N03 153w03 10:12:12
Pounrevik 23 6 62N32 164w52 10:59:28
Pribilof Islands 1 7 57N24'00 169w33'03 11:18:12
Prince of Wales 18 4 55N44 133w15 8:53:00
Prudhoe Bay 16 5 70N15 148w22 9:53:28
Quartz Creek 10 5 60N29 149w50 9:59:20
Quinhagak 4 3 59N44'56 161w54'57 10:47:40
Rainbow 3 5 61N00 149w39 9:58:36
Rampart 25 5 65N30'18 150w10'12 10:00:41
Red Devil 4 5 61N45'40 157w18'45 10:29:15
Red Salmon 6 5 58N44 157w01 10:28:04
Rego 7 5 64N51 147w47 9:51:08
Rodman 19 4 57N03 135w20 9:01:20
Rogers Park 3 5 61N11'53 149w50'57 9:59:24
Ruby 25 5 64N44'22 155w29'13 10:21:57
Russian Mission 23 3 61N47 161w19 10:45:16
Saint George 1 7 57N24'00 169w33'03 11:18:12
Saint George Island 1 7 57N24'00 169w33'03 11:18:12
Saint Marys 23 6 62N03'11 163w09'57 10:52:40
Saint Michael 15 6 63N28'41 162w02'21 10:48:09
Saint Paul 1 7 57N24'00 170w16'54 11:21:08
Saint Terese 9 4 58N28'20 134w46'49 8:59:07
Salmon Creek 9 4 58N20 134w28 8:57:52
Salt Chuck 18 4 55N37'35 132w33'13 8:50:13
Sanak 1 6 54N30 162w49 10:51:16
Sand Lake 3 5 61N09 149w57 9:59:48
Sand Point 1 2 55N20'23 160w29'50 10:41:59
San Juan Cannery 22 5 60N03 148w04 9:52:16
Savonoski 5 5 58N43'02 156w51'50 10:27:27
Savoonga 15 7 63N42 170w29 11:21:56
Saxman 11 4 55N19'06 131w35'45 8:46:23
Scammon Bay 23 6 61N50'34 165w34'54 11:02:20
Scow Bay 24 4 56N46'13 132w57'37 8:51:50
Seatons Stop 21 5 62N58 141w56 9:27:44
Selawik 17 2 66N36'14 160w00'25 10:40:02
Seldovia 10 5 59N26'17 151w42'41 10:06:51
Seversens 13 5 59N45'13 154w49'02 10:19:16
Seward 10 5 60N06'15 149w26'32 9:57:46
Shageluk 25 2 62N40'56 159w33'43 10:38:15
Shaktoolik 15 3 64N20 161w09 10:44:36
Shanly 7 5 64N51 147w47 9:51:08
Sheldon Point 23 6 62N32 164w52 10:59:28
Sheldons Point 23 6 62N32'01 164w50'28 10:59:22
Shemya Island 1 2 52N43 174w07 11:36:28
Sheshalik 17 6 66N59'39 162w49'41 10:51:19
Shishmaref 15 6 66N15'24 166w04'19 11:04:17
Shoreline Drive 11 4 55N24 132w08 8:48:32
Shuman House 25 5 66N54 143w46 9:35:04
Shungnak 17 5 66N53'17 157w08'11 10:28:33
Silvertip 3 5 60N45 149w22 9:57:28
Sinuk 15 6 64N35'34 166w15'10 11:05:01
Sitka 19 4 57N03'11 135w19'48 9:01:19
Situk 20 1 59N26'07 139w33'17 9:18:13
Skagway 20 4 59N27'30 135w18'50 9:01:15
Skwentna 14 5 61N58 151w11 10:04:44
Slaterville 7 5 64N50'53 147w43'25 9:50:54
Sleetmute 4 5 61N42'09 157w10'11 10:28:41
Snowball 7 5 64N51 147w47 9:51:08
Snug Harbor 10 5 60N29 149w50 9:59:20
Soldotna 10 5 60N29'16 151w03'30 10:04:14
Solomon 15 6 64N33'39 164w26'21 10:57:45
Sourdough 22 5 62N26 144w59 9:39:56
South Bjerremark 7 5 64N50 147w53 9:51:32
South Fairbanks 7 5 64N51 147w47 9:51:08
South Naknek 5 5 58N42'56 156w59'53 10:28:00
Spenard 3 5 61N11'19 149w54'23 9:59:38
Sprucewood 7 5 64N51 147w47 9:51:08
Squaw Harbor 1 2 55N14'36 160w33'12 10:42:13
Standard 25 5 64N47 148w32 9:54:08
Stebbins 15 6 63N31'20 162w17'17 10:49:09
Sterling 10 5 60N32 150w46 10:03:04
Stevens Village 25 5 66N00'23 149w05'27 9:56:22
Stony River 4 5 61N46'59 156w35'17 10:26:21
Strelna 22 5 61N30'41 144w04'08 9:36:17
Stuyahok 25 3 62N03'37 160w57'03 10:43:48
Summit 14 5 63N20 149w07 9:56:28
Summit Lodge 22 5 62N26 144w59 9:39:56
Sunnyside 20 4 57N59 136w15 9:05:00
Sunshine 14 2 62N10 150w04 10:00:16
Suntrana 25 5 63N51'15 148w50'54 9:55:24
Susitna 14 5 61N32'37 150w30'45 10:02:03
Sutton 14 5 61N42'41 148w53'39 9:55:35
Takotna 25 5 62N59'19 156w03'51 10:24:15
Takshak 23 6 61N57'28 162w10'37 10:48:42
Taku Lodge 9 4 58N21 134w33 8:58:12
Talkeetna 14 5 62N19'26 150w06'34 10:00:26
Tanacross 21 5 63N23'07 143w20'47 9:33:23
Tanana 25 5 65N10'19 152w04'44 10:08:19
Tanani 8 4 59N16'12 135w26'36 9:01:46
Tanunak (Tununak P O) 4 6 60N35'08 165w15'21 11:01:01
Tatitlek 22 5 60N51'53 146w40'43 9:46:43
Taylor 15 6 65N43'38 164w50'55 10:59:24
Tazlina 22 5 62N04 146w27 9:45:48
Tee Harbor 9 4 58N25 134w46 8:59:04
Telida 25 5 63N23 153w16 10:13:04
Teller 15 6 65N15'49 166w21'39 11:05:27
Teller Mission 15 6 65N20 166w29 11:05:56
Tenakee Springs 20 4 57N46'51 135w13'08 9:00:53
Terminal Reservation 20 4 59N30 135w26 9:01:44
Tetlin 21 5 63N08 142w31 9:30:04
Thane 9 4 58N15'51 134w19'49 8:57:19
The Harbor 9 4 58N24'37 134w45'21 8:59:01
Thorne Bay 18 4 55N41 132w27 8:49:48
Tin City 15 6 65N33'31 167w56'53 11:11:48
Todd 19 4 57N27'40 135w02'23 9:00:10
Togiak 6 2 59N03'43 160w22'35 10:41:30
Tok 21 5 63N20'12 142w59'08 9:31:57
Tokeen 18 4 55N56 133w20 8:53:20
Toksook Bay 4 6 60N31'49 165w06'09 11:00:25
Tonsina 22 5 61N39'21 145w10'31 9:40:42
Totem Bight 11 4 55N24 132w08 8:48:32
Totem Park 7 5 64N51'46 147w46'41 9:51:07
Tuluksak 4 2 61N06'09 160w57'42 10:43:51
Tuntutuliak 4 6 60N22 162w38 10:50:32
Tununak 4 6 60N37 165w15 11:01:00
Tuomi 3 5 61N16'48 149w49'48 9:59:19
Turnagain Heights 3 5 61N11'45 149w56'29 9:59:46
Twin Hills 6 2 59N21 160w00 10:40:00
Tyee 20 4 57N02'26 134w32'36 8:58:10
Tyonek 10 5 61N04'05 151w08'13 10:04:33
Ugashik 13 5 57N30'47 157w23'51 10:29:35
Ukak 4 6 60N43'39 164w55'57 10:59:44
Umiat 16 5 69N22'01 152w08'39 10:08:35
Umkumiut 4 6 60N29'54 165w11'56 11:00:48
Unalakleet 15 2 63N52'23 160w47'17 10:43:09
Unalaska 1 6 53N53 166w32 11:06:08
Unga 1 2 55N10'58 160w30'23 10:42:02
Ungalik 15 2 63N52 160w47 10:43:08
University Park 7 5 64N51 147w47 9:51:08
Upper Kalskag 25 2 61N32 160w18 10:41:12
Upper Mendenhall Valley 9 4 58N24 134w34 8:58:16
Upper Nickeyville 11 4 55N24 132w08 8:48:32
Upper Yukon 25 5 66N27 144w19 9:37:16
Usibelli 25 5 63N51'41 148w46'49 9:55:07
Uyak 12 5 57N38 154w00 10:16:00
Valdez 22 5 61N07'51 146w20'54 9:45:24
Vanderbilt Hill 9 4 58N20'42 134w29'32 8:57:58
Vank Island 24 4 56N28 132w23 8:49:32
Venetie 25 5 67N00'50 146w25'07 9:45:40
Wacker 11 4 55N25 131w44 8:46:56
Wade Hampton 23 6 62N18 164w41 10:58:44
Wainwright 16 2 70N38'13 160w02'18 10:40:09
Wales 15 6 65N37 168w05 11:12:20
Ward Cove 11 4 55N24'43 131w43'22 8:46:53
Wasilla 14 5 61N34'53 149w26'22 9:57:45
Waterfall 18 4 55N17'50 133w14'26 8:52:58
Wells 8 4 59N25'00 135w55'59 9:03:44
West Fairwest 7 5 64N51 147w47 9:51:08
Westgate 7 5 64N50'14 147w47'45 9:51:11
West Juneau 9 4 58N17'42 134w25'46 8:57:43
West Petersburg 24 4 56N48'51 132w59'35 8:51:58
Westwood 7 5 64N51 147w47 9:51:08
Wevok 16 6 68N52'19 166w05'25 11:04:22
White Mountain 15 6 64N40'53 163w24'20 10:53:37
Whitney 3 5 61N15 149w49 9:59:16
Whitshed 22 5 60N28 145w57 9:43:48
Whittier 22 5 60N46'23 148w41'02 9:54:44
Wilburs Place 23 6 62N05 163w28 10:53:52
Wilcox 7 5 64N51 147w47 9:51:08
Wilcox Estates 7 5 64N51 147w47 9:51:08
Wild Lake 25 5 66N56 151w30 10:06:00
Wildwood Station 10 5 60N35 151w18 10:05:12
Willow 14 5 61N45 150w03 10:00:12
Willow Lake 14 5 61N44'40 150w02'11 10:00:09
Wilson Village 3 5 61N14'11 149w49'09 9:59:17
Windham (P O) 20 4 57N35'46 133w20'15 8:53:21
Wiseman 17 5 67N24'36 150w06'27 10:00:26
Woodchopper 21 5 64N51 147w47 9:51:08
Woodland Park 3 5 61N12 149w53 9:59:32
Wood River 6 2 59N04'09 158w26'28 10:33:46
Woodrow 10 5 60N11'30 149w22'30 9:57:30
Woody Island 12 5 57N47 152w21 10:09:24
Wortmanns 22 5 61N06'40 145w48'59 9:43:16
Wrangell 24 4 56N28'15 132w22'36 8:49:30
Yakutat 20 1 59N32'49 139w43'38 9:18:55
Yankee Creek 25 5 62N56 156w04 10:24:16
Yistletaw 25 2 64N49'21 157w22'21 10:29:29

TIME TABLES

Arizona has declined to observe daylight time, except as noted in the time tables. During World War II wartime ended early in the MST portions of Arizona. The shift to MST for Yuma County (Table #3) has been estimated from incomplete information. Some publications circa 1900 show southern Arizona as far north as Phoenix on Pacific time.

AZ # 1

Before 11/18/1883		LMT
11/18/1883	12:00	MST
3/31/1918	02:00	MWT
10/27/1918	02:00	MST
3/30/1919	02:00	MWT
10/26/1919	02:00	MST
2/09/1942	02:00	MWT
1/01/1944	00:01	MST
3/17/1944	00:01	MWT
10/01/1944	00:01	MST
4/30/1967	02:00	MDT
10/29/1967	02:00	MST
....		

AZ # 2

Before 11/18/1883		LMT
11/18/1883	12:00	PST
3/31/1918	02:00	PWT
10/27/1918	02:00	PST
3/30/1919	02:00	PWT
10/26/1919	02:00	PST
2/09/1942	02:00	PWT
3/07/1945	00:01	MST
4/30/1967	02:00	MDT
10/29/1967	02:00	MST
....		

AZ # 3

Before 11/18/1883		LMT
11/18/1883	12:00	PST
3/31/1918	02:00	PWT
10/27/1918	02:00	PST
3/30/1919	02:00	PWT
10/26/1919	02:00	PST
3/06/1921	02:00	PDT
10/30/1921	02:00	PST
1/01/1929	00:00	MST
2/09/1942	02:00	MWT
1/01/1944	00:01	MST
3/17/1944	00:01	MWT
10/01/1944	00:01	MST
4/30/1967	02:00	MDT
10/29/1967	02:00	MST

COUNTIES

1 Apache
2 Cochise
3 Coconino
4 Gila
5 Graham
6 Greenlee
7 La Paz (was in Yuma Co)
8 Maricopa
9 Mohave
10 Navajo
11 Pima
12 Pinal
13 Santa Cruz
14 Yavapai
15 Yuma

A and F Trailer Court 8 1 33N17'45 111w50'28 7:27:22
A and F Trailer Park 8 1 33N29'40 112w06'37 7:28:26
Abra 14 1 34N54'07 112w26'46 7:29:47
Achi 11 1 32N20'40 112w00'51 7:28:03
Adamana 1 1 34N58'36 109w49'18 7:19:17
Adamsville 12 1 33N00'46 111w26'29 7:25:46
Admiral Trailer Park 8 1 33N27'03 111w59'30 7:27:58
Adobe 8 1 33N41'21 112w07'19 7:28:29
Adobe Mountain Trailer Park 8 1 33N41'10 112w06'52 7:28:27
Agua Caliente 8 1 32N59'07 113w19'25 7:33:18
Agua Fria 8 1 33N36'20 112w18'50 7:29:15
Agua Fria 14 1 34N32 112w28 7:29:52
Agua Linda 13 1 31N40'44 111w03'40 7:24:15
Aguila 8 1 33N56'34 113w10'24 7:32:42
Ahan Owuch 11 1 32N08'33 112w20'34 7:29:22
Ahwatukee 8 1 33N20'30 111w59'00 7:27:56
Aire Libre Mobile Home Park 8 1 33N38'16 112w01'02 7:28:04
Ajo 11 1 32N22'18 112w51'36 7:31:26
Ak 11 1 31N55 112w02 7:28:08
Akchin 11 1 31N55 111w53 7:27:32
Ak Chin 12 1 33N01'58 112w04'21 7:28:17
Ak Chut Vaya 11 1 31N37'50 111w48'32 7:27:14
Ak Komelik 11 1 31N43'04 112w12'02 7:28:48
Alamo Crossing 9 2 34N15'36 113w34'55 7:34:20
Alchesay Flat 10 1 33N50 109w58 7:19:52
Alhambra 8 1 33N29'54 112w08'01 7:28:32
Ali Ak Chin 11 1 31N51'29 112w32'24 7:30:10
Ali Chuk 11 1 31N48'54 112w33'22 7:30:13
Ali Chukson 11 1 31N54'49 111w47'55 7:27:12
Ali Molina 11 1 31N54'00 111w46'25 7:27:06
Ali Oidak 11 1 32N18'15 112w01'30 7:28:06
Allah 8 1 33N55'41 112w41'24 7:30:46
Allan Lake Landing 3 1 34N49'31 111w26'09 7:25:45
Allentown 1 1 35N17'31 109w09'28 7:16:38
Allenville 8 1 33N21'07 112w35'09 7:30:21
Alma Gardens 8 1 33N24'17 111w51'14 7:27:25
Alma Meadows Mobile Home Pk 8 1 33N24'17 111w51'25 7:27:26
Alpine 1 1 33N50'53 109w08'33 7:16:34
Alta Mira 8 1 33N19'32 111w54'25 7:27:38
Alto 13 1 31N36'16 110w52'39 7:23:31
Amado 13 1 31N42'28 111w03'50 7:24:15
Ambassador Downs Mobile Home 8 1 33N24'24 111w46'49 7:27:07
Amberwood 8 1 33N21'42 111w52'07 7:27:28
Amberwood II 8 1 33N20'45 111w50'41 7:27:23
Amberwood North 8 1 33N39'35 112w08'45 7:28:35
Ambrosia Mill 8 1 33N47'59 113w10'54 7:32:44
Amphitheater 11 1 32N16'20 110w58'18 7:23:53
Andalusia 8 1 33N34'10 111w52'10 7:27:29
Anegam 11 1 32N22'22 112w01'49 7:28:07
Angell 3 1 35N11'44 111w18'12 7:25:13
Antares 9 2 35N25'11 113w48'28 7:35:14
Apache 2 1 31N41'25 109w07'54 7:16:32
Apache 10 1 33N57 110w05 7:20:20
Apache Acres Trailer Park 8 1 33N25'20 111w36'05 7:26:24
Apache Flats 2 1 31N33'29 110w21'43 7:21:27
Apache Grove 6 1 32N52'11 109w11'23 7:16:46
Apache Ho 12 1 33N25 111w34 7:26:16
Apache Junction 12 1 33N24'54 111w32'56 7:26:12
Apache Wells 8 1 33N27'34 111w42'37 7:26:50
Apache West Mobile Village 8 1 33N24'50 111w51'14 7:27:25
Apex 3 1 35N56'35 112w11'06 7:28:44
Apollo Mobile Home Park 8 1 33N34'59 112w16'06 7:29:04
Apron Crossing 14 1 34N29'00 113w02'49 7:32:11
Araby 15 3 32N40'32 114w31'17 7:38:05
Aragon Place 6 1 32N58'20 109w21'25 7:17:26
Aravaipa 5 1 32N57'26 110w21'16 7:21:25
Arcadia 8 1 33N30 112w00 7:28:00
Arcosanti 14 1 34N20'34 112w05'41 7:28:23
Aripine 10 1 34N24'30 110w25'49 7:21:43
Aristocrat Trailer Park 8 1 33N29'41 112w03'45 7:28:15
Arivaca 11 1 31N34'29 111w19'54 7:25:20
Arivaca Junction 11 1 31N43'38 111w03'38 7:24:15
Arizola 12 1 32N51'04 111w42'49 7:26:51
Arizona Acres Mobile Home Re 8 1 33N24'46 111w37'35 7:26:30
Arizona City 12 1 32N45'21 111w40'13 7:26:41
Arizona Shores 7 3 34N09 114w17 7:37:08
Arizona State Teachers Coll 3 1 35N12 111w37 7:26:28
Arizona Sun Sites 2 1 31N55'00 109w57'30 7:19:50
Arlington 8 1 33N19'32 112w45'48 7:31:03
Arnold Place 14 1 34N27'12 111w55'03 7:27:40
Arntz 10 1 34N56'09 110w02'31 7:20:10
Arrowhead Mall 8 1 33N33 112w13 7:28:52
Arrowhead Ranch 8 1 33N40'06 112w11'30 7:28:46
Artesa 11 1 31N53'58 111w51'06 7:27:24
Artesia 5 1 32N41'53 109w42'25 7:18:50
Asher 15 3 32N40'32 114w04'22 7:36:17
Ash Fork 14 1 35N13'30 112w29'00 7:29:56
Ashurst 5 1 32N59'03 109w55'54 7:19:44
Athos 9 2 34N57'00 114w08'19 7:36:33
A-1 Trailer Park 8 1 33N26'55 112w00'30 7:28:02
Audley 14 1 35N24'06 113w02'18 7:32:09
Aultman 14 1 34N36'59 111w54'49 7:27:39
Autumn Ridge 8 1 33N39'11 112w09'11 7:28:37
Avondale 8 1 33N26'08 112w20'56 7:29:24
Avra 11 1 32N19'40 111w13'03 7:24:52
Avra 12 1 32N33'07 111w18'10 7:25:13
Aztec 15 3 32N49'28 113w26'57 7:33:48
Aztec Lodge 4 1 33N50'42 110w58'06 7:23:52
Babbit Winter 3 1 34N37'31 110w49'57 7:23:20
Baby Rock 10 1 36N46'31 110w00'30 7:20:02
Bacabi 10 1 35N55'25 110w39'24 7:22:38
Bagdad 14 1 34N34'52 113w12'14 7:32:49
Bakerville 2 1 31N25'22 109w53'12 7:19:33
Baldwin Place 14 1 34N17'08 112w29'05 7:29:56
Baldwins Crossing 14 1 34N49'26 111w48'25 7:27:14
Bapchule 12 1 33N08'11 111w52'21 7:27:29
Barkerville 11 1 32N49'54 110w56'41 7:23:47
Barts Crossing 3 1 34N28'20 110w55'50 7:23:43
Basking Ridge 8 1 33N38'22 111w56'09 7:27:45
Bayless Shopping Center 12 1 33N25 111w34 7:26:16
Bear Canyon Junction 4 1 33N32'11 110w23'37 7:21:34
Beardsley 8 1 33N39'41 112w22'42 7:29:31
Beaver Dam 9 2 36N53 113w56 7:35:44
Belaire Manor 8 1 33N30'55 112w10'45 7:28:43
Bel-Aire Trailer Park 8 1 33N29'05 112w06'52 7:28:27
Bell 10 1 34N16'20 109w54'51 7:19:39
Bella Vista Estates 2 1 31N33 110w17 7:21:08
Bellemont 3 1 35N14'17 111w49'58 7:27:20
Bellevue 4 1 33N19'55 110w56'34 7:23:46
Benson 2 1 31N58'04 110w17'38 7:21:11
Benson Highway 11 1 32N03 110w51 7:23:24
Benson Junction 2 1 31N44'21 110w11'51 7:20:47
Bernardino 2 1 31N30'38 109w18'44 7:17:15
Berry 9 2 35N15'10 114w58'16 7:39:53
Betatakin Overlook 10 1 36N40'54 110w31'51 7:22:07
Bethany Grand Mobile Home Pk 8 1 33N31'34 112w09'52 7:28:39
Bethany Villa Adult Mobile H 8 1 33N31'34 112w09'48 7:28:39
Beverly Trailer Park 8 1 33N24'22 111w51'13 7:27:25
Beyerville 13 1 31N23'25 110w52'40 7:23:31
Bidahochi 10 1 35N24'37 110w03'50 7:20:15
Big Horn 8 1 32N51'34 112w23'31 7:29:34
Big Palm Trailer Park 8 1 33N27'45 111w58'45 7:27:55
Big Pine Mobile Home Park 8 1 33N27'38 111w58'45 7:27:55
Big Reef Mill 14 1 33N57'53 112w29'03 7:29:56
Big Springs 3 1 36N36'06 112w20'57 7:29:24
Biltmore Gates 8 1 33N31'21 112w01'00 7:28:04
Biltmore Greens III 8 1 33N31'43 112w00'45 7:28:03
Biltmore Villas 8 1 33N30'45 112w01'15 7:28:05
Bisbee 2 1 31N26'53 109w55'40 7:19:43
Bisbee Junction 2 1 31N21'05 109w53'08 7:19:33
Bishop Place 3 1 35N27'37 112w43'20 7:30:53
Bitahochee 10 1 35N24 110w05 7:20:20
Bitlabito 1 1 36N50'28 109w01'11 7:16:05
Bitter Springs 3 1 36N37'43 111w39'13 7:26:37
Black Bear Spring 2 1 31N23'10 110w17'15 7:21:09
Black Canyon City 14 1 34N04'15 112w09'00 7:28:36
Black Diamond 2 1 31N50'37 109w54'22 7:19:37
Black Falls Crossing 3 1 35N34'13 111w16'30 7:25:06
Black River Crossing 4 1 33N42'46 110w12'40 7:20:51
Blackwater 12 1 33N01'52 111w34'55 7:26:20
Blaisdell 15 3 32N42'45 114w25'33 7:37:42
Blake Place 12 1 32N48'27 110w31'18 7:22:05
Bledsoe 2 1 31N26'52 110w18'22 7:21:13
Blue 6 1 33N36'36 109w06'22 7:16:25
Blue Bell Mobile Home Park 8 1 33N26'16 112w07'36 7:28:30
Blue Gap 1 1 36N10'15 109w56'45 7:19:47
Blue Hills Farms 14 1 34N31'15 112w17'45 7:29:11
Blue Palm Mobile Home Park 8 1 33N27'03 112w07'11 7:28:29
Blue Sky Mobile Estates 8 1 33N32'10 112w09'40 7:28:39
Blue Star Mobile Home Park 8 1 33N25'02 111w35'41 7:26:23
Blue Vista 6 1 33N37'09 109w04'57 7:16:20
Bon 12 1 32N58'17 111w54'28 7:27:38
Bona Venture Mobile Home Pk 8 1 33N38'55 112w03'47 7:28:15
Bonds Trailer Park 8 1 33N24'56 111w50'40 7:27:23
Bonelli Landing 9 2 36N05'00 114w28'52 7:37:55
Boneyard 1 1 33N52'45 109w16'18 7:17:05
Bonita 5 1 32N35'23 109w58'07 7:19:52
Bonita Trading Post 1 1 35N44'11 109w04'11 7:16:17
Bonnie Blink 2 1 31N32'48 110w22'18 7:21:29
Bootlegger Crossing 3 1 35N14'20 112w06'49 7:28:27
Booze Crossing 9 1 36N49'00 112w36'01 7:30:24
Boquillas 2 1 31N46'19 110w13'39 7:20:55
Borree Corner 12 1 32N58'24 111w33'29 7:26:14
Bosque 8 1 32N57'59 112w35'51 7:30:23
Bouse 7 3 33N55'57 114w00'18 7:36:01
Bowie 2 1 32N19'35 109w29'11 7:17:57
Bowie Junction (historical) 2 1 32N21'45 109w37'30 7:18:30
Boys Ranch 8 1 33N18 111w46 7:27:04

Bradberry 2 1 32N24'37 110w18'43 7:21:15
Bradshaw City 14 1 34N11'48 112w21'18 7:29:25
Braemar VII 8 1 33N34'35 112w12'20 7:28:49
Branaman 12 1 33N03'05 110w54'40 7:23:39
Brandywine 8 1 33N38'17 112w08'25 7:28:34
Breckenridge Manor 8 1 33N21'46 111w47'45 7:27:11
Brenda 7 3 33N40'47 113w56'38 7:35:47
Brentwood Mobile Manor 8 1 33N25'09 111w45'04 7:27:00
Brentwood West 8 1 33N24'36 111w45'35 7:27:02
Bridge Canyon Country Est 14 1 35N20 112w53 7:31:32
Bridgeport 8 1 33N20'52 111w52'00 7:27:28
Bridgeport 14 1 34N43'17 111w59'45 7:27:59
Briggs 2 1 31N25'06 109w53'47 7:19:35
Briggs 14 1 34N03'39 112w28'30 7:29:54
Brighton Place 8 1 33N20'17 111w51'47 7:27:27
Bristol Square 8 1 33N35'24 112w11'23 7:28:46
Broadway Trailer Court 8 1 33N24'27 112w06'14 7:28:25
Bronze Boot 8 1 33N29'09 112w02'39 7:28:11
Browns Crossing 9 1 34N17'39 113w32'44 7:34:11
Bryce 5 1 32N55'44 109w49'38 7:19:19
Buckeye 8 1 33N22'13 112w34'59 7:30:20
Buckeye Mill 2 1 32N15'22 109w34'54 7:18:20
Buckhorn 8 1 33N24'56 111w42'04 7:26:48
Buenavante 8 1 33N35'56 111w55'17 7:27:41
Buena Vista 5 1 32N50'37 109w33'41 7:18:15
Buenos Aires 11 1 31N31'16 111w39'24 7:26:38
Buffalo Crossing 6 1 33N45'47 109w21'16 7:17:25
Buffalo Crossing Camp 6 1 33N46'04 109w21'16 7:17:25
Bullhead City 9 2 35N08'52 114w34'03 7:38:16
Bumble Bee 14 1 34N12'03 112w09'08 7:28:37
Bumstead 8 1 33N34'24 112w21'22 7:29:25
Burch 4 1 33N26'38 110w49'53 7:23:20
Burgundy Hill 8 1 33N21'48 111w58'35 7:27:54
Burns 12 1 33N00'46 111w50'01 7:27:20
Burnt Water 1 1 35N13 109w20 7:17:20
Burro John 14 1 34N07'49 112w21'37 7:29:26
Burton 10 1 34N19'56 110w08'50 7:20:35
Bushman Acres 10 1 35N01'27 110w40'46 7:22:43
Bush Pit 7 3 33N45'05 113w46'07 7:35:04
Buzzard Gulch Trailer Park 10 1 34N55'09 110w09'04 7:20:36
Bylas 5 1 33N08'19 110w07'28 7:20:30
Byrds Mobile Park 8 1 33N25'37 112w21'05 7:29:24
Cactus 8 1 33N35'55 112w01'47 7:28:07
Cactus Cove Trailer Park 8 1 33N27'08 112w06'54 7:28:28
Cactus Flat 5 1 32N45'30 109w42'56 7:18:52
Cactus Forest 12 1 32N57'36 111w19'09 7:25:17
Cactus Gale V 8 1 33N36'00 112w09'51 7:28:39
Cactus Gardens Mobile Home P 8 1 33N36'39 112w02'13 7:28:09
Cactus Villa 8 1 33N35'18 111w51'16 7:27:25
Cactus Wren Mobile Park 8 1 33N25'12 111w37'52 7:26:31
Calabasas 13 1 31N28'02 110w58'29 7:23:54
Calumet 2 1 31N21'15 109w36'25 7:18:26
Calva 5 1 33N10'50 110w11'09 7:20:45
Cambridge Heights 8 1 33N21'15 111w58'47 7:27:55
Camel 8 1 33N03'00 113w16'35 7:33:06
Camelback Estates IV 8 1 33N33'51 111w58'25 7:27:54
Camelback Trailer Ranch 8 1 33N28'12 112w02'14 7:28:09
Camelot Luxury Homes 8 1 33N21'37 111w55'23 7:27:42
Camel View Plaza 8 1 33N29 111w56 7:27:44
Cameron 3 1 35N52'33 111w24'44 7:25:39
Camp Creek 8 1 33N54'42 111w48'58 7:27:16
Campo Bonito 3 1 34N26'10 111w02'46 7:24:11
Campo Bonito 12 1 32N33'49 110w44'16 7:22:57
Campstone 2 1 31N38'36 110w20'45 7:21:23
Camp Verde 14 1 34N33'49 111w51'13 7:27:25
Camp Verde Indian Res 14 1 34N34 111w51 7:27:24
Cane 3 1 36N34'04 112w00'11 7:28:01
Cane Beds 9 1 36N56'47 112w53'37 7:31:34
Canelo 13 1 31N32'34 110w30'50 7:22:03
Canyon Day 4 1 33N47'05 110w01'33 7:20:06
Canyon Diablo 3 1 35N09'46 111w07'01 7:24:28
Canyon Run 8 1 33N19'58 111w52'54 7:27:32
Canyon Trails Mobile Home Pk 8 1 33N41'29 112w06'36 7:28:26
Canyon View 8 1 33N39'21 112w09'11 7:28:37
Canyon Village 8 1 33N35'37 112w06'54 7:28:28
Capitol 8 1 33N30 112w05 7:28:20
Capri Village 8 1 33N27'19 112w08'55 7:28:36
Carefree 8 1 33N49'20 111w55'03 7:27:40
Carlton Vista 6 1 33N42'12 109w09'09 7:16:37
Carmen 13 1 31N35'14 111w03'08 7:24:13
Carrizo 4 1 33N59'38 110w17'17 7:21:09
Cartwright 8 1 33N28'50 112w11'11 7:28:45
Casa Blanca 12 1 33N07'13 111w53'15 7:27:33
Casa de Francisco Mobile Hom 8 1 33N22'20 112w04'10 7:28:17
Casa del Oro 12 1 32N34'39 110w50'38 7:23:23
Casa del Sol Resorts 8 1 33N35'05 112w12'15 7:28:49
Casa del Sol Resorts Number 8 1 33N35'15 112w15'10 7:29:01
Casa Grande 12 1 32N52'46 111w45'24 7:27:02
Casa Linda 8 1 33N20'25 111w51'16 7:27:25
Casa Piedra 13 1 31N23'21 111w15'00 7:25:00
Casa Rica 8 1 33N35'20 111w51'30 7:27:26
Casa Rosa 14 1 33N56'51 112w20'06 7:29:20
Casas Adobes 11 1 32N19'24 110w59'40 7:23:59
Casas del Campo Mobile Home 8 1 33N19'44 111w50'15 7:27:21
Casa Serena Mobile Home Park 8 1 33N24'15 111w38'42 7:26:35
Casas Grande Mall 12 1 32N53 111w44 7:26:56
Cascabel 2 1 32N17'29 110w22'44 7:21:31
Cashion 8 1 33N26'07 112w17'50 7:29:11
Castillo Nuevo Mobile Home P 8 1 33N24'36 111w45'35 7:27:02
Castle Butte 10 1 35N18'17 110w20'53 7:21:24
Castle Canyon Mesa 14 1 34N35'27 112w21'18 7:29:25
Castle Dome Landing 15 3 32N57'54 114w27'46 7:37:51
Castle Hot Springs 14 1 33N59'00 112w21'35 7:29:26
Castle Rock Shores 7 3 34N09 114w17 7:37:08
Catalina 11 1 32N29'50 110w55'25 7:23:42
Catalina Foothills 11 1 32N17'52 110w55'05 7:23:40
Catalina Village 8 1 33N27'35 112w08'46 7:28:35
Catfish Paradise 9 2 34N44'42 114w29'12 7:37:57
Cavalay Park 2 1 31N33'08 110w21'45 7:21:27
Cave Creek 8 1 33N50'00 111w57'00 7:27:48
Cazador 2 1 31N29'29 109w25'18 7:17:41
Cedar 9 2 34N46'43 113w47'37 7:35:10
Cedar Creek 4 1 33N53'44 110w10'23 7:20:42
Cedar Creek Crossing 4 1 33N51'55 110w12'02 7:20:48
Cedar Mill 14 1 34N28'19 111w59'45 7:27:59
Cedar Ridge 3 1 35N53 111w25 7:25:40
Cedar Ridge 8 1 33N20'00 111w50'42 7:27:23
Cedar Springs 10 1 35N27'06 110w21'49 7:21:27
Centerville 14 1 34N45'35 112w03'21 7:28:13
Central 5 1 32N52'03 109w47'32 7:19:10
Central Heights 4 1 33N24'45 110w48'51 7:23:15
Central Park Village 8 1 33N38'19 112w04'32 7:28:18
Central Ridge 8 1 33N19'10 111w53'09 7:27:33
Centura West 8 1 33N27'38 112w11'15 7:28:45
Cerbat 9 2 35N18'11 114w08'20 7:36:33
Chador Mobile Home Park 8 1 33N34'47 112w15'05 7:29:00
Chair Crossing 3 1 36N52'22 111w35'40 7:26:23
Chakpahu 10 1 35N45'43 110w10'20 7:20:41
Chalender 3 1 35N14'04 112w01'28 7:28:06
Chambers 1 1 35N11'19 109w25'57 7:17:44
Chamiso 2 1 31N59'34 110w21'14 7:21:25
Chandler 8 1 33N18'22 111w50'26 7:27:22
Chandler Gardens Mobile Home 8 1 33N18'36 111w49'58 7:27:20
Chandler Heights 8 1 33N12'43 111w41'08 7:26:45
Chandler Meadows Mobile Home 8 1 33N19'04 111w50'02 7:27:20
Chaney Place 5 1 32N29'00 109w20'48 7:17:23
Chaparral 8 1 33N38'36 112w10'44 7:28:43
Chapparal Mobile Village 8 1 33N22'42 112w04'46 7:28:19
Charco 11 1 32N15'02 112w36'19 7:30:25
Charleston 2 1 31N37'55 110w10'25 7:20:42
Charlie Moore Place 6 1 33N23'23 109w02'47 7:16:11
Chavez Crossing Campground 3 1 34N50'36 111w46'34 7:27:06
Cherokee Mobile Village 8 1 33N25'02 111w36'34 7:26:26
Cherry 14 1 34N35'17 112w02'28 7:28:10
Chetco 1 1 35N12'59 109w20'01 7:17:20
Chevelon 3 1 35N12 111w37 7:26:28
Chevelon Crossing 3 1 34N35'36 110w47'14 7:23:09
Cheyenne Village 8 1 33N36'00 112w08'15 7:28:33
Chiapuk 12 1 32N32'09 112w08'04 7:28:32
Chiawuli Tak 11 1 31N56'08 111w46'49 7:27:07
Chico Shunie 11 1 32N19'40 112w56'46 7:31:47
Chilchinbito 10 1 36N31'38 110w04'54 7:20:20
Childs 11 1 32N27'10 112w50'34 7:31:22
Chilean Mill 14 1 34N09'04 112w23'33 7:29:34
Chimney Hill 8 1 33N35'05 111w51'20 7:27:25
Chinle 1 1 36N09'16 109w33'07 7:18:12
Chino Valley 14 1 34N45'27 112w27'11 7:29:49
Chiricahua 2 1 31N35'32 109w14'24 7:16:58
Chiulikam 8 1 32N34'28 112w31'31 7:30:06
Chiuli Shaik 11 1 31N49'43 111w38'46 7:26:35
Chloride 9 2 35N24'52 114w11'55 7:36:48
Choulic 11 1 31N40'02 111w46'34 7:27:06
Christmas 4 1 33N03'44 110w44'31 7:22:58
Christopher Creek 4 1 34N18'55 111w00'59 7:24:04
Chris-Town 8 1 33N30'46 112w06'00 7:28:24
Chrysotile 4 1 33N44'25 110w33'58 7:22:16
Chuichu 12 1 32N45'07 111w46'57 7:27:08
Chukson 11 1 31N54'47 111w47'46 7:27:11
Chukut Kuk 11 1 31N45'56 112w06'16 7:28:25
Chutum Vaya 11 1 31N42'59 111w38'46 7:26:35
Chuwut Murk 11 1 31N53'14 112w08'42 7:28:35
Cibecue 10 1 34N02'41 110w29'05 7:21:56
Cibecue Creek 10 1 34N05'47 110w30'09 7:22:01
Cibola 7 3 33N18'59 114w39'51 7:38:39
Ciela Grande Mobile Home Pk 8 1 33N24'24 111w37'33 7:26:30
Cienega Springs 7 3 34N11'19 114w13'26 7:36:54
Cimarron 8 1 33N23'15 111w59'29 7:27:58
Cinco Soles 8 1 33N31'30 111w57'10 7:27:49
Circle City 8 1 33N48'57 112w34'46 7:30:19
Citrus Gardens 8 1 33N25'17 111w44'33 7:26:58
Citrus Grove Trailer Court 8 1 33N24'52 111w51'07 7:27:24
Citrus Grove Trailer Park 8 1 33N33'20 112w04'25 7:28:18
Citrus Hills 8 1 33N22'45 112w02'30 7:28:10
Citrus Park 8 1 33N32'55 112w26'37 7:29:46
Claremont Place 8 1 33N31'42 112w02'30 7:28:10
Clarkdale 14 1 34N46'16 112w03'26 7:28:14
Claypool 4 1 33N24'40 110w50'31 7:23:22
Clay Springs 10 1 34N21'42 110w17'41 7:21:11
Clear Creek 14 1 34N31'19 111w49'04 7:27:16
Clearview Heights 10 1 34N54'30 110w08'44 7:20:35
Clearview Hills 8 1 33N32'03 111w59'05 7:27:56
Clearwater Hills 8 1 33N29 111w56 7:27:44
Cleator 14 1 34N16'43 112w13'56 7:28:56
Cleaveland 6 1 33N43'18 109w16'50 7:17:07
Clemenceau 14 1 34N43'55 112w01'33 7:28:06
Clifton 6 1 33N03'03 109w17'44 7:17:11
Clints Well 3 1 34N33'16 111w18'44 7:25:15
Cloverleaf 8 1 33N20'40 111w51'45 7:27:27
Coal Mine Mesa 3 1 35N57'35 110w56'20 7:23:45
Cobblestone Square 8 1 33N36'05 111w58'19 7:27:53
Cochise 2 1 32N06'49 109w55'16 7:19:41
Cochran 12 1 33N06'34 111w08'57 7:24:36
Coconino 3 1 35N59'40 112w11'51 7:28:47
Cocopah Indian Reservation 7 3 34N34 111w51 7:27:24
Coffeepot 4 1 34N02'22 111w11'10 7:24:45
Cogdill Center 3 1 35N11'09 111w38'36 7:26:34
Colcord Mountain Estates 4 1 34N15'50 110w54'01 7:23:36
Colfred 15 3 32N42'16 113w54'03 7:35:36
College Park 8 1 33N37'39 112w10'40 7:28:43
Colonial Coronita 8 1 33N18'16 111w47'45 7:27:11
Colony Biltmore IV 8 1 33N30'55 112w01'26 7:28:06
Colony South 8 1 33N37'17 112w06'37 7:28:26
Colorado City 9 1 36N59'25 112w58'30 7:31:54
Colorado River Indian Res 7 3 34N09 114w17 7:37:08
Columbia 14 1 34N02'01 112w18'35 7:29:14
Commerce 8 1 33N27 112w04 7:28:16
Comobabi 11 1 32N03'29 111w47'58 7:27:12
Concho 1 1 34N28'31 109w36'19 7:18:25
Conger 8 1 33N22'23 112w39'27 7:30:38
Congress 14 1 34N09'45 112w51'00 7:31:24
Congress Junction 14 1 34N09'46 112w50'39 7:31:23
Contempo Tempe 8 1 33N23'25 111w58'20 7:27:53
Contention 2 1 31N46'08 110w12'05 7:20:48
Continental 11 1 31N51'08 110w58'27 7:23:54
Continental Tempe 8 1 33N21'05 111w54'46 7:27:39
Continental Village 8 1 33N34'10 111w51'29 7:27:26
Coolidge 12 1 32N58'40 111w31'01 7:26:04
Coolidge Dam 4 1 33N10'55 110w31'33 7:22:06
Co-op Village 8 1 33N20'11 112w12'26 7:28:50
Copper Creek 12 1 32N45'03 110w28'33 7:21:54
Copper Hill 4 1 33N25'49 110w45'50 7:23:03
Copper Kettle Trailer Villa 8 1 33N37'55 112w00'38 7:28:03
Copper Mine 1 1 36N50'06 109w03'38 7:16:15
Copper Mines 3 1 35N53 111w25 7:25:40
Copperopolis 14 1 34N04'49 112w28'10 7:29:53
Copper Queen 2 1 31N25 109w54 7:19:36
Coral Sands Mobile Estates 8 1 33N25'15 111w34'58 7:26:20
Cordes 14 1 34N18'12 112w09'58 7:28:40
Cordes Junction 14 1 34N19'56 112w07'11 7:28:29
Cordes Junction Interchange 14 1 34N19'45 112w07'12 7:28:29
Cordes Lakes 14 1 34N18'28 113w06'10 7:32:25
Cork 5 1 32N57'25 109w55'05 7:19:40
Corner Windmill 11 1 32N07'08 111w19'16 7:25:17
Cornfields 1 1 35N39'08 109w40'43 7:18:43
Cornville 14 1 34N43'04 111w55'15 7:27:41
Coronada Foothills Estates 11 1 32N18 110w56 7:23:44
Corona de Tucson 11 1 31N57'55 110w46'30 7:23:06
Coronado 11 1 32N13 110w53 7:23:32
Coronado Mobile Home Park 8 1 33N24'48 111w46'19 7:27:05
Coronado Village 2 1 31N32'55 110w20'50 7:21:23
Corona Village 8 1 33N19'05 111w55'28 7:27:42
Correjo Crossing 1 1 34N05'30 109w12'11 7:16:49
Corta Junction 2 1 31N23'46 109w52'59 7:19:32
Cortaro 11 1 32N21'22 111w05'16 7:24:21
Corva 3 1 35N16'31 112w20'55 7:29:24

Cosnino 3 1 35N12'20 111w28'27 7:25:54
Cotton Center 8
1 33N05'14 112w39'58 7:30:40
Cottonwood 1 1 36N04'23 109w53'30 7:19:34
Cottonwood 12 1 33N04'26 111w42'00 7:26:48
Cottonwood 14 1 34N44'21 112w00'33 7:28:02
Cottonwood Ranch 8
1 33N36'20 112w13'50 7:28:55
Cottonwood Station 1
1 36N09 109w33 7:18:12
Country Club Trailer Grove 8
1 33N28'52 112w00'30 7:28:02
Country Club Village Mobile 8
1 33N27'11 111w49'54 7:27:20
Country Cousins Mobile Mecca 8
1 33N23'33 111w49'58 7:27:20
Country Estates 14
1 34N32'15 111w50'57 7:27:24
Country Greens at Villa de P 8
1 33N30'08 112w17'09 7:29:09
Country Hills Mobile Estates 8
1 33N27'45 112w18'56 7:29:16
Country Horizons 8
1 33N34'25 111w53'30 7:27:34
Country Life 8 1 33N26 111w50 7:27:20
Country Meadows 8
1 33N33'57 112w17'02 7:29:08
Country Ridge 8
1 33N39'24 112w07'22 7:28:29
Countryside Mobile Home Park 8
1 33N22'34 112w06'05 7:28:24
Country Trace 8
1 33N38'05 111w55'35 7:27:42
Country Villa 8
1 33N26'28 112w20'16 7:29:21
County Fair West 8
1 33N28'40 112w11'45 7:28:47
Courtland 2 1 31N46'12 109w48'29 7:19:14
Cove 1 1 36N33'55 109w13'02 7:16:52
Covered Wagon Mobile Home Pk 8
1 33N31'55 112w06'45 7:28:27
Covered Wells 11
1 31N55 111w53 7:27:32
Cowlic 11 1 31N48'30 111w59'18 7:27:57
Cow Springs 3 1 36N24'47 110w49'18 7:23:17
Coyote Basin Ranch 3
1 34N50'33 111w25'49 7:25:43
Coyote Field 11
1 32N11'55 111w39'47 7:26:39
Coyote Springs 1
1 36N15'38 109w42'56 7:18:52
Crag 8 1 33N18'04 112w54'05 7:31:36
Craycroft 11 1 32N12'25 110w52'29 7:23:30
Crestview 2 1 31N25 109w54 7:19:36
Crestview 8 1 33N18'11 111w56'30 7:27:46
Crookton 14 1 35N17'43 112w42'26 7:30:50
Crosby Crossing 1
1 33N54'42 109w20'40 7:17:23
Cross Canyon 1 1 35N39 109w06 7:16:24
Crown King 14 1 34N12'20 112w20'16 7:29:21
Crozier 9 2 35N25'30 113w38'55 7:34:36
Cucamonga Junction 3
1 35N18'09 112w23'05 7:29:32
Cuckelbur 12 1 32N53 111w44 7:26:56
Currys Corner 8
1 33N41'55 111w55'28 7:27:42
Curtiss 2 1 31N53'04 110w13'45 7:20:55
Cutter 4 1 33N21'10 110w39'07 7:22:36
Cyclopic 9 2 35N46'58 114w14'43 7:36:59
Cypress Estates 8
1 33N24'58 111w45'20 7:27:01
Dagger 4 1 33N41'40 110w48'45 7:23:15
Dam View 7 3 34N09 114w17 7:37:08
Danas Trailer Ranch 8
1 33N24'59 111w36'19 7:26:25
Dandrea 14 1 34N21'53 112w22'34 7:29:30
Darling 3 1 35N12'02 111w23'59 7:25:36
Date 14 1 34N18'55 112w55'03 7:31:40
Dateland 15 3 32N47'47 113w32'25 7:34:10
Davis Dam 9 2 35N10'48 114w33'56 7:38:16
Davis-Monthan AFB 11
1 32N11 110w53 7:23:32
Daze 3 1 35N14'56 112w24'13 7:29:37
De Anza Village 2
1 31N33'06 110w20'30 7:21:22
Deer Creek 8 1 33N35'00 112w13'03 7:28:52
Deering Park Estates 14
1 34N32'10 112w33'56 7:30:16
Deer Valley 8 1 33N41'02 112w08'03 7:28:32
Dehorn 4 1 33N31'37 110w10'44 7:20:43
Del Muerto 1 1 36N11'05 109w26'32 7:17:46
Del Rio 14 1 34N49'23 112w26'34 7:29:46
DeLuxe Trailer Court 8
1 33N27'06 112w06'15 7:28:25
Dennehotso 1 1 36N51 109w51 7:19:24
Dennison 3 1 35N05'12 110w54'15 7:23:37
Deserama Mobile Ranch 8
1 33N25'03 111w46'42 7:27:07
Desert Bell Estates II 8
1 33N39'24 112w03'04 7:28:12
Desert Carmel 12
1 32N53 111w44 7:26:56
Desert Gem Mobile Home Park 8
1 33N27'11 112w11'51 7:28:47
Desert Highlands 8
1 33N43'10 111w52'55 7:27:32
Desert Pines 8 1 33N38'15 112w08'35 7:28:34
Desert Ridge 8 1 33N38'03 111w55'51 7:27:43
Desert Sage Mobile Manor 8
1 33N27'48 111w58'49 7:27:55
Desert Sands 8 1 33N26 111w50 7:27:20
Desert Sands Mobile Home Pk 8
1 33N41'33 112w07'04 7:28:28
Desert Valley Estates 8
1 33N39'18 112w05'52 7:28:23
Desert View 3 1 36N03 112w08 7:28:32
Desert Village Mobile Home P 8
1 33N24'45 111w37'21 7:26:29
Desert Villas 8
1 33N21'10 111w58'25 7:27:54
Desert Vista Estates III 8
1 33N25'25 111w37'44 7:26:31
Desert Wells 7 3 33N42'30 113w49'15 7:35:17

Desert Wind II 8
1 33N36'16 111w55'21 7:27:41
Dewey 14 1 34N31'48 112w14'26 7:28:58
Diamond Bell Ranch 11
1 31N58'24 111w16'54 7:25:08
Diamond Creek Junction Campg 10
1 33N53'37 109w56'01 7:19:44
Diamond Fields 1
1 36N48'46 109w53'22 7:19:33
Diamond Valley 14
1 34N34'05 112w22'28 7:29:30
Dilkon 10 1 35N23'07 110w19'12 7:21:17
Dimario Place 4
1 33N22'40 110w48'59 7:23:16
Dixie 8 1 33N21'34 112w45'25 7:31:02
Dobson 11 1 32N28'24 111w17'30 7:25:10
Dobson Ranch 8 1 33N22'14 111w52'25 7:27:30
Dobson Shores 8
1 33N22'37 111w52'48 7:27:31
Dolan Springs 9
2 35N35'31 114w16'21 7:37:05
Dollbeer Mobile Home Ranch 8
1 33N24'45 111w38'52 7:26:35
Dome 15 3 32N45'19 114w21'41 7:37:27
Don Luis 2 1 31N24'09 109w54'58 7:19:40
Dos Cabezas 2 1 32N10'31 109w36'46 7:18:27
Double Adobe 2 1 31N28'00 109w41'22 7:18:45
Doubletree Canyon 8
1 33N33'50 111w58'56 7:27:56
Douglas 2 1 31N20'40 109w32'41 7:18:11
Dragoon 2 1 32N01'41 110w02'17 7:20:09
Drake 9 2 35N02'24 114w07'16 7:36:29
Drake 14 1 34N58'53 112w22'32 7:29:30
Dreamland Villa 8
1 33N25'17 111w42'36 7:26:50
Drexel Heights 11
1 32N08'28 111w01'40 7:24:07
Dublin 5 1 32N53'46 109w50'01 7:19:20
Dudleyville 12 1 32N58'19 110w46'33 7:23:06
Dugas 14 1 34N21'43 111w58'40 7:27:55
Duncan 6 1 32N43'17 109w06'17 7:16:25
Dunhill Meadows 8
1 33N30'19 112w13'29 7:28:54
Dunhill Place 8
1 33N38'35 112w09'10 7:28:37
Duquesne 13 1 31N22'15 110w41'05 7:22:44
Durfee Crossing 3
1 34N34'26 110w48'15 7:23:13
Dusk File 8 1 33N20'54 111w55'05 7:27:40
Duval 11 1 31N55'54 110w57'27 7:23:50
Dysart (historic town) 8
1 33N36'52 112w19'28 7:29:18
Eagar 1 1 34N06'40 109w17'27 7:17:10
Eagle Creek 6 1 33N03 109w18 7:17:12
East Flagstaff 3
1 35N12'41 111w36'45 7:26:27
East Fork 10 1 33N47'53 109w55'47 7:19:43
East Fort 14 1 34N09'49 112w15'16 7:29:01
East Mesa 8 1 33N24'55 111w39'26 7:26:38
East Pershing Plaza 2
1 31N33'18 110w20'35 7:21:22
East Plantsite 6
1 33N02'49 109w19'05 7:17:16
Eastway Mobile Home Park 8
1 33N27'12 111w49'03 7:27:16
Echinique Place 3
1 34N43'04 110w57'58 7:23:52
Eddy Place 14 1 34N57'38 112w36'07 7:30:24
Eden 5 1 32N57'40 109w53'41 7:19:35
Ehrenberg 7 3 33N36'15 114w31'28 7:38:06
Eighteen Bells Mobile Home P 8
1 33N38'32 112w02'34 7:28:10
El Camino Mobile Home Park 8
1 33N38'48 112w01'39 7:28:07
Elden Pueblo 3 1 35N14'33 111w34'02 7:26:16
El Dorado Mobile Home Resort 8
1 33N27'51 111w59'20 7:27:57
Eleven Mile Corner 12
1 32N52'46 111w33'59 7:26:16
Elfrida 2 1 31N41'07 109w41'11 7:18:45
Elgin 13 1 31N39'35 110w31'29 7:22:06
Elik 12 1 32N31 111w57 7:27:48
Ellison Place 5
1 33N00'35 110w18'54 7:21:16
El Mar Trailer Court 8
1 33N24'48 111w45'30 7:27:02
El Mirage 8 1 33N36'47 112w19'26 7:29:18
Elmwood Trailer Park 8
1 33N18'23 111w49'45 7:27:19
Eloy 12 1 32N45'21 111w33'15 7:26:13
El Paseo 8 1 33N33'42 111w53'44 7:27:35
El Pueblecito 15
3 32N44 114w35 7:38:20
El Rio 11 1 32N14'07 110w59'20 7:23:57
El San Juan Trailer Park 8
1 33N35'00 112w15'15 7:29:01
El Sereno-La Rosa 8
1 33N27'59 112w01'51 7:28:07
El Tule 1 1 34N22'47 109w23'48 7:17:35
Emery 5 1 33N04'11 110w00'59 7:20:04
Emery Park 11 1 32N08'28 110w57'19 7:23:49
Emika 11 1 32N26'00 112w29'09 7:29:57
Emmanuel Mission 1
1 36N48'08 109w23'48 7:17:35
Empire Landing 7
3 34N09 114w17 7:37:08
Engesser Junction 15
3 33N12'04 113w52'18 7:35:29
Enid 12 1 33N04'21 112w12'04 7:28:48
Ensenada del Oro 8
1 33N34'47 111w52'10 7:27:29
Entro 14 1 34N36'25 112w24'12 7:29:37
Escalante Crossing 2
1 31N51'40 110w12'33 7:20:50
Esmond 11 1 32N05'36 110w45'51 7:23:03
Esplanada 8 1 33N21'09 111w50'49 7:27:23
Estados de La Mancha II 8
1 33N34'35 111w54'05 7:27:36
Estate Monterra 8
1 33N31'55 112w02'25 7:28:10
Estates La Colina 8
1 33N20'17 111w54'04 7:27:36
Estrella 8 1 33N00'04 112w25'00 7:29:40

Estrella Camp 8
1 33N26'55 112w22'26 7:29:30
Estrella Estates Family Park 8
1 33N28'07 112w05'23 7:28:22
Evergreen Villa Mobile Home 8
1 33N19'42 111w51'13 7:27:25
Fairbank 2 1 31N42'54 110w11'05 7:20:44
Fair Oaks 14 1 34N43'25 112w45'40 7:31:03
Fairwood VIII 8
1 33N35'16 112w12'20 7:28:49
Falcon Estates 8
1 33N26 111w50 7:27:20
Falfa 8 1 33N20'46 111w49'55 7:27:20
Feaster 1 1 33N59'30 109w08'41 7:16:35
Fennemore 8 1 33N34'13 112w25'36 7:29:42
Fenner 2 1 31N58'12 110w13'50 7:20:55
Ferguson Place Windmill 14
1 34N20'48 112w43'58 7:30:56
Fiesta Park 8 1 33N25'17 111w44'54 7:27:00
Firebrand Ranch 8
1 33N34'36 111w58'53 7:27:56
Fish Creek (historical town) 8
1 33N32'00 111w18'20 7:25:13
Fishers Landing 15
3 32N58'22 114w27'46 7:37:51
Fivemile Landing 9
2 34N47'43 114w30'18 7:38:01
Flagstaff 3 1 35N11'53 111w39'02 7:26:36
Flamingo Mobile Home Resort 8
1 33N31'34 112w09'56 7:28:40
Flat Rock 1 1 36N00'20 109w33'18 7:18:13
Flecha Caida Estates 11
1 32N18 110w56 7:23:44
Florence 12 1 33N01'53 111w23'12 7:25:33
Florence Junction 12
1 33N15'34 111w20'11 7:25:21
Flores 14 1 34N03'45 112w49'15 7:31:17
Flower Pot 14 1 34N30'12 111w58'12 7:27:53
Forbing Park 14
1 34N33'56 112w29'42 7:29:59
Fordville 12 1 32N42'16 110w41'37 7:22:46
Forepaugh 8 1 33N58'17 113w02'44 7:32:11
Forest Lakes Estates 3
1 34N20'20 110w47'57 7:23:12
Forrest 2 1 31N22'00 109w43'37 7:18:54
Fort Apache 10 1 33N47'26 109w59'17 7:19:57
Fort Apache Indian Res 10
1 33N50 109w58 7:19:52
Fort Apache Junction 4
1 33N47'23 110w00'04 7:20:00
Fort Defiance 1
1 35N44'40 109w04'33 7:16:18
Fort Huachuca 2
1 31N33 110w21 7:21:24
Fort McDonald 4
1 34N14'06 111w20'51 7:25:23
Fort McDowell 8
1 33N38'12 111w40'26 7:26:42
Fort McDowell Indian Res 8
1 33N38 111w40 7:26:40
Fort Misery 14 1 34N08'25 112w21'57 7:29:28
Fort River Caves 14
1 34N34'05 111w50'47 7:27:23
Fort Thomas 5 1 33N02'13 109w57'53 7:19:52
Fort Tule 14 1 34N00'12 112w16'02 7:29:04
Fort Tuthill 3 1 35N08'30 111w41'37 7:26:46
Fortuna 15 3 32N41'26 114w27'08 7:37:49
Fort Verde Estates 14
1 34N32'26 111w51'22 7:27:25
Fort Whipple 14
1 34N33'17 112w27'07 7:29:48
Fountain East 8
1 33N24'37 111w41'58 7:26:48
Fountain Hills 8
1 33N36'42 111w43'00 7:26:52
Fountain of the Sun 8
1 33N24'41 111w39'19 7:26:37
Fountain View 8
1 33N36'28 111w43'52 7:26:55
Fowler 8 1 33N27'05 112w12'11 7:28:49
Fox 6 1 32N44'35 109w08'16 7:16:33
Foxboro 8 1 33N33'15 112w15'05 7:29:00
Fox Glen 8 1 33N35'32 112w12'56 7:28:52
Franconia 9 2 34N44'22 114w16'03 7:37:04
Franklin 6 1 32N40'39 109w04'43 7:16:19
Frazier Wells 3
2 35N46'57 113w04'17 7:32:17
Fredonia 9 1 36N56'44 112w31'33 7:30:06
Freeman 8 1 32N50'45 112w17'45 7:29:11
Fresnal Canyon 11
1 31N55 111w53 7:27:32
Friendly Corners 12
1 32N37'04 111w33'01 7:26:12
Fry 2 1 31N33'24 110w17'40 7:21:11
Fuller Ranch 8 1 33N24'17 111w47'02 7:27:08
Gadsden 15 3 32N33'16 114w47'03 7:39:08
Gainey Ranch 8 1 33N34'16 111w55'00 7:27:40
Galena 2 1 31N25'19 109w53'33 7:19:34
Galeyville 2 1 31N57'01 109w13'04 7:16:52
Gallups 4 1 34N04'43 111w11'09 7:24:45
Ganado 1 1 35N42'41 109w32'29 7:18:10
Gatewood Housing 2
1 31N33'18 110w20'05 7:21:20
Germann 8 1 33N16'41 111w40'07 7:26:40
Geronimo 5 1 33N04'37 110w02'04 7:20:08
Getz 9 2 35N12'17 114w01'10 7:36:05
Gibson 11 1 32N22'43 112w52'20 7:31:29
Gila Bend 8 1 32N56'52 112w42'58 7:30:52
Gila Bend Indian Reservation 8
1 31N55 111w53 7:27:32
Gila Crossing 8
1 33N16'36 112w09'58 7:28:40
Gila River Indian Res 8
1 33N05 111w44 7:26:56
Gilbert 8 1 33N21'10 111w47'18 7:27:09
Gillespie 8 1 33N15'42 112w58'50 7:31:55
Gillette 14 1 34N01'08 112w09'46 7:28:39
Gisela 4 1 34N06'06 111w16'45 7:25:07
Gladden 7 1 33N54'09 113w17'55 7:33:12
Gleeson 2 1 31N44'02 109w49'45 7:19:19
Glenbar 5 1 32N55'00 109w51'27 7:19:26
Glen Canyon Trailer Park 8
1 33N32'20 112w06'48 7:28:27

Glendale 8 1 33N32'19 112w11'07 7:28:44
Glendale West Mobile Home Pk 8
1 33N32'23 112w13'50 7:28:55
Glen Ilah 14 1 34N12'54 112w45'30 7:31:02
Glen Oaks 14 1 34N26'35 112w32'52 7:30:11
Glenview Estates 8
1 33N18'15 111w55'24 7:27:42
Globe 4 1 33N23'39 110w47'09 7:23:09
Goldbadge 8 1 33N36'39 112w20'18 7:29:21
Golden Hills 8 1 33N26 111w50 7:27:20
Golden West Estates 8
1 33N25'20 111w45'30 7:27:02
Goldfield 12 1 33N27'32 111w29'12 7:25:57
Goodwater 10 1 34N59'31 109w56'39 7:19:47
Goodwin 14 1 34N21'21 112w22'45 7:29:31
Goodyear 8 1 33N26'07 112w21'27 7:29:26
Goodyear Farms 8
1 34N30 112w41 7:30:44
Government Hill 4
1 33N40'28 111w08'58 7:24:36
Graham 5 1 32N52'30 109w44'24 7:18:58
Grand Canyon 3 1 36N03'16 112w08'19 7:28:33
Grand Canyon Caverns 3
2 35N31'43 113w13'50 7:32:55
Grand Canyon Estates 3
1 36N03 112w08 7:28:32
Grand Missouri Adult Mobile 8
1 33N31'06 112w09'10 7:28:37
Grand View 14 1 34N25'11 112w49'21 7:31:17
Grandview Mobile Home Park 8
1 33N28'34 112w00'40 7:28:03
Granite 14 1 34N41'44 112w24'31 7:29:38
Granite Basin Summer Homes 14
1 34N36'48 112w33'12 7:30:13
Granite Dells 14
1 34N36'21 112w24'42 7:29:39
Granite Reef Estates 8
1 33N26'21 111w41'01 7:26:44
Granville 6 1 33N11'20 109w22'55 7:17:32
Grapevine 4 1 33N39'04 111w02'54 7:24:12
Grasshopper 10 1 34N04'32 110w37'47 7:22:31
Grasshopper Junction 9
2 35N23'49 114w15'32 7:37:02
Gray Mountain 3
1 35N44'45 111w28'22 7:25:53
Greasewood 10 1 35N31'21 109w51'24 7:19:26
Greasewood Springs 1
1 36N35 109w05 7:16:20
Greaterville 9 1 31N45'51 110w45'03 7:23:00
Green Acres Mobile and Recre 8
1 33N27'01 112w06'55 7:28:28
Green Acres Trailer Court 8
1 33N24'55 111w52'56 7:27:32
Greenbriar 8 1 33N35'03 112w09'50 7:28:39
Greenbrier East 8
1 33N36'55 111w58'00 7:27:52
Greenfield Estates 8
1 33N25'25 111w44'06 7:26:56
Greenfield Park 8
1 33N25'17 111w43'47 7:26:55
Greenhaven Mobile Park 8
1 33N27'27 111w58'46 7:27:55
Greenlaw Village 3
1 35N12 111w37 7:26:28
Green Spot 1 1 34N11'23 109w24'11 7:17:37
Greentrails 8 1 33N38'23 112w03'46 7:28:15
Green Tree Mobile Home Park 8
1 33N18'30 111w49'47 7:27:19
Green Valley 11
1 31N52'00 110w59'35 7:23:58
Green Valley Trailer Park 8
1 33N23'37 112w00'33 7:28:02
Greenway Center 8
1 33N35 112w23 7:29:32
Greenway Park V 8
1 33N37'44 111w57'51 7:27:51
Greenwood 9 2 34N30'28 113w35'38 7:34:23
Greer 1 1 34N00'36 109w27'29 7:17:50
Greer Place 1 1 34N36'12 109w36'16 7:18:25
Griffith 9 2 35N04'00 114w06'57 7:36:28
Gripe 5 1 32N48'45 109w36'05 7:18:24
Grizzles Orchard 2
1 31N45'15 109w44'53 7:19:00
Groom Creek 14 1 34N28'32 112w25'50 7:29:43
Growler 15 3 32N48'56 113w47'54 7:35:12
Gu Achi 11 1 32N19'25 112w02'26 7:28:10
Guadalupe 8 1 33N22'15 111w57'44 7:27:51
Gu Chuapo 11 1 31N53'40 111w39'50 7:26:39
Guevavi Mission (ruins) 13
1 31N24'36 110w54'06 7:23:36
Gu Komelik 12 1 31N55 111w53 7:27:32
Gunsight 11 1 32N22 112w51 7:31:24
Gu Oidak 11 1 31N55'18 112w02'34 7:28:10
Gurli Put Vo 11
1 32N12'14 112w01'08 7:28:05
Guthrie 6 1 32N56'46 109w15'09 7:17:01
Gu Vo 11 1 32N03'56 112w33'36 7:30:14
Hacienda de Valencia 8
1 33N24'36 111w44'01 7:26:56
Hacienda Los Encino 13
1 31N39'32 110w38'48 7:22:35
Haciendas del Lago 8
1 33N34'40 111w52'16 7:27:29
Hacienda Solano Park 8
1 33N18'18 111w47'25 7:27:10
Hackberry 9 2 35N22'09 113w43'35 7:34:54
Haivana Nakya 11
1 32N00'24 111w42'47 7:26:51
Haivan Vaya 11 1 31N36'35 111w52'22 7:27:29
Hali Murk 11 1 32N00'04 112w17'37 7:29:10
Hamilton Corner 8
1 33N14'52 111w50'26 7:27:22
Hamilton Crossing 3
1 34N39'17 110w59'49 7:23:59
Hannagan Meadow 6
1 33N38'32 109w19'24 7:17:18
Hano 10 1 35N50'13 110w23'30 7:21:34
Happy Jack 3 1 34N44'36 111w24'24 7:25:38
Happy Valley Ranch 8
1 33N42'57 111w53'57 7:27:36
Harcuvar 7 3 33N45'36 113w39'09 7:34:37
Hard Rocks 10 1 36N04'42 110w26'18 7:21:45
Harmony Villa 8
1 33N27'38 111w41'32 7:26:46
Harqua 8 1 33N14'35 112w59'54 7:32:00
Harrington Place 11
1 32N02'33 110w32'46 7:22:11
Harris 9 2 35N08'13 114w04'59 7:36:20
Harshaw 13 1 31N28'02 110w42'23 7:22:50
Hashan Chuchg 11
1 31N34'02 111w46'20 7:27:05
Hassayampa 8 1 33N20'54 112w43'29 7:30:54
Havana Nakya 11
1 31N55 111w53 7:27:32
Havasupai Indian Reservation 3
1 34N09 114w17 7:37:08
Haviland 9 2 34N48'08 114w10'35 7:36:42
Hawaiian Village Mobile Home 8
1 33N27'16 111w50'24 7:27:22
Hawkins 14 1 34N16'02 112w54'06 7:31:36
Hawley Lake 1 1 33N59'02 109w44'47 7:18:59
Hayden 4 1 33N00'17 110w47'05 7:23:08
Hayden Junction 12
1 33N00'35 110w48'53 7:23:16
Headquarters 10
1 34N48'51 109w51'51 7:19:27
Heap Place 1 1 34N35'01 109w24'27 7:17:38
Heatherbrook 8 1 33N20'52 111w53'27 7:27:34
Heaton 12 1 33N04'44 112w08'02 7:28:32
Heber 10 1 34N25'53 110w35'36 7:22:22
Hecla 14 1 34N32'17 112w07'15 7:28:29
Helena 8 1 33N21'22 111w56'34 7:27:46
Helvetia 11 1 31N51'28 110w47'17 7:23:09
Hereford 2 1 31N26'18 110w05'50 7:20:23
Heritage Court 8
1 33N34'54 111w51'26 7:27:26
Heritage Highlands 8
1 33N36'22 112w04'42 7:28:19
Heritage North Ranch 8
1 33N38'20 111w55'55 7:27:44
Heritage Terrace 8
1 33N34'00 111w54'06 7:27:36
Hibbard 10 1 34N58'12 110w31'04 7:22:04
Hickiwan 11 1 32N22'08 112w28'29 7:29:54
Hidden Acres Mobile Home Pk 8
1 33N27'10 112w12'01 7:28:48
Hidden Springs 3
1 35N53 111w25 7:25:40
Hidden Springs Mission 3
1 36N11'21 111w23'39 7:25:35
Highjinks 12 1 32N34'16 110w44'16 7:22:57
Highland Park 2
1 31N27'02 109w56'25 7:19:46
Highland Park 14
1 34N33'33 112w34'06 7:30:16
Highland Terrace Mobile Home 8
1 33N35'38 112w05'50 7:28:23
Hightown 8 1 33N18'16 111w54'31 7:27:38
Higley 8 1 33N18'26 111w43'13 7:26:53
Hillside 14 1 34N25'06 112w54'59 7:31:40
Hilltop 2 1 32N16 109w14 7:16:56
Hilltop 9 2 35N12'29 114w01'27 7:36:06
Hi View Mobile Home Park 8
1 33N35'33 112w05'49 7:28:23
Hoa Murk 11 1 32N16'47 112w40'00 7:30:40
Hohokam Village 8
1 33N26'26 111w49'10 7:27:17
Hoi Oidak 11 1 32N18'12 111w52'17 7:27:29
Hoka Tiki Mobile Village 8
1 33N34'09 112w12'27 7:28:50
Ho-Kay-Gan 14 1 34N32 112w28 7:29:52
Holbrook 10 1 34N54'08 110w09'27 7:20:38
Holiday 7 3 34N09 114w17 7:37:08
Holiday Palms Mobile Home Pk 8
1 33N24'32 111w37'39 7:26:31
Holiday Spa Mobile Home Park 8
1 33N34'48 112w02'55 7:28:12
Holiday Village Mobile Home 8
1 33N24'07 111w51'12 7:27:25
Hollywood 5 1 32N49'46 109w40'58 7:18:44
Homestead 8 1 33N27'20 111w45'54 7:27:04
Hookers Hot Springs 2
1 32N20'19 110w14'20 7:20:57
Hooper 14 1 34N15'58 112w22'56 7:29:32
Hope 7 3 33N43'23 113w42'06 7:34:48
Hopi 10 1 35N56 110w22 7:21:28
Hopi Indian Reservation 3
1 35N50 110w30 7:22:00
Horn 15 3 32N56'41 113w30'09 7:34:01
Horse Crossing 3
1 34N35'04 111w07'47 7:24:31
Horse Mesa 1 1 36N42'18 109w02'45 7:16:11
Horse Mesa 8 1 33N34'59 111w21'17 7:25:25
Horseshoe Mobile Home Park 8
1 33N24'48 111w54'10 7:27:37
Horse Thief 14 1 34N24 112w14 7:28:56
Hortons Place 12
1 32N52'40 110w34'59 7:22:20
Hotason Vo 11 1 32N14'47 112w36'15 7:30:25
Hotevilla 10 1 35N55'40 110w40'20 7:22:41
Houck 1 1 35N16'59 109w12'23 7:16:50
House Rock 3 1 36N57 112w31 7:30:04
Huachuca City 2
1 31N37'40 110w20'00 7:21:20
Huachuca Terrace 2
1 31N23'48 109w55'28 7:19:42
Hualapai 9 2 35N12 114w02 7:36:08
Hualapai Indian Reservation 3
1 34N34 111w51 7:27:24
Hubbell 1 1 35N43 109w33 7:18:12
Huck Ovi 10 1 35N53'30 110w41'13 7:22:45
Humboldt 14 1 34N30'03 112w14'12 7:28:57
Humburg 14 1 34N03'17 112w19'21 7:29:17
Hunt 1 1 34N36'36 109w37'37 7:18:30
Hunters Point 1
1 35N32'52 109w06'16 7:16:25
Hyde Park 8 1 33N37'14 111w58'00 7:27:52
Hyde Park Lodge 8
1 33N27'51 111w59'28 7:27:58
Hyder 15 3 33N00'59 113w20'53 7:33:24
Immanuel Mission 1
1 36N58 109w02 7:16:08
Imperial Mobile Home Park 8
1 33N24'48 111w46'30 7:27:06
Indian Gardens 3
1 34N54'50 111w43'35 7:26:54
Indian Hot Springs 5
1 32N59'54 109w54'00 7:19:36
Indian Moccasin 9
1 36N53'50 112w44'30 7:30:58
Indian Pine 10 1 34N04'48 109w54'17 7:19:37
Indian Ridge Estates 11
1 32N15'16 110w50'32 7:23:22
Indian School 8
1 33N30 112w05 7:28:20
Indian Springs 8
1 33N30'26 112w12'50 7:28:51
Indian Wells 10
1 35N24'20 110w05'03 7:20:20
Inscription House 3
1 36N19 110w56 7:23:44
Inspiration 4 1 33N24'45 110w52'58 7:23:32
Iron Springs 14
1 34N35'05 112w34'09 7:30:17
Ironwood Terrace 8
1 33N30'46 112w12'20 7:28:49
Itak 11 1 31N41'41 112w00'23 7:28:02
Jackrabbit 12 1 32N53 111w44 7:26:56
Jackrabbit House 12
1 32N36'19 111w53'43 7:27:35
Jackson Acres 14
1 34N32 112w28 7:29:52
Jacob Lake 3 1 36N42'48 112w12'56 7:28:52
Jadito 10 1 35N46'28 110w08'10 7:20:33
Jakes Corner 4 1 34N00'38 111w19'07 7:25:16
J and M Trailer Park 8
1 33N27'06 112w15'22 7:29:01
Jaynes 11 1 32N17'45 111w01'42 7:24:07
Jeddito 10 1 35N49 110w12 7:20:48
Jerome 14 1 34N44'56 112w06'47 7:28:27
Johnson 2 1 32N06'11 110w03'56 7:20:16
Jones Crossing 3
1 34N31'47 111w16'59 7:25:08
Jops Landing 9 2 34N32'38 114w21'52 7:37:27
Jordan Meadows 14
1 34N32'27 111w51'55 7:27:28
Joseph City 10 1 34N57'21 110w20'00 7:21:20
Juanita Mobile Home Park 8
1 33N25'15 111w39'12 7:26:37
Junction Interstate Nineteen 11
1 32N11'40 110w58'34 7:23:54
Junction Overlook 1
1 36N08'14 109w29'32 7:17:58
Junction State Route Eightfo 12
1 32N43'23 111w30'55 7:26:04
Juniper Heights 14
1 34N31'18 112w27'44 7:29:51
Kahachi Miliuk 11
1 31N48'09 111w41'45 7:26:47
Kaibab 9 1 36N54 112w44 7:30:56
Kaibab Indian Reservation 9
1 35N49 110w12 7:20:48
Kaibito 3 1 36N35'50 111w04'25 7:24:18
Kaihon Kug 11 1 32N00'58 112w04'44 7:28:19
Kaka 8 1 32N30'35 112w18'57 7:29:16
Kansas Settlement 2
1 32N03'54 109w45'44 7:19:03
Karmella Mobile Home Park 8
1 33N24'05 111w50'25 7:27:22
Katherine 9 2 35N13'20 114w33'40 7:38:15
Kawaika-A 10 1 35N44'41 110w13'12 7:20:53
Kay-Bee Mobile Villa 8
1 33N27'11 111w49'35 7:27:18
Kayenta 10 1 36N43'40 110w15'14 7:21:01
Keams Canyon 10
1 35N48'45 110w11'40 7:20:47
Kearny 12 1 33N03'25 110w54'36 7:23:38
Keats Crossing 8
1 33N22'36 111w51'43 7:27:27
Kelvin 12 1 33N06'41 110w58'22 7:23:53
Kensington 8 1 33N37'00 111w58'25 7:27:54
Kerwo 11 1 31N55 111w53 7:27:32
Kim 15 3 32N44'05 113w42'06 7:34:48
Kimball 5 1 32N53'46 109w46'29 7:19:06
Kinder Crossing 3
1 34N33'59 111w08'32 7:24:34
Kingman 9 2 35N11'22 114w03'08 7:36:13
Kingsgate 8 1 33N22'50 111w47'40 7:27:11
Kingston Knolls Terrace 11
1 32N13'42 110w50'42 7:23:23
Kin-li-Chee 1 1 35N44'35 109w26'22 7:17:45
Kinney Junction 1
1 33N55'02 109w46'24 7:19:06
Kino 11 1 32N20'05 111w03'41 7:24:15
Kino Springs 13
1 31N21'47 110w48'34 7:23:14
Kinsley Ranch 11
1 31N42 111w04 7:24:16
Kinter 15 3 32N45'26 114w23'50 7:37:35
Kirkland 14 1 34N25'03 112w42'47 7:30:51
Kirkland Junction 14
1 34N22'09 112w39'52 7:30:39
Klagetoh 1 1 35N30'07 109w31'39 7:18:07
Klondyke 5 1 32N50'07 110w19'54 7:21:20
Knoell East 8 1 33N22'38 111w53'11 7:27:33
Knoell Mesa 8 1 33N23'27 111w46'59 7:27:08
Kofa 15 3 32N52'55 113w38'45 7:34:35
Kohatk 12 1 32N34'42 112w00'18 7:28:01
Kohls Ranch 4 1 34N19'31 111w05'37 7:24:22
Kokopnyama 10 1 35N46'49 110w07'36 7:20:30
Komak Wuacho 11
1 32N13'25 112w19'46 7:29:19
Komatke 8 1 33N17'36 112w10'29 7:28:42
Komelik 11 1 31N55 111w53 7:27:32
Kom Kug 11 1 31N36'38 111w40'13 7:26:41
Kom Vo 11 1 31N57'35 112w20'54 7:29:24
Kon Tiki Mobile Home Park 8
1 33N20'03 111w51'03 7:27:24
Kool Corner 15 3 32N48'02 114w29'55 7:38:00
Ko Vaya 11 1 32N04'37 111w53'41 7:27:35
Kuakatch 11 1 32N08'15 112w39'44 7:30:39
Kui Tatk 11 1 32N02'18 112w04'50 7:28:19
Kuit Vaya 11 1 31N40'42 111w40'49 7:26:43
Kupk 11 1 31N55'25 112w12'47 7:28:51
Kykotsmovi 10 1 35N52 110w36 7:22:24
Kyrene 8 1 33N20'05 111w56'42 7:27:47

La Casa Trail Mobile Villa 8
1 33N24'58 111w35'20 7:26:21
La Casita Mobile Park 8
1 33N26'59 111w49'13 7:27:17
La Fontana Heights 8
1 33N30'47 112w12'40 7:28:51
Laguna 12 1 32N35'14 111w37'43 7:26:31
Laguna 15 3 32N49'08 114w29'05 7:37:56
Lake Biltmore Estates 8
1 33N35'12 112w07'25 7:28:30
Lake Havasu City 9
2 34N29'02 114w19'18 7:37:17
Lake Mary 3 1 35N12 111w37 7:26:28
Lake Mead Rancheros 9
2 35N12 114w02 7:36:08
Lake Mohave 9 2 35N09 114w34 7:38:16
Lake Mohave Recreation Site 9
2 35N13'18 114w33'46 7:38:15
Lake Montezuma 14
1 34N37'56 111w46'38 7:27:07
Lake of the Woods 10
1 34N09'50 109w59'20 7:19:57
Lakeside 10 1 34N09'16 109w58'22 7:19:53
Lakeside 7 3 34N09 114w17 7:37:08
Lakeview 3 1 34N54'33 111w26'47 7:25:47
LaLoma Ranch 8 1 33N30'48 112w21'31 7:29:26
La Montana Del Sur 8
1 33N22'20 112w04'03 7:28:16
Lancaster 14 1 34N18'49 111w42'53 7:26:52
La Palma 12 1 32N52'45 111w30'52 7:26:03
Lapham 14 1 34N10'50 112w24'05 7:29:36
Lariat Tra-Tel Trailer Court 8
1 33N28'00 111w59'18 7:27:57
Larneds Landing 9
3 34N18'30 114w03'05 7:36:12
La Ronde Shopping Center 8
1 33N35 112w23 7:29:32
Las Alegres 8 1 33N27'37 111w41'22 7:26:45
Las Guijas 11 1 31N40'13 111w22'53 7:25:32
Las Villas 8 1 33N31'20 111w55'15 7:27:41
La Terraza 8 1 33N27'50 112w11'17 7:28:45
Laveen 8 1 33N21'46 112w10'07 7:28:40
Lawrence Crossing 14
1 34N39'11 111w43'55 7:26:56
Lazona Trailer Court 8
1 33N24'50 111w48'00 7:27:12
Lazy Daze Mobile Home Park 8
1 33N27'08 112w08'59 7:28:36
Lazy D Trailer Ranch 8
1 33N22'50 112w03'53 7:28:16
Lazy J Trailer Lodge 8
1 33N32'28 112w11'55 7:28:48
Lebanon 5 1 32N44'43 109w42'56 7:18:52
Legante Paseo 8
1 33N22'17 111w51'54 7:27:28
Legend Estates 8
1 33N28'02 112w09'11 7:28:37
Lehi 8 1 33N27'32 111w48'46 7:27:15
Lehman Mill 14 1 34N05'45 112w27'42 7:29:51
Leisure Time Mobile Park 8
1 33N33'39 112w12'30 7:28:50
Leisure World 8
1 33N24'04 111w41'21 7:26:45
Lemontree 8 1 33N24'35 111w44'34 7:26:58
Leupp 3 1 35N17'02 110w57'52 7:23:51
Leupp Corner 3 1 35N04'27 110w51'26 7:23:26
Lewis Springs 2
1 31N34'52 110w08'29 7:20:34
Lexington Place 8
1 33N38'15 112w12'00 7:28:48
Liberty 8 1 33N22'39 112w29'10 7:29:57
Liberty Mobile Home Park 8
1 33N40'04 112w01'28 7:28:06
Liberty Village 8
1 33N29'47 112w16'34 7:29:06
Ligurta 15 3 32N40'28 114w17'39 7:37:11
Lincon 11 1 31N55 111w53 7:27:32
Linden 10 1 34N17'06 110w09'23 7:20:38
Links Point 8 1 33N35'36 111w58'05 7:27:52
Lisitzky 10 1 34N55'41 110w08'09 7:20:33
Litchfield 8 1 33N25'36 112w21'16 7:29:25
Litchfield Junction 8
1 33N25'21 112w21'43 7:29:27
Litchfield Park 8
1 33N29'36 112w21'26 7:29:26
Little Acres 4 1 33N23'41 110w49'13 7:23:17
Little Colorado 10
1 34N56 110w29 7:21:56
Littlefield 9 2 36N53'14 113w55'44 7:35:43
Little Franks 5
1 32N25'57 109w12'53 7:16:52
Little Spring 3
1 34N35'55 111w13'42 7:24:55
Littletown 11 1 32N07'22 110w52'25 7:23:30
Little Tucson 11
1 31N55 111w53 7:27:32
Lizard 8 1 33N38'07 112w20'40 7:29:23
Lizard Acres 8 1 33N38'51 112w20'16 7:29:21
Lochiel 13 1 31N20'08 110w37'24 7:22:30
Loma Linda 11 1 32N26'53 110w45'16 7:23:01
Lone Butte Ranch 8
1 33N13'57 112w02'47 7:28:11
Lone Star 5 1 32N48'59 109w40'50 7:18:43
Longhaven West 8
1 33N30'26 112w10'15 7:28:41
Longhorn Ranch II 8
1 33N36'04 112w11'53 7:28:48
Long Valley 3 1 34N31'15 111w19'44 7:25:19
Lookout Mountain 8
1 33N37'24 112w01'38 7:28:07
Los Burros 1 1 34N08'29 109w46'35 7:19:06
Los Gatos 8 1 33N29 111w56 7:27:44
Los Maderas 8 1 33N26'57 111w47'00 7:27:08
Lost Dutchman Mobile Home Pk 8
1 33N25'02 111w35'56 7:26:24
Lost Eden 3 1 34N37'54 111w15'37 7:25:02
Los Tesoros 8 1 33N19'43 111w54'44 7:27:39
Love 7 3 33N51'08 113w27'54 7:33:52
Lowell 2 1 31N25'40 109w53'35 7:19:34
Lower Miami 4 1 33N24'24 110w51'18 7:23:25
Lower Tillman 3
1 34N37'42 110w47'45 7:23:11
Lower Wheatfields 1
1 36N12'15 109w08'07 7:16:32
Low Mountain 10
1 35N56'25 110w06'46 7:20:27
Lukachukai 1 1 36N25'01 109w13'41 7:16:55
Luke 8 1 33N33 112w21 7:29:24
Luke Air Force Base 8
1 33N33 112w11 7:28:44
Lukeville 11 1 31N52'57 112w48'54 7:31:16
Lupton 1 1 35N21'14 109w03'11 7:16:13
Luzena 2 1 32N21'17 109w37'34 7:18:30
Lynx Estates 14
1 34N32 112w28 7:29:52
Macks Crossing 3
1 34N37'06 111w05'31 7:24:22
Madera Canyon 13
1 31N43'30 110w52'46 7:23:31
Magma 12 1 33N07'54 111w29'55 7:26:00
Maine 3 1 35N15'11 111w56'16 7:27:45
Maish Vaya 11 1 32N10'01 112w07'36 7:28:30
Makgum Havoka 11
1 32N16'29 111w57'37 7:27:50
Mammoth 12 1 32N43'21 110w38'24 7:22:34
Mangum Springs 3
1 36N37'34 112w20'55 7:29:24
Manila 10 1 34N57'54 110w24'46 7:21:39
Many Farms 1 1 36N21'10 109w37'02 7:18:28
Manzoro 2 1 32N02'41 109w58'13 7:19:53
Maques Place 6 1 32N58'33 109w21'57 7:17:28
Marana 11 1 32N26'12 111w13'29 7:24:54
Marble Canyon 3
1 36N48'56 111w38'13 7:26:33
Maricopa 12 1 33N03'29 112w02'49 7:28:11
Maricopa Indian Reservation 12
1 33N05 112w00 7:28:00
Maricopa Village 8
1 33N22'17 112w14'13 7:28:57
Maricopa Wells 12
1 33N09'43 112w05'00 7:28:20
Marine Corps Air Station 15
3 32N44 114w35 7:38:20
Marinette 8 1 33N36 112w17 7:29:08
Marlborough Meadows 8
1 33N35'40 112w10'29 7:28:42
Marlborough Mesa 8
1 33N21'41 111w51'11 7:27:25
Marlborough Park 8
1 33N26'51 111w55'44 7:27:43
Martinez Lake 15
3 32N44 114w35 7:38:20
Maryland West Mobile Home Pk 8
1 33N31'46 112w10'58 7:28:44
Maryvale 8 1 33N30'07 112w10'37 7:28:42
Maryvale Terrace 8
1 33N29'34 112w11'40 7:28:47
Ma Shon Pi 10 1 35N56'14 110w40'13 7:22:41
Matthie 8 1 33N59'36 112w48'32 7:31:14
Maverick 1 1 33N44'34 109w32'48 7:18:11
Mayer 14 1 34N23'52 112w14'08 7:28:57
Mayflower Terrace 8
1 33N36'55 112w00'06 7:28:00
McClintock Manor 8
1 33N23'22 111w54'17 7:27:37
McConnico 9 2 35N08'38 114w05'34 7:36:22
McCormick Ranch 8
1 33N33'09 111w54'05 7:27:36
McDowell 8 1 33N28 112w00 7:28:00
McDowell Trailer Village 8
1 33N27'56 112w00'27 7:28:02
McGuire Crossing 3
1 34N27'19 111w01'12 7:24:05
McGuireville 14
1 34N38'17 111w48'59 7:27:16
McMicken 8 1 33N29'50 112w25'35 7:29:42
McMillianville 4
1 33N33'26 110w40'45 7:22:43
McNary 1 1 34N04'25 109w51'23 7:19:26
McNary Place 14
1 34N17'46 112w29'25 7:29:58
McNeal 2 1 31N36'04 109w40'10 7:18:41
McQueen 8 1 33N22'48 111w49'50 7:27:19
McVay 7 3 33N48'14 113w50'17 7:35:21
Meadow Brook 15
3 32N44 114w35 7:38:20
Meadowvale 8 1 33N26'05 111w46'28 7:27:06
Mennonite Mission 1
1 35N43 109w33 7:18:12
Meridiancheri Mobile Home Pk 8
1 33N25'15 111w34'50 7:26:19
Mesa 8 1 33N25'20 111w49'19 7:27:17
Mesa Gardens Mobile Home Pk 8
1 33N24'57 111w51'10 7:27:25
Mesa Grande Trailer Ranch 8
1 33N27'13 111w46'01 7:27:04
Mesa Patios 8 1 33N25'47 111w49'07 7:27:16
Mesa Shadows East Mobile Hom 8
1 33N24'40 111w42'28 7:26:50
Mesa Shadows Mobile Home Pk 8
1 33N24'40 111w43'03 7:26:52
Mesa Travelodge Mobile Home 8
1 33N23'33 111w50'08 7:27:21
Mesa Verde Estates 14
1 34N35'05 111w51'34 7:27:26
Mescal 2 1 31N59'24 110w26'05 7:21:44
Meteor City 3 1 35N05'40 110w56'05 7:23:44
Mexican Town 11
1 32N22'05 112w51'47 7:31:27
Mexican Water 1
1 36N58'01 109w38'14 7:18:33
Mexican Water Trading Post 1
1 36N55'27 109w36'11 7:18:25
Miami 4 1 33N23'57 110w52'05 7:23:28
Miami Gardens 4
1 33N24'37 110w49'40 7:23:19
Michigan Palms Mobile Home P 8
1 33N39'11 112w02'01 7:28:08
Michigan Trailer Park 8
1 33N29'17 112w07'36 7:28:30
Middle Verde 14
1 34N37'12 111w53'27 7:27:34
Midges Court 8 1 33N30'52 112w09'19 7:28:37
Midland City 4 1 33N24'43 110w49'25 7:23:18
Midway 8 1 32N38'01 112w51'16 7:31:25
Midway 7 3 34N04'14 113w53'09 7:35:33
Miles Manor 2 1 31N33'30 110w20'21 7:21:21
Milkwater 1 1 36N03'10 109w06'36 7:16:26
Miller Valley 14
1 34N33'11 112w28'31 7:29:54
Mineral Creek 12
1 33N03 110w54 7:23:36
Mingus Mountain 14
1 34N41 112w07 7:28:28
Minnehaha 14 1 34N09'48 112w24'24 7:29:38
Minnesota Court 8
1 33N27'05 111w58'05 7:27:52
Mint 14 1 34N42'10 112w34'18 7:30:17
Miracle Valley 2
1 31N22'45 110w09'10 7:20:37
Mirador 8 1 33N34'40 111w51'50 7:27:27
Miramonte Acres 2
1 31N25 109w54 7:19:36
Mishongnovi 10 1 35N48'18 110w29'31 7:21:58
Mission Monterey 8
1 33N34'26 111w52'00 7:27:28
Mission Valley 8
1 33N21'09 111w51'05 7:27:24
Mobile 8 1 33N03 112w16 7:29:04
Moccasin (P O) 9
1 36N54'34 112w45'29 7:31:02
Moenave 3 1 36N08'19 111w20'12 7:25:21
Moenkopi 3 1 36N06'40 111w13'18 7:24:53
Mohave Crossing 9
2 35N20'00 114w35'17 7:38:21
Mohave Valley 9
2 34N52 114w09 7:36:36
Mohawk 15 3 32N43'36 113w45'16 7:35:01
Moi Vaya 8 1 32N33'48 112w27'29 7:29:50
Mojave City 9 2 35N02'40 114w37'20 7:38:29
MonDak Mobile Home Park 8
1 33N25'10 111w44'58 7:27:00
Montara 8 1 33N35'40 112w11'30 7:28:46
Montclair Terrace 8
1 33N37'50 111w59'33 7:27:58
Montecito Mobile Home Est 8
1 33N25'18 111w52'51 7:27:31
Montezuma 8 1 33N04'33 113w13'20 7:32:53
Moon Valley Canyon 8
1 33N38'15 112w04'51 7:28:19
Moon Valley Mobile Home Est 8
1 33N38'33 112w03'14 7:28:13
Moqui 3 1 35N03'38 110w48'55 7:23:16
Morado Encanto 8
1 33N39'03 112w08'07 7:28:32
Morenci 6 1 33N04'43 109w21'53 7:17:28
Mormon Crossing 3
1 34N37'01 110w47'13 7:23:09
Mormon Lake 3 1 34N54'30 111w27'45 7:25:51
Morristown 8 1 33N51'24 112w37'21 7:30:29
Mountainaire 3 1 35N05'07 111w39'55 7:26:40
Mountain Gate Mobile Home Pk 8
1 33N21'37 112w05'20 7:28:21
Mountain Meadow 4
1 34N19'22 111w00'20 7:24:01
Mountain Shadows Mobile Home 8
1 33N41'25 112w07'14 7:28:29
Mountain View 2
1 31N25 109w54 7:19:36
Mountain View 11
1 32N00'09 110w40'52 7:22:43
Mountain View Estates 14
1 34N32'15 111w50'15 7:27:21
Mountain View Meadows 8
1 33N33'22 112w11'15 7:28:45
Mountain View Mobile Home Pk 8
1 33N28'39 111w54'35 7:27:38
Mountain View Trailer Court 8
1 33N34'25 112w05'29 7:28:22
Mountain Vista 8
1 33N38'37 112w01'04 7:28:04
Mount Elden 3 1 35N12 111w37 7:26:28
Mount Lemmon 11
1 32N27 110w45 7:23:00
Mule Crossing 3
1 34N27'27 111w00'01 7:24:00
Munds Park 3 1 34N56'44 111w38'22 7:26:33
Na-Ab-Tee Canyon 10
1 35N24 110w05 7:20:20
Na Ah Tee 10 1 35N29'25 110w08'38 7:20:35
Naco 2 1 31N20'07 109w56'51 7:19:47
Nagles Crossing 9
1 36N51'50 112w34'44 7:30:19
Narcho Santos 11
1 32N08'43 112w08'28 7:28:34
Nariska 12 1 32N30'16 111w15'46 7:25:03
Natches 5 1 33N12'39 110w17'58 7:21:12
Navajo 1 1 35N07'27 109w32'15 7:18:09
Navajo Gospel Mission 10
1 36N02'10 110w30'32 7:22:02
Navajo Indian Reservation 1
1 35N41 109w03 7:16:12
Navajo Monument 10
1 36N41 110w21 7:21:24
Navajo Mountain Mission 3
1 36N56'05 110w46'32 7:23:06
Navajo Mountain Trading Post 3
1 36N19 110w56 7:23:44
Navajo Station 1
1 35N43 109w33 7:18:12
Naviska 11 1 32N29'33 111w15'16 7:25:01
Nawt Vaya 11 1 32N01'59 111w29'18 7:25:57
Nazlini 1 1 35N53'47 109w26'53 7:17:48
Neff 2 1 31N28'45 109w58'45 7:19:55
Nelson 11 1 32N25'44 111w16'08 7:25:05
Nelson 14 2 35N30'51 113w19'10 7:33:17
Nesuftanga 10 1 35N46'49 110w08'26 7:20:34
Newfield 11 1 31N32'51 111w43'58 7:26:56
New Home Mobile Park 8
1 33N30'58 112w06'54 7:28:28
New Hope 8 1 33N26 111w50 7:27:20
New Hope Trailer Park 8
1 33N24'46 111w42'09 7:26:49
New Horizons 8 1 33N21'29 111w50'57 7:27:24
New Oraibi 10 1 35N53 110w37 7:22:28
New River 8 1 33N54'57 112w08'07 7:28:32
New Tucson 11 1 31N58'38 110w42'14 7:22:49
Nicksville 2 1 31N26'18 110w14'54 7:21:00

Noah 15 3 32N41'05 114w01'17 7:36:05
Nogales 13 1 31N20'25 110w56'01 7:23:44
Noipa Kam 11 1 32N17'06 112w08'53 7:28:36
Nolia 11 1 31N55 111w53 7:27:32
Nolic 11 1 32N02'07 111w57'07 7:27:48
Nommel Place 7 3 33N04'56 114w41'11 7:38:45
Normal Jct 8 1 33N24'39 111w54'53 7:27:40
Northeast 8 1 33N31 112w02 7:28:08
Northern Hills 11
1 32N19 110w57 7:23:48
North Komelik 12
1 32N30'28 111w56'45 7:27:47
North Mammoth 12
1 32N44'01 110w38'47 7:22:35
North Rim 3 1 36N57 112w31 7:30:04
Northwest 8 1 33N30 112w08 7:28:32
Northwoods 1 1 34N01'42 109w27'22 7:17:49
Norton 15 3 32N48'38 113w47'53 7:35:12
Nortons Corner 8
1 33N18'24 111w47'20 7:27:09
Nortons Landing 7
3 33N03'02 114w38'36 7:38:34
Nutrioso 1 1 33N57'11 109w12'31 7:16:50
Oak Creek 14 1 34N46'45 111w45'45 7:27:03
Oak Grove 9 2 36N09'10 113w34'59 7:34:20
Oakhurst 8 1 33N38'33 111w57'04 7:27:48
Oak Knoll Village 14
1 34N30'55 112w26'38 7:29:47
Oak Springs 1 1 35N28'32 109w07'37 7:16:30
Oak Wells 12 1 32N47'20 110w56'13 7:23:45
Oasis Park 8 1 33N25 111w34 7:26:16
Oatman 9 2 35N01'35 114w22'58 7:37:32
Ocotillo 8 1 33N14'37 111w51'28 7:27:26
Ocotillo 14 1 34N21'49 112w12'04 7:28:48
Octave 14 1 34N08'30 112w41'21 7:30:45
Oit Ihuk 11 1 32N18'56 112w14'42 7:28:59
Olberg 12 1 33N05'32 111w41'08 7:26:45
Old Columbine 5
1 32N42'26 109w54'32 7:19:38
Old Glory 13 1 31N26'03 111w15'11 7:25:01
Old Oraibi 10 1 35N52'35 110w38'23 7:22:34
Old Shongopavi (site) 10
1 35N48'16 110w31'11 7:22:05
Old Sopori School 11
1 31N42'09 111w11'08 7:24:45
Old Tucson 11 1 32N13'05 111w07'46 7:24:31
Olga 2 1 32N17'59 109w21'31 7:17:26
Olive West 8 1 33N34'10 112w12'54 7:28:52
One Mile 3 1 36N48'18 112w03'13 7:28:13
Oracle 12 1 32N36'39 110w46'13 7:23:05
Oracle Foothills Estates 11
1 32N17'59 110w57'10 7:23:49
Oracle Junction 12
1 32N33'18 110w55'58 7:23:44
Oracle Place (shopping ctr) 11
1 32N20'11 110w58'35 7:23:54
Oraibi 10 1 35N52'31 110w37'11 7:22:29
Orange Grove Estates 11
1 32N19'16 111w02'24 7:24:10
Orangetree 8 1 33N20'13 111w53'40 7:27:35
Orangetree Estates 8
1 33N35'11 111w57'51 7:27:51
Orangewood Village Mobilehom 8
1 33N39'24 112w07'06 7:28:28
Oregon Trail Mobile Home Pk 8
1 33N33'28 112w06'52 7:28:27
Oro Blanco 13 1 31N29'45 111w16'45 7:25:07
Oro Valley 11 1 32N23'27 110w57'57 7:23:52
Otero 13 1 31N31'50 111w00'51 7:24:03
Out West Trailer Park 8
1 33N27'03 112w07'41 7:28:31
Overgaard 10 1 34N23'27 110w33'09 7:22:13
Overland Trail 8
1 33N39'20 112w09'36 7:28:38
Owl 15 3 32N43'19 113w47'29 7:35:10
Pacific Mobile Manor 8
1 33N24'58 111w57'04 7:26:28
Packer 14 1 34N05'54 112w16'07 7:29:04
Page 3 1 36N54'31 111w28'22 7:25:53
Page Springs 14
1 34N46'03 111w53'34 7:27:34
Palamino Acres 8
1 33N21 111w47 7:27:08
Palmaritas 8 1 33N33'32 112w07'55 7:28:32
Palmas del Sol 8
1 33N27'03 111w41'46 7:26:47
Palmas Royale 8
1 33N33'25 112w05'00 7:28:20
Palm Gardens Mobile Home Man 8
1 33N24'47 111w46'05 7:27:04
Palm Lakes Village 8
1 33N38'07 112w00'30 7:28:02
Palm Shadows Mobile Home Pk 8
1 33N32'38 112w10'12 7:28:41
Palm Springs 12
1 33N24'17 111w32'16 7:26:09
Palms Trailer Park 8
1 33N27'59 112w02'15 7:28:09
Palomas 15 3 32N54'32 113w28'50 7:33:55
Palominas 2 1 31N22'47 110w07'04 7:20:28
Palo Verde 8 1 33N20'53 112w40'36 7:30:42
Palo Verde Mobile Home and R 8
1 33N29'23 112w56'08 7:31:45
Palo Verde Mobile Manor 8
1 33N27'51 111w59'25 7:27:58
Palo Verde Stand 11
1 32N20'11 112w01'56 7:28:08
P and E Junction 14
1 34N36'22 112w24'14 7:29:37
Pan Tak 11 1 32N00'42 111w33'53 7:26:16
Pantano 11 1 31N59'58 110w34'46 7:22:19
Papago 8 1 33N06'15 113w08'18 7:32:33
Papago 11 1 31N59 112w00 7:28:00
Papago Farms 11
1 31N47'09 112w18'30 7:29:14
Papago Indian Reservation 8
1 31N55 111w53 7:27:32
Papago Peaks Village 8
1 33N27'23 111w57'59 7:27:52
Paradise 2 1 31N56'05 109w13'06 7:16:52
Paradise Acres 14
1 34N32'12 111w50'56 7:27:24
Paradise City 8
1 33N38'26 112w01'49 7:28:07
Paradise Grove Family Park 8
1 33N33'38 112w12'39 7:28:51
Paradise Grove Trailer Park 8
1 33N32'02 112w11'10 7:28:45
Paradise North Mobile Home P 8
1 33N39'13 112w01'46 7:28:07
Paradise Palms Trailer Resor 8
1 33N24'58 111w47'42 7:27:11
Paradise Shadows Mobile Home 8
1 33N39'36 112w01'29 7:28:06
Paradise Valley 8
1 33N31'52 111w56'31 7:27:46
Paradise Valley Miranda 8
1 33N38'21 111w58'42 7:27:55
Paradise Valley Mobilhome Pa 8
1 33N38'07 112w01'01 7:28:04
Paradise Valley Oasis 8
1 33N37'27 112w00'06 7:28:00
Paradise View Mobile Home Pk 8
1 33N28'52 111w58'53 7:27:56
Paradise Village North II 8
1 33N36'48 111w58'25 7:27:54
Parker 7 3 34N09'00 114w17'18 7:37:09
Parker Creek 4 1 33N24 110w48 7:23:12
Park Place Travel Resort 8
1 33N24'32 111w42'10 7:26:49
Parks 3 1 35N15'38 111w56'53 7:27:48
Parkside 8 1 33N21'00 111w59'15 7:27:57
Parkview Estates 8
1 33N42'12 112w09'54 7:28:40
Parkview Mesa 8
1 33N22'50 111w50'36 7:27:22
Parkview North 8
1 33N38'15 112w08'55 7:28:36
Parkview Village Mobile Home 8
1 33N27'04 111w57'57 7:27:52
Parkwood 8 1 33N28'42 112w09'13 7:28:37
Parque Vista Estates 8
1 33N39'20 112w00'42 7:28:03
Parsons Grove 12
1 32N49'28 110w28'32 7:21:54
Partridge (historical) 13
1 31N28'47 111w16'29 7:25:06
Pascua Yaqui Indian Village 11
1 32N14'54 110w59'01 7:23:56
Patagonia 13 1 31N32'22 110w45'20 7:23:01
Patrick Park 8 1 33N23'37 112w01'12 7:28:05
Paulcell Place 1
1 34N57'43 109w49'31 7:19:18
Paulden 14 1 34N53'08 112w28'03 7:29:52
Paul Spur 2 1 31N21'58 109w44'02 7:18:56
Paxton Place 14
1 34N10'20 112w29'02 7:29:56
Payson 4 1 34N13'51 111w19'28 7:25:18
Peach Pu 11 1 32N03'39 112w18'59 7:29:16
Peach Springs 9
2 35N31'45 113w25'29 7:33:42
Peacock Village 8
1 33N38'45 112w14'20 7:28:57
Pearce 2 1 31N54'18 109w49'12 7:19:17
Pecan Grove Trailer Park 8
1 33N29'16 112w06'57 7:28:28
Peeples Valley 14
1 34N16'08 112w43'35 7:30:54
Pensfield Place 8
1 33N35'26 112w12'20 7:28:49
Penzance 10 1 34N54'19 110w15'15 7:21:01
Peoria 8 1 33N34'50 112w14'12 7:28:57
Peoria Estates 8
1 33N35'02 112w14'17 7:28:57
Peoria Polynesian Village 8
1 33N35'05 112w15'10 7:29:01
Pepper Ridge 8 1 33N38'35 112w01'46 7:28:07
Pepper Tree Mobile Home Park 8
1 33N31'48 112w11'45 7:28:47
Pepperwood 8 1 33N18'33 111w54'12 7:27:37
Peralta Estates 12
1 33N25 111w34 7:26:16
Peridot 4 1 33N18'37 110w27'17 7:21:49
Peri-Winkle Mobile Home Park 8
1 33N30'50 112w07'04 7:28:28
Perkinsville 14
1 34N54'06 112w11'26 7:28:46
Perryville 8 1 33N26'08 112w27'38 7:29:51
Peters Corner 12
1 32N52'33 112w02'53 7:28:12
Peterson 8 1 33N22'42 111w56'34 7:27:46
Petrified Forest National Pk 10
1 34N55 110w09 7:20:36
Phoenix 8 1 33N26'54 112w04'24 7:28:18
Phoenix Acres Trailer Park 8
1 33N26'28 112w08'14 7:28:33
Phoenix Mobile Home Park 8
1 33N41'34 112w06'40 7:28:27
Phoenix West Mobile Home Pk 8
1 33N32'25 112w07'35 7:28:30
Pia Oik 11 1 31N56'48 112w32'28 7:30:10
Piato Vaya 11 1 32N03'02 112w09'26 7:28:38
Pica 14 2 35N27'26 113w08'11 7:32:33
Picacho 12 1 32N42'58 111w29'41 7:25:59
Piedmont 14 1 34N14'20 112w51'49 7:31:27
Piedra 8 1 32N54'17 112w59'05 7:31:56
Pilgrim Playground 3
1 34N57'43 111w28'52 7:25:55
Pima 5 1 32N53'46 109w49'37 7:19:18
Pinal 4 1 33N22'34 110w45'11 7:23:01
Pinaveta 14 1 35N13'38 112w34'20 7:30:17
Pine 4 1 34N23'04 111w27'16 7:25:49
Pinecrest 5 1 32N49 109w43 7:18:52
Pinedale 10 1 34N18'27 110w15'03 7:21:00
Pine Springs 1 1 35N24'19 109w16'46 7:17:07
Pine Tank 3 1 35N14'31 112w03'55 7:28:16
Pinetop 10 1 34N07'33 109w56'13 7:19:45
Pink Arrow 10 1 35N46'37 110w09'24 7:20:38
Pinnacle Paradise 8
1 33N42'05 111w53'38 7:27:35
Pinnacle Peak Country Club E 8
1 33N41'13 111w53'38 7:27:35
Pinnacle Peak Estates I 8
1 33N42'27 111w54'20 7:27:37
Pinnacle Peak Estates II 8
1 33N41'22 111w54'20 7:27:37
Pinnacle Peak Estates III 8
1 33N42'37 111w53'48 7:27:35
Pinnacle Peak Heights 8
1 33N41'44 111w51'50 7:27:27
Pinnacle Peak Heights IV 8
1 33N41'56 111w51'52 7:27:27
Pinnacle Peak Heights V-VI 8
1 33N41'30 111w51'50 7:27:27
Pinnacle Peak Shadows 8
1 33N41'46 111w52'45 7:27:31
Pinnacle Peak Village 8
1 33N42'00 111w54'04 7:27:36
Pinon 10 1 36N06'03 110w13'31 7:20:54
Pinta 1 1 35N04'56 109w37'48 7:18:31
Pioneer 7 3 33N41'31 113w53'40 7:35:35
Pioneer Acres 14
1 34N33'35 111w50'35 7:27:22
Pioneer Estates 8
1 33N38'15 112w10'15 7:28:41
Pioneer Village II 8
1 33N34'45 112w12'38 7:28:51
Pipyak 11 1 32N18'49 111w47'20 7:27:09
Pirtleville 2 1 31N21'25 109w33'40 7:18:15
Pisinimo 11 1 32N02'06 112w18'52 7:29:15
Pitoikam 11 1 31N48'40 111w40'44 7:26:43
Pi Va Hon Kia Pi 10
1 35N53'22 110w41'56 7:22:48
Planet 7 3 34N14'51 113w57'51 7:35:51
Plantsite 6 1 33N03'23 109w19'55 7:17:20
Plaza 3 1 35N12 111w37 7:26:28
Plaza Trailer Inn 8
1 33N27'02 112w00'11 7:28:01
Plomosa 7 3 33N38'03 114w07'02 7:36:28
Point of Pines 5
1 33N21'57 109w45'03 7:19:00
Point of Rocks 8
1 32N59'38 112w45'26 7:31:02
Polacca 10 1 35N50'12 110w22'51 7:21:31
Poland Junction 14
1 34N27'03 112w16'07 7:29:04
Polo Village 11
1 32N14'23 110w56'51 7:23:47
Polvo 11 1 32N11'13 110w54'31 7:23:38
Pomerene 2 1 31N59'58 110w17'08 7:21:09
Ponderosa Park 14
1 34N28'17 112w29'12 7:29:57
Po Ni Vi 10 1 35N52'53 110w42'48 7:22:51
Pony Acres Mobile Home Park 8
1 33N24'48 111w54'19 7:27:37
Portal 2 1 31N54'49 109w08'27 7:16:34
Poston 7 3 33N59'26 114w23'44 7:37:35
Potato Patch 14
1 34N25'48 112w24'48 7:29:39
Potter Place 1 1 34N48'40 109w39'18 7:18:37
Powell 9 2 34N44'14 114w22'34 7:37:30
Pozo 8 1 33N16'37 111w50'26 7:27:22
Prado del Sol 8
1 33N18'53 111w57'00 7:27:48
Prescott 14 1 34N32'24 112w28'04 7:29:52
Prescott Valley 14
1 34N36'36 112w18'54 7:29:16
Presidential Estates 2
1 31N37 110w19 7:21:16
Preston Hills 8
1 33N35'05 111w52'00 7:27:28
Price 12 1 33N05'44 111w13'54 7:24:56
Prinston Park 8
1 33N21 111w47 7:27:08
Pueblo Alto 8 1 33N18 111w46 7:27:04
Pueblo Gardens 11
1 32N11'46 110w56'19 7:23:45
Pueblo Sereno Mobile Home Pk 8
1 33N27'12 111w54'06 7:27:36
Puertocito 11 1 31N36'35 111w29'47 7:25:59
Pumpkin Center 3
1 35N24'53 111w54'55 7:27:40
Pumpkin Center 4
1 33N52 111w19 7:25:16
Punkin Center 4
1 33N52'20 111w18'45 7:25:15
Purple Sage Mobile Home Park 8
1 33N32'21 112w11'55 7:28:48
Quail Country Place 8
1 33N39'05 112w04'12 7:28:17
Quail Lane 8 1 33N35'00 112w11'42 7:28:47
Quail Place 8 1 33N20'47 111w52'20 7:27:29
Quail Valley 8 1 33N37'42 111w58'45 7:27:55
Quartzsite 7 3 33N39'50 114w13'45 7:36:55
Queen Creek 8 1 33N14'55 111w38'01 7:26:32
Queen Valley 12
1 33N17'55 111w17'20 7:25:09
Querino 1 1 35N17 109w12 7:16:48
Quijotoa 11 1 32N07'38 112w08'15 7:28:33
Quinlin 11 1 32N15'22 111w36'21 7:26:25
Quivero 3 1 35N31'57 112w11'24 7:28:46
Radium 4 1 33N27'01 110w49'26 7:23:18
Rainbow Mines 3
1 34N19'37 110w46'10 7:23:05
Rainbow Valley 8
1 33N13'55 112w23'11 7:29:33
Raintree 8 1 33N20'10 111w54'31 7:27:38
Raintree Luxury Homes 8
1 33N19'53 111w55'46 7:27:43
Rambler Mobile Park 8
1 33N24'50 111w37'51 7:26:31
Rambling Rons Mobile Home Pk 8
1 33N31'34 112w09'51 7:28:39
Ramsey 2 1 31N26'45 110w18'39 7:21:15
Ranch del Sol 8
1 33N21 111w47 7:27:08
Rancho de Arboleda 8
1 33N27'25 111w46'50 7:27:07
Rancho de Chandler 8
1 33N17'20 111w49'10 7:27:17
Rancho del Rio 7
3 34N09 114w17 7:37:08
Rancho Encanto 8
1 33N38'10 112w07'50 7:28:31
Rancho Hermoso 8
1 33N27'26 112w00'40 7:28:03

Rancho Mobile Estates 8 1 33N28'31 112w00'40 7:28:03
Rancho Rio Vista Mobile Home 8 1 33N25'25 111w58'03 7:27:52
Rancho San Carlos 8 1 33N36'00 112w01'02 7:28:04
Rancho Santa Fe 8 1 33N38'13 111w59'31 7:27:58
Rancho Tempe Family and Adul 8 1 33N23'02 111w57'28 7:27:50
Rancho Vista Estates 14 1 34N31'23 112w30'31 7:30:02
Randolph 12 1 32N55'01 111w30'51 7:26:03
Rankin 11 1 32N08'34 110w50'15 7:23:21
Rare Metals 3 1 36N08'58 111w08'08 7:24:33
Raso 2 1 32N20'22 109w45'09 7:19:01
Ray 12 1 33N11'00 110w59'49 7:23:59
Ray Junction 12 1 33N06'25 110w57'45 7:23:51
Ray Place 9 2 35N49'21 114w00'11 7:36:01
Reata Pass 8 1 33N44'00 111w50'39 7:27:23
Reddell's Ranch Acres 14 1 34N34'20 111w51'45 7:27:27
Redington 11 1 32N25'39 110w29'33 7:21:58
Red Lake 3 1 35N22'45 112w09'35 7:28:38
Red Mesa 1 1 36N59'47 109w22'06 7:17:28
Red Rock 1 1 36N36'16 109w03'36 7:16:14
Red Rock 12 1 32N34'34 111w19'30 7:25:18
Red Rock 14 1 34N49'32 111w48'57 7:27:16
Redwood Gardens Mobile Home 8 1 33N24'45 111w52'46 7:27:31
Renaissance 8 1 33N21'06 111w55'25 7:27:42
Reymert 12 1 33N13'47 111w12'31 7:24:50
Reynolds Trailer Court 8 1 33N24'50 111w53'45 7:27:35
Richville 1 1 34N17'10 109w21'17 7:17:25
Ridgegate 8 1 33N36'54 112w03'44 7:28:15
Rileys El Encinar 2 1 31N29'23 109w59'20 7:19:57
Rillito 11 1 32N24'53 111w09'20 7:24:37
Rimmy Jims 3 1 35N06'36 111w01'49 7:24:07
Rimrock 14 1 34N39'02 111w44'42 7:26:59
Rincon 11 1 32N04'34 111w55'02 7:27:40
Riordan 3 1 36N11'33 111w44'11 7:26:57
Rio Rico 13 1 31N28'17 110w58'33 7:23:54
Rio Verde 8 1 33N43'21 111w40'30 7:26:42
Rittenhouse 8 1 33N15'24 111w38'04 7:26:32
Riverside 12 1 33N06'19 110w57'26 7:23:50
Riverside Stage Stop 12 1 33N03 110w54 7:23:36
Riverside Terrace 11 1 32N19 110w57 7:23:48
Riviera 9 2 35N06'03 114w37'14 7:38:29
Riviera Mobile Home Park 8 1 33N27'15 111w54'32 7:27:38
Road Junction Windmill 8 1 34N00'37 111w57'18 7:27:49
Roadrunner Mobile Home Park 8 1 33N24'05 112w04'30 7:28:18
Robbers Roost 3 2 35N39'38 113w09'08 7:32:37
Robinson Trail Crossing 10 1 34N21'34 110w05'24 7:20:22
Robles Junction 11 1 32N04'38 111w18'40 7:25:15
Rock Crossing 9 1 36N43'34 113w20'28 7:33:22
Rock Crossing Campground 3 1 34N33'45 111w12'56 7:24:52
Rockledge 3 1 34N58'05 111w28'12 7:25:53
Rock Point 1 1 36N43'05 109w37'31 7:18:30
Rock Springs 14 1 34N02'56 112w08'52 7:28:35
Rocky Junction 4 1 33N28'39 110w14'54 7:21:00
Rocky Point 8 1 32N32'01 112w50'51 7:31:23
Roles Inn of America 8 1 33N32'41 112w10'01 7:28:40
Roll 15 3 32N45'06 113w59'18 7:35:57
Rolling Hills Country Club E 11 1 32N12'04 110w48'41 7:23:15
Rollin' W Mobile Home Ranch 8 1 33N38'47 112w02'27 7:28:10
Roosevelt 4 1 33N40'03 111w08'01 7:24:32
Rosebud 1 1 34N00'02 109w16'00 7:17:04
Rose Creek Lodge 4 1 33N50'03 110w58'39 7:23:55
Rosedale Heights 10 1 34N54'33 110w09'10 7:20:37
Rose Garden Place 8 1 33N40'05 112w06'55 7:28:28
Rose Garden Place III 8 1 33N40'12 112w06'37 7:28:26
Rose Lane Trailer Park 8 1 33N26'55 112w07'30 7:28:30
Rosemont Camp 11 1 31N49'30 110w44'03 7:22:56
Rosemont Junction 11 1 31N50'03 110w43'56 7:22:56
Rose Terrace Trailer Park 8 1 33N30'53 112w09'18 7:28:37
Rose Well 3 1 35N44'31 112w52'19 7:31:29
Rough Rock 1 1 36N24'26 109w52'20 7:19:29
Round Rock 1 1 36N30'47 109w28'22 7:17:53
Roundy Crossing 10 1 34N17'45 110w05'33 7:20:22
Rowood 11 1 32N22'06 112w50'43 7:31:23
Royal Estates West 8 1 33N36'30 112w11'20 7:28:45
Royal Glen Mobile Home Park 8 1 33N32'35 112w09'07 7:28:36
Royal Palm Travel Trailer an 8 1 33N34'12 112w06'06 7:28:24
Royal Palm Village 8 1 33N24'45 111w44'48 7:26:59
Ruby 13 1 31N27'40 111w14'13 7:24:57
Rush Place Windmill 14 1 34N16'34 112w36'36 7:30:26
Ryan 3 1 36N41'18 112w20'55 7:29:24
Rye 4 1 34N06'34 111w21'11 7:25:25
Sacate 12 1 33N10'38 112w04'48 7:28:19
Sacaton 12 1 33N04'36 111w44'19 7:26:57
Sacaton Flats 12 1 33N04'12 111w40'04 7:26:40
Sacred Mountain 3 1 35N12 111w37 7:26:28
Saddle 8 1 33N09'28 113w04'46 7:32:19
Saddlehorn Ranch 8 1 33N38'28 112w11'16 7:28:45
Safford 5 1 32N50'02 109w42'25 7:18:50
Sagewood 8 1 33N23'17 111w50'10 7:27:21
Saginaw 2 1 31N25'45 109w52'58 7:19:32
Sahara Mobile Home Park 8 1 33N32'15 112w08'52 7:28:35
Sahuarita 11 1 31N57'27 110w57'18 7:23:49
Sahuarita Heights 11 1 31N57'00 110w55'29 7:23:42
Saint David 2 1 31N54'15 110w12'49 7:20:51
Saint Johns 1 1 34N30'21 109w21'37 7:17:26
Saint Johns Mission 8 1 33N17'25 112w10'21 7:28:41
Saint Joseph Youth Camp 3 1 34N56'45 111w29'32 7:25:58
Saint Michaels 1 1 35N38'41 109w05'42 7:16:23
Salado 1 1 34N26'01 109w24'36 7:17:38
Salina 1 1 36N01'20 109w52'00 7:19:28
Salome 7 3 33N46'52 113w36'50 7:34:27
Salt River 8 1 33N32 111w45 7:27:00
Salt River Indian Res 8 1 33N30 111w44 7:26:56
Salt River Powder District 4 1 33N40 111w09 7:24:36
San Agustin 11 1 31N36'08 111w53'39 7:27:35
San Carlos 4 1 33N20'43 110w27'09 7:21:49
San Carlos 8 1 33N20'45 111w51'00 7:27:24
San Carlos Indian Res 4 1 33N20 110w27 7:21:48
Sanchez 5 1 32N52'10 109w32'32 7:18:10
Sandalwood 8 1 33N37'42 111w59'52 7:27:59
Sanders 1 1 35N12'59 109w19'59 7:17:20
Sand Mill 14 1 34N04'40 112w44'36 7:30:58
Sand Springs 1 1 36N50'22 109w42'06 7:18:48
Sand Springs 3 1 35N43'08 110w55'57 7:23:44
Sandwash Mill 11 1 31N28'56 111w24'55 7:25:40
San Gabriel 8 1 33N38'58 112w09'11 7:28:37
San Jose 2 1 31N25 109w54 7:19:36
San Jose 5 1 32N49'12 109w35'29 7:18:22
San Lucy Village 8 1 32N57'50 112w43'02 7:30:52
San Luis 11 1 32N04'49 111w57'16 7:27:49
San Luis 15 3 32N29'13 114w46'53 7:39:08
San Manuel 12 1 32N35'59 110w37'49 7:22:31
San Miguel 8 1 33N37'01 112w11'15 7:28:45
San Miguel 11 1 31N36'46 111w46'53 7:27:08
Sanokai Village 8 1 33N14'00 111w40'15 7:26:41
San Pedro 11 1 32N05'00 111w29'15 7:25:57
San Rafael 11 1 31N44'14 112w01'25 7:28:06
San Rafael Terrace 2 1 31N25 109w54 7:19:36
San Serafin 11 1 32N17'15 112w00'30 7:28:02
San Simon 2 1 32N16'04 109w13'37 7:16:54
Santa Claus 9 2 35N20'12 114w12'56 7:36:52
Santa Cruz 11 1 32N02'04 111w54'23 7:27:38
Santa Cruz 12 1 33N13'41 112w09'57 7:28:40
Santa Grande Mobile Home Pk 8 1 33N30'57 112w09'14 7:28:37
Santa Lucia 11 1 32N04'02 111w56'56 7:27:48
Santa Maria 8 1 33N25'22 112w12'12 7:28:49
Santan 12 1 33N10'33 111w47'55 7:27:12
San Tan Mobile Village 8 1 33N18'12 111w47'25 7:27:10
Santa Rita 13 1 31N42 111w04 7:24:16
Santiago 8 1 33N37'15 111w58'25 7:27:54
Santo Tomas 8 1 33N32'54 111w54'57 7:27:40
San Vicente 11 1 32N00'42 111w38'11 7:26:33
San Xavier 11 1 31N58'25 111w05'40 7:24:23
San Xavier Indian Res 11 1 32N02 111w05 7:24:20
Sapano Vaya 11 1 31N35'49 111w39'44 7:26:39
Sasabe 11 1 31N29'19 111w32'29 7:26:10
Sawmill 1 1 35N54'09 109w09'55 7:16:40
Sawmill 4 1 33N37'05 110w23'45 7:21:35
Schoens Crossing 10 1 34N24'35 110w06'58 7:20:28
Schuchk 11 1 32N07'16 111w40'57 7:26:44
Schuchuli 11 1 32N13'20 112w41'15 7:30:45
Scottsdale 8 1 33N30'33 111w53'54 7:27:36
Scottsdale Mobile Home Park 8 1 33N27'12 111w54'57 7:27:40
Scottsdale Ranch 8 1 33N34'30 111w51'27 7:27:26
Scottsdale Trailer Corral 8 1 33N29'03 111w55'28 7:27:42
S C Townhouse Mobile Home Es 8 1 33N34'37 112w16'14 7:29:05
Second Mesa 10 1 35N47'36 110w30'16 7:22:01
Secundino 11 1 31N41'38 111w26'32 7:25:46
Security Acres 14 1 34N33'03 111w51'50 7:27:27
Sedona 3 1 34N52'11 111w45'37 7:27:02
Seligman 14 1 35N19'32 112w52'36 7:31:30
Sells 11 1 31N54'43 111w52'50 7:27:31
Seneca 4 1 33N45'24 110w30'44 7:22:03
Sentinel 8 1 32N51'29 113w12'45 7:32:51
Serape 8 1 33N13'58 111w50'11 7:27:21
Sereno 3 1 35N14'22 112w16'21 7:29:05
Sereno Spring 3 1 35N14'20 112w16'47 7:29:07
Sevenmile 10 1 33N47'07 109w57'22 7:19:49
Seven Palms Mobile Home Est 8 1 33N38'33 112w03'52 7:28:15
Shadow Canyon 8 1 33N39'11 112w07'16 7:28:29
Shadow Hills 8 1 33N37'51 112w10'38 7:28:43
Shadow Mountain 8 1 33N36'20 112w01'10 7:28:05
Shadow Mountain Village Scot 8 1 33N27'12 111w53'50 7:27:35
Shadow Ridge II 8 1 33N37'26 111w58'25 7:27:54
Shady Ranch Trailer Lodge 8 1 33N29'00 111w59'06 7:27:56
Shady Rest Mobile Home Park 8 1 33N24'17 111w34'56 7:26:20
Shamrock Mobile Home Park 8 1 33N32'09 112w14'28 7:28:58
Shaotkam 11 1 31N46'10 112w24'35 7:29:38
Shawmut 8 1 32N59'49 112w30'11 7:30:01
Sheep Crossing Campground 1 1 33N57'35 109w30'21 7:18:01
Sheffield Place 8 1 33N29'15 112w15'10 7:29:01
Sheldon 6 1 32N48'53 109w10'18 7:16:41
Shelley 14 1 34N11'35 112w24'22 7:29:37
Sherwood 8 1 33N26 111w50 7:27:20
Sherwood Forest Estates 3 1 35N14'26 112w02'39 7:28:11
Shiloh Canyon 8 1 33N35'05 111w50'44 7:27:23
Shipolovi 10 1 35N48'30 110w29'44 7:21:59
Shongopovi 10 1 35N48'20 110w31'38 7:22:07
Shonto 10 1 36N35'40 110w38'30 7:22:34
Shopishik 12 1 32N43'17 111w46'52 7:27:07
Short Creek 9 1 36N59 112w59 7:31:56
Show Low 10 1 34N15'15 110w01'45 7:20:07
Shumway 10 1 34N24'22 110w04'20 7:20:17
Sichomovi 10 1 35N50'07 110w23'37 7:21:34
Sierra Bonita 5 1 32N15 109w50 7:19:20
Sierra Plaza 10 1 34N54'38 110w09'54 7:20:40
Sierra Vista 2 1 31N33'16 110w18'11 7:21:13
Sierra Vista Estates 2 1 31N29'00 110w15'00 7:21:00
Sif Vaya 12 1 32N37'05 112w06'50 7:28:27
Signal 9 2 34N28'27 113w37'59 7:34:32
Signal Village 2 1 31N33'00 110w21'20 7:21:25
Sikort Chuapo 11 1 32N18'55 112w40'16 7:30:41
Sikul Himatk 11 1 32N06'54 112w02'06 7:28:08
Sil Murk (Papago) 8 1 32N59'00 112w43'40 7:30:55
Sil Nakya 11 1 32N13'18 111w48'57 7:27:16
Silver Bell 11 1 32N23'00 111w30'00 7:26:00
Silver Bell Trailer Park 8 1 33N30'15 112w03'45 7:28:15
Silver Creek 10 1 34N20'24 109w56'56 7:19:48
Silvergate II 8 1 33N20'25 111w52'24 7:27:30
Silvergate Trails 8 1 33N19'42 111w52'41 7:27:31
Silver Spur Ranch 8 1 33N25'00 111w37'45 7:26:31
Silver Spur Village 8 1 33N25'12 111w37'38 7:26:31
Singing Spur Mobile Park 8 1 33N30'10 112w02'00 7:28:08
Siovi Shuatak 11 1 31N57'03 112w35'51 7:30:23
Site Six 9 2 34N30 114w20 7:37:20
Sivili Chuchg 11 1 31N44'39 112w09'36 7:28:38
Six Mile Crossing 9 1 34N33'40 113w21'04 7:33:24
Skoksonak 11 1 32N17'44 111w32'13 7:26:09
Skull Valley 14 1 34N30'19 112w41'05 7:30:44
Skyline Bel Aire Estates 11 1 32N19'13 110w53'20 7:23:33
Skyline Heights 8 1 33N32'52 112w02'44 7:28:11
Sky Ridge Mobile Homes 8 1 33N22'20 112w04'00 7:28:16
Skyway Village 8 1 33N26 111w50 7:27:20
Sleepy Hollow Trailer Villag 8 1 33N24'01 112w04'24 7:28:18
Smelter City 14 1 34N44 112w01 7:28:04
Smelter Town 12 1 33N17'28 111w16'35 7:25:06
Smoke Signal 10 1 35N58'48 110w02'40 7:20:11
Smurr 8 1 32N55'43 112w49'14 7:31:17
Snaketown 12 1 33N10'59 111w55'08 7:27:41
Snowflake 10 1 34N30'48 110w04'40 7:20:19
Soap Creek 3 1 36N49 111w38 7:26:32
Soldier Camp 11 1 32N25'37 110w44'26 7:22:58
Solomon 5 1 32N48'45 109w38'00 7:18:32
Sombrero Butte 12 1 32N43'34 110w28'54 7:21:56
Somerton 15 3 32N35'47 114w42'32 7:38:50
Sonoita 13 1 31N40'46 110w39'17 7:22:37
Sonora 12 1 33N09'55 110w59'43 7:23:59
Sonora Town 8 1 33N20'07 111w47'20 7:27:09
Sotos Crossing (historical) 13 1 31N37'50 111w02'08 7:24:09
South Bisbee 2 1 31N25'01 109w54'11 7:19:37
South Central 8 1 33N24 112w03 7:28:12
South Cove 9 2 36N05'26 114w05'50 7:36:23
Southern Acres Mobile Home P 8 1 33N23'36 112w00'23 7:28:02
Southern Palms Trailer Park 8 1 33N23'33 111w49'54 7:27:20
South Fort 14 1 34N08'48 112w15'59 7:29:04
Southgate Mall 15 3 32N44 114w35 7:38:20
South Komelik 11 1 31N43'20 111w46'20 7:27:05
South Mountain Trailer Park 8 1 33N22'10 112w04'25 7:28:18
South Phoenix 8 1 33N24'24 112w04'22 7:28:17
South Santan 12 1 33N07'03 111w44'44 7:26:59
South Tucson 11 1 32N11'58 110w58'04 7:23:52
Speedway 11 1 32N15 110w55 7:23:40
Sponseller 10 1 34N11'47 109w53'12 7:19:33

Springerville 1 1 34N08'00 109W17'07 7:17:08
Spring Valley 14 1 34N20'42 112W09'30 7:28:38
Sprucedale 6 1 33N44'25 109W19'35 7:17:18
Spur Cross 6 1 33N11'00 109W27'26 7:17:50
Spurlock 4 1 34N08'54 111W01'54 7:24:08
Squaw Peak Terrace 8 1 33N29'45 112W00'53 7:28:04
Stagecoach Trailer Park 8 1 33N27'08 112W08'56 7:28:36
Stanfield 12 1 32N52'57 111W57'41 7:27:51
Stan Shuatuk 11 1 31N47'56 112W17'59 7:29:12
Stanton 14 1 34N09'55 112W43'43 7:30:55
Stanwix 8 1 32N50'23 113W19'20 7:33:17
Stargo 6 1 33N04'04 109W21'34 7:17:26
Stark 2 1 31N22'17 110W02'10 7:20:09
Starlite Trailer Park 8 1 33N27'00 111W59'30 7:27:58
Star Valley 4 1 34N15'18 111W15'28 7:25:02
Steam 15 3 32N43'40 114W42'00 7:38:48
Steamboat 1 1 35N45 109W51 7:19:24
Steamboat Canyon 1 1 35N44'53 109W51'00 7:19:24
Steamboat Canyon Trading Pos 1 1 35N44'48 109W51'30 7:19:26
Steeplechase 8 1 33N38'41 112W07'25 7:28:30
Stewart Mountain Trailer Par 8 1 33N24'58 111W37'41 7:26:31
Stoa Pitk 11 1 32N29'06 112W30'58 7:30:04
Stockham 11 1 32N16'27 111W00'25 7:24:02
Stockton 9 2 35N18'34 114W05'21 7:36:21
Stonegate Crossing 8 1 33N19'55 111W50'13 7:27:21
Stoneman Lake 3 1 34N46'53 111W30'43 7:26:03
Stony Mountain Villas 8 1 33N35'24 112W01'50 7:28:07
Stotonic 12 1 33N09'29 111W47'55 7:27:12
Stotonyak 11 1 32N09'18 112W22'05 7:29:28
Stoval 15 3 32N45'54 113W37'17 7:34:29
Strawberry 4 1 34N24'28 111W29'34 7:25:58
Strayhorse 6 1 33N33'02 109W19'03 7:17:16
Stringfield 14 1 34N41'42 112W33'21 7:30:13
Student Union 11 1 32N14 110W57 7:23:48
Summerhaven 11 1 32N26'19 110W45'33 7:23:02
Summer Mesa 8 1 33N24'06 111W44'56 7:27:00
Summerplace Green 8 1 33N23'48 111W46'30 7:27:06
Summer Place Trails 8 1 33N23'45 111W46'55 7:27:08
Summer Place Village 8 1 33N24'00 111W47'03 7:27:08
Sunburst Homes 8 1 33N28'03 112W11'15 7:28:45
Sun City 8 1 33N35'51 112W16'16 7:29:05
Sun City West 8 1 33N39'43 112W20'26 7:29:22
Suncrest Villas Chandler 8 1 33N18'10 111W56'17 7:27:45
Suncrest Villas East 8 1 33N38'19 112W01'59 7:28:08
Suncrest Villas Mesa 8 1 33N23'20 111W46'47 7:27:07
Suncrest Villas West 8 1 33N40'28 112W08'50 7:28:35
Sundad 8 1 33N10'53 113W14'07 7:32:56
Sundial Mobile Park 8 1 33N27'13 111W49'44 7:27:19
Sunflower 8 1 33N51'51 111W28'01 7:25:52
Sun Grove Mobile Home Park 8 1 33N33'25 112W16'45 7:29:07
Sunizona 2 1 31N25'05 109W39'10 7:18:37
Sun Lakes 8 1 33N12'40 111W52'29 7:27:30
Sunny Acres Trailer Village 8 1 33N24'45 111W39'52 7:26:39
Sunnyside 2 1 31N26'02 110W24'16 7:21:37
Sunnyslope 8 1 33N33'57 112W03'52 7:28:15
Sunny Slope Mobile Home Park 8 1 33N34'13 112W04'54 7:28:20
Sunray Manor 8 1 33N36'44 112W08'25 7:28:34
Sunridge IV 8 1 33N21'10 111W51'20 7:27:25
Sunrise 3 1 35N17'55 110W59'19 7:23:57
Sunrise Heights Mobile Home 8 1 33N38'53 112W02'50 7:28:11
Sunrise Springs 1 1 35N36'13 109W44'41 7:18:59
Sunrise Terrace 8 1 33N29'45 112W14'03 7:28:56
Sunrise Trading Post 1 1 35N36'39 109W44'31 7:18:58
Sunrise Village Mobile Home 8 1 33N27'34 111W42'32 7:26:50
Sunrise Vista Mobile Home Pk 8 1 33N24'36 111W45'19 7:27:01
Sunscape Homes 8 1 33N27'40 112W11'40 7:28:47
Sunset 5 1 32N31'26 110W12'24 7:20:50
Sunset Acres 2 1 31N25 109W54 7:19:36
Sunset Hills 8 1 33N37'40 112W02'06 7:28:08
Sunset North 8 1 33N37'23 112W05'10 7:28:21
Sunset Ridge I 8 1 33N37'36 111W56'50 7:27:47
Sunset Trail Ranch 8 1 33N24'48 111W38'40 7:26:35
Sunset Village 8 1 33N35'33 112W15'34 7:29:02
Sunset Vista 8 1 33N38'55 112W11'18 7:28:45
Sunshine 3 1 35N07'26 111W01'51 7:24:07
Sunshine Acres 8 1 33N28'37 111W42'50 7:26:51
Sunshine Valley Mobile Home 8 1 33N16'54 111W50'40 7:27:23
Sun Tech 8 1 33N19'48 111W51'49 7:27:27
Sun Terra Acres 8 1 33N21 111W47 7:27:08
Sun Trailer Park 8 1 33N27'06 112W06'22 7:28:25
Suntrails 8 1 33N23'50 111W45'26 7:27:02
Suntree 8 1 33N23'00 111W45'55 7:27:04
Sun Valley 10 1 34N58'50 110W03'27 7:20:14
Sun Valley Mobile Home Park 8 1 33N35'33 111W59'06 7:27:56
Sun Valley Trailer Park 8 1 33N27'53 112W00'32 7:28:02
Sunview 8 1 33N22'35 111W47'40 7:27:11
Supai 3 1 36N14'13 112W41'18 7:30:45
Superior 12 1 33N17'38 111W05'44 7:24:23
Superstition Country 8 1 33N24'01 111W37'45 7:26:31
Superstition Estates 12 1 33N25 111W34 7:26:16
Superstition Shadows Mobile 8 1 33N25'00 111W35'27 7:26:22
Supi Oidak 11 1 31N55 111W53 7:27:32
Surprise 8 1 33N37'50 112W19'57 7:29:20
Swansea 7 3 34N10'12 113W50'43 7:35:23
Sweetwater 11 1 31N57'39 112W35'00 7:30:20
Sweetwater 12 1 33N07'55 111W50'24 7:27:22
Sweetwater Garden 8 1 33N36'15 111W59'35 7:27:58
Sweetwater Ranch 8 1 33N36'15 111W53'15 7:27:33
Swift Trail Junction 5 1 32N43'47 109W42'48 7:18:51
Sycamore 14 1 34N51'50 112W05'57 7:28:24
Tacna 15 3 32N41'50 113W57'25 7:35:50
Tahchee 1 1 36N13'43 109W53'38 7:19:35
Taliesin West 8 1 33N36'25 111W50'33 7:27:22
Taliverde 8 1 33N31'05 112W01'40 7:28:07
Tanners Crossing 3 1 35N51'50 111W23'11 7:25:33
Tanner Springs 1 1 35N17'18 109W41'06 7:18:44
Tanque 5 1 32N36'32 109W32'15 7:18:09
Tanque Verde 11 1 32N15'06 110W44'12 7:22:57
Tapco 14 1 34N47'41 112W02'46 7:28:11
Tarton 8 1 32N52'44 113W05'57 7:32:24
Tatai Toak 11 1 32N23'47 112W29'45 7:29:59
Tatk Kam Vo 11 1 31N59'24 112W20'35 7:29:22
Tatkum Vo 11 1 31N40'05 112W07'23 7:28:30
Tat Momoli 12 1 32N36'14 111W51'40 7:27:27
Tatria Toak 11 1 31N55 111W53 7:27:32
Taylor 10 1 34N27'54 110W05'26 7:20:22
Taylor Place 2 1 32N04'34 109W19'27 7:17:18
Teec Nos Pas 1 1 36N54'30 109W06'00 7:16:24
Tees To 10 1 35N02 110W42 7:22:48
Tees Toh 10 1 35N29'58 110W24'18 7:21:37
Tempe 8 1 33N24'53 111W54'31 7:27:38
Tempe Camp 3 1 34N54'28 111W26'30 7:25:46
Tempe Cascade 8 1 33N25'27 111W53'12 7:27:33
Tempe Junction 8 1 33N24'51 111W56'34 7:27:46
Tempe Royal Palms 8 1 33N20'54 111W54'15 7:27:37
Tempe Travel Trailer Villa 8 1 33N24'48 111W54'22 7:27:37
Temple Bar Marina 9 2 34N52 114W09 7:36:36
Tes Nez Iah 1 1 36N56'35 109W42'30 7:18:50
Tewa 10 1 35N51'20 110W23'00 7:21:32
Thatcher 5 1 32N50'57 109W45'31 7:19:02
Theba 8 1 32N55'10 112W53'38 7:31:35
The Citadel 8 1 33N34'20 112W12'05 7:28:48
The Covey 8 1 33N37'10 111W58'49 7:27:55
The Gap 3 1 35N53 111W25 7:25:40
The Haciendas 8 1 33N17'35 111W49'15 7:27:17
The Home Place 8 1 33N18'54 111W52'41 7:27:31
The Lakes 8 1 33N22'16 111W55'10 7:27:41
The Landings 8 1 33N22'00 111W54'28 7:27:38
The Pointe 8 1 33N33'15 112W02'45 7:28:11
The Pointe at South Mountain 8 1 33N22'28 111W58'32 7:27:54
The Preserve 8 1 33N34'49 112W01'15 7:28:05
The Town Square 8 1 33N38'29 112W04'07 7:28:16
The Trails III 8 1 33N27'11 111W53'40 7:27:35
The West Winds Trailer Court 8 1 33N18'20 111W49'54 7:27:20
Thomas Trailer Court 8 1 33N28'51 112W02'22 7:28:09
Three Forks 1 1 33N51'17 109W18'49 7:17:15
Three Fountains 8 1 33N31'07 112W11'17 7:28:45
Three Points 11 1 32N04'36 111W18'47 7:25:15
Three Way 6 1 32N56'54 109W13'47 7:16:55
Thunderbird Palms II 8 1 33N36'34 112W10'59 7:28:44
Thunderbird Valley II 8 1 33N36'55 112W06'44 7:28:27
Tiburon 8 1 33N19'49 111W53'20 7:27:33
Tierra Madre 8 1 33N21 111W47 7:27:08
Tiger 12 1 32N42'28 110W40'54 7:22:44
Tiis Holoni 3 1 35N33'54 111W03'12 7:24:13
Tiki Tai Village 8 1 33N31'50 112W10'50 7:28:43
Tin House 3 1 35N41'52 112W32'43 7:30:11
Tintown 2 1 31N24'51 109W53'52 7:19:35
Tolacon 1 1 36N58 109W02 7:16:08
Tolani 3 1 35N26'05 110W50'38 7:23:23
Tolchico 3 1 35N23'36 111W06'26 7:24:26
Tolleson 8 1 33N27'00 112W15'31 7:29:02
Toltec 12 1 32N47'32 111W36'51 7:26:27
Tombstone 2 1 31N42'46 110W04'01 7:20:16
Tonalea 3 1 36N19 110W56 7:23:44
Tonopah 8 1 33N29'37 112W56'11 7:31:45
Tonto Basin 4 1 33N52 111W19 7:25:16
Tonto Village 4 1 34N18'58 111W07'53 7:24:32
Topawa 11 1 31N48'50 111W49'30 7:27:18
Topock 9 2 34N43'06 114W29'11 7:37:57
Toreva 10 1 35N48'15 110W29'47 7:21:59
Tortilla Flat 8 1 33N31'35 111W23'21 7:25:33
Totacon 1 1 36N51'00 109W25'30 7:17:42
Totopitk 8 1 32N33'48 112W12'44 7:28:51
Tovrea 8 1 33N26'36 111W58'34 7:27:54
Toyei 1 1 35N42'09 109W56'15 7:19:45
Trailer Corral 8 1 33N27'08 112W08'48 7:28:35
Trailing R Mobile Park 8 1 33N25'04 111W38'31 7:26:34
Trail Inn Lodge 8 1 33N27'06 112W07'25 7:28:30
Trail-R-Dale Mobile Home Pk 8 1 33N25'30 112W20'57 7:29:24
Trail Riders Holiday Park 8 1 33N25'03 111W46'33 7:27:06
Trails West Mobile Home Park 8 1 33N24'31 111W35'21 7:26:21
Tremaine 8 1 33N21'32 111W49'54 7:27:20
Trench Camp 13 1 31N27'52 110W43'43 7:22:55
Tres Rios 14 1 34N33'50 111W50'51 7:27:23
Triple T Mobilcity 8 1 33N32'28 112W11'55 7:28:48
Troweek 1 1 33N55'44 109W03'36 7:16:14
Troy 12 1 33N08'37 110W53'55 7:23:36
Truxton 9 2 35N29'06 113W33'46 7:34:15
Tsaile 1 1 36N16'47 109W10'02 7:16:40
Tse Bonita 1 1 35N41 109W03 7:16:12
Tsegi 10 1 36N38'58 110W25'43 7:21:43
Tsintaa Yiti Ii 1 1 35N49'32 109W48'42 7:19:15
Tubac 13 1 31N36'45 111W02'43 7:24:11
Tuba City 3 1 36N08'06 111W14'21 7:24:57
Tucker 4 1 33N38'27 110W36'24 7:22:26
Tucson 11 1 32N13'18 110W55'33 7:23:42
Tucson Country Club Estates 11 1 32N15'33 110W51'29 7:23:26
Tucson Estates 11 1 32N11'15 111W05'25 7:24:22
Tucson National Estates 11 1 32N21'11 111W01'30 7:24:06
Tully 2 1 31N58'58 110W07'22 7:20:29
Tumacacori 13 1 31N34'07 111W03'06 7:24:12
Turf Mobile Manor 8 1 33N37'38 112W05'51 7:28:23
Turf Trailer Lodge 8 1 33N38'30 112W05'40 7:28:23
Turkey Crossing 3 1 34N25'41 111W01'19 7:24:05
Turkey Flat 5 1 32N37'51 109W49'14 7:19:17
Turtle Creek 8 1 33N38'18 112W04'14 7:28:17
Tusayan 3 1 35N58'25 112W07'33 7:28:30
Tusconita 11 1 32N08 110W56 7:23:44
Tutt 14 1 34N39'38 112W24'51 7:29:39
Tuweep 9 1 36N24'57 113W03'57 7:32:16
Twin Acres Family Mobile Pk 8 1 33N24'49 111W36'57 7:26:28
Twin Arrows 3 1 35N12 111W37 7:26:28
Twin Buttes 10 1 35N26'07 109W54'12 7:19:37
Twin Buttes 11 1 31N54'09 111W03'36 7:24:14
Twin Falls 1 1 36N51'49 109W06'07 7:16:24
Twin Knolls 8 1 33N24'48 111W39'02 7:26:36
Two Guns 3 1 35N07'04 111W05'34 7:24:22
Two Story 1 1 35N39 109W06 7:16:24
Tyson 15 3 32N47'48 113W52'51 7:35:31
Ubank Place 10 1 34N54'39 109W57'03 7:19:48
Uhs Kug 11 1 31N57'58 111W33'07 7:26:12
Union Hills Manor 8 1 33N39'12 112W08'07 7:28:32
University Mobile Home Park 8 1 33N25'01 111W55'22 7:27:41
University of Arizona 11 1 32N13 110W55 7:23:40
Upper Greasewood Trading Pos 1 1 36N35 109W05 7:16:20
Upper Wheatfields 1 1 36N13'23 109W04'45 7:16:19
Utevak 11 1 31N42'08 111W44'56 7:27:00
Utting 7 3 33N50'20 113W53'10 7:35:33
Vahki 12 1 33N12 111W50 7:27:20
Vail 11 1 32N02'52 110W42'41 7:22:51
Vainom Kug 11 1 32N02'48 112W03'26 7:28:14
Vaiva Vo 12 1 32N43'04 111W55'33 7:27:42
Vakamok 11 1 31N42'20 112W01'49 7:28:07
Valencia 8 1 33N22'46 112W35'00 7:30:20
Valentine 9 2 35N23'15 113W39'25 7:34:38
Valle 3 1 35N39'06 112W11'55 7:28:48
Valley Farms 12 1 32N59'18 111W26'48 7:25:47
Valley Gardens Trailer Park 8 1 33N27'00 112W00'20 7:28:01
Valley Mobile Homes Estate 8 1 33N19'03 111W50'15 7:27:21
Valley Palms Mobile Home Pk 8 1 33N24'52 111W37'15 7:26:29
Valley View 8 1 33N39'17 112W04'43 7:28:19
Valley View 11 1 32N19'06 110W58'02 7:23:52
Val Vista Trailer Park 8 1 33N39'34 112W01'56 7:28:08
Vamori 11 1 31N43'16 111W54'17 7:27:37
Vanar 2 1 32N14'28 109W05'40 7:16:23
Vandenburg Village 11 1 32N10'49 110W52'02 7:23:28
Vaya Chin 11 1 32N20'50 112W19'34 7:29:18
Velda Rose Estates 8 1 33N25'10 111W41'21 7:26:45
Velda Rose Gardens 8 1 33N24'45 111W42'46 7:26:51
Venezia 14 1 34N23'35 112W24'58 7:29:40
Ventana 11 1 32N27'58 112W14'33 7:28:58
Venture Out 8 1 33N24'42 111W43'24 7:26:54
Verde 14 1 34N38 111W47 7:27:08
Verde Real 8 1 33N37'36 112W08'54 7:28:36
Verde River Meadows One 14 1 34N34'58 111W52'13 7:27:29
Vernon 1 1 34N15'27 109W41'32 7:18:46
Viason Chin 11 1 32N00'55 112W17'23 7:29:10
Vicksburg 7 3 33N44'40 113W45'05 7:35:00
Vicksburg Junction 7 3 33N43'08 113W46'00 7:35:04
Victorine Crossing 3 1 34N34'16 111W04'03 7:24:16
Villa Carmel Mobile Home Pk 8 1 33N38'03 112W01'40 7:28:07
Villa de Paz 8 1 33N29'59 112W16'57 7:29:08
Village Fairways 8 1 33N35'42 111W58'50 7:27:55

Village Meadows 2 1 31N33 110w17 7:21:08
Village of Gila Springs 8 1 33N18'42 111w56'19 7:27:45
Village on the Lakes 8 1 33N30'55 112w00'45 7:28:03
Village Park 8 1 33N35'03 112w12'00 7:28:48
Villa Monte Vista 8 1 33N23'40 112w03'20 7:28:13
Villa Novena 8 1 33N31'40 112w05'06 7:28:20
Villas Plaza 8 1 33N40'18 112w07'15 7:28:29
Villa Vista 8 1 33N35'23 112w15'20 7:29:01
Villiage Meadows 2 1 31N33'00 110w16'15 7:21:05
Vista Alegre 8 1 33N22'25 111w50'17 7:27:21
Vista Catalina 11 1 32N30'05 110w55'24 7:23:42
Vista del Cerro 8 1 33N34'19 111w59'50 7:27:59
Vista Encantada 3 1 36N13'50 111w58'22 7:27:53
Vopolo Havoka 11 1 31N45'33 111w55'25 7:27:42
Wabash Trailer Court 8 1 33N34'13 112w03'51 7:28:15
Waddell 8 1 33N36'41 112w25'35 7:29:42
Wagoner 14 1 34N12'49 112w32'06 7:30:08
Wagon Wheel Mobile Ranch 8 1 33N27'35 111w58'52 7:27:55
Wahak Hotrontk (San Simon In 11 1 32N10'58 112w21'54 7:29:28
Wahweap 3 1 36N59'48 111w29'22 7:25:57
Walapai 9 2 35N20'40 113w53'00 7:35:32
Walker 14 1 34N27'21 112w22'39 7:29:31
Walker Place Windmill 14 1 34N20'38 112w37'18 7:30:29
Walnut Grove 14 1 34N16'59 112w32'52 7:30:11
Walpi 10 1 35N49'56 110w23'50 7:21:35
Warner Park 8 1 33N20'00 111w51'20 7:27:25
Warren 2 1 31N24'39 109w52'40 7:19:31
Washington Camp 13 1 31N22'55 110w41'26 7:22:46
Washington Park 4 1 34N25'28 111w16'01 7:25:04
Washington Trailer Park 8 1 33N26'55 112w00'25 7:28:02
Wayne 8 1 33N33'58 112w24'32 7:29:38
Webb 8 1 33N33'09 112w21'59 7:29:28
Weedville 8 1 33N36'50 112w12'53 7:28:52
Welcome Home Mobile Park 8 1 33N30'57 112w06'45 7:28:27
Wellington Court 8 1 33N35'35 112w11'55 7:28:48
Wellton 15 3 32N40'22 114w08'46 7:36:35
Wenden 7 3 33N49'21 113w32'27 7:34:10
Wepo Village 10 1 35N53'36 110w22'24 7:21:30
Westbriar 8 1 33N29'53 112w15'06 7:29:00
Westbrook Village 8 1 33N39'26 112w16'39 7:29:07
West Chandler 8 1 33N18'19 111w56'42 7:27:47
West Chevelon Crossing 3 1 34N28'17 110w55'28 7:23:42
Westcliff Park 8 1 33N36'47 112w09'14 7:28:37
West End 8 1 33N29'40 112w15'16 7:29:01
Western Acres Mobile Home Pk 8 1 33N27'10 112w11'59 7:28:48
Western Acres Mobile Park 8 1 33N24'52 111w37'27 7:26:30
Western Palms Mobile Home Co 8 1 33N27'18 112w12'18 7:28:49
Westerra 8 1 33N35'55 112w11'22 7:28:45
Westgreen Estates 8 1 33N33'55 112w15'05 7:29:00
West Mesa Trailer Court 8 1 33N24'51 111w50'57 7:27:24
West Pershing Plaza 2 1 31N33'18 110w20'55 7:21:24
Westridge Park 8 1 33N27'35 112w12'16 7:28:49
West Sedona 14 1 34N30 112w41 7:30:44
Westward Quest 8 1 33N26 111w50 7:27:20
Westwind 8 1 33N35'55 112w11'54 7:28:48
West Winslow 10 1 35N02'25 110w44'30 7:22:58
West Yuma 15 3 32N43 114w40 7:38:40
Wheatfields 1 1 36N14'16 109w07'41 7:16:31
Wheeler Place 2 1 32N15'53 109w04'58 7:16:20
Wheel Inn Ranch 8 1 33N27'33 111w55'43 7:27:43
Whetstone 2 1 31N57'26 110w20'29 7:21:22
Whipple 14 1 34N33'24 112w26'56 7:29:48
Whispering Hills 2 1 31N33 110w17 7:21:08
Whispering Pines 6 1 33N43'49 109w03'20 7:16:13
White Clay 1 1 36N03'54 109w13'05 7:16:52
White Cone 10 1 35N36'19 110w04'03 7:20:16
White Hills 9 2 35N44'17 114w23'48 7:37:35
White Mountain Lake 10 1 34N15 110w02 7:20:08
White Mountain Lakes Estates 10 1 34N21'19 109w59'43 7:19:59
Whiteriver 10 1 33N50'13 109w57'49 7:19:51
White Tanks 8 1 33N36'15 112w17'55 7:29:12
Whitlock Cienega 5 1 32N33'10 109w20'07 7:17:20
Whitted Place 3 1 34N43'55 110w57'35 7:23:50
Why 11 1 32N16'07 112w44'17 7:30:57
Wickchoupai 11 1 32N00'14 111w55'16 7:27:41
Wickenburg 8 1 33N58'07 112w43'44 7:30:55
Wide Ruins 1 1 35N25'10 109w29'45 7:17:59
Wiggins Crossing 3 1 34N31'00 110w59'16 7:23:57
Wigwam Villa Mobile Home Pk 8 1 33N28'07 112w05'23 7:28:22
Wikieup 9 2 34N42'12 113w36'38 7:34:27
Wild Cow Campground 9 2 35N03'55 113w52'12 7:35:29
Wild Flower 8 1 33N40'13 112w04'49 7:28:19
Wildwood Estates 14 1 34N34'27 112w30'27 7:30:02
Wilhoit 14 1 34N25'33 112w35'10 7:30:21
Willaha 3 1 35N45'43 112w15'48 7:29:03
Willcox 2 1 32N15'10 109w49'53 7:19:20
Williams 3 1 35N14'58 112w11'25 7:28:46
Williams Air Force Base 8 1 33N21 111w50 7:27:20
Williams Junction 3 1 35N14'35 112w08'05 7:28:32
Willow 4 1 33N42'53 110w58'40 7:23:55
Willow Beach 9 2 35N58 114w50 7:39:20
WillowBrook II 8 1 33N35'14 112w10'58 7:28:44
Willow Canyon 11 1 32N23'19 110w41'53 7:22:48
Willow Spring 14 1 34N40'12 112w51'45 7:31:27
Willow Springs 3 1 36N11'22 111w23'35 7:25:34
Willows West 8 1 33N29'53 112w13'22 7:28:53
Willow Valley Estates 9 2 34N52 114w09 7:36:36
Wilmot 11 1 32N07'20 110w50'38 7:23:23
Windemere 8 1 33N31'55 111w54'12 7:27:37
Windmill 8 1 33N35'50 112w13'41 7:28:55
Window Rock 1 1 35N40'50 109w03'07 7:16:12
Windsong 8 1 33N38'34 111w55'41 7:27:43
Windsor Mobile Home Park 8 1 33N24'46 111w46'41 7:27:07
Windsor Square 8 1 33N33'56 112w10'30 7:28:42
Wingfield 3 1 34N34'15 111w18'17 7:25:13
Winkelman 4 1 32N59'15 110w46'13 7:23:05
Winnwood Homes 8 1 33N26'56 112w20'30 7:29:22
Winona 3 1 35N12'18 111w24'27 7:25:38
Winslow 10 1 35N01'27 110w41'48 7:22:47
Wintercone Park 8 1 33N26'58 111w49'06 7:27:16
Wintersburg 8 1 33N25'28 112w52'02 7:31:28
Winwood 2 1 31N25 109w54 7:19:36
Wishing Well Trailer Park 8 1 33N18'23 111w49'40 7:27:19
Wittmann 8 1 33N46'35 112w31'40 7:30:07
Wolf Crossing 3 1 35N23'40 111w06'27 7:24:26
Womack East 8 1 33N20'49 111w51'15 7:27:25
Wonder Rift 8 1 33N21'01 112w01'08 7:28:05
Woodbridge Crossing 8 1 33N23'05 111w47'45 7:27:11
Woodcreek 8 1 33N23'00 111w52'12 7:27:29
Woodglen 8 1 33N21'11 111w52'17 7:27:29
Woodin 3 1 35N50'56 112w15'18 7:29:01
Woodland Heights 8 1 33N23'25 111w45'27 7:27:02
Woodleaf 8 1 33N31'20 111w54'14 7:27:37
Woodleaf II 8 1 33N35'36 111w57'45 7:27:51
Woodridge Lakes 8 1 33N26'20 111w48'08 7:27:13
Woodridge VI 8 1 33N39'30 112w10'10 7:28:41
Woodruff 10 1 34N46'53 110w02'34 7:20:10
Woodside 8 1 33N23'25 111w45'55 7:27:04
Wood Springs 1 1 35N48'45 109w27'41 7:17:51
Wood Trap 14 1 34N36'28 112w47'56 7:31:12
Wranglers Roost 8 1 33N55'27 112w06'45 7:28:27
Wymola 12 1 32N39'29 111w24'14 7:25:37
Yampai 14 2 35N29'22 113w11'59 7:32:48
Yaqui Indian Settlement 8 1 33N25 112w00 7:28:00
Yarnell 14 1 34N13'18 112w44'48 7:30:59
Yava 14 1 34N28'19 112w53'23 7:31:34
Yavapai Hills 14 1 34N33'42 112w22'58 7:29:32
Yavapai Indian Reservation 14 1 34N34 112w28 7:29:52
Yazzi 1 1 36N34'45 109w13'25 7:16:54
Yellow Hammer Mill 2 1 32N21'48 109w17'17 7:17:09
York 6 1 32N53'37 109w12'08 7:16:49
Young 4 1 34N06'05 110w57'47 7:23:51
Young America Homes 8 1 33N28'34 112w09'08 7:28:37
Young America West 8 1 33N29'34 112w15'36 7:29:02
Youngberg 12 1 33N27'27 111w29'25 7:25:58
Youngtown 8 1 33N35'38 112w18'08 7:29:13
Yucca 9 2 34N52'20 114w08'55 7:36:36
Yuma 15 3 32N43'31 114w37'25 7:38:30
Yuma Proving Ground 15 3 32N52 114w26 7:37:44
Yuma Station 15 3 32N39 114w35 7:38:20
Zeniff 10 1 34N34'38 110w22'39 7:21:31

TIME TABLES

Before 11/18/1883		LMT
11/18/1883	12:00	CST
3/31/1918	02:00	CWT
10/27/1918	02:00	CST
3/30/1919	02:00	CWT
10/26/1919	02:00	CST
2/09/1942	02:00	CWT
9/30/1945	02:00	CST
4/30/1967	02:00	US#1

COUNTIES

1 Arkansas
2 Ashley
3 Baxter
4 Benton
5 Boone
6 Bradley
7 Calhoun
8 Carroll
9 Chicot
10 Clark
11 Clay
12 Cleburne
13 Cleveland
14 Columbia
15 Conway
16 Craighead
17 Crawford
18 Crittenden
19 Cross
20 Dallas
21 Desha
22 Drew
23 Faulkner
24 Franklin
25 Fulton
26 Garland
27 Grant
28 Greene
29 Hempstead
30 Hot Spring
31 Howard
32 Independence
33 Izard
34 Jackson
35 Jefferson
36 Johnson
37 Lafayette
38 Lawrence
39 Lee
40 Lincoln
41 Little River
42 Logan
43 Lonoke
44 Madison
45 Marion
46 Miller
47 Mississippi
48 Monroe
49 Montgomery
50 Nevada
51 Newton
52 Ouachita
53 Perry
54 Phillips
55 Pike
56 Poinsett
57 Polk
58 Pope
59 Prairie
60 Pulaski
61 Randolph
62 St Francis
63 Saline
64 Scott
65 Searcy
66 Sebastian
67 Sevier
68 Sharp
69 Stone
70 Union
71 Van Buren
72 Washington
73 White
74 Woodruff
75 Yell

Place	Latitude	Longitude	Time
Aa Junction 38	36N04'47	90W56'23	6:03:46
Abbott 64	35N04'24	94W11'37	6:16:46
Aberdeen 48	34N36'12	91W20'30	6:05:22
Acorn 57	34N38'34	94W12'03	6:16:48
Ada 15	35N06'25	92W52'24	6:11:30
Adona 53	35N02'17	92W53'52	6:11:35
Advance 3	36N09'19	92W22'56	6:09:32
Aetna 16	35N55'47	90W33'17	6:02:13
Afton 25	36N23	91W31	6:06:04
Agnos 25	36N16'38	91W41'29	6:06:46
Airport Village 34	35N38'16	91W11'42	6:04:47
Alabam 44	36N09'09	93W40'52	6:14:43
Alabama 50	33N29	93W24	6:13:36
Alamo 49	34N28'26	93W28'07	6:13:52
Albany 50	33N40	93W22	6:13:28
Albert 49	34N22'16	93W52'28	6:15:30
Albert Pike 26	34N30	93W03	6:12:12
Albion 73	35N20'33	91W47'22	6:07:09
Alco 69	35N53'15	92W22'01	6:09:28
Alexander 28	36N04	90W32	6:02:08
Alexander 60	34N37'46	92W26'28	6:09:46
Alf 49	34N29'23	93W52'13	6:15:29
Alfrey 48	34N49'44	91W09'18	6:04:37
Algoa 34	35N30'21	91W07'00	6:04:28
Alicia 38	35N53'35	91W04'58	6:04:20
Alix 24	35N25'29	93W43'49	6:14:55
Allbrook 31	33N53	93W55	6:15:40
Alleene 41	33N46'12	94W15'37	6:17:02
Allen 58	35N36	93W08	6:12:32
Allendale 48	34N48'37	91W15'59	6:05:04
Allfriend 51	36N11	93W24	6:13:36
Allis 22	33N37'40	91W54'18	6:07:37
Allison 69	35N56'12	92W07'02	6:08:28
Allport 43	34N32'31	91W47'02	6:07:08
Alma 17	35N28'40	94W13'18	6:16:53
Almond 12	35N41'45	91W47'54	6:07:12
Almyra 1	34N24'22	91W24'34	6:05:38
Alpena 5	36N17'41	93W17'31	6:13:10
Alpha 75	35N06'56	93W16'50	6:13:07
Alpine 10	34N13'44	93W22'44	6:13:31
Alread 71	35N37'58	92W40'47	6:10:43
Altheimer 35	34N19'09	91W50'50	6:07:23
Alto 56	35N34'12	90W19'52	6:01:19
Altus 24	35N26'46	93W45'44	6:15:03
Aly 75	34N59	93W18	6:13:12
Amagon 34	35N33'43	91W06'37	6:04:26
Amanca 18	35N06'30	90W13'47	6:00:55
Amboy 60	34N48'21	92W17'29	6:09:10
Ames 50	33N34'29	93W13'01	6:12:52
Amity 10	34N15'53	93W27'39	6:13:51
Amy 52	33N43'55	92W48'55	6:11:16
Anderson 4	36N18	94W17	6:17:08
Anderson 64	34N54'44	94W07'17	6:16:29
Anderson Tully 56	35N29'07	90W36'06	6:02:24
Andrews 73	35N11'02	91W34'05	6:06:16
Andrews Landing 47	35N25'11	90W02'42	6:00:11
Annieville 38	36N09'18	91W14'25	6:04:58
Anthony 29	33N42	93W35	6:14:20
Antioch 16	35N55'46	90W34'37	6:02:18
Antioch 30	34N18'42	92W59'12	6:11:57
Antioch 53	34N57'28	92W45'31	6:11:02
Antioch 73	35N08'08	91W55'01	6:07:40
Antoine 55	34N02'10	93W25'14	6:13:41
Apalco 37	33N21'30	93W27'36	6:13:50
Apex 66	34N59'59	94W26'09	6:17:45
Aplin 53	34N58'26	92W58'43	6:11:55
Appleby 72	36N01'16	94W14'46	6:16:59
Applegate Ford 8	36N15'47	93W36'39	6:14:27
Apple Glenn 4	36N27	94W32	6:18:08
Appleton 58	35N25'28	92W52'29	6:11:30
Apt 16	35N46'27	90W40'20	6:02:41
Arbaugh 51	35N46'54	93W30'05	6:14:00
Arbor Grove 38	36N01'06	91W02'51	6:04:11
Arcadia 29	33N50'32	93W27'57	6:13:52
Archey Valley 71	35N42	92W44	6:10:56
Ard 75	35N14	93W10	6:12:40
Arden 41	33N41'22	94W17'08	6:17:09
Arkadelphia 10	34N07'15	93W03'13	6:12:13
Arkana 3	36N14'18	92W18'59	6:09:16
Arkana 37	33N06	93W39	6:14:36
Arkansas 1	34N04	91W22	6:05:28
Arkansas City 21	33N36'31	91W12'24	6:04:50
Arkansas Fuel Oil Company Vi 14	33N16	93W14	6:12:56
Arkansas Post 1	34N01	91W21	6:05:24
Arkawana 3	36N24'13	92W27'39	6:09:51
Arkinda 41	33N46'49	94W28'07	6:17:52
Arkola 66	35N05'05	94W18'32	6:17:14
Arkoma 66	35N21'15	94W26'08	6:17:45
Arlberg 69	35N44'01	92W23'21	6:09:33
Armorel 47	35N55'12	89W47'53	5:59:12
Armstrong 68	36N22'22	91W19'02	6:05:16
Arnett 72	35N53'42	94W02'22	6:16:09
Artesian 7	33N24'06	92W28'08	6:09:53
Artex 46	33N23'15	93W49'55	6:15:20
Arthur 15	35N15	92W41	6:10:44
Artist Point 17	35N43'11	94W08'14	6:16:33
Ashdown 41	33N40'27	94W07'52	6:16:31
Asher 44	35N56'33	93W51'01	6:15:24
Asher 60	34N44	92W20	6:09:20
Ash Flat 68	36N13'26	91W36'30	6:06:26
Ashland 38	35N58	91W01	6:04:04
Ashley 32	35N51	91W37	6:06:28
Ashton 9	33N18'46	91W20'21	6:05:21
Athelstan 47	35N41'53	90W10'42	6:00:43
Athens 31	34N18'52	93W58'36	6:15:54
Atkins 58	35N14'47	92W56'11	6:11:45
Atlanta 14	33N07'07	93W03'09	6:12:13
Attica 61	36N21'03	90W59'43	6:03:59
Atwood 31	34N05'54	94W04'21	6:16:17
Aubrey 39	34N43'00	90W54'01	6:03:36
Auburn 40	34N02	91W31	6:06:04
Augsburg 58	35N24'52	93W14'17	6:12:57
Augusta 74	35N16'56	91W21'55	6:05:28
Aurelle 70	33N02'53	92W24'20	6:09:37
Aurora 44	35N59'50	93W42'09	6:14:49
Austin 15	35N26'31	92W31'35	6:10:06
Austin 43	34N59'54	91W59'01	6:07:56
Auvergne 34	35N30'49	91W13'50	6:04:55
Avant 26	34N38'45	93W20'23	6:13:22
Avant Landing 26	34N38'10	93W23'00	6:13:32
Avery 40	33N55'47	91W39'25	6:06:38
Avilla 63	34N40'57	92W35'06	6:10:20
Avoca 4	36N24'07	94W04'14	6:16:17
Avon 67	34N04'29	94W19'22	6:17:17
Azor 50	33N35'30	93W25'29	6:13:42
Back Gate 21	33N55'57	91W23'34	6:05:34
Bailey 32	35N32'29	91W29'45	6:05:59
Bain 26	34N32	93W09	6:12:36
Baker 37	33N27'53	93W32'45	6:14:11
Baker 65	35N54'49	92W35'51	6:10:23
Baker 68	36N16'50	91W24'50	6:05:39
Baker Ford 25	36N22'35	91W33'40	6:06:15
Baker Hollow 65	35N56'05	92W42'38	6:10:51
Baker Springs 31	34N18'45	94W10'03	6:16:40
Balch 34	35N31'54	91W03'56	6:04:16
Bald Knob 73	35N18'35	91W34'04	6:06:16
Baldwin 72	36N02'54	94W05'48	6:16:23
Ball 4	36N07	94W28	6:17:52
Ballard 68	36N14'06	91W40'07	6:06:40
Ballard Landing 23	34N57'48	92W24'40	6:09:39
Band Mill 33	36N08'01	91W58'44	6:07:55
Bangs Landing 7	33N19'14	92W27'42	6:09:51
Banks 6	33N34'29	92W16'08	6:09:05
Banner 12	35N38'30	91W49'53	6:07:20
Banyard 72	35N45'36	94W12'24	6:16:50
Barber 42	35N07'42	94W03'12	6:16:13
Barcelona 17	35N37'14	94W27'21	6:17:49
Bard 28	36N04'28	90W22'37	6:01:30
Bardstown 47	35N32'08	90W09'36	6:00:38
Barfield 47	35N54'18	89W46'04	5:59:04
Barham 24	35N26	93W57	6:15:48
Barham 52	33N43'25	93W03'14	6:12:13
Barkada 22	33N40'23	91W54'08	6:07:37
Barling 66	35N19'32	94W18'05	6:17:12
Barnes 24	35N38'07	93W49'13	6:15:17
Barnes 74	35N19	91W11	6:04:44
Barnett 71	35N23	92W25	6:09:40
Barney 23	35N15'06	92W12'24	6:08:50
Barraque 35	34N27	92W10	6:08:40
Barren Fork 33	35N58	91W44	6:06:56
Barrentine Corner 73	35N04'08	91W56'42	6:07:47
Barringer 10	33N50'53	93W08'02	6:12:32
Barson 74	35N09'05	91W04'23	6:04:18
Barton 54	34N32'51	90W46'05	6:03:04
Base Line 60	34N40'05	92W19'04	6:09:16
Bashe 66	35N18'45	94W26'03	6:17:44
Bass 51	35N54'15	92W59'52	6:11:59
Bassett 47	35N32'11	90W07'36	6:00:30
Bass Little 66	35N12	94W19	6:17:16
Batavia 5	36N15'18	93W13'21	6:12:53
Bateman 34	35N36	91W20	6:05:20
Bates 64	34N54'29	94W23'12	6:17:33
Batesville 32	35N46'11	91W38'27	6:06:34
Batson 36	35N37'20	93W38'50	6:14:35
Battlefield 29	33N35'36	93W41'18	6:14:45
Battles (P O) 33	36N02'44	91W45'05	6:07:00
Baucum 60	34N43'44	92W07'48	6:08:31
Bauxite 63	34N33'20	92W31'16	6:10:05
Bauxite Junction 63	34N35'06	92W30'56	6:10:04
Baxter 22	33N31'45	91W29'49	6:05:59
Baxter 26	34N42	93W18	6:13:12
Bay 16	35N44'32	90W33'44	6:02:15
Bayless 48	34N49'28	91W13'28	6:04:54
Bayliss 58	35N24	93W14	6:12:56
Bayou Meto 1	34N13'25	91W31'16	6:06:05
Bayou Metro 43	34N47	91W54	6:07:36
Bay Village 56	35N26'59	90W40'33	6:02:42
B B Junction 49	34N34'53	91W06'17	6:04:25
Beach Grove 24	35N40'43	93W44'30	6:14:58
Beacon Addition 4	36N20'00	93W59'54	6:16:00
Bear 26	34N32'04	93W16'25	6:13:06
Bear Creek 65	35N49'53	92W46'05	6:11:04
Bear Creek Springs 5	36N17'51	93W10'59	6:12:44
Bearden 52	33N43'28	92W36'56	6:10:28
Bear Hollow Village 66	35N22	94W23	6:17:32
Bear Wallow 42	35N12	93W32	6:14:08
Beasley 56	35N28'04	90W19'22	6:01:17
Beatie 4	36N25	94W35	6:18:20
Beaton 30	34N18'19	93W15'41	6:13:03
Beaty 4	36N27'05	94W31'30	6:18:06
Beauchamp 64	34N48'18	94W16'14	6:17:05
Beaudry 26	34N42	93W04	6:12:16
Beaver 8	36N28'25	93W46'02	6:15:04
Beaver Shores 4	36N19'22	94W01'09	6:16:05
Beck 18	34N57	90W28	6:01:52
Beck 46	33N24'33	93W44'40	6:14:59
Becton 74	35N03'51	91W14'54	6:05:00
Bedford 19	35N13	90W52	6:03:28
Beebe 73	35N04'14	91W52'46	6:07:31
Bee Branch 71	35N27'03	92W23'40	6:09:35
Beech 46	33N14	93W52	6:15:28
Beech Creek 2	33N08	91W38	6:06:32
Beech Creek Crossing 2	33N19'06	91W56'13	6:07:45
Beech Grove 20	33N48'47	92W26'54	6:09:48
Beech Grove 28	36N10'20	90W37'09	6:02:29
Beechwood 51	36N00'29	93W22'08	6:13:29
Beedeville 34	35N25'44	91W06'35	6:04:26
Behestian 52	33N44	92W57	6:11:48
Beirne 10	33N53'19	93W12'14	6:12:49
Belcher 73	35N04'54	91W36'07	6:06:24
Belfast 27	34N24'52	92W27'32	6:09:50
Belk Corner 23	35N02'58	92W29'25	6:09:58
Bellaire 9	33N32	91W26	6:05:44
Bella Vista 4	36N28'53	94W16'23	6:17:06
Bell City 11	36N17'16	90W07'19	6:00:29
Bellefonte 5	36N12'03	93W02'54	6:12:12
Belle Meade 62	34N55'46	90W26'04	6:01:44
Belleville 75	35N05'35	93W26'54	6:13:48
Bellmore 69	35N44	91W52	6:07:28
Bells Chapel 58	35N14	92W55	6:11:40
Bellville 5	36N28'02	93W03'32	6:12:14
Bellville 67	33N56'19	94W10'29	6:16:42
Belton 29	33N57	93W51	6:15:24
Belview 33	36N05'25	91W55'10	6:07:41
Bemis 74	35N09'45	91W04'03	6:04:16
Ben 69	35N43'16	91W56'54	6:07:48
Bend 36	35N21'15	93W23'14	6:13:33
Bend Ford 65	35N57'33	92W51'42	6:11:27
Benedict 23	35N00	92W32	6:10:08
Bengall 34	35N37	91W16	6:05:04
Ben Gay 68	36N05	91W29	6:05:56
Bengel 34	35N27'09	91W19'23	6:05:18
Ben Hur 51	35N43'49	92W58'22	6:11:53
Ben Lomond 67	33N50'07	94W07'06	6:16:28
Bennett 11	36N28	90W24	6:01:36

Place	Latitude	Longitude	Time
Bennett Bayou 25	36N26	92w04	6:08:16
Bentley 15	35N06	92w46	6:11:04
Benton 63	34N33'52	92w35'12	6:10:21
Bentonville 4	36N22'22	94w12'31	6:16:50
Benzal 1	33N59'56	91w09'41	6:04:39
Berea 2	33N20'21	91w42'02	6:06:48
Berger 60	34N39'46	92w18'28	6:09:14
Bergman 5	36N18'58	93w00'27	6:12:02
Berlin 2	33N04'50	91w45'47	6:07:03
Bernice 58	35N15'00	93w07'46	6:12:31
Berryville 8	36N21'53	93w34'04	6:14:16
Bertig 28	36N04'16	90w19'51	6:01:19
Beryl 23	35N04'59	92w15'36	6:09:02
Bethany 31	34N04'39	94w01'11	6:16:05
Bethel 10	34N01'10	93w17'15	6:13:09
Bethel 14	33N25'27	93w19'39	6:13:19
Bethel 28	35N59'16	90w31'45	6:02:07
Bethel 58	35N14'56	93w06'32	6:12:26
Bethel Grove 72	36N02	94w15	6:17:00
Bethel Heights 4	36N12'51	94w07'45	6:16:31
Bethesda 32	35N47'29	91w47'18	6:07:09
Bethlehem 15	35N17'01	92w35'15	6:10:21
Beulah 59	43N52'23	91w24'32	6:05:38
Beulah Island Landing 21	33N48'09	91w01'31	6:04:06
Beverage Town 71	35N25	92w43	6:10:52
Beverly 66	35N21	94w07	6:16:28
Bevis Corner 43	34N43'14	92w00'25	6:08:02
Bexar 25	36N17'12	91w59'44	6:07:59
Biddle 60	34N43'10	92w15'33	6:09:02
Bidville 17	35N44'23	93w58'54	6:15:56
Big Bottom 32	35N41	91w27	6:05:48
Big Creek Corner 39	34N40'22	90w53'24	6:03:34
Bigelow 53	35N00'04	92w37'47	6:10:31
Big Flat 3	36N00'18	92w24'15	6:09:37
Big Fork 57	34N29'11	93w58'11	6:15:53
Biggers 61	36N19'57	90w48'22	6:03:13
Biggs Landing 18	35N03'30	90w12'07	6:00:48
Big Hill 7	33N39'56	92w24'55	6:09:40
Big Lake 47	35N51'07	90w08'27	6:00:34
Big Rock 60	34N41	92w20	6:09:20
Big Rock 66	35N10'28	94w16'41	6:17:07
Big Spring Mill 32	35N49'38	91w43'25	6:06:54
Big Springs 45	36N11	92w45	6:11:00
Big Springs 69	35N52	92w07	6:08:28
Billingsleys Corner 41	33N50	94w21	6:17:24
Billstown 55	33N58'51	93w34'15	6:14:17
Bingen 29	33N58'32	93w47'02	6:15:08
Birdell 61	36N14'40	91w04'41	6:04:19
Birdeye 19	35N22'43	90w41'14	6:02:45
Birdsong 47	35N27'30	90w15'45	6:01:03
Birdtown 15	35N18'22	92w36'27	6:10:26
Birmac 35	34N10'17	91w37'10	6:06:29
Birta 58	35N01'02	93w08'00	6:12:32
Biscoe (Fredonia) 59	34N49'15	91w24'15	6:05:37
Bismarck 30	34N18'58	93w10'14	6:12:41
Blackburn 72	35N48'59	94w13'10	6:16:53
Black Cat Landing 47	35N27'58	90w01'22	6:00:05
Black Diamond 46	33N08'09	93w54'35	6:15:38
Blackfish 62	35N03'58	90w34'55	6:02:20
Black Fork 64	34N46'01	94w25'51	6:17:43
Black Jack 28	36N10'43	90w42'03	6:02:48
Blackjack Corner 4	36N27'26	94w08'22	6:16:33
Blackland 31	33N49	93w53	6:15:32
Blackland 41	33N43	94w24	6:17:36
Black Oak 16	35N50'20	90w22'05	6:01:28
Black Oak 56	35N27'18	90w24'47	6:01:39
Black Oak 72	35N59'00	94w04'46	6:16:19
Black Rock 38	36N06'30	91w05'50	6:04:23
Black Springs 49	34N27'40	93w42'45	6:14:51
Blackton 49	34N40'03	91w06'15	6:04:25
Blackville 34	35N29'00	91w09'53	6:04:40
Blackwell 15	35N13'20	92w50'28	6:11:22
Blakely 26	34N41'48	93w04'09	6:12:17
Blakemore 43	34N33	91w53	6:07:32
Blanchard Springs 70	33N01	92w43	6:10:52
Blanco 65	35N55'43	92w48'43	6:11:15
Blansett 64	34N47'24	94w13'12	6:16:53
Blanton 18	35N10'29	90w09'59	6:00:40
Blanville 68	36N04	91w37	6:06:28
Bledsoe 39	34N54'19	90w31'27	6:02:06
Blevins 29	33N52'18	93w34'37	6:14:18
Bloomer 66	35N17'38	94w08'19	6:16:33
Bloomfield 4	36N16'34	94w32'17	6:18:09
Blossom 62	34N55'52	91w02'44	6:04:11
Blue Ball 75	34N57'44	93w42'30	6:14:50
Blue Bayou 31	33N58'10	93w57'20	6:15:49
Blue Cane 11	36N14	90w13	6:00:52
Blue Eye 8	36N29'55	93w23'50	6:13:35
Blue Hill 60	34N52'19	92w20'42	6:09:23
Blue Mountain 42	35N07'49	93w42'41	6:14:51
Blue Ridge 31	34N11	94w02	6:16:08
Blue Springs 26	34N40'25	93w04'22	6:12:17
Bluff City 50	33N43'06	93w08'02	6:12:32
Bluffton 75	34N54'19	93w36'02	6:14:24
Blytheville 47	35N55'38	89w55'08	5:59:41
Blytheville Air Force Base 47	35N57	89w57	5:59:48
Board Camp 57	34N32'16	94w05'43	6:16:23
Boas 38	36N02	90w57	6:03:48
Boat Run 56	35N27'44	90w31'12	6:02:05
Bob Ward 18	35N05	90w20	6:01:20
Bodcaw 50	33N33'30	93w24'25	6:13:38
Boeuf 9	33N11'55	91w22'47	6:05:31
Boggy 46	33N13'29	93w53'12	6:15:33
Bog Springs 57	34N19'46	94w25'44	6:17:43
Bogy 35	34N13	91w45	6:07:00
Bohannon 44	36N05	93w50	6:15:20
Bois d'Arc 29	33N38	93w48	6:15:12
Bolding 70	33N05'01	92w13'45	6:08:55
Boles 64	34N46'46	94w02'56	6:16:12
Bonair 62	34N56'58	90w47'27	6:03:10
Bonanza 66	35N14'21	94w25'33	6:17:42
Bondsville 47	35N38'28	90w14'55	6:01:00
Bonnerdale 30	34N23'05	93w22'54	6:13:32
Bono 16	35N54'31	90w48'09	6:03:13
Bono 23	35N15'22	92w28'34	6:09:54
Booker 18	35N18'26	90w17'22	6:01:09
Booker 60	34N47'46	92w11'46	6:08:47
Boone 5	36N28'25	93w01'15	6:12:05
Booneville 42	35N08'24	93w55'17	6:15:41
Booster 65	35N44'58	92w39'36	6:10:38
Boothe 64	35N02'38	94w07'02	6:16:28
Boston 44	35N50'26	93w36'04	6:14:24
Boswell 10	34N02'39	93w16'45	6:13:07
Boswell 33	36N02'25	92w03'20	6:08:13
Botkinburg 71	35N41'56	92w31'01	6:10:04
Boueff 9	33N07	91w16	6:05:04
Boughton 10	33N51'00	93w19'32	6:13:18
Bovine 2	33N10'42	91w52'54	6:07:32
Bowen 55	33N58'09	93w29'39	6:13:59
Bowman 9	33N27'14	91w18'11	6:05:13
Bowman 13	34N01	92w07	6:08:28
Bowman 16	35N49'23	90w29'33	6:01:58
Boxelder 47	35N56	90w15	6:01:00
Boxley 51	35N58'36	93w24'07	6:13:36
Box Springs 14	33N15'42	93w22'05	6:13:28
Boyd 46	33N20'30	93w55'38	6:15:43
Boydell 2	33N21'56	91w29'28	6:05:58
Boyd Hill 37	33N26'41	93w40'15	6:14:41
Boydsville 11	36N20'03	90w23'01	6:01:32
Boynton 47	35N58'53	90w14'54	6:01:00
Bradford 73	35N25'23	91w27'21	6:05:49
Bradley 37	33N05'53	93w39'17	6:14:37
Bradley Quarters 6	33N37	92w04	6:08:16
Bradshaw 11	36N24	90w21	6:01:24
Brady 60	34N45	92w22	6:09:28
Bragg City 52	33N39'56	92w59'09	6:11:57
Brakebill 61	36N27'28	90w57'47	6:03:51
Branch 24	35N18'20	93w57'12	6:15:49
Branchville 40	33N54'08	91w52'51	6:07:31
Brandon 22	33N43'09	91w55'12	6:07:41
Brandywine Landing 18	35N22'00	90w07'10	6:00:29
Brannon 44	35N49'04	93w56'46	6:15:47
Brasfield 59	34N49'58	91w22'50	6:05:31
Brashears 44	35N50	93w50	6:15:20
Brawley 64	34N51'16	94w18'45	6:17:15
Bredlow Corner 60	34N32'03	92w06'04	6:08:24
Brentwood 72	35N51'36	94w06'25	6:16:26
Brewer 12	35N40'12	92w10'46	6:08:43
Briar 31	34N05'24	93w52'34	6:15:30
Briark 18	35N08'48	90w07'33	6:00:30
Brice 18	35N05'03	90w16'59	6:01:08
Brickeys 39	34N51'38	90w35'32	6:02:22
Bridge Creek 52	33N25	92w52	6:11:28
Bridge Junction 18	35N08'33	90w05'38	6:00:23
Briggsville 75	34N56'02	93w29'39	6:13:59
Brighton 28	36N04'03	90w21'22	6:01:25
Bright Star 31	33N53	93w55	6:15:40
Brightstar 46	33N06'55	93w59'22	6:15:57
Brightwater 4	36N25'04	94w03'24	6:16:14
Brinkley 48	34N53'16	91w11'40	6:04:47
Brister 14	33N08'26	93w11'31	6:12:46
Bristol 23	35N09	92w08	6:08:32
Bristow 61	36N11	90w59	6:03:56
Brittain 60	34N39'25	92w19'21	6:09:17
Broad 6	33N17'34	92w04'27	6:08:18
Brockett 61	36N20'19	90w56'34	6:03:46
Brockington Corner 23	34N58'14	92w17'42	6:09:11
Brockwell 33	36N08'34	91w55'35	6:07:42
Brookings 11	36N17'06	90w43'14	6:02:53
Brookland 16	35N54'00	90w34'55	6:02:20
Brooks 63	34N33'58	92w26'51	6:09:47
Brown 47	35N53	90w10	6:00:40
Brown Ford 25	36N19'55	91w36'05	6:06:24
Browns 18	35N05'35	90w23'13	6:01:33
Brown Springs 30	34N09'25	92w55'14	6:11:41
Brownstown 67	33N49'04	94w04'01	6:16:16
Brownsville 12	35N35'53	92w03'55	6:08:16
Bruins 18	34N52'40	90w20'05	6:01:20
Bruins Landing 18	34N57	90w28	6:01:52
Brumley 23	35N03'45	92w25'33	6:09:42
Brummitt 43	34N32'20	91w39'42	6:06:39
Bruno 45	36N08'39	92w46'41	6:11:07
Brush Creek 27	34N13'04	92w39'12	6:10:37
Brush Creek 72	36N11	93w58	6:15:52
Brushey Lake 56	35N29'09	90w54'48	6:03:39
Brushy 64	34N51	93w52	6:15:28
Brutonville 34	35N37	90w54	6:03:36
Bryant 32	35N44'30	91w39'07	6:06:36
Bryant 63	34N35'45	92w29'20	6:09:57
Brymar 47	35N42	89w58	5:59:52
Buckeye 44	36N06'23	93w54'07	6:15:36
Buckeye 47	35N57'36	90w09'32	6:00:38
Buckhorn 49	34N44'03	91w02'59	6:04:12
Buckner 37	33N21'30	93w26'09	6:13:45
Buck Range 31	33N51'24	93w50'56	6:15:24
Bucks Landing 59	34N52'14	91w27'58	6:05:52
Bucksnort 20	33N50'44	92w28'27	6:09:54
Buckville 26	34N39	93w20	6:13:20
Buddys Landing 49	34N37'27	93w32'35	6:14:10
Buell 66	35N18'11	94w22'54	6:17:32
Buena Vista 52	33N29'14	92w57'18	6:11:49
Buffalo City 3	36N10'04	92w26'31	6:09:46
Buford 3	36N14'44	92w25'42	6:09:43
Buie 27	34N21'07	92w33'50	6:10:15
Bullard 59	35N00	91w39	6:06:36
Bullfrog Valley 58	35N24	93w07	6:12:28
Bull Shoals 45	36N23'02	92w34'53	6:10:20
Bulltown 74	35N08'03	91w10'35	6:04:42
Bunker Hill 53	35N04'11	92w40'07	6:10:40
Bunn 20	34N00'05	92w29'43	6:09:59
Bunney 16	35N43'21	90w23'04	6:01:32
Burdette 47	35N49'02	89w56'21	5:59:45
Burg 31	34N14'13	94w04'12	6:16:17
Burke 41	33N46	94w16	6:17:04
Burks 1	34N18'06	91w24'08	6:05:37
Burlington 5	36N22'46	93w13'41	6:12:55
Burma 66	35N05	94w16	6:17:04
Burnett 58	35N19	92w52	6:11:28
Burnt Cane Crossing 62	34N59'24	90w36'51	6:02:27
Burnt Hill 16	35N52'41	90w30'55	6:02:04
Burnville 66	35N11'19	94w11'20	6:16:45
Burton 47	35N55'15	89w51'20	5:59:25
Burton Mill 37	33N10'26	93w38'06	6:14:32
Burtsell 10	33N57'18	93w17'23	6:13:10
Busch 8	36N27'51	93w49'50	6:15:19
Bussey 14	33N09'20	93w27'22	6:13:49
Butler 47	35N36'42	89w56'19	5:59:45
Butlerville 43	34N58'33	91w50'00	6:07:20
Butterfield 30	34N25'38	92w48'49	6:11:15
Buttermilk 58	35N23'14	92w53'49	6:11:35
Buzzard Roost Landing 3	36N20'59	92w17'31	6:09:10
Byran 64	34N56'07	94w13'30	6:16:54
Byron 25	36N19'21	91w57'27	6:07:50
Cabanal 8	36N16'42	93w31'55	6:14:08
Cabot 43	34N58'28	92w00'59	6:08:04
Cache Lake 11	36N17'44	90w31'59	6:02:08
Caddo Gap 49	34N24'00	93w37'09	6:14:29
Caddo Valley 10	34N10'55	93w04'15	6:12:17
Cades 40	34N00'55	91w35'11	6:06:21
Caglesville 58	35N23'43	92w57'52	6:11:51
Cain 17	35N35'59	94w10'39	6:16:43
Cairo 70	33N13'12	92w52'11	6:11:29
Calamine 68	36N00'41	91w23'56	6:05:36
Caldwell 62	35N04'28	90w49'00	6:03:16
Cale 50	33N37'34	93w14'25	6:12:58
Caledonia 70	33N03'20	92w39'13	6:10:37
Calf Creek 65	35N55	92w49	6:11:16
Calhoun 14	33N13'10	93w09'16	6:12:37
Calhoun 40	33N53'34	91w47'19	6:07:09
Calhoun 59	35N00	91w26	6:05:44
Calhoun Junction 14	33N15'04	93w08'53	6:12:36
Calico Rock 33	36N07'10	92w08'09	6:08:33
Calion 70	33N19'44	92w32'18	6:10:09
Calmer 13	33N56'15	92w01'50	6:08:07
Calumet 47	35N58'54	89w59'10	5:59:57
Calvert 27	34N13	92w25	6:09:40
Calvin 38	35N55'48	91w03'31	6:04:14
Camark 52	33N37'56	92w46'00	6:11:04
Camden 52	33N35'04	92w50'03	6:11:20
Cammack Village 60	34N46'41	92w20'56	6:09:24
Camp 25	36N24'51	91w44'05	6:06:56
Campbell 65	35N52'15	92w28'30	6:09:54
Campbell Station 34	35N40'06	91w14'41	6:04:59
Camp Joseph T Robinson 23	34N45	92w22	6:09:28
Canaan 39	34N51'17	90w47'34	6:03:10
Canaan 65	35N52'01	92w42'12	6:10:49
Canadian 47	35N54	89w47	5:59:08
Canale 37	33N04'00	93w48'50	6:15:15
Cane 73	35N10	91w51	6:07:24
Cane Creek 27	34N26'35	92w21'13	6:09:25
Canehill 72	35N54'31	94w23'47	6:17:35
Caney 23	35N03'40	92w23'04	6:09:32
Caney 30	34N15'25	93w04'32	6:12:18
Caney 45	36N06'18	92w37'46	6:10:31
Caney 50	33N34	93w24	6:13:36
Caney Fork 55	34N13	93w31	6:14:04
Caney Valley 55	34N15'44	93w32'23	6:14:10
Canfield 37	33N10'58	93w37'57	6:14:32
Cannon Creek 44	35N54'17	93w56'24	6:15:46
Canoe Landing 13	33N56'38	92w15'54	6:09:04
Capps 5	36N14'08	93w11'21	6:12:45
Capps City 46	33N01'12	93w58'35	6:15:54
Caraway 16	35N45'29	90w19'20	6:01:17
Carbon City 42	35N17'51	93w47'30	6:15:10
Carden Bottoms 75	35N08'54	93w00'49	6:12:03
Careyville Landing 70	33N15'48	92w18'32	6:09:14
Cargile 70	33N09'26	92w39'06	6:10:36
Cargile 71	35N23	92w18	6:09:12
Carlisle 43	34N46'59	91w44'47	6:06:59
Carlton 9	33N19	91w19	6:05:16
Carmel 6	33N32'41	92w04'17	6:08:17
Carmi 47	35N53'19	90w16'23	6:01:06
Carnis 66	35N14'53	94w12'10	6:16:49
Carolan 42	35N05'37	93w58'45	6:15:55
Caroline 43	34N59	91w58	6:07:52
Carpenter 11	36N28	90w44	6:02:56
Carrol Corner 47	35N43'43	90w10'43	6:00:43
Carroll 52	33N44	92w50	6:11:20
Carroll's Corner 47	35N53	90w10	6:00:40
Carrollton 8	36N15'45	93w19'18	6:13:17
Carryville 11	36N20'32	90w06'14	6:00:25
Carson 47	35N37'58	90w02'36	6:00:10
Carson Lake 47	35N38	90w03	6:00:12
Carter 2	33N14	91w47	6:07:08
Carter Cove Use Area 75	34N59	93w18	6:13:12
Carthage 20	34N04'30	92w33'19	6:10:13
Cartney 3	36N11'40	92w22'56	6:09:32
Carver 27	34N12'59	92w37'06	6:10:28
Carver 51	35N59'10	93w02'30	6:12:10
Cary 16	35N43'12	90w41'17	6:02:45
Casa 53	35N01'22	93w02'51	6:12:11
Case 28	36N12'29	90w45'45	6:03:03
Casey 74	35N02'46	91w11'50	6:04:47
Cash 16	35N47'39	90w56'11	6:03:45
Cass 24	35N41'15	93w49'09	6:15:17
Casscoe 1	34N31'32	91w19'33	6:05:18
Cassidy 56	35N35'00	90w29'01	6:01:56
Caswell 7	33N45	92w32	6:10:08
Catalpa 36	35N41'29	93w31'35	6:14:06
Catcher 17	35N24'27	94w16'35	6:17:06
Catholic Point 15	35N20'39	92w33'10	6:10:13
Cato 23	34N55'42	92w15'40	6:09:03
Catron Spur 54	34N14'14	90w57'06	6:03:48
Caulksville 42	35N18'07	93w51'50	6:15:27
Cauthron 64	34N55'15	94w17'50	6:17:11
Cavanaugh 66	35N18'44	94w25'32	6:17:42
Cave City 68	35N56'30	91w32'54	6:06:12
Cave Creek 51	35N55'45	92w58'45	6:11:55
Cavell 74	35N15'36	91w15'39	6:05:03
Caverna 4	36N29'57	94w16'09	6:17:05
Cave Springs 4	36N15'48	94w13'54	6:16:56
Cazort Springs 36	35N38'34	93w25'11	6:13:41
Cecil 24	35N26'19	93w56'40	6:15:47
Cedar Creek 15	35N19'21	92w32'07	6:10:08
Cedar Creek 64	34N47'07	93w51'59	6:15:28
Cedar Falls 15	35N08	92w55	6:11:40

Place	Latitude	Longitude	Time
Cedar Fourche Landing 26	34N39'27	93w16'45	6:13:07
Cedar Grove 32	35N34'39	91w43'31	6:06:54
Cedar Grove 61	36N16	90w58	6:03:52
Cedarville 17	35N34'11	94w22'00	6:17:28
Center 68	36N08'59	91w30'39	6:06:03
Center Grove 27	34N19'05	92w17'32	6:09:10
Center Hill 28	36N03'35	90w32'38	6:02:11
Center Hill 73	35N15'45	91w53'02	6:07:32
Center Point 10	33N55	93w09	6:12:36
Center Point 31	34N01'35	93w56'51	6:15:47
Center Point 59	34N47	91w34	6:06:16
Center Post 12	35N29	92w12	6:08:48
Center Ridge 10	34N16	93w28	6:13:52
Center Ridge 15	35N22'26	92w33'46	6:10:15
Centerton 4	36N21'35	94w17'06	6:17:08
Center Valley 58	35N19'48	93w05'04	6:12:20
Centerville 23	35N16'23	92w15'23	6:09:02
Centerville 29	33N38'39	93w29'21	6:13:57
Centerville 34	35N48'42	91w13'20	6:04:53
Centerville 75	35N06'46	93w10'07	6:12:40
Central 19	35N15'07	90w56'01	6:03:44
Central 30	34N17'46	92w51'10	6:11:25
Central 67	33N57	94w21	6:17:24
Central Baptist College 23	35N05	92w27	6:09:48
Central City 26	34N30	93w03	6:12:12
Central City 66	35N19'09	94w15'07	6:17:00
Cerrogordo 41	33N55'11	94w28'33	6:17:54
Chalk Bluff 11	36N27	90w12	6:00:48
Chalybeate Springs 69	35N46'49	91w57'29	6:07:50
Chalybeate Springs 75	34N59'12	93w34'20	6:14:17
Chambersville 7	33N44'52	92w25'52	6:09:43
Champagnolle 70	33N18'39	92w31'18	6:10:05
Chance 51	35N45'09	93w08'42	6:12:35
Chandler 26	34N27'49	93w15'49	6:13:03
Chanticleer 9	33N20	91w17	6:05:08
Chapel Hill 67	34N02'03	94w23'46	6:17:35
Charleston 24	35N17'49	94w02'10	6:16:09
Charlotte 32	35N49'06	91w26'19	6:05:45
Chatfield 18	35N00'21	90w23'50	6:01:35
Cheatham 67	34N06'16	94w28'05	6:17:52
Chelford 47	35N31'00	90w14'12	6:00:57
Cherokee City 4	36N17'54	94w34'39	6:18:19
Cherokee Village 68	36N17'52	91w30'57	6:06:04
Cherry Hill 53	34N59'24	92w52'27	6:11:30
Cherry Hill 57	34N35'09	93w59'53	6:16:00
Cherry Valley 19	35N24'07	90w45'11	6:03:01
Chester 17	35N40'51	94w10'30	6:16:42
Chickalah 75	35N09'51	93w16'42	6:13:07
Chickasawba 47	35N56	89w51	5:59:24
Chicot 9	33N12'20	91w17'11	6:05:09
Chicot Terrace 60	34N41	92w21	6:09:24
Chidester 52	33N42'08	93w01'13	6:12:05
Childers 59	34N55'14	91w33'51	6:06:15
Childress 16	35N57'42	90w20'32	6:01:22
Childress 59	34N58	91w30	6:06:00
Chilson 16	35N48	90w56	6:03:44
Chimes 71	35N41'53	92w44'18	6:10:57
Chismville 42	35N13'02	93w56'25	6:15:46
Choctaw 71	35N31'39	92w26'23	6:09:46
Chrisp 73	35N07	91w53	6:07:32
Christian 32	35N36	91w29	6:05:56
Chula 75	34N47'12	93w34'16	6:14:17
Cicalla 62	35N04'27	90w31'43	6:02:07
Cigarette Landing 18	35N18'16	90w06'55	6:00:28
Cincinnati 72	36N02'14	94w30'39	6:18:03
Cisco 8	36N22'33	93w29'38	6:13:59
Claiborne 33	36N06	92w05	6:08:20
Clantonville 4	36N28'53	93w54'32	6:15:38
Clarendon 48	34N41'35	91w18'49	6:05:15
Clarkedale 18	35N18'33	90w14'10	6:00:57
Clarkridge 3	36N28'40	92w21'04	6:09:24
Clarks Corner 62	35N07'24	90w36'43	6:02:27
Clarksville 36	35N28'17	93w27'59	6:13:52
Claude 71	35N28'22	92w36'08	6:10:25
Clay 73	35N23'48	91w47'10	6:07:09
Clear Lake 47	35N51'48	89w52'24	5:59:30
Clear Lake Junction 46	33N31'15	93w55'25	6:15:42
Clear Point 4	36N17'44	94w00'37	6:16:02
Clear Spring 10	34N04'15	93w22'55	6:13:32
Clearwater 47	35N55'24	90w15'25	6:01:02
Cleveland 15	35N25'17	92w42'34	6:10:50
Clifton 23	35N12	92w28	6:09:52
Clifty 44	36N14'14	93w47'46	6:15:11
Clinton 71	35N35'29	92w27'37	6:09:50
Clipper 46	33N34'19	93w51'11	6:15:25
Cloar 18	35N18'35	90w27'28	6:01:50
Clover Bend 38	36N03	90w59	6:03:56
Cloverdale 60	34N40'23	92w21'02	6:09:24
Clow 29	33N53'23	93w46'21	6:15:05
Clyde 72	35N53'29	94w24'23	6:17:38
Coal 64	34N55	94w23	6:17:32
Coaldale 64	34N53'39	94w26'55	6:17:48
Coal Hill 36	35N26'14	93w40'22	6:14:41
Cobbs 43	34N37'42	92w00'32	6:08:02
Cody 39	34N50'38	90w38'23	6:02:34
Coffeeville 34	35N29'28	91w24'01	6:05:36
Coffey 73	35N12	91w58	6:07:52
Coffman 28	36N02'17	90w24'29	6:01:38
Coffman 38	36N03'49	91w04'42	6:04:19
Coin 8	36N19'49	93w20'52	6:13:23
Coldwater 19	35N21'52	90w34'44	6:02:19
Coldwell 73	35N23	91w37	6:06:28
Cole 41	33N39'03	93w59'11	6:15:57
Cole 66	35N12	94w24	6:17:36
Coleman 22	33N46'28	91w44'56	6:07:00
Coler 29	33N34'29	93w35'21	6:14:21
Cole Ridge 47	35N50'34	89w59'57	6:00:00
Cole Spur 40	33N59	91w34	6:06:16
Colfax 3	36N18'39	92w25'22	6:09:41
College City 38	36N07'31	90w56'21	6:03:45
College Heights 22	33N35'25	91w48'02	6:07:12
College Hill 14	33N24'21	93w12'03	6:12:48
Collegeville 63	34N38'12	92w28'31	6:09:54
Collier 28	36N01	90w29	6:01:56
Collietown 32	35N52'11	91w49'51	6:07:19
Collins 22	33N31'53	91w33'55	6:06:16
Colona 74	35N11'30	91w14'08	6:04:57
Colt 62	35N07'53	90w48'40	6:03:15
Colton Crossing 19	35N21'55	90w36'44	6:02:27
Columbia 61	36N22	90w56	6:03:44
Columbus 29	33N46'33	93w49'01	6:15:16
Colville 4	36N15	94w12	6:16:48
Comal 45	36N14'14	92w46'20	6:11:05
Combs 44	35N49'32	93w50'11	6:15:21
Comet 41	33N41'02	94w14'36	6:16:58
Cominto 22	33N32'44	91w37'36	6:06:30
Compton 51	36N05'48	93w18'09	6:13:13
Conant 73	35N09'17	91w40'23	6:06:42
Concord 12	35N39'49	91w50'51	6:07:23
Concord 17	35N28'14	94w15'27	6:17:02
Congo 63	34N39'32	92w35'14	6:10:21
Connells Point 48	34N24'35	91w00'05	6:04:00
Conner 8	36N14'28	93w26'41	6:13:47
Convenience 58	35N20	92w57	6:11:48
Conway 23	35N05'19	92w26'31	6:09:46
Cooleyville 55	34N01'18	93w46'00	6:15:04
Cooney 20	34N07'56	92w31'54	6:10:08
Copeland 71	35N40'17	92w38'11	6:10:33
Copper Mine 4	36N19'52	93w58'07	6:15:52
Cord 32	35N48'43	91w20'36	6:05:22
Corinth 31	34N02'34	93w50'28	6:15:22
Corinth 75	35N04'24	93w25'45	6:13:43
Corley 42	35N12'48	93w38'04	6:14:32
Cornerstone 35	34N13'49	91w44'42	6:06:59
Cornertown 25	36N29'53	91w45'30	6:07:02
Cornerville 40	33N50'39	91w56'25	6:07:46
Cornhill 67	33N53	94w05	6:16:20
Cornie 70	33N04'04	92w43'33	6:10:54
Corning 11	36N24'28	90w34'47	6:02:19
Cosgrove 9	33N18'23	91w23'58	6:05:36
Cotter 3	36N16'16	92w32'07	6:10:08
Cotton Belt 28	36N05'35	90w27'42	6:01:51
Cotton Belt Junction 48	34N48	91w09	6:04:36
Cottondale 35	34N10'49	91w51'37	6:07:26
Cotton Plant 74	35N00'29	91w15'04	6:05:00
Cotton Town 42	35N22'03	93w38'39	6:14:35
Cotton Town 75	35N06'47	93w03'11	6:12:13
Cottonwood Corner 16	35N49'52	90w18'18	6:01:13
Cottonwood Corner 47	35N42'19	90w03'12	6:00:13
Cottonwood Corner 62	35N05'11	90w38'05	6:02:32
Council 39	34N52'20	90w29'22	6:01:57
Countiss 54	34N16'49	90w52'41	6:03:31
County Line 31	33N57	93w56	6:15:44
Cove 57	34N26'06	94w24'40	6:17:39
Cove City 17	35N41	94w21	6:17:24
Cove Creek 72	35N50	94w18	6:17:12
Cowan 45	36N10'31	92w38'46	6:10:35
Cowell 51	35N49'14	93w09'51	6:12:39
Cow Lake 34	35N25	91w05	6:04:20
Cowlingsville 67	33N50'54	94w04'04	6:16:16
Coy 43	34N32'19	91w52'26	6:07:30
Cozahome 65	36N02'42	92w30'05	6:10:00
Crabtree 71	35N37'13	92w34'30	6:10:18
Crafton Landing 23	34N58'28	92w24'27	6:09:38
Craig 71	35N32	92w36	6:10:24
Crain City 70	33N16'03	92w30'26	6:10:02
Craney 6	33N31'10	92w13'28	6:08:54
Cranfield Landing 3	36N24'11	92w19'14	6:09:17
Cravens 24	35N32'54	93w55'00	6:15:40
Crawford 5	36N10'36	92w54'37	6:11:38
Crawfordsville 18	35N13'30	90w19'30	6:01:18
Creech 4	36N13'35	94w02'07	6:16:08
Creigh 48	34N26'44	91w00'02	6:04:00
Crest 5	36N29'00	93w12'19	6:12:49
Creswell 33	36N05'27	92w07'27	6:08:30
Cricket 5	36N26'56	93w12'08	6:12:49
Crigler 40	33N57'32	91w46'09	6:07:05
Crittenden 18	35N14'39	90w27'20	6:01:49
Critten Ridge 41	33N43	94w24	6:17:36
Crockett 11	36N22'33	90w19'50	6:01:19
Crocketts Bluff 1	34N26'38	91w13'12	6:04:53
Croker 33	35N52'58	91w51'41	6:07:27
Crook 22	33N28	91w57	6:07:48
Crosby 73	35N16'55	91w50'00	6:07:20
Cross 8	36N29	93w38	6:14:32
Crosses 44	35N52'27	93w54'40	6:15:39
Crossett 2	33N07'41	91w57'40	6:07:51
Cross Hollow 4	36N16'42	94w06'47	6:16:27
Cross Lanes 17	35N23'24	94w12'21	6:16:49
Crossroad 2	33N13'46	91w55'29	6:07:42
Crossroad 59	34N56'01	91w43'10	6:06:53
Cross Roads 6	33N36'11	92w11'09	6:08:45
Crossroads 12	35N27'53	92w12'55	6:08:52
Cross Roads 27	34N13'29	92w24'21	6:09:37
Crossroads 29	33N43'38	93w43'48	6:14:55
Cross Roads 30	34N22'40	93w23'56	6:13:36
Crossroads 33	36N11'37	92w05'39	6:08:23
Crossroads 34	35N36'55	91w15'35	6:05:02
Cross Roads 41	33N50'07	94w23'20	6:17:33
Cross Roads 44	36N04'31	93w54'30	6:15:38
Cross Roads 48	34N25'38	91w04'10	6:04:17
Cross Roads 52	33N25'15	92w43'08	6:10:53
Crossroads 59	34N58	91w30	6:06:00
Crossroads 66	35N06'43	94w11'53	6:16:48
Crossroads 75	35N11'39	93w29'36	6:13:58
Crow Creek 62	35N01	90w47	6:03:08
Crowley 28	36N12	90w37	6:02:28
Crows 63	34N36'51	92w46'09	6:11:05
Crumrod 54	34N08'55	90w58'54	6:03:56
Crystal Springs 26	34N31'19	93w20'09	6:13:21
Crystal Springs Landing 26	34N32'50	93w21'40	6:13:27
Cullendale 52	33N32'21	92w49'20	6:11:17
Culp 3	36N06'35	92w13'08	6:08:53
Culpepper 71	35N30'58	92w30'59	6:10:04
Cumi 3	36N24'23	92w11'00	6:08:44
Cummings Springs 50	33N45'10	93w11'01	6:12:44
Current River 61	36N19	90w49	6:03:16
Current View 11	36N29'54	90w46'45	6:03:07
Curtis 10	33N59'52	93w06'20	6:12:25
Cushman 32	35N52'22	91w45'14	6:07:01
Cushman Junction 32	35N46'08	91w41'22	6:06:45
Cut Off 46	33N14	93w45	6:15:00
Cypert 54	34N29'24	90w57'22	6:03:49
Cypress Corner 39	34N39'25	90w46'04	6:03:04
Cypress Ridge 48	34N45	91w09	6:04:36
Cypress Valley 15	35N16'15	92w37'48	6:10:31
Dabney 71	35N37'54	92w47'11	6:11:09
Dacus 18	35N08	90w11	6:00:44
Daggett 74	35N02'03	91w19'11	6:05:17
Dagmar 48	34N51'22	91w18'02	6:05:12
Daisy 55	34N14'14	93w44'31	6:14:58
Dalark 20	34N02'14	92w53'09	6:11:33
Dale Place 66	35N06'35	94w17'22	6:17:09
Dallas 7	33N35	92w24	6:09:36
Dallas 57	34N32'09	94w13'08	6:16:53
Dalton 61	36N25'16	91w08'29	6:04:34
Damascus 14	33N15'44	93w01'05	6:12:04
Damascus 23	35N22'02	92w24'34	6:09:38
Danley 23	34N58	92w24	6:09:36
Dansby 39	34N53'39	90w38'25	6:02:34
Danville 75	35N03'14	93w23'36	6:13:34
Darcy 12	35N32	92w06	6:08:24
Dardanelle 75	35N13'23	93w09'28	6:12:38
Darysaw 27	34N13	92w18	6:09:12
Datto 11	36N23'30	90w43'51	6:02:55
Dave 29	33N38'33	93w52'51	6:15:31
Davenport 73	35N26	91w50	6:07:20
Davidson 17	35N42'00	94w28'36	6:17:54
Davis Ford 31	34N14'07	94w00'56	6:16:04
Davis Spur 16	35N43'35	90w32'40	6:02:11
Day 33	36N14'19	91w43'39	6:06:55
Days Creek 46	33N19	94w00	6:16:00
Dayton 66	35N06'51	94w13'35	6:16:54
Dean 8	36N11'31	93w32'01	6:14:08
Deane 22	33N34'13	91w41'49	6:06:47
Deaneyville 29	33N48	93w23	6:13:32
Dean Island Landing 47	35N25'27	90w02'22	6:00:09
De Ann 29	33N46'41	93w33'45	6:14:15
Deans Market 17	35N31'56	94w13'14	6:16:53
Dean Springs 17	35N32'08	94w11'42	6:16:47
Deanyville 29	33N51'43	93w29'57	6:14:00
Dearman 47	35N52'21	90w00'31	6:00:02
De Bastrop 2	33N07	91w31	6:06:04
Deberrie 53	34N56'27	93w00'54	6:12:04
Decatur 4	36N20'09	94w27'38	6:17:51
Deckerville 56	35N26'42	90w18'18	6:01:13
Deep Elm 9	33N29'28	91w23'58	6:05:36
Deep Elm 48	34N32'19	91w10'26	6:04:42
Deep Landing 16	35N44'49	90w25'18	6:01:41
Deer 51	35N49'36	93w12'33	6:12:50
Deerfield 21	34N05'10	90w59'02	6:03:56
Degelow 16	35N44'39	90w21'28	6:01:26
Deglow 16	35N45'05	90w22'34	6:01:30
De Gray 10	34N10'30	93w08'51	6:12:35
Dekalb 27	34N24	92w31	6:10:04
Delaney 44	35N51'08	93w54'00	6:15:36
Delaplaine 28	36N14'01	90w43'35	6:02:54
Delaware 42	35N17'01	93w17'55	6:13:12
Delfore 16	35N55'13	90w17'47	6:01:11
Delight 55	34N01'53	93w30'10	6:14:01
Dell 47	35N51'19	90w02'30	6:00:10
Delmar 8	36N09'38	93w20'27	6:13:22
Delpro 47	35N33'08	90w05'04	6:00:20
Delta 50	33N28'18	93w17'05	6:13:08
Deluce 1	34N12'31	91w14'48	6:04:59
Democrat 62	35N01'13	90w25'30	6:01:42
Demun 61	36N17	90w58	6:03:52
Denmark 34	35N29'03	91w34'59	6:06:20
Dennard 71	35N45'24	92w31'28	6:10:06
Denning 24	35N25'45	93w45'25	6:15:02
Dennison Heights 32	35N44'15	91w38'21	6:06:33
Denny Ford 44	36N12'20	93w52'49	6:15:31
Denton 38	36N05'43	91w12'28	6:04:50
Denton 64	34N53	94w11	6:16:44
Denton Island 16	35N45'19	91w01'48	6:04:07
Denver 8	36N23'33	93w18'53	6:13:16
Denwood 47	35N29'17	90w15'03	6:01:00
Departee 32	35N34	91w25	6:05:40
De Queen 67	34N02'16	94w20'28	6:17:22
Dermott 9	33N31'31	91w26'09	6:05:45
De Roane 29	33N39	93w34	6:14:16
De Roche 30	34N19'40	93w03'24	6:12:14
Des Arc 59	34N58'37	91w29'42	6:05:59
Desha 32	35N44'10	91w40'47	6:06:43
De Soto 45	36N05	92w36	6:10:24
DeSoto Landing 21	33N41'34	91w13'45	6:04:55
Detonti 63	34N29'50	92w30'31	6:10:02
DeValls Bluff 59	34N47'05	91w27'30	6:05:50
DeView 74	35N13'26	91w11'35	6:04:46
Dewey 9	33N28'27	91w14'33	6:04:58
Dewey 73	35N25'16	91w45'29	6:07:02
Dewey Mill 56	35N30'31	90w23'03	6:01:32
De Witt 1	34N17'34	91w20'16	6:05:21
Dexter 35	34N19'00	92w06'30	6:08:26
Dialion 13	33N58	92w11	6:08:44
Diamond 66	35N05	94w17	6:17:08
Diamond Cave 51	35N59'06	93w13'57	6:12:56
Diamond City 5	36N27'52	92w55'12	6:11:41
Diamond Grove 66	35N18'43	94w11'55	6:16:48
Diamondhead 30	34N26'23	92w56'42	6:11:47
Dian 50	33N48	93w23	6:13:32
Diaz 34	35N38'18	91w15'54	6:05:04
Dickerson 36	35N41	93w39	6:14:36
Dickey Junction 51	35N50'15	92w57'16	6:11:49
Dickson 4	36N26	94w20	6:17:20
Dicus 38	36N05'18	90w55'40	6:03:43
Dierks 31	34N07'09	94w00'59	6:16:04
Dill 12	35N34	91w56	6:07:44
Dillard 31	33N54	93w56	6:15:44
Dillen 36	35N42'29	93w11'19	6:12:45
Dills Mills 50	33N40'04	93w12'17	6:12:49
Dilworth 67	33N56'23	94w14'57	6:17:00
Dimple 47	35N28'06	90w15'02	6:01:00
Dinsmore 51	36N06'52	93w28'24	6:13:54
Divide 15	35N02	93w03	6:12:12
Dixie 16	35N55'15	90w27'05	6:01:48
Dixie 18	35N10'23	90w29'21	6:01:57

Dixie 28 36N14'42 90W19'10 6:01:17
Dixie 60 34N45'51 92W13'41 6:08:55
Dixie 74 35N04'36 91W21'47 6:05:27
Dixon 48 34N52 91W08 6:04:32
Dobbs Landing 48 34N45'19 91W18'21 6:05:13
Dobell 56 35N40'58 90W30'43 6:02:03
Dobson 56 35N41 91W00 6:04:00
Dobyville 10 34N00'43 93W15'14 6:13:01
Dodd City 45 36N19'38 92W47'34 6:11:10
Doddridge 46 33N05'30 93W54'29 6:15:38
Dodge City 70 33N01'10 92W58'06 6:11:52
Dodson 14 33N14'30 93W20'46 6:13:23
Dodsons Corner 62 35N01 90W47 6:03:08
Dogpatch 51 36N06'35 93W08'05 6:12:32
Dogwood 27 34N14'12 92W31'35 6:10:06
Dogwood 47 35N53'32 89W55'07 5:59:40
Dogwood 73 35N06 91W36 6:06:24
Dollar Junction 70
33N04'12 92W11'16 6:08:45
Dollarway 35 34N13 92W02 6:08:08
Dolph 33 36N13'42 92W06'45 6:08:27
Donald 24 35N19 93W56 6:15:44
Donaldson 30 34N14'12 92W55'24 6:11:42
Dongola 65 35N54'31 92W45'30 6:11:02
Doniphan 73 35N14'52 91W40'10 6:06:41
Donnick 56 35N38'45 90W26'46 6:01:47
Dooley 46 33N28'07 93W51'26 6:15:26
Dora 17 35N27'15 94W26'26 6:17:46
Dorothy 16 35N54'31 90W49'09 6:03:17
Dortch 43 34N43 92W03 6:08:12
Dota 32 35N47'40 91W22'40 6:05:31
Dotson 29 33N55'21 93W35'54 6:14:24
Douglas 40 34N02'31 91W32'04 6:06:08
Dover 58 35N24'05 93W06'51 6:12:27
Dowdy 32 35N51'06 91W18'15 6:05:13
Dowell 38 35N56 90W57 6:03:48
Doylestown 35 34N16'12 92W12'13 6:08:49
Drakes Creek 44 36N01'14 93W51'35 6:15:26
Drasco 12 35N37'53 91W56'49 6:07:47
Driftwood 38 35N58'16 91W15'07 6:05:00
Driggs 42 35N14'11 93W46'20 6:15:05
Dripping Springs 17
35N31'59 94W23'53 6:17:36
Driver 47 35N36'44 90W00'43 6:00:03
Dryden 16 35N50'03 90W54'32 6:03:38
Dryfork 8 36N09'12 93W29'20 6:13:57
Dry Run 20 33N49 92W22 6:09:28
Drytown 33 35N58 91W48 6:07:12
Dub 56 35N31'20 90W21'27 6:01:26
Dublin 42 35N21'43 93W28'16 6:13:53
Duckett 31 34N17 94W13 6:16:52
Duckett Ford 31 34N15'47 94W11'36 6:16:46
Dudley Lake 35 34N27 91W52 6:07:28
Duff 65 36N00'02 92W45'45 6:11:03
Dugger 5 36N07'33 92W55'03 6:11:40
Dumas 21 33N53'13 91W29'30 6:05:58
Dumas City 70 33N15'32 92W45'18 6:11:01
Duncan 48 34N37'15 91W15'04 6:05:00
Dunlap 29 33N51'09 93W32'20 6:14:09
Dunn 61 36N14'26 91W06'20 6:04:25
Dunnington 32 35N37'31 91W25'43 6:05:43
Dunnington 35 34N22 91W47 6:07:08
Durham 72 35N56'58 93W58'49 6:15:55
Durian 30 34N23 92W49 6:11:16
Dutch Creek 75 35N00 93W39 6:14:36
Dutch Mills 72 35N52'32 94W29'29 6:17:58
Dutton 44 35N49'00 93W41'37 6:14:46
Duty 38 36N04 91W04 6:04:16
Duvall 19 35N12'30 90W33'36 6:02:14
Dyer 17 35N29'32 94W08'15 6:16:33
Dyess 47 35N35'23 90W12'48 6:00:51
Eagle Mills 52 33N40'57 92W42'16 6:10:49
Eagletie 20 33N52'57 92W36'27 6:10:26
Eagleton 57 34N40'49 94W18'00 6:17:12
Earle 18 35N16'30 90W28'00 6:01:52
Earl Prairie 42 35N06'36 93W59'31 6:15:58
Earnheart 32 35N44'50 91W46'05 6:07:04
East Black Oak 18 35N29 90W21 6:01:24
East Camden 52 33N36'28 92W44'24 6:10:58
East End 63 34N33'02 92W20'27 6:09:22
East Fork 23 35N11 92W23 6:09:32
East Pocahontas 61
36N16 90W58 6:03:52
Eastport 41 33N47'19 94W28'53 6:17:56
East Richwood 69 35N50'45 92W08'04 6:08:32
East Richwoods 69 35N52 92W07 6:08:28
East Sullivan 68 35N59 91W36 6:06:24
Eastview 47 35N43'11 90W07'35 6:00:30
East Wilson 47 35N36 90W03 6:00:12
Eaton 38 36N02'24 91W12'58 6:04:52
Ebenezer 14 33N18'03 93W03'30 6:12:14
Ebony 18 35N11'51 90W15'41 6:01:03
Echo 42 35N05'50 94W08'05 6:16:32
Economy 58 35N18'00 92W53'34 6:11:34
Ecore Fabre 52 33N34 92W53 6:11:32
Eden 48 34N51'49 91W16'28 6:05:06
Eden Isle 12 35N32 92W06 6:08:24
Edgemont 12 35N36'08 92W11'46 6:08:47
Edmondson 18 35N06'23 90W18'37 6:01:14
Edmonson 32 35N53'28 91W48'58 6:07:16
Edna 36 35N33'17 93W37'55 6:14:32
Edwards 59 35N01'24 91W47'50 6:07:11
Edwards Junction 51
35N50'54 93W21'40 6:13:27
Edwards Landing 23
34N57'52 92W24'42 6:09:39
Efay 72 36N04 94W09 6:16:36
Eglantine 71 35N34'46 92W18'22 6:09:13
Egypt 16 35N52'05 90W56'44 6:03:47
Elaine 54 34N18'30 90W51'07 6:03:24
Elba 71 35N46'08 92W26'45 6:09:47
Elberta 65 35N51'00 92W30'07 6:10:00
Elberta 75 35N10'49 93W09'25 6:12:38
El Dorado 70 33N12'27 92W39'58 6:10:40
Eldridge Corner 1 34N17'50 91W28'25 6:05:54
Eleven Points 61 36N22 91W04 6:04:16
Elgin 34 35N45'50 91W17'33 6:05:10
Elixir 5 36N20 93W01 6:12:04
Elizabeth 25 36N19'53 92W05'45 6:08:23
Elkhorn Tavern 4 36N27'13 94W00'56 6:16:04
Elkins 72 36N00'05 94W00'29 6:16:02
Elkins Park 61 36N24'35 90W53'57 6:03:36
Elk Ranch 8 36N24 93W44 6:14:56
Elliott 52 33N27'26 92W49'40 6:11:19
Ellis 3 36N14'43 92W15'54 6:09:04
Ellis 19 35N13 90W56 6:03:44
Ellis Chapel 19 35N11'35 90W53'58 6:03:36
Ellison 35 34N20'37 91W54'07 6:07:36
Ellsworth 42 35N17 93W33 6:14:12
Elm 10 34N16 93W28 6:13:52
Elm Grove 16 35N43'44 90W29'03 6:01:56
Elmo 32 35N37'15 91W23'30 6:05:34
Elm Park 64 35N01'17 94W07'08 6:16:29
Elm Springs 72 36N12'22 94W14'03 6:16:56
Elm Store 61 36N28'51 91W11'14 6:04:45
Elmwood 5 36N08'39 93W06'19 6:12:25
Elmwood 9 33N27'55 91W16'59 6:05:08
Elmwood 35 34N13'42 91W43'14 6:06:53
Elnora 61 36N10'20 90W57'47 6:03:51
Elon 2 33N03 91W54 6:07:36
El Paso 73 35N07'34 92W05'43 6:08:23
Emanuel 1 34N24'03 91W19'21 6:05:17
Emerson 14 33N05'51 93W11'34 6:12:46
Eminence 9 33N13'39 91W11'21 6:04:45
Emmet 50 33N43'34 93W28'13 6:13:53
Emmons 48 34N48'31 91W09'18 6:04:37
Emon 14 33N21'16 93W14'16 6:12:57
Empire 9 33N07'19 91W26'07 6:05:44
Enders 23 35N19'36 92W13'42 6:08:55
Engelberg 61 36N20'16 90W54'33 6:03:38
England 43 34N32'39 91W58'08 6:07:53
England Junction 35
34N45 92W21 6:09:24
English 35 34N10'36 91W39'18 6:06:37
English Place 35 34N23'27 92W11'03 6:08:44
Enola 23 35N11'43 92W12'11 6:08:49
Enon 22 33N35'18 91W40'40 6:06:43
Enright 73 35N09'16 91W30'08 6:06:01
Enterprise 66 35N15'56 94W25'44 6:17:43
Erbie 51 36N05'01 93W13'59 6:12:56
Eros 45 36N11'00 92W51'02 6:11:24
Erwin 34 35N33'43 91W13'33 6:04:54
Erwin 59 34N58 91W30 6:06:00
Esculapia 4 36N21 94W06 6:16:24
Estes 60 34N33 91W53 6:07:32
Estico 34 35N37'23 91W06'48 6:04:27
Ethel 1 34N17'11 91W09'49 6:04:39
Etna 24 35N29 93W50 6:15:20
Etowah 47 35N43'44 90W13'56 6:00:56
Euclid 31 34N10'25 94W01'06 6:16:04
Euclid Heights 26 34N30'09 93W01'42 6:12:07
Eudora 9 33N06'34 91W15'43 6:05:03
Eula 65 35N54'08 92W53'45 6:11:35
Eureka Springs 8 36N24'04 93W44'16 6:14:57
Evadale 47 35N33'04 90W06'22 6:00:25
Evansville 72 35N47'43 94W29'48 6:17:59
Evelyn Hills 72 36N04 94W09 6:16:36
Evening Shade 68 36N04'18 91W37'09 6:06:29
Evening Star 28 36N14 90W43 6:02:52
Everton 5 36N09'19 92W54'24 6:11:38
Ewal 54 34N21'54 90W49'52 6:03:19
Ewing 5 36N09 93W03 6:12:12
Excelsior 66 35N12'00 94W18'51 6:17:15
Experiment 14 33N12'09 93W27'57 6:13:52
Extra 2 33N06 91W45 6:07:00
Faber 30 34N10'06 92W56'10 6:11:45
Fairbanks 71 35N26'40 92W16'19 6:09:05
Fair Field 19 35N19'37 90W49'33 6:03:18
Fairfield 35 34N12'45 91W53'42 6:07:35
Fairfield 60 34N41 92W21 6:09:24
Fairfield Bay 71 35N35'39 92W16'40 6:09:07
Fairindale 20 34N04 92W33 6:10:12
Fair Landing 54 34N15'24 90W50'22 6:03:21
Fairman 60 34N46'44 92W12'43 6:08:51
Fairmount 59 34N35'44 91W35'56 6:06:24
Fair Oaks 19 35N14'36 91W01'52 6:04:07
Fairplay 63 34N30 92W42 6:10:48
Fairview 9 33N17'01 91W15'38 6:05:03
Fairview 20 33N58'23 92W52'46 6:11:31
Fairview 25 36N18'35 91W49'41 6:07:19
Fairview 45 36N20'00 92W36'16 6:10:25
Fairview 52 33N32'11 92W50'16 6:11:21
Fairview 60 34N42'08 92W16'37 6:09:06
Fairview 65 35N56'43 92W29'13 6:09:57
Fairview 67 34N10 94W19 6:17:16
Faith 35 34N06'13 92W06'12 6:08:25
Falcon 50 33N27'52 93W24'48 6:13:39
Falls Chapel 67 33N53 94W05 6:16:20
Fallsville 51 35N46'35 93W27'55 6:13:52
Fancy Hill 49 34N24 93W37 6:14:28
Fannie 49 34N41'58 93W26'58 6:13:48
Farelly Lake 35 34N06'17 91W31'50 6:06:07
Farewell 8 36N23'32 93W22'10 6:13:29
Fargo 48 34N57'05 91W10'48 6:04:43
Farindale 20 34N05'34 92W24'30 6:09:38
Farmington 72 36N02'31 94W14'49 6:16:59
Farmville 6 33N30'56 92W11'25 6:08:46
Farris 69 35N57 92W22 6:09:28
Farris Springs 36 35N38'41 93W27'48 6:13:51
Faulknerville 28 36N10 90W37 6:02:28
Fayette 7 33N21 92W27 6:09:48
Fayette Junction 72
36N02'30 94W10'49 6:16:43
Fayetteville 72 36N03'45 94W09'26 6:16:38
Feenyville 40 33N58'38 91W54'33 6:07:38
Felce 18 35N13'50 90W23'57 6:01:36
Felker 4 36N14 94W28 6:17:52
Felsenthal 70 33N03'34 92W09'24 6:08:38
Felton 39 34N48'15 90W47'46 6:03:11
Fender 61 36N10'30 90W53'45 6:03:35
Fendley 10 34N13'56 93W20'00 6:13:20
Fenter 27 34N22'36 92W38'15 6:10:33
Ferda 35 34N27'32 91W57'16 6:07:49
Ferguson 54 34N08'17 90W59'02 6:03:56
Ferguson 75 35N07 93W26 6:13:44
Ferguson Crossroads 46
33N19'58 93W57'11 6:15:49
Ferguson Landing 54
34N07'39 90W57'50 6:03:51
Fern 24 35N38'20 94W00'58 6:16:04
Ferndale 60 34N46'44 92W33'27 6:10:14
Fiftysix 69 35N57'27 92W13'06 6:08:52
Figure Five 17 35N31'01 94W21'13 6:17:25
Finch 28 36N04 90W32 6:02:08
Fir 49 34N37 93W28 6:13:52
Fisher 16 35N46'50 90W58'49 6:03:55
Fisher 56 35N29'29 90W58'27 6:03:54
Fitzgerald 34 35N39'09 91W17'19 6:05:09
Fitzgerald Crossing 19
35N10'43 90W48'12 6:03:13
Fitzhugh 74 35N21'29 91W19'22 6:05:17
Fivemile 12 35N40'25 91W57'34 6:07:50
Flag 69 35N49'09 92W23'39 6:09:35
Flag Lake Crossing 19
35N13'25 90W38'35 6:02:34
Flat 51 35N57'34 92W59'09 6:11:57
Flat Creek 38 36N06 91W13 6:04:52
Flat Rock 36 35N20 93W15 6:13:00
Flatwoods 51 36N00'26 93W08'04 6:12:32
Fleener 39 34N52 91W01 6:04:04
Flint 4 36N16 94W25 6:17:40
Flippin 45 36N16'44 92W35'49 6:10:23
Floodway 47 35N53 90W10 6:00:40
Floral 32 35N35'14 91W45'25 6:07:02
Florence 22 33N45'56 91W38'44 6:06:35
Floss 72 35N47'42 94W21'39 6:17:27
Floyd 73 35N11'41 91W58'03 6:07:52
Fogel 57 34N42'25 94W27'15 6:17:49
Fogleman 18 35N24 90W15 6:01:00
Fomby 41 33N41 94W08 6:16:32
Fontaine 28 36N00'02 90W48'48 6:03:15
Fordyce 20 33N48'49 92W24'46 6:09:39
Foreman (New Rocky Comfort) 41
33N43'18 94W23'48 6:17:35
Forest Grove 14 33N02'32 93W09'52 6:12:39
Forest Park 60 34N46 92W23 6:09:32
Formosa 71 35N27'47 92W30'36 6:10:02
Forrest Bonner 20 33N50'21 92W32'40 6:10:11
Forrest City 62 35N00'29 90W47'23 6:03:10
Fort Chaffee 66 35N18'44 94W18'21 6:17:13
Fort Douglas 36 35N41'03 93W14'30 6:12:58
Fort Lynn 46 33N09'54 93W53'02 6:15:32
Fort Smith 66 35N23'09 94W23'54 6:17:36
Forty Four 33 36N08'37 92W03'39 6:08:15
Forum 44 36N10'54 93W42'53 6:14:52
Foster 61 36N21 90W59 6:03:56
Foster Hill 70 33N07'23 92W43'34 6:10:54
Fouke 46 33N15'40 93W53'07 6:15:32
Fountain Hill 2 33N21'28 91W51'01 6:07:24
Fountain Lake 30 34N34'22 92W59'15 6:11:57
Fountain Prairie 2
33N14 91W48 6:07:12
Fourche 53 34N59'38 92W37'15 6:10:29
Fourche Junction 53
34N57'23 93W09'25 6:12:38
Fourche Lafave 53 35N00 92W49 6:11:16
Four Forks 39 34N46 90W46 6:03:04
Four Forks 74 35N03'44 91W14'20 6:04:57
Four Gums 62 35N00'50 91W00'47 6:04:03
Fourmile Corner 59
34N58'42 91W33'49 6:06:15
Fourmile Hill 73 35N17'26 91W46'13 6:07:05
Fowler 75 35N08'54 93W01'12 6:12:05
Fox 69 35N47'29 92W17'51 6:09:11
Fox Hill 66 35N05'45 94W17'28 6:17:10
Francis 5 36N14 93W04 6:12:16
Francis 12 35N35 92W04 6:08:16
Francure 73 35N09 91W29 6:05:56
Franklin 33 36N10'13 91W46'33 6:07:06
Freck 45 36N06'26 92W42'00 6:10:48
Fredonia 59 34N49 91W24 6:05:36
Freedom 57 34N38 94W23 6:17:32
Free Hope 14 33N17'30 93W09'50 6:12:39
Freeo 52 33N46 92W41 6:10:44
French 25 36N21'38 91W41'36 6:06:46
French 37 33N04 93W33 6:14:12
Frenchmans Bayou 47
35N27'58 90W10'51 6:00:43
Frenchport 52 33N28'16 92W46'40 6:11:07
Frenchport Landing 52
33N29'00 92W45'14 6:11:01
Fresno 40 33N57'47 91W42'25 6:06:50
Friendship 13 33N58'37 92W02'36 6:08:10
Friendship 14 33N22 93W30 6:14:00
Friendship 15 35N22'31 92W30'29 6:10:02
Friendship 30 34N13'23 93W00'10 6:12:01
Friley 36 35N43'45 93W37'40 6:14:31
Frisco 4 36N15'23 94W04'41 6:16:19
Frisco Junction 47
35N56 90W15 6:01:00
Fritz 28 36N11'09 90W17'07 6:01:08
Frog Town 66 35N02'23 94W21'15 6:17:25
Fryatt 25 36N27'49 91W39'04 6:06:36
Frys Mill 56 35N32'54 90W20'05 6:01:20
Fulton 29 33N36'52 93W48'48 6:15:15
Funston 23 35N03'26 92W11'13 6:08:45
Furlow 43 34N49'59 91W58'49 6:07:55
Furry 17 35N28'50 94W18'08 6:17:13
Gainesboro 32 35N46 91W37 6:06:28
Gaines Landing 9 33N27'34 91W13'45 6:04:55
Gainesville 28 36N09'53 90W30'38 6:02:03
Gainsboro 32 35N47'48 91W31'53 6:06:08
Gaither 5 36N08'37 93W10'00 6:12:40
Galena 31 34N15'05 94W06'46 6:16:27
Galet 18 35N06'55 90W12'47 6:00:51
Galilee 18 35N26'10 90W23'06 6:01:32
Galla Creek 58 35N14 93W03 6:12:12
Galla Rock 58 35N10'40 92W58'10 6:11:53
Gallatin 4 36N12'22 94W25'37 6:17:42
Galloway 60 34N46'47 92W07'43 6:08:31
Gamaliel 3 36N27'24 92W13'59 6:08:56
Gamaliel Landing 3
36N25'19 92W13'25 6:08:54
Gammon 18 35N14'53 90W09'09 6:00:37
Gap 49 34N25 93W37 6:14:28
Gap Springs 57 34N27 94W07 6:16:28
Garber 36 35N39'54 93W22'03 6:13:28
Garden 74 35N05 91W23 6:05:32
Gardner 70 33N06'22 92W22'51 6:09:31
Garfield 4 36N26'54 93W58'26 6:15:54
Garland 46 33N22 93W43 6:14:52
Garland City Station 46
33N21'46 93W42'35 6:14:50
Garland Springs 23
35N13'39 92W09'10 6:08:37
Garlandville 29 33N48'42 93W29'04 6:13:56
Garner 73 35N08'29 91W47'10 6:07:09
Garnett 40 33N50'39 91W46'39 6:07:07
Garret Grove 39 34N48 91W00 6:04:00

Place	Latitude	Longitude	Time
Garrett 36	35N24'20	93w21'34	6:13:26
Garrett Bridge 40	33N52'01	91w39'18	6:06:37
Garrett Grove 39	34N48'02	91w04'58	6:04:20
Garson 47	35N58'26	90w13'39	6:00:55
Gassett 39	34N52'26	90w33'44	6:02:15
Gassville 3	36N16'59	92w29'38	6:09:59
Gaston 49	34N33	93w46	6:15:04
Gateway 4	36N29'25	93w55'54	6:15:44
Gaulett 56	35N39'01	90w42'36	6:02:50
Gavin 18	35N11'27	90w13'11	6:00:53
Gayler 69	35N55'38	92w10'12	6:08:41
Gaylor 69	35N52	92w07	6:08:28
Geneva 67	34N01'15	94w14'31	6:16:58
Genevia 60	34N42'29	92w13'16	6:08:53
Genoa 46	33N23'01	93w54'34	6:15:38
Gentry 4	36N16'03	94w29'04	6:17:56
Gentry Corner 23	34N57'27	92w17'27	6:09:10
George 51	36N04'47	93w24'01	6:13:36
Georges Creek 45	36N15'03	92w45'41	6:11:03
Georgetown 44	35N59'44	93w49'52	6:15:19
Georgetown 58	35N20'00	93w16'33	6:13:06
Georgetown 73	35N07'37	91w27'18	6:05:49
Georgia 50	33N41	93w16	6:13:04
Gepp 25	36N23'16	92w06'15	6:08:25
Geridge 43	34N32'24	91w42'22	6:06:49
Gernada Chapel 24	35N29	93w50	6:15:20
Gertrude 46	33N24'32	93w58'42	6:15:55
Gethsemane 35	34N25'00	91w52'02	6:07:28
Geyer Springs 60	34N42'05	92w20'06	6:09:20
Gibbs 49	34N40	93w41	6:14:44
Gibson 16	35N46'37	90w48'56	6:03:16
Gibson 60	34N53'03	92w14'08	6:08:57
Gid 33	35N58'47	91w51'23	6:07:26
Gieseck 19	35N10'48	90w33'37	6:02:14
Gifford 30	34N22'32	92w44'39	6:10:59
Gilbert 65	35N59'16	92w42'58	6:10:52
Gilchrist 47	35N45	89w56	5:59:44
Giles 12	35N35	92w08	6:08:32
Giles Spur 38	36N06	90w57	6:03:48
Gilkerson 16	35N48'14	90w48'23	6:03:14
Gilkey 75	34N59	93w21	6:13:24
Gill 39	34N52'39	90w54'27	6:03:38
Gillam Park 60	34N42'24	92w15'21	6:09:01
Gillett 1	34N07'02	91w22'35	6:05:30
Gillham 67	34N10'09	94w18'58	6:17:16
Gillian Settlement 36	35N37'54	93w24'06	6:13:36
Gilmore 18	35N24'42	90w16'42	6:01:07
Gin City 37	33N06'25	93w43'22	6:14:53
Gipson 64	34N53'54	94w23'13	6:17:33
Gladden 19	35N16	90w28	6:01:52
Glade 4	36N22'05	93w54'50	6:15:39
Glaize 34	35N29	91w25	6:05:40
Glass 34	35N51	91w07	6:04:28
Gleason 23	35N06'39	92w30'57	6:10:04
Gleghorn 11	36N23	90w31	6:02:04
Glencoe 25	36N17'39	91w44'50	6:06:59
Glendale 40	33N57'46	91w57'33	6:07:50
Glenlake 35	34N11'36	91w53'21	6:07:33
Glen Rose 30	34N27'20	92w43'46	6:10:55
Glenville 50	33N29'29	93w11'44	6:12:47
Glenwood 55	34N19'36	93w33'02	6:14:12
Gobbler 8	36N11'19	93w27'22	6:13:49
Gobblers Point 15	35N25'22	92w46'43	6:11:07
Godfrey Log 6	33N14'32	92w05'18	6:08:21
Gold Creek 23	35N00'43	92w24'50	6:09:39
Golden City 42	35N03'33	93w55'33	6:15:42
Golden Lake 47	35N32'45	90w02'44	6:00:11
Gold Lake Estates 23	35N05	92w27	6:09:48
Goldman 1	34N27'17	91w36'15	6:06:25
Goobertown 16	35N57'05	90w34'32	6:02:18
Good Hope 52	33N38'38	93w03'35	6:12:14
Goodman 63	34N33'37	92w28'12	6:09:53
Goodrich 74	35N19'54	91w13'49	6:04:55
Goodrum 43	34N53	92w00	6:08:00
Goodwin 62	34N56'17	91w01'15	6:04:05
Goose Camp 36	35N26	93w37	6:14:28
Gorby 33	36N06'07	92w04'33	6:08:18
Goshen 72	36N06'04	93w59'28	6:15:58
Gosnell 47	35N57'35	89w58'19	5:59:53
Gospoda 59	34N53'19	91w29'42	6:05:59
Gould 40	33N59'06	91w33'39	6:06:15
Gourd 40	33N50'37	91w35'48	6:06:23
Grady 40	34N04'48	91w42'02	6:06:48
Grandfield 55	34N13'06	93w54'42	6:15:39
Grand Glaise 34	35N28'30	91w24'35	6:05:38
Grand Lake 9	33N05'32	91w12'38	6:04:51
Grandview 8	36N26'02	93w37'16	6:14:29
Grandview 15	35N21'11	92w35'50	6:10:23
Grange 68	35N56	91w33	6:06:12
Grannis 57	34N14'26	94w20'05	6:17:20
Grants 37	33N09'22	93w39'26	6:14:38
Grapevine 27	34N08'44	92w18'55	6:09:16
Graphic 17	35N34'24	94w08'36	6:16:34
Grassy 12	35N39	91w50	6:07:20
Grassy Lake 18	35N16	90w28	6:01:52
Grassy Lake Bottom 18	35N16'05	90w23'45	6:01:35
Gravel Hill 71	35N28'49	92w38'14	6:10:33
Gravel Hill 73	35N15'43	91w58'38	6:07:55
Gravel Junction 10	34N02'43	92w56'33	6:11:46
Gravelly 75	34N52'59	93w41'14	6:14:45
Gravelridge 6	33N26'47	92w13'08	6:08:53
Gravel Ridge 60	34N52'06	92w11'26	6:08:46
Graves Chapel 67	33N53	94w05	6:16:20
Gravesville 71	35N23'21	92w20'52	6:09:23
Gravette 4	36N25'19	94w27'12	6:17:49
Gray Rock 42	35N20'24	93w44'40	6:14:59
Grays 74	35N13'35	91w14'02	6:04:56
Grayson 42	35N03'20	93w52'10	6:15:29
Graysonia 10	34N07'37	93w26'23	6:13:46
Greasy Corner 62	35N00'26	90w26'54	6:01:48
Greenbrier 23	35N14'02	92w23'15	6:09:33
Greene High 28	36N04	90w32	6:02:08
Greenfield 56	35N37'56	90w42'45	6:02:51
Green Forest 8	36N20'07	93w26'09	6:13:45
Green Hill 22	33N33'53	91w53'52	6:07:35
Greenland 72	35N59'39	94w10'30	6:16:42
Greenway 11	36N20'28	90w13'13	6:00:53
Greenwood 24	35N24'28	93w46'16	6:15:05
Greenwood 66	35N12'56	94w15'20	6:17:01
Greenwood Junction 17	35N26'53	94w26'23	6:17:46
Greer Place 39	34N45'10	90w40'21	6:02:41
Greers Ferry 12	35N34	92w11	6:08:44
Gregory 74	35N09'19	91w20'35	6:05:22
Grider 47	35N38'19	89w58'50	5:59:55
Griffin 15	35N24	92w49	6:11:16
Griffith Spring 40	33N56	91w50	6:07:20
Griffithtown 10	34N03'17	92w57'34	6:11:50
Griffithville 73	35N07'25	91w38'42	6:06:35
Grove 51	36N05	92w58	6:11:52
Grubbs 34	35N38'59	91w04'26	6:04:18
Grubb Springs 5	36N12'54	93w09'16	6:12:37
Guernsey 29	33N42	93w35	6:14:20
Guion 33	35N55'31	91w56'26	6:07:46
Gulledge 2	33N04'15	91w52'16	6:07:29
Gum Grove 50	33N42'08	93w10'45	6:12:43
Gum Log 58	35N17	92w59	6:11:56
Gum Point 16	35N46'45	90w32'07	6:02:08
Gum Pond 1	34N32	91w32	6:06:08
Gum Springs 10	34N04'02	93w05'30	6:12:22
Gum Springs 13	33N58'43	92w16'26	6:09:06
Gum Springs 60	34N41'57	92w19'32	6:09:18
Gum Tree 75	35N11'12	93w27'10	6:13:49
Gum Woods 43	34N32	91w58	6:07:52
Gurdon 10	33N55'15	93w09'14	6:12:37
Guy 23	35N19'31	92w20'03	6:09:20
Habberton 72	36N06'54	94w03'05	6:16:12
Hackett 66	35N11'25	94w24'39	6:17:39
Hadley 37	33N22	93w26	6:13:44
Hagarville 36	35N30'56	93w19'29	6:13:18
Hagler 1	34N15'15	91w31'41	6:06:07
Haig 60	34N49'08	92w18'59	6:09:16
Hale 26	34N35	93w10	6:12:40
Haleside 39	34N43'04	90w39'19	6:02:37
Half Moon 47	35N54'43	90w00'52	6:00:03
Half Moon Lake 47	35N55	90w01	6:00:04
Halfway 10	34N05'05	93w19'18	6:13:17
Halley 21	33N32'08	91w19'29	6:05:18
Halley Junction 9	33N31'58	91w22'31	6:05:30
Halliday 28	36N07'17	90w26'03	6:01:44
Hallsville 59	34N49'00	91w29'43	6:05:59
Halstead 60	34N45	92w22	6:09:28
Hamburg 2	33N13'41	91w47'51	6:07:11
Hamil 61	36N24'11	91w03'55	6:04:16
Hamilton 26	34N42'17	93w07'59	6:12:32
Hamilton 43	34N37'19	91w43'09	6:06:53
Hamiter 43	34N39'44	92w04'02	6:08:16
Hamlet 23	35N04'41	92w18'18	6:09:13
Hamlin 19	35N14'06	90w55'39	6:03:43
Hammons 46	33N05'44	94w02'29	6:16:10
Hammonsville 73	35N14	92w07	6:08:28
Hampton 7	33N32'16	92w28'11	6:09:53
Hancock 16	35N48'05	90w17'46	6:01:11
Hancock Junction 16	35N46'50	90w18'17	6:01:13
Hand 3	36N20	92w06	6:08:24
Hand Landing 3	36N17'10	92w12'13	6:08:49
Hand Valley 45	36N12'18	92w29'40	6:09:59
Hannaberry 35	34N07'21	91w33'32	6:06:14
Hanover 18	35N15'00	90w23'19	6:01:33
Hanover 69	35N48'12	92w07'25	6:08:30
Happy 73	35N09'55	91w38'39	6:06:35
Happy Bend 58	35N15'50	92w52'02	6:11:28
Happy Corners 47	35N56	90w15	6:01:00
Hardin 23	35N14	92w21	6:09:24
Hardin 35	34N16'52	92w09'00	6:08:36
Hardy 68	36N18'57	91w28'57	6:05:56
Haretown 10	34N01'15	93w22'27	6:13:30
Hargrave Corner 11	36N15'33	90w13'45	6:00:55
Hargraves Junction 11	36N16	90w18	6:01:12
Harlow 7	33N44'53	92w34'01	6:10:16
Harmon 5	36N12'47	92w55'16	6:11:41
Harmon 72	36N09'13	94w16'37	6:17:06
Harmontown 32	35N45'40	91w48'50	6:07:15
Harmony 5	36N14	93w04	6:12:16
Harmony 6	33N37	92w04	6:08:16
Harmony 14	33N08'33	93w21'18	6:13:25
Harmony 36	35N32'53	93w33'20	6:14:13
Harmony 44	36N06'29	93w42'44	6:14:51
Harmony 50	33N39'15	93w23'56	6:13:36
Harmony 73	35N14'15	91w54'24	6:07:38
Harmony Grove 52	33N39'07	92w46'51	6:11:07
Harness 69	35N50'35	92w24'19	6:09:37
Haroldton 17	35N21'44	94w15'36	6:17:02
Harp 30	34N19'36	92w47'19	6:11:09
Harper 13	33N49	92w02	6:08:08
Harrell 7	33N30'36	92w23'55	6:09:36
Harriet 65	35N59'36	92w31'13	6:10:05
Harris 69	35N57	92w09	6:08:36
Harris 72	36N01'52	94w02'51	6:16:11
Harrisburg 56	35N33'51	90w43'00	6:02:52
Harrison 5	36N13'47	93w06'27	6:12:26
Hart 73	35N17'55	92w03'06	6:08:12
Hartford 66	35N01'22	94w22'52	6:17:31
Hartley 57	34N22'06	94w10'14	6:16:41
Hartman 36	35N25'57	93w36'55	6:14:28
Hartsell 73	35N28	91w41	6:06:44
Hartsugg 71	35N41	92w37	6:10:28
Hartwell 44	36N07'13	93w48'06	6:15:12
Harvard 18	35N14'02	90w12'26	6:00:50
Harve 23	35N10	92w16	6:09:04
Harvey 64	34N50'45	93w47'06	6:15:08
Harwood 9	33N09'46	91w07'41	6:04:31
Haskell 63	34N30'05	92w38'11	6:10:33
Hasty 51	36N00'54	93w02'51	6:12:11
Hatchie Coon 56	35N38'06	90w29'31	6:01:58
Hatfield 57	34N29'08	94w22'42	6:17:31
Hattieville 15	35N17'15	92w47'12	6:11:09
Hatton 31	34N21'30	94w22'18	6:17:29
Havana 75	35N06'40	93w31'46	6:14:07
Hawkins 62	35N03'37	90w55'19	6:03:41
Hayley 59	34N59'45	91w39'17	6:06:37
Haynes 39	34N53'27	90w47'31	6:03:10
Hays 28	36N03	90w23	6:01:32
Haywood 11	36N20	90w13	6:00:52
Haywood 35	34N21'46	91w55'29	6:07:42
Hazel 49	34N31	93w40	6:14:40
Hazel Grove 32	35N52'20	91w21'38	6:05:27
Hazel Valley 72	35N51'40	93w59'32	6:15:58
Hazen 59	34N46'51	91w34'51	6:06:19
Heafer 18	35N21'59	90w20'23	6:01:22
Healing Springs 4	36N15'17	94w16'41	6:17:07
Healing Springs 12	35N40	91w56	6:07:44
Health 44	35N47'21	93w56'34	6:15:46
Hearn 10	34N05	93w02	6:12:08
Heart 25	36N19'25	91w42'53	6:06:52
Heber 12	35N30	92w00	6:08:00
Heber Springs 12	35N29'29	92w01'52	6:08:07
Hebron 13	33N46	92w14	6:08:56
Hector 58	35N28'02	92w58'29	6:11:54
Heelstring 11	36N21'13	90w41'40	6:02:47
Heffington 34	35N26'58	91w30'47	6:06:03
Helena 54	34N31'46	90w35'29	6:02:22
Helena Crossing 54	34N30'12	90w37'12	6:02:29
Helfer Log Landing 47	35N38'49	90w16'14	6:01:05
Hempwallace 26	34N26'38	93w12'37	6:12:50
Henderson 3	36N22'50	92w13'39	6:08:55
Henderson College 10	34N05	93w02	6:12:08
Hendrix College 23	35N05	92w27	6:09:48
Henslee Heights 35	34N15'44	92w04'58	6:08:20
Hensley 60	34N30'19	92w12'20	6:08:49
Hensley Ford 65	35N51'35	92w45'13	6:11:01
Henton 1	34N25	91w40	6:06:40
Herbert 52	33N33'04	92w50'17	6:11:21
Herbine 13	33N49'16	92w02'02	6:08:08
Herd 69	36N04	92w11	6:08:44
Hergett 16	35N46'03	90w35'28	6:02:22
Herma 70	33N15'39	92w37'21	6:10:29
Herman 16	35N42'54	90w31'56	6:02:08
Hermitage 6	33N26'47	92w10'26	6:08:42
Hermitage 60	34N43	92w16	6:09:04
Herndon 16	35N56	90w43	6:02:52
Herpel 69	35N54'27	92w01'36	6:08:06
Herring 75	35N00	93w31	6:14:04
Hervey 46	33N29'53	93w46'37	6:15:06
Heth 62	35N04'39	90w29'42	6:01:59
Heubner 11	36N13'01	90w18'43	6:01:15
Hickey 36	35N30	93w15	6:13:00
Hickeytown 36	35N24'17	93w18'38	6:13:15
Hickman 47	35N56'39	89w43'59	5:58:56
Hickman Landing 47	35N56'34	89w41'14	5:58:45
Hickoria 11	36N23'28	90w26'36	6:01:46
Hickory 8	36N21	93w26	6:13:44
Hickory Creek 4	36N15'15	94w02'04	6:16:08
Hickory Flat 73	35N29'21	91w45'13	6:07:01
Hickory Grove 51	35N50	93w17	6:13:08
Hickory Grove 75	35N09'37	93w28'12	6:13:53
Hickory Hill 15	35N14'35	92w43'59	6:10:56
Hickory Plains 59	34N59'24	91w44'12	6:06:57
Hickory Ridge 19	35N23'50	90w59'47	6:03:59
Hickory Valley 32	35N53'45	91w33'23	6:06:14
Hicks 54	34N33'54	90w58'52	6:03:55
Hicks 72	35N56'20	94w02'53	6:16:12
Hicks Station 62	35N05'39	90w36'46	6:02:27
Hicksville 54	34N35	91w01	6:04:04
Hico 4	36N11	94w31	6:18:04
Hidden Valley 68	36N16'31	91w30'46	6:06:03
Higden 12	35N34'24	92w12'11	6:08:49
Higgins 15	35N06	92w52	6:11:28
Higgins 60	34N39'05	92w14'02	6:08:56
Higginson 73	35N11'41	91w42'45	6:06:51
Highfill 4	36N15'41	94w21'27	6:17:26
Highland 55	34N02'07	93w46'19	6:15:05
Highland 57	34N37'37	93w57'47	6:15:51
Highland 68	36N16	91w30	6:06:00
Highland Farm 18	34N58'00	90w23'05	6:01:32
Hightower 47	35N48'51	90w01'01	6:00:04
Hilburn 44	35N48	93w47	6:15:08
Hill Creek 15	35N12'41	92w37'08	6:10:29
Hillcrest 36	35N28	93w30	6:14:00
Hillcrest 60	34N45	92w22	6:09:28
Hillemann 74	35N07'21	91w05'20	6:04:21
Hillsboro 70	33N08'08	92w29'52	6:09:59
Hilo 6	33N21'42	92w16'21	6:09:05
Hilton 47	35N38'45	90w05'25	6:00:22
Hindman 48	34N40	91w05	6:04:20
Hindsville 44	36N08'39	93w51'43	6:15:27
Hinkle 36	35N25'40	93w35'00	6:14:20
Hiram 12	35N28'09	91w52'04	6:07:28
Hiwasse 4	36N25'54	94w20'01	6:17:20
Hixson 69	36N02	92w08	6:08:32
H Lake Landing 1	34N10'40	91w05'41	6:04:23
Hobbs 17	35N32	94w16	6:17:04
Hobbtown 17	35N34'27	94w18'11	6:17:13
Hogan 38	36N09'28	91w07'54	6:04:32
Hogeye 72	35N55'13	94w16'03	6:17:04
Hog Jaw 49	34N35'57	93w45'24	6:15:02
Holdridge 1	34N25'54	91w26'34	6:05:46
Holiday Island 8	36N24	93w44	6:14:56
Holla Bend 58	35N09'58	93w03'06	6:12:12
Holland 23	35N10'17	92w16'25	6:09:06
Holland 43	34N55'27	92w03'12	6:08:13
Hollis 53	34N52'28	93w06'37	6:12:26
Holly 71	35N40	92w24	6:09:36
Holly Corner 11	36N16	90w18	6:01:12
Holly Creek 31	34N08	93w57	6:15:48
Holly Grove 48	34N35'45	91w11'59	6:04:48
Holly Island 11	36N16	90w18	6:01:12
Holly Island Community 11	36N15'33	90w09'29	6:00:38
Holly Springs 15	35N17'55	92w31'09	6:10:05
Holly Springs 20	33N48'55	92w42'34	6:10:50
Holly Springs 73	35N15	91w43	6:06:52
Hollywood 10	34N06'14	93w14'48	6:12:59
Holman 36	35N29'04	93w18'39	6:13:15
Holmes 61	36N16	90w58	6:03:52
Holub 39	34N50'52	90w54'29	6:03:38
Homan 46	33N32'34	93w53'10	6:15:33
Homewood 53	35N01'48	92w58'35	6:11:54
Hon 64	34N56'21	94w10'52	6:16:43
Hooker 28	36N13'24	90w31'54	6:02:08
Hooker 35	34N07'11	91w52'51	6:07:31
Hoop Spur 54	34N20'38	90w50'12	6:03:21
Hoover 4	36N15	94w20	6:17:20
Hoover Landing 61	36N11'17	90w59'22	6:03:57

Place	Latitude	Longitude	Time
Hope 29	33N40'01	93w35'29	6:14:22
Hopeville 7	33N47'23	92w33'26	6:10:14
Hopewell 5	36N20'06	93w05'32	6:12:22
Hopewell 12	35N23'53	92w03'54	6:08:16
Hopewell 28	36N14'41	90w21'12	6:01:25
Hopewell 38	35N58'42	91w05'20	6:04:21
Hopper 39	34N51'09	91w03'06	6:04:12
Hopper 49	34N21'31	93w41'19	6:14:45
Horatio 67	33N56'18	94w21'25	6:17:26
Hornor 54	34N33	90w41	6:02:44
Horsehead 14	33N06'35	93w15'49	6:13:03
Horsehead 36	35N33	93w34	6:14:16
Horseshoe 34	35N30'46	91w16'28	6:05:06
Horseshoe Bend 33	36N12	91w43	6:06:52
Hortons Landing 1	34N17'43	91w06'45	6:04:27
Hot Springs 26	34N30'13	93w03'18	6:12:13
Hot Springs Junction 60	34N42'48	92w17'07	6:09:08
Hot Springs National Park 26	34N30	93w03	6:12:12
Hot Springs Village 26	34N40'19	92w59'55	6:12:00
Hough 8	36N18'32	93w21'54	6:13:28
Houston 53	35N02'00	92w41'40	6:10:47
Howard 15	35N09	92w37	6:10:28
Howard 57	34N42'21	94w26'13	6:17:45
Howell 74	35N06'49	91w14'43	6:04:59
Hoxie 38	36N03'01	90w58'30	6:03:54
Hoyt 36	35N25'35	93w33'49	6:14:15
Hubbard 72	35N54'19	94w19'11	6:17:17
Huddleston 49	34N37	93w47	6:15:08
Hudgin 13	33N59	91w59	6:07:56
Hudson 51	35N56	93w14	6:12:56
Hudsons Landing Campground 54	34N13'08	91w03'34	6:04:14
Hudspeth 9	33N26'13	91w27'09	6:05:49
Huey 7	33N39	92w28	6:09:52
Huff 32	35N37'25	91w36'21	6:06:25
Huffman 47	35N58'24	89w44'02	5:58:56
Hughes 62	34N56'57	90w28'17	6:01:53
Hulbert 18	35N07'51	90w11'35	6:00:46
Huma 54	34N32'05	90w40'23	6:02:42
Humnoke 43	34N32'29	91w45'25	6:07:02
Humphrey 1	34N25'19	91w42'22	6:06:49
Hunt 14	33N10'41	93w21'20	6:13:25
Hunt 36	35N31'44	93w39'31	6:14:38
Hunt 64	34N57	93w45	6:15:00
Hunter 74	35N03'10	91w07'34	6:04:30
Huntington 66	35N04'56	94w15'47	6:17:03
Huntsville 44	36N05'10	93w44'28	6:14:58
Hurds 9	33N32'02	91w21'22	6:05:25
Hurricane Grove 49	34N33	93w38	6:14:32
Hutchinson 32	35N38'41	91w40'27	6:06:42
Hutson 32	35N38	91w28	6:05:52
Huttig 70	33N02'22	92w10'57	6:08:44
Hyden 1	34N11'20	91w21'39	6:05:27
Hydrick 56	35N26'47	90w44'37	6:02:58
Ida 12	35N35'17	91w55'40	6:07:43
Imboden 38	36N12'09	91w10'28	6:04:42
Imo 65	35N46'43	92w45'02	6:11:00
Index 46	33N32'49	94w02'30	6:16:10
Indian 9	33N03'09	91w17'22	6:05:09
Indian Bay 48	34N22'58	91w04'01	6:04:16
Indian Bayou 43	34N32	91w52	6:07:28
Indianhead Lake Estates 60	34N48	92w14	6:08:56
Industrial 60	34N41	92w21	6:09:24
Ingalls 6	33N23'00	92w09'03	6:08:36
Ingleside 34	35N29'22	91w19'11	6:05:17
Ingram 61	36N23'56	91w00'27	6:04:02
Ink 57	34N35'14	94w07'26	6:16:30
Ione 42	35N08	93w55	6:15:40
Ionia 4	36N19'57	94w30'52	6:18:03
Ions Creek 75	34N48	93w36	6:14:24
Irma 50	33N33'19	93w17'00	6:13:08
Irons Fork Landing 26	34N41'24	93w21'51	6:13:27
Iron Springs 50	33N52'21	93w24'16	6:13:37
Iron Springs 60	34N35'22	92w19'32	6:09:18
Ironton 60	34N37'55	92w16'38	6:09:07
Isbell 43	34N34	91w42	6:06:48
Island 66	35N24	94w07	6:16:28
Island No 39 Landing 18	35N20'52	90w06'34	6:00:26
Island Town 34	35N34'43	91w15'53	6:05:04
Iuka 33	36N12'15	92w09'18	6:08:37
Ivan 20	33N54'42	92w25'28	6:09:42
Ivesville 60	34N48'09	92w25'57	6:09:44
Ivy 20	34N07'41	92w31'46	6:10:07
Ivy 24	35N30	94w00	6:16:00
Jacinto 20	33N54'16	92w38'17	6:10:33
Jacks Bay Landing 1	34N05'43	91w10'12	6:04:41
Jacks Landing 23	34N59'22	92w24'14	6:09:37
Jackson Ford 12	35N22'33	91w55'30	6:07:42
Jackson Heights 60	34N55	92w07	6:08:28
Jackson Landing 16	35N56'32	90w22'45	6:01:31
Jacksonport 34	35N38'30	91w18'34	6:05:14
Jacksonville 60	34N51'58	92w06'36	6:08:26
James 64	34N55	93w51	6:15:24
James Creek 45	36N20	92w36	6:10:24
James Mill 18	35N15'46	90w13'03	6:00:52
James R Bush 54	34N27	90w44	6:02:56
Jamestown 32	35N41'48	91w42'16	6:06:49
Jamestown 36	35N26'31	93w27'45	6:13:51
Janes Creek 61	36N19	91w13	6:04:52
Japton 44	35N57'43	93w48'15	6:15:13
Jasmine 59	35N03'51	91w35'01	6:06:20
Jasper 51	36N00'29	93w11'11	6:12:45
Jeanette 18	35N10'41	90w25'45	6:01:43
Jeannette 18	35N04	90w30	6:02:00
Jeff Davis 41	33N48	94w23	6:17:32
Jefferson 14	33N21'04	93w22'07	6:13:28
Jefferson 35	34N22'50	92w09'50	6:08:39
Jefferson Square 35	34N13	92w02	6:08:08
Jeffersonville 39	34N43'17	90w40'38	6:02:43
Jeffrey 60	34N49'19	92w19'17	6:09:17
Jennie 9	33N15'22	91w17'10	6:05:09
Jenny Lind 66	35N15'03	94w19'05	6:17:16
Jenson 66	35N11'50	94w26'20	6:17:45
Jericho 18	35N17'09	90w13'37	6:00:54
Jerome 22	33N23'58	91w28'12	6:05:53
Jerrett 61	36N25	90w54	6:03:36
Jersey 6	33N25'42	92w18'51	6:09:15
Jerusalem 15	35N24'17	92w49'00	6:11:16
Jessieville 26	34N42'04	93w03'41	6:12:15
Jesup 38	36N01'01	91w20'10	6:05:21
Jethro 24	35N36'27	93w53'14	6:15:33
Jewell 41	33N51'22	94w25'26	6:17:42
Jim Fork 66	35N07	94w21	6:17:24
Joan 10	34N06'52	92w56'25	6:11:46
Joe Burleson 45	36N15	92w45	6:11:00
Johnson 42	35N20'34	93w27'13	6:13:49
Johnson 72	36N07'58	94w09'55	6:16:40
Johnston 14	33N15'57	93w10'01	6:12:40
Johnstown 34	35N34'42	91w09'45	6:04:39
Johnsville 6	33N22'23	92w00'57	6:08:04
Joiner 47	35N30'28	90w08'49	6:00:35
Jolliff Store 47	35N56	90w15	6:01:00
Jonesboro 16	35N50'32	90w42'15	6:02:49
Jones Mills 30	34N26'15	92w53'15	6:11:33
Jonesville 46	33N16	93w53	6:15:32
Jonquil 62	35N04'55	90w27'15	6:01:49
Joplin 49	34N32'32	93w27'09	6:13:49
Jordan 3	36N13'58	92w11'03	6:08:44
Jordan Landing 3	36N16'14	92w11'27	6:08:46
Joy 73	35N17'15	91w57'01	6:07:48
Joyce City 52	33N22'33	92w38'56	6:10:36
Joyland 56	35N28'27	90w26'56	6:01:48
Joyland Park 42	35N08	93w55	6:15:40
Judd Hill 56	35N36'08	90w31'09	6:02:05
Judsonia 73	35N16'12	91w38'23	6:06:34
Julius 18	35N11'21	90w18'26	6:01:14
Jumbo 33	36N03'36	91w58'46	6:07:55
Junction City 70	33N00'58	92w43'27	6:10:54
Jurden 62	34N57	90w28	6:01:52
Kahoka 69	35N52	92w07	6:08:28
Kalamazoo 42	35N22'05	93w41'40	6:14:47
Kansas 10	33N51'29	92w59'17	6:11:57
Kate 18	35N02'41	90w21'41	6:01:27
Kay 59	34N35'46	91w32'47	6:06:11
Kay 65	35N47'10	92w41'31	6:10:46
Kearney 35	34N24'47	92w10'19	6:08:41
Keaton 1	34N27	91w20	6:05:20
Kedron 13	34N02'40	92w08'25	6:08:34
Keeler Corner 73	35N21'36	91w29'04	6:05:56
Keener 5	36N18'46	92w59'14	6:11:57
Keesee 45	36N29	92w50	6:11:20
Keeter 45	36N24	92w43	6:10:52
Keevil 48	34N48	91w14	6:04:56
Keiser 47	35N40'28	90w05'59	6:00:24
Kellum 67	34N06'59	94w26'23	6:17:46
Kelso 21	33N47'51	91w16'14	6:05:05
Kenney 53	34N58	92w39	6:10:36
Kenova 70	33N21'26	92w41'50	6:10:47
Kensett 73	35N13'54	91w40'03	6:06:40
Kent 52	33N37'32	92w48'47	6:11:15
Kentucky 63	34N30	92w35	6:10:20
Kenwood 15	35N11'59	92w48'45	6:11:15
Kenyon 34	35N47'32	91w13'24	6:04:54
Keo 43	34N36'10	92w00'32	6:08:02
Kerlin 14	33N11'01	93w13'31	6:12:54
Kerr 43	34N47'12	92w03'30	6:08:14
Kiblah 46	33N03'05	93w53'45	6:15:35
Kibler 17	35N25'49	94w13'53	6:16:56
Kilgore 11	36N24	90w39	6:02:36
Killin 22	33N36'44	91w44'28	6:06:58
Kimball 2	33N01'34	91w36'34	6:06:26
Kimberley 55	34N02'37	93w41'20	6:14:45
Kimbrough 40	34N08	91w41	6:06:44
Kinard 70	33N11'37	92w30'57	6:10:04
Kindall 54	34N33'19	90w49'16	6:03:17
King 25	36N24'13	91w31'35	6:06:06
King 36	35N32	93w29	6:13:56
King 67	34N08'38	94w18'00	6:17:12
King Mills 68	36N18	91w31	6:06:04
Kings 67	34N10	94w19	6:17:16
Kingsland 13	33N51'30	92w17'38	6:09:11
Kingsland Landing 47	35N29'00	90w02'33	6:00:10
Kingsley Crossing 62	34N58'35	90w36'55	6:02:28
Kingston 44	36N03'02	93w31'06	6:14:04
Kingston 75	35N01'00	93w18'54	6:13:16
Kingtown 54	34N29'48	90w53'29	6:03:34
Kinton 62	35N08'32	90w38'01	6:02:32
Kirby 55	34N15'01	93w38'28	6:14:34
Kirkland 52	33N24'55	92w48'49	6:11:15
Kittle 25	36N16'00	91w37'41	6:06:31
Kittlers 1	34N22'22	91w24'35	6:05:38
Kizer 37	33N03'54	93w39'45	6:14:39
Knob 11	36N17	90w27	6:01:48
Knob Creek 33	36N05'03	91w59'17	6:07:57
Knobel 11	36N19'12	90w36'07	6:02:24
Knowlton 21	34N06'26	90w57'49	6:03:51
Knoxville 10	34N06'58	92w59'31	6:11:58
Knoxville 36	35N22'55	93w21'51	6:13:27
Knoxville Junction 36	35N24'32	93w23'04	6:13:32
Koch Ridge 71	35N35	92w28	6:09:52
Kokomo 39	34N52'55	90w32'58	6:02:12
Kramer 74	35N17	91w22	6:05:28
Kress City 37	33N17'39	93w36'17	6:14:25
Kurdo 21	33N50	91w16	6:05:04
Lacey 22	33N27'18	91w50'48	6:07:23
Laconia 21	34N03'11	90w57'15	6:03:49
Laconia Landing 21	34N01'39	90w57'59	6:03:52
LaCrosse 33	36N05'26	91w50'29	6:07:22
Ladd 35	34N08'27	91w54'32	6:07:38
Ladelle 22	33N27'52	91w47'37	6:07:10
La Fave 64	34N51	93w47	6:15:08
Lafe 28	36N12'15	90w30'50	6:02:03
Lafferty 33	35N54'51	91w49'30	6:07:18
LaGrange 39	34N39'23	90w43'58	6:02:56
La Grue 1	34N17	91w20	6:05:20
LaGrue Springs 1	34N12'28	91w12'42	6:04:51
Lake Catherine 26	34N30	93w03	6:12:12
Lake City 16	35N48'58	90w26'03	6:01:44
Lake Dick 35	34N15'07	91w50'19	6:07:21
Lake Elmdale 72	36N11	94w09	6:16:36
Lake Farm 35	34N13'28	91w42'13	6:06:49
Lake Frances 4	36N08	94w33	6:18:12
Lakehall 9	33N19'42	91w16'14	6:05:05
Lake Hamilton 26	34N25'28	93w05'42	6:12:23
Lakeport 9	33N13'30	91w07'36	6:04:30
Lake Ridge 54	34N33'08	90w48'11	6:03:13
Lakeside 26	34N30	93w03	6:12:12
Lakeside 52	33N34'41	92w44'17	6:10:57
Lakeside 62	34N58'12	90w37'20	6:02:29
Lakeside 63	34N32'12	92w15'55	6:09:04
Lakeview 3	36N22'07	92w32'43	6:10:11
Lake View 16	35N53'32	90w27'09	6:01:49
Lake View 54	34N32	90w37	6:02:28
Lakeview 75	35N08'02	93w01'23	6:12:06
Lake Village 9	33N19'43	91w16'54	6:05:08
Lakeway 45	36N20'19	92w46'06	6:11:04
Lakewood 60	34N47'40	92w14'38	6:08:59
Lamar 36	35N26'26	93w23'16	6:13:33
Lamartine 14	33N23'35	93w17'19	6:13:09
Lamb 64	34N52	94w00	6:16:00
Lambert 30	34N18'29	93w12'23	6:12:50
Lambethville 18	35N22'43	90w10'53	6:00:44
Lambrook 54	34N20'08	90w58'03	6:03:52
Lamont 27	34N06	92w17	6:09:08
Lanark 6	33N31'52	92w15'52	6:09:03
Lancaster 17	35N34	94w14	6:16:56
Landers 30	34N15'48	92w45'04	6:11:00
Landers 56	35N34'09	90w36'30	6:02:26
Landis 65	35N56'22	92w26'31	6:09:46
Laneburg 50	33N41'06	93w20'48	6:13:23
Lanesport 41	33N38'57	94w28'22	6:17:53
Langford 35	34N10'03	91w35'44	6:06:23
Langley 55	34N18'46	93w50'30	6:15:22
L'Anguille 19	35N14'12	90w53'39	6:03:35
Lansing 18	35N15'01	90w23'12	6:01:33
Lanty 15	35N20'11	92w41'08	6:10:45
Lapile 70	33N05'36	92w16'07	6:09:04
Larkin 33	36N06'42	91w52'04	6:07:28
Larue 4	36N20'30	93w56'45	6:15:47
Latour 54	34N34'34	90w44'28	6:02:58
Laughlin 14	33N20'12	93w05'50	6:12:23
Lauratown 38	36N01'12	91w05'18	6:04:21
Lavaca 66	35N20'10	94w10'23	6:16:42
Lave Creek 68	36N08	91w37	6:06:28
Lawrenceville 48	34N30'33	91w10'51	6:04:43
Lawson 70	33N11'48	92w28'58	6:09:56
Layne 68	36N04	91w37	6:06:28
Leachville 47	35N56'09	90w15'28	6:01:02
Lead Hill 5	36N25'11	92w54'53	6:11:40
Leake 50	33N30	93w10	6:12:40
Lebanon 65	35N55	92w38	6:10:32
Lebanon 67	34N06'23	94w05'52	6:16:23
Ledwidge 53	34N57'26	92w33'58	6:10:16
Lee Creek 17	35N40'53	94w20'57	6:17:24
Lehi 18	35N08'50	90w17'33	6:01:10
Leitner 35	34N15'00	92w04'00	6:08:16
Leland 9	33N22'20	91w09'23	6:04:38
Lemmons 11	36N24	90w26	6:01:44
Lenham 27	34N18'01	92w38'20	6:10:33
Lennie 47	35N46'03	90w10'39	6:00:43
Lenox 10	34N14'56	93w16'06	6:13:04
Leola 27	34N10'10	92w35'27	6:10:22
Leonard 11	36N13'11	90w14'58	6:01:00
Lepanto 56	35N36'40	90w19'47	6:01:19
Lepanto Junction 16	35N44'17	90w20'00	6:01:20
Lerch 37	33N15'13	93w29'33	6:13:58
Leslie 65	35N49'49	92w33'28	6:10:14
Lester 16	35N52'40	90w27'12	6:01:49
Lester 52	33N38'55	92w55'12	6:11:41
Lester Junction 52	33N37'40	92w56'13	6:11:45
Lesterville 61	36N09'03	90w57'23	6:03:50
Letchworth 59	34N54'39	91w29'39	6:05:59
Letona 73	35N21'42	91w49'45	6:07:19
Leverney 49	34N42	93w27	6:13:48
Levesque 19	35N14'57	90w42'38	6:02:51
Levy 60	34N47'19	92w16'35	6:09:06
Lewis 22	33N29'15	91w47'27	6:07:10
Lewis 64	35N03'12	94w07'30	6:16:30
Lewisburg 15	35N08	92w45	6:11:00
Lewisville 37	33N21'30	93w34'39	6:14:19
Lexa 54	34N35'52	90w45'08	6:03:01
Lexa Junction 54	34N35'56	90w46'05	6:03:04
Lexington 69	35N43	92w25	6:09:40
Liberty 42	35N17'06	93w22'56	6:13:32
Liberty 49	34N40'48	93w26'44	6:13:47
Liberty 52	33N24'16	92w50'11	6:11:21
Liberty 66	35N01'39	94w13'51	6:16:55
Liberty Hall 75	35N14	93w10	6:12:40
Liberty Valley 73	35N18	91w34	6:06:16
Lick Branch 5	36N19'48	93w13'43	6:12:55
Lick Creek 41	33N44	94w12	6:16:48
Lick Mountain 15	35N23	92w35	6:10:20
Liddell 11	36N27	90w09	6:00:36
Light 28	36N04'12	90w44'52	6:02:59
Lignite 63	34N33'43	92w29'15	6:09:57
Limedale 32	35N47'38	91w43'09	6:06:53
Limedale Junction 32	35N48'57	91w42'48	6:06:51
Limestone 51	35N47'02	93w17'00	6:13:08
Lincoln 72	35N56'58	94w25'24	6:17:42
Linder 23	35N11'25	92w22'22	6:09:29
Lindsey 38	35N59'27	91w00'59	6:04:04
Linn Creek 71	35N45	92w27	6:09:48
Linwood 35	34N09'13	91w47'50	6:07:11
Lisbon 70	33N16'21	92w49'38	6:11:19
Litteral 72	36N06	94w16	6:17:04
Little Arkansaw 5	36N17'21	93w14'11	6:12:57
Little Bay 7	33N45'45	92w31'56	6:10:08
Little Black 61	36N27	90w51	6:03:24
Little Dixie 74	35N00'26	91w21'53	6:05:28
Little Fir Landing 49	34N37'50	93w28'27	6:13:54
Little Flock 4	36N19	94w08	6:16:32
Little Garnett 40	33N51'47	91w48'13	6:07:13
Little Green Store 47	35N57'08	90w02'10	6:00:09
Little Italy 53	34N56'15	92w35'09	6:10:21
Little Red 73	35N26'48	91w44'10	6:06:57
Little River 47	35N48'27	90w06'01	6:00:24
Little River Country Club 41	33N50	94w21	6:17:24
Little Rock 60	34N44'47	92w17'22	6:09:09

Little Texas 64	34N50'33	93w43'32	6:14:54
Littrel Ford 8	36N15'05	93w35'52	6:14:23
Live Oak 22	33N45	91w34	6:06:16
Lloyd Ford 7	33N21'33	92w22'41	6:09:31
Loafer 51	35N47'00	93w28'59	6:13:56
Locke 17	35N40'26	94w04'24	6:16:18
Lockesburg 67	33N58'02	94w10'06	6:16:40
Lockheart 32	35N50'12	91w14'47	6:04:59
Locust Bayou 7	33N33'24	92w40'08	6:10:41
Locust Grove 32	35N43'15	91w44'18	6:06:57
Locust Grove 69	35N54	92w23	6:09:32
Lodge Corner 1	34N18'00	91w31'30	6:06:06
Lodi 55	34N18'39	93w42'26	6:14:50
Lofton 26	34N24'02	93w13'52	6:12:55
Logan 4	36N12'03	94w23'14	6:17:33
Lollie 23	34N59'17	92w35'03	6:10:20
London 58	35N19'44	93w15'10	6:13:01
Lone 42	35N03'49	94w02'50	6:16:11
Lone Elm 24	35N32'48	93w57'54	6:15:52
Lone Grove 15	35N18'54	92w42'06	6:10:48
Lone Hill 30	34N21	92w55	6:11:40
Lonelm 24	35N31	94w05	6:16:20
Lone Pine 40	33N51	91w49	6:07:16
Lone Pine 65	35N58'23	92w33'45	6:10:15
Lone Pine 75	35N06'14	93w19'18	6:13:17
Lone Rock 3	36N10'50	92w20'40	6:09:23
Lone Star 8	36N20'38	93w45'10	6:15:01
Lone Star 33	36N00'13	91w59'23	6:07:58
Long 41	33N39'30	94w01'36	6:16:06
Longino 62	34N58'58	90w52'14	6:03:29
Longview 6	33N22'51	91w58'13	6:07:53
Longview Crossing 2	33N20'49	91w55'03	6:07:40
Lon Norris 66	35N18	94w25	6:17:40
Lono 30	34N12'29	92w42'36	6:10:50
Lonoke 43	34N47'02	91w53'59	6:07:36
Lonsdale 26	34N32'40	92w48'29	6:11:14
Lookout 1	34N33'48	91w22'35	6:05:30
Lookout Store 48	34N38	91w23	6:05:32
Lorado 28	35N59'21	90w43'03	6:02:52
Lorays 21	34N06'38	90w59'02	6:03:56
Lorine 61	36N16	90w58	6:03:52
Lost Bridge Village 4	36N23'18	93w54'24	6:15:38
Lost Corner 15	35N24'45	92w39'16	6:10:37
Lost Corner 58	35N34'18	92w50'02	6:11:20
Louann 52	33N23'27	92w47'30	6:11:10
Louise 18	35N04'35	90w17'37	6:01:10
Love 33	36N04	91w37	6:06:28
Love Creek 10	34N01'31	93w18'53	6:13:16
Love Place 19	35N18'59	90w34'25	6:02:18
Lowden 47	35N48'52	90w03'39	6:00:15
Lowell 4	36N15'19	94w07'50	6:16:31
Lower Poplar Ridge 16	35N50	90w22	6:01:28
Lower Surrounded Hill 59	34N50	91w24	6:05:36
Lowes Boydsville 11	36N16	90w18	6:01:12
Low Gap 51	36N00	93w11	6:12:44
Lowry 5	36N28'18	93w03'15	6:12:13
Loy 44	36N00'52	93w33'08	6:14:13
Luber 69	35N45'56	92w05'01	6:08:20
Lucas 18	34N56	90w20	6:01:20
Lucas 42	35N04'11	94w06'55	6:16:28
Lucca Landing 21	33N42'55	91w12'54	6:04:52
Lucerne 62	35N04'17	90w33'29	6:02:14
Ludwig 36	35N30'39	93w25'45	6:13:43
Lumber 14	33N21'01	93w20'50	6:13:23
Luna 9	33N22'59	91w12'18	6:04:49
Luna Landing 9	33N23'25	91w11'37	6:04:46
Lundell 54	34N11'31	90w57'44	6:03:51
Lundsford Corner 60	34N54'26	92w32'58	6:10:12
Lunenburg 33	36N00'09	91w54'27	6:07:38
Lunet 52	33N45'48	92w54'31	6:11:38
Lunsford 16	35N45'26	90w28'49	6:01:55
Lurton 51	35N46'17	93w04'39	6:12:19
Lutherville 36	35N29'02	93w16'40	6:13:07
Luxora 47	35N45'22	89w55'41	5:59:43
Lydalisk 69	35N44'38	92w20'03	6:09:20
Lydesdale 14	33N19'15	93w07'05	6:12:28
Lynn 38	36N00'26	91w15'08	6:05:01
Mabelvale 60	34N39'18	92w23'11	6:09:33
Maberry 74	35N01'19	91w19'33	6:05:18
Macedonia 14	33N10'35	93w18'00	6:13:12
Macedonia 15	35N19'51	92w45'45	6:11:03
Macedonia 75	35N00'21	93w27'57	6:13:52
Macey 16	35N54	90w21	6:01:24
Macks 34	35N36'45	91w21'45	6:05:27
Macon 60	34N55'13	92w10'06	6:08:40
Macon Lake 9	33N25'43	91w19'28	6:05:18
Madding 35	34N13'29	91w50'01	6:07:20
Maddox 26	34N29'33	93w18'11	6:13:13
Madison 62	35N00'47	90w43'21	6:02:53
Magazine 42	35N09'03	93w48'24	6:15:14
Magic Springs 65	35N48'54	92w51'32	6:11:26
Magnesia Springs 14	33N20'33	93w10'27	6:12:42
Magness 32	35N42'08	91w28'49	6:05:55
Magnet 30	34N27'14	92w50'38	6:11:23
Magnet Cove 30	34N23	92w49	6:11:16
Magnolia 14	33N16'01	93w14'21	6:12:57
Main Shore 28	36N00	90w25	6:01:40
Main Street 60	34N47	92w15	6:09:00
Majors 10	34N13'18	93w28'23	6:13:54
Mallet Town 15	35N16	92w34	6:10:16
Mallory Spur 18	35N00'56	90w23'07	6:01:32
Malvern 30	34N21'44	92w48'46	6:11:15
Mammoth Spring 25	36N29'44	91w32'26	6:06:10
Manchester 20	34N00	92w52	6:11:28
Mandalay 47	35N46'45	90w14'09	6:00:57
Mandeville 46	33N28'54	93w57'50	6:15:51
Manfred 49	34N24'28	93w38'54	6:14:36
Mangrum 16	35N47'16	90w21'27	6:01:26
Manila 47	35N52'48	90w10'01	6:00:40
Manning 20	34N01'16	92w47'34	6:11:10
Mansfield 66	35N03'34	94w15'09	6:17:01
Manson 61	36N11'39	90w57'45	6:03:51
Many Islands 25	36N23'20	91w31'45	6:06:07
Maple 8	36N26'05	93w29'50	6:13:59
Maple Corner 54	34N33'19	90w51'30	6:03:26
Maple Grove 56	35N38'31	90w33'15	6:02:13
Maple Springs 32	35N38'07	91w30'38	6:06:03
Marble 44	36N08'23	93w35'14	6:14:21
Marble City 51	36N05	93w10	6:12:40
Marcella 69	35N47'17	91w53'01	6:07:32
Marche 60	34N51'48	92w21'44	6:09:27
Marianna 39	34N46'25	90w45'27	6:03:02
Marie 47	35N36'37	90w04'51	6:00:19
Marie Saline 2	33N02	92w00	6:08:00
Marion 18	35N12'52	90w11'47	6:00:47
Marked Tree 56	35N31'58	90w25'14	6:01:41
Marmaduke 28	36N11'13	90w22'59	6:01:32
Marrs Hill 72	36N02	94w20	6:17:20
Marsden 6	33N19'40	92w13'21	6:08:53
Marsena 65	35N52'49	92w47'40	6:11:11
Marshall 65	35N54'32	92w37'52	6:10:31
Marshell 32	35N52	91w17	6:05:08
Mars Hill 37	33N16	93w33	6:14:12
Mars Hill 58	35N16'34	92w59'57	6:12:00
Martindale 60	34N52'54	92w41'17	6:10:45
Martin Spring 36	35N32'40	93w26'09	6:13:45
Martinville 23	35N19'30	92w28'56	6:09:56
Marvell 54	34N33'20	90w54'46	6:03:39
Marvinville 75	35N07'05	93w33'00	6:14:12
Mary Spur 54	34N16'00	90w54'56	6:03:40
Marysville 70	33N13'38	92w57'26	6:11:50
Mason 75	35N02	93w07	6:12:28
Mason Valley 4	36N17'57	94w20'26	6:17:22
Masonville 21	33N35'05	91w24'18	6:05:37
Massard 66	35N20'54	94w20'26	6:17:22
Matchetts Landing 23	34N58'13	92w24'34	6:09:38
Matney 3	36N08	92w23	6:09:32
Matthews 23	35N15	92w16	6:09:04
Maumee 65	36N03'10	92w38'49	6:10:35
Maumee Crossing 65	36N02'20	92w38'13	6:10:33
Maumelle 60	34N48'49	92w26'33	6:09:46
Maxey 17	35N33	94w03	6:16:12
Maxville 68	35N56	91w33	6:06:12
Mayfield 72	36N08'01	93w56'38	6:15:47
Mayflower 23	34N57'25	92w25'38	6:09:43
Maynard 61	36N25'11	90w53'50	6:03:35
Maysville 4	36N24'13	94w36'06	6:18:24
Mayton 46	33N22'35	93w44'09	6:14:57
Mayview 1	34N12'33	91w21'24	6:05:26
Mazarn 26	34N25'51	93w26'01	6:13:44
McAlmont 60	34N48'30	92w10'54	6:08:44
McArthur 21	33N41'22	91w20'05	6:05:20
McBee Landing 45	36N16'47	92w32'00	6:10:08
McCaskill 29	33N55'00	93w38'29	6:14:34
McClelland 74	35N06'15	91w24'24	6:05:38
McClendons Corner 47	35N32'24	90w13'53	6:00:56
McCormick 56	35N35'52	90w24'58	6:02:19
McCreanor 43	34N47'00	91w47'42	6:07:11
McCrory 74	35N15'22	91w12'00	6:04:48
McDonald 19	35N16'12	90w36'07	6:02:24
McDougal 11	36N26'24	90w23'29	6:01:34
McElroy 19	35N12'53	90w50'15	6:03:21
McFadden 34	35N24'23	91w05'31	6:04:22
McFall 1	34N31	91w26	6:05:44
McFerrin 47	35N46'40	90w02'32	6:00:10
McGavock 47	35N30	90w08	6:00:32
McGehee 21	33N37'44	91w23'58	6:05:36
McGintytown 23	35N14'50	92w17'30	6:09:10
McGlendon Mill 70	33N11'31	92w17'37	6:09:10
McGregor 74	35N01'02	91w13'35	6:04:54
McHue 32	35N41'34	91w39'29	6:06:38
McIlroy 24	35N41	93w46	6:15:04
McJester 12	35N28'26	91w49'06	6:07:16
McKamie 37	33N16'06	93w29'56	6:14:00
McKennon 36	35N22	93w19	6:13:16
McKennon Ford 8	36N20'55	93w35'26	6:14:22
McKinney 6	33N38'12	92w10'44	6:08:43
McKinney 46	33N23'20	93w47'43	6:15:11
McLaren 15	35N20	92w40	6:10:40
McMillan Corner 9	33N23'13	91w18'30	6:05:14
McNab 29	33N39'40	93w49'57	6:15:20
McNair 72	36N03'01	94w10'34	6:16:42
McNeil 14	33N20'52	93w12'35	6:12:50
McPherson 3	36N08'25	92w15'09	6:09:01
McRae 73	35N06'46	91w49'20	6:07:17
Meadowcliff 60	34N41'48	92w21'03	6:09:24
Meadow Cliff 62	35N01	90w47	6:03:08
Meadows 17	35N29'35	94w16'01	6:17:04
Medina 1	33N57'51	91w11'55	6:04:48
Medlock 14	33N21'00	93w01'30	6:12:06
Meeks Settlement 10	34N02'30	93w23'30	6:13:34
Meg 24	35N29	93w50	6:15:20
Melbourne 33	36N03'34	91w54'30	6:07:38
Mellwood 54	34N13'11	90w57'01	6:03:48
Melrose 69	35N44'37	91w50'57	6:07:24
Melton 35	34N08	91w53	6:07:32
Mena 57	34N35'10	94w14'22	6:16:57
Mendenhall 50	33N33'19	93w07'32	6:12:30
Meneshea 18	35N25'35	90w12'52	6:00:51
Menifee 15	35N08'54	92w33'14	6:10:13
Meridian 2	33N02'05	91w58'43	6:07:55
Meroney 40	33N57'37	91w44'02	6:06:56
Merrivale 60	34N44	92w20	6:09:20
Merry Green 27	34N19	92w23	6:09:32
Mersman 19	35N21'32	90w45'15	6:03:01
Mesa 59	34N46'54	91w29'37	6:05:58
Metalton 8	36N13'23	93w31'47	6:14:07
Meto 43	34N47'08	91w59'45	6:07:59
Meyers 26	34N27'33	93w21'14	6:13:25
Mickles 75	35N04'08	93w17'24	6:13:10
Middle 24	35N27	93w50	6:15:20
Middlebrook 61	36N27'31	90w55'34	6:03:42
Middleton 15	35N20'10	92w38'10	6:10:33
Midland 66	35N05'35	94w21'11	6:17:25
Midway 3	36N23'07	92w27'42	6:09:51
Midway 30	34N15'15	92w57'48	6:11:51
Midway 34	35N33'36	91w03'08	6:04:13
Midway 35	34N17'49	92w11'20	6:08:45
Midway 37	33N27'42	93w37'29	6:14:30
Midway 39	34N53'36	90w27'15	6:01:49
Midway 42	35N17'29	93w31'38	6:14:07
Midway 45	36N24'38	92w39'46	6:10:39
Midway 47	35N58'53	90w01'07	6:00:04
Midway 50	33N48'40	93w27'23	6:13:50
Midway 62	35N07'46	90w34'39	6:02:19
Midway 73	35N17'34	91w36'28	6:06:26
Midway Corner 18	35N04'07	90w17'37	6:01:10
Milford 67	33N55'07	94w05'07	6:16:20
Mill Bayou 1	34N25	91w27	6:05:48
Mill Creek 58	35N17	93w09	6:12:36
Mill Creek 66	35N20'21	94w25'22	6:17:41
Miller 28	35N58'49	90w25'24	6:01:42
Miller 41	33N47	94w28	6:17:52
Millers 18	35N03'46	90w13'48	6:00:55
Millers Bluff 52	33N23'45	92w38'02	6:10:32
Millers Crossing 67	33N48'20	94w09'58	6:16:40
Millerville 27	34N10'52	92w23'55	6:09:36
Mill Ford 6	33N26'42	92w19'46	6:09:19
Milligan Ridge 47	35N53	90w10	6:00:40
Milltown 66	35N09'25	94w08'58	6:16:36
Millville 52	33N42'41	92w39'23	6:10:38
Millwood 41	33N40'17	93w58'58	6:15:56
Milo 2	33N17'43	91w57'00	6:07:48
Milrose 67	33N55'12	94w11'09	6:16:45
Milton Ford 24	35N37'38	93w53'13	6:15:33
Mine Creek 29	33N55	93w47	6:15:08
Mineola 31	34N18'48	94w01'50	6:16:07
Mineral 67	34N11'22	94w19'58	6:17:20
Mineral Springs 24	35N38'33	93w43'52	6:14:55
Mineral Springs 31	33N52'30	93w54'49	6:15:39
Minorca 61	36N25	90w54	6:03:36
Minorea 61	36N29'39	90w50'46	6:03:23
Minturn 38	35N58'28	91w01'39	6:04:07
Mist 2	33N16'26	91w41'29	6:06:46
Mitchell 11	36N20'13	90w14'04	6:00:56
Mitchell 19	35N24	90w45	6:03:00
Mitchell 25	36N19'25	92w00'45	6:08:03
Mitchell Corner 73	35N13'58	91w29'01	6:05:56
Mitchell Mill 28	36N11'51	90w14'28	6:00:58
Mitchellville 21	33N54'20	91w29'56	6:06:00
Mixon 42	35N05'26	93w52'47	6:15:31
Moark 11	36N29'00	90w31'30	6:02:06
Modoc 54	34N20'09	90w46'46	6:03:07
Modoc Landing 54	34N17'48	90w47'37	6:03:10
Moffit 72	35N59	94w19	6:17:16
Moko 25	36N28'03	91w50'23	6:07:22
Monarch 45	36N22'38	92w50'44	6:11:23
Monette 16	35N53'26	90w20'39	6:01:23
Monkey Run 3	36N20'43	92w28'47	6:09:55
Monnie Springs 60	34N55'10	92w29'09	6:09:57
Monroe 49	34N44'05	91w06'16	6:04:25
Montana 36	35N25'30	93w32'41	6:14:11
Monte Ne 4	36N17'14	94w04'08	6:16:17
Monte Ne Shores 4	36N17'03	94w04'34	6:16:18
Monterey 19	35N25'21	90w36'02	6:02:24
Monticello 22	33N37'44	91w47'27	6:07:10
Montongo 22	33N33	91w47	6:07:08
Montreal 66	35N07'03	94w20'54	6:17:24
Montrose 2	33N17'51	91w29'37	6:05:58
Mont Sandals 66	35N19	94w14	6:16:56
Mooney 54	34N12	91w00	6:04:00
Moore 51	35N45'18	92w58'41	6:11:55
Moorefield 32	35N46'06	91w34'13	6:06:17
Moores Mill 6	33N17'38	92w00'27	6:08:02
Moran 47	35N44'28	89w57'49	5:59:51
Moreland 58	35N22'03	92w59'54	6:12:00
Morgan 60	34N53'11	92w22'20	6:09:29
Morganton 71	35N28'21	92w20'22	6:09:21
Morning Star 28	36N04'01	90w25'40	6:01:43
Morning Star 30	34N30'19	92w59'20	6:11:57
Morning Star 65	35N58'22	92w35'38	6:10:23
Morning Sun 73	35N11'42	91w43'50	6:06:55
Moro 39	34N47'42	90w59'28	6:03:58
Moro Bay 6	33N18'23	92w21'01	6:09:24
Morrilton 15	35N09'03	92w44'38	6:10:59
Morris 1	34N26	91w34	6:06:16
Morris 50	33N40'12	93w14'47	6:12:59
Morrison Bluff 42	35N22	93w32	6:14:08
Morriston 25	36N15'57	91w46'49	6:07:07
Morrow 72	35N51'30	94w26'14	6:17:45
Morton 74	35N15'04	91w05'36	6:04:22
Mosby 54	34N13	90w57	6:03:48
Mosby Spur 54	34N10'46	90w58'02	6:03:52
Moscow 35	34N08'47	91w47'42	6:07:11
Mosley 75	35N10'52	93w15'06	6:13:00
Mossville 51	35N53'42	93w23'24	6:13:34
Mound City 18	35N11'25	90w07'45	6:00:31
Mound Place Lodge 39	34N40'01	90w35'02	6:02:20
Mounds 19	35N06'54	90w16'01	6:01:04
Mounds 28	36N09'26	90w17'38	6:01:11
Mountainburg 17	35N38'08	94w10'02	6:16:40
Mountain Crest 24	35N45'30	93w53'15	6:15:33
Mountain Fork 57	34N38'30	94w25'43	6:17:43
Mountain Grove 24	35N32'07	93w48'19	6:15:13
Mountain Home 3	36N20'07	92w23'06	6:09:32
Mountain Home 73	35N23'12	91w48'32	6:07:14
Mountain Pine 26	34N34'19	93w10'23	6:12:42
Mountain Springs 43	35N01'34	92w04'13	6:08:17
Mountain Top 24	35N29	93w50	6:15:20
Mountain Valley 26	34N37'45	93w03'24	6:12:14
Mountain View 69	35N52'06	92w07'03	6:08:28
Mount Calm 25	36N28	91w59	6:07:56
Mount Carmel 32	35N44'39	91w26'26	6:05:46
Mount Elba 13	33N51'03	92w09'30	6:08:38
Mount Gaylor 17	35N45'11	94w06'54	6:16:28
Mount George 75	35N06'47	93w14'30	6:12:58
Mount Hersey 51	36N00'49	92w57'00	6:11:48
Mount Holly 70	33N18'09	92w57'17	6:11:49
Mount Ida 49	34N33'24	93w38'02	6:14:32
Mount Judea 51	35N55'17	93w03'36	6:12:14
Mount Moriah 30	34N23'42	93w21'13	6:13:25
Mount Moriah 50	33N38'19	93w18'51	6:13:15
Mount Moriah 55	34N06'32	93w41'27	6:14:46
Mount Olive 6	33N25'44	92w03'32	6:08:14
Mount Olive 23	35N11'48	92w33'18	6:10:13
Mount Olive 33	36N00'02	92w05'34	6:08:22
Mount Olive 56	35N28'57	90w24'46	6:01:39
Mount Olive 72	36N00	94w01	6:16:04
Mount Pilgrim 60	34N53'40	92w26'29	6:09:46
Mount Pisgah 73	35N19	91w50	6:07:20
Mount Pleasant 25	36N17'33	91w53'08	6:07:33

Mount Pleasant 33 35N57'42 91W45'20 6:07:01
Mount Pleasant 46 33N22'37 93W58'52 6:15:55
Mount Pleasant 50 33N27'31 93W29'37 6:13:58
Mount Sherman 51 36N01'51 93W15'22 6:13:01
Mount Tabor 22 33N33 91W47 6:07:08
Mount Tabor 26 34N42'27 93W20'16 6:13:21
Mount Vernon 14 33N19'46 93W22'48 6:13:31
Mount Vernon 23 35N13'35 92W07'26 6:08:30
Mount Vernon 36 35N26 93W37 6:14:28
Mount Zion 13 34N01'36 92W06'43 6:08:27
Mozart 21 34N00'53 91W06'35 6:04:26
Mozart 69 35N50'08 92W19'04 6:09:16
Muddy Fork 31 34N08'09 93W53'41 6:15:35
Mud Lake 62 34N54'44 90W30'50 6:02:03
Muir 47 35N31'53 90W10'58 6:00:44
Mulberry 17 35N30'02 94W03'05 6:16:12
Mulligan 56 35N42'05 90W41'46 6:02:47
Murfreesboro 55 34N03'44 93W41'23 6:14:46
Murphys Corner 34 35N36'29 91W11'05 6:04:44
Murray 51 35N55'48 93W18'42 6:13:15
Murta 38 36N06'48 90W53'37 6:03:34
Mustin Lake 52 33N35 92W47 6:11:08
Myatt 25 36N23 91W39 6:06:36
Myersville 33 35N53'06 91W52'34 6:07:30
Myron 33 36N11'01 91W42'20 6:06:49
Myrtle 5 36N21'41 93W05'04 6:12:20
Myrtle Grove 9 33N18'37 91W16'16 6:05:05
Nady 1 34N00 91W15 6:05:00
Nail 51 35N49'28 93W17'34 6:13:10
Nalle 16 35N53'44 90W50'14 6:03:21
Nance 63 34N32'53 92W46'14 6:11:05
Nance Ford 27 34N23'48 92W37'10 6:10:29
Nasco 33 35N57'51 91W59'06 6:07:56
Nash Corner 39 34N52'52 91W04'50 6:04:19
Nashville 31 33N56'44 93W50'49 6:15:23
Nathan 55 34N06'22 93W48'49 6:15:15
Natural Dam 17 35N38'55 94W23'40 6:17:35
Natural Steps 60 34N51'43 92W28'31 6:09:54
Naylor 23 35N09'31 92W11'14 6:08:45
Neal 47 35N58 90W12 6:00:48
Neal Springs 67 33N55'28 94W22'26 6:17:30
Nebo 4 36N25'00 94W26'27 6:17:46
Nebo 40 34N00'10 91W48'51 6:07:15
Needham 16 35N49'21 90W32'06 6:02:08
Needmore 33 36N02'27 91W41'28 6:06:46
Needmore 64 34N48'32 94W02'19 6:16:09
Neely 75 35N14 93W10 6:12:40
Negro Head Corner 74 35N20'38 91W21'27 6:05:26
Nella 64 34N45'37 94W09'48 6:16:39
Nelson 11 36N22 90W44 6:02:56
Nelsonville 68 36N04'12 91W25'35 6:05:42
Nemo 16 35N52'23 90W51'36 6:03:26
Nettleton 16 35N49'10 90W39'04 6:02:36
Neuhardt 18 35N03'40 90W19'44 6:01:19
Nevark 50 33N33'22 93W10'01 6:12:40
Newark 32 35N42'06 91W26'29 6:05:46
New Augusta 74 35N16'16 91W21'31 6:05:26
New Blaine 42 35N17'22 93W25'12 6:13:41
Newburg 33 36N06'56 91W56'59 6:07:48
New Caledonia 70 33N01 92W43 6:10:52
Newcastle 62 35N07'15 90W42'44 6:02:51
Newcomb 63 34N34 92W39 6:10:36
New Dixie 53 35N02'33 92W36'43 6:10:27
New Edinburg 13 33N45'26 92W14'18 6:08:57
Newell 70 33N09'57 92W44'40 6:10:59
New Gascony 35 34N13'35 91W46'35 6:07:06
New Haroldton 17 35N22'15 94W14'31 6:16:58
New Hope 5 36N27'38 93W07'55 6:12:32
New Hope 20 33N53'45 92W47'52 6:11:11
New Hope 22 33N31'54 91W52'31 6:07:30
New Hope 28 35N59'44 90W29'14 6:01:57
New Hope 32 35N46 91W37 6:06:28
Newhope 55 34N13'49 93W52'48 6:15:31
New Hope 58 35N13'17 93W06'49 6:12:27
New Hope 62 34N57 90W28 6:01:52
New Hope 70 33N03'53 92W55'31 6:11:42
New Jenny Lind 66 35N15'03 94W19'05 6:17:16
New London 70 33N11'18 92W20'21 6:09:21
Newnata 69 35N53'22 92W15'06 6:09:00
New Neely 75 35N06'57 93W04'52 6:12:19
Newport 7 33N25'47 92W41'42 6:10:47
Newport 34 35N36'17 91W16'54 6:05:08
New Salme 74 35N17 91W22 6:05:28
New Spadra 36 35N25'13 93W30'58 6:14:04
New Summit 63 34N33 92W30 6:10:00
New Tennessee 53 34N58 93W06 6:12:24
Newton 23 35N09 92W12 6:08:48
Newton Landing 3 36N20'39 92W12'59 6:08:52
New Town 17 35N25'10 94W12'18 6:16:49
Newtown 35 34N20'02 91W50'23 6:07:22
Nichols 15 35N24 92W42 6:10:48
Nick Springs 70 33N11'54 92W33'37 6:10:14
Nimmo 73 35N11'05 91W28'25 6:05:54
Nimmons 11 36N18'24 90W05'40 6:00:23
Nimrod 53 34N57'33 93W04'35 6:12:18
Ninetysix Corner 18 35N01'25 90W20'15 6:01:21
Nix 20 34N00 92W47 6:11:08
Noahs 65 35N48'57 92W33'01 6:10:12
Noble Lake 35 34N10'23 91W51'15 6:07:25
Nodena 47 35N33'25 89W56'58 5:59:48
Nogal 53 35N04'33 92W34'02 6:10:16
Nogo 58 35N40'32 92W51'46 6:11:27
Nola 64 34N52'40 93W44'28 6:14:58
Noland 61 36N11'36 91W03'02 6:04:12
Norden 47 35N33'15 90W08'03 6:00:32
Norfork 3 36N12'34 92W17'03 6:09:08
Norman 49 34N27'18 93W40'48 6:14:43
Norphlet 70 33N18'57 92W39'46 6:10:39
Norristown 58 35N16 93W10 6:12:40
North Big Rock 68 36N05 91W29 6:05:56
North Bingen 29 33N59'17 93W47'16 6:15:09
North Boothe 64 35N08 94W03 6:16:12
North Brinkley 48 34N48 91W09 6:04:36
North Cedar 35 34N13 92W02 6:08:08
North Crossett 2 33N09'56 91W56'29 6:07:46
North Dardanelle 58 35N13'46 93W08'28 6:12:34
Northern Ohio 56 35N30'12 90W27'13 6:01:49
North Harrison 5 36N15 93W06 6:12:24
North Heights 46 33N26 94W04 6:16:16
North Hughes 62 34N57 90W20 6:01:52
North Lebanon 68 36N11 91W25 6:05:40
North Lewisville 37 33N22 93W35 6:14:20
North Lexa 54 34N36'40 90W45'20 6:03:01
North Little Rock 60 34N46'10 92W16'01 6:09:04
North Pitts 56 35N40'41 91W01'39 6:04:07
Northpoint 60 34N54 92W30 6:10:00
North Union 68 36N22 91W19 6:05:16
Northwest 69 36N00 92W15 6:09:00
Norvell 18 35N16'46 90W28'39 6:01:55
Nowland 29 33N46 93W30 6:14:00
Noxburn 28 36N06'30 90W28'53 6:01:56
Noxobe 14 33N08'43 93W06'15 6:12:25
Nuckles 34 35N34'04 91W21'26 6:05:26
Nugulf 70 33N14'57 92W37'54 6:10:32
Number Nine 47 35N59'16 89W48'27 5:59:14
Nunley 57 34N32'26 94W09'36 6:16:38
Nutts 55 34N11'56 93W27'41 6:13:51
Oak Bluff 11 36N17 90W17 6:01:08
Oak Forest 39 34N48'10 90W54'29 6:03:38
Oak Forest 60 34N44'31 92W19'46 6:09:19
Oakgrove 8 36N27'22 93W26'11 6:13:45
Oak Grove 13 33N56'56 92W01'56 6:08:08
Oak Grove 17 35N25'16 94W17'39 6:17:11
Oak Grove 30 34N20'54 92W54'14 6:11:37
Oak Grove 43 34N55'50 91W54'42 6:07:39
Oak Grove 50 33N35'54 93W14'30 6:12:58
Oak Grove 58 35N21'32 92W57'33 6:11:50
Oak Grove 60 34N50'32 92W19'29 6:09:18
Oak Grove 67 33N53'09 94W08'00 6:16:32
Oak Grove 72 36N11'23 94W11'13 6:16:45
Oakhaven 29 33N43'45 93W37'14 6:14:29
Oak Hill 8 36N28'38 93W41'54 6:14:48
Oakland 45 36N27'39 92W34'15 6:10:17
Oakland Heights 35 34N16'19 92W07'45 6:08:31
Oakland Heights 58 35N17 93W09 6:12:36
Oaklawn 26 34N30 93W03 6:12:12
Oak Park 35 34N13 92W02 6:08:08
Oak Park 66 35N25'50 94W23'29 6:17:34
Oark 36 35N41'22 93W34'20 6:14:17
Oconee 61 36N25 91W08 6:04:32
Odell 72 35N46'21 94W25'05 6:17:40
Oden 49 34N37'08 93W46'36 6:15:06
O'Donnell Bend 47 35N47'49 89W48'12 5:59:13
Offutt Landing 54 34N11'18 90W54'09 6:03:37
Ogden 41 33N34'57 94W02'33 6:16:10
Ogemaw 52 33N27'45 93W01'30 6:12:06
Oil Trough 32 35N37'51 91W27'37 6:05:50
Okay 31 33N46'03 93W55'26 6:15:42
O'Kean 61 36N10'09 90W48'51 6:03:15
Okolona 10 33N59'50 93W20'16 6:13:21
Ola 75 35N01'56 93W13'23 6:12:54
Old Alabam 44 36N08'04 93W40'46 6:14:43
Old Austin 43 34N59'12 91W57'50 6:07:51
Old Bonnerdale 26 34N24'11 93W23'32 6:13:34
Old Botkinburg 71 35N40'34 92W29'17 6:09:57
Old Buffalo 45 36N10'06 92W27'24 6:09:50
Old Cove 57 34N26'50 94W22'26 6:17:30
Old Grand Glaise 34 35N29'23 91W22'31 6:05:30
Old Hickory 15 35N19'36 92W48'10 6:11:13
Old Jenny Lind 66 35N14'24 94W19'36 6:17:18
Old Joe 3 36N10'28 92W13'53 6:08:56
Old Lapile 70 33N04'07 92W14'50 6:08:59
Old Lexington 69 35N43'11 92W24'39 6:09:39
Old Martin Mill Place 38 35N56'24 91W11'53 6:04:48
Old Milo 2 33N17'41 91W53'24 6:07:34
Old Neely 75 35N09'02 93W05'39 6:12:23
Old River 35 34N11 91W40 6:06:40
Old Town 37 33N23'05 93W34'32 6:14:18
Old Union 70 33N13 92W40 6:10:40
Old Weona 56 35N32'07 90W34'23 6:02:18
Olena 1 34N20'10 91W24'37 6:05:38
Olio 64 34N54'53 93W50'54 6:15:24
Oliver 64 34N55'54 94W15'38 6:17:03
Oliver Springs 17 35N31 94W18 6:17:12
Olmstead 60 34N56'35 92W12'44 6:08:51
Olvey 5 36N11'27 92W57'57 6:11:52
Olyphant 34 35N31'28 91W22'56 6:05:32
Oma 26 34N23'46 93W15'52 6:13:03
Omaha 5 36N27'08 93W11'18 6:12:45
Omega 8 36N13 93W32 6:14:08
Omega 21 33N49'17 91W28'39 6:05:55
Omega 75 35N08'51 93W13'25 6:12:54
Onda 72 35N51'59 94W17'30 6:17:10
O'Neal 32 35N46'35 91W51'34 6:07:26
One Horse Store 1 34N29 91W33 6:06:12
Oneida 54 34N27'41 90W46'59 6:03:08
Onia 69 35N55'08 92W19'37 6:09:18
Onyx 75 34N51'05 93W24'28 6:13:38
Opal 43 35N05'50 92W00'10 6:08:01
Opal 57 34N32'22 93W59'22 6:15:57
Oppelo 15 35N06'04 92W46'03 6:11:04
Optimus 69 36N02'41 92W07'30 6:08:30
Orion 27 34N28'27 92W15'11 6:09:01
Orlando 13 33N43'11 92W08'28 6:08:34
Orton 41 33N38'46 93W55'24 6:15:42
Osage 8 36N10'57 93W24'16 6:13:37
Osage Mills 4 36N16'52 94W16'07 6:17:04
Osceola 47 35N42'18 89W58'10 5:59:53
Ott 25 36N29'55 92W04'45 6:08:19
Otter 63 34N36 92W24 6:09:36
Otto 23 35N01'46 92W11'33 6:08:46
Otwell 16 35N43'33 90W50'16 6:03:21
Ouachita 20 33N51'08 92W49'45 6:11:19
Ouachita College 10 34N05 93W02 6:12:08
Ouita 58 35N17 93W09 6:12:36
Overcup 15 35N13'30 92W41'31 6:10:46
Overcup 74 35N21'15 91W13'49 6:04:55
Owens 14 33N01'31 93W03'16 6:12:13
Owensville 63 34N36'57 92W49'17 6:11:17
Oxford 33 36N13'16 91W55'45 6:07:43
Oxford Ford 25 36N28'01 91W35'56 6:06:24
Oxley 65 35N50'32 92W27'25 6:09:50
Ozan 29 33N50'52 93W43'08 6:14:53
Ozark 24 35N29'13 93W49'39 6:15:19
Ozark Acres 68 36N17'41 91W22'58 6:05:32
Ozark Lithia 26 34N35'44 93W00'44 6:12:03
Ozone 36 35N38'28 93W26'35 6:13:46
Pace City 52 33N24'10 92W54'43 6:11:39
Packard Springs 8 36N20 93W45 6:15:00
Palarm 23 34N54'18 92W26'51 6:09:47
Palatka 11 36N27'59 90W39'28 6:02:38
Palestine 62 34N58'20 90W54'09 6:03:37
Palmer 49 34N34'34 91W03'56 6:04:16
Palmyra 40 33N55'22 91W55'49 6:07:43
Pangburn 73 35N25'36 91W50'12 6:07:21
Pankey 60 34N48'01 92W25'13 6:09:41
Pankov 41 33N42'16 94W20'23 6:17:22
Pansy 13 33N49'19 92W00'10 6:08:01
Panther Forest 9 33N20 91W17 6:05:08
Paraclifta 67 33N53 94W11 6:16:44
Paradise 22 33N32 91W48 6:07:12
Paradise 24 35N37'56 93W50'02 6:15:20
Paradise Landing 18 35N21'39 90W07'39 6:00:31
Paradise Landing 23 34N58'38 92W24'31 6:09:38
Paragould 28 36N03'30 90W30'00 6:02:00
Paraloma 67 33N47'52 94W01'08 6:16:05
Paris 42 35N17'31 93W43'47 6:14:55
Park 64 34N48 93W58 6:15:52
Parkdale 2 33N07'17 91W32'44 6:06:11
Parker 50 33N34 93W23 6:13:32
Parker Ford 44 36N12'03 93W50'09 6:15:21
Parkers 60 34N37'06 92W18'56 6:09:16
Parkers Chapel 70 33N13 92W40 6:10:40
Parkers Corner 43 34N39'27 91W43'07 6:06:52
Park Grove 48 34N41'32 91W12'42 6:04:51
Park Hill 60 34N47'09 92W15'37 6:09:02
Parkin 19 35N15'48 90W34'16 6:02:17
Park Place 39 34N49'44 90W35'46 6:02:23
Parks 64 34N48'07 93W57'38 6:15:51
Parma 69 35N43'09 92W10'44 6:08:43
Parnell 43 34N59 92W01 6:08:04
Paron 63 34N46'22 92W45'30 6:11:02
Paroquet 32 35N40'28 91W21'49 6:05:27
Partain 12 35N37'40 92W14'23 6:08:58
Partee 14 33N14'32 93W14'40 6:12:59
Parthenon 51 35N57'11 93W14'31 6:12:58
Pastoria 35 34N21'29 92W02'24 6:08:10
Patmos 29 33N30'42 93W33'58 6:14:16
Patoka 18 35N04'24 90W18'40 6:01:15
Patrick 44 35N50'35 93W53'01 6:15:32
Patsville 6 33N27 92W10 6:08:40
Patterson 11 36N16'20 90W07'18 6:00:29
Patterson 66 34N59'31 94W21'39 6:17:27
Patterson 74 35N15'24 91W14'06 6:04:56
Pattonville 32 35N47'34 91W42'51 6:06:51
Pattsville 6 33N26'31 92W06'24 6:08:26
Pauls Switch 16 35N57'08 90W49'30 6:03:18
Paup 46 33N30'07 93W56'33 6:15:46
Pawheen 47 35N56 90W15 6:01:00
Payne 11 36N17 90W07 6:00:28
Payne 70 33N08'51 92W25'51 6:09:43
Payneway 56 35N32'35 90W30'10 6:02:01
Peach Orchard 11 36N16'43 90W39'46 6:02:39
Peanut 24 35N40'31 93W42'17 6:14:49
Pearcy 26 34N25'43 93W17'23 6:13:10
Pea Ridge 4 36N27'14 94W06'54 6:16:28
Pea Ridge 21 33N55'14 91W20'12 6:05:21
Pearson 12 35N26'26 92W07'40 6:08:31
Pecan 47 35N29 90W03 6:00:12
Pecan Grove 60 34N46'23 92W12'24 6:08:50
Pecan Point 47 35N28'39 90W02'21 6:00:09
Pecan Point Landing 47 35N28'29 90W01'54 6:00:08
Pedro 4 36N10'06 94W24'14 6:17:37
Peel 45 36N25'56 92W46'07 6:11:04
Pelsor 58 35N43 93W04 6:12:16
Pencil Bluff 49 34N37'47 93W44'03 6:14:56
Pendleton 21 33N58'38 91W22'55 6:05:32
Penjur 62 34N58'30 90W25'41 6:01:43
Pennington 6 33N37 92W06 6:08:24
Pennington 34 35N35'21 91W03'40 6:04:15
Pennys 67 33N52'41 94W09'54 6:16:40
Penrose 74 35N11'34 91W03'03 6:04:12
Perkins 31 34N04'36 93W51'35 6:15:26
Perla 30 34N21'52 92W46'17 6:11:05
Perry 53 35N02'51 92W47'38 6:11:11
Perrytown 29 33N41'47 93W32'13 6:14:09
Perryville 53 35N00'17 92W48'09 6:11:13
Peter Creek 12 35N35 91W57 6:07:48
Peter Pender 24 35N21'36 93W56'03 6:15:44
Peters 39 34N49'10 90W28'44 6:01:55
Petit Jean 58 35N05'26 93W10'49 6:12:43
Pettigrew 44 35N49'04 93W38'54 6:14:36
Pettus 43 34N40'01 91W54'22 6:07:37
Pettyview 26 34N24'18 93W10'01 6:12:40
Pettyville 47 35N50'45 90W07'10 6:00:29
Peytonville 41 33N41'37 94W04'41 6:16:19
Pfeiffer 32 35N49'26 91W35'16 6:06:21
Phenix 40 34N02'00 91W46'15 6:07:05
Philadelphia 14 33N12'14 93W18'43 6:13:15
Philadelphia 16 35N52'44 90W42'09 6:02:49
Philander Smith College 60 34N44 92W19 6:09:16
Phillips 16 35N48'59 90W35'03 6:02:20
Phillips 26 34N33 92W50 6:11:20
Phillips Bayou 39 34N38'53 90W38'23 6:02:34
Phoenix 58 35N24 93W01 6:12:04
Pickens 21 33N50'48 91W28'47 6:05:55
Pickens 73 35N20'51 91W52'27 6:07:30
Piercetown 51 35N57'59 93W04'17 6:12:17
Pigeon 3 36N27 92W21 6:09:24
Piggott 11 36N22'58 90W11'26 6:00:46
Pike City 55 34N06'44 93W34'30 6:14:18
Pike Junction 10 34N02'06 93W24'38 6:13:39
Pilgrims Rest 54 34N23'25 90W52'10 6:03:29
Pilgrims Rest 72 36N11'14 93W59'38 6:15:59
Pillar 54 34N32'46 90W42'57 6:02:52
Pilot Rock 36 35N40 93W13 6:12:52
Pinckney 18 34N58'36 90W18'19 6:01:13
Pindall 65 36N03'58 92W52'52 6:11:31
Pine 12 35N29 91W52 6:07:28
Pinebergen 35 34N06'10 91W59'32 6:07:58
Pine Bluff 35 34N13'42 92W00'11 6:08:01
Pine City 49 34N34'58 91W06'47 6:04:27
Pinecrest 35 34N13 92W02 6:08:08
Pine Grove 20 33N52'56 92W46'18 6:11:05

Pine Grove Valley 64 35N04 94w15 6:17:00
Pine Haven 63 34N33'53 92w29'22 6:09:57
Pine Island Landing 6 33N15'05 92w04'22 6:08:17
Pine Log 4 36N24 93w54 6:15:36
Pine Mountain 23 35N01 92w27 6:09:48
Pine Ridge 48 34N41 91w11 6:04:44
Pine Ridge 49 34N35'09 93w54'36 6:15:38
Pine Top 4 36N19'28 93w52'40 6:15:31
Pinetree 62 35N07'36 90w55'41 6:03:43
Pine Valley 32 35N56 91w33 6:06:12
Pineville 33 36N09'46 92w06'25 6:08:26
Piney 24 35N35'09 94w03'27 6:16:14
Piney 26 34N30'11 93w07'33 6:12:30
Piney 36 35N20'40 93w19'31 6:13:18
Piney Fork 68 36N04 91w38 6:06:32
Piney Grove 37 33N26'16 93w36'22 6:14:25
Piney Grove 55 33N58'17 93w27'21 6:13:49
Pinnacle 60 34N49'32 92w29'48 6:09:59
Pisgah 55 33N58'45 93w31'33 6:14:06
Pisgah 75 35N14 93w10 6:12:40
Pitkin Corner 72 35N53'07 94w10'29 6:16:42
Pitman 61 36N28'42 90w49'21 6:03:17
Pittinger 19 35N26'32 90w59'11 6:03:57
Pitts 56 35N40'28 91w01'53 6:04:08
Pittsburg 36 35N26 93w22 6:13:28
Pittston Junction 24 35N38'56 93w43'52 6:14:55
Plainfield 14 33N02'52 93w19'07 6:13:16
Plainview 42 35N18'53 93w35'22 6:14:21
Plainview 73 35N18'45 91w40'37 6:06:42
Plainview 75 34N59'22 93w17'50 6:13:11
Plant 71 35N35 92w28 6:09:52
Planters 9 33N08 91w18 6:05:12
Plantersville 22 33N46'01 91w52'50 6:07:31
Plata 49 34N27'09 93w32'48 6:14:11
Pleasant Grove 16 35N50 90w48 6:03:12
Pleasant Grove 69 35N48'59 91w54'33 6:07:38
Pleasant Grove 71 35N29'34 92w36'53 6:10:28
Pleasant Hill 15 35N23'06 92w35'13 6:10:21
Pleasant Hill 17 35N31'18 94w02'56 6:16:12
Pleasant Hill 19 35N13 90w47 6:03:08
Pleasant Hill 26 34N27'20 93w09'41 6:12:39
Pleasant Hill 42 35N20'14 93w36'50 6:14:27
Pleasant Hill 50 33N51'54 93w25'40 6:13:43
Pleasant Hill 75 34N53'21 93w32'16 6:14:09
Pleasant Hills 69 35N55 92w19 6:09:16
Pleasant Plains 32 35N33'00 91w37'34 6:06:30
Pleasant Ridge 5 36N13'31 92w54'28 6:11:38
Pleasant Ridge 8 36N28'54 93w38'38 6:14:35
Pleasant Ridge 25 36N18 91w39 6:06:36
Pleasant Valley 8 36N23'13 93w36'35 6:14:26
Pleasant Valley 23 35N10'44 92w26'58 6:09:48
Pleasant Valley 33 36N08'18 92w09'50 6:08:39
Pleasant Valley 37 33N06'31 93w48'45 6:15:15
Pleasant Valley 53 34N58'17 92w40'27 6:10:42
Pleasant Valley 58 35N26'27 93w08'00 6:12:32
Pleasant View 24 35N29'01 94w01'03 6:16:04
Pleasure Heights 4 36N14'10 94w00'55 6:16:04
Pless 58 35N24'15 93w15'54 6:13:04
Plum Bayou 35 34N20 91w54 6:07:36
Plumerville 15 35N09'36 92w38'26 6:10:34
Plumlee 51 36N05 93w18 6:13:12
Plunketts 59 34N49 91w24 6:05:36
Pocahontas 61 36N15'41 90w58'16 6:03:53
Poff 12 35N40 92w11 6:08:44
Point 74 35N09 91w21 6:05:24
Point Cedar 30 34N19'39 93w18'26 6:13:14
Point De Luce 1 34N12 91w17 6:05:08
Point Peter 65 35N57'20 92w54'33 6:11:38
Poker Point Landing 18 35N20'10 90w07'00 6:00:28
Poland 28 36N00 90w37 6:02:28
Pollard 11 36N25'51 90w16'06 6:01:04
Polo 8 36N26 93w33 6:14:12
Ponca 51 36N01'27 93w21'52 6:13:27
Ponders 38 36N00'03 90w53'49 6:03:35
Pontoon 15 35N02 93w03 6:12:12
Pooles Landing 23 34N58'33 92w24'55 6:09:40
Poping 24 35N27'10 93w53'22 6:15:33
Poplar Corner 47 35N55'51 90w10'38 6:00:43
Poplar Grove 54 34N32'52 90w51'11 6:03:25
Poplar Ridge 16 35N49'47 90w24'16 6:01:37
Porter 17 35N44 94w08 6:16:32
Portia 38 36N05'11 91w04'02 6:04:16
Portland 2 33N14'16 91w30'41 6:06:03
Posey 62 34N57'19 91w06'58 6:04:28
Possum Fork 21 33N46 91w16 6:05:04
Possum Grape 34 35N28'33 91w24'40 6:05:39
Postal Landing 74 35N08'17 91w25'36 6:05:42
Postelle 54 34N34'12 91w01'22 6:04:05
Potter 57 34N33'13 94w20'20 6:17:21
Potter Junction 57 34N33'02 94w18'21 6:17:13
Pottsville 58 35N14'53 93w02'56 6:12:12
Poughkeepsie 68 36N04'36 91w28'45 6:05:55
Poven 27 34N19'27 92w38'23 6:10:34
Powell 16 35N56 90w38 6:02:32
Powell 45 36N14'15 92w49'00 6:11:16
Powers 29 33N39'59 93w43'32 6:14:54
Powhatan 38 36N04'56 91w07'06 6:04:28
Poyen 27 34N20 92w38 6:10:32
Prague 27 34N17'12 92w16'50 6:09:07
Prairie Creek 4 36N20'31 94w03'42 6:16:15
Prairie Creek 66 35N03'08 94w21'00 6:17:24
Prairie Grove 72 35N58'33 94w19'03 6:17:16
Prairie Landing 1 34N04'49 91w11'18 6:04:45
Prairie View 42 35N20'04 93w31'04 6:14:04
Prattsville 27 34N18'53 92w33'12 6:10:13
Prescott 50 33N48'09 93w22'51 6:13:31
Presley Junction 18 35N10'43 90w11'14 6:00:45
Preston 23 35N01'32 92w25'20 6:09:41
Preston Ferry 1 34N32'05 91w18'13 6:05:13
Preston Place 54 34N28'32 90w38'37 6:02:34
Price 26 34N30 93w03 6:12:12
Price 45 36N27 92w38 6:10:32
Price 72 35N58 94w29 6:17:56
Price Ford 12 35N22'30 91w57'22 6:07:49
Prim 12 35N41'38 92w06'30 6:08:26
Princedale 19 35N15'50 90w38'49 6:02:35
Princeton 20 33N58'54 92w37'28 6:10:30
Princeton Landing 74 35N10'32 91w25'38 6:05:43
Process City 67 34N01'16 94w21'55 6:17:28
Proctor 18 35N05'42 90w22'24 6:01:30
Promised Land 47 35N53'57 89w51'11 5:59:25
Promised Land 56 35N41 90w31 6:02:04
Pronton 15 35N06'43 93w00'37 6:12:02
Prosperity 5 36N19'58 93w12'03 6:12:48
Prosperity 75 35N09'24 93w09'55 6:12:40
Protho Junction 60 34N46'03 92w11'55 6:08:48
Providence 73 35N22'13 91w40'34 6:06:42
Provo 67 34N02'15 94w06'27 6:16:26
Pruitt 51 36N03'44 93w08'12 6:12:33
Pryor 73 35N10'30 91w32'55 6:06:12
Pugh 2 33N14'22 91w57'43 6:07:51
Pulaski 60 34N46'06 92w18'35 6:09:14
Pulaski Heights 60 34N45'25 92w19'00 6:09:16
Pullman 67 34N06'52 94w18'59 6:17:16
Pumpkin Bend 74 35N18 91w06 6:04:24
Purdy 44 36N05'29 93w34'25 6:14:18
Puryear 64 34N47'25 94w25'34 6:17:42
Pyatt 45 36N14'45 92w50'41 6:11:23
Quarles 18 35N06'04 90w14'43 6:00:59
Quarry Heights 75 35N06'36 93w41'47 6:14:47
Quarry Landing 3 36N15'40 92w14'28 6:08:58
Quinn 70 33N16'54 92w36'52 6:10:27
Quitman 12 35N23'03 92w12'56 6:08:52
Ragan 54 34N17'34 90w51'34 6:03:26
Raggio 39 34N49'56 90w36'18 6:02:25
Rago 4 36N27'02 94w11'45 6:16:47
Ragsdale 53 34N56'25 92w53'42 6:11:35
Ragtown 49 34N32'25 91w06'36 6:04:26
Rally Hill 5 36N09'39 92w57'09 6:11:49
Ralph 45 36N10'19 92w40'27 6:10:42
Ramsey 20 33N52'27 92w33'13 6:10:13
Ramsey Hill 32 35N46 91w37 6:06:28
Randall 13 34N01'24 92w02'28 6:08:10
Randolph 21 33N55 91w31 6:06:04
Random Shot Landing 47 35N29'32 90w02'47 6:00:11
Ranger 75 35N07'19 93w20'35 6:13:22
Rankin 53 34N58 92w44 6:10:56
Raspberry 58 35N41'11 92w56'05 6:11:44
Rasts Landing 18 35N22'43 90w07'42 6:00:31
Ratcliff 42 35N18'30 93w53'00 6:15:32
Ratio 54 34N15'40 90w55'55 6:03:44
Ravanna 46 33N03'55 94w02'27 6:16:10
Ravenden 38 36N14'00 91w15'06 6:05:00
Ravenden Springs 61 36N18'59 91w13'21 6:04:53
Rawlinson 62 34N55'45 90w35'23 6:02:22
Rawlison 62 34N57 90w28 6:01:52
Rawls 2 33N00'38 91w51'18 6:07:25
Raymond 48 34N37 91w07 6:04:28
Reader 50 33N45'07 93w06'18 6:12:25
Readland 9 33N03'56 91w12'48 6:04:51
Reamey 34 35N39'52 91w18'33 6:05:14
Rea Valley 45 36N13'16 92w32'28 6:10:10
Rector 11 36N15'47 90w17'33 6:01:10
Red Bank 5 36N11'46 93w16'00 6:13:04
Red Bank Landing 3 36N26'58 92w16'03 6:09:04
Red Bluff 41 33N38'45 93w57'29 6:15:50
Red Colony 67 33N58 94w09 6:16:36
Redding 24 35N40'48 93w46'37 6:15:06
Redemption 53 35N00 92w37 6:10:28
Redfern 62 34N59'36 90w50'07 6:03:20
Redfield 35 34N26'42 92w10'59 6:08:44
Red Fork 21 33N56'11 91w16'12 6:05:05
Red Gate 60 34N38'47 92w26'39 6:09:47
Red Gum Farm 62 34N57'50 90w28'48 6:01:55
Red Hill 52 33N44'36 93w01'28 6:12:06
Redland 50 33N48'24 93w16'39 6:13:07
Red Leaf 9 33N16'20 91w11'47 6:04:47
Red Lick 36 35N33 93w25 6:13:40
Red Line 47 35N42'53 90w05'28 6:00:22
Redman Point 18 35N14'26 90w06'47 6:00:27
Red Oak 26 34N25'13 93w01'16 6:12:05
Red Onion 16 35N59'45 90w20'33 6:01:22
Red Rock 51 35N54'52 93w08'07 6:12:32
Red Springs 10 33N54'08 93w03'51 6:12:15
Red Star 44 35N52'00 93w31'50 6:14:07
Redstripe 69 35N49 91w55 6:07:40
Red Wing 67 34N02'46 94w14'34 6:16:58
Reed 21 33N42 91w27 6:05:48
Reed Keathly 75 35N03 93w29 6:13:56
Reeds Creek 38 35N56 91w18 6:05:12
Reedville 21 33N55'49 91w31'06 6:06:04
Reese 39 34N53'50 90w26'48 6:01:47
Reeves 51 35N54'49 93w29'55 6:14:00
Reform 63 34N47'23 92w50'00 6:11:20
Rehms Corner 15 35N05'13 92w47'56 6:11:12
Relfs Bluff 40 33N48'04 91w50'34 6:07:22
Relief 32 35N39 91w42 6:06:48
Remmel 34 35N32'49 91w09'47 6:04:39
Rena 17 35N29 94w21 6:17:24
Rendezvous 52 33N30'36 92w49'52 6:11:19
Republican 23 35N16'53 92w25'30 6:09:42
Retta 58 35N31'00 92w56'56 6:11:48
Revel 74 35N13'48 91w16'53 6:05:08
Revilee 42 35N11 93w47 6:15:08
Rex 71 35N36'09 92w42'21 6:10:49
Reydell 35 34N09'26 91w34'03 6:06:16
Reyno 61 36N21'46 90w45'13 6:03:01
Reynolds 28 36N11 90w20 6:01:20
Reynolds 44 35N58'55 93w35'58 6:14:24
Rhea 72 36N00'51 94w24'10 6:17:37
Rheas Mill 72 36N01 94w24 6:17:36
Rhyne 11 36N21'29 90w08'22 6:00:33
Riceville 18 35N07'23 90w13'33 6:00:54
Rich 48 34N45'52 91w08'14 6:04:33
Richardson 35 34N13'05 91w44'17 6:06:57
Richardson 61 36N24 90w52 6:03:28
Richland 60 34N43 92w16 6:09:04
Richland View 72 36N00 94w01 6:16:04
Richmond 41 33N38'15 94w12'26 6:16:50
Rich Mountain 57 34N41'26 94w20'13 6:17:21
Richwood 10 34N05 93w02 6:12:08
Richwoods 10 34N02'13 93w05'07 6:12:20
Richwoods 38 36N08'33 91w00'42 6:04:03
Ridge 16 35N44'50 90w41'13 6:02:45
Ridgeway 5 36N19'04 93w12'16 6:12:49
Riffe Ford 10 33N46'20 93w02'07 6:12:08
Riggs 16 35N46'14 90w57'16 6:03:49
Riley 2 33N21'47 91w42'59 6:06:52
Riley 75 35N07 93w32 6:14:08
Rington 47 35N59'46 90w11'17 6:00:45
Rio Vista 73 35N17'26 91w28'15 6:05:53
Risher 16 35N44'48 90w58'25 6:03:54
Rison 13 33N57'30 92w11'24 6:08:46
Ritchie 70 33N17'10 92w32'30 6:10:10
Ritz 64 34N45'11 94w14'10 6:16:57
Riverdale 66 35N25'25 94w06'14 6:16:25
River Front 19 35N15'46 90w40'00 6:02:40
River Mountain 42 35N17 93w19 6:13:16
Riverside 42 35N17'56 93w17'12 6:13:09
Riverside 74 35N17'37 91w14'28 6:04:58
Rivervale 56 35N40'26 90w20'24 6:01:22
Riverview 15 35N06'57 92w47'03 6:11:08
Rixey 60 34N48'57 92w10'08 6:08:41
Roane 37 33N07 93w41 6:14:44
Roanoke 61 36N13 91w04 6:04:16
Roark 2 33N21'42 91w49'12 6:07:17
Roasting Ear 69 35N56 92w18 6:09:12
Roberts 35 34N27 91w43 6:06:52
Robertsville 15 35N22'04 92w47'24 6:11:10
Robinson 4 36N10'09 94w21'31 6:17:26
Robinson Point Landing 3 36N21'06 92w14'18 6:08:57
Rob Roy 35 34N16'52 91w53'49 6:07:35
Rock 44 36N16'18 93w51'58 6:15:28
Rock Creek 65 36N02 92w31 6:10:04
Rock Hill 28 36N04 90w32 6:02:08
Rock Hill 67 33N53 94w05 6:16:20
Rockhouse 44 36N16'55 93w40'22 6:14:41
Rock Island Junction 6 33N27 92w10 6:08:40
Rock Island Quarters 70 33N13 92w40 6:10:40
Rockport 30 34N23'15 92w49'31 6:11:18
Rock Springs 22 33N45'40 91w54'29 6:07:38
Rock Springs 65 35N56'41 92w32'07 6:10:08
Rockwell 26 34N30 93w03 6:12:12
Rocky 47 35N56 90w15 6:01:00
Rocky 57 34N35'30 94w22'09 6:17:29
Rocky Crossing 53 34N54'42 93w03'20 6:12:13
Rocky Ford 44 36N09'40 93w45'37 6:15:02
Rocky Hill 71 35N45 92w31 6:10:04
Rocky Mound 14 33N08'27 93w21'53 6:13:28
Rocky Mound 29 33N40'08 93w31'47 6:14:07
Rocky Mound 46 33N16 93w53 6:15:32
Rodney 3 36N14'34 92w09'40 6:08:39
Roe 48 34N38'00 91w23'06 6:05:32
Rogers 4 36N19'55 94w07'06 6:16:28
Rohwer 21 33N45'39 91w16'32 6:05:06
Rokey 47 35N51'34 90w16'29 6:01:06
Roland 60 34N54'02 92w29'53 6:10:00
Rolfe Junction 2 33N07'25 91w52'21 6:07:29
Rolla 30 34N12'29 92w43'50 6:10:55
Roller Ridge 4 36N29 93w55 6:15:40
Romance 73 35N14'27 92w03'04 6:08:12
Rondo 39 34N39'33 90w49'14 6:03:17
Rondo 46 33N26'40 93w58'39 6:15:55
Rone 35 34N04'11 92w07'40 6:08:31
Roosevelt 73 35N30'59 91w40'09 6:06:41
Rosa 47 35N46'10 89w50'59 5:59:24
Rosboro 55 34N17'15 93w30'30 6:14:02
Rose Bud 73 35N19'53 92w04'52 6:08:19
Rose City 60 34N45'29 92w12'27 6:08:50
Rose Creek 53 35N04 93w00 6:12:00
Rosedale 60 34N43'15 92w22'22 6:09:29
Roseland 47 35N50'47 90w06'04 6:00:24
Rose Meadow 60 34N43 92w16 6:09:04
Rose Place 19 35N14'19 90w35'45 6:02:23
Rosetta 36 35N42'32 93w20'40 6:13:23
Roseville 42 35N22'57 93w46'31 6:15:06
Rosie 32 35N40'06 91w32'18 6:06:09
Ross 58 35N27'18 93w15'11 6:13:01
Rosston 50 33N35'33 93w16'35 6:13:06
Rotan 47 35N37'30 89w59'31 5:59:58
Rottaken 60 34N34'23 92w12'39 6:08:51
Roughedge Ford 65 35N58'20 92w54'16 6:11:37
Round Hill 20 34N07'56 92w47'39 6:11:11
Round Mountain 15 35N02 93w03 6:12:12
Round Pond 62 35N04 90w37 6:02:28
Round Prairie 4 36N16 94w33 6:18:12
Rover 75 34N56'47 93w24'19 6:13:37
Rowell 13 33N53'10 92w01'06 6:08:04
Roxton 44 36N02'13 93w47'53 6:15:12
Roy 47 35N39'37 90w05'41 6:00:23
Roy 55 34N00'30 93w41'49 6:14:47
Royal 26 34N30'41 93w14'27 6:12:58
Royal 73 35N06 92w01 6:08:04
Royal Oak 63 34N40 92w22 6:09:28
Rubicon 63 34N37'52 92w45'58 6:11:04
Rudd 8 36N12'49 93w29'09 6:13:57
Ruddell 32 35N47 91w41 6:06:44
Ruddle Mill 32 35N46 91w37 6:06:28
Rudy 17 35N31'40 94w16'14 6:17:05
Rule 8 36N16'40 93w27'35 6:13:50
Rumley 71 35N47'20 92w30'49 6:10:03
Running Lake 61 36N19 90w53 6:03:32
Rupert 71 35N38'03 92w41'27 6:10:46
Rush 45 36N07'59 92w34'15 6:10:17
Rushing 69 35N44'07 92w15'52 6:09:03
Russell 73 35N21'45 91w30'27 6:06:02
Russellville 58 35N16'42 93w08'01 6:12:32
Ruth 25 36N22'12 92w08'10 6:08:33
Rutherford 32 35N43'22 91w32'19 6:06:09
Ryan 43 34N32'37 91w49'39 6:07:19
Rye 13 33N44'46 91w59'52 6:07:59
Rye Hill 66 35N22 94w23 6:17:32
Ryker 51 35N53'17 93w28'24 6:13:54
Sacred Heart 36 35N26 93w37 6:14:28
Saddle 25 36N21'18 91w38'19 6:06:33
Saffell 38 35N55'11 91w17'24 6:05:10
Sage 33 36N02'45 91w48'58 6:07:16

Place	Latitude	Longitude	Time
Saginaw 30	34N18'01	92w56'10	6:11:45
Saint Charles 1	34N22'18	91w08'11	6:04:33
Saint Claire 18	35N13'07	90w07'07	6:00:28
Saint Francis 11	36N27'12	90w08'43	6:00:35
Saint James 69	35N50'18	91w55'04	6:07:40
Saint Joe 65	36N01'48	92w48'16	6:11:13
Saint Paul 44	35N49'27	93w45'50	6:15:03
Saint Thomas 47	35N26'31	90w08'34	6:00:34
Saint Vincent 15	35N18'04	92w43'53	6:10:56
Salado 32	35N41'28	91w35'44	6:06:23
Salem 25	36N22'16	91w49'21	6:07:17
Salem 52	33N41'27	92w39'26	6:10:38
Salem 55	34N18'40	93w37'03	6:14:28
Salem 63	34N37'44	92w33'29	6:10:14
Salem Landing 3	36N22'00	92w14'40	6:08:59
Salesville 3	36N15	92w16	6:09:04
Saline 13	35N52'24	92w16'01	6:09:04
Saline Landing 31	33N45'30	93w57'40	6:15:51
Saltillo 23	35N01'39	92w19'35	6:09:18
Salus 36	35N43'51	93w24'21	6:13:37
Samples 35	34N20'46	92w08'26	6:08:34
Sanders 50	33N28'50	93w21'26	6:13:26
Sand Gap 58	35N43'15	93w05'45	6:12:23
Sand Hill 59	35N00'31	91w26'05	6:05:44
Sandiff 12	35N38'52	92w13'23	6:08:54
Sand Point 17	35N39	94w05	6:16:20
Sand Ridge 42	35N17'35	93w34'45	6:14:19
Sand Spring 58	35N27	93w16	6:13:04
Sandtown 15	35N08	92w45	6:11:00
Sandtown 32	35N54'17	91w38'06	6:06:32
Sandy 16	35N45'57	90w26'09	6:01:45
Sandy Bend 70	33N06	92w22	6:09:28
Sandy Land 70	33N20'05	92w42'04	6:10:48
Sandy Ridge 47	35N57	89w57	5:59:48
Sans Souci 47	35N39'11	89w56'58	5:59:48
Sans Souci Landing 47	35N39'43	89w56'05	5:59:44
Saratoga 31	33N45'06	93w54'09	6:15:37
Sardis 63	34N31'54	92w24'28	6:09:38
Satuma 53	34N54'09	92w51'33	6:11:26
Saulsburg 48	34N58'12	91w12'58	6:04:52
Savoy 72	36N06'20	94w19'57	6:17:20
Sawmill 70	33N09'30	92w15'19	6:09:01
Sayre 52	33N45'07	93w05'31	6:12:22
Schaal 31	33N53	93w55	6:15:40
Schaberg 17	35N43'38	94w10'10	6:16:41
Schug 16	35N57'57	90w26'31	6:01:46
Scipio 22	35N23'46	91w47'38	6:07:11
Scotia 58	35N19'52	93w17'32	6:13:10
Scotland 71	35N31'39	92w36'42	6:10:27
Scott 43	34N41'47	92w05'46	6:08:23
Scottsville 58	35N26'55	93w02'47	6:12:11
Scott Valley 39	34N43'48	90w46'04	6:03:04
Scranton 42	35N21'40	93w32'08	6:14:09
Screeton 59	34N46'53	91w40'02	6:06:40
Searcy 73	35N15'02	91w44'10	6:06:57
Seaton 43	34N33	91w53	6:07:32
Seba 4	36N22'22	94w17'37	6:17:10
Sedgwick 38	35N58'40	90w51'50	6:03:27
Segur 49	34N21'22	93w30'13	6:14:01
Self 5	36N23'53	93w06'29	6:12:26
Self Creek 55	34N15	93w42	6:14:48
Sellers Store 68	36N20'30	91w24'35	6:05:38
Selma 22	33N41'50	91w34'03	6:06:16
Seyppel 18	34N57	90w28	6:01:52
Shady 57	34N26'59	94w07'12	6:16:29
Shady Grove 3	36N15'05	92w22'45	6:09:31
Shady Grove 25	36N22'00	91w54'46	6:07:39
Shady Grove 36	35N27'46	93w31'26	6:14:06
Shady Grove 42	35N13'48	93w24'54	6:13:40
Shady Grove 47	35N49'49	90w10'43	6:00:43
Shady Grove 50	33N48	93w23	6:13:32
Shady Grove 56	35N40'41	90w36'23	6:02:26
Shady Grove 60	34N45'43	92w28'19	6:09:53
Shakertown 10	33N56'03	92w58'54	6:11:56
Shannon 40	34N05	91w42	6:06:48
Shannon 61	36N12'32	90w57'29	6:03:50
Shannondale 62	34N55'09	90w30'27	6:02:02
Shannon Hills 63	34N37'12	92w23'43	6:09:35
Shannon Tank 40	34N05'21	91w43'07	6:06:52
Shannonville 18	35N15'59	90w28'53	6:01:56
Shark 75	34N59'42	93w30'53	6:14:04
Sharman 14	33N11'24	93w24'39	6:13:39
Sharp Ford 4	36N14'22	93w54'52	6:15:39
Sharum 61	36N13'22	90w51'14	6:03:25
Shaw 63	34N29'53	92w32'17	6:10:09
Shawmut 55	34N09'06	93w26'58	6:13:48
Shawnee 47	35N29'43	90w07'00	6:00:28
Shearerville 62	35N08'53	90w24'02	6:01:36
Shelbyville 68	35N57'32	91w23'58	6:05:36
Shell Lake 62	35N04	90w30	6:02:00
Shepherd 17	35N44	93w59	6:15:56
Sheppard 29	33N37'35	93w43'19	6:14:53
Sheppard Point 1	34N11'28	91w12'42	6:04:51
Shepperd Crossing 62	34N59'16	90w36'01	6:02:24
Sheridan 27	34N18'25	92w24'04	6:09:36
Sherman 36	35N40	93w26	6:13:44
Sherrill 35	34N23'07	91w57'02	6:07:48
Sherwood 60	34N48'54	92w13'27	6:08:54
Sherwood Hills 30	34N23	92w49	6:11:16
Shibley 17	35N27'01	94w17'37	6:17:10
Shiloh 14	33N23'34	93w16'16	6:13:05
Shiloh 31	33N52'15	94w00'01	6:16:00
Shiloh 37	33N23'19	93w27'35	6:13:50
Shiloh 58	35N17	93w09	6:12:36
Shiloh 61	36N18	91w02	6:04:08
Shipp 3	36N12'43	92w21'36	6:09:26
Shippen 47	35N41'26	90w05'58	6:00:24
Shirley 71	35N39'22	92w19'09	6:09:17
Shives 9	33N16'31	91w10'15	6:04:41
Shoal Creek 42	35N17	93w26	6:13:44
Shoffner 34	35N28'17	91w13'51	6:04:55
Shorewood Hills 30	34N26'15	92w53'45	6:11:35
Short Mountain 42	35N18	93w45	6:15:00
Shover Springs 29	33N37'22	93w31'49	6:14:07
Shuler 70	33N10'43	92w54'05	6:11:36
Shumaker 52	33N40'18	92w43'32	6:10:54
Sidney 68	36N00'11	91w39'35	6:06:38
Sidon 73	35N20'40	91w56'21	6:07:45
Siedenstricker 59	34N43'42	91w33'10	6:06:13
Signal Hill 69	35N45	92w04	6:08:16
Silex 58	35N30'02	93w12'54	6:12:52
Sills 75	35N16'40	93w16'37	6:13:06
Siloam 61	36N27	90w56	6:03:44
Siloam Springs 4	36N11'17	94w32'25	6:18:10
Silver 49	34N32'05	93w30'36	6:14:02
Silver Hill 65	35N58'14	92w44'45	6:10:59
Silver Lake 21	33N56	91w26	6:05:44
Silver Ridge 67	33N53	94w05	6:16:20
Simmons 32	35N48'22	91w43'22	6:06:53
Simmons Ford 8	36N19'48	93w35'16	6:14:21
Simpson 6	33N27'31	92w06'15	6:08:25
Simpson 27	34N25	92w18	6:09:12
Simpson 58	35N36'26	93w03'57	6:12:16
Sims 49	34N39'33	93w41'27	6:14:46
Simsboro 18	35N01'31	90w22'23	6:01:30
Sisemore 43	34N47'01	91w51'05	6:07:24
Sitka 68	36N11'18	91w25'17	6:05:41
Skaggs 61	36N14'16	90w54'26	6:03:38
Skunkhollow 23	35N05	92w27	6:09:48
Skylight 72	35N50'32	94w23'39	6:17:35
Slaytonville 66	35N06'38	94w26'18	6:17:45
Slick Rock Ford 12	35N22'40	91w53'30	6:07:34
Sloan 38	36N09'58	91w08'39	6:04:35
Slonikers Mill 62	35N00'28	90w55'00	6:03:40
Slovak 59	34N38'55	91w34'55	6:06:20
Smackover 70	33N21'53	92w43'29	6:10:54
Smale 49	34N42'37	91w06'14	6:04:25
Smalley 48	34N25	91w01	6:04:04
Smart 69	35N44	92w09	6:08:36
Smead 52	33N47'41	92w49'03	6:11:16
Smearney 6	33N23	92w09	6:08:36
Smearny 6	33N23'50	92w00'58	6:08:04
Smeltzer 17	35N27'28	94w18'40	6:17:15
Smith 70	33N08'08	92w39'00	6:10:36
Smith Corner 39	34N46'31	90w54'30	6:03:38
Smithdale 19	35N15'39	90w31'23	6:02:06
Smiths Corner 39	34N48	91w00	6:04:00
Smithton 10	33N57	93w08	6:12:32
Smithville 38	36N04'49	91w18'13	6:05:13
Smithville 46	33N03'14	93w52'03	6:15:28
Smithville 70	33N13'30	92w34'29	6:10:18
Smyrna 10	34N03'44	93w20'19	6:13:21
Smyrna 58	35N39'03	92w55'11	6:11:41
Snipe 14	33N19'28	93w02'53	6:12:12
Snow 45	36N15'10	92w48'07	6:11:12
Snowball 65	35N54'23	92w49'18	6:11:17
Snow Hill 52	33N23'16	92w39'14	6:10:37
Snow Lake 21	34N03'39	91w01'23	6:04:06
Snyder 2	33N17'37	91w37'16	6:06:29
Social Hill 30	34N19'55	92w54'47	6:11:39
Solgohachia 15	35N15'22	92w40'34	6:10:42
Solo 58	35N35'14	92w57'48	6:11:51
Sonora 72	36N09'55	94w02'41	6:16:11
Sorrells 35	34N09'39	92w03'57	6:08:16
Soudan 39	34N49'34	90w39'33	6:02:38
Southall 20	33N55	92w26	6:09:44
South Big Rock 68	36N00	91w29	6:05:56
South Crossett 2	33N06'20	91w57'13	6:07:49
Southerlands Crossroads 24	35N29	93w50	6:15:20
Southern State College 14	33N16	93w14	6:12:56
South Fort Smith 66	35N19'53	94w24'03	6:17:36
South Harrison 5	36N12	93w07	6:12:28
South Hot Springs 26	34N30	93w03	6:12:12
South Jacksonville 60	34N47	92w12	6:08:48
Southland 16	35N49'17	90w27'52	6:01:51
Southland 54	34N35'07	90w39'14	6:02:37
South Lead Hill 5	36N23'41	92w54'38	6:11:39
South Lebanon 68	36N08	91w25	6:05:40
South Ozark 24	35N28'49	93w49'51	6:15:19
South Pine Bluff 35	34N13	92w02	6:08:08
South Sheridan 27	34N19	92w24	6:09:36
Southside 32	35N41'54	91w37'24	6:06:30
South Side 60	34N43	92w16	6:09:04
Southside 71	35N25'35	92w23'23	6:09:34
South Union 68	36N17	91w18	6:05:12
Southwest Little Rock 60	34N44	92w20	6:09:20
Spadra 36	35N25'30	93w29'37	6:13:58
Sparkman 20	33N55'00	92w50'53	6:11:24
Spear Lake 56	35N32'53	90w19'18	6:01:17
Spencer Place 39	34N47'23	90w35'52	6:02:23
Spillway Landing 26	34N34'18	93w12'56	6:12:52
Spirit Lake 37	33N22	93w35	6:14:20
Sport Haven Landing 23	34N58'16	92w24'13	6:09:37
Spotville 14	33N16	93w14	6:12:56
Spriggs Mill 34	35N27'09	91w19'11	6:05:17
Spring Creek 39	34N41'19	90w53'53	6:03:36
Springdale 72	36N11'12	94w07'43	6:16:31
Springfield 15	35N16'03	92w33'27	6:10:14
Spring Grove 28	36N03	90w34	6:02:16
Springhill 23	35N11'19	92w23'32	6:09:34
Spring Hill 29	33N35'15	93w38'54	6:14:36
Spring Hill 52	33N30'23	93w01'17	6:12:05
Springtown 4	36N15'39	94w25'23	6:17:42
Spring Valley 60	34N43'58	92w26'34	6:09:46
Spring Valley 72	36N10'34	93w56'05	6:15:44
Sprotville 14	33N11'26	93w01'14	6:12:05
Sprudel 29	33N36'59	93w45'59	6:15:04
Spur Four 47	35N37'09	90w05'20	6:00:21
Stacy 18	35N24'16	90w13'57	6:00:56
Stacy 56	35N40'42	90w34'15	6:02:17
Stafford 75	35N09'23	93w25'48	6:13:43
Stamps 37	33N21'55	93w29'42	6:13:59
Standard Umpstead 52	33N22'23	92w40'29	6:10:42
Stanford 28	36N05'50	90w39'49	6:02:39
Stanley 1	34N10	91w23	6:05:32
Star City 40	33N56'34	91w50'36	6:07:22
Stark 12	35N32	92w06	6:08:24
Stark City 47	35N56'16	90w02'11	6:00:09
Starr Hill 72	35N57	94w25	6:17:40
State Capital 60	34N44	92w16	6:09:04
State College of Arkansas 23	35N05	92w27	6:09:48
State Line 14	33N06	93w12	6:12:48
State Services 63	34N45	92w43	6:10:52
State University 16	35N50	90w43	6:02:52
Staves 13	34N02'21	92w16'38	6:09:07
Steel 37	33N20	93w38	6:14:32
Steele 15	35N13	92w37	6:10:28
Stegall 34	35N36'26	91w08'24	6:04:34
Stella 33	36N00'39	91w48'01	6:07:12
Stelltown 55	34N02'48	93w32'57	6:14:12
Stephens 52	33N24'40	93w04'10	6:12:17
Steprock 73	35N25'44	91w41'15	6:06:45
Sterling Springs 16	35N55'23	90w42'38	6:02:51
Steve 75	34N52'14	93w19'19	6:13:17
Stevens Creek 73	35N18	91w34	6:06:16
Stevens Landing 56	35N40'42	90w27'50	6:01:51
Stewart 56	35N28'40	90w36'05	6:02:24
Stier 16	35N42'16	90w20'29	6:01:22
Stillions 2	33N15'10	92w02'32	6:08:10
Stillwater 75	34N45'10	93w24'47	6:13:39
Stimson 21	34N01'46	91w04'23	6:04:18
Stockton 50	33N26'57	93w18'37	6:13:14
Stokes 61	36N21'21	90w56'03	6:03:44
Stonewall 28	36N14'35	90w33'08	6:02:13
Stony Point 53	35N04'37	92w36'16	6:10:25
Stony Point 73	35N04	91w53	6:07:32
Story 49	34N41'35	93w31'03	6:14:04
Stoverville 51	36N01'52	93w23'53	6:13:36
Stow Landing 70	33N16'35	92w26'48	6:09:47
Strangers Home 38	35N54	91w05	6:04:20
Strawberry 36	35N32'52	93w21'15	6:13:25
Strawberry 38	35N58'03	91w19'16	6:05:17
Strickler 72	35N50'01	94w18'47	6:17:15
Stringers Mill 34	35N31'21	91w06'59	6:04:28
Stringtown 67	33N56'11	94w14'38	6:16:59
Strong 70	33N06'27	92w20'05	6:09:20
Stuart 68	36N15'50	91w31'06	6:06:04
Stumptoe 71	35N27'57	92w49'47	6:11:19
Sturkie 25	36N27'26	91w52'23	6:07:30
Stuttgart 1	34N30'01	91w33'09	6:06:13
Subiaco 42	35N17'34	93w38'04	6:14:32
Success 11	36N27'16	90w43'17	6:02:53
Sugar Camp 12	35N40	92w07	6:08:28
Sugar Grove 42	35N04'55	93w48'04	6:15:12
Sugar Hill 72	35N57	94w25	6:17:40
Sugar Loaf 5	36N26	92w55	6:11:40
Sugarloaf Lake 66	35N11	94w25	6:17:40
Sulphur City 72	35N57'54	94w03'01	6:16:12
Sulphur Rock 32	35N45'04	91w30'02	6:06:00
Sulphur Springs 2	33N04'18	92w01'52	6:08:07
Sulphur Springs 4	36N29'00	94w27'30	6:17:50
Sulphur Springs 35	34N10'50	92w07'24	6:08:30
Sulphur Springs 36	35N28'39	93w33'50	6:14:15
Sulphur Springs 75	35N11'33	93w19'33	6:13:18
Summers 72	35N58'52	94w29'29	6:17:58
Summers Ford 8	36N27'45	93w35'44	6:14:23
Summerville 7	33N31'13	92w21'20	6:09:25
Summerville Ford 27	34N24'30	92w37'39	6:10:31
Summit 45	36N15'08	92w41'26	6:10:46
Sumpter 6	33N29'08	92w02'57	6:08:12
Sunnydale 73	35N26'51	91w41'45	6:06:47
Sunny Hill 73	35N15	91w43	6:06:52
Sunnyside 9	33N17'40	91w10'50	6:04:43
Sunnyside 15	35N22'07	92w37'39	6:10:31
Sunset 18	35N13'18	90w12'20	6:00:49
Sunset 72	35N48'37	94w00'47	6:16:03
Sunshine 2	33N11'13	91w31'46	6:06:07
Sunshine 26	34N28'28	93w14'09	6:12:57
Supply 61	36N27'25	90w50'29	6:03:22
Sutherland Crossroads 24	35N32'05	93w46'14	6:15:05
Suttle 72	35N58'34	94w23'53	6:17:36
Sutton 50	33N38'41	93w23'54	6:13:36
Swain 51	35N50'57	93w20'23	6:13:22
Swan Lake 35	34N10'56	91w41'38	6:06:47
Swayne 47	35N48	89w51	5:59:24
Sweden 35	34N11'35	91w43'27	6:06:54
Sweet Home 53	35N01'18	92w45'28	6:11:02
Sweet Home 60	34N41'11	92w14'32	6:08:58
Swifton 34	35N49'18	91w07'42	6:04:31
Sycamore 5	36N26'42	92w57'37	6:11:50
Sycamore 10	33N50'33	93w09'44	6:12:39
Sycamore Bend 62	34N57	90w28	6:01:52
Sycamore Bend Farm 62	34N59'05	90w27'08	6:01:49
Sylamore 33	35N56'29	92w06'29	6:08:26
Sylvan Hills 60	34N50'11	92w13'52	6:08:55
Sylvania 43	34N58'20	91w55'42	6:07:43
Tafton 60	34N37'10	92w13'16	6:08:53
Tag 58	35N31'53	93w02'29	6:12:10
Talbert Landing 3	36N24'18	92w13'15	6:08:53
Talladega 35	34N07	92w07	6:08:28
Talley 14	33N09'44	93w04'25	6:12:18
Tamo 35	34N06'37	91w45'33	6:07:02
Tappan 54	34N19	90w55	6:03:40
Tarry 40	34N04'33	91w50'29	6:07:22
Tarsus 62	35N05'24	90w24'26	6:01:38
Tate 42	35N01'36	93w59'48	6:15:59
Tates Bluff 52	33N47'56	92w54'03	6:11:36
Taylor 14	33N06'01	93w27'39	6:13:51
Tech 58	35N17	93w09	6:12:36
Telico 62	35N07	90w48	6:03:12
Temperanceville 31	33N58'13	93w52'58	6:15:32
Temple 41	33N34'56	93w59'26	6:15:58
Tennessee 22	33N33	91w47	6:07:08
Tennessee 27	34N12	92w37	6:10:28
Terre Noire 10	34N04	93w17	6:13:08
Terrytown 60	34N39'13	92w25'38	6:09:43
Texarkana 46	33N26'30	94w02'15	6:16:09
Thacker 38	36N14	91w16	6:05:04
Thebes 2	33N17'10	91w35'03	6:06:20
The Pines 64	34N52'00	94w04'13	6:16:17
The Quarry 32	35N47'31	91w45'04	6:07:00
Thida 32	35N34'16	91w28'44	6:05:55
Thiel 27	34N14'43	92w36'57	6:10:28
Thola 65	35N53'12	92w25'45	6:09:43

Thomasville 39 34N44'45 90w56'02 6:03:44
Thompson 18 35N00'18 90w20'20 6:01:21
Thompson 44 35N55'18 93w56'46 6:15:47
Thompson 55 34N05 93w41 6:14:44
Thornburg 53 34N56'03 92w48'23 6:11:14
Thorney 44 35N59'43 93w55'56 6:15:44
Thornton 7 33N46'44 92w29'30 6:09:58
Three Brothers 3 36N27'09 92w27'56 6:09:52
Three Creeks 70 33N05'40 92w51'13 6:11:25
Three Forks 18 35N20'16 90w26'44 6:01:47
Three Sisters Landing 26 34N37'26 93w10'17 6:12:41
Three Way 47 35N41'56 90w14'38 6:00:59
Tichnor 1 34N08'25 91w16'14 6:05:05
Tide Water 14 33N12'52 93w08'23 6:12:34
Tillar 22 33N42'44 91w27'10 6:05:49
Tilly 58 35N43 92w50 6:11:20
Tilton 19 35N19'02 91w00'50 6:04:03
Tily 58 35N43'12 92w49'58 6:11:20
Timbo 69 35N52'15 92w19'01 6:09:16
Tinsman 7 33N37'47 92w21'18 6:09:25
Tintop 64 34N45'12 94w16'15 6:17:05
Tip 74 35N09'46 91w10'02 6:04:40
Tipperary 11 36N20'03 90w28'21 6:01:53
Tisdale Ford 72 36N04'25 93w59'31 6:15:58
Titsworth 42 35N21 93w41 6:14:44
Toad Suck 53 35N04'32 92w33'35 6:10:14
Tobin 55 34N02 93w30 6:14:00
Togo 19 35N20'27 90w32'55 6:02:12
Tokalon 42 35N22'35 93w28'16 6:13:53
Tokio 29 34N00'12 93w45'03 6:15:00
Toledo 13 35N55'35 92w09'40 6:08:39
Tollette 31 33N49'11 93w53'39 6:15:35
Tollville 59 34N43'11 91w32'07 6:06:08
Toltec 43 34N39'04 92w03'21 6:08:13
Tolu 72 35N48'52 94w29'42 6:17:59
Tomahawk 65 36N03'38 92w42'23 6:10:50
Tomato 47 35N50'37 89w44'28 5:58:58
Tomberlins 43 34N30'57 91w52'17 6:07:29
Tomlinson 42 35N05 94w05 6:16:20
Toney 24 35N31'05 93w57'45 6:15:51
Toneyville 60 34N53'58 92w06'07 6:08:24
Tongin 39 34N51'22 90w36'29 6:02:26
Tontitown 72 36N10'40 94w14'00 6:16:56
Topaz 18 35N02'11 90w21'33 6:01:26
Totten 43 34N53 91w46 6:07:04
Trace 10 33N50'13 92w57'07 6:11:48
Traceys Landing 3 36N17'56 92w16'00 6:09:04
Trafalgar 2 33N21'15 91w35'42 6:06:23
Trammellville 11 36N16 90w18 6:01:12
Traskwood 63 34N26'57 92w39'14 6:10:37
Treat 58 35N36'45 93w09'40 6:12:39
Trenton 54 34N29'59 90w51'55 6:03:28
Trippe 21 33N35'43 91w20'04 6:05:20
Troy 47 35N36 89w58 5:59:52
Troy 52 33N30'03 93w05'13 6:12:21
Trumann 56 35N40'25 90w30'26 6:02:02
Tubal 70 33N04 92w56 6:11:44
Tuck 16 35N50 90w48 6:03:12
Tucker 35 34N26'40 91w57'16 6:07:49
Tuckerman 34 35N43'50 91w11'54 6:04:48
Tuckertown 47 35N48'35 89w56'09 5:59:45
Tulip 20 34N04'56 92w39'13 6:10:37
Tull 27 34N26'52 92w34'34 6:10:18
Tully 56 35N41 90w31 6:02:04
Tulot 56 35N37'08 90w28'33 6:01:54
Tumbling Shoals 12 35N32'31 91w58'02 6:07:52
Tunis 28 35N57'58 90w32'16 6:02:09
Tupelo 34 35N23'35 91w13'50 6:04:55
Turkey 45 36N14'40 92w45'49 6:11:03
Turkey Creek 69 35N45'59 92w12'35 6:08:50
Turkey Scratch 54 34N38'38 90w55'38 6:03:43
Turner 47 35N50'13 90w03'42 6:00:15
Turner 54 34N28'34 91w01'07 6:04:04
Turrell 18 35N22'47 90w15'28 6:01:02
Tuttle 72 36N02'01 93w58'20 6:15:53
Twentythree 73 35N22'34 91w33'34 6:06:14
Twin Creek 33 35N56'44 92w02'10 6:08:09
Twin Springs 60 34N45 92w22 6:09:28
Twist 19 35N22'34 90w30'26 6:02:02
Tyro 40 33N50'08 91w43'14 6:06:53
Tyronza 56 35N29'24 90w21'31 6:01:26
Tyronza Junction 56 35N30'44 90w23'21 6:01:33
Ulm 59 34N34'33 91w27'38 6:05:51
Umpire 31 34N16'44 94w03'02 6:16:12
Unco 7 33N29'01 92w25'16 6:09:41
Union 25 36N15'35 91w55'16 6:07:41
Union 42 35N19'14 93w40'02 6:14:40
Union 67 34N03'41 94w21'39 6:17:27
Union 70 33N04'33 92w20'05 6:09:20
Union 74 35N18'10 91w16'05 6:05:04
Union Hill 32 35N32'03 91w30'42 6:06:03
Union Ridge 66 35N08 94w03 6:16:12
Uniontown 17 35N35'04 94w26'38 6:17:47
Union Valley 43 34N45'53 92w00'12 6:08:01
Union Valley 53 34N58 92w49 6:11:16
Unity 28 36N05'48 90w29'00 6:01:56
University of Arkansas at Mo 22 33N33 91w47 6:07:08
Uno 56 35N38'55 91w01'39 6:04:07
Upper Surrounded Hill 59 34N53 91w25 6:05:40
Urbana 70 33N09'34 92w26'45 6:09:47
Urbanette 8 36N25'11 93w32'00 6:14:08
Ursula 66 35N19'26 94w05'34 6:16:22
Vaden 10 33N52'19 92w56'13 6:11:45
Vail 47 35N49'48 90w17'02 6:01:08
Valentine 60 34N49'18 92w09'43 6:08:39
Valley Hill 12 35N32 92w06 6:08:24
Valley Junction 22 33N26'43 91w47'37 6:07:10
Valley Springs 5 36N09'27 92w59'34 6:11:58
Valley View 16 35N50 90w48 6:03:12
Vallier 1 34N19'35 91w38'02 6:06:32
Van 1 34N19'36 91w14'03 6:04:56
Van Buren 17 35N26'12 94w20'53 6:17:24
Vance 34 35N46'38 91w09'49 6:04:39
Vandervoort 57 34N22'53 94w21'56 6:17:28
Vanduzer 52 36N19'35 93w54'20 6:15:37
Vanity Corner 73 35N15 91w43 6:06:52
Vanndale 19 35N18'48 90w46'26 6:03:06
Vanness Crossing 39 34N51'43 90w39'08 6:02:37
Varner 40 34N02'18 91w37'08 6:06:29
Vaucluse 9 33N20'47 91w11'55 6:04:48
Vaughan 32 35N41 91w23 6:05:32
Vaughn 4 36N18'55 94w18'14 6:17:13
Vaugine 35 34N13 92w00 6:08:00
Veasey 22 33N29 91w49 6:07:16
Velie 52 33N41'58 92w49'13 6:11:17
Velvet Ridge 73 35N24'47 91w34'34 6:06:18
Vendor 51 35N56'50 93w04'38 6:12:19
Venice 2 33N02'13 92w01'40 6:08:07
Venus 44 35N55'31 93w36'13 6:14:25
Verona 45 36N06'33 92w49'38 6:11:19
Vesta 24 35N22'45 94w02'30 6:16:10
Vick 6 33N19'43 92w06'20 6:08:25
Victor 58 35N39'02 93w00'09 6:12:01
Victoria 47 35N45'24 90w03'21 6:00:13
Victoria 70 33N04'29 92w19'51 6:09:19
Vidette 25 36N25'38 92w07'06 6:08:28
Village 14 33N15'48 93w03'14 6:12:13
Village Junction 14 33N14'57 93w03'03 6:12:12
Villemont 35 34N10 91w34 6:06:16
Vilonia 23 35N05'02 92w12'28 6:08:50
Vimy Ridge 63 34N36'04 92w24'48 6:09:39
Vincent 18 35N12'44 90w18'03 6:01:12
Vine Prairie 17 35N31 94w05 6:16:20
Vineyard 39 34N39'28 90w52'12 6:03:29
Vineyard 72 35N48 94w29 6:17:56
Viney Grove 72 36N00'30 94w19'48 6:17:19
Vinity Corner 73 35N04'47 91w44'35 6:06:58
Viola 25 36N23'48 91w58'57 6:07:56
Violet Hill 33 36N09'13 91w50'29 6:07:22
Wabash 54 34N23'19 90w49'43 6:03:19
Wabbaseka 35 34N21'39 91w47'45 6:07:11
Wade 67 35N59'03 94w22'57 6:17:32
Wager 4 36N15 94w17 6:17:08
Wagnon 6 33N39'55 92w17'19 6:09:09
Wakefield Village 60 34N41'10 92w19'40 6:09:19
Walcott 28 36N02'36 90w40'16 6:02:41
Waldenburg 56 35N33'55 90w56'01 6:03:44
Waldo 14 33N21'05 93w17'44 6:13:11
Waldron 64 34N53'54 94w05'26 6:16:22
Walker 14 33N13'35 93w13'30 6:12:54
Walker 73 35N07'19 91w41'22 6:06:45
Walker Creek 37 33N07 93w31 6:14:04
Walkers Corner 43 34N42'48 92w05'28 6:08:22
Walkerville 14 33N05'22 93w18'50 6:13:15
Wallace 2 33N14'59 91w44'38 6:06:59
Wallace 41 33N40'54 94w21'30 6:17:26
Wallaceburg 29 33N53'35 93w32'50 6:14:11
Walls 43 34N40 91w59 6:07:56
Walnut 51 35N47'26 93w21'33 6:13:26
Walnut Corner 28 36N02'25 90w46'32 6:03:06
Walnut Corner 54 34N33'18 90w46'05 6:03:04
Walnut Grove 11 36N25 90w35 6:02:20
Walnut Grove 14 33N04'21 93w23'37 6:13:34
Walnut Grove 32 35N50'13 91w23'09 6:05:33
Walnut Grove 41 33N41 94w08 6:16:32
Walnut Grove 56 35N41 90w31 6:02:04
Walnut Grove 71 35N33'44 92w33'20 6:10:13
Walnut Grove 72 36N00'13 94w16'01 6:17:04
Walnut Grove 75 35N05'02 93w35'50 6:14:23
Walnut Grove Corner 56 35N37'39 90w37'03 6:02:28
Walnut Hill 37 33N06'35 93w41'02 6:14:44
Walnut Lake 21 33N50 91w30 6:06:00
Walnut Ridge 27 34N24'07 92w14'15 6:08:57
Walnut Ridge 38 36N04'06 90w57'21 6:03:49
Walnut Springs 67 33N56'57 94w17'32 6:17:10
Walters 47 35N52'25 90w16'38 6:01:07
Waltreak 75 34N59'02 93w36'44 6:14:27
Wampler 35 34N13 92w02 6:08:08
Wampoo 60 34N33'09 92w05'00 6:08:20
Wappanocca 18 35N18 90w16 6:01:04
Warbritton 35 34N16'35 92w01'51 6:08:07
Ward 43 35N01'49 91w57'01 6:07:48
Ward 60 34N40'30 92w18'14 6:09:13
Wardell 47 35N32'20 90w10'42 6:00:43
Wards Crossing 75 34N56'40 93w19'40 6:13:19
Ware 14 33N01'46 93w04'16 6:12:17
War Eagle 4 36N16'04 93w56'27 6:15:46
Wargo Landing 21 33N49'11 91w09'00 6:04:36
Warm Springs 61 36N28'49 91w03'05 6:04:12
Warner 52 33N38'17 92w47'51 6:11:11
Warnock Springs 14 33N18'36 93w08'30 6:12:34
Warren 6 33N36'45 92w03'52 6:08:15
Warsaw 60 34N57'08 92w09'18 6:08:37
Washburn 66 35N10'06 94w05'36 6:16:22
Washington 29 33N46'26 93w40'57 6:14:44
Washington Square 62 35N01 90w47 6:03:08
Washita 49 34N39'10 93w32'00 6:14:08
Watalula 24 35N34'24 93w49'38 6:15:19
Watensaw 59 34N45 91w28 6:05:52
Water Can Crossing 31 34N09'20 93w56'34 6:15:46
Waterloo 50 33N32'35 93w14'45 6:12:59
Water Valley 61 36N20 91w08 6:04:32
Watkins 73 35N15 91w43 6:06:52
Watkins Corner 54 34N28'07 90w57'21 6:03:49
Watson 7 33N38'50 92w22'26 6:09:30
Watson 21 33N53'42 91w15'22 6:05:01
Watson Chapel 35 34N11'21 92w03'56 6:08:16
Wattensaw 43 34N54'27 91w50'53 6:07:24
Watts 65 35N49'06 92w39'33 6:10:38
Wave 20 34N01'39 92w41'18 6:10:45
Waveland 75 35N07'25 93w37'41 6:14:31
Waverly 18 35N02'49 90w14'20 6:00:57
Wayton 51 35N54'13 93w15'14 6:13:01
Weathers 44 35N57'34 93w31'13 6:14:05
Weaver 24 35N22 94w02 6:16:08
Webb City 24 35N28'05 93w49'54 6:15:20
Weber 1 34N08'45 91w10'36 6:04:42
Weddington 72 36N05'21 94w25'10 6:17:41
Wedington 72 36N04 94w25 6:17:40
Weeks 6 33N40'09 92w12'36 6:08:50
Weeks 64 34N52'52 94w25'07 6:17:40
Weiner 56 35N37'13 90w53'54 6:03:36
Welborn 15 35N10 92w45 6:11:00
Welcome 14 33N01'16 93w27'57 6:13:52
Welcome 58 35N26'58 92w54'14 6:11:37
Weldon 34 35N26'43 91w13'53 6:04:56
Wells Bayou 40 33N55 91w37 6:06:28
Welsh 49 34N21'22 93w28'25 6:13:54
Weona 56 35N32'49 90w35'51 6:02:23
Weona Junction 56 35N30'27 90w35'59 6:02:24
Wesley 44 36N01'38 93w55'12 6:15:41
Wesley Chapel 15 35N08 92w45 6:11:00
Wesson 70 33N06'55 92w45'45 6:11:03
West Bauxite 63 34N33 92w30 6:10:00
West Camden Heights 52 33N35 92w47 6:11:08
West Cobb 24 35N43'34 93w45'19 6:15:01
West Crossett 2 33N08'27 91w59'38 6:07:59
West End 35 34N13'25 92w03'36 6:08:14
Western Grove 51 36N06'03 92w57'13 6:11:49
West Fork 72 35N55'27 94w11'18 6:16:45
West Gum Springs 10 34N05 93w02 6:12:08
West Hartford 66 35N00'16 94w24'36 6:17:38
West Helena 54 34N33'02 90w38'30 6:02:34
West Kennett 11 36N15'35 90w07'18 6:00:29
West Liberty 44 36N17'17 93w45'47 6:15:03
West Line 67 34N02 94w34 6:18:16
West Marche 60 34N52'49 92w24'28 6:09:38
West Memphis 18 35N08'47 90w11'04 6:00:44
Westor 39 34N50'27 90w51'49 6:03:27
West Otis 67 33N57'11 94w26'10 6:17:45
Westover 47 35N31'16 90w12'48 6:00:51
West Pangburn 12 35N25'54 91w53'12 6:07:33
West Point 4 36N15'10 94w33'58 6:18:16
West Point 73 35N12'25 91w36'51 6:06:27
West Prairie 56 35N37 90w52 6:03:28
West Richwoods 69 35N49'35 92w10'18 6:08:41
West Ridge 47 35N40'59 90w15'45 6:01:03
West Sullivan 68 35N59 91w39 6:06:36
Westville 17 35N25'13 94w15'30 6:17:02
Westwood 60 34N42'24 92w22'12 6:09:29
Wharton 44 36N01'29 93w37'49 6:14:31
Wharton Creek 44 36N02 93w37 6:14:28
Wheatley 62 34N54'46 91w06'36 6:04:26
Wheeler 71 35N37 92w43 6:10:52
Wheeler 72 36N06'51 94w15'32 6:17:02
Wheeling 25 36N19'13 91w51'47 6:07:27
Whelen Springs 10 33N49'51 93w07'34 6:12:30
Whipple 71 35N25'19 92w27'43 6:09:51
Whiskerville 38 36N07'11 90w48'47 6:03:15
Whisp 47 35N52'40 90w16'30 6:01:06
Whispering Springs 12 35N33'15 92w13'53 6:08:56
Whistleville 47 35N46'17 90w07'34 6:00:30
Whitaker 56 35N34 90w43 6:02:52
White 2 33N00'50 91w59'44 6:07:59
White Cliffs 67 33N47'49 94w03'36 6:16:14
White Eagle 15 35N06 92w57 6:11:48
Whitefield 40 34N03'52 91w45'24 6:07:02
White Hall 35 34N16'26 92w05'27 6:08:22
Whitehall 39 34N45'51 90w32'49 6:02:11
Whitehall 56 35N28'49 90w44'08 6:02:57
Whitehall 75 35N08'55 92w59'49 6:11:59
Whitehead Ford 12 35N22'38 91w58'18 6:07:53
Whitener 44 36N08'28 93w53'45 6:15:35
White Oak 24 35N32'46 93w51'32 6:15:26
White Oak 36 35N34'34 93w40'34 6:14:42
White Oak Bluff 13 34N01'53 92w18'21 6:09:13
White Rock 24 35N34'54 93w58'09 6:15:53
White Rock 72 36N04'46 94w15'08 6:17:01
Whitetown 49 34N37'47 93w44'42 6:14:59
Whiteville 3 36N17 92w30 6:10:00
Whitley 17 35N35 94w07 6:16:28
Whitlow 2 33N13'08 91w59'09 6:07:57
Whitlow Junction 2 33N11'59 91w57'55 6:07:52
Whitmore 62 35N04'10 90w34'05 6:02:16
Whittington 30 34N36'51 92w53'18 6:11:33
Whitton 47 35N30'41 90w16'06 6:01:04
Wickes 57 34N18'11 94w20'17 6:17:21
Wick Mill 19 35N09'47 90w56'09 6:03:45
Wideman 33 36N11'11 92w00'31 6:08:02
Widener 62 35N01'24 90w41'05 6:02:44
Wilbeth 56 35N32'04 90w20'23 6:01:22
Wilburn 12 35N30'26 91w53'17 6:07:33
Wild Cherry 25 36N15'50 92w03'24 6:08:14
Wiley 61 36N11 90w55 6:03:40
Wiley Crossing 56 35N27'38 90w44'24 6:02:58
Wileys Cove 65 35N50'15 92w34'25 6:10:18
Wilkins 35 34N15'35 91w55'47 6:07:43
Williams 43 34N40 92w04 6:08:16
Williams Junction 53 34N52'53 92w46'24 6:11:06
Williamson 67 33N57 94w21 6:17:24
Williford 68 36N15'10 91w21'21 6:05:25
Willis 5 36N22'41 92w59'11 6:11:57
Willis 56 35N39 90w31 6:02:04
Willisville 50 33N31'01 93w17'53 6:13:12
Willow 20 34N08'01 92w44'46 6:10:59
Willow Belle 43 34N38'09 92w01'46 6:08:07
Willow Creek 71 35N27 92w24 6:09:36
Wilmar 22 33N37'44 91w55'53 6:07:44
Wilmington 70 33N13 92w26 6:09:44
Wilmington Landing 70 33N16'21 92w25'19 6:09:41
Wilmot 2 33N03'26 91w34'24 6:06:18
Wilson 47 35N34'05 90w02'31 6:00:10
Wilson 58 35N12'37 92w55'46 6:11:43
Wilson Junction 47 35N50'50 90w03'42 6:00:15
Wilton 41 33N44'28 94w08'53 6:16:36
Winchester 22 33N46'28 91w28'28 6:05:54
Winesburg 16 35N50'39 90w54'03 6:03:36
Winfield 64 34N53'11 94w11'10 6:16:45
Winfrey 17 35N44'04 94w05'58 6:16:24
Wing 75 34N56'41 93w27'51 6:13:51
Winington 5 36N21'21 92w54'27 6:11:38
Winona 8 36N22 93w41 6:14:44
Winrock 15 35N08'17 92w56'37 6:11:46
Winslow 72 35N48'03 94w08'05 6:16:32
Winston Terrace 60 34N44 92w20 6:09:20
Winthrop 41 33N49'54 94w21'16 6:17:25
Wirth 68 36N27'02 91w22'49 6:05:31

Place	Latitude	Longitude	Time
Wiseman 33	36N14'04	91w48'55	6:07:16
Witcherville 66	35N08'15	94w15'51	6:17:03
Witherspoon 30	34N09'32	92w59'20	6:11:57
Witter 44	35N56'15	93w41'00	6:14:44
Wittich 24	35N22	93w52	6:15:28
Wittsburg 19	35N13'08	90w42'06	6:02:48
Witts Springs 65	35N46'05	92w52'00	6:11:28
Wiville 74	35N08'53	91w14'27	6:04:58
Wolf Bayou 12	35N39'17	91w54'38	6:07:39
Wolf Creek 55	34N02	93w28	6:13:52
Wolquarry 33	35N53'51	91w54'34	6:07:38
Womble 49	34N28	93w40	6:14:40
Wonderview 15	35N19'40	92w43'47	6:10:55
Woodberry 7	33N34'56	92w30'57	6:10:04
Wooden Hills 5	36N20'13	93w03'37	6:12:14
Woodland 36	35N31'27	93w31'14	6:14:05
Woodland Corner 47	35N58'00	90w02'12	6:00:09
Woodland Heights 60	34N47'37	92w23'54	6:09:36
Woodland Hills 25	36N22'42	91w27'47	6:05:51
Woodrow 12	35N39'48	92w04'50	6:08:19
Woodson 60	34N31'45	92w12'39	6:08:51
Woods Point Landing 3	36N17'39	92w10'20	6:08:41
Woodyardville 60	34N39'56	92w16'11	6:09:05
Woolsey 72	35N53'07	94w10'06	6:16:40
Woolum 65	35N58'20	92w53'00	6:11:32
Woolum 71	35N42'39	92w39'49	6:10:39
Wooster 23	35N12'07	92w27'21	6:09:49
Worden 73	35N17'39	91w29'28	6:05:58
Worthen 58	35N14'37	93w01'21	6:12:05
Wright 35	34N26'06	92w03'58	6:08:16
Wrightland 39	34N50'14	90w47'47	6:03:11
Wrights Corner 73	35N21'19	91w37'22	6:06:29
Wrightsville 60	34N36'08	92w13'00	6:08:52
Wright Town 17	35N24'24	94w17'40	6:17:11
Wyanoke 18	35N06'14	90w11'24	6:00:46
Wycamp 54	34N33'17	90w42'56	6:02:52
Wycough 32	35N45	91w26	6:05:44
Wye 60	34N56'21	92w38'30	6:10:34
Wylie Spur 18	35N11'55	90w14'55	6:01:00
Wyman 72	36N04'30	94w04'09	6:16:17
Wynne 19	35N13'28	90w47'12	6:03:09
Wyola 72	35N52'44	94w02'49	6:16:11
Yale 36	35N40'16	93w39'02	6:14:36
Yancopin 21	33N56'26	91w13'07	6:04:52
Yancy 29	33N50'03	93w48'35	6:15:14
Yarbo 47	35N58'45	89w54'37	5:59:38
Yarbo Place 19	35N21'26	90w31'10	6:02:05
Yardelle 51	36N04'01	93w00'14	6:12:01
Y City 64	34N44'05	94w04'37	6:16:18
Yell 4	36N11	94w23	6:17:32
Yellow Banks 56	35N29'13	90w26'38	6:01:47
Yellow Bayou 9	33N24'29	91w15'14	6:05:01
Yellville 45	36N13'34	92w41'05	6:10:44
Yocum 8	36N25'10	93w24'47	6:13:39
Yoder 1	34N27'14	91w29'17	6:05:57
Yoestown 17	35N25'43	94w10'41	6:16:43
York 43	34N57	92w03	6:08:12
Yorktown 40	34N01'15	91w49'00	6:07:16
Young 50	33N34'28	93w10'51	6:12:43
Young Gravelly 75	34N54'55	93w39'30	6:14:38
Youngstown 22	33N25'24	91w47'37	6:07:10
Yukon 21	33N47'49	91w28'44	6:05:55
Zack 65	35N57'31	92w39'58	6:10:40
Zent 48	34N48	91w09	6:04:36
Zinc 5	36N17'07	92w54'51	6:11:39
Zion 33	36N04'49	91w46'11	6:07:05
Zont 48	34N59'01	91w09'47	6:04:39

TIME TABLES

Date	Time	Zone	Date	Time	Zone	Date	Time	Zone	Date	Time	Zone	Date	Time	Zone
Before 11/18/1883		LMT	4/30/1950	02:00	PDT	4/24/1955	02:00	PDT	4/24/1960	02:00	PDT	4/25/1965	02:00	PDT
11/18/1883	12:00	PST	9/24/1950	02:00	PST	9/25/1955	02:00	PST	9/25/1960	02:00	PST	10/31/1965	02:00	PST
3/31/1918	02:00	PWT	4/29/1951	02:00	PDT	4/29/1956	02:00	PDT	4/30/1961	02:00	PDT	4/24/1966	02:00	PDT
10/27/1918	02:00	PST	9/30/1951	02:00	PST	9/30/1956	02:00	PST	9/24/1961	02:00	PST	10/30/1966	02:00	PST
3/30/1919	02:00	PWT	4/27/1952	02:00	PDT	4/28/1957	02:00	PDT	4/29/1962	02:00	PDT	4/30/1967	02:00	US#1
10/26/1919	02:00	PST	9/28/1952	02:00	PST	9/29/1957	02:00	PST	10/28/1962	02:00	PST			
2/09/1942	02:00	PWT	4/26/1953	02:00	PDT	4/27/1958	02:00	PDT	4/28/1963	02:00	PDT			
9/30/1945	02:00	PST	9/27/1953	02:00	PST	9/28/1958	02:00	PST	10/27/1963	02:00	PST			
3/14/1948	02:00	PDT	4/25/1954	02:00	PDT	4/26/1959	02:00	PDT	4/26/1964	02:00	PDT			
1/01/1949	02:00	PST	9/26/1954	02:00	PST	9/27/1959	02:00	PST	10/25/1964	02:00	PST			

COUNTIES

1 Alameda
2 Alpine
3 Amador
4 Butte
5 Calaveras
6 Colusa
7 Contra Costa
8 Del Norte
9 El Dorado
10 Fresno
11 Glenn
12 Humboldt
13 Imperial
14 Inyo
15 Kern
16 Kings
17 Lake
18 Lassen
19 Los Angeles
20 Madera
21 Marin
22 Mariposa
23 Mendocino
24 Merced
25 Modoc
26 Mono
27 Monterey
28 Napa
29 Nevada
30 Orange
31 Placer
32 Plumas
33 Riverside
34 Sacramento
35 San Benito
36 San Bernardino
37 San Diego
38 San Francisco
39 San Joaquin
40 San Luis Obispo
41 San Mateo
42 Santa Barbara
43 Santa Clara
44 Santa Cruz
45 Shasta
46 Sierra
47 Siskiyou
48 Solano
49 Sonoma
50 Stanislaus
51 Sutter
52 Tehama
53 Trinity
54 Tulare
55 Tuolumne
56 Ventura
57 Yolo
58 Yuba

Place	Latitude	Longitude	Time
Abalone Cove 19	33N46	118w21	7:53:24
Abbott 51	39N01'14	121w37'28	8:06:30
Aberdeen 14	36N58'41	118w15'09	7:53:01
Academy 10	36N49	119w43	7:58:52
Acampo 39	38N10'29	121w16'39	8:05:07
Acolita 13	33N04'16	115w11'02	7:40:44
Actis 15	34N57'31	118w08'52	7:52:35
Actis Gardens 15	35N08	117w59	7:51:56
Acton 19	34N28'12	118w11'45	7:52:47
Adams 17	38N51'23	122w43'07	8:10:52
Adams Square 19	34N08'01	118w14'25	7:52:58
Adela 50	37N47'19	120w51'44	8:03:27
Adelaida 40	35N38'44	120w52'21	8:03:29
Adelanto 36	34N34'58	117w24'30	7:49:38
Adin 25	41N11'38	120w56'39	8:03:47
Adobe Corner 41	37N25'34	122w15'55	8:09:04
Advance 54	36N30'57	118w54'06	7:55:36
Aerial Acres 15	35N05'16	117w47'28	7:51:10
Aetna Springs 28	38N39'13	122w28'54	8:09:56
Afton 11	39N25'12	121w57'55	8:07:52
Afton 36	35N02'11	116w22'44	7:45:31
Ager 47	41N51'59	122w27'34	8:09:50
Agnew 43	37N23'41	121w57'29	8:07:50
Agoura 19	34N08'35	118w44'13	7:54:57
Agoura Hills 19	34N08'35	118w44'13	7:54:57
Agra 37	33N20'00	117w29'57	7:50:00
Agua Caliente 49	38N19'27	122w29'13	8:09:57
Agua Caliente Indian Res 33	33N49	116w32	7:46:08
Agua Caliente Springs 37	33N05	116w36	7:46:24
Agua Dulce 19	34N29'47	118w19'29	7:53:18
Agua Fria 22	37N29'06	120w01'09	8:00:05
Aguanga 33	33N26'36	116w51'51	7:47:27
Ahwahnee 20	37N21'56	119w43'31	7:58:54
Ainsworth Corner 47	41N59'55	121w33'31	8:06:14
Akers 39	37N59'54	121w16'57	8:05:08
Alabama Hill 5	38N21'18	120w35'27	8:02:22
Alameda 1	37N45'55	122w14'26	8:08:58
Alameda 15	35N14'16	119w00'08	7:56:01
Alamitos 43	37N15'02	121w51'58	8:07:28
Alamo 7	37N51'01	122w01'52	8:08:07
Alamo Oaks 7	37N50'22	121w59'31	8:07:58
Alamorio 13	32N58'45	115w27'38	7:41:51
Alba 39	37N47'53	121w02'19	8:04:09
Albany 1	37N53'13	122w17'48	8:09:11
Alberhill 33	33N43'38	117w23'56	7:49:36
Albion 23	39N13'25	123w46'03	8:15:04
Albrae 1	37N29'44	121w59'18	8:07:57
Alderbrook Tract 43	37N19	122w02	8:08:08
Alder Creek 34	38N38'05	121w12'02	8:04:48
Aldercroft Heights 43	37N09'39	121w58'04	8:07:52
Alderglen Springs 49	38N50'07	123w03'06	8:12:12
Alderpoint 12	40N10'35	123w36'38	8:14:27
Alder Springs 10	37N03'58	119w24'04	7:57:36
Alder Springs 11	39N39'04	122w43'28	8:10:54
Alemandra 51	39N08'56	121w41'13	8:06:45
Alessandro 33	33N53'10	117w16'10	7:49:05
Alexander Valley 49	38N42	122w54	8:11:36
Alford Place 52	40N13'06	122w39'56	8:10:40
Algerine 55	37N54'40	120w22'56	8:01:32
Algoma 47	41N15'24	121w52'56	8:07:32
Algoso 15	35N21'35	118w55'27	7:55:42
Alhambra 19	34N05'43	118w07'34	7:52:30
Alhambra Valley 7	37N59	122w07	8:08:28
Alicia 58	39N06'10	121w34'50	8:06:19
Alico 14	36N34'11	117w57'44	7:51:51
Alisal 27	36N41	121w39	8:06:36
Alla 19	33N58'52	118w25'44	7:53:43
All American 43	37N19	122w02	8:08:08
Alleghany 46	39N28'11	120w50'32	8:03:22
Allen 3	38N37'02	120w06'35	8:00:26
Allendale 48	38N26'41	121w56'31	8:07:46
Allensworth 54	35N51'49	119w23'17	7:57:33
Alliance 12	40N53'19	124w05'12	8:16:21
Alliance Redwood 49	38N26'02	122w58'19	8:11:53
Almanor 32	40N13'03	121w10'23	8:04:42
Almondale 19	34N30	117w55	7:51:40
Almonte 21	37N53'24	122w31'26	8:10:06
Alondra 19	33N54	118w19	7:53:16
Alondra Park 19	33N54	118w20	7:53:20
Alpaugh 54	35N53'16	119w29'11	7:57:57
Alpine 23	39N26'11	123w34'56	8:14:20
Alpine 37	32N50'06	116w45'56	7:47:04
Alpine Heights 37	32N49'05	116w46'48	7:47:07
Alpine Hills 41	37N27	122w11	8:08:44
Alpine Village 54	36N08	118w49	7:55:16
Alray 36	34N19'42	117w28'55	7:49:56
Alsace 19	33N58'43	118w24'53	7:53:40
Alta 31	39N12'24	120w48'37	8:03:14
Altadena 19	34N11'23	118w07'49	7:52:31
Alta Hill 29	39N13'48	121w04'32	8:04:18
Al Tahoe 9	38N56'31	119w58'57	7:59:56
Alta Loma 36	34N07'20	117w35'50	7:50:23
Alta Mesa 43	37N23'56	122w08'01	8:08:32
Altamont 1	37N44'38	121w39'42	8:06:39
Alta Sierra 15	35N43'45	118w32'55	7:54:12
Alta Sierra Estates 29	39N13	121w04	8:04:16
Altaville 5	38N05'33	120w34'26	8:02:18
Alto 21	37N54'16	122w31'28	8:10:06
Alton 12	40N32'51	124w08'23	8:16:34
Alturas 25	41N29'14	120w32'29	8:02:10
Alum Rock 43	37N21'58	121w49'34	8:07:18
Alvarado 1	37N36	122w01	8:08:04
Alviso 43	37N25'34	121w58'27	8:07:54
Amador City 3	38N25'10	120w49'23	8:03:18
Ambassador 19	34N04	118w18	7:53:12
Ambler 54	36N18'29	119w16'53	7:57:08
Ambler Park 27	36N41	121w39	8:06:36
Amboy 36	34N33'28	115w44'37	7:42:58
Ambrose 7	38N02	121w58	8:07:52
Ambrose 25	41N30'07	120w58'49	8:03:55
American Canyon 28	38N07	122w14	8:08:56
Amos 13	33N07'05	115w15'18	7:41:01
Ampere 39	38N06'09	121w14'32	8:04:58
Amphibious Base 37	32N40	117w10	7:48:40
Amsterdam 24	37N25'49	120w32'28	8:02:10
Anaheim 30	33N50'07	117w54'49	7:51:39
Anchor Bay 23	38N48'10	123w34'36	8:14:18
Anderson 45	40N26'54	122w17'48	8:09:11
Andersonia 23	39N58'41	123w48'22	8:15:13
Anderson Landing (Abandoned) 27	36N08'42	121w39'26	8:06:38
Anderson Springs 17	38N45	122w37	8:10:28
Andesite 47	41N31'57	122w12'13	8:08:49
Andover 31	39N18'38	120w14'46	8:00:59
Andrade 13	32N43	114w43	7:38:52
Andrade Corner 19	34N38'55	118w22'34	7:53:30
Andrew Jackson P O 37	32N45	117w04	7:48:16
Angels Camp 5	38N04'37	120w33'08	8:02:13
Angelus Oaks 36	34N09	116w59	7:47:56
Angiola 54	35N59'21	119w28'30	7:57:54
Angwin 28	38N34'33	122w26'56	8:09:48
Anita 4	39N48'39	121w58'38	8:07:55
Annapolis 49	38N43'19	123w22'07	8:13:28
Annette 15	35N39'03	120w10'41	8:00:43
Ansel 15	34N54'18	118w09'12	7:52:37
Antelope 34	38N42'30	121w19'44	8:05:19
Antelope Acres 19	34N45'16	118w17'19	7:53:09
Antelope Center 19	34N34'48	117w58'06	7:51:52
Antes 54	36N18'31	119w07'47	7:56:31
Antioch 7	38N00'18	121w48'17	8:07:13
Antlers 45	40N53'44	122w22'12	8:09:29
Antonio 42	34N50'07	120w34'08	8:02:17
Anza 13	32N48'01	115w29'51	7:41:59
Anza 33	33N33'18	116w40'22	7:46:41
Apex 9	38N43'37	120w49'20	8:03:17
Applegate 31	39N00'03	120w59'29	8:03:58
Apple Valley 36	34N30'03	117w11'06	7:48:44
Aptos 44	36N58'38	121w53'54	8:07:36
Arastraville 55	37N59'53	120w13'33	8:00:54
Araz Junction 13	32N44'50	114w42'49	7:38:51
Arbee 6	39N12'40	121w59'41	8:07:59
Arbios 10	36N46'36	120w23'49	8:01:35
Arboga 58	39N03'05	121w33'17	8:06:13
Arbolada 56	34N26'59	119w15'26	7:57:02
Arbuckle 6	39N01'03	122w03'24	8:08:14
Arcade 19	34N05	118w22	7:53:28
Arcade 57	38N28'33	121w34'43	8:06:19
Arcadia 19	34N08'23	118w02'04	7:52:08
Arcata 12	40N52'00	124w04'54	8:16:20
Arch Beach Heights 30	33N32	117w47	7:51:08
Archer 36	34N25'14	115w21'53	7:41:28
Arcilla 33	33N47'00	117w28'43	7:49:55
Arden 34	38N36	121w23	8:05:32
Arden Town 34	38N34'27	121w22'55	8:05:32
Ardmore 19	33N56	118w11	7:52:44
Arena 24	37N22'15	120w40'31	8:02:42
Argos 36	34N43'33	116w15'00	7:45:00
Arguello 42	34N34'42	120w38'31	8:02:34
Argus 36	35N44'50	117w23'40	7:49:35
Arlanza 33	33N56'34	117w27'53	7:49:52
Arlanza Village 33	33N56	117w29	7:49:56
Arleta 19	34N15	118w25	7:53:40
Arlight 42	34N34'40	120w38'18	8:02:33
Arlington 33	33N55'13	117w26'44	7:49:47
Arlington Station 33	33N54'51	117w26'25	7:49:46
Arlynda Corners 12	40N35'42	124w15'14	8:17:01
Armistead 15	35N32'52	117w55'36	7:51:42
Armona 16	36N18'57	119w42'27	7:58:50
Armstrong 39	38N05'21	121w16'25	8:05:06
Army Point 48	38N03	122w09	8:08:36
Army Terminal 1	37N48	122w13	8:08:52
Arnold 5	38N15'20	120w21'00	8:01:24
Arnold 23	39N31'08	123w23'33	8:13:34
Arnold Heights 33	33N53'37	117w16'41	7:49:07
Aromas 35	36N53'19	121w38'31	8:06:34
Arrowbear Lake 36	34N12'39	117w04'57	7:48:20
Arrowhead 36	34N17	117w14	7:48:56
Arrowhead Highlands 36	34N13'48	117w15'43	7:49:03
Arrowhead Junction 36	34N56'34	114w49'25	7:39:18
Arrowhead Springs 36	34N11'12	117w15'39	7:49:03
Arrow Mall 19	34N06	117w53	7:51:32
Arroyo Grande 40	35N07'07	120w35'23	8:02:22
Arroz 57	38N37'15	121w58'12	8:07:53
Artesia 19	33N51'57	118w04'56	7:52:20
Artois 11	39N37'11	122w11'34	8:08:46
Arvin 15	35N12'33	118w49'39	7:55:19
Arvin Farm Labor Center 15	35N24	119w02	7:56:08
Asco 1	37N40'59	121w52'18	8:07:29
Ash Creek Junction 47	41N16'03	122w04'36	8:08:18
Ashford Junction 14	35N54'35	116w40'21	7:46:41
Ashford Mill 14	35N55'08	116w41'02	7:46:44
Ash Hill 36	34N42'25	116w03'15	7:44:13
Ashland 1	37N41'41	122w06'46	8:08:27
Ashlan Park 10	36N48	119w46	7:59:04
Ashrama 43	37N18'26	121w28'07	8:05:52
Asilomar 27	36N37	121w56	8:07:44
Aspendell 14	37N22	118w24	7:53:36
Aspen Valley 55	37N49'39	119w46'13	7:59:05
Asti 49	38N45'47	122w58'19	8:11:53
Asuncion 40	35N30'54	120w40'42	8:02:43
Asylum 23	39N08'01	123w11'58	8:12:48
Atascadero 40	35N29'22	120w40'11	8:02:41
Athens 19	33N55'12	118w16'49	7:53:07
Atherton 41	37N27'41	122w11'48	8:08:47
Athlone 24	37N12'29	120w21'25	8:01:26
Atlanta 39	37N48'47	121w07'11	8:04:29
Atlas 28	38N25'45	122w14'49	8:08:59
Atolia 36	35N18'53	117w36'30	7:50:26
Atwater 19	34N06'59	118w15'20	7:53:01
Atwater 24	37N20'49	120w36'40	8:02:27
Atwood 30	33N51'56	117w49'48	7:51:19
Auberry 10	37N04'51	119w29'04	7:57:56
Auburn 31	38N53'48	121w04'33	8:04:18
Auckland 54	36N35'17	119w06'21	7:56:25
August School Area 39	37N59	121w16	8:05:04
Aukum 9	38N33'26	120w43'32	8:02:54
Aurant 19	34N04'41	118w09'48	7:52:39
Aurora 50	37N39'36	121w00'06	8:04:00
Avalon 19	33N20'34	118w19'37	7:53:18
Avalon Village 19	33N48'46	118w15'47	7:53:03
Avena 39	37N50'35	121w03'55	8:04:16
Avenal 16	36N00'15	120w07'41	8:00:31
Avery 5	38N12'16	120w22'08	8:01:29
Avery Place 52	40N10'55	121w46'46	8:07:07

Avila Beach 40	35N10'48	120w43'51	8:02:55
Avila Place 18	41N02'35	120w52'00	8:03:28
Avinsino Corner 9	38N41'37	120w40'32	8:02:42
Avocado 10	36N47'22	119w24'11	7:57:37
Avocado Heights 19	34N02	118w00	7:52:00
Avon (Associated P O) 7	38N01'58	122w04'27	8:08:18
Azalea 47	41N16'42	122w18'04	8:09:12
Azure Vista 37	32N43'10	117w15'44	7:49:03
Azusa 19	34N08'01	117w54'24	7:51:38
Babcock Crossing 32	40N07'37	120w37'33	8:02:30
Baden 41	37N39	122w26	8:09:44
Badger 54	36N37'53	119w00'44	7:56:03
Badwater 14	36N13'47	116w45'58	7:47:04
Bagby 22	37N43	120w12	8:00:48
Bagdad 36	34N34'58	115w52'29	7:43:30
Bahia 48	38N05'48	122w06'07	8:08:24
Bailey 19	33N58	118w01	7:52:04
Bailhache 49	38N36'13	122w51'13	8:11:25
Baker 36	35N15'54	116w04'25	7:44:18
Bakersfield 15	35N22'24	119w01'04	7:56:04
Balance Rock 54	35N48'22	118w39'04	7:54:36
Balboa 30	33N35'13	117w54'00	7:51:36
Balboa Island 30	33N35'40	117w53'27	7:51:34
Balch 36	35N02'34	116w01'36	7:44:06
Balch Camp 10	36N54'11	119w07'20	7:56:29
Balderson Station 9	38N56'05	120w45'11	8:03:01
Baldwin Lake 36	34N16	116w51	7:47:24
Baldwin Park 19	34N05'07	117w57'36	7:51:50
Baldy, Mount 36	34N14'10	117w39'33	7:50:38
Ballarat 14	36N02'52	117w13'21	7:48:53
Ballard 42	34N38'09	120w06'44	8:00:27
Ballico 24	37N27'16	120w42'18	8:02:49
Ballou 36	34N02'57	117w36'22	7:50:25
Ballroad 30	33N49	118w02	7:52:08
Balls Ferry 45	40N27	122w18	8:09:12
Baltimore Park 21	37N55'51	122w31'53	8:10:08
Baltimore Town 29	39N23'16	120w32'21	8:02:09
Bancroft 7	37N56'02	122w02'46	8:08:11
Bancroft Point 37	32N44'13	116w59'05	7:47:56
Bandini 19	33N58'56	118w07'02	7:52:28
Bangor 4	39N23'19	121w24'15	8:05:37
Bankhead Springs 37	32N38'59	116w14'35	7:44:58
Banner 37	33N04'08	116w32'43	7:46:11
Banning 33	33N55'32	116w52'32	7:47:30
Bannister 15	35N15'56	119w05'59	7:56:24
Bannock 36	34N56'12	114w51'47	7:39:27
Banta 39	37N45'16	121w22'11	8:05:29
Barber 4	39N42'53	121w50'04	8:07:20
Barber City 30	33N45'32	118w01'24	7:52:06
Bard 13	32N47'21	114w33'19	7:38:13
Bardi 39	37N45'53	121w09'51	8:04:39
Bardsdale 56	34N22'18	118w55'55	7:55:44
Barkerville 17	39N09'16	122w33'41	8:10:15
Barlett Springs 17	39N11'02	122w42'12	8:10:49
Barlow 49	38N25'30	122w51'27	8:11:26
Barnwell 36	35N17'35	115w14'06	7:40:56
Baroda 42	34N41'12	120w35'30	8:02:22
Barona 37	32N56'09	116w52'02	7:47:28
Barona Ranch Indian Res 37	32N56	116w52	7:47:28
Barrett 22	37N38'24	120w17'05	8:01:08
Barrett 37	32N37'45	116w27'35	7:45:50
Barrett Junction 37	32N36'41	116w42'23	7:46:50
Barrington 19	34N04	118w29	7:53:56
Barro 28	38N31'34	122w29'30	8:09:58
Barron Park 43	37N25	122w08	8:08:32
Barstow 10	36N48'55	119w58'08	7:59:53
Barstow 36	34N53'55	117w01'19	7:48:05
Barstow Colony 10	36N48	119w50	7:59:20
Barsug 42	34N57'27	120w34'19	8:02:17
Bartle 47	41N15'28	121w49'12	8:07:17
Bartlett 14	36N28'36	118w01'48	7:52:07
Bartolo 19	34N00'23	118w03'41	7:52:15
Barton 3	38N27'17	120w31'45	8:02:07
Barton 10	36N44	119w45	7:59:00
Base Line 36	34N07	117w18	7:49:12
Bassett 19	34N02'59	117w59'45	7:51:59
Bassetts 46	39N37'11	120w35'11	8:02:21
Bass Lake 20	37N19'12	119w33'24	7:58:14
Batavia 48	38N23'23	121w51'30	8:07:26
Batto 49	38N17'01	122w26'09	8:09:45
Baumberg 1	37N37'15	122w05'57	8:08:24
Baxter 31	39N12'47	120w46'48	8:03:07
Bay 36	34N15	116w53	7:47:32
Bayley 25	41N17'17	120w32'13	8:02:09
Bayliss 11	39N34'58	122w02'41	8:08:11
Bay Meadows Race Track 41	37N33	122w18	8:09:12
Bayo Vista 7	38N02'13	122w15'37	8:09:02
Bay Park 37	32N46'54	117w12'20	7:48:49
Bayshore 41	37N42'23	122w24'42	8:09:39
Bayside 12	40N50'33	124w03'45	8:16:15
Bayview 12	40N46'22	124w10'58	8:16:44
Bay View 38	37N44	122w24	8:09:36
Bayview District 38	37N44'54	122w27'16	8:09:49
Bayview Park 7	37N58	122w20	8:09:20
Bay View Park 27	36N37	121w50	8:07:20
Baywood Park 40	35N19'35	120w50'03	8:03:20
Beach Center 30	33N41	118w00	7:52:00
Beale Air Force Base 58	39N07	121w22	8:05:28
Beale East 58	39N07	121w22	8:05:28
Beale West 58	39N07	121w25	8:05:40
Beall Place (Site) 12	40N01'39	123w49'43	8:15:19
Beal Place 45	40N35'52	121w44'55	8:07:00
Bealville 15	35N16'20	118w37'31	7:54:30
Bear Creek 24	37N17'50	120w24'59	8:01:40
Bear Creek 39	38N05'02	121w14'30	8:04:58
Bear River 29	38N54	121w04	8:04:16
Bear River Lake 3	38N25	120w33	8:02:12
Bear River Pines 29	39N10'10	120w58'01	8:03:52
Bear Valley 2	38N27'53	120w02'20	8:00:09
Bear Valley 22	37N34'08	120w07'06	8:00:28
Beatrice 12	40N40'12	124w12'05	8:16:48
Beatrice 57	38N38'36	121w35'42	8:06:23
Beatty Junction 14	36N35'17	116w56'32	7:47:46
Beaumont 33	33N55'46	116w58'35	7:47:54
Beckwourth 32	39N49'13	120w22'40	8:01:31
Beegum 52	40N20'42	122w51'25	8:11:26
Beeks Place 30	33N49'13	117w38'16	7:50:33
Bee Rock 27	35N47'14	120w56'17	8:03:45
Bel Air 19	34N05'00	118w26'52	7:53:47
Bel Aire Estates 21	37N53	122w29	8:09:56
Belden 32	40N00'22	121w14'53	8:05:00
Beldons Landing 48	38N11'20	121w58'26	8:07:54
Belfast 18	40N26'37	120w27'02	8:01:48
Belfort 26	38N24'59	119w15'58	7:57:04
Bell 19	33N58'39	118w11'10	7:52:45
Bellaire 7	38N00	121w51	8:07:24
Bella Vista 7	38N00	121w51	8:07:24
Bella Vista 19	34N01	118w09	7:52:36
Bella Vista 45	40N38'27	122w13'53	8:08:56
Bella Vista 54	35N39'08	118w19'18	7:53:17
Belle Haven 41	37N27	122w11	8:08:44
Belle Monte 41	37N31'09	122w17'45	8:09:11
Belleview 12	40N30'22	124w07'11	8:16:29
Belleview 55	38N00'47	120w17'23	8:01:10
Bellevue 49	38N24'07	122w42'45	8:10:51
Bellflower 19	33N52'54	118w06'58	7:52:28
Bell Gardens 19	33N57'55	118w09'02	7:52:36
Bell Mountain 36	34N37'27	117w12'22	7:48:49
Bellota 39	38N03'11	121w00'46	8:04:03
Bell Springs 23	39N55'25	123w28'21	8:13:53
Bells Station 43	36N51	121w24	8:05:36
Belltown 33	34N01	117w23	7:49:32
Bellview 12	40N30	124w06	8:16:24
Bel Marin Keys 21	38N06	122w34	8:10:16
Belmont 41	37N31'13	122w16'29	8:09:06
Belmont Shore 19	33N45'26	118w08'10	7:52:33
Beltown 33	34N00'42	117w22'57	7:49:32
Belvedere 19	34N02'26	118w10'06	7:52:40
Belvedere 21	37N52'22	122w27'48	8:09:51
Belvedere Gardens 19	34N01	118w09	7:52:36
Belvedere Heights 33	33N59'01	117w18'36	7:49:14
Belvernon Gardens 21	37N53	122w29	8:09:56
Bena 15	35N19'36	118w44'20	7:54:57
Ben Ali 34	38N37'19	121w25'17	8:05:41
Benbow 12	40N04'07	123w47'00	8:15:08
Bend 52	40N15'19	122w12'27	8:08:50
Ben Hur 22	37N21'06	119w57'24	7:59:50
Benicia 48	38N02'58	122w09'27	8:08:38
Benito 10	36N49'18	120w26'07	8:01:44
Ben Lomond 44	37N05'21	122w05'07	8:08:20
Benton 26	37N49'09	118w28'32	7:53:54
Benton Crossing 26	37N41'57	118w45'47	7:55:03
Benton Hot Springs 26	37N48'01	118w31'41	7:54:07
Berenda 20	37N02'25	120w09'09	8:00:37
Berg 51	39N10'51	121w37'35	8:06:30
Berkeley 1	37N52'18	122w16'18	8:09:05
Berkeley Highlands 7	37N54	122w17	8:09:08
Bernal 38	37N45	122w26	8:09:44
Berros 40	35N04'41	120w32'20	8:02:09
Berry Creek 4	39N38'43	121w24'08	8:05:37
Berryessa 28	38N40	122w19	8:09:16
Berryessa 43	37N23'11	121w51'34	8:07:26
Berryessa Park 28	38N18	122w18	8:09:12
Berry Glenn 12	41N19'03	124w02'24	8:16:10
Berry Hill Estates 19	33N46	118w21	7:53:24
Berteleda 8	41N46	124w12	8:16:48
Bertram 13	33N22'25	115w46'32	7:43:06
Bertsch Terrace 8	41N46	124w12	8:16:48
Bestville 47	41N18'03	123w08'31	8:12:34
Beswick 47	41N58'01	122w13'15	8:08:53
Bethany 33	37N43	121w26	8:05:44
Bethel Island 7	38N00'54	121w38'22	8:06:33
Bethel Tract 10	36N37	119w31	7:58:04
Betteravia 42	34N55'04	120w30'50	8:02:03
Betteravia Junction 42	34N55'39	120w31'58	8:02:08
Beulah Picnic Ground 37	32N50'56	116w32'59	7:46:12
Beverly Glen 19	34N06'28	118w26'41	7:53:47
Beverly Hills 19	34N04'25	118w23'58	7:53:36
Bicknell 42	34N49'00	120w23'32	8:01:34
Bieber 18	41N07'17	121w08'35	8:04:34
Big Bar 5	38N18'43	120w43'08	8:02:53
Big Bar 53	40N44'28	123w15'17	8:13:01
Big Basin (P O) 44	37N10'21	122w13'15	8:08:53
Big Bear 36	34N12	116w58	7:47:52
Big Bear City 36	34N15'40	116w50'39	7:47:23
Big Bear Highlands 36	34N15	116w53	7:47:32
Big Bear Lake 36	34N14'38	116w54'38	7:47:39
Big Bear Pines 36	34N15	116w53	7:47:32
Big Bear Pinewoods 36	34N15	116w53	7:47:32
Big Bend 4	39N41'54	121w27'35	8:05:50
Big Bend 31	39N18'20	120w31'01	8:02:04
Big Bend 45	41N01	121w55	8:07:40
Big Bend 49	38N14'11	122w27'40	8:09:51
Big Bunch 10	36N45'26	119w32'14	7:58:09
Big Chief 31	39N20	120w12	8:00:48
Big Creek 10	37N12'18	119w14'42	7:56:59
Bigelow 14	37N20'07	118w18'48	7:53:15
Big Flat 47	41N00	122w41	8:10:44
Biggs 4	39N24'45	121w42'42	8:06:51
Big Lagoon 12	41N09'38	124w07'57	8:16:32
Big Lagoon Park 12	41N04	124w08	8:16:32
Big Meadow 5	38N24'54	120w06'51	8:00:27
Big Oak Flat 55	37N49'25	120w15'26	8:01:02
Big Pine (Bigpine P O) 14	37N09'54	118w17'19	7:53:09
Big Pine Indian Reservation 14	37N10	118w17	7:53:08
Big Pines 19	34N22'44	117w41'21	7:50:45
Big Rock Springs 19	34N26'07	117w50'05	7:51:20
Big Springs 47	41N35'44	122w24'14	8:09:37
Big Sur 27	36N16'13	121w48'23	8:07:14
Big Trees 5	38N16'39	120w18'34	8:01:14
Big Trees 44	37N03	122w04	8:08:16
Big Valley 18	41N04	121w07	8:04:28
Bijou 9	38N56'48	119w58'03	7:59:52
Bijou Park 9	38N56'58	119w57'28	7:59:50
Binghamton 48	38N21'05	121w49'18	8:07:17
Binney Junction 58	39N09'27	121w35'21	8:06:21
Biola 10	36N48'08	120w00'55	8:00:04
Biola Junction 10	36N48'03	119w52'04	7:59:28
Birch Hill 37	33N20	116w55	7:47:40
Birchville 29	39N19'40	121w08'36	8:04:34
Birds Landing 48	38N07'58	121w52'11	8:07:29
Bishop 14	37N21'49	118w23'39	7:53:35
Bishop Acres 15	35N30	119w16	7:57:04
Bishop Creek 14	37N22	118w24	7:53:36
Bishop Indian Reservation 14	37N22	118w24	7:53:36
Biskra Palms 33	33N47'24	116w15'08	7:45:01
Bismarck 36	34N57'57	116w51'31	7:47:26
Bissell 15	34N59'41	118w00'05	7:52:00
Bitney Corner 29	39N13'55	121w06'28	8:04:26
Bitterwater 35	36N22'49	121w00'06	8:04:00
Bivalve 21	38N05'33	122w49'34	8:11:18
Bixby 19	33N50	118w11	7:52:44
Bixby Knolls 19	33N50'08	118w10'33	7:52:42
Bixby Landing 27	36N22'20	121w54'21	8:07:37
Bixler 7	37N56'25	121w37'16	8:06:29
Black Butte 47	41N23'30	122w21'36	8:09:26
Black Lands 39	38N03'27	121w14'30	8:04:58
Black Meadow Landing 36	34N21'07	114w11'49	7:36:47
Black Oaks 49	38N49'51	122w49'53	8:11:20
Black Point 21	38N06'37	122w30'16	8:10:01
Black Point Landing 49	38N40'46	123w25'38	8:13:43
Blackslough Landing 39	37N59'40	121w25'04	8:05:40
Blackwells Corner 15	35N36'54	119w52'01	7:59:28
Blairsden 32	39N46'52	120w36'56	8:02:28
Blakes Landing 21	38N11'40	122w55'06	8:11:40
Blanchard 22	37N43'53	120w19'28	8:01:18
Blanco 27	36N40'43	121w44'30	8:06:58
Blanco 54	36N02'10	119w30'37	7:58:02
Blavo 42	39N34'18	121w43'56	8:06:56
Blocksburg 12	40N16'34	123w38'07	8:14:32
Bloomfield 49	38N18'50	122w51'00	8:11:24
Bloomfield Acres 12	40N52	124w05	8:16:20
Bloomington 36	34N04'13	117w23'42	7:49:35
Blossom Hill 43	37N15	121w51	8:07:24
Blossom Valley 43	37N23	122w05	8:08:20
Blue Canyon (Blue Canon P O) 31	39N15'26	120w42'36	8:02:50
Blue Hills 43	37N17'17	122w01'52	8:08:07
Blue Jay 36	34N14'46	117w12'32	7:48:50
Blue Lake 12	40N52'59	123w58'58	8:15:56
Bluff Creek 12	41N03	123w40	8:14:40
Blunkall Crossing 52	40N08'30	121w51'04	8:07:24
Blunt 52	40N14'31	122w17'24	8:09:10
Bly 33	34N00	117w26	7:49:44
Blythe 33	33N36'37	114w35'44	7:38:23
Boal 37	32N36'49	117w05'18	7:48:21
Boards Crossing 55	38N18'16	120w13'59	8:00:56
Bob Hoaglin Place 53	40N05'40	123w19'39	8:13:19
Bob Rabbit Place (Site) 15	35N33'58	118w16'51	7:53:07
Boca 29	39N23'10	120w05'35	8:00:22
Bodega 49	38N20'43	122w58'22	8:11:53
Bodega Bay 49	38N20'00	123w02'49	8:12:11
Bodfish 15	35N35'17	118w29'28	7:53:58
Bodie 26	38N12'44	119w00'40	7:56:03
Bogue 51	39N05'53	121w37'26	8:06:30
Boiling Point 19	34N31'20	118w15'41	7:53:03
Bolam 47	41N30'51	122w14'53	8:09:00
Boles 25	41N32'21	121w03'29	8:04:14
Bolinas 21	37N54'34	122w41'07	8:10:44
Bollinger Place 52	39N50'37	122w52'43	8:11:31
Bolsa 30	33N45	117w59	7:51:56
Bolsa Knolls 27	36N44'02	121w38'13	8:06:33
Bombay 34	38N41'13	121w28'45	8:05:55
Bombay Beach 13	33N14	115w31	7:42:04
Bonanza Springs 17	38N51'52	122w41'09	8:10:45
Bonds Corner 13	32N41'37	115w20'11	7:41:21
Bonetti 9	38N40'29	120w27'13	8:01:49
Bonilla 49	38N16'41	122w26'12	8:09:45
Bonita 20	36N57'09	120w12'03	8:00:48
Bonita 37	32N39'28	117w01'45	7:48:07
Bonnefoy 3	38N21'38	120w45'00	8:03:00
Bonnie Bell 33	33N56'57	116w38'34	7:46:34
Bonnie Doon 44	37N02'30	122w08'58	8:08:36
Bonnie View 6	39N22'57	122w41'02	8:10:44
Bonnyview 45	40N32	122w23	8:09:32
Bonsall 37	33N17'20	117w13'29	7:48:54
Boonville 23	39N00'33	123w21'54	8:13:28
Booth Crossing 17	39N30'10	122w59'30	8:11:58
Bootjack 22	37N27'54	119w53'08	7:59:33
Borden 20	36N55'48	120w01'32	8:00:06

Border City 19 34N30 117w50 7:51:20
Boron 15 34N59'58 117w38'56 7:50:36
Borosolvay 36 35N44'06 117w24'03 7:49:36
Borrego 37 33N13'16 116w20'00 7:45:20
Borrego Springs 37
33N15'21 116w22'27 7:45:30
Bostonia 37 32N48'27 116w56'08 7:47:45
Boston Ravine 29 39N12'29 121w04'07 8:04:16
Boulder Bay 36 34N14'23 116w56'44 7:47:47
Boulder Creek 44 37N07'34 122w07'16 8:08:29
Boulder Oaks 37 32N43'54 116w29'02 7:45:56
Boulder Park 13 32N39'32 116w06'00 7:44:24
Boulevard 37 32N40 116w16 7:45:04
Bouquet Junction 19
34N25'22 118w32'23 7:54:10
Bourns Landing 23
38N47'06 123w33'42 8:14:15
Bowerbank 15 35N23'58 119w24'27 7:57:38
Bowles 10 36N36'15 119w45'00 7:59:00
Bowling Green 34 38N36 121w26 8:05:44
Bowman 31 38N56'31 121w02'47 8:04:11
Bowman Place 23 39N47'22 123w33'42 8:14:15
Box Springs 33 33N56'48 117w17'44 7:49:11
Boyers Landing 6 38N57'06 121w50'17 8:07:21
Boyes Hot Springs 49
38N18'50 122w28'51 8:09:55
Boyle 19 34N04 118w13 7:52:52
Boyle Heights 19 34N02'02 118w12'16 7:52:49
Boys Republic 36 33N59'49 117w43'25 7:50:54
Brackney 44 37N04'08 122w04'52 8:08:19
Bracut 12 40N49'39 124w04'56 8:16:20
Bradbury 19 34N08'49 117w58'12 7:51:53
Bradford 1 37N40 122w05 8:08:20
Bradley 27 35N51'48 120w47'59 8:03:12
Bragur 42 34N56'07 120w32'44 8:02:11
Brainard 12 40N48'44 124w06'33 8:16:26
Bramlet Place 53 40N15'38 123w09'43 8:12:39
Brandeis 56 34N21 119w04 7:56:16
Brandon Corner 9 38N35'09 120w56'00 8:03:44
Brandy City 46 39N32'16 121w01'27 8:04:06
Branscomb 23 39N39'13 123w37'28 8:14:30
Brant 36 35N17'30 115w22'11 7:41:29
Brawley 13 32N58'43 115w31'46 7:42:07
Bray 47 41N38'39 121w58'11 8:07:53
Brazos 28 38N12'30 122w18'18 8:09:13
Brea 30 33N55'00 117w53'57 7:51:36
Brea Chem 30 33N55'01 117w52'06 7:51:28
Bredehoft Place 23
39N46'58 122w56'18 8:11:45
Brela 9 38N34'31 120w57'53 8:03:52
Brents Junction 19
34N08'54 118w41'49 7:54:47
Brentwood 7 37N55'55 121w41'41 8:06:47
Brentwood 19 34N03'07 118w28'23 7:53:54
Brentwood Heights 19
34N03'49 118w28'26 7:53:54
Bretz Mill 10 37N02'15 119w14'20 7:56:57
Briceburg 22 37N36'18 119w57'57 7:59:52
Briceland 12 40N06'29 123w53'56 8:15:36
Bridge Haven 49 38N26'01 123w05'59 8:12:24
Bridgehead 7 38N00'18 121w45'16 8:07:01
Bridge House 34 38N30 121w12 8:04:48
Bridgeport 22 37N26'00 120w00'12 8:00:01
Bridgeport 26 38N15'21 119w13'49 7:56:55
Bridgeport 29 39N17'30 121w11'37 8:04:46
Bridgeport Landing (Site) 23
39N03'46 123w41'38 8:14:47
Bridgeville 12 40N28'10 123w47'55 8:15:12
Briggs 19 34N04 118w22 7:53:28
Briggs Terrace 19
34N14'27 118w13'33 7:52:54
Brighton 34 38N32'58 121w24'58 8:05:40
Briones 7 37N59 122w12 8:08:48
Brisbane 41 37N40'51 122w23'56 8:09:36
Bristol 30 33N45 117w55 7:51:40
Brito 24 36N59'33 120w42'28 8:02:50
Broadmoor 41 37N41 122w29 8:09:56
Broadview Farms 10
36N49'19 120w30'21 8:02:01
Broadway 34 38N33 121w29 8:05:56
Broadway 41 37N35 122w22 8:09:28
Broadwell 36 34N52'26 116w11'33 7:44:46
Brockman 18 40N57'50 120w29'53 8:02:00
Brockmans Corner 14
37N22'34 118w25'53 7:53:44
Brockway 31 39N13'36 120w00'40 8:00:03
Broderick 57 38N35'28 121w30'58 8:06:04
Bromela 40 35N01'04 120w34'58 8:02:20
Brookdale 44 37N06'23 122w06'18 8:08:25
Brookhurst Center 30
33N49 117w59 7:51:56
Brooks 57 38N44'30 122w08'49 8:08:35
Brookside Park 41
37N27 122w11 8:08:44
Brooks Mill 25 41N16'46 120w18'35 8:01:14
Brown 15 35N46'25 117w50'57 7:51:24
Browning 30 33N44'00 117w48'05 7:51:12
Browns Corner 57 38N40'40 121w40'05 8:07:12
Browns Flat 55 38N00'14 120w23'03 8:01:32
Browns Valley 58 39N14'32 121w24'29 8:05:38
Brownsville 58 39N28'24 121w16'05 8:05:04
Bruce Crossing 3 38N27'42 120w22'36 8:01:30
Bruceville 34 38N20'09 121w24'58 8:05:40
Brush Creek 4 39N41'26 121w20'17 8:05:21
Bryant 19 33N52 118w10 7:52:40
Bryants 9 38N43'08 120w28'32 8:01:54
Bryman 36 34N40'29 117w20'41 7:49:23
Bryn Mawr 36 34N02'54 117w13'48 7:48:55
Bryson 27 35N48'24 121w05'22 8:04:21
Bryte 57 38N35'41 121w32'26 8:06:10
Buchanan 55 37N54'53 120w11'15 8:00:45
Buchli 28 38N12'54 122w19'54 8:09:20
Buckeye 9 38N55'26 120w47'49 8:03:11
Buckeye 32 39N47'44 121w18'11 8:05:13
Buckeye 45 40N38'37 122w23'47 8:09:35
Buckhorn 56 34N24'03 118w48'53 7:55:16
Buckingham Park 17
39N00'56 122w45'25 8:11:02
Buck Meadows 22 37N48'46 120w03'48 8:00:15
Bucks Bar 9 38N44 120w48 8:03:12
Bucks Lake 32 39N56 120w55 8:03:40
Bucks Lodge 32 39N52'32 121w10'25 8:04:42
Bucksport 12 40N46'31 124w11'28 8:16:46
Bucktown 48 38N23'27 122w01'23 8:08:06
Buellton 42 34N36'49 120w11'30 8:00:46
Buena 37 33N10'24 117w12'28 7:48:50
Buena Park 30 33N52'03 117w59'50 7:51:59
Buena Vista 3 38N17'40 120w54'44 8:03:39
Buena Vista 22 37N42'40 119w47'34 7:59:10
Buena Vista 49 38N17'23 122w26'02 8:09:44
Buena Vista 52 40N03'20 121w51'59 8:07:28
Buffalo Hill 9 38N54'31 120w50'47 8:03:23
Buhach 24 37N20'11 120w34'51 8:02:19
Bullard 9 38N36'33 120w57'37 8:03:50
Bullard 10 36N49 119w49 7:59:16
Bull Creek 12 40N20'09 124w01'31 8:16:06
Bullion, Mount 22
37N30'25 120w02'33 8:00:10
Bullock's Fashion Square 19
34N09 118w26 7:53:44
Bully Hill 45 40N47'52 122w11'31 8:08:46
Bumblebee 55 38N13'35 119w59'46 7:59:59
Bummerville 5 38N24'05 120w30'17 8:02:01
Bunker 48 38N21'03 121w45'26 8:07:02
Bunker Hill 3 38N25'36 120w49'38 8:03:19
Buntingville 18 40N17'09 120w29'02 8:01:56
Burbank 19 34N10'51 118w18'29 7:53:14
Burbank 43 37N19'24 121w55'50 8:07:43
Burbank Junction 19
34N11'07 118w19'02 7:53:16
Burbeck 23 39N25'48 123w26'33 8:13:46
Burdell 21 38N09'29 122w33'51 8:10:15
Burke 19 33N59 118w05 7:52:20
Burkett Acres 39 37N58 121w15 8:05:00
Burkett Gardens 39
37N58 121w15 8:05:00
Burlingame 41 37N35'03 122w21'54 8:09:28
Burlingame Hills 41
37N35 122w22 8:09:28
Burlington 12 40N18'31 123w54'29 8:15:38
Burness 10 36N45'54 119w39'27 7:58:38
Burney 45 40N52'57 121w39'35 8:06:38
Burnham 39 37N53'31 121w08'52 8:04:35
Burnt Ranch 53 40N48'33 123w28'23 8:13:54
Burr 54 36N14'43 119w06'51 7:56:27
Burrel 10 36N29'18 119w59'03 7:59:56
Burrough 10 37N01 119w24 7:57:36
Burson (Helisma Station) 5
38N11'02 120w53'22 8:03:33
Burton Mill 15 35N30'02 118w24'22 7:53:37
Bush 36 34N09'00 115w42'08 7:42:49
Butano Park 41 37N14'00 122w19'34 8:09:18
Butler 19 34N07'57 117w57'52 7:51:51
Butte City 11 39N27'53 121w59'20 8:07:57
Butte Creek 4 39N44 121w50 8:07:20
Butte Meadows 4 40N04'53 121w33'00 8:06:12
Butte Saint Junction 19
34N01'05 118w13'51 7:52:55
Butte Valley 47 41N50 121w58 8:07:52
Buttonwillow 15 35N24'02 119w28'07 7:57:52
Byron 7 37N52'02 121w38'13 8:06:33
Cabazon 33 33N55'03 116w47'11 7:47:09
Cabin Cove 54 36N27'56 118w39'11 7:54:37
Cable 15 35N10'09 118w28'31 7:53:54
Cabrillo 19 33N50 118w14 7:52:56
Cabrillo Estates 40
35N18 120w45 8:03:00
Cache Creek 15 35N08 117w59 7:51:56
Cachuma Village 42
34N35'10 119w59'24 7:59:58
Cactus 13 32N51'44 114w53'46 7:39:35
Cactus City 33 33N40'42 115w57'47 7:43:51
Cadenasso 57 38N42'52 122w07'41 8:08:31
Cadiz 36 34N31'12 115w30'43 7:42:03
Cadwell 49 38N21'30 122w46'36 8:11:06
Cahuilla 33 33N33 116w43 7:46:52
Cahuilla Estates 33
33N33 116w43 7:46:52
Cahuilla Hills 33
33N41'19 116w24'56 7:45:40
Cahuilla Indian Reservation 33
33N30 116w40 7:46:40
Cain Rock 12 40N08'13 123w35'30 8:14:22
Cain Rock Crossing 12
40N08'49 123w36'07 8:14:24
Cairns Corner 54 36N12'45 119w08'05 7:56:32
Cajon 36 34N17'56 117w27'20 7:49:49
Cajon Junction 36
34N18'42 117w28'26 7:49:54
Calabasas 19 34N09'28 118w38'15 7:54:33
Calabasas Highlands 19
34N07'51 118w38'40 7:54:35
Calabasas Park 19
34N08 118w39 7:54:36
Calada 36 35N34'47 115w22'14 7:41:29
Calaveras 39 38N00 121w20 8:05:20
Calaveras Yacht and Country 39
37N58 121w19 8:05:16
Calaveritas 5 38N09'29 120w36'32 8:02:26
Calavo Gardens 37
32N45'46 116w57'37 7:47:50
Calders Corner 15
35N23'01 119w15'01 7:57:00
Caldor 9 38N36'22 120w25'54 8:01:44
Caldors Corner 15
35N21 118w59 7:55:56
Caldwell Pines 17
38N50'44 122w48'25 8:11:14
Calexico 13 32N40'44 115w29'53 7:42:00
Calexico Lodge 37
32N39'58 116w16'48 7:45:07
Calflax 10 36N20'33 120w06'07 8:00:24
Calgro 54 36N29'23 119w17'05 7:57:08
Calico 15 35N37'58 119w12'20 7:56:49
Calico 36 34N56'56 116w51'51 7:47:27
Cal-Ida 46 39N31'34 121w00'53 8:04:04
Caliente 15 35N17'28 118w37'37 7:54:30
California City 15
35N07'33 117w59'06 7:51:56
California Heights 19
33N49'36 118w10'33 7:52:42
California Hot Springs 54
35N52'49 118w40'22 7:54:41
California Rehabilitation Ce 33
33N53 117w33 7:50:12
California Valley 40
35N19'12 120w00'21 8:00:01
Calimesa 33 34N00'14 117w03'40 7:48:15
Calipatria 13 33N07'32 115w30'48 7:42:03
Calistoga 28 38N34'44 122w34'43 8:10:19
Calla 39 37N46'33 121w10'55 8:04:44
Callahan 47 41N18'35 122w48'01 8:11:12
Callender 40 35N03'11 120w35'43 8:02:23
Calneva 18 40N09'10 120w00'28 8:00:02
Calpack 24 37N17'49 120w21'04 8:01:24
Calpella 23 39N14'01 123w12'10 8:12:49
Calpine 46 39N39'59 120w26'19 8:01:45
Calville 12 40N56'11 124w05'57 8:16:24
Calwa 10 36N42'38 119w45'27 7:59:02
Calzona 36 34N07'44 114w24'37 7:37:38
Camanche 5 38N12'48 120w56'03 8:03:44
Camarillo 56 34N12'59 119w02'12 7:56:09
Camarillo Heights 56
34N15 119w03 7:56:12
Cambria 40 35N33'51 121w04'47 8:04:19
Cambrian Park 43 37N15'25 121w55'47 8:07:43
Cambrian Park Plaza 43
37N15 121w56 8:07:44
Cambria Pines 40 35N33 121w05 8:04:20
Cambria Pines Manor 40
35N33 121w05 8:04:20
Camden 10 36N25'52 119w47'49 7:59:11
Camellia Station 34
38N34 121w26 8:05:44
Cameo 10 36N45'53 119w42'08 7:58:49
Cameo Acres 7 37N50 122w00 8:08:00
Cameron 15 35N05'48 118w17'48 7:53:11
Cameron 23 39N16'21 123w33'12 8:14:13
Cameron Corners 37
32N37'44 116w28'13 7:45:53
Cameron Creek Colony 54
36N19'02 119w12'14 7:56:49
Cameron Park 9 38N40 120w56 8:03:44
Camino 9 38N44'18 120w40'26 8:02:42
Camino Heights 9 38N44 120w41 8:02:44
Campana 9 38N53'03 120w31'10 8:02:05
Camp Angelus (Angelus Oaks P 36
34N08'45 116w58'54 7:47:56
Camp Barlett 56 34N25'41 119w06'26 7:56:26
Campbell 43 37N17'14 121w56'56 8:07:48
Campbell Hot Springs 46
39N34'30 120w20'49 8:01:23
Campbellville 52 40N01'33 121w43'19 8:06:53
Camp Connell 5 38N18'34 120w16'38 8:01:07
Camp Earnest 55 38N00'47 120w13'30 8:00:54
Camp Eighteen 4 39N37'37 121w10'09 8:04:41
Camp Evers 44 37N02'34 122w01'26 8:08:06
Camphora 27 36N27'11 121w22'12 8:05:29
Camp Irwin 36 35N15'39 116w41'12 7:46:45
Camp Kaweah 54 36N34 118w46 7:55:04
Camp Meeker 49 38N25'31 122w57'30 8:11:50
Camp Nelson 54 36N08'34 118w36'30 7:54:26
Campo 37 32N36'23 116w28'05 7:45:52
Campo Indian Reservation 37
32N38 116w20 7:45:20
Campo Seco 5 38N13'38 120w51'08 8:03:25
Campo Seco 55 37N56'20 120w24'54 8:01:40
Camp Owens 15 35N46'07 118w25'48 7:53:43
Camp Pardee 5 38N14'53 120w50'36 8:03:22
Camp Pendleton 37
33N19 117w18 7:49:12
Camp Pendola 55 38N12'53 120w08'53 8:00:36
Camp Richardson 9
38N56'04 120w02'21 8:00:09
Camp Rose 49 38N36'55 122w49'48 8:11:19
Camp Sabrina 14 37N22 118w24 7:53:36
Camp Sierra 10 37N11'26 119w15'32 7:57:02
Camp Spaulding 29
39N19'09 120w38'13 8:02:33
Campton Heights 12
40N35 124w08 8:16:32
Camptonville 58 39N27'07 121w02'51 8:04:11
Camp Wishon 54 36N08 118w49 7:55:16
Camulos 56 34N24'24 118w45'21 7:55:01
Canby 25 41N26'38 120w52'09 8:03:29
Canby Cross 47 41N49'08 121w32'33 8:06:10
Canebrake 15 35N43'42 118w08'15 7:52:33
Cannery Row 27 36N36'48 121w53'48 8:07:35
Cannon 48 38N18'16 121w56'46 8:07:47
Canoga Annex 19 34N12 118w37 7:54:28
Canoga Park 19 34N12'04 118w35'50 7:54:23
Cantil 15 35N18'32 117w58'03 7:51:52
Cantrall Mill 25 41N19'09 120w19'35 8:01:18
Cantua Creek 10 36N30'05 120w18'55 8:01:16
Canyon 7 37N50 122w11 8:08:44
Canyon Acres 30 33N33'11 117w46'18 7:51:05
Canyon City 37 32N35'42 116w31'37 7:46:06
Canyon Country 19
34N25 118w32 7:54:08
Canyon Crest 33 33N59 117w21 7:49:24
Canyon Crest Heights 33
33N58'50 117w19'41 7:49:19
Canyondam 32 40N10'19 121w04'18 8:04:17
Canyon Lake 33 33N45 117w10 7:48:40
Capay 11 39N47'48 122w05'00 8:08:20
Capay 57 38N42'28 122w02'49 8:08:11
Cape Horn 2 38N29'27 119w57'57 7:59:52
Cape Horn 31 39N07'45 120w55'25 8:03:42
Capetown 12 40N27'59 124w21'58 8:17:28
Capistrano Beach 30
33N27'49 117w40'42 7:50:43
Capistrano Highlands 30
33N34 117w45 7:51:00
Capital Hill 40 35N37'40 120w40'47 8:02:43
Capitan 42 34N27'48 120w02'32 8:00:10
Capitola 44 36N58'31 121w57'08 8:07:49
Capps Crossing 9 38N38'51 120w23'40 8:01:35
Carbona 39 37N41'46 121w24'40 8:05:39
Carbon Canyon 36 34N01 117w41 7:50:44
Carbondale 3 38N24'32 121w00'21 8:04:01
Cardiff 37 33N01'18 117w16'49 7:49:07
Cardiff-by-the-Sea (Cardiff) 37
33N01'18 117w16'49 7:49:07
Card Place 23 39N48'29 123w24'13 8:13:37
Cardwell 10 36N46 119w47 7:59:08
Caribou 32 40N04'50 121w09'24 8:04:38
Carlotta 12 40N32'15 124w03'34 8:16:14
Carlsbad 37 33N09'29 117w20'59 7:49:24

Place	Latitude	Longitude	Time
Carlton 30	33N54'07	117w50'11	7:51:21
Carlton Hills 37	32N51'10	116w59'38	7:47:59
Carmel 27	36N33'18	121w55'06	8:07:40
Carmel by the Sea 27	36N33'18	121w55'06	8:07:40
Carmel Highlands 27	36N30'12	121w55'46	8:07:43
Carmel Hills 27	36N33	121w53	8:07:32
Carmel Point 27	36N33	121w53	8:07:32
Carmel Valley 27	36N28'47	121w43'53	8:06:56
Carmel Valley Village 27	36N29	121w44	8:06:56
Carmel Woods 27	36N33	121w53	8:07:32
Carmen City 5	38N02'51	120w41'23	8:02:46
Carmenita 19	33N53'29	118w02'43	7:52:11
Carmet 49	38N22'28	123w04'31	8:12:18
Carmichael 34	38N37'02	121w19'38	8:05:19
Carnadero 43	36N58'35	121w32'32	8:06:10
Carnelian Bay 31	39N13'37	120w04'51	8:00:19
Carpenter 1	37N36'48	122w02'36	8:08:10
Carpenter Place 23	39N44'05	122w55'43	8:11:43
Carpinteria 42	34N23'56	119w31'03	7:58:04
Carpinteria Valley 42	34N25	119w33	7:58:12
Carquinez Heights 48	38N04'35	122w14'20	8:08:57
Carr 42	34N55'52	120w30'39	8:02:03
Carrick Addition 47	41N26	122w23	8:09:32
Carrolton 39	37N47'55	121w04'09	8:04:17
Carrville 53	41N03'54	122w42'11	8:10:49
Carson 19	33N49'53	118w16'52	7:53:07
Carson Hill 5	38N01'42	120w30'20	8:02:01
Cartago 14	36N19'15	118w01'32	7:52:06
Caruthers 10	36N32'34	119w49'56	7:59:20
Carvin Creek Homesites 46	39N37'43	120w34'37	8:02:18
Carwood 19	33N51	118w09	7:52:36
Casa Blanca 33	33N55'59	117w24'06	7:49:36
Casa Conejo 56	34N11	118w55	7:55:40
Casa Correo 7	37N58	121w59	8:07:56
Casa de Oro 37	32N44'56	116w58'48	7:47:55
Casa Loma 31	39N12'02	120w46'32	8:03:06
Cascade 32	39N42'00	121w10'38	8:04:43
Casey Corner 29	39N11'50	121w10'37	8:04:42
Casitas Springs 56	34N22'17	119w18'20	7:57:13
Casmalia 42	34N50'17	120w31'49	8:02:07
Caspar 23	39N21'49	123w48'53	8:15:16
Cassel 45	40N55'09	121w32'48	8:06:11
Castaic 19	34N29'20	118w37'19	7:54:29
Castaic Junction 19	34N26'27	118w36'20	7:54:25
Castella 45	41N08'19	122w19'00	8:09:16
Castellammare 19	34N05	118w30	7:54:00
Castle 24	37N23	120w34	8:02:16
Castle Air Force Base 24	37N23	120w34	8:02:16
Castle Crag 45	41N09'46	122w17'27	8:09:10
Castle Garden 24	37N23	120w34	8:02:16
Castle Gardens 24	37N21'24	120w34'47	8:02:19
Castle Park 37	32N36'37	117w04'00	7:48:16
Castle Rock Springs 17	38N46'13	122w42'56	8:10:52
Castlewood 1	37N42	121w54	8:07:36
Castro City 43	37N24'09	122w06'09	8:08:25
Castro Valley 1	37N41'39	122w05'07	8:08:20
Castroville 27	36N45'57	121w45'25	8:07:02
Caswell 19	34N43'20	118w47'51	7:55:11
Catalina 19	34N09	118w07	7:52:28
Cathedral City 33	33N46'47	116w27'52	7:45:51
Catheys Valley 22	37N25'57	120w05'49	8:00:23
Catlett 51	38N50'43	121w32'15	8:06:09
Cave City 5	38N12'09	120w30'27	8:02:02
Cavin 56	34N23'43	118w50'55	7:55:24
Cawelo 15	35N29'58	119w09'53	7:56:40
Cayley 6	37N43'49	121w35'58	8:06:24
Cayton 45	40N53	121w40	8:06:40
Cayucos 40	35N26'34	120w53'28	8:03:34
Cazadero 49	38N32'00	123w05'03	8:12:20
Cecile 10	36N42'03	119w43'00	7:58:52
Cecilville 47	41N08'28	123w08'20	8:12:33
Cedar 19	37N12	119w09	7:56:36
Cedarbrook 10	36N42'25	119w00'26	7:56:02
Cedar Crest 10	37N12	119w09	7:56:36
Cedar Crossing 52	40N13'47	121w50'11	8:07:21
Cedar Flat 31	39N14	120w05	8:00:20
Cedar Glen 36	34N15'14	117w09'50	7:48:39
Cedar Grove 9	38N44	120w41	8:02:44
Cedar Grove 10	36N47'27	118w40'10	7:54:41
Cedar Mill 32	39N56'39	120w55'20	8:03:41
Cedarpines Park 36	34N15'00	117w19'30	7:49:18
Cedar Ridge 29	39N11'56	121w01'12	8:04:05
Cedar Ridge 55	38N03'57	120w16'33	8:01:06
Cedar Rock Lodge 55	38N01'18	120w14'45	8:00:59
Cedar Slope 54	36N08'43	118w34'39	7:54:19
Cedar Springs 19	34N21'02	117w53'03	7:51:32
Cedarville 25	41N31'45	120w10'20	8:00:41
Cedarville Indian Res 25	41N32	120w10	8:00:40
Cella 10	36N41'30	119w27'14	7:57:49
Ceneda 15	35N21'16	117w53'47	7:51:35
Centerville 4	39N47'16	121w39'15	8:06:37
Centerville 10	36N44	119w30	7:58:00
Centerville 45	40N31'06	122w29'03	8:09:56
Centerville District 1	37N33'15	121w59'53	8:08:00
Centeville 10	36N44'02	119w29'49	7:57:59
Central 57	38N23'34	121w34'19	8:06:17
Central Camp 20	37N20'58	119w28'58	7:57:56
Central Coast 30	33N39	117w51	7:51:24
Central Colusa 6	39N08	122w06	8:08:24
Central District 19	34N03	117w47	7:51:08
Centralia 34	38N19'13	121w14'37	8:04:58
Central Shasta 45	40N37	122w00	8:08:00
Central Valley 45	40N40'50	122w22'12	8:09:29
Centre 34	38N35	121w25	8:05:40
Century City 19	34N03'20	118w25'01	7:53:40
Ceres 50	37N35'42	120w57'24	8:03:50
Cerritos 19	33N52	118w05	7:52:20
Cerro 21	37N59'30	122w31'49	8:10:07
Cerro Villa Heights 30	33N49'36	117w48'12	7:51:13
Chabot Terrace 48	38N08'50	122w14'42	8:08:59
Chadbourne 48	38N14'38	122w04'58	8:08:20
Chaffee 15	35N04'00	118w10'13	7:52:41
Chalfant 26	37N22	118w24	7:53:36
Chalk Bank Landing 47	41N54'44	121w38'30	8:06:34
Challenge 58	39N29'15	121w13'21	8:04:53
Chambers Lodge 31	39N04'24	120w08'25	8:00:34
Chambless 36	34N33'41	115w32'38	7:42:11
Chamisa Gap 17	38N58'41	122w40'53	8:10:44
Champagne 36	34N02'04	117w33'45	7:50:15
Champagne Fountain 43	37N16'33	122w00'27	8:08:02
Chaney Ranch 10	36N39'21	120w34'41	8:02:19
Chapman 19	34N08'54	118w04'57	7:52:20
Chapmantown 4	39N43'14	121w48'56	8:07:16
Chapman Woods 19	34N09	118w05	7:52:20
Chappo 37	33N17'35	117w21'40	7:49:27
Charter Oak 19	34N06'11	117w50'42	7:51:23
Chase 36	35N11'02	115w30'09	7:42:01
Chatsworth 19	34N15'26	118w36'01	7:54:24
Chatsworth Lake Manor 56	34N14'27	118w38'10	7:54:33
Chawanakee 10	37N05	119w29	7:57:56
Cheeseville 47	41N31'16	122w53'55	8:11:36
Chemeketa Park 43	37N09'45	121w58'47	8:07:55
Chemurgic 50	37N27'51	120w55'04	8:03:40
Cherokee 4	39N38'47	121w32'14	8:06:09
Cherokee 29	39N22'13	121w02'31	8:04:10
Cherokee 39	38N09'31	121w14'32	8:04:58
Cherokee 55	37N58'54	120w14'48	8:00:59
Cherokee Strip 15	35N28'02	119w15'35	7:57:02
Cherry Creek Acres 29	39N06'15	121w04'54	8:04:20
Cherryland 1	37N42	122w06	8:08:24
Cherry Valley 33	33N58'21	116w58'35	7:47:54
Chester 32	40N18'23	121w13'51	8:04:55
Chestnut 41	37N39	122w26	8:09:44
Chianti 49	38N44'14	122w56'28	8:11:46
Chicago Park 29	39N09	120w58	8:03:52
Chico 4	39N43'43	121w50'11	8:07:21
Chico Landing 4	39N42'45	121w56'40	8:07:47
Chico Vecino 4	39N44	121w50	8:07:20
Chilcoot 32	39N47'52	120w08'19	8:00:33
Childrens Fairyland 1	37N49	122w14	8:08:56
Childs Meadows 52	40N19	121w32	8:06:08
China 38	37N47	122w26	8:09:44
China Lake 15	35N39'03	117w39'39	7:50:39
Chinatown 38	37N47'48	122w24'27	8:09:38
Chinese Camp 55	37N52'16	120w25'56	8:01:44
Chino 36	34N00'44	117w41'17	7:50:45
Chinowths Corner 54	36N19'37	119w20'05	7:57:20
Chipps 48	38N03'05	121w54'50	8:07:39
Chiquita 49	38N38'06	122w52'24	8:11:30
Chiriaco Summit 33	33N39'39	115w43'14	7:42:53
Chittenden 35	36N54'12	121w36'26	8:06:26
Chloride City 14	36N42'24	116w52'53	7:47:32
Cholame 40	35N43'26	120w17'44	8:01:11
Chorro 40	35N19'36	120w40'36	8:02:42
Chowchilla 20	37N07'23	120w15'33	8:01:02
Chrisman 56	34N17'52	119w18'04	7:57:12
Christie 7	38N00'11	122w12'20	8:08:49
Chrome 23	39N43'45	122w32'54	8:10:12
Chualar 27	36N34'14	121w31'03	8:06:04
Chubbuck 36	34N21'54	115w17'07	7:41:08
Chuckwalla 33	33N42	115w11	7:40:44
Chula Vista 37	32N38'24	117w05'00	7:48:20
Church of God Colony 10	36N37	119w31	7:58:04
Cienega 19	34N01'16	118w19'39	7:53:19
Cienega Mirth 14	37N08'08	118w27'58	7:53:52
Cima 36	35N14'16	115w29'54	7:42:00
Cimarron 16	36N17'55	119w48'46	7:59:15
Cinco 15	35N15'48	118w02'07	7:52:08
Cincotta 10	36N45'41	119w45'13	7:59:01
Cisco 31	39N18'06	120w32'45	8:02:11
Cisco Grove 31	39N18'36	120w32'20	8:02:09
Citro 54	36N23'34	119w01'25	7:56:06
Citrona 57	38N38'01	121w58'13	8:07:53
Citrus 34	38N36'24	121w15'56	8:05:04
Citrus Heights 34	38N42'26	121w16'48	8:05:07
City Hall 38	37N47	122w26	8:09:44
City of Commerce 19	33N58'20	118w07'19	7:52:29
City of Industry 19	34N01'11	117w57'28	7:51:50
City Terrace 19	34N03'00	118w10'55	7:52:44
Civic Center 19	34N11	118w27	7:53:48
Civic Center 21	38N01	122w33	8:10:12
Civic Center 30	33N45	117w51	7:51:24
Civic Center Annex 1	37N48	122w13	8:08:52
Clairemont 37	32N47'50	117w11'30	7:48:46
Clam Beach 12	40N59'41	124w06'39	8:16:27
Claraville 15	35N26'32	118w19'43	7:53:19
Claraville Flat 15	35N26'32	118w19'22	7:53:17
Clare Mill 23	39N24'59	123w25'37	8:13:42
Claremont 19	34N05'48	117w43'08	7:50:53
Claribel 50	37N42'52	120w49'28	8:03:18
Clarksburg 57	38N25'14	121w31'34	8:06:06
Clarks Crossing 49	38N39'56	123w18'45	8:13:15
Clarksville 9	38N39'18	121w03'05	8:04:12
Clarsona 3	38N22'26	120w58'57	8:03:56
Claus 50	37N41'12	120w55'08	8:03:41
Claussenius 9	38N50'48	120w36'46	8:02:27
Clay 34	38N20'10	121w09'30	8:04:38
Clayton 7	37N56'28	121w56'05	8:07:44
Clayton 31	38N54'29	121w18'40	8:05:15
Clear Creek 18	40N17'53	121w02'51	8:04:11
Clear Creek 47	41N42'34	123w26'57	8:13:48
Clear Creek Junction 32	40N17'39	121w03'58	8:04:16
Clearing House 22	37N39'54	119w51'59	7:59:28
Clearlake Highlands 17	38N57'22	122w38'48	8:10:35
Clearlake Oaks 17	39N01'27	122w40'26	8:10:42
Clearlake Park 17	38N58'04	122w39'14	8:10:37
Clement Junction 19	34N00'51	118w14'16	7:52:57
Clements 39	38N11'27	121w05'14	8:04:21
Cleone 23	39N29'24	123w47'04	8:15:08
Clifton 19	33N49'39	118w22'44	7:53:31
Clima 48	38N14'58	122w04'14	8:08:17
Clint 10	36N25'53	119w46'21	7:59:05
Clinter 10	36N46	119w45	7:59:00
Clinton 3	38N22'34	120w40'02	8:02:40
Clio 32	39N44'36	120w34'45	8:02:19
Clipper Gap 31	38N58'10	121w00'59	8:04:04
Clipper Mills 4	39N31'58	121w09'23	8:04:38
Clotho 10	36N43'17	119w36'32	7:58:26
Cloverdale 45	40N28'25	122w28'29	8:09:54
Cloverdale 49	38N48'20	123w00'58	8:12:04
Clover Flat 37	32N39'43	116w24'49	7:45:39
Clovis 10	36N49'31	119w42'07	7:58:48
Clyde 7	38N01'32	122w01'42	8:08:07
Clyde 13	32N53'15	114w55'40	7:39:43
Coachella 33	33N40'49	116w10'23	7:44:42
Coachella Valley 33	33N39	116w11	7:44:44
Coahuila 33	33N32'27	116w44'35	7:46:58
Coalinga 10	36N08'23	120w21'33	8:01:26
Coarsegold 20	37N15'44	119w42'00	7:58:48
Coastal 27	36N15	121w44	8:06:56
Cobb 17	38N49'20	122w43'19	8:10:53
Coburn 27	36N17'19	121w09'06	8:04:36
Cochrane 39	37N43'52	121w21'31	8:05:26
Cockatoo Grove 37	32N38'35	116w58'59	7:47:56
Coddingtown 49	38N27	122w42	8:10:48
Codora 11	39N27'32	122w01'16	8:08:05
Coffee 53	41N00	122w41	8:10:44
Cohasset 4	39N55'32	121w43'48	8:06:55
Cold Fork 52	40N10'19	122w40'20	8:10:41
Cold Springs 9	38N44'31	120w52'09	8:03:29
Cold Springs 55	38N09'45	120w03'08	8:00:13
Cole 19	34N06	118w22	7:53:28
Cole 47	42N00'08	122w38'21	8:10:33
Coleville 26	38N33'59	119w30'22	7:58:01
Colfax 31	39N06'03	120w57'08	8:03:49
Colfax Spring 55	37N49'15	120w01'36	8:00:06
Colima 19	33N56'41	118w00'46	7:52:03
College Center 15	35N23	118w59	7:55:56
College City 6	39N00'21	122w00'30	8:08:02
College Grove Center 37	32N45	117w04	7:48:16
College Heights 19	34N06'24	117w41'18	7:50:45
College Heights 44	36N59	121w54	8:07:36
College Park 43	37N20'32	121w53'55	8:07:36
College Park 56	34N12	118w53	7:55:32
Collegeville 39	37N54'18	121w08'47	8:04:35
Collier 19	34N12	118w37	7:54:28
Collierville 39	38N12'53	121w16'04	8:05:04
Collins 28	38N09'57	122w15'05	8:09:00
Collins Landing 23	38N47'40	123w34'06	8:14:16
Collinsville 48	38N04'37	121w50'56	8:07:24
Colma 41	37N40'37	122w27'28	8:09:50
Coloma 9	38N48'00	120w53'21	8:03:33
Colonial 34	38N32	121w27	8:05:48
Colonial Juarez 30	33N44	117w57	7:51:48
Colton 36	34N04'26	117w18'46	7:49:15
Columbia 55	38N02'11	120w24'01	8:01:36
Colusa 6	39N12'52	122w00'30	8:08:02
Colusa Junc 51	39N08'52	121w39'33	8:06:38
Cometa 39	37N51'24	120w56'42	8:03:47
Commerce 19	33N58'20	118w07'19	7:52:29
Commonwealth 30	33N53	117w56	7:51:44
Community Center 56	34N16'09	118w44'12	7:54:57
Como 30	33N41'56	117w47'34	7:51:10
Comptche 23	39N16	123w35	8:14:20
Compton 19	33N53'45	118w13'09	7:52:53
Compton Landing 6	39N20'11	122w01'50	8:08:07
Conant 45	41N06'46	122w19'28	8:09:18
Conaway 57	38N40'38	121w40'19	8:06:41
Concepcion 42	34N27'13	120w27'14	8:01:49
Concord 7	37N58'41	122w01'48	8:08:07
Concord Naval Weapons Statio 7	37N58	122w01	8:08:04
Conejo 10	36N31'06	119w43'05	7:58:52
Conejo Village 56	34N12	118w53	7:55:32
Confederate Corners 27	36N38'41	121w39'48	8:06:39
Confidence 55	38N02'51	120w12'01	8:00:48
Conner 15	35N10'48	119w06'54	7:56:28
Convict Lake 26	37N22	118w24	7:53:36
Cooks Valley 12	40N00'05	123w47'06	8:15:08
Cool 9	38N53	121w01	8:04:04
Cooley Landing 41	37N28'36	122w07'14	8:08:29
Coolidge Springs 13	33N23'39	116w02'58	7:44:12
Cooper 17	39N13'11	123w00'11	8:12:01
Cooper 27	36N42'52	121w42'58	8:06:52

Coopers Corner 39 38N10 121W13 8:04:52
Cooperstown 50 37N44'36 120W32'37 8:02:10
Copco 25 41N29'57 120W31'57 8:02:08
Copco 47 41N59'00 122W21'37 8:09:26
Copic 25 41N51'55 121W20'27 8:05:22
Copper City 11 39N43'23 122W48'30 8:11:14
Copper City 36 35N21'03 117W11'05 7:48:44
Copperopolis 5 37N58'52 120W38'27 8:02:34
Copple Place 52 40N00'31 122W37'43 8:10:31
Coram 45 40N42'37 122W26'25 8:09:46
Corcoran 16 36N05'53 119W33'34 7:58:14
Cordelia 48 38N12'38 122W08'05 8:08:32
Cordelia Junction 48 38N13'01 122W08'19 8:08:33
Cordero Junction 48 38N17'16 121W57'12 8:07:49
Cordova 34 38N30'37 121W28'27 8:05:54
Cordova Town West 34 38N35 121W20 8:05:20
Cornell 19 34N06'52 118W46'37 7:55:06
Cornell 25 41N47'58 121W19'06 8:05:16
Corning 52 39N55'40 122W10'41 8:08:43
Coromar 42 34N26'03 119W52'00 7:59:28
Corona 33 33N52'31 117W33'56 7:50:16
Corona del Mar 30 33N35'53 117W52'20 7:51:29
Coronado 37 32N41'09 117W10'56 7:48:44
Coronita 33 33N53 117W33 7:50:12
Corporal 43 36N55'47 121W32'49 8:06:11
Corralitos 44 36N59'19 121W48'19 8:07:13
Corte Madera 21 37N55'32 122W31'35 8:10:06
Cortena 6 39N13'09 122W11'06 8:08:44
Cortez 24 37N28'31 120W44'19 8:02:57
Cory 11 39N46'06 122W08'55 8:08:36
Coso 14 35N58'42 117W55'43 7:51:43
Coso Junction 14 36N02'42 117W56'47 7:51:47
Costa Mesa 30 33N38'28 117W55'04 7:51:40
Cosunme 34 38N29'33 121W10'26 8:04:42
Cosy Dell 36 34N16'44 117W27'10 7:49:49
Cotati 49 38N19'37 122W42'22 8:10:49
Cotners Corner 36 34N28'17 117W10'15 7:48:41
Cottage Corners 35 36N52'10 121W23'58 8:05:36
Cottage Grove 47 41N36'10 123W30'16 8:14:01
Cottage Springs 5 38N21'22 120W12'39 8:00:51
Cotton Center 54 36N03'58 119W08'31 7:56:34
Cottonwood 45 40N23'09 122W16'47 8:09:07
Cougar 47 41N35'00 122W11'03 8:08:44
Coulterville 22 37N42'38 120W11'49 8:00:47
Counsman 51 38N44'58 121W29'29 8:05:58
Country Club Estates 40 35N18 120W45 8:03:00
Country Modern 15 35N08 117W59 7:51:56
County Strip 19 34N06 118W23 7:53:32
Court 7 37N59 122W07 8:08:28
Courtland 34 38N19'52 121W34'03 8:06:16
Covelo 23 39N47'35 123W14'49 8:12:59
Covina 19 34N05'24 117W53'22 7:51:33
Covington Mill 53 40N43 122W48 8:11:12
Cowan Heights 30 33N46'40 117W46'23 7:51:06
Cow Creek 55 38N14'26 119W59'28 7:59:58
Cowell 7 37N57'10 121W59'18 8:07:57
Cox 33 33N50'20 114W46'19 7:39:05
Coyote 43 37N13'00 121W44'22 8:06:57
Coyoteville 9 38N33'05 120W41'20 8:02:45
Coyote Wells 13 32N44'19 115W58'00 7:43:52
Crabtree 10 36N50'37 119W05'20 7:56:21
Crabtree Place 53 40N09'13 123W21'01 8:13:24
Craf 36 34N05 117W08 7:48:32
Crafton 36 34N03'47 117W07'15 7:48:29
Craig 4 39N20'15 121W33'47 8:06:15
Cranmore 51 38N59'17 121W48'20 8:07:13
Crannell 12 41N00'43 124W05'01 8:16:20
Crater 14 37N12'58 117W41'11 7:50:45
Cray Mill 26 38N13'07 118W59'03 7:55:56
Creed 48 38N14'36 121W51'15 8:07:25
Creegan 24 37N17'31 120W27'43 8:01:51
Crenshaw 19 33N59 118W22 7:53:28
Crescent 19 34N06 118W23 7:53:32
Crescent City 8 41N45'22 124W12'02 8:16:48
Crescent Mills 32 40N05'48 120W54'35 8:03:38
Cressey 24 37N25'11 120W39'59 8:02:40
Crest 18 40N43'29 120W22'09 8:01:29
Crest 37 32N48 116W57 7:47:48
Cresta 4 39N50'37 121W24'12 8:05:37
Crest Forest 36 34N14 117W17 7:49:08
Crestline 36 34N14'31 117W17'05 7:49:08
Crestmore 33 34N01'27 117W23'14 7:49:33
Crestmore Heights 33 34N00 117W26 7:49:44
Creston 28 38N12'33 122W12'11 8:08:49
Creston 40 35N31'08 120W31'22 8:02:05
Crest Park 36 34N14'02 117W11'44 7:48:47
Crestview 26 37N45'09 118W59'00 7:55:56
Crocker Place 17 39N33'25 123W03'14 8:12:13
Crockett 7 38N03'09 122W12'43 8:08:51
Croft 9 38N34'54 120W26'01 8:01:44
Cromberg 32 39N51'37 120W41'26 8:02:46
Crome 15 35N26'30 119W11'57 7:56:48
Cromir 10 36N48'16 120W25'15 8:01:41
Cronese Valley 36 35N06'00 116W16'21 7:45:05
Cross Roads 36 34N12'52 114W12'54 7:36:52
Crowley 23 39N24'33 123W25'28 8:13:42
Crowley 54 36N20 119W18 7:57:12
Crowley Lake 26 37N22 118W24 7:53:36
Crown 49 38N16'00 122W39'21 8:10:37
Crown Jewel 36 34N04'38 117W12'33 7:48:50
Crows Landing 50 37N23'38 121W04'14 8:04:17
Crucero 36 35N02'50 116W09'53 7:44:40
Crutcher 19 33N54 118W10 7:52:40
Crystal Cove 30 33N34'31 117W50'26 7:51:22
Crystal Lake 29 39N19'22 120W34'09 8:02:17
Cubbler Place 23 39N45'10 123W08'55 8:12:36
Cucamonga 36 34N06'23 117W35'32 7:50:22
Cudahy 19 33N57'38 118W11'04 7:52:44
Cuesta-by-the-Sea 40 35N19'06 120W50'45 8:03:23
Culver City 19 34N01'16 118W23'44 7:53:35
Culver Junc 19 34N01'42 118W23'22 7:53:33
Cummings 23 39N50'00 123W37'51 8:14:31
Cunard 51 38N48'50 121W41'05 8:06:44
Cunningham 49 38N21'45 122W46'36 8:11:06
Cupertino 43 37N19'23 122W01'52 8:08:07
Curlew 13 32N56'00 115W24'17 7:41:37
Curry Village 22 37N44'17 119W34'22 7:58:17
Curtis 47 41N12'02 121W45'56 8:07:04
Curtiss Heights 12 40N52 124W05 8:16:20
Curtner 1 37N28'11 121W55'21 8:07:41
Cushenbury 36 34N21'14 116W51'27 7:47:26
Cushing 40 35N25'34 120W36'11 8:02:25
Cutler 54 36N31'24 119W17'09 7:57:09
Cutten 12 40N46'12 124W08'30 8:16:34
Cutter Place Campground 45 40N39'42 121W43'36 8:06:54
Cuttings Wharf 28 38N13'36 122W18'28 8:09:14
Cuyama 42 34N56'07 119W36'51 7:58:27
Cygnus 48 38N09'10 122W05'17 8:08:21
Cypress 30 33N49'01 118W02'11 7:52:09
Cypress Grove 21 38N09'57 122W53'58 8:11:36
Daggett 36 34N51'48 116W53'14 7:47:33
Dagon 3 38N20'41 120W57'37 8:03:50
Dairyland 20 37N01'06 120W18'34 8:01:14
Dairy Valley 19 33N51'30 118W03'50 7:52:15
Dairyville 52 40N07'48 122W07'12 8:08:29
Dales 52 40N18'50 122W04'14 8:08:17
Dalewood 30 33N47 117W59 7:51:56
Daley Mill 15 35N20'19 117W55'53 7:51:44
Dalton 25 41N56'11 121W25'06 8:05:40
Daly City 41 37N43'13 122W31'33 8:10:06
Dana 45 41N06'42 121W33'49 8:06:15
Dana Point 30 33N28'01 117W41'50 7:50:47
Danby 36 34N38'08 115W20'50 7:41:23
Danielson 48 38N14'18 122W06'14 8:08:25
Dan Ryan Place 18 41N08'59 120W48'58 8:03:16
Dantoni 58 39N09'54 121W30'55 8:06:04
Dantuma Place 52 40N17'37 121W47'56 8:07:12
Danville 7 37N49'18 121W59'56 8:08:00
Daphnedale Park 25 41N30'33 120W32'38 8:02:11
Dardanelle 55 38N20'28 119W49'58 7:59:20
Darlington 9 38N43'45 120W24'02 8:01:36
Darlingtonia 8 41N50'11 123W56'31 8:15:46
Darrah 22 37N31'05 119W50'03 7:59:20
Darwin 14 36N16'05 117W35'27 7:50:22
Darwin Mines 14 36N16'38 117W35'46 7:50:23
Date City 13 32N47'35 115W18'33 7:41:14
Daulton 20 37N07'09 119W58'52 7:59:55
Davenport 44 37N00'42 122W11'27 8:08:46
Davenport Landing 44 37N01'28 122W12'53 8:08:52
Davis 57 38N32'42 121W44'22 8:06:57
Davis Creek 25 41N44'00 120W22'15 8:01:29
Dawson Place 52 39N55'26 122W42'23 8:10:50
Day 25 41N12'42 121W22'31 8:05:30
Dayton 4 39N38'55 121W52'16 8:07:29
Dayton Avenue 19 34N05'02 118W13'18 7:52:53
Daywalt 49 38N24 122W50 8:11:20
Deacon Lee Place 47 41N28'51 122W55'41 8:11:43
Deadman Crossing 52 40N09'27 122W34'52 8:10:19
Deadwood 4 39N44'33 121W31'25 8:06:06
Deadwood 53 40N43'10 122W43'57 8:10:56
Deadwood 55 38N00'15 120W06'26 8:00:26
Deane Brothers Subdivision 19 34N25 118W32 7:54:08
Dean Place 51 39N13'24 121W46'48 8:07:07
Dearborn Park 41 37N15'32 122W19'01 8:09:16
Death Valley 14 36N27 116W52 7:47:28
Death Valley Junction 14 36N18'08 116W24'46 7:45:39
Debon 47 41N26 122W23 8:09:32
Declezville 36 34N02'40 117W28'50 7:49:55
Decoto 1 37N36 122W01 8:08:04
Dedrick 53 40N51'46 123W02'08 8:12:09
Deep Springs 14 37N22'18 117W59'03 7:51:56
Deer Creek 52 40N15'36 121W23'31 8:05:34
Deer Creek Colony 54 35N58'42 118W59'57 7:56:00
Deer Creek Crossing 52 40N03'15 121W46'59 8:07:08
Deer Crossing 10 36N41'24 119W02'52 7:56:11
Deer Lake Highlands 19 34N17'02 118W35'45 7:54:23
Deer Lick Springs 53 40N22 122W53 8:11:32
Deer Park 28 38N32 122W28 8:09:52
Deer View 9 38N50'36 120W40'00 8:02:40
Deetz 47 41N21'29 122W22'56 8:09:32
DeHaven 23 39N39'37 123W47'02 8:15:08
Del Aire 19 33N55 118W22 7:53:28
Delano 15 35N46'08 119W14'46 7:56:59
Del Cerro 37 32N47 117W04 7:48:16
Del Dios 37 33N04'22 117W07'06 7:48:28
Delevan (P O) 6 39N21'15 122W11'24 8:08:46
Delft Colony 54 36N30'43 119W26'42 7:57:47
Delhi 24 37N25'56 120W46'39 8:03:07
Delkern 15 35N21 119W03 7:56:12
Delleker 32 39N48'32 120W29'49 8:01:59
DelLoma 53 40N46'43 123W19'52 8:13:19
Del Mar 37 32N57'34 117W15'52 7:49:03
Del Mar 44 36N59 122W00 8:08:00
Del Mar Heights 37 32N56'54 117W15'36 7:49:02
Del Mar Heights 40 35N22 120W51 8:03:24
Del Mar Landing 49 38N44'28 123W30'17 8:14:01
Del Mar Race Track 37 32N59 117W16 7:49:04
Del Mesa 21 37N58 122W31 8:10:04
Delmonico Place 23 39N58'32 123W19'02 8:13:16
Delmonte 27 36N36'03 121W52'05 8:07:28
Del Monte Center 27 36N36 121W53 8:07:32
Del Monte Forest 27 36N35 121W56 8:07:44
Del Monte Heights 27 36N36'42 121W49'52 8:07:19
Del Monte Park 27 36N37 121W56 8:07:44
Del Paso 34 38N39'10 121W28'20 8:05:53
Del Paso Heights 34 38N38'10 121W25'09 8:05:41
Delphos 6 39N11'25 122W10'08 8:08:41
Del Rey 10 36N39'33 119W35'34 7:58:22
Del Rey Oaks 27 36N35'36 121W50'02 8:07:20
Del Rio Woods 49 38N37'23 122W50'18 8:11:21
Del Rosa 36 34N08'56 117W14'33 7:48:58
Del Sur 19 34N41'23 118W17'16 7:53:09
Delta 19 33N55'11 118W19'15 7:53:17
Delta 39 38N13 121W33 8:06:12
Delta 45 40N56'40 122W25'25 8:09:42
DeLuz 37 33N21'32 117W16'12 7:49:05
Del Valle 19 34N25'10 118W39'20 7:54:37
Democrat Hot Springs 15 35N23 119W01 7:56:04
Demuth 25 41N20'16 121W15'54 8:05:04
Denair 50 37N31'35 120W47'45 8:03:11
Denis 19 34N37'34 118W07'27 7:52:30
Denny 53 40N56'39 123W23'08 8:13:33
Denverton 48 38N13'29 121W53'47 8:07:35
Derby Acres 15 35N14'50 119W35'40 7:58:23
DeSabla 4 39N52'26 121W36'06 8:06:24
Descanso 37 32N51'10 116W36'54 7:46:28
Descanso Junction 37 32N50'28 116W36'43 7:46:27
Desert 36 35N28 115W16 7:41:04
Desert Beach 33 33N30'46 115W55'35 7:43:42
Desert Camp 33 33N32'01 115W58'57 7:43:56
Desert Center 33 33N42'45 115W24'05 7:41:36
Desert Heights 36 34N12'04 116W08'27 7:44:34
Desert Hot Springs 33 33N57'40 116W30'03 7:46:00
Desert Lake 15 35N00'09 117W41'53 7:50:48
Desert Lodge 37 33N12'38 116W19'35 7:45:18
Desert Shores 13 33N39 116W09 7:44:36
Desert View 33 33N48'05 116W38'24 7:46:34
Desert View Highlands 19 34N36 118W09 7:52:36
Des Moines 30 33N55'55 117W58'01 7:51:52
Devils Den 15 35N46 119W58 7:59:52
Devils Elbow 6 39N20'45 122W25'40 8:09:43
Devon 42 34N50'31 120W31'06 8:02:04
Devore 36 34N12'59 117W24'02 7:49:36
Devore Heights 36 34N14'14 117W24'53 7:49:40
Dew Drop 29 39N05'14 121W05'08 8:04:21
Diablo 7 37N50'06 121W57'25 8:07:50
Diablo Range 43 37N05 121W25 8:05:40
Diamond 30 33N44 117W54 7:51:36
Diamond Bar 19 34N01'43 117W48'34 7:51:14
Diamond Crossing 31 39N06'35 120W17'24 8:01:10
Diamond Heights 38 37N45 122W26 8:09:44
Diamond Springs 9 38N41'41 120W48'50 8:03:15
Diamond Springs Heights 9 38N42 120W49 8:03:16
Dibble Place 25 41N11'22 120W53'45 8:03:35
Di Giorgio 15 35N15'10 118W51'02 7:55:24
Dillard 34 38N24'05 121W15'21 8:05:01
Dillon Beach 21 38N15'03 122W57'51 8:11:51
Dimond 1 37N48 122W13 8:08:52
Dinkey Creek 10 37N05'10 119W09'24 7:56:38
Dinsmore 12 40N29'30 123W36'21 8:14:25
Dinsmores 12 40N43'12 123W44'16 8:14:57
Dinuba 54 36N32'36 119W23'10 7:57:33
Dirigo 45 41N08'58 122W18'34 8:09:14
Ditch Camp Five 9 38N45'55 120W32'50 8:02:11
Dixie 18 40N56'39 121W10'15 8:04:41
Dixie Crossing 18 40N53'14 121W06'55 8:04:28
Dixieland 13 32N47'27 115W46'10 7:43:05
Dixon 48 38N19'26 121W49'16 8:07:17
Dobbins 58 39N22'18 121W12'18 8:04:49
Doble 36 34N17'55 116W49'15 7:47:17
Dockweiler 19 34N02 118W19 7:53:16
Doghouse Junction 37 32N36'01 116W50'25 7:47:22
Dogtown 11 39N35'19 122W42'42 8:10:51
Dogtown 22 37N42'08 120W07'37 8:00:30
Dogtown 39 38N12'50 121W05'15 8:04:21
Doheny Park 30 33N28 117W40 7:50:40
Dolanco Junction 19 33N50'42 118W17'57 7:53:12
Dollar Ranch 7 37N53 122W03 8:08:12
Dolomite 14 36N33'11 117W56'40 7:51:47
Dolores 19 33N49'59 118W13'32 7:52:54
Dominguez 19 33N50'05 118W13'04 7:52:52
Dominguez Junction 19 33N51'48 118W13'01 7:52:52
Donlon 56 34N12 119W10 7:56:40
Donner 29 39N22 120W18 8:01:12
Donner Lake 29 39N20 120W12 8:00:48
Don Pedro Camp 55 37N40 120W28 8:01:52
Dora Belle 10 37N06'46 119W19'12 7:57:17
Dorrington 5 38N18'05 120W16'34 8:01:06
Dorris 47 41N58'03 121W55'01 8:07:40
Dorr Place 49 38N37'14 123W05'26 8:12:22
Dos Cabezas 37 32N44'45 116W08'22 7:44:33
Dos Palmas Corners 33 33N55'29 116W30'04 7:46:00
Dos Palos 24 36N59'10 120W37'32 8:02:30
Dos Palos Y 24 37N02'56 120W38'04 8:02:32
Dos Rios 23 39N43'01 123W21'08 8:13:25
Douds Landing 5 38N12'46 120W19'28 8:01:18
Dougherty 1 37N42'40 121W54'31 8:07:38
Dougherty 39 38N09'45 121W14'32 8:04:58
Douglas 19 34N01 118W28 7:53:52
Douglas City 53 40N39'08 122W56'37 8:11:46
Douglas Flat 5 38N06'52 120W27'14 8:01:49

Place	Latitude	Longitude	Time
Douglas Junction 19	33N51'21	118w09'50	7:52:39
Douglas Park 8	41N47'15	124w03'42	8:16:15
Downey 19	33N56'24	118w07'54	7:52:32
Downieville 46	39N33'34	120w49'33	8:03:18
Doyle 18	40N01'41	120w06'10	8:00:25
Doyle Center 37	32N41'44	117w05'56	7:48:24
Doyle Crossing 32	40N06'47	120w28'58	8:01:56
Doyles Corner 45	40N52'39	121w33'33	8:06:14
Dozier 48	38N17'08	121w48'56	8:07:16
Drake 42	34N28'14	120w18'10	8:01:13
Drakesbad 32	40N26'40	121w24'12	8:05:37
Drawbridge 1	37N27'59	121w58'26	8:07:54
Dresser 1	37N35'33	121w57'17	8:07:49
Drytown 3	38N26'28	120w51'12	8:03:25
Duarte 19	34N08'22	117w58'35	7:51:54
Dublin 1	37N42'08	121w56'05	8:07:44
Ducor 54	35N53'30	119w02'47	7:56:11
Dudmore 19	33N51'24	118w21'00	7:53:24
Dufour 57	38N45'43	121w50'31	8:07:22
Dugan 9	38N36'16	120w57'28	8:03:50
Dulah 56	34N18'45	119w21'32	7:57:26
Dulzura 37	32N38'39	116w46'50	7:47:07
Dumont 36	35N41'35	116w10'30	7:44:42
Duncans Mills 49	38N27'14	123w03'14	8:12:13
Duncan Springs 23	38N57'08	123w07'25	8:12:30
Dunderberg Mill 26	38N06'14	119w14'58	7:57:00
Dunes 13	32N46'59	114w47'47	7:39:11
Dunlap 10	36N44'18	119w07'12	7:56:29
Dunlap Acres 36	34N01'52	117w06'24	7:48:26
Dunlap Place 23	39N51'14	123w25'51	8:13:43
Dunmovin 14	36N05'19	117w57'37	7:51:50
Dunn 36	35N02'42	116w26'13	7:45:45
Dunneville 35	36N56'26	121w24'34	8:05:38
Dunnigan 57	38N53'07	121w58'07	8:07:52
Dunsmuir 47	41N13'11	122w16'26	8:09:06
Durham 4	39N38'47	121w47'56	8:07:12
Durmid 33	33N25'51	115w49'56	7:43:20
Dustin Acres 15	35N13'10	119w23'23	7:57:34
Dutch Flat 31	39N12'22	120w50'12	8:03:21
Dutch Village 19	33N51	118w09	7:52:36
Dutton 48	38N04'34	121w52'56	8:07:32
Dutton Landing 28	38N12'41	122w18'21	8:09:13
Eagle Lake Resort 18	40N25	120w39	8:02:36
Eagle Mountain 33	33N51'27	115w29'11	7:41:57
Eagle Rock 19	34N08'20	118w12'47	7:52:51
Eagles Nest 37	33N17'17	116w35'36	7:46:22
Eagle Tree 39	38N15	121w31	8:06:04
Eagleville 25	41N18'59	120w06'53	8:00:28
Eagleville 58	39N34'46	121w05'43	8:04:23
Earlimart 54	35N53'03	119w16'17	7:57:05
Earp 36	34N09'53	114w18'01	7:37:12
East Acres 20	36N51	120w27	8:01:48
East Antioch 7	38N00'37	121w46'17	8:07:05
East Applegate 31	39N06	120w59	8:03:56
East Arboga 58	39N03'25	121w33'02	8:06:12
East Biggs 4	39N24'55	121w39'10	8:06:37
East Blythe 33	33N36'38	114w34'23	7:38:18
East Colusa 6	39N14	121w59	8:07:56
East Compton 19	33N54	118w12	7:52:48
Easter Cross 37	32N50'23	117w14'37	7:48:58
East Farmersville 54	36N18'06	119w11'38	7:56:47
East Firebaugh 20	36N58	120w04	8:00:16
East Fresno 10	36N46	119w43	7:58:52
East Garrison 27	36N39'11	121w43'53	8:06:56
Eastgate 19	34N04	118w23	7:53:32
East Gate 33	33N56	117w14	7:48:56
East Gridley 4	39N21'48	121w39'39	8:06:39
East Guernewood 49	38N30	123w00	8:12:00
East Highlands 36	34N06'35	117w10'11	7:48:41
East Hopland 23	38N58	123w07	8:12:28
East Imperial 13	32N55	114w49	7:39:16
East Irvine 30	33N40'33	117w45'32	7:51:02
East Kern 15	35N13	117w56	7:51:44
East La Mirada 19	33N55	117w59	7:51:56
Eastland 19	34N04	117w56	7:51:44
East Long Beach 19	33N47	118w09	7:52:36
East Los Angeles 19	34N01'26	118w10'16	7:52:41
East Lynwood 19	33N55	118w12	7:52:48
Eastman Place 45	40N30'41	121w43'53	8:06:56
East Modesto 50	37N38	120w59	8:03:56
Eastmont 1	37N46	122w11	8:08:44
East Nicolaus 51	38N54'37	121w32'38	8:06:11
Easton 10	36N39'01	119w47'23	7:59:10
East Orosi 54	36N32'53	119w15'35	7:57:02
East Palo Alto 41	37N28'08	122w08'24	8:08:34
East Pasadena 19	34N08'46	118w05'36	7:52:22
East Pleasanton 1	37N40'25	121w49'44	8:07:19
Eastport 7	37N50'23	122w10'46	8:08:43
East Porterville 54	36N03	118w59	7:55:56
East Quincy 32	39N56'03	120w53'49	8:03:35
East Richmond 7	37N57	122w19	8:09:16
East San Diego 37	32N44'58	117w06'33	7:48:26
East San Gabriel Valley 19	34N06	117w53	7:51:32
East Santa Cruz 44	36N59	122w00	8:08:00
East Shasta 45	41N00	121w30	8:06:00
East Side 39	38N08'07	121w14'32	8:04:58
Eastside Acres 20	36N51	120w27	8:01:48
Eastside Ranch 20	36N51	120w27	8:01:48
East Sierra 46	39N36	120w12	8:00:48
East Stockton 39	37N58	121w15	8:05:00
East Tehama 52	40N21	121w49	8:07:16
East Tulare 54	36N13	119w20	7:57:20
East Tustin 30	33N45	117w49	7:51:16
East Vallejo 48	38N07	122w14	8:08:56
East Ventura 56	34N16	119w13	7:56:52
East View 19	33N45	118w19	7:53:16
East Whittier 19	33N57'48	118w01'02	7:52:04
East Windsor 49	38N32'39	122w48'03	8:11:12
Eastwood Village 19	34N02	117w56	7:51:44
East Yolo 57	38N33	121w33	8:06:12
Eberly 1	37N34'21	121w59'32	8:07:58
Echo Lake 9	38N50'02	120w02'26	8:00:10
Echo Park 19	34N05	118w16	7:53:04
Eckley 7	38N03'14	122w12'06	8:08:48
Edendale 19	34N05	118w16	7:53:04
Edendale 49	38N29'06	123w00'06	8:12:00
Eden Gardens 37	32N59'14	117w15'26	7:49:02
Eden Hot Springs 33	33N53'44	117w03'16	7:48:13
Edenvale 43	37N15'54	121w49'01	8:07:16
Eder 31	39N17'59	120w17'29	8:01:10
Edgar 13	32N47'20	115w43'57	7:42:56
Edgemar 41	37N39'14	122w29'23	8:09:58
Edgemont 18	40N18	120w32	8:02:08
Edgemont 33	33N55'13	117w16'40	7:49:07
Edgemont Acres 15	34N56	117w57	7:51:48
Edgewood 47	41N27'30	122w25'50	8:09:43
Edison 15	35N20'51	118w52'15	7:55:29
Edmiston 10	36N46'44	119w32'22	7:58:09
Edmundson Acres 15	35N13'44	118w49'20	7:55:17
Edna 40	35N12'14	120w36'43	8:02:27
Edom 33	33N48'25	116w23'25	7:45:34
Edwards 15	34N55'34	117w56'03	7:51:44
Edwards Air Force Base 15	34N54	117w52	7:51:28
Edwards Crossing 29	39N19'49	120w58'59	8:03:56
Edwards Estates 15	34N56	117w57	7:51:48
Edwards Palisades 15	34N56	117w57	7:51:48
Edwin 3	38N22'43	120w59'12	8:03:57
Eel Rock 12	40N16	123w53	8:15:32
Egan 33	33N43'56	117w00'40	7:48:03
Eight Mile House 9	38N44	120w41	8:02:44
El Bonita 49	38N30'44	122w58'58	8:11:56
El Cajon 37	32N47'41	116w57'42	7:47:51
El Camino 52	40N02'28	122w10'10	8:08:41
El Campo 21	37N53'51	122w27'51	8:09:51
El Casco 33	33N58'52	117w07'03	7:48:28
El Centro 13	32N47'31	115w33'44	7:42:15
El Cerrito 7	37N54'57	122w18'38	8:09:15
El Cerrito 33	33N50'26	117w31'19	7:50:05
Elders Corner 31	38N57'24	121w06'00	8:04:24
Elderwood 54	36N28'18	119w07'17	7:56:29
El Dorado 9	38N40'58	120w50'48	8:03:23
El Dorado Hills 9	38N41	121w11	8:04:44
Eldridge 49	38N21	122w31	8:10:04
Electra 3	38N19'56	120w40'13	8:02:41
El Encanto Heights 42	34N26	119w53	7:59:32
Elftman 19	33N50'25	118w13'20	7:52:53
El Granada 41	37N30'10	122w28'06	8:09:52
Elizabeth Lake 19	34N40	118w21	7:53:24
Elk 10	36N45'01	119w29'31	7:57:58
Elk 23	39N07'49	123w43'00	8:14:52
Elk Creek 11	39N36'19	122w32'17	8:10:09
Elk Grove 34	38N24'32	121w22'14	8:05:29
Elkhorn 27	36N49'28	121w44'22	8:06:57
Elkhorn Village 57	38N36	121w32	8:06:08
Elk River 12	40N44'11	124w10'23	8:16:42
Ellicott 44	36N55'18	121w50'09	8:07:21
Elliott Corner 22	37N27'46	119w46'25	7:59:06
Ellis 33	33N46'19	117w13'06	7:48:52
Ellis Place 54	36N31'16	119w01'05	7:56:04
Ellwood 42	34N25'54	119w53'13	7:59:33
El Macero 57	38N32'49	121w41'35	8:06:46
Elmco 54	35N59'33	119w02'31	7:56:10
Elmhurst 1	37N44	122w10	8:08:40
Elmira 48	38N20'54	121w54'32	8:07:38
El Mirador 54	36N10'40	119w01'03	7:56:04
El Mirage 36	34N36'08	117w37'49	7:50:31
Elmo 15	35N40'46	119w19'46	7:57:19
El Modena 30	33N47'16	117w48'31	7:51:14
El Monte 7	37N58	121w59	8:07:56
El Monte 19	34N04'07	118w01'36	7:52:06
Elmore Desert Ranch 13	33N06'13	115w47'59	7:43:12
Elm View 10	36N32'51	119w47'25	7:59:10
Elmwood 1	37N52	122w15	8:09:00
El Nido 19	33N51'56	118w21'38	7:53:27
El Nido 24	37N08'06	120w29'28	8:01:58
Elora 36	35N08'17	115w31'41	7:42:07
El Paso De Robles 40	35N38	120w41	8:02:44
El Pinal 39	37N58'50	121w16'52	8:05:07
El Portal 22	37N40'29	119w46'59	7:59:08
El Porto Beach 19	33N53	118w24	7:53:36
El Pueblo 7	38N00	121w51	8:07:24
El Rio 56	34N13'56	119w10'18	7:56:41
El Rio Villa 57	38N32'05	121w56'35	8:07:46
El Roble 23	39N05'23	123w10'47	8:12:43
Elsa 27	36N15'03	121w08'16	8:04:33
El Segundo 19	33N55'09	118w24'56	7:53:40
El Sereno 19	34N04'52	118w10'37	7:52:42
Elsey 4	39N36'27	121w35'36	8:06:22
Elsinore 33	33N40'05	117w19'35	7:49:18
Elsinore Valley 33	33N44	117w26	7:49:44
El Sobrante 7	37N58'38	122w17'39	8:09:11
El Sueno 42	34N26'37	119w46'13	7:59:05
El Toro 30	33N37'33	117w41'34	7:50:46
El Toro Marine Corps Air Sta 30	33N41	117w42	7:50:48
Elvas 34	38N35'00	121w26'51	8:05:47
El Verano 49	38N17'52	122w29'26	8:09:58
Elverta 34	38N42'50	121w27'42	8:05:51
El Viejo 50	37N40	121w00	8:04:00
Elvira 37	32N50'15	117w13'57	7:48:56
Emandal 23	39N25	123w21	8:13:24
Emerald Bay 9	38N57'36	120w05'49	8:00:23
Emerald Bay 30	33N33'09	117w48'30	7:51:14
Emerald Lake 41	37N28	122w14	8:08:56
Emeryville 1	37N49'53	122w17'03	8:09:08
Emigrant Gap 31	39N17'49	120w40'18	8:02:41
Emmaton 34	38N04'49	121w43'52	8:06:55
Empire 50	37N38'18	120w54'04	8:03:36
Encanto 37	32N42'43	117w02'58	7:48:12
Enchanted Hills 28	38N22'59	122w25'30	8:09:42
Encinal 43	37N21	122w02	8:08:08
Encinal 51	39N12'56	121w39'38	8:06:39
Encinitas 37	33N02'13	117w17'28	7:49:10
Encino 19	34N09'33	118w30'01	7:54:00
Engineer Springs 37	32N37'41	116w45'51	7:47:03
Englewood 12	40N23'48	123w56'16	8:15:45
English Town 43	37N10'46	121w50'17	8:07:21
Ennis 33	34N00'34	117w25'43	7:49:43
Ensley 51	38N48'27	121w40'18	8:06:41
Enson 54	36N33'33	119w22'27	7:57:30
Enterprise 3	38N32'25	120w50'46	8:03:23
Enterprise 17	39N21'48	122w56'58	8:11:48
Enterprise 45	40N33'50	122w20'30	8:09:22
Epworth 56	34N18'54	118w53'28	7:55:34
Erickson 47	41N39'01	122w06'48	8:08:27
Escalon 39	37N47'51	120w59'44	8:03:59
Escondido 37	33N07'09	117w05'08	7:48:21
Escondido Junction 37	33N10'54	117w22'04	7:49:28
Escondido Village Mall 37	33N04	117w03	7:48:12
Esex 36	34N44'01	115w14'39	7:40:59
Esparto 57	38N41'32	122w00'58	8:08:04
Esperanza 30	33N52'32	117w45'21	7:51:01
Esquon 4	39N36'21	121w45'57	8:07:04
Essex 12	40N54'22	124w02'03	8:16:08
Essex 36	34N44	115w15	7:41:00
Estelle 13	33N10'35	115w30'28	7:42:02
Estrella 40	35N42'20	120w36'33	8:02:26
Estudillo 1	37N43	122w09	8:08:36
Etheda Springs 10	36N41'39	119w00'23	7:56:02
Etiwanda 36	34N07'34	117w31'22	7:50:05
Etna 47	41N27'25	122w53'37	8:11:34
Ettawa Springs 17	38N51'04	122w41'42	8:10:47
Ettersburg 12	40N08'19	123w59'46	8:15:59
Eucalyptus Hills 37	32N52'47	116w56'45	7:47:47
Eugene 50	37N53'35	120w50'45	8:03:23
Eureka 12	40N48'08	124w09'45	8:16:39
Evans Place 18	41N03'36	120w13'43	8:00:55
Evelyn 14	36N08'48	116w18'55	7:45:16
Everglade 51	38N58'57	121w45'59	8:07:04
Evergreen 43	37N18'35	121w46'57	8:07:08
Evergreen Acres 42	34N54	120w26	8:01:44
Exeter 54	36N17'46	119w08'28	7:56:34
Facht Place 52	40N14'33	121w57'44	8:07:51
Fagan 4	39N20'10	121w40'57	8:06:44
Fairbanks 9	38N51'57	120w40'09	8:02:41
Fairfax 21	37N59'14	122w35'16	8:10:21
Fairfield 48	38N14'58	122w02'20	8:08:09
Fairhaven 12	40N47'07	124w12'06	8:16:48
Fairmead 20	37N04'35	120w11'31	8:00:46
Fairmont 19	34N44'05	118w25'26	7:53:42
Fairmont Terrace 1	37N43	122w09	8:08:36
Fairmount 7	37N55	122w18	8:09:12
Fair Oaks 34	38N38'41	121w16'16	8:05:05
Fair Oaks 39	37N57'19	121w15'27	8:05:02
Fair Oaks 40	35N07	120w35	8:02:20
Fair Play 9	38N35'37	120w39'34	8:02:38
Fairview 1	37N40	122w03	8:08:12
Fairview 10	36N42	119w33	7:58:12
Fairview 30	33N41	117w54	7:51:36
Fairview 50	37N38	120w59	8:03:56
Fairview 54	35N55'33	118w29'38	7:53:59
Fairview 56	34N18'55	118w54'50	7:55:39
Fairville 49	38N10'41	122w26'40	8:09:47
Fales Hot Springs 26	38N21'04	119w23'57	7:57:36
Falk 12	40N47	124w10	8:16:40
Fallbrook 37	33N22'35	117w15'01	7:49:00
Fallen Leaf 9	38N52'59	120w04'18	8:00:17
Falling Springs 19	34N18'06	117w50'18	7:51:21
Fallon 21	38N16'29	122w54'17	8:11:37
Fall River Mills 45	41N00'17	121w26'14	8:05:45
Fallrock Junction 37	33N13'24	117w23'36	7:49:34
Fallsvale 36	34N06	116w57	7:47:48
Famoso 15	35N35'53	119w12'26	7:56:50
Fancher 10	36N44	119w45	7:59:00
Fane 54	36N22'12	119w08'01	7:56:32
Farley 23	39N36'53	123w21'58	8:13:28
Farmers Market 19	34N04	118w21	7:53:24
Farmersville 54	36N17'52	119w12'21	7:56:49
Farmington 39	37N55'48	120w59'57	8:04:00
Farr 37	33N07'49	117w19'43	7:49:19
Farwell 1	37N35'54	121w56'39	8:07:47
Fashion Square La Habra 30	33N56	117w56	7:51:44
Favinger Place 52	40N02'41	121w58'35	8:07:54
Fawnskin 36	34N16'05	116w56'30	7:47:46
Fayette 54	36N12'07	119w03'50	7:56:15
Feather Falls 4	39N35'36	121w15'19	8:05:01
Feather River Inn 32	39N47	120w37	8:02:28
Feather River Park 32	39N46'42	120w37'43	8:02:31
Federal 19	34N06	117w53	7:51:32

Federal Building 38 37N47 122W26 8:09:44
Federal Building 56 34N12 119W10 7:56:40
Federal Terrace 48 38N07 122W14 8:08:56
Felix 5 38N01'42 120W42'53 8:02:52
Fellows 15 35N10'43 119W32'25 7:58:10
Felton 44 37N03'05 122W04'20 8:08:17
Felton Grove 44 37N03 122W04 8:08:16
Femmons 55 37N56'18 120W01'17 8:00:05
Fenner 36 34N48'57 115W10'42 7:40:43
Fergus 24 37N19'10 120W32'14 8:02:09
Fern 45 40N41'18 121W55'50 8:07:43
Fern Ann Falls 19 34N17'05 118W36'56 7:54:28
Fernbridge 12 40N36'59 124W12'00 8:16:48
Fernbrook 37 32N58'05 116W54'39 7:47:39
Ferndale 12 40N34'35 124W15'46 8:17:03
Fern Valley 33 33N45'31 116W41'50 7:46:47
Fernwood 12 40N52'09 123W50'58 8:15:24
Fernwood 19 34N04'46 118W36'06 7:54:24
Ferrum 33 33N27'31 115W51'36 7:43:26
Fetters Hot Springs 49 38N19'12 122W29'06 8:09:56
Fiddlers Green 11 39N43'44 122W42'51 8:10:51
Fiddletown 3 38N30'14 120W45'16 8:03:01
Fieldbrook 12 40N57'57 124W02'04 8:16:08
Fields Landing 12 40N43'29 124W12'50 8:16:51
Figarden 10 36N49'22 119W51'41 7:59:27
Fig Garden 10 36N48 119W48 7:59:12
Fig Orchard 15 35N18'31 118W34'54 7:54:20
Figueroa 19 34N11 118W08 7:52:32
Fillmore 56 34N23'57 118W55'02 7:55:40
Finley 17 39N00'16 122W52'28 8:11:30
Finley Place 52 40N17'36 121W47'31 8:07:10
Firebaugh 10 36N51'32 120W27'18 8:01:49
Firebrick 3 38N20'04 120W55'27 8:03:42
Fire Mountain 52 40N19 121W32 8:06:08
Firestone 19 33N56 118W11 7:52:44
Firestone Park 19 33N57'47 118W13'54 7:52:56
First Street 37 33N12 117W20 7:49:20
Fish Camp 22 37N28'43 119W38'22 7:58:33
Fishel 36 34N18'45 115W14'29 7:40:58
Fisher 12 40N56'30 124W07'02 8:16:28
Fisher 45 41N02'11 122W23'32 8:09:34
Fisher Place 5 38N14'07 120W26'59 8:01:48
Fish Rock 23 38N48'18 123W35'03 8:14:20
Fish Springs 14 37N04'30 118W15'10 7:53:01
Fisk 38 37N46 122W28 8:09:52
Fitchburg 1 37N46 122W11 8:08:44
Five Brooks 21 38N00'04 122W45'24 8:11:02
Five Corners 39 37N49'37 121W08'35 8:04:34
Five Mile Terrace 9 38N44'18 120W42'43 8:02:51
Five Points 10 36N25'46 120W06'07 8:00:24
Five Points 15 35N03'05 118W30'42 7:54:03
Five Points 19 34N03'44 118W01'06 7:52:04
Five Points 32 39N52'16 120W34'17 8:02:17
Five Points 37 32N44'35 117W11'02 7:48:44
Five Points 48 38N17'27 121W38'36 8:06:34
Flamingo Heights 36 34N14'26 116W26'17 7:45:45
Fleener Place 47 41N50'52 121W35'22 8:06:21
Fleet 37 32N45 117W09 7:48:36
Fleetridge 37 32N43'40 117W14'50 7:48:59
Fleta 15 35N00'12 118W09'26 7:52:38
Fletcher 25 41N26'45 120W45'12 8:03:01
Fletcher Place 25 41N44'15 120W30'49 8:02:03
Flinn Springs 37 32N48 116W57 7:47:48
Flintridge 19 34N11'11 118W11'12 7:52:45
Flonellis 9 38N34'10 120W57'49 8:03:51
Florence 19 33N58'28 118W14'50 7:52:59
Florin 34 38N29'46 121W24'28 8:05:38
Florin Crossing 47 41N11'05 121W37'51 8:06:31
Floriston 29 39N23'41 120W01'13 8:00:05
Flosden Acres 48 38N08'11 122W15'04 8:09:00
Flournoy 52 39N55'14 122W26'06 8:09:44
Flower Village 15 35N23 118W59 7:55:56
Fluhr 24 37N21'46 120W34'36 8:02:18
Flumeville 23 38N55'46 123W42'31 8:14:50
Fly in Acres 5 38N15 120W21 8:01:24
Flynn 36 34N58'43 115W43'53 7:42:56
Folsom 34 38N40'41 121W10'30 8:04:42
Folsom Junction 34 38N40'06 121W10'52 8:04:43
Fondo 13 33N06'41 115W37'25 7:42:30
Fontana 36 34N05'32 117W26'03 7:49:44
Foote Crossing 46 39N25'01 120W57'02 8:03:48
Foothill Center 19 34N07 117W54 7:51:36
Foothill Farms 34 38N40'35 121W20'07 8:05:20
Foppiano 39 38N01'19 121W14'25 8:04:58
Forbestown 4 39N31'02 121W15'58 8:05:04
Ford City 15 35N09'16 119W27'19 7:57:49
Forebay 31 39N14'12 120W44'08 8:02:57
Forest 46 39N29'29 120W51'07 8:03:24
Foresta 22 37N41'54 119W45'15 7:59:01
Forest Falls 36 34N05'09 116W54'33 7:47:38
Forest Glen 53 40N22'24 123W19'27 8:13:18
Foresthill 31 39N01'13 120W49'01 8:03:16
Forest Hills 49 38N30'29 122W55'24 8:11:42
Forest Home 3 38N29 120W51 8:03:24
Forest Home 36 34N06 116W57 7:47:48
Forest Knolls 21 38N00'55 122W41'15 8:10:45
Forest Lake 17 38N49'05 122W43'00 8:10:52
Forest Lake 39 38N10 121W13 8:04:52
Forest Park 19 34N26'50 118W25'40 7:53:43
Forest Park 44 37N07 122W07 8:08:28
Forest Ranch 4 39N52'56 121W40'18 8:06:41
Forest Springs 29 39N13 121W04 8:04:16
Forest Springs 44 37N08'20 122W08'52 8:08:35
Forestville 49 38N28'25 122W53'21 8:11:33
Forks of Salmon 47 41N16 123W19 8:13:16
Fornis 9 38N53'33 120W51'37 8:03:26
Fort Baker 21 37N52 122W30 8:10:00
Fort Barry 21 37N52 122W30 8:10:00
Fort Bidwell 25 41N51'38 120W09'01 8:00:36
Fort Bidwell Indian Res 25 41N52 120W12 8:00:48
Fort Bragg 23 39N26'45 123W48'15 8:15:13
Fort Bragg Landing 23 39N26'26 123W48'48 8:15:15
Fort Cronkhite 21 37N52 122W30 8:10:00
Fort Dick 8 41N52'05 124W08'52 8:16:35
Fort Goff 47 41N51'44 123W15'20 8:13:01
Fort Independence Indian Res 14 36N51 118W13 7:52:52
Fort Irwin 36 35N15 116W42 7:46:48
Fort Jones 47 41N36'28 122W50'21 8:11:21
Fort Macarthur 19 33N44 118W18 7:53:12
Fort McDowell 38 37N51'46 122W25'18 8:09:41
Fort Mohave Indian Res 36 35N02 114W38 7:38:32
Fort Ord 27 36N38 121W46 8:07:04
Fort Ord Village 27 36N37 121W50 8:07:20
Fort Orford 42 34N28'13 120W13'39 8:00:55
Fort Piute 36 35N06'54 114W59'04 7:39:56
Fort Romie 27 36N24'01 121W20'43 8:05:23
Fort Rosecrans 37 32N41'03 117W14'43 7:48:59
Fort Ross 49 38N30'51 123W14'33 8:12:58
Fort Scott 38 37N48'06 122W28'21 8:09:53
Fort Seward 12 40N13'23 123W38'32 8:14:34
Fort Sutter 34 38N34 121W28 8:05:52
Fortuna 12 40N35'54 124W09'22 8:16:37
Fort Yuma 13 32N44 114W38 7:38:32
Fort Yuma Indian Reservation 13 32N44 114W38 7:38:32
Foster 37 32N54'30 116W55'31 7:47:42
Foster 47 41N15'14 122W57'28 8:11:50
Foster City 41 37N33'31 122W16'12 8:09:05
Fountain Place 9 38N51'04 119W55'59 7:59:44
Fountain Springs 54 35N53'28 118W54'53 7:55:40
Fountain Valley 30 33N42'33 117W57'10 7:51:49
Four Corners 7 37N57'23 122W02'18 8:08:09
Four Corners 36 34N11 116W04 7:44:16
Four Corners 37 32N58'40 116W46'35 7:47:06
Four Corners 49 38N16'33 122W27'35 8:09:50
Four Pines 17 39N36'36 123W00'42 8:12:03
Four Points 19 34N32'33 118W01'45 7:52:07
Fourth Crossing 5 38N07'53 120W38'01 8:02:32
Fouts Springs 6 39N21'12 122W39'50 8:10:39
Fowler 10 36N37'50 119W40'39 7:58:43
Foy 19 34N00 118W16 7:53:04
Frances 30 33N42'43 117W45'49 7:51:03
Franciscan Park 41 37N42 122W28 8:09:52
Franklin 28 38N18 122W18 8:09:12
Franklin 34 38N22'45 121W27'12 8:05:49
Frazier Park 15 34N49'22 118W56'38 7:55:47
Fraziers Landing 6 39N00'18 121W49'05 8:07:16
Freda 36 34N06'08 114W54'35 7:39:38
Fredalba 36 34N12'06 117W07'53 7:48:32
Fredericksburg 2 38N49'44 119W47'09 7:59:09
Freedom 44 36N56'07 121W46'19 8:07:05
Freeman Junction 15 35N36'06 117W54'07 7:51:36
Freemans Crossing 46 39N23'20 121W05'04 8:04:20
Freeport 34 38N27'43 121W30'02 8:06:00
Freestone 49 38N22'21 122W54'52 8:11:39
Fremont 1 37N32'54 121W59'15 8:07:57
Fremont 36 35N11'30 117W34'33 7:50:18
Fremont 57 38N40'36 121W38'02 8:06:32
Fremont Landing (Site) 57 38N46'58 121W37'04 8:06:28
French Camp 39 37N53'03 121W16'12 8:05:05
French Corral 29 39N18'22 121W09'37 8:04:38
French Gulch 45 40N42'03 122W38'14 8:10:33
Frenchtown 9 38N38'29 120W54'37 8:03:38
Frenchtown 58 39N23'17 121W15'14 8:05:01
Fresh Pond 9 38N45'37 120W31'44 8:02:07
Freshwater 12 40N45'42 124W03'38 8:16:15
Freshwater Corners 12 40N47'08 124W05'03 8:16:20
Fresno 10 36N44'52 119W46'17 7:59:05
Fresno Crossing 20 37N14'14 119W46'27 7:59:06
Friant 10 36N59'16 119W42'39 7:58:51
Friendly Hills 19 33N57'13 118W00'10 7:52:01
Friendly Hills 36 34N08 116W19 7:45:16
Friend Place 53 40N29'09 123W21'45 8:13:27
Frink 13 33N21'45 115W38'50 7:42:35
Frost 36 34N30'39 117W16'36 7:49:06
Fruitland 12 40N17'45 123W49'27 8:15:18
Fruitridge Manor 34 38N31'30 121W26'28 8:05:46
Fruitvale 1 37N47 122W13 8:08:52
Fruitvale 15 35N23'00 119W04'56 7:56:20
Fruto 11 39N35'24 122W26'56 8:09:48
Frying Pan 53 40N05'03 122W58'39 8:11:55
Fuller 13 32N51'37 115W24'19 7:41:37
Fuller Acres 15 35N18'00 118W54'39 7:55:39
Fullerton 30 33N52'13 117W55'28 7:51:42
Fulton 49 38N29'47 122W46'08 8:11:05
Gabilan 27 36N42 121W32 8:06:08
Gabilan Acres 27 36N45'19 121W37'06 8:06:28
Gale 36 34N51'22 116W50'29 7:47:22
Galivan 30 33N34'10 117W40'23 7:50:42
Gallinas 21 38N01'13 122W31'27 8:10:06
Galt 34 38N15'17 121W17'56 8:05:12
Ganns 5 38N24'16 120W09'29 8:00:38
Ganser Bar 32 40N00 121W15 8:05:00
Garberville 12 40N06'01 123W47'38 8:15:11
Gardena 19 33N53'18 118W18'29 7:53:14
Garden Acres 39 37N58 121W14 8:04:56
Gardena Village 41 37N41 122W29 8:09:56
Garden Farms 40 35N25'05 120W36'19 8:02:25
Garden Gate Village 43 37N19 122W02 8:08:08
Garden Grove 30 33N46'26 117W56'26 7:51:46
Gardenland 34 38N36'40 121W28'26 8:05:54
Garden Valley 9 38N51'15 120W51'30 8:03:26
Garden Village 41 37N41 122W29 8:09:56
Garey 42 34N53'19 120W18'50 8:01:15
Garfield 15 35N36 118W30 7:54:00
Garlock 15 35N24'09 117W47'21 7:51:09
Garnet 33 33N54'07 116W32'41 7:46:11
Garvanza 19 34N06'59 118W10'46 7:52:43
Gasoline Alley 31 38N54 121W04 8:04:16
Gas Point 45 40N24'56 122W32'00 8:10:08
Gasquet 8 41N50'44 123W58'06 8:15:52
Gaston 29 39N23'39 120W44'26 8:02:58
Gateley 7 38N00'26 122W18'32 8:09:14
Gate Place (Site) 32 39N55'45 120W34'36 8:02:18
Gates 48 38N21 121W59 8:07:56
Gateway 19 34N00 118W24 7:53:36
Gateway 29 39N19'34 120W12'09 8:00:49
Gato 42 34N27'27 120W22'36 8:01:30
Gaviota 42 34N28'18 120W12'50 8:00:51
Gazelle 47 41N31'15 122W31'09 8:10:05
Geary 38 37N47 122W26 8:09:44
Gemco 19 34N12'33 118W26'12 7:53:45
Gene 36 34N10 114W18 7:37:12
Genesee 32 40N02'35 120W45'10 8:03:01
Genevra 6 39N04'12 122W05'26 8:08:22
George 36 34N35 117W23 7:49:32
George Air Force Base 36 34N35 117W22 7:49:28
Georgetown 9 38N54'25 120W50'15 8:03:21
George Washington 37 32N45 117W09 7:48:36
Gepford 16 36N23'54 119W48'30 7:59:14
Gerber 52 40N03'23 122W08'57 8:08:36
Geyser Resort 49 38N48 123W01 8:12:04
Geyserville 49 38N42'28 122W54'05 8:11:36
Giant 7 37N59'26 122W21'22 8:09:25
Gibson 45 41N00'43 122W24'28 8:09:38
Gibsonville 46 39N44'25 120W54'28 8:03:38
Giffen Cantua Ranch 10 36N28'29 120W23'29 8:01:34
Gilberts 9 38N38'13 120W29'30 8:01:58
Gillete 54 36N10'26 119W02'07 7:56:08
Gillis 39 37N56'03 121W22'55 8:05:32
Gillis 47 41N57'30 122W05'45 8:08:23
Gilman Hot Springs 33 33N50'09 116W59'17 7:47:57
Gilroy 43 37N00'21 121W34'02 8:06:16
Gilroy Hot Springs 43 37N01 121W35 8:06:20
Girvan 45 40N30'46 122W22'44 8:09:31
Glacier Lodge 14 37N10 118W17 7:53:08
Glamis 13 32N59'51 115W04'16 7:40:17
Glasgow 36 34N59'01 115W52'08 7:43:29
Glassell 19 34N07 118W14 7:52:56
Glen Arbor 44 37N04'28 122W04'52 8:08:19
Glen Avon 33 34N00'42 117W29'02 7:49:56
Glen Avon Heights 33 34N01 117W29 7:49:56
Glenblair 23 39N27'28 123W43'27 8:14:54
Glenbrook 17 38N51'06 122W45'27 8:11:02
Glenbrook 29 39N14'32 121W02'04 8:04:08
Glenbrook Heights 29 39N13 121W04 8:04:16
Glenburn 45 41N03'41 121W29'21 8:05:57
Glencoe 5 38N21'15 120W35'02 8:02:20
Glencove 48 38N04'07 122W12'21 8:08:49
Glendale 12 40N54'00 124W00'57 8:16:04
Glendale 19 34N08'33 118W15'15 7:53:01
Glendale Junction 19 34N04'31 118W13'27 7:52:54
Glendora 19 34N08'10 117W51'52 7:51:27
Glen Ellen 49 38N21'51 122W31'23 8:10:06
Glen Frazer 7 37N59'54 122W09'42 8:08:39
Glenhaven 17 39N01'35 122W43'55 8:10:56
Glen Martin 36 34N09 116W59 7:47:56
Glenn 11 39N31'19 122W00'46 8:08:03
Glennville 15 35N43'44 118W42'10 7:54:49
Glenoaks 19 34N11 118W20 7:53:20
Glen Oaks 37 32N50'18 116W48'11 7:47:13
Glenshire 29 39N20 120W12 8:00:48
Glen Valley 33 33N51'43 117W19'31 7:49:18
Glenview 17 38N54'00 122W45'29 8:11:02
Glenview 19 34N07'28 118W36'02 7:54:24
Glenview 37 32N49'56 116W54'18 7:47:37
Glenwood 44 37N06'30 121W59'08 8:07:57
Globe 54 36N06'04 118W49'38 7:55:19
Globe Mill 53 40N53'04 123W01'22 8:12:05
Glorietta 7 37N51'44 122W10'01 8:08:40
Glorietta 10 36N50'16 119W42'31 7:58:50
Goat Rock 49 38N34'54 123W07'13 8:12:29
Goffs 36 34N55'09 115W03'43 7:40:15
Golden Gate Race Track 1 37N53 122W19 8:09:16
Golden Hills 37 32N44 117W07 7:48:28
Golden Trout Crossing 4 39N36'27 121W09'02 8:04:36
Gold Flat 29 39N14'46 121W01'24 8:04:06
Gold Gulch 44 37N03 122W04 8:08:16
Gold Hill 31 38N54'06 121W10'50 8:04:43
Goldleaf 10 36N43'20 119W43'01 7:58:52
Gold Run 31 39N10'51 120W51'17 8:03:25
Goldstone 36 35N17'50 116W54'47 7:47:39
Goldtree 40 35N19'19 120W40'53 8:02:44
Goler Heights 15 35N25'37 117W44'42 7:50:59
Goleta 42 34N26'09 119W49'36 7:59:18
Goleta Valley 42 34N27 119W50 7:59:20
Gonzales 27 36N30'24 121W26'36 8:05:46
Goodale 54 36N22'41 119W02'36 7:56:10
Goodmans Corner 5 38N12'18 120W59'10 8:03:57
Goodmill 10 36N46'51 119W01'21 7:56:05
Goodyears Bar 46 39N32'24 120W53'00 8:03:32
Gorda 27 35N55'57 121W28'04 8:05:52

Gordola 44 36N58'31 122w08'00 8:08:32
Gordon 10 36N53'46 119w43'44 7:58:55
Gorman 19 34N47'46 118w51'06 7:55:24
Gosford 15 35N18'40 119w05'26 7:56:22
Goshen 54 36N21'04 119w25'09 7:57:41
Gottsville 47 41N52'03 122w44'24 8:10:58
Government Island 1 37N47 122w16 8:09:04
Grabtown 41 37N25'20 122w20'34 8:09:22
Graeagle 32 39N45'59 120w37'03 8:02:28
Graham 19 33N57 118w14 7:52:56
Graham Place 53 40N25'36 123w24'25 8:13:38
Graino 6 39N02'09 121w57'40 8:07:51
Granada Hills 19 34N15'53 118w31'20 7:54:05
Grand Avenue 33 33N55 117w44 7:50:56
Grand Central 19 34N10 118w16 7:53:04
Grand Island 6 39N03'58 121w52'02 8:07:28
Grand Lake 1 37N49 122w14 8:08:56
Grand Terrace 36 34N02'02 117w18'46 7:49:15
Grandview 36 34N53'24 117w06'21 7:48:25
Grandview-Palos Verdes 19 33N46 118w21 7:53:24
Grangeville 16 36N20'37 119w42'28 7:58:50
Granite Bay Vista 31 38N45 121w17 8:05:08
Granite Springs 22 37N42'04 120w17'41 8:01:11
Graniteville 29 39N26'27 120w44'19 8:02:57
Grant 49 38N35'25 122w50'48 8:11:23
Grantville 37 32N47'15 117w05'47 7:48:23
Grape 36 34N05'53 117w27'48 7:49:51
Grapeland 36 34N07'30 117w33'42 7:50:15
Grapevine 15 34N55'37 118w55'30 7:55:42
Grapevine Crossing 52 40N06'22 121w46'46 8:07:07
Grapit 11 39N40'52 122w11'35 8:08:46
Grass Flat 46 39N40'33 120w56'03 8:03:44
Grass Lake 47 41N38'06 122w11'25 8:08:46
Grass Valley 29 39N13'09 121w03'36 8:04:14
Graton 49 38N26'11 122w52'07 8:11:28
Gravenstein 49 38N24'17 122w48'24 8:11:14
Gravesboro 10 36N46'23 119w24'38 7:57:39
Grays Crossing 2 38N35'31 119w39'21 7:58:37
Grays Flat 32 40N01'04 121w03'45 8:04:15
Grayson 50 37N33'50 121w10'42 8:04:43
Greeley 15 35N21 118w59 7:55:56
Green 19 34N00 118w17 7:53:08
Greenacres 15 35N23'00 119w06'32 7:56:26
Green Brae 21 37N56'55 122w31'25 8:10:06
Greenbrook 7 37N50 122w00 8:08:00
Greendale 57 38N22'25 121w35'06 8:06:20
Greenfield (Delkern P O) 15 35N16'08 119w00'07 7:56:00
Greenfield 27 36N19'15 121w14'34 8:04:58
Greenmead 19 33N56 118w15 7:53:00
Greenspot 36 34N05 117w08 7:48:32
Green Valley 19 34N37'18 118w24'47 7:53:39
Green Valley Estates 48 38N14 122w02 8:08:08
Green Valley Lake 36 34N14'27 117w04'35 7:48:18
Greenview 47 41N33'03 122w54'16 8:11:37
Greenview Acres 12 40N52 124w05 8:16:20
Greenville 32 40N08'23 120w57'00 8:03:48
Greenville 58 39N26'12 121w10'35 8:04:42
Greenwater 14 36N10'46 116w36'56 7:46:28
Greenwich Village 56 34N10'53 118w51'49 7:55:27
Greenwood 9 38N53'48 120w54'42 8:03:39
Greenwood 11 39N41'46 122w11'36 8:08:46
Gregg 20 36N52'54 119w56'09 7:59:45
Grenada 47 41N38'50 122w31'08 8:10:05
Gridley 4 39N21'50 121w41'33 8:06:46
Griffin Place 52 39N58'10 122w47'07 8:11:08
Griffith 19 34N06 118w16 7:53:04
Grimes 6 39N04'28 121w53'34 8:07:34
Griminger 9 38N43'11 120w24'33 8:01:38
Grizzlie Place 25 41N54'04 120w38'22 8:02:33
Grizzly Flat 9 38N38'11 120w31'35 8:02:06
Grossmont 37 32N46'42 116w59'15 7:47:57
Grove 23 39N26'13 123w39'30 8:14:38
Grove Highlands 27 36N37 121w56 8:07:44
Groveland 55 37N50'18 120w13'54 8:00:56
Grover City 40 35N07'18 120w37'13 8:02:29
Guadalcanal Village 48 38N07'07 122w17'34 8:09:10
Guadalupe 42 34N58'18 120w34'15 8:02:17
Gualala 23 38N45'57 123w31'37 8:14:06
Guasti 36 34N03'54 117w35'08 7:50:21
Guatay 37 32N50'56 116w33'23 7:46:14
Guerneville 49 38N30'07 122w59'42 8:11:59
Guernewood 49 38N29'34 123w00'50 8:12:03
Guernewood Park 49 38N29'49 123w00'41 8:12:03
Guernsey 16 36N12'47 119w38'24 7:58:34
Guernsey Mill 54 35N50'03 118w36'56 7:54:28
Guild 39 38N08'43 121w14'33 8:04:58
Guinda 57 38N49'45 122w11'34 8:08:46
Gulf 15 35N10'46 119w09'33 7:56:38
Gum 42 34N55'12 120w31'14 8:02:05
Gustine 24 37N15'28 120w59'52 8:03:59
Gypsite 15 35N19'52 117w55'49 7:51:43
Hacienda 49 38N30'41 122w55'36 8:11:42
Hacienda Del Florasol 37 32N37'02 116w29'58 7:46:00
Hacienda Heights 19 34N00'25 117w57'49 7:51:51
Hackamore 25 41N33'07 121w07'21 8:04:29
Hacketsville 12 40N29'15 124w10'13 8:16:41
Hagginwood 34 38N37'39 121w25'53 8:05:44
Haight 39 38N05'34 121w14'31 8:04:58
Haines 56 34N19'29 119w06'07 7:56:24
Haiwee 14 36N09 117w59 7:51:56
Halcyon 40 35N06'12 120w35'41 8:02:23
Hale Place 49 38N30'30 123w02'08 8:12:09
Hales Grove 23 39N49'04 123w46'52 8:15:07
Half Moon Bay 41 37N27'49 122w25'39 8:09:43
Halfway House 15 35N35'23 118w57'34 7:55:50
Hall 1 37N36 122w01 8:08:04
Hall 27 36N51'55 121w44'02 8:06:56
Hallelujah Junction 18 39N46'32 120w02'18 8:00:09
Halloran Springs 36 35N16 116w04 7:44:16
Halls Corner 16 36N20'33 119w48'20 7:59:13
Halls Flat 18 40N45'22 121w15'29 8:05:02
Hall Station 1 37N35'12 122w03'51 8:08:15
Hallwood 58 39N09 121w32 8:06:08
Halsted Flat 32 40N01'13 121w04'15 8:04:17
Hamblin 16 36N19'47 119w36'32 7:58:26
Hambone 47 41N20'06 121w41'48 8:06:47
Hamburg 47 41N46'59 123w03'33 8:12:14
Hamburg Farms 24 36N52'46 120w45'46 8:03:03
Hamilton Air Force Base 21 38N03 122w31 8:10:04
Hamilton City 11 39N44'34 122w00'45 8:08:03
Hamlet 21 38N12'28 122w55'28 8:11:42
Hammer Place 52 40N07'11 122w42'58 8:10:52
Hammil 26 37N40'43 118w24'10 7:53:37
Hammond 10 36N45'35 119w47'10 7:59:09
Hammond 54 36N27'56 118w51'37 7:55:26
Hammond Crossing 47 41N11'05 121w35'26 8:06:22
Hammonton 58 39N11'35 121w25'11 8:05:41
Hancock 19 33N57 118w17 7:53:08
Hanford 16 36N19'39 119w38'41 7:58:35
Hansen 30 33N49'02 118w00'35 7:52:02
Happy Camp 47 41N47'36 123w22'42 8:13:31
Happy Valley 9 38N40'55 120w33'44 8:02:15
Happy Valley 19 34N05'01 118w11'58 7:52:48
Harbin Springs 17 38N47'16 122w39'16 8:10:37
Harbin Springs Annex 17 38N47'32 122w39'37 8:10:38
Harbison Canyon 37 32N49'13 116w49'45 7:47:19
Harbor 56 34N12 119w10 7:56:40
Harbor City 19 33N47'24 118w17'49 7:53:11
Harbor Hills 19 33N46'49 118w18'50 7:53:15
Harbor Side 37 32N36'36 117w04'50 7:48:19
Harden Flat 55 37N48'40 119w56'47 7:59:47
Hardman Center 33 33N57 117w24 7:49:36
Hardwick 16 36N24'05 119w43'04 7:58:52
Hardy 23 39N42'45 123w48'07 8:15:12
Hardy Place 23 39N48'04 122w56'59 8:11:48
Harlem 27 36N23'57 121w15'09 8:05:01
Harlem Springs 36 34N07'17 117w13'31 7:48:54
Harlow Place 45 41N08'43 121w40'33 8:06:42
Harmony 40 35N30'31 121w01'18 8:04:05
Harmony Acres 36 35N08'37 116w06'31 7:44:26
Harmony Grove 37 33N05'46 117w08'04 7:48:32
Harold 19 34N32'42 118w06'31 7:52:26
Harp 50 37N34'50 120w59'02 8:03:56
Harpertown 15 35N17'41 118w55'21 7:55:41
Harrington 6 38N57'32 122w00'59 8:08:04
Harris 12 40N05'03 123w39'27 8:14:38
Harrisburg 14 36N21'50 117w06'38 7:48:27
Harrison Park 37 33N01'34 116w34'06 7:46:16
Harry Floyd Terrace 48 38N07'45 122w14'13 8:08:57
Hart 36 35N17'20 115w06'09 7:40:25
Hartland 54 36N39'16 118w57'24 7:55:50
Hartley 48 38N25'02 121w56'45 8:07:47
Harts Place 15 35N30'03 117w56'52 7:51:47
Harvard 36 34N57'04 116w39'50 7:46:39
Haskell Creek Homesites 46 39N38'05 120w33'06 8:02:12
Hatch 50 37N29'23 120w57'16 8:03:49
Hat Creek (P O) 45 40N47'28 121w30'17 8:06:01
Hatfield 47 41N59'53 121w31'06 8:06:04
Hathaway Pines 5 38N11'31 120w21'52 8:01:27
Hathaway Place 40 35N10'01 120w17'54 8:01:12
Hatton Fields 27 36N33 121w53 8:07:32
Havasu Lake 36 34N28'56 114w24'47 7:37:39
Havasu Palms 36 34N23'56 114w16'47 7:37:07
Haven Place 52 40N10'57 122w40'29 8:10:42
Havilah 15 35N31'04 118w31'04 7:54:04
Hawaiian Gardens 19 33N49'53 118w04'19 7:52:17
Hawkins Bar 53 40N52'13 123w31'18 8:14:05
Hawkinsville 47 41N45'39 122w37'15 8:10:29
Hawley 32 39N48'39 120w21'14 8:01:25
Hawthorne 19 33N54'59 118w21'06 7:53:24
Hayden 36 35N02'41 115w36'37 7:42:26
Hayden Hill 18 40N59'44 120w53'10 8:03:33
Hayfield 33 33N42'17 115w38'01 7:42:32
Hayfork 53 40N33'16 123w10'55 8:12:44
Hays Place 23 39N40'38 122w54'36 8:11:38
Haystack 49 38N13'24 122w36'32 8:10:26
Hayward 1 37N40'08 122w04'47 8:08:19
Hayward 22 37N38'34 120w22'13 8:01:29
Hayward Highlands 1 37N40 122w03 8:08:12
Hayward Landing 1 37N38'41 122w09'18 8:08:37
Hayward Park 41 37N33'16 122w18'44 8:09:15
Hazard 19 34N03 118w11 7:52:44
Hazelton 15 35N02'32 119w23'01 7:57:32
Healdsburg 49 38N36'38 122w52'05 8:11:28
Hearst 23 39N29'30 123w12'49 8:12:51
Heart Bar Campground 36 34N09'31 116w47'09 7:47:09
Heather Glen 31 39N01'06 120w58'51 8:03:55
Heath Place 23 39N49'27 123w22'48 8:13:31
Heber 13 32N43'51 115w31'44 7:42:07
Hector 36 34N48'14 116w27'06 7:45:48
Helena 53 40N46'25 123w07'38 8:12:31
Helendale 36 34N44'38 117w19'25 7:49:18
Hellhole Palms 37 33N14'12 116w26'22 7:45:45
Helltown 4 39N48'42 121w39'31 8:06:38
Helm 10 36N31'54 120w05'50 8:00:23
Helm Corner 16 36N05'53 119w38'34 7:58:34
Hemet 33 33N44'51 116w58'16 7:47:53
Hemlock Crossing 20 37N38'18 119w13'23 7:56:54
Henderson 41 37N28'46 122w09'52 8:08:39
Henderson Center 12 40N47 124w10 8:16:40
Henderson Village 39 38N06'03 121w18'16 8:05:13
Henley 47 41N54'08 122w33'44 8:10:15
Henleyville 52 39N57'43 122w19'32 8:09:18
Henry 40 35N29'23 120w38'49 8:02:35
Herald 34 38N17'45 121w14'36 8:04:58
Hercules 7 38N01'02 122w17'15 8:09:09
Herlong 18 40N08'37 120w08'01 8:00:32
Herlong Junction 18 40N07'29 120w14'44 8:00:59
Hermosa Beach 19 33N51'44 118w23'55 7:53:36
Hernandez 35 36N51 121w24 8:05:36
Herndon 10 36N50'12 119w54'59 7:59:40
Herpoco 7 38N00'42 122w16'12 8:09:05
Hershey 57 38N55'32 121w59'44 8:07:59
Hesperia 36 34N25'35 117w18'00 7:49:12
Hessel 49 38N20'54 122w46'34 8:11:06
Hess Mill 55 38N06'09 120w14'12 8:00:57
Hetch Hetchy Junction 55 37N48'04 120w29'12 8:01:57
Hewitt 19 34N11'59 118w23'21 7:53:33
Heyer 1 37N39 122w04 8:08:16
Hickman 50 37N37'25 120w45'10 8:03:01
Hidden Hills 19 34N09'37 118w39'05 7:54:36
Hidden Meadows 37 33N04 117w03 7:48:12
Hidden Palms 33 33N49'13 116w18'02 7:45:12
Hidden River 36 34N10'42 116w18'26 7:45:14
Hidden Springs 19 34N19'06 118w07'49 7:52:31
Hidden Valley 31 38N45'51 121w09'44 8:04:39
Higby 54 36N17'06 119w17'13 7:57:09
Higgins Corner 29 39N02'34 121w05'38 8:04:23
Highcroft 49 38N30'07 122w56'33 8:11:46
Highgrove 33 34N00'57 117w19'57 7:49:20
Highland 36 34N07'42 117w12'28 7:48:50
Highland Manor 15 35N24 119w02 7:56:08
Highland Park 15 35N24 119w02 7:56:08
Highland Park 19 34N06'43 118w11'53 7:52:48
Highland Springs 17 38N56'14 122w54'21 8:11:37
Highland Springs 33 33N58'10 116w56'29 7:47:46
Hights Corner 15 35N26'36 119w12'05 7:56:48
Highway City 10 36N48'39 119w53'02 7:59:32
Hilarita 21 37N53'03 122w28'15 8:09:53
Hildreth 20 37N06'32 119w37'55 7:58:32
Hillcrest 15 35N23 118w57 7:55:48
Hillcrest 37 32N44'52 117w09'24 7:48:38
Hillcrest 45 40N51'50 121w54'27 8:07:38
Hillcrest Center 15 35N23 118w57 7:55:48
Hillcrest Park 48 38N07 122w14 8:08:56
Hillgrove 19 34N01'00 117w58'45 7:51:55
Hillmaid 54 36N24'50 119w08'02 7:56:32
Hillsborough 41 37N34'27 122w22'42 8:09:31
Hillsborough Park 41 37N33'18 122w21'28 8:09:26
Hillsdale 37 32N46'45 116w55'38 7:47:43
Hillsdale 41 37N32'11 122w18'16 8:09:13
Hills Ferry 50 37N20'56 120w58'43 8:03:55
Hills Flat 29 39N13'27 121w03'08 8:04:13
Hilltop 15 35N23 119w01 7:56:04
Hilmar 24 37N24'31 120w50'57 8:03:24
Hilt 47 41N59'42 122w37'20 8:10:29
Hilton 49 38N30'17 122w56'21 8:11:45
Hinda 33 33N57'10 117w03'26 7:48:14
Hinkley 36 34N56'05 117w11'54 7:48:48
Hinsdale 51 39N00'55 121w46'40 8:07:07
Hinton 29 39N22'31 120w04'22 8:00:17
Hiouchi 8 41N47'34 124w04'15 8:16:17
Hiouchi Valley 8 41N46 124w12 8:16:48
Hirschdale 29 39N22'07 120w04'30 8:00:18
Hite Cove 22 37N38'27 119w50'53 7:59:24
Hi Vista 19 34N44'06 117w46'35 7:51:06
Hoaglin 53 40N12 123w30 8:14:00
Hobart 19 34N00'44 118w12'14 7:52:49
Hobart Mills 29 39N24'02 120w10'58 8:00:44
Hobergs 17 38N50'37 122w43'24 8:10:54
Hoboken 53 40N52'59 123w26'01 8:13:44
Hodge 36 34N48'56 117w11'33 7:48:46
Hoffman Point 10 36N41'32 119w11'50 7:56:47
Holcomb Village 37 33N21'03 116w44'12 7:46:57
Holiday Forest 36 34N15 116w53 7:47:32
Hollenbeck 25 41N27'43 121w16'56 8:05:08
Hollis 15 35N40'03 119w11'25 7:56:46
Hollister 35 36N51'09 121w24'02 8:05:36
Hollydale 19 33N54'53 118w09'39 7:52:39
Hollydale 49 38N30'19 122w55'08 8:11:41
Hollywood 19 34N05'54 118w19'33 7:53:18
Hollywood Beach 56 34N10'02 119w13'47 7:56:55
Hollywood by the Sea 56 34N09'38 119w13'30 7:56:54
Hollywood Park Race Track 19 33N57 118w20 7:53:20
Hollywood Riviera 19 33N48'51 118w22'56 7:53:32
Holmes 12 40N25'07 123w56'22 8:15:45
Holt 39 37N56'04 121w25'34 8:05:42
Holtville 13 32N48'40 115w22'46 7:41:31
Holy City 43 37N09'25 121w58'40 8:07:55
Home Acres 7 38N00 121w51 8:07:24
Home Gardens 19 33N56 118w11 7:52:44
Home Gardens 33 33N52'41 117w31'12 7:50:05
Home Junc 19 34N02'09 118w26'02 7:53:44
Homeland 33 33N44'35 117w06'30 7:48:26
Homelands 37 32N44'30 116w58'18 7:47:53
Homer 36 34N55'12 114w56'10 7:39:45
Homestead 25 41N54'49 121w25'19 8:05:41
Homestead 33 33N33 116w43 7:46:52
Homestead 39 37N56 121w16 8:05:04
Homestead Valley 21 37N54 122w32 8:10:08
Homewood 31 39N05'13 120w09'33 8:00:38
Honby 19 34N25'16 118w29'29 7:53:58
Honcut 4 39N19'45 121w31'58 8:06:08
Honda 42 34N36'56 120w37'57 8:02:32

Honeydew 12	40N14'40	124w07'18	8:16:29
Honey Lake 18	40N05	120w06	8:00:24
Hood 34	38N22'06	121w30'59	8:06:04
Hood Junction 34	38N21'49	121w30'31	8:06:02
Hooker 52	40N18'03	122w19'33	8:09:18
Hookston 7	37N56'29	122w03'06	8:08:12
Hookton 12	40N40'24	124w13'02	8:16:52
Hoopa 12	41N03'02	123w40'24	8:14:42
Hoopa Valley Indian Res 12	41N03	123w40	8:14:40
Hooper 47	41N16'05	122w09'38	8:08:39
Hooperville 47	41N40'44	122w50'52	8:11:23
Hope Ranch 42	34N25'19	119w46'12	7:59:05
Hopeton 24	37N29'30	120w31'48	8:02:07
Hope Valley 2	41N54	120w21	8:01:24
Hopland 23	38N58'23	123w06'55	8:12:28
Hoppaw 8	41N31'28	124w01'44	8:16:07
Horizon Hills 56	34N12	118w53	7:55:32
Hornbrook 47	41N54'37	122w33'17	8:10:13
Hornitos 22	37N30'08	120w14'14	8:00:57
Horse Creek 47	41N49'27	122w59'45	8:11:59
Horse Flat 8	41N54'02	123w46'09	8:15:05
Horse Lake 18	40N40'27	120w24'11	8:01:37
Horstville 58	39N01'41	121w23'26	8:05:34
Hotlum 47	41N28'27	122w18'48	8:09:15
Hough Springs 17	39N09'45	122w36'40	8:10:27
Houghton Place 52	39N48'18	122w40'38	8:10:43
Houze Place 36	34N46'07	117w37'30	7:50:30
Hovley 13	33N00'09	115w31'15	7:42:05
Howard 47	41N18'47	122w16'33	8:09:06
Howard Landing 34	38N13'44	121w36'00	8:06:24
Howard Landing Ferry 34	38N14'12	121w36'09	8:06:25
Howard Springs 17	38N51'30	122w40'25	8:10:42
Howell Place 56	34N28'09	119w07'08	7:56:29
Howells Landing 6	38N55'51	121w50'08	8:07:21
Howest 41	37N35	122w22	8:09:28
Howland Flat 46	39N42'54	120w53'08	8:03:33
Hoxie Crossing 53	40N01'04	123w06'44	8:12:27
Hoyt Crossing 29	39N18'16	121w04'39	8:04:19
Huasna 40	35N07'22	120w23'33	8:01:34
Hub 16	36N24'08	119w48'29	7:59:14
Hub City 19	33N53	118w15	7:53:00
Hubert Place 40	35N10'08	120w15'09	8:01:04
Hudner 35	36N54'00	121w27'01	8:05:48
Hudson 50	37N38	120w59	8:03:56
Hughes Mill 31	39N05'28	120w46'43	8:03:07
Hughes Place 4	39N43'40	121w24'04	8:05:36
Hughson 50	37N35'49	120w51'54	8:03:28
Hulburd Grove 37	32N51'43	116w37'20	7:46:29
Hume 10	36N47'06	118w54'46	7:55:39
Humphreys 19	34N24'37	118w26'23	7:53:46
Humphreys Station 10	36N49	119w43	7:58:52
Hunter Place 12	40N10'46	124w00'51	8:16:03
Hunters Valley 22	37N30	120w14	8:00:56
Huntington Beach 30	33N39'37	117w59'54	7:52:00
Huntington Lake 10	37N13'54	119w14'06	7:56:56
Huntington Park 19	33N58'54	118w13'27	7:52:54
Huntley 39	37N45'31	120w56'46	8:03:47
Hurleton 4	39N29'51	121w23'11	8:05:33
Huron 10	36N12'10	120w06'07	8:00:24
Hutt 36	34N54'28	117w04'28	7:48:18
Hyampom 53	40N37'03	123w27'05	8:13:48
Hyde Park 19	33N58'50	118w19'47	7:53:19
Hydesville 12	40N32'52	124w05'46	8:16:23
Hydril 16	36N00'46	120w05'51	8:00:23
Ibis 36	34N56'24	114w47'30	7:39:10
Iceland 29	39N22'32	120w01'30	8:00:06
Idlewild 31	39N06'32	120w09'30	8:00:38
Idlewild 54	35N48'39	118w40'16	7:54:41
Idria 35	36N25'01	120w40'24	8:02:42
Idyllwild 33	33N44'24	116w43'05	7:46:52
Idylwood Acres 7	37N55	122w03	8:08:12
Igerna 47	41N24'06	122w22'42	8:09:31
Ignacio 21	38N04'13	122w32'15	8:10:09
Igo 45	40N30'20	122w32'26	8:10:10
Ilmon 15	35N18'45	118w41'35	7:54:46
Imola 28	38N16'43	122w16'46	8:09:07
Imperial 13	32N50'51	115w34'07	7:42:16
Imperial Beach 37	32N35'02	117w06'44	7:48:27
Imperial Crest 19	33N54	118w05	7:52:20
Inca 33	33N48'03	114w45'56	7:39:04
Incline 22	37N39'38	119w51'06	7:59:24
Independence 5	38N20'57	120w30'45	8:02:03
Independence 14	36N48'10	118w11'57	7:52:48
Indian Falls 32	40N03'25	120w57'46	8:03:51
Indian Gulch 22	37N26'22	120w11'45	8:00:47
Indian Mission 10	37N05	119w29	7:57:56
Indianola 12	40N48'46	124w04'55	8:16:20
Indian Springs 19	34N19'56	118w19'58	7:53:20
Indian Springs 20	37N03'02	119w43'53	7:58:56
Indian Springs 23	39N44'01	123w22'22	8:13:29
Indian Springs 37	32N43'13	116w52'48	7:47:31
Indian Village 14	36N26'57	116w52'24	7:47:30
Indian Wells 15	35N39'55	117w52'20	7:51:29
Indian Wells 33	33N43'07	116w18'27	7:45:14
Indio 33	33N43'14	116w12'53	7:44:52
Industry (City of Industry) 19	34N01'11	117w57'28	7:51:50
Ingle 10	36N43'17	120w15'20	8:01:01
Inglenook 23	39N31'47	123w45'28	8:15:02
Ingleside 38	37N44'15	122w31'00	8:10:04
Inglewood 19	33N57'42	118w21'08	7:53:25
Ingomar 24	37N10'49	120w58'02	8:03:52
Ingot 45	40N43'40	122w04'41	8:08:19
Inperial Gables 13	33N07'39	114w55'42	7:39:43
Inskip 4	39N59'24	121w32'24	8:06:10
Inspiration Point 9	38N56'47	120w05'58	8:00:24
Inverness 21	38N06'04	122w51'21	8:11:25
Inverness Park 21	38N03'50	122w49'18	8:11:17
Inwood 45	40N31'27	121w57'22	8:07:49
Inyokern 15	35N38'49	117w48'42	7:51:15
Ione 3	38N21'10	120w55'54	8:03:44
Iowa City 58	39N17'30	121w28'35	8:05:54
Iowa Hill 31	39N06'31	120w51'30	8:03:26
Iremel 42	34N55'24	120w31'32	8:02:06
Iris 13	33N11'43	115w24'13	7:41:37
Irmulco 23	39N25'20	123w30'59	8:14:04
Iron Mountain 36	34N07	114w31	7:38:04
Iron Mountain 45	40N40'15	122w31'23	8:10:06
Ironsides 19	33N48'40	118w18'19	7:53:13
Irrigosa 20	36N53'28	119w59'11	7:59:57
Irvine 30	33N40'10	117w49'20	7:51:17
Irvings Crest 37	32N58'47	116w54'41	7:47:39
Irvington 1	37N31'22	121w58'14	8:07:53
Irwin 24	37N23'49	120w50'56	8:03:24
Irwindale 19	34N06'25	117w56'04	7:51:44
Island Crossing 10	37N32'06	119w04'02	7:56:16
Island Mountain 53	40N01'35	123w29'21	8:13:57
Isla Vista 42	34N25	119w51	7:59:24
Isleton 34	38N09'43	121w36'38	8:06:27
Italian Swiss Colony 20	36N58	120w04	8:00:16
Ivanhoe 54	36N23'14	119w13'01	7:56:52
Ivanpah 36	35N20'26	115w18'35	7:41:14
Iversen Landing 23	38N50'44	123w38'43	8:14:35
Ivesta 10	36N43'19	119w38'08	7:58:33
Ivory 54	36N34'07	119w25'21	7:57:41
Jacinto 11	39N34'52	122w00'20	8:08:01
Jacinto Grange 11	39N31	122w01	8:08:04
Jacksnipe 48	38N11'34	122w04'01	8:08:16
Jackson 3	38N20'56	120w46'23	8:03:06
Jackson Gate 3	38N21	120w46	8:03:04
Jacksonville 55	37N52	120w26	8:01:44
Jacobs Corner 57	38N40'18	121w53'36	8:07:34
Jacumba 37	32N37'03	116w11'20	7:44:45
Jalama 42	34N29'53	120w29'37	8:01:58
Jamacha 37	32N44'30	116w54'38	7:47:39
Jamacha Junction 37	32N44'23	116w56'33	7:47:46
James 4	39N39'12	121w32'55	8:06:12
Jamesan 10	36N43'12	120w12'32	8:00:50
Jamesburg 27	36N22'11	121w35'21	8:06:21
Jameson Beach 9	38N55	120w00	8:00:00
Jamestown 55	37N57'12	120w25'18	8:01:41
Jamul 37	32N43'01	116w52'31	7:47:30
Janes Place 12	40N47'22	123w42'56	8:14:52
Janesville 18	40N17'48	120w31'23	8:02:06
Jarbo 4	39N30	121w33	8:06:12
Jarvis Landing 1	37N31'46	122w03'45	8:08:15
Jasmin 15	35N44'34	119w08'38	7:56:35
Jastro 15	35N22'36	119w04'17	7:56:17
Java 36	34N53'15	114w43'35	7:38:54
Jefferson 19	34N01'06	118w16'16	7:53:05
Jellico 18	40N50'42	121w17'30	8:05:10
Jelly 52	40N11	122w16	8:09:04
Jenks Place 11	39N42'31	122w50'50	8:11:23
Jenner 49	38N26'59	123w06'52	8:12:27
Jenny Lind 5	38N05'42	120w52'08	8:03:29
Jerome 47	41N43'54	121w59'57	8:08:00
Jerseydale 22	37N33'49	119w51'23	7:59:26
Jesmond Dene 37	33N10'49	117w06'30	7:48:26
Jesus Maria 5	38N17'08	120w38'47	8:02:35
Jet 50	37N25'58	121w05'56	8:04:24
Jewell 21	38N02'12	122w44'41	8:10:59
Jimgrey 36	34N58'37	117w28'00	7:49:52
Jim Leggett Place 23	39N51'46	123w25'10	8:13:41
Jimtown 49	38N40'00	122w49'07	8:11:16
Joes Landing 51	38N46'48	121w36'09	8:06:25
Joesphine 51	39N05'39	121w48'00	8:07:12
Jofegan 37	33N18'54	117w19'53	7:49:20
Johannesburg 15	35N22'22	117w38'02	7:50:32
John Adams P O 37	32N46	117w07	7:48:28
Johnsondale 54	35N58'29	118w32'24	7:54:10
Johnson Landing 1	37N37'45	122w09'08	8:08:37
Johnson Park 45	40N53	121w40	8:06:40
Johnsons 12	41N21'02	123w52'15	8:15:29
Johnson Tract 54	36N20	119w18	7:57:12
Johnston Corner 44	36N55'43	121w42'15	8:06:49
Johnstons Corner 36	34N49'49	117w10'46	7:48:43
Johnstonville 18	40N23'04	120w35'11	8:02:21
Johnstown 37	32N50'17	116w53'45	7:47:35
Johnsville 32	39N45'39	120w41'40	8:02:47
Joint Union High School 24	36N59'05	120w37'20	8:02:29
Jolon 27	35N58	121w11	8:04:44
Jones Corner 54	36N03'57	119w06'22	7:56:25
Jones Place 9	38N50'59	120w22'10	8:01:29
Jonesville 4	40N06'45	121w27'58	8:05:52
Joshua 36	35N16'16	115w26'55	7:41:48
Joshua Tree 36	34N08'05	116w18'44	7:45:15
Jovista 54	35N47'51	119w10'55	7:56:44
Juan 36	35N21'59	115w05'14	7:40:21
Julian 37	33N04'43	116w36'04	7:46:24
Junction Camp 7	37N51'58	121w55'53	8:07:44
Junction Camp 42	34N43'54	119w58'45	7:59:55
Junction City 53	40N44'00	123w03'09	8:12:13
Junction House (Site) 4	39N44'26	121w17'27	8:05:10
Junction House 29	39N19'00	120w48'36	8:03:14
Junction Ranch 14	36N04'26	117w30'43	7:50:03
June Lake 26	37N46'47	119w04'28	7:56:18
June Lake Junction 26	37N48'45	119w03'12	7:56:13
Juniper 25	41N28'48	120w34'18	8:02:17
Juniper Hills 19	34N26'39	117w56'04	7:51:44
Juniper Lake Resort 18	40N18	121w14	8:04:56
Juniper Springs 33	33N45'58	117w05'00	7:48:20
Jupiter 55	38N07'21	120w16'54	8:01:08
Jurupa 33	33N59	117w29	7:49:56
Kadota 24	37N17'42	120w24'40	8:01:39
Kaiser 36	34N05'38	117w29'17	7:49:57
Kaiser Center 1	37N48	122w16	8:09:04
Kaiser's Eagle Mountain 33	33N51	115w29	7:41:56
Kalina 25	41N59'43	121w25'09	8:05:41
Kamp Klamath 8	41N32	124w02	8:16:08
Kanawyers 10	36N47'43	118w35'02	7:54:20
Kandra 25	41N49'34	121w23'56	8:05:36
Kane Spring 13	33N06'33	115w50'07	7:43:20
Karlo 18	40N33'02	120w18'52	8:01:15
Karnak 51	38N47'06	121w39'16	8:06:37
Kathryn 30	33N42'15	117w45'09	7:51:01
Kaweah 54	36N28'11	118w55'03	7:55:40
Kayandee 15	35N20'51	118w59'39	7:55:59
Kearny Mesa 37	32N49	117w09	7:48:36
Kearsarge 14	36N48'25	118w06'59	7:52:28
Kecks Corner 15	35N40'15	120w04'51	8:00:19
Keddie 32	40N00'54	120w57'36	8:03:50
Keeler 14	36N29'14	117w52'23	7:51:30
Keenbrook 36	34N14'58	117w27'24	7:49:50
Keene 15	35N13'25	118w33'41	7:54:15
Keene Summit 23	39N16	123w35	8:14:20
Kegg 47	41N41'22	121w59'09	8:07:57
Keith 56	34N23'39	118w57'33	7:55:50
Kekawaka 53	40N05'44	123w31'05	8:14:04
Keller Place 11	39N42'56	122w54'24	8:11:38
Kellog 49	38N35	122w35	8:10:20
Kellogg 49	38N37'56	122w40'22	8:10:41
Kelsey 9	38N47'56	120w49'11	8:03:17
Kelseyville 17	38N58'41	122w50'18	8:11:21
Kelso 36	35N00'45	115w39'10	7:42:37
Kennedy Meadow 55	37N59	120w23	8:01:32
Kenny 23	39N55'19	123w53'51	8:15:35
Kensington 7	37N54'38	122w16'45	8:09:07
Kensington 37	32N46	117w06	7:48:24
Kentfield 21	37N57'08	122w33'22	8:10:13
Kenton Mill 36	34N38'23	116w21'16	7:45:25
Kentwood-in-the-Pines 37	33N04'18	116w34'29	7:46:18
Kent Woodlands 21	37N58	122w31	8:10:04
Kenwood 49	38N24'50	122w32'42	8:10:11
Keough Hot Springs 14	37N15'17	118w22'34	7:53:30
Kephart 25	41N35'21	121w18'47	8:05:15
Kerens 36	34N57'59	115w48'21	7:43:13
Kerman 10	36N43'25	120w03'32	8:00:14
Kern City 15	35N21'14	119w04'21	7:56:17
Kernell 15	35N45'25	119w20'35	7:57:22
Kern Homes 15	35N24	119w02	7:56:08
Kern Lake 15	35N08'24	119w04'26	7:56:18
Kernvale 15	35N39	118w28	7:53:52
Kernville 15	35N45'17	118w25'28	7:53:42
Kester 19	34N12	118w27	7:53:48
Keswick 45	40N37'21	122w27'53	8:09:52
Kett 45	40N36'26	122w27'46	8:09:51
Kettenpom 53	40N09'27	123w27'35	8:13:50
Kettleman 39	38N06'58	121w14'32	8:04:58
Kettleman City 16	36N00'30	119w57'39	7:59:51
Kettleman Station 16	35N59'56	119w57'46	7:59:51
Kevet 56	34N21'44	119w02'22	7:56:09
Keyes 50	37N33'24	120w54'52	8:03:39
Keyesville 15	35N37'33	118w30'36	7:54:02
Keystone 19	33N49'31	118w16'46	7:53:07
Keystone 55	37N50'07	120w30'24	8:02:02
Kibesillah 23	39N35'25	123w46'36	8:15:06
Kiesel 57	38N39'47	121w36'56	8:06:28
Kilaga Springs 31	38N58'16	121w14'49	8:04:59
Kilkare Woods 1	37N37'42	121w54'40	8:07:39
Kilowatt 15	35N23'56	119w26'47	7:57:47
Kimball 56	34N15'24	119w11'18	7:56:45
Kincaid 19	34N07'43	117w56'05	7:51:44
King 30	33N46	117w53	7:51:32
King City 27	36N12'46	121w07'30	8:04:30
King Farms 57	38N43'36	121w41'25	8:06:46
King Salmon 12	40N44'22	124w13'03	8:16:52
Kings Beach 31	39N14'16	120w01'32	8:00:06
Kingsburg 10	36N30'50	119w33'11	7:58:13
Kings Canyon National Park 54	36N44	118w58	7:55:52
Kingsville 9	38N40'36	120w52'29	8:03:30
Kingvale 29	39N19'16	120w25'40	8:01:43
Kinyon 47	41N16'17	121w53'35	8:07:34
Kirkville 51	38N54'32	121w47'30	8:07:10
Kirkwood 2	38N42'10	120w04'18	8:00:17
Kirkwood 11	39N51'19	122w09'39	8:08:39
Kiska 52	40N04'06	122w09'34	8:08:38
Kismet 20	37N02'50	120w05'33	8:00:22
Kister 4	39N49'20	121w21'44	8:05:27
Kit Carson 3	38N41	120w07	8:00:28
Kiva Beach 9	38N56'26	120w03'00	8:00:12
Klamath 8	41N31'36	124w02'14	8:16:09
Klamath Glen 8	41N30'46	123w59'34	8:15:58
Klamath River (P O) 47	41N51'41	122w49'18	8:11:17
Klau 40	35N37'31	120w53'26	8:03:34
Klinefelter 36	34N54'02	114w45'58	7:39:04
Klondike 36	34N40'06	116w00'08	7:44:01
Klondike Mine 53	40N24'01	123w23'27	8:13:34
Kneeland 12	40N45'41	123w59'37	8:15:58
Knightsen 7	37N58'08	121w40'01	8:06:40
Knights Ferry 50	37N49'11	120w40'16	8:02:41
Knights Landing 57	38N47'59	121w43'02	8:06:52
Knob 45	40N23'20	122w59'13	8:11:57
Knowles 20	37N13'12	119w52'23	7:59:30
Knowles Corner 49	38N21'09	122w48'51	8:11:15
Knowles Junction 20	37N12'10	119w54'29	7:59:38

Knoxville 28 38N49'40 122w20'22 8:09:21
Komandorski Village 1 37N42'58 121w54'28 8:07:38
Korbel 12 40N52'14 123w57'26 8:15:50
Korbel 49 38N30'28 122w57'48 8:11:51
Korblex 12 40N54'13 124w04'13 8:16:17
Kramer Hills 36 34N55'15 117w28'04 7:49:52
Kramer Junction 36 34N59'33 117w32'27 7:50:10
Kramm 4 39N33'11 121w35'01 8:06:20
Krug 28 38N31'05 122w28'50 8:09:55
Kyburz 9 38N46'29 120w17'45 8:01:11
La Ballona 19 34N00 118w24 7:53:36
La Barr Meadows 29 39N10'29 121w02'39 8:04:11
La Canada 19 34N12'16 118w12'00 7:52:48
La Casita del Arroyo 19 34N08'29 118w09'57 7:52:40
Lacjac 10 36N36'42 119w28'59 7:57:56
Lackey Place 15 35N37'56 118w38'45 7:54:35
La Costa 19 34N06 118w44 7:54:56
La Crescenta 19 34N13'27 118w14'21 7:52:57
La Cresta 15 35N23 118w59 7:55:56
La Cresta 37 32N48'40 116w51'45 7:47:27
La Delta 36 34N38'32 117w20'37 7:49:22
Ladera 41 37N24 122w12 8:08:48
Ladera Heights 19 33N59 118w22 7:53:28
Lafayette 7 37N53'09 122w07'01 8:08:28
La Fetra 19 34N08 117w51 7:51:24
La Fresa 19 33N52'22 118w20'06 7:53:20
Lagol 56 34N16'10 118w56'59 7:55:48
LaGrange 50 37N39'49 120w27'45 8:01:51
Laguna 19 33N58'36 118w08'20 7:52:33
Laguna Beach 30 33N32'32 117w46'56 7:51:08
Laguna Dam 13 32N44 114w35 7:38:20
Laguna Hills 30 33N36'45 117w42'43 7:50:51
Laguna Junction 37 32N48'34 116w30'42 7:46:03
Laguna Lake 40 35N18 120w45 8:03:00
Laguna Niguel 30 33N31'21 117w42'24 7:50:50
Lagunitas 21 38N00'41 122w42'04 8:10:48
La Habra 30 33N55'55 117w56'43 7:51:47
La Habra Heights 19 33N57'39 117w56'59 7:51:48
La Honda 41 37N19'09 122w16'23 8:09:06
La Honda Park 5 38N07'14 120w29'43 8:01:59
Laird Landing 47 41N52'23 121w43'23 8:06:54
Lairds Corner 54 36N03'05 119w13'52 7:56:55
Lairds Landing 21 38N09'34 122w54'41 8:11:39
Lairport 19 33N55'20 118w22'40 7:53:31
La Jolla 30 33N51'27 117w52'32 7:51:30
La Jolla 37 32N50'50 117w16'24 7:49:06
La Jolla Amago 37 33N16'58 116w51'45 7:47:27
La Jolla Indian Reservation 37 33N17 116w54 7:47:36
La Jolla Ranch 10 36N43'42 120w36'07 8:02:24
Lake Alpine 2 38N28'43 120w00'10 8:00:01
Lake Arrowhead 36 34N14'54 117w11'18 7:48:45
Lake City 25 41N38'34 120w12'57 8:00:52
Lake City 29 39N21'31 120w56'26 8:03:46
Lake Elsinore 33 33N55 117w44 7:50:56
Lake Forest 31 39N11'04 120w06'49 8:00:27
Lakehead 45 40N54'19 122w22'41 8:09:31
Lake Henshaw 37 33N07 116w40 7:46:40
Lake Hills Estates 9 38N41 121w11 8:04:44
Lake Hughes 19 34N40'37 118w26'40 7:53:47
Lake Isabella 15 35N36'33 118w28'58 7:53:56
Lake Kirkwood 9 38N42 120w04 8:00:16
Lakeland Village 33 33N38'19 117w20'35 7:49:22
Lake Los Angeles 19 34N35 118w06 7:52:24
Lake Mary 26 37N38 118w58 7:55:52
Lake Mathews 33 33N52 117w19 7:49:16
Lake Morena Village 37 32N37 116w28 7:45:52
Lake Nokopen 18 40N18 121w01 8:04:04
Lake of The Woods 15 34N49 118w57 7:55:48
Lakeport 17 39N02'35 122w54'53 8:11:40
Lake San Marcos 37 33N07'34 117w12'27 7:48:50
Lake Shastina 47 41N29 122w25 8:09:40
Lakeshore 10 37N15'11 119w10'26 7:56:42
Lakeshore 45 40N52'48 122w23'15 8:09:33
Lakeside 37 32N51'26 116w55'17 7:47:41
Lakeside Farms 37 32N52'01 116w56'21 7:47:45
Lakeside Park 19 34N13'41 118w38'45 7:54:35
Lake Tahoe 31 39N14 120w07 8:00:28
Lake Tamarisk 33 33N43 115w24 7:41:36
Lake Valley 9 38N55'48 120w00'13 8:00:01
Lakeview 15 35N05'41 119w06'31 7:56:26
Lakeview 33 33N50'19 117w07'02 7:48:28
Lakeview 37 32N50'34 116w54'12 7:47:37
Lakeview Hot Springs 33 33N50'18 117w08'41 7:48:35
Lakeview Junction 25 41N28'34 120w32'12 8:02:09
Lake View Terrace 19 34N17 118w27 7:53:48
Lakeville 49 38N11'57 122w32'46 8:10:11
Lakewood 19 33N51'13 118w07'59 7:52:32
Lakin 47 41N22'42 121w33'40 8:06:15
La Loma 50 37N38 120w59 8:03:56
Lamanda Park 19 34N08'53 118w05'35 7:52:22
Lambert 49 38N37 122w52 8:11:28
La Mesa 37 32N46'04 117w01'20 7:48:05
La Mirada 19 33N55'02 118w00'40 7:52:03
Lamoine 45 40N58'41 122w25'47 8:09:43
Lamont 15 35N15'35 118w54'48 7:55:39
Lanare 10 36N25'50 119w55'48 7:59:43
Lancaster 19 34N41'53 118w08'09 7:52:33
Lancha Plana 3 38N13'29 120w54'03 8:03:36
Landco 15 35N22'46 119w03'37 7:56:14
Lander Crossing 31 39N04'09 120w58'39 8:03:55

Landers 36 34N15'58 116w23'32 7:45:34
Land Park 34 38N32 121w28 8:05:52
Landscape 1 37N54 122w17 8:09:08
Lane 39 38N00'10 121w14'57 8:05:00
Lane Mill 14 36N16'55 117w34'12 7:50:17
Lanfair 36 35N07'33 115w10'58 7:40:44
Lang 19 34N25'54 118w22'36 7:53:30
Lansdale 21 37N59 122w35 8:10:20
La Palma 30 33N50'47 118w02'45 7:52:11
La Paloma 30 33N46'51 117w48'13 7:51:13
La Panza 40 35N21'40 120w12'52 8:00:51
La Patera 42 34N26'15 119w50'28 7:59:22
La Playa 37 32N42'44 117w14'40 7:48:59
La Porte 32 39N40'56 120w58'59 8:03:56
La Presa 37 32N42'29 116w59'47 7:47:59
La Puente 19 34N01'12 117w56'55 7:51:48
LaQuinta 33 33N39'48 116w18'33 7:45:14
Larabee 12 40N24'22 123w55'41 8:15:43
Larabee Ranch 12 40N21 123w55 8:15:40
Larchmont Riviera 34 38N33 121w22 8:05:28
Largo 23 39N01'18 123w07'44 8:12:31
Largo Vista 19 34N25'37 117w45'55 7:51:04
Larkfield 49 38N26 122w43 8:10:52
Larkmead 28 38N33'32 122w31'19 8:10:05
Larkspur 21 37N56'03 122w32'03 8:10:08
Larwin Plaza-Vallejo 48 38N07 122w14 8:08:56
Larwin Square-Tustin 30 33N45 117w49 7:51:16
La Salle 42 34N38'52 120w31'31 8:02:06
Lasco 18 40N25'21 120w58'18 8:03:53
Las Cruces 42 34N30'29 120w13'41 8:00:55
La Selva Beach 44 36N56'12 121w51'49 8:07:27
Las Flores (Malibu P O) 19 34N02'14 118w38'06 7:54:32
Las Flores 37 33N17'09 117w27'05 7:49:48
Las Flores 52 40N04'19 122w09'42 8:08:39
Las Gallinas 21 38N01'14 122w32'15 8:10:09
La Sierra 33 33N55'15 117w29'44 7:49:59
La Sierra Heights 33 33N56'39 117w29'08 7:49:57
Las Juntas 7 37N55'55 122w03'12 8:08:13
Las Lomas 27 36N55 121w47 8:07:08
Las Lomas 49 38N40'38 123w08'03 8:12:32
Las Palmas 10 36N45'27 119w41'58 7:58:48
Las Posas 56 34N17 119w02 7:56:08
Las Posas Estates 56 34N14 119w02 7:56:08
Last Chance 31 39N06'41 120w37'25 8:02:30
Lathrop 39 37N49'22 121w16'32 8:05:06
La Tijera 19 33N59 118w20 7:53:20
Laton 10 36N26'00 119w41'09 7:58:45
Latrobe 9 38N33'35 120w58'58 8:03:56
Laughlin 23 39N16'47 123w14'00 8:12:56
Laurel 41 37N31'55 122w18'24 8:09:14
Laurel 44 37N07'00 121w57'55 8:07:52
Laurel Canyon 19 34N12 118w24 7:53:36
La Verne 19 34N06'03 117w46'01 7:51:04
Lavic 36 34N43'40 116w18'45 7:45:15
La Vina 20 36N52'50 120w06'34 8:00:26
Lawndale 19 33N53'14 118w21'06 7:53:24
Lawndale 49 38N25'17 122w34'09 8:10:17
Lawrence 43 37N22'12 121w59'41 8:07:59
Laws 14 37N24'03 118w20'41 7:53:23
Laytonville 23 39N41'18 123w28'54 8:13:56
Leadfield 14 36N50'48 117w03'30 7:48:14
Leaf 47 41N38'32 122w00'03 8:08:00
Leavitt 18 40N23'46 120w31'30 8:02:06
Lebec 15 34N50'12 118w51'48 7:55:27
Leesdale 56 34N11'48 119w05'56 7:56:24
Leesville 6 39N11'24 122w25'04 8:09:40
Lee Vining 26 37N57'27 119w07'15 7:56:29
Leggett 23 39N51'57 123w42'47 8:14:51
Le Grand 24 37N13'43 120w14'50 8:00:59
Leisure Town 48 38N21'58 121w56'37 8:07:46
Leisure World 30 33N46 118w05 7:52:20
Lemona 33 33N58'49 117w19'30 7:49:18
Lemoncove 54 36N22'58 119w01'25 7:56:06
Lemon Grove 37 32N44'33 117w01'50 7:48:07
Lemon Heights 30 33N45'32 117w46'52 7:51:07
Lemoore 16 36N18'03 119w46'55 7:59:08
Lemoore Station 16 36N16 119w54 7:59:36
Lennox 19 33N56'17 118w21'06 7:53:24
Lento 42 34N28'22 120w09'34 8:00:38
Lenwood 36 34N52'36 117w06'11 7:48:25
Leon 36 34N33'29 117w18'20 7:49:13
Leonardi 9 38N52'55 120w32'07 8:02:08
Leona Valley 19 34N37'06 118w17'14 7:53:09
Lerdo 15 35N29'25 119w09'06 7:56:36
Lerona 10 37N07'46 119w25'49 7:57:43
Letterman 38 37N47 122w27 8:09:48
Leucadia 37 33N04'05 117w18'09 7:49:13
Levis 10 36N37'25 120w24'19 8:01:37
Lewiston 53 40N42'27 122w48'23 8:11:14
Lexington 43 37N10 121w58 8:07:52
Liberty 49 38N17'04 122w42'03 8:10:48
Liberty Acres 19 33N55 118w21 7:53:24
Liberty Farms 48 38N19 121w42 8:06:48
Libfarm 48 38N19 121w42 8:06:48
Lick 43 37N17'14 121w50'41 8:07:23
Lido Isle 30 33N36'14 117w54'59 7:51:40
Likely 25 41N13'50 120w30'11 8:02:01
Lilac 37 33N17'16 117w04'59 7:48:20
Limco 56 34N21 119w04 7:56:16
Limon 56 34N19'14 119w06'25 7:56:26
Limoneira 56 34N19'49 119w07'29 7:56:30
Lincoln 31 38N53'30 121w17'31 8:05:10
Lincoln Acres 37 32N40'04 117w04'19 7:48:17
Lincoln Crest 19 34N35'13 118w18'14 7:53:13
Lincoln Heights 19 34N04'14 118w12'15 7:52:49
Lincoln Village 19 33N49'40 118w13'19 7:52:53
Lincoln Village 34 38N35 121w20 8:05:20
Lincoln Village 39 38N00'19 121w19'38 8:05:19
Linda 58 39N07'40 121w32'59 8:06:12
Linda Mar 41 37N38 122w29 8:09:56

Linda Mar Gardens 37 32N59 117w16 7:49:04
Linda Vista 19 34N10'17 118w10'34 7:52:42
Linda Vista 37 32N47'00 117w10'14 7:48:41
Linda Vista 43 37N22 121w49 8:07:16
Lindbergh Field 37 32N44 117w11 7:48:44
Lindcove 54 36N21'28 119w03'49 7:56:15
Linden 39 38N01'17 121w04'58 8:04:20
Linden Avenue 41 37N39 122w26 8:09:44
Lindenwood 41 37N27 122w11 8:08:44
Lindsay 54 36N12'11 119w05'14 7:56:21
Lingard 24 37N14'25 120w23'47 8:01:35
Lingos Landing 48 38N09'34 121w55'29 8:07:42
Linne 40 35N34'21 120w34'05 8:02:16
Linnell 54 36N20 119w18 7:57:12
Linnie 14 35N49'59 117w51'58 7:51:28
Lira 51 39N08'43 121w52'00 8:07:28
Liskey 25 41N50'56 121w24'32 8:05:38
Lisko 54 36N05'49 119w02'11 7:56:09
List 54 36N16'34 119w07'37 7:56:30
Litchfield 18 40N22'58 120w23'10 8:01:33
Little Hayen 32 40N00'34 121w13'45 8:04:55
Little Lake 14 35N56'12 117w54'21 7:51:37
Little Lake 33 33N45 116w56 7:47:44
Little Morongo Heights 36 34N05'44 116w31'09 7:46:05
Little Norway 9 38N49 120w03 8:00:12
Little Paradise 33 33N40'11 116w31'14 7:46:05
Little Penny 23 38N55'22 123w27'24 8:13:50
Little Reed Heights 21 37N53 122w29 8:09:56
Little River 23 39N16'15 123w47'14 8:15:09
Littlerock 19 34N31'16 117w58'58 7:51:56
Little Shasta 47 41N42'43 122w23'25 8:09:34
Little Valley 18 40N53'40 121w10'35 8:04:42
Live Oak 34 38N29'03 121w04'23 8:04:18
Live Oak 51 39N16'33 121w39'32 8:06:38
Live Oak Acres 56 34N24'25 119w18'27 7:57:14
Live Oak Canyon 19 34N07 117w46 7:51:04
Live Oak Springs 37 32N41'26 116w20'01 7:45:20
Livermore 1 37N40'55 121w46'01 8:07:04
Livingston 24 37N23'13 120w43'21 8:02:53
Llanada 35 36N36'33 120w54'56 8:03:40
Llano 19 34N30 117w50 7:51:20
Llano 49 38N24'43 122w47'36 8:11:10
Lobitos 41 37N22'59 122w23'57 8:09:36
Lobo 30 33N48 117w59 7:51:56
Locans 10 36N43'25 119w39'44 7:58:39
Loch Lomond 17 38N51'48 122w43'06 8:10:52
Locke 34 38N15'02 121w30'30 8:06:02
Lockeford 39 38N09'49 121w08'56 8:04:36
Lockhart 36 35N00'53 117w19'48 7:49:19
Lockwood 27 35N56'39 121w04'49 8:04:19
Locust 21 37N54 122w32 8:10:08
Lodge Pole 54 36N34 118w46 7:55:04
Lodi 39 38N07'49 121w16'17 8:05:05
Lodi Junction 39 38N07'42 121w14'32 8:04:58
Lodi Rural 39 38N09 121w18 8:05:12
Lodoga 6 39N18'07 122w29'17 8:09:57
Loftus 45 40N54 122w23 8:09:32
Logan 35 36N54'25 121w37'50 8:06:31
Logandale 11 39N26'14 122w11'27 8:08:46
Loganville 46 39N34'05 120w39'58 8:02:40
Log Landing 25 41N57'48 120w29'46 8:01:59
Lois 54 36N01'07 119w01'36 7:56:06
Lokern 15 35N24'00 119w32'42 7:58:11
Lokoya 28 38N22'24 122w25'36 8:09:42
Loleta 12 40N38'28 124w13'27 8:16:54
Loma 19 33N46 118w08 7:52:32
Loma 54 36N15'28 119w17'11 7:57:09
Loma Linda 36 34N02'54 117w15'37 7:49:02
Loma Mar 41 37N16'16 122w18'27 8:09:14
Loma Portal 37 32N44'38 117w13'05 7:48:52
Loma Rica 58 39N18'43 121w25'00 8:05:40
Lomas Santa Fe 37 32N59 117w16 7:49:04
Loma Verde 21 38N06 122w34 8:10:16
Lombard 28 38N11'27 122w15'18 8:09:01
Lomita 19 33N47'32 118w18'51 7:53:15
Lomita Park 41 37N37'00 122w24'12 8:09:37
Lomo 4 40N02'19 121w36'54 8:06:28
Lomo 51 39N13'15 121w38'26 8:06:34
Lompico 44 37N06'20 122w03'06 8:08:12
Lompoc 42 34N38'21 120w27'25 8:01:50
Lompoc Landing (Site) 42 34N43'12 120w36'25 8:02:26
Lompoc Valley 42 34N40 120w24 8:01:36
London 54 36N28'34 119w26'32 7:57:46
Lone Pine 14 36N36'22 118w03'43 7:52:15
Lone Pine Indian Reservation 14 36N36 118w04 7:52:16
Lone Star 10 36N42'02 119w40'49 7:58:43
Lone Star 11 39N42'34 122w48'29 8:11:14
Lone Star Junction 12 40N37'58 123w52'34 8:15:30
Lone Wolf Colony 36 34N28'14 117w09'18 7:48:37
Long Barn 55 38N05'35 120w08'00 8:00:32
Long Beach 19 33N46'01 118w11'18 7:52:45
Long Beach Naval Shipyard 19 33N49 118w10 7:52:40
Longvale 23 39N33'19 123w25'43 8:13:43
Longview 19 34N30 117w55 7:51:40
Longville 32 40N08'52 121w14'37 8:04:58
Lonoak 27 36N16'39 120w56'31 8:03:46
Lonoke 43 37N01'33 121w34'37 8:06:18
Lonsmith 15 35N20'25 118w55'21 7:55:41
Lookout 25 41N12'29 121w09'15 8:04:37
Lookout Junction 25 41N15'31 121w14'01 8:04:56
Loomis 31 38N49'17 121w11'31 8:04:46
Loomis Corners 45 40N35'18 122w18'17 8:09:13
Loop 19 33N56 118w11 7:52:44
Loope 2 38N39'55 119w41'42 7:58:47
Loraine 15 35N18'17 118w26'09 7:53:45
Loree Estates 43 37N19 122w02 8:08:08

Place	Latitude	Longitude	Time
Lorenzo Station 1	37N41'33	122w07'44	8:08:31
Lort 54	36N20'34	119w09'12	7:56:37
Los Alamitos 30	33N48'11	118w04'18	7:52:17
Los Alamitos Junction 30	33N48'21	117w59'54	7:52:00
Los Alamos 42	34N44'40	120w16'38	8:01:07
Los Altos 19	33N47'38	118w07'28	7:52:30
Los Altos 43	37N23'07	122w06'47	8:08:27
Los Altos Hills 43	37N22'47	122w08'11	8:08:33
Los Angeles 19	34N03'08	118w14'34	7:52:58
Los Banos 24	37N03'30	120w50'56	8:03:24
Los Berros 40	35N07	120w35	8:02:20
Los Coyotes Indian Res 37	33N18	116w31	7:46:04
Los Deltos 10	36N51	120w27	8:01:48
Los Feliz 19	34N06	118w18	7:53:12
Los Gatos 43	37N13'36	121w58'25	8:07:54
Los Medanos 7	38N00'44	121w51'01	8:07:24
Los Molinos 52	40N01'17	122w05'57	8:08:24
Los Nietos 19	33N58'06	118w04'11	7:52:17
Los Nietos Junction 19	33N57'41	118w04'10	7:52:17
Los Olivos 42	34N40'04	120w06'50	8:00:27
Los Osos 40	35N18'40	120w49'53	8:03:20
Los Padres 56	34N41	119w14	7:56:56
Los Posas Park 56	34N14	119w02	7:56:08
Los Ranchitos 21	38N01	122w33	8:10:12
Los Serranos 36	33N58'22	117w42'26	7:50:50
Lost City 5	38N05'12	120w44'55	8:03:00
Los Terrentos 37	32N50'05	116w37'16	7:46:29
Lost Hills 15	35N36'59	119w41'36	7:58:46
Lost Lake 33	33N37	114w35	7:38:20
Los Trancos Woods 41	37N20'58	122w11'54	8:08:48
Los Tules 37	33N17'00	116w37'13	7:46:29
Lotus 9	38N48'06	120w54'27	8:03:38
Lovdal 57	38N36'01	121w33'05	8:06:12
Lovelock 4	39N53'29	121w34'36	8:06:18
Lowell 28	38N10'27	122w15'08	8:09:01
Lower Crossing (Site) 47	41N55'41	122w09'31	8:08:38
Lower Forni 9	38N48'11	120w13'41	8:00:55
Lower Lake 17	38N54'38	122w36'33	8:10:26
Lower Town 26	38N22'03	119w07'08	7:56:29
Lower Trinity 53	40N49	123w26	8:13:44
Lowes Corner 54	36N05'40	119w13'52	7:56:55
Lowrey 52	40N00'50	122w33'08	8:10:13
Loyalton 46	39N40'35	120w14'24	8:00:58
Loyola 43	37N22	122w06	8:08:24
Loyola Corners 43	37N21'08	122w05'06	8:08:20
Lucas Valley 21	38N01	122w33	8:10:12
Lucca 54	36N14'43	119w05'20	7:56:21
Lucerne 16	36N22'51	119w39'48	7:58:39
Lucerne 17	39N05'25	122w47'43	8:11:11
Lucerne Valley 36	34N26'38	116w58'01	7:47:52
Lucia 27	36N01'15	121w32'58	8:06:12
Ludlow 36	34N43'16	116w09'33	7:44:38
Lugo 19	34N01	118w12	7:52:48
Lugo 36	34N22'02	117w20'29	7:49:22
Lumer 54	36N02'15	118w59'25	7:55:58
Lumpkin 4	39N36'36	121w12'28	8:04:50
Lundy 26	38N01'39	119w14'26	7:56:58
Lushmeadows Mountain Estates 22	37N29	119w58	7:59:52
Luther Burbank 49	38N27	122w42	8:10:48
Luzon 7	38N00'52	122w15'01	8:09:00
Lynwood 19	33N55'49	118w12'38	7:52:51
Lynwood Gardens 19	33N54'37	118w11'28	7:52:46
Lynwood Hills 37	32N38'43	117w03'03	7:48:12
Lyons Crossing 13	32N43'02	115w36'12	7:42:25
Lyonsville 52	40N18'34	121w44'13	8:06:57
Lyoth 39	37N42'57	121w22'50	8:05:31
Lytle Creek 36	34N15'33	117w29'57	7:50:00
Lytton 49	38N39'34	122w52'14	8:11:29
Mabie 32	39N47'37	120w31'13	8:02:05
Macdoel 47	41N49'37	122w00'15	8:08:01
Maclay 19	34N17	118w27	7:53:48
Macomber Palms 33	33N47'55	116w15'16	7:45:01
Madeline 18	41N03'04	120w28'28	8:01:54
Madeline Plains 18	40N52	120w22	8:01:28
Madera 20	36N57'41	120w03'35	8:00:14
Madera Acres 20	36N58	120w04	8:00:16
Madera Rural 20	36N59	120w05	8:00:20
Madera West 20	36N54	120w21	8:01:24
Madison 57	38N40'46	121w58'02	8:07:52
Madonna Road Plaza 40	35N18	120w45	8:03:00
Mad River 53	40N18	123w26	8:13:44
Madrone 43	37N09'02	121w40'14	8:06:41
Magalia 4	39N48'44	121w34'38	8:06:19
Magnolia 13	32N59	115w32	7:42:08
Magnolia 54	36N01'22	118w59'39	7:55:59
Magnolia Avenue 33	33N57'26	117w25'03	7:49:40
Magnolia Center 33	33N57	117w23	7:49:32
Magnolia Park 19	34N10'04	118w20'47	7:53:23
Magra 31	39N08'57	120w53'44	8:03:35
Magunden 15	35N21'54	118w56'02	7:55:44
Mahou Riviera 19	34N00'48	118w48'20	7:55:13
Maine Prairie 48	38N18'29	121w45'28	8:07:02
Majors 44	36N58'57	122w08'32	8:08:34
Malaga 10	36N41'01	119w43'58	7:58:56
Malby Crossing 34	38N36'48	121w04'12	8:04:17
Malibu 19	34N02	118w41	7:54:44
Malibu Beach 19	34N02	118w41	7:54:44
Malibu Bowl 19	34N03'40	118w44'22	7:54:57
Malibu Canyon Homes 19	34N08	118w39	7:54:36
Malibu Hills 19	34N02'51	118w44'36	7:54:58
Malibu Junction 19	34N08'36	118w45'22	7:55:01
Malibu Vista 19	34N02'52	118w46'24	7:55:06
Mallagh Landing 40	35N10'27	120w42'56	8:02:52
Malott 7	37N55	122w18	8:09:12
Maltby 7	38N00'54	122w04'09	8:08:17
Maltha 15	35N25'17	118w59'47	7:55:59
Mammoth 25	41N43'50	121w21'14	8:05:25
Mammoth Lakes 26	37N38'55	118w58'16	7:55:53
Manchester 23	38N58'13	123w41'13	8:14:45
Manhattan Beach 19	33N53'05	118w24'36	7:53:38
Manila 12	40N51'07	124w09'40	8:16:39
Manix 36	34N58'55	116w35'36	7:46:22
Mankas Corner 48	38N17'11	122w06'21	8:08:25
Manlove 34	38N33'15	121w22'16	8:05:29
Manly Fall 14	35N56'15	117w11'07	7:48:44
Manor 21	37N59'27	122w35'23	8:10:22
Manteca 39	37N47'51	121w12'54	8:04:52
Manteca Junction 39	37N51'49	121w13'40	8:04:55
Manton 52	40N26'07	121w52'08	8:07:29
Manuel Mill 5	38N15'40	120w21'36	8:01:26
Manzana 49	38N26'42	122w52'15	8:11:29
Manzanar 14	36N44'24	118w04'47	7:52:19
Manzanita 4	39N22	121w42	8:06:48
Manzanita 21	37N52'54	122w30'59	8:10:04
Manzanita 37	32N40'08	116w17'20	7:45:09
Manzanita Indian Reservation 37	32N44	116w18	7:45:12
Manzanita Lake 45	40N32'08	121w33'35	8:06:14
Maple Creek 12	40N45'45	123w52'05	8:15:28
Maple Grove 12	40N28'09	123w49'57	8:15:20
Maravilla Park 19	34N01	118w09	7:52:36
Marble Place 23	39N27'30	123w34'17	8:14:17
Marcel 15	35N11'25	118w30'59	7:54:04
Marcelina 19	33N50	118w19	7:53:16
March 33	33N54	117w16	7:49:04
March Air Force Base 33	33N54	117w15	7:49:00
Marchant 51	38N49'23	121w40'44	8:06:43
March Field 33	33N54'00	117w15'15	7:49:01
Marconi 21	38N08'38	122w52'38	8:11:31
Maredith Mill 46	39N38'23	120w52'52	8:03:31
Mare Island 48	38N06	122w16	8:09:04
Mariani Mall 43	37N19	122w02	8:08:08
Marian Place 52	40N18'36	121w49'13	8:07:17
Maricopa 15	35N03'32	119w24'00	7:57:36
Marigold 36	34N04'40	117w14'26	7:48:58
Marina 27	36N41'04	121w48'04	8:07:12
Marina 38	37N48	122w26	8:09:44
Marina Del Rey 19	33N58	118w27	7:53:48
Marina District 38	37N48'11	122w26'11	8:09:45
Marin City 21	37N52'07	122w30'29	8:10:02
Marin Country Club Estates 21	38N06	122w34	8:10:16
Marine Corps Base 36	34N08	116w04	7:44:16
Marine Corps Recruit Depot 37	32N45	117w09	7:48:36
Marine Corps Supply Center 36	34N58	116w55	7:47:40
Mariner 30	33N46	118w05	7:52:20
Marinwood 21	38N02	122w32	8:10:08
Mariposa 22	37N29'06	119w57'55	7:59:52
Market 19	34N02	118w15	7:53:00
Markleeville 2	38N41'42	119w46'45	7:59:07
Marks Place 23	39N42'12	123w09'24	8:12:38
Mark West 49	38N27	122w42	8:10:48
Mark West Springs 49	38N32'57	122w43'09	8:10:53
Marlboro 30	33N48'45	117w51'29	7:51:26
Marloma 19	33N46	118w21	7:53:24
Marne 19	34N00'20	117w54'20	7:51:37
Marshall 21	38N09'38	122w53'35	8:11:34
Marshall Junction 10	37N00'50	119w34'05	7:58:16
Marshall Station 10	36N49	119w43	7:58:52
Marsh Creek Springs 7	37N53'34	121w51'10	8:07:25
Marsh Mill 29	39N26'40	120w42'09	8:02:49
Martell 3	38N22'01	120w47'42	8:03:11
Martinez 7	38N01'10	122w07'59	8:08:32
Martinez 33	33N33'46	116w09'08	7:44:37
Martinez 55	38N01'24	120w22'43	8:01:31
Martinez Place 40	35N17'17	120w09'54	8:00:40
Martins 19	34N33'58	118w39'32	7:54:38
Martins Beach 41	37N22'30	122w24'25	8:09:38
Martinus Corner 27	35N56'24	121w07'05	8:04:28
Mart of Montebello 19	34N01	118w07	7:52:28
Mar Vista 19	34N00'17	118w25'48	7:53:43
Mary Ellen Place 52	40N07'12	122w37'52	8:10:31
Marysville 58	39N08'45	121w35'25	8:06:22
Mascorini Place 27	36N21'22	121w31'22	8:06:05
Massack 32	39N55'34	120w50'12	8:03:21
Matchin 54	36N19'31	119w07'45	7:56:31
Mather 34	38N34	121w21	8:05:24
Mather 55	37N52'56	119w51'17	7:59:25
Mather Air Force Base 34	38N33	121w17	8:05:08
Mather Field 34	38N34'00	121w17'45	8:05:11
Mather Heights 34	38N33	121w17	8:05:08
Matheson 45	40N39'47	122w27'36	8:09:50
Mathews Mill 10	37N07'24	119w22'19	7:57:29
Matilija Springs 56	34N29'00	119w18'16	7:57:13
Mattei 10	36N42'01	119w41'27	7:58:46
Maxwell 6	39N16'35	122w11'25	8:08:46
May 33	33N53'42	117w29'24	7:49:58
Mayaro 4	39N49'27	121w25'16	8:05:41
Mayfair 15	35N20'11	118w54'48	7:55:39
Mayflower Village 19	34N08	118w00	7:52:00
Mayhew 34	38N33'55	121w20'59	8:05:24
Maywood 19	33N59'12	118w11'04	7:52:44
McArthur 25	41N19'54	120w32'11	8:02:09
McArthur 45	41N03'01	121w23'53	8:05:36
McAvoy 7	38N02'19	121w57'33	8:07:50
McCann 12	40N19'25	123w50'06	8:15:20
McClellan Air Force Base 34	38N40	121w23	8:05:32
McClellan Place 53	40N29'14	123w25'08	8:13:41
McCloud 47	41N15'21	122w08'18	8:08:33
McClure Place 23	39N47'34	123w02'03	8:12:08
McClure Place 52	40N16'03	121w49'27	8:07:18
McColl 45	40N43'38	122w19'43	8:09:19
McConnel 34	38N21'45	121w20'45	8:05:23
McConnel Place 9	38N47'49	120w26'49	8:01:47
McCulloh 31	38N57'16	120w31'30	8:02:06
McFarland 15	35N40'41	119w13'42	7:56:55
McGill 49	38N11'55	122w26'08	8:09:45
McHenry 50	37N42'27	121w00'11	8:04:01
McIntosh Landing (Site) 11	39N46'33	122w01'47	8:08:07
McKay 5	38N14'49	120w18'26	8:01:14
McKay 40	35N47'01	120w43'27	8:02:54
McKenzie Place 52	40N17'41	121w54'03	8:07:36
McKeon 31	38N54	121w04	8:04:16
McKinleyville 12	40N56'48	124w05'58	8:16:24
McKittrick 15	35N18'20	119w37'18	7:58:29
McKnight Acres 28	38N07	122w14	8:08:56
McLane 10	36N46	119w45	7:59:00
McLaren 38	37N43	122w25	8:09:40
McManus 9	38N47'57	120w31'59	8:02:08
McMillan Manor 56	34N12	119w10	7:56:40
McNear 49	38N13'43	122w36'47	8:10:27
McNears Beach 21	37N59'36	122w27'08	8:09:49
McPherson 30	33N47'16	117w49'34	7:51:18
Meadow Brook 9	38N51'34	120w49'59	8:03:20
Meadowbrook 33	33N47	117w14	7:48:56
Meadowbrook Woods 36	34N14'04	117w12'05	7:48:48
Meadow Lake Park 29	39N20	120w12	8:00:48
Meadow Lakes 10	37N04'49	119w25'47	7:57:43
Meadowsweet 21	37N55'23	122w30'30	8:10:02
Meadow Valley 32	39N55'47	121w03'35	8:04:14
Meadow Vista 31	39N00'04	121w01'15	8:04:05
Mead Valley 33	33N47	117w14	7:48:56
Meares 25	41N37'15	121w11'52	8:04:47
Mecca 33	33N34'18	116w04'35	7:44:18
Medicine Lake Lodge 47	41N57	121w28	8:05:52
Meeks Bay 9	39N02'04	120w07'23	8:00:30
Meiners Oak 56	34N26'49	119w16'42	7:57:07
Meinert 7	37N56'39	122w01'35	8:08:06
Meins Landing 48	38N08'23	121w54'22	8:07:37
Meiss 9	38N38'18	120w20'07	8:01:20
Melbourne 23	39N17'00	123w38'59	8:14:36
Melita 49	38N27'24	122w38'09	8:10:33
Mello 58	39N12'24	121w33'44	8:06:15
Melody Oaks Trailer Park 3	38N21	120w46	8:03:04
Meloland 13	32N48'11	115w26'48	7:41:47
Melones 5	38N00'45	120w29'51	8:01:59
Melsons Corner 9	38N36'37	120w42'13	8:02:49
Melvin 10	36N48'31	119w42'00	7:58:48
Mendocino 23	39N18'28	123w47'54	8:15:12
Mendota 10	36N45'13	120w22'50	8:01:31
Menifee 33	33N43'42	117w08'44	7:48:35
Menlo Baths 25	41N15'57	120w04'58	8:00:20
Menlo Park 41	37N27'14	122w10'52	8:08:43
Mentone 36	34N04'12	117w08'01	7:48:32
Merazo 28	38N13'03	122w22'19	8:09:29
Merced 24	37N18'08	120w28'55	8:01:56
Merced Falls 24	37N31'23	120w19'53	8:01:20
Mercey Hot Springs 10	36N42'15	120w51'33	8:03:26
Mercuryville 49	38N46'34	122w49'15	8:11:17
Meridian 6	39N08'36	121w54'48	8:07:39
Meridian 15	35N06'27	118w54'48	7:55:39
Meridian 43	37N19'23	121w58'07	8:07:52
Merlin 32	39N53'18	121w21'57	8:05:28
Merrill 36	34N06	117w28	7:49:52
Merrills Landing 4	39N52'42	122w02'19	8:08:09
Merrimac 4	39N45'58	121w18'23	8:05:14
Merritt 57	38N36'51	121w45'34	8:07:02
Merritt-Peck Colonies 10	36N36	119w27	7:57:48
Merryman 54	36N19'33	119w06'16	7:56:25
Mesa Camp 26	37N30'28	118w34'21	7:54:17
Mesa Center 30	33N39	117w55	7:51:40
Mesa Grande 37	33N10'49	116w46'06	7:47:04
Mesa Verde 33	33N37	114w35	7:38:20
Mesaville 33	33N41'39	114w38'57	7:38:36
Mesquite 13	33N01'17	115w06'27	7:40:26
Mesquite Oasis 37	32N55'11	116w13'04	7:44:52
Metcalf Grove 8	41N45'59	124w07'44	8:16:31
Metro Main 34	38N33	121w28	8:05:52
Metropolitan 12	40N35	124w08	8:16:32
Metropolitan 19	34N05	118w22	7:53:28
Mettler 15	35N03'50	118w58'09	7:55:53
Metz 27	36N21'18	121w12'38	8:04:51
Mevers 9	38N51'22	120w00'43	8:00:03
Mexican Colony 15	35N28'08	119w16'04	7:57:04
Meyers 39	37N45'31	121w00'06	8:04:00
Meyers Place 11	39N37'09	122w41'28	8:10:46
Meyers Place 52	40N16'01	121w55'10	8:07:41
Michigan Bluff 31	39N02'35	120w44'25	8:02:58
Michillinda 19	34N09	118w05	7:52:20
Midas 31	39N13'00	120w45'24	8:03:02
Mid City 39	37N57	121w17	8:05:08
Midco 42	34N56'11	120w27'42	8:01:51
Middlefield Road 41	37N28	122w14	8:08:56
Middle River 39	37N56	121w26	8:05:44
Middleton 28	38N12'24	122w15'43	8:09:03
Middletown 17	38N45'09	122w36'50	8:10:27

Midlake 17	39N09	123W12	8:12:48
Midland 33	33N51'40	114W48'05	7:39:12
Midoil 15	35N09'30	119W31'18	7:58:05
Midpines 22	37N32'40	119W55'10	7:59:41
Midtown 4	39N44	121W50	8:07:20
Midtown Center 19	34N03	118W20	7:53:20
Midvalley 54	36N17'53	119W23'14	7:57:33
Midway 6	37N42'53	121W33'25	8:06:14
Midway 36	35N01'58	116W28'14	7:45:53
Midway 45	40N30'08	121W57'55	8:07:52
Midway City 30	33N44'41	117W59'18	7:51:57
Midway Wells 13	33N00	115W04	7:40:16
Mikon 57	38N35'15	121W32'14	8:06:09
Mile High 19	34N24'46	117W46'23	7:51:06
Miles 40	35N11'08	120W42'08	8:02:49
Miley 10	36N37'20	119W32'46	7:58:11
Milford 18	40N10'17	120W22'17	8:01:29
Millbrae 41	37N35'55	122W23'10	8:09:33
Millbrae Meadows 41	37N36'08	122W24'58	8:09:40
Mill City 26	37N37'22	118W59'29	7:55:58
Mill Creek 52	40N19'35	121W31'18	8:06:05
Mill Creek Park 36	34N05	117W08	7:48:32
Miller 43	36N57'26	121W32'37	8:06:10
Miller Crossing 20	37N30'38	119W11'59	7:56:48
Miller Place 53	40N27'57	123W25'42	8:13:43
Millers Corners 20	36N58	120W04	8:00:16
Millers Landing 6	38N57'24	121W50'19	8:07:21
Millers Ranch 27	36N15'07	121W25'44	8:05:43
Millersville 15	35N18'14	118W27'25	7:53:50
Millerton 21	38N06'33	122W50'40	8:11:23
Milligan 36	34N16'36	115W10'10	7:40:41
Mills 38	37N47	122W25	8:09:40
Mills College 1	37N47	122W11	8:08:44
Millsdale 41	37N35	122W22	8:09:28
Mills Landing 19	33N22'06	118W28'53	7:53:56
Mills Orchard 11	39N44'16	122W03'19	8:08:13
Mills Orchards 6	39N16'39	122W16'26	8:09:06
Millspaugh 14	36N02'46	117W27'36	7:49:50
Millux 15	35N10'49	119W11'52	7:56:47
Mill Valley 21	37N54'22	122W32'38	8:10:11
Millville 45	40N32'58	122W10'27	8:08:42
Milo 54	36N13'13	118W48'59	7:55:16
Milpas 42	34N26	119W41	7:58:44
Milpitas 43	37N25'42	121W54'20	8:07:37
Milton 5	38N01'55	120W51'04	8:03:24
Mina 23	39N57'54	123W21'26	8:13:26
Mineral 52	40N20'52	121W35'38	8:06:23
Mineral King 54	36N27'03	118W35'38	7:54:23
Mineral Slide 4	39N47'07	121W37'08	8:06:29
Minkler 10	36N43'26	119W27'26	7:57:50
Minneola 36	34N50'46	116W46'34	7:47:06
Minnesota 45	40N39'44	122W29'16	8:09:57
Minnesota Flat 46	39N26'58	120W49'48	8:03:19
Mint Canyon 19	34N25'45	118W26'29	7:53:46
Minter Village 15	35N30'13	119W10'55	7:56:44
Minturn 20	37N08'23	120W16'24	8:01:06
Mirabel Heights 49	38N29'26	122W53'22	8:11:33
Mirabel Park 49	38N29'36	122W53'41	8:11:35
Miracle Hot Springs 15	35N34'33	118W32'01	7:54:08
Miracle Manor 15	35N08	117W59	7:51:56
Mirador 54	36N10'01	119W02'06	7:56:08
Miraleste 19	33N45'08	118W19'31	7:53:18
Mira Loma 33	33N59'33	117W30'56	7:50:04
Miramar 37	32N52'36	117W10'25	7:48:42
Miramar 41	37N29'35	122W27'20	8:09:49
Mira Mesa 37	32N54'56	117W08'35	7:48:34
Miramonte 10	36N41'33	119W03'05	7:56:12
Mira Monte 56	34N26'01	119W17'03	7:57:08
Miranda 12	40N14'05	123W49'21	8:15:17
Mira Vista 7	37N57	122W19	8:09:16
Missile View 42	34N54	120W26	8:01:44
Mission 43	37N21	121W59	8:07:56
Mission Annex 38	37N46	122W26	8:09:44
Mission Bay 37	32N47	117W14	7:48:56
Mission Beach 37	32N46'57	117W15'05	7:49:00
Mission Canyon 42	34N27	119W43	7:58:52
Mission District 38	37N45'36	122W25'05	8:09:40
Mission Highlands 49	38N19'11	122W27'24	8:09:50
Mission Hills 19	34N15'26	118W27'58	7:53:52
Mission Hills 37	32N45'10	117W11'10	7:48:45
Mission Hills 42	34N42	120W29	8:01:56
Mission Junction 19	34N03'45	118W13'36	7:52:54
Mission Rafael 21	37N59	122W32	8:10:08
Mission San Jose 1	37N32	121W58	8:07:52
Mission San Jose District 1	37N31'59	121W55'09	8:07:41
Mission Soledad 27	36N24'17	121W21'18	8:05:25
Mission Valley 37	32N46	117W09	7:48:36
Mission Viejo 30	33N36'00	117W40'16	7:50:41
Mission Village 37	32N48	117W08	7:48:32
Misson Springs 44	37N03'59	122W01'53	8:08:08
Missouri Triangle 15	35N26'20	119W41'21	7:58:45
Mitchell Corner 54	36N19'36	119W12'19	7:56:49
Mitchell Mill 5	38N23	120W31	8:02:04
Mitchell Place 52	39N57'33	122W43'01	8:10:52
Mitchells Corner 15	35N13'25	118W50'29	7:55:22
Mi-Wuk Village 55	38N03'57	120W11'02	8:00:44
Moccasin 32	40N04'37	120W56'07	8:03:44
Moccasin 55	37N48'39	120W17'56	8:01:12
Mock 14	36N32'37	117W55'57	7:51:44
Mococo 7	38N01'32	122W06'54	8:08:28
Modesto 50	37N38'21	120W59'45	8:03:59
Modjeska 30	33N42'33	117W37'31	7:50:30
Moffett Field 43	37N25	122W03	8:08:12
Mohawk 32	39N46'44	120W38'04	8:02:32
Mojave 15	35N03'09	118W10'23	7:52:42
Mojave Heights 36	34N34'07	117W19'29	7:49:18
Mojave Valley 36	34N53	117W07	7:48:28
Mokelumne City 39	38N15'11	121W26'17	8:05:45
Mokelumne Hill 5	38N18'02	120W42'19	8:02:49
Molena 48	38N07'33	121W52'32	8:07:30
Molino 49	38N25'33	122W50'49	8:11:23
Molus 27	36N28'05	121W23'35	8:05:34
Monaco 19	33N52'23	118W21'30	7:53:26
Monada 39	38N02'13	121W16'38	8:05:07
Monarch Bay 30	33N31	117W43	7:50:52
Mona Vista 55	37N59	120W23	8:01:32
Monmouth 10	36N33'58	119W44'21	7:58:57
Mono Crossing 10	37N20'31	119W03'25	7:56:14
Mono Hot Springs 10	37N19'36	119W01'00	7:56:04
Monola 14	37N08'37	118W14'34	7:52:58
Mono Lake (P O) 26	37N59'26	119W08'37	7:56:34
Monolith 15	35N07'14	118W22'19	7:53:29
Mono Mills 26	37N53'15	118W57'30	7:55:50
Mono Village 26	38N08'59	119W22'34	7:57:30
Mono Vista 55	37N59'52	120W16'08	8:01:05
Monroe 49	38N27'10	122W45'01	8:11:00
Monrovia 19	34N08'53	117W59'53	7:52:00
Mons 33	33N55'14	116W44'47	7:46:59
Monsanto 7	38N01'34	122W03'16	8:08:13
Monson 54	36N29'32	119W20'08	7:57:21
Montague 47	41N43'42	122W31'36	8:10:06
Montair 7	37N50	122W00	8:08:00
Montalvin Manor 7	37N58	122W20	8:09:20
Montalvo 56	34N15'14	119W12'10	7:56:49
Montana 19	34N02	118W30	7:54:00
Montara 41	37N32'32	122W30'54	8:10:04
Monta Vista 43	37N19'22	122W03'25	8:08:14
Montclair 36	34N03	117W42	7:50:48
Montclair Plaza 36	34N05	117W41	7:50:44
Montebello 19	34N00'34	118W06'16	7:52:25
Montebello Gardens 19	33N59	118W05	7:52:20
Montecito 42	34N26'12	119W37'52	7:58:31
Monte Nido 19	34N04'51	118W41'10	7:54:45
Monterey 27	36N36'01	121W53'37	8:07:34
Monterey Park 19	34N03'45	118W07'19	7:52:29
Monterey Peninsula 27	36N36	121W56	8:07:44
Monte Rio 49	38N27'56	123W00'28	8:12:02
Monte Rosa 49	38N30'14	123W01'34	8:12:06
Montesano 49	38N29'14	123W00'58	8:12:04
Monte Sereno 43	37N14'11	121W59'29	8:07:58
Monte Toyon 44	36N59'47	121W53'42	8:07:35
Monte Vista 31	39N11'12	120W49'54	8:03:20
Montezuma 48	38N10'03	121W53'16	8:07:33
Montezuma 55	37N54'17	120W27'09	8:01:49
Montgomery 23	39N14'01	123W23'19	8:13:33
Montgomery City 26	37N49'43	118W25'48	7:53:43
Montgomery Creek 45	40N50'30	121W55'21	8:07:41
Montgomery Field 37	32N49	117W08	7:48:32
Montgomery Village 49	38N26'40	122W41'15	8:10:45
Montpehier 50	37N32'42	120W42'18	8:02:49
Montrose 19	34N12'23	118W13'24	7:52:54
Moody 30	33N49	118W02	7:52:08
Mooney Flat 29	39N12'56	121W16'24	8:05:06
Moonridge 36	34N14'07	116W51'17	7:47:25
Moonstone 12	41N01'49	124W06'30	8:16:26
Moore 36	35N23'22	115W15'49	7:41:03
Moores Flat 29	39N25'09	120W50'59	8:03:24
Moorpark 56	34N17'08	118W52'52	7:55:31
Moorpark Home Acres 56	34N15'56	118W54'51	7:55:39
Morada 39	38N02	121W15	8:05:00
Moraga 7	37N50'06	122W07'43	8:08:31
Moran 18	40N54'06	120W29'21	8:01:57
Mora Villa 42	34N26	119W42	7:58:48
Moreland Mill 15	35N30'26	118W21'15	7:53:25
Morena 37	32N46'51	117W12'25	7:48:50
Morena Village 37	32N40'46	116W30'15	7:46:01
Moreno 33	33N55'03	117W09'25	7:48:38
Moreno 37	32N52'24	116W55'27	7:47:42
Moreno Valley 33	33N56	117W15	7:49:00
Morettis Junction 37	33N11'59	116W42'31	7:46:50
Morgan Hill 43	37N07'50	121W39'12	8:06:37
Morgans Landing 57	38N19'42	121W34'29	8:06:18
Morgan Springs 52	40N21'44	121W30'36	8:06:02
Mormon 39	37N57'01	121W15'53	8:05:04
Mormon Bar 22	37N27'44	119W56'49	7:59:47
Morningside Park 19	33N57'35	118W19'32	7:53:18
Morongo Indian Reservation 33	33N57	116W48	7:47:12
Morongo Valley 36	34N02'49	116W34'48	7:46:19
Morrison 9	38N42'35	120W19'24	8:01:18
Morristown 46	39N39'09	120W54'13	8:03:37
Morro Bay 40	35N21'57	120W50'56	8:03:24
Morro Palisades 40	35N18	120W45	8:03:00
Morse 35	36N50'16	121W29'32	8:05:58
Mortero Palms 37	32N43'09	116W09'03	7:44:36
Mortmar 33	33N31'18	115W56'06	7:43:44
Moss 13	32N59'52	115W24'25	7:41:38
Moss Beach 41	37N31'39	122W30'44	8:10:03
Mossdale 39	37N47'05	121W18'27	8:05:14
Moss Landing 27	36N48'16	121W47'09	8:07:09
Motion 45	40N40'28	122W27'34	8:09:50
Motor City 9	38N44'02	120W44'22	8:02:57
Mott 47	41N15'36	122W16'28	8:09:06
Mountain Center 33	33N42'16	116W43'26	7:46:54
Mountain Empire 37	32N42	116W28	7:45:52
Mountain Gate 45	40N42'59	122W19'50	8:09:19
Mountain Home Village 36	34N06'02	116W59'54	7:48:00
Mountain House 6	37N45'15	121W34'28	8:06:18
Mountain Mesa 15	35N38'22	118W24'17	7:53:37
Mountain Pass 36	35N28	115W16	7:41:04
Mountain Ranch 5	38N13'42	120W32'23	8:02:10
Mountain Spring 37	32N37	116W11	7:44:44
Mountain Top Junction 36	34N23'25	117W34'31	7:50:18
Mountain View 15	35N21	118W59	7:55:56
Mountain View 36	34N30'23	117W21'28	7:49:26
Mountain View 43	37N23'10	122W04'58	8:08:20
Mountain View Acres 36	34N33	117W21	7:49:24
Mount Aukum 9	38N33	120W44	8:02:56
Mount Baldy 36	34N14	117W40	7:50:40
Mount Bullion 22	37N29	119W58	7:59:52
Mountclef Village 56	34N14'04	118W53'07	7:55:32
Mount Eden 1	37N38'10	122W05'56	8:08:24
Mount Eden Station 1	37N38'09	122W06'47	8:08:27
Mount Hamilton 43	37N21	121W50	8:07:20
Mount Hannah Lodge 17	38N53'16	122W43'46	8:10:55
Mount Hebron 47	41N47'14	122W00'11	8:08:01
Mount Helix 37	32N46	116W59	7:47:56
Mount Hermon 44	37N03'04	122W03'27	8:08:14
Mount Jackson 49	38N30'48	122W54'14	8:11:37
Mount Laguna 37	32N52'20	116W25'03	7:45:40
Mount San Antonio 19	34N00	117W51	7:51:24
Mount Shasta 47	41N18'36	122W18'34	8:09:14
Mount Signal 13	32N40'42	115W38'18	7:42:33
Mount View 7	37N59	122W07	8:08:28
Mount Washington 19	34N05'57	118W13'10	7:52:53
Mount Wilson 19	34N13'35	118W03'55	7:52:16
Mowry Landing 1	37N30'22	122W01'04	8:08:04
Mugginsville 47	41N34'25	122W57'02	8:11:48
Muir 7	37N59'26	122W07'45	8:08:31
Muir 23	39N23'54	123W20'38	8:13:23
Muir Beach 21	38N04	122W48	8:11:12
Muir Woods 21	37N54	122W32	8:10:08
Mulberry 4	39N44	121W49	8:07:16
Mulford Gardens 1	37N42'17	122W10'43	8:08:43
Mulford Landing 1	37N41'44	122W11'24	8:08:46
Mulkey Place 25	41N51'54	120W38'16	8:02:33
Mundo 13	33N16'25	115W34'06	7:42:16
Munyon 13	33N02'26	115W24'51	7:41:39
Murdock Crossing (Ford) 32	40N07'05	120W32'02	8:02:08
Murietta Farm 10	36N39'06	120W27'30	8:01:50
Murphy Crossing 27	36N54'20	121W40'31	8:06:42
Murphy Place 53	40N17'36	123W13'13	8:12:53
Murphys 5	38N08'15	120W27'31	8:01:50
Murray 16	36N05'39	120W00'09	8:00:01
Murray Park 21	37N56'40	122W33'09	8:10:13
Murrieta 33	33N33'14	117W12'47	7:48:51
Murrieta Hot Springs 33	33N33'38	117W09'26	7:48:38
Muscatel 10	36N47'34	119W51'30	7:59:26
Muscoy 36	34N09'15	117W20'36	7:49:22
Myers Flat 12	40N15'59	123W52'09	8:15:29
Myoma 33	33N45'05	116W16'39	7:45:07
Myricks Corner 15	35N30'59	119W17'24	7:57:10
Myrtletowne 12	40N47	124W10	8:16:40
Mystic 29	39N26'15	120W01'08	8:00:05
Nacimiento 27	35N48'33	120W44'26	8:02:58
Nadeau 19	33N57'56	118W14'32	7:52:58
Nanceville 54	36N04'10	119W04'20	7:56:17
Napa 28	38N17'50	122W17'04	8:09:08
Napa Junction 28	38N11'15	122W14'59	8:09:00
Napa Soda Springs 28	38N23'27	122W16'42	8:09:07
Naples 19	33N45'16	118W07'22	7:52:29
Naples 42	34N26'27	119W57'29	7:59:50
Naranjo 54	36N24'17	119W03'42	7:56:15
Narlon 42	34N48'38	120W35'52	8:02:23
Narod 36	34N03'29	117W41'01	7:50:44
Nashmead 23	39N49'21	123W24'49	8:13:39
Nashua 27	36N44'29	121W45'53	8:07:04
Nashville 9	38N34'44	120W50'39	8:03:23
National City 37	32N40'41	117W05'54	7:48:24
Natividad 27	36N43'58	121W35'44	8:06:23
Natoma 34	38N39'18	121W10'49	8:04:43
Naud Junction 19	34N03'38	118W14'07	7:52:56
Navajo 37	32N47	117W02	7:48:08
Naval 37	32N45	117W09	7:48:36
Naval 56	34N10	119W12	7:56:48
Naval Air Station 1	37N47	122W16	8:09:04
Naval Air Station 16	36N17	119W51	7:59:24
Naval Hospital 1	37N48	122W13	8:08:52
Naval Hospital 37	32N45	117W09	7:48:36
Naval Supply Center 1	37N48	122W13	8:08:52
Naval Training Center 37	32N45	117W09	7:48:36
Navarro 23	39N09'07	123W32'27	8:14:10
Navelencia 10	36N41'00	119W23'05	7:57:32
Navy Landing 19	33N45'47	118W11'55	7:52:48
Neal 43	37N24'49	122W08'34	8:08:34
Nealeys Corner 36	34N11'14	117W26'18	7:49:45
Nebelhorn 9	38N48'41	120W02'00	8:00:08
Nebo 36	34N52'48	116W57'24	7:47:50

Need 34 38N18'08 121w19'25 8:05:18
Needles 36 34N50'53 114w36'48 7:38:27
Neenach 19 34N40 118w11 7:52:44
Nelson 4 39N33'08 121w45'52 8:07:03
Nelsons Crossing 4 39N39'50 121w12'53 8:04:52
Neponset 27 36N43'43 121w47'00 8:07:08
Nervo 49 38N41'16 122w52'45 8:11:31
Nestor 37 32N34'33 117w05'00 7:48:20
Neufeld 15 35N37'10 119w19'54 7:57:20
Nevada 29 39N19 120w59 8:03:56
Nevada 36 34N03'56 117w13'02 7:48:52
Nevada City 29 39N15'42 121w00'54 8:04:04
Nevin 19 34N00'51 118w14'43 7:52:59
New Almaden 43 37N10'34 121w49'11 8:07:17
Newark 1 37N31'47 122w02'21 8:08:09
New Auberry 10 37N05'36 119w29'46 7:57:59
Newberry Springs 36 34N49'37 116w41'13 7:46:45
Newburg 12 40N36'02 124w07'28 8:16:30
Newbury Park 56 34N11'03 118w54'35 7:55:38
Newcastle 31 38N52'27 121w07'56 8:04:32
New Chicago 3 38N26'14 120w50'07 8:03:20
New Cuyama 42 34N56'49 119w41'04 7:58:44
New Dunn 36 35N02'58 116w25'31 7:45:42
Newell 25 41N53'18 121w22'16 8:05:29
Newhall 19 34N23'05 118w31'48 7:54:07
Newhall Ranch 19 34N25 118w32 7:54:08
New Hope Landing 39 38N13'41 121w29'23 8:05:58
Newlove 7 37N59'38 121w45'42 8:07:03
Newman 50 37N18'50 121w01'11 8:04:05
Newman Springs 17 39N11'47 122w42'53 8:10:52
New Monterey 27 36N36'53 121w54'04 8:07:36
New Pine Creek 25 41N59'35 120w17'53 8:01:12
Newport 23 39N34'39 123w46'25 8:15:06
Newport Beach 30 33N37'08 117w55'41 7:51:43
Newport Heights 30 33N37'09 117w55'21 7:51:41
Newtown 9 38N42'16 120w40'41 8:02:43
Newtown 29 39N15'10 121w06'08 8:04:25
Newtown 45 40N39'26 122w23'43 8:09:35
Newville 11 39N47'28 122w31'38 8:10:07
Nicasio 21 38N03'42 122w41'51 8:10:47
Nice 17 39N07'24 122w50'50 8:11:23
Nicholls Warm Springs 33 33N36'21 114w43'49 7:38:55
Nichols 7 38N02'29 121w59'13 8:07:57
Nicklin 33 33N56'37 117w00'48 7:48:03
Nicks Cove 21 38N11'59 122w55'12 8:11:41
Nicolaus 51 38N54'12 121w34'36 8:06:18
Nielsburg 31 38N57'26 121w01'56 8:04:08
Nielson Place 53 40N00'25 123w20'36 8:13:22
Nigger Hill 9 38N44 120w48 8:03:12
Nightingale 33 33N35'22 116w27'07 7:45:48
Niguel Terrace 30 33N31 117w43 7:50:52
Niland 13 33N14'24 115w31'05 7:42:04
Niles 1 37N34'44 121w58'36 8:07:54
Nimbus 34 38N37'45 121w12'51 8:04:51
Nimshew 4 39N50'37 121w37'05 8:06:28
Nineth Street Junction 19 34N01'13 118w13'11 7:52:53
Ninetynine Oaks 19 34N28'33 118w36'57 7:54:28
Nipinnawassee 20 37N24'12 119w43'56 7:58:56
Nipomo 40 35N02'34 120w28'30 8:01:54
Nipton 36 35N28'00 115w16'17 7:41:05
Nitro 7 38N00'33 122w21'49 8:09:27
Noel Heights 49 38N29'38 122w57'40 8:11:51
Noe Valley 38 37N45 122w26 8:09:44
Norco 33 33N56 117w33 7:50:12
Nord 4 39N46'47 121w57'22 8:07:49
Norden 29 39N19'05 120w21'18 8:01:25
Normal Heights 37 32N45'48 117w07'19 7:48:29
Norman 11 39N24'29 122w11'27 8:08:46
North Annex 19 34N18 118w26 7:53:44
North Antelope Valley 19 34N42 118w12 7:52:48
North Bay View Park 27 36N37 121w50 8:07:20
North Beach 38 37N48'21 122w24'40 8:09:39
North Belridge 15 34N50 120w32 8:02:08
North Berkeley 1 37N53 122w16 8:09:04
North Bloomfield 29 39N22'06 120w53'54 8:03:36
North Carlsbad 37 33N12 117w20 7:49:20
North City 37 33N03 117w04 7:48:16
North Clairemont 37 32N49'58 117w11'57 7:48:48
North Coastal 12 41N00 124w04 8:16:16
North Columbia 29 39N22'22 120w59'10 8:03:57
Northcrest 8 41N46 124w12 8:16:48
North Cucamonga 36 34N06 117w35 7:50:20
North Dinuba 54 36N34'03 119w23'37 7:57:34
North Downey 19 33N57 118w08 7:52:32
Northeast Modesto 50 37N38 120w59 8:03:56
North Edwards 15 35N01'01 117w50'05 7:51:20
North El Dorado 9 38N48 120w44 8:02:56
North Elsinore 33 33N41'24 117w20'18 7:49:21
North Fair Oaks 41 37N29 122w12 8:08:48
North Fillmore 56 34N24'24 118w55'57 7:55:44
North Fork 20 37N13'47 119w30'31 7:58:02
North Gardena 19 33N53 118w17 7:53:08
North Glendale 19 34N09'38 118w15'49 7:53:03
North Highlands 34 38N41'09 121w22'16 8:05:29
North Hills 19 34N16 118w30 7:54:00
North Hollywood 19 34N10'20 118w22'41 7:53:31
North Inglewood 19 33N58 118w21 7:53:24
North Island 37 32N42 117w14 7:48:56
North Jamul 37 32N43'32 116w52'07 7:47:28
North Landing 26 37N38'07 118w44'37 7:54:58
North Loma Linda 36 34N04 117w16 7:49:04
North Long Beach 19 33N51'36 118w11'05 7:52:44
North Oaks 19 34N25 118w32 7:54:08
North Palm Springs 33 33N55'22 116w32'32 7:46:10
North Park 37 32N44'27 117w07'47 7:48:31
North Pomona 19 34N05'24 117w44'58 7:51:00
North Redondo Beach 19 33N52 118w22 7:53:28
North Richmond 7 37N57'32 122w21'59 8:09:28
Northridge 19 34N13'42 118w32'09 7:54:09
North Sacramento 34 38N36'22 121w27'23 8:05:50
North San Juan 29 39N22'10 121w06'10 8:04:25
North Santa Maria 42 34N57'25 120w26'37 8:01:46
North Seal Beach 30 33N46 118w05 7:52:20
North Shafter 15 35N30'41 119w17'01 7:57:08
North Shore 33 33N34 116w05 7:44:20
North Shore 36 34N16'05 117w11'00 7:48:44
Northspur 23 39N25'22 123w33'03 8:14:12
North Star 58 39N35'12 121w04'33 8:04:18
North Torrance 19 33N52 118w20 7:53:20
North Turlock 50 37N29 120w50 8:03:20
North Valley Plaza 4 39N44 121w50 8:07:20
North Wawona 22 37N32'55 119w38'24 7:58:34
Northwest 21 38N13 122w50 8:11:20
North Whittier 19 34N03 117w59 7:51:56
North Whittier Heights 19 34N00 117w57 7:51:48
Northwood 49 38N28'32 123w00'02 8:12:00
Northwood Heights 49 38N28'47 122w59'54 8:12:00
Northwood Lodge 49 38N28'38 122w59'48 8:11:59
Norton 39 38N04'51 121w14'30 8:04:58
Norton 57 38N35'10 121w58'12 8:07:53
Norton Air Force Base 36 34N06 117w15 7:49:00
Nortonville 7 37N57'28 121w52'46 8:07:31
Norvell 18 40N29'11 121w00'16 8:04:01
Norwalk 19 33N54'08 118w04'51 7:52:19
Norwalk Manor 19 33N54 118w05 7:52:20
Norwood Center 19 34N17 118w27 7:53:48
Notarb 20 37N00'40 120w07'05 8:00:28
Notleys Landing 27 36N23'54 121w54'09 8:07:37
Novato 21 38N06'27 122w34'07 8:10:16
Noyo 23 39N25'42 123w48'08 8:15:13
Nubieber 18 41N05'45 121w10'55 8:04:44
Nuestro 51 39N11'02 121w39'40 8:06:39
Nuevo 33 33N48'05 117w08'42 7:48:35
Nut Tree 48 38N21 121w59 8:07:56
Nyland 56 34N13'32 119w08'03 7:56:32
Nyland Acres 56 34N12 119w10 7:56:40
Oak Bottom 45 40N38 122w33 8:10:12
Oakdale 50 37N46'00 120w50'46 8:03:23
Oak Glen 12 40N16'57 123w44'24 8:14:58
Oak Glen 36 34N02'58 116w56'49 7:47:47
Oak Grove 4 39N25'38 121w36'15 8:06:25
Oak Grove 5 38N07'01 120w53'09 8:03:33
Oak Grove 37 33N23'06 116w47'18 7:47:09
Oak Grove 54 36N27'02 118w47'28 7:55:10
Oakhurst 20 37N19'41 119w38'54 7:58:36
Oak Knoll 19 34N07'28 118w08'06 7:52:32
Oak Knoll 28 38N21'30 122w20'02 8:09:20
Oak Knoll Hills 43 37N19 122w02 8:08:08
Oak Knolls 42 34N54 120w26 8:01:44
Oakland 1 37N48'16 122w16'11 8:09:05
Oakland Recreational Camp 55 37N50 120w14 8:00:56
Oakley 7 37N59'51 121w42'41 8:06:51
Oakmont 49 38N26'27 122w36'12 8:10:25
Oak Park 34 38N33'05 121w28'12 8:05:53
Oak Park 40 35N38'52 120w41'23 8:02:46
Oak Run 45 40N41'07 122w01'25 8:08:06
Oaks 40 35N07'08 120w35'38 8:02:23
Oak Valley 56 34N09 118w48 7:55:12
Oak Valley 58 39N29'55 121w02'13 8:04:09
Oak View 56 34N24'00 119w17'57 7:57:12
Oak Village 56 34N23'32 118w57'45 7:55:51
Oakville 28 38N26'13 122w24'04 8:09:36
Oakwood 19 34N05 118w18 7:53:12
Oasis 33 33N27'57 116w05'53 7:44:24
Oban 19 34N46'28 118w08'50 7:52:35
Obie 45 41N10'11 121w42'49 8:06:51
Obregon 13 32N51'29 114w47'18 7:39:09
O'Brien 45 40N48'44 122w19'23 8:09:18
Occidental 49 38N24'27 122w56'50 8:11:47
Ocean Beach 37 32N44'43 117w15'16 7:49:01
Oceano 40 35N05'56 120w36'41 8:02:27
Ocean Park 19 34N00'08 118w28'58 7:53:56
Ocean Roar 21 38N12'58 122w55'26 8:11:42
Oceanside 37 33N11'45 117w22'43 7:49:31
Ocean View 30 33N42'56 117w59'16 7:51:57
Ocean View 49 38N20 123w03 8:12:12
Ockenden 10 37N05'20 119w19'00 7:57:16
Ocotillo 13 32N44'19 115w59'36 7:43:58
Ocotillo Wells 37 33N08'38 116w07'55 7:44:32
Octol 54 36N07'26 119w19'39 7:57:19
Odd Fellows Park 49 38N30'08 122w56'46 8:11:47
Ogilby 13 32N49'01 114w50'17 7:39:21
Ohm 50 37N37'36 121w16'59 8:05:08
Oil City 15 35N25'35 118w57'34 7:55:50
Oildale 15 35N25'11 119w01'13 7:56:05
Oil Junction 15 35N25'11 119w03'22 7:56:13
Ojai 56 34N26'53 119w14'31 7:56:58
Ojala 56 34N29'04 119w17'54 7:57:12
Olancha 14 36N16'55 118w00'20 7:52:01
Olcott 48 38N16'38 121w49'23 8:07:18
Old Adobe 40 35N44'16 120w41'56 8:02:48
Old Bailey Place 23 39N10'05 123w28'53 8:13:56
Old Bretz Mill 10 37N04'54 119w17'52 7:57:11
Old Dale 36 34N07'21 115w47'40 7:43:11
Old Fellows Park 49 38N30 123w00 8:12:00
Old Forbestown 4 39N31'41 121w16'47 8:05:07
Old Fort Jim 9 38N42'38 120w43'04 8:02:52
Old Fort Tejon 15 34N52'25 118w53'36 7:55:34
Old Gilroy 43 36N59'59 121w31'31 8:06:06
Old Hilltown 27 36N37'53 121w40'06 8:06:40
Old Hopland 23 38N58'33 123w05'59 8:12:24
Old Hulbert Place 25 41N26'18 121w03'06 8:04:12
Old Mammoth 26 37N38 118w58 7:55:52
Old Pino 9 38N49'05 120w38'46 8:02:35
Old Point Comfort 19 34N24'55 117w49'58 7:51:20
Old Red Rock Place 23 38N47'35 123w26'27 8:13:46
Old River 15 35N16'02 119w06'29 7:56:26
Old San Diego 37 32N46 117w11 7:48:44
Old Station 45 40N40'31 121w25'47 8:05:43
Old Town 15 35N08'34 118w29'38 7:53:59
Old Town 42 34N24'16 119w31'45 7:58:07
Old Town San Diego 37 32N45'15 117w11'46 7:48:47
Oleander 10 36N38'04 119w45'14 7:59:01
Olema 21 38N02'27 122w47'13 8:11:09
Oleum 7 38N02'41 122w14'50 8:08:59
Olga 19 34N06'45 118w09'53 7:52:40
Olinda 30 33N55 117w53 7:51:32
Olinda 45 40N26'38 122w24'23 8:09:38
Olive 30 33N50'10 117w50'43 7:51:23
Olive Hill 58 39N17'18 121w28'09 8:05:53
Olivehurst 58 39N05'44 121w33'04 8:06:12
Olivenhain 37 33N02'46 117w14'02 7:48:56
Olive View 19 34N19'28 118w26'34 7:53:46
Olsen Crossing 12 40N34'57 123w39'41 8:14:39
Olympia 44 37N04'11 122w03'27 8:08:14
Olympic 19 34N04 118w24 7:53:36
Olympic Valley 31 39N09 120w09 8:00:36
Omega 29 39N20'00 120w44'54 8:03:00
Omira 18 39N58'01 120w04'35 8:00:18
Omo Ranch 9 38N34'53 120w34'20 8:02:17
Omus 49 38N43'11 122w55'07 8:11:40
O'Neals 20 37N07'42 119w41'36 7:58:46
Onehundred Palms 33 33N33'43 116w10'18 7:44:41
O'Neil Place 23 39N41'56 122w57'33 8:11:50
Ono 45 40N28'31 122w37'01 8:10:28
Ontario 36 34N03'48 117w39'00 7:50:36
Ontario Intl Airport 36 34N04 117w35 7:50:20
Onyx 15 35N41'25 118w13'11 7:52:53
Opal Cliffs 44 36N57'39 121w57'47 8:07:51
Ophir 31 38N53'28 121w07'21 8:04:29
Ora 10 36N09'05 120w19'32 8:01:18
Orange 30 33N47'16 117w51'08 7:51:25
Orange Avenue Junction 19 34N05'33 117w56'32 7:51:46
Orange Cove 10 36N37'28 119w18'46 7:57:15
Orange Heights 36 34N06 117w38 7:50:32
Orangehurst 30 33N52 117w58 7:51:52
Orange Park Acres 30 33N48'07 117w46'53 7:51:08
Orangevale 34 38N40'43 121w13'29 8:04:54
Orcutt 42 34N51'55 120w26'06 8:01:44
Ordbend 11 39N37'47 122w00'16 8:08:01
Ordway 33 34N00'15 117w10'01 7:48:40
Oregon City 4 39N35'38 121w31'42 8:06:07
Oregon House 58 39N21'23 121w16'41 8:05:07
Orford 39 37N58'38 121w11'18 8:04:45
Orick 12 41N17'13 124w03'31 8:16:14
Orinda 7 37N52'38 122w10'43 8:08:43
Orinda Village 7 37N53'15 122w11'40 8:08:47
Orita 13 32N58'38 115w24'16 7:41:37
Orland 11 39N44'51 122w11'43 8:08:47
Orleans 12 41N18'06 123w32'24 8:14:10
Orleans Flat 29 39N25'44 120w50'02 8:03:20
Ormand 33 34N00'40 117w25'03 7:49:40
Oro Fino 47 41N34'50 122w55'13 8:11:41
Oro Grande 36 34N35'56 117w20'00 7:49:20
Oroleve 4 39N31'36 121w10'42 8:04:43
Oro Loma 10 36N53'27 120w41'22 8:02:45
Orosi 54 36N32'42 119w17'11 7:57:09
Oroville 4 39N30'50 121w33'19 8:06:13
Oroville Jct (Tres Vias) 4 39N30'35 121w38'58 8:06:36
Orris 54 35N51'14 119w03'37 7:56:14
Orrs Springs 23 39N13'46 123w21'49 8:13:27
Ortega 39 37N54'17 121w16'16 8:05:05
Ortega 42 34N24'59 119w35'05 7:58:20
Ortonville 56 34N19'17 119w17'26 7:57:10
Orwood 7 37N56'24 121w34'04 8:06:16
Osbourne 19 34N06 118w20 7:53:20
Ostrom 58 39N04'10 121w30'38 8:06:03
Oswald 51 39N04'09 121w37'30 8:06:30
Otay 37 32N35'41 117w03'49 7:48:15
Oteys Sierra Village 14 37N21'31 118w27'30 7:53:50
Otterbein 19 33N59'15 117w53'02 7:51:32
Outingdale 9 38N37'00 120w43'44 8:02:55
Oval 54 36N20 119w18 7:57:12
Owenyo 14 36N40'42 118w02'36 7:52:10
Owl 33 33N55'40 116w49'00 7:47:16
Oxalis 10 36N54'43 120w32'56 8:02:12
Oxford 48 38N18'26 121w37'11 8:06:29
Oxford Mill 46 39N34'19 120w49'28 8:03:18
Oxnard 56 34N11'51 119w10'34 7:56:42
Oxnard Beach 56 34N09'48 119w13'37 7:56:54
Ozol 7 38N01'36 122w09'43 8:08:39
Pabrico 1 37N34'58 122w00'19 8:08:01
Pacer 42 34N56'07 120w29'20 8:01:57

Pachappa 33	33N56'48	117w23'03	7:49:32
Pacheco 7	37N59'01	122w04'27	8:08:18
Pacific 9	38N45'37	120w30'22	8:02:01
Pacific 19	33N48	118w11	7:52:44
Pacifica 41	37N36'50	122w29'09	8:09:57
Pacific Beach 37	32N47'52	117w14'22	7:48:57
Pacific Gardens 39	37N58	121w19	8:05:16
Pacific Grove 27	36N37	121w55	8:07:40
Pacific Grove Acres 27	36N37'44	121w55'44	8:07:43
Pacific House 9	38N46	120w30	8:02:00
Pacific Manor 12	40N52	124w05	8:16:20
Pacific Manor 41	37N39'01	122w29'19	8:09:57
Pacific Palisades 19	34N02'53	118w31'32	7:54:06
Pacific Villas 39	37N58	121w19	8:05:16
Pacoima 19	34N15'45	118w25'34	7:53:42
Paddison Square 19	33N54	118w05	7:52:20
Paddon 48	38N21	121w59	8:07:56
Paicines 35	36N43'43	121w16'39	8:05:07
Paige 54	36N10'55	119w25'11	7:57:41
Paintersville 34	38N19'12	121w34'30	8:06:18
Pajaro 27	36N54'15	121w44'51	8:06:59
Pala 37	33N21'55	117w04'33	7:48:18
Pala Indian Reservation 37	33N21	117w03	7:48:12
Pala Mesa 37	33N19'56	117w09'46	7:48:39
Pala Mesa Village 37	33N23	117w21	7:49:24
Palermo 4	39N26'08	121w32'13	8:06:09
Pallett 19	34N26	117w50	7:51:20
Palm Beach 44	36N52'02	121w49'01	8:07:16
Palm City 33	33N43	116w19	7:45:16
Palm City 37	32N35'01	117w05'00	7:48:20
Palmdale 19	34N34'46	118w06'56	7:52:28
Palm Desert 33	33N43'17	116w23'15	7:45:33
Palmer Creek 12	40N35	124w08	8:16:32
Palmetto 32	39N49'26	121w19'05	8:05:16
Palm Grove 37	32N44'07	116w12'32	7:44:50
Palmo 15	35N33'33	119w19'49	7:57:19
Palms 19	34N01'22	118w24'17	7:53:37
Palm Springs 33	33N49'49	116w32'40	7:46:11
Palm Wells 36	34N03	116w35	7:46:20
Palo Alto 43	37N26'31	122w08'31	8:08:34
Palo Cedro 45	40N33'50	122w14'16	8:08:57
Paloma 5	38N15'34	120w45'44	8:03:03
Palomares 1	37N42	122w05	8:08:20
Palomar Mountain (P O) 37	33N19'22	116w52'40	7:47:31
Palomar Park 41	37N28	122w15	8:09:00
Palos Verdes 19	33N43	118w21	7:53:24
Palos Verdes Estates 19	33N48'02	118w23'21	7:53:33
Palos Verdes Peninsula 19	33N46	118w22	7:53:28
Palo Verde 13	33N25'58	114w43'53	7:38:56
Panama 15	35N16'01	119w03'21	7:56:13
Panamint 14	36N07'06	117w05'40	7:48:23
Panamint Springs 14	36N20'23	117w28'01	7:49:52
Panoche 35	36N35'49	120w49'57	8:03:20
Panoche Junction 10	36N32'46	120w29'13	8:01:57
Panorama City 19	34N13'29	118w26'56	7:53:48
Panorama Heights 30	33N46'40	117w47'50	7:51:11
Panorama Heights 36	34N07'27	116w13'12	7:44:53
Panorama Heights 54	35N48'18	118w37'42	7:54:31
Paola 25	41N27'19	120w31'39	8:02:07
Pape Place 52	40N10'17	121w48'06	8:07:12
Paradise 4	39N44'47	121w38'10	8:06:33
Paradise 50	37N38	121w01	8:04:04
Paradise Camp 26	37N22	118w24	7:53:36
Paradise Cay 21	37N53	122w29	8:09:56
Paradise Clay 21	37N54'47	122w28'27	8:09:54
Paradise Park 44	37N00'37	122w02'33	8:08:10
Paradise Springs 19	34N23'45	117w48'20	7:51:13
Paramount 19	33N53'22	118w09'32	7:52:38
Parchers Camp 14	37N22	118w24	7:53:36
Pardee 19	34N24'54	118w32'23	7:54:10
Paris 19	34N28'19	118w10'48	7:52:43
Park 1	37N52	122w17	8:09:08
Park Central 1	37N47	122w16	8:09:04
Parker Dam 36	34N17'14	114w08'32	7:36:34
Parker Junction 36	34N46'13	114w35'43	7:38:23
Parkfield 27	35N53'59	120w25'54	8:01:44
Parkfield Junction 10	36N04'55	120w28'46	8:01:55
Parkhill 4	39N43'21	121w29'44	8:05:59
Parklabrea 19	34N03'57	118w21'15	7:53:25
Parkmoor 43	37N19	121w55	8:07:40
Parkside 38	37N45	122w29	8:09:56
Park Siding 49	38N13	122w38	8:10:32
Park Village 14	36N30'40	116w51'17	7:47:25
Parkway 34	38N29'46	121w27'28	8:05:50
Parkway Estates 34	38N29	121w27	8:05:48
Parkwood 20	36N58	120w04	8:00:16
Parlier 10	36N36'42	119w31'34	7:58:06
Parramore Springs 17	39N18'49	122w52'44	8:11:31
Parrott Landing 4	39N37'05	121w58'44	8:07:55
Parsley Bar Crossing 31	39N01'42	120w26'05	8:01:44
Pasadena 19	34N08'52	118w08'37	7:52:34
Pasatiempo 44	37N00'16	122w01'29	8:08:06
Paskenta 52	39N53'05	122w32'41	8:10:11
Paso Robles 40	35N37'36	120w41'24	8:02:46
Patata 19	33N56	118w11	7:52:44
Patch 15	35N15'10	118w53'42	7:55:35
Patricks Point 12	41N07'25	124w09'20	8:16:37
Patterson 50	37N28'18	121w07'43	8:04:31
Patton 36	34N08'09	117w13'23	7:48:54
Patton Village 18	40N09	120w08	8:00:32
Paulsell 50	37N43'06	120w41'22	8:02:45
Pauma Valley 37	33N18'12	116w58'50	7:47:55
Paxton 32	40N02'17	120w59'38	8:03:59
Paymaster Landing 13	33N14'45	114w41'20	7:38:45
Payne 53	40N14'35	123w05'30	8:12:22
Payne Place 52	40N14'00	121w52'35	8:07:30
Paynes Creek 52	40N20'08	121w54'50	8:07:39
Paynesville 2	38N48'33	119w46'42	7:59:07
P-38 Crossing 52	40N10'10	121w53'45	8:07:35
Peaceful Pines 2	38N24'22	119w47'18	7:59:09
Peachton 4	39N22'50	121w39'37	8:06:38
Peachtree Crossing 17	38N56'12	122w34'05	8:10:16
Peanut 53	40N28'05	123w10'03	8:12:40
Pearblossom 19	34N30'23	117w54'32	7:51:38
Peardale 29	39N11'28	120w59'56	8:04:00
Pearland 19	34N33'40	118w02'22	7:52:09
Pearson 39	38N07'49	121w14'46	8:04:59
Pearson 58	39N03'43	121w34'35	8:06:18
Pearsonville 14	35N39	117w49	7:51:16
Peavine 46	39N40'40	120w00'20	8:00:01
Pebble Beach 27	36N34	121w57	8:07:48
Pecwan 12	41N03	123w40	8:14:40
Pedley 33	33N58'31	117w28'30	7:49:54
Pedro Valley 41	37N35'36	122w29'49	8:09:59
Peethill 57	38N35'03	121w31'16	8:06:05
Peligreen Place 52	40N12'32	121w47'14	8:07:09
Pellow Place 52	39N58'36	122w37'43	8:10:31
Peltier 39	38N11'19	121w14'35	8:04:58
Penasquitos 37	32N59	117w07	7:48:28
Pendleton 37	33N22	117w25	7:49:40
Peninsula Center 19	33N46	118w21	7:53:24
Peninsula Village 32	40N16'24	121w07'46	8:04:31
Penney 53	40N11'54	123w06'02	8:12:24
Penngrove 49	38N17'59	122w39'56	8:10:40
Pennington 51	39N17'28	121w47'32	8:07:10
Penn Valley 29	39N13	121w04	8:04:16
Penoyar 47	41N40'03	122w03'42	8:08:15
Penryn 31	38N51'08	121w10'06	8:04:40
Pentland 15	34N59'08	119w21'20	7:57:25
Pentz 4	39N39'19	121w34'58	8:06:20
Penvir 27	36N32'19	121w28'59	8:05:56
Pepper Corner 33	33N51'06	117w32'59	7:50:12
Pepperwood 12	40N26'46	123w59'30	8:15:58
Pepperwood Grove 17	39N03'29	122w46'49	8:11:07
Peral 54	36N25'41	119w17'09	7:57:09
Peralta Hills 30	33N50'40	117w49'01	7:51:16
Perez 25	41N40'35	121w15'11	8:05:01
Perkins 34	38N32'47	121w23'50	8:05:35
Perks Corner 9	38N42'41	120w50'17	8:03:21
Permanente 14	36N22'27	118w00'28	7:52:02
Perris 33	33N46'57	117w13'40	7:48:55
Perris Valley 33	33N48	117w12	7:48:48
Perry 19	33N51'56	118w20'37	7:53:22
Perry 43	37N11'01	121w42'19	8:06:49
Perrys Corner 13	32N51'42	115w22'45	7:41:31
Pescadero 41	37N15'18	122w22'49	8:09:31
Petaluma 49	38N13'57	122w38'08	8:10:33
Petaluma Rural 49	38N16	122w41	8:10:44
Peters 39	37N58'51	121w02'49	8:04:11
Peterson Mill 14	37N15'16	118w28'39	7:53:55
Peterson Place 52	39N52'42	122w45'46	8:11:03
Petrolia 12	40N19'32	124w17'09	8:17:09
Pettit Place (Site) 15	35N38'23	118w37'00	7:54:28
Pettyjohn Place 52	40N10'25	122w40'29	8:10:42
Phelan 36	34N25'34	117w34'17	7:50:17
Phelps Corner 37	32N43'20	116w48'35	7:47:14
Philbrick Mill 23	39N04'56	123w29'39	8:13:59
Phillips 9	38N49'05	120w04'36	8:00:18
Phillipsville 12	40N12'33	123w47'05	8:15:08
Philo 23	39N03'57	123w26'38	8:13:47
Picacho 13	33N01'23	114w36'37	7:38:26
Pico 19	34N22'39	118w36'40	7:54:27
Pico Heights 19	34N03	118w18	7:53:12
Pico Rivera 19	33N58'59	118w05'45	7:52:23
Piedmont 1	37N49'28	122w13'50	8:08:55
Piedra 10	36N48'37	119w22'52	7:57:31
Piedra PO 10	36N49'22	119w21'52	7:57:27
Pierce 47	41N16'07	122w12'49	8:08:51
Pierce 48	38N07'32	122w05'58	8:08:24
Piercy 23	39N57'59	123w47'39	8:15:11
Pierpont Bay 56	34N15'35	119w16'06	7:57:04
Pike 46	39N26'21	120w59'49	8:03:59
Pilibos Ranch 10	36N41'01	120w30'48	8:02:03
Pilliken 9	38N41'11	120w21'12	8:01:25
Pilot Hill 9	38N50'06	121w00'48	8:04:03
Pine Bluff 34	38N41	121w11	8:04:44
Pine Cove 33	33N45'38	116w44'13	7:46:57
Pinecrest 55	38N11'19	119w59'23	7:59:58
Pinecroft 31	39N04'35	120w58'37	8:03:54
Pinedale 10	36N50'34	119w47'20	7:59:09
Pine Flat 54	35N52'41	118w39'02	7:54:36
Pine Grove 3	38N24'47	120w39'28	8:02:38
Pine Grove 17	38N49'42	122w43'48	8:10:55
Pine Grove 23	39N20'58	123w48'47	8:15:15
Pine Grove 37	32N56'43	116w42'42	7:46:51
Pine Grove 45	40N39'54	122w21'08	8:09:25
Pine Hill 12	40N45'53	124w10'24	8:16:42
Pine Hills 37	33N02'54	116w37'48	7:46:31
Pinehurst 10	36N41'43	119w00'56	7:56:04
Pineridge 10	37N04	119w22	7:57:28
Pine Valley 37	32N49'17	116w31'42	7:46:07
Pine Wood 33	33N48'51	116w44'12	7:46:57
Pinewood Camp 54	36N34'26	118w45'54	7:55:04
Pinezanita 36	34N09'52	116w57'09	7:47:49
Pinnacles 35	36N31'51	121w08'39	8:04:35
Pinnio 18	41N04'27	120w28'06	8:01:52
Pino Grande 9	38N52'13	120w37'30	8:02:30
Pinole 7	38N00'16	122w17'52	8:09:11
Pinon Hills 36	34N26'00	117w38'44	7:50:35
Pinto Wye 33	34N01'15	116w01'07	7:44:04
Pinyon Crest 33	33N36'31	116w26'11	7:45:45
Pinyon Pines 33	33N48	116w44	7:46:56
Pioneer 3	38N25'55	120w34'15	8:02:17
Pioneer 47	41N17'33	122w18'33	8:09:14
Pioneer Point 36	35N47'09	117w21'45	7:49:27
Pioneertown 36	34N09'24	116w29'43	7:45:59
Pippin Corner 40	35N17'56	120w24'07	8:01:36
Piru 56	34N24'55	118w47'35	7:55:10
Pisgah 36	34N45'35	116w21'16	7:45:25
Pismo Beach 40	35N08'34	120w38'25	8:02:34
Pitco 16	36N21'24	119w39'46	7:58:39
Pittsburg 7	38N01'41	121w53'01	8:07:32
Pittville 45	41N02'55	121w20'00	8:05:20
Pixley 54	35N58'07	119w17'27	7:57:10
Pizona 26	37N58'18	118w33'26	7:54:14
Placentia 30	33N52'20	117w52'10	7:51:29
Place of the Oaks 53	40N46'53	122w44'55	8:11:00
Placerville 9	38N43'47	120w47'51	8:03:11
Plainfield 57	38N35'27	121w47'45	8:07:11
Plainsburg 24	37N13'59	120w19'24	8:01:18
Plainview 54	36N08'39	119w07'59	7:56:32
Planada 24	37N17'27	120w19'03	8:01:16
Planehaven 34	38N40	121w23	8:05:32
Plano 54	36N02'37	119w00'27	7:56:02
Plantation 49	38N32	123w05	8:12:20
Plaskett 27	35N55'00	121w28'04	8:05:52
Plasse 3	38N38'14	120w07'32	8:00:30
Plaster City 13	32N47'33	115w51'28	7:43:26
Platina 45	40N22	122w53	8:11:32
Playa del Rey 19	33N56'56	118w26'41	7:53:47
Playmor 37	32N37	117w04	7:48:16
Plaza 30	33N47	117w50	7:51:20
Plaza Camino Real 37	33N01	117w17	7:49:08
Plaza Center 36	34N03	117w39	7:50:36
Pleasant Grove 51	38N49'26	121w28'58	8:05:56
Pleasant Hill 7	37N56'53	122w03'35	8:08:14
Pleasant Hill 12	40N52	124w05	8:16:20
Pleasanton 1	37N39'45	121w52'25	8:07:30
Pleasant Valley 9	38N40'59	120w39'43	8:02:39
Pleasant View 54	35N48'20	118w38'24	7:54:34
Pleyto 27	35N51'37	120w59'33	8:03:58
Plumbago 46	39N27'08	120w49'00	8:03:16
Plumtree Crossing 31	39N04'49	120w59'36	8:03:58
Plymouth 3	38N28'55	120w50'37	8:03:22
Poe 4	39N44'40	121w28'13	8:05:53
Poffenbergers Landing 51	38N56'20	121w49'46	8:07:19
Poinsettia Tract 7	38N00	121w51	8:07:24
Point Arena 23	38N54'32	123w41'31	8:14:46
Point Firmin 19	33N44	118w18	7:53:12
Point Loma 37	32N44	117w14	7:48:56
Point McCloud 45	40N55'26	122w14'33	8:08:58
Point Mugu 56	34N07	119w06	7:56:24
Point Pleasant 34	38N19'54	121w27'46	8:05:51
Point Reyes Station 21	38N04'09	122w48'21	8:11:13
Point Richmond 7	37N55'27	122w23'17	8:09:33
Poker Flat 46	39N41'36	120w50'37	8:03:22
Polaris 29	39N20'21	120w08'05	8:00:32
Pole Garden 17	39N13'11	122w38'11	8:10:33
Polk 34	38N31'56	121w24'28	8:05:38
Polk Springs 52	40N07'02	121w39'51	8:06:39
Pollard Flat 45	40N59'45	122w25'02	8:09:40
Pollock 34	38N29'22	121w28'03	8:05:52
Pollock 45	40N55'00	122w23'05	8:09:32
Pollock Pines 9	38N45'41	120w35'08	8:02:21
Pomo 23	39N18'24	123w05'41	8:12:23
Pomona 19	34N03'19	117w45'05	7:51:00
Ponca 54	36N02'31	119w00'58	7:56:04
Pond 15	35N43'04	119w19'40	7:57:19
Pondosa 47	41N11'58	121w41'16	8:06:45
Pope 13	33N21'57	115w43'19	7:42:53
Pope 39	38N08'30	121w14'33	8:04:58
Pope Valley 28	38N36'55	122w25'36	8:09:42
Poplar 54	36N03'12	119w08'32	7:56:34
Porphyry 33	33N52'33	117w32'20	7:50:09
Portal Inn 45	40N44'09	122w19'06	8:09:16
Port Chicago 7	38N02'46	122w01'11	8:08:05
Port Costa 7	38N02'47	122w10'56	8:08:44
Porter 5	38N23'39	120w25'27	8:01:42
Porterville 54	36N03'55	119w00'57	7:56:04
Port Hueneme 56	34N08'52	119w11'39	7:56:47
Port Kenyon 12	40N35'43	124w16'43	8:17:07
Portola 32	39N48'38	120w28'05	8:01:52
Portola Terrace 41	37N27	122w11	8:08:44
Portola Valley 41	37N23'03	122w14'03	8:08:56
Port San Luis 40	35N10'30	120w45'15	8:03:01
Portuguese Bend 19	33N44'23	118w22'07	7:53:28
Posey 54	35N48'17	118w40'55	7:54:44
Poso Park 54	35N48'39	118w38'02	7:54:32
Posts 27	36N13'42	121w45'48	8:07:03
Potrero 37	32N36'17	116w36'44	7:46:27
Potrero District 38	37N45'35	122w23'49	8:09:35
Potter Valley 23	39N19'20	123w06'43	8:12:27
Potwisha 54	36N31'03	118w47'56	7:55:12
Poverty Hill 46	39N37'21	121w00'21	8:04:01
Poway 37	32N57'46	117w02'06	7:48:08
Powellton 4	39N55'44	121w34'17	8:06:17
Pozo 40	35N18'13	120w22'32	8:01:30
Prairie City 34	38N38'32	121w09'17	8:04:37
Prather 10	37N02'15	119w30'47	7:58:03
Prattco 27	36N37	121w50	8:07:20
Pratton 10	36N44'48	119w53'55	7:59:36
Pratt Place 23	39N54'47	123w43'14	8:14:53
Prattville 32	40N12'36	121w09'33	8:04:38
Prenda 33	33N55'17	117w23'15	7:49:33
Presidio 38	37N47	122w27	8:09:48
Presidio of Monterey 27	36N36	121w53	8:07:32
Presswood 23	39N10'06	123w12'17	8:12:49
Preston 49	38N50'07	123w00'59	8:12:04

Preston Heights 12 40N52 124w05 8:16:20
Preuss 19 34N03 118w23 7:53:32
Priest 55 37N48'51 120w16'18 8:01:05
Priest Valley 27 36N08 120w22 8:01:28
Princeton 6 39N24'12 122w00'32 8:08:02
Princeton 41 37N30'18 122w29'09 8:09:57
Princeton-by-the-Sea 41 37N30 122w28 8:09:52
Proberta 52 40N04'54 122w10'10 8:08:41
Progress 51 39N03'48 121w48'00 8:07:12
Project City 45 40N40'48 122w21'03 8:09:24
Prospect 18 39N52'57 120w00'04 8:00:00
Prospect 32 39N45'08 120w47'39 8:03:11
Prospero 15 35N28'16 119w07'33 7:56:30
Prosser Lakeview Estates 29 39N20 120w12 8:00:48
Prunedale 27 36N46'33 121w40'07 8:06:40
Pudding Creek 23 39N27 123w48 8:15:12
Puente Junction 19 34N00'51 117w57'34 7:51:50
Pulga 4 39N48'11 121w26'51 8:05:47
Pumpkin Center 15 35N16'01 119w01'57 7:56:08
Pumpkin Center 18 41N06'36 121w06'20 8:04:25
Punta 56 34N21'45 119w26'45 7:57:47
Punta Gorda 56 34N21'24 119w26'27 7:57:46
Purdon Crossing 29 39N19'39 121w02'43 8:04:11
Pushawalla Palms 33 33N49'27 116w16'51 7:45:07
Quail 54 36N00'35 119w18'09 7:57:13
Quail Valley 33 33N42'25 117w14'39 7:48:59
Quaker Meadow 54 36N06'37 118w33'13 7:54:13
Quaking Aspen 54 36N08 118w49 7:55:16
Quality 15 35N47'02 119w07'07 7:56:28
Quartz 55 37N55'41 120w25'11 8:01:41
Quartz Hill 19 34N38'43 118w13'02 7:52:52
Queen City 46 39N39'53 120w56'21 8:03:45
Quincy 32 39N56'13 120w56'46 8:03:47
Quincy Junction 32 39N57'48 120w53'50 8:03:35
Quintette 9 38N54'54 120w41'10 8:02:45
Quito 43 37N17 122w01 8:08:04
Rackerby 58 39N26'23 121w20'25 8:05:22
Raco 10 36N48'02 119w58'41 7:59:55
Radec 33 33N27'51 116w54'47 7:47:39
Radnor 54 35N49'49 119w15'39 7:57:03
Radum 1 37N40'13 121w51'29 8:07:26
Rafael Village 21 38N04'08 122w32'55 8:10:12
Raffetto 9 38N51'49 120w26'25 8:01:46
Ragby 22 37N36'43 120w08'03 8:00:32
Ragtown 36 34N39'54 116w09'04 7:44:36
Rail Road Flat 5 38N20 120w30 8:02:00
Rainbow 31 39N18'37 120w30'27 8:02:02
Rainbow 37 33N24'37 117w08'49 7:48:35
Rainbow Spring 45 41N06'50 121w32'56 8:06:12
Rainbow Wells 36 35N12'17 115w39'03 7:42:36
Raisin 10 36N36'09 119w54'11 7:59:37
Raisin City (Raisin P O) 10 36N36'09 119w54'11 7:59:37
Ralph 55 37N57'56 120w16'12 8:01:05
Ralph Leggett Place 23 39N51'33 123w24'04 8:13:36
Ramada 4 39N33'20 121w42'36 8:06:50
Ramal 49 38N13'17 122w23'37 8:09:34
Ramirez 19 34N00 118w17 7:53:08
Ramirez 58 39N16'03 121w32'16 8:06:09
Ramona 34 38N32'51 121w24'28 8:05:38
Ramona 37 33N02'30 116w52'02 7:47:28
Ramona Bowl 33 33N43'11 116w56'58 7:47:48
Rampart 31 39N09'53 120w10'38 8:00:43
Ramsey 23 39N58'21 123w26'46 8:13:47
Ramsey Crossing 31 38N59'54 120w33'12 8:02:13
Rana 36 34N05'22 117w19'09 7:49:17
Ranch Club Estates 33 33N49 116w32 7:46:08
Ranch House 37 33N15 117w18 7:49:12
Ranchita 37 33N12'36 116w30'57 7:46:04
Rancho Bernardo 37 33N01'07 117w03'36 7:48:14
Rancho California 33 33N46 117w29 7:49:56
Rancho Cordova 34 38N35'21 121w18'06 8:05:12
Rancho Cucamonga 36 34N06'23 117w35'32 7:50:22
Rancho Del Campo 37 32N36'06 116w28'06 7:45:52
Rancho Del Mar 28 38N07 122w14 8:08:56
Rancho Del Rey 37 32N37 117w04 7:48:16
Rancho Dos Palmas 33 33N29'55 115w49'49 7:43:19
Rancho La Costa 37 33N05 117w17 7:49:08
Rancho Llano Seco 4 39N36'30 121w57'07 8:07:48
Rancho Mirage 33 33N44'23 116w24'43 7:45:39
Rancho Palos Verdes 19 33N46 118w21 7:53:24
Rancho Park 19 34N02 118w26 7:53:44
Rancho Penasquitos 37 32N59 117w07 7:48:28
Rancho Rinconado 43 37N19 122w02 8:08:08
Rancho San Fernando Rey 42 34N25 119w42 7:58:48
Rancho Santa Clarita 19 34N26'24 118w31'52 7:54:07
Rancho Santa Fe 37 33N01'13 117w12'07 7:48:48
Rancho Seco 15 35N16'59 117w59'20 7:51:57
Rand 15 35N25'19 117w41'30 7:50:46
Randall 9 38N46 120w30 8:02:00
Randall Island 34 38N20 121w34 8:06:16
Randolph 46 39N34'47 120w22'11 8:01:29
Randsburg 15 35N22'07 117w39'26 7:50:38
Ratto Landing 28 38N13'55 122w17'18 8:09:09
Ravendale 18 40N47'55 120w21'51 8:01:27
Ravenna 19 34N26'19 118w13'28 7:52:54
Ravenswood 41 37N28'35 122w08'03 8:08:32
Rawhide 55 37N59 120w23 8:01:32
Rawson 52 40N07'04 122w11'36 8:08:46
Raymer 19 34N12'53 118w27'52 7:53:51
Raymond 20 37N13'02 119w54'16 7:59:37
Rayo 54 36N27'00 119w11'14 7:56:45
Rector 54 36N18'19 119w14'31 7:56:58
Red Apple 5 38N10'44 120w22'50 8:01:31
Red Bank 52 40N05'58 122w26'39 8:09:47
Redbanks 54 36N25'20 119w08'36 7:56:34
Red Bluff 52 40N10'43 122w14'05 8:08:56
Redcrest 12 40N24'02 123w56'56 8:15:48
Redding 45 40N35'12 122w23'26 8:09:34
Red Dog 29 39N13'00 120w53'54 8:03:36
Red Hill 30 33N45 117w49 7:51:16
Redlands 36 34N03'43 117w10'54 7:48:44
Redlands Heights 36 34N04 117w12 7:48:48
Redman 19 34N45'50 117w58'08 7:51:53
Red Mountain 36 35N21'30 117w36'57 7:50:28
Redondo Beach 19 33N50'57 118w23'15 7:53:33
Redondo Junction 19 34N00'57 118w13'35 7:52:54
Redshank 33 33N41'48 116w39'48 7:46:39
Reds Meadow 26 37N38 118w58 7:55:52
Red Top 20 37N18 120w29 8:01:56
Redway 12 40N07'13 123w49'20 8:15:17
Redwood City 41 37N29'10 122w14'00 8:08:56
Redwood Corral 54 35N58'57 118w39'42 7:54:39
Redwood Estates 43 37N09'23 121w59'08 8:07:57
Redwood Grove 44 37N09'27 122w07'59 8:08:32
Redwood Junction 41 37N28'38 122w13'13 8:08:53
Redwood Lodge 23 39N27 123w48 8:15:12
Redwood Lodge 44 37N06'28 121w56'37 8:07:46
Redwoods 45 40N35'47 121w56'04 8:07:44
Redwood Terrace 41 37N18'53 122w17'38 8:09:11
Redwood Valley 23 39N15'56 123w12'12 8:12:49
Reed 21 37N54'18 122w29'58 8:10:00
Reedley 10 36N35'47 119w26'58 7:57:48
Reef Station 16 35N54'06 120w03'14 8:00:13
Reeves Place 23 39N53'21 123w06'45 8:12:27
Reeves Place 40 35N09'54 120w18'32 8:01:14
Regina Heights 23 39N08'54 123w10'21 8:12:41
Reilly Heights 23 39N06'35 123w30'53 8:14:04
Relief 29 39N21'41 120w51'35 8:03:26
Remnoy 16 36N20'23 119w33'12 7:58:13
Reno Junction 18 39N47'31 120w05'56 8:00:24
Renoville 36 35N33'10 116w11'18 7:44:45
Renshaw Place 40 35N10'20 120w15'42 8:01:03
Requa 8 41N32'49 124w03'55 8:16:16
Rescue 9 38N43 120w57 8:03:48
Reseda 19 34N12'04 118w32'08 7:54:09
Reward 14 36N44'51 118w03'15 7:52:13
Reward 15 35N19'21 119w40'42 7:58:43
Rex 42 34N56'43 120w22'34 8:01:30
Reyes Place 23 39N50'46 123w24'24 8:13:38
Reynolds 21 38N08'54 122w52'55 8:11:32
Reynolds 23 39N59 123w48 8:15:12
Rheem 7 37N51'39 122w07'34 8:08:30
Rheem Valley 7 37N51'36 122w07'22 8:08:29
Rhodes 39 37N43 121w26 8:05:44
Rialto 36 34N06'23 117w22'10 7:49:29
Ribbonwood 33 33N34'13 116w29'53 7:46:00
Ribie 15 35N15'10 118w52'43 7:55:31
Ricardo 15 35N22'26 117w59'18 7:51:57
Riccas Corner 49 38N25'24 122w47'13 8:11:09
Rice 36 34N05'01 114w50'56 7:39:24
Rice Crossing 29 39N18'46 121w12'13 8:04:49
Riceton 4 39N26'58 121w43'28 8:06:54
Rich 15 34N58'35 117w43'36 7:50:54
Richardson Grove 12 40N06 123w48 8:15:12
Richardson Springs 4 39N50'24 121w46'33 8:07:06
Rich Bar 32 40N01 121w10 8:04:40
Richfield 52 39N58'30 122w10'32 8:08:42
Richgrove 54 35N47'48 119w06'25 7:56:26
Rich Gulch 5 38N19'49 120w37'48 8:02:31
Richmond 7 37N56'09 122w20'48 8:09:23
Richmond District 38 37N46'50 122w28'17 8:09:53
Richmond Square 41 37N36 122w24 8:09:36
Richvale 4 39N29'38 121w44'37 8:06:58
Rico 13 32N48'24 115w23'48 7:41:35
Ridge 23 39N20'12 123w18'00 8:13:12
Ridgecrest 15 35N37'21 117w40'12 7:50:41
Ridgeville 53 40N51'53 122w48'07 8:11:12
Ridgewoods Heights 12 40N44'08 124w08'50 8:16:35
Riego 51 38N45'05 121w29'01 8:05:56
Rimcrest 33 33N49 116w32 7:46:08
Rimforest 36 34N13'47 117w13'27 7:48:54
Rimlon 33 33N50'15 116w26'33 7:45:46
Rimpau 19 34N03 118w20 7:53:20
Rimrock 36 34N11'53 116w33'13 7:46:13
Rinckel 45 41N08'00 122w04'27 8:08:18
Rincon 37 33N17'17 116w57'27 7:47:50
Rincon 44 37N00'44 122w03'05 8:08:12
Rincon Annex 38 37N46 122w27 8:09:48
Rincon Indian Reservation 37 33N17'17 116w57'27 7:47:50
Rio Bonito 4 34N04 118w22 7:53:28
Rio Bravo 15 35N23'53 119w17'24 7:57:10
Rio Campo 49 38N28 123w00 8:12:00
Rio Dell 12 40N29'58 124w06'19 8:16:25
Rio Dell 49 38N29'57 122w54'22 8:11:37
Rio Del Mar 44 36N58'06 121w53'57 8:07:36
Rio Linda 34 38N41'28 121w26'51 8:05:47
Rio Nido 49 38N31'16 122w58'33 8:11:54
Rio Oso 51 38N57'40 121w32'36 8:06:10
Rio Vista 48 38N09'21 121w41'25 8:06:46
Rio Vista Junction 48 38N12'26 121w52'29 8:07:30
Ripley 33 33N31'31 114w39'19 7:38:37
Ripon 39 37N44'30 121w07'24 8:04:30
Ripperdan 20 36N51'05 120w03'18 8:00:13
Rivera 19 33N59 118w05 7:52:20
Riverbank 50 37N44'10 120w56'04 8:03:44
Riverbend 10 36N45'25 119w30'37 7:58:02
Riverdale 10 36N25'52 119w51'31 7:59:26
Riverdale 23 39N53'16 123w44'47 8:14:59
River Kern 15 35N43 118w26 7:53:44
River Oaks 35 36N53'59 121w35'36 8:06:22
River Pines 3 38N32'47 120w44'35 8:02:58
River Road 50 37N38 120w59 8:03:56
Riverside 33 33N57'12 117w23'43 7:49:35
Riverside Grove 44 37N10'26 122w08'32 8:08:34
Riverside Junction 33 33N59'07 117w21'37 7:49:26
Riverside Park 12 40N29'43 123w59'30 8:15:58
Riverton 9 38N46'16 120w26'54 8:01:48
Riverview 15 35N24 119w02 7:56:08
Riverview 37 32N51'21 116w55'52 7:47:43
Riverview 45 40N55'22 122w24'06 8:09:36
Riverview 57 38N30'13 121w33'32 8:06:14
Riverview Farms 37 32N50'42 116w55'52 7:47:43
Riviera 19 34N03'28 118w30'02 7:54:00
Riviera Cliff 39 37N58 121w19 8:05:16
Roads End 54 35N56 118w30 7:54:00
Robbers Creek 18 40N22'13 121w00'14 8:04:01
Robbins 51 38N52'13 121w42'19 8:06:49
Roberts Landing 1 37N40'23 122w09'50 8:08:39
Roberts Place 52 40N02'28 121w51'23 8:07:26
Robertsville 43 37N15'48 121w52'31 8:07:30
Robinson Mills 4 39N29'42 121w19'11 8:05:17
Robinsons Corner 4 39N21'52 121w36'25 8:06:26
Robla 34 38N39'41 121w26'44 8:05:47
Roblar 49 38N19'17 122w45'28 8:11:02
Robles Del Rio 27 36N28'12 121w43'56 8:06:56
Rob Roy Junction 44 36N58'15 121w52'23 8:07:30
Rochester 36 34N05'30 117w32'48 7:50:11
Rockaway Beach 41 37N36'31 122w29'39 8:09:59
Rock City 7 37N50'59 121w56'04 8:07:44
Rock Creek 32 39N54'10 121w21'07 8:05:24
Rock Creek Camp 32 39N55'36 121w18'54 8:05:16
Rock Creek Crossing 32 39N56'19 121w21'46 8:05:27
Rock Crest 32 39N55 121w20 8:05:20
Rock Haven 10 37N07'33 119w19'06 7:57:16
Rocking Horse Ranchos 19 33N44 118w18 7:53:12
Rockland Landing (Aban'd) 27 36N00'29 121w31'06 8:06:04
Rocklin 31 38N47'27 121w14'05 8:04:56
Rockport 23 39N44'20 123w48'54 8:15:16
Rockridge 1 37N50 122w14 8:08:56
Rocktram 28 38N15'27 122w16'46 8:09:07
Rockville 48 38N14'39 122w07'16 8:08:29
Rockwood 13 33N02'56 115w30'43 7:42:03
Rocky Hill 54 36N18'05 119w07'00 7:56:28
Rodeo 7 38N01'59 122w15'57 8:09:04
Rodgers Crossing 10 36N51'43 119w07'12 7:56:29
Rogers Flat 32 39N55 121w20 8:05:20
Rogerville 4 39N36'41 121w13'17 8:04:53
Rogina Heights 23 39N09 123w12 8:12:48
Rohnert Park 49 38N20'23 122w42'00 8:10:48
Rohnerville 12 40N34'02 124w08'04 8:16:32
Rolands 49 38N30'39 122w58'46 8:11:55
Rolinda 10 36N44'07 119w57'39 7:59:51
Rolling Hills 19 33N45'25 118w21'11 7:53:25
Rolling Hills 33 33N33 116w43 7:46:52
Rolling Hills Estates 19 33N47'16 118w21'26 7:53:26
Rolling Hills Estates 40 35N18 120w45 8:03:00
Rolling Hills Riviera 19 33N44 118w18 7:53:12
Rollingwood 7 37N58 122w20 8:09:20
Romie Lane 27 36N41 121w39 8:06:36
Romoland 33 33N44'45 117w10'27 7:48:42
Roosevelt 19 34N43'10 118w00'17 7:52:01
Roosevelt Corner 19 34N40 118w11 7:52:44
Roosevelt Terrace 48 38N07 122w14 8:08:56
Rosamond 15 34N51'51 118w09'45 7:52:39
Rose Bowl 19 34N10 118w10 7:52:40
Rosedale 15 35N23'01 119w08'40 7:56:35
Roseland 49 38N25 122w44 8:10:56
Rosemary 42 34N56'44 120w23'37 8:01:34
Rosemead 19 34N04'50 118w04'19 7:52:17
Rosemont 34 38N33'07 121w21'49 8:05:27
Rosemont 37 33N00'03 116w55'27 7:47:42
Rose Place 17 39N09'57 122w49'00 8:11:16
Roseville 31 38N45'08 121w17'13 8:05:09
Roseville 37 32N43'41 117w13'53 7:48:56
Roseville Square 31 38N45 121w17 8:05:08
Rosewood 12 40N46'05 124w09'52 8:16:39
Rosewood 52 40N16'11 122w33'19 8:10:13
Ross 21 37N57'45 122w33'14 8:10:13
Ross 49 38N27'31 122w53'05 8:11:32
Ross Corner 13 32N46'53 114w35'22 7:38:21
Ross Crossing 10 36N59'16 119w07'39 7:56:31
Rossi 16 36N17'44 119w49'54 7:59:20
Rossmoor 30 33N47'08 118w05'03 7:52:20
Rossmoor Highlands 30 33N48 118w04 7:52:16
Ross Valley 21 37N58 122w32 8:10:08
Rotavele 11 39N41'04 121w59'57 8:08:00
Rough and Ready 29 39N13'49 121w08'06 8:04:32

Place	Latitude	Longitude	Time
Round Hill Country Club 7	37n51	122w01	8:08:04
Round Mountain 45	40n47'39	121w56'27	8:07:46
Round Valley 14	37n22	118w24	7:53:36
Round Valley 52	40n14'23	121w30'20	8:06:01
Round Valley Indian Res 23	39n50	123w18	8:13:12
Rovana 14	37n24'46	118w36'52	7:54:27
Rowen 15	35n14'27	118w34'33	7:54:18
Rowland 19	34n00'06	117w55'44	7:51:43
Rowland Heights 19	33n58'34	117w54'16	7:51:37
Rubidoux 33	33n59'46	117w24'17	7:49:37
Rucker 43	37n03'15	121w35'28	8:06:22
Rumsey 57	38n53'18	122w14'11	8:08:57
Running Springs 36	34n12'28	117w06'30	7:48:26
Rupert 58	39n09	121w32	8:06:08
Rush Landing 48	38n13'01	122w01'42	8:08:07
Russ 19	34n26'23	118w18'50	7:53:15
Russell 48	38n14'20	122w05'41	8:08:23
Russell City 1	37n39'10	122w07'57	8:08:32
Russian River Terrace 49	38n30'17	122w55'32	8:11:42
Russ Place 53	40n08'45	123w16'40	8:13:07
Ruth 53	40n16'11	123w19'13	8:13:17
Rutherford 28	38n27'31	122w25'17	8:09:41
Ruthven 13	32n57'09	115w00'38	7:40:03
Ryan 14	36n19'23	116w40'14	7:46:41
Ryans Slough 12	40n47	124w09	8:16:36
Ryde 34	38n14'19	121w33'34	8:06:14
Sablon 36	34n10'29	114w59'37	7:39:58
Sabre City 31	38n45	121w17	8:05:08
Sacate 42	34n28'20	120w17'33	8:01:10
Saco 15	35n26'40	119w05'29	7:56:22
Sacramento 34	38n34'54	121w29'36	8:05:58
Sacramento Army Depot 34	38n33	121w28	8:05:52
Sacramento Canyon 45	40n58	122w21	8:09:24
Sacramento Landing 21	38n08'59	122w54'19	8:11:37
Sacramento South 34	38n32	121w27	8:05:48
Saddle Junction 33	33n46'26	116w40'24	7:46:42
Sage 33	33n34'54	116w55'53	7:47:44
Sage Hen 18	41n06'39	120w28'37	8:01:54
Sageland 15	35n28'48	118w12'42	7:52:51
Saint Bernard 52	40n15'36	121w22'15	8:05:29
Saint Francis Heights 41	37n41	122w29	8:09:56
Saint Helena 28	38n30'19	122w28'09	8:09:53
Saint James Park 43	37n20	121w53	8:07:32
Saint Johns 54	36n23'05	119w05'51	7:56:23
Saint Lawrence Terrace 40	35n45	120w42	8:02:48
Saint Louis 46	39n41'55	120w55'26	8:03:42
Saint Marys College 7	37n51	122w06	8:08:24
Saint Matthew 41	37n34	122w19	8:09:16
Salida 50	37n42'21	121w05'02	8:04:20
Salinas 27	36n40'40	121w39'16	8:06:37
Salminas Resort 17	38n52'33	122w43'39	8:10:55
Salmon Creek 49	38n21'02	123w03'40	8:12:15
Salt Creek 45	40n54	122w23	8:09:32
Saltdale 15	35n21'33	117w53'12	7:51:33
Salton 33	33n28'26	115w53'02	7:43:32
Salton City 13	33n20	116w00	7:44:00
Salton Sea Beach 13	33n22'30	116w00'40	7:44:03
Saltus 36	34n32'16	115w41'21	7:42:45
Salvador 28	38n20'27	122w19'11	8:09:17
Salvia 33	33n52'21	116w30'03	7:46:00
Salyer 53	40n53'25	123w35'00	8:14:20
Samoa 12	40n49'08	124w11'07	8:16:44
San Andreas 5	38n11'46	120w40'46	8:02:43
San Anselmo 21	37n58'29	122w33'38	8:10:15
San Antonio 43	37n23	122w05	8:08:20
San Antonio Heights 36	34n09'20	117w39'20	7:50:37
San Ardo 27	36n01'14	120w54'15	8:03:37
San Augustine 42	34n27'34	120w21'26	8:01:26
San Benito 35	36n30'35	121w04'51	8:04:19
San Bernardino 36	34n07'17	117w18'08	7:49:13
Sanborn 15	35n00'02	118w06'20	7:52:25
San Bruno 41	37n37'50	122w24'36	8:09:38
San Carlos 37	32n47	117w02	7:48:08
San Carlos 41	37n30'26	122w15'34	8:09:02
San Clemente 30	33n25'37	117w36'40	7:50:27
Sandberg 19	34n44'28	118w42'31	7:54:50
Sand City 27	36n37	121w51	8:07:24
Sanders 51	39n12'10	121w39'39	8:06:39
Sand Hill 7	37n58'25	121w41'40	8:06:47
Sandia 13	32n53'08	115w24'18	7:41:37
San Diego 37	32n42'55	117w09'23	7:48:38
San Dieguito 37	33n03	117w16	7:49:04
San Dimas 19	34n06'24	117w48'21	7:51:13
Sands 36	35n00'55	115w56'31	7:43:46
Sandy Gulch 5	38n22'49	120w31'54	8:02:08
Sandy Korner 33	33n38'32	116w10'49	7:44:43
Sandyland 42	34n25	119w33	7:58:12
Sandyland Cove 42	34n23'48	119w31'49	7:58:07
San Emidio 15	34n39'56	119w18'13	7:57:13
San Felipe 37	33n11'57	116w35'52	7:46:23
San Felipe 43	36n58'15	121w25'05	8:05:40
San Fernando 19	34n16'55	118w26'17	7:53:45
Sanford 19	34n04	118w18	7:53:12
San Francisco 38	37n46'30	122w25'06	8:09:40
San Francisco Intl Airport 41	37n37	122w23	8:09:32
San Francisco Recreation Cam 55	38n33	121w17	8:05:08
San Gabriel 19	34n05'46	118w06'18	7:52:25
Sanger 10	36n42'29	119w33'18	7:58:13
San Geronimo 21	38n00'48	122w39'46	8:10:39
San Geronimo Valley 21	38n00	122w39	8:10:36
San Gorgonio Pass 33	33n59	117w02	7:48:08
San Gregorio 41	37n19'38	122w23'08	8:09:33
San Ignacio 37	33n18'17	116w31'03	7:46:04
Sanitarium 28	38n32'42	122w28'28	8:09:54
San Jacinto 33	33n47'02	116w57'28	7:47:50
San Joaquin 10	36n36'24	120w11'17	8:00:45
San Joaquin Bridge 39	37n49	121w17	8:05:08
San Joaquin River Club 39	37n40'51	121w16'19	8:05:05
San Jose 43	37n20'07	121w53'38	8:07:35
San Juan Bautista 35	36n50'44	121w32'13	8:06:09
San Juan Capistrano 30	33n30'06	117w39'42	7:50:39
San Juan Hot Springs 30	33n35'27	117w30'31	7:50:02
Sankey 51	38n46'42	121w29'53	8:06:00
San Lawrence Terrace 40	35n44'45	120w40'57	8:02:44
San Leandro 1	37n43'30	122w09'18	8:08:37
San Lorenzo 1	37n40'52	122w07'24	8:08:30
San Lorenzo Park 44	37n11'46	122w08'40	8:08:35
San Lorenzo Valley 44	37n07	122w06	8:08:24
San Lucas 27	36n07'44	121w01'10	8:04:05
San Luis Obispo 40	35n16'58	120w39'31	8:02:38
San Luis Obispo Bay 40	35n12	120w41	8:02:44
San Luis Obispo Rural 40	35n17	120w37	8:02:28
San Luis Rey 37	33n13'55	117w19'22	7:49:17
San Luis Rey Downs 37	33n14	117w20	7:49:20
San Luis Rey Heights 37	33n19'08	117w12'30	7:48:50
San Marcos 37	33n08'36	117w09'55	7:48:40
San Marin 21	38n06	122w34	8:10:16
San Marino 19	34n07'17	118w06'20	7:52:25
San Martin 43	37n05'06	121w36'33	8:06:26
San Mateo 41	37n33'47	122w19'28	8:09:18
San Mateo Park 41	37n34'00	122w20'39	8:09:23
San Miguel 40	35n45'09	120w41'43	8:02:47
San Onofre 37	33n22'52	117w34'20	7:50:17
San Pablo 7	37n57'44	122w20'40	8:09:23
San Pasqual 37	33n05'30	116w57'11	7:47:49
San Pasqual Indian Res 37	33n13	116w58	7:47:52
San Pedro 19	33n44'09	118w17'29	7:53:10
San Pedro Hill 19	33n44'46	118w20'07	7:53:20
San Quentin 21	37n56'29	122w29'02	8:09:56
San Rafael 21	37n58'25	122w31'48	8:10:07
San Ramon 7	37n46'48	121w58'37	8:07:54
San Ramon Village 1	37n43'17	121w55'44	8:07:43
San Roque 42	34n26	119w44	7:58:56
Sans Crainte 7	37n55	122w03	8:08:12
San Simeon 15	35n38'38	121w11'23	8:04:46
Santa Ana 30	33n44'44	117w52'01	7:51:28
Santa Ana Air Facility 30	33n42	117w49	7:51:16
Santa Ana Canyon 30	33n53	117w44	7:50:56
Santa Ana Heights 30	33n39'09	117w53'41	7:51:35
Santa Anita 19	34n08	118w02	7:52:08
Santa Anita Race Track 19	34n08	118w03	7:52:12
Santa Barbara 42	34n25'24	119w42'12	7:58:49
Santa Clara 43	37n20'51	121w15'63	8:05:04
Santa Cruz 44	36n58'27	122w01'47	8:08:07
Santa Cruz Gardens 44	36n59	122w00	8:08:00
Santa Fe Springs 19	33n56'50	118w05'04	7:52:20
Santa Margarita 40	35n23'24	120w36'29	8:02:26
Santa Maria 42	34n57'11	120w26'05	8:01:44
Santa Maria Valley 42	34n54	120w24	8:01:36
Santa Monica 19	34n01'10	118w29'25	7:53:58
Santa Nella 24	37n15	121w00	8:04:00
Santa Nella 49	38n29'50	122w57'56	8:11:52
Santa Nella Village 24	37n05'52	121w00'57	8:04:04
Santa Paula 56	34n21'15	119w03'30	7:56:14
Santa Rita 27	36n43'26	121w39'18	8:06:37
Santa Rita 42	34n42	120w29	8:01:56
Santa Rita Park 24	37n03	120w36	8:02:24
Santa Rosa 49	38n26'26	122w42'48	8:10:51
Santa Rosa Indian Res 33	33n34	116w31	7:46:04
Santa Rosa Race Track 49	38n26	122w42	8:10:48
Santa Susana 56	34n16'18	118w42'29	7:54:50
Santa Susana Knolls 56	34n15'44	118w40'22	7:54:41
Santa Venetia 21	37n59'55	122w31'27	8:10:06
Santa Western 19	34n05	118w22	7:53:28
Santa Ynez 42	34n36'52	120w04'44	8:00:19
Santa Ynez Valley 42	34n37	120w07	8:00:28
Santa Ysabel 37	33n06'33	116w40'20	7:46:41
Santa Ysabel Indian Res 37	33n10	116w37	7:46:28
Santee 37	32n50'18	116w58'23	7:47:54
San Tomas 43	37n16'08	121w58'28	8:07:54
San Ysidro 37	33n15'19	116w33'56	7:46:16
Saranap 7	37n53	122w05	8:08:20
Saratoga 43	37n15'50	122w01'19	8:08:05
Saratoga Springs 17	39n10'31	122w58'47	8:11:55
Sargent 43	36n55'10	121w32'49	8:06:11
Sather Gate 1	37n52	122w16	8:09:04
Saticoy 56	34n16'59	119w08'56	7:56:36
Sattley 46	39n36'58	120w25'34	8:01:42
Saugus 19	34n24'41	118w32'21	7:54:09
Saunders Landing 23	38n51'04	123w38'53	8:14:36
Sausalito 21	37n51'33	122w29'03	8:09:56
Savercool Place 52	40n11'23	121w41'31	8:06:46
Saviers 56	34n12	119w10	7:56:40
Savoy 19	34n06	117w53	7:51:32
Sawmill Flat 10	36n58'10	119w00'59	7:56:04
Sawyers Bar 47	41n18	123w07	8:12:28
Saxon 57	38n28'00	121w39'19	8:06:37
Scales 46	39n35'54	120w59'29	8:03:58
Scarface 25	41n24'42	121w17'38	8:05:11
Scenic Brook Estates 55	37n59	120w23	8:01:32
Scenic Center 50	37n38	120w59	8:03:56
Scheelite 14	37n22'41	118w40'33	7:54:42
Scheideck 56	35n04	119w24	7:57:36
Schellville 49	38n14'46	122w26'19	8:09:45
Schilling 10	36n24'32	119w54'46	7:59:39
Schooner Landing (Site) 21	38n03'51	122w55'45	8:11:43
Sciots Camp 9	38n47'10	120w09'09	8:00:37
Scissors Crossing 37	33n05'47	116w28'28	7:45:54
Scotia 12	40n28'57	124w05'59	8:16:24
Scotland 36	34n14'32	117w29'50	7:49:59
Scott Bar 47	41n45	123w00	8:12:00
Scott Place 12	40n12'24	124w01'56	8:16:08
Scotts 18	39n50'47	120w05'29	8:00:22
Scotts Corner 1	37n35'20	121w52'12	8:07:29
Scotts Valley 44	37n03'04	122w00'49	8:08:03
Scotts Valley Center 44	36n59	122w00	8:08:00
Scottsville 3	38n20'05	120w45'17	8:03:01
Scotty Place 18	41n07'27	120w52'22	8:03:29
Scranton 14	36n27'07	116w30'10	7:46:01
Scripps Ranch 37	32n55	117w06	7:48:24
Seacliff 44	36n59	121w54	8:07:36
Sea Cliff 56	34n20'40	119w25'02	7:57:40
Seahaven 21	38n06	122w51	8:11:24
Seal Beach 30	33n44'29	118w06'14	7:52:25
Seal Beach Naval Weapons Sta 30	33n46	118w05	7:52:20
Seal Cove 41	37n31'09	122w30'42	8:10:03
Searles 15	35n29'02	117w38'04	7:50:32
Searles Valley 36	35n46	117w23	7:49:32
Sears Point 49	38n09'04	122w26'48	8:09:47
Seaside 27	36n36'40	121w51'02	8:07:24
Sebastiani 49	38n17	122w28	8:09:52
Sebastopol 29	39n21'46	121w07'12	8:04:29
Sebastopol 49	38n24'08	122w49'22	8:11:17
Second Crossing 10	37n32'01	119w00'42	7:56:03
Second Garrotte 55	37n49'30	120w11'47	8:00:47
Secret Town 31	39n09'26	120w52'36	8:03:30
Sedco Hills 33	33n38'30	117w17'24	7:49:10
Seeley 13	32n47'35	115w41'25	7:42:46
Seguro 15	35n25'11	119w01'13	7:56:05
Seiad Valley 47	41n50'26	123w11'29	8:12:46
Seigler Springs 17	38n52'28	122w41'23	8:10:46
Selby 7	38n03'24	122w14'34	8:08:58
Selma 10	36n34'15	119w36'40	7:58:27
Seminole Hot Springs 19	34n06'26	118w47'23	7:55:10
Semitropic 15	35n36'07	119w30'27	7:58:02
Seneca 32	40n06'38	121w05'01	8:04:20
Sentous 19	34n01'35	118w22'16	7:53:29
Sepulveda 19	34n09'42	118w16'55	7:53:08
Sequoia 54	36n25'39	119w06'58	7:56:28
Sequoia Crest 54	36n08	118w49	7:55:16
Sequoia National Park 54	36n33'51	118w46'22	7:55:05
Serena 42	34n24'45	119w33'19	7:58:13
Serena Park 42	34n25'07	119w34'18	7:58:17
Serra Mesa 37	32n48'10	117w08'15	7:48:33
Serramonte 41	37n41	122w29	8:09:56
Serrano 40	35n20'06	120w39'13	8:02:37
Serrano Place 30	33n38'49	117w41'20	7:50:45
Serra Reirea 19	34n02'43	118w40'52	7:54:43
Sespe 56	34n24'00	118w56'58	7:55:48
Sespe Village 56	34n23'11	118w57'17	7:55:49
Seven Oaks 36	34n11'11	116w54'48	7:47:39
Seven Pines 14	36n47'08	118w17'35	7:53:10
Seville 54	36n29'09	119w13'20	7:56:53
Shady Dell 37	32n58'22	116w54'58	7:47:40
Shady Glen 31	39n07'05	120w56'55	8:03:48
Shafter 15	35n30'02	119w16'15	7:57:05
Shafter 21	38n00'16	122w42'27	8:10:50
Shake City 23	39n25'52	123w27'58	8:13:52
Shandon 40	35n39'19	120w22'28	8:01:30
Shannon Place 53	40n09'17	123w21'40	8:13:27
Sharon 20	37n05'53	120w07'44	8:00:31
Sharon Valley 58	39n28'56	121w14'45	8:04:59
Sharpe Army Depot 39	37n49	121w17	8:05:08
Sharp Park 41	37n38'10	122w29'13	8:09:57
Shasta 45	40n35'58	122w29'27	8:09:58
Shasta Dam 45	40n40	122w23	8:09:32
Shasta Retreat 47	41n14'08	122w16'17	8:09:05
Shasta Springs 47	41n14'49	122w15'36	8:09:02
Shaver Lake 10	37n09	119w18	7:57:12
Shaver Lake Heights 10	37n06'26	119w19'08	7:57:17
Shaver Lake Point 10	37n09	119w18	7:57:12
Shaws Flat 55	38n00'28	120w24'30	8:01:38
Sheep Crossing 20	37n33'41	119w12'30	7:56:50
Sheep Ranch 5	38n12'34	120w27'47	8:01:51
Sheepshead 18	40n51'20	120w49'24	8:03:18
Sheldon 34	38n25'51	121w17'57	8:05:12
Shell 16	36n19'44	119w37'20	7:58:29
Shell Beach 40	35n09'19	120w40'17	8:02:41
Shelter Cove 12	40n01'50	124w04'19	8:16:17
Shelter Cove 41	37n35'47	122w30'42	8:10:03
Sheridan 31	38n58'47	121w22'28	8:05:30
Sheridan 46	38n27'56	123w02'06	8:12:08
Sherman Acres 5	38n26'49	120w04'23	8:00:18

Sherman Island 34 38N10 121w42 8:06:48
Sherman Oaks 19 34N09'04 118w26'54 7:53:48
Sherwin Plaza 26 37N38 118w58 7:55:52
Sherwood Forest 7 37N58 122w18 8:09:12
Shiloh 49 38N31'25 122w47'41 8:11:11
Shingle Springs 9 38N39'57 120w55'30 8:03:42
Shingletown 45 40N29'33 121w53'17 8:07:33
Shinn 1 37N34'00 121w58'56 8:07:56
Shippee 4 39N32'24 121w41'13 8:06:45
Shipyard Acres 28 38N15'36 122w16'12 8:09:05
Shirley 16 36N23'55 119w39'48 7:58:39
Shirley 30 33N49 118w02 7:52:08
Shirley Meadows 15 35N42'39 118w33'20 7:54:13
Shively 12 40N25'51 123w58'07 8:15:52
Shore Acres 7 38N02'09 121w57'52 8:07:51
Short Acres 16 36N20 119w39 7:58:36
Short Place 9 38N46'48 120w28'23 8:01:54
Shoshone 14 35N58'23 116w16'13 7:45:05
Shrub 9 38N35'33 120w57'13 8:03:49
Shuman 42 34N52'01 120w31'18 8:02:05
Shumway 18 40N41'49 120w29'24 8:01:58
Siberia 36 34N37'36 115w59'06 7:43:56
Sicard Flat 58 39N13'52 121w20'42 8:05:23
Sidds Landing 11 39N33'27 122w00'11 8:08:01
Sierra 10 36N59 119w20 7:57:20
Sierra City 46 39N33'57 120w37'58 8:02:32
Sierra Glen 54 36N38'22 118w59'57 7:56:00
Sierra Heights 54 36N11'14 119w03'40 7:56:15
Sierra Madre 19 34N09'42 118w03'07 7:52:12
Sierra Sky Park 10 36N50'32 119w51'53 7:59:28
Sierra Village No 1 55 38N05 120w13 8:00:52
Sierraville 46 39N35'23 120w21'59 8:01:28
Signal Butte 47 41N16'49 122w11'15 8:08:45
Signal Hill 19 33N47'59 118w09'45 7:52:39
Silt 15 34N59'59 117w44'55 7:51:00
Silverado 30 33N44'46 117w38'10 7:50:33
Silver Canyon Landing 19 33N19'10 118w23'34 7:53:34
Silver City 54 36N27'58 118w38'42 7:54:35
Silver Creek Church 10 36N44'07 120w34'03 8:02:16
Silver Fork 9 38N47 120w18 8:01:12
Silver Lake 3 38N21 120w46 8:03:04
Silver Strand 56 34N09'10 119w13'03 7:56:52
Silverthorn 45 40N38'52 122w23'26 8:09:34
Simi 49 38N38'24 122w52'24 8:11:30
Simi 56 34N16'10 118w46'48 7:55:07
Simi Valley 56 34N16 118w45 7:55:00
Simmler 40 35N21'05 119w59'10 7:59:57
Simms 39 37N47'53 121w05'39 8:04:23
Sims 45 41N04'19 122w21'14 8:09:25
Singing Springs 19 34N19'16 118w07'40 7:52:31
Sisquoc 42 34N51'53 120w17'26 8:01:10
Sites 6 39N18'32 122w20'15 8:09:21
Six-Bit Crossing 52 40N05'53 121w48'51 8:07:15
Skidoo 14 36N26'08 117w08'48 7:48:35
Skinner Mill Place 52 40N09'24 122w42'07 8:10:48
Skinners 9 38N41'57 120w59'39 8:03:59
Skyforest 36 34N14'07 117w10'42 7:48:43
Skyhigh 5 38N25'36 120w05'55 8:00:24
Skyland 36 34N14'00 117w17'07 7:49:08
Sky Londa 41 37N23'01 122w15'42 8:09:03
Skytop 36 35N42'05 117w29'53 7:50:00
Sky Valley 33 33N58 116w30 7:46:00
Slagger 47 41N19'33 121w43'19 8:06:53
Slater 15 35N32'58 119w11'47 7:56:47
Sleepy Hollow 21 37N59 122w35 8:10:20
Sleepy Hollow 36 33N56'52 117w46'40 7:51:07
Sleepy Valley 19 34N30'33 118w21'52 7:53:27
Sloat 32 39N52'00 120w43'35 8:02:54
Sloughhouse 34 38N31 121w06 8:04:24
Smartville 58 39N12'27 121w17'51 8:05:11
Smeltzer 30 33N43'49 117w59'37 7:51:58
Smiley Heights 36 34N04 117w12 7:48:48
Smiley Park 36 34N11'54 117w07'36 7:48:30
Smith Corner 15 35N28'42 119w16'40 7:57:07
Smithflat 9 38N44'12 120w45'15 8:03:01
Smith Mill 54 36N05'25 118w39'27 7:54:38
Smith River 8 41N55'43 124w08'43 8:16:35
Smoke Tree 33 33N49 116w32 7:46:08
Smoke Tree 36 35N08'07 116w05'22 7:44:21
Snelling 24 37N31'09 120w26'11 8:01:45
Snoboy 1 37N30'41 121w56'43 8:07:47
Snow Bend 10 37N16'02 119w07'31 7:56:30
Snow Creek 33 33N53'24 116w41'00 7:46:44
Snowden 47 41N21'17 123w02'09 8:12:09
Snowdon 47 41N47'36 122w28'33 8:09:54
Snowline Camp 9 38N44 120w41 8:02:44
Soapweed 9 38N50'31 120w40'37 8:02:42
Soboba Hot Springs 33 33N47'59 116w55'42 7:47:43
Sobrante 7 38N00'08 122w20'54 8:09:24
Soda Bay 17 39N00'04 122w47'17 8:11:09
Soda Springs 4 40N05'17 121w35'12 8:06:21
Soda Springs 23 39N25'22 123w25'59 8:13:44
Soda Springs 29 39N19'24 120w22'44 8:01:31
Soda Springs 54 36N02'21 118w45'26 7:55:02
Solana Beach 37 32N59'28 117w16'13 7:49:05
Solano Race Track 48 38N08 122w14 8:08:56
Soledad 27 36N25'29 121w19'31 8:05:18
Solemint 19 34N24'59 118w27'05 7:53:48
Solinsky Crossing 5 38N23'18 120w18'33 8:01:14
Solromar 56 34N03'00 118w57'10 7:55:49
Solvang 42 34N35'45 120w08'12 8:00:33
Solyo 50 37N36'34 121w15'48 8:05:03
Somerset 9 38N38'52 120w41'05 8:02:44
Somerset 47 41N51'09 121w59'24 8:07:58
Somersville 7 37N57'25 121w51'48 8:07:27
Somes Bar 47 41N23 123w29 8:13:56
Somis 56 34N15'26 118w59'43 7:55:59
Sonoma 49 38N17'31 122w27'25 8:09:50
Sonoma Vista 49 38N17 122w28 8:09:52
Sonora 55 37N59'03 120w22'52 8:01:31
Sonora Junction 26 38N20'55 119w27'03 7:57:48
Soquel 44 36N59'17 121w57'20 8:07:49
Sorensens 2 38N46'28 119w54'07 7:59:36
Sorrento 37 32N54'03 117w13'20 7:48:53
Sorroca 57 38N20'32 121w36'32 8:06:26
Soto 19 33N58 118w13 7:52:52
Soto Saint Junction 19 34N01'08 118w13'06 7:52:52
Souas Corner 49 38N26'47 122w51'37 8:11:26
Soulsbyville 55 37N59'05 120w15'46 8:01:03
South Alhambra 19 34N04 118w08 7:52:32
South Anaheim 30 33N48'32 117w54'01 7:51:36
South Antelope Valley 19 34N31 118w07 7:52:28
South Bay Cities 19 33N51 118w23 7:53:32
South Belridge 15 35N18 119w37 7:58:28
South Berkeley 1 37N52 122w16 8:09:04
South Coast 30 33N34 117w44 7:50:56
South Coastside 41 37N25 122w22 8:09:28
South Corona 33 33N53 117w33 7:50:12
South Coyote 43 37N11'56 121w43'14 8:06:53
South Dos Palos (Dos Palos S 24 36N57'52 120w39'08 8:02:37
South Downey 19 33N55 118w09 7:52:36
Southeast 19 34N00 118w14 7:52:56
Southeastern 37 32N42 117w07 7:48:28
South El Dorado 9 38N39 120w51 8:03:24
South El Monte 19 34N03'07 118w02'45 7:52:11
South Fontana 36 34N03'46 117w29'17 7:49:57
South Fork 12 40N21 123w55 8:15:40
South Fork 20 37N13'52 119w29'36 7:57:58
South Fork 23 39N25'34 123w43'34 8:14:54
South Fresno 10 36N41 119w48 7:59:12
South Gardena 19 33N53 118w17 7:53:08
South Gate 19 33N57'17 118w12'40 7:52:51
South Laguna 30 33N30'02 117w44'32 7:50:58
South Lake 54 35N38'13 118w21'58 7:53:28
South Lake Tahoe 9 38N56'45 119w58'13 7:59:53
Southland 1 37N38 122w07 8:08:28
South Landing 26 37N34'55 118w43'58 7:54:56
South Leggett 23 39N50'55 123w42'23 8:14:50
South Los Angeles 19 33N55'39 118w16'38 7:53:07
South Main 30 33N43 117w52 7:51:28
South Modesto 50 37N36 120w59 8:03:56
South Oceanside 37 33N10'38 117w21'20 7:49:25
South Oroville 4 39N29'48 121w33'04 8:06:12
South Park 37 32N43'12 117w07'42 7:48:31
South Park 49 38N26 122w43 8:10:52
South Pasadena 19 34N06'58 118w08'58 7:52:36
Southport 57 38N34 121w32 8:06:08
Southport Landing 12 40N41'42 124w14'52 8:16:59
South San Diego 37 32N35'01 117w05'46 7:48:23
South San Francisco 41 37N39'17 122w24'24 8:09:38
South San Gabriel 19 34N03'45 118w05'22 7:52:21
South San Jose Hills 19 34N01 117w54 7:51:36
South San Leandro 1 37N42 122w08 8:08:32
South Santa Ana 30 33N42'41 117w52'02 7:51:28
South Shafter 15 35N30 119w16 7:57:04
South Shores Shopping Center 1 37N47 122w16 8:09:04
South Sutter 51 38N52 121w32 8:06:08
South Taft 15 35N08'05 119w27'19 7:57:49
South Trona 36 35N42'56 117w23'47 7:49:35
South Turlock 50 37N29 120w50 8:03:20
South Vista 37 33N11 117w15 7:49:00
South Wawona 22 37N32'29 119w38'27 7:58:34
Southwest Village 19 33N50'48 118w18'34 7:53:14
South Whittier 19 33N57'39 118w02'27 7:52:10
South Whittier Heights 19 33N56 118w02 7:52:08
South Yuba 58 39N07'32 121w35'04 8:06:20
Spadra 19 34N03'08 117w47'57 7:51:12
Spalding Corner 45 41N07'55 121w34'36 8:06:18
Spangler 36 35N32'56 117w27'02 7:49:48
Spanish Creek 32 39N56 120w55 8:03:40
Spanish Flat 9 38N49'24 120w48'30 8:03:14
Spanish Flat 28 38N18 122w18 8:09:12
Spanish Ranch 32 39N57'03 121w03'22 8:04:13
Sparkle 7 37N55'42 122w03'20 8:08:13
Spaulding 18 40N25 120w39 8:02:36
Spaulding Tract 18 40N39'11 120w46'15 8:03:05
Spear Creek 54 35N49'12 118w35'36 7:54:22
Spellacy 15 35N06'47 119w28'14 7:57:53
Spence 27 36N36'46 121w33'56 8:06:16
Sperry 36 35N44'30 116w13'17 7:44:53
Spicer City 15 35N30'04 119w36'13 7:58:25
Spinks Corner 54 36N12'43 119w13'56 7:56:56
Spoonbill 48 38N03'38 121w54'10 8:07:37
Spreckels 27 36N37'19 121w38'45 8:06:35
Spreckels Junction 27 36N39'30 121w37'47 8:06:31
Springfield 55 38N01'15 120w24'41 8:01:39
Spring Gap 55 38N10'07 120w06'04 8:00:24
Spring Garden 32 39N53'42 120w47'06 8:03:08
Spring Hill 29 39N13'57 121w02'35 8:04:10
Springtowne 48 38N07 122w14 8:08:56
Spring Valley 9 38N46'46 120w31'36 8:02:06
Spring Valley 37 32N44'41 116w59'53 7:48:00
Springville 54 36N07'49 118w49'02 7:55:16
Springville 56 34N13'14 119w05'42 7:56:23
Spruce Point 12 40N44'36 124w11'48 8:16:47
Spurgeon 43 33N45 117w53 7:51:32
Spyrock 23 39N52'36 123w26'34 8:13:46
Squab 28 38N11'50 122w16'35 8:09:06
Squabbletown 55 38N00'53 120w23'07 8:01:32
Squaw Hill 52 39N54'29 122w05'31 8:08:22
Squaw Valley 10 36N44'27 119w14'44 7:56:59
Squirrel Mountain Valley 15 35N37'24 118w24'32 7:53:38
Squirrel Valley 15 35N39 118w28 7:53:52
Stacy 18 40N13'48 120w01'13 8:00:05
Stafford 12 40N27'15 124w03'09 8:16:13
Standard 55 37N58'00 120w18'39 8:01:15
Standish 18 40N21'55 120w25'16 8:01:41
Stanfield Hill 58 39N20'33 121w19'55 8:05:20
Stanford 43 37N25 122w10 8:08:40
Stanislaus 55 38N08'18 120w22'09 8:01:29
Stanley 28 38N14'41 122w17'34 8:09:10
Stanton 30 33N48'09 117w59'32 7:51:58
State Capitol 34 38N34 121w29 8:05:56
Stateline 9 38N57'30 119w56'34 7:59:46
Stauffer 56 34N45'16 119w03'57 7:56:16
Steamboat Landing 34 38N18'20 121w34'23 8:06:18
Stedman 36 34N37'48 116w10'02 7:44:40
Steele Park 28 38N18 122w18 8:09:12
Steelhead 12 40N10'13 123w38'39 8:14:35
Steelhead 47 41N46'37 123w02'17 8:12:09
Steens Landing 23 38N49'42 123w37'04 8:14:28
Steeplehollow Crossing 29 39N11'46 120w53'07 8:03:32
Stege 7 37N55'00 122w19'34 8:09:18
Stegeman 6 39N21'28 122w01'39 8:08:07
Stent 55 37N55'04 120w24'44 8:01:39
Stephens 19 33N56 118w04 7:52:16
Sterling Park 41 37N42 122w28 8:09:52
Steuben Place 52 39N57'52 122w44'37 8:10:58
Stevens 15 35N18'51 119w11'23 7:56:46
Stevinson 24 37N19'40 120w51'02 8:03:24
Stewarts Point 49 38N39'07 123w23'53 8:13:36
Stewartville 7 37N56'47 121w50'51 8:07:23
Stills Landing (Ruins) 33 34N01'42 116w42'53 7:46:52
Stinson Beach 21 37N54'02 122w38'36 8:10:34
Stirling City 4 39N54'28 121w31'37 8:06:06
Stirling Junction 4 39N42'51 121w48'44 8:07:15
Stockton 39 37N57'28 121w17'23 8:05:10
Stoil 54 35N55'05 119w25'28 7:57:42
Stokdale 15 35N21 119w03 7:56:12
Stomar 50 37N21'43 121w02'41 8:04:11
Stone 12 40N30'44 124w06'47 8:16:27
Stonebreaker Crossing 18 41N04'05 120w58'27 8:03:54
Stonegate 41 37N27 122w11 8:08:44
Stonehurst 19 34N15'04 118w22'10 7:53:29
Stone Lagoon 12 41N04 124w08 8:16:32
Stoneman 19 34N05'19 118w07'17 7:52:29
Stone Place (Ruins) 54 35N54'09 118w44'00 7:54:56
Stonestown 38 37N44'34 122w32'38 8:10:11
Stonyford 6 39N22'31 122w32'35 8:10:10
Stony Point 49 38N18'39 122w44'02 8:10:56
Storey 20 36N58'27 120w01'05 8:00:04
Storrie 32 39N55'03 121w19'20 8:05:17
Stout 54 36N10'58 119w04'46 7:56:19
Stout Grove 8 41N47'26 124w04'54 8:16:20
Stove Pipe Wells 14 36N18 116w45 7:47:00
Stratford 16 36N11'22 119w49'20 7:59:17
Strathearn 56 34N16'52 118w47'54 7:55:12
Strathmore 54 36N08'44 119w03'35 7:56:14
Strawberry 9 38N47'49 120w08'39 8:00:35
Strawberry 55 38N11'54 120w00'30 8:00:02
Strawberry Manor 21 37N54 122w32 8:10:08
Strawberry Point 21 37N54 122w31 8:10:04
Strawberry Valley 58 39N33'51 121w06'21 8:04:25
Stronghold 25 41N54'20 121w24'31 8:05:38
Stuart 37 33N15'04 117w25'12 7:49:41
Studebaker 19 33N55'11 118w05'43 7:52:23
Studio City 19 34N08'55 118w23'44 7:53:35
Studio Village 19 34N00 118w24 7:53:36
Styx 33 33N52'41 114w47'40 7:39:11
Subaco 51 38N55'43 121w44'18 8:06:57
Subeet 48 38N13'42 122w04'48 8:08:19
Success 54 36N04 119w04 7:56:16
Sucker Flat 58 39N12'43 121w17'46 8:05:11
Sucro 48 38N14'57 121w48'08 8:07:13
Sugarfield 57 38N42'50 121w45'09 8:07:01
Sugarloaf 36 34N14'36 116w49'41 7:47:19
Sugarloaf 45 40N51'24 122w23'48 8:09:35
Sugarloaf Mountain Park 54 35N50'20 118w36'13 7:54:25
Sugar Pine 20 37N26'28 119w38'00 7:58:32
Sugarpine 55 38N03'30 120w12'02 8:00:48
Suisun 48 38N14'18 122w02'21 8:08:09
Suisun City 48 38N14'18 122w02'21 8:08:09
Sullivan 51 39N12'12 121w38'04 8:06:32
Sulphur Springs 19 34N28'46 118w36'48 7:54:27
Sulphur Springs 35 36N17'35 120w59'01 8:03:56
Sulphur Springs 56 34N25'37 119w05'37 7:56:22
Sultana 54 36N32'44 119w20'21 7:57:21
Summer Home 39 37N50'51 121w11'05 8:04:44
Summerhome 49 38N29'52 122w56'24 8:11:46
Summerhome Park 49 38N28 122w53 8:11:32
Summerland 42 34N25'17 119w35'44 7:58:23
Summertown 45 40N32'40 121w33'59 8:06:16
Summerville 47 41N05'56 123w04'00 8:12:16

Summit 15 35N07'40 118w24'47 7:53:39
Summit 36 34N20 117w25 7:49:40
Summit City 29 39N24'32 120w30'05 8:02:00
Summit City 45 40N41'10 122w24'02 8:09:36
Summit Inn 22 37N29 119w58 7:59:52
Sun City 33 33N42'33 117w11'47 7:48:47
Suncrest 37 32N48'15 116w51'49 7:47:27
Sunfair 36 34N09'50 116w14'47 7:44:59
Sunfair Heights 36 34N14'25 116w13'05 7:44:52
Sunkist 30 33N50 117w52 7:51:28
Sunkist 36 34N04'38 117w11'24 7:48:46
Sunland 19 34N16'01 118w18'05 7:53:12
Sunland 54 36N01'21 118w58'53 7:55:56
Sunny Brae 12 40N51'30 124w03'55 8:16:16
Sunnybrook 3 38N20'35 120w52'33 8:03:30
Sunny Hills 30 33N54'04 117w56'08 7:51:45
Sunnymead 33 33N56'24 117w14'34 7:48:58
Sunnyside 10 36N44'57 119w41'54 7:58:48
Sunnyside 31 39N08'36 120w09'09 8:00:37
Sunnyside 37 32N40'27 117w00'56 7:48:04
Sunnyside 52 39N50'39 122w51'51 8:11:27
Sunnyslope 4 39N22'03 121w25'51 8:05:43
Sunnyslope 33 34N00'43 117w25'57 7:49:44
Sunnyvale 43 37N22'08 122w02'07 8:08:08
Sunnyvale Plaza 43 37N23 122w01 8:08:04
Sunny Vista 37 32N38'41 117w04'02 7:48:16
Sunol 1 37N36 121w53 8:07:32
Sunrise 19 34N40'23 118w07'51 7:52:31
Sunrise Oasis 33 33N49 116w32 7:46:08
Sunrise Vista 17 38N52'48 122w43'59 8:10:56
Sunset 12 40N52 124w05 8:16:20
Sunset 38 37N46 122w28 8:09:52
Sunset 51 39N15'02 121w39'03 8:06:36
Sunset Beach 30 33N42'59 118w04'05 7:52:16
Sunset Beach 44 36N55 121w47 8:07:08
Sunset Cliffs 37 32N43'44 117w15'39 7:49:03
Sunset District 38 37N45'13 122w29'39 8:09:59
Sunset Hills 19 34N00 117w57 7:51:48
Sunset Terrace 40 35N18 120w45 8:03:00
Sunset Tract 56 34N24 119w18 7:57:12
Sunset View 29 39N13'46 121w05'43 8:04:23
Sunset-Whitney Ranch 31 38N48 121w14 8:04:56
Sunshine Camp 55 37N59'16 120w16'54 8:01:08
Sunshine Homes 19 34N25 118w32 7:54:08
Sunsweet 36 34N03'36 117w41'02 7:50:44
Sun Valley 19 34N13'03 118w22'10 7:53:29
Sun Village 19 34N35 118w06 7:52:24
Surf 42 34N41'04 120w36'09 8:02:25
Surfside 30 33N43'40 118w04'53 7:52:20
Surprise 25 41N34'26 120w26'07 8:01:44
Surprise Valley 25 41N33 120w09 8:00:36
Susana Knolls 56 34N16 118w45 7:55:00
Susanville 18 40N24'59 120w39'07 8:02:36
Suscol 28 38N14'38 122w17'02 8:09:08
Sutter 51 39N09'35 121w44'52 8:06:59
Sutter Creek 3 38N23'35 120w48'05 8:03:12
Sutter Hill 3 38N22'42 120w48'02 8:03:12
Sutter Island 34 38N20 121w34 8:06:16
Suval 48 38N14'48 122w04'36 8:08:18
Sveadal 43 37N05'01 121w47'17 8:07:09
Swall 54 36N14'27 119w17'10 7:57:09
Swansea 14 36N31'29 117w54'11 7:51:37
Swanston 34 38N36'18 121w26'09 8:05:45
Swanton 44 37N03'51 122w13'35 8:08:54
Sweeneys Crossing 9 38N39'10 120w37'26 8:02:30
Sweetbriar 45 41N07'48 122w19'09 8:09:17
Sweet Brier 45 41N09 122w19 8:09:16
Sweetland 29 39N20'35 121w07'09 8:04:29
Swingle 57 38N33'30 121w40'28 8:06:42
Swobe 47 41N16'37 121w54'48 8:07:39
Sycamore 6 39N08'02 121w56'27 8:07:46
Sycamore 7 37N50 122w00 8:08:00
Sycamore Flat 27 36N16'00 121w23'33 8:05:34
Sycamore Springs 40 35N11'11 120w42'48 8:02:51
Sykes 14 36N02'12 117w57'34 7:51:50
Sylmar 19 34N18'28 118w26'54 7:53:48
Sylvan Lodge 55 38N05'03 120w09'22 8:00:37
Sylvia Park 19 34N06'54 118w34'51 7:54:19
Syndicate Mill 26 38N13'24 118w59'37 7:55:58
Taft 15 35N08'33 119w27'20 7:57:49
Taft Heights 15 35N08'05 119w28'18 7:57:53
Tagus 54 36N16'17 119w22'02 7:57:28
Tahoe City 31 39N10'20 120w08'16 8:00:33
Tahoe Keys 9 38N56 119w59 7:59:56
Tahoe Paradise 9 38N56 119w59 7:59:56
Tahoe Pines 31 39N06'17 120w09'33 8:00:38
Tahoe Valley 9 38N54'49 120w00'12 8:00:01
Tahoe Vista 31 39N14'24 120w03'00 8:00:12
Tahoma 31 39N04'03 120w07'38 8:00:31
Tajiguas 42 34N28'00 120w06'27 8:00:26
Talica 37 33N12 117w20 7:49:20
Talich 37 33N12'00 117w19'00 7:49:16
Tallac Village 9 38N55'19 120w01'15 8:00:05
Tall Timber Camp 55 38N04'25 120w10'17 8:00:41
Talmage 23 39N07'51 123w09'54 8:12:40
Talus 14 36N05'13 117w58'19 7:51:53
Tamalpais Valley 21 37N52'47 122w32'41 8:10:11
Tamalpais Valley Junction 21 37N52'55 122w31'25 8:10:06
Tamarack 5 38N26'20 120w04'30 8:00:18
Tambo 58 39N14'22 121w34'34 8:06:18
Tambs Station 55 37N59 120w23 8:01:32
Tancred 57 38N45'55 122w09'45 8:08:39
Tanforan 41 37N39 122w26 8:09:44
Tangair 42 34N45'16 120w36'36 8:02:26
Tanglewood 44 37N03 122w04 8:08:16
Tan Oak Park 23 39N49'40 123w36'11 8:14:25
Tara Hills 7 37N58 122w20 8:09:20
Tarke 51 39N08'43 121w50'53 8:07:24
Tarpey 10 36N47'16 119w41'59 7:58:48
Tarpey Village 10 36N47'35 119w42'00 7:58:48
Tarzana 19 34N10'24 118w33'11 7:54:13
Tassajara 7 37N47'48 121w51'47 8:07:27
Tassajara Hot Springs 27 36N14'03 121w32'52 8:06:11
Tatu 23 39N39'30 123w20'37 8:13:22
Taurusa 54 36N25'04 119w15'09 7:57:01
Taylor 33 33N35'54 116w25'03 7:45:40
Taylor Crossing 31 39N06'37 120w59'01 8:03:56
Taylor Junction 19 34N03'47 118w13'20 7:52:53
Taylorsville 32 40N04'32 120w50'19 8:03:21
Teakettle Junction 14 36N45'37 117w32'30 7:50:10
Teal 48 38N10'24 122w04'40 8:08:19
Tecate 37 32N34'38 116w37'36 7:46:30
Tecnor 47 41N47 122w00 8:08:00
Tecopa 14 35N50'54 116w13'32 7:44:54
Tecopa Hot Springs 14 35N51 116w13 7:44:52
Tehachapi 15 35N07'56 118w26'53 7:53:48
Tehama 52 40N01'38 122w07'20 8:08:29
Telegraph City 5 37N56'04 120w44'20 8:02:57
Temecula 33 33N29'37 117w08'51 7:48:35
Temescal 1 37N50 122w16 8:09:04
Temple City 19 34N06'26 118w03'25 7:52:14
Templeton 40 35N32'59 120w42'18 8:02:49
Tennant 47 41N35'02 121w54'44 8:07:39
Tent City 37 32N41 117w11 7:48:44
Terminal Island 19 33N44 118w18 7:53:12
Terminous 39 38N06'48 121w29'40 8:05:59
Termo 18 40N51'57 120w27'33 8:01:50
Terra Bella 54 35N57'45 119w02'36 7:56:10
Terra Cotta 33 33N42'11 117w22'26 7:49:30
Terra Linda 21 38N01 122w33 8:10:12
Terra Loma 41 37N41 122w29 8:09:56
Tewksbury Heights 7 37N57 122w19 8:09:16
Textile 19 34N02 118w18 7:53:12
The Cedars 31 39N15'11 120w21'08 8:01:25
The Crossing 18 40N29'11 120w28'23 8:01:54
The Forks 23 39N11'28 123w12'24 8:12:50
The Geysers 49 38N48 123w01 8:12:04
The Grove 24 37N24'14 120w35'38 8:02:23
The Homestead 39 37N56'20 121w17'05 8:05:08
Thenard 19 33N47'12 118w14'30 7:52:58
The Oaks 19 34N30'38 118w21'16 7:53:25
The Oaks 23 38N54'17 123w13'30 8:12:54
The Oaks 29 39N13'10 121w04'48 8:04:19
The Pines 20 37N19'08 119w33'08 7:58:13
The Plaza 36 35N09'01 116w03'12 7:44:13
Thermal 33 33N38'25 116w08'19 7:44:33
Thermalito 4 39N29'54 121w36'03 8:06:24
The Sea Ranch 49 40N12 123w30 8:14:00
The Willows 37 32N50'05 116w43'18 7:46:53
The Willows 44 37N06'10 121w55'25 8:07:42
Thoman 28 38N29'28 122w27'03 8:09:48
Thomas Lane 15 35N29'15 119w17'02 7:57:08
Thomas Mountain 14 33N36'45 116w37'34 7:46:30
Thomasson 48 38N13'02 122w06'23 8:08:26
Thompson 28 38N14'21 122w16'50 8:09:07
Thompson Place 52 40N09'37 121w58'22 8:07:53
Thorn 36 34N28'33 117w16'48 7:49:07
Thorn Junction 12 40N03'49 123w57'45 8:15:51
Thornton 39 38N13'34 121w25'25 8:05:42
Thousand Oaks 56 34N10'14 118w50'12 7:55:21
Thousand Palms 33 33N49'12 116w23'22 7:45:33
Three Arch Bay 30 33N29'27 117w43'53 7:50:56
Three Crossing 17 39N19'00 122w55'13 8:11:41
Three Point 19 34N40 118w26 7:53:44
Three Points 19 34N44'10 118w35'52 7:54:23
Three Rivers 54 36N26'20 118w54'13 7:55:37
Three Rocks 10 36N30 120w19 8:01:16
Thyle 40 35N20'28 120w37'57 8:02:32
Tiber 40 35N10'42 120w37'03 8:02:28
Tiburon 21 37N52'25 122w27'20 8:09:49
Tierra Buena 51 39N08'56 121w39'57 8:06:40
Tierra del School 37 32N37'23 116w19'15 7:45:17
Tierra del Sol 37 32N40 116w16 7:45:04
Tierra Santa 37 32N47 117w06 7:48:24
Tiger Lily 9 38N40'52 120w46'26 8:03:06
Timba 50 37N20'34 121w01'48 8:04:07
Timber Lodge 22 37N33 119w56 7:59:44
Timbuctoo 58 39N13'01 121w19'03 8:05:16
Tionesta 25 41N38'46 121w19'37 8:05:18
Tipton 54 36N03'34 119w18'40 7:57:15
Tisdale 51 39N02'26 121w47'06 8:07:08
Titus 37 32N37'57 116w10'44 7:44:43
Tivy Valley 10 36N42 119w33 7:58:12
Toadtown 4 39N53'17 121w35'22 8:06:21
Tobin 32 39N56'17 121w18'27 8:05:14
Tocaloma 21 38N03'01 122w45'30 8:11:02
Todd Place 40 35N16'27 120w09'45 8:00:39
Todd Valley 31 38N59'53 120w51'02 8:03:24
Todos Santos 7 37N58 122w01 8:08:04
Tokay 54 36N33'07 119w21'29 7:57:26
Toland Landing 48 38N05'18 121w45'01 8:07:00
Tolenas 48 38N15'55 122w00'16 8:08:01
Tollhouse 10 37N01'08 119w23'54 7:57:36
Toluca Lake 19 34N09 118w22 7:53:28
Tomales 21 38N14'47 122w54'16 8:11:37
Toms Place 26 37N33'41 118w40'49 7:54:43
Tomspur 39 38N03'26 121w16'33 8:05:06
Tonyville 54 36N14'55 119w05'23 7:56:22
Toolville 54 36N17'15 119w07'00 7:56:28
Toomey 36 34N55'15 116w44'40 7:46:59
Topanga 19 34N05'37 118w36'02 7:54:24
Topanga Beach 19 34N02'24 118w34'43 7:54:19
Topanga Oaks 19 34N05 118w37 7:54:28
Topanga Park 19 34N06'27 118w37'42 7:54:31
Topa Topa 56 34N21 119w04 7:56:16
Topaz 26 38N36'40 119w31'04 7:58:04
Top of the World 30 33N32'54 117w45'12 7:51:01
Tormey 7 38N03'02 122w14'53 8:09:00
Toro 27 36N34 121w40 8:06:40
Torrance 19 33N50'09 118w20'23 7:53:22
Torres Martinez Indian Res 33 33N28 116w02 7:44:08
Torrey Crossing 12 40N36'33 123w35'48 8:14:23
Torrey Pines Homes 37 32N50 117w14 7:48:56
Tortuga 13 33N10'04 115w20'31 7:41:22
Tower 10 36N46 119w47 7:59:08
Towle 31 39N12'15 120w47'53 8:03:12
Town and Country 7 37N50 122w00 8:08:00
Town and Country Trailer Pk 33 33N56 117w14 7:48:56
Town and Country Village 34 38N37'05 121w23'59 8:05:36
Town Center 54 36N20 119w18 7:57:12
Town Talk 29 39N14'36 121w01'47 8:04:07
Toyon 5 38N12'18 120w45'52 8:03:03
Toyon 45 40N33 122w22 8:09:28
Trabuco 30 33N41 117w36 7:50:24
Trabuco Canyon 30 33N39'50 117w35'22 7:50:21
Tracy 39 37N44'23 121w25'27 8:05:42
Trancas 19 34N01'52 118w50'32 7:55:22
Tranquillity 10 36N38'56 120w15'06 8:01:00
Traver 54 36N27'19 119w29'02 7:57:56
Travis Air Force Base 48 38N16 121w55 8:07:40
Travis Field 48 38N16'20 121w55'54 8:07:44
Treasure Island 38 37N46 122w27 8:09:48
Trent 24 37N04'39 120w52'47 8:03:31
Trenton 49 38N29'07 122w51'03 8:11:24
Tres Pinos 35 36N47'24 121w19'12 8:05:17
Trevarno 1 37N41'26 121w44'47 8:06:59
Trigo 20 36N54'47 119w57'34 7:59:50
Trimmer 10 36N54'18 119w17'43 7:57:11
Trinidad 12 41N03'34 124w08'31 8:16:34
Trinity Alps 53 40N51'27 122w53'21 8:11:33
Trinity Center 53 41N00 122w41 8:10:44
Trinity Village 53 40N52'32 123w31'38 8:14:07
Triple R Estates 54 36N04 119w04 7:56:16
Triunfo Corner 56 34N09'27 118w49'26 7:55:18
Trocha 54 35N47'53 119w08'46 7:56:35
Trona 36 35N45'46 117w22'19 7:49:29
Tropico 19 34N08 118w16 7:53:04
Tropico Village 15 34N52 118w10 7:52:40
Trowbridge 51 38N54'39 121w31'27 8:06:06
Troy 31 39N18'42 120w27'43 8:01:51
Truckee 29 39N19'41 120w10'56 8:00:44
Truckhaven 13 33N17'49 115w58'35 7:43:54
Trull 39 37N56'19 121w30'02 8:06:00
Tryon Corner 8 41N52'39 124w08'43 8:16:35
Tuber 25 41N56'13 121w27'01 8:05:48
Tudor 51 39N00'18 121w37'21 8:06:29
Tujunga 19 34N15'08 118w17'15 7:53:09
Tulare 54 36N12'28 119w20'47 7:57:23
Tulelake 47 41N57'22 121w28'35 8:05:54
Tule River Indian Res 54 36N02 118w43 7:54:52
Tunitas 41 37N23 122w23 8:09:32
Tunnel Inn 45 40N43'35 122w19'25 8:09:18
Tuolumne 55 37N57'39 120w14'11 8:00:57
Tuolumne Meadows 55 37N45 119w35 7:58:20
Tupman 15 35N17'53 119w21'01 7:57:24
Turk 10 36N10'16 120w13'16 8:00:53
Turlock 50 37N29'41 120w50'44 8:03:23
Turner 39 37N51'36 121w13'02 8:04:52
Turner 49 38N20'28 122w46'35 8:11:06
Turner Station 39 37N48 121w11 8:04:44
Tustin 30 33N44'45 117w49'31 7:51:18
Tustin-Foothills 30 33N46 117w48 7:51:12
Tuttle 24 37N17'46 120w22'40 8:01:31
Tuttletown 55 37N59'30 120w27'31 8:01:50
Tuxedo Country Club Estates 39 37N58 121w19 8:05:16
Tuxedo Park 39 37N58 121w19 8:05:16
T V Bell 24 37N18 120w29 8:01:56
Twain 32 40N01'08 121w01'58 8:04:08
Twain Harte 55 38N02'23 120w13'54 8:00:56
Tweedy 19 33N56 118w11 7:52:44
Twentymile Crossing 52 40N06'50 121w48'59 8:07:16
Twentynine Palms 36 34N08'08 116w03'12 7:44:13
Twentynine Palms Base 36 34N14 116w04 7:44:16
Twentynine Palms Indian Res 36 34N07 116w02 7:44:08
Twin Bridges 9 38N48'41 120w07'23 8:00:30
Twin Buttes 54 36N28'00 119w12'20 7:56:49
Twin Cities 34 38N17'28 121w18'36 8:05:14
Twin Creeks 43 37N09'22 121w50'35 8:07:22
Twin Lakes 15 34N59'14 118w30'49 7:54:03
Twin Lakes 19 34N16'41 118w36'02 7:54:24
Twin Lakes 44 36N58'03 121w59'49 8:07:59
Twin Oaks 15 35N18'45 118w24'32 7:53:38
Twin Oaks 37 33N11'07 117w09'14 7:48:37
Twin Peaks 36 34N14'20 117w13'58 7:48:56
Twin Pines 31 39N01'32 120w58'42 8:03:55
Two Rivers 32 39N49'23 120w40'09 8:02:41
Two Rock 49 38N15'59 122w47'28 8:11:10
Tyee City 12 40N55'21 124w07'32 8:16:30
Tylers Corner 9 38N31'42 120w41'07 8:02:44
Tyndall Landing 57 38N52'59 121w49'01 8:07:16
Tyrone 49 38N26'57 122w59'58 8:12:00
Ueland Place (Site) 53 40N18'47 123w23'44 8:13:35

Ukiah 23 39N09'01 123w12'24 8:12:50
Ulmar 1 37N42'11 121w42'54 8:06:52
Ultra 54 35N57'51 118w59'51 7:55:59
Una 15 35N25'28 119w10'37 7:56:42
Underwood Park 23 39N51'36 123w42'57 8:14:52
Union 28 38N19'17 122w18'32 8:09:14
Union City (Alvarado) 1 37N35'47 122w04'50 8:08:19
Union Hill 29 39N12'20 121w02'15 8:04:09
Union Hill 46 39N35'50 121w00'08 8:04:01
Union Landing 23 39N41'58 123w48'02 8:15:12
Union Mills 29 39N21'14 120w06'22 8:00:25
Universal City 19 34N08'20 118w21'09 7:53:25
University City 37 32N51'17 117w12'11 7:48:49
University Heights 37 32N45'20 117w08'19 7:48:33
University Heights 41 37N27 122w11 8:08:44
University of Cal-Davis 57 38N37 121w43 8:06:52
University of Santa Clara 43 37N21 121w58 8:07:52
University Park 30 33N37 117w54 7:51:36
Upland 36 34N05'51 117w38'51 7:50:35
Upper Crossing 47 41N52'50 122w09'54 8:08:40
Upper Forni 9 38N49'20 120w10'18 8:00:41
Upper Lake 17 39N09'53 122w54'34 8:11:38
Upper San Gabriel Valley 19 34N06 118w01 7:52:04
Upper Scheelite 14 37N22 118w24 7:53:36
Upper Soda Springs 47 41N13 122w16 8:09:04
Upper Town 26 38N21'16 119w07'01 7:56:28
Upton 47 41N20'28 122w20'49 8:09:23
Uptown 36 34N08 117w18 7:49:12
Urgon 39 38N09'29 121w16'14 8:05:05
U S Naval Hospital 19 33N49 118w10 7:52:40
U S Naval Postgrad School 27 36N36 121w53 8:07:32
Uva 10 36N37'08 119w29'20 7:57:57
Vacation 49 38N30 123w00 8:12:00
Vacation Beach 49 38N29'23 123w00'44 8:12:03
Vacaville 48 38N21'24 121w59'12 8:07:57
Vacaville Junction 48 38N17'44 121w57'51 8:07:51
Vade 9 38N49 120w03 8:00:12
Valdez 57 38N19'34 121w36'44 8:06:27
Vale 48 38N19'13 121w47'04 8:07:08
Valencia 19 34N26'37 118w36'31 7:54:26
Valerie 33 33N34'08 116w10'46 7:44:43
Valinda 19 34N02'43 117w56'34 7:51:46
Valjean 36 35N35'08 116w07'26 7:44:30
Valla 19 33N57'29 118w03'31 7:52:14
Vallecito 5 38N05'14 120w28'19 8:01:53
Vallejo 48 38N06'15 122w15'20 8:09:01
Vallemar 41 37N36'49 122w28'47 8:09:55
Valleton 27 35N53'22 120w42'17 8:02:49
Valle Vista 7 37N49'22 122w08'16 8:08:33
Valle Vista 33 33N44'52 116w53'33 7:47:34
Valley Acres 15 35N12'22 119w24'21 7:57:37
Valley Center 37 33N13'06 117w02'00 7:48:08
Valley Crossing 49 38N41'59 123w24'45 8:13:39
Valleydale 19 34N07 117w54 7:51:36
Valley Fair 43 37N19 121w56 8:07:44
Valley Ford 49 38N19'05 122w55'23 8:11:42
Valley Home 50 37N49'44 120w54'40 8:03:39
Valley of Enchantment 36 34N14'48 117w18'14 7:49:13
Valley of the Moon 36 34N14 117w17 7:49:08
Valley Plaza 19 34N05 118w22 7:53:28
Valley Springs 5 38N11'30 120w49'41 8:03:19
Valley View Park 36 34N14'06 117w18'26 7:49:14
Valley Village 19 34N10 118w24 7:53:36
Valley Wells 14 35N49'42 117w19'51 7:49:19
Valley Wells 36 35N28 115w16 7:41:04
Valley Wells Station 36 35N26'05 115w42'05 7:42:48
Valona 7 38N03'08 122w13'24 8:08:54
Val Verde 19 34N26'42 118w39'24 7:54:38
Val Verde 33 33N50'54 117w15'11 7:49:01
Val Verde Park 19 34N25 118w32 7:54:08
Valyermo 19 34N26'46 117w51'05 7:51:24
Van Allen 39 37N47'54 121w03'05 8:04:12
Vance 54 36N13'27 119w06'09 7:56:25
Vanden 48 38N21 121w59 8:07:56
Vandenberg Air Force Base 42 34N41 120w29 8:01:56
Vandenberg Village 42 34N42 120w29 8:01:56
Vandenburg 42 34N41 120w29 8:01:56
Vanderbilt 36 35N19'50 115w15'01 7:41:00
Van Duzen 12 40N28 123w48 8:15:12
Vanguard 10 36N15'19 119w57'29 7:59:50
Vann 17 39N15'10 122w57'16 8:11:49
Van Ness 19 33N58'57 118w19'07 7:53:16
Van Nuys 19 34N11'12 118w26'53 7:53:48
Vanowen 19 34N05 118w22 7:53:28
Van Vleck 9 38N46'41 120w30'52 8:02:03
Vasona Junction 43 37N15'26 121w57'49 8:07:51
Vasquez Crossing 35 36N19'04 120w51'13 8:03:25
Vega 19 34N11'31 118w21'00 7:53:24
Venado 49 38N36'20 123w00'25 8:12:02
Venice 19 33N59'27 118w27'33 7:53:50
Venida 54 36N19'58 119w07'45 7:56:31
Venola 15 35N18'39 119w03'12 7:56:13
Ventucopa 42 34N49'53 119w28'08 7:57:53
Ven-tu Park 56 34N11 118w55 7:55:40
Ventura 56 34N16'42 119w17'32 7:57:10
Verano 49 38N18'10 122w28'26 8:09:54
Verdant 13 33N07'03 115w33'29 7:42:14
Verde 40 35N10'18 120w33'25 8:02:14
Verdemont 36 34N11'36 117w21'51 7:49:27
Verdi Sierra Pines 46 39N31 119w59 7:59:56
Verdugo City 19 34N12'41 118w14'19 7:52:57
Verdugo Viejo 19 34N10 118w15 7:53:00
Vermont Avenue 19 34N05 118w18 7:53:12
Vernalis 39 37N37'51 121w17'10 8:05:09
Vernon 19 34N00'14 118w13'45 7:52:55
Verona 51 38N47'10 121w37'03 8:06:28
Verona Landing 51 38N54 121w35 8:06:20
Vestal 54 35N50'23 119w05'02 7:56:20
Veteran Heights 28 38N34'27 122w26'06 8:09:44
Veterans Administration Hosp 19 33N49 118w10 7:52:40
Veterans Bureau Hospital 43 37N24 122w09 8:08:36
Veterans Home 28 38N24 122w22 8:09:28
Vichy Springs 23 39N10'01 123w09'25 8:12:38
Vichy Springs 28 38N20'16 122w15'36 8:09:02
Victor 39 38N08'17 121w12'18 8:04:49
Victoria Park 19 33N53 118w17 7:53:08
Victorville 36 34N32'10 117w17'25 7:49:10
Victory Center Annex 19 34N05 118w22 7:53:28
Victory Plams 33 33N42'20 115w45'04 7:43:00
Vidal 36 34N07'08 114w30'34 7:38:02
Vidal Junction 36 34N11'19 114w34'24 7:38:18
Viewland 18 40N25'49 120w16'45 8:01:07
View Park 19 34N00'00 118w20'30 7:53:22
Viking 19 33N49 118w07 7:52:28
Village 19 34N04 118w26 7:53:44
Villa Grande 49 38N28'23 123w01'28 8:12:06
Villa Montalvo 43 37N14'38 122w01'47 8:08:07
Villa Park 30 33N48'52 117w48'44 7:51:15
Villa Verona 4 39N30 121w33 8:06:12
Villinger 39 38N08'39 121w22'21 8:05:29
Vina 52 39N55'59 122w03'10 8:08:13
Vincent 19 34N30'02 118w06'56 7:52:28
Vincent Landing 21 38N13'10 122w56'27 8:11:46
Vineburg 49 38N16'21 122w26'15 8:09:45
Vine Hill 7 38N00'31 122w05'42 8:08:23
Vineyard 36 34N05 117w31 7:50:04
Vinland 15 35N42'54 119w14'02 7:56:56
Vinton 32 39N48'16 120w10'38 8:00:43
Vinvale 19 33N57'13 118w09'46 7:52:39
Viola 45 40N31'05 121w40'36 8:06:42
Virgilia 32 40N01'07 121w06'16 8:04:25
Virginia Colony 56 34N17'16 118w51'27 7:55:26
Virginiatown 31 38N54'02 121w12'49 8:04:51
Virner 9 38N54 120w50 8:03:20
Visalia 54 36N19'49 119w17'28 7:57:10
Visitacion 38 37N43 122w25 8:09:40
Vista 37 33N12'00 117w14'30 7:48:58
Vista del Mar 19 33N49'08 118w11'52 7:52:47
Vista del Morro 40 35N18 120w45 8:03:00
Vista Grande 41 37N41 122w27 8:09:48
Vista La Mesa 37 32N46 117w00 7:48:00
Vista Park 15 35N21 118w59 7:55:56
Vista Robles 4 39N25'15 121w33'05 8:06:12
Volcano 3 38N26'35 120w37'47 8:02:31
Volcanoville 9 38N58'55 120w47'17 8:03:09
Vollmers 45 40N56'35 122w26'20 8:09:45
Volta 24 37N05'51 120w55'30 8:03:42
Vorden 34 38N16'38 121w32'24 8:06:10
Voss 9 38N39'26 120w23'12 8:01:33
Waddington 12 40N34'02 124w12'02 8:16:48
Wade Place 52 40N17'46 121w54'51 8:07:39
Wadstrom 56 34N18'58 119w17'26 7:57:10
Wagner 19 33N57 118w18 7:53:12
Wagner 39 37N47'53 121w04'49 8:04:19
Wagner 55 38N21'31 119w52'37 7:59:30
Wagy Flats 15 35N39 118w28 7:53:52
Wahtoke 10 36N40'37 119w27'25 7:57:50
Waldo 21 37N52'16 122w30'09 8:10:01
Waldo Junction 58 39N06'40 121w18'29 8:05:14
Waldorf 42 34N54'40 120w33'15 8:02:13
Waldorf Crossing 53 40N50'05 123w09'35 8:12:38
Waldrue Heights 49 38N21'52 122w33'36 8:10:14
Walerga 34 38N40'30 121w21'53 8:05:28
Walker 19 33N58 118w10 7:52:40
Walker 26 38N33 119w30 7:58:00
Walker 47 41N52 122w44 8:10:56
Walker Landing 34 38N12'55 121w36'15 8:06:25
Wallace 5 38N11'39 120w58'37 8:03:54
Wallace Center 15 35N10'11 119w27'53 7:57:52
Walltown 34 38N34'27 121w06'10 8:04:25
Walmort 34 38N22'50 121w14'35 8:04:58
Walnut 19 34N01'13 117w51'52 7:51:27
Walnut Creek 7 37N54'23 122w03'50 8:08:15
Walnut Grove 34 38N14'32 121w30'38 8:06:03
Walnut Heights 7 37N53 122w03 8:08:12
Walnut Park 19 33N58'05 118w13'27 7:52:54
Walong 15 35N11'51 118w32'13 7:54:09
Walsh Landing 49 38N33'20 123w17'58 8:13:12
Walsh Station 34 38N31'44 121w20'01 8:05:20
Walteria 19 33N48'18 118w21'01 7:53:24
Walter Springs 28 38N39'13 122w21'25 8:09:26
Walthal 39 37N58'43 121w08'43 8:04:35
Warm Springs 1 37N34 121w59 8:07:56
Warm Springs District 1 37N29'14 121w55'41 8:07:43
Warner 36 34N03'39 117w08'44 7:48:35
Warner Ranch 33 33N56 117w14 7:48:56
Warner Springs 37 33N16'56 116w37'58 7:46:32
Warnerville 50 37N43'57 120w35'44 8:02:23
Wasco 15 35N35'39 119w20'24 7:57:22
Waseck 12 41N13'01 123w45'15 8:15:01
Washington 19 34N01 118w16 7:53:04
Washington 29 39N21'34 120w47'53 8:03:12
Washington Manor 1 37N42 122w08 8:08:32
Waterford 50 37N38'29 120w45'34 8:03:02
Waterloo 39 38N02'05 121w11'09 8:04:45
Watermans Corner 13 32N46'52 115w26'49 7:41:47
Wathier Landing 36 34N02'38 116w42'45 7:46:51
Watson 19 33N48'30 118w14'02 7:52:56
Watson Junction 19 33N47'58 118w15'11 7:53:01
Watsonville 44 36N54'37 121w45'21 8:07:01
Watsonville Junction 27 36N53'42 121w44'41 8:06:59
Watts 19 33N56'26 118w14'31 7:52:58
Watts Valley 10 37N01 119w24 7:57:36
Waukena 54 36N08'19 119w30'31 7:58:02
Waverly Park 56 34N12 118w53 7:55:32
Wawona 22 37N32'13 119w39'19 7:58:37
Wayne 43 37N23'09 121w53'52 8:07:35
Weaverville 53 40N43'52 122w56'27 8:11:46
Weber Grove 8 41N48'23 124w07'50 8:16:31
Webster 57 38N33'44 121w39'15 8:06:37
Webster Street 1 37N47 122w16 8:09:04
Weed 47 41N25'22 122w23'06 8:09:32
Weed Patch 15 35N14'17 118w54'51 7:55:39
Weeds Point 58 39N28'39 121w02'55 8:04:12
Weimar 31 39N02'15 120w58'17 8:03:53
Weisel 33 33N48'36 117w29'56 7:50:00
Weitchpec 12 41N11'18 123w42'26 8:14:50
Welby 27 36N11'19 121w04'07 8:04:16
Weldon 54 35N39'57 118w17'22 7:53:09
Weldons 56 34N20'42 119w17'46 7:57:11
Wellington Heights 19 34N02'10 118w11'05 7:52:44
Wellsona 40 35N41'50 120w41'33 8:02:46
Wells Place (Site) 52 40N11'53 121w55'52 8:07:43
Wendel 18 40N20'54 120w13'57 8:00:56
Wengler 45 40N54'51 121w54'27 8:07:38
Weott 12 40N19'19 123w55'14 8:15:41
Werner 7 37N56'26 121w36'29 8:06:26
West 21 37N59 122w45 8:11:00
West Adams 19 34N02 118w19 7:53:16
West Anaheim 30 33N49'56 117w56'30 7:51:46
West Arcadia 19 34N07'34 118w03'14 7:52:13
West Athens 19 33N55 118w18 7:53:12
West Butte 6 39N11'14 121w53'13 8:07:33
West Carson 19 33N50 118w18 7:53:12
Westchester 19 33N57'35 118w23'59 7:53:36
West Colton 36 34N04'01 117w21'07 7:49:24
West Colusa 6 39N12 122w25 8:09:40
West Compton 19 33N54 118w16 7:53:04
West Covina 19 34N04'07 117w56'17 7:51:45
Westend 36 35N42'25 117w23'29 7:49:34
Western Addition 38 37N47'07 122w26'45 8:09:47
Western Avenue 19 33N45 118w19 7:53:16
Western Village 15 35N08 117w59 7:51:56
Westfield 19 33N46 118w21 7:53:24
West Fresno 10 36N45 119w50 7:59:20
West Garden Grove 30 33N47 117w59 7:51:56
Westgate 43 37N19 121w58 8:07:52
Westgate 56 34N12 118w53 7:55:32
West Glendale 19 34N08'54 118w16'21 7:53:05
West Guernewood 49 38N30 123w00 8:12:00
West Hartley 7 37N56'26 121w48'42 8:07:15
Westhaven 10 36N13'36 119w59'38 7:59:59
Westhaven 12 41N02'10 124w06'36 8:16:26
West Highlands 36 34N08'22 117w13'50 7:48:55
West Hills 56 34N27 119w16 7:57:04
West Hollywood 19 34N05'24 118w21'39 7:53:27
West Imperial 13 32N50 115w45 7:43:00
Westlake 41 37N42'44 122w32'42 8:10:11
Westlake Village 56 34N12 118w53 7:55:32
Westley 50 37N32'58 121w11'53 8:04:48
West Los Angeles 19 34N02'47 118w26'50 7:53:47
Westlund Place 12 40N14'02 124w00'58 8:16:04
West Manteca 39 37N47'50 121w15'03 8:05:00
West March 33 33N54'12 117w16'37 7:49:06
West Menlo Park 41 37N27 122w11 8:08:44
Westminster 30 33N45'33 118w00'21 7:52:01
West Modesto 50 37N37 121w01 8:04:04
Westmont 19 33N57 118w18 7:53:12
Westmorland 13 33N02'14 115w37'14 7:42:29
West Napa 28 38N18 122w18 8:09:12
West Orange 30 33N47 117w53 7:51:32
West Palm Springs 33 33N56 116w38 7:46:32
West Park 10 36N42'37 119w51'01 7:59:24
West Pittsburg 7 38N01'37 121w56'10 8:07:45
West Point 5 38N23'57 120w31'35 8:02:06
Westport 23 39N38'09 123w46'55 8:15:08
West Portal 38 37N44 122w27 8:09:48
West Puente Valley 19 34N03 117w58 7:51:52
Westridge 41 37N41 122w29 8:09:56
West Sacramento 57 38N34'50 121w31'45 8:06:07
West Saticoy 56 34N17'07 119w09'34 7:56:38
Westside 10 36N24'02 120w08'17 8:00:33
Westside 15 35N09 119w23 7:57:32
Westside 50 37N38 120w59 8:03:56
West Sierra 46 39N35 120w45 8:03:00
West Tehama 52 40N03 122w30 8:10:00
West Valley 31 38N55 121w19 8:05:16
West Venida 54 36N20'28 119w07'44 7:56:31
Westvern 19 34N00 118w19 7:53:16
Westville 31 39N10'30 120w38'49 8:02:35

West Whittier 19 33N59'19 118w03'22 7:52:13
Westwood 18 40N18'22 121w00'17 8:04:01
Westwood 19 34N03'22 118w25'47 7:53:43
Westwood Acres 43 37N01 121w35 8:06:20
Westwood Junction 18 40N25'55 120w56'44 8:03:47
Westwood Village 12 40N52 124w05 8:16:20
Westwood Village 19 34N03'34 118w26'36 7:53:46
Wheatland 58 39N00'36 121w25'19 8:05:41
Wheaton Springs 36 35N27'44 115w28'31 7:41:54
Wheeler 23 39N53'08 123w54'36 8:15:38
Wheeler Ridge 15 35N00'16 118w56'55 7:55:48
Wheeler Springs 56 34N30'29 119w17'26 7:57:10
Whiskey Springs 23 39N21'48 123w39'56 8:14:40
Whiskeytown 45 40N38'20 122w33'31 8:10:14
Whisky Falls 20 37N17'13 119w26'18 7:57:45
Whispering Pines 17 38N48'49 122w42'41 8:10:51
Whispering Pines 37 33N05'10 116w35'06 7:46:20
White Hall 9 38N46'31 120w24'15 8:01:37
White Heather 19 34N31'13 118w18'21 7:53:13
Whitehorse 25 41N18'43 121w23'58 8:05:36
White Pines 5 38N15'58 120w20'23 8:01:22
White River 54 35N48'40 118w50'31 7:55:22
White River Summer Home Trac 54 35N50'58 118w37'34 7:54:30
White Rock 34 38N37'38 121w05'28 8:04:22
Whitesboro 23 39N12'53 123w45'48 8:15:03
Whites Landing 19 33N23'40 118w22'08 7:53:29
White Spot 29 39N16'53 121w00'35 8:04:02
Whitethorn 12 40N01'26 123w56'31 8:15:46
White Water (P O) 33 33N55'30 116w38'09 7:46:33
White Wolf 55 37N52'09 119w38'52 7:58:35
Whitley Gardens 40 35N39'33 120w30'24 8:02:02
Whitlock Place 52 39N50'07 122w41'55 8:10:48
Whitlow 12 40N18'55 123w47'46 8:15:11
Whitmore 45 40N37'46 121w54'56 8:07:40
Whitmore Hot Springs 26 37N37'57 118w48'41 7:55:15
Whitner Heights 10 36N37 119w31 7:58:04
Whitney 31 38N50'01 121w18'21 8:05:13
Whitney Portal 14 36N35'21 118w13'30 7:52:54
Whittier 19 33N58'45 118w01'55 7:52:08
Whittier Downs 19 33N59 118w04 7:52:16
Whittier Junction 19 34N00'18 118w03'51 7:52:15
Whittington Place (Site) 45 40N42'32 121w40'50 8:06:43
Wible Orchard 15 35N19'04 119w01'13 7:56:05
Wicks Corner 4 39N34'56 121w37'11 8:06:29
Wiest 13 33N03'31 115w26'51 7:41:47
Wilbur Springs 6 39N02'22 122w25'07 8:09:40
Wilcox 19 34N05 118w20 7:53:20
Wildasin 19 33N59'20 118w17'57 7:53:12
Wild Bill Place 17 39N13'51 122w46'50 8:11:07
Wild Crossing 36 34N46'48 117w16'27 7:49:06
Wilder Place 52 39N49'34 122w37'50 8:10:31
Wildflower 10 36N30'14 119w40'56 7:58:44
Wildomar 33 33N35'52 117w16'40 7:49:07
Wildrose 14 35N46 117w23 7:49:32
Wildwood 12 40N30 124w06 8:16:24
Wildwood 19 34N17'44 118w14'28 7:52:58
Wildwood 44 37N09'05 122w08'06 8:08:32
Wildwood 53 40N24'01 123w03'11 8:12:13
Wilfred 49 38N22'02 122w42'47 8:10:51
Willaura Estates 29 39N13 121w04 8:04:16
William H Taft 37 32N48 117w11 7:48:44
Williams 6 39N09'17 122w08'54 8:08:36
Willie Hoaglin Place 53 40N06'51 123w20'07 8:13:20
Willis Palms 33 33N49'38 116w19'43 7:45:19
Willits 23 39N24'35 123w21'16 8:13:25
Willota 48 38N14'40 122w06'21 8:08:25
Willow Brook 19 33N54'58 118w13'50 7:52:55
Willow Creek 12 40N56'23 123w37'49 8:14:31
Willow Creek Crossing 33 33N47'00 116w39'15 7:46:37
Willow Glen 43 37N18'31 121w53'19 8:07:33
Willow Ranch 25 41N54'09 120w21'26 8:01:26
Willows 11 39N31'28 122w11'33 8:08:46
Willow Springs 15 34N52'42 118w17'45 7:53:11
Willow Springs 18 40N52'44 121w14'48 8:04:59
Willow Springs 26 38N11'19 119w12'13 7:56:49
Willow Springs 55 37N59 120w16 8:01:04
Willow Valley 29 39N16 121w01 8:04:04
Will Rogers 19 34N01 118w29 7:53:56
Wilmar 19 34N04 118w05 7:52:20
Wilmington 19 33N46'48 118w15'42 7:53:03
Wilseyville 5 38N22'45 120w30'49 8:02:03
Wilshire-La Brea 19 34N04 118w21 7:53:24
Wilsie 13 32N48'00 115w36'08 7:42:25
Wilson 51 38N58'42 121w37'29 8:06:30
Wilsona 19 34N40 118w11 7:52:44
Wilsona Gardens 19 34N40'04 117w49'29 7:51:18
Wilson Corner 40 35N28'07 120w22'41 8:01:31
Wilson Grove 49 38N31'00 122w51'13 8:11:25
Wilsonia 54 36N44'06 118w57'20 7:55:49
Wilson Landing (Site) 4 39N47'49 122w01'16 8:08:05
Wilson Place 11 39N40'24 122w24'06 8:09:36
Wilton 34 38N24'43 121w16'16 8:05:05
Wimp 54 36N30'02 119w14'35 7:56:58
Winchester 33 33N42'25 117w05'01 7:48:20
Windsor 49 38N32'50 122w48'55 8:11:16
Windsor Hills 19 33N59'20 118w21'11 7:53:25
Wineland 10 36N32'30 119w34'58 7:58:20
Wingfoot 19 33N59'21 118w15'06 7:53:00
Wingo 49 38N12'33 122w25'32 8:09:42
Winnetka 19 34N12'48 118w34'16 7:54:17
Winter Gardens 37 32N49'52 116w55'57 7:47:44
Winterhaven 13 32N44'22 114w38'02 7:38:32
Winters 57 38N31'30 121w58'11 8:07:53
Wintersburg 30 33N42'57 117w59'49 7:51:59
Winterwarm 37 33N20'27 117w13'17 7:48:53
Winton 24 37N23'22 120w36'44 8:02:27
Wise 19 33N55 118w25 7:53:40
Wiseburn 19 33N55 118w21 7:53:24
Wishon 20 37N18 119w32 7:58:08
Wister 13 33N18'55 115w36'09 7:42:25
Witch Creek 37 33N03 116w54 7:47:36
Witter Springs (P O) 17 39N10'48 122w57'44 8:11:51
Wofford Heights 15 35N42'25 118w27'19 7:53:49
Wolf 10 36N41'43 119w38'13 7:58:33
Wolf 29 39N03'31 121w08'14 8:04:33
Wonderland 32 40N33 122w22 8:09:28
Woodacre 21 38N00'46 122w38'39 8:10:35
Woodbridge 39 38N09'15 121w18'01 8:05:12
Woodcrest 33 33N52'56 117w21'23 7:49:26
Woodford 15 35N12'46 118w33'06 7:54:12
Woodfords 2 38N46'40 119w49'15 7:59:17
Woodlake 39 38N09'08 121w14'32 8:04:58
Woodlake Junction 54 36N24'49 119w06'52 7:56:27
Woodland 54 36N24'49 119w05'52 7:56:23
Woodland 57 38N40'43 121w46'20 8:07:05
Woodland Acres 56 34N27 119w16 7:57:04
Woodland Hills 19 34N10'06 118w36'18 7:54:25
Woodlands 36 34N14'42 116w48'02 7:47:12
Woodleaf 58 39N31'03 121w11'26 8:04:46
Woodman 23 39N46'16 123w23'20 8:13:33
Wood Ranch 10 36N44'58 120w38'17 8:02:33
Woodruff Avenue 19 33N53 118w08 7:52:32
Woodside 41 37N25'48 122w15'10 8:09:01
Woodside Glens 41 37N26'26 122w15'20 8:09:01
Woodside Highlands 41 37N28 122w15 8:09:00
Woodville 21 37N56'41 122w42'19 8:10:49
Woodville 54 36N05'37 119w11'53 7:56:48
Woody 15 35N42'15 118w50'00 7:55:20
Woolsey Flat 29 39N24'41 120w52'01 8:03:28
Workfield 27 36N37 121w50 8:07:20
Workman 19 33N55'47 118w10'02 7:52:40
Worldway Postal Center 19 34N05 118w19 7:53:16
Worswick 12 40N36'43 124w11'26 8:16:46
Worth 54 36N03'09 118w56'10 7:55:45
Wright Place (Site) 12 41N16'40 123w40'38 8:14:43
Wrightwood 36 34N21'39 117w37'57 7:50:32
Wunpost 27 35N55'52 120w51'44 8:03:27
Wyandotte 4 39N27'29 121w28'00 8:05:52
Wyeth 54 36N31'10 119w15'57 7:57:04
Wynola 37 33N05'51 116w38'41 7:46:35
Wyntoon 47 41N11'30 122w03'48 8:08:15
Wyo 11 39N46'14 122w11'25 8:08:46
Yager Junction 12 40N32'54 123w49'24 8:15:18
Yale 33 33N45 116w56 7:47:44
Yankee Hill 4 39N42'13 121w31'16 8:06:05
Yankee Hill 55 38N02'23 120w22'37 8:01:30
Yankee Jims 31 39N01'46 120w51'38 8:03:27
Yellowjacket 52 40N14'26 121w41'24 8:06:46
Yellowjacket Place 53 40N10'10 123w19'21 8:13:17
Yermo 36 34N54'18 116w49'10 7:47:17
Yettem 54 36N29'11 119w15'31 7:57:02
Ygnacio Valley 7 37N56 122w02 8:08:08
Yokohl 54 36N19'32 119w04'53 7:56:20
Yolanda 21 37N59 122w35 8:10:20
Yolano 48 38N24'37 121w42'16 8:06:49
Yolo 57 38N43'55 121w48'24 8:07:14
Yontocket 8 41N54'28 124w11'52 8:16:47
Yorba 30 33N51'55 117w48'29 7:51:14
Yorba Linda 30 33N53'19 117w48'44 7:51:15
York 19 34N05 118w22 7:53:28
Yorkville 23 38N53'53 123w12'48 8:12:51
Yosemite 22 37N45 119w35 7:58:20
Yosemite Forks 20 37N22'02 119w37'51 7:58:31
Yosemite Junction 55 37N53'27 120w29'14 8:01:57
Yosemite Lodge 22 37N45 119w35 7:58:20
Yosemite National Park 22 37N45 119w35 7:58:20
Yosemite Village 22 37N44'43 119w35'50 7:58:23
You Bet 29 39N12'33 120w53'56 8:03:36
Youngstown 39 38N10'26 121w14'31 8:04:58
Yountville 28 38N24'06 122w21'35 8:09:26
Yreka 47 41N44'08 122w38'00 8:10:32
Yreka City 47 41N40 122w36 8:10:24
Yuba City 51 39N08'26 121w36'57 8:06:28
Yuba Foothills 58 39N25 121w13 8:04:52
Yuba Pass 29 39N19'23 120w35'57 8:02:24
Yucaipa 36 34N02'01 117w02'32 7:48:10
Yucca Grove 36 35N24'09 115w47'29 7:43:10
Yucca Inn 36 34N24'35 117w35'19 7:50:21
Yucca Valley 36 34N07'09 116w26'42 7:45:47
Zamora 57 38N47'48 121w52'51 8:07:31
Zante 54 36N06'53 119w02'41 7:56:11
Zayante 44 37N05'31 122w02'33 8:08:10
Zediker 10 36N45'26 119w31'23 7:58:06
Zenia 53 40N12'20 123w29'27 8:13:58
Zentner 15 35N42'11 119w10'06 7:56:40
Zinfandel 28 38N28'58 122w26'28 8:09:46
Zurich 14 37N10'58 118w15'33 7:53:02
Zuver 31 38N58'27 120w35'56 8:02:24
Zzyzx 36 35N16 116w04 7:44:16

TIME TABLES

CO # 1
Before 11/18/1883 LMT
11/18/1883 12:00 MST
3/31/1918 02:00 MWT
10/27/1918 02:00 MST
3/30/1919 02:00 MWT
10/26/1919 02:00 MST
2/09/1942 02:00 MWT
9/30/1945 02:00 MST
4/25/1965 02:00 MDT
10/31/1965 02:00 MST
4/24/1966 02:00 MDT
10/30/1966 02:00 MST
4/30/1967 02:00 US#1

CO # 2
Before 11/18/1883 LMT
11/18/1883 12:00 MST
3/31/1918 02:00 MWT
10/27/1918 02:00 MST
3/30/1919 02:00 MWT
10/26/1919 02:00 MST
3/28/1920 02:00 MDT
10/31/1920 02:00 MST
3/27/1921 02:00 MDT
5/22/1921 02:00 MST
2/09/1942 02:00 MWT
9/30/1945 02:00 MST
4/25/1965 02:00 MDT
10/31/1965 02:00 MST
4/24/1966 02:00 MDT
10/30/1966 02:00 MST
4/30/1967 02:00 US#1

CO # 3
Before 11/18/1883 LMT
11/18/1883 12:00 MST
3/31/1918 02:00 MWT
10/27/1918 02:00 MST
3/30/1919 02:00 MWT
10/26/1919 02:00 MST
2/09/1942 02:00 MWT
9/30/1945 02:00 MST
5/02/1964 02:00 MDT
9/27/1964 02:00 MST
4/25/1965 02:00 MDT
10/31/1965 02:00 MST
4/24/1966 02:00 MDT
10/30/1966 02:00 MST
4/30/1967 02:00 US#1

COUNTIES

1 Adams
2 Alamosa
3 Arapahoe
4 Archuleta
5 Baca
6 Bent
7 Boulder
8 Chaffee
9 Cheyenne
10 Clear Creek
11 Conejos
12 Costilla
13 Crowley
14 Custer
15 Delta
16 Denver
17 Dolores
18 Douglas
19 Eagle
20 Elbert
21 El Paso
22 Fremont
23 Garfield
24 Gilpin
25 Grand
26 Gunnison
27 Hinsdale
28 Huerfano
29 Jackson
30 Jefferson
31 Kiowa
32 Kit Carson
33 Lake
34 La Plata
35 Larimer
36 Las Animas
37 Lincoln
38 Logan
39 Mesa
40 Mineral
41 Moffat
42 Montezuma
43 Montrose
44 Morgan
45 Otero
46 Ouray
47 Park
48 Phillips
49 Pitkin
50 Prowers
51 Pueblo
52 Rio Blanco
53 Rio Grande
54 Routt
55 Saguache
56 San Juan
57 San Miguel
58 Sedgwick
59 Summit
60 Teller
61 Washington
62 Weld
63 Yuma

Place		Lat	Long	Time
Abarr 63	1	39N51'02	102w42'24	6:50:50
Abbet Place 19	1	39N55'18	106w25'17	7:05:41
Abbeyville 26	1	38N46'39	106w29'30	7:05:58
Abeyta 36	1	37N04'47	104w11'09	6:56:45
Able 6	1	38N03'38	102w52'09	6:51:29
Acequia 18	2	39N31'25	105w01'39	7:00:07
Ackerman 38	1	40N40'13	103w10'35	6:52:42
Acres Green Homes 18	2	39N37	105w00	7:00:00
Adams City 1	2	39N50	104w56	6:59:44
Adelaide 22	1	38N33'36	105w05'25	7:00:22
Adelaide 33	1	39N14'50	106w15'27	7:05:02
Adena 44	1	40N00'30	104w53'10	6:59:33
Adna 62	1	40N20'22	104w49'40	6:59:19
Adobe Park 8	1	38N32	106w00	7:04:00
Agate 20	1	39N27'42	103w56'30	6:55:46
Agua Ramon 53	1	37N42'42	106w33'20	7:06:13
Aguilar 36	1	37N24'10	104w39'10	6:58:37
Akin 39	1	39N15'17	108w15'45	7:13:03
Akron 61	1	40N09'38	103w12'50	6:52:51
Alamo 28	1	37N39'20	104w57'29	6:59:50
Alamo Placita 16	2	39N43'15	104w58'31	6:59:54
Alamosa 17	1	37N28'10	105w52'10	7:03:29
Alcott 16	2	39N47	105w03	7:00:12
Alden 62	1	40N27'27	104w34'53	6:58:20
Alder 55	1	38N22'10	106w02'20	7:04:09
Alice 10	1	39N49'06	105w38'32	7:02:34
Allen 23	1	39N36'39	107w08'34	7:08:34
Allens Park 7	1	40N11'40	105w31'30	7:02:06
Allison 34	1	37N01'28	107w29'15	7:09:57
Alma 47	1	39N17'02	106w03'44	7:04:15
Alma Junction 47	1	39N16'03	106w02'41	7:04:11
Almont 26	1	38N39'53	106w50'44	7:07:23
Alpine 8	1	38N42'40	106w16'35	7:05:06
Alpine 53	1	37N41'21	106w35'18	7:06:21
Alta 57	1	37N53'11	107w51'08	7:11:25
Alta Vista 21	1	39N01'37	104w06'43	6:56:27
Altman 60	1	38N44'10	105w08'00	7:00:32
Altona 7	1	40N08'02	105w16'56	7:01:00
Altura 3	2	39N44'25	104w48'14	6:59:13
Altura 4	1	37N11'00	107w11'26	7:08:46
Alvin 63	1	40N18'28	102w04'31	6:48:18
American City 24	1	39N52'21	105w35'12	7:02:21
Americus 8	1	38N54'09	106w09'54	7:04:40
Ames 57	1	37N51'53	107w52'54	7:11:32
Amherst 48	1	40N40'58	102w09'56	6:48:40
Anaconda 60	1	38N43'55	108w09'45	7:12:39
Andersonville 35	1	40N35'38	105w03'24	7:00:14
Andrix 36	1	37N16'46	103w11'32	6:52:46
Angel Acres 30	1	39N30	105w20	7:01:20
Angora 52	1	40N10'36	108w34'30	7:14:18
Animas City 34	1	37N17	107w52	7:11:28
Animas Forks 56	1	37N55'52	107w34'15	7:10:17
Ansel 53	1	37N42'11	106w06'07	7:04:24
Antelope Springs 5	1	37N29'41	102w56'07	6:51:44
Antero Junction 47	1	38N55'24	105w57'53	7:03:52
Antlers 23	1	39N32'36	107w43'38	7:10:55
Anton 61	1	39N44'30	103w13'00	6:52:52
Antonio 11	1	37N04'45	106w00'29	7:04:02
Antonito 11	1	37N05	105w54	7:03:36
Anvil Points 23	1	39N30'58	107w55'20	7:11:41
Apache City 28	1	37N51'30	104w49'50	6:59:19
Apex 24	1	39N49	105w31	7:02:04
Appleton 39	1	39N07'15	108w36'27	7:14:26
Applewood 30	2	39N45	105w10	7:00:40
Aqua Ramon 53	1	37N32	106w21	7:05:24
Ara 7	1	40N01'30	105w14'59	7:01:00
Arabian Acres 60	1	38N57	105w17	7:01:08
Arapahoe 9	1	38N51	102w11	6:48:44
Arboles 4	1	37N01'41	107w25'07	7:09:40
Argo Mill 10	1	39N44'34	105w30'22	7:02:01
Arickaree 61	1	39N41'57	103w03'56	6:52:16
Aristocrat Ranchettes 62	1	40N05	104w49	6:59:16
Arlington 31	1	38N20'10	103w20'34	6:53:22
Arlington Park 62	1	40N24	104w42	6:58:48
Armel 63	1	39N47'50	102w06'28	6:48:26
Aroya 9	1	38N51'15	103w07'30	6:52:30
Arriba 37	1	39N17'10	103w16'30	6:53:06
Arriola 42	1	37N26'33	108w38'44	7:14:35
Arrowhead 35	1	40N34'45	105w01'26	7:00:06
Artesia 40	1	40N20	108w34	7:14:16
Arvada 30	2	39N48'10	105w05'13	7:00:21
Arvada Heights 30	2	39N48	105w06	7:00:24
Ashcroft 49	1	39N03'13	106w47'57	7:07:12
Aspen 49	3	39N11'28	106w49'01	7:07:16
Aspen Park 30	1	39N32'21	105w17'39	7:01:11
Association Camp 35	1	40N20	105w34	7:02:16
Atchee 23	1	39N33'47	108w54'44	7:15:39
Atlanta 5	1	37N30'13	102w59'44	6:51:59
Atwood 38	1	40N32'52	103w16'09	6:53:05
Auburn 62	1	40N22'05	104w38'10	6:58:33
Ault 62	1	40N34'57	104w43'53	6:58:56
Aurora 1	2	39N43'46	104w49'53	6:59:20
Austin 15	1	38N46'52	107w57'01	7:11:48
Avalo 62	1	40N48'12	103w38'59	6:54:36
Avon 19	1	39N37'53	106w31'18	7:06:05
Avondale 51	1	38N14'15	104w21'02	6:57:24
Axial 41	1	40N17'07	107w47'29	7:11:10
Ayer 45	1	37N45'29	103w50'45	6:55:23
Azure 25	1	39N59'44	106w30'27	7:06:02
Bachelor 40	1	37N52'40	106w56'27	7:07:46
Badito 28	1	37N43'38	105w00'49	7:00:03
Bailey 47	1	39N24'20	105w28'22	7:01:53
Bailey Place 41	1	40N18'08	108w36'22	7:14:25
Balarat 7	1	40N09'33	105w23'45	7:01:35
Bald Mountain 7	1	40N02	105w25	7:01:40
Baldwin 26	1	38N45'50	107w02'50	7:08:11
Balfour 47	1	38N54'26	105w43'26	7:02:54
Balltown 33	1	39N04'40	106w16'50	7:05:07
Baltimore 24	1	39N54'12	105w34'26	7:02:18
Balzac 44	1	40N24'25	103w28'15	6:53:53
Barela 36	1	37N06'56	104w15'40	6:57:03
Barnesville 62	1	40N28'45	104w28'45	6:57:55
Barr 1	2	39N57	104w58	6:59:52
Barr Lake 1	2	39N56'40	104w46'29	6:59:06
Bartlett 5	1	37N26'00	102w08'37	6:48:34
Barton 50	1	38N04	102w18	6:49:12
Basalt 19	1	39N22'08	107w01'56	7:08:08
Basin 57	1	38N03'57	108w32'10	7:14:09
Battle Creek 54	1	41N00'05	107w14'40	7:08:59
Baxter 51	1	38N16'33	104w29'28	6:57:58
Baxterville 53	1	37N40'27	106w39'26	7:06:38
Bayfield 34	1	37N13'32	107w35'51	7:10:23
Beacon Hill 60	1	38N43'21	105w09'52	7:00:39
Beards Corner 57	1	38N03'57	108w36'41	7:14:27
Bear Mine 26	1	38N56	107w16	7:09:04
Bear River 54	1	40N29'02	107w07'00	7:08:28
Beartown 56	1	37N43'22	107w30'12	7:10:01
Beaver Point 35	1	40N21'52	105w32'38	7:02:11
Beaver Ridge 47	1	39N14	106w00	7:04:00
Beck Sand Draw Crossing 20	1	39N01'37	104w03'10	6:56:13
Bedrock 43	1	38N18'54	108w53'25	7:15:34
Beecher Island 63	1	39N52'20	102w11'02	6:48:44
Belden 19	1	39N31'32	106w23'08	7:05:33
Belle Plain 51	1	38N17	104w35	6:58:20
Belleview 8	1	38N34'09	106w02'12	7:04:09
Bellvue 35	1	40N37'35	105w10'16	7:00:41
Belmar (P O) 30	2	39N41'49	105w05'07	7:00:20
Belmont 51	1	38N17	104w35	6:58:20
Bendemeer Valley 10	1	39N38	105w20	7:01:20
Bennett 1	1	39N45'32	104w25'37	6:57:42
Benton 45	1	37N54'18	103w39'24	6:54:38
Bergen Park 30	1	39N41'29	105w21'40	7:01:27
Berthoud 35	1	40N18'30	105w04'50	7:00:19
Berthoud Falls 10	1	39N46	105w42	7:02:48
Berthoud Pass 10	1	39N45	105w32	7:02:08
Berts Corner 35	1	40N18'28	105w06'08	7:00:25
Beshoar 36	1	37N13'05	104w24'22	6:57:37
Beta 38	1	40N27'58	103w22'42	6:53:31
Beta 50	1	38N05'10	102w41'24	6:50:46
Bethune 32	1	39N18'15	102w25'27	6:49:42
Beulah 51	1	38N04'30	104w59'10	6:59:57
Beverly Grove 63	1	39N54'53	102w41'43	6:50:47
Beverly Hills 18	1	39N28'30	104w52'45	6:59:31
Big Bend 6	1	38N12'05	102w45'01	6:51:00
Big Elk Meadows 7	1	40N15'43	105w25'47	7:01:43
Bighorn 19	1	39N38'12	106w17'48	7:05:11
Bijou 20	1	39N25'21	104w11'52	6:56:47
Bijou 44	1	40N14'38	103w53'11	6:55:33
Binco Place 25	1	40N16'48	106w31'30	7:06:06
Birdseye 33	1	39N18'40	106w13'37	7:04:54
Bisonte 5	1	37N15'08	102w35'28	6:50:22
Black Eagle Mill 10	1	39N43'35	105w32'49	7:02:11
Black Forest 21	1	39N00'47	104w42'01	6:58:48
Black Hawk 24	1	39N47'49	105w29'36	7:01:58
Black Hollow Junction 35	1	40N35'46	105w01'44	7:00:07
Blakeland 18	2	39N33'35	105w02'10	7:00:09
Blanca 11	1	37N26'17	105w30'55	7:02:04
Blende 51	1	38N14'45	104w34'05	6:58:16
Bloom 45	1	37N41'15	103w57'22	6:55:49
Blue Mountain 41	1	40N14'54	108w51'40	7:15:27
Blue Mountain Estates 30	2	39N45	105w11	7:00:44
Blue River 59	1	39N25'47	106w02'36	7:04:10
Blue Valley 10	1	39N41'59	105w29'19	7:01:57
Blue Valley Acres 10	1	39N45	105w32	7:02:08
Bockman Lumber Camp 29	1	40N33'30	105w57'55	7:03:52
Boettcher 35	1	40N39'46	105w06'28	7:00:26
Boggsville 6	1	38N02'30	103w12'44	6:52:51
Bonanza 55	1	38N17'41	106w08'30	7:04:34
Boncarbo 36	1	37N13'00	104w41'40	6:58:47
Bond 19	1	39N52'28	106w41'12	7:06:45
Bondad 34	1	37N02'45	107w52'32	7:11:30
Bonita 55	1	38N13'58	106w12'52	7:04:51
Boone 51	1	38N14'55	104w15'23	6:57:02
Bordenville 47	1	39N16'34	105w40'59	7:02:44
Boulder 7	1	40N00'54	105w16'12	7:01:05
Boulder Junction 7	1	40N01'00	105w12'30	7:00:50
Bountiful 11	1	37N13'45	105w58'35	7:03:54
Bovina 37	1	39N16'49	103w23'05	6:53:32
Bower Place 41	1	40N35'10	108w41'17	7:14:45
Bowie 15	1	38N55'17	107w32'22	7:10:09
Bow Mar 3	2	39N37'42	105w02'58	7:00:12
Boxelder Estates 35	1	40N35	105w06	7:00:24
Box Prairie 35	1	40N34'53	105w28'06	7:01:52
Boyero 37	1	38N56'34	103w16'15	6:53:05
Bracewell 62	1	40N27'34	104w49'00	6:59:16
Bradford 28	1	37N52'53	105w19'57	7:01:20
Bragdon 51	1	38N24'07	104w36'40	6:58:27
Brandon 31	1	38N26'47	102w26'21	6:49:45
Branson 36	1	37N01'03	103w53'02	6:55:32
Breckenridge 59	1	39N28'54	106w02'16	7:04:09
Breen 34	1	37N11'33	108w04'38	7:12:19
Brewster 22	1	38N23	105w08	7:00:32
Bridgeport 39	1	38N50'12	108w22'48	7:13:31
Bridges Switch 39	1	39N05'55	108w24'12	7:13:37
Briggsdale 62	1	40N38'05	104w19'35	6:57:18
Brighton 1	2	39N59'07	104w49'12	6:59:17
Brimstone Corner 15	1	38N56'17	107w58'29	7:11:54
Bristol 50	1	38N07'20	102w18'40	6:49:15
Broadmoor 21	1	38N47'44	104w50'27	6:59:22
Broadway Estates 3	2	39N37	105w00	7:00:00
Brocker Place 29	1	40N28'14	106w07'27	7:04:30
Broken Arrow Acres 30	1	39N30'10	105w19'34	7:01:18
Bronquist 51	1	38N12'07	104w53'28	6:59:34
Brookfield 5	1	37N35'38	102w50'30	6:51:22
Brook Forest 10	1	39N34'46	105w22'53	7:01:32

Brook Forest Estates 10
1 39N38 105w20 7:01:20
Brookridge 3 2 39N37 105w00 7:00:00
Brookside 22 1 38N24'55 105w11'29 7:00:46
Brookvale 10 1 39N37'47 105w25'07 7:01:40
Brookwood 21 1 38N53 104w48 6:59:12
Broomfield 7 2 39N55'14 105w05'10 7:00:21
Broughton 15 1 38N48'48 108w19'35 7:13:18
Brown 57 1 38N03'55 108w01'20 7:12:05
Brownlee 29 1 40N47'05 106w17'10 7:05:09
Browns Canyon 8
1 38N36'43 106w03'34 7:04:14
Browns Corner 35
1 40N24'27 105w03'30 7:00:14
Bruce 62 1 40N29'45 104w51'50 6:59:27
Brumley 33 1 39N05'22 106w32'32 7:06:10
Brush 44 1 40N15'32 103w37'24 6:54:30
Buchanan 38 1 40N49'55 103w10'05 6:52:40
Buckeye 35 1 40N49'38 105w05'40 7:00:23
Buckeye Crossroads 5
1 37N33'27 102w07'42 6:48:31
Buckingham 35 1 40N35'26 105w03'56 7:00:16
Buckingham 62 1 40N37'17 103w58'38 6:55:55
Buckingham Square 3
2 39N43 104w51 6:59:24
Buckskin Joe 22
1 38N28'35 105w19'35 7:01:18
Buda 62 1 40N19'43 104w58'38 6:59:55
Buena Vista 8 1 38N50'32 106w07'50 7:04:31
Buffalo Creek 30
1 39N23'12 105w16'11 7:01:05
Buffham Place 41
1 40N45'19 108w53'42 7:15:35
Buford 52 1 39N59'14 107w36'58 7:10:28
Bulger 35 1 40N47'37 104w58'55 6:59:56
Bulkley Mine 26
1 38N50'38 106w58'10 7:07:53
Bunyan 62 1 40N17'25 104w54'53 6:59:40
Burdett 61 1 40N21'56 102w57'02 6:51:48
Burland Ranchettes 47
1 39N25 105w20 7:01:20
Burlington 32 1 39N18'22 102w16'08 6:49:05
Burlington Square 7
1 40N11 105w07 7:00:28
Burns 19 1 39N52'26 106w53'06 7:07:32
Burnt Mill 51 1 38N03'06 104w47'45 6:59:11
Buttes 21 1 38N35'14 104w40'00 6:58:40
Byers 3 1 39N42'41 104w13'38 6:56:55
Cabin Creek 1 1 39N44'26 104w01'48 6:56:07
Caddoa 6 1 38N03'41 102w55'36 6:51:42
Cahone 17 1 37N39'32 108w48'26 7:15:14
Calcite 22 1 38N26'10 105w53'12 7:03:33
Caldwell Place 41
1 40N26'07 108w58'31 7:15:54
Calhan 21 1 39N02'08 104w17'48 6:57:11
Calhoun 61 1 40N08'33 102w53'24 6:51:34
California Oil Camp 52
1 40N05 108w47 7:15:08
Calloway Place 41
1 40N51'19 108w55'57 7:15:44
Calumet 28 1 37N41'34 104w51'33 6:59:26
Camden 44 1 40N18'15 103w32'55 6:54:12
Cameltown 26 1 38N36'46 106w33'54 7:06:16
Cameo 39 1 39N08'55 108w19'13 7:13:17
Camp Bird 46 1 37N58'22 107w43'33 7:10:54
Camp George West 30
2 39N45 105w11 7:00:44
Campion 35 1 40N20'58 105w04'38 7:00:19
Campo 5 1 37N06'18 102w34'45 6:50:19
Canfield 7 2 40N03'13 105w04'27 7:00:18
Canon 11 1 37N02'36 106w08'43 7:04:35
Canon City 22 1 38N24'00 105w13'00 7:00:52
Canton 62 1 40N18'57 104w20'44 6:57:23
Capitol City 27
1 38N00'26 107w27'58 7:09:52
Capitol Hill 16
2 39N44 104w58 6:59:52
Capulin 11 1 37N17'02 106w06'39 7:04:27
Carbonate 23 1 39N44'35 107w20'46 7:09:23
Carbondale 23 1 39N24'08 107w12'38 7:08:51
Carbonera 23 1 39N27'32 108w57'30 7:15:50
Carbon Junction 34
1 37N14'15 107w51'58 7:11:28
Cardiff 23 1 39N30'22 107w18'37 7:09:14
Cardinal 7 1 39N58'11 105w32'50 7:02:11
Caribou 7 1 39N58'51 105w34'41 7:02:19
Carlton (P O) 50
1 38N05'09 102w25'05 6:49:40
Carr 62 1 40N53'46 104w52'28 6:59:30
Carracas 4 1 37N00'18 107w15'29 7:09:02
Carrizo Springs 5
1 37N09'49 103w02'04 6:52:08
Carr Place 41 1 40N45'25 108w54'06 7:15:36
Carson 27 1 37N52'09 107w21'42 7:09:27
Carterville 19 1 39N37'51 106w38'44 7:06:35
Casa 45 1 38N00'33 103w28'18 6:53:53
Cascade 21 1 38N53'48 104w58'18 6:59:53
Cascade 34 1 37N36'12 107w45'43 7:11:03
Castiel 45 1 38N06'26 103w27'45 6:53:51
Castle Oaks 18 1 39N22 104w52 6:59:28
Castle Rock 18 1 39N22'20 104w51'20 6:59:25
Cathedral 27 1 38N05'45 107w02'00 7:08:08
Catherine 23 1 39N24'26 107w09'08 7:08:37
Cattle Creek 23
1 39N27'30 107w15'43 7:09:03
Cedar 57 1 38N10 108w25 7:13:40
Cedar Cove 35 1 40N24'57 105w15'54 7:01:04
Cedar Creek 43 1 38N28'44 107w42'50 7:10:51
Cedar Crest 51 1 37N48'25 104w17'53 6:57:12
Cedaredge 15 1 38N54'06 107w55'33 7:11:42
Cedar Grove 51 1 38N04'30 104w56'18 6:59:45
Cedar Point 20 1 39N20'43 103w52'12 6:55:29
Cedarwood 51 1 37N56'30 104w37'01 6:58:28
Centennial 3 2 39N38 104w59 6:59:56
Center 55 1 37N45'11 106w06'29 7:04:26
Centerville 8 1 38N42'32 106w05'28 7:04:22
Central City 24
1 39N48'07 105w30'49 7:02:03
Centro 11 1 37N17'02 106w08'49 7:04:35
Chacra 23 1 39N34'31 107w26'46 7:09:47
Chaddsford 3 2 39N43 104w51 6:59:24
Chama 12 1 37N09'43 105w22'40 7:01:31
Chama 28 1 37N43'08 105w17'54 7:01:12

Champion Mill 33
1 39N08'15 106w30'14 7:06:01
Chance 26 1 38N26'14 106w50'57 7:07:24
Channing 50 1 38N08'37 102w32'56 6:50:12
Chapel Hills 21
1 38N53 104w48 6:59:12
Chattanooga 56 1 37N52'25 107w43'29 7:10:54
Chautauqua 7 1 40N00 105w16 7:01:04
Cheraw 45 1 38N06'25 103w30'35 6:54:02
Cherrelyn 3 2 39N38 104w59 6:59:56
Cherry 18 1 39N22 104w52 6:59:28
Cherry Creek 16
2 39N36 104w53 6:59:32
Cherry Hills Crest 3
2 39N37 105w00 7:00:00
Cherry Hills Manor 3
2 39N37 105w00 7:00:00
Cherry Hills Village 3
2 39N38'30 104w57'32 6:59:50
Cherry Knolls 3
2 39N37 105w00 7:00:00
Cherry Ridge 3 2 39N38 104w59 6:59:56
Cherry Valley 18
1 39N23 104w45 6:59:00
Cherrywood Village 3
2 39N37 105w00 7:00:00
Chester 55 1 38N22'25 106w18'04 7:05:12
Cheyenne Canon 21
1 38N53 104w48 6:59:12
Cheyenne Wells 9
1 38N49'17 102w21'10 6:49:25
Chimney Rock (P O) 4
1 37N13'43 107w20'45 7:09:23
Chipeta 15 1 38N40'52 108w00'30 7:12:02
Chipita Park 21
1 38N55'28 105w00'22 7:00:01
Chivington 31 1 38N26'11 102w32'35 6:50:10
Chromo 4 1 37N02'11 106w50'34 7:07:22
Chula Vista 24 2 39N45 105w11 7:00:44
Cimarron 43 1 38N26'33 107w33'22 7:10:13
Cinderella City 3
2 39N38 104w59 6:59:56
Circle East Mall 21
1 38N51 104w47 6:59:08
Citadel 21 1 38N51 104w47 6:59:08
Clark 54 1 40N42'22 106w55'07 7:07:40
Clark 62 1 40N19'40 104w55'30 6:59:42
Clarkville 63 1 40N23'42 102w37'32 6:50:30
Clay 30 2 39N51'31 105w15'48 7:01:03
Cleora 8 1 38N30'48 105w58'10 7:03:53
Cliffdale 30 1 39N24'31 105w22'33 7:01:30
Clifford 37 1 39N02'38 103w21'03 6:53:24
Clifton 39 1 39N05'31 108w26'54 7:13:48
Climax 33 1 39N22'41 106w10'59 7:04:44
Cloverly 62 1 40N27'24 104w37'33 6:58:30
Coal Creek 22 1 38N21'40 105w08'52 7:00:35
Coaldale 22 1 38N21'56 105w45'26 7:03:02
Coalmont 29 1 40N33'45 106w26'38 7:05:47
Coburn 15 1 38N50'48 107w38'07 7:10:32
Cochetopa 55 1 38N13 106w45 7:07:00
Codo 28 1 37N30'08 105w08'48 7:00:35
Cody Park 30 2 39N42'57 105w16'11 7:01:05
Cokedale 36 1 37N08'43 104w37'14 6:58:29
Colby 15 1 38N55'54 107w58'29 7:11:54
Cold Spring 14 1 38N08'58 105w14'31 7:00:58
Collbran 39 1 39N14'26 107w57'38 7:11:51
College 62 1 40N24 104w42 6:58:48
College Heights 34
1 37N17 107w52 7:11:28
College View 16
2 39N39'47 105w01'16 7:00:05
Colona 46 1 38N19'30 107w46'45 7:11:07
Colorado City 51
1 37N56'43 104w50'05 6:59:20
Colorado Mountain Estates 60
1 38N57 105w17 7:01:08
Colorado Springs 21
1 38N50'02 104w49'15 6:59:17
Columbine 3 2 39N37 105w00 7:00:00
Columbine 54 1 40N51'15 106w57'55 7:07:52
Columbine Hills 30
2 39N37 105w00 7:00:00
Columbine Knolls 3
2 39N37 105w00 7:00:00
Columbine Manor 3
2 39N37 105w00 7:00:00
Columbine Valley 3
2 39N36'04 105w01'54 7:00:08
Columbus 34 1 37N19'40 107w37'46 7:10:31
Comanche 1 1 39N59'08 104w18'00 6:57:12
Comer 62 1 40N28'04 104w51'14 6:59:25
Commerce City 1
2 39N48'80 104w56'00 6:59:44
Como 47 1 39N18'58 105w53'32 7:03:34
Concrete 22 1 38N23'00 104w59'50 6:59:59
Conejos 11 1 37N05'18 106w01'09 7:04:05
Conifer 30 1 39N31'16 105w18'17 7:01:13
Conifer Mountain 30
1 39N30 105w20 7:01:20
Conifer Park 30
1 39N30 105w20 7:01:20
Cooper 44 1 40N21'38 103w31'43 6:54:07
Cope 61 1 39N39'50 102w51'02 6:51:24
Copperdale 7 1 39N54'51 105w20'56 7:01:24
Copper Spur 19 1 39N54'38 106w41'16 7:06:45
Cordova Plaza 36
1 37N08'00 104w49'45 6:59:19
Cornelia 6 1 38N05'34 103w17'16 6:53:09
Corner Windmill 36
1 37N33'25 104w06'52 6:56:27
Cornish 62 1 40N31'23 104w24'46 6:57:39
Corona 25 1 39N56'04 105w41'05 7:02:44
Coronado 1 2 39N50 104w57 6:59:48
Corson Place 55
1 38N19'27 106w46'52 7:07:07
Cortez 42 1 37N20'56 108w35'07 7:14:20
Cory 15 1 38N47'17 107w59'12 7:11:57
Cotopaxi 22 1 38N22'13 105w41'15 7:02:45
Cottonwood 24 1 39N45'48 105w25'27 7:01:42
Cottonwood 55 1 37N56'04 105w38'37 7:02:34
Cottonwood Crossing 36
1 37N37'15 103w26'05 6:53:44

Country Club Estates 35
1 40N35 105w06 7:00:24
Country Club Park 7
1 40N00 105w16 7:01:04
Coventry 43 1 38N09'36 108w22'27 7:13:30
Cowdrey 29 1 40N51'35 106w18'45 7:05:15
Cozy Corner 1 2 39N54'50 105w01'31 7:00:06
Cragmor 21 1 38N53 104w48 6:59:12
Craig 41 1 40N30'55 107w32'45 7:10:11
Craig Place 41 1 40N43'13 108w57'13 7:15:49
Craig South Highlands 41
1 40N29'06 107w33'45 7:10:15
Crawford 15 1 38N42'14 107w36'30 7:10:26
Creede 40 1 37N50'57 106w55'33 7:07:42
Crescent 7 1 39N55'42 105w20'32 7:01:22
Crescent Village 7
1 39N55'11 105w21'38 7:01:27
Cresta Vista 21
1 38N48 104w49 6:59:16
Crested Butte 26
1 38N52'11 106w59'14 7:07:57
Crestmoor 3 2 39N41 104w56 6:59:44
Crestone 55 1 37N59'47 105w41'57 7:02:48
Cripple Creek 60
1 38N44'48 105w10'40 7:00:43
Crisman 7 1 40N02'27 105w21'39 7:01:27
Critchell 30 1 39N29'42 105w12'22 7:00:49
Crook 38 1 40N51'32 102w48'02 6:51:12
Crossons 30 1 39N23'57 105w23'09 7:01:33
Crowley 13 1 38N11'35 103w51'20 6:55:25
Crystal 26 1 39N03'33 107w06'02 7:08:24
Crystola 21 1 38N57'21 105w01'36 7:00:06
Cuchara 28 1 37N22'45 105w05'59 7:00:24
Cuchara Junction 28
1 37N40'01 104w41'08 6:58:45
Cuerna Verde Park 51
1 37N55'19 104w58'15 6:59:53
Culp 50 1 38N08'09 102w36'32 6:50:26
Cumbres 11 1 37N01'11 106w26'50 7:05:47
Dacono 62 1 40N05'05 104w56'20 6:59:45
Dailey 38 1 40N39'24 102w43'24 6:50:54
Dalerose 36 1 37N15 103w21 6:53:24
Dallas 46 1 38N11'00 107w44'39 7:10:59
Dearfield 62 1 40N17'26 104w15'32 6:57:02
De Beque 39 1 39N20'04 108w12'52 7:12:51
Deckers 18 2 39N15'17 105w13'35 7:00:54
Deepcreek 54 1 40N43 106w55 7:07:40
Deer Creek Valley Ranchos 47
1 39N25 105w20 7:01:20
Deermont 30 1 39N30'27 105w11'02 7:00:44
Deer Park 54 1 40N16 106w57 7:07:48
Deer Trail 3 1 39N36'54 104w02'38 6:56:11
Delagua 36 1 37N20'24 104w39'45 6:58:39
Delcarbon 28 1 37N42'45 104w52'35 6:59:30
Delhi 36 1 37N38'32 104w01'03 6:56:04
Dell 19 1 39N53'08 106w51'21 7:07:25
Del Norte 53 1 37N40'44 106w21'10 7:05:25
Delta 15 1 38N44'32 108w04'06 7:12:16
Dent 62 1 40N18'35 104w50'00 6:59:20
Denver 16 2 39N44'21 104w59'03 6:59:56
Denver Merchandise Mart 1
2 39N48 104w57 6:59:48
Deora 5 1 37N34'49 102w57'58 6:51:52
Derby 1 2 39N50 104w55 6:59:40
Derby Junction 19
1 39N52'08 106w54'18 7:07:37
Devine 51 1 38N16'30 104w27'25 6:57:50
Dick 62 1 40N01'53 104w56'12 6:59:45
Dillon 59 1 39N37'49 106w02'34 7:04:10
Dinosaur 41 1 40N14'37 109w00'50 7:16:03
Divide 60 1 38N56'31 105w09'24 7:00:38
Dixon 35 1 40N44'20 105w00'12 7:00:01
Dodd 44 1 40N17'14 103w42'25 6:54:50
Doenz Place 59 1 39N54'18 106w24'04 7:05:36
Dolores 42 1 37N28'26 108w30'14 7:14:01
Dome Rock 30 1 39N25'18 105w11'49 7:00:47
Dominguez 15 1 38N47'50 108w19'18 7:13:17
Dominion 7 1 40N08'35 105w07'35 7:00:30
Donald Wall Place 41
1 40N26'52 108w59'05 7:15:56
Dorey Lakes 24 2 39N45 105w11 7:00:44
Dorsey 58 1 40N54'44 102w36'12 6:50:25
Dory Hill 24 2 39N45 105w11 7:00:44
Dotsero 19 1 39N38'59 107w03'35 7:08:14
Dove Creek 17 1 37N45'58 108w54'19 7:15:37
Dover 62 1 40N46'46 104w48'43 6:59:15
Dowds Junction 19
1 39N36'30 106w26'50 7:05:47
Downieville 10 1 39N46'00 105w36'50 7:02:27
Downtown 3 2 39N38 104w59 6:59:56
Doyleville 26 1 38N27'06 106w36'32 7:06:26
Drake 35 1 40N25'55 105w20'23 7:01:22
Drakes 35 1 40N33'15 105w04'46 7:00:19
Dream House Acres 3
2 39N37 105w00 7:00:00
Dry Creek Basin 57
1 38N10 108w25 7:13:40
Dudley 47 1 39N17'49 106w04'16 7:04:17
Duffield 21 1 38N44'32 104w54'43 6:59:39
Dumont 10 1 39N45'53 105w35'59 7:02:24
Duncan 55 1 37N52'27 105w36'50 7:02:27
Dunckley 54 1 40N18'03 107w11'37 7:08:46
Dunton 17 1 37N46'22 108w05'36 7:12:22
Dunul 53 1 37N39'44 106w06'07 7:04:24
Dupont 1 2 39N50'17 104w54'41 6:59:39
Durango 34 1 37N16'31 107w52'46 7:11:31
Durham 39 1 39N05'16 108w35'54 7:14:24
Dyersville 59 1 39N25'14 105w59'00 7:03:56
Dyke 4 1 37N13'35 107w11'41 7:08:47
Eads 31 1 38N28'50 102w46'53 6:51:08
Eagle 19 1 39N39'19 106w49'41 7:07:19
Eagles Nest 19 1 37N37'06 106w23'08 7:05:33
Earl 36 1 37N20'00 104w16'40 6:57:07
East Adams 1 1 39N53 104w11 6:56:44
East Alamosa 2 1 37N28 105w51 7:03:24
East Arapahoe 3
1 39N41 104w17 6:57:08
East Canon 22 1 38N27'10 105w12'45 7:00:51
Eastdale 12 1 37N01'43 105w39'01 7:02:36
Eastlake 1 2 39N55'26 104w57'39 6:59:51
Eastlake 51 1 38N14 104w38 6:58:32
East La Salle 62
1 40N21'17 104w40'55 6:58:44

Place		Latitude	Longitude	Time
Eastonville 21	1	39N03'40	104W33'42	6:58:15
East Portal 24	1	39N54'12	105W38'38	7:02:35
Eastridge 3	2	39N39	104W51	6:59:24
East Vancorum 43	1	38N13'40	108W35'40	7:14:23
East Weston 36	1	37N08	104W48	6:59:12
Eaton 62	1	40N31'49	104W42'39	6:58:51
Echo 22	1	38N26'34	105W32'18	7:02:09
Echo House 42	1	37N10'04	108W29'58	7:14:00
Echo Lake 10	1	39N45	105W32	7:02:08
Eckert 15	1	38N50'34	107W57'44	7:11:51
Eckley 63	1	40N06'50	102W29'25	6:49:58
Eden 51	1	38N18'59	104W36'57	6:58:28
Edgemont 30	2	39N43'52	105W07'49	7:00:31
Edgewater 30	2	39N45'11	105W03'49	7:00:15
Edison 21	1	38N50	104W13	6:56:52
Edith 4	1	37N00'20	106W54'35	7:07:38
Edler 5	1	37N11	102W47	6:51:08
Edwards 19	1	39N38'42	106W35'37	7:06:22
Egeria 54	1	40N01'52	106W46'20	7:07:05
Eggers 30	1	40N41'27	105W29'13	7:01:57
Egnar 57	1	37N54'59	108W56'22	7:15:45
Elba 61	1	39N56'54	103W13'04	6:52:52
Elbert 20	1	39N13'10	104W32'12	6:58:09
Elder 5	1	37N10'35	102W46'40	6:51:07
Elder 45	1	38N07'24	103W58'00	6:55:52
Eldora 7	1	39N56'55	105W33'48	7:02:15
Eldorado Springs 7	1	39N55'57	105W16'35	7:01:06
Eldredge 46	1	38N17'16	107W46'00	7:11:04
Elephant Park 30	1	39N37'44	105W21'44	7:01:27
Elesmere 21	1	38N51'53	104W42'36	6:58:50
Eleven Mile Village 47	1	38N59	105W22	7:01:28
Elizabeth 20	1	39N21'37	104W35'47	6:58:23
El Jebel 19	1	39N23'42	107W05'23	7:08:22
Elk Creek Acres 30	1	39N25	105W20	7:01:20
Elk Creek Highlands 47	1	39N25	105W20	7:01:20
Elkdale 25	1	40N02'25	105W52'50	7:03:31
Elkhead 54	1	40N38'55	107W12'25	7:08:50
Elkhorn Acres 47	1	39N25	105W20	7:01:20
Elk River 54	1	40N30	106W50	7:07:20
Elk Springs 41	1	40N21'20	108W26'52	7:13:47
Elkton 26	1	38N57'49	107W01'58	7:08:08
Elkton 60	1	38N43'20	105W09'00	7:00:36
Ellicott 21	1	38N50'18	104W23'11	6:57:33
Elm 62	1	40N21'13	104W47'00	6:59:08
El Moro 36	1	37N13'28	104W27'58	6:57:52
El Rancho 30	2	39N41'55	105W19'59	7:01:20
Elsmere 21	1	38N53	104W42	6:58:48
El Vado 7	1	40N00'21	105W20'45	7:01:23
Elwell 62	1	40N20'10	104W56'29	6:59:46
Emma 49	1	39N21'54	107W03'40	7:08:15
Empire 10	1	39N45'41	105W41'02	7:02:44
Engleville 36	1	37N08'58	104W28'29	6:57:54
Englewood 3	2	39N38'52	104W59'14	6:59:57
Eno 1	2	39N53'14	104W50'37	6:59:22
Erie 7	2	40N03'01	105W02'58	7:00:12
Escalante 15	1	38N45'28	108W15'40	7:13:03
Escalante Forks 39	1	38N44	108W04	7:12:16
Espinosa 11	1	37N07'50	105W56'44	7:03:47
Estabrook 47	1	39N22'59	105W25'44	7:01:43
Estes Park 35	1	40N22'38	105W31'16	7:02:05
Estrella 2	1	37N21'58	105W55'26	7:03:42
Eureka 56	1	37N52'47	107W33'52	7:10:15
Evans 62	1	40N22'35	104W41'30	6:58:46
Evanston 62	1	40N06'25	104W56'17	6:59:45
Evansville 53	1	37N40'16	106W19'06	7:05:16
Everett 33	1	39N04'04	106W30'05	7:06:00
Evergreen 30	1	39N38'00	105W19'00	7:01:16
Ever Green Hills 30	1	39N38	105W20	7:01:20
Evergreen West 10	1	39N38	105W20	7:01:20
Fairplay 47	1	39N13'29	106W00'05	7:04:00
Fairview 14	1	38N04'04	105W05'55	7:00:24
Fairview 23	1	39N33	107W39	7:10:36
Fairview 43	1	38N29'20	107W48'09	7:11:13
Fairview 60	1	38N44'38	105W09'28	7:00:38
Fairway Estates 35	1	40N35	105W06	7:00:24
Falcon 21	1	38N55'59	104W36'29	6:58:26
Falcon Estates 21	1	38N51	104W48	6:59:12
Falfa 34	1	37N12'47	107W47'25	7:11:10
Fall Creek 57	1	38N00	108W00	7:12:00
Farisita 28	1	37N44'41	105W04'15	7:00:17
Farmers 62	1	40N27'07	104W46'43	6:59:07
Fayette 45	1	38N04'22	103W46'08	6:55:05
Fearnowville 51	1	38N16'45	104W33'35	6:58:14
Federal Heights 1	2	39N51'05	104W59'53	7:00:00
Fenders 30	2	39N34'26	105W12'59	7:00:52
Ferncliff 7	1	40N11'27	105W30'45	7:02:03
Ferndale 30	1	39N24'22	105W15'18	7:01:01
Fink 22	1	38N29'20	105W22'50	7:01:31
Fir 12	1	37N29'07	105W10'44	7:00:43
Fire Clay 30	2	39N51'07	105W15'25	7:01:02
Firestone 62	1	40N06'45	104W56'10	6:59:45
First View 9	1	38N49	102W21	6:49:24
Fishers Crossing 36	1	37N15'07	104W14'28	6:56:58
Fitzsimons 1	2	39N45	104W48	6:59:12
Flagler 32	1	39N17'35	103W04'00	6:52:16
Fleming 38	1	40N40'48	102W50'20	6:51:21
Flintwood Hills 18	1	39N23	104W45	6:59:00
Florence 22	1	38N23'25	105W07'05	7:00:28
Floresta 26	1	38N50'31	107W07'20	7:08:29
Florida 34	1	37N12'54	107W45'07	7:11:00
Florissant 60	1	38N56'45	105W17'20	7:01:09
Florissant Heights 60	1	38N57	105W17	7:01:08
Fondis 20	1	39N12'57	104W20'48	6:57:23
Forder 37	1	38N40'51	103W42'19	6:54:49
Forest Hills 24	2	39N45	105W11	7:00:44
Fort Big Spring 9	1	38N56'00	102W49'45	6:51:19
Fort Boettcher 29	1	40N48'16	106W32'36	7:06:10
Fort Carson 21	1	38N45	104W47	6:59:08
Fort Collins 35	1	40N35'07	105W05'02	7:00:20
Fort Garland 12	1	37N25'44	105W26'00	7:01:44
Fort Julesburg 58	1	40N56'35	102W21'28	6:49:26
Fort Logan 3	2	39N39	105W02	7:00:08
Fort Lupton 62	1	40N05'05	104W48'45	6:59:15
Fort Lyon 6	1	39N06'00	103W09'00	6:52:36
Fort Morgan 44	1	40N15'01	103W47'58	6:55:12
Fort Reynolds 51	1	38N13'50	104W18'10	6:57:13
Fort Saint Vrain 62	1	40N16'44	104W51'16	6:59:25
Fort Sedgwick 58	1	40N56'35	102W22'48	6:49:31
Fosston 62	1	40N34'07	104W21'34	6:57:26
Fountain 21	1	38N40'56	104W42'01	6:58:48
Four Corners Crossing 6	1	38N01'36	102W46'39	6:51:07
Fowler 45	1	38N07'45	104W01'22	6:56:05
Foxborough 7	2	39N55	105W06	7:00:24
Fox Creek 11	1	37N03'56	106W12'03	7:04:48
Foxton 30	1	39N25'28	105W14'08	7:00:57
Franktown 18	1	39N23'29	104W45'08	6:59:01
Fraser 25	1	39N56'42	105W49'00	7:03:16
Frederick 62	1	40N05'57	104W56'12	6:59:45
Fred Wall Place 41	1	40N26'17	108W58'34	7:15:54
Freeland 10	1	39N44'39	105W35'42	7:02:23
Freeman 53	1	37N32	106W21	7:05:24
Freshwater 47	1	38N46	105W32	7:02:08
Frick 5	1	37N35'07	102W57'18	6:51:49
Friendship Ranch 47	1	39N25	105W20	7:01:20
Frisco 59	1	39N34'28	106W05'49	7:04:23
Frost 43	1	38N34'02	107W58'10	7:11:53
Fruita 39	1	39N09'32	108W43'42	7:14:55
Fruitvale 39	1	39N04'54	108W29'46	7:13:59
Fulford 19	1	39N30'54	106W39'21	7:06:37
Funston 23	1	39N33'38	107W20'55	7:09:24
Futurity 8	1	38N44'11	105W57'12	7:03:49
Galatea 31	1	38N30'16	103W01'27	6:52:06
Galena 22	1	38N15'43	105W16'38	7:01:07
Galeton 62	1	40N31'15	104W35'07	6:58:20
Gallen 38	1	40N41'16	103W00'28	6:52:02
Garcia 12	1	37N00'15	105W32'12	7:02:09
Garden City 62	1	40N23'38	104W41'20	6:58:45
Gardner 28	1	37N47'00	105W09'54	7:00:40
Garfield 8	1	38N33'06	106W17'30	7:05:10
Garland City 12	1	37N27'09	105W20'30	7:01:22
Garo 47	1	39N06'28	105W53'23	7:03:34
Gary 44	1	40N04'26	103W35'04	6:54:20
Gaskil 25	1	40N19'50	105W51'42	7:03:27
Gates 62	1	40N31'53	104W45'17	6:59:01
Gateview 26	1	38N17'37	107W13'05	7:08:52
Gateway 39	1	38N41	108W59	7:15:56
Gato 4	1	37N03	107W12	7:08:48
Gem Village 34	1	37N13'09	107W38'12	7:10:33
Genesee 30	2	39N45	105W11	7:00:44
Genoa 37	1	39N16'42	103W29'59	6:54:00
Georgetown 10	1	39N42'22	105W41'49	7:02:47
Gerrard 53	1	37N40'38	106W35'33	7:06:22
Giddings 35	1	40N37'17	105W00'36	7:00:02
Gilcrest 62	1	40N16'55	104W46'38	6:59:07
Gill 62	1	40N27'15	104W32'30	6:58:10
Gillet 60	1	38N46'55	105W07'20	7:00:29
Gilman 19	1	39N31'58	106W23'36	7:05:34
Gilpin 24	1	39N53'27	105W30'27	7:02:02
Gilpin 6	1	37N56'46	103W11'03	6:52:44
Gilson Gulch 10	1	39N45'42	105W30'27	7:02:02
Gilsonite 39	1	39N10'37	108W46'41	7:15:07
Glacier Gorge Junction 35	1	40N18'28	105W38'34	7:02:34
Gladel 56	1	38N01	108W47	7:15:08
Glade Park 39	1	39N00	108W44	7:14:56
Gladstone 56	1	37N53'25	107W38'59	7:10:36
Glen Comfort 35	1	40N23'37	105W26'23	7:01:46
Glen Cove 60	1	38N52'33	105W04'20	7:00:17
Glendale 3	2	39N42'18	104W55'59	6:59:44
Glendale 7	1	40N04'55	105W21'57	7:01:28
Glendevey 35	1	40N48'37	105W56'04	7:03:44
Glen Echo 35	1	40N41'55	105W35'05	7:02:20
Glen Eden 54	1	40N43'02	106W54'52	7:07:39
Glenelk 30	1	39N27'48	105W21'15	7:01:25
Glen Eyie 21	1	38N53'30	104W53'02	6:59:32
Glen Haven 35	1	40N27'14	105W26'55	7:01:48
Glenisle 47	1	39N24'32	105W30'33	7:02:02
Glen Park 21	1	39N06'52	104W55'11	6:59:41
Glentivar 47	1	39N14	106W00	7:04:00
Glenwood Springs 23	1	39N33'02	107W19'27	7:09:18
Golconda 42	1	37N27'27	108W09'06	7:12:36
Golden 30	2	39N45'20	105W13'14	7:00:53
Goldfield 60	1	38N43'04	105W07'32	7:00:30
Gold Hill 7	1	40N03'47	105W24'13	7:01:37
Goodale 50	1	38N07'05	102W26'05	6:49:44
Goodell Corner 35	1	40N44'07	105W34'50	7:02:19
Gooding 7	2	40N04'25	105W04'57	7:00:20
Goodnight 51	1	38N15'40	104W40'10	6:58:41
Goodpasture 51	1	38N05'00	104W55'10	6:59:41
Goodrich 44	1	40N21'04	104W03'40	6:56:15
Gordon 28	1	37N40'54	104W51'16	6:59:25
Gothic 26	1	38N57'33	106W59'21	7:07:57
Gould 29	1	40N31'35	106W01'34	7:04:06
Gove 62	1	40N24'38	104W55'36	6:59:42
Gowanda 62	1	40N12'17	104W54'00	6:59:36
Graft 5	1	37N26'52	102W53'31	6:51:34
Granada 50	1	38N03'50	102W18'36	6:49:14
Granby 25	1	40N05'10	105W56'20	7:03:45
Grand Island 7	1	39N58'15	105W36'10	7:02:25
Grand Junction 39	1	39N03'50	108W33'00	7:14:12
Grand Lake 25	1	40N15'08	105W49'21	7:03:17
Grand Mesa 15	1	39N02'25	107W56'57	7:11:48
Grand Valley 23	1	39N27'07	108W03'08	7:12:13
Grandview 34	1	37N13'39	107W49'35	7:11:18
Grandview Estates 18	2	39N32'37	104W49'14	6:59:17
Granite 8	1	39N02'37	106W15'46	7:05:03
Grant 47	1	39N27'35	105W39'40	7:02:39
Grate 50	1	38N05'14	102W24'55	6:49:40
Graymont 10	1	39N41'40	105W48'00	7:03:12
Greeley 62	1	40N25'24	104W42'31	6:58:50
Greeley Junction 62	1	40N27'20	104W41'38	6:58:47
Greeley Mall 62	1	40N24	104W42	6:58:48
Greenhorn 51	1	37N54'25	104W51'10	6:59:25
Greenland 18	1	39N10'57	104W51'17	6:59:25
Green Mountain 30	2	39N41	105W08	7:00:32
Green Mountain Camp 59	1	40N04	106W24	7:05:36
Green Mountain Estates 30	2	39N41	105W08	7:00:32
Green Mountain Falls 60	1	38N56'06	105W00'59	7:00:04
Green Mountain Village 30	2	39N41'53	105W07'55	7:00:32
Green Towers 51	1	37N55	104W56	6:59:44
Green Valley Acres 30	1	39N30'08	105W18'41	7:01:15
Greenway Park 30	2	39N55	105W06	7:00:24
Greenwood 14	1	38N12'18	105W05'47	7:00:23
Greenwood Village 3	2	39N37'02	104W57'01	6:59:48
Gresham 7	1	40N08'25	105W25'54	7:01:44
Greystone 41	1	40N36'34	108W40'24	7:14:42
Griff 38	1	40N46'56	103W00'24	6:52:02
Griffin 44	1	40N14'33	103W56'42	6:55:47
Grizzly 23	1	39N33'28	107W14'50	7:08:59
Grover 62	1	40N52'17	104W13'29	6:56:54
Guadalupe 11	1	37N05'43	106W01'30	7:04:06
Guffey 47	1	38N45'04	105W31'15	7:02:05
Gulnare 36	1	37N19'02	104W45'05	6:59:00
Gunbarrel Estates 7	1	40N11	105W07	7:00:28
Gunbarrel Meadows 7	1	40N00	105W16	7:01:04
Gunnison 26	1	38N32'45	106W55'29	7:07:42
Guston 46	1	37N54'59	107W41'23	7:10:46
Gypsum 19	1	39N38'49	106W57'04	7:07:48
Hadley 45	1	38N02'18	103W24'10	6:53:37
Hahns Peak 54	1	40N43	106W55	7:07:40
Hale 63	1	39N37'47	102W08'32	6:48:34
Hallcraft Town Houses 30	2	39N41	105W08	7:00:32
Hambert 62	1	40N18'54	104W44'15	6:58:57
Hamilton 8	1	38N55'28	106W27'30	7:05:50
Hamilton 41	1	40N22'02	107W36'45	7:10:27
Hamlet 51	1	38N09'17	104W05'36	6:56:22
Hancock 8	1	38N38'25	106W21'55	7:05:28
Hanna 53	1	37N40'46	106W27'30	7:05:50
Hanover 21	1	38N51	104W47	6:59:08
Happy Canyon 18	1	39N26'06	104W52'12	6:59:29
Harboro 5	1	37N29'51	102W48'52	6:51:15
Hardin 62	1	40N21'04	104W25'30	6:57:42
Hardman 62	1	40N21'57	104W54'53	6:59:40
Harmony 35	1	40N31'24	105W02'35	7:00:10
Harney 62	1	40N09'05	104W56'25	6:59:46
Harris Park 47	1	39N30'42	105W29'26	7:01:58
Harry Parker Place 26	1	39N03'08	107W28'07	7:09:52
Hartman 50	1	38N07'13	102W13'10	6:48:53
Hartner 2	1	37N23'33	105W54'34	7:03:38
Hartsel 47	1	39N01'18	105W47'43	7:03:11
Hasty 6	1	38N06'45	102W57'25	6:51:50
Haswell 31	1	38N27'08	103W09'45	6:52:39
Haver 47	1	38N57'54	105W55'37	7:03:42
Hawkins 31	1	38N29'38	102W55'55	6:51:44
Hawley 45	1	37N58'58	103W42'38	6:54:51
Haxtun 48	1	40N38'28	102W37'35	6:50:30
Haybro 54	1	40N19'56	106W57'32	7:07:50
Hayden 54	1	40N29'31	107W15'25	7:09:02
Hayford 38	1	40N40'42	103W09'50	6:52:39
Hays 45	1	38N04'23	103W37'07	6:54:28
Hazeltine 1	2	39N53'48	104W52'57	6:59:32
Hazeltine Heights 1	2	39N53'08	104W53'21	6:59:33
Heartstrong 63	1	39N56'51	102W34'35	6:50:18
Heath 31	1	38N16'20	103W28'10	6:53:53
Heatherwood 7	1	40N00	105W16	7:01:04
Hebron 29	1	40N35'46	106W24'23	7:05:38
Heeney 59	1	40N04	106W24	7:05:36
Heiberger 39	1	39N16'08	107W48'06	7:11:12
Henderson 1	2	39N55'14	104W51'55	6:59:28
Henery 2	1	37N23'54	105W54'23	7:03:38
Henkel 21	1	38N31'12	104W37'33	6:58:30
Henson 27	1	38N01'15	107W22'35	7:09:30
Hereford 62	1	40N58'30	104W18'19	6:57:13
Hermosa 34	1	37N24'55	107W50'05	7:11:20
Herzman Mesa 30	1	39N36'38	105W18'35	7:01:14
Hesperus 34	1	37N17'10	108W02'20	7:12:09
Hessie 7	1	39N57'18	105W35'58	7:02:24
Hiawatha 41	1	40N59'18	108W37'11	7:14:29
Hidden Valley 30	1	39N41'41	105W20'19	7:01:21
Hideaway Park 25	1	39N55'05	105W47'06	7:03:08
Hierro 26	1	38N29'41	107W01'51	7:08:07
Higbee 45	1	37N46'35	103W27'32	6:53:50
Higby 23	1	39N34'11	107W13'32	7:08:54
High Chateau Ranches 60	1	38N57	105W17	7:01:08
Highland 7	1	40N14'20	105W04'58	7:00:20
Highland Acres 62	1	40N24	104W42	6:58:48
Highland Lake 62	1	40N14'52	105W00'50	7:00:03
Highland Lakes 60	1	38N56	105W09	7:00:36

Highland Park 39 1 39N05'31 108w28'51 7:13:55
Highland Park 47 1 39N29'56 105w31'43 7:02:07
Highlands 16 2 39N46 105w01 7:00:04
High-mar 7 1 40N00 105w16 7:01:04
Hi-Land Acres 1 2 39N59'18 104w52'37 6:59:30
Hill and Park 62 1 40N24 104w42 6:58:48
Hillrose 44 1 40N19'33 103w31'17 6:54:05
Hillsboro 62 1 40N19'58 104w51'50 6:59:27
Hillside 14 1 38N15'55 105w36'40 7:02:27
Hilltop 18 2 39N27'06 104w40'51 6:58:43
Hilton 6 1 38N04'13 103w03'38 6:52:15
Hitchens 54 1 40N30 106w50 7:07:20
Hiwan Hills 30 1 39N38'25 105w19'46 7:01:19
Hobson 51 1 38N20'27 104w56'02 6:59:44
Hoehne 36 1 37N16'52 104w22'50 6:57:31
Hoffman Heights 3 2 39N43 104w51 6:59:24
Holiday Hills 60 1 39N00 105w04 7:00:16
Hollowell Corner 35 1 40N22'42 105w03'31 7:00:14
Holly 50 1 38N03'08 102w07'20 6:48:29
Hollywood 60 1 38N42'34 105w07'58 7:00:32
Holy Cross City 19 1 39N24'54 106w28'39 7:05:55
Holyoke 48 1 40N35'04 102w18'07 6:49:12
Homelake 53 1 37N34'32 106w05'47 7:04:23
Homewood Park 30 2 39N32'34 105w11'50 7:00:47
Hooks 19 1 39N22'27 107w05'17 7:08:21
Hooper 2 1 37N44'34 105w52'29 7:03:30
Hoopup 36 1 37N15 103w21 6:53:24
Hoovers Corner 43 1 38N36'25 108w03'30 7:12:14
Horseshoe 47 1 39N12'14 106w05'05 7:04:20
Horsetooth Heights 35 1 40N30'16 105w09'13 7:00:37
Hotchkiss 15 1 38N47'59 107w43'08 7:10:53
Hot Creek 11 1 37N16 106w15 7:05:00
Hot Sulphur Springs 25 1 40N04'23 106w06'08 7:04:25
Houghton 36 1 37N35'22 104w02'34 6:56:10
Houston 62 1 40N15'17 104w48'23 6:59:14
Howard 22 1 38N26'55 105w50'05 7:03:20
Howard Place 29 1 40N29'16 106w12'59 7:04:52
Howardsville 56 1 37N50'08 107w35'37 7:10:22
Hoyt 44 1 40N00'56 104w04'28 6:56:18
Hudson 62 1 40N04'25 104w38'33 6:58:34
Huerfano Valley 51 1 38N02 104w17 6:57:08
Huff 15 1 38N45'25 108w15'20 7:13:01
Hugo 37 1 39N08'10 103w28'10 6:53:53
Hurley 44 1 40N16'27 103w45'40 6:55:03
Hurrich 62 1 40N31'52 104w47'36 6:59:10
Husted 21 1 38N59 104w52 6:59:28
Hyde 61 1 40N08'09 102w49'56 6:51:20
Hygiene 7 1 40N11'19 105w10'49 7:00:43
Hyland Hills 10 1 39N38 105w20 7:01:20
Idaho Creek 62 1 40N07'20 105w00'45 7:00:03
Idaho Springs 10 1 39N44'33 105w00'47 7:00:03
Idalia 63 1 39N42'14 102w17'36 6:49:10
Idledale 30 2 39N39'58 105w14'37 7:00:58
Idylwilde 35 1 40N42'03 105w39'15 7:02:37
Ignacio 34 1 37N06'54 107w37'57 7:10:32
Iles Grove 41 1 40N20'07 107w41'12 7:10:45
Iliff 38 1 40N45'33 103w03'58 6:52:16
Ilium 57 1 37N55'47 107w53'50 7:11:35
Ilse 14 1 38N26 105w13 7:00:52
Independence 49 1 39N06'26 106w36'19 7:06:25
Independence 60 1 38N43'56 105w08'10 7:00:33
Indian Agency 34 1 37N07 107w38 7:10:32
Indian Creek 60 1 38N57 105w17 7:01:08
Indian Hills 30 2 39N37 105w14 7:00:56
Indian Meadows 35 1 40N42'02 105w33'05 7:02:12
Indians Hills 30 2 39N37'58 105w15'33 7:01:02
Indian Springs Village 30 1 39N25'55 105w19'12 7:01:17
Insmont 47 1 39N23'31 105w27'09 7:01:49
Iola 26 1 38N29 107w06 7:08:24
Ione 62 1 40N08'56 104w48'37 6:59:14
Iris 55 1 38N24'58 106w49'42 7:07:19
Iron City 8 1 38N42'31 106w20'15 7:05:21
Irondale 1 2 39N50'58 104w53'48 6:59:35
Ironton 46 1 37N55'58 107w40'47 7:10:43
Irwin 26 1 38N52'25 107w05'47 7:08:23
Ivywild 21 1 38N48'38 104w50'05 6:59:20
Jackson Field 62 1 40N24'25 104w41'09 6:58:45
Jack Springs 41 1 40N21'04 108w42'09 7:14:49
Jamestown 7 1 40N06'56 105w23'17 7:01:33
Jansen 36 1 37N08'58 104w32'18 6:58:09
Jaroso 12 1 37N00'10 105w37'25 7:02:30
Jasper 53 1 37N25'04 106w27'43 7:05:51
Jefferson 47 1 39N22'38 105w48'00 7:03:12
Jefferson Heights 47 1 39N23 105w48 7:03:12
Jessica 38 1 40N45'38 103w10'17 6:52:41
Jessum 62 1 40N08'20 105w01'28 7:00:06
Joes 63 1 39N39'23 102w40'42 6:50:43
John Held Corner 39 1 39N08'12 108w08'08 7:12:33
Johnson 62 1 40N05'15 104w26'32 6:57:46
Johnsons Corner 39 1 39N05'31 108w29'46 7:13:59
Johnson Village 8 1 38N50 106w08 7:04:32
Johnstown 62 1 40N20'13 104w54'42 6:59:39
Juanita 4 1 37N01'38 107w09'00 7:08:36
Juanita Junction 15 1 38N55'29 107w31'39 7:10:07
Julesburg 58 1 40N59'18 102w15'50 6:49:03
Juniper Hot Springs 41 1 40N28'02 107w57'11 7:11:49
Kahler 62 1 40N19'42 104w59'53 7:00:00
Kaibab 19 1 39N39 106w50 7:07:20
Kannah 39 1 38N56'21 108w26'47 7:13:47
Karl 50 1 38N08'15 102w31'10 6:50:05
Karval 37 1 38N44 103w32 6:54:08
Kassler 30 1 39N29'26 105w05'39 7:00:23
Kearns 4 1 37N07'52 107w09'35 7:08:38
Keenesburg 62 1 40N06'30 104w31'10 6:58:05
Keesee 6 1 38N08'11 102w46'42 6:51:07
Kelim 35 1 40N34'24 104w57'01 6:59:48
Kelker 21 1 38N47'45 104w46'51 6:59:07
Keller 6 1 38N03'46 103w08'45 6:52:35
Kellytown 18 2 39N28'53 104w59'35 6:59:58
Kenyon Corner 35 1 40N38'22 105w04'20 7:00:17
Keota 62 1 40N42'10 104w04'29 6:56:18
Kerns 35 1 40N30'27 104w56'38 6:59:47
Kerper City 55 1 38N16'58 106w08'30 7:04:34
Kersey 62 1 40N23'15 104w33'40 6:58:15
Keyhole 15 1 38N41'35 108w18'30 7:13:14
Keystone 54 1 40N18'04 106w57'45 7:07:51
Keystone 57 1 37N56'59 107w52'37 7:11:30
Keystone 59 1 39N35'58 105w59'12 7:03:57
Kiggin 23 1 39N25'35 107w14'20 7:08:57
Kim 36 1 37N14'48 103w21'06 6:53:24
King Center 13 1 38N10'37 103w54'25 6:55:38
Kings Canyon 29 1 40N56 106w14 7:04:56
Kings Corner 35 1 40N22'42 105w04'22 7:00:17
Kinikinik 35 1 40N42'45 105w44'15 7:02:57
Kiowa 20 1 39N20'50 104w27'50 6:57:51
Kirk 63 1 39N36'48 102w35'28 6:50:22
Kirkland 62 1 40N11'16 105w00'55 7:00:04
Kit Carson 9 1 38N45'40 102w47'20 6:51:09
Kittredge 30 2 39N39'17 105w17'57 7:01:12
Kkrval 37 1 38N44'03 103w32'07 6:54:08
Kline 34 1 37N08'39 108w07'08 7:12:29
Kluver 62 1 40N34'25 104w56'36 6:59:46
Knob Hill 21 1 38N50'24 104w46'56 6:59:08
Kobe 33 1 39N07'46 106w18'51 7:05:15
Koen 50 1 38N04'17 102w20'47 6:49:23
Koenig 62 1 40N23'08 104w55'38 6:59:43
Kokomo 59 1 39N25'27 106w11'21 7:04:45
Kornman 50 1 38N09'01 102w36'42 6:50:27
Krammes 45 1 38N02'27 103w41'20 6:54:45
Krauss 62 1 40N06'25 104w26'32 6:57:46
Kremmling 25 1 40N03'32 106w23'18 7:05:33
Kreybill 6 1 38N06'50 103w06'00 6:52:24
Kuhlmann Heights 7 2 39N45 105w11 7:00:44
Kuhns Crossing 20 1 39N16'55 104w07'25 6:56:30
Kuner 62 1 40N22'34 104w29'24 6:57:58
Kutch 20 1 37N54'38 103w52'08 6:55:29
K-Z Ranchettes 47 1 39N25 105w20 7:01:20
La Boca 34 1 37N00'40 107w36'05 7:10:24
Lacy 23 1 39N30'33 107w52'08 7:11:29
Lafayette 7 2 39N59'37 105w05'21 7:00:21
La Foret 21 1 39N00'34 104w42'50 6:58:51
La Fruto 2 1 37N24'53 105w53'53 7:03:36
La Garita 55 1 37N50'27 106w14'46 7:04:59
Laird 63 1 40N04'57 102w06'11 6:48:25
La Jara 11 1 37N16'30 105w57'35 7:03:50
La Junta 45 1 37N59'06 103w32'36 6:54:10
La Junta Gardens 45 1 37N59'58 103w33'11 6:54:13
La Junta Village 45 1 38N02'15 103w31'50 6:54:07
Lakeborough 30 2 39N38 105w04 7:00:16
Lake City 27 1 38N01'48 107w18'53 7:09:16
Lake George 47 1 38N58'47 105w21'25 7:01:26
Lakeside 16 2 39N46'42 105w03'32 7:00:14
Lake View 24 2 39N45 105w11 7:00:44
Lakewood 30 2 39N42'17 105w04'51 7:00:19
Lamar 50 1 38N05'14 102w37'13 6:50:29
Lamartine 10 1 39N43'46 105w36'58 7:02:28
Lamb 44 1 40N14'42 103w50'50 6:55:23
Lambert Place 49 1 39N19'44 107w20'46 7:09:23
La Montana Mesa 60 1 38N57 105w17 7:01:08
La Plata 34 1 37N23'50 108w03'45 7:12:15
Laporte 35 1 40N37'35 105w08'14 7:00:33
La Posta 34 1 37N07'31 107w53'40 7:11:35
Larand 29 1 40N37'21 106w17'32 7:05:10
Lariat 53 1 37N34 106w09 7:04:36
Larkspur 18 1 39N13'43 104w53'12 6:59:33
La Salle 62 1 40N20'56 104w42'05 6:58:48
Las Animas 6 1 38N04'00 103w13'20 6:52:53
Las Animas Junction 6 1 38N03'45 103w10'25 6:52:42
Lasauses 12 1 37N16'00 105w44'45 7:02:59
Lascar 28 1 37N49'30 104w44'53 6:59:00
Las Mesitas 11 1 37N03'52 106w06'36 7:04:26
Last Chance 61 1 39N44'27 103w35'28 6:54:22
La Valley 12 1 37N06'07 105w20'50 7:01:23
La Veta 28 1 37N30'18 105w00'26 7:00:02
La Veta Pass 12 1 37N35'35 105w12'10 7:00:49
Lawson 10 1 39N45'57 105w37'37 7:02:30
Lay 41 1 40N31'36 107w52'53 7:11:32
Lazear 15 1 38N46'48 107w46'52 7:11:07
Leader 1 1 39N53'58 104w03'21 6:56:13
Leadville 33 1 39N15'03 106w17'31 7:05:10
Leadville Junction 33 1 39N15'31 106w20'21 7:05:21
Leal 25 1 39N48'37 106w02'38 7:04:11
Leavick 47 1 39N11'42 106w08'13 7:04:33
Lebanon 42 1 37N27'26 108w35'27 7:14:22
Leisure Living 62 2 40N03 105w04 7:00:16
Lenado 49 1 39N14'33 106w45'43 7:07:03
Leon 19 1 39N23'05 107w05'55 7:08:24
Leonard 57 1 38N03'50 108w01'35 7:12:06
Leroy 38 1 40N31'34 102w54'49 6:51:39
Lester 28 1 37N30'06 104w42'46 6:58:51
Lewis 42 1 37N29'59 108w40'07 7:14:40
Leyden 30 2 39N50'41 105w11'01 7:00:44
Leyden Junction 30 2 39N50'46 105w08'52 7:00:35
Leyner 7 2 40N02'59 105w06'07 7:00:24
Liberty 5 1 37N18'29 102w43'24 6:50:54
Liberty 55 1 37N51'37 105w35'43 7:02:23
Liberty 62 1 40N12'22 105w00'31 7:00:02
Liberty Bell 57 1 37N56'07 107w47'42 7:11:11
Liggett 16 2 40N02'42 105w08'00 7:00:32
Lime 51 1 38N08'55 104w37'27 6:58:30
Lime 57 1 37N57'18 107w55'49 7:11:43
Limon 37 1 39N15'50 103w41'30 6:54:46
Lincoln 59 1 39N29'15 105w59'06 7:03:56
Lincoln Hills 24 1 39N55'21 105w27'28 7:01:50
Lincoln Park 22 1 38N25'45 105w13'10 7:00:53
Lindon 61 1 39N44'22 103w24'48 6:53:39
Little Dam 35 1 40N25'20 105w13'20 7:00:53
Littleton 3 2 39N36'48 105w00'58 7:00:04
Livengood Hills 18 2 39N31 104w46 6:59:04
Livermore 35 1 40N47'40 105w13'00 7:00:52
Living Springs 1 1 39N53'29 104w18'00 6:57:12
Lobatos 11 1 37N04'46 105w56'54 7:03:48
Lochbuie 62 2 39N57 104w58 6:59:52
Lochwood 30 2 39N41 105w00 7:00:00
Lodi 44 1 40N15'04 103w42'12 6:54:49
Logan 38 1 40N34'43 103w21'28 6:53:26
Log Lane Village 44 1 40N16 103w50 6:55:20
Logtown 34 1 37N33'06 107w35'27 7:10:22
Loma 39 1 39N11'45 108w48'45 7:15:15
Loma Linda 34 1 37N13'27 107w47'43 7:11:11
Lombard Village 51 1 38N13'30 104w32'40 6:58:11
Lone Oak 36 1 37N03'18 103w37'58 6:54:32
Lone Pine Estates 30 2 39N35'42 105w14'41 7:00:59
Lone Star 61 1 40N21'07 102w51'03 6:51:24
Lonetree 4 1 37N10'05 107w10'20 7:08:41
Longmont 7 1 40N10'02 105w06'05 7:00:24
Longview 30 1 39N25'03 105w11'36 7:00:46
Lookout Mountain 30 2 39N45 105w11 7:00:44
Loretto Heights 16 2 39N39 105w02 7:00:08
Lory 62 1 40N25'17 104w54'35 6:59:38
Los Cerritos 11 1 37N08'54 105w54'37 7:03:38
Los Fuertes 12 1 37N08'04 105w22'45 7:01:31
Louisville 7 2 39N58'40 105w07'53 7:00:32
Louviers 18 2 39N28'40 105w00'24 7:00:02
Loveland 35 1 40N23'52 105w04'28 7:00:18
Loveland Heights 35 1 40N23'23 105w27'49 7:01:51
Lowe 62 1 40N29'33 104w35'42 6:58:23
Lowery Air Force Base 16 2 39N43 104w53 6:59:32
Loyd 41 1 40N18'13 107w42'15 7:10:49
Lubers 6 1 38N07'44 102w55'26 6:51:42
Lucerne 62 1 40N28'55 104w41'57 6:58:48
Ludlow 36 1 37N20'00 104w34'58 6:58:20
Lujane 43 1 38N29'14 107w43'59 7:10:56
Lulu City 25 1 40N26'44 105w50'51 7:03:23
Lycan 5 1 37N36'55 102w12'01 6:48:48
Lynn 36 1 37N25'38 104w38'26 6:58:34
Lyons 7 1 40N13'29 105w16'15 7:01:05
Lyons Park Estates 7 1 40N14 105w17 7:01:08
Mack 39 1 39N13'26 108w51'52 7:15:27
Maddux 62 1 40N11'32 104w49'09 6:59:17
Madison Hill 30 2 39N50 105w01 7:00:04
Madrid 36 1 37N07'37 106w38'30 7:06:34
Magee 1 2 39N45'20 104w46'51 6:59:07
Magnolia 7 1 39N59'38 105w21'53 7:01:28
Maher 43 1 38N38'42 107w35'03 7:10:20
Malachite 28 1 37N45'16 105w15'37 7:01:02
Maloy 62 1 40N14'40 104w58'10 6:59:53
Malta 33 1 39N13'46 106w21'01 7:05:24
Manassa 11 1 37N10'27 105w56'13 7:03:45
Mancos 42 1 37N20'42 108w17'19 7:13:09
Mancos Creek 42 1 37N21 108w34 7:14:16
Mandalay Gardens 30 2 39N55 105w06 7:00:24
Manhattan 35 1 40N43'56 105w35'58 7:02:24
Manila 1 1 39N45'23 104w31'19 6:58:05
Manitou Springs 21 1 38N51'35 104w55'00 6:59:40
Manzanola 45 1 38N06'34 103w51'56 6:55:28
Marble 26 1 39N04'20 107w11'18 7:08:45
Marcott 38 1 40N52'43 102w43'25 6:50:54
Mariano 42 1 37N10'46 108w52'22 7:15:29
Marlman 6 1 38N05'37 103w20'55 6:53:24
Marnel 51 1 38N03'20 104w37'43 6:58:31
Marnett 7 1 40N10'06 105w08'00 7:00:32
Marshall 7 2 39N57'20 105w13'45 7:00:55
Marshdale 30 1 39N35'33 105w18'42 7:01:15
Marshdale Park 30 1 39N38 105w20 7:01:20
Marvel 34 1 37N06'45 108w07'34 7:12:30
Maryvale 25 1 39N55'59 105w47'12 7:03:09
Mason Corner 62 1 40N28'01 104w42'05 6:58:48
Masonic Park 53 1 37N40 106w37 7:06:28
Masontown 59 1 39N33'59 106w05'59 7:04:24
Masonville 35 1 40N29'15 105w12'37 7:00:50
Massadona 41 1 40N15'10 108w38'23 7:14:34
Masters 62 1 40N18'34 104w14'40 6:56:59
Matheson 20 1 39N10'18 103w58'30 6:55:54
Matthews 62 1 40N28'47 104w29'50 6:57:59
Maxeyville 53 1 37N37'05 106w08'56 7:04:36
Maybell 41 1 40N31'04 108w05'11 7:12:21
Mayday 34 1 37N21'02 108w04'34 7:12:18
Mayne 28 1 37N33'06 104w43'07 6:58:52
Maysville 8 1 38N32'19 106w11'23 7:04:46

May Valley 50 1 38N12'06 102W36'48 6:50:27
McClave 6 1 38N08'15 102W51'00 6:51:24
Mc Clellands 35 1 40N31'41 105W04'49 7:00:19
Mc Clintock 2 1 37N25'40 105W31'33 7:02:06
Mc Coy 19 1 39N54'58 106W43'30 7:06:54
McCoy Hills 1 2 39N50 104W57 6:59:48
McCoy Subdivision 8 1 38N32 106W00 7:04:00
McElmo 42 1 37N21 108W34 7:14:16
Mc Gregor 54 1 40N28'46 107W02'04 7:08:08
Mc Kenzie Junction 14 1 38N09'51 105W11'25 7:00:46
Mead 62 1 40N14'00 104W59'53 7:00:00
Meadow Brook Heights 30 2 39N37 105W00 7:00:00
Mears Junction 8 1 38N26'50 106W06'30 7:04:26
Medina Plaza 36 1 37N07'40 104W47'30 6:59:10
Meeker 52 1 40N02'15 107W54'45 7:11:39
Meeker Park 7 1 40N14'02 105W31'49 7:02:07
Melina 6 1 38N05'58 103W11'10 6:52:45
Meredith 49 1 39N21'47 106W43'46 7:06:55
Merino 38 1 40N28'57 103W21'03 6:53:24
Mesa 39 1 39N09'59 108W08'18 7:12:33
Mesa 51 1 38N15 104W39 6:58:36
Mesa Verde National Park 42 1 37N11 108W29 7:13:56
Mesita 12 1 37N05'54 105W36'05 7:02:24
Messex 61 1 40N25'46 103W26'10 6:53:45
Meyers Corner 35 1 40N40'05 105W01'08 7:00:05
Middleton 56 1 37N51'18 107W34'18 7:10:17
Midland 60 1 38N51'30 105W09'40 7:00:39
Mid Vail 19 1 39N36'54 106W22'02 7:05:28
Midway 5 1 37N08'57 102W11'08 6:48:45
Midway 21 1 38N50'33 104W58'24 6:59:54
Midway 26 1 38N20'38 107W03'12 7:08:13
Midway 35 1 40N25'49 105W19'20 7:01:17
Midway 60 1 38N44'24 105W08'32 7:00:34
Midway 61 1 40N13'35 103W23'50 6:53:35
Miles Place 41 1 40N39'57 108W59'31 7:15:58
Milliken 62 1 40N19'46 104W51'17 6:59:25
Millwood 42 1 37N25'18 108W19'59 7:13:20
Milner 54 1 40N29'05 107W01'08 7:08:05
Mindeman 45 1 37N42'25 103W54'58 6:55:40
Mineral Hot Springs 55 1 38N10'08 105W55'31 7:03:42
Minnehaha 21 1 38N50'58 104W57'32 6:59:50
Minturn 19 1 39N35'11 106W25'49 7:05:43
Mirage 55 1 38N06'10 105W51'50 7:03:27
Miramonte 7 1 39N55'50 105W22'20 7:01:29
Mishawaka 35 1 40N41'14 105W21'55 7:01:28
Missouri Park 8 1 38N32 106W00 7:04:00
Mitchell 19 1 39N23'30 106W19'07 7:05:16
Mitchel Place 52 1 39N47'17 108W38'48 7:14:35
Mobley Place 41 1 40N16'32 108W36'13 7:14:25
Model 36 1 37N22'20 104W14'40 6:56:59
Moffat 41 1 40N20 107W36 7:10:24
Moffat 55 1 37N59'56 105W54'34 7:03:38
Mogote 11 1 37N03'34 106W05'30 7:04:22
Molina 39 1 39N11'21 108W03'35 7:12:14
Monarch 8 1 38N32'26 106W18'49 7:05:15
Monson 28 1 37N30'58 104W42'13 6:58:49
Montbello 16 2 39N47'37 104W49'59 6:59:20
Montclair 16 2 39N44 104W54 6:59:36
Monte Vista 53 1 37N34'45 106W08'51 7:04:35
Monte Vista Estates 18 1 39N21'55 104W55'15 6:59:41
Montezuma 59 1 39N34'52 105W52'00 7:03:28
Montrose 43 1 38N28'42 107W52'32 7:11:30
Monument 21 1 39N05'30 104W52'20 6:59:29
Monument Lake Park 36 1 37N08 104W48 6:59:12
Monument Park 36 1 37N12'25 105W02'45 7:00:11
Moonridge 18 2 39N21'55 105W07'01 7:00:28
Moore 62 1 40N11'22 104W50'48 6:59:23
Moore Dale 47 1 39N25 105W29 7:01:56
Morey 7 1 40N13'03 105W05'32 7:00:22
Morgan 11 1 37N19'40 106W01'10 7:04:05
Morley 36 1 37N01'55 104W30'15 6:58:01
Morning Glory 28 1 37N40'12 104W50'44 6:59:23
Morrison 30 2 39N39'13 105W11'26 7:00:46
Mortimer 12 1 37N27'52 105W20'26 7:01:22
Mosca 2 1 37N39 105W52 7:03:28
Mosea 2 1 37N39'04 105W52'08 7:03:29
Moseley 44 1 40N14'56 103W45'13 6:55:01
Mountain Park 30 2 39N45 105W11 7:00:44
Mountain View 30 2 39N46'28 105W03'18 7:00:13
Mountain View 35 1 40N35'33 105W07'43 7:00:31
Mountain View 43 1 38N18'19 108W29'00 7:13:56
Mountain View Acres 2 1 37N28 105W51 7:03:24
Mountain View Lakes 30 1 39N25 105W20 7:01:20
Mount Crested Butte 26 1 38N52 106W59 7:07:56
Mount Harris 54 1 40N29'01 107W08'39 7:08:35
Mount Lincoln 39 1 39N06'22 108W22'58 7:13:32
Mount Massive Lakes 33 1 39N09'08 106W18'00 7:05:12
Mount Olivet 30 2 39N47'15 105W08'30 7:00:34
Mount Pearl 9 1 38N57'45 102W47'20 6:51:09
Mount Princeton 8 1 38N45 106W05 7:04:20
Mount Vernon Club Place 30 2 39N43'22 105W17'36 7:01:10
Muleshoe 28 1 37N35'23 105W10'55 7:00:44
Mulford 23 1 39N24'00 107W09'05 7:08:36
Mumper Corner 62 1 40N27'07 104W41'48 6:58:47
Murray Place 5 1 37N30'58 102W59'48 6:51:59
Mutual 28 1 37N37 104W47 6:59:08
Mystic 54 1 40N34'12 106W59'43 7:07:59
Nast 49 1 39N17'30 106W36'03 7:06:24
Nathrop 8 1 38N44'50 106W04'30 7:04:18
Naturita 43 1 38N13'06 108W34'05 7:14:16
Nederland 7 1 39N57'41 105W30'37 7:02:02
Needleton 56 1 37N38'26 107W41'27 7:10:46
Nelson 44 1 40N15'10 103W39'37 6:54:38
Nepesta 51 1 38N10'08 104W08'33 6:56:34
Nevadaville 24 1 39N47'43 105W31'55 7:02:08
New Castle 23 1 39N34'22 107W32'09 7:10:09
Newdale 45 1 38N01'44 103W39'48 6:54:39
Newett 8 1 38N52'00 105W59'18 7:03:57
New Haven 38 1 40N28'59 102W50'09 6:51:21
New Raymer 62 1 40N36 103W51 6:55:24
Nighthawk 18 2 39N21'17 105W10'08 7:00:41
Ninaview 6 1 37N38'38 103W14'25 6:52:58
Ninemile Corner 7 2 40N00'55 105W06'11 7:00:25
Ninemile Corner 44 1 40N08'47 103W35'02 6:54:20
Ninetyfour 10 1 39N49'39 105W38'09 7:02:33
Niwot 7 1 40N06'14 105W10'13 7:00:41
Noel 57 1 38N05'59 107W54'44 7:11:39
Noland 7 1 40N15'33 105W15'14 7:01:01
Norfolk 35 1 40N54'39 104W58'09 6:59:53
Norrie 49 1 39N19'29 106W39'18 7:06:37
North Aurora 1 2 39N45 104W47 6:59:08
North Avondale 51 1 38N15'43 104W20'44 6:57:23
North Boulder 7 1 40N00 105W16 7:01:04
North Cherry Creek Valley 3 2 39N42 104W53 6:59:32
North Creede 40 1 37N51'51 106W55'31 7:07:42
Northdale 17 1 37N48'34 109W00'58 7:16:04
North Delta 15 1 38N45'31 108W04'07 7:12:16
North End 21 1 38N53 104W48 6:59:12
Northgate 29 1 40N53'09 106W17'37 7:05:10
Northglenn 1 2 39N53'08 104W59'12 6:59:57
North La Junta 45 1 37N59'49 103W31'53 6:54:08
North Pecos 1 2 39N50 105W01 7:00:04
North Pole 21 1 38N54 104W58 6:59:52
North Valley 1 2 39N50 104W57 6:59:48
North Washington Heights 1 2 39N50 104W57 6:59:48
Norwood 57 1 38N07'50 108W17'30 7:13:10
Nucla 43 1 38N16'10 108W32'50 7:14:11
Nugget 24 1 39N51'49 105W35'16 7:02:21
Numa 13 1 38N13 103W45 6:55:00
Nunn 62 1 40N42'13 104W46'49 6:59:07
Nutria 4 1 37N13'51 107W07'30 7:08:30
Nyberg 51 1 38N16'06 104W23'51 6:57:35
Oak Creek 54 1 40N16'30 106W57'28 7:07:50
Oak Grove 43 1 38N27'36 107W55'39 7:11:43
Occidental 28 1 37N30'54 105W06'23 7:00:26
Oehlmann Park 30 1 39N31'08 105W15'31 7:01:02
Offield Place 41 1 40N59'09 108W39'45 7:14:39
Ohio 26 1 38N34'00 106W36'40 7:06:27
Olathe 43 1 38N36'18 107W58'54 7:11:56
Old Fort Bent 45 1 38N02'26 103W25'44 6:53:43
Old Fort Lyon 6 1 38N06'02 103W07'25 6:52:30
Old Fort Lyons 6 1 38N05'45 102W46'20 6:51:05
Old Fort Vasquez 62 1 40N11'40 104W49'14 6:59:17
Old Haines Place 26 1 38N24'03 107W09'54 7:08:40
Old Homestead 29 1 40N26'25 106W08'35 7:04:34
Old Roach 35 1 40N55'28 106W07'00 7:04:28
Old Wells 9 1 38N54'00 102W19'33 6:49:18
Olinger Gardens 30 2 39N45 105W03 7:00:12
Oliver 26 1 38N56 107W16 7:09:04
Olney Springs 13 1 38N09'58 103W56'39 6:55:47
Olson Place 26 1 39N08'45 107W25'33 7:09:42
Olympus Heights 35 1 40N22'40 105W29'00 7:01:56
Omega 35 1 40N32'23 105W04'48 7:00:19
Ophir 57 1 37N51'25 107W49'55 7:11:20
Ophir Loop 57 1 37N51'35 107W52'04 7:11:28
Orchard 44 1 40N19'52 104W07'04 6:56:28
Orchard City 15 1 38N49'42 107W58'13 7:11:53
Orchard Corner 43 1 38N30'30 107W43'46 7:10:55
Orchard Mesa 39 1 39N02'35 108W33'06 7:14:12
Orchard Park 22 1 38N28'20 105W13'40 7:00:55
Ordway 13 1 38N13'05 103W45'20 6:55:01
Orestod 19 1 39N52'05 106W41'01 7:06:44
Ormandale 51 1 38N15 104W39 6:58:36
Ormega 45 1 37N57'39 103W35'09 6:54:21
Oro 33 1 39N14'07 106W15'06 7:05:00
Orodell 7 1 40N00'54 105W19'29 7:01:18
Orr 45 1 38N06'27 103W32'05 6:54:08
Orsa 18 1 39N25'20 104W54'48 6:59:39
Ortiz 11 1 37N00'15 106W02'37 7:04:10
Osier 11 1 37N00'48 106W20'09 7:05:21
Otis 61 1 40N08'56 102W57'45 6:51:51
Ouray 46 1 38N01'22 107W40'15 7:10:41
Ovid 58 1 40N57'38 102W23'15 6:49:33
Owl Canyon 35 1 40N45'45 105W10'30 7:00:42
Oxford 34 1 37N10'08 107W42'49 7:10:51
Oxyoke 30 2 39N18'11 105W11'52 7:00:47
Pactolus 24 2 39N55'04 105W27'50 7:01:51
Padroni 38 1 40N46'40 103W10'20 6:52:41
Pagoda 54 1 40N20'13 107W24'55 7:09:40
Pagosa 4 1 37N16 107W00 7:08:00
Pagosa Junction 4 1 37N02'17 107W11'55 7:08:48
Pagosa Springs 4 1 37N16'10 107W00'33 7:08:02
Paisaje 11 1 37N04'04 106W03'36 7:04:14
Palisade 39 1 39N06'37 108W21'01 7:13:24
Palmer Lake 18 1 39N07'20 104W55'00 6:59:40
Pando 19 1 39N27'26 106W19'59 7:05:20
Pandora 57 1 37N56'00 107W47'06 7:11:08
Paoli 48 1 40N36'44 102W28'20 6:49:53
Paonia 15 1 38N52'06 107W35'29 7:10:22
Papeton 21 1 38N52'35 104W48'05 6:59:12
Paradise Hills 30 2 39N42'45 105W15'04 7:01:00
Paradox 43 1 38N22'06 108W57'42 7:15:51
Paragon Estates 7 2 39N58'55 105W10'27 7:00:42
Park Center 22 1 38N28'40 105W12'20 7:00:49
Park City 47 1 39N16'42 106W05'33 7:04:22
Parkdale 22 1 38N29'10 105W22'20 7:01:29
Parker 18 2 39N31'07 104W45'39 6:59:03
Park Hill 16 2 39N45 104W55 6:59:40
Parkville 55 1 38N13'38 106W06'00 7:04:24
Parkville 59 1 39N29'56 106W56'58 7:07:48
Parlin 26 1 38N30'10 106W43'40 7:06:55
Parma 2 1 37N32'14 106W02'17 7:04:09
Parras Plaza 36 1 37N10'38 104W57'21 6:59:49
Parrish 50 1 38N07'18 102W23'03 6:49:32
Parshall 25 1 40N03'25 106W10'29 7:04:42
Patt 36 1 37N15 103W21 6:53:24
Patterson Crossing 36 1 37N13'03 104W12'28 6:56:50
Patterson Place 26 1 39N06'50 107W25'01 7:09:40
Payne 15 1 38N48'06 107W54'05 7:11:36
Peabodys 47 1 39N20'53 105W55'36 7:03:42
Peaceful Valley 7 1 40N07'53 105W29'50 7:01:59
Pea Green Corner 43 1 38N39'00 108W05'40 7:12:23
Pearl 29 1 40N59'07 106W32'47 7:06:11
Pear Park 39 1 39N04'13 108W28'17 7:13:53
Peckham 62 1 40N18'14 104W45'02 6:59:00
Peconic 32 1 39N19'15 102W08'54 6:48:36
Peeples 15 1 38N49'19 108W20'28 7:13:22
Peetz 38 1 40N57'46 103W06'43 6:52:27
Penitentiary 22 1 38N26 105W13 7:00:52
Penrose 22 1 38N25'30 105W01'20 7:00:05
Peoples 1 2 39N43 104W51 6:59:24
Peoria 3 1 39N40'47 104W06'49 6:56:27
Perigo 24 1 39N52'45 105W31'49 7:02:07
Perl-Mack 1 2 39N50 105W01 7:00:04
Peterson Field 21 1 38N49 104W43 6:58:52
Petes Place 41 1 40N33'15 108W42'40 7:14:51
Peyton 21 1 39N01'44 104W28'57 6:57:56
Pheasant Run 3 2 39N43 104W51 6:59:24
Phillipsburg 30 2 39N32'18 105W11'11 7:00:45
Phippsburg 54 1 40N13'56 106W56'35 7:07:46
Phoenix 24 1 39N55'43 105W32'06 7:02:08
Pictou 28 1 37N38'19 104W48'47 6:59:15
Piedmont 36 1 37N08'16 104W33'05 6:58:12
Piedmont 46 1 38N09 107W45 7:11:00
Piedra 4 1 37N13'25 107W20'25 7:09:22
Pieplant Mill 26 1 38N56'17 106W33'32 7:06:14
Pierce 62 1 40N38'08 104W45'17 6:59:01
Pike-San Isabel Village 47 1 39N03'07 105W43'12 7:02:53
Pikes Peak 21 1 38N54 104W58 6:59:52
Pikeview 21 1 38N54'55 104W49'18 6:59:17
Pine 30 1 39N24'36 105W19'24 7:01:18
Pinecliff 7 1 39N56 105W26 7:01:44
Pinecliffe 24 1 39N55'55 105W25'40 7:01:43
Pine Crest 21 1 39N06'45 104W54'28 6:59:38
Pine Nook 18 2 39N23'03 105W04'15 7:00:17
Pine Park Estates 30 2 39N40 105W07 7:00:28
Pinewood Springs 35 1 40N16'24 105W21'22 7:01:25
Piney Crossing Campground 19 1 39N42'37 106W25'12 7:05:41
Pinnacle Park 62 1 40N24 104W42 6:58:48
Pinneo 61 1 40N12'34 103W26'17 6:53:45
Pinon 43 1 38N16'00 108W24'00 7:13:36
Pinon 51 1 38N26'00 104W36'25 6:58:26
Pinon Acres 34 1 37N13'40 107W49'00 7:11:16
Pinon Canyon 36 1 37N10 104W30 6:58:00
Pitkin 26 1 38N36'33 106W30'58 7:06:04
Pittsburg 26 1 38N57'08 107W03'43 7:08:15
Placerville 57 1 38N01'00 108W03'10 7:12:13
Placita 49 1 39N07'56 107W15'44 7:09:03
Plainview 30 2 39N53'37 105W16'33 7:01:06
Plastic 30 1 39N51'39 105W13'41 7:00:55
Plateau City 39 1 39N14'14 107W58'52 7:11:55
Platner 61 1 40N09'19 103W04'01 6:52:16
Platoro 11 1 37N21'07 106W31'56 7:06:08
Platte Springs 47 1 39N03'49 105W21'29 7:01:26
Platteville 62 1 40N12'54 104W49'20 6:59:17
Plaza 53 1 37N32 106W21 7:05:24
Pleasanton 22 1 38N21'54 105W44'50 7:02:59
Pleasant View 30 2 39N44'03 105W10'16 7:00:41
Pleasant View 42 1 37N35'22 108W45'52 7:15:03
Pleasant View Ridge 7 1 40N07'00 105W03'18 7:00:13
Plumbs 62 2 40N05'16 105W02'36 7:00:10
Poncha Springs 8 1 38N30'46 106W04'36 7:04:18
Ponderosa Park 20 1 39N24'30 104W39'02 6:58:36
Portland 22 1 38N23'28 105W01'28 7:00:06
Portland 46 1 38N04'53 107W42'03 7:10:48
Poudre Park 35 1 40N41'10 105W18'15 7:01:13
Powars 62 1 40N02'27 104W48'27 6:59:14
Powderhorn (P O) 26 1 38N16'58 107W06'58 7:08:28

Powder Wash 41 1 40N56'45 108W18'39 7:13:15
Powell 38 1 40N47'20 102W59'22 6:51:57
Price Creek 41 1 40N16'38 108W05'46 7:12:23
Primero 36 1 37N08'33 104W44'28 6:58:58
Princeton 8 1 38N59'36 106W13'10 7:04:53
Pritchett 5 1 37N22'13 102W51'33 6:51:26
Proctor 38 1 40N48'25 102W57'04 6:51:48
Prospect 62 1 40N07 104W31 6:58:04
Prospect Heights 22 1 38N25'35 105W14'13 7:00:57
Prospect Valley 62 1 40N04'25 104W24'52 6:57:39
Prowers 6 1 38N04'55 102W46'02 6:51:04
Pryor 28 1 37N30'29 104W42'49 6:58:51
Pueblo 51 1 38N15'16 104W36'31 6:58:26
Pueblo Army Depot 51 1 38N17 104W35 6:58:20
Pulliam 62 1 40N19'14 104W56'36 6:59:46
Pultney 13 1 38N09'44 104W02'50 6:56:11
Purcell 62 1 40N38'18 104W36'04 6:58:24
Purgatoire Valley 6 1 37N52 103W06 6:52:24
Puritan 62 1 40N05'06 104W59'55 7:00:00
Quartzville 47 1 39N20'42 106W04'36 7:04:18
Querida 14 1 38N07'34 105W20'02 7:01:20
Quimby 1 2 39N52'24 104W56'36 6:59:46
Radium 25 1 39N57'10 106W33'29 7:06:14
Ragged Mountain 26 1 38N56 107W16 7:09:04
Rago 61 1 40N00'07 103W24'54 6:53:40
Rainbow Valley 60 1 38N56 105W09 7:00:36
Ramah 21 1 39N07'18 104W09'55 6:56:40
Rand 29 1 40N27'14 106W10'51 7:04:43
Randall 45 1 38N05'44 103W34'45 6:54:19
Rangely 52 1 40N05'16 108W48'12 7:15:13
Range View Estates 62 1 40N24 104W42 6:58:48
Rattlesnake Buttes 28 1 37N37 104W47 6:59:08
Raymer 62 1 40N36'29 103W50'31 6:55:22
Raymond 7 1 40N09'18 105W27'50 7:01:51
Read 15 1 38N45'58 107W58'32 7:11:54
Redcliff 19 1 39N30'44 106W22'03 7:05:28
Red Feather Lakes 35 1 40N48'09 105W35'28 7:02:22
Redlands 39 1 39N04'44 108W38'06 7:14:32
Red Lion 38 1 40N53'30 102W40'35 6:50:42
Redmesa 34 1 37N05'40 108W10'11 7:12:41
Redmond 35 1 40N28'44 105W02'25 7:00:10
Red Mountain 46 1 37N54'13 107W42'07 7:10:48
Reds Place 35 1 40N43'50 105W52'16 7:03:29
Redstone 49 1 39N10'51 107W14'21 7:08:57
Redvale 43 1 38N10'30 108W25'00 7:13:40
Red Wing 28 1 37N44'10 105W17'22 7:01:09
Reilly Canyon 36 1 37N15'16 104W42'34 6:58:50
Rembrandt Place 3 2 39N35 104W56 6:59:44
Resurrection Mill 33 1 39N14'07 106W16'35 7:05:06
Rex 35 1 40N47'20 105W10'40 7:00:43
Rezago 36 1 37N10 104W30 6:58:00
Rhone 39 1 39N07'36 108W40'40 7:14:43
Richfield 11 1 37N16'40 105W56'40 7:03:47
Rico 17 1 37N41'34 108W01'47 7:12:07
Ridgeway 46 1 38N09'10 107W45'90 7:11:06
Rifle 23 1 39N32'05 107W46'57 7:11:08
Rinn 62 1 40N08'20 104W59'54 7:00:00
Rio Blanco 52 1 39N44'16 107W56'41 7:11:47
Riverdale 6 1 38N03'31 103W18'58 6:53:16
Riverside 7 1 40N10'32 105W26'12 7:01:45
Riverside 8 1 38N56'18 106W11'00 7:04:44
Riverview 30 1 39N23'51 105W16'03 7:01:04
Robb 63 1 40N06'09 102W22'17 6:49:29
Roberta 45 1 37N59'47 103W40'31 6:54:42
Robinson Place 41 1 40N24'21 108W59'07 7:15:56
Rock Creek Pprk 21 1 38N42'09 104W50'19 6:59:21
Rock Crossing 36 1 37N25'53 103W56'44 6:55:47
Rock Crossing 51 1 37N46'12 104W07'25 6:56:30
Rockdale 8 1 38N59'29 106W24'40 7:05:39
Rockland 38 1 40N30'38 102W43'10 6:50:53
Rockport 62 1 40N53'55 104W47'46 6:59:11
Rockvale 22 1 38N07'10 105W09'50 7:00:39
Rockwood 34 1 37N29'27 107W48'05 7:11:12
Rocky 30 2 39N51'39 105W14'49 7:00:59
Rocky Ford 45 1 38N03'09 103W43'11 6:54:53
Rocky Mountain Arsenal 1 2 39N45 104W48 6:59:12
Roe 43 1 38N32'16 107W56'39 7:11:47
Rogers Mesa 15 1 38N46'45 107W47'33 7:11:10
Roggen 62 1 40N10'03 104W22'18 6:57:29
Roland Valley 47 1 39N25 105W20 7:01:20
Rolla 1 2 39N52'09 104W53'27 6:59:34
Rolling Hills 7 1 40N00 105W16 7:01:04
Rollinsville 24 1 39N55'02 105W30'02 7:02:00
Romeo 11 1 37N10'20 105W59'05 7:03:56
Romley 8 1 38N40'30 106W22'10 7:05:29
Rosedale 30 1 39N38'24 105W22'57 7:01:32
Rosedale 62 1 40N23'07 104W41'53 6:58:48
Rosemont 60 1 38N44'32 104W57'23 6:59:50
Rosevale 39 1 39N03'36 108W34'47 7:14:19
Rosita 14 1 38N05'50 105W20'08 7:01:21
Roswell 21 1 38N52'25 104W49'08 6:59:17
Roubideau 15 1 38N44'08 108W09'00 7:12:36
Roundup Junction 42 1 37N28'58 108W09'42 7:12:39
Rouse 28 1 37N29'27 104W42'40 6:58:51
Rowena 7 1 40N04'37 105W23'20 7:01:33
Roy 62 1 40N06'35 104W33'54 6:58:16
Royal Gorge 22 1 38N28 105W19 7:01:16
Royal Ranch 47 1 39N25 105W20 7:01:20
Roydale 16 2 39N46'12 104W52'22 6:59:29
Ruby 26 1 38N51'58 107W05'42 7:08:23
Ruby 39 1 39N12'10 108W55'59 7:15:44
Ruby 49 1 39N01'15 106W36'31 7:06:26
Ruedi 19 1 39N21'59 106W47'51 7:07:11
Rugby 36 1 37N28'12 104W39'52 6:58:39
Rulison 23 1 39N29'50 107W56'24 7:11:46
Rush 21 1 38N50'24 104W05'30 6:56:22
Russell 12 1 37N33'19 105W17'14 7:01:09
Russell Gulch 24 1 39N46'43 105W32'11 7:02:09
Rustic 35 1 40N34'49 105W41'58 7:02:48
Ruxton 6 1 37N44'53 103W08'46 6:52:35
Rye 51 1 37N55'25 104W55'47 6:59:43
Sable 1 2 39N45'59 104W49'50 6:59:19
Sacramento 47 1 39N13'17 106W06'25 7:04:26
Saguache 55 1 38N05'15 106W05'40 7:04:23
Saint Charles Mesa 51 1 38N14 104W33 6:58:12
Saint Elmo 8 1 38N42'17 106W20'51 7:05:23
Saint Peters 38 1 40N41 102W50 6:51:20
Saint Petersburg 38 1 40N33'20 102W49'00 6:51:16
Saints John 59 1 39N34'18 105W52'52 7:03:31
Saint Thomas 36 1 37N08'04 104W33'25 6:58:14
Saint Vrains 62 1 40N02'13 104W57'15 6:59:49
Salida 8 1 38N32'05 105W59'54 7:04:00
Salina 7 1 40N03'02 105W22'19 7:01:29
Salt Creek 51 1 38N14'30 104W34'30 6:58:18
Sample 22 1 38N28'20 105W21'18 7:01:25
Sams 57 1 38N06'14 107W57'25 7:11:50
San Acacio 12 1 37N12'50 105W33'50 7:02:15
San Antonio 11 1 37N01'15 106W01'39 7:04:07
Sandown 16 2 39N46'21 104W54'03 6:59:36
Sand Park 8 1 38N32 106W00 7:04:00
Sanford 11 1 37N15'30 105W54'15 7:03:37
San Francisco 12 1 37N09 105W24 7:01:36
Sangre De Cristo Ranches 12 1 37N26 105W26 7:01:44
San Isabel 14 1 37N59'15 105W03'14 7:00:13
San Juan 36 1 37N07 104W45 6:59:00
San Luis 12 1 37N12'03 105W25'24 7:01:42
San Miguel 36 1 37N05'58 104W23'42 6:57:35
San Miguel 57 1 37N56'49 107W50'07 7:11:20
San Pablo 12 1 37N08'57 105W23'47 7:01:35
San Pedro 12 1 37N09'35 105W24'07 7:01:36
Santa Clara 28 1 37N26'20 104W47'14 6:59:09
Santa Fe Drive 16 2 39N44 105W01 7:00:04
Santa Maria 47 1 39N26'59 105W37'58 7:02:32
Sapinero 26 1 38N27'34 107W18'06 7:09:12
Sarcillo 36 1 37N07'32 104W45'32 6:59:02
Sarcillo Canon 36 1 37N08 104W48 6:59:12
Sargent 53 1 37N41 106W08 7:04:32
Sargents 55 1 38N24'15 106W24'52 7:05:39
Sargents School 53 1 37N34 106W09 7:04:36
Satank 23 1 39N24'50 107W13'40 7:08:55
Saunders 15 1 38N45'37 108W00'34 7:12:02
Sawpit 57 1 37N59'43 108W00'04 7:12:00
Saxton 15 1 38N46'06 107W58'15 7:11:53
Schofield 26 1 39N02'28 107W03'16 7:08:13
Schramm 63 1 40N06'50 102W36'20 6:50:25
S Crossing 5 1 37N31'19 102W57'54 6:51:52
Security 21 1 38N45'30 104W44'33 6:58:58
Sedalia 18 2 39N26'13 102W57'43 6:51:51
Sedgewick 55 1 38N16'45 106W08'50 7:04:35
Sedgwick 58 1 40N56'11 102W31'30 6:50:06
Segundo 36 1 37N08 104W45 6:59:00
Seibert 9 1 39N17'57 102W52'07 6:51:28
Selma 38 1 40N46'17 103W01'50 6:52:07
Semper 30 2 39N51'22 105W03'51 7:00:15
Sequndo 36 1 37N07'15 104W43'18 6:58:53
Seven Lakes 60 1 38N46'54 105W00'29 7:00:02
Sevenmile Plaza 53 1 37N38'53 106W14'13 7:04:57
Severance 62 1 40N31'27 104W51'02 6:59:24
Shadow Mountain 25 1 40N15 105W50 7:03:20
Shaffers Crossing 30 1 39N28'43 105W22'04 7:01:28
Shamballah-Ashrama 18 2 39N20'35 105W01'58 7:00:08
Shamrock 1 1 39N53'07 103W48'57 6:55:16
Sharpsdale 28 1 37N43'10 105W21'40 7:01:27
Shauano Vista 8 1 38N32 106W00 7:04:00
Shavano 8 1 38N36'10 106W17'23 7:05:10
Shaw 37 1 39N33'02 103W21'37 6:53:26
Shaw Heights 1 2 39N50 105W01 7:00:04
Shaw Heights Mesa 1 2 39N50 105W01 7:00:04
Shawnee 47 1 39N25'16 105W33'13 7:02:13
Sheehan 62 1 40N03'30 104W26'30 6:57:46
Sheephorn 19 1 39N53'32 106W27'59 7:05:52
Shelton 45 1 38N05'00 103W36'21 6:54:25
Sheridan 3 2 39N38'49 105W01'29 7:00:06
Sheridan Lake 31 1 38N28'00 102W17'30 6:49:10
Sherman 27 1 37N54'10 107W25'20 7:09:41
Sherrelwood 1 2 39N50 105W00 7:00:00
Sherrelwood Estates 1 2 39N50 105W01 7:00:04
Shirley 8 1 38N25'28 106W07'40 7:04:31
Shirley 21 1 38N54'04 104W39'10 6:58:37
Shoshone 23 1 39N35'26 107W11'09 7:08:45
Sidney 54 1 40N23'13 106W50'55 7:07:24
Sierra 12 1 37N31'21 105W16'08 7:01:05
Sierra Vista 51 1 37N55 104W56 6:59:44
Sikes 22 1 38N15'30 105W04'27 7:00:18
Sillsville 26 1 38N26'48 106W45'38 7:07:03
Siloam 51 1 38N15'05 104W58'31 6:59:54
Silt 23 1 39N32'55 107W39'20 7:10:37
Silver Cliff 14 1 38N08'07 105W26'45 7:01:47
Silverdale 10 1 39N41'30 105W41'44 7:02:47
Silver Heights 18 1 39N25'05 104W51'55 6:59:28
Silver Plume 10 1 39N41'46 105W43'31 7:02:54
Silver Springs 47 1 39N27'33 105W23'44 7:01:35
Silver Spruce 7 1 40N00'17 105W20'50 7:01:23
Silverthorne 59 1 39N38'15 106W03'41 7:04:15
Silverton 56 1 37N48'43 107W39'50 7:10:39
Simla 20 1 39N08'30 104W05'00 6:56:20
Simpson 1 1 39N35 104W03 6:56:12
Simpson 36 1 37N29'52 104W10'00 6:56:40
Singleton 47 1 39N26'35 105W36'05 7:02:24
Sinnard 35 1 40N35'18 105W00'10 7:00:01
Skinners 21 1 38N46'08 104W45'39 6:59:03
Skyland Village 1 2 39N50 105W01 7:00:04
Skyline 3 2 39N41 104W56 6:59:44
Sky Village 30 2 39N33'02 105W14'48 7:00:59
Skyway 21 1 38N48 104W49 6:59:16
Skyway 39 1 39N03'00 108W05'30 7:12:22
Skyway Estates 21 1 38N48 104W49 6:59:16
Skyway Park 21 1 38N48 104W49 6:59:16
Slater 41 1 41N00 107W23 7:09:32
Slick Rock 57 1 38N03 108W54 7:15:36
Sloan 62 1 40N03'06 104W29'15 6:57:57
Smelter Place 41 1 40N34'14 108W40'04 7:14:40
Smeltertown 8 1 38N32'51 106W00'50 7:04:03
Smith Hill 24 1 39N46'42 105W27'29 7:01:50
Smith Place 26 1 38N12'06 107W03'33 7:08:14
Sneffels 46 1 37N58'31 107W44'57 7:11:00
Snowmass 49 1 39N19'54 106W59'08 7:07:57
Snow Water Springs 30 2 39N15'53 105W12'59 7:00:52
Snyder 44 1 40N19'45 103W35'45 6:54:23
Somerset 26 1 38N55'35 107W28'11 7:09:53
Sopris 36 1 37N08'05 104W33'50 6:58:15
Sopris Plaza 36 1 37N08'26 104W34'30 6:58:18
Sorrento 9 1 38N46'50 102W54'20 6:51:37
South 63 1 39N40 102W25 6:49:40
South Aurora 3 2 39N40 104W53 6:59:32
South Boulder 7 1 40N00 105W16 7:01:04
South Canon 22 1 38N22 105W17 7:01:08
South Denver 16 2 39N43 104W58 6:59:52
Southern Ute Indian Res 34 1 37N07 107W38 7:10:32
South Fork 53 1 37N40'12 106W38'21 7:06:33
South Forty 59 1 39N38 106W04 7:04:16
Southglenn 3 2 39N37 105W00 7:00:00
South Jefferson 30 2 39N35 105W12 7:00:48
South Park City 47 1 39N14 106W00 7:04:00
South Platte 30 1 39N24'27 105W10'15 7:00:41
South Roggen 62 1 40N06'08 104W20'17 6:57:21
Southwind 3 2 39N37 105W00 7:00:00
Southwood 3 2 39N37 105W00 7:00:00
Spanish Colony 62 1 40N24 104W42 6:58:48
Spanish Village 62 1 40N23'04 104W32'45 6:58:11
Spar City 40 1 37N42'26 106W58'04 7:07:52
Sparks 41 1 40N55'05 108W48'59 7:15:16
Spencer 26 1 38N21'17 107W06'42 7:08:27
Spencer Heights 35 1 40N40'27 105W47'02 7:03:08
Sphinx Park 30 1 39N25'28 105W18'52 7:01:15
Spicer 29 1 40N28'00 106W27'20 7:05:49
Spike Buck 22 1 38N27'32 105W28'00 7:01:52
Spitzie Place 41 1 40N52'10 108W56'57 7:15:48
Spivak 30 2 39N44'41 105W04'03 7:00:16
Spook City 55 1 38N13'48 106W11'48 7:04:47
Springdale 7 1 40N06'35 105W21'28 7:01:26
Springfield 5 1 37N24'30 102W36'50 6:50:27
Spring Valley 60 1 38N56 105W09 7:00:36
Spruce 18 1 39N09'24 104W52'40 6:59:31
Sprucedale 30 1 39N35'20 105W21'06 7:01:24
Sprucewood 18 2 39N20'56 105W07'13 7:00:29
Squaw Point 17 1 37N46 108W54 7:15:36
Stage 62 1 40N36'42 104W44'32 6:58:58
Stanley Park 30 2 39N37'06 105W17'32 7:01:10
Stapleton 42 1 37N29'56 108W24'15 7:13:37
Starkville 36 1 37N06'55 104W31'25 6:58:06
State Bridge 19 1 39N51'28 106W38'57 7:06:36
State Coal Mine Junction 62 1 40N03'30 104W59'32 6:59:58
Steamboat Springs 54 1 40N29'06 106W49'52 7:07:19
Steamboat Village 54 1 40N09 106W54 7:07:36
Stelbars Lindland 29 1 40N34'28 106W03'51 7:04:15
Stem Beach 51 1 38N09'50 104W38'35 6:58:34
Sterling 38 1 40N37'32 103W12'26 6:52:50
Sterling Place 41 1 40N49'14 108W53'29 7:15:34
Stockyards 16 2 39N48 104W57 6:59:48
Stollsteimer 4 1 37N08'30 107W21'15 7:09:25
Stone City 51 1 38N26'55 104W51'38 6:59:27
Stoneham 62 1 40N36'20 103W39'58 6:54:40
Stoner 42 1 37N35'22 108W19'10 7:13:17
Stonewall 36 1 37N09'08 105W01'00 7:00:04
Stonewall Gap 36 1 37N09'05 105W02'17 7:00:09
Stonington 5 1 37N17'37 102W11'13 6:48:45
Stove Prairie Landing 35 1 40N40'57 105W23'19 7:01:33
Strasburg 1 1 39N44'18 104W19'22 6:57:17
Stratmoor Hills 21 1 38N46'59 104W47'38 6:59:11
Stratton 32 1 39N18'12 102W36'15 6:50:25
Stratton 60 1 38N44'52 105W08'58 7:00:36
Stratton Meadows 21 1 38N48'12 104W48'40 6:59:15

 COLORADO

Stratton Park 21 1 38N53 104w48 6:59:12
Stringtown 33 1 39N14'01 106w19'07 7:05:16
Strong 28 1 37N42'45 104w54'06 6:59:36
Stuart 31 1 38N28'17 102w11'39 6:48:47
Sublette 62 1 40N18'28 104w10'48 6:56:43
Sugar 50 1 38N09'01 102w40'05 6:50:40
Sugar City 13 1 38N13'55 103w39'45 6:54:39
Sugar Junction 53 1 37N34'04 106w06'43 7:04:27
Sugarloaf 7 1 40N01'01 105w24'24 7:01:38
Sullivan 3 2 39N40'17 104w53'51 6:59:35
Summerville 7 1 40N03'25 105w23'38 7:01:35
Summit Cove 59 1 39N38 106w04 7:04:16
Summitville 53 1 37N25'50 106w35'30 7:06:22
Sunbeam 41 1 40N33'03 108w11'43 7:12:47
Sunnyside 7 1 40N00'13 105w22'52 7:01:31
Sunnyside 34 1 37N17 107w52 7:11:28
Sunnyside 40 1 37N50'46 106w57'35 7:07:50
Sunnyslopes 1 2 39N55 105w06 7:00:24
Sunset 7 1 40N02'09 105w28'06 7:01:52
Sunset City 22 1 38N24'45 105w25'00 7:01:40
Sunshine 7 1 40N03'57 105w21'58 7:01:28
Superior 7 2 39N57'10 105w10'05 7:00:40
Surrey Ridge 18 1 39N22 104w52 6:59:28
Sutank 23 1 39N24 107w13 7:08:52
Swallows 51 1 38N18'08 104w51'35 6:59:26
Swallows Nest 42 1 37N09'26 108w28'02 7:13:52
Swan 8 1 38N40'48 106w02'29 7:04:10
Swandyke 59 1 39N30'30 105w53'30 7:03:34
Swede Corners 55 1 38N05 106w09 7:04:36
Sweet Place 41 1 40N32'10 108w40'44 7:14:43
Sweetwater 19 1 39N39 106w57 7:07:48
Swink 45 1 38N00'52 103w37'40 6:54:31
Swissvale 22 1 38N29'02 105w54'00 7:03:36
Switzerland Park 7 1 40N00'05 105w26'03 7:01:44
Switzerland Village 30 1 39N25 105w20 7:01:20
Sylvan 42 1 37N35 108w46 7:15:04
Tabernash 25 1 39N59'37 105w50'33 7:03:22
Table Land 58 1 40N50 102w17 6:49:08
Tabor 7 2 40N03'05 105w04'25 7:00:18
Tacoma 34 1 37N31'25 107w46'53 7:11:08
Tamarron 34 1 37N17 107w52 7:11:28
Tampa 62 1 40N09'00 104w27'18 6:57:49
Tanglewood Acres 14 1 38N05'38 105w33'40 7:02:15
Tarryall 47 1 39N07'19 105w28'30 7:01:54
Taylor Park 26 1 38N40 106w51 7:07:24
Teds Place 35 1 40N39'50 105w11'20 7:00:45
Telluride 57 1 37N56'15 107w48'42 7:11:15
Tennyson Heights 35 1 40N35 105w06 7:00:24
Tercio 36 1 37N03'07 104w59'46 6:59:59
Terminal Annex 16 2 39N43 104w59 6:59:56
Texas Creek 22 1 38N24'47 105w34'48 7:02:19
Texas Oil Camp 52 1 40N05 108w47 7:15:08
Thatcher 36 1 37N32'45 104w06'30 6:56:26
The Mesa 21 1 38N51 104w52 6:59:28
The Pinery 18 2 39N31 104w46 6:59:04
Thistledown 46 1 37N59'37 107w41'57 7:10:48
Thomasville 49 1 39N21'37 106w42'07 7:06:48
Thornburgh 52 1 40N12'25 107w41'43 7:10:47
Thornton 1 2 39N52'05 104w58'17 6:59:53
Three Forks 11 1 37N16'36 106w37'16 7:06:29
Thurman 61 1 39N18 103w04 6:52:16
Tiffany 34 1 37N01'58 107w32'15 7:10:09
Tijeras 36 1 37N07'33 104w39'45 6:58:39
Timbers 3 2 39N39 104w51 6:59:24
Timnath 35 1 40N31'45 104w59'05 6:59:56
Timpas 45 1 37N49'05 103w46'25 6:55:06
Tincup 26 1 38N45'16 106w28'40 7:05:55
Tiny Town 30 2 39N36'15 105w13'21 7:00:53
Tioga 28 1 37N41'56 104w55'37 6:59:42
Tisdels Place 41 1 40N35'41 108w46'34 7:15:06
Tobe 36 1 37N13'09 103w36'40 6:54:27
Tobin 38 1 40N50'03 102w52'20 6:51:29
Tolan Place 26 1 39N09'08 107w28'01 7:09:52
Tolland 24 1 39N54'18 105w35'19 7:02:21
Toltec 28 1 37N37 104w47 6:59:08
Tomah 18 1 39N18'07 104w53'22 6:59:33
Tomboy 57 1 37N56'12 107w45'14 7:11:01
Tonnerville 6 1 38N04 103w13 6:52:52
Tonville 62 1 40N00'33 104w42'12 6:58:49
Toonerville 6 1 37N46'30 103w09'49 6:52:39
Toponas 54 1 40N03'37 106w48'27 7:07:14
Torres 36 1 37N04'10 105w03'20 7:00:13
Torres 53 1 37N36'24 106w12'14 7:04:49
Towaoc 42 1 37N12'16 108w43'44 7:14:55
Towner 31 1 38N28'15 102w04'45 6:48:19
Trail Junction Picnic Ground 21 1 38N54'10 104w54'48 6:59:39
Tranquil Acres 60 1 39N00 105w04 7:00:16
Trapper 54 1 40N06'14 106w52'45 7:07:31
Trilby Corner 35 1 40N29'41 105w04'37 7:00:18
Trimble 34 1 37N23'25 107w50'45 7:11:23
Trinchera 36 1 37N02'32 104w02'49 6:56:11
Trinidad 36 1 37N10'10 104w30'00 6:58:00
Troublesome 25 1 40N03'39 106w17'28 7:05:10
Troutdale 30 1 39N38'13 105w20'51 7:01:23
Trout Haven 60 1 38N56 105w09 7:00:36
Trout Lake 57 1 37N52 107w52 7:11:28
Troy 36 1 37N15 103w21 6:53:24
Truckton 21 1 38N44'17 104w10'54 6:56:44
Trujillo 4 1 37N06'02 107w02'47 7:08:11
Trumbull 30 2 39N15'47 105w13'08 7:00:53
Trump 47 1 38N50'57 105w47'16 7:03:09
Tuber 62 1 40N31'52 104w46'27 6:59:06
Tuckerville 34 1 37N29'33 107w29'05 7:09:56
Tungsten 7 1 39N58'19 105w28'32 7:01:54
Turkey Creek 51 1 38N23 104w46 6:59:04
Turret 8 1 38N38'25 105w59'18 7:03:57
Twelvemile Corner 44 1 40N04'24 103w47'32 6:55:10
Twin Cedars 18 2 39N21'35 105w10'00 7:00:40
Twin Crossing 34 1 37N01'47 107w52'40 7:11:31
Twin Forks 30 2 39N35'34 105w13'09 7:00:53
Twin Lakes 33 1 39N04'58 106w22'53 7:05:32
Twin Mills 38 1 40N34'25 103w07'33 6:52:30
Twin Rock 60 1 38N57 105w17 7:01:08
Twin Spruce 30 2 39N53'21 105w21'29 7:01:26
Two Butte Creek 50 1 37N52 102w19 6:49:16
Two Buttes 5 1 37N33'40 102w23'50 6:49:35
Tyrone 36 1 37N27'15 104w12'28 6:56:50
Una 23 1 39N23'59 108w06'29 7:12:26
Unaweep 39 1 38N59 108w27 7:13:48
Uncompahgre 43 1 38N22'41 107w49'05 7:11:16
Union 44 1 40N22'36 103w30'02 6:54:00
University Park 16 2 39N41 104w58 6:59:52
Upper Saint Vrain 7 1 40N12 105w30 7:02:00
Uravan 43 1 38N22'06 108w44'09 7:14:57
U S Air Force Academy 21 1 38N59 104w52 6:59:28
Utah Junction 1 2 39N48'02 104w59'51 6:59:59
Utaline 39 1 39N07'37 109w02'30 7:16:10
Ute 43 1 38N15'20 108w16'14 7:13:05
Ute Heights 8 1 38N32 106w00 7:04:00
Ute Mountain 42 1 37N10 108w40 7:14:40
Ute Mountain Indian Res 42 1 37N12 108w44 7:14:56
Utleyville 36 1 37N16'16 103w01'51 6:52:07
Vail 19 1 39N38'25 106w22'25 7:05:30
Valdez 36 1 37N07'20 104w42'05 6:58:48
Vallecito 34 1 37N23 107w35 7:10:20
Valley Hi Mountain Estates 60 1 38N57 105w17 7:01:08
Valley View 51 1 38N04'06 104w58'35 6:59:54
Vallie 22 1 38N23'39 105w46'19 7:03:05
Vallorso 36 1 37N16'58 104w38'40 6:58:35
Valmont 7 1 40N01'55 105w12'50 7:00:51
Vanadium 57 1 37N58'01 107w58'16 7:11:53
Vance Junction 57 1 37N56'08 107w53'53 7:11:36
Vance Place 46 1 38N03'36 107w50'27 7:11:22
Vancorum 43 1 38N14 108w36 7:14:24
Vastine 53 1 37N38'04 106w06'10 7:04:25
Velasquez Plaza 36 1 37N07'25 104w46'55 6:59:08
Venetian Village 21 1 38N53 104w48 6:59:12
Vernal 43 1 38N23'23 107w49'43 7:11:19
Vernon 63 1 39N56'47 102w18'54 6:49:16
Vicksburg 8 1 38N59'57 106w22'38 7:05:31
Victor 60 1 38N42'36 105w08'22 7:00:33
Viejo San Acacio 12 1 37N12'10 105w30'28 7:02:02
Vigil 36 1 37N09'40 107w56'28 7:11:46
Vilas 5 1 37N22'25 102w26'45 6:49:47
Village East 3 2 39N43 104w51 6:59:24
Villa Grove 55 1 38N14'55 105w56'55 7:03:48
Villa Italia 30 2 39N42 105w05 7:00:20
Villegreen 36 1 37N18'21 103w31'11 6:54:05
Vineland 51 1 38N14'44 104w27'32 6:57:50
Viola 36 1 37N08'00 104w36'00 6:58:24
Virginia Dale 35 1 40N57'17 105w20'55 7:01:24
Vista Verde 3 2 39N37 105w00 7:00:00
Vollmar 62 1 40N08'06 104w50'18 6:59:21
Vona 32 1 39N18'13 102w44'33 6:50:58
Vroman 45 1 38N05'23 103w48'35 6:55:14
Vulcan 26 1 38N20'44 107w00'03 7:08:00
Wagner Manor 7 1 40N00 105w16 7:01:04
Wagon Wheel Gap 40 1 37N46 106w49 7:07:16
Wahatoya 28 1 37N30 105w00 7:00:00
Wah Keeney Park 30 1 39N39'37 105w20'24 7:01:22
Wahketa Village 44 1 40N16 103w49 6:55:16
Walden 29 1 40N43'54 106w16'59 7:05:08
Walker 62 1 40N15'52 104w57'06 6:59:48
Wallace Village 7 2 39N53'00 105w05'32 7:00:22
Wallstreet 7 1 40N02'20 105w23'25 7:01:34
Walnut Hills 3 2 39N38 104w59 6:59:56
Walsenburg 28 1 37N37'27 104w46'47 6:59:07
Walsh 5 1 37N23'10 102w16'40 6:49:07
Waltonia 35 1 40N24'50 105w21'45 7:01:27
Walts Corner 36 1 37N10'08 103w52'46 6:55:31
Wamblee Park 30 1 39N30 105w20 7:01:20
Wamblee Valley 30 1 39N30 105w20 7:01:20
Wandcrest Park 30 1 39N26'08 105w23'36 7:01:34
Ward 7 1 40N04'20 105w30'28 7:02:02
Wareland 6 1 39N05'33 103w12'55 6:52:52
Warren 62 1 40N57'35 104w53'30 6:59:34
Warwick 50 1 38N07'26 102w16'25 6:49:06
Waterton 30 1 39N29'37 105w05'17 7:00:21
Watkins 1 1 39N44'43 104w36'25 6:58:26
Watson Place 41 1 40N48'03 108w55'00 7:15:40
Wattenberg 62 1 40N01'40 104w50'10 6:59:21
Wauneta 63 1 40N17'35 102w15'15 6:49:01
Waunita Hot Springs 26 1 38N30'51 106w30'28 7:06:02
Waverly 2 1 37N25'47 106w00'20 7:04:01
Waverly 35 1 40N44'11 105w04'34 7:00:18
Weaver 40 1 37N53'00 106w55'30 7:07:42
Webster 47 1 39N27'27 105w43'11 7:02:53
Weir Place 41 1 40N17'10 108w36'37 7:14:26
Welby 1 2 39N50'12 104w57'31 6:59:50
Weldona 44 1 40N20'46 103w58'07 6:55:52
Weller 47 1 39N26'51 105w37'12 7:02:29
Wellington 35 1 40N42'14 105w00'29 7:00:02
Wellshire 16 2 39N41 104w56 6:59:44
Wellsville 22 2 38N29'12 105w54'34 7:03:38
Welty 62 1 40N19'40 105w01'02 7:00:04
West Burlington 32 1 39N18'12 102w18'33 6:49:14
Westcliffe 14 1 38N08'05 105w27'55 7:01:52
West Creek 18 2 39N09'09 105w09'47 7:00:39
West End 21 1 38N51 104w52 6:59:28
Western Hills 1 2 39N49'56 104w59'48 6:59:59
West Farm 50 1 38N05'34 102w33'29 6:50:14
Westland 30 2 39N45 105w06 7:00:24
Westminster 1 2 39N50'12 105w02'12 7:00:09
Westminster Plaza 1 2 39N50 105w01 7:00:04
Weston 36 1 37N07'58 104w50'54 6:59:24
Westplains 38 1 40N51'53 103w29'50 6:53:59
West Vail 19 1 39N37'49 106w24'51 7:05:39
West Vancorum 43 1 38N13'40 108w36'00 7:14:24
West Village 49 1 39N12 106w50 7:07:20
Westwood 16 2 39N42 105w02 7:00:08
Westwood Lake 60 1 39N00 105w04 7:00:16
Wetmore 14 1 38N14'17 105w05'03 7:00:20
Wezel 37 1 38N47'54 103w27'15 6:53:49
Wheat Ridge 30 2 39N45'58 105w04'36 7:00:18
Wheeler 24 2 39N45 105w11 7:00:44
Wheeler Junction 59 1 39N30'22 106w08'30 7:04:34
Wheelman 7 1 40N00'13 105w22'24 7:01:30
Whitehorn 22 1 38N38'38 105w52'40 7:03:31
Whitepine 26 1 38N32'30 106w23'35 7:05:34
White River City 52 1 40N05'27 108w13'25 7:12:54
Whiterock 51 1 37N51'57 104w06'50 6:56:27
Whitewater 39 1 38N59'28 108w27'10 7:13:49
Wideawake 24 1 39N51'00 105w31'16 7:02:05
Widefield 21 1 38N44'00 104w43'10 6:58:53
Wiggins 44 1 40N13'50 104w04'20 6:56:17
Wigwam 21 1 38N32'22 104w38'06 6:58:32
Wiladel 61 1 39N44'35 103w00'34 6:52:02
Wildcat 62 1 40N15'33 104w53'03 6:59:32
Wild Horse 9 1 38N49'33 103w00'40 6:52:03
Wild Horse 51 1 38N19'45 104w40'05 6:58:40
Wiley 50 1 38N09'15 102w43'09 6:50:53
Willard 38 1 40N33'16 103w29'09 6:53:57
Willey Lumber Camp 29 1 40N30'10 105w53'55 7:03:36
Williamsburg 22 1 38N22'55 105w09'05 7:00:36
Will-o-the-Wisp 47 1 39N27'41 105w24'35 7:01:38
Willowbrook 30 2 39N40 105w07 7:00:28
Willow Creek 3 2 39N38 104w59 6:59:56
Willow Gulch 17 1 38N08 108w17 7:13:08
Wilmor 19 1 39N39'19 106w37'45 7:06:31
Wilson Crossing 28 1 37N50'52 104w34'09 6:58:17
Wilson Lake Estates 60 1 38N57 105w17 7:01:08
Wilson Place 41 1 40N45'43 108w53'35 7:15:34
Windsor 62 1 40N28'39 104w54'03 6:59:36
Winfield 8 1 38N59'05 106w26'25 7:05:46
Wingo 49 1 39N20'45 107w00'35 7:08:02
Winter Park 25 1 39N53 105w46 7:03:04
Wolcott 19 1 39N42'10 106w40'41 7:06:43
Wolhurst 3 2 39N34'14 105w01'58 7:00:08
Wondervu 7 1 39N55'32 105w23'40 7:01:35
Woodglen 1 2 39N53 104w58 6:59:52
Woodland Acres 51 1 37N55 104w56 6:59:44
Woodland Park 60 1 38N59'38 105w03'23 7:00:14
Woodrow 61 1 39N59'18 103w35'28 6:54:22
Woody Creek 49 1 39N16'13 106w53'08 7:07:33
Wootton 36 1 36N59'57 104w29'14 6:57:57
Wray 63 1 40N04'33 102w13'22 6:48:53
Xenia 61 1 40N09'40 103w20'40 6:53:23
Yampa 54 1 40N09'09 106w54'29 7:07:38
Yankee 10 1 39N49'35 105w37'24 7:02:30
Yarmony 19 1 39N53'22 106w37'09 7:06:29
Yellow Jacket 42 1 37N32'04 108w43'00 7:14:52
Yoder 21 1 38N50'22 104w13'17 6:56:53
Yorkborough 1 2 39N50 104w57 6:59:48
Yorkville 22 1 38N17'32 105w17'23 7:01:10
Yuma 61 1 40N07'20 102w43'29 6:50:54
Zamara 36 1 37N09'14 104w55'12 6:59:41
Zinzer 53 1 37N33'37 106w05'38 7:04:23
Zuni 1 2 39N48'12 105w01'16 7:00:05

TIME TABLES

Standard time was "obligatory" in Connecticut until 1938. Nevertheless, daylight time was widely observed, beginning in 1920 in the larger cities, and generally after 1926. Caution is advised from 1920 to 1930.

CT # 1

Date	Time	Zone
Before 11/18/1883		LMT
11/18/1883	12:00	EST
3/31/1918	02:00	EWT
10/27/1918	02:00	EST
3/30/1919	02:00	EWT
10/26/1919	02:00	EST
4/25/1926	02:00	EDT
9/26/1926	02:00	EST
4/24/1927	02:00	EDT
9/25/1927	02:00	EST
4/29/1928	02:00	EDT
9/30/1928	02:00	EST
4/28/1929	02:00	EDT
9/29/1929	02:00	EST
4/27/1930	02:00	EDT
9/28/1930	02:00	EST
4/26/1931	02:00	EDT
9/27/1931	02:00	EST
4/24/1932	02:00	EDT
9/25/1932	02:00	EST
4/30/1933	02:00	EDT
9/24/1933	02:00	EST
4/29/1934	02:00	EDT
9/30/1934	02:00	EST
4/28/1935	02:00	EDT
9/29/1935	02:00	EST
4/26/1936	02:00	EDT
9/27/1936	02:00	EST
4/25/1937	02:00	EDT
9/26/1937	02:00	EST
4/24/1938	02:00	EDT
10/02/1938	02:00	EST
4/30/1939	02:00	EDT
9/24/1939	02:00	EST
4/28/1940	02:00	EDT
9/29/1940	02:00	EST
4/27/1941	02:00	EDT
9/28/1941	02:00	EST
2/09/1942	02:00	EWT
9/30/1945	02:00	EST
4/28/1946	02:00	US#2

CT # 2

Date	Time	Zone
Before 11/18/1883		LMT
11/18/1883	12:00	EST
3/31/1918	02:00	EWT
10/27/1918	02:00	EST
3/30/1919	02:00	EWT
10/26/1919	02:00	EST
4/25/1920	02:00	EDT
10/31/1920	02:00	EST
4/24/1921	02:00	EDT
9/25/1921	02:00	EST
4/30/1922	02:00	EDT
9/24/1922	02:00	EST
4/29/1923	02:00	EDT
9/30/1923	02:00	EST
4/27/1924	02:00	EDT
9/28/1924	02:00	EST
4/26/1925	02:00	EDT
9/27/1925	02:00	EST
4/25/1926	02:00	EDT
9/26/1926	02:00	EST
4/24/1927	02:00	EDT
9/25/1927	02:00	EST
4/29/1928	02:00	EDT
9/30/1928	02:00	EST
4/28/1929	02:00	EDT
9/29/1929	02:00	EST
4/27/1930	02:00	EDT
9/28/1930	02:00	EST
4/26/1931	02:00	EDT
9/27/1931	02:00	EST
4/24/1932	02:00	EDT
9/25/1932	02:00	EST
4/30/1933	02:00	EDT
9/24/1933	02:00	EST
4/29/1934	02:00	EDT
9/30/1934	02:00	EST
4/28/1935	02:00	EDT
9/29/1935	02:00	EST
4/26/1936	02:00	EDT
9/27/1936	02:00	EST
4/25/1937	02:00	EDT
9/26/1937	02:00	EST
4/24/1938	02:00	EDT
10/02/1938	02:00	EST
4/30/1939	02:00	EDT
9/24/1939	02:00	EST
4/28/1940	02:00	EDT
9/29/1940	02:00	EST
4/27/1941	02:00	EDT
9/28/1941	02:00	EST
2/09/1942	02:00	EWT
9/30/1945	02:00	EST
4/28/1946	02:00	US#2

CT # 3

Date	Time	Zone
Before 11/18/1883		LMT
11/18/1883	12:00	EST
3/31/1918	02:00	EWT
10/27/1918	02:00	EST
3/30/1919	02:00	EWT
10/26/1919	02:00	EST
4/25/1920	02:00	EDT
10/31/1920	02:00	EST
4/25/1926	02:00	EDT
9/26/1926	02:00	EST
4/24/1927	02:00	EDT
9/25/1927	02:00	EST
4/29/1928	02:00	EDT
9/30/1928	02:00	EST
4/28/1929	02:00	EDT
9/29/1929	02:00	EST
4/27/1930	02:00	EDT
9/28/1930	02:00	EST
4/26/1931	02:00	EDT
9/27/1931	02:00	EST
4/24/1932	02:00	EDT
9/25/1932	02:00	EST
4/30/1933	02:00	EDT
9/24/1933	02:00	EST
4/29/1934	02:00	EDT
9/30/1934	02:00	EST
4/28/1935	02:00	EDT
9/29/1935	02:00	EST
4/26/1936	02:00	EDT
9/27/1936	02:00	EST
4/25/1937	02:00	EDT
9/26/1937	02:00	EST
4/24/1938	02:00	EDT
10/02/1938	02:00	EST
4/30/1939	02:00	EDT
9/24/1939	02:00	EST
4/28/1940	02:00	EDT
9/29/1940	02:00	EST
4/27/1941	02:00	EDT
9/28/1941	02:00	EST
2/09/1942	02:00	EWT
9/30/1945	02:00	EST
4/28/1946	02:00	US#2

CT # 4

Date	Time	Zone
Before 11/18/1883		LMT
11/18/1883	12:00	EST
3/31/1918	02:00	EWT
10/27/1918	02:00	EST
3/30/1919	02:00	EWT
10/26/1919	02:00	EST
4/24/1921	02:00	EDT
9/25/1921	02:00	EST
4/25/1926	02:00	EDT
9/26/1926	02:00	EST
4/24/1927	02:00	EDT
9/25/1927	02:00	EST
4/29/1928	02:00	EDT
9/30/1928	02:00	EST
4/28/1929	02:00	EDT
9/29/1929	02:00	EST
4/27/1930	02:00	EDT
9/28/1930	02:00	EST
4/26/1931	02:00	EDT
9/27/1931	02:00	EST
4/24/1932	02:00	EDT
9/25/1932	02:00	EST
4/30/1933	02:00	EDT
9/24/1933	02:00	EST
4/29/1934	02:00	EDT
9/30/1934	02:00	EST
4/28/1935	02:00	EDT
9/29/1935	02:00	EST
4/26/1936	02:00	EDT
9/27/1936	02:00	EST
4/25/1937	02:00	EDT
9/26/1937	02:00	EST
4/24/1938	02:00	EDT
10/02/1938	02:00	EST
4/30/1939	02:00	EDT
9/24/1939	02:00	EST
4/28/1940	02:00	EDT
9/29/1940	02:00	EST
4/27/1941	02:00	EDT
9/28/1941	02:00	EST
2/09/1942	02:00	EWT
9/30/1945	02:00	EST
4/28/1946	02:00	US#2

CT # 5

Date	Time	Zone
Before 11/18/1883		LMT
11/18/1883	12:00	EST
3/31/1918	02:00	EWT
10/27/1918	02:00	EST
3/30/1919	02:00	EWT
10/26/1919	02:00	EST
4/24/1921	02:00	EDT
9/25/1921	02:00	EST
4/30/1922	02:00	EDT
9/24/1922	02:00	EST
4/29/1923	02:00	EDT
9/30/1923	02:00	EST
4/27/1924	02:00	EDT
9/28/1924	02:00	EST
4/26/1925	02:00	EDT
9/27/1925	02:00	EST
4/25/1926	02:00	EDT
9/26/1926	02:00	EST
4/24/1927	02:00	EDT
9/25/1927	02:00	EST
4/29/1928	02:00	EDT
9/30/1928	02:00	EST
4/28/1929	02:00	EDT
9/29/1929	02:00	EST
4/27/1930	02:00	EDT
9/28/1930	02:00	EST
4/26/1931	02:00	EDT
9/27/1931	02:00	EST
4/24/1932	02:00	EDT
9/25/1932	02:00	EST
4/30/1933	02:00	EDT
9/24/1933	02:00	EST
4/29/1934	02:00	EDT
9/30/1934	02:00	EST
4/28/1935	02:00	EDT
9/29/1935	02:00	EST
4/26/1936	02:00	EDT
9/27/1936	02:00	EST
4/25/1937	02:00	EDT
9/26/1937	02:00	EST
4/24/1938	02:00	EDT
10/02/1938	02:00	EST
4/30/1939	02:00	EDT
9/24/1939	02:00	EST
4/28/1940	02:00	EDT
9/29/1940	02:00	EST
4/27/1941	02:00	EDT
9/28/1941	02:00	EST
2/09/1942	02:00	EWT
9/30/1945	02:00	EST
4/28/1946	02:00	US#2

COUNTIES

1 Fairfield
2 Hartford
3 Litchfield
4 Middlesex
5 New Haven
6 New London
7 Tolland
8 Windham

Place	CT	Lat	Long	Time
Abington 8	1	41N51'38	72w00'26	4:48:02
Addison 2	2	41N43'06	72w34'38	4:50:19
Agua Vista 1	4	41N24	73w27	4:53:48
Aljen Heights 6	1	41N34	71w53	4:47:32
Allerton Farms 5	1	41N30	73w03	4:52:12
Allingtown 5	2	41N17'51	72w57'38	4:51:51
Allyns Point 6	2	41N26'30	72w04'45	4:48:19
Almyville 8	1	41N43'05	71w52'00	4:47:28
Alsop Corner 2	1	41N48'19	72w49'05	4:51:16
Amenia Union 3	1	41N49'28	73w30'20	4:54:01
Amesville 3	1	41N57'46	73w22'35	4:53:30
Amity 5	2	41N23	73w00	4:52:00
Amston 7	1	41N37'31	72w20'37	4:49:22
Andover 7	1	41N44'14	72w22'15	4:49:29
Ansonia 5	1	41N20'46	73w04'46	4:52:19
Aqua Vista 1	4	41N26'46	73w26'40	4:53:47
Arnolds 4	1	41N27'57	72w30'54	4:50:04
Ashford 8	1	41N52'23	72w07'19	4:48:29
Ashford Lake 8	1	41N50	72w16	4:49:04
Aspetuck 1	3	41N13'05	73w19'17	4:53:17
Attawan Beach 6	1	41N18'11	72w12'26	4:48:50
Attawaugan 8	1	41N52'02	71w52'54	4:47:32
Atwoodville 7	1	41N47'05	72w10'30	4:48:42
Augerville 5	2	41N22'19	72w54'23	4:51:38
Avery Corner 6	1	41N35'56	72w12'41	4:48:51
Avery Heights 3	1	41N35	73w25	4:53:40
Avery Hill 6	1	41N34	71w53	4:47:32
Avon 2	1	41N48'35	72w49'52	4:51:19
Baccus Corner 6	1	41N30'52	72w06'18	4:48:25
Bahre Corner 2	1	41N50'42	72w54'02	4:51:36
Baileyville 4	1	41N30'47	72w43'30	4:50:54
Bakersville 3	1	41N49'55	73w01'50	4:52:07
Baldwins Crossing 5	2	41N14'24	73w05'36	4:52:22
Ballouville 8	1	41N52'36	71w51'42	4:47:27
Ball Pond 1	4	41N24	73w27	4:53:48
Baltic 6	1	41N37'01	72w05'06	4:48:20
Banksville 1	1	41N02	73w37	4:54:28
Bantam 3	1	41N43'28	73w14'12	4:52:57
Barkhampsted Center 3	1	41N55'44	72w58'01	4:51:52
Barkhamsted 3	1	41N55'45	72w54'52	4:51:39
Barnum 1	2	41N10	73w13	4:52:52
Barry Square 2	2	41N45	72w41	4:50:44
Bashan 4	1	41N30'47	72w26'02	4:49:44
Bayview 5	2	41N12'44	73w01'50	4:52:07
Beacon Falls 5	1	41N26'34	73w03'47	4:52:15
Beardsley 1	2	41N12	73w12	4:52:48
Beaverbrook 1	4	41N24'40	73w25'13	4:53:41
Beaver Head Corner 5	1	41N23'22	72w44'05	4:50:56
Beckettville 1	4	41N23'35	73w28'23	4:53:54
Bedlam Corner 8	1	41N46'47	72w09'18	4:48:37
Bel Aire Estates 6	1	41N21	71w59	4:47:56
Belden 1	1	41N07	73w26	4:53:44
Belle Haven 1	1	41N00'32	73w37'55	4:54:32
Belltown 1	1	41N04'37	73w31'45	4:54:07
Bensted Corner 2	1	41N42'23	72w52'49	4:51:31
Berkshire 1	1	41N24'31	73w15'36	4:53:02
Berkshire Estates 3	1	41N26'33	73w15'32	4:53:02
Berkshire Shopping Center 1	4	41N24	73w27	4:53:48
Berlin 2	1	41N37'17	72w44'46	4:50:59
Beseck Lake 4	1	41N31'07	72w44'07	4:50:56
Best View 6	2	41N24	72w07	4:48:28
Bethany 5	1	41N25'18	72w59'51	4:51:59
Bethel 1	1	41N22'16	73w24'52	4:53:39
Bethlehem 3	1	41N38'23	73w12'32	4:52:50
Bigelow Corners 1	4	41N28'19	73w30'18	4:54:01
Birch Groves 3	1	41N32'49	73w26'30	4:53:46
Birch Hill 3	1	41N43	73w29	4:53:56
Birch Mountain 7	1	41N47	72w31	4:50:04
Birchwood 2	2	41N53'52	72w43'18	4:50:53
Birdland 2	1	41N59	72w34	4:50:16
Bishops Corner 2	2	41N34'52	72w52'10	4:51:29
Bissell 2	2	41N49	72w37	4:50:28
Black Hall 6	1	41N17'55	72w19'08	4:49:17
Black Point 6	1	41N17'10	72w12'21	4:48:49
Black Point Beach Club 6	1	41N17'48	72w12'16	4:48:49
Black Rock 1	2	41N09'31	73w13'33	4:52:54
Blackstone Acres 5	2	41N17	72w48	4:51:12
Bloomfield 2	2	41N49'35	72w43'50	4:50:55
Blue Hills 2	2	41N47	72w41	4:50:44
Boardmans Bridge 3	1	41N35	73w25	4:53:40
Bolton 7	1	41N46'08	72w26'02	4:49:44
Bonny Brook 3	1	41N35	73w25	4:53:40
Borough 6	2	41N21	72w03	4:48:12
Boston 1	1	41N16'41	73w24'28	4:53:38
Botsford 1	1	41N21'59	73w15'27	4:53:02
Boulder Lake 4	1	41N17	72w32	4:50:08
Bozrah 6	1	41N33	72w10	4:48:40
Bradford Hill 8	1	41N41	71w55	4:47:40
Bradleyville 5	1	41N31'24	73w04'57	4:52:20
Branchville 1	1	41N16'03	73w26'32	4:53:46
Brandy Hill 8	1	41N40	73w21	4:53:24
Branford 5	2	41N16'46	72w48'56	4:51:16
Branford Hills 5	2	41N17	72w48	4:51:12
Branford Point 5	2	41N17	72w48	4:51:12
Breakneck 2	2	41N53'12	72w39'35	4:50:38
Brendan Heights 7	1	41N59	72w39	4:50:36
Bretton Heights 4	3	41N32'37	72w39'36	4:50:38
Bridgeport 1	2	41N10'01	73w12'19	4:52:49
Bridgewater 3	1	41N32'06	73w22'00	4:53:28
Brighton Beach 6	1	41N19	72w20	4:49:20
Brightview 5	2	41N16'18	72w53'50	4:51:35
Bristol 2	3	41N40'18	72w56'59	4:51:48
Bristol Terrace 5	1	41N30	73w03	4:52:12
Broad Brook 2	1	41N54'44	72w32'44	4:50:11
Brockway 6	1	41N23'40	72w22'50	4:49:31
Brockway Landing 6	1	41N23'19	72w23'20	4:49:33
Bromica 3	1	41N43	73w29	4:53:56
Brookfield 1	1	41N28'57	73w24'36	4:53:38
Brookfield Center 1	1	41N27'58	73w23'17	4:53:33
Brooklyn 8	1	41N47'17	71w57'01	4:47:48
Brooksvale 5	1	41N28'09	72w54'59	4:51:40
Browns Corner 3	1	41N49'41	72w58'37	4:51:54
Bruce Park 1	1	41N02	73w37	4:54:28
Brush Island 1	1	41N05	73w29	4:53:56
Buckingham 2	2	41N42'44	72w31'22	4:50:05
Buckland 2	1	41N47'46	72w33'04	4:50:12
Bucks Corners 2	2	41N41	72w35	4:50:20
Bull Run Corner 2	1	41N55'47	72w40'13	4:50:41
Bulls Bridge 3	1	41N40'32	73w30'28	4:54:02
Bundy Hill 6	1	41N37	71w59	4:47:56
Bungay 5	1	41N24	73w04	4:52:16
Bunker Hill 5	1	41N34'16	73w03'50	4:52:15
Burlington 2	1	41N46'09	72w57'54	4:51:52
Burnetts Corner 6	1	41N23'21	71w58'49	4:47:55
Burnham 2	2	41N47'57	72w37'07	4:50:28
Burnside 2	2	41N46'47	72w36'27	4:50:26
Burnt Hill 5	1	41N34'27	73w02'04	4:52:08
Burr Hill 4	1	41N23	72w26	4:49:44
Burrville 3	1	41N52'06	73w05'07	4:52:20
Burwells Beach 5	2	41N13	73w03	4:52:12
Byram 1	1	41N00'15	73w39'15	4:54:37
Calhoun Corners 3	1	41N48'13	73w22'56	4:53:32
Camp Bethel 4	1	41N29	72w31	4:50:04
Camptown 5	1	41N19	73w04	4:52:16
Campville 3	1	41N44'14	73w06'22	4:52:25
Canaan 3	1	42N01'38	73w19'47	4:53:19
Canaan Valley 3	1	42N02'26	73w15'26	4:53:02
Candleset Cove 3	1	41N35	73w25	4:53:40
Candlewood Hill 1	4	41N24	73w27	4:53:48

Candlewood Hill 4
1 41N30 72w34 4:50:16
Candlewood Isle 1
4 41N24 73w27 4:53:48
Candlewood Knolls 1
4 41N28'46 73w27'50 4:53:51
Candlewood Lake Club 3
1 41N29'40 73w26'27 4:53:46
Candlewood Lake Estates 1
1 41N35 73w30 4:54:00
Candlewood Orchards 1
1 41N28'07 73w26'12 4:53:45
Candlewood Pines 1
4 41N27'24 73w27'12 4:53:49
Candlewood Point 3
1 41N32'11 73w26'28 4:53:46
Candlewood Shores 1
1 41N28'55 73w26'33 4:53:46
Candlewood Springs 3
1 41N33'35 73w26'24 4:53:46
Candlewood Trails 3
1 41N35 73w25 4:53:40
Cannondale 1 1 41N12'59 73w25'33 4:53:42
Canterbury 8 1 41N41'54 71w58'17 4:47:53
Canton 2 1 41N49'28 72w53'39 4:51:35
Canton Center 2 1 41N51'23 72w54'56 4:51:40
Carmel, Mount 5 2 41N25'27 72w54'21 4:51:37
Cedar Beach 5 2 41N10'42 73w05'54 4:52:24
Cedar Heights 1 4 41N26'53 73w26'10 4:53:45
Cedarhurst 1 1 41N25'36 73w13'18 4:52:53
Cedar Knolls 3 1 41N35 73w25 4:53:40
Cedar Lake 2 3 41N41 72w56 4:51:44
Cedar Land 5 1 41N28'26 73w13'35 4:52:54
Cedar Springs 2 1 41N36 72w53 4:51:32
Center 1 2 41N15 73w13 4:52:52
Centerbrook 4 1 41N21'05 72w24'59 4:49:40
Center Groton 6 2 41N23'01 72w01'42 4:48:07
Center Hill 2 1 41N53 72w59 4:51:56
Centerville 5 2 41N23'02 72w54'27 4:51:38
Central 2 2 41N46 72w41 4:50:44
Central Village 8
1 41N43'22 71w54'26 4:47:38
Chaffeeville 7 1 41N47'41 72w12'32 4:48:50
Chalkers Beach 4
1 41N17 72w22 4:49:28
Chaplin 8 1 41N47'41 72w07'40 4:48:31
Chapman Beach 4 1 41N17 72w26 4:49:44
Cherry Brook 2 1 41N51 72w55 4:51:40
Cherry Hill 3 1 41N52 73w22 4:53:28
Cherry Park 2 1 41N48'41 72w53'15 4:51:33
Cheshire 5 1 41N29'56 72w54'04 4:51:36
Chester 4 1 41N24'11 72w27'05 4:49:48
Chesterfield 6 1 41N25'38 72w12'54 4:48:52
Chickahominy 1 1 41N02 73w37 4:54:28
Chippens Hill 2 3 41N41 72w56 4:51:44
Christy Hill Estates 6
2 41N26 72w05 4:48:20
Churchwood 6 1 41N19 72w12 4:48:48
Circle Beach 5 1 41N17 72w36 4:50:24
City Point 5 2 41N16'59 72w55'44 4:51:43
Clarks Corner 8 1 41N46'05 72w05'35 4:48:22
Clarks Falls 6 1 41N27'22 71w48'53 4:47:16
Clarks Village 6
1 41N21'37 71w50'42 4:47:23
Clayville 6 1 41N37'02 71w58'41 4:47:55
Clearview Heights 7
1 41N57 72w18 4:49:12
Clifton 5 1 41N24 73w04 4:52:16
Clinton 4 1 41N16'43 72w31'41 4:50:07
Clinton Beach 4 1 41N15'59 72w30'03 4:50:00
Clintonville 5 2 41N23'39 72w49'03 4:51:16
Cobalt 4 1 41N33'44 72w33'21 4:50:13
Cobalt Landing 4
1 41N33'22 72w33'42 4:50:15
Colburn Hill 7 1 41N57 72w18 4:49:12
Colchester 6 1 41N34'32 72w19'57 4:49:20
Colebrook 3 1 41N59'22 73w05'46 4:52:23
Collinsville 2 1 41N48'46 72w55'14 4:51:41
Colonial Manor 6
1 41N32 72w05 4:48:20
Colonial Plaza 5
1 41N34 73w04 4:52:16
Columbia 7 1 41N42'07 72w18'06 4:49:12
Compo 1 3 41N06'41 73w21'20 4:53:25
Compo Beach 1 3 41N08 73w21 4:53:24
Compo Hill 1 3 41N08 73w21 4:53:24
Conantville 7 1 41N44'19 72w12'09 4:48:49
Congamond Lakes 2
1 42N00 72w42 4:50:48
Connecticut Post Shop Ctr 5
2 41N13 73w03 4:52:12
Connings Park 6 2 41N23 72w04 4:48:16
Conning Towers 6
2 41N21 72w03 4:48:12
Copaco Shopping Center 2
2 41N49 72w42 4:50:48
Corbin's Corner Shopping Pk 2
2 41N44 72w44 4:50:56
Corner of The Pines 3
1 41N50'19 73w19'44 4:53:19
Cornwall 3 1 41N50'37 73w19'47 4:53:19
Cornwall Bridge 3
1 41N49'07 73w22'17 4:53:29
Cornwall Center 3
1 41N52 73w22 4:53:28
Cornwall Hollow 3
1 42N02 73w20 4:53:20
Cos Cob 1 1 41N02'00 73w36'00 4:54:24
Cottage Grove 2 2 41N49'17 72w41'46 4:50:47
Country Club Heights 2
1 41N35 72w53 4:51:32
Coventry 7 1 41N46'12 72w18'20 4:49:13
Cranbury 1 3 41N08'50 73w23'44 4:53:35
Cranska Village 8
1 41N43 71w53 4:47:32
Crescent Beach 6
1 41N18'54 72w12'09 4:48:49
Crescent Park 6 1 41N18'37 72w12'13 4:48:49
Cromwell 4 3 41N35'42 72w38'45 4:50:35
Crowley Corner 4
1 41N28'38 72w18'42 4:49:15
Crowleys Corner 2
1 41N49'00 72w52'04 4:51:28

Crystal Lake 7 1 41N55'54 72w22'44 4:49:31
Daleville 7 1 41N53 72w18 4:49:12
Damascus 5 2 41N17 72w48 4:51:12
Danbury 1 4 41N23'41 73w27'16 4:53:49
Danbury Quarter 3
1 41N55 73w04 4:52:16
Danielson 8 1 41N48'09 71w53'11 4:47:33
Darien 1 1 41N04'43 73w28'11 4:53:53
Davidsons Corner 5
1 41N25'43 72w58'36 4:51:54
Dayville 8 1 41N50'47 71w53'17 4:47:33
Deep River 4 1 41N23'08 72w26'10 4:49:45
Deerfield 2 2 41N51 72w39 4:50:36
Deer Island 3 1 41N41 73w15 4:53:00
Deer Run Shores 1
1 41N35 73w30 4:54:00
Dempsey Landing 3
1 41N42'45 73w13'39 4:52:55
Derby 5 1 41N19'14 73w05'22 4:52:21
Derby Neck 5 1 41N19 73w04 4:52:16
Devil's Backbone 3
1 41N38 73w13 4:52:52
Devon 5 2 41N12'08 73w06'08 4:52:25
Diamond Lake 2 2 41N41 72w35 4:50:20
Dibble Hill 3 1 41N52 73w22 4:53:28
Dickerman's Corner 2
1 41N35 72w53 4:51:32
Doaneville 6 1 41N34'18 71w52'32 4:47:30
Dodgingtown 1 1 41N22'45 73w21'24 4:53:26
Dolphin Gardens 6
2 41N21 72w03 4:48:12
Double Beach 5 2 41N15'29 72w49'57 4:51:20
Dowd's Corner 2 1 41N49 72w54 4:51:36
Drakeville 3 1 41N51'18 73w09'28 4:52:38
Durham 4 1 41N28'54 72w40'54 4:50:44
Durham Center 4 1 41N28'29 72w40'51 4:50:43
Eagleville 7 1 41N47'12 72w16'37 4:49:06
East Berlin 2 1 41N37'06 72w42'51 4:50:51
East Bridgeport 1
2 41N10'27 73w10'51 4:52:43
East Bristol 2 3 41N39'59 72w54'44 4:51:39
East Brooklyn 8 1 41N47'48 71w53'52 4:47:35
East Canaan 3 1 42N00'48 73w17'03 4:53:08
East Cornwall 3 1 41N48'33 73w18'28 4:53:14
East Derby 5 1 41N18'50 73w04'41 4:52:19
East End 5 1 41N33 73w01 4:52:04
Eastern Point 6 2 41N21 72w03 4:48:12
East Farmington Heights 2
1 41N43'54 72w46'36 4:51:06
East Farms 5 1 41N32'46 72w58'59 4:51:56
Eastford 8 1 41N54'07 72w04'49 4:48:19
East Glastonbury 2
2 41N41'39 72w32'03 4:50:08
East Granby 2 1 41N56'28 72w43'40 4:50:55
East Great Plain 6
1 41N32 72w05 4:48:20
East Haddam 4 1 41N27'11 72w27'42 4:49:51
East Haddam Landing 4
1 41N27 72w28 4:49:52
East Hampton 4 1 41N34'33 72w30'11 4:50:01
East Hartford 2 2 41N46'56 72w36'45 4:50:27
East Hartford Gardens 2
2 41N44'07 72w36'48 4:50:27
East Hartland 2 1 41N59'56 72w54'21 4:51:37
East Haven 5 2 41N16'34 72w52'08 4:51:29
East Hill 2 1 41N49 72w54 4:51:36
East Kent 3 1 41N44'04 73w24'15 4:53:37
East Killingly 8
1 41N50'57 71w49'09 4:47:17
East Litchfield 3
1 41N45'43 73w07'08 4:52:29
East Lyme 6 1 41N22'04 72w13'09 4:48:53
East Morris 3 1 41N41'18 73w10'50 4:52:43
East Mountain 5 1 41N31'48 73w00'50 4:52:03
East New London 6
2 41N21'69 72w05'59 4:48:24
East Norwalk 1 3 41N06'20 73w23'56 4:53:36
Easton 1 2 41N15'10 73w17'52 4:53:11
East Plymouth 2 3 41N41'35 72w59'55 4:52:00
East Port Chester 1
1 41N02 73w37 4:54:28
East Putnam 8 1 41N54'49 71w49'02 4:47:16
East River 5 1 41N17'07 72w38'20 4:50:33
East River Beach 5
1 41N17 72w36 4:50:24
East Thompson 8 1 42N00'32 71w48'33 4:47:14
Eastview Acres 5
1 41N24 73w04 4:52:16
East Village 5 1 41N21'30 73w11'13 4:52:45
East Wallingford 5
1 41N26'37 72w47'22 4:51:09
East Willington 7
1 41N52'25 72w14'15 4:48:57
East Windsor 2 1 41N55 72w35 4:50:20
East Windsor Hill 2
2 41N51'37 72w36'13 4:50:25
East Woodstock 8
1 41N59'01 71w58'40 4:47:55
Ebbs Corner 2 1 42N01'07 72w44'54 4:51:00
Edgewood 2 3 41N42'09 72w55'29 4:51:42
Edgewood 7 1 41N57 72w18 4:49:12
Ekonk 8 1 41N38'44 71w50'53 4:47:24
Ekonk Hill 6 1 41N34 71w52 4:47:28
Ellington 7 1 41N54'14 72w28'13 4:49:53
Elliotts 8 1 41N50'00 72w00'44 4:48:03
Ellithorpe 7 1 41N59'42 72w18'52 4:49:15
Ellsworth 3 1 41N49'48 73w25'39 4:53:43
Elm Hill 2 2 41N41 72w44 4:50:56
Elmville 8 1 41N49'53 71w52'37 4:47:30
Elmwood 1 4 41N22 73w25 4:53:40
Elmwood 4 2 41N43'59 72w43'23 4:50:54
Enders Island 6 1 41N21 71w58 4:47:52
Enfield 2 1 41N58'34 72w35'32 4:50:22
Erickson Corner 3
1 41N39'49 73w25'21 4:53:41
Essex 4 1 41N21'12 72w23'28 4:49:34
Ethel Acres 6 1 41N37 71w59 4:47:56
Ettadore Park 5 2 41N13 73w03 4:52:12
Exeter 6 1 41N37'11 72w15'53 4:49:04
Fabyan 8 1 42N00'49 71w56'25 4:47:46
Fairfield 1 2 41N08'28 73w15'51 4:53:03
Fairground 6 1 41N32 72w05 4:48:20
Fair Haven 5 2 41N18'40 72w53'46 4:51:35

Fair Haven East 5
2 41N17'52 72w53'16 4:51:33
Fair Lawn 5 1 41N32'45 73w00'14 4:52:01
Fairmount 5 1 41N35'10 73w03'21 4:52:13
Fairy Lake 6 1 41N28 72w10 4:48:40
Fall Mountain 2 3 41N41 72w56 4:51:44
Fall Mountain Lake 3
3 41N40 73w01 4:52:04
Falls Switch 6 1 41N32 72w05 4:48:20
Falls Village 3 1 41N57'21 73w21'49 4:53:27
Farmington 2 1 41N43'11 72w49'57 4:51:20
Farmington Station 2
1 41N43'15 72w51'48 4:51:27
Farnhams 2 1 41N51'46 72w33'36 4:50:14
Far View Beach 5
2 41N13 73w03 4:52:12
Fenwick 4 1 41N16'15 72w21'15 4:49:25
Fenwood 4 1 41N16'09 72w22'01 4:49:28
Ferris Estates 3
1 41N35 73w25 4:53:40
Ferry Point 4 1 41N17 72w22 4:49:28
Ferry View Heights 6
2 41N26 72w05 4:48:20
Field Crest Estates 6
1 41N21 71w59 4:47:56
Firetown 2 1 41N54'18 72w49'24 4:51:18
Fitch Corner 6 2 41N27'17 72w06'22 4:48:25
Fitchville 6 1 41N33'53 72w09'16 4:48:37
Five City Plaza Shopping Ctr 2
2 41N46 72w45 4:51:00
Five Points 1 1 41N19'20 73w21'25 4:53:26
Five Points 2 1 41N59'44 72w47'45 4:51:11
Flanders 3 1 41N44'26 73w27'20 4:53:49
Flanders 6 1 41N22'08 72w13'05 4:48:52
Flat Rock 8 1 41N41 71w55 4:47:40
Flax Hill 1 1 41N07 73w26 4:53:44
Floral Park 4 1 41N17 72w22 4:49:28
Floydville 2 1 41N55'43 72w46'49 4:51:07
Fogelmarks Corners 4
3 41N36'08 72w36'13 4:50:25
Forbes Village 2
2 41N44'00 72w36'00 4:50:24
Forest Glen 4 1 41N17 72w22 4:49:28
Forest Heights 5
2 41N14'21 73w02'38 4:52:11
Forest Hills 2 1 41N36 72w53 4:51:32
Forest Park 7 1 41N39 72w22 4:49:28
Forest Village 2
2 41N44'52 72w35'49 4:50:23
Forestville 2 3 41N40'36 72w55'14 4:51:41
Forestville 7 1 41N57 72w18 4:49:12
Fort Hill 3 1 41N35 73w25 4:53:40
Fort Trumbull 5 2 41N12'35 73w03'25 4:52:14
Fort Trumbull 6 2 41N20'37 72w05'37 4:48:22
Fort Trumbull Beach 5
2 41N13 73w03 4:52:12
Four Corners 6 1 41N26'58 72w11'43 4:48:47
Fox Den 2 1 41N49 72w50 4:51:20
Foxon 5 2 41N19'28 72w50'09 4:51:21
Foxtown 4 1 41N34 72w20 4:49:20
Fox Village 7 1 41N57 72w18 4:49:12
Franklin 6 1 41N36'32 72w08'47 4:48:35
Franklin Square 6
1 41N32 72w05 4:48:20
Frog Hollow 7 1 41N54 72w28 4:49:52
Furnace Hollow 7
1 41N57 72w18 4:49:12
Gales Ferry 6 2 41N25'47 72w04'57 4:48:20
Gallows Hill 1 1 41N20 73w26 4:53:44
Garden City 5 1 41N24 73w04 4:52:16
Gaylordsville 3 1 41N38'47 73w29'05 4:53:56
Georgetown 1 1 41N15'20 73w26'07 4:53:44
Germantown 1 4 41N24'29 73w26'34 4:53:46
Giants Neck 6 1 41N18'01 72w13'59 4:48:56
Gilbert Corners 1
1 41N10'32 73w26'24 4:53:46
Gildersleeve 4 3 41N35'48 72w37'17 4:50:29
Gilead 7 1 41N40'24 72w24'32 4:49:38
Gilman 6 1 41N34'37 72w11'59 4:48:48
Glasgo 6 1 41N33'21 71w53'19 4:47:33
Glastonbury 2 2 41N42'44 72w36'31 4:50:26
Glen 1 1 41N20 73w26 4:53:44
Glenbrook 1 1 41N03'53 73w31'36 4:54:06
Glen Ridge 5 1 41N30'04 73w03'57 4:52:16
Glenville 1 1 41N02'07 73w39'37 4:54:38
Glynville 7 1 41N57 72w18 4:49:12
Golden Spur 6 2 41N22'09 72w11'49 4:48:47
Good Hill 3 1 41N33 73w12 4:52:48
Goodrich Heights 4
3 41N37'35 72w39'10 4:50:37
Goodrichville 2 1 41N58'40 72w48'51 4:51:15
Goodsell Point 5
2 41N17 72w48 4:51:12
Goodwives Shopping Plaza 1
1 41N05 73w29 4:53:56
Goshen 3 1 41N49'54 73w13'32 4:52:54
Goshen Hills 6 1 41N38 72w13 4:48:52
Governor's Hill 5
1 41N24 73w04 4:52:16
Granbrook Park 2
1 41N56'10 72w46'16 4:51:05
Granby 2 1 41N57'14 72w47'21 4:51:09
Granite Bay 5 2 41N17 72w48 4:51:12
Graniteville 6 2 41N20'06 72w09'15 4:48:37
Grantville 3 1 41N57'04 73w09'25 4:52:38
Grapeville 3 1 41N43'15 73w13'43 4:52:55
Grappaville 3 1 41N44 73w14 4:52:56
Grasmere 1 2 41N10 73w15 4:53:00
Grassy Hill 3 1 41N33 73w12 4:52:48
Grassy Plain 1 4 41N22 73w25 4:53:40
Great Hammock 4 1 41N17 72w22 4:49:28
Great Harbor 5 2 41N23 72w51 4:51:24
Great Meadows 1 4 41N24 73w27 4:53:48
Greenfield Hill 1
2 41N10'35 73w17'32 4:53:10
Green Manorville 2
1 41N59 72w34 4:50:16
Greens Farms 1 2 41N07'26 73w19'11 4:53:17
Greenville 6 1 41N32'01 72w03'28 4:48:14
Greenwich 1 1 41N01'35 73w37'44 4:54:31
Greystone 3 3 41N40 73w01 4:52:04
Griswold 6 1 41N35 71w56 4:47:44
Griswoldville 4 2 41N41'37 72w40'16 4:50:41

Grosvenor Dale 8 1 41N58'06 71W53'43 4:47:35
Groton 6 2 41N21'00 72W04'44 4:48:19
Groton Heights 6 2 41N21 72W03 4:48:12
Groton Lake Shores 6 1 41N19 72W12 4:48:48
Groton Long Point 6 2 41N18'52 72W00'30 4:48:02
Groton Shopping Mall 6 2 41N21 72W03 4:48:12
Grove Beach 4 1 41N16'29 72W29'02 4:49:56
Grove Beach Point 4 1 41N17 72W26 4:49:44
Grove Beach Terrace 4 1 41N17 72W26 4:49:44
Grover Hill 1 2 41N08'47 73W13'44 4:52:55
Guilford 5 1 41N17'20 72W40'56 4:50:44
Gurleyville 7 1 41N48'51 72W13'18 4:48:53
Haddam 4 1 41N28'38 72W30'45 4:50:03
Haddam Neck 4 1 41N35 72W30 4:50:00
Hadlyme 6 1 41N25'13 72W24'25 4:49:38
Hale Court 1 3 41N07'17 73W21'05 4:53:24
Hallville 6 1 41N29'36 72W02'01 4:48:08
Hamburg 6 1 41N23'04 72W21'02 4:49:24
Hamden 5 2 41N23'45 72W53'50 4:51:35
Hammertown 3 1 42N02'35 73W24'47 4:53:39
Hampsted 2 1 41N57'01 72W53'45 4:51:35
Hampton 8 1 41N47'02 72W03'19 4:48:13
Hancock 3 3 41N38'11 73W01'27 4:52:06
Hank Hill 7 1 41N48 72W15 4:49:00
Hanover 6 1 41N38'33 72W03'57 4:48:16
Happyland 6 1 41N28'22 72W03'54 4:48:16
Harborview 1 1 41N04'55 73W24'33 4:53:38
Harbor View 4 1 41N15'48 72W30'57 4:50:04
Harrisons 6 2 41N23'12 72W06'03 4:48:24
Harrisville 8 1 41N55'34 71W56'14 4:47:45
Hartford 2 2 41N45'49 72W41'08 4:50:45
Hartland 2 1 41N59'46 72W58'48 4:51:55
Harwinton 3 1 41N46'16 73W03'37 4:52:14
Hattertown 1 1 41N20'28 73W18'34 4:53:14
Hawks Nest Beach 6 1 41N17'00 72W17'02 4:49:08
Hawleyville 1 1 41N25'39 73W21'20 4:53:25
Hawthorne Terrace 1 4 41N27'32 73W25'50 4:53:43
Hayden 2 2 41N53'21 72W37'47 4:50:31
Hayestown 1 4 41N25'12 73W27'15 4:53:49
Hazardville 2 1 41N59'14 72W32'43 4:50:11
Hebron 7 1 41N39'28 72W21'59 4:49:28
Heilwield Corner 6 1 41N30'46 72W15'04 4:49:00
Hickory Haven 3 1 41N37'30 73W23'41 4:53:35
Hidden Lake 4 1 41N30 72W34 4:50:16
Higganum 4 1 41N29'49 72W33'27 4:50:14
Highland 4 3 41N33'56 72W44'19 4:50:57
Highland Park 2 1 41N45'54 72W29'47 4:49:59
High Ridge 1 1 41N10'08 73W33'51 4:54:15
Highwood 5 2 41N22 72W55 4:51:40
Hillcrest 5 1 41N32'39 73W06'09 4:52:25
Hilliardville 2 1 41N47'03 72W33'21 4:50:13
Hillside 1 2 41N12 73W10 4:52:40
Hitchcock Lake 5 1 41N36 72W59 4:51:56
Hoadley Neck 5 2 41N15'46 72W43'59 4:50:56
Hockanum 4 2 41N44'26 72W38'03 4:50:32
Holiday Homes 6 1 41N34 72W20 4:49:20
Hollywyle Park 1 4 41N27'50 73W27'35 4:53:50
Honeypot Glen 5 1 41N31'21 72W53'13 4:51:33
Hope Valley 7 1 41N38'01 72W22'32 4:49:30
Hopeville 5 1 41N31'53 73W02'09 4:52:09
Hopeville 6 1 41N36'45 71W56'20 4:47:45
Hopewell 1 1 41N20'50 73W20'13 4:53:21
Hopewell 2 2 41N39'52 72W35'02 4:50:20
Horse Heaven 3 1 41N37'02 73W17'03 4:53:08
Hoskins 2 1 41N54'01 72W47'11 4:51:09
Hotchkissville 3 1 41N34'02 73W13'03 4:52:52
Huckleberry Hill 2 1 41N49 72W50 4:51:20
Hungary 2 1 41N58'36 72W46'46 4:51:07
Hungary Hill 8 1 41N42 71W50 4:47:20
Hunting Ridge 1 1 41N08'18 73W34'23 4:54:18
Huntington 1 1 41N17'47 73W08'48 4:52:35
Huntingtown 1 1 41N21'29 73W17'09 4:53:09
Huntsville 3 1 41N56'41 73W18'47 4:53:15
Hurds Corner 3 1 41N37'19 73W25'21 4:53:41
Hydeville 7 1 41N59'35 72W16'36 4:49:06
Indian Cove 5 2 41N23 72W51 4:51:24
Indian Neck 5 2 41N15'40 72W48'04 4:51:12
Ives Corner 5 1 41N28'02 72W54'23 4:51:38
Ivoryton 4 1 41N20'54 72W26'23 4:49:46
Jericho 6 1 41N20'12 72W17'56 4:49:12
Jericho Hill 6 1 41N19 72W20 4:49:20
Jewett City 6 1 41N36'24 71W58'53 4:47:56
Jordan (Waterford P O) 6 2 41N20'21 72W08'41 4:48:35
Jordan Village 6 2 41N20 72W09 4:48:36
Joyceville 3 1 42N03'01 73W25'34 4:53:42
Kelly Corner 3 1 41N52'42 73W12'25 4:52:50
Kelseytown 4 1 41N17'48 72W31'58 4:50:08
Kensington 2 3 41N38'07 72W46'09 4:51:05
Kent 3 1 41N43'29 73W28'39 4:53:55
Kent Furnace 3 1 41N44'15 73W28'11 4:53:53
Kenyonville 8 1 41N55'46 72W04'59 4:48:20
Kilby 5 2 41N18 72W56 4:51:44
Killingly Center 8 1 41N50'19 71W52'11 4:47:29
Killingworth 4 1 41N21'29 72W33'51 4:50:15
Kings Corner 2 1 41N56'40 72W36'10 4:50:25
Kitemaug 6 2 41N26'44 72W05'20 4:48:21
Knollcrest 1 4 41N29'55 73W28'01 4:53:52
Knollwood 4 1 41N16'00 72W23'02 4:49:32
Lake Bashan 4 1 41N27 72W28 4:49:52
Lake Beseck 4 1 41N31 72W43 4:50:52
Lake Garda 2 1 41N45 72W53 4:51:32
Lake Hayward 4 1 41N34 72W20 4:49:20
Lake Pocotopaug 4 1 41N36 72W31 4:50:04
Lakeridge Heights 4 3 41N33 72W39 4:50:36
Lakeside 3 1 41N40'56 73W14'16 4:52:57
Lakeside 5 1 41N25'59 73W13'36 4:52:54
Lake View Terrace 7 1 41N56'49 72W22'02 4:49:28
Lakeville 3 1 41N57'52 73W26'26 4:53:46
Lakewood 5 1 41N34'47 73W01'49 4:52:07
Lamson Corner 2 3 41N44'33 72W58'18 4:51:53
Lanesville 3 1 41N32'08 73W25'24 4:53:42
Lattins Landing 1 4 41N26'57 73W25'46 4:53:43
Laurel Beach 5 2 41N10'58 73W05'39 4:52:23
Laurel Glen 6 1 41N28'20 71W48'55 4:47:16
Laurel Hill 6 1 41N55 71W55 4:47:40
Laysville 6 1 41N20'55 72W17'56 4:49:12
Lebanon 6 1 41N38'10 72W12'47 4:48:51
Ledyard Center 6 2 41N26'23 72W00'53 4:48:04
Leesville 4 1 41N30'42 72W28'54 4:49:56
Leetes Island 5 2 41N15'55 72W42'53 4:50:52
Leffingwell 6 1 41N32 72W05 4:48:20
Liberty Hill 6 1 41N39'56 72W15'19 4:49:01
Lime Rock 3 1 41N56'01 73W23'23 4:53:34
Lisbon 6 1 41N35 72W01 4:48:04
Litchfield 3 1 41N44'50 73W11'21 4:52:45
Little Boston 1 1 41N18 73W23 4:53:32
Little City 4 1 41N26'51 72W36'02 4:50:24
Little Haddam 4 1 41N28'51 72W26'47 4:49:47
Long Hill 1 2 41N14'38 73W13'18 4:52:53
Long Hill 5 1 41N33'56 73W01'24 4:52:06
Long Hill 6 2 41N21 72W03 4:48:12
Long Ridge 1 1 41N09'20 73W35'48 4:54:23
Long Society 6 1 41N32 72W05 4:48:20
Lordship 1 2 41N09'11 73W07'43 4:52:31
Lords Point 6 1 41N20'09 71W55'39 4:47:43
Lower City 3 1 41N55'29 73W16'36 4:53:06
Lower Merryall 3 1 41N38'48 73W24'58 4:53:40
Lydallville 2 1 41N47'43 72W29'27 4:49:58
Lyme 6 1 41N24 72W21 4:49:24
Lyme Station 6 1 41N18'06 72W19'38 4:49:19
Lyons Plain 1 1 41N13'30 73W20'48 4:53:23
Macedonia 3 1 41N44'34 73W29'58 4:54:00
Madison 5 1 41N16'46 72W35'56 4:50:24
Manchester 2 1 41N46'33 72W31'19 4:50:05
Manchester Green 2 1 41N47'06 72W30'03 4:50:00
Manitock Spring 6 2 41N21'10 72W09'44 4:48:39
Mansfield Center 7 1 41N45'55 72W11'55 4:48:48
Mansfield City 7 1 41N45'57 72W14'03 4:48:56
Mansfield Depot 7 1 41N48'05 72W18'25 4:49:14
Mansfield Four Corners 7 1 41N49'38 72W16'00 4:49:04
Mansfield Hollow 7 1 41N45'27 72W11'11 4:48:45
Maple Hill 2 2 41N41 72W44 4:50:56
Marble Dale 3 1 41N39'49 73W22'10 4:53:29
Margerie Manor 1 4 41N27'08 73W28'04 4:53:52
Marion 2 1 41N33'49 72W55'34 4:51:42
Marlborough 2 1 41N37'53 72W27'37 4:49:50
Maromas 4 3 41N32'26 72W33'40 4:50:15
Mashapaug 7 1 42N01'38 72W08'19 4:48:33
Massapeag 6 2 41N27'28 72W04'53 4:48:20
Mayberry Village 2 2 41N46'43 72W35'13 4:50:21
McClaveville 3 1 42N02'23 73W05'48 4:52:23
Mechanicsville 2 1 41N58'08 72W47'39 4:51:11
Mechanicsville 8 1 41N56'24 71W53'39 4:47:35
Melrose 2 1 41N56'15 72W31'18 4:50:05
Melville Village 1 2 41N11'28 73W14'06 4:52:56
Meriden 5 3 41N32'17 72W48'27 4:51:14
Merrow 7 1 41N49'28 72W18'39 4:49:15
Merwinsville 3 1 41N38'51 73W29'00 4:53:56
Mianus 1 1 41N02'38 73W35'30 4:54:22
Middle Beach 5 1 41N16'13 72W35'41 4:50:23
Middlebury 5 1 41N31'40 73W07'41 4:52:31
Middlefield 4 1 41N31'02 72W42'45 4:50:51
Middle Haddam 4 1 41N33'14 72W33'02 4:50:12
Middletown 4 3 41N33'44 72W39'04 4:50:36
Midway 6 2 41N20'29 72W02'02 4:48:08
Milbrook 1 1 41N02 73W37 4:54:28
Milestone Corner 6 1 41N30'54 72W16'31 4:49:06
Milford 5 2 41N13'20 73W03'25 4:52:14
Milford Lawns 5 2 41N13'29 73W00'29 4:52:02
Mill Brook 3 1 41N57'48 73W07'12 4:52:29
Millbrook 5 2 41N22'45 72W53'36 4:51:34
Milldale 2 1 41N33'57 72W53'32 4:51:34
Mill Hill 1 2 41N10'38 73W09'38 4:52:39
Millington 4 1 41N29'09 72W21'21 4:49:25
Mill Plain 1 2 41N08'55 73W16'15 4:53:05
Mill Plain 5 1 41N33'18 73W00'47 4:52:03
Millstone 6 1 41N18'39 72W10'01 4:48:40
Millville 5 1 41N29'27 73W04'03 4:52:16
Milton 3 1 41N46'12 73W16'23 4:53:06
Minortown 3 1 41N34'34 73W10'29 4:52:42
Miramichi 4 3 41N32'59 72W42'04 4:50:48
Miry Brook 1 4 41N21'59 73W28'58 4:53:56
Mitcheltown 3 1 41N51'30 73W27'39 4:53:51
Mixville 5 1 41N31'20 72W56'10 4:51:45
Mohegan 6 2 41N28'36 72W06'01 4:48:24
Momauguin 5 2 41N15'07 72W52'36 4:51:30
Monroe 1 1 41N19'57 73W12'28 4:52:50
Montowese 5 2 41N21'01 72W51'37 4:51:26
Montville Center 6 1 41N28'44 72W09'06 4:48:36
Moodus 4 1 41N30'10 72W27'02 4:49:48
Mooreville 3 1 41N54'34 73W03'38 4:52:15
Moosup 8 1 41N42'46 71W52'53 4:47:32
Morningside 5 2 41N12'46 73W00'37 4:52:02
Morningside Park 6 2 41N20'53 72W07'40 4:48:31
Morris 3 1 41N41'03 73W11'48 4:52:47
Morris Cove 5 2 41N15'29 72W53'31 4:51:34
Mount Carmel 5 2 41N25'27 72W54'21 4:51:37
Mount Hope 8 1 41N49'26 72W10'17 4:48:41
Mount Parnassus 4 1 41N28'18 72W24'48 4:49:39
Murray 1 2 41N11'40 73W17'10 4:53:09
Myrtle Beach 5 2 41N11'46 73W04'37 4:52:18
Mystic 6 1 41N21'15 71W58'01 4:47:52
Mystic Seaport 6 1 41N21'40 71W58'01 4:47:52
Naugatuck 5 1 41N29'09 73W03'04 4:52:12
Naugatuck Gardens 5 2 41N12'46 73W05'45 4:52:23
Naugatuck Junction 5 2 41N12'27 73W06'22 4:52:25
Naugatuck Valley Mall 5 1 41N33 73W01 4:52:04
Nautilus Park 6 2 41N21 72W03 4:48:12
Nelsons Corner 3 1 41N56'46 73W03'03 4:52:12
Nepaug 3 1 41N49'47 72W59'58 4:52:00
Newberry Corner 3 1 41N47'21 73W08'26 4:52:34
New Britain 2 3 41N39'40 72W46'48 4:51:07
New Canaan 1 1 41N08'48 73W29'43 4:53:59
Newent 6 1 41N36'16 72W01'06 4:48:04
New Fairfield 1 1 41N27'59 73W29'10 4:53:57
Newfield 1 2 41N10'41 73W10'00 4:52:40
Newfield 3 1 41N51'28 73W07'47 4:52:31
Newfield Heights 4 3 41N33'27 72W40'32 4:50:42
New Hartford 3 1 41N52'56 72W58'39 4:51:55
New Haven 5 2 41N18'29 72W55'43 4:51:43
Newington 4 2 41N41'52 72W43'27 4:50:54
Newington Junction 4 2 41N42'51 72W44'15 4:50:57
New London 6 2 41N21'20 72W06'00 4:48:24
New Milford 3 1 41N34'37 73W24'32 4:53:38
New Preston 3 1 41N40'30 73W21'08 4:53:25
Newtown 1 1 41N24'50 73W18'14 4:53:13
New Village 8 1 41N41 71W55 4:47:40
Niantic 6 2 41N19'31 72W11'37 4:48:46
Nichols 1 2 41N14'27 73W09'42 4:52:39
Noank 6 2 41N19'40 71W59'28 4:47:58
Noble 1 2 41N11 73W11 4:52:44
Norfolk 3 1 41N59'38 73W12'09 4:52:49
Noroton 1 1 41N03'52 73W29'21 4:53:57
Noroton Heights 1 1 41N04'30 73W29'32 4:53:58
North Ashford 8 1 41N57'15 72W06'19 4:48:25
North Bloomfield 2 2 41N53'10 72W44'49 4:50:59
North Branford 5 1 41N19'39 72W46'04 4:51:04
North Canaan 3 1 42N01 73W18 4:53:12
North Canton 2 1 41N53'52 72W53'35 4:51:34
North Colebrook 3 1 42N01'03 73W06'55 4:52:28
North Cornwall 3 1 41N52'15 73W18'54 4:53:16
North Coventry 7 1 41N47'54 72W22'20 4:49:29
North Cromwell 4 3 41N36'41 72W38'39 4:50:35
Northfield 3 1 41N41'41 73W06'40 4:52:27
Northford 5 1 41N23'37 72W47'30 4:51:10
North Franklin 6 1 41N38'00 72W09'50 4:48:39
North Glenwood 6 2 41N26 72W05 4:48:20
North Goshen 3 1 41N53'55 73W12'46 4:52:51
North Granby 2 1 41N59'45 72W49'48 4:51:19
North Greenwich 1 1 41N05'45 73W41'23 4:54:46
North Grosvenor Dale 8 1 41N59'08 71W53'57 4:47:36
North Guilford 5 2 41N22'01 72W43'03 4:50:52
North Haven 5 2 41N23'27 72W51'36 4:51:26
North Hollow 2 1 42N02'02 72W55'50 4:51:43
North Kent 3 1 41N46'01 73W25'44 4:53:43
North Lyme 6 1 41N24'43 72W20'14 4:49:21
North Madison 5 1 41N21'35 72W38'14 4:50:33
North Mianus 1 1 41N03'29 73W34'55 4:54:20
North Somers 7 1 42N00'58 72W26'55 4:49:48
North Stamford 1 1 41N08'17 73W32'38 4:54:11
North Sterling 8 1 41N42 71W50 4:47:20
North Stonington 6 1 41N26'27 71W52'54 4:47:32
North Thompsonville 2 1 42N00'58 72W35'34 4:50:22
Northville 3 1 41N37'45 73W23'37 4:53:34
North Westchester 6 1 41N34'51 72W24'06 4:49:36
North Wilton 1 1 41N12'44 73W28'00 4:53:52
North Windham 8 1 41N44'58 72W09'18 4:48:37
North Woodbury 3 1 41N33'01 73W12'21 4:52:49
North Woodstock 8 1 41N59'25 71W59'51 4:47:59
Norwalk 1 3 41N07'03 73W24'30 4:53:38
Norwalk Mall 1 3 41N08 73W24 4:53:36
Norwich 6 1 41N31'27 72W04'35 4:48:18
Norwichtown 6 1 41N33'11 72W06'21 4:48:25
Nut Plains 5 2 41N19'28 72W41'05 4:50:44
Oakdale 6 1 41N27'58 72W09'28 4:48:38
Oakdale Manor 3 1 41N26'40 73W15'10 4:53:01
Oakland 2 1 41N48'22 72W31'06 4:50:04
Oakland Gardens 2 1 41N44'33 72W47'12 4:51:09
Oakville 3 1 41N35'36 73W05'09 4:52:21
Obtuse Hill 1 1 41N27'59 73W21'43 4:53:27
Occum 6 1 41N35'42 72W03'04 4:48:12
Olde Mistick Village 6 1 41N21 71W59 4:47:56
Old Greenwich 1 1 41N01'22 73W33'55 4:54:16
Old Lyme 6 1 41N18'57 72W19'46 4:49:19
Old Lyme Shores 6 1 41N17'25 72W16'31 4:49:06
Old Mystic 6 1 41N23'29 71W57'44 4:47:51
Old Saybrook 4 1 41N17'30 72W22'36 4:49:30
Oneco 8 1 41N41'37 71W48'32 4:47:14
Orange 5 2 41N16'42 73W01'34 4:52:06
Orcutts 7 1 41N58'36 72W19'20 4:49:17

Place		Lat.	Long.	Time
Ore Hill 3	1	41N57'26	73w28'03	4:53:52
Oronoke 5	1	41N32'29	73w05'23	4:52:22
Oronoque 1	2	41N14'52	73w06'07	4:52:24
Oswegatchie 6	2	41N21'18	72w10'36	4:48:42
Oswegatchie Hills 6	1	41N19	72w12	4:48:48
Otter Cove Estates 4	1	41N20'14	72w22'16	4:49:29
Overlook 5	1	41N34'00	73w02'55	4:52:12
Owenoke 1	3	41N06'24	73w21'39	4:53:27
Oxford 5	1	41N26'02	73w07'02	4:52:28
Ox Hill 1	2	41N13'42	73w13'10	4:52:53
Ox Hill 6	1	41N32	72w05	4:48:20
Oxoboxo Lake 6	1	41N28	72w10	4:48:40
Pachaug 6	1	41N35'03	71w56'28	4:47:46
Packer 8	1	41N39'59	71w57'10	4:47:49
Packerville 8	1	41N42	71w58	4:47:52
Palestine 1	1	41N21'56	73w19'13	4:53:17
Palmers Hill 1	1	41N03'49	73w33'59	4:54:16
Palmertown 6	2	41N26'51	72w07'53	4:48:32
Paradise Green 1	2	41N12	73w08	4:52:32
Pawcatuck 6	1	41N22'38	71w50'03	4:47:20
Paynes Corners 5	2	41N22'43	73w00'06	4:52:00
Pegville 2	1	41N58'23	72w48'26	4:51:14
Pemberwick 1	1	41N01'32	73w39'40	4:54:39
Pequabuck 3	3	41N40'22	72w59'37	4:51:58
Pequot Indian Reservation 6	1	41N27'26	71w58'17	4:47:53
Perkins Corner 8	1	41N44'22	72w15'36	4:49:02
Phoenixville 8	1	41N52'37	72w05'11	4:48:21
Pine Bridge 5	1	41N25'41	73w04'05	4:52:16
Pine Grove 3	1	42N00'00	73w21'18	4:53:25
Pine Grove 6	1	41N20'10	72w11'08	4:48:45
Pine Hill 2	1	41N51'44	72w48'44	4:51:15
Pine Meadow 3	1	41N52'35	72w58'03	4:51:52
Pine Orchard 5	2	41N16'01	72w46'39	4:51:07
Pine Rock Park 1	1	41N15'42	73w05'45	4:52:23
Pineville 8	1	41N52'58	71w51'06	4:47:24
Pinneys Corners 1	1	41N11'11	73w31'23	4:54:06
Plainfield 8	1	41N40'35	71w54'56	4:47:40
Plainville 2	1	41N40'28	72w51'31	4:51:26
Plantsville 2	1	41N35'01	72w53'34	4:51:34
Platts Mills 5	1	41N30'52	73w03'09	4:52:13
Plattsville 1	2	41N13'22	73w15'24	4:53:02
Plaza 5	1	41N34	73w02	4:52:08
Pleasant Acres 1	4	41N25'51	73w26'53	4:53:48
Pleasant Valley 3	1	41N54'44	72w59'18	4:51:57
Pleasant Valley 6	2	41N22'17	72w04'26	4:48:18
Pleasure Beach 6	2	41N18'36	72w08'45	4:48:35
Plymouth 3	3	41N40'19	73w03'12	4:52:13
Pocotopaug Lake 4	1	41N35'54	72w30'39	4:50:03
Podunk 5	1	41N19'20	72w39'08	4:50:37
Point Beach 5	2	41N13	73w03	4:52:12
Point O'Woods 6	1	41N17'35	72w15'18	4:49:01
Pomeraug 3	1	41N31'34	73w12'41	4:52:51
Pomfret 8	1	41N53'51	71w57'47	4:47:51
Pomfret Center 8	1	41N53'14	71w57'45	4:47:51
Pomfret Landing 8	1	41N50'58	71w56'11	4:47:45
Pomperaug 3	1	41N33	73w12	4:52:48
Pond Meadow 4	1	41N19'39	72w28'06	4:49:52
Pond Point 5	2	41N13	73w03	4:52:12
Ponset 4	1	41N27'54	72w33'24	4:50:14
Ponus 1	1	41N07'36	73w31'13	4:54:05
Pootatuck Park 1	1	41N25'45	73w15'37	4:53:02
Poquetanuck 6	1	41N29'11	72w02'27	4:48:10
Poquonock 2	2	41N54'17	72w40'45	4:50:43
Poquonock Bridge 6	2	41N20'42	72w01'31	4:48:06
Portland 4	3	41N34'22	72w38'28	4:50:34
Pratts Corner 2	1	41N33'29	72w51'14	4:51:25
Presidential 2	1	41N59	72w34	4:50:16
Preston 6	1	41N31	72w01	4:48:04
Prospect 5	1	41N30'08	72w58'45	4:51:55
Prospect Beach 5	2	41N16	72w58	4:51:52
Prospect Hill 2	1	41N56	72w37	4:50:28
Puddle Town 3	1	41N52'00	72w57'31	4:51:50
Putnam 8	2	41N54'54	71w54'34	4:47:38
Putnam Heights 8	1	41N53'32	71w52'07	4:47:28
Putney 1	2	41N14'06	73w06'44	4:52:27
Quaddick 8	1	41N56'18	71w49'16	4:47:17
Quaker Farms 5	1	41N25'39	73w09'22	4:52:37
Quaker Hill 6	2	41N24'12	72w06'23	4:48:26
Quakertown 6	1	41N24'36	72w00'17	4:48:01
Quarryville 7	1	41N51'52	72w25'18	4:49:41
Quebec 8	1	41N47'57	71w53'18	4:47:33
Quinebaug 8	1	42N01'25	71w57'01	4:47:48
Quinnipiac 5	1	41N26'00	72w50'04	4:51:20
Rainbow 2	2	41N55'05	72w41'35	4:50:46
Rawson 8	1	41N48'25	72w04'11	4:48:17
Redding 1	1	41N18'09	73w23'02	4:53:32
Redding Ridge 1	1	41N18'50	73w21'03	4:53:24
Reynolds Bridge 3	1	41N39'26	73w04'49	4:52:19
Richards Corner 5	1	41N28'57	72w54'20	4:51:37
Ridgebury 1	1	41N21'38	73w31'29	4:54:06
Ridgefield 1	1	41N16'53	73w29'55	4:54:00
Ridgeway 1	1	41N04'00	73w33'22	4:54:13
Ridgewood 4	1	41N15'34	72w30'36	4:50:02
Ridgewood 6	2	41N18'45	72w06'17	4:48:25
Ridgewood Park 6	2	41N20	72w09	4:48:36
Rising Corner 2	1	42N02'09	72w42'45	4:50:51
Riverbank 1	1	41N06'17	73w35'13	4:54:21
Rivercliff 5	2	41N11'41	73w06'17	4:52:25
Riverdale 4	1	41N33'41	72w35'00	4:50:20
River Glen 2	1	41N44'41	72w51'47	4:51:27
Riverside 1	1	41N02'01	73w34'43	4:54:19
Riverside 2	1	41N49	72w55	4:51:40
Riverside 5	1	41N23'17	73w10'23	4:52:42
Riversville 1	1	41N03'40	73w40'32	4:54:42
Riverton 3	1	41N57'46	73w01'02	4:52:04
Robertsville 3	1	41N58'44	73w02'40	4:52:11
Rockfall 4	3	41N32	72w42	4:50:48
Rockland 5	1	41N24'42	72w39'23	4:50:38
Rock Landing 4	1	41N29'49	72w31'15	4:50:05
Rock Raymond 1	2	41N17'27	73w16'29	4:53:06
Rock Ridge 1	1	41N02'06	73w38'47	4:54:35
Rockville 7	3	41N52'00	72w27'00	4:49:48
Rocky Glen 1	1	41N25'57	73w16'17	4:53:05
Rocky Hill 4	2	41N39'53	72w38'23	4:50:34
Rogers 8	1	41N50'25	71w54'24	4:47:38
Romford 3	1	41N40'31	73w17'29	4:53:10
Roseland Park 8	1	41N57'01	71w57'24	4:47:50
Round Beach 1	3	41N04'44	73w23'47	4:53:35
Round Hill 1	1	41N02	73w37	4:54:28
Rowayton 1	1	41N03'50	73w26'13	4:53:45
Roxbury 3	1	41N33'23	73w18'33	4:53:14
Roxbury Falls 3	1	41N30'30	73w18'40	4:53:15
Roxbury Station 3	1	41N33'27	73w19'54	4:53:20
Russian Village 3	1	41N26'46	73w15'10	4:53:01
Sachem Head 5	2	41N14'45	72w42'15	4:50:49
Salem 6	1	41N29'25	72w16'33	4:49:06
Salem Four Corners 6	1	41N34	72w20	4:49:20
Salisbury 3	1	41N59'00	73w25'18	4:53:41
Sandy Beach 3	1	41N41'40	73w13'12	4:52:53
Sandy Hook 1	1	41N25'12	73w16'57	4:53:08
Sandy Point 6	2	41N20'54	72w11'04	4:48:44
Sanfordtown 1	1	41N17'41	73w21'46	4:53:27
Saugatuck 1	3	41N07'21	73w22'14	4:53:29
Saugatuck Shores 1	3	41N05'50	73w22'16	4:53:29
Saunders Point 6	1	41N20'27	72w11'10	4:48:45
Savin Rock 5	2	41N16	72w58	4:51:52
Saybrook Manor 4	1	41N17'07	72w23'58	4:49:36
Saybrook Point 4	1	41N17'02	72w21'16	4:49:25
Scantic 2	1	41N53'46	72w33'11	4:50:13
Scitico 2	1	41N59'05	72w30'58	4:50:04
Scotland 8	1	41N41'54	72w04'55	4:48:20
Sea Bluff 5	2	41N15'14	72w57'55	4:51:52
Seaside 6	2	41N18'14	72w07'59	4:48:32
Seaview Beach 5	1	41N16'23	72w35'04	4:50:20
Secret Lake 2	1	41N49	72w50	4:51:20
Sellecks Corners 1	1	41N11'07	73w32'04	4:54:08
Seymour 5	1	41N23'48	73w04'35	4:52:18
Shady Rest 5	1	41N26'59	73w16'36	4:53:06
Shailerville 4	1	41N28'15	72w29'45	4:49:59
Sharon 3	1	41N52'45	73w28'38	4:53:55
Sharon Valley 3	1	41N53'02	73w29'34	4:53:58
Shelton 1	1	41N18'59	73w05'37	4:52:22
Sherman 1	1	41N34'45	73w29'46	4:53:59
Sherman Corner 7	1	41N46'13	72w08'12	4:48:33
Sherwood Manor 2	1	41N59	72w34	4:50:16
Shewville 6	1	41N29'18	71w59'42	4:47:59
Shippan Point 1	1	41N01'40	73w31'27	4:54:06
Shorehaven 1	3	41N05'30	73w23'20	4:53:33
Short Beach 5	2	41N15'41	72w50'27	4:51:22
Silver Beach 5	2	41N12'06	73w03'53	4:52:16
Silvermine 1	1	41N09'05	73w26'44	4:53:47
Simsbury 2	1	41N52'33	72w48'06	4:51:12
Skiff Mountain 3	1	41N43	73w29	4:53:56
Smith Corner 6	1	41N35'29	72w07'46	4:48:31
Snug Harbor 1	4	41N26'34	73w27'05	4:53:48
Sodom 3	1	42N02'09	73w17'53	4:53:12
Somers 7	1	41N59'07	72w26'48	4:49:47
Somersville 7	1	41N58'58	72w29'18	4:49:57
Sound View 6	1	41N17'20	72w17'17	4:49:09
South Britain 5	1	41N28'15	73w15'07	4:53:00
Southbury 5	1	41N28'53	73w12'49	4:52:51
South Canaan 3	1	41N57'42	73w20'02	4:53:20
South Canterbury 8	1	41N42	71w58	4:47:52
South Chaplin 8	1	41N46'36	72w07'54	4:48:32
South Coventry 7	1	41N46	72w19	4:49:16
South Ellsworth 3	1	41N49'08	73w25'47	4:53:43
South End 1	1	41N02'23	73w32'15	4:54:09
South End 5	2	41N14'38	72w53'40	4:51:35
South Farms 4	3	41N33'15	72w38'36	4:50:34
Southford 5	1	41N27'52	73w09'44	4:52:39
South Glastonbury 2	2	41N40'01	72w35'50	4:50:23
South Glenwoods 6	2	41N26	72w05	4:48:20
Southington 2	1	41N35'47	72w52'41	4:51:31
South Kent 3	1	41N40'46	73w28'16	4:53:53
South Killingly 8	1	41N47'28	71w50'01	4:47:20
South Lyme 6	1	41N18'19	72w15'32	4:49:02
South Manchester 2	1	41N47	72w31	4:50:04
South Meriden 5	3	41N30'58	72w50'03	4:51:20
South Norfolk 3	1	41N55'23	73w12'28	4:52:50
South Norwalk 1	3	41N05'37	73w25'09	4:53:41
Southport 1	2	41N08'11	73w17'02	4:53:08
South Wethersfield 4	2	41N41'25	72w39'22	4:50:37
South Willington 7	1	41N51'19	72w18'07	4:49:12
South Wilton 1	1	41N10'05	73w25'00	4:53:40
South Windham 8	1	41N40'46	72w10'15	4:48:41
South Windsor 2	1	41N49'25	72w37'18	4:50:29
Southwood Acres 2	1	41N59	72w34	4:50:16
South Woodstock 8	1	41N56'20	71w57'36	4:47:50
Sport Hill 1	2	41N14	73w16	4:53:04
Sprague 6	1	41N37	72w05	4:48:20
Springdale 1	1	41N05'16	73w31'29	4:54:06
Spring Glen 5	2	41N21'48	72w54'33	4:51:38
Spring Hill 7	1	41N47'13	72w13'28	4:48:54
Stafford 7	1	41N59'05	72w17'22	4:49:09
Stafford Springs 7	1	41N57'15	72w18'10	4:49:13
Staffordville 7	1	41N59'38	72w15'33	4:49:02
Stamford 1	1	41N03'12	73w32'21	4:54:09
Stanwich 1	1	41N07'10	73w37'11	4:54:29
State Line 7	1	41N57	72w18	4:49:12
Stepney 1	1	41N18'14	73w15'17	4:53:01
Sterling 8	1	41N42'27	71w49'45	4:47:19
Sterling Hill 8	1	41N43	71w53	4:47:32
Stetson Corner 8	1	41N47'10	72w00'30	4:48:02
Stevenson 1	1	41N22'59	73w11'06	4:52:44
Stillmans Corner 2	1	41N33'45	72w51'53	4:51:28
Stonington 6	1	41N20'09	71w54'23	4:47:38
Stony Corners 2	1	41N49	72w50	4:51:20
Stony Creek 5	2	41N15'52	72w44'48	4:50:59
Storrs 7	1	41N48'30	72w15'00	4:49:00
Straitsville 5	1	41N28'11	73w02'01	4:52:08
Stratfield 1	2	41N12'24	73w14'11	4:52:57
Stratford 1	2	41N11'04	73w08'01	4:52:32
Submarine Base 6	2	41N21	72w03	4:48:12
Suffield 2	1	41N58'54	72w39'04	4:50:36
Sunnyside 1	1	41N17'50	73w04'23	4:52:18
Sunrise Hill 5	2	41N23	73w00	4:52:00
Ta'agan Point 1	4	41N26'15	73w27'13	4:53:49
Taconic 3	1	42N02'08	73w24'30	4:53:38
Taftville 6	1	41N34'11	72w02'52	4:48:11
Talcott Village 2	1	41N43	72w50	4:51:20
Talcottville 7	1	41N49'07	72w30'04	4:50:00
Talmadge Hill 1	1	41N07'07	73w29'58	4:54:00
Tariffville 2	1	41N54'31	72w45'38	4:51:03
Taylor Corners 1	4	41N26'48	73w31'31	4:54:06
Terminal 5	2	41N19	72w55	4:51:40
Terryville 3	3	41N40'41	73w00'41	4:52:03
Thames View 6	2	41N23'40	72w06'34	4:48:26
Thamesville 6	1	41N30'36	72w05'19	4:48:21
The Cedars 3	1	41N55'56	73w27'20	4:53:49
The Dock 1	2	41N12	73w08	4:52:32
Thomaston 3	1	41N40'26	73w04'25	4:52:18
Thompson 8	1	41N57'31	71w51'47	4:47:27
Thompsonville 2	1	41N59'49	72w35'58	4:50:24
Thralltown 2	2	41N52'56	72w39'19	4:50:37
Titicus 1	1	41N17'32	73w30'14	4:54:01
Toilsome Hill 1	2	41N12'07	73w13'23	4:52:54
Tokeneke 1	1	41N04'00	73w28'00	4:53:52
Tolland 7	1	41N52'17	72w22'09	4:49:29
Tolles 3	3	41N38'39	73w00'36	4:52:02
Topstone 1	1	41N17'45	73w26'58	4:53:48
Torringford 3	1	41N49'16	73w04'50	4:52:19
Torrington 3	1	41N48'02	73w07'18	4:52:29
Totoket 5	2	41N19'42	72w48'50	4:51:15
Town Hill 3	1	41N51'11	72w59'58	4:52:00
Town Landing 6	1	41N17'45	72w19'42	4:49:19
Town Line Plaza 2	2	41N40	72w39	4:50:36
Town Plot Hill 5	1	41N32'20	73w03'12	4:52:13
Tracy 5	1	41N30'08	72w48'44	4:51:15
Trails Corner 6	2	41N20'29	72w03'28	4:48:14
Tri-City Shopping Plaza 7	1	41N51	72w28	4:49:52
Trumbull 1	2	41N14'34	73w12'04	4:52:48
Tunxis Hill 1	2	41N10'34	73w14'28	4:52:58
Turkey Cobble 3	1	41N55'44	73w11'35	4:52:46
Turn of River 1	1	41N06'11	73w32'55	4:54:12
Twin Lakes 3	1	42N01'06	73w23'14	4:53:33
Tyler Lake Heights 3	1	41N50'16	73w16'15	4:53:05
Uncasville 6	2	41N26'04	72w06'37	4:48:26
Union 7	1	41N59'27	72w09'28	4:48:38
Union City 5	1	41N29'48	73w02'56	4:52:12
Unionville 2	1	41N45'28	72w53'12	4:51:33
Upper Merryall 3	1	41N39'44	73w25'21	4:53:41
Upper Stepney 1	1	41N19'21	73w15'56	4:53:04
U S Coast Guard Academy 6	2	41N21	72w06	4:48:24
Vernon 7	1	41N49'07	72w28'48	4:49:55
Vernon Center 7	3	41N50'13	72w28'21	4:49:53
Versailles 6	1	41N36'06	72w02'16	4:48:09
Village Hill 6	1	41N40'59	72w14'19	4:48:57
Voluntown 6	1	41N34'14	71w52'15	4:47:29
Wallingford 5	1	41N27'25	72w49'25	4:51:18
Wallingford Plaza 5	1	41N28	72w49	4:51:16
Walnut Beach 5	2	41N11'35	73w05'01	4:52:20
Walnut Hill 6	1	41N22	72w13	4:48:52
Walnut Tree Hill 1	1	41N25	73w17	4:53:08
Wamphassuc Point 6	1	41N21	71w58	4:47:52
Wapping 2	2	41N49'38	72w33'13	4:50:13
Warehouse Point 2	1	41N55'45	72w37'07	4:50:28
Warren 3	1	41N44'34	73w20'57	4:53:24
Warrenville 8	1	41N51'48	72w09'47	4:48:39
Washington 3	1	41N37'53	73w18'40	4:53:15
Washington Hill 3	1	41N49	72w54	4:51:36
Washington Square 6	1	41N32	72w05	4:48:20
Waterbury 5	1	41N33'29	73w03'07	4:52:12
Waterford 6	2	41N21	72w09	4:48:36
Watertown 3	1	41N36'22	73w07'07	4:52:28
Waterville 5	1	41N35'25	73w03'05	4:52:12
Wauregan 8	1	41N44'39	71w54'35	4:47:38
Wauregan Station 8	1	41N44'29	71w53'47	4:47:35
Wauwecus Hill 6	1	41N32	72w05	4:48:20
Weatogue 2	1	41N51	72w50	4:51:20
Weatogue 3	1	42N02'35	73w20'44	4:53:23
Webster Square Shopping Ctr 2	3	41N38	72w46	4:51:04
Weekeempee 3	1	41N33	73w12	4:52:48
Welles Village 2	2	41N43'40	72w36'00	4:50:24

Place		Latitude	Longitude	Time
Wells Quarter Village 2	2	41N43	72w41	4:50:44
Wellsville 3	1	41N35'49	73w24'55	4:53:40
Wequetequock 6	1	41N21'32	71w52'47	4:47:31
Wesleyan 4	3	41N33	72w39	4:50:36
West Ashford 8	1	41N51'24	72w10'44	4:48:43
West Avon 2	1	41N47'23	72w51'50	4:51:27
West Bantam 3	1	41N44	73w14	4:52:56
Westbrook 4	1	41N17'07	72w26'53	4:49:48
West Cheshire 5	1	41N29'51	72w55'13	4:51:41
Westchester 6	1	41N33'02	72w24'45	4:49:39
West Cornwall 3	1	41N52'17	73w21'44	4:53:27
West End 2	3	41N41	72w56	4:51:44
West Farms Mall 2	1	41N43	72w50	4:51:20
Westfield 4	3	41N35'05	72w42'04	4:50:48
Westford 8	1	41N55'13	72w10'36	4:48:42
West Goshen 3	1	41N49'38	73w15'08	4:53:01
West Granby 2	1	41N57'22	72w50'35	4:51:22
West Haddam 4	1	41N25'49	72w33'36	4:50:14
West Hartford 2	2	41N45'43	72w44'33	4:50:58
West Hartland 2	1	42N00'27	72w58'16	4:51:53
West Haven 5	2	41N16'14	72w56'51	4:51:47
West Lakes 5	2	41N23	72w51	4:51:24
Westminster 8	1	41N42'34	72w01'07	4:48:04
West Morris 3	1	41N41'19	73w15'46	4:53:03
West Mystic 6	1	41N21'02	71w58'57	4:47:56
West Norfolk 3	1	42N00'11	73w13'29	4:52:54
West Norwalk 1	1	41N06'30	73w27'46	4:53:51
Weston 1	1	41N12'03	73w22'52	4:53:31
Westport 1	5	41N08'29	73w21'30	4:53:26
West Putnam Avenue 1	1	41N02	73w37	4:54:28
West Redding 1	1	41N19'35	73w26'05	4:53:44
West Shore 5	2	41N14'32	72w58'16	4:51:53
West Side 6	1	41N32	72w05	4:48:20
West Side Hill 5	1	41N33'14	73w03'42	4:52:15
West Simsbury 2	1	41N52'23	72w51'31	4:51:26
West Stafford 7	1	41N58'14	72w21'20	4:49:25
West Suffield 2	1	41N59'19	72w41'33	4:50:46
West Thompson 8	1	41N56'42	71w54'41	4:47:39
West Torrington 3	1	41N49'06	73w08'39	4:52:35
Westview Acres 5	1	41N24	73w04	4:52:16
Westview Heights 5	1	41N32'07	73w05'41	4:52:23
Westville 5	2	41N19'50	72w58'20	4:51:53
West Wauregan 8	1	41N44'55	71w54'58	4:47:40
West Willington 7	1	41N52'52	72w18'09	4:49:13
Westwood Park 6	1	41N32	72w05	4:48:20
West Woods 3	1	41N48'33	73w28'31	4:53:54
West Woodstock 8	1	41N57'16	72w02'45	4:48:11
Wethersfield 4	2	41N42'51	72w39'11	4:50:37
Wheeler Farms 5	2	41N13	73w03	4:52:12
Whigville 2	3	41N43'59	72w56'33	4:51:46
Whipstick 1	1	41N17	73w30	4:54:00
Whisconier 1	1	41N28	73w23	4:53:32
Whitacres 2	1	41N59	72w34	4:50:16
Whitcomb Hill 3	1	41N49	73w22	4:53:28
White Sands Beach 6	1	41N17'00	72w18'17	4:49:13
Whitings Corner 2	2	41N47'14	72w46'00	4:51:04
Whitneyville 5	2	41N20'39	72w54'46	4:51:39
Wildermere Beach 5	2	41N11'22	73w05'16	4:52:21
Wildmans Landing 1	4	41N25'29	73w27'20	4:53:49
Williams Crossing 6	1	41N39'24	72w09'32	4:48:38
Willimantic 8	1	41N42'38	72w12'31	4:48:50
Willington 7	1	41N52	72w16	4:49:04
Willington Hill 7	1	41N52'30	72w15'52	4:49:03
Willow Point 6	1	41N21	71w58	4:47:52
Wilson 2	2	41N48'43	72w39'28	4:50:38
Wilsonville 8	1	42N00'44	71w53'26	4:47:34
Wilton 1	1	41N11'43	73w26'18	4:53:45
Winchester Center 3	1	41N54'00	73w08'07	4:52:32
Windermere 7	1	41N52'40	72w29'05	4:49:56
Windham 8	1	41N41'59	72w09'27	4:48:38
Winding Lanes 2	1	41N49	72w50	4:51:20
Windsor 2	2	41N51'09	72w38'39	4:50:35
Windsor Locks 2	1	41N55'45	72w37'40	4:50:31
Windsorville 2	1	41N53'27	72w32'09	4:50:09
Winnipauk 1	3	41N08'47	73w25'20	4:53:41
Winsted 3	1	41N55'16	73w03'38	4:52:15
Winthrop 4	1	41N21'42	72w29'21	4:49:57
Wolcott 5	1	41N36'08	72w59'14	4:51:57
Woodbridge 5	2	41N21'09	73w00'32	4:52:02
Woodbury 3	1	41N32'40	73w12'34	4:52:50
Woodmont 5	2	41N13'41	72w59'31	4:51:58
Woodstock 8	1	41N56'54	71w58'28	4:47:54
Woodstock Valley 8	1	41N56'27	72w04'20	4:48:17
Woodtick 5	1	41N34'44	72w58'43	4:51:55
Woodville 3	1	41N42'17	73w17'51	4:53:11
Wopowog 4	1	41N31'23	72w29'08	4:49:57
Wormwood Hill 7	1	41N49'20	72w11'44	4:48:47
Wrightville 3	1	41N49'43	73w08'58	4:52:36
Yale 5	2	41N19	72w56	4:51:44
Yalesville 5	1	41N29'37	72w49'27	4:51:18
Yale University 5	2	41N19	72w56	4:51:44
Yantic 6	1	41N33'35	72w07'27	4:48:30
Yelping Hill 3	1	41N54'17	73w17'57	4:53:12
Zoar 1	1	41N25	73w17	4:53:08

TIME TABLES

DE # 1
Before 11/18/1883 LMT
11/18/1883 12:00 EST
3/31/1918 02:00 EWT
10/27/1918 02:00 EST
3/30/1919 02:00 EWT
10/26/1919 02:00 EST
3/28/1920 02:00 EDT
10/31/1920 02:00 EST
4/24/1921 02:00 EDT
9/25/1921 02:00 EST
4/30/1922 02:00 EDT
9/24/1922 02:00 EST
4/29/1923 02:00 EDT
9/30/1923 02:00 EST
4/27/1924 02:00 EDT
9/28/1924 02:00 EST
4/26/1925 02:00 EDT
9/27/1925 02:00 EST
4/25/1926 02:00 EDT
9/26/1926 02:00 EST
4/24/1927 02:00 EDT
9/25/1927 02:00 EST
4/29/1928 02:00 EDT
9/30/1928 02:00 EST
4/28/1929 02:00 EDT
9/29/1929 02:00 EST
4/27/1930 02:00 EDT
9/28/1930 02:00 EST
4/26/1931 02:00 EDT
9/27/1931 02:00 EST
4/24/1932 02:00 EDT
9/25/1932 02:00 EST
4/30/1933 02:00 EDT
9/24/1933 02:00 EST
4/29/1934 02:00 EDT
9/30/1934 02:00 EST
4/28/1935 02:00 EDT
9/29/1935 02:00 EST
4/26/1936 02:00 EDT
9/27/1936 02:00 EST
4/25/1937 02:00 EDT
9/26/1937 02:00 EST
4/24/1938 02:00 EDT
9/25/1938 02:00 EST
4/30/1939 02:00 EDT
9/24/1939 02:00 EST
4/28/1940 02:00 EDT
9/29/1940 02:00 EST
4/27/1941 02:00 EDT
9/28/1941 02:00 EST
2/09/1942 02:00 EWT
9/30/1945 02:00 EST
4/28/1946 02:00 EDT
9/29/1946 02:00 EST
4/27/1947 02:00 EDT
9/28/1947 02:00 EST
4/25/1948 02:00 EDT
9/26/1948 02:00 EST
4/24/1949 02:00 EDT
9/25/1949 02:00 EST
4/30/1950 02:00 EDT
9/24/1950 02:00 EST
4/29/1951 02:00 EDT
9/30/1951 02:00 EST
4/27/1952 02:00 EDT
9/28/1952 02:00 EST
4/26/1953 02:00 EDT
9/27/1953 02:00 EST
4/25/1954 02:00 EDT
9/26/1954 02:00 EST
4/24/1955 02:00 EDT
9/25/1955 02:00 EST
4/29/1956 02:00 US#2

DE # 2
Before 11/18/1883 LMT
11/18/1883 12:00 EST
3/31/1918 02:00 EWT
10/27/1918 02:00 EST
3/30/1919 02:00 EWT
10/26/1919 02:00 EST
2/09/1942 02:00 EWT
9/30/1945 02:00 EST
4/28/1946 02:00 DE#1
4/29/1956 02:00 US#2

DE # 3
Before 11/18/1883 LMT
11/18/1883 12:00 EST
3/31/1918 02:00 EWT
10/27/1918 02:00 EST
3/30/1919 02:00 EWT
10/26/1919 02:00 EST
2/09/1942 02:00 EWT
9/30/1945 02:00 EST
4/27/1947 02:00 US#3

DE # 4
Before 11/18/1883 LMT
11/18/1883 12:00 EST
3/31/1918 02:00 EWT
10/27/1918 02:00 EST
3/30/1919 02:00 EWT
10/26/1919 02:00 EST
2/09/1942 02:00 EWT
9/30/1945 02:00 EST
4/25/1948 02:00 US#3

DE # 5
Before 11/18/1883 LMT
11/18/1883 12:00 EST
3/31/1918 02:00 EWT
10/27/1918 02:00 EST
3/30/1919 02:00 EWT
10/26/1919 02:00 EST
2/09/1942 02:00 EWT
9/30/1945 02:00 EST
4/29/1951 02:00 DE#1
4/29/1956 02:00 US#2

DE # 6
Before 11/18/1883 LMT
11/18/1883 12:00 EST
3/31/1918 02:00 EWT
10/27/1918 02:00 EST
3/30/1919 02:00 EWT
10/26/1919 02:00 EST
2/09/1942 02:00 EWT
9/30/1945 02:00 EST
4/26/1953 02:00 US#3

DE # 7
Before 11/18/1883 LMT
11/18/1883 12:00 EST
3/31/1918 02:00 EWT
10/27/1918 02:00 EST
3/30/1919 02:00 EWT
10/26/1919 02:00 EST
2/09/1942 02:00 EWT
9/30/1945 02:00 EST
4/28/1946 02:00 EDT
9/29/1946 02:00 EST
4/27/1947 02:00 EDT
9/28/1947 02:00 EST
4/25/1948 02:00 EDT
9/26/1948 02:00 EST
4/24/1949 02:00 EDT
9/25/1949 02:00 EST
4/30/1950 02:00 EDT
9/24/1950 02:00 EST
4/29/1951 02:00 EDT
9/30/1951 02:00 EST
4/27/1952 02:00 EDT
9/28/1952 02:00 EST
4/24/1955 02:00 EDT
9/25/1955 02:00 EST
4/29/1956 02:00 US#2

DE # 8
Before 11/18/1883 LMT
11/18/1883 12:00 EST
3/31/1918 02:00 EWT
10/27/1918 02:00 EST
3/30/1919 02:00 EWT
10/26/1919 02:00 EST
2/09/1942 02:00 EWT
9/30/1945 02:00 EST
4/27/1947 02:00 EDT
9/28/1947 02:00 EST
4/25/1948 02:00 EDT
9/26/1948 02:00 EST
4/24/1949 02:00 EDT
9/25/1949 02:00 EST
4/30/1950 02:00 EDT
9/24/1950 02:00 EST
4/29/1951 02:00 EDT
9/30/1951 02:00 EST
4/27/1952 02:00 EDT
9/28/1952 02:00 EST
4/24/1955 02:00 EDT
9/25/1955 02:00 EST
4/29/1956 02:00 US#2

DE # 9
Before 11/18/1883 LMT
11/18/1883 12:00 EST
3/31/1918 02:00 EWT
10/27/1918 02:00 EST
3/30/1919 02:00 EWT
10/26/1919 02:00 EST
2/09/1942 02:00 EWT
9/30/1945 02:00 EST
4/28/1946 02:00 EDT
9/29/1946 02:00 EST
4/25/1948 02:00 DE#1
4/29/1956 02:00 US#2

DE # 10
Before 11/18/1883 LMT
11/18/1883 12:00 EST
3/31/1918 02:00 EWT
10/27/1918 02:00 EST
3/30/1919 02:00 EWT
10/26/1919 02:00 EST
4/26/1931 02:00 DE#1
4/29/1956 02:00 US#2

DE # 11
Before 11/18/1883 LMT
11/18/1883 12:00 EST
3/31/1918 02:00 EWT
10/27/1918 02:00 EST
3/30/1919 02:00 EWT
10/26/1919 02:00 EST
2/09/1942 02:00 EWT
9/30/1945 02:00 EST
4/28/1946 02:00 EDT
9/29/1946 02:00 EST
4/26/1953 02:00 DE#1
4/29/1956 02:00 US#2

DE # 12
Before 11/18/1883 LMT
11/18/1883 12:00 EST
3/31/1918 02:00 EWT
10/27/1918 02:00 EST
3/30/1919 02:00 EWT
10/26/1919 02:00 EST
4/24/1938 02:00 DE#1
4/29/1956 02:00 US#2

DE # 13
Before 11/18/1883 LMT
11/18/1883 12:00 DE#2
4/27/1947 02:00 DE#1
4/29/1956 02:00 US#2

DE # 14
Before 11/18/1883 LMT
11/18/1883 12:00 DE#2
4/25/1948 02:00 DE#1
4/29/1956 02:00 US#2

DE # 15
Before 11/18/1883 LMT
11/18/1883 12:00 DE#2
4/26/1953 02:00 DE#1
4/29/1956 02:00 US#2

DE # 16
Before 11/18/1883 LMT
11/18/1883 12:00 EST
3/31/1918 02:00 EWT
10/27/1918 02:00 EST
3/30/1919 02:00 EWT
10/26/1919 02:00 EST
2/09/1942 02:00 EWT
9/30/1945 02:00 EST
4/24/1955 02:00 EDT
9/25/1955 02:00 EST
4/29/1956 02:00 US#2

COUNTIES

1 Kent　2 New Castle　3 Sussex

Abbotts Mill 3 9 38N53'11 75w28'37 5:01:54
Adams Crossroads 3 7 38N47'50 75w42'06 5:02:48
Adamsville 1 7 38N49'53 75w41'22 5:02:45
Addick Estates 2 1 39N48'10 75w27'00 5:01:48
Afton 2 1 39N49'37 75w28'52 5:01:55
Airport Villa 2 1 39N41 75w34 5:02:16
Alapocas 2 1 39N46'15 75w33'35 5:02:14
Alban Park 2 1 39N43'45 75w34'30 5:02:18
Albertson 2 1 39N44'25 75w37'40 5:02:31
Albertson Park 2 1 39N44 75w39 5:02:36
Albion 2 1 39N42'50 75w39'45 5:02:39
Analine Village 2 1 39N48 75w28 5:01:52
Anderson Crossroads 3 6 38N51'31 75w22'13 5:01:29
Andersons Corner 3 16 38N41'55 75w15'35 5:01:02
Andrewsville 1 7 38N51'41 75w38'07 5:02:32
Anglesey 2 1 39N45'32 75w36'59 5:02:28
Angola Beach 3 16 38N43 75w17 5:01:08
Angola by the Bay 3 16 38N40'15 75w10'30 5:00:42
Angola Landing 3 16 38N38'38 75w07'38 5:00:31
Anna Acres 3 16 38N43 75w05 5:00:20
Anneville 1 1 39N07'45 75w31'10 5:02:05
Arbour Park 2 10 39N39'15 75w45'55 5:03:04
Arc Corner 2 10 39N43'19 75w46'26 5:03:06
Arden 2 1 39N48'33 75w29'13 5:01:57
Ardencroft 2 1 39N48'15 75w29'30 5:01:58
Ardentown 2 1 39N48'30 75w29'00 5:01:56
Argo Corners 3 6 38N52'17 75w20'45 5:01:23
Armstrong 2 12 39N28'50 75w43'01 5:02:52
Arundel 2 1 39N44'10 75w40'05 5:02:40
Ashbourne Hills 2 1 39N48'35 75w28'05 5:01:52
Ashland 2 1 39N47'59 75w39'27 5:02:38
Ashley 2 1 39N43'45 75w35'00 5:02:20
Atlanta 3 16 38N42'31 75w40'42 5:02:43
Atlanta Estates 3 16 38N39'50 75w38'00 5:02:32
Auburn Hills 2 10 39N48'15 75w41'35 5:02:46
Augustine 2 1 39N45'50 75w33'15 5:02:13
Augustine Beach 2 12 39N31 75w35 5:02:20
Avalon 2 1 39N43'50 75w37'20 5:02:29
Bacon 3 4 38N27 75w35 5:02:20
Bacons 3 6 39N05'11 75w34'12 5:02:17
Baileys Landing 3 2 38N34'20 75w38'38 5:02:35
Baldton 2 1 39N41 75w34 5:02:16
Barkers Landing 1 6 39N05'06 75w27'27 5:01:50
Barkley 2 1 39N49'55 75w31'08 5:02:05
Basin Corner 2 1 39N40'50 75w35'25 5:02:22
Bayard 3 4 38N30'01 75w07'55 5:00:32
Bayview Manor 2 1 39N38'20 75w36'45 5:02:27
Bay View Park 3 16 38N30'27 75w03'35 5:00:14
Bayville 3 3 38N28'06 75w05'21 5:00:21
Bay Vista 3 3 38N41'50 75w05'53 5:00:24
Bear 2 12 39N37'45 75w39'31 5:02:38
Beaver Brook 2 1 39N41 75w34 5:02:16
Beaver Dam Heights 3 16 38N39'15 75w35'20 5:02:21
Beaver Valley 2 1 39N50'21 75w33'52 5:02:15
Beech Haven 1 1 39N11'45 75w35'45 5:02:23
Bellefonte 2 1 39N45'58 75w30'35 5:02:02
Bellevue 2 1 39N46'15 75w29'02 5:01:56
Bellevue Manor 2 1 39N46 75w30 5:02:00
Belltown 3 16 38N44'49 75w10'42 5:00:43
Belmoor 2 1 39N43'30 75w35'35 5:02:22
Belvidere 2 1 39N43'19 75w36'57 5:02:28
Bennum 3 4 38N42'40 75w18'52 5:01:15
Ben Robins Landing 3 16 38N39'29 75w09'25 5:00:38
Berrytown 1 3 39N00'45 75w35'40 5:02:23
Bestfield 2 1 39N43'10 75w36'30 5:02:26
Bethany Beach 3 16 38N32'22 75w03'20 5:00:13
Bethel 1 1 39N14'03 75w34'55 5:02:20
Bethel 3 16 38N34'14 75w37'11 5:02:29
Bethesda 1 6 39N08'15 75w41'35 5:02:46
Bicentennial Village 1 1 39N09'55 75w33'15 5:02:13
Biddles Corner 2 12 39N31'30 75w38'58 5:02:36
Big Oak Corners 1 11 39N16'10 75w35'20 5:02:21
Big Pine 1 7 38N51'02 75w41'41 5:02:47
Big Stone Beach 1 9 38N55 75w22 5:01:28
Binns Village 2 10 39N41 75w43 5:02:52
Birchwood Park 2 10 39N40'35 75w41'25 5:02:46
Birds Corner 2 12 39N33'48 75w38'26 5:02:34
Bishops Corner 1 6 39N13'25 75w34'34 5:02:18
Blackbird 2 14 39N22'15 75w39'34 5:02:38
Blackbird Landing 2 14 39N23'20 75w38'10 5:02:33
Black Hog Landing 3 16 38N46'26 75w11'27 5:00:46
Blackiston 1 2 39N16'14 75w42'03 5:02:48
Blackwater 3 16 38N32'45 75w09'45 5:00:39
Blackwater Beach 3 16 38N34'48 75w09'29 5:00:38
Blades 3 16 38N38'08 75w36'37 5:02:26
Blanchard 3 7 38N49'14 75w39'09 5:02:37
Blue Ball 2 1 39N46'38 75w32'42 5:02:11
Blue Hen Mall 1 1 39N09 75w31 5:02:04
Blue Rock Manor 2 1 39N47'45 75w32'35 5:02:10
Bookhammer Landing 3 16 38N40'40 75w08'11 5:00:33
Bottom Hills 3 16 38N37'02 75w04'17 5:00:17
Bowen Landing 3 9 38N55'13 75w24'34 5:01:38
Bowers 1 6 39N04 75w24 5:01:36
Bowers Beach 1 9 39N03'35 75w24'06 5:01:36
Boxwood 2 1 39N43'35 75w35'50 5:02:23
Boyds Corner 2 12 39N30'00 75w38'58 5:02:36
Brackenville 2 12 39N46'50 75w41'00 5:02:44
Brackenville Woods 2 12 39N47'25 75w39'42 5:02:39
Brack-Ex 2 1 39N45 75w35 5:02:20
Branchview 3 16 38N38'23 75w40'12 5:02:41
Brandon 2 1 39N49'33 75w31'28 5:02:06
Brandywine 2 1 39N49'46 75w32'05 5:02:08
Brandywine Estates 2 1 39N47'20 75w29'00 5:01:56
Brandywine Hills 2 1 39N46'05 75w31'30 5:02:06
Brandywine Springs 2 1 39N44'40 75w38'40 5:02:35
Brandywine Springs Manor 2 1 39N44'55 75w38'15 5:02:33
Brandywood 2 1 39N49'15 75w30'30 5:02:02
Breezewood 1 3 39N03'22 75w33'19 5:02:13
Breezewood 2 10 39N41 75w43 5:02:52
Brenford 1 11 39N15'23 75w36'40 5:02:27
Briar Park 1 1 39N06'22 75w32'40 5:02:11
Brick Store 2 11 39N19'19 75w34'23 5:02:18
Bridgeville 3 3 38N44'33 75w36'17 5:02:25
Bridgeville Manor 3 3 38N44'00 75w35'45 5:02:23
Broad Acres 3 16 38N38'23 75w34'34 5:02:18
Broad Creek 3 6 38N35'08 75w35'03 5:02:20
Broadkill Beach 3 16 38N49'41 75w12'44 5:00:51
Brookbend 2 10 39N41 75w43 5:02:52
Brookdale Heights 1 1 39N05'02 75w29'34 5:01:58
Brookfield 1 1 39N05'46 75w32'20 5:02:09
Brookhaven 2 10 39N41 75w43 5:02:52
Brookhill Farms 2 12 39N46'33 75w41'10 5:02:45
Brookland Terrace 2 1 39N44'36 75w37'26 5:02:30
Brookside 2 10 39N40'01 75w43'38 5:02:55
Brookside Park 2 10 39N40 75w43 5:02:52
Brookview Apartments 2 1 39N48 75w28 5:01:52
Browns Corner 1 1 39N05'28 75w31'09 5:02:05
Brownsville 1 16 38N54'49 75w40'48 5:02:43
Bryan Park 3 16 38N41'23 75w35'15 5:02:21
Bryans Store 3 4 38N35'33 75w24'35 5:01:38
Buck Hill Landing 3 4 38N33'35 75w13'20 5:00:53
Buckingham Heights 2 1 39N48'23 75w29'50 5:01:59
Bullseye 3 16 38N35'30 75w13'25 5:00:54
Bunting 3 3 38N27'48 75w09'16 5:00:37
Burwood 1 1 39N05'34 75w33'44 5:02:15
Bush Manor 1 1 39N12'28 75w33'49 5:02:15

Buttonwood 2 1 39N41'00 75w33'25 5:02:14
Cains Landing 1 9 38N57'28 75w21'37 5:01:26
Calhoun Landing 3 16 38N35'33 75w07'15 5:00:29
Camden 1 1 39N06'48 75w32'32 5:02:10
Canby Park Estates 2 1 39N44'20 75w34'55 5:02:20
Cannon 3 6 38N41'58 75w36'55 5:02:28
Canterbury 1 3 39N02'33 75w33'21 5:02:13
Canterbury Hills 2 1 39N45'45 75w39'15 5:02:37
Capitol Green 1 1 39N09'18 75w31'02 5:02:04
Capitol Park 1 1 39N08'29 75w30'16 5:02:01
Caravel Farms 2 15 39N35'45 75w43'15 5:02:53
Cardiff 2 1 39N45 75w33 5:02:12
Carlisle Village 1 1 39N11'15 75w34'45 5:02:19
Carpenter 2 1 39N49'06 75w27'53 5:01:52
Carpenters Corner 3 16 38N44'33 75w09'02 5:00:36
Carrcroft 2 1 39N47'15 75w30'23 5:02:02
Carrcroft Crest 2 1 39N47'30 75w30'15 5:02:01
Carter 1 1 39N09 75w31 5:02:04
Carter Development 1 1 39N07'11 75w31'49 5:02:07
Casson Corner 1 1 39N09'38 75w36'31 5:02:26
Castle Hills 2 1 39N41'11 75w33'54 5:02:16
Catalina Gardens 2 10 39N39'05 75w44'45 5:02:59
Cave Colony 3 16 38N45'50 75w17'25 5:01:10
Cedarbrook Acres 1 2 39N16'45 75w36'35 5:02:26
Cedar Heights 2 1 39N43'15 75w37'00 5:02:28
Cedars 2 1 39N44'30 75w38'15 5:02:33
Centennial Village 2 12 39N38'23 75w39'35 5:02:38
Center Green 2 1 39N48 75w28 5:01:52
Centerville 2 12 39N49'17 75w37'01 5:02:28
Central Kent 1 6 39N04 75w33 5:02:12
Central Pencader 2 15 39N35 75w44 5:02:56
Centreville 2 1 39N46 75w35 5:02:20
Chalfonte 2 1 39N45 75w33 5:02:12
Chambersville 2 14 39N21'49 75w34'45 5:02:19
Channin 2 1 39N48 75w31 5:02:04
Chapel Hill 2 10 39N42'05 75w43'53 5:02:56
Chapeltown 1 6 39N05'59 75w41'50 5:02:47
Chaplecroft 1 1 39N07'15 75w32'20 5:02:09
Chatham 2 1 39N48'15 75w31'00 5:02:04
Chelsea Estates 2 1 39N41'30 75w35'45 5:02:23
Cherokee Woods 2 10 39N40'30 75w42'35 5:02:50
Cherry Hill 2 10 39N40'55 75w46'23 5:03:06
Cherrytree Landing 3 16 38N38'35 75w35'29 5:02:22
Chestnut Grove 1 1 39N10'10 75w34'19 5:02:17
Chestnut Hill Estates 2 10 39N40'45 75w42'25 5:02:50
Chestnut Knoll 3 9 38N57'27 75w27'10 5:01:49
Cheswold 1 6 39N13'09 75w35'10 5:02:21
Choate 2 10 39N42'08 75w41'45 5:02:47
Choptank Mills 1 3 39N04'01 75w44'08 5:02:57
Christiana 2 10 39N39'54 75w39'37 5:02:38
Christiana Acres 2 1 39N41'20 75w37'10 5:02:29
Christine Manor 2 10 39N41 75w43 5:02:52
Church Hill 2 1 39N46'20 75w40'25 5:02:42
Church Hill Village 1 9 38N56'04 75w28'34 5:01:54
Clarksons Crossroads 3 16 38N42'52 75w39'10 5:02:37
Clarksville 3 16 38N32'56 75w08'53 5:00:36
Claymont 2 1 39N48'02 75w27'36 5:01:50
Claymont Addition 2 1 39N47'55 75w28'15 5:01:53
Claymont Heights 2 1 39N47'45 75w28'15 5:01:53
Clayton 1 2 39N17'26 75w38'05 5:02:32
Clearfield 2 1 39N48 75w28 5:01:52
Clearview Manor 2 1 39N42'20 75w34'05 5:02:16
Cleland Heights 2 1 39N44'05 75w34'30 5:02:18
Clifton Park Manor 2 1 39N45'30 75w30'45 5:02:03
Club House Landing 3 16 38N33'45 75w05'28 5:00:22
Cocked Hat 3 16 38N46'00 75w36'40 5:02:27
College Park 2 10 39N40'25 75w46'10 5:03:05
Collins Beach 2 14 39N23'07 75w31'20 5:02:05
Collins Park 2 1 39N41'10 75w33'24 5:02:14
Collins Pond Acres 3 16 38N42'38 75w30'50 5:02:03
Colmar Manor 1 2 39N17'00 75w36'35 5:02:26
Colonial Heights 2 1 39N44'50 75w05'05 5:00:20
Colonial Park 2 1 39N45 75w35 5:02:20
Colony Hills 2 1 39N42'40 75w36'35 5:02:26
Columbia 3 4 38N29'52 75w40'41 5:02:43
Concord 2 1 39N45'51 75w32'35 5:02:10
Concord 3 16 38N38'31 75w33'20 5:02:13
Concord Hills 2 1 39N50'02 75w32'45 5:02:11
Concord Manor 2 1 39N48'20 75w32'30 5:02:10
Cool Spring 3 6 38N43'55 75w14'55 5:01:00
Cool Spring Farms 3 16 38N43'33 75w15'10 5:01:01
Cooper Farm 2 1 39N44'25 75w38'30 5:02:34
Coopers Corner 1 1 39N08'20 75w31'20 5:02:05
Corbit 2 12 39N35'17 75w39'35 5:02:38
Corner Ketch 2 1 39N44'57 75w44'29 5:02:58
Cornish Hills 2 10 39N46'15 75w42'30 5:02:50
Cottage Mill 2 10 39N39'12 75w45'18 5:03:01
Cottonpatch Hill 3 16 38N32 75w04 5:00:16
Country Club Estates 3 9 38N54'08 75w24'35 5:01:38
Coventry 2 1 39N40'20 75w38'10 5:02:33
Coverdale Crossroads 3 16 38N42'37 75w31'53 5:02:08
Covered Bridge Farms 2 10 39N42'00 75w47'00 5:03:08
Cowgills Corner 1 1 39N11'45 75w28'50 5:01:55
Cragmere 2 1 39N46 75w30 5:02:00
Cragmere Woods 2 1 39N46 75w30 5:02:00
Craigs Mill 3 16 38N37'36 75w38'54 5:02:36
Cranston Heights 2 1 39N44'00 75w37'51 5:02:31
Cristine Manor 2 10 39N41'20 75w47'00 5:03:08
Crossgates 1 1 39N08'20 75w32'10 5:02:09
Cross Keys 3 16 38N33'57 75w22'06 5:01:28
Dagsboro 3 4 38N32'57 75w14'46 5:00:59
Darley Woods 2 1 39N49'00 75w28'25 5:01:54
Dartmouth Woods 2 1 39N50'00 75w30'40 5:02:03
Davis Corner 1 6 39N09'55 75w40'55 5:02:44
Davis Landing 3 9 38N54'02 75w20'11 5:01:21
Deakyneville 2 11 39N22'09 75w32'41 5:02:11
Deerhurst 2 1 39N47'00 75w32'30 5:02:10
Delaire 2 1 39N46'30 75w29'15 5:01:57
Delaneys Corner 2 14 39N17'57 75w44'51 5:02:59
Delaplane Manor 2 10 39N41'46 75w42'33 5:02:50
Delaware City 2 15 39N34'40 75w35'21 5:02:21
Delaware Heights 2 1 39N49'30 75w37'15 5:02:29
Delaware Junction 2 1 39N43'23 75w34'37 5:02:18
Del Haven Estates 1 6 39N03'21 75w30'04 5:02:00
Delmar 3 4 38N27'23 75w34'39 5:02:19
Delpark Manor 2 1 39N43'00 75w39'30 5:02:38
Del Shire 1 1 39N12'33 75w33'55 5:02:16
Derby Shores 1 6 39N05'11 75w34'12 5:02:17
Devon 2 1 39N49'40 75w32'25 5:02:10
Devonshire 2 1 39N49'30 75w32'25 5:02:10
Dewey Beach 3 3 38N41'34 75w04'30 5:00:18
Dexter Corners 2 14 39N20'04 75w42'00 5:02:48
Dinahs Corner 1 2 39N11'09 75w38'42 5:02:35
Dobbinsville 2 1 39N39'23 75w34'46 5:02:19
Donas Landing 1 1 39N12'45 75w25'53 5:01:44
Douglas Forge 3 16 38N38'45 75w34'40 5:02:19
Dover 1 1 39N09'29 75w31'29 5:02:06
Dover Air Force Base 1 1 39N07 75w29 5:01:56
Doverbrook Gardens 1 1 39N09 75w31 5:02:04
Downs Chapel 1 2 39N12'43 75w43'11 5:02:53
Drawbridge 3 16 38N47'27 75w15'08 5:01:01
Drummond North 2 10 39N41 75w43 5:02:52
Dublin Hill 3 16 38N45'11 75w39'14 5:02:37
Dunleith 2 1 39N42'31 75w33'21 5:02:13
Dunlinden Acres 2 1 39N44'10 75w38'45 5:02:35
Dupont 1 1 39N11'40 75w33'50 5:02:15
Dupont Manor 1 1 39N11'47 75w32'57 5:02:12
Duponts Landing 2 1 39N45'05 75w29'40 5:01:59
Duross Heights 2 1 39N40'50 75w37'22 5:02:29
Dutch Neck Crossroads 1 1 39N17'10 75w30'58 5:02:04
Eagles Nest Landing 2 14 39N20'43 75w33'49 5:02:15
Eastburn Acres 2 10 39N42'20 75w41'00 5:02:44
Eastburn Heights 2 10 39N42'33 75w40'52 5:02:43
East Lake Gardens 1 1 39N10'25 75w31'30 5:02:06
Eastman Heights 3 6 38N53'23 75w25'00 5:01:40
East Minquadale 2 1 39N42'15 75w33'52 5:02:15
Eastover Hills 1 1 39N09 75w31 5:02:04
East Side Village 3 16 38N46'27 75w18'07 5:01:12
Eberton 1 1 39N13'15 75w34'20 5:02:17
Eden Park 2 1 39N41 75w34 5:02:16
Eden Park Gardens 2 1 39N43'12 75w32'38 5:02:11
Edenridge 2 1 39N47'55 75w33'45 5:02:15
Eden Roc 1 1 39N12'00 75w35'49 5:02:23
Edgebrooke 2 10 39N40'10 75w39'47 5:02:39
Edge Hill 1 1 39N10'05 75w31'02 5:02:04
Edgehill Acres 1 1 39N09 75w31 5:02:04
Edgemoor 2 1 39N45'00 75w30'00 5:02:00
Edgemoor Gardens 2 1 39N45'30 75w29'50 5:01:59
Edgemoor Terrace 2 1 39N45'20 75w30'15 5:02:01
Edgewater Acres 3 3 38N28 75w13 5:00:52
Edgewood Hills 2 1 39N45'30 75w30'15 5:02:01
Edwardsville 1 3 38N59'47 75w42'51 5:02:51
Ellendale 3 4 38N48'25 75w25'23 5:01:42
Elliott Heights 2 10 39N41 75w43 5:02:52
Elmhurst 2 1 39N43'50 75w35'25 5:02:22
Elsmere 2 1 39N44'21 75w35'54 5:02:24
English Village 2 10 39N41 75w43 5:02:52
Everetts Corner 1 2 39N12'02 75w44'47 5:02:59
Evergreen Acres 3 9 38N54'20 75w26'53 5:01:48
Fairfax 2 1 39N47'11 75w32'37 5:02:10
Fairfield 2 10 39N41'45 75w46'15 5:03:05
Fairfield Crest 2 10 39N41'45 75w45'45 5:03:03
Fairfield Farms 1 1 39N07'23 75w31'35 5:02:06
Fairmount 3 16 38N39'59 75w13'18 5:00:53
Fairview 1 1 39N10'10 75w32'10 5:02:09
Fairwinds 2 12 39N38'37 75w38'36 5:02:34
Farmington 1 6 38N52'09 75w34'44 5:02:19
Farnhurst 2 1 39N41'35 75w34'40 5:02:19
Faulkland 2 1 39N44'51 75w38'09 5:02:33
Faulkland Heights 2 1 39N44'35 75w37'50 5:02:31
Faulkwoods 2 1 39N45 75w33 5:02:12
Federal 2 10 39N41 75w43 5:02:52
Federalsburg 3 16 38N49'41 75w25'47 5:01:43
Felton 3 3 39N01 75w35 5:02:20
Felton Manor 1 3 39N00'25 75w34'05 5:02:16
Felton Station 1 3 39N00'29 75w34'30 5:02:18
Fennimore Landing 2 14 39N26'42 75w35'34 5:02:22
Fenwick Island 3 16 38N27'44 75w03'06 5:00:12
Fern Hook 2 1 39N42'10 75w34'20 5:02:17
Fernwood 3 16 38N39'12 75w34'20 5:02:17
Ferry Landing 3 4 38N35'32 75w14'40 5:00:59
Fieldsboro 2 14 39N25'02 75w39'32 5:02:38
Fireside Park 2 10 39N41 75w43 5:02:52
Fisher Landing 3 16 38N42'45 75w10'32 5:00:42
Five Points 3 16 38N44'55 75w10'25 5:00:42
Flea Hill 3 4 38N39'44 75w26'10 5:01:45
Fleming Corners 1 16 38N55'06 75w35'54 5:02:24
Flemings Corner 1 16 38N55 75w35 5:02:20
Flemings Landing 2 14 39N21'14 75w32'56 5:02:12
Flemings Landings 2 14 39N24 75w41 5:02:44
Florence 1 6 39N05'00 75w27'50 5:01:51
Foord Landing 3 16 38N50'06 75w15'29 5:01:02
Fords Corner 1 2 39N11'33 75w42'00 5:02:48
Forest 2 14 39N22'00 75w40'40 5:02:43
Forest Brook Glen 2 1 39N43'00 75w36'00 5:02:24
Forest Hills Park 2 1 39N47'15 75w31'30 5:02:06
Forest Landing 1 1 39N07'03 75w30'13 5:02:01
Forest Park 2 1 39N44'15 75w36'30 5:02:26
Fort Delaware 2 15 39N35'22 75w34'00 5:02:16
Fort Saulsbury 3 9 38N56'02 75w19'55 5:01:20
Foulk Woods 2 1 39N48'45 75w31'15 5:02:05
Four Seasons 2 10 39N41 75w43 5:02:52
Fox Chase Park 2 10 39N40'30 75w41'00 5:02:44
Foxfield 2 10 39N40'35 75w46'40 5:03:07
Fox Hall 1 1 39N10'25 75w33'35 5:02:14
Foxhall Courtside 1 1 39N10'36 75w35'17 5:02:21
Fox Meadow Farm 2 12 39N48'10 75w41'55 5:02:48
Frankford 3 4 38N31'02 75w14'07 5:00:56
Frasers Corner 2 10 39N34'47 75w46'00 5:03:04
Frederica 1 16 39N00'32 75w27'58 5:01:52
Galewood 2 1 39N48 75w31 5:02:04
Gams Crest 2 12 39N33'00 75w38'50 5:02:35
Garfield Park 2 1 39N42'07 75w33'22 5:02:13
Garton Development 1 1 39N06'45 75w33'35 5:02:14
Gateway Farms 2 12 39N46'37 75w41'24 5:02:46
Generals Greene 1 1 39N07'33 75w15'00 5:01:00
George Read Village 2 10 39N41 75w43 5:02:52
Georgetown 3 4 38N41'24 75w23'09 5:01:33
Ginns Corner 2 14 39N24 75w41 5:02:44
Glasgow 2 10 39N36'17 75w44'44 5:02:59
Glasgow Pines 2 10 39N37'00 75w42'40 5:02:51
Glen Burne Estate 2 1 39N43'00 75w38'00 5:02:32
Glendale 2 10 39N37'37 75w40'08 5:02:41
Glenville 2 1 39N42'45 75w38'25 5:02:34
Goose Point 2 15 39N32'33 75w46'27 5:03:06
Gordon Heights 2 1 39N45'35 75w30'35 5:02:02
Gordy Estates 2 1 39N43'30 75w36'45 5:02:27
Goslee Mill 3 1 39N43'06 75w11'21 5:00:45
Granogue 2 1 39N49'54 75w35'12 5:02:21
Gravel Hill 3 4 38N42'51 75w18'58 5:01:16
Graylyn Crest 2 1 39N47'45 75w31'00 5:02:04
Greater Newark 2 10 39N41 75w44 5:02:56
Green Acres 2 1 39N47'25 75w29'50 5:01:59
Greenbank 2 1 39N44'20 75w38'10 5:02:33
Green Briar 1 6 39N08'48 75w40'30 5:02:42
Greenbriar 2 1 39N41 75w34 5:02:16
Greenbridge 2 10 39N40'30 75w43'23 5:02:54
Green Hill 3 16 38N47'28 75w10'03 5:00:40
Greenleaf Manor 2 10 39N40'52 75w42'15 5:02:49
Green Meadow 2 1 39N47'25 75w31'05 5:02:04
Greens Corner 1 3 38N59'25 75w40'55 5:02:44
Greens Landing 3 16 38N39'19 75w09'46 5:00:39
Green Spring 2 14 39N19'03 75w38'57 5:02:36
Greentop 3 16 38N51'12 75w25'08 5:01:41
Greentree 2 1 39N48 75w28 5:01:52
Greenview 1 1 39N07'05 75w31'30 5:02:06
Greenville 1 16 38N53'10 75w39'44 5:02:39
Greenville 2 1 39N46'44 75w35'55 5:02:24

Greenville Manor 2 1 39N46'53 75w35'45 5:02:23
Greenwood 3 7 38N48'25 75w35'30 5:02:22
Grendon Farms 2 1 39N43'30 75w40'40 5:02:43
Greylag 2 12 39N29'03 75w40'05 5:02:40
Grubbs Corner 2 1 39N49'45 75w29'27 5:01:58
Grubbs Landing 2 1 39N47'10 75w28'10 5:01:53
Gumboro 3 4 38N28'39 75w21'56 5:01:28
Gum Crossroads 3 16 38N39'14 75w28'24 5:01:54
Gumwood 2 1 39N48 75w31 5:02:04
Guyencourt 2 1 39N48'49 75w35'12 5:02:21
Gwinhurst 2 1 39N47'30 75w28'45 5:01:55
Hall Estates 1 9 38N56'23 75w27'45 5:01:51
Hambys Corner 2 1 39N49'21 75w29'15 5:01:57
Hamilton Park 2 1 39N43'02 75w32'46 5:02:11
Hammville 1 1 39N13'38 75w34'42 5:02:19
Harbeson 3 16 38N43'29 75w17'07 5:01:08
Hardscrabble 3 16 38N36'53 75w28'44 5:01:55
Hares Corner 2 1 39N39'55 75w36'16 5:02:25
Harmony 2 10 39N41'43 75w41'35 5:02:46
Harmony Hills 2 10 39N41'35 75w41'00 5:02:44
Harrington 1 4 38N55'25 75w34'41 5:02:19
Hartly 1 6 39N10'07 75w42'49 5:02:51
Haverford 2 12 39N47'00 75w41'40 5:02:47
Hayden Park 2 1 39N43 75w37 5:02:28
Hay Point Landing 1 11 39N21'05 75w32'55 5:02:12
Hazeldell 2 1 39N42'45 75w32'50 5:02:11
Hazelwood 1 1 39N13'06 75w31'35 5:02:06
Hazlettville 1 6 39N06'59 75w38'33 5:02:34
Hazzard Landing 3 16 38N48'37 75w12'50 5:00:51
Hearns Crossroads 3 2 38N31'59 75w33'02 5:02:12
Hearns Mill 3 16 38N40'42 75w35'40 5:02:23
Heather Valley 2 1 39N45'40 75w40'48 5:02:43
Henlopen Acres 3 16 38N43'47 75w05'12 5:00:21
Henry Clay 2 1 39N46'13 75w34'50 5:02:19
Heritage 2 10 39N43'15 75w40'40 5:02:43
Heritage Village 3 16 38N39'27 75w37'55 5:02:32
Herring Landing 3 16 38N39'00 75w08'08 5:00:33
Hickman 1 16 38N49'59 75w43'23 5:02:54
Hickory Dale Acres 1 1 39N12'42 75w33'45 5:02:15
Hickory Hill 2 12 39N46'48 75w41'35 5:02:46
Hickory Hill 3 16 38N32'19 75w18'25 5:01:14
Hickory Ridge 1 11 39N18 75w36 5:02:24
Hideaway Acres 1 1 39N05'12 75w29'48 5:01:59
Highland Acres 1 1 39N07'15 75w31'20 5:02:05
Highland Acres 3 16 38N45'55 75w09'20 5:00:37
Highland Meadows 2 12 39N47'10 75w40'20 5:02:41
Highland West 2 1 39N44 75w39 5:02:36
Highland Woods 2 1 39N49'00 75w28'50 5:01:55
High Point 2 1 39N46'15 75w30'30 5:02:02
Hillcrest 2 1 39N45'46 75w30'25 5:02:02
Hilldale 1 1 39N11'45 75w28'55 5:01:56
Hillendale 2 1 39N47'45 75w29'10 5:01:57
Hillside Heights 2 10 39N40'50 75w41'15 5:02:45
Hilltop Manor 2 1 39N46'45 75w29'00 5:01:56
Hitchens Crossroads 3 2 38N34'37 75w27'44 5:01:51
Hoars Addition 1 6 39N12'50 75w35'00 5:02:20
Hockessin 2 12 39N47'15 75w41'49 5:02:47
Holiday Acres 3 4 38N34'20 75w15'57 5:01:04
Holiday Hills 2 1 39N49'00 75w30'15 5:02:01
Holiday Pines 3 16 38N38'03 75w12'35 5:00:50
Hollandsville 1 3 38N59'07 75w39'59 5:02:40
Holletts Corners 1 2 39N17'22 75w43'59 5:02:56
Holloway Terrace 2 1 39N42'06 75w32'48 5:02:11
Holly Knoll 2 12 39N47'18 75w42'15 5:02:49
Hollymount 3 16 38N40'31 75w13'19 5:00:53
Holly Oak 2 1 39N47'18 75w28'45 5:01:55
Holly Oak 3 16 38N37 75w39 5:02:36
Holly Oak Terrace 2 1 39N47'00 75w29'20 5:01:57
Hollyville 3 16 38N40'18 75w14'33 5:00:58
Holts Landing 3 16 38N35'29 75w07'38 5:00:31
Hopkins Corners 1 16 38N57'18 75w40'37 5:02:42
Hourglass 1 6 39N07'37 75w40'57 5:02:44
Houston 1 4 38N55'03 75w30'20 5:02:01
Houston 3 16 38N47'15 75w14'27 5:00:58
Hudson Pond Acres 3 16 38N50'30 75w26'25 5:01:46
Hughes Crossing 1 1 39N12'08 75w34'17 5:02:17
Hughes Crossroads 1 3 38N58'16 75w41'50 5:02:47
Hunting Hills 2 10 39N40'40 75w47'05 5:03:08
Huntley 1 1 39N08'13 75w31'13 5:02:05
Hyde Park 2 1 39N44'45 75w39'00 5:02:36
Idela 2 1 39N43'30 75w35'25 5:02:22
Indian Beach 3 16 38N41'08 75w04'25 5:00:18
Indian Field 2 1 39N48'45 75w28'35 5:01:54
Indian Mission 3 16 38N40'24 75w14'08 5:00:57
Indian River Acres 3 4 38N33 75w15 5:01:00
Iron Hill 2 10 39N38'00 75w45'15 5:03:01
Irons Lane Landing 3 16 38N35'12 75w08'40 5:00:35
Israel Haul 3 16 38N34'41 75w11'14 5:00:45
Ivy Ridge 2 1 39N40'30 75w38'00 5:02:32
Jacobs Crossroads 3 16 38N44'35 75w41'11 5:02:45
Jamisons Corner 2 12 39N30'13 75w41'05 5:02:44
Jefferson Crossroads 3 16 38N50'03 75w20'44 5:01:23
Jefferson Farms 2 1 39N40'44 75w34'17 5:02:17
Jimtown 3 16 38N43'55 75w11'13 5:00:45
John Marsh Landing 3 16 38N39'31 75w09'54 5:00:40
Johnson 3 4 38N28'31 75w08'20 5:00:33
Johnson Corner 3 3 38N28 75w13 5:00:52
Johnstown 3 7 38N48'18 75w34'33 5:02:18
Jones Crossroads 3 2 38N36'16 75w26'50 5:01:47
Keeney 2 12 39N37'08 75w42'13 5:02:49
Keen-Wik 3 3 38N27'38 75w05'26 5:00:22
Kenilworth 2 1 39N48 75w28 5:01:52
Kenmore Park 3 16 38N39'30 75w34'40 5:02:19
Kent Acres 1 1 39N07'54 75w31'31 5:02:06
Kentmere 2 1 39N46'00 75w33'42 5:02:15
Kenton 1 6 39N13'39 75w39'48 5:02:39
Keystone 2 1 39N43'35 75w36'20 5:02:25
Kiamensi 2 1 39N43'25 75w38'25 5:02:34
Killens Addition 3 16 38N43 75w05 5:00:20
Kings Crossroads 3 4 38N44'46 75w27'12 5:01:49
Kirkwood 2 13 39N34'18 75w41'48 5:02:47
Kirkwood Gardens 2 1 39N44'55 75w39'15 5:02:37
Kitts Hummock 1 1 39N06'09 75w24'09 5:01:37
Klair Estates 2 1 39N43'15 75w39'15 5:02:37
Knowles Crossroads 3 16 38N39'13 75w27'08 5:01:49
Kynlyn Apartments 2 1 39N46 75w30 5:02:00
Laffertys Corner 1 1 39N09'02 75w29'10 5:01:57
Lake Pines 3 2 38N33'20 75w32'56 5:02:12
Lake Shores 3 16 38N41'00 75w35'45 5:02:23
Lakeside Manor 3 2 38N33'45 75w33'45 5:02:15
Lakewood 3 9 38N54'28 75w27'20 5:01:49
Lamatan 2 10 39N41 75w43 5:02:52
Lancashire 2 1 39N45 75w33 5:02:12
Lancaster Court 2 1 39N45'05 75w36'00 5:02:24
Lancaster Village 2 1 39N44'40 75w35'22 5:02:21
Landenberg Junction 2 1 39N43'49 75w37'09 5:02:29
Landers Park 2 1 39N41'40 75w34'05 5:02:16
Landlith 2 1 39N44'38 75w31'47 5:02:07
Latimer Estates 2 1 39N43'55 75w34'30 5:02:18
Laurel 3 2 38N33'23 75w34'18 5:02:17
Laurel Bend 1 1 39N08'11 75w30'40 5:02:03
Lauren Farms 2 12 39N36'05 75w41'05 5:02:44
Lawndale 1 11 39N16'35 75w35'27 5:02:22
Layton Corners 1 16 38N53'56 75w41'36 5:02:46
Lebanon 1 1 39N06'41 75w30'03 5:02:00
Leedom Estates 2 1 39N41 75w34 5:02:16
Leedon Estates 2 1 39N41'30 75w35'05 5:02:20
Leipsic 1 1 39N14'27 75w31'02 5:02:04
Lewes 3 5 38N46'28 75w08'23 5:00:34
Lewes Beach 3 5 38N47'06 75w08'54 5:00:36
Lexington Mill 1 6 39N02'18 75w30'34 5:02:02
Liberty 2 1 39N43'43 75w37'03 5:02:28
Liftwood 2 1 39N46'40 75w31'20 5:02:05
Lightfoots Furnace 3 16 38N38'27 75w34'43 5:02:19
Limestone Acres 2 1 39N43'30 75w40'00 5:02:40
Limestone Gap 2 1 39N43'40 75w39'35 5:02:38
Limestone Gardens 2 1 39N44 75w39 5:02:36
Lincoln 3 6 38N52'11 75w25'24 5:01:42
Lindamere 2 1 39N45'40 75w29'35 5:01:58
Linden Hill 2 1 39N43'48 75w41'38 5:02:47
Lindenmere 2 1 39N46 75w30 5:02:00
Lingo Landing 3 16 38N38'01 75w07'28 5:00:30
Little Creek 1 1 39N10'01 75w26'55 5:01:48
Little Creek Landing 1 1 39N09'39 75w26'43 5:01:47
Little Heaven 1 6 39N02'30 75w27'25 5:01:50
Llangollen Estates 2 1 39N38'50 75w37'08 5:02:29
Locustville 1 1 39N04'26 75w29'40 5:01:59
London Village 1 6 39N04'10 75w31'52 5:02:07
Long Point Landing 1 11 39N18'27 75w37'15 5:02:29
Longview Farms 2 1 39N45 75w33 5:02:12
Longwood 2 1 39N48'35 75w32'20 5:02:09
Lords Corner 1 3 39N00'52 75w43'25 5:02:54
Lorewood Grove 2 13 39N32'25 75w41'15 5:02:45
Loveville 2 1 39N46'15 75w39'53 5:02:40
Lowe 3 2 38N31'29 75w30'33 5:02:02
Lower Christiana 2 1 39N44 75w36 5:02:24
Lower Moores Corner 1 1 39N10'53 75w35'10 5:02:21
Lowes Crossroads 3 16 38N31'24 75w24'24 5:01:38
Lumbrook 2 10 39N41'07 75w43'59 5:02:56
Lynch Heights 1 9 38N57'08 75w25'33 5:01:42
Lyndalia 2 1 39N43'05 75w36'10 5:02:25
Lynnfield 2 1 39N47'20 75w30'30 5:02:02
Magnolia 1 6 39N04'16 75w28'35 5:01:54
Mahan 1 3 39N03'57 75w43'04 5:02:52
Maloneys Landing 1 9 38N57'40 75w22'17 5:01:29
Manette Heights 2 1 39N42'55 75w39'25 5:02:38
Manor 2 1 39N41 75w34 5:02:16
Manor Park 2 1 39N41'15 75w35'45 5:02:23
Maplecrest 2 1 39N43'45 75w39'15 5:02:37
Maplewood 2 10 39N41 75w43 5:02:52
Marabou Meadows 2 15 39N35'25 75w44'45 5:02:59
Marker Estates 1 1 39N12'28 75w34'12 5:02:17
Marshallton 2 1 39N43'32 75w39'16 5:02:37
Marshtown 3 16 38N41'36 75w09'51 5:00:39
Marvels Crossroads 1 4 38N55'39 75w31'03 5:02:04
Marydel 1 8 39N06'44 75w44'41 5:02:59
Masonicville 2 1 39N43'15 75w36'50 5:02:27
Massey Landing 3 16 38N37'34 75w06'16 5:00:25
Mastens Corner 1 16 38N58'07 75w37'04 5:02:28
Mayfair 1 1 39N08'00 75w32'15 5:02:09
Mayfield 2 1 39N47'50 75w30'30 5:02:02
Mayview Manor 2 1 39N41 75w34 5:02:16
McClellandville 2 10 39N42'34 75w46'38 5:03:07
McDaniel Heights 2 1 39N48'08 75w32'54 5:02:12
McDonalds Crossroads 3 16 38N40'03 75w26'52 5:01:47
McDonough 2 12 39N29'29 75w39'00 5:02:36
McKnatt Corners 1 16 38N56'27 75w40'44 5:02:43
Meadow Acres 3 16 38N39'30 75w34'03 5:02:16
Meadowbrook 2 1 39N45'10 75w43'25 5:02:54
Meadowbrook Acres 1 6 39N03'53 75w32'25 5:02:10
Meadowood 2 10 39N42'30 75w41'15 5:02:45
Mechanicsville 2 10 39N43'01 75w47'02 5:03:08
Meeting House Hill 2 10 39N47'30 75w41'33 5:02:46
Melvin Crossroads 1 16 38N55'07 75w43'17 5:02:53
Melvins 1 4 38N56'36 75w31'23 5:02:06
Melvins Crossroads 1 3 38N57'52 75w31'33 5:02:06
Mermaid 2 1 39N44'34 75w41'36 5:02:46
Middleboro Manor 2 1 39N43'25 75w35'00 5:02:20
Middleford 3 16 38N40'00 75w34'03 5:02:16
Middlesex Beach 3 16 38N31'21 75w03'16 5:00:13
Middletown 2 12 39N26'58 75w43'00 5:02:52
Midnight Thicket 3 2 38N34'35 75w32'20 5:02:09
Midvale 2 1 39N39'35 75w36'39 5:02:27
Midway 3 16 38N43'41 75w07'47 5:00:31
Midway Park 3 16 38N44'23 75w08'35 5:00:34
Milford 3 9 38N54'45 75w25'42 5:01:43
Milford Crossroads 2 10 39N42'56 75w44'28 5:02:58
Milford Meadows 2 10 39N42'23 75w43'45 5:02:55
Milford Plaza 3 9 38N55 75w22 5:01:28
Mill Creek 2 12 39N47'05 75w42'19 5:02:49
Millpond Acres 3 16 38N45'52 75w12'15 5:00:49
Millsboro 3 3 38N35'29 75w17'30 5:01:10
Millside 2 1 39N43'05 75w33'10 5:02:13
Milltown 2 1 39N43'51 75w39'59 5:02:40
Millville 3 16 38N32'58 75w07'25 5:00:30
Milton 3 16 38N46'39 75w18'37 5:01:14
Minners Corners 1 16 38N58'14 75w37'50 5:02:31
Minquadale 2 1 39N42'25 75w34'01 5:02:16
Mispillion Light 3 9 38N56'50 75w18'55 5:01:16
Mission 3 16 38N32'47 75w21'17 5:01:25
Mockingbird Hills 2 1 39N45'37 75w40'40 5:02:43
Monroe Park 2 1 39N46'20 75w35'47 5:02:23
Montchanin 2 1 39N47'23 75w35'22 5:02:21
Monterey Farms 2 1 39N41 75w34 5:02:16
Moores Corner 1 6 39N12'34 75w36'21 5:02:25
Morris Estates 1 1 39N08'47 75w31'13 5:02:05
Morris Mill 3 16 38N38'20 75w19'02 5:01:16
Mount Cuba 2 1 39N47'29 75w38'24 5:02:34
Mount Joy 3 16 38N37'55 75w17'47 5:01:11
Mount Pleasant 2 13 39N30'39 75w42'42 5:02:51
Mulberry Landing 3 3 38N29'09 75w04'36 5:00:18
Murrays Corner 3 16 38N45'07 75w09'02 5:00:36
Murry Landing 3 16 38N34'14 75w05'36 5:00:22
Naaman 2 1 39N48'43 75w26'39 5:01:47
Naamans Gardens 2 1 39N49'30 75w31'00 5:02:04
Naamans Manor 2 1 39N49'22 75w30'03 5:02:00
Nandains Landing 1 1 39N15'45 75w31'40 5:02:07
Nanticoke Acres 3 16 38N38'22 75w35'06 5:02:20
Nanticoke Estates 3 16 38N37'23 75w37'15 5:02:29
Nassau 3 6 38N45'07 75w11'17 5:00:45
Newark 2 10 39N41'01 75w45'00 5:03:00
New Castle 2 1 39N39'43 75w34'00 5:02:16
New Castle Manor 2 1 39N41 75w34 5:02:16
Newkirk Estates 2 10 39N41 75w43 5:02:52
New Market 3 4 38N48'26 75w23'50 5:01:35
Newport 2 1 39N42'49 75w36'35 5:02:26
Newport Heights 2 1 39N42'50 75w36'15 5:02:25
Nonatum Mills 2 10 39N41'23 75w45'15 5:03:01
Northcrest 2 1 39N45 75w33 5:02:12
North Hills 2 1 39N46 75w30 5:02:00

North Ridge 2 1 39N48 75w28 5:01:52
North Seaford Heights 3 2 38N39'18 75w36'15 5:02:25
Northshire 2 1 39N49'05 75w30'10 5:02:01
North Shores 1 16 38N54'55 75w26'53 5:01:48
North Shores 3 16 38N39'12 75w35'00 5:02:20
North Star 2 10 39N45'40 75w43'10 5:02:53
Northwest Dover Heights 1 1 39N09 75w31 5:02:04
Northwood 2 1 39N47'45 75w30'10 5:02:01
Nottingham Green 2 10 39N41'10 75w46'43 5:03:07
Nottingham Manor 2 10 39N41'05 75w46'00 5:03:04
Oakdale 2 10 39N39'57 75w41'53 5:02:48
Oak Grove 1 1 39N09'23 75w29'23 5:01:58
Oak Grove 2 1 39N45 75w35 5:02:20
Oak Grove 3 16 38N39'39 75w42'24 5:02:50
Oak Hill 2 1 39N45 75w35 5:02:20
Oakland 2 10 39N40'50 75w45'55 5:03:04
Oak Lane Manor 2 1 39N47'35 75w31'50 5:02:07
Oakley 3 16 38N48'23 75w29'21 5:01:57
Oakmont 2 1 39N41 75w34 5:02:16
Oak Orchard 3 16 38N35'46 75w10'23 5:00:42
Oakwood Hills 2 1 39N45'45 75w40'05 5:02:40
Ocean View 3 16 38N32'42 75w05'22 5:00:21
Ocean Village 3 16 38N33'25 75w03'35 5:00:14
Odessa 2 12 39N27'26 75w39'42 5:02:39
Odessa Heights 2 12 39N27'08 75w39'45 5:02:39
Ogletown 2 10 39N40'41 75w41'52 5:02:47
Old Furnace 3 16 38N40'00 75w31'00 5:02:04
Old Landing 3 16 38N41'13 75w07'42 5:00:31
Old Mill Manor 2 10 39N41'30 75w42'15 5:02:49
Omar 3 4 38N31'38 75w12'00 5:00:48
Overbrook 3 16 38N46'03 75w12'55 5:00:52
Overlook 2 1 39N48 75w28 5:01:52
Overlook Colony 2 1 39N48'15 75w28'10 5:01:53
Overview Gardens 2 1 39N41 75w34 5:02:16
Owens 3 16 38N48'20 75w31'35 5:02:06
Owls Nest Estates 2 1 39N46 75w35 5:02:20
Oyster Rocks 3 16 38N48'07 75w12'11 5:00:49
Packing House Corner 3 4 38N27'57 75w40'25 5:02:42
Paden Corner 1 1 39N09'20 75w36'46 5:02:27
Palmer Park 1 1 39N06'10 75w32'25 5:02:10
Palm Spring Manor 2 10 39N41 75w43 5:02:52
Paris Villa 1 6 39N03'53 75w31'45 5:02:07
Parkside 2 12 39N33'23 75w42'15 5:02:49
Pearson Grove 1 2 39N13'44 75w45'13 5:03:01
Pearsons Corner 1 6 39N09'14 75w39'00 5:02:36
Pembrey 2 1 39N48'20 75w31'35 5:02:06
Penarth 2 1 39N48'25 75w31'05 5:02:04
Pencader 2 10 39N40'23 75w44'33 5:02:58
Pendrew Manor 2 1 39N43'05 75w39'55 5:02:40
Penn Acres 2 1 39N40'48 75w34'57 5:02:20
Pennrock 2 10 39N42'52 75w41'15 5:02:45
Penn Rose 2 1 39N45'30 75w31'20 5:02:05
Pennwood 1 1 39N07'38 75w30'48 5:02:03
Pennyhill 2 1 39N46'07 75w30'53 5:02:04
Pennyhill Terrace 2 1 39N45'50 75w30'30 5:02:02
Penrock 2 1 39N47'30 75w29'15 5:01:57
Pepper 3 2 38N32'30 75w28'39 5:01:55
Pepperbox 3 4 38N29'55 75w26'24 5:01:46
Peppers Landing 3 3 38N28'35 75w04'42 5:00:19
Perry Park 2 1 39N45 75w33 5:02:12
Perth 2 1 39N48 75w31 5:02:04
Petersburg 1 3 39N02'57 75w38'55 5:02:36
Phillips Heights 2 1 39N46'00 75w30'30 5:02:02
Phillips Hill 3 16 38N34'08 75w20'00 5:01:20
Pickering Beach 1 1 39N09 75w31 5:02:04
Piedmont 2 12 39N47 75w39 5:02:36
Piermont Woods 2 10 39N38'45 75w42'25 5:02:50
Pilottown 3 16 38N46'47 75w09'10 5:00:37
Pinecrest 2 1 39N42'53 75w40'15 5:02:41
Pine Swamp Corner 2 10 39N40'31 75w40'49 5:02:43
Pinetown 3 16 38N44'43 75w13'27 5:00:54
Pine Tree Corners 2 14 39N24'26 75w39'42 5:02:39
Pine Water Landing 3 16 38N39'23 75w10'18 5:00:41
Piney Grove 3 4 38N37'52 75w23'14 5:01:33
Piney Grove Manor 3 4 38N38'35 75w22'15 5:01:29
Pleasant Hill 2 1 39N44'26 75w43'40 5:02:55
Pleasant Hills 2 1 39N42'40 75w37'25 5:02:30
Pleasanton Acres 1 1 39N12'00 75w30'15 5:02:01
Pleasantville 2 10 39N39'50 75w37'35 5:02:30
Plymouth 1 3 39N01'52 75w33'43 5:02:15
Point Breeze 2 14 39N22'37 75w39'55 5:02:40
Polly Drummond 2 10 39N41 75w43 5:02:52
Porter 2 12 39N36'01 75w41'25 5:02:46
Port Mahon 1 1 39N11'07 75w24'05 5:01:36
Port Penn 2 12 39N31'00 75w34'37 5:02:18
Portsville 3 2 38N33'43 75w37'49 5:02:31
Postles Corner 1 1 39N08'05 75w26'54 5:01:48
Powelton 1 6 38N53'13 75w34'32 5:02:18
Prices Corner 2 1 39N44'13 75w37'21 5:02:29
Prices Corner Center 2 1 39N44'08 75w37'31 5:02:30
Primehook Beach 3 16 38N51'20 75w14'35 5:00:58
Pusey Crossroads 3 16 38N33'29 75w24'35 5:01:38
Quaker Hill 2 10 39N47'50 75w41'35 5:02:46
Quakertown 3 16 38N45'19 75w09'35 5:00:38
Quarryville 2 1 39N46'45 75w29'15 5:01:57
Radnor Green 2 1 39N48'30 75w28'23 5:01:54
Radnor Woods 2 1 39N48 75w28 5:01:52
Ralphs 3 4 38N30'03 75w38'12 5:02:33
Rambleton Acres 2 1 39N41 75w34 5:02:16
Ramblewood 2 1 39N45 75w33 5:02:12
Redden 3 4 38N44'29 75w25'03 5:01:40
Redden Crossroads 3 4 38N44'21 75w25'24 5:01:42
Red Lion 2 15 39N36'30 75w39'51 5:02:39
Reeves Crossing 1 3 38N59'00 75w34'42 5:02:19
Rehoboth Beach 3 3 38N43'15 75w04'35 5:00:18
Rehoboth Manor 3 3 38N43 75w05 5:00:20
Reliance 3 16 38N38'07 75w42'24 5:02:50
Revills Landing 3 9 38N56'48 75w21'05 5:01:24
Reybold 2 15 39N35'32 75w37'50 5:02:31
Reynolds Mill 3 16 38N48'47 75w20'40 5:01:23
Richard Heights 3 16 38N40'30 75w38'20 5:02:33
Richardson Estates 1 1 39N06'50 75w31'00 5:02:04
Richardson Park 2 1 39N43'55 75w35'10 5:02:21
Ridgewood 2 4 37N46'00 75w30'45 5:02:03
Rising Sun 1 1 39N06'01 75w30'57 5:02:04
Riverdale 3 16 38N35'38 75w11'30 5:00:46
Riverside 2 1 39N47'45 75w28'00 5:01:52
Riverside Gardens 2 1 39N48 75w28 5:01:52
Riverview 3 3 38N34'57 75w16'30 5:01:06
Robbins 3 4 38N45'43 75w25'19 5:01:41
Robertson Landing 3 16 38N48'19 75w14'36 5:00:58
Robinson Landing 3 16 38N41'35 75w08'31 5:00:34
Robinsonville 3 16 38N42'49 75w11'33 5:00:46
Robscott Manor 2 10 39N39'25 75w44'50 5:02:59
Rockland 2 1 39N47'46 75w34'21 5:02:17
Rock Manor 2 1 39N46'10 75w32'45 5:02:11
Rodney Village 1 1 39N07'55 75w31'58 5:02:08
Rodric Village 1 1 39N07'53 75w31'05 5:02:04
Roesville 1 3 38N59'52 75w31'43 5:02:07
Rogers Corners 2 1 39N42'40 75w32'50 5:02:11
Rogers Haven 3 16 38N33'35 75w05'40 5:00:23
Rogers Manor 2 1 39N40'25 75w33'41 5:02:15
Rolling Hills 2 1 39N43'05 75w39'00 5:02:36
Rolling Park 2 1 39N47'15 75w28'15 5:01:53
Rosedale Beach 3 16 38N35 75w17 5:01:08
Rosegate 2 1 39N42'35 75w32'50 5:02:11
Rose Hill 2 1 39N41 75w34 5:02:16
Rose Hill Gardens 2 1 39N41 75w34 5:02:16
Roselle 2 1 39N45 75w35 5:02:20
Roselle Terrace 2 1 39N44'20 75w36'50 5:02:27
Roseville Park 2 10 39N41'58 75w42'48 5:02:51
Ross 3 2 38N39'24 75w37'17 5:02:29
Roxana 3 4 38N29'47 75w10'12 5:00:41
Royal Grant 1 1 39N06'44 75w31'34 5:02:06
Runnymeade 2 12 39N46'18 75w41'30 5:02:46
Ruthby 2 10 39N41'08 75w42'09 5:02:49
Rutherford 2 10 39N41'20 75w40'50 5:02:43
Sabarto East 1 1 39N12'38 75w34'09 5:02:17
Saint George 3 4 38N29'56 75w35'06 5:02:20
Saint Georges 2 12 39N33'18 75w39'02 5:02:36
Saint Georges Heights 2 12 39N33'50 75w39'08 5:02:37
Sand Hill 3 4 38N43'55 75w21'38 5:01:27
Sandtown 1 3 39N02'00 75w43'09 5:02:53
Sandy Brae 3 16 38N44'15 75w08'55 5:00:36
Sandy Fork 3 2 38N33'14 75w31'57 5:02:08
Sandy Landing 3 4 38N34'15 75w10'45 5:00:43
Sassafras Landing 3 16 38N29'56 75w04'59 5:00:20
Saulsbury Switch 3 4 38N42'06 75w20'37 5:01:22
Schoolview 1 1 39N09'15 75w30'10 5:02:01
Schultie Crossroads 1 3 38N59'43 75w44'07 5:02:56
Scottfield 2 10 39N41 75w43 5:02:52
Scotts Corner 3 7 38N46'51 75w40'03 5:02:40
Scrap Tavern Crossroads 1 3 39N00'22 75w31'41 5:02:07
Seabreeze 3 16 38N41'45 75w04'55 5:00:20
Seaford 3 2 38N38'28 75w36'41 5:02:27
Seaford Heights 3 2 38N39'00 75w36'30 5:02:26
Sedgley Farms 2 1 39N45'54 75w37'26 5:02:30
Seeneytown 1 2 39N11'59 75w39'58 5:02:40
Selbyville 3 3 38N27'37 75w13'16 5:00:53
Seven Hickories 1 11 39N12'58 75w37'47 5:02:31
Shady Lane 1 1 39N07'08 75w31'05 5:02:04
Shaft Ox Corner 3 16 38N31'29 75w21'26 5:01:26
Sharpley 2 1 39N48'00 75w33'20 5:02:13
Shawnee 3 9 38N53'23 75w27'25 5:01:50
Shawnee Acres 3 9 38N53'40 75w24'10 5:01:37
Shaws Corner 1 2 39N12'11 75w38'57 5:02:36
Shawtown 2 1 39N41 75w34 5:02:16
Sheep Pen Landing 3 16 38N38'34 75w08'53 5:00:36
Sheffield Manor 2 10 39N41'53 75w41'24 5:02:46
Shellburne 2 1 39N46'50 75w30'45 5:02:03
Sherwood 1 1 39N08'35 75w32'05 5:02:08
Sherwood Acres 3 16 38N32'10 75w08'45 5:00:35
Sherwood Forest 2 10 39N40'15 75w41'25 5:02:46
Sherwood Park 2 1 39N44'10 75w39'30 5:02:38
Shingle Landing 2 12 39N32'36 75w35'39 5:02:23
Shipley Heights 2 1 39N47'00 75w31'30 5:02:06
Shockley Manor 3 16 38N43'00 75w06'03 5:00:24
Shortly 3 4 38N36'26 75w23'42 5:01:35
Shorts Corner 1 2 39N12'23 75w40'22 5:02:41
Shorts Landing 1 11 39N20'59 75w32'09 5:02:09
Silver Brook 2 10 39N39'23 75w45'15 5:03:01
Silverbrook Gardens 2 1 39N44'30 75w35'00 5:02:20
Silver Lake Shores 3 16 38N43 75w05 5:00:20
Silverside 2 1 39N47'35 75w29'26 5:01:58
Silverside Heights 2 1 39N47'05 75w28'50 5:01:55
Silview 2 1 39N42'46 75w37'20 5:02:29
Simonds Gardens 2 1 39N42'20 75w32'38 5:02:11
Six Forks 1 4 38N53'18 75w31'48 5:02:07
Skyline Crest 2 1 39N43'30 75w41'05 5:02:44
Slaughter 1 6 39N09'34 75w42'55 5:02:52
Slaughter Beach 3 6 38N54'46 75w18'16 5:01:13
Slaytonville 3 16 38N55 75w35 5:02:20
Sloan Landing 3 16 38N39'18 75w07'58 5:00:32
Smith Crossroads 1 8 39N05'42 75w42'58 5:02:52
Smith Hill 3 2 38N29'42 75w30'48 5:02:03
Smyrna 1 11 39N17'59 75w36'18 5:02:25
Smyrna Landing 1 11 39N18'29 75w35'38 5:02:23
Snug Harbor 3 16 38N39'30 75w34'25 5:02:18
South Bethany 3 16 38N30'59 75w03'12 5:00:13
South Bowers 1 9 39N03'26 75w23'52 5:01:35
South Dover Acres 1 1 39N09 75w31 5:02:04
South Wilmington 2 1 39N43'45 75w32'40 5:02:11
Southwood 2 12 39N47'05 75w43'27 5:02:54
Springfield Crossroads 3 4 38N40'57 75w18'29 5:01:14
Spring Hill 1 9 38N58'00 75w25'55 5:01:44
Spring Valley 2 1 39N46'15 75w38'50 5:02:35
Spruance City 1 11 39N17'40 75w37'00 5:02:28
Stanley Manor 3 9 38N54'10 75w27'35 5:01:50
Stanton 2 1 39N42'56 75w38'28 5:02:34
Stanton Estates 2 1 39N42'48 75w38'50 5:02:35
Star Hill 1 1 39N06'19 75w32'27 5:02:10
Star Hill Village 1 1 39N06'00 75w32'15 5:02:09
Star Landing 3 16 38N45'39 75w12'10 5:00:49
Stave Landing 2 14 39N25'53 75w36'05 5:02:24
Staytonville 3 16 38N50'58 75w31'09 5:02:05
Stockdale 2 1 39N48'00 75w27'30 5:01:50
Stockley 3 16 38N38'27 75w20'25 5:01:22
Stockly 3 4 38N41 75w23 5:01:32
Stockton 2 1 39N41 75w34 5:02:16
Stonehaven 2 1 39N45'55 75w30'45 5:02:03
Stratford 2 1 39N40'05 75w37'55 5:02:32
Strawberry Landing 3 16 38N30'03 75w04'18 5:00:17
Summit Bridge 2 13 39N32'07 75w43'35 5:02:54
Surrey Park 2 1 39N48'15 75w31'50 5:02:07
Susan Beach Corner 3 4 38N28'05 75w39'10 5:02:37
Sussex Shores 3 16 38N33'00 75w03'27 5:00:14
Swain Acres 3 4 38N41'30 75w24'00 5:01:36
Swallow Hill 2 1 39N47'38 75w38'08 5:02:33
Swann Keys 3 3 38N28'48 75w05'12 5:00:21
Swanwyck 2 1 39N41'37 75w33'39 5:02:15
Swanwyck Estates 2 1 39N41 75w34 5:02:16
Swanwyck Gardens 2 1 39N41 75w34 5:02:16
Sycamore 3 2 38N35'45 75w29'27 5:01:58
Sycamore Gardens 2 10 39N41'45 75w42'25 5:02:50
Talleys Corner 2 1 39N48'29 75w30'57 5:02:04
Talleyville 2 1 39N48'32 75w32'57 5:02:12
Tanglewood 2 10 39N41 75w43 5:02:52
Tarleton 2 1 39N48 75w31 5:02:04
Tavistock 2 1 39N48'20 75w33'30 5:02:14
Taylor Estates 1 1 39N07'40 75w31'48 5:02:07
Taylors Bridge 2 14 39N24 75w41 5:02:44
Taylors Corner 2 14 39N23'15 75w42'58 5:02:52
Taylors Gut Landing 1 11 39N19'39 75w30'55 5:02:04
Taylortown 2 12 39N38'50 75w40'18 5:02:41
Tent 2 11 39N21'26 75w36'23 5:02:26
Thatchers Landing 3 4 38N33'23 75w12'08 5:00:49
The Beeches 1 1 39N09 75w31 5:02:04
The Blades 1 1 39N07'00 75w31'45 5:02:07
The Cedars 2 1 39N44 75w39 5:02:36
The Hamlet 1 1 39N10'10 75w32'55 5:02:12
The Heath 3 9 38N54'25 75w27'30 5:01:50
The Highlands 2 10 39N43'15 75w41'00 5:02:44
The Island 3 16 38N37 75w39 5:02:36
The Landing 3 16 38N35'34 75w12'51 5:00:51
The Oaks 3 16 38N39'50 75w35'55 5:02:24
The Timbers 2 1 39N48 75w31 5:02:04

Thomas Landing 2 14 39N26'53 75w36'48 5:02:27
Thompsonville 1 9 38N59'58 75w23'24 5:01:34
Thowrntown 2 12 39N31'04 75w36'11 5:02:25
Tidbury Manor 1 1 39N06'58 75w30'53 5:02:04
Todd Estates 2 10 39N40'15 75w42'45 5:02:51
Tower Trailer Park 2 1 39N48 75w28 5:01:52
Towne Point 1 1 39N10'40 75w31'00 5:02:04
Townsend 2 14 39N23'42 75w41'31 5:02:46
Trepagnier 2 12 39N46'45 75w40'08 5:02:41
Trinity 3 16 38N37'28 75w11'13 5:00:45
Truitts Park 3 3 38N42'20 75w05'30 5:00:22
Turnkey 1 1 39N05'17 75w32'52 5:02:11
Tuxedo Park 2 1 39N43'05 75w37'15 5:02:29
Twin Eagle Farms 1 2 39N16'50 75w42'45 5:02:51
Twin Oaks 2 1 39N47'05 75w32'10 5:02:09
Tybouts Corner 2 15 39N37'12 75w38'33 5:02:34
Tybrook 2 1 39N44'55 75w37'55 5:02:32
Underwood Corner 1 2 39N14'40 75w40'50 5:02:43
Union Street 2 1 39N45 75w35 5:02:20
Upper Christiana 2 10 39N41 75w41 5:02:44
Vagabond Trailer Park 2 1 39N48 75w28 5:01:52
Valley Run 2 1 39N45 75w33 5:02:12
Vandyke 2 14 39N21'26 75w44'43 5:02:59
Van Dyke Village 2 1 39N41 75w34 5:02:16
Varlano 2 10 39N39'33 75w40'25 5:02:42
Vaughn Landing 3 16 38N46'43 75w16'57 5:01:08
Vernon 1 16 38N53'36 75w39'11 5:02:37
Village of Drummond Hill 2 10 39N41 75w43 5:02:52
Villa Monterey 2 1 39N46 75w30 5:02:00
Viola 1 3 39N02'34 75w34'20 5:02:17
Voshell Cove 1 1 39N10'08 75w36'18 5:02:25
Voshell Mill 1 1 39N05'53 75w31'44 5:02:07
Voshels Cove 1 1 39N09 75w31 5:02:04
Walker 2 11 39N20'30 75w36'11 5:02:25
Walnut Ridge 2 1 39N48'10 75w37'53 5:02:32
Waples 3 16 38N49'33 75w18'28 5:01:14
Ward 3 4 38N29'07 75w28'41 5:01:55
Warren Landing 1 6 39N03'47 75w25'33 5:01:42
Warwick 3 16 38N36'11 75w13'51 5:00:55
Washington Heights 2 1 39N43'35 75w38'20 5:02:33
Washington Heights 3 16 38N42'45 75w05'45 5:00:23
Washington Park 2 1 39N39'40 75w34'52 5:02:19
Waterview Acres 3 16 38N38'27 75w32'45 5:02:11
Wawaset Park 2 1 39N45'20 75w34'30 5:02:18
Waynes Corner 2 1 39N49'29 75w30'05 5:02:00
Webb Landing 1 9 39N02'46 75w23'37 5:01:34
Webb Landing 3 16 38N42'41 75w10'50 5:00:43
Webb Manor 3 9 38N54'08 75w26'48 5:01:47
Webster Farms 2 1 39N47'40 75w30'40 5:02:03
Wedgewood 1 1 39N08'00 75w32'35 5:02:10
Wedgewood 2 12 39N38'45 75w38'30 5:02:34
Wedgewood Acres 2 1 39N41 75w34 5:02:16
Weisman Acres 3 9 38N55 75w22 5:01:28
Wellington Hills 2 12 39N47'23 75w42'30 5:02:50
Welshire 2 1 39N47'05 75w31'00 5:02:04
Wescoats Corner 3 16 38N45'06 75w09'53 5:00:40
West Beach 3 4 38N34'27 75w10'15 5:00:41
West Farm 2 1 39N47'15 75w36'10 5:02:25
Westfield 2 1 39N43'05 75w38'30 5:02:34
Westgate Farms 2 1 39N46'00 75w39'40 5:02:39
West Haven 2 1 39N45'35 75w35'30 5:02:22
West Meadow 2 10 39N42'20 75w44'00 5:02:56
West Minquadale 2 1 39N42'45 75w34'03 5:02:16
Westminster 2 1 39N45'25 75w38'50 5:02:35
Westover Hills 2 1 39N45'48 75w35'28 5:02:22
West Park 2 1 39N45'20 75w35'57 5:02:24
Westview 2 1 39N43 75w37 5:02:28
Westwood Manor 2 1 39N48'00 75w30'05 5:02:00
Westwoods 3 4 38N29'42 75w22'19 5:01:29
Whaleys Corners 3 4 38N39'08 75w25'50 5:01:43
Whaleys Crossroads 3 16 38N31'55 75w27'02 5:01:48
Whigville 1 6 39N13'20 75w40'20 5:02:41
White Briar 2 12 39N47'18 75w41'10 5:02:45
White Hall 1 3 39N02'27 75w35'45 5:02:23
Whitehall Crossroads 1 1 39N16'06 75w31'18 5:02:05
Whitehall Landing 1 1 39N15'02 75w28'37 5:01:54
White House Landing 1 6 39N05'15 75w28'00 5:01:52
Whiteleysburg 1 3 38N57'27 75w43'55 5:02:56
White Oak Farms 1 1 39N10'30 75w30'35 5:02:02
White River Estates 3 16 38N33'50 75w39'20 5:02:37
Whitesville 3 4 38N27'31 75w25'38 5:01:43
Wiggins Mill 2 14 39N24'12 75w42'19 5:02:49
Williamsburg 2 12 39N35'07 75w41'05 5:02:44
Williamsville 1 4 38N53'44 75w30'37 5:02:02
Williamsville 3 3 38N27'36 75w08'01 5:00:32
Willow Grove 1 1 39N04'15 75w37'43 5:02:31
Willow Run 2 1 39N44'40 75w36'35 5:02:26
Wilmington 2 1 39N44'45 75w32'49 5:02:11
Wilmington Manor 2 1 39N41'12 75w35'05 5:02:20
Wilmington Manor Gardens 2 1 39N40'22 75w34'54 5:02:20
Wilmont 2 1 39N48'25 75w32'15 5:02:09
Wilson 2 10 39N39'39 75w44'18 5:02:57
Wiltbank Landing 3 16 38N48'31 75w14'26 5:00:58
Windermer 2 1 39N43 75w37 5:02:28
Windsor Hills 2 1 39N48'00 75w31'45 5:02:07
Windy Bush 2 1 39N48'00 75w29'30 5:01:58
Windy Hills 2 10 39N41'20 75w43'00 5:02:52
Winterbury 2 1 39N45'40 75w39'30 5:02:38
Winterthur 2 1 39N48'10 75w35'31 5:02:22
Wisseman Acres 3 9 38N54'20 75w27'20 5:01:49
Woodbine 2 1 39N48'45 75w31'45 5:02:07
Wood Branch 3 4 38N40'01 75w21'40 5:01:27
Woodbrook 1 1 39N09 75w31 5:02:04
Woodbrook 2 1 39N47'38 75w33'30 5:02:14
Woodcrest 1 1 39N10'25 75w32'30 5:02:10
Woodcrest 2 1 39N43'15 75w36'10 5:02:25
Wooddale 2 1 39N45'58 75w38'14 5:02:33
Woodenhawk 3 7 38N47'30 75w41'26 5:02:46
Woodland 2 1 39N44'45 75w37'00 5:02:28
Woodland 3 16 38N36'00 75w39'30 5:02:38
Woodland Beach 1 11 39N20'00 75w28'30 5:01:54
Woodland Heights 3 6 38N33'48 75w34'30 5:02:18
Woodland Homes 2 1 39N43 75w37 5:02:28
Woodshade 2 12 39N39'15 75w41'00 5:02:44
Woods Haven 1 9 38N55'50 75w24'50 5:01:39
Woodside 1 3 39N04'17 75w34'07 5:02:16
Woodside Hills 2 1 39N47'15 75w29'25 5:01:58
Woodside Manor 2 10 39N35'20 75w43'30 5:02:54
Woods Manor 1 1 39N09 75w31 5:02:04
Woods Manor East 1 1 39N07'51 75w30'32 5:02:02
Worthland 2 1 39N48'30 75w27'00 5:01:48
Wrange Hill Estates 2 12 39N35'30 75w42'00 5:02:48
Wrangle Hill 2 12 39N34'45 75w39'28 5:02:38
Wrights Crossroads 1 6 39N09'06 75w43'50 5:02:55
Wyoming 1 1 39N07'05 75w33'33 5:02:14
York Beach 3 16 38N30'34 75w03'12 5:00:13
Yorklyn 2 12 39N48'29 75w40'33 5:02:42
Zoar 3 16 38N38'49 75w17'51 5:01:11

TIME TABLES

Date	Time	Zone
Before 3/13/1884		LMT
3/13/1884	12:00	EST
3/31/1918	02:00	EWT
10/27/1918	02:00	EST
3/30/1919	02:00	EWT
10/26/1919	02:00	EST
5/02/1922	02:00	EDT
9/04/1922	02:00	EST
2/09/1942	02:00	EWT
9/30/1945	02:00	EST
5/11/1947	02:00	EDT
9/28/1947	02:00	EST
5/02/1948	02:00	EDT
9/26/1948	02:00	EST
4/24/1949	02:00	EDT
9/25/1949	02:00	EST
5/04/1950	02:00	EDT
9/24/1950	02:00	EST
4/29/1951	02:00	EDT
9/30/1951	02:00	EST
4/27/1952	02:00	EDT
9/28/1952	02:00	EST
4/30/1953	02:00	EDT
9/27/1953	02:00	EST
4/25/1954	02:00	EDT
9/26/1954	02:00	EST
4/24/1955	02:00	EDT
9/25/1955	02:00	EST
4/29/1956	02:00	EDT
10/28/1956	02:00	EST
4/28/1957	02:00	EDT
10/27/1957	02:00	EST
4/27/1958	02:00	EDT
10/26/1958	02:00	EST
4/26/1959	02:00	EDT
10/25/1959	02:00	EST
4/24/1960	02:00	EDT
10/30/1960	02:00	EST
4/30/1961	02:00	EDT
10/29/1961	02:00	EST
4/29/1962	02:00	EDT
10/28/1962	02:00	EST
4/28/1963	02:00	EDT
10/27/1963	02:00	EST
4/26/1964	02:00	EDT
10/25/1964	02:00	EST
4/25/1965	02:00	EDT
10/31/1965	02:00	EST
4/24/1966	02:00	EDT
10/30/1966	02:00	EST
4/30/1967	02:00	US#1

COUNTIES

1 District of Columbia

Place	Latitude	Longitude	Time
Anacostia 1	38N51'59	76w59'03	5:07:56
Barnaby Terrace 1	38N50'00	76w59'22	5:07:57
Barnaby Woods 1	38N58'29	77w03'36	5:08:14
Bellevue 1	38N49'36	77w01'12	5:08:05
Benjamin Franklin 1	38N53	77w00	5:08:00
Benning 1	38N53'42	76w56'57	5:07:48
Benning Heights 1	38N52'54	76w56'11	5:07:45
Bolling Air Force Base 1	38N51	77w01	5:08:04
Brightwood 1	38N57'40	77w01'40	5:08:07
Brightwood Park 1	38N57'25	77w01'31	5:08:06
Brookland 1	38N55'58	76w59'04	5:07:56
Burleith 1	38N54'55	77w04'22	5:08:17
Calvert 1	38N55	77w04	5:08:16
Capitol Building 1	38N53'18	77w00'36	5:08:02
Capitol View 1	38N53'22	76w55'54	5:07:44
Cardinal 1	38N56	77w00	5:08:00
Chillum Station 1	38N57'20	77w00'16	5:08:01
Cleveland Park 1	38N56'10	77w03'57	5:08:16
Colonial Village 1	38N59'33	77w02'25	5:08:10
Columbia Heights 1	38N55'32	77w01'47	5:08:07
Congress Heights 1	38N50'34	77w00'02	5:08:00
Congress Park 1	38N50'28	76w59'28	5:07:58
Crestwood 1	38N56'30	77w02'27	5:08:10
Customs House 1	38N56	76w59	5:07:56
Deanewood 1	38N53'54	76w55'47	5:07:43
Douglass Dwellings 1	38N50'54	76w58'41	5:07:55
Eagle 1	38N57	77w06	5:08:24
Eckington 1	38N54'45	77w00'34	5:08:02
Fairfax Village 1	38N51'43	76w57'05	5:07:48
Fort Bayard 1	38N57'19	77w05'28	5:08:22
Fort Carroll 1	38N50'16	77w00'24	5:08:02
Fort Davis 1	38N51'59	76w57'02	5:07:48
Fort De Russey 1	38N57'48	77w03'01	5:08:12
Fort Dupont 1	38N52'21	76w56'20	5:07:45
Fort Greble 1	38N49'38	77w00'53	5:08:04
Fort Lincoln New Town 1	38N55'20	76w57'24	5:07:50
Foxhall Village 1	38N54'42	77w05'05	5:08:20
Friendship 1	38N57	77w06	5:08:24
Garfield Heights 1	38N51'20	76w58'11	5:07:53
Georgetown 1	38N54'17	77w03'46	5:08:15
Glover Park 1	38N55'15	77w04'39	5:08:19
Good Hope 1	38N51'45	76w57'51	5:07:51
Greenway 1	38N53'15	76w57'18	5:07:49
Hawthorne 1	38N58'49	77w03'18	5:08:13
Hillcrest 1	38N51'43	76w57'30	5:07:50
Hoya 1	38N55	77w04	5:08:16
Ivy City 1	38N54'40	76w59'06	5:07:56
Kendall Green 1	38N54	77w00	5:08:00
Kenilworth 1	38N54'21	76w56'26	5:07:46
Kent 1	38N56'01	77w06'14	5:08:25
Knox Hill Dwellings 1	38N51'12	76w58'02	5:07:52
Lamond 1	38N57'59	77w00'28	5:08:02
Langdon 1	38N55'23	76w58'27	5:07:54
LeDroit Park 1	38N54'57	77w00'58	5:08:04
L'Enfant Plaza 1	38N53	77w01	5:08:04
Manor Park 1	38N57'50	77w00'58	5:08:04
Marshall Heights 1	38N53'10	76w55'42	5:07:43
McLean Gardens 1	38N56'14	77w04'32	5:08:18
Mount Pleasant 1	38N55'50	77w02'28	5:08:10
Naval Observatory 1	38N55'12	77w03'54	5:08:16
Naval Research Laboratory 1	38N52	77w00	5:08:00
Naval Station 1	38N52	77w00	5:08:00
Naylor Gardens 1	38N51'24	76w58'01	5:07:52
North Gate 1	38N59'14	77w02'08	5:08:09
Palisades 1	38N57	77w06	5:08:24
Park View 1	38N55'55	77w01'26	5:08:06
Petworth 1	38N56'45	77w01'31	5:08:06
Potomac Heights 1	38N55'39	77w06'29	5:08:26
Randle 1	38N52	76w59	5:07:56
River Terrace 1	38N53'31	76w57'28	5:07:50
Shepherds Landing 1	38N48'57	77w01'41	5:08:07
Spring Valley 1	38N56'22	77w05'57	5:08:24
State Department 1	38N53	77w00	5:08:00
Temple Heights 1	38N55	77w02	5:08:08
Tenleytown 1	38N56'58	77w05'10	5:08:21
Terra Cotta 1	38N57'13	76w59'55	5:08:00
The Palisades 1	38N55'30	77w06'06	5:08:24
Treasury 1	38N53	77w00	5:08:00
Trinidad 1	38N54'20	76w59'05	5:07:56
Truxton Circle 1	38N54	77w00	5:08:00
Twining 1	38N52'18	76w57'58	5:07:52
Walter Reed 1	38N59	77w01	5:08:04
Washington 1	38N53'42	77w02'12	5:08:09
Washington Highlands 1	38N49'55	76w59'42	5:07:59
Watergate 1	38N54	77w03	5:08:12
Wesley Heights 1	38N55'52	77w05'18	5:08:21
West End 1	38N54	77w03	5:08:12
White House 1	38N54	77w02	5:08:08
Woodley Park 1	38N55'43	77w03'22	5:08:13
Woodley Road 1	38N56	77w03	5:08:12
Woodridge 1	38N55'52	76w58'17	5:07:53

TIME TABLES

FL # 1

Date	Time	Zone
Before 5/30/1889		LMT
5/30/1889	12:00	CST
3/31/1918	02:00	CWT
10/27/1918	02:00	CST
3/30/1919	02:00	CWT
10/26/1919	02:00	CST
2/09/1942	02:00	CWT
9/30/1945	02:00	CST
4/30/1967	02:00	US#1

FL # 2

Date	Time	Zone
Before 5/30/1889		LMT
5/30/1889	12:00	CST
3/31/1918	02:00	CWT
10/27/1918	02:00	CST
3/30/1919	02:00	CWT
10/26/1919	02:00	CST
2/09/1942	02:00	CWT
9/30/1945	02:00	CST
4/28/1946	02:00	CDT
9/29/1946	02:00	CST
4/27/1947	02:00	CDT
9/28/1947	02:00	CST
4/25/1948	02:00	CDT
9/26/1948	02:00	CST
4/24/1949	02:00	CDT
9/25/1949	02:00	CST
4/30/1950	02:00	CDT
9/24/1950	02:00	CST
4/29/1951	02:00	CDT
9/30/1951	02:00	CST
4/27/1952	02:00	CDT
9/28/1952	02:00	CST
4/26/1953	02:00	CDT
9/27/1953	02:00	CST
4/25/1954	02:00	CDT
9/26/1954	02:00	CST
4/24/1955	02:00	CDT
9/25/1955	02:00	CST
4/29/1956	02:00	CDT
10/28/1956	02:00	CST
4/28/1957	02:00	CDT
10/27/1957	02:00	CST
4/27/1958	02:00	CDT
10/26/1958	02:00	CST
4/26/1959	02:00	CDT
10/25/1959	02:00	CST
4/24/1960	02:00	CDT
10/30/1960	02:00	CST
4/30/1961	02:00	CDT
10/29/1961	02:00	CST
4/29/1962	02:00	CDT
10/28/1962	02:00	CST
4/28/1963	02:00	CDT
10/27/1963	02:00	CST
4/26/1964	02:00	CDT
10/25/1964	02:00	CST
4/25/1965	02:00	CDT
10/31/1965	02:00	CST
4/30/1967	02:00	US#1

FL # 3

Date	Time	Zone
Before 5/30/1889		LMT
5/30/1889	12:00	CST
3/31/1918	02:00	CWT
10/27/1918	02:00	CST
3/30/1919	02:00	CWT
10/26/1919	02:00	CST
4/27/1941	02:00	CDT
9/28/1941	02:00	CST
2/09/1942	02:00	CWT
9/30/1945	02:00	CST
4/28/1946	02:00	CDT
9/29/1946	02:00	CST
5/04/1947	02:00	CDT
9/28/1947	02:00	CST
4/25/1948	02:00	CDT
9/26/1948	02:00	CST
4/24/1949	02:00	CDT
9/25/1949	02:00	CST
4/30/1950	02:00	CDT
9/24/1950	02:00	CST
4/29/1951	02:00	CDT
9/30/1951	02:00	CST
4/27/1952	02:00	CDT
9/28/1952	02:00	CST
4/26/1953	02:00	CDT
9/27/1953	02:00	CST
4/25/1954	02:00	CDT
9/26/1954	02:00	CST
4/24/1955	02:00	CDT
10/30/1955	02:00	CST
4/29/1956	02:00	CDT
10/28/1956	02:00	CST
4/28/1957	02:00	CDT
10/27/1957	02:00	CST
4/27/1958	02:00	CDT
9/01/1958	02:00	CST
4/26/1959	02:00	CDT
10/25/1959	02:00	CST
4/24/1960	02:00	CDT
10/30/1960	02:00	CST
4/30/1961	02:00	CDT
10/29/1961	02:00	CST
4/29/1962	02:00	CDT
10/28/1962	02:00	CST
4/28/1963	02:00	CDT
10/27/1963	02:00	CST
4/26/1964	02:00	CDT
10/25/1964	02:00	CST
4/25/1965	02:00	CDT
10/31/1965	02:00	CST
4/30/1967	02:00	US#1

FL # 4

Date	Time	Zone
Before 5/30/1889		LMT
5/30/1889	12:00	CST
3/31/1918	02:00	CWT
10/27/1918	02:00	CST
3/30/1919	02:00	CWT
10/26/1919	02:00	CST
4/26/1931	02:00	CDT
9/27/1931	02:00	CST
4/27/1941	02:00	CDT
9/28/1941	02:00	CST
2/09/1942	02:00	CWT
9/30/1945	02:00	CST
4/28/1946	02:00	CDT
9/29/1946	02:00	CST
5/04/1947	02:00	CDT
9/28/1947	02:00	CST
4/25/1948	02:00	CDT
9/26/1948	02:00	CST
4/24/1949	02:00	CDT
9/25/1949	02:00	CST
4/30/1950	02:00	CDT
9/24/1950	02:00	CST
4/29/1951	02:00	CDT
9/30/1951	02:00	CST
4/27/1952	02:00	CDT
9/28/1952	02:00	CST
4/26/1953	02:00	CDT
9/27/1953	02:00	CST
4/25/1954	02:00	CDT
9/26/1954	02:00	CST
4/24/1955	02:00	CDT
10/30/1955	02:00	CST
4/29/1956	02:00	CDT
10/28/1956	02:00	CST
4/28/1957	02:00	CDT
10/27/1957	02:00	CST
4/27/1958	02:00	CDT
9/01/1958	02:00	CST
4/26/1959	02:00	CDT
10/25/1959	02:00	CST
4/24/1960	02:00	CDT
10/30/1960	02:00	CST
4/30/1961	02:00	CDT
10/29/1961	02:00	CST
4/29/1962	02:00	CDT
10/28/1962	02:00	CST
4/28/1963	02:00	CDT
10/27/1963	02:00	CST
4/26/1964	02:00	CDT
10/25/1964	02:00	CST
4/25/1965	02:00	CDT
10/31/1965	02:00	CST
4/30/1967	02:00	US#1

FL # 5

Date	Time	Zone
Before 5/30/1889		LMT
5/30/1889	12:00	CST
3/31/1918	02:00	CWT
10/27/1918	02:00	CST
1/01/1919	02:00	EST
3/30/1919	02:00	EWT
10/26/1919	02:00	EST
2/09/1942	02:00	EWT
9/30/1945	02:00	EST
4/30/1967	02:00	US#1

FL # 6

Date	Time	Zone
Before 5/30/1889		LMT
5/30/1889	12:00	CST
3/31/1918	02:00	CWT
10/27/1918	02:00	CST
1/01/1919	02:00	EST
3/30/1919	02:00	EWT
10/26/1919	02:00	EST
2/09/1942	02:00	EWT
9/30/1945	02:00	EST
4/28/1946	02:00	EDT
9/29/1946	02:00	EST
4/30/1967	02:00	US#1

COUNTIES

1 Alachua
2 Baker
3 Bay
4 Bradford
5 Brevard
6 Broward
7 Calhoun
8 Charlotte
9 Citrus
10 Clay
11 Collier
12 Columbia
13 Dade
14 De Soto
15 Dixie
16 Duval
17 Escambia
18 Flagler
19 Franklin
20 Gadsden
21 Gilchrist
22 Glades
23 Gulf
24 Hamilton
25 Hardee
26 Hendry
27 Hernando
28 Highlands
29 Hillsborough
30 Holmes
31 Indian River
32 Jackson
33 Jefferson
34 Lafayette
35 Lake
36 Lee
37 Leon
38 Levy
39 Liberty
40 Madison
41 Manatee
42 Marion
43 Martin
44 Monroe
45 Nassau
46 Okaloosa
47 Okeechobee
48 Orange
49 Osceola
50 Palm Beach
51 Pasco
52 Pinellas
53 Polk
54 Putnam
55 St Johns
56 St Lucie
57 Santa Rosa
58 Sarasota
59 Seminole
60 Sumter
61 Suwannee
62 Taylor
63 Union
64 Volusia
65 Wakulla
66 Walton
67 Washington

Abe Springs 7 1 30N21'56 85w08'51 5:40:35
Achan 53 5 27N51'33 81w58'07 5:27:52
Acline 8 5 26N53'05 82w00'55 5:28:04
Acres of Diamond 5
5 28N05 80w38 5:22:32
Adams 24 5 30N27'54 83w02'46 5:32:11
Adamsville 29 5 27N48'52 82w23'03 5:29:32
Adamsville 60 5 28N47'58 82w01'15 5:28:05
Agricola 53 5 27N47'15 81w53'30 5:27:34
Airport 13 6 25N48 80w15 5:21:00
Airport Siding 16
5 30N27 81w34 5:26:16
Alachua 1 5 29N47'44 82w29'40 5:29:59
Aladdin City 13 5 25N34'13 80w27'16 5:21:49
Alafia 29 5 28N01 82w08 5:28:32
Alamana 64 5 28N56'34 81w06'10 5:24:25
Alameda 13 6 25N45'47 80w17'52 5:21:11
Alaqua 66 1 30N43 86w07 5:44:28
Alcoma 53 5 27N53'41 81w28'57 5:25:56
Alderene Park 59
5 28N48'40 81w21'57 5:25:28
Alderman Park 16
5 30N20 81w35 5:26:20
Alexander Springs 35
5 29N04'48 81w34'42 5:26:19
Alford 32 1 30N41'37 85w23'32 5:41:34
Allandale 64 5 29N07'17 80w58'36 5:23:54
Allanton 3 1 30N01'53 85w27'28 5:41:50
Allapattah 13 6 25N48'51 80w13'27 5:20:54
Allenhurst 5 5 28N44'10 80w45'21 5:23:01
Allen Landing 65
5 30N08'53 84w40'11 5:38:41
Allentown 57 1 30N45'45 87w02'32 5:48:10
Alliance 32 1 30N36'35 85w06'49 5:40:27
Alligator Lake 49
5 28N15 81w17 5:25:08
Alligator Point Marina 19
5 30N11 84w23 5:37:32
Alma 33 5 30N36'39 83w54'23 5:35:38
Alpine 28 5 27N37'55 81w28'35 5:25:54
Alpine Heights 66
1 30N44'41 86w12'36 5:44:50
Altamonte Springs 59
5 28N39'39 81w21'57 5:25:28
Alta Vista 8 5 26N57 82w00 5:28:00
Altha 7 1 30N34'13 85w07'38 5:40:31
Alton 34 5 30N03'10 83w08'17 5:32:33
Altoona 35 5 28N57'56 81w38'56 5:26:36
Altschul 20 5 30N37 84w25 5:37:40
Alturas 53 5 27N52'17 81w42'55 5:26:52
Alva 36 5 26N42'55 81w36'37 5:26:26
Amelia City 45 5 30N35'24 81w27'27 5:25:50
American Beach 45
5 30N34'29 81w26'39 5:25:47
Anastasia 55 5 29N53'15 81w17'23 5:25:10
Anclote 51 5 28N10'33 82w46'51 5:31:07
Anclote Acres 51
5 28N13 82w43 5:30:52
Andalusia 18 5 29N29'59 81w29'06 5:25:56
Andover Golf Estates 13
6 25N57'50 80w12'31 5:20:50
Andover Lake Estates 13
6 25N57'57 80w12'08 5:20:49
Andrews 45 5 30N44'06 81w56'53 5:27:48
Andytown 6 6 26N08'44 80w26'31 5:21:46
Angel City 5 5 28N20'39 80w39'39 5:22:39
Angler Park 44 5 25N08 80w25 5:21:40
Anglers Park 44 5 25N08'23 80w23'51 5:21:35
Ankona 56 5 27N20'25 80w16'31 5:21:06
Anna Maria 41 5 27N31'51 82w44'01 5:30:56
Anona 52 5 27N53'42 82w49'51 5:31:19
Anthony 42 5 29N17'21 82w06'43 5:28:27
Antioch 29 5 28N02'48 82w14'57 5:29:00
Apalachicola 19 5 29N43'32 84w59'00 5:39:56
Apollo Beach 29 5 27N46 82w24 5:29:36
Apopka 48 5 28N40'49 81w30'35 5:26:02
Aqui Esta 8 5 26N54'22 82w02'50 5:28:11
Araquey 55 5 29N56'46 81w20'15 5:25:21
Arcadia 14 5 27N12'56 81w51'31 5:27:26
Arcadia West 14 5 27N38 82w08 5:28:32
Archbold 28 5 27N10'52 81w21'08 5:25:25
Archer 1 5 29N31'47 82w31'09 5:30:05
Ards Crossroads 30
1 30N57'33 85w41'36 5:42:46
Argyle 66 1 30N43'10 86w02'40 5:44:11
Ariel 64 5 28N54'01 80w51'50 5:23:27
Aripeka 51 5 28N25'55 82w39'52 5:30:39
Arlington 9 5 28N52'09 82w21'37 5:29:26
Arlington 16 5 30N20'08 81w36'11 5:26:25
Arlington Green 16
5 30N20 81w35 5:26:20
Arlington Heights 16
5 30N20 81w35 5:26:20
Arlington Park 6
6 26N18'24 80w06'26 5:20:26
Arlingwood 16 5 30N20 81w35 5:26:20
Armstrong 55 5 29N45'43 81w26'53 5:25:48
Arran 65 5 30N11'25 84w24'58 5:37:40
Arrant Settlement 30
1 30N51'33 85w58'27 5:43:54
Arredondo 1 5 29N36'17 82w24'34 5:29:38
Arundel 43 5 27N05'16 80w17'55 5:21:12
Ashmore 65 5 30N05'07 84w28'13 5:37:53
Ashton 49 5 28N14'46 81w14'39 5:24:59
Ashville 33 5 30N36'59 83w38'48 5:34:35
Aspalaga Landing 20
5 30N37'05 84w54'28 5:39:38
Astatula 35 5 28N42'34 81w43'59 5:26:56
Astor 35 5 29N09'44 81w31'32 5:26:06
Astor Farms 59 5 28N49'45 81w21'48 5:25:27
Astor Park 35 5 29N09'12 81w34'20 5:26:17
Astronaut Trail 5
5 28N36 80w49 5:23:16
Athena 62 5 29N59'16 83w29'40 5:33:59
Atlantic Beach 16
5 30N20'03 81w23'56 5:25:36
Atlantic Boulevard Estates 16
5 30N20 81w35 5:26:20
Atlantic Heights 13
6 25N51'18 80w07'15 5:20:29
Atlantis 50 6 26N37 80w06 5:20:24
Auburn 46 1 30N49'12 86w32'16 5:46:09
Auburndale 53 5 28N03'54 81w47'20 5:27:09
Aucilla 33 5 30N28'47 83w45'16 5:35:01
Audubon 5 5 28N26'13 80w39'36 5:22:38
Aurantia 5 5 28N43'40 80w53'16 5:23:33
Aurora 5 5 28N08'08 80w41'06 5:22:44
Auxiliary Field No 9 46
1 30N26 86w37 5:46:28
Avalon Beach 57 1 30N31'48 87w06'06 5:48:24
Avoca 24 5 30N34'40 83w01'37 5:32:06
Avondale 16 5 30N18'15 81w42'41 5:26:51
Avon Park 28 5 27N35'44 81w30'23 5:26:02
Avon Park Lakes 28
5 27N37'41 81w32'55 5:26:12
Ayers 27 5 28N27'47 82w26'38 5:29:47
Azalea Park 48 5 28N32'27 81w18'03 5:25:12
Azalea Terrace 16
5 30N17 81w35 5:26:20
Babson Park 53 5 27N49'54 81w31'21 5:26:05
Bagdad 57 3 30N35'55 87w01'52 5:48:07
Bagwell Landing 20
5 30N27'35 84w27'10 5:37:49
Bahama Beach 3 1 30N11'50 85w50'33 5:43:22
Bahia Beach 29 5 27N44 82w24 5:29:36
Bahia-mar 6 6 26N05 80w09 5:20:36
Bahoma 67 1 30N48'52 85w30'29 5:42:02
Bailey 40 5 30N34'05 83w35'31 5:34:22
Baird 53 5 27N41'14 81w57'22 5:27:49
Bairs Den 28 5 27N12'29 81w19'43 5:25:19
Baker 3 1 30N09'57 85w41'09 5:42:45
Baker 46 1 30N47'49 86w40'53 5:46:44
Baker Settlement 30
1 30N52'01 85w54'18 5:43:37
Bakers Mill 24 5 30N34'46 82w56'22 5:31:45
Bakersville 55 5 29N54'21 81w29'29 5:25:58
Baldwin 16 5 30N18'09 81w58'32 5:27:54
Bal Harbour 13 6 25N53'29 80w07'38 5:20:31
Ballantine Manor 41
5 27N20 82w32 5:30:08
Ballard Pines 5 5 27N54'56 80w28'43 5:21:55
Ballentine Manor 41
5 27N24'04 82w33'56 5:30:16
Balm 29 5 27N45'33 82w15'41 5:29:03
Bamboo 60 5 28N49'21 81w57'57 5:27:52
Barber Quarters 47
5 27N15'08 80w50'22 5:23:21
Barberville 64 5 29N11'13 81w25'16 5:25:41
Bar Dee Homes 52
5 27N53 82w46 5:31:04

Bardin 54 5 29N42'51 81W43'30 5:26:54
Bare Beach 50 5 26N45 80W58 5:23:52
Barefoot Bay 5 5 27N47 80W29 5:21:56
Barker Store 30 1 30N54'51 85W54'58 5:43:40
Barrineau Park 17 1 30N42 87W26 5:49:44
Barrs Landing 64 5 29N20'16 81W33'54 5:26:16
Barry College 13 6 25N53 80W11 5:20:44
Barth 17 1 30N45'41 87W19'49 5:49:19
Bartow 53 5 27N53'46 81W50'36 5:27:22
Barwal 6 6 26N18'31 80W05'24 5:20:22
Bascom 32 1 30N55'40 85W07'07 5:40:28
Basinger 47 5 27N24'00 81W01'00 5:24:04
Baskin 52 5 27N53'48 82W47'43 5:31:11
Bass 12 5 30N06'30 82W41'46 5:30:47
Bassville Park 35 5 28N50'25 81W46'08 5:27:05
Basswood Estates 47 5 27N16'40 80W51'27 5:23:26
Battle Ground Forks 66 1 30N30'16 85W56'59 5:43:48
Baum 37 5 30N30'50 84W04'49 5:36:19
Baxter 2 5 30N30'48 82W14'02 5:28:56
Bay Acres 58 5 27N12 82W30 5:30:00
Bayard 16 5 30N08'36 81W30'47 5:26:03
Bay City 19 1 29N45'23 85W01'14 5:40:05
Bay Harbor 3 1 30N08'49 85W36'53 5:42:28
Bay Harbor 6 6 26N09'02 80W07'05 5:20:28
Bay Harbor Islands 13 6 25N53'14 80W07'53 5:20:32
Bayhead 3 1 30N18'26 85W34'55 5:42:20
Bay Heights 13 6 25N44'44 80W13'19 5:20:53
Bay Hill 60 5 28N42'36 82W14'24 5:28:58
Bay Lake 35 5 28N28'38 81W54'22 5:27:37
Bay Lake 42 5 29N26'45 81W58'29 5:27:54
Bay Lake 48 5 28N33 81W23 5:25:32
Bayou Crossing 30 1 30N45'51 85W54'01 5:43:36
Bayou George 3 1 30N15'45 85W32'24 5:42:10
Bay Pines 52 5 27N48'50 82W46'42 5:31:07
Bay Point 44 5 24N37'35 81W35'33 5:26:22
Bayport 27 5 28N32'44 82W38'32 5:30:34
Bay Ridge 48 5 28N45'23 81W33'36 5:26:14
Bayshore 13 6 25N49'43 80W11'08 5:20:45
Bayshore 36 5 26N42'54 81W49'25 5:27:18
Bay Shore Estates 58 5 27N04 82W20 5:29:20
Bayshore Gardens 41 5 27N25'30 82W35'26 5:30:22
Bayshore Manor 36 5 26N40'36 81W51'53 5:27:28
Bayshore Park 8 5 26N57 82W00 5:28:00
Bay Springs 17 1 30N46'24 87W28'45 5:49:55
Bayview 3 1 30N11'33 85W42'46 5:42:51
Bayview 52 5 27N57'34 82W42'40 5:30:51
Bay Vista 52 5 27N45 82W39 5:30:36
Baywood 54 5 29N43'08 81W48'59 5:27:16
Beach 31 5 27N40 80W24 5:21:36
Beach Haven 17 4 30N23'05 87W18'28 5:49:14
Beachville 61 5 29N59'52 82W51'41 5:31:27
Beachwood 16 5 30N17'30 81W31'01 5:26:04
Beacon Beach 3 1 30N05'47 85W38'51 5:42:35
Beacon Hill 23 1 29N55'22 85W23'09 5:41:33
Beacon Hills 16 5 30N22'56 81W30'27 5:26:02
Beacon Light 6 6 26N17 80W09 5:20:36
Beacon Squier 51 5 28N13 82W45 5:31:00
Bealsville 29 5 28N01 82W08 5:28:32
Bean City 50 5 26N40'54 80W45'43 5:23:03
Bear Creek 3 1 30N09 85W39 5:42:36
Bear Head 66 1 30N43 86W07 5:44:28
Bear Hollow 28 5 27N12'30 81W17'17 5:25:09
Bear Lake 59 5 28N41 81W28 5:25:52
Bearpen Landing 30 1 30N52'20 85W52'40 5:43:31
Beattys Corner 29 5 27N58'00 82W10'15 5:28:41
Beauclere Gardens 16 5 30N11'56 81W37'56 5:26:32
Beauclere Manor 16 5 30N14 81W38 5:26:32
Beaver Creek 46 1 30N52'48 86W46'43 5:47:07
Becker 45 5 30N40'16 81W38'29 5:26:34
Beck Hammock 59 5 28N47'12 81W13'07 5:24:52
Beckhamtown 1 5 29N39'21 82W04'38 5:28:19
Beeghly Heights 16 5 30N29'26 81W40'27 5:26:42
Bee Ridge 58 5 27N17'01 82W28'51 5:29:55
Beetree Ford 38 5 29N13'49 82W38'56 5:30:36
Belair 37 5 30N22'48 84W16'06 5:37:04
Bel-Air 59 5 28N47'41 81W15'17 5:25:01
Belandville 57 1 30N58'54 86W50'56 5:47:24
Bell 21 5 29N45'19 82W51'46 5:31:27
Bellair 10 5 30N10'27 81W44'27 5:26:58
Belleair 52 5 27N56'08 82W48'23 5:31:14
Belleair Beach 52 5 27N55'22 82W50'36 5:31:22
Belleair Bluffs 52 5 27N55'16 82W49'02 5:31:16
Belleair Shores 52 5 27N54'59 82W50'44 5:31:23
Belle Ayre Estates 35 5 28N48 81W39 5:26:36
Belle Glade 50 5 26N41'03 80W40'04 5:22:40
Belle Glade Camp 50 5 26N39 80W41 5:22:44
Belle Haven 52 5 28N00 82W46 5:31:04
Belle Isle 48 5 28N27'29 81W21'34 5:25:26
Belle Meade 11 5 26N02'58 81W41'59 5:26:48
Belleview 17 4 30N26 87W17 5:49:08
Belleview 42 5 29N03'18 82W03'45 5:28:15
Belleview Heights 42 5 29N01'13 82W04'12 5:28:17
Bells Mill 67 1 30N39'43 85W34'29 5:42:18
Bellview 17 4 30N27'41 87W18'54 5:49:16
Bellville 24 5 30N35'46 83W15'27 5:33:02
Bellwood 5 5 28N30'17 80W47'05 5:23:08
Bellwood Estates 37 5 30N30'14 84W19'42 5:37:19
Bel Marra 50 6 26N24'21 80W04'20 5:20:17
Belmont 24 5 30N29'53 82W45'03 5:31:00
Belmont 52 5 27N56 82W46 5:31:04
Belmore 10 5 29N53'11 81W53'56 5:27:36
Belvedere Homes 50 6 26N42 80W05 5:20:20
Benbow 22 5 26N48'53 81W02'47 5:24:11
Bennett 3 1 30N23'30 85W31'56 5:42:08
Bennett Landing 64 5 29N06'02 81W26'02 5:25:44
Ben's Lake 46 1 30N28 86W32 5:46:08
Benson Junction 64 5 28N51'54 81W19'47 5:25:19
Benton 12 5 30N29'11 82W39'39 5:30:39
Bereah 53 5 27N39'39 81W37'33 5:26:30
Beresford 64 5 29N00'08 81W20'51 5:25:23
Beresford Manor 64 5 29N02 81W18 5:25:12
Berkeley 27 5 28N30'09 82W35'20 5:30:21
Bermont 8 5 26N56'43 81W45'39 5:27:03
Berry 53 5 28N19'07 81W51'44 5:27:27
Berrydale 57 1 30N53'57 87W00'50 5:48:03
Bertha 59 5 28N37'06 81W15'59 5:25:04
Bessemer 43 5 27N00'26 80W36'05 5:22:24
Bessent 2 5 30N13'16 82W06'53 5:28:28
Bethany 41 5 27N21 82W10 5:28:40
Bethel 65 5 30N15'07 84W19'27 5:37:18
Bethlehem 30 1 30N55'28 85W44'21 5:42:57
Bethune Beach 64 5 29N02 80W55 5:23:40
Betts 3 1 30N32'15 85W23'36 5:41:34
Betty Lou Beach 3 1 30N09 85W39 5:42:36
Beulah 17 4 30N32'03 87W24'06 5:49:36
Beulah 48 5 28N32'04 81W34'22 5:26:17
Bevell Place 60 5 28N28'47 82W02'36 5:28:10
Bevens 9 5 28N57'59 82W24'04 5:29:36
Beverley Beach 6 6 25N59'41 80W07'07 5:20:28
Beverley Terrace 58 5 27N22'08 82W30'26 5:30:02
Beverly 19 5 29N51'10 84W58'07 5:39:52
Beverly Beach 18 5 29N30'52 81W08'41 5:24:35
Beverly Hills 9 5 28N51 82W29 5:29:56
Beverly Hills 16 5 30N24'39 81W42'29 5:26:50
Beverly Terrace 58 5 27N21 82W31 5:30:04
Beville Heights 1 5 29N39'23 82W23'59 5:29:36
Bevilles Corner 60 5 28N38'58 82W03'17 5:28:13
Bid-A-Wee 3 1 30N12'09 85W51'00 5:43:24
Big Bayou 52 5 27N47 82W40 5:30:40
Big Bend Farm 37 5 30N25 84W20 5:37:20
Big Blackjack Landing 19 5 29N54'59 84W35'01 5:38:20
Big Coppitt Key 44 5 24N34 81W44 5:26:56
Big Cypress 26 5 26N45 80W58 5:23:52
Big Cypress Seminole Indian 6 6 26N01 80W13 5:20:52
Biggar 36 5 26N31'13 81W53'28 5:27:34
Big Pine Key 44 5 24N40 81W21 5:25:24
Biltmore 16 5 30N21'39 81W43'46 5:26:55
Biltmore Beach 3 1 30N08'37 85W45'29 5:43:02
Bimini 18 5 29N28'56 81W21'21 5:25:25
Birch Ocean Front 6 6 26N07'51 80W06'23 5:20:26
Biscayne Facility 13 6 25N47 80W13 5:20:52
Biscayne Gardens 13 6 25N54'47 80W12'38 5:20:51
Biscayne Park 13 6 25N52'56 80W10'51 5:20:43
Biscayne Village 16 5 30N26'10 81W43'08 5:26:53
Bithlo 48 5 28N33'16 81W06'24 5:24:26
Black Acres 1 5 29N40 82W20 5:29:20
Black Creek 37 5 30N30'29 84W05'18 5:36:21
Blackman 46 1 30N55'28 86W38'12 5:46:33
Black Point 18 5 29N26'49 81W18'19 5:25:13
Blacks Ford 55 5 30N02'49 81W33'38 5:26:15
Blacks Still 24 5 30N28'00 82W48'08 5:31:13
Bland 1 5 29N54'07 82W29'57 5:30:00
Blanton 51 5 28N24'41 82W14'48 5:28:59
Blazed Pine Landing 7 1 30N15'47 85W09'29 5:40:38
Blazed Pine Landing 39 5 30N13'35 84W41'59 5:38:48
Blichton 42 5 29N16'56 82W20'13 5:29:21
Blocker 37 5 30N35'14 84W16'25 5:37:06
Blood Landing 45 5 30N47'20 81W48'57 5:27:16
Bloody Bluff 19 5 30N23 84W48 5:39:12
Bloomingdale 29 5 27N53'36 82W14'26 5:28:58
Blountstown 7 1 30N26'36 85W02'43 5:40:11
Blowing Rocks 43 5 26N58'36 80W04'55 5:20:20
Bloxham 37 5 30N23'18 84W37'51 5:38:31
Bluefield 43 5 27N11'59 80W35'15 5:22:21
Blue Gulf Beach 66 1 30N20'28 86W12'21 5:44:49
Blue Inlet 50 6 26N22'41 80W04'26 5:20:18
Blue Lake 51 5 28N18'10 82W03'27 5:28:14
Blue Lake 64 5 29N02 81W18 5:25:12
Blue Lakes Ridge 35 5 28N59'06 81W31'52 5:26:07
Blue Mountain 66 1 30N20 86W12 5:44:48
Blue Mountain Beach 66 1 30N20'14 86W11'50 5:44:47
Blue Springs 24 5 30N29'11 83W13'12 5:32:53
Blue Springs 35 5 28N44 81W49 5:27:16
Blue Springs 64 5 28N55 81W17 5:25:08
Blue Springs Landing 64 5 28N56'35 81W20'24 5:25:22
Bluff Landing 16 5 30N12'55 81W43'02 5:26:52
Bluff Landing 46 1 30N49'05 86W44'40 5:46:59
Bluff Springs 17 1 30N56'10 87W17'41 5:49:11
Bluffton 64 5 29N07'34 81W30'07 5:26:00
Boardman 42 5 29N28'02 82W12'51 5:28:51
Boca Chica 44 5 24N34 81W42 5:26:48
Boca Ciega 52 5 27N45'37 82W45'59 5:31:04
Boca Grande 36 5 26N44'55 82W15'44 5:29:03
Boca Harbour 50 6 26N24'44 80W04'21 5:20:17
Boca Raton 50 6 26N21'30 80W05'00 5:20:20
Bogia 17 1 30N50'32 87W19'28 5:49:18
Bohemia 17 4 30N29'00 87W09'36 5:48:38
Bokeelia 36 5 26N42'19 82W09'33 5:28:38
Bon Ami 39 5 30N06'52 84W59'14 5:39:57
Bonaventure 5 5 28N16'25 80W41'37 5:22:46
Bonifay 30 1 30N47'30 85W40'47 5:42:43
Bonita Beach 36 5 26N20 81W47 5:27:08
Bonita Shores 36 5 26N19'50 81W49'37 5:27:18
Bonita Springs 36 5 26N20'22 81W46'44 5:27:07
Bonnie 53 5 27N51'47 81W55'53 5:27:44
Bonnie Lock 6 6 26N16'45 80W07'41 5:20:31
Bon Terra 18 5 29N34'53 81W11'18 5:24:45
Bookertown 59 5 28N49'41 81W19'55 5:25:20
Booth Landing 55 5 30N04'02 81W21'50 5:25:27
Bostwick 54 5 29N46'26 81W38'14 5:26:33
Botts 57 1 30N39 87W05 5:48:20
Boulevard 52 5 28N00 82W46 5:31:04
Boulogne 45 5 30N46'17 81W58'34 5:27:54
Bounds Crossing 30 1 30N47'53 85W54'45 5:43:39
Bowden 16 5 30N15'57 81W37'06 5:26:28
Bowling Green 25 5 27N38'17 81W49'27 5:27:18
Boyd 62 5 30N11'20 83W36'24 5:34:26
Boyette 29 5 27N49'02 82W13'22 5:28:53
Boynton Beach 50 6 26N31'30 80W04'00 5:20:16
Boys Ranch 61 5 30N18 82W59 5:31:56
Braden Castle 41 5 27N29'46 82W31'50 5:30:07
Bradenton 41 5 27N29'55 82W34'30 5:30:18
Bradenton Beach 41 5 27N28'00 82W42'15 5:30:49
Bradford 67 1 30N39'18 85W33'06 5:42:12
Bradfordville 37 5 30N33'40 84W13'04 5:36:52
Bradley Junction 53 5 27N47'42 81W58'50 5:27:55
Branchborough 51 5 28N15'32 82W05'22 5:28:21
Branchton 29 5 28N08'04 82W17'14 5:29:09
Branchville 20 5 30N39'14 84W28'58 5:37:56
Brandon 29 5 27N56'15 82W17'10 5:29:09
Branford 61 5 29N57'32 82W55'42 5:31:43
Brannonville 3 1 30N13'28 85W35'34 5:42:22
Braswells 33 5 30N33 83W52 5:35:28
Bratt 17 1 30N57'56 87W25'39 5:49:43
Breezeswept Park Estates 6 6 26N07'44 80W12'46 5:20:51
Brent 17 4 30N28'07 87W14'10 5:48:57
Brentwood 16 5 30N21'32 81W39'32 5:26:38
Brentwood Estates 6 6 26N11'21 80W08'50 5:20:35
Brewers Landing 10 5 29N52'23 81W37'15 5:26:29
Brewster 53 5 27N45'09 81W58'47 5:27:55
Brickell Hammock 13 6 25N44'59 80W12'17 5:20:49
Brickton 17 1 30N44'01 87W19'17 5:49:17
Brickyard 19 5 29N57'45 85W01'19 5:40:05
Brickyard Landing 19 5 29N56'56 85W00'54 5:40:04
Brickyard Landing 45 5 30N45'42 81W47'01 5:27:08
Bridgeport 52 5 28N01'37 82W41'28 5:30:46
Bridgeport 54 5 29N45'11 81W34'13 5:26:17
Bridges 25 5 27N24'30 81W54'25 5:27:38
Bridle Path Acres 37 5 30N30'32 84W15'45 5:37:03
Bright 13 6 25N50 80W17 5:21:08
Brighton 28 5 27N13'32 81W05'43 5:24:23
Brighton Indian Reservation 22 6 27N04 81W04 5:24:16
Briney Breezes 50 6 26N31 80W03 5:20:12
Bristol 39 5 30N25'55 84W58'33 5:39:54
Broad Branch 7 1 30N18'41 85W17'44 5:41:11
Broadview Country Club Est 6 6 26N09 80W13 5:20:52
Broadview Park 6 6 26N07 80W13 5:20:52
Brock Crossroad 67 1 30N41'25 85W37'46 5:42:31
Bronson 38 5 29N26'51 82W38'33 5:30:34
Brooker 4 5 29N53'19 82W19'58 5:29:20
Brooklyn 16 5 30N19'24 81W40'29 5:26:42
Brookside 31 5 27N46'02 80W33'06 5:22:12
Brooksville 27 5 28N33'18 82W23'17 5:29:33
Brooksville West 27 5 28N31 82W29 5:29:56
Browardale 6 6 26N08 80W14 5:20:56
Broward Gardens 6 6 26N03'25 80W12'28 5:20:50
Broward Highlands 6 6 26N17'53 80W06'40 5:20:27
Brownsdale 57 1 30N52'56 87W13'32 5:48:54
Browns Landing 12 5 30N22'09 82W39'42 5:30:39
Browns Landing 54 5 29N35'49 81W38'18 5:26:33
Browns Still 63 5 29N59'03 82W29'27 5:29:58
Browns Village 13 6 25N49 80W14 5:20:56
Brownsville 13 6 25N49 80W14 5:20:56
Brownsville 17 4 30N25'30 87W15'07 5:49:00
Browntown 32 1 30N58'56 85W28'02 5:41:52
Brownville 14 5 27N17'52 81W49'27 5:27:18
Broxson 57 1 30N34'03 86W55'19 5:47:41
Bruce 66 1 30N28'20 85W57'55 5:43:52
Bruceville 42 5 29N14'01 81W56'50 5:27:47

Brushy Crossing 39 5 30N13'41 84w59'09 5:39:57
Bryant 50 5 26N50'58 80w37'00 5:22:28
Bryants Landing 23 1 30N01'01 85w08'48 5:40:35
Bryceville 45 5 30N23'04 81w56'20 5:27:45
Brynwood 36 5 26N36 81w52 5:27:28
Buccaneer Estates 13 6 25N55 80w15 5:21:00
Bucell Junction 62 5 30N04'10 83w33'21 5:34:13
Buchanan 25 5 27N24'42 81w47'34 5:27:10
Buckhead Ridge 22 5 27N07'48 80w53'38 5:23:35
Buckhorn 65 5 30N04'01 84w27'07 5:37:48
Buckingham 36 5 26N40'29 81w43'56 5:26:56
Buckingham West 1 5 29N39'30 82w26'07 5:29:44
Buckville 34 5 30N07'44 83w17'33 5:33:10
Buda 1 5 29N45'32 82w37'34 5:30:30
Buena Vista 13 6 25N48'46 80w11'31 5:20:46
Buena Vista 32 1 30N52'46 85w02'06 5:40:08
Buena Vista 51 5 28N11 82w45 5:31:00
Buffalo Bluff 54 5 29N34'46 81w40'26 5:26:42
Bull Headley Public Landing 37 5 30N37'04 84w15'10 5:37:01
Bunche Park 13 6 25N55'13 80w14'14 5:20:57
Bunker 14 5 27N13 81w52 5:27:28
Bunker 66 1 30N23'14 86w04'58 5:44:20
Bunnell 18 5 29N27'57 81w15'29 5:25:02
Burbank 42 5 29N17'26 82w00'04 5:28:00
Burgess Landing 23 1 30N02'27 85w10'11 5:40:41
Burnetts Lake 1 5 29N47'14 82w28'40 5:29:55
Bushnell 60 5 28N39'53 82w06'47 5:28:27
Butcher Pen Landing 19 5 29N48'11 84w57'59 5:39:52
Butter Landing 57 1 30N42'44 86w49'48 5:47:19
Byrd 55 5 29N40'39 81w27'40 5:25:51
Byrneville 17 1 30N57'58 87w19'37 5:49:18
Cabbage Grove 62 5 30N12'34 83w52'26 5:35:30
Cadillac 1 5 29N44'29 82w32'20 5:30:09
Cairo 3 1 30N18'17 85w28'38 5:41:55
Caldwell Landing 42 5 29N14'41 81w57'56 5:27:52
Caleb 16 5 30N16'36 81w49'55 5:27:20
Calhoun West 7 1 30N26 85w16 5:41:04
Callahan 45 5 30N33'43 81w49'51 5:27:19
Callaway 3 1 30N09'10 85w34'12 5:42:17
Calphos 9 5 28N54'43 82w23'04 5:29:32
Cambon 16 5 30N20'45 81w48'23 5:27:14
Camellia Gardens 48 5 28N29 81w22 5:25:28
Cameron City 59 5 28N45'24 81w13'08 5:24:53
Campbell 49 5 28N15'31 81w27'24 5:25:50
Campbellton 32 1 30N56'57 85w24'08 5:41:37
Camp Blanding 10 5 29N57 82w06 5:28:24
Camp Echockotee 10 5 30N09'08 81w43'38 5:26:55
Camp Ocala 35 5 29N06'27 81w37'52 5:26:31
Camp Roosevelt 42 5 29N08'45 82w06'56 5:28:28
Camps 27 5 28N35'28 82w25'51 5:29:43
Camps Mine 27 5 28N32 82w29 5:29:56
Camps Still 24 5 30N25'56 82w52'02 5:31:28
Campton 46 1 30N52'24 86w31'06 5:46:04
Campville 1 5 29N39'58 82w07'07 5:28:28
Cana 56 5 27N17'00 80w29'36 5:21:58
Canaan 59 5 28N47'24 81w13'22 5:24:53
Canal Point 50 5 26N51'32 80w38'02 5:22:32
Candler 42 5 29N04'16 81w58'06 5:27:52
Caney Creek 66 1 30N53'59 86w12'31 5:44:50
Cannon Town 46 1 30N51'17 86w40'27 5:46:42
Canova Beach 5 5 28N08 80w35 5:22:20
Cantonment 17 1 30N36'30 87w20'24 5:49:22
Cape Canaveral 5 5 28N24'20 80w36'18 5:22:25
Cape Coral 36 5 26N33'45 81w56'59 5:27:48
Cape Haze 8 5 26N51'00 82w17'40 5:29:11
Cape Sable 44 5 25N33 81w01 5:24:04
Cape Vista 41 5 27N28 82w35 5:30:20
Capitola 37 5 30N27'03 84w05'17 5:36:21
Capps 33 5 30N24'37 83w54'40 5:35:39
Captiva 36 5 26N31'18 82w11'22 5:28:45
Caraway Landing 1 5 29N32'51 82w08'30 5:28:34
Carbur 62 5 29N55'05 83w25'41 5:33:43
Cardwell 50 5 26N45'56 80w39'36 5:22:38
Caribbean Key 50 6 26N23'59 80w04'21 5:20:17
Carleton 54 5 29N36 82w05 5:28:20
Carl Fisher 13 6 25N48 80w09 5:20:36
Carlson 60 5 28N49'27 82w10'55 5:28:44
Carlton 52 5 28N00 82w46 5:31:04
Carlton Village 35 5 28N55'56 81w53'08 5:27:33
Carnestown 11 5 25N54'38 81w21'52 5:25:27
Carol City 13 6 25N56'25 80w14'45 5:20:59
Carr 7 1 30N34 85w08 5:40:32
Carrabelle 19 5 29N51'11 84w39'52 5:38:39
Carrabelle Beach 19 5 29N49'55 84w41'03 5:38:44
Carrabelle Lighthouse 19 5 29N49'38 84w42'04 5:38:48
Carraway 54 5 29N42'32 81w47'12 5:27:09
Carr Landing 46 1 30N40'23 86w41'51 5:46:47
Carrollwood 29 5 28N04 82w29 5:29:56
Carter Landing 7 1 30N17'32 85w08'53 5:40:36
Carters 53 5 28N03 81w56 5:27:44
Carters Bulkhead 5 5 28N01'49 80w32'43 5:22:11
Carters Corner 53 5 28N02'38 81w51'31 5:27:26
Carver 16 5 30N22 81w41 5:26:44
Carver 60 5 28N39'25 82w06'09 5:28:25
Carver Heights 6 6 26N18'53 80w06'14 5:20:25
Carver Manor 16 5 30N22'40 81w43'42 5:26:55
Carver Ranches 6 6 25N59'17 80w11'33 5:20:46
Carver Ranch Estates 6 6 25N59 80w12 5:20:48
Carver Village 6 6 26N15'07 80w08'37 5:20:34
Cary 16 5 30N27'45 81w47'04 5:27:08
Caryville 67 1 30N46'23 85w48'51 5:43:15
Casa Blanco 33 5 30N30'58 83w53'16 5:35:33
Casa Cola 55 5 29N58'19 81w20'47 5:25:23
Cassadaga 64 5 28N57'58 81w14'10 5:24:57
Casselberry 59 5 28N40'39 81w19'41 5:25:19
Cassia 35 5 28N53'21 81w27'56 5:25:52
Castle Hill 35 5 28N32'44 81w41'04 5:26:44
Catawba 9 5 28N41'18 82w22'36 5:29:30
Cecil Field Naval Air Statio 16 5 30N19 81w39 5:26:36
Cedar Creek 42 5 29N16'25 81w54'07 5:27:36
Cedar Creek Landing 42 5 29N18'10 81w54'11 5:27:37
Cedar Grove 3 1 30N10'15 85w37'31 5:42:30
Cedar Hammock 41 5 27N28 82w35 5:30:20
Cedar Hills 16 5 30N15'46 81w44'51 5:26:59
Cedar Hills Estates 16 5 30N16'38 81w44'44 5:26:59
Cedar Key 38 5 29N08'18 83w02'07 5:32:08
Cedar Landing 42 5 29N30'47 81w51'55 5:27:28
Cedar Landing 55 5 29N43'26 81w15'14 5:25:01
Cedar Point 16 5 30N26'37 81w27'50 5:25:51
Cedar Tree Landing 66 1 30N28'14 85w52'31 5:43:30
Center Fait Landing 57 1 30N42'37 86w50'21 5:47:21
Center Hill 60 5 28N38'59 81w59'34 5:27:58
Center Park 16 5 30N17'24 81w30'05 5:26:00
Centerville 37 5 30N33'25 84w10'35 5:36:42
Central City 39 5 30N11'17 84w55'33 5:39:42
Central Pasco 51 5 28N18 82w24 5:29:36
Central Volusia 64 5 29N06 81w06 5:24:24
Century 17 1 30N58'23 87w15'50 5:49:03
Century 21 36 5 26N36 81w52 5:27:28
Century Corners 50 6 26N42 80w05 5:20:20
Cerrogordo 30 1 30N49'54 85w53'15 5:43:33
Chain O Lakes 35 5 28N59'01 81w30'43 5:26:03
Chaires 37 5 30N26'10 84w07'03 5:36:28
Chancey 34 5 30N14'25 83w15'38 5:33:03
Channell 35 5 28N48 81w39 5:26:36
Chantilly Acres 1 5 29N42'50 82w25'05 5:29:40
Chapel Hill 50 6 26N29'52 80w04'28 5:20:18
Charlotte Beach 8 5 26N56 82w14 5:28:56
Charlotte Harbor 8 5 26N57'29 82w04'02 5:28:16
Charlotte Park 8 5 26N54'35 82w03'15 5:28:13
Chaseville 16 5 30N20 81w35 5:26:20
Chason 7 1 30N32'06 85w11'31 5:40:46
Chassahowitzka 9 5 28N42'46 82w34'28 5:30:18
Chatham 44 5 25N42'50 81w14'39 5:24:59
Chatmar 42 5 29N04'01 82w27'11 5:29:49
Chattahoochee 20 5 30N42'18 84w50'35 5:39:22
Cherry Lake 40 5 30N33'00 83w25'40 5:33:43
Cherry Lake 60 5 28N54'38 81w57'14 5:27:49
Chester 45 5 30N40'58 81w32'25 5:26:10
Chiefland 38 5 29N30'13 82w52'19 5:31:29
Childs 28 5 27N12'34 81w20'42 5:25:23
Chipley 67 1 30N46'54 85w32'19 5:42:09
Chipola 7 1 30N18'05 85w07'06 5:40:28
Chipola Park 7 1 30N47 85w14 5:40:56
Chipola Terrace 32 1 30N49'38 85w09'57 5:40:40
Choctaw 66 1 30N22'02 86w06'22 5:44:25
Choctaw Beach 66 1 30N28'16 86w20'36 5:45:22
Chokoloskee 11 5 25N48'45 81w21'44 5:25:27
Chosen 50 5 26N40 80w41 5:22:44
Chosen Labor Camp 50 5 26N40 80w41 5:22:44
Christina 53 5 28N03 81w56 5:27:44
Christmas 48 5 28N32'10 81w01'04 5:24:04
Chuluota 59 5 28N38'30 81w07'25 5:24:30
Chumuckla 57 1 30N46'35 87w14'14 5:48:57
Chumuckla Springs 57 1 30N50'01 87w17'46 5:49:11
Cinco Bayou 46 1 30N25 86w36 5:46:24
Cisky Park 35 5 28N47'40 81w50'58 5:27:24
Citra 42 5 29N24'42 82w06'36 5:28:26
Citronelle 9 5 28N58'42 82w34'08 5:30:17
Citrus Center 22 5 26N50 81w06 5:24:24
Citrus Park 29 5 28N04'41 82w34'12 5:30:17
Citrus Springs 9 5 29N03 82w27 5:29:48
Citrus Tower 35 5 28N33 81w45 5:27:00
City Point 5 5 28N24'21 80w45'20 5:23:01
City View 36 5 26N36 81w52 5:27:28
Clair-Mel City 29 5 27N57 82w24 5:29:36
Clara 62 5 29N47'49 83w19'13 5:33:17
Clarcona 48 5 28N36'45 81w29'56 5:26:00
Clark 1 5 29N46'23 82w37'34 5:30:30
Clarksville 7 1 30N26'12 85w11'10 5:40:45
Clarkwild 29 5 28N03'03 82w19'11 5:29:17
Clay Island 35 5 28N39'49 81w41'46 5:26:47
Clay Landing 16 5 30N32'01 81w44'34 5:26:58
Clay Landing 38 5 29N31'24 82w58'07 5:31:52
Clay Landing 54 5 29N46'28 81w33'43 5:26:15
Clayno 4 5 29N54'22 82w15'01 5:29:00
Clay Sink 51 5 28N28'20 82w04'01 5:28:16
Clear Lake 1 5 29N40 82w20 5:29:20
Clear Springs 46 1 30N52'25 86w34'12 5:46:17
Clear Springs 66 1 30N58'47 86w20'43 5:45:23
Clearview 52 5 27N49 82w41 5:30:44
Clearwater 52 5 27N57'56 82w48'01 5:31:12
Clearwater Beach 52 5 27N58'37 82w49'41 5:31:19
Clermont 35 5 28N32'57 81w46'23 5:27:06
Cleveland 8 5 26N57'41 81w59'03 5:27:56
Cleveland Street 52 5 27N58 82w47 5:31:08
Clewiston 26 5 26N45'14 80w56'02 5:23:44
Clifton 16 5 30N20 81w35 5:26:20
Cliftonville 63 5 30N02'40 82w23'32 5:29:34
Clinton Heights 51 5 28N19'46 82w11'23 5:28:46
Clio 39 5 30N19'09 84w49'34 5:39:18
Cloud Lake 50 6 26N40'33 80w04'27 5:20:18
Cluster Springs 66 1 30N50'18 86w12'19 5:44:49
Coach Light Manor 36 5 26N36 81w52 5:27:28
Coachman 52 5 27N58'39 82w44'17 5:30:57
Cobb Creek 57 1 30N57'29 87w05'34 5:48:22
Cobb Cross Roads 30 1 30N58'50 85w32'51 5:42:11
Cobbtown 57 1 30N52'58 87w07'11 5:48:29
Cockran Landing 23 1 30N06'01 85w10'54 5:40:44
Cocoa 5 5 28N23'09 80w44'32 5:22:58
Cocoa Beach 5 5 28N19'11 80w36'28 5:22:26
Coconut 36 5 26N23'57 81w50'23 5:27:22
Coconut Creek 6 6 26N15 80w11 5:20:44
Coconut Creek Park 6 6 26N14'30 80w10'57 5:20:44
Coconut Grove 13 6 25N42'44 80w15'26 5:21:02
Cody 33 5 30N21'38 84w03'04 5:36:12
Codys Corner 18 5 29N20'35 81w18'40 5:25:15
Coes Landing 37 5 30N27'07 84w28'58 5:37:56
Coker 25 5 27N33'54 81w48'54 5:27:16
Coldwater 57 1 30N39 87w05 5:48:20
Colee 6 6 26N08 80w11 5:20:44
Coleman 60 5 28N47'58 82w04'13 5:28:17
Coleman Landing 60 5 28N47'54 82w06'11 5:28:25
College Park 6 6 26N19'27 80w06'23 5:20:26
College Park 16 5 30N20'41 81w40'41 5:26:43
College Park 48 5 28N35 81w24 5:25:36
College Park 55 5 29N52'59 81w21'11 5:25:25
College Point 3 1 30N09 85w39 5:42:36
Collier City 6 6 26N15 80w09 5:20:36
Collier Manor 6 6 26N17 80w09 5:20:36
Collier Park 6 6 26N14'02 80w09'34 5:20:38
Collins Landing 37 5 30N25'05 84w33'13 5:38:13
Collins Mill 32 1 30N57'57 85w31'52 5:42:07
Collins Park Estates 56 5 27N22'18 80w19'09 5:21:17
Colonial Hills 51 5 28N13 82w44 5:30:56
Colonial Manor 16 5 30N19 81w43 5:26:52
Colonialtown 48 5 28N33 81w21 5:25:24
Columbia 12 5 30N04'25 82w41'45 5:30:47
Combee Settlement 53 5 28N04 81w54 5:27:36
Compass Lake 32 1 30N35'33 85w23'34 5:41:34
Conant 35 5 28N56'15 81w55'41 5:27:43
Conch Key 44 5 24N47'24 80w53'23 5:23:34
Concord 20 5 30N39'27 84w21'54 5:37:28
Concord 37 5 30N33'49 84w02'44 5:36:11
Conner 42 5 29N14'24 81w57'41 5:27:51
Conner Landing 42 5 29N14'19 81w57'59 5:27:52
Conners Ford 39 5 30N19'34 84w51'50 5:39:27
Connersville 53 5 27N54'32 81w47'11 5:27:09
Connersville 64 5 29N16'31 81w28'34 5:25:54
Conway 48 5 28N30'09 81w19'51 5:25:19
Cooglers Beach 27 5 28N33'11 82w39'01 5:30:36
Cook Landing 55 5 30N05'06 81w21'49 5:25:27
Cooks Hammock 34 5 29N55'46 83w16'36 5:33:06
Cooper City 6 6 26N03'25 80w16'19 5:21:05
Coopertown 13 6 25N45'37 80w33'40 5:22:15
Copeland 11 5 25N57'12 81w21'22 5:25:25
Copeland Settlement 1 5 29N40'33 82w14'40 5:28:59
Copelands Landing 31 5 27N43'37 80w25'00 5:21:40
Coquina Gables 55 5 29N50'34 81w15'56 5:25:04
Cora 57 1 30N57 87w09 5:48:36
Coral Cove 58 5 27N15 82w31 5:30:04
Coral Estates 6 6 26N09'37 80w07'40 5:20:31
Coral Gables 13 6 25N43'16 80w16'07 5:21:04
Coral Gardens 43 5 27N08'22 80w12'41 5:20:51
Coral Heights 6 6 26N10'46 80w07'45 5:20:31
Coral Hills 6 6 26N11'17 80w07'19 5:20:29
Coral Manor 6 6 26N18'00 80w06'14 5:20:25
Coral Point 6 6 26N09 80w11 5:20:44
Coral Ridge 6 6 26N09'36 80w06'36 5:20:26
Coral Ridge Isles 6 6 26N11'33 80w07'05 5:20:28
Coral Springs 6 6 26N16 80w15 5:21:00
Coral Way Village 13 6 25N44'35 80w19'39 5:21:19
Coral Woods 6 6 26N10'01 80w07'39 5:20:31
Corkscrew 11 5 26N28'18 81w33'34 5:26:14
Cornwell 28 5 27N22'42 81w05'49 5:24:23
Coronado 64 5 29N02 80w55 5:23:40
Coronet 29 5 27N59'14 82w04'51 5:28:19
Corry Field 17 1 30N04 87w12 5:48:48
Cortez 41 5 27N28'08 82w41'11 5:30:45
Cosme 29 5 28N06'31 82w34'22 5:30:17
Cosmo 16 5 30N21'52 81w30'56 5:26:04
Cosson Mill 66 1 30N42'00 86w10'52 5:44:43
Cottage Hill 17 1 30N37'57 87w19'12 5:49:17
Cottage Hill Landing 17 1 30N37'26 87w15'51 5:49:03
Cottage Point 36 5 26N36 81w52 5:27:28

Cottondale 32 1 30N47'49 85w22'36 5:41:30
Cotton Landing 39 5 30N03'05 85w04'24 5:40:18
Cottonplant 42 5 29N11 82w09 5:28:36
Council 36 5 26N22'32 81w48'14 5:27:13
Country Club Acres 50 6 26N27 80w05 5:20:20
Country Club Estates 12 5 30N17 81w24 5:25:36
Country Club Estates 53 5 28N32 81w22 5:25:28
Country Club Isles 6 6 26N14'57 80w05'36 5:20:22
Country Club Manor 59 5 28N47'26 81w17'02 5:25:08
Country Estates 51 5 28N11 82w44 5:30:56
County Club Acres 50 6 26N27'00 80w07'40 5:20:31
County Line Landing 3 1 30N18'40 85w59'39 5:43:59
Courtenay 5 5 28N27'24 80w42'35 5:22:50
Cove 3 1 30N08'44 85w38'57 5:42:36
Cow Creek 64 5 28N50'14 81w01'40 5:24:07
Cox 7 1 30N36'05 85w08'21 5:40:33
Cox Corner 53 5 27N52'44 81w45'40 5:27:03
Coytown 48 5 28N33 81w21 5:25:24
Cracker Landing 42 5 29N27'40 81w55'10 5:27:41
Crackertown 38 5 29N02'10 82w41'12 5:30:45
Craggs 21 5 29N46'43 82w44'28 5:30:58
Crandall 45 5 30N43'15 81w37'20 5:26:29
Crawford 45 5 30N30'31 81w52'52 5:27:31
Crawfordville 65 5 30N10'33 84w22'31 5:37:30
Creels 19 5 29N49'18 84w54'33 5:39:38
Creighton 64 5 28N53'14 80w55'20 5:23:41
Crescent Beach 55 5 29N46'07 81w15'14 5:25:01
Crescent Beach 58 5 27N19 82w31 5:30:04
Crescent City 54 5 29N25'48 81w30'39 5:26:03
Crescent City Station 54 5 29N24'54 81w32'00 5:26:08
Cresthaven 6 6 26N17 80w09 5:20:36
Cresthaven Villas 50 6 26N40 80w06 5:20:24
Crestview 13 6 25N55 80w15 5:21:00
Crestview 46 1 30N45'43 86w34'14 5:46:17
Crewsville 25 5 27N25'10 81w34'57 5:26:20
Cromanton 3 1 30N06'58 85w38'06 5:42:32
Crooked Lake Park 53 5 27N49'44 81w35'03 5:26:20
Croom 27 5 28N35'15 82w13'40 5:28:55
Cross Bayou 52 5 27N51'27 82w44'02 5:30:56
Cross City 15 5 29N38'03 83w07'31 5:32:30
Cross Creek 1 5 29N29'10 82w09'55 5:28:40
Crossley 54 5 29N35'20 81w59'36 5:27:58
Crown Point 48 5 28N35'17 81w34'02 5:26:16
Crows Bluff 35 5 29N00'27 81w23'22 5:25:33
Crystal Beach 52 5 28N05'28 82w46'48 5:31:07
Crystal Lake 53 5 28N02 81w57 5:27:48
Crystal Lake 67 1 30N26'38 85w41'19 5:42:45
Crystal River 9 5 28N54'08 82w35'34 5:30:22
Crystal Springs 51 5 28N10'52 82w09'28 5:28:38
Cubitis 14 5 27N15'35 81w50'27 5:27:22
Cudjoe 44 5 24N45 81w20 5:25:20
Cumbee 53 5 28N03 81w56 5:27:44
Cummings 31 5 27N47'50 80w27'44 5:21:51
Cumpressco 60 5 28N21'31 82w02'22 5:28:09
Cunningham Estates 51 5 28N15'50 82w12'26 5:28:50
Curlew 52 5 28N03'10 82w44'35 5:30:58
Curtis 21 5 29N45 82w52 5:31:28
Curtis Mill 65 5 30N00'30 84w31'34 5:38:06
Cutler 13 5 25N36'53 80w18'39 5:21:15
Cutler Ridge 13 5 25N34'49 80w20'49 5:21:23
Cutlers 9 5 28N51'45 82w34'59 5:30:20
Cypress 32 1 30N42'47 85w04'26 5:40:18
Cypress Creek 24 5 30N34'24 82w47'39 5:31:11
Cypress Gardens 53 5 27N59'37 81w41'25 5:26:46
Cypress Harbor 6 6 26N12'52 80w07'12 5:20:29
Cypress Isles Estates 6 6 26N13'17 80w06'41 5:20:27
Cypress Lake Estates 64 5 29N03'38 81w15'40 5:25:03
Cypress Point 54 5 29N41'52 81w35'25 5:26:22
Cypress Quarters 47 5 27N15'06 80w48'51 5:23:15
Dade City 51 5 28N21'52 82w11'46 5:28:47
Dahlberg 50 5 26N40'11 80w42'01 5:22:48
Dahoma 45 5 30N28'11 81w54'31 5:27:38
Daisy Lake 64 5 29N01'28 81w22'45 5:25:31
Dalhousie Acres 35 5 28N54'06 81w37'49 5:26:31
Dalkeith 23 1 30N00'20 85w09'15 5:40:37
Dallas 42 5 28N58'15 82w02'28 5:28:10
Dallus Creek Landing 62 5 29N43'16 83w29'12 5:33:57
Dame Point Manor 16 5 30N23'47 81w34'02 5:26:16
Dames Point 16 5 30N23'18 81w33'29 5:26:14
Dania 6 6 26N03'07 80w08'39 5:20:35
Dania Indian Reservation 6 6 26N01 80w13 5:20:52
Danks Corner 42 5 29N00'39 82w07'12 5:28:29
Danville 63 5 30N00'04 82w22'17 5:29:29
Darby 51 5 28N21'30 82w21'30 5:29:26
Darlington 66 1 30N56'37 86w03'27 5:44:14
Darsey 20 5 30N41'16 84w22'47 5:37:31
Davenport 53 5 28N09'40 81w36'07 5:26:24
Davie 6 6 26N03'52 80w13'56 5:20:56
Davis Shores 55 5 29N53'49 81w17'50 5:25:11
Day 34 5 30N11'38 83w17'29 5:33:10
Daysville 1 5 29N37'39 82w22'11 5:29:29
Daytona Beach 64 5 29N12'38 81w01'23 5:24:06
Daytona Beach Shores 64 5 29N10'33 80w58'59 5:23:56
Daytona Highbridge Estates 64 5 29N13 81w02 5:24:08
Daytona Highridge Estates 64 5 29N08'06 81w08'05 5:24:32
Daytona Park Estates 64 5 29N03'16 81w14'47 5:24:59
Deadman Landing 64 5 29N15'42 81w32'05 5:26:08
Deanville 18 5 29N20'34 81w21'10 5:25:25
DeBary 64 5 28N52'58 81w18'32 5:25:14
Deem City 50 6 26N20'12 80w32'28 5:22:10
Deep Creek 12 5 30N22'22 82w37'23 5:30:30
Deep Lake 11 5 26N02'32 81w20'39 5:25:23
Deerfield Beach 6 6 26N19'05 80w06'00 5:20:24
Deerland 46 1 30N45'06 86w26'09 5:45:45
Deer Park 49 5 28N05'28 80w53'53 5:23:36
Deerwood Club 16 5 30N13'51 81w32'59 5:26:12
De Funiak Springs 66 1 30N43'17 86w06'56 5:44:28
Dekle Beach 62 5 29N50'56 83w37'10 5:34:29
Delaco 46 1 30N46 86w34 5:46:16
De Land 64 5 29N01'41 81w18'12 5:25:13
De Land Highlands 64 5 29N04'14 81w15'52 5:25:03
De Leon Springs 64 5 29N07'09 81w21'06 5:25:24
De Leon Springs Heights 64 5 29N08'24 81w19'12 5:25:17
Delespine 5 5 28N29'25 80w46'46 5:23:07
Dell 61 5 30N08'11 83w14'24 5:32:58
Dellwood 32 1 30N49'25 85w02'59 5:40:12
Dellwood 52 5 27N58'57 82w42'33 5:30:50
Delray Beach 50 6 26N27'40 80w04'23 5:20:18
Delray Gardens 50 6 26N28'47 80w07'22 5:20:29
Delray Shores 50 6 26N28'15 80w05'51 5:20:23
Delta 50 6 26N51'29 80w13'32 5:20:54
Deltona 64 5 28N54'01 81w15'50 5:25:03
Delwood Beach 3 1 30N08'40 85w42'48 5:42:51
Demere Landing 36 5 26N35'33 82w07'36 5:28:30
Denaud 26 5 26N44'31 81w30'37 5:26:02
Dennet 40 5 30N32'10 83w36'41 5:34:27
Denver 54 5 29N24'15 81w31'37 5:26:06
De Soto City 28 5 27N26'32 81w24'19 5:25:37
Desoto Lakes 58 5 27N20 82w32 5:30:08
Destin 46 1 30N23'36 86w29'45 5:45:59
Devils Garden 26 5 26N45 80w58 5:23:52
Dewey Park 16 5 30N13'54 81w42'10 5:26:49
Dickerson City 57 1 30N39 87w05 5:48:20
Dickert 61 5 30N20'21 83w04'50 5:32:19
Dills 33 5 30N37'23 83w46'20 5:35:05
Dinner Island 18 5 29N33'39 81w23'05 5:25:32
Dinsmore 16 5 30N24'21 81w44'41 5:26:59
Diregо Park 3 1 30N11'30 85w38'22 5:42:33
Disston Plaza 52 5 27N47 82w43 5:30:52
Dixie 27 5 28N26'05 82w18'10 5:29:13
Dixie Grove 51 5 28N15 82w45 5:31:00
Dixieland 53 5 28N02 81w57 5:27:48
Dixie Ranch Acres 47 5 27N19'24 80w54'28 5:23:38
Dixie Village 48 5 28N31 81w21 5:25:24
Dixonville 57 1 30N59'56 87w02'11 5:48:09
Doctors Inlet 10 5 30N06'00 81w46'35 5:27:06
Doctor's Lake Estates 10 5 30N08 81w42 5:26:48
Dogtown 20 5 30N40'43 84w30'12 5:38:01
Dogwood Lake Estates 30 1 30N53 85w40 5:42:40
Dona Vista 35 5 28N53'40 81w41'15 5:26:45
Donner 16 5 30N20'24 81w24'42 5:25:39
Dorcas 46 1 30N47'53 86w24'57 5:45:40
Dorset 50 5 26N49 80w40 5:22:40
Douglas City 20 5 30N35 84w35 5:38:20
Douglas Crossroads 66 1 30N43 85w57 5:43:48
Douglas Landing 23 1 30N00'40 85w08'00 5:40:32
Douglass Crossroads 66 1 30N41'15 85w58'36 5:43:54
Dover 29 5 27N59'38 82w13'11 5:28:53
Dover Shores 48 5 28N31 81w21 5:25:24
Dowling Park 61 5 30N14'36 83w14'11 5:32:57
Drayton Island 54 5 29N23 81w38 5:26:32
Dreamworld 59 5 28N47'02 81w16'34 5:25:06
Drew Park 29 5 27N59'01 82w30'48 5:30:03
Drexel 51 5 28N15 82w28 5:29:52
Drifton 33 5 30N29'43 83w52'46 5:35:31
Driftwood Acres 6 6 26N01'40 80w13'36 5:20:54
Druid Hills 59 5 28N38 81w22 5:25:28
Dublin 35 5 28N47'21 81w37'37 5:26:30
Duck Key 44 5 24N42 81w05 5:24:20
Duette 41 5 27N35'24 82w07'23 5:28:30
Dukes 63 5 29N57'58 82w24'27 5:29:38
Dummit Grove 5 5 28N42'24 80w43'41 5:22:55
Dundee 53 5 28N01'20 81w37'10 5:26:29
Dunedin 52 5 28N01'10 82w46'19 5:31:05
Dunedin Isles 52 5 28N01'39 82w47'26 5:31:10
Dunlawton 64 5 29N09 80w59 5:23:56
Dunn Creek 16 5 30N29'10 81w35'27 5:26:22
Dunnellon 42 5 29N02'56 82w27'40 5:29:51
Dupont 18 5 29N25'36 81w13'22 5:24:53
Dupont Center 55 5 29N45'22 81w18'48 5:25:15
Dupree Gardens 51 5 28N14'15 82w26'49 5:29:47
Durant 29 5 27N54'30 82w11'11 5:28:45
Durant Estates 1 5 29N39'23 82w24'17 5:29:37
Durbin 55 5 30N05'14 81w27'41 5:25:51
Durham 7 1 30N26'33 85w04'31 5:40:18
Durisoe Landing 42 5 29N15'48 81w56'47 5:27:47
Duval 16 5 30N29'05 81w37'19 5:26:29
Dyal 45 5 30N37'16 81w52'13 5:27:29
Eagle Island 47 5 27N26'31 80w50'37 5:23:22
Eagle Lake 53 5 27N58'41 81w45'24 5:27:02
Earleton 1 5 29N45 82w06 5:28:24
Early Bird 42 5 29N12'56 82w22'04 5:29:28
East Alachua 1 5 29N47 82w30 5:30:00
East Auburndale 53 5 28N04 81w46 5:27:04
East Avenue 58 5 27N19 82w31 5:30:04
Eastbrook 48 5 28N34 81w35 5:26:20
Eastern Shores 13 6 25N56'00 80w08'09 5:20:33
East Flagler 18 5 29N32 81w14 5:24:56
Eastgate 41 5 27N26'30 82w30'22 5:30:01
Eastgate 48 5 28N36 81w21 5:25:24
Eastgate 58 5 27N05'50 82w25'17 5:29:41
East Gate Park 6 6 26N09'23 80w11'49 5:20:47
East Hill 17 4 30N26 87w15 5:49:00
East Lake Park 29 5 28N00 82w25 5:29:40
Eastlake Weir 42 5 29N01'12 81w54'30 5:27:38
East Liberty 39 5 30N21 84w48 5:39:12
East Mandarin 16 5 30N09'11 81w38'29 5:26:34
East Marion 42 5 29N12 81w50 5:27:20
East Milton 57 3 30N36'54 87w01'18 5:48:05
East Mims 5 5 28N39'32 80w49'41 5:23:19
East Mulberry 53 5 27N53'40 81w57'55 5:27:52
East Naples 11 5 26N08'17 81w46'00 5:27:04
East Okeechobee 47 5 27N18 80w45 5:23:00
East Orange 48 5 28N33 81w11 5:24:44
East Palatka 54 5 29N39'29 81w35'55 5:26:24
East Pensacola Heights 17 4 30N25'43 87w10'48 5:48:43
Eastpoint 19 5 29N44'11 84w52'43 5:39:31
Eastport 16 5 30N25'23 81w35'57 5:26:24
East Rockland Key 44 5 24N34 81w44 5:26:56
East Tampa 29 5 27N51'51 82w22'49 5:29:31
East Venice 58 5 27N04 82w20 5:29:20
Eastway Park 6 6 26N17'37 80w05'27 5:20:22
East Williston 38 5 29N23 82w27 5:29:48
East Winter Haven 53 5 28N02 81w42 5:26:48
Eastwood 53 5 28N01'26 81w40'14 5:26:41
Eaton Park 53 5 28N00'30 81w54'28 5:27:38
Eatonville 48 5 28N36'52 81w22'51 5:25:31
Eau Gallie 5 5 28N07'44 80w37'50 5:22:31
Ebb 40 5 30N21'12 83w39'07 5:34:36
Ebro 67 1 30N26'52 85w52'27 5:43:30
Econfina 3 1 30N24'43 85w32'09 5:42:09
Econfina Landing 62 5 30N03'32 83w54'23 5:35:38
Eddy 2 5 30N32'36 82w20'20 5:29:21
Eden 56 5 27N16'35 80w14'35 5:20:58
Edgar 54 5 29N35'41 81w57'03 5:27:48
Edgeville 41 5 27N18'51 82w06'30 5:28:26
Edgewater 64 5 28N59'19 80w54'09 5:23:37
Edgewater Gulf Beach 3 1 30N11'10 85w49'15 5:43:17
Edgewater Junction 64 5 28N58'36 80w56'48 5:23:47
Edgewood 16 5 30N18 81w38 5:26:32
Edgewood 48 5 28N29'09 81w22'21 5:25:29
Edison 29 5 27N51'54 82w04'00 5:28:16
Edison Center 13 6 25N50'00 80w12'05 5:20:48
Eggleston Heights 16 5 30N20'26 81w35'54 5:26:24
Eglin 46 2 30N32 86w36 5:46:24
Eglin Air Force Base 46 2 30N29 86w30 5:46:00
Eglin Village 46 2 30N27'46 86w32'22 5:46:09
Egypt Lake 29 5 28N00 82w30 5:30:00
Ehren 51 5 28N15'58 82w26'53 5:29:48
Elbow Landing 45 5 30N49'03 81w55'45 5:27:43
Elder Springs 59 5 28N44'27 81w17'36 5:25:10
El Destinado 37 5 30N30'19 84w16'39 5:37:07
Eldora 64 5 28N54'32 80w49'12 5:23:17
Eldorado 35 5 28N47'45 81w49'30 5:27:18
El Dorado Acres 36 5 26N20 81w47 5:27:08
Eldridge 64 5 29N12 81w27 5:25:48
Electra 42 5 29N07'37 81w53'16 5:27:33
Eleven Mile 19 5 29N42'36 85w09'14 5:40:37
Elfers 51 5 28N12'59 82w43'21 5:30:53
El Jobean 8 5 26N57'51 82w12'39 5:28:51
Elkton 55 5 29N46'58 81w25'34 5:25:42
Ellaville 32 1 30N58'29 85w22'36 5:41:30
Ellaville 61 5 30N22'52 83w10'22 5:32:41
Ellenton 41 5 27N31'17 82w31'40 5:30:07
Ellerslie 51 5 28N18'37 82w08'57 5:28:36
Ellinor Village 64 5 29N16'47 81w02'28 5:24:10
Ellison Acres 64 5 29N02 80w55 5:23:40
Ellisville 12 5 30N00'13 82w35'51 5:30:23
Ellsworth Junction 35 5 28N45'48 81w43'33 5:26:54
Ellyson Field 17 3 30N31 87w12 5:48:48
Ellzey 38 5 29N18'39 82w47'37 5:31:10
Eloise 53 5 27N59'40 81w44'18 5:26:57
Eloise Woods 53 5 28N00'10 81w41'48 5:26:47
El Portal 13 6 25N51'18 80w11'36 5:20:46
El Rancho Village 41 5 27N28 82w35 5:30:20
Elwood 55 5 29N59'55 81w32'36 5:26:10

Elwood Park 41 5 27N28'08 82w30'22 5:30:01
Emanuel Landing 64 5 28N52'43 81w21'43 5:25:27
Empire Point 16 5 30N19 81w39 5:26:36
Emporia 64 5 29N11'56 81w28'06 5:25:52
Enchanted Park 16 5 30N14'44 81w46'13 5:27:05
Englewood 16 5 30N17'14 81w37'35 5:26:30
Englewood 58 5 26N57'42 82w21'10 5:29:25
Englewood Beach 58 5 26N56 82w16 5:29:04
Englewood Manor 50 6 26N36 80w05 5:20:20
Enon 17 1 30N47'34 87w31'28 5:50:06
Ensley 17 3 30N31'07 87w16'22 5:49:05
Enterprise 64 5 28N52'08 81w16'01 5:25:04
Eridu 62 5 30N18'06 83w44'50 5:34:59
Errol Estates 48 5 28N58 81w39 5:26:36
Escambia Farms 46 1 30N57'28 86w37'59 5:46:32
Espanola 18 5 29N30'25 81w18'35 5:25:14
Estero 36 5 26N26'16 81w48'25 5:27:14
Estero River Heights 36 5 26N26 81w49 5:27:16
Estiffanulga 39 5 30N18'29 85w01'57 5:40:08
Esto 30 1 30N59'14 85w38'46 5:42:35
Ethel 35 5 28N48'07 81w26'37 5:25:46
Eucheeanna 66 1 30N38'44 86w02'42 5:44:11
Euclid 52 5 27N47 82w40 5:30:40
Eugene 15 5 29N36'41 83w05'17 5:32:21
Eureka 42 5 29N22'19 81w54'17 5:27:37
Eustis 35 5 28N51'09 81w41'08 5:26:45
Eva 53 5 28N19'34 81w50'01 5:27:20
Everglades 11 5 25N52 81w23 5:25:32
Everglades City 11 5 25N51'35 81w22'50 5:25:31
Evergreen 45 5 30N42'00 81w45'08 5:27:01
Evinston 1 5 29N29'12 82w13'53 5:28:56
Ewell 53 5 27N53'35 81w55'30 5:27:42
Facil 24 5 30N21'56 82w47'30 5:31:10
Fairbanks 1 5 29N43'28 82w15'51 5:29:03
Fairfield 16 5 30N21 81w39 5:26:36
Fairfield 42 5 29N22'00 82w15'05 5:29:00
Fair Gate 6 6 26N13'41 80w12'37 5:20:50
Fairlane Estates 59 5 28N45'11 81w17'49 5:25:11
Fairlawn 6 6 26N17'57 80w06'02 5:20:24
Fairmont 16 5 30N17 81w35 5:26:20
Fairview 12 5 30N27'04 82w31'08 5:30:05
Fairview Shores 48 5 28N35'27 81w23'40 5:25:35
Fairvilla 48 5 28N34'43 81w24'32 5:25:38
Fairyland 5 5 28N14 80w40 5:22:40
Fakahatchee 11 5 25N52'05 81w29'22 5:25:57
Falmouth 61 5 30N21'46 83w07'53 5:32:32
Fanlew 33 5 30N16'17 84w03'27 5:36:14
Fannin 38 5 29N36 82w55 5:31:40
Farmdale 3 1 30N01'04 85w28'11 5:41:53
Farm Hill 17 1 30N36'49 87w21'13 5:49:25
Farmton 64 5 28N50'48 81w03'39 5:24:15
Fatio 64 5 28N58'51 81w19'56 5:25:20
Faulks Ferry Landing 57 1 30N34'16 86w56'04 5:47:44
Favoretta (Favorita Station) 18 5 29N22'00 81w10'30 5:24:42
Favorita 18 5 29N22 81w11 5:24:44
Fawn Ford 39 5 30N18'18 84w54'52 5:39:39
Federal Point 54 5 29N44'52 81w32'40 5:26:11
Fedhaven 53 5 27N51'25 81w24'46 5:25:39
Felda 26 5 26N32'22 81w26'09 5:25:45
Felicia 9 5 28N55'47 82w23'44 5:29:35
Felkel 37 5 30N35'49 84w07'04 5:36:28
Fellowship 42 5 29N14'49 82w17'32 5:29:10
Fellowship Park 10 5 30N01'18 81w43'20 5:26:53
Fellsmere 31 5 27N46'03 80w36'06 5:22:24
Fenholloway 62 5 30N04'38 83w29'49 5:33:59
Fernandina Beach 45 5 30N40'10 81w27'46 5:25:51
Fern Crest Village 6 6 26N05'20 80w13'10 5:20:53
Ferndale 35 5 28N37'18 81w42'13 5:26:49
Fern Park 59 5 28N38'56 81w21'05 5:25:24
Ferry Pass 17 4 30N30'36 87w12'45 5:48:51
Festus 33 5 30N36'05 83w58'08 5:35:53
Fidelis 57 1 30N56'10 87w01'27 5:48:06
Fiftone 16 5 30N14'56 81w59'46 5:27:59
Fig Tree Landing 65 5 30N08'59 84w12'49 5:36:51
Fincher 33 5 30N39'36 83w57'58 5:35:52
Fish Creek 62 5 29N47'10 83w34'20 5:34:17
Fisher Corner 7 1 30N22'53 85w12'55 5:40:52
Fisher Island 13 6 25N48 80w09 5:20:36
Fish Lake 49 5 28N18 81w25 5:25:40
Fivay Junction 51 5 28N19'25 82w31'07 5:30:04
Five Points 5 5 28N22 80w45 5:23:00
Five Points 12 5 30N12'32 82w38'15 5:30:33
Five Points 67 1 30N42'46 85w45'05 5:43:00
Flagami 13 6 25N45'43 80w18'59 5:21:16
Flagler 13 5 25N36 80w13 5:20:52
Flagler 44 5 24N34 81w44 5:26:56
Flagler Beach 18 5 29N28'29 81w07'38 5:24:31
Flamingo 44 5 25N08'29 80w55'32 5:23:42
Flamingo 48 5 28N22'54 81w22'26 5:25:30
Flamingo Bay 36 5 26N34'18 82w06'15 5:28:25
Flamingo Village 6 6 26N09'24 80w10'54 5:20:44
Flat Landing 45 5 30N49'17 81w56'07 5:27:44
Fleming Heights 48 5 28N34 81w27 5:25:48
Flemington 42 5 29N24'27 82w17'52 5:29:11
Fletcher 15 5 29N44'27 82w59'06 5:31:56
Fletcher Landing 38 5 29N21'02 83w03'32 5:32:14
Florahome 54 5 29N43'57 81w53'01 5:27:32
Floral Bluff 16 5 30N20'34 81w36'29 5:26:26
Floral City 9 5 28N45'00 82w17'49 5:29:11
Floral Park 50 6 26N36 80w05 5:20:20
Flordale 16 5 30N22 81w41 5:26:44
Florence 20 5 30N35'37 84w28'58 5:37:56
Florence Villa 53 5 28N02'36 81w43'01 5:26:52
Floresta 50 6 26N21'13 80w06'09 5:20:25
Floresta Estates 6 6 26N17'56 80w05'15 5:20:21
Florida Beach 3 1 30N12'03 85w51'05 5:43:24
Florida City 13 5 25N26'51 80w28'46 5:21:55
Florida Gardens 50 6 26N36 80w05 5:20:20
Florida Hills 35 5 28N56'47 81w25'32 5:25:42
Floridale 57 1 30N40'53 86w50'13 5:47:21
Floridana Beach 5 5 27N56'46 80w29'45 5:21:59
Florida Ridge 31 5 27N35 80w25 5:21:40
Florida Southern College 53 5 28N33 81w23 5:25:32
Floridatown 57 1 30N34'52 87w09'17 5:48:37
Floritan 53 5 27N54'11 81w37'29 5:26:30
Florosa 46 1 30N25 86w39 5:46:36
Flower Bluff 38 5 29N29 82w52 5:31:28
Flowers Field Landing 57 1 30N36'32 86w50'13 5:47:21
Flowersville 66 1 30N57'13 86w20'18 5:45:21
Fluffy Landing 66 1 30N25'51 86w08'10 5:44:33
Foley 62 5 30N04'09 83w31'51 5:34:07
Footman 5 5 28N19'49 80w41'27 5:22:46
Fordville 58 5 27N20'16 82w24'58 5:29:40
Forest City 59 5 28N39'41 81w25'09 5:25:41
Forest Grove 1 5 29N44'30 82w34'56 5:30:20
Forest Highlands 66 1 30N42'25 86w23'02 5:45:32
Forest Hills 29 5 28N03 82w27 5:29:48
Forest Hills 35 5 29N00'10 81w25'34 5:25:42
Forest Ridge 1 5 29N40 82w20 5:29:20
Forrest Hills 64 5 29N18 81w03 5:24:12
Fort Barrancas 17 4 30N20'52 87w17'50 5:49:11
Fort Basinger 28 5 27N21'43 81w03'26 5:24:14
Fort Brook Landing 42 5 29N30'52 81w54'28 5:27:38
Fort Caroline 16 5 30N23'12 81w30'02 5:26:00
Fort Caroline Club Estates 16 5 30N20 81w35 5:26:20
Fort Centre 22 5 26N57'16 81w09'43 5:24:39
Fort De Soto 52 5 27N36'55 82w44'11 5:30:57
Fort Drum 47 5 27N31'35 80w48'25 5:23:14
Fort Gadsden 19 1 29N55'01 84w58'38 5:39:55
Fort Gates 54 5 29N25'02 81w39'29 5:26:38
Fort George Island 16 5 30N24'10 81w25'49 5:25:43
Fort Green 25 5 27N36'44 81w56'37 5:27:46
Fort Green Springs 25 5 27N35'29 81w56'22 5:27:45
Fort Hamer 41 5 27N31'30 82w25'49 5:29:43
Fort Jefferson 44 5 24N37'39 82w52'23 5:31:30
Fort King Acres 51 5 28N15'42 82w12'00 5:28:48
Fort Kissimmee 47 5 27N35'09 81w09'38 5:24:39
Fort Lauderdale 6 6 26N07'19 80w08'37 5:20:34
Fort Lonesome 29 5 27N42'16 82w08'46 5:28:35
Fort Mason 35 5 28N52'36 81w42'04 5:26:48
Fort Matanzas 55 5 29N42'53 81w14'20 5:24:57
Fort McCoy 42 5 29N21'53 81w58'02 5:27:52
Fort McRee 17 4 30N19'30 87w18'54 5:49:16
Fort Meade 53 5 27N45'07 81w48'07 5:27:12
Fort Myers 36 5 26N38'25 81w52'21 5:27:29
Fort Myers Beach 36 5 26N27'06 81w56'54 5:27:48
Fort Myers Shores 36 5 26N42'32 81w44'46 5:26:59
Fort Myers Villas 36 5 26N33'40 81w51'50 5:27:27
Fort Ogden 14 5 27N05'13 81w57'09 5:27:49
Fort Pierce 56 5 27N26'47 80w19'33 5:21:18
Fort Pierce Beach 56 5 27N21 80w19 5:21:16
Fort Pierce Shores 56 5 27N21 80w19 5:21:16
Fort Redoubt 17 4 30N21'19 87w17'49 5:49:11
Fort San Carlos 17 4 30N20'49 87w17'49 5:49:11
Fort Taylor 44 5 24N32'51 81w48'36 5:27:14
Fort Union 61 5 30N24'26 83w02'51 5:32:11
Fort Walton Beach 46 1 30N24'20 86w37'08 5:46:29
Fort White 12 5 29N55'23 82w42'50 5:30:51
Fortymile Bend 13 6 25N45'40 80w49'38 5:23:19
Fountain 2 1 30N28'43 85w25'11 5:41:41
Fountain Heights 53 5 27N59'35 81w57'24 5:27:50
Four Corners 52 5 27N54'57 82w43'47 5:30:55
Four Mile Village 66 1 30N22'20 86w19'19 5:45:17
Four Points 37 5 30N24'00 84w16'51 5:37:07
Four Points 50 6 26N40 80w06 5:20:24
Fowler Bluff 38 5 29N23'47 83w01'28 5:32:06
Foxleigh 41 5 27N29'55 82w26'01 5:29:44
Fox Town 53 5 28N09'08 81w55'34 5:27:42
Francis 54 5 29N38'03 81w42'29 5:26:50
Franjo 13 5 25N34'45 80w20'11 5:21:21
Franklin 19 1 29N44'53 85w01'41 5:40:07
Franklintown 45 5 30N33'22 81w26'59 5:25:48
Franwood Pines 50 6 26N27'48 80w07'02 5:20:28
Freemont 20 5 30N36'45 84w27'02 5:37:48
Freeport 66 1 30N29'53 86w08'10 5:44:33
Frink 7 1 30N22'06 85w12'51 5:40:51
Frog City 13 6 25N45'35 80w35'57 5:22:24
Frontenac 5 5 28N27'41 80w45'49 5:23:03
Frostproof 53 5 27N44'44 81w31'51 5:26:07
Fruit Cove 55 5 30N06'39 81w38'31 5:26:34
Fruitland 54 5 29N25'37 81w38'38 5:26:35
Fruitland Park 35 5 28N51'40 81w54'24 5:27:38
Fruitville 58 5 27N19'46 82w27'28 5:29:50
Fuller Heights 53 5 27N54'32 81w59'54 5:28:00
Fullers 48 5 28N35'57 81w33'14 5:26:13
Fullerton 64 5 28N52 80w51 5:23:24
Fullerville 35 5 29N00'31 81w27'16 5:25:49
Fulton 16 5 30N18 81w38 5:26:32
Fussells Corner 53 5 28N04'10 81w51'01 5:27:24
Gaberonne 17 4 30N28'07 87w09'39 5:48:39
Gabriella 59 5 28N37'34 81w14'41 5:24:59
Gainesville 1 5 29N39'05 82w19'30 5:29:18
Galliver 46 1 30N43'27 86w42'26 5:46:50
Galloway 53 5 28N05'46 82w00'24 5:28:02
Galt City 57 1 30N35'21 87w03'29 5:48:14
Gandyville 17 1 30N59'49 87w17'18 5:49:09
Gardena 59 5 28N40 81w12 5:24:48
Garden City 16 5 30N26'26 81w41'57 5:26:48
Garden City 46 1 30N49'56 86w32'00 5:46:08
Garden Cove 44 5 25N10'22 80w22'06 5:21:28
Garden Grove 27 5 28N28'48 82w26'07 5:29:44
Garden Isles 6 6 26N13'25 80w07'08 5:20:29
Gardenville 29 5 27N50'46 82w22'55 5:29:32
Gardner 25 5 27N21'05 81w48'00 5:27:12
Gardner 37 5 30N29'29 84w07'32 5:36:30
Gardner Landing 19 1 29N49'03 84w59'14 5:39:57
Garnier 46 1 30N36 86w36 5:46:24
Garnier Landing 57 1 30N38'31 86w48'06 5:47:12
Gary 29 5 27N57'20 82w25'42 5:29:43
Gaskin 66 1 30N58'15 86w08'08 5:44:33
Gaskins Still 23 1 30N02'17 85w10'53 5:40:44
Gasparilla 36 5 26N48'16 82w16'37 5:29:06
Gateway Mall 52 5 27N51 82w40 5:30:40
Geigers Landing 59 5 28N47'21 81w08'53 5:24:36
General Mail Center 16 5 30N19 81w39 5:26:36
Geneva 59 5 28N44'22 81w06'55 5:24:28
Genoa 24 5 30N24'01 82w50'06 5:31:20
Georgetown 54 5 29N23'28 81w38'20 5:26:33
Georgiana 5 5 28N17'17 80w40'31 5:22:42
Gibson 20 5 30N33'58 84w23'58 5:37:36
Gibsonia 53 5 28N06'52 81w58'26 5:27:54
Gibsonton 29 5 27N51'12 82w22'52 5:29:32
Gifford 31 5 27N40'30 80w24'34 5:21:38
Gilberts Mill 67 1 30N38'03 85w29'33 5:41:58
Gilchrist 8 5 26N46'30 81w53'33 5:27:34
Gillette 41 5 27N36'03 82w31'38 5:30:07
Gilmore 16 5 30N21'54 81w33'25 5:26:14
Ginco Bayou 46 1 30N25'19 86w36'34 5:46:26
Gin Hole Landing 46 1 30N40'48 86w39'10 5:46:37
Glades 50 5 26N41 80w32 5:22:08
Glass 32 1 30N51'51 85w25'43 5:41:43
Glencoe 64 5 29N01'32 80w58'20 5:23:53
Glendale 66 1 30N51'46 86w06'52 5:44:27
Glen Ridge 50 6 26N40'09 80w04'28 5:20:18
Glen Saint Mary 2 5 30N16'32 82w09'39 5:28:39
Glenvar Heights 13 6 25N42'26 80w19'33 5:21:18
Glenwood 3 1 30N09'49 85w38'14 5:42:33
Glenwood 45 5 30N39'39 81w31'37 5:26:06
Glenwood 64 5 29N05'09 81w21'16 5:25:25
Glenwood Heights 13 6 25N49'51 80w14'13 5:20:57
Glidden Park 56 5 27N26'16 80w20'03 5:21:20
Glory 20 5 30N35 84w35 5:38:20
Glynlea 16 5 30N17 81w35 5:26:20
Golden Beach 13 6 25N57'53 80w07'21 5:20:29
Golden Beach 58 5 27N04 82w20 5:29:20
Golden Gate 11 5 26N11'15 81w41'43 5:26:47
Golden Gate 43 5 27N09'44 80w12'59 5:20:52
Golden Heights 35 5 28N48 81w39 5:26:36
Golden Isles 6 6 25N58'46 80w07'44 5:20:31
Goldenrod (Golden Rod Sta) 59 5 28N36'36 81w17'20 5:25:09
Golden Shores 13 6 25N56 80w09 5:20:36
Golf 50 6 26N30 80w06 5:20:24
Golfair Manor 16 5 30N26 81w39 5:26:36
Golf Estates 6 6 26N09'33 80w11'53 5:20:48
Golf Lake Estates 41 5 27N28 82w35 5:30:20
Golf View 50 6 26N41'19 80w06'46 5:20:27
Golfview Heights 50 6 26N40 80w06 5:20:24
Gomez 43 5 27N05'04 80w08'37 5:20:34
Gonzalez 17 3 30N34'53 87w17'29 5:49:10
Goodbys 16 5 30N12'09 81w37'01 5:26:28
Good Hope 46 1 30N58'08 86w37'53 5:46:32
Goodland 11 5 25N55'28 81w38'45 5:26:35
Goodno 22 5 26N46'06 81w18'43 5:25:15
Gopher Ridge 55 5 29N39'54 81w24'52 5:25:39
Gordon 66 1 30N53'22 86w16'48 5:45:07
Gordon Chapel 54 5 29N36 82w05 5:28:20
Gordonville 53 5 27N56'44 81w48'02 5:27:12
Gores Landing 42 5 29N17'21 81w55'34 5:27:42
Gotha 48 5 28N31'39 81w31'24 5:26:06
Goulding 17 4 30N26'34 87w13'21 5:48:53
Goulds 13 5 25N33'44 80w22'57 5:21:32
Graceville 32 1 30N57'24 85w31'00 5:42:04
Grady 34 5 29N57'14 82w55'56 5:31:44
Graham 4 5 29N51'36 82w13'07 5:28:52
Grahamsville 42 5 29N13'54 81w57'59 5:27:52
Grahamville Landing 42 5 29N13'36 81w58'38 5:27:55
Grand Crossing 16 5 30N21'31 81w43'16 5:26:53
Grandin 54 5 29N43'39 81w55'07 5:27:40

Grand Island 35 5 28N52'56 81w43'45 5:26:55
Grand Park 16 5 30N21'10 81w41'58 5:26:48
Grand Ridge 32 1 30N42'44 85w01'13 5:40:05
Grandview 54 5 29N41'58 81w35'59 5:26:24
Grangers Mill 12 5 30N17 81w24 5:25:36
Grant 5 5 27N55'43 80w31'36 5:22:06
Gratigny 13 6 25N54 80w13 5:20:52
Grayton Beach 66 1 30N19'50 86w09'54 5:44:40
Grayvik 44 5 25N19'00 80w17'13 5:21:09
Greenacres City 50 6 26N37'24 80w07'32 5:20:30
Green Bay 53 5 27N50'09 81w55'23 5:27:42
Greenbriar 59 5 28N46'33 81w19'05 5:25:16
Green Cove Springs 10 5 29N59'30 81w40'42 5:26:43
Greenfield 12 5 30N18'49 82w33'46 5:30:15
Greenfield 16 5 30N21'07 81w26'49 5:25:47
Greenfield 51 5 28N21'12 82w30'18 5:30:01
Greenfield Manor 16 5 30N17 81w35 5:26:20
Greenhead 67 1 30N30'16 85w39'36 5:42:38
Green Hills 3 1 30N29 85w25 5:41:40
Green Hills 13 5 25N36 80w22 5:21:28
Greenland 16 5 30N10'18 81w32'42 5:26:11
Green-Mar Acres 13 6 25N40'14 80w20'35 5:21:22
Green Point 19 5 29N45'27 84w49'55 5:39:20
Greensboro 20 5 30N34'09 84w44'36 5:38:58
Greenville 40 5 30N28'09 83w37'49 5:34:31
Greenwood 32 1 30N52'12 85w09'43 5:40:39
Greenwood 57 1 30N57 87w09 5:48:36
Gretna 20 5 30N37'01 84w39'36 5:38:38
Greyhound Key 44 5 24N51 80w47 5:23:08
Griffin 53 5 28N05'02 81w59'43 5:27:59
Griffins Corner 25 5 27N32'22 81w43'52 5:26:55
Gritney 30 1 30N50'17 85w49'49 5:43:19
Grocery Place 11 5 25N57'07 81w36'58 5:26:28
Gross 45 5 30N42'57 81w40'32 5:26:42
Grove City 8 5 26N54'50 82w19'38 5:29:19
Groveland 35 5 28N33'28 81w51'05 5:27:24
Grove Park 1 5 29N36'00 82w09'13 5:28:37
Grove Park 16 5 30N17 81w35 5:26:20
Grove Park 29 5 28N00 82w30 5:30:00
Grove Park 53 5 28N02 81w57 5:27:48
Grove Park Estates 29 5 28N00 82w30 5:30:00
Guilford 63 5 30N03'16 82w24'45 5:29:39
Gulf Beach 17 4 30N17'53 87w25'39 5:49:43
Gulf Beach Heights 17 4 30N18'52 87w26'22 5:49:45
Gulf Breeze 57 4 30N21'25 87w09'50 5:48:39
Gulf City 29 5 27N42'20 82w27'43 5:29:51
Gulf Gate Estates 58 5 27N16 82w31 5:30:04
Gulf Hammock 38 5 29N15'10 82w43'52 5:30:55
Gulf Harbors 51 5 28N14'05 82w45'30 5:31:02
Gulf Lagoon Beach 3 1 30N09'52 85w47'13 5:43:09
Gulf Pines 66 1 30N22'17 86w20'07 5:45:20
Gulfport 52 5 27N44'53 82w42'13 5:30:49
Gulf Resort Beach 3 1 30N13'24 85w53'30 5:43:34
Gulf Shores 58 5 27N04 82w20 5:29:20
Gulf Stream 50 6 26N29'36 80w03'19 5:20:13
Gum Creek Landing 67 1 30N42'43 85w50'04 5:43:20
Gum Landing 57 1 30N56'58 86w58'54 5:47:56
Gunn Landing 38 5 29N13'34 82w43'58 5:30:56
Gunn Landing 39 5 30N15'16 85w04'06 5:40:16
Habor Bluffs 52 5 27N54'23 82w49'31 5:31:18
Hacienda Village 6 6 26N05'06 80w12'05 5:20:48
Hague 1 5 29N46'13 82w25'17 5:29:41
Haile 1 5 29N41'25 82w34'25 5:30:18
Haines City 53 5 28N06'50 81w37'05 5:26:28
Hainesworth 1 5 29N49'10 82w26'41 5:29:47
Half Moon 1 5 29N39 82w36 5:30:24
Halifax Estates 64 5 29N08'50 80w58'01 5:23:52
Hallandale 6 6 25N58'51 80w08'55 5:20:36
Hall City 22 5 26N52'41 81w19'36 5:25:18
Halsema 16 5 30N18'44 81w51'55 5:27:28
Hamburg 40 5 30N33'56 83w31'37 5:34:06
Hamilton 6 6 26N15 80w09 5:20:36
Hammond 54 5 29N26 81w31 5:26:04
Hammondville 6 6 26N14'39 80w12'05 5:20:48
Hampton 4 5 29N51'51 82w07'52 5:28:31
Hampton Beach 4 5 29N52'17 82w10'01 5:28:40
Hampton Springs 62 5 30N05'07 83w39'18 5:34:37
Hancock 54 5 29N47'23 81w37'53 5:26:32
Hanson 40 5 30N33'05 83w22'02 5:33:28
Happy Valley 17 1 30N58'52 87w14'54 5:49:00
Harbinwood Estates 37 5 30N30'51 84w20'07 5:37:20
Harbor Beach 6 6 26N06'20 80w06'57 5:20:28
Harbor Bluffs 52 5 27N53 82w46 5:31:04
Harbor East 50 6 26N22'33 80w04'26 5:20:18
Harbor Heights 6 6 26N05'49 80w06'46 5:20:27
Harbor Oaks 64 5 29N06'28 80w58'09 5:23:53
Harbor Palms 52 5 28N02'36 82w41'32 5:30:46
Harbor Point 64 5 29N13 81w02 5:24:08
Harbor Shores 35 5 28N52'08 81w44'45 5:26:59
Harbor View 8 5 26N58'08 82w02'29 5:28:10
Harbor View 16 5 30N23'53 81w42'58 5:26:52
Harbor Village 6 6 26N14'15 80w05'45 5:20:23
Harbour Heights 8 5 26N59'26 82w00'09 5:28:01
Hardaway 20 5 30N38 84w44 5:38:56
Hardeetown 38 5 29N29'29 82w51'50 5:31:27
Hardin Heights 20 5 30N40'27 84w50'19 5:39:21
Hardway 20 5 30N37'49 84w44'08 5:38:57
Harker 11 5 26N20'35 81w20'37 5:25:22
Harlem 26 5 26N44'14 80w57'04 5:23:48
Harlem Heights 48 5 28N30'36 81w37'15 5:26:29
Harney 29 5 28N00'53 82w22'29 5:29:30
Harold 57 1 30N39'32 86w52'49 5:47:31
Harp 57 1 30N33'37 87w06'29 5:48:26
Harper 57 1 30N26'43 86w52'45 5:47:31
Harrisburg 22 5 26N55'44 81w19'02 5:25:16
Harrison 9 5 28N58'33 82w24'25 5:29:38
Hart Haven 16 5 30N19'31 81w45'53 5:27:04
Harvey Heights 36 5 26N36 81w52 5:27:28
Hasan 1 5 29N51'31 82w26'17 5:29:45
Hastings 55 5 29N43'04 81w30'30 5:26:02
Hatchbend 34 5 29N50'49 82w55'06 5:31:40
Hathaway Mill 30 1 30N48'49 85w48'05 5:43:12
Havana 20 5 30N37'25 84w24'53 5:37:40
Haven Beach 52 5 27N54 82w51 5:31:24
Haverhill 50 6 26N41'27 80w07'13 5:20:29
Hawkins Shop Landing 45 5 30N48'32 81w57'41 5:27:51
Hawley Heights 13 6 25N39'39 80w20'41 5:21:23
Hawthorne 1 5 29N35'30 82w05'15 5:28:21
Haynes 32 1 30N52'06 84w57'27 5:39:50
Hays Place 19 5 29N50'27 84w56'45 5:39:47
Hedges 45 5 30N35'56 81w35'55 5:26:24
Heilbronn 4 5 30N01'08 82w09'03 5:28:36
Heilbron Springs 4 5 29N57 82w06 5:28:24
Helen 37 5 30N18'26 84w24'00 5:37:36
Hell Gate 43 5 26N58'35 80w05'12 5:20:21
Henderson Landing 16 5 30N30'35 81w33'29 5:26:14
Henderson Mill 7 1 30N34'04 85w04'11 5:40:17
Hen Scratch 28 5 27N18'44 81w28'07 5:25:52
Hercules 16 5 30N14 81w57 5:27:48
Hermitage 20 5 28N14 80w36 5:22:24
Hernando 9 5 28N54'02 82w22'29 5:29:30
Herndon 48 5 28N33 81w23 5:25:32
Hero 45 5 30N37'01 81w39'22 5:26:37
Hesperides 53 5 27N53'02 81w27'33 5:25:50
Hialeah 13 6 25N51'26 80w16'42 5:21:07
Hialeah Estates 13 6 25N51'27 80w17'29 5:21:10
Hialeah Gardens 13 6 25N51'53 80w19'29 5:21:18
Hialeah Lakes 13 6 25N54 80w18 5:21:12
Hibernia 10 5 30N03'54 81w41'52 5:26:47
Hibiscus Mobile Park 35 5 28N48 81w39 5:26:36
Hickory Hill 30 1 30N49'19 85w55'30 5:43:42
Hickory Landing 19 1 29N59'18 85w00'51 5:40:03
Hicoria 28 5 27N09'04 81w21'11 5:25:25
Hidden River 58 5 27N17'55 82w15'45 5:29:03
High Bluff 19 5 29N49'09 84w49'31 5:39:18
High Bluff Landing 20 5 30N27'23 84w29'54 5:38:00
Highland 10 5 30N06'44 82w02'45 5:28:11
Highland Beach 50 6 26N23'57 80w03'57 5:20:16
Highland City 53 5 27N57'54 81w52'41 5:27:31
Highland Court Manor 1 5 29N40 82w20 5:29:20
Highland Lakes 13 6 25N58'05 80w09'48 5:20:39
Highland Lakes 28 5 27N38'01 81w31'19 5:26:05
Highland Park 52 5 27N53 82w46 5:31:04
Highland Park 53 5 27N51'53 81w33'43 5:26:15
Highland Park 59 5 28N47'33 81w16'16 5:25:05
Highlands 6 6 26N17 80w09 5:20:36
Highlands 16 5 30N25'31 81w40'41 5:26:43
Highlands Park Estates 28 5 27N18'40 81w19'13 5:25:17
Highland View 23 5 29N50'16 85w18'57 5:41:16
High Point 52 5 27N54'51 82w42'20 5:30:49
High Ridge Estates 6 6 26N12'43 80w06'57 5:20:28
High Springs 1 5 29N49'36 82w35'49 5:30:23
Hiland Park 3 1 30N12'03 85w37'37 5:42:30
Hilden 55 5 30N03'56 81w26'25 5:25:46
Hildreth 61 5 29N57'09 82w48'20 5:31:13
Hillcoat 24 5 30N28'20 82w54'33 5:31:38
Hillcrest Heights 53 5 27N49'15 81w31'51 5:26:07
Hilldale 29 5 28N00 82w30 5:30:00
Hilliard 45 5 30N41'27 81w55'03 5:27:40
Hilliardville 65 5 30N17'15 84w23'58 5:37:36
Hill N Dale 27 5 28N32 82w29 5:29:56
Hillsboro Beach 6 6 26N17'37 80w04'45 5:20:19
Hilolo 47 5 27N26'56 80w46'17 5:23:05
Hines 15 5 29N44'21 83w14'12 5:32:57
Hinson 20 5 30N38'50 84w25'00 5:37:40
Hinsons Cross Roads 67 1 30N40'07 85w50'33 5:43:22
Hobbs Crossroads 30 1 30N54'55 85w57'36 5:43:50
Hobe Sound 43 5 27N03'33 80w08'12 5:20:33
Hodgson 38 5 29N24'13 82w27'22 5:29:49
Hogan 16 5 30N17'28 81w34'55 5:26:20
Hog Valley 42 5 29N29'39 81w53'44 5:27:35
Holden Heights 48 5 28N31 81w24 5:25:36
Holder (Ladonia Station) 9 5 28N58'00 82w25'15 5:29:41
Holiday 51 5 28N11'15 82w44'23 5:30:58
Holiday Gardens 51 5 28N12 82w44 5:30:56
Holiday Harbor 16 5 30N18'17 81w26'38 5:25:47
Holiday Heights 44 5 25N08 80w25 5:21:40
Holiday Hills 51 5 28N14 82w45 5:31:00
Holiday Manor 53 5 28N09'32 81w41'11 5:26:45
Holiday Plaza 3 1 30N09 85w39 5:42:36
Holland 37 5 30N25'39 84w31'58 5:38:08
Holland Crossroads 30 1 30N57'55 85w38'48 5:42:35
Holley 57 1 30N26'48 86w54'25 5:47:38
Hollingsworth Bluff 12 5 29N52'08 82w44'35 5:30:58
Hollister 54 5 29N37'21 81w48'50 5:27:15
Holly Ford 16 5 30N24'40 81w39'13 5:26:37
Holly Hill 64 5 29N14'36 81w02'16 5:24:09
Holly Point 10 5 30N09'19 81w41'46 5:26:47
Hollywood 6 6 26N00'39 80w08'59 5:20:36
Hollywood Beach 3 1 30N15'14 85w57'25 5:43:50
Hollywood Beach Gardens 6 6 26N00'49 80w12'14 5:20:49
Hollywood Hills 6 6 26N01 80w11 5:20:44
Hollywood Ridge Farms 6 6 25N58'30 80w11'40 5:20:47
Hollywood Seminole Indian Re 6 6 26N01 80w13 5:20:52
Holmes Beach 41 5 27N29'50 82w42'33 5:30:50
Holmes Valley 67 1 30N34'36 85w44'35 5:42:58
Holmes West 30 1 30N52 85w56 5:43:44
Holopaw 49 5 28N08'08 81w04'35 5:24:18
Holt 46 1 30N42'56 86w44'45 5:46:59
Homeland 53 5 27N49'03 81w49'29 5:27:18
Homer Landing 45 5 30N35'24 81w33'30 5:26:14
Homestead 13 5 25N28'06 80w28'40 5:21:55
Homestead Air Force Base 13 5 25N30 80w24 5:21:36
Homestead Ridge 37 5 30N30'05 84w07'13 5:36:29
Homosassa 9 5 28N46'52 82w36'55 5:30:28
Homosassa Springs 9 5 28N48'12 82w34'34 5:30:18
Honeyville 23 1 30N03'28 85w11'24 5:40:46
Honore 58 5 27N14'33 82w15'48 5:29:03
Hontoon Landing 64 5 28N58'33 81w21'38 5:25:27
Hooker Point 26 5 26N44'23 80w55'01 5:23:40
Hoover Mill 30 1 30N52'10 85w41'10 5:42:45
Hopewell 29 5 27N55'42 82w07'26 5:28:30
Hopewell 40 5 30N28 83w25 5:33:40
Hopkins 5 5 28N05 80w38 5:22:32
Hopkins Landing 20 5 30N24'54 84w38'07 5:38:32
Hornsville 32 1 30N56'28 85w00'13 5:40:01
Horse Landing 54 5 29N32'27 81w42'23 5:26:50
Horseshoe Beach 15 5 29N26'28 83w17'15 5:33:09
Hosford 39 5 30N23'11 84w47'53 5:39:12
Houston 61 5 30N15'24 82w54'10 5:31:37
Howard 13 5 25N38'49 80w20'04 5:21:20
Howell Place 62 5 29N46'17 83w30'30 5:34:02
Howey Height 35 5 28N39'57 81w43'52 5:26:55
Howey In The Hills 35 5 28N43'00 81w46'25 5:27:06
Hoyt 42 5 29N09'56 82w23'52 5:29:35
Hubs Landing 5 5 28N35'19 80w41'01 5:22:44
Huckleberry Landing 23 5 29N46'10 85w05'04 5:40:20
Hucomer 64 5 28N56'12 80w53'19 5:23:33
Hudson 30 1 30N51'44 85w56'36 5:43:46
Hudson 51 5 28N21'51 82w41'37 5:30:46
Hugh 10 5 30N09'56 82w01'59 5:28:08
Hulaw 67 1 30N46'45 85w33'30 5:42:14
Hull 14 5 27N07'08 81w56'33 5:27:46
Hunter 54 5 29N36'23 81w45'48 5:27:03
Huntington 54 5 29N26'25 81w33'10 5:26:13
Hurlburt 46 1 30N25 86w41 5:46:44
Hurst Landing 17 4 30N27'36 87w24'33 5:49:38
Hyde Grove 16 5 30N17'03 81w45'34 5:27:02
Hyde Park 16 5 30N16'49 81w44'56 5:27:00
Hyde Park 65 5 34N41'11 84w15'43 5:37:03
Hypoluxo 50 6 26N33'58 80w03'13 5:20:13
Iamonia 37 5 30N40'05 84w09'49 5:36:39
Iddo 62 5 30N16'39 83w43'30 5:34:54
Idylwild 1 5 29N40 82w20 5:29:20
Ilexhurst 41 5 27N29'25 82w42'27 5:30:50
Immokalee 11 5 26N25'06 81w25'03 5:25:40
Imperial Estates 48 5 28N29 81w22 5:25:28
Imperial Point 6 6 26N11'55 80w07'08 5:20:29
Indialantic 5 5 28N05'21 80w33'57 5:22:16
Indian Creek 13 6 25N52 80w08 5:20:32
Indian Creek Village 13 6 25N52'40 80w08'11 5:20:33
Indian Ford 57 1 30N42'48 86w55'26 5:47:42
Indian Harbour Beach 5 5 28N08'55 80w35'19 5:22:21
Indian Lake Estates 53 5 27N48'49 81w22'43 5:25:31
Indian Mound Village 59 5 28N48'11 81w13'01 5:24:52
Indianola 5 5 28N23'46 80w42'53 5:22:52
Indian Pass 23 5 29N41'25 85w15'52 5:41:03
Indian River City 5 5 28N33'34 80w47'58 5:23:12
Indian River Shores 31 5 27N42'59 80w23'04 5:21:32
Indian Rocks Beach 52 5 27N52'30 82w51'05 5:31:24
Indian Shores 52 5 27N51'45 82w50'55 5:31:24
Indiantown 43 5 27N01'37 80w29'09 5:21:57
Indrio 56 5 27N31'13 80w21'11 5:21:25
Ingle 45 5 30N25'08 81w55'40 5:27:43
Inglis 38 5 29N01'48 82w40'08 5:30:41
Inlet Beach 66 1 30N16'36 86w00'29 5:44:02
Inlikita 13 5 25N36'08 80w28'58 5:21:56

Innisbrook 52 5 28N06'41 82w45'23 5:31:02
Interbay 29 5 27N53 82w31 5:30:04
Intercession City 49 5 28N15'44 81w30'29 5:26:02
Interior County 58 5 27N10 82w21 5:29:24
Interlachen 54 5 29N37'25 81w53'26 5:27:34
Inverness 9 5 28N50'08 82w19'50 5:29:19
Inverrary 6 6 26N09 80w13 5:20:52
Inwood 32 1 30N42'01 84w58'27 5:39:54
Inwood 53 5 28N02'12 81w45'55 5:27:04
Iola 23 1 30N08'55 85w09'55 5:40:40
Iona 36 5 26N31'12 81w57'51 5:27:51
Iona Gardens 36 5 26N36 81w52 5:27:28
Irvine 42 5 29N24'19 82w15'05 5:29:00
Islamorada 44 5 24N55'26 80w37'41 5:22:31
Island Grove 1 5 29N27'12 82w06'24 5:28:26
Islandia 13 5 25N25 80w13 5:20:52
Isleboro 64 5 29N03'55 80w56'50 5:23:47
Isle of Normandy 13 6 25N51'09 80w08'07 5:20:32
Isle of Psalms 16 5 30N17'02 81w25'46 5:25:43
Isle of Psalms South 16 5 30N16'03 81w25'58 5:25:44
Isles of Capri 11 5 25N58'57 81w43'40 5:26:55
Isleworth 48 5 28N30 81w32 5:26:08
Istachatta 27 5 28N39'35 82w16'40 5:29:07
Istokpoga 28 5 27N24'48 81w21'05 5:25:24
Istokpoga Shores 28 5 27N27 81w15 5:25:00
Italia 45 5 30N36'59 81w43'02 5:26:52
Ivan 65 5 30N13'24 84w21'44 5:37:27
Ives Estates 13 6 25N57'43 80w10'37 5:20:42
Izagora 30 1 30N54'36 85w50'30 5:43:22
Jackson Bluff 37 5 30N23'20 84w38'31 5:38:34
Jackson Still 66 1 30N43 86w07 5:44:28
Jacksonville 16 5 30N19'55 81w39'21 5:26:37
Jacksonville Beach 16 5 30N17'40 81w23'36 5:25:34
Jacksonville Heights 16 5 30N15'07 81w47'10 5:27:09
Jacksonville Naval Air Sta 16 5 30N19 81w39 5:26:36
Jacksonville Navy Fuel Depot 16 5 30N23 81w41 5:26:44
Jacksonville University 16 5 30N20 81w35 5:26:20
Jacob 32 1 30N54 85w24 5:41:36
Jacobs 32 1 30N53'41 85w23'52 5:41:35
Jamestown 59 5 28N37'50 81w14'26 5:24:58
Jamieson 20 5 30N39'45 84w27'02 5:37:48
JanPhyl Village 53 5 28N00'52 81w46'19 5:27:05
Jarrott 33 5 30N37'25 83w56'03 5:35:44
Jasmine Estates 51 5 28N19 82w42 5:30:48
Jasper 24 5 30N31'05 82w56'54 5:31:48
Jassamine 51 5 28N22 82w11 5:28:44
Jay 57 1 30N57'10 87w09'05 5:48:36
Jay Jay 5 5 28N38'44 80w49'12 5:23:17
Jena 15 5 29N39'48 83w22'13 5:33:29
Jenada Isles 6 6 26N09'47 80w09'27 5:20:38
Jennings 24 5 30N36'14 83w05'53 5:32:24
Jensen Beach 43 5 27N15'15 80w13'48 5:20:55
Jensen Place 39 5 30N13'48 84w55'37 5:39:42
Jerome 11 5 25N59'49 81w20'49 5:25:23
Jerry Landing 45 5 30N36'04 81w34'07 5:26:16
Jessamine 51 5 28N24'48 82w16'13 5:29:05
Jessie Willies 6 6 26N01'08 80w42'45 5:22:51
Jiggs Landing 41 5 27N25'55 82w28'55 5:29:56
Joels Landing 16 5 30N33'06 81w40'08 5:26:41
Johnson 54 5 29N35'04 81w58'24 5:27:54
Johnson Crossroad 67 1 30N43'46 85w39'49 5:42:39
Johnsons Corner 35 5 28N58'32 81w32'31 5:26:10
Johns Pass 52 5 27N50 82w48 5:31:12
Jolly Corner 29 5 28N00'14 82w17'25 5:29:10
Jonesboro 15 5 29N42'39 83w17'50 5:33:11
Jones Corner 53 5 28N01'59 81w48'52 5:27:15
Jones Landing 59 5 28N42'15 81w12'23 5:24:50
Jonesville 1 5 29N39'14 82w31'24 5:30:06
Joshua 14 5 27N13 81w52 5:27:28
Judson 38 5 29N37 82w49 5:31:16
June Park 5 5 28N04'19 80w40'49 5:22:43
Juniper 20 5 30N32'33 84w45'12 5:39:01
Juno Beach 50 6 26N52'46 80w03'13 5:20:13
Jupiter 50 6 26N56'02 80w05'40 5:20:23
Jupiter Inlet Beach Colony 50 6 26N56'55 80w04'30 5:20:18
Jupiter Island 43 5 27N05 80w07 5:20:28
Kalamazoo 64 5 28N50'45 81w06'37 5:24:26
Kanapaha 1 5 29N35'49 82w25'22 5:29:41
Kathleen 53 5 28N07'14 82w01'24 5:28:06
Keaton Beach 62 5 30N07 83w35 5:34:20
Keela 50 5 26N41'23 80w52'43 5:23:31
Keene 45 5 30N28'59 81w50'49 5:27:23
Keentown 41 5 27N34'16 82w08'16 5:28:33
Kelly Park 48 5 28N46 81w30 5:26:00
Kellys Mill 46 1 30N44'16 86w46'34 5:47:06
Kenansville 49 5 27N52'34 80w59'17 5:23:57
Kendall 13 6 25N40'44 80w19'03 5:21:16
Kendrick 42 5 29N15'12 82w10'05 5:28:40
Kennedy Hill 29 5 28N00'06 82w18'09 5:29:13
Kennedy Still 24 5 30N32'40 82w53'15 5:31:33
Kenneth City 52 5 27N49 82w43 5:30:52
Kenny 2 5 30N21'21 82w14'34 5:28:58
Kensington Park 58 5 27N22 82w30 5:30:00
Kent 45 5 30N31'17 81w58'00 5:27:52
Kent Mill 32 1 30N40'10 85w25'39 5:41:43

Kentucky Landing 23 1 30N08'55 85w08'23 5:40:34
Keri 26 5 26N35'50 81w22'48 5:25:31
Kern 39 5 30N07'47 84w59'20 5:39:57
Kerr City 42 5 29N22'12 81w47'00 5:27:08
Keuka 54 5 29N36'16 81w54'46 5:27:39
Key Biscayne 13 6 25N41'36 80w09'47 5:20:39
Key Colony Beach 44 5 24N43'14 81w01'08 5:24:05
Key Largo 44 5 25N08 80w25 5:21:40
Key Largo Park 44 5 25N08 80w25 5:21:40
Key Largo Village 44 5 25N08 80w25 5:21:40
Keystone Heights 10 5 29N47'09 82w01'54 5:28:08
Keystone Islands 13 6 25N53'39 80w09'15 5:20:37
Keysville 29 5 27N52'08 82w05'45 5:28:23
Key West 44 5 24N33'19 81w46'58 5:27:08
Kilarney Shores 16 5 30N17 81w35 5:26:20
Killarney 48 5 28N32'49 81w39'02 5:26:36
Killearn Estates 37 5 30N28 84w18 5:37:12
Killingsworth Crossroads 46 1 30N45'02 86w27'31 5:45:50
Kinard 7 1 30N15'53 85w14'30 5:40:58
Kincaid Hills 1 5 29N38'01 82w17'01 5:29:08
Kings Bay 13 5 25N38'13 80w18'05 5:21:12
Kings Ferry 45 5 30N47'06 81w50'21 5:27:21
Kingsford 53 5 27N52'47 81w58'24 5:27:54
Kingsland 50 6 26N27'48 80w06'11 5:20:25
Kingsley 10 5 29N58'54 81w59'46 5:27:59
Kingsley Beach 10 5 29N58'44 81w59'45 5:27:59
Kingsley Lake 10 5 29N57 82w06 5:28:24
Kingsley Village 10 5 29N58'18 82w00'59 5:28:04
Kings Road 16 5 30N19 81w43 5:26:52
Kingswood Manor 48 5 28N35 81w24 5:25:36
Kinsey 25 5 27N20'24 81w53'42 5:27:35
Kirby Loop 56 5 27N21 80w19 5:21:16
Kirkwood 1 5 29N32'10 82w19'49 5:29:19
Kissimmee 49 5 28N17'30 81w24'28 5:25:38
Kissimmee Park 49 5 28N15 81w17 5:25:08
Knights 29 5 28N04'34 82w08'16 5:28:33
Knoxhill 66 1 30N43 85w57 5:43:48
Koerber 66 1 30N43'38 86w04'17 5:44:17
Korona 18 5 29N24'24 81w11'48 5:24:47
Kossuthville 53 5 28N02'39 81w50'46 5:27:23
Kuhlman 28 5 27N23'44 81w24'59 5:25:40
Kynesville 32 1 30N43'52 85w21'17 5:41:25
La Belle 26 5 26N45'41 81w26'19 5:25:45
LaBuena 2 5 30N14'32 82w05'58 5:28:24
Lackawanna 16 5 30N17'41 81w45'41 5:27:03
Lacoochee 51 5 28N27'56 82w10'20 5:28:41
Lacota 42 5 29N13'59 81w55'34 5:27:42
LaCrosse 1 5 29N50'35 82w24'18 5:29:37
Lady Lake 35 5 28N55'02 81w55'23 5:27:42
Lafayette 37 5 30N25'40 84w12'59 5:36:52
La Gorce Island 13 6 25N48 80w09 5:20:36
La Grange 5 5 28N38'10 80w49'50 5:23:19
Laguna Beach 3 1 30N14'22 85w55'27 5:43:42
Laird 3 1 30N18'50 85w55'07 5:43:40
Lake Alfred 53 5 28N05'30 81w43'25 5:26:54
Lake Ashby Shores 64 5 28N56'21 81w05'40 5:24:23
Lake Bird 62 5 30N14 83w37 5:34:28
Lake Bradford 37 5 30N26 84w17 5:37:08
Lake Brantley 59 5 28N42 81w20 5:25:20
Lake Buena Vista 48 5 28N33 81w23 5:25:32
Lake Butler 63 5 30N01'21 82w20'23 5:29:22
Lake Cain Hills 48 5 28N29'01 81w28'39 5:25:55
Lake Carroll 29 5 28N03 82w30 5:30:00
Lake Charm 59 5 28N40'24 81w11'54 5:24:48
Lake City 12 5 30N11'22 82w38'22 5:30:33
Lake Clarke Shores 50 6 26N38'42 80w04'34 5:20:18
Lake Como 54 5 29N29'01 81w34'23 5:26:18
Lake Fern 29 5 28N08'58 82w34'47 5:30:19
Lake Forest 6 6 25N58'38 80w11'00 5:20:44
Lake Forest 16 5 30N23'52 81w40'26 5:26:42
Lake Forest Hills 16 5 30N23'28 81w41'25 5:26:46
Lake Forest Manor 16 5 30N23'35 81w39'58 5:26:40
Lake Frances 35 5 28N48 81w44 5:26:56
Lake Garfield 53 5 27N53'25 81w45'41 5:27:03
Lake Geneva 10 5 29N46'19 82w00'37 5:28:02
Lake Hamilton 53 5 28N02'39 81w37'41 5:26:31
Lake Harbor 50 5 26N41'34 80w48'53 5:23:16
Lake Helen 64 5 28N58'50 81w14'01 5:24:56
Lake Holloway 53 5 28N02 81w55 5:27:40
Lake Jackson 37 5 30N31'56 84w21'42 5:37:27
Lake Jem 35 5 28N44'46 81w40'02 5:26:40
Lake Joanna 35 5 28N51 81w41 5:26:44
Lake Juniata 35 5 28N48 81w44 5:26:56
Lake Kathryn Estates 59 5 28N40 81w20 5:25:20
Lake Kathryn Heights 35 5 29N00'49 81w29'21 5:25:57
Lake Kathryn Village 59 5 28N40 81w20 5:25:20
Lakeland 53 5 28N03 81w57 5:27:48
Lake Lindsey 27 5 28N32 82w29 5:29:56
Lake Lucerne 13 6 25N57'53 80w14'30 5:20:58
Lake Lucina 16 5 30N20 81w35 5:26:20
Lake Mack Park 35 5 28N59'22 81w26'11 5:25:45
Lake Magdalene 29 5 28N04 82w28 5:29:52

Lake Maitland 48 5 28N37 81w23 5:25:32
Lake Marian Highlands 49 5 27N52'34 81w02'35 5:24:10
Lake Mary 59 5 28N45'31 81w19'05 5:25:16
Lake Maude 53 5 28N01 81w44 5:26:56
Lake Mendelin Estates 48 5 28N41 81w28 5:25:52
Lake Monroe 59 5 28N49'28 81w19'38 5:25:19
Lakemont 28 5 27N32'34 81w27'14 5:25:49
Lake of the Hills 53 5 27N57'18 81w35'41 5:26:23
Lake Ola 35 5 28N48 81w39 5:26:36
Lake Panasoffkee 60 5 28N45'20 82w05'42 5:28:23
Lake Park 50 6 26N48'00 80w04'00 5:20:16
Lake Park Estates 16 5 30N23'14 81w41'36 5:26:46
Lake Pasadena Heights 51 5 28N19'40 82w13'21 5:28:53
Lake Placid 28 5 27N17'34 81w21'47 5:25:27
Lakeport 22 5 26N58'34 81w07'39 5:24:31
Lake Rogers Isle 50 6 26N22'52 80w04'27 5:20:18
Lake Saunders Trailer Park 35 5 28N48 81w39 5:26:36
Lake Ship Heights 53 5 28N00 81w44 5:26:56
Lake Shore 16 5 30N16'51 81w43'34 5:26:54
Lake Shore Estates 52 5 27N57 82w45 5:31:00
Lakeside 37 5 30N22'33 84w18'03 5:37:12
Lake Tarpon 52 5 27N57 82w45 5:31:00
Lake Tarpon Mobile Homes 52 5 27N57 82w45 5:31:00
Lakeview 6 6 26N17'57 80w09'37 5:20:38
Lake View Point 20 5 30N25'26 84w35'52 5:38:23
Lake Wales 53 5 27N54'04 81w35'10 5:26:21
Lake Weir 42 5 29N03 81w56 5:27:44
Lakewood 16 5 30N15'39 81w38'06 5:26:32
Lakewood 37 5 30N26 84w17 5:37:08
Lakewood 66 1 30N59'18 86w16'55 5:45:08
Lakewood Park 56 5 27N32'34 80w24'09 5:21:37
Lake Worth 50 6 26N36'56 80w03'26 5:20:14
Lamont 33 5 30N22'37 83w48'47 5:35:15
Lanair Park 50 6 26N36 80w05 5:20:20
Lanark 19 5 29N53 84w36 5:38:24
Lanark Village 19 5 29N53'00 84w35'45 5:38:23
Lancaster 61 5 30N14'56 83w12'11 5:32:49
Land o' Lakes 51 5 28N13'07 82w27'28 5:29:50
Landrum 9 5 28N45'17 82w23'06 5:29:32
Lands End Ranch 54 5 29N32'34 81w54'08 5:27:37
Lane Landing 55 5 29N51'26 81w33'11 5:26:13
Lane Park 35 5 28N46'19 81w45'28 5:27:02
Langmar 16 5 30N20'47 81w46'21 5:27:05
Lansing 14 5 27N15'23 81w53'21 5:27:33
Lantana 50 6 26N35'11 80w03'08 5:20:13
Largo 52 5 27N54'33 82w47'15 5:31:09
Larsen 16 5 30N16'42 81w37'57 5:26:32
Lauderdale-by-the-Sea 6 6 26N11'30 80w05'48 5:20:23
Lauderdale Isles 6 6 26N06 80w12 5:20:48
Lauderdale Lakes 6 6 26N09'58 80w12'31 5:20:50
Lauderhill 6 6 26N08'24 80w12'49 5:20:51
Launch Complex 5 5 5 28N26'21 80w34'25 5:22:18
Launch Complex 6 5 5 28N26'26 80w34'22 5:22:17
Launch Complex 11 5 5 28N28'30 80w32'23 5:22:10
Launch Complex 12 5 5 28N28'50 80w32'32 5:22:10
Launch Complex 13 5 5 28N29'09 80w32'41 5:22:11
Launch Complex 14 5 5 28N29'27 80w32'49 5:22:11
Launch Complex 15 5 5 28N29'46 80w32'58 5:22:12
Launch Complex 16 5 5 28N30'05 80w33'07 5:22:12
Launch Complex 17 5 5 28N26'46 80w33'57 5:22:16
Launch Complex 18 5 5 28N26'56 80w33'43 5:22:15
Launch Complex 19 5 5 28N30'23 80w33'16 5:22:13
Launch Complex 20 5 5 28N30'42 80w33'24 5:22:14
Launch Complex 25 5 5 28N25'55 80w34'28 5:22:18
Launch Complex 26 5 5 28N26'35 80w34'18 5:22:17
Launch Complex 29 5 5 28N25'48 80w34'32 5:22:18
Launch Complex 30 5 5 28N26'17 80w34'50 5:22:19
Launch Complex 31 5 5 28N27'04 80w33'19 5:22:13
Launch Complex 32 5 5 28N27'11 80w33'16 5:22:13
Launch Complex 34 5 5 28N31'17 80w33'41 5:22:15
Launch Complex 37 5 5 28N31'49 80w34'03 5:22:16
Launch Complex 40 5 5 28N33'43 80w34'38 5:22:19
Launch Complex 41 5 5 28N35'00 80w35'00 5:22:20
Launch Complex 36A 5 5 28N28'17 80w32'17 5:22:09
Launch Complex 39A 5 5 28N36'28 80w36'15 5:22:25
Launch Complex 36B 5 5 28N28'05 80w32'28 5:22:10
Launch Complex 39B 5 5 28N37'28 80w37'17 5:22:29

Laurel 58 5 27N07'48 82w27'12 5:29:49
Laurel Grove 10 5 30N09'19 81w42'05 5:26:48
Laurel Hill 46 1 30N57'56 86w27'35 5:45:50
Laurel Park 17 4 30N26 87w15 5:49:00
Lawhons Mill 65 5 30N09'58 84w24'08 5:37:37
Lawtey 4 5 30N02'38 82w04'19 5:28:17
Layton 44 5 24N49'25 80w48'50 5:23:15
Lazy Lake 6 6 26N09'21 80w08'42 5:20:35
Lealman (Lellman Station) 52 5 27N49'15 82w40'46 5:30:43
Lebanon 38 5 29N06 82w38 5:30:32
Lecanto 9 5 28N51'05 82w29'16 5:29:57
Lee 40 5 30N25'10 83w18'02 5:33:12
Lee Cypress 11 5 25N56'38 81w21'47 5:25:27
Leesburg 35 5 28N48'38 81w52'41 5:27:31
Lehigh Acres 36 5 26N37'30 81w37'30 5:26:30
Leisure City 13 5 25N29'42 80w25'46 5:21:43
Leland 40 5 30N36'37 83w19'32 5:33:18
Lely Golf Estates 11 5 26N11 81w48 5:27:12
Lelyland 11 5 26N11 81w48 5:27:12
Lely Tropical Estates 11 5 26N11 81w48 5:27:12
Lemon Bluff 64 5 28N48'22 81w07'56 5:24:32
Lemon City 13 6 25N49'48 80w11'35 5:20:46
Lemon Grove 25 5 27N33'29 81w40'42 5:26:43
Leno 10 5 29N53'22 81w38'27 5:26:34
Leon 37 5 30N28 84w18 5:37:12
Leonards 7 1 30N28'48 85w06'17 5:40:25
Leon Hamilton Place 44 5 25N31'16 81w12'22 5:24:49
Leonia 30 1 30N55 86w01 5:44:04
Leonton 33 5 30N33 83w52 5:35:28
Leroy 42 5 29N08'03 82w19'47 5:29:19
Lessie 45 5 30N43'30 81w46'38 5:27:07
Leto 29 5 28N00 82w31 5:30:04
Lewis 39 5 30N12'49 85w03'33 5:40:14
Libby Heights 1 5 29N40 82w20 5:29:20
Liberty 39 5 30N16'54 84w50'30 5:39:22
Liberty 66 1 30N49'13 86w12'49 5:44:51
Liberty Point 22 5 26N48'40 80w59'11 5:23:57
Liberty Square 13 6 25N49'53 80w13'01 5:20:52
Lido Beach 52 5 27N45 82w42 5:30:48
Lighthouse Point 6 6 26N16'31 80w05'15 5:20:21
Lighthouse Point 43 5 27N12'07 80w16'25 5:21:06
Lily 25 5 27N21'58 81w57'57 5:27:52
Limestone 25 5 27N21'55 81w53'57 5:27:36
Limestone 33 5 30N21'04 84w01'41 5:36:07
Limona 29 5 27N56'43 82w18'15 5:29:13
Lincoln 13 6 25N48 80w09 5:20:36
Lincoln City 4 5 29N57 82w06 5:28:24
Lincoln Estates 1 5 29N38'23 82w18'04 5:29:12
Lincoln Park 60 5 28N39'12 82w06'30 5:28:26
Linda Loma 36 5 26N36 81w52 5:27:28
Linden 60 5 28N33'42 82w02'03 5:28:08
Lindgren 13 5 25N36'01 80w25'47 5:21:43
Lisbon 35 5 28N52'13 81w47'23 5:27:10
Lithia 29 5 27N51'00 82w10'30 5:28:42
Little Harbor on the Hillsbo 6 6 26N19'02 80w05'18 5:20:21
Little Lake City 21 5 29N49'34 82w53'31 5:31:34
Little River 13 6 25N50'50 80w11'34 5:20:46
Little Torch Key 44 5 24N45 81w20 5:25:20
Littman 20 5 30N35'31 84w30'52 5:38:03
Live Oak 61 5 30N17'41 82w59'03 5:31:56
Live Oak 67 1 30N34'46 85w51'53 5:43:28
Live Oak Island 65 5 30N03'42 84w16'37 5:37:06
Live Oak Point 65 5 30N11 84w23 5:37:32
Lloyd 33 5 30N28'38 84w01'19 5:36:05
Loch Lommond 10 5 29N48'05 82w00'49 5:28:03
Lochloosa 1 5 29N30'41 82w06'02 5:28:24
Lock Arbor 59 5 28N47'11 81w18'59 5:25:16
Lockhart 48 5 28N37'09 81w26'34 5:25:46
Lockwood Ridge 58 5 27N19 82w31 5:30:04
Log Landing 21 5 29N44'45 82w56'14 5:31:45
Lois 33 5 30N31'34 83w54'57 5:35:40
Lokosee 49 5 27N45'19 80w54'44 5:23:39
Lona 12 5 30N12 82w44 5:30:56
Londonderry 48 5 28N34 81w27 5:25:48
Longbeach 41 5 27N26'13 82w41'00 5:30:44
Long Beach Resort 3 1 30N10'45 82w48'30 5:31:14
Longboat Key 41 5 27N24'44 82w39'33 5:30:38
Long Branch 24 5 30N22'21 82w41'36 5:30:46
Longdale 59 5 28N42'39 81w20'02 5:25:20
Long Hammock 60 5 28N55'37 82w06'12 5:28:25
Long Key 44 5 24N49 80w49 5:23:16
Long Point 3 1 30N06'54 85w35'53 5:42:24
Longwood 46 1 30N27'38 86w35'19 5:46:21
Longwood 59 5 28N42'10 81w20'19 5:25:21
Loretto 16 5 30N09'25 81w35'42 5:26:23
Lorida 28 5 27N26'35 81w15'14 5:25:01
Lorraine 41 5 27N25'54 82w23'44 5:29:35
Los Trancos Woods 1 5 29N41'59 82w29'34 5:29:58
Lottieville 21 5 29N36'43 82w53'53 5:31:36
Lotus 5 5 28N14'50 80w39'25 5:22:38
Loughman 53 5 28N14'30 81w34'01 5:26:16
Louise 1 5 29N50'14 82w13'53 5:28:56
Lovedale 32 1 30N52'47 85w02'35 5:40:10
Loveridge Heights 5 5 28N10 80w38 5:22:32
Lovett 40 5 30N37'41 83w34'24 5:34:18
Lovewood 32 1 30N48 85w22 5:41:28
Lowell 42 5 29N19'49 82w11'30 5:28:46
Lower Boca Ciega 52 5 27N45 82w44 5:30:56
Lower Clay Landing 38 5 29N27'43 82w59'24 5:31:58
Lower Keys 44 5 24N37 81w39 5:26:36
Lower Langston Landing 39 5 30N07'43 84w40'17 5:38:41
Lowry 39 5 30N25'28 84w46'34 5:39:06
Loxahatchee 50 6 26N41'00 80w16'48 5:21:07
Loyce 51 5 28N22'49 82w29'12 5:29:57
Lucerne Park 53 5 28N04'51 81w40'32 5:26:42
Ludlam 13 6 25N44 80w18 5:21:12
Lullwater Beach 3 1 30N09 85w39 5:42:36
Lulu 12 5 30N06'26 82w29'29 5:29:58
Lumberton 51 5 28N15'57 82w08'12 5:28:33
Lundy 54 5 29N37'05 81w38'52 5:26:35
Luraville 61 5 30N07'20 83w10'10 5:32:41
Lutterloh 37 5 30N19'42 84w15'11 5:37:01
Lutz 29 5 28N09'03 82w27'42 5:29:51
Lyle Corner 53 5 27N54'46 81w52'11 5:27:29
Lynchburg 53 5 28N05'16 81w45'19 5:27:01
Lynne 42 5 29N11'32 81w55'03 5:27:40
Lynn Haven 3 1 30N14'43 85w38'54 5:42:36
Mabel 60 5 28N34'45 81w58'38 5:27:55
Macclenny 2 5 30N16'55 82w07'20 5:28:29
MacDill Air Force Base 29 5 27N51 82w30 5:30:00
Mack Bayou 66 1 30N23 86w14 5:44:56
Madeira Beach 52 5 27N47'52 82w47'51 5:31:11
Madison 40 5 30N28'09 83w24'47 5:33:39
Magnet Cove 20 5 30N37 84w25 5:37:40
Magnolia Beach 3 1 30N09'30 85w43'26 5:42:54
Magnolia Bluffs 19 5 29N44'05 84w54'00 5:39:36
Magnolia Gardens 16 5 30N22'39 81w42'12 5:26:49
Magnolia Landing 55 5 29N54'40 81w35'32 5:26:22
Magnolia Springs 10 5 30N00'42 81w41'44 5:26:47
Mainland 64 5 29N18 81w03 5:24:12
Maitland (Lake Maitland) 48 5 28N37'39 81w21'48 5:25:27
Malabar 5 5 28N00'12 80w33'57 5:22:16
Malone 32 1 30N57'27 85w09'44 5:40:39
Manalapan 50 6 26N34'08 80w02'42 5:20:11
Manasota 58 5 27N00'54 82w24'10 5:29:37
Manasota Beach 58 5 27N00'37 82w24'46 5:29:39
Manasota Key 58 5 26N56 82w16 5:29:04
Manatee 41 5 27N29'46 82w32'23 5:30:10
Mandarin 16 5 30N09'37 81w39'34 5:26:38
Mango 29 5 27N58'46 82w18'24 5:29:14
Mango Hills 29 5 27N59'32 82w17'41 5:29:11
Mangonia Park 50 6 26N45'36 80w04'26 5:20:18
Manhattan 41 5 27N30'26 82w19'08 5:29:17
Manhattan Beach 16 5 30N22'00 81w23'56 5:25:36
Manning 2 5 30N10'30 82w10'29 5:28:42
Manns Spur 2 5 30N14'04 82w19'11 5:29:17
Mannville 54 5 29N37'43 81w52'06 5:27:28
Marathon 44 5 24N42'48 81w05'26 5:24:22
Marathon Shores 44 5 24N43'31 81w02'55 5:24:12
Maravilla 56 5 27N21 80w19 5:21:16
Marco 11 5 25N58'20 81w43'45 5:26:55
Marcy 43 5 27N08'31 80w39'08 5:22:37
Margaretta 2 5 30N15'55 82w13'15 5:28:53
Margate 6 6 26N14'39 80w12'24 5:20:50
Margate Estates 6 6 26N13'21 80w12'00 5:20:48
Marianna 32 1 30N46'27 85w13'37 5:40:54
Maricamp 42 5 29N09'44 82w05'33 5:28:22
Marietta 16 5 30N19'08 81w47'00 5:27:08
Marineland 18 5 29N40 81w13 5:24:52
Marion 24 5 30N26'28 82w56'48 5:31:47
Marion Oaks 42 5 29N11 82w09 5:28:36
Marland 28 5 27N20'20 81w14'27 5:24:58
Martel 42 5 29N11'11 82w14'48 5:28:59
Martin 42 5 29N17'37 82w11'26 5:28:46
Mart Law Seminole Village 13 6 25N56'39 80w49'07 5:23:16
Mary Esther 46 1 30N24'35 86w39'47 5:46:39
Masaryktown 27 5 28N26'29 82w27'26 5:29:50
Mascotte 35 5 28N34'41 81w53'13 5:27:33
Mason 12 5 30N02'23 82w35'53 5:30:24
Mason Landing 46 1 30N38'31 86w47'10 5:47:09
Masters Landing 36 5 26N33'36 82w04'47 5:28:19
Matanzas 55 5 29N49 81w18 5:25:12
Matlacha 36 5 26N37'46 82w04'16 5:28:17
Matoaka 41 5 27N24'10 82w31'49 5:30:07
Mattox 45 5 30N17'35 82w02'24 5:28:10
Maxcy Quarters 53 5 27N42'53 81w32'47 5:26:11
Maxville 16 5 30N11'54 82w00'40 5:28:03
Mayo 34 5 30N03'10 83w10'30 5:32:42
Mayo Junction 34 5 30N12'20 83w16'00 5:33:04
Mayo West 34 5 30N08 83w16 5:33:04
Mayport 16 5 30N23'35 81w25'51 5:25:43
Mayport Naval Housing 16 5 30N23 81w25 5:25:40
Mayport Naval Station 16 5 30N19 81w39 5:26:36
Maysland 40 5 30N35'46 83w34'21 5:34:17
Maytown 64 5 28N48'25 80w57'37 5:23:50
McAllaster Landing 3 1 30N19'55 85w33'27 5:42:14
McAllister 42 5 29N20 82w12 5:28:48
McAlpin 61 5 30N08'20 82w57'07 5:31:48
McAlpin Landing 24 5 30N21'42 82w40'32 5:30:42
McCoy Air Force Base 48 5 28N26 81w21 5:25:24
McCrabb Landing 15 5 29N40'15 82w57'36 5:31:50
McDavid 17 1 30N51'58 87w19'11 5:49:17
McGregor Gardens 36 5 26N36 81w52 5:27:28
McGregor Groves 36 5 26N36 81w52 5:27:28
McIntosh 42 5 29N26'55 82w13'20 5:28:53
McIntyre 19 5 29N58'52 84w31'34 5:38:06
McKenzie Landing 45 5 30N48'59 81w54'18 5:27:37
McKinnon 17 1 30N47'20 87w28'24 5:49:54
McLellan 57 1 30N59'11 86w53'11 5:47:33
McMeekin 54 5 29N35'42 82w00'47 5:28:03
McNeal 7 1 30N25'42 85w01'58 5:40:08
McPherson 2 5 30N14'51 82w04'49 5:28:19
McRae 10 5 29N47 82w02 5:28:08
Meadowbrook 10 5 30N08 81w42 5:26:48
Meadowbrook 48 5 28N34 81w27 5:25:48
Meadowbrook Terrace 10 5 30N10'38 81w44'05 5:26:56
Mecca 59 5 28N48 81w15 5:25:00
Medart 65 5 30N04'57 84w23'14 5:37:33
Medley 13 6 25N50'25 80w19'36 5:21:18
Medulla 53 5 27N58'03 81w58'25 5:27:54
Melaleuca Isle 6 6 26N07 80w13 5:20:52
Melbourne 5 5 28N04'43 80w36'10 5:22:25
Melbourne Beach 5 5 28N04'05 80w33'38 5:22:15
Melbourne Gardens 5 5 28N05 80w38 5:22:32
Melbourne Shores 5 5 28N05 80w36 5:22:24
Melbourne Village 5 5 28N05'06 80w40'00 5:22:40
Meldrim Park 55 5 29N53'12 81w33'41 5:26:15
Melrose 54 5 29N42'33 82w03'00 5:28:12
Melrose Park 6 6 26N08 80w12 5:20:48
Melrose Park 12 5 30N17 81w24 5:25:36
Memphis 41 5 27N32'08 82w33'41 5:30:15
Memphis Heights 41 5 27N32'11 82w33'16 5:30:13
Mercer 61 5 30N16'37 83w06'51 5:32:27
Meredith Manor 59 5 28N42 81w20 5:25:20
Merediths 38 5 29N28'42 82w36'11 5:30:25
Meridan 37 5 30N26 84w17 5:37:08
Meridian 37 5 30N38'18 84w16'55 5:37:08
Meritt Landing 46 1 30N47'06 86w37'49 5:46:31
Merritt Island 5 5 28N21 80w42 5:22:48
Mexico Beach 3 1 29N56'52 85w25'05 5:41:40
Miami 13 6 25N46'26 80w11'38 5:20:47
Miami Beach 13 6 25N47'25 80w07'49 5:20:31
Miami Gardens 6 6 25N58'46 80w12'10 5:20:49
Miami Lakes 13 6 25N54 80w18 5:21:12
Miami Shores 13 6 25N51'46 80w11'35 5:20:46
Miami Springs 13 6 25N49'19 80w17'23 5:21:10
Micanopy 1 5 29N30'16 82w16'48 5:29:07
Micanopy Junction 1 5 29N31'20 82w13'50 5:28:55
Micco 5 5 27N52'49 80w30'02 5:22:00
Miccosukee 37 5 30N35'40 84w02'29 5:36:10
Mickler Landing 55 5 30N09'41 81w21'22 5:25:25
Middleburg 10 5 30N04'07 81w51'38 5:27:27
Middle Keys 44 5 24N46 80w57 5:23:48
Middle River 6 6 26N09'49 80w10'02 5:20:40
Middle River Manor 6 6 26N09'23 80w07'24 5:20:30
Middle River Vista 6 6 26N09'02 80w09'26 5:20:38
Midway 20 5 30N29'43 84w27'16 5:37:49
Midway 29 5 28N03'56 82w05'49 5:28:23
Midway 34 5 30N00'42 83w04'44 5:32:19
Midway 59 5 28N47'24 81w13'52 5:24:55
Midway West 13 6 25N51 80w15 5:21:00
Mikesville 12 5 29N56'47 82w36'08 5:30:25
Mildred 47 5 27N16'59 80w55'57 5:23:44
Miles City 11 5 26N09'14 81w20'41 5:25:23
Military Park 50 6 26N42'58 80w06'47 5:20:27
Millcreek 55 5 29N48 81w16 5:25:04
Miller 63 5 29N58'03 82w27'58 5:29:52
Miller Bend 66 1 30N28'23 85w53'06 5:43:32
Miller Crossroads 30 1 30N56'57 85w44'30 5:42:58
Miller Landing 66 1 30N28'20 85w53'21 5:43:33
Millers Ferry 67 1 30N34'20 85w50'40 5:43:23
Millers Public Landing 37 5 30N32'22 84w19'35 5:37:18
Milligan 46 1 30N45'08 86w38'27 5:46:34
Millspring 32 1 30N43 85w01 5:40:04
Milltown 23 1 29N49'57 85w17'50 5:41:11
Millview 17 4 30N25'04 87w21'22 5:49:25
Millville 3 1 30N09'04 85w37'50 5:42:31
Milton 57 3 30N37'56 87w02'23 5:48:10
Mims 5 5 28N39'54 80w50'42 5:23:23
Mineral Springs 57 1 30N57 87w09 5:48:36
Minneola 35 5 28N34'27 81w44'47 5:26:59
Mintons Corner 5 5 28N04'42 80w40'15 5:22:41
Miracle Mile 36 5 26N36 81w52 5:27:28
Miramar 6 6 25N59'13 80w13'57 5:20:56
Miramar Beach 66 1 30N22'27 86w21'31 5:45:26
Miramar Terrace 16 5 30N16'46 81w39'31 5:26:38
Mission City 64 5 29N01'17 80w56'49 5:23:47
Missouri Landing 19 1 29N54'50 84w59'10 5:39:57
Mitchell Beach 52 5 27N47'14 82w47'07 5:31:08
Mitchell Lake Estates 13 6 25N54'20 80w13'41 5:20:55
Mobile Haven Estates 36 5 26N36 81w52 5:27:28
Mobile Home Park 58 5 27N19 82w31 5:30:04
Mobile Manor 59 5 28N42 81w20 5:25:20
Moccasin Landing 54 5 29N32'22 81w33'19 5:26:13
Modello 13 5 25N30'08 80w26'36 5:21:46
Moffitt 25 5 27N27'16 81w47'49 5:27:11
Mohawk 35 5 28N34'19 81w43'48 5:26:55
Molasses Junction 55 5 29N51'03 81w29'38 5:25:59
Molino 17 1 30N43'26 87w18'51 5:49:15

Molino Crossroads 17 1 30N43'04 87w20'20 5:49:21
Monet 50 6 26N50'16 80w05'40 5:20:23
Money Bayou 23 1 29N48 85w18 5:41:12
Monkey Box 22 5 26N55'58 81w03'22 5:24:13
Monroe 11 5 25N54 81w17 5:25:08
Monroes Corner 42 5 29N01'31 82w07'12 5:28:29
Montague 42 5 29N09'01 82w04'30 5:28:18
Montbrook 38 5 29N19'37 82w27'02 5:29:48
Montclair 35 5 28N49'18 81w54'59 5:27:40
Monteocha 1 5 29N47'46 82w17'08 5:29:09
Monterey 16 5 30N20 81w35 5:26:20
Monticello 33 5 30N32'42 83w52'13 5:35:29
Montivilla 33 5 30N32'51 83w53'19 5:35:33
Montverde 35 5 28N36'00 81w40'27 5:26:42
Montverde Junction 35 5 28N33'43 81w40'57 5:26:44
Moore Haven 22 5 26N49'58 81w05'36 5:24:22
Moreland Park 60 5 28N53'21 82w02'31 5:28:10
Morgan Place 19 5 30N00'35 84w45'20 5:39:01
Morgantown 8 5 27N00'21 81w58'04 5:27:52
Moriczville 29 5 28N07'09 82w09'00 5:28:36
Morningside Park 48 5 28N26'35 81w24'25 5:25:38
Morrison Home 50 6 26N40 80w06 5:20:24
Morriston 38 5 29N16'53 82w26'17 5:29:45
Morse Shores 36 5 26N39 81w50 5:27:20
Mosley Hall 40 5 30N28 83w38 5:34:32
Mosquito Grove 35 5 29N03'47 81w27'24 5:25:50
Mosquito Landing 39 5 30N16'34 85w03'25 5:40:14
Moss Bluff 42 5 29N04'59 81w53'02 5:27:32
Moss Town 51 5 28N27'32 82w10'50 5:28:43
Mossy Head 66 1 30N44'35 86w18'54 5:45:16
Mott 50 5 26N41'21 80w52'07 5:23:28
Moultrie 55 5 29N49'12 81w19'22 5:25:17
Moultrie Junction 55 5 29N53'28 81w20'05 5:25:20
Mound Grove 64 5 29N24'07 81w06'47 5:24:27
Mountain Lake 53 5 27N53 81w34 5:26:16
Mountain Lake Station 53 5 27N56'58 81w35'43 5:26:23
Mount Carmel 57 1 30N58'51 87w07'07 5:48:28
Mount Carrie 12 5 30N11'42 82w30'14 5:30:01
Mount Dora 35 5 28N48'08 81w38'41 5:26:35
Mount Enon 29 5 28N02'13 82w04'21 5:28:17
Mount Homer 35 5 28N49'43 81w42'03 5:26:48
Mount Olive 42 5 29N12'05 82w17'06 5:29:08
Mount Pine 61 5 30N09'48 82w57'16 5:31:49
Mount Pleasant 20 5 30N39'26 84w41'28 5:38:46
Mount Plymouth 35 5 28N48'28 81w32'00 5:26:08
Mount Royal 54 5 29N29 81w41 5:26:44
Muce 22 5 26N49'39 81w29'46 5:25:59
Muddy Ford 57 1 30N27'34 86w53'42 5:47:35
Mud Landing 65 5 29N59'54 84w26'06 5:37:44
Mulat 57 1 30N33'04 87w07'24 5:48:30
Mulberry 53 5 27N53'42 81w58'25 5:27:54
Mullet Lake Park 59 5 28N47'20 81w08'19 5:24:33
Mullinsville 53 5 27N45 81w32 5:26:08
Mullis City 29 5 28N02'23 82w30'33 5:30:02
Mulloy Landing 33 5 30N20'19 83w59'06 5:35:56
Munson 57 1 30N51'27 86w52'23 5:47:30
Munson Island 44 5 24N34 81w44 5:26:56
Murdock 8 5 27N00'45 82w08'47 5:28:35
Murray Hill 16 5 30N18'44 81w42'37 5:26:50
Muscogee 17 1 30N36'20 87w23'48 5:49:35
Muscogee Landing 39 5 30N17'14 85w03'06 5:40:12
Myakka City 41 5 27N20'58 82w09'42 5:28:39
Myakka Head 41 5 27N28'04 82w04'33 5:28:18
Myakka River Manor 58 5 27N04 82w20 5:29:20
Myerlee 36 5 26N36 81w52 5:27:28
Myrtis 12 5 30N03'55 82w36'01 5:30:24
Myrtle Grove 17 4 30N25'15 87w18'27 5:49:14
Myrtle Island 18 5 29N35'07 81w26'29 5:25:46
Nalcrest 53 5 27N51'29 81w25'31 5:25:42
Naples 11 5 26N08'30 81w47'42 5:27:11
Naples Manor 11 5 26N05'18 81w43'35 5:26:54
Naples Park 11 5 26N15'41 81w48'34 5:27:14
Naranja 13 5 25N31'04 80w25'23 5:21:42
Narcoossee 49 5 28N17'53 81w14'21 5:24:57
Nash 33 5 30N27'15 83w53'35 5:35:34
Nashua 54 5 29N31'06 81w40'16 5:26:41
Nassauville 45 5 30N34'09 81w31'11 5:26:05
National Gardens 64 5 29N19'56 81w07'36 5:24:30
Naval Air Medical Center 17 4 30N30 87w15 5:49:00
Naval Air Station 17 4 30N21 87w16 5:49:04
Naval Hospital 16 5 30N19 81w39 5:26:36
Naval Technical Training Ctr 17 1 30N04 87w12 5:48:48
Naval Training Center 48 5 28N34 81w19 5:25:16
Navarre 57 1 30N24'05 86w51'49 5:47:27
Navy Point 17 4 30N22'47 87w17'36 5:49:10
Neals 21 5 29N46'07 82w42'46 5:30:51
Neheb 59 5 28N41'30 81w12'02 5:24:48
Neilhurst 10 5 30N07'15 81w43'39 5:26:55
Neilson 53 5 27N40'41 81w30'04 5:26:00
Neoga 18 5 29N31'34 81w20'12 5:25:21
Neptune Beach 16 5 30N18'42 81w23'48 5:25:35
Nevins 31 5 27N36'41 80w23'07 5:21:32
New Berlin 16 5 30N23'54 81w33'10 5:26:13
Newbern 29 5 28N09 82w28 5:29:52
Newberry 1 5 29N38'46 82w36'24 5:30:26
Newburn 61 5 30N16'20 83w08'27 5:32:34
Newcastle 16 5 30N22'19 81w35'09 5:26:21
New Clay Landing 38 5 29N31'06 82w58'12 5:31:53
New Eden 49 5 28N16'40 81w10'47 5:24:43
New Harmony 66 1 30N51'12 86w16'48 5:45:07
New Home 66 1 30N36'32 86w13'11 5:44:53
New Hope 7 1 30N21'30 85w03'56 5:40:16
New Hope 30 1 30N56'51 85w52'46 5:43:31
New Hope 67 1 30N34'40 85w48'32 5:43:14
New Liberty City 13 6 25N55 80w15 5:21:00
Newnans Lake Homesites 1 5 29N38'59 82w14'23 5:28:58
New Pierce 41 5 27N24 82w32 5:30:08
New Pine Landing 15 5 29N31'44 82w58'39 5:31:55
New Point Comfort 8 5 26N55'50 82w20'28 5:29:22
Newport 44 5 25N06'13 80w25'53 5:21:44
Newport 65 5 30N11'57 84w10'51 5:36:43
New Port Richey 51 5 28N14'38 82w43'10 5:30:53
New River 4 5 29N57'39 82w15'56 5:29:04
New River 6 6 26N08 80w11 5:20:44
New Smyrna 64 5 28N59 80w56 5:23:44
New Smyrna Beach 64 5 29N01'32 80w55'38 5:23:43
Newtown Heights 58 5 27N19 82w31 5:30:04
New Upsala 59 5 28N47'46 81w19'00 5:25:16
New York 57 1 30N50'18 87w12'03 5:48:48
Niceville 46 1 30N31'00 86w28'56 5:45:56
Nichols 53 5 27N53'24 82w01'54 5:28:08
Niles 23 1 29N47'13 85w16'27 5:41:06
Nine Mile 19 5 29N43'00 85w07'17 5:40:29
Ninemile Bend 50 5 26N40'39 80w32'28 5:22:10
Nixon 3 1 30N19'20 85w27'05 5:41:48
Nobles 17 4 30N29 87w12 5:48:48
Nobleton 27 5 28N38'43 82w15'51 5:29:03
Nocatee 14 5 27N09'36 81w52'57 5:27:32
Nokomis 58 5 27N07'08 82w26'40 5:29:47
Nokomis Beach 58 5 27N07'34 82w28'16 5:29:53
Noma 30 1 30N58'55 85w37'07 5:42:28
Noma Junction 30 1 30N58'21 85w37'04 5:42:28
Norfleet 37 5 30N26'33 84w23'31 5:37:34
Norin Plaza 13 6 25N53 80w11 5:20:44
Norland 13 6 25N56 80w13 5:20:52
Normandy 13 6 25N51 80w08 5:20:32
Normandy 16 5 30N18'20 81w45'39 5:27:03
Normandy Isle 13 6 25N48 80w09 5:20:36
Normandy Manor 16 5 30N19 81w43 5:26:52
Normandy Shores 13 6 25N51'34 80w08'21 5:20:33
Normandy Village 16 5 30N16'46 81w46'53 5:27:08
North Andrews Gardens 6 6 26N11 80w09 5:20:36
North Andrews Terrace 6 6 26N12 80w09 5:20:36
North Babcock 5 5 28N05 80w38 5:22:32
North Bal Harbor 6 6 26N09'13 80w06'59 5:20:28
North Bay Village 13 6 25N50'45 80w09'15 5:20:37
North Columbia 12 5 30N23 82w35 5:30:20
North Crest 48 5 28N41 81w28 5:25:52
Northeast Park 52 5 27N48 82w39 5:30:36
North Fort Myers 36 5 26N40'01 81w52'49 5:27:31
North Lauderdale 6 6 26N13 80w13 5:20:52
North Meadowbrook Terrace 10 5 30N10'42 81w45'05 5:27:00
North Miami 13 6 25N53'23 80w11'13 5:20:45
North Miami Beach 13 6 25N55'58 80w09'46 5:20:39
North Naples 11 5 26N13'08 81w47'31 5:27:10
North Oak Hill 16 5 30N15'12 81w46'23 5:27:06
North Orlando 59 5 28N41 81w17 5:25:08
North Palm Beach 50 6 26N49'02 80w04'56 5:20:20
North Peninsula 64 5 29N23 81w05 5:24:20
North Pompano Beach 6 6 26N16'43 80w06'11 5:20:25
North Port 58 5 27N03'00 82w15'00 5:29:00
North Port Charlotte 58 5 27N02'38 82w13'57 5:28:56
North Redington Beach 52 5 27N48'57 82w49'15 5:31:17
North River Shores 56 5 27N13'02 80w16'12 5:21:05
North Ruskin 29 5 27N45'52 82w23'41 5:29:35
North Saint Johns 55 5 30N08 81w29 5:25:56
North Shore 16 5 30N23'03 81w39'25 5:26:38
Northside 58 5 27N19 82w31 5:30:04
Northwest 13 6 25N51 80w14 5:20:56
North Westside 13 6 25N48 80w19 5:21:16
North Winter Haven 53 5 28N03 81w44 5:26:56
Northwood 1 5 29N42'08 82w22'10 5:29:29
Northwood 16 5 30N26'00 81w39'45 5:26:39
Northwood 50 6 26N45 80w05 5:20:20
Norwalk 54 5 29N26'05 81w43'00 5:26:52
Norwalk Landing 54 5 29N25'49 81w40'40 5:26:43
Norwood 13 6 25N57 80w13 5:20:52
Norwood 16 5 30N22'36 81w40'05 5:26:40
Nova Road 64 5 29N18 81w03 5:24:12
Nowatney 29 5 28N04'25 82w26'49 5:29:47
NTC Annex 48 5 28N26 81w21 5:25:24
Nubbin Ridge 46 1 30N50'25 86w40'29 5:46:42
Nurmi Isles 6 6 26N07'20 80w07'02 5:20:28
Nutal Rise 33 5 30N09'01 83w57'51 5:35:51
Oak 42 5 29N15'07 82w06'57 5:28:28
Oak Crest 1 5 29N36 82w05 5:28:20
Oakdale 32 1 30N42'37 85w11'07 5:40:44
Oak Grove 17 1 30N54'31 87w25'39 5:49:43
Oak Grove 20 5 30N41'30 84w44'00 5:38:56
Oak Grove 23 1 29N47'25 85w17'49 5:41:11
Oak Grove 25 5 27N28'55 81w52'18 5:27:29
Oak Grove 46 1 30N55'29 86w34'03 5:46:16
Oak Grove 60 5 28N35'59 82w02'37 5:28:10
Oak Harbor 16 5 30N21'36 81w25'30 5:25:42
Oak Haven 16 5 30N17 81w35 5:26:20
Oak Hill 16 5 30N14'46 81w45'05 5:27:00
Oak Hill 64 5 28N51'51 80w51'17 5:23:25
Oak Hill Park 16 5 30N14'41 81w46'41 5:27:07
Oakhurst 52 5 27N53 82w46 5:31:04
Oak Knoll 41 5 27N30'41 82w16'40 5:29:07
Oak Knoll Estates 37 5 30N31'25 84w15'59 5:37:04
Oakland 48 5 28N33'17 81w38'00 5:26:32
Oakland Hills 59 5 28N37 81w25 5:25:40
Oak Landing 16 5 30N15'12 81w26'04 5:25:44
Oakland Park 6 6 26N10'19 80w07'56 5:20:32
Oakland Park 35 5 28N48'13 81w40'39 5:26:43
Oakland Shores 48 5 28N38 81w22 5:25:28
Oak Park 65 5 30N06'08 84w29'45 5:37:59
Oak Terrace 53 5 27N50'20 81w58'39 5:27:55
Oakwood Villa 16 5 30N19'04 81w34'45 5:26:19
O'Brien 61 5 30N02'17 82w56'25 5:31:46
Ocala 42 5 29N11'13 82w08'25 5:28:34
Ocala Ridge 42 5 29N11'35 82w12'50 5:28:51
Ocean Beach 5 5 28N20 80w37 5:22:28
Ocean Breeze 43 5 27N15 80w13 5:20:52
Ocean Breeze Park 43 5 27N14'08 80w13'15 5:20:53
Ocean City 46 1 30N26'27 86w36'49 5:46:27
Ocean Ridge 50 6 26N31'36 80w02'55 5:20:12
Ocean View 13 6 25N50 80w08 5:20:32
Ocean View Heights 13 6 25N44'11 80w14'17 5:20:57
Ocean Vue 6 6 26N19'04 80w04'38 5:20:19
Oceanway 16 5 30N28'00 81w37'57 5:26:32
Ocheesee 7 1 30N34'32 85w01'01 5:40:04
Ocheesee Landing 7 1 30N34'55 84w57'58 5:39:52
Ochlockonee 37 5 30N28'20 84w24'25 5:37:38
Ochopee 11 5 25N54'04 81w18'13 5:25:13
Ocoee 48 5 28N34'08 81w32'39 5:26:11
Octahatchee 24 5 30N34'45 83w11'26 5:32:46
Odena 23 5 29N44'24 85w11'11 5:40:45
Odessa 51 5 28N11'37 82w35'31 5:30:22
Ojus 13 6 25N56'53 80w09'03 5:20:36
Okahumpka 35 5 28N44'51 81w53'46 5:27:35
Okaloo 46 1 30N54'56 86w29'10 5:45:57
Okeechobee 47 5 27N14'37 80w49'48 5:23:19
Okeelanta 50 5 26N36'34 80w42'42 5:22:51
Oklawaha 42 5 29N02'33 81w55'46 5:27:43
Old Callaway 3 1 30N08'36 85w34'18 5:42:17
Old Fernandina 45 5 30N41'22 81w27'09 5:25:49
Old Grove 11 5 25N57'31 81w36'32 5:26:26
Old Henley Place 51 5 28N23'52 82w08'32 5:28:34
Old Landing 19 5 29N41'28 84w47'25 5:39:10
Old Land Place 57 1 30N33'13 86w56'20 5:47:45
Old Marco Junction 11 5 26N01'21 81w42'03 5:26:48
Old Myakka 58 5 27N18'46 82w16'01 5:29:04
Old Plantation Landing 38 5 29N13'16 82w44'21 5:30:57
Oldsmar 52 5 28N02'02 82w39'55 5:30:40
Old Town 15 5 29N36'04 82w58'55 5:31:56
Old Warehouse Landing 30 1 30N53'25 85w52'53 5:43:32
Olga 36 5 26N43'07 81w42'45 5:26:51
Olive 17 4 30N30'31 87w15'19 5:49:01
Olso 31 5 27N35'11 80w22'50 5:21:31
Olustee 63 5 30N12'14 82w25'44 5:29:43
Olympia Heights 13 6 25N43'35 80w21'20 5:21:25
Ona 25 5 27N28'54 81w55'09 5:27:41
Oneco 41 5 27N26'50 82w32'47 5:30:11
O'Neil 45 5 30N37'02 81w30'52 5:26:03
Opa-Locka 13 6 25N54'07 80w15'02 5:21:00
Open Air 52 5 27N47 82w40 5:30:40
Open Sands 3 1 30N12'18 85w51'28 5:43:26
Orange 39 5 30N13'39 85w01'30 5:40:06
Orange Bend 35 5 28N51'39 81w47'56 5:27:12
Orange Blossom 35 5 28N41'16 81w47'12 5:27:09
Orange Blossom Hills 42 5 28N59'42 82w00'03 5:28:00
Orange Blossom Hills South 35 5 28N55'41 81w56'54 5:27:48
Orange City 64 5 28N56'55 81w17'56 5:25:12
Orange City Hills 64 5 28N55'43 81w17'47 5:25:11
Orangedale 53 5 28N09'26 81w54'19 5:27:37
Orangedale 55 5 30N00'30 81w36'48 5:26:27
Orange Grove Villas 51 5 28N17'11 82w11'19 5:28:45
Orange Hammock 18 5 29N28 81w15 5:25:00
Orange Heights 1 5 29N43'10 82w08'22 5:28:33
Orange Hill 67 1 30N47 85w32 5:42:08
Orange Home 60 5 28N49'45 81w59'45 5:27:59
Orange Lake 42 5 29N25 82w13 5:28:52
Orange Mills 54 5 29N41'05 81w34'24 5:26:18
Orange Mountain 35 5 28N30'10 81w43'12 5:26:53
Orange Park 10 5 30N09'57 81w42'24 5:26:50
Orange Park Landing 10 5 30N10'06 81w41'45 5:26:47
Orange Springs 42 5 29N30'21 81w56'44 5:27:47
Orchid 31 5 27N46 80w25 5:21:40

Orienta Gardens 59 5 28N39'26 81w22'56 5:25:32
Orient Park 29 5 27N58'20 82w22'23 5:29:30
Oriole Beach 57 4 30N22'25 87w05'29 5:48:22
Orlando 48 5 28N32'17 81w22'46 5:25:31
Orlando Naval Hospital 48 5 28N34 81w19 5:25:16
Orlovista 48 5 28N32'17 81w27'38 5:25:51
Ormond Beach 64 5 29N17'08 81w03'22 5:24:13
Ormond-by-the-Sea 64 5 29N20'56 81w04'00 5:24:16
Orsino 5 5 28N31'39 80w39'56 5:22:40
Ortega 16 5 30N16'13 81w42'30 5:26:50
Ortega Farms 16 5 30N15'07 81w43'20 5:26:53
Ortega Forest 16 5 30N15'41 81w42'39 5:26:51
Ortega Hills 16 5 30N19 81w39 5:26:36
Ortega Terrace 16 5 30N15'50 81w42'03 5:26:48
Ortona 22 5 26N48'46 81w18'57 5:25:16
Ortona 64 5 29N15'08 81w01'33 5:24:06
Osceola 59 5 28N47'34 81w03'34 5:24:14
Osceola Forest 16 5 30N23 81w41 5:26:44
Osceola Landing 42 5 29N15'55 81w56'34 5:27:46
Oslo 31 5 27N35 80w23 5:21:32
Osowaw Junction 47 5 27N34'45 80w50'06 5:23:20
Osprey 58 5 27N11'45 82w29'26 5:29:58
Osteen 64 5 28N50'45 81w09'46 5:24:39
Otis 16 5 30N18'33 81w53'43 5:27:35
Otter Creek 38 5 29N19'29 82w46'19 5:31:05
Outer West 13 6 25N47 80w24 5:21:36
Overbrook Gardens 58 5 26N56 82w16 5:29:04
Overstreet 23 1 29N59'53 85w22'08 5:41:29
Oviedo 59 5 28N40'11 81w12'30 5:24:50
Owl Landing 39 5 30N01'05 85w00'58 5:40:04
Oxford 60 5 28N55'38 82w02'15 5:28:09
Oyster Bayou 51 5 28N14 82w44 5:30:56
Ozello 9 5 28N49'32 82w39'26 5:30:38
Ozona 52 5 28N04'09 82w46'33 5:31:06
Pablo Keys 16 5 30N16'19 81w25'26 5:25:42
Pace 57 3 30N35'57 87w09'40 5:48:39
Paces Landing 5 5 28N38'04 80w49'09 5:23:17
Packwood Place 64 5 28N56'16 80w52'11 5:23:29
Padlock 61 5 30N13'52 82w58'00 5:31:52
Page Park 36 5 26N34'44 81w51'44 5:27:27
Pahokee 50 5 26N49'11 80w39'56 5:22:40
Painters Hill 18 5 29N31'57 81w09'14 5:24:37
Paisley 35 5 28N59'00 81w32'31 5:26:10
Palatka 54 5 29N38'54 81w38'16 5:26:33
Palm 29 5 27N56'33 82w23'52 5:29:35
Palma Ceia 29 5 27N55'14 82w29'44 5:29:59
Palm Acres 36 5 26N36 81w52 5:27:28
Palma Sola 41 5 27N30'43 82w37'56 5:30:32
Palma Sola Park 41 5 27N29'29 82w38'13 5:30:33
Palm Bay 5 5 28N02'03 80w35'20 5:22:21
Palm Beach 50 6 26N42'19 80w02'12 5:20:09
Palm Beach Air Force Base 50 6 26N40 80w06 5:20:24
Palm Beach Farms 50 6 26N40'08 80w08'59 5:20:36
Palm Beach Gardens 50 6 26N50 80w06 5:20:24
Palm Beach Shores 50 6 26N46'40 80w02'09 5:20:09
Palm City 43 5 27N10'03 80w15'59 5:21:04
Palmdale 22 5 26N56'42 81w18'59 5:25:16
Palmetto 41 5 27N31'16 82w34'21 5:30:17
Palmetto Estates 13 5 25N36 80w22 5:21:28
Palmetto Landing 42 5 29N18'28 81w54'31 5:27:38
Palm Harbor 52 5 28N04'40 82w45'50 5:31:03
Palmo 55 5 29N57'58 81w34'03 5:26:16
Palm River 29 5 27N57 82w24 5:29:36
Palm River Estates 11 5 26N16'41 81w46'41 5:27:07
Palm Shadows 59 5 28N47'18 81w08'35 5:24:34
Palm Shores 5 5 28N11'03 80w39'11 5:22:37
Palm Springs 13 6 25N52'13 80w17'57 5:21:12
Palm Springs 50 6 26N37 80w06 5:20:24
Palm Springs Estates 13 6 25N52'56 80w18'23 5:21:14
Palm Springs North 13 6 25N55'50 80w19'43 5:21:19
Palm Valley 55 5 30N10'38 81w23'16 5:25:33
Palm Valley Landing 55 5 30N10'32 81w24'02 5:25:36
Palm View 41 5 27N34'06 82w33'26 5:30:14
Palm Village 13 6 25N53 80w17 5:21:08
Paloma Park 36 5 26N39 81w53 5:27:32
Panacea 65 5 30N02'14 84w23'16 5:37:33
Panacea Park 65 5 30N01'44 84w23'56 5:37:36
Panacoochee Retreats 60 5 28N48'00 82w08'08 5:28:33
Panama City 3 1 30N09'31 85w39'37 5:42:38
Panama City Beach 3 1 30N10'35 85w48'20 5:43:13
Panama Heights 67 1 30N31'18 85w39'01 5:42:36
Panama Park 16 5 30N23'05 81w38'27 5:26:34
Paola 59 5 28N47'37 81w21'47 5:25:27
Paolita Station 11 5 25N52 81w23 5:25:32
Paradise 1 5 29N42'17 82w20'44 5:29:23
Paradise Bay 41 5 27N28 82w35 5:30:20
Paradise Beach 17 1 30N24'02 87w25'14 5:49:41
Paradise Palms 50 6 26N21'11 80w07'35 5:20:30
Paradise Park 56 5 27N28'18 80w20'36 5:21:22
Paradise Point 9 5 28N53'00 82w35'32 5:30:22
Paradise Shores 36 5 26N39 81w50 5:27:20
Parch Landing 42 5 29N17'38 81w54'48 5:27:39
Park City 6 6 26N07 80w13 5:20:52
Parker 3 1 30N07'51 85w36'12 5:42:25
Parker Island 28 5 27N14'40 81w17'54 5:25:12
Parkerville 57 1 30N37'26 86w50'54 5:47:24
Park Haven 6 6 26N17'41 80w06'42 5:20:27
Parkland 6 6 26N19 80w15 5:21:00
Parmalee 41 5 27N22'15 82w13'06 5:28:52
Paront 32 1 30N43 85w01 5:40:04
Parramore 32 1 30N52'19 84w59'35 5:39:58
Parrish 41 5 27N35'14 82w25'31 5:29:42
Pasadena 52 5 27N46'13 82w43'58 5:30:56
Pasadena Shores 51 5 28N18'53 82w12'21 5:28:49
Pasco 51 5 28N19'28 82w20'14 5:29:21
Pass-a-Grille Beach 52 5 27N44 82w45 5:31:00
Pass Station 10 5 29N58'51 81w46'24 5:27:06
Patersonville 54 5 29N41'19 81w35'05 5:26:20
Patrick Air Force Base 5 5 28N14 80w36 5:22:24
Paxon 16 5 30N19 81w43 5:26:52
Paxton 66 1 30N58'53 86w18'27 5:45:14
Peace River Shores 8 5 27N01'48 81w57'46 5:27:51
Peach Orchard 1 5 29N33'00 82w29'47 5:29:59
Peaden 46 1 30N54'30 86w34'59 5:46:20
Pearl Court 16 5 30N22'28 81w38'43 5:26:35
Pebbledale 53 5 27N50'31 81w56'36 5:27:46
Pecan Park 16 5 30N30'42 81w37'22 5:26:29
Peck 37 5 30N32'23 84w05'30 5:36:22
Peddys Mill 53 5 27N54 81w58 5:27:52
Pedro 42 5 28N58'53 82w07'12 5:28:29
Peeks Landing 38 5 29N13'45 82w43'58 5:30:56
Pelican Lake 50 5 26N48'40 80w36'38 5:22:27
Pembroke 53 5 27N47'10 81w48'19 5:27:13
Pembroke Park 6 6 25N59'15 80w10'30 5:20:42
Pembroke Pines 6 6 26N00'10 80w13'27 5:20:54
Peniel 54 5 29N37'11 81w40'47 5:26:43
Peninsula 29 5 27N56 82w30 5:30:00
Peninsula 64 5 29N11 81w00 5:24:00
Penney Farms 10 5 29N58'46 81w48'38 5:27:15
Pennichaw 64 5 28N47'55 81w00'21 5:24:01
Pennsuco 13 6 25N53'41 80w22'42 5:21:31
Pensacola 17 4 30N25'16 87w13'01 5:48:52
Pensacola Beach 17 4 30N20'00 87w08'15 5:48:33
Pensacola Shores 57 4 30N22 87w11 5:48:44
Peoples City 42 5 29N25 82w13 5:28:52
Peppertree Bay 58 5 27N20 82w32 5:30:08
Perdido Bay 17 4 30N19'58 87w25'14 5:49:41
Perdido Heights 17 1 30N24'01 87w25'23 5:49:42
Perkins 37 5 30N27'14 84w13'21 5:36:53
Perky 44 5 24N38'54 81w34'19 5:26:17
Perrine 13 5 25N36'17 80w21'14 5:21:25
Perry 62 5 30N07'02 83w34'55 5:34:20
Peters 13 5 25N35'53 80w21'16 5:21:25
Peterson 34 5 30N05'33 83w12'55 5:32:52
Phifer 1 5 29N35'28 82w11'17 5:28:45
Philips Plaza 16 5 30N18 81w38 5:26:32
Phillipi Gardens 58 5 27N17 82w31 5:30:04
Pickettville 16 5 30N21'54 81w44'30 5:26:58
Picnic 29 5 28N00 82w31 5:30:04
Picolata 55 5 29N54'53 81w35'35 5:26:22
Piedmont 48 5 28N38'16 81w27'29 5:25:50
Pierce 53 5 27N50'05 81w58'18 5:27:53
Pierson 64 5 29N14'21 81w27'57 5:25:52
Pine Air 50 6 26N40 80w06 5:20:24
Pine Bluff 55 5 30N07'27 81w35'10 5:26:21
Pine Bluff 57 1 30N33'34 86w58'42 5:47:55
Pine Castle 48 5 28N28'18 81w22'05 5:25:28
Pinecrest 29 5 27N50'59 82w08'45 5:28:35
Pinecrest 44 5 25N44'47 80w56'23 5:23:46
Pinecrest 59 5 28N46'28 81w16'13 5:25:05
Pineda 5 5 28N14'13 80w40'43 5:22:43
Pine Dale 53 5 27N51'17 81w58'16 5:27:53
Pine Forest 17 4 30N31'10 87w18'59 5:49:16
Pine Grove 5 5 28N05 80w38 5:22:32
Pine Grove 49 5 28N15'34 81w11'05 5:24:44
Pine Grove 62 5 30N18 82w59 5:31:56
Pine Hill Estates 1 5 29N39'43 82w27'23 5:29:50
Pine Hills 35 5 28N56'58 81w25'06 5:25:40
Pine Hills 48 5 28N33'27 81w27'13 5:25:49
Pine Island 27 5 28N34'30 82w39'10 5:30:37
Pine Island Center 36 5 26N36'48 82w07'06 5:28:28
Pine Island Landing 64 5 29N18'37 81w32'48 5:26:11
Pine Lakes 35 5 28N56'27 81w25'49 5:25:43
Pineland 36 5 26N39'37 82w09'13 5:28:37
Pineland 62 5 30N07 83w35 5:34:20
Pineland Gardens 16 5 30N17 81w35 5:26:20
Pine Landing 15 5 29N32'01 82w58'50 5:31:55
Pine Level 14 5 27N15'54 81w59'31 5:27:58
Pinellas Park 52 5 27N50'33 82w41'59 5:30:48
Pine Log 3 1 30N24'13 85w54'42 5:43:39
Pine Manor 36 5 26N34'21 81w52'42 5:27:31
Pine Mount 61 5 30N09'46 83w57'17 5:35:49
Pineola 9 5 28N41'19 82w16'23 5:29:06
Pine Ridge Country Estates 9 5 28N51 82w29 5:29:56
Pine Shores 58 5 27N16 82w32 5:30:08
Pinesville 1 5 29N35'15 82w31'25 5:30:06
Pine Top 2 5 30N16'22 82w10'53 5:28:44
Pinetta 40 5 30N35'38 83w21'09 5:33:25
Pineville 17 1 30N53'55 87w34'57 5:50:20
Pinewood 13 6 25N54 80w13 5:20:52
Pinewood Park 13 6 25N51'56 80w12'50 5:20:51
Piney Bluff Landing 54 5 29N33'06 81w34'22 5:26:17
Piney Grove 66 1 30N48'14 86w07'51 5:44:31
Piney Island Landing 42 5 29N21'14 81w53'20 5:27:33
Piney Point 41 5 27N38'02 82w32'26 5:30:10
Pinland 62 5 30N01'04 83w31'41 5:34:07
Pioneer Village 36 5 26N39 81w53 5:27:32
Pirate Harbor 8 5 26N48'09 82w02'43 5:28:11
Pittman 30 1 30N56'32 85w49'12 5:43:17
Pittman 35 5 28N59'59 81w38'31 5:26:34
Pittsburg 53 5 27N39'13 81w30'10 5:26:01
Placida 8 5 26N49'55 82w15'54 5:29:04
Plains 28 5 27N24'33 81w11'04 5:24:44
Plantation 6 6 26N07'38 80w14'00 5:20:56
Plantation 44 5 25N01 80w31 5:22:04
Plantation Acres 6 6 26N07 80w13 5:20:52
Plantation Gardens 6 6 26N07'46 80w14'16 5:20:57
Plantation Isles 6 6 26N06'07 80w13'42 5:20:55
Plantation Park 6 6 26N07'07 80w13'38 5:20:55
Plant City 29 5 28N01'06 82w06'47 5:28:27
Platt 14 5 27N05'30 82w00'07 5:28:00
Playland Estates 6 6 26N01'56 80w12'15 5:20:49
Playland Isles 6 6 26N03'40 80w12'16 5:20:49
Playland Village 6 6 26N04'26 80w13'30 5:20:54
Plaza 42 5 29N11 82w09 5:28:36
Pleasant Grove 17 4 30N21'32 87w20'43 5:49:23
Pleasant Grove 29 5 27N54'19 82w10'14 5:28:41
Pleasant Grove 66 1 30N49'26 86w03'49 5:44:15
Pleasant Ridge 66 1 30N41'34 86w10'27 5:44:42
Plummer 16 5 30N26'37 81w48'28 5:27:14
Plummers 16 5 30N11'22 81w37'54 5:26:32
Plum Orchard 65 5 30N09'05 84w08'53 5:36:36
Plymouth 48 5 28N41'31 81w32'51 5:26:11
Poinciana 49 5 28N18 81w25 5:25:40
Poinsettia Park 53 5 28N02'45 81w41'10 5:26:45
Point Baker 57 1 30N41'24 87w03'13 5:48:13
Point O'Rocks 58 5 27N14'43 82w32'08 5:30:09
Point Pleasant 42 5 29N21'34 81w48'33 5:27:14
Point Washington 66 1 30N22'12 86w06'54 5:44:28
Polk City 53 5 28N10'56 81w49'27 5:27:18
Polly Town 16 5 30N26'20 81w35'43 5:26:23
Polo Club Estates 50 6 26N40 80w06 5:20:24
Pomona Landing 54 5 29N30'23 81w33'31 5:26:14
Pomona Park 54 5 29N30'00 81w35'30 5:26:22
Pompano Beach 6 6 26N14'15 80w07'30 5:20:30
Pompano Beach Highlands 6 6 26N16'57 80w06'26 5:20:26
Pompano Isles 6 6 26N13'01 80w06'05 5:20:24
Pompano Park 6 6 26N11'56 80w12'31 5:20:50
Ponce 13 6 25N45 80w16 5:21:04
Ponce de Leon 30 1 30N43'22 85w56'15 5:43:45
Ponce Inlet 64 5 29N05'46 80w56'14 5:23:45
Ponce Park 64 5 29N05 80w55 5:23:40
Pond Creek 66 1 30N47'31 86w23'15 5:45:33
Ponte Vedra 55 5 30N13'38 81w22'49 5:25:31
Ponte Vedra Beach 55 5 30N14'22 81w23'09 5:25:33
Poplar Head 67 1 30N43'05 85w38'51 5:42:35
Port Boca Grande 36 5 26N43'13 82w15'34 5:29:02
Port Charlotte 8 5 26N58'33 82w05'27 5:28:22
Port Everglades 6 6 26N05'48 80w07'39 5:20:31
Port Everglades Junction 6 6 26N04'48 80w10'08 5:20:41
Port Inglis 38 5 28N59'39 82w45'40 5:31:03
Portland 66 1 30N30'44 86w11'45 5:44:47
Port Leon 65 5 30N07'51 84w11'42 5:36:47
Port Lonesome 51 5 28N16'26 82w05'30 5:28:22
Port Malabar 5 5 28N04 80w37 5:22:28
Port Mayaca 43 5 26N59 80w36 5:22:24
Port of Palm Beach Junction 50 6 26N47 80w04 5:20:16
Port Orange 64 5 29N08'03 81w00'34 5:24:02
Port Richey 51 5 28N16'17 82w43'11 5:30:53
Port Saint Joe 23 5 29N48'42 85w18'11 5:41:13
Port Saint John 5 5 28N22 80w45 5:23:00
Port Saint Lucie 56 5 27N17'37 80w21'02 5:21:24
Port Salerno 43 5 27N08'38 80w12'03 5:20:48
Port Sewall 43 5 27N11 80w12 5:20:48
Port Sutton 29 5 27N54'23 82w25'15 5:29:41
Port Tampa 29 5 27N51'48 82w31'37 5:30:06
Port Tampa City 29 5 27N52 82w31 5:30:04
Postil 46 1 30N28'43 86w29'06 5:45:56
Pottsburg 16 5 30N17 81w35 5:26:20
Pouchers Corner 61 5 30N18'51 82w49'17 5:31:17
Powell 27 5 28N29'32 82w25'43 5:29:43
Power Landing 7 1 30N16'51 85w04'55 5:40:20
Poyner 53 5 28N18'08 81w51'23 5:27:26
Prairie Junction 53 5 27N54'48 81w59'01 5:27:56
Princeton 13 5 25N32'17 80w24'33 5:21:38
Prine 53 5 28N07 81w37 5:26:28
Proctors Landing 57 1 30N42'27 87w16'05 5:49:04
Produce 29 5 28N00 82w25 5:29:40

Progress Village 29 5 27N54 82W22 5:29:28
Prospect Landing 45 5 30N48'59 81W55'14 5:27:41
Prospect Road 6 6 26N09 80W12 5:20:48
Prosperity 30 1 30N51'06 85W56'49 5:43:47
Providence 53 5 28N09'13 81W58'25 5:27:54
Providence 63 5 30N00'14 82W32'51 5:30:11
Pumpkin Center 35 5 28N43'05 81W49'46 5:27:19
Punta Gorda 8 5 26N55'46 82W02'44 5:28:11
Punta Gorda Beach 8 5 26N55'23 82W21'36 5:29:26
Punta Gorda Isles 8 5 26N55'02 82W04'43 5:28:19
Punta Rassa 36 5 26N29'15 82W00'45 5:28:03
Purvis Still 24 5 30N25'41 82W45'38 5:31:03
Putnam Hall 54 5 29N44 81W58 5:27:52
Quinavista 17 4 30N19'42 87W21'23 5:49:26
Quincy 20 5 30N35'13 84W35'00 5:38:20
Quinlan 16 5 30N26 81W39 5:26:36
Quintette 17 1 30N39'58 87W18'46 5:49:15
Raccoon Key 44 5 24N34 81W44 5:26:56
Race Track Landing 57 1 30N40'58 86W56'16 5:47:45
Raiford 63 5 30N03'49 82W14'12 5:28:57
Rainbow Falls 42 5 29N06'11 82W26'20 5:29:45
Rainbow Homes 50 6 26N26'30 80W05'43 5:20:23
Rainbow Lakes 42 5 29N03 82W27 5:29:48
Raleigh 38 5 29N26'29 82W27'59 5:29:52
Ralston Beach 29 5 28N00 82W30 5:30:00
Rambo 32 1 30N59'48 85W24'14 5:41:37
Ramrod Key 44 5 24N45 81W20 5:25:20
Ramsey Beach 17 4 30N26'47 87W21'04 5:49:24
Ratliff 45 5 30N30'27 81W48'01 5:27:12
Rattlesnake 29 5 27N53'21 82W31'28 5:30:06
Ravenna Park 59 5 28N47'25 81W18'30 5:25:14
Rawls 24 5 30N32'53 82W58'42 5:31:55
Rawls Park 53 5 28N03 81W56 5:27:44
Reavills Corner 35 5 28N33'46 81W41'39 5:26:47
Redbay 66 1 30N35'32 85W56'42 5:43:47
Reddick 42 5 29N21'59 82W11'51 5:28:47
Red Head 67 1 30N29'11 85W50'31 5:43:22
Redington Beach 52 5 27N48'30 82W48'41 5:31:15
Redington Shores 52 5 27N49'33 82W49'45 5:31:19
Redland 13 5 25N31'41 80W29'26 5:21:58
Red Level 9 5 28N58'10 82W38'11 5:30:33
Relay 18 5 29N18'29 81W16'14 5:25:05
Remlap 29 5 27N49'55 82W22'55 5:29:32
Remley Heights 35 5 28N48 81W39 5:26:36
Remuda Ranch Grants 11 5 25N55 81W39 5:26:36
Rerdell 27 5 28N34'02 82W09'23 5:28:38
Resota Beach 3 1 30N18'12 85W35'37 5:42:22
Rex 1 5 29N37'48 82W05'51 5:28:23
Ribault Manor 16 5 30N23'42 81W42'12 5:26:49
Rice Creek 54 5 29N42'10 81W39'51 5:26:39
Rich Bay 20 5 30N36'16 84W23'31 5:37:34
Richey Lakes 51 5 28N14 82W44 5:30:56
Richland 51 5 28N16'58 82W08'35 5:28:34
Richloam 27 5 28N30'04 82W06'47 5:28:27
Richmond Heights 13 5 25N37'52 80W22'09 5:21:29
Richter Crossroads 32 1 30N50'12 85W30'08 5:42:01
Rideout 10 5 30N06 81W47 5:27:08
Ridge Harbor 8 5 26N59'25 81W57'17 5:27:49
Ridge Manor 27 5 28N30'26 82W10'14 5:28:41
Ridgewood 1 5 29N40 82W20 5:29:20
Ridgewood 10 5 30N08'19 81W47'04 5:27:08
Ridgewood 53 5 27N53'28 81W54'50 5:27:39
Ridge Wood Heights 58 5 27N17 82W31 5:30:04
Riley Landing 57 1 30N43'05 86W48'35 5:47:14
Rileys Park 35 5 28N48 81W39 5:26:36
Rio 43 5 27N13'09 80W14'22 5:20:57
Riomar 31 5 27N38'41 80W21'23 5:21:26
Rio Vista Isles 6 6 26N06'37 80W07'23 5:20:30
Rital 27 5 28N31'20 82W13'04 5:28:52
Ritta 50 5 26N45 80W58 5:23:52
Riverdale 51 5 28N28'57 82W11'47 5:28:47
Riverdale 55 5 29N49'17 81W33'07 5:26:12
River Forest 35 5 29N00'47 81W23'31 5:25:34
River Junction 20 5 30N41'08 84W50'29 5:39:22
Riverland Village 6 6 26N06 80W12 5:20:48
River Lawn 36 5 26N39 81W50 5:27:20
River Park 56 5 27N18'50 80W20'51 5:21:23
River Ranch 53 5 27N53 81W34 5:26:16
River Ranch Shores 53 5 27N53 81W34 5:26:16
Riverside 13 6 25N46 80W14 5:20:56
Riverside 16 5 30N18'43 81W41'04 5:26:44
Riverside Acres 48 5 28N38'09 81W24'56 5:25:40
Riverview 16 5 30N24'21 81W41'15 5:26:45
Riverview 17 4 30N32'33 87W11'48 5:48:47
Riverview 29 5 27N51'57 82W19'36 5:29:18
Riviera Beach 50 6 26N46'30 80W03'30 5:20:14
Riviera Colony 11 5 26N11 81W48 5:27:12
Rixford 61 5 30N21'11 82W57'51 5:31:51
Roan 35 5 28N33'10 81W40'57 5:26:44
Roberts Landing 65 5 30N04'41 84W38'07 5:38:32
Robin Hill 59 5 28N40 81W22 5:25:28
Robinson Heights 1 5 29N36'54 82W18'19 5:29:13
Robinson Point 57 1 30N39 87W05 5:48:20
Rochelle 1 5 29N35'47 82W13'04 5:28:52
Rock Bluff 39 5 30N32'36 84W54'46 5:39:39
Rock Bluff Landing 21 5 29N47'40 82W55'11 5:31:41
Rock Bluff Landing 39 5 30N33'38 84W57'48 5:39:51
Rock Creek 32 1 30N39'06 85W09'37 5:40:38
Rock Creek 46 1 30N57'43 86W46'44 5:47:07
Rockdale 13 5 25N37'43 80W20'28 5:21:22
Rockdale Keys 13 5 25N36 80W22 5:21:28
Rock Harbor 44 5 25N04'35 80W27'38 5:21:51
Rock Hill 6 6 26N07 80W13 5:20:52
Rock Hill 66 1 30N36'02 86W06'22 5:44:25
Rock Island 11 5 26N06'44 81W20'40 5:25:23
Rock Island Village 6 6 26N09'37 80W10'28 5:20:42
Rock Landing 19 5 29N58'48 84W34'06 5:38:16
Rock Landing 65 5 30N01'35 84W23'11 5:37:33
Rockledge 5 5 28N21'02 80W43'32 5:22:54
Rock Ridge 53 5 28N18'08 81W56'14 5:27:45
Rocksprings 42 5 29N07'02 82W23'01 5:29:32
Rock Springs 48 5 28N41 81W28 5:25:52
Rockwell 5 5 28N17'39 80W40'29 5:22:42
Rocky Creek 29 5 28N00'15 82W34'47 5:30:19
Rocky Point 1 5 29N35'39 82W20'20 5:29:21
Rodman 54 5 29N32'17 81W45'23 5:27:02
Roeville 57 3 30N40'36 86W59'37 5:47:58
Ro-Len Lake Gardens 6 6 25N58'39 80W09'55 5:20:40
Rolling Acres 27 5 28N32 82W29 5:29:56
Rolling Hills 16 5 30N19 81W43 5:26:52
Rolling Hills 53 5 27N49'24 81W58'08 5:27:53
Rolling Oak Acres 6 6 26N07 80W13 5:20:52
Rollins Corner 7 1 30N26'13 85W13'18 5:40:53
Romeo 42 5 29N12'22 82W26'11 5:29:45
Rood 50 6 26N56'56 80W11'50 5:20:47
Roosevelt Estates 50 6 26N40 80W06 5:20:24
Rose 38 5 30N20'57 84W08'01 5:36:32
Rosedale 20 5 30N39'19 84W48'31 5:39:14
Roseland 31 5 27N50'08 80W29'36 5:21:58
Rosemont Hills 48 5 28N35 81W24 5:25:36
Rosewood 38 5 29N14'20 82W55'56 5:31:44
Rotonda 8 5 26N53'00 82W17'25 5:29:10
Rotonda West 8 5 26N50 82W16 5:29:04
Round Lake 32 1 30N39'05 85W23'20 5:41:33
Roux Quarters 53 5 27N53'37 81W46'21 5:27:05
Roy 18 5 29N37'02 81W29'20 5:25:57
Royal 60 5 28N53'39 82W05'43 5:28:23
Royal Gardens Estates 41 5 27N28 82W35 5:30:20
Royal Oak Hills 50 6 26N20'43 80W06'02 5:20:24
Royal Palm Beach 50 6 26N41 80W15 5:21:00
Royal Palm Beach Plaza 50 6 26N40 80W06 5:20:24
Royal Palm Hammock 11 5 25N59'38 81W35'31 5:26:22
Royal Palm Isles 6 6 26N10'08 80W10'08 5:20:41
Royal Palms Park 6 6 26N09'07 80W11'02 5:20:44
Royal Pal Village 36 5 26N36 81W52 5:27:28
Royal Poinciana Park 31 5 27N36'44 80W24'06 5:21:36
Royals Crossroads 30 1 30N58'32 85W59'52 5:43:59
Royal Terrace 16 5 30N22'25 81W41'30 5:26:46
Royster 53 5 27N53'17 81W56'45 5:27:47
Rubonia 41 5 27N34'43 82W33'10 5:30:13
Runnymede 49 5 28N16'52 81W14'39 5:24:59
Runyon 50 5 26N43'57 80W40'01 5:22:40
Ruskin 29 5 27N43'14 82W26'00 5:29:44
Russell 10 5 30N03'22 81W44'51 5:26:59
Russell Landing 10 5 30N04'02 81W44'03 5:26:56
Rutland 60 5 28N51'10 82W12'49 5:28:51
Rutledge 1 5 29N40'54 82W24'36 5:29:38
Rye 41 5 27N30'51 82W22'05 5:29:28
Sabal Palms Estates 6 6 26N12'21 80W12'40 5:20:51
Safety Harbor 52 5 27N59'26 82W41'36 5:30:46
Saint Andrew 3 1 30N10'25 85W41'58 5:42:48
Saint Armand's 58 5 27N19 82W31 5:30:04
Saint Augustine 55 5 29N53'40 81W18'53 5:25:16
Saint Augustine Beach 55 5 29N51'01 81W15'56 5:25:04
Saint Augustine Shores 55 5 29N48 81W16 5:25:04
Saint Catherine 27 5 28N36'36 82W08'18 5:28:33
Saint Cloud 49 5 28N14'55 81W16'53 5:25:08
Saint Francis 35 5 29N02'09 81W25'11 5:25:41
Saint George 52 5 28N03'22 82W43'41 5:30:55
Saint Georges Island 19 5 29N45 84W53 5:39:32
Saint James City 36 5 26N29'50 82W04'43 5:28:19
Saint Johns Park 16 5 30N17'01 81W42'56 5:26:52
Saint Johns Park 18 5 29N25'22 81W25'53 5:25:44
Saint Johns River Estates 59 5 28N50'21 81W20'09 5:25:21
Saint Joseph 51 5 28N22'32 82W17'13 5:29:09
Saint Josephs 59 5 28N48'40 81W19'22 5:25:17
Saint Leo 51 5 28N20'13 82W15'31 5:29:02
Saint Lucie 56 5 27N29'21 80W20'24 5:21:22
Saint Marks 65 5 30N09'39 84W12'23 5:36:50
Saint Nicholas 16 5 30N18'19 81W38'09 5:26:33
Saint Peter 37 5 30N29'08 84W13'45 5:36:55
Saint Petersburg 52 5 27N46'14 82W40'46 5:30:43
Saint Petersburg Beach 52 5 27N43'30 82W44'29 5:30:58
Saint Teresa 19 5 29N55'50 84W27'15 5:37:49
Salem 62 5 29N53'12 83W24'47 5:33:39
Salerno 43 5 27N09 80W12 5:20:48
Salt Springs 42 5 29N21'03 81W44'07 5:26:56
Salvista 36 5 26N40'58 81W52'05 5:27:28
Samoset 41 5 27N28'09 82W32'30 5:30:10
Sampson 4 5 29N54'59 82W12'29 5:28:50
Sampson 55 5 30N03'52 81W30'07 5:26:00
Samsula 64 5 29N01'33 81W03'02 5:24:12
San Antonio 51 5 28N20'09 82W16'29 5:29:06
San Blas 3 1 30N05'21 85W36'36 5:42:26
Sanborn 65 5 30N04'18 84W36'16 5:38:25
San Carlos Park 36 5 26N28'01 81W48'06 5:27:12
Sandalfoot Cove 50 6 26N23 80W05 5:20:20
Sandalwood 16 5 30N19'03 81W31'04 5:26:04
Sand Cut 17 4 30N25'17 87W19'41 5:49:19
Sand Cut 50 5 26N49 80W40 5:22:40
Sanders Beach 17 4 30N23'58 87W14'17 5:48:57
Sanderson 2 5 30N15'07 82W16'23 5:29:06
Sanders Park 6 6 26N15'16 80W07'58 5:20:32
Sandestin 46 1 30N25 86W33 5:46:12
Sandpiper Cove 46 1 30N25 86W33 5:46:12
Sandy 41 5 27N16'24 82W06'57 5:28:28
Sandy Point 61 5 29N54'32 82W51'56 5:31:28
Sanford 59 5 28N48'01 81W16'24 5:25:06
Sanford Farms 59 5 28N49'42 81W20'28 5:25:22
Sangully 53 5 28N03 81W56 5:27:44
Sanibel 36 5 26N26'55 82W01'21 5:28:05
San Jose 16 5 30N15'02 81W38'23 5:26:34
San Jose Estates 16 5 30N14 81W38 5:26:32
San Jose Forest 16 5 30N15'05 81W37'45 5:26:31
Sanlando Springs 59 5 28N41'00 81W22'55 5:25:32
Sanlanta 59 5 28N47'52 81W15'54 5:25:04
San Marco 16 5 30N18'42 81W39'36 5:26:38
San Mateo 16 5 30N26'36 81W37'57 5:26:32
San Mateo 54 5 29N36'23 81W35'05 5:26:20
San Pablo 16 5 30N17'43 81W26'16 5:25:45
San Pedro Junction 34 5 30N00'39 83W12'54 5:32:52
San Souci 16 5 30N17 81W35 5:26:20
San Souci Estates 13 6 25N53'03 80W09'29 5:20:38
Sans Pareil 16 5 30N16'59 81W29'40 5:25:59
Sans Souci 8 5 26N59'06 81W58'04 5:27:52
Santa Barbara Shores 6 6 26N13'13 80W06'02 5:20:24
Santa Clara 20 5 30N35'01 84W33'44 5:38:15
Santa Fe 1 5 29N53'00 82W25'50 5:29:43
Santa Fe Beach 1 5 29N45'04 82W05'53 5:28:24
Santa Fe Lake 1 5 29N45 82W06 5:28:24
Santa Monica 3 1 30N15 85W57 5:43:48
Santa Monica 16 5 30N17 81W35 5:26:20
Santa Rosa Beach 66 1 30N23'45 86W13'44 5:44:55
Santos 42 5 29N06'32 82W05'35 5:28:22
Sapp 2 5 30N08'50 82W11'09 5:28:45
Sarabay Acres 58 5 27N12 82W30 5:30:00
Sarasota 58 5 27N20'10 82W31'51 5:30:07
Sarasota Beach 58 5 27N16 82W33 5:30:12
Sarasota Colony 22 5 27N00'18 81W03'16 5:24:13
Sarasota Heights 58 5 27N18'46 82W31'47 5:30:07
Sarasota Springs 58 5 27N18 82W28 5:29:52
Saratoga 54 5 29N31'55 81W41'02 5:26:44
Sargent 2 5 30N34'26 82W25'46 5:29:43
Sarno Plaza 5 5 28N10 80W38 5:22:32
Satellite Beach 5 5 28N10'33 80W35'25 5:22:22
Satsuma 54 5 29N33'17 81W39'22 5:26:37
Saufley Field 17 3 30N28 87W21 5:49:24
Sawdust 20 5 30N32'53 84W40'37 5:38:42
Sawgrass 55 5 30N15 81W23 5:25:32
Saxton 4 5 30N00'42 82W05'01 5:28:20
Scanlon 62 5 30N07'49 83W53'46 5:35:35
School of the Resurrection 16 5 30N21'38 81W36'09 5:26:25
Sconiers Mill 66 1 30N40'46 86W09'50 5:44:39
Scotland 20 5 30N34'35 84W25'49 5:37:43
Scotts Ferry 7 1 30N27 85W03 5:40:12
Scottsmoor 5 5 28N46'00 80W52'42 5:23:31
Seabreeze 64 5 29N13'57 81W00'50 5:24:03
Seacoll 9 5 28N56'21 82W23'39 5:29:35
Seaglades 17 4 30N19'29 87W22'58 5:49:32
Seagrove Beach 66 1 30N19'06 86W07'49 5:44:31
Sea Ranch Lakes 6 6 26N12'08 80W05'39 5:20:23
Sears 26 5 26N38'47 81W22'33 5:25:30
Searstown 53 5 28N03 81W56 5:27:44
Seaside 44 5 25N08 80W25 5:21:40
Seaton Landing 16 5 30N32'43 81W39'38 5:26:39
Sebastian 31 5 27N48'58 80W28'15 5:21:53
Sebastian Highlands 31 5 27N47 80W29 5:21:56
Sebring 28 5 27N29'43 81W26'28 5:25:46
Sebring Southgate 28 5 27N30 81W27 5:25:48
Secotan 62 5 30N10'34 83W38'04 5:34:32

Seffner 29 5 27N59'00 82W16'33 5:29:06
Sellersville 57 1 30N59'30 86W55'41 5:47:43
Selman 7 1 30N32'09 85W01'43 5:40:07
Seminole 46 1 30N28'44 86W24'36 5:45:38
Seminole 52 5 27N50'22 82W47'29 5:31:10
Seminole Heights 29 5 27N59 82W28 5:29:52
Seminole Hills 3 1 30N22'13 85W55'55 5:43:44
Seminole Lake Country Club 52 5 27N53 82W46 5:31:04
Seminole Manor 50 6 26N36 80W05 5:20:20
Seminole Park 52 5 27N53 82W46 5:31:04
Seminole Shores 43 5 27N10'53 80W09'57 5:20:40
Seminole Springs 35 5 28N50'43 81W31'42 5:26:07
Seneca 35 5 28N51'57 81W36'05 5:26:24
Seven Springs 51 5 28N12'43 82W39'58 5:30:40
Seville 64 5 29N19'00 81W29'34 5:25:58
Sewalls Point 43 5 27N11'57 80W12'09 5:20:49
Shackleford 17 4 30N27 87W13 5:48:52
Shadeville 65 5 30N11'57 84W18'32 5:37:14
Shadow Lawn Estates 1 5 29N41'02 82W22'34 5:29:30
Shady 42 5 29N05'43 82W10'09 5:28:41
Shady Grove 32 1 30N39'10 84W59'47 5:39:59
Shady Grove 62 5 30N17'16 83W37'55 5:34:32
Shady Rest 16 5 30N30'00 81W32'22 5:26:09
Shady Rest 20 5 30N35'17 84W29'13 5:37:57
Shalimar 46 1 30N26'44 86W34'45 5:46:19
Shamrock 15 5 29N38'35 83W08'42 5:32:35
Shangri-la 52 5 27N53 82W46 5:31:04
Shannon Wood 1 5 29N37'58 82W26'21 5:29:45
Sharpes 5 5 28N25'55 80W45'37 5:23:02
Sharpstown 7 1 30N21'59 85W06'01 5:40:24
Shawano 50 5 26N33'16 80W30'42 5:22:03
Shawnee 22 5 26N46'37 80W57'55 5:23:52
Shell Bluff 18 5 29N30'23 81W29'34 5:25:58
Shell Bluff Landing 18 5 29N29'36 81W29'16 5:25:57
Shell Bluff Landing 55 5 30N00'56 81W20'46 5:25:23
Shell Ferry Landing 67 1 30N32'14 85W51'37 5:43:26
Shell Island 11 5 26N01'26 81W43'58 5:26:56
Shell Island 65 5 30N09'34 84W13'00 5:36:52
Shell Land 52 5 27N56 82W46 5:31:04
Shell Point Village 36 5 26N36 81W52 5:27:28
Sheltering Pines 36 5 26N36 81W52 5:27:28
Shenandoah 13 6 25N45'33 80W13'21 5:20:53
Shenks 1 5 29N45'43 82W08'31 5:28:34
Sherman 47 5 27N12'37 80W45'20 5:23:01
Sherwood Forest 16 5 30N24'35 81W43'28 5:26:54
Sherwood Park 50 6 26N26'42 80W06'42 5:20:27
Shiloh 1 5 29N47 82W30 5:30:00
Shiloh 5 5 28N47'25 80W48'17 5:23:13
Shilow 29 5 28N02'24 82W07'38 5:28:31
Shiney Town 58 5 27N11'37 82W20'46 5:29:23
Shingle Creek 49 5 28N18 81W25 5:25:40
Shingle Landing 39 5 30N15'44 85W03'29 5:40:14
Shired Island 15 5 29N23'49 83W12'04 5:32:48
Shore Acres 52 5 27N49'04 82W36'13 5:30:25
Shorewood 6 6 26N18'11 80W05'59 5:20:24
Siesta 58 5 27N18 82W33 5:30:12
Siesta Key 58 5 27N17 82W33 5:30:12
Sills 32 1 30N56'42 85W17'00 5:41:08
Silver Beach Heights 35 5 28N57'02 81W39'32 5:26:38
Silver Bluff Estates 13 6 25N44'55 80W14'11 5:20:57
Silver Palm 13 5 25N33'02 80W26'29 5:21:46
Silver Sands 3 1 30N09 85W39 5:42:36
Silver Shores 6 6 26N11'22 80W06'04 5:20:24
Silver Springs 42 5 29N12'59 82W03'28 5:28:14
Silver Springs 46 1 30N48'23 86W33'09 5:46:13
Silver Springs Shores 42 5 29N11 82W09 5:28:36
Simmons Crossing 57 1 30N54'50 86W57'52 5:47:51
Simms Landing 34 5 29N51'15 82W53'12 5:31:33
Simpson Yard 16 5 30N21 81W39 5:26:36
Simsville 32 1 30N40'50 85W10'27 5:40:42
Sinai 32 1 30N39'42 84W54'37 5:39:38
Singer Island 50 6 26N47 80W04 5:20:16
Sink Creek 32 1 30N37'21 85W09'06 5:40:36
Sipes 59 5 28N48 81W15 5:25:00
Sirmans 40 5 30N21 83W39 5:34:36
Sisco 54 5 29N31'15 81W37'38 5:26:31
Sixmile Bend 50 5 26N38'44 80W34'43 5:22:19
Sixmile Creek 29 5 27N57'59 82W21'39 5:29:27
Skipper 65 5 30N02'53 84W21'37 5:37:26
Skycrest 52 5 28N00 82W46 5:31:04
Sky Lake 48 5 28N27'25 81W23'30 5:25:34
Skyland Heights 1 5 29N40 82W20 5:29:20
Skytop 35 5 28N34'01 81W43'00 5:26:52
Slater 36 5 26N44'22 81W51'04 5:27:24
Slaughter 51 5 28N37 82W03 5:28:12
Slavia 59 5 28N38'52 81W13'50 5:24:55
Sloans Ridge 35 5 28N34'43 81W56'41 5:27:47
Slones Ridge 35 5 28N34 81W52 5:27:28
Smallpox Tommies Old Place 13 6 25N50'37 80W46'13 5:23:05
Smith 40 5 30N37'41 83W21'13 5:33:25
Smith Creek 65 5 30N11 84W39 5:38:36
Smith Creek Landing 19 1 29N55'06 85W00'52 5:40:03
Smith Crossroads 30 1 30N59'00 85W46'18 5:43:05
Smith Landing 7 1 30N18'01 85W08'58 5:40:36
Smiths Corner 30 1 30N53 85W40 5:42:40
Smiths Crossroads 30 1 31N01 85W44 5:42:56
Smokehouse Crossing 39 5 30N16'15 84W58'28 5:39:54
Snake Creek 6 6 25N59 80W12 5:20:48
Snapper Creek Park 13 6 25N42 80W19 5:21:16
Sneads 32 1 30N42'27 84W55'28 5:39:42
Snow Hill 59 5 28N42'11 81W06'53 5:24:28
Snows Corner 29 5 28N00'09 82W13'12 5:28:53
Snug Harbor 43 5 27N12'08 80W13'17 5:20:53
Socrum 53 5 28N10'04 82W01'09 5:28:05
Solana 8 5 26N56'48 82W01'34 5:28:06
Sopchoppy 65 5 30N03'35 84W29'20 5:37:57
Soroka Shores 6 6 26N09'09 80W06'33 5:20:26
Sorrento 35 5 28N48'27 81W33'50 5:26:15
Sorrento Shores 58 5 27N12 82W30 5:30:00
South Allapattah 13 5 25N31'59 80W21'58 5:21:28
South and East Junction 59 5 28N48 81W15 5:25:00
South and East Osceola 49 5 28N06 81W04 5:24:16
South Apopka 48 5 28N39'42 81W30'35 5:26:02
South Bay 50 5 26N39'49 80W42'59 5:22:52
South Bay Estates 13 6 25N44'22 80W14'32 5:20:58
Southboro 50 6 26N41 80W04 5:20:16
South Boyette 29 5 28N00 82W31 5:30:04
South Clermont 35 5 28N29'52 81W46'21 5:27:05
South Clewiston 26 5 26N42'34 80W54'08 5:23:37
South Clinton Heights 51 5 28N19'17 82W11'01 5:28:44
South Cocoa Beach 5 5 28N16'52 80W36'24 5:22:26
South Daytona 64 5 29N09'56 81W00'17 5:24:01
Southeast 53 5 28N01 81W44 5:26:56
South Flomaton 17 1 30N59'30 87W15'27 5:49:02
Southfort 14 5 27N04'04 81W57'51 5:27:51
South Fort Myers 36 5 26N36 81W52 5:27:28
Southgate 58 5 27N19 82W32 5:30:08
South Gate Ridge 58 5 27N17 82W30 5:30:00
South Jacksonville 16 5 30N18'39 81W38'45 5:26:35
Southmere 5 5 28N39'54 80W57'23 5:23:50
South Miami 13 6 25N42'26 80W17'37 5:21:10
South Miami Heights 13 5 25N35'50 80W22'51 5:21:31
South Mulberry 53 5 27N53'08 81W58'30 5:27:54
South Ocala 42 5 29N11 82W09 5:28:36
South Palm Beach 50 6 26N35'19 80W02'20 5:20:09
South Pasadena 52 5 27N45'17 82W44'16 5:30:57
South Patrick 5 5 28N11'54 80W35'45 5:22:23
South Patrick Shores 5 5 28N12 80W36 5:22:24
South Peninsula 64 5 29N08 80W57 5:23:48
South Pine Lakes 35 5 28N55'53 81W25'56 5:25:44
South Ponte Vedra Beach 55 5 30N01'20 81W19'26 5:25:18
Southport 3 1 30N17'21 85W38'26 5:42:34
South Port 49 5 28N08'18 81W21'09 5:25:25
South Punta Gorda Heights 8 5 26N51'55 81W59'28 5:27:58
Southridge 16 5 30N17'35 81W30'13 5:26:01
South Shore 50 5 26N45 80W58 5:23:52
Southside 6 6 26N05 80W09 5:20:36
Southside 35 5 28N56 81W40 5:26:40
Southside 53 5 28N02 81W57 5:27:48
Southside 58 5 27N19 82W31 5:30:04
Southside Estates 16 5 30N17'53 81W33'30 5:26:14
South Tampa 29 5 27N56'56 82W21'16 5:29:25
South Trail 58 5 27N17'54 82W31'50 5:30:07
South Venice 58 5 27N03'10 82W25'28 5:29:42
Southwest 50 6 26N40 80W06 5:20:24
South Westside 13 6 25N44 80W21 5:21:24
Southwood 48 5 28N29 81W22 5:25:28
Spanish Landing 55 5 30N04'07 81W22'16 5:25:29
Sparr 42 5 29N20'18 82W06'46 5:28:27
Spaulding 16 5 30N24'43 81W46'30 5:27:06
Spray 40 5 30N30'50 83W37'14 5:34:29
Spring Creek 65 5 30N04'50 84W19'40 5:37:19
Springfield 3 1 30N09'11 85W36'41 5:42:27
Springfield 16 5 30N20'44 81W39'13 5:26:37
Spring Glen 16 5 30N17'46 81W36'35 5:26:26
Springhead 29 5 28N01 82W08 5:28:32
Spring Hill 1 5 29N49'57 82W31'42 5:30:07
Spring Hill 27 5 28N33'20 82W27'02 5:29:48
Spring Hill 37 5 30N20'21 84W23'17 5:37:33
Spring Hill 57 1 30N46'02 86W56'30 5:47:46
Spring Lake 27 5 28N29'36 82W18'11 5:29:13
Spring Lake 28 5 27N30 81W27 5:25:48
Spring Park 16 5 30N18 81W38 5:26:32
Spring Run Landing 67 1 30N30'35 85W51'18 5:43:25
Springside 54 5 29N40'30 81W42'54 5:26:52
Springville 12 5 30N17'33 82W45'49 5:31:03
Spuds 55 5 29N44'22 81W28'18 5:25:53
Stanton 42 5 28N59'46 81W54'55 5:27:40
Starke 4 5 29N56'38 82W06'36 5:28:26
Starkes Ferry 42 5 28N59'30 81W49'56 5:27:20
Starks Landing 64 5 28N56'48 81W20'39 5:25:23
Starr 61 5 30N17'03 83W04'49 5:32:19
State Highway 59 5 28N37 81W19 5:25:16
Steckert 2 5 30N12'37 82W07'31 5:28:30
Steele Church 66 1 30N43 86W07 5:44:28
Steele City 32 1 30N43'27 85W23'16 5:41:33
Steinhatchee 62 5 29N40'15 83W23'16 5:33:33
Stemper 29 5 28N09 82W28 5:29:52
Stephensville 62 5 29N41 83W23 5:33:32
Stetson 64 5 29N02 81W18 5:25:12
Stockade 16 5 30N13'16 81W30'20 5:26:01
Stock Island 44 5 24N34 81W44 5:26:56
Stokes Landing 54 5 29N34'19 81W41'55 5:26:48
Stokley Landing 65 5 30N03'21 84W21'40 5:37:27
Storey Crossing 49 5 28N16'16 81W03'19 5:24:13
Story Landing 66 1 30N35'58 85W54'55 5:43:40
Stoutamire Landing 37 5 30N20'42 84W41'40 5:38:47
Streamline 50 5 26N49 80W40 5:22:40
Strickland Landing 65 5 30N09'53 84W11'26 5:36:46
Strickland Landing 67 1 30N26'59 85W53'29 5:43:34
Strouds Landing 42 5 29N15'59 81W57'25 5:27:50
Stuart 43 5 27N11'50 80W15'11 5:21:01
Sturkey 51 5 28N23'43 82W04'14 5:28:17
Suburban Heights 1 5 29N40'04 82W23'30 5:29:34
Sugar Junction 26 5 26N44'10 80W55'15 5:23:41
Sugarloaf Shores 44 5 24N38'38 81W33'44 5:26:15
Sugarmill Woods 9 5 28N47 82W37 5:30:28
Sugarton 26 5 26N45'54 80W57'38 5:23:51
Sulphur Springs 29 5 28N01'30 82W27'04 5:29:48
Sumatra 39 5 30N01'12 84W58'45 5:39:55
Summerfield 42 5 29N00'30 82W02'06 5:28:08
Summer Haven 55 5 29N41'56 81W13'25 5:24:54
Summerland Key 44 5 24N40 81W27 5:25:48
Summerport Beach 48 5 28N29'24 81W33'53 5:26:16
Sumner 38 5 29N13'00 82W58'04 5:31:52
Sumterville 60 5 28N44'41 82W03'49 5:28:15
Sunbeam 16 5 30N12'21 81W34'44 5:26:19
Sun City 29 5 27N40'41 82W28'44 5:29:55
Sun City Center 29 5 27N43 82W21 5:29:24
Suncoast Estates 36 5 26N39 81W53 5:27:32
Sun Garden 10 5 29N59 81W41 5:26:44
Sun Haven 58 5 27N21 82W31 5:30:04
Suniland 13 6 25N40 80W20 5:21:20
Sunland 59 5 28N48 81W15 5:25:00
Sunland Estates 59 5 28N45'15 81W16'54 5:25:08
Sunland Gardens 56 5 27N27'45 80W21'44 5:21:27
Sunniland 11 5 26N16'08 81W20'31 5:25:22
Sun 'n Lakes Estates 28 5 27N18 81W22 5:25:28
Sunny Hills 67 1 30N47 85W32 5:42:08
Sunny Isles 13 6 25N57'01 80W07'23 5:20:30
Sunnyland 58 6 27N17'07 82W29'36 5:29:58
Sunnyside 3 1 30N15'01 85W56'52 5:43:47
Sunnyside 35 5 28N47'55 81W50'08 5:27:21
Sun Ray Homes 53 5 27N45 81W32 5:26:08
Sunrise 6 6 26N08'01 80W06'48 5:20:27
Sunrise Golf Village 6 6 26N08 80W14 5:20:56
Sunrise Harbor 13 6 25N42'19 80W14'53 5:21:00
Sunrise Heights 6 6 26N08'32 80W14'42 5:20:59
Sunrise Key 6 6 26N07'48 80W07'00 5:20:28
Sunset Beach 52 5 27N45'07 82W45'48 5:31:03
Sunset Corners 13 6 25N42'06 80W20'03 5:21:20
Sunset Gardens 5 5 28N05 80W38 5:22:32
Sunset Harbor 42 5 28N59'30 81W58'46 5:27:55
Sunset Island 13 6 25N48 80W09 5:20:36
Sunset Point 44 5 25N01 80W31 5:22:04
Sunset Public Landing 37 5 30N31'59 84W21'25 5:37:26
Sunshine 29 5 28N00 82W34 5:30:16
Sunshine Beach 52 5 27N46'36 82W46'43 5:31:07
Sunshine Park 6 6 26N01'45 80W12'42 5:20:51
Sunshine Parkway 50 6 26N36 80W13 5:20:52
Sunshine Ranches 6 6 26N07 80W13 5:20:52
Sun Swept Isles 6 6 25N58'26 80W09'09 5:20:37
Sun-Tan Village 13 6 25N49'49 80W15'57 5:21:04
Suntree 5 5 28N05 80W38 5:22:32
Sunvale 28 5 27N18'37 81W16'01 5:25:04
Surf 65 5 29N59'05 84W25'16 5:37:41
Surfside 13 6 25N52'41 80W07'33 5:20:30
Suwanee Valley 12 5 30N17 81W24 5:25:36
Suwannee 15 5 29N19'43 83W08'40 5:32:35
Suwannee 61 5 30N23'20 82W57'24 5:31:50
Suwannee River 21 5 29N35'26 82W55'46 5:31:43

Suwannee Springs 61 5 30N23'38 82w56'15 5:31:45
Suwannee Valley 12 5 30N17'56 82w42'30 5:30:50
Svea 46 1 30N58'03 86w24'12 5:45:37
Swamp Field Landing 30 1 30N51'11 85w52'55 5:43:32
Sweet Gum Head 30 1 30N46 85w51 5:43:24
Sweetgum Landing 46 1 30N38'16 86w47'32 5:47:10
Sweetwater 13 6 25N45'47 80w22'24 5:21:30
Sweetwater 16 5 30N16'10 81w45'52 5:27:03
Sweetwater 25 5 27N24'33 81w42'10 5:26:49
Sweetwater 39 5 30N30'28 84w58'20 5:39:53
Sweetwater Creek 29 5 28N00 82w34 5:30:16
Sweetwater Oaks 59 5 28N42 81w20 5:25:20
Switzerland 55 5 30N04'33 81w38'51 5:26:35
Sycamore 20 5 30N35'02 84w49'44 5:39:19
Sydney 29 5 27N57'47 82w12'27 5:28:50
Sykes Landing 54 5 29N32'15 81w32'21 5:26:09
Sylvania 67 1 30N37'00 85w40'29 5:42:42
Sylvan Lake 59 5 28N47'43 81w21'47 5:25:27
Sylvan Shores 35 5 28N48 81w39 5:26:36
Tacoma 1 5 29N31'40 82w19'09 5:29:17
Taft 48 5 28N25'46 81w21'55 5:25:28
Tahitian Gardens 51 5 28N12 82w45 5:31:00
Tallahassee 37 5 30N26'17 84w16'51 5:37:07
Tallevast 41 5 27N24'05 82w32'35 5:30:10
Talleyrand 16 5 30N27 81w34 5:26:16
Tall Palm Landing 35 5 28N58'53 81w21'57 5:25:28
Tallyrand 16 5 30N21'34 81w37'58 5:26:32
Tamarac 6 6 26N11 80w13 5:20:52
Tamiami 13 6 25N46 80w19 5:21:16
Tampa 29 5 27N56'50 82w27'31 5:29:50
Tancrede 53 5 27N57'24 81w58'23 5:27:54
Tangelo Park 48 5 28N27'20 81w26'46 5:25:47
Tangerine 48 5 28N45'53 81w37'51 5:26:31
Tang-o-Mar Beach 66 1 30N25 86w33 5:46:12
Tarpon 29 5 28N02'22 82w34'00 5:30:16
Tarpon Point 58 5 27N01'18 82w16'37 5:29:06
Tarpon Springs 52 5 28N08'45 82w45'25 5:31:02
Tarrytown 60 5 28N33'17 82w03'17 5:28:13
Tatum 58 5 27N19'05 82w25'34 5:29:42
Tavares 35 5 28N48'14 81w43'33 5:26:54
Tavernier 44 5 25N00'40 80w30'55 5:22:04
Taylor 2 5 30N26'25 82w17'29 5:29:10
Tee and Green Estates 8 5 26N56'41 82w00'09 5:28:01
Telegraph Estates 36 5 26N43'54 81w41'18 5:26:45
Telogia 39 5 30N21'02 84w49'09 5:39:17
Temple Terrace 29 5 28N02'06 82w23'22 5:29:33
Temple Terrace Junction 29 5 28N01'52 82w21'09 5:29:25
Tendil Crossing 30 1 30N57'50 85w34'47 5:42:19
Tenile 17 1 30N43'53 87w27'52 5:49:51
Tenille 62 5 29N47 83w20 5:33:20
Tenmile Corner 13 5 25N36'56 80w51'27 5:23:26
Tennille 62 5 29N46'40 83w19'34 5:33:18
Tensulate 16 5 30N14 81w57 5:27:48
Tequesta 50 6 26N58 80w06 5:20:24
Terra Ceia 41 5 27N34'45 82w34'50 5:30:19
Terra Mana 41 5 27N31'28 82w36'32 5:30:26
Terra Mar 6 6 26N12'57 80w05'44 5:20:23
Terrytown 50 6 26N20'09 80w32'22 5:22:09
The Cove 6 6 26N18'40 80w05'06 5:20:20
The Jungle 52 5 27N47'18 82w45'09 5:31:01
The Pines 13 6 25N44'44 80w14'28 5:20:58
Theressa 4 5 29N50'06 82w04'15 5:28:17
The Watson Place 34 5 25N42'36 81w14'41 5:24:59
Thomas City 33 5 30N21'18 83w58'23 5:35:54
Thompson 44 5 25N02'31 80w29'34 5:21:58
Thonotosassa 29 5 28N03'40 82w18'09 5:29:13
Thunderbird 36 5 26N36 81w52 5:27:28
Tibbits Park Palms 10 5 29N47'34 82w02'19 5:28:09
Tice 36 5 26N40'28 81w48'55 5:27:16
Tidewater 38 5 29N07'43 82w34'13 5:30:17
Tierra Verda 52 5 27N43 82w42 5:30:48
Tiger Bay 53 5 27N45'32 81w50'50 5:27:23
Tildenville 48 5 28N33'34 81w36'31 5:26:26
Tilton 19 1 29N44'20 85w04'56 5:40:20
Tisonia 16 5 30N32'03 81w37'17 5:26:29
Titusville 5 5 28N36'43 80w48'28 5:23:14
Tobacco Patch Landing 42 5 29N25'49 81w55'31 5:27:42
Tocoi 55 5 29N50'41 81w33'29 5:26:14
Tocoi Junction 55 5 29N47 81w26 5:25:44
Tommytown 51 5 28N22'33 82w12'14 5:28:49
Tomoka Estates 64 5 29N18'53 81w05'57 5:24:24
Tooke Lake Junction 27 5 28N31'54 82w23'14 5:29:33
Torrey 25 5 27N36'38 81w49'35 5:27:18
Towers 48 5 28N36 81w21 5:25:24
Town and Country Plaza 17 4 30N26 87w15 5:49:00
Town Park Estates 13 6 25N45'16 80w21'06 5:21:24
Townsend 34 5 30N07'44 83w20'22 5:33:21
Trail Center 34 5 25N48'16 80w52'34 5:23:30
Trailer City 37 5 30N26 84w17 5:37:08
Trailer Estates 41 5 27N25'27 82w34'49 5:30:19
Trailer Haven 5 5 28N05 80w38 5:22:32
Trailtown 11 5 25N51'20 81w01'24 5:24:06
Tranquility Park 53 5 28N00'30 81w44'44 5:26:59
Trapnell 29 5 27N58'00 82w06'17 5:28:25
Traxler 1 5 29N52'14 82w32'25 5:30:10
Treasure Hill Park 17 4 30N19'26 87w24'24 5:49:38
Treasure Island 13 6 25N51 80w08 5:20:32
Treasure Island 52 5 27N46'08 82w46'09 5:31:05
Trenton 21 5 29N36'47 82w49'04 5:31:16
Triangle 35 5 28N48 81w39 5:26:36
Triangle Acres 35 5 28N48 81w39 5:26:36
Trilby 51 5 28N27'44 82w11'42 5:28:47
Trilcoochee 51 5 28N27'49 82w11'00 5:28:44
Tri Par Estates 58 5 27N23 82w32 5:30:08
Tropic 5 5 28N09'51 80w36'58 5:22:28
Tropical Gulf Acres 8 5 26N50'30 81w59'28 5:27:58
Tropical Shores Manor 35 5 28N48 81w44 5:26:56
Tropicanna Mobile Manor 36 5 26N36 81w52 5:27:28
Tropic Heights 8 5 26N57 82w00 5:28:00
Tropic Isle 50 6 26N26'06 80w04'05 5:20:16
Truck Corner 59 5 28N41'30 81w10'47 5:24:43
Truckland 36 5 26N29'55 81w58'05 5:27:52
Tuckers Corner 8 5 26N51'27 81w45'35 5:27:02
Turkey Creek 29 5 27N58'40 82w11'06 5:28:44
Turkey Foot 11 5 26N05'14 81w01'55 5:24:08
Turkey Landing 42 5 29N14'08 81w58'15 5:27:53
Turnbull 5 5 28N42'36 80w51'45 5:23:27
Turner River 11 5 25N54 81w17 5:25:08
Tuscanooga 35 5 28N37'11 81w56'47 5:27:47
Twentymile 55 5 30N07'35 81w25'19 5:25:41
Twentymile Bend 50 6 26N41'10 80w23'19 5:21:33
Twin Lake 29 5 28N01 82w27 5:29:48
Twin Palms 36 5 26N36 81w52 5:27:28
Twin Pole 39 5 30N06'08 84w50'59 5:39:24
Two Egg 32 1 30N51'09 85w04'35 5:40:18
Tyler 21 5 29N39'03 82w45'51 5:31:03
Tyndall 3 1 30N05 85w37 5:42:28
Tyndall Air Force Base 3 1 30N09 85w39 5:42:36
Uleta 13 6 25N47 80w13 5:20:52
Umatilla 35 5 28N55'45 81w39'57 5:26:40
Underwood Crossing 30 1 30N58'28 85w35'01 5:42:20
Union Park 48 5 28N34'17 81w14'26 5:24:58
University of Florida 1 5 29N40 82w20 5:29:20
University of Miami 13 6 25N44 80w16 5:21:04
University of South Florida 29 5 28N04 82w25 5:29:40
University of Tampa 29 5 27N56 82w29 5:29:56
University of West Florida 17 4 30N29 87w12 5:48:48
University Park 16 5 30N20 81w35 5:26:20
University Park 50 6 26N23'00 80w07'30 5:20:30
Upper Key Largo 44 5 25N08 80w25 5:21:40
Upper Keys 44 5 25N01 80w32 5:22:08
Upper Langston Landing 65 5 30N12'51 84w40'52 5:38:43
U S A F Hospital 46 1 30N28 86w32 5:46:08
Useppa Island 36 5 26N45 82w16 5:29:04
Usher 38 5 29N24'26 82w49'01 5:31:16
Usinas Beach 55 5 29N57'10 81w18'17 5:25:13
U S Navy Mine Defense Labor 3 1 30N09 85w39 5:42:36
Utopia 58 5 27N17'23 82w21'37 5:29:26
Valdez 64 5 28N50'42 81w19'21 5:25:17
Valkaria 5 5 27N57'48 80w32'38 5:22:11
Valley Church 66 1 30N43 86w07 5:44:28
Valparaiso 46 2 30N30'43 86w29'38 5:45:59
Valrico 29 5 27N56'44 82w15'29 5:29:02
Vamo 58 5 27N13'18 82w29'53 5:30:00
Vanderbilt Beach 11 5 26N16'13 81w47'24 5:27:10
Vanderbilt Park 13 6 25N47'55 80w21'31 5:21:26
Vandolah 25 5 27N30'55 81w55'32 5:27:42
Van Horn Landing 19 1 29N53'44 85w00'42 5:40:03
Vaughn 50 5 26N37'56 80w52'09 5:23:29
Vaughn Landing 45 5 30N37'41 81w34'24 5:26:18
Vause Landing 37 5 30N26'18 84w31'47 5:38:07
Venetia 16 5 30N14'50 81w41'38 5:26:47
Venetian Gardens 58 5 27N08 82w27 5:29:48
Venetian Islands 13 6 25N48 80w09 5:20:36
Venetia Terrace 16 5 30N14'10 81w43'05 5:26:52
Venice 58 5 27N05'58 82w27'16 5:29:49
Venice Beach 58 5 27N05'59 82w27'28 5:29:50
Venice Beach Park 58 5 27N04 82w20 5:29:20
Venice East 58 5 27N03'24 82w22'43 5:29:31
Venice Gardens 58 5 27N04'22 82w24'28 5:29:38
Venice Groves 58 5 27N03'09 82w24'17 5:29:37
Venus 28 5 27N04'01 81w21'25 5:25:26
Verdie 45 5 30N26'06 81w55'17 5:27:41
Vereen 65 5 30N16'22 84w14'28 5:36:58
Vermont Heights 55 5 29N48'36 81w23'50 5:25:35
Verna 41 5 27N23'13 82w16'06 5:29:04
Vernon 67 1 30N37'22 85w42'44 5:42:51
Vero Beach 31 5 27N38'18 80w23'51 5:21:35
Vero Beach Highlands 31 5 27N40 80w24 5:21:36
Vero Beach South 31 5 27N40 80w24 5:21:36
Vero Lake Estates 31 5 27N44'42 80w31'41 5:22:07
Vero Shores 31 5 27N40 80w24 5:21:36
Vicksburg 3 1 30N19'32 85w39'53 5:42:40
Victor 52 5 28N10'10 82w46'24 5:31:06
Victory Gardens 13 5 25N34 80w22 5:21:28
Viking 56 5 27N32'29 80w21'44 5:21:27
Vilano Beach 55 5 29N55'07 81w17'35 5:25:10
Vilas 39 5 30N13'08 84w53'09 5:39:33
Village Green 1 5 29N40 82w20 5:29:20
Village Green 5 5 28N20 80w44 5:22:56
Villa Rica 50 6 26N23 80w05 5:20:20
Villa Sabine 17 4 30N19'54 87w09'33 5:48:38
Villa Tasso 66 1 30N27'36 86w23'17 5:45:33
Vineland 48 5 28N23'42 81w30'12 5:26:01
Vinzant Landing 12 5 29N55'15 82w33'57 5:30:16
Virginia Gardens 13 6 25N48'36 80w18'09 5:21:13
Vista 38 5 29N22'36 83w02'54 5:32:12
Vitis 51 5 28N16'51 82w08'39 5:28:35
Volusia 64 5 29N10'06 81w31'16 5:26:05
Wabasso 31 5 27N44'53 80w26'11 5:21:45
Wabasso Beach 31 5 27N45'52 80w23'57 5:21:36
Wacahoota 1 5 29N33'23 82w23'28 5:29:34
Wacissa 33 5 30N21'30 83w59'14 5:35:57
Waddells Mill 32 1 30N52'13 85w19'32 5:41:18
Wade 1 5 29N44'28 82w37'10 5:30:29
Wadesboro 37 5 30N30'18 84w03'57 5:36:16
Wagner 59 5 28N42'17 81w16'57 5:25:08
Wagon Wheel 11 5 26N06'02 81w03'54 5:24:16
Wahneta 53 5 27N57'09 81w43'38 5:26:55
Wahoo 60 5 28N41'25 82w11'45 5:28:47
Wainright Landing 37 5 30N24'08 84w36'40 5:38:27
Waits Junction 35 5 28N34'19 81w41'26 5:26:46
Wakulla 65 5 30N14'12 84w13'52 5:36:55
Wakulla Beach 65 5 30N06'33 84w15'33 5:37:02
Wakulla Gardens 65 5 30N10'35 84w18'28 5:37:14
Wakulla Springs 65 5 30N14'00 84w18'19 5:37:13
Walden Lake 29 5 28N01 82w08 5:28:32
Waldo 1 5 29N47'22 82w10'03 5:28:40
Walkers Landing 45 5 30N48'55 81w54'29 5:27:38
Walkill 10 5 29N56'16 81w39'44 5:26:39
Wallace 57 1 30N40'38 87w10'48 5:48:43
Wall Springs 52 5 28N06'04 82w46'19 5:31:05
Walnut Hill 17 1 30N53'07 87w30'36 5:50:02
Walsingham 52 5 27N52'37 82w47'52 5:31:11
Walter Hamilton Place 44 5 25N33'29 81w10'19 5:24:41
Walton 56 5 27N17'59 80w15'23 5:21:02
Wannee 21 5 29N43'06 82w56'28 5:31:46
Ward 37 5 30N18'14 84w42'11 5:38:49
Ward Basin 57 1 30N35'06 86w59'49 5:47:59
Ward Ridge 23 5 29N47 85w17 5:41:08
Warm Mineral Springs 58 5 27N03'22 82w15'51 5:29:03
Warrington 17 4 30N23'02 87w16'30 5:49:06
Washington Park 6 6 26N07 80w13 5:20:52
Washington Park 22 5 26N50'30 81w05'47 5:24:23
Waterbury 41 5 27N26'43 82w18'12 5:29:13
Waters Lake 21 5 29N42'32 82w43'58 5:30:56
Watertown 12 5 30N11'32 82w36'53 5:30:28
Watson 50 5 26N41'25 80w49'51 5:23:19
Wauchula 25 5 27N32'49 81w48'42 5:27:15
Wauchula Hills 25 5 27N33 81w49 5:27:16
Waukeenah 33 5 30N24'40 83w57'11 5:35:49
Wausau 67 1 30N37'55 85w35'20 5:42:21
Waveland 56 5 27N16'03 80w12'25 5:20:50
Waverly 53 5 27N58'43 81w36'51 5:26:27
Weathersfield 59 5 28N39'42 81w23'57 5:25:36
Webb Landing 57 1 30N43'53 87w17'10 5:49:09
Webb's City 52 5 27N46 82w38 5:30:32
Webster 60 5 28N36'35 82w03'19 5:28:13
Weeki Wachee 27 5 28N30'55 82w34'23 5:30:18
Week Landing 15 5 29N23'49 83w02'08 5:32:09
Weirsdale 42 5 28N58'54 81w55'28 5:27:42
Wekiva 35 5 28N47'33 81w25'27 5:25:42
Wekiwa Manor 48 5 28N41 81w28 5:25:52
Wekiwa Springs 48 5 28N41 81w28 5:25:52
Welaka 54 5 29N28'44 81w40'18 5:26:41
Welcome 29 5 27N50'09 82w06'16 5:28:25
Wellborn 61 5 30N13'51 82w49'11 5:31:17
Wells Landing 42 5 29N25'00 81w55'06 5:27:40
Wesconnett 16 5 30N14'48 81w43'50 5:26:55
Wesley Chapel 51 5 28N14 82w11 5:28:44
Wesley Manor 55 5 30N12 81w35 5:26:20
Wesley Manor Retirement Vill 55 5 30N07'37 81w37'26 5:26:30
West Auburndale 53 5 28N04 81w49 5:27:16
West Augustine 55 5 29N48 81w16 5:25:04
Westbay 3 1 30N18 85w52 5:43:28
West Bay 16 5 30N24 81w45 5:27:00
West Bradenton 41 5 27N29 82w37 5:30:28
Westchester 13 6 25N45'16 80w19'39 5:21:19
West Deerfield Beach 6 6 26N18'49 80w09'01 5:20:36
West Dixie Bend 6 6 26N18'56 80w12'06 5:20:48
West Eau Gallie 5 5 28N08'08 80w40'19 5:22:41

West End 32 1 30N47 85w14 5:40:56
West End 42 5 29N11 82w10 5:28:40
Western Acres 36 5 26N39 81w53 5:27:32
West Farm 40 5 30N28 83w25 5:33:40
West Flagler 18 5 29N26 81w20 5:25:20
West Frostproof 53 5 27N44'00 81w35'00 5:26:20
West Gate 50 6 26N42'08 80w05'54 5:20:24
Westgate Lake Manor 6 6 26N07'23 80w12'23 5:20:50
West Hills 1 5 29N39'58 82w24'29 5:29:38
West Holly Hill 64 5 29N14 81w02 5:24:08
West Hollywood 6 6 26N01 80w12 5:20:48
West Jacksonville 16 5 30N20'24 81w43'21 5:26:53
West Lake 24 5 30N30'10 83w06'53 5:32:28
West Lake Wales 53 5 27N53'24 81w38'48 5:26:35
West Landing 45 5 30N33'44 81w42'13 5:26:49
West Lantana 50 6 26N35 80w04 5:20:16
West Liberty 39 5 30N25 84w59 5:39:56
West Melbourne 5 5 28N04'17 80w39'13 5:22:37
West Miami 13 6 25N45'47 80w17'47 5:21:11
Westmoreland Estates 1 5 29N40 82w20 5:29:20
West Okeechobee 47 5 27N19 80w54 5:23:36
West Palm Beach 50 6 26N42'54 80w03'13 5:20:13
West Palm Beach Farms 50 6 26N40'43 80w07'46 5:20:31
West Palmetto Park 50 6 26N23 80w05 5:20:20
West Panama City Beach 3 1 30N13 85w53 5:43:32
West Pensacola 17 4 30N25'35 87w16'47 5:49:07
West Saint Lucie 56 5 27N28 80w27 5:21:48
West Scenic Park 53 5 27N55'13 81w38'33 5:26:34
Westside 64 5 29N13 81w02 5:24:08
West Tampa 29 5 27N57'11 82w29'22 5:29:57
West Tocoi 10 5 29N51'00 81w37'03 5:26:28
West Vero Beach 31 5 27N40 80w24 5:21:36
Westview 13 6 25N54 80w13 5:20:52
Westville 30 1 30N46'28 85w51'06 5:43:24
West Wakulla County 65 5 30N05 84w26 5:37:44
West Winter Haven 53 5 28N03 81w47 5:27:08
Westwood 16 5 30N14'27 81w45'37 5:27:02
Westwood 48 5 28N34 81w27 5:25:48
Westwood Lake 13 6 25N43'44 80w22'23 5:21:30
Westwood Lakes 13 6 25N44 80w23 5:21:32
Wetumpka 20 5 30N28'58 84w37'23 5:38:30
Wewahitchka 23 1 30N06'45 85w12'02 5:40:48
Whidden Corner 26 5 26N45'14 81w04'56 5:24:20
Whispering Hills Golf Estate 5 5 28N35'42 80w49'20 5:23:17
Whispering Palms 50 6 26N36 80w05 5:20:20
Whispering Pines 47 5 27N16'38 80w50'23 5:23:22
White Beach 58 5 27N14'24 82w31'35 5:30:06
White City 23 5 29N53'02 85w13'12 5:40:53
White City 56 5 27N22'25 80w20'03 5:21:20
Whitehead Crossroads 67 1 30N42'15 85w46'04 5:43:04
Whitehouse 16 5 30N18'58 81w50'47 5:27:23
White Oak Landing 39 5 30N05'53 85w06'47 5:40:27
White Sand Landing 45 5 30N49'02 81w57'49 5:27:51
Whites Ford 55 5 30N01'33 81w31'30 5:26:06
Whites Landing 59 5 28N41'59 81w14'20 5:24:57
White Springs 24 5 30N19'46 82w45'33 5:31:02
White Springs 39 5 30N26 84w59 5:39:56
Whitfield Estates 41 5 27N24'35 82w34'10 5:30:17
Whiting Field 57 3 30N43 87w01 5:48:04
Whitney 35 5 28N49'01 81w56'14 5:27:45
Whitney Beach 41 5 27N25'46 82w40'50 5:30:43
Whittier 49 5 27N52'22 81w00'23 5:24:02
Wilbur-by-the-Sea 64 5 29N07'52 80w57'28 5:23:50
Wilburn 12 5 30N11'26 82w34'44 5:30:19
Wilcox 21 5 29N36'39 82w55'18 5:31:41
Wilcox Junction 21 5 29N36'41 82w56'25 5:31:46
Wild Island 28 5 27N22'21 81w12'14 5:24:49
Wildwood 60 5 28N51'54 82w02'21 5:28:09
Wiley 5 5 28N40'25 80w49'44 5:23:19
Williams Ditch Landing 17 1 30N38'59 87w16'37 5:49:06
Williams Landing 37 5 30N26'54 84w31'16 5:38:05
Williams Point 5 5 28N26'53 80w45'47 5:23:03
Williford 21 5 29N47'10 82w47'29 5:31:10
Willis 7 1 30N33'11 85w11'12 5:40:45
Willis Landing 23 1 29N58'32 85w04'23 5:40:18
Williston 38 5 29N23'14 82w26'49 5:29:47
Willow 41 5 27N38'39 82w20'48 5:29:23
Wilma 39 5 30N09'15 84w57'52 5:39:51
Wilson 5 5 28N38'35 80w41'48 5:22:47
Wilson Corner 59 5 28N48'29 81w21'47 5:25:27
Wilson Haven 51 5 28N32 82w29 5:29:56
Wilson Place 59 5 28N48'28 81w21'13 5:25:25
Wilton Manors 6 6 26N09'36 80w08'21 5:20:33
Wimauma 29 5 27N42'44 82w17'57 5:29:12
Wimberly Estates 1 5 29N41'26 82w22'38 5:29:31
Windermere 48 5 28N29'43 81w32'06 5:26:08
Windmill Village Trailer Par 11 5 26N11 81w48 5:27:12
Windsor 1 5 29N38'47 82w11'11 5:28:45
Windy Hill 16 5 30N17 81w35 5:26:20
Winfield 12 5 30N15'46 82w41'10 5:30:45
Winslow Beach 5 5 28N20 80w37 5:22:28
Winston 53 5 28N01'53 82w00'54 5:28:04
Winter Beach 31 5 27N43'08 80w25'15 5:21:41
Winter Garden 48 5 28N33'54 81w35'11 5:26:21
Winter Haven 53 5 28N01'19 81w43'59 5:26:56
Winter Park 48 5 28N35'59 81w20'22 5:25:21
Winter Springs 59 5 28N41'55 81w18'30 5:25:14
Wiscon 27 5 28N32'26 82w27'44 5:29:51
Withla 53 5 28N20'23 81w52'16 5:27:29
Wolfolk 53 5 27N48'00 81w37'49 5:26:31
Wonderwood 16 5 30N22'07 81w24'48 5:25:39
Woodland Acres 16 5 30N20 81w35 5:26:20
Woodland Park 36 5 26N38 81w52 5:27:28
Woodlawn 3 1 30N09 85w39 5:42:36
Woodlawn 55 5 29N55'52 81w20'39 5:25:23
Woodlawn Beach 57 4 30N23'17 86w59'27 5:47:58
Woodmere 58 5 27N01'13 82w23'27 5:29:34
Woodruff Springs 59 5 28N48'28 81w20'42 5:25:23
Woods 39 5 30N20'50 84w58'49 5:39:55
Woodside Heights 37 5 30N26 84w17 5:37:08
Woodville 3 1 30N09 85w39 5:42:36
Woodville 38 5 30N18'50 84w14'51 5:36:59
Worthington 63 5 29N58 82w29 5:29:56
Worthington Springs 63 5 29N55'45 82w25'25 5:29:42
Wright 46 1 30N27'20 86w38'18 5:46:33
Wright Landing 19 5 29N59'57 85w00'31 5:40:02
Wulfert 36 5 26N28'48 82w10'41 5:28:43
Wynnehaven Beach 46 1 30N24'36 86w46'56 5:47:08
Wynwood 59 5 28N47'22 81w15'09 5:25:01
Yacht Harbor 50 6 26N47 80w04 5:20:16
Yalaha 35 5 28N44'18 81w48'32 5:27:14
Yamato 50 6 26N24'34 80w05'25 5:20:22
Yankeetown 38 5 29N01'47 82w42'58 5:30:52
Ybel 36 5 26N25'27 82w04'16 5:28:17
Ybor City 29 5 27N57'53 82w26'07 5:29:44
Yeehaw Junction 49 5 27N42'00 80w54'16 5:23:37
Yellow Bluff Fort 16 5 30N23'58 81w33'22 5:26:13
Yellow Jacket 15 5 29N27'47 83w00'05 5:32:00
Yelvington 54 5 29N37'52 81w31'27 5:26:06
Yent Place 19 5 29N51'49 84w42'01 5:38:48
Yniestra 17 4 30N30'06 87w09'37 5:48:38
Yon's Lakeside Estates 37 5 30N26 84w17 5:37:08
Yon's Subdivision 23 1 29N48 85w18 5:41:12
York 42 5 29N09'00 82w18'01 5:29:12
Youmans 29 5 28N01'30 82w04'06 5:28:16
Youngstown 3 1 30N21'51 85w26'18 5:41:45
Yukon 16 5 30N14'04 81w41'54 5:26:48
Yulee 45 5 30N37'54 81w36'24 5:26:26
Yulee Heights 45 5 30N36'26 81w35'52 5:26:23
Zana 43 5 27N07'11 80w37'11 5:22:29
Zellwood 48 5 28N43'51 81w36'05 5:26:24
Zephyrhills 51 5 28N14'00 82w10'53 5:28:44
Zolfo Springs 25 5 27N29'35 81w47'46 5:27:11
Zuber 42 5 29N16'01 82w10'52 5:28:43

TIME TABLES

There is considerable confusion about shifts from Central to Eastern time, and the reverse. These shifts for rural areas have not been documented and may not always be correct, particularly at the boundaries between Eastern and Central time zone areas.

GA # 1		
Before 1/01/1903		LMT
1/01/1903	12:00	EST
3/31/1918	02:00	EWT
10/27/1918	02:00	EST
3/30/1919	02:00	EWT
10/26/1919	02:00	EST
2/09/1942	02:00	EWT
9/30/1945	02:00	EST
4/30/1967	02:00	US#1

GA # 2		
Before 1/01/1903		LMT
1/01/1903	12:00	EST
3/31/1918	02:00	EWT
10/27/1918	02:00	EST
3/30/1919	02:00	EWT
10/26/1919	02:00	EST
8/04/1941	02:00	EDT
2/09/1942	02:00	EWT
9/30/1945	02:00	EST
4/30/1967	02:00	US#1

GA # 3		
Before 1/01/1888		LMT
1/01/1888	12:00	EST
3/31/1918	02:00	EWT
10/27/1918	02:00	EST
3/30/1919	02:00	EWT
10/26/1919	02:00	EST
2/09/1942	02:00	EWT
9/30/1945	02:00	EST
4/30/1967	02:00	US#1

GA # 4		
Before 3/25/1888		LMT
3/25/1888	12:00	EST
3/31/1918	02:00	EWT
10/27/1918	02:00	EST
3/30/1919	02:00	EWT
10/26/1919	02:00	EST
2/09/1942	02:00	EWT
9/30/1945	02:00	EST
4/30/1967	02:00	US#1

GA # 5		
Before 1/01/1903		LMT
1/01/1903	12:00	CST
3/31/1918	02:00	CWT
10/27/1918	02:00	CST
3/30/1919	02:00	CWT
10/26/1919	02:00	CST
3/22/1941	00:00	EST
2/09/1942	02:00	EWT
1/29/1943	00:01	CWT
9/30/1945	02:00	EST
4/30/1967	02:00	US#1

GA # 6		
Before 1/01/1903		LMT
1/01/1903	12:00	EST
1/01/1918	12:00	CST
3/31/1918	02:00	CWT
10/27/1918	02:00	CST
3/30/1919	02:00	CWT
10/26/1919	02:00	CST
3/22/1941	00:00	EST
2/09/1942	02:00	EWT
1/29/1943	00:01	CWT
9/30/1945	02:00	EST
4/30/1967	02:00	US#1

GA # 7		
Before 1/01/1903		LMT
1/01/1903	12:00	EST
1/01/1918	12:00	CST
3/31/1918	02:00	CWT
10/27/1918	02:00	CST
3/30/1919	02:00	CWT
10/26/1919	02:00	CST
4/28/1935	01:00	CDT
9/29/1935	02:00	CST
4/26/1936	00:00	CDT
9/27/1936	02:00	CST
4/25/1937	00:00	CDT
9/26/1937	00:00	CST
4/24/1938	00:00	CDT
9/25/1938	00:00	CST
4/30/1939	00:00	CDT
9/24/1939	00:00	CST
4/28/1940	00:00	CDT
9/29/1940	00:00	CST
3/22/1941	00:00	EST
2/09/1942	02:00	EWT
1/29/1943	00:01	CWT
9/30/1945	02:00	EST
4/30/1967	02:00	US#1

GA # 8		
Before 1/01/1903		LMT
1/01/1903	12:00	CST
3/31/1918	02:00	CWT
10/27/1918	02:00	CST
3/30/1919	02:00	CWT
10/26/1919	02:00	CST
3/21/1941	11:35	EST
2/09/1942	02:00	EWT
1/28/1943	12:30	CWT
9/30/1945	02:00	EST
4/30/1967	02:00	US#1

GA # 9		
Before 1/01/1903		LMT
1/01/1903	12:00	CST
3/31/1918	02:00	CWT
10/27/1918	02:00	CST
3/30/1919	02:00	CWT
10/26/1919	02:00	CST
4/25/1937	00:00	CDT
9/26/1937	00:00	CST
4/24/1938	00:00	CDT
9/25/1938	00:00	CST
4/30/1939	00:00	CDT
9/24/1939	00:00	CST
4/28/1940	00:00	CDT
9/29/1940	00:00	CST
3/21/1941	11:35	EST
2/09/1942	02:00	EWT
1/28/1943	12:30	CWT
9/30/1945	02:00	EST
4/30/1967	02:00	US#1

GA # 10		
Before 1/01/1903		LMT
1/01/1903	12:00	CST
3/31/1918	02:00	CWT
10/27/1918	02:00	CST
3/30/1919	02:00	CWT
10/26/1919	02:00	CST
4/28/1935	01:00	CDT
9/29/1935	02:00	CST
4/26/1936	00:00	CDT
9/27/1936	02:00	CST
4/25/1937	00:00	CDT
9/26/1937	00:00	CST
4/24/1938	00:00	CDT
9/25/1938	00:00	CST
4/30/1939	00:00	CDT
9/24/1939	00:00	CST
4/28/1940	00:00	CDT
9/29/1940	00:00	CST
3/21/1941	11:35	EST
2/09/1942	02:00	EWT
1/28/1943	12:30	CWT
9/30/1945	02:00	EST
4/30/1967	02:00	US#1

GA # 11		
Before 1/01/1903		LMT
1/01/1903	12:00	CST
3/31/1918	02:00	CWT
10/27/1918	02:00	CST
3/30/1919	02:00	CWT
10/26/1919	02:00	CST
4/19/1936	00:00	CDT
9/12/1936	00:00	CST
4/25/1937	00:00	CDT
8/29/1937	00:00	CST
5/29/1938	00:00	CDT
9/10/1938	00:00	CST
5/27/1939	00:00	CDT
9/09/1939	00:00	CST
5/27/1940	00:00	CDT
9/08/1940	00:00	CST
3/21/1941	11:35	EST
2/09/1942	02:00	EWT
1/28/1943	12:30	CWT
9/30/1945	02:00	EST
4/30/1967	02:00	US#1

GA # 12		
Before 1/01/1903		LMT
1/01/1903	12:00	CST
3/31/1918	02:00	CWT
10/27/1918	02:00	CST
3/30/1919	02:00	CWT
10/26/1919	02:00	CST
2/09/1942	02:00	CWT
9/30/1945	02:00	EST
4/30/1967	02:00	US#1

GA # 13		
Before 1/01/1903		LMT
1/01/1903	12:00	CST
3/31/1918	02:00	CWT
10/27/1918	02:00	CST
3/30/1919	02:00	CWT
10/26/1919	02:00	CST
7/20/1941	02:00	CDT
2/09/1942	02:00	CWT
9/30/1945	02:00	EST
4/30/1967	02:00	US#1

GA # 14		
Before 1/01/1903		LMT
1/01/1903	12:00	CST
3/31/1918	02:00	CWT
10/27/1918	02:00	CST
3/30/1919	02:00	CWT
10/26/1919	02:00	CST
3/22/1941	00:00	EST
2/09/1942	02:00	EWT
1/28/1943	12:30	CWT
9/30/1945	02:00	EST
4/30/1967	02:00	US#1

GA # 15		
Before 1/01/1903		LMT
1/01/1903	12:00	CST
3/31/1918	02:00	CWT
10/27/1918	02:00	CST
3/30/1919	02:00	CWT
10/26/1919	02:00	CST
4/25/1937	00:00	CDT
9/26/1937	00:00	CST
4/24/1938	00:00	CDT
9/25/1938	00:00	CST
6/01/1939	00:00	CDT
9/01/1939	00:00	CST
4/28/1940	00:00	CDT
9/29/1940	00:00	CST
3/22/1941	00:00	EST
2/09/1942	02:00	EWT
1/28/1943	12:30	CWT
9/30/1945	02:00	EST
4/30/1967	02:00	US#1

GA # 16		
Before 1/01/1903		LMT
1/01/1903	12:00	CST
3/31/1918	02:00	CWT
10/27/1918	02:00	CST
3/30/1919	02:00	CWT
10/26/1919	02:00	CST
3/23/1941	12:00	EST
2/09/1942	02:00	EWT
2/14/1943	02:00	CWT
9/30/1945	02:00	EST
4/30/1967	02:00	US#1

GA # 17		
Before 1/01/1903		LMT
1/01/1903	12:00	CST
3/31/1918	02:00	CWT
10/27/1918	02:00	CST
3/30/1919	02:00	CWT
10/26/1919	02:00	CST
4/30/1939	00:00	CDT
9/24/1939	00:00	CST
3/23/1941	12:00	EST
2/09/1942	02:00	EWT
2/14/1943	02:00	CWT
9/30/1945	02:00	EST
4/30/1967	02:00	US#1

GA # 18		
Before 1/01/1903		LMT
1/01/1903	12:00	CST
3/31/1918	02:00	CWT
10/27/1918	02:00	CST
3/30/1919	02:00	CWT
10/26/1919	02:00	CST
4/26/1936	00:00	CDT
9/27/1936	02:00	CST
4/25/1937	00:00	CDT
9/26/1937	00:00	CST
3/24/1941	02:00	EST
2/09/1942	02:00	EWT
1/28/1943	12:30	CWT
9/30/1945	02:00	EST
4/30/1967	02:00	US#1

GA # 19		
Before 1/01/1903		LMT
1/01/1903	12:00	CST
3/31/1918	02:00	CWT
10/27/1918	02:00	CST
3/30/1919	02:00	CWT
10/26/1919	02:00	CST
3/21/1941	11:35	EST
2/09/1942	02:00	EWT
9/27/1942	02:00	CWT
9/30/1945	02:00	EST
4/30/1967	02:00	US#1

GA # 20		
Before 1/01/1903		LMT
1/01/1903	12:00	EST
3/31/1918	02:00	EWT
10/27/1918	02:00	EST
3/30/1919	02:00	EWT
10/26/1919	02:00	EST
2/09/1942	02:00	EWT
1/28/1943	12:30	CWT
9/30/1945	02:00	EST
4/30/1967	02:00	US#1

GA # 21		
Before 1/01/1903		LMT
1/01/1903	12:00	EST
3/31/1918	02:00	EWT
10/27/1918	02:00	EST
3/30/1919	02:00	EWT
10/26/1919	02:00	EST
4/25/1937	00:00	EDT
9/26/1937	00:00	EST
4/24/1938	00:00	EDT
9/25/1938	00:00	EST
4/30/1939	00:00	EDT
9/24/1939	00:00	EST
4/28/1940	00:00	EDT
9/29/1940	00:00	EST
2/09/1942	02:00	EWT
1/28/1943	12:30	CWT
9/30/1945	02:00	EST
4/30/1967	02:00	US#1

GA # 22		
Before 1/01/1903		LMT
1/01/1903	12:00	EST
3/31/1918	02:00	EWT
10/27/1918	02:00	EST
3/30/1919	02:00	EWT
10/26/1919	02:00	EST
8/04/1941	02:00	EDT
2/09/1942	02:00	EWT
1/28/1943	12:30	CWT
9/30/1945	02:00	EST
4/30/1967	02:00	US#1

GA # 23		
Before 5/01/1888		LMT
5/01/1888	12:00	EST
3/31/1918	02:00	EWT
10/27/1918	02:00	EST
3/30/1919	02:00	EWT
10/26/1919	02:00	EST
2/09/1942	02:00	EWT
1/28/1943	12:30	CWT
9/30/1945	02:00	EST
4/30/1967	02:00	US#1

GA # 24		
Before 1/01/1903		LMT
1/01/1903	12:00	EST
3/31/1918	02:00	EWT
10/27/1918	02:00	EST
3/30/1919	02:00	EWT
10/26/1919	02:00	EST
2/09/1942	02:00	EWT
1/28/1943	12:00	CWT
2/04/1943	12:00	EWT
9/30/1945	02:00	EST
4/30/1967	02:00	US#1

GA # 25		
Before 1/01/1903		LMT
1/01/1903	12:00	EST
3/31/1918	02:00	EWT
10/27/1918	02:00	EST
3/30/1919	02:00	EWT
10/26/1919	02:00	EST
2/09/1942	02:00	EWT
2/05/1943	02:00	CWT
9/30/1945	02:00	EST
4/30/1967	02:00	US#1

COUNTIES

1 Appling
2 Atkinson
3 Bacon
4 Baker
5 Baldwin
6 Banks
7 Barrow
8 Bartow
9 Ben Hill
10 Berrien
11 Bibb
12 Bleckley
13 Brantley
14 Brooks
15 Bryan
16 Bulloch
17 Burke
18 Butts
19 Calhoun
20 Camden
21 Candler
22 Carroll
23 Catoosa
24 Charlton
25 Chatham
26 Chattahoochee
27 Chattooga
28 Cherokee
29 Clarke
30 Clay
31 Clayton
32 Clinch
33 Cobb
34 Coffee
35 Colquitt
36 Columbia
37 Cook
38 Coweta
39 Crawford
40 Crisp
41 Dade
42 Dawson
43 Decatur
44 De Kalb
45 Dodge
46 Dooly
47 Dougherty
48 Douglas
49 Early
50 Echols
51 Effingham
52 Elbert
53 Emanuel
54 Evans
55 Fannin
56 Fayette
57 Floyd
58 Forsyth
59 Franklin
60 Fulton
61 Gilmer
62 Glascock
63 Glynn
64 Gordon
65 Grady
66 Greene
67 Gwinnett
68 Habersham
69 Hall
70 Hancock
71 Haralson
72 Harris
73 Hart
74 Heard
75 Henry
76 Houston
77 Irwin
78 Jackson
79 Jasper
80 Jeff Davis
81 Jefferson
82 Jenkins
83 Johnson
84 Jones
85 Lamar
86 Lanier
87 Laurens
88 Lee
89 Liberty
90 Lincoln
91 Long
92 Lowndes
93 Lumpkin
94 McDuffie
95 McIntosh
96 Macon
97 Madison
98 Marion
99 Meriwether
100 Miller
101 Mitchell
102 Monroe
103 Montgomery
104 Morgan
105 Murray
106 Muscogee
107 Newton
108 Oconee
109 Oglethorpe
110 Paulding
111 Peach
112 Pickens
113 Pierce
114 Pike
115 Polk
116 Pulaski
117 Putnam
118 Quitman
119 Rabun
120 Randolph
121 Richmond
122 Rockdale
123 Schley
124 Screven
125 Seminole
126 Spalding
127 Stephens
128 Stewart
129 Sumter
130 Talbot
131 Taliaferro
132 Tattnall
133 Taylor
134 Telfair
135 Terrell
136 Thomas
137 Tift
138 Toombs
139 Towns
140 Treutlen
141 Troup
142 Turner
143 Twiggs
144 Union
145 Upson
146 Walker
147 Walton
148 Ware
149 Warren
150 Washington
151 Wayne
152 Webster
153 Wheeler
154 White
155 Whitfield
156 Wilcox
157 Wilkes
158 Wilkinson
159 Worth

Aaron 16	20	32N34'05	81w59'33	5:27:58
Abac 137	20	31N27	83w31	5:34:04
Abba 77	20	31N45'24	83w22'14	5:33:29
Abbeville 156	20	31N59'31	83w18'25	5:33:14
Abbottsford 141	8	33N02'50	85w10'47	5:40:43
Abercorn Heights 25	20	32N01'57	81w06'25	5:24:26
Aberdeen 56	8	33N24'32	84w36'07	5:38:24
Abernathys Mill 71	8	33N51'51	85w12'35	5:40:50
Abilene 22	8	33N38'57	85w02'59	5:40:12
Achord 45	20	32N06'22	82w58'08	5:31:53
Acorn Pond 159	20	31N48'37	83w51'19	5:35:25
Acree 47	20	31N33'19	83w59'46	5:35:59
Acworth 33	8	34N03'57	84w40'37	5:38:42
Adabelle 16	20	32N17'29	81w55'38	5:27:43
Adairsville 8	8	34N22'07	84w56'03	5:39:44
Adams Crossroads 67	20	33N57'51	84w08'23	5:36:34
Adamson 74	8	33N16'04	85w13'56	5:40:56
Adams Park 143	20	32N48	83w30	5:34:00
Adamsville 60	8	33N45'33	84w30'19	5:38:01
Adasburg 157	20	33N42'22	82w32'54	5:30:12
Adel 37	20	31N08'13	83w25'25	5:33:42
Adgateville 79	20	33N13'23	83w40'16	5:34:41
Adrian 53	20	32N31'50	82w35'22	5:30:21
Aerial 68	20	34N39'52	83w38'40	5:34:35
Afton 42	8	34N30'01	84w14'44	5:36:59
Agnes 90	20	33N48	82w29	5:29:56
Agnes Scott College 44	20	33N47	84w17	5:37:08
Agricola 62	20	33N11'40	82w43'14	5:30:53
Ai 61	8	34N50'01	84w27'10	5:37:49
Aid 59	20	34N22	83w14	5:32:56
Ailey 103	20	32N11'14	82w33'57	5:30:16
Airline 73	20	34N22	83w05	5:32:20
Akes 115	8	33N58'02	85w19'05	5:41:16
Akin 16	20	32N23	81w40	5:26:40
Akin 151	20	31N27'21	81w42'16	5:26:49
Akins 16	20	32N18'22	81w37'14	5:26:29
Akins Mill 16	20	32N30'51	81w48'58	5:27:16
Akridge 65	8	30N58'59	84w09'38	5:36:39
Alabama Junction 25	20	32N04'33	81w08'25	5:24:34
Alaculsy 105	8	34N59'19	84w37'59	5:38:32
Alamo 153	20	32N08'49	82w46'41	5:31:07
Alapaha 10	20	31N23'06	83w13'23	5:32:54
Albany 47	11	31N34'42	84w09'21	5:36:37
Albion Acres 121	20	33N26	82w01	5:28:04
Alcorns 87	20	32N24'34	83w06'37	5:32:26
Alcovy 107	20	33N38'23	83w47'13	5:35:09
Alcovy Mountain 147	20	33N44'26	83w45'59	5:35:04
Alcovy Shores 79	20	33N23'22	83w49'58	5:35:20
Alderman Landing 16	20	32N19'42	81w28'55	5:25:56
Aldora 85	15	33N03'07	84w10'33	5:36:42
Alexander 17	20	33N01'19	81w52'37	5:27:30
Alexis 50	20	30N44'31	82w55'07	5:31:40
Alford 73	20	34N21	82w56	5:31:44
Alfords 159	20	31N27'44	83w55'26	5:35:42
Aline 21	20	32N21'39	82w09'38	5:28:39
Allatoona 8	8	34N06'29	84w42'41	5:38:51
Allen City 67	20	34N00	84w10	5:36:40
Allendale 67	20	33N59'21	83w59'02	5:35:56
Allendale 106	17	32N31'40	84w55'32	5:39:42
Allenhurst 89	20	31N47'02	81w36'28	5:26:26
Allentown 143	20	32N35'35	83w13'33	5:32:54
Allenville 10	20	31N07'44	83w12'51	5:32:51
Allenwood 5	20	33N04'11	83w15'41	5:33:03
Allie 99	8	33N05'57	84w43'44	5:38:55
Alligood 87	20	32N26'10	83w00'15	5:32:01
Allon 39	8	32N38'15	83w59'02	5:35:56
Alma 3	20	31N32'21	82w27'45	5:29:51
Almira 81	20	32N56'41	82w31'34	5:30:06
Almon 107	20	33N37'09	83w55'20	5:35:41
Alpharetta 60	7	34N04'31	84w17'39	5:37:11
Alpine 27	8	34N27'21	85w29'30	5:41:58
Alps 99	8	33N08'53	84w36'12	5:38:25
Alps Road 29	20	33N55	83w20	5:33:20
Alston 103	20	32N04'50	82w28'40	5:29:55
Altamaha 132	20	31N57'41	82w12'27	5:28:50
Altamaha Park 63	20	31N25'35	81w36'26	5:26:26
Altamaha River 1	20	31N53	82w18	5:29:12
Alta Vista 106	17	32N28'53	84w55'30	5:39:42
Altman 124	20	32N49	81w39	5:26:36
Alto 6	20	34N28'02	83w34'26	5:34:18
Alto Park 57	8	34N17	85w12	5:40:48
Alvaton 99	8	33N10'15	84w34'50	5:38:19
Alvin 97	20	34N14'03	83w19'27	5:33:18
Amboy 142	20	31N43	83w39	5:34:36
Ambrose 34	20	31N35'37	83w00'52	5:32:03
Americus 129	18	32N04'20	84w13'58	5:36:56
Amicalola 42	8	34N33'17	84w15'09	5:37:01
Amity 90	20	33N40'33	82w29'23	5:29:58
Amos Mill 41	8	34N43'03	85w31'08	5:42:05
Amsterdam 43	8	30N43'38	84w26'09	5:37:45
Amzi 105	8	34N46	84w48	5:39:12
Anderson City 159	20	31N22'17	83w51'17	5:35:25
Anderson Mill 16	20	32N13'11	81w48'14	5:27:13
Andersons Corner 141	8	32N52'36	84w57'06	5:39:48
Andersonville 28	8	34N07'46	84w29'51	5:37:59
Andersonville 129	8	32N11'45	84w08'24	5:36:34
Andrews Crossroads 99	8	32N59'00	84w39'40	5:38:39
Angelville 64	8	34N35'20	84w53'24	5:39:34
Anguilla 63	20	31N15'19	81w36'13	5:26:25
Ansley Mill 94	20	33N31'10	82w24'49	5:29:39
Antioch 115	8	33N57'12	85w09'41	5:40:39
Antioch 119	20	34N53'28	83w17'57	5:33:12
Antioch 141	8	33N06'27	85w10'12	5:40:41
Aonia 157	20	33N40'31	82w37'24	5:30:30
Apalachee 104	20	33N41'11	83w25'52	5:33:43
Apple Valley 78	20	34N09'31	83w30'34	5:34:02
Appling 36	20	33N32'45	82w18'58	5:29:16
Arabi 40	20	31N49'53	83w44'17	5:34:57
Aragon 115	8	34N02'44	85w03'22	5:40:13
Aragon Park 121	20	33N28	81w59	5:27:56
Arcade 78	20	34N04'40	83w33'42	5:34:15
Arch City 64	8	34N30	84w57	5:39:48
Archery 152	8	32N01'36	84w26'54	5:37:48
Arco 63	20	31N12'04	81w30'23	5:26:02
Arcola 16	20	32N20'36	81w36'08	5:26:25
Ardick 95	20	31N27'40	81w26'01	5:25:44
Ardmore 51	20	32N29'42	81w25'44	5:25:43
Argyle 32	20	31N04'26	82w38'55	5:30:36
Arkwright 11	25	32N55'58	83w42'11	5:34:49
Arles 129	18	32N07'05	84w11'51	5:36:47
Arlington 19	8	31N26'23	84w43'30	5:38:54
Armboy 142	20	31N47'32	83w35'15	5:34:21
Armena 88	20	31N40'51	84w17'05	5:37:08
Armuchee 57	8	34N23'20	85w10'55	5:40:44
Arnco Mills 38	8	33N24'53	84w51'13	5:39:25
Arnold Mill 60	8	34N07'03	84w23'17	5:37:33
Arnoldsville 109	20	33N54'18	83w13'01	5:32:52
Arp 77	20	31N45'21	83w24'25	5:33:38
Arrowhead Village 31	8	33N31	84w21	5:37:24
Ashburn 142	20	31N42'21	83w39'12	5:34:37
Ashford Park 44	20	33N52	84w20	5:37:20
Ashintilly 95	20	31N23'37	81w24'33	5:25:38
Ashland 59	20	34N19'32	83w21'21	5:33:25
Ashton 9	20	31N42'17	83w09'22	5:32:37
Aska 55	8	34N46'04	84w15'44	5:37:03
Aspinwall 113	20	31N26'05	82w10'27	5:28:42
Astoria 148	1	31N08'54	82w17'31	5:29:10
Atco 8	8	34N10'50	84w49'12	5:39:17
Athens 29	3	33N57'39	83w22'41	5:33:31
Atkinson 13	20	31N13'23	81w51'10	5:27:25
Atlanta 60	7	33N44'56	84w23'17	5:37:33
Atlanta Junction 57	8	34N12'50	85w10'58	5:40:44
Attapulgus 43	8	30N44'56	84w29'02	5:37:56
Attica 78	3	34N01'07	83w29'31	5:33:58
Atwater 145	8	32N58'06	84w22'10	5:37:29
Atwell 81	20	33N08'26	82w17'11	5:29:09
Aubrey 8	8	34N15'52	84w45'10	5:39:01
Aubrey 74	8	33N11'56	85w08'10	5:40:33
Auburn 7	20	34N00'49	83w49'40	5:35:19
Audubon 64	8	34N33'58	84w49'09	5:39:17
Augusta 121	2	33N28'00	82w01'00	5:28:04
Auraria 93	8	34N28'28	84w01'24	5:36:06
Ausmac 43	8	30N59'46	84w37'27	5:38:30
Austell 33	8	33N48'45	84w38'04	5:38:32
Austin 104	20	33N38	83w37	5:34:28
Autreyville 35	20	31N03'44	83w45'54	5:35:04
Autry 69	1	34N18	83w49	5:35:16
Avalon 25	20	32N00	81w05	5:24:20
Avalon 127	20	34N30'07	83w11'43	5:32:47
Avans 41	8	34N52	85w31	5:42:04
Avants 153	20	32N06'36	82w51'34	5:31:26
Avera 81	20	33N11'38	82w31'38	5:30:07
Avert Acres 47	11	31N34	84w11	5:36:44
Avery 28	8	34N11'44	84w25'21	5:37:41
Avondale 11	25	32N41'30	83w38'15	5:34:33
Avondale 25	20	32N03'10	81w03'28	5:24:14
Avondale 94	20	33N21'19	82w19'34	5:29:18
Avondale 106	17	32N27'30	84w58'31	5:39:54
Avondale Estates 44	20	33N46'17	84w16'02	5:37:04
Avon Park 25	20	32N03'20	81w03'36	5:24:14
Axson 2	20	31N16'34	82w44'04	5:30:56
Aycock Mill 120	8	31N38'14	84w36'47	5:38:27
Ayersville 127	20	34N33'39	83w24'48	5:33:39
Babcock 100	8	31N06'44	84w38'30	5:38:34
Back Landing 63	23	31N09'01	81w28'38	5:25:55
Bacon Park 25	20	32N00	81w05	5:24:20
Baconton 101	20	31N22'46	84w09'40	5:36:39
Baden 14	20	30N43'02	83w33'55	5:34:16
Baileys Park 12	20	32N18'41	83w21'09	5:33:25
Bainbridge 43	8	30N54'13	84w34'32	5:38:18
Bairdstown 66	20	33N41'53	83w07'08	5:32:29
Bakers Crossing 25	20	31N59'13	81w04'20	5:24:17
Baker Village 106	17	32N25'28	84w56'20	5:39:45
Baldwin 68	20	34N29'30	83w32'15	5:34:09
Baldwinville 130	8	32N39'02	84w26'59	5:37:48
Ballew Mill 55	8	34N50'21	84w20'57	5:37:24
Ball Ground 28	8	34N20'17	84w22'36	5:37:30
Ball Ground 105	8	34N46	84w48	5:39:12
Balls Ferry 83	20	32N43	82w47	5:31:08
Baltimore 157	20	33N44	82w45	5:31:00
Bamburg 50	20	30N46'38	82w54'51	5:31:39
Bancroft 49	8	31N24'53	84w50'24	5:39:22
Banning 22	8	33N30'43	84w55'52	5:39:43
Banning Mills 22	8	33N31'34	84w55'28	5:39:42
Bannockburn 10	20	31N17'05	83w03'27	5:32:14
Barbers 35	20	31N13'18	83w43'17	5:34:53

Barbers Landing 148 20 31N04'26 82w18'52 5:29:15
Barkers Crossroads 74 8 33N22'26 85w10'16 5:40:41
Barker Spring 145 8 32N55'17 84w26'18 5:37:45
Barksdale 150 20 33N00 82w53 5:31:32
Barnes Crossroads 99 8 32N58'01 84w41'25 5:38:46
Barnesdale 37 20 31N11'11 83w22'24 5:33:30
Barnesville 85 8 33N03'16 84w09'21 5:36:37
Barnett 149 20 33N30'14 82w48'28 5:31:14
Barnett Shoals 108 3 33N59 83w23 5:33:32
Barney 14 20 31N00'29 83w30'47 5:34:03
Barneyville 37 20 31N12'50 83w27'15 5:33:49
Barnhill 140 20 32N19'35 82w40'09 5:30:41
Barnsley 8 8 34N14 84w57 5:39:48
Barretts 92 20 31N00'05 83w11'58 5:32:48
Barretts Mill 29 3 34N00'28 83w21'53 5:33:28
Barrettsville 42 8 34N20'23 84w09'25 5:36:38
Barrons Lane 96 8 32N22'00 83w59'47 5:35:59
Barrow Heights 7 20 33N59'30 83w44'40 5:34:59
Bartlett 96 8 32N20'08 84w06'55 5:36:28
Bartletts Ferry 72 17 32N29 84w57 5:39:48
Bartonwoods 44 7 33N46 84w21 5:37:24
Bartow 8 8 34N07'17 84w44'56 5:39:00
Bartow 81 20 32N52'43 82w28'26 5:29:54
Barwick 136 20 30N53'24 83w44'27 5:34:58
Bascom 124 20 32N50'25 81w40'06 5:26:40
Bass Crossroads 141 8 33N08'33 84w54'05 5:39:36
Bastonville 62 20 33N18'28 82w31'54 5:30:08
Batesville 28 8 34N09'48 84w22'42 5:37:31
Batesville 68 20 34N44'53 83w36'41 5:34:27
Bath 121 20 33N20'19 82w10'36 5:28:42
Battery Point 25 20 32N03 81w04 5:24:16
Battle Hill Haven 60 7 33N45'21 84w26'46 5:37:47
Battle Park 106 17 32N26 84w57 5:39:48
Baughs Crossroads 141 8 32N54'57 85w01'12 5:40:05
Baughville 130 8 32N39'10 84w40'14 5:38:41
Baxley 1 20 31N46'41 82w20'55 5:29:24
Baxter 144 8 34N44'19 84w04'29 5:36:18
Bay 35 20 31N11'30 83w55'36 5:35:42
Bayvale 121 20 33N26'54 82w03'07 5:28:12
Bayview 91 20 31N43 81w45 5:27:00
Beach 148 20 31N26'23 82w30'14 5:30:01
Beachton 65 8 30N43'37 84w08'23 5:36:34
Beacon Heights 104 20 33N34'41 83w28'39 5:33:55
Beall 130 8 32N44'16 84w33'12 5:38:13
Beall Springs 149 20 33N18'32 82w42'59 5:30:52
Beallwood 106 17 32N29 84w57 5:39:48
Beards Creek 91 20 31N51'58 81w53'08 5:27:33
Beasley Gap 28 8 34N20'56 84w35'50 5:38:23
Beatrice 128 8 32N03 84w48 5:39:12
Beatum 27 8 34N34'45 85w08'57 5:40:36
Beaulieu 25 20 31N55'57 81w06'47 5:24:27
Beaumount 23 8 34N50'17 85w11'31 5:40:46
Beaverdale 155 8 34N55'16 84w50'33 5:39:22
Beech Cove Vista 139 20 34N56'02 83w44'44 5:34:59
Beech Hill 158 20 32N49'20 83w00'33 5:32:02
Beechwood 133 8 32N32'56 84w04'10 5:36:17
Beechwood Hills 29 3 33N59 83w23 5:33:32
Belair 121 20 33N26'31 82w07'17 5:28:29
Belfast 15 20 31N49'27 81w17'31 5:25:10
Bell 52 20 33N59'18 82w46'35 5:31:06
Belleview 130 8 32N46'19 84w33'28 5:38:14
Belle Vista 63 20 31N21'27 81w44'15 5:26:57
Bellevue 17 20 32N55'49 82w01'16 5:28:05
Bells Ferry Landing 103 20 31N58'52 82w33'13 5:30:13
Bells Landing 17 20 33N02'26 81w48'15 5:27:13
Bellton 69 1 34N23 83w40 5:34:40
Bellview 100 8 31N09'26 84w35'58 5:38:24
Bellville 30 8 31N35'41 84w53'58 5:39:36
Bellville 54 20 32N09'08 81w58'28 5:27:54
Bellville Bluff 95 20 31N32 81w31 5:26:04
Bellville Point 95 20 31N31'52 81w21'58 5:25:28
Belmont 44 20 33N43'24 84w09'59 5:36:40
Belmont 69 1 34N11'08 83w45'41 5:35:03
Belmont Hills 33 8 33N53 84w32 5:38:08
Belvedere Park 44 20 33N45'17 84w16'03 5:37:04
Belvedere Plaza 44 20 33N44 84w16 5:37:04
Belvins Acres 23 8 35N01 85w11 5:40:44
Bemiss 92 20 30N55'59 83w14'29 5:32:58
Bender 87 20 32N33 83w04 5:32:16
Benedict 63 20 31N12'57 81w30'06 5:26:00
Benedict 115 8 33N58'26 85w15'26 5:41:02
Benefit 154 20 34N33'27 83w43'48 5:34:55
Benevolence 120 8 31N52'54 84w44'05 5:38:56
Ben Hill 60 10 33N41'26 84w30'41 5:38:03
Bennetts Landing 82 20 32N48'07 82w02'37 5:28:10
Benning Hills 106 17 32N24'43 84w56'07 5:39:44
Benning Park 106 17 32N25'56 84w56'26 5:39:46
Bentley Place 146 8 34N57 85w18 5:41:12
Benton 57 8 34N15'43 85w17'54 5:41:12
Berginville 98 8 32N17'04 84w35'22 5:38:21
Berkeley Lake 67 20 33N59 84w11 5:36:44
Berkshire Woods 25 20 32N00 81w05 5:24:20
Berlin 35 20 31N04'05 83w37'26 5:34:30
Bermuda 19 8 31N29'20 84w29'30 5:37:58
Berner 102 8 33N09'17 83w49'43 5:35:19
Berry Hill 57 8 34N19 85w14 5:40:56
Berry Landing 51 20 32N25'16 81w12'15 5:24:49
Berryton 27 8 34N27'00 85w23'11 5:41:33
Berryville 51 20 32N25'42 81w15'32 5:25:02
Berwin 57 8 34N17'46 85w07'04 5:40:28
Berzelia 36 20 33N24'24 82w15'06 5:29:00
Bethany 4 8 31N18'27 84w35'59 5:38:24
Bethany 43 8 30N51'26 84w43'27 5:38:54
Bethel 1 20 31N49'23 82w08'54 5:28:36
Bethel 30 8 31N40'46 84w57'33 5:39:50
Bethel 34 20 31N27'58 82w52'54 5:31:32
Bethel 51 20 32N24'49 81w21'18 5:25:25
Bethel 79 20 33N20'41 83w45'16 5:35:01
Bethel 142 20 31N39'30 83w34'00 5:34:16
Bethesda 25 20 31N57'47 81w05'39 5:24:23
Bethesda 66 20 33N38'03 83w00'35 5:32:02
Bethesda 67 20 33N55'17 84w05'03 5:36:20
Bethlehem 7 20 33N55'55 83w42'50 5:34:51
Bethlehem 144 8 34N54'07 84w04'39 5:36:19
Betts 99 8 32N57'06 84w35'15 5:38:21
Between 147 20 33N49 83w48 5:35:12
Beulah 70 20 33N08'33 83w03'21 5:32:13
Beulah 90 20 33N55'57 82w37'44 5:30:31
Beulah 110 8 33N52'43 85w00'15 5:40:01
Beulah Heights 60 7 33N44'06 84w21'03 5:37:24
Beverly 52 20 34N05'44 82w43'44 5:30:55
Beverly Heights 106 17 32N29 84w57 5:39:48
Beverly Hills 146 8 34N58'09 85w16'16 5:41:05
Bexton 38 8 33N15'48 84w44'12 5:38:57
Bibb City 106 17 32N29'44 84w59'31 5:39:58
Bibb Mills 102 8 33N02 83w56 5:35:44
Bickley 148 20 31N24'19 82w36'11 5:30:25
Big Canoe 112 8 34N28 84w26 5:37:44
Big Creek 58 8 34N06'59 84w10'31 5:36:42
Big Creek 61 8 34N44'06 84w16'51 5:37:07
Big Oak 13 20 31N03'36 81w56'11 5:27:45
Big Slough Boat Landing 43 8 30N55'53 84w33'17 5:38:13
Big Springs 141 8 32N59'42 84w54'18 5:39:37
Billarp 48 8 33N41 84w46 5:39:04
Bill Davis 17 20 32N58 81w45 5:27:00
Billyville 20 20 30N55'31 81w40'57 5:26:44
Binghams Chapel 72 8 32N39'41 84w57'26 5:39:50
Birdie 126 8 33N19'11 84w20'40 5:37:23
Birds 51 20 32N20'26 81w14'39 5:24:59
Birdsong Crossroads 145 8 32N48'31 84w15'26 5:37:02
Birdsville 82 20 32N52'17 82w04'41 5:28:19
Birmingham 60 7 34N09'59 84w19'59 5:37:20
Bishop 108 20 33N49'09 83w26'20 5:33:45
Biss 111 8 32N35'11 83w50'45 5:35:23
Blackjack 38 8 33N16'10 84w39'00 5:38:36
Blackshear 113 20 31N18'21 82w14'32 5:28:58
Blackshear Place 69 1 34N13'15 83w51'40 5:35:27
Blacks Landing 124 20 32N52'31 81w28'14 5:25:53
Blacksville 75 20 33N26'01 84w08'56 5:36:36
Blackville 140 20 32N28'55 82w35'54 5:30:24
Blackwell 33 8 34N01'13 84w31'43 5:38:07
Blackwell 79 20 33N21'59 83w40'53 5:34:44
Blackwells 33 8 33N59'41 84w31'05 5:38:04
Blackwood 64 8 34N27'23 84w54'10 5:39:37
Bladen 63 20 31N14'40 81w42'08 5:26:49
Blaine 112 8 34N30'38 84w33'25 5:38:14
Blairsville 144 8 34N52'34 83w57'30 5:35:50
Blair Village 60 7 33N39'27 84w22'13 5:37:29
Blakely 49 8 31N22'39 84w56'03 5:39:44
Blandford 51 20 32N16'42 81w15'48 5:25:03
Bland Villa 40 20 31N58 83w47 5:35:08
Blandy 5 20 33N04'31 83w18'19 5:33:13
Blanton 92 20 30N49'48 83w07'08 5:32:29
Blantons Mill 126 8 33N13'14 84w26'04 5:37:44
Blaylock Mill 146 8 34N40'01 85w18'00 5:41:12
Blevins Acre 23 8 34N57'11 85w11'14 5:40:45
Blitch 16 20 32N35'22 81w46'57 5:27:08
Blitchton 15 20 32N11'49 81w26'17 5:25:45
Bloodtown 105 8 34N37'34 84w41'20 5:38:45
Bloomingdale 25 20 32N07'56 81w17'57 5:25:12
Blount 102 8 33N10'49 83w57'34 5:35:50
Blountsville 84 20 33N06'35 83w28'55 5:33:56
Blowing Spring 146 8 34N58'27 85w20'15 5:41:21
Blue Ridge 55 8 34N51'50 84w19'27 5:37:18
Blue Springs 14 20 30N47'23 83w27'24 5:33:50
Blue Springs 124 20 32N37'59 81w25'18 5:25:41
Blue Springs Landing 124 20 32N37'43 81w25'09 5:25:41
Bluffton 30 8 31N31'22 84w52'04 5:39:28
Blun 53 20 32N42'04 82w17'50 5:29:11
Blundale 53 20 32N44'53 82w23'29 5:29:34
Blythe 121 20 33N17'33 82w12'06 5:28:48
Bobo 64 8 34N28'36 84w40'31 5:38:42
Bogart 108 20 33N56'57 83w32'05 5:34:08
Boggy 24 20 30N31'19 82w09'06 5:28:36
Bohanon Crossroad 38 8 33N16'14 84w52'04 5:39:28
Bold Springs 147 20 33N54'03 83w48'06 5:35:12
Bolen 148 20 31N23'23 82w27'52 5:29:51
Bolingbroke 102 8 32N56'57 83w48'12 5:35:13
Bolivar 8 8 34N22'11 84w42'42 5:38:51
Bolton 60 7 33N48'51 84w27'12 5:37:49
Bona Bella 25 20 32N00'50 81w03'58 5:24:16
Bon Acre Landing 26 16 32N17'09 84w55'18 5:39:41
Bonair 121 20 33N31'20 82w02'54 5:28:12
Bonaire 76 20 32N32'37 83w35'46 5:34:23
Bond 97 20 34N13'47 83w11'15 5:32:45
Bonds 143 20 32N48 83w30 5:34:00
Boneville 44 20 33N26'00 82w26'20 5:29:45
Bonneyman 113 1 31N14'26 82w19'11 5:29:17
Boozeville 57 8 34N10'17 85w10'31 5:40:42
Boston 136 20 30N47'30 83w47'24 5:35:10
Bostwick 104 20 33N44'14 83w30'52 5:34:03
Bottsford 129 8 31N58'50 84w26'17 5:37:45
Bowdon 22 8 33N32'16 85w15'12 5:41:01
Bowdon Junction 22 8 33N39'47 85w08'49 5:40:35
Bowen Mill 16 20 32N14'27 81w49'50 5:27:19
Bowens Mill 9 20 31N50'33 83w12'34 5:32:50
Bowersville 73 20 34N22'22 83w04'58 5:32:20
Bowman 52 20 34N12'17 83w01'51 5:32:07
Box Ankle 102 8 33N07'00 83w58'24 5:35:54
Box Springs 130 8 32N31'57 84w39'40 5:38:39
Boyd Highlands 23 8 34N58'52 85w10'53 5:40:44
Boydville 65 8 30N52'53 84w21'19 5:37:25
Boydville 127 20 34N32'24 83w21'59 5:33:28
Boykin 100 8 31N06'16 84w41'12 5:38:45
Boynton 23 8 34N55'24 85w11'27 5:40:46
Boynton Ridge 23 8 34N55 85w12 5:40:48
Boys Estate 63 20 31N18'59 81w28'22 5:25:53
Bradley 84 20 33N03'14 83w33'31 5:34:14
Braganza 148 20 31N07'05 82w15'11 5:29:01
Branchville 101 8 31N09'01 84w18'56 5:37:16
Brantley 98 8 32N22'13 84w33'44 5:38:15
Braselton 78 20 34N06'33 83w45'46 5:35:03
Braswell 104 20 33N45'36 83w33'15 5:34:13
Braswell 110 8 33N59'21 84w57'47 5:39:51
Bremen 71 8 33N43'16 85w08'44 5:40:35
Brent 102 8 32N58'54 84w00'37 5:36:02
Brentwood 47 11 31N34 84w11 5:36:44
Brentwood 151 20 31N41'40 82w06'49 5:28:27
Brest 101 20 31N23 84w10 5:36:40
Brewton 87 20 32N35'37 82w47'53 5:31:12
Briarcliff 44 20 33N50 84w19 5:37:16
Briarwood 60 7 33N41 84w27 5:37:48
Briar Wood Estates 33 8 33N56 84w32 5:38:08
Brice 57 8 34N06'34 85w09'12 5:40:37
Brickston 95 20 31N36'44 81w29'25 5:25:58
Brick Store 107 20 33N39 83w43 5:34:52
Bridgeboro 159 20 31N24'05 83w58'30 5:35:54
Bridgeman Heights 11 25 32N50 83w37 5:34:28
Bridges Crossroad 135 8 31N45'57 84w21'14 5:37:25
Bridgetown 34 20 31N26'11 83w03'24 5:32:14
Brier Creek Landing 124 20 32N46'55 81w25'54 5:25:44
Briggston 92 20 30N43'17 83w18'21 5:33:13
Brighams Landing 17 20 33N05'50 81w39'10 5:26:37
Brighton 137 20 31N27 83w31 5:34:04
Brinson 43 8 30N58'36 84w44'16 5:38:57
Brinson Crossing 81 20 33N12'37 82w21'36 5:29:26
Brisbon 15 20 31N55'01 81w18'23 5:25:14
Bristol 113 20 31N26'54 82w12'53 5:28:52
Broad 157 20 33N56'49 82w42'24 5:30:50
Broadfield 63 20 31N18'25 81w27'43 5:25:51
Broadhurst 151 20 31N28'26 81w55'03 5:27:40
Brobston 63 20 31N15'36 81w33'29 5:26:14
Brockton 78 20 34N07'12 83w29'41 5:33:59
Bronco 146 8 34N39'36 85w20'34 5:41:22
Bronwood 135 8 31N49'51 84w21'52 5:37:27
Brooker 80 20 31N44'50 82w41'08 5:30:45
Brookfield 137 20 31N25'06 83w23'28 5:33:34
Brookhaven 11 25 32N49 83w41 5:34:44
Brookhaven 44 6 33N51'30 84w20'25 5:37:22
Brookhaven 106 17 32N27'02 84w56'40 5:39:47
Brooklet 16 20 32N22'46 81w39'48 5:26:39
Brooklyn 128 8 32N10'25 84w42'31 5:38:50
Brookman 63 20 31N11'27 81w39'33 5:26:38
Brooks 31 8 33N17'27 84w27'34 5:37:50
Brooks 158 20 32N54'35 83w22'54 5:33:32
Brooks Crossing 29 3 33N59 83w23 5:33:32
Brook Springs 150 20 32N58'14 82w56'46 5:31:47
Brooksville 120 8 31N52'24 84w39'24 5:38:38
Brookton 69 1 34N26'42 83w46'46 5:35:07
Brookvale Estates 23 8 34N58'17 85w14'05 5:40:56
Brookwood 58 8 34N05'42 84w10'36 5:36:42
Brookwood 87 20 32N33 82w54 5:31:36
Brotherton Field 146 8 34N54'52 85w16'04 5:41:04
Broughton 79 20 33N30'19 83w39'12 5:34:37
Browndale 116 20 32N18'18 83w35'15 5:34:21
Brown Ford 50 20 30N39'32 82w50'09 5:31:21
Browning 156 20 31N55'02 83w16'21 5:33:05
Brown Mill 55 8 34N55'26 84w14'47 5:36:59
Browns 5 20 33N05 83w14 5:32:56
Brownsand 130 8 32N34'23 84w26'32 5:37:46
Browns Crossing 5 20 33N02'50 83w21'27 5:33:26
Brownsville 110 8 33N47'58 84w45'27 5:39:02
Browntown 13 20 31N20'14 81w46'55 5:27:08
Brownwood 104 20 33N33'41 83w33'21 5:34:13
Broxton 34 20 31N37'30 82w53'13 5:31:33
Brunswick 63 23 31N08'59 81w29'30 5:25:58
Bryan Mill 55 8 34N53'52 84w10'21 5:36:41
Bryant 45 20 32N21'13 83w08'05 5:32:32
Buchanan 71 8 33N48'09 85w11'19 5:40:45
Buckhead 25 20 31N47'37 81w07'47 5:24:31
Buckhead 60 7 33N50'22 84w22'46 5:37:31
Buckhead 104 20 33N34'06 83w21'45 5:33:27
Buckhorn Tavern 93 8 34N31'23 84w02'15 5:36:09
Budapest 71 8 33N42'54 85w13'05 5:40:52
Buena Vista 98 8 32N19'08 84w31'02 5:38:04
Buffington 28 8 34N14'29 84w25'15 5:37:41
Buford 67 20 34N07'14 84w00'16 5:36:01
Bugaboo Landing 148 20 30N46'44 82w14'04 5:28:56

Bullard 143 20 32N37'49 83W29'50 5:33:59
Bullard Landing 143 20 32N37'32 83W32'33 5:34:10
Bullhead Bluff 20 20 30N53'07 81W50'45 5:27:23
Bull Hole Landing 82 20 32N48'36 82W07'11 5:28:29
Bulloch Crossroads 99 8 32N52'23 84W37'57 5:38:32
Bumphead 123 8 32N11'21 84W12'13 5:36:49
Bunker Hill 144 8 34N50'22 84W03'04 5:36:12
Burket Ferry Landing 134 20 31N52'10 82W45'15 5:31:01
Burnett 61 8 34N49'25 84W24'26 5:37:38
Burnett 151 20 31N39'12 81W59'42 5:27:59
Burney Hill 37 20 31N09'58 83W31'43 5:34:07
Burning Bush 23 8 34N53'55 85W12'53 5:40:52
Burnside 25 20 31N56'38 81W06'39 5:24:27
Burnt Fort 20 20 30N56'43 81W53'54 5:27:36
Burrell Ford 119 20 34N58'08 83W07'12 5:32:29
Burris Crossroads 28 8 34N19'48 84W29'15 5:37:57
Burroughs 25 20 31N58'29 81W14'52 5:24:59
Burtons Ferry Landing 124 20 32N56'12 81W30'15 5:26:01
Burtsboro 93 8 34N28'42 84W05'23 5:36:22
Burwell 22 8 33N34'45 85W12'23 5:40:50
Bushnell 34 20 31N33'36 82W57'36 5:31:50
Bussey Crossroads 99 8 32N52'37 84W38'39 5:38:35
Butler 47 11 31N34 84W11 5:36:44
Butler 133 8 32N33'25 84W14'18 5:36:57
Butts 82 20 32N43'33 82W01'35 5:28:06
Buxton Landing 17 20 33N06'54 81W41'48 5:26:47
Byers Crossroads 22 8 33N31'39 84W51'44 5:39:27
Byne Crossroads 88 20 31N41'51 84W13'10 5:36:53
Byromville 46 20 32N12'07 83W54'31 5:35:38
Byron 111 8 32N39'13 83W45'35 5:35:02
Cabaniss 102 8 33N09'12 83W52'46 5:35:31
Cabin Bluff 20 20 30N53'21 81W31'00 5:26:04
Cadley 149 20 33N32'01 82W39'35 5:30:38
Cadwell 87 20 32N20'22 83W02'32 5:32:10
Cagle 112 8 34N23'48 84W25'59 5:37:44
Cairo 65 8 30N52'38 84W12'05 5:36:48
Caleb 67 20 33N46'57 84W00'44 5:36:03
Calhoun 64 8 34N30'09 84W57'04 5:39:48
Callaway Mill 155 8 34N49'59 85W03'37 5:40:14
Calvary 65 8 30N43'36 84W20'59 5:37:24
Calvin 79 20 33N22'47 83W42'15 5:34:49
Camak 149 20 33N27'12 82W38'46 5:30:35
Camelot 29 3 33N59 83W23 5:33:32
Camelot 31 8 33N31 84W21 5:37:24
Cameron 124 20 32N33'28 81W40'26 5:26:42
Camilla 101 20 31N13'52 84W12'38 5:36:51
Campania 36 20 33N24'38 82W17'25 5:29:10
Campbellton 60 10 33N39'01 84W40'10 5:38:41
Campton 147 20 33N52'18 83W43'13 5:34:53
Canal Lake 144 8 34N53'43 83W59'53 5:36:00
Candler 69 1 34N12'37 83W46'53 5:35:08
Cane Creek 93 8 34N34'19 84W00'43 5:36:03
Cannon Crossing 146 8 34N57'13 85W16'42 5:41:07
Cannon Gate 36 20 33N29 82W02 5:28:08
Cannonville 141 8 32N57'59 85W06'19 5:40:25
Canon 73 20 34N20'46 83W06'36 5:32:26
Canoochee 53 20 32N40'19 82W10'45 5:28:43
Canoochee 54 20 32N13 81W55 5:27:40
Canton 28 8 34N14'12 84W29'27 5:37:58
Capel 65 8 30N58'23 84W11'55 5:36:48
Capitol Hill 60 7 33N45 84W23 5:37:32
Captolo 124 20 32N37'31 81W35'50 5:26:23
Carbondale 155 8 34N38'40 84W59'38 5:39:59
Carey 66 20 33N32'51 83W16'09 5:33:05
Carey Park 60 7 33N47'01 84W28'19 5:37:53
Carl 7 20 34N00'20 83W48'41 5:35:15
Carlan 6 20 34N20'03 83W24'02 5:33:36
Carlton 97 20 34N02'35 83W02'02 5:32:08
Carmel 99 8 33N06 84W35 5:38:20
Carmichael Crossroads 28 8 34N12'44 84W23'48 5:37:35
Carnegie 120 8 31N38'34 84W46'45 5:39:07
Carnes Creek 127 20 34N32'14 83W19'43 5:33:19
Carnesville 59 20 34N22'11 83W14'07 5:32:56
Carnigan 95 20 31N26'03 81W23'39 5:25:35
Carns Mill 112 8 34N31'33 84W30'31 5:38:02
Caroline Park 106 17 32N30'52 84W58'37 5:39:54
Carrolls 99 8 33N00'44 84W33'58 5:38:16
Carrollton 22 8 33N35 85W05 5:40:20
Carrols Crossing 67 20 34N04'57 84W02'48 5:36:11
Carrs 70 20 33N17 82W58 5:31:52
Carsonville 133 8 32N42'47 84W17'23 5:37:10
Cartecay 61 8 34N37'35 84W23'01 5:37:32
Carter Acres 106 17 32N24'29 84W57'59 5:39:52
Carters 105 8 34N36'32 84W41'35 5:38:46
Carters Bight Landing 1 20 31N51'41 82W06'56 5:28:28
Carters Grove 131 20 33N41'36 82W56'36 5:31:46
Cartersville 8 8 34N09'54 84W48'00 5:39:12
Caruso 126 8 33N19'47 84W17'14 5:37:09
Caruthers Mill 147 20 33N52'48 83W35'35 5:34:22
Carver Village 25 20 32N04'14 81W07'14 5:24:29
Cary 12 20 32N30'53 83W18'18 5:33:13
Cascade Heights 60 10 33N43'20 84W27'48 5:37:51
Cascade Hills 106 17 32N30'33 84W59'03 5:39:56
Casey Springs 105 8 34N40 84W51 5:39:24
Caseyville 115 8 33N54'47 85W17'53 5:41:12
Cash 64 8 34N29'23 84W49'07 5:39:16
Cass 8 8 34N13 84W51 5:39:24
Cassandra 146 8 34N47'03 85W23'53 5:41:36
Cassville 8 8 34N14'41 84W51'08 5:39:25
Cataula 72 8 32N39'19 84W52'07 5:39:28
Catlett 146 8 34N44'58 85W11'33 5:40:46
Catlin 87 20 32N30'40 82W49'19 5:31:17
Catoosa Springs 23 8 34N55 85W03 5:40:12
Cave Spring 57 8 34N14'31 85W20'09 5:41:21
Cecil 37 20 31N02'43 83W23'32 5:33:34
Cedar Bluff Landing 51 20 32N33'36 81W19'42 5:25:19
Cedar Cliff 139 20 34N58'50 83W47'36 5:35:10
Cedar Creek Park 29 3 33N59 83W23 5:33:32
Cedar Crossing 138 20 32N01'32 82W24'29 5:29:38
Cedar Grove 25 20 31N57'37 81W09'13 5:24:37
Cedar Grove 44 20 33N39'38 84W18'08 5:37:13
Cedar Grove 60 10 33N37'36 84W41'15 5:38:45
Cedar Grove 87 20 32N15'00 82W52'56 5:31:32
Cedar Grove 146 8 34N43'00 85W25'34 5:41:42
Cedar Hammock 25 20 31N58'29 81W05'01 5:24:20
Cedarpark 134 20 31N58'31 82W50'15 5:31:21
Cedar Point 95 20 31N29'50 81W20'58 5:25:24
Cedar Rock 149 20 33N30'09 82W36'56 5:30:28
Cedar Springs 49 8 31N11'00 85W02'17 5:40:09
Cedartown 115 8 34N03'13 85W15'18 5:41:01
Cedar Valley 155 8 34N51'15 84W54'40 5:39:39
Celeste 157 20 33N46'58 82W50'42 5:31:23
Cenchat 146 8 34N54'46 85W20'45 5:41:23
Centennial 104 20 33N35'09 83W36'45 5:34:27
Center 8 8 34N11'59 84W44'26 5:38:58
Center 78 20 34N03'21 83W25'10 5:33:41
Center 138 20 32N07'40 82W23'49 5:29:35
Center Hill 35 20 31N08'20 83W53'53 5:35:36
Center Hill 60 7 33N46'29 84W28'19 5:37:53
Center Point 22 8 33N44 85W02 5:40:08
Centerpoint 152 8 31N59'06 84W31'49 5:38:07
Center Post 146 8 34N36'29 85W21'11 5:41:25
Centerville 49 8 31N16'29 84W53'46 5:39:35
Centerville 52 20 34N12'23 82W53'30 5:31:34
Centerville 67 20 33N48'13 84W02'35 5:36:10
Centerville 76 8 32N37'48 83W41'23 5:34:46
Centerville 130 8 32N41'41 84W27'20 5:37:49
Centerville 157 20 33N48'04 82W55'22 5:31:41
Centralhatchee 74 8 33N22'08 85W06'13 5:40:25
Central Junction 25 20 32N05'24 81W09'52 5:24:39
Central Toombs 138 20 32N01 82W21 5:29:24
Century 88 20 31N40'38 84W09'46 5:36:39
Ceylon 20 20 30N57'41 81W39'03 5:26:36
Chalybeate Springs 99 8 32N51'24 84W34'49 5:38:19
Chamberlain 146 8 34N42 85W22 5:41:28
Chamblee 44 20 33N53'31 84W17'56 5:37:12
Chamblis Mill 129 18 32N08'11 84W03'54 5:36:16
Chambliss 135 8 31N55'10 84W32'39 5:38:11
Champion Crossroad 72 8 32N51'04 84W52'13 5:39:29
Chapel Hill 48 8 33N41'10 84W42'57 5:38:52
Chappel 85 8 33N10'40 84W05'51 5:36:23
Chappells Mill 87 20 32N39'41 83W03'10 5:32:13
Charing 133 8 32N27'41 84W21'42 5:37:27
Charles 128 8 32N07'36 84W49'44 5:39:19
Charles 138 20 32N13'18 82W25'44 5:29:43
Charlotteville 103 20 32N00'40 82W31'21 5:30:05
Chaserville 37 20 31N13'01 83W21'27 5:33:26
Chastain 136 20 31N01'57 83W55'50 5:35:43
Chatham City 25 20 32N06'01 81W09'16 5:24:37
Chatham Villas 25 20 32N06 81W09 5:24:36
Chatsworth 105 8 34N45'57 84W46'12 5:39:05
Chattahoochee 60 8 33N48'30 84W28'55 5:37:56
Chattahoochee Plantation 33 8 33N56 84W32 5:38:08
Chattanooga Valley 146 8 34N57 85W19 5:41:16
Chatterton 34 20 31N30'41 82W44'11 5:30:57
Chattoogaville 27 8 34N20'42 85W26'49 5:41:47
Chauncey 45 20 32N06'16 83W03'53 5:32:16
Checkero 119 20 34N53 83W24 5:33:36
Chelsea 27 8 34N31'24 85W26'25 5:41:46
Chennault 90 20 33N54'27 82W36'08 5:30:25
Cherokee 28 8 34N10'05 84W34'15 5:38:17
Cherrying 61 8 34N46'49 84W23'27 5:37:34
Cherrylog 61 8 34N47 84W24 5:37:36
Chestatee 58 8 34N17'39 83W59'59 5:36:00
Chester 45 20 32N23'37 83W09'11 5:32:37
Chestnutflat 146 8 34N42 85W22 5:41:28
Chestnut Gap 55 8 34N53'44 84W24'48 5:37:39
Chestnut Mountain 69 1 34N10'21 83W50'17 5:35:21
Chickamauga 146 8 34N52'16 85W17'27 5:41:10
Chickasawhatchee 135 8 31N42'04 84W22'29 5:37:30
Chicopee 69 1 34N15'12 83W50'37 5:35:22
Childs Place 128 8 32N07'41 84W58'58 5:39:56
China Hill 134 20 31N51'10 83W05'04 5:32:20
Chipley 72 8 32N50 85W00 5:40:00
Chippewa Terrace 25 20 31N59'55 81W06'59 5:24:28
Choestoe 144 8 34N47'43 83W53'14 5:35:33
Chokee 88 20 31N53'37 84W02'59 5:36:12
Chopped Oak 61 8 34N47'03 84W27'41 5:37:51
Christopher 26 8 32N19'37 84W43'50 5:38:55
Chubbtown 57 8 34N21'15 85W16'57 5:41:08
Chula 137 20 31N32'58 83W32'51 5:34:11
Church Hill 98 8 32N09'47 84W32'44 5:38:11
Cinderella Hills 23 8 34N57'16 85W11'54 5:40:48
Cisco 105 8 34N57'04 84W44'11 5:38:57
City Village 106 17 32N29'19 84W59'17 5:39:57
Civic Center 60 7 33N47 84W23 5:37:32
Clabber Landing 87 20 32N19'48 82W44'49 5:30:59
Clarkdale 33 8 33N49'51 84W38'59 5:38:36
Clarke Dale 29 3 33N59 83W23 5:33:32
Clarkesville 68 20 34N36'45 83W31'30 5:34:06
Clarking 24 20 30N30'58 82W07'06 5:28:28
Clarks Bluff 20 20 30N56'22 81W48'42 5:27:15
Clarksboro 78 3 34N02'28 83W29'54 5:34:00
Clarks Landing 20 20 30N55'48 81W54'20 5:27:37
Clarks Mill 135 8 31N38'39 84W27'59 5:37:52
Clarkston 44 20 33N48'34 84W14'23 5:36:58
Claxton 54 20 32N09'41 81W54'15 5:27:37
Clayfields 158 20 32N51'13 83W15'05 5:33:00
Clay Hill 90 20 33N39'52 82W26'40 5:29:47
Clayton 119 20 34N52'41 83W24'04 5:33:36
Clearview 25 20 32N05'28 81W07'14 5:24:29
Clearview 96 8 32N14'51 84W04'28 5:36:18
Clearwater Springs 114 15 33N00'55 84W19'29 5:37:18
Clem 22 8 33N31'41 85W00'48 5:40:03
Clermont 69 1 34N28'40 83W46'25 5:35:06
Cleveland 154 20 34N35'49 83W45'48 5:35:03
Cliftondale 60 10 33N38 84W26 5:37:44
Climax 43 8 30N52'33 84W25'53 5:37:44
Clinchfield 76 20 32N24'48 83W38'18 5:34:33
Clinton 84 20 32N59'55 83W33'20 5:34:13
Clito 16 20 32N30'44 81W45'14 5:27:01
Clopine 111 20 32N29'02 83W48'07 5:35:12
Cloudland 27 8 34N30'57 85W29'40 5:41:59
Clover 56 8 33N22'26 84W34'36 5:38:18
Cloverdale 41 8 34N43'16 85W31'41 5:42:07
Clubview Heights 106 17 32N29'43 84W57'12 5:39:49
Clyattville 92 20 30N41'29 83W18'55 5:33:16
Clyo 51 20 32N29'02 81W16'02 5:25:04
Coal Mountain 58 8 34N16'17 84W06'03 5:36:24
Cobb 129 20 31N57'31 83W59'19 5:35:57
Cobbham 94 20 33N34'07 82W25'58 5:29:44
Cobbham Crossroads 94 20 33N33'10 82W26'14 5:29:45
Cobbtown 132 20 32N16'49 82W08'20 5:28:33
Cobbville 134 20 31N55'04 82W58'57 5:31:56
Cochran 12 20 32N23'12 83W21'17 5:33:25
Cody Landing 26 16 32N16'36 84W54'34 5:39:38
Coffee 3 20 31N30'27 82W18'42 5:29:15
Coffee Bluff 25 20 31N56'12 81W09'12 5:24:37
Coffinton 128 8 32N00'35 85W01'21 5:40:05
Cogdell 32 20 31N09'53 82W43'05 5:30:52
Cohentown 157 20 33N47'38 82W43'07 5:30:52
Cohutta 155 8 34N57'34 84W57'10 5:39:49
Cohutta Springs 105 8 34N53'16 84W43'38 5:38:55
Colbert 97 20 34N02'16 83W12'46 5:32:51
Coldbrook 51 20 32N14'15 81W14'31 5:24:58
Coldwater Creek 52 20 34N12 82W50 5:31:20
Cole City 41 8 34N57'07 85W34'05 5:42:16
Coleman 120 8 31N40'22 84W53'21 5:39:33
Colemans Lake 53 20 32N49'15 82W16'31 5:29:06
Colerain 20 20 30N49'58 81W54'03 5:27:36
Colesburg 20 20 30N55'24 81W42'59 5:26:52
Coles Crossing 55 8 34N56'45 84W15'01 5:37:00
Coley 12 20 32N25'41 83W23'20 5:33:33
Colfax 16 20 32N26 81W47 5:27:08
Colima 64 8 34N32'35 84W42'26 5:38:50
College 111 8 32N33 83W53 5:35:32
Collegeboro 16 20 32N25 81W47 5:27:08
College Heights 47 11 31N34 84W11 5:36:44
College Park 60 7 33N39'12 84W26'58 5:37:48
Collier 102 8 33N02'49 84W01'01 5:36:04
Collins 132 20 32N10'52 82W06'33 5:28:26
Collinsville 44 6 33N42'08 84W05'19 5:36:21
Colomokee 49 8 31N27'37 84W52'46 5:39:31
Colon 32 20 30N45'21 82W37'20 5:30:29
Colonial Oaks 25 20 32N00 81W05 5:24:20
Colonial Place 47 11 31N34 84W10 5:36:40
Colquitt 100 8 31N10'16 84W44'00 5:38:56
Colson Store 68 20 34N34 83W33 5:34:12
Columbia Heights 36 20 33N29 82W02 5:28:08
Columbus 106 17 32N27'39 84W59'16 5:39:57
Colwell 55 8 34N53'49 84W28'21 5:37:53
Comer 97 20 34N03'49 83W07'32 5:32:30
Commerce 78 20 34N12'14 83W27'26 5:33:50
Commissary Hill 19 8 31N26'59 84W39'58 5:38:40
Comolli 52 20 34N08 82W50 5:31:20
Concord 114 8 33N05'28 84W26'15 5:37:45
Concord 123 8 32N19'52 84W20'33 5:37:22
Concord 129 8 32N08'24 84W22'53 5:37:32
Condor 87 20 32N32'33 82W50'12 5:31:21
Coney 40 20 31N58 83W47 5:35:08
Coniston 105 8 34N38'16 84W42'33 5:38:50
Conley 31 20 33N38'41 84W19'33 5:37:18
Constitution 44 7 33N41'20 84W20'33 5:37:22
Conyers 122 20 33N40'03 84W01'04 5:36:04
Cooks Crossing 60 10 33N37'36 84W28'28 5:37:54
Cooksville 74 8 33N14'21 84W59'52 5:39:59
Cooktown 100 8 31N12'25 84W33'37 5:38:14
Cooktown 158 20 32N38'11 83W08'00 5:32:32
Coolidge 136 20 31N00'40 83W51'59 5:35:28
Cool Springs 35 20 31N13'44 83W36'06 5:34:24

Cooneys Landing 24
20 30N49'38 81W56'05 5:27:44
Cooper Branch Landing 8
8 34N10'13 84W43'43 5:38:55
Cooper Creek 55 8 34N44'36 84W08'22 5:36:33
Cooper Heights 146
8 34N48'26 85W23'21 5:41:33
Coopers 5 20 32N58'42 83W17'07 5:33:08
Coopervile 124
20 32N35'26 81W42'15 5:26:49
Coosa 57 8 34N15'16 85W21'16 5:41:25
Copeland 45 20 31N59'17 83W14'22 5:32:57
Copeland Crossing 23
8 34N52'01 85W04'53 5:40:20
Corbin 8 8 34N13'12 84W41'44 5:38:47
Cordele 40 20 31N57'48 83W46'57 5:35:08
Cordrays Mill 19
8 31N35'20 84W33'48 5:38:15
Corea 100 8 31N14'03 84W43'38 5:38:55
Corinth 74 8 33N13'48 84W56'44 5:39:47
Cork 18 20 33N13'00 83W51'48 5:35:27
Cornelia 68 20 34N30'41 83W31'38 5:34:07
Cottle 10 20 31N12'05 83W18'53 5:33:16
Cotton 101 20 31N09'41 84W04'01 5:36:16
Cotton Hill 30 8 31N43'51 84W58'01 5:39:52
Cottons Crossroads 141
8 32N52'41 85W07'04 5:40:28
Council 32 20 30N36'50 82W30'40 5:30:03
Country Club Hills 121
20 33N29'25 82W01'00 5:28:04
County Line 7 20 33N59 83W43 5:34:52
County Line 128 8 32N03 84W48 5:39:12
Court Square 87
20 32N33 82W54 5:31:36
Covena 53 20 32N29'49 82W26'33 5:29:46
Coverdale 142 20 31N37'41 83W43'09 5:34:53
Covington 107 20 33N35'48 83W51'37 5:35:26
Covington Mills 107
20 33N40 83W52 5:35:28
Cox 95 20 31N27'18 81W33'49 5:26:15
Coxs Crossing 31
8 33N38'46 84W23'27 5:37:34
Crabapple 60 8 34N05'24 84W20'19 5:37:21
Crandall 105 8 34N52'00 84W44'44 5:38:59
Crane Eater 64 8 34N31'30 84W52'21 5:39:29
Cravey 134 20 32N01 83W04 5:32:16
Crawford 109 20 33N52'58 83W09'17 5:32:37
Crawfordville 131
20 33N33'14 82W53'46 5:31:35
Crawley 148 20 31N23'09 82W27'13 5:29:49
Credit Hill 95 20 31N30'41 81W30'02 5:26:00
Creek Island 89
20 31N49'14 81W39'25 5:26:38
Crescent 95 20 31N30'33 81W22'11 5:25:29
Crest 145 8 32N55'55 84W26'41 5:37:47
Crest Hill Gardens 25
20 32N00 81W05 5:24:20
Crestview 4 8 31N19'58 84W37'10 5:38:29
Crestwell Heights 11
25 32N51 83W41 5:34:44
Crestwood 159 20 31N28'03 83W59'15 5:35:57
Crews Crossing 148
20 31N11'08 82W35'43 5:30:23
Cromers 59 20 34N16'33 83W15'56 5:33:04
Crosland 35 20 31N18'15 83W38'35 5:34:34
Cross Keys 11 25 32N51'07 83W35'17 5:34:21
Cross Plains 22 8 33N33'33 84W58'27 5:39:54
Crossroads 8 8 34N07'21 85W00'51 5:40:03
Crossroads 49 8 31N20'15 84W44'25 5:38:58
Cross Roads 73 20 34N23'17 83W01'13 5:32:05
Crossroads 89 20 31N44'50 81W27'48 5:25:51
Cross Roads 110 8 34N00'36 84W45'20 5:39:01
Crossroads 118 8 31N50'03 84W59'28 5:39:58
Crowders Crossing 99
8 32N56'07 84W43'53 5:38:56
Crowville 110 8 34N02'41 84W46'33 5:39:06
Croxton Crossroads 129
20 31N57'31 84W19'29 5:37:18
Cruse 67 20 34N00 84W10 5:36:40
Crystal Springs 11
25 32N50 83W37 5:34:28
Crystal Springs 57
8 34N24'43 85W13'37 5:40:54
Crystal Valley 106
16 32N30'57 84W53'08 5:39:33
Cuba 49 8 31N17'32 84W51'51 5:39:27
Cuffietown 159 20 31N44'08 83W48'59 5:35:16
Culloden 102 8 32N51'47 84W05'38 5:36:23
Culverton 70 20 33N18'30 82W53'43 5:31:35
Cumming 58 8 34N12'26 84W08'25 5:36:34
Cumslo 84 25 32N56'50 83W31'00 5:34:04
Cunningham 57 8 34N09'54 85W15'48 5:41:03
Cunningham Corner 81
20 32N50'43 82W21'31 5:29:26
Cunningham Crossroads 130
8 32N49'21 84W34'13 5:38:17
Curry Hill 90 20 33N50'35 82W31'50 5:30:07
Curryville 64 8 34N26'37 85W04'44 5:40:19
Curtis 55 8 34N55'32 84W20'09 5:37:21
Cusseta 26 8 32N18'19 84W46'22 5:39:05
Custer Road Terrace 106
17 32N23'21 84W56'30 5:39:46
Custer Terrace 106
17 32N26 84W57 5:39:48
Cutcane 55 8 34N56'11 84W14'14 5:36:57
Cuthbert 120 8 31N46'16 84W47'22 5:39:09
Cutoff 96 8 32N16'35 84W03'14 5:36:13
Cutting 32 20 31N00'52 82W48'13 5:31:13
Cypress Mills 63
20 31N11'25 81W28'11 5:25:53
Cypress Siding 24
20 30N57'56 82W06'55 5:28:28
Cyrene 43 8 30N57'45 84W41'32 5:38:46
Dacula 67 20 33N59'19 83W53'53 5:35:36
Daffin Heights 25
20 32N01'42 81W04'52 5:24:19
Dahlonega 93 8 34N31'57 83W59'06 5:35:56
Daisy 54 20 32N09'06 81W50'05 5:27:20
Dakota 142 20 31N46'33 83W41'36 5:34:46
Dallas 110 8 33N55'25 84W50'27 5:39:22
Dallondale 23 8 34N57'48 85W14'56 5:41:00
Dalton 155 19 34N46'11 84W58'13 5:39:53
Damascus 49 8 31N17'56 84W43'08 5:38:53
Damascus 64 8 34N33'00 84W56'09 5:39:45
Dames Ferry 102
20 33N01 83W44 5:34:56
Danburg 157 20 33N52'06 82W39'08 5:30:37
Daniel 15 20 31N54'49 81W21'52 5:25:27
Daniel Landing 17
20 33N06'22 81W40'16 5:26:41
Daniels 54 20 32N04'52 81W58'49 5:27:55
Daniel Springs 66
20 33N38'58 82W58'30 5:31:54
Danielsville 97
20 34N07'27 83W13'17 5:32:53
Danville 143 20 32N36'20 83W14'44 5:32:59
Darien 95 20 31N22'12 81W26'03 5:25:44
Dasha Landing 51
20 32N18'29 81W10'52 5:24:43
Dasher 92 20 30N44'50 83W13'15 5:32:53
David 62 20 33N13 82W28 5:29:52
Davis 1 20 31N53'54 82W15'24 5:29:02
Davis Academy 6
20 34N16 83W25 5:33:40
Davis Boat Landing 24
20 30N47'09 82W09'03 5:28:36
Davisboro 150 20 32N58'44 82W36'29 5:30:26
Davis Crossroads 33
8 33N58'36 84W41'24 5:38:46
Davis Crossroads 146
8 34N45'19 85W22'05 5:41:28
Davis Landing 1
20 31N54'55 82W14'55 5:29:00
Davis Mill 159 20 31N45'31 83W55'11 5:35:41
Davis Park 125 8 31N01'50 84W52'31 5:39:30
Dawesville 136 20 30N55'20 84W00'33 5:36:02
Dawnville 155 8 34N49'09 84W52'45 5:39:31
Dawson 135 8 31N46'24 84W26'48 5:37:47
Dawsonville 42 8 34N25'16 84W07'09 5:36:29
Days Crossroads 30
8 31N43'18 85W02'39 5:40:11
Deans Crossing 54
20 32N05'33 81W54'19 5:27:37
Dearing 44 20 33N24'47 82W23'07 5:29:32
Decatur 44 7 33N46'29 84W17'47 5:37:11
Dedrich 158 20 32N51'09 83W13'46 5:32:55
Deenwood 148 20 31N14 82W23 5:29:32
Deepstep 150 20 33N01'05 82W58'09 5:31:53
Deerwood Park 44
20 33N44 84W16 5:37:04
Delhi 157 20 33N54'49 82W40'27 5:30:42
Dellwood 53 20 32N40'22 82W23'01 5:29:32
Delmar 92 20 30N53'07 83W08'16 5:32:33
Delowe 60 7 33N41 84W27 5:37:48
Delray 145 15 32N57'07 84W18'05 5:37:12
Delux 143 20 32N29'43 83W29'14 5:33:57
Demorest 68 20 34N33'54 83W32'43 5:34:11
Denmark 16 20 32N17'04 81W43'27 5:26:54
Dennis 5 20 33N12'51 83W20'33 5:33:22
Dennis 105 8 34N42'07 84W42'32 5:38:50
Denton 80 20 31N43'21 82W41'38 5:30:47
Denver 74 8 33N11'29 85W10'28 5:40:42
DeSoto 129 20 31N57'19 84W03'44 5:36:15
De Soto Park 57 8 34N12 85W13 5:40:52
Desser 125 8 30N53'10 84W51'46 5:39:27
Devereux 70 20 33N13'19 83W04'25 5:32:18
Devils Den 60 8 33N34'27 84W50'50 5:39:23
Dewberry 69 1 34N18 83W49 5:35:16
Dewberry 146 8 34N57 85W18 5:41:12
Dewey Crossroads 8
8 34N19'47 84W47'31 5:39:10
DeWitt 101 20 31N25'11 84W08'24 5:36:34
Dewy Rose 52 20 34N10'11 82W57'11 5:31:49
Dexter 87 20 32N25'56 83W03'41 5:32:15
Dial 55 8 34N45'35 84W13'01 5:36:52
Dialtown 107 20 33N38'50 83W51'48 5:35:27
Diamond 61 8 34N40'27 84W16'34 5:37:06
Diamond Hill 97
20 34N03'48 83W16'41 5:33:07
Diamond Landing 87
20 32N23'29 82W46'53 5:31:08
Dickerson Mill 119
20 34N56'16 83W26'34 5:33:46
Dickey 19 8 31N33'25 84W39'37 5:38:38
Dicks Hill 68 20 34N35'00 83W25'35 5:33:42
Dickson 104 20 33N34'15 83W36'25 5:34:26
Digbey 31 8 33N15'27 84W29'22 5:37:57
Dillard 119 20 34N58'12 83W23'14 5:33:33
Dillon 136 20 30N53'58 83W53'33 5:35:34
Dingler Crossroads 22
8 33N32'40 84W56'05 5:39:44
Dinglewood 106 17 32N28'07 84W58'14 5:39:53
District Path 143
20 32N36'46 83W22'45 5:33:31
Divide 110 8 33N58'21 84W57'44 5:39:51
Dixie 14 20 30N47'08 83W39'52 5:34:39
Dixie 107 20 33N34'24 83W46'13 5:35:05
Dixie Union 148
20 31N20'21 82W27'48 5:29:51
Dixon Crossroads 68
20 34N37'31 83W29'51 5:33:59
Dobbins Air Force Base 33
8 33N56 84W32 5:38:08
Dock Junction 63
20 31N12 81W30 5:26:00
Doctortown 151 20 31N39'12 81W49'46 5:27:19
Dodge High 45 20 32N13'49 83W13'45 5:32:55
Dodges Lake Landing 134
20 31N52'31 83W10'32 5:32:42
Doerun 35 20 31N19'10 83W55'02 5:35:40
Dog Crossing 145
15 32N58'53 84W15'41 5:37:03
Doles 159 20 31N41'57 83W53'07 5:35:32
Donald 91 20 31N49'17 81W51'01 5:27:24
Donalsonville 125
8 31N02'25 84W52'45 5:39:31
Donegal 16 20 32N33'48 81W43'27 5:26:54
Donovan 83 20 32N46'16 82W42'47 5:30:51
Doogan 105 8 34N57 84W44 5:38:56
Dooling 46 20 32N13'49 83W55'41 5:35:43
Doraville 44 20 33N53'53 84W17'00 5:37:08
Dorchester 89 20 31N47'43 81W24'19 5:25:37
Dorsey 104 20 33N36'19 83W33'10 5:34:13
Dosaga 47 11 31N33'40 84W06'50 5:36:27
Dosia 137 20 31N27 83W31 5:34:04
Dot 22 8 33N32 85W15 5:41:00
Double Branches 90
20 33N45'07 82W19'59 5:29:20
Doublegate 47 11 31N34 84W11 5:36:44
Double Run 156 20 31N51'29 83W33'30 5:34:14
Dougherty 42 8 34N22'56 84W03'54 5:36:16
Douglas 34 20 31N30'31 82W51'00 5:31:24
Douglass Crossroads 49
8 31N18'12 84W40'24 5:38:42
Douglasville 48 8 33N45'05 84W44'52 5:38:59
Douglasville 49 8 31N21'35 84W40'13 5:38:41
Dove Creek 52 20 34N04'47 82W56'32 5:31:46
Dover 124 20 32N34'37 81W42'55 5:26:52
Dover Bluff 20 20 31N01'01 81W31'38 5:26:07
Doverel 135 8 31N42'05 84W31'20 5:38:05
Downs 150 20 33N03'58 82W40'25 5:30:42
Downtown 60 7 33N45 84W20 5:37:20
Dows Landing 16
20 32N32'17 81W39'19 5:26:37
Doyle 98 8 32N17'03 84W26'38 5:37:47
Draketown 71 8 33N49'34 85W02'39 5:40:11
Draneville 98 8 32N12'38 84W29'14 5:37:57
Drayton 46 20 32N04'26 83W57'20 5:35:49
Dresden 38 8 33N21'05 84W55'07 5:39:40
Drew 58 8 34N12'30 84W13'11 5:36:53
Drexel 104 20 33N38 83W37 5:34:28
Drone 17 20 33N03'19 82W09'32 5:28:38
Druid Hills 44 7 33N46'49 84W20'10 5:37:21
Drum Point Landing 89
20 31N41'01 81W16'27 5:25:06
Dry Branch 82 20 32N55 81W57 5:27:48
Dry Branch 143 20 32N48'02 83W29'55 5:34:00
Dry Pond 78 20 34N11'29 83W34'30 5:34:18
Dublin 87 20 32N32'25 82W54'14 5:31:37
Dubois 45 20 32N18'12 83W16'24 5:33:06
Ducker 47 11 31N31'34 84W21'58 5:37:28
Ducktown 58 8 34N14'38 84W14'58 5:37:00
Dudley 87 20 32N32'32 83W04'14 5:32:17
Due West 33 8 33N56 84W32 5:38:08
Duffee 101 20 31N14 84W13 5:36:52
Dugdown 71 8 33N54'00 85W15'18 5:41:01
Duluth 67 20 34N00'10 84W08'41 5:36:35
Dumas 152 8 32N02'22 84W29'29 5:37:58
Dunaire 44 20 33N44 84W16 5:37:04
Dunaway Gardens 38
8 33N28'42 84W49'09 5:39:17
Duncan Park 23 8 35N01 85W14 5:40:56
Duncanville 65 8 30N44 84W08 5:36:32
Dungeness 20 20 30N44'53 81W28'03 5:25:52
Dunlap 109 20 33N57'12 83W15'13 5:33:01
Dunn 55 8 34N56'37 84W27'36 5:37:50
Dunn Store 105 8 34N53 84W45 5:39:00
Dunwoody 44 20 33N56'46 84W20'05 5:37:20
DuPont 32 20 30N59'18 82W52'18 5:31:29
Durand 99 8 32N55'01 84W46'26 5:39:06
Durden 14 20 30N47'30 83W28'25 5:33:54
Durdenville 53 20 32N32'11 82W11'37 5:28:46
Durham 146 8 34N51'29 85W25'57 5:41:44
Durham Town 66 20 33N39'42 83W01'57 5:32:08
Dyas 102 8 32N51'58 83W59'40 5:35:59
Dye 52 20 34N12 83W02 5:32:08
Dyes Crossroad 17
20 33N12'38 82W08'46 5:28:35
Dyke 61 8 34N35'59 84W24'42 5:37:39
Eagle Cliff 146 8 34N55'42 85W21'10 5:41:25
Eagle Grove 73 20 34N17'46 83W00'25 5:32:02
Eagle Pond 88 20 31N51'29 84W13'53 5:36:56
Earls Ford 119 20 34N52'46 83W13'43 5:32:55
Eason 136 20 30N48'39 83W50'58 5:35:24
Eason Bluff 1 20 31N53'59 82W10'55 5:28:44
East Albany 47 11 31N34'32 84W06'21 5:36:25
Eastanollee 127
20 34N31'13 83W15'20 5:33:01
East Armuchee 146
8 34N37'35 85W07'49 5:40:31
East Atlanta 44 7 33N44'24 84W20'42 5:37:23
East Boynton 23 8 34N55'32 85W10'20 5:40:41
East Crisp 40 20 31N57'24 83W40'47 5:34:43
East Dougherty 159
20 31N31'27 83W59'22 5:35:57
East Dublin 87 20 32N32'53 82W52'19 5:31:29
East Edgewood 106
17 32N28'58 84W55'07 5:39:40
East Ellijay 61 8 34N41'02 84W28'22 5:37:53
East Griffin 126
8 33N14'37 84W13'44 5:36:55
East Highlands 106
17 32N28'44 84W58'19 5:39:53
East Juliette 84
20 33N06'31 83W47'33 5:35:10
East Lake 44 20 33N45'09 84W18'16 5:37:13
Eastland Heights 44
7 33N43'08 84W19'48 5:37:19
Eastman 45 20 32N11'51 83W10'40 5:32:43
Eastman Mills 45
20 32N12 83W11 5:32:44
East Marietta 33
8 33N56 84W32 5:38:08
East Meadow 29 3 33N59 83W23 5:33:32
East Moultrie 35
20 31N11 83W48 5:35:12
East Newnan 38 8 33N21'02 84W46'36 5:39:06
East Point 60 7 33N40'46 84W26'22 5:37:45
East River 86 20 31N01 83W00 5:32:00
East Thomaston 145
8 32N53'22 84W18'56 5:37:16
East Trion 27 8 34N32'47 85W17'30 5:41:10
Eastville 108 20 33N52'39 83W30'18 5:34:01
East Warrenton 131
20 33N24'24 82W38'24 5:30:34
Eastwood 44 7 33N44 84W20 5:37:20
Eastwood Apartments 11
25 32N49 83W41 5:34:44
Eatonton 117 20 33N19'36 83W23'19 5:33:33
Ebenezer 147 20 33N42'40 83W37'19 5:34:29
Ebenezer Landing 51
20 32N22'43 81W10'57 5:24:44
Ebernezer 147 20 33N39 83W43 5:34:52
Ebo Landing 63 20 31N11'17 81W23'14 5:25:33
Echeconnee 111 8 32N41'06 83W42'02 5:34:48
Echota 64 8 34N31 84W55 5:39:40
Eden 51 20 32N10'25 81W23'27 5:25:34
Edgars 158 20 32N50'42 83W12'45 5:32:51
Edgehill 62 20 33N09'08 82W37'28 5:30:30

Edgemere 25 20 32N02'21 81W05'16 5:24:21
Edgewater Park 25
20 32N00 81W05 5:24:20
Edgewood 36 20 33N29 82W02 5:28:08
Edgewood 44 7 33N45'42 84W20'29 5:37:22
Edgewood 106 17 32N29'28 84W55'30 5:39:42
Edgewood Crossroads 131
20 33N36'47 82W52'39 5:31:31
Edison 19 8 31N33'29 84W44'18 5:38:57
Edith 32 20 30N40'42 82W33'05 5:30:12
Edman 99 8 33N02'11 84W33'52 5:38:15
Edna 54 20 32N13'52 81W49'51 5:27:19
Eelbeck 26 8 32N26'30 84W45'10 5:39:01
Egypt 51 20 32N27'42 81W28'27 5:25:54
Eightmile Still 32
20 31N04'05 82W52'49 5:31:31
Elberta 76 20 32N39'33 83W37'08 5:34:29
Elberton 52 20 34N06'40 82W52'02 5:31:28
Elder 108 20 33N46'05 83W20'50 5:33:23
Elders 61 8 34N41'51 84W34'26 5:38:18
Elders Mill 38 8 33N16'28 84W37'44 5:38:31
Eldora 15 20 32N07 81W29 5:25:56
Eldorado 137 20 31N21'32 83W29'10 5:33:57
Eldorendo 43 8 31N02'38 84W39'07 5:38:36
Eleanor Village 47
11 31N34 84W11 5:36:44
Elery 74 8 33N21'19 85W08'02 5:40:32
Elim 91 20 31N47'41 81W40'29 5:26:42
Elizabeth 33 8 33N58'34 84W32'51 5:38:11
Elko 76 20 32N19'51 83W42'23 5:34:50
Ellabell 15 20 32N07'24 81W29'09 5:25:57
Ella Gap 61 8 34N38'31 84W29'57 5:38:00
Ellaville 123 8 32N14'17 84W18'33 5:37:14
Ellenton 35 20 31N10'33 83W35'15 5:34:21
Ellenwood 31 20 33N36'36 84W17'17 5:37:09
Ellerbeetown 145
8 32N54'36 84W27'25 5:37:50
Ellerslie 72 8 32N37'53 84W48'05 5:39:12
Ellijay 61 8 34N41'41 84W28'56 5:37:56
Elliotts Bluff 20
20 30N50'44 81W33'42 5:26:15
Ellisons Landing 17
20 33N05'35 81W38'46 5:26:35
Ellis Plantation 81
20 33N06'34 82W20'19 5:29:21
Ellwood 121 20 33N18'15 82W07'46 5:28:31
Elmodel 4 8 31N20'44 84W28'21 5:37:53
Elmview 98 8 32N18'40 84W33'47 5:38:15
Elmwood 87 20 32N33 82W54 5:31:36
Elpino 65 8 30N59'49 84W13'53 5:36:56
Elrod Mill 55 8 34N52'01 84W17'49 5:37:11
Elza 132 20 32N05 82W07 5:28:28
Ematia Island 79
20 33N13 83W40 5:34:40
Embry 110 8 33N55 84W50 5:39:20
Embry Hills 44 20 33N53 84W18 5:37:12
Emerich 46 20 32N17'00 83W47'38 5:35:11
Emerson 8 8 34N07'37 84W45'20 5:39:01
Emerson 14 20 30N46'33 83W37'55 5:34:32
Emerson Park 148
20 31N11'19 82W23'52 5:29:35
Emit 16 20 32N20'37 81W44'24 5:26:58
Emma 42 8 34N30'28 84W13'27 5:36:54
Emmalane 82 20 32N45'35 81W59'54 5:28:00
Emory University 44
7 33N47 84W21 5:37:24
Empire 45 20 32N20'25 83W17'47 5:33:11
Empress 14 20 30N40'17 83W33'57 5:34:16
Eneck Landing 124
20 32N36'16 81W23'53 5:25:36
Englewood 106 17 32N27'23 84W54'49 5:39:39
English Eddy 138
20 31N58'09 82W21'24 5:29:26
Enigma 10 20 31N24'46 83W19'45 5:33:19
Ennis 150 20 32N54'38 82W58'56 5:31:56
Enon Grove 74 8 33N20'23 85W00'57 5:40:04
Enterprise 100 8 31N07'22 84W49'33 5:39:18
Enterprise 109 20 33N55'34 82W58'12 5:31:53
Ephesus 74 8 33N24'25 85W15'16 5:41:01
Epworth 55 8 34N57'02 84W23'06 5:37:32
Erastus 6 20 34N15'09 83W20'28 5:33:22
Erick 153 20 32N07'23 82W49'54 5:31:20
Ernest 32 20 30N46'44 82W39'37 5:30:38
Esmond 126 8 33N15'56 84W20'00 5:37:20
Esom Hill 115 8 33N56'56 85W23'16 5:41:33
Estelle 146 8 34N44'49 85W20'28 5:41:22
Ethridge 52 20 34N06'15 82W55'12 5:31:41
Ethridge 84 20 33N08'04 83W28'06 5:33:52
Etna 115 8 34N00'27 85W23'44 5:41:35
Eton 105 8 34N49'30 84W45'48 5:39:03
Eudora 79 20 33N25 83W43 5:34:52
Euharlee 8 8 34N08'41 84W55'59 5:39:44
Eulonia 95 20 31N31'59 81W25'38 5:25:43
Evans 36 20 33N32'01 82W07'51 5:28:31
Evans Landing 124
20 32N32'40 81W40'01 5:26:40
Evansville 141 8 33N03'58 85W13'27 5:40:54
Evelyn 63 20 31N18'53 81W28'18 5:25:53
Everett 63 20 31N23'25 81W38'20 5:26:33
Everett 136 20 30N42'14 83W48'16 5:35:13
Everett Springs 57
8 34N29'41 85W06'50 5:40:27
Evermay 99 8 33N06 84W35 5:38:20
Excelsior 21 20 32N18'48 81W57'58 5:27:52
Excelsior 137 20 31N24'16 83W36'29 5:34:26
Exley 51 20 32N14'44 81W13'45 5:24:55
Experiment 126 8 33N15'55 84W16'54 5:37:08
Faceville 43 8 30N45'11 84W38'24 5:38:34
Faceville Landing 43
8 30N47'18 84W40'00 5:38:40
Fagan 111 8 32N31'11 83W51'49 5:35:27
Fain 144 8 34N49'28 83W52'17 5:35:29
Fairburn 60 10 33N34'01 84W34'52 5:38:19
Fairchild 125 8 30N49'28 84W54'24 5:39:38
Fairfax 148 20 31N15'37 82W36'28 5:30:26
Fairfield 25 20 32N01'57 81W05'27 5:24:22
Fairhope 95 20 31N32'14 81W23'20 5:25:33
Fairlawn Acres 23
8 34N56'46 85W15'14 5:41:01
Fairmount 64 8 34N26'10 84W42'00 5:38:48
Fair Oaks 33 8 33N54'59 84W32'41 5:38:11
Fairplay 48 8 33N37'24 84W51'36 5:39:26
Fairplay 104 20 33N41'16 83W34'59 5:34:20
Fairview 59 20 34N24'37 83W09'54 5:32:40
Fairview 68 20 34N36'04 83W36'49 5:34:27
Fairview 146 8 34N56'44 85W17'04 5:41:08
Fairway Oaks 25
20 32N01'11 81W05'46 5:24:23
Fairyland 146 8 34N53 85W24 5:41:36
Falling Rocks 1
20 31N56'24 82W22'24 5:29:30
Fancy Bluff 63 20 31N08'23 81W33'30 5:26:14
Fancy Hall 15 20 31N46'07 81W14'42 5:24:59
Fantasy Hills 146
8 34N56'45 85W19'51 5:41:19
Fargo 32 20 30N41'06 82W33'43 5:30:15
Farmdale 124 20 32N41'58 81W36'37 5:26:26
Farmers High 22 8 33N31'57 85W11'18 5:40:45
Farmersville 27 8 34N29'10 85W13'51 5:40:55
Farmington 108 20 33N46'34 83W25'25 5:33:42
Farmville 64 8 34N26'54 84W50'40 5:39:23
Farrar 79 20 33N27'46 83W38'03 5:34:32
Fashion 105 8 34N46 84W48 5:39:12
Faulkner 112 8 34N20 84W23 5:37:32
Fayetteville 56 8 33N26'55 84W27'18 5:37:49
Federal 47 11 31N35 84W10 5:36:40
Federal Annex 60
7 33N45 84W20 5:37:20
Federal Reserve 60
7 33N45 84W23 5:37:32
Felton 71 8 33N53'17 85W13'25 5:40:54
Fence 67 20 34N01 83W49 5:35:16
Fender 137 20 31N22 83W29 5:33:56
Fendig 13 20 31N20'24 81W50'26 5:27:22
Fernwood 25 20 32N01'55 81W03'52 5:24:15
Ferrell Crossroads 49
8 31N29'03 84W54'58 5:39:40
Ferry Lake 137 20 31N28'02 83W28'23 5:33:54
Ferry Landing 24
20 30N46'58 82W01'29 5:28:06
Ficklin 157 20 33N38'03 82W46'46 5:31:07
Fickling Mill 133
8 32N39'14 84W10'40 5:36:43
Ficklings Mill 133
8 32N33 84W14 5:36:56
Fidelle 64 8 34N36'15 84W49'14 5:39:17
Fields Crossroads 60
7 34N06'52 84W18'48 5:37:15
Fields Landing 28
8 34N11'49 84W34'26 5:38:18
Fife 60 10 33N32'05 84W32'44 5:38:11
Fighting Pine 127
20 34N33'53 83W14'44 5:32:59
Fincherville 18
20 33N24'33 83W57'12 5:35:49
Findlay 46 20 32N09'14 83W46'18 5:35:05
Finleyson 116 20 32N07'47 83W30'03 5:34:00
Fish 115 8 33N59'55 85W08'27 5:40:34
Fish Creek 115 8 34N00'36 85W07'54 5:40:32
Fishtrap Cut Landing 87
20 32N28'14 82W51'28 5:31:26
Fitzgerald 9 20 31N42'53 83W15'10 5:33:01
Fitzgerald Cotton Mill 9
20 31N43 83W15 5:33:00
Fitzpatrick 143
20 32N44'55 83W26'15 5:33:45
Five Forks 8 8 34N08'38 84W58'41 5:39:55
Five Forks 67 20 33N53'11 84W03'36 5:36:14
Five Forks 136 20 30N52'38 83W47'54 5:35:12
Fivemile Still 32
20 31N05'15 82W48'18 5:31:13
Five Points 6 20 34N14'28 83W23'26 5:33:34
Five Points 22 8 33N40'00 84W57'10 5:39:49
Five Points 45 20 32N04'23 83W10'53 5:32:44
Five Points 47 11 31N34'29 84W05'35 5:36:22
Five Points 60 7 33N45'15 84W23'23 5:37:34
Five Points 62 20 33N17'15 82W39'41 5:30:39
Five Points 84 20 33N01'10 83W39'26 5:34:38
Five Points 85 8 33N07'30 84W12'56 5:36:52
Five Points 87 20 32N26'29 83W07'13 5:32:29
Five Points 92 20 30N52'28 83W17'28 5:33:10
Five Points 96 8 32N17'29 83W54'58 5:35:40
Five Points 98 8 32N27'14 84W26'41 5:37:47
Five Points 120 8 31N42'05 84W33'29 5:38:14
Five Points 132
20 31N55'19 82W02'03 5:28:08
Five Points 133 8 32N41'33 84W15'55 5:37:04
Five Points 140
20 32N25'22 82W27'57 5:29:52
Five Points 142
20 31N38'38 83W45'35 5:35:02
Five Points 156
20 32N05'41 83W35'08 5:34:21
Five Springs 155
8 34N42'46 84W58'28 5:39:54
Flat Branch 61 8 34N46'09 84W29'24 5:37:58
Flat Ford 37 20 31N13'16 83W30'14 5:34:01
Flat Ford 77 20 31N40'53 83W27'48 5:33:51
Flatlands 144 8 34N44'05 84W01'24 5:36:06
Flat Rock 117 20 33N14'14 83W19'03 5:33:16
Flat Rock 106 17 32N33'03 84W52'14 5:39:29
Flat Shoals 73 20 34N21'20 82W59'15 5:31:57
Flat Tub Landing 34
20 31N47'15 82W51'28 5:31:26
Flea Hill 20 20 30N47'34 81W50'22 5:27:21
Fleetwood 25 20 32N01'52 81W04'24 5:24:18
Fleming 89 20 31N52'50 81W25'36 5:25:42
Flemington 89 20 31N51'34 81W33'51 5:26:15
Flint 101 20 31N18'59 84W10'45 5:36:43
Flint Hill 107 20 33N40'13 83W51'04 5:35:24
Flint Hill 130 8 32N48 84W42 5:38:48
Flintside 129 20 31N57 84W01 5:36:04
Flintstone 146 8 34N56'30 85W20'37 5:41:22
Flippen 75 20 33N28'59 84W11'15 5:36:45
Floral Hill 157
20 33N50'02 82W37'31 5:30:30
Florence 128 8 32N05'28 85W02'28 5:40:10
Florida Junction 25
20 32N04'13 81W07'47 5:24:31
Flovilla 18 20 33N15'13 83W53'55 5:35:36
Flowery Branch 69
1 34N11'06 83W55'31 5:35:42
Flowery Gap Landing 17
20 33N11'53 81W45'33 5:27:02
Floyd 33 8 33N50'49 84W35'08 5:38:21
Floyd Springs 57
8 34N25'36 85W09'18 5:40:37
Fodie 14 20 30N50'57 83W32'27 5:34:10
Folkston 24 20 30N49'49 82W00'36 5:28:02
Folsom 8 8 34N22'58 84W49'43 5:39:19
Forest Hills 67
20 33N56'21 83W59'34 5:35:58
Forest Hills 121
20 33N28'52 82W02'23 5:28:10
Forest Lake 11 25 32N51 83W41 5:34:44
Forest Park 31 20 33N37'19 84W22'09 5:37:29
Forest Park 47 11 31N34 84W11 5:36:44
Forest River Farms 25
20 32N00 81W05 5:24:20
Forestview 20 20 30N55'36 81W35'35 5:26:22
Forge Mill 55 8 34N53'36 84W14'47 5:36:59
Forrester 88 20 31N38'59 84W09'46 5:36:39
Forrest Hills 25
20 32N01'19 81W04'53 5:24:20
Forsyth 102 8 33N02'03 83W56'18 5:35:45
Fort Barrington Landing 95
20 31N28'49 81W36'57 5:26:28
Fort Benning 26
16 32N21'08 84W58'08 5:39:53
Fort Gaines 30 8 31N36'32 85W02'50 5:40:11
Fort Gordon 121
20 33N25'15 82W09'44 5:28:39
Fort Lamar 97 20 34N14'24 83W16'26 5:33:06
Fort McAllister 15
20 31N53'26 81W11'46 5:24:47
Fort McPherson 60
7 33N42'26 84W26'01 5:37:44
Fort Mudge 13 20 31N03'51 82W11'12 5:28:45
Fort Oglethorpe 23
8 34N56'55 85W15'25 5:41:02
Fort Screven 25
20 32N01'15 80W50'40 5:23:23
Fort Smith 93 8 34N37'47 83W58'23 5:35:54
Fortson 72 8 32N36'25 84W56'14 5:39:45
Fortsonia 52 20 34N00'54 82W46'45 5:31:07
Fort Stewart 89
20 31N52 81W35 5:26:20
Fort Valley 111 8 32N33'13 83W53'15 5:35:33
Fortville 84 20 33N03'12 83W27'27 5:33:50
Foster Hills 23 8 34N58'08 85W10'55 5:40:44
Foster Mills 57 8 34N09'58 85W20'34 5:41:22
Fouche 57 8 34N21'44 85W18'43 5:41:15
Fountainville 96
8 32N17'00 84W09'26 5:36:38
Four Points 47 11 31N33'35 84W08'23 5:36:34
Four Points 82 20 32N40'18 81W59'36 5:27:58
Four Points 96 8 32N19'04 83W59'31 5:35:58
Fouts Mill 48 8 33N38'58 84W46'34 5:39:06
Fowlertown 127 20 34N33'09 83W19'16 5:33:17
Fowlstown 43 8 30N48 84W33 5:38:12
Fowlstown Fowltown 43
8 30N48'09 84W32'50 5:38:11
Franklin 74 8 33N16'39 85W05'53 5:40:24
Franklin Springs 59
20 34N17'05 83W08'40 5:32:35
Franklinton 11 20 32N48'15 83W32'08 5:34:09
Frazers Crossing 63
20 31N17'55 81W34'03 5:26:16
Frazier 12 20 32N20'57 83W18'10 5:33:13
Free Home 28 8 34N14'19 84W17'20 5:37:09
Freeman 49 8 31N21'38 85W03'46 5:40:15
Friendship 39 8 32N40'26 83W51'40 5:35:27
Friendship 70 20 33N04'53 83W01'53 5:32:08
Friendship 115 8 34N11'51 85W17'47 5:41:11
Friendship 129 8 32N09'00 84W25'17 5:37:41
Friendship 139 20 34N57'50 83W47'14 5:35:09
Frolona 74 8 33N19'28 85W14'10 5:40:57
Fruitland 50 20 30N49'24 82W51'18 5:31:25
Fry 55 8 34N59'13 84W23'35 5:37:34
Frying Pan Landing 51
20 32N26'15 81W12'33 5:24:50
Fullerville 22 8 33N44 84W55 5:39:40
Fullwood Springs 115
8 33N55'09 85W18'48 5:41:15
Funkhouser 8 8 34N23'13 84W42'07 5:38:48
Funston 35 20 31N11'59 83W52'25 5:35:30
Furniture 33 8 33N48'17 84W36'39 5:38:27
Furniture City 33
8 33N48 84W37 5:38:28
Gabbettville 141
8 32N56'40 85W08'00 5:40:32
Gaddistown 144 8 34N42'14 84W04'44 5:36:19
Gaffneys Landing 51
20 32N25'45 81W12'23 5:24:50
Gaillard 39 8 32N38'36 84W00'19 5:36:01
Gaines Community 29
3 33N59 83W23 5:33:32
Gainesville 69 1 34N17'52 83W49'27 5:35:18
Galloway 55 8 34N56'09 84W21'19 5:37:25
Galloway Mill 55
8 34N54'05 84W23'06 5:37:32
Galts Ferry Landing 28
8 34N07'51 84W38'16 5:38:33
Garden City 25 20 32N06'51 81W09'15 5:24:37
Garden Lakes 57 8 34N17 85W12 5:40:48
Garden Valley 96
8 32N26'23 84W07'06 5:36:28
Gardi 151 20 31N32'17 81W47'54 5:27:12
Gardner 150 20 32N51'12 82W57'46 5:31:51
Garfield 53 20 32N38'59 82W05'54 5:28:24
Garnersville 30 8 31N45'06 85W00'02 5:40:00
Garretta 87 20 32N27'00 82W56'39 5:31:47
Gary 53 20 32N33'27 82W19'07 5:29:16
Gass 41 8 34N51'49 85W32'57 5:42:12
Gates City 60 7 33N45 84W23 5:37:32
Gatewood 129 18 32N01'23 84W10'33 5:36:42
Gay 99 8 33N05'37 84W34'26 5:38:18
Geneva 130 8 32N34'47 84W33'03 5:38:12
Gentian 106 17 32N30'39 84W55'45 5:39:43
Georgetown 63 20 31N12'49 81W40'26 5:26:42
Georgetown 107 20 33N38 83W52 5:35:28
Georgetown 118 8 31N53'04 85W06'27 5:40:26
Georgia Southern 16
20 32N26 81W47 5:27:08
Georgia Southwestern College 129
18 32N04 84W14 5:36:56
German Village 63
20 31N13'18 81W21'28 5:25:26

Germany 119 20 34N53'45 83w28'00 5:33:52
Gertrude 17 20 32N50'41 82w17'48 5:29:11
Gholston Stand Crossroads 97 20 34N05'34 83w08'45 5:32:35
Gibson 62 20 33N14'00 82w35'44 5:30:23
Gilbert Landing 49 8 31N28'27 85w04'01 5:40:16
Gill 90 20 33N52 82w39 5:30:36
Gillionville 47 8 31N35'13 84w26'00 5:37:44
Gillis Place 128 8 32N10'17 84w58'34 5:39:54
Gillis Springs 140 20 32N27'33 82w29'30 5:29:58
Gillsville 6 20 34N18'28 83w38'01 5:34:32
Gilmore 33 8 33N50'53 84w29'39 5:37:59
Girard 17 20 33N02'25 81w42'44 5:26:51
Glades 69 1 34N25'43 83w43'52 5:34:55
Glades 117 20 33N23 83w26 5:33:44
Gladesville 79 20 33N11'38 83w46'42 5:35:07
Gladys 10 20 31N28'12 83w14'16 5:32:57
Glasgow 136 20 30N48 83w48 5:35:12
Glen Alta 98 8 32N18'24 84w39'05 5:38:36
Glen Arden 106 17 32N28'25 84w55'01 5:39:40
Glencliff 145 8 32N54'27 84w25'30 5:37:42
Glencoe 20 20 31N08'08 81w43'28 5:26:54
Glendale 121 20 33N28 81w59 5:27:56
Glen Haven 44 20 33N44'38 84w13'05 5:36:52
Glenloch 74 8 33N24'33 85w05'10 5:40:21
Glenloch Village 56 8 33N19 84w17 5:37:08
Glenmore 148 20 31N07'25 82w31'48 5:30:07
Glenn 74 8 33N09'15 85w12'11 5:40:49
Glenn Field 146 8 34N54'12 85w15'49 5:41:03
Glenns 106 17 32N31'50 84w57'03 5:39:48
Glennville 132 20 31N56'11 81w55'43 5:27:43
Glenwood 57 8 34N18'44 85w10'20 5:40:41
Glenwood 153 20 32N10'47 82w40'11 5:30:41
Glenwood Hills 44 20 33N44'19 84w17'18 5:37:09
Glory 10 20 31N22'04 83w08'37 5:32:34
Gloster 67 20 33N54'35 84w03'55 5:36:16
Glovers Millpond 62 20 33N08'18 82w34'58 5:30:20
Gloverton 38 8 33N23'57 84w49'47 5:39:19
Glynco 63 20 31N15 81w28 5:25:52
Glynn Camp 63 20 31N12'36 81w34'03 5:26:16
Glynn Haven 63 20 31N11'18 81w22'37 5:25:30
Goat Town 150 20 33N01'07 82w58'52 5:31:55
Gobar Landing 16 20 32N28'03 81w32'31 5:26:10
Gobblers Hill 26 8 32N16'54 84w43'09 5:38:53
Gober 28 8 34N18'20 84w24'26 5:37:38
Godfrey 104 20 33N27'12 83w30'18 5:34:01
Godley Landing 20 20 30N57'36 81w53'31 5:27:34
Godwinsville 45 20 32N08'08 83w07'38 5:32:31
Goffs Mill 120 8 31N42'19 84w41'45 5:38:47
Goggins 85 8 33N04'33 84w05'31 5:36:22
Goldmine 73 20 34N17'26 83w02'46 5:32:11
Goldsboro 12 20 32N28'21 83w13'40 5:32:55
Goldson 133 8 32N33'39 84w15'32 5:37:02
Goloid 124 20 32N41'29 81w40'21 5:26:41
Goodes 60 10 33N31'57 84w43'42 5:38:55
Good Hope 147 20 33N47'05 83w36'33 5:34:26
Goolsby 79 20 33N14'07 83w37'26 5:34:30
Goose Island 61 8 34N47'07 84w24'09 5:37:37
Goose Neck 116 20 32N14'54 83w27'08 5:33:49
Gorday 159 20 31N29 83w53 5:35:32
Gordon 158 20 32N52'55 83w19'57 5:33:20
Gordon Road 60 7 33N44 84w25 5:37:40
Gordon Springs 155 8 34N48 85w01 5:40:04
Gordonston 25 20 32N03'18 81w03'59 5:24:16
Gordy 159 20 31N28'49 83w52'48 5:35:31
Gore 27 8 34N27'66 85w16'09 5:41:05
Goshen 90 20 33N51'49 82w30'29 5:30:02
Goss 52 20 34N09'02 82w55'19 5:31:41
Gough 17 20 33N05'30 82w13'36 5:28:54
Gould Landing 95 20 31N37'19 81w15'45 5:25:03
Graball 90 20 33N55'47 82w33'53 5:30:16
Gracewood 121 20 33N22'21 82w01'56 5:28:08
Grady 115 8 34N01 85w15 5:41:00
Graham 1 20 31N49'53 82w30'09 5:30:01
Grandview 112 8 34N29'44 84w23'38 5:37:35
Grange 81 20 33N00 82w24 5:29:36
Grangerville 159 20 31N29 81w44 5:26:56
Granite Hill 70 20 33N17 82w58 5:31:52
Grantville 38 8 33N14'05 84w50'09 5:39:21
Grassdale 8 8 34N16'22 84w47'13 5:39:09
Gratis 147 20 33N52'57 83w39'48 5:34:39
Graves 135 8 31N46'05 84w31'09 5:38:05
Gray 84 20 33N00'34 83w32'02 5:34:08
Gray Hill 141 8 32N55'29 85w04'56 5:40:20
Graymont 53 20 32N35 82w09 5:28:36
Grays Landing 138 20 31N58'04 82w26'04 5:29:44
Grayson 67 20 33N53'39 83w57'21 5:35:49
Graysville 23 8 34N58'35 85w08'29 5:40:34
Greeley 28 8 34N19 84w33 5:38:12
Greely 28 8 34N23'35 84w38'42 5:38:35
Green Acres 23 8 34N57'51 85w15'11 5:41:01
Green Acres 25 20 32N02'43 81w03'42 5:24:15
Green Acres 29 3 33N55'05 83w20'14 5:33:21
Green Acres Estate 87 20 32N33 82w54 5:31:36
Greenberry Crossroads 84 20 32N57'14 83w26'59 5:33:48
Green Island Hills 106 17 32N32'06 85w00'26 5:40:02
Greenough 101 20 31N18'59 84w06'06 5:36:24
Greensboro 66 20 33N34'32 83w10'57 5:32:44
Greens Crossing 92 20 30N54'59 83w03'26 5:32:14
Greens Cut 17 20 33N10 81w59 5:27:56
Greens Mill 55 8 34N50'32 84w18'00 5:37:12
Greens Mill 130 8 32N46'02 84w34'22 5:38:17
Greenville 20 20 30N48'05 81w50'00 5:27:20
Greenville 99 8 33N01'43 84w42'47 5:38:51
Greenway 53 20 32N34 82w15 5:29:00
Greenway 60 7 34N03'33 84w23'00 5:37:32
Greenwood 75 20 33N23'34 84w10'08 5:36:41
Greenwood 86 20 30N56'55 82w58'27 5:31:54
Greenwood 101 20 31N11'52 84w20'24 5:37:22
Greenwood Forest 32 20 30N56 83w00 5:32:00
Greggs 37 20 31N04'07 83w29'24 5:33:58
Gregory 105 8 34N57'12 84w46'57 5:39:08
Gresham Park 44 7 33N44 84w20 5:37:20
Greshamville 66 20 33N37'35 83w19'26 5:33:18
Gresston 45 20 32N17'10 83w15'09 5:33:01
Greyfield 20 20 30N46'41 81w27'59 5:25:52
Griffin 126 15 33N14'48 84w15'51 5:37:03
Griffins Landing 17 20 33N06'56 81w42'16 5:26:49
Grimball Park 25 20 32N00 81w05 5:24:20
Grimshaw 16 20 32N23'56 81w41'56 5:26:48
Griswold 84 25 32N50 83w37 5:34:28
Griswoldville 84 20 32N52'14 83w29'20 5:33:57
Grizzletown 8 8 34N04 84w40 5:38:40
Grogan 111 8 32N35'07 83w55'32 5:35:42
Grooverville 136 20 30N43'15 83w43'37 5:34:54
Grovania 76 20 32N21'57 83w39'48 5:34:39
Groveland 15 20 32N08'39 81w44'45 5:26:59
Groveland 25 20 32N01'30 81w06'27 5:24:26
Grove Level 78 20 34N15'26 83w29'26 5:33:58
Grove Park 25 20 32N00 81w05 5:24:20
Grove Park 60 7 33N46'24 84w26'44 5:37:47
Grove Park 76 20 32N22'40 83w43'33 5:34:54
Grove Point 25 20 31N57'05 81w12'15 5:24:49
Grovetown 36 20 33N27'01 82w11'54 5:28:48
Grubbs 25 20 32N00'37 81w10'52 5:24:43
Guild 146 8 34N42 85w22 5:41:28
Gum Branch 89 20 31N51'29 81w43'37 5:26:54
Gum Log 144 8 34N53 83w58 5:35:52
Gum Springs 8 8 34N21'37 84w47'12 5:39:09
Gum Stump Landing 20 20 30N48'43 81w53'02 5:27:32
Guysie 3 20 31N32'39 82w31'54 5:30:08
Guyton 51 20 32N20'10 81w23'30 5:25:34
Habersham 68 20 34N35'23 83w33'38 5:34:15
Haddock 84 20 33N01'57 83w25'45 5:33:43
Haddock Landing 80 20 31N49'47 82w48'02 5:31:12
Haddonville 51 20 32N26'04 81w13'49 5:24:55
Hagan 54 20 32N09'21 81w56'02 5:27:44
Hahira 92 20 30N59'28 83w22'22 5:33:29
Halcyondale 124 20 32N32'20 81w35'54 5:26:24
Hales Landing 43 8 30N50'51 84w39'36 5:38:38
Half Moon Landing 80 20 31N57'29 82w28'53 5:29:56
Halfmoon Landing 89 20 31N41'58 81w16'43 5:25:07
Halifax 20 20 30N57'53 81w41'54 5:26:48
Hall Mill 146 8 34N47'00 85w21'21 5:41:25
Halls 8 8 34N18 84w56 5:39:44
Halls Crossing 150 20 33N01'26 82w38'51 5:30:35
Halls Ferry Landing 138 20 31N58'16 82w28'55 5:29:56
Halls Landing 158 20 32N42'14 82w58'02 5:31:52
Hallwood 117 20 33N14'49 83w21'48 5:33:27
Halycon Bluff 25 20 32N04 81w07 5:24:28
Hamer 25 20 32N05'38 81w12'28 5:24:50
Hamilton 72 8 32N45'28 84w52'30 5:39:30
Hamilton Crossroads 94 20 33N33'55 82w29'41 5:29:59
Hammett 39 8 32N39'23 84w01'08 5:36:05
Hampton 75 8 33N23'13 84w16'59 5:37:08
Hancock Landing 17 20 33N09'33 81w45'51 5:27:03
Handy 38 8 33N22'35 84w58'09 5:39:53
Haney 57 8 34N05'04 85w25'12 5:41:41
Hanlin 110 8 33N56'42 84w54'59 5:39:40
Hannah 48 8 33N35'13 84w51'49 5:39:27
Hannahs Mill 145 8 32N55'58 84w20'58 5:37:24
Hannatown 43 8 30N42'38 84w40'13 5:38:41
Hanover 43 8 30N56'33 84w38'56 5:38:36
Hapeville 60 7 33N39'36 84w24'37 5:37:38
Happy Hollow 8 8 34N10'52 84w42'39 5:38:51
Happy Hollow 156 20 31N58 83w36 5:34:24
Happy Landing 13 20 31N09'47 81w51'24 5:27:26
Haralson 141 8 33N13'35 84w34'17 5:38:17
Harbin 67 20 33N56'51 83w51'15 5:35:25
Hard Cash 52 20 34N11'05 82w58'16 5:31:53
Harding 138 20 31N31'39 83w25'45 5:33:43
Hardwick 5 20 33N04'05 83w13'25 5:32:54
Hardys Crossroads 79 20 33N22'51 83w48'58 5:35:16
Harlem 36 22 33N24'52 82w18'46 5:29:15
Harllee 117 20 33N05 83w14 5:32:56
Harlow 87 20 32N29'38 82w58'35 5:31:54
Harmony 28 8 34N14'52 84w24'25 5:37:38
Harmony 117 20 33N27'08 83w21'08 5:33:25
Harmony Church 106 17 32N26 84w57 5:39:48
Harp 56 8 33N24'15 84w26'36 5:37:46
Harrietts Bluff 20 20 30N52'16 81w35'09 5:26:21
Harrington 63 20 31N12'23 81w22'13 5:25:29
Harris 99 8 33N04 84w45 5:39:00
Harrisburg 5 20 33N02'54 83w14'26 5:32:58
Harrisburg 146 8 34N35'28 85w23'23 5:41:34
Harris City 99 8 32N58'05 84w42'46 5:38:51
Harrison 97 20 34N12'50 83w07'28 5:32:30
Harrison 150 20 32N49'34 82w43'31 5:30:54
Harrisons Mill 30 8 31N32'53 84w53'09 5:39:33
Harrisonville 141 8 33N10'33 84w59'19 5:39:57
Harrock Hall 25 20 32N00 81w05 5:24:20
Hartford 116 20 32N17'08 83w26'57 5:33:48
Hartley 111 8 32N34'46 83w54'53 5:35:40
Harts 62 20 33N19'03 82w33'33 5:30:14
Hartsfield 35 20 31N13'00 83w58'34 5:35:54
Hartwell 73 20 34N21'10 82w55'56 5:31:44
Harvest 68 20 34N37'36 83w36'26 5:34:26
Haskins 87 20 32N33 83w04 5:32:16
Haskins Crossing 87 20 32N32'47 83w07'03 5:32:28
Hassler Mill 155 8 34N48'07 85w01'05 5:40:04
Hasslers Mill 105 8 34N48'44 84w41'43 5:38:47
Hastings 31 8 33N26'55 84w19'31 5:37:18
Hasty 148 20 31N15'27 82w34'23 5:30:18
Hatcher 118 8 31N48'53 85w00'49 5:40:03
Hatley 40 20 31N53'57 83w36'48 5:34:27
Hawkins 146 8 34N36'15 85w22'28 5:41:30
Hawkins Crossroads 130 8 32N45'42 84w36'30 5:38:26
Hawkins Shop Landing 24 20 30N48'33 81w57'43 5:27:51
Hawkinstown 4 8 31N15'47 84w27'00 5:37:48
Hawkinsville 116 20 32N17'01 83w28'20 5:33:53
Hayes Crossing 127 20 34N31'52 83w17'36 5:33:10
Hayesville Landing 49 8 31N08'20 85w03'40 5:40:15
Haylow 50 20 30N49'33 82w54'19 5:31:37
Hayner 63 20 31N09'43 81w43'24 5:26:54
Hayneville 76 20 32N23'00 83w37'15 5:34:29
Hayston 107 20 33N31'09 83w46'04 5:35:04
Haysville 146 8 34N52'49 85w21'47 5:41:27
Haywood 148 20 31N21'28 82w25'56 5:29:44
Hazard 150 20 32N52'13 82w53'12 5:31:33
Hazlehurst 20 20 30N54'48 81w50'19 5:27:21
Hazlehurst 80 20 31N52'10 82w35'40 5:30:23
Head River 41 8 34N39'25 85w30'27 5:42:02
Heardmont 52 20 34N06'38 82w41'44 5:30:47
Heard Place 128 8 32N10'06 84w59'25 5:39:58
Heardville 58 8 34N16'50 84w14'10 5:36:57
Hebardville 148 20 31N14'27 82w22'05 5:29:28
Hebron 6 20 34N17'05 83w21'52 5:33:27
Hebron 150 20 32N57'51 82w59'51 5:31:59
Heights 106 17 32N29'20 84w56'58 5:39:48
Helen 154 20 34N42'05 83w43'54 5:34:56
Helena 134 20 32N04'25 82w54'53 5:31:40
Hemp 55 8 34N53'00 84w10'19 5:36:41
Henderson 76 20 32N20'28 83w47'22 5:35:09
Hendersons Landing 124 20 32N32'49 81w40'32 5:26:42
Henderson Still 2 20 31N11'14 82w58'06 5:31:52
Hendricks 145 8 32N56'21 84w28'00 5:37:52
Hentown 49 8 31N16'47 84w50'13 5:39:21
Hephzibah 121 20 33N18'50 82w05'49 5:28:23
Hermitage 57 8 34N19'32 85w03'56 5:40:16
Herndon 82 20 32N49'13 82w07'46 5:28:31
Herndonville 147 20 33N42'40 83w41'59 5:34:48
Herod 135 8 31N41'55 84w26'29 5:37:46
Hiawassee 139 20 34N56'57 83w45'27 5:35:02
Hickman Forks 145 8 32N54'18 84w27'14 5:37:49
Hickory Bluff 20 20 31N05'30 81w34'15 5:26:17
Hickory Flat 6 20 34N23 83w40 5:34:40
Hickory Flat 28 8 34N10'12 84w25'22 5:37:41
Hickory Level 22 8 33N35 85w05 5:40:20
Hickox 13 20 31N09'01 81w59'48 5:27:59
Hicks 96 8 32N28'57 84w06'45 5:36:23
Higdon 55 8 34N53'47 84w26'20 5:37:45
Higdon Mill 61 8 34N49'22 84w24'34 5:37:38
Higgins Mill 102 8 33N07'42 84w00'16 5:36:01
Higgston 103 20 32N12'59 82w28'02 5:29:52
High Falls 102 8 33N10'32 84w01'32 5:36:06
Highland Heights 92 20 30N52'44 83w16'29 5:33:06
Highland Mills 126 8 33N16'40 84w16'58 5:37:08
Highland Park 25 20 32N00'34 81w06'02 5:24:24
Highland Park 106 17 32N29'16 84w56'13 5:39:45
Highland Pines 106 17 32N33'28 84w56'49 5:39:47
High Point 20 20 30N54'54 81w25'21 5:25:41
High Point 107 20 33N31'40 83w51'07 5:35:24
High Point 146 8 34N51'48 85w22'01 5:41:28
High Shoals 108 20 33N49'15 83w30'22 5:34:01
Hightower 58 8 34N18'22 84w12'53 5:36:52
Hill City 64 8 34N35'56 85w00'20 5:40:01
Hillcrest 141 8 33N07'45 85w02'25 5:40:10
Hillman 131 20 33N36'03 82w47'52 5:31:11
Hills 68 20 34N40 83w27 5:33:48
Hillsboro 79 20 33N10'47 83w38'28 5:34:34
Hillsdale 137 20 31N28'03 83w35'57 5:34:24
Hillside Cottages 60 7 33N47'23 84w21'53 5:37:28
Hills Store 17 20 33N01'09 81w36'04 5:26:24
Hilltonia 124 20 32N53'00 81w39'30 5:26:38
Hilton 49 8 31N17'17 85w03'55 5:40:16
Hilyer 141 8 32N58'53 84w59'35 5:39:58
Hinesville 89 20 31N50'48 81w35'46 5:26:23
Hinkles 146 8 34N54'30 85w23'40 5:41:35
Hinson Crossing 148 20 31N10'23 82w39'58 5:30:40
Hinsonton 101 20 31N10'46 84w01'43 5:36:07
Hinton 112 8 34N28'51 84w34'58 5:38:20
Hiram 110 8 33N52'32 84w45'44 5:39:03
Hi Roc Shores 122 20 33N41 84w00 5:36:00
Hix 97 20 34N10'57 83w20'30 5:33:22
Hobby 142 20 31N39'45 83w44'27 5:34:58
Hoboken 13 20 31N10'51 82w08'06 5:28:32
Hogan 109 20 33N49'59 83w02'55 5:32:12

Hogansville 141 8 33N10'23 84w54'54 5:39:40
Hog Mountain 67 20 34N02'58 83w55'45 5:35:43
Holbrook 28 8 34N12'46 84w16'16 5:37:05
Holcomb 112 8 34N24'46 84w16'50 5:37:07
Holland 27 8 34N21'07 85w22'21 5:41:29
Holland Landing 95 20 31N25'59 81w30'30 5:26:02
Hollingsworth 6 20 34N26'19 83w30'30 5:34:02
Hollis 14 20 30N55'21 83w44'21 5:34:57
Hollonville 114 8 33N09'56 84w27'38 5:37:51
Holly Spring 8 8 34N14'05 84w44'18 5:38:57
Holly Springs 28 8 34N10'26 84w30'05 5:38:00
Holly Springs 78 20 34N15 83w34 5:34:16
Hollywood 68 20 34N38'58 83w26'51 5:33:47
Holmes 46 20 32N14'35 83w39'59 5:34:40
Holt 19 8 31N30'14 84w27'13 5:37:49
Holt 77 20 31N35'44 83w09'03 5:32:36
Homeland 24 20 30N51'21 82w01'16 5:28:05
Homer 6 20 34N20'01 83w29'57 5:34:00
Homerville 32 20 31N02'11 82w44'50 5:30:59
Homestead 113 20 31N16'33 82w16'38 5:29:07
Honeygall Landing 63 20 31N20'38 81w32'09 5:26:09
Honora 90 20 33N54'26 82w30'36 5:30:02
Hood 144 8 34N45'49 83w52'27 5:35:30
Hooker 41 8 34N58'44 85w26'02 5:41:44
Hooper 71 8 33N44'18 85w20'15 5:41:21
Hopeful 101 20 31N10'07 84w23'35 5:37:34
Hopeulikit 16 20 32N31'17 81w51'02 5:27:24
Hopewell 20 20 30N58'59 81w45'04 5:27:00
Hopewell 60 8 34N09'10 84w17'08 5:37:09
Hopewell 72 8 32N49'21 84w57'15 5:39:49
Hopkins 148 20 30N58'17 82w25'50 5:29:43
Horns 39 8 32N40'31 84w00'13 5:36:01
Horse Ford 91 20 31N34'46 81w40'39 5:26:43
Horseleg Estates 57 8 34N17 85w12 5:40:48
Horseshoe Bend 74 8 33N16'42 85w15'16 5:41:01
Hortense 13 20 31N20'11 81w57'23 5:27:50
Hoschton 78 20 34N05'47 83w45'41 5:35:03
Hothouse 55 8 34N56'04 84w18'14 5:37:13
Houston 74 8 33N09'34 85w08'16 5:40:33
Houston Lake 76 20 32N29'44 83w40'34 5:34:42
Howard 133 8 32N35'45 84w23'04 5:37:32
Howards Mill 49 8 31N09'22 84w59'41 5:39:59
Howell 36 20 33N33'23 82w19'05 5:29:16
Howell 50 20 30N49'39 83w03'14 5:32:13
Howell Grove 70 20 33N19'25 83w05'21 5:32:21
Huber 143 20 32N42'15 83w33'23 5:34:14
Hubert 16 20 32N18'23 81w29'31 5:25:58
Hub Junction 107 20 33N35'58 83w45'01 5:35:00
Hudson Ferry Landing 124 20 32N37'06 81w24'44 5:25:39
Hudson Mill 72 8 32N39 84w51 5:39:24
Huffaker 57 8 34N16'48 85w14'37 5:40:58
Huffer 34 20 31N33'46 82w47'39 5:31:11
Hughland 132 20 32N02'42 82w03'18 5:28:13
Hulett 22 8 33N35 85w05 5:40:20
Hull 97 20 34N00'53 83w17'38 5:33:11
Hulmeville 52 20 34N08 82w50 5:31:20
Hunter 124 20 32N39 81w33 5:26:12
Hunter Army Airfield 25 20 32N01 81w06 5:24:24
Hunters 124 20 32N39'16 81w33'02 5:26:12
Hunters Crossroad 99 8 32N57'33 84w45'38 5:39:03
Huntington 129 18 32N00'08 84w08'28 5:36:34
Hunts Corner 64 8 34N31'48 84w50'44 5:39:23
Huntsville 110 8 34N00 84w49 5:39:16
Hurst 55 8 34N50'28 84w11'21 5:36:45
Hutchins 109 20 33N50'26 83w10'05 5:32:40
Hutchins Landing 49 8 31N25'56 85w03'48 5:40:15
Hutchinson Landing 43 8 30N46'00 84w44'12 5:38:57
Huxford 95 20 31N33'33 81w30'37 5:26:02
Hyatts Landing 51 20 32N16'24 81w26'21 5:25:45
Ida Vesper 26 8 32N19'04 84w41'46 5:38:47
Ideal 96 8 32N22'10 84w11'17 5:36:45
Idlewood 17 20 33N00'55 81w58'49 5:27:55
Ila 97 20 34N10'21 83w17'32 5:33:10
Imlac 99 8 33N01'28 84w33'46 5:38:15
Imperial 117 20 33N20'38 83w24'18 5:33:37
Inaha 142 20 31N37'07 83w36'22 5:34:25
Indianola 92 20 30N51'51 83w11'22 5:32:45
Indian Springs 18 8 33N14'33 83w55'15 5:35:41
Indian Springs 23 8 34N57'28 85w09'52 5:40:39
Industrial 60 10 33N44 84w32 5:38:08
Inman 56 8 33N23'07 84w24'43 5:37:39
Inman Park 60 7 33N45'27 84w21'46 5:37:27
International 68 20 34N31 83w32 5:34:08
International Office Park 60 7 33N40 84w23 5:37:32
Ione 14 20 31N00'44 83w44'02 5:34:56
Iron City 125 8 31N00'48 84w47'47 5:39:15
Iron Stab 115 8 34N02'07 84w56'37 5:39:46
Irwins 150 20 32N56 82w49 5:31:16
Irwins Crossroads 150 20 32N51'26 82w50'58 5:31:24
Irwinton 158 20 32N48'40 83w10'22 5:32:41
Irwinville 77 20 31N38'53 83w22'58 5:33:32
Isabella 159 20 31N34'06 83w51'14 5:35:25
Isle of Hope 25 20 31N58'54 81w03'40 5:24:15
Ithaca 22 8 33N40'50 84w56'53 5:39:48
Ivanhoe 16 20 32N17'02 81w28'39 5:25:55
Ivey 158 20 32N54'25 83w17'27 5:33:10
Iveys Mill 4 8 31N23'28 84w35'10 5:38:21
Ivylog 144 8 34N57'43 84w03'32 5:36:14
Jackson 18 20 33N17'40 83w57'58 5:35:52
Jacksons Crossroads 157 20 33N53'25 82w50'42 5:31:23
Jacksonville 66 20 33N37'57 83w02'17 5:32:09
Jacksonville 134 20 31N48'45 82w58'45 5:31:55
Jacksonville 139 20 34N55'04 83w51'27 5:35:26
Jacobsons Landing 124 20 32N48'44 81w31'42 5:26:07
Jake 22 8 33N39'07 85w13'39 5:40:55
Jakin 49 8 31N05'27 84w58'56 5:39:56
Jamaica 63 20 31N15'06 81w39'09 5:26:37
James 84 20 32N57'59 83w28'26 5:33:54
Jamestown 26 8 32N16'20 84w50'21 5:39:21
Jamestown 32 20 30N55'41 82w35'05 5:30:20
Jamestown 148 20 31N16'13 82w23'00 5:29:32
Jarrell 133 8 32N39'48 84w16'53 5:37:08
Jarrett 127 20 34N36'33 83w14'34 5:32:58
Jasper 112 8 34N28'04 84w25'45 5:37:43
Jay Bird Springs 45 20 32N07'52 83w00'20 5:32:01
Jeff 30 8 31N33'22 84w48'36 5:39:14
Jefferson 20 20 30N57'59 81w47'25 5:27:10
Jefferson 78 20 34N07'01 83w34'21 5:34:17
Jefferson 117 20 33N26'57 83w18'42 5:33:15
Jefferson Mill 109 20 33N53 83w09 5:32:36
Jeffersonville 143 20 32N41'15 83w20'48 5:33:23
Jekyll Island 63 20 31N12 81w29 5:25:56
Jenkinsburg 18 20 33N19'28 84w02'09 5:36:09
Jennie 54 20 32N03'02 81w53'21 5:27:33
Jersey 147 20 33N42'56 83w47'56 5:35:12
Jerusalem 20 20 30N58'41 81w50'45 5:27:23
Jerusalem 112 8 34N26'30 84w34'56 5:38:20
Jesup 151 20 31N36'26 81w53'08 5:27:33
Jeterville 100 8 31N14'34 84w42'22 5:38:49
Jewell 131 20 33N17'46 82w46'39 5:31:07
Jewelville 6 20 34N22'19 83w24'14 5:33:37
Jewtown 63 20 31N09'43 81w23'49 5:25:35
Jimps 16 20 32N23'08 81w50'08 5:27:21
Jinks 43 8 30N42'59 84w49'26 5:39:18
Joe Cone Landing 16 20 32N16'35 81w26'45 5:25:47
Joel 22 8 33N28'32 85w14'17 5:40:57
Johnson Corner 138 20 32N03'54 82w18'05 5:29:12
Johnson Crossroads 99 8 32N54'04 84w35'57 5:38:24
Johnstonville 85 8 33N05'22 84w04'28 5:36:18
Jolly 114 8 33N07'20 84w23'24 5:37:34
Jones 95 20 31N38'01 81w28'49 5:25:55
Jones Acres 84 25 32N50 83w37 5:34:28
Jonesboro 31 9 33N31'17 84w21'14 5:37:25
Jones Creek 144 8 34N50'41 84w06'25 5:36:26
Jones Crossing 30 8 31N38'29 84w58'20 5:39:53
Jones Crossroads 49 8 31N10'27 84w56'13 5:39:45
Jones Crossroads 141 8 32N52'10 85w02'05 5:40:08
Jones Mill 55 8 34N54'24 84w31'27 5:38:06
Jones Settlement 145 8 32N59'01 84w28'16 5:37:53
Jonesville 22 8 33N33'36 85w13'54 5:40:56
Jordan 153 20 32N02'05 82w40'08 5:30:41
Jordan Place 88 20 31N45'21 84w12'31 5:36:50
Jot Em Down Store 113 20 31N18 82w15 5:29:00
Julienton 95 20 31N33'37 81w18'07 5:25:12
Juliette 102 20 33N06'26 83w48'01 5:35:12
Junction City 130 8 32N36'12 84w27'34 5:37:50
Juniper 98 8 32N31'52 84w36'16 5:38:25
Juno 42 8 34N28'33 84w11'39 5:36:47
Kansas 22 8 33N42 85w11 5:40:44
Kaolin 150 20 33N01'34 82w52'51 5:31:31
Kartah 27 8 34N26'52 85w14'55 5:41:00
Kathleen 76 20 32N29'45 83w36'28 5:34:26
Keith 23 8 34N55'05 85w02'31 5:40:10
Keithsburg 28 8 34N16'28 84w27'06 5:37:48
Keiths Mill 155 8 34N44'35 84w52'52 5:39:31
Keller 15 20 31N50'35 81w15'14 5:25:01
Kelley Hill 106 17 32N26 84w57 5:39:48
Kelleytown 75 20 33N32'14 84w05'21 5:36:21
Kelly 79 20 33N26'25 83w37'10 5:34:29
Kellytown 75 20 33N27 84w09 5:36:36
Kemp 53 20 32N31 82w19 5:29:16
Kennesaw 33 8 34N01'24 84w36'56 5:38:28
Kensington 146 8 34N46'27 85w22'22 5:41:29
Kensington Park 25 20 32N01'24 81w06'07 5:24:24
Kents Landing 82 20 32N48'10 82w01'05 5:28:04
Kenwood 56 8 33N30'41 84w26'10 5:37:45
Kenzie 145 8 32N53 84w20 5:37:20
Kewanee 87 20 32N29'36 83w05'25 5:32:22
Keysville 17 20 33N14'01 82w13'57 5:28:56
Kibbee 103 20 32N17'15 82w31'31 5:30:06
Kiker 61 8 34N40'00 84w30'03 5:38:00
Kilby Mill 119 20 34N57'01 83w29'34 5:33:58
Kildare 51 20 32N32'03 81w27'20 5:25:49
Killarney 100 8 31N08'14 84w56'29 5:39:46
Kimbrough 152 8 32N00'22 84w39'00 5:38:36
Kinderlou 92 20 30N48'03 83w22'03 5:33:28
Kings 107 20 33N40 83w52 5:35:28
Kings Boat Landing 24 20 30N57'17 82w08'14 5:28:33
Kingsboro 72 8 32N42'30 84w52'10 5:39:29
Kingsland 20 20 30N47'59 81w41'24 5:26:46
Kingston 8 8 34N14'13 84w56'39 5:39:47
King's Wood 25 20 32N04 81w07 5:24:28
Kingwood 35 20 31N11 83w48 5:35:12
Kinlaw 20 20 30N50'40 81w40'33 5:26:42
Kinseytown 154 20 34N35'17 83w39'02 5:34:36
Kirkland 2 20 31N18'29 82w54'30 5:31:38
Kirkland 80 20 31N47'54 82w45'46 5:31:03
Kirkwood 44 7 33N45'22 84w19'24 5:37:18
Kitchens Landing 13 20 31N02'30 82w13'30 5:28:54
Kite 78 20 32N41'32 82w30'53 5:30:04
Kittles Landing 124 20 32N48'31 81w31'12 5:26:05
Klondike 44 20 33N38'44 84w07'36 5:36:30
Klondike 69 1 34N11'43 83w46'42 5:35:07
Klondike 76 20 32N20'53 83w34'34 5:34:18
Knot 141 8 33N00'42 84w56'17 5:39:45
Knott 141 8 33N02 85w02 5:40:08
Knoxville 39 8 32N43'27 83w59'52 5:35:59
Kramer 156 20 31N57'21 83w23'24 5:33:34
Krannert 57 8 34N15'26 85w19'39 5:41:19
K'Ville 151 20 31N33'23 82w07'33 5:28:30
Kyle 55 8 34N57'25 84w21'25 5:37:26
Laboon 147 20 33N47 83w37 5:34:28
Laconte 37 20 31N12'47 83w26'57 5:33:48
La Crosse 123 8 32N11'12 84w14'25 5:36:58
Ladds 8 8 34N08'55 84w49'46 5:39:19
La Fayette 146 8 34N42'17 85w16'55 5:41:08
Laffingal 28 8 34N11'29 84w38'55 5:38:36
La Grange 141 8 33N02'21 85w01'53 5:40:08
Laingkat 43 8 30N43'09 84w29'18 5:37:57
Lake 115 8 34N01 85w15 5:41:00
Lake Arrowhead 28 8 34N19 84w33 5:38:12
Lake Capri Estates 122 20 33N43 84w06 5:36:24
Lake Cindy 75 8 33N23 84w17 5:37:08
Lake City 31 8 33N36'23 84w20'07 5:37:20
Lake Creek 115 8 34N04'13 85w13'02 5:40:52
Lakehills 38 8 33N24'32 84w46'18 5:39:05
Lake Howard 146 8 34N42 85w22 5:41:28
Lakeland 86 20 31N02'27 83w04'31 5:32:18
Lake Lucerne 67 20 33N53 84w08 5:36:32
Lakemont 119 20 34N46'55 83w24'59 5:33:40
Lakemount 119 20 34N47 83w25 5:33:40
Lake Park 92 20 30N40'55 83w10'47 5:32:43
Lakeshore Estates 69 1 34N18'05 83w51'32 5:35:26
Lakeside 11 25 32N50'28 83w34'26 5:34:18
Lakeside Park 25 20 32N00 81w05 5:24:20
Lake Talmadge 75 8 33N23 84w17 5:37:08
Lake Tara 31 8 33N32'30 84w21'00 5:37:24
Lakeview 23 8 34N58'45 85w15'32 5:41:02
Lakeview 57 8 34N16'28 85w16'30 5:41:06
Lakeview 111 8 32N34'40 83w44'59 5:35:00
Lakeview Estates 122 20 33N42'24 84w01'54 5:36:08
Lakewood 60 7 33N43 84w23 5:37:32
Lakewood Heights 60 7 33N42'17 84w22'43 5:37:31
Lamar 129 20 32N00'58 84w04'19 5:36:17
Lamara Heights 25 20 32N02'00 81w06'13 5:24:25
Lamarville 25 20 32N02'01 81w08'55 5:24:36
Lamkin 36 20 33N30'51 82w05'52 5:28:23
Lance Mill 144 8 34N56'52 84w08'35 5:36:34
Landrum 42 8 34N24'51 84w01'10 5:36:05
Lands Crossroads 77 20 31N43'10 83w23'05 5:33:32
Lane Landing 82 20 32N47'40 82w00'44 5:28:03
Laney 101 20 31N13 84w02 5:36:08
Langdon 99 8 32N56'43 84w36'03 5:38:24
Lanier 15 20 32N07'47 81w32'13 5:26:09
Lanier Heights 11 25 32N48'59 83w34'07 5:34:16
Lashley 76 20 32N32'45 83w36'41 5:34:27
Lathemtown 28 8 34N14'46 84w18'26 5:37:14
Laurel Hills 106 17 32N31'04 84w59'14 5:39:57
Laurens Hill 87 20 32N34 83w09 5:32:36
Lavender 57 8 34N17'31 85w20'28 5:41:22
La Vista 44 7 33N49 84w20 5:37:20
Lavonia 59 20 34N26'09 83w06'25 5:32:26
Lawrences Mill 114 8 32N59'00 84w29'59 5:38:00
Lawrenceville 67 20 33N57'22 83w59'17 5:35:57
Lawton 82 20 32N52'18 81w56'44 5:27:47
Lax 77 20 31N28'23 83w07'18 5:32:29
Leaf 154 20 34N34'28 83w39'40 5:34:39
Leah 36 20 33N39'47 82w20'08 5:29:21
Leary 19 8 31N29'08 84w30'50 5:38:03
Leathersville 90 20 33N43'00 82w26'24 5:29:46
Lebanon (Toonigh Station) 28 8 34N08'34 84w30'34 5:38:02
Lecount 89 20 31N40'47 81w27'32 5:25:50
Leefield 16 20 32N25'05 81w36'49 5:26:27
Lee Pope 39 8 32N36'43 83w57'21 5:35:49
Leesburg 88 20 31N43'55 84w10'15 5:36:41
Lees Crossing 141 8 33N01'51 85w03'40 5:40:15
Lees Mill 56 8 33N25 84w31 5:38:04
Lehigh 34 20 31N39'55 82w42'56 5:30:52
Lela 125 8 30N58'59 84w51'47 5:39:27
Leland 33 8 33N48'44 84w33'32 5:38:14
Leliaton 2 20 31N19'29 82w59'36 5:31:58
Lena 33 8 34N04 84w40 5:38:40
Lenox 37 20 31N16'17 83w27'54 5:33:52
Lenox Square 60 7 33N51 84w22 5:37:28
Leo 154 20 34N32'28 83w44'26 5:34:58
LePageville 25 20 32N04'18 81w03'33 5:24:14
Leslie 129 20 31N57'19 84w05'12 5:36:21
Lester 101 20 31N22'10 84w02'42 5:36:11
Letford 15 20 32N02'19 81w36'05 5:26:24
Leverett 90 20 33N48'38 82w23'28 5:29:34
Leveretts 152 8 31N56'34 84w34'12 5:38:17
Lewis 124 20 32N48'06 81w40'54 5:26:44
Lewis Corner 64 8 34N30'54 84w48'37 5:39:14
Lewiston 36 20 33N30'36 82w12'08 5:28:49
Lewiston 158 20 32N53'47 83w24'08 5:33:37
Lewistown 36 20 33N32 82w08 5:28:32
Lewner 144 8 34N56'56 84w09'28 5:36:38
Lexington 109 20 33N52'11 83w06'43 5:32:27
Lexsy 53 20 32N28'06 82w17'51 5:29:11
Liberty 66 20 33N25'17 83w08'14 5:32:33

Liberty City 25 20 32N02'51 81W08'16 5:24:33
Liberty Hill 85 8 33N09'12 84W08'03 5:36:32
Liberty Hill 159 20 31N24'03 83W56'23 5:35:46
Lifsey 114 8 33N02'12 84W22'24 5:37:30
Lightfoot 158 20 32N49 83W05 5:32:20
Lilburn 67 20 33N53'24 84W08'35 5:36:34
Lilly 46 20 32N08'49 83W52'39 5:35:31
Lilypond 64 8 34N26'02 84W57'07 5:39:48
Limerick 89 20 31N50'12 81W23'10 5:25:33
Lime Sink 65 8 31N02 84W19 5:37:16
Limestone 12 20 32N23 83W21 5:33:24
Lincoln Hills 106 17 32N31'40 84W56'45 5:39:47
Lincoln Landing 15 20 31N46'31 81W12'25 5:24:50
Lincoln Park 145 8 32N52'04 84W19'50 5:37:19
Lincolnton 90 20 33N47'32 82W28'45 5:29:55
Lindale 57 8 34N11'12 85W10'29 5:40:42
Linden 106 17 32N27'41 84W55'26 5:39:42
Lind Landing 153 20 31N56'27 82W35'11 5:30:21
Lindsey Creek 106 17 32N29 84W57 5:39:48
Linesville 157 20 33N50'38 82W51'55 5:31:28
Linton 70 20 33N06'59 82W59'34 5:31:58
Linwood 146 8 34N42'46 85W17'21 5:41:09
Listonia 40 20 31N57'51 83W39'34 5:34:38
Lithia Springs 48 8 33N47'38 84W39'38 5:38:39
Lithonia 44 6 33N42'44 84W06'19 5:36:25
Little Hope 125 8 31N00'46 84W54'34 5:39:38
Little House Creek 9 20 31N45 83W18 5:33:12
Little Miami 92 20 30N48'51 83W15'38 5:33:03
Little River 117 20 33N16 83W25 5:33:40
Little River 157 20 33N39'19 82W46'01 5:31:04
Little River Landing 28 8 34N09'53 84W34'52 5:38:19
Little Sand Mountain 27 8 34N29 85W14 5:40:56
Livingston 57 8 34N12'46 85W20'55 5:41:24
Livingston 159 20 31N24'58 83W56'36 5:35:46
Lizella 11 8 32N48'25 83W49'12 5:35:17
Loce 90 20 33N43'21 82W28'39 5:29:55
Lockett Crossing 47 11 31N33'27 84W15'15 5:37:01
Loco 90 20 33N48 82W29 5:29:56
Locust Grove 75 20 33N20'45 84W06'33 5:36:26
Loftin 99 8 32N53'06 84W35'53 5:38:24
Logan 157 20 33N43'30 82W42'47 5:30:51
Loganville 147 20 33N50'20 83W54'03 5:35:36
Log Landing 50 20 30N38'00 82W37'49 5:30:31
Log Landing 151 20 31N27'13 81W37'34 5:26:30
Logtown 145 8 32N51'01 84W11'19 5:36:45
Lollie 87 20 32N29 82W46 5:31:04
Lombard 53 20 32N25'32 82W19'31 5:29:18
Lone Oak 99 8 33N10'18 84W48'58 5:39:16
Long Cane 141 8 32N57'23 85W08'27 5:40:34
Long Pond 153 20 32N04'52 82W32'44 5:30:11
Longstreet 38 8 33N23'01 84W39'52 5:38:39
Longstreet Bleckley 12 20 32N23 83W21 5:33:24
Lookout Mountain 146 8 34N58'39 85W21'28 5:41:26
Lorane 11 25 32N54'50 83W46'27 5:35:06
Lorenzo 51 20 32N26'15 81W22'37 5:25:30
Lorwood 25 20 32N00 81W05 5:24:20
Lost Mountain 33 8 33N56'26 84W42'09 5:38:49
Lothair 140 20 32N21'18 82W39'20 5:30:37
Lotts 34 20 31N35'15 82W51'30 5:31:26
Louise 141 8 33N05'02 84W56'09 5:39:45
Louisville 81 20 33N00'05 82W24'41 5:29:39
Louvale 128 8 32N10'30 84W49'31 5:39:18
Louvale Station 128 8 32N09'05 84W50'11 5:39:21
Love Hill 23 8 34N55'07 85W08'47 5:40:35
Lovejoy 31 8 33N26'10 84W18'52 5:37:15
Lovelace 90 20 33N47'28 82W34'16 5:30:17
Lovett 87 20 32N38'17 82W46'04 5:31:04
Loving 55 8 34N55'12 84W13'16 5:36:53
Lowell 22 8 33N27'59 85W02'42 5:40:11
Lower Sansavilla 151 20 31N29'43 81W38'56 5:26:36
Lower Sister Bluff Landing 1 20 31N50'23 82W04'25 5:28:18
Lowery 87 20 32N21'17 82W47'58 5:31:12
Lowes Crossing 96 8 32N23'30 83W58'49 5:35:55
Lowry 31 8 33N18'42 84W23'47 5:37:35
Lucile 49 8 31N14'36 84W55'02 5:39:40
Lucius 61 8 34N48'06 84W22'46 5:37:31
Ludowici 91 20 31N42'28 81W44'33 5:26:58
Ludville 112 8 34N28'10 84W36'35 5:38:26
Luella 75 8 33N21'07 84W10'43 5:36:43
Luke 49 8 31N20'16 85W00'01 5:40:00
Lula 69 20 34N23'15 83W39'59 5:34:40
Lulaton 13 20 31N12'56 81W54'14 5:27:37
Lumber City 134 20 31N55'45 82W40'47 5:30:43
Lumber City Landing 134 20 31N55'12 82W40'38 5:30:43
Lumpkin 42 8 34N22'02 84W02'27 5:36:10
Lumpkin 128 8 32N03'03 84W47'57 5:39:12
Lundberg 157 20 33N39'00 82W43'36 5:30:54
Luthersville 99 8 33N12'36 84W44'40 5:38:59
Luvdale 47 11 31N34 84W11 5:36:44
Luxomni 67 20 33N53'46 84W06'59 5:36:28
Lyerly 27 8 34N24'24 85W24'12 5:41:37
Lyneville 131 20 33N38'09 82W55'47 5:31:43
Lynhaven 38 8 33N23'02 84W50'01 5:39:20
Lyn Hills 106 17 32N32'18 84W55'49 5:39:43
Lynhurst 25 20 31N59'32 81W06'42 5:24:27
Lynn 43 8 30N58'49 84W36'54 5:38:28
Lynn 132 20 31N58'21 81W57'43 5:27:51
Lynnwood 23 8 34N57 85W18 5:41:12
Lyons 138 20 32N12'15 82W19'19 5:29:17
Lytle 146 8 34N54'59 85W16'30 5:41:06
Mableton 33 8 33N49'07 84W34'57 5:38:20
Macedonia 28 8 34N15'13 84W21'38 5:37:27
Macedonia 100 8 31N14'49 84W39'41 5:38:39
Macedonia 139 20 34N55'05 83W43'30 5:34:54
Mac Fishery Landing 151 20 31N34'52 81W46'13 5:27:05
Machen 79 20 33N23'31 83W35'24 5:34:22
Macland 33 8 33N54'08 84W40'21 5:38:41
Macon 11 25 32N50'26 83W37'57 5:34:32
Maddox 129 20 31N59'49 84W14'33 5:36:58
Madison 104 20 33N35'44 83W28'05 5:33:52
Madola 55 8 34N55'40 84W25'47 5:37:43
Madras 38 8 33N26'24 84W44'32 5:38:58
Madray Springs 151 20 31N44'02 81W58'44 5:27:55
Magby Gap 41 8 34N52 85W31 5:42:04
Magnet 122 20 33N33'54 84W00'56 5:36:04
Magnolia 12 20 32N25'48 83W27'14 5:33:49
Magnolia Park 25 20 32N01'07 81W04'58 5:24:20
Magruder 17 20 32N55'12 82W14'30 5:28:58
Mahailey Crossroads 74 8 33N21'32 85W13'07 5:40:52
Major 38 8 33N27'12 84W39'23 5:38:38
Mallets Landing 20 20 30N47'44 81W51'10 5:27:25
Mallorysville 157 20 33N52 82W44 5:30:56
Malvern 53 20 32N48 81W57 5:27:48
Manassas 132 20 32N09'37 82W01'11 5:28:05
Manchester 99 8 32N51'35 84W37'12 5:38:29
Mandeville 22 8 33N39'16 85W08'13 5:40:33
Manningtown 151 20 31N24'47 81W51'31 5:27:26
Manor 148 20 31N06'13 82W34'24 5:30:18
Mansfield 107 20 33N31'04 83W44'04 5:34:56
Manta 26 8 32N17'09 84W42'49 5:38:51
Maple Grove 55 8 34N54'37 84W10'16 5:36:41
Marblehill 112 8 34N25'50 84W20'13 5:37:21
Maretts 73 20 34N25'23 82W59'09 5:31:57
Margret 55 8 34N45'16 84W08'46 5:36:35
Marietta 33 10 33N57'09 84W33'00 5:38:12
Marine Corps Center 47 20 31N33 84W03 5:36:12
Marion 61 8 34N38'09 84W15'35 5:37:02
Marion 143 20 32N39'44 83W26'14 5:33:45
Marlow 51 20 32N16'08 81W23'27 5:25:34
Marshall 40 20 31N52'06 83W53'18 5:35:33
Marshallville 96 8 32N27'22 83W56'25 5:35:46
Marsh Crossing 146 8 34N43'02 85W19'42 5:41:19
Mars Hill 33 8 34N02'06 84W41'30 5:38:46
Marsh Landing 95 20 31N25'01 81W17'45 5:25:11
Martech 60 7 33N47 84W26 5:37:44
Martin 127 20 34N29'13 83W11'06 5:32:44
Martindale 146 8 34N37'22 85W18'08 5:41:13
Martinez 36 20 33N31'02 82W04'33 5:28:18
Martins Crossroads 90 20 33N46'20 82W22'19 5:29:29
Martins Crossroads 120 8 31N41'49 84W38'20 5:38:33
Mashburn Mill 55 8 34N53'26 84W08'08 5:36:33
Mason 74 8 33N15'57 85W15'40 5:41:03
Massee 37 20 31N11'24 83W21'26 5:33:26
Massey Hill 158 20 32N51'36 83W20'48 5:33:23
Masseyville 146 8 34N43'36 85W27'48 5:41:51
Match 52 20 34N12 83W02 5:32:08
Mathews 81 20 33N12'39 82W18'28 5:29:14
Matt 58 8 34N17'55 84W09'11 5:36:37
Matthews 81 20 33N13 82W18 5:29:12
Mattox 24 20 30N55'03 82W05'05 5:28:20
Mattox Ford 32 20 30N43'59 82W41'24 5:30:46
Mauk 133 8 32N30'06 84W25'16 5:37:41
Maxeys 109 20 33N45'15 83W10'25 5:32:42
Maxim 90 20 33N47'35 82W20'27 5:29:22
Maxwell 55 8 34N49'34 84W21'33 5:37:26
Maxwell 79 20 33N25'00 83W39'40 5:34:39
Mayday 50 8 30N49'38 83W00'33 5:32:02
Mayfair 25 20 32N04 81W07 5:24:28
Mayfield 70 20 33N21'18 82W48'03 5:31:12
Mayhaw 100 8 31N10'35 84W52'31 5:39:30
Mays Bluff 20 20 30N54'19 81W53'16 5:27:33
Maysville 6 20 34N15'10 83W33'42 5:34:15
McAfee 44 20 33N44 84W16 5:37:04
McBean 121 20 33N14'36 81W57'03 5:27:48
McBride 38 8 33N23'33 84W46'46 5:39:07
McCaysville 55 8 34N59'10 84W22'17 5:37:29
McCollum 38 8 33N27'01 84W42'01 5:38:48
McCrary Settlement 145 8 32N59'32 84W28'22 5:37:53
McCullough 55 8 34N58'11 84W12'48 5:36:51
McCutchen 155 8 34N48 85W01 5:40:04
McDainels 64 8 34N27'18 84W56'48 5:39:47
McDaniel 112 8 34N30'30 84W37'50 5:38:31
McDaniels 64 8 34N27 84W58 5:39:52
McDonald Acres 23 8 34N57'35 85W14'23 5:40:58
McDonough 75 21 33N26'50 84W08'49 5:36:35
McEachins Landing 153 20 31N57'03 82W34'32 5:30:18
McElheneys Crossroads 79 20 33N14'36 83W45'38 5:35:03
McElroys Mill 122 20 33N46'35 83W59'08 5:35:57
McGregor 103 20 32N11'47 82W30'18 5:30:01
McIntosh 89 20 31N49'32 81W31'26 5:26:06
McIntosh Mill Village 38 8 33N22 84W47 5:39:08
McIntyre 158 20 32N50'46 83W11'27 5:32:46
McKee 42 8 34N27'35 84W08'31 5:36:34
McKinney 145 15 32N55'33 84W17'31 5:37:10
McKinnon 151 20 31N25'30 81W55'37 5:27:42
McLendon Crossroads 99 8 32N59'33 84W37'36 5:38:30
McLeods Mill 24 20 30N58'17 82W23'20 5:29:33
McNatt Falls 138 20 31N58'12 82W28'18 5:29:53
McPherson 110 8 33N56'51 84W54'24 5:39:38
McRae 134 20 32N04'04 82W54'03 5:31:36
McTier 1 20 31N48'21 82W14'46 5:28:59
McWhorter 48 8 33N36'47 84W50'12 5:39:21
Meadow 67 20 33N58'41 84W05'51 5:36:23
Meadowdale 76 20 32N26'40 83W46'33 5:35:06
Meansville 114 15 33N02'57 84W18'25 5:37:14
Mechanic Hill 121 20 33N17'51 81W57'31 5:27:50
Mechanicsville 67 20 33N55'39 84W14'33 5:36:58
Meda 117 20 33N16'52 83W22'01 5:33:28
Meeks 83 20 32N37'07 82W33'25 5:30:14
Meigs 136 20 31N04'20 84W05'21 5:36:21
Meinhard 25 20 32N10'53 81W12'40 5:24:51
Meldrim 51 20 32N08'35 81W22'41 5:25:31
Melrose 92 8 30N38'27 83W08'09 5:32:33
Melson 57 8 34N10'16 85W24'34 5:41:38
Melton 121 20 33N20'26 82W04'39 5:28:19
Mendes 132 20 31N59'55 81W58'27 5:27:54
Menlo 27 8 34N29'05 85W28'35 5:41:54
Meridian 95 20 31N27'06 81W22'41 5:25:31
Meriwether 5 20 33N09'18 83W19'09 5:33:17
Meriwether White Sulphur Spr 99 8 32N53 84W50 5:39:20
Merrillville 136 20 30N56'56 83W52'48 5:35:31
Mershon 113 20 31N27'50 82W15'27 5:29:02
Mesena 149 20 33N27'35 82W35'25 5:30:22
Metasville 157 20 33N46'04 82W36'06 5:30:24
Metcalf 136 20 30N42'00 83W59'17 5:35:57
Methvins 129 18 32N06'45 84W04'09 5:36:17
Metter 21 20 32N23'49 82W03'37 5:28:14
Mexico Crossing 32 20 31N08'30 82W47'11 5:31:09
Miami Valley 111 8 32N33'13 83W47'48 5:35:11
Mica 28 8 34N21'28 84W16'22 5:37:05
Middle Oconee 29 20 33N57 83W27 5:33:48
Middle Place 25 20 31N48'05 81W06'44 5:24:27
Middle Rockdale 122 20 33N40 84W02 5:36:08
Middleton 52 20 34N05'57 82W46'03 5:31:04
Midland 106 8 32N34'29 84W49'38 5:39:19
Midriver 20 20 30N58'32 81W52'03 5:27:28
Midville 17 20 32N49'08 82W14'06 5:28:56
Midway 23 8 34N57'47 85W15'34 5:41:02
Midway 32 20 30N59'24 82W41'00 5:30:44
Midway 68 20 34N32'30 83W32'25 5:34:10
Midway 87 20 32N38'44 82W47'47 5:31:11
Midway 89 20 31N48'20 81W25'51 5:25:43
Midway 90 20 33N52'42 82W33'09 5:30:13
Midway 132 20 32N01'53 81W53'37 5:27:34
Milan 134 20 32N01'02 83W03'46 5:32:15
Milford 4 8 31N22'54 84W32'37 5:38:10
Mill Creek 155 8 34N43'57 85W02'32 5:40:10
Milledgeville 5 20 33N04'48 83W13'56 5:32:56
Millen 82 20 32N48'14 81W56'58 5:27:48
Millers Mill 75 20 33N32'06 84W08'29 5:36:34
Millhaven 124 20 32N56'01 81W38'59 5:26:36
Millwood 148 20 31N15'56 82W39'38 5:30:39
Milner 85 8 33N07'00 84W11'48 5:36:47
Milner Crossroads 85 8 33N03'39 84W12'27 5:36:50
Milstead 122 20 33N41'16 83W59'32 5:35:58
Mimsville 4 8 31N15'20 84W31'43 5:38:07
Mineola 92 20 30N54'27 83W20'37 5:33:22
Mineral Bluff 55 8 34N54'52 84W16'36 5:37:06
Minnesota 35 20 31N18'42 83W54'37 5:35:38
Minneta 79 20 33N17'08 83W42'42 5:34:51
Minter 87 20 32N29'09 82W45'38 5:31:03
Minton 159 20 31N21'18 83W49'08 5:35:17
Mission Ridge 146 8 34N57 85W18 5:41:12
Mitchell 62 20 33N13'11 82W42'12 5:30:49
Mitchell Forks 16 20 32N14'36 81W42'09 5:26:49
Mize 127 20 34N28'24 83W20'13 5:33:21
Mizell 133 8 32N34'34 84W18'22 5:37:13
Mobley Crossing 116 20 32N19'23 83W24'28 5:33:38
Modoc 53 20 32N39'20 82W18'34 5:29:14
Mogul 11 25 32N50'59 83W33'54 5:34:16
Molena 114 8 33N00'43 84W30'01 5:38:00
Moncrief 65 8 30N26 84W17 5:37:08
Moniac 24 20 30N31'05 82W13'31 5:28:54
Monks Crossing 92 20 30N53'55 83W06'11 5:32:25
Monroe 147 20 33N47'41 83W42'48 5:34:51
Montclair 121 20 33N29 82W02 5:28:08
Monteith 25 20 32N10'49 81W11'25 5:24:46
Montevideo 52 20 34N16'20 82W49'19 5:31:17
Montezuma 96 8 32N18'18 84W01'39 5:36:07
Montgomery 25 20 31N56'25 81W07'20 5:24:29
Montgomery Corner 139 20 34N59'09 83W37'13 5:34:29
Monticello 79 20 33N18'17 83W41'00 5:34:44
Montreal 44 20 33N49 84W17 5:37:08
Montrose 87 20 32N33'34 83W09'12 5:32:37
Moody 92 20 30N59 83W12 5:32:48
Moody Field 86 20 30N51 83W15 5:33:00
Moody Landing 24 20 30N47'13 82W01'29 5:28:06
Moons 146 8 34N55'50 85W20'55 5:41:24
Moores 87 20 32N31'06 82W59'23 5:31:58
Moores Crossroads 30 8 31N44'40 85W01'02 5:40:04
Mora 34 20 31N24'50 82W57'14 5:31:49
Moran 39 8 32N50'55 83W55'55 5:35:44
Moreland 38 8 33N17'12 84W46'04 5:39:04
Morgan 19 8 31N32'15 84W35'58 5:38:24
Morgan 71 8 33N44'49 85W04'23 5:40:18
Morganton 55 8 34N52'29 84W14'39 5:36:59
Morganville 41 8 34N56'11 85W27'13 5:41:49
Morningside 57 8 34N15'52 85W16'57 5:41:08
Morningside 60 7 33N47'48 84W22'08 5:37:29

Morningside Heights 69 1 34N18 83w49 5:35:16
Morning Side Hills 69 1 34N17'33 83w47'35 5:35:10
Morris 118 8 31N47'39 84w56'47 5:39:47
Morris Brown 60 7 33N45 84w25 5:37:40
Morris Estates 23 8 34N58'32 85w10'36 5:40:42
Morrow 31 8 33N34'59 84w20'22 5:37:21
Morton 84 20 32N58'41 83w31'33 5:34:06
Morven 14 20 30N56'29 83w29'58 5:34:00
Mosquito Crossing 66 20 33N28'28 83w07'02 5:32:28
Moss Oak 76 20 32N25'10 83w46'28 5:35:06
Mossy Creek 154 20 34N32'28 83w41'08 5:34:45
Mossy Dell 88 20 31N45'38 84w06'48 5:36:27
Moultrie 35 20 31N10'47 83w47'21 5:35:09
Mountainbrook 72 8 32N51'31 84w51'02 5:39:24
Mountain City 119 20 34N55'05 83w23'08 5:33:33
Mountain Hill 72 8 32N43'23 85w01'22 5:40:05
Mountain Park 60 8 34N04'51 84w24'41 5:37:39
Mountain Scene 139 20 34N51'26 83w43'20 5:34:53
Mountain Springs 84 20 32N53'57 83w27'21 5:33:49
Mountain View 31 8 33N38'30 84w23'25 5:37:34
Mountain View 146 8 34N54'44 85w19'08 5:41:17
Mount Airy 68 20 34N31'07 83w30'03 5:34:00
Mount Berry 57 8 34N17 85w11 5:40:44
Mount Bethel 60 8 33N57'58 84w24'41 5:37:39
Mount Carmel 146 8 34N39'46 85w18'36 5:41:14
Mount Herman 25 20 31N57'12 81w08'44 5:24:35
Mount Olivet 73 20 34N24'01 82w59'08 5:31:57
Mount Park 67 20 33N53 84w08 5:36:32
Mount Pleasant 6 20 34N22'04 83w26'32 5:33:46
Mount Pleasant 25 20 31N56'50 81w08'47 5:24:35
Mount Pleasant 43 8 31N01'26 84w27'37 5:37:50
Mount Pleasant 151 20 31N26'02 81w40'46 5:26:43
Mount Vernon 103 20 32N10'42 82w35'41 5:30:23
Mount Vernon 147 20 33N50'08 83w38'40 5:34:35
Mount Vernon 155 8 34N48 85w01 5:40:04
Mountville 141 8 33N02'21 84w52'51 5:39:31
Mount Wilkinson 33 8 33N52'07 84w28'00 5:37:52
Mount Zion 22 8 33N38'03 85w11'14 5:40:45
Mouth of The Branch Landing 13 20 31N18'58 81w55'52 5:27:43
Mouth of The Swamp Landing 13 20 31N17'01 81w56'58 5:27:48
Moxley 81 20 32N55'10 82w23'29 5:29:34
Moye 19 8 31N36'39 84w46'37 5:39:06
Mud Creek 68 20 34N30 83w36 5:34:24
Mud Valley 32 20 30N53'25 82w41'34 5:30:46
Mulberry 7 20 33N59 83w43 5:34:52
Mulberry Grove 25 20 32N11'22 81w09'34 5:24:38
Mulberry Grove 72 8 32N39'46 84w57'27 5:39:50
Mundys Mill 31 9 33N29'24 84w23'22 5:37:33
Munnerlyn 17 20 32N57'12 81w57'44 5:27:51
Murdock McRaes Landing 134 20 31N54'13 82w42'01 5:30:48
Murphy 35 20 31N04'15 83w49'25 5:35:18
Murphy Junction 55 8 34N53'05 84w18'30 5:37:14
Murray Hill 17 20 32N57'34 81w43'01 5:26:52
Murray Hills 121 20 33N29'06 82w02'55 5:28:12
Murrays Crossroads 123 8 32N19'15 84w17'40 5:37:11
Murray's Lake 31 8 33N37 84w22 5:37:28
Murrayville 69 1 34N25'07 83w54'21 5:35:37
Musella 39 8 32N47'52 84w01'56 5:36:08
Musselwhite 40 20 31N57'00 83w41'56 5:34:48
Myricks Mill 143 20 32N47'03 83w22'36 5:33:30
Myrtle 111 20 32N29'14 83w48'56 5:35:16
Myrtle Grove 15 20 31N53'04 81w14'45 5:24:59
Mystic 77 20 31N37'19 83w20'09 5:33:21
Nacoochee 154 20 34N41'06 83w42'38 5:34:51
Nahunta 13 20 31N12'15 81w58'53 5:27:56
Nails Creek 6 20 34N22 83w14 5:32:56
Nakomis 39 8 32N32'48 84w00'04 5:36:00
Nance Springs 155 8 34N37'21 84w56'24 5:39:46
Nankin 14 20 30N39'57 83w28'05 5:33:52
Nankipooh 106 17 32N33'23 84w56'42 5:39:47
Naomi 146 8 34N41'35 85w12'28 5:40:50
Nashville 10 20 31N12'26 83w15'01 5:33:00
National Colony Apartments 31 8 33N31 84w21 5:37:24
National Hills 121 20 33N28 82w01 5:28:04
Navy Yard Landing 49 8 31N05'58 85w01'48 5:40:07
Naylor 92 20 30N54'31 83w04'42 5:32:19
Neal 76 20 32N26'24 83w47'18 5:35:09
Neal 114 8 33N03'03 84w29'09 5:37:57
Neal Crossing 27 8 34N33'10 85w24'54 5:41:40
Neals Landing 125 8 30N58'38 85w00'19 5:40:01
Nebo 110 8 33N50'18 84w49'54 5:39:20
Nebula 99 8 32N51'01 84w40'38 5:38:43
Neco 121 20 33N24'52 82w00'25 5:28:02
Needham 148 20 31N09'21 82w25'43 5:29:43
Needmore 13 20 31N20'00 81w54'01 5:27:36
Needmore 50 20 30N40'44 82w42'42 5:30:51
Neese 97 20 34N04'39 83w18'55 5:33:16
Nelson 112 8 34N22'55 84w22'16 5:37:29
Nevils 16 20 32N15'49 81w45'40 5:27:03
Newark 136 20 30N49'25 83w54'35 5:35:38
Newborn 107 20 33N31'01 83w41'46 5:34:47
New Branch 138 20 32N04'55 82w15'06 5:29:00
New Cotton Mill 28 8 34N14 84w29 5:37:56
Newell 24 20 30N56'29 82w01'20 5:28:05
New Elm 35 20 31N17'37 83w49'09 5:35:17
New England 41 8 34N54'37 85w28'49 5:41:55
New Era 129 18 32N06'51 84w08'11 5:36:33
New Ford 50 20 30N46'55 82w50'02 5:31:20
New Georgia 110 8 33N48'32 84w53'24 5:39:34
New Holland 69 1 34N18'25 83w48'09 5:35:13
New Home 41 8 34N52 85w31 5:42:04
New Hope 16 20 32N20'17 81w53'49 5:27:35
New Hope 61 8 34N43'39 84w30'32 5:38:02
New Hope 63 20 31N17'14 81w26'39 5:25:47
New Hope 67 20 33N55'23 83w54'59 5:35:40
New Hope 90 20 33N44'57 82w23'31 5:29:34
New Hope 110 8 33N57'29 84w47'22 5:39:09
Newington 124 20 32N35'24 81w30'15 5:26:01
Newington Landing 51 20 32N17'14 81w10'49 5:24:43
New Lacy 3 20 31N32'21 82w22'18 5:29:29
New Lois 10 20 31N05'06 83w16'06 5:33:04
Newnan 38 14 33N22'50 84w47'59 5:39:12
New Point 129 8 32N03'17 84w18'09 5:37:13
Newport 55 8 34N43'22 84w14'02 5:36:56
New Rock Hill 14 20 31N00'04 83w34'28 5:34:18
New Salem 6 20 34N20 83w30 5:34:00
New Sirmans 32 20 31N02 83w04 5:32:16
Newton 4 8 31N18'46 84w20'09 5:37:21
Newton Factory 107 20 33N40 83w52 5:35:28
Newtown 60 7 34N01'16 84w16'12 5:37:05
New Town 64 8 34N31'50 84w54'21 5:39:37
New Town 157 20 33N48'43 82w48'39 5:31:15
New York 115 8 34N03 85w03 5:40:12
Neyami 88 20 31N49'25 84w12'55 5:36:52
Nicholasville 49 8 31N24'14 84w40'12 5:38:41
Nicholasville 147 20 33N52'05 83w45'17 5:35:01
Nicholls 34 20 31N31'02 82w38'06 5:30:32
Nicholson 78 20 34N06'50 83w25'54 5:33:44
Nicholsonville 25 20 31N57'33 81w08'16 5:24:33
Nickelsville 64 8 34N36'06 84w52'01 5:39:28
Nicklesville 158 20 32N41'10 83w05'08 5:32:21
Nickleville 65 8 30N48'20 84w20'07 5:37:20
Nickville 52 20 34N06'48 83w00'06 5:32:00
Nimblewill 93 8 34N33'48 84w08'25 5:36:34
Nixon 121 20 33N20'13 81w57'22 5:27:49
Noah 81 20 33N12'55 82w17'10 5:29:09
Noble 146 8 34N46'50 85w15'16 5:41:01
Noonday 33 8 34N03'43 84w31'17 5:38:05
Norcross 67 20 33N56'28 84w12'49 5:36:51
Norman 157 20 33N56'02 82w45'48 5:31:03
Norman Park 35 20 31N16'08 83w41'14 5:34:45
Normantown 138 20 32N18'22 82w22'11 5:29:29
Norris 149 20 33N22'57 82w43'27 5:30:54
Norristown 53 20 32N30'24 82w29'40 5:29:59
Norristown Junction 53 20 32N33'27 82w29'19 5:29:57
North Atlanta 44 6 33N51'54 84w20'12 5:37:21
North Buena Vista 98 8 32N26 84w31 5:38:04
North Canton 28 8 34N14'38 84w29'38 5:37:59
North Central 155 8 34N49 84w55 5:39:40
North Clayton 31 8 33N34'55 84w18'12 5:37:13
Northcutt 61 8 34N43'49 84w25'50 5:37:43
North Dade 41 8 34N55 85w27 5:41:48
North Decatur 44 7 33N47'25 84w18'22 5:37:13
North Druid Hills 44 20 33N50 84w19 5:37:16
North Dublin 87 20 32N33 82w54 5:31:36
North Echols 50 20 30N46 82w57 5:31:48
North Elberton 52 20 34N07'37 82w51'32 5:31:26
North Highlands 106 17 32N29'40 84w59'07 5:39:56
North High Shoals 108 20 33N49 83w30 5:34:00
North Kirkwood 44 7 33N45'42 84w19'44 5:37:19
North Ogeechee 82 20 32N51 81w55 5:27:40
North Rockdale 122 20 33N44 83w59 5:35:56
North Roswell 60 7 34N01 84w21 5:37:24
North Side 60 7 33N50 84w23 5:37:32
North West Point 141 8 32N54'11 85w09'36 5:40:38
North Whitfield 155 8 34N55 84w56 5:39:44
Northwoods 44 20 33N52'39 84w17'16 5:37:09
Norton 155 8 34N51'17 84w51'00 5:39:24
Norwich 133 8 32N32'11 84w26'40 5:37:47
Norwood 149 20 33N27'45 82w42'19 5:30:49
Notalee Orchards 144 8 34N52'42 84w00'19 5:36:01
Note 117 20 33N16'03 83w27'50 5:33:51
Nuberg 73 20 34N15'52 82w53'42 5:31:35
Nunez 53 20 32N29'28 82w20'50 5:29:23
Oakdale 33 8 33N49'07 84w29'52 5:37:59
Oakfield 159 20 31N46'40 83w58'17 5:35:53
Oak Grove 22 8 33N27'36 85w07'31 5:40:30
Oak Grove 28 8 34N06 84w31 5:38:04
Oak Grove 103 20 32N07'47 82w31'36 5:30:06
Oak Grove 141 8 32N54'17 84w55'23 5:39:42
Oak Grove 157 20 33N43'41 82w34'00 5:30:16
Oak Hill 19 8 31N36'09 84w28'38 5:37:55
Oak Hill 61 8 34N39'03 84w25'46 5:37:43
Oak Hill 107 20 33N32'19 84w00'36 5:36:02
Oakhurst 25 20 31N59'43 81w07'27 5:24:30
Oakhurst 44 7 33N45'48 84w18'39 5:37:15
Oak Knolls 76 20 32N29'19 83w47'17 5:35:09
Oakland 61 8 34N38'03 84w23'15 5:37:33
Oakland 88 20 31N40'26 84w15'36 5:37:02
Oakland 99 8 33N06'30 84w35'28 5:38:22
Oakland Heights 8 8 34N12'44 84w47'43 5:39:11
Oak Landing 151 20 31N34'01 81w45'25 5:27:02
Oakland Park 106 17 32N24'47 84w57'38 5:39:51
Oaklawn 14 20 30N50'57 83w44'16 5:34:57
Oaklawn 38 8 33N19'47 84w46'51 5:39:07
Oak Level 15 20 31N51'20 81w13'31 5:24:54
Oakman 64 8 34N33'59 84w42'30 5:38:50
Oak Mountain 22 8 33N33'38 85w01'15 5:40:05
Oak Mountain 72 8 32N44'33 84w43'31 5:38:54
Oak Park 53 20 32N21'29 82w18'53 5:29:16
Oak Ridge 137 20 31N24 83w30 5:34:00
Oakton 146 8 34N35'58 85w17'13 5:41:09
Oakville 135 8 31N51'09 84w27'51 5:37:51
Oakwood 69 1 34N13'39 83w53'04 5:35:32
Oaky 51 20 32N31'29 81w23'28 5:25:34
Oasis 55 8 34N54'55 84w28'56 5:37:56
Oberry 2 20 31N23'06 82w58'51 5:31:55
Ocee 60 8 34N03'52 84w12'46 5:36:51
Ochillee 26 17 32N23'39 84w50'40 5:39:23
Ochlocknee 136 20 30N58'25 84w03'11 5:36:13
Ochwalkee 153 20 32N11'37 82w38'24 5:30:34
Ocilla 77 20 31N35'39 83w15'02 5:33:00
Oconee 150 20 32N51'19 82w57'00 5:31:48
Oconee Heights 29 3 33N59'23 83w25'33 5:33:42
Oconee Springs Park 117 20 33N17'20 83w11'58 5:32:48
Odessa 151 20 31N33'27 81w49'13 5:27:17
Odessadale 99 8 33N00'57 84w48'47 5:39:15
Odis Crossroads 6 20 34N23'41 83w23'42 5:33:35
Odum 151 20 31N39'57 82w01'41 5:28:07
Offerman 113 20 31N24'34 82w06'43 5:28:27
Ogeechee 124 20 32N37'11 81w45'54 5:27:04
Ogeecheeton 25 20 32N03'35 81w07'50 5:24:31
Oglesby 52 20 34N04'32 82w58'02 5:31:52
Oglesby 150 20 33N05 82w58 5:31:52
Oglethorpe 25 20 32N00 81w05 5:24:20
Oglethorpe 96 8 32N17'37 84w03'40 5:36:15
Oglethorpe Park 25 20 32N03 81w07 5:24:28
Oglethorpe University 44 20 33N52 84w20 5:37:20
Ohoopee 138 20 32N10'48 82w13'11 5:28:53
Okefenokee 148 20 31N14 82w22 5:29:28
Ola 75 20 33N26'09 84w02'31 5:36:10
Old Airport Community 57 8 34N17 85w12 5:40:48
Old Damascus 49 8 31N18'26 84w44'14 5:38:57
Old Dellwood 53 20 32N40'06 82w21'57 5:29:28
Old Landing 91 20 31N35'45 81w43'30 5:26:54
Old Log Landing 51 20 32N23'47 81w10'59 5:24:44
Old Town 81 20 32N54'50 82w18'33 5:29:14
Old Wood Landing 51 20 32N21'28 81w10'04 5:24:40
O'Leary 25 20 32N12'38 81w10'34 5:24:42
Olifftown 21 20 32N29'40 82w05'51 5:28:23
Olive Branch 130 8 32N40'21 84w36'35 5:38:26
Oliver 124 20 32N31'17 81w32'00 5:26:08
Olivers Mill 135 8 31N52'20 84w20'11 5:37:21
Ollie 61 8 34N44'54 84w36'03 5:38:24
Olney 16 20 32N15'19 81w27'39 5:25:51
Omaha 128 8 32N08'46 85w00'48 5:40:03
Omaha Springs 81 20 33N10'10 82w32'36 5:30:10
Omega 137 20 31N20'27 83w35'37 5:34:22
O Neal 151 20 31N24'01 81w56'11 5:27:45
O'Neals Crossroads 74 8 33N11'39 85w13'25 5:40:54
Oostanaula 64 8 34N28'53 85w00'52 5:40:03
Ophir 28 8 34N19'46 84w15'54 5:37:04
Opies Landing 124 20 32N33'51 81w41'56 5:26:48
Orange 28 8 34N15'20 84w20'29 5:37:22
Orchard Hill 126 8 33N11'11 84w12'41 5:36:51
Orchard Hills 146 8 34N57'00 85w17'17 5:41:09
Ordway 106 17 32N29 84w57 5:39:48
Oreburg 57 8 34N15'43 85w18'46 5:41:15
Orianna 140 20 32N28'26 82w38'43 5:30:35
Orland 140 20 32N26'00 82w40'21 5:30:41
Ormewood 60 7 33N43'48 84w21'25 5:37:26
Orsman 57 8 34N22'00 85w14'20 5:40:57
Oscarville 58 8 34N14'54 83w58'30 5:35:54
Osierfield 77 20 31N40'01 83w06'58 5:32:28
Ossahatchie 72 8 32N39'14 84w46'36 5:39:06
Otter Creek 113 20 31N19'25 82w08'04 5:28:32
Ousley 92 20 30N47'39 83w25'51 5:33:43
Overbrook 16 20 32N14'15 81w48'44 5:27:15
Owen 113 20 31N20'37 82w11'24 5:28:46
Owensboro 156 20 31N52'38 83w25'41 5:33:43
Owensbyville 74 8 33N11'14 85w05'10 5:40:21
Owltown 144 8 34N48'47 83w56'24 5:35:46
Oxford 107 20 33N37'08 83w52'03 5:35:28
Oxlot Landing 151 20 31N33'22 81w43'31 5:26:54
Pabst 76 20 32N26'25 83w37'39 5:34:31
Pace 107 20 33N34'43 83w57'47 5:35:51
Pachitla 120 8 31N45'46 84w40'53 5:38:44
Padena 55 8 34N51'10 84w13'08 5:36:53
Paintertown 55 8 34N59'11 84w20'53 5:37:24
Palato 79 20 33N22'58 83w44'40 5:34:59

Place		Lat.	Long.	Time
Palmetto 60	10	33N31'04	84w40'11	5:38:41
Palmetto 109	20	33N54'21	82w55'23	5:31:42
Palmyra 88	20	31N38'15	84w11'40	5:36:47
Pancras 5	20	33N00'07	83w15'20	5:33:01
Panhandle 133	8	32N33'28	84w10'54	5:36:44
Panhandle 149	20	33N19	82w29	5:29:56
Pannell 147	20	33N46'06	83w40'30	5:34:42
Panola 44	20	33N38'46	84w11'15	5:36:45
Pantertown 55	8	34N55	84w17	5:37:08
Panthersville 44	6	33N42'26	84w16'19	5:37:05
Paoli 97	20	34N05'32	83w05'30	5:32:22
Paradise Park 25	20	32N00	81w05	5:24:20
Paradise Park 151	20	31N33'09	81w42'32	5:26:50
Paramore Hill 82	20	32N45'30	81w53'17	5:27:33
Pardue Mill 68	20	34N35'32	83w35'07	5:34:20
Parhams 59	20	34N25'36	83w14'26	5:32:58
Parish 21	20	32N23'38	81w59'20	5:27:57
Parkchester 106	17	32N27'20	84w56'00	5:39:44
Park City 146	8	34N56'44	85w16'01	5:41:04
Parker Courthouse 43	8	30N59'17	84w25'08	5:37:41
Parkers 43	8	31N01	84w28	5:37:52
Parkers 124	20	32N41'59	81w48'36	5:27:14
Parkersburg 25	20	31N59'04	81w03'08	5:24:13
Parkertown 73	20	34N27'27	83w02'24	5:32:10
Parkertown Mill 73	20	34N27'14	83w02'36	5:32:10
Parkerville 159	20	31N26'22	83w55'51	5:35:43
Park Hill 69	1	34N18	83w49	5:35:16
Parks Mill 104	20	33N30'10	83w17'18	5:33:09
Parksville 19	8	31N30'34	84w45'49	5:39:03
Parkwood 25	20	32N01'42	81w03'51	5:24:15
Parrett Crossing 155	8	34N58'33	84w57'29	5:39:50
Parrott 135	8	31N53'36	84w30'48	5:38:03
Pasco 136	20	30N54'41	83w59'45	5:35:59
Pateville 40	20	31N50'09	83w49'26	5:35:18
Patillo 85	8	33N12'06	84w05'33	5:36:22
Patmos 4	8	31N22'33	84w33'54	5:38:16
Patten 136	20	30N55'01	83w48'53	5:35:16
Patterson 97	20	34N01'47	83w14'43	5:32:59
Patterson 113	20	31N23'14	82w08'25	5:28:34
Paulk 12	20	32N23'09	83w24'19	5:33:37
Paulk Landing 49	8	31N23'30	85w04'46	5:40:19
Pavo 14	20	30N57'35	83w44'17	5:34:57
Paxton 24	20	30N50'56	82w04'23	5:28:18
Payne 11	25	32N51'10	83w41'17	5:34:45
Payne 28	8	34N06'34	84w38'57	5:38:36
Paynes Mill 145	8	32N55'19	84w19'15	5:37:17
Peach Orchard 121	20	33N26	82w01	5:28:04
Peachtree Center 60	7	33N45	84w20	5:37:20
Peachtree City 56	8	33N23'48	84w35'45	5:38:23
Peacocks Crossing 150	20	32N52'13	82w45'21	5:31:01
Pearl 52	20	34N06'30	82w43'15	5:30:53
Pearly 87	20	32N33	82w54	5:31:36
Pearson 2	20	31N17'51	82w51'09	5:31:25
Pebblebrook Estates 33	8	33N49'14	84w31'39	5:38:07
Pebble City 101	20	31N14'51	84w04'40	5:36:19
Pebble Hill 14	20	30N55'02	83w34'41	5:34:19
Pecan 30	8	31N38'26	84w59'32	5:39:58
Pecan City 47	20	31N31'03	84w04'12	5:36:17
Pedenville 114	8	33N07'22	84w29'47	5:37:59
Peeks Crossing 38	8	33N18'22	84w35'53	5:38:24
Pelham 101	20	31N07'39	84w09'07	5:36:36
Pembroke 15	20	32N08'09	81w37'20	5:26:29
Pendarvis 151	20	31N30'11	81w45'30	5:27:02
Pendergrass 78	20	34N09'44	83w40'41	5:34:43
Pendley Hills 44	20	33N44	84w16	5:37:04
Penfield 66	20	33N40'02	83w10'39	5:32:43
Penia 40	20	31N58'11	83w42'01	5:34:48
Pennick 63	20	31N18'46	81w33'33	5:26:14
Pennington 104	20	33N29'05	83w33'39	5:34:15
Pennington 129	8	32N09'36	84w05'14	5:36:21
Pennville 27	8	34N30'44	85w19'17	5:41:17
Peoples Still 65	8	30N53	84w19	5:37:16
Pepperton 18	8	33N17'36	83w56'42	5:35:47
Perennial 27	8	34N27'13	85w24'57	5:41:40
Perkins 82	20	32N54'34	81w57'11	5:27:49
Perkins Place 128	8	32N08'12	84w59'37	5:39:58
Perry 76	20	32N27'29	83w43'54	5:34:56
Perry Homes 60	7	33N47	84w26	5:37:44
Persico 99	8	32N54'55	84w36'15	5:38:25
Persimmon 119	20	34N53'46	83w30'43	5:34:03
Petersburg 64	8	34N35'12	84w42'56	5:38:52
Peterson Hill 120	8	31N46'54	84w50'54	5:39:24
Petross 103	20	32N08'52	82w28'01	5:29:52
Pew Landing 82	20	32N48'29	82w06'53	5:28:28
Pfeiffers Landing 124	20	32N46'05	81w25'58	5:25:44
Phelps 155	8	34N41'53	84w59'00	5:39:56
Philema 88	20	31N45'14	84w01'01	5:36:04
Phillips 121	20	33N29	82w02	5:28:08
Phillipsburg 137	20	31N26'22	83w31'10	5:34:05
Philomath 109	20	33N43'38	82w59'29	5:31:58
Phinizy 36	20	33N36'37	82w19'35	5:29:18
Phoenix 117	20	33N21'57	83w16'40	5:33:07
Pickard 145	8	32N55'16	84w24'50	5:37:39
Pidcock 14	20	30N47'03	83w42'28	5:34:50
Piddleville 16	20	32N33'20	81w57'35	5:27:50
Piedmont 85	15	33N01'01	84w15'03	5:37:00
Piedmont Heights 141	8	32N59'29	85w12'28	5:40:50
Pierceville 55	8	34N59	84w22	5:37:28
Pineboro 35	20	31N10'40	83w40'22	5:34:41
Pine Chapel 64	8	34N30	84w57	5:39:48
Pinefield Crossroads 6	20	34N25'17	83w26'27	5:33:46
Pine Gardens 25	20	32N03'58	81w03'37	5:24:14
Pine Grove 1	20	31N48'47	82w26'51	5:29:47
Pine Grove 92	20	30N56	83w15	5:33:00
Pine Harbor 95	20	31N32'50	81w22'32	5:25:30
Pine Hill 81	20	32N56'57	82w23'58	5:29:36
Pine Hill 106	17	32N25'40	84w56'09	5:39:45
Pinehurst 46	20	32N11'45	83w45'47	5:35:03
Pinehurst 75	20	33N33	84w14	5:36:56
Pine Lake 44	20	33N47'37	84w12'22	5:36:49
Pineland 50	20	30N42'47	82w45'56	5:31:04
Pine Log 8	8	34N20'34	84w43'56	5:38:56
Pine Mountain 72	8	32N51'53	84w51'15	5:39:25
Pine Mountain 119	20	34N56'25	83w11'14	5:32:45
Pine Mountain Valley 72	8	32N47'55	84w49'24	5:39:18
Pineora 51	20	32N17'12	81w23'30	5:25:34
Pine Park 65	8	30N51'04	84w06'07	5:36:24
Pinesville 84	20	33N01'22	83w29'21	5:33:57
Pinetree Plaza 44	20	33N54	84w16	5:37:04
Pinetta 77	20	31N35'35	83w21'30	5:33:26
Pine Valley 37	20	31N05'14	83w28'24	5:33:54
Pine Valley 121	20	33N28	81w59	5:27:56
Pine Valley 148	20	31N12'04	82w31'07	5:30:04
Pineview 156	20	32N06'36	83w30'04	5:34:00
Piney Bluff 20	20	31N01'10	81w32'18	5:26:09
Piney Grove 72	17	32N29	84w57	5:39:48
Piney Grove 151	20	31N44'13	82w01'08	5:28:05
Pink 154	20	34N35'29	83w42'45	5:34:51
Pin Point 25	20	31N57'11	81w05'33	5:24:22
Pinson 57	8	34N21'47	85w03'49	5:40:15
Pio Nono 11	25	32N51	83w36	5:34:24
Pirkle Woods 58	8	34N13'25	84w07'48	5:36:31
Piscola 136	20	30N41'24	83w40'34	5:34:42
Pisgah 61	8	34N42'29	84w17'42	5:37:11
Pittman 67	20	33N58'19	84w10'11	5:36:41
Pitts 156	20	31N56'40	83w32'27	5:34:10
Pittsburg 44	20	33N52'50	84w13'10	5:36:53
Plainfield 45	20	32N17'19	83w06'44	5:32:27
Plains 129	8	32N02'02	84w23'34	5:37:34
Plainview 59	20	34N22'00	83w21'22	5:33:25
Plainview 149	20	33N25'04	82w37'36	5:30:30
Plainview 155	8	34N52'40	84w56'40	5:39:47
Plainville 64	8	34N24'18	85w02'14	5:40:09
Plank Landing 151	20	31N34'17	81w45'50	5:27:03
Planter 97	20	34N07'10	83w20'26	5:33:22
Plaza 31	8	33N37	84w22	5:37:28
Pleasant Grove 141	8	32N58	85w00	5:40:00
Pleasant Grove 144	8	34N50'31	84w01'24	5:36:06
Pleasant Grove 155	8	34N49'46	84w56'31	5:39:46
Pleasant Hill 55	8	34N56'43	84w16'23	5:37:06
Pleasant Hill 61	8	34N45'14	84w36'08	5:38:25
Pleasant Hill 67	20	33N56'27	84w07'20	5:36:29
Pleasant Hill 130	8	32N48'22	84w29'56	5:38:00
Pleasant Hill 135	8	31N52'42	84w24'10	5:37:37
Pleasant Valley 8	8	34N20'22	84w51'47	5:39:27
Pleasant Valley 46	20	32N06	83w48	5:35:12
Pleasant Valley 61	8	34N34'28	84w27'32	5:37:50
Po Biddy Crossroads 130	8	32N41'25	84w28'19	5:37:53
Pocataligo 97	20	34N11'59	83w17'05	5:33:08
Point Peter 109	20	33N59'45	83w00'48	5:32:03
Pollards Corner 36	20	33N37'15	82w16'31	5:29:06
Pomona 126	8	33N19'09	84w17'02	5:37:08
Ponderosa 138	20	32N11'44	82w15'16	5:29:01
Pond Spring 146	8	34N49'20	85w19'32	5:41:18
Pooler 25	20	32N06'55	81w14'50	5:24:59
Poor Robin Landing 124	20	32N42'09	81w25'43	5:25:43
Pope City 156	20	31N57	83w27	5:33:48
Popes Ferry 102	8	33N07	83w48	5:35:12
Poplar Crossroads 130	8	32N42'17	84w23'55	5:37:36
Poplar Grove 59	20	34N30'51	83w06'56	5:32:28
Poplar Hill 45	20	31N59'27	83w06'04	5:32:24
Poplar Springs 71	8	33N48'44	85w17'23	5:41:10
Popwellville 13	20	31N18'57	81w44'43	5:26:59
Portal 16	20	32N32'17	81w55'57	5:27:44
Porter 12	20	32N24'46	83w23'59	5:33:36
Porterdale 107	20	33N34'30	83w53'38	5:35:35
Porter Springs 93	8	34N37'41	83w56'54	5:35:48
Portland 115	8	34N03'26	85w02'11	5:40:09
Port Royal 15	20	31N54'13	81w17'45	5:25:11
Port Wentworth 25	20	32N08'56	81w09'48	5:24:39
Port Wentworth Junction 25	20	32N08'37	81w11'32	5:24:46
Postell 84	25	32N54'56	83w31'36	5:34:06
Potter 50	20	30N38'48	82w56'00	5:31:44
Potters Landing 49	8	31N09'38	85w04'57	5:40:20
Potterville 133	8	32N30'52	84w07'03	5:36:28
Poulan 159	20	31N30'46	83w47'16	5:35:09
Powder Springs 33	8	33N51'34	84w41'02	5:38:44
Powell Landing 49	8	31N24'23	85w04'35	5:40:18
Powell Place 47	11	31N34	84w11	5:36:44
Powelltown 159	20	31N24'34	83w47'05	5:35:08
Powelton 70	20	33N25'43	82w52'15	5:31:29
Power Place 128	8	32N08'09	84w59'54	5:40:00
Powerville 111	8	32N36'14	83w47'34	5:35:10
Prater Mill 155	8	34N53'43	84w55'12	5:39:41
Pratersville 155	8	34N37'38	84w57'19	5:39:49
Prather 157	20	33N48'05	82w48'01	5:31:12
Prattsburg 130	8	32N42'45	84w21'28	5:37:26
Prentiss 1	20	31N47'38	82w23'45	5:29:35
Presley 139	20	34N57	83w45	5:35:00
Preston 152	8	32N03'57	84w32'15	5:38:09
Pretoria 16	20	32N24'35	81w43'50	5:26:55
Pretoria 47	11	31N30'15	84w19'02	5:37:16
Price 69	1	34N23'11	83w55'16	5:35:41
Pridgen 34	20	31N41'48	82w55'23	5:31:42
Priest Landing 25	20	31N57'31	81w00'42	5:24:03
Primrose 99	8	33N08'36	84w44'31	5:38:58
Princeton 29	3	33N59	83w23	5:33:32
Pringle 150	20	32N48'00	82w38'05	5:30:32
Prior 115	8	34N00'52	85w22'44	5:41:31
Pritchetts 159	20	31N21'50	83w57'21	5:35:49
Privette Heights 33	8	33N56	84w32	5:38:08
Prosperity 13	20	31N12'38	81w56'14	5:27:45
Pulaski 21	20	32N23'24	81w57'25	5:27:50
Pumpkin Center 36	20	33N25	82w19	5:29:16
Putnam 98	8	32N15'31	84w25'05	5:37:40
Putney 47	20	31N28'12	84w07'04	5:36:28
Pyles Marsh 63	20	31N14'34	81w33'39	5:26:15
Pyne 141	8	33N02'02	85w07'34	5:40:30
Quality 136	20	31N02'26	84w04'25	5:36:18
Queensland 9	20	31N47'56	83w14'11	5:32:57
Quill 61	8	34N38'34	84w18'01	5:37:12
Quitman 14	20	30N47'05	83w33'36	5:34:14
Rabbit Hill 15	20	31N54'22	81w16'10	5:25:05
Rabun Gap 119	20	34N58	83w23	5:33:32
Raccoon Bluff 95	20	31N27'57	81w14'07	5:24:56
Racepond 24	20	31N00'10	82w07'47	5:28:31
Radio Springs 57	8	34N13'19	85w14'34	5:40:58
Radium Springs 47	11	31N31'34	84w08'08	5:36:33
Rahns 51	20	32N18'51	81w16'53	5:25:08
Raines 40	20	31N53'27	83w51'52	5:35:27
Rains Landing 20	20	30N59'50	81w54'25	5:27:38
Raleigh 99	8	32N56'12	84w38'11	5:38:33
Ramhurst 105	8	34N41'53	84w43'51	5:38:55
Randall 128	8	32N03'58	84w43'10	5:38:53
Ranger 64	8	34N30'04	84w42'35	5:38:50
Raoul 68	20	34N28	83w34	5:34:16
Raulerson 13	20	31N23	82w08	5:28:32
Ravenwood 121	20	33N29	82w02	5:28:08
Raybon 13	20	31N15'46	81w58'20	5:27:53
Ray City 10	20	31N04'28	83w11'58	5:32:48
Rayle 157	20	33N47'23	82w54'00	5:31:36
Raymond 38	8	33N20'19	84w42'53	5:38:52
Raysville 94	20	33N37'08	82w28'55	5:29:56
Raytown 131	20	33N34'09	82w45'09	5:31:01
Rebecca 142	20	31N48'23	83w29'13	5:33:57
Rebie 12	20	32N27'43	83w10'34	5:32:42
Recovery 43	8	30N45'23	84w44'15	5:38:57
Redan 44	20	33N44'43	84w07'54	5:36:32
Red Bluff 9	20	31N46'29	83w00'07	5:32:00
Red Bluff 20	20	31N03'03	81w41'45	5:26:47
Red Bluff Landing 80	20	31N57'44	82w27'21	5:29:49
Red Bluff Landing 124	20	32N55'03	81w39'23	5:26:38
Redbone 85	8	32N59'24	84w05'51	5:36:23
Redbone Crossroads 145	8	32N52'09	84w15'20	5:37:01
Redbud 64	8	34N31'58	84w48'59	5:39:16
Red Clay 155	8	34N59'05	84w56'46	5:39:47
Red Hill 59	20	34N26'06	83w15'38	5:33:03
Red Hill 128	8	32N05	84w40	5:38:40
Redland 151	20	31N38'23	81w57'16	5:27:49
Red Lane 69	1	34N18	83w49	5:35:16
Red Oak 60	8	33N37'29	84w29'55	5:38:00
Red Rock 33	8	33N58'46	84w42'58	5:38:52
Red Rock 159	20	31N34'57	83w56'15	5:35:45
Red Stone 78	20	34N06	83w34	5:34:16
Red Store Crossroads 4	8	31N24'16	84w16'34	5:37:06
Redwine 60	8	33N30'45	84w48'48	5:39:15
Reed Creek 73	20	34N26'45	82w55'30	5:31:42
Reese 104	20	33N32'24	83w37'26	5:34:30
Reese 149	20	33N20'41	82w34'44	5:30:19
Reeseburg 57	8	34N07'53	85w10'42	5:40:43
Reeves 64	8	34N27'41	85w00'46	5:40:03
Register 16	20	32N22'01	81w53'03	5:27:32
Rehobeth 72	8	32N38'27	84w53'02	5:39:32
Rehoboth 44	20	33N49'27	84w15'53	5:37:04
Reids 143	20	32N43'05	83w34'02	5:34:16
Reidsboro 114	8	33N08'15	84w23'01	5:37:32
Reids Crossroads 117	20	33N24'33	83w25'36	5:33:42
Reidsville 132	20	32N06'12	82w07'05	5:28:28
Reka 15	20	32N08'21	81w40'39	5:26:43
Relay 57	8	34N05'56	85w11'30	5:40:46
Relee 34	20	31N45'39	82w55'59	5:31:44
Remerton 92	20	30N50'38	83w18'38	5:33:15
Renfroe 26	8	32N13'57	84w42'45	5:38:51
Reno 65	8	30N46'25	84w17'32	5:37:10
Rentz 87	20	32N23'00	82w59'29	5:31:58
Reo 146	8	34N42'55	85w06'29	5:40:26
Resaca 64	8	34N34'49	84w56'36	5:39:46
Resseaus Crossroads 117	20	33N12'04	83w26'04	5:33:44
Rest Haven 67	20	34N07'59	83w58'36	5:35:54
Retreat 89	20	31N42'10	81w24'51	5:25:39
Rex 31	20	33N35'31	84w16'12	5:37:05
Reynolds 133	8	32N33'35	84w05'47	5:36:23
Reynoldsville 125	8	30N51'25	84w46'41	5:39:07

Place		Latitude	Longitude	Time
Rhine 45	20	31N59'22	83w12'01	5:32:48
Riceboro 89	20	31N44'07	81w26'01	5:25:44
Rice Landing 124	20	32N54'24	81w38'59	5:26:36
Richfield 25	20	32N02'27	81w07'58	5:24:32
Richland 128	8	32N05'16	84w40'03	5:38:40
Richmond Hill 15	20	31N56'17	81w18'13	5:25:13
Richwood 46	20	32N02'30	83w47'11	5:35:09
Ricks Place 30	8	31N45'44	85w05'58	5:40:24
Rico 60	10	33N34'52	84w46'08	5:39:05
Riddleyville 150	20	32N54'24	82w39'57	5:30:40
Ridgeville 95	20	31N24'22	81w24'06	5:25:36
Ridgeway 72	8	32N38'07	84w43'18	5:38:53
Ridgewood 25	20	32N02'00	81w05'55	5:24:24
Ridley 74	8	33N18'04	85w12'01	5:40:48
Rincon 51	20	32N17'45	81w14'08	5:24:57
Ringgold 23	8	34N54'57	85w06'33	5:40:26
Rio 126	8	33N16'48	84w22'55	5:37:32
Rio Vista 25	20	31N55'45	81w05'17	5:24:21
Ripley 143	20	32N43'30	83w25'02	5:33:40
Rising Fawn 41	8	34N45'36	85w31'52	5:42:07
Ritch 151	20	31N32'23	82w06'23	5:28:26
River Bend 47	20	31N26'36	84w08'09	5:36:33
Riverbend 77	20	31N29'26	83w15'48	5:33:03
Riverdale 31	8	33N34'21	84w24'48	5:37:39
Riverland Terrace 106	17	32N25'18	84w57'17	5:39:49
Rivers End 25	20	31N59'12	81w06'56	5:24:28
Riverside 11	25	32N51	83w41	5:34:44
Riverside 25	20	32N02'43	81w00'40	5:24:03
Riverside 35	20	31N10'48	83w48'23	5:35:14
Riverside 57	8	34N17	85w12	5:40:48
Riverside 60	7	33N48'44	84w28'03	5:37:52
Rivertown 60	10	33N36'56	84w44'15	5:38:57
Riverturn 125	8	30N59'23	84w56'51	5:39:47
Rives Landing 32	20	30N42'28	82w31'38	5:30:07
Roanoke 9	20	31N43	83w15	5:33:00
Roberta 39	8	32N43'18	84w00'48	5:36:03
Roberts Cross Road 69	1	34N07	84w00	5:36:00
Roberts Crossroads 69	1	34N08'02	83w56'07	5:35:44
Robertstown 154	20	34N42'36	83w44'27	5:34:58
Robertsville 146	8	34N52'58	85w17'47	5:41:11
Robinson 57	8	34N15'48	85w17'15	5:41:09
Robinson 131	20	33N35'07	82w59'32	5:31:58
Rochelle 156	20	31N57'03	83w27'23	5:33:50
Rockalo 74	8	33N22'33	85w12'21	5:40:49
Rock Branch 52	20	34N14'23	82w48'00	5:31:12
Rock Creek 127	20	34N34	83w16	5:33:04
Rock Cut 31	8	33N36	84w20	5:37:20
Rockdale 60	7	33N47'13	84w26'06	5:37:44
Rock Fence Crossroads 17	20	33N01'34	81w34'41	5:26:19
Rock Hill 49	8	31N19'41	85w01'54	5:40:08
Rockingham 3	20	31N32'52	82w25'00	5:29:40
Rock Landing 53	20	32N49'28	82w17'13	5:29:09
Rockledge 87	20	32N26'34	82w41'52	5:30:47
Rockmart 115	8	34N00'09	85w02'30	5:40:10
Rockridge 74	8	33N18'19	85w08'02	5:40:32
Rock Spring 146	8	34N49'27	85w14'34	5:40:58
Rock Springs 138	20	32N04'23	82w24'53	5:29:40
Rock Springs Landing 87	20	32N24'07	82w49'02	5:31:16
Rockville 117	20	33N19'39	83w13'08	5:32:53
Rocky Creek 64	8	34N30	84w57	5:39:48
Rocky Face 155	8	34N48'18	85w01'39	5:40:07
Rocky Ford 124	20	32N39'48	81w49'47	5:27:19
Rocky Hammock Landing 80	20	31N48'51	82w49'23	5:31:18
Rocky Hill 65	8	30N42'09	84w12'37	5:36:50
Rocky Mount 99	8	33N09'55	84w40'24	5:38:42
Rocky Plains 107	20	33N29'50	83w55'06	5:35:40
Roddenberry 65	8	30N52'37	84w15'36	5:37:02
Roddy 45	20	32N21'09	83w15'02	5:33:00
Rodgers 8	8	34N12'08	84w49'40	5:39:19
Rogers 82	20	32N49'09	82w04'26	5:28:18
Rogers 97	20	34N09'16	83w20'26	5:33:22
Rogers Crossing 82	20	32N48'56	82w04'25	5:28:18
Rogers Mill 154	20	34N30'13	83w40'40	5:34:43
Roland 145	8	32N51'34	84w24'57	5:37:40
Rolston 61	8	34N40'25	84w20'40	5:37:23
Rome 57	5	34N15'25	85w09'53	5:40:40
Roopville 22	8	33N27'23	85w07'51	5:40:31
Roosevelt 61	8	34N42'11	84w33'02	5:38:12
Roosterville 74	8	33N24'12	85w11'02	5:40:44
Roper 32	20	30N49	82w39	5:30:36
Roper 80	20	31N48'43	82w39'06	5:30:36
Ropers Crossroads 36	20	33N30'26	82w08'29	5:28:34
Roscoe 38	8	33N29'41	84w49'20	5:39:17
Rosebud 67	20	33N47'55	83w58'00	5:35:52
Rosedale 57	8	34N26'18	85w06'29	5:40:26
Rose Dhu 25	20	32N00	81w05	5:24:20
Rose Hill 25	20	31N59'22	81w06'41	5:24:27
Rose Hill 106	17	32N29'15	84w58'59	5:39:56
Rose Hill 108	20	33N46'44	83w18'41	5:33:15
Rose Hill 114	15	33N01'56	84w20'00	5:37:20
Rose Hill Heights 106	17	32N29'46	84w58'26	5:39:54
Rosemont 36	20	33N37'10	82w14'34	5:28:58
Rosemont Park 57	8	34N17	85w12	5:40:48
Rosier 17	20	32N58'41	82w14'34	5:28:58
Rosin Ford 151	20	31N24'01	81w49'06	5:27:16
Ross 97	20	34N02'45	83w04'00	5:32:16
Rossignol Hill 25	20	32N05'43	81w08'55	5:24:36
Rossville 146	12	34N58'59	85w17'10	5:41:09
Roswell 60	7	34N01'23	84w21'42	5:37:27
Round Bluff Landing 80	20	31N56'06	82w35'12	5:30:21
Round Oak 84	20	33N06'39	83w36'55	5:34:28
Roundtop 61	8	34N36'13	84w33'58	5:38:16
Routons Crossroads 99	8	32N53'36	84w37'57	5:38:32
Rover 126	8	33N12'23	84w20'06	5:37:20
Rowena 49	8	31N22'51	84w42'47	5:38:51
Rowland 45	20	32N26'11	83w10'07	5:32:40
Rowland Spring 8	8	34N13'10	84w44'24	5:38:58
Roxanna 110	8	33N55	84w50	5:39:20
Roy 61	8	34N39'18	84w21'12	5:37:25
Royal 12	20	32N26'44	83w22'44	5:33:31
Royston 73	20	34N17'13	83w06'37	5:32:26
Ruckersville 52	20	34N09'53	82w47'18	5:31:09
Rudden 117	20	33N26'18	83w20'01	5:33:20
Rupert 133	8	32N26'25	84w16'48	5:37:07
Ruskin 148	20	31N09'04	82w26'42	5:29:47
Russell 7	20	33N58'43	83w42'01	5:34:48
Russellville 102	8	32N54'09	83w59'29	5:35:58
Rutland 11	8	32N44'27	83w39'17	5:34:37
Rutledge 104	20	33N37'33	83w36'45	5:34:27
Rydal 8	8	34N20'07	84w42'56	5:38:52
Ryo 64	8	34N27'14	84w40'26	5:38:42
Sadlers Landing 20	20	30N52'16	81w36'30	5:26:26
Saffold 49	8	31N07'12	85w02'00	5:40:08
Saginaw 34	20	31N30'57	82w40'11	5:30:41
Saint Charles 38	8	33N16'07	84w46'33	5:39:06
Saint Clair 17	20	33N09'03	82w13'05	5:28:52
Saint George 24	20	30N31'15	82w02'16	5:28:09
Saint Louis 96	8	32N27'55	83w52'01	5:35:28
Saint Marks 99	8	33N07'31	84w49'16	5:39:17
Saint Marys 20	20	30N43'49	81w32'48	5:26:11
Saint Marys Hills 106	17	32N27'04	84w56'05	5:39:44
Saint Simons 63	20	31N08'06	81w23'25	5:25:34
Saint Simons Island 63	20	31N09'01	81w22'11	5:25:29
Salacoa 28	8	34N23'26	84w36'41	5:38:27
Sale City 101	20	31N15'51	84w01'17	5:36:05
Salem 12	20	32N29	83w15	5:33:00
Salem 23	8	34N57'25	85w02'33	5:40:10
Salem 108	20	33N43'22	83w23'11	5:33:33
Salter 13	20	31N08'43	81w47'27	5:27:10
Sanborn 47	11	31N34	84w11	5:36:44
Sandalwood 47	11	31N34	84w11	5:36:44
Sand Bed 76	20	32N27'24	83w37'06	5:34:28
Sandersville 150	20	32N58'53	82w48'37	5:31:14
Sandersville Rural 150	20	33N01	82w47	5:31:08
Sandfly 25	20	31N59'22	81w04'35	5:24:18
Sand Hill 14	20	30N59'05	83w39'03	5:34:36
Sand Hill 22	8	33N38'21	84w58'21	5:39:53
Sand Hill 148	20	31N06'40	82w32'22	5:30:09
Sand Mountain 41	8	34N55	85w33	5:42:12
Sand Town 33	8	33N56	84w32	5:38:08
Sandtown 157	20	33N50'10	82w41'16	5:30:45
Sandy 18	20	33N14'06	83w55'25	5:35:30
Sandy Bottom 2	20	31N11'27	82w45'25	5:31:02
Sandy Cross 59	20	34N17'14	83w13'34	5:32:54
Sandy Cross 109	20	33N56'35	83w04'00	5:32:16
Sandy Ford 119	20	34N51'38	83w14'49	5:32:59
Sandy Hill 157	20	33N51'46	82w41'55	5:30:48
Sandy Plains 33	8	34N00'47	84w29'44	5:37:59
Sandy Point 39	8	32N46'08	83w56'23	5:35:46
Sandy Run 70	20	33N13'47	83w07'42	5:32:31
Sandy Springs 60	20	33N55'27	84w22'43	5:37:31
Sanford 97	20	34N04'43	83w20'54	5:33:24
Sanford 128	8	31N58'46	84w56'37	5:39:46
Santa Claus 138	20	32N10'17	82w19'54	5:29:20
Santaluca 61	8	34N47'13	84w26'05	5:37:44
Sapelo 95	20	31N23	81w17	5:25:08
Sapelo Island 95	20	31N23'50	81w16'44	5:25:07
Sapp 12	20	32N23	83w21	5:33:24
Sapps Still 34	20	31N42'57	82w56'15	5:31:45
Sappville 148	20	31N15'16	82w32'32	5:30:10
Sarah 144	8	34N40'03	84w02'09	5:36:09
Sardis 17	20	32N58'30	81w45'28	5:27:02
Sargent 38	8	33N25'56	84w52'10	5:39:29
Sasser 135	8	31N43'11	84w20'50	5:37:23
Satilla 80	20	31N47'14	82w34'05	5:30:16
Satilla Creek 1	20	31N42	82w23	5:29:32
Satolah 119	20	34N59'25	83w11'35	5:32:46
Sautee 154	20	34N41'04	83w40'51	5:34:43
Sautee-Nacoochee 154	20	34N41	83w40	5:34:40
Savannah 25	4	32N05'00	81w06'00	5:24:24
Savannah Beach 25	20	31N59'37	80w50'55	5:23:24
Sawdust 36	22	33N25'08	82w19'56	5:29:20
Sawhatchee 49	8	31N16'36	85w01'40	5:40:07
Saxon 109	20	33N59'10	82w53'32	5:31:34
Scarboro 82	20	32N42'47	81w52'32	5:27:30
Scarbrough Cross Roads 75	20	33N37'50	84w13'08	5:36:53
Scarlet 20	20	30N56'02	81w45'50	5:27:03
Scenic Hills 23	8	34N55'23	85w09'34	5:40:38
Schatulga 106	17	32N30'50	84w52'14	5:39:29
Schlatterville 13	20	31N10'19	82w12'00	5:28:48
Schley 35	20	31N14'07	83w49'38	5:35:19
Scooterville 159	20	31N22'55	83w41'24	5:34:46
Scotchville 20	20	30N46'08	81w37'03	5:26:28
Scotland 134	20	32N02'55	82w49'02	5:31:16
Scott 83	20	32N33'06	82w40'01	5:30:40
Scottdale 44	20	33N47'23	84w15'51	5:37:03
Scottsboro 5	20	33N01'29	83w14'05	5:32:56
Scotts Corner 17	20	32N54'02	82w10'36	5:28:42
Screven 151	20	31N29'10	82w01'02	5:28:04
Screven Fork 89	20	31N46'23	81w29'29	5:25:58
Scrutchins 88	20	31N51'51	84w11'48	5:36:47
Scuffletown 94	20	33N31'40	82w28'31	5:29:54
Seabrook 89	20	31N44'36	81w19'44	5:25:19
Sea Island 63	20	31N11'00	81w21'00	5:25:24
Seals 20	20	30N52'22	81w42'15	5:26:49
Seines Landing 51	20	32N24'49	81w11'52	5:24:47
Sells 78	20	34N06	83w46	5:35:04
Seney 115	8	34N05'05	85w07'16	5:40:29
Senoia 38	8	33N18'08	84w33'14	5:38:13
Sessoms 3	20	31N30'56	82w34'59	5:30:20
Seville 156	20	31N57'37	83w36'04	5:34:24
Seymour 117	20	33N19	83w23	5:33:32
Shackleford Landing 49	8	31N12'02	85w06'21	5:40:25
Shady Dale 79	20	33N24'02	83w35'25	5:34:22
Shady Field Landing 87	20	32N23'43	82w48'01	5:31:12
Shady Grove 22	8	33N38'34	85w01'32	5:40:06
Shake Rag 56	8	33N25'03	84w33'34	5:38:14
Shake Rag 60	7	34N03'23	84w07'54	5:36:32
Shannon 57	8	34N20'12	85w04'17	5:40:17
Sharon 131	20	33N33'35	82w47'42	5:31:11
Sharon Park 25	20	32N05'25	81w10'14	5:24:41
Sharphagen 125	8	31N01'14	84w49'44	5:39:19
Sharpsburg 38	8	33N20'21	84w38'55	5:38:36
Sharps Spur 103	20	32N12	82w31	5:30:04
Sharp Top 28	8	34N21'47	84w28'59	5:37:56
Shawnee 51	20	32N28'32	81w24'30	5:25:38
Shellbine 20	20	30N54'27	81w31'04	5:26:04
Shell Bluff 17	20	33N08'52	81w53'53	5:27:36
Shell Bluff Landing 17	20	33N13'36	81w49'24	5:27:18
Shellman 120	8	31N45'22	84w36'55	5:38:28
Shellman Bluff 95	20	31N34'21	81w19'24	5:25:18
Shelly 14	20	30N59'58	83w44'14	5:34:57
Sheppards 124	20	32N38'14	81w32'07	5:26:08
Sherwood 31	8	33N31	84w21	5:37:24
Sherwood Forest 38	8	33N24'27	84w48'33	5:39:14
Sherwood Forest 57	8	34N15'51	85w07'18	5:40:29
Shewmake 87	20	32N30'50	83w02'05	5:32:08
Shields Crossroads 146	8	34N52	85w23	5:41:32
Shiloh 72	8	32N48'36	84w41'46	5:38:47
Shiloh 92	20	30N56'24	83w24'28	5:33:38
Shiloh 97	20	34N13'01	83w13'41	5:32:55
Shiloh 129	8	32N09'09	84w18'35	5:37:14
Shingler 159	20	31N34'41	83w47'05	5:35:08
Shirley Grove 68	20	34N42'58	83w24'55	5:33:40
Shirley Park 25	20	32N01'26	81w04'46	5:24:19
Shiver 14	20	30N49'41	83w32'31	5:34:10
Shivers Mill 120	8	31N40'36	84w44'24	5:38:58
Shoal Creek 73	20	34N26'22	83w02'05	5:32:08
Shoals 149	20	33N08	82w42	5:30:48
Shookville 23	8	34N54'42	85w05'11	5:40:21
Shorts Mill 68	20	34N34'21	83w29'34	5:33:58
Shoulderbone 70	20	33N20'22	83w04'48	5:32:19
Shurlington 11	25	32N50	83w37	5:34:28
Sibbie 156	20	31N51'16	83w18'18	5:33:13
Sibley 142	20	31N47'53	83w42'37	5:34:50
Sigsbee 35	20	31N15'54	83w51'34	5:35:26
Silco 20	20	30N52'05	81w49'52	5:27:19
Silica Hills 47	11	31N34	84w10	5:36:40
Silk Hope 25	20	32N02'34	81w11'31	5:24:46
Silk Mills 52	20	34N06'18	82w50'49	5:31:23
Siloam 66	20	33N32'12	83w04'52	5:32:19
Silver City 42	8	34N20'03	84w06'58	5:36:28
Silver Creek 57	8	34N10'34	85w09'41	5:40:39
Silver Hill 24	20	30N50'16	82w07'35	5:28:30
Silver Hill 27	8	34N24'06	85w18'26	5:41:14
Silver Pines 11	25	32N49	83w41	5:34:44
Silvertown 145	8	32N54'15	84w20'36	5:37:22
Silvertown 149	20	33N25'20	82w38'41	5:30:35
Simpson 74	8	33N20'50	85w10'19	5:40:41
Simpson Crossroads 8	8	34N17'51	84w48'01	5:39:12
Sims Landing 17	20	33N03'21	81w49'29	5:27:18
Sirmans 32	20	31N04'52	82w58'10	5:31:53
Six Mile 57	8	34N10'38	85w12'23	5:40:50
Skipperton 11	8	32N44'37	83w41'33	5:34:46
Skullhead 148	20	31N05'26	82w19'43	5:29:19
Skyland 44	20	33N52	84w20	5:37:20
Skyland Terrace 25	20	32N04	81w07	5:24:28
Slover 151	20	31N33'13	81w56'25	5:27:46
Smarr 102	8	32N59'07	83w52'56	5:35:32
Smiley Crossroads 91	20	31N51'47	81w46'02	5:27:04
Smithboro 79	20	33N18'19	83w35'02	5:34:20
Smithonia 109	20	34N00'10	83w10'34	5:32:42
Smiths Crossroad 141	8	32N57'17	85w01'11	5:40:05
Smiths Crossroads 72	8	32N50'15	84w56'03	5:39:44
Smiths Landing 43	8	30N53'41	84w44'59	5:39:00
Smiths Mill 141	8	32N54'30	84w57'59	5:39:52
Smithsonia 11	20	32N48'12	83w34'06	5:34:16
Smithsonia 109	20	34N01	83w12	5:32:48
Smithville 88	20	31N54'01	84w15'07	5:37:00
Smyrna 33	8	33N53'02	84w30'52	5:38:03
Snake Nation 55	8	34N52	84w19	5:37:16
Snapfinger 44	20	33N41'13	84w12'06	5:36:48
Snapping Shoals 107	20	33N40	83w52	5:35:28
Snead 36	20	33N33'56	82w07'15	5:28:29
Snellville 67	20	33N51'26	84w01'12	5:36:05
Snelsons Crossroads 99	8	32N58'30	84w39'59	5:38:40
Snipesville 80	20	31N45'42	82w45'04	5:31:00

Snows Mill 147 20 33N50'23 83w33'29 5:34:14
Snow Spring 46 20 32N15'15 83w46'54 5:35:08
Snow Springs 8 8 34N20'25 84w58'35 5:39:54
Soapstick 64 8 34N34'50 84w52'47 5:39:31
Social Circle 147 20 33N39'22 83w43'06 5:34:52
Sofkee 11 25 32N43'27 83w39'12 5:34:37
Somerset Park 25 20 32N00 81w05 5:24:20
Sonoraville 64 8 34N26'53 84w48'32 5:39:14
Soperton 140 20 32N22'37 82w35'33 5:30:22
South Base 76 20 32N37 83w39 5:34:36
South Canton 28 8 34N13'00 84w30'17 5:38:01
South Cobb 33 8 33N48 84w38 5:38:32
South Decatur 44 20 33N44 84w16 5:37:04
South De Kalb 44 20 33N43 84w17 5:37:08
South Echols 50 20 30N39 82w56 5:31:44
Southern Junction 63 20 31N13'53 81w31'08 5:26:05
Southern Tech 33 8 33N56 84w32 5:38:08
South Jackson 78 20 34N03 83w30 5:34:00
South Kirkwood 44 7 33N45'07 84w19'24 5:37:18
Southland 121 20 33N26 82w01 5:28:04
Southland 133 8 32N24'03 84w13'39 5:36:55
South Lincolnton 90 20 33N45 82w25 5:29:40
South Macon 11 25 32N47 83w41 5:34:44
South Moultrie 35 20 31N11 83w48 5:35:12
South Nellsville 121 20 33N27 81w57 5:27:48
South Newport 95 20 31N38'05 81w23'47 5:25:35
South Ogeechee 82 20 32N43 82w00 5:28:00
Southover 25 20 32N02'48 81w07'38 5:24:31
South Rockdale 122 20 33N35 84w04 5:36:16
South Rossville 146 8 34N58'09 85w17'41 5:41:11
South Thompson 138 20 32N06'29 82w22'15 5:29:29
Southward 15 20 32N08'28 81w42'13 5:26:49
Spain 14 20 30N51'52 83w32'17 5:34:09
Spalding 96 8 32N17'35 83w59'52 5:35:59
Spann 83 20 32N39'56 82w44'56 5:31:00
Sparks 37 20 31N10'00 83w26'15 5:33:45
Sparks 150 20 33N05'16 82w44'16 5:30:57
Sparks Mill 55 8 34N53'42 84w08'42 5:36:35
Sparta 70 20 33N16'32 82w58'35 5:31:54
Spell Landing 13 20 31N18'19 81w54'11 5:27:37
Spence 65 8 31N01'57 84w09'52 5:36:39
Spencer Hills 146 8 34N58'01 85w18'35 5:41:14
Spilo 144 8 34N53 83w58 5:35:52
Split Silk 147 20 33N39'46 83w50'30 5:35:22
Spooner 32 20 30N58'21 82w32'39 5:30:11
Spout Spring Crossroads 69 1 34N10'36 83w54'36 5:35:38
Spring Bluff 20 20 31N06'20 81w37'48 5:26:31
Spring Branch 1 20 31N50'29 82w21'07 5:29:24
Spring Creek 57 8 34N10 85w08 5:40:32
Springfield 51 20 32N22'20 81w18'42 5:25:15
Springfield 70 20 33N24'49 82w56'36 5:31:46
Springfield 131 20 33N37'40 82w56'57 5:31:48
Spring Hill 153 20 32N00'47 82w43'32 5:30:54
Spring Place 105 8 34N45'29 84w49'16 5:39:17
Springvale 120 8 31N49'41 84w52'47 5:39:31
Spring View Acres 69 1 34N19'48 83w50'23 5:35:22
Sprite 27 8 34N17'18 85w23'45 5:41:35
Stafford 20 20 30N48'55 81w28'02 5:25:52
Stalco 124 20 32N32'00 81w33'32 5:26:14
Staley Heights 25 20 32N01'58 81w07'14 5:24:29
Stallings Crossroad 38 8 33N20'19 84w58'48 5:39:55
Standleys Store 30 8 31N37 85w03 5:40:12
Stanfordville 117 20 33N13'23 83w30'03 5:34:00
Stanley Landing 24 20 30N45'17 82w02'15 5:28:09
Stanley Mill 61 8 34N44'36 84w17'28 5:37:10
Stanleys Store 138 20 32N11 82w17 5:29:08
Stapleton 81 20 33N12'56 82w28'06 5:29:52
Stapletons Crossroads 81 20 33N06'03 82w30'15 5:30:01
Stark 18 8 33N20'00 83w54'24 5:35:38
Starksville 88 20 31N46'19 84w08'44 5:36:35
Starling Ford 50 20 30N46'46 82w49'29 5:31:18
Star Point 22 8 33N27'24 85w05'03 5:40:20
Starrs Mill 56 8 33N19'38 84w30'45 5:38:03
Starrsville 107 20 33N32'22 83w49'10 5:35:17
State College 25 20 32N03 81w04 5:24:16
Statenville 50 20 30N42'11 83w01'40 5:32:07
Statesboro 16 20 32N26'55 81w47'00 5:27:08
Statesborough 16 20 32N13'03 81w43'26 5:26:54
Statham 7 20 33N57'54 83w35'48 5:34:23
Statham Shoals 156 20 31N58'00 83w16'59 5:33:08
Staunton 37 20 31N16'52 83w28'01 5:33:52
Stave Landing 87 20 32N22'33 82w44'16 5:30:57
Steadman 71 8 33N45 85w17 5:41:08
Steam Mill 125 8 30N58'12 84w58'07 5:39:52
Steeles Mill 126 20 33N18'27 84w08'13 5:36:33
Stellaville 81 20 33N11'24 82w19'53 5:29:20
Stephens 109 20 33N47'41 83w09'42 5:32:39
Stephensville 41 8 34N53'07 85w32'39 5:42:11
Stergeon Creek 9 20 31N44 83w11 5:32:44
Sterling 63 20 31N16'20 81w33'42 5:26:15
Stevens Crossing 53 20 32N46'21 82w15'17 5:29:01
Stevens Pottery 5 20 32N57 83w17 5:33:08
Stewart 107 20 33N25'19 83w51'08 5:35:25
Stewart Mill 55 8 34N49'15 84w19'01 5:37:16
Stewart Town 41 8 34N49'16 85w33'47 5:42:15
Stewartville 85 8 33N06 84w20 5:37:20
Stilesboro 8 8 34N06'17 84w54'57 5:39:40
Stillmore 53 20 32N26'31 82w12'55 5:28:52
Stillwell 51 20 32N22'40 81w15'02 5:25:00
Stilson 16 20 32N19'33 81w33'12 5:26:13
Stockbridge 75 20 33N32'39 84w14'02 5:36:56
Stock Hill 55 8 34N42'27 84w13'46 5:36:55
Stocks 88 20 31N44 84w10 5:36:40
Stockton 86 20 30N56'21 82w59'59 5:32:00
Stokesville 2 20 31N21'40 82w42'49 5:30:51
Stokesville 24 20 30N22'59 82w04'06 5:28:16
Stone Mountain 44 20 33N48'29 84w10'13 5:36:41
Stones Crossroads 94 20 33N31'22 82w26'05 5:29:44
Stonewall 60 8 33N35'52 84w32'51 5:38:11
Stoney Point 22 8 33N26'35 85w11'35 5:40:46
Stony Bluff Landing 17 20 33N02'35 81w33'20 5:26:13
Stop 56 8 33N28'47 84w35'20 5:38:21
Stovall 68 20 34N31 83w32 5:34:08
Stovall 99 8 32N57'39 84w51'07 5:39:24
Stovall Mill 154 20 34N36'40 83w40'20 5:34:41
Stratford 60 10 33N45'15 84w28'50 5:37:55
Strickland Landing 13 20 31N17'09 81w54'27 5:27:38
Strouds 102 8 32N55'13 84w03'58 5:36:16
Stuckey 153 20 32N10'15 82w42'37 5:30:50
Subligna 27 8 34N33'36 85w11'15 5:40:45
Suches 144 8 34N41'20 84w01'20 5:36:05
Sudie 110 8 33N52'02 84w50'29 5:39:22
Sugar Creek 55 8 34N52'42 84w21'37 5:37:26
Sugar Hill 46 20 32N17'20 83w39'14 5:34:37
Sugar Hill 67 20 34N06'23 84w02'01 5:36:08
Sugartown 23 8 34N53'10 85w04'18 5:40:17
Sugar Valley 64 8 34N33'29 85w00'43 5:40:03
Sulphur Springs 41 8 34N46 85w32 5:42:08
Sulphur Springs Station 41 8 34N41'18 85w32'29 5:42:10
Sumac 105 8 34N53'01 84w47'58 5:39:12
Summertown 53 20 32N44'45 82w16'35 5:29:06
Summerville 27 8 34N28'50 85w20'52 5:41:23
Summit 53 20 32N35 82w09 5:28:36
Summit Hill 23 8 34N57'26 85w09'19 5:40:37
Sumner 159 20 31N30'46 83w44'19 5:34:57
Sumter 129 20 31N56'57 84w15'18 5:37:01
Sunbury 89 20 31N46'05 81w16'52 5:25:07
Sun Hill 150 20 32N57'05 82w43'46 5:30:55
Sun Hill 151 20 31N27'04 81w55'16 5:27:41
Sunlight Park 121 20 33N28 81w59 5:27:56
Sunny Side 126 8 33N20'26 84w17'27 5:37:10
Sunnyside 139 20 34N55'59 83w46'38 5:35:07
Sunnyside 148 20 31N14 82w22 5:29:28
Sunset 35 20 31N11 83w48 5:35:12
Sunset Heights 69 1 34N20'30 83w49'06 5:35:16
Sunset Park 25 20 32N02'05 81w03'58 5:24:16
Sunset Terrace 106 17 32N26'48 84w55'10 5:39:41
Sunset Village 145 8 32N53'52 84w24'14 5:37:37
Sunsweet 137 20 31N34'09 83w33'57 5:34:16
Suomi 45 20 32N06 83w04 5:32:16
Surrency 1 20 31N43'25 82w11'53 5:28:48
Sutallee 28 8 34N13'22 84w37'05 5:38:28
Suttles Mill 146 8 34N37'30 85w11'00 5:40:44
Suttons Corner 30 8 31N36'02 84w50'39 5:39:23
Suwanee 67 20 34N03'05 84w04'17 5:36:17
Swainsboro 53 20 32N35'50 82w20'02 5:29:20
Swan 55 8 34N45'19 84w11'24 5:36:46
Swan Lake 75 20 33N33 84w14 5:36:56
Swanson Mill 23 8 34N58'38 85w08'44 5:40:35
Sweden 112 8 34N32'36 84w38'31 5:38:34
Sweet Gum 55 8 34N58'52 84w12'03 5:36:48
Swift Creek 11 25 32N49 83w33 5:34:12
Swords 104 20 33N32'39 83w18'25 5:33:14
Sybert 90 20 33N48'53 82w33'18 5:30:13
Sycamore 142 20 31N40'27 83w38'15 5:34:33
Sylvan Hills 60 7 33N42'33 84w25'04 5:37:40
Sylvania 124 20 32N45'01 81w38'13 5:26:33
Sylvester 159 20 31N31'50 83w50'08 5:35:21
Sylvester Drive 35 20 31N11 83w48 5:35:12
Symons Landing 51 20 32N21'47 81w10'33 5:24:42
Tabernacle 150 20 32N58'16 82w55'00 5:31:40
Tadmore 69 1 34N14 83w46 5:35:04
Tahoma 121 20 33N18'35 81w55'41 5:27:43
Tails Creek 61 8 34N41'23 84w36'56 5:38:28
Talbotton 130 8 32N40'39 84w32'22 5:38:09
Talking Rock 112 8 34N30'33 84w30'18 5:38:01
Tallahassee 80 20 31N55'08 82w34'09 5:30:17
Tallapoosa 71 8 33N44'40 85w17'17 5:41:09
Tallulah Falls 68 20 34N43'50 83w23'40 5:33:35
Talmadge 112 8 34N25'27 84w35'15 5:38:21
Talmo 78 20 34N11'06 83w43'15 5:34:53
Talmo 148 20 31N18'47 82w34'09 5:30:17
Talona 61 8 34N35'50 84w30'43 5:38:03
Tanner 150 20 32N58'31 82w44'32 5:30:58
Tanner Mill 69 1 34N10'41 83w47'09 5:35:09
Tarboro 20 20 31N01'03 81w48'20 5:27:13
Tarrytown 103 20 32N19'07 82w33'34 5:30:14
Tarver 50 20 30N42'05 82w55'28 5:31:42
Tarversville 143 20 32N32'24 83w26'24 5:33:46
Tate 112 8 34N25'06 84w22'58 5:37:32
Tate City 139 20 34N58'54 83w33'16 5:34:13
Tattnall Square 11 25 32N50'00 83w38'49 5:34:35
Tatum 141 8 33N01 85w06 5:40:24
Tatumsville 25 20 32N02'14 81w06'54 5:24:28
Tax 130 8 32N48 84w42 5:38:48
Tax Crossroads 130 8 32N48'42 84w35'54 5:38:24
Taylor Landing 51 20 32N21'07 81w29'26 5:25:58
Taylors Landing 148 20 31N04'56 82w19'53 5:29:20
Taylors Mill 111 8 32N36'21 83w52'26 5:35:30
Taylorsville 8 8 34N05'10 84w59'15 5:39:57
Tazewell 98 8 32N22'49 84w26'27 5:37:46
Teeterville 86 20 31N06'45 83w08'38 5:32:35
Telfair Junction 25 20 32N04'44 81w08'46 5:24:35
Telfair Woods 17 20 33N05'36 81w49'26 5:27:18
Tell 60 8 33N39'05 84w35'40 5:38:23
Teloga 27 8 34N33'36 85w24'35 5:41:38
Temperance 134 20 31N53'22 83w08'47 5:32:35
Temperance Bell 66 20 33N40'34 83w02'53 5:32:12
Temple 22 8 33N44'13 85w01'57 5:40:08
Temple Grove 105 8 34N55'42 84w46'18 5:39:05
Tempy 159 20 31N26'55 83w49'03 5:35:16
Ten Mile Still Landing 43 8 30N47'55 84w43'51 5:38:55
Tennga 105 8 34N59'12 84w44'19 5:38:57
Tennille 150 20 32N56'09 82w48'42 5:31:15
Terra Cotta 11 25 32N47'37 83w38'32 5:34:34
Terrell 159 20 31N37'04 83w44'43 5:34:59
Tetlow 151 20 31N40'47 82w04'17 5:28:17
Texas 74 8 33N14'27 85w11'56 5:40:48
Thalean 129 8 32N01'06 84w17'37 5:37:10
Thalmann 63 20 31N17'26 81w41'20 5:26:45
The Hill 121 20 33N28 82w01 5:28:04
The Rock 145 15 32N57'50 84w14'28 5:36:58
Thirteen Forks 52 20 34N12'47 82w55'45 5:31:43
Thomasboro 124 20 32N43'10 81w47'25 5:27:10
Thomas Crossroads 38 8 33N24'28 84w40'56 5:38:44
Thomas Landing 95 20 31N38'27 81w15'25 5:25:02
Thomas Mill 144 8 34N55'52 84w08'17 5:36:33
Thomaston 145 14 32N53'17 84w19'36 5:37:18
Thomasville 60 7 33N41'50 84w20'59 5:37:24
Thomasville 136 20 30N50'11 83w58'44 5:35:55
Thompson Crossroad 99 8 33N04'30 84w46'20 5:39:05
Thompsons Mill 7 20 34N06'46 83w49'04 5:35:16
Thompsons Mills 78 20 34N06 83w46 5:35:04
Thompsonville 146 8 34N51'48 85w24'27 5:41:38
Thomson 94 20 33N28'14 82w30'17 5:30:01
Three Forks 55 8 34N39'50 84w11'05 5:36:44
Three Forks 119 20 34N58'04 83w12'49 5:32:51
Three Points 53 20 32N47'01 82w14'43 5:28:59
Three Points 140 20 31N04'18 82w28'46 5:29:55
Three Runs 81 20 32N54'27 82w20'22 5:29:21
Three Sisters Mountain 93 8 34N33 83w56 5:35:44
Thrift 82 20 32N41'56 82w03'22 5:28:13
Thunder 145 8 33N01 84w30 5:38:00
Thunderbolt 25 20 32N02'00 81w03'00 5:24:12
Thurston 66 20 33N35 83w11 5:32:44
Thurston 145 8 32N55 84w26 5:37:44
Thyatira 78 20 34N08'28 83w32'00 5:34:08
Tickanetley 61 8 34N39'14 84w17'38 5:37:11
Ticknor 35 20 31N20'02 83w56'36 5:35:46
Tidings 27 8 34N25'26 85w14'51 5:40:59
Tifton 137 20 31N27'01 83w30'31 5:34:02
Tiger 119 20 34N50'49 83w25'59 5:33:44
Tignall 157 20 33N52'03 82w44'29 5:30:58
Tillman 92 20 30N55'26 83w20'59 5:33:24
Tilton 155 8 34N39'54 84w56'22 5:39:45
Timothy 29 3 33N59 83w23 5:33:32
Tioga 61 8 34N36'36 84w30'15 5:38:01
Tippetts 116 20 32N15'51 83w29'11 5:33:57
Tippettville 46 20 32N05'55 83w36'51 5:34:27
Tison 132 20 31N56'18 82w01'15 5:28:05
Titus 139 20 34N56'49 83w37'54 5:34:32
Toccoa 127 20 34N34'38 83w19'57 5:33:20
Toccoa Creek 127 20 34N36 83w20 5:33:20
Toccoa Falls 127 20 34N35'37 83w21'30 5:33:26
Toco Hills 44 20 33N50 84w19 5:37:16
Toledo 24 20 30N38'09 82w03'10 5:28:13
Tom 83 20 32N42'34 82w29'17 5:29:57
Tompkins 20 20 30N54'41 81w47'34 5:27:10
Toms Creek 127 20 34N28'47 83w14'38 5:32:59
Toombs Central 138 20 32N02'50 82w20'53 5:29:24
Toomsboro 158 20 32N49'36 83w04'46 5:32:19
Toonigh 28 8 34N08'34 84w30'34 5:38:02
Toonerville 155 8 34N52'05 84w53'16 5:39:33
Topeka Junction 145 15 32N58'28 84w12'31 5:36:50
Torreys Landing 25 20 31N50'25 81w05'20 5:24:21
Towalaga 126 8 33N18'51 84w12'17 5:36:49
Towaliga 18 8 33N14 84w03 5:36:12

Town and Country 33
8 33N56 84w32 5:38:08
Town Bluff Landing 80
20 31N56'54 82w30'14 5:30:01
Town Creek 144 8 34N49'20 83w52'12 5:35:29
Towns 134 20 32N00'15 82w45'17 5:31:01
Townsend 95 20 31N32'21 81w31'22 5:26:05
Townsend Mill 144
20 34N55'13 83w52'02 5:35:28
Traders Hill 24
20 30N46'46 82w01'52 5:28:07
Traisville 32 20 31N03'34 82w41'07 5:30:44
Trans 146 8 34N42 85w22 5:41:28
Tremont 40 20 32N00'48 83w36'48 5:34:27
Tremont 121 20 33N29 82w02 5:28:08
Tremont Park 25
20 32N03'35 81w08'17 5:24:33
Trenton 41 8 34N52'19 85w30'33 5:42:02
Trice 145 8 32N53 84w20 5:37:20
Trickem 67 20 33N50'26 84w07'52 5:36:31
Trickum 155 8 34N47'46 85w04'58 5:40:20
Trimble 141 8 33N12'07 84w53'32 5:39:34
Trinity 89 20 31N55'47 81w33'24 5:26:14
Trion 27 8 34N32'38 85w18'38 5:41:15
Troup Spring Landing 87
20 32N27'27 82w50'14 5:31:21
Troupville 92 20 30N50'56 83w20'15 5:33:21
Troutman 128 8 31N56'12 84w41'49 5:38:47
Truckers 16 20 32N21'20 81w38'03 5:26:32
Trudie 13 20 31N18'00 81w57'52 5:27:51
Tuckasee King Landing 51
20 32N31'55 81w16'34 5:25:06
Tucker 44 20 33N51'16 84w13'02 5:36:52
Tuckers Crossroad 87
20 32N42'03 82w51'55 5:31:28
Tugaloo 68 20 34N42'27 83w22'01 5:33:28
Tunnel Hill 155 8 34N50'26 85w02'34 5:40:10
Turin 38 8 33N19'35 84w38'09 5:38:33
Turkey Creek Landing 87
20 32N25'40 82w49'54 5:31:20
Turman 19 8 31N30'05 84w43'46 5:38:55
Turner City 47 11 31N35'52 84w06'29 5:36:26
Turner Lake Ford 77
20 31N41'40 83w27'38 5:33:51
Turners Corner 93
8 34N39'47 83w54'03 5:35:36
Turners Rock 25
20 32N00'47 81w00'20 5:24:01
Turnerville 68 20 34N41'12 83w25'34 5:33:42
Turntime Crossroads 72
8 32N41'25 84w47'19 5:39:09
Turpin Place 121
20 33N27 82w00 5:28:00
Tusculum 51 20 32N23'34 81w25'51 5:25:43
Tuxedo Park 121
20 33N27 82w01 5:28:04
Twin City 53 20 32N34'58 82w09'19 5:28:37
Twin Lakes 92 20 30N43 83w13 5:32:52
Tybee Island 25
20 32N00'00 80w50'45 5:23:23
Tyrone 56 8 33N28'16 84w35'50 5:38:23
Tyrone 157 20 33N40'20 82w51'41 5:31:27
Ty Ty 137 20 31N28'18 83w38'49 5:34:35
Tyus 22 8 33N28'03 85w12'08 5:40:49
Unadilla 46 20 32N15'41 83w44'12 5:34:57
Underwood 5 20 33N07'39 83w06'53 5:32:28
Undine 54 20 32N13'38 81w58'47 5:27:55
Union 21 20 32N28'57 82w03'14 5:28:13
Union 41 8 34N50'42 85w31'30 5:42:06
Union 45 20 32N05'52 83w15'02 5:33:00
Union 55 8 34N57'13 84w18'59 5:37:16
Union 98 8 32N20'50 84w37'48 5:38:31
Union 110 8 33N50'36 84w58'52 5:39:55
Union 118 8 31N52'32 84w56'16 5:39:45
Union 128 8 32N09'23 84w54'13 5:39:37
Unionburg 137 20 31N27 83w31 5:34:04
Union City 60 10 33N35'13 84w32'33 5:38:10
Union Hill 28 8 34N11'42 84w22'53 5:37:32
Union Hill 127 20 34N30'08 83w17'00 5:33:08
Union Junction 25
20 32N03'00 81w07'36 5:24:30
Union Point 66 20 33N36'56 83w04'29 5:32:18
Union Point 155
19 34N45'59 84w55'36 5:39:42
Union Springs 122
20 33N34'42 84w08'14 5:36:33
Unionville 85 8 33N09'39 84w03'00 5:36:12
Unionville 137 20 31N26'05 83w30'35 5:34:02
Unity 59 20 34N22'32 83w19'29 5:33:18
University 11 25 32N51 83w36 5:34:24
Univeter 28 8 34N11'46 84w30'02 5:38:00
Upatoi 106 8 32N32'55 84w44'24 5:38:58
Upper Bradley Place 128
8 32N12'18 84w56'45 5:39:47
Upper Lookout Creek 41
8 34N46 85w30 5:42:00
Upper Sansavilla Landing 151
20 31N30'28 81w39'33 5:26:38
Upton 34 20 31N31'17 82w53'36 5:31:34
Upton Mill 133 8 32N33 84w14 5:36:56
Uptonville 24 20 30N53'58 82w04'06 5:28:16
Uvalda 153 20 32N02'08 82w30'30 5:30:02
Vada 43 8 31N04'43 84w24'48 5:37:39
Valdosta 92 24 30N49'57 83w16'43 5:33:07
Valley 119 20 34N57 83w23 5:33:32
Valley Point 155
8 34N43 84w58 5:39:52
Valley View 146 8 34N55'22 85w21'05 5:41:24
Valona 95 20 31N28'41 81w20'39 5:25:23
Vanceville 137 20 31N25'58 83w26'27 5:33:46
Vandiver 59 20 34N24'04 83w15'09 5:33:01
Vandiver Heights 33
8 33N56 84w32 5:38:08
Vanna 59 20 34N14'29 83w04'18 5:32:17
Vans Valley 57 8 34N07'53 85w19'24 5:41:18
Van Wert 115 8 33N59'14 85w02'36 5:40:10
Varnell 155 8 34N54'04 84w58'26 5:39:54
Vaughn 126 8 33N16'51 84w23'30 5:37:34
Veal 22 8 33N26'09 85w13'49 5:40:55
Veazey 66 20 33N30'16 83w08'28 5:32:34
Vega 114 15 33N01'24 84w17'19 5:37:09
Veribest 109 20 33N56'39 82w59'43 5:31:59
Vernon 141 8 33N03'36 85w09'29 5:40:38
Vernonburg 25 20 31N57'56 81w07'13 5:24:29
Vernon View 25 20 31N55'43 81w05'56 5:24:24
Vessels Ford 32
20 30N51'15 82w35'02 5:30:20
Vesta 109 20 33N57'23 82w56'19 5:31:45
Veterans Hospital 121
20 33N28 82w01 5:28:04
Vickers Crossing 32
20 30N44'02 82w35'43 5:30:23
Victoria 28 8 34N08'13 84w36'34 5:38:26
Victoria Landing 28
8 34N09'13 84w37'19 5:38:29
Victory 22 8 33N30'40 85w12'37 5:40:50
Victory Heights 25
20 32N02'31 81w03'43 5:24:15
Vidalia 138 20 32N13'03 82w24'49 5:29:39
Vidette 17 20 33N02'15 82w14'51 5:28:59
Vienna 46 20 32N05'29 83w47'44 5:35:11
View 68 20 34N31 83w32 5:34:08
Villanow 146 8 34N40'25 85w06'53 5:40:28
Villa Rica 22 8 33N43'55 84w55'09 5:39:41
Vincent 87 20 32N28'24 83w00'02 5:32:00
Vineyard Crossroads 38
8 33N22'52 84w40'17 5:38:41
Vinings 33 8 33N51'53 84w27'52 5:37:51
Viola 74 8 33N15'17 85w08'56 5:40:36
Vista-Grove 44 20 33N47 84w17 5:37:08
Vista Terrace 106
17 32N27'57 84w53'54 5:39:36
Vulcan 146 8 34N46 85w32 5:42:08
Waco 71 8 33N42'10 85w11'00 5:40:44
Wades 120 8 31N51'00 84w45'26 5:39:02
Wadley 81 20 32N52'00 82w24'15 5:29:37
Wagon Wheel 37 20 31N14'12 83w27'43 5:33:51
Wahoma 148 20 31N09'38 82w25'40 5:29:43
Wahoo 93 8 34N32 83w59 5:35:56
Walden 11 25 32N42'29 83w39'56 5:34:40
Waleska 28 8 34N18'59 84w33'08 5:38:13
Walker 47 11 31N32'25 84w18'54 5:37:16
Walker Ford 77 20 31N41'20 83w27'41 5:33:51
Walker Mill 126 8 33N16'14 84w10'18 5:36:41
Walker Park 147
20 33N50'13 83w44'06 5:34:56
Walkersville 113
20 31N23'37 82w16'34 5:29:06
Walkinshaw 121 20 33N16'37 81w53'41 5:27:35
Wallace 116 20 32N11'49 83w29'50 5:33:59
Wallaceville 146
8 34N53'52 85w19'08 5:41:17
Walls Crossing 123
8 32N15'13 84w22'14 5:37:29
Walnut Grove 146
8 34N38'30 85w17'41 5:41:11
Walnut Grove 147
20 33N44'33 83w51'09 5:35:25
Waltertown 148 20 31N17'58 82w24'09 5:29:37
Walthourville 89
20 31N46'26 81w37'58 5:26:32
Warehouse Landing 80
20 31N57'15 82w30'53 5:30:04
Waresboro 148 20 31N14'52 82w28'26 5:29:54
Wares Crossroads 141
8 33N06'23 85w04'29 5:40:18
Waresville 74 8 33N13'43 85w14'18 5:40:57
Warfield 117 20 33N17'58 83w23'02 5:33:32
Waring 155 8 34N50'04 84w58'17 5:39:53
Warm Springs 99 8 32N53'25 84w40'52 5:38:43
Warner Robins 76
20 32N37'15 83w36'00 5:34:24
Warren Terrace 146
8 34N55'59 85w17'16 5:41:09
Warrenton 149 20 33N24'25 82w39'44 5:30:39
Warsaw 60 20 34N01'05 84w11'25 5:36:46
Warsaw 95 20 31N35'23 81w29'43 5:25:59
Warthen 150 20 33N06'07 82w48'14 5:31:13
Warwick 159 20 31N49'51 83w55'08 5:35:41
Warwoman Dell 119
20 34N52'53 83w21'08 5:33:25
Washington 157 20 33N44'12 82w44'22 5:30:57
Waterloo 77 20 31N35'36 83w28'28 5:33:54
Waterport 147 20 33N51 83w54 5:35:36
Watkinsville 108
20 33N51'46 83w24'32 5:33:38
Watson Crossroads 30
8 31N43'46 85w01'04 5:40:04
Waverly 20 20 31N05'44 81w43'22 5:26:53
Waverly Hall 72 8 32N41'00 84w44'18 5:38:57
Waverly Park 23 8 34N58'19 85w14'58 5:41:00
Wax 57 8 34N08'35 85w06'12 5:40:25
Wayback 19 8 31N33 84w42 5:38:48
Waycross 148 1 31N12'48 82w21'15 5:29:25
Waynesboro 17 20 33N05'23 82w00'57 5:28:04
Waynesville 13 20 31N13'45 81w47'22 5:27:09
Wayside 84 20 33N03'40 83w36'18 5:34:25
Weaver 114 8 33N06 84w20 5:37:20
Webb 60 7 34N05'50 84w15'34 5:37:02
Weber 10 20 31N14'13 83w08'24 5:32:34
Wefanie 91 20 31N46'14 81w48'59 5:27:16
Welcome 38 8 33N23'47 84w52'25 5:39:30
Welcome Hill 27 8 34N34'29 85w19'07 5:41:16
Wells Spring Landing 87
20 32N24'41 82w49'34 5:31:18
Wenona 40 20 31N54'19 83w46'01 5:35:04
Weracoba Heights 106
17 32N28'26 84w58'08 5:39:53
Wesley 53 20 32N29'00 82w19'52 5:29:19
Wesley 133 8 32N39'32 84w19'49 5:37:19
Wesleyan 11 25 32N50 83w37 5:34:28
Wesleyan Estates 11
25 32N51 83w41 5:34:44
West Bainbridge 43
8 30N55'30 84w35'00 5:38:20
West Bremen 71 8 33N45'20 85w08'52 5:40:35
West Brow 41 8 34N55'22 85w24'55 5:41:40
West Cordele 40
20 31N58 83w47 5:35:08
West Crisp 40 20 31N56 83w50 5:35:20
West Crossing 71
8 33N43'50 85w14'41 5:40:59
West Dougherty 47
11 31N32 84w14 5:36:56
West Dublin 87 20 32N33 82w54 5:31:36
West End 57 8 34N17 85w12 5:40:48
West End 60 7 33N44'17 84w24'59 5:37:40
Wester 52 20 34N08 82w50 5:31:20
Westgate Park 29
3 33N59 83w23 5:33:32
West Georgia College 22
8 33N35 85w05 5:40:20
West Green 34 20 31N36'46 82w44'05 5:30:56
West Jackson 78
20 34N09 83w43 5:34:52
Westlake 143 20 32N29'20 83w29'01 5:33:56
West Newnan 38 8 33N23'08 84w49'41 5:39:19
Westoak 33 8 33N59'16 84w31'54 5:38:08
Weston 152 8 31N58'33 84w36'54 5:38:28
Westover 121 20 33N23'41 81w59'26 5:27:58
West Point 141 13 32N52'40 85w11'00 5:40:44
West Savannah 25
20 32N03 81w09 5:24:36
Westside 23 8 34N57'29 85w13'24 5:40:54
Westside 69 1 34N18 83w49 5:35:16
West Summerville 27
8 34N28'21 85w22'10 5:41:29
West Valdosta 92
20 30N48'56 83w18'54 5:33:16
West Vidalia 138
20 32N15 82w24 5:29:36
Westview Cemetery 40
20 31N57'15 83w47'30 5:35:10
Westwick 121 20 33N29'06 82w03'17 5:28:13
Westwood 9 20 31N44'05 83w17'33 5:33:10
Wheat Hill 25 20 32N06'21 81w09'23 5:24:38
Wheeler Heights 11
25 32N49'34 83w33'31 5:34:14
Wheless 121 20 33N27'06 82w02'48 5:28:11
Whigham 65 8 30N52'58 84w19'26 5:37:18
Whipples Crossing 87
20 32N31'45 83w03'31 5:32:14
Whispering Pines 74
8 33N18'44 85w06'14 5:40:25
Whistleville 7 20 33N59'37 83w46'59 5:35:08
White 8 8 34N16'58 84w44'43 5:38:59
White Bluff 25 20 31N59'15 81w07'44 5:24:31
White City 28 8 34N14'58 84w22'38 5:37:31
White City 48 8 33N43'52 84w48'16 5:39:13
Whitehall 29 3 33N54'25 83w21'26 5:33:26
White Hill 124 20 32N40'47 81w34'24 5:26:18
Whitehouse 75 20 33N32'35 84w08'15 5:36:33
Whitemarsh Island 25
20 32N03 81w04 5:24:16
White Oak 20 20 31N01'52 81w43'50 5:26:55
White Path 61 8 34N45'01 84w24'47 5:37:39
White Plains 66
20 33N28'19 83w02'08 5:32:09
White Sand Landing 24
20 30N49'01 81w57'52 5:27:51
Whitesburg 22 8 33N29'38 84w54'50 5:39:39
Whitestone 61 8 34N33'37 84w30'42 5:38:03
White Sulphur 69
1 34N21'22 83w46'01 5:35:04
White Sulphur Springs 99
8 32N54'28 84w48'12 5:39:13
Whitesville 72 8 32N49'03 85w01'53 5:40:08
Whitfield 141 8 33N04'37 84w56'53 5:39:48
Whitney 147 20 33N43'20 83w42'43 5:34:51
Whitworth 59 20 34N29'02 83w05'42 5:32:23
Wildwood 41 8 34N57'48 85w24'40 5:41:39
Wiley 119 20 34N47'54 83w25'13 5:33:41
Willacoochee 2 20 31N20'26 83w02'46 5:32:11
Willard 117 20 33N18'26 83w29'02 5:33:56
Willett 106 17 32N26'54 84w57'25 5:39:50
Williams 25 20 32N06'22 81w15'08 5:25:01
Williamsburg 19 8 31N27'50 84w35'53 5:38:24
Williamsburg 32
20 30N46'57 82w30'46 5:30:03
Williamsburg 47
20 31N29'53 84w06'55 5:36:28
Williams Landing 16
20 32N31'40 81w38'57 5:26:36
Williamson 114 8 33N10'56 84w21'42 5:37:27
Willie 89 20 32N00'50 81w40'03 5:26:40
Willis Plaza 106
17 32N25'32 84w55'52 5:39:43
Wilmington Island 25
20 32N00 80w59 5:23:56
Wilmington Park 25
20 31N59'37 80w59'18 5:23:57
Wilshire 25 20 32N00 81w05 5:24:20
Wilshire Estates 25
20 32N00 81w05 5:24:20
Wilson Mill 55 8 34N43'01 84w14'53 5:37:00
Wilsons Church 78
20 34N12 83w27 5:33:48
Wilsonville 34 20 31N24'38 82w40'52 5:30:43
Winchester 96 8 32N25'05 83w57'28 5:35:50
Winder 7 20 33N59'33 83w43'13 5:34:53
Windsor 147 20 33N52'48 83w50'30 5:35:22
Windsor Estates 38
8 33N25'38 84w48'41 5:39:15
Windsor Forest 25
20 31N58'35 81w07'57 5:24:32
Windsor Park 106
17 32N29 84w57 5:39:48
Windsor Spring 121
20 33N23'05 82w04'09 5:28:17
Windward 25 20 31N58'28 81w11'11 5:24:45
Windy Ridge 55 8 34N55'36 84w17'20 5:37:09
Winfield 36 20 33N36'22 82w23'49 5:29:35
Winfield Hill 36
20 33N38'22 82w25'49 5:29:43
Winokur 24 20 31N02'17 82w01'13 5:28:05
Winona Park 148
20 31N13'44 82w23'15 5:29:33
Winston 48 8 33N43'30 84w49'30 5:39:18
Winterville 29 20 33N58'01 83w16'42 5:33:07
Withers 32 20 30N51'17 82w54'12 5:31:37
Wofford Crossroads 8
8 34N17 84w45 5:39:00
Woodbine 20 20 30N57'49 81w43'22 5:26:53
Woodbury 99 8 32N59'01 84w34'58 5:38:20
Woodcliff 124 20 32N44'26 81w45'48 5:27:03
Woodfin Mill 85 8 33N06'37 84w13'52 5:36:55
Woodland 130 8 32N47'14 84w33'43 5:38:15
Woodland Hills 87
20 32N33 82w54 5:31:36

Woodland Hills 146	8	34N57	85w18	5:41:12
Woodlawn 90	20	33N42'14	82w26'39	5:29:47
Woodlawn Estates 106	17	32N29'43	84w54'55	5:39:40
Woodlawn Terrace 25	20	32N05'33	81w10'44	5:24:43
Woods Grove 139	20	34N56	83w51	5:35:24
Woods Station 23	8	35N01	85w11	5:40:44
Woodstock 28	8	34N06'05	84w31'10	5:38:05
Woodville 25	20	32N05'30	81w08'44	5:24:35
Woodville 66	20	33N40'17	83w06'22	5:32:25
Woolsey 31	8	33N21'44	84w24'44	5:37:39
Wooster 99	8	33N08'30	84w37'49	5:38:31
Workmore 134	20	31N56'06	82w56'22	5:31:45
Worley Crossroads 28	8	34N22'41	84w27'48	5:37:51
Wormsloe 25	20	31N58'35	81w03'46	5:24:15
Worth 142	20	31N45'02	83w40'33	5:34:42
Worthville 18	20	33N23'23	83w55'17	5:35:41
Wray 77	20	31N37'20	83w03'18	5:32:13
Wrayswood 66	20	33N41'36	83w18'53	5:33:16
Wrens 81	20	33N12'27	82w23'31	5:29:34
Wright Mill 55	8	34N54'36	84w11'32	5:36:46
Wrightsboro 94	20	33N33'01	82w34'09	5:30:17
Wright Square 25	20	32N03	81w06	5:24:24
Wrightsville 83	20	32N43'45	82w43'12	5:30:53
Wriley 158	20	32N50'54	83w09'30	5:32:38
Wymberley 25	20	32N00	81w05	5:24:20
Wynnton 106	17	32N28'03	84w57'03	5:39:48
Yahoola 93	8	34N32	83w59	5:35:56
Yankee Landing 63	20	31N07'33	81w39'45	5:26:39
Yarbroughs Mill 64	8	34N25'38	84w46'27	5:39:06
Yates 38	8	33N27'48	84w53'42	5:39:35
Yates Crossroads 74	8	33N22'04	85w13'56	5:40:56
Yatesville 145	8	32N54'49	84w08'34	5:36:34
Yellow Bluff Fishing Village 89	20	31N48	81w26	5:25:44
Yellowdirt 74	8	33N24'50	85w02'27	5:40:10
Yellow River 107	20	33N28	83w52	5:35:28
Yeomans 135	8	31N50'07	84w28'01	5:37:52
Yonah 154	1	34N38'28	83w45'13	5:35:01
Yonkers 45	20	32N21'58	83w13'00	5:32:52
York 119	20	34N56'07	83w23'21	5:33:33
Yorkville 110	8	33N55'27	84w59'44	5:39:59
Youngcane 144	8	34N53	83w58	5:35:52
Young Harris 139	20	34N55'59	83w50'50	5:35:23
Youngs 115	8	34N01	85w15	5:41:00
Youngstown 144	8	34N52'47	83w58'44	5:35:55
Youth 147	20	33N47'07	83w51'22	5:35:25
Ypsilanti 130	8	32N44'33	84w24'48	5:37:39
Yukon 61	8	34N37'38	84w28'05	5:37:52
Zaidee 140	20	32N22'26	82w31'45	5:30:07
Zebina 81	20	33N09'52	82w21'14	5:29:25
Zebulon 70	20	33N11'01	83w00'03	5:32:00
Zebulon 114	8	33N06'08	84w20'34	5:37:22
Zeigler 124	20	32N45'06	81w43'49	5:26:55
Zellobee 98	8	32N17'46	84w37'14	5:38:29
Zenith 39	8	32N36'42	83w58'40	5:35:55
Zetella 126	8	33N14'27	84w22'56	5:37:32
Zetto 30	8	31N35'36	84w56'13	5:39:45
Zingara 122	20	33N44'52	83w58'27	5:35:54
Zion 1	20	31N51'49	82w10'48	5:28:43
Zuta 63	20	31N19'14	81w35'03	5:26:20

TIME TABLES

Hawaii has not observed daylight time, except for the period shown in 1933 and during World War II.

Before 1/01/1900		LMT
1/01/1900	12:00	HST
4/30/1933	02:00	HDT
5/21/1933	02:00	HST
2/09/1942	02:00	HWT
9/30/1945	02:00	HST
6/08/1947	02:00	AHST

COUNTIES

1 Hawaii
2 Honolulu (Oahu)
3 Kauai
4 Maui (incl. Molokai)

Ah Fong Village 4 20N51'12 156w27'53 10:25:52
Ahole Heiau 1 19N08'24 155w26'36 10:21:46
Ahualoa 1 20N05 155w28 10:21:52
Ahuena Heiau 1 19N38'32 156w00'01 10:24:00
Ahuimanu 2 21N26'41 157w50'16 10:31:21
Ahukini Landing 3 21N59'43 159w20'08 10:37:21
Aiea 2 21N22'56 157w56'01 10:31:44
Aiea Heights 2 21N23'27 157w55'13 10:31:41
Aina Haina 2 21N16'55 157w45'09 10:31:01
Ainapo 1 19N21'33 155w25'27 10:21:42
Airport Village 4 20N49'20 156w27'15 10:25:49
Akona 1 20N06'13 155w36'42 10:22:27
Akupu 2 21N23'39 158w06'11 10:32:25
Alabama Village 4 20N51'57 156w27'15 10:25:49
Alasaki Camp 1 20N01 155w17 10:21:08
Alewa Heights 2 21N20'35 157w51'10 10:31:25
Aliamanu 2 21N21'17 157w55'39 10:31:43
Amauulu Camps 1 19N42 155w05 10:20:20
Anaehoomalu 1 19N55'01 155w53'25 10:23:34
Anahola 3 22N08'43 159w18'56 10:37:16
Anaki 3 22N09'02 159w43'05 10:38:52
Andrade 1 19N51 155w06 10:20:24
Barbers Point Housing 2 21N20 158w05 10:32:20
Camp H M Smith 2 21N23 157w56 10:31:44
Canoe Landing Site 1 19N21'08 154w58'40 10:19:55
Captain Cook 1 19N29'49 155w55'18 10:23:41
Central Power Plant Village 4 20N57 156w40 10:26:40
Chinatown 2 21N20 157w52 10:31:28
Chin Chuck 1 19N54 155w08 10:20:32
City of Refuge 1 19N26 155w55 10:23:40
Coconut Grove 2 21N24 157w47 10:31:08
Cod Fish Village 4 20N53'47 156w25'16 10:25:41
Cooks Heiau 1 19N29'20 155w56'46 10:23:47
Coral Gardens 2 21N25 157w48 10:31:12
Corn Mill Camp 4 20N50'15 156w19'57 10:25:20
Crater Maui 4 20N57 156w40 10:26:40
Crater Village 4 20N54'03 156w39'54 10:26:40
Crestview 2 21N24'32 157w59'58 10:32:00
Dillingham Ranch 2 21N34 158w10 10:32:40
East Molokai 4 21N05 156w57 10:27:48
Eleele 3 21N54'37 159w35'14 10:38:21
Elevenmile Homestead 1 19N36'23 155w04'31 10:20:18
Ewa 2 21N20'33 158w02'25 10:32:10
Ewa Beach 2 21N18'56 158w00'26 10:32:02
Ewa-Schofield Junction 2 21N23'58 157w58'53 10:31:56
Fernandez Village 2 21N21'01 158w02'00 10:32:08
Filipino Camp 4 20N50'25 156w19'41 10:25:19
Ford Island 2 21N21 157w56 10:31:44
Fort Shafter 2 21N19 157w50 10:31:20
Foster Village 2 21N21'55 157w55'40 10:31:43
Glenwood 1 19N29'27 155w09'14 10:20:37
Haaheo 1 19N42 155w05 10:20:20
Haena 1 19N38'44 154w59'16 10:19:57
Haena 3 22N13'28 159w33'53 10:38:16
Haiku 4 20N55'03 156w19'33 10:25:18
Haina 1 20N05'46 155w28'19 10:21:53
Hakalau 1 19N53'59 155w07'45 10:20:31
Halaula 1 20N14'16 155w46'48 10:23:07
Halawa 1 20N13'37 155w46'06 10:23:04
Halawa 2 21N23 157w56 10:31:44
Halawa 4 21N09'35 156w44'32 10:26:58
Halawa Heights 2 21N22'54 157w55'06 10:31:40
Halawa Hills 2 21N23 157w56 10:31:44
Haleaha 2 21N37 157w55 10:31:40
Hale Homaha 3 22N13'33 159w32'59 10:38:12
Haleiwa 2 21N35'30 158w06'51 10:32:27
Haleiwa Army Beach 2 21N35'31 158w07'00 10:32:28
Halekii Heiau 4 20N54'30 156w29'42 10:25:59
Halena 4 21N05'33 157w14'04 10:28:56
Hale o Kane Heiau 4 20N39'08 156w07'54 10:24:32
Hale o Lono Heiau 1 19N40'14 156w01'49 10:24:07
Hale o Mano Heiau 1 19N40'24 156w01'48 10:24:07
Halepalaoa Landing 4 20N50'03 156w48'53 10:27:16
Hale Pili 1 19N37'45 155w52'14 10:23:29
Halepiula 1 19N55'52 155w23'40 10:21:35
Halimaile 4 20N52'16 156w20'38 10:25:23
Hamakuapoko 4 20N55'19 156w20'53 10:25:24
Hamoa 4 20N43'24 155w59'19 10:23:57
Hana 4 20N45'29 155w59'25 10:23:58
Hanaipoe 1 19N56'54 155w27'42 10:21:51
Hanalei 3 22N12'19 159w30'10 10:38:01
Hanalei Homesteads 3 22N11'07 159w27'59 10:37:52
Hanalei Landing 3 22N12'58 159w30'01 10:38:00
Hanamaulu 3 21N59'51 159w21'26 10:37:26
Hanapepe 3 21N54'43 159w35'43 10:38:23
Hanapepe Heights 3 21N55'13 159w35'32 10:38:22
Haou 4 20N41'51 156w00'25 10:24:02
Happy Valley 4 20N53'42 156w30'35 10:26:02
Hauula 2 21N36'38 157w54'39 10:31:39
Hawaiian Ocean View Estates 1 19N30 155w55 10:23:40
Hawaiian-Spanish Village 4 20N54'32 156w22'29 10:25:30
Hawaiian Village 2 21N19 157w51 10:31:24
Hawaiian Village 4 20N54'21 156w25'02 10:25:40
Hawaii Kai 2 21N16'58 157w42'19 10:30:49
Hawaii National Park 1 19N26 155w15 10:21:00
Hawi 1 20N14'29 155w49'58 10:23:20
Heeia 2 21N25'51 157w48'38 10:31:15
Hickam Air Force Base 2 21N20 157w54 10:31:36
Hickam Village 2 21N20'43 157w56'42 10:31:47
Highway Village 1 19N52 155w07 10:20:28
Hikapoloa 1 20N14'32 155w51'34 10:23:26
Hikiau Heiau 1 19N28'43 155w55'19 10:23:41
Hikina o ka la Heiau 3 22N02'44 159w20'18 10:37:21
Hilea 1 19N08'19 155w32'12 10:22:09
Hilo 1 19N43'47 155w05'24 10:20:22
Hoaeae 2 21N24 158w01 10:32:04
Hoai Heiau 3 21N53'07 159w28'37 10:37:54
Hoea 1 20N14 155w50 10:23:20
Hokamahoe House Lot 1 19N59 155w14 10:20:56
Hokuula 4 20N43'38 155w59'14 10:23:57
Holualoa 1 19N37'22 155w57'08 10:23:49
Honalo 1 19N32'47 155w55'55 10:23:44
Honaunau 1 19N25'37 155w54'47 10:23:39
Honohina 1 19N55'38 155w09'25 10:20:38
Honoipu Landing (Site) 1 20N14'45 155w53'33 10:23:34
Honokaa 1 20N04'58 155w28'21 10:21:53
Honokaa Landing 1 20N06'16 155w28'27 10:21:54
Honokahua (Honokohua P O) 4 21N00'11 156w39'28 10:26:38
Honokai Hale 2 21N20'33 158w06'39 10:32:27
Honokohau 1 19N40'25 156w01'45 10:24:07
Honokohau 4 21N01'08 156w36'41 10:26:27
Honokowai 4 20N57'15 156w41'23 10:26:46
Honolua 4 21N00'59 156w38'26 10:26:34
Honolulu 2 21N18'25 157w51'30 10:31:26
Honolulu Intl Airport 2 21N24 157w54 10:31:36
Honolulu Landing 1 19N33'30 154w53'01 10:19:32
Honomaele 4 20N48'04 156w02'20 10:24:09
Honomakau 1 20N14'24 155w49'14 10:23:17
Honomalino 1 19N30 155w55 10:23:40
Honomu 1 19N52'24 155w07'03 10:20:28
Honopu 1 19N07'33 155w47'16 10:23:09
Honouliuli 2 21N22'04 158w02'10 10:32:09
Honuapo 1 19N05'36 155w33'04 10:22:12
Hookena 1 19N22'59 155w54'03 10:23:36
Hoolehua 4 21N10'16 157w04'17 10:28:17
Hoopuloa 1 19N12'02 155w54'25 10:23:38
Hopoi 4 20N54 156w30 10:26:00
Hopoi Village 4 20N52'56 156w30'39 10:26:03
Hopuwai 1 19N50'57 155w20'26 10:21:22
Hospital Village 4 20N52 156w27 10:25:48
Huehue 1 19N37 155w57 10:23:48
Huelo 4 20N54'30 156w13'39 10:24:55
Hyashi Village 4 20N50'27 156w30'33 10:26:02
Iroquois Point 2 21N20 157w59 10:31:56
Iwasaki Camp 1 19N36 155w04 10:20:16
Iwilei 2 21N18'59 157w52'41 10:31:31
Japanese Village One 4 20N54'19 156w25'17 10:25:41
Kaaawa 2 21N33'26 157w51'13 10:31:25
Kaalaea 2 21N29 157w51 10:31:24
Kaalawai 2 21N15'43 157w48'03 10:31:12
Kaalualu 1 18N58'23 155w36'52 10:22:27
Kaana 3 22N06'11 159w40'46 10:38:43
Kaanapali 4 20N55'54 156w41'50 10:26:47
Kaapahu 1 20N03 155w22 10:21:28
Kaau 1 20N06'33 155w36'41 10:22:27
Kaauhuhu Homesteads 1 20N14 155w50 10:23:20
Kaawaloa 1 19N28'57 155w56'12 10:23:45
Kaawanui Village 3 21N56'46 159w37'54 10:38:32
Kaeleku 4 20N47'11 156w01'34 10:24:06
Kahakuloa 4 20N59'59 156w33'14 10:26:13
Kahala 2 21N16'11 157w47'11 10:31:09
Kahaluu 1 19N35'00 155w58'09 10:23:53
Kahaluu 2 21N27'48 157w50'12 10:31:21
Kahana 2 21N33'29 157w52'45 10:31:31
Kahana 4 20N58'48 156w40'48 10:26:43
Kahei Homesteads 1 20N14 155w50 10:23:20
Kaheka Village 4 20N53'44 156w21'56 10:25:28
Kahua 1 20N08 155w48 10:23:12
Kahuku 2 21N40'49 157w57'04 10:31:48
Kahului 4 20N53'41 156w28'12 10:25:53
Kaiaakea 1 19N56 155w11 10:20:44
Kaiele Heiau 1 19N07'51 155w30'52 10:22:03
Kailiili 4 20N50'51 156w16'21 10:25:05
Kailua 1 19N38'26 155w59'44 10:23:59
Kailua 2 21N24'08 157w44'22 10:30:57
Kailua 4 20N53'40 156w13'01 10:24:52
Kailua Kona 1 19N39 155w59 10:23:56
Kailua Village 4 20N52'17 156w21'54 10:25:28
Kai Malino 1 19N30 155w55 10:23:40
Kaimu 1 19N21'53 154w58'20 10:19:53
Kaimuki 2 21N16'58 157w48'06 10:31:12
Kainaliu 1 19N32'06 155w55'44 10:23:43
Kainalu 4 21N06 157w01 10:28:04
Kaiwiki 1 19N42 155w05 10:20:20
Kakio 4 20N42'48 155w59'48 10:23:59
Kalae 4 21N09'55 157w00'30 10:28:02
Kalaheo 3 21N55'43 159w31'49 10:38:07
Kalamaula 4 21N06 157w01 10:28:04
Kalaoa 1 19N43'43 155w58'54 10:23:56
Kalaoa Homesteads 1 19N37 155w57 10:23:48
Kalapana 1 19N21'15 154w58'43 10:19:55
Kalauao 2 21N23'05 157w56'53 10:31:48
Kalaupapa 4 21N11'33 156w59'10 10:27:57
Kalawao 4 21N10'49 156w57'04 10:27:48
Kalepolepo 4 20N46'01 156w27'45 10:25:51
Kalihi 2 21N20'11 157w52'35 10:31:30
Kalihi Kai 2 21N19'36 157w53'19 10:31:33
Kalihiwai 3 22N13'03 159w25'57 10:37:44
Kalopa Mauka 1 20N05 155w28 10:21:52
Kaluaaha 4 21N04'12 156w49'16 10:27:17
Kaluanui Heiau 4 20N43'27 155w59'35 10:23:58
Kamaili 1 19N24'53 154w54'06 10:19:36
Kamalino 3 21N50'15 160w14'01 10:40:56
Kamalo 4 21N03'02 156w52'37 10:27:30
Kamehameha Heights 2 21N20'06 157w51'53 10:31:28
Kamiloloa 4 21N05'02 157w00'08 10:28:01
Kamooloa 2 21N34'22 158w06'51 10:32:27
Kamuela 1 20N01'23 155w40'18 10:22:41
Kanahena 4 20N37'18 156w26'29 10:25:46
Kaneeleele Heiau 1 19N08'21 155w30'17 10:22:01
Kaneohe 2 21N25'05 157w48'13 10:31:13
Kaneohe Marine Corps Air Sta 2 21N24 157w47 10:31:08
Kaniahiku Village 1 19N29'22 154w55'38 10:19:43
Kaonoulu 4 20N44'25 156w20'08 10:25:21
Kapaa 3 22N04'42 159w19'19 10:37:17
Kapaahu 1 19N20'30 155w00'50 10:20:03
Kapaau 1 20N14'01 155w48'05 10:23:12
Kapahi 3 22N06'01 159w21'38 10:37:27
Kapahulu 2 21N16'41 157w48'56 10:31:16
Kapaia 3 21N59'36 159w22'08 10:37:29
Kapaka 3 21N55'25 159w37'01 10:38:28
Kapalama 2 21N20 157w52 10:31:28
Kapalaoa 1 19N54'45 155w53'56 10:23:36
Kapalawai 3 21N56'56 159w39'26 10:38:38
Kapapala 1 19N12 155w29 10:21:56
Kapaula Heiau 3 22N05'27 159w45'05 10:39:00
Kapehu 1 19N59 155w14 10:20:56
Kapinao Heiau 3 22N11'29 159w23'17 10:37:33
Kapoho 1 19N30'22 154w50'55 10:19:24
Kapulena 1 20N06'21 155w31'44 10:22:07
Kapunakea 4 20N53'27 156w41'03 10:26:44
Kau 1 19N19 155w25 10:21:40
Kaueleau 1 19N26'40 154w54'55 10:19:40
Kaukohoku 1 19N34'33 155w51'43 10:23:27
Ka Ulu a Paoa Heiau 3 22N13'22 159w35'16 10:38:21
Kaumakani 3 21N55'08 159w37'20 10:38:29
Kaumalapau 4 20N47 156w59 10:27:56
Kaumana 1 19N41'19 155w08'39 10:20:35
Kaunakakai 4 21N05'36 157w01'26 10:28:06
Kaunalewa 3 22N00'11 159w44'28 10:38:58
Kaunene 1 19N25'17 155w46'47 10:23:07
Kaupakulua 4 20N53'25 156w17'52 10:25:11
Kaupo 4 20N38'22 156w07'31 10:24:30

Place	Latitude	Longitude	Code
Kaupulehu 1	19N50'05	155W59'21	10:23:57
Kawaihae 1	20N02'28	155W49'50	10:23:19
Kawaihua 3	22N04	159W20	10:37:20
Kawailiula 1	20N01'38	155W42'23	10:22:50
Kawailoa 2	21N36	158W05	10:32:20
Kawailoa Beach 2	21N37'41	158W04'48	10:32:19
Kawainui 1	19N49'44	155W05'55	10:20:24
Kawanui 1	19N31	155W55	10:23:40
Kawela 2	21N42'03	158W00'37	10:32:02
Keaalu 2	21N25'04	157W46'08	10:31:05
Keaau 1	19N37'32	155W02'30	10:20:10
Keaau Camp 1	19N38	155W02	10:20:08
Keaau Ranch 1	19N38	155W02	10:20:08
Keahua 4	20N51'37	156W23'07	10:25:32
Kealahou 4	20N46	156W20	10:25:20
Kealakehe Homesteads 1	20N31	156W52	10:27:28
Kealakekua 1	19N31'15	155W55'21	10:23:41
Kealakomo 1	19N16'27	155W09'18	10:20:37
Kealapuali 1	19N37'36	155W51'47	10:23:27
Kealia 1	19N24'01	155W52'55	10:23:32
Kealia 3	22N06'07	159W18'31	10:37:14
Keamuku 1	19N50'35	155W43'16	10:22:53
Keanae 4	20N51'41	156W09'06	10:24:36
Keanakolu 1	19N55'06	155W20'17	10:21:21
Keanapaakai 1	19N26'42	155W47'52	10:23:11
Keauhou 1	19N33'55	155W57'54	10:23:52
Keauhou Landing (Site) 1	19N16'04	155W14'14	10:20:57
Keaukaha 1	19N43'49	155W02'47	10:20:11
Keawaiki 1	19N53'24	155W54'30	10:23:38
Keawakapu 4	20N42'27	156W26'52	10:25:47
Keawanui 3	22N09'10	159W43'33	10:38:54
Keehia 1	20N01	155W17	10:21:08
Keei 1	19N27'52	155W55'38	10:23:43
Keeku Heiau 1	19N06'58	155W31'34	10:22:06
Keelinawi 3	21N48'15	160W13'42	10:40:55
Kehena 1	19N23'44	154W55'59	10:19:44
Kekaha 3	21N58'16	159W42'54	10:38:52
Kekaloa Heiau 1	19N21'30	154W58'37	10:19:54
Kelawea 4	20N53'06	156W40'30	10:26:42
Keokea 1	19N25'12	155W52'58	10:23:32
Keokea 4	20N42'31	156W21'30	10:25:26
Keolu Hills 2	21N22'46	157W43'54	10:30:56
Keomuku 4	20N50'19	156W55'15	10:27:41
Keoneoio 4	20N36'11	156W25'24	10:25:42
Kepuhi 4	21N11'28	157W15'01	10:29:00
Kiekie 3	21N53'11	160W12'46	10:40:51
Kihalani Homestead 1	19N59	155W14	10:20:56
Kihei 4	20N47'06	156W27'56	10:25:52
Kiholo 1	19N51'27	155W55'27	10:23:42
Kii Landing 3	21N58'38	160W03'32	10:40:14
Kilauea 3	22N12'43	159W24'44	10:37:39
Kilauea Military Camp 1	19N26	155W15	10:21:00
Kilauea Settlement 1	19N26	155W16	10:21:04
Kiolakaa Keaa Homesteads 1	19N04	155W35	10:22:20
Kipahulu 4	20N39'24	156W03'31	10:24:14
Kipapa Heiau 3	22N13'21	159W23'20	10:37:33
Kipu 3	21N57'15	159W25'36	10:37:42
Kipu 4	21N09'57	157W01'22	10:28:05
Kipuka Nahuaopala 1	19N02'43	155W37'05	10:22:28
Kipuka Nene 1	19N19'48	155W16'54	10:21:08
Koae 1	19N31'36	154W50'48	10:19:23
Koali 4	20N41'20	156W01'26	10:24:06
Koele 4	20N50'23	156W55'13	10:27:41
Kohala 1	20N14	155W48	10:23:12
Koheo 4	21N05'14	157W00'58	10:28:04
Koholalele Landing 1	20N03'07	155W20'54	10:21:24
Kokee 3	21N58	159W43	10:38:52
Kokokahi 2	21N24'51	157W46'44	10:31:07
Kokomo 4	20N52'12	156W18'32	10:25:14
Kolo 1	19N30	155W55	10:23:40
Koloa 3	21N54'24	159W28'09	10:37:53
Koloa Landing 3	21N52'56	159W28'17	10:37:53
Koloa Mill 3	21N54'12	159W26'51	10:37:47
Komakawai 1	19N23'52	155W46'34	10:23:06
Kona 1	19N25	155W55	10:23:40
Kona Coast 1	19N25	155W55	10:23:40
Koolauloa 2	21N38	158W00	10:32:00
Koolaupoko 2	21N24	157W49	10:31:16
Kualapuu 4	21N09'19	157W02'23	10:28:10
Kualoa 2	21N32	157W53	10:31:32
Kuau 4	20N55'46	156W22'16	10:25:29
Kuhio Village 1	20N01'28	155W39'45	10:22:39
Kuhua 4	20N57	156W40	10:26:40
Kukaiau 1	20N01'58	155W21'01	10:21:24
Kukanono 2	21N24	157W47	10:31:08
Kukii Heiau 1	19N30'54	154W50'12	10:19:21
Kukio 1	19N49'17	156W00'07	10:24:00
Kukui 1	19N34'37	155W05'28	10:20:22
Kukuihaele 1	20N07'17	155W34'15	10:22:17
Kukuihaele Landing 1	20N07'53	155W33'33	10:22:14
Kukuiula 3	21N53'19	159W29'20	10:37:57
Kukui Village 1	20N01'00	155W16'50	10:21:07
Kula 4	20N45	156W20	10:25:20
Kuliouou 2	21N17'18	157W43'45	10:30:55
Kumukumu 3	22N06'39	159W18'36	10:37:14
Kunia 2	21N27'48	158W03'55	10:32:16
Kunia Camp 2	21N27'48	158W03'55	10:32:16
Kupolo 3	21N58'03	159W21'48	10:37:27
Kurtistown 1	19N36'13	155W03'26	10:20:14
Laeapuki 1	19N19'02	155W04'07	10:20:16
Lahaina 4	20N52'42	156W40'57	10:26:44
Lahainaluna 4	20N53'37	156W39'44	10:26:39
Lahuipuaa 1	19N56'45	155W52'15	10:23:29
Laie 2	21N39'13	157W55'38	10:31:43
Lalakoa 4	20N49'32	156W54'44	10:27:39
Lanai City 4	20N49'50	156W55'20	10:27:41
Laniakea 1	19N38'20	155W59'44	10:23:59
Lanikai 2	21N23'31	157W42'57	10:30:52
Lanikai Heights 2	21N24	157W47	10:31:08
Launiupoko 4	20N51'20	156W38'59	10:26:36
Laupahoehoe 1	19N59'13	155W14'06	10:20:56
Lawai 3	21N55'19	159W30'34	10:38:02
Leahi 3	21N47'34	160W13'26	10:40:54
Lehua Landing 3	21N59'48	160W06'01	10:40:24
Lihue 3	21N58'52	159W22'16	10:37:29
Loaloa Heiau 4	20N38'36	156W07'29	10:24:30
Lopa 4	20N48'12	156W48'45	10:27:15
Lower Paia 4	20N55'09	156W23'04	10:25:32
Lower Village 2	21N21'37	158W01'43	10:32:07
Lower Village Three 4	20N53'45	156W25'45	10:25:43
Lualualei 2	21N24	158W10	10:32:40
Lualualei Homesteads 2	21N26	158W11	10:32:44
Lunaville 4	20N52'37	156W40'25	10:26:42
Maalaea 4	20N47'47	156W30'51	10:26:03
Maalehu 4	21N10'01	157W01'25	10:28:06
Mahaiula 1	19N47'10	156W02'21	10:24:09
Mahana 4	21N09'14	157W08'54	10:28:36
Mahinahina Camp 4	20N57'36	156W39'31	10:26:38
Mahinui 2	21N24'52	157W46'26	10:31:06
Mahukona 1	20N11'15	155W54'09	10:23:37
Maili 2	21N25'19	158W10'49	10:32:43
Makaha 2	21N28'10	158W13'03	10:32:52
Makahalau 1	19N58'34	155W33'06	10:22:12
Makakilo City 2	21N20'49	158W05'09	10:32:21
Makalawena 1	19N47'43	156W01'46	10:24:07
Makapala 1	20N13'28	155W45'08	10:23:01
Makawao 4	20N51'25	156W18'47	10:25:15
Makaweli 3	21N56'13	159W39'08	10:38:37
Makaweli Landing 3	21N56'27	159W39'07	10:38:36
Makena 4	20N39'27	156W26'43	10:25:47
Makiki Heights 2	21N19'03	157W50'18	10:31:21
Makole 3	22N07'17	159W44'26	10:38:58
Mala 4	20N53'26	156W41'16	10:26:45
Malae 2	21N25'42	157W45'58	10:31:04
Maluhia Camp 4	20N57'24	156W32'16	10:26:09
Mana 1	20N00'02	155W33'37	10:22:14
Mana 3	22N02'17	159W46'20	10:39:05
Marconi Area 2	21N40	157W59	10:31:56
Mauka Loa 1	19N51	155W06	10:20:24
Maulua 1	19N59	155W14	10:20:56
Maunalani Heights 2	21N17'48	157W47'33	10:31:10
Mauna Loa 4	21N08'09	157W12'59	10:28:52
Maunawili 2	21N22'22	157W46'14	10:31:05
McGerrow Village 4	20N51'59	156W27'40	10:25:51
McGrew Point 2	21N23	157W56	10:31:44
Meyer Camp 1	19N13'15	155W29'35	10:21:58
Middle Moaula Camp 1	19N12'09	155W31'14	10:22:05
Middle Village Three 4	20N53'41	156W25'36	10:25:42
Mikilua 2	21N26	158W11	10:32:44
Mililani Town 2	21N27'29	158W01'04	10:32:04
Mill Camps 2	21N35	158W06	10:32:24
Milolii 1	19N11'12	155W54'35	10:23:38
Milo Village 1	20N00'59	155W17'06	10:21:08
Moa Heiau 1	19N19'20	155W03'25	10:20:14
Moiliili 2	21N17'26	157W49'45	10:31:19
Mokae 4	20N43'15	155W59'45	10:23:59
Mokae Landing 4	20N43'22	155W59'15	10:23:57
Mokaoku 1	19N43'53	155W04'04	10:20:16
Mokapu 2	21N27	157W45	10:31:00
Moku 4	21N04'13	156W57'33	10:27:50
Mokulau 4	20N38'44	156W06'38	10:24:27
Mokulau Landing 4	20N38'35	156W06'44	10:24:27
Mokuleia 2	21N35'03	158W09'07	10:32:36
Moloaa 3	22N11	159W21	10:37:24
Monohaa 1	19N33'08	155W51'30	10:23:26
Mookini Heiau 1	20N15'39	155W52'46	10:23:31
Moomomi 4	21N12'00	157W09'22	10:28:37
Mopua 4	20N48'51	156W36'52	10:26:27
Mountain View 1	19N33'21	155W06'29	10:20:26
Muolea 4	20N41'23	156W01'13	10:24:05
Naalehu 1	19N03'50	155W35'09	10:22:21
Nahiku 4	20N49'40	156W05'40	10:24:23
Nanakuli 2	21N23'26	158W09'17	10:32:37
Napili 4	20N57	156W40	10:26:40
Napoopoo 1	19N30	155W55	10:23:40
Nashiwa Village 4	20N54'06	156W22'06	10:25:28
Nawiliwili 3	21N57'57	159W21'23	10:37:26
Niihau 3	21N54	160W08	10:40:32
Nine Miles 1	19N38	155W02	10:20:08
Ninole 1	19N08'02	155W30'45	10:22:03
Niu 2	21N17'06	157W44'32	10:30:58
Niukapu Heiau 3	21N54'01	159W30'00	10:38:00
Niukukahi Heiau 1	19N22'01	154W59'03	10:19:56
Niulii 1	20N13'32	155W44'45	10:22:59
Niumalu 3	21N57'19	159W21'54	10:37:28
Niu Village 1	20N00'48	155W16'32	10:21:06
Nonopahu Village 3	21N58'17	159W38'20	10:38:33
Nonopapa 3	21N52'03	160W13'23	10:40:54
North Hilo 1	19N42	155W18	10:21:12
North Kohala 1	20N11	155W49	10:23:16
North Kona 1	19N38	155W53	10:23:32
Numila 3	21N54'06	159W33'35	10:38:14
Nuu 4	20N37'55	156W11'11	10:24:45
Nuu Landing 4	20N37'43	156W10'51	10:24:43
Ohiapili 4	21N06'18	157W03'18	10:28:13
Oiamoi 3	21N50'21	160W10'07	10:40:40
Okoe 1	19N30	155W55	10:23:40
Olaa 1	19N38	155W02	10:20:08
Olaa Summer Lots 1	19N26	155W16	10:21:04
Old Keanae Landing 4	20N51'58	156W09'04	10:24:36
Olinda 4	20N51	156W19	10:25:16
Olomana 2	21N24	157W47	10:31:08
Olowalu 4	20N48'53	156W37'30	10:26:30
Omao 3	21N55'57	159W29'21	10:37:57
Omapio 4	20N46	156W20	10:25:20
Oneula Beach 2	21N18'34	158W01'44	10:32:07
Onomea 1	19N49'00	155W06'13	10:20:25
Ookala 1	20N01'03	155W17'14	10:21:09
Opaeula Camp 2	21N35	158W06	10:32:24
Opihikao 1	19N25'47	154W53'00	10:19:32
Orpheum Village 4	20N54'11	156W22'20	10:25:29
Paauhau 1	20N05'07	155W26'26	10:21:46
Paauhau Landing 1	20N05'40	155W26'34	10:21:46
Paauhau Mauka 1	20N05	155W28	10:21:52
Paauilo 1	20N02'31	155W22'16	10:21:29
Pacific Heights 2	21N19'36	157W50'33	10:31:22
Pacific Palisades 2	21N25'32	157W57'39	10:31:51
Pahala 1	19N12'19	155W28'48	10:21:55
Pahoa 1	19N29'51	154W57'03	10:19:48
Pahoehoe 1	19N30	155W55	10:23:40
Paholoi 4	20N52'49	156W20'44	10:25:23
Paia 4	20N54'12	156W22'10	10:25:29
Pakala Village (Makaweli) 3	21N56'13	159W39'08	10:38:37
Palani Junction 1	19N41'29	155W58'43	10:23:55
Palehua 2	21N23'58	158W06'11	10:32:25
Paliaalii 1	19N59'09	155W33'00	10:22:12
Palihooukapapa 1	19N58'17	155W31'57	10:22:08
Panaewa 1	19N42	155W05	10:20:20
Papa 1	19N12'33	155W52'00	10:23:28
Papaaloa 1	19N58'44	155W13'16	10:20:53
Papaikou 1	19N47'20	155W05'45	10:20:23
Papakonani Boat Landing 1	19N57'08	155W52'06	10:23:28
Papaloa 1	19N30'34	155W47'54	10:23:12
Papaloa 3	22N03'29	159W19'59	10:37:20
Pauahi 1	19N30'26	155W49'35	10:23:18
Paukaa 1	19N45'56	155W05'42	10:20:23
Paukukalo 4	20N54'31	156W29'16	10:25:57
Paumalu 2	21N36	158W05	10:32:20
Pauwalu 4	21N05'29	156W46'36	10:27:06
Pauwela 4	20N56'02	156W19'12	10:25:17
Pawaa 2	21N18	157W50	10:31:20
Pawaina 1	19N30'19	155W51'36	10:23:26
Peahi 4	20N55	156W19	10:25:16
Pearl City 2	21N23'50	157W58'24	10:31:54
Pearl City Heights 2	21N24	157W58	10:31:52
Pearl Harbor Naval Sta 2	21N21	157W56	10:31:44
Pelekunu 4	21N09'51	156W52'58	10:27:32
Pepeekeo 1	19N50'01	155W06'26	10:20:26
Pepeekeo Mill 1	19N51'03	155W05'17	10:20:21
Pepeekeo Mill Camp 1	19N51	155W06	10:20:24
Pihana 4	20N54	156W30	10:26:00
Pihana Heiau 4	20N54'22	156W29'46	10:25:59
Piihonua 1	19N42'57	155W08'20	10:20:33
Poamoho Camp 2	21N31	158W02	10:32:08
Pohakea Homesteads 1	20N03	155W22	10:21:28
Pohakupu 2	21N23'05	157W45'15	10:31:01
Pohoiki 1	19N27'39	154W50'49	10:19:23
Poipu 3	21N52'35	159W27'14	10:37:49
Pokii 3	21N58'59	159W43'15	10:38:53
Poliahu Heiau 3	22N02'58	159W21'30	10:37:26
Polihale Heiau 3	22N06'01	159W44'50	10:38:59
Pomoho 2	21N30	158W03	10:32:12
Popoiwi Heiau 4	20N38'35	156W06'57	10:24:28
Port Allen 3	21N54'22	159W35'21	10:38:21
Portlock 2	21N16'43	157W42'39	10:30:51
Pua Akala 1	19N47'24	155W20'05	10:21:20
Puako 1	19N58'30	155W50'38	10:23:23
Pualaa 1	19N28'18	154W50'11	10:19:21
Pualaea Homestead 1	19N59	155W14	10:20:56
Pua Loke 3	21N58'20	159W22'33	10:37:30
Puhi 3	21N58'07	159W23'58	10:37:36
Pukalani 4	20N50'12	156W20'12	10:25:21
Pukoo 4	21N04'35	156W47'45	10:27:11
Pulehu 4	20N46'48	156W19'43	10:25:19
Punaluu 1	19N08'21	155W30'26	10:22:02
Punaluu 2	21N37	157W55	10:31:40
Punaluu Kahawai 1	19N15'03	155W36'33	10:22:26
Puohala 2	21N25	157W48	10:31:12
Puohala Village 2	21N24'22	157W48'09	10:31:13
Puopelu 1	20N01'24	155W41'06	10:22:44
Pupukea 2	21N45	157W57	10:31:48
Puuanahulu 1	19N49'07	155W50'47	10:23:23
Puueo 1	19N44'01	155W05'32	10:20:22
Puu Hue 1	20N14	155W50	10:23:20
Puuiki 4	20N42'18	156W00'08	10:24:01
Puukolii 4	20N56'04	156W40'37	10:26:42
Puunene 4	20N51'49	156W27'11	10:25:49
Puunoa 4	20N52'56	156W41'09	10:26:45
Puunui 2	21N20'13	157W51'03	10:31:24
Puuohala 4	20N54	156W30	10:26:00
Puuohala Village 4	20N53'58	156W30'42	10:26:03
Puu Waawaa Ranch 1	20N31	156W52	10:27:28
Puuwai 3	21N54'08	160W11'39	10:40:47
Ranch Camp 2	21N33'56	158W07'41	10:32:31
Renton 2	21N21	158W02	10:32:08
Renton Village 2	21N20'41	158W02'16	10:32:09
Russian Village 4	20N54'23	156W25'29	10:25:42
Saddle Road Junction 1	19N56'21	155W41'25	10:22:46
Saint Louis Heights 2	21N18'11	157W48'25	10:31:14
Saki Mana 3	22N03'37	159W45'48	10:39:03
Sam Sing Village 4	20N52'17	156W26'46	10:25:47
Sand Hills 4	20N53'44	156W29'51	10:25:59
Schofield Barracks 2	21N30	158W04	10:32:16
School Village 4	20N54'20	156W22'13	10:25:29
South Kohala 1	20N04	155W43	10:22:52
South Kona 1	19N21	155W49	10:23:16
Spanish B Village 4	20N52'06	156W26'54	10:25:48

Spreckelsville 4	20N53'49	156w24'54	10:25:40
Store Village 4	20N54'24	156w22'27	10:25:30
Submarine Base 2	21N21	157w56	10:31:44
Sunset Beach 2	21N40'23	158w02'53	10:32:12
Tenney Village 2	21N20'33	158w02'41	10:32:11
Thompson Corner 2	21N33'55	158w06'57	10:32:28
Tripler Army Hospital 2	21N21	157w53	10:31:32
Ualapue 4	21N03'56	156w49'57	10:27:20
Ulaino 4	20N48'31	156w03'32	10:24:14
Ulumalu 4	20N54'34	156w17'12	10:25:09
Ulupalakua 4	20N38'57	156w24'04	10:25:36
Umikoa (Kukaiau Ranch) 1	19N58'57	155w23'04	10:21:32
Umipaa 4	21N06'35	157w03'20	10:28:13
Union Mill 1	20N14	155w47	10:23:08
University 2	21N19	157w50	10:31:20
Upper Village Three 4	20N53'14	156w25'17	10:25:41
Varona Village 2	21N20'13	158w02'45	10:32:11
Village Eight 4	20N51'28	156w26'28	10:25:46
Village Five 4	20N51'34	156w27'30	10:25:50
Village Four 4	20N52'30	156w26'23	10:25:46
Village Six 4	20N50'22	156w28'21	10:25:53
Village Ten 4	20N51'42	156w24'01	10:25:36
Village Thirteen 4	20N50'13	156w26'06	10:25:44
Village Two 4	20N53'41	156w24'19	10:25:37
Volcano 1	19N25'51	155w14'16	10:20:57
Wahiawa 2	21N30'10	158w01'25	10:32:06
Wahiawa 3	21N54	159w35	10:38:20
Wahilauhue 4	21N10'15	157w15'27	10:29:02
Waiahole 2	21N29'09	157w51'24	10:31:26
Waiahukini 1	18N57'01	155w42'13	10:22:49
Waiaka 1	20N01'47	155w42'07	10:22:48
Waiaka Heiau 1	19N20'25	155w00'39	10:20:03
Waiakea 1	19N43'01	155w04'15	10:20:17
Waiakoa 4	20N45'45	156w19'48	10:25:19
Waialae 2	21N16'45	157w47'27	10:31:10
Waialee 2	21N41'23	158w01'35	10:32:06
Waialua 2	21N34'36	158w07'49	10:32:31
Waialua 4	21N06'01	156w45'41	10:27:03
Waialua Mill 2	21N35	158w06	10:32:24
Waianae 2	21N26'41	158w11'24	10:32:46
Waianae Homesteads 2	21N26	158w11	10:32:44
Waianae Uka 2	21N26	158w11	10:32:44
Waiau 2	21N23'35	157w57'45	10:31:51
Waiehu 4	20N55'17	156w29'49	10:25:59
Waiehu Village 4	20N55'03	156w30'56	10:26:04
Waihee 4	20N56'02	156w30'53	10:26:04
Waihou 1	19N32'24	155w54'12	10:23:37
Waikane 2	21N30'02	157w51'18	10:31:25
Waikapu 4	20N51'29	156w30'25	10:26:02
Waikapuna 1	19N01'29	155w34'56	10:22:20
Waikapu Reservoir Village 4	20N54	156w30	10:26:00
Waikele 2	21N24	158w01	10:32:04
Waikii 1	19N51'38	155w39'08	10:22:37
Waikiki 2	21N16'58	157w49'46	10:31:19
Waikui 1	20N01'30	155w49'27	10:23:18
Wailau 4	21N10'07	156w49'51	10:27:19
Wailea 1	19N53'15	155w07'25	10:20:30
Wailua 3	22N03'08	159w20'16	10:37:21
Wailua 4	20N50'55	156w08'11	10:24:33
Wailua House Lots 3	22N03'44	159w20'46	10:37:23
Wailuku 4	20N53'28	156w30'17	10:26:01
Wailuku Heights 4	20N52'39	156w31'10	10:26:05
Wailupe 2	21N16'47	157w45'35	10:31:02
Waimalu 2	21N24	157w57	10:31:48
Waimanalo 2	21N21'00	157w43'15	10:30:53
Waimanalo Beach 2	21N20'25	157w42'10	10:30:49
Waimea (Kamuela P O) 1	20N01'23	155w40'18	10:22:41
Waimea 2	21N38'56	158w03'58	10:32:16
Waimea 3	21N57'30	159w40'15	10:38:41
Wainaku 1	19N44'41	155w05'42	10:20:23
Wainee 4	20N52'27	156w40'14	10:26:41
Wainiha 3	22N12'58	159w32'36	10:38:10
Waiohinu 1	19N04'13	155w36'51	10:22:27
Waiopili Heiau 3	21N53'35	159w25'25	10:37:42
Waipahoehoe 1	19N36'15	155w00'40	10:20:03
Waipahu 2	21N23'12	158w00'33	10:32:02
Waipio 1	20N06'40	155w35'55	10:22:24
Waipio Acres 2	21N28'03	158w00'59	10:32:04
Waipouli 3	22N03'50	159w19'29	10:37:18
Waipunalei Homesteads 1	22N04	159w20	10:37:20
Weliweli 1	19N54'04	155w54'26	10:23:38
Weloka 1	19N57'38	155w12'03	10:20:48
West Molokai 4	21N11	157w06	10:28:24
Wheeler Air Force Base 2	21N30	158w03	10:32:12
Wheeler Field 2	21N29'20	158w02'19	10:32:09
Whitmore Village 2	21N30'50	158w01'23	10:32:06
Wilhelmina Rise 2	21N17'26	157w47'50	10:31:11
Woodlawn 2	21N19'04	157w48'19	10:31:13
Wood Valley Homesteads 1	19N12	155w29	10:21:56
Yung Hee Village 4	20N51'41	156w27'20	10:25:49

TIME TABLES

Some informal reports show Pacific time observed in southern Idaho later than most sources indicate, but this has not been documented. Southern Idaho changed to daylight time on February 3, 1974, rather than January 6, 1974 with the rest of the country.

ID # 1

Before 11/18/1883		LMT
11/18/1883	12:00	PST
3/31/1918	02:00	PWT
10/27/1918	02:00	PST
3/30/1919	02:00	PWT
10/26/1919	02:00	PST
2/09/1942	02:00	PWT
9/30/1945	02:00	PST
4/30/1961	02:00	PDT
10/29/1961	02:00	PST
4/29/1962	02:00	PDT
10/28/1962	02:00	PST
4/28/1963	02:00	PDT
10/27/1963	02:00	PST
4/26/1964	02:00	PDT
10/25/1964	02:00	PST
4/25/1965	02:00	PDT
10/31/1965	02:00	PST
4/24/1966	02:00	PDT
10/30/1966	02:00	PST
4/30/1967	02:00	US#1

ID # 2

Before 11/18/1883		LMT
11/18/1883	12:00	PST
3/31/1918	02:00	PWT
10/27/1918	02:00	PST
3/30/1919	02:00	PWT
10/26/1919	02:00	PST
2/09/1942	02:00	PWT
9/30/1945	02:00	PST
4/26/1964	02:00	PDT
10/25/1964	02:00	PST
4/24/1966	02:00	US#1

ID # 3

Before 11/18/1883		LMT
11/18/1883	12:00	PST
3/31/1918	02:00	PWT
10/27/1918	02:00	PST
3/30/1919	02:00	PWT
10/26/1919	02:00	PST
5/01/1938	02:00	PDT
10/01/1938	02:00	PST
5/07/1939	02:00	PDT
10/01/1939	02:00	PST
5/05/1940	02:00	PDT
9/29/1940	02:00	PST
5/04/1941	02:00	PDT
9/28/1941	02:00	PST
2/09/1942	02:00	PWT
9/30/1945	02:00	PST
4/26/1964	02:00	PDT
10/25/1964	02:00	PST
4/24/1966	02:00	US#1

ID # 4

Before 11/18/1883		LMT
11/18/1883	12:00	PST
3/31/1918	02:00	PWT
10/27/1918	02:00	PST
3/30/1919	02:00	PWT
10/26/1919	02:00	PST
2/09/1942	02:00	PWT
9/30/1945	02:00	PST
4/30/1961	02:00	PDT
10/29/1961	02:00	PST
4/29/1962	02:00	PDT
10/28/1962	02:00	PST
4/28/1963	02:00	PDT
10/27/1963	02:00	PST
4/26/1964	02:00	PDT
10/25/1964	02:00	PST
4/24/1966	02:00	US#1

ID # 5

Before 11/18/1883		LMT
11/18/1883	12:00	PST
3/31/1918	02:00	PWT
10/27/1918	02:00	PST
3/30/1919	02:00	PWT
10/26/1919	02:00	PST
2/09/1942	02:00	PWT
9/30/1945	02:00	PST
4/26/1964	02:00	PDT
10/25/1964	02:00	PST
4/25/1965	02:00	PDT
10/31/1965	02:00	PST
4/24/1966	02:00	PDT
10/30/1966	02:00	PST
4/30/1967	02:00	US#1

ID # 6

Before 11/18/1883		LMT
11/18/1883	12:00	PST
3/31/1918	02:00	PWT
10/27/1918	02:00	PST
3/30/1919	02:00	PWT
10/26/1919	02:00	PST
5/01/1938	02:00	PDT
10/01/1938	02:00	PST
5/07/1939	02:00	PDT
10/01/1939	02:00	PST
5/05/1940	02:00	PDT
9/29/1940	02:00	PST
5/04/1941	02:00	PDT
9/28/1941	02:00	PST
2/09/1942	02:00	PWT
9/30/1945	02:00	PST
4/30/1961	02:00	PDT
10/29/1961	02:00	PST
4/29/1962	02:00	PDT
10/28/1962	02:00	PST
4/28/1963	02:00	PDT
10/27/1963	02:00	PST
4/26/1964	02:00	PDT
10/25/1964	02:00	PST
4/24/1966	02:00	US#1

ID # 7

Before 11/18/1883		LMT
11/18/1883	12:00	PST
3/31/1918	02:00	PWT
10/27/1918	02:00	PST
3/30/1919	02:00	PWT
10/26/1919	02:00	PST
2/09/1942	02:00	PWT
9/30/1945	02:00	PST
4/27/1952	02:00	PDT
9/01/1952	02:00	PST
4/30/1961	02:00	PDT
10/29/1961	02:00	PST
4/29/1962	02:00	PDT
10/28/1962	02:00	PST
4/28/1963	02:00	PDT
10/27/1963	02:00	PST
4/26/1964	02:00	PDT
10/25/1964	02:00	PST
4/25/1965	02:00	PDT
10/31/1965	02:00	PST
4/24/1966	02:00	PDT
10/30/1966	02:00	PST
4/30/1967	02:00	US#1

ID # 8

Before 4/01/1893		LMT
4/01/1893	12:00	PST
3/31/1918	02:00	PWT
10/27/1918	02:00	PST
3/30/1919	02:00	PWT
10/26/1919	02:00	PST
5/15/1931	02:00	PDT
10/15/1931	02:00	PST
4/30/1933	02:00	PDT
9/24/1933	02:00	PST
4/29/1934	02:00	PDT
9/30/1934	02:00	PST
4/28/1935	02:00	PDT
9/29/1935	02:00	PST
4/26/1936	02:00	PDT
9/27/1936	02:00	PST
4/25/1937	02:00	PDT
9/26/1937	02:00	PST
5/01/1938	02:00	PDT
10/01/1938	02:00	PST
5/07/1939	02:00	PDT
10/01/1939	02:00	PST
5/05/1940	02:00	PDT
9/29/1940	02:00	PST
5/04/1941	02:00	PDT
9/28/1941	02:00	PST
2/09/1942	02:00	PWT
9/30/1945	02:00	PST
4/30/1961	02:00	PDT
10/29/1961	02:00	PST
4/29/1962	02:00	PDT
10/28/1962	02:00	PST
4/28/1963	02:00	PDT
10/27/1963	02:00	PST
4/26/1964	02:00	PDT
10/25/1964	02:00	PST
4/24/1966	02:00	US#1

ID # 9

Before 4/01/1893		LMT
4/01/1893	12:00	PST
3/31/1918	02:00	PWT
10/27/1918	02:00	PST
3/30/1919	02:00	PWT
10/26/1919	02:00	PST
4/30/1933	02:00	PDT
9/24/1933	02:00	PST
4/29/1934	02:00	PDT
9/30/1934	02:00	PST
4/28/1935	02:00	PDT
9/29/1935	02:00	PST
4/26/1936	02:00	PDT
9/27/1936	02:00	PST
4/25/1937	02:00	PDT
9/26/1937	02:00	PST
4/24/1938	02:00	PDT
9/24/1938	02:00	PST
5/07/1939	02:00	PDT
10/01/1939	02:00	PST
5/05/1940	02:00	PDT
9/29/1940	02:00	PST
5/04/1941	02:00	PDT
9/28/1941	02:00	PST
2/09/1942	02:00	PWT
9/30/1945	02:00	PST
4/26/1964	02:00	PDT
10/25/1964	02:00	PST
4/24/1966	02:00	US#1

ID # 10

Before 4/01/1893		LMT
4/01/1893	12:00	PST
3/31/1918	02:00	PWT
10/27/1918	02:00	PST
3/30/1919	02:00	PWT
10/26/1919	02:00	PST
4/26/1936	02:00	PDT
9/27/1936	02:00	PST
4/25/1937	02:00	PDT
9/26/1937	02:00	PST
4/24/1938	02:00	PDT
9/24/1938	02:00	PST
5/07/1939	02:00	PDT
10/01/1939	02:00	PST
5/05/1940	02:00	PDT
9/29/1940	02:00	PST
5/04/1941	02:00	PDT
9/28/1941	02:00	PST
2/09/1942	02:00	PWT
9/30/1945	02:00	PST
4/30/1961	02:00	PDT
10/29/1961	02:00	PST
4/29/1962	02:00	PDT
10/28/1962	02:00	PST
4/28/1963	02:00	PDT
10/27/1963	02:00	PST
4/26/1964	02:00	PDT
10/25/1964	02:00	PST
4/24/1966	02:00	US#1

ID # 11

Before 4/01/1893		LMT
4/01/1893	12:00	PST
3/31/1918	02:00	PWT
10/27/1918	02:00	PST
3/30/1919	02:00	PWT
10/26/1919	02:00	PST
5/10/1931	02:00	PDT
10/04/1931	02:00	PST
4/29/1934	02:00	PDT
9/30/1934	02:00	PST
4/28/1935	02:00	PDT
9/29/1935	02:00	PST
4/26/1936	02:00	PDT
9/27/1936	02:00	PST
4/25/1937	02:00	PDT
10/02/1937	02:00	PST
5/01/1938	02:00	PDT
10/01/1938	02:00	PST
5/07/1939	02:00	PDT
10/01/1939	02:00	PST
5/05/1940	02:00	PDT
9/29/1940	02:00	PST
5/04/1941	02:00	PDT
9/28/1941	02:00	PST
2/09/1942	02:00	PWT
9/30/1945	02:00	PST
4/26/1964	02:00	PDT
10/25/1964	02:00	PST
4/24/1966	02:00	US#1

ID # 12

Before 11/18/1883		LMT
11/18/1883	12:00	PST
3/31/1918	02:00	PWT
10/27/1918	02:00	PST
3/30/1919	02:00	PWT
10/26/1919	02:00	PST
2/09/1942	02:00	PWT
9/30/1945	02:00	PST
4/30/1950	02:00	PDT
9/24/1950	02:00	PST
4/30/1961	02:00	PDT
10/29/1961	02:00	PST
4/29/1962	02:00	PDT
10/28/1962	02:00	PST
4/28/1963	02:00	PDT
10/27/1963	02:00	PST
4/26/1964	02:00	PDT
10/25/1964	02:00	PST
4/24/1966	02:00	US#1

ID # 13

Before 11/18/1883		LMT
11/18/1883	12:00	PST
3/31/1918	02:00	PWT
10/27/1918	02:00	PST
1/01/1919	02:00	MST
3/30/1919	02:00	MWT
10/26/1919	02:00	MST
2/09/1942	02:00	MWT
9/30/1945	02:00	MST
4/30/1961	02:00	MDT
10/29/1961	02:00	MST
4/29/1962	02:00	MDT
10/28/1962	02:00	MST
4/28/1963	02:00	MDT
10/27/1963	02:00	MST
4/30/1967	02:00	MDT
10/29/1967	02:00	MST
4/28/1968	02:00	MDT
10/27/1968	02:00	MST
4/27/1969	02:00	MDT
10/26/1969	02:00	MST
4/26/1970	02:00	MDT
10/25/1970	02:00	MST
4/25/1971	02:00	MDT
10/31/1971	02:00	MST
4/30/1972	02:00	MDT
10/29/1972	02:00	MST
4/29/1973	02:00	MDT
10/28/1973	02:00	MST
2/03/1974	02:00	MDT
10/27/1974	02:00	US#1

ID # 14

Before 11/18/1883		LMT
11/18/1883	12:00	PST
3/31/1918	02:00	PWT
10/27/1918	02:00	PST
1/01/1919	02:00	MST
3/30/1919	02:00	MWT
10/26/1919	02:00	MST
2/09/1942	02:00	MWT
9/30/1945	02:00	MST
4/30/1967	02:00	MDT
10/29/1967	02:00	MST
4/28/1968	02:00	MDT
10/27/1968	02:00	MST
4/27/1969	02:00	MDT
10/26/1969	02:00	MST
4/26/1970	02:00	MDT
10/25/1970	02:00	MST
4/25/1971	02:00	MDT
10/31/1971	02:00	MST
4/30/1972	02:00	MDT
10/29/1972	02:00	MST
4/29/1973	02:00	MDT
10/28/1973	02:00	MST
2/03/1974	02:00	MDT
10/27/1974	02:00	US#1

ID # 15

Before 11/18/1883		LMT
11/18/1883	12:00	PST
3/31/1918	02:00	PWT
10/27/1918	02:00	PST
3/30/1919	02:00	PWT
6/01/1919	02:00	MWT
10/26/1919	02:00	MST
2/09/1942	02:00	MWT
9/30/1945	02:00	MST
4/26/1964	02:00	MDT
10/25/1964	02:00	MST
4/25/1965	02:00	MDT
10/31/1965	02:00	MST
4/30/1967	02:00	MDT
10/29/1967	02:00	MST
4/28/1968	02:00	MDT
10/27/1968	02:00	MST
4/27/1969	02:00	MDT
10/26/1969	02:00	MST
4/26/1970	02:00	MDT
10/25/1970	02:00	MST
4/25/1971	02:00	MDT
10/31/1971	02:00	MST
4/30/1972	02:00	MDT
10/29/1972	02:00	MST
4/29/1973	02:00	MDT
10/28/1973	02:00	MST
2/03/1974	02:00	MDT
10/27/1974	02:00	US#1

ID # 16

Before 11/18/1883		LMT
11/18/1883	12:00	PST
3/31/1918	02:00	PWT
10/27/1918	02:00	PST
3/30/1919	02:00	PWT
6/01/1919	02:00	MWT
10/26/1919	02:00	MST
2/09/1942	02:00	MWT
9/30/1945	02:00	MST
4/30/1967	02:00	MDT
10/29/1967	02:00	MST
4/28/1968	02:00	MDT
10/27/1968	02:00	MST
4/27/1969	02:00	MDT
10/26/1969	02:00	MST
4/26/1970	02:00	MDT
10/25/1970	02:00	MST
4/25/1971	02:00	MDT
10/31/1971	02:00	MST
4/30/1972	02:00	MDT
10/29/1972	02:00	MST
4/29/1973	02:00	MDT
10/28/1973	02:00	MST
2/03/1974	02:00	MDT
10/27/1974	02:00	US#1

ID # 17

Before 11/18/1883		LMT
11/18/1883	12:00	PST
3/31/1918	02:00	PWT
10/27/1918	02:00	PST
3/30/1919	02:00	PWT
10/26/1919	02:00	PST
5/13/1923	02:00	MST
2/09/1942	02:00	MWT
9/30/1945	02:00	MST
4/30/1961	02:00	MDT
10/29/1961	02:00	MST
4/29/1962	02:00	MDT
10/28/1962	02:00	MST
4/28/1963	02:00	MDT
10/27/1963	02:00	MST
4/30/1967	02:00	MDT
10/29/1967	02:00	MST
4/28/1968	02:00	MDT
10/27/1968	02:00	MST
4/27/1969	02:00	MDT
10/26/1969	02:00	MST
4/26/1970	02:00	MDT
10/25/1970	02:00	MST
4/25/1971	02:00	MDT
10/31/1971	02:00	MST
4/30/1972	02:00	MDT
10/29/1972	02:00	MST
4/29/1973	02:00	MDT
10/28/1973	02:00	MST
2/03/1974	02:00	MDT
10/27/1974	02:00	US#1

ID # 18

Before 11/18/1883		LMT
11/18/1883	12:00	PST
3/31/1918	02:00	PWT
10/27/1918	02:00	PST
3/30/1919	02:00	PWT
10/26/1919	02:00	PST
5/13/1923	02:00	MST
2/09/1942	02:00	MWT
9/30/1945	02:00	MST
4/30/1967	02:00	MDT
10/29/1967	02:00	MST
4/28/1968	02:00	MDT
10/27/1968	02:00	MST
4/27/1969	02:00	MDT
10/26/1969	02:00	MST
4/26/1970	02:00	MDT
10/25/1970	02:00	MST
4/25/1971	02:00	MDT
10/31/1971	02:00	MST
4/30/1972	02:00	MDT
10/29/1972	02:00	MST
4/29/1973	02:00	MDT
10/28/1973	02:00	MST
2/03/1974	02:00	MDT
10/27/1974	02:00	US#1

COUNTIES

1 Ada
2 Adams
3 Bannock
4 Bear Lake
5 Benewah
6 Bingham
7 Blaine
8 Boise
9 Bonner
10 Bonneville
11 Boundary
12 Butte
13 Camas
14 Canyon
15 Caribou
16 Cassia
17 Clark
18 Clearwater
19 Custer
20 Elmore
21 Franklin
22 Fremont
23 Gem
24 Gooding
25 Idaho
26 Jefferson
27 Jerome
28 Kootenai
29 Latah
30 Lemhi
31 Lewis
32 Lincoln
33 Madison
34 Minidoka
35 Nez Perce
36 Oneida
37 Owyhee
38 Payette
39 Power
40 Shoshone
41 Teton
42 Twin Falls
43 Valley
44 Washington

Aberdeen 6 16 42N56'39 112w50'15 7:31:21
Aberdeen Junction 6
16 43N13'23 112w28'12 7:29:53
Abstein Place 43
18 44N58'15 115w29'09 7:41:57
Acequia 34 18 42N40'05 113w35'46 7:34:23
Adair 40 2 47N20'32 115w36'40 7:42:27
Addie 11 4 48N57'13 116w09'55 7:44:40
Adelaide 34 18 42N48'26 113w43'16 7:34:53
Agatha 35 2 46N30'39 116w34'33 7:46:18
Ahsahka 18 2 46N30'08 116w19'23 7:45:18
Aiken 6 14 43N12'33 112w24'21 7:29:37
Alameda 3 16 42N57 112w28 7:29:52
Albion 16 18 42N24'46 113w34'38 7:34:19
Alder Creek 5 2 47N13'22 116w36'24 7:46:26
Alexander 15 14 42N39'04 111w42'30 7:26:50
Algoma 9 2 48N11'49 116w34'16 7:46:17
Allendale 14 17 43N40'35 116w52'26 7:47:30
Allens Spur 11 2 48N44'26 116w21'55 7:45:28
Almo 16 18 42N06'01 113w37'58 7:34:32
Alpha 43 18 44N23'28 116w00'25 7:44:02
Alpine 2 18 44N34 116w40 7:46:40
Alridge 6 14 43N12'40 111w58'32 7:27:54
Alton 4 14 42N13'39 111w09'03 7:24:36
Amalga 34 18 42N34'37 113w43'26 7:34:54
American Falls 39
18 42N47'10 112w51'13 7:31:25
Ammon 10 14 43N28'11 111w57'57 7:27:52
Amsco 14 18 43N45'53 116w38'54 7:46:36
Amsterdam 42 18 42N17'45 114w35'02 7:38:20
Anderson 21 14 42N01'14 111w57'22 7:27:49
Anderson Dam 20
18 43N08 115w42 7:42:48
Anderson Place 42
18 42N14'41 114w57'00 7:39:48
Annis 26 14 43N43'42 111w56'07 7:27:44
Antelope 10 14 43N38 111w45 7:27:00
Appleton 24 18 42N44'53 114w38'04 7:38:32
Apple Valley 14
18 43N50'24 116w59'44 7:47:59
Arbon 39 18 42N27'21 112w34'03 7:30:16
Arbon Crossing 39
14 42N52'23 112w38'00 7:30:32
Arbon PO 39 18 42N29'19 112w32'52 7:30:11
Archabal 43 18 44N50'49 116w07'16 7:44:29
Archer 33 14 43N42'49 111w46'55 7:27:08
Arco 12 16 43N38'12 113w17'58 7:33:12
Argora 17 14 44N10 112w14 7:28:56
Arimo 3 14 42N33'36 112w10'14 7:28:41
Arling 43 18 44N37'31 116w02'57 7:44:12
Arrow 35 2 46N28'41 116w46'01 7:47:04
Artesian City 42
18 42N25'02 114w09'37 7:36:38
Asbestos Point 25
2 45N49'05 115w56'23 7:43:46
Ashton 22 13 44N04'18 111w26'51 7:25:47
Athol 28 4 47N56'53 116w42'25 7:46:50
Atlanta 20 18 43N48'06 115w07'33 7:40:30
Atlas 28 2 47N42'02 116w49'43 7:47:19
Atomic City 6 16 43N26'42 112w48'43 7:31:15
Avery 40 2 47N15'02 115w48'15 7:43:13
Avon 29 2 46N49'34 116w36'46 7:46:27
Baker 30 16 45N05'41 113w44'01 7:34:56
Bancroft 15 14 42N43'13 111w53'06 7:27:32
Banida 21 14 42N13'52 111w56'30 7:27:46
Banks 8 18 44N04'50 116w07'23 7:44:30
Bannock 39 14 42N51'41 112w43'19 7:30:53
Barber 1 18 43N34'34 116w08'12 7:44:33
Barite 7 18 43N33'23 114w19'32 7:37:18
Barlow 26 14 43N40'16 112w00'44 7:28:03
Barrymore 27 18 42N40'51 114w27'44 7:37:51
Barton 44 18 44N23'04 116w47'56 7:47:12
Basalt 6 14 43N18'56 112w09'49 7:28:39
Basin 16 18 42N14'44 113w47'01 7:35:08
Bassett 26 14 43N39'04 112w05'15 7:28:21
Bates 41 14 40N03'50 79w57'08 5:19:49
Bayhorse 19 18 44N23'52 114w18'39 7:37:15
Bayview 28 2 47N58'49 116w33'33 7:46:14
Beachs Corner 10
14 43N32'33 111w57'48 7:27:51
Bear 2 18 45N01'28 116w40'16 7:46:41
Bear Lake Hot Springs 4
14 42N06'31 111w15'52 7:25:03
Bear Lake Sands 4
14 42N03'06 111w15'10 7:25:01
Beatty 1 18 43N36'30 116w20'24 7:45:22
Bedstead Corner 22
14 44N16'33 111w47'32 7:27:10
Beer Bottle Crossing 2
18 44N36'31 116w13'48 7:44:55
Beetville 16 18 42N29'19 113w49'50 7:35:19
Bellevue 7 18 43N27'49 114w15'35 7:37:02
Bellgrove 28 1 47N32'02 116w54'50 7:47:39
Belmont 28 2 47N55'34 116w38'19 7:46:33
Belvidere 43 18 44N28'32 116w01'57 7:44:08
Bench 15 14 42N30'13 111w40'46 7:26:43
Benewah 5 2 47N13'40 116w47'00 7:47:08
Bengoechea Place 37
18 42N18'17 115w50'49 7:43:23
Bennington 4 14 42N23'28 111w19'15 7:25:17
Berenice 12 16 43N49'40 112w58'24 7:31:54
Berger 42 18 42N28'11 114w34'26 7:38:18
Bergstrom Place 42
18 42N11'40 114w56'09 7:39:45
Bern 4 14 42N20'23 111w23'07 7:25:32
Bessien 32 18 42N54'31 114w10'22 7:36:41
Best Corner 18 2 46N33'43 116w08'59 7:44:36
Bickel 42 18 42N31'41 114w12'35 7:36:50
Big Cedar 25 2 46N04'52 115w48'48 7:43:15
Big Creek 43 18 45N07'38 115w19'24 7:41:18
Big Eddy 8 18 44N12'58 116w06'23 7:44:26
Big George 35 2 46N30'10 116w29'31 7:45:58
Big Springs 22
14 44N29'54 111w15'18 7:25:01
Bills 42 18 42N31'56 114w17'08 7:37:09
Bingo Creek Landing 18
2 46N45'26 116w44'09 7:42:57
Black Bear 40 3 47N30'58 115w51'05 7:43:24
Blackbird Townsite 30
18 45N05'35 114w13'51 7:36:55
Black Canyon 23
18 43N55'36 116w26'29 7:45:46
Black Cloud 40 2 47N28 115w55 7:43:40
Blackfoot 6 13 43N11'26 112w20'39 7:29:23
Black Lake 28 2 47N19 116w34 7:46:16
Black Pine 36 18 42N04'21 112w58'46 7:31:55
Blackrock 3 14 42N47'49 112w19'34 7:29:18
Black Rock Crossing 37
18 42N03'34 115w39'06 7:42:36
Blacks Creek 1
18 43N28'40 116w08'14 7:44:33
Blacktail 9 2 48N07'14 116w29'07 7:45:56
Blackwell 28 1 47N41'52 116w48'25 7:47:14
Blaine 13 18 43N20'33 114w35'41 7:38:23
Blaine 29 2 46N39'26 116w56'52 7:47:47
Blanchard 9 2 48N01'01 116w58'58 7:47:56
Bliss 24 18 42N55'37 114w56'55 7:39:48
Bloomington 4 14 42N11'31 111w24'02 7:25:36
Blue Creek Crossing 37
18 42N27'28 116w15'09 7:45:01
Blue Dome 17 16 44N09'37 112w54'38 7:31:39
Boehls 18 2 46N52'29 115w54'16 7:43:37
Boise 1 18 43N36'49 116w12'09 7:44:49
Boise Hills Village 1
18 43N37'57 116w11'20 7:44:45
Boise Junction 1
18 43N36'18 116w15'21 7:45:01
Boles 25 2 45N54'38 116w30'11 7:46:01
Bonanza 19 18 44N22'14 114w43'37 7:38:54
Bone 10 14 43N18'45 111w47'40 7:27:11
Bonners Ferry 11
1 48N41'29 116w18'55 7:45:16
Borah 1 18 43N38 116w13 7:44:52
Border 4 14 42N10'59 111w02'48 7:24:11
Boulder 7 18 43N50'26 114w30'20 7:38:01
Bovard 29 2 46N39'55 116w42'05 7:46:48
Bovill 29 2 46N51'32 116w23'33 7:45:34
Bowmont 14 18 43N27'22 116w32'24 7:46:10
Box Canyon 22 14 44N22'44 111w24'17 7:25:37
Bradley 40 6 47N32 116w08 7:44:32
Bramwell 23 18 43N50'18 116w34'55 7:46:20
Bridge 16 18 42N07'46 113w20'30 7:33:22
Broadford 7 18 43N28'11 114w16'46 7:37:07
Bronx 9 2 48N21'07 116w32'47 7:46:11
Broten 9 2 48N13'16 116w24'59 7:45:40
Brownlee 8 18 44N00'32 116w14'40 7:44:59
Bruce Eddy 18 2 46N30'49 116w17'23 7:45:10
Bruneau 37 18 42N52'50 115w47'47 7:43:11
Buckingham 38 18 43N59'21 116w53'33 7:47:34
Budge 34 18 42N36'32 113w49'25 7:35:18
Buhl 42 18 42N35'57 114w45'31 7:39:02
Buist 36 18 42N19'38 112w36'17 7:30:25
Bull Creek Crossing 37
18 42N07'42 115w55'19 7:43:41
Bull Pasture 36
18 42N09'41 112w31'39 7:30:07
Buncel Place 37
18 42N33'01 116w01'25 7:44:06
Bundy 35 2 46N21'41 116w45'23 7:47:02
Bunn 40 3 47N30'40 115w53'53 7:43:36
Burgdorf 25 18 45N16'38 115w54'43 7:43:39
Burke 40 8 47N31'13 115w49'09 7:43:17
Burley 16 18 42N32'09 113w47'31 7:35:10
Burmah 32 18 43N07'46 114w15'34 7:37:02
Burns 11 2 48N37'34 116w23'38 7:45:35
Burton 33 14 43N47'51 111w51'26 7:27:26
Butler Bay 5 2 47N19 116w34 7:46:16
Butte City 12 16 43N36'36 113w14'36 7:32:58
Butte Creek Landing 18
2 46N51'53 115w44'14 7:42:57
Byrne 33 14 43N41'31 111w44'45 7:26:59
Cabarton 43 18 44N26'08 116w02'21 7:44:09
Cabinet 9 2 48N05'04 116w04'21 7:44:17
Cable Car Crossing 25
18 45N27'14 115w56'31 7:43:46
Cache 41 14 43N47'17 111w09'44 7:24:39
Calder 40 2 47N16'40 116w11'25 7:44:46
Caldwell 14 18 43N39'47 116w41'11 7:46:45
Calendar 25 2 45N37'27 115w40'08 7:42:41
Camas 26 13 44N00'27 112w13'13 7:28:53
Cambridge 3 14 42N27'02 112w06'57 7:28:28
Cambridge 44 18 44N34 116w41 7:46:44
Cameron 35 2 46N36'21 116w34'16 7:46:17
Canyon Creek 33
14 43N53 111w36 7:26:24
Carbonate 40 10 47N27'19 115w45'50 7:43:03
Carbon Center 40
3 47N33'30 115w54'00 7:43:36
Cardiff 18 4 46N34'28 115w48'41 7:43:15
Cardiff Mill 18
2 46N28'15 115w47'37 7:43:10
Cardwell 5 2 47N12'33 116w33'45 7:46:15
Carey 7 18 43N18'28 113w56'38 7:35:47
Careywood 9 2 48N02'05 116w38'32 7:46:34
Caribel 25 2 46N15'29 115w56'37 7:43:46
Caribou City 10
14 43N06'11 111w15'50 7:25:03
Carlin Bay 28 2 47N27 116w47 7:47:08
Carl Ratliff Place 37
18 42N04'25 115w56'33 7:43:46
Carmen 30 16 45N14'33 113w53'33 7:35:34
Carothers Place 37
18 42N53'01 116w25'55 7:45:44
Carrietown 13 18 43N36'18 114w41'58 7:38:48
Cascade 43 18 44N30'59 116w02'27 7:44:10
Castleford 42 18 42N31'15 114w52'03 7:39:28
Castle Rocks 20
18 43N19'42 115w18'49 7:41:15
Casto 19 18 44N34'05 114w50'52 7:39:23
Cataldo 40 2 47N32'56 116w19'43 7:45:19
Cat Creek Crossing 37
18 42N08'58 115w44'59 7:43:00
Cathedral Pines 7
18 43N46'39 114w31'33 7:38:06
Cavendish 35 2 46N33'37 116w25'59 7:45:44
Cayuse Junction 18
2 46N35'57 114w51'11 7:39:25
Cedar 42 18 42N35'38 114w42'17 7:38:49
Cedar Creek 9 2 48N01'06 116w26'43 7:45:47
Cedarhill 36 18 42N16'01 112w43'50 7:30:55
Cedron 41 14 40N00'19 79w56'53 5:19:46
Centerville 8 18 43N54'46 115w53'29 7:43:34
Central 15 14 42N38'06 111w48'39 7:27:15
Central Cove 14
18 43N36'26 116w51'42 7:47:27
Cerro Grande 6
16 43N26'28 112w55'57 7:31:44
Chalk Cut 20 18 42N58'52 115w31'56 7:42:08
Challis 19 18 44N30'17 114w13'51 7:36:55
Chapin 41 14 43N38'36 111w06'36 7:24:26
Chatcolet 5 2 47N22'20 116w45'45 7:47:03
Chausse 4 14 42N10'51 111w04'59 7:24:20
Cherry Creek 36
18 42N05'54 112w13'41 7:28:55
Cherrylane 35 2 46N30'58 116w40'50 7:46:43
Cherryville 21
14 42N02'26 111w44'55 7:27:00
Chesley 35 2 46N20'57 116w33'07 7:46:12
Chester 22 14 43N59'58 111w34'09 7:26:17
Chesterfield 15
14 42N52'01 111w54'04 7:27:36
Chilco 28 2 47N51'50 116w44'44 7:46:59
Chilly 19 16 44N04'40 113w52'41 7:35:31
China Hat 37 18 42N06'06 115w56'21 7:43:45
China Hill 15 14 42N33'10 111w49'36 7:27:18
Chubbuck 3 14 42N55'15 112w27'55 7:29:52
Churchill 16 18 42N15 113w53 7:35:32
Clagstone 9 2 48N01'11 116w48'20 7:47:13
Clarendon Hot Springs 7
18 43N33'34 114w24'51 7:37:39
Clark Fork 9 2 48N08'43 116w10'29 7:44:42
Clarkia 40 2 47N00'39 116w15'07 7:45:00
Clarks Fork 9 2 48N11 116w10 7:44:40
Clarkson 6 14 43N12'42 112w25'04 7:29:40
Clarksville 28 1 47N45'14 116w43'55 7:46:56
Clark Tree 25 2 46N17'49 115w42'38 7:42:51
Clarkville 28 1 47N46 116w46 7:47:04
Clawson 41 14 43N47'53 111w06'36 7:24:26
Clay Caves 27 18 42N36'59 114w17'38 7:37:11
Clayton 19 18 44N15'34 114w24'03 7:37:36
Claytonia 37 18 43N34'03 116w49'55 7:47:20
Clearwater 25 2 46N01'21 115w53'24 7:43:34
Cleft 20 18 43N14'22 115w50'59 7:43:24
Clementsville 41
14 43N52'36 111w22'09 7:25:29
Cleveland 21 14 42N25 111w44 7:26:56
Clicks 31 2 46N16'49 116w32'02 7:46:08
Cliff 19 16 43N52'33 113w40'38 7:34:43
Cliffs 37 18 42N38'21 116w58'46 7:47:55
Clifton 21 14 42N11'24 112w00'26 7:28:02
Clover 42 18 42N30'51 114w41'12 7:38:45
Cloverdale 1 18 43N37'11 116w19'59 7:45:20
Clyde 12 15 44N08'09 113w14'46 7:32:59
Cobalt 30 18 45N00'15 114w20'00 7:37:20
Cocolalla 9 2 48N06'29 116w36'59 7:46:28
Coconut Grove 25
18 45N19'06 116w27'58 7:45:52
Coeur d'Alene 28
1 47N40'40 116w46'46 7:47:07
Coeur d'Alene Indian Res 5
2 47N20 116w50 7:47:20
Coeur d'Alene Junction 28
5 47N45'24 116w54'41 7:47:39
Coffee Point 6
16 43N09'23 112w58'02 7:31:52
Colburn 9 2 48N23'50 116w32'03 7:46:08
Coleman 9 2 48N00'15 116w54'21 7:47:37
Collier Place 37
18 42N34'45 116w14'22 7:44:57
Collins 6 14 43N12'08 112w22'30 7:29:30
Collister 1 18 43N36 115w39 7:42:36
Coltman 10 14 43N37'04 112w00'41 7:28:03
Comical Turn 37
18 42N33'41 116w08'37 7:44:34
Concord 25 2 45N35'05 115w40'58 7:42:44
Concrete 44 17 44N21'19 116w47'40 7:47:11
Conda 15 14 42N43'42 111w31'54 7:26:08
Conkling Park 28
2 47N24'16 116w45'26 7:47:02
Conner 16 18 42N19 113w22 7:33:28
Connor 16 18 42N16'52 113w30'02 7:34:00
Conrad Crossing Campground 40
2 47N09'31 115w24'57 7:41:40
Coolin 9 2 48N28'47 116w50'54 7:47:24
Cooperville 25 2 45N46 116w18 7:45:12
Copeland 11 2 48N54'08 116w23'16 7:45:33
Copperville 25 2 45N45'11 116w19'24 7:45:18
Cora 29 2 47N00'14 116w57'50 7:47:51
Corbin Junction 28
2 47N53'28 116w43'11 7:46:53
Cornwall 29 5 46N42'32 116w51'53 7:47:28
Corral 13 18 43N21 114w57 7:39:48
Cotterel 16 18 42N31'02 113w27'30 7:33:50
Cotton 10 13 43N25'35 112w05'15 7:28:21
Cottonwood 25 4 46N02'55 116w20'55 7:45:24
Cottonwood 37 18 42N29'10 116w00'26 7:44:02
Coulam 3 14 42N16'01 111w59'00 7:27:56
Council 43 18 44N43'48 116w26'14 7:45:45
Cow Creek 18 2 46N29'45 115w55'55 7:43:44
Craig Junction 31
2 46N16'32 116w31'58 7:46:08
Craigmont 31 2 46N14'29 116w27'58 7:45:52
Cranes Nest 37
18 42N03'16 116w03'37 7:44:14
Crawford Place (site) 44
18 44N21'57 117w08'52 7:48:35
Cream Can Junction 7
18 42N56'19 113w23'05 7:33:32
Crescent 29 2 46N38'36 116w25'28 7:45:42
Crill Place 37
18 42N49'33 116w27'10 7:45:49
Crossport 11 2 48N42'04 116w13'13 7:44:53
Cross Trails 25
2 45N28'35 115w41'27 7:42:46
Crouch 8 18 44N06'55 115w58'12 7:43:53
Crutcher Crossing 37
18 42N15'36 116w52'09 7:47:29
Crystal 39 14 42N39'14 112w29'44 7:29:59
Crystal 44 18 44N10'02 116w53'24 7:47:34
Culdesac 35 2 46N22'29 116w40'20 7:46:41
Culver 9 2 48N16 116w33 7:46:12
Cuprum 2 18 45N05'12 116w41'18 7:46:45
Curry 42 18 42N33'50 114w33'16 7:38:13
Custer 19 18 44N23'15 114w41'42 7:38:47
Dairy Creek 36
18 42N27'45 112w25'45 7:29:43
Dalton Gardens 28
1 47N43'47 116w46'09 7:47:05

Place		Lat	Long	Time
Daniels 36	18	42N22'23	112w24'44	7:29:39
Dans Place 37	18	42N16'21	115w49'53	7:43:20
Darby 41	14	43N41'39	111w03'55	7:24:16
Darlington 12	16	43N48'49	113w24'50	7:33:39
Davidson 25	2	45N50'35	116w35'40	7:46:23
Davis Elbow 40	3	47N44'55	116w01'41	7:44:07
Dayton 21	14	42N06'47	111w59'34	7:27:58
Deal 14	18	43N30'24	116w32'26	7:46:10
Deary 29	2	46N47'58	116w33'18	7:46:13
Declo 16	17	42N31'06	113w37'38	7:34:31
Deep Creek 11	2	48N37'24	116w23'32	7:45:34
Deep Creek 42	18	42N35'37	114w50'43	7:39:23
Dehlin 10	14	43N23'04	111w42'32	7:26:50
DeLamar 37	18	43N01'28	116w49'50	7:47:19
DelMonte 23	17	43N52'08	116w32'32	7:46:10
Delta 40	3	47N36'28	115w56'25	7:43:46
Democrat 37	18	43N05'47	116w46'28	7:47:06
Dent 18	2	46N37'26	116w12'08	7:44:49
Denver 25	2	45N59'54	116w14'06	7:44:56
De Smet 5	2	47N08'46	116w54'53	7:47:40
DeVeny Place 25	18	45N21'27	116w23'39	7:45:35
Devils Ladder 2	18	45N10'42	116w26'04	7:45:44
Dew Drop 37	18	42N01'28	115w56'38	7:43:47
Dewey 37	18	43N02'25	116w45'41	7:47:03
DeWoff 7	18	42N42'24	113w15'35	7:33:02
Diamond 44	18	44N24'51	116w46'30	7:47:06
Dickensheet Junction 9	2	48N27'07	116w54'25	7:47:38
Dickens Place 37	18	42N08'59	115w58'17	7:43:53
Dickey 19	16	44N08'04	113w54'16	7:35:37
Dickshooter 37	18	42N23'30	116w30'03	7:46:00
Dietrich 32	18	42N54'34	114w15'52	7:37:03
Dingle 4	14	42N13'10	111w16'02	7:25:04
Dixie 20	18	43N19'02	115w26'46	7:41:47
Dixie 25	2	45N50	115w26	7:41:44
Doles 14	18	43N40'11	116w46'58	7:47:08
Don 39	14	42N54'34	112w31'45	7:30:07
Doniphan 7	18	43N24'39	114w29'01	7:37:56
Donnelly 43	18	44N43'54	116w04'48	7:44:19
Dorsey 40	10	47N27'46	115w44'50	7:42:59
Dover 9	2	48N15'06	116w36'36	7:46:26
Downata Hot Springs 3	14	42N23'19	112w05'18	7:28:21
Downey 3	14	42N25'43	112w07'25	7:28:30
Doyle Place 37	18	42N50'43	116w19'59	7:45:20
Driggs 41	14	43N43'24	111w06'38	7:24:27
Drummond 22	14	43N59'55	111w20'40	7:25:23
Dryden 25	2	46N08'10	116w12'02	7:44:48
Dry Forty 37	18	42N27'04	116w24'45	7:45:39
Dubois 17	14	44N10'35	112w13'48	7:28:55
Dudley 28	2	47N32'31	116w25'24	7:45:42
Dufort 9	2	48N09'55	116w35'45	7:46:23
Duncan Creek Crossing 37	18	42N27'14	116w03'31	7:44:14
Duncan Place 42	18	42N02'08	114w48'32	7:39:14
Dwight 41	14	43N49	111w10	7:24:40
Eagle 1	18	43N41'44	116w21'11	7:45:25
Eagle 40	2	47N38'37	115w55'01	7:43:40
Eagle Nest 43	18	44N36'26	115w56'32	7:43:46
Eagle Rock 10	14	43N29	112w00	7:28:00
Easley Hot Springs 7	18	43N46'50	114w32'32	7:38:10
East Camas 13	18	43N20	114w42	7:38:48
East Clark 17	14	44N23	111w55	7:27:40
East Greenacres 28	5	47N45'09	116w58'08	7:47:53
East Hope 9	2	48N14'31	116w17'40	7:45:11
East Kamiah 25	2	46N12'10	116w00'25	7:44:02
East Lewiston 35	12	46N24	116w59	7:47:56
Eastport 11	4	49N00'01	116w10'49	7:44:43
Eaton 44	18	44N16'33	117w04'49	7:48:19
Eccles 22	14	44N19'37	111w18'03	7:25:12
Echo Beach 28	2	47N53'16	116w52'32	7:47:30
Eddyville 28	1	47N36'58	116w43'50	7:46:55
Eden 27	18	42N36'21	114w12'36	7:36:50
Edgemere 9	2	48N04'33	116w48'51	7:47:15
Edmonds 33	14	43N54'47	111w52'48	7:27:31
Edwardsburg 43	18	45N07'08	115w19'30	7:41:18
Egin 22	14	43N56'12	111w50'12	7:27:21
Egypt 21	14	42N05'48	111w50'12	7:27:21
Effie 38	18	44N01'32	116w55'02	7:47:40
Eighteenmile 17	14	44N18'01	111w54'06	7:27:36
Eileen 11	2	48N46'35	116w09'45	7:44:39
Elba 16	18	42N14'54	113w33'38	7:34:15
Elk City 25	2	45N49'37	115w26'09	7:41:45
Elkhorn 40	2	40N46'39	116w02'30	7:44:10
Elk River 18	2	46N47'01	116w10'44	7:44:43
Elk Summit 25	2	46N19'26	114w38'56	7:38:36
Ellis 19	18	44N41'31	114w02'51	7:36:11
Elmira 9	2	48N28'47	116w27'41	7:45:51
Emerald Creek 40	2	47N04'19	116w19'38	7:45:19
Emida 5	2	47N06'57	116w35'49	7:46:23
Emigrant Crossing 20	18	43N02'53	115w17'08	7:41:09
Emigrant Crossing 37	18	42N55'05	115w52'26	7:43:30
Emmett 23	17	43N52'26	116w29'54	7:46:00
Enaville 40	3	47N33'45	116w14'57	7:45:00
Enrose 14	18	43N42'06	116w44'45	7:46:59
Era 12	16	43N34'50	113w34'43	7:34:19
Erlmo 40	2	47N15'35	116w02'57	7:44:12
Estes 29	5	46N46'40	117w01'08	7:48:05
Ethelton 40	2	47N15'18	115w54'17	7:43:37
Evans Landing 9	2	48N04'32	116w31'50	7:46:07
Evergreen 2	18	44N53'25	116w23'21	7:45:33
Excelsior Beach 28	2	47N52'49	116w52'33	7:47:30
Fairfield 13	18	43N20'48	114w47'27	7:39:10
Fairview 21	14	42N00'48	111w52'33	7:27:30
Fairview 39	18	42N51'01	112w52'07	7:31:28
Fairview 42	18	42N32'06	114w47'21	7:39:09
Fairylawn 37	18	42N34'11	116w59'18	7:47:57
Falcon 40	2	47N20'56	115w40'26	7:42:42
Fall Creek 25	2	45N48'44	115w39'06	7:42:36
Falls City 27	18	42N40'50	114w25'24	7:37:42
Featherville 20	18	43N36'36	115w15'26	7:41:02
Felt 41	14	43N52'23	111w11'02	7:24:44
Feltham 44	18	44N12'26	116w55'48	7:47:43
Fenn 25	2	45N57'48	116w15'19	7:45:01
Ferdinand 25	2	46N09'09	116w23'18	7:45:33
Ferguson 40	3	47N33'36	115w55'24	7:43:42
Fernan Lake 28	1	47N41	116w45	7:47:00
Fernwood 5	2	47N06'44	116w23'30	7:45:34
Filer 42	18	42N34'13	114w36'25	7:38:26
Fingal 6	16	42N58'05	112w48'32	7:31:14
Firth 6	14	43N18'19	112w10'56	7:28:44
Fischer 14	18	43N34'27	116w34'37	7:46:18
Fish Haven 4	14	42N02'13	111w23'44	7:25:35
Five Corners 18	2	46N38'24	116w10'20	7:44:41
Five Points 15	14	42N56'21	112w07'38	7:28:31
Flat Creek 5	2	47N13'56	116w29'25	7:45:58
Fletcher 31	2	46N17'22	116w24'36	7:45:38
Flint 37	18	42N55'00	116w46'55	7:47:08
Florence 25	18	45N30'04	116w01'39	7:44:07
Forebay 35	12	46N25'25	116w57'33	7:47:50
Forest 31	2	46N08'53	116w39'24	7:46:38
Forney 30	18	45N13	114w16	7:37:04
Fort Hall 6	14	43N02'00	112w26'15	7:29:45
Fort Hall Indian Reservation 3	14	43N02	112w27	7:29:48
Fort Wilson 38	18	44N01'45	116w50'39	7:47:23
Four Corners 9	2	48N17'18	116w59'21	7:47:57
Four Corners 37	18	42N06'19	116w36'25	7:46:26
Fourway Junction 25	18	45N19'58	115w21'44	7:41:27
Fox Creek 41	14	43N39'02	111w06'36	7:24:26
France 22	14	43N58'21	111w16'28	7:25:06
Franklin 21	14	42N00'49	111w48'23	7:27:14
Fraser 18	2	46N23'28	116w08'15	7:44:33
Freedom 15	14	42N58'58	111w02'41	7:24:11
French Corner 38	18	44N03'27	116w34'46	7:46:19
French Creek 25	18	45N25'24	116w01'35	7:44:06
Frisco 40	3	47N30'44	115w51'30	7:43:26
Fritser Ford 43	18	45N05'12	115w37'40	7:42:31
Frost Place 37	18	42N11'33	115w56'24	7:43:46
Fruitland 38	18	44N00'28	116w54'56	7:47:40
Fruitvale 2	18	44N48'55	116w26'21	7:45:45
Fuller 24	18	42N55'46	114w49'21	7:39:17
Fullmer 6	14	43N18'31	112w40'08	7:30:41
Galena 7	18	43N52'17	114w39'23	7:38:38
Gannett 13	18	43N21'36	114w10'30	7:36:42
Gardena 8	18	43N58'33	116w11'24	7:44:46
Garden City 1	18	43N37'20	116w14'14	7:44:57
Garden Valley 8	18	44N05'24	115w57'04	7:43:48
Garfield 26	14	43N29	112w00	7:28:00
Garrard Branch 16	18	42N19'00	114w00'03	7:36:00
Garwood 28	1	47N49'55	116w46'35	7:47:06
Gay 6	14	43N02'54	112w07'03	7:28:28
Gayway Corner 38	18	44N01'33	116w55'21	7:47:41
Gem 40	3	47N30'30	115w52'01	7:43:28
Genesee 29	2	46N33'03	116w55'28	7:47:42
Geneva 4	14	42N21'31	111w03'52	7:24:15
Gentry 40	11	47N28'27	115w53'39	7:43:35
Georgetown 4	14	42N28'56	111w22'12	7:25:29
German Settlement 35	2	46N25'07	116w30'03	7:46:00
Gerrard 10	14	43N23'04	112w02'21	7:28:09
Gerrit 22	14	44N12'31	111w16'13	7:25:05
Gibbonsville 30	16	45N33'20	113w55'20	7:35:41
Gibbs 28	1	47N41'27	116w48'10	7:47:13
Gibson 6	14	43N06'02	112w25'03	7:29:40
Gibson City 40	2	47N32	116w14	7:44:56
Gifford 35	2	46N26'36	116w33'20	7:46:13
Gilmore 30	16	44N27'32	113w16'08	7:33:05
Gimlet 7	18	43N36'15	114w20'56	7:37:24
Givens Hot Springs 37	18	43N25'20	116w42'50	7:46:51
Giveout 4	14	42N25'07	111w09'28	7:24:38
Glencoe 4	14	42N14	111w24	7:25:36
Glendale 21	14	42N11	111w57	7:27:48
Glengary 9	2	48N13'19	116w22'25	7:45:30
Glenns Ferry 20	18	42N57'18	115w18'00	7:41:12
Glenwood 18	2	46N29	116w15	7:45:00
Glenwood 25	2	46N14'39	115w49'55	7:43:20
Godwin 42	18	42N30'46	114w34'26	7:38:18
Golconda Mill 40	3	47N28'29	115w52'12	7:43:29
Goldburg 19	16	44N23'08	113w38'42	7:34:35
Gold Creek 40	2	47N08'14	115w24'25	7:41:38
Golden 25	2	45N48'44	115w40'44	7:42:43
Gold Point 25	2	45N46'59	115w23'34	7:41:34
Good Grief 11	4	48N56'58	116w10'35	7:44:42
Gooding 24	18	42N56'20	114w42'44	7:38:51
Goodrich 2	18	44N39'13	116w33'25	7:46:14
Goshen 6	14	43N18'35	112w04'57	7:28:20
Goshen Junction 6	14	43N18'30	112w10'43	7:28:43
Grace 15	14	42N34'34	111w43'47	7:26:55
Graham 8	18	43N58'08	115w16'25	7:41:06
Grainville 22	14	44N01'38	111w22'02	7:25:28
Grand Junction 28	5	47N43'45	116w58'22	7:47:53
Grandview 6	16	43N03'11	112w47'15	7:31:09
Grand View 37	18	42N59'23	116w05'33	7:44:22
Grangemont 18	2	46N29	116w15	7:45:00
Grangeville 25	4	45N55'36	116w07'17	7:44:29
Granite 8	18	43N56'27	115w58'00	7:43:52
Granite 9	2	48N05'16	116w25'29	7:45:42
Grant 26	14	43N38'27	112w00'45	7:28:03
Grasmere 37	18	42N23	115w53	7:43:32
Gray 10	14	42N58	111w23	7:25:32
Greencreek 25	2	46N06'26	116w15'48	7:45:03
Greenleaf 14	18	43N40'17	116w48'55	7:47:16
Greenwood 27	18	42N34'36	114w02'55	7:36:12
Greer 18	2	46N23'24	116w10'27	7:44:42
Greys Landing 42	18	42N07'58	114w43'42	7:38:55
Grimes Pass 8	18	44N02'41	115w51'23	7:43:26
Gross 23	18	44N18'48	116w18'24	7:45:14
Grouse 19	16	43N41	113w37	7:34:28
Groveland 6	14	43N13'12	112w22'18	7:29:29
Guyaz 10	14	43N28'54	111w38'45	7:26:35
Gwenford 36	18	42N08'11	112w19'45	7:29:19
Hagerman 24	18	42N48'44	114w53'52	7:39:35
Hahn 30	16	44N22'20	113w13'00	7:32:52
Hailey 7	18	43N31'11	114w18'52	7:37:15
Haley 18	2	46N29'43	115w55'28	7:43:42
Hamer 26	14	43N55'38	112w12'19	7:28:49
Hamilton Corner 38	18	43N57'10	116w46'17	7:47:05
Hammett 20	18	42N56'45	115w27'55	7:41:52
Hampton 29	2	46N54'52	116w50'54	7:47:24
Hand Place 42	18	42N08'41	114w58'07	7:39:52
Hansen 42	18	42N31'47	114w18'19	7:37:13
Hardscrabble Campground 8	18	44N14'23	115w53'54	7:43:36
Harer 4	14	42N11'22	111w10'15	7:24:41
Harlem 9	2	48N02'21	116w48'41	7:47:15
Harpster 25	2	45N59'12	115w57'45	7:43:51
Harrell Place 42	18	42N04'39	114w47'07	7:39:08
Harrisburg 25	2	46N17'49	116w01'29	7:44:06
Harris Landing 28	1	47N47'06	116w42'06	7:46:48
Harrison 28	2	47N27'16	116w47'04	7:47:08
Harvard 29	2	46N55'03	116w43'43	7:46:55
Harvey Place 37	18	42N30'46	116w04'39	7:44:19
Hatch 15	14	42N49'10	111w51'05	7:27:24
Hatwai 35	12	46N26'11	116w58'02	7:47:52
Hauser 28	2	47N46'23	117w01'37	7:48:06
Hauser Lake 28	2	47N44	117w00	7:48:00
Havens 6	14	43N16'14	112w35'24	7:30:22
Hawgood 26	14	43N52'11	112w09'02	7:28:36
Hawkins 3	14	42N32'37	112w20'29	7:29:22
Hawley 7	18	42N44'03	113w23'42	7:33:35
Hawleys Landing 5	2	47N21'21	116w46'00	7:47:04
Haycrop 28	2	47N45'59	116w53'34	7:47:34
Hayden 28	5	47N45'58	116w47'08	7:47:09
Hayden Lake 28	5	47N45'32	116w45'21	7:47:01
Haytown 27	18	42N41'34	114w30'05	7:38:00
Hazelton 27	18	42N35'47	114w08'07	7:36:32
Headquarters 18	4	46N37'48	115w48'30	7:43:14
Heglar 16	18	42N28'25	113w08'47	7:32:35
Heise 26	14	43N38'31	111w41'01	7:26:44
Helena 2	18	45N10'13	116w39'05	7:46:36
Hellhole 4	14	42N19'20	111w12'05	7:24:48
Helmer 29	2	46N48'03	116w28'09	7:45:53
Heman 22	14	43N57'23	111w47'48	7:27:11
Henry 15	14	42N54'25	111w31'48	7:26:07
Herbert 33	14	43N42'23	111w39'33	7:26:38
Herman 10	14	43N08'26	111w25'48	7:25:43
Herrick 40	2	47N16'22	116w06'20	7:44:25
Heyburn 34	18	42N33'31	113w45'47	7:35:03
Hibbard 33	14	43N51'19	111w50'16	7:27:21
Highlands 1	18	43N38'46	116w11'34	7:44:46
Hill City 13	18	43N18'02	115w03'01	7:40:12
Hillcrest 1	18	43N33'49	116w10'55	7:44:44
Hillview 10	14	43N29	112w00	7:28:00
Hinckley 33	14	43N51'54	111w51'27	7:27:26
Hobson 16	18	42N31'55	113w55'23	7:35:42
Hoelzle Place 42	18	42N12'02	114w57'08	7:39:49
Holbrook 36	18	42N09'43	112w39'11	7:30:37
Holbrook Summit 36	18	42N09'55	112w27'10	7:29:49
Hollister 42	18	42N21'12	114w34'27	7:38:18
Hollywood 18	2	46N33'19	115w50'08	7:43:21
Homedale 37	18	43N37'04	116w55'58	7:47:44
Honeysuckle Hills 28	1	47N46	116w46	7:47:04
Hoover 2	18	44N45'09	116w26'26	7:45:46
Hope 9	2	48N14'52	116w18'22	7:45:13
Hornet 2	18	44N44	116w26	7:45:44
Horsecamp 40	2	47N11'29	115w52'51	7:43:31
Horseshoe Bend 8	18	43N54'53	116w11'49	7:44:47
Hot Spring 37	18	42N47'31	115w43'01	7:42:52
Hot Springs Landing 7	18	43N19'48	114w23'58	7:37:36
Houston 19	16	43N52'59	113w34'33	7:34:18
Howe 12	16	43N47'01	113w00'14	7:32:01
Howell 29	5	46N44'09	116w48'57	7:47:16
Howelltown 28	2	47N47'09	116w58'48	7:47:55
Hoyt 40	2	47N15'11	115w55'02	7:43:40
Huetter 28	2	47N42'04	116w51'01	7:47:24
Humphrey 17	14	44N29'18	112w13'58	7:28:56
Hunt 27	18	42N40'42	114w14'57	7:37:00
Huston 14	18	43N36'37	116w46'56	7:47:08
Hydra 27	18	42N41'58	114w31'05	7:38:04
Hynes 34	18	42N36'44	113w53'27	7:35:34
Idaho City 8	18	43N49'43	115w50'01	7:43:20
Idaho Falls 10	13	43N28'00	112w02'00	7:28:08
Idahome 16	18	42N24'56	113w23'56	7:33:36
Idavada 42	18	41N59'50	114w38'29	7:38:34
Idmon 17	14	44N21'39	111w54'39	7:27:39
Indian Cove 37	18	42N57	115w28	7:41:52
Indian Grove 16	18	42N06'46	113w43'39	7:34:55
Indian Head Rock 13	18	43N33'19	114w48'02	7:39:12
Indian Jim Place 42	18	42N10'04	114w54'46	7:39:39
Indian Valley 2	18	44N33'26	116w25'59	7:45:44
Ingard 38	18	44N02'01	116w55'20	7:47:41
Inkom 3	14	42N47'47	112w15'12	7:29:01
Iona 10	14	43N31'35	111w55'56	7:27:44
Ireland Springs 36	18	42N09'54	112w29'41	7:29:59

Irwin 10 14 43N24'31 111W17'55 7:25:12
Isabella Landing 18 2 46N50'59 115W37'41 7:42:31
Island Park 22 14 44N25'28 111W22'13 7:25:29
Iversons 16 18 42N18'17 114W00'36 7:36:02
Jacks Creek Crossing 37 18 42N27'01 116W08'47 7:44:35
Jackson 16 18 42N38'02 113W34'11 7:34:17
Jackson Landing Campground 22 14 44N26'46 111W26'11 7:25:45
Jacques 35 2 46N22'18 116W43'35 7:46:54
James Place 37 18 42N16'37 115W46'45 7:43:07
Jamestown 6 14 43N23 112W08 7:28:32
Jaype 18 2 46N31'49 115W49'44 7:43:19
Jenkins Crossing 25 18 45N17'06 116W02'39 7:44:11
Jenkins Will 22 14 44N04'36 111W57'35 7:27:50
Jenness 23 18 43N49'56 116W37'27 7:46:30
Jensen 33 14 43N44'34 111W44'47 7:26:59
Jerome 27 18 42N43'27 114W31'04 7:38:04
Jim Moore Place 25 2 45N29'11 115W20'18 7:41:21
Joel 29 5 46N42'38 116W52'37 7:47:30
Johnson Grade 24 18 42N49'36 114W52'22 7:39:29
Johnsons Mill 18 2 46N25'38 115W55'02 7:43:40
Jolley 33 14 43N50'32 111W46'38 7:27:07
Jonathan 44 18 44N16'03 117W03'09 7:48:13
Jones Crossing 17 14 44N05'13 112W13'07 7:28:52
Joseph 25 2 45N47'50 116W28'37 7:45:54
Josephson 14 18 43N44'56 116W38'15 7:46:33
Judge Town 18 2 46N28'32 115W47'46 7:43:11
Judkins 41 14 43N55'19 111W08'56 7:24:36
Juliaetta 29 2 46N34'44 116W42'18 7:46:49
Juniper 36 18 42N09'12 112W58'09 7:31:53
Kameron 18 2 46N46'21 116W15'11 7:45:01
Kamiah 31 2 46N13'38 116W01'42 7:44:07
Karcher Junction 14 18 43N35'10 116W36'07 7:46:24
Katies Place 37 18 42N05'27 115W56'49 7:43:47
Katka 11 2 48N41'23 116W08'04 7:44:32
Keeler 40 2 46N57'26 116W18'25 7:45:14
Keenan City 10 14 43N08'27 111W20'22 7:25:21
Kellogg 40 9 47N32'18 116W07'06 7:44:28
Kendrick 29 2 46N36'51 116W38'44 7:46:35
Kenyon 16 18 42N24'56 113W52'10 7:35:29
Keogh 16 18 42N13'24 113W19'58 7:33:20
Ketchum 7 18 43N40'51 114W21'46 7:37:27
Keuterville 25 2 46N02'03 116W26'26 7:45:46
Kidder 25 2 46N09 115W59 7:43:56
Kilgore 17 14 44N24'08 111W53'35 7:27:34
Kimama 32 18 42N50'17 113W47'41 7:35:11
Kimball 6 14 43N16'25 112W13'07 7:28:52
Kimberly 42 18 42N32'02 114W21'50 7:37:27
King Hill 20 18 43N00'15 115W12'11 7:40:49
Kings Corner 14 18 43N31'05 116W32'01 7:46:08
Kingston 40 3 47N32'57 116W16'11 7:45:05
Kinport 15 14 42N45'16 111W56'27 7:27:46
Kippen 31 2 46N18'40 116W32'55 7:46:12
Knowlton Heights 14 18 43N32'43 116W46'19 7:47:05
Knull 42 18 42N31'35 114W33'16 7:38:13
Kooskia 25 2 46N08'42 115W58'37 7:43:54
Kootenai 9 2 48N18'37 116W30'45 7:46:03
Kuna 1 18 43N29'31 116W25'09 7:45:41
Kyle 40 2 47N19'41 115W45'24 7:43:02
Labelle 26 14 43N42'12 111W51'36 7:27:26
Laclede 9 2 48N10'13 116W45'18 7:47:01
Lago 15 14 42N27'05 111W41'45 7:26:47
Lake 22 14 44N40'01 111W23'34 7:25:34
Lake Creek 28 2 47N27 117W08 7:48:32
Lake Fork 43 18 44N49'58 116W05'02 7:44:20
Lakeview 9 2 47N58'13 116W26'44 7:45:47
Lamb Creek 9 2 48N30'59 116W55'35 7:47:42
Lamont 22 14 43N58'11 111W12'55 7:24:52
Lanark 4 14 42N16'54 111W25'40 7:25:43
Landmark 43 18 44N39'23 115W32'39 7:42:11
Landore 2 18 45N07'24 116W37'39 7:46:31
Lane 28 2 47N33 116W20 7:45:20
Lane Cemetery 28 2 47N30'27 116W32'13 7:46:09
Lapwai 35 2 46N24'18 116W48'14 7:47:13
Lardo 43 18 44N55 116W08 7:44:32
Larson 40 10 47N28'15 115W44'44 7:42:59
Last Chance 22 14 44N22'00 111W24'05 7:25:36
Last Chance Resort 22 14 44N31 111W20 7:25:20
Lava Hot Springs 3 13 42N37'10 112W00'37 7:28:02
Lawman Ford 43 18 45N06'36 115W36'32 7:42:26
Leadore 30 16 44N40'49 113W21'26 7:33:26
Leadville 30 16 44N42'21 113W18'26 7:33:14
Leesburg 30 18 45N13'26 114W06'47 7:36:27
Leland 35 2 46N34'41 116W36'21 7:46:25
Lemhi 30 16 44N51'06 113W37'08 7:34:29
Lemhi Range 30 16 44N31'08 113W29'23 7:33:58
Lenore 35 2 46N30'31 116W33'00 7:46:12
Leon 35 12 46N31'55 117W02'21 7:48:09
Leone 1 17 43N24'28 116W05'34 7:44:22
Leonia 11 2 48N37'00 116W02'55 7:44:12
Leslie 19 16 43N51'57 113W28'00 7:33:52
Letha 23 18 43N53'40 116W38'48 7:46:35
Lewiston 35 12 46N25'00 117W01'00 7:48:04
Lewiston Orchards 35 12 46N22'50 116W58'28 7:47:54
Lewisville 26 14 43N41'45 112W00'35 7:28:02
Liberty 4 14 42N19'02 111W27'05 7:25:48
Liberty 6 14 43N10'08 112W33'16 7:30:13
Lidy Hot Springs 17 14 44N10 112W14 7:28:56
Lifton 4 14 42N07'24 111W18'45 7:25:15
Lincoln 10 14 43N30'47 111W57'49 7:27:51
Linfor 40 3 47N36'30 116W14'05 7:44:56
Linrose 21 14 42N02 111W59 7:27:56
Little Rock 23 18 43N55'01 116W41'34 7:46:46
Little Sugarloaf 37 18 43N05'46 116W42'13 7:46:49
Lone Pine 17 16 44N11'10 112W56'03 7:31:44
Lone Rock 39 18 42N46'03 112W49'13 7:31:17
Lone Star 32 18 42N56 114W24 7:37:36
Lookout 35 2 46N31 116W33 7:46:12
Lorenzo 26 14 43N43'42 111W52'14 7:27:29
Lost River 12 16 43N41'21 113W22'14 7:33:29
Lotus 5 2 47N13'48 116W36'59 7:46:28
Lowell 25 2 46N08'39 115W35'41 7:42:23
Lower Battle Creek Crossing 37 18 42N22'58 116W21'54 7:45:28
Lower Pittsburg Landing 25 2 45N37'57 116W28'27 7:45:54
Lower Stanley 19 18 44N13'37 114W55'40 7:39:43
Lowman 8 18 44N05'01 115W37'11 7:42:29
Lucile 25 2 45N32'07 116W18'34 7:45:14
Lund 15 14 42N38'34 111W53'16 7:27:33
Lyman 33 14 43N44'21 111W49'01 7:27:16
Mace 40 8 47N31'06 115W49'16 7:43:17
Mackay 19 16 43N54'53 113W36'45 7:34:27
Mackay Bar 25 18 45N22'34 115W30'19 7:42:01
Mackey Bar 25 18 44N55 116W06 7:44:24
Macks Inn 22 14 44N29'57 111W20'13 7:25:21
Macon 13 18 43N19'36 114W32'39 7:38:11
Maddens 14 18 43N39'43 116W35'49 7:46:23
Magic 13 18 43N15'19 114W23'09 7:37:33
Magic City 7 18 43N17'26 114W21'53 7:37:28
Magic Resort 7 18 43N16'57 114W23'20 7:37:33
Malad City 36 18 42N11'30 112W15'00 7:29:00
Malta 16 18 42N18'23 113W22'06 7:33:28
Manson 4 14 42N34'11 111W29'53 7:26:00
Mapleton 21 14 42N05'02 111W44'53 7:27:00
Marble Creek 40 2 47N15'10 116W01'51 7:44:07
Marion 16 18 42N17'12 113W54'37 7:35:38
Mark 33 14 43N46'31 111W49'52 7:27:19
Marsing 37 18 43N32'44 116W48'44 7:47:15
Martin 12 16 43N31'08 113W33'59 7:34:16
Marysville 22 14 44N04'17 111W25'10 7:25:41
Mashburn 5 2 47N10'45 116W29'42 7:45:59
Masonia 40 3 47N27'06 116W10'47 7:44:43
May 30 16 44N36'16 113W54'40 7:35:39
Mayfield 20 18 43N25'05 115W54'02 7:43:36
May Place 42 18 42N12'04 114W53'23 7:39:34
McArthur 11 2 48N34 116W24 7:45:36
McCall 43 17 44N54'40 116W05'52 7:44:23
McCammon 3 13 42N39'02 112W11'32 7:28:46
McCarthy 40 2 47N29'35 115W54'32 7:43:38
McCrea Place 25 18 45N18'14 116W28'35 7:45:54
McDonaldville 6 16 43N15'36 112W22'27 7:29:30
McGuire 28 5 47N42'45 116W59'25 7:47:58
McGuires 28 2 47N44 117W00 7:48:00
McHenry 27 18 42N35'44 114W03'05 7:36:12
McMillan 42 18 42N32'36 114W25'14 7:37:41
Meadow Creek 11 2 48N49'14 116W09'30 7:44:38
Meadows 2 18 44N57'40 116W14'34 7:44:58
Medimont 28 2 47N28'34 116W36'12 7:46:25
Melba 14 18 43N22'32 116W31'41 7:46:07
Melrose 35 2 46N24'30 116W27'13 7:45:49
Menan 26 14 43N43'15 111W59'21 7:27:57
Meridian 1 18 43N36'44 116W23'26 7:45:34
Mesa 43 18 44N37'44 116W26'59 7:45:48
Meteor 37 18 42N06'47 114W40'48 7:38:43
Mexican Place 25 2 45N48'46 116W30'20 7:46:01
Mica 28 2 47N37'14 116W52'13 7:47:29
Michaud 39 14 42N53'25 112W36'49 7:30:27
Midas 9 2 48N16 116W33 7:46:12
Midasville 25 2 45N33'37 115W28'09 7:41:53
Middleton 14 18 43N42'25 116W37'09 7:46:29
Midnight 43 18 44N55'23 115W19'47 7:41:19
Midvale 44 18 44N28'17 116W44'01 7:46:56
Midway 14 18 43N37'32 116W37'53 7:46:32
Midway 26 14 43N42'25 112W00'15 7:28:01
Miller Creek Settlement 37 18 42N04'54 116W07'38 7:44:31
Milner 42 18 42N31'07 114W01'19 7:36:05
Milo 10 14 43N36'39 111W52'59 7:27:32
Mineral 44 18 44N33'55 117W04'36 7:48:18
Minidoka 34 17 42N45'14 113W29'22 7:33:57
Mink Creek 21 14 42N13'42 111W42'54 7:26:52
Mitchell 6 14 43N23'50 112W06'36 7:28:26
Mohler 31 2 46N17'23 116W20'43 7:45:23
Montana Junction 3 14 42N54 112W27 7:29:48
Monteview 26 16 43N58'19 112W32'08 7:30:09
Montour 23 18 43N55'30 116W19'40 7:45:19
Montpelier 4 13 42N19'20 111W17'49 7:25:11
Moody 33 14 43N50'13 111W38'03 7:26:32
Moody Creek 33 14 43N47 111W28 7:25:52
Moore 12 16 43N44'09 113W21'56 7:33:28
Moose City 18 2 46N47'13 115W06'27 7:40:26
Mora 1 18 43N27'35 116W21'08 7:45:25
Moravia 11 2 48N38'54 116W22'41 7:45:31
Moreland 6 16 43N13'22 112W26'30 7:29:46
Morgan 6 14 43N03'38 111W55'36 7:27:42
Morgan Place 37 18 43N06'29 116W16'26 7:45:06
Morrow 31 2 46N07'37 116W31'21 7:46:05
Morton 9 2 48N12'05 116W41'29 7:46:46
Moscow 29 1 46N43'57 116W59'57 7:48:00
Moss 14 18 43N36'57 116W37'09 7:46:29
Mound Valley 21 14 42N21'26 111W42'42 7:26:51
Mountain Home 20 18 43N07'59 115W41'25 7:42:46
Mountain Home Air Force Base 20 18 43N03 115W52 7:43:28
Mountain View 1 18 43N37 116W15 7:45:00
Mount Idaho 25 2 45N54'14 116W04'52 7:44:19
Mowry 5 2 47N18'34 116W59'42 7:47:59
Moyie Springs 11 2 48N43'35 116W11'15 7:44:45
Mozart 28 2 47N24'40 116W56'09 7:47:45
Mud Lake 26 16 43N50'29 112W28'31 7:29:54
Mud Springs 25 2 45N51'49 115W35'07 7:42:20
Muldoon 7 18 43N18 113W57 7:35:48
Mullan 40 10 47N28'13 115W48'03 7:43:12
Murphy 37 18 43N13'06 116W33'05 7:46:12
Murphy Hot Springs 37 18 42N01'49 115W22'05 7:41:28
Murray 40 3 47N37'38 115W51'27 7:43:26
Murtaugh 42 18 42N29'33 114W09'41 7:36:39
Musselshell 18 2 46N21'26 115W44'34 7:42:58
Myers 34 18 42N36'32 113W45'14 7:35:01
Myrtle 35 2 46N29'49 116W43'30 7:46:54
Naf 16 18 42N00'37 113W17'05 7:33:08
Nampa 14 18 43N32'27 116W33'45 7:46:15
Naples 11 2 48N34'16 116W23'29 7:45:34
Neeley 39 18 42N44'01 112W54'51 7:31:39
Neva 18 2 46N47'55 116W17'48 7:45:11
New Centerville 8 18 43N52'52 115W54'33 7:43:38
Newdale 22 14 43N53'00 111W36'20 7:26:25
New Meadows 2 17 44N58'17 116W16'59 7:45:08
New Plymouth 38 18 43N58'12 116W49'05 7:47:16
Newsome 25 2 45N54'27 115W37'45 7:42:31
New Sweden 10 14 43N29 112W00 7:28:00
Nezperce 31 4 46N14'06 116W14'23 7:44:58
Nez Perce Indian Reservation 18 2 46N14 116W14 7:44:56
Nicholia 30 16 44N21'36 113W00'39 7:32:03
Niter 15 14 42N30'13 111W43'48 7:26:55
Nordman 9 2 48N38'02 116W56'41 7:47:47
Norland 34 18 42N47'41 113W40'21 7:34:41
North Fork 30 16 45N24'22 113W59'35 7:35:58
North Kenyon 16 18 42N25'56 113W51'37 7:35:26
North Lapwai 35 2 46N26'38 116W50'06 7:47:20
North Lewiston 35 12 46N25'29 117W00'11 7:48:01
North Pole 28 2 47N54'16 116W44'28 7:46:58
Norwood 43 18 44N48'31 116W06'08 7:44:25
Notus 14 18 43N43'32 116W48'01 7:47:12
Nounan 4 14 42N28'40 111W27'01 7:25:48
Oakley 16 17 42N14'36 113W52'52 7:35:31
Obsidian 19 18 44N04'44 114W50'47 7:39:23
Oden 9 2 48N19'20 116W24'42 7:45:39
Ola 23 18 44N11 116W18 7:45:12
Old Beaver 17 14 44N24'38 112W11'47 7:28:47
Old Fort 43 18 44N48'42 116W09'24 7:44:38
Old Golden 25 2 45N47'21 115W39'10 7:42:37
Oldtown 9 2 48N10'49 117W02'34 7:48:10
Olsen 6 14 43N17'07 112W37'16 7:30:29
Omega 5 2 47N20'02 116W28'39 7:45:55
Omill 18 2 46N29'38 115W55'33 7:43:42
Onaway 29 2 46N55'42 116W53'24 7:47:34
Orchard 1 17 43N18'53 116W01'31 7:44:06
Oreana 37 18 43N03'13 116W23'39 7:45:35
Orofino 18 4 46N28'46 116W15'15 7:45:01
Orogrande 25 2 45N42'20 115W32'33 7:42:10
Orvin 10 14 43N32'00 112W00'31 7:28:02
Osburn 40 4 47N30'22 115W59'54 7:44:00
Osgood 10 14 43N34'13 112W06'08 7:28:25
Outlet Bay 9 2 48N29'40 116W53'32 7:47:34
Ovid 4 14 42N17'20 111W23'51 7:25:35
Owinza 32 18 42N53'58 114W03'21 7:36:13
Owyhee 1 18 43N25'06 116W11'59 7:44:48
Owyhee Heights 37 18 43N37'29 116W59'23 7:47:58
Oxford 21 14 42N15'32 112W01'14 7:28:05
Pagari 32 18 43N07'05 114W04'19 7:36:17
Page 40 3 47N31'58 116W12'10 7:44:49
Palisades 10 14 43N21'07 111W13'01 7:24:52
Palisades Corner 38 18 43N58'31 116W54'42 7:47:39
Paradise Hot Springs 20 18 43N33'14 115W16'22 7:41:05
Pardee 25 2 46N17'55 116W07'28 7:44:30
Pardee Corner 25 2 46N18'53 116W05'45 7:44:23
Paris 4 14 42N13'38 111W24'01 7:25:36
Park 29 2 46N48 116W33 7:46:12
Parker 22 14 43N57'34 111W45'25 7:27:02
Parkers Place 37 18 42N07'08 115W55'57 7:43:44
Parkinson 33 14 43N48'58 111W39'30 7:26:38
Parma 14 18 43N47'07 116W56'32 7:47:46
Patterson 30 16 44N31'25 113W42'41 7:34:51
Paul 34 18 42N36'29 113W46'57 7:35:08
Pauline 39 18 42N34'15 112W33'34 7:30:14
Payette 38 17 44N04'42 116W55'58 7:47:44
Payette Heights 38 17 44N04'19 116W54'50 7:47:39
Payne 10 14 43N34'22 112W03'09 7:28:13
Pearl 23 18 43N51'21 116W18'59 7:45:16
Pearson 40 2 47N21'16 115W43'44 7:42:55
Peavey 42 18 42N35'01 114W39'07 7:38:36
Pebble 15 14 42N44'39 111W59'59 7:28:00
Peck 18 2 46N29'56 116W25'57 7:45:44
Pedee 5 2 47N21'04 116W46'26 7:47:06
Pegram 4 14 42N08'34 111W07'41 7:24:31
Pella 16 18 42N28'31 113W50'16 7:35:21
Perkins 1 18 43N36'18 116W16'22 7:45:05
Perrine 27 18 42N39'14 114W18'58 7:37:16
Peterson 18 16 43N14 112W23 7:29:32
Petersons Crossing 37 18 43N07'21 116W52'32 7:47:30
Picabo 13 18 43N18'21 114W04'01 7:36:16
Pierce 18 2 46N29'28 115W47'53 7:43:12
Pilgrim Stage Station Histor 20 18 42N52'44 115W07'51 7:40:31
Pine 20 18 43N29'03 115W18'40 7:41:15
Pine Creek 40 3 47N32'55 116W13'17 7:44:53
Pinehurst 2 18 45N15'10 116W20'00 7:45:20
Pinehurst 40 2 47N32'20 116W14'11 7:44:57
Pine Ridge 2 18 44N56'20 116W22'54 7:45:32
Pineview 22 14 44N17'11 111W18'36 7:25:14
Pingree 7 16 43N07'00 112W35'52 7:30:23
Pioneerville 8 18 43N58'08 115W50'45 7:43:23
Placerville 8 18 43N56'36 115W56'46 7:43:47

Plano 33	14	43N53'28	111w53'27	7:27:34
Player Place 42	18	42N01'12	114w49'00	7:39:16
Plaza 23	18	43N54'41	116w25'55	7:45:44
Pleasant Valley 1	18	43N26'41	116w14'46	7:44:59
Pleasant Valley Place 37	18	42N32'26	116w50'11	7:47:21
Pleasant View 28	2	47N41'13	117w00'41	7:48:03
Pleasantview 36	18	42N09'22	112w20'13	7:29:21
Plummer 5	4	47N20'07	116w53'15	7:47:33
Plummer Junction 5	4	47N20'24	116w52'07	7:47:28
Pocatello 3	13	42N52'17	112w26'41	7:29:47
Pocono 40	2	47N14'48	116w02'52	7:44:11
Polaris 40	2	47N30	116w00	7:44:00
Pollock 25	18	45N18'45	116w21'29	7:45:26
Ponderay 9	2	48N18'20	116w31'58	7:46:08
Ponds Resort 22	14	44N31	111w20	7:25:20
Poplar 10	14	43N37'13	111w41'06	7:26:44
Porthill 11	2	48N59'54	116w29'49	7:45:59
Portneuf 3	14	42N47'42	112w21'46	7:29:27
Post Falls 28	5	47N43'05	116w57'02	7:47:48
Potlatch 29	2	46N55'18	116w53'50	7:47:35
Potlatch Junction 29	2	46N55'46	116w55'57	7:47:44
Potter Place 25	18	45N18'28	116w26'23	7:45:46
Powell Junction 25	2	46N34'45	114w43'04	7:38:52
Prairie 20	18	43N30'18	115w34'23	7:42:18
Preston 21	13	42N05'47	111w52'33	7:27:30
Prichard 40	3	47N39'23	115w58'31	7:43:54
Priest Lake 9	2	48N31'31	116w56'16	7:47:45
Priest River 9	2	48N10'51	117w02'09	7:48:09
Princeton 29	2	46N54'51	116w49'59	7:47:20
Punkin Corner 13	18	43N18'48	114w54'33	7:39:38
Pyke 22	14	43N57'34	111w43'24	7:26:54
Quartzburg 8	18	43N57'40	115w59'15	7:43:57
Quigley 39	18	42N44'18	113w04'09	7:32:17
Raft River 16	18	42N47	112w51	7:31:24
Ramey 38	18	44N00'10	116w56'13	7:47:45
Ramsdell 5	2	47N21'10	116w40'32	7:46:42
Ramsey 28	1	47N51'52	116w48'26	7:47:14
Rands 13	18	43N20'40	114w39'06	7:38:36
Rankin Mill 2	18	45N15'59	116w32'41	7:46:11
Rathdrum 28	2	47N48'45	116w53'44	7:47:35
Raymond 4	14	42N16'29	111w03'29	7:24:14
Reas Pass 22	14	44N33'58	111w11'27	7:24:46
Rebecca 44	18	44N14'27	116w51'25	7:47:26
Reclamation Village 20	18	43N20'08	115w29'16	7:41:57
Redfish Lake 19	18	44N13	114w56	7:39:44
Red River Hot Springs 25	2	45N47'16	115w11'57	7:40:48
Red Rock Junction 3	14	42N21'16	112w02'57	7:28:12
Regina 1	18	43N23'23	115w58'43	7:43:55
Renfrew 5	2	47N08'39	116w26'15	7:45:45
Reno 17	14	44N10	112w14	7:28:56
Reno 30	16	44N16'16	112w58'49	7:31:55
Reubens 31	2	46N20	116w33	7:46:12
Reverse 20	18	43N01'33	115w36'21	7:42:25
Rexburg 33	14	43N49'34	111w47'20	7:27:09
Reynolds 37	18	43N12'05	116w44'36	7:46:58
Richfield 32	18	43N02'55	114w09'17	7:36:37
Rickard Crossing 37	18	42N15'32	116w40'54	7:46:44
Riddle 37	18	42N11'13	116w06'34	7:44:26
Ridgedale 36	18	42N01'23	112w28'45	7:29:55
Rigby 26	14	43N40'21	111w54'51	7:27:39
Riggins 25	18	45N25'20	116w18'52	7:45:15
Riggins Hot Springs 25	18	45N25'01	116w10'15	7:44:41
Ririe 26	14	43N37'55	111w46'22	7:27:05
Rising River 6	14	43N19'26	112w19'51	7:29:19
Ritz 11	2	48N46'44	116w22'07	7:45:28
Riverdale 5	2	47N19	116w34	7:46:16
Riverdale 21	14	42N09'41	111w50'13	7:27:21
Riverside 6	14	43N11'49	112w26'04	7:29:44
Riverside 14	18	43N30'07	116w45'23	7:47:02
Riverside 18	2	46N29'44	116w17'47	7:45:11
Roberts 26	14	43N43'13	112w07'32	7:28:30
Robin 3	14	42N34'38	112w14'45	7:28:59
Robinson Bar 19	18	44N14'49	114w40'34	7:38:42
Rockaway Beach 28	1	47N47'19	116w41'56	7:46:48
Rock Creek 42	18	42N25'56	114w18'17	7:37:13
Rockford 6	14	43N11'23	112w32'02	7:30:08
Rockford Bay 28	1	47N30'19	116w52'39	7:47:31
Rock House Place 42	18	42N10'22	114w46'50	7:39:07
Rockland 39	18	42N34'24	112w52'35	7:31:30
Rocky Bar 20	18	43N41'21	115w17'21	7:41:09
Rocky Point 5	2	47N21'21	116w44'43	7:46:59
Rogerson 42	18	42N13'05	114w35'36	7:38:22
Roland 40	2	47N22'48	115w40'05	7:42:40
Rookstool Corner 14	18	43N46'42	116w51'09	7:47:25
Rose 6	14	43N15'16	112w19'31	7:29:18
Rose 15	14	42N36'13	111w32'13	7:26:09
Roseberry 43	18	44N43'51	116w02'56	7:44:12
Rose Lake 28	2	47N32'20	116w28'15	7:45:53
Roseworth 42	18	42N22'01	114w55'17	7:39:41
Roswell 14	18	43N44'57	116w57'39	7:47:51
Rouse 6	16	43N13'36	112w28'42	7:29:55
Rover 5	2	47N12'12	116w34'31	7:46:18
Roy 39	18	42N21'50	112w49'49	7:31:19
Roy Summit 36	18	42N19'03	112w48'05	7:31:12
Rubicon 2	18	44N58'56	116w22'04	7:45:28
Ruby 16	18	42N30'14	113w49'19	7:35:17
Rudo 18	2	46N29'21	116w00'41	7:44:03
Rupert 34	18	42N37'09	113w40'35	7:34:42
Sage Junction 26	14	43N49'51	112w11'40	7:28:47
Sagle 9	2	48N12'09	116w32'48	7:46:11
Saint Anthony 22	13	43N57'59	111w40'53	7:26:44
Saint Charles 4	14	42N06'50	111w23'17	7:25:33
Saint Joe 5	2	47N18'40	116w21'07	7:45:24
Saint Johns 36	18	42N12'50	112w17'28	7:29:10
Saint Leon 10	14	43N29	112w00	7:28:00
Saint Maries 5	2	47N18'52	116w33'42	7:46:15
Salem 33	14	43N52'36	111w46'20	7:27:05
Salmon 30	16	45N10'33	113w53'42	7:35:35
Sam 41	14	43N43'09	111w18'11	7:25:13
Samaria 36	18	42N07'04	112w20'10	7:29:21
Samuels 9	2	48N25'46	116w29'34	7:45:58
Sanders 5	2	47N06'23	116w47'43	7:47:11
Sand Hollow 38	18	43N48'25	116w44'48	7:46:59
Sandpoint 9	7	48N16'36	116w33'08	7:46:13
Santa 5	2	47N09'01	116w26'53	7:45:48
Sawtooth City 7	18	43N53'48	114w50'22	7:39:21
Sawyer 9	2	48N08'40	116w45'17	7:47:01
Schiller 39	14	42N52'47	112w39'27	7:30:38
Schnoors 11	1	48N41'23	116w20'19	7:45:21
Schodde 27	18	42N36'26	113w59'25	7:35:58
Schow 34	18	42N35'13	113w42'38	7:34:51
Scott Place 25	18	45N26'05	116w00'22	7:44:01
Scoville 6	16	43N28'50	112w59'43	7:31:59
Seaburg 25	2	45N28'34	116w01'48	7:44:07
Sebree 20	18	43N11'09	115w47'23	7:43:10
Sego Place 37	18	42N23'03	115w55'08	7:43:41
Selby 13	18	43N20'38	114w42'35	7:38:50
Selle 9	2	48N21'25	116w29'19	7:45:57
Seneacquoteen 9	2	48N09'06	116w45'16	7:47:01
Setters 28	2	47N28'05	117w00'26	7:48:02
Sharon 4	14	42N21'02	111w28'42	7:25:55
Shelley 6	14	43N22'53	112w07'21	7:28:29
Shells Lick 25	2	45N42'24	116w07'37	7:44:30
Shelton 26	14	43N29	112w00	7:28:00
Sherwin 29	2	46N56'52	116w20'49	7:45:23
Sherwood Beach 9	2	48N29'48	116w50'22	7:47:21
Shoshone 32	18	42N56'10	114w24'18	7:37:37
Shoup 30	18	45N22'37	114w16'34	7:37:06
Silver Beach 28	2	47N56'54	116w53'28	7:47:34
Silver City 37	18	43N01'01	116w43'56	7:46:56
Silver Creek Plunge 43	18	44N07	115w58	7:43:52
Silver Sands Beach 28	2	47N53'32	116w53'01	7:47:32
Silvertip Landing 5	2	47N21'42	116w41'30	7:46:46
Silverton 40	2	47N29'35	115w57'16	7:43:49
Simplot 14	18	43N40'11	116w43'57	7:46:56
Sinclair 11	4	48N55'45	116w10'33	7:44:42
Skyline 10	14	43N29	112w00	7:28:00
Slacks Corner 37	18	43N04'55	116w44'28	7:46:58
Slate Creek 25	2	45N38'18	116w16'46	7:45:07
Slickpoo 31	2	46N19'01	116w42'36	7:46:50
Small 17	14	44N10	112w14	7:28:56
Smelter Heights 40	2	47N32'21	116w09'31	7:44:38
Smelterville 40	2	47N32'34	116w10'50	7:44:43
Smith Corrals 12	16	43N19'36	113w14'43	7:32:59
Smiths Ferry 43	18	44N18'05	116w05'19	7:44:21
Smith Springs 7	18	42N38'15	113w18'38	7:33:15
Smokehouse 25	2	45N21'23	115w15'04	7:41:00
Soda Springs 15	14	42N39'16	111w36'14	7:26:25
Soldier 13	18	43N22'13	114w47'27	7:39:10
Sonna 1	18	43N36'35	116w27'21	7:45:49
South Gate Plaza 35	12	46N24	116w59	7:47:56
South Mountain 37	18	42N45'08	116w55'21	7:47:41
Southside 1	18	43N36	116w12	7:44:48
Southwick 35	2	46N36'13	116w28'16	7:45:53
Spalding 35	2	46N26'49	116w48'59	7:47:16
Spanish Town 20	18	43N42'35	115w15'15	7:41:01
Spencer 17	14	44N21'38	112w11'10	7:28:45
Spirit Lake 28	2	47N57'59	116w52'03	7:47:28
Spiry Place 37	18	42N54'37	116w24'23	7:45:38
Springdale 16	18	42N30'56	113w41'24	7:34:46
Springfield 7	16	43N04'54	112w40'52	7:30:43
Springston 28	2	47N28'42	116w43'55	7:46:56
Squaw Bay 28	2	47N27	116w47	7:47:08
Squirrel 22	14	44N01'38	111w17'54	7:25:12
Staley Springs 22	14	44N39'37	111w26'04	7:25:44
Standrod 16	18	41N59'38	113w25'16	7:33:41
Stanford 29	2	46N49'58	116w38'37	7:46:34
Stanley 19	18	44N12'41	114w56'42	7:39:47
Stanton Crossing 7	18	43N19'40	114w18'42	7:37:15
Star 1	18	43N41'32	116w29'33	7:45:58
Starkey 2	18	44N51'02	116w26'51	7:45:47
Starrhs Ferry 16	18	42N33	113w48	7:35:12
State Line 28	2	47N42	117w02	7:48:08
State Line Village 28	2	47N42'16	117w02'11	7:48:09
Steamboat Rock 20	18	43N26'54	115w37'35	7:42:30
Steamboat Rocks 40	2	47N54'53	116w07'32	7:44:30
Steel Place 42	18	42N07'18	114w58'53	7:39:56
Steirman 8	18	43N50	115w50	7:43:20
Sterling 7	16	43N02'17	112w43'51	7:30:55
Stetson 40	2	47N17'06	115w46'24	7:43:06
Stevens 2	18	44N50'55	116w22'40	7:45:31
Stibnite 43	18	44N53'54	115w20'18	7:41:21
Stites 25	4	46N05'30	115w58'31	7:43:54
Stoddard 14	17	43N23	116w32	7:46:08
Stone 36	18	42N00'59	112w41'40	7:30:47
Stout Crossing 20	18	43N09'16	115w18'33	7:41:14
Strevell 16	18	42N00'22	113w12'10	7:32:49
Stull 40	3	47N28'20	115w51'49	7:43:27
Sturgeon 28	2	47N50'59	116w51'35	7:47:26
Sublett 16	18	42N18'44	113w08'10	7:32:33
Suckpoo 31	2	46N22	116w40	7:46:40
Sugar City 33	14	43N52'23	111w44'51	7:26:59
Sugar Loaf 27	18	42N40'53	114w22'37	7:37:30
Sully 42	18	42N32'21	114w23'00	7:37:32
Sunbeam 19	18	44N16'16	114w44'00	7:38:56
Sunnydell 33	14	43N41'04	111w45'15	7:27:01
Sunnyside 9	2	48N16'49	116w23'46	7:45:35
Sunnyside 40	2	47N32	116w08	7:44:32
Sunnyslope 14	18	43N35'19	116w47'32	7:47:10
Sun Valley 7	18	43N41'50	114w21'03	7:37:24
Swan Lake 3	14	42N18'28	111w59'53	7:28:00
Swan Valley 10	14	43N27'04	111w22'48	7:25:31
Swartz Corner 14	18	43N30'05	116w33'15	7:46:13
Sweeney 40	2	47N32'25	116w10'07	7:44:40
Sweet 23	18	43N58'23	116w19'25	7:45:18
Sweetwater 35	2	46N22'21	116w47'31	7:47:10
Syringa 25	2	46N09'03	115w43'34	7:42:54
Taber 6	14	43N19'05	112w41'17	7:30:45
Talache 9	2	48N08'27	116w29'03	7:45:56
Talache Landing 9	2	48N07'43	116w28'40	7:45:55
Talmage 15	14	42N40'44	111w47'12	7:27:09
Tamarack 2	18	44N57'19	116w23'05	7:45:32
Tate Place 37	18	42N05'14	115w58'53	7:43:56
Taylor 10	14	43N29	112w00	7:28:00
Teakean 18	2	46N33'04	116w22'47	7:45:31
Teepee Creek 43	18	44N56'25	115w44'18	7:42:57
Telegraph Hill 37	18	43N00'56	116w44'48	7:46:59
Tendoy 30	16	44N57'34	113w38'38	7:34:35
Ten Mile 1	14	43N18	112w09	7:28:36
Tensed 5	2	47N09'36	116w55'15	7:47:41
Tepee Circles 12	16	43N26'36	113w31'35	7:34:06
Terreton 26	16	43N50'30	112w26'08	7:29:45
Teton 22	14	43N53'12	111w40'37	7:26:42
Tetonia 41	14	43N49'09	111w09'43	7:24:39
Thain Road 35	12	46N24	116w59	7:47:56
Thama 9	2	48N09'12	116w50'48	7:47:23
Thatcher 21	14	42N24'32	111w43'34	7:26:54
The Cedars 18	2	46N52'22	115w04'34	7:40:18
Thiard 40	3	47N36'56	115w54'15	7:43:37
Thomas 6	14	43N10'58	112w30'14	7:30:01
Thompson Place 25	2	45N33'59	116w19'29	7:45:18
Thornton 33	14	43N45'30	111w50'40	7:27:23
Three Creek 37	18	42N04'17	115w09'31	7:40:38
Three Forks 37	18	42N05'27	116w01'45	7:44:07
Three Forks 41	14	40N06'42	79w57'00	5:19:48
Three Island Crossing 20	18	42N56'08	115w19'55	7:41:20
Threemile Corner 11	2	48N43'53	116w17'55	7:45:12
Threemile Crossing 42	18	42N14'52	114w51'50	7:39:27
Ticeska 20	18	42N55'32	115w05'21	7:40:21
Tiegs Corner 14	18	43N30'50	116w30'47	7:46:03
Tikura 7	18	43N12'53	114w00'43	7:36:03
Tipperary Corner 27	18	42N34'38	114w17'44	7:37:11
Topaz 3	14	42N37	112w01	7:28:04
Torreys 19	18	44N15'13	114w36'05	7:38:24
Tramway 25	2	46N17'05	116w06'25	7:44:26
Transfer 35	12	46N25'45	117w01'46	7:48:07
Travers 34	18	42N36'33	113w44'10	7:34:57
Treasureton 21	14	42N15'55	111w50'44	7:27:23
Trestle Creek 9	2	48N17'00	116w20'59	7:45:24
Triangle 37	18	42N46'56	116w37'59	7:46:32
Triumph 7	18	43N38'42	114w15'12	7:37:01
Trout 16	18	42N19'21	113w54'01	7:35:36
Troy 29	5	46N44'13	116w46'07	7:47:04
Trude 22	14	44N27'40	111w20'43	7:25:23
Tuanna Crossing 42	18	42N25'39	114w58'48	7:39:55
Tunupa 32	18	42N57'18	114w34'42	7:38:19
Turner 15	14	42N34'36	111w49'05	7:27:16
Turner Bay 28	2	47N27	116w47	7:47:08
Turnpike 4	14	42N06'36	111w15'46	7:25:03
Tuttle 24	18	42N51'30	114w50'21	7:39:21
Twin Beaches 28	1	47N37'12	116w47'50	7:47:11
Twin Falls 42	18	42N33'47	114w27'36	7:37:50
Twin Forks 41	14	40N06'20	79w56'45	5:19:47
Twin Groves 22	14	43N58'28	111w37'37	7:26:30
Twin Lakes 28	2	47N49	116w54	7:47:36
Twinlow 28	2	47N52'38	116w51'19	7:47:25
Twin Springs 8	18	43N40'10	115w42'01	7:42:48
Two Forks 41	14	40N05'11	79w55'49	5:19:43
Tyhee 3	14	42N57'06	112w27'56	7:29:52
Ucon 10	14	43N35'47	111w57'47	7:27:51
Ulysses 30	18	45N27'28	114w09'02	7:36:36
Underkoflers Corner 14	18	43N37'09	116w40'18	7:46:41
Unincorp 15	14	42N59'20	111w22'35	7:25:30
Unity 16	18	42N31'07	113w44'33	7:34:58
University 29	5	46N44	117w00	7:48:00
Upper Battle Creek Crossing 37	18	42N28'41	116w19'21	7:45:17
Upper Crossing 25	18	45N38'40	114w42'22	7:38:49
Upper Pittsburg Landing 25	2	45N37'32	116w28'12	7:45:53

```
Ustick 1          18 43N38'01 116w19'15 7:45:17
Valley View Heights 35
                  12 46N25'24 116w58'11 7:47:53
Vans Corner (Priest Lake PO) 9
                   2 48N31'31 116w56'16 7:47:45
Vassar 29          2 46N49'45 116w36'58 7:46:28
Vay 9              2 48N06'56 116w46'37 7:47:06
Vernon 1          18 43N35'19 116w09'36 7:44:38
Victor 41         13 43N36'10 111w06'38 7:24:27
View 16           18 42N27'03 113w41'47 7:34:47
Viola 29           5 46N50'19 117w01'25 7:48:06
Virginia 3        14 42N29'39 112w09'53 7:28:40
Vosburg Place 42
                  18 42N11'28 114w49'00 7:39:16
Waha 35           12 46N12'48 116w51'04 7:47:24
Walker 33         14 43N46'20 111w42'28 7:26:50
Wallace 40        11 47N28'27 115w55'37 7:43:42
Walters Ferry 14
                  18 43N20'26 116w35'55 7:46:24
Wapello 6         14 43N14'49 112w15'22 7:29:01
Wapi 7            18 42N42'56 113w10'56 7:32:44
Wardboro 4        14 42N15'21 111w16'35 7:25:06
Wardner 40         3 47N31'22 116w07'59 7:44:32
Warm Lake 43      18 44N39'15 115w40'00 7:42:40
Warm River 22     14 44N06'54 111w19'12 7:25:17
Warren 25         18 45N15'51 115w40'32 7:42:42
Warrens 14        18 43N19'43 116w32'21 7:46:09
Washington Mill 8
                  18 43N53'32 115w45'27 7:43:02
Washoe 38         17 44N03'16 116w56'50 7:47:47
Wayan (Unincorp) 15
                  14 42N59'20 111w22'35 7:25:30
Wayland 5          2 47N10'09 116w28'09 7:45:53
Weavers Hole 13
                  18 43N18'00 114w56'51 7:39:47
Webb 35            2 46N20'38 116w49'56 7:47:20
Webb 40            3 47N29'18 115w53'26 7:43:34
Weippe 18          2 46N22'34 115w56'14 7:43:45
Weiser 44         17 44N15'04 116w58'06 7:47:52
Weitz 14          18 43N40'10 116w45'31 7:47:02
Wendell 24        18 42N46'33 114w42'12 7:38:49
West Camas 13     18 43N19    115w01    7:40:04
West Clark 17     16 44N17    112w34    7:30:16
Western Shoshone 37
                  18 42N05    116w11    7:44:44
Westlake 25        2 46N07'19 116w30'22 7:46:01
Westma 14         17 43N24'57 116w32'28 7:46:10
Westmond 9         2 48N08'24 116w36'09 7:46:25
West Mountain 43
                  18 44N31    116w03    7:44:12
Weston 21         14 42N02'14 111w58'43 7:27:55
West Salmon Falls 42
                  18 42N33    114w57    7:39:48
Whipsaw Saddle 25
                   2 45N47'34 116w20'54 7:45:24
White Bird 25      2 45N45'42 116w17'59 7:45:12
Whitney 1         18 43N35    116w15    7:45:00
Whitney 21        14 42N03'57 111w50'13 7:27:21
Wickahoney 37     18 42N27'36 115w58'57 7:43:56
Wickahoney Crossing 37
                  18 42N32'32 115w58'38 7:43:55
Wilder 14         17 43N40'36 116w54'39 7:47:39
Wilford 22        14 43N54'46 111w40'37 7:26:42
Willard 5          2 47N14'26 117w02'17 7:48:09
Willola 35         2 46N30'18 116w34'09 7:46:17
Willow 38         18 44N06    116w44    7:46:56
Winchester 31      4 46N14'24 116w37'24 7:46:30
Winder 21         14 42N10'35 111w54'54 7:27:40
Windy Devil 19
                  16 43N54'40 113w41'18 7:34:45
Windy Gap 20      18 43N19'15 115w24'47 7:41:39
Winona 25          2 46N07'56 116w06'25 7:44:26
Winsper 17        16 44N07'50 112w30'52 7:30:03
Wolf Lodge 28      1 47N38'29 116w36'57 7:46:28
Wolverine 6       14 43N16'53 111w56'07 7:27:44
Wood 38           18 44N07'32 116w54'22 7:47:37
Woodland 2        18 44N55'49 116w22'55 7:45:32
Woodland 25        2 46N18'40 116w04'03 7:44:16
Woodland Park 40
                   2 47N28    115w55    7:43:40
Woodlawn Park 40
                   2 47N29'10 115w54'04 7:43:36
Woodruff 36       18 42N02'10 112w12'50 7:28:51
Woods Crossing 33
                  14 43N46'27 111w37'47 7:26:31
Woodville 6       14 43N25'01 112w08'31 7:28:34
Worley 28          2 47N24'03 116w54'58 7:47:40
Wrencoe 9          2 48N13'44 116w42'07 7:46:48
Yale 16           18 42N35'50 113w14'07 7:32:56
Yale 29            2 46N51'44 116w41'44 7:46:47
Yellowjacket 30
                  18 44N58'47 114w31'51 7:38:07
Yellow Pine 43
                  18 44N57'54 115w29'34 7:41:58
Zaza 35            2 46N03'44 116w50'43 7:47:23
Zenda 3           14 42N22'40 112w03'28 7:28:14
```

TIME TABLES

State law required all birth times to be recorded in CST until July 1, 1959, except during World War II when CWT was recorded officially. But this law was not always observed, leading to considerable confusion about actual time of birth for summer births. In 1936 the greater Chicago area is shown as CDT instead of the official EST. However, these are equivalent in their effect. Small towns are assumed to follow nearby larger towns, which may not always be correct.

IL # 1		
Before 11/18/1883		LMT
11/18/1883	12:00	CST
3/31/1918	02:00	CWT
10/27/1918	02:00	CST
3/30/1919	02:00	CWT
10/26/1919	02:00	CST
6/13/1920	02:00	CDT
10/31/1920	02:00	CST
3/27/1921	02:00	CDT
10/30/1921	02:00	CST
4/30/1922	02:00	CDT
9/24/1922	02:00	CST
4/29/1923	02:00	CDT
9/30/1923	02:00	CST
4/27/1924	02:00	CDT
9/28/1924	02:00	CST
4/26/1925	02:00	CDT
9/27/1925	02:00	CST
4/25/1926	02:00	CDT
9/26/1926	02:00	CST
4/24/1927	02:00	CDT
9/25/1927	02:00	CST
4/29/1928	02:00	CDT
9/30/1928	02:00	CST
4/28/1929	02:00	CDT
9/29/1929	02:00	CST
4/27/1930	02:00	CDT
9/28/1930	02:00	CST
4/26/1931	02:00	CDT
9/27/1931	02:00	CST
4/24/1932	02:00	CDT
9/25/1932	02:00	CST
4/30/1933	02:00	CDT
9/24/1933	02:00	CST
4/29/1934	02:00	CDT
9/30/1934	02:00	CST
4/28/1935	02:00	CDT
9/29/1935	02:00	CST
3/01/1936	02:00	CDT
11/15/1936	02:00	CST
4/25/1937	02:00	US#2

IL # 2		
Before 11/18/1883		LMT
11/18/1883	12:00	CST
3/31/1918	02:00	CWT
10/27/1918	02:00	CST
3/30/1919	02:00	CWT
10/26/1919	02:00	CST
6/13/1920	02:00	CDT
10/31/1920	02:00	CST
3/27/1921	02:00	CDT
10/30/1921	02:00	CST
4/30/1922	02:00	CDT
9/24/1922	02:00	CST
4/29/1923	02:00	CDT
9/30/1923	02:00	CST
4/27/1924	02:00	CDT
9/28/1924	02:00	CST
4/26/1925	02:00	CDT
9/27/1925	02:00	CST
4/25/1926	02:00	CDT
9/26/1926	02:00	CST
4/24/1927	02:00	CDT
9/25/1927	02:00	CST
4/29/1928	02:00	CDT
9/30/1928	02:00	CST
4/28/1929	02:00	CDT
9/29/1929	02:00	CST
4/27/1930	02:00	CDT
9/28/1930	02:00	CST
4/26/1931	02:00	CDT
9/27/1931	02:00	CST
4/24/1932	02:00	CDT
9/25/1932	02:00	CST
4/30/1933	02:00	CDT
9/24/1933	02:00	CST
4/29/1934	02:00	CDT
9/30/1934	02:00	CST
4/28/1935	02:00	CDT
9/29/1935	02:00	CST
3/01/1936	02:00	CDT
11/15/1936	02:00	CST
4/25/1937	02:00	CDT
9/26/1937	02:00	CST
4/24/1938	02:00	CDT
9/25/1938	02:00	CST
4/30/1939	02:00	CDT
9/24/1939	02:00	CST
4/28/1940	02:00	CDT
9/29/1940	02:00	CST
4/27/1941	02:00	CDT
9/28/1941	02:00	CST
2/09/1942	02:00	CWT
9/30/1945	02:00	CST
4/28/1946	02:00	CDT
9/29/1946	02:00	CST
4/27/1947	02:00	CDT
9/28/1947	02:00	CST
4/25/1948	02:00	CDT
9/26/1948	02:00	CST
4/24/1949	02:00	CDT
9/25/1949	02:00	CST
4/30/1950	02:00	CDT
9/24/1950	02:00	CST
4/29/1951	02:00	CDT
9/30/1951	02:00	CST
4/27/1952	02:00	CDT
9/28/1952	02:00	CST
4/26/1953	02:00	CDT
9/27/1953	02:00	CST
4/25/1954	02:00	CDT
9/26/1954	02:00	CST
4/24/1955	02:00	CDT
9/25/1955	02:00	CST
4/29/1956	02:00	US#2

IL # 3		
Before 11/18/1883		LMT
11/18/1883	12:00	CST
3/31/1918	02:00	CWT
10/27/1918	02:00	CST
3/30/1919	02:00	CWT
10/26/1919	02:00	CST
6/13/1920	02:00	CDT
10/31/1920	02:00	CST
3/27/1921	02:00	CDT
10/30/1921	02:00	CST
4/30/1922	02:00	CDT
9/24/1922	02:00	CST
4/29/1923	02:00	CDT
9/30/1923	02:00	CST
4/27/1924	02:00	CDT
9/28/1924	02:00	CST
4/26/1925	02:00	CDT
9/27/1925	02:00	CST
4/25/1926	02:00	CDT
9/26/1926	02:00	CST
4/24/1927	02:00	CDT
9/25/1927	02:00	CST
4/29/1928	02:00	CDT
9/30/1928	02:00	CST
4/28/1929	02:00	CDT
9/29/1929	02:00	CST
4/27/1930	02:00	CDT
9/28/1930	02:00	CST
4/26/1931	02:00	CDT
9/27/1931	02:00	CST
4/24/1932	02:00	CDT
9/25/1932	02:00	CST
4/30/1933	02:00	CDT
9/24/1933	02:00	CST
4/29/1934	02:00	CDT
9/30/1934	02:00	CST
4/28/1935	02:00	CDT
9/29/1935	02:00	CST
3/01/1936	02:00	CDT
11/15/1936	02:00	CST
4/25/1937	02:00	CDT
9/26/1937	02:00	CST
4/24/1938	02:00	CDT
9/25/1938	02:00	CST
4/30/1939	02:00	CDT
9/24/1939	02:00	CST
4/28/1940	02:00	CDT
9/29/1940	02:00	CST
4/27/1941	02:00	CDT
9/28/1941	02:00	CST
2/09/1942	02:00	CWT
9/30/1945	02:00	CST
4/28/1946	02:00	CDT
9/29/1946	02:00	CST
4/27/1947	02:00	CDT
9/28/1947	02:00	CST
4/25/1948	02:00	CDT
9/26/1948	02:00	CST
4/24/1949	02:00	CDT
9/25/1949	02:00	CST
4/30/1950	02:00	CDT
9/24/1950	02:00	CST
4/29/1951	02:00	CDT
9/30/1951	02:00	CST
4/27/1952	02:00	CDT
9/28/1952	02:00	CST
4/26/1953	02:00	CDT
9/27/1953	02:00	CST
4/25/1954	02:00	CDT
9/26/1954	02:00	CST
4/24/1955	02:00	CDT
9/25/1955	02:00	CST
4/29/1956	02:00	CDT
9/30/1956	02:00	CST
4/28/1957	02:00	CDT
9/29/1957	02:00	CST
4/27/1958	02:00	CDT
9/28/1958	02:00	CST
4/26/1959	02:00	US#2

IL # 4		
Before 11/18/1883		LMT
11/18/1883	12:00	CST
3/31/1918	02:00	CWT
10/27/1918	02:00	CST
3/30/1919	02:00	CWT
10/26/1919	02:00	CST
2/09/1942	02:00	CWT
9/30/1945	02:00	CST
7/01/1959	02:00	US#2

IL # 5		
Before 11/18/1883		LMT
11/18/1883	12:00	CST
3/31/1918	02:00	CWT
10/27/1918	02:00	CST
3/30/1919	02:00	CWT
10/26/1919	02:00	CST
2/09/1942	02:00	CWT
9/30/1945	02:00	CST
4/27/1947	02:00	US#2

IL # 6		
Before 11/18/1883		LMT
11/18/1883	12:00	CST
3/31/1918	02:00	CWT
10/27/1918	02:00	CST
3/30/1919	02:00	CWT
10/26/1919	02:00	CST
2/09/1942	02:00	CWT
9/30/1945	02:00	CST
4/28/1946	02:00	US#2

IL # 7		
Before 11/18/1883		LMT
11/18/1883	12:00	CST
3/31/1918	02:00	CWT
10/27/1918	02:00	CST
3/30/1919	02:00	CWT
10/26/1919	02:00	CST
2/09/1942	02:00	CWT
9/30/1945	02:00	CST
4/28/1946	02:00	CDT
9/29/1946	02:00	CST
4/27/1947	02:00	CDT
9/28/1947	02:00	CST
4/25/1948	02:00	CDT
9/26/1948	02:00	CST
4/24/1949	02:00	CDT
9/25/1949	02:00	CST
4/30/1950	02:00	CDT
9/24/1950	02:00	CST
4/29/1951	02:00	CDT
9/30/1951	02:00	CST
4/27/1952	02:00	CDT
9/28/1952	02:00	CST
4/26/1953	02:00	CDT
9/27/1953	02:00	CST
4/25/1954	02:00	CDT
9/26/1954	02:00	CST
4/24/1955	02:00	CDT
9/25/1955	02:00	CST
4/29/1956	02:00	CDT
9/30/1956	02:00	CST
4/28/1957	02:00	CDT
9/29/1957	02:00	CST
4/27/1958	02:00	CDT
9/28/1958	02:00	CST
4/26/1959	02:00	US#2

IL # 8		
Before 11/18/1883		LMT
11/18/1883	12:00	CST
3/31/1918	02:00	CWT
10/27/1918	02:00	CST
3/30/1919	02:00	CWT
10/26/1919	02:00	CST
2/09/1942	02:00	CWT
9/30/1945	02:00	CST
4/27/1952	02:00	CDT
9/28/1952	02:00	CST
4/26/1953	02:00	CDT
9/27/1953	02:00	CST
4/25/1954	02:00	CDT
9/26/1954	02:00	CST
4/24/1955	02:00	CDT
9/25/1955	02:00	CST
4/29/1956	02:00	CDT
9/30/1956	02:00	CST
4/28/1957	02:00	CDT
9/29/1957	02:00	CST
4/27/1958	02:00	CDT
9/28/1958	02:00	CST
4/26/1959	02:00	US#2

IL # 9		
Before 11/18/1883		LMT
11/18/1883	12:00	IL#1
9/29/1935	02:00	CST
4/26/1936	02:00	CDT
9/27/1936	02:00	CST
4/25/1937	02:00	IL#2
4/29/1956	02:00	US#2

IL # 10		
Before 11/18/1883		LMT
11/18/1883	12:00	IL#1
10/31/1920	02:00	CST
4/30/1933	02:00	IL#2
4/29/1956	02:00	US#2

IL # 11		
Before 11/18/1883		LMT
11/18/1883	12:00	IL#1
9/27/1931	02:00	CST
4/24/1938	02:00	CDT
9/25/1938	02:00	CST
4/30/1939	02:00	CDT
9/24/1939	02:00	CST
4/28/1940	02:00	CDT
9/29/1940	02:00	CST
4/27/1941	02:00	CDT
9/28/1941	02:00	IL#2
4/29/1956	02:00	US#2

IL # 12		
Before 11/18/1883		LMT
11/18/1883	12:00	CST
3/31/1918	02:00	CWT
10/27/1918	02:00	CST
3/30/1919	02:00	CWT
10/26/1919	02:00	CST
4/26/1931	02:00	IL#1
9/28/1941	02:00	US#2

IL # 13		
Before 11/18/1883		LMT
11/18/1883	12:00	CST
3/31/1918	02:00	CWT
10/27/1918	02:00	CST
3/30/1919	02:00	CWT
10/26/1919	02:00	CST
4/24/1938	02:00	CDT
9/25/1938	02:00	IL#4
7/01/1959	02:00	US#2

IL # 14		
Before 11/18/1883		LMT
11/18/1883	12:00	CST
3/31/1918	02:00	CWT
10/27/1918	02:00	CST
3/30/1919	02:00	CWT
10/26/1919	02:00	CST
4/26/1931	02:00	CDT
9/27/1931	02:00	CST
4/24/1932	02:00	CDT
9/25/1932	02:00	CST
4/30/1933	02:00	CDT
9/24/1933	02:00	CST
4/29/1934	02:00	CDT
9/30/1934	02:00	CST
4/28/1935	02:00	CDT
9/29/1935	02:00	CST
3/01/1936	02:00	CDT
11/15/1936	02:00	CST
4/25/1937	02:00	CDT
9/26/1937	02:00	CST
4/24/1938	02:00	CDT
9/25/1938	02:00	IL#3
4/26/1959	02:00	US#2

IL # 15		
Before 11/18/1883		LMT
11/18/1883	12:00	CST
3/31/1918	02:00	CWT
10/27/1918	02:00	CST
3/30/1919	02:00	CWT
10/26/1919	02:00	CST
4/24/1938	02:00	CDT
9/25/1938	02:00	CST
4/30/1939	02:00	CDT
9/24/1939	02:00	CST
4/28/1940	02:00	CDT
9/29/1940	02:00	CST
4/27/1941	02:00	CDT
9/28/1941	02:00	IL#2
4/29/1956	02:00	US#2

IL # 16		
Before 11/18/1883		LMT
11/18/1883	12:00	CST
3/31/1918	02:00	CWT
10/27/1918	02:00	CST
3/30/1919	02:00	CWT
10/26/1919	02:00	CST
4/26/1931	02:00	IL#3
4/26/1959	02:00	US#2

IL # 17		
Before 11/18/1883		LMT
11/18/1883	12:00	IL#4
4/24/1932	02:00	CDT
9/25/1932	02:00	CST
4/30/1933	02:00	CDT
9/24/1933	02:00	CST
4/29/1934	02:00	CDT
9/30/1934	02:00	CST
4/28/1935	02:00	CDT
9/29/1935	02:00	CST
3/01/1936	02:00	CDT
11/15/1936	02:00	CST
4/25/1937	02:00	CDT
9/26/1937	02:00	CST
4/24/1938	02:00	CDT
9/25/1938	02:00	CST
4/30/1939	02:00	CDT
9/24/1939	02:00	CST
4/28/1940	02:00	CDT
9/29/1940	02:00	CST
4/27/1941	02:00	CDT
9/28/1941	02:00	IL#2
4/29/1956	02:00	US#2

IL # 18		
Before 11/18/1883		LMT
11/18/1883	12:00	CST
3/31/1918	02:00	CWT
10/27/1918	02:00	CST
3/30/1919	02:00	CWT
10/26/1919	02:00	CST
4/24/1938	02:00	CDT
9/25/1938	02:00	CST
4/30/1939	02:00	CDT
9/24/1939	02:00	CST
4/28/1940	02:00	CDT
9/29/1940	02:00	CST
4/27/1941	02:00	CDT
9/28/1941	02:00	CST
2/09/1942	02:00	CWT
9/30/1945	02:00	CST
4/28/1946	02:00	IL#2
4/29/1956	02:00	US#2

IL # 19		
Before 11/18/1883		LMT
11/18/1883	12:00	IL#4
4/26/1931	02:00	CDT
9/27/1931	02:00	CST
4/24/1932	02:00	CDT
9/25/1932	02:00	CST
4/30/1933	02:00	CDT
9/24/1933	02:00	CST
4/29/1934	02:00	CDT
9/30/1934	02:00	CST
4/28/1935	02:00	CDT
9/29/1935	02:00	CST
3/01/1936	02:00	CDT
11/15/1936	02:00	CST
4/25/1937	02:00	CDT
9/26/1937	02:00	CST
4/24/1938	02:00	CDT
9/25/1938	02:00	CST
4/30/1939	02:00	CDT
9/24/1939	02:00	CST
4/28/1940	02:00	CDT
9/29/1940	02:00	CST
4/27/1941	02:00	CDT
9/28/1941	02:00	IL#2
4/29/1956	02:00	US#2

IL # 20		
Before 11/18/1883		LMT
11/18/1883	12:00	CST
3/31/1918	02:00	CWT
10/27/1918	02:00	CST
3/30/1919	02:00	CWT
10/26/1919	02:00	CST
5/05/1940	02:00	CDT
9/29/1940	02:00	CST
2/09/1942	02:00	CWT
9/30/1945	02:00	CST
4/28/1946	02:00	US#2

IL # 21		
Before 11/18/1883		LMT
11/18/1883	12:00	CST
3/31/1918	02:00	CWT
10/27/1918	02:00	CST
3/30/1919	02:00	CWT
10/26/1919	02:00	CST
4/27/1941	02:00	CDT
9/28/1941	02:00	IL#2
4/29/1956	02:00	US#2

IL # 22		
Before 11/18/1883		LMT
11/18/1883	12:00	CST
3/31/1918	02:00	CWT
10/27/1918	02:00	CST
3/30/1919	02:00	CWT
10/26/1919	02:00	CST
4/27/1941	02:00	US#2

IL # 23		
Before 11/18/1883		LMT
11/18/1883	12:00	IL#6
9/29/1946	02:00	CST
7/01/1959	02:00	US#2

IL # 24		
Before 11/18/1883		LMT
11/18/1883	12:00	IL#6
10/27/1957	02:00	CST
7/01/1959	02:00	US#2

IL # 25		
Before 11/18/1883		LMT
11/18/1883	12:00	CST
3/31/1918	02:00	CWT
10/27/1918	02:00	CST
3/30/1919	02:00	CWT
10/26/1919	02:00	CST
2/09/1942	02:00	CWT
9/30/1945	02:00	CST
4/29/1946	02:00	US#4

IL # 26		
Before 11/18/1883		LMT
11/18/1883	12:00	IL#6
4/28/1946	02:00	IL#2
4/29/1956	02:00	US#2

IL # 27		
Before 11/18/1883		LMT
11/18/1883	12:00	IL#4
4/29/1934	02:00	IL#2
4/29/1956	02:00	US#2

IL # 28		
Before 11/18/1883		LMT
11/18/1883	12:00	CST
3/31/1918	02:00	CWT
10/27/1918	02:00	CST
3/30/1919	02:00	CWT
10/26/1919	02:00	CST
2/09/1942	02:00	CWT

TIME TABLES

9/30/1945 02:00 CST
4/28/1946 02:00 CDT
9/29/1946 02:00 CST
4/27/1947 02:00 CDT
9/28/1947 02:00 CST
4/25/1948 02:00 CDT
9/26/1948 02:00 CST
4/24/1949 02:00 CDT
9/25/1949 02:00 CST
4/30/1950 02:00 CDT
9/24/1950 02:00 CST
4/29/1951 02:00 CDT
9/30/1951 02:00 CST
4/27/1952 02:00 CDT
9/28/1952 02:00 CST
4/26/1953 02:00 CDT
9/27/1953 02:00 CST
4/25/1954 02:00 CDT
9/26/1954 02:00 CST
4/24/1955 02:00 CDT
9/25/1955 02:00 CST
4/29/1956 02:00 CDT
10/28/1956 02:00 CST
4/28/1957 02:00 CDT
10/27/1957 02:00 CST
4/27/1958 02:00 CDT
9/28/1958 02:00 CST
4/26/1959 02:00 US#2

IL # 29
Before 11/18/1883 LMT
11/18/1883 12:00 IL#5
4/27/1947 02:00 IL#3
4/26/1959 02:00 US#2

IL # 30
Before 11/18/1883 LMT
11/18/1883 12:00 CST
3/31/1918 02:00 CWT
10/27/1918 02:00 CST
3/30/1919 02:00 CWT
10/26/1919 02:00 CST
2/09/1942 02:00 CWT
9/30/1945 02:00 CST
4/27/1947 02:00 IL#2
4/29/1956 02:00 US#2

IL # 31
Before 11/18/1883 LMT
11/18/1883 12:00 IL#5
4/24/1955 02:00 CDT
9/25/1955 02:00 CST
4/29/1956 02:00 CDT
10/28/1956 02:00 CST
4/28/1957 02:00 CDT
10/27/1957 02:00 CST
4/27/1958 02:00 CDT
9/28/1958 02:00 CST
4/26/1959 02:00 US#2

IL # 32
Before 11/18/1883 LMT
11/18/1883 12:00 IL#5
9/28/1947 02:00 CST
7/01/1959 02:00 US#2

IL # 33
Before 11/18/1883 LMT
11/18/1883 12:00 IL#5
9/26/1948 02:00 CST
7/01/1959 02:00 US#2

IL # 34
Before 11/18/1883 LMT
11/18/1883 12:00 IL#4
4/24/1932 02:00 IL#1
9/28/1941 02:00 US#2

IL # 35
Before 11/18/1883 LMT
11/18/1883 12:00 IL#5
4/24/1955 02:00 US#4

IL # 36
Before 11/18/1883 LMT
11/18/1883 12:00 CST
3/31/1918 02:00 CWT
10/27/1918 02:00 CST
3/30/1919 02:00 CWT
10/26/1919 02:00 CST
2/09/1942 02:00 CWT
9/30/1945 02:00 CST
4/25/1948 02:00 IL#2
4/29/1956 02:00 US#2

IL # 37
Before 11/18/1883 LMT
11/18/1883 12:00 CST
3/31/1918 02:00 CWT
10/27/1918 02:00 CST
3/30/1919 02:00 CWT
10/26/1919 02:00 CST
2/09/1942 02:00 CWT
9/30/1945 02:00 CST
4/25/1948 02:00 IL#3
4/26/1959 02:00 US#2

IL # 38
Before 11/18/1883 LMT
11/18/1883 12:00 CST
3/31/1918 02:00 CWT
10/27/1918 02:00 CST
3/30/1919 02:00 CWT
10/26/1919 02:00 CST
2/09/1942 02:00 CWT
9/30/1945 02:00 CST
4/30/1950 02:00 US#4

IL # 39
Before 11/18/1883 LMT
11/18/1883 12:00 CST
3/31/1918 02:00 CWT
10/27/1918 02:00 CST
3/30/1919 02:00 CWT
10/26/1919 02:00 CST
2/09/1942 02:00 CWT
9/30/1945 02:00 CST
4/30/1950 02:00 IL#3
4/26/1959 02:00 US#2

IL # 40
Before 11/18/1883 LMT
11/18/1883 12:00 CST
3/31/1918 02:00 CWT
10/27/1918 02:00 CST
3/30/1919 02:00 CWT
10/26/1919 02:00 CST
2/09/1942 02:00 CWT
9/30/1945 02:00 CST
4/30/1950 02:00 CDT
9/24/1950 02:00 CST
4/29/1951 02:00 CDT
9/30/1951 02:00 CST
4/27/1952 02:00 CDT
9/28/1952 02:00 CST
4/26/1953 02:00 CDT
9/27/1953 02:00 CST
4/25/1954 02:00 CDT
9/26/1954 02:00 CST
4/24/1955 02:00 CDT
9/25/1955 02:00 CST
4/29/1956 02:00 CDT
10/28/1956 02:00 CST
4/28/1957 02:00 CDT
4/29/1957 02:00 IL#3
4/26/1959 02:00 US#2

IL # 41
Before 11/18/1883 LMT
11/18/1883 12:00 CST
3/31/1918 02:00 CWT
10/27/1918 02:00 CST
3/30/1919 02:00 CWT
10/26/1919 02:00 CST
2/09/1942 02:00 CWT
9/30/1945 02:00 CST
4/29/1951 02:00 IL#3
4/26/1959 02:00 US#2

IL # 42
Before 11/18/1883 LMT
11/18/1883 12:00 IL#4
4/29/1934 02:00 IL#1
9/28/1941 02:00 US#2

IL # 43
Before 11/18/1883 LMT
11/18/1883 12:00 CST
3/31/1918 02:00 CWT
10/27/1918 02:00 CST
3/30/1919 02:00 CWT
10/26/1919 02:00 CST
2/09/1942 02:00 CWT
9/30/1945 02:00 CST
4/29/1951 02:00 IL#2
4/29/1956 02:00 US#2

IL # 44
Before 11/18/1883 LMT
11/18/1883 12:00 CST
3/31/1918 02:00 CWT
10/27/1918 02:00 CST
3/30/1919 02:00 CWT
10/26/1919 02:00 CST
2/09/1942 02:00 CWT
9/30/1945 02:00 CST
4/29/1951 02:00 US#4

IL # 45
Before 11/18/1883 LMT
11/18/1883 12:00 IL#8
9/26/1954 02:00 CST
7/01/1959 02:00 US#2

IL # 46
Before 11/18/1883 LMT
11/18/1883 12:00 CST
3/31/1918 02:00 CWT
10/27/1918 02:00 CST
3/30/1919 02:00 CWT
10/26/1919 02:00 CST
2/09/1942 02:00 CWT
9/30/1945 02:00 CST
4/27/1952 02:00 US#4

IL # 47
Before 11/18/1883 LMT
11/18/1883 12:00 IL#8
8/28/1955 02:00 CST
4/29/1956 02:00 IL#3
4/26/1959 02:00 US#2

IL # 48
Before 11/18/1883 LMT
11/18/1883 12:00 CST
3/31/1918 02:00 CWT
10/27/1918 02:00 CST
3/30/1919 02:00 CWT
10/26/1919 02:00 CST
2/09/1942 02:00 CWT
9/30/1945 02:00 CST
4/27/1952 02:00 US#3

IL # 49
Before 11/18/1883 LMT
11/18/1883 12:00 CST
3/31/1918 02:00 CWT
10/27/1918 02:00 CST
3/30/1919 02:00 CWT
10/26/1919 02:00 CST
2/09/1942 02:00 CWT
9/30/1945 02:00 CST
4/26/1953 02:00 CDT
9/27/1953 02:00 CST
4/25/1954 02:00 CDT
9/26/1954 02:00 CST
4/24/1955 02:00 CDT
9/25/1955 02:00 CST
4/29/1956 02:00 CDT
9/30/1956 02:00 CST
4/28/1957 02:00 CDT
9/29/1957 02:00 CST
7/01/1959 02:00 US#2

IL # 50
Before 11/18/1883 LMT
11/18/1883 12:00 CST
3/31/1918 02:00 CWT
10/27/1918 02:00 CST
3/30/1919 02:00 CWT
10/26/1919 02:00 CST
2/09/1942 02:00 CWT
9/30/1945 02:00 CST
4/26/1953 02:00 IL#3
4/26/1959 02:00 US#2

IL # 51
Before 11/18/1883 LMT
11/18/1883 12:00 CST
3/31/1918 02:00 CWT
10/27/1918 02:00 CST
3/30/1919 02:00 CWT
10/26/1919 02:00 CST
2/09/1942 02:00 CWT
9/30/1945 02:00 CST
4/25/1954 02:00 US#2

IL # 52
Before 11/18/1883 LMT
11/18/1883 12:00 CST
3/31/1918 02:00 CWT
10/27/1918 02:00 CST
3/30/1919 02:00 CWT
10/26/1919 02:00 CST
2/09/1942 02:00 CWT
9/30/1945 02:00 CST
4/25/1954 02:00 CDT
9/26/1954 02:00 CST
7/01/1959 02:00 US#2

IL # 53
Before 11/18/1883 LMT
11/18/1883 12:00 CST
3/31/1918 02:00 CWT
10/27/1918 02:00 CST
3/30/1919 02:00 CWT
10/26/1919 02:00 CST
2/09/1942 02:00 CWT
9/30/1945 02:00 CST
4/25/1954 02:00 IL#3
4/26/1959 02:00 US#2

IL # 54
Before 11/18/1883 LMT
11/18/1883 12:00 CST
3/31/1918 02:00 CWT
10/27/1918 02:00 CST
3/30/1919 02:00 CWT
10/26/1919 02:00 CST
2/09/1942 02:00 CWT
9/30/1945 02:00 CST
4/24/1955 02:00 US#2

IL # 55
Before 11/18/1883 LMT
11/18/1883 12:00 CST
3/31/1918 02:00 CWT
10/27/1918 02:00 CST
3/30/1919 02:00 CWT
10/26/1919 02:00 CST
2/09/1942 02:00 CWT
9/30/1945 02:00 CST
4/24/1955 02:00 IL#3
4/26/1959 02:00 US#2

IL # 56
Before 11/18/1883 LMT
11/18/1883 12:00 CST
3/31/1918 02:00 CWT
10/27/1918 02:00 CST
3/30/1919 02:00 CWT
10/26/1919 02:00 CST
2/09/1942 02:00 CWT
9/30/1945 02:00 CST
4/24/1955 02:00 US#4

IL # 57
Before 11/18/1883 LMT
11/18/1883 12:00 CST
3/31/1918 02:00 CWT
10/27/1918 02:00 CST
3/30/1919 02:00 CWT
10/26/1919 02:00 CST
2/09/1942 02:00 CWT
9/30/1945 02:00 CST
4/24/1955 02:00 IL#2
4/29/1956 02:00 US#2

IL # 58
Before 11/18/1883 LMT
11/18/1883 12:00 CST
3/31/1918 02:00 CWT
10/27/1918 02:00 CST
3/30/1919 02:00 CWT
10/26/1919 02:00 CST
2/09/1942 02:00 CWT
9/30/1945 02:00 CST
4/24/1955 02:00 CDT
9/25/1955 02:00 CST
4/29/1956 02:00 CDT
10/28/1956 02:00 CST
4/28/1957 02:00 CDT
10/27/1957 02:00 CST
4/27/1958 02:00 CDT
9/28/1958 02:00 CST
4/26/1959 02:00 US#2

IL # 59
Before 11/18/1883 LMT
11/18/1883 12:00 CST
3/31/1918 02:00 CWT
10/27/1918 02:00 CST
3/30/1919 02:00 CWT
10/26/1919 02:00 CST
2/09/1942 02:00 CWT
9/30/1945 02:00 CST
4/24/1955 02:00 CDT
9/25/1955 02:00 CST
7/01/1959 02:00 US#2

IL # 60
Before 11/18/1883 LMT
11/18/1883 12:00 CST
3/31/1918 02:00 CWT
10/27/1918 02:00 CST
3/30/1919 02:00 CWT
10/26/1919 02:00 CST
2/09/1942 02:00 CWT
9/30/1945 02:00 CST
4/30/1950 02:00 US#3

IL # 61
Before 11/18/1883 LMT
11/18/1883 12:00 CST
3/31/1918 02:00 CWT
10/27/1918 02:00 CST
3/30/1919 02:00 CWT
10/26/1919 02:00 CST
2/09/1942 02:00 CWT
9/30/1945 02:00 CST
4/24/1955 02:00 CDT
9/25/1955 02:00 CST
4/29/1956 02:00 CDT
10/28/1956 02:00 CST
4/28/1957 02:00 CDT
9/29/1957 02:00 IL#3
4/26/1959 02:00 US#2

IL # 62
Before 11/18/1883 LMT
11/18/1883 12:00 CST
3/31/1918 02:00 CWT
10/27/1918 02:00 CST
3/30/1919 02:00 CWT
10/26/1919 02:00 CST
2/09/1942 02:00 CWT
9/30/1945 02:00 CST
4/29/1956 02:00 US#2

IL # 63
Before 11/18/1883 LMT
11/18/1883 12:00 CST
3/31/1918 02:00 CWT
10/27/1918 02:00 CST
3/30/1919 02:00 CWT
10/26/1919 02:00 CST
2/09/1942 02:00 CWT
9/30/1945 02:00 CST
4/29/1956 02:00 IL#3
4/26/1959 02:00 US#2

IL # 64
Before 11/18/1883 LMT
11/18/1883 12:00 CST
3/31/1918 02:00 CWT
10/27/1918 02:00 CST
3/30/1919 02:00 CWT
10/26/1919 02:00 CST
2/09/1942 02:00 CWT
9/30/1945 02:00 CST
4/28/1957 02:00 US#2

IL # 65
Before 11/18/1883 LMT
11/18/1883 12:00 CST
3/31/1918 02:00 CWT
10/27/1918 02:00 CST
3/30/1919 02:00 CWT
10/26/1919 02:00 CST
2/09/1942 02:00 CWT
9/30/1945 02:00 CST
4/28/1957 02:00 IL#3
4/26/1959 02:00 US#2

IL # 66
Before 11/18/1883 LMT
11/18/1883 12:00 CST
3/31/1918 02:00 CWT
10/27/1918 02:00 CST
3/30/1919 02:00 CWT
10/26/1919 02:00 CST
2/09/1942 02:00 CWT
9/30/1945 02:00 CST
4/27/1958 02:00 CDT
9/28/1958 02:00 CST
4/26/1959 02:00 US#2

IL # 67
Before 11/18/1883 LMT
11/18/1883 12:00 CST
3/31/1918 02:00 CWT
10/27/1918 02:00 CST
3/30/1919 02:00 CWT
10/26/1919 02:00 CST
2/09/1942 02:00 CWT
9/30/1945 02:00 CST
4/27/1958 02:00 US#2

IL # 68
Before 11/18/1883 LMT
11/18/1883 12:00 CST
3/31/1918 02:00 CWT
10/27/1918 02:00 CST
3/30/1919 02:00 CWT
10/26/1919 02:00 CST
2/09/1942 02:00 CWT
9/30/1945 02:00 CST
4/25/1948 02:00 CDT
9/26/1948 02:00 CST
4/24/1949 02:00 CDT
9/25/1949 02:00 CST
4/30/1950 02:00 CDT
9/24/1950 02:00 CST
4/29/1951 02:00 CDT
9/30/1951 02:00 CST
4/27/1952 02:00 CDT
9/28/1952 02:00 CST
4/26/1953 02:00 CDT
9/27/1953 02:00 CST
4/25/1954 02:00 CDT
9/26/1954 02:00 CST
4/24/1955 02:00 CDT
9/25/1955 02:00 CST
4/29/1956 02:00 CDT
9/30/1956 02:00 CST
4/28/1957 02:00 US#2

IL # 69
Before 11/18/1883 LMT
11/18/1883 12:00 CST
3/31/1918 02:00 CWT
10/27/1918 02:00 CST
3/30/1919 02:00 CWT
10/26/1919 02:00 CST
5/04/1941 02:00 CDT
9/28/1941 02:00 CST
2/09/1942 02:00 CWT
9/30/1945 02:00 CST
4/24/1955 02:00 IL#2
4/29/1956 02:00 US#2

IL # 70
Before 11/18/1883 LMT
11/18/1883 12:00 CST
3/31/1918 02:00 CWT
10/27/1918 02:00 CST
3/30/1919 02:00 CWT
10/26/1919 02:00 CST
5/04/1941 02:00 CDT
9/28/1941 02:00 CST
2/09/1942 02:00 CWT
9/30/1945 02:00 CST
4/25/1948 02:00 IL#2
4/29/1956 02:00 US#2

IL # 71
Before 11/18/1883 LMT
11/18/1883 12:00 CST
3/31/1918 02:00 CWT
10/27/1918 02:00 CST
3/30/1919 02:00 CWT
10/26/1919 02:00 CST
4/27/1941 02:00 CDT
9/28/1941 02:00 CST
2/09/1942 02:00 CWT
9/30/1945 02:00 CST
4/24/1955 02:00 US#2

IL # 72
Before 11/18/1883 LMT
11/18/1883 12:00 CST
3/31/1918 02:00 CWT
10/27/1918 02:00 CST
3/30/1919 02:00 CWT
10/26/1919 02:00 CST
4/24/1929 02:00 US#3

IL # 73
Before 11/18/1883 LMT
11/18/1883 12:00 CST
3/31/1918 02:00 CWT
10/27/1918 02:00 CST
3/30/1919 02:00 CWT
10/26/1919 02:00 CST
2/09/1942 02:00 CWT
9/30/1945 02:00 CST
4/25/1954 02:00 CDT
9/26/1954 02:00 CST
4/24/1955 02:00 CDT
9/25/1955 02:00 CST
7/01/1959 02:00 US#2

IL # 74
Before 11/18/1883 LMT
11/18/1883 12:00 IL#6
9/25/1949 02:00 CST
7/01/1959 02:00 US#2

IL # 75
Before 11/18/1883 LMT
11/18/1883 12:00 CST
3/31/1918 02:00 CWT
10/27/1918 02:00 CST
3/30/1919 02:00 CWT
10/26/1919 02:00 CST
2/09/1942 02:00 CWT
9/30/1945 02:00 CST
4/28/1946 02:00 CDT
9/29/1946 02:00 CST
4/24/1955 02:00 IL#3
4/26/1959 02:00 US#2

IL # 76
Before 11/18/1883 LMT
11/18/1883 12:00 CST
3/31/1918 02:00 CWT
10/27/1918 02:00 CST
3/30/1919 02:00 CWT
10/26/1919 02:00 CST
2/09/1942 02:00 CWT

TIME TABLES

9/30/1945 02:00 CST
4/28/1957 02:00 CDT
9/29/1957 02:00 CST
5/25/1958 02:00 CDT
9/28/1958 02:00 CST
4/26/1959 02:00 US#2

IL # 77
Before 11/18/1883 LMT
11/18/1883 12:00 CST
3/31/1918 02:00 CWT
10/27/1918 02:00 CST
3/30/1919 02:00 CWT
10/26/1919 02:00 CST
5/01/1938 02:00 IL#3
4/26/1959 02:00 US#2

IL # 78
Before 11/18/1883 LMT
11/18/1883 12:00 CST
3/31/1918 02:00 CWT
10/27/1918 02:00 CST
3/30/1919 02:00 CWT
10/26/1919 02:00 CST
2/09/1942 02:00 CWT
9/30/1945 02:00 CST
4/25/1954 02:00 CDT
9/26/1954 02:00 CST
4/24/1955 02:00 CDT
9/25/1955 02:00 CST
4/29/1956 02:00 US#2

IL # 79
Before 11/18/1883 LMT
11/18/1883 12:00 CST
3/31/1918 02:00 CWT
10/27/1918 02:00 CST
3/30/1919 02:00 CWT
10/26/1919 02:00 CST
2/09/1942 02:00 CWT
9/30/1945 02:00 CST
4/24/1949 02:00 CDT
9/25/1949 02:00 CST
4/30/1950 02:00 CDT
9/24/1950 02:00 CST
4/29/1951 02:00 CDT
9/30/1951 02:00 CST
4/27/1952 02:00 CDT
9/28/1952 02:00 CST
4/26/1953 02:00 CDT
9/27/1953 02:00 CST
4/25/1954 02:00 CDT
9/26/1954 02:00 CST
4/24/1955 02:00 CDT
9/25/1955 02:00 CST
4/29/1956 02:00 CDT
10/28/1956 02:00 CST
4/28/1957 02:00 CDT
9/29/1957 02:00 IL#3
4/26/1959 02:00 US#2

IL # 80
Before 11/18/1883 LMT
11/18/1883 12:00 CST
3/31/1918 02:00 CWT
10/27/1918 02:00 CST
3/30/1919 02:00 CWT
10/26/1919 02:00 CST
2/09/1942 02:00 CWT
9/30/1945 02:00 CST
4/28/1946 02:00 CDT
9/29/1946 02:00 CST
4/27/1947 02:00 CDT
9/28/1947 02:00 CST
4/25/1948 02:00 CDT
9/26/1948 02:00 CST
4/24/1949 02:00 CDT
9/25/1949 02:00 CST
4/30/1950 02:00 CDT
9/24/1950 02:00 CST
4/29/1951 02:00 CDT
9/30/1951 02:00 CST
4/27/1952 02:00 CDT
9/28/1952 02:00 CST
4/26/1953 02:00 CDT
9/27/1953 02:00 CST
4/25/1954 02:00 CDT
9/26/1954 02:00 CST
4/24/1955 02:00 CDT
9/25/1955 02:00 CST
4/29/1956 02:00 CDT
10/28/1956 02:00 CST
4/28/1957 02:00 IL#3
4/26/1959 02:00 US#2

IL # 81
Before 11/18/1883 LMT
11/18/1883 12:00 CST
3/31/1918 02:00 CWT
10/27/1918 02:00 CST
3/30/1919 02:00 CWT
10/26/1919 02:00 CST
2/09/1942 02:00 CWT
9/30/1945 02:00 CST
4/29/1951 02:00 CDT
9/30/1951 02:00 CST
4/27/1952 02:00 CDT
9/28/1952 02:00 CST
4/26/1953 02:00 CDT
9/27/1953 02:00 CST
4/25/1954 02:00 CDT
9/26/1954 02:00 CST
4/24/1955 02:00 CDT
9/25/1955 02:00 CST
4/29/1956 02:00 CDT
10/28/1956 02:00 CST
4/28/1957 02:00 IL#3
4/26/1959 02:00 US#2

IL # 82
Before 11/18/1883 LMT
11/18/1883 12:00 CST
3/31/1918 02:00 CWT
10/27/1918 02:00 CST
3/30/1919 02:00 CWT
10/26/1919 02:00 CST
4/27/1941 02:00 CDT
9/28/1941 02:00 CST
2/09/1942 02:00 IL#3
4/26/1959 02:00 US#2

IL # 83
Before 11/18/1883 LMT
11/18/1883 12:00 CST
3/31/1918 02:00 CWT
10/27/1918 02:00 CST
3/30/1919 02:00 CWT
10/26/1919 02:00 CST
4/27/1941 02:00 CDT
9/28/1941 02:00 CST
2/09/1942 02:00 CWT
9/30/1945 02:00 CST
4/28/1946 02:00 CDT
9/29/1946 02:00 CST
4/27/1947 02:00 CDT
9/28/1947 02:00 CST
4/25/1948 02:00 CDT
9/26/1948 02:00 CST
4/24/1949 02:00 CDT
9/25/1949 02:00 CST
4/30/1950 02:00 CDT
9/24/1950 02:00 CST
4/29/1951 02:00 CDT
9/30/1951 02:00 CST
4/27/1952 02:00 CDT
9/28/1952 02:00 CST
4/26/1953 02:00 CDT
9/27/1953 02:00 CST
4/25/1954 02:00 CDT
9/26/1954 02:00 CST
4/24/1955 02:00 CDT
9/25/1955 02:00 CST
4/29/1956 02:00 CDT
10/28/1956 02:00 CST
4/28/1957 02:00 IL#3
4/26/1959 02:00 US#2

IL # 84
Before 11/18/1883 LMT
11/18/1883 12:00 CST
3/31/1918 02:00 CWT
10/27/1918 02:00 CST
3/30/1919 02:00 CWT
10/26/1919 02:00 CST
2/09/1942 02:00 CWT
9/30/1945 02:00 CST
4/27/1947 02:00 US#5

IL # 85
Before 11/18/1883 LMT
11/18/1883 12:00 CST
3/31/1918 02:00 CWT
10/27/1918 02:00 CST
3/30/1919 02:00 CWT
10/26/1919 02:00 CST
2/09/1942 02:00 CWT
9/30/1945 02:00 CST
4/29/1956 02:00 CDT
9/30/1956 02:00 CST
4/27/1958 02:00 CDT
9/28/1958 02:00 CST
4/26/1959 02:00 US#2

IL # 86
Before 11/18/1883 LMT
11/18/1883 12:00 CST
3/31/1918 02:00 CWT
10/27/1918 02:00 CST
3/30/1919 02:00 CWT
10/26/1919 02:00 CST
2/09/1942 02:00 CWT
9/30/1945 02:00 CST
4/27/1947 02:00 CDT
9/28/1947 02:00 CST
4/25/1948 02:00 CDT
9/26/1948 02:00 CST
4/24/1949 02:00 CDT
9/25/1949 02:00 CST
4/30/1950 02:00 CDT
9/24/1950 02:00 CST
4/29/1951 02:00 CDT
9/30/1951 02:00 CST
4/27/1952 02:00 CDT
9/28/1952 02:00 CST
4/26/1953 02:00 CDT
9/27/1953 02:00 CST
4/25/1954 02:00 CDT
9/26/1954 02:00 CST
4/24/1955 02:00 CDT
9/25/1955 02:00 CST
4/29/1956 02:00 CDT
10/28/1956 02:00 CST
4/28/1957 02:00 IL#3
4/26/1959 02:00 US#2

IL # 87
Before 11/18/1883 LMT
11/18/1883 12:00 CST
3/31/1918 02:00 CWT
10/27/1918 02:00 CST
3/30/1919 02:00 CWT
10/26/1919 02:00 CST
4/27/1941 02:00 CDT
9/28/1941 02:00 IL#4
7/01/1959 02:00 US#2

IL # 88
Before 11/18/1883 LMT
11/18/1883 12:00 CST
3/31/1918 02:00 CWT
10/27/1918 02:00 CST
3/30/1919 02:00 CWT
10/26/1919 02:00 CST
2/09/1942 02:00 CWT
9/30/1945 02:00 CST
4/29/1956 02:00 CDT
9/30/1956 02:00 CST
7/01/1959 02:00 US#2

IL # 89
Before 11/18/1883 LMT
11/18/1883 12:00 CST
3/31/1918 02:00 CWT
10/27/1918 02:00 CST
3/30/1919 02:00 CWT
10/26/1919 02:00 CST
2/09/1942 02:00 CWT
9/30/1945 02:00 CST
4/24/1955 02:00 CDT
10/30/1955 02:00 CST
4/29/1956 02:00 CDT
10/28/1956 02:00 CST
4/28/1957 02:00 CDT
10/27/1957 02:00 CST
4/27/1958 02:00 CDT
9/28/1958 02:00 CST
4/26/1959 02:00 US#2

IL # 90
Before 11/18/1883 LMT
11/18/1883 12:00 CST
3/31/1918 02:00 CWT
10/27/1918 02:00 CST
3/30/1919 02:00 CWT
10/26/1919 02:00 CST
2/09/1942 02:00 CWT
9/30/1945 02:00 CST
4/24/1955 02:00 CDT
9/25/1955 02:00 CST
4/29/1956 02:00 CDT
9/30/1956 02:00 CST
4/28/1957 02:00 CDT
9/29/1957 02:00 CST
4/27/1958 02:00 US#2

IL # 91
Before 11/18/1883 LMT
11/18/1883 12:00 CST
3/31/1918 02:00 CWT
10/27/1918 02:00 CST
3/30/1919 02:00 CWT
10/26/1919 02:00 CST
2/09/1942 02:00 CWT
9/30/1945 02:00 CST
4/27/1952 02:00 CDT
9/28/1952 02:00 CST
4/26/1953 02:00 CDT
9/27/1953 02:00 CST
4/25/1954 02:00 CDT
9/26/1954 02:00 CST
4/24/1955 02:00 CDT
9/25/1955 02:00 CST
4/29/1956 02:00 CDT
10/28/1956 02:00 CST
4/28/1957 02:00 CDT
10/27/1957 02:00 CST
4/27/1958 02:00 CDT
9/28/1958 02:00 CST
4/26/1959 02:00 US#2

IL # 92
Before 11/18/1883 LMT
11/18/1883 12:00 CST
3/31/1918 02:00 CWT
10/27/1918 02:00 CST
3/30/1919 02:00 CWT
10/26/1919 02:00 CST
4/27/1941 02:00 CDT
9/28/1941 02:00 CST
2/09/1942 02:00 CWT
9/30/1945 02:00 CST
4/28/1946 02:00 CDT
9/29/1946 02:00 CST
4/27/1947 02:00 CDT
9/28/1947 02:00 CST
4/25/1948 02:00 CDT
9/26/1948 02:00 CST
4/24/1949 02:00 CDT
9/25/1949 02:00 CST
4/30/1950 02:00 CDT
9/24/1950 02:00 CST
4/29/1951 02:00 CDT
9/30/1951 02:00 CST
4/27/1952 02:00 CDT
9/28/1952 02:00 CST
4/26/1953 02:00 CDT
9/27/1953 02:00 CST
4/25/1954 02:00 CDT
9/26/1954 02:00 CST
4/24/1955 02:00 US#4

IL # 93
Before 11/18/1883 LMT
11/18/1883 12:00 CST
3/31/1918 02:00 CWT
10/27/1918 02:00 CST
3/30/1919 02:00 CWT
10/26/1919 02:00 CST
2/09/1942 02:00 CWT
9/30/1945 02:00 CST
4/26/1953 02:00 CDT
9/27/1953 02:00 CST
4/25/1954 02:00 CDT
9/26/1954 02:00 CST
4/24/1955 02:00 CDT
9/25/1955 02:00 CST
4/29/1956 02:00 US#2

IL # 94
Before 11/18/1883 LMT
11/18/1883 12:00 CST
3/31/1918 02:00 CWT
10/27/1918 02:00 CST
3/30/1919 02:00 CWT
10/26/1919 02:00 CST
2/09/1942 02:00 CWT
9/30/1945 02:00 CST
4/24/1955 02:00 CDT
9/25/1955 02:00 CST
4/29/1956 02:00 CDT
9/30/1956 02:00 CST
7/01/1959 02:00 US#2

IL # 95
Before 11/18/1883 LMT
11/18/1883 12:00 CST
3/31/1918 02:00 CWT
10/27/1918 02:00 CST
3/30/1919 02:00 CWT
10/26/1919 02:00 CST
6/13/1920 02:00 CDT
10/31/1920 02:00 CST
3/27/1921 02:00 CDT
10/30/1921 02:00 CST
4/30/1922 02:00 CDT
9/24/1922 02:00 CST
4/29/1923 02:00 CDT
9/30/1923 02:00 CST
4/27/1924 02:00 CDT
9/28/1924 02:00 CST
4/26/1925 02:00 CDT
9/27/1925 02:00 CST
4/25/1926 02:00 CDT
9/26/1926 02:00 CST
4/24/1927 02:00 CDT
9/25/1927 02:00 CST
4/29/1928 02:00 CDT
9/30/1928 02:00 CST
4/28/1929 02:00 CDT
9/29/1929 02:00 CST
4/27/1930 02:00 CDT
9/28/1930 02:00 CST
4/26/1931 02:00 CDT
9/27/1931 02:00 CST
4/24/1932 02:00 CDT
9/25/1932 02:00 CST
4/30/1933 02:00 CDT
9/24/1933 02:00 CST
4/29/1934 02:00 CDT
9/30/1934 02:00 CST
4/28/1935 02:00 CDT
9/29/1935 02:00 CST
4/26/1936 02:00 CDT
9/27/1936 02:00 CST
4/25/1937 02:00 CDT
9/26/1937 02:00 CST
4/24/1938 02:00 CDT
9/25/1938 02:00 CST
4/30/1939 02:00 CDT
9/24/1939 02:00 CST
4/28/1940 02:00 CDT
9/29/1940 02:00 CST
4/27/1941 02:00 CDT
9/28/1941 02:00 IL#3
4/26/1959 02:00 US#2

IL # 96
Before 11/18/1883 LMT
11/18/1883 12:00 CST
3/31/1918 02:00 CWT
10/27/1918 02:00 CST
3/30/1919 02:00 CWT
10/26/1919 02:00 CST
2/09/1942 02:00 CWT
9/30/1945 02:00 CST
4/24/1949 02:00 CDT
9/25/1949 02:00 CST
4/30/1950 02:00 CDT
9/24/1950 02:00 CST
4/29/1951 02:00 CDT
9/30/1951 02:00 CST
4/27/1952 02:00 CDT
9/28/1952 02:00 CST
4/26/1953 02:00 CDT
9/27/1953 02:00 CST
4/25/1954 02:00 CDT
9/26/1954 02:00 CST
4/24/1955 02:00 IL#3
4/26/1959 02:00 US#2

IL # 97
Before 11/18/1883 LMT
11/18/1883 12:00 CST
3/31/1918 02:00 CWT
10/27/1918 02:00 CST
3/30/1919 02:00 CWT
10/26/1919 02:00 CST
2/09/1942 02:00 CWT
9/30/1945 02:00 CST
4/27/1947 02:00 CDT
9/28/1947 02:00 CST
4/25/1948 02:00 CDT
9/26/1948 02:00 CST
4/24/1949 02:00 CDT
9/25/1949 02:00 CST
4/30/1950 02:00 CDT
9/30/1950 02:00 IL#2
4/29/1956 02:00 US#2

IL # 98
Before 11/18/1883 LMT
11/18/1883 12:00 CST
3/31/1918 02:00 CWT
10/27/1918 02:00 CST
3/30/1919 02:00 CWT
10/26/1919 02:00 CST
5/05/1940 02:00 CDT
9/29/1940 02:00 CST
4/27/1941 02:00 CDT
9/28/1941 02:00 IL#2
4/29/1956 02:00 US#2

IL # 99
Before 11/18/1883 LMT
11/18/1883 12:00 CST
3/31/1918 02:00 CWT
10/27/1918 02:00 CST
3/30/1919 02:00 CWT
10/26/1919 02:00 CST
5/05/1940 02:00 CDT
9/29/1940 02:00 CST
4/27/1941 02:00 CDT
9/28/1941 02:00 CST
2/09/1942 02:00 US#4

IL # 100
Before 11/18/1883 LMT
11/18/1883 12:00 IL#1
4/26/1931 02:00 CDT
10/25/1931 02:00 IL#1
9/28/1941 02:00 US#2

IL # 101
Before 11/18/1883 LMT
11/18/1883 12:00 CST
3/31/1918 02:00 CWT
10/27/1918 02:00 CST
3/30/1919 02:00 CWT
10/26/1919 02:00 CST
6/13/1920 00:01 CDT
10/31/1920 00:01 CST
3/27/1921 00:01 CDT
10/30/1921 00:01 CST
4/30/1922 00:01 CDT
9/24/1922 00:01 CST
4/29/1923 00:01 CDT
9/30/1923 00:01 CST
4/27/1924 00:01 CDT
9/28/1924 00:01 CST
4/26/1925 00:01 CDT
9/27/1925 00:01 CST
4/25/1926 00:01 CDT
9/26/1926 00:01 CST
4/24/1927 00:01 CDT
9/25/1927 00:01 CST
4/29/1928 00:01 CDT
9/30/1928 00:01 CST
4/28/1929 00:01 CDT
9/29/1929 00:01 CST
4/27/1930 00:01 CDT
9/28/1930 00:01 CST
4/26/1931 00:01 CDT
9/27/1931 00:01 CST
4/24/1932 00:01 CDT
9/25/1932 00:01 CST
4/30/1933 00:01 CDT
9/24/1933 00:01 CST
4/29/1934 00:01 CDT
9/30/1934 00:01 CST
4/28/1935 00:01 CDT
9/29/1935 00:01 CST
3/01/1936 00:01 CDT
11/01/1936 00:01 CST
5/08/1937 00:01 CDT
9/26/1937 00:01 CST
5/01/1938 00:01 CDT
9/25/1938 00:01 CST
5/07/1939 00:01 CDT
9/24/1939 00:01 CST
5/05/1940 00:01 CDT
9/29/1940 00:01 CST
5/04/1941 00:01 CDT
9/28/1941 00:01 CST
9/28/1941 02:00 IL#3
4/26/1959 02:00 US#2

IL # 102
Before 11/18/1883 LMT
11/18/1883 12:00 CST
3/31/1918 02:00 CWT
10/27/1918 02:00 CST
3/30/1919 02:00 CWT
10/26/1919 02:00 CST
4/30/1933 00:01 CDT
9/24/1933 00:01 CST
4/29/1934 00:01 CDT
9/30/1934 00:01 CST
4/28/1935 00:01 CDT
9/29/1935 00:01 CST
4/26/1936 00:01 CDT
9/27/1936 00:01 CST
5/08/1937 00:01 CDT
9/26/1937 00:01 CST
5/01/1938 00:01 CDT
9/25/1938 00:01 CST
5/07/1939 00:01 CDT
9/24/1939 00:01 CST
5/05/1940 00:01 CDT
9/29/1940 00:01 CST
5/04/1941 00:01 CDT
9/28/1941 00:01 CST
9/28/1941 02:00 US#3

IL # 103
Before 11/18/1883 LMT
11/18/1883 12:00 CST
3/31/1918 02:00 CWT
10/27/1918 02:00 CST
3/30/1919 02:00 CWT
10/26/1919 02:00 CST
4/29/1928 02:00 CDT
9/30/1928 02:00 CST
4/24/1932 02:00 CDT
9/25/1932 02:00 CST
4/30/1933 02:00 CDT
9/24/1933 02:00 CST
4/29/1934 02:00 CDT
9/30/1934 02:00 CST
4/28/1935 02:00 CDT
9/29/1935 02:00 CST

TIME TABLES

4/26/1936 02:00 CDT
9/27/1936 02:00 CST
4/25/1937 02:00 CDT
9/26/1937 02:00 CST
4/24/1938 02:00 CDT
9/25/1938 02:00 CST
4/30/1939 02:00 CDT
9/24/1939 02:00 CST
4/28/1940 02:00 CDT
9/29/1940 02:00 CST
4/27/1941 02:00 CDT
9/28/1941 02:00 CST
2/09/1942 02:00 CWT
9/30/1945 02:00 CST
4/28/1946 02:00 CDT
9/29/1946 02:00 CST
4/27/1947 02:00 CDT
9/28/1947 02:00 CST
4/25/1948 02:00 CDT
9/26/1948 02:00 CST
4/24/1949 02:00 CDT
9/25/1949 02:00 CST
4/30/1950 02:00 CDT
9/24/1950 02:00 CST
4/29/1951 02:00 CDT
9/30/1951 02:00 CST
4/27/1952 02:00 CDT
9/28/1952 02:00 CST
4/26/1953 02:00 CDT
9/27/1953 02:00 CST
4/25/1954 02:00 CDT
9/26/1954 02:00 CST
4/24/1955 02:00 CDT
9/25/1955 02:00 CST
4/29/1956 02:00 US#2
....
IL # 104
Before 11/18/1883 LMT
11/18/1883 12:00 CST
3/31/1918 02:00 CWT
10/27/1918 02:00 CST
3/30/1919 02:00 CWT
10/26/1919 02:00 CST
5/17/1940 02:00 CDT
9/29/1940 02:00 CST
4/27/1941 02:00 CDT
9/28/1941 02:00 IL#2
4/29/1956 02:00 US#2
....
IL # 105
Before 11/18/1883 LMT
11/18/1883 12:00 CST
3/31/1918 02:00 CWT
10/27/1918 02:00 CST
3/30/1919 02:00 CWT
10/26/1919 02:00 CST
6/13/1920 02:00 CDT
10/31/1920 02:00 CST
4/30/1933 00:01 CDT
9/24/1933 00:01 CST
4/29/1934 00:01 CDT
9/30/1934 00:01 CST
4/28/1935 00:01 CDT
9/29/1935 00:01 CST
4/26/1936 00:01 CDT
9/27/1936 00:01 CST
5/08/1937 00:01 CDT
9/26/1937 00:01 CST
5/01/1938 00:01 CDT
9/25/1938 00:01 CST
5/07/1939 00:01 CDT
9/24/1939 00:01 CST
5/05/1940 00:01 CDT
9/29/1940 00:01 CST
4/27/1941 00:01 CDT
9/28/1941 00:01 IL#7
4/26/1959 02:00 US#2
....
IL # 106
Before 11/18/1883 LMT
11/18/1883 12:00 CST
3/31/1918 02:00 CWT
10/27/1918 02:00 CST
3/30/1919 02:00 CWT
10/26/1919 02:00 CST
2/09/1942 02:00 CWT
9/30/1945 02:00 CST
5/05/1946 02:00 CDT
9/29/1946 02:00 CST
4/27/1947 02:00 IL#3
4/26/1959 02:00 US#2
....
IL # 107
Before 11/18/1883 LMT
11/18/1883 12:00 IL#1
10/31/1920 02:00 CST
4/30/1933 00:01 CDT
9/24/1933 00:01 CST
4/29/1934 00:01 CDT
9/30/1934 00:01 CST
4/28/1935 00:01 CDT
9/29/1935 00:01 CST
4/26/1936 00:01 CDT
9/27/1936 00:01 CST
4/25/1937 00:01 CDT
9/26/1937 00:01 CST
4/24/1938 00:01 CDT
9/25/1938 00:01 CST
4/30/1939 00:01 CDT
9/24/1939 00:01 CST
4/28/1940 00:01 CDT
9/29/1940 00:01 CST
4/27/1941 00:01 CDT
9/28/1941 00:01 CST
2/09/1942 02:00 CWT
9/30/1945 02:00 CST
4/28/1946 02:00 IL#2
4/29/1956 02:00 US#2
....
IL # 108
Before 11/18/1883 LMT
11/18/1883 12:00 CST
3/31/1918 02:00 CWT
10/27/1918 02:00 CST
3/30/1919 02:00 CWT
10/26/1919 02:00 CST
2/09/1942 02:00 CWT
9/30/1945 02:00 CST
4/28/1946 02:00 CDT
9/29/1946 02:00 CST
4/27/1947 02:00 CDT
10/25/1947 02:00 CST
4/25/1948 02:00 IL#2
4/29/1956 02:00 US#2
....
IL # 109
Before 11/18/1883 LMT
11/18/1883 12:00 IL#1
4/27/1941 02:00 CDT
9/28/1941 02:00 CST
2/09/1942 02:00 CWT
9/30/1945 02:00 CST
4/28/1946 02:00 CDT
9/29/1946 02:00 CST
4/27/1947 02:00 CDT
10/29/1947 02:00 IL#2
4/29/1956 02:00 US#2
....
IL # 110
Before 11/18/1883 LMT
11/18/1883 12:00 CST
3/31/1918 02:00 CWT
10/27/1918 02:00 CST
3/30/1919 02:00 CWT
10/26/1919 02:00 CST
2/09/1942 02:00 CWT
9/30/1945 02:00 CST
4/27/1947 02:00 CDT
10/29/1947 02:00 CST
4/25/1948 02:00 CDT
9/26/1948 02:00 CST
4/24/1949 02:00 CDT
9/25/1949 02:00 CST
4/30/1950 02:00 CDT
9/24/1950 02:00 CST
4/29/1951 02:00 CDT
9/30/1951 02:00 CST
4/27/1952 02:00 CDT
9/28/1952 02:00 CST
4/26/1953 02:00 CDT
9/27/1953 02:00 CST
4/25/1954 02:00 CDT
9/26/1954 02:00 CST
4/24/1955 02:00 CDT
9/25/1955 02:00 CST
4/29/1956 02:00 IL#3
4/26/1959 02:00 US#2
....
IL # 111
Before 11/18/1883 LMT
11/18/1883 12:00 IL#7
9/26/1948 02:00 CST
5/29/1949 02:00 CDT
9/03/1949 02:00 CST
4/30/1950 02:00 IL#7
4/26/1959 02:00 US#2
....
IL # 112
Before 11/18/1883 LMT
11/18/1883 12:00 CST
3/31/1918 02:00 CWT
10/27/1918 02:00 CST
3/30/1919 02:00 CWT
10/26/1919 02:00 CST
2/09/1942 02:00 CWT
9/30/1945 02:00 CST
4/27/1947 02:00 CDT
9/28/1947 02:00 CST
4/25/1948 02:00 CDT
10/30/1948 02:00 IL#3
4/26/1959 02:00 US#2
....
IL # 113
Before 11/18/1883 LMT
11/18/1883 12:00 CST
3/31/1918 02:00 CWT
10/27/1918 02:00 CST
3/30/1919 02:00 CWT
10/26/1919 02:00 CST
5/05/1940 02:00 CDT
9/29/1940 02:00 CST
2/09/1942 02:00 CWT
9/30/1945 02:00 CST
4/28/1946 02:00 CDT
9/29/1946 02:00 CST
4/27/1947 02:00 CDT
9/28/1947 02:00 CST
4/25/1948 02:00 CDT
9/26/1948 02:00 CST
4/24/1949 02:00 CDT
9/26/1949 02:00 US#4
....
IL # 114
Before 11/18/1883 LMT
11/18/1883 12:00 CST
3/31/1918 02:00 CWT
10/27/1918 02:00 CST
3/30/1919 02:00 CWT
10/26/1919 02:00 CST
4/28/1935 02:00 CDT
9/29/1935 02:00 CST
4/26/1936 02:00 CDT
9/27/1936 02:00 CST
4/25/1937 02:00 CDT
9/26/1937 02:00 CST
4/24/1938 02:00 CDT
9/25/1938 02:00 CST
4/30/1939 02:00 CDT
9/24/1939 02:00 CST
4/28/1940 02:00 CDT
9/29/1940 02:00 CST
4/27/1941 02:00 CDT
10/26/1941 02:00 CST
2/09/1942 02:00 CWT
9/30/1945 02:00 CST
4/28/1946 02:00 IL#2
4/29/1956 02:00 US#2
....
IL # 115
Before 11/18/1883 LMT
11/18/1883 12:00 CST
3/31/1918 02:00 CWT
10/27/1918 02:00 CST
3/30/1919 02:00 CWT
10/26/1919 02:00 CST
4/27/1941 02:00 CDT
10/26/1941 02:00 CST
2/09/1942 02:00 CWT
9/30/1945 02:00 CST
4/28/1946 02:00 IL#2
4/29/1956 02:00 US#2
....
IL # 116
Before 11/18/1883 LMT
11/18/1883 12:00 IL#1
10/04/1936 02:00 CST
4/25/1937 02:00 CDT
9/26/1937 02:00 CST
4/24/1938 02:00 CDT
9/25/1938 02:00 CST
4/30/1939 02:00 CDT
9/24/1939 02:00 CST
4/28/1940 02:00 CDT
9/29/1940 02:00 CST
4/27/1941 02:00 CDT
9/28/1941 02:00 CST
2/09/1942 02:00 CWT
9/30/1945 02:00 CST
4/28/1946 02:00 CDT
9/29/1946 02:00 CST
4/27/1947 02:00 CDT
9/28/1947 02:00 CST
4/25/1948 02:00 CDT
9/26/1948 02:00 CST
4/24/1949 02:00 CDT
9/25/1949 02:00 CST
4/30/1950 02:00 CDT
9/24/1950 02:00 CST
4/29/1951 02:00 CDT
9/30/1951 02:00 CST
4/27/1952 02:00 CDT
9/28/1952 02:00 CST
4/26/1953 02:00 CDT
9/27/1953 02:00 CST
4/25/1954 02:00 CDT
9/26/1954 02:00 CST
4/24/1955 02:00 CDT
9/25/1955 02:00 CST
4/29/1956 02:00 US#2
....
IL # 117
Before 11/18/1883 LMT
11/18/1883 12:00 CST
3/31/1918 02:00 CWT
10/27/1918 02:00 CST
3/30/1919 02:00 CWT
10/26/1919 02:00 CST
5/25/1941 02:00 CDT
9/28/1941 02:00 IL#6
4/28/1946 02:00 US#2
....
IL # 118
Before 11/18/1883 LMT
11/18/1883 12:00 CST
3/31/1918 02:00 CWT
10/27/1918 02:00 CST
3/30/1919 02:00 CWT
10/26/1919 02:00 CST
5/13/1940 02:00 CDT
9/29/1940 02:00 CST
4/27/1941 02:00 CDT
9/28/1941 02:00 IL#2
4/29/1956 02:00 US#2
....
IL # 119
Before 11/18/1883 LMT
11/18/1883 12:00 CST
3/31/1918 02:00 CWT
10/27/1918 02:00 CST
3/30/1919 02:00 CWT
10/26/1919 02:00 CST
5/12/1941 02:00 CDT
10/26/1941 02:00 CST
2/09/1942 02:00 CWT
9/30/1945 02:00 CST
4/28/1946 02:00 IL#2
4/29/1956 02:00 US#2
....
IL # 120
Before 11/18/1883 LMT
11/18/1883 12:00 CST
3/31/1918 02:00 CWT
10/27/1918 02:00 CST
3/30/1919 02:00 CWT
10/26/1919 02:00 CST
5/25/1941 02:00 CDT
9/25/1941 02:00 IL#7
4/26/1959 02:00 US#2
....
IL # 121
Before 11/18/1883 LMT
11/18/1883 12:00 CST
3/31/1918 02:00 CWT
10/27/1918 02:00 CST
3/30/1919 02:00 CWT
10/26/1919 02:00 CST
2/09/1942 02:00 CWT
9/30/1945 02:00 CST
4/27/1947 02:00 CDT
9/28/1947 02:00 CST
4/25/1948 02:00 CDT
9/26/1948 02:00 CST
4/24/1949 02:00 CDT
9/25/1949 02:00 CST
4/30/1950 02:00 CDT
9/24/1950 02:00 CST
4/29/1951 02:00 CDT
9/30/1951 02:00 CST
4/27/1952 02:00 CDT
9/28/1952 02:00 CST
4/26/1953 02:00 CDT
9/27/1953 02:00 CST
4/25/1954 02:00 CDT
9/26/1954 02:00 CST
4/24/1955 02:00 CDT
9/25/1955 02:00 CST
6/01/1956 02:00 CDT
9/01/1956 02:00 CST
4/28/1957 02:00 IL#3
4/26/1959 02:00 US#2
....
IL # 122
Before 11/18/1883 LMT
11/18/1883 12:00 CST
3/31/1918 02:00 CWT
10/27/1918 02:00 CST
3/30/1919 02:00 CWT
10/26/1919 02:00 CST
2/09/1942 02:00 CWT
9/30/1945 02:00 CST
4/25/1954 02:00 CDT
9/26/1954 02:00 CST
4/24/1955 02:00 CDT
9/25/1955 02:00 CST
4/29/1956 02:00 CDT
9/30/1956 02:00 CST
4/28/1957 02:00 CDT
9/29/1957 02:00 CST
5/01/1958 02:00 CDT
10/01/1958 02:00 CST
4/26/1959 02:00 US#2
....
IL # 123
Before 11/18/1883 LMT
11/18/1883 12:00 CST
3/31/1918 02:00 CWT
10/27/1918 02:00 CST
3/30/1919 02:00 CWT
10/26/1919 02:00 CST
6/04/1941 02:00 CDT
9/28/1941 02:00 CST
2/09/1942 02:00 CWT
9/30/1945 02:00 CST
4/28/1946 02:00 IL#2
4/29/1956 02:00 US#2
....
IL # 124
Before 11/18/1883 LMT
11/18/1883 12:00 CST
3/31/1918 02:00 CWT
10/27/1918 02:00 CST
3/30/1919 02:00 CWT
10/26/1919 02:00 CST
6/01/1941 02:00 CDT
9/18/1941 02:00 IL#7
4/26/1959 02:00 US#2
....
IL # 125
Before 11/18/1883 LMT
11/18/1883 12:00 CST
3/31/1918 02:00 CWT
10/27/1918 02:00 CST
3/30/1919 02:00 CWT
10/26/1919 02:00 CST
5/11/1941 02:00 CDT
10/26/1941 02:00 CST
2/09/1942 02:00 CWT
9/30/1945 02:00 CST
4/28/1946 02:00 IL#2
4/29/1956 02:00 US#2
....
IL # 126
Before 11/18/1883 LMT
11/18/1883 12:00 CST
3/31/1918 02:00 CWT
10/27/1918 02:00 CST
3/30/1919 02:00 CWT
10/26/1919 02:00 CST
4/24/1938 02:00 CDT
9/25/1938 02:00 CST
4/30/1939 02:00 CDT
9/24/1939 02:00 CST
4/28/1940 02:00 CDT
9/29/1940 02:00 CST
4/27/1941 02:00 CDT
10/26/1941 02:00 CST
2/09/1942 02:00 CWT
9/30/1945 02:00 CST
4/28/1946 02:00 US#2
....
IL # 127
Before 11/18/1883 LMT
11/18/1883 12:00 CST
3/31/1918 02:00 CWT
10/27/1918 02:00 CST
3/30/1919 02:00 CWT
10/26/1919 02:00 CST
6/08/1941 02:00 CDT
9/28/1941 02:00 IL#7
4/26/1959 02:00 US#2
....
IL # 128
Before 11/18/1883 LMT
11/18/1883 12:00 IL#6
9/27/1953 02:00 CST
5/01/1954 02:00 CDT
10/02/1954 02:00 CST
4/24/1955 02:00 IL#3
4/26/1959 02:00 US#2
....
IL # 129
Before 11/18/1883 LMT
11/18/1883 12:00 IL#6
9/26/1948 02:00 CST
5/29/1949 02:00 CDT
9/03/1949 02:00 CST
4/30/1950 02:00 CDT
9/01/1950 02:00 CST
4/29/1951 02:00 IL#2
4/29/1956 02:00 US#2
....
IL # 130
Before 11/18/1883 LMT
11/18/1883 12:00 CST
3/31/1918 02:00 CWT
10/27/1918 02:00 CST
3/30/1919 02:00 CWT
10/26/1919 02:00 CST
6/01/1941 00:01 CDT
9/28/1941 00:01 IL#6
4/28/1946 02:00 US#2
....
IL # 131
Before 11/18/1883 LMT
11/18/1883 12:00 IL#7
9/07/1958 02:00 CST
1/01/1959 02:00 US#2
....
IL # 132
Before 11/18/1883 LMT
11/18/1883 12:00 CST
3/31/1918 02:00 CWT
10/27/1918 02:00 CST
3/30/1919 02:00 CWT
10/26/1919 02:00 CST
2/09/1942 02:00 CWT
9/30/1945 02:00 CST
4/27/1947 02:00 CDT
9/28/1947 02:00 CST
4/25/1948 02:00 CDT
9/26/1948 02:00 CST
4/24/1949 02:00 CDT
9/03/1949 02:00 CST
4/30/1950 02:00 CDT
9/03/1950 02:00 CST
4/29/1951 02:00 IL#2
4/29/1956 02:00 US#2
....
IL # 133
Before 11/18/1883 LMT
11/18/1883 12:00 CST
3/31/1918 02:00 CWT
10/27/1918 02:00 CST
3/30/1919 02:00 CWT
10/26/1919 02:00 CST
5/24/1940 02:00 CDT
9/29/1940 02:00 CST
2/09/1942 02:00 CWT
9/30/1945 02:00 CST
4/28/1946 02:00 CDT
9/29/1946 02:00 CST
4/27/1947 02:00 CDT
9/28/1947 02:00 CST
4/25/1948 02:00 CDT
9/26/1948 02:00 CST
4/24/1949 02:00 CDT
10/02/1949 02:00 CST
4/30/1950 02:00 CDT
9/24/1950 02:00 CST
4/29/1951 02:00 CDT
9/30/1951 02:00 CST
4/27/1952 02:00 CDT
9/28/1952 02:00 CST
4/26/1953 02:00 CDT
9/27/1953 02:00 CST
4/25/1954 02:00 CDT
9/26/1954 02:00 CST
4/24/1955 02:00 CDT
10/30/1955 02:00 CST
4/29/1956 02:00 IL#3
4/26/1959 02:00 US#2
....
IL # 134
Before 11/18/1883 LMT
11/18/1883 12:00 CST
3/31/1918 02:00 CWT
10/27/1918 02:00 CST
3/30/1919 02:00 CWT
10/26/1919 02:00 CST
6/01/1941 02:00 CDT
9/28/1941 02:00 CST
2/09/1942 02:00 CWT
9/30/1945 02:00 CST
4/28/1946 02:00 IL#2
4/29/1956 02:00 US#2
....
IL # 135
Before 11/18/1883 LMT
11/18/1883 12:00 CST
3/31/1918 02:00 CWT
10/27/1918 02:00 CST
3/30/1919 02:00 CWT
10/26/1919 02:00 CST
5/25/1941 02:00 CDT
9/28/1941 02:00 CST
2/09/1942 02:00 CWT
9/30/1945 02:00 CST
4/28/1946 02:00 CDT
9/29/1946 02:00 CST
4/27/1947 02:00 CDT
9/28/1947 02:00 CST
4/25/1948 02:00 CDT
9/26/1948 02:00 CST
4/24/1949 02:00 CDT
9/25/1949 02:00 CST
4/30/1950 02:00 CDT
9/24/1950 02:00 CST
4/29/1951 02:00 CDT
9/30/1951 02:00 CST
4/27/1952 02:00 CDT

TIME TABLES

9/28/1952 02:00 CST
4/26/1953 02:00 CDT
9/27/1953 02:00 CST
4/25/1954 02:00 CDT
9/26/1954 02:00 CST
4/24/1955 02:00 US#4
....
IL # 136
Before 11/18/1883 LMT
11/18/1883 12:00 CST
3/31/1918 02:00 CWT
10/27/1918 02:00 CST
3/30/1919 02:00 CWT
10/26/1919 02:00 CST
6/08/1941 02:00 CDT
9/28/1941 02:00 CST
2/09/1942 02:00 CWT
9/30/1945 02:00 CST
4/28/1946 02:00 CDT
9/29/1946 02:00 CST
4/27/1947 02:00 CDT
9/28/1947 02:00 CST
4/25/1948 02:00 CDT
9/26/1948 02:00 CST
4/24/1949 02:00 CDT
9/25/1949 02:00 CST
4/30/1950 02:00 CDT
9/24/1950 02:00 CST
4/29/1951 02:00 CDT
9/30/1951 02:00 CST
4/27/1952 02:00 CDT
9/28/1952 02:00 CST
4/26/1953 02:00 CDT
9/27/1953 02:00 CST
4/25/1954 02:00 CDT
9/26/1954 02:00 CST
4/24/1955 02:00 IL#2
4/29/1956 02:00 US#2
....
IL # 137
Before 11/18/1883 LMT
11/18/1883 12:00 CST
3/31/1918 02:00 CWT
10/27/1918 02:00 CST
3/30/1919 02:00 CWT
10/26/1919 02:00 CST
2/09/1942 02:00 CWT
9/30/1945 02:00 CST
4/29/1956 02:00 CDT
9/30/1956 02:00 CST
4/28/1957 02:00 CDT
9/29/1957 02:00 CST
5/01/1958 02:00 CDT
8/31/1958 02:00 CST
1/01/1959 02:00 US#2
....
IL # 138
Before 11/18/1883 LMT
11/18/1883 12:00 CST
3/31/1918 02:00 CWT
10/27/1918 02:00 CST
3/30/1919 02:00 CWT
10/26/1919 02:00 CST
5/26/1940 02:00 CDT
9/29/1940 02:00 IL#6
4/28/1946 02:00 US#2
....
IL # 139
Before 11/18/1883 LMT
11/18/1883 12:00 CST
3/31/1918 02:00 CWT
10/27/1918 02:00 CST
3/30/1919 02:00 CWT
10/26/1919 02:00 CST
2/09/1942 02:00 CWT
9/30/1945 02:00 CST
4/28/1946 02:00 CDT
9/29/1946 02:00 CST
5/01/1947 02:00 CDT
9/01/1947 02:00 CST
4/24/1955 02:00 CDT
10/30/1955 02:00 CST
4/29/1956 02:00 CDT
10/28/1956 02:00 CST
4/25/1957 02:00 IL#3
4/26/1959 02:00 US#2
....
IL # 140
Before 11/18/1883 LMT
11/18/1883 12:00 IL#1
10/26/1919 02:00 CST
4/27/1921 02:00 CDT
10/03/1921 02:00 CST
4/30/1922 02:00 IL#2
4/29/1956 02:00 US#2
....
IL # 141
Before 11/18/1883 LMT
11/18/1883 12:00 CST
3/31/1918 02:00 CWT
10/27/1918 02:00 CST
3/30/1919 02:00 CWT
10/26/1919 02:00 CST
2/09/1942 02:00 CWT
9/30/1945 02:00 CST
4/27/1952 02:00 CDT
9/28/1952 02:00 CST
5/01/1955 02:00 CDT
9/25/1955 02:00 CST
4/29/1956 02:00 IL#3
4/26/1959 02:00 US#2
....
IL # 142
Before 11/18/1883 LMT
11/18/1883 12:00 CST
3/31/1918 02:00 CWT
10/27/1918 02:00 CST
3/30/1919 02:00 CWT
10/26/1919 02:00 CST
6/21/1920 00:01 CDT
10/04/1920 00:01 CST
3/27/1921 02:00 IL#2
4/29/1956 02:00 US#2

COUNTIES

1 Adams
2 Alexander
3 Bond
4 Boone
5 Brown
6 Bureau
7 Calhoun
8 Carroll
9 Cass
10 Champaign
11 Christian
12 Clark
13 Clay
14 Clinton
15 Coles
16 Cook
17 Crawford
18 Cumberland
19 De Kalb
20 De Witt
21 Douglas
22 Du Page
23 Edgar
24 Edwards
25 Effingham
26 Fayette
27 Ford
28 Franklin
29 Fulton
30 Gallatin
31 Greene
32 Grundy
33 Hamilton
34 Hancock
35 Hardin
36 Henderson
37 Henry
38 Iroquois
39 Jackson
40 Jasper
41 Jefferson
42 Jersey
43 Jo Daviess
44 Johnson
45 Kane
46 Kankakee
47 Kendall
48 Knox
49 Lake
50 La Salle
51 Lawrence
52 Lee
53 Livingston
54 Logan
55 McDonough
56 McHenry
57 McLean
58 Macon
59 Macoupin
60 Madison
61 Marion
62 Marshall
63 Mason
64 Massac
65 Menard
66 Mercer
67 Monroe
68 Montgomery
69 Morgan
70 Moultrie
71 Ogle
72 Peoria
73 Perry
74 Piatt
75 Pike
76 Pope
77 Pulaski
78 Putnam
79 Randolph
80 Richland
81 Rock Island
82 St Clair
83 Saline
84 Sangamon
85 Schuyler
86 Scott
87 Shelby
88 Stark
89 Stephenson
90 Tazewell
91 Union
92 Vermilion
93 Wabash
94 Warren
95 Washington
96 Wayne
97 White
98 Whiteside
99 Will
100 Williamson
101 Winnebago
102 Woodford

Abbot 76 4 37N33'26 88w41'56 5:54:48
Abingdon 48 24 40N48'16 90w24'06 6:01:36
Abington 66 4 41N07 90w50 6:03:20
Acacia Acres 16 1 41N48 87w52 5:51:28
Acme Station 72 98 40N40 89w40 5:58:40
Adair 55 4 40N25'08 90w29'48 6:01:59
Adams 1 66 39N51'55 91w11'53 6:04:48
Adams 50 26 41N35 88w45 5:55:00
Adams Corner 93 4 38N30'47 87w44'31 5:50:58
Addatorata Village 16 21 42N08'54 87w56'25 5:51:46
Addieville 95 4 38N23'29 89w29'24 5:57:58
Addison 22 17 41N55'54 87w59'20 5:51:57
Addison Lake Manor 22 17 41N56 88w00 5:52:00
Adeline 71 63 42N08'36 89w29'25 5:57:58
Aden 33 4 38N14'30 88w27'30 5:53:50
Adrian 34 4 40N31'15 91w10'01 6:04:40
Advance 40 4 39N09'24 88w01'44 5:52:07
Aero Estates 22 12 41N47 88w09 5:52:36
Aetna 15 63 39N24 88w19 5:53:16
Aetna 54 55 40N05 89w12 5:56:48
Afolkey 89 4 42N25'57 89w34'28 5:58:18
Afton 19 60 41N51 88w46 5:55:04
Agnew 98 26 41N47'12 89w48'00 5:59:12
Ahern 46 82 41N09'15 87w36'17 5:50:25
Aiken 43 4 42N21'09 90w24'55 6:01:40
Akin 28 4 37N59'16 88w45'08 5:55:01
Akin Junction 28 4 38N00'36 88w45'41 5:55:03
Akron 72 57 40N54'14 89w39'14 5:58:37
Aladdin 75 66 39N42'59 91w19'23 6:05:18
Alan Dale 60 7 38N57 90w11 6:00:44
Alba 37 4 41N26 89w55 5:59:40
Albany 98 4 41N47'22 90w13'09 6:00:53
Albers 14 49 38N32'36 89w36'44 5:58:27
Albion 24 4 38N22'39 88w03'22 5:52:13
Albright 12 55 39N23 87w42 5:50:48
Alda 95 4 38N27'46 89w14'12 5:56:57
Alden 56 7 42N27'32 88w31'04 5:54:04
Aldridge 91 4 37N33'30 89w28'12 5:57:53
Aledo 66 4 41N11'59 90w44'57 6:03:00
Alexander 69 4 39N43'28 90w02'17 6:00:09
Alexis 94 4 41N03'48 90w33'21 6:02:13
Alexis Junction 94 4 41N04'02 90w38'18 6:02:33
Algonquin 56 1 42N09'56 88w17'39 5:53:11
Algonquin Trails 16 6 42N04 87w57 5:51:48
Alhambra 60 37 38N53'18 89w43'53 5:58:56
Aliceville 37 4 41N33'08 89w52'46 5:59:31
Allen 50 56 41N09 88w38 5:54:32
Allen 63 29 40N18'18 89w38'58 5:58:36
Allendale 60 7 38N57 90w11 6:00:44
Allendale 93 4 38N31'36 87w42'35 5:50:50
Allen Grove 63 29 40N16 89w40 5:58:40
Allens Corners 45 29 42N05'58 88w28'53 5:53:56
Allens Spring 76 4 37N22'08 88w39'25 5:54:38
Allentown 90 98 40N33'21 89w23'48 5:57:35
Allenville 70 7 39N33'20 88w31'47 5:54:07
Allerton 10 55 39N54'42 87w56'11 5:51:45
Allin 57 4 40N27 89w12 5:56:48
Allison 51 4 38N44 87w34 5:50:16
Allright 12 55 39N17'50 87w44'56 5:51:00
Alma 61 4 38N43'18 88w54'33 5:55:38
Almora 45 107 42N03'39 88w20'10 5:53:21
Alonzo 38 80 40N34'00 87w43'52 5:50:55
Alorton 82 25 38N35'23 90w07'12 6:00:29
Alpha 37 4 41N11'30 90w22'48 6:01:31
Alpine 16 1 41N35'11 87w52'53 5:51:32
Alsey 86 63 39N33'38 90w26'02 6:01:44
Alsip 16 1 41N40'08 87w44'19 5:50:57
Alsip Woods 16 1 41N40 87w43 5:50:52
Alta 72 98 40N48'39 89w38'03 5:58:32
Altamont 25 56 39N03'43 88w44'53 5:55:00
Altamont 60 7 38N57 90w11 6:00:44
Altgeld Gardens 16 1 41N39'16 87w36'07 5:50:24
Altmar 50 4 41N08'31 88w53'33 5:55:34
Alto 52 56 41N51 89w00 5:56:00
Alton 60 7 38N53'26 90w11'03 6:00:44
Altona 48 4 41N06'53 90w09'52 6:00:39
Alton Siding 59 47 39N18 89w52 5:59:28
Alto Pass 91 4 37N34'13 89w19'03 5:57:16
Altorf 46 115 41N11'25 87w57'44 5:51:51
Alvin 92 26 40N18'30 87w36'30 5:50:26
Alworth 101 48 42N14'37 89w14'44 5:56:59
Amboy 52 29 41N42'51 89w19'43 5:57:19
Amenia 74 4 40N01'19 88w39'59 5:54:40
America 77 4 37N08'18 89w07'25 5:56:30
Americana Village 22 2 41N53 88w04 5:52:16
Ames 67 55 38N08'48 90w03'16 6:00:13
Amity 53 55 40N58 88w45 5:55:00
Amity 80 4 38N46'35 87w55'27 5:51:42
Anchor 57 55 40N34'05 88w32'08 5:54:09
Anchorage 16 1 42N06 87w50 5:51:20
Ancient Tree 16 2 42N07 87w49 5:51:16
Ancona 53 55 41N02'26 88w52'21 5:55:29
Andalusia 81 4 41N26'21 90w43'03 6:02:52
Anderman Acres 99 82 41N35 88w11 5:52:44
Anderson 9 29 39N58'56 90w09'32 6:00:38
Anderson 12 55 39N19 87w44 5:50:56
Anderson 59 4 39N20'38 89w50'42 5:59:23
Andover 37 4 41N17'38 90w17'31 6:01:10
Andres 99 30 41N22'18 87w52'57 5:51:32
Andrew 84 133 39N53'44 89w38'24 5:58:34
Anna 91 4 37N27'37 89w14'49 5:56:59
Annapolis 17 4 39N08'40 87w49'00 5:51:16
Annawan 37 4 41N23'50 89w54'16 5:59:37
Antioch 49 22 42N28'38 88w05'44 5:52:23
Appanoose 34 4 40N35 91w18 6:05:12
Apple Canyon Lake 43 4 42N30 90w06 6:00:24
Applegate 51 4 38N47'34 87w47'48 5:51:11
Apple River 43 66 42N30'18 90w05'55 6:00:24
Appleton 48 4 40N56'09 90w09'39 6:00:39
Appletree 16 6 41N35 87w46 5:51:04
Apple Valley 16 1 42N04 87w48 5:51:12
Aptakisic 49 26 42N10'57 87w56'50 5:51:47
Arboretum Villages 22 12 41N47 88w05 5:52:20
Arbor Trails 99 1 41N30 87w41 5:50:44
Arbury Hills 99 4 41N32'08 87w50'51 5:51:23
Arcadia 16 1 41N31 87w42 5:50:48
Arcadia 69 63 39N50'21 90w14'41 6:00:59
Archer 84 133 39N46'53 89w44'09 5:58:57
Archie 92 96 39N53'39 87w49'42 5:51:19
Arcola 21 63 39N41'05 88w18'23 5:53:14
Ardenmoor 12 55 39N21'57 87w47'48 5:51:11
Arden Shores 49 116 42N17 87w51 5:51:24
Arenzville 9 66 39N52'37 90w22'24 6:01:30
Argenta 58 57 39N58'55 88w49'22 5:55:17
Argo 8 4 42N06 89w58 5:59:52
Argo 16 1 41N47 87w50 5:51:20
Argyle 101 28 42N21'36 88w56'24 5:55:46
Arispie 6 4 41N16 89w27 5:57:48
Arlington 6 54 41N28'25 89w14'57 5:57:00
Arlington Heights 16 100 42N05'18 87w58'50 5:51:55
Arlington Heights 84 29 39N49'11 89w36'05 5:58:24
Arlington Ridge 16 6 42N06 87w58 5:51:52
Armington 90 55 40N20'20 89w18'41 5:57:15
Armstrong 92 54 40N18'23 87w52'40 5:51:31
Arnold 8 4 42N10'12 90w13'35 6:00:54
Arnold 69 63 39N43'16 90w08'42 6:00:35
Aroma 46 5 41N05 87w47 5:51:08
Aroma Park 46 5 41N04'47 87w48'41 5:51:15
Arpee 66 4 41N10'59 90w56'49 6:03:47
Arrington 96 4 38N22 88w31 5:54:04
Arrowhead 22 2 41N53 88w05 5:52:20
Arrowhead 55 4 40N28 90w41 6:02:44
Arrowsmith 57 97 40N26'58 88w37'54 5:54:32
Arrow Wood 60 7 38N57 90w11 6:00:44
Arsenal 99 114 41N31 88w07 5:52:28
Artesia 38 4 40N37 88w03 5:52:12
Arthur 21 50 39N42'53 88w28'20 5:53:53
Asbury 30 4 37N53 88w12 5:52:48
Ashburn 16 14 41N45 87w44 5:50:56
Ashdale Junction 8 4 42N05'06 89w55'28 5:59:42
Ashkum 38 31 40N52'49 87w57'18 5:51:49
Ashland 9 65 39N53'16 90w00'28 6:00:02
Ashley 96 4 38N19'46 89w11'27 5:56:46
Ashmore 15 63 39N31'59 88w01'20 5:52:05
Ashton 52 31 41N51'58 89w13'16 5:56:53
Assumption 11 61 39N31'13 89w02'56 5:56:12
Astoria 29 66 40N13'39 90w21'34 6:01:26
Athenia 16 1 41N31 87w42 5:50:48
Athens 65 55 39N57'39 89w43'26 5:58:54
Athensville 31 63 39N27'20 90w11'21 6:00:45
Atkinson 37 4 41N25'15 90w00'54 6:00:04
Atlanta 54 37 40N15'34 89w14'00 5:56:56
Atlas 75 4 39N30'50 90w58'10 6:03:53
Atlee Ogles 82 25 38N31 89w59 5:59:56
Atrium 22 27 41N54 87w57 5:51:48
Atterberry 65 4 40N03'39 89w55'25 5:59:42
Attila 100 4 37N46'11 88w46'16 5:55:05
Atwater 59 4 39N19'58 89w43'30 5:58:54
Atwood 21 55 39N47'58 88w27'44 5:53:51

Atwood Heights 16 1 41N40 87W43 5:50:52
Auburn 84 101 39N35'30 89W44'47 5:58:59
Auburn Park 16 1 41N44 87W39 5:50:36
Audubon 68 7 39N17 89W12 5:56:48
Auer Landing 7 65 38N54'05 90W31'22 6:02:05
Augerville 10 138 40N08'23 88W10'18 5:52:41
Augsburg 26 4 38N52'00 89W00'48 5:56:03
Augusta 34 4 40N13'48 90W57'00 6:03:48
Aurora 45 102 41N45'38 88W19'12 5:53:17
Austin 16 1 41N58 87W40 5:50:40
Austin 58 55 40N00 89W05 5:56:20
Austin View 16 12 41N40 87W47 5:51:08
Aux Sable 32 48 41N23'41 88W19'43 5:53:19
Ava 39 4 37N53'18 89W29'41 5:57:59
Avena 26 56 39N00'27 88W55'40 5:55:43
Avery Hill 82 25 38N33'11 90W01'37 6:00:06
Aviston 14 55 38N36'24 89W36'27 5:58:26
Avoca 53 72 40N48 88W31 5:54:04
Avon 29 4 40N39'51 90W26'05 6:01:44
Ayers 3 63 38N57'49 89W27'07 5:57:48
Ayers 8 23 42N03'14 90W06'56 6:00:28
Ayers 10 54 39N55 87W58 5:51:52
Babcock 81 87 41N30 90W26 6:01:44
Babson 45 95 41N54 88W19 5:53:16
Babylon 29 63 40N35'27 90W20'57 6:01:24
Baden Baden 3 90 38N46'35 89W31'13 5:58:05
Bader 85 66 40N10'23 90W22'07 6:01:28
Baileyville 71 63 42N11'50 89W35'36 5:58:22
Bainbridge 85 7 40N03 90W30 6:02:00
Baker 50 26 41N33'20 88W48'40 5:55:15
Bakerville 41 4 38N15'30 88W53'51 5:55:35
Balcom 91 4 37N24'47 89W12'22 5:56:49
Bald Bluff 36 4 41N01'07 90W51'13 6:03:25
Bald Hill 41 4 38N10 89W06 5:56:24
Bald Mound 45 60 41N50'46 88W24'23 5:53:38
Baldwin 79 55 38N10'59 89W50'33 5:59:22
Baldwin Beach 63 55 40N20'45 90W01'55 6:00:08
Baldwin Heights 41 4 38N26'59 89W08'41 5:56:35
Bales Lake 38 43 40N31 88W05 5:52:20
Ball 84 30 39N40 89W39 5:58:36
Ballou 99 7 41N16'39 88W06'07 5:52:24
Banklick 100 4 37N49'38 88W42'08 5:54:49
Banner 29 4 40N31'01 89W54'30 5:59:38
Bannister 61 4 38N36 88W57 5:55:48
Bannockburn 49 2 42N11'36 87W51'59 5:51:28
Barbers Corners 99 4 41N42'39 88W04'06 5:52:16
Barclay 84 29 39N52'29 89W31'04 5:58:04
Bardolph 55 4 40N29'42 90W33'52 6:02:15
Bargerville 64 4 37N09 88W44 5:54:56
Barlow Park 92 26 40N18'34 87W37'23 5:50:30
Barnes 57 79 40N30'10 88W54'06 5:55:36
Barnett 20 55 40N11 89W05 5:56:20
Barnett 60 25 38N51'16 89W53'04 5:59:32
Barnett 68 37 39N15'52 89W41'50 5:58:47
Barney Ford 15 67 39N33'07 88W06'07 5:52:24
Barnhill 96 4 38N17'04 88W21'51 5:53:27
Barr 59 63 39N24'17 90W06'15 6:00:25
Barr 84 55 39N57'43 89W41'49 5:58:47
Barren 28 4 38N05 88W59 5:55:56
Barreville 56 6 42N16'32 88W15'45 5:53:03
Barrington 16 1 42N09'14 88W08'10 5:52:33
Barrington Center 45 6 42N06'38 88W11'39 5:52:47
Barrington Highlands 49 1 42N09 88W06 5:52:24
Barrington Hills 16 1 42N08'41 88W09'20 5:52:37
Barrington Woods 16 1 42N09'08 88W03'21 5:52:13
Barrow 31 4 39N30'22 90W24'05 6:01:36
Barry 75 4 39N41'39 91W02'20 6:04:09
Barstow 81 63 41N31'06 90W21'25 6:01:26
Bartelso 14 55 38N32'11 89W27'59 5:57:52
Bartlett 16 27 41N59'42 88W11'08 5:52:45
Bartonville 72 98 40N39'01 89W39'07 5:58:36
Basco 34 4 40N19'40 91W12'00 6:04:48
Base 10 29 40N19 88W08 5:52:32
Batavia 45 103 41N51'00 88W18'45 5:53:15
Batavia Highlands 45 103 41N52 88W19 5:53:16
Batchtown 7 65 39N01'59 90W39'27 6:02:38
Bates 84 55 39N43'27 89W50'58 5:59:24
Batestown 92 54 40N07'12 87W41'47 5:50:47
Bath 63 63 40N11'36 90W08'27 6:00:34
Battery Rock 35 4 37N32 88W07 5:52:28
Baum 31 55 39N19'39 90W18'56 6:01:16
Bay City 76 4 37N14'56 88W29'48 5:53:59
Bay Colony 16 6 42N03 87W55 5:51:40
Bayle City 26 4 39N06'50 89W09'58 5:56:40
Baylestown 59 55 39N05'29 89W52'46 5:59:31
Baylis 75 4 39N43'42 90W54'29 6:03:38
Bay View Garden 102 56 40N48'32 89W31'14 5:58:05
Beach 49 140 42N25 87W49 5:51:16
Beach Station 49 140 42N25'16 87W50'57 5:51:24
Beacon Hill 16 1 41N31 87W38 5:50:32
Beamington 84 55 39N40'15 89W35'30 5:58:22
Beardstown 9 7 40N01'03 90W25'27 6:01:42
Bear Grove 26 139 38N58 89W11 5:56:44
Bearsdale 58 26 39N53'49 89W00'40 5:56:03
Beason 54 55 40N08'37 89W11'36 5:56:46
Beaty 29 66 40N16'30 90W14'45 6:00:59
Beau Bien 22 12 41N47 88W05 5:52:20
Beaucoup 95 4 38N20'59 89W17'31 5:57:10
Beaver 38 57 40N54 87W36 5:50:24
Beaver Creek (Wisetown) 3 55 38N46'03 89W23'37 5:57:34
Beaver Creek 33 4 38N10 88W26 5:53:44
Beaverton Crossroads 4 91 42N24'28 88W49'18 5:55:17
Beaver Valley 16 12 41N38 87W51 5:51:24
Beaverville 38 55 40N57'16 87W39'16 5:50:37
Beckemeyer 14 55 38N36'20 89W26'09 5:57:45
Bedford 75 63 39N31'45 90W35'03 6:02:20
Bedford 96 4 38N31 88W25 5:53:40
Bedford Park 16 1 41N45'46 87W48'00 5:51:12
Beecher 99 22 41N20'26 87W37'17 5:50:29
Beecher City 25 4 39N11'17 88W47'12 5:55:09
Beech Landing 7 65 38N58'25 90W40'21 6:02:41
Beechville 7 65 38N58'17 90W38'51 6:02:35
Bee Creek 75 4 39N24'01 90W38'09 6:02:33
Bel Air Gardens 16 1 42N04 87W48 5:51:12
Belden 56 48 42N28'27 88W20'50 5:53:23
Belgium 92 26 40N03'41 87W38'17 5:50:33
Belgium Row 92 54 40N07'59 87W45'13 5:51:01
Belknap 44 4 37N19'30 88W56'20 5:55:45
Bell 54 29 40N11'31 89W23'15 5:57:33
Bellair 17 4 39N08'31 87W56'43 5:51:47
Belle Prairie 53 55 40N39 88W31 5:54:04
Belle Prairie City 33 4 38N13'21 88W33'19 5:54:13
Belle Rive 41 4 38N13'58 88W44'26 5:54:58
Belleview 7 4 39N21'03 90W46'52 6:03:07
Belleville 82 25 38N31'12 89W59'02 5:59:56
Bellevue 72 98 40N41'04 89W40'48 5:58:43
Bellflower 57 56 40N20'24 88W31'37 5:54:06
Bellmont 93 13 38N23'04 87W54'41 5:51:39
Bell Plain 62 56 41N02 89W13 5:56:52
Bells Landing 29 4 40N30'16 89W53'07 5:59:32
Belltown 31 4 39N22'57 90W24'28 6:01:38
Bellwood 16 2 41N52'53 87W52'59 5:51:32
Belmont 22 12 41N47'34 88W02'16 5:52:09
Belmont 38 16 40N44 87W43 5:50:52
Belmont Village 60 7 38N57 90W11 6:00:44
Beltrees 42 4 38N57'34 90W19'32 6:01:18
Belvidere 4 26 42N15'50 88W50'39 5:55:23
Bement 74 30 39N55'19 88W34'19 5:54:17
Benedale Green 22 12 41N47 88W05 5:52:20
Benevolent Heights 82 25 38N31 89W59 5:59:56
Benld 59 55 39N05'34 89W48'14 5:59:13
Bennett 92 54 40N03'51 87W48'22 5:51:13
Bennett Landing 91 4 37N32'02 89W29'54 5:58:00
Bennington 24 4 38N31'27 88W07'53 5:52:32
Bennington 62 54 41N02 89W06 5:56:24
Bensenville 22 17 41N57'18 87W56'24 5:51:46
Benson 102 21 40N51'02 89W07'20 5:56:29
Bentley 34 4 40N20'40 91W06'42 6:04:27
Benton 28 4 37N59'48 88W55'12 5:55:41
Benton City Park 28 4 38N00 88W56 5:55:44
Benton Park 28 4 38N03'35 88W54'53 5:55:40
Bentown 57 79 40N28'19 88W48'23 5:55:14
Benville 5 66 39N51'51 90W51'53 6:03:28
Berdan 31 55 39N21'54 90W23'43 6:01:35
Berger 16 1 41N37 87W40 5:50:40
Berkeley 16 2 41N53'20 87W54'12 5:51:37
Berlin 84 55 39N45'32 89W54'11 5:59:37
Bernadotte 29 63 40N25 90W16 6:01:04
Bernice 16 19 41N34'45 87W32'53 5:50:12
Berreman 43 4 42N14 89W57 5:59:48
Berry 84 55 39N45 89W32 5:58:08
Berry 96 4 38N26 88W32 5:54:08
Berryville 80 4 38N35'58 87W55'43 5:51:43
Berryville 91 4 37N27'25 89W17'16 5:57:09
Berwick 94 4 40N47'57 90W32'18 6:02:09
Berwyn 16 1 41N51'02 87W47'37 5:51:10
Bessie 28 4 37N59'50 88W48'45 5:55:15
Bethalto 60 55 38N54'33 90W02'26 6:00:10
Bethany 70 56 39N38'44 88W44'17 5:54:57
Bethel 13 4 38N38 88W38 5:54:32
Bethel 55 4 40N20 90W44 6:02:56
Bethel 69 4 39N46'35 90W25'29 6:01:42
Bethel 92 54 39N53'50 87W32'40 5:50:11
Bethlehem 25 4 39N04 88W45 5:55:00
Beulah Heights 83 4 37N49 88W27 5:53:48
Beverly 1 66 39N47'36 90W59'27 6:03:58
Beverly Manor 90 98 40N41'42 89W28'03 5:57:52
Bible Grove 13 4 38N52'19 88W26'46 5:53:47
Biddleborn 95 55 38N17'52 89W41'05 5:58:44
Big Bay 64 4 37N19'00 88W43'18 5:54:53
Big Foot 56 7 42N25 88W37 5:54:28
Big Foot Prairie 56 7 42N29'42 88W35'56 5:54:24
Big Grove 47 55 41N30 88W32 5:54:08
Biggs 63 63 40N14'29 89W54'15 5:59:37
Biggsville 36 4 40N51'13 90W51'53 6:03:28
Big Hollow 49 27 42N23 88W09 5:52:36
Big Mound 96 4 38N20 88W25 5:53:40
Bigneck 1 53 40N09 91W13 6:04:52
Big Rock 45 25 41N45'50 88W32'49 5:54:11
Big Spring 87 1 39N19 88W32 5:54:08
Billett 51 4 38N39'52 87W39'08 5:50:37
Bingham 26 4 39N06'51 89W12'48 5:56:51
Binghampton 52 29 41N43'00 89W18'14 5:57:13
Bingman Station 97 4 38N04'59 88W14'41 5:52:59
Binney 60 7 38N59'24 89W43'38 5:58:55
Birch Island 7 65 39N07'53 90W40'52 6:02:43
Bird 59 63 39N19 89W59 5:59:56
Birds 51 4 38N50'13 87W40'04 5:50:40
Birds 99 82 41N28'30 88W11'50 5:52:47
Birkbeck 20 8 40N10'37 88W52'06 5:55:28
Birkner 82 25 38N33'44 90W01'45 6:00:07
Birmingham 85 4 40N15'51 90W49'15 6:03:17
Bishop 25 4 39N03 88W25 5:53:40
Bishop 63 7 40N20'45 89W52'29 5:59:30
Bishop Hill 37 4 41N12'06 90W07'08 6:00:29
Bismarck 92 26 40N15'50 87W36'29 5:50:26
Bissell 84 133 39N50'46 89W34'54 5:58:20
Bixby 82 46 38N29'35 90W13'25 6:00:54
Black 24 4 38N28'04 88W06'10 5:52:25
Blackberry 45 55 41N49 88W27 5:53:48
Blackberry Heights 45 102 41N46 88W20 5:53:20
Blackberry Woods 45 41 41N45 88W27 5:53:48
Blackhawk 8 4 42N11'15 90W13'26 6:00:54
Black Hawk 81 87 41N27 90W34 6:02:16
Blackhawk Heights 22 2 41N47 87W57 5:51:48
Blackland 58 57 39N45'41 89W06'14 5:56:25
Blackstone 53 55 41N05'04 88W41'27 5:54:46
Blaine 4 91 42N26'49 88W48'11 5:55:13
Blair 53 36 41N06'12 88W18'31 5:53:14
Blair 79 63 38N02'41 89W44'31 5:58:58
Blairsville 33 4 38N10'06 88W27'51 5:53:51
Blairsville 100 4 37N48'40 89W07'25 5:56:30
Blakes 50 41 41N27'31 88W45'10 5:55:01
Blanding 43 4 42N16'29 90W23'09 6:01:33
Blanding Landing Recreation 43 4 42N17'09 90W24'12 6:01:37
Blandinsville 55 4 40N33'22 90W51'57 6:03:28
Blissville 41 4 38N15 89W06 5:56:24
Block 10 54 39N58'06 88W05'08 5:52:21
Blodgett 49 1 42N11 87W49 5:51:16
Blodgett 99 7 41N22'39 88W11'24 5:52:46
Bloom 16 1 41N31 87W35 5:50:20
Bloomfield 1 66 40N01'15 91W18'25 6:05:14
Bloomfield 23 7 39N45'34 87W40'57 5:50:44
Bloomfield 44 4 37N27'09 88W52'30 5:55:30
Bloomingdale 22 27 41N57'27 88W04'51 5:52:19
Bloomington 57 104 40N29'03 88W59'37 5:55:58
Bloomington Heights 57 104 40N28'50 89W02'01 5:56:08
Blossom Hill 56 1 42N14 88W15 5:53:00
Blount 92 26 40N12 87W41 5:50:44
Blue Fountain 60 7 38N57 90W11 6:00:44
Blue Island 16 2 41N39'26 87W40'48 5:50:43
Blue Mound 58 58 39N42'04 89W07'23 5:56:30
Blue Point 25 4 39N07 88W33 5:54:12
Blue Ridge 74 55 40N16'04 88W29'17 5:53:57
Bluff 67 55 38N17 90W15 6:01:00
Bluff City 26 139 38N57'50 89W02'47 5:56:11
Bluff City 85 66 40N10'49 90W13'49 6:00:55
Bluffdale 31 63 39N19 90W33 6:02:12
Bluff Hall 1 85 39N49 91W15 6:05:00
Bluff Junction 60 25 38N49'06 89W58'57 5:59:56
Bluffs 86 65 39N45'07 90W32'06 6:02:08
Bluffside 82 46 38N29'02 90W09'17 6:00:37
Bluff Springs 9 7 39N59'16 90W20'45 6:01:23
Bluff View Park 82 25 38N37 90W01 6:00:04
Bluford 41 4 38N19'51 88W43'33 5:54:54
Blyton 29 63 40N33'51 90W16'35 6:01:06
Boaz 64 4 37N17'30 88W53'59 5:55:36
Bobtown 65 66 40N04'34 89W59'17 5:59:57
Boden 66 4 41N15'30 90W35'13 6:02:21
Bodmann 74 30 39N52'58 88W34'45 5:54:19
Bogan's 25 4 39N07 88W33 5:54:12
Bogota 40 4 38N55'06 88W14'24 5:52:58
Bohleysville 82 55 38N24'55 90W07'07 6:00:28
Bois d'Arc 68 63 39N29 89W37 5:58:28
Boles 44 4 37N26 88W58 5:55:52
Bolingbrook 99 4 41N41'55 88W04'06 5:52:16
Boling Green 99 1 41N40 88W00 5:52:00
Bolivia 11 8 39N44'32 89W20'49 5:57:23
Bolo 95 4 38N15 89W19 5:57:16
Bolton 89 4 42N14'31 89W43'31 5:58:54
Bond 51 4 38N49 87W42 5:50:48
Bondville 10 23 40N06'48 88W22'10 5:53:29
Bone Gap 24 4 38N26'51 87W59'45 5:51:59
Bonfield 46 55 41N08'48 88W03'28 5:52:14
Bongard 10 54 39N55'27 88W07'25 5:52:30
Bonnie 41 4 38N12'10 88W54'12 5:55:37
Bonnie Brea 99 114 41N35 88W03 5:52:12
Bonpas 80 4 38N37 87W58 5:51:52
Bonus 4 26 42N16 88W46 5:55:04
Boody 58 57 39N45'59 89W02'57 5:56:12
Boone 4 8 42N22 88W45 5:55:00
Boos 40 4 38N55'48 88W06'39 5:52:27
Booster Station 82 25 38N36 89W58 5:59:52
Boothby 28 4 38N00'08 88W46'43 5:55:07
Borton 23 65 39N39'21 87W56'02 5:51:44
Boskydell 39 4 37N40'16 89W12'49 5:56:51
Boulder 14 4 38N41'48 89W13'32 5:56:54
Boulder Hill 47 102 41N44 88W19 5:53:16
Boulevard Manor 16 1 41N51 87W46 5:51:04
Bourbon 21 55 39N44'44 88W22'44 5:53:31
Bourbonnais 46 115 41N08'30 87W52'30 5:51:30
Bowdre 21 65 39N44 88W09 5:52:36
Bowen 34 4 40N14'00 91W03'45 6:04:15
Bowes 45 54 42N00'29 88W23'27 5:53:34
Bowlesville 30 4 37N39 88W12 5:52:48
Bowling 81 4 41N23 90W37 6:02:28
Bowling Green 26 63 39N11 88W57 5:55:48
Bowman 42 25 39N08'15 90W14'40 6:00:59
Bowman Ford 18 55 39N15'58 88W09'38 5:52:39
Boyd 41 4 38N24'49 89W00'48 5:56:03
Boyd Ford 15 65 39N36'38 88W04'15 5:52:17
Boyle 31 63 39N17'00 90W34'38 6:02:19
Boyleston 96 4 38N21'41 88W26'33 5:53:46
Boynton 90 72 40N21'08 89W26'07 5:57:44
Braceville 32 37 41N13'37 88W15'53 5:53:04
Bradbury 18 4 39N19'27 88W14'34 5:52:58
Braden 33 4 37N59'47 88W36'58 5:54:28
Bradford 88 4 41N10'38 89W39'27 5:58:38
Bradfordton 84 133 39N49'24 89W44'22 5:58:57
Bradley 32 125 41N22 88W25 5:53:40
Bradley 46 7 41N08'31 87W51'40 5:51:27
Braeside 16 3 42N09'09 87W46'20 5:51:05
Braidwood 99 36 41N15'54 88W12'44 5:52:51
Branding 7 65 38N57 90W36 6:02:24
Brandywine 22 21 41N53 87W58 5:51:52
Branigar Estates 16 27 42N01 88W00 5:52:00
Breckenridge 34 4 40N14'37 91W17'11 6:05:09
Breckenridge 84 55 39N41'56 89W26'51 5:57:47
Breeds 29 4 40N33'19 89W55'13 5:59:41
Breese 14 55 38N36'38 89W31'37 5:58:06

Bremen 43 4 42N24'02 90w24'49 6:01:39
Bremen 79 66 37N58'16 89w44'50 5:58:59
Brenton 27 30 40N43 88w11 5:52:44
Brentwood Estates 16
6 42N06 88w02 5:52:08
Brereton 29 4 40N36'39 90w01'33 6:00:06
Brettwood 58 26 39N52 88w57 5:55:48
Brewerville 79 63 38N02 90w00 6:00:00
Briar Bluff 37 87 41N27'35 90w21'48 6:01:27
Briarbrook Village 22
2 41N53 88w05 5:52:20
Briarcliffe 22 2 41N53 88w05 5:52:20
Briarwoods Estates 49
6 42N10 87w53 5:51:32
Briarwood Trace 100
4 37N43 89w14 5:56:56
Brickman Manor 16
6 42N04 87w57 5:51:48
Bridgelane 81 87 41N30 90w30 6:02:00
Bridgeport 51 4 38N42'21 87w45'36 5:51:02
Bridgeview 16 1 41N45'00 87w48'15 5:51:13
Bridgeway Addition 81
87 41N28'24 90w30'15 6:02:01
Briergate 49 1 42N10'34 87w48'53 5:51:16
Bright Oaks 56 1 42N14 88w15 5:53:00
Brighton 59 37 39N02'23 90w08'26 6:00:34
Brimfield 72 58 40N50'20 89w53'11 5:59:33
Brisbane 99 1 41N29'33 87w57'28 5:51:50
Bristol 47 7 41N41'08 88w25'41 5:53:43
Bristol Lake 47
25 41N39 88w27 5:53:48
Bristol Ridge 47
25 41N39 88w27 5:53:48
Broadlands 10 54 39N54'31 87w59'39 5:51:59
Broadmoor 88 4 41N08'44 89w37'43 5:58:31
Broadview 16 2 41N51'50 87w51'12 5:51:25
Broadway 101 28 42N17 89w04 5:56:16
Broadwell 54 29 40N04'05 89w26'35 5:57:46
Brock Landing 7
65 38N53'24 90w31'51 6:02:07
Brocton 23 55 39N42'56 87w55'57 5:51:44
Brokaw 57 79 40N27'04 88w54'09 5:55:37
Bronson 92 54 40N06'54 87w48'19 5:51:13
Brooke Estates 49
1 42N11 87w49 5:51:16
Brookeridge 22 12 41N48 88w01 5:52:04
Brookfield 16 1 41N49'26 87w51'06 5:51:24
Brook Forest 22 2 41N48 87w56 5:51:44
Brookforest North 99
114 41N33 88w07 5:52:28
Brookhaven 98 4 41N40 89w56 5:59:44
Brookhaven Manor 22
19 41N47 87w59 5:51:56
Brookhill 49 42 42N16 87w56 5:51:44
Brooklyn 82 25 38N39'31 90w09'57 6:00:40
Brooklyn 85 4 40N13'33 90w45'57 6:03:03
Brookport 64 62 37N07'25 88w37'49 5:54:31
Brooks 60 4 38N46'27 90w05'24 6:00:22
Brookside 14 4 38N32 89w12 5:56:48
Brooks Isle 71 28 42N01 89w20 5:57:20
Brookview 72 98 40N45 89w37 5:58:28
Brookville 71 63 42N02'55 89w41'02 5:58:44
Brookville 92 54 40N03'53 87w36'23 5:50:26
Brookwood 16 1 42N07 87w56 5:51:44
Brookwood Estates 22
17 41N57 87w59 5:51:56
Brothers 92 54 40N08'40 87w48'31 5:51:14
Broughton 33 4 37N56'05 88w27'43 5:53:51
Brouilletts Creek 23
4 39N45 87w35 5:50:20
Brown 10 54 40N21 88w24 5:53:36
Brownfield 76 4 37N20'44 88w36'25 5:54:26
Browning 85 66 40N07'44 90w22'19 6:01:29
Browns 24 4 38N22'37 87w58'59 5:51:56
Browns Crossing 84
55 39N43'26 89w59'02 5:59:56
Browns Mill 89 46 42N16'56 89w31'15 5:58:05
Brownstown 26 56 38N59'45 88w57'10 5:55:49
Brownsville 97 4 38N02'29 88w14'41 5:52:59
Brownton 69 113 39N45'49 90w11'28 6:00:46
Brownwood 90 72 40N23'46 89w28'29 5:57:54
Brubaker 61 4 38N41'35 88w52'35 5:55:30
Bruce 50 135 41N10 88w50 5:55:20
Bruce 70 7 39N31'08 88w35'40 5:54:23
Brunkhorst Landing 39
4 37N41'54 89w31'05 5:58:04
Brunning 99 114 41N35 88w03 5:52:12
Brunswick 87 63 39N31 88w45 5:55:00
Brushy 83 4 37N47 88w39 5:54:36
Brushy Mound 59
47 39N13 89w53 5:59:32
Brussels 7 65 38N56'58 90w35'19 6:02:21
Bryant 29 7 40N27'58 90w05'30 6:00:22
Bryce 38 7 40N38'04 87w45'24 5:51:02
Buck 23 67 39N39 87w50 5:51:20
Buckeye 89 61 42N25 89w39 5:58:36
Buckhart 84 55 39N44'59 89w26'41 5:57:47
Buckheart 29 7 40N30 90w03 6:00:12
Buckhorn 5 66 39N56'12 90w50'09 6:03:21
Buckhorn Corners 89
61 42N25'29 89w38'18 5:58:33
Buckingham 46 36 41N02'49 88w10'31 5:52:42
Buckley 38 43 40N35'49 88w02'17 5:52:09
Buckner 28 4 37N58'59 89w00'58 5:56:04
Bucks 20 35 40N15'54 88w58'12 5:55:53
Bucktown 92 54 40N06'48 87w44'41 5:50:59
Buda 6 63 41N19'34 89w40'44 5:58:43
Budd 53 55 41N05'56 88w37'23 5:54:30
Buena Vista 83 4 37N44'18 88w34'34 5:54:18
Buena Vista 85 65 40N09 90w37 6:02:28
Buena Vista 89 4 42N25'32 89w40'40 5:58:43
Buffalo 84 8 39N51'09 89w24'31 5:57:38
Buffalo Grove 16
6 42N09'05 87w57'35 5:51:50
Buffalo Grove 71
4 41N59 89w35 5:58:20
Buffalo Hart 84 8 39N54'50 89w26'51 5:57:47
Buffalo Prairie 81
4 41N20'18 90w51'17 6:03:25
Bull Creek 49 42 42N16 87w56 5:51:44
Bulldog Crossing 58
26 39N47'44 89w00'45 5:56:03
Bulpitt 11 26 39N35'30 89w25'26 5:57:42

Buncombe 44 4 37N28'17 88w58'37 5:55:54
Bungay 33 4 38N10'45 88w24'31 5:53:38
Bunje 3 63 38N59'33 89w35'28 5:58:22
Bunker Hill 59 55 39N02'34 89w57'06 5:59:48
Bunker Hill Estates 16
1 42N02 87w49 5:51:16
Bunkum 82 4 38N37'15 90w02'41 6:00:11
Bunsenville 92 54 39N58 87w38 5:50:32
Burbank 16 1 41N44 87w45 5:51:00
Bureau 6 55 41N17'21 89w21'59 5:57:28
Burgess 66 4 41N07'38 90w38'29 6:02:34
Burke 8 4 42N03'04 90w02'12 6:00:09
Burksville 67 8 38N16'02 90w09'09 6:00:37
Burlingame 9 63 39N55'25 90w09'48 6:00:39
Burlington 45 41 42N03'10 88w32'53 5:54:12
Burnett 6 63 41N16'38 89w39'49 5:58:39
Burnham 16 6 41N38'20 87w33'24 5:50:14
Burnham Mill 45
107 42N02 88w17 5:53:08
Burns 37 4 41N16 90w02 6:00:08
Burns 57 35 40N24'01 88w58'42 5:55:55
Burnside 16 1 41N43'13 87w35'53 5:50:24
Burnside 34 4 40N30'14 91w06'00 6:04:24
Burnside 44 4 37N33 88w46 5:55:04
Burnside 48 33 40N46'10 90w16'24 6:01:06
Burnside's Lakewood 16
29 41N29 87w43 5:50:52
Burnt Prairie 97
4 38N15'06 88w15'41 5:53:03
Burritt 101 4 42N20 89w13 5:56:52
Burr Oak 16 1 41N39 87w42 5:50:48
Burr Oaks 99 114 41N33 88w07 5:52:28
Burrowsville 58
55 39N47'58 88w37'59 5:54:32
Burr Ridge 22 2 41N44'56 87w55'06 5:51:40
Burt 90 86 40N20'17 89w22'06 5:57:28
Burton 1 92 39N54'17 91w14'56 6:05:00
Burtons Bridge 56
1 42N16'47 88w13'44 5:52:55
Burton View 54 4 40N10'15 89w29'05 5:57:56
Busenville 92 54 39N59'14 87w40'32 5:50:42
Bush 100 4 37N50'36 89w07'52 5:56:31
Bushnell 55 4 40N33'10 90w30'22 6:02:01
Bushton 15 106 39N35'32 88w08'19 5:52:33
Butler 68 7 39N11'58 89w32'02 5:58:08
Butler Grove 68 7 39N13 89w32 5:58:08
Butterfield 22 83 41N53 88w01 5:52:04
Butterfield West 22
2 41N53 88w04 5:52:16
Button 27 43 40N27 88w00 5:52:00
Buzzville 63 55 40N18 90w04 6:00:16
Bybee 29 4 40N35'52 90w11'05 6:00:44
Byron 71 57 42N07'37 89w15'20 5:57:01
Byron Hills 81 4 41N37 90w20 6:01:20
Caber 27 38 40N59'45 88w12'19 5:52:49
Cabery 46 38 41N00 88w12 5:52:48
Cable 66 4 41N17'02 90w30'26 6:02:02
Cache 2 4 37N06'00 89w15'41 5:57:03
Cadiz 35 4 37N34'45 88w13'35 5:52:54
Cadwell 70 50 39N40'52 88w31'18 5:54:05
Cahokia 82 25 38N34'15 90w11'24 6:00:46
Cairo 2 4 37N00'19 89w10'35 5:56:42
Cairo Junction 2
4 37N02'27 89w11'30 5:56:46
Caldwell 90 98 40N38'32 89w30'56 5:58:04
Caledonia 4 45 42N22'10 88w53'33 5:55:34
Caledonia Landing 77
4 37N10'45 89w04'19 5:56:17
Calhoun 80 4 38N39'01 88w02'37 5:52:10
Calloway 11 7 39N33'44 89w21'19 5:57:25
Calumet City 16
21 41N36'56 87w31'46 5:50:07
Calumet Park 16 1 41N39'46 87w39'38 5:50:39
Calvin 97 4 38N12'29 88w01'07 5:52:04
Camargo 21 65 39N48'01 88w09'50 5:52:39
Cambon 28 4 37N53'58 88w59'53 5:56:00
Cambria 100 4 37N46'53 89w07'09 5:56:29
Cambridge 37 4 41N18'13 90w11'34 6:00:46
Cambridge 49 42 42N16 87w56 5:51:44
Cambridge-on-the-Lake 16
6 42N09 87w57 5:51:48
Camden 85 4 40N09'13 90w46'14 6:03:05
Cameo Terrace 16
6 42N09 87w57 5:51:48
Cameron 94 4 40N53'20 90w31'02 6:02:04
Camp Algonquin 56
1 42N10'59 88w16'04 5:53:04
Campbell 15 63 39N25 88w18 5:53:12
Campbell 92 26 40N11'28 87w34'46 5:50:19
Campbell Hill 39
63 37N55'48 89w32'56 5:58:12
Campbells Island 81
87 41N30 90w26 6:01:44
Camp Epworth 4 26 42N15 88w44 5:54:56
Camp Ground 41 4 38N20'20 88w50'06 5:55:20
Camp Grove 62 4 41N04'44 89w37'59 5:58:32
Camp Point 1 66 40N02'21 91w04'09 6:04:17
Campton 45 60 41N54 88w26 5:53:44
Camp Travis 13 4 38N39'36 88w19'53 5:53:20
Campus 53 36 41N01'24 88w18'22 5:53:13
Campus Walk 45
107 42N02 88w17 5:53:08
Candlewood Estates 10
54 40N12 88w24 5:53:36
Canoe Creek 81 4 41N37 90w12 6:00:48
Canteen 82 25 38N38 90w04 6:00:16
Canterbury Lane 16
1 42N04 87w48 5:51:12
Canton 29 7 40N33'29 90w02'06 6:00:08
Cantrall 84 55 39N56'16 89w40'33 5:58:42
Capitol 84 133 39N48 89w39 5:58:36
Capitol Oaks 82
25 38N35 89w58 5:59:52
Capri Gardens 16
6 42N06 88w02 5:52:08
Capri Village 16
6 42N06 88w02 5:52:08
Capron 4 8 42N23'59 88w44'25 5:54:58
Carbon 82 25 38N35'38 89w56'21 5:59:45
Carbon Cliff 81
87 41N29'41 90w23'26 6:01:34
Carbondale 39 4 37N43'38 89w13'00 5:56:52
Carbon Hill 32 30 41N17'49 88w18'00 5:53:12

Cardiff 53 26 41N03'06 88w17'14 5:53:09
Carle Springs 20
35 40N15'13 88w58'01 5:55:52
Carlin Prec 7 4 39N21 90w39 6:02:36
Carlinville 59 47 39N16'47 89w52'54 5:59:32
Carlock 57 32 40N34'56 89w07'55 5:56:32
Carlsburg 59 7 39N05'00 89w43'20 5:58:53
Carlyle 14 55 38N36'37 89w22'21 5:57:29
Carman 36 4 40N44'26 91w03'34 6:04:14
Carmi 97 4 38N05'27 88w09'31 5:52:38
Carol Stream 22 2 41N54'45 88w08'05 5:52:32
Carpenter 60 25 38N53'31 89w53'39 5:59:35
Carpentersville 45
105 42N07'16 88w15'28 5:53:02
Carriage Creek 16
29 41N29 87w43 5:50:52
Carrier Mills 83
4 37N41'03 88w37'58 5:54:32
Carrigan 61 4 38N38 89w05 5:56:20
Carroll 92 72 39N55 87w45 5:51:00
Carrollton 31 55 39N18'08 90w24'25 6:01:38
Carrollwood 60 29 38N52 90w05 6:00:20
Carson 26 63 39N09 89w00 5:56:00
Carterville 100 4 37N45'36 89w04'38 5:56:19
Carthage 34 23 40N24'59 91w08'10 6:04:33
Carthage 71 28 41N55'08 89w18'49 5:57:15
Carthage Lake 36
4 40N47'26 91w04'31 6:04:18
Cartter 61 4 38N32'28 88w54'44 5:55:39
Cartwright 84 29 39N51 89w54 5:59:36
Cary 56 1 42N12'43 88w14'17 5:52:57
Cascade 84 55 39N40'13 89w29'31 5:57:58
Casey 12 56 39N17'57 87w59'33 5:51:58
Caseyville 82 25 38N38'12 90w01'32 6:00:06
Casner 41 4 38N21 89w05 5:56:20
Casner 58 54 39N48'01 88w47'28 5:55:10
Cass 9 63 39N58'05 90w16'09 6:01:05
Cass 29 63 40N30 90w16 6:01:04
Castle Fin 12 55 39N28'12 87w44'00 5:50:56
Castle Junction 81
4 41N23'33 90w34'40 6:02:19
Castleton 88 4 41N07'04 89w42'22 5:58:49
Catharine 50 4 41N31'23 88w43'09 5:54:53
Catlin 92 54 40N03'54 87w42'07 5:50:48
Caton Farm 99 82 41N33'55 88w14'21 5:52:57
Cave 28 4 37N54 88w46 5:55:04
Cave in Rock 35 4 37N28'09 88w09'59 5:52:40
Cayuga 53 127 40N56'28 88w35'01 5:54:20
Cazenovia 102 4 40N51'01 89w19'55 5:57:20
Cedar 48 4 40N51 90w23 6:01:32
Cedar Glen 47 4 41N41 88w21 5:53:24
Cedar Grove 100 4 37N46 88w56 5:55:44
Cedar Island 49 6 42N24 88w11 5:52:44
Cedar Park 60 4 38N45'20 90w06'14 6:00:25
Cedar Point 50 57 41N15'47 89w07'32 5:56:30
Cedar Run 16 6 42N09 87w57 5:51:48
Cedarville 89 61 42N22'33 89w37'59 5:58:32
Center Hill 8 4 42N04'51 90w02'46 6:00:11
Centerville 7 65 38N55'49 90w34'18 6:02:17
Centerville 48 4 41N03'52 90w03'15 6:00:13
Centerville 59 4 39N06'03 89w58'41 5:59:55
Centerville 74 55 40N07'24 88w29'46 5:53:59
Centerville 97 4 38N12'02 88w09'58 5:52:40
Central 47 55 41N28'26 88w26'02 5:53:44
Central City 32
37 41N14'16 88w16'54 5:53:08
Central City 61
55 38N32'56 89w07'37 5:56:30
Centralia 61 4 38N31'30 89w08'00 5:56:32
Central Park 92
54 40N17 87w41 5:50:44
Centreville 82 25 38N35'00 90w07'30 6:00:30
Century Oaks West 45
107 42N02 88w17 5:53:08
Cereal 53 4 40N42'30 88w21'04 5:53:24
Cermak Plaza 16 1 41N51 87w48 5:51:12
Cerro Gordo 74 54 39N53'26 88w43'41 5:54:55
Chadwick 8 4 42N00'48 89w53'26 5:59:34
Chalfin Bridge 67
63 38N12'43 90w16'07 6:01:04
Challacombe 59 4 39N13'06 90w07'16 6:00:29
Chalmers 55 4 40N25 90w43 6:02:52
Chambersburg 75
65 39N49'02 90w39'26 6:02:38
Chambord 22 2 41N48 87w56 5:51:44
Champaign 10 21 40N06'59 88w14'36 5:52:58
Champlin 53 72 40N46'59 88w32'45 5:54:11
Chana 71 4 41N58'50 89w13'11 5:56:53
Chandlerville 9
29 40N02'53 90w09'18 6:00:37
Channahon 99 48 41N25'46 88w13'43 5:52:55
Channel Lake 49 6 42N29 88w09 5:52:36
Chantilly 49 1 42N11 87w49 5:51:16
Chanute Air Force Base 10
29 40N18 88w09 5:52:36
Chapin 69 65 39N45'57 90w23'56 6:01:36
Chapman 68 4 39N06'20 89w19'01 5:57:16
Charleston 15 106 39N29'46 88w10'34 5:52:42
Charlotte 53 44 40N49'11 88w17'20 5:53:09
Charter Grove 19
6 42N03'59 88w37'53 5:54:32
Chasco 44 4 37N19'09 89w01'17 5:56:05
Chateau Terrace 82
25 38N32 90w00 6:00:00
Chatham 84 30 39N40'34 89w42'16 5:58:49
Chatsworth 53 58 40N45'13 88w17'31 5:53:10
Chatton 1 66 40N09'03 91w01'58 6:04:08
Chauncey 51 4 38N50'07 87w52'15 5:51:29
Chautauqua 42 4 38N57'52 90w23'08 6:01:33
Chautauqua Park 63
55 40N19'22 90w03'07 6:00:12
Chebanse 46 57 41N00'11 87w54'29 5:51:38
Checkrow 29 63 40N33'15 90w22'41 6:01:31
Chelsea Cove 16 6 42N09 87w57 5:51:48
Chemung 56 7 42N24'55 88w40'00 5:54:40
Cheney Grove 57
36 40N26 88w31 5:54:04
Cheneyville 92 80 40N28'09 87w35'05 5:50:20
Chenoa 57 35 40N44'30 88w43'11 5:54:53
Chenot Place 82
25 38N31 89w59 5:59:56
Cherry 6 58 41N25'37 89w12'48 5:56:51
Cherry Grove 8 4 42N09 89w48 5:59:12

Cherry Hill 99 114 41N31'24 88W00'52 5:52:03
Cherry Point 23 7 39N47'57 87W43'16 5:50:53
Cherry Valley 101 28 42N14'05 88W56'56 5:55:48
Cherrywood 11 7 39N34 89W21 5:57:24
Cherrywood 99 1 41N40 88W00 5:52:00
Cherwood Ford 18 54 39N12'07 88W12'48 5:52:51
Chester 79 66 37N54'49 89W49'19 5:59:17
Chesterfield 59 63 39N15'18 90W03'47 6:00:15
Chestervale 54 29 40N05'32 89W19'18 5:57:17
Chesterville 21 50 39N42'12 88W23'28 5:53:34
Chestline 1 66 39N50'41 90W57'35 6:03:50
Chestnut 48 33 40N46 90W17 6:01:08
Chestnut 54 55 40N03'13 89W11'07 5:56:44
Chicago 16 1 41N51'00 87W39'00 5:50:36
Chicago Heights 16 1 41N30'22 87W38'08 5:50:33
Chicago Lawn 16 1 41N47 87W43 5:50:52
Chicago Ridge 16 1 41N42'05 87W46'45 5:51:07
Chili 34 4 40N13'04 91W08'29 6:04:34
Chillicothe 72 51 40N55'20 89W29'10 5:57:57
Chilon Chalet 16 1 41N31 87W38 5:50:32
China 52 37 41N49 89W19 5:57:16
Chinatown 60 7 38N43'37 89W56'49 5:59:47
Chippendale 49 6 42N09 88W06 5:52:24
Chippewa 16 1 41N40 87W43 5:50:52
Chipps 70 7 39N37'59 88W34'52 5:54:19
Chittenden 49 140 42N22 87W53 5:51:32
Chittyville 100 4 37N49'46 89W01'40 5:56:07
Choat 64 65 37N12'48 88W47'55 5:55:12
Choctaw 12 4 39N16'56 87W43'17 5:50:53
Chouteau 60 4 38N47 90W05 6:00:20
Chrisman 23 7 39N48'13 87W40'25 5:50:42
Christopher 28 4 37N58'21 89W03'12 5:56:13
Christy 51 4 38N42 87W51 5:51:24
Churchill 6 134 41N23'15 89W10'20 5:56:41
Churchville 22 27 41N56'06 87W57'14 5:51:49
Cicero 16 1 41N50'44 87W45'14 5:51:01
Cimic 84 37 39N35'24 89W39'21 5:58:37
Cincinnati Landing 75 4 39N35'54 91W10'29 6:04:42
Cinnamon Creek 99 1 41N40 88W00 5:52:00
Cisco 74 57 40N00'41 88W43'34 5:54:54
Cisne 96 4 38N30'57 88W26'15 5:53:45
Cissna Park 38 132 40N33'53 87W53'35 5:51:34
Citation Lake Estates 16 2 42N07 87W49 5:51:16
City Park 11 7 39N34 89W21 5:57:24
Clank 2 4 37N11'18 89W19'30 5:57:18
Clare 19 40 42N00'58 88W49'45 5:55:19
Claremont 80 4 38N43'10 87W58'17 5:51:53
Clarence 27 132 40N27'50 87W58'15 5:51:53
Clarendon Hills 22 2 41N47'51 87W57'17 5:51:49
Clarion 6 54 41N30'18 89W11'31 5:56:46
Clark 31 63 39N15'35 90W34'40 6:02:19
Clark Center 12 55 39N21'45 87W46'55 5:51:08
Clarke City 46 36 41N09'29 88W14'34 5:52:58
Clarksburg 87 7 39N19'48 88W44'30 5:54:58
Clarksdale 11 63 39N29'23 89W22'04 5:57:28
Clarksville 12 55 39N27'06 87W47'52 5:51:11
Clarksville 57 7 40N39'02 88W50'54 5:55:24
Clarmin 95 55 38N13'16 89W41'58 5:58:48
Claus 99 22 41N22'11 87W36'36 5:50:26
Clay City 13 4 38N41'19 88W21'15 5:53:25
Claypool 32 125 41N22 88W25 5:53:40
Clays Prairie 23 128 39N41'13 87W33'48 5:50:15
Claysville 84 29 39N52'02 89W54'01 5:59:36
Clayton 1 63 40N01'53 90W57'38 6:03:51
Claytonville 38 7 40N34'01 87W49'23 5:51:18
Clearing 16 1 41N46'41 87W45'42 5:51:03
Clear Lake 9 7 40N03'02 90W18'32 6:01:14
Clear Lake 84 29 39N48'49 89W34'07 5:58:16
Cleburne 28 4 37N56'09 89W03'13 5:56:13
Clement 14 55 38N36 89W18 5:57:12
Clements 69 63 39N37'08 90W09'03 6:00:36
Cleone 12 4 39N25'23 87W54'27 5:51:38
Cleveland 37 63 41N30'22 90W18'53 6:01:16
Cliffdale 7 4 39N21'38 90W37'35 6:02:30
Clifford 100 4 37N49'25 89W04'38 5:56:19
Clifton 38 35 40N56'07 87W56'04 5:51:44
Clifton Terrace 60 7 38N55'46 90W15'20 6:01:01
Clifty Heights 100 4 37N46 88W56 5:55:44
Clinch 73 4 38N01 89W14 5:56:56
Clinton 20 8 40N09'13 88W57'52 5:55:51
Clintonia 20 8 40N10 88W59 5:55:56
Clover 37 4 41N12 90W16 6:01:04
Cloverdale 22 1 41N56'22 88W07'13 5:52:29
Cloverdale 90 98 40N38'25 89W30'58 5:58:04
Cloverleaf 60 25 38N41 90W07 6:00:28
Cloverleaf 81 87 41N30 90W30 6:02:00
Clyde 16 1 41N51 87W46 5:51:04
Clyde 98 55 41N53 89W55 5:59:40
Coach Light Manor 16 6 42N04 87W57 5:51:48
Coal City 32 30 41N17'16 88W17'08 5:53:09
Coaler 38 16 40N44'50 87W43'59 5:50:56
Coal Hollow 6 41 41N21'56 89W21'48 5:57:27
Coalton 68 7 39N16'58 89W18'04 5:57:12
Coalton 92 80 40N25'57 87W35'24 5:50:22
Coal Valley 81 87 41N25'43 90W27'39 6:01:51
Coatsburg 1 63 40N01'58 91W09'27 6:04:38
Cobblestone 16 1 42N04 87W48 5:51:12
Cobblewood 16 2 42N07 87W49 5:51:16
Cobden 91 4 37N31'53 89W15'12 5:57:01
Coe 81 4 41N37 90W16 6:01:04
Coello (North City) 28 4 37N59'39 89W04'02 5:56:16
Coffee 93 4 38N20 87W52 5:51:28
Coffeen 68 63 39N05'21 89W23'26 5:57:34
Colby Point 56 27 42N17'47 88W14'24 5:52:58
Colchester 55 4 40N25'35 90W47'33 6:03:10
Coldbrook 94 4 40N56'51 90W31'02 6:02:04
Cold Spring 87 63 39N18 88W58 5:55:52
Coleman 45 107 41N58'43 88W17'50 5:53:11
Coles 15 63 39N31'13 88W28'16 5:53:53
Coleta 98 4 41N54'08 89W48'08 5:59:13
Colfax 57 55 40N34'01 88W36'59 5:54:28
College Heights 83 4 37N49 88W27 5:53:48
College Park 45 107 42N02 88W17 5:53:08
College View 99 114 41N35 88W03 5:52:12
Collins 79 55 38N01'15 89W56'52 5:59:47
Collins 99 82 41N35 88W11 5:52:44
Collins 101 4 42N29 89W02 5:56:08
Collinsville 60 7 38N40'13 89W59'04 5:59:56
Collison 92 38 40N13'30 87W48'14 5:51:13
Colmar 55 4 40N20'43 90W53'28 6:03:34
Coloma 98 26 41N47 89W41 5:58:44
Colona 37 63 41N29'02 90W21'11 6:01:25
Colonial Gardens 101 55 42N19 89W02 5:56:08
Colonial Heights 16 6 42N04 87W57 5:51:48
Colonial Ridge 16 6 42N03 87W53 5:51:32
Colonial Village 60 7 38N57 90W11 6:00:44
Colonial Village 99 1 41N40 88W00 5:52:00
Colony Park 22 2 41N53 88W05 5:52:20
Colony Point 49 6 42N10 87W53 5:51:32
Colp 100 4 37N48'19 89W04'48 5:56:19
Columbia 67 46 38N26'37 90W12'04 6:00:48
Columbus 1 63 39N59'17 91W08'48 6:04:35
Colusa 34 4 40N34'15 91W10'04 6:04:40
Colvin Park 19 110 42N08'17 88W47'00 5:55:08
Combs 74 55 40N07'10 88W36'37 5:54:26
Comer 59 47 39N17'35 89W58'14 5:59:53
Como 98 26 41N45'59 89W46'01 5:59:04
Compro 84 101 39N35'23 89W46'57 5:59:08
Compromise 10 54 40N16 88W00 5:52:00
Compton 52 57 41N41'40 89W04'52 5:56:19
Conant 73 4 38N03'21 89W28'56 5:57:56
Concord 69 66 39N49'00 90W22'22 6:01:29
Concord Green 49 42 42N16 87W56 5:51:44
Condit 10 54 40N16 88W17 5:53:08
Confidence 26 4 38N55'22 88W55'35 5:55:42
Congerville 102 5 40N37'01 89W12'15 5:56:49
Congress Park 16 1 41N50 87W51 5:51:24
Conlogue 25 128 39N35'24 87W47'25 5:51:10
Connelly Ford 12 4 39N15'09 87W55'30 5:51:42
Conover 47 25 41N39 88W27 5:53:48
Conover 63 66 40N10'38 90W01'26 6:00:06
Conrad 7 65 38N55'31 90W37'01 6:02:28
Continental Village 49 140 42N23 87W52 5:51:28
Cooks Mills 15 65 39N34'57 88W24'22 5:53:37
Cooksville 57 57 40N32'35 88W42'59 5:54:52
Cooper 84 8 39N45 89W26 5:57:44
Cooper 90 98 40N39'37 89W24'15 5:57:37
Cooperstown 5 65 39N57'50 90W36'23 6:02:26
Copley 48 4 41N01 90W09 6:00:36
Cora 39 50 37N49'26 89W40'13 5:58:41
Coral 56 29 42N13'02 88W33'52 5:54:15
Coral Gable 82 25 38N36 89W58 5:59:52
Cordes 95 4 38N17'46 89W27'26 5:57:50
Cordova 81 4 41N40'49 90W19'08 6:01:17
Corinth 100 4 37N49'08 88W46'35 5:55:06
Cornell 53 55 40N59'24 88W43'45 5:54:55
Cornerville 33 4 37N54'25 88W37'24 5:54:30
Cornland 54 4 39N56'14 89W24'08 5:57:37
Cornwall 37 4 41N22 90W02 6:00:08
Cortese 46 115 41N05 87W53 5:51:32
Cortland 19 6 41N55'12 88W41'19 5:54:45
Corwin 54 63 40N06 89W32 5:58:08
Costin 57 104 40N29 88W59 5:55:56
Cottage 83 4 37N44 88W25 5:53:40
Cottage Grove 83 4 37N44'53 88W24'38 5:53:39
Cottage Hills 60 29 38N54'11 90W04'12 6:00:17
Cotton Hill 84 55 39N40 89W33 5:58:12
Cottonwood 30 4 37N53'21 88W12'47 5:52:51
Coughlin 72 51 40N53'45 89W29'47 5:57:59
Coulterville 79 55 38N11'11 89W36'20 5:58:25
Council Hill 43 4 42N29'19 90W21'13 6:01:25
Country Acres 82 25 38N31 89W59 5:59:56
Country Aire 45 107 42N02 88W17 5:53:08
Country Club Hills 16 6 41N34'05 87W43'13 5:50:53
Country Club Manor 16 6 41N35 87W46 5:51:04
Country Club Place 82 25 38N31 89W59 5:59:56
Country Club Terrace 82 25 38N31 89W59 5:59:56
Country Courts 81 87 41N30 90W30 6:02:00
Country Esquire 10 138 40N06 88W12 5:52:48
Country Fair 10 21 40N07 88W15 5:53:00
Country Gardens 16 1 42N07 87W56 5:51:44
Country Heights 41 4 38N18 88W55 5:55:40
Country Knolls 45 107 42N02 88W17 5:53:08
Country Lake 22 12 41N47 88W09 5:52:36
Country Manor 25 4 39N07 88W33 5:54:12
Countryside 16 1 41N46'58 87W52'41 5:51:31
Countryside 45 25 41N39 88W27 5:53:48
Countryside Lake 49 126 42N14 87W59 5:51:56
Countryside Manor 49 42 42N16 87W56 5:51:44
Country View Estates 99 12 41N47 88W09 5:52:36
Covel 57 104 40N29 88W59 5:55:56
Covell 57 4 40N26'34 89W06'30 5:56:26
Coventry 56 9 42N14 88W21 5:53:24
Covington 95 4 38N27'17 89W26'09 5:57:45
Cowden 87 63 39N14'54 88W51'44 5:55:27
Cowling 93 4 38N18'41 87W56'21 5:51:45
Coyne 56 21 42N11'01 88W27'07 5:53:48
Coyne Center 81 4 41N24'17 90W33'33 6:02:14
Coynes 99 114 41N34'32 88W08'34 5:52:34
Crab Orchard 100 4 37N43'45 88W48'15 5:55:13
Crab Orchard Estates 100 4 37N44'58 89W08'51 5:56:35
Cragin 16 2 41N55 87W45 5:51:00
Craig Place 22 83 41N53 88W01 5:52:04
Crain 39 4 37N46'48 89W30'28 5:58:02
Crainville 100 4 37N45'07 89W04'04 5:56:16
Cramer 72 60 40N41'28 89W56'49 5:59:47
Crandall 90 98 40N37'58 89W25'55 5:57:44
Crane Creek 63 63 40N10 89W53 5:59:32
Crater Prec 7 63 39N16 90W38 6:02:32
Cravat 41 4 38N25'25 89W05'35 5:56:22
Crawford Countryside 16 29 41N31'15 87W42'48 5:50:51
Creal Springs 100 4 37N37'10 88W50'12 5:55:21
Creek 20 4 40N06 88W51 5:55:24
Creekside 16 29 41N30 87W42 5:50:48
Creekwood 16 1 41N40 88W00 5:52:00
Crenshaw 100 4 37N46 88W56 5:55:44
Crenshaw Crossing 100 4 37N46'26 88W58'46 5:55:55
Crescent 38 7 40N44 87W50 5:51:20
Crescent 90 98 40N32'50 89W39'56 5:58:40
Cresent (Cresent City P O) 38 7 40N46'12 87W51'32 5:51:26
Cress Creek 22 12 41N47 88W09 5:52:36
Crest Haven 82 25 38N31 89W59 5:59:56
Crest Hill 99 114 41N33'17 88W05'55 5:52:24
Creston 71 6 41N55'51 88W57'52 5:55:51
Crestview Terrace 96 4 38N23 88W22 5:53:28
Crestwood 16 26 41N39'40 87W45'09 5:51:01
Crestwood Estates 100 4 37N46 88W56 5:55:44
Crete 49 1 41N26'40 87W37'53 5:50:32
Creve Coeur 90 98 40N38'50 89W35'28 5:58:22
Cricket Hill 16 29 41N30 87W42 5:50:48
Crisp 96 4 38N26'22 88W35'44 5:54:23
Crittenden 10 54 39N55 88W11 5:52:44
Crocketts Estates 49 27 42N23 88W09 5:52:36
Croft 65 29 40N02'53 89W35'18 5:58:21
Crook 33 4 38N05 88W26 5:53:44
Crooked Lake 49 6 42N25 88W04 5:52:16
Crooked Lake Oaks 49 6 42N25 88W04 5:52:16
Cropsey 57 55 40N36'33 88W28'43 5:53:55
Crossroads 44 4 37N20'56 88W49'03 5:55:16
Crossroads 82 25 38N35'33 89W57'59 5:59:52
Crossroad Terrace 82 25 38N37 90W01 6:00:04
Crossville 97 4 38N09'42 88W03'55 5:52:16
Crouch 33 4 38N13 88W31 5:54:04
Crown Estates 22 27 41N54 87W57 5:51:48
Cruger 102 71 40N43'19 89W18'36 5:57:14
Cruse 13 4 38N49'18 88W40'40 5:54:43
Crystal Gardens 56 9 42N14'01 88W22'48 5:53:31
Crystal Lake 56 9 42N14'28 88W18'58 5:53:16
Crystal Lake 60 7 38N57 90W11 6:00:44
Crystal Lake Estates 56 9 42N14 88W21 5:53:24
Crystal Lawns 99 114 41N32 88W05 5:52:20
Crystal Manor 56 9 42N13'23 88W17'30 5:53:10
Crystal Vista 56 9 42N14'19 88W22'16 5:53:29
Cuba 29 62 40N29'34 90W11'26 6:00:46
Cuba 49 1 42N11'02 88W11'27 5:52:46
Cufty Heights 100 4 37N46 88W56 5:55:44
Cullom 53 44 40N52'40 88W16'09 5:53:05
Culver 65 55 40N00'24 89W41'14 5:58:45
Cumberland Green 45 95 41N54 88W19 5:53:16
Cumberland Heights 96 4 38N23 88W22 5:53:28
Cunningham Courts 16 6 42N06 88W02 5:52:08
Curran 84 55 39N44'32 89W46'19 5:59:05
Curtis 65 29 40N03'44 89W47'25 5:59:10
Cushman 70 61 39N39'36 88W37'27 5:54:30
Custer 62 54 41N02'14 89W09'13 5:56:37
Custer 99 37 41N14 88W09 5:52:36
Custer Park 99 37 41N15 88W08 5:52:32
Cutler 73 63 38N01'56 89W33'56 5:58:16
Cutmer 38 7 40N39'01 87W36'00 5:50:24
Cypress 44 4 37N21'54 89W01'05 5:56:04
d'Adrian Gardens 60 7 38N57 90W11 6:00:44
Daggett 8 4 42N01'57 89W58'25 5:59:54
Dahinda 48 4 40N55'29 90W06'32 6:00:26
Dahlgren 33 4 38N11'53 88W41'04 5:54:44
Dailey 10 54 40N14'20 87W56'51 5:51:47
Dakota 89 67 42N23'19 89W31'34 5:58:06
Dale 33 4 37N59'42 88W29'30 5:53:58
Dale 57 4 40N26 89W05 5:56:20
Dallasania 83 4 37N41 88W38 5:54:32
Dallas City 34 4 40N38'10 91W10'02 6:04:40
Dalton City 70 55 39N42'43 88W48'16 5:55:13
Dalzell 6 134 41N21'28 89W10'34 5:56:42
Damascus 89 61 42N22'20 89W42'22 5:58:49

Damiansville 14
49 38N30'36 89W37'10 5:58:29
Damon 5 66 40N04'59 90W49'48 6:03:19
Dana 50 55 40N57'28 88W57'00 5:55:48
Danforth 38 29 40N49'13 87W58'40 5:51:55
Danley 79 55 38N05'44 90W06'56 6:00:28
Danvers 57 20 40N31'46 89W10'38 5:56:43
Danville 92 26 40N07'28 87W37'48 5:50:31
Danway 50 120 41N25'57 88W41'30 5:54:46
Dareville 41 4 38N11'54 88W58'35 5:55:54
Darien 22 54 41N45 87W58 5:51:52
Darmstadt 82 39 38N19'15 89W43'54 5:58:56
Darrow 38 56 40N43'08 87W36'11 5:50:25
Darwin 12 4 39N17'00 87W36'43 5:50:27
Davis 69 113 39N40'46 90W13'06 6:00:52
Davis 89 65 42N25'21 89W24'49 5:57:39
Davis Junction 71
57 42N06'06 89W05'35 5:56:22
Dawleys 2 4 37N12'45 89W17'46 5:57:11
Dawson 84 29 39N51'10 89W27'48 5:57:51
Daysville 71 28 41N59'04 89W19'06 5:57:16
Dayton 37 63 41N29'21 90W19'17 6:01:17
Dayton 50 6 41N23'05 88W47'39 5:55:11
Dearborn Heights 16
1 41N43 87W45 5:51:00
Decatur 58 26 39N50'25 88W57'17 5:55:49
Decker 80 4 38N38 88W13 5:52:52
Decorra 36 4 40N43'40 90W58'12 6:03:53
Deep Lake 49 6 42N25 88W04 5:52:16
Deep Spring Woods 56
15 42N23 88W26 5:53:44
Deep Woods 49 126 42N14 87W59 5:51:56
Deer Creek 90 112 40N37'48 89W19'57 5:57:20
Deerfield 49 2 42N10'16 87W50'40 5:51:23
Deer Grove 98 29 41N36'28 89W41'22 5:58:45
Deering City 28
59 37N54'59 88W53'31 5:55:34
Dee Road 16 1 42N02 87W51 5:51:24
Deer Park 49 6 42N09'39 88W04'53 5:52:20
Deerpath 49 2 42N14'53 87W51'34 5:51:26
Deer Plain 7 65 38N55'54 90W31'59 6:02:08
Deers 10 54 40N03'18 88W07'21 5:52:29
Dees 18 55 39N13'23 88W09'33 5:52:38
Degognia 39 50 37N51'40 89W37'49 5:58:31
De Kalb 19 36 41N55'46 88W45'01 5:55:00
Delafield 33 4 38N08'52 88W36'10 5:54:25
De Land 74 55 40N07'20 88W38'43 5:54:35
Delavan 90 35 40N22'21 89W32'50 5:58:11
Delhi 42 25 39N02'43 90W15'21 6:01:01
Dellwood Highlands 99
114 41N35 88W03 5:52:12
Delmar 46 82 41N10'39 87W36'18 5:50:25
Del Mar Woods 49
2 42N12 87W51 5:51:24
DeLong 48 33 40N49'00 90W18'16 6:01:13
De Long 92 43 40N06'47 87W54'07 5:51:36
Delrey 38 29 40N40'22 88W01'02 5:52:04
Delta 83 4 37N41'03 88W42'10 5:54:49
Delwood 76 4 37N34'47 88W34'17 5:54:17
Dement 71 6 41N56 89W00 5:56:00
Democrat Spring 42
55 39N05'02 90W29'01 6:01:56
Denison 51 4 38N38 87W42 5:50:48
Denmark 73 63 37N59'51 89W29'50 5:57:59
Denning 28 4 37N54 88W58 5:55:52
Dennison 12 56 39N27'39 87W35'52 5:50:23
Denny 73 4 38N02'51 89W19'37 5:57:18
Denrock 98 4 41N41'59 89W58'32 5:59:54
Denver 34 4 40N17'26 91W06'25 6:04:26
Denver 80 4 38N48 88W12 5:52:48
Depler Springs 29
7 40N25'59 90W11'04 6:00:44
Depue 6 48 41N19'27 89W18'24 5:57:14
Derby 27 111 40N26'30 88W26'33 5:53:46
Derby 83 4 37N37'44 88W23'08 5:53:33
Derinda 43 4 42N14 90W09 6:00:36
Derinda Center 43
4 42N19 90W13 6:00:52
Derry 75 4 39N37 90W58 6:03:52
Deselm 46 26 41N14'58 87W58'28 5:51:54
De Soto 39 4 37N49'03 89W13'40 5:56:55
Des Plaines 16 1 42N02'00 87W53'00 5:51:32
Detroit 75 4 39N37'14 90W40'36 6:02:42
Devereux Heights 84
133 39N50'59 89W36'43 5:58:27
Dewey 10 54 40N19'08 88W16'55 5:53:08
Dewey Park 60 25 38N48 89W57 5:59:48
DeWitt 20 63 40N10'52 88W47'10 5:55:09
Dewmaine 100 4 37N46'50 89W04'37 5:56:18
Dexter 25 56 39N04'51 88W41'00 5:54:44
Diamond 32 37 41N17'19 88W15'06 5:53:00
Diamond City 33 4 38N05'21 88W33'09 5:54:13
Diamond Lake 49 6 42N14'40 88W00'36 5:52:02
Diana 28 4 38N05'59 88W45'05 5:55:00
Dickerson 10 54 40N19'06 88W25'20 5:53:41
Dickeys 46 60 41N03'03 88W02'14 5:52:09
Dieterich 25 4 39N03'43 88W22'47 5:53:31
Dillon 90 35 40N28'36 89W32'17 5:58:09
Dillsburg 57 29 40N18'59 88W04'46 5:52:19
Dimmick 50 55 41N26'25 89W06'59 5:56:28
Diona 15 4 39N22'36 88W08'21 5:52:33
Disco 34 4 40N37'13 91W01'16 6:04:05
Diswood 2 4 37N13'53 89W19'22 5:57:17
Divernon 84 37 39N33'56 89W39'26 5:58:38
Divide 41 4 38N26'49 88W49'47 5:55:19
Divine 32 48 41N23'09 88W17'43 5:53:11
Dix 41 4 38N26'30 88W56'15 5:55:45
Dixmoor 16 2 41N37'54 87W39'39 5:50:39
Dixon 52 25 41N50'20 89W28'46 5:57:55
Dixon Springs 76
4 37N23'04 88W40'07 5:54:40
Dobbins Downs 10
138 40N06 88W12 5:52:48
Dodds 41 4 38N15 88W53 5:55:32
Doddsville 55 4 40N16'42 90W39'06 6:02:36
Dogtown Landing 7
65 38N58'59 90W40'16 6:02:41
Dog Walk 100 4 37N45'33 88W55'58 5:55:44
Dogwood 17 4 39N03'50 87W53'27 5:51:34
Dollville 87 63 39N26'13 88W59'30 5:55:58
Dolson 12 4 39N26 87W51 5:51:24
Dolton 16 1 41N38'20 87W36'26 5:50:26
Doney 46 82 41N04'00 87W37'30 5:50:30
Dongola 91 23 37N21'40 89W09'57 5:56:40
Donnellson 68 63 39N01'40 89W28'24 5:57:54
Donovan 38 57 40N53'00 87W36'58 5:50:28
Dora 70 55 39N43 88W44 5:54:56
Dorans 15 63 39N33'04 88W20'40 5:53:23
Dorchester 59 55 39N05'08 89W53'15 5:59:33
Dorr 56 15 42N17 88W24 5:53:36
Dorris Heights 83
4 37N44'58 88W33'11 5:54:13
Dorrisville 83 4 37N44 88W33 5:54:12
Dorsey 60 4 38N58'25 90W00'05 6:00:00
Douglas 48 60 40N47 90W01 6:00:04
Douglas 82 29 38N25'28 89W58'57 5:59:56
Douglass 48 60 40N47'10 90W05'03 6:00:20
Dover 6 55 41N26'12 89W23'36 5:57:34
Dow 42 37 39N00'48 90W20'29 6:01:22
Dowell 39 4 37N56'23 89W14'16 5:56:57
Downers Fairview 22
12 41N48 88W01 5:52:04
Downers Grove 22
12 41N48'32 88W00'40 5:52:03
Downers Grove Estates 22
12 41N48 88W01 5:52:04
Downey 49 140 42N19 87W51 5:51:24
Downs 57 79 40N23'49 88W52'14 5:55:29
Downtown 84 133 39N48 89W39 5:58:36
Dozaville 79 63 37N54'25 89W57'23 5:59:50
Drake 31 4 39N27'32 90W28'14 6:01:53
Dresden Acres 32
125 41N22 88W25 5:53:40
Dressor 26 63 39N10'23 89W03'04 5:56:12
Drew Dell Acres 60
7 38N57 90W11 6:00:44
Drexel 16 1 41N51 87W46 5:51:04
Drivers 41 4 38N19'50 88W59'35 5:55:58
Druce Lake 49 6 42N22'18 88W00'09 5:52:01
Drummer 27 111 40N28 88W24 5:53:36
Drummond 99 48 41N24'21 88W10'36 5:52:42
Drury 81 4 41N23 90W58 6:03:52
Dry Grove 57 4 40N32 89W06 5:56:24
Dry Hill 39 4 37N49'02 89W33'12 5:58:13
Dry Point 87 63 39N14 88W52 5:55:28
Du Bois 95 4 38N13'26 89W12'44 5:56:51
DuBois Center 95
4 38N15'06 89W12'41 5:56:51
Duck Lake Woods 49
27 42N23 88W09 5:52:36
Dudley 25 128 39N34'36 87W51'00 5:51:24
Dudleyville 3 55 38N49'26 89W25'05 5:57:40
Duncan 66 4 41N17 90W51 6:03:24
Duncan 88 55 40N59'01 89W47'21 5:59:09
Duncan Mills 29 4 40N20'24 90W11'27 6:00:46
Duncanville 17 4 38N57'17 87W41'44 5:50:47
Dundas 80 4 38N50'06 88W05'06 5:52:20
Dundee Station 45
10 42N05'56 88W16'17 5:53:05
Dunes Park 49 140 42N25'15 87W49'32 5:51:18
Dunfermline 29 7 40N29'28 90W01'54 6:00:08
Dunham 56 7 42N23 88W38 5:54:32
Dunham Castle 45
26 41N57'08 88W16'17 5:53:05
Dunham Woods 45 2 41N57 88W16 5:53:04
Dunhurst 16 6 42N09 87W57 5:51:48
Dunkle 11 61 39N28'05 89W03'46 5:56:15
Dunlap 72 57 40N51'42 89W40'43 5:58:43
Dunlap Lake 60 25 38N48 89W57 5:59:48
Dunleith 43 4 42N29 90W37 6:02:28
Dunn 70 56 39N37'34 88W41'30 5:54:46
Dunning 16 1 41N57'10 87W47'47 5:51:11
Du Page 99 4 41N41 88W04 5:52:16
Dupo 82 46 38N30'58 90W12'37 6:00:50
Du Quoin 73 4 37N59'58 89W15'08 5:57:01
Durand 101 55 42N26'11 89W19'55 5:57:20
Durham 34 4 40N35'48 91W05'22 6:04:21
Durley 3 55 38N56'04 89W22'05 5:57:28
Dutch Creek Woodlands 56
27 42N21 88W14 5:52:56
Dutch Hollow 82
25 38N34'03 90W01'51 6:00:07
Dutch Mills 91 4 37N24'55 89W16'22 5:57:05
Dutton 75 4 39N40'28 90W47'59 6:03:12
Duvall 87 7 39N28'45 88W47'25 5:55:10
Dwight 53 26 41N05'40 88W25'30 5:53:42
Dykersburg 100 4 37N41'32 88W44'23 5:54:58
Eagerville 59 55 39N06'42 89W47'02 5:59:08
Eagle 50 4 41N09 88W54 5:55:36
Eagle 83 4 37N39'04 88W23'34 5:53:34
Eagle Creek 30 4 37N39 88W19 5:53:16
Eagle Heights 45
107 42N02 88W17 5:53:08
Eagle Lake 99 22 41N21 87W37 5:50:28
Eagle Park 60 25 38N41 90W07 6:00:28
Eagle Point 71 4 41N59'37 89W41'05 5:58:44
Eagle Point Bay 44
4 37N33 88W58 5:55:52
Earl 50 28 41N35 88W52 5:55:28
Earlville 50 28 41N35'22 88W55'19 5:55:41
East Alton 60 29 38N52'49 90W06'40 6:00:27
East Bend 10 54 40N21 88W17 5:53:08
East Brooklyn 32
36 41N10'24 88W15'50 5:53:03
Eastburn 38 56 40N46'23 87W38'08 5:50:33
East Cape Girardeau 2
4 37N19 89W26 5:57:44
East Carondelet 82
46 38N32'31 90W13'58 6:00:56
East Chicago Heights 16
1 41N30'23 87W35'30 5:50:22
East Clinton 98 4 41N50'13 90W09'54 6:00:40
East Dubuque 43 4 42N29'32 90W38'34 6:02:34
East Dundee (Dundee Station) 45
10 42N05'56 88W16'17 5:53:05
East Eldorado 83
4 37N49 88W26 5:53:44
Eastern 28 4 37N59 88W46 5:55:04
East Fulton 98 4 41N52 90W09 6:00:36
East Galena 43 4 42N25 90W23 6:01:32
East Galesburg 48
74 40N56'52 90W18'36 6:01:14
East Gillespie 59
55 39N08'27 89W48'44 5:59:15
East Grove 52 55 41N38 89W27 5:57:48
East Hannibal 75
4 39N43'47 91W21'03 6:05:24
East Hardin 31 55 39N09'36 90W36'32 6:02:26
East Hazel Crest 16
1 41N34'25 87W38'47 5:50:35
East Joliet 99
114 41N32'06 88W03'06 5:52:12
East Keokuk 34 4 40N24 91W24 6:05:36
East Lincoln 54 4 40N11 89W18 5:57:12
East Loon Lake 49
6 42N28 88W07 5:52:28
East Lynn 92 132 40N27'59 87W48'00 5:51:12
East Marion 100 4 37N44 88W52 5:55:28
East Meadowbrook 60
25 38N54 90W01 6:00:04
East Meadowview 46
115 41N09 87W52 5:51:28
East Moline 81 87 41N30'03 90W26'39 6:01:47
East Monroe 35 4 37N34 88W18 5:53:12
East Nelson 70 7 39N34 88W32 5:54:08
East Newbern 42 4 39N00'52 90W18'48 6:01:15
East Oakland 15
65 39N38 88W01 5:52:04
Easton 63 63 40N13'57 89W50'33 5:59:22
East Peoria 90 98 40N39'58 89W34'48 5:58:19
East River 46 26 41N01 87W43 5:50:52
East Rockford 101
28 42N17 89W04 5:56:16
East Saint Louis 82
25 38N37'28 90W09'03 6:00:36
East Side 16 1 41N42'44 87W31'55 5:50:08
East Wenona 50 29 41N04 89W03 5:56:12
East Winchester 86
63 39N37 90W25 6:01:40
Eastwood Manor 56
27 42N20'44 88W14'28 5:52:58
Eaton 17 4 39N05'23 87W48'05 5:51:12
Eberle 25 4 38N56'33 88W27'25 5:53:50
Ebner 8 4 41N55'55 90W06'27 6:00:26
Echo Lake 49 6 42N12 88W03 5:52:12
Eckard 63 55 40N19'11 89W59'20 5:59:57
Eddy 49 17 42N27'41 87W53'54 5:51:36
Eddyville 76 4 37N29'56 88W35'16 5:54:21
Edelstein 72 57 40N56'27 89W37'45 5:58:31
Eden 50 136 41N14 89W06 5:56:24
Eden 72 57 40N41'20 89W49'58 5:59:20
Eden 79 63 38N07'14 89W40'03 5:58:40
Eden Park 100 4 37N45'18 89W01'26 5:56:06
Edford 37 4 41N27 90W15 6:01:00
Edgar 23 7 39N45'20 87W42'04 5:50:48
Edgebrook 16 2 42N00 87W46 5:51:04
Edgemont 82 25 38N35'37 90W03'49 6:00:15
Edgetown 46 82 41N10'46 87W34'32 5:50:18
Edgewood 10 138 40N06 88W12 5:52:48
Edgewood 25 4 38N55'14 88W39'41 5:54:39
Edgewood 60 7 38N57 90W11 6:00:44
Edgewood 102 71 40N43 89W17 5:57:08
Edgewood Heights 4
28 42N16 89W00 5:56:00
Edgington 81 4 41N23 90W44 6:02:56
Edginton 81 4 41N23'13 90W45'49 6:03:03
Edinburg 11 55 39N39'26 89W23'22 5:57:33
Edison Square 49
140 42N23 87W52 5:51:28
Edwards 72 4 40N44'45 89W44'39 5:58:59
Edwardsville 60
25 38N48'41 89W57'11 5:59:49
Effingham 25 59 39N07'12 88W32'36 5:54:10
Effner 38 56 40N46'14 87W31'34 5:50:06
Egan 71 4 42N11'18 89W24'21 5:57:37
Egyptian Hills 100
4 37N37 88W50 5:55:20
Egyptian Shores 100
4 37N37 88W50 5:55:20
Eichorn 35 4 37N29'28 88W24'19 5:53:37
Eileen 32 36 41N17'39 88W16'16 5:53:05
Ela 49 6 42N12 88W04 5:52:16
Elba 30 4 37N49'35 88W19'35 5:53:18
Elba 48 4 40N51 90W03 6:00:12
Elba Center 48 60 40N50'39 90W02'35 6:00:10
Elbow 80 4 38N38'32 88W07'18 5:52:29
Elbridge 23 56 39N30'45 87W34'58 5:50:20
Elburn 45 84 41N53'32 88W28'20 5:53:53
Elco 2 4 37N18'02 89W15'57 5:57:04
El Dara 75 4 39N37'21 90W59'30 6:03:58
Eldena 52 29 41N46'16 89W24'36 5:57:38
Elderville 34 4 40N19'49 91W17'40 6:05:11
Eldorado 83 4 37N48'49 88W26'17 5:53:45
Eldred 31 63 39N17'15 90W33'08 6:02:13
Eldridge 46 82 41N09'34 87W43'12 5:50:53
Eleanor 94 4 40N58'58 90W41'42 6:02:47
Eleroy 89 4 42N19'57 89W45'38 5:59:03
Elgin 45 107 42N02'14 88W16'52 5:53:07
Eliza 66 4 41N17'45 90W58'03 6:03:52
Elizabeth 43 4 42N19'04 90W13'17 6:00:53
Elizabethtown 35
4 37N26'45 88W18'18 5:53:13
Elk 39 4 37N54 89W14 5:56:56
Elk Grove 16 27 41N59'54 88W00'13 5:52:01
Elk Grove Village 16
27 42N00'14 87W58'13 5:51:53
Elkhart 54 29 40N01'14 89W28'58 5:57:56
Elkhorn 5 65 39N53 90W44 6:02:56
Elkhorn Grove 8 4 42N00'29 89W44'04 5:58:56
Elk Prairie 41 4 38N10 88W59 5:55:56
Elk Ridge Villa 16
6 42N04 87W57 5:51:48
Elkton 95 4 38N17'30 89W33'24 5:58:14
Elkville 39 4 37N54'36 89W14'09 5:56:57
Ellery 96 4 38N21'17 88W08'55 5:52:36
Ellington 1 92 39N58 91W20 6:05:20
Elliott 27 39 40N27'53 88W16'20 5:53:05
Elliottstown 25 4 39N00'04 88W27'10 5:53:49
Ellis 11 4 39N35'24 89W31'44 5:58:07
Ellis 84 29 39N56'48 89W35'55 5:58:24
Ellis 92 38 40N21'19 87W53'06 5:51:32
Ellis Grove 79 63 38N00'32 89W54'21 5:59:37
Ellison 94 4 40N46 90W43 6:02:52
Ellisville 29 4 40N37'36 90W18'18 6:01:13
Ellsworth 57 29 40N27'01 88W43'00 5:54:52
Ellwood 19 110 42N06 88W42 5:54:48
Elm Estates 22 27 41N54 87W57 5:51:48
Elm Grove 90 21 40N32 89W34 5:58:16

Elmhurst 22 2 41N53'58 87w56'25 5:51:46
Elmira 88 4 41N10'47 89w49'54 5:59:20
Elmore 88 58 40N57'24 89w58'37 5:59:54
El Morro 16 6 41N36 87w45 5:51:00
Elmoville 43 4 42N15'56 90w02'49 6:00:11
Elm River 96 4 38N31 88w19 5:53:16
Elmwood 72 60 40N46'40 89w57'59 5:59:52
Elmwood Park 16 2 41N55'16 87w48'33 5:51:14
El Paso 102 69 40N44'21 89w00'59 5:56:04
El-Rancho 46 115 41N05 87w53 5:51:32
Elsah 42 55 38N57'22 90w21'35 6:01:26
Elsdon 16 1 41N47'37 87w43'18 5:50:53
El Sierra 22 12 41N48 88w01 5:52:04
Elva 19 36 41N51'51 88w46'34 5:55:06
Elvaston 34 4 40N23'42 91w14'58 6:05:00
Elvira 44 4 37N29'36 89w01'46 5:56:07
El Vista 16 6 41N36 87w45 5:51:00
El Vista 72 98 40N43'44 89w37'45 5:58:31
Elwin 58 26 39N46'44 88w58'48 5:55:55
Elwood 99 70 41N24'14 88w06'42 5:52:27
Embarrass 15 67 39N31'02 88w05'28 5:52:22
Emden 54 29 40N17'55 89w29'06 5:57:56
Emerald Green 22 26 41N49 88w11 5:52:44
Emerald Park 56 27 42N19'08 88w15'01 5:53:00
Emerald Terrace 82 25 38N31 89w59 5:59:56
Emerson 98 26 41N48'22 89w45'53 5:59:04
Emerson City 41 4 38N08'22 89w02'43 5:56:11
Emery 58 26 39N58'45 88w57'04 5:55:48
Eminence 54 4 40N17 89w19 5:57:16
Emington 53 36 40N58'11 88w21'29 5:53:26
Emma 97 4 37N58'29 88w07'13 5:52:29
Emmet 55 4 40N30 90w44 6:02:56
Empire 57 4 40N18'20 88w42'27 5:54:50
Enchanted Forest 72 98 40N42 89w38 5:58:32
Energy 100 63 37N46'26 89w01'35 5:56:06
Enfield 97 4 38N05'58 88w20'15 5:53:21
Englemann 82 55 38N26 89w46 5:59:04
Englewood 16 1 41N46'47 87w38'45 5:50:35
English 42 55 39N08 90w26 6:01:44
Enion 29 55 40N16'30 90w10'38 6:00:43
Enos 59 47 39N18'04 90w00'27 6:00:02
Enright 57 4 40N44'23 88w58'01 5:55:52
Enterprise 96 4 38N31'20 88w21'27 5:53:26
Eola 22 19 41N46'39 88w14'34 5:52:58
Eppards Point 53 127 40N48 88w38 5:54:32
Epplyanna 89 65 42N25'30 89w26'39 5:57:47
Epworth 97 4 38N04'14 88w06'22 5:52:25
Equality 30 4 37N44'02 88w20'36 5:53:22
Erie 98 88 41N39'23 90w04'45 6:00:19
Erienna 32 46 41N21 88w32 5:54:08
Erin 89 4 42N20 89w46 5:59:04
Ernst 12 4 39N18'58 87w40'23 5:50:42
Erwin 85 4 40N07'55 90w42'32 6:02:50
Esmen 53 55 40N59 88w39 5:54:36
Esmond 19 40 42N02'01 88w56'08 5:55:45
Essex 46 29 41N10'38 88w11'08 5:52:45
Estate Lane 16 1 42N04 87w48 5:51:12
Etherton 39 4 37N41'07 89w19'16 5:57:17
Etna 15 63 39N23'22 88w25'11 5:53:41
Euclid Lake 16 6 42N04 87w57 5:51:48
Eureka 102 71 40N43'17 89w16'22 5:57:05
Evans 54 29 40N13'18 89w21'50 5:57:27
Evans 62 54 41N02'17 89w06'20 5:56:25
Evanston 16 1 42N02'28 87w41'24 5:50:46
Evansville 79 63 38N05'25 89w56'18 5:59:45
Evarts 89 4 42N15'11 89w28'28 5:57:54
Evergreen Park 16 1 41N43'14 87w42'06 5:50:48
Evers 25 4 39N05'53 88w27'12 5:53:49
Ewbanks 1 92 39N58'43 91w19'10 6:05:17
Ewing 28 4 38N05'19 88w51'08 5:55:25
Exermont 82 7 38N38'52 90w02'47 6:00:11
Exeter 86 63 39N43'15 90w29'47 6:01:59
Exline 46 115 41N09'00 87w46'06 5:51:04
Exposition View 45 7 41N47'33 88w20'37 5:53:22
Eylar 53 36 40N54'44 88w27'10 5:53:49
Ezra 28 4 37N54 88w55 5:55:40
Fairbanks 70 55 39N43'02 88w31'48 5:54:07
Fairbury 53 72 40N44'50 88w30'53 5:54:04
Fairdale 19 56 42N06'00 88w55'58 5:55:44
Fairfield 49 6 42N13'09 88w03'41 5:52:15
Fairfield 96 4 38N22'44 88w21'35 5:53:26
Fairgrange 15 106 39N34'43 88w10'18 5:52:41
Fairhaven 8 4 41N56'44 89w55'45 5:59:43
Fairland 21 65 39N52'35 88w06'06 5:52:24
Fairman 61 4 38N40'40 89w06'17 5:56:25
Fairmont 60 7 38N54'32 90w12'51 6:00:51
Fairmont 99 114 41N33'22 88w03'33 5:52:14
Fairmont City 82 25 38N38'59 90w05'35 6:00:22
Fairmount 64 4 37N09 88w44 5:54:56
Fairmount 92 54 40N02'44 87w49'50 5:51:19
Fair Oaks 16 27 41N58 88w06 5:52:24
Fairview 11 7 39N34 89w21 5:57:24
Fairview 16 1 41N59 87w52 5:51:28
Fairview 29 65 40N38'00 90w09'49 6:00:39
Fairview 82 25 38N35'30 90w00'51 6:00:03
Fairview Addition 83 4 37N49 88w27 5:53:48
Fairview Gardens 16 6 42N04 87w57 5:51:48
Fairview Heights 82 25 38N36 90w00 6:00:00
Fairview Park Plaza 14 4 38N31 89w08 5:56:32
Fairway Estates 22 2 41N53 88w05 5:52:20
Fairway Trace 16 6 42N03 87w53 5:51:32
Faithorn 99 1 41N25'41 87w36'29 5:50:26
Fall Creek 1 66 39N46'44 91w18'08 6:05:13
Falling Spring 82 46 38N31'57 90w11'12 6:00:45
Fall River 50 6 41N18 88w46 5:55:04
Falmouth 40 4 39N03'17 88w08'44 5:52:35
Fancher 87 63 39N16'03 88w46'23 5:55:06
Fancy Creek 84 133 39N54 89w39 5:58:36
Fancy Prairie 65 29 39N59'51 89w35'58 5:58:24
Fandon 55 4 40N22'06 90w45'41 6:03:03
Fargo 5 66 39N58'25 90w51'17 6:03:25
Farina 26 4 38N50'03 88w46'20 5:55:05
Farmdale 90 98 40N39'57 89w30'40 5:58:03
Farmer City 20 57 40N14'36 88w38'33 5:54:34
Farmers 29 63 40N25 90w24 6:01:36
Farmersville 68 63 39N26'36 89w39'06 5:58:36
Farmingdale 22 19 41N47 87w59 5:51:56
Farmingdale 84 29 39N49'22 89w48'22 5:59:13
Farmingdale South 22 19 41N47 87w59 5:51:56
Farmingdale Terrace 22 19 41N47 87w59 5:51:56
Farmingdale Village 22 19 41N47 87w59 5:51:56
Farmington 15 63 39N23'45 88w12'40 5:52:51
Farmington 29 61 40N41'53 90w00'21 6:00:01
Farmington 45 95 41N54 88w19 5:53:16
Farm Ridge 50 41 41N15 88w52 5:55:28
Farmsted 22 12 41N47 88w09 5:52:36
Farnsworth 49 140 42N19 87w50 5:51:20
Farrington 12 56 39N28'12 87w32'46 5:50:11
Farrington 41 4 38N26 88w45 5:55:00
Farrow 72 98 40N41 89w37 5:58:28
Fay 8 4 42N00'12 90w00'58 6:00:04
Fayette 31 55 39N19'12 90w09'13 6:00:37
Fayette 53 72 40N42 88w24 5:53:36
Fayetteville 82 55 38N22'39 89w47'43 5:59:11
Fayville 2 4 37N09'53 89w25'36 5:57:42
Feehanville 16 6 42N04 87w57 5:51:48
Felix 32 30 41N19 88w17 5:53:08
Felker 90 98 40N42 89w25 5:57:40
Fenton 98 8 41N43'50 90w01'48 6:00:07
Ferber 28 4 37N54'25 88w44'32 5:54:58
Fergestown 100 4 37N47'33 88w57'53 5:55:52
Ferguson Ford 5 66 39N51'40 90w54'12 6:03:37
Ferndale 56 27 42N18'07 88w14'29 5:52:58
Fernway 16 6 41N34 87w49 5:51:16
Fernway Park 16 6 41N35'13 87w49'48 5:51:19
Ferrel 23 56 39N29'46 87w35'06 5:50:20
Ferrin 14 55 38N36'34 89w14'00 5:56:56
Ferris 34 4 40N28'08 91w10'13 6:04:41
Fiatt 29 4 40N33'37 90w10'47 6:00:43
Ficklin 21 7 39N47'55 88w21'19 5:53:25
Fiday View 99 114 41N33 88w07 5:52:28
Fidelity 42 4 39N09'10 90w09'52 6:00:39
Field 41 4 38N26 88w52 5:55:28
Fieldcrest 16 6 41N36 87w45 5:51:00
Fieldon 42 55 39N06'31 90w29'54 6:02:00
Fillmore 68 66 39N06'55 89w16'44 5:57:07
Filson 21 63 39N41'22 88w13'55 5:52:56
Findlay 87 63 39N31'21 88w45'13 5:55:01
Finney Heights 14 4 38N31 89w08 5:56:32
Finneyville 35 4 37N32'40 88w06'19 5:52:25
First Pommier 46 26 41N01 87w43 5:50:52
Fisher 10 57 40N18'53 88w21'00 5:53:24
Fishhook 75 4 39N48'20 90w53'07 6:03:32
Fitchmoor 50 54 41N27'43 89w09'54 5:56:40
Fithian 92 43 40N06'50 87w52'23 5:51:30
Five Islands Park 45 55 41N58'18 88w18'35 5:53:14
Five Point 65 29 39N59'21 89w52'59 5:59:32
Five Points 19 6 42N00'09 88w44'25 5:54:58
Flag Center 71 6 41N56'26 89w07'20 5:56:29
Flagg 71 6 41N53'45 89w08'27 5:56:34
Flanagan 53 55 40N52'41 88w51'40 5:55:27
Flannigan 33 4 38N00 88w39 5:54:36
Flat Branch 87 57 39N34 88w58 5:55:52
Flat Rock 17 4 38N54'06 87w40'18 5:50:41
Flatville 10 30 40N14'22 88w03'33 5:52:14
Flatwoods 44 4 37N25'25 88w43'27 5:54:54
Fletchers 57 68 40N31'37 88w47'01 5:55:08
Flickerville 46 115 41N13'12 87w57'22 5:51:49
Flint 33 4 38N03'48 88w37'38 5:54:31
Flint 75 4 39N42 90w40 6:02:40
Flora 13 4 38N40'08 88w29'08 5:53:57
Floraville 82 55 38N22'35 90w03'22 6:00:13
Florence 86 4 39N37'38 90w36'38 6:02:27
Florence 89 4 42N12'52 89w39'35 5:58:38
Florid 78 41 41N13'43 89w16'51 5:57:07
Flossmoor 16 1 41N32'34 87w41'05 5:50:44
Flossmoor Highlands 16 1 41N32'46 87w42'48 5:50:51
Flowerfield 22 2 41N52'02 88w02'02 5:52:08
Flowerfield Acres 22 83 41N53 88w01 5:52:04
Floyd 94 4 40N51 90w30 6:02:00
Fondulac 90 98 40N42 89w31 5:58:04
Fon-Du-Lac 99 82 41N35 88w11 5:52:44
Foosland 10 54 40N21'41 88w25'41 5:53:43
Forest Acres 82 25 38N38 90w08 6:00:32
Forest City 63 7 40N22'12 89w49'39 5:59:19
Forest Estates 16 6 42N06 88w02 5:52:08
Forest Gardens 49 6 42N16 88w08 5:52:32
Foresthaven 49 2 42N14 87w53 5:51:32
Forest Heights 16 1 41N31 87w38 5:50:32
Forest Hills 16 1 41N44 87w50 5:51:20
Forest Homes 60 29 38N54'52 90w05'09 6:00:21
Forest Lake 49 6 42N12'27 88w03'20 5:52:13
Forest Manor 99 114 41N35 88w03 5:52:12
Forest Park 16 1 41N52'46 87w48'49 5:51:15
Forest Park 99 114 41N32'45 88w03'23 5:52:14
Forest River 16 1 42N05 87w54 5:51:36
Forest View 16 1 41N48'31 87w47'36 5:51:10
Forest View Hills 16 6 41N36 87w45 5:51:00
Forman 64 4 37N20'48 88w54'26 5:55:38
Formosa Junction 60 7 38N42'26 89w55'41 5:59:43
Forrest 53 72 40N45'07 88w24'40 5:53:39
Forrestal Village 49 140 42N19 87w50 5:51:20
Forreston 71 58 42N07'34 89w34'45 5:58:19
Forsyth 58 26 39N55'57 88w57'04 5:55:48
Fort Dearborn 16 1 41N54 87w37 5:50:28
Fort Gage 79 63 37N57'38 89w54'16 5:59:37
Fort Russell 60 25 38N53 89w59 5:59:56
Fort Sheridan 49 26 42N09 87w58 5:51:52
Foss Acres 49 140 42N19 87w50 5:51:20
Fossland 49 17 42N29'40 87w57'06 5:51:48
Fosterburg 60 29 38N58'18 90w04'30 6:00:18
Foster Pond 67 8 38N18'42 90w13'39 6:00:55
Fountain 67 55 38N21'45 90w16'58 6:01:08
Fountain Bluff 39 4 37N44 89w33 5:58:12
Fountain Creek 38 7 40N30'58 87w48'39 5:51:15
Fountain Gap 67 46 38N23'15 90w15'18 6:01:01
Fountain Green 34 4 40N28'33 90w58'09 6:03:53
Four Corners 60 7 38N43'06 90w04'32 6:00:18
Four Lakes 22 12 41N47 88w05 5:52:20
Four Mile 96 4 38N19 88w39 5:54:36
Fowler 1 66 40N00'28 91w15'30 6:05:02
Fox 47 25 41N37'23 88w29'42 5:53:59
Foxcroft 22 2 41N53 88w04 5:52:16
Fox Lake 49 1 42N23'48 88w11'01 5:52:44
Fox Lake Hills 49 1 42N24'29 88w07'54 5:52:32
Fox Lake Vista 49 1 42N26 88w14 5:52:56
Fox Lawn 47 25 41N39 88w27 5:53:48
Fox Point 16 6 42N09 88w06 5:52:24
Fox River 49 1 42N13 88w12 5:52:48
Fox River Estates 45 95 41N57'36 88w18'35 5:53:14
Fox River Grove 56 1 42N12'03 88w12'52 5:52:51
Fox River Heights 45 95 41N54 88w19 5:53:16
Fox River Valley Gardens 56 1 42N14'33 88w12'07 5:52:48
Francis 83 4 37N53'59 88w27'11 5:53:49
Frankfort 99 55 41N29'45 87w50'55 5:51:24
Frankfort Heights 28 4 37N54 88w55 5:55:40
Franklin 69 63 39N37'13 90w02'38 6:00:11
Franklin Corners 98 55 41N55'01 89w54'38 5:59:39
Franklin Grove 52 40 41N50'30 89w18'01 5:57:12
Franklin Park 16 1 41N56'07 87w51'56 5:51:28
Franklin Square 99 55 41N30 87w51 5:51:24
Franklinville 56 11 42N16'36 88w30'40 5:54:03
Franks 19 7 41N42'39 88w40'47 5:54:43
Fravet 90 72 40N26'56 89w22'14 5:57:29
Frederick 85 7 40N04'12 90w25'44 6:01:43
Freeburg 82 29 38N25'39 89w54'49 5:59:39
Freeman Spur 100 4 37N51'40 88w59'50 5:55:59
Freeport 89 108 42N17'48 89w37'16 5:58:29
Fremont Center 49 6 42N17'52 88w04'17 5:52:17
Fremont Junction 16 27 41N58 88w06 5:52:24
French Creek 24 4 38N18 88w01 5:52:04
Frenchman's Cove 16 6 42N06 87w58 5:51:52
French Village 82 7 38N36'01 90w03'00 6:00:12
Frielings 46 39 41N09'38 88w06'47 5:52:27
Friends Creek 58 57 40N00 88w49 5:55:16
Friendsville 93 4 38N30'11 87w48'59 5:51:16
Frisco 28 4 38N06'48 88w46'42 5:55:07
Frog City 2 4 37N06 89w16 5:57:04
Frogtown 95 4 38N26'32 89w29'30 5:57:58
Frontenac 22 12 41N44'41 88w13'58 5:52:56
Frontenac Place 60 7 38N57 90w11 6:00:44
Fruit 60 25 38N49'51 89w51'45 5:59:27
Fruitland 81 87 41N28'17 90w31'00 6:02:04
Fruitland Landing 7 4 38N52'18 90w34'03 6:02:16
Fry's Wheatland View 99 12 41N47 88w09 5:52:36
Fulkerson Landing 42 65 38N58'21 90w32'45 6:02:11
Fuller 70 65 39N35'38 88w28'12 5:53:53
Fullerton 20 63 40N12'37 88w44'40 5:54:59
Fulls 10 138 40N06'48 88w05'25 5:52:22
Fulton 98 4 41N52'02 90w09'34 6:00:38
Fults 67 63 38N09'58 90w12'57 6:00:52
Funkhouser 25 56 39N05'39 88w37'16 5:54:29
Funks Grove 57 73 40N21'49 89w06'52 5:56:27
Furman 82 25 38N36'05 89w58'00 5:59:52
Future City 2 4 37N01'44 89w11'17 5:56:45
Gages Lake 49 27 42N21 88w01 5:52:04
Galatia 83 4 37N50'26 88w36'33 5:54:26
Gale 2 4 37N14'56 89w26'51 5:57:47
Galena 43 4 42N25'00 90w25'44 6:01:43
Galena Junction 43 4 42N22'26 90w26'35 6:01:46
Galesburg 48 74 40N56'52 90w22'16 6:01:29
Galesville 74 55 40N09'19 88w33'23 5:54:14
Gallagher 80 4 38N38'04 88w10'02 5:52:40
Galt 98 26 41N47'22 89w45'44 5:59:03
Galton 21 63 39N44'22 88w18'01 5:53:12
Galva 37 4 41N10'03 90w02'33 6:00:10
Ganeer 46 82 41N09 87w41 5:50:44
Ganntown 44 4 37N21'48 88w47'03 5:55:08
Garber 27 111 40N30'57 88w22'54 5:53:32

Gard 60 25 38N51'44 89w57'36 5:59:50
Gardena 90 98 40N38'11 89w30'19 5:58:01
Garden Heights 83
4 37N43'13 88w31'37 5:54:06
Garden Hill 96 4 38N35 88w38 5:54:32
Garden Homes 16 1 41N42 87w42 5:50:48
Garden of Eden 46
82 41N10'11 87w33'42 5:50:15
Garden Plain 98 4 41N48'03 90w07'49 6:00:31
Garden Prairie 4
30 42N15'12 88w43'29 5:54:54
Garden Quarter 45
107 42N02 88w17 5:53:08
Gardner 32 72 41N11'08 88w18'35 5:53:14
Gards Point 93 4 38N28'28 87w54'40 5:51:39
Garfield 32 36 41N09 88w19 5:53:16
Garfield 50 29 41N05'06 88w57'22 5:55:49
Garfield Park 16
1 41N52 87w43 5:50:52
Garland 23 55 39N43'06 87w48'41 5:51:15
Garnerville 97 4 38N06'52 88w03'11 5:52:13
Garrett 21 55 39N47'55 88w25'27 5:53:42
Garrison 33 4 38N14'54 88w31'09 5:54:05
Gartside 82 25 38N32'38 90w02'10 6:00:09
Gary Gardens 22 2 41N53 88w05 5:52:20
Gas Light Village 32
125 41N22 88w25 5:53:40
Gays 70 63 39N27'29 88w29'38 5:53:59
Gears Ferry 43 4 42N23'21 90w27'54 6:01:52
Geff (Jeffersonville) 96
4 38N26'33 88w24'15 5:53:37
Genesee 98 4 41N53 89w48 5:59:12
Geneseo 37 4 41N26'53 90w09'15 6:00:37
Geneva 45 109 41N53'15 88w18'19 5:53:13
Geneva Road 22 30 41N53'17 88w09'05 5:52:36
Genoa 19 110 42N05'50 88w41'34 5:54:46
Gent City 100 4 37N46 88w56 5:55:44
Georges Creek 64
4 37N19 88w47 5:55:08
Georgetown 8 4 42N08'23 89w49'43 5:59:19
Georgetown 55 4 40N28 90w41 6:02:44
Georgetown 92 57 39N58'31 87w38'09 5:50:33
Gerald 10 54 40N16'14 87w55'48 5:51:43
Gerlaw 94 4 40N59'13 90w36'06 6:02:24
German 80 4 38N48 87w58 5:51:52
German Corner 37
4 41N17'37 90w01'51 6:00:07
Germantown 14 50 38N33'13 89w32'18 5:58:09
Germantown 102 57 40N47 89w25 5:57:40
Germantown Hills 102
4 40N45'59 89w28'04 5:57:52
German Valley 89
66 42N12'56 89w28'24 5:57:54
Germanville 53 4 40N42 88w17 5:53:08
Gibson City 27
111 40N27'55 88w22'33 5:53:30
Gibsonia 30 4 37N38'49 88w15'45 5:53:03
Gifford 57 54 40N18'21 88w01'16 5:52:05
Gila 40 4 39N06'46 88w15'37 5:53:02
Gilberts 45 8 42N06'12 88w22'22 5:53:29
Gilbirds 5 65 39N55'23 90w42'05 6:02:48
Gilchrist 29 7 40N38'50 90w02'23 6:00:10
Gilchrist 66 4 41N12'19 90w37'27 6:02:30
Gilead 7 65 39N07'27 90w40'02 6:02:40
Gilead Landing 7
65 39N07'23 90w40'59 6:02:44
Gillespie 59 55 39N07'47 89w49'10 5:59:17
Gilletts 99 1 41N31'02 87w56'13 5:51:45
Gillum 57 104 40N24'28 88w53'58 5:55:36
Gilman 38 29 40N46'00 87w59'32 5:51:58
Gilmer 1 63 39N59 91w12 6:04:48
Gilmer 49 6 42N14'06 88w02'46 5:52:11
Gilmore 3 63 38N58'40 89w37'12 5:58:29
Gilmore 25 4 38N59'15 88w43'03 5:54:52
Gilmore Lake 67
46 38N27 90w12 6:00:48
Gilson 48 4 40N51'42 90w12'05 6:00:48
Ginger Creek 22 2 41N48 87w56 5:51:44
Ginger Hill 81 87 41N26'17 90w34'02 6:02:16
Gingle Corners 66
4 41N15'47 90w44'09 6:02:57
Girard 59 29 39N26'47 89w46'51 5:59:07
Gladstone 36 4 40N51'52 90w57'40 6:03:51
Gladstone Commons 16
6 42N04 87w57 5:51:48
Glasford 72 55 40N34'21 89w48'48 5:59:15
Glasgow 86 4 39N33'02 90w28'48 6:01:55
Glass Works 60 7 38N54 90w10 6:00:40
Glen 60 7 38N45 89w59 5:59:56
Glen Acres 16 1 42N01 87w54 5:51:36
Glenarm 84 30 39N37'25 89w38'56 5:58:36
Glen Arms 49 27 42N23 88w09 5:52:36
Glen Avon 57 30 40N20'46 88w35'33 5:54:22
Glenayre 16 2 42N04 87w48 5:51:12
Glenayre Gardens 16
2 42N04 87w48 5:51:12
Glenbrook Countryside 16
2 42N07 87w49 5:51:16
Glenburn 92 54 40N08'34 87w46'06 5:51:04
Glen Carbon 60 7 38N44'54 89w58'59 5:59:56
Glen Carbon Crossing 60
7 38N45'08 89w57'19 5:59:49
Glencoe 16 1 42N08'06 87w45'29 5:51:02
Glendale 76 4 37N27'20 88w40'17 5:54:41
Glendale 81 87 41N29'08 90w24'56 6:01:40
Glendale Gardens 60
29 38N53 90w05 6:00:20
Glendale Heights 22
2 41N54'37 88w04'18 5:52:17
Glen Ellyn 22 26 41N52'39 88w04'01 5:52:16
Glen Ellyn Countryside 22
26 41N53 88w04 5:52:16
Glen Ellyn Woods 22
26 41N53 88w04 5:52:16
Glengarry 45 1 41N56 87w53 5:51:32
Glen Hill 22 2 41N53 88w04 5:52:16
Glenn 16 1 41N48'17 87w46'39 5:51:07
Glenn 39 50 37N48'13 89w34'50 5:58:19
Glennshire 49 6 42N12 88w03 5:52:12
Glen Oak 22 2 41N52'54 88w02'21 5:52:09
Glen Park 50 4 41N31 88w41 5:54:44
Glen Ridge 16 29 41N30 87w42 5:50:48
Glenshire 16 1 42N04 87w48 5:51:12
Glenview 16 1 42N04'11 87w47'16 5:51:09
Glenview 82 25 38N35'13 89w56'14 5:59:45
Glenview Countryside 16
1 42N04 87w48 5:51:12
Glenview Estates 16
1 42N04 87w48 5:51:12
Glenview Terrace 16
1 42N04 87w48 5:51:12
Glenview Woodlands 16
1 42N04 87w48 5:51:12
Glenwood 16 1 41N32'33 87w36'08 5:50:25
Glenwood Estates 16
1 41N33 87w37 5:50:28
Glover 10 8 40N06'49 88w01'08 5:52:05
Godfrey 60 7 38N57'28 90w11'12 6:00:45
Godley 99 37 41N14'12 88w14'37 5:52:58
Goeselville 16 6 41N37'27 87w47'06 5:51:08
Golconda 76 4 37N22'02 88w29'11 5:53:57
Gold 6 63 41N27 89w48 5:59:12
Golden 1 66 40N06'33 91w01'03 6:04:04
Golden Acres 16 1 42N04 87w48 5:51:12
Golden Acres 72
98 40N44'38 89w37'54 5:58:32
Golden Eagle 7 4 38N53'36 90w34'44 6:02:19
Golden Gardens 82
25 38N35'22 90w06'24 6:00:26
Golden Gate 96 4 38N21'34 88w12'15 5:52:49
Golden Lily 2 4 37N04'32 89w11'09 5:56:45
Gold Hill 30 4 37N44 88w13 5:52:52
Golena Knolls 72
51 40N55 89w30 5:58:00
Golf 16 1 42N03'32 87w47'33 5:51:10
Golf Park Terrace 16
6 42N03 87w55 5:51:40
Golfview Hills 22
2 41N48 87w56 5:51:44
Goode 28 4 38N05 89w04 5:56:16
Goodenow 49 22 41N23'29 87w38'12 5:50:33
Goodfarm 32 26 41N09 88w25 5:53:40
Goodfield 102 112 40N37'47 89w16'29 5:57:06
Good Hope 55 4 40N33'28 90w40'24 6:02:42
Goodings Grove 99
1 41N37'45 87w55'51 5:51:43
Goodrich 46 4 41N06'32 88w03'29 5:52:14
Goodwine 38 7 40N34'02 87w47'04 5:51:08
Goofy Ridge 63
137 40N20 89w56 5:59:44
Goose Creek 74 4 40N06 88w38 5:54:32
Goose Lake 32 48 41N22 88w18 5:53:12
Gordon 17 32 39N00'29 87w41'05 5:50:44
Goreville 44 4 37N33'16 88w58'20 5:55:53
Gorham 39 4 37N43'06 89w29'09 5:57:57
Gorman 32 30 41N15'40 88w20'30 5:53:22
Goshen 88 4 41N07 89w56 5:59:44
Gossett 97 4 37N55'24 88w22'09 5:53:29
Gougars 99 114 41N31'25 88w00'17 5:52:01
Gowins 76 4 37N26'37 88w28'04 5:53:52
Grafton 42 77 38N58'12 90w25'53 6:01:44
Grand 39 4 37N39 89w28 5:57:52
Grand Chain 77 4 37N15 89w01 5:56:04
Grand Chain Landing 77
4 37N13'35 88w59'35 5:55:58
Grand Crossing 16
1 41N45 87w36 5:50:24
Grand Detour 71
25 41N53'48 89w24'42 5:57:39
Grand Pass 31 63 39N27'28 90w35'46 6:02:23
Grand Pier 76 4 37N34 88w27 5:53:48
Grand Prairie 41
4 38N25 89w05 5:56:20
Grand Rapids 50
41 41N14 88w45 5:55:00
Grand Ridge 50 41 41N14'13 88w49'53 5:55:20
Grand Tower 39 4 37N37'35 89w29'52 5:57:59
Grandview 8 4 41N31 89w55 5:59:40
Grandview 25 55 39N32'28 87w50'46 5:51:23
Grandview 84 133 39N48'59 89w37'07 5:58:28
Grandville 40 4 39N08 88w00 5:52:00
Grandwood Park 49
140 42N22 87w53 5:51:32
Graney 60 25 38N50'01 89w54'49 5:59:39
Grange 10 36 39N58 88w21 5:53:24
Granite City 60 7 38N42'05 90w08'55 6:00:36
Grantfork 60 63 38N49'48 89w39'56 5:58:40
Grant Park 46 21 41N14 87w39 5:50:36
Grantsburg 44 4 37N23'27 88w44'49 5:54:59
Granville 78 41 41N15'40 89w13'39 5:56:55
Grape Creek 92 54 40N04'04 87w35'55 5:50:24
Grass Lake 49 6 42N26 88w09 5:52:36
Grassy 100 4 37N38 89w06 5:56:24
Gray 97 4 38N14 88w03 5:52:12
Gray Ford 92 38 40N17'01 87w47'43 5:51:11
Graymont 53 55 40N52'40 88w46'37 5:55:06
Graymoor 16 1 41N31 87w42 5:50:48
Grays Corner 51 4 38N38'36 87w43'19 5:50:53
Grayslake 49 27 42N20'40 88w02'30 5:52:10
Grays Siding 92
54 40N07 87w47 5:51:08
Grayville 24 4 38N15'27 87w59'37 5:51:58
Greathouse Ford 96
4 38N27'28 88w37'49 5:54:31
Great Lakes 49
116 42N18 87w50 5:51:20
Green Acres 55 4 40N28 90w41 6:02:44
Green Acres 84
133 39N53'36 89w40'24 5:58:42
Greenbriar 99 1 41N31 87w58 5:51:52
Green Brier 17 4 38N54'31 87w54'26 5:51:38
Greenbrook Country 16
27 41N58 88w06 5:52:24
Greenbush 94 4 40N42'43 90w32'07 6:02:08
Green Creek 25 4 39N12'10 88w31'24 5:54:06
Greendale 13 4 38N37'47 88w41'52 5:54:47
Greenfield 31 55 39N20'37 90w12'45 6:00:51
Green Garden 99
30 41N25 87w51 5:51:24
Green Meadows 16
27 41N58 88w06 5:52:24
Greenoak 6 55 41N28'49 89w24'30 5:57:38
Green Oaks 49 27 42N17 87w54 5:51:36
Greenpond 75 63 39N29'43 90w38'34 6:02:34
Greenridge 59 53 39N25'10 89w47'40 5:59:11
Green River 37 63 41N28'32 90w19'09 6:01:17
Green Rock 37 63 41N28'23 90w21'27 6:01:26
Greentree 49 42 42N16 87w56 5:51:44
Greenup 18 55 39N14'52 88w09'48 5:52:39
Green Valley 22
83 41N53 88w01 5:52:04
Green Valley 90
21 40N24'27 89w38'34 5:58:34
Greenview 65 29 40N04'59 89w44'17 5:58:57
Greenville 3 55 38N53'32 89w24'47 5:57:39
Greenwich 46 115 41N07'06 87w55'37 5:51:42
Greenwood 56 11 42N23'33 88w23'21 5:53:33
Greenwood Meadows 60
7 38N57 90w11 6:00:44
Greer 38 80 40N31'59 87w35'41 5:50:23
Gretna 22 2 41N53'53 88w06'05 5:52:24
Gridley 57 57 40N44'36 88w52'53 5:55:32
Griffin 66 4 41N14'25 90w29'22 6:01:57
Grigg 79 93 38N11'26 89w54'28 5:59:38
Griggsville 75 53 39N42'32 90w43'28 6:02:54
Grimes Addition 98
26 41N48 89w43 5:58:52
Grimsby 39 4 37N45'01 89w26'57 5:57:48
Grinnell 64 4 37N16'45 88w52'20 5:55:29
Grisham 68 63 39N03 89w32 5:58:08
Griswold 53 44 40N54'47 88w21'14 5:53:25
Groat 28 4 37N58'04 88w52'16 5:55:29
Gross 35 4 37N31'59 88w17'26 5:53:10
Gross Point 16 2 42N04'44 87w43'21 5:50:53
Grove 40 4 39N07 88w17 5:53:08
Grove City 11 55 39N42'24 89w17'49 5:57:11
Groveland 90 98 40N35'33 89w32'04 5:58:08
Grover 96 4 38N22 88w19 5:53:16
Guilford 43 4 42N25'03 90w18'01 6:01:12
Gulfport 36 4 40N48'50 91w05'10 6:04:21
Gurnee 49 34 42N22'13 87w54'07 5:51:36
Gurney 9 4 39N53'57 90w03'00 6:00:12
Guthrie 27 111 40N30'30 88w19'30 5:53:18
Hadley 51 4 38N43'10 87w54'31 5:51:38
Hadley 75 4 39N42'20 90w58'21 6:03:53
Hadley Landing Public Access 7
65 39N02'46 90w35'24 6:02:22
Haegers Bend 56 1 42N11'20 88w15'38 5:53:03
Hafer 100 4 37N46 89w04 5:56:16
Hagaman 59 63 39N18'37 90w04'41 6:00:19
Hagarstown 26 139 38N56'36 89w10'06 5:56:40
Hagener 9 66 39N55'33 90w23'50 6:01:35
Hahnaman 98 29 41N37'54 89w38'06 5:58:32
Haines 54 29 40N14'51 89w35'30 5:58:22
Haines 61 4 38N31 88w52 5:55:28
Hainesville 49 27 42N20'42 88w04'04 5:52:16
Haldane 71 63 42N03'45 89w34'26 5:58:18
Hale 94 4 40N56 90w43 6:02:52
Half Day 49 2 42N12'04 87w56'00 5:51:44
Hall 6 134 41N22 89w13 5:56:52
Hallidayboro 39 4 37N53'20 89w14'13 5:56:57
Hallock 38 80 40N33'41 87w35'46 5:50:23
Hallock 72 51 40N55 89w34 5:58:16
Halls Ford 15 4 39N26'14 88w09'25 5:52:38
Hallsville 20 55 40N09'03 89w05'34 5:56:22
Hallville 20 8 40N09 88w57 5:55:48
Halsey 91 4 37N34'02 89w27'10 5:57:49
Halsey Village 49
140 42N19 87w50 5:51:20
Hamburg 3 4 38N51'58 89w16'29 5:57:06
Hamburg 7 65 39N13'48 90w43'03 6:02:52
Hamburg Landing 91
4 37N24'23 89w24'44 5:57:39
Hamel 60 29 38N53'20 89w50'43 5:59:23
Hamilton 34 4 40N23'47 91w20'20 6:05:21
Hamilton Corners 98
4 41N42'27 89w57'58 5:59:52
Hamlet 66 4 41N18'50 90w44'06 6:02:56
Hamletsburg 76 4 37N08'19 88w25'54 5:53:44
Hammond 74 55 39N47'49 88w35'30 5:54:22
Hampshire 45 55 42N05'52 88w31'49 5:54:07
Hampshire Manor 45
29 42N05 88w28 5:53:52
Hampton 81 4 41N33'21 90w24'33 6:01:38
Hampton Court 16
6 41N35 87w46 5:51:04
Hampton Park 99
114 41N35 88w03 5:52:12
Hanaford 28 4 37N57'21 88w50'25 5:55:22
Hanley Ford 15 4 39N23'45 88w09'52 5:52:39
Hanna 37 4 41N30 90w16 6:01:04
Hanna City 72 57 40N41'30 89w47'42 5:59:11
Hannon 11 7 39N34 89w21 5:57:24
Hanover 43 4 42N15'23 90w16'46 6:01:07
Hanover Highlands 16
27 41N58 88w06 5:52:24
Hanover Park 22
27 41N59'58 88w08'42 5:52:35
Hanover Square 16
27 41N58 88w06 5:52:24
Hanson 87 63 39N13'02 89w06'39 5:56:27
Harbor Dell 60 7 38N57 90w11 6:00:44
Harbor Estates 49
6 42N09 88w06 5:52:24
Harco 100 4 37N47'45 88w39'00 5:54:36
Hardin 7 55 39N09'24 90w37'04 6:02:28
Harding 50 28 41N30'54 88w50'58 5:55:24
Hardinville 17 4 38N54'58 87w50'13 5:51:21
Harlem 101 4 42N20'25 89w01'04 5:56:04
Harlem-Irving Plaza 16
1 41N57 87w47 5:51:08
Harmon 52 55 41N43'22 89w33'14 5:58:13
Harmony 34 4 40N19 91w07 6:04:28
Harmony 41 23 38N24'26 88w47'34 5:55:10
Harmony 56 29 42N09'40 88w31'35 5:54:06
Harmony Village 16
6 42N09 87w57 5:51:48
Harp 20 63 40N11 88w51 5:55:24
Harper 71 63 42N08'29 89w38'50 5:58:35
Harpster 27 54 40N24'20 88w26'55 5:53:48
Harris 23 7 39N40'35 87w42'19 5:50:49
Harris 29 63 40N30 90w23 6:01:32
Harris 74 57 40N13'57 88w35'33 5:54:22
Harrisburg 83 4 37N44'18 88w32'26 5:54:10
Harrison 39 4 37N47'48 89w20'13 5:57:21
Harrison 101 4 42N25'38 89w11'29 5:56:46
Harrisonville 32
30 41N17'14 88w18'17 5:53:13

Harrisonville 67
55 38N16'39 90W21'00 6:01:24
Harrisonville Landing 67
55 38N16'44 90W21'53 6:01:28
Harristown 58 26 39N51'14 89W05'02 5:56:20
Harrisville 101 4 42N09'25 89W01'57 5:56:08
Harter 13 4 38N41 88W32 5:54:08
Hartford 60 29 38N50'00 90W05'45 6:00:23
Hartford 100 4 37N48'17 88W39'56 5:54:40
Hartland 56 15 42N21'49 88W30'26 5:54:02
Hartsburg 54 29 40N15'03 89W26'27 5:57:46
Hartshorn 92 54 40N07'47 87W42'19 5:50:49
Hartsville 76 4 37N32'09 88W28'58 5:53:56
Harvard 56 7 42N25'20 88W36'49 5:54:27
Harvard Hills 90
98 40N43'43 89W28'53 5:57:56
Harvel 68 63 39N21'22 89W31'56 5:58:08
Harvey 16 2 41N36'36 87W38'48 5:50:35
Harwood 10 30 40N22 88W03 5:52:12
Harwood Heights 16
2 41N58'02 87W48'27 5:51:14
Hastings 16 1 41N40'52 87W58'18 5:51:53
Hastings 92 96 39N54'33 87W53'29 5:51:34
Hastings Landing 7
65 38N57'56 90W40'15 6:02:41
Hatcher Woods 32
125 41N22 88W25 5:53:40
Havana 63 55 40N18'00 90W03'39 6:00:15
Haw Creek 48 4 40N51 90W10 6:00:40
Hawthorne 16 1 41N51 87W43 5:50:52
Hawthorn Woods 49
6 42N13'01 88W02'58 5:52:12
Hayes 21 7 39N51'45 88W16'52 5:53:07
Haymarket 16 1 41N53 87W38 5:50:32
Haynes 84 29 39N50'58 89W17'47 5:57:11
Haypress 31 63 39N21'41 90W32'05 6:02:08
Hazel Crest 16 2 41N34'18 87W41'40 5:50:47
Hazelcrest Highlands 16
2 41N35 87W40 5:50:40
Hazel Dell 18 4 39N12'08 88W02'28 5:52:10
Hazelgreen 16 1 41N41'00 87W44'24 5:50:58
Hazelhurst 8 4 41N57'48 89W41'10 5:58:45
Headyville 25 4 39N04 88W23 5:53:32
Heapsville 36 4 40N45'35 91W04'18 6:04:17
Heathercrest 16 2 42N07 87W49 5:51:16
Heatherlea 16 6 42N06 88W02 5:52:08
Heatherridge 49
140 42N22 87W53 5:51:32
Heathsville 17 4 38N53'48 87W34'04 5:50:16
Heaton 92 80 40N24'39 87W35'22 5:50:21
Hebron 56 48 42N28'18 88W25'56 5:53:44
Hecker 67 55 38N18'18 89W59'39 5:59:59
Hegeler 6 134 41N22'21 89W10'56 5:56:44
Hegeler 92 54 40N04'32 87W38'06 5:50:32
Hegewisch 16 26 41N39'13 87W32'49 5:50:11
Helena 51 4 38N36'51 87W51'50 5:51:27
Helm 61 4 38N30'40 88W42'31 5:54:50
Helmar 47 55 41N32'42 88W29'02 5:53:56
Helvetia 60 56 38N42 89W39 5:58:36
Heman 58 57 39N56'49 89W06'20 5:56:25
Henderson 48 74 41N01'30 90W21'22 6:01:25
Henderson 59 55 39N09'21 89W47'43 5:59:11
Henderson Grove 48
74 41N01'11 90W24'41 6:01:39
Hendrix 57 35 40N25'10 88W58'40 5:55:55
Hendryx Manor 72
98 40N45 89W37 5:58:28
Henkel 52 57 41N36'01 89W10'25 5:56:42
Hennepin 78 41 41N15'15 89W20'32 5:57:22
Henning 92 26 40N18'18 87W42'03 5:50:48
Henry 62 30 41N06'41 89W21'23 5:57:26
Hensley 10 54 40N11 88W17 5:53:08
Henton 87 7 39N27'49 88W54'16 5:55:37
Herald 97 4 37N57'59 88W10'53 5:52:44
Heralds Prairie 97
4 37N58 88W12 5:52:48
Herbert 4 110 42N09'17 88W46'34 5:55:06
Herborn 87 63 39N21 88W37 5:54:28
Heritage 81 87 41N30 90W30 6:02:00
Hermon 48 4 40N45'25 90W19'11 6:01:17
Herod 76 4 37N34'49 88W26'10 5:53:45
Herrick 87 63 39N13'13 88W59'04 5:55:56
Herrin 100 4 37N48'11 89W01'39 5:56:07
Herrin Junction 100
4 37N49'27 89W00'40 5:56:03
Herscher 46 39 41N02'57 88W05'52 5:52:23
Hersman 5 76 39N57'00 90W44'28 6:02:58
Hervey City 58 55 39N45'20 88W51'03 5:55:24
Hettick 59 63 39N21'18 90W02'13 6:00:09
Hewittsville 11 7 39N32'14 89W18'50 5:57:15
Heyworth 57 35 40N18'48 88W58'25 5:55:54
Hickman 38 7 40N34'03 87W45'52 5:51:03
Hickory 85 66 40N10 90W17 6:01:08
Hickory Corners 28
4 37N59'40 89W00'08 5:56:01
Hickory Corners 49
6 42N27'58 88W01'01 5:52:04
Hickory Falls 56
15 42N23 88W26 5:53:44
Hickory Grove 1
92 39N56'11 91W18'39 6:05:15
Hickory Grove 8 4 42N03'35 90W04'03 6:00:16
Hickory Hill 96 4 38N25 88W39 5:54:36
Hickory Hills 16
12 41N43'32 87W49'30 5:51:18
Hickory Point 58
26 39N54 88W58 5:55:52
Hicks 35 4 37N32'35 88W22'32 5:53:30
Hidalgo 40 4 39N09'21 88W08'49 5:52:35
Hidden Cove 16 1 41N45 87W50 5:51:20
Hidden Creek 16 6 42N06 88W02 5:52:08
Hidden Hills 55 4 40N28 90W41 6:02:44
Higginsville 92
38 40N14'31 87W45'26 5:51:02
High Lake 22 1 41N53 88W12 5:52:48
Highland 60 56 38N44'22 89W40'16 5:58:41
Highland Hills 22
83 41N50'57 88W00'16 5:52:01
Highland Lake 49
27 42N21 88W01 5:52:04
Highland Park 49
1 42N10'54 87W48'01 5:51:12
Highland Park 83
4 37N49 88W27 5:53:48
Highlands 22 2 41N48 87W56 5:51:44
Highland Shores 56
15 42N23 88W26 5:53:44
Highlawn 16 1 41N38 87W38 5:50:32
High Meadows 72
98 40N40 89W40 5:58:40
Highmoor 49 2 42N11'59 87W50'32 5:51:22
Highview Estates 22
2 41N47 87W57 5:51:48
Highway Village 90
98 40N39'57 89W32'45 5:58:11
Highwood 49 6 42N11'59 87W48'33 5:51:14
Highwood 82 25 38N32 90W00 6:00:00
Highwood Terrace 82
25 38N32 90W00 6:00:00
Hilcrest 68 7 39N08 89W30 5:58:00
Hildreth 23 96 39N51'56 87W50'08 5:51:21
Hill 25 4 38N55'49 88W31'16 5:54:05
Hillcrest 7 4 39N14 90W43 6:02:52
Hillcrest 16 1 41N40 88W00 5:52:00
Hillcrest 71 6 41N57'04 89W03'52 5:56:15
Hillerman 64 4 37N14'12 88W53'23 5:55:34
Hillery 92 54 40N07'52 87W41'40 5:50:47
Hillsboro 68 7 39N09'40 89W29'37 5:57:58
Hillsdale 81 4 41N36'49 90W10'22 6:00:41
Hillside 16 2 41N52'40 87W54'10 5:51:37
Hillside 46 115 41N05 87W53 5:51:32
Hillside Manor 46
115 41N05 87W53 5:51:32
Hills, Lake in the 1
66 40N08'53 91W00'07 6:04:00
Hills, Lake in the 56
9 42N10'54 88W19'49 5:53:19
Hindsboro 21 65 39N41'06 88W08'01 5:52:32
Hines 16 1 41N51'13 87W50'22 5:51:21
Hinsdale 22 2 41N48'03 87W56'13 5:51:45
Hinswood 22 19 41N47 87W59 5:51:56
Hire 55 4 40N30 90W51 6:03:24
Hitt 8 4 41N59'41 89W44'08 5:58:57
Hitt 50 6 41N19'00 88W51'22 5:55:25
Hittle 90 72 40N22 89W20 5:57:20
Hodges Park Station 2
4 37N08'59 89W16'22 5:57:05
Hodgeville 76 4 37N20'44 88W33'37 5:54:14
Hodgkins 16 1 41N46'08 87W51'28 5:51:26
Hoffman 14 4 38N32'29 89W15'49 5:57:03
Hoffman Estates 16
6 42N02'34 88W04'47 5:52:19
Hogue Town 12 4 39N11'25 87W55'41 5:51:43
Hogville Landing 7
65 39N04'58 90W40'49 6:02:43
Holbrook 16 1 41N32 87W38 5:50:32
Holcomb 71 57 42N03'53 89W05'44 5:56:23
Holcombville Corners 56
9 42N17'30 88W19'12 5:53:17
Holden 73 4 38N01 89W14 5:56:56
Holder 57 79 40N27'04 88W48'15 5:55:13
Holiday Hills 56
6 42N17'24 88W13'29 5:52:54
Holiday Shores 60
25 38N55'19 89W56'26 5:59:46
Holland 25 63 39N12'57 88W44'56 5:55:00
Hollandia 82 25 38N32 90W00 6:00:00
Hollenback 32 125 41N22 88W25 5:53:40
Hollendale 16 1 41N36 87W38 5:50:32
Holliday 26 4 39N12'59 88W49'29 5:55:18
Hollis 72 98 40N35'48 89W40'12 5:58:41
Hollowayville 6
134 41N21'54 89W17'49 5:57:11
Hollydale 16 2 41N34 87W40 5:50:40
Hollywood 16 1 41N50 87W51 5:51:24
Hollywood Heights 82
25 38N37'57 89W59'47 5:59:59
Hollywood Ridge 16
6 42N09 87W57 5:51:48
Holmes 90 35 40N23'01 89W35'07 5:58:20
Holmes Center 72
51 40N55 89W30 5:58:00
Holmes Corner 76
4 37N19'31 88W38'01 5:54:32
Holmes Landing 85
66 40N10'37 90W12'10 6:00:49
Homberg 76 4 37N19'31 88W33'07 5:54:12
Home Gardens 92
54 40N17 87W41 5:50:44
Homer 10 57 40N02'05 87W57'29 5:51:50
Homestead 82 25 38N36 89W58 5:59:52
Hometown 16 2 41N44'04 87W43'53 5:50:56
Homewood 16 2 41N33'26 87W39'56 5:50:40
Homewood Acres 16
2 41N34 87W40 5:50:40
Homewood Shores 16
2 41N34 87W40 5:50:40
Homewood Terrace 16
2 41N34 87W40 5:50:40
Honey Bend 68 37 39N15'19 89W37'22 5:58:29
Honey Creek 71 4 41N59'25 89W16'47 5:57:07
Honey Point 59 4 39N13 89W47 5:59:08
Hononegah Heights 101
4 42N25 89W01 5:56:04
Hoodville 33 4 38N02'57 88W31'38 5:54:07
Hookdale 3 4 38N49'35 89W18'41 5:57:15
Hooper 38 57 40N56'09 87W36'24 5:50:26
Hoopeston 92 80 40N28'02 87W40'06 5:50:40
Hooppole 37 4 41N31'20 89W54'35 5:59:38
Hoosier 13 4 38N47 88W25 5:53:40
Hope 50 43 41N09 89W06 5:56:24
Hope 92 54 40N12'20 87W54'15 5:51:37
Hopedale 90 72 40N25'15 89W24'52 5:57:39
Hopewell 62 30 41N04 89W20 5:57:20
Hop Hollow 60 7 38N57 90W11 6:00:44
Hopkins 98 4 41N48 89W48 5:59:12
Hopkins Park 46
82 41N03'48 87W37'30 5:50:30
Hopper 36 4 40N47'08 90W59'26 6:03:58
Horace 23 7 39N43'13 87W42'24 5:50:50
Horatio Gardens 49
6 42N09'52 87W56'32 5:51:46
Hord 13 4 38N53'04 88W31'16 5:54:05
Hornsby 59 37 39N10'14 89W44'42 5:58:59
Horseshoe 83 4 37N41'56 88W22'44 5:53:31
Hospital 46 115 41N05 87W53 5:51:32
Houston 1 66 40N09 91W06 6:04:20
Houston 79 63 38N09'33 89W46'52 5:59:07
Howardton 39 4 37N37'45 89W27'52 5:57:51
Howe 6 134 41N20 89W18 5:57:12
Hoyleton 95 4 38N26'30 89W16'27 5:57:06
Hubbard 96 4 38N19'43 88W21'36 5:53:26
Hubbard Woods 16
1 42N06'56 87W44'34 5:50:58
Hubbard Woods 61
4 38N30'52 89W01'23 5:56:06
Hubly 65 4 40N08'08 89W39'32 5:58:38
Hudgens 100 4 37N39'18 88W56'27 5:55:46
Hudson 57 41 40N36'21 88W59'14 5:55:57
Huegely 95 4 38N24'20 89W19'06 5:57:16
Huey 14 55 38N36'16 89W17'28 5:57:10
Huffaker 84 55 39N40'29 89W57'23 5:59:50
Hughes 23 55 39N46'28 87W53'28 5:51:34
Hugh's Addition 84
133 39N49 89W37 5:58:28
Hugo 21 7 39N45'14 88W08'56 5:52:36
Hull 75 4 39N42'25 91W12'24 6:04:50
Humboldt 15 65 39N36'15 88W19'08 5:53:17
Hume 23 55 39N47'48 87W52'07 5:51:28
Humm Wye 35 4 37N27'38 88W24'22 5:53:37
Humrick 92 54 39N54'56 87W32'56 5:50:12
Hunt 40 4 39N03'04 88W01'24 5:52:06
Hunt City 40 4 39N03'04 88W01'24 5:52:06
Hunter 4 28 42N25'44 88W52'15 5:55:29
Hunter 23 56 39N40 87W35 5:50:20
Huntington 22 12 41N47 88W09 5:52:36
Huntington Commons 16
6 42N04 87W57 5:51:48
Huntinton Park 60
7 38N57 90W11 6:00:44
Huntley 56 21 42N10'05 88W25'41 5:53:43
Huntsville 85 4 40N11'28 90W51'52 6:03:27
Hurlbut 54 29 40N01 89W32 5:58:08
Hurricane 26 4 39N11 89W11 5:56:44
Hurricane 31 55 39N17'30 90W29'24 6:01:58
Hurst 100 4 37N49'59 89W08'34 5:56:34
Hustle 92 132 40N28'00 87W49'55 5:51:20
Hutchins Park 101
28 42N22'46 89W03'57 5:56:16
Hutsonville 17 4 39N06'34 87W39'23 5:50:38
Hutton 15 4 39N24'45 88W05'04 5:52:20
Hyde Park 16 1 41N48 87W36 5:50:24
Idaville Corner 38
132 40N34 87W54 5:51:36
Idlewild 49 27 42N21'11 87W59'34 5:51:58
Idlewood 41 4 38N22'49 88W55'22 5:55:41
Idylside 99 114 41N31'08 88W07'19 5:52:29
Illiana 92 54 40N11'47 87W31'55 5:50:08
Illiana Heights 46
82 41N10'08 87W32'35 5:50:10
Illini 58 57 39N55 89W05 5:56:20
Illinois City 81
4 41N23'51 90W53'58 6:03:36
Illinois Veterans Home 1
92 39N55 91W23 6:05:32
Illiopolis 84 29 39N51'13 89W14'31 5:56:58
Imbs 82 46 38N31'25 90W08'07 6:00:32
Imperial 49 42 42N16 87W56 5:51:44
Ina 41 4 38N09'04 88W54'14 5:55:37
Independence 75 4 39N31'53 90W47'29 6:03:10
Independence 83 4 37N39 88W32 5:54:08
Indian Creek 49
126 42N13'37 87W58'47 5:51:55
Indian Grove 53
72 40N43 88W31 5:54:04
Indian Head Park 16
1 41N46'13 87W54'08 5:51:37
Indian Hill 16 1 41N30'06 87W38'52 5:50:35
Indian Hill 22 12 41N47 88W09 5:52:36
Indian Hills 16 1 41N31 87W38 5:50:32
Indian Oaks 46
115 41N11'30 87W51'05 5:51:24
Indian Oaks 99 1 41N40 88W00 5:52:00
Indianola 92 72 39N55'38 87W44'24 5:50:58
Indian Point 48 4 40N46 90W23 6:01:32
Indian Point 49 6 42N28 88W07 5:52:28
Indian Prairie 96
4 38N31 88W32 5:54:08
Indian Ridge 56
15 42N23 88W26 5:53:44
Indiantown 6 55 41N17 89W34 5:58:16
Indian Trail Estates 49
6 42N10 87W53 5:51:32
Industry 55 4 40N19'40 90W36'25 6:02:26
Ingalls Park 99
114 41N31'21 88W02'34 5:52:10
Ingalton 22 54 41N54'22 88W12'13 5:52:49
Ingleside 49 27 42N22'52 88W08'23 5:52:34
Ingleside Shore 49
27 42N24'06 88W08'39 5:52:35
Ingraham 13 4 38N50'10 88W20'02 5:53:20
Ingram Hill 83 4 37N44 88W33 5:54:12
Inman 30 4 37N50'16 88W10'23 5:52:42
International Village 22
83 41N53 88W01 5:52:04
Inverness 16 6 42N07'05 88W05'46 5:52:23
Iola 13 4 38N50'04 88W37'41 5:54:31
Iowa Junc 72 98 40N39'28 89W38'17 5:58:33
Iowa Junction 36
4 40N41'14 91W03'36 6:04:14
Ipava 29 66 40N21'05 90W19'28 6:01:18
Irene 4 28 42N10'13 88W54'01 5:55:36
Irish Grove 65 4 40N05 89W37 5:58:28
Irishtown 14 55 38N42 89W20 5:57:20
Iron 97 4 37N58'26 88W14'29 5:52:58
Iroquois 38 56 40N49'39 87W34'55 5:50:20
Irving 68 7 39N12'21 89W24'16 5:57:37
Irving Park 16 2 41N57 87W45 5:51:00
Irvington 95 4 38N26'21 89W09'46 5:56:39
Irwin 46 60 41N03'08 87W59'02 5:51:56
Irwins Park 84
101 39N37'34 89W43'34 5:58:54
Isabel 23 65 39N39'19 87W57'00 5:51:48
Isabel 29 4 40N19 90W10 6:00:40
Island Grove 40 4 39N08 88W28 5:53:52
Island Grove 84
55 39N43'27 89W57'39 5:59:51
Island Lake 49 1 42N16'34 88W11'31 5:52:46

Itasca 22 17 41N58'30 88w00'26 5:52:02
Itasca Ranchettes 22 17 41N58 88w01 5:52:04
Iuka 61 4 38N36'58 88w47'25 5:55:10
Ivanhoe 16 1 41N38 87w38 5:50:32
Ivanhoe 49 6 42N16'44 88w02'31 5:52:10
Ivesdale 10 57 39N56'36 88w27'19 5:53:49
Ivy 67 63 38N09'05 90w14'03 6:00:56
Ivy Glen 45 7 41N47 88w20 5:53:20
Ivy Heights 60 29 38N53 90w05 6:00:20
Jackson Heights 60 7 38N57 90w11 6:00:44
Jackson Park 16 1 41N47 87w36 5:50:24
Jacksonville 69 113 39N44'02 90w13'44 6:00:55
Jacob 39 4 37N44'42 89w32'13 5:58:09
Jalapa 31 55 39N13'14 90w19'27 6:01:18
Jamaica 92 54 39N59'28 87w48'24 5:51:14
Jamesburg 92 38 40N15'44 87w44'56 5:51:00
Jamestown 14 63 38N44'02 89w30'52 5:58:03
Jamestown 73 63 38N02'59 89w31'45 5:58:07
Janesville 18 4 39N22'27 88w14'37 5:52:58
Jaques 5 65 39N53'02 90w44'35 6:02:58
Jarvis 60 4 38N42 89w53 5:59:32
Jasper 96 4 38N26 88w19 5:53:16
Jefferson 16 2 41N58 87w45 5:51:00
Jeffersonville 96 4 38N26'33 88w24'15 5:53:37
Jeffries 100 65 37N49 88w56 5:55:44
Jeiseyville 11 26 39N35 89w24 5:57:36
Jeisyville 11 26 39N34'38 89w24'18 5:57:37
Jenkins 20 8 40N09'10 89w02'01 5:56:08
Jenkins 100 65 37N51'15 88w55'39 5:55:43
Jerome 84 133 39N46'03 89w40'50 5:58:43
Jersey 42 25 39N09 90w18 6:01:12
Jerseyville 42 25 39N07'12 90w19'42 6:01:19
Jewell Road 22 2 41N52'36 88w08'09 5:52:33
Jewett 18 54 39N12'28 88w14'45 5:52:59
Jimtown 26 139 38N59'16 89w12'45 5:56:51
Joetta 34 4 40N26'01 90w55'53 6:03:44
Johannisburg 95 55 38N23'04 89w39'11 5:58:37
Johnsburg 56 27 42N22'48 88w14'31 5:52:58
Johnsonville 92 26 40N12'38 87w40'11 5:50:41
Johnsonville 96 4 38N31'20 88w32'13 5:54:09
Johnston City 100 63 37N49'14 88w55'39 5:55:43
Johnstown 18 63 39N21'48 88w17'13 5:53:09
Joliet 99 114 41N31'30 88w04'54 5:52:20
Jonathan Creek 70 7 39N39 88w32 5:54:08
Jones 15 63 39N27'09 88w20'09 5:53:21
Jonesboro 91 4 37N27'06 89w16'05 5:57:04
Jones Ridge 39 50 37N48'01 89w37'31 5:58:30
Jonesville 50 117 41N18'41 89w04'17 5:56:17
Joppa 64 65 37N12'23 88w50'41 5:55:23
Joppa Junction 44 4 37N19'47 89w01'53 5:56:08
Jordan 98 4 41N53 89w41 5:58:44
Joshua 29 4 40N35 90w09 6:00:36
Joslin 81 4 41N33'26 90w13'19 6:00:53
Joy 66 4 41N11'48 90w52'49 6:03:31
Joy Prairie 69 63 39N47'12 90w17'53 6:01:12
Jubilee 72 58 40N51 89w49 5:59:16
Jules 9 63 39N58'05 90w15'37 6:01:02
Julien Hill 76 4 37N28'30 88w28'43 5:53:55
Junction 30 4 37N43'24 88w14'12 5:52:57
Junction City (Glen Ridge) 61 4 38N34'49 89w07'40 5:56:31
Junction City 72 98 40N45 89w37 5:58:28
Justice 16 1 41N44'40 87w50'16 5:51:21
Kahm 31 55 39N19'40 90w15'39 6:01:03
Kampsville 7 63 39N17'52 90w36'32 6:02:26
Kane 31 55 39N11'24 90w21'13 6:01:25
Kaneville 45 55 41N50'07 88w31'19 5:54:05
Kangley 50 135 41N09 88w52 5:55:28
Kangly 50 135 41N08'45 88w52'25 5:55:30
Kankakee 46 115 41N07'12 87w51'40 5:51:27
Kankakee Valley 46 26 41N01 87w43 5:50:52
Kansas 23 66 39N33'10 87w56'22 5:51:45
Kaolin 91 4 37N30'42 89w18'00 5:57:12
Kappa 102 41 40N40'33 89w00'28 5:56:02
Karbers Ridge 35 4 37N34'47 88w20'00 5:53:20
Karnak 77 4 37N17'37 88w58'31 5:55:54
Kasbeer 6 55 41N30'18 89w27'48 5:57:51
Kaser 31 55 39N17'58 90w27'51 6:01:51
Kaskaskia 79 63 37N55'17 89w54'47 5:59:39
Kaufman 60 37 38N51'45 89w46'38 5:59:07
Kedron 30 4 37N39'56 88w20'29 5:53:22
Kedron 37 4 41N28'06 89w52'35 5:59:30
Kedzie Grace 16 2 41N57 87w42 5:50:48
Keene 1 53 40N09 91w12 6:04:48
Keenes 96 4 38N20'17 88w38'35 5:54:34
Keenesville 96 4 38N24'08 88w38'53 5:54:36
Keeneyville 22 27 41N58'03 88w07'13 5:52:29
Keensburg 93 4 38N21'02 87w52'07 5:51:28
Kegley 28 4 37N54'34 88w44'35 5:54:58
Keith 96 4 38N35 88w28 5:53:52
Keithsburg 66 66 41N05'58 90w56'33 6:03:46
Kell 61 4 38N29'28 88w54'23 5:55:38
Keller 72 98 40N45'41 89w35'50 5:58:23
Kellerville 1 63 39N55'52 90w56'04 6:03:44
Kelleyville 92 26 40N03 87w38 5:50:32
Kellogg 79 55 38N00'57 90w03'16 6:00:13
Kelly 94 4 41N01 90w30 6:02:00
Kellyville 92 96 40N03'21 87w38'21 5:50:33
Kelsey 63 55 40N14'37 90w02'37 6:00:10
Kemp 21 63 39N41'44 88w11'07 5:52:44
Kemper 42 55 39N12'58 90w09'52 6:00:39
Kemper Landing 67 63 38N09'43 90w16'30 6:01:06
Kempside 95 4 38N19'02 89w25'36 5:57:42
Kempton 27 44 40N56'08 88w14'14 5:52:57
Kendall 47 7 41N36 88w25 5:53:40
Kendall Hills 60 29 38N53 90w05 6:00:20
Keneddy 101 4 42N29 89w02 5:56:08
Kenilwicke 16 6 42N06 88w02 5:52:08
Kenilworth 16 2 42N05'09 87w43'03 5:50:52

Kennedy 49 2 42N14'33 87w52'17 5:51:29
Kenner 13 4 38N38'45 88w34'05 5:54:16
Kenney 20 55 40N05'48 89w05'09 5:56:21
Ken Rock 101 28 42N13 89w04 5:56:16
Kensington 16 1 41N40'41 87w36'26 5:50:26
Kent 89 4 42N18'31 89w54'07 5:59:36
Kentland 47 55 41N32'47 88w26'02 5:53:44
Kentucky 23 128 39N35'36 87w36'40 5:50:27
Kenwood 10 21 40N06'22 88w17'40 5:53:11
Keptown 25 4 39N04'44 88w40'11 5:54:41
Kernan 50 135 41N08'34 88w44'23 5:54:58
Kerr 10 54 40N21 87w58 5:51:52
Kerrick 57 104 40N33'11 88w59'15 5:55:57
Kerton 29 66 40N15 90w11 6:00:44
Kewanee 37 4 41N14'44 89w55'29 5:59:42
Keyesport 14 4 38N44'31 89w16'25 5:57:06
Keyesport Landing 3 4 38N45'24 89w16'22 5:57:05
Keys 84 55 39N46'48 89w34'23 5:58:18
Key West 16 6 42N03 87w53 5:51:32
Kibbie 17 4 39N04'11 87w56'17 5:51:45
Kickapoo 72 4 40N47'24 89w45'04 5:59:00
Kidd 67 55 38N07'02 90w10'22 6:00:41
Kidley 23 7 39N44'42 87w32'29 5:50:10
Kilbourne 63 66 40N09'07 90w00'36 6:00:02
Kildeer 49 6 42N10'14 88w02'52 5:52:11
Kimberly Heights 16 6 41N35 87w46 5:51:04
Kincaid 11 26 39N35'19 89w24'52 5:57:39
Kinderhook 75 4 39N42'08 91w09'11 6:04:37
King 11 63 39N26 89w30 5:58:00
King 31 55 39N13'51 90w34'44 6:02:19
Kingdom 52 25 41N53'37 89w23'37 5:57:34
Kingman 87 63 39N18'01 88w33'35 5:54:14
Kings 15 65 39N40'45 87w59'07 5:51:56
Kings 71 6 42N00'15 89w06'21 5:56:25
Kings Cove 49 6 42N10 87w53 5:51:32
Kings Island 49 6 42N23'03 88w10'51 5:52:43
Kings Park 99 1 41N40 88w00 5:52:00
Kingston 1 66 39N49'00 91w01'40 6:04:07
Kingston 19 64 42N05'59 88w45'32 5:55:02
Kingston Mines 72 57 40N33'30 89w46'29 5:59:06
Kinkaid 39 4 37N49 89w32 5:58:08
Kinmundy 61 4 38N46'24 88w50'48 5:55:23
Kinsman 32 55 41N11'23 88w34'10 5:54:17
Kirkland 19 56 42N05'33 88w51'04 5:55:24
Kirksville 70 7 39N34'14 88w40'06 5:54:40
Kirkwood 94 4 40N51'57 90w44'54 6:03:00
Kisch 9 63 39N54'57 90w12'03 6:00:48
Kise Crossing 67 46 38N25'13 90w15'28 6:01:02
Kishwaukee 101 28 42N09'54 89w09'00 5:56:36
Kishwaukee Glen 101 28 42N13 89w04 5:56:16
Kittredge 8 4 42N07'59 89w46'44 5:59:07
Klein Acres 10 29 40N19 88w08 5:52:32
Klines Corner 96 4 38N22'18 88w15'32 5:53:02
Klondike 2 4 37N03'46 89w13'54 5:56:56
Klondike 49 6 42N25'27 88w08'57 5:52:36
Klondyke 51 4 38N43 87w52 5:51:28
Knapp 84 55 39N42'53 89w49'00 5:59:16
Knapp's Noll 101 4 42N28 89w05 5:56:20
Knight Prairie 33 4 38N05 88w39 5:54:36
Knob Hill 47 25 41N36'03 88w29'50 5:53:59
Knollcrest 16 2 41N35 87w40 5:50:40
Knollwood 49 27 42N17'10 87w53'08 5:51:33
Knollwood 84 133 39N49 89w37 5:58:28
Knottingham 22 12 41N48 88w01 5:52:04
Knox 48 4 40N56'03 90w15'17 6:01:01
Knoxville 48 74 40N54'30 90w17'05 6:01:08
Kortcamp 68 7 39N10 89w28 5:57:52
Kramm 72 4 40N45'29 89w46'55 5:59:08
Kritesville 7 65 39N05'57 90w39'51 6:02:39
Kuhn 60 25 38N46'55 89w52'35 5:59:30
Kumler 57 56 40N17'59 88w34'41 5:54:19
Lace 22 54 41N45'07 87w58'03 5:51:52
La Clede 26 4 38N52'47 88w42'55 5:54:52
Lacon 62 30 41N01'29 89w24'40 5:57:39
La Crosse 34 4 40N31'44 91w01'22 6:04:05
Ladd 6 134 41N22'57 89w13'08 5:56:53
Laenna 54 29 40N01 89w12 5:56:48
Lafayette 79 63 37N54 89w56 5:59:44
Lafayette 88 4 41N06'29 89w58'17 5:59:53
La Fontaine 16 1 42N04 87w48 5:51:12
La Fox 45 60 41N53'11 88w24'32 5:53:38
La Grange 5 65 39N56'50 90w32'14 6:02:09
La Grange 16 1 41N48'18 87w52'09 5:51:29
La Grange Highlands 16 1 41N47 87w53 5:51:32
La Grange Park 16 1 41N50'05 87w51'42 5:51:27
Laguna Woods 16 2 41N36 87w40 5:50:40
La Harpe 34 4 40N35'00 90w58'09 6:03:53
LaHogue 27 29 40N45'48 88w05'17 5:52:21
Lake 14 55 38N32 89w19 5:57:16
Lake Barrington 49 1 42N12'45 88w09'09 5:52:37
Lake Bluff 49 116 42N16'44 87w50'03 5:51:20
Lake Boulevard Addition 92 54 40N17 87w41 5:50:44
Lake Bracken 48 74 40N57 90w22 6:01:28
Lake Briarwood 16 27 42N04 87w59 5:51:56
Lake Camelot 72 98 40N34 89w44 5:58:56
Lake Carlinville 59 47 39N18 89w52 5:59:28
Lake Catherine 49 6 42N29 88w08 5:52:32
Lake Centralia 61 55 39N16 90w12 6:00:48
Lake Charleston 15 106 39N29 88w13 5:52:52
Lake Charlotte 45 95 41N54 88w19 5:53:16
Lake City 70 4 39N45'16 88w43'12 5:54:53
Lake Corner 49 6 42N14'19 88w06'42 5:52:27
Lake Creek 28 4 37N52'34 89w01'37 5:56:06

Lakecrest 68 7 39N10 89w28 5:57:52
Lake Crest 100 4 37N37 88w50 5:55:20
Lake Estates 100 4 37N46 88w56 5:55:44
Lake Forest 49 2 42N12'40 87w53'12 5:51:33
Lake Forest Estates 82 25 38N32 90w00 6:00:00
Lake Fork 54 29 39N58'14 89w21'00 5:57:24
Lake Holiday 19 25 41N40 88w35 5:54:20
Lakehurst 49 140 42N23 87w52 5:51:28
Lake in the Hills 1 66 40N08'53 91w00'07 6:04:00
Lake in the Hills 56 9 42N10'54 88w19'49 5:53:19
Lake in the Woods 22 12 41N48 88w01 5:52:04
Lake Iroquois 38 43 40N31 88w05 5:52:20
Lake Killarney 56 1 42N14 88w15 5:53:00
Lake Lancelot 72 98 40N34 89w44 5:58:56
Lakeland Hills 82 25 38N32 90w00 6:00:00
Lakeland Park 56 27 42N21 88w14 5:52:56
Lake Lawrence 51 4 38N45 87w31 5:50:04
Lake Lynwood 16 1 41N31 87w38 5:50:32
Lake Marie 49 6 42N28 88w07 5:52:28
Lake Marion 61 105 42N07 88w16 5:53:04
Lakemoor 56 18 42N19'43 88w11'56 5:52:48
Lake of the Winds 16 6 42N09 87w57 5:51:48
Lake of the Woods 72 57 40N52 89w41 5:58:44
Lake Pana 11 63 39N23 89w04 5:56:16
Lake Park Estates 16 6 42N06 88w02 5:52:08
Lake Park Forest 16 6 42N06 88w02 5:52:08
Lake Petersburg 65 29 40N01 89w51 5:59:24
Lake Piasa 42 37 39N02 90w09 6:00:36
Lakeside Knolls 68 7 39N10 89w28 5:57:52
Lakeside Villas 16 6 42N09 87w57 5:51:48
Lake Summerset 101 4 42N27'16 89w23'22 5:57:33
Lake Tacoma 100 4 37N43 89w14 5:56:56
Lake Thunderbird 78 4 41N11 89w24 5:57:36
Lakeview 16 1 41N57 87w40 5:50:40
Lakeview 60 7 38N42'56 89w56'40 5:59:47
Lakeview Acres 60 7 38N40 90w00 6:00:00
Lake View Estates 100 4 37N37 89w13 5:56:52
Lakeview Heights 96 4 38N23 88w22 5:53:28
Lake Villa 49 7 42N25'01 88w04'26 5:52:18
Lake Wildwood 62 56 41N07 89w12 5:56:48
Lakewood 16 29 41N29 87w43 5:50:52
Lakewood 22 54 41N55'00 88w11'51 5:52:47
Lakewood 56 56 42N13'45 88w21'18 5:53:25
Lakewood 60 7 38N57 90w11 6:00:44
Lakewood 63 55 40N14'50 90w05'06 6:00:20
Lakewood 87 7 39N19'30 88w53'58 5:55:36
Lakewood Park 100 4 37N43 89w14 5:56:56
Lakewood Shores 99 7 41N16'54 88w08'41 5:52:35
Lakewood Village 45 105 42N07 88w16 5:53:04
Lake Zurich 49 6 42N11'49 88w05'36 5:52:22
Lamard 96 4 38N26 88w25 5:53:40
Lamb 35 4 37N31'54 88w07'29 5:52:30
Lambert 16 1 41N40 88w00 5:52:00
LaMoille 6 55 41N31'54 89w16'47 5:57:07
Lamoine 55 4 40N20 90w51 6:03:24
Lamotte 17 4 39N00 87w37 5:50:28
Lamplighter 57 104 40N34 88w54 5:55:36
Lanark 8 4 42N06'08 89w50'00 5:59:20
Lancaster 72 55 40N34'49 89w50'14 5:59:21
Lancaster 93 4 38N32'52 87w51'55 5:51:28
Landes 17 4 38N51'53 87w53'21 5:51:33
Lane 20 63 40N07'21 88w51'20 5:55:25
Lanesville 84 55 39N51'09 89w20'56 5:57:24
Langham 32 4 41N17'48 88w32'04 5:54:08
Langley 6 63 41N22'09 89w41'17 5:58:45
Langleyville 11 7 39N34 89w21 5:57:24
Lansdowne 82 25 38N38 90w04 6:00:16
Lansing 16 12 41N33'53 87w32'20 5:50:09
Lanton 70 55 39N46'07 88w36'21 5:54:25
Laona 101 4 42N28 89w20 5:57:20
LaPlace 58 54 39N48'00 88w43'03 5:54:52
La Prairie 1 66 40N09 91w00 6:04:00
La Prairie Center 62 48 41N03 89w26 5:57:44
Larchland 94 4 40N49'12 90w39'10 6:02:37
Larkdale 49 6 42N16 88w08 5:52:32
Larkdale 58 26 39N53'18 88w54'43 5:55:39
Larkinsburg 13 4 38N52 88w38 5:54:32
LaRose 62 56 40N58'56 89w14'07 5:56:56
La Rue 91 4 37N32'44 89w27'13 5:57:49
La Salle 50 117 41N20 89w06 5:56:24
Latham 54 56 39N58'07 89w09'44 5:56:39
Latham Park 101 4 42N22'06 89w03'46 5:56:15
Latona 40 4 38N58'50 88w18'42 5:53:15
Laura 88 58 40N55'17 89w55'35 5:59:42
Laurette 57 56 40N19'31 88w32'36 5:54:10
La Vergne 16 1 41N51 87w48 5:51:12
Lawler 30 4 37N43'41 88w17'09 5:53:09
Lawndale 54 36 40N13'05 89w16'57 5:57:08
Lawn Ridge 62 4 40N58'26 89w37'45 5:58:31
Lawrence 4 7 42N26'28 88w38'28 5:54:34
Lawrenceville 51 4 38N43'45 87w40'54 5:50:44

Lawrencewood 16 1 42N02 87W49 5:51:16
Layfield 73 4 38N06'23 89W26'07 5:57:44
Layton 85 65 40N07 90W34 6:02:16
Leaf River 71 55 42N07'32 89W24'13 5:57:37
Leamington 30 4 37N38'22 88W18'25 5:53:14
Lebanon 82 7 38N36'14 89W48'26 5:59:14
Le Claire 60 25 38N47'44 89W57'25 5:59:50
Ledford 83 4 37N42'00 88W35'24 5:54:22
Lee 52 43 41N47'42 88W56'29 5:55:46
Lee Center 52 29 41N44'51 89W16'43 5:57:07
Leech 96 4 38N20 88W12 5:52:48
Leeds 50 29 41N01'15 88W59'17 5:55:57
Leef 60 63 38N52 89W40 5:58:40
Leepertown 6 41 41N18 89W22 5:57:28
Leesburg 29 66 40N14'50 90W19'02 6:01:16
Leesville 46 26 41N01'29 87W37'30 5:50:30
Lehigh 46 115 41N06'37 88W01'05 5:52:04
Leisure City 76 4 37N29'25 88W26'33 5:53:46
Leisure Village 49
6 42N24 88W11 5:52:44
Leithton 49 126 42N14'47 87W58'46 5:51:55
Leland 50 26 41N36'45 88W47'58 5:55:12
Leland Grove 84
133 39N46'37 89W40'45 5:58:43
Lementon 82 29 38N26 89W54 5:59:36
Lemmon 84 29 39N31'53 89W47'39 5:59:11
Lemont 16 1 41N40'25 88W00'06 5:52:00
Lena 89 65 42N22'46 89W49'20 5:59:17
Lenox 94 4 40N51 90W37 6:02:28
Lenzburg 82 39 38N17'14 89W49'02 5:59:16
Leonard 38 55 40N46'07 87W55'19 5:51:41
Leon Corners 98 4 41N35'39 89W55'13 5:59:41
Leonore 50 57 41N11'22 88W58'50 5:55:55
L'Erable 38 35 40N54'12 87W50'49 5:51:23
Lerna 15 63 39N25'06 88W17'19 5:53:09
Le Roy 57 81 40N21'07 88W45'51 5:55:03
Lester 61 4 38N48'09 88W58'35 5:55:54
Levan 39 4 37N49 89W26 5:57:44
Levee 75 66 39N44 91W18 6:05:12
Leverett 10 29 40N11'21 88W12'35 5:52:50
Levings 77 4 37N13'02 89W03'42 5:56:15
Lewisburg 65 29 39N58'12 89W49'57 5:59:20
Lewis Corner 76 4 37N16'21 88W34'46 5:54:19
Lewistown 29 7 40N23'35 90W09'17 6:00:37
Lewood 99 82 41N35 88W11 5:52:44
Lexington 57 7 40N38'29 88W47'00 5:55:08
Leyden 16 1 41N56 87W53 5:51:32
Liberty 1 66 39N52'46 91W06'28 6:04:26
Liberty 83 4 37N43'12 88W34'18 5:54:17
Liberty Acres 49
42 42N16 87W56 5:51:44
Liberty Lake 49
42 42N16 87W56 5:51:44
Liberty Park 22
19 41N47 87W59 5:51:56
Libertyville 49
42 42N16'59 87W57'11 5:51:49
Lick 84 30 39N41 89W42 5:58:48
Lick Creek 91 4 37N31'21 89W04'30 5:56:18
Licking 17 4 39N08 87W54 5:51:36
Lick Prairie 93 4 38N29 87W54 5:51:36
Lidice 99 114 41N33'17 88W05'25 5:52:22
Lifers Landing 34
4 40N14'54 91W29'09 6:05:57
Lightsville 71 4 42N08'49 89W24'15 5:57:37
Lilac Circle Homes 22
83 41N53 88W01 5:52:04
Lilly 90 4 40N32'15 89W17'12 5:57:09
Lillyville 18 4 39N11'23 88W27'07 5:53:48
Lily Cache 99 82 41N35'25 88W10'53 5:52:44
Lily Cache Acres 99
82 41N35 88W11 5:52:44
Lily Lake 45 84 41N56'56 88W28'40 5:53:55
Lilymoor 56 27 42N19'50 88W12'47 5:52:51
Lima 1 63 40N10'39 91W22'42 6:05:31
Limerick 6 55 41N29'41 89W28'01 5:57:52
Lincoln 54 29 40N08'54 89W21'53 5:57:28
Lincoln Addition 60
29 38N52 90W05 6:00:20
Lincoln Estates 99
4 41N30'09 87W48'25 5:51:14
Lincoln Gardens 60
7 38N54 90W10 6:00:40
Lincoln Hills 22
2 41N53 88W04 5:52:16
Lincoln Park 16 1 41N55 87W39 5:50:36
Lincolnshire 49 2 42N11 87W55 5:51:40
Lincolnshire 99 1 41N28 87W37 5:50:28
Lincoln's New Salem 65
29 39N59 89W49 5:59:16
Lincolnwood 16 1 42N00'16 87W43'48 5:50:55
Lincolnwood Hills 99
1 41N30'41 87W54'45 5:51:39
Lindenhurst 49 6 42N24'38 88W01'34 5:52:06
Lindenwood 71 57 42N03'11 89W01'50 5:56:07
Linder 31 55 39N18 90W19 6:01:16
Linn 93 4 38N32 87W43 5:50:52
Linn 102 4 40N53 89W13 5:56:52
Lintner 58 55 39N48'00 88W40'04 5:54:40
Lioncrest 16 29 41N29 87W43 5:50:52
Lipsey 15 63 39N29'29 88W25'04 5:53:40
Lis 40 4 39N01'12 88W15'37 5:53:02
Lisbon 47 55 41N28'53 88W28'56 5:53:56
Lisbon Center 47
25 41N31'28 88W26'02 5:53:44
Lisle 22 12 41N48'04 88W04'29 5:52:18
Litchfield 46 82 41N09'48 87W35'12 5:50:21
Litchfield 68 37 39N10'31 89W39'15 5:58:37
Literberry 69 63 39N51'15 90W11'58 6:00:48
Lithia 87 7 39N25'39 88W43'04 5:54:52
Little America 29
7 40N24'21 90W02'04 6:00:08
Little Indian 9
63 39N53'15 90W12'04 6:00:48
Little Mackinaw 90
72 40N27 89W20 5:57:20
Little Rock 47 25 41N43'03 88W34'34 5:54:18
Littleton 85 4 40N14'02 90W37'20 6:02:29
Little York 94 4 41N00'40 90W44'46 6:02:59
Lively Grove 95
55 38N18'23 89W36'41 5:58:27
Liverpool 29 66 40N23'30 90W00'03 6:00:00
Livingston 12 55 39N24'24 87W38'46 5:50:35
Livingston 60 26 38N58'03 89W45'50 5:59:03
Loami 84 55 39N40'32 89W50'48 5:59:23
Loch Lomond 49
126 42N14 87W59 5:51:56
Lockhaven 42 7 38N56'26 90W17'17 6:01:09
Lockport 99 114 41N35'22 88W03'28 5:52:14
Locust 11 63 39N29 89W12 5:56:48
Loda 38 41 40N31'03 88W04'19 5:52:17
Lodemia 53 72 40N48'26 88W33'57 5:54:16
Lodge 74 55 40N06'22 88W33'36 5:54:14
Logan 23 7 39N44'14 87W36'18 5:50:25
Logan 28 4 37N57 88W50 5:55:20
Logan Square 16 1 41N55 87W42 5:50:48
Log Cabin Camp 46
82 41N09'42 87W34'56 5:50:20
Lomax 36 4 40N40'44 91W04'22 6:04:17
Lombard 22 83 41N52'48 88W00'28 5:52:02
Lombardville 88 4 41N13'16 89W39'30 5:58:38
London Mills 29 4 40N42'38 90W15'58 6:01:04
Lone Grove 26 4 38N53 88W52 5:55:28
Lone Tree 6 55 41N18 89W30 5:58:00
Lone Tree 36 4 40N50'13 91W01'05 6:04:04
Long Branch 63 55 40N13'02 90W02'16 6:00:09
Long Branch 83 4 37N53'06 88W34'38 5:54:19
Long Creek 58 4 39N48'43 88W50'51 5:55:23
Long Grove 49 6 42N10'42 87W59'52 5:51:59
Long Lake 49 27 42N22'47 88W07'05 5:52:28
Long Meadow 22 12 41N48 88W01 5:52:04
Long Point 53 55 41N00'17 88W53'30 5:55:34
Long Shore Park 72
98 40N45'22 89W33'39 5:58:15
Longview 10 65 39N53'12 88W03'59 5:52:16
Longwood Farms 16
1 41N31 87W38 5:50:32
Longwood Manor 22
12 41N47 88W09 5:52:36
Loogootee 26 4 38N54'17 88W51'13 5:55:25
Looking Glass 14
55 38N31 89W39 5:58:36
Lookout Point 56
15 42N23 88W26 5:53:44
Loon Lake 49 6 42N26'49 88W05'24 5:52:22
Loose Pulley Junction 71
57 42N07'34 89W13'26 5:56:54
Loraine 1 53 40N09'15 91W13'20 6:04:53
Loran 89 4 42N14'06 89W54'37 5:59:38
Lords' Park Manor 16
107 42N02 88W17 5:53:08
Lorenzo 99 7 41N20'50 88W12'56 5:52:52
Loretto 53 127 40N58'40 88W26'05 5:53:44
Lorraine Park 22
2 41N53 88W05 5:52:20
Lostant 50 43 41N08'34 89W03'36 5:56:14
Lost Nation 71 25 41N50 89W30 5:58:00
Lotus 10 54 40N19'08 88W27'21 5:53:49
Lotus Woods 49 6 42N25'19 88W10'23 5:52:42
Lou Del 67 8 38N20 90W09 6:00:36
Loudon 26 4 39N09 88W53 5:55:32
Louisville 13 4 38N46'20 88W30'09 5:54:01
Love 6 4 41N34'09 89W48'21 5:59:13
Love 92 54 39N55 87W34 5:50:16
Lovejoy 38 80 40N32 87W43 5:50:52
Lovejoy 82 25 38N39 90W10 6:00:40
Loves Corner 35 4 37N29'44 88W10'14 5:52:41
Loves Park 101 55 42N19'12 89W03'29 5:56:14
Lovilla 33 4 38N09'24 88W40'00 5:54:40
Lovington 70 61 39N42'56 88W37'57 5:54:32
Lowder 84 55 39N33'03 89W50'45 5:59:23
Lowe 70 55 39N44 88W32 5:54:08
Lowell 50 136 41N15'02 89W00'38 5:56:03
Low Point 102 4 40N52'21 89W18'48 5:57:15
Loxa 15 106 39N29'50 88W16'02 5:53:04
Lucas 25 4 38N57 88W25 5:53:40
Lucas 54 29 40N18'24 89W22'03 5:57:28
Ludlow 57 30 40N23'13 88W07'39 5:52:31
Lukin 51 4 38N37 87W50 5:51:20
Lumaghi Heights 60
7 38N40'13 89W56'52 5:59:47
Lusk 76 4 37N28'58 88W28'27 5:53:54
Luther 63 4 40N11'36 89W39'11 5:58:37
Lyman 27 30 40N38 88W11 5:52:44
Lynchburg 63 66 40N06 90W14 6:00:56
Lyndon 98 4 41N43'03 89W55'33 5:59:42
Lynn Center 37 4 41N17'45 90W21'28 6:01:26
Lynn Gardens 46
115 41N05 87W53 5:51:32
Lynnville 69 113 39N41'13 90W20'45 6:01:23
Lynnwood 47 4 41N41 88W21 5:53:24
Lynwood 16 12 41N31'35 87W32'19 5:50:09
Lyons 16 2 41N48'48 87W49'05 5:51:16
Mabel 23 54 39N52'35 87W41'32 5:50:46
Macedonia 28 4 38N03'07 88W42'19 5:54:49
Mackinaw 90 118 40N32'13 89W21'27 5:57:26
Mackinaw Dells 102
5 40N37'26 89W13'51 5:56:55
Mackler Heights 16
1 41N31 87W38 5:50:32
Macomb 55 66 40N27'33 90W40'18 6:02:41
Macon 58 57 39N42'46 88W59'49 5:55:59
Macoupin 59 51 39N12'48 89W57'26 5:59:50
Madison 60 35 38N40'37 90W09'25 6:00:38
Madonnaville 67 8 38N15'54 90W14'48 6:00:59
Maeystown 67 63 38N13'29 90W14'00 6:00:56
Magnet 15 63 39N26'21 88W23'52 5:53:35
Magnolia 78 56 41N06'49 89W11'40 5:56:47
Mahomet 10 54 40N11'43 88W24'15 5:53:37
Maizetown 92 54 39N57'15 87W48'16 5:51:13
Makanda 39 4 37N37'03 89W12'32 5:56:50
Malden 6 55 41N25'28 89W22'09 5:57:29
Malone 90 29 40N22 89W40 5:58:40
Malta 19 40 41N55'47 88W51'39 5:55:27
Malvern 98 75 41N51'19 89W53'12 5:59:33
Manchester 86 63 39N32'32 90W19'56 6:01:20
Manhattan 99 82 41N25'21 87W59'09 5:51:57
Manito 63 7 40N25'33 89W46'45 5:59:07
Manley 29 4 40N35'02 90W25'32 6:01:42
Manlius 6 55 41N27'23 89W40'08 5:58:41
Mannheim 16 1 41N56 87W53 5:51:32
Mannon 66 4 41N13'52 90W57'24 6:03:50
Mansfield 74 55 40N12'41 88W30'22 5:54:01
Manson Ford 76 4 37N27'03 88W34'03 5:54:16
Manteno 46 26 41N15'02 87W49'53 5:51:20
Manville 53 55 41N03'18 88W45'58 5:55:04
Maple 60 25 38N51'37 89W52'35 5:59:30
Maplebrook 22 12 41N47 88W09 5:52:36
Maple Grove 24 4 38N32'00 88W05'38 5:52:23
Maple Lane 98 26 41N48 89W43 5:58:52
Maple Park 45 84 41N54'27 88W35'57 5:54:24
Maple Point 18 4 39N19'56 88W06'47 5:52:27
Maples Mill 29 7 40N25'42 90W01'50 6:00:07
Mapleton 72 98 40N33'59 89W43'54 5:58:56
Maplewood 82 25 38N34 90W08 6:00:32
Maplewood Park 82
25 38N34'32 90W10'34 6:00:42
Maquon 48 4 40N47'56 90W09'56 6:00:40
Marblehead 1 92 39N50'23 91W22'06 6:05:28
Marcelline 1 53 40N07'05 91W22'02 6:05:28
Marcoe 41 4 38N16'01 88W57'59 5:55:52
Marcus 8 4 42N09'30 90W11'45 6:00:47
Mardell Manor 72
98 40N40 89W40 5:58:40
Marengo 56 119 42N14'55 88W36'30 5:54:26
Marietta 29 63 40N30'04 90W23'33 6:01:34
Marigold 79 63 38N04'47 90W00'23 6:00:02
Marina Terrace 47
4 41N41 88W21 5:53:24
Marina Village 47
4 41N41 88W21 5:53:24
Marine 60 55 38N47'11 89W46'39 5:59:07
Marion 100 63 37N43'50 88W55'59 5:55:44
Marion Circle 45
41 41N45 88W27 5:53:48
Marion Hills 22
54 41N46 87W57 5:51:48
Marissa 82 53 38N15'00 89W45'00 5:59:00
Mark 78 41 41N15'52 89W15'00 5:57:00
Market Place 10
21 40N07 88W15 5:53:00
Market Place Shopping Center 16
6 42N02'46 87W56'21 5:51:45
Markham 16 1 41N35'37 87W41'41 5:50:47
Markham 69 113 39N44'45 90W19'40 6:01:19
Markham City 41 4 38N20 88W44 5:54:56
Marley 23 128 39N30'46 87W36'54 5:50:28
Marley 99 1 41N32'55 87W55'32 5:51:42
Marlow 41 4 38N19'15 88W47'36 5:55:10
Maroa 58 8 40N02'11 88W57'25 5:55:50
Marquette 6 48 41N19'51 89W15'45 5:57:03
Marquette Heights 90
98 40N37'03 89W36'01 5:58:24
Marrowbone 70 55 39N38 88W45 5:55:00
Marseilles 50 120 41N19'51 88W42'29 5:54:50
Marshall 12 55 39N23'29 87W41'37 5:50:46
Marshall Landing 7
65 38N57'27 90W30'21 6:02:01
Marston 66 4 41N20 90W40 6:02:40
Martin Landing 7
65 38N54'37 90W38'17 6:02:33
Martinsburg 75 4 39N30'57 90W50'33 6:03:22
Martinsville 12
55 39N20'08 87W52'55 5:51:32
Martinton 38 30 40N54'57 87W43'31 5:50:54
Marydale 14 55 38N41'51 89W22'19 5:57:29
Marydale Manor 16
1 41N37 87W40 5:50:40
Maryland 71 63 42N03'56 89W32'50 5:58:11
Maryland Place 60
7 38N43'54 90W06'36 6:00:26
Maryville 60 7 38N43'25 89W57'21 5:59:49
Marywood 45 102 41N47'37 88W17'25 5:53:10
Mascoutah 82 55 38N29'25 89W47'35 5:59:10
Mason 25 4 38N57'11 88W37'25 5:54:30
Mason City 63 121 40N12'08 89W41'53 5:58:48
Massbach 43 4 42N14'46 90W07'18 6:00:29
Massilon 96 4 38N26 88W13 5:52:52
Matanzas 63 55 40N13'52 90W05'58 6:00:24
Matanzas Beach 63
55 40N14'35 90W06'14 6:00:25
Mathersville 66 4 41N16 90W36 6:02:24
Matherville 66 4 41N15'35 90W36'28 6:02:26
Matteson 16 2 41N30'14 87W42'47 5:50:51
Matthews 73 4 37N58'03 89W22'26 5:57:30
Matthews Junction 39
4 37N57'09 89W22'26 5:57:30
Mattoon 15 63 39N28'59 88W22'22 5:53:29
Maud 93 4 38N23'51 87W51'19 5:51:25
Maunie 97 4 38N02'08 88W02'44 5:52:11
Maxwell 72 98 40N41'19 89W42'01 5:58:48
Maxwell 84 55 39N37'59 89W53'57 5:59:36
Mayberry 96 4 38N16'14 88W32'55 5:54:12
Mayfair 90 98 40N37 89W29 5:57:56
Mayfield 19 36 42N01 88W46 5:55:04
Maynard Lake 10
21 40N07 88W15 5:53:00
Mayngaite 16 1 41N31 87W42 5:50:48
Mays 23 128 39N37'44 87W47'32 5:51:10
Maysville 75 4 39N42'27 90W47'57 6:03:12
Maytown 52 29 41N37'42 89W22'04 5:57:28
Mayview 10 138 40N06'48 88W06'37 5:52:26
Maywood 16 1 41N52'45 87W50'35 5:51:22
Mazon 32 122 41N14'29 88W25'10 5:53:41
Mazonia 32 37 41N12'33 88W16'52 5:53:07
McCall 34 4 40N27'10 91W11'49 6:04:47
McCann Ford 18 4 39N22'24 88W10'37 5:52:42
McClay Orchard 31
63 39N28'00 90W31'30 6:02:06
McClellan 41 4 38N15 88W59 5:55:56
McClure 2 4 37N19'04 89W25'53 5:57:44
McClusky 42 25 39N02'36 90W19'13 6:01:17
McConnell 89 4 42N26'04 89W43'53 5:58:56
McCook 16 1 41N47'52 87W50'41 5:51:23
McCormick 76 4 37N33'02 88W40'14 5:54:41
McCormick Place 16
1 41N51'10 87W36'42 5:50:27
McCown 23 55 39N47'57 87W55'41 5:51:43
McCullom Lake 56
62 42N22'06 88W17'33 5:53:10
McDowell 53 127 40N49'50 88W35'06 5:54:20
McFarlan 35 4 37N29 88W18 5:53:12
McGirr 19 60 41N49'03 88W48'08 5:55:13
McHenry 56 30 42N20'41 88W16'26 5:53:06
McHenry Shores 56
30 42N19'08 88W15'29 5:53:02
McKee 1 66 39N53 90W59 6:03:56
McKeen 12 55 39N27'30 87W36'50 5:50:27
McKendree 92 54 40N00 87W34 5:50:16

McKinley 95 4 38N13'57 89w32'54 5:58:12
McLean 57 72 40N18'52 89w10'11 5:56:41
McLeansboro 33 4 38N05'36 88w32'08 5:54:09
McNabb 78 41 41N10'37 89w12'33 5:56:50
McNulta 57 54 40N22'15 88w29'21 5:53:57
McQueen 45 54 42N03'43 88w23'05 5:53:32
McVey 59 29 39N23'23 89w44'47 5:58:59
Meacham 61 4 38N42 88w45 5:55:00
Meadowbrook 55 4 40N28 90w41 6:02:44
Meadowbrook 60 25 38N53'54 90w00'24 6:00:02
Meadowdale 45 105 42N07 88w16 5:53:04
Meadowdale Shopping Center 45 105 42N07 88w16 5:53:04
Meadow Heights 60 7 38N41'30 89w59'28 5:59:58
Meadow Mart 101 55 42N19 89w02 5:56:08
Meadows 57 35 40N44'40 88w48'17 5:55:13
Meadowview 46 115 41N05 87w53 5:51:32
Mechanicsburg 84 8 39N48'34 89w23'50 5:57:35
Medalist Park 16 6 42N06 88w02 5:52:08
Media 36 4 40N46'30 90w49'55 6:03:20
Medina 72 57 40N50 89w35 5:58:20
Medinah 22 27 41N58'53 88w03'04 5:52:12
Medinah on the Lake 22 27 41N58 88w05 5:52:20
Medora 59 55 39N10'28 90w08'35 6:00:34
Meeks 92 54 39N59'59 87w35'04 5:50:20
Meersman 81 87 41N30 90w26 6:01:44
Melody 49 2 42N14'25 87w52'57 5:51:32
Melrose 12 4 39N13'24 87w45'51 5:51:03
Melrose Park 16 1 41N54'02 87w51'24 5:51:26
Melville 60 7 38N56'13 90w14'45 6:00:59
Melvin 27 30 40N34'03 88w14'52 5:52:59
Melwood 23 55 39N45'42 87w51'49 5:51:27
Menard 79 66 37N54'36 89w50'23 5:59:22
Mendon 1 53 40N05'18 91w17'01 6:05:08
Mendota 50 123 41N32'50 89w07'03 5:56:28
Menominee 43 4 42N29'16 90w31'59 6:02:08
Meppen 7 65 38N59'49 90w36'17 6:02:25
Mercer 66 4 41N12 90w43 6:02:52
Merchandise Mart 16 1 41N54 87w38 5:50:32
Meredith 45 84 41N53'58 88w32'25 5:54:10
Meredosia 69 65 39N49'52 90w33'34 6:02:14
Meriden 50 56 41N34'17 89w02'00 5:56:08
Meridian 14 4 38N37 89w12 5:56:48
Meridian Heights 77 4 37N07 89w12 5:56:48
Mermet 64 4 37N16'23 88w50'46 5:55:23
Merna 57 68 40N31'00 88w49'33 5:55:18
Merriam 96 4 38N21'45 88w16'38 5:53:07
Merrimac 67 55 38N18 90w19 6:01:16
Merrionette Park 16 1 41N41'03 87w42'01 5:50:48
Merritt 86 4 39N42'52 90w24'57 6:01:40
Merry Oaks 81 87 41N30 90w26 6:01:44
Mesa Lake 93 4 38N33 87w52 5:51:28
Metamora 102 57 40N47'26 89w21'38 5:57:27
Metcalf 23 55 39N48'04 87w48'26 5:51:14
Metropolis 64 62 37N09'04 88w43'55 5:54:56
Mettawa 49 126 42N14'00 87w55'33 5:51:42
Meyer 1 66 40N08'52 91w30'12 6:06:01
Meyer 28 4 38N02'53 89w02'34 5:56:10
Meyer 46 115 41N05 87w53 5:51:32
Meyers Bay 49 6 42N23 88w11 5:52:44
Michael 7 55 39N14'07 90w37'24 6:02:30
Michael Landing Public Acces 7 55 39N14'07 90w36'29 6:02:26
Michigan Beach 99 114 41N30'53 88w03'44 5:52:15
Mid City 31 55 39N13'19 90w23'29 6:01:34
Middeal 8 4 41N58'30 89w59'17 5:59:57
Middlebury 45 6 42N08'39 88w14'17 5:52:57
Middle Creek 34 4 40N22'22 91w01'38 6:04:07
Middlefork 92 38 40N19 87w50 5:51:20
Middlegrove 29 4 40N42'16 90w05'58 6:00:24
Middlepoint 97 4 37N56'02 88w17'47 5:53:11
Middleport 38 30 40N50 87w44 5:50:56
Middlesworth 87 7 39N24'44 88w42'55 5:54:52
Middleton 96 4 38N17'35 88w40'11 5:54:41
Middletown 54 63 40N06'01 89w35'27 5:58:22
Midland City 20 55 40N08'43 89w08'01 5:56:32
Midland Hills 39 4 37N37 89w13 5:56:52
Midlothian 16 1 41N37'31 87w43'03 5:50:52
Midway 60 4 38N55'43 89w58'19 5:59:53
Midway 64 4 37N14'23 88w38'02 5:54:32
Midway 90 98 40N31'10 89w39'43 5:58:39
Midway 92 26 40N00'58 87w38'16 5:50:33
Mid-West 16 1 41N53 87w41 5:50:44
Milam 58 55 39N41 88w52 5:55:28
Milan 81 87 41N27'11 90w34'19 6:02:17
Mildred 84 133 39N46 89w38 5:58:32
Miles 59 37 39N04'10 90w06'26 6:00:26
Milford 38 7 40N37'42 87w41'46 5:50:47
Milks Grove 38 35 40N53 87w58 5:51:52
Milla 50 57 41N08'29 88w59'00 5:55:56
Millbrook 47 25 41N35'54 88w33'10 5:54:13
Millbrook 72 4 40N56 89w57 5:59:48
Millburn 49 6 42N25'33 88w00'14 5:52:01
Mill Creek 16 6 42N09 87w57 5:51:48
Mill Creek 91 4 37N20'30 89w15'09 5:57:01
Milledgeville 8 63 41N57'48 89w46'28 5:59:06
Miller 50 55 41N25 88w39 5:54:36
Miller 82 25 38N32'06 89w56'12 5:59:45
Miller City 2 4 37N06'39 89w21'22 5:57:25
Miller Lake 41 4 38N18 88w55 5:55:40
Millersburg 66 4 41N14'29 90w49'06 6:03:16
Millersville 11 63 39N27'04 89w09'29 5:56:38
Miller Woods 16 1 41N31 87w38 5:50:32
Millhurst 50 25 41N37'22 88w33'08 5:54:13
Millington 47 7 41N33'45 88w35'54 5:54:24
Mills 3 55 38N48 89w25 5:57:40
Millsdale 99 70 41N26'06 88w09'51 5:52:39
Mill Shoals 97 4 38N14'55 88w20'48 5:53:23
Mill Spring 60 7 38N57 90w11 6:00:44
Millstadt 82 56 38N27'41 90w05'30 6:00:22
Millstadt Junction 67 46 38N27'42 90w13'04 6:00:52
Millville 43 4 42N26'56 90w03'05 6:00:12
Millville 59 55 39N03'25 89w56'13 5:59:45
Milmine 74 54 39N54'27 88w39'01 5:54:36
Milne 87 63 39N15'47 88w47'32 5:55:10
Milo 6 4 41N11'33 89w34'56 5:58:20
Milroy 36 4 41N01'07 90w55'15 6:03:41
Milton 75 4 39N33'52 90w39'01 6:02:36
Mindale 90 72 40N25'33 89w22'11 5:57:29
Mineral 6 63 41N22'57 89w50'11 5:59:21
Mineral Springs 98 26 41N48 89w43 5:58:52
Minier 90 86 40N26'01 89w18'47 5:57:15
Minonk 102 124 40N54'16 89w02'04 5:56:08
Minooka 32 48 41N27'19 88w15'42 5:53:03
Mira 10 138 40N05'02 88w09'44 5:52:39
Misenheimer 91 4 37N23 89w18 5:57:12
Missa 53 55 41N05'54 88w44'32 5:54:58
Missal 53 135 41N08 88w50 5:55:20
Mission 50 55 41N30 88w38 5:54:32
Missionfield 92 54 40N06'17 87w45'13 5:51:01
Mission Hills 16 2 42N07 87w49 5:51:16
Mississippi 42 37 39N02 90w19 6:01:16
Missouri 5 76 40N04 90w45 6:03:00
Mitchell 28 4 37N55'08 89w02'46 5:56:11
Mitchell 60 4 38N45'43 90w05'07 6:00:20
Mitchellsville 83 4 37N39'02 88w32'16 5:54:09
Mitchie 67 63 38N12'37 90w20'00 6:01:20
Mobet Meadows 81 4 41N37 90w20 6:01:20
Moccasin 25 4 39N08'50 88w45'28 5:55:02
Mode 87 63 39N15'59 88w44'01 5:54:56
Modena 88 4 41N08'07 89w45'47 5:59:03
Modesto 59 63 39N28'42 89w58'55 5:59:56
Modoc 79 55 38N03'09 90w02'14 6:00:09
Moecherville 45 102 41N46 88w20 5:53:20
Moellenbrocks 60 7 38N42'23 90w04'20 6:00:17
Mohawk 22 17 41N57 87w58 5:51:52
Mokena 99 3 41N31'34 87w53'21 5:51:33
Moline 81 87 41N30'24 90w30'54 6:02:04
Momence 46 82 41N10'00 87w39'46 5:50:39
Mona 27 44 40N54 88w11 5:52:44
Monaville 49 1 42N23'58 88w06'41 5:52:27
Monee 49 26 41N25'12 87w44'30 5:50:58
Money Creek 57 7 40N38 88w52 5:55:28
Monica 88 55 40N55'25 89w49'23 5:59:18
Monmouth 94 23 40N54'41 90w38'50 6:02:35
Monroe Center 71 57 42N05'54 89w00'02 5:56:00
Monroe City 67 8 38N15'21 90w15'57 6:01:04
Mont 60 25 38N46'02 89w55'49 5:59:43
Montague Forest 45 107 42N02 88w17 5:53:08
Montebello 34 4 40N25 91w18 6:05:12
Monterey 29 4 40N31'52 89w56'45 5:59:47
Monterey Village 99 1 41N30 87w41 5:50:44
Montezuma 75 4 39N33'07 90w34'47 6:02:19
Montgomery 45 7 41N43'50 88w20'45 5:53:23
Monticello 74 30 40N01'40 88w34'24 5:54:18
Montmorency 98 4 41N43 89w41 5:58:44
Montrose 25 56 39N09'55 88w22'45 5:53:31
Moon 53 55 41N04'04 88w51'21 5:55:25
Moonshine 12 4 39N11'26 87w53'44 5:51:35
Moores Corner 92 26 40N15'59 87w39'07 5:50:36
Moores Prairie 41 4 38N10 88w46 5:55:04
Mooseheart 45 2 41N49'26 88w20'05 5:53:20
Morea 17 4 38N55'36 87w37'56 5:50:32
Moredock 67 55 38N22 90w18 6:01:12
Morehaven 101 4 42N25'28 89w01'24 5:56:06
Morgan 15 65 39N36 88w06 5:52:24
Morgan Park 16 1 41N42 87w40 5:50:40
Moriah 12 4 39N13'02 87w56'22 5:51:45
Moro 60 4 38N55'29 90w01'19 6:00:05
Moronts 78 48 41N17'10 89w17'40 5:57:11
Morreville 5 65 39N51'01 90w48'01 6:03:12
Morris 32 125 41N21'26 88w25'16 5:53:41
Morris Hills 82 7 38N40 90w00 6:00:00
Morrison 98 75 41N48'35 89w57'54 5:59:52
Morrisonville 11 63 39N25'12 89w27'20 5:57:49
Morristown 37 4 41N23'47 90w17'55 6:01:12
Morristown 101 4 42N10'21 89w04'01 5:56:16
Morse 88 4 41N13'49 89w38'42 5:58:35
Morseville (Plum River) 43 4 42N18'20 89w58'45 5:59:55
Mortimer 23 7 39N51'19 87w43'28 5:50:54
Morton 90 98 40N36'46 89w27'33 5:57:50
Morton Grove 16 1 42N02'26 87w46'57 5:51:08
Morton Park 16 1 41N51 87w46 5:51:04
Moscow 91 4 37N24'41 89w03'09 5:56:13
Moser Highlands 22 12 41N47 88w09 5:52:36
Mosquito 11 55 39N45 89w12 5:56:48
Mossville 72 4 40N48'56 89w34'04 5:58:16
Moulton 87 7 39N24 88w48 5:55:12
Mound City 77 4 37N05'07 89w09'45 5:56:39
Mound Station (Timewell P O) 5 66 40N00'28 90w52'25 6:03:30
Mountain 83 4 37N40 88w26 5:53:44
Mountain Glen 91 4 37N31'39 89w17'23 5:57:10
Mount Hope 57 72 40N21 89w12 5:56:48
Mount Joy 54 37 40N17'12 89w16'55 5:57:08
Mount Morris 71 28 42N03'01 89w25'52 5:57:43
Mount Olive 59 7 39N04'20 89w43'38 5:58:55
Mount Palatine 50 43 41N11'33 89w09'47 5:56:39
Mount Pleasant 91 4 37N27'07 89w04'25 5:56:18
Mount Pleasant 98 75 41N48 89w55 5:59:40
Mount Prospect 16 1 42N03'59 87w56'14 5:51:45
Mount Prospect Gardens 16 1 42N04 87w57 5:51:48
Mount Pulaski 54 29 40N00'39 89w16'56 5:57:08
Mount Sterling 5 76 39N59'14 90w45'48 6:03:03
Mount Vernon 41 4 38N19'02 88w54'11 5:55:37
Mount Zion 58 55 39N46'17 88w52'27 5:55:30
Moweaqua 87 57 39N37'29 89w01'08 5:56:05
Mozier 7 4 39N17'33 90w44'57 6:03:00
Mozier Landing 7 4 39N15'20 90w43'33 6:02:54
Mudds Landing 79 55 38N00'33 90w03'13 6:00:13
Muddy 83 4 37N45'54 88w31'00 5:54:04
Mulberry Grove 3 54 38N55'30 89w16'08 5:57:05
Mulkeytown 28 4 37N58'15 89w06'41 5:56:27
Muncie 92 43 40N06'56 87w50'41 5:51:23
Mundelein 49 126 42N15'47 88w00'14 5:52:01
Mundelein Ridge Estates 49 126 42N14 87w59 5:51:56
Munger 22 27 41N57'52 88w13'22 5:52:53
Munger 75 66 39N45'26 91w19'19 6:05:17
Munson 37 4 41N22 90w09 6:00:36
Munstel 53 55 41N06'20 88w54'10 5:55:37
Munster 50 135 41N08 88w50 5:55:20
Murdock 21 65 39N48'03 88w04'42 5:52:19
Murphy Acres 99 114 41N33 88w07 5:52:28
Murphysboro 39 4 37N45'52 89w20'06 5:57:20
Murrayville 69 63 39N35'08 90w15'07 6:01:00
Mylith Park 49 6 42N15'51 88w11'30 5:52:46
Myrtle 71 4 42N10'05 89w21'24 5:57:26
Naausay 47 82 41N35 88w19 5:53:16
Nachusa 52 37 41N49'53 89w23'23 5:57:34
Nameoki 60 7 38N43'54 90w07'40 6:00:31
Naperville 22 12 41N47'09 88w08'50 5:52:35
Naplate 50 6 41N20'01 88w52'41 5:55:31
Naples 86 65 39N45'26 90w36'26 6:02:26
Narita 54 29 39N58'59 89w13'08 5:56:53
Nashua 71 28 41N58 89w19 5:57:16
Nashville 95 4 38N20'37 89w22'50 5:57:31
Nason 41 4 38N10'34 88w58'03 5:55:52
Natalie Estates 16 6 41N36 87w45 5:51:00
National City 82 25 38N38'44 90w09'39 6:00:39
National Stock Yards 82 25 38N39 90w09 6:00:36
Natrona 63 29 40N16'15 89w37'56 5:58:32
Nauvoo 34 4 40N33'00 91w23'05 6:05:32
Navajo Hills 16 12 41N40 87w47 5:51:08
Naval Air Station 16 1 42N06 87w50 5:51:20
Neadmore 12 4 39N14'57 87w51'37 5:51:26
Neal 18 4 39N18'07 88w20'30 5:53:22
Nebo 75 4 39N26'33 90w47'27 6:03:10
Nebraska 53 55 40N53 88w52 5:55:28
Neelys 69 65 39N44 90w31 6:02:04
Neelyville 69 65 39N45'23 90w28'35 6:01:54
Neilson 100 4 37N37'49 88w57'38 5:55:51
Nekoma 37 4 41N10'22 90w11'19 6:00:45
Nelson 52 86 41N47'47 89w36'06 5:58:24
Neoga 18 63 39N19'10 88w27'10 5:53:49
Neponset 6 63 41N17'45 89w47'25 5:59:10
Nettle Creek 32 55 41N26'33 88w34'41 5:54:19
Neunert 39 4 37N43'22 89w32'44 5:58:11
Nevada 53 127 41N05'09 88w33'05 5:54:12
Nevins 23 128 39N32'02 87w38'19 5:50:33
Newark 47 55 41N32'13 88w35'00 5:54:20
New Athens 82 35 38N19'35 89w52'37 5:59:30
New Baden 14 41 38N32'06 89w42'02 5:58:48
New Bedford 6 88 41N30'46 89w43'14 5:58:53
New Berlin 84 55 39N43'31 89w54'38 5:59:39
Newbern 42 4 39N00'25 90w20'13 6:01:21
New Blossom Hill 56 1 42N14 88w15 5:53:00
New Boston 66 4 41N10'13 90w59'48 6:03:59
Newburg 58 57 39N58'52 88w48'14 5:55:13
Newburg 75 4 39N37 90w44 6:02:56
New Burnside 44 4 37N34'45 88w46'15 5:55:05
Newby 15 63 39N26'27 88w19'05 5:53:16
New Camp 100 4 37N48 89w05 5:56:20
New Canton 75 4 39N38'10 91w05'45 6:04:23
Newcastle 83 4 37N39'02 88w40'17 5:54:41
New City 84 55 39N40'13 89w32'07 5:58:08
New Columbia 64 4 37N18'38 88w46'31 5:55:06
Newcomb 10 54 40N16 88w24 5:53:36
New Delhi 42 25 39N05 90w22 6:01:28
New Dennison 100 4 37N41'34 88w51'20 5:55:25
New Design (Burksville Sta) 67 8 38N16'05 90w07'06 6:00:28
New Douglas 60 7 38N58'12 89w39'59 5:58:40
Newell 92 26 40N09'47 87w35'01 5:50:20
New Grand Chain (Grand Chain 77 4 37N15'07 89w01'16 5:56:05
New Hanover 67 46 38N23'12 90w13'38 6:00:55
New Hartford 75 4 39N34'32 90w54'36 6:03:38
New Haven 30 4 37N54'31 88w07'45 5:52:31
New Hebron 17 4 38N57'00 87w44'40 5:50:59
New Holland 54 63 40N11'05 89w34'51 5:58:19
New Hope 100 4 37N47'38 88w41'20 5:54:45
New La Grange 5 65 39N53 90w39 6:02:36
New Lebanon 19 29 42N05'56 88w36'11 5:54:25
New Lenox 99 1 41N30'43 87w57'56 5:51:52
New Liberty 76 4 37N07'19 88w26'52 5:53:47
Newman 21 55 39N47'55 87w59'09 5:51:57
Newmansville 9 29 40N00'12 90w00'42 6:00:03
New Memphis 14 55 38N28'45 89w40'42 5:58:43
New Milford 101 28 42N11'13 89w04'04 5:56:16
New Minden 95 4 38N26'29 89w22'13 5:57:29
New Palatine 79 63 38N05 89w51 5:59:24
New Palestine 79 63 37N59'47 89w49'14 5:59:17
New Philadelphia 55 63 40N29'22 90w28'20 6:01:53

Newport 49 17 42N28 87W56 5:51:44
Newport 60 25 38N40'51 90W10'33 6:00:42
New Salem 75 4 39N42'27 90W50'51 6:03:23
Newton 40 4 38N59'27 88W09'45 5:52:39
Newton Corners 98
4 41N44'11 90W06'59 6:00:28
Newtown 53 55 41N04 88W45 5:55:00
Newtown 92 54 40N10'02 87W46'09 5:51:05
New Trier 16 1 42N05 87W45 5:51:00
New Virginia 100
4 37N49 88W56 5:55:44
New Windsor (Windsor) 66
4 41N12'08 90W26'32 6:01:46
Niantic 11 30 39N51'14 89W09'58 5:56:40
Nifa 45 103 41N50 88W19 5:53:16
Niles 16 2 42N01'08 87W48'10 5:51:13
Nilwood 59 53 39N23'53 89W48'31 5:59:14
Niota 34 4 40N37'03 91W17'16 6:05:09
Nipper Corner 33
4 38N02'19 88W28'13 5:53:53
Nippersink Terrace 49
6 42N26 88W14 5:52:56
Nixon 20 55 40N07 88W45 5:55:00
Nixon's Greenwood-Central 16
1 42N04 87W48 5:51:12
Noble 80 4 38N41'51 88W13'25 5:52:54
Nokomis 68 7 39N18'04 89W17'06 5:57:08
Noltings 95 4 38N29'16 89W11'57 5:56:48
Nora 43 4 42N27'21 89W56'43 5:59:47
Nordic Park 22 17 41N58 88W01 5:52:04
Normal 57 104 40N30'51 88W59'26 5:55:58
Norman 32 4 41N18 88W31 5:54:04
Normandale 90 98 40N35 89W37 5:58:28
Normandy 6 29 41N33'43 89W38'57 5:58:36
Normandy Hill 16
2 42N07 87W49 5:51:16
Normandy Villa 16
1 41N31 87W38 5:50:32
Normantown 99 82 41N39'17 88W13'56 5:52:56
Norpaul 16 1 41N56 87W53 5:51:32
Norridge 16 2 41N57'48 87W49'38 5:51:19
Norris 29 7 40N37'33 90W01'55 6:00:08
Norris City 97 4 37N58'52 88W19'45 5:53:19
North 16 1 42N03 87W42 5:50:48
North Alton 60 7 38N55'20 90W11'47 6:00:47
North Aurora 45
102 41N48'22 88W19'38 5:53:19
North Barrington 49
6 42N12'28 88W08'26 5:52:34
Northbelt Homesites 82
25 38N32 90W00 6:00:00
North Bluffs 86
65 39N46 90W31 6:02:04
Northbrook 16 1 42N07'39 87W49'44 5:51:19
Northbrook Knolls 16
2 42N07 87W49 5:51:16
Northbrook West 16
2 42N07 87W49 5:51:16
North Chicago 49
140 42N19'32 87W50'28 5:51:22
North Chillicothe 72
51 40N55'51 89W30'05 5:58:00
North City 28 4 37N59'39 89W04'02 5:56:16
North Dixon 52 25 41N50 89W30 5:58:00
North Dupo 82 46 38N32'58 90W12'02 6:00:48
Northeast 1 66 40N09 90W58 6:03:52
Northern 28 4 38N05 88W46 5:55:04
Northfield 16 1 42N05'59 87W46'51 5:51:07
Northfield Woods 16
6 42N05 87W53 5:51:32
North Fork 30 4 37N49 88W19 5:53:16
Northgate 16 27 41N58 88W06 5:52:24
North Glen Ellyn 22
2 41N53'31 88W03'47 5:52:15
North Hampton 72
51 40N55'52 89W32'20 5:58:09
North Hanover 43
4 42N17'37 90W16'43 6:01:07
North Harvey 16 2 41N36 87W40 5:50:40
North Henderson 66
4 41N05'21 90W28'31 6:01:54
North Hills 49
126 42N14 87W59 5:51:56
North Hooper 38
57 40N57'02 87W36'25 5:50:26
Northlake 16 2 41N55'02 87W53'44 5:51:35
North Libertyville Estates 49
42 42N16 87W56 5:51:44
North Litchfield 68
37 39N13 89W39 5:58:36
Northmore 60 7 38N57 90W11 6:00:44
Northmore Heights 25
4 39N07 88W33 5:54:12
North Mounds 77 4 37N07'23 89W12'01 5:56:48
North Muddy 40 4 39N01 88W19 5:53:16
North Northfield 16
1 42N08'18 87W52'53 5:51:32
North Okaw 15 65 39N36 88W24 5:53:36
North Ottawa 50 6 41N21 88W51 5:55:24
North Otter 59 4 39N29 89W53 5:59:32
North Palmyra 59
55 39N28 90W00 6:00:00
North Park 101 28 42N20'34 89W03'07 5:56:12
North Pekin 90 98 40N36'54 89W37'20 5:58:29
North Plato 45 29 42N03'18 88W27'51 5:53:51
North Quincy 1 92 39N58'14 91W23'46 6:05:35
North Riverside 16
1 41N50'34 87W49'23 5:51:18
North Shore 56 9 42N14'24 88W21'41 5:53:27
North Shoreland 100
4 37N46 88W56 5:55:44
North Town 16 1 42N00 87W42 5:50:48
North Utica 50 89 41N20 89W00 5:56:00
North Venice 60
25 38N40'51 90W09'59 6:00:40
Northville 50 7 41N33'48 88W42'19 5:54:49
North Winchester 86
63 39N39 90W29 6:01:56
Northwoods 19 110 42N06 88W42 5:54:48
North Woods 22 54 41N52 88W11 5:52:44
Northwoods Place 60
29 38N53 90W05 6:00:20
Norton 46 36 41N03 88W11 5:52:44
Nortonville 69 63 39N33'44 90W08'23 6:00:34
Norway 50 4 41N27'56 88W39'52 5:54:39
Norwood 66 4 41N05'21 90W38'17 6:02:33
Norwood 72 98 40N42 89W41 5:58:44
Norwood Park 16 1 41N59 87W50 5:51:20
Norwood Park 72
98 40N42'20 89W41'55 5:58:48
Nottingham Park 16
1 41N47 87W46 5:51:04
Nottingham Woods 45
55 41N49'47 88W27'55 5:53:52
Novak Park 45 95 41N57'32 88W19'04 5:53:16
Nubbin Ridge 97 4 38N06 88W20 5:53:20
Nunda 56 6 42N17 88W15 5:53:00
Nutwood 42 55 39N05'05 90W33'21 6:02:13
Oak 76 4 37N34'35 88W31'04 5:54:04
Oak Brook 22 21 41N49'58 87W55'44 5:51:43
Oak Brook Shopping Center 22
2 41N48 87W56 5:51:44
Oakbrook Terrace 22
21 41N51'00 87W57'52 5:51:51
Oakdale 95 4 38N15'42 89W30'05 5:58:00
Oakdale Woods 22
17 41N57 87W58 5:51:52
Oakford 65 66 40N06'09 89W57'47 5:59:51
Oak Forest 16 1 41N36'10 87W44'38 5:50:59
Oakglen 16 19 41N33'47 87W33'30 5:50:14
Oak Grove 49 27 42N17'47 87W55'00 5:51:40
Oak Grove 60 7 38N57 90W11 6:00:44
Oak Grove 81 4 41N24'38 90W34'14 6:02:17
Oak Hill 72 58 40N47'15 89W51'59 5:59:28
Oak Hills 82 7 38N38'17 89W58'50 5:59:55
Oak Hills Estates 4
28 42N16 89W00 5:56:00
Oakland 15 65 39N39'14 88W01'34 5:52:06
Oakland Center 85
65 40N14'02 90W30'30 6:02:02
Oak Lawn 16 1 41N43'15 87W45'15 5:51:01
Oaklawn 92 54 40N17 87W41 5:50:44
Oakley 58 54 39N52'34 88W48'21 5:55:13
Oak Meadows 22 54 41N52 88W11 5:52:44
Oak Park 16 1 41N53'06 87W47'04 5:51:08
Oak Ridge 102 57 40N48'41 89W26'15 5:57:45
Oak Run 48 4 40N55 90W07 6:00:28
Oak Spring Woods 49
42 42N16 87W56 5:51:44
Oakton 16 1 42N01 87W54 5:51:36
Oakwood 22 19 41N47 87W59 5:51:56
Oakwood 72 98 40N41 89W37 5:58:28
Oakwood 92 56 40N06'58 87W46'42 5:51:07
Oakwood Heights 60
29 38N52'54 90W04'06 6:00:16
Oakwood Hills 56
1 42N14'47 88W14'34 5:52:58
Oakwood Knolls 49
6 42N28 88W07 5:52:28
Oakwood Shores 56
15 42N23 88W26 5:53:44
Oautoga Bluff 60
7 38N57 90W11 6:00:44
Obed 87 63 39N33'55 88W35'40 5:55:37
Oblong 17 4 39N00'07 87W54'32 5:51:38
Oconee 87 63 39N17'08 89W06'27 5:56:26
Ocoya 53 127 40N48'18 88W41'02 5:54:44
Odell 53 127 41N00'13 88W31'31 5:54:06
Odgen 93 4 38N27'07 87W49'37 5:51:18
Odin 61 4 38N37'02 89W03'08 5:56:13
O'Fallon 82 25 38N35'32 89W54'40 5:59:39
Ogden 10 54 40N06'50 87W57'22 5:51:49
Ogden Park 16 1 41N47 87W40 5:50:40
Ogle 66 4 41N06'26 90W53'01 6:03:32
Ogles 82 25 38N32'48 90W03'17 6:00:13
Oglesby 50 117 41N17'43 89W03'34 5:56:14
O'Hare Airport 16
1 41N59 87W52 5:51:28
Ohio 6 55 41N33'27 89W27'39 5:57:51
Ohio Grove 66 4 41N07 90W43 6:02:52
Ohlman 68 7 39N20'42 89W13'07 5:56:52
Oil Center 17 4 38N58'05 87W49'58 5:51:20
Oil Center 61 4 38N31 89W08 5:56:32
Oilfield 12 4 39N23'38 87W59'19 5:51:57
Oil Grove 17 4 38N51'46 87W38'30 5:50:34
Okaw 87 7 39N29 88W45 5:55:00
Okawville 95 4 38N26'03 89W33'01 5:58:12
Old Brownfield 76
4 37N21'32 88W35'47 5:54:23
Old Camp 100 4 37N48 89W05 5:56:20
Old Du Quoin 73 4 37N58'30 89W10'59 5:56:44
Oldenburg 60 29 38N47'49 90W06'05 6:00:24
Olde Salem 16 27 41N58 88W06 5:52:24
Old Farm 22 12 41N47 88W09 5:52:36
Old Gilchrist 66
4 41N13'52 90W37'30 6:02:30
Old Kane 31 55 39N11'20 90W22'21 6:01:29
Old Kaskaskia 79
63 37N56'56 89W55'19 5:59:41
Old Marissa 82 55 38N15'30 89W45'15 5:59:01
Old Mill Creek 49
6 42N25'19 87W58'21 5:51:53
Old Mill Grove 49
6 42N12 88W03 5:52:12
Old Niota 34 4 40N36'48 91W18'07 6:05:12
Old Pearl 75 63 39N26'30 90W38'53 6:02:36
Old Princeton 9
63 39N52'41 90W09'50 6:00:39
Old Ripley 3 63 38N53'46 89W34'12 5:58:17
Old Salem Chautauqua 65
29 39N59'32 89W50'07 5:59:20
Old Shawneetown 30
4 37N41'49 88W08'12 5:52:33
Old Stonington 11
4 39N38 89W11 5:56:44
Oldtown 57 79 40N26 88W52 5:55:28
Oldtown 83 4 37N36'08 88W41'18 5:54:45
Olena 36 4 40N47'08 90W56'19 6:03:45
Olga 33 4 37N59'29 88W34'37 5:54:18
Olin 72 4 40N45'10 89W46'06 5:59:04
Olio 102 71 40N43 89W14 5:56:56
Olive 60 26 38N58 89W45 5:59:00
Olive Branch 2 4 37N10'07 89W21'06 5:57:24
Oliver 23 56 39N29'02 87W40'53 5:50:44
Olivet 92 54 39N56'31 87W38'37 5:50:34
Olmsted 77 4 37N10'50 89W05'20 5:56:21
Olney 80 63 38N43'51 88W05'07 5:52:20
Olympia Fields 16
1 41N30'48 87W40'27 5:50:42
Olympia Gardens 16
1 41N31 87W38 5:50:32
Olympic Terrace 22
12 41N47 88W09 5:52:36
Olympic Village 16
1 41N31 87W38 5:50:32
Omaha 30 4 37N53'25 88W18'11 5:53:13
Omar 44 4 37N30'06 88W58'07 5:55:52
Omega 61 4 38N42'16 88W46'50 5:55:07
Omphghent 60 55 38N58 89W52 5:59:28
Onarga 38 29 40N42'54 88W00'22 5:52:01
Oneco 89 4 42N29'15 89W39'51 5:58:39
Oneida 48 4 41N04'20 90W13'31 6:00:54
Ontario 48 4 41N04'43 90W18'27 6:01:14
Ontarioville 22
27 41N59'15 88W09'00 5:52:36
Opdyke 41 4 38N15'35 88W47'26 5:55:10
Opheim 37 4 41N15 90W23 6:01:32
Ophiem 37 4 41N15'09 90W23'15 6:01:33
Ophir 50 56 41N30 88W59 5:55:56
Oquawka 36 4 40N55'55 90W56'49 6:03:47
Ora 39 4 37N55 89W26 5:57:44
Oran 54 55 40N11 89W12 5:56:48
Orange 12 4 39N12'24 87W49'17 5:51:17
Orangemans Hall 66
4 41N18'49 90W36'29 6:02:26
Orange Prairie 72
98 40N46'39 89W40'11 5:58:41
Orangeville 89 65 42N28'06 89W38'38 5:58:35
Oraville 39 4 37N51'54 89W23'00 5:57:32
Orchard 96 4 38N35 88W38 5:54:32
Orchard Acres 56
9 42N14 88W21 5:53:24
Orchard Heights 80
4 38N44 88W05 5:52:20
Orchard Mines 72
98 40N35'21 89W40'40 5:58:43
Orchard Valley 49
140 42N22 87W53 5:51:32
Orchardville 96 4 38N30'23 88W39'01 5:54:36
Oreana 58 57 39N56'19 88W51'56 5:55:28
Oregon 71 28 42N00'53 89W19'56 5:57:20
Orel 96 4 38N18 88W34 5:54:16
Orient 28 4 37N55'06 88W58'39 5:55:55
Orio 93 4 38N33'16 87W46'44 5:51:07
Orion 37 4 41N21'17 90W22'53 6:01:32
Orland 16 1 41N36 87W52 5:51:28
Orland Hills 16
12 41N38 87W51 5:51:24
Orland Park 16 12 41N37'49 87W51'14 5:51:25
Orleans 69 4 39N43'25 90W04'46 6:00:19
Orleans Terrace 22
17 41N56 88W00 5:52:00
Ormonde 94 4 40N51'18 90W36'47 6:02:27
Orvil 54 29 40N16 89W26 5:57:44
Osage 28 4 37N53 89W07 5:56:28
Osage 50 4 41N04 88W59 5:55:56
Osbernville 11 55 39N45'40 89W10'43 5:56:43
Osborn 81 4 41N31'21 90W16'23 6:01:06
Osceola 88 4 41N12'47 89W46'47 5:59:07
Osco 37 4 41N20'52 90W16'49 6:01:07
Oskaloosa 13 4 38N45'35 88W38'56 5:54:36
Osman 57 55 40N17'45 88W28'19 5:53:53
Ospur 20 8 40N05'19 88W57'19 5:55:49
Ossami Lake 90 98 40N37 89W29 5:57:56
Oswego 47 43 41N40'58 88W21'05 5:53:24
Otego 26 4 38N58 88W58 5:55:52
Ottawa 50 6 41N20'44 88W50'33 5:55:22
Otterville 42 37 39N03'02 90W23'54 6:01:36
Otto 46 26 41N02'50 87W53'28 5:51:34
Ottoville 6 134 41N20 89W12 5:56:48
Ottville 6 134 41N20'53 89W15'31 5:57:02
Owaneco 11 63 39N28'56 89W11'37 5:56:46
Owego 53 127 40N53 88W32 5:54:08
Owen 101 28 42N22 89W06 5:56:24
Owen Center 101
28 42N22'06 89W07'01 5:56:28
Oxford 37 4 41N12 90W23 6:01:32
Oxville 86 65 39N42'17 90W33'40 6:02:15
Ozark 44 4 37N32'33 88W45'46 5:55:03
Pacesetter Park 16
1 41N36 87W38 5:50:32
Paderborn 82 8 38N21'37 90W02'33 6:00:10
Padua 57 29 40N27'01 88W45'50 5:55:03
Paineville 100 4 37N48'32 89W00'06 5:56:00
Palatine 16 1 42N06'37 88W02'03 5:52:08
Palermo 23 96 39N51'56 87W52'51 5:51:31
Palestine 17 4 39N00'13 87W36'46 5:50:27
Palisades 22 1 41N42'49 87W56'01 5:51:44
Palm Beach 56 6 42N22'36 88W11'50 5:52:47
Palmer 11 63 39N27'28 89W24'14 5:57:37
Palmerton 9 29 40N00'02 90W08'56 6:00:36
Palmyra 52 25 41N51'06 89W34'40 5:58:19
Palmyra 59 55 39N26'05 89W59'45 5:59:59
Paloma 1 63 40N01'22 91W11'42 6:04:47
Palos Gardens 16
12 41N40 87W47 5:51:08
Palos Heights 16
12 41N40'05 87W47'47 5:51:11
Palos Hills 16 12 41N41'48 87W49'01 5:51:16
Palos Park 16 12 41N40'02 87W49'49 5:51:19
Palos Westgate 16
12 41N40 87W47 5:51:08
Palsgrove 8 4 42N10'06 90W01'25 6:00:06
Pam Anne Estates 16
1 42N04 87W48 5:51:12
Pana 11 63 39N23'20 89W04'48 5:56:19
Panama 3 63 39N01'46 89W31'27 5:58:06
Pankeyville 83 4 37N42'30 88W32'10 5:54:09
Panola 102 55 40N47'01 89W01'16 5:56:05
Panther Creek 9
29 40N00 90W07 6:00:28
Papineau 38 26 40N58'09 87W42'59 5:50:52
Paradise 15 63 39N24'37 88W26'12 5:53:45
Paris 23 128 39N36'40 87W41'46 5:50:47
Park City 49 140 42N20'54 87W53'03 5:51:32
Parker 12 4 39N24 87W57 5:51:48
Parker 44 4 37N34'13 88W48'00 5:55:12
Parkersburg 80 4 38N35'23 88W03'24 5:52:14

Parkfield Terrace 82 25 38N34 90W08 6:00:32
Park Forest 99 1 41N29'29 87W40'28 5:50:42
Park Forest South 16 1 41N30 87W41 5:50:44
Park Hills 25 4 39N07 88W33 5:54:12
Parkhome 16 1 41N51 87W46 5:51:04
Parkland 72 7 40N27'45 89W45'05 5:59:00
Park Lane 46 26 41N01 87W43 5:50:52
Park Meadows 16 6 42N04 88W00 5:52:00
Park Ridge 16 1 42N00'40 87W50'26 5:51:22
Park Ridge Manor 16 1 42N02 87W51 5:51:24
Parkville 10 36 39N54'06 88W21'49 5:53:27
Parkwood 45 107 42N02 88W17 5:53:08
Parkwood Village 16 107 42N02 88W17 5:53:08
Parnell 20 63 40N13'23 88W43'14 5:54:53
Parrish 28 4 37N56'29 88W48'46 5:55:15
Parrish Addition 83 4 37N49 88W27 5:53:48
Partridge 102 51 40N52 89W26 5:57:44
Passport 80 4 38N47'21 88W14'37 5:52:58
Patoka 61 4 38N45'19 89W05'43 5:56:23
Patterson 31 63 39N28'50 90W28'58 6:01:56
Patterson Heights 60 7 38N57 90W11 6:00:44
Patterson Springs 21 54 39N47'32 88W11'34 5:52:46
Patton 12 56 39N28'37 87W33'31 5:50:14
Patton 93 4 38N28'37 87W45'13 5:51:01
Pattonsburg 62 54 40N56'16 89W11'04 5:56:44
Pauline 10 54 40N07'39 88W00'21 5:52:01
Paulton 100 4 37N45'50 88W48'14 5:55:13
Pavillion 47 25 41N36'38 88W28'30 5:53:54
Pawnee 84 55 39N35'30 89W34'49 5:58:19
Pawnee Junction 84 37 39N35'23 89W38'46 5:58:35
Paw Paw 52 56 41N41'20 88W58'52 5:55:55
Paxton 27 129 40N27'37 88W05'43 5:52:23
Paynes Point 71 4 42N01'26 89W12'24 5:56:50
Payson 1 85 39N49'01 91W14'32 6:04:58
Paytonville 32 125 41N20'12 88W25'52 5:53:43
Peach Orchard 27 30 40N34 88W16 5:53:04
Pea Ridge 5 66 40N04 90W51 6:03:24
Pearl 75 4 39N27'35 90W37'33 6:02:30
Pearl City 89 66 42N15'55 89W49'33 5:59:18
Pebble Beach 32 125 41N22 88W25 5:53:40
Pecatonica 101 30 42N18'50 89W21'33 5:57:26
Peerless 99 82 41N35 88W11 5:52:44
Pegram 31 55 39N20'47 90W23'49 6:01:35
Pekin 90 98 40N34'03 89W38'26 5:58:34
Pekin Heights 90 98 40N32'47 89W36'15 5:58:25
Pella 27 57 40N48 88W11 5:52:44
Pembroke 46 82 41N04 87W35 5:50:20
Pendleton 41 4 38N15 88W46 5:55:04
Penfield 10 54 40N18'12 87W56'48 5:51:47
Pennington Point 55 4 40N23'38 90W33'14 6:02:13
Pennsylvania 63 7 40N16 89W46 5:59:04
Penny Oaks 55 4 40N28 90W41 6:02:44
Penrose 98 26 41N53'15 89W40'04 5:58:40
Peoria 72 98 40N41'37 89W35'20 5:58:21
Peoria Heights 72 98 40N44'50 89W34'26 5:58:18
Peotone 99 30 41N19'56 87W47'07 5:51:08
Pepper Tree 16 6 42N06 88W02 5:52:08
Pequot 32 30 41N17 88W17 5:53:08
Percy 79 63 38N00'59 89W37'07 5:58:28
Perdueville 27 129 40N27'56 88W10'45 5:52:43
Perks 77 4 37N18'35 89W04'51 5:56:19
Perry 75 4 39N46'59 90W44'43 6:02:59
Perryton 66 4 41N17 90W44 6:02:56
Perryville 101 28 42N13'18 88W58'46 5:55:55
Pershing 28 4 37N52'48 88W57'55 5:55:52
Persifer 48 4 40N56 90W10 6:00:40
Peru 50 130 41N19'39 89W07'44 5:56:31
Pesotum 10 36 39N54'53 88W16'24 5:53:06
Peters 60 7 38N45 89W59 5:59:56
Petersburg 51 4 38N35'30 87W49'52 5:51:19
Petersburg 65 29 40N00'42 89W50'53 5:59:24
Petersburg 82 25 38N35'32 89W55'16 5:59:41
Peters Creek 35 4 37N29'16 88W14'29 5:52:58
Peterstown 50 123 41N29'53 89W08'48 5:56:35
Petersville 66 4 41N16'46 90W56'18 6:03:45
Petite Lake 49 6 42N26 88W08 5:52:32
Petrolia 51 4 38N45'38 87W46'44 5:51:07
Petty 51 4 38N48 87W50 5:51:20
Pharoah's Gardens 100 4 37N55 89W15 5:57:00
Pheasant Creek 16 2 42N07 87W49 5:51:16
Pheasant Meadows 99 22 41N21 87W37 5:50:28
Pheasant Ridge 99 3 41N32 87W52 5:51:28
Phelps 82 46 38N29'21 90W13'00 6:00:52
Phelps 94 4 40N50'55 90W34'29 6:02:18
Phenix 37 4 41N32 90W09 6:00:36
Philadelphia 9 63 39N55'26 90W07'02 6:00:28
Phillippe 16 6 42N04 88W00 5:52:00
Phillipstown 97 4 38N08'31 88W01'18 5:52:05
Philo 10 57 40N00'25 88W09'29 5:52:38
Phinney 10 138 40N06 88W12 5:52:48
Phoenix 16 26 41N36'40 87W38'05 5:50:32
Piasa 59 37 39N06'57 90W07'25 6:00:30
Piasa Hills 60 7 38N57 90W11 6:00:44
Picadilly Terrace 22 2 41N47 87W57 5:51:48
Pickaway 87 63 39N34 88W52 5:55:28
Pierce 19 43 41N51 88W39 5:54:36
Pierceburg 17 4 38N55'50 87W54'28 5:51:38
Pierron 3 90 38N46'48 89W35'53 5:58:24
Pierson 74 55 39N47'53 88W31'42 5:54:07
Piety Hill 50 117 41N18 89W03 5:56:12
Pigeon Grove 38 132 40N32 87W56 5:51:44
Pike 53 35 40N48 88W45 5:55:00
Pike 75 4 39N27'35 91W02'06 6:04:08
Pilot Knob 95 4 38N16 89W25 5:57:40
Pilsen 16 1 41N51 87W40 5:50:40
Pinckneyville 73 4 38N04'49 89W22'55 5:57:32
Pine Creek 71 4 41N59 89W27 5:57:48
Pinecrest 99 114 41N33 88W07 5:52:28
Pine Grove 32 125 41N22 88W25 5:53:40
Pinelands 22 95 41N54 88W19 5:53:16
Pine Meadow 99 1 41N40 88W00 5:52:00
Pine Rock 71 4 41N59 89W13 5:56:52
Pingree Grove 45 29 42N04'07 88W24'48 5:53:39
Pinkstaff 51 4 38N47'40 87W40'09 5:50:41
Pin Oak 60 25 38N47 89W53 5:59:32
Pioneer 72 98 40N46'58 89W39'17 5:58:37
Piopolis 33 4 38N11'01 88W33'41 5:54:15
Piper City 27 57 40N45'24 88W11'28 5:52:46
Pisgah 69 63 39N40'07 90W07'32 6:00:30
Pistakee 49 6 42N25 88W12 5:52:48
Pistakee Heights 49 6 42N21 88W14 5:52:56
Pistakee Highlands 56 27 42N24'31 88W12'23 5:52:50
Pistakee Hills 56 27 42N21 88W14 5:52:56
Pistaqua Heights 49 6 42N21 88W14 5:52:56
Pitchin 38 132 40N36'11 87W51'59 5:51:28
Pitman 68 63 39N24 89W39 5:58:36
Pittsburg 26 139 38N52'17 89W12'42 5:56:51
Pittsburg 100 4 37N46'37 88W50'58 5:55:24
Pittsfield 75 65 39N36'28 90W48'18 6:03:13
Pittwood 38 30 40N51'39 87W43'46 5:50:55
Pixley 13 4 38N48 88W18 5:53:12
Plainfield 99 82 41N37'37 88W12'14 5:52:49
Plainfield Acres 99 82 41N35 88W11 5:52:44
Plainview 59 53 39N09'33 89W59'23 5:59:58
Plainville 1 66 39N47'09 91W11'07 6:04:44
Plano 47 25 41N39'46 88W32'13 5:54:09
Plato Center 45 29 42N01'36 88W25'48 5:53:43
Plattville 47 25 41N31'54 88W22'53 5:53:32
Pleak 87 63 39N35'44 88W56'18 5:55:45
Pleasant 29 66 40N19 90W17 6:01:08
Pleasant Dale 16 1 41N48 87W52 5:51:28
Pleasantdale Estates 22 1 41N40 88W00 5:52:00
Pleasant Grove 15 63 39N24 88W16 5:53:04
Pleasant Grove 44 4 37N26'27 89W01'47 5:56:07
Pleasant Hill 22 2 41N53 88W05 5:52:20
Pleasant Hill 57 7 40N36'47 88W44'49 5:54:59
Pleasant Hill 75 4 39N26'36 90W52'20 6:03:29
Pleasant Hills 16 27 41N58 88W04 5:52:16
Pleasant Mound 3 4 38N51'47 89W17'25 5:57:10
Pleasant Plains 84 29 39N52'22 89W55'16 5:59:41
Pleasant Ridge 53 72 40N48 88W24 5:53:36
Pleasant Ridge 60 63 38N43'21 89W58'40 5:59:55
Pleasant Run 16 6 42N09 87W57 5:51:48
Pleasant Vale 75 4 39N37 91W05 6:04:20
Pleasant Valley 43 4 42N13'33 90W01'37 6:00:06
Pleasant View 58 57 39N41 89W05 5:56:20
Pleasantview 85 7 40N06'11 90W27'53 6:01:52
Plumfield 28 4 37N53'29 89W00'24 5:56:02
Plum Grove Countryside 16 6 42N04 88W00 5:52:00
Plum Grove Estates 16 6 42N06 88W02 5:52:08
Plum Grove Hills 16 6 42N04 88W00 5:52:00
Plum Grove Village 16 6 42N04 88W00 5:52:00
Plum Grove Woods 16 6 42N06 88W02 5:52:08
Plum Hill 95 4 38N21'46 89W30'31 5:58:02
Plum River 43 4 42N18'20 89W58'45 5:59:55
Plymouth 34 52 40N17'30 90W55'08 6:03:41
Poag 60 25 38N47'49 90W02'20 6:00:09
Pocahontas 3 55 38N49'40 89W32'24 5:58:10
Poe 67 93 38N10 90W00 6:00:00
Point Prec 7 65 38N55 90W35 6:02:20
Point West 22 83 41N53 88W01 5:52:04
Polk 99 22 41N18'42 87W36'30 5:50:26
Polo 71 7 41N59'10 89W34'45 5:58:19
Pomona 39 4 37N37'41 89W20'12 5:57:21
Pond 44 4 37N25 88W54 5:55:36
Ponemah 94 4 40N49'14 90W42'20 6:02:49
Pontiac 53 127 40N52'51 88W37'47 5:54:31
Pontiac 82 25 38N35'14 89W59'05 5:59:56
Pontoon Beach 60 7 38N43'54 90W04'49 6:00:19
Pontoosuc 34 4 40N37'44 91W12'19 6:04:49
Pope 26 4 38N47 89W11 5:56:44
Poplar City 63 63 40N14'50 89W56'23 5:59:46
Poplar Grove 4 91 42N22'06 88W49'19 5:55:17
Poplar Grove 81 87 41N27'28 90W27'23 6:01:50
Poplar Ridge 39 4 37N42'01 89W22'14 5:57:29
Poppleton Landing 7 65 38N54'25 90W38'01 6:02:32
Portage 43 4 42N22'58 90W27'23 6:01:50
Port Byron 81 4 41N36'23 90W20'07 6:01:20
Porterfield 62 56 41N05'03 89W09'43 5:56:39
Porterville (Eaton P O) 17 4 39N05'23 87W48'05 5:51:12
Port Jackson 17 4 38N51'49 87W46'42 5:51:07
Portland 98 4 41N37 90W02 6:00:08
Portland Corners 98 4 41N39'48 89W58'44 5:59:55
Port Ridge 99 114 41N35 88W03 5:52:12
Portuguese Hill 69 113 39N45'21 90W12'55 6:00:52
Posen 16 1 41N37'54 87W40'53 5:50:44
Posen 95 4 38N15'30 89W20'08 5:57:21
Posen Junction 16 1 41N39 87W42 5:50:48
Posey 14 55 38N32'13 89W21'09 5:57:25
Post Oak 26 4 39N05'25 88W54'33 5:55:38
Potomac 92 38 40N18'18 87W48'02 5:51:12
Pottawattamie Hills 16 2 41N35 87W40 5:50:40
Pottstown 72 98 40N43'05 89W39'37 5:58:38
Pottsville 91 4 37N25'19 89W21'27 5:57:26
Powder Creek 82 25 38N31 89W59 5:59:56
Powder Mill Woods 82 25 38N31 89W59 5:59:56
Powellton 34 4 40N32'09 91W16'07 6:05:04
Powerton 90 98 40N32'17 89W40'44 5:58:43
Prairie 79 93 38N10'23 89W56'35 5:59:46
Prairie 87 63 39N17 88W38 5:54:32
Prairie Center 50 6 41N28'08 88W56'04 5:55:44
Prairie City 55 4 40N37'16 90W27'43 6:01:51
Prairie Creek 54 29 40N16 89W33 5:58:12
Prairie du Pont 82 46 38N32 90W14 6:00:56
Prairie du Rocher 79 55 38N04'59 90W05'45 6:00:23
Prairie Green 22 2 41N53 88W05 5:52:20
Prairie Green 38 80 40N32 87W36 5:50:24
Prairie Grove 56 27 42N21 88W14 5:52:56
Prairie Hill 58 55 39N45'17 88W47'08 5:55:09
Prairie Home 87 55 39N39 88W44 5:54:56
Prairieton 11 57 39N37 89W04 5:56:16
Prairietown 60 8 38N57'59 89W55'19 5:59:41
Prairie View 49 26 42N11'57 87W57'20 5:51:49
Prairieville 52 25 41N50'29 89W36'43 5:58:27
Preemption 66 4 41N18'46 90W35'04 6:02:20
Prentice 69 4 39N51'25 90W02'37 6:00:10
Prestbury 45 102 41N46 88W20 5:53:20
Preston 79 63 38N06'22 89W51'36 5:59:26
Preston Heights 99 114 41N30 88W05 5:52:20
Prestwick 99 4 41N30 87W51 5:51:24
Prickett 60 25 38N48 89W57 5:59:48
Prince Crossing 22 54 41N54'18 88W11'04 5:52:44
Princeton 6 131 41N22'05 89W27'53 5:57:52
Princeville 88 55 40N55'47 89W45'27 5:59:02
Proctor 27 54 40N24'44 88W24'06 5:53:36
Prophetstown 98 23 41N40'17 89W56'10 5:59:45
Prospect 57 29 40N19'10 88W12'46 5:52:51
Prospect Heights 16 6 42N05'43 87W56'15 5:51:45
Prospect Meadows 16 6 42N04 87W57 5:51:48
Prospect Park 82 25 38N38 90W04 6:00:16
Prouty 84 55 39N40'56 89W55'43 5:59:43
Providence 6 55 41N16'41 89W35'33 5:58:22
Provincetown 16 6 41N35 87W46 5:51:04
Proving Ground 8 4 42N05 90W09 6:00:36
Prudential Plaza 16 1 41N53 87W37 5:50:28
Pruett 26 4 39N03'53 88W54'39 5:55:39
Pryortown 77 4 37N11'25 89W08'55 5:56:36
Puder 46 21 41N14'42 87W36'24 5:50:26
Pujol 79 63 37N54 89W56 5:59:44
Pulaski 77 4 37N12'49 89W12'21 5:56:49
Pulleys Mill 100 4 37N33 88W58 5:55:52
Pullman 16 1 41N41'34 87W36'21 5:50:25
Pureton 80 4 38N43'50 88W13'28 5:52:54
Putman 29 4 40N30 90W10 6:00:40
Putnam 78 8 41N11'06 89W23'47 5:57:35
Pyatts 73 4 38N00'11 89W22'16 5:57:29
Pyramid 95 4 38N20'03 89W13'40 5:56:55
Quarry 42 77 38N59 90W27 6:01:48
Quentin Corners 49 6 42N09'59 88W03'47 5:52:15
Quincy 1 92 39N56'08 91W24'35 6:05:38
Quincy Junction 75 4 39N27'04 91W01'30 6:04:06
Quiver 63 137 40N23 89W56 5:59:44
Quiver Beach 63 55 40N19'48 90W02'50 6:00:11
Raccoon 61 4 38N30 88W58 5:55:52
Raddle 39 4 37N46'44 89W35'12 5:58:21
Radford 11 57 39N34'39 89W02'04 5:56:08
Radley 52 28 41N38'16 88W56'28 5:55:46
Radnor 72 57 40N50 89W42 5:58:48
Radom 95 4 38N16'55 89W11'32 5:56:46
Rafetown 40 4 38N51'29 88W00'08 5:52:01
Rainbow Hills 45 95 41N55'10 88W22'12 5:53:29
Raleigh 83 4 37N49'37 88W31'55 5:54:08
Ramona Place 60 7 38N57 90W11 6:00:44
Ramsey 26 4 39N08'40 89W06'31 5:56:26
Randall Park 49 140 42N23 87W52 5:51:28
Randolph 57 35 40N22'34 88W58'49 5:55:55
Rankin 92 132 40N27'54 87W53'47 5:51:35
Ransom 50 56 41N09'22 88W38'58 5:54:36
Ransom Ridge Estates 16 1 42N02 87W51 5:51:24
Rantoul 57 29 40N18'30 88W09'21 5:52:37
Rapatee 48 4 40N42'54 90W09'29 6:00:38
Rapids City 81 4 41N34'54 90W20'36 6:01:22
Rardin 15 65 39N36'15 88W06'06 5:52:24

Raritan 36 4 40N41'45 90W49'38 6:03:19
Raum 76 4 37N27'46 88W31'15 5:54:05
Raven 23 7 39N48'14 87W32'46 5:50:11
Ravenswood 16 2 41N58 87W42 5:50:48
Ravinia 49 3 42N09'49 87W47'13 5:51:09
Rawalts 29 4 40N33'12 89W58'47 5:59:55
Rawlins 43 4 42N27 90W27 6:01:48
Rawson Bridge 56 1 42N14'32 88W12'54 5:52:52
Ray 85 65 40N12'22 90W28'32 6:01:54
Raymond 68 62 39N19'10 89W34'19 5:58:17
Raynor Park 99 114 41N33'04 88W05'40 5:52:23
Rayville 92 26 40N18'24 87W39'30 5:50:38
Reading 53 55 41N04 88W52 5:55:28
Rector 83 4 37N53 88W26 5:53:44
Red Bud 79 93 38N12'42 89W59'39 5:59:59
Reddick 53 36 41N05'50 88W15'02 5:53:00
Red Landing 7 65 39N10'07 90W42'26 6:02:50
Redmon 23 67 39N38'43 87W51'42 5:51:27
Red Oak 89 4 42N23'32 89W40'18 5:58:41
Red Oak Terrace 49 1 42N11 87W49 5:51:16
Reed 99 37 41N15 88W13 5:52:52
Reeders 59 47 39N18'20 90W02'27 6:00:10
Reeds 36 4 40N55'02 90W49'31 6:03:18
Reeds Station 39 4 37N46'40 89W09'39 5:56:39
Rees 69 63 39N38'08 90W05'33 6:00:22
Reeseville 44 4 37N20'35 88W43'11 5:54:53
Regency Grove 22 12 41N48 88W01 5:52:04
Regency Terrace 22 27 41N58 88W05 5:52:20
Reich Landing 5 65 39N58'45 90W30'47 6:02:03
Reilly 92 132 40N24'57 87W51'16 5:51:25
Reily Lake 79 63 37N58'45 89W55'15 5:59:41
Renault 67 55 38N09'13 90W08'02 6:00:32
Renchville 72 51 40N55 89W30 5:58:00
Rend City 28 4 38N01'37 88W59'05 5:55:56
Rennerville 87 7 39N27'24 88W48'26 5:55:14
Reno 3 63 38N58'30 89W30'50 5:58:03
Renshaw 76 4 37N21'16 88W40'42 5:54:43
Rentchler 82 25 38N29'29 89W52'23 5:59:30
Reseda 16 6 42N06 88W02 5:52:08
Resthaven 99 7 41N15'43 88W08'10 5:52:33
Reynolds 81 4 41N19'47 90W40'13 6:02:41
Reynoldsburg 44 4 37N30'55 88W46'33 5:55:06
Reynoldsville 91 4 37N22'02 89W23'42 5:57:35
Rice 43 4 42N20'21 90W23'40 6:01:35
Rice 73 4 38N12'02 89W23'01 5:57:32
Rich 16 6 41N31 87W45 5:51:00
Richards 50 135 41N10'43 88W50'10 5:55:21
Richardson 45 84 41N57'59 88W35'08 5:54:21
Richfield 1 66 39N48'55 91W06'59 6:04:28
Richland 84 29 39N50'45 89W51'29 5:59:26
Richland 87 63 39N23 88W38 5:54:32
Richland Grove 66 4 41N18 90W30 6:02:00
Richmond 56 48 42N28'33 88W18'21 5:53:13
Richmond 90 72 40N21'39 89W22'08 5:57:29
Richton Hills 16 22 41N29 87W43 5:50:52
Richton Park 16 22 41N29'04 87W42'12 5:50:49
Richview 95 4 38N22'42 89W10'48 5:56:43
Richwood 42 55 39N08 90W33 6:02:12
Richwoods 17 4 38N57'29 87W33'15 5:50:13
Richwoods 72 98 40N47 89W37 5:58:28
Ricks 11 63 39N24 89W25 5:57:40
Riddle Hill 84 133 39N47'12 89W45'52 5:59:03
Riddleville 51 4 38N51'07 87W39'05 5:50:36
Ridge 87 63 39N29 88W52 5:55:28
Ridgecrest 32 125 41N22 88W25 5:53:40
Ridge Farm 92 54 39N53'44 87W39'07 5:50:36
Ridgefield 56 9 42N16'06 88W21'41 5:53:27
Ridgeland 38 29 40N43 88W05 5:52:20
Ridgemoor 22 2 41N48 87W56 5:51:44
Ridge Prairie Heights 82 25 38N36 89W58 5:59:52
Ridgeville 38 29 40N42'49 88W04'04 5:52:16
Ridgewood 99 114 41N32'08 88W02'25 5:52:10
Ridgway 30 4 37N47'57 88W15'40 5:53:03
Ridott 89 46 42N17'47 89W28'31 5:57:54
Ridott Corners 89 46 42N16'31 89W28'32 5:57:54
Riehl 60 7 38N56'09 90W16'26 6:01:06
Riffel 13 4 38N46 88W30 5:54:00
Riffle 13 4 38N48'19 88W33'51 5:54:15
Riggston 86 63 39N41'43 90W25'23 6:01:42
Riley 56 29 42N11'29 88W37'57 5:54:32
Rileyville 100 4 37N51'02 88W40'22 5:54:41
Rinard 96 4 38N34'14 88W27'56 5:53:52
Ringwood 56 45 42N23'32 88W17'49 5:53:11
Rio 48 4 41N06'33 90W23'59 6:01:36
Ripley 5 67 40N01'22 90W38'19 6:02:33
Rising 10 23 40N09'26 88W20'01 5:53:20
Rising Sun 76 4 37N24'25 88W34'41 5:54:19
Rising Sun 97 4 38N00'01 88W01'41 5:52:07
Risk 53 55 40N40'15 88W24'19 5:53:37
Ritchie 99 7 41N15'18 88W06'19 5:52:25
River 46 82 41N09'33 87W35'36 5:50:22
Riverair 60 7 38N57 90W11 6:00:44
Riverdale 16 1 41N38'00 87W37'59 5:50:32
Riverdale 101 4 42N25'12 89W01'46 5:56:07
River Forest 16 1 41N53'52 87W48'50 5:51:15
River Glen 49 6 42N09 88W06 5:52:24
River Grove 16 1 41N55'33 87W50'09 5:51:21
River Heights 83 54 40N17 87W41 5:50:44
River Ridge 47 25 41N39 88W27 5:53:48
Riverside 16 1 41N50'06 87W49'22 5:51:17
Riverside Island 49 6 42N24 88W11 5:52:44
Riverside Lawns 16 1 41N51 87W50 5:51:20
Riverside Park 56 27 42N21 88W14 5:52:56
Riverstream 56 27 42N20'17 88W15'28 5:53:02
Riverton 84 29 39N50'39 89W32'22 5:58:09
Riverview 8 4 41N58 90W06 6:00:24
Riverview Heights 47 4 41N41 88W21 5:53:24
Riverwoods 49 6 42N10'03 87W53'49 5:51:35
Rivoli 66 4 41N12 90W30 6:02:00
Roaches 41 4 38N19'30 89W04'34 5:56:18
Roachtown 82 55 38N27'47 90W02'27 6:00:10
Roanoke 102 21 40N47'46 89W11'50 5:56:47
Robbins 16 22 41N38'38 87W42'13 5:50:49
Robbs 76 4 37N27'32 88W41'59 5:54:48
Robein 90 98 40N41'18 89W30'40 5:58:03
Roberts 27 30 40N36'46 88W11'00 5:52:44
Roberts Park 16 1 41N43 87W45 5:51:00
Robin Hill 99 114 41N33 88W07 5:52:28
Robinson 17 32 39N00'19 87W44'21 5:50:57
Roby 11 8 39N44'21 89W23'57 5:57:36
Rochelle 71 6 41N55'26 89W04'07 5:56:16
Rochester 84 55 39N44'58 89W31'54 5:58:08
Rochester 93 4 38N20'44 87W49'41 5:51:19
Rock 76 4 37N24'46 88W37'10 5:54:29
Rockbridge 31 55 39N16'09 90W12'15 6:00:49
Rock City 89 65 42N24'48 89W28'05 5:57:52
Rock Creek 1 53 40N02'45 91W23'58 6:05:36
Rock Creek 35 4 37N32'12 88W13'38 5:52:55
Rockdale 99 114 41N30'22 88W06'52 5:52:27
Rockdale Junction 99 114 41N33'51 88W06'24 5:52:26
Rock Falls 98 60 41N46'47 89W41'20 5:58:45
Rockford 101 28 42N16'16 89W05'38 5:56:23
Rockgate Estates 60 7 38N57 90W11 6:00:44
Rock Grove 89 4 42N27'47 89W30'43 5:58:03
Rock Island 81 87 41N30'34 90W34'43 6:02:19
Rockport 75 4 39N32'20 91W00'31 6:04:02
Rock Run 89 4 42N23 89W27 5:57:48
Rockton 101 65 42N27'09 89W04'20 5:56:17
Rockvale 71 28 42N04 89W19 5:57:16
Rockville 46 4 41N15 87W58 5:51:52
Rockwell 50 117 41N20 89W06 5:56:24
Rockwood 79 50 37N50'26 89W42'02 5:58:48
Rocky Ford 18 4 39N18'41 88W10'20 5:52:41
Rocky Run 34 63 40N15 91W24 6:05:36
Rodden 43 4 42N19'41 90W19'13 6:01:17
Rodemich 82 55 38N26'27 90W08'16 6:00:33
Rogers 27 38 40N58 88W11 5:52:44
Rogers Park 16 2 42N00 87W40 5:50:40
Rohrer 69 63 39N31'46 89W57'35 5:59:50
Roland 97 4 37N55'48 88W15'48 5:53:03
Rolling Acres 10 29 40N19 88W08 5:52:32
Rolling Acres 72 98 40N45 89W37 5:58:28
Rolling Meadows 16 6 42N05'03 88W00'47 5:52:03
Rolling Meadows 55 4 40N28 90W41 6:02:44
Rollins 49 27 42N22'46 88W03'46 5:52:15
Rollo 19 28 41N40'23 88W53'10 5:55:33
Rome 72 51 40N52'59 89W30'09 5:58:01
Rome Heights 72 51 40N55 89W30 5:58:00
Romeo 99 78 41N38'26 88W03'30 5:52:14
Romeoville 99 78 41N38'51 88W05'22 5:52:21
Romine 61 4 38N31 88W45 5:55:00
Rondout 49 27 42N16'48 87W53'43 5:51:35
Roodhouse 31 63 39N29'02 90W22'17 6:01:29
Rooks Creek 53 4 40N53 88W45 5:55:00
Rooney Heights 99 114 41N33 88W07 5:52:28
Roots 79 55 38N01'04 89W58'20 5:59:53
Root Spring 56 1 42N14 88W15 5:53:00
Ropers Landing 76 4 37N18'14 88W30'32 5:54:02
Rosamond 11 63 39N22'47 89W09'37 5:56:38
Roscoe 101 4 42N24'48 89W00'33 5:56:02
Rose 87 7 39N23 88W52 5:55:28
Rosebud 76 4 37N16'42 88W35'02 5:54:20
Rosecrans 49 17 42N27'55 87W57'09 5:51:49
Rosedale 42 65 39N02'39 90W32'53 6:02:12
Rosefield 72 58 40N46 89W49 5:59:16
Rose Ford 76 4 37N29'13 88W32'10 5:54:09
Rose Hill 22 12 41N48 88W01 5:52:04
Rose Hill 40 59 39N06'13 88W08'50 5:52:35
Rose Lake 82 25 38N38'24 90W06'26 6:00:26
Roseland 16 1 41N42 87W37 5:50:28
Roselle 22 17 41N59'05 88W04'47 5:52:19
Rosemont 16 1 41N59'43 87W53'04 5:51:32
Rosemont 82 25 38N37'37 90W05'50 6:00:23
Roseville 94 4 40N43'56 90W39'52 6:02:39
Rosewood 60 29 38N53 90W05 6:00:20
Rosewood Heights 60 29 38N53'16 90W05'05 6:00:20
Rosiclare 35 4 37N25'25 88W20'46 5:53:23
Roslyn 18 4 39N13'46 88W22'41 5:53:31
Rossville 92 80 40N22'45 87W40'07 5:50:40
Rossville Junction 92 80 40N21'28 87W38'37 5:50:34
Roth 2 4 37N06'01 89W18'26 5:57:14
Round Grove 53 36 41N04 88W18 5:53:12
Round Grove 98 75 41N47'06 89W52'19 5:59:29
Round Knob 64 4 37N14'50 88W44'15 5:54:57
Round Lake 49 27 42N21'12 88W05'36 5:52:22
Round Lake Beach 49 27 42N22'18 88W05'24 5:52:22
Round Lake Heights 49 27 42N22'48 88W06'15 5:52:25
Round Lake Park 49 27 42N21'25 88W04'36 5:52:18
Round Prairie 96 4 38N27'26 88W32'21 5:54:09
Rountree 68 4 39N18 89W25 5:57:40
Rowe 53 127 40N55'56 88W40'11 5:54:41
Rowell 20 55 40N04'19 89W01'46 5:56:07
Roxana 60 29 38N50'54 90W04'34 6:00:18
Roxbury 52 56 41N42'02 89W02'22 5:56:09
Royal 10 57 40N11'34 87W58'22 5:51:53
Royal Heights 82 25 38N32'39 90W00'49 6:00:03
Royal Lake 59 4 39N06'37 89W57'41 5:59:51
Royal Lake Resort 3 4 38N56 89W16 5:57:04
Royal Lakes Village 59 4 39N07 90W03 6:00:12
Royalton 28 94 37N52'37 89W06'52 5:56:27
Rozetta 36 4 40N56'30 90W51'49 6:03:27
Rubicon 31 55 39N23 90W12 6:00:48
Rudement 83 4 37N38'11 88W29'25 5:53:58
Rugby 53 36 40N54'43 88W29'25 5:53:58
Ruma 79 55 38N08'06 89W59'52 5:59:59
Rural Hill 33 4 37N57'38 88W39'04 5:54:36
Rush 43 4 42N25 90W02 6:00:08
Rushville 85 65 40N07'16 90W33'47 6:02:15
Russell 49 17 42N29'26 87W54'45 5:51:39
Russellville 4 91 42N19'41 88W47'01 5:55:08
Russellville 51 4 38N49'08 87W31'54 5:50:08
Rust 28 4 38N00'09 88W45'40 5:55:03
Rutherford 10 54 40N01'29 88W03'09 5:52:13
Rutland 50 39 40N59'03 89W02'30 5:56:10
Rutledge 20 63 40N15 88W45 5:55:00
Ruyle 42 55 39N12 90W11 6:00:44
Ryan 92 54 40N03'01 87W48'22 5:51:13
Sabina 57 30 40N20'50 88W39'02 5:54:36
Sacramento 97 4 38N01'54 88W20'15 5:53:21
Sadorus 10 36 39N58'01 88W20'47 5:53:23
Sag Bridge 16 1 41N41'18 87W55'59 5:51:44
Saidora 63 29 40N06'18 90W08'41 6:00:35
Sailor Springs 13 4 38N45'50 88W21'47 5:53:27
Saint Albans 34 53 40N14 91W12 6:04:48
Saint Anne 46 26 41N01'30 87W42'50 5:50:51
Saint Anne Woods 46 26 41N02'15 87W37'30 5:50:30
Saint Augustine 48 4 40N43'06 90W24'39 6:01:39
Saint Charles 45 95 41N54'51 88W18'31 5:53:14
Saint Clair 82 25 38N32 89W59 5:59:56
Saint Clair Square 82 25 38N38 90W04 6:00:16
Saint David 29 7 40N29'36 90W02'55 6:00:12
Saint Elmo 26 56 39N01'38 88W50'53 5:55:24
Sainte Marie 40 4 38N56 88W01 5:52:04
Saint Francis 25 4 39N08 88W25 5:53:40
Saint Francisville 51 4 38N35'28 87W38'48 5:50:35
Saint George 46 115 41N11'33 87W46'32 5:51:06
Saint Jacob 60 7 38N42'50 89W46'05 5:59:04
Saint James 26 4 38N57'16 88W51'04 5:55:24
Saint James Estates 16 1 41N31 87W38 5:50:32
Saint Joe 67 8 38N13'58 90W09'13 6:00:37
Saint Johns 73 4 38N01'51 89W14'27 5:56:58
Saint Joseph 10 8 40N06'42 88W02'30 5:52:10
Saint Libory 82 55 38N21'45 89W42'35 5:58:50
Saint Mary 34 52 40N20'46 90W56'02 6:03:44
Saint Marys 25 4 39N07 88W33 5:54:12
Saint Morgan 60 55 38N39'44 89W41'15 5:58:45
Saint Paul 26 4 38N51'10 88W57'12 5:55:49
Saint Paul Junction 16 1 41N39 87W42 5:50:48
Saint Peter 26 4 38N52'05 88W51'14 5:55:25
Saint Regis 22 83 41N53 88W01 5:52:04
Saint Rose 14 55 38N41'03 89W33'16 5:58:13
Saint Thomas 60 4 38N45'43 90W07'01 6:00:28
Salem 61 4 38N37'37 88W56'44 5:55:47
Salina 46 39 41N10 88W04 5:52:16
Saline 60 63 38N47 89W39 5:58:36
Saline 83 4 37N38'43 88W41'45 5:54:47
Saline Landing 35 4 37N34'12 88W07'49 5:52:31
Saline Mines 30 4 37N42 88W09 5:52:36
Salisbury 84 55 39N53'23 89W47'53 5:59:12
Salt Creek 63 63 40N10 89W46 5:59:04
Saluda 48 4 40N52'19 90W23'39 6:01:35
Samoth 64 4 37N19'58 88W47'15 5:55:09
Samsville 24 4 38N29'23 88W03'27 5:52:14
Sand Barrens 51 4 38N35'24 87W41'38 5:50:47
Sandburn 44 4 37N30'33 88W50'32 5:55:22
Sandoval 61 4 38N36'56 89W06'51 5:56:27
Sandpebble Walk 16 6 42N09 87W57 5:51:48
Sand Prairie 90 21 40N26 89W40 5:58:40
Sandra Heights 16 1 41N31 87W38 5:50:32
Sand Ridge 32 48 41N25'26 88W19'35 5:53:18
Sand Ridge 39 4 37N44'24 89W26'33 5:57:46
Sands 98 75 41N45'04 89W51'43 5:59:27
Sandusky 2 4 37N12'09 89W16'20 5:57:05
Sandwich 19 25 41N38'45 88W37'18 5:54:29
Sandy 86 4 39N37 90W21 6:01:24
Sandy Ford 50 4 41N10'42 88W54'42 5:55:39
Sangamon 58 26 39N52'00 88W51'21 5:55:25
Sangamon Valley 9 63 40N01 90W13 6:00:52
San Jose 54 29 40N18'20 89W36'10 5:58:25
Sankoty 72 98 40N45'34 89W33'54 5:58:16
Santa Anna 20 57 40N15 88W39 5:54:36
Santa Fe 14 4 38N32 89W26 5:57:44
Santa Fe Park 16 2 41N43'27 87W54'16 5:51:37
Saratoga 32 125 41N27'33 88W25'53 5:53:44
Saratoga 91 4 37N30'32 89W09'25 5:56:38
Saratoga Center 62 30 41N06'42 89W35'31 5:58:22
Sargent 21 65 39N43 88W03 5:52:12
Sato 39 4 37N54'32 89W25'50 5:57:43
Sauganash 16 2 41N59'24 87W44'32 5:50:58
Sauget 82 25 38N35'47 90W11'05 6:00:44
Sauk 16 1 41N32 87W37 5:50:28
Sauk Village 16 6 41N29'18 87W34'03 5:50:16
Saunders 84 29 39N51'07 89W18'26 5:57:14
Saunemin 53 36 40N53'35 88W24'19 5:53:37
Savage 69 113 39N46'53 90W12'39 6:00:51
Savanna 8 23 42N05'40 90W09'24 6:00:38
Savoy 10 25 40N03'17 88W15'06 5:53:00
Sawyerville 59 55 39N04'42 89W48'26 5:59:14
Say Brook 22 12 41N47 88W09 5:52:36
Saybrook 57 36 40N25'36 88W31'34 5:54:06
Scales Mound 43 4 42N28'33 90W15'10 6:01:01
Scarboro 52 56 41N46'53 89W02'03 5:56:08

Schaeferville 90 98 40N32'52 89w37'52 5:58:31
Schapville 43 4 42N23'49 90w12'19 6:00:49
Schaumburg 16 6 42N02'00 88w05'00 5:52:20
Scheller 41 4 38N11'11 88w05'42 5:56:23
Schick 22 27 41N57'06 88w09'51 5:52:39
Schiller Park 16 1 41N57'21 87w52'15 5:51:29
Schmieder Landing 7 65 38N53'41 90w31'40 6:02:07
Schnell 80 4 38N38'09 88w14'58 5:53:00
Schoper 59 4 39N20'17 89w47'03 5:59:08
Schram City 68 7 39N09'51 89w27'49 5:57:51
Schrodts Station 93 4 38N22'57 87w49'30 5:51:18
Schrum 16 19 41N36'04 87w32'56 5:50:12
Schuline 79 63 38N05'22 89w46'44 5:59:07
Schwer 38 7 40N39'38 87w47'17 5:51:09
Sciota 55 4 40N33'39 90w45'06 6:03:00
Scioto Mills 89 61 42N21'23 89w40'07 5:58:40
Scotland 23 7 39N48 87w41 5:50:44
Scotland 55 4 40N24 90w37 6:02:28
Scotsboro 100 6 37N46 88w56 5:55:44
Scott Air Force Base 82 6 38N32 89w52 5:59:28
Scottland 23 4 39N48'16 87w36'18 5:50:25
Scottsburg 55 4 40N33'14 90w35'37 6:02:22
Scottsville 59 63 39N28'49 90w06'17 6:00:25
Scottsville 96 4 38N19'45 88w10'20 5:52:41
Scottswood 10 138 40N06 88w12 5:52:48
Scottville 59 63 39N28 90w05 6:00:20
Scovel 53 36 40N54'42 88w23'54 5:53:36
Scraper-Moecherville 45 102 41N44'47 88w16'51 5:53:07
Seaton 66 4 41N06'08 90w48'05 6:03:12
Seatonville 6 134 41N21'53 89w16'35 5:57:06
Sebastopol 60 56 38N42'40 89w36'02 5:58:24
Secor 102 55 40N44'31 89w08'07 5:56:32
Seehorn 75 66 39N45'19 91w15'40 6:05:03
Sefton 26 4 39N04'15 88w57'20 5:55:49
Selby 6 41 41N22 89w20 5:57:20
Sellers 10 54 40N11'11 88w06'17 5:52:25
Selmaville 61 4 38N36'25 88w59'43 5:55:59
Selsor Ford 92 38 40N15'32 87w47'42 5:51:11
Seminary 26 4 38N52 89w12 5:56:48
Seminary 80 4 38N35'01 88w07'35 5:52:30
Senachwine 78 4 41N12 89w24 5:57:36
Seneca 50 46 41N18'40 88w36'35 5:54:26
Sepo 29 7 40N20'37 90w07'09 6:00:29
Serena 50 41 41N29'10 88w43'53 5:54:56
Sesser 28 4 38N05'30 89w03'01 5:56:12
Seven Hickory 15 106 39N35 88w11 5:52:44
Seven Hills 49 6 42N25 88w04 5:52:16
Seville 29 63 40N29'08 90w20'37 6:01:22
Seward 101 4 42N14'20 89w21'28 5:57:26
Sexson 87 1 39N23'22 88w31'05 5:54:04
Sexson Corner 87 63 39N28 88w30 5:54:00
Seymour 10 54 40N06'25 88w25'36 5:53:42
Shabbona 19 60 41N46'05 88w52'37 5:55:30
Shabbona Grove 19 28 41N43'57 88w51'20 5:55:25
Shadetree 16 6 41N36 87w45 5:51:00
Shadow Lawn 46 82 41N09'35 87w34'18 5:50:17
Shady Beach 37 4 41N32'20 90w11'48 6:00:47
Shady Grove 64 4 37N07'26 88w33'57 5:54:16
Shady Hill 49 6 42N09 88w06 5:52:24
Shafter 26 4 39N00'49 89w11'06 5:56:44
Shakerag 100 4 37N49'20 88w54'32 5:55:38
Shale City 66 4 41N13'11 90w38'26 6:02:34
Shamrock 57 104 40N25'07 88w53'58 5:55:36
Shanghai 94 4 41N03'03 90w29'48 6:01:59
Shanghai City 94 4 41N04 90w33 6:02:12
Shannon 8 66 42N09'17 89w44'23 5:58:58
Sharon 26 139 39N02 89w06 5:56:24
Sharpsburg 11 7 39N36'50 89w21'04 5:57:24
Shattuc 14 4 38N36'38 89w11'34 5:56:46
Shaw 49 6 42N23 88w07 5:52:28
Shaw 94 4 41N02'45 90w38'13 6:02:33
Shawnee 30 4 37N44 88w08 5:52:32
Shawneetown 30 4 37N42'47 88w11'12 5:52:45
Shaws 52 29 41N42'27 89w14'07 5:56:56
Shaws Point 59 4 39N19 89w46 5:59:04
Sheffield 6 63 41N21'30 89w44'14 5:58:57
Sheffield Green 4 28 42N16 89w00 5:56:00
Shelby 24 4 38N30 88w06 5:52:24
Shelbyville 87 7 39N24'23 88w47'24 5:55:10
Sheldon 38 7 40N46'09 87w33'50 5:50:15
Sheldons Grove 85 66 40N10'00 90w17'39 6:01:11
Shepherd 75 4 39N43'30 91w20'40 6:05:23
Sherburnville 46 21 41N13'44 87w32'41 5:50:11
Sheridan 50 57 41N31'48 88w40'47 5:54:43
Sheridan Village 72 98 40N45 89w37 5:58:28
Sherman 84 53 39N53'37 89w36'17 5:58:25
Sherrard 66 4 41N19'08 90w30'21 6:02:01
Sherwood Forest 22 17 41N57 87w59 5:51:56
Shetlerville 35 4 37N25'50 88w24'27 5:53:38
Shields 41 4 38N28'04 88w42'48 5:54:51
Shields 49 116 42N17 87w52 5:51:28
Shiloh 82 25 38N33'41 89w53'50 5:59:35
Shiloh Hill 39 63 37N55'31 89w37'16 5:58:29
Shiloh Station 82 25 38N32'02 89w53'53 5:59:36
Shiloh Valley 82 25 38N31 89w53 5:59:32
Shinn 75 4 39N40'35 91w10'02 6:04:40
Shipman 59 53 39N07'30 90w02'39 6:00:11
Shirland 101 4 42N26'40 89w11'51 5:56:47
Shirley 41 4 38N17'06 88w50'17 5:55:21
Shirley 57 37 40N24'26 89w03'45 5:56:15
Shoal Creek 3 63 38N58 89w33 5:58:12
Shobonier 26 4 38N52'10 89w05'19 5:56:21
Shokokon 36 4 40N44'51 91w04'27 6:04:18
Shop Creek 68 4 39N16'33 89w38'44 5:58:35
Shore Acres 98 26 41N46 89w41 5:58:44
Shore Hills 56 15 42N23 88w26 5:53:44
Shorewood 46 26 41N01 87w43 5:50:52
Shorewood 99 82 41N31'12 88w12'06 5:52:48
Shorewood Village 16 6 42N03 87w55 5:51:40
Shull's Urban Estates 10 29 40N19 88w08 5:52:32
Shumway 25 63 39N11'06 88w39'08 5:54:37
Sibley 27 55 40N35'13 88w22'52 5:53:31
Sicily 11 4 39N35'24 89w29'28 5:57:58
Sidell 92 96 39N54'35 87w49'16 5:51:17
Sidney 10 54 40N01'30 88w04'24 5:52:18
Sigel 87 1 39N13'34 88w29'39 5:53:59
Signal Hill 82 25 38N34'38 90w03'24 6:00:14
Siloam 5 66 39N53'17 90w54'57 6:03:40
Silver Creek 89 4 42N15 89w34 5:58:16
Silver Lake 56 1 42N14'06 88w14'41 5:52:59
Silvis 81 87 41N30'44 90w24'54 6:01:40
Silvis Heights 81 87 41N30 90w24 6:01:36
Simpson 44 4 37N28'02 88w45'18 5:55:01
Simpson 97 4 38N09 88w02 5:52:08
Sims 96 4 38N21'37 88w31'50 5:54:07
Sinclair 69 63 39N48'08 90w07'18 6:00:29
Six Mile 28 4 37N55 89w04 5:56:16
Skelton 54 55 40N08'34 89w15'14 5:57:01
Ski Hill 56 1 42N12'07 88w12'25 5:52:50
Skokie 16 1 42N02'00 87w44'00 5:50:56
Skokie Junction 49 116 42N15'33 87w51'13 5:51:25
Skokie Manor 49 116 42N14'38 87w51'28 5:51:26
Slap Out 61 4 38N35 88w47 5:55:08
Sleepy Hollow 45 10 42N05'39 88w18'09 5:53:13
Smallwood 40 4 38N54 88w12 5:52:48
Smithboro 3 55 38N53'46 89w20'26 5:57:22
Smithdale 53 55 41N05'05 88w46'30 5:55:06
Smithfield 29 63 40N28'24 90w17'30 6:01:10
Smithshire 94 4 40N47'34 90w46'47 6:03:07
Smithton 82 25 38N24'31 89w59'31 5:59:58
Smithville 72 57 40N39'37 89w47'59 5:59:12
Smithville 96 4 38N16'14 88w35'30 5:54:22
Snicarte 63 63 40N07'24 90w13'53 6:00:56
Snider 92 26 40N12'15 87w41'52 5:50:47
Snyder 12 4 39N16'57 87w40'03 5:50:40
Sollitt 46 22 41N17'36 87w38'05 5:50:32
Solomon 20 63 40N14'56 88w49'22 5:55:17
Solon Mills 56 48 42N26'32 88w16'24 5:53:06
Somer 10 29 40N10 88w12 5:52:48
Somerset 22 2 41N48 87w56 5:51:44
Somerset 39 4 37N48 89w20 5:57:20
Somerset 56 9 42N14 88w21 5:53:24
Somerset 83 4 37N39'16 88w27'26 5:53:50
Somonauk 19 7 41N38'01 88w40'52 5:54:43
Songer 13 4 38N42 88w38 5:54:32
Sonora 34 4 40N30 91w18 6:05:12
Soperville 48 74 41N00'31 90w23'52 6:01:35
Sorento 3 63 38N59'56 89w34'25 5:58:18
South 16 1 42N02 87w41 5:50:44
South Addison 22 21 41N54'18 87w59'19 5:51:57
South Barrington 16 6 42N05'29 88w07'18 5:52:29
South Beloit 101 65 42N29'35 89w02'12 5:56:09
South Bluffs 86 65 39N44 90w32 6:02:08
South Bridgeview 16 1 41N44 87w48 5:51:12
South Chicago 16 1 41N43'22 87w32'11 5:50:09
South Chicago Heights 16 1 41N28'51 87w38'16 5:50:33
South Clinton 20 8 40N09 88w57 5:55:48
South Crouch 33 4 38N09 88w31 5:54:04
South Danville 92 54 40N06'54 87w38'15 5:50:33
South Deering 16 1 41N41'32 87w33'30 5:50:14
South Dixon 52 25 41N48 89w27 5:57:48
South Elgin 45 107 41N59'39 88w17'32 5:53:10
South Elkhorn 8 4 41N58'00 89w42'44 5:58:51
Southern 100 4 37N38 88w58 5:55:52
Southern View 84 133 39N45'26 89w39'13 5:58:37
South Fillmore 68 4 39N03 89w18 5:57:12
South Flannigan 33 4 37N56 88w39 5:54:36
South Fork 11 26 39N34 89w26 5:57:44
South Freeport 89 4 42N14'27 89w34'21 5:58:17
Southgate 16 6 42N04 88w00 5:52:00
South Grove 19 40 42N01 88w53 5:55:32
South Holland 16 19 41N36'03 87w36'25 5:50:26
South Homer 10 54 40N02 87w59 5:51:56
South Hurricane 26 4 39N07 89w12 5:56:48
South Jacksonville 69 113 39N42'31 90w13'41 6:00:55
Southlawn 84 133 39N45'13 89w37'17 5:58:29
South Litchfield 68 37 39N08 89w39 5:58:36
South Lockport 99 114 41N34'23 88w03'16 5:52:13
South Macon 58 57 39N42 88w59 5:55:56
South Moline 81 87 41N28'41 90w31'28 6:02:06
South Moline Gardens 81 87 41N30 90w30 6:02:00
Southmoor 16 12 41N39'09 87w49'47 5:51:19
Southmoor 60 7 38N57 90w11 6:00:44
South Mounds 77 4 37N44 88w33 5:54:12
South Muddy 40 4 38N54 88w19 5:53:16
South Oak Park 16 1 41N52 87w47 5:51:08
South Ottawa 50 6 41N19'54 88w50'13 5:55:21
South Otter 59 4 39N24 89w53 5:59:32
South Palmyra 59 63 39N24 89w59 5:59:56
South Park 45 102 41N44'08 88w18'13 5:53:13
South Pekin 90 98 40N29'40 89w39'06 5:58:36
Southport 72 58 40N47'33 89w53'55 5:59:36
South Rock Island 81 87 41N28'46 90w34'58 6:02:20
South Rome 72 51 40N50'59 89w32'15 5:58:09
South Ross 92 26 40N18 87w39 5:50:36
South Roxana 60 29 38N49'46 90w03'46 6:00:15
South Shore 16 1 41N46 87w34 5:50:16
South Standard 59 4 39N21 89w48 5:59:12
South Stickney 16 1 41N44 87w48 5:51:12
South Streator 53 135 41N06 88w50 5:55:20
South Twigg 33 4 37N56 88w32 5:54:08
South Waukegan 49 140 42N19 87w51 5:51:24
Southwest 17 4 38N52 87w52 5:51:28
South Wheatland 58 26 39N48 88w58 5:55:52
South Wilmington 32 36 41N10'22 88w16'36 5:53:06
South Winchester 86 63 39N36 90w30 6:02:00
Spanish Court 49 1 42N11 87w49 5:51:16
Spankey 42 55 39N11'20 90w33'02 6:02:12
Sparks Hill 35 4 37N35'05 88w17'13 5:53:09
Sparland 62 48 41N01'43 89w26'18 5:57:45
Sparta 79 55 38N07'23 89w42'06 5:58:48
Spaulding 16 107 42N00'10 88w14'07 5:52:56
Spaulding 84 29 39N51'58 89w32'25 5:58:10
Spaulding Corners 49 34 42N22'14 87w52'52 5:51:31
Speer 88 4 40N59'18 89w39'01 5:58:36
Spencer 75 66 39N42'39 91w15'57 6:05:04
Spencer 99 1 41N29'53 87w56'30 5:51:46
Spencer Heights 77 4 37N07'38 89w11'41 5:56:47
Spillertown 100 4 37N45'59 88w55'10 5:55:41
Spin Lake 57 20 40N32 89w11 5:56:44
Spires 50 55 40N52'35 88w57'37 5:55:50
Sportsman Lake 61 4 38N36 88w57 5:55:48
Spring 4 26 42N12 88w46 5:55:04
Spring Bay 102 56 40N49'28 89w31'20 5:58:05
Spring Creek 75 4 39N27 90w44 6:02:56
Springerton 97 4 38N10'46 88w21'15 5:53:25
Springfield 84 133 39N48'06 89w38'37 5:58:34
Spring Garden 41 4 38N09'47 88w51'20 5:55:25
Spring Grove 56 6 42N26'37 88w14'11 5:52:57
Springhaven 60 7 38N57 90w11 6:00:44
Spring Hill 98 88 41N36'45 90w02'42 6:00:11
Spring Lake 10 54 40N12 88w24 5:53:36
Spring Lake 90 55 40N29 89w47 5:59:08
Spring Point 18 4 39N13 88w24 5:53:36
Spring Valley 6 134 41N19'39 89w11'59 5:56:48
Springville 91 4 37N22'28 89w16'03 5:57:04
Squaw Grove 19 43 41N46 88w39 5:54:36
Staley 10 23 40N06'47 88w18'45 5:53:15
Stallings 60 7 38N43'29 90w03'47 6:00:15
Standard 78 57 41N15'24 89w10'51 5:56:43
Standard City 59 65 39N21'08 89w47'15 5:59:09
Stanford 57 36 40N26'05 89w13'04 5:56:52
Stanton 10 54 40N11 88w04 5:52:16
Stanton Point 49 27 42N23 88w09 5:52:36
Staples Corner 16 1 42N08'21 88w01'18 5:52:05
Star City 7 65 39N08'03 90w40'25 6:02:42
Stark 88 55 40N59'44 89w44'38 5:58:59
Starks 45 29 42N05'18 88w27'24 5:53:50
Starne 84 29 39N49'27 89w36'18 5:58:25
Starnes 84 133 39N48 89w38 5:58:32
State Park Place 60 7 38N39'31 90w02'50 6:00:11
Staunton 59 26 39N00'44 89w47'28 5:59:10
Stavanger 50 46 41N23'55 88w36'50 5:54:27
Steel City 28 4 37N59'53 88w52'45 5:55:31
Steele 99 1 41N30'21 87w57'44 5:51:51
Steeleville 79 63 38N00'26 89w39'30 5:58:38
Steelton 92 54 40N00'34 87w40'44 5:50:43
Steelton 98 26 41N48 89w43 5:58:52
Steeple Run 22 12 41N47 88w09 5:52:36
Steger 16 1 41N28'12 87w38'11 5:50:33
Stelle 46 38 41N00 88w12 5:52:48
Ste Marie 40 4 38N55'56 88w01'24 5:52:06
Sterling 98 26 41N47'19 89w41'46 5:58:47
Sterling Place 82 25 38N37'35 90w02'23 6:00:10
Steuben 62 48 41N03 89w28 5:57:52
Stevenson 61 4 38N34 88w53 5:55:32
Steward 52 6 41N50'52 89w01'12 5:56:05
Stewardson 87 63 39N15'47 88w37'47 5:54:31
Stickney 16 1 41N49'17 87w46'58 5:51:08
Stillman Valley 71 56 42N06'26 89w10'45 5:56:43
Stillwell 34 4 40N13'07 91w10'58 6:04:44
Stiritz 100 4 37N50'10 88w56'54 5:55:48
Stockdale 32 4 41N21'04 88w29'33 5:53:58
Stockland 38 7 40N36'52 87w35'34 5:50:22
Stockton 43 66 42N20'59 90w00'24 6:00:02
Stock Yards 16 1 41N49 87w39 5:50:36
Stoehrs 90 98 40N31'23 89w41'37 5:58:46
Stokes 91 4 37N27 89w06 5:56:24
Stolle 82 25 38N32'36 90w10'11 6:00:41
Stolletown 14 4 38N41'36 89w26'48 5:57:47
Stonebridge 16 2 41N35 87w40 5:50:40
Stone Church 35 4 37N28 88w22 5:53:28
Stone Church 95 55 38N21'01 89w37'31 5:58:30
Stone Fort 39 4 37N37'24 89w11'48 5:56:47
Stonefort 100 4 37N36'51 88w42'29 5:54:50
Stonelake 56 11 42N19 88w27 5:53:48
Stone Park 16 2 41N54'20 87w53'01 5:51:32

Stoneyville 50 6 41N18'17 88w50'11 5:55:21
Stonington 11 55 39N38'24 89w11'34 5:56:46
Stony Island 16 1 41N43'21 87w34'30 5:50:18
Stookey 82 25 38N33 90w04 6:00:16
Storeyland 60 7 38N57 90w11 6:00:44
Storybrook 47 25 41N39 88w27 5:53:48
Stoy 17 4 38N59'51 87w49'59 5:51:20
Strasburg 87 63 39N21'09 88w37'09 5:54:29
Stratford 71 4 41N59'49 89w29'27 5:57:58
Stratford Hills 22 27 41N54 87w57 5:51:48
Strathmore Grove 16 6 42N09 87w57 5:51:48
Stratton 23 128 39N36 87w36 5:50:24
Stratton 41 4 38N26'44 88w42'48 5:54:51
Straut 75 63 39N26'36 90w42'21 6:02:49
Strawn 53 55 40N39'09 88w23'47 5:53:35
Strawns Crossing 69 63 39N47'09 90w09'03 6:00:36
Streamwood 16 27 42N01'32 88w10'42 5:52:43
Streator 50 135 41N07'15 88w50'07 5:55:20
Streator Junction 102 71 40N43 89w17 5:57:08
Stringtown 80 4 38N49'30 87w59'01 5:51:56
Stronghurst 36 4 40N44'49 90w54'14 6:03:37
Stubblefield 3 55 38N50'54 89w27'59 5:57:52
Sublette 52 57 41N38'35 89w13'40 5:56:55
Suburban Estates 22 12 41N48 88w01 5:52:04
Suburban Heights 95 4 38N31 89w08 5:56:32
Sudduth 84 55 39N42'18 89w48'57 5:59:16
Suez 66 4 41N07 90w36 6:02:24
Sugar Brook 99 1 41N40 88w00 5:52:00
Sugar Creek 14 55 38N37 89w39 5:58:36
Sugar Grove 45 41 41N45'41 88w26'37 5:53:46
Sugar Grove 66 4 41N14'06 90w43'54 6:02:56
Sugar Island 46 57 41N00'23 87w49'25 5:51:18
Sugar Loaf 82 46 38N31 90w11 6:00:44
Sugarloaf Heights 82 46 38N29'46 90w12'45 6:00:51
Sullivan 70 7 39N35'58 88w36'28 5:54:26
Sullivant 27 55 40N34 88w23 5:53:32
Sulphur Springs 50 41 41N25'09 88w46'27 5:55:06
Summerfield 82 7 38N35'50 89w45'06 5:59:00
Summerhill 16 2 42N07 87w49 5:51:16
Summer Hill 75 4 39N32'47 90w55'09 6:03:41
Summerlakes 22 26 41N49 88w11 5:52:44
Summersville 41 4 38N19'40 88w52'01 5:55:28
Summerville 59 4 39N11'20 90w07'25 6:00:30
Summit 16 1 41N47'17 87w48'37 5:51:14
Summit 82 25 38N33'04 90w00'17 6:00:01
Summit Heights 68 7 39N08 89w30 5:58:00
Summum 29 66 40N16'04 90w16'42 6:01:07
Sumner 51 4 38N43'01 87w51'41 5:51:27
Sumpter 18 4 39N17 88w16 5:53:04
Sunbeam 66 4 41N07'38 90w44'06 6:02:56
Sunbury 53 56 41N06'03 88w31'39 5:54:07
Sunfield 73 4 38N03'52 89w14'24 5:56:58
Sunny Crest 16 6 41N32'09 87w41'38 5:50:47
Sunny Hill 37 4 41N23'56 90w24'57 6:01:40
Sunny Hill 75 4 39N37'23 90w46'15 6:03:05
Sunny Hills Estates 22 12 41N48 88w01 5:52:04
Sunnyland 90 98 40N41'29 89w30'29 5:58:02
Sunny Land 99 114 41N33 88w07 5:52:28
Sunnyside 56 27 42N23'22 88w13'34 5:52:54
Sunnyside 89 4 42N21'24 89w54'49 5:59:39
Sunnyside 100 4 37N48'13 89w03'15 5:56:13
Sunrise Ridge 56 15 42N23 88w26 5:53:44
Sunrise Ridge 99 114 41N35 88w03 5:52:12
Sunset Acres 49 42 42N16 87w56 5:51:44
Sunset Harbor 100 4 37N46 88w56 5:55:44
Sunset Hills 16 17 41N58 88w04 5:52:16
Sunset Lake 59 29 39N27 89w47 5:59:08
Sunset Landing 7 65 38N56'45 90w39'49 6:02:39
Surrey 94 4 40N54'42 90w28'05 6:01:52
Sutter 34 4 40N16'45 91w20'36 6:05:22
Sutter 90 72 40N23'48 89w22'10 5:57:29
Sutton 45 6 42N05'45 88w11'39 5:52:47
Sutton Point 16 2 42N07 87w49 5:51:16
Swan 94 4 40N40 90w37 6:02:28
Swan Creek 94 4 40N40'04 90w39'17 6:02:37
Swansea 82 25 38N32'02 89w59'20 5:59:57
Swanwick 73 4 38N10'11 89w32'10 5:58:09
Swedona 66 4 41N16'46 90w26'41 6:01:47
Sweet Water 65 4 40N03'14 89w41'38 5:58:47
Swift 22 2 41N55'13 88w02'32 5:52:10
Swiss Valley 99 1 41N28 87w37 5:50:28
Swissville 52 25 41N50 89w30 5:58:00
Swygert 53 127 40N54'42 88w31'46 5:54:07
Sycamore 19 6 41N59'20 88w41'12 5:54:45
Sylvan 9 29 39N59'06 90w04'16 6:00:17
Sylvan Hill 16 12 41N38 87w51 5:51:24
Sylvan Lake 49 6 42N14'38 88w03'10 5:52:13
Symerton 99 7 41N19'43 88w03'09 5:52:13
Symmes 23 128 39N32 87w42 5:50:48
Table Grove 29 66 40N21'51 90w25'30 6:01:42
Tabor 20 55 40N10'50 89w08'05 5:56:32
Taft 16 2 41N53 87w55 5:51:40
Talbott 90 55 40N30'37 89w47'04 5:59:08
Talkington 84 55 39N34 89w52 5:59:28
Tallmadge 46 82 41N06'41 87w37'30 5:50:30
Tall Trees 16 1 42N04 87w48 5:51:12
Tallula 65 29 39N56'40 89w56'14 5:59:45
Tamalco 3 4 38N46'15 89w17'29 5:57:10
Tamarac 16 1 41N32 87w41 5:50:44
Tamarack 99 82 41N39'03 88w15'10 5:53:01
Tamaroa 73 4 38N08'16 89w13'48 5:56:55
Tamms 2 4 37N14'06 89w16'12 5:57:05
Tampico 98 29 41N37'49 89w47'10 5:59:09
Tanglewood 16 27 41N58 88w06 5:52:24
Tankville 2 4 37N07'37 89w23'01 5:57:32
Tansill 76 4 37N18'22 88w32'16 5:54:09
Tate 83 4 37N53 88w39 5:54:36
Tatumville 2 4 37N15'28 89w16'46 5:57:07
Taylor 71 28 41N55 89w20 5:57:20
Taylor 75 4 39N36'01 90w57'48 6:03:51
Taylor Ridge 81 4 41N23'12 90w40'05 6:02:40
Taylor Springs 68 7 39N07'51 89w29'31 5:57:58
Taylorville 11 7 39N32'56 89w17'40 5:57:11
Tazewell 90 72 40N29'04 89w19'57 5:57:20
Techny 16 2 42N07 87w49 5:51:16
Teheran 63 4 40N13'28 89w47'56 5:59:12
Temple Hill 76 4 37N18'26 88w37'49 5:54:31
Tennessee 55 4 40N24'43 90w50'21 6:03:21
Terminal Junction 81 87 41N29 90w34 6:02:16
Terra Cotta 56 9 42N16'54 88w18'02 5:53:12
Terre Haute 36 4 40N39'59 90w58'52 6:03:55
Teutopolis 25 56 39N07'59 88w28'19 5:53:53
Texas 20 8 40N06 88w59 5:55:56
Texas City 83 4 37N52'42 88w23'36 5:53:34
Texico 41 4 38N26'22 88w53'49 5:55:35
Thackeray 33 4 38N07'12 88w27'11 5:53:49
Thawville 38 30 40N40'33 88w06'58 5:52:28
Thayer 84 29 39N32'17 89w45'47 5:59:03
Thebes 2 4 37N13'15 89w27'39 5:57:51
The Burg 52 56 41N42'23 89w05'55 5:56:24
The Clusters 99 1 41N40 88w00 5:52:00
The Covered Bridges 22 2 41N53 88w05 5:52:20
The Crossroads 7 4 38N54'03 90w33'45 6:02:15
The Fairway of Country Lakes 22 12 41N47 88w09 5:52:36
The Greens 16 6 42N03 87w53 5:51:32
The Greens of Woodgate 16 29 41N30 87w42 5:50:48
The Ledges 101 4 42N25 89w01 5:56:04
The Meadows 22 12 41N47 88w05 5:52:20
The Terrace 49 116 42N17 87w51 5:51:24
Third Lake 49 27 42N22'26 88w00'39 5:52:03
Thomas 6 29 41N30'42 89w49'10 5:59:17
Thomasboro 10 30 40N14'30 88w11'03 5:52:44
Thomasville 68 63 39N29'23 89w39'16 5:58:37
Thompson 43 4 42N25 90w10 6:00:40
Thompsonville 28 4 37N55'03 88w45'44 5:55:03
Thomson 8 4 41N57'32 90w05'57 6:00:24
Thornton 16 1 41N34'05 87w36'29 5:50:26
Thornton Junction 16 19 41N35'21 87w36'25 5:50:26
Thornwilde 22 26 41N49 88w11 5:52:44
Thurber 33 4 38N04'57 88w25'39 5:53:43
Tice 65 29 39N59'07 89w47'41 5:59:11
Ticona 50 136 41N13'27 89w03'09 5:56:13
Tierra Grande 16 6 41N35 87w46 5:51:04
Tilden 79 55 38N12'43 89w40'57 5:58:44
Tillman 82 46 38N32'11 90w09'08 6:00:37
Tilton 92 26 40N05'43 87w38'51 5:50:35
Timber 72 55 40N35 89w50 5:59:20
Timber Lake 8 4 42N06 89w58 5:59:52
Timber Lake 49 6 42N09 88w06 5:52:24
Timberlake Estates 22 2 41N48 87w56 5:51:44
Timberlake Village 16 6 42N04 87w57 5:51:48
Timberline 99 114 41N33 88w07 5:52:28
Timber Ridge 16 1 41N44 87w50 5:51:20
Timber Trails 22 2 41N48 87w56 5:51:44
Time 75 4 39N33'41 90w43'27 6:02:54
Times Square 41 4 38N18 88w55 5:55:40
Timewell 5 66 40N00'28 90w52'25 6:03:30
Timothy 18 4 39N18'11 88w07'46 5:52:31
Tinley Park 16 1 41N34'24 87w47'04 5:51:08
Tinley Terrace 16 1 41N35 87w46 5:51:04
Tioga 34 53 40N12'40 91w20'49 6:05:23
Tipton 10 54 40N04'11 88w02'06 5:52:08
Tipton 67 8 38N14'09 90w06'04 6:00:24
Tiskilwa 6 55 41N17'32 89w30'22 5:58:01
Tison 83 4 37N53'23 88w30'52 5:54:03
Titus 31 55 39N11'36 90w34'43 6:02:19
Todds Mill 73 4 38N12'09 89w21'57 5:57:28
Todds Point 87 63 39N34'37 88w45'57 5:55:04
Toledo 18 4 39N16'25 88w14'37 5:52:58
Tolono 10 36 39N59'10 88w15'32 5:53:02
Toluca 62 54 41N00'08 89w08'00 5:56:32
Tomahawk Bluff 50 117 41N20 89w06 5:56:24
Tomlinson 57 29 40N19'08 88w13'59 5:52:56
Tompkins 94 4 40N51 90w43 6:02:52
Toms Prairie 96 4 38N24'28 88w15'31 5:53:02
Tonica 50 136 41N12'57 89w04'00 5:56:16
Tonti 61 4 38N39'53 88w58'42 5:55:55
Topeka 63 137 40N19'49 89w55'52 5:59:43
Torino 99 37 41N12'21 88w14'05 5:52:56
Toronto 84 133 39N42'50 89w37'47 5:58:31
Toulon 88 4 41N05'37 89w51'53 5:59:28
Tovey 11 26 39N35 89w27 5:57:48
Tovey Humphrey Station 11 26 39N35'23 89w27'18 5:57:49
Towanda 57 68 40N33'50 88w53'56 5:55:36
Tower Hill 87 63 39N23'16 88w57'38 5:55:51
Tower Lake 49 6 42N13'55 88w09'07 5:52:36
Towne Oaks 90 98 40N35'00 89w32'53 5:58:12
Trago Lake 13 4 38N40 88w28 5:53:52
Trailpark Gardens 90 98 40N44'02 89w31'06 5:58:04
Tremont 60 7 38N57 90w11 6:00:44
Tremont 90 98 40N31'39 89w29'33 5:57:58
Trenton 14 7 38N36'20 89w40'55 5:58:44
Triezenbers 16 12 41N40 87w47 5:51:08
Trilla 15 4 39N22'30 88w21'01 5:53:24
Trimble 17 4 39N03'48 87w41'04 5:50:44
Triple Lance Heights 100 4 37N43 89w14 5:56:56
Tri-state Village 22 2 41N48 87w56 5:51:44
Triumph 50 56 41N29'58 89w01'19 5:56:05
Triumvera 16 1 42N04 87w48 5:51:12
Trivoli 72 57 40N41'26 89w53'31 5:59:34
Troster 57 55 40N19'06 88w28'47 5:53:55
Trout Valley 56 1 42N14 88w15 5:53:00
Trowbridge 87 1 39N18'37 88w31'04 5:54:04
Troxel 45 84 41N50'03 88w35'47 5:54:23
Troy 60 90 38N43'45 89w52'59 5:59:32
Troy Crossing 60 7 38N42'20 89w57'25 5:59:50
Troy Grove 50 123 41N28'04 89w04'59 5:56:20
Troy Junction 60 7 38N44'04 89w55'41 5:59:43
Tru Lock Acres 55 4 40N28 90w41 6:02:44
Truro 48 4 40N57'27 90w02'32 6:00:10
Tuckers Corners 33 4 37N59'27 88w35'44 5:54:23
Tullamore 49 126 42N14 87w59 5:51:56
Tunbridge 20 55 40N06'49 89w02'55 5:56:12
Tunnel Hill 44 4 37N31'25 88w50'19 5:55:21
Turnberry 56 9 42N14 88w21 5:53:24
Turner Camp 56 1 42N11'21 88w15'02 5:53:00
Turner Landing 7 65 39N04'13 90w41'43 6:02:47
Turpin 58 55 39N47'19 88w55'09 5:55:41
Tuscarora 72 98 40N36'19 89w40'02 5:58:40
Tuscola 21 7 39N47'57 88w16'59 5:53:08
Twelvemile Corner 52 56 41N45'34 89w05'00 5:56:20
Twigg 33 4 38N00 88w33 5:54:12
Twilight Terrace 82 25 38N31 89w59 5:59:56
Twin City 10 138 40N06 88w12 5:52:48
Twin Grove 57 104 40N29'36 89w04'47 5:56:19
Twin Lakes 60 4 38N44 89w53 5:59:32
Twin Oaks 16 6 42N03 87w55 5:51:40
Twin Oaks 99 114 41N33 88w07 5:52:28
Tyrone 28 4 37N59 89w06 5:56:24
Udina 45 54 42N02'36 88w22'34 5:53:30
Ulah 37 4 41N16'09 90w08'46 6:00:35
Ullin 77 4 37N16'37 89w11'00 5:56:44
Ullrich 70 4 39N44'27 88w40'53 5:54:44
Union 54 29 40N17'15 89w22'01 5:57:28
Union 56 29 42N13'59 88w32'32 5:54:10
Union 63 7 40N23'27 89w48'34 5:59:14
Union 99 114 41N29'49 88w01'24 5:52:06
Union Center 18 4 39N19'58 88w04'53 5:52:20
Union Grove 98 8 41N50'03 90w01'35 6:00:06
Union Hill 46 39 41N06'27 88w08'48 5:52:35
Union Hill 82 25 38N35'17 90w00'21 6:00:01
Uniontown 48 60 40N44'51 90w05'55 6:00:24
Union Town 61 4 38N31'08 88w45'01 5:55:00
Unionville 64 4 37N07'20 88w32'48 5:54:11
Unionville 92 26 40N01'30 87w38'17 5:50:33
Unionville 98 75 41N49'09 89w58'57 5:59:56
Unity (Hodges Park Station) 2 4 37N08'59 89w16'22 5:57:05
Unity 74 55 39N50 88w32 5:54:08
University 10 138 40N06 88w12 5:52:48
University 33 4 37N56'11 88w36'34 5:54:26
University Heights 15 106 39N29 88w13 5:52:52
University Mall 39 57 39N59 88w49 5:55:16
Upper Alton 60 7 38N54 90w10 6:00:40
Uptown 16 1 41N58 87w40 5:50:40
Urbain 28 4 37N58'28 89w02'26 5:56:10
Urban 11 7 39N34 89w21 5:57:24
Urbana 10 138 40N06'38 88w12'26 5:52:50
Urbandale 2 4 37N03'10 89w11'09 5:56:45
Ursa 1 53 40N04'29 91w22'02 6:05:28
Ustick 98 55 41N53'02 89w59'31 5:59:58
Utah 94 4 40N59'03 90w29'16 6:01:57
Utica 50 8 41N20'26 89w00'36 5:56:02
Utopia 22 21 41N51'04 87w58'22 5:51:53
Valier 28 4 38N00'55 89w02'33 5:56:10
Valier Patch 28 4 38N01'36 89w02'12 5:56:09
Valley 88 4 41N01 89w42 5:58:48
Valley City 75 4 39N42'25 90w39'09 6:02:37
Valley Lo 16 1 42N04 87w48 5:51:12
Valley Mission 91 4 37N21'29 89w20'21 5:57:21
Valley View 22 12 41N49'49 88w04'04 5:52:16
Valley View 45 95 41N57'58 88w17'56 5:53:12
Valley View 90 98 40N39 89w34 5:58:16
Valmeyer 67 55 38N17'40 90w18'57 6:01:16
Van Burensburg 68 4 39N02'10 89w16'46 5:57:07
Vance 92 54 40N03 87w53 5:51:32
Vandalia 26 139 38N57'38 89w05'37 5:56:22
Vanderville 11 63 39N25'31 89w17'51 5:57:11
Van Orin 6 54 41N33'00 89w21'12 5:57:25
Van Petten 52 26 41N42'15 89w37'19 5:58:29
Van Wood 84 29 39N57'41 89w35'55 5:58:24
Varna 62 56 41N02'11 89w13'34 5:56:54
Velma 11 63 39N30'53 89w13'57 5:56:56
Venedy 95 55 38N23'42 89w38'45 5:58:35
Venetian Village 49 6 42N23'55 88w03'09 5:52:13
Venice 60 96 38N40'20 90w10'11 6:00:41
Vera 26 139 39N02'03 89w06'47 5:56:27
Vergennes 39 4 37N54'08 89w20'08 5:57:21
Vermilion 23 56 39N34'52 87w35'20 5:50:21
Vermilion Grove 92 54 39N55'30 87w39'18 5:50:37
Vermilion Heights 92 54 40N07'25 87w39'12 5:50:37
Vermilionville 50 136 41N15'34 88w59'44 5:55:59
Vermillion 50 136 41N13 89w00 5:56:00
Vermillion Estates 53 127 40N53 88w38 5:54:32
Vermont 29 66 40N17'39 90w25'40 6:01:43
Vernal 92 54 40N15'49 87w41'58 5:50:48
Vernon 61 4 38N48'08 89w05'13 5:56:21
Vernon Hills 49 126 42N13'10 87w58'46 5:51:55
Verona 32 55 41N13'04 88w30'05 5:54:00
Versailles 5 65 39N53'06 90w39'21 6:02:37
Vets Row 72 51 40N55 89w30 5:58:00
Vevay Park 18 4 39N16'45 88w03'13 5:52:13
Vicic 90 98 40N39 89w34 5:58:16
Victor 19 26 41N40 88w46 5:55:04
Victoria 48 4 41N02'01 90w05'54 6:00:24
Vienna 44 4 37N24'55 88w53'52 5:55:35

Vienna Woods 16 1 41N31 87W42 5:50:48
Village Square 22 12 41N48 88W01 5:52:04
Villagrove 21 50 39N51'46 88W09'44 5:52:39
Villa Hills 82 25 38N32 90W05 6:00:20
Villa Marie 60 7 38N57 90W11 6:00:44
Villa Park 22 21 41N53'23 87W59'20 5:51:57
Villa Ridge 60 7 38N57 90W11 6:00:44
Villa Ridge 77 4 37N09'31 89W11'41 5:56:47
Villas 17 4 38N53'58 87W45'13 5:51:01
Villas Salceda 16 2 42N07 87W49 5:51:16
Villa Verde 16 6 42N09 87W57 5:51:48
Villa West 16 12 41N38 87W51 5:51:24
Villa Westbrook 55 4 40N28 90W41 6:02:44
Vinegar Hill 43 4 42N29 90W26 6:01:44
Viola 66 4 41N12'11 90W35'13 6:02:21
Virden 59 29 39N30'03 89W46'04 5:59:04
Virgil 45 84 41N57'21 88W32'14 5:54:09
Virginia 9 63 39N57'04 90W12'44 6:00:51
Volo 49 6 42N19'34 88W10'04 5:52:40
Vonachen Knolls 72 51 40N55 89W30 5:58:00
Voorhies 74 30 39N52'01 88W34'48 5:54:19
Vulcan 82 46 38N31'44 90W14'32 6:00:58
Wacker 8 4 42N03'29 90W02'46 6:00:11
Waddams 89 4 42N25 89W45 5:59:00
Waddams Grove 89 64 42N25'03 89W53'03 5:59:32
Wadsworth 49 17 42N25'43 87W55'26 5:51:42
Waggoner 68 63 39N22'39 89W39'11 5:58:37
Wakefield 80 4 38N50'24 88W14'38 5:52:59
Waldo 53 55 40N48 88W52 5:55:28
Walker 34 4 40N15 91W18 6:05:12
Walker 58 57 39N40'35 89W00'24 5:56:02
Walker 99 82 41N37'04 88W12'23 5:52:50
Walker Ford 15 4 39N25'20 88W10'35 5:52:42
Walkerville 31 63 39N23'13 90W29'43 6:01:59
Wall 27 30 40N32 88W11 5:52:44
Wallace 50 6 41N25 88W53 5:55:32
Walla Walla 18 54 39N12'03 88W11'32 5:52:46
Wallingford 99 82 41N25 87W59 5:51:56
Walnut 6 29 41N33'24 89W35'36 5:58:22
Walnut 90 72 40N29'02 89W22'17 5:57:29
Walnut Grove 55 4 40N36'58 90W33'33 6:02:14
Walnut Hill 61 4 38N28'38 89W02'36 5:56:10
Walnut Prairie 12 4 39N14'24 87W39'58 5:50:40
Walpole 33 4 37N56'12 88W33'17 5:54:13
Walsh 79 63 38N05'22 89W51'03 5:59:24
Walshville 68 7 39N04'15 89W37'08 5:58:29
Waltersburg 76 4 37N22'44 88W33'51 5:54:15
Waltham 50 56 41N26'00 89W00'37 5:56:02
Walton 52 25 41N42'54 89W26'18 5:57:45
Waltonville 41 4 38N12'32 89W02'20 5:56:09
Walz 92 26 40N08'12 87W34'01 5:50:16
Wamac 14 4 38N30'32 89W08'26 5:56:34
Wanda 60 25 38N50'04 90W02'19 6:00:09
Wanlock 66 4 41N13'09 90W37'31 6:02:30
Wapella 20 8 40N13'13 88W57'43 5:55:51
Ward 39 4 37N51'00 89W14'07 5:56:56
Wards Grove 43 4 42N20 89W57 5:59:48
Ware 91 4 37N26'52 89W23'38 5:57:35
Warner 37 4 41N24'37 90W22'33 6:01:30
Warnock 67 46 38N23'44 90W16'09 6:01:05
Warren 43 65 42N29'47 89W59'22 5:59:57
Warrenhurst 22 26 41N49'22 88W12'51 5:52:51
Warren Park 16 1 41N51 87W46 5:51:04
Warrensburg 58 57 39N55'58 89W03'43 5:56:15
Warrenville 22 26 41N49'04 88W10'24 5:52:42
Warsaw 34 4 40N21'33 91W26'04 6:05:44
Wartburg 67 8 38N17'26 90W11'44 6:00:47
Wartrace 44 4 37N23'57 88W46'43 5:55:07
Wasco 45 29 41N56'17 88W24'16 5:53:37
Washburn 102 55 40N55'09 89W17'28 5:57:10
Washington 90 98 40N42'13 89W24'26 5:57:38
Washington Park 82 99 38N38'06 90W05'34 6:00:22
Wasson 83 4 37N47'17 88W29'05 5:53:56
Wataga 48 4 41N01'31 90W16'47 6:01:07
Waterford 29 7 40N21 90W07 6:00:28
Waterloo 67 8 38N20'09 90W08'59 6:00:36
Waterman 19 60 41N46'18 88W46'25 5:55:06
Watertown 71 28 41N59'07 89W17'40 5:57:11
Watertown 81 87 41N30 90W26 6:01:44
Water Valley 91 4 37N33'31 89W10'31 5:56:42
Watkins 20 4 40N16'51 88W40'38 5:54:43
Watkins Ford 76 4 37N32'09 88W37'52 5:54:31
Watseka 38 7 40N46'34 87W44'11 5:50:57
Watson 25 4 39N01'31 88W34'11 5:54:17
Wauconda 49 22 42N15'32 88W08'21 5:52:33
Waukegan 49 140 42N21'49 87W50'41 5:51:23
Wauponsee 32 125 41N16'28 88W29'40 5:53:59
Waverly 69 55 39N35'30 89W57'10 5:59:49
Waycinden Park 16 6 42N03 87W53 5:51:32
Wayland 85 4 40N12'16 90W42'25 6:02:50
Wayne 22 26 41N57'03 88W14'32 5:52:58
Wayne Center 22 27 41N56'34 88W10'25 5:52:42
Wayne City 96 4 38N20'43 88W35'16 5:54:21
Waynesville 20 55 40N14'20 89W07'23 5:56:30
Weaver 12 56 39N25'05 87W35'58 5:50:24
Webber 41 23 38N21 88W45 5:55:00
Webster 34 4 40N27'59 91W00'02 6:04:00
Webster 38 7 40N46'25 87W36'14 5:50:26
Webster 76 4 37N23 88W40 5:54:40
Webster Park 6 134 41N20 89W12 5:56:48
Wedges Corner 49 6 42N23'10 88W00'15 5:52:01
Wedron 50 41 41N26'10 88W46'24 5:55:06
Weedman 57 57 40N16'53 88W36'11 5:54:25
Wee-ma-tuk Hills 29 4 40N30 90W11 6:00:44
Welco Corners 99 1 41N41'50 88W02'29 5:52:10
Weldon 20 55 40N07'16 88W44'43 5:54:59
Welge 79 63 37N57'23 89W42'45 5:58:51
Welland 52 56 41N37'36 89W04'15 5:56:17
Weller 37 4 41N12 90W09 6:00:36
Wellington 38 80 40N32'21 87W40'48 5:50:43
Wellington Heights 99 114 41N33 88W07 5:52:28
Wempletown 101 4 42N20'36 89W12'15 5:56:49
Wendel 6 54 41N31'59 89W12'36 5:56:50
Wendelin 13 4 38N50'00 88W16'22 5:53:05
Wenona 62 29 41N03'09 89W03'01 5:56:12
Wenonah 68 7 39N19'37 89W17'20 5:57:09
Wertenberg 14 55 38N26'46 89W39'53 5:58:40
Wesley 90 98 40N39'11 89W36'15 5:58:25
Wesley 99 30 41N15 88W06 5:52:24
Westaway 45 102 41N46 88W20 5:53:20
Westbrook Estates 82 25 38N36 89W58 5:59:52
West Brooklyn 52 55 41N41'34 89W08'49 5:56:35
West Brook Village 55 4 40N28 90W41 6:02:44
Westbury 99 1 41N40 88W00 5:52:00
Westchester 16 1 41N51'02 87W52'55 5:51:32
West Chicago 22 1 41N53'05 88W12'14 5:52:49
West City 28 4 38N00'11 88W56'18 5:55:45
Westdale 16 1 41N54 87W52 5:51:28
Westdale Gardens 16 27 41N54 87W57 5:51:48
West Deerfield 49 2 42N11 87W52 5:51:28
West Dundee (Dundee PO) 45 10 42N05'53 88W16'58 5:53:08
West DuPage Park 22 30 41N52'22 88W10'57 5:52:44
West End 83 4 37N53'24 88W42'20 5:54:49
West End 101 28 42N16 89W09 5:56:36
Western 37 4 41N22 90W23 6:01:32
Western Mound 59 63 39N18 90W06 6:00:24
Western Springs 16 1 41N48'35 87W54'02 5:51:36
Westervelt 87 63 39N28'44 88W51'42 5:55:27
Westfield 12 4 39N27'23 87W59'46 5:51:59
Westfield 99 114 41N33 88W07 5:52:28
Westfield Corners 101 48 42N12'30 89W13'51 5:56:55
West Frankfort 28 4 37N53'52 88W55'53 5:55:44
West Frankfort Lake 28 4 37N54 88W55 5:55:40
West Galena 43 4 42N24 90W27 6:01:48
Westgate 100 4 37N46 88W56 5:55:44
West Glen 72 98 40N45 89W37 5:58:28
West Glenview 16 1 42N04 87W48 5:51:12
West Hallock 72 57 40N55'15 89W38'21 5:58:33
Westhaven 16 6 41N35'07 87W50'35 5:51:22
West Jersey 88 4 41N01'08 89W55'37 5:59:42
West Junction 89 61 42N18'53 89W39'32 5:58:38
West Kankakee 46 115 41N07'07 87W53'17 5:51:33
West Lake 17 4 39N00 87W44 5:50:56
Westlake 22 2 41N53 88W04 5:52:16
West Lake Forest 49 2 42N13'19 87W52'23 5:51:30
West Liberty 40 4 38N51'12 88W05'04 5:52:20
West Lincoln 54 4 40N11 89W26 5:57:44
West Marion 100 4 37N44 88W58 5:55:52
West Meadowview 46 115 41N05 87W53 5:51:32
West Miltmore 49 6 42N25 88W04 5:52:16
West Monroe 35 4 37N33 88W23 5:53:32
Westmont 22 19 41N47'45 87W58'32 5:51:54
Westmore 22 83 41N53 88W01 5:52:04
West Newell 92 26 40N12'12 87W36'55 5:50:28
Weston 57 35 40N44'50 88W37'19 5:54:29
West Peoria 72 98 40N41'33 89W37'40 5:58:31
West Point 34 4 40N15'18 91W10'57 6:04:44
West Point Landing 29 66 40N12'49 90W10'13 6:00:41
Westport 51 4 38N41'08 87W32'23 5:50:10
West Pullman 16 1 41N40'46 87W38'31 5:50:34
Westridge 16 1 42N07 87W56 5:51:44
West Ridge 21 7 39N49'33 88W13'01 5:52:52
West Rosiclare 35 4 37N26 88W22 5:53:28
West Rural Hill 33 4 37N57'56 88W41'18 5:54:45
West Salem 24 4 38N31'15 88W00'17 5:52:01
West Union 12 4 39N12'57 87W39'58 5:50:40
West Vienna 44 4 37N25'43 88W58'10 5:55:53
Westview 82 25 38N32'13 90W06'06 6:00:24
Westville 92 96 40N02'32 87W38'19 5:50:33
Westwood 22 17 41N56 88W00 5:52:00
West York 17 4 39N10'16 87W40'25 5:50:42
Wetaug 77 4 37N19'26 89W10'00 5:56:40
Wethersfield 37 4 41N12 89W55 5:59:40
Wetzel 23 7 39N42'22 87W42'22 5:50:49
Wheatfield 14 4 38N42 89W26 5:57:44
Wheaton 22 2 41N51'58 88W06'25 5:52:26
Wheaton Center 22 2 41N53 88W05 5:52:20
Wheeler 40 4 39N02'48 88W18'59 5:53:16
Wheeling 16 21 42N08'21 87W55'44 5:51:43
Whiskey Corners 56 48 42N29 88W18 5:53:12
Whispering Hills 56 27 42N21 88W14 5:52:56
Whispering Oaks 49 2 42N14 87W53 5:51:32
Whitaker 46 21 41N15'05 87W43'40 5:50:55
White Ash 100 4 37N47'22 88W55'29 5:55:42
White City 59 26 39N03'53 89W45'48 5:59:03
White City 63 29 40N06'18 90W06'27 6:00:26
White Cliffs 60 7 38N57 90W11 6:00:44
Whitefield 6 48 41N08'55 89W30'17 5:58:01
Whitehall 16 6 42N04 87W57 5:51:48
White Hall 31 55 39N26'13 90W24'11 6:01:37
White Heath 74 30 40N05'10 88W30'46 5:54:03
White Hill (Chasco) 44 4 37N19'09 89W01'17 5:56:05
White Oak 57 4 40N36 89W06 5:56:24
White Oak 68 63 39N30'35 89W34'16 5:58:17
White Oaks Bay 56 15 42N23 88W26 5:53:44
White Pigeon 98 75 41N53'25 89W53'28 5:59:34
White Pines 22 17 41N57 87W58 5:51:52
White Rock 71 6 42N02'11 89W08'02 5:56:32
Whites Addition 81 87 41N30 90W26 6:01:44
Whitford Place 60 7 38N57 90W11 6:00:44
Whitley 70 63 39N29 88W32 5:54:08
Whitmore 58 57 39N56 88W51 5:55:24
Whittington 28 4 38N05'21 88W54'10 5:55:37
Whitton 43 4 42N13'33 90W18'30 6:01:14
Wichert 46 26 41N03'26 87W42'15 5:50:49
Wicker Park 16 1 41N54 87W40 5:50:40
Wickmore 60 7 38N57 90W11 6:00:44
Wilbern 62 56 40N56'48 89W19'25 5:57:18
Wilberton 26 4 38N52 88W57 5:55:48
Wilbur Heights 10 21 40N08'33 88W14'08 5:52:57
Wilcox 13 4 38N41 88W21 5:53:24
Wilcox 34 4 40N19 91W25 6:05:40
Wilderman 82 29 38N28'25 89W56'21 5:59:45
Wildrose 45 95 41N54 88W19 5:53:16
Wildwood 45 102 41N46 88W20 5:53:20
Wildwood 49 27 42N20'34 87W59'53 5:52:00
Wilkinson 19 36 42N00'24 88W46'58 5:55:08
Will 99 30 41N20 87W43 5:50:52
Willard 2 4 37N05'11 89W21'08 5:57:25
Willard 82 25 38N36 89W58 5:59:52
Willard Landing 91 4 37N27'19 89W27'03 5:57:48
Willeys 11 7 39N35'49 89W14'00 5:56:56
Williams 84 29 39N55 89W32 5:58:08
Williamsburg 41 4 38N13'40 89W03'31 5:56:14
Williamsburg 70 55 39N43'03 88W34'19 5:54:17
Williamsburg Hill 87 63 39N18'01 88W56'05 5:55:44
Williamsfield 48 4 40N55'21 90W00'52 6:00:03
Williamson 60 26 38N59'08 89W45'50 5:59:03
Williams Park 49 1 42N15'15 88W11'00 5:52:44
Williams Place 60 7 38N57 90W11 6:00:44
Williamsville 84 29 39N57'15 89W32'55 5:58:12
Willisville 73 63 37N59'02 89W35'22 5:58:21
Willow 43 4 42N16'41 89W56'59 5:59:48
Willoway 22 12 41N47 88W09 5:52:36
Willow Bar Landing 7 65 39N06'44 90W40'48 6:02:43
Willow Branch 74 4 39N59 88W41 5:54:44
Willowbrook 22 2 41N44'52 87W56'07 5:51:44
Willow Brooke 101 4 42N29 89W02 5:56:08
Willow Creek 52 56 41N46 89W00 5:56:00
Willow Estates 19 110 42N06 88W42 5:54:48
Willow Estates 38 26 40N57 87W39 5:50:36
Willow Hill 40 4 38N59'45 88W01'21 5:52:05
Willow's East 16 1 42N04 87W48 5:51:12
Willow Springs 16 1 41N44'27 87W51'37 5:51:26
Willow Wood 16 6 42N06 88W02 5:52:08
Wilmette 16 1 42N04'20 87W43'22 5:50:53
Wilmington 99 30 41N18'28 88W08'48 5:52:35
Wilsman 50 4 41N10'16 88W55'55 5:55:44
Wilson 49 34 42N22'20 88W08'23 5:52:34
Wilson Ford 75 4 39N50'22 90W51'52 6:03:27
Wilson Heights 60 7 38N42'46 89W56'01 5:59:44
Wilson Landing 7 65 39N01'35 90W41'31 6:02:46
Wilsonville 59 55 39N04'15 89W51'22 5:59:25
Wilton 99 4 41N22'46 87W56'03 5:51:44
Wilton Center 99 4 41N21'05 87W57'35 5:51:50
Winchester 86 63 39N37'47 90W27'22 6:01:49
Winden Oak 45 55 41N51 88W28 5:53:52
Windham Manor 16 2 42N07 87W49 5:51:16
Windsor 87 63 39N26'27 88W35'41 5:54:23
Windsor Park 10 138 40N06 88W12 5:52:48
Wine Hill 79 63 37N56'56 89W40'28 5:58:42
Winfield 22 30 41N51'42 88W09'39 5:52:39
Wing 53 141 40N49'10 88W24'04 5:53:36
Winkel 90 29 40N20'56 89W37'53 5:58:32
Winkle 73 4 38N09'00 89W29'19 5:57:57
Winnebago 101 48 42N15'58 89W14'28 5:56:58
Winneberger 7 4 38N52'47 90W35'07 6:02:20
Winneshiek 89 4 42N20'40 89W31'38 5:58:07
Winnetka 16 2 42N06'29 87W44'09 5:50:57
Winslow 89 64 42N29'33 89W47'32 5:59:10
Winston 43 4 42N20'04 90W21'49 6:01:27
Winston Hills 22 12 41N48 88W01 5:52:04
Winston Park 16 6 42N06 88W02 5:52:08
Winston Village 99 1 41N40 88W00 5:52:00
Winston Woods 99 1 41N40 88W00 5:52:00
Winterrowd 25 4 38N56'27 88W22'30 5:53:30
Winthrop Harbor 49 142 42N28'44 87W49'25 5:51:18
Winthrop Harbor Station 49 142 42N28'44 87W50'42 5:51:23
Wireton 16 1 41N39 87W42 5:50:48
Wisetown 3 55 38N46'03 89W23'37 5:57:34
Witt 68 7 39N15'23 89W20'53 5:57:24
Woburn 3 55 38N57'31 89W20'47 5:57:23
Wolf Creek 100 4 37N37'36 89W03'10 5:56:13
Wolf Lake 63 29 40N05'12 90W08'43 6:00:35
Wolf Lake 91 4 37N30'15 89W26'18 5:57:45
Wolfs 47 12 41N41'45 88W15'39 5:53:03
Womac 59 47 39N16'17 89W47'17 5:59:09

Wonder Lake 56 15 42N23'36 88w20'25 5:53:22
Wonder View 56 15 42N23 88w26 5:53:44
Wonder Woods 56 15 42N23 88w26 5:53:44
Woodbine 43 4 42N20'32 90w08'43 6:00:35
Woodborough 16 2 41N34 87w40 5:50:40
Woodburn 59 55 39N02'51 90w00'43 6:00:03
Woodbury 18 56 39N11'45 88w18'11 5:53:13
Woodcrest 82 25 38N35'16 90w03'07 6:00:12
Wood Dale 22 17 41N57'48 87w58'44 5:51:55
Wooddale 72 98 40N40 89w40 5:58:40
Wooded Shores 56 15 42N23 88w26 5:53:44
Woodford 102 124 40N50'48 89w01'41 5:56:07
Wood Hill 99 1 41N30 87w41 5:50:44
Woodhull 37 4 41N10'44 90w18'57 6:01:16
Woodland 38 29 40N42'52 87w43'52 5:50:55
Woodland 46 82 41N09'44 87w32'57 5:50:12
Woodland Addition 50 6 41N17'57 88w50'00 5:55:20
Woodland Heights 16 27 41N58 88w06 5:52:24
Woodland Hills 45 2 41N50'58 88w16'53 5:53:08
Woodland Junction 38 29 40N41'50 87w43'51 5:50:55
Woodland Lake 92 54 40N04 87w42 5:50:48
Woodland Shores 52 25 41N50 89w30 5:58:00
Woodlawn 41 4 38N19'48 89w01'57 5:56:08
Woodlawn Heights 98 26 41N48 89w43 5:58:52
Woodmere 49 42 42N16 87w56 5:51:44
Woodridge 22 43 41N44'49 88w03'01 5:52:12
Woodridge 49 2 42N09'10 87w48'33 5:51:14
Wood River 60 29 38N51'40 90w05'51 6:00:23
Woodruff Corners 89 4 42N16'39 89w25'36 5:57:42
Woodside 84 55 39N43'12 89w40'44 5:58:43
Woodside Estates 22 2 41N48 87w56 5:51:44
Woodson 69 63 39N37'44 90w13'08 6:00:53
Woodstock 56 11 42N18'53 88w26'55 5:53:48
Woodvale 94 4 41N01'26 90w38'39 6:02:35
Woodview Manor 16 1 42N07 87w56 5:51:44
Woodville 1 4 40N11'18 91w10'58 6:04:44
Woodville 31 63 39N14 90w31 6:02:04
Woodworth 38 7 40N39'35 87w50'45 5:51:23
Woody 31 55 39N15'49 90w29'06 6:01:56
Woodyard 23 54 39N51'56 87w39'22 5:50:37
Woodyard 26 4 38N52 89w05 5:56:20
Wooster Lake 49 27 42N23 88w09 5:52:36
Woosung 71 4 41N54'12 89w32'27 5:58:10
Worden 60 8 38N55'53 89w50'20 5:59:21
Worth 16 12 41N41'23 87w47'50 5:51:11
Wrights 31 4 39N22'33 90w17'39 6:01:11
Wrights Corner 26 4 39N07'46 88w51'59 5:55:28
Wyanet 6 55 41N21'55 89w35'02 5:58:20
Wyckles 58 26 39N51'11 89w01'44 5:56:07
Wyckles Corners 58 26 39N50'38 89w01'44 5:56:07
Wynoose 80 4 38N35'55 88w13'19 5:52:53
Wyoming 88 4 41N03'42 89w46'23 5:59:06
Wysox 8 4 41N58 89w48 5:59:12
Wythe 34 4 40N20 91w36 6:06:24
Wyton 92 54 40N07'46 87w38'36 5:50:34
Xenia 13 4 38N38'09 88w38'05 5:54:32
Yale 40 4 39N07'11 88w01'29 5:52:06
Yantisville 87 63 39N32'11 88w53'00 5:55:32
Yard Center 16 1 41N37 87w40 5:50:40
Yates 57 4 40N43 88w38 5:54:32
Yates City 48 60 40N46'43 90w00'53 6:00:04
Yatesville 69 4 39N50'45 90w03'37 6:00:14
Yeager 46 82 41N12'28 87w42'08 5:50:49
Yellow Banks 36 4 40N43'49 91w04'52 6:04:19
Yellowhead 46 21 41N15 87w36 5:50:24
Yeomans 69 63 39N39'02 90w02'27 6:00:10
Yeoward Addition 98 26 41N45'29 89w39'38 5:58:39
York 12 4 39N10'17 87w38'21 5:50:33
York Center 22 21 41N51'25 87w59'16 5:51:57
Yorkfield 22 21 41N52 87w57 5:51:48
Yorkshire Woods 22 2 41N48 87w56 5:51:44
Yorktown 6 4 41N34'11 89w51'00 5:59:24
Yorkville 47 25 41N38'28 88w26'50 5:53:47
Young America 23 55 39N51 87w51 5:51:24
Young Hickory 29 4 40N40 90w15 6:01:00
Youngsdale 45 55 41N59'26 88w20'26 5:53:22
Youngstown 94 4 40N39'38 90w37'02 6:02:28
Yuton 57 4 40N32'00 89w03'37 5:56:14
Zanesville 68 4 39N19'20 89w39'11 5:58:37
Zearing 6 55 41N26'44 89w19'02 5:57:16
Zeigler 28 4 37N53'58 89w03'07 5:56:12
Zenith 96 4 38N32'55 88w37'21 5:54:29
Zenobia 84 55 39N31'43 89w32'01 5:58:08
Zier Cors 8 4 42N09'14 89w49'25 5:59:18
Zif 96 4 38N35 88w19 5:53:16
Zion 8 4 42N05 90w09 6:00:36
Zion 49 142 42N26'46 87w49'58 5:51:20
Zuma 81 4 41N33 90w16 6:01:04

TIME TABLES

This state has a very complex time zone picture and not all of the time shifts are documented. Even newspaper reports present contradictory information. Time changes for smaller towns are not complete. In such instances, it is advisable to consider also the practice of nearby larger towns. As a general rule the CST portions of Indiana observe daylight time in the summer, while the EST portions do not observe daylight time. The exceptions are 1969 and 1970 when the entire state observed daylight time and the areas near Cincinnati and Louisville which observe EDT in the summer.

IN # 1		
Before 11/18/1883		LMT
11/18/1883	12:00	IN#2
6/13/1920	02:00	CDT
10/31/1920	02:00	CST
3/27/1921	02:00	CDT
10/30/1921	02:00	CST
4/30/1922	02:00	CDT
9/24/1922	02:00	CST
4/29/1923	02:00	CDT
9/30/1923	02:00	CST
4/27/1924	02:00	CDT
9/28/1924	02:00	CST
4/26/1925	02:00	CDT
9/27/1925	02:00	CST
4/25/1926	02:00	CDT
9/26/1926	02:00	CST
4/24/1927	02:00	CDT
9/25/1927	02:00	CST
4/29/1928	02:00	CDT
9/30/1928	02:00	CST
4/28/1929	02:00	CDT
9/29/1929	02:00	CST
4/27/1930	02:00	CDT
9/28/1930	02:00	CST
4/26/1931	02:00	CDT
9/27/1931	02:00	CST
4/24/1932	02:00	CDT
9/25/1932	02:00	CST
4/30/1933	02:00	CDT
9/24/1933	02:00	CST
4/29/1934	02:00	CDT
9/30/1934	02:00	CST
4/28/1935	02:00	CDT
9/29/1935	02:00	CST
4/26/1936	02:00	CDT
9/27/1936	02:00	CST
4/25/1937	02:00	CDT
9/26/1937	02:00	CST
4/24/1938	02:00	CDT
9/25/1938	02:00	CST
4/30/1939	02:00	CDT
9/24/1939	02:00	CST
4/28/1940	02:00	CDT
9/29/1940	02:00	CST
4/27/1941	02:00	CDT
9/28/1941	02:00	CST
2/09/1942	02:00	CWT
9/30/1945	02:00	CST
4/28/1946	02:00	CDT
9/29/1946	02:00	CST
4/27/1947	02:00	CDT
9/28/1947	02:00	CST
4/25/1948	02:00	CDT
9/26/1948	02:00	CST
4/24/1949	02:00	CDT
9/25/1949	02:00	CST
4/30/1950	02:00	CDT
9/24/1950	02:00	CST
4/29/1951	02:00	CDT
9/30/1951	02:00	CST
4/27/1952	02:00	CDT
9/28/1952	02:00	CST
4/26/1953	02:00	CDT
9/27/1953	02:00	CST
4/25/1954	02:00	CDT
9/26/1954	02:00	CST
4/24/1955	02:00	CDT
9/25/1955	02:00	CST
4/29/1956	02:00	CDT
9/30/1956	02:00	CST
4/28/1957	02:00	CDT
9/29/1957	02:00	CST
4/27/1958	02:00	CDT
9/28/1958	02:00	CST
4/26/1959	02:00	CDT
9/27/1959	02:00	CST
4/24/1960	02:00	CDT
9/25/1960	02:00	CST
4/30/1961	02:00	CDT
10/29/1961	02:00	CST
4/29/1962	02:00	CDT
10/28/1962	02:00	CST
4/28/1963	02:00	CDT
10/27/1963	02:00	CST
4/26/1964	02:00	CDT
10/25/1964	02:00	CST
4/25/1965	02:00	CDT
10/31/1965	02:00	CST
4/24/1966	02:00	CDT
10/30/1966	02:00	CST
4/30/1967	02:00	CDT
10/29/1967	02:00	CST
4/28/1968	02:00	CDT
10/27/1968	02:00	CST
4/27/1969	02:00	CDT
10/26/1969	02:00	CST
4/26/1970	02:00	CDT
10/25/1970	02:00	CST
4/25/1971	02:00	CDT
10/31/1971	02:00	CST
4/30/1972	02:00	CDT
10/29/1972	02:00	CST
4/29/1973	02:00	CDT
10/28/1973	02:00	CST
1/06/1974	02:00	CDT
10/27/1974	02:00	CST
2/23/1975	02:00	CDT
10/26/1975	02:00	CST
4/25/1976	02:00	US#1

IN # 2		
Before 11/18/1883		LMT
11/18/1883	12:00	CST
3/31/1918	02:00	CWT
10/27/1918	02:00	CST
3/30/1919	02:00	CWT
10/26/1919	02:00	CST
2/09/1942	02:00	CWT
9/30/1945	02:00	CST
4/24/1955	02:00	CDT
10/30/1955	02:00	CST
4/29/1956	02:00	CDT
10/28/1956	02:00	CST
4/28/1957	02:00	US#2

IN # 3		
Before 11/18/1883		LMT
11/18/1883	12:00	CST
3/31/1918	02:00	CWT
10/27/1918	02:00	CST
3/30/1919	02:00	CWT
10/26/1919	02:00	CST
2/09/1942	02:00	CWT
9/30/1945	02:00	CST
4/28/1946	02:00	CDT
9/29/1946	02:00	CST
4/27/1947	02:00	CDT
9/28/1947	02:00	CST
4/25/1948	02:00	CDT
9/26/1948	02:00	CST
4/24/1949	02:00	CDT
9/25/1949	02:00	CST
4/24/1955	02:00	CDT
10/30/1955	02:00	CST
4/29/1956	02:00	CDT
10/28/1956	02:00	CST
4/28/1957	02:00	CDT
9/29/1957	02:00	CST
4/27/1958	02:00	CDT
9/28/1958	02:00	CST
4/26/1959	02:00	CDT
9/27/1959	02:00	CST
4/24/1960	02:00	CDT
9/25/1960	02:00	CST
4/30/1961	02:00	US#1

IN # 4		
Before 11/18/1883		LMT
11/18/1883	12:00	CST
3/31/1918	02:00	CWT
10/27/1918	02:00	CST
3/30/1919	02:00	CWT
10/26/1919	02:00	CST
4/28/1929	02:00	CDT
9/29/1929	02:00	CST
4/27/1930	02:00	CDT
9/28/1930	02:00	CST
4/26/1931	02:00	CDT
9/27/1931	02:00	CST
4/24/1932	02:00	CDT
9/25/1932	02:00	CST
4/30/1933	02:00	CDT
9/24/1933	02:00	CST
4/29/1934	02:00	CDT
9/30/1934	02:00	CST
4/28/1935	02:00	CDT
9/29/1935	02:00	CST
4/26/1936	02:00	CDT
9/27/1936	02:00	CST
4/25/1937	02:00	CDT
9/26/1937	02:00	CST
4/24/1938	02:00	CDT
9/25/1938	02:00	CST
4/30/1939	02:00	CDT
9/24/1939	02:00	CST
4/28/1940	02:00	CDT
9/29/1940	02:00	CST
4/27/1941	02:00	CDT
9/28/1941	02:00	CST
2/09/1942	02:00	CWT
9/30/1945	02:00	CST
4/28/1946	02:00	CDT
9/29/1946	02:00	CST
4/27/1947	02:00	CDT
9/28/1947	02:00	CST
4/25/1948	02:00	CDT
9/26/1948	02:00	CST
4/24/1949	02:00	CDT
9/25/1949	02:00	CST
4/30/1950	02:00	CDT
9/24/1950	02:00	CST
4/29/1951	02:00	CDT
9/30/1951	02:00	CST
4/27/1952	02:00	CDT
9/28/1952	02:00	CST
4/26/1953	02:00	CDT
9/27/1953	02:00	CST
4/25/1954	02:00	CDT
9/26/1954	02:00	CST
4/24/1955	02:00	CDT
10/30/1955	02:00	CST
4/29/1956	02:00	CDT
10/28/1956	02:00	CST
4/28/1957	02:00	CDT
9/29/1957	02:00	CST
4/27/1958	02:00	US#1

IN # 5		
Before 11/18/1883		LMT
11/18/1883	12:00	IN#2
4/26/1925	02:00	CDT
9/27/1925	02:00	CST
4/25/1926	02:00	CDT
9/26/1926	02:00	CST
4/24/1927	02:00	CDT
9/25/1927	02:00	CST
4/29/1928	02:00	CDT
9/30/1928	02:00	CST
4/28/1929	02:00	CDT
9/29/1929	02:00	CST
4/27/1930	02:00	CDT
9/28/1930	02:00	CST
4/26/1931	02:00	CDT
9/27/1931	02:00	CST
4/24/1932	02:00	CDT
9/25/1932	02:00	CST
4/30/1933	02:00	CDT
9/24/1933	02:00	CST
4/29/1934	02:00	CDT
9/30/1934	02:00	CST
4/28/1935	02:00	CDT
9/29/1935	02:00	CST
3/01/1936	02:00	CDT
11/15/1936	02:00	CST
4/25/1937	02:00	CDT
9/26/1937	02:00	CST
4/24/1938	02:00	CDT
9/25/1938	02:00	CST
4/30/1939	02:00	CDT
9/24/1939	02:00	CST
4/28/1940	02:00	CDT
9/29/1940	02:00	CST
4/27/1941	02:00	CDT
9/28/1941	02:00	CST
2/09/1942	02:00	CWT
9/30/1945	02:00	CST
5/01/1946	02:00	CDT
10/01/1946	02:00	US#2

IN # 6		
Before 11/18/1883		LMT
11/18/1883	12:00	CST
3/31/1918	02:00	CWT
10/27/1918	02:00	CST
3/30/1919	02:00	CWT
10/26/1919	02:00	CST
6/13/1920	02:00	CDT
10/31/1920	02:00	CST
3/27/1921	02:00	CDT
10/30/1921	02:00	CST
4/30/1922	02:00	CDT
9/24/1922	02:00	CST
4/29/1923	02:00	CDT
9/30/1923	02:00	CST
4/27/1924	02:00	CDT
9/28/1924	02:00	CST
4/26/1925	02:00	CDT
9/27/1925	02:00	CST
4/25/1926	02:00	CDT
9/26/1926	02:00	CST
4/24/1927	02:00	CDT
9/25/1927	02:00	CST
4/29/1928	02:00	CDT
9/30/1928	02:00	CST
4/28/1929	02:00	CDT
9/29/1929	02:00	CST
4/27/1930	02:00	CDT
9/28/1930	02:00	CST
4/26/1931	02:00	CDT
9/27/1931	02:00	CST
4/24/1932	02:00	CDT
9/25/1932	02:00	CST
4/30/1933	02:00	CDT
9/24/1933	02:00	CST
4/29/1934	02:00	CDT
9/30/1934	02:00	CST
4/28/1935	02:00	CDT
9/29/1935	02:00	CST
3/01/1936	02:00	CDT
11/15/1936	02:00	CST
4/25/1937	02:00	US#2

IN # 7		
Before 11/18/1883		LMT
11/18/1883	12:00	IN#2
5/01/1938	02:00	CDT
10/01/1938	02:00	CST
2/09/1942	02:00	CWT
9/30/1945	02:00	CST
4/28/1946	02:00	CDT
9/29/1946	02:00	CST
4/27/1947	02:00	CDT
9/28/1947	02:00	CST
4/25/1948	02:00	CDT
9/26/1948	02:00	CST
4/24/1949	02:00	CDT
9/25/1949	02:00	CST
4/30/1950	02:00	CDT
9/24/1950	02:00	CST
4/29/1951	02:00	CDT
9/30/1951	02:00	CST
4/27/1952	02:00	CDT
9/28/1952	02:00	CST
4/26/1953	02:00	CDT
9/27/1953	02:00	CST
4/25/1954	02:00	CDT
9/26/1954	02:00	CST
4/24/1955	02:00	CDT
10/30/1955	02:00	CST
4/29/1956	02:00	CDT
10/28/1956	02:00	CST
4/28/1957	02:00	CDT
9/29/1957	02:00	CST
4/27/1958	02:00	US#1

IN # 8		
Before 11/18/1883		LMT
11/18/1883	12:00	IN#2
4/27/1930	00:01	CDT
9/28/1930	00:01	CST
4/26/1931	00:01	CDT
9/27/1931	00:01	CST
4/24/1932	00:01	CDT
9/25/1932	00:01	CST
4/30/1933	00:01	CDT
10/01/1933	00:01	CST
4/29/1934	00:01	CDT
9/30/1934	00:01	CST
4/28/1935	00:01	CDT
9/29/1935	00:01	CST
4/26/1936	02:00	CDT
9/27/1936	02:00	CST
4/25/1937	02:00	CDT
9/26/1937	02:00	CST
4/24/1938	02:00	CDT
9/25/1938	02:00	CST
4/30/1939	02:00	CDT
9/24/1939	02:00	CST
4/28/1940	02:00	CDT
9/29/1940	02:00	CST
4/27/1941	02:00	CDT
9/28/1941	02:00	CST
2/09/1942	02:00	CWT
9/30/1945	02:00	CST
4/28/1946	02:00	US#3

IN # 9		
Before 11/18/1883		LMT
11/18/1883	12:00	IN#2
4/27/1930	02:00	CDT
9/28/1930	02:00	CST
4/26/1931	02:00	CDT
9/27/1931	02:00	CST
4/24/1932	02:00	CDT
9/25/1932	02:00	CST
4/30/1933	02:00	CDT
9/24/1933	02:00	CST
4/29/1934	02:00	CDT
9/30/1934	02:00	CST
4/28/1935	02:00	CDT
9/29/1935	02:00	CST
4/26/1936	02:00	CDT
9/27/1936	02:00	CST
4/25/1937	02:00	CDT
9/26/1937	02:00	CST
4/24/1938	02:00	CDT
9/25/1938	02:00	CST
4/30/1939	02:00	CDT
9/24/1939	02:00	CST
4/28/1940	02:00	CDT
9/29/1940	02:00	CST
4/27/1941	02:00	CDT
9/28/1941	02:00	CST
2/09/1942	02:00	CWT
9/30/1945	02:00	CST
4/28/1946	02:00	US#3

IN # 10		
Before 11/18/1883		LMT
11/18/1883	12:00	IN#2
4/27/1947	02:00	CDT
9/28/1947	02:00	CST
4/25/1948	02:00	CDT
9/26/1948	02:00	CST
4/24/1949	02:00	CDT
9/25/1949	02:00	CST
4/30/1950	02:00	CDT
9/24/1950	02:00	CST
4/29/1951	02:00	CDT
9/30/1951	02:00	CST
4/27/1952	02:00	CDT
9/28/1952	02:00	CST
4/26/1953	02:00	CDT
9/27/1953	02:00	CST
4/25/1954	02:00	CDT
9/26/1954	02:00	CST
4/24/1955	02:00	CDT
10/30/1955	02:00	CST
4/29/1956	02:00	CDT
10/28/1956	02:00	CST
4/28/1957	02:00	CDT
9/29/1957	02:00	CST
4/27/1958	02:00	CDT
9/28/1958	02:00	CST
4/26/1959	02:00	US#1

IN # 11		
Before 11/18/1883		LMT
11/18/1883	12:00	CST
3/31/1918	02:00	CWT
10/27/1918	02:00	CST
3/30/1919	02:00	CWT
10/26/1919	02:00	CST
4/28/1929	02:00	CDT
9/29/1929	02:00	CST
4/27/1930	02:00	CDT
9/28/1930	02:00	CST
4/26/1931	02:00	CDT
9/27/1931	02:00	CST
4/24/1932	02:00	CDT
9/25/1932	02:00	CST
4/30/1933	02:00	CDT
9/24/1933	02:00	CST
4/29/1934	02:00	CDT
9/30/1934	02:00	CST
4/28/1935	02:00	CDT
9/29/1935	02:00	CST
4/26/1936	02:00	CDT
9/27/1936	02:00	CST
4/25/1937	02:00	CDT
9/26/1937	02:00	CST
4/24/1938	02:00	CDT
9/25/1938	02:00	CST
4/30/1939	02:00	CDT
9/24/1939	02:00	CST
4/28/1940	02:00	CDT
9/29/1940	02:00	CST
4/27/1941	02:00	CDT
9/28/1941	02:00	CST
2/09/1942	02:00	CWT
9/30/1945	02:00	CST
4/28/1946	02:00	CDT
9/29/1946	02:00	CST
4/27/1947	02:00	CDT
9/28/1947	02:00	CST
4/25/1948	02:00	CDT
9/26/1948	02:00	CST
4/24/1949	02:00	CDT
9/25/1949	02:00	CST
4/30/1950	02:00	CDT
9/24/1950	02:00	CST
4/29/1951	02:00	CDT
9/30/1951	02:00	CST
4/27/1952	02:00	CDT
9/28/1952	02:00	CST
4/26/1953	02:00	CDT
9/27/1953	02:00	CST
4/25/1954	02:00	CDT
9/26/1954	02:00	CST
4/24/1955	02:00	CDT
10/30/1955	02:00	CST
4/29/1956	02:00	CDT
10/28/1956	02:00	CST
4/28/1957	02:00	CDT
9/29/1957	02:00	CST
4/27/1958	02:00	US#1

IN # 12		
Before 11/18/1883		LMT
11/18/1883	12:00	IN#2
5/13/1927	02:00	CDT
9/25/1927	02:00	CST
4/29/1928	02:00	CDT
9/30/1928	02:00	CST
4/28/1929	02:00	CDT
9/29/1929	02:00	CST
4/27/1930	02:00	CDT
9/28/1930	02:00	CST
4/26/1931	02:00	CDT
9/27/1931	02:00	CST
4/24/1932	02:00	CDT
9/25/1932	02:00	CST
4/30/1933	02:00	CDT
9/24/1933	02:00	CST
4/29/1934	02:00	CDT
9/30/1934	02:00	CST
4/28/1935	02:00	CDT
9/29/1935	02:00	CST
3/01/1936	02:00	CDT
11/15/1936	02:00	CST
4/25/1937	02:00	CDT
9/26/1937	02:00	CST
4/24/1938	02:00	CDT
9/25/1938	02:00	CST
4/30/1939	02:00	CDT
9/24/1939	02:00	CST
4/28/1940	02:00	CDT
9/29/1940	02:00	CST
4/27/1941	02:00	CDT
9/28/1941	02:00	CST
2/09/1942	02:00	CWT
9/30/1945	02:00	CST
4/28/1946	02:00	CDT
9/29/1946	02:00	CST

TIME TABLES

4/27/1947 02:00 CDT
9/28/1947 02:00 CST
4/25/1948 02:00 CDT
9/26/1948 02:00 CST
4/24/1949 02:00 CDT
9/25/1949 02:00 CST
4/30/1950 02:00 CDT
9/24/1950 02:00 CST
4/29/1951 02:00 CDT
9/30/1951 02:00 CST
4/27/1952 02:00 CDT
9/28/1952 02:00 CST
4/26/1953 02:00 CDT
9/27/1953 02:00 CST
4/25/1954 02:00 CDT
9/26/1954 02:00 CST
4/24/1955 02:00 CDT
10/30/1955 02:00 CST
4/29/1956 02:00 CDT
10/28/1956 02:00 CST
4/28/1957 02:00 CDT
9/29/1957 02:00 CST
4/27/1958 02:00 US#3
....
IN # 13
Before 11/18/1883 LMT
11/18/1883 12:00 IN#2
4/28/1946 02:00 CDT
9/29/1946 02:00 CST
4/27/1947 02:00 CDT
9/28/1947 02:00 CST
4/25/1948 02:00 CDT
9/26/1948 02:00 CST
4/24/1949 02:00 CDT
9/25/1949 02:00 CST
4/30/1950 02:00 CDT
9/24/1950 02:00 CST
4/29/1951 02:00 CDT
9/30/1951 02:00 CST
4/27/1952 02:00 CDT
9/28/1952 02:00 CST
4/26/1953 02:00 CDT
9/27/1953 02:00 CST
4/25/1954 02:00 CDT
9/26/1954 02:00 CST
4/24/1955 02:00 CDT
10/30/1955 02:00 CST
4/29/1956 02:00 CDT
10/28/1956 02:00 CST
4/28/1957 02:00 CDT
9/29/1957 02:00 CST
4/27/1958 02:00 US#1
....
IN # 14
Before 11/18/1883 LMT
11/18/1883 12:00 IN#2
4/30/1922 02:00 CDT
9/24/1922 02:00 CST
4/29/1923 02:00 CDT
9/30/1923 02:00 CST
4/27/1924 02:00 CDT
9/28/1924 02:00 CST
4/26/1925 02:00 CDT
9/27/1925 02:00 CST
4/25/1926 02:00 CDT
9/26/1926 02:00 CST
4/24/1927 02:00 CDT
9/25/1927 02:00 CST
4/29/1928 02:00 CDT
9/30/1928 02:00 CST
4/28/1929 02:00 CDT
9/29/1929 02:00 CST
4/27/1930 02:00 CDT
9/28/1930 02:00 CST
4/26/1931 02:00 CDT
9/27/1931 02:00 CST
4/24/1932 02:00 CDT
9/25/1932 02:00 CST
4/30/1933 02:00 CDT
9/24/1933 02:00 CST
4/29/1934 02:00 CDT
9/30/1934 02:00 CST
4/28/1935 02:00 CDT
9/29/1935 02:00 CST
3/01/1936 02:00 CDT
11/15/1936 02:00 CST
4/25/1937 02:00 US#2
....
IN # 15
Before 11/18/1883 LMT
11/18/1883 12:00 IN#2
4/24/1932 02:00 CDT
9/25/1932 02:00 CST
2/09/1942 02:00 CWT
9/30/1945 02:00 CST
4/25/1948 02:00 CDT
9/26/1948 02:00 CST
4/27/1952 02:00 CDT
9/28/1952 02:00 CST
4/26/1953 02:00 CDT
9/27/1953 02:00 CST
4/25/1954 02:00 CDT
9/26/1954 02:00 CST
4/24/1955 02:00 CDT
10/30/1955 02:00 CST
4/29/1956 02:00 CDT
10/28/1956 02:00 CST
4/28/1957 02:00 CDT
9/29/1957 02:00 CST
4/27/1958 02:00 US#1
....
IN # 16
Before 11/18/1883 LMT
11/18/1883 12:00 IN#2
4/26/1931 02:00 CDT
9/27/1931 02:00 CST
4/30/1939 02:00 CDT
9/24/1939 02:00 CST
4/28/1940 02:00 CDT
9/29/1940 02:00 CST
4/27/1941 02:00 CDT
9/28/1941 02:00 CST
2/09/1942 02:00 CWT
9/30/1945 02:00 CST
4/28/1946 02:00 CDT
9/29/1946 02:00 CST
4/25/1948 02:00 CDT
9/26/1948 02:00 CST
4/27/1952 02:00 CDT
9/28/1952 02:00 CST
4/26/1953 02:00 CDT
9/27/1953 02:00 CST
4/25/1954 02:00 CDT
9/26/1954 02:00 CST
4/24/1955 02:00 CDT
10/30/1955 02:00 CST
4/29/1956 02:00 CDT
10/28/1956 02:00 CST
4/28/1957 02:00 CDT
9/29/1957 02:00 CST
4/27/1958 02:00 US#1
....
IN # 17
Before 11/18/1883 LMT
11/18/1883 12:00 CST
3/31/1918 02:00 CWT
10/27/1918 02:00 CST
3/30/1919 02:00 CWT
10/26/1919 02:00 CST
6/13/1920 02:00 CDT
10/31/1920 02:00 CST
3/27/1921 02:00 CDT
10/30/1921 02:00 CST
4/30/1922 02:00 CDT
9/24/1922 02:00 CST
4/29/1923 02:00 CDT
9/30/1923 02:00 CST
4/27/1924 02:00 CDT
9/28/1924 02:00 CST
4/26/1925 02:00 CDT
9/27/1925 02:00 CST
4/25/1926 02:00 CDT
9/26/1926 02:00 CST
4/24/1927 02:00 CDT
9/25/1927 02:00 CST
4/29/1928 02:00 CDT
9/30/1928 02:00 CST
4/28/1929 02:00 CDT
9/29/1929 02:00 CST
4/27/1930 02:00 CDT
9/28/1930 02:00 CST
4/26/1931 02:00 CDT
9/27/1931 02:00 CST
5/01/1932 02:00 CDT
11/01/1932 01:00 CST
4/30/1933 02:00 CDT
9/24/1933 02:00 CST
4/29/1934 02:00 CDT
9/30/1934 02:00 CST
4/28/1935 02:00 CDT
9/29/1935 02:00 CST
3/01/1936 02:00 CDT
11/15/1936 02:00 CST
4/25/1937 02:00 CDT
9/26/1937 02:00 CST
4/24/1938 02:00 CDT
9/25/1938 02:00 CST
4/30/1939 02:00 CDT
9/24/1939 02:00 CST
4/28/1940 02:00 CDT
9/29/1940 02:00 CST
4/27/1941 02:00 CDT
10/27/1941 02:00 US#2
....
IN # 18
Before 11/18/1883 LMT
11/18/1883 12:00 IN#2
4/24/1938 02:00 CDT
9/25/1938 02:00 CST
4/30/1939 02:00 CDT
9/24/1939 02:00 CST
4/28/1940 02:00 CDT
9/29/1940 02:00 CST
4/27/1941 02:00 CDT
9/28/1941 02:00 CST
2/09/1942 02:00 CWT
9/30/1945 02:00 CST
4/26/1953 02:00 CDT
9/27/1953 02:00 CST
4/25/1954 02:00 CDT
9/26/1954 02:00 CST
4/24/1955 02:00 CDT
10/30/1955 02:00 CST
4/29/1956 02:00 CDT
10/28/1956 02:00 CST
4/28/1957 02:00 CDT
9/29/1957 02:00 CST
4/27/1958 02:00 US#1
....
IN # 19
Before 11/18/1883 LMT
11/18/1883 12:00 IN#2
4/28/1940 02:00 CDT
9/29/1940 02:00 CST
4/27/1941 02:00 CDT
9/28/1941 02:00 CST
2/09/1942 02:00 CWT
9/30/1945 02:00 CST
4/26/1953 02:00 CDT
9/27/1953 02:00 CST
4/25/1954 02:00 CDT
9/26/1954 02:00 CST
4/24/1955 02:00 CDT
10/30/1955 02:00 CST
4/29/1956 02:00 CDT
10/28/1956 02:00 CST
4/28/1957 02:00 CDT
9/29/1957 02:00 CST
4/27/1958 02:00 US#1
....
IN # 20
Before 11/18/1883 LMT
11/18/1883 12:00 CST
3/31/1918 02:00 CWT
10/27/1918 02:00 CST
3/30/1919 02:00 CWT
10/26/1919 02:00 CST
6/13/1920 02:00 CDT
10/31/1920 02:00 CST
3/27/1921 02:00 CDT
10/30/1921 02:00 CST
4/30/1922 02:00 CDT
9/24/1922 02:00 CST
4/29/1923 02:00 CDT
9/30/1923 02:00 CST
4/27/1924 02:00 CDT
9/28/1924 02:00 CST
4/26/1925 02:00 CDT
9/27/1925 02:00 CST
4/25/1926 02:00 CDT
9/26/1926 02:00 CST
4/24/1927 02:00 CDT
9/25/1927 02:00 CST
4/29/1928 02:00 CDT
9/30/1928 02:00 CST
4/28/1929 02:00 CDT
9/29/1929 02:00 CST
4/27/1930 02:00 CDT
9/28/1930 02:00 CST
4/26/1931 02:00 CDT
9/27/1931 02:00 CST
4/24/1932 02:00 CDT
9/25/1932 02:00 CST
4/30/1933 02:00 CDT
10/01/1933 02:00 CST
4/29/1934 02:00 CDT
9/30/1934 02:00 CST
4/28/1935 02:00 CDT
9/29/1935 02:00 CST
3/01/1936 02:00 CDT
11/15/1936 02:00 CST
4/25/1937 02:00 US#2
....
IN # 21
Before 11/18/1883 LMT
11/18/1883 12:00 IN#2
4/24/1938 02:00 CDT
9/25/1938 02:00 CST
4/30/1939 02:00 CDT
9/24/1939 02:00 CST
4/28/1940 02:00 CDT
9/29/1940 02:00 CST
4/27/1941 02:00 CDT
9/28/1941 02:00 CST
2/09/1942 02:00 CWT
9/30/1945 02:00 CST
4/28/1946 02:00 CDT
9/29/1946 02:00 CST
4/27/1947 02:00 CDT
9/28/1947 02:00 CST
4/25/1948 02:00 CDT
9/26/1948 02:00 CST
4/24/1949 02:00 CDT
9/25/1949 02:00 CST
4/30/1950 02:00 CDT
9/24/1950 02:00 CST
4/29/1951 02:00 CDT
9/30/1951 02:00 CST
4/27/1952 02:00 CDT
9/28/1952 02:00 CST
4/26/1953 02:00 CDT
9/27/1953 02:00 CST
4/25/1954 02:00 CDT
9/26/1954 02:00 CST
4/24/1955 02:00 CDT
10/30/1955 02:00 CST
4/29/1956 02:00 CDT
10/28/1956 02:00 CST
4/28/1957 02:00 CDT
9/29/1957 02:00 CST
4/27/1958 02:00 US#1
....
IN # 22
Before 11/18/1883 LMT
11/18/1883 12:00 IN#2
4/24/1938 02:00 CDT
9/25/1938 02:00 CST
4/30/1939 02:00 CDT
9/24/1939 02:00 CST
4/28/1940 02:00 CDT
9/29/1940 02:00 CST
4/27/1941 02:00 CDT
9/28/1941 02:00 CST
2/09/1942 02:00 CWT
9/30/1945 02:00 CST
4/28/1946 02:00 CDT
9/29/1946 02:00 CST
4/25/1948 02:00 CDT
9/26/1948 02:00 CST
4/24/1955 02:00 CDT
10/30/1955 02:00 CST
4/29/1956 02:00 CDT
10/28/1956 02:00 CST
4/28/1957 02:00 CDT
9/29/1957 02:00 CST
4/27/1958 02:00 US#1
....
IN # 23
Before 11/18/1883 LMT
11/18/1883 12:00 IN#2
4/26/1931 02:00 CDT
9/27/1931 02:00 CST
4/24/1932 02:00 CDT
9/25/1932 02:00 CST
4/30/1933 02:00 CDT
9/24/1933 02:00 CST
4/29/1934 02:00 CDT
9/30/1934 02:00 CST
4/28/1935 02:00 CDT
9/29/1935 02:00 CST
3/01/1936 02:00 CDT
11/15/1936 02:00 CST
4/25/1937 02:00 US#2
....
IN # 24
Before 11/18/1883 LMT
11/18/1883 12:00 IN#2
4/28/1946 02:00 CDT
9/29/1946 02:00 CST
4/27/1947 02:00 CDT
9/28/1947 02:00 CST
4/25/1948 02:00 CDT
9/26/1948 02:00 CST
4/24/1949 02:00 CDT
9/25/1949 02:00 CST
4/30/1950 02:00 CDT
9/24/1950 02:00 CST
4/29/1951 02:00 CDT
9/30/1951 02:00 CST
4/27/1952 02:00 CDT
9/28/1952 02:00 CST
4/26/1953 02:00 CDT
9/27/1953 02:00 CST
4/25/1954 02:00 CDT
9/26/1954 02:00 CST
4/24/1955 02:00 CDT
10/30/1955 02:00 CST
4/29/1956 02:00 CDT
10/28/1956 02:00 CST
4/28/1957 02:00 CDT
9/29/1957 02:00 CST
4/27/1958 02:00 US#1
....
IN # 25
Before 11/18/1883 LMT
11/18/1883 12:00 CST
3/31/1918 02:00 CWT
10/27/1918 02:00 CST
3/30/1919 02:00 CWT
10/26/1919 02:00 CST
2/09/1942 02:00 CWT
9/30/1945 02:00 CST
4/28/1946 02:00 CDT
9/29/1946 02:00 CST
4/27/1947 02:00 CDT
9/28/1947 02:00 CST
4/25/1948 02:00 CDT
9/26/1948 02:00 CST
4/24/1955 02:00 CDT
10/30/1955 02:00 CST
4/29/1956 02:00 CDT
10/28/1956 02:00 CST
4/28/1957 02:00 CDT
9/29/1957 02:00 CST
4/27/1958 02:00 CDT
9/28/1958 02:00 CST
4/26/1959 02:00 CDT
9/27/1959 02:00 CST
4/24/1960 02:00 CDT
9/25/1960 02:00 CST
4/30/1961 02:00 US#1
....
IN # 26
Before 11/18/1883 LMT
11/18/1883 12:00 CST
3/31/1918 02:00 CWT
10/27/1918 02:00 CST
3/30/1919 02:00 CWT
10/26/1919 02:00 CST
2/09/1942 02:00 CWT
9/30/1945 02:00 CST
4/27/1947 02:00 CDT
9/28/1947 02:00 CST
4/25/1948 02:00 CDT
9/26/1948 02:00 CST
4/24/1955 02:00 CDT
10/30/1955 02:00 CST
4/29/1956 02:00 CDT
10/28/1956 02:00 CST
4/28/1957 02:00 CDT
9/29/1957 02:00 CST
4/27/1958 02:00 CDT
9/28/1958 02:00 CST
4/26/1959 02:00 CDT
9/27/1959 02:00 CST
4/24/1960 02:00 CDT
9/25/1960 02:00 CST
4/30/1961 02:00 US#1
....
IN # 27
Before 11/18/1883 LMT
11/18/1883 12:00 IN#2
4/30/1950 02:00 CDT
9/24/1950 02:00 CST
4/29/1951 02:00 CDT
9/30/1951 02:00 CST
4/27/1952 02:00 CDT
9/28/1952 02:00 CST
4/26/1953 02:00 CDT
9/27/1953 02:00 CST
4/25/1954 02:00 CDT
9/26/1954 02:00 CST
4/24/1955 02:00 CDT
10/30/1955 02:00 CST
4/29/1956 02:00 CDT
10/28/1956 02:00 CST
4/28/1957 02:00 CDT
9/29/1957 02:00 CST
4/27/1958 02:00 CDT
9/28/1958 02:00 CST
4/26/1959 02:00 CDT
9/27/1959 02:00 CST
4/24/1960 02:00 CDT
9/25/1960 02:00 CST
4/30/1961 02:00 US#1
....
IN # 28
Before 11/18/1883 LMT
11/18/1883 12:00 IN#2
4/25/1954 02:00 CDT
9/26/1954 02:00 CST
4/24/1955 02:00 CDT
10/30/1955 02:00 CST
4/29/1956 02:00 CDT
10/28/1956 02:00 CST
4/28/1957 02:00 CDT
9/29/1957 02:00 CST
4/27/1958 02:00 CDT
9/28/1958 02:00 CST
4/26/1959 02:00 CDT
9/27/1959 02:00 CST
4/24/1960 02:00 CDT
9/25/1960 02:00 CST
4/30/1961 02:00 US#1
....
IN # 29
Before 11/18/1883 LMT
11/18/1883 12:00 IN#2
4/26/1953 02:00 CDT
9/27/1953 02:00 CST
4/25/1954 02:00 CDT
9/26/1954 02:00 CST
4/24/1955 02:00 CDT
10/30/1955 02:00 CST
4/29/1956 02:00 CDT
10/28/1956 02:00 CST
4/28/1957 02:00 CDT
9/29/1957 02:00 CST
4/27/1958 02:00 CDT
9/28/1958 02:00 CST
4/26/1959 02:00 CDT
9/27/1959 02:00 CST
4/24/1960 02:00 CDT
9/25/1960 02:00 CST
4/30/1961 02:00 US#1
....
IN # 30
Before 11/18/1883 LMT
11/18/1883 12:00 CST
3/31/1918 02:00 CWT
10/27/1918 02:00 CST
3/30/1919 02:00 CWT
10/26/1919 02:00 CST
2/09/1942 02:00 CWT
9/30/1945 02:00 CST
4/25/1954 02:00 EST
4/27/1969 02:00 EDT
10/26/1969 02:00 EST
4/26/1970 02:00 EDT
10/25/1970 02:00 EST
....
IN # 31
Before 11/18/1883 LMT
11/18/1883 12:00 CST
3/31/1918 02:00 CWT
10/27/1918 02:00 CST
3/30/1919 02:00 CWT
10/26/1919 02:00 CST
4/30/1933 02:00 CDT
9/24/1933 02:00 CST
5/05/1934 02:00 CDT
10/01/1934 02:00 CST
4/28/1935 02:00 CDT
9/01/1935 02:00 CST
4/26/1936 02:00 CDT
8/29/1936 02:00 CST
4/25/1937 02:00 CDT
8/28/1937 02:00 CST
4/24/1938 02:00 CDT
9/25/1938 02:00 CST
4/30/1939 02:00 CDT
10/01/1939 02:00 CST
4/28/1940 02:00 CDT
9/29/1940 02:00 CST
4/27/1941 02:00 CDT
9/28/1941 02:00 CST
2/09/1942 02:00 CWT
9/30/1945 02:00 CST
4/27/1947 02:00 CDT
9/28/1947 02:00 CST
4/25/1948 02:00 CDT
9/26/1948 02:00 CST
4/24/1949 02:00 CDT
9/25/1949 02:00 CST
4/30/1950 02:00 CDT
9/24/1950 02:00 CST
4/29/1951 02:00 CDT
9/30/1951 02:00 CST
4/27/1952 02:00 CDT
9/28/1952 02:00 CST
4/26/1953 02:00 CDT
9/27/1953 02:00 CST
4/25/1954 02:00 EST
4/27/1969 02:00 EDT
10/26/1969 02:00 EST
4/26/1970 02:00 EDT
10/25/1970 02:00 EST
....
IN # 32
Before 11/18/1883 LMT
11/18/1883 12:00 CST
3/31/1918 02:00 CWT
10/27/1918 02:00 CST
3/30/1919 02:00 CWT
10/26/1919 02:00 CST
4/27/1941 02:00 CDT
9/28/1941 02:00 CST
2/09/1942 02:00 CWT
9/30/1945 02:00 CST
4/25/1954 02:00 EST
4/27/1969 02:00 EDT
10/26/1969 02:00 EST
4/26/1970 02:00 EDT
10/25/1970 02:00 EST
....
IN # 33
Before 11/18/1883 LMT
11/18/1883 12:00 CST
3/31/1918 02:00 CWT
10/27/1918 02:00 CST

TIME TABLES

Date	Time	Zone
3/30/1919	02:00	CWT
10/26/1919	02:00	CST
2/09/1942	02:00	CWT
9/30/1945	02:00	CST
4/25/1954	02:00	EST
4/28/1968	02:00	US#1

IN # 34

Date	Time	Zone
Before 11/18/1883		LMT
11/18/1883	12:00	CST
3/31/1918	02:00	CWT
10/27/1918	02:00	CST
3/30/1919	02:00	CWT
10/26/1919	02:00	CST
4/28/1940	02:00	CDT
9/02/1940	02:00	CST
4/27/1941	02:00	CDT
9/28/1941	02:00	CST
2/09/1942	02:00	CWT
9/30/1945	02:00	CST
4/28/1946	02:00	CDT
9/29/1946	02:00	CST
4/27/1947	02:00	CDT
9/28/1947	02:00	CST
4/25/1948	02:00	CDT
9/26/1948	02:00	CST
4/24/1949	02:00	CDT
9/25/1949	02:00	CST
4/30/1950	02:00	CDT
9/24/1950	02:00	CST
4/29/1951	02:00	CDT
9/30/1951	02:00	CST
4/27/1952	02:00	CDT
9/28/1952	02:00	CST
4/26/1953	02:00	CDT
9/27/1953	02:00	CST
4/25/1954	02:00	EST
4/27/1969	02:00	EDT
10/26/1969	02:00	EST
4/26/1970	02:00	EDT
10/25/1970	02:00	EST

IN # 35

Date	Time	Zone
Before 11/18/1883		LMT
11/18/1883	12:00	CST
3/31/1918	02:00	CWT
10/27/1918	02:00	CST
3/30/1919	02:00	CWT
10/26/1919	02:00	CST
2/09/1942	02:00	CWT
9/30/1945	02:00	CST
4/25/1954	02:00	EST
4/27/1969	02:00	EDT
10/26/1969	02:00	EST
4/26/1970	02:00	EDT
10/25/1970	02:00	EST
4/25/1971	02:00	EDT
10/31/1971	02:00	EST
4/30/1972	02:00	EDT
10/29/1972	02:00	EST

IN # 36

Date	Time	Zone
Before 11/18/1883		LMT
11/18/1883	12:00	CST
3/31/1918	02:00	CWT
10/27/1918	02:00	CST
3/30/1919	02:00	CWT
10/26/1919	02:00	CST
2/09/1942	02:00	CWT
9/30/1945	02:00	CST
4/26/1953	02:00	CDT
9/27/1953	02:00	CST
4/25/1954	02:00	EST
4/27/1969	02:00	EDT
10/26/1969	02:00	EST
4/26/1970	02:00	EDT
10/25/1970	02:00	EST

IN # 37

Date	Time	Zone
Before 11/18/1883		LMT
11/18/1883	12:00	CST
3/31/1918	02:00	CWT
10/27/1918	02:00	CST
3/30/1919	02:00	CWT
10/26/1919	02:00	CST
2/09/1942	02:00	CWT
9/30/1945	02:00	CST
4/27/1947	02:00	CDT
9/28/1947	02:00	CST
4/25/1948	02:00	CDT
9/26/1948	02:00	CST
4/24/1949	02:00	CDT
9/25/1949	02:00	CST
4/30/1950	02:00	CDT
9/24/1950	02:00	CST
4/29/1951	02:00	CDT
9/30/1951	02:00	CST
4/27/1952	02:00	CDT
9/28/1952	02:00	CST
4/26/1953	02:00	CDT
9/27/1953	02:00	CST
4/25/1954	02:00	EST
4/30/1967	02:00	US#1

IN # 38

Date	Time	Zone
Before 11/18/1883		LMT
11/18/1883	12:00	CST
3/31/1918	02:00	CWT
10/27/1918	02:00	CST
3/30/1919	02:00	CWT
10/26/1919	02:00	CST
2/09/1942	02:00	CWT
9/30/1945	02:00	CST
4/24/1949	02:00	CDT
9/25/1949	02:00	CST
4/30/1950	02:00	CDT
9/24/1950	02:00	CST
4/29/1951	02:00	CDT
9/30/1951	02:00	CST
4/27/1952	02:00	CDT
9/28/1952	02:00	CST
4/26/1953	02:00	CDT
9/27/1953	02:00	CST
4/25/1954	02:00	EST
4/30/1967	02:00	US#1

IN # 39

Date	Time	Zone
Before 11/18/1883		LMT
11/18/1883	12:00	CST
3/31/1918	02:00	CWT
10/27/1918	02:00	CST
3/30/1919	02:00	CWT
10/26/1919	02:00	CST
4/30/1933	02:00	CDT
9/24/1933	02:00	CST
4/26/1936	02:00	CDT
9/27/1936	02:00	CST
5/02/1937	02:00	CDT
10/01/1937	02:00	CST
4/24/1938	02:00	CDT
9/25/1938	02:00	CST
4/30/1939	02:00	CDT
9/24/1939	02:00	CST
4/28/1940	02:00	CDT
9/29/1940	02:00	CST
2/09/1942	02:00	CWT
9/30/1945	02:00	CST
4/27/1947	02:00	CDT
9/28/1947	02:00	CST
4/25/1948	02:00	CDT
9/26/1948	02:00	CST
4/24/1949	02:00	CDT
9/25/1949	02:00	CST
4/30/1950	02:00	CDT
9/24/1950	02:00	CST
4/29/1951	02:00	CDT
9/30/1951	02:00	CST
4/27/1952	02:00	CDT
9/28/1952	02:00	CST
4/26/1953	02:00	CDT
9/27/1953	02:00	CST
4/25/1954	02:00	EST
4/27/1969	02:00	EDT
10/26/1969	02:00	EST
4/26/1970	02:00	EDT
10/25/1970	02:00	EST

IN # 40

Date	Time	Zone
Before 11/18/1883		LMT
11/18/1883	12:00	CST
3/31/1918	02:00	CWT
10/27/1918	02:00	CST
3/30/1919	02:00	CWT
10/26/1919	02:00	CST
4/26/1931	00:01	CDT
9/27/1931	00:01	CST
4/24/1932	00:01	CDT
9/25/1932	00:01	CST
4/30/1933	00:01	CDT
10/01/1933	00:01	CST
4/29/1934	00:01	CDT
9/30/1934	00:01	CST
4/28/1935	00:01	CDT
9/29/1935	00:01	CST
4/26/1936	02:00	CDT
9/27/1936	02:00	CST
4/25/1937	02:00	CDT
9/26/1937	02:00	CST
4/24/1938	02:00	CDT
9/25/1938	02:00	CST
4/30/1939	02:00	CDT
9/24/1939	02:00	CST
4/28/1940	02:00	CDT
9/29/1940	02:00	CST
4/27/1941	02:00	CDT
9/28/1941	02:00	CST
2/09/1942	02:00	CWT
9/30/1945	02:00	CST
4/28/1946	02:00	CDT
9/29/1946	02:00	CST
4/27/1947	02:00	CDT
9/28/1947	02:00	CST
4/25/1948	02:00	CDT
9/26/1948	02:00	CST
4/24/1949	02:00	CDT
9/25/1949	02:00	CST
4/30/1950	02:00	CDT
9/24/1950	02:00	CST
4/29/1951	02:00	CDT
9/30/1951	02:00	CST
4/27/1952	02:00	CDT
9/28/1952	02:00	CST
4/26/1953	02:00	CDT
9/27/1953	02:00	CST
4/25/1954	02:00	EST
4/27/1969	02:00	EDT
10/26/1969	02:00	EST
4/26/1970	02:00	EDT
10/25/1970	02:00	EST

IN # 41

Date	Time	Zone
Before 11/18/1883		LMT
11/18/1883	12:00	CST
3/31/1918	02:00	CWT
10/27/1918	02:00	CST
3/30/1919	02:00	CWT
10/26/1919	02:00	CST
4/28/1935	02:00	CDT
9/29/1935	02:00	CST
4/26/1936	02:00	CDT
9/27/1936	02:00	CST
4/25/1937	02:00	CDT
9/26/1937	02:00	CST
4/24/1938	02:00	CDT
9/11/1938	02:00	CST
5/01/1939	02:00	CDT
9/01/1939	02:00	CST
4/27/1941	02:00	CDT
11/23/1941	02:00	CST
2/09/1942	02:00	CWT
9/30/1945	02:00	CST
4/26/1953	02:00	CDT
9/27/1953	02:00	CST
4/25/1954	02:00	EST
4/27/1969	02:00	EDT
10/26/1969	02:00	EST
4/26/1970	02:00	EDT
10/25/1970	02:00	EST

IN # 42

Date	Time	Zone
Before 11/18/1883		LMT
11/18/1883	12:00	CST
3/31/1918	02:00	CWT
10/27/1918	02:00	CST
3/30/1919	02:00	CWT
10/26/1919	02:00	CST
4/28/1940	02:00	CDT
9/29/1940	02:00	CST
5/04/1941	00:01	CDT
9/01/1941	00:01	CST
2/09/1942	02:00	CWT
9/30/1945	02:00	CST
4/27/1947	02:00	CDT
9/28/1947	02:00	CST
4/25/1954	02:00	EST
4/27/1969	02:00	EDT
10/26/1969	02:00	EST
4/26/1970	02:00	EDT
10/25/1970	02:00	EST

IN # 43

Date	Time	Zone
Before 11/18/1883		LMT
11/18/1883	12:00	CST
3/31/1918	02:00	CWT
10/27/1918	02:00	CST
3/30/1919	02:00	CWT
10/26/1919	02:00	CST
4/24/1938	02:00	CDT
9/04/1938	02:00	CST
5/13/1939	02:00	CDT
10/01/1939	02:00	CST
4/27/1941	02:00	CDT
10/26/1941	02:00	CST
2/09/1942	02:00	CWT
9/30/1945	02:00	CST
4/28/1946	02:00	CDT
9/29/1946	02:00	CST
4/27/1947	02:00	CDT
9/28/1947	02:00	CST
4/25/1948	02:00	CDT
9/26/1948	02:00	CST
4/26/1953	02:00	CDT
9/27/1953	02:00	CST
4/25/1954	02:00	EST
4/27/1969	02:00	EDT
10/26/1969	02:00	EST
4/26/1970	02:00	EDT
10/25/1970	02:00	EST

IN # 44

Date	Time	Zone
Before 11/18/1883		LMT
11/18/1883	12:00	CST
3/31/1918	02:00	CWT
10/27/1918	02:00	CST
3/30/1919	02:00	CWT
10/26/1919	02:00	CST
4/29/1939	02:00	CDT
9/01/1939	02:00	CST
4/28/1940	02:00	CDT
9/02/1940	02:00	CST
4/27/1941	02:00	CDT
9/28/1941	02:00	CST
2/09/1942	02:00	CWT
9/30/1945	02:00	CST
4/28/1946	02:00	CDT
9/29/1946	02:00	CST
4/27/1947	02:00	CDT
9/28/1947	02:00	CST
4/25/1948	02:00	CDT
9/26/1948	02:00	CST
4/24/1949	02:00	CDT
9/25/1949	02:00	CST
4/30/1950	02:00	CDT
9/24/1950	02:00	CST
4/29/1951	02:00	CDT
9/30/1951	02:00	CST
4/27/1952	02:00	CDT
9/28/1952	02:00	CST
4/26/1953	02:00	CDT
9/27/1953	02:00	CST
4/25/1954	02:00	EST
4/27/1969	02:00	EDT
10/26/1969	02:00	EST
4/26/1970	02:00	EDT
10/25/1970	02:00	EST

IN # 45

Date	Time	Zone
Before 11/18/1883		LMT
11/18/1883	12:00	CST
3/31/1918	02:00	CWT
10/27/1918	02:00	CST
3/30/1919	02:00	CWT
10/26/1919	02:00	CST
4/28/1935	02:00	CDT
9/29/1935	02:00	CST
4/26/1936	02:00	CDT
9/27/1936	02:00	CST
4/25/1937	02:00	CDT
9/26/1937	02:00	CST
4/24/1938	02:00	CDT
9/25/1938	02:00	CST
4/30/1939	02:00	CDT
10/01/1939	02:00	CST
4/28/1940	02:00	CDT
9/29/1940	02:00	CST
4/27/1941	02:00	CDT
9/28/1941	02:00	CST
2/09/1942	02:00	CWT
9/30/1945	02:00	CST
4/25/1954	02:00	EST
4/27/1969	02:00	EDT
10/26/1969	02:00	EST
4/26/1970	02:00	EDT
10/25/1970	02:00	EST

IN # 46

Date	Time	Zone
Before 11/18/1883		LMT
11/18/1883	12:00	CST
3/31/1918	02:00	CWT
10/27/1918	02:00	CST
3/30/1919	02:00	CWT
10/26/1919	02:00	CST
4/25/1937	02:00	CDT
9/26/1937	02:00	CST
4/24/1938	02:00	CDT
9/25/1938	02:00	CST
4/30/1939	02:00	CDT
9/24/1939	02:00	CST
2/09/1942	02:00	CWT
9/30/1945	02:00	CST
4/28/1946	02:00	CDT
9/29/1946	02:00	CST
4/26/1953	02:00	CDT
9/27/1953	02:00	CST
4/25/1954	02:00	EST
4/27/1969	02:00	EDT
10/26/1969	02:00	EST
4/26/1970	02:00	EDT
10/25/1970	02:00	EST

IN # 47

Date	Time	Zone
Before 11/18/1883		LMT
11/18/1883	12:00	CST
3/31/1918	02:00	CWT
10/27/1918	02:00	CST
3/30/1919	02:00	CWT
10/26/1919	02:00	CST
4/28/1940	02:00	CDT
9/29/1940	02:00	CST
4/27/1941	02:00	CDT
9/28/1941	02:00	CST
2/09/1942	02:00	CWT
9/30/1945	02:00	CST
4/28/1946	02:00	CDT
9/29/1946	02:00	CST
4/27/1947	02:00	CDT
9/28/1947	02:00	CST
4/25/1948	02:00	CDT
9/26/1948	02:00	CST
4/24/1949	02:00	CDT
9/25/1949	02:00	CST
4/30/1950	02:00	CDT
9/24/1950	02:00	CST
4/29/1951	02:00	CDT
9/30/1951	02:00	CST
4/27/1952	02:00	CDT
9/28/1952	02:00	CST
4/26/1953	02:00	CDT
9/27/1953	02:00	CST
4/25/1954	02:00	EST
4/27/1969	02:00	EDT
10/26/1969	02:00	EST
4/26/1970	02:00	EDT
10/25/1970	02:00	EST

IN # 48

Date	Time	Zone
Before 11/18/1883		LMT
11/18/1883	12:00	CST
3/31/1918	02:00	CWT
10/27/1918	02:00	CST
3/30/1919	02:00	CWT
10/26/1919	02:00	CST
4/24/1938	02:00	CDT
9/25/1938	02:00	CST
4/30/1939	02:00	CDT
9/24/1939	02:00	CST
4/28/1940	02:00	CDT
9/29/1940	02:00	CST
4/27/1941	02:00	CDT
9/28/1941	02:00	CST
2/09/1942	02:00	CWT
9/30/1945	02:00	CST
4/27/1947	02:00	CDT
9/28/1947	02:00	CST
4/25/1948	02:00	CDT
9/26/1948	02:00	CST
4/26/1953	02:00	CDT
9/27/1953	02:00	CST
4/25/1954	02:00	EST
4/27/1969	02:00	EDT
10/26/1969	02:00	EST
4/26/1970	02:00	EDT
10/25/1970	02:00	EST

IN # 49

Date	Time	Zone
Before 11/18/1883		LMT
11/18/1883	12:00	CST
3/31/1918	02:00	CWT
10/27/1918	02:00	CST
3/30/1919	02:00	CWT
10/26/1919	02:00	CST
6/01/1937	02:00	CDT
9/01/1937	02:00	CST
5/15/1938	02:00	CDT
9/01/1938	02:00	CST
6/01/1939	02:00	CDT
9/01/1939	02:00	CST
4/28/1940	02:00	CDT
9/29/1940	02:00	CST
4/27/1941	02:00	CDT
9/28/1941	02:00	CST
2/09/1942	02:00	CWT
9/30/1945	02:00	CST
4/25/1954	02:00	EST
4/27/1969	02:00	EDT
10/26/1969	02:00	EST
4/26/1970	02:00	EDT
10/25/1970	02:00	EST

IN # 50

Date	Time	Zone
Before 11/18/1883		LMT
11/18/1883	12:00	CST
3/31/1918	02:00	CWT
10/27/1918	02:00	CST
3/30/1919	02:00	CWT
10/26/1919	02:00	CST
4/24/1938	02:00	CDT
9/25/1938	02:00	CST
4/30/1939	02:00	CDT
9/24/1939	02:00	CST
4/28/1940	02:00	CDT
9/29/1940	02:00	CST
4/27/1941	02:00	CDT
9/28/1941	02:00	CST
2/09/1942	02:00	CWT
9/30/1945	02:00	CST
4/25/1954	02:00	EST
4/27/1969	02:00	EDT
10/26/1969	02:00	EST
4/26/1970	02:00	EDT
10/25/1970	02:00	EST

IN # 51

Date	Time	Zone
Before 11/18/1883		LMT
11/18/1883	12:00	CST
3/31/1918	02:00	CWT
10/27/1918	02:00	CST
3/30/1919	02:00	CWT
10/26/1919	02:00	CST
2/09/1942	02:00	CWT
9/30/1945	02:00	CST
4/25/1954	02:00	EST
4/30/1967	02:00	US#1

IN # 52

Date	Time	Zone
Before 11/18/1883		LMT
11/18/1883	12:00	CST
3/31/1918	02:00	CWT
10/27/1918	02:00	CST
3/30/1919	02:00	CWT
10/26/1919	02:00	CST
2/09/1942	02:00	CWT
9/30/1945	02:00	CST
4/26/1953	02:00	CDT
9/27/1953	02:00	CST
4/25/1954	02:00	CDT
9/26/1954	02:00	CST
4/24/1955	02:00	CDT
9/25/1955	02:00	CST
4/29/1956	02:00	CDT
9/30/1956	02:00	CST
4/28/1957	02:00	CDT
9/29/1957	02:00	CST
4/27/1958	02:00	CDT
9/28/1958	02:00	CST
4/26/1959	02:00	CDT
9/27/1959	02:00	CST
4/24/1960	02:00	CDT
9/25/1960	02:00	CST
4/30/1961	02:00	CDT
10/29/1961	02:00	CST
4/29/1962	02:00	CDT
10/28/1962	02:00	CST
4/28/1963	02:00	CDT
10/27/1963	02:00	CST
4/26/1964	02:00	CDT
10/25/1964	02:00	CST
4/25/1965	02:00	EST
10/30/1966	02:00	CST
4/30/1967	02:00	US#1

IN # 53

Date	Time	Zone
Before 11/18/1883		LMT
11/18/1883	12:00	CST
3/31/1918	02:00	CWT
10/27/1918	02:00	CST
3/30/1919	02:00	CWT
10/26/1919	02:00	CST
2/09/1942	02:00	CWT
9/30/1945	02:00	CST
4/24/1955	02:00	CDT
9/25/1955	02:00	CST
4/29/1956	02:00	CDT
9/30/1956	02:00	CST
4/28/1957	02:00	CDT
9/29/1957	02:00	CST
4/27/1958	02:00	CDT
9/28/1958	02:00	CST
4/26/1959	02:00	CDT
9/27/1959	02:00	CST
4/24/1960	02:00	CDT
9/25/1960	02:00	CST
4/30/1961	02:00	CDT
10/29/1961	02:00	CST
4/29/1962	02:00	CDT
10/28/1962	02:00	CST
4/28/1963	02:00	CDT
10/27/1963	02:00	CST
4/26/1964	02:00	CDT
10/25/1964	02:00	CST
4/25/1965	02:00	EST
10/30/1966	02:00	CST
4/30/1967	02:00	US#1

IN # 54

Date	Time	Zone
Before 11/18/1883		LMT
11/18/1883	12:00	CST
3/31/1918	02:00	CWT
10/27/1918	02:00	CST
3/30/1919	02:00	CWT
10/26/1919	02:00	CST
2/09/1942	02:00	CWT
9/30/1945	02:00	CST
4/26/1953	02:00	CDT
9/27/1953	02:00	CST
4/25/1954	02:00	CDT
9/26/1954	02:00	CST
5/01/1955	00:00	CDT
9/04/1955	00:00	CST
4/29/1956	02:00	CDT

TIME TABLES

9/02/1956 02:00 CST
4/28/1957 02:00 CDT
9/29/1957 02:00 CST
4/27/1958 02:00 CDT
9/28/1958 02:00 CST
4/26/1959 02:00 CDT
9/27/1959 02:00 CST
4/24/1960 02:00 CDT
9/25/1960 02:00 CST
4/30/1961 02:00 CDT
10/29/1961 02:00 CST
4/29/1962 02:00 CDT
10/28/1962 02:00 CST
4/28/1963 02:00 CDT
10/27/1963 02:00 CST
4/26/1964 02:00 CDT
10/25/1964 02:00 CST
4/25/1965 02:00 EST
10/30/1966 02:00 CST
4/30/1967 02:00 US#1

IN # 55
Before 11/18/1883 LMT
11/18/1883 12:00 CST
3/31/1918 02:00 CWT
10/27/1918 02:00 CST
3/30/1919 02:00 CWT
10/26/1919 02:00 CST
2/09/1942 02:00 CWT
9/30/1945 02:00 CST
5/02/1948 02:00 CDT
10/26/1948 02:00 CST
4/29/1951 02:00 CDT
9/30/1951 02:00 CST
4/24/1955 02:00 CDT
9/25/1955 02:00 CST
4/29/1956 02:00 CDT
9/30/1956 02:00 CST
4/28/1957 02:00 CDT
9/29/1957 02:00 CST
4/27/1958 02:00 CDT
10/26/1958 02:00 CST
4/26/1959 02:00 CDT
9/27/1959 02:00 CST
4/24/1960 02:00 CDT
9/25/1960 02:00 CST
4/30/1961 02:00 CDT
9/24/1961 02:00 CST
4/29/1962 02:00 CDT
10/28/1962 02:00 CST
4/28/1963 02:00 CDT
10/27/1963 02:00 CST
4/26/1964 02:00 CDT
10/25/1964 02:00 CST
4/25/1965 02:00 EST
10/30/1966 02:00 CST
4/30/1967 02:00 US#1

IN # 56
Before 11/18/1883 LMT
11/18/1883 12:00 CST
3/31/1918 02:00 CWT
10/27/1918 02:00 CST
3/30/1919 02:00 CWT
10/26/1919 02:00 CST
2/09/1942 02:00 CWT
9/30/1945 02:00 CST
5/01/1955 00:00 CDT
9/25/1955 02:00 CST
4/29/1956 02:00 CDT
9/30/1956 02:00 CST
4/28/1957 02:00 CDT
9/29/1957 02:00 CST
4/27/1958 02:00 CDT
10/01/1958 02:00 CST
4/26/1959 02:00 CDT
9/27/1959 02:00 CST
4/24/1960 02:00 CDT
9/25/1960 02:00 CST
4/30/1961 02:00 CDT
10/29/1961 02:00 CST
4/29/1962 02:00 CDT
10/28/1962 02:00 CST
4/28/1963 02:00 CDT
10/27/1963 02:00 CST
4/26/1964 02:00 CDT
10/25/1964 02:00 CST
4/25/1965 02:00 EST
10/30/1966 02:00 CST
4/30/1967 02:00 US#1

IN # 57
Before 11/18/1883 LMT
11/18/1883 12:00 CST
3/31/1918 02:00 CWT
10/27/1918 02:00 CST
3/30/1919 02:00 CWT
10/26/1919 02:00 CST
2/09/1942 02:00 CWT
9/30/1945 02:00 CST
5/01/1955 02:00 CDT
9/25/1955 02:00 CST
5/01/1956 02:00 CDT
9/25/1956 02:00 CST
4/28/1957 02:00 CDT
9/29/1957 02:00 CST
4/27/1958 02:00 CDT
9/28/1958 02:00 CST
4/26/1959 02:00 CDT
9/27/1959 02:00 CST
4/24/1960 02:00 CDT
9/25/1960 02:00 CST
4/30/1961 02:00 CDT
10/29/1961 02:00 CST
4/29/1962 02:00 CDT
10/28/1962 02:00 CST
4/28/1963 02:00 CDT
10/27/1963 02:00 CST
4/26/1964 02:00 CDT
10/25/1964 02:00 CST
4/25/1965 02:00 EST
10/30/1966 02:00 CST
4/30/1967 02:00 US#1

IN # 58
Before 11/18/1883 LMT
11/18/1883 12:00 CST
3/31/1918 02:00 CWT
10/27/1918 02:00 CST
3/30/1919 02:00 CWT
10/26/1919 02:00 CST
2/09/1942 02:00 CWT
9/30/1945 02:00 CST
4/24/1955 02:00 CDT
9/25/1955 02:00 CST
4/29/1956 02:00 CDT
10/28/1956 02:00 CST
4/28/1957 02:00 CDT
9/29/1957 02:00 CST
4/27/1958 02:00 CDT
9/28/1958 02:00 CST
4/26/1959 02:00 CDT
9/27/1959 02:00 CST
4/24/1960 02:00 CDT
9/25/1960 02:00 CST
4/30/1961 02:00 CDT
10/29/1961 02:00 CST
4/29/1962 02:00 CDT
10/28/1962 02:00 CST
4/28/1963 02:00 CDT
10/27/1963 02:00 CST
4/26/1964 02:00 CDT
10/25/1964 02:00 CST
4/25/1965 02:00 EST
10/30/1966 02:00 CST
4/30/1967 02:00 US#1

IN # 59
Before 11/18/1883 LMT
11/18/1883 12:00 CST
3/31/1918 02:00 CWT
10/27/1918 02:00 CST
3/30/1919 02:00 CWT
10/26/1919 02:00 CST
2/09/1942 02:00 CWT
9/30/1945 02:00 CST
5/01/1955 00:00 CDT
9/25/1955 02:00 CST
4/29/1956 02:00 CDT
9/30/1956 02:00 CST
4/28/1957 02:00 CDT
9/29/1957 02:00 CST
4/27/1958 02:00 CDT
9/28/1958 02:00 CST
4/26/1959 02:00 CDT
9/27/1959 02:00 CST
4/24/1960 02:00 CDT
9/25/1960 02:00 CST
4/30/1961 02:00 CDT
10/29/1961 02:00 CST
4/29/1962 02:00 CDT
10/28/1962 02:00 CST
4/28/1963 02:00 CDT
10/27/1963 02:00 CST
4/26/1964 02:00 CDT
10/25/1964 02:00 CST
4/25/1965 02:00 EST
10/30/1966 02:00 CST
4/30/1967 02:00 US#1

IN # 60
Before 11/18/1883 LMT
11/18/1883 12:00 CST
3/31/1918 02:00 CWT
10/27/1918 02:00 CST
3/30/1919 02:00 CWT
10/26/1919 02:00 CST
2/09/1942 02:00 CWT
9/30/1945 02:00 CST
5/01/1955 00:00 CDT
9/25/1955 02:00 CST
4/29/1956 02:00 CDT
10/28/1956 02:00 CST
4/28/1957 02:00 CDT
9/29/1957 02:00 CST
4/27/1958 02:00 CDT
9/28/1958 02:00 CST
4/26/1959 02:00 CDT
9/27/1959 02:00 CST
4/24/1960 02:00 CDT
9/25/1960 02:00 CST
4/30/1961 02:00 CDT
10/29/1961 02:00 CST
4/29/1962 02:00 CDT
10/28/1962 02:00 CST
4/28/1963 02:00 CDT
10/27/1963 02:00 CST
4/26/1964 02:00 CDT
10/25/1964 02:00 CST
4/25/1965 02:00 EST
10/30/1966 02:00 CST
4/30/1967 02:00 US#1

IN # 61
Before 11/18/1883 LMT
11/18/1883 12:00 CST
3/31/1918 02:00 CWT
10/27/1918 02:00 CST
3/30/1919 02:00 CWT
10/26/1919 02:00 CST
2/09/1942 02:00 CWT
9/30/1945 02:00 CST
5/01/1955 00:00 CDT
8/28/1955 00:00 CST
4/29/1956 02:00 CDT
9/30/1956 02:00 CST
4/28/1957 02:00 CDT
9/29/1957 02:00 CST
4/27/1958 02:00 CDT
9/28/1958 02:00 CST
4/26/1959 02:00 CDT
9/27/1959 02:00 CST
4/24/1960 02:00 CDT
9/25/1960 02:00 CST
4/30/1961 02:00 CDT
10/29/1961 02:00 CST
4/29/1962 02:00 CDT
10/28/1962 02:00 CST
4/28/1963 02:00 CDT
10/27/1963 02:00 CST
4/26/1964 02:00 CDT
10/25/1964 02:00 CST
4/25/1965 02:00 EST
10/30/1966 02:00 CST
4/30/1967 02:00 US#1

IN # 62
Before 11/18/1883 LMT
11/18/1883 12:00 CST
3/31/1918 02:00 CWT
10/27/1918 02:00 CST
3/30/1919 02:00 CWT
10/26/1919 02:00 CST
2/09/1942 02:00 CWT
9/30/1945 02:00 CST
5/01/1955 00:00 CDT
8/29/1955 00:00 CST
4/29/1956 02:00 CDT
9/30/1956 02:00 CST
4/28/1957 02:00 CDT
9/29/1957 02:00 CST
4/27/1958 02:00 CDT
9/28/1958 02:00 CST
4/26/1959 02:00 CDT
9/27/1959 02:00 CST
4/24/1960 02:00 CDT
9/25/1960 02:00 CST
4/30/1961 02:00 CDT
10/29/1961 02:00 CST
4/29/1962 02:00 CDT
10/28/1962 02:00 CST
4/28/1963 02:00 CDT
10/27/1963 02:00 CST
4/26/1964 02:00 CDT
10/25/1964 02:00 CST
4/25/1965 02:00 EST
10/30/1966 02:00 CST
4/30/1967 02:00 US#1

IN # 63
Before 11/18/1883 LMT
11/18/1883 12:00 CST
3/31/1918 02:00 CWT
10/27/1918 02:00 CST
3/30/1919 02:00 CWT
10/26/1919 02:00 CST
2/09/1942 02:00 CWT
9/30/1945 02:00 CST
4/24/1955 02:00 CDT
9/25/1955 02:00 CST
4/29/1956 02:00 CDT
9/30/1956 02:00 CST
4/28/1957 02:00 CDT
9/29/1957 02:00 CST
4/27/1958 02:00 CDT
9/28/1958 02:00 CST
4/26/1959 02:00 CDT
9/27/1959 02:00 CST
4/24/1960 02:00 CDT
9/25/1960 02:00 CST
4/30/1961 02:00 CDT
10/29/1961 02:00 CST
4/29/1962 02:00 CDT
10/28/1962 02:00 CST
4/28/1963 02:00 CDT
10/27/1963 02:00 CST
4/26/1964 02:00 EST
10/30/1966 02:00 CST
4/30/1967 02:00 US#1

IN # 64
Before 11/18/1883 LMT
11/18/1883 12:00 CST
3/31/1918 02:00 CWT
10/27/1918 02:00 CST
3/30/1919 02:00 CWT
10/26/1919 02:00 CST
2/09/1942 02:00 CWT
9/30/1945 02:00 CST
5/01/1955 00:00 CDT
8/28/1955 00:00 CST
4/29/1956 02:00 CDT
9/30/1956 02:00 CST
4/28/1957 02:00 CDT
9/29/1957 02:00 CST
4/27/1958 02:00 CDT
9/28/1958 02:00 CST
4/26/1959 02:00 CDT
9/27/1959 02:00 CST
4/24/1960 02:00 CDT
9/25/1960 02:00 CST
4/30/1961 02:00 CDT
10/29/1961 02:00 CST
4/29/1962 02:00 CDT
10/28/1962 02:00 CST
4/28/1963 02:00 CDT
10/27/1963 02:00 CST
4/26/1964 02:00 EST
10/30/1966 02:00 CST
4/30/1967 02:00 US#1

IN # 65
Before 11/18/1883 LMT
11/18/1883 12:00 CST
3/31/1918 02:00 CWT
10/27/1918 02:00 CST
3/30/1919 02:00 CWT
10/26/1919 02:00 CST
2/09/1942 02:00 CWT
9/30/1945 02:00 CST
4/26/1953 02:00 CDT
9/27/1953 02:00 CST
4/25/1954 02:00 CDT
9/26/1954 02:00 CST
5/01/1955 00:00 CDT
8/28/1955 00:00 CST
4/29/1956 02:00 CDT
9/30/1956 02:00 CST
4/28/1957 02:00 CDT
9/29/1957 02:00 CST
4/27/1958 02:00 CDT
9/28/1958 02:00 CST
4/26/1959 02:00 CDT
9/27/1959 02:00 CST
4/24/1960 02:00 CDT
9/25/1960 02:00 CST
4/30/1961 02:00 CDT
10/29/1961 02:00 CST
4/29/1962 02:00 CDT
10/28/1962 02:00 CST
4/28/1963 02:00 CDT
10/27/1963 02:00 CST
4/26/1964 02:00 EST
10/30/1966 02:00 CST
4/30/1967 02:00 US#1

IN # 66
Before 11/18/1883 LMT
11/18/1883 12:00 CST
3/31/1918 02:00 CWT
10/27/1918 02:00 CST
3/30/1919 02:00 CWT
10/26/1919 02:00 CST
2/09/1942 02:00 CWT
9/30/1945 02:00 CST
4/29/1951 02:00 CDT
9/30/1951 02:00 CST
5/01/1955 00:00 CDT
9/04/1955 00:00 CST
4/29/1956 02:00 CDT
9/30/1956 02:00 CST
4/28/1957 02:00 CDT
9/29/1957 02:00 CST
4/27/1958 02:00 CDT
9/28/1958 02:00 CST
4/26/1959 02:00 CDT
9/27/1959 02:00 CST
4/24/1960 02:00 CDT
9/25/1960 02:00 CST
4/30/1961 02:00 CDT
10/29/1961 02:00 CST
4/29/1962 02:00 CDT
10/28/1962 02:00 CST
4/28/1963 02:00 CDT
10/27/1963 02:00 CST
4/26/1964 02:00 EST
10/30/1966 02:00 CST
4/30/1967 02:00 CDT
10/29/1967 02:00 CST
4/28/1968 02:00 CDT
10/27/1968 02:00 CST
4/27/1969 02:00 EDT
10/26/1969 02:00 EST
4/26/1970 02:00 EDT
10/25/1970 02:00 EST

IN # 67
Before 11/18/1883 LMT
11/18/1883 12:00 CST
3/31/1918 02:00 CWT
10/27/1918 02:00 CST
3/30/1919 02:00 CWT
10/26/1919 02:00 CST
2/09/1942 02:00 CWT
9/30/1945 02:00 CST
5/01/1955 00:00 CDT
9/04/1955 00:00 CST
4/29/1956 02:00 CDT
9/30/1956 02:00 CST
4/28/1957 02:00 CDT
9/29/1957 02:00 CST
4/27/1958 02:00 CDT
9/28/1958 02:00 CST
4/26/1959 02:00 CDT
9/27/1959 02:00 CST
4/24/1960 02:00 CDT
9/25/1960 02:00 CST
4/30/1961 02:00 CDT
10/29/1961 02:00 CST
4/29/1962 02:00 CDT
10/28/1962 02:00 CST
4/28/1963 02:00 CDT
10/27/1963 02:00 CST
4/26/1964 02:00 EST
10/30/1966 02:00 CST
4/30/1967 02:00 CDT
10/29/1967 02:00 CST
4/28/1968 02:00 CDT
10/27/1968 02:00 CST
4/27/1969 02:00 EDT
10/26/1969 02:00 EST
4/26/1970 02:00 EDT
10/25/1970 02:00 EST

IN # 68
Before 11/18/1883 LMT
11/18/1883 12:00 CST
3/31/1918 02:00 CWT
10/27/1918 02:00 CST
3/30/1919 02:00 CWT
10/26/1919 02:00 CST
2/09/1942 02:00 CWT
9/30/1945 02:00 CST
5/01/1955 02:00 CDT
9/25/1955 02:00 CST
4/29/1956 02:00 CDT
9/30/1956 02:00 CST
4/28/1957 02:00 CDT
9/29/1957 02:00 CST
4/27/1958 02:00 CDT
9/28/1958 02:00 CST
4/26/1959 02:00 CDT
9/27/1959 02:00 CST
4/24/1960 02:00 CDT
9/25/1960 02:00 CST
4/30/1961 02:00 CDT
10/29/1961 02:00 CST
4/29/1962 02:00 CDT
10/28/1962 02:00 CST
4/28/1963 02:00 CDT
10/27/1963 02:00 CST
4/26/1964 02:00 EST
10/29/1967 02:00 CST
4/28/1968 02:00 CDT
10/27/1968 02:00 CST
4/27/1969 02:00 EDT
10/26/1969 02:00 EST
4/26/1970 02:00 EDT
10/25/1970 02:00 EST

IN # 69
Before 11/18/1883 LMT
11/18/1883 12:00 CST
3/31/1918 02:00 CWT
10/27/1918 02:00 CST
3/30/1919 02:00 CWT
10/26/1919 02:00 CST
2/09/1942 02:00 CWT
9/30/1945 02:00 CST
5/01/1955 00:00 CDT
8/28/1955 00:00 CST
4/29/1956 02:00 CDT
9/30/1956 02:00 CST
4/28/1957 02:00 CDT
9/29/1957 02:00 CST
4/27/1958 02:00 CDT
9/28/1958 02:00 CST
4/26/1959 02:00 CDT
9/27/1959 02:00 CST
4/24/1960 02:00 CDT
9/25/1960 02:00 CST
4/30/1961 02:00 CDT
10/29/1961 02:00 CST
4/29/1962 02:00 CDT
10/28/1962 02:00 CST
4/28/1963 02:00 CDT
10/27/1963 02:00 CST
4/26/1964 02:00 EST
10/29/1967 02:00 CST
4/28/1968 02:00 CDT
10/27/1968 02:00 CST
4/27/1969 02:00 EDT
10/26/1969 02:00 EST
4/26/1970 02:00 EDT
10/25/1970 02:00 EST

IN # 70
Before 11/18/1883 LMT
11/18/1883 12:00 CST
3/31/1918 02:00 CWT
10/27/1918 02:00 CST
3/30/1919 02:00 CWT
10/26/1919 02:00 CST
2/09/1942 02:00 CWT
9/30/1945 02:00 CST
4/27/1952 02:00 CDT
9/28/1952 02:00 CST
4/24/1955 02:00 CDT
9/25/1955 02:00 CST
4/29/1956 02:00 CDT
9/30/1956 02:00 CST
4/28/1957 02:00 CDT
9/29/1957 02:00 CST
4/27/1958 02:00 CDT
9/28/1958 02:00 CST
4/26/1959 02:00 CDT
9/27/1959 02:00 CST
4/24/1960 02:00 CDT
9/25/1960 02:00 CST
4/30/1961 02:00 CDT
10/29/1961 02:00 CST
4/29/1962 02:00 CDT
10/28/1962 02:00 CST
4/28/1963 02:00 CDT
10/27/1963 02:00 CST
4/26/1964 02:00 EST
4/27/1969 02:00 EDT
10/26/1969 02:00 EST
4/26/1970 02:00 EDT
10/25/1970 02:00 EST

IN # 71
Before 11/18/1883 LMT
11/18/1883 12:00 CST
3/31/1918 02:00 CWT
10/27/1918 02:00 CST
3/30/1919 02:00 CWT
10/26/1919 02:00 CST
2/09/1942 02:00 CWT
9/30/1945 02:00 CST
4/30/1950 02:00 CDT
9/24/1950 02:00 CST
4/27/1952 02:00 CDT
9/28/1952 02:00 CST
4/26/1953 02:00 CDT
9/27/1953 02:00 CST
4/25/1954 02:00 CDT
9/26/1954 02:00 CST
4/24/1955 02:00 CDT
9/25/1955 02:00 CST
4/29/1956 02:00 CDT
10/28/1956 02:00 CST
4/28/1957 02:00 CDT
9/29/1957 02:00 CST
4/27/1958 02:00 CDT
10/26/1958 02:00 CST
4/26/1959 02:00 CDT
10/25/1959 02:00 CST
4/24/1960 02:00 CDT
10/30/1960 02:00 CST

TIME TABLES

4/30/1961 02:00 CDT
10/29/1961 02:00 CST
4/29/1962 02:00 CDT
10/28/1962 02:00 CST
4/28/1963 02:00 CDT
10/27/1963 02:00 CST
4/26/1964 02:00 EST
4/27/1969 02:00 EDT
10/26/1969 02:00 EST
4/26/1970 02:00 EDT
10/25/1970 02:00 EST

....

IN # 72
Before 11/18/1883 LMT
11/18/1883 12:00 CST
3/31/1918 02:00 CWT
10/27/1918 02:00 CST
3/30/1919 02:00 CWT
10/26/1919 02:00 CST
2/09/1942 02:00 CWT
9/30/1945 02:00 CST
4/26/1953 02:00 CDT
9/27/1953 02:00 CST
4/25/1954 02:00 CDT
9/26/1954 02:00 CST
4/24/1955 02:00 CDT
9/25/1955 02:00 CST
4/29/1956 02:00 CDT
9/30/1956 02:00 CST
4/28/1957 02:00 CDT
9/29/1957 02:00 CST
4/27/1958 02:00 CDT
9/28/1958 02:00 CST
4/26/1959 02:00 CDT
9/27/1959 02:00 CST
4/24/1960 02:00 CDT
9/25/1960 02:00 CST
4/30/1961 02:00 CDT
10/29/1961 02:00 CST
4/29/1962 02:00 CDT
10/28/1962 02:00 CST
4/28/1963 02:00 CDT
10/27/1963 02:00 CST
4/26/1964 02:00 EST
4/27/1969 02:00 EDT
10/26/1969 02:00 EST
4/26/1970 02:00 EDT
10/25/1970 02:00 EST

....

IN # 73
Before 11/18/1883 LMT
11/18/1883 12:00 CST
3/31/1918 02:00 CWT
10/27/1918 02:00 CST
3/30/1919 02:00 CWT
10/26/1919 02:00 CST
2/09/1942 02:00 CWT
9/30/1945 02:00 CST
4/24/1955 02:00 CDT
9/25/1955 02:00 CST
4/29/1956 02:00 CDT
9/30/1956 02:00 CST
4/28/1957 02:00 CDT
9/29/1957 02:00 CST
4/27/1958 02:00 CDT
9/28/1958 02:00 CST
4/26/1959 02:00 CDT
9/27/1959 02:00 CST
4/24/1960 02:00 CDT
9/25/1960 02:00 CST
4/30/1961 02:00 CDT
10/29/1961 02:00 CST
4/29/1962 02:00 CDT
10/28/1962 02:00 CST
4/28/1963 02:00 CDT
10/27/1963 02:00 CST
4/26/1964 02:00 EST
4/27/1969 02:00 EDT
10/26/1969 02:00 EST
4/26/1970 02:00 EDT
10/25/1970 02:00 EST

....

IN # 74
Before 11/18/1883 LMT
11/18/1883 12:00 CST
3/31/1918 02:00 CWT
10/27/1918 02:00 CST
3/30/1919 02:00 CWT
10/26/1919 02:00 CST
2/09/1942 02:00 CWT
9/30/1945 02:00 CST
4/26/1953 02:00 CDT
9/27/1953 02:00 CST
4/25/1954 02:00 CDT
9/26/1954 02:00 CST
5/01/1955 00:00 CDT
9/04/1955 00:00 CST
4/29/1956 02:00 CDT
9/02/1956 02:00 CST
4/28/1957 02:00 CDT
9/29/1957 02:00 CST
4/27/1958 02:00 CDT
9/28/1958 02:00 CST
4/26/1959 02:00 CDT
9/27/1959 02:00 CST
4/24/1960 02:00 CDT
9/25/1960 02:00 CST
4/30/1961 02:00 CDT
10/29/1961 02:00 CST
4/29/1962 02:00 CDT
10/28/1962 02:00 CST
4/28/1963 02:00 CDT
10/27/1963 02:00 CST
4/26/1964 02:00 EST
4/27/1969 02:00 EDT
10/26/1969 02:00 EST
4/26/1970 02:00 EDT
10/25/1970 02:00 EST

....

IN # 75
Before 11/18/1883 LMT
11/18/1883 12:00 CST
3/31/1918 02:00 CWT
10/27/1918 02:00 CST
3/30/1919 02:00 CWT
10/26/1919 02:00 CST
2/09/1942 02:00 CWT
9/30/1945 02:00 CST
5/01/1946 02:00 CDT
9/29/1946 02:00 CST
4/26/1953 02:00 CDT
9/27/1953 02:00 CST
4/25/1954 02:00 CDT
9/26/1954 02:00 CST
4/24/1955 02:00 CDT
9/25/1955 02:00 CST
4/29/1956 02:00 CDT
10/28/1956 02:00 CST
4/28/1957 02:00 CDT
9/29/1957 02:00 CST
4/27/1958 02:00 CDT
10/26/1958 02:00 CST
4/26/1959 02:00 CDT
10/25/1959 02:00 CST
4/24/1960 02:00 CDT
10/30/1960 02:00 CST
4/30/1961 02:00 CDT
10/29/1961 02:00 CST
4/29/1962 02:00 CDT
10/28/1962 02:00 CST
4/28/1963 02:00 CDT
10/27/1963 02:00 CST
4/26/1964 02:00 EST
4/27/1969 02:00 EDT
10/26/1969 02:00 EST
4/26/1970 02:00 EDT
10/25/1970 02:00 EST

....

IN # 76
Before 11/18/1883 LMT
11/18/1883 12:00 CST
3/31/1918 02:00 CWT
10/27/1918 02:00 CST
3/30/1919 02:00 CWT
10/26/1919 02:00 CST
2/09/1942 02:00 CWT
9/30/1945 02:00 CST
4/28/1946 02:00 CDT
9/29/1946 02:00 CST
4/30/1950 02:00 CDT
9/24/1950 02:00 CST
4/27/1952 02:00 CDT
9/28/1952 02:00 CST
4/26/1953 02:00 CDT
9/27/1953 02:00 CST
4/25/1954 02:00 CDT
9/26/1954 02:00 CST
4/24/1955 02:00 CDT
9/25/1955 02:00 CST
4/29/1956 02:00 CDT
10/28/1956 02:00 CST
4/28/1957 02:00 CDT
9/29/1957 02:00 CST
4/27/1958 02:00 CDT
10/26/1958 02:00 CST
4/26/1959 02:00 CDT
10/05/1959 00:01 CST
4/24/1960 02:00 CDT
9/25/1960 02:00 CST
4/30/1961 02:00 CDT
10/29/1961 02:00 CST
4/29/1962 02:00 CDT
10/28/1962 02:00 CST
4/28/1963 02:00 CDT
10/27/1963 02:00 CST
4/26/1964 02:00 EST
4/27/1969 02:00 EDT
10/26/1969 02:00 EST
4/26/1970 02:00 EDT
10/25/1970 02:00 EST

....

IN # 77
Before 11/18/1883 LMT
11/18/1883 12:00 CST
3/31/1918 02:00 CWT
10/27/1918 02:00 CST
3/30/1919 02:00 CWT
10/26/1919 02:00 CST
2/09/1942 02:00 CWT
9/30/1945 02:00 CST
4/28/1946 02:00 CDT
9/29/1946 02:00 CST
4/30/1950 02:00 CDT
9/24/1950 02:00 CST
4/29/1951 02:00 CDT
9/30/1951 02:00 CST
4/27/1952 02:00 CDT
9/28/1952 02:00 CST
4/26/1953 02:00 CDT
9/27/1953 02:00 CST
4/25/1954 02:00 CDT
9/26/1954 02:00 CST
4/24/1955 02:00 CDT
9/25/1955 02:00 CST
4/29/1956 02:00 CDT
10/28/1956 02:00 CST
4/28/1957 02:00 CDT
9/29/1957 02:00 CST
4/27/1958 02:00 CDT
10/26/1958 02:00 CST
4/26/1959 02:00 CDT
4/27/1959 02:00 C T
9/27/1959 02:00 CST
4/24/1960 02:00 CDT
9/25/1960 02:00 CST
4/30/1961 02:00 CDT
10/29/1961 02:00 CST
4/29/1962 02:00 CDT
10/28/1962 02:00 CST
4/28/1963 02:00 CDT
10/27/1963 02:00 CST
4/26/1964 02:00 EST
4/27/1969 02:00 EDT
10/26/1969 02:00 EST
4/26/1970 02:00 EDT
10/25/1970 02:00 EST

....

IN # 78
Before 11/18/1883 LMT
11/18/1883 12:00 CST
3/31/1918 02:00 CWT
10/27/1918 02:00 CST
3/30/1919 02:00 CWT
10/26/1919 02:00 CST
2/09/1942 02:00 CWT
9/30/1945 02:00 CST
4/28/1946 02:00 CDT
9/29/1946 02:00 CST
4/26/1953 02:00 CDT
9/27/1953 02:00 CST
4/25/1954 02:00 CDT
9/26/1954 02:00 CST
5/01/1955 00:00 CDT
9/25/1955 02:00 CST
4/29/1956 02:00 CDT
9/30/1956 02:00 CST
4/28/1957 02:00 CDT
9/29/1957 02:00 CST
4/27/1958 02:00 CDT
9/28/1958 02:00 CST
4/26/1959 02:00 CDT
9/27/1959 02:00 CST
4/24/1960 02:00 CDT
10/30/1960 02:00 CST
4/30/1961 02:00 CDT
9/24/1961 02:00 CST
4/29/1962 02:00 CDT
10/28/1962 02:00 CST
4/28/1963 02:00 CDT
10/27/1963 02:00 CST
4/26/1964 02:00 EST
4/27/1969 02:00 EDT
10/26/1969 02:00 EST
4/26/1970 02:00 EDT
10/25/1970 02:00 EST

....

IN # 79
Before 11/18/1883 LMT
11/18/1883 12:00 CST
3/31/1918 02:00 CWT
10/27/1918 02:00 CST
3/30/1919 02:00 CWT
10/26/1919 02:00 CST
2/09/1942 02:00 CWT
9/30/1945 02:00 CST
4/30/1950 02:00 CDT
9/24/1950 02:00 CST
4/24/1955 02:00 CDT
9/25/1955 02:00 CST
4/29/1956 02:00 CDT
9/30/1956 02:00 CST
4/28/1957 02:00 CDT
9/29/1957 02:00 CST
4/27/1958 02:00 CDT
9/28/1958 02:00 CST
4/26/1959 02:00 CDT
9/27/1959 02:00 CST
4/24/1960 02:00 CDT
9/25/1960 02:00 CST
4/30/1961 02:00 CDT
10/29/1961 02:00 CST
4/29/1962 02:00 CDT
10/28/1962 02:00 CST
4/28/1963 02:00 CDT
10/27/1963 02:00 CST
4/26/1964 02:00 EST
4/27/1969 02:00 EDT
10/26/1969 02:00 EST
4/26/1970 02:00 EDT
10/25/1970 02:00 EST

....

IN # 80
Before 11/18/1883 LMT
11/18/1883 12:00 CST
3/31/1918 02:00 CWT
10/27/1918 02:00 CST
3/30/1919 02:00 CWT
10/26/1919 02:00 CST
2/09/1942 02:00 CWT
9/30/1945 02:00 CST
4/26/1953 02:00 CDT
9/27/1953 02:00 CST
4/25/1954 02:00 CDT
9/26/1954 02:00 CST
4/24/1955 02:00 CDT
9/25/1955 02:00 CST
4/29/1956 02:00 CDT
10/28/1956 02:00 CST
4/28/1957 02:00 CDT
9/29/1957 02:00 CST
4/27/1958 02:00 CDT
10/26/1958 02:00 CST
4/26/1959 02:00 CDT
10/25/1959 02:00 CST
4/24/1960 02:00 CDT
10/30/1960 02:00 CST
4/30/1961 02:00 CDT
10/29/1961 02:00 CST
4/29/1962 02:00 CDT
10/28/1962 02:00 CST
4/28/1963 02:00 CDT
10/27/1963 02:00 CST
4/26/1964 02:00 EST
4/27/1969 02:00 EDT
10/26/1969 02:00 EST
4/26/1970 02:00 EDT
10/25/1970 02:00 EST

....

IN # 81
Before 11/18/1883 LMT
11/18/1883 12:00 CST
3/31/1918 02:00 CWT
10/27/1918 02:00 CST
3/30/1919 02:00 CWT
10/26/1919 02:00 CST
2/09/1942 02:00 CWT
9/30/1945 02:00 CST
4/28/1946 02:00 CDT
9/29/1946 02:00 CST
4/30/1950 02:00 CDT
9/24/1950 02:00 CST
4/26/1953 02:00 CDT
9/27/1953 02:00 CST
4/25/1954 02:00 CDT
9/26/1954 02:00 CST
4/24/1955 02:00 CDT
9/25/1955 02:00 CST
4/29/1956 02:00 CDT
10/28/1956 02:00 CST
4/28/1957 02:00 CDT
9/29/1957 02:00 CST
4/27/1958 02:00 CDT
10/26/1958 02:00 CST
4/26/1959 02:00 CDT
10/25/1959 02:00 CST
4/24/1960 02:00 CDT
10/30/1960 02:00 CST
4/30/1961 02:00 CDT
10/29/1961 02:00 CST
4/29/1962 02:00 CDT
10/28/1962 02:00 CST
4/28/1963 02:00 CDT
10/27/1963 02:00 CST
4/26/1964 02:00 EST
4/27/1969 02:00 EDT
10/26/1969 02:00 EST
4/26/1970 02:00 EDT
10/25/1970 02:00 EST

....

IN # 82
Before 11/18/1883 LMT
11/18/1883 12:00 CST
3/31/1918 02:00 CWT
10/27/1918 02:00 CST
3/30/1919 02:00 CWT
10/26/1919 02:00 CST
2/09/1942 02:00 CWT
9/30/1945 02:00 CST
4/24/1955 02:00 CDT
9/25/1955 02:00 CST
4/29/1956 02:00 CDT
10/28/1956 02:00 CST
4/28/1957 02:00 CDT
9/29/1957 02:00 CST
4/27/1958 02:00 CDT
9/28/1958 02:00 CST
4/26/1959 02:00 CDT
9/27/1959 02:00 CST
4/24/1960 02:00 CDT
9/25/1960 02:00 CST
4/30/1961 02:00 CDT
10/29/1961 02:00 CST
4/29/1962 02:00 CDT
10/28/1962 02:00 CST
4/28/1963 02:00 CDT
10/27/1963 02:00 CST
4/26/1964 02:00 EST
4/27/1969 02:00 EDT
10/26/1969 02:00 EST
4/26/1970 02:00 EDT
10/25/1970 02:00 EST

....

IN # 83
Before 11/18/1883 LMT
11/18/1883 12:00 CST
3/31/1918 02:00 CWT
10/27/1918 02:00 CST
3/30/1919 02:00 CWT
10/26/1919 02:00 CST
2/09/1942 02:00 CWT
9/30/1945 02:00 CST
4/26/1953 02:00 CDT
9/27/1953 02:00 CST
4/25/1954 02:00 CDT
9/26/1954 02:00 CST
4/24/1955 02:00 CDT
9/25/1955 02:00 CST
4/29/1956 02:00 CDT
10/28/1956 02:00 CST
4/28/1957 02:00 CDT
9/29/1957 02:00 CST
4/27/1958 02:00 CDT
9/28/1958 02:00 CST
4/26/1959 02:00 CDT
9/27/1959 02:00 CST
4/24/1960 02:00 CDT
9/25/1960 02:00 CST
4/30/1961 02:00 CDT
10/29/1961 02:00 CST
4/29/1962 02:00 CDT
10/28/1962 02:00 CST
4/28/1963 02:00 CDT
10/27/1963 02:00 CST
4/26/1964 02:00 EST
4/27/1969 02:00 EDT
10/26/1969 02:00 EST
4/26/1970 02:00 EDT
10/25/1970 02:00 EST

....

IN # 84
Before 11/18/1883 LMT
11/18/1883 12:00 CST
3/31/1918 02:00 CWT
10/27/1918 02:00 CST
3/30/1919 02:00 CWT
10/26/1919 02:00 CST
2/09/1942 02:00 CWT
9/30/1945 02:00 CST
4/25/1954 02:00 CDT
9/26/1954 02:00 CST
4/24/1955 02:00 CDT
9/25/1955 02:00 CST
4/29/1956 02:00 CDT
10/01/1956 00:00 CST
4/28/1957 02:00 CDT
9/29/1957 02:00 CST
4/27/1958 02:00 CDT
9/28/1958 02:00 CST
4/26/1959 02:00 CDT
9/27/1959 02:00 CST
4/24/1960 02:00 CDT
9/25/1960 02:00 CST
4/30/1961 02:00 CDT
10/29/1961 02:00 CST
4/29/1962 02:00 CDT
10/28/1962 02:00 CST
4/28/1963 02:00 CDT
10/27/1963 02:00 CST
4/26/1964 02:00 EST
4/27/1969 02:00 EDT
10/26/1969 02:00 EST
4/26/1970 02:00 EDT
10/25/1970 02:00 EST

....

IN # 85
Before 11/18/1883 LMT
11/18/1883 12:00 CST
3/31/1918 02:00 CWT
10/27/1918 02:00 CST
3/30/1919 02:00 CWT
10/26/1919 02:00 CST
2/09/1942 02:00 CWT
9/30/1945 02:00 CST
5/01/1955 00:00 CDT
9/04/1955 00:00 CST
4/29/1956 02:00 CDT
9/30/1956 02:00 CST
4/28/1957 02:00 CDT
9/29/1957 02:00 CST
4/27/1958 02:00 CDT
9/28/1958 02:00 CST
4/26/1959 02:00 CDT
9/27/1959 02:00 CST
4/24/1960 02:00 CDT
9/25/1960 02:00 CST
4/30/1961 02:00 CDT
10/29/1961 02:00 CST
4/29/1962 02:00 CDT
10/28/1962 02:00 CST
4/28/1963 02:00 CDT
10/27/1963 02:00 CST
4/26/1964 02:00 EST
4/27/1969 02:00 EDT
10/26/1969 02:00 EST
4/26/1970 02:00 EDT
10/25/1970 02:00 EST

....

IN # 86
Before 11/18/1883 LMT
11/18/1883 12:00 CST
3/31/1918 02:00 CWT
10/27/1918 02:00 CST
3/30/1919 02:00 CWT
10/26/1919 02:00 CST
2/09/1942 02:00 CWT
9/30/1945 02:00 CST
5/01/1955 00:00 CDT
9/25/1955 02:00 CST
4/29/1956 02:00 CDT
9/30/1956 02:00 CST
4/28/1957 02:00 CDT
9/29/1957 02:00 CST
4/27/1958 02:00 CDT
9/28/1958 02:00 CST
4/26/1959 02:00 CDT
9/27/1959 02:00 CST
4/24/1960 02:00 CDT
9/25/1960 02:00 CST
4/30/1961 02:00 CDT
10/29/1961 02:00 CST
4/29/1962 02:00 CDT
10/28/1962 02:00 CST
4/28/1963 02:00 CDT
10/27/1963 02:00 CST
4/26/1964 02:00 EST
4/27/1969 02:00 EDT
10/26/1969 02:00 EST
4/26/1970 02:00 EDT
10/25/1970 02:00 EST

....

IN # 87
Before 11/18/1883 LMT
11/18/1883 12:00 CST
3/31/1918 02:00 CWT
10/27/1918 02:00 CST
3/30/1919 02:00 CWT
10/26/1919 02:00 CST
2/09/1942 02:00 CWT
9/30/1945 02:00 CST
4/26/1953 02:00 CDT
9/27/1953 02:00 CST
4/25/1954 02:00 CDT
9/26/1954 02:00 CST
5/01/1955 00:00 CDT
9/25/1955 02:00 CST
4/29/1956 02:00 CDT
9/30/1956 02:00 CST
4/28/1957 02:00 CDT
9/29/1957 02:00 CST
4/27/1958 02:00 CDT
9/28/1958 02:00 CST
4/26/1959 02:00 CDT
9/27/1959 02:00 CST
4/24/1960 02:00 CDT
9/25/1960 02:00 CST
4/30/1961 02:00 CDT
10/29/1961 02:00 CST
4/29/1962 02:00 CDT
10/28/1962 02:00 CST
4/28/1963 02:00 CDT

TIME TABLES

10/27/1963	02:00	CST
4/26/1964	02:00	EST
4/27/1969	02:00	EDT
10/26/1969	02:00	EST
4/26/1970	02:00	EDT
10/25/1970	02:00	EST

IN # 88

Before 11/18/1883		LMT
11/18/1883	12:00	CST
3/31/1918	02:00	CWT
10/27/1918	02:00	CST
3/30/1919	02:00	CWT
10/26/1919	02:00	CST
2/09/1942	02:00	CWT
9/30/1945	02:00	CST
4/26/1953	02:00	CDT
9/27/1953	02:00	CST
4/25/1954	02:00	CDT
9/26/1954	02:00	CST
4/24/1955	02:00	CDT
9/25/1955	02:00	CST
4/29/1956	02:00	CDT
9/30/1956	02:00	CST
4/28/1957	02:00	CDT
9/29/1957	02:00	CST
4/27/1958	02:00	CDT
9/28/1958	02:00	CST
4/26/1959	02:00	CDT
9/27/1959	02:00	CST
4/24/1960	02:00	CDT
9/25/1960	02:00	CST
4/30/1961	02:00	CDT
10/29/1961	02:00	CST
4/29/1962	02:00	CDT
10/28/1962	02:00	CST
4/28/1963	02:00	EST
4/27/1969	02:00	EDT
10/26/1969	02:00	EST
4/26/1970	02:00	EDT
10/25/1970	02:00	EST

IN # 89

Before 11/18/1883		LMT
11/18/1883	12:00	CST
3/31/1918	02:00	CWT
10/27/1918	02:00	CST
3/30/1919	02:00	CWT
10/26/1919	02:00	CST
2/09/1942	02:00	CWT
9/30/1945	02:00	CST
4/24/1955	02:00	CDT
9/25/1955	02:00	CST
4/29/1956	02:00	CDT
9/30/1956	02:00	CST
4/28/1957	02:00	CDT
9/29/1957	02:00	CST
4/27/1958	02:00	CDT
9/28/1958	02:00	CST
4/26/1959	02:00	CDT
9/27/1959	02:00	CST
4/24/1960	02:00	CDT
9/25/1960	02:00	CST
4/30/1961	02:00	CDT
10/29/1961	02:00	CST
4/29/1962	02:00	CDT
10/28/1962	02:00	CST
4/28/1963	02:00	EST
4/27/1969	02:00	EDT
10/26/1969	02:00	EST
4/26/1970	02:00	EDT
10/25/1970	02:00	EST

IN # 90

Before 11/18/1883		LMT
11/18/1883	12:00	CST
3/31/1918	02:00	CWT
10/27/1918	02:00	CST
3/30/1919	02:00	CWT
10/26/1919	02:00	CST
2/09/1942	02:00	CWT
9/30/1945	02:00	CST
4/28/1946	02:00	CDT
9/29/1946	02:00	CST
4/26/1953	02:00	CDT
9/27/1953	02:00	CST
4/25/1954	02:00	CDT
9/26/1954	02:00	CST
4/24/1955	02:00	CDT
9/25/1955	02:00	CST
4/29/1956	02:00	CDT
9/30/1956	02:00	CST
4/28/1957	02:00	CDT
9/29/1957	02:00	CST
4/27/1958	02:00	CDT
9/28/1958	02:00	CST
4/26/1959	02:00	CDT
9/27/1959	02:00	CST
4/24/1960	02:00	CDT
9/25/1960	02:00	CST
4/30/1961	02:00	CDT
10/29/1961	02:00	CST
4/29/1962	02:00	CDT
10/28/1962	02:00	CST
4/28/1963	02:00	EST
4/27/1969	02:00	EDT
10/26/1969	02:00	EST
4/26/1970	02:00	EDT
10/25/1970	02:00	EST

IN # 91

Before 11/18/1883		LMT
11/18/1883	12:00	CST
3/31/1918	02:00	CWT
10/27/1918	02:00	CST
3/30/1919	02:00	CWT
10/26/1919	02:00	CST
2/09/1942	02:00	CWT
9/30/1945	02:00	CST
5/01/1955	00:00	CDT
9/04/1955	00:00	CST
4/29/1956	02:00	CDT
9/30/1956	02:00	CST
4/28/1957	02:00	CDT
9/29/1957	02:00	CST
4/27/1958	02:00	CDT
9/28/1958	02:00	CST
4/26/1959	02:00	CDT
9/27/1959	02:00	CST
4/24/1960	02:00	CDT
9/25/1960	02:00	CST
4/30/1961	02:00	CDT
10/29/1961	02:00	CST
4/29/1962	02:00	CDT
10/28/1962	02:00	CST
4/28/1963	02:00	EST
4/27/1969	02:00	EDT
10/26/1969	02:00	EST
4/26/1970	02:00	EDT
10/25/1970	02:00	EST

IN # 92

Before 11/18/1883		LMT
11/18/1883	12:00	CST
3/31/1918	02:00	CWT
10/27/1918	02:00	CST
3/30/1919	02:00	CWT
10/26/1919	02:00	CST
2/09/1942	02:00	CWT
9/30/1945	02:00	CST
5/01/1955	00:00	CDT
9/01/1955	00:00	CST
4/29/1956	02:00	CDT
9/30/1956	02:00	CST
4/28/1957	02:00	CDT
9/29/1957	02:00	CST
4/27/1958	02:00	CDT
9/28/1958	02:00	CST
4/26/1959	02:00	CDT
10/25/1959	02:00	CST
4/24/1960	02:00	EST
10/29/1961	02:00	CST
4/29/1962	02:00	CDT
10/28/1962	02:00	CST
4/28/1963	02:00	CDT
10/27/1963	02:00	CST
4/26/1964	02:00	EST
4/27/1969	02:00	EDT
10/26/1969	02:00	EST
4/26/1970	02:00	EDT
10/25/1970	02:00	EST

IN # 93

Before 11/18/1883		LMT
11/18/1883	12:00	CST
3/31/1918	02:00	CWT
10/27/1918	02:00	CST
3/30/1919	02:00	CWT
10/26/1919	02:00	CST
2/09/1942	02:00	CWT
9/30/1945	02:00	CST
5/08/1955	02:00	CDT
9/04/1955	00:00	CST
4/29/1956	02:00	CDT
9/30/1956	02:00	CST
4/28/1957	02:00	CDT
9/29/1957	02:00	CST
4/27/1958	02:00	CDT
9/28/1958	02:00	CST
4/26/1959	02:00	CDT
9/27/1959	02:00	CST
4/24/1960	02:00	EST
10/29/1961	02:00	CST
4/29/1962	02:00	CDT
10/28/1962	02:00	CST
4/28/1963	02:00	CDT
10/27/1963	02:00	CST
4/26/1964	02:00	EST
4/27/1969	02:00	EDT
10/26/1969	02:00	EST
4/26/1970	02:00	EDT
10/25/1970	02:00	EST

IN # 94

Before 11/18/1883		LMT
11/18/1883	12:00	CST
3/31/1918	02:00	CWT
10/27/1918	02:00	CST
3/30/1919	02:00	CWT
10/26/1919	02:00	CST
2/09/1942	02:00	CWT
9/30/1945	02:00	CST
5/01/1955	00:00	CDT
9/01/1955	00:00	CST
4/29/1956	02:00	CDT
9/30/1956	02:00	CST
4/28/1957	02:00	CDT
9/29/1957	02:00	CST
4/27/1958	02:00	CDT
9/28/1958	02:00	CST
4/26/1959	02:00	CDT
9/27/1959	02:00	CST
4/24/1960	02:00	EST
10/29/1961	02:00	CST
4/29/1962	02:00	CDT
10/28/1962	02:00	CST
4/28/1963	02:00	CDT
10/27/1963	02:00	CST
4/26/1964	02:00	EST
4/27/1969	02:00	EDT
10/26/1969	02:00	EST
4/26/1970	02:00	EDT
10/25/1970	02:00	EST

IN # 95

Before 11/18/1883		LMT
11/18/1883	12:00	CST
3/31/1918	02:00	CWT
10/27/1918	02:00	CST
3/30/1919	02:00	CWT
10/26/1919	02:00	CST
2/09/1942	02:00	CWT
9/30/1945	02:00	CST
4/26/1953	02:00	CDT
9/27/1953	02:00	CST
4/25/1954	02:00	CDT
9/26/1954	02:00	CST
5/10/1955	02:00	CDT
9/04/1955	00:00	CST
4/29/1956	02:00	CDT
9/30/1956	02:00	CST
4/28/1957	02:00	CDT
9/29/1957	02:00	CST
4/27/1958	02:00	CDT
9/28/1958	02:00	CST
4/26/1959	02:00	CDT
9/27/1959	02:00	CST
4/24/1960	02:00	EST
10/29/1961	02:00	CST
4/29/1962	02:00	CDT
10/28/1962	02:00	CST
4/28/1963	02:00	CDT
10/27/1963	02:00	CST
4/26/1964	02:00	EST
4/27/1969	02:00	EDT
10/26/1969	02:00	EST
4/26/1970	02:00	EDT
10/25/1970	02:00	EST

IN # 96

Before 11/18/1883		LMT
11/18/1883	12:00	CST
3/31/1918	02:00	CWT
10/27/1918	02:00	CST
3/30/1919	02:00	CWT
10/26/1919	02:00	CST
2/09/1942	02:00	CWT
9/30/1945	02:00	CST
4/26/1953	02:00	CDT
9/27/1953	02:00	CST
4/25/1954	02:00	CDT
9/26/1954	02:00	CST
5/08/1955	00:00	CDT
9/04/1955	00:00	CST
4/29/1956	02:00	CDT
9/30/1956	02:00	CST
4/28/1957	02:00	CDT
9/29/1957	02:00	CST
4/27/1958	02:00	CDT
9/28/1958	02:00	CST
4/26/1959	02:00	CDT
9/27/1959	02:00	CST
4/24/1960	02:00	EST
10/29/1961	02:00	CST
4/29/1962	02:00	CDT
10/28/1962	02:00	CST
4/28/1963	02:00	CDT
10/27/1963	02:00	CST
4/26/1964	02:00	EST
4/27/1969	02:00	EDT
10/26/1969	02:00	EST
4/26/1970	02:00	EDT
10/25/1970	02:00	EST

IN # 97

Before 11/18/1883		LMT
11/18/1883	12:00	CST
3/31/1918	02:00	CWT
10/27/1918	02:00	CST
3/30/1919	02:00	CWT
10/26/1919	02:00	CST
2/09/1942	02:00	CWT
9/30/1945	02:00	CST
4/24/1955	02:00	EST
9/29/1957	02:00	CST
4/27/1958	02:00	EST
4/27/1969	02:00	EDT
10/26/1969	02:00	EST
4/26/1970	02:00	EDT
10/25/1970	02:00	EST

IN # 98

Before 11/18/1883		LMT
11/18/1883	12:00	CST
3/31/1918	02:00	CWT
10/27/1918	02:00	CST
3/30/1919	02:00	CWT
10/26/1919	02:00	CST
2/09/1942	02:00	CWT
9/30/1945	02:00	CST
4/26/1953	02:00	CDT
9/27/1953	02:00	CST
4/25/1954	02:00	CDT
9/26/1954	02:00	CST
4/24/1955	02:00	EST
9/29/1957	02:00	CST
4/27/1958	02:00	EST
4/27/1969	02:00	EDT
10/26/1969	02:00	EST
4/26/1970	02:00	EDT
10/25/1970	02:00	EST

IN # 99

Before 11/18/1883		LMT
11/18/1883	12:00	CST
3/31/1918	02:00	CWT
10/27/1918	02:00	CST
3/30/1919	02:00	CWT
10/26/1919	02:00	CST
2/09/1942	02:00	CWT
9/30/1945	02:00	CST
4/27/1947	02:00	CDT
9/06/1947	02:00	CST
4/25/1948	02:00	CDT
9/26/1948	02:00	CST
4/29/1951	02:00	CDT
9/30/1951	02:00	CST
4/24/1955	02:00	EST
9/29/1957	02:00	CST
4/27/1958	02:00	EST
4/27/1969	02:00	EDT
10/26/1969	02:00	EST
4/26/1970	02:00	EDT
10/25/1970	02:00	EST

IN # 100

Before 11/18/1883		LMT
11/18/1883	12:00	CST
3/31/1918	02:00	CWT
10/27/1918	02:00	CST
3/30/1919	02:00	CWT
10/26/1919	02:00	CST
6/22/1941	02:00	CDT
9/28/1941	02:00	CST
2/09/1942	02:00	CWT
9/30/1945	02:00	CST
4/28/1946	02:00	CDT
9/29/1946	02:00	CST
4/27/1947	02:00	CDT
9/28/1947	02:00	CST
4/25/1948	02:00	CDT
9/26/1948	02:00	CST
4/24/1949	02:00	CDT
9/25/1949	02:00	CST
4/30/1950	02:00	CDT
9/24/1950	02:00	CST
4/29/1951	02:00	CDT
9/30/1951	02:00	CST
4/27/1952	02:00	CDT
9/28/1952	02:00	CST
4/26/1953	02:00	CDT
9/27/1953	02:00	CST
4/25/1954	02:00	CDT
9/26/1954	02:00	CST
4/24/1955	02:00	EST
9/29/1957	02:00	CST
4/27/1958	02:00	EST
4/27/1969	02:00	EDT
10/26/1969	02:00	EST
4/26/1970	02:00	EDT
10/25/1970	02:00	EST

IN # 101

Before 11/18/1883		LMT
11/18/1883	12:00	CST
3/31/1918	02:00	CWT
10/27/1918	02:00	CST
3/30/1919	02:00	CWT
10/26/1919	02:00	CST
2/09/1942	02:00	CWT
9/30/1945	02:00	CST
4/24/1955	02:00	EST
9/29/1957	02:00	CST
4/27/1958	02:00	CDT
9/28/1958	02:00	CST
4/26/1959	02:00	EST
4/27/1969	02:00	EDT
10/26/1969	02:00	EST
4/26/1970	02:00	EDT
10/25/1970	02:00	EST

IN # 102

Before 11/18/1883		LMT
11/18/1883	12:00	CST
3/31/1918	02:00	CWT
10/27/1918	02:00	CST
3/30/1919	02:00	CWT
10/26/1919	02:00	CST
4/30/1933	02:00	CDT
9/24/1933	02:00	CST
4/29/1934	02:00	CDT
9/30/1934	02:00	CST
4/28/1935	02:00	CDT
9/29/1935	02:00	CST
4/26/1936	02:00	CDT
9/27/1936	02:00	CST
4/25/1937	02:00	CDT
9/26/1937	02:00	CST
4/24/1938	02:00	CDT
9/25/1938	02:00	CST
4/30/1939	02:00	CDT
9/24/1939	02:00	CST
4/28/1940	02:00	CDT
9/29/1940	02:00	CST
4/27/1941	02:00	CDT
9/28/1941	02:00	CST
2/09/1942	02:00	CWT
9/30/1945	02:00	CST
4/28/1946	02:00	CDT
9/29/1946	02:00	CST
4/27/1947	02:00	CDT
9/28/1947	02:00	CST
4/25/1948	02:00	CDT
9/26/1948	02:00	CST
4/24/1949	02:00	CDT
9/25/1949	02:00	CST
4/30/1950	02:00	CDT
9/24/1950	02:00	CST
4/29/1951	02:00	CDT
9/30/1951	02:00	CST
4/27/1952	02:00	CDT
9/28/1952	02:00	CST
4/26/1953	02:00	CDT
9/27/1953	02:00	CST
4/25/1954	02:00	CDT
9/26/1954	02:00	CST
4/24/1955	02:00	EST
9/29/1957	02:00	CST
4/27/1958	02:00	CDT
9/28/1958	02:00	CST
4/26/1959	02:00	EST
4/27/1969	02:00	EDT
10/26/1969	02:00	EST
4/26/1970	02:00	EDT
10/25/1970	02:00	EST

IN # 103

Before 11/18/1883		LMT
11/18/1883	12:00	CST
3/31/1918	02:00	CWT
10/27/1918	02:00	CST
3/30/1919	02:00	CWT
10/26/1919	02:00	CST
2/09/1942	02:00	CWT
9/30/1945	02:00	CST
4/28/1946	02:00	CDT
9/29/1946	02:00	CST
4/27/1947	02:00	CDT
9/28/1947	02:00	CST
4/25/1948	02:00	CDT
9/26/1948	02:00	CST
4/24/1949	02:00	CDT
9/25/1949	02:00	CST
4/30/1950	02:00	CDT
9/24/1950	02:00	CST
4/29/1951	02:00	CDT
9/30/1951	02:00	CST
4/27/1952	02:00	CDT
9/28/1952	02:00	CST
4/26/1953	02:00	CDT
9/27/1953	02:00	CST
4/25/1954	02:00	CDT
9/26/1954	02:00	CST
4/24/1955	02:00	EST
9/29/1957	02:00	CST
4/27/1958	02:00	CDT
9/28/1958	02:00	CST
4/26/1959	02:00	EST
4/27/1969	02:00	EDT
10/26/1969	02:00	EST
4/26/1970	02:00	EDT
10/25/1970	02:00	EST

IN # 104

Before 11/18/1883		LMT
11/18/1883	12:00	CST
3/31/1918	02:00	CWT
10/27/1918	02:00	CST
3/30/1919	02:00	CWT
10/26/1919	02:00	CST
2/09/1942	02:00	CWT
9/30/1945	02:00	CST
4/28/1946	02:00	CDT
9/29/1946	02:00	CST
4/27/1947	02:00	CDT
9/28/1947	02:00	CST
4/26/1953	02:00	CDT
9/27/1953	02:00	CST
4/25/1954	02:00	CDT
9/26/1954	02:00	CST
4/24/1955	02:00	EST
9/29/1957	02:00	CST
4/27/1958	02:00	CDT
9/28/1958	02:00	CST
4/26/1959	02:00	EST
4/27/1969	02:00	EDT
10/26/1969	02:00	EST
4/26/1970	02:00	EDT
10/25/1970	02:00	EST

IN # 105

Before 11/18/1883		LMT
11/18/1883	12:00	CST
3/31/1918	02:00	CWT
10/27/1918	02:00	CST
3/30/1919	02:00	CWT
10/26/1919	02:00	CST
2/09/1942	02:00	CWT
9/30/1945	02:00	CST
4/28/1946	02:00	CDT
9/29/1946	02:00	CST
4/27/1947	02:00	CDT
9/28/1947	02:00	CST
4/25/1948	02:00	CDT
9/26/1948	02:00	CST
4/27/1952	02:00	CDT
9/28/1952	02:00	CST
4/26/1953	02:00	CDT
9/27/1953	02:00	CST
4/25/1954	02:00	CDT
9/26/1954	02:00	CST
4/24/1955	02:00	EST
9/29/1957	02:00	CST
4/27/1958	02:00	CDT
9/28/1958	02:00	CST
4/26/1959	02:00	EST
4/27/1969	02:00	EDT
10/26/1969	02:00	EST
4/26/1970	02:00	EDT
10/25/1970	02:00	EST

IN # 106

Before 11/18/1883		LMT
11/18/1883	12:00	CST
3/31/1918	02:00	CWT
10/27/1918	02:00	CST
3/30/1919	02:00	CWT
10/26/1919	02:00	CST
2/09/1942	02:00	CWT
9/30/1945	02:00	CST
4/28/1946	02:00	CDT
9/29/1946	02:00	CST
4/29/1951	02:00	CDT
9/30/1951	02:00	CST
4/27/1952	02:00	CDT
9/28/1952	02:00	CST
4/26/1953	02:00	CDT
9/27/1953	02:00	CST
4/25/1954	02:00	CDT
9/26/1954	02:00	CST
4/24/1955	02:00	EST
9/29/1957	02:00	CST
4/27/1958	02:00	CDT
9/28/1958	02:00	CST
4/26/1959	02:00	EST
4/27/1969	02:00	EDT
10/26/1969	02:00	EST
4/26/1970	02:00	EDT
10/25/1970	02:00	EST

TIME TABLES

IN # 107

Before 11/18/1883		LMT
11/18/1883	12:00	CST
3/31/1918	02:00	CWT
10/27/1918	02:00	CST
3/30/1919	02:00	CWT
10/26/1919	02:00	CST
2/09/1942	02:00	CWT
9/30/1945	02:00	CST
4/27/1947	02:00	CDT
9/28/1947	02:00	CST
4/25/1948	02:00	CDT
9/26/1948	02:00	CST
4/26/1953	02:00	CDT
9/27/1953	02:00	CST
4/25/1954	02:00	CDT
9/26/1954	02:00	CST
4/24/1955	02:00	EST
9/29/1957	02:00	CST
4/27/1958	02:00	CDT
9/28/1958	02:00	CST
4/26/1959	02:00	EST
4/27/1969	02:00	EDT
10/26/1969	02:00	EST
4/26/1970	02:00	EDT
10/25/1970	02:00	EST

IN # 108

Before 11/18/1883		LMT
11/18/1883	12:00	CST
3/31/1918	02:00	CWT
10/27/1918	02:00	CST
3/30/1919	02:00	CWT
10/26/1919	02:00	CST
2/09/1942	02:00	CWT
9/30/1945	02:00	CST
4/26/1953	02:00	CDT
9/27/1953	02:00	CST
4/25/1954	02:00	CDT
9/26/1954	02:00	CST
4/24/1955	02:00	EST
9/29/1957	02:00	CST
4/27/1958	02:00	CDT
9/28/1958	02:00	CST
4/26/1959	02:00	EST
4/27/1969	02:00	EDT
10/26/1969	02:00	EST
4/26/1970	02:00	EDT
10/25/1970	02:00	EST

IN # 109

Before 11/18/1883		LMT
11/18/1883	12:00	CST
3/31/1918	02:00	CWT
10/27/1918	02:00	CST
3/30/1919	02:00	CWT
10/26/1919	02:00	CST
2/09/1942	02:00	CWT
9/30/1945	02:00	CST
4/25/1954	02:00	CDT
9/26/1954	02:00	CST
4/24/1955	02:00	EST
9/29/1957	02:00	CST
4/27/1958	02:00	CDT
9/28/1958	02:00	CST
4/26/1959	02:00	EST
4/27/1969	02:00	EDT
10/26/1969	02:00	EST
4/26/1970	02:00	EDT
10/25/1970	02:00	EST

IN # 110

Before 11/18/1883		LMT
11/18/1883	12:00	CST
3/31/1918	02:00	CWT
10/27/1918	02:00	CST
3/30/1919	02:00	CWT
10/26/1919	02:00	CST
2/09/1942	02:00	CWT
9/30/1945	02:00	CST
4/27/1947	02:00	CDT
10/01/1947	02:00	CST
4/25/1948	02:00	CDT
9/26/1948	02:00	CST
4/29/1951	02:00	CDT
9/30/1951	02:00	CST
4/24/1955	02:00	EST
9/29/1957	02:00	CST
4/27/1958	02:00	CDT
9/28/1958	02:00	CST
4/26/1959	02:00	EST
4/27/1969	02:00	EDT
10/26/1969	02:00	EST
4/26/1970	02:00	EDT
10/25/1970	02:00	EST

IN # 111

Before 11/18/1883		LMT
11/18/1883	12:00	CST
3/31/1918	02:00	CWT
10/27/1918	02:00	CST
3/30/1919	02:00	CWT
10/26/1919	02:00	CST
2/09/1942	02:00	CWT
9/30/1945	02:00	CST
4/28/1946	02:00	CDT
9/29/1946	02:00	CST
5/01/1947	02:00	CDT
10/01/1947	02:00	CST
4/29/1951	02:00	CDT
9/30/1951	02:00	CST
4/27/1952	02:00	CDT
9/28/1952	02:00	CST
4/26/1953	02:00	CDT
9/27/1953	02:00	CST
4/25/1954	02:00	CDT
9/26/1954	02:00	CST
4/24/1955	02:00	EST
9/29/1957	02:00	CST
4/27/1958	02:00	CDT
9/28/1958	02:00	CST
4/26/1959	02:00	EST
4/27/1969	02:00	EDT
10/26/1969	02:00	EST
4/26/1970	02:00	EDT
10/25/1970	02:00	EST

IN # 112

Before 11/18/1883		LMT
11/18/1883	12:00	CST
3/31/1918	02:00	CWT
10/27/1918	02:00	CST
3/30/1919	02:00	CWT
10/26/1919	02:00	CST
2/09/1942	02:00	CWT
9/30/1945	02:00	CST
4/30/1950	02:00	CDT
10/01/1950	02:00	CST
4/24/1955	02:00	EST
9/29/1957	02:00	CST
4/27/1958	02:00	CDT
9/28/1958	02:00	CST
4/26/1959	02:00	EST
4/27/1969	02:00	EDT
10/26/1969	02:00	EST
4/26/1970	02:00	EDT
10/25/1970	02:00	EST

IN # 113

Before 11/18/1883		LMT
11/18/1883	12:00	CST
3/31/1918	02:00	CWT
10/27/1918	02:00	CST
3/30/1919	02:00	CWT
10/26/1919	02:00	CST
2/09/1942	02:00	CWT
9/30/1945	02:00	CST
4/24/1955	02:00	EST
9/29/1957	02:00	CST
4/27/1958	02:00	CDT
9/28/1958	02:00	CST
4/26/1959	02:00	CDT
9/27/1959	02:00	CST
4/24/1960	02:00	EST
4/27/1969	02:00	EDT
10/26/1969	02:00	EST
4/26/1970	02:00	EDT
10/25/1970	02:00	EST

IN # 114

Before 11/18/1883		LMT
11/18/1883	12:00	CST
3/31/1918	02:00	CWT
10/27/1918	02:00	CST
3/30/1919	02:00	CWT
10/26/1919	02:00	CST
2/09/1942	02:00	CWT
9/30/1945	02:00	CST
4/26/1953	02:00	CDT
9/27/1953	02:00	CST
4/24/1955	02:00	EST
9/29/1957	02:00	CST
4/27/1958	02:00	CDT
9/28/1958	02:00	CST
4/26/1959	02:00	CDT
9/27/1959	02:00	CST
4/24/1960	02:00	EST
4/27/1969	02:00	EDT
10/26/1969	02:00	EST
4/26/1970	02:00	EDT
10/25/1970	02:00	EST

IN # 115

Before 11/18/1883		LMT
11/18/1883	12:00	CST
3/31/1918	02:00	CWT
10/27/1918	02:00	CST
3/30/1919	02:00	CWT
10/26/1919	02:00	CST
2/09/1942	02:00	CWT
9/30/1945	02:00	CST
4/26/1953	02:00	CDT
9/27/1953	02:00	CST
4/25/1954	02:00	CDT
9/26/1954	02:00	CST
4/24/1955	02:00	EST
9/29/1957	02:00	CST
4/27/1958	02:00	CDT
9/28/1958	02:00	CST
4/26/1959	02:00	CDT
9/27/1959	02:00	CST
4/24/1960	02:00	EST
4/27/1969	02:00	EDT
10/26/1969	02:00	EST
4/26/1970	02:00	EDT
10/25/1970	02:00	EST

IN # 116

Before 11/18/1883		LMT
11/18/1883	12:00	CST
3/31/1918	02:00	CWT
10/27/1918	02:00	CST
3/30/1919	02:00	CWT
10/26/1919	02:00	CST
2/09/1942	02:00	CWT
9/30/1945	02:00	CST
4/24/1955	02:00	EST
12/02/1956	02:00	CST
4/28/1957	02:00	CDT
9/29/1957	02:00	CST
4/27/1958	02:00	CDT
9/28/1958	02:00	CST
4/26/1959	02:00	EST
4/27/1969	02:00	EDT
10/26/1969	02:00	EST
4/26/1970	02:00	EDT
10/25/1970	02:00	EST

IN # 117

Before 11/18/1883		LMT
11/18/1883	12:00	CST
3/31/1918	02:00	CWT
10/27/1918	02:00	CST
3/30/1919	02:00	CWT
10/26/1919	02:00	CST
2/09/1942	02:00	CWT
9/30/1945	02:00	CST
4/30/1950	02:00	CDT
9/24/1950	02:00	CST
4/29/1951	02:00	CDT
9/30/1951	02:00	CST
4/27/1952	02:00	CDT
9/28/1952	02:00	CST
4/26/1953	02:00	CDT
9/27/1953	02:00	CST
4/25/1954	02:00	CDT
9/26/1954	02:00	CST
4/24/1955	02:00	EST
12/02/1956	02:00	CST
4/28/1957	02:00	CDT
9/29/1957	02:00	CST
4/27/1958	02:00	CDT
9/28/1958	02:00	CST
4/26/1959	02:00	EST
4/27/1969	02:00	EDT
10/26/1969	02:00	EST
4/26/1970	02:00	EDT
10/25/1970	02:00	EST

IN # 118

Before 11/18/1883		LMT
11/18/1883	12:00	CST
3/31/1918	02:00	CWT
10/27/1918	02:00	CST
3/30/1919	02:00	CWT
10/26/1919	02:00	CST
2/09/1942	02:00	CWT
9/30/1945	02:00	CST
4/25/1948	02:00	CDT
9/26/1948	02:00	CST
4/30/1950	02:00	CDT
9/24/1950	02:00	CST
4/29/1951	02:00	CDT
9/30/1951	02:00	CST
4/26/1953	02:00	CDT
9/27/1953	02:00	CST
4/24/1955	02:00	EST
12/02/1956	02:00	CST
4/28/1957	02:00	CDT
9/29/1957	02:00	CST
4/27/1958	02:00	CDT
9/28/1958	02:00	CST
4/26/1959	02:00	EST
4/27/1969	02:00	EDT
10/26/1969	02:00	EST
4/26/1970	02:00	EDT
10/25/1970	02:00	EST

IN # 119

Before 11/18/1883		LMT
11/18/1883	12:00	CST
3/31/1918	02:00	CWT
10/27/1918	02:00	CST
3/30/1919	02:00	CWT
10/26/1919	02:00	CST
2/09/1942	02:00	CWT
9/30/1945	02:00	CST
4/26/1953	02:00	CDT
9/27/1953	02:00	CST
4/25/1954	02:00	CDT
9/26/1954	02:00	CST
4/24/1955	02:00	EST
12/02/1956	02:00	CST
4/28/1957	02:00	CDT
9/29/1957	02:00	CST
4/27/1958	02:00	CDT
9/28/1958	02:00	CST
4/26/1959	02:00	EST
4/27/1969	02:00	EDT
10/26/1969	02:00	EST
4/26/1970	02:00	EDT
10/25/1970	02:00	EST

IN # 120

Before 11/18/1883		LMT
11/18/1883	12:00	CST
3/31/1918	02:00	CWT
10/27/1918	02:00	CST
3/30/1919	02:00	CWT
10/26/1919	02:00	CST
2/09/1942	02:00	CWT
9/30/1945	02:00	CST
4/29/1951	02:00	CDT
9/30/1951	02:00	CST
4/26/1953	02:00	CDT
9/27/1953	02:00	CST
4/24/1955	02:00	EST
12/02/1956	02:00	CST
4/28/1957	02:00	CDT
9/29/1957	02:00	CST
4/27/1958	02:00	CDT
9/28/1958	02:00	CST
4/26/1959	02:00	EST
4/27/1969	02:00	EDT
10/26/1969	02:00	EST
4/26/1970	02:00	EDT
10/25/1970	02:00	EST

IN # 121

Before 11/18/1883		LMT
11/18/1883	12:00	CST
3/31/1918	02:00	CWT
10/27/1918	02:00	CST
3/30/1919	02:00	CWT
10/26/1919	02:00	CST
2/09/1942	02:00	CWT
9/30/1945	02:00	CST
4/28/1946	02:00	CDT
9/29/1946	02:00	CST
4/27/1947	02:00	CDT
9/28/1947	02:00	CST
4/25/1948	02:00	CDT
9/26/1948	02:00	CST
4/24/1949	02:00	CDT
9/25/1949	02:00	CST
4/30/1950	02:00	CDT
10/01/1950	02:00	CST
4/29/1951	02:00	CDT
9/30/1951	02:00	CST
4/27/1952	02:00	CDT
9/28/1952	02:00	CST
4/26/1953	02:00	CDT
9/27/1953	02:00	CST
4/25/1954	02:00	CDT
9/26/1954	02:00	CST
4/24/1955	02:00	EST
12/02/1956	02:00	CST
4/28/1957	02:00	CDT
9/29/1957	02:00	CST
4/27/1958	02:00	CDT
9/28/1958	02:00	CST
4/26/1959	02:00	EST
4/27/1969	02:00	EDT
10/26/1969	02:00	EST
4/26/1970	02:00	EDT
10/25/1970	02:00	EST

IN # 122

Before 11/18/1883		LMT
11/18/1883	12:00	CST
3/31/1918	02:00	CWT
10/27/1918	02:00	CST
3/30/1919	02:00	CWT
10/26/1919	02:00	CST
2/09/1942	02:00	CWT
9/30/1945	02:00	CST
4/28/1946	02:00	CDT
9/29/1946	02:00	CST
4/27/1947	02:00	CDT
9/28/1947	02:00	CST
4/25/1948	02:00	CDT
9/26/1948	02:00	CST
4/24/1949	02:00	CDT
9/25/1949	02:00	CST
4/30/1950	02:00	CDT
9/24/1950	02:00	CST
4/29/1951	02:00	CDT
9/30/1951	02:00	CST
4/27/1952	02:00	CDT
9/28/1952	02:00	CST
4/26/1953	02:00	CDT
9/27/1953	02:00	CST
4/25/1954	02:00	CDT
9/26/1954	02:00	CST
4/24/1955	02:00	CDT
9/25/1955	02:00	CST
4/29/1956	02:00	CDT
9/30/1956	02:00	CST
4/28/1957	02:00	CDT
9/29/1957	02:00	CST
4/27/1958	02:00	CDT
9/28/1958	02:00	CST
4/26/1959	02:00	CDT
9/27/1959	02:00	CST
4/24/1960	02:00	EST
4/27/1969	02:00	EDT
10/26/1969	02:00	EST
4/26/1970	02:00	EDT
10/25/1970	02:00	EST

IN # 123

Before 11/18/1883		LMT
11/18/1883	12:00	CST
3/31/1918	02:00	CWT
10/27/1918	02:00	CST
3/30/1919	02:00	CWT
10/26/1919	02:00	CST
2/09/1942	02:00	CWT
9/30/1945	02:00	CST
4/27/1947	02:00	CDT
9/28/1947	02:00	CST
4/25/1948	02:00	CDT
9/26/1948	02:00	CST
4/30/1950	02:00	CDT
9/24/1950	02:00	CST
4/24/1955	02:00	CDT
10/30/1955	02:00	CST
4/29/1956	02:00	CDT
10/28/1956	02:00	CST
4/28/1957	02:00	CDT
9/29/1957	02:00	CST
4/27/1958	02:00	CDT
9/28/1958	02:00	CST
4/26/1959	02:00	CDT
9/27/1959	02:00	CST
4/24/1960	02:00	EST
4/27/1969	02:00	EDT
10/26/1969	02:00	EST
4/26/1970	02:00	EDT
10/25/1970	02:00	EST

IN # 124

Before 11/18/1883		LMT
11/18/1883	12:00	CST
3/31/1918	02:00	CWT
10/27/1918	02:00	CST
3/30/1919	02:00	CWT
10/26/1919	02:00	CST
2/09/1942	02:00	CWT
9/30/1945	02:00	CST
4/25/1948	02:00	CDT
10/01/1948	02:00	CST
4/24/1949	02:00	CDT
9/25/1949	02:00	CST
4/30/1950	02:00	CDT
9/24/1950	02:00	CST
4/24/1955	02:00	CDT
10/30/1955	02:00	CST
4/29/1956	02:00	CDT
10/28/1956	02:00	CST
4/28/1957	02:00	CDT
9/29/1957	02:00	CST
4/27/1958	02:00	CDT
9/28/1958	02:00	CST
4/26/1959	02:00	CDT
9/27/1959	02:00	CST
4/24/1960	02:00	EST
4/27/1969	02:00	EDT
10/26/1969	02:00	EST
4/26/1970	02:00	EDT
10/25/1970	02:00	EST

IN # 125

Before 11/18/1883		LMT
11/18/1883	12:00	CST
3/31/1918	02:00	CWT
10/27/1918	02:00	CST
3/30/1919	02:00	CWT
10/26/1919	02:00	CST
2/09/1942	02:00	CWT
9/30/1945	02:00	CST
4/27/1952	02:00	CDT
9/28/1952	02:00	CST
4/26/1953	02:00	CDT
9/27/1953	02:00	CST
4/25/1954	02:00	CDT
9/26/1954	02:00	CST
4/24/1955	02:00	CDT
9/25/1955	02:00	CST
4/29/1956	02:00	CDT
9/30/1956	02:00	CST
4/28/1957	02:00	CDT
9/29/1957	02:00	CST
4/27/1958	02:00	CDT
9/28/1958	02:00	CST
4/26/1959	02:00	CDT
9/27/1959	02:00	CST
4/24/1960	02:00	EST
4/27/1969	02:00	EDT
10/26/1969	02:00	EST
4/26/1970	02:00	EDT
10/25/1970	02:00	EST

IN # 126

Before 11/18/1883		LMT
11/18/1883	12:00	CST
3/31/1918	02:00	CWT
10/27/1918	02:00	CST
3/30/1919	02:00	CWT
10/26/1919	02:00	CST
2/09/1942	02:00	CWT
9/30/1945	02:00	CST
4/26/1953	02:00	CDT
9/27/1953	02:00	CST
4/25/1954	02:00	CDT
9/26/1954	02:00	CST
4/24/1955	02:00	CDT
9/25/1955	02:00	CST
4/29/1956	02:00	CDT
9/30/1956	02:00	CST
4/28/1957	02:00	CDT
9/29/1957	02:00	CST
4/27/1958	02:00	CDT
9/28/1958	02:00	CST
4/26/1959	02:00	CDT
9/27/1959	02:00	CST
4/24/1960	02:00	EST
4/27/1969	02:00	EDT
10/26/1969	02:00	EST
4/26/1970	02:00	EDT
10/25/1970	02:00	EST

IN # 127

Before 11/18/1883		LMT
11/18/1883	12:00	CST
3/31/1918	02:00	CWT
10/27/1918	02:00	CST
3/30/1919	02:00	CWT
10/26/1919	02:00	CST
2/09/1942	02:00	CWT
9/30/1945	02:00	CST
4/25/1954	02:00	CDT
9/26/1954	02:00	CST
4/24/1955	02:00	CDT
9/25/1955	02:00	CST
4/29/1956	02:00	CDT
9/30/1956	02:00	CST
4/28/1957	02:00	CDT
9/29/1957	02:00	CST
4/27/1958	02:00	CDT
9/28/1958	02:00	CST
4/26/1959	02:00	CDT
9/27/1959	02:00	CST
4/24/1960	02:00	EST
4/27/1969	02:00	EDT
10/26/1969	02:00	EST
4/26/1970	02:00	EDT
10/25/1970	02:00	EST

IN # 128

Before 11/18/1883		LMT
11/18/1883	12:00	CST
3/31/1918	02:00	CWT
10/27/1918	02:00	CST
3/30/1919	02:00	CWT
10/26/1919	02:00	CST
2/09/1942	02:00	CWT
9/30/1945	02:00	CST
4/24/1955	02:00	CDT
9/25/1955	02:00	CST
4/29/1956	02:00	CDT
9/30/1956	02:00	CST
4/28/1957	02:00	CDT
9/29/1957	02:00	CST
4/27/1958	02:00	CDT
9/28/1958	02:00	CST
4/26/1959	02:00	CDT
9/27/1959	02:00	CST
4/24/1960	02:00	EST
4/27/1969	02:00	EDT

TIME TABLES

10/26/1969 02:00 EST
4/26/1970 02:00 EDT
10/25/1970 02:00 EST

IN # 129
Before 11/18/1883 LMT
11/18/1883 12:00 CST
3/31/1918 02:00 CWT
10/27/1918 02:00 CST
3/30/1919 02:00 CWT
10/26/1919 02:00 CST
2/09/1942 02:00 CWT
9/30/1945 02:00 CST
4/27/1952 02:00 CDT
9/28/1952 02:00 CST
4/26/1953 02:00 CDT
9/27/1953 02:00 CST
4/24/1955 02:00 CDT
9/25/1955 02:00 CST
4/29/1956 02:00 CDT
10/01/1956 02:00 CST
4/28/1957 02:00 CDT
9/29/1957 02:00 CST
4/27/1958 02:00 CDT
9/28/1958 02:00 CST
4/26/1959 02:00 CDT
9/27/1959 02:00 CST
4/24/1960 02:00 EST
4/27/1969 02:00 EDT
10/26/1969 02:00 EST
4/26/1970 02:00 EDT
10/25/1970 02:00 EST

IN # 130
Before 11/18/1883 LMT
11/18/1883 12:00 CST
3/31/1918 02:00 CWT
10/27/1918 02:00 CST
3/30/1919 02:00 CWT
10/26/1919 02:00 CST
6/29/1941 02:00 CDT
10/26/1941 02:00 CST
2/09/1942 02:00 CWT
9/30/1945 02:00 CST
4/27/1947 02:00 CDT
9/28/1947 02:00 CST
4/26/1953 02:00 CDT
9/27/1953 02:00 CST
4/25/1954 02:00 CDT
9/26/1954 02:00 CST
4/24/1955 02:00 CDT
10/30/1955 02:00 CST
4/29/1956 02:00 CDT
11/19/1956 01:00 CST
4/28/1957 02:00 CDT
9/29/1957 02:00 CST
4/27/1958 02:00 CDT
10/26/1958 02:00 CST
4/26/1959 02:00 CDT
10/25/1959 02:00 CST
4/24/1960 02:00 EST
4/27/1969 02:00 EDT
10/26/1969 02:00 EST
4/26/1970 02:00 EDT
10/25/1970 02:00 EST

IN # 131
Before 11/18/1883 LMT
11/18/1883 12:00 CST
3/31/1918 02:00 CWT
10/27/1918 02:00 CST
3/30/1919 02:00 CWT
10/26/1919 02:00 CST
4/26/1936 02:00 CDT
9/27/1936 02:00 CST
4/24/1938 02:00 CDT
9/25/1938 02:00 CST
4/30/1939 02:00 CDT
9/24/1939 02:00 CST
4/28/1940 02:00 CDT
9/29/1940 02:00 CST
4/27/1941 02:00 CDT
9/28/1941 02:00 CST
2/09/1942 02:00 CWT
9/30/1945 02:00 CST
4/28/1946 02:00 CDT
9/29/1946 02:00 CST
4/25/1948 02:00 CDT
9/26/1948 02:00 CST
4/30/1950 02:00 CDT
9/24/1950 02:00 CST
4/29/1951 02:00 CDT
9/30/1951 02:00 CST
4/27/1952 02:00 CDT
9/28/1952 02:00 CST
4/26/1953 02:00 CDT
9/27/1953 02:00 CST
4/25/1954 02:00 CDT
9/26/1954 02:00 CST
4/24/1955 02:00 CDT
10/30/1955 02:00 CST
4/29/1956 02:00 CDT
9/29/1957 02:00 CST
4/27/1958 02:00 CDT
9/28/1958 02:00 CST
4/26/1959 02:00 CDT
9/27/1959 02:00 CST
4/24/1960 02:00 EST
4/27/1969 02:00 EDT
10/26/1969 02:00 EST
4/26/1970 02:00 EDT
10/25/1970 02:00 EST

IN # 132
Before 11/18/1883 LMT
11/18/1883 12:00 CST
3/31/1918 02:00 CWT
10/27/1918 02:00 CST
3/30/1919 02:00 CWT
10/26/1919 02:00 CST
2/09/1942 02:00 CWT
9/30/1945 02:00 CST
4/27/1947 02:00 CDT
9/28/1947 02:00 CST
4/24/1949 02:00 CDT
9/25/1949 02:00 CST
4/23/1950 02:00 CDT
9/09/1950 02:00 CST
4/28/1957 02:00 CDT
9/29/1957 02:00 CST
4/27/1958 02:00 CDT
9/28/1958 02:00 CST
4/26/1959 02:00 CDT
9/27/1959 02:00 CST
4/24/1960 02:00 EST
4/27/1969 02:00 EDT
10/26/1969 02:00 EST
4/26/1970 02:00 EDT
10/25/1970 02:00 EST

IN # 133
Before 11/18/1883 LMT
11/18/1883 12:00 CST
3/31/1918 02:00 CWT
10/27/1918 02:00 CST
3/30/1919 02:00 CWT
10/26/1919 02:00 CST
2/09/1942 02:00 CWT
9/30/1945 02:00 CST
4/27/1952 02:00 CDT
9/28/1952 02:00 CST
4/26/1953 02:00 CDT
9/27/1953 02:00 CST
4/25/1954 02:00 CDT
9/26/1954 02:00 CST
4/24/1955 02:00 CDT
9/25/1955 02:00 CST
4/29/1956 02:00 CDT
10/28/1956 02:00 CST
4/28/1957 02:00 CDT
9/29/1957 02:00 CST
4/27/1958 02:00 CDT
10/26/1958 02:00 CST
4/26/1959 02:00 CDT
10/25/1959 02:00 CST
4/24/1960 02:00 EST
4/27/1969 02:00 EDT
10/26/1969 02:00 EST
4/26/1970 02:00 EDT
10/25/1970 02:00 EST

IN # 134
Before 11/18/1883 LMT
11/18/1883 12:00 CST
3/31/1918 02:00 CWT
10/27/1918 02:00 CST
3/30/1919 02:00 CWT
10/26/1919 02:00 CST
6/29/1941 01:00 CDT
10/26/1941 01:00 CST
2/09/1942 02:00 CWT
9/30/1945 02:00 CST
5/04/1946 02:00 CDT
10/05/1946 02:00 CST
4/27/1947 02:00 CDT
9/28/1947 02:00 CST
4/25/1948 02:00 CDT
9/26/1948 02:00 CST
4/24/1949 02:00 CDT
9/25/1949 02:00 CST
4/23/1950 02:00 CDT
9/09/1950 02:00 CST
4/29/1951 02:00 CDT
9/30/1951 02:00 CST
4/27/1952 02:00 CDT
9/28/1952 02:00 CST
4/26/1953 02:00 CDT
9/27/1953 02:00 CST
4/25/1954 02:00 CDT
9/26/1954 02:00 CST
4/24/1955 02:00 CDT
10/30/1955 02:00 CST
4/29/1956 02:00 CDT
10/28/1956 01:00 CST
4/28/1957 02:00 CDT
9/29/1957 02:00 CST
4/27/1958 02:00 CDT
9/28/1958 02:00 CST
4/26/1959 02:00 CDT
9/27/1959 02:00 CST
4/24/1960 02:00 EST
4/27/1969 02:00 EDT
10/26/1969 02:00 EST
4/26/1970 02:00 EDT
10/25/1970 02:00 EST

IN # 135
Before 11/18/1883 LMT
11/18/1883 12:00 CST
3/31/1918 02:00 CWT
10/27/1918 02:00 CST
3/30/1919 02:00 CWT
10/26/1919 02:00 CST
4/27/1941 02:00 CDT
10/28/1941 02:00 CST
2/09/1942 02:00 CWT
9/30/1945 02:00 CST
4/25/1948 02:00 CDT
9/26/1948 02:00 CST
4/30/1950 02:00 CDT
9/24/1950 02:00 CST
4/24/1955 02:00 CDT
10/30/1955 02:00 CST
4/29/1956 02:00 CDT
10/28/1956 02:00 CST
4/28/1957 02:00 CDT
9/29/1957 02:00 CST
4/27/1958 02:00 CDT
9/28/1958 02:00 CST
4/26/1959 02:00 CDT
9/27/1959 02:00 CST
4/24/1960 02:00 EST
4/27/1969 02:00 EDT
10/26/1969 02:00 EST
4/26/1970 02:00 EDT
10/25/1970 02:00 EST

IN # 136
Before 11/18/1883 LMT
11/18/1883 12:00 CST
3/31/1918 02:00 CWT
10/27/1918 02:00 CST
3/30/1919 02:00 CWT
10/26/1919 02:00 CST
2/09/1942 02:00 CWT
9/30/1945 02:00 CST
4/26/1953 02:00 CDT
9/27/1953 02:00 CST
4/25/1954 02:00 CDT
9/26/1954 02:00 CST
4/24/1955 02:00 CDT
9/25/1955 02:00 CST
4/02/1956 02:00 CDT
9/29/1956 02:00 CST
4/28/1957 02:00 CDT
9/29/1957 02:00 CST
4/27/1958 02:00 CDT
9/28/1958 02:00 CST
4/26/1959 02:00 CDT
9/27/1959 02:00 CST
4/24/1960 02:00 EST
4/27/1969 02:00 EDT
10/26/1969 02:00 EST
4/26/1970 02:00 EDT
10/25/1970 02:00 EST

IN # 137
Before 11/18/1883 LMT
11/18/1883 12:00 CST
3/31/1918 02:00 CWT
10/27/1918 02:00 CST
3/30/1919 02:00 CWT
10/26/1919 02:00 CST
2/09/1942 02:00 CWT
9/30/1945 02:00 CST
5/01/1950 02:00 CDT
9/30/1950 02:00 CST
4/28/1957 02:00 CDT
9/29/1957 02:00 CST
4/27/1958 02:00 CDT
9/28/1958 02:00 CST
4/26/1959 02:00 CDT
9/27/1959 02:00 CST
4/24/1960 02:00 EST
4/27/1969 02:00 EDT
10/26/1969 02:00 EST
4/26/1970 02:00 EDT
10/25/1970 02:00 EST

IN # 138
Before 11/18/1883 LMT
11/18/1883 12:00 CST
3/31/1918 02:00 CWT
10/27/1918 02:00 CST
3/30/1919 02:00 CWT
10/26/1919 02:00 CST
6/29/1941 02:00 CDT
10/26/1941 02:00 CST
2/09/1942 02:00 CWT
9/30/1945 02:00 CST
4/30/1950 02:00 CDT
9/24/1950 02:00 CST
4/29/1951 02:00 CDT
9/30/1951 02:00 CST
4/27/1952 02:00 CDT
9/28/1952 02:00 CST
4/26/1953 02:00 CDT
9/27/1953 02:00 CST
4/25/1954 02:00 CDT
9/26/1954 02:00 CST
4/24/1955 02:00 CDT
10/30/1955 02:00 CST
4/29/1956 02:00 CDT
9/23/1956 00:01 CST
4/28/1957 02:00 CDT
9/29/1957 02:00 CST
4/27/1958 02:00 CDT
9/28/1958 02:00 CST
4/26/1959 02:00 CDT
9/27/1959 02:00 CST
4/24/1960 02:00 EST
4/27/1969 02:00 EDT
10/26/1969 02:00 EST
4/26/1970 02:00 EDT
10/25/1970 02:00 EST

IN # 139
Before 11/18/1883 LMT
11/18/1883 12:00 CST
3/31/1918 02:00 CWT
10/27/1918 02:00 CST
3/30/1919 02:00 CWT
10/26/1919 02:00 CST
2/09/1942 02:00 CWT
9/30/1945 02:00 CST
4/26/1953 02:00 CDT
9/27/1953 02:00 CST
4/25/1954 02:00 CDT
9/26/1954 02:00 CST
4/24/1955 02:00 CDT
10/30/1955 02:00 CST
4/29/1956 02:00 CDT
11/18/1956 02:00 CST
4/28/1957 02:00 CDT
9/29/1957 02:00 CST
4/27/1958 02:00 CDT
9/28/1958 02:00 CST
4/26/1959 02:00 CDT
9/27/1959 02:00 CST
4/24/1960 02:00 EST
4/27/1969 02:00 EDT
10/26/1969 02:00 EST
4/26/1970 02:00 EDT
10/25/1970 02:00 EST

IN # 140
Before 11/18/1883 LMT
11/18/1883 12:00 CST
3/31/1918 02:00 CWT
10/27/1918 02:00 CST
3/30/1919 02:00 CWT
10/26/1919 02:00 CST
2/09/1942 02:00 CWT
9/30/1945 02:00 CST
5/05/1946 02:00 CDT
9/27/1946 02:00 CST
4/27/1947 02:00 CDT
9/28/1947 02:00 CST
4/25/1954 02:00 CDT
9/26/1954 02:00 CST
4/24/1955 02:00 CDT
9/25/1955 02:00 CST
4/29/1956 02:00 CDT
10/28/1956 02:00 CST
4/28/1957 02:00 CDT
9/29/1957 02:00 CST
4/27/1958 02:00 CDT
10/26/1958 02:00 CST
4/26/1959 02:00 CDT
10/25/1959 02:00 CST
4/24/1960 02:00 EST
4/27/1969 02:00 EDT
10/26/1969 02:00 EST
4/26/1970 02:00 EDT
10/25/1970 02:00 EST

IN # 141
Before 11/18/1883 LMT
11/18/1883 12:00 CST
3/31/1918 02:00 CWT
10/27/1918 02:00 CST
3/30/1919 02:00 CWT
10/26/1919 02:00 CST
2/09/1942 02:00 CWT
9/30/1945 02:00 CST
4/24/1955 02:00 CDT
10/30/1955 02:00 CST
4/29/1956 02:00 CDT
11/18/1956 02:00 CST
4/28/1957 02:00 CDT
9/29/1957 02:00 CST
4/27/1958 02:00 CDT
9/28/1958 02:00 CST
4/26/1959 02:00 CDT
9/27/1959 02:00 CST
4/24/1960 02:00 EST
4/27/1969 02:00 EDT
10/26/1969 02:00 EST
4/26/1970 02:00 EDT
10/25/1970 02:00 EST

IN # 142
Before 11/18/1883 LMT
11/18/1883 12:00 CST
3/31/1918 02:00 CWT
10/27/1918 02:00 CST
3/30/1919 02:00 CWT
10/26/1919 02:00 CST
2/09/1942 02:00 CWT
9/30/1945 02:00 CST
4/30/1950 02:00 CDT
9/24/1950 02:00 CST
4/25/1954 02:00 CDT
9/26/1954 02:00 CST
4/24/1955 02:00 CDT
9/25/1955 02:00 CST
4/29/1956 02:00 CDT
10/28/1956 02:00 CST
4/28/1957 02:00 CDT
9/29/1957 02:00 CST
4/27/1958 02:00 CDT
10/26/1958 02:00 CST
4/26/1959 02:00 CDT
10/25/1959 02:00 CST
4/24/1960 02:00 EST
4/27/1969 02:00 EDT
10/26/1969 02:00 EST
4/26/1970 02:00 EDT
10/25/1970 02:00 EST

IN # 143
Before 11/18/1883 LMT
11/18/1883 12:00 CST
3/31/1918 02:00 CWT
10/27/1918 02:00 CST
3/30/1919 02:00 CWT
10/26/1919 02:00 CST
2/09/1942 02:00 CWT
9/30/1945 02:00 CST
4/25/1954 02:00 CDT
9/26/1954 02:00 CST
4/24/1955 02:00 CDT
9/25/1955 02:00 CST
4/29/1956 02:00 CDT
10/28/1956 02:00 CST
4/28/1957 02:00 CDT
9/29/1957 02:00 CST
4/27/1958 02:00 CDT
10/26/1958 02:00 CST
4/26/1959 02:00 CDT
10/25/1959 02:00 CST
4/24/1960 02:00 EST
4/27/1969 02:00 EDT
10/26/1969 02:00 EST
4/26/1970 02:00 EDT
10/25/1970 02:00 EST

IN # 144
Before 11/18/1883 LMT
11/18/1883 12:00 CST
3/31/1918 02:00 CWT
10/27/1918 02:00 CST
3/30/1919 02:00 CWT
10/26/1919 02:00 CST
2/09/1942 02:00 CWT
9/30/1945 02:00 CST
4/26/1953 02:00 CDT
9/27/1953 02:00 CST
4/25/1954 02:00 CDT
9/26/1954 02:00 CST
4/24/1955 02:00 CDT
9/25/1955 02:00 CST
4/29/1956 02:00 CDT
10/28/1956 02:00 CST
4/28/1957 02:00 CDT
9/29/1957 02:00 CST
4/27/1958 02:00 CDT
10/26/1958 02:00 CST
4/26/1959 02:00 CDT
10/25/1959 02:00 CST
4/24/1960 02:00 EST
4/27/1969 02:00 EDT
10/26/1969 02:00 EST
4/26/1970 02:00 EDT
10/25/1970 02:00 EST

IN # 145
Before 11/18/1883 LMT
11/18/1883 12:00 CST
3/31/1918 02:00 CWT
10/27/1918 02:00 CST
3/30/1919 02:00 CWT
10/26/1919 02:00 CST
2/09/1942 02:00 CWT
9/30/1945 02:00 CST
4/24/1955 02:00 CDT
10/30/1955 02:00 CST
4/29/1956 02:00 CDT
11/19/1956 01:00 CST
4/28/1957 02:00 CDT
9/29/1957 02:00 CST
4/27/1958 02:00 CDT
9/28/1958 02:00 CST
4/26/1959 02:00 CDT
9/27/1959 02:00 CST
4/24/1960 02:00 EST
4/27/1969 02:00 EDT
10/26/1969 02:00 EST
4/26/1970 02:00 EDT
10/25/1970 02:00 EST

IN # 146
Before 11/18/1883 LMT
11/18/1883 12:00 CST
3/31/1918 02:00 CWT
10/27/1918 02:00 CST
3/30/1919 02:00 CWT
10/26/1919 02:00 CST
2/09/1942 02:00 CWT
9/30/1945 02:00 CST
4/24/1955 02:00 CDT
9/25/1955 02:00 CST
4/29/1956 02:00 CDT
10/28/1956 02:00 CST
4/28/1957 02:00 CDT
9/29/1957 02:00 CST
4/27/1958 02:00 CDT
9/28/1958 02:00 CST
4/26/1959 02:00 CDT
9/27/1959 02:00 CST
4/24/1960 02:00 EST
4/27/1969 02:00 EDT
10/26/1969 02:00 EST
4/26/1970 02:00 EDT
10/25/1970 02:00 EST

IN # 147
Before 11/18/1883 LMT
11/18/1883 12:00 CST
3/31/1918 02:00 CWT
10/27/1918 02:00 CST
3/30/1919 02:00 CWT
10/26/1919 02:00 CST
2/09/1942 02:00 CWT
9/30/1945 02:00 CST
4/24/1955 02:00 CDT
10/30/1955 02:00 CST
4/29/1956 02:00 CDT
10/28/1956 02:00 CST
4/28/1957 02:00 CDT
9/29/1957 02:00 CST
4/27/1958 02:00 CDT
9/28/1958 02:00 CST
4/26/1959 02:00 CDT
9/27/1959 02:00 CST
4/24/1960 02:00 EST
4/27/1969 02:00 EDT
10/26/1969 02:00 EST
4/26/1970 02:00 EDT
10/25/1970 02:00 EST

IN # 148
Before 11/18/1883 LMT
11/18/1883 12:00 CST
3/31/1918 02:00 CWT
10/27/1918 02:00 CST
3/30/1919 02:00 CWT
10/26/1919 02:00 CST
2/09/1942 02:00 CWT
9/30/1945 02:00 CST
4/25/1954 02:00 CDT
9/26/1954 02:00 CST
4/24/1955 02:00 CDT
10/30/1955 02:00 CST
4/29/1956 02:00 CDT
10/28/1956 02:00 CST
4/28/1957 02:00 CDT
9/29/1957 02:00 CST
4/27/1958 02:00 CDT
9/28/1958 02:00 CST

TIME TABLES

4/26/1959 02:00 CDT
9/27/1959 02:00 CST
4/24/1960 02:00 EST
4/27/1969 02:00 EDT
10/26/1969 02:00 EST
4/26/1970 02:00 EDT
10/25/1970 02:00 EST

....

IN # 149

Before 11/18/1883 LMT
11/18/1883 12:00 CST
3/31/1918 02:00 CWT
10/27/1918 02:00 CST
3/30/1919 02:00 CWT
10/26/1919 02:00 CST
2/09/1942 02:00 CWT
9/30/1945 02:00 CST
4/26/1953 02:00 CDT
9/27/1953 02:00 CST
4/25/1954 02:00 CDT
9/26/1954 02:00 CST
4/24/1955 02:00 CDT
10/30/1955 02:00 CST
4/29/1956 02:00 CDT
10/28/1956 02:00 CST
4/28/1957 02:00 CDT
9/29/1957 02:00 CST
4/27/1958 02:00 CDT
9/28/1958 02:00 CST
4/26/1959 02:00 CDT
9/27/1959 02:00 CST
4/24/1960 02:00 EST
4/27/1969 02:00 EDT
10/26/1969 02:00 EST
4/26/1970 02:00 EDT
10/25/1970 02:00 EST

....

IN # 150

Before 11/18/1883 LMT
11/18/1883 12:00 CST
3/31/1918 02:00 CWT
10/27/1918 02:00 CST
3/30/1919 02:00 CWT
10/26/1919 02:00 CST
2/09/1942 02:00 CWT
9/30/1945 02:00 CST
4/25/1948 02:00 CDT
9/26/1948 02:00 CST
4/24/1955 02:00 CDT
10/30/1955 02:00 CST
4/29/1956 02:00 CDT
10/28/1956 02:00 CST
4/28/1957 02:00 CDT
9/29/1957 02:00 CST
4/27/1958 02:00 CDT
9/28/1958 02:00 CST
4/26/1959 02:00 CDT
9/27/1959 02:00 CST
4/24/1960 02:00 EST
4/27/1969 02:00 EDT
10/26/1969 02:00 EST
4/26/1970 02:00 EDT
10/25/1970 02:00 EST

....

IN # 151

Before 11/18/1883 LMT
11/18/1883 12:00 CST
3/31/1918 02:00 CWT
10/27/1918 02:00 CST
3/30/1919 02:00 CWT
10/26/1919 02:00 CST
2/09/1942 02:00 CWT
9/30/1945 02:00 CST
4/29/1951 02:00 CDT
9/30/1951 02:00 CST
4/28/1957 02:00 CDT
9/29/1957 02:00 CST
4/27/1958 02:00 CDT
9/28/1958 02:00 CST
4/26/1959 02:00 CDT
9/27/1959 02:00 CST
4/24/1960 02:00 EST
4/27/1969 02:00 EDT
10/26/1969 02:00 EST
4/26/1970 02:00 EDT
10/25/1970 02:00 EST

....

IN # 152

Before 11/18/1883 LMT
11/18/1883 12:00 CST
3/31/1918 02:00 CWT
10/27/1918 02:00 CST
3/30/1919 02:00 CWT
10/26/1919 02:00 CST
2/09/1942 02:00 CWT
9/30/1945 02:00 CST
4/24/1955 02:00 CDT
10/30/1955 02:00 CST
4/29/1956 02:00 CDT
10/28/1956 02:00 CST
4/28/1957 02:00 CDT
9/29/1957 02:00 CST
4/27/1958 02:00 CDT
10/26/1958 02:00 CST
4/26/1959 02:00 CDT
10/25/1959 02:00 CST
4/24/1960 02:00 EST
4/27/1969 02:00 EDT
10/26/1969 02:00 EST
4/26/1970 02:00 EDT
10/25/1970 02:00 EST

....

IN # 153

Before 11/18/1883 LMT
11/18/1883 12:00 CST
3/31/1918 02:00 CWT
10/27/1918 02:00 CST
3/30/1919 02:00 CWT
10/26/1919 02:00 CST
2/09/1942 02:00 CWT
9/30/1945 02:00 CST
4/27/1947 02:00 CDT
9/28/1947 02:00 CST
4/27/1952 02:00 CDT
9/28/1952 02:00 CST
4/26/1953 02:00 CDT
9/27/1953 02:00 CST
4/25/1954 02:00 CDT
9/26/1954 02:00 CST
4/24/1955 02:00 CDT
10/30/1955 02:00 CST
4/29/1956 02:00 CDT
10/28/1956 02:00 CST
4/28/1957 02:00 CDT
9/29/1957 02:00 CST
4/27/1958 02:00 CDT
9/28/1958 02:00 CST
4/26/1959 02:00 CDT
9/27/1959 02:00 CST
4/24/1960 02:00 EST
4/27/1969 02:00 EDT
10/26/1969 02:00 EST
4/26/1970 02:00 EDT
10/25/1970 02:00 EST

....

IN # 154

Before 11/18/1883 LMT
11/18/1883 12:00 CST
3/31/1918 02:00 CWT
10/27/1918 02:00 CST
3/30/1919 02:00 CWT
10/26/1919 02:00 CST
2/09/1942 02:00 CWT
9/30/1945 02:00 CST
4/27/1952 02:00 CDT
9/28/1952 02:00 CST
4/26/1953 02:00 CDT
9/27/1953 02:00 CST
4/25/1954 02:00 CDT
9/26/1954 02:00 CST
4/24/1955 02:00 CDT
10/30/1955 02:00 CST
4/29/1956 02:00 CDT
10/28/1956 02:00 CST
4/28/1957 02:00 CDT
9/29/1957 02:00 CST
4/27/1958 02:00 CDT
9/28/1958 02:00 CST
4/26/1959 02:00 CDT
9/27/1959 02:00 CST
4/24/1960 02:00 EST
4/27/1969 02:00 EDT
10/26/1969 02:00 EST
4/26/1970 02:00 EDT
10/25/1970 02:00 EST

....

IN # 155

Before 11/18/1883 LMT
11/18/1883 12:00 CST
3/31/1918 02:00 CWT
10/27/1918 02:00 CST
3/30/1919 02:00 CWT
10/26/1919 02:00 CST
2/09/1942 02:00 CWT
9/30/1945 02:00 CST
4/24/1955 02:00 CDT
10/30/1955 02:00 CST
4/29/1956 02:00 CDT
10/01/1956 00:00 CST
4/28/1957 02:00 CDT
9/29/1957 02:00 CST
4/27/1958 02:00 CDT
9/28/1958 02:00 CST
4/26/1959 02:00 CDT
9/27/1959 02:00 CST
4/24/1960 02:00 EST
4/27/1969 02:00 EDT
10/26/1969 02:00 EST
4/26/1970 02:00 EDT
10/25/1970 02:00 EST

....

IN # 156

Before 11/18/1883 LMT
11/18/1883 12:00 CST
3/31/1918 02:00 CWT
10/27/1918 02:00 CST
3/30/1919 02:00 CWT
10/26/1919 02:00 CST
2/09/1942 02:00 CWT
9/30/1945 02:00 CST
4/24/1955 02:00 CDT
9/25/1955 02:00 CST
4/29/1956 02:00 CDT
10/01/1956 02:00 CST
4/28/1957 02:00 CDT
9/29/1957 02:00 CST
4/27/1958 02:00 CDT
9/28/1958 02:00 CST
4/26/1959 02:00 CDT
9/27/1959 02:00 CST
4/24/1960 02:00 EST
4/27/1969 02:00 EDT
10/26/1969 02:00 EST
4/26/1970 02:00 EDT
10/25/1970 02:00 EST

....

IN # 157

Before 11/18/1883 LMT
11/18/1883 12:00 CST
3/31/1918 02:00 CWT
10/27/1918 02:00 CST
3/30/1919 02:00 CWT
10/26/1919 02:00 CST
2/09/1942 02:00 CWT
9/30/1945 02:00 CST
4/26/1953 02:00 CDT
9/27/1953 02:00 CST
4/25/1954 02:00 CDT
9/26/1954 02:00 CST
4/24/1955 02:00 CDT
9/25/1955 02:00 CST
4/29/1956 02:00 CDT
10/28/1956 02:00 CST
4/28/1957 02:00 CDT
9/29/1957 02:00 CST
4/27/1958 02:00 CDT
9/28/1958 02:00 CST
4/26/1959 02:00 CDT
9/27/1959 02:00 CST
4/24/1960 02:00 EST
4/27/1969 02:00 EDT
10/26/1969 02:00 EST
4/26/1970 02:00 EDT
10/25/1970 02:00 EST

....

IN # 158

Before 11/18/1883 LMT
11/18/1883 12:00 CST
3/31/1918 02:00 CWT
10/27/1918 02:00 CST
3/30/1919 02:00 CWT
10/26/1919 02:00 CST
2/09/1942 02:00 CWT
9/30/1945 02:00 CST
4/26/1953 02:00 CDT
9/27/1953 02:00 CST
4/25/1954 02:00 CDT
9/26/1954 02:00 CST
4/24/1955 02:00 CDT
9/25/1955 02:00 CST
4/29/1956 02:00 CDT
10/01/1956 02:00 CST
4/28/1957 02:00 CDT
9/29/1957 02:00 CST
4/27/1958 02:00 CDT
9/28/1958 02:00 CST
4/26/1959 02:00 CDT
9/27/1959 02:00 CST
4/24/1960 02:00 EST
4/27/1969 02:00 EDT
10/26/1969 02:00 EST
4/26/1970 02:00 EDT
10/25/1970 02:00 EST

....

IN # 159

Before 11/18/1883 LMT
11/18/1883 12:00 CST
3/31/1918 02:00 CWT
10/27/1918 02:00 CST
3/30/1919 02:00 CWT
10/26/1919 02:00 CST
2/09/1942 02:00 CWT
9/30/1945 02:00 CST
5/01/1955 00:00 CDT
9/04/1955 00:00 CST
4/29/1956 02:00 CDT
9/30/1956 02:00 CST
4/28/1957 02:00 CDT
9/29/1957 02:00 CST
4/27/1958 02:00 CDT
9/28/1958 02:00 CST
4/26/1959 02:00 CDT
9/27/1959 02:00 CST
4/24/1960 02:00 EST
4/27/1969 02:00 EDT
10/26/1969 02:00 EST
4/26/1970 02:00 EDT
10/25/1970 02:00 EST

....

IN # 160

Before 11/18/1883 LMT
11/18/1883 12:00 CST
3/31/1918 02:00 CWT
10/27/1918 02:00 CST
3/30/1919 02:00 CWT
10/26/1919 02:00 CST
2/09/1942 02:00 CWT
9/30/1945 02:00 CST
4/24/1955 02:00 CDT
9/04/1955 00:00 CST
4/29/1956 02:00 CDT
9/30/1956 02:00 CST
4/28/1957 02:00 CDT
9/29/1957 02:00 CST
4/27/1958 02:00 CDT
9/28/1958 02:00 CST
4/26/1959 02:00 CDT
9/27/1959 02:00 CST
4/24/1960 02:00 EST
4/27/1969 02:00 EDT
10/26/1969 02:00 EST
4/26/1970 02:00 EDT
10/25/1970 02:00 EST

....

IN # 161

Before 11/18/1883 LMT
11/18/1883 12:00 CST
3/31/1918 02:00 CWT
10/27/1918 02:00 CST
3/30/1919 02:00 CWT
10/26/1919 02:00 CST
2/09/1942 02:00 CWT
9/30/1945 02:00 CST
4/26/1953 02:00 CDT
9/27/1953 02:00 CST
4/25/1954 02:00 CDT
9/26/1954 02:00 CST
4/24/1955 02:00 CDT
9/25/1955 02:00 CST
4/29/1956 02:00 CDT
9/30/1956 02:00 CST
4/28/1957 02:00 CDT
9/29/1957 02:00 CST
4/27/1958 02:00 CDT
9/28/1958 02:00 CST
4/26/1959 02:00 EST
4/27/1969 02:00 EDT
10/26/1969 02:00 EST
4/26/1970 02:00 EDT
10/25/1970 02:00 EST

....

IN # 162

Before 11/18/1883 LMT
11/18/1883 12:00 CST
3/31/1918 02:00 CWT
10/27/1918 02:00 CST
3/30/1919 02:00 CWT
10/26/1919 02:00 CST
2/09/1942 02:00 CWT
9/30/1945 02:00 CST
4/25/1948 02:00 CDT
9/26/1948 02:00 CST
4/27/1952 02:00 CDT
9/28/1952 02:00 CST
4/26/1953 02:00 CDT
9/27/1953 02:00 CST
4/25/1954 02:00 CDT
9/26/1954 02:00 CST
4/24/1955 02:00 CDT
9/25/1955 02:00 CST
4/29/1956 02:00 CDT
10/28/1956 02:00 CST
4/28/1957 02:00 CDT
9/29/1957 02:00 CST
4/27/1958 02:00 CDT
10/26/1958 02:00 CST
4/26/1959 02:00 CDT
10/25/1959 02:00 CST
4/24/1960 02:00 CDT
10/30/1960 02:00 CST
4/30/1961 02:00 EST
4/27/1969 02:00 EDT
10/26/1969 02:00 EST
4/26/1970 02:00 EDT
10/25/1970 02:00 EST

....

IN # 163

Before 11/18/1883 LMT
11/18/1883 12:00 CST
3/31/1918 02:00 CWT
10/27/1918 02:00 CST
3/30/1919 02:00 CWT
10/26/1919 02:00 CST
2/09/1942 02:00 CWT
9/30/1945 02:00 CST
4/25/1948 02:00 CDT
9/26/1948 02:00 CST
4/24/1955 02:00 CDT
9/25/1955 02:00 CST
4/29/1956 02:00 CDT
10/28/1956 02:00 CST
4/28/1957 02:00 CDT
9/29/1957 02:00 CST
4/27/1958 02:00 CDT
9/28/1958 02:00 CST
4/26/1959 02:00 CDT
9/27/1959 02:00 CST
4/24/1960 02:00 CDT
9/25/1960 02:00 CST
4/30/1961 02:00 EST
4/27/1969 02:00 EDT
10/26/1969 02:00 EST
4/26/1970 02:00 EDT
10/25/1970 02:00 EST

....

IN # 164

Before 11/18/1883 LMT
11/18/1883 12:00 CST
3/31/1918 02:00 CWT
10/27/1918 02:00 CST
3/30/1919 02:00 CWT
10/26/1919 02:00 CST
2/09/1942 02:00 CWT
9/30/1945 02:00 CST
4/26/1953 02:00 CDT
9/27/1953 02:00 CST
4/25/1954 02:00 CDT
9/26/1954 02:00 CST
4/24/1955 02:00 CDT
9/25/1955 02:00 CST
4/29/1956 02:00 CDT
9/30/1956 02:00 CST
4/28/1957 02:00 CDT
9/29/1957 02:00 CST
4/27/1958 02:00 CDT
9/28/1958 02:00 CST
4/26/1959 02:00 CDT
9/27/1959 02:00 CST
4/24/1960 02:00 CDT
9/25/1960 02:00 CST
4/30/1961 02:00 EST
4/27/1969 02:00 EDT
10/26/1969 02:00 EST
4/26/1970 02:00 EDT
10/25/1970 02:00 EST

....

IN # 165

Before 11/18/1883 LMT
11/18/1883 12:00 CST
3/31/1918 02:00 CWT
10/27/1918 02:00 CST
3/30/1919 02:00 CWT
10/26/1919 02:00 CST
2/09/1942 02:00 CWT
9/30/1945 02:00 CST
4/24/1955 02:00 CDT
9/25/1955 02:00 CST
4/29/1956 02:00 CDT
9/30/1956 02:00 CST
4/28/1957 02:00 CDT
9/29/1957 02:00 CST
4/27/1958 02:00 CDT
9/28/1958 02:00 CST
4/26/1959 02:00 CDT
9/27/1959 02:00 CST
4/24/1960 02:00 CDT
9/25/1960 02:00 CST
4/30/1961 02:00 EST
4/27/1969 02:00 EDT
10/26/1969 02:00 EST
4/26/1970 02:00 EDT
10/25/1970 02:00 EST

....

IN # 166

Before 11/18/1883 LMT
11/18/1883 12:00 CST
3/31/1918 02:00 CWT
10/27/1918 02:00 CST
3/30/1919 02:00 CWT
10/26/1919 02:00 CST
2/09/1942 02:00 CWT
9/30/1945 02:00 CST
4/24/1955 02:00 CDT
9/25/1955 02:00 CST
4/29/1956 02:00 CDT
9/30/1956 02:00 CST
4/28/1957 02:00 CDT
9/29/1957 02:00 CST
4/27/1958 02:00 CDT
9/28/1958 02:00 CST
4/26/1959 02:00 CDT
9/27/1959 02:00 CST
4/24/1960 02:00 CDT
9/25/1960 02:00 CST
4/30/1961 02:00 EST
4/27/1969 02:00 EDT
10/26/1969 02:00 EST
4/26/1970 02:00 EDT
10/25/1970 02:00 EST
4/25/1971 02:00 EDT
10/31/1971 02:00 EST
4/30/1972 02:00 EDT
10/29/1972 02:00 EST
4/29/1973 02:00 EDT
10/28/1973 02:00 EST
2/23/1975 02:00 US#1

....

IN # 167

Before 11/18/1883 LMT
11/18/1883 12:00 CST
3/31/1918 02:00 CWT
10/27/1918 02:00 CST
3/30/1919 02:00 CWT
10/26/1919 02:00 CST
4/27/1941 02:00 CDT
9/28/1941 02:00 CST
2/09/1942 02:00 CWT
9/30/1945 02:00 CST
4/27/1952 02:00 CDT
9/28/1952 02:00 CST
4/26/1953 02:00 CDT
9/27/1953 02:00 CST
4/25/1954 02:00 CDT
9/26/1954 02:00 CST
4/24/1955 02:00 CDT
9/25/1955 02:00 CST
4/29/1956 02:00 CDT
9/30/1956 02:00 CST
4/28/1957 02:00 CDT
9/29/1957 02:00 CST
4/27/1958 02:00 CDT
9/28/1958 02:00 CST
4/26/1959 02:00 CDT
10/25/1959 02:00 CST
4/24/1960 02:00 CDT
10/30/1960 02:00 CST
4/30/1961 02:00 EST
4/27/1969 02:00 EDT
10/26/1969 02:00 EST
4/26/1970 02:00 EDT
10/25/1970 02:00 EST
4/25/1971 02:00 EDT
10/31/1971 02:00 EST
4/30/1972 02:00 EDT
10/29/1972 02:00 EST
4/29/1973 02:00 EDT
10/28/1973 02:00 EST
2/23/1975 02:00 US#1

....

IN # 168

Before 11/18/1883 LMT
11/18/1883 12:00 CST
3/31/1918 02:00 CWT
10/27/1918 02:00 CST
3/30/1919 02:00 CWT
10/26/1919 02:00 CST
2/09/1942 02:00 CWT
9/30/1945 02:00 CST
4/25/1954 02:00 CDT
9/26/1954 02:00 CST
4/24/1955 02:00 CDT
9/25/1955 02:00 CST
4/29/1956 02:00 CDT
9/29/1957 02:00 CST
4/27/1958 02:00 CDT
10/26/1958 02:00 CST
4/26/1959 02:00 CDT
10/25/1959 02:00 CST
4/24/1960 02:00 CDT
10/30/1960 02:00 CST
4/30/1961 02:00 EST
4/27/1969 02:00 EDT
10/26/1969 02:00 EST
4/26/1970 02:00 EDT
10/25/1970 02:00 EST
4/25/1971 02:00 EDT
10/31/1971 02:00 EST
4/30/1972 02:00 EDT
10/29/1972 02:00 EST
4/29/1973 02:00 EDT
10/28/1973 02:00 EST
2/23/1975 02:00 US#1

....

IN # 169

Before 11/18/1883 LMT
11/18/1883 12:00 CST
3/31/1918 02:00 CWT
10/27/1918 02:00 CST
3/30/1919 02:00 CWT
10/26/1919 02:00 CST

TIME TABLES

2/09/1942 02:00 CWT
9/30/1945 02:00 CST
4/24/1955 02:00 CDT
9/25/1955 02:00 CST
4/29/1956 02:00 CDT
9/30/1956 02:00 CST
4/28/1957 02:00 CDT
9/29/1957 02:00 CST
4/27/1958 02:00 CDT
9/28/1958 02:00 CST
4/26/1959 02:00 CDT
9/27/1959 02:00 CST
4/24/1960 02:00 CDT
9/25/1960 02:00 CST
4/30/1961 02:00 EST
4/27/1969 02:00 EDT
10/26/1969 02:00 EST
4/26/1970 02:00 EDT
10/25/1970 02:00 EST
4/25/1971 02:00 EDT
10/31/1971 02:00 EST
4/30/1972 02:00 EDT
10/29/1972 02:00 EST
4/29/1973 02:00 EDT
10/28/1973 02:00 EST
2/23/1975 02:00 EDT
10/26/1975 02:00 EST
....

IN # 170
Before 11/18/1883 LMT
11/18/1883 12:00 CST
3/31/1918 02:00 CWT
10/27/1918 02:00 CST
3/30/1919 02:00 CWT
10/26/1919 02:00 CST
2/09/1942 02:00 CWT
9/30/1945 02:00 CST
4/26/1953 02:00 CDT
9/27/1953 02:00 CST
4/25/1954 02:00 CDT
9/26/1954 02:00 CST
4/24/1955 02:00 CDT
9/25/1955 02:00 CST
4/29/1956 02:00 CDT
11/04/1956 02:00 CST
4/28/1957 02:00 CDT
9/29/1957 02:00 CST
4/27/1958 02:00 CDT
9/28/1958 02:00 CST
4/26/1959 02:00 CDT
9/27/1959 02:00 CST
4/24/1960 02:00 CDT
9/25/1960 02:00 CST
4/30/1961 02:00 EST
4/27/1969 02:00 EDT
10/26/1969 02:00 EST
4/26/1970 02:00 EDT
10/25/1970 02:00 EST
....

IN # 171
Before 11/18/1883 LMT
11/18/1883 12:00 CST
3/31/1918 02:00 CWT
10/27/1918 02:00 CST
3/30/1919 02:00 CWT
10/26/1919 02:00 CST
4/27/1941 02:00 CDT
9/28/1941 02:00 CST
2/09/1942 02:00 CWT
9/30/1945 02:00 CST
4/28/1946 02:00 CDT
9/29/1946 02:00 CST
4/27/1947 02:00 CDT
9/28/1947 02:00 CST
4/25/1948 02:00 CDT
9/26/1948 02:00 CST
4/24/1949 02:00 CDT
9/10/1949 02:00 CST
4/30/1950 02:00 CDT
9/24/1950 02:00 CST
4/29/1951 02:00 CDT
9/30/1951 02:00 CST
4/27/1952 02:00 CDT
9/28/1952 02:00 CST
4/26/1953 02:00 CDT
9/27/1953 02:00 CST
4/25/1954 02:00 CDT
9/26/1954 02:00 CST
4/24/1955 02:00 CDT
10/30/1955 02:00 CST
4/02/1956 02:00 CDT
10/28/1956 02:00 CST
4/28/1957 02:00 CDT
9/29/1957 02:00 CST
4/27/1958 02:00 CDT
9/28/1958 02:00 CST
4/26/1959 02:00 CDT
9/27/1959 02:00 CST
4/24/1960 02:00 CDT
9/25/1960 02:00 CST
4/30/1961 02:00 EST
4/27/1969 02:00 EDT
10/26/1969 02:00 EST
4/26/1970 02:00 EDT
10/25/1970 02:00 EST
....

IN # 172
Before 11/18/1883 LMT
11/18/1883 12:00 CST
3/31/1918 02:00 CWT
10/27/1918 02:00 CST
3/30/1919 02:00 CWT
10/26/1919 02:00 CST
2/09/1942 02:00 CWT
9/30/1945 02:00 CST
5/29/1947 02:00 CDT
9/28/1947 02:00 CST
4/25/1948 02:00 CDT
9/26/1948 02:00 CST
4/29/1951 02:00 CDT
9/30/1951 02:00 CST
4/28/1957 02:00 CDT
9/29/1957 02:00 CST
4/27/1958 02:00 CDT
9/28/1958 02:00 CST
4/26/1959 02:00 CDT
9/27/1959 02:00 CST
4/24/1960 02:00 CDT
9/25/1960 02:00 CST
4/30/1961 02:00 EST
4/27/1969 02:00 EDT
10/26/1969 02:00 EST
4/26/1970 02:00 EDT
10/25/1970 02:00 EST
....

IN # 173
Before 11/18/1883 LMT
11/18/1883 12:00 CST
3/31/1918 02:00 CWT
10/27/1918 02:00 CST
3/30/1919 02:00 CWT
10/26/1919 02:00 CST
4/27/1941 02:00 CDT
9/28/1941 02:00 CST
2/09/1942 02:00 CWT
9/30/1945 02:00 CST
4/07/1946 02:00 CDT
9/01/1946 02:00 CST
4/27/1947 02:00 CDT
9/28/1947 02:00 CST
4/25/1948 02:00 CDT
9/26/1948 02:00 CST
4/24/1949 02:00 CDT
9/25/1949 02:00 CST
4/30/1950 02:00 CDT
9/24/1950 02:00 CST
4/29/1951 02:00 CDT
9/30/1951 02:00 CST
4/27/1952 02:00 CDT
9/28/1952 02:00 CST
4/26/1953 02:00 CDT
9/27/1953 02:00 CST
4/25/1954 02:00 CDT
9/26/1954 02:00 CST
4/24/1955 02:00 CDT
9/25/1955 02:00 CST
4/29/1956 02:00 CDT
11/04/1956 02:00 CST
4/28/1957 02:00 CDT
9/29/1957 02:00 CST
4/27/1958 02:00 CDT
9/28/1958 02:00 CST
4/26/1959 02:00 CDT
9/27/1959 02:00 CST
4/24/1960 02:00 CDT
9/25/1960 02:00 CST
4/30/1961 02:00 EST
....

IN # 174
Before 11/18/1883 LMT
11/18/1883 12:00 CST
3/31/1918 02:00 CWT
10/27/1918 02:00 CST
3/30/1919 02:00 CWT
10/26/1919 02:00 CST
2/09/1942 02:00 CWT
9/30/1945 02:00 CST
4/24/1955 02:00 CDT
9/25/1955 02:00 CST
4/29/1956 02:00 CDT
9/30/1956 02:00 CST
4/28/1957 02:00 CDT
9/29/1957 02:00 CST
4/27/1958 02:00 CDT
10/26/1958 02:00 CST
4/26/1959 02:00 CDT
9/27/1959 02:00 CST
4/24/1960 02:00 CDT
9/25/1960 02:00 CST
4/30/1961 02:00 EST
4/27/1969 02:00 EDT
10/26/1969 02:00 EST
4/26/1970 02:00 EDT
10/25/1970 02:00 EST
....

IN # 175
Before 11/18/1883 LMT
11/18/1883 12:00 CST
3/31/1918 02:00 CWT
10/27/1918 02:00 CST
3/30/1919 02:00 CWT
10/26/1919 02:00 CST
2/09/1942 02:00 CWT
9/30/1945 02:00 CST
4/27/1947 02:00 CDT
9/30/1947 02:00 CST
4/25/1948 02:00 CDT
9/26/1948 02:00 CST
4/24/1949 02:00 CDT
9/10/1949 02:00 CST
4/30/1950 02:00 CDT
9/24/1950 02:00 CST
4/24/1955 02:00 CDT
10/30/1955 02:00 CST
4/29/1956 02:00 CDT
10/28/1956 02:00 CST
4/28/1957 02:00 CDT
9/29/1957 02:00 CST
4/27/1958 02:00 CDT
9/28/1958 02:00 CST
4/26/1959 02:00 CDT
9/27/1959 02:00 CST
4/24/1960 02:00 CDT
9/25/1960 02:00 CST
4/30/1961 02:00 EST
4/27/1969 02:00 EDT
10/26/1969 02:00 EST
4/26/1970 02:00 EDT
10/25/1970 02:00 EST
....

IN # 176
Before 11/18/1883 LMT
11/18/1883 12:00 CST
3/31/1918 02:00 CWT
10/27/1918 02:00 CST
3/30/1919 02:00 CWT
10/26/1919 02:00 CST
4/27/1941 02:00 CDT
9/28/1941 02:00 CST
2/09/1942 02:00 CWT
9/30/1945 02:00 CST
4/28/1946 02:00 CDT
9/29/1946 02:00 CST
4/30/1950 02:00 CDT
9/24/1950 02:00 CST
4/29/1951 02:00 CDT
9/30/1951 02:00 CST
4/27/1952 02:00 CDT
9/28/1952 02:00 CST
4/26/1953 02:00 CDT
9/27/1953 02:00 CST
4/25/1954 02:00 CDT
9/26/1954 02:00 CST
4/24/1955 02:00 CDT
9/25/1955 02:00 CST
4/29/1956 02:00 CDT
10/28/1956 02:00 CST
4/28/1957 02:00 CDT
9/29/1957 02:00 CST
4/27/1958 02:00 CDT
10/26/1958 02:00 CST
4/26/1959 02:00 CDT
10/25/1959 02:00 CST
4/24/1960 02:00 CDT
10/30/1960 02:00 CST
4/30/1961 02:00 EST
4/28/1968 02:00 US#1
....

IN # 177
Before 11/18/1883 LMT
11/18/1883 12:00 CST
3/31/1918 02:00 CWT
10/27/1918 02:00 CST
3/30/1919 02:00 CWT
10/26/1919 02:00 CST
2/09/1942 02:00 CWT
9/30/1945 02:00 CST
4/29/1951 02:00 CDT
9/30/1951 02:00 CST
4/25/1954 02:00 CDT
9/26/1954 02:00 CST
4/24/1955 02:00 CDT
9/25/1955 02:00 CST
4/29/1956 02:00 CDT
9/30/1956 02:00 CST
4/28/1957 02:00 CDT
9/29/1957 02:00 CST
4/27/1958 02:00 CDT
9/28/1958 02:00 CST
4/26/1959 02:00 CDT
9/27/1959 02:00 CST
4/24/1960 02:00 CDT
9/25/1960 02:00 CST
4/30/1961 02:00 EST
4/27/1969 02:00 EDT
10/26/1969 02:00 EST
4/26/1970 02:00 EDT
10/25/1970 02:00 EST
4/25/1971 02:00 EDT
10/31/1971 02:00 EST
4/30/1972 02:00 EDT
10/29/1972 02:00 EST
4/29/1973 02:00 EDT
10/28/1973 02:00 EST
2/23/1975 02:00 EDT
10/26/1975 02:00 EST
....

IN # 178
Before 11/18/1883 LMT
11/18/1883 12:00 CST
3/31/1918 02:00 CWT
10/27/1918 02:00 CST
3/30/1919 02:00 CWT
10/26/1919 02:00 CST
2/09/1942 02:00 CWT
9/30/1945 02:00 CST
4/29/1951 02:00 CDT
9/30/1951 02:00 CST
4/27/1952 02:00 CDT
9/28/1952 02:00 CST
4/26/1953 02:00 CDT
9/27/1953 02:00 CST
4/25/1954 02:00 CDT
9/26/1954 02:00 CST
4/24/1955 02:00 CDT
9/25/1955 02:00 CST
4/29/1956 02:00 CDT
9/30/1956 02:00 CST
4/28/1957 02:00 CDT
9/29/1957 02:00 CST
4/27/1958 02:00 CDT
9/28/1958 02:00 CST
4/26/1959 02:00 CDT
9/27/1959 02:00 CST
4/24/1960 02:00 CDT
9/25/1960 02:00 CST
4/30/1961 02:00 EST
4/27/1969 02:00 EDT
10/26/1969 02:00 EST
4/26/1970 02:00 EDT
10/25/1970 02:00 EST
4/25/1971 02:00 EDT
10/31/1971 02:00 EST
4/30/1972 02:00 EDT
10/29/1972 02:00 EST
4/29/1973 02:00 EDT
10/28/1973 02:00 EST
2/23/1975 02:00 EDT
10/26/1975 02:00 EST
....

IN # 179
Before 11/18/1883 LMT
11/18/1883 12:00 CST
3/31/1918 02:00 CWT
10/27/1918 02:00 CST
3/30/1919 02:00 CWT
10/26/1919 02:00 CST
2/09/1942 02:00 CWT
9/30/1945 02:00 CST
4/26/1953 02:00 CDT
9/27/1953 02:00 CST
4/25/1954 02:00 CDT
9/26/1954 02:00 CST
4/24/1955 02:00 CDT
9/25/1955 02:00 CST
4/29/1956 02:00 CDT
9/30/1956 02:00 CST
4/28/1957 02:00 CDT
9/29/1957 02:00 CST
4/27/1958 02:00 CDT
9/28/1958 02:00 CST
4/26/1959 02:00 CDT
9/27/1959 02:00 CST
4/24/1960 02:00 CDT
9/25/1960 02:00 CST
4/30/1961 02:00 EST
4/27/1969 02:00 US#1
....

IN # 180
Before 11/18/1883 LMT
11/18/1883 12:00 CST
3/31/1918 02:00 CWT
10/27/1918 02:00 CST
3/30/1919 02:00 CWT
10/26/1919 02:00 CST
2/09/1942 02:00 CWT
9/30/1945 02:00 CST
4/24/1955 02:00 CDT
9/25/1955 02:00 CST
4/29/1956 02:00 CDT
9/30/1956 02:00 CST
4/28/1957 02:00 CDT
9/29/1957 02:00 CST
4/27/1958 02:00 CDT
9/28/1958 02:00 CST
4/26/1959 02:00 CDT
9/27/1959 02:00 CST
4/24/1960 02:00 CDT
10/30/1960 02:00 CST
4/30/1961 02:00 EST
4/27/1969 02:00 EDT
10/26/1969 02:00 EST
4/26/1970 02:00 EDT
10/25/1970 02:00 EST
....

IN # 181
Before 11/18/1883 LMT
11/18/1883 12:00 CST
3/31/1918 02:00 CWT
10/27/1918 02:00 CST
3/30/1919 02:00 CWT
10/26/1919 02:00 CST
2/09/1942 02:00 CWT
9/30/1945 02:00 CST
4/24/1955 02:00 CDT
10/30/1955 02:00 CST
4/29/1956 02:00 CDT
10/28/1956 02:00 CST
4/28/1957 02:00 CDT
9/29/1957 02:00 CST
4/27/1958 02:00 CDT
9/28/1958 02:00 CST
4/26/1959 02:00 CDT
9/27/1959 02:00 CST
4/24/1960 02:00 CDT
9/25/1960 02:00 CST
4/30/1961 02:00 EST
4/27/1969 02:00 EDT
10/26/1969 02:00 EST
4/26/1970 02:00 EDT
10/25/1970 02:00 EST
....

IN # 182
Before 11/18/1883 LMT
11/18/1883 12:00 CST
3/31/1918 02:00 CWT
10/27/1918 02:00 CST
3/30/1919 02:00 CWT
10/26/1919 02:00 CST
2/09/1942 02:00 CWT
9/30/1945 02:00 CST
4/25/1954 02:00 CDT
9/26/1954 02:00 CST
4/24/1955 02:00 CDT
10/30/1955 02:00 CST
4/29/1956 02:00 CDT
10/28/1956 02:00 CST
4/28/1957 02:00 CDT
9/29/1957 02:00 CST
4/27/1958 02:00 CDT
9/28/1958 02:00 CST
4/26/1959 02:00 CDT
9/27/1959 02:00 CST
4/24/1960 02:00 CDT
9/25/1960 02:00 CST
4/30/1961 02:00 EST
4/27/1969 02:00 EDT
10/26/1969 02:00 EST
4/26/1970 02:00 EDT
10/25/1970 02:00 EST
....

IN # 183
Before 11/18/1883 LMT
11/18/1883 12:00 CST
3/31/1918 02:00 CWT
10/27/1918 02:00 CST
3/30/1919 02:00 CWT
10/26/1919 02:00 CST
2/09/1942 02:00 CWT
9/30/1945 02:00 CST
4/26/1953 02:00 CDT
9/27/1953 02:00 CST
4/25/1954 02:00 CDT
9/26/1954 02:00 CST
4/24/1955 02:00 CDT
10/30/1955 02:00 CST
4/29/1956 02:00 CDT
10/28/1956 02:00 CST
4/28/1957 02:00 CDT
9/29/1957 02:00 CST
4/27/1958 02:00 CDT
9/28/1958 02:00 CST
4/26/1959 02:00 CDT
9/27/1959 02:00 CST
4/24/1960 02:00 CDT
9/25/1960 02:00 CST
4/30/1961 02:00 EST
4/27/1969 02:00 EDT
10/26/1969 02:00 EST
4/26/1970 02:00 EDT
10/25/1970 02:00 EST
....

IN # 184
Before 11/18/1883 LMT
11/18/1883 12:00 CST
3/31/1918 02:00 CWT
10/27/1918 02:00 CST
3/30/1919 02:00 CWT
10/26/1919 02:00 CST
2/09/1942 02:00 CWT
9/30/1945 02:00 CST
4/29/1951 02:00 CDT
9/30/1951 02:00 CST
4/28/1957 02:00 CDT
9/29/1957 02:00 CST
4/27/1958 02:00 CDT
9/28/1958 02:00 CST
4/26/1959 02:00 CDT
9/27/1959 02:00 CST
4/24/1960 02:00 CDT
9/25/1960 02:00 CST
4/30/1961 02:00 EST
4/27/1969 02:00 EDT
10/26/1969 02:00 EST
4/26/1970 02:00 EDT
10/25/1970 02:00 EST
....

IN # 185
Before 11/18/1883 LMT
11/18/1883 12:00 CST
3/31/1918 02:00 CWT
10/27/1918 02:00 CST
3/30/1919 02:00 CWT
10/26/1919 02:00 CST
2/09/1942 02:00 CWT
9/30/1945 02:00 CST
4/26/1953 02:00 CDT
9/27/1953 02:00 CST
4/25/1954 02:00 CDT
9/26/1954 02:00 CST
4/24/1955 02:00 CDT
9/25/1955 02:00 CST
4/29/1956 02:00 CDT
10/28/1956 02:00 CST
4/28/1957 02:00 CDT
9/29/1957 02:00 CST
4/27/1958 02:00 CDT
10/26/1958 02:00 CST
4/26/1959 02:00 CDT
10/25/1959 02:00 CST
4/24/1960 02:00 CDT
10/30/1960 02:00 CST
4/30/1961 02:00 EST
4/27/1969 02:00 US#1
....

IN # 186
Before 11/18/1883 LMT
11/18/1883 12:00 CST
3/31/1918 02:00 CWT
10/27/1918 02:00 CST
3/30/1919 02:00 CWT
10/26/1919 02:00 CST
2/09/1942 02:00 CWT
9/30/1945 02:00 CST
4/28/1946 02:00 CDT
9/29/1946 02:00 CST
4/27/1947 02:00 CDT
9/28/1947 02:00 CST
4/25/1948 02:00 CDT
9/26/1948 02:00 CST
4/24/1949 02:00 CDT
9/25/1949 02:00 CST
4/30/1950 02:00 CDT
9/24/1950 02:00 CST
4/29/1951 02:00 CDT
9/30/1951 02:00 CST
4/27/1952 02:00 CDT
9/28/1952 02:00 CST
4/26/1953 02:00 CDT
9/27/1953 02:00 CST
4/25/1954 02:00 CDT
9/26/1954 02:00 CST
4/24/1955 02:00 CDT
10/30/1955 02:00 CST
4/29/1956 02:00 CDT
10/28/1956 02:00 CST
4/28/1957 02:00 CDT
9/29/1957 02:00 CST
4/27/1958 02:00 CDT
9/28/1958 02:00 CST
4/26/1959 02:00 CDT
9/27/1959 02:00 CST
4/24/1960 02:00 CDT
9/25/1960 02:00 CST
4/30/1961 02:00 EST
4/27/1969 02:00 EDT
10/26/1969 02:00 EST
4/26/1970 02:00 EDT
10/25/1970 02:00 EST
....

TIME TABLES

IN # 187

Date	Time	Zone
Before 11/18/1883		LMT
11/18/1883	12:00	CST
3/31/1918	02:00	CWT
10/27/1918	02:00	CST
3/30/1919	02:00	CWT
10/26/1919	02:00	CST
2/09/1942	02:00	CWT
9/30/1945	02:00	CST
4/24/1955	02:00	CDT
9/25/1955	02:00	CST
4/29/1956	02:00	CDT
10/01/1956	02:00	CST
4/28/1957	02:00	CDT
9/29/1957	02:00	CST
4/27/1958	02:00	CDT
9/28/1958	02:00	CST
4/26/1959	02:00	CDT
9/27/1959	02:00	CST
4/24/1960	02:00	CDT
9/25/1960	02:00	CST
4/30/1961	02:00	EST
4/27/1969	02:00	EDT
10/26/1969	02:00	EST
4/26/1970	02:00	EDT
10/25/1970	02:00	EST

IN # 188

Date	Time	Zone
Before 11/18/1883		LMT
11/18/1883	12:00	CST
3/31/1918	02:00	CWT
10/27/1918	02:00	CST
3/30/1919	02:00	CWT
10/26/1919	02:00	CST
2/09/1942	02:00	CWT
9/30/1945	02:00	CST
4/24/1955	02:00	CDT
9/25/1955	02:00	CST
4/29/1956	02:00	CDT
10/28/1956	02:00	CST
4/28/1957	02:00	CDT
9/29/1957	02:00	CST
4/27/1958	02:00	CDT
9/28/1958	02:00	CST
4/26/1959	02:00	CDT
9/27/1959	02:00	CST
4/24/1960	02:00	CDT
9/25/1960	02:00	CST
4/30/1961	02:00	EST
4/27/1969	02:00	EDT
10/26/1969	02:00	EST
4/26/1970	02:00	EDT
10/25/1970	02:00	EST
4/25/1971	02:00	EDT
10/31/1971	02:00	EST
4/30/1972	02:00	EDT
10/29/1972	02:00	EST
4/29/1973	02:00	EDT
10/28/1973	02:00	EST
2/23/1975	02:00	US#1

IN # 189

Date	Time	Zone
Before 11/18/1883		LMT
11/18/1883	12:00	CST
3/31/1918	02:00	CWT
10/27/1918	02:00	CST
3/30/1919	02:00	CWT
10/26/1919	02:00	CST
2/09/1942	02:00	CWT
9/30/1945	02:00	CST
4/24/1955	02:00	CDT
9/25/1955	02:00	CST
4/05/1956	02:00	CDT
10/28/1956	02:00	CST
4/28/1957	02:00	CDT
9/29/1957	02:00	CST
4/27/1958	02:00	CDT
9/28/1958	02:00	CST
4/26/1959	02:00	CDT
9/27/1959	02:00	CST
4/24/1960	02:00	CDT
9/25/1960	02:00	CST
4/30/1961	02:00	EST
4/27/1969	02:00	EDT
10/26/1969	02:00	EST
4/26/1970	02:00	EDT
10/25/1970	02:00	EST
4/25/1971	02:00	EDT
10/31/1971	02:00	EST
4/30/1972	02:00	EDT
10/29/1972	02:00	EST
4/29/1973	02:00	EDT
10/28/1973	02:00	EST
2/23/1975	02:00	US#1

IN # 190

Date	Time	Zone
Before 11/18/1883		LMT
11/18/1883	12:00	CST
3/31/1918	02:00	CWT
10/27/1918	02:00	CST
3/30/1919	02:00	CWT
10/26/1919	02:00	CST
2/09/1942	02:00	CWT
9/30/1945	02:00	CST
4/24/1955	02:00	CDT
9/25/1955	02:00	CST
4/29/1956	02:00	CDT
10/01/1956	02:00	CST
4/28/1957	02:00	CDT
9/29/1957	02:00	CST
4/27/1958	02:00	CDT
10/26/1958	02:00	CST
4/26/1959	02:00	CDT
9/27/1959	02:00	CST
4/24/1960	02:00	CDT
9/25/1960	02:00	CST
4/30/1961	02:00	EST
4/27/1969	02:00	EDT
10/26/1969	02:00	EST
4/26/1970	02:00	EDT
10/25/1970	02:00	EST

IN # 191

Date	Time	Zone
Before 11/18/1883		LMT
11/18/1883	12:00	CST
3/31/1918	02:00	CWT
10/27/1918	02:00	CST
3/30/1919	02:00	CWT
10/26/1919	02:00	CST
2/09/1942	02:00	CWT
9/30/1945	02:00	CST
4/28/1957	02:00	CDT
9/29/1957	02:00	CST
4/27/1958	02:00	CDT
9/28/1958	02:00	CST
4/26/1959	02:00	CDT
9/27/1959	02:00	CST
4/24/1960	02:00	EST
10/29/1961	02:00	CST
4/29/1962	02:00	EST
4/27/1969	02:00	EDT
10/26/1969	02:00	EST
4/26/1970	02:00	EDT
10/25/1970	02:00	EST

IN # 192

Date	Time	Zone
Before 11/18/1883		LMT
11/18/1883	12:00	CST
3/31/1918	02:00	CWT
10/27/1918	02:00	CST
3/30/1919	02:00	CWT
10/26/1919	02:00	CST
2/09/1942	02:00	CWT
9/30/1945	02:00	CST
5/08/1955	00:00	CDT
9/04/1955	00:00	CST
4/29/1956	02:00	CDT
9/02/1956	02:00	CST
4/28/1957	02:00	CDT
9/29/1957	02:00	CST
4/27/1958	02:00	CDT
9/28/1958	02:00	CST
4/26/1959	02:00	CDT
9/27/1959	02:00	CST
4/24/1960	02:00	EST
10/29/1961	02:00	CST
4/29/1962	02:00	EST
4/27/1969	02:00	EDT
10/26/1969	02:00	EST
4/26/1970	02:00	EDT
10/25/1970	02:00	EST

IN # 193

Date	Time	Zone
Before 11/18/1883		LMT
11/18/1883	12:00	CST
3/31/1918	02:00	CWT
10/27/1918	02:00	CST
3/30/1919	02:00	CWT
10/26/1919	02:00	CST
2/09/1942	02:00	CWT
9/30/1945	02:00	CST
5/08/1955	02:00	CDT
9/04/1955	00:00	CST
4/29/1956	02:00	CDT
9/30/1956	02:00	CST
4/28/1957	02:00	CDT
9/29/1957	02:00	CST
4/27/1958	02:00	CDT
9/28/1958	02:00	CST
4/26/1959	02:00	CDT
9/27/1959	02:00	CST
4/24/1960	02:00	EST
10/29/1961	02:00	CST
4/29/1962	02:00	EST
4/27/1969	02:00	EDT
10/26/1969	02:00	EST
4/26/1970	02:00	EDT
10/25/1970	02:00	EST

IN # 194

Date	Time	Zone
Before 11/18/1883		LMT
11/18/1883	12:00	CST
3/31/1918	02:00	CWT
10/27/1918	02:00	CST
3/30/1919	02:00	CWT
10/26/1919	02:00	CST
2/09/1942	02:00	CWT
9/30/1945	02:00	CST
4/26/1953	02:00	CDT
9/27/1953	02:00	CST
4/25/1954	02:00	CDT
9/26/1954	02:00	CST
5/10/1955	02:00	CDT
9/04/1955	00:00	CST
4/29/1956	02:00	CDT
9/30/1956	02:00	CST
4/28/1957	02:00	CDT
9/29/1957	02:00	CST
4/27/1958	02:00	CDT
9/28/1958	02:00	CST
4/26/1959	02:00	CDT
9/27/1959	02:00	CST
4/24/1960	02:00	EST
10/29/1961	02:00	CST
4/29/1962	02:00	EST
4/27/1969	02:00	EDT
10/26/1969	02:00	EST
4/26/1970	02:00	EDT
10/25/1970	02:00	EST

IN # 195

Date	Time	Zone
Before 11/18/1883		LMT
11/18/1883	12:00	CST
3/31/1918	02:00	CWT
10/27/1918	02:00	CST
3/30/1919	02:00	CWT
10/26/1919	02:00	CST
2/09/1942	02:00	CWT
9/30/1945	02:00	CST
4/26/1953	02:00	CDT
9/27/1953	02:00	CST
4/25/1954	02:00	CDT
9/26/1954	02:00	CST
5/08/1955	00:00	CDT
9/04/1955	00:00	CST
4/29/1956	02:00	CDT
9/30/1956	02:00	CST
4/28/1957	02:00	CDT
9/29/1957	02:00	CST
4/27/1958	02:00	CDT
9/28/1958	02:00	CST
4/26/1959	02:00	CDT
9/27/1959	02:00	CST
4/24/1960	02:00	EST
10/29/1961	02:00	CST
4/29/1962	02:00	EST
4/27/1969	02:00	EDT
10/26/1969	02:00	EST
4/26/1970	02:00	EDT
10/25/1970	02:00	EST

IN # 196

Date	Time	Zone
Before 11/18/1883		LMT
11/18/1883	12:00	CST
3/31/1918	02:00	CWT
10/27/1918	02:00	CST
3/30/1919	02:00	CWT
10/26/1919	02:00	CST
2/09/1942	02:00	CWT
9/30/1945	02:00	CST
11/14/1954	02:00	EST
9/29/1957	02:00	CST
4/27/1958	02:00	CDT
9/28/1958	02:00	CST
4/26/1959	02:00	EST
4/27/1969	02:00	EDT
10/26/1969	02:00	EST
4/26/1970	02:00	EDT
10/25/1970	02:00	EST

IN # 197

Date	Time	Zone
Before 11/18/1883		LMT
11/18/1883	12:00	CST
3/31/1918	02:00	CWT
10/27/1918	02:00	CST
3/30/1919	02:00	CWT
10/26/1919	02:00	CST
2/09/1942	02:00	CWT
9/30/1945	02:00	CST
4/27/1947	02:00	CDT
9/28/1947	02:00	CST
4/27/1952	02:00	CDT
9/28/1952	02:00	CST
4/26/1953	02:00	CDT
9/27/1953	02:00	CST
4/25/1954	02:00	CDT
9/26/1954	02:00	CST
11/14/1954	02:00	EST
9/29/1957	02:00	CST
4/27/1958	02:00	CDT
9/28/1958	02:00	CST
4/26/1959	02:00	EST
4/27/1969	02:00	EDT
10/26/1969	02:00	EST
4/26/1970	02:00	EDT
10/25/1970	02:00	EST

IN # 198

Date	Time	Zone
Before 11/18/1883		LMT
11/18/1883	12:00	CST
3/31/1918	02:00	CWT
10/27/1918	02:00	CST
3/30/1919	02:00	CWT
10/26/1919	02:00	CST
2/09/1942	02:00	CWT
9/30/1945	02:00	CST
4/26/1953	02:00	CDT
9/27/1953	02:00	CST
4/25/1954	02:00	CDT
9/26/1954	02:00	CST
11/14/1954	02:00	EST
9/29/1957	02:00	CST
4/27/1958	02:00	CDT
9/28/1958	02:00	CST
4/26/1959	02:00	EST
4/27/1969	02:00	EDT
10/26/1969	02:00	EST
4/26/1970	02:00	EDT
10/25/1970	02:00	EST

IN # 199

Date	Time	Zone
Before 11/18/1883		LMT
11/18/1883	12:00	CST
3/31/1918	02:00	CWT
10/27/1918	02:00	CST
3/30/1919	02:00	CWT
10/26/1919	02:00	CST
2/09/1942	02:00	CWT
9/30/1945	02:00	CST
4/24/1955	02:00	CDT
9/25/1955	02:00	CST
4/29/1956	02:00	CDT
9/30/1956	02:00	CST
4/28/1957	02:00	CDT
9/29/1957	02:00	CST
4/27/1958	02:00	CDT
9/28/1958	02:00	CST
4/26/1959	02:00	CDT
9/27/1959	02:00	CST
4/24/1960	02:00	CDT
9/25/1960	02:00	CST
4/30/1961	02:00	CDT
10/29/1961	02:00	CST
4/29/1962	02:00	EST
4/27/1969	02:00	EDT
10/26/1969	02:00	EST
4/26/1970	02:00	EDT
10/25/1970	02:00	EST

IN # 200

Date	Time	Zone
Before 11/18/1883		LMT
11/18/1883	12:00	CST
3/31/1918	02:00	CWT
10/27/1918	02:00	CST
3/30/1919	02:00	CWT
10/26/1919	02:00	CST
2/09/1942	02:00	CWT
9/30/1945	02:00	CST
5/01/1955	00:00	CDT
9/04/1955	00:00	CST
4/29/1956	02:00	CDT
9/30/1956	02:00	CST
4/28/1957	02:00	CDT
9/29/1957	02:00	CST
4/27/1958	02:00	CDT
9/28/1958	02:00	CST
4/26/1959	02:00	CDT
9/27/1959	02:00	CST
4/24/1960	02:00	CDT
9/25/1960	02:00	CST
4/30/1961	02:00	CDT
10/29/1961	02:00	CST
4/29/1962	02:00	EST
4/27/1969	02:00	EDT
10/26/1969	02:00	EST
4/26/1970	02:00	EDT
10/25/1970	02:00	EST

IN # 201

Date	Time	Zone
Before 11/18/1883		LMT
11/18/1883	12:00	CST
3/31/1918	02:00	CWT
10/27/1918	02:00	CST
3/30/1919	02:00	CWT
10/26/1919	02:00	CST
4/30/1933	02:00	CDT
9/24/1933	02:00	CST
4/28/1935	02:00	CDT
9/29/1935	02:00	CST
4/26/1936	02:00	CDT
9/27/1936	02:00	CST
4/24/1938	02:00	CDT
9/25/1938	02:00	CST
4/30/1939	02:00	CDT
9/24/1939	02:00	CST
4/28/1940	02:00	CDT
9/29/1940	02:00	CST
4/27/1941	02:00	CDT
9/28/1941	02:00	CST
2/09/1942	02:00	CWT
9/30/1945	02:00	CST
4/28/1946	02:00	CDT
9/29/1946	02:00	CST
4/27/1947	02:00	CDT
9/28/1947	02:00	CST
4/25/1948	02:00	CDT
9/26/1948	02:00	CST
4/24/1949	02:00	CDT
9/25/1949	02:00	CST
4/30/1950	02:00	CDT
9/24/1950	02:00	CST
11/28/1954	02:00	EST
10/30/1955	02:00	CST
4/29/1956	02:00	CDT
9/30/1956	02:00	CST
4/28/1957	02:00	CDT
9/29/1957	02:00	CST
4/27/1958	02:00	CDT
9/28/1958	02:00	CST
4/26/1959	02:00	CDT
9/27/1959	02:00	CST
4/24/1960	02:00	CDT
9/25/1960	02:00	CST
4/30/1961	02:00	CDT
10/29/1961	02:00	CST
4/29/1962	02:00	EST
10/30/1966	02:00	CST
4/30/1967	02:00	CDT
10/29/1967	02:00	CST
4/28/1968	02:00	CDT
10/27/1968	02:00	CST
4/27/1969	02:00	EDT
10/26/1969	02:00	EST
4/26/1970	02:00	EDT
10/25/1970	02:00	EST

IN # 202

Date	Time	Zone
Before 11/18/1883		LMT
11/18/1883	12:00	CST
3/31/1918	02:00	CWT
10/27/1918	02:00	CST
3/30/1919	02:00	CWT
10/26/1919	02:00	CST
2/09/1942	02:00	CWT
9/30/1945	02:00	CST
4/28/1946	02:00	CDT
9/29/1946	02:00	CST
4/27/1947	02:00	CDT
9/28/1947	02:00	CST
4/25/1948	02:00	CDT
9/26/1948	02:00	CST
11/28/1954	02:00	EST
10/30/1955	02:00	CST
4/29/1956	02:00	CDT
9/30/1956	02:00	CST
4/28/1957	02:00	CDT
9/29/1957	02:00	CST
4/27/1958	02:00	CDT
9/28/1958	02:00	CST
4/26/1959	02:00	CDT
9/27/1959	02:00	CST
4/24/1960	02:00	CDT
9/25/1960	02:00	CST
4/30/1961	02:00	CDT
10/29/1961	02:00	CST
4/29/1962	02:00	EST
10/30/1966	02:00	CST
4/30/1967	02:00	CDT
10/29/1967	02:00	CST
4/28/1968	02:00	CDT
10/27/1968	02:00	CST
4/27/1969	02:00	EDT
10/26/1969	02:00	EST
4/26/1970	02:00	EDT
10/25/1970	02:00	EST

IN # 203

Date	Time	Zone
Before 11/18/1883		LMT
11/18/1883	12:00	CST
3/31/1918	02:00	CWT
10/27/1918	02:00	CST
3/30/1919	02:00	CWT
10/26/1919	02:00	CST
2/09/1942	02:00	CWT
9/30/1945	02:00	CST
4/26/1953	02:00	CDT
9/27/1953	02:00	CST
4/25/1954	02:00	CDT
9/26/1954	02:00	CST
11/28/1954	02:00	EST
10/30/1955	02:00	CST
4/29/1956	02:00	CDT
9/30/1956	02:00	CST
4/28/1957	02:00	CDT
9/29/1957	02:00	CST
4/27/1958	02:00	CDT
9/28/1958	02:00	CST
4/26/1959	02:00	CDT
9/27/1959	02:00	CST
4/24/1960	02:00	CDT
9/25/1960	02:00	CST
4/30/1961	02:00	CDT
10/29/1961	02:00	CST
4/29/1962	02:00	EST
10/30/1966	02:00	CST
4/30/1967	02:00	CDT
10/29/1967	02:00	CST
4/28/1968	02:00	CDT
10/27/1968	02:00	CST
4/27/1969	02:00	EDT
10/26/1969	02:00	EST
4/26/1970	02:00	EDT
10/25/1970	02:00	EST

IN # 204

Date	Time	Zone
Before 11/18/1883		LMT
11/18/1883	12:00	CST
3/31/1918	02:00	CWT
10/27/1918	02:00	CST
3/30/1919	02:00	CWT
10/26/1919	02:00	CST
2/09/1942	02:00	CWT
9/30/1945	02:00	CST
11/28/1954	02:00	EST
10/30/1955	02:00	CST
4/29/1956	02:00	CDT
9/30/1956	02:00	CST
4/28/1957	02:00	CDT
9/29/1957	02:00	CST
4/27/1958	02:00	CDT
9/28/1958	02:00	CST
4/26/1959	02:00	CDT
9/27/1959	02:00	CST
4/24/1960	02:00	CDT
9/25/1960	02:00	CST
4/30/1961	02:00	CDT
10/29/1961	02:00	CST
4/29/1962	02:00	EST
10/30/1966	02:00	CST
4/30/1967	02:00	CDT
10/29/1967	02:00	CST
4/28/1968	02:00	CDT
10/27/1968	02:00	CST
4/27/1969	02:00	EDT
10/26/1969	02:00	EST
4/26/1970	02:00	EDT
10/25/1970	02:00	EST

IN # 205

Date	Time	Zone
Before 11/18/1883		LMT
11/18/1883	12:00	CST
3/31/1918	02:00	CWT
10/27/1918	02:00	CST
3/30/1919	02:00	CWT
10/26/1919	02:00	CST
5/05/1940	02:00	CDT
10/01/1940	02:00	CST
5/01/1941	02:00	CDT
10/01/1941	02:00	CST
2/09/1942	02:00	CWT
9/30/1945	02:00	CST
5/01/1946	02:00	CDT
10/01/1946	02:00	CST
4/27/1947	02:00	CDT
9/28/1947	02:00	CST
4/25/1948	02:00	CDT
9/26/1948	02:00	CST
4/24/1949	02:00	CDT
9/25/1949	02:00	CST
4/30/1950	02:00	CDT
9/24/1950	02:00	CST
4/29/1951	02:00	CDT
9/30/1951	02:00	CST
4/27/1952	02:00	CDT
9/28/1952	02:00	CST
4/26/1953	02:00	CDT
9/27/1953	02:00	CST
4/25/1954	02:00	CDT
9/26/1954	02:00	CST
11/28/1954	02:00	EST
10/30/1955	02:00	CST
4/29/1956	02:00	CDT
10/28/1956	02:00	CST
4/28/1957	02:00	CDT
10/27/1957	02:00	CST
4/27/1958	02:00	CDT
10/26/1958	02:00	CST
4/26/1959	02:00	CDT
10/25/1959	02:00	CST
4/24/1960	02:00	CDT

TIME TABLES

Date	Time	Zone
10/30/1960	02:00	CST
4/30/1961	02:00	CDT
10/29/1961	02:00	CST
4/29/1962	02:00	EST
10/30/1966	02:00	CST
4/30/1967	02:00	CDT
10/29/1967	02:00	CST
4/28/1968	02:00	CDT
10/27/1968	02:00	CST
4/27/1969	02:00	EDT
10/26/1969	02:00	EST
4/26/1970	02:00	EDT
10/25/1970	02:00	EST

IN # 206

Date	Time	Zone
Before 11/18/1883		LMT
11/18/1883	12:00	CST
3/31/1918	02:00	CWT
10/27/1918	02:00	CST
3/30/1919	02:00	CWT
10/26/1919	02:00	CST
4/28/1940	02:00	CDT
9/29/1940	02:00	CST
4/27/1941	02:00	CDT
9/28/1941	02:00	CST
2/09/1942	02:00	CWT
9/30/1945	02:00	CST
4/28/1946	02:00	CDT
9/29/1946	02:00	CST
4/27/1947	02:00	CDT
9/28/1947	02:00	CST
4/25/1948	02:00	CDT
9/26/1948	02:00	CST
4/24/1949	02:00	CDT
9/25/1949	02:00	CST
4/30/1950	02:00	CDT
9/24/1950	02:00	CST
4/29/1951	02:00	CDT
9/30/1951	02:00	CST
4/27/1952	02:00	CDT
9/28/1952	02:00	CST
4/26/1953	02:00	CDT
9/27/1953	02:00	CST
4/25/1954	02:00	CDT
9/26/1954	02:00	CST
11/28/1954	02:00	EST
10/30/1955	02:00	CST
4/29/1956	02:00	CDT
10/28/1956	02:00	CST
4/28/1957	02:00	CDT
10/27/1957	02:00	CST
4/27/1958	02:00	CDT
10/26/1958	02:00	CST
4/26/1959	02:00	CDT
10/25/1959	02:00	CST
4/24/1960	02:00	CDT
10/30/1960	02:00	CST
4/30/1961	02:00	CDT
10/29/1961	02:00	CST
4/29/1962	02:00	EST
10/30/1966	02:00	CST
4/30/1967	02:00	CDT
10/29/1967	02:00	CST
4/28/1968	02:00	CDT
10/27/1968	02:00	CST
4/27/1969	02:00	EDT
10/26/1969	02:00	EST
4/26/1970	02:00	EDT
10/25/1970	02:00	EST

IN # 207

Date	Time	Zone
Before 11/18/1883		LMT
11/18/1883	12:00	CST
3/31/1918	02:00	CWT
10/27/1918	02:00	CST
3/30/1919	02:00	CWT
10/26/1919	02:00	CST
5/15/1929	02:00	CDT
9/30/1929	02:00	CST
5/10/1930	02:00	CDT
9/27/1930	02:00	CST
4/26/1931	02:00	CDT
9/28/1931	02:00	CST
4/24/1932	02:00	CDT
10/01/1932	02:00	CST
4/30/1933	02:00	CDT
9/24/1933	02:00	CST
4/29/1934	02:00	CDT
9/30/1934	02:00	CST
4/28/1935	02:00	CDT
9/29/1935	02:00	CST
4/26/1936	02:00	CDT
9/27/1936	02:00	CST
4/25/1937	02:00	CDT
9/26/1937	02:00	CST
4/24/1938	02:00	CDT
9/25/1938	02:00	CST
4/30/1939	02:00	CDT
9/24/1939	02:00	CST
4/28/1940	02:00	CDT
9/29/1940	02:00	CST
4/27/1941	02:00	CDT
9/28/1941	02:00	CST
2/09/1942	02:00	CWT
9/30/1945	02:00	CST
4/28/1946	02:00	CDT
9/29/1946	02:00	CST
4/27/1947	02:00	CDT
9/28/1947	02:00	CST
4/25/1948	02:00	CDT
9/26/1948	02:00	CST
4/24/1949	02:00	CDT
9/25/1949	02:00	CST
4/30/1950	02:00	CDT
9/24/1950	02:00	CST
4/29/1951	02:00	CDT
9/30/1951	02:00	CST
4/27/1952	02:00	CDT
9/28/1952	02:00	CST
4/26/1953	02:00	CDT
9/27/1953	02:00	CST
4/25/1954	02:00	CDT
9/26/1954	02:00	CST
11/28/1954	02:00	EST
10/30/1955	02:00	CST
4/29/1956	02:00	CDT
10/28/1956	02:00	CST
4/28/1957	02:00	CDT
9/29/1957	02:00	CST
4/27/1958	02:00	CDT
10/26/1958	02:00	CST
4/26/1959	02:00	CDT
10/25/1959	02:00	CST
4/24/1960	02:00	CDT
10/30/1960	02:00	CST
4/30/1961	02:00	CDT
10/29/1961	02:00	CST
4/29/1962	02:00	EST
10/30/1966	02:00	CST
4/30/1967	02:00	CDT
10/29/1967	02:00	CST
4/28/1968	02:00	CDT
10/27/1968	02:00	CST
4/27/1969	02:00	EDT
10/26/1969	02:00	EST
4/26/1970	02:00	EDT
10/25/1970	02:00	EST

IN # 208

Date	Time	Zone
Before 11/18/1883		LMT
11/18/1883	12:00	CST
3/31/1918	02:00	CWT
10/27/1918	02:00	CST
3/30/1919	02:00	CWT
10/26/1919	02:00	CST
4/26/1931	02:00	CDT
9/27/1931	02:00	CST
4/30/1932	00:01	CDT
10/02/1932	00:01	CST
4/30/1933	00:01	CDT
9/24/1933	00:01	CST
4/29/1934	02:00	CDT
9/30/1934	02:00	CST
4/28/1935	02:00	CDT
9/29/1935	02:00	CST
4/26/1936	02:00	CDT
9/27/1936	02:00	CST
4/25/1937	02:00	CDT
9/26/1937	02:00	CST
4/24/1938	02:00	CDT
9/25/1938	02:00	CST
4/30/1939	02:00	CDT
9/24/1939	02:00	CST
4/28/1940	02:00	CDT
9/29/1940	02:00	CST
4/27/1941	02:00	CDT
9/28/1941	02:00	CST
2/09/1942	02:00	CWT
9/30/1945	02:00	CST
4/28/1946	02:00	CDT
9/29/1946	02:00	CST
4/28/1947	02:00	CDT
9/29/1947	02:00	CST
4/25/1948	02:00	CDT
9/26/1948	02:00	CST
4/24/1949	02:00	CDT
9/25/1949	02:00	CST
4/30/1950	02:00	CDT
9/24/1950	02:00	CST
4/29/1951	02:00	CDT
9/30/1951	02:00	CST
4/27/1952	02:00	CDT
9/28/1952	02:00	CST
4/26/1953	02:00	CDT
9/27/1953	02:00	CST
4/25/1954	02:00	CDT
9/26/1954	02:00	CST
11/28/1954	02:00	EST
10/30/1955	02:00	CST
3/25/1956	02:00	CDT
10/28/1956	02:00	CST
4/28/1957	02:00	CDT
10/27/1957	02:00	CST
4/27/1958	02:00	CDT
10/26/1958	02:00	CST
4/26/1959	02:00	CDT
10/25/1959	02:00	CST
4/24/1960	02:00	CDT
10/30/1960	02:00	CST
4/30/1961	02:00	CDT
10/29/1961	02:00	CST
4/29/1962	02:00	EST
10/30/1966	02:00	CST
4/30/1967	02:00	CDT
10/29/1967	02:00	CST
4/28/1968	02:00	CDT
10/27/1968	02:00	CST
4/27/1969	02:00	EDT
10/26/1969	02:00	EST
4/26/1970	02:00	EDT
10/25/1970	02:00	EST

IN # 209

Date	Time	Zone
Before 11/18/1883		LMT
11/18/1883	12:00	CST
3/31/1918	02:00	CWT
10/27/1918	02:00	CST
3/30/1919	02:00	CWT
10/26/1919	02:00	CST
4/28/1940	02:00	CDT
9/29/1940	02:00	CST
2/09/1942	02:00	CWT
9/30/1945	02:00	CST
4/25/1948	02:00	CDT
9/26/1948	02:00	CST
4/25/1954	02:00	CDT
9/26/1954	02:00	CST
11/28/1954	02:00	EST
10/30/1955	02:00	CST
4/29/1956	02:00	CDT
9/30/1956	02:00	CST
4/28/1957	02:00	CDT
9/29/1957	02:00	CST
4/27/1958	02:00	CDT
9/28/1958	02:00	CST
4/26/1959	02:00	CDT
9/27/1959	02:00	CST
4/24/1960	02:00	CDT
10/30/1960	02:00	CST
4/30/1961	02:00	CDT
10/29/1961	02:00	CST
4/29/1962	02:00	EST
10/30/1966	02:00	CST
4/30/1967	02:00	CDT
10/29/1967	02:00	CST
4/28/1968	02:00	CDT
10/27/1968	02:00	CST
4/27/1969	02:00	EDT
10/26/1969	02:00	EST
4/26/1970	02:00	EDT
10/25/1970	02:00	EST

IN # 210

Date	Time	Zone
Before 11/18/1883		LMT
11/18/1883	12:00	CST
3/31/1918	02:00	CWT
10/27/1918	02:00	CST
3/30/1919	02:00	CWT
10/26/1919	02:00	CST
4/27/1941	02:00	CDT
9/28/1941	02:00	CST
2/09/1942	02:00	CWT
9/30/1945	02:00	CST
4/27/1947	02:00	CDT
9/28/1947	02:00	CST
4/25/1948	02:00	CDT
9/26/1948	02:00	CST
4/24/1949	02:00	CDT
9/25/1949	02:00	CST
4/30/1950	02:00	CDT
9/24/1950	02:00	CST
4/29/1951	02:00	CDT
9/30/1951	02:00	CST
4/27/1952	02:00	CDT
9/28/1952	02:00	CST
4/26/1953	02:00	CDT
9/27/1953	02:00	CST
4/25/1954	02:00	CDT
9/26/1954	02:00	CST
11/28/1954	02:00	EST
10/30/1955	02:00	CST
4/29/1956	02:00	CDT
9/30/1956	02:00	CST
4/28/1957	02:00	CDT
9/29/1957	02:00	CST
4/27/1958	02:00	CDT
10/26/1958	02:00	CST
4/26/1959	02:00	CDT
10/25/1959	02:00	CST
4/24/1960	02:00	CDT
10/30/1960	02:00	CST
4/30/1961	02:00	CDT
10/29/1961	02:00	CST
4/29/1962	02:00	EST
10/30/1966	02:00	CST
4/30/1967	02:00	CDT
10/29/1967	02:00	CST
4/28/1968	02:00	CDT
10/27/1968	02:00	CST
4/27/1969	02:00	EDT
10/26/1969	02:00	EST
4/26/1970	02:00	EDT
10/25/1970	02:00	EST

IN # 211

Date	Time	Zone
Before 11/18/1883		LMT
11/18/1883	12:00	CST
3/31/1918	02:00	CWT
10/27/1918	02:00	CST
3/30/1919	02:00	CWT
10/26/1919	02:00	CST
2/09/1942	02:00	CWT
9/30/1945	02:00	CST
11/28/1954	02:00	EST
10/30/1955	02:00	CST
4/28/1957	02:00	CDT
9/29/1957	02:00	CST
4/27/1958	02:00	CDT
9/28/1958	02:00	CST
4/26/1959	02:00	CDT
9/27/1959	02:00	CST
4/24/1960	02:00	CDT
9/25/1960	02:00	CST
4/30/1961	02:00	EST
10/30/1966	02:00	CST
4/30/1967	02:00	EST
4/27/1969	02:00	EDT
10/26/1969	02:00	EST
4/26/1970	02:00	EDT
10/25/1970	02:00	EST

IN # 212

Date	Time	Zone
Before 11/18/1883		LMT
11/18/1883	12:00	CST
3/31/1918	02:00	CWT
10/27/1918	02:00	CST
3/30/1919	02:00	CWT
10/26/1919	02:00	CST
2/09/1942	02:00	CWT
9/30/1945	02:00	CST
4/28/1946	02:00	CDT
9/29/1946	02:00	CST
4/24/1949	02:00	CDT
9/25/1949	02:00	CST
11/28/1954	02:00	EST
10/30/1955	02:00	CST
4/28/1957	02:00	CDT
9/29/1957	02:00	CST
4/27/1958	02:00	CDT
9/28/1958	02:00	CST
4/26/1959	02:00	CDT
9/27/1959	02:00	CST
4/24/1960	02:00	CDT
9/25/1960	02:00	CST
4/30/1961	02:00	EST
10/30/1966	02:00	CST
4/30/1967	02:00	EST
4/27/1969	02:00	EDT
10/26/1969	02:00	EST
4/26/1970	02:00	EDT
10/25/1970	02:00	EST

IN # 213

Date	Time	Zone
Before 11/18/1883		LMT
11/18/1883	12:00	CST
3/31/1918	02:00	CWT
10/27/1918	02:00	CST
3/30/1919	02:00	CWT
10/26/1919	02:00	CST
2/09/1942	02:00	CWT
9/30/1945	02:00	CST
4/25/1948	02:00	CDT
10/01/1948	02:00	CST
4/24/1949	02:00	CDT
9/25/1949	02:00	CST
4/30/1950	02:00	CDT
9/24/1950	02:00	CST
11/28/1954	02:00	EST
10/30/1955	02:00	CST
4/29/1956	02:00	CDT
10/28/1956	02:00	CST
4/28/1957	02:00	CDT
9/29/1957	02:00	CST
4/27/1958	02:00	CDT
9/28/1958	02:00	CST
4/26/1959	02:00	CDT
9/27/1959	02:00	CST
4/24/1960	02:00	CDT
9/25/1960	02:00	CST
4/30/1961	02:00	EST
10/30/1966	02:00	CST
4/30/1967	02:00	EST
4/27/1969	02:00	EDT
10/26/1969	02:00	EST
4/26/1970	02:00	EDT
10/25/1970	02:00	EST

IN # 214

Date	Time	Zone
Before 11/18/1883		LMT
11/18/1883	12:00	CST
3/31/1918	02:00	CWT
10/27/1918	02:00	CST
3/30/1919	02:00	CWT
10/26/1919	02:00	CST
2/09/1942	02:00	CWT
9/30/1945	02:00	CST
4/26/1953	02:00	CDT
9/27/1953	02:00	CST
4/25/1954	02:00	CDT
9/26/1954	02:00	CST
11/28/1954	02:00	EST
10/30/1955	02:00	CST
4/29/1956	02:00	CDT
9/30/1956	02:00	CST
4/28/1957	02:00	CDT
9/29/1957	02:00	CST
4/27/1958	02:00	CDT
9/28/1958	02:00	CST
4/26/1959	02:00	CDT
9/27/1959	02:00	CST
4/24/1960	02:00	CDT
9/25/1960	02:00	CST
4/30/1961	02:00	EST
10/30/1966	02:00	CST
4/30/1967	02:00	EST
4/27/1969	02:00	EDT
10/26/1969	02:00	EST
4/26/1970	02:00	EDT
10/25/1970	02:00	EST

IN # 215

Date	Time	Zone
Before 11/18/1883		LMT
11/18/1883	12:00	CST
3/31/1918	02:00	CWT
10/27/1918	02:00	CST
3/30/1919	02:00	CWT
10/26/1919	02:00	CST
4/27/1941	02:00	CDT
9/28/1941	02:00	CST
2/09/1942	02:00	CWT
9/30/1945	02:00	CST
4/28/1946	02:00	CDT
9/29/1946	02:00	CST
4/27/1947	02:00	CDT
10/25/1947	02:00	CST
4/25/1948	02:00	CDT
9/26/1948	02:00	CST
4/24/1949	02:00	CDT
9/25/1949	02:00	CST
4/30/1950	02:00	CDT
9/24/1950	02:00	CST
4/29/1951	02:00	CDT
9/30/1951	02:00	CST
4/27/1952	02:00	CDT
9/28/1952	02:00	CST
4/26/1953	02:00	CDT
9/27/1953	02:00	CST
4/25/1954	02:00	CDT
9/26/1954	02:00	CST
11/28/1954	02:00	EST
10/30/1955	02:00	CST
4/29/1956	02:00	CDT
9/30/1956	02:00	CST
4/28/1957	02:00	CDT
9/29/1957	02:00	CST
4/27/1958	02:00	CDT
9/28/1958	02:00	CST
4/26/1959	02:00	CDT
9/27/1959	02:00	CST
4/24/1960	02:00	CDT
9/25/1960	02:00	CST
4/30/1961	02:00	EST
10/30/1966	02:00	CST
4/30/1967	02:00	EST
4/27/1969	02:00	EDT
10/26/1969	02:00	EST
4/26/1970	02:00	EDT
10/25/1970	02:00	EST

IN # 216

Date	Time	Zone
Before 11/18/1883		LMT
11/18/1883	12:00	CST
3/31/1918	02:00	CWT
10/27/1918	02:00	CST
3/30/1919	02:00	CWT
10/26/1919	02:00	CST
2/09/1942	02:00	CWT
9/30/1945	02:00	CST
4/28/1946	02:00	CDT
9/29/1946	02:00	CST
4/27/1947	02:00	CDT
10/25/1947	02:00	CST
4/25/1948	02:00	CDT
9/26/1948	02:00	CST
4/24/1949	02:00	CDT
9/25/1949	02:00	CST
4/30/1950	02:00	CDT
9/24/1950	02:00	CST
4/29/1951	02:00	CDT
9/30/1951	02:00	CST
4/27/1952	02:00	CDT
9/28/1952	02:00	CST
4/26/1953	02:00	CDT
9/27/1953	02:00	CST
4/25/1954	02:00	CDT
9/26/1954	02:00	CST
11/28/1954	02:00	EST
10/30/1955	02:00	CST
3/25/1956	02:00	CDT
10/27/1956	02:00	CST
4/28/1957	02:00	CDT
9/29/1957	02:00	CST
4/27/1958	02:00	CDT
9/28/1958	02:00	CST
4/26/1959	02:00	CDT
9/27/1959	02:00	CST
4/24/1960	02:00	CDT
9/25/1960	02:00	CST
4/30/1961	02:00	EST
10/30/1966	02:00	CST
4/30/1967	02:00	EST
4/27/1969	02:00	EDT
10/26/1969	02:00	EST
4/26/1970	02:00	EDT
10/25/1970	02:00	EST

IN # 217

Date	Time	Zone
Before 11/18/1883		LMT
11/18/1883	12:00	CST
3/31/1918	02:00	CWT
10/27/1918	02:00	CST
3/30/1919	02:00	CWT
10/26/1919	02:00	CST
4/28/1940	02:00	CDT
9/29/1940	02:00	CST
4/27/1941	02:00	CDT
9/28/1941	02:00	CST
2/09/1942	02:00	CWT
9/30/1945	02:00	CST
4/28/1946	02:00	CDT
9/29/1946	02:00	CST
4/27/1947	02:00	CDT
9/28/1947	02:00	CST
4/25/1948	02:00	CDT
9/26/1948	02:00	CST
4/24/1949	02:00	CDT
9/25/1949	02:00	CST
4/30/1950	02:00	CDT
9/24/1950	02:00	CST
4/29/1951	02:00	CDT
9/30/1951	02:00	CST
4/27/1952	02:00	CDT
9/28/1952	02:00	CST
4/26/1953	02:00	CDT
9/27/1953	02:00	CST
4/25/1954	02:00	CDT
9/26/1954	02:00	CST
11/28/1954	02:00	EST
10/30/1955	02:00	CST
4/29/1956	02:00	CDT
10/28/1956	02:00	CST
4/28/1957	02:00	CDT
10/27/1957	02:00	CST
4/27/1958	02:00	CDT
10/26/1958	02:00	CST
4/26/1959	02:00	CDT
10/25/1959	02:00	CST
4/24/1960	02:00	CDT
10/30/1960	02:00	CST
4/30/1961	02:00	EST
10/30/1966	02:00	CST
4/30/1967	02:00	EST
4/27/1969	02:00	EDT
10/26/1969	02:00	EST
4/26/1970	02:00	EDT
10/25/1970	02:00	EST

IN # 218

Date	Time	Zone
Before 11/18/1883		LMT
11/18/1883	12:00	CST
3/31/1918	02:00	CWT
10/27/1918	02:00	CST
3/30/1919	02:00	CWT
10/26/1919	02:00	CST
4/24/1938	02:00	CDT
9/25/1938	02:00	CST
4/30/1939	02:00	CDT
9/24/1939	02:00	CST
4/28/1940	02:00	CDT
9/29/1940	02:00	CST

TIME TABLES

4/27/1941 02:00 CDT
9/28/1941 02:00 CST
2/09/1942 02:00 CWT
9/30/1945 02:00 CST
4/28/1946 02:00 CDT
9/29/1946 02:00 CST
4/27/1947 02:00 CDT
9/28/1947 02:00 CST
4/25/1948 02:00 CDT
9/26/1948 02:00 CST
4/24/1949 02:00 CDT
9/25/1949 02:00 CST
4/30/1950 02:00 CDT
9/24/1950 02:00 CST
4/29/1951 02:00 CDT
9/30/1951 02:00 CST
4/27/1952 02:00 CDT
9/28/1952 02:00 CST
4/26/1953 02:00 CDT
9/27/1953 02:00 CST
4/25/1954 02:00 CDT
9/26/1954 02:00 CST
11/28/1954 02:00 EST
10/30/1955 02:00 CST
4/29/1956 02:00 CDT
10/28/1956 02:00 CST
4/28/1957 02:00 CDT
10/27/1957 02:00 CST
4/27/1958 02:00 CDT
10/26/1958 02:00 CST
4/26/1959 02:00 CDT
10/25/1959 02:00 CST
4/24/1960 02:00 CDT
10/30/1960 02:00 CST
4/30/1961 02:00 EST
10/30/1966 02:00 CST
4/30/1967 02:00 EST
4/27/1969 02:00 EDT
10/26/1969 02:00 EST
4/26/1970 02:00 EDT
10/25/1970 02:00 EST

....

IN # 219
Before 11/18/1883 LMT
11/18/1883 12:00 CST
3/31/1918 02:00 CWT
10/27/1918 02:00 CST
3/30/1919 02:00 CWT
10/26/1919 02:00 CST
4/24/1938 02:00 CDT
10/02/1938 02:00 CST
4/23/1939 02:00 CDT
10/01/1939 02:00 CST
4/28/1940 02:00 CDT
9/29/1940 02:00 CST
4/27/1941 02:00 CDT
9/28/1941 02:00 CST
2/09/1942 02:00 CWT
9/30/1945 02:00 CST
4/28/1946 02:00 CDT
9/29/1946 02:00 CST
4/27/1947 02:00 CDT
9/28/1947 02:00 CST
4/25/1948 02:00 CDT
9/26/1948 02:00 CST
4/24/1949 02:00 CDT
9/25/1949 02:00 CST
4/30/1950 02:00 CDT
9/24/1950 02:00 CST
4/29/1951 02:00 CDT
9/30/1951 02:00 CST
4/27/1952 02:00 CDT
9/28/1952 02:00 CST
4/26/1953 02:00 CDT
9/27/1953 02:00 CST
4/25/1954 02:00 CDT
9/26/1954 02:00 CST
11/28/1954 02:00 EST
10/30/1955 02:00 CST
4/29/1956 02:00 CDT
10/28/1956 02:00 CST
4/28/1957 02:00 CDT
9/29/1957 02:00 CST
4/27/1958 02:00 CDT
10/26/1958 02:00 CST
4/26/1959 02:00 CDT
10/25/1959 02:00 CST
4/24/1960 02:00 CDT
10/30/1960 02:00 CST
4/30/1961 02:00 EST
10/30/1966 02:00 CST
4/30/1967 02:00 EST
4/27/1969 02:00 EDT
10/26/1969 02:00 EST
4/26/1970 02:00 EDT
10/25/1970 02:00 EST

....

IN # 220
Before 11/18/1883 LMT
11/18/1883 12:00 CST
3/31/1918 02:00 CWT
10/27/1918 02:00 CST
3/30/1919 02:00 CWT
10/26/1919 02:00 CST
2/09/1942 02:00 CWT
9/30/1945 02:00 CST
4/27/1947 02:00 CDT
9/28/1947 02:00 CST
4/25/1948 02:00 CDT
9/26/1948 02:00 CST
4/24/1949 02:00 CDT
9/25/1949 02:00 CST
4/30/1950 02:00 CDT
9/24/1950 02:00 CST
4/29/1951 02:00 CDT
9/30/1951 02:00 CST
4/27/1952 02:00 CDT
9/28/1952 02:00 CST
4/26/1953 02:00 CDT
9/27/1953 02:00 CST
4/25/1954 02:00 CDT
9/26/1954 02:00 CST
4/24/1955 02:00 CDT
10/30/1955 02:00 CST
4/29/1956 02:00 CDT
10/28/1956 02:00 CST
4/28/1957 02:00 CDT
9/29/1957 02:00 CST
4/27/1958 02:00 CDT
9/28/1958 02:00 CST
4/26/1959 02:00 CDT
10/25/1959 02:00 CST
4/24/1960 02:00 CDT
10/30/1960 02:00 CST
4/30/1961 02:00 CDT
10/29/1961 02:00 CST
4/29/1962 02:00 EST
10/27/1963 02:00 CST
4/26/1964 02:00 US#1

....

IN # 221
Before 11/18/1883 LMT
11/18/1883 12:00 CST
3/31/1918 02:00 CWT
10/27/1918 02:00 CST
3/30/1919 02:00 CWT
10/26/1919 02:00 CST
2/09/1942 02:00 CWT
9/30/1945 02:00 CST
4/24/1955 02:00 CDT
10/30/1955 02:00 CST
4/29/1956 02:00 CDT
10/28/1956 02:00 CST
4/28/1957 02:00 CDT
9/29/1957 02:00 CST
4/27/1958 02:00 CDT
9/28/1958 02:00 CST
4/26/1959 02:00 CDT
9/27/1959 02:00 CST
4/24/1960 02:00 CDT
9/25/1960 02:00 CST
4/30/1961 02:00 CDT
10/29/1961 02:00 CST
4/29/1962 02:00 EST
10/27/1963 02:00 CST
4/26/1964 02:00 US#1

....

IN # 222
Before 11/18/1883 LMT
11/18/1883 12:00 CST
3/31/1918 02:00 CWT
10/27/1918 02:00 CST
3/30/1919 02:00 CWT
10/26/1919 02:00 CST
2/09/1942 02:00 CWT
9/30/1945 02:00 CST
4/25/1954 02:00 CDT
9/26/1954 02:00 CST
4/24/1955 02:00 CDT
10/30/1955 02:00 CST
4/29/1956 02:00 CDT
10/28/1956 02:00 CST
4/28/1957 02:00 CDT
9/29/1957 02:00 CST
4/27/1958 02:00 CDT
9/28/1958 02:00 CST
4/26/1959 02:00 CDT
9/27/1959 02:00 CST
4/24/1960 02:00 CDT
9/25/1960 02:00 CST
4/30/1961 02:00 CDT
10/29/1961 02:00 CST
4/29/1962 02:00 EST
10/27/1963 02:00 CST
4/26/1964 02:00 US#1

....

IN # 223
Before 11/18/1883 LMT
11/18/1883 12:00 CST
3/31/1918 02:00 CWT
10/27/1918 02:00 CST
3/30/1919 02:00 CWT
10/26/1919 02:00 CST
2/09/1942 02:00 CWT
9/30/1945 02:00 CST
4/26/1953 02:00 CDT
9/27/1953 02:00 CST
4/25/1954 02:00 CDT
9/26/1954 02:00 CST
4/24/1955 02:00 CDT
10/30/1955 02:00 CST
4/29/1956 02:00 CDT
10/28/1956 02:00 CST
4/28/1957 02:00 CDT
9/29/1957 02:00 CST
4/27/1958 02:00 CDT
9/28/1958 02:00 CST
4/26/1959 02:00 CDT
9/27/1959 02:00 CST
4/24/1960 02:00 CDT
9/25/1960 02:00 CST
4/30/1961 02:00 CDT
10/29/1961 02:00 CST
4/29/1962 02:00 EST
10/27/1963 02:00 CST
4/26/1964 02:00 US#1

....

IN # 224
Before 11/18/1883 LMT
11/18/1883 12:00 CST
3/31/1918 02:00 CWT
10/27/1918 02:00 CST
3/30/1919 02:00 CWT
10/26/1919 02:00 CST
2/09/1942 02:00 CWT
9/30/1945 02:00 CST
4/24/1955 02:00 CDT
10/30/1955 02:00 CST
4/29/1956 02:00 CDT
10/28/1956 02:00 CST
4/28/1957 02:00 CDT
9/29/1957 02:00 CST
4/27/1958 02:00 CDT
9/28/1958 02:00 CST
4/26/1959 02:00 CDT
9/27/1959 02:00 CST
4/24/1960 02:00 CDT
9/25/1960 02:00 CST
4/30/1961 02:00 EST
4/27/1969 02:00 EDT
10/26/1969 02:00 CST
4/26/1970 02:00 CDT
10/25/1970 02:00 CST
4/25/1971 02:00 US#1

....

IN # 225
Before 11/18/1883 LMT
11/18/1883 12:00 CST
3/31/1918 02:00 CWT
10/27/1918 02:00 CST
3/30/1919 02:00 CWT
10/26/1919 02:00 CST
2/09/1942 02:00 CWT
9/30/1945 02:00 CST
4/26/1953 02:00 CDT
9/27/1953 02:00 CST
4/25/1954 02:00 CDT
9/26/1954 02:00 CST
4/24/1955 02:00 CDT
10/30/1955 02:00 CST
4/29/1956 02:00 CDT
10/28/1956 02:00 CST
4/28/1957 02:00 CDT
9/29/1957 02:00 CST
4/27/1958 02:00 CDT
9/28/1958 02:00 CST
4/26/1959 02:00 CDT
9/27/1959 02:00 CST
4/24/1960 02:00 CDT
9/25/1960 02:00 CST
4/30/1961 02:00 EST
4/27/1969 02:00 EDT
10/26/1969 02:00 CST
4/26/1970 02:00 CDT
10/25/1970 02:00 CST
4/25/1971 02:00 US#1

....

IN # 226
Before 11/18/1883 LMT
11/18/1883 12:00 CST
3/31/1918 02:00 CWT
10/27/1918 02:00 CST
3/30/1919 02:00 CWT
10/26/1919 02:00 CST
2/09/1942 02:00 CWT
9/30/1945 02:00 CST
4/24/1955 02:00 CDT
10/30/1955 02:00 CST
4/29/1956 02:00 CDT
10/28/1956 02:00 CST
4/28/1957 02:00 CDT
9/29/1957 02:00 CST
4/27/1958 02:00 CDT
9/28/1958 02:00 CST
4/26/1959 02:00 CDT
9/27/1959 02:00 CST
4/24/1960 02:00 CDT
9/25/1960 02:00 CST
4/30/1961 02:00 EST
10/27/1963 02:00 CST
4/26/1964 02:00 CDT
10/25/1964 02:00 CST
4/25/1965 02:00 EST
10/30/1966 02:00 CST
4/30/1967 02:00 US#1

....

IN # 227
Before 11/18/1883 LMT
11/18/1883 12:00 CST
3/31/1918 02:00 CWT
10/27/1918 02:00 CST
3/30/1919 02:00 CWT
10/26/1919 02:00 CST
2/09/1942 02:00 CWT
9/30/1945 02:00 CST
4/26/1953 02:00 CDT
9/27/1953 02:00 CST
4/25/1954 02:00 CDT
9/26/1954 02:00 CST
4/24/1955 02:00 CDT
10/30/1955 02:00 CST
4/29/1956 02:00 CDT
10/28/1956 02:00 CST
4/28/1957 02:00 CDT
9/29/1957 02:00 CST
4/27/1958 02:00 CDT
9/28/1958 02:00 CST
4/26/1959 02:00 CDT
9/27/1959 02:00 CST
4/24/1960 02:00 CDT
9/25/1960 02:00 CST
4/30/1961 02:00 EST
10/27/1963 02:00 CST
4/26/1964 02:00 CDT
10/25/1964 02:00 CST
4/25/1965 02:00 EST
10/30/1966 02:00 CST
4/30/1967 02:00 US#1

....

IN # 228
Before 11/18/1883 LMT
11/18/1883 12:00 CST
3/31/1918 02:00 CWT
10/27/1918 02:00 CST
3/30/1919 02:00 CWT
10/26/1919 02:00 CST
2/09/1942 02:00 CWT
9/30/1945 02:00 CST
10/31/1954 00:01 EST
4/27/1969 02:00 EDT
10/26/1969 02:00 EST
4/26/1970 02:00 EDT
10/25/1970 02:00 EST

....

IN # 229
Before 11/18/1883 LMT
11/18/1883 12:00 CST
3/31/1918 02:00 CWT
10/27/1918 02:00 CST
3/30/1919 02:00 CWT
10/26/1919 02:00 CST
2/09/1942 02:00 CWT
9/30/1945 02:00 CST
10/31/1954 00:01 EST
4/28/1968 02:00 US#1

....

IN # 230
Before 11/18/1883 LMT
11/18/1883 12:00 CST
3/31/1918 02:00 CWT
10/27/1918 02:00 CST
3/30/1919 02:00 CWT
10/26/1919 02:00 CST
2/09/1942 02:00 CWT
9/30/1945 02:00 CST
4/26/1953 02:00 CDT
9/27/1953 02:00 CST
4/25/1954 02:00 CDT
9/26/1954 02:00 CST
10/31/1954 00:01 EST
4/27/1969 02:00 EDT
10/26/1969 02:00 EST
4/26/1970 02:00 EDT
10/25/1970 02:00 EST

....

IN # 231
Before 11/18/1883 LMT
11/18/1883 12:00 CST
3/31/1918 02:00 CWT
10/27/1918 02:00 CST
3/30/1919 02:00 CWT
10/26/1919 02:00 CST
2/09/1942 02:00 CWT
9/30/1945 02:00 CST
4/25/1954 02:00 CDT
9/26/1954 02:00 CST
10/31/1954 00:01 EST
4/27/1969 02:00 EDT
10/26/1969 02:00 EST
4/26/1970 02:00 EDT
10/25/1970 02:00 EST

....

IN # 232
Before 11/18/1883 LMT
11/18/1883 12:00 CST
3/31/1918 02:00 CWT
10/27/1918 02:00 CST
3/30/1919 02:00 CWT
10/26/1919 02:00 CST
4/26/1931 02:00 CDT
9/27/1931 02:00 CST
5/01/1932 00:01 CDT
9/25/1932 00:01 CST
4/30/1933 02:00 CDT
9/24/1933 02:00 CST
4/29/1934 02:00 CDT
9/30/1934 02:00 CST
4/28/1935 02:00 CDT
9/29/1935 02:00 CST
4/26/1936 02:00 CDT
9/27/1936 02:00 CST
4/25/1937 02:00 CDT
9/26/1937 02:00 CST
4/24/1938 02:00 CDT
9/25/1938 02:00 CST
4/30/1939 02:00 CDT
9/24/1939 02:00 CST
4/28/1940 02:00 CDT
9/29/1940 02:00 CST
4/27/1941 02:00 CDT
9/28/1941 02:00 CST
2/09/1942 02:00 CWT
9/30/1945 02:00 CST
4/28/1946 02:00 CDT
9/29/1946 02:00 CST
4/27/1947 02:00 CDT
9/28/1947 02:00 CST
4/25/1948 02:00 CDT
9/26/1948 02:00 CST
4/24/1949 02:00 CDT
9/25/1949 02:00 CST
4/30/1950 02:00 CDT
9/24/1950 02:00 CST
4/29/1951 02:00 CDT
9/30/1951 02:00 CST
4/27/1952 02:00 CDT
9/28/1952 02:00 CST
4/26/1953 02:00 CDT
9/27/1953 02:00 CST
4/25/1954 02:00 CDT
9/26/1954 02:00 CST
10/31/1954 00:01 EST
4/27/1969 02:00 EDT
10/26/1969 02:00 EST
4/26/1970 02:00 EDT
10/25/1970 02:00 EST

....

IN # 233
Before 11/18/1883 LMT
11/18/1883 12:00 CST
3/31/1918 02:00 CWT
10/27/1918 02:00 CST
3/30/1919 02:00 CWT
10/26/1919 02:00 CST
4/29/1928 00:01 CDT
9/30/1928 00:01 CST
4/28/1929 00:01 CDT
9/29/1929 00:01 CST
4/27/1930 00:01 CDT
9/28/1930 00:01 CST
4/26/1931 00:01 CDT
9/27/1931 00:01 CST
4/24/1932 00:01 CDT
9/25/1932 00:01 CST
4/30/1933 00:01 CDT
10/01/1933 00:01 CST
4/29/1934 00:01 CDT
9/30/1934 00:01 CST
4/28/1935 00:01 CDT
9/29/1935 00:01 CST
4/26/1936 02:00 CDT
9/27/1936 02:00 CST
4/25/1937 02:00 CDT
9/26/1937 02:00 CST
4/24/1938 02:00 CDT
9/25/1938 02:00 CST
4/30/1939 02:00 CDT
10/01/1939 02:00 CST
4/28/1940 02:00 CDT
9/29/1940 02:00 CST
4/27/1941 02:00 CDT
9/28/1941 02:00 CST
2/09/1942 02:00 CWT
9/30/1945 02:00 CST
4/28/1946 02:00 CDT
9/29/1946 02:00 CST
4/27/1947 02:00 CDT
9/28/1947 02:00 CST
4/25/1948 02:00 CDT
9/26/1948 02:00 CST
5/01/1949 02:00 CDT
9/25/1949 02:00 CST
4/30/1950 02:00 CDT
10/01/1950 02:00 CST
4/29/1951 02:00 CDT
9/30/1951 02:00 CST
4/27/1952 02:00 CDT
9/28/1952 02:00 CST
4/26/1953 02:00 CDT
9/27/1953 02:00 CST
4/25/1954 02:00 CDT
9/26/1954 02:00 CST
10/31/1954 00:01 EST
4/27/1969 02:00 EDT
10/26/1969 02:00 EST
4/26/1970 02:00 EDT
10/25/1970 02:00 EST

....

IN # 234
Before 11/18/1883 LMT
11/18/1883 12:00 CST
3/31/1918 02:00 CWT
10/27/1918 02:00 CST
3/30/1919 02:00 CWT
10/26/1919 02:00 CST
4/28/1929 02:00 CDT
9/29/1929 02:00 CST
4/27/1930 02:00 CDT
9/28/1930 02:00 CST
4/26/1931 02:00 CDT
9/27/1931 02:00 CST
4/24/1932 02:00 CDT
9/25/1932 02:00 CST
4/30/1933 02:00 CDT
10/01/1933 02:00 CST
4/29/1934 02:00 CDT
9/30/1934 02:00 CST
4/28/1935 02:00 CDT
9/29/1935 02:00 CST
4/26/1936 02:00 CDT
9/27/1936 02:00 CST
4/25/1937 02:00 CDT
9/26/1937 02:00 CST
4/24/1938 02:00 CDT
9/25/1938 02:00 CST
4/30/1939 02:00 CDT
9/24/1939 02:00 CST
4/28/1940 02:00 CDT
9/29/1940 02:00 CST
4/27/1941 02:00 CDT
9/28/1941 02:00 CST
2/09/1942 02:00 CWT
9/30/1945 02:00 CST
4/28/1946 02:00 CDT
9/29/1946 02:00 CST
4/27/1947 02:00 CDT
9/28/1947 02:00 CST
4/25/1948 02:00 CDT
9/26/1948 02:00 CST
4/24/1949 02:00 CDT
9/25/1949 02:00 CST
4/30/1950 02:00 CDT
9/24/1950 02:00 CST
4/29/1951 02:00 CDT
9/30/1951 02:00 CST
4/27/1952 02:00 CDT
9/28/1952 02:00 CST
4/26/1953 02:00 CDT
9/27/1953 02:00 CST
4/25/1954 02:00 CDT
9/26/1954 02:00 CST
10/31/1954 00:01 EST
4/27/1969 02:00 EDT
10/26/1969 02:00 EST
4/26/1970 02:00 EDT
10/25/1970 02:00 EST

....

IN # 235
Before 11/18/1883 LMT
11/18/1883 12:00 CST
3/31/1918 02:00 CWT
10/27/1918 02:00 CST
3/30/1919 02:00 CWT
10/26/1919 02:00 CST
5/01/1938 02:00 CDT
10/01/1938 02:00 CST
4/30/1939 02:00 CDT
9/30/1939 02:00 CST
4/27/1941 02:00 CDT
9/28/1941 02:00 CST

TIME TABLES

2/09/1942 02:00 CWT
9/30/1945 02:00 CST
4/26/1953 02:00 CDT
9/27/1953 02:00 CST
4/25/1954 02:00 CDT
9/26/1954 02:00 CST
10/31/1954 00:01 EST
4/27/1969 02:00 EDT
10/26/1969 02:00 EST
4/26/1970 02:00 EDT
10/25/1970 02:00 EST

IN # 236

Before 11/18/1883 LMT
11/18/1883 12:00 CST
3/31/1918 02:00 CWT
10/27/1918 02:00 CST
3/30/1919 02:00 CWT
10/26/1919 02:00 CST
4/28/1940 02:00 CDT
9/29/1940 02:00 CST
4/27/1941 02:00 CDT
9/28/1941 02:00 CST
2/09/1942 02:00 CWT
9/30/1945 02:00 CST
4/28/1946 02:00 CDT
9/29/1946 02:00 CST
4/27/1947 02:00 CDT
9/28/1947 02:00 CST
4/25/1948 02:00 CDT
9/26/1948 02:00 CST
4/24/1949 02:00 CDT
9/25/1949 02:00 CST
4/30/1950 02:00 CDT
9/24/1950 02:00 CST
4/29/1951 02:00 CDT
9/30/1951 02:00 CST
4/27/1952 02:00 CDT
9/28/1952 02:00 CST
4/26/1953 02:00 CDT
9/27/1953 02:00 CST
4/25/1954 02:00 CDT
9/26/1954 02:00 CST
10/31/1954 00:01 EST
4/27/1969 02:00 EDT
10/26/1969 02:00 EST
4/26/1970 02:00 EDT
10/25/1970 02:00 EST

IN # 237

Before 11/18/1883 LMT
11/18/1883 12:00 CST
3/31/1918 02:00 CWT
10/27/1918 02:00 CST
3/30/1919 02:00 CWT
10/26/1919 02:00 CST
5/01/1938 02:00 CDT
10/02/1938 02:00 CST
4/30/1939 02:00 CDT
10/01/1939 02:00 CST
4/28/1940 02:00 CDT
9/29/1940 02:00 CST
4/27/1941 02:00 CDT
9/28/1941 02:00 CST
2/09/1942 02:00 CWT
9/30/1945 02:00 CST
4/28/1946 02:00 CDT
9/29/1946 02:00 CST
4/27/1947 02:00 CDT
9/28/1947 02:00 CST
4/25/1948 02:00 CDT
9/26/1948 02:00 CST
4/24/1949 02:00 CDT
9/25/1949 02:00 CST
4/30/1950 02:00 CDT
9/24/1950 02:00 CST
4/29/1951 02:00 CDT
9/30/1951 02:00 CST
4/27/1952 02:00 CDT
9/28/1952 02:00 CST
4/26/1953 02:00 CDT
9/27/1953 02:00 CST
4/25/1954 02:00 CDT
9/26/1954 02:00 CST
10/31/1954 00:01 EST
4/27/1969 02:00 EDT
10/26/1969 02:00 EST
4/26/1970 02:00 EDT
10/25/1970 02:00 EST

IN # 238

Before 11/18/1883 LMT
11/18/1883 12:00 CST
3/31/1918 02:00 CWT
10/27/1918 02:00 CST
3/30/1919 02:00 CWT
10/26/1919 02:00 CST
6/13/1920 02:00 CDT
10/31/1920 02:00 CST
3/27/1921 02:00 CDT
10/30/1921 02:00 CST
4/30/1922 02:00 CDT
9/24/1922 02:00 CST
4/29/1923 02:00 CDT
9/30/1923 02:00 CST
4/27/1924 02:00 CDT
9/28/1924 02:00 CST
4/26/1925 02:00 CDT
9/27/1925 02:00 CST
4/25/1926 02:00 CDT
9/26/1926 02:00 CST
4/24/1927 02:00 CDT
9/25/1927 02:00 CST
4/29/1928 02:00 CDT
9/30/1928 02:00 CST
4/28/1929 02:00 CDT
9/29/1929 02:00 CST
4/27/1930 02:00 CDT
9/28/1930 02:00 CST
4/26/1931 02:00 CDT
9/27/1931 02:00 CST
4/30/1932 02:00 CDT
10/01/1932 02:00 CST
4/30/1933 02:00 CDT
10/01/1933 02:00 CST
4/29/1934 02:00 CDT
9/30/1934 02:00 CST
4/28/1935 02:00 CDT
9/29/1935 02:00 CST
4/26/1936 02:00 CDT
9/27/1936 02:00 CST
4/25/1937 02:00 CDT
9/26/1937 02:00 CST
4/24/1938 02:00 CDT
9/25/1938 02:00 CST
4/30/1939 02:00 CDT
9/24/1939 02:00 CST
4/28/1940 02:00 CDT
9/29/1940 02:00 CST
4/27/1941 02:00 CDT
9/28/1941 02:00 CST
2/09/1942 02:00 CWT
9/30/1945 02:00 CST
4/28/1946 02:00 CDT
9/29/1946 02:00 CST
4/27/1947 02:00 CDT
9/28/1947 02:00 CST
4/25/1948 02:00 CDT
9/26/1948 02:00 CST
4/24/1949 02:00 CDT
9/25/1949 02:00 CST
4/30/1950 02:00 CDT
9/24/1950 02:00 CST
4/29/1951 02:00 CDT
9/30/1951 02:00 CST
4/27/1952 02:00 CDT
9/28/1952 02:00 CST
4/26/1953 02:00 CDT
9/27/1953 02:00 CST
4/25/1954 02:00 CDT
9/26/1954 02:00 CST
10/31/1954 00:01 EST
4/27/1969 02:00 EDT
10/26/1969 02:00 EST
4/26/1970 02:00 EDT
10/25/1970 02:00 EST

IN # 239

Before 11/18/1883 LMT
11/18/1883 12:00 CST
3/31/1918 02:00 CWT
10/27/1918 02:00 CST
3/30/1919 02:00 CWT
10/26/1919 02:00 CST
4/25/1937 02:00 CDT
9/26/1937 02:00 CST
4/24/1938 02:00 CDT
9/25/1938 02:00 CST
4/30/1939 02:00 CDT
9/24/1939 02:00 CST
2/09/1942 02:00 CWT
9/30/1945 02:00 CST
4/27/1947 02:00 CDT
9/28/1947 02:00 CST
4/25/1948 02:00 CDT
9/26/1948 02:00 CST
4/26/1953 02:00 CDT
9/27/1953 02:00 CST
4/25/1954 02:00 CDT
9/26/1954 02:00 CST
10/31/1954 00:01 EST
4/27/1969 02:00 EDT
10/26/1969 02:00 EST
4/26/1970 02:00 EDT
10/25/1970 02:00 EST

IN # 240

Before 11/18/1883 LMT
11/18/1883 12:00 CST
3/31/1918 02:00 CWT
10/27/1918 02:00 CST
3/30/1919 02:00 CWT
10/26/1919 02:00 CST
2/09/1942 02:00 CWT
9/30/1945 02:00 CST
4/26/1953 02:00 CDT
9/27/1953 02:00 CST
4/25/1954 02:00 CDT
9/26/1954 02:00 CST
4/24/1955 02:00 CDT
10/30/1955 02:00 CST
4/29/1956 02:00 CDT
10/28/1956 02:00 CST
4/28/1957 02:00 CDT
9/29/1957 02:00 CST
4/27/1958 02:00 CDT
9/28/1958 02:00 CST
4/26/1959 02:00 CDT
9/27/1959 02:00 CST
4/24/1960 02:00 CDT
9/25/1960 02:00 CST
4/30/1961 02:00 EST
10/27/1963 02:00 CST
4/26/1964 02:00 EST
4/27/1969 02:00 EDT
10/26/1969 02:00 CST
4/26/1970 02:00 CDT
10/25/1970 02:00 CST
4/25/1971 02:00 US#1

IN # 241

Before 11/18/1883 LMT
11/18/1883 12:00 CST
3/31/1918 02:00 CWT
10/27/1918 02:00 CST
3/30/1919 02:00 CWT
10/26/1919 02:00 CST
2/09/1942 02:00 CWT
9/30/1945 02:00 CST
4/26/1953 02:00 CDT
9/27/1953 02:00 CST
4/25/1954 02:00 CDT
9/26/1954 02:00 CST
4/24/1955 02:00 CDT
10/30/1955 02:00 CST
4/29/1956 02:00 CDT
10/28/1956 02:00 CST
4/28/1957 02:00 CDT
9/29/1957 02:00 CST
4/27/1958 02:00 CDT
9/28/1958 02:00 CST
4/26/1959 02:00 CDT
9/27/1959 02:00 CST
4/24/1960 02:00 CDT
9/25/1960 02:00 CST
4/30/1961 02:00 EST
10/27/1963 02:00 CST
4/26/1964 02:00 CDT
10/25/1964 02:00 CST
4/25/1965 02:00 EST
4/27/1969 02:00 EDT
10/26/1969 02:00 CST
4/26/1970 02:00 CDT
10/25/1970 02:00 CST
4/25/1971 02:00 US#1

IN # 242

Before 11/18/1883 LMT
11/18/1883 12:00 CST
3/31/1918 02:00 CWT
10/27/1918 02:00 CST
3/30/1919 02:00 CWT
10/26/1919 02:00 CST
2/09/1942 02:00 CWT
9/30/1945 02:00 CST
4/25/1954 02:00 CDT
9/26/1954 02:00 CST
11/28/1954 02:00 EST
9/29/1957 02:00 CST
4/27/1958 02:00 CDT
9/28/1958 02:00 CST
4/26/1959 02:00 CDT
9/27/1959 02:00 CST
4/24/1960 02:00 CDT
9/25/1960 02:00 CST
4/30/1961 02:00 EST
4/27/1969 02:00 EDT
10/26/1969 02:00 EST
4/26/1970 02:00 EDT
10/25/1970 02:00 EST

IN # 243

Before 11/18/1883 LMT
11/18/1883 12:00 CST
3/31/1918 02:00 CWT
10/27/1918 02:00 CST
3/30/1919 02:00 CWT
10/26/1919 02:00 CST
2/09/1942 02:00 CWT
9/30/1945 02:00 CST
4/30/1950 02:00 CDT
9/01/1950 02:00 CST
11/07/1954 00:01 EST
9/29/1957 02:00 CST
4/27/1958 02:00 EST
9/27/1959 02:00 CST
4/24/1960 02:00 EST
4/27/1969 02:00 EDT
10/26/1969 02:00 EST
4/26/1970 02:00 EDT
10/25/1970 02:00 EST

IN # 244

Before 11/18/1883 LMT
11/18/1883 12:00 CST
3/31/1918 02:00 CWT
10/27/1918 02:00 CST
3/30/1919 02:00 CWT
10/26/1919 02:00 CST
2/09/1942 02:00 CWT
9/30/1945 02:00 CST
4/24/1955 02:00 EST
9/29/1957 02:00 CST
4/27/1958 02:00 CDT
9/28/1958 02:00 CST
10/01/1958 02:00 EST
4/27/1969 02:00 EDT
10/26/1969 02:00 EST
4/26/1970 02:00 EDT
10/25/1970 02:00 EST

IN # 245

Before 11/18/1883 LMT
11/18/1883 12:00 CST
3/31/1918 02:00 CWT
10/27/1918 02:00 CST
3/30/1919 02:00 CWT
10/26/1919 02:00 CST
2/09/1942 02:00 CWT
9/30/1945 02:00 CST
4/28/1946 02:00 CDT
9/29/1946 02:00 CST
4/26/1953 02:00 CDT
9/27/1953 02:00 CST
4/25/1954 02:00 CDT
9/26/1954 02:00 CST
4/24/1955 02:00 EST
9/29/1957 02:00 CST
4/27/1958 02:00 CDT
9/28/1958 02:00 CST
10/13/1958 02:00 EST
4/27/1969 02:00 EDT
10/26/1969 02:00 EST
4/26/1970 02:00 EDT
10/25/1970 02:00 EST

IN # 246

Before 11/18/1883 LMT
11/18/1883 12:00 CST
3/31/1918 02:00 CWT
10/27/1918 02:00 CST
3/30/1919 02:00 CWT
10/26/1919 02:00 CST
2/09/1942 02:00 CWT
9/30/1945 02:00 CST
4/27/1947 02:00 CDT
9/28/1947 02:00 CST
4/24/1955 02:00 CDT
9/25/1955 02:00 CST
4/29/1956 02:00 CDT
9/03/1956 02:00 CST
4/28/1957 02:00 CDT
9/29/1957 02:00 CST
4/27/1958 02:00 CDT
9/28/1958 02:00 CST
4/26/1959 02:00 CDT
9/27/1959 02:00 CST
4/24/1960 02:00 CDT
9/25/1960 02:00 CST
12/05/1960 02:00 EST
12/07/1960 00:00 CST
4/30/1961 02:00 CDT
10/29/1961 02:00 CST
4/29/1962 02:00 EST
4/27/1969 02:00 EDT
10/26/1969 02:00 EST
4/26/1970 02:00 EDT
10/25/1970 02:00 EST

IN # 247

Before 11/18/1883 LMT
11/18/1883 12:00 CST
3/31/1918 02:00 CWT
10/27/1918 02:00 CST
3/30/1919 02:00 CWT
10/26/1919 02:00 CST
2/09/1942 02:00 CWT
9/30/1945 02:00 CST
4/24/1955 02:00 EST
10/28/1956 02:00 CST
4/28/1957 02:00 CDT
9/29/1957 02:00 CST
4/27/1958 02:00 EST
4/27/1969 02:00 EDT
10/26/1969 02:00 EST
4/26/1970 02:00 EDT
10/25/1970 02:00 EST

IN # 248

Before 11/18/1883 LMT
11/18/1883 12:00 CST
3/31/1918 02:00 CWT
10/27/1918 02:00 CST
3/30/1919 02:00 CWT
10/26/1919 02:00 CST
2/09/1942 02:00 CWT
9/30/1945 02:00 CST
4/26/1953 02:00 CDT
9/27/1953 02:00 CST
4/25/1954 02:00 CDT
9/26/1954 02:00 CST
4/24/1955 02:00 EST
10/28/1956 02:00 CST
4/28/1957 02:00 CDT
9/29/1957 02:00 CST
4/27/1958 02:00 EST
4/27/1969 02:00 EDT
10/26/1969 02:00 EST
4/26/1970 02:00 EDT
10/25/1970 02:00 EST

IN # 249

Before 11/18/1883 LMT
11/18/1883 12:00 CST
3/31/1918 02:00 CWT
10/27/1918 02:00 CST
3/30/1919 02:00 CWT
10/26/1919 02:00 CST
6/22/1941 02:00 CDT
9/28/1941 02:00 CST
2/09/1942 02:00 CWT
9/30/1945 02:00 CST
4/28/1946 02:00 CDT
9/29/1946 02:00 CST
4/27/1947 02:00 CDT
9/28/1947 02:00 CST
4/25/1948 02:00 CDT
9/26/1948 02:00 CST
4/24/1949 02:00 CDT
9/25/1949 02:00 CST
4/30/1950 02:00 CDT
9/24/1950 02:00 CST
4/29/1951 02:00 CDT
9/30/1951 02:00 CST
4/27/1952 02:00 CDT
9/28/1952 02:00 CST
4/26/1953 02:00 CDT
9/27/1953 02:00 CST
4/25/1954 02:00 CDT
9/26/1954 02:00 CST
4/24/1955 02:00 EST
10/28/1956 02:00 CST
4/28/1957 02:00 CDT
9/29/1957 02:00 CST
4/27/1958 02:00 EST
4/27/1969 02:00 EDT
10/26/1969 02:00 EST
4/26/1970 02:00 EDT
10/25/1970 02:00 EST

IN # 250

Before 11/18/1883 LMT
11/18/1883 12:00 CST
3/31/1918 02:00 CWT
10/27/1918 02:00 CST
3/30/1919 02:00 CWT
10/26/1919 02:00 CST
2/09/1942 02:00 CWT
9/30/1945 02:00 CST
4/28/1946 02:00 CDT
9/29/1946 02:00 CST
4/27/1947 02:00 CDT
9/28/1947 02:00 CST
4/25/1948 02:00 CDT
9/26/1948 02:00 CST
4/24/1949 02:00 CDT
9/25/1949 02:00 CST
4/30/1950 02:00 CDT
9/24/1950 02:00 CST
4/29/1951 02:00 CDT
9/30/1951 02:00 CST
4/27/1952 02:00 CDT
9/28/1952 02:00 CST
4/26/1953 02:00 CDT
9/27/1953 02:00 CST
4/25/1954 02:00 CDT
9/26/1954 02:00 CST
4/24/1955 02:00 EST
10/28/1956 02:00 CST
4/28/1957 02:00 CDT
9/29/1957 02:00 CST
4/27/1958 02:00 EST
4/27/1969 02:00 EDT
10/26/1969 02:00 EST
4/26/1970 02:00 EDT
10/25/1970 02:00 EST

IN # 251

Before 11/18/1883 LMT
11/18/1883 12:00 CST
3/31/1918 02:00 CWT
10/27/1918 02:00 CST
3/30/1919 02:00 CWT
10/26/1919 02:00 CST
2/09/1942 02:00 CWT
9/30/1945 02:00 CST
4/24/1955 02:00 EST
10/28/1956 02:00 CST
4/28/1957 02:00 CDT
9/29/1957 02:00 CST
4/27/1958 02:00 CDT
9/28/1958 02:00 CST
4/26/1959 02:00 EST
4/27/1969 02:00 EDT
10/26/1969 02:00 EST
4/26/1970 02:00 EDT
10/25/1970 02:00 EST

IN # 252

Before 11/18/1883 LMT
11/18/1883 12:00 CST
3/31/1918 02:00 CWT
10/27/1918 02:00 CST
3/30/1919 02:00 CWT
10/26/1919 02:00 CST
2/09/1942 02:00 CWT
9/30/1945 02:00 CST
4/26/1953 02:00 CDT
9/27/1953 02:00 CST
4/25/1954 02:00 CDT
9/26/1954 02:00 CST
4/24/1955 02:00 EST
10/28/1956 02:00 CST
4/28/1957 02:00 CDT
9/29/1957 02:00 CST
4/27/1958 02:00 CDT
9/28/1958 02:00 CST
4/26/1959 02:00 EST
4/27/1969 02:00 EDT
10/26/1969 02:00 EST
4/26/1970 02:00 EDT
10/25/1970 02:00 EST

IN # 253

Before 11/18/1883 LMT
11/18/1883 12:00 CST
3/31/1918 02:00 CWT
10/27/1918 02:00 CST
3/30/1919 02:00 CWT
10/26/1919 02:00 CST
2/09/1942 02:00 CWT
9/30/1945 02:00 CST
12/12/1954 02:00 EST
9/29/1957 02:00 CST
4/27/1958 02:00 CDT
9/28/1958 02:00 CST
4/26/1959 02:00 EST
4/27/1969 02:00 EDT
10/26/1969 02:00 EST
4/26/1970 02:00 EDT
10/25/1970 02:00 EST

IN # 254

Before 11/18/1883 LMT
11/18/1883 12:00 CST
3/31/1918 02:00 CWT
10/27/1918 02:00 CST
3/30/1919 02:00 CWT
10/26/1919 02:00 CST
4/30/1939 02:00 CDT
9/24/1939 02:00 CST
4/28/1940 02:00 CDT
9/29/1940 02:00 CST
2/09/1942 02:00 CWT
9/30/1945 02:00 CST
4/28/1946 02:00 CDT
9/29/1946 02:00 CST
4/27/1947 02:00 CDT
9/28/1947 02:00 CST
4/25/1948 02:00 CDT
9/26/1948 02:00 CST
4/24/1949 02:00 CDT
9/25/1949 02:00 CST
4/30/1950 02:00 CDT
9/24/1950 02:00 CST
4/29/1951 02:00 CDT
9/30/1951 02:00 CST
4/27/1952 02:00 CDT
9/28/1952 02:00 CST
4/26/1953 02:00 CDT

TIME TABLES

9/27/1953 02:00 CST
4/25/1954 02:00 CDT
9/26/1954 02:00 CST
12/12/1954 02:00 EST
9/29/1957 02:00 CST
4/27/1958 02:00 CDT
9/28/1958 02:00 CST
4/26/1959 02:00 EST
4/27/1969 02:00 EDT
10/26/1969 02:00 EST
4/26/1970 02:00 EDT
10/25/1970 02:00 EST

IN # 255
Before 11/18/1883 LMT
11/18/1883 12:00 CST
3/31/1918 02:00 CWT
10/27/1918 02:00 CST
3/30/1919 02:00 CWT
10/26/1919 02:00 CST
2/09/1942 02:00 CWT
9/30/1945 02:00 CST
4/28/1946 02:00 CDT
9/29/1946 02:00 CST
4/27/1947 02:00 CDT
9/28/1947 02:00 CST
4/25/1948 02:00 CDT
9/26/1948 02:00 CST
4/24/1949 02:00 CDT
9/25/1949 02:00 CST
4/30/1950 02:00 CDT
9/24/1950 02:00 CST
4/29/1951 02:00 CDT
9/30/1951 02:00 CST
4/27/1952 02:00 CDT
9/28/1952 02:00 CST
4/26/1953 02:00 CDT
9/27/1953 02:00 CST
4/25/1954 02:00 CDT
9/26/1954 02:00 CST
12/12/1954 02:00 EST
9/29/1957 02:00 CST
4/27/1958 02:00 CDT
9/28/1958 02:00 CST
4/26/1959 02:00 EST
4/27/1969 02:00 EDT
10/26/1969 02:00 EST
4/26/1970 02:00 EDT
10/25/1970 02:00 EST

IN # 256
Before 11/18/1883 LMT
11/18/1883 12:00 CST
3/31/1918 02:00 CWT
10/27/1918 02:00 CST
3/30/1919 02:00 CWT
10/26/1919 02:00 CST
2/09/1942 02:00 CWT
9/30/1945 02:00 CST
4/27/1947 02:00 CDT
9/28/1947 02:00 CST
4/25/1948 02:00 CDT
9/26/1948 02:00 CST
4/24/1949 02:00 CDT
9/25/1949 02:00 CST
4/30/1950 02:00 CDT
9/24/1950 02:00 CST
4/29/1951 02:00 CDT
9/30/1951 02:00 CST
4/27/1952 02:00 CDT
9/28/1952 02:00 CST
4/26/1953 02:00 CDT
9/27/1953 02:00 CST
4/25/1954 02:00 CDT
9/26/1954 02:00 CST
12/12/1954 02:00 EST
9/29/1957 02:00 CST
4/27/1958 02:00 CDT
9/28/1958 02:00 CST
4/26/1959 02:00 EST
4/27/1969 02:00 EDT
10/26/1969 02:00 EST
4/26/1970 02:00 EDT
10/25/1970 02:00 EST

IN # 257
Before 11/18/1883 LMT
11/18/1883 12:00 CST
3/31/1918 02:00 CWT
10/27/1918 02:00 CST
3/30/1919 02:00 CWT
10/26/1919 02:00 CST
2/09/1942 02:00 CWT
9/30/1945 02:00 CST
4/26/1953 02:00 CDT
9/27/1953 02:00 CST
4/25/1954 02:00 CDT
9/26/1954 02:00 CST
12/12/1954 02:00 EST
9/29/1957 02:00 CST
4/27/1958 02:00 CDT
9/28/1958 02:00 CST
4/26/1959 02:00 EST
4/27/1969 02:00 EDT
10/26/1969 02:00 EST
4/26/1970 02:00 EDT
10/25/1970 02:00 EST

IN # 258
Before 11/18/1883 LMT
11/18/1883 12:00 CST
3/31/1918 02:00 CWT
10/27/1918 02:00 CST
3/30/1919 02:00 CWT
10/26/1919 02:00 CST
6/13/1920 02:00 CDT
10/31/1920 02:00 CST
3/27/1921 02:00 CDT
10/30/1921 02:00 CST
4/30/1922 02:00 CDT
9/24/1922 02:00 CST
4/29/1923 02:00 CDT
9/30/1923 02:00 CST
4/27/1924 02:00 CDT
9/28/1924 02:00 CST
4/26/1925 02:00 CDT
9/27/1925 02:00 CST
4/25/1926 02:00 CDT
9/26/1926 02:00 CST
4/24/1927 02:00 CDT
9/25/1927 02:00 CST
4/29/1928 02:00 CDT
9/30/1928 02:00 CST
4/28/1929 02:00 CDT
9/29/1929 02:00 CST
4/27/1930 02:00 CDT
9/28/1930 02:00 CST
4/26/1931 02:00 CDT
9/27/1931 02:00 CST
4/24/1932 02:00 CDT
9/25/1932 02:00 CST
4/30/1933 02:00 CDT
9/24/1933 02:00 CST
4/29/1934 02:00 CDT
9/30/1934 02:00 CST
4/28/1935 02:00 CDT
9/29/1935 02:00 CST
4/26/1936 02:00 CDT
9/27/1936 02:00 CST
4/25/1937 02:00 CDT
9/26/1937 02:00 CST
4/24/1938 02:00 CDT
9/25/1938 02:00 CST
4/30/1939 02:00 CDT
9/24/1939 02:00 CST
4/28/1940 02:00 CDT
9/29/1940 02:00 CST
4/27/1941 02:00 CDT
9/28/1941 02:00 CST
2/09/1942 02:00 CWT
9/30/1945 02:00 CST
4/28/1946 02:00 CDT
9/29/1946 02:00 CST
4/27/1947 02:00 CDT
9/28/1947 02:00 CST
4/25/1948 02:00 CDT
9/26/1948 02:00 CST
4/24/1949 02:00 CDT
9/25/1949 02:00 CST
4/30/1950 02:00 CDT
9/24/1950 02:00 CST
4/29/1951 02:00 CDT
9/30/1951 02:00 CST
4/27/1952 02:00 CDT
9/28/1952 02:00 CST
4/26/1953 02:00 CDT
9/27/1953 02:00 CST
4/25/1954 02:00 CDT
9/26/1954 02:00 CST
11/14/1954 02:00 EST
4/27/1969 02:00 EDT
10/26/1969 02:00 EST
4/26/1970 02:00 EDT
10/25/1970 02:00 EST

IN # 259
Before 11/18/1883 LMT
11/18/1883 12:00 CST
3/31/1918 02:00 CWT
10/27/1918 02:00 CST
3/30/1919 02:00 CWT
10/26/1919 02:00 CST
2/09/1942 02:00 CWT
9/30/1945 02:00 CST
11/14/1954 02:00 EST
4/27/1969 02:00 EDT
10/26/1969 02:00 EST
4/26/1970 02:00 EDT
10/25/1970 02:00 EST

IN # 260
Before 11/18/1883 LMT
11/18/1883 12:00 CST
3/31/1918 02:00 CWT
10/27/1918 02:00 CST
3/30/1919 02:00 CWT
10/26/1919 02:00 CST
4/30/1938 02:00 CDT
10/01/1938 02:00 CST
4/28/1940 02:00 CDT
9/29/1940 02:00 CST
4/27/1941 02:00 CDT
9/28/1941 02:00 CST
2/09/1942 02:00 CWT
9/30/1945 02:00 CST
4/28/1946 02:00 CDT
9/29/1946 02:00 CST
4/27/1947 02:00 CDT
9/28/1947 02:00 CST
11/14/1954 02:00 EST
4/27/1969 02:00 EDT
10/26/1969 02:00 EST
4/26/1970 02:00 EDT
10/25/1970 02:00 EST

IN # 261
Before 11/18/1883 LMT
11/18/1883 12:00 CST
3/31/1918 02:00 CWT
10/27/1918 02:00 CST
3/30/1919 02:00 CWT
10/26/1919 02:00 CST
4/27/1941 02:00 CDT
9/28/1941 02:00 CST
2/09/1942 02:00 CWT
9/30/1945 02:00 CST
11/14/1954 02:00 EST
4/27/1969 02:00 EDT
10/26/1969 02:00 EST
4/26/1970 02:00 EDT
10/25/1970 02:00 EST

IN # 262
Before 11/18/1883 LMT
11/18/1883 12:00 CST
3/31/1918 02:00 CWT
10/27/1918 02:00 CST
3/30/1919 02:00 CWT
10/26/1919 02:00 CST
4/26/1936 02:00 CDT
9/27/1936 02:00 CST
4/24/1938 02:00 CDT
9/25/1938 02:00 CST
4/30/1939 02:00 CDT
9/24/1939 02:00 CST
4/28/1940 02:00 CDT
9/29/1940 02:00 CST
4/27/1941 02:00 CDT
9/28/1941 02:00 CST
2/09/1942 02:00 CWT
9/30/1945 02:00 CST
4/28/1946 02:00 CDT
9/29/1946 02:00 CST
4/25/1948 02:00 CDT
9/26/1948 02:00 CST
11/14/1954 02:00 EST
4/27/1969 02:00 EDT
10/26/1969 02:00 EST
4/26/1970 02:00 EDT
10/25/1970 02:00 EST

IN # 263
Before 11/18/1883 LMT
11/18/1883 12:00 CST
3/31/1918 02:00 CWT
10/27/1918 02:00 CST
3/30/1919 02:00 CWT
10/26/1919 02:00 CST
4/26/1936 02:00 CDT
9/27/1936 02:00 CST
4/24/1938 02:00 CDT
9/25/1938 02:00 CST
4/30/1939 02:00 CDT
9/24/1939 02:00 CST
4/28/1940 02:00 CDT
9/29/1940 02:00 CST
4/27/1941 02:00 CDT
9/28/1941 02:00 CST
2/09/1942 02:00 CWT
9/30/1945 02:00 CST
11/14/1954 02:00 EST
4/27/1969 02:00 EDT
10/26/1969 02:00 EST
4/26/1970 02:00 EDT
10/25/1970 02:00 EST

IN # 264
Before 11/18/1883 LMT
11/18/1883 12:00 CST
3/31/1918 02:00 CWT
10/27/1918 02:00 CST
3/30/1919 02:00 CWT
10/26/1919 02:00 CST
2/09/1942 02:00 CWT
9/30/1945 02:00 CST
11/14/1954 02:00 EST
9/29/1957 02:00 CST
4/27/1958 02:00 EST
4/27/1969 02:00 EDT
10/26/1969 02:00 EST
4/26/1970 02:00 EDT
10/25/1970 02:00 EST

IN # 265
Before 11/18/1883 LMT
11/18/1883 12:00 CST
3/31/1918 02:00 CWT
10/27/1918 02:00 CST
3/30/1919 02:00 CWT
10/26/1919 02:00 CST
4/26/1936 02:00 CDT
9/27/1936 02:00 CST
4/24/1938 02:00 CDT
9/25/1938 02:00 CST
4/30/1939 02:00 CDT
9/24/1939 02:00 CST
4/28/1940 02:00 CDT
9/29/1940 02:00 CST
4/27/1941 02:00 CDT
9/28/1941 02:00 CST
2/09/1942 02:00 CWT
9/30/1945 02:00 CST
4/28/1946 02:00 CDT
9/29/1946 02:00 CST
4/27/1947 02:00 CDT
9/28/1947 02:00 CST
4/25/1948 02:00 CDT
9/26/1948 02:00 CST
4/24/1949 02:00 CDT
9/25/1949 02:00 CST
4/30/1950 02:00 CDT
9/24/1950 02:00 CST
4/29/1951 02:00 CDT
9/30/1951 02:00 CST
4/27/1952 02:00 CDT
9/28/1952 02:00 CST
4/26/1953 02:00 CDT
9/27/1953 02:00 CST
11/14/1954 02:00 EST
9/29/1957 02:00 CST
4/27/1958 02:00 EST
4/27/1969 02:00 EDT
10/26/1969 02:00 EST
4/26/1970 02:00 EDT
10/25/1970 02:00 EST

IN # 266
Before 11/18/1883 LMT
11/18/1883 12:00 CST
3/31/1918 02:00 CWT
10/27/1918 02:00 CST
3/30/1919 02:00 CWT
10/26/1919 02:00 CST
4/26/1936 02:00 CDT
9/27/1936 02:00 CST
4/24/1938 02:00 CDT
9/25/1938 02:00 CST
4/30/1939 02:00 CDT
9/24/1939 02:00 CST
4/28/1940 02:00 CDT
9/29/1940 02:00 CST
4/27/1941 02:00 CDT
9/28/1941 02:00 CST
2/09/1942 02:00 CWT
9/30/1945 02:00 CST
4/28/1946 02:00 CDT
9/29/1946 02:00 CST
4/25/1948 02:00 CDT
9/26/1948 02:00 CST
4/29/1951 02:00 CDT
9/30/1951 02:00 CST
4/27/1952 02:00 CDT
9/28/1952 02:00 CST
4/26/1953 02:00 CDT
9/27/1953 02:00 CST
4/25/1954 02:00 CDT
9/26/1954 02:00 CST
11/14/1954 02:00 EST
9/29/1957 02:00 CST
4/27/1958 02:00 EST
4/27/1969 02:00 EDT
10/26/1969 02:00 EST
4/26/1970 02:00 EDT
10/25/1970 02:00 EST

IN # 267
Before 11/18/1883 LMT
11/18/1883 12:00 CST
3/31/1918 02:00 CWT
10/27/1918 02:00 CST
3/30/1919 02:00 CWT
10/26/1919 02:00 CST
2/09/1942 02:00 CWT
9/30/1945 02:00 CST
4/27/1947 02:00 CDT
9/28/1947 02:00 CST
4/25/1948 02:00 CDT
9/26/1948 02:00 CST
4/30/1950 02:00 CDT
9/24/1950 02:00 CST
4/26/1953 02:00 CDT
9/27/1953 02:00 CST
4/25/1954 02:00 CDT
9/26/1954 02:00 CST
11/14/1954 02:00 EST
9/29/1957 02:00 CST
4/27/1958 02:00 EST
4/27/1969 02:00 EDT
10/26/1969 02:00 EST
4/26/1970 02:00 EDT
10/25/1970 02:00 EST

IN # 268
Before 11/18/1883 LMT
11/18/1883 12:00 CST
3/31/1918 02:00 CWT
10/27/1918 02:00 CST
3/30/1919 02:00 CWT
10/26/1919 02:00 CST
2/09/1942 02:00 CWT
9/30/1945 02:00 CST
4/25/1948 02:00 CDT
9/26/1948 02:00 CST
11/14/1954 02:00 EST
9/29/1957 02:00 CST
4/27/1958 02:00 EST
4/27/1969 02:00 EDT
10/26/1969 02:00 EST
4/26/1970 02:00 EDT
10/25/1970 02:00 EST

IN # 269
Before 11/18/1883 LMT
11/18/1883 12:00 CST
3/31/1918 02:00 CWT
10/27/1918 02:00 CST
3/30/1919 02:00 CWT
10/26/1919 02:00 CST
2/09/1942 02:00 CWT
9/30/1945 02:00 CST
4/26/1953 02:00 CDT
9/27/1953 02:00 CST
4/25/1954 02:00 CDT
9/26/1954 02:00 CST
11/14/1954 02:00 EST
9/29/1957 02:00 CST
4/27/1958 02:00 EST
4/27/1969 02:00 EDT
10/26/1969 02:00 EST
4/26/1970 02:00 EDT
10/25/1970 02:00 EST

IN # 270
Before 11/18/1883 LMT
11/18/1883 12:00 CST
3/31/1918 02:00 CWT
10/27/1918 02:00 CST
3/30/1919 02:00 CWT
10/26/1919 02:00 CST
2/09/1942 02:00 CWT
9/30/1945 02:00 CST
4/25/1954 02:00 CDT
9/26/1954 02:00 CST
11/14/1954 02:00 EST
9/29/1957 02:00 CST
4/27/1958 02:00 EST
4/27/1969 02:00 EDT
10/26/1969 02:00 EST
4/26/1970 02:00 EDT
10/25/1970 02:00 EST

IN # 271
Before 11/18/1883 LMT
11/18/1883 12:00 CST
3/31/1918 02:00 CWT
10/27/1918 02:00 CST
3/30/1919 02:00 CWT
10/26/1919 02:00 CST
5/08/1932 02:00 CDT
9/25/1932 02:00 CST
4/30/1933 02:00 CDT
9/24/1933 02:00 CST
4/29/1934 02:00 CDT
9/30/1934 02:00 CST
4/28/1935 02:00 CDT
9/29/1935 02:00 CST
4/26/1936 02:00 CDT
9/27/1936 02:00 CST
4/25/1937 02:00 CDT
9/26/1937 02:00 CST
4/24/1938 02:00 CDT
9/25/1938 02:00 CST
4/30/1939 02:00 CDT
9/24/1939 02:00 CST
4/28/1940 02:00 CDT
9/29/1940 02:00 CST
4/27/1941 02:00 CDT
9/28/1941 02:00 CST
2/09/1942 02:00 CWT
9/30/1945 02:00 CST
4/28/1946 02:00 CDT
9/29/1946 02:00 CST
4/27/1947 02:00 CDT
9/28/1947 02:00 CST
4/25/1948 02:00 CDT
9/26/1948 02:00 CST
4/24/1949 02:00 CDT
9/25/1949 02:00 CST
4/30/1950 02:00 CDT
9/24/1950 02:00 CST
4/29/1951 02:00 CDT
9/30/1951 02:00 CST
4/27/1952 02:00 CDT
9/28/1952 02:00 CST
4/26/1953 02:00 CDT
9/27/1953 02:00 CST
4/25/1954 02:00 CDT
9/26/1954 02:00 CST
11/14/1954 02:00 EST
9/29/1957 02:00 CST
4/27/1958 02:00 EST
4/27/1969 02:00 EDT
10/26/1969 02:00 EST
4/26/1970 02:00 EDT
10/25/1970 02:00 EST

IN # 272
Before 11/18/1883 LMT
11/18/1883 12:00 CST
3/31/1918 02:00 CWT
10/27/1918 02:00 CST
3/30/1919 02:00 CWT
10/26/1919 02:00 CST
2/09/1942 02:00 CWT
9/30/1945 02:00 CST
1/02/1955 00:01 EST
9/29/1957 02:00 CST
4/27/1958 02:00 EST
4/27/1969 02:00 EDT
10/26/1969 02:00 EST
4/26/1970 02:00 EDT
10/25/1970 02:00 EST

IN # 273
Before 11/18/1883 LMT
11/18/1883 12:00 CST
3/31/1918 02:00 CWT
10/27/1918 02:00 CST
3/30/1919 02:00 CWT
10/26/1919 02:00 CST
4/28/1935 02:00 CDT
9/29/1935 02:00 CST
4/26/1936 02:00 CDT
9/27/1936 02:00 CST
4/25/1937 02:00 CDT
10/03/1937 02:00 CST
4/30/1939 02:00 CDT
9/24/1939 02:00 CST
4/28/1940 02:00 CDT
9/29/1940 02:00 CST
4/27/1941 02:00 CDT
9/28/1941 02:00 CST
2/09/1942 02:00 CWT
9/30/1945 02:00 CST
4/30/1950 02:00 CDT
9/24/1950 02:00 CST
4/29/1951 02:00 CDT
9/30/1951 02:00 CST
4/27/1952 02:00 CDT
9/28/1952 02:00 CST
4/26/1953 02:00 CDT
9/27/1953 02:00 CST
4/25/1954 02:00 CDT
9/26/1954 02:00 CST
1/02/1955 00:01 EST
9/29/1957 02:00 CST
4/27/1958 02:00 EST
4/27/1969 02:00 EDT
10/26/1969 02:00 EST
4/26/1970 02:00 EDT
10/25/1970 02:00 EST

IN # 274
Before 11/18/1883 LMT
11/18/1883 12:00 CST
3/31/1918 02:00 CWT
10/27/1918 02:00 CST
3/30/1919 02:00 CWT
10/26/1919 02:00 CST
2/09/1942 02:00 CWT

TIME TABLES

9/30/1945 02:00 CST
1/02/1955 00:01 EST
9/29/1957 02:00 CST
4/27/1958 02:00 CDT
9/28/1958 02:00 CST
4/26/1959 02:00 EST
4/27/1969 02:00 EDT
10/26/1969 02:00 EST
4/26/1970 02:00 EDT
10/25/1970 02:00 EST

IN # 275
Before 11/18/1883 LMT
11/18/1883 12:00 CST
3/31/1918 02:00 CWT
10/27/1918 02:00 CST
3/30/1919 02:00 CWT
10/26/1919 02:00 CST
2/09/1942 02:00 CWT
9/30/1945 02:00 CST
4/25/1954 02:00 EST
9/29/1957 02:00 CST
4/27/1958 02:00 EST
4/27/1969 02:00 EDT
10/26/1969 02:00 EST
4/26/1970 02:00 EDT
10/25/1970 02:00 EST

IN # 276
Before 11/18/1883 LMT
11/18/1883 12:00 CST
3/31/1918 02:00 CWT
10/27/1918 02:00 CST
3/30/1919 02:00 CWT
10/26/1919 02:00 CST
2/09/1942 02:00 CWT
9/30/1945 02:00 CST
4/28/1946 02:00 CDT
9/29/1946 02:00 CST
4/27/1947 02:00 CDT
9/28/1947 02:00 CST
4/25/1948 02:00 CDT
9/26/1948 02:00 CST
4/24/1949 02:00 CDT
9/25/1949 02:00 CST
4/30/1950 02:00 CDT
9/24/1950 02:00 CST
4/29/1951 02:00 CDT
9/30/1951 02:00 CST
4/27/1952 02:00 CDT
9/28/1952 02:00 CST
4/26/1953 02:00 CDT
9/27/1953 02:00 CST
4/25/1954 02:00 EST
9/29/1957 02:00 CST
4/27/1958 02:00 EST
4/27/1969 02:00 EDT
10/26/1969 02:00 EST
4/26/1970 02:00 EDT
10/25/1970 02:00 EST

IN # 277
Before 11/18/1883 LMT
11/18/1883 12:00 CST
3/31/1918 02:00 CWT
10/27/1918 02:00 CST
3/30/1919 02:00 CWT
10/26/1919 02:00 CST
2/09/1942 02:00 CWT
9/30/1945 02:00 CST
4/27/1947 02:00 CDT
9/28/1947 02:00 CST
4/25/1948 02:00 CDT
9/26/1948 02:00 CST
4/24/1949 02:00 CDT
9/25/1949 02:00 CST
4/30/1950 02:00 CDT
9/24/1950 02:00 CST
4/29/1951 02:00 CDT
9/30/1951 02:00 CST
4/27/1952 02:00 CDT
9/28/1952 02:00 CST
4/26/1953 02:00 CDT
9/27/1953 02:00 CST
4/25/1954 02:00 EST
9/29/1957 02:00 CST
4/27/1958 02:00 EST
4/27/1969 02:00 EDT
10/26/1969 02:00 EST
4/26/1970 02:00 EDT
10/25/1970 02:00 EST

IN # 278
Before 11/18/1883 LMT
11/18/1883 12:00 CST
3/31/1918 02:00 CWT
10/27/1918 02:00 CST
3/30/1919 02:00 CWT
10/26/1919 02:00 CST
2/09/1942 02:00 CWT
9/30/1945 02:00 CST
4/25/1948 02:00 CDT
9/26/1948 02:00 CST
4/25/1954 02:00 EST
9/29/1957 02:00 CST
4/27/1958 02:00 EST
4/27/1969 02:00 EDT
10/26/1969 02:00 EST
4/26/1970 02:00 EDT
10/25/1970 02:00 EST

IN # 279
Before 11/18/1883 LMT
11/18/1883 12:00 CST
3/31/1918 02:00 CWT
10/27/1918 02:00 CST
3/30/1919 02:00 CWT
10/26/1919 02:00 CST
2/09/1942 02:00 CWT
9/30/1945 02:00 CST
4/27/1947 02:00 CDT
9/28/1947 02:00 CST
4/26/1953 02:00 CDT
9/27/1953 02:00 CST
4/25/1954 02:00 EST
9/29/1957 02:00 CST
4/27/1958 02:00 EST
4/01/1960 02:00 EDT
10/01/1960 02:00 EST
4/30/1961 02:00 EDT
10/01/1961 02:00 E T
10/29/1961 02:00 EST
4/27/1969 02:00 EDT
10/26/1969 02:00 EST
4/26/1970 02:00 EDT
10/25/1970 02:00 EST

IN # 280
Before 11/18/1883 LMT
11/18/1883 12:00 CST
3/31/1918 02:00 CWT
10/27/1918 02:00 CST
3/30/1919 02:00 CWT
10/26/1919 02:00 CST
2/09/1942 02:00 CWT
9/30/1945 02:00 CST
11/28/1954 02:00 EST
9/29/1957 02:00 CST
4/27/1958 02:00 CDT
9/28/1958 02:00 CST
4/26/1959 02:00 EST
4/27/1969 02:00 EDT
10/26/1969 02:00 EST
4/26/1970 02:00 EDT
10/25/1970 02:00 EST

IN # 281
Before 11/18/1883 LMT
11/18/1883 12:00 CST
3/31/1918 02:00 CWT
10/27/1918 02:00 CST
3/30/1919 02:00 CWT
10/26/1919 02:00 CST
2/09/1942 02:00 CWT
9/30/1945 02:00 CST
4/28/1946 02:00 CDT
9/29/1946 02:00 CST
4/27/1947 02:00 CDT
9/28/1947 02:00 CST
4/25/1948 02:00 CDT
9/26/1948 02:00 CST
4/24/1949 02:00 CDT
9/25/1949 02:00 CST
4/30/1950 02:00 CDT
9/24/1950 02:00 CST
4/29/1951 02:00 CDT
9/30/1951 02:00 CST
4/27/1952 02:00 CDT
9/28/1952 02:00 CST
4/26/1953 02:00 CDT
9/27/1953 02:00 CST
4/25/1954 02:00 CDT
9/26/1954 02:00 CST
11/28/1954 02:00 EST
9/29/1957 02:00 CST
4/27/1958 02:00 CDT
9/28/1958 02:00 CST
4/26/1959 02:00 EST
4/27/1969 02:00 EDT
10/26/1969 02:00 EST
4/26/1970 02:00 EDT
10/25/1970 02:00 EST

IN # 282
Before 11/18/1883 LMT
11/18/1883 12:00 CST
3/31/1918 02:00 CWT
10/27/1918 02:00 CST
3/30/1919 02:00 CWT
10/26/1919 02:00 CST
2/09/1942 02:00 CWT
9/30/1945 02:00 CST
4/25/1948 02:00 CDT
9/26/1948 02:00 CST
4/24/1949 02:00 CDT
9/25/1949 02:00 CST
4/30/1950 02:00 CDT
9/24/1950 02:00 CST
4/29/1951 02:00 CDT
9/30/1951 02:00 CST
4/27/1952 02:00 CDT
9/28/1952 02:00 CST
4/26/1953 02:00 CDT
9/27/1953 02:00 CST
4/25/1954 02:00 CDT
9/26/1954 02:00 CST
11/28/1954 02:00 EST
9/29/1957 02:00 CST
4/27/1958 02:00 CDT
9/28/1958 02:00 CST
4/26/1959 02:00 EST
4/27/1969 02:00 EDT
10/26/1969 02:00 EST
4/26/1970 02:00 EDT
10/25/1970 02:00 EST

IN # 283
Before 11/18/1883 LMT
11/18/1883 12:00 CST
3/31/1918 02:00 CWT
10/27/1918 02:00 CST
3/30/1919 02:00 CWT
10/26/1919 02:00 CST
2/09/1942 02:00 CWT
9/30/1945 02:00 CST
4/30/1950 02:00 CDT
9/24/1950 02:00 CST
4/29/1951 02:00 CDT
9/30/1951 02:00 CST
4/27/1952 02:00 CDT
9/28/1952 02:00 CST
4/26/1953 02:00 CDT
9/27/1953 02:00 CST
4/25/1954 02:00 CDT
9/26/1954 02:00 CST
11/28/1954 02:00 EST
9/29/1957 02:00 CST
4/27/1958 02:00 CDT
9/28/1958 02:00 CST
4/26/1959 02:00 EST
4/27/1969 02:00 EDT
10/26/1969 02:00 EST
4/26/1970 02:00 EDT
10/25/1970 02:00 EST

IN # 284
Before 11/18/1883 LMT
11/18/1883 12:00 CST
3/31/1918 02:00 CWT
10/27/1918 02:00 CST
3/30/1919 02:00 CWT
10/26/1919 02:00 CST
2/09/1942 02:00 CWT
9/30/1945 02:00 CST
4/26/1953 02:00 CDT
9/27/1953 02:00 CST
4/25/1954 02:00 CDT
9/26/1954 02:00 CST
11/28/1954 02:00 EST
9/29/1957 02:00 CST
4/27/1958 02:00 CDT
9/28/1958 02:00 CST
4/26/1959 02:00 EST
4/27/1969 02:00 EDT
10/26/1969 02:00 EST
4/26/1970 02:00 EDT
10/25/1970 02:00 EST

IN # 285
Before 11/18/1883 LMT
11/18/1883 12:00 CST
3/31/1918 02:00 CWT
10/27/1918 02:00 CST
3/30/1919 02:00 CWT
10/26/1919 02:00 CST
2/09/1942 02:00 CWT
9/30/1945 02:00 CST
11/28/1954 02:00 EST
4/29/1956 02:00 E T
10/28/1956 02:00 EST
9/29/1957 02:00 CST
4/27/1958 02:00 CDT
9/28/1958 02:00 CST
4/26/1959 02:00 EST
4/27/1969 02:00 EDT
10/26/1969 02:00 EST
4/26/1970 02:00 EDT
10/25/1970 02:00 EST

IN # 286
Before 11/18/1883 LMT
11/18/1883 12:00 CST
3/31/1918 02:00 CWT
10/27/1918 02:00 CST
3/30/1919 02:00 CWT
10/26/1919 02:00 CST
2/09/1942 02:00 CWT
9/30/1945 02:00 CST
11/28/1954 02:00 EST
9/29/1957 02:00 CST
4/27/1958 02:00 CDT
9/28/1958 02:00 CST
4/26/1959 02:00 EST
4/27/1969 02:00 EDT
10/26/1969 02:00 EST
4/26/1970 02:00 EDT
10/25/1970 02:00 EST

IN # 287
Before 11/18/1883 LMT
11/18/1883 12:00 CST
3/31/1918 02:00 CWT
10/27/1918 02:00 CST
3/30/1919 02:00 CWT
10/26/1919 02:00 CST
2/09/1942 02:00 CWT
9/30/1945 02:00 CST
11/07/1954 00:01 EST
4/27/1969 02:00 EDT
10/26/1969 02:00 EST
4/26/1970 02:00 EDT
10/25/1970 02:00 EST

IN # 288
Before 11/18/1883 LMT
11/18/1883 12:00 CST
3/31/1918 02:00 CWT
10/27/1918 02:00 CST
3/30/1919 02:00 CWT
10/26/1919 02:00 CST
2/09/1942 02:00 CWT
9/30/1945 02:00 CST
4/26/1953 02:00 CDT
9/27/1953 02:00 CST
4/25/1954 02:00 CDT
9/26/1954 02:00 CST
11/07/1954 00:01 EST
4/27/1969 02:00 EDT
10/26/1969 02:00 EST
4/26/1970 02:00 EDT
10/25/1970 02:00 EST

IN # 289
Before 11/18/1883 LMT
11/18/1883 12:00 CST
3/31/1918 02:00 CWT
10/27/1918 02:00 CST
3/30/1919 02:00 CWT
10/26/1919 02:00 CST
2/09/1942 02:00 CWT
9/30/1945 02:00 CST
4/25/1954 02:00 CDT
9/26/1954 02:00 CST
11/07/1954 00:01 EST
4/27/1969 02:00 EDT
10/26/1969 02:00 EST
4/26/1970 02:00 EDT
10/25/1970 02:00 EST

IN # 290
Before 11/18/1883 LMT
11/18/1883 12:00 CST
3/31/1918 02:00 CWT
10/27/1918 02:00 CST
3/30/1919 02:00 CWT
10/26/1919 02:00 CST
5/01/1929 02:00 CDT
10/01/1929 02:00 CST
5/01/1930 02:00 CDT
10/01/1930 02:00 CST
4/28/1940 02:00 CDT
9/29/1940 02:00 CST
4/27/1941 02:00 CDT
9/28/1941 02:00 CST
2/09/1942 02:00 CWT
9/30/1945 02:00 CST
4/28/1946 02:00 CDT
9/29/1946 02:00 CST
4/27/1947 02:00 CDT
9/28/1947 02:00 CST
4/25/1948 02:00 CDT
9/26/1948 02:00 CST
4/24/1949 02:00 CDT
9/25/1949 02:00 CST
4/30/1950 02:00 CDT
9/29/1950 02:00 CST
4/29/1951 02:00 CDT
9/30/1951 02:00 CST
4/27/1952 02:00 CDT
9/28/1952 02:00 CST
4/26/1953 02:00 CDT
9/27/1953 02:00 CST
4/25/1954 02:00 CDT
9/26/1954 02:00 CST
11/07/1954 00:01 EST
4/27/1969 02:00 EDT
10/26/1969 02:00 EST
4/26/1970 02:00 EDT
10/25/1970 02:00 EST

IN # 291
Before 11/18/1883 LMT
11/18/1883 12:00 CST
3/31/1918 02:00 CWT
10/27/1918 02:00 CST
3/30/1919 02:00 CWT
10/26/1919 02:00 CST
2/09/1942 02:00 CWT
9/30/1945 02:00 CST
11/07/1954 00:01 EST
9/29/1957 02:00 CST
4/27/1958 02:00 EST
4/27/1969 02:00 EDT
10/26/1969 02:00 EST
4/26/1970 02:00 EDT
10/25/1970 02:00 EST

IN # 292
Before 11/18/1883 LMT
11/18/1883 12:00 CST
3/31/1918 02:00 CWT
10/27/1918 02:00 CST
3/30/1919 02:00 CWT
10/26/1919 02:00 CST
2/09/1942 02:00 CWT
9/30/1945 02:00 CST
4/27/1947 02:00 CDT
9/28/1947 02:00 CST
4/25/1948 02:00 CDT
9/26/1948 02:00 CST
4/24/1949 02:00 CDT
9/25/1949 02:00 CST
4/30/1950 02:00 CDT
9/24/1950 02:00 CST
4/29/1951 02:00 CDT
9/30/1951 02:00 CST
4/27/1952 02:00 CDT
9/28/1952 02:00 CST
4/26/1953 02:00 CDT
9/27/1953 02:00 CST
11/07/1954 00:01 EST
9/29/1957 02:00 CST
4/27/1958 02:00 EST
4/27/1969 02:00 EDT
10/26/1969 02:00 EST
4/26/1970 02:00 EDT
10/25/1970 02:00 EST

IN # 293
Before 11/18/1883 LMT
11/18/1883 12:00 CST
3/31/1918 02:00 CWT
10/27/1918 02:00 CST
3/30/1919 02:00 CWT
10/26/1919 02:00 CST
2/09/1942 02:00 CWT
9/30/1945 02:00 CST
4/27/1947 02:00 CDT
9/28/1947 02:00 CST
4/25/1948 02:00 CDT
9/26/1948 02:00 CST
4/27/1952 02:00 CDT
9/28/1952 02:00 CST
4/26/1953 02:00 CDT
9/27/1953 02:00 CST
11/07/1954 00:01 EST
9/29/1957 02:00 CST
4/27/1958 02:00 EST
4/27/1969 02:00 EDT
10/26/1969 02:00 EST
4/26/1970 02:00 EDT
10/25/1970 02:00 EST

IN # 294
Before 11/18/1883 LMT
11/18/1883 12:00 CST
3/31/1918 02:00 CWT
10/27/1918 02:00 CST
3/30/1919 02:00 CWT
10/26/1919 02:00 CST
2/09/1942 02:00 CWT
9/30/1945 02:00 CST
4/25/1948 02:00 CDT
9/26/1948 02:00 CST
11/07/1954 00:01 EST
9/29/1957 02:00 CST
4/27/1958 02:00 EST
4/27/1969 02:00 EDT
10/26/1969 02:00 EST
4/26/1970 02:00 EDT
10/25/1970 02:00 EST

IN # 295
Before 11/18/1883 LMT
11/18/1883 12:00 CST
3/31/1918 02:00 CWT
10/27/1918 02:00 CST
3/30/1919 02:00 CWT
10/26/1919 02:00 CST
2/09/1942 02:00 CWT
9/30/1945 02:00 CST
4/26/1953 02:00 CDT
9/27/1953 02:00 CST
4/25/1954 02:00 CDT
9/26/1954 02:00 CST
11/07/1954 00:01 EST
9/29/1957 02:00 CST
4/27/1958 02:00 EST
4/27/1969 02:00 EDT
10/26/1969 02:00 EST
4/26/1970 02:00 EDT
10/25/1970 02:00 EST

IN # 296
Before 11/18/1883 LMT
11/18/1883 02:00 CST
3/31/1918 02:00 CWT
10/27/1918 02:00 CST
3/30/1919 02:00 CWT
10/26/1919 02:00 CST
2/09/1942 02:00 CWT
9/30/1945 02:00 CST
5/01/1947 02:00 CDT
9/16/1947 02:00 CST
4/25/1948 02:00 CDT
9/26/1948 02:00 CST
4/24/1949 02:00 CDT
9/25/1949 02:00 CST
4/30/1950 02:00 CDT
9/24/1950 02:00 CST
4/26/1953 02:00 CDT
9/27/1953 02:00 CST
11/07/1954 00:01 EST
9/29/1957 02:00 CST
4/27/1958 02:00 EST
4/27/1969 02:00 EDT
10/26/1969 02:00 EST
4/26/1970 02:00 EDT
10/25/1970 02:00 EST

IN # 297
Before 11/18/1883 LMT
11/18/1883 12:00 CST
3/31/1918 02:00 CWT
10/27/1918 02:00 CST
3/30/1919 02:00 CWT
10/26/1919 02:00 CST
4/24/1938 02:00 CDT
10/01/1938 02:00 CST
4/28/1940 02:00 CDT
9/29/1940 02:00 CST
4/27/1941 02:00 CDT
9/28/1941 02:00 CST
2/09/1942 02:00 CWT
9/30/1945 02:00 CST
4/28/1946 02:00 CDT
9/29/1946 02:00 CST
4/27/1947 02:00 CDT
9/28/1947 02:00 CST
4/25/1948 02:00 CDT
9/26/1948 02:00 CST
4/24/1949 02:00 CDT
9/25/1949 02:00 CST
4/30/1950 02:00 CDT
9/24/1950 02:00 CST
4/29/1951 02:00 CDT
9/30/1951 02:00 CST
4/27/1952 02:00 CDT
9/28/1952 02:00 CST
4/26/1953 02:00 CDT
9/27/1953 02:00 CST
4/25/1954 02:00 CDT
9/26/1954 02:00 CST
11/07/1954 00:01 EST
9/29/1957 02:00 CST
4/27/1958 02:00 EST
4/26/1959 02:00 EDT
10/25/1959 02:00 EST
4/27/1969 02:00 EDT
10/26/1969 02:00 EST
4/26/1970 02:00 EDT
10/25/1970 02:00 EST

IN # 298
Before 11/18/1883 LMT
11/18/1883 12:00 CST
3/31/1918 02:00 CWT
10/27/1918 02:00 CST
3/30/1919 02:00 CWT
10/26/1919 02:00 CST

TIME TABLES

4/30/1939 02:00 CDT
10/01/1939 02:00 CST
4/28/1946 02:00 CDT
9/29/1946 02:00 CST
4/27/1947 02:00 CDT
9/28/1947 02:00 CST
4/25/1948 02:00 CDT
9/26/1948 02:00 CST
4/24/1949 02:00 CDT
9/25/1949 02:00 CST
4/30/1950 02:00 CDT
9/24/1950 02:00 CST
4/29/1951 02:00 CDT
9/30/1951 02:00 CST
4/27/1952 02:00 CDT
9/28/1952 02:00 CST
4/26/1953 02:00 CDT
9/27/1953 02:00 CST
4/25/1954 02:00 CDT
9/26/1954 02:00 CST
11/07/1954 00:01 EST
9/29/1957 02:00 CST
4/27/1958 02:00 EST
4/27/1969 02:00 EDT
10/26/1969 02:00 EST
4/26/1970 02:00 EDT
10/25/1970 02:00 EST

IN # 299
Before 11/18/1883 LMT
11/18/1883 12:00 CST
3/31/1918 02:00 CWT
10/27/1918 02:00 CST
3/30/1919 02:00 CWT
10/26/1919 02:00 CST
4/24/1938 02:00 CDT
9/25/1938 02:00 CST
4/30/1939 02:00 CDT
9/24/1939 02:00 CST
4/28/1940 02:00 CDT
9/02/1940 02:00 CST
2/09/1942 02:00 CWT
9/30/1945 02:00 CST
4/28/1946 02:00 CDT
9/29/1946 02:00 CST
4/27/1947 02:00 CDT
9/28/1947 02:00 CST
4/25/1948 02:00 CDT
9/26/1948 02:00 CST
4/24/1949 02:00 CDT
9/25/1949 02:00 CST
4/30/1950 02:00 CDT
9/24/1950 02:00 CST
4/29/1951 02:00 CDT
9/30/1951 02:00 CST
4/27/1952 02:00 CDT
9/28/1952 02:00 CST
4/26/1953 02:00 CDT
9/27/1953 02:00 CST
4/25/1954 02:00 CDT
9/26/1954 02:00 CST
11/07/1954 00:01 EST
9/29/1957 02:00 CST
4/27/1958 02:00 EST
4/27/1969 02:00 EDT
10/26/1969 02:00 EST
4/26/1970 02:00 EDT
10/25/1970 02:00 EST

IN # 300
Before 11/18/1883 LMT
11/18/1883 12:00 CST
3/31/1918 02:00 CWT
10/27/1918 02:00 CST
3/30/1919 02:00 CWT
10/26/1919 02:00 CST
2/09/1942 02:00 CWT
9/30/1945 02:00 CST
4/25/1948 02:00 CDT
9/26/1948 02:00 CST
4/24/1949 02:00 CDT
9/25/1949 02:00 CST
4/30/1950 02:00 CDT
9/24/1950 02:00 CST
4/29/1951 02:00 CDT
9/30/1951 02:00 CST
4/27/1952 02:00 CDT
9/28/1952 02:00 CST
4/26/1953 02:00 CDT
9/27/1953 02:00 CST
4/25/1954 02:00 CDT
9/26/1954 02:00 CST
11/07/1954 00:01 EST
9/29/1957 02:00 CST
4/27/1958 02:00 CDT
9/28/1958 02:00 CST
4/26/1959 02:00 EST
4/27/1969 02:00 EDT
10/26/1969 02:00 EST
4/26/1970 02:00 EDT
10/25/1970 02:00 EST

IN # 301
Before 11/18/1883 LMT
11/18/1883 12:00 CST
3/31/1918 02:00 CWT
10/27/1918 02:00 CST
3/30/1919 02:00 CWT
10/26/1919 02:00 CST
2/09/1942 02:00 CWT
9/30/1945 02:00 CST
4/25/1948 02:00 CDT
9/26/1948 02:00 CST
4/30/1950 02:00 CDT
9/24/1950 02:00 CST
4/29/1951 02:00 CDT
9/30/1951 02:00 CST
4/26/1953 02:00 CDT
9/27/1953 02:00 CST
4/25/1954 02:00 CDT
9/26/1954 02:00 CST
11/07/1954 00:01 EST
9/29/1957 02:00 CST
4/27/1958 02:00 CDT
9/28/1958 02:00 CST
4/26/1959 02:00 EST
4/27/1969 02:00 EDT
10/26/1969 02:00 EST
4/26/1970 02:00 EDT
10/25/1970 02:00 EST

IN # 302
Before 11/18/1883 LMT
11/18/1883 12:00 CST
3/31/1918 02:00 CWT
10/27/1918 02:00 CST
3/30/1919 02:00 CWT
10/26/1919 02:00 CST
2/09/1942 02:00 CWT
9/30/1945 02:00 CST
4/26/1953 02:00 CDT
9/27/1953 02:00 CST
4/25/1954 02:00 CDT
9/26/1954 02:00 CST
4/24/1955 02:00 EST
10/30/1955 00:01 CST
4/29/1956 02:00 EST
9/29/1957 02:00 CST
4/27/1958 02:00 CDT
9/28/1958 02:00 CST
4/26/1959 02:00 EST
4/27/1969 02:00 EDT
10/26/1969 02:00 EST
4/26/1970 02:00 EDT
10/25/1970 02:00 EST

IN # 303
Before 11/18/1883 LMT
11/18/1883 12:00 CST
3/31/1918 02:00 CWT
10/27/1918 02:00 CST
3/30/1919 02:00 CWT
10/26/1919 02:00 CST
2/09/1942 02:00 CWT
9/30/1945 02:00 CST
4/27/1952 02:00 EST
4/27/1969 02:00 EDT
10/26/1969 02:00 EST
4/26/1970 02:00 EDT
10/25/1970 02:00 EST

IN # 304
Before 11/18/1883 LMT
11/18/1883 12:00 CST
3/31/1918 02:00 CWT
10/27/1918 02:00 CST
3/30/1919 02:00 CWT
10/26/1919 02:00 CST
2/09/1942 02:00 CWT
9/30/1945 02:00 CST
4/27/1952 02:00 EST
4/25/1954 02:00 EDT
9/26/1954 02:00 EST
4/30/1967 02:00 EDT
10/29/1967 02:00 EST
4/28/1968 02:00 EDT
10/27/1968 02:00 EST
4/27/1969 02:00 EDT
10/26/1969 02:00 EST
4/26/1970 02:00 EDT
10/25/1970 02:00 EST

IN # 305
Before 11/18/1883 LMT
11/18/1883 12:00 CST
3/31/1918 02:00 CWT
10/27/1918 02:00 CST
3/30/1919 02:00 CWT
10/26/1919 02:00 CST
2/09/1942 02:00 CWT
9/30/1945 02:00 CST
11/28/1954 00:01 EST
9/29/1957 02:00 CST
4/27/1958 02:00 EST
4/27/1969 02:00 EDT
10/26/1969 02:00 EST
4/26/1970 02:00 EDT
10/25/1970 02:00 EST

IN # 306
Before 11/18/1883 LMT
11/18/1883 12:00 CST
3/31/1918 02:00 CWT
10/27/1918 02:00 CST
3/30/1919 02:00 CWT
10/26/1919 02:00 CST
2/09/1942 02:00 CWT
9/30/1945 02:00 CST
4/26/1953 02:00 CDT
9/27/1953 02:00 CST
4/25/1954 02:00 CDT
9/26/1954 02:00 CST
11/28/1954 00:01 EST
9/29/1957 02:00 CST
4/27/1958 02:00 EST
4/27/1969 02:00 EDT
10/26/1969 02:00 EST
4/26/1970 02:00 EDT
10/25/1970 02:00 EST

IN # 307
Before 11/18/1883 LMT
11/18/1883 12:00 CST
3/31/1918 02:00 CWT
10/27/1918 02:00 CST
3/30/1919 02:00 CWT
10/26/1919 02:00 CST
2/09/1942 02:00 CWT
9/30/1945 02:00 CST
11/28/1954 00:01 EST
9/29/1957 02:00 CST
4/27/1958 02:00 CDT
9/28/1958 02:00 CST
4/26/1959 02:00 EST
4/27/1969 02:00 EDT
10/26/1969 02:00 EST
4/26/1970 02:00 EDT
10/25/1970 02:00 EST

IN # 308
Before 11/18/1883 LMT
11/18/1883 12:00 CST
3/31/1918 02:00 CWT
10/27/1918 02:00 CST
3/30/1919 02:00 CWT
10/26/1919 02:00 CST
2/09/1942 02:00 CWT
9/30/1945 02:00 CST
4/28/1946 02:00 CDT
9/29/1946 02:00 CST
4/27/1947 02:00 CDT
9/28/1947 02:00 CST
4/25/1948 02:00 CDT
9/26/1948 02:00 CST
4/24/1949 02:00 CDT
9/25/1949 02:00 CST
4/30/1950 02:00 CDT
9/24/1950 02:00 CST
4/29/1951 02:00 CDT
9/30/1951 02:00 CST
4/27/1952 02:00 CDT
9/28/1952 02:00 CST
4/26/1953 02:00 CDT
9/27/1953 02:00 CST
4/25/1954 02:00 CDT
9/26/1954 02:00 CST
11/28/1954 00:01 EST
9/29/1957 02:00 CST
4/27/1958 02:00 CDT
9/28/1958 02:00 CST
4/26/1959 02:00 EST
4/27/1969 02:00 EDT
10/26/1969 02:00 EST
4/26/1970 02:00 EDT
10/25/1970 02:00 EST

IN # 309
Before 11/18/1883 LMT
11/18/1883 12:00 CST
3/31/1918 02:00 CWT
10/27/1918 02:00 CST
3/30/1919 02:00 CWT
10/26/1919 02:00 CST
2/09/1942 02:00 CWT
9/30/1945 02:00 CST
4/27/1947 02:00 CDT
9/28/1947 02:00 CST
4/30/1950 02:00 CDT
9/24/1950 02:00 CST
4/29/1951 02:00 CDT
9/30/1951 02:00 CST
4/27/1952 02:00 CDT
9/28/1952 02:00 CST
4/26/1953 02:00 CDT
9/27/1953 02:00 CST
4/25/1954 02:00 CDT
9/26/1954 02:00 CST
11/28/1954 00:01 EST
9/29/1957 02:00 CST
4/27/1958 02:00 CDT
9/28/1958 02:00 CST
4/26/1959 02:00 EST
4/27/1969 02:00 EDT
10/26/1969 02:00 EST
4/26/1970 02:00 EDT
10/25/1970 02:00 EST

IN # 310
Before 11/18/1883 LMT
11/18/1883 12:00 CST
3/31/1918 02:00 CWT
10/27/1918 02:00 CST
3/30/1919 02:00 CWT
10/26/1919 02:00 CST
2/09/1942 02:00 CWT
9/30/1945 02:00 CST
4/26/1953 02:00 CDT
9/27/1953 02:00 CST
4/25/1954 02:00 CDT
9/26/1954 02:00 CST
11/28/1954 00:01 EST
9/29/1957 02:00 CST
4/27/1958 02:00 CDT
9/28/1958 02:00 CST
4/26/1959 02:00 EST
4/27/1969 02:00 EDT
10/26/1969 02:00 EST
4/26/1970 02:00 EDT
10/25/1970 02:00 EST

IN # 311
Before 11/18/1883 LMT
11/18/1883 12:00 CST
3/31/1918 02:00 CWT
10/27/1918 02:00 CST
3/30/1919 02:00 CWT
10/26/1919 02:00 CST
2/09/1942 02:00 CWT
9/30/1945 02:00 CST
11/28/1954 00:01 EST
4/27/1969 02:00 EDT
10/26/1969 02:00 EST
4/26/1970 02:00 EDT
10/25/1970 02:00 EST

IN # 312
Before 11/18/1883 LMT
11/18/1883 12:00 CST
3/31/1918 02:00 CWT
10/27/1918 02:00 CST
3/30/1919 02:00 CWT
10/26/1919 02:00 CST
2/09/1942 02:00 CWT
9/30/1945 02:00 CST
4/26/1953 02:00 CDT
9/27/1953 02:00 CST
4/25/1954 02:00 CDT
9/26/1954 02:00 CST
11/21/1954 01:00 EST
9/29/1957 02:00 CST
4/27/1958 02:00 CDT
9/28/1958 02:00 CST
4/26/1959 02:00 EST
4/27/1969 02:00 EDT
10/26/1969 02:00 EST
4/26/1970 02:00 EDT
10/25/1970 02:00 EST

IN # 313
Before 11/18/1883 LMT
11/18/1883 12:00 CST
3/31/1918 02:00 CWT
10/27/1918 02:00 CST
3/30/1919 02:00 CWT
10/26/1919 02:00 CST
2/09/1942 02:00 CWT
9/30/1945 02:00 CST
11/28/1954 02:00 EST
9/29/1957 02:00 CST
4/27/1958 02:00 EST
4/27/1969 02:00 EDT
10/26/1969 02:00 EST
4/26/1970 02:00 EDT
10/25/1970 02:00 EST

IN # 314
Before 11/18/1883 LMT
11/18/1883 12:00 CST
3/31/1918 02:00 CWT
10/27/1918 02:00 CST
3/30/1919 02:00 CWT
10/26/1919 02:00 CST
2/09/1942 02:00 CWT
9/30/1945 02:00 CST
4/25/1948 02:00 CDT
9/26/1948 02:00 CST
4/30/1950 02:00 CDT
9/24/1950 02:00 CST
11/28/1954 02:00 EST
9/29/1957 02:00 CST
4/27/1958 02:00 EST
4/27/1969 02:00 EDT
10/26/1969 02:00 EST
4/26/1970 02:00 EDT
10/25/1970 02:00 EST

IN # 315
Before 11/18/1883 LMT
11/18/1883 12:00 CST
3/31/1918 02:00 CWT
10/27/1918 02:00 CST
3/30/1919 02:00 CWT
10/26/1919 02:00 CST
2/09/1942 02:00 CWT
9/30/1945 02:00 CST
4/25/1948 02:00 CDT
9/26/1948 02:00 CST
4/24/1949 02:00 CDT
9/25/1949 02:00 CST
4/30/1950 02:00 CDT
9/24/1950 02:00 CST
4/29/1951 02:00 CDT
9/30/1951 02:00 CST
4/27/1952 02:00 CDT
9/28/1952 02:00 CST
4/26/1953 02:00 CDT
9/27/1953 02:00 CST
4/25/1954 02:00 CDT
9/26/1954 02:00 CST
12/12/1954 00:01 EST
9/29/1957 02:00 CST
4/27/1958 02:00 CDT
9/28/1958 02:00 CST
4/26/1959 02:00 EST
4/27/1969 02:00 EDT
10/26/1969 02:00 EST
4/26/1970 02:00 EDT
10/25/1970 02:00 EST

IN # 316
Before 11/18/1883 LMT
11/18/1883 12:00 CST
3/31/1918 02:00 CWT
10/27/1918 02:00 CST
3/30/1919 02:00 CWT
10/26/1919 02:00 CST
2/09/1942 02:00 CWT
9/30/1945 02:00 CST
4/25/1948 02:00 CDT
9/26/1948 02:00 CST
4/24/1949 02:00 CDT
9/25/1949 02:00 CST
4/30/1950 02:00 CDT
9/24/1950 02:00 CST
4/29/1951 02:00 CDT
9/30/1951 02:00 CST
4/27/1952 02:00 CDT
9/28/1952 02:00 CST
4/26/1953 02:00 CDT
9/27/1953 02:00 CST
4/25/1954 02:00 CDT
9/26/1954 02:00 CST
11/28/1954 01:00 EST
9/29/1957 02:00 CST
4/27/1958 02:00 CDT
9/28/1958 02:00 CST
4/26/1959 02:00 EST
4/27/1969 02:00 EDT
10/26/1969 02:00 EST
4/26/1970 02:00 EDT
10/25/1970 02:00 EST

IN # 317
Before 11/18/1883 LMT
11/18/1883 12:00 CST
3/31/1918 02:00 CWT
10/27/1918 02:00 CST
3/30/1919 02:00 CWT
10/26/1919 02:00 CST
2/09/1942 02:00 CWT
9/30/1945 02:00 CST
4/25/1948 02:00 CDT
9/26/1948 02:00 CST
4/24/1949 02:00 CDT
9/25/1949 02:00 CST
4/30/1950 02:00 CDT
9/24/1950 02:00 CST
4/29/1951 02:00 CDT
9/30/1951 02:00 CST
4/27/1952 02:00 CDT
9/28/1952 02:00 CST
4/26/1953 02:00 CDT
9/27/1953 02:00 CST
4/25/1954 02:00 CDT
9/26/1954 02:00 CST
12/12/1954 01:00 EST
9/29/1957 02:00 CST
4/27/1958 02:00 CDT
9/28/1958 02:00 CST
4/26/1959 02:00 EST
4/27/1969 02:00 EDT
10/26/1969 02:00 EST
4/26/1970 02:00 EDT
10/25/1970 02:00 EST

IN # 318
Before 11/18/1883 LMT
11/18/1883 12:00 CST
3/31/1918 02:00 CWT
10/27/1918 02:00 CST
3/30/1919 02:00 CWT
10/26/1919 02:00 CST
6/01/1932 02:00 CDT
9/05/1932 02:00 CST
6/02/1933 02:00 CDT
9/04/1933 02:00 CST
6/03/1934 02:00 CDT
9/03/1934 02:00 CST
6/02/1935 02:00 CDT
9/02/1935 02:00 CST
4/30/1939 02:00 CDT
9/24/1939 02:00 CST
2/09/1942 02:00 CWT
9/30/1945 02:00 CST
4/28/1946 02:00 CDT
9/29/1946 02:00 CST
4/27/1947 02:00 CDT
9/28/1947 02:00 CST
4/25/1948 02:00 CDT
9/26/1948 02:00 CST
4/24/1949 02:00 CDT
9/25/1949 02:00 CST
4/30/1950 02:00 CDT
9/24/1950 02:00 CST
4/29/1951 02:00 CDT
9/30/1951 02:00 CST
4/27/1952 02:00 CDT
9/28/1952 02:00 CST
4/26/1953 02:00 CDT
9/27/1953 02:00 CST
4/25/1954 02:00 CDT
9/26/1954 02:00 CST
11/21/1954 02:00 EST
9/29/1957 02:00 CST
4/27/1958 02:00 CDT
9/28/1958 02:00 CST
4/26/1959 02:00 EST
4/27/1969 02:00 EDT
10/26/1969 02:00 EST
4/26/1970 02:00 EDT
10/25/1970 02:00 EST

IN # 319
Before 11/18/1883 LMT
11/18/1883 12:00 CST
3/31/1918 02:00 CWT
10/27/1918 02:00 CST
3/30/1919 02:00 CWT
10/26/1919 02:00 CST
2/09/1942 02:00 CWT
9/30/1945 02:00 CST
4/26/1953 02:00 CDT
9/27/1953 02:00 CST
4/25/1954 02:00 CDT
9/26/1954 02:00 CST
4/24/1955 02:00 CDT
9/25/1955 02:00 CST
4/29/1956 02:00 CDT
9/30/1956 02:00 CST
4/28/1957 02:00 CDT
9/29/1957 02:00 CST
4/27/1958 02:00 CDT
9/28/1958 02:00 CST
4/26/1959 02:00 CDT
9/27/1959 02:00 CST
4/24/1960 02:00 CDT
9/25/1960 02:00 CST
11/28/1960 00:00 EST
4/27/1969 02:00 EDT
10/26/1969 02:00 EST
4/26/1970 02:00 EDT
10/25/1970 02:00 EST

IN # 320
Before 11/18/1883 LMT
11/18/1883 12:00 CST
3/31/1918 02:00 CWT
10/27/1918 02:00 CST
3/30/1919 02:00 CWT
10/26/1919 02:00 CST

TIME TABLES

2/09/1942 02:00 CWT
9/30/1945 02:00 CST
4/24/1955 02:00 CDT
9/25/1955 02:00 CST
4/29/1956 02:00 CDT
9/30/1956 02:00 CST
4/28/1957 02:00 CDT
9/29/1957 02:00 CST
4/27/1958 02:00 CDT
9/28/1958 02:00 CST
4/26/1959 02:00 CDT
9/27/1959 02:00 CST
4/24/1960 02:00 CDT
9/25/1960 02:00 CST
11/28/1960 00:00 EST
4/27/1969 02:00 EDT
10/26/1969 02:00 EST
4/26/1970 02:00 EDT
10/25/1970 02:00 EST

IN # 321
Before 11/18/1883 LMT
11/18/1883 12:00 CST
3/31/1918 02:00 CWT
10/27/1918 02:00 CST
3/30/1919 02:00 CWT
10/26/1919 02:00 CST
2/09/1942 02:00 CWT
9/30/1945 02:00 CST
4/30/1950 02:00 CDT
9/24/1950 02:00 CST
4/26/1953 02:00 CDT
9/27/1953 02:00 CST
4/25/1954 02:00 CDT
9/26/1954 02:00 CST
4/24/1955 02:00 CDT
9/25/1955 02:00 CST
4/29/1956 02:00 CDT
10/08/1956 00:00 CST
4/28/1957 02:00 CDT
9/29/1957 02:00 CST
4/27/1958 02:00 CDT
9/28/1958 02:00 CST
4/26/1959 02:00 CDT
9/27/1959 02:00 CST
4/24/1960 02:00 CDT
9/25/1960 02:00 CST
11/28/1960 00:00 EST
4/27/1969 02:00 EDT
10/26/1969 02:00 EST
4/26/1970 02:00 EDT
10/25/1970 02:00 EST

IN # 322
Before 11/18/1883 LMT
11/18/1883 12:00 CST
3/31/1918 02:00 CWT
10/27/1918 02:00 CST
3/30/1919 02:00 CWT
10/26/1919 02:00 CST
2/09/1942 02:00 CWT
9/30/1945 02:00 CST
5/01/1955 00:00 CDT
9/04/1955 00:00 CST
4/29/1956 02:00 CDT
9/30/1956 02:00 CST
4/28/1957 02:00 CDT
9/29/1957 02:00 CST
4/27/1958 02:00 CDT
9/28/1958 02:00 CST
4/26/1959 02:00 CDT
9/27/1959 02:00 CST
4/24/1960 02:00 CDT
9/25/1960 02:00 CST
11/27/1960 02:00 EST
4/27/1969 02:00 EDT
10/26/1969 02:00 EST
4/26/1970 02:00 EDT
10/25/1970 02:00 EST

IN # 323
Before 11/18/1883 LMT
11/18/1883 12:00 CST
3/31/1918 02:00 CWT
10/27/1918 02:00 CST
3/30/1919 02:00 CWT
10/26/1919 02:00 CST
2/09/1942 02:00 CWT
9/30/1945 02:00 CST
5/08/1955 02:00 CDT
9/04/1955 00:00 CST
4/29/1956 02:00 CDT
9/30/1956 02:00 CST
4/28/1957 02:00 CDT
9/29/1957 02:00 CST
4/27/1958 02:00 CDT
9/28/1958 02:00 CST
4/26/1959 02:00 CDT
9/27/1959 02:00 CST
4/24/1960 02:00 CDT
9/25/1960 02:00 CST
11/27/1960 02:00 EST
10/29/1961 02:00 CST
4/29/1962 02:00 EST
4/27/1969 02:00 EDT
10/26/1969 02:00 EST
4/26/1970 02:00 EDT
10/25/1970 02:00 EST

IN # 324
Before 11/18/1883 LMT
11/18/1883 12:00 CST
3/31/1918 02:00 CWT
10/27/1918 02:00 CST
3/30/1919 02:00 CWT
10/26/1919 02:00 CST
2/09/1942 02:00 CWT
9/30/1945 02:00 CST
4/28/1946 02:00 CDT
9/29/1946 02:00 CST
4/27/1947 02:00 CDT
9/28/1947 02:00 CST
4/25/1948 02:00 CDT
9/26/1948 02:00 CST
4/24/1949 02:00 CDT
9/25/1949 02:00 CST
4/30/1950 02:00 CDT
9/24/1950 02:00 CST
4/29/1951 02:00 CDT
9/30/1951 02:00 CST
4/27/1952 02:00 CDT
9/28/1952 02:00 CST
4/26/1953 02:00 CDT
9/27/1953 02:00 CST
4/25/1954 02:00 CDT
9/26/1954 02:00 CST
11/28/1954 02:00 EST
10/30/1955 02:00 CST
4/29/1956 02:00 CDT
9/30/1956 02:00 CST
4/28/1957 02:00 CDT
9/29/1957 02:00 CST
4/27/1958 02:00 CDT
9/28/1958 02:00 CST
4/26/1959 02:00 CDT
9/27/1959 02:00 CST
4/24/1960 02:00 CDT
9/25/1960 02:00 CST
4/30/1961 02:00 EST
4/27/1969 02:00 EDT
10/26/1969 02:00 EST
4/26/1970 02:00 EDT
10/25/1970 02:00 EST

IN # 325
Before 11/18/1883 LMT
11/18/1883 12:00 CST
3/31/1918 02:00 CWT
10/27/1918 02:00 CST
3/30/1919 02:00 CWT
10/26/1919 02:00 CST
2/09/1942 02:00 CWT
9/30/1945 02:00 CST
4/25/1948 02:00 CDT
9/26/1948 02:00 CST
4/24/1949 02:00 CDT
9/25/1949 02:00 CST
4/30/1950 02:00 CDT
9/24/1950 02:00 CST
4/29/1951 02:00 CDT
9/30/1951 02:00 CST
4/27/1952 02:00 CDT
9/28/1952 02:00 CST
4/26/1953 02:00 CDT
9/27/1953 02:00 CST
4/25/1954 02:00 CDT
9/26/1954 02:00 CST
11/28/1954 02:00 EST
10/30/1955 02:00 CST
4/29/1956 02:00 CDT
9/30/1956 02:00 CST
4/28/1957 02:00 CDT
9/29/1957 02:00 CST
4/27/1958 02:00 CDT
9/28/1958 02:00 CST
4/26/1959 02:00 CDT
9/27/1959 02:00 CST
4/24/1960 02:00 CDT
9/25/1960 02:00 CST
4/30/1961 02:00 EST
4/27/1969 02:00 EDT
10/26/1969 02:00 EST
4/26/1970 02:00 EDT
10/25/1970 02:00 EST

IN # 326
Before 11/18/1883 LMT
11/18/1883 12:00 CST
3/31/1918 02:00 CWT
10/27/1918 02:00 CST
3/30/1919 02:00 CWT
10/26/1919 02:00 CST
4/27/1941 02:00 CDT
9/28/1941 02:00 CST
2/09/1942 02:00 CWT
9/30/1945 02:00 CST
4/25/1948 02:00 CDT
9/26/1948 02:00 CST
4/26/1953 02:00 CDT
9/27/1953 02:00 CST
4/25/1954 02:00 CDT
9/26/1954 02:00 CST
11/28/1954 02:00 EST
10/30/1955 02:00 CST
4/29/1956 02:00 CDT
10/28/1956 02:00 CST
4/28/1957 02:00 CDT
9/29/1957 02:00 CST
4/27/1958 02:00 CDT
10/26/1958 02:00 CST
4/26/1959 02:00 CDT
10/25/1959 02:00 CST
4/24/1960 02:00 CDT
10/30/1960 02:00 CST
4/30/1961 02:00 EST
4/27/1969 02:00 EDT
10/26/1969 02:00 EST
4/26/1970 02:00 EDT
10/25/1970 02:00 EST

IN # 327
Before 11/18/1883 LMT
11/18/1883 12:00 CST
3/31/1918 02:00 CWT
10/27/1918 02:00 CST
3/30/1919 02:00 CWT
10/26/1919 02:00 CST
2/09/1942 02:00 CWT
9/30/1945 02:00 CST
4/26/1953 02:00 CDT
9/27/1953 02:00 CST
4/25/1954 02:00 CDT
9/26/1954 02:00 CST
11/28/1954 02:00 EST
10/30/1955 02:00 CST
4/29/1956 02:00 CDT
9/30/1956 02:00 CST
4/28/1957 02:00 CDT
9/29/1957 02:00 CST
4/27/1958 02:00 CDT
9/28/1958 02:00 CST
4/26/1959 02:00 CDT
9/27/1959 02:00 CST
4/24/1960 02:00 CDT
9/25/1960 02:00 CST
4/30/1961 02:00 EST
4/27/1969 02:00 EDT
10/26/1969 02:00 EST
4/26/1970 02:00 EDT
10/25/1970 02:00 EST

IN # 328
Before 11/18/1883 LMT
11/18/1883 12:00 CST
3/31/1918 02:00 CWT
10/27/1918 02:00 CST
3/30/1919 02:00 CWT
10/26/1919 02:00 CST
2/09/1942 02:00 CWT
9/30/1945 02:00 CST
4/25/1954 02:00 CDT
9/26/1954 02:00 CST
11/28/1954 02:00 EST
10/30/1955 02:00 CST
4/29/1956 02:00 CDT
9/30/1956 02:00 CST
4/28/1957 02:00 CDT
9/29/1957 02:00 CST
4/27/1958 02:00 CDT
9/28/1958 02:00 CST
4/26/1959 02:00 CDT
9/27/1959 02:00 CST
4/24/1960 02:00 CDT
9/25/1960 02:00 CST
4/30/1961 02:00 EST
4/27/1969 02:00 EDT
10/26/1969 02:00 EST
4/26/1970 02:00 EDT
10/25/1970 02:00 EST

IN # 329
Before 11/18/1883 LMT
11/18/1883 12:00 CST
3/31/1918 02:00 CWT
10/27/1918 02:00 CST
3/30/1919 02:00 CWT
10/26/1919 02:00 CST
2/09/1942 02:00 CWT
9/30/1945 02:00 CST
4/28/1946 02:00 CDT
9/29/1946 02:00 CST
4/27/1947 02:00 CDT
9/28/1947 02:00 CST
4/25/1948 02:00 CDT
9/26/1948 02:00 CST
4/27/1952 02:00 CDT
9/28/1952 02:00 CST
4/26/1953 02:00 CDT
9/27/1953 02:00 CST
4/25/1954 02:00 CDT
9/26/1954 02:00 CST
11/28/1954 02:00 EST
10/30/1955 02:00 CST
4/02/1956 02:00 CDT
11/04/1956 02:00 CST
4/28/1957 02:00 CDT
9/29/1957 02:00 CST
4/27/1958 02:00 CDT
9/28/1958 02:00 CST
4/26/1959 02:00 CDT
10/25/1959 02:00 CST
4/24/1960 02:00 CDT
10/30/1960 02:00 CST
4/30/1961 02:00 EST
4/27/1969 02:00 EDT
10/26/1969 02:00 EST
4/26/1970 02:00 EDT
10/25/1970 02:00 EST

IN # 330
Before 11/18/1883 LMT
11/18/1883 12:00 CST
3/31/1918 02:00 CWT
10/27/1918 02:00 CST
3/30/1919 02:00 CWT
10/26/1919 02:00 CST
2/09/1942 02:00 CWT
9/30/1945 02:00 CST
4/26/1953 02:00 CDT
9/27/1953 02:00 CST
4/25/1954 02:00 CDT
9/26/1954 02:00 CST
1/02/1955 00:00 EST
2/13/1955 02:00 CST
4/24/1955 02:00 CDT
9/25/1955 02:00 CST
4/29/1956 02:00 CDT
9/30/1956 02:00 CST
4/28/1957 02:00 CDT
9/29/1957 02:00 CST
4/27/1958 02:00 CDT
9/28/1958 02:00 CST
4/26/1959 02:00 CDT
9/27/1959 02:00 CST
4/24/1960 02:00 CDT
9/25/1960 02:00 CST
4/30/1961 02:00 EST
4/27/1969 02:00 EDT
10/26/1969 02:00 EST
4/26/1970 02:00 EDT
10/25/1970 02:00 EST

IN # 331
Before 11/18/1883 LMT
11/18/1883 12:00 CST
3/31/1918 02:00 CWT
10/27/1918 02:00 CST
3/30/1919 02:00 CWT
10/26/1919 02:00 CST
2/09/1942 02:00 CWT
9/30/1945 02:00 CST
1/02/1955 00:00 EST
2/13/1955 02:00 CST
4/24/1955 02:00 CDT
9/25/1955 02:00 CST
4/29/1956 02:00 CDT
9/30/1956 02:00 CST
4/28/1957 02:00 CDT
9/29/1957 02:00 CST
4/27/1958 02:00 CDT
9/28/1958 02:00 CST
4/26/1959 02:00 CDT
9/27/1959 02:00 CST
4/24/1960 02:00 CDT
9/25/1960 02:00 CST
4/30/1961 02:00 EST
4/27/1969 02:00 EDT
10/26/1969 02:00 EST
4/26/1970 02:00 EDT
10/25/1970 02:00 EST

IN # 332
Before 11/18/1883 LMT
11/18/1883 12:00 CST
3/31/1918 02:00 CWT
10/27/1918 02:00 CST
3/30/1919 02:00 CWT
10/26/1919 02:00 CST
2/09/1942 02:00 CWT
9/30/1945 02:00 CST
4/28/1946 02:00 CDT
9/29/1946 02:00 CST
4/27/1947 02:00 CDT
9/28/1947 02:00 CST
4/25/1948 02:00 CDT
9/26/1948 02:00 CST
4/24/1949 02:00 CDT
9/25/1949 02:00 CST
4/30/1950 02:00 CDT
9/24/1950 02:00 CST
4/29/1951 02:00 CDT
9/30/1951 02:00 CST
4/27/1952 02:00 CDT
9/28/1952 02:00 CST
4/26/1953 02:00 CDT
9/27/1953 02:00 CST
4/25/1954 02:00 CDT
9/26/1954 02:00 CST
1/02/1955 00:00 EST
2/13/1955 02:00 CST
4/24/1955 02:00 CDT
9/25/1955 02:00 CST
4/29/1956 02:00 CDT
11/15/1956 02:00 CST
4/28/1957 02:00 CDT
9/29/1957 02:00 CST
4/27/1958 02:00 CDT
9/28/1958 02:00 CST
4/26/1959 02:00 CDT
9/27/1959 02:00 CST
4/24/1960 02:00 CDT
9/25/1960 02:00 CST
4/30/1961 02:00 EST
4/27/1969 02:00 EDT
10/26/1969 02:00 EST
4/26/1970 02:00 EDT
10/25/1970 02:00 EST

IN # 333
Before 11/18/1883 LMT
11/18/1883 12:00 CST
3/31/1918 02:00 CWT
10/27/1918 02:00 CST
3/30/1919 02:00 CWT
10/26/1919 02:00 CST
2/09/1942 02:00 CWT
9/30/1945 02:00 CST
4/27/1947 02:00 CDT
9/28/1947 02:00 CST
4/26/1953 02:00 CDT
9/27/1953 02:00 CST
4/25/1954 02:00 CDT
9/26/1954 02:00 CST
1/02/1955 00:00 EST
9/25/1955 02:00 CST
4/29/1956 02:00 CDT
9/30/1956 02:00 CST
4/28/1957 02:00 CDT
9/29/1957 02:00 CST
4/27/1958 02:00 CDT
9/28/1958 02:00 CST
4/26/1959 02:00 CDT
9/27/1959 02:00 CST
4/24/1960 02:00 CDT
9/25/1960 02:00 CST
4/30/1961 02:00 EST
4/27/1969 02:00 EDT
10/26/1969 02:00 EST
4/26/1970 02:00 EDT
10/25/1970 02:00 EST

IN # 334
Before 11/18/1883 LMT
11/18/1883 12:00 CST
3/31/1918 02:00 CWT
10/27/1918 02:00 CST
3/30/1919 02:00 CWT
10/26/1919 02:00 CST
2/09/1942 02:00 CWT
9/30/1945 02:00 CST
1/02/1955 00:00 EST
9/25/1955 02:00 CST
4/29/1956 02:00 CDT
9/30/1956 02:00 CST
4/28/1957 02:00 CDT
9/29/1957 02:00 CST
4/27/1958 02:00 CDT
9/28/1958 02:00 CST
4/26/1959 02:00 CDT
9/27/1959 02:00 CST
4/24/1960 02:00 CDT
9/25/1960 02:00 CST
4/30/1961 02:00 EST
4/27/1969 02:00 EDT
10/26/1969 02:00 EST
4/26/1970 02:00 EDT
10/25/1970 02:00 EST

IN # 335
Before 11/18/1883 LMT
11/18/1883 12:00 CST
3/31/1918 02:00 CWT
10/27/1918 02:00 CST
3/30/1919 02:00 CWT
10/26/1919 02:00 CST
2/09/1942 02:00 CWT
9/30/1945 02:00 CST
1/02/1955 00:00 EST
9/25/1955 02:00 CST
4/28/1957 02:00 CDT
9/29/1957 02:00 CST
4/27/1958 02:00 CDT
9/28/1958 02:00 CST
4/26/1959 02:00 CDT
9/27/1959 02:00 CST
4/24/1960 02:00 CDT
9/25/1960 02:00 CST
4/30/1961 02:00 EST
4/27/1969 02:00 EDT
10/26/1969 02:00 EST
4/26/1970 02:00 EDT
10/25/1970 02:00 EST

IN # 336
Before 11/18/1883 LMT
11/18/1883 12:00 CST
3/31/1918 02:00 CWT
10/27/1918 02:00 CST
3/30/1919 02:00 CWT
10/26/1919 02:00 CST
2/09/1942 02:00 CWT
9/30/1945 02:00 CST
4/28/1946 02:00 CDT
9/29/1946 02:00 CST
4/27/1947 02:00 CDT
9/28/1947 02:00 CST
4/25/1948 02:00 CDT
9/26/1948 02:00 CST
4/24/1949 02:00 CDT
9/25/1949 02:00 CST
4/30/1950 02:00 CDT
9/24/1950 02:00 CST
4/29/1951 02:00 CDT
9/30/1951 02:00 CST
4/27/1952 02:00 CDT
9/28/1952 02:00 CST
4/26/1953 02:00 CDT
9/27/1953 02:00 CST
4/25/1954 02:00 CDT
9/26/1954 02:00 CST
1/02/1955 00:00 EST
9/25/1955 02:00 CST
4/29/1956 02:00 CDT
9/30/1956 02:00 CST
4/28/1957 02:00 CDT
9/29/1957 02:00 CST
4/27/1958 02:00 CDT
9/28/1958 02:00 CST
4/26/1959 02:00 CDT
9/27/1959 02:00 CST
4/24/1960 02:00 CDT
9/25/1960 02:00 CST
4/30/1961 02:00 EST
4/27/1969 02:00 EDT
10/26/1969 02:00 EST
4/26/1970 02:00 EDT
10/25/1970 02:00 EST

IN # 337
Before 11/18/1883 LMT
11/18/1883 12:00 CST
3/31/1918 02:00 CWT
10/27/1918 02:00 CST
3/30/1919 02:00 CWT
10/26/1919 02:00 CST
2/09/1942 02:00 CWT
9/30/1945 02:00 CST
4/27/1947 02:00 CDT
9/28/1947 02:00 CST
4/26/1953 02:00 CDT
9/27/1953 02:00 CST
4/25/1954 02:00 CDT
9/26/1954 02:00 CST
1/02/1955 00:00 EST
9/25/1955 02:00 CST
4/29/1956 02:00 CDT
9/30/1956 02:00 CST
4/28/1957 02:00 CDT
9/29/1957 02:00 CST
4/27/1958 02:00 CDT
9/28/1958 02:00 CST
4/26/1959 02:00 CDT
9/27/1959 02:00 CST
4/24/1960 02:00 CDT
9/25/1960 02:00 CST
4/30/1961 02:00 EST
4/27/1969 02:00 EDT
10/26/1969 02:00 EST
4/26/1970 02:00 EDT
10/25/1970 02:00 EST

TIME TABLES

IN # 338		
Before 11/18/1883		LMT
11/18/1883	12:00	CST
3/31/1918	02:00	CWT
10/27/1918	02:00	CST
3/30/1919	02:00	CWT
10/26/1919	02:00	CST
2/09/1942	02:00	CWT
9/30/1945	02:00	CST
4/26/1953	02:00	CDT
9/27/1953	02:00	CST
4/25/1954	02:00	CDT
9/26/1954	02:00	CST
1/02/1955	00:00	EST
9/25/1955	02:00	CST
4/29/1956	02:00	CDT
9/30/1956	02:00	CST
4/28/1957	02:00	CDT
9/29/1957	02:00	CST
4/27/1958	02:00	CDT
9/28/1958	02:00	CST
4/26/1959	02:00	CDT
9/27/1959	02:00	CST
4/24/1960	02:00	CDT
9/25/1960	02:00	CST
4/30/1961	02:00	EST
4/27/1969	02:00	EDT
10/26/1969	02:00	EST
4/26/1970	02:00	EDT
10/25/1970	02:00	EST

IN # 339		
Before 11/18/1883		LMT
11/18/1883	12:00	CST
3/31/1918	02:00	CWT
10/27/1918	02:00	CST
3/30/1919	02:00	CWT
10/26/1919	02:00	CST
2/09/1942	02:00	CWT
9/30/1945	02:00	CST
4/28/1946	02:00	CDT
9/29/1946	02:00	CST
4/25/1948	02:00	CDT
9/26/1948	02:00	CST
4/24/1949	02:00	CDT
9/25/1949	02:00	CST
4/26/1953	02:00	CDT
9/27/1953	02:00	CST
4/25/1954	02:00	CDT
9/26/1954	02:00	CST
1/02/1955	00:00	EST
9/25/1955	02:00	CST
4/29/1956	02:00	CDT
11/04/1956	02:00	CST
4/28/1957	02:00	CDT
9/29/1957	02:00	CST
4/27/1958	02:00	CDT
10/26/1958	02:00	CST
4/26/1959	02:00	CDT
9/27/1959	02:00	CST
4/24/1960	02:00	CDT
9/25/1960	02:00	CST
4/30/1961	02:00	EST
4/27/1969	02:00	EDT
10/26/1969	02:00	EST
4/26/1970	02:00	EDT
10/25/1970	02:00	EST

IN # 340		
Before 11/18/1883		LMT
11/18/1883	12:00	CST
3/31/1918	02:00	CWT
10/27/1918	02:00	CST
3/30/1919	02:00	CWT
10/26/1919	02:00	CST
4/26/1931	02:00	CDT
9/27/1931	02:00	CST
4/24/1932	02:00	CDT
9/25/1932	02:00	CST
2/09/1942	02:00	CWT
9/30/1945	02:00	CST
4/28/1946	02:00	CDT
9/29/1946	02:00	CST
4/30/1950	02:00	CDT
9/24/1950	02:00	CST
4/29/1951	02:00	CDT
9/30/1951	02:00	CST
4/27/1952	02:00	CDT
9/28/1952	02:00	CST
4/26/1953	02:00	CDT
9/27/1953	02:00	CST
4/25/1954	02:00	CDT
9/26/1954	02:00	CST
4/24/1955	02:00	CDT
9/25/1955	02:00	CST
4/29/1956	02:00	CDT
11/18/1956	00:00	CST
4/28/1957	02:00	CDT
9/29/1957	02:00	CST
4/27/1958	02:00	CDT
10/26/1958	02:00	CST
4/26/1959	02:00	CDT
10/25/1959	02:00	CST
4/24/1960	02:00	EST
11/13/1960	02:00	CST
4/30/1961	02:00	EST
4/27/1969	02:00	EDT
10/26/1969	02:00	EST
4/26/1970	02:00	EDT
10/25/1970	02:00	EST

IN # 341		
Before 11/18/1883		LMT
11/18/1883	12:00	CST
3/31/1918	02:00	CWT
10/27/1918	02:00	CST
3/30/1919	02:00	CWT
10/26/1919	02:00	CST
2/09/1942	02:00	CWT
9/30/1945	02:00	CST
4/29/1951	02:00	CDT
9/30/1951	02:00	CST
4/27/1952	02:00	CDT
9/28/1952	02:00	CST
4/26/1953	02:00	CDT
9/27/1953	02:00	CST
4/25/1954	02:00	CDT
9/26/1954	02:00	CST
4/24/1955	02:00	CDT
9/25/1955	02:00	CST
4/29/1956	02:00	CDT
9/30/1956	02:00	CST
4/28/1957	02:00	CDT
9/29/1957	02:00	CST
4/27/1958	02:00	CDT
9/28/1958	02:00	CST
4/26/1959	02:00	CDT
9/27/1959	02:00	CST
4/24/1960	02:00	EST
11/13/1960	02:00	CST
4/30/1961	02:00	EST
4/27/1969	02:00	EDT
10/26/1969	02:00	EST
4/26/1970	02:00	EDT
10/25/1970	02:00	EST

IN # 342		
Before 11/18/1883		LMT
11/18/1883	12:00	CST
3/31/1918	02:00	CWT
10/27/1918	02:00	CST
3/30/1919	02:00	CWT
10/26/1919	02:00	CST
2/09/1942	02:00	CWT
9/30/1945	02:00	CST
4/26/1953	02:00	CDT
9/27/1953	02:00	CST
4/25/1954	02:00	CDT
9/26/1954	02:00	CST
4/24/1955	02:00	CDT
9/25/1955	02:00	CST
4/29/1956	02:00	CDT
9/30/1956	02:00	CST
4/28/1957	02:00	CDT
9/29/1957	02:00	CST
4/27/1958	02:00	CDT
9/28/1958	02:00	CST
4/26/1959	02:00	CDT
9/27/1959	02:00	CST
4/24/1960	02:00	EST
11/13/1960	02:00	CST
4/30/1961	02:00	EST
4/27/1969	02:00	EDT
10/26/1969	02:00	EST
4/26/1970	02:00	EDT
10/25/1970	02:00	EST

IN # 343		
Before 11/18/1883		LMT
11/18/1883	12:00	CST
3/31/1918	02:00	CWT
10/27/1918	02:00	CST
3/30/1919	02:00	CWT
10/26/1919	02:00	CST
2/09/1942	02:00	CWT
9/30/1945	02:00	CST
4/25/1954	02:00	CDT
9/26/1954	02:00	CST
4/24/1955	02:00	CDT
9/25/1955	02:00	CST
4/29/1956	02:00	CDT
9/30/1956	02:00	CST
4/28/1957	02:00	CDT
9/29/1957	02:00	CST
4/27/1958	02:00	CDT
9/28/1958	02:00	CST
4/26/1959	02:00	CDT
9/27/1959	02:00	CST
4/24/1960	02:00	EST
11/13/1960	02:00	CST
4/30/1961	02:00	EST
4/27/1969	02:00	EDT
10/26/1969	02:00	EST
4/26/1970	02:00	EDT
10/25/1970	02:00	EST

IN # 344		
Before 11/18/1883		LMT
11/18/1883	12:00	CST
3/31/1918	02:00	CWT
10/27/1918	02:00	CST
3/30/1919	02:00	CWT
10/26/1919	02:00	CST
2/09/1942	02:00	CWT
9/30/1945	02:00	CST
4/24/1955	02:00	CDT
9/25/1955	02:00	CST
4/29/1956	02:00	CDT
9/30/1956	02:00	CST
4/28/1957	02:00	CDT
9/29/1957	02:00	CST
4/27/1958	02:00	CDT
9/28/1958	02:00	CST
4/26/1959	02:00	CDT
9/27/1959	02:00	CST
4/24/1960	02:00	EST
11/13/1960	02:00	CST
4/30/1961	02:00	EST
4/27/1969	02:00	EDT
10/26/1969	02:00	EST
4/26/1970	02:00	EDT
10/25/1970	02:00	EST

IN # 345		
Before 11/18/1883		LMT
11/18/1883	12:00	CST
3/31/1918	02:00	CWT
10/27/1918	02:00	CST
3/30/1919	02:00	CWT
10/26/1919	02:00	CST
2/09/1942	02:00	CWT
9/30/1945	02:00	CST
4/27/1947	02:00	CDT
9/28/1947	02:00	CST
4/02/1948	02:00	CDT
9/26/1948	02:00	CST
4/30/1950	02:00	CDT
9/24/1950	02:00	CST
4/29/1951	02:00	CDT
9/30/1951	02:00	CST
4/27/1952	02:00	CDT
9/28/1952	02:00	CST
4/26/1953	02:00	CDT
9/27/1953	02:00	CST
4/25/1954	02:00	CDT
9/26/1954	02:00	CST
4/24/1955	02:00	CDT
9/25/1955	02:00	CST
4/29/1956	02:00	CDT
11/11/1956	02:00	CST
4/28/1957	02:00	CDT
9/29/1957	02:00	CST
4/27/1958	02:00	CDT
10/26/1958	02:00	CST
4/26/1959	02:00	CDT
10/25/1959	02:00	CST
4/24/1960	02:00	EST
11/13/1960	02:00	CST
4/30/1961	02:00	EST
4/27/1969	02:00	EDT
10/26/1969	02:00	EST
4/26/1970	02:00	EDT
10/25/1970	02:00	EST

COUNTIES

1 Adams
2 Allen
3 Bartholomew
4 Benton
5 Blackford
6 Boone
7 Brown
8 Carroll
9 Cass
10 Clark
11 Clay
12 Clinton
13 Crawford
14 Daviess
15 Dearborn
16 Decatur
17 De Kalb
18 Delaware
19 Dubois
20 Elkhart
21 Fayette
22 Floyd
23 Fountain
24 Franklin
25 Fulton
26 Gibson
27 Grant
28 Greene
29 Hamilton
30 Hancock
31 Harrison
32 Hendricks
33 Henry
34 Howard
35 Huntington
36 Jackson
37 Jasper
38 Jay
39 Jefferson
40 Jennings
41 Johnson
42 Knox
43 Kosciusko
44 La Grange
45 Lake
46 La Porte
47 Lawrence
48 Madison
49 Marion
50 Marshall
51 Martin
52 Miami
53 Monroe
54 Montgomery
55 Morgan
56 Newton
57 Noble
58 Ohio
59 Orange
60 Owen
61 Parke
62 Perry
63 Pike
64 Porter
65 Posey
66 Pulaski
67 Putnam
68 Randolph
69 Ripley
70 Rush
71 St Joseph
72 Scott
73 Shelby
74 Spencer
75 Starke
76 Steuben
77 Sullivan
78 Switzerland
79 Tippecanoe
80 Tipton
81 Union
82 Vanderburgh
83 Vermillion
84 Vigo
85 Wabash
86 Warren
87 Warrick
88 Washington
89 Wayne
90 Wells
91 White
92 Whitley

Place	County	Elev	Lat	Long	Time
Aaron	78	35	38N52'59	85W07'33	5:40:30
Abbey Dell	59	160	38N35	86W32	5:46:08
Abels Acres	3	147	39N13	85W54	5:43:36
Aberdeen	58	33	38N54'19	84W59'15	5:39:57
Abington	89	315	39N43'59	84W57'47	5:39:51
Aboite	2	228	41N00'03	85W19'05	5:41:16
Abydel	59	160	38N34'14	86W33'40	5:46:15
Acme	36	147	38N58'41	86W03'32	5:44:14
Acton	49	100	39N39'20	85W58'01	5:43:52
Adams	16	108	39N22'57	85W33'36	5:42:14
Adams	55	101	39N28'56	86W21'20	5:45:25
Adamsboro	9	164	40N47'04	86W16'01	5:45:04
Adams Lake	44	30	41N32	85W22	5:41:28
Adams Mill	8	165	40N28'50	86W30'32	5:46:02
Addison	73	101	39N32	85W46	5:43:04
Addmore	10	166	38N18	85W45	5:43:00
Ade	56	2	40N52'06	87W26'41	5:49:47
Adel	60	344	39N11'31	86W47'45	5:47:11
Advance	6	251	39N59'45	86W37'12	5:46:29
Adyeville	62	64	38N11'27	86W46'10	5:47:05
Aetna	45	20	41N35'31	87W17'22	5:49:09
Africa	74	57	37N50'25	87W04'22	5:48:17
Ainsworth	45	6	41N29	87W16	5:49:04
Air Mail Field	49	100	39N45	86W14	5:44:56
Aix	37	2	41N02'29	87W09'05	5:48:36
Akron	25	242	41N02'18	86W01'41	5:44:07
Aladdin	48	101	40N16	85W41	5:42:44
Alamo	54	147	39N58'55	87W03'26	5:48:14
Alaska	60	113	39N28'13	86W38'29	5:46:34
Albany	18	255	40N18'03	85W14'31	5:40:58
Albion	57	44	41N23'44	85W25'28	5:41:42
Albion	72	320	38N44'37	85W44'03	5:42:56
Aldine	75	28	41N12'03	86W40'28	5:46:42
Alert	16	101	39N09'37	85W40'42	5:42:43
Alexandria	48	105	40N15'46	85W40'33	5:42:42
Alfont	48	101	39N57'05	85W48'53	5:43:16
Alford	63	59	38N29'29	87W14'34	5:48:58
Alfordsville	14	85	38N33'38	86W56'54	5:47:48
Algiers	63	59	38N29'14	87W10'30	5:48:42
Alida	46	9	41N30'38	86W54'11	5:47:37
Allen Crossing	69	275	39N06'14	85W19'01	5:41:16
Allendale	84	77	39N23'30	87W23'45	5:49:35
Allens Acres	6	100	39N53	86W16	5:45:04
Allensville	78	35	38N52'23	85W01'13	5:40:05
Alliance	48	101	40N02'00	85W39'00	5:42:36
Allisonville	49	100	39N54'18	86W04'42	5:44:19
Allman	55	101	39N37'02	86W25'52	5:45:43
Alma Lake	61	89	39N31	87W08	5:48:32
Alpine	21	272	39N33'14	85W10'33	5:40:42
Alquina	21	272	39N36'46	85W03'17	5:40:13
Alta	83	73	39N46'20	87W23'12	5:49:33
Alto	34	331	40N26'24	86W09'56	5:44:40
Alton	62	169	38N07'21	86W25'04	5:45:40
Altona	17	228	41N21'05	85W09'18	5:40:37
Alvarado	76	30	41N34'36	84W50'16	5:39:21
Amber Valley	84	77	39N29	87W22	5:49:28
Ambia	4	150	40N29'24	87W31'01	5:50:04
Ambler	46	9	41N42'57	86W47'48	5:47:11
Amboy	52	338	40N36'05	85W55'44	5:43:43
Americus	79	147	40N31'33	86W45'29	5:47:02
Ames	69	149	40N02'00	86W53'13	5:47:33
Amity	41	108	39N25'34	86W00'04	5:44:00
Amo	32	115	39N41'17	86W36'49	5:46:27
Amsworth	45	6	41N29'16	87W15'31	5:49:02
Anderson	48	102	40N06'19	85W40'49	5:42:43
Andersonville	18	254	40N13'07	85W25'52	5:41:43
Andersonville	24	275	39N29'51	85W17'20	5:41:09
Andrews	35	288	40N51'45	85W36'06	5:42:24
Andrews Manor	27	284	40N34	85W42	5:42:48
Andry	46	8	41N43'04	86W45'29	5:47:02
Angola	76	45	41N38'05	84W59'58	5:40:00
Anita	41	97	39N25'33	86W11'29	5:44:46
Annandale Estates	7	145	39N13'04	86W15'58	5:45:04
Annapolis	61	128	39N51'09	87W15'02	5:49:00
Anoka	9	164	40N43'19	86W16'57	5:45:08
Ansley Acres	2	233	41N04'42	85W12'44	5:40:51
Anthony	18	254	40N16'40	85W26'10	5:41:45
Anthony Wayne Village	2	233	41N02'22	85W06'20	5:40:25
Antioch	12	181	40N13'41	86W30'21	5:46:01
Antioch	28	93	39N10	87W12	5:48:48
Antioch	38	291	40N22'04	84W56'32	5:39:46
Antioch	78	35	38N51'34	84W53'02	5:39:32
Antiville	38	291	40N29'51	84W58'43	5:39:55
Apache Acres	84	82	39N42	86W51	5:47:24
Apalona	62	69	38N09'16	86W37'56	5:46:32
Arba	68	307	40N00'39	84W52'01	5:39:28
Arcadia	29	97	40N10'33	86W01'18	5:44:05
Arcana	27	284	40N32'19	85W30'12	5:42:01
Arcitc Spring	10	176	38N16'59	85W42'41	5:42:51
Arcola	2	230	41N06'13	85W17'39	5:41:11
Arctic Springs	10	166	38N18	85W45	5:43:00
Arda	63	59	38N31'02	87W15'02	5:49:00

Ardmore 71 202 41N41'21 86W19'03 5:45:16
Argos 50 212 41N41'50 86W14'42 5:44:59
Ari 67 230 41N15'49 85W14'58 5:41:00
Ar'les Acres 29 97 40N03 86W01 5:44:04
Arlington 53 344 39N11'02 86W33'00 5:46:12
Arlington 70 101 39N38'33 85W34'35 5:42:18
Armiesburg 61 128 39N45'48 87W21'04 5:49:24
Armstrong 82 53 38N06'33 87W38'50 5:50:35
Armuth Acres 3 147 39N13 85W54 5:43:36
Arney 60 344 39N13'07 86W55'54 5:47:44
Aroma 29 97 40N11'58 85W52'27 5:43:30
Arrowhead Park 43 297 41N16'44 85W47'24 5:43:10
Art 11 89 39N24'10 87W09'19 5:48:37
Arthur 63 59 38N20'26 87W14'45 5:48:59
Artic 17 228 41N28'25 84W48'53 5:39:16
Artist Point 13 169 38N09'39 86W22'14 5:45:29
Ashboro 61 89 39N23'56 87W06'21 5:48:25
Ashby Yards 63 59 38N28'28 87W17'05 5:49:08
Asherville 61 89 39N28'28 87W03'43 5:48:15
Ash Grove 79 147 40N32'52 86W50'52 5:47:23
Ash Iron Springs 87 53 38N02'07 87W11'12 5:48:45
Ashland 33 253 39N55'34 85W18'16 5:41:13
Ashland 55 115 39N29 86W36 5:46:24
Ashley 76 30 41N31'38 85W03'56 5:40:16
Asphaltum 37 226 41N06'01 86W59'53 5:48:00
Athens 25 328 41N03'13 86W07'31 5:44:30
Atherton 84 82 39N36'29 87W21'43 5:49:27
Atkinson 4 147 40N33'46 87W14'48 5:48:59
Atkinsonville 60 344 39N22'40 86W52'24 5:47:30
Atlanta 29 97 40N12'55 86W01'35 5:44:06
Attica 23 129 40N17'39 87W14'56 5:49:00
Atwood 43 295 41N15'39 85W58'31 5:43:54
Aubbeenaubbee 25 328 41N08 86W24 5:45:36
Auburn 17 234 41N22'01 85W03'32 5:40:14
Auburn Junction 17 234 41N21'07 85W04'29 5:40:18
Augusta 49 100 39N53'24 86W12'44 5:44:51
Augusta 63 59 38N19'53 87W11'27 5:48:46
Aultshire 18 254 40N12'43 85W20'46 5:41:23
Aurora 15 38 39N03'25 84W54'05 5:39:36
Austin 72 319 38N45'30 85W48'29 5:43:14
Avalon 2 233 41N00'58 85W09'28 5:40:38
Avalon Hills 49 100 39N52'41 86W03'21 5:44:13
Avery 12 181 40N18'32 86W26'26 5:45:46
Avilla 67 46 41N21'57 85W14'20 5:40:57
Avoca 47 344 38N54'43 86W32'52 5:46:11
Avon 32 97 39N45'46 86W23'59 5:45:36
Avonburg 78 35 38N53'11 85W10'20 5:40:41
Avondale 27 284 40N34 85W42 5:42:48
Aylesworth 23 144 40N12'11 87W14'35 5:48:58
Aylesworth 64 28 41N19'06 87W06'48 5:48:27
Ayr 50 218 41N27 86W05 5:44:20
Ayrshire 63 59 38N22'39 87W14'39 5:48:59
Azalia 3 147 39N05'30 85W50'50 5:43:23
Babcock 64 6 41N34'21 87W06'18 5:48:25
Bacon 59 160 38N24'38 86W26'00 5:45:44
Badger Grove 91 147 40N35'01 86W57'49 5:47:51
Baileys Corner 37 226 41N04'15 86W59'54 5:48:00
Bainbridge 67 128 39N45'40 86W48'43 5:47:15
Bainter Town 20 260 41N31'01 85W49'02 5:43:16
Bakalar Air Force Base 3 147 39N15'09 85W53'42 5:43:35
Baker 55 113 39N22 86W32 5:46:08
Bakers Corner 29 97 40N07'50 86W08'15 5:44:33
Bakertown 67 30 41N21'59 85W21'26 5:41:26
Balbec 38 291 40N31'51 85W08'56 5:40:36
Balbee 38 291 40N30 85W09 5:40:36
Bald Knobs 36 139 39N01'12 86W10'14 5:44:41
Baldridge 13 80 39N13'23 87W22'20 5:49:29
Baldwin Heights 26 59 38N24 87W35 5:50:20
Ball State University 18 254 40N13 85W24 5:41:36
Ballstown 69 275 39N15'02 85W14'39 5:40:59
Bandmill 42 59 38N32'18 87W36'10 5:50:25
Bandon 62 69 38N08'14 86W36'01 5:46:24
Banning Corner 86 129 40N21'59 87W09'45 5:48:39
Banquo 35 287 40N41'47 85W37'11 5:42:29
Banta 55 97 39N31'26 86W15'01 5:45:00
Bar-Barry Heights 79 147 40N27'22 86W54'57 5:47:40
Barbee 43 291 41N17'27 85W42'44 5:42:51
Barbersville 39 97 38N54'21 85W16'51 5:41:07
Barce 4 147 40N37'15 87W16'36 5:49:06
Bargersville 41 99 39N31'15 86W10'04 5:44:40
Barkley 37 2 41N02 87W04 5:48:16
Barnaby Acres 3 147 39N13 85W54 5:43:36
Barnard 67 128 39N50'55 86W42'02 5:46:48
Barnhart Town 84 77 39N30'14 87W26'08 5:49:45
Barr 14 85 38N41 87W01 5:48:04
Barrett 65 58 38N12'02 87W52'10 5:51:29
Barrick Corner 11 89 39N15'22 87W04'24 5:48:18
Bartlettsville 47 344 38N58'13 86W26'31 5:45:46
Bartley 84 82 39N42 86W51 5:47:24
Barton 26 59 38N15 87W23 5:49:32
Bartonia 68 307 40N06'55 84W51'04 5:39:24
Bascom Corner 58 33 38N54'32 84W58'07 5:39:52
Bass Lake 75 222 41N12'26 86W36'07 5:46:24
Bass Station 75 222 41N11'07 86W36'08 5:46:25
Batesville 69 276 39N18'00 85W13'20 5:40:53
Bath 24 30 39N30'30 84W51'45 5:39:27
Battle Ground 79 147 40N30'30 86W50'30 5:47:22
Baugh City 87 53 37N57'29 87W24'42 5:49:39
Baugo 20 271 41N40 86W02 5:44:08
Bayfield 43 291 41N16'29 85W42'25 5:42:50
Beal 42 86 38N35 87W38 5:50:32
Beanblossom 53 147 39N16'01 86W14'57 5:45:00
Bear Branch 58 33 38N54'46 85W04'30 5:40:18
Bearcreek 38 287 40N32 84W56 5:39:44
Beard 12 181 40N22'25 86W27'02 5:45:48
Beardstown 66 181 41N08'17 86W36'09 5:46:25
Bear Lake 57 30 41N24 85W26 5:41:44
Bear Wallow 7 147 39N19'25 86W22'08 5:45:29
Beatrice 64 2 41N25'37 87W11'22 5:48:45
Beattys Corner 46 9 41N37'20 86W53'38 5:47:35
Beatys Beach 44 30 41N41'03 85W36'13 5:42:25
Beaver City 56 2 40N54'25 87W24'56 5:49:40
Beaver Dam 43 291 41N04 86W00 5:44:00
Becks Grove 7 147 39N04'45 86W07'00 5:44:28
Becks Mill 88 165 38N32'07 86W09'20 5:44:37
Beckville 54 147 40N00'38 86W42'35 5:46:50
Bedford 47 345 38N51'40 86W29'14 5:45:57
Bedford Heights 47 345 38N51 86W30 5:46:00
Beecamp 39 97 38N45 85W19 5:41:16
Beech Brook 73 101 39N33'08 85W47'52 5:43:11
Beech Creek 28 193 39N07 86W45 5:47:00
Beech Grove 49 100 39N43'19 86W05'24 5:44:22
Beech Grove 55 101 39N31'02 86W26'47 5:45:47
Beechwood 13 169 38N12'24 86W25'28 5:45:42
Beehunter 28 194 38N57'22 87W07'16 5:48:29
Bee Ridge 11 89 39N32'13 87W10'10 5:48:41
Beesons 89 317 39N43'19 85W11'55 5:40:48
Behlmer Corner 69 275 39N12'09 85W10'11 5:40:41
Belknap 10 166 38N19 85W44 5:42:56
Belknap 82 55 37N59'00 87W41'17 5:50:45
Bell Center 91 181 40N52'07 86W38'21 5:46:33
Belle Arbor 49 100 39N43'13 85W59'15 5:43:57
Belle Union 67 128 39N34'23 86W42'22 5:46:49
Belleview 39 97 38N51'21 85W22'41 5:41:31
Belleville 32 247 39N40'38 86W29'18 5:45:57
Bellfountain 38 291 40N26'00 84W51'49 5:39:27
Bellmore 61 128 39N45'33 87W06'19 5:48:25
Bell Rohr Park 43 291 41N19'54 85W46'52 5:43:07
Belmont 7 145 39N09'07 86W20'50 5:45:23
Belmont 33 253 39N55'18 85W20'59 5:41:24
Belshaw 45 26 41N15'23 87W27'12 5:49:49
Ben Davis 49 100 39N45 86W14 5:44:56
Benefiel Corner 13 71 39N07'42 87W24'32 5:49:38
Bengal 73 101 39N28'24 85W55'22 5:43:41
Benham 69 275 38N59'01 85W15'01 5:41:00
Bennetts Switch 52 331 40N35'06 86W06'46 5:44:27
Bennettsville 10 166 38N25'32 85W48'31 5:43:14
Bennington 78 35 38N51'32 85W08'26 5:40:34
Benton 20 261 41N30'33 85W45'40 5:43:03
Bentonville 21 274 39N44'43 86W11'39 5:44:47
Benwood 11 89 39N33'40 87W06'51 5:48:27
Berlien 76 30 41N38'12 84W52'36 5:39:30
Berne 1 230 40N39'28 84W57'07 5:39:48
Berwick Manor 73 101 39N33 85W48 5:43:12
Bethany 3 147 39N10'26 86W03'55 5:44:16
Bethany 55 101 39N31'57 86W22'33 5:45:30
Bethany 61 126 39N51'15 87W08'50 5:48:35
Bethel 18 253 40N15'00 85W32'02 5:42:08
Bethel 65 58 38N13 87W56 5:51:44
Bethel 89 315 39N59'12 84W49'49 5:39:19
Bethel Village 3 147 39N09'07 85W55'29 5:43:42
Bethlehem 10 166 38N32'21 85W25'14 5:41:41
Between-the-Lakes Park 43 291 41N19'29 85W44'12 5:42:57
Beverly Hill 64 4 41N32'56 86W59'08 5:47:57
Beverly Shores 64 9 41N41'33 86W58'39 5:47:55
Bicknell 42 74 38N46'27 87W18'28 5:49:14
Big Creek 91 147 40N41 86W52 5:47:28
Bigger 40 128 38N57 85W30 5:42:00
Big Hill 25 328 41N02'43 86W11'45 5:44:47
Big Lake 57 30 41N12 85W28 5:41:52
Big Springs 6 97 40N04'13 86W15'38 5:45:03
Billingsville 81 313 39N33'21 84W54'35 5:39:38
Billtown 11 89 39N30'36 87W11'10 5:48:45
Billville 11 89 39N30'13 87W07'32 5:48:30
Bippus 35 289 40N56'39 85W37'26 5:42:30
Birchim 46 2 41N42'37 86W36'10 5:46:25
Birdseye 19 67 38N19'00 86W41'45 5:46:47
Birmingham 52 335 40N56'16 86W06'34 5:44:26
Black 65 58 37N58 87W54 5:51:36
Blackhawk 2 233 41N06 85W08 5:40:32
Blackhawk 84 82 39N18'32 87W18'01 5:49:12
Blackhawk Beach 64 6 41N31'04 87W02'28 5:48:10
Blackhawk Forest 2 233 41N06 85W08 5:40:32
Blackiston Heights 10 166 38N18 85W45 5:43:00
Blackiston Mill 22 166 38N20'08 85W47'53 5:43:12
Blackiston Village 10 166 38N18 85W45 5:43:00
Black Oak 14 85 38N39'45 87W04'52 5:48:19
Black Oak 45 6 41N33'58 87W23'37 5:49:34
Black Point 43 291 41N24'18 85W41'01 5:42:44
Black Rock 86 129 40N22'04 87W05'49 5:48:23
Blaine 38 291 40N24'09 85W03'22 5:40:13
Blairsville 65 58 38N04'44 87W45'43 5:51:03
Blanford 83 73 39N39'54 87W31'14 5:50:05
Blocher 72 320 38N43'05 85W39'24 5:42:38
Bloods Wood Crossing 42 86 38N32'19 87W37'49 5:50:31
Bloomer 48 101 40N05'02 85W46'05 5:43:04
Bloomfield 28 192 39N01'37 86W56'15 5:47:45
Bloomfield 38 291 40N30'42 84W58'26 5:39:54
Bloomfield 74 61 38N01'28 87W05'47 5:48:23
Bloomingdale 61 128 39N50'00 87W14'59 5:49:00
Blooming Grove 24 275 39N30'08 85W03'53 5:40:16
Bloomingport 68 307 40N01'37 84W59'41 5:39:59
Bloomington 53 340 39N09'55 86W31'35 5:46:06
Blountsville 33 253 40N03'36 85W14'25 5:40:58
Blue 58 33 38N55'30 85W00'17 5:40:01
Blue Creek 1 228 40N42 84W51 5:39:24
Blue Creek 24 30 39N14 85W06 5:40:24
Bluegrass 25 328 41N01 86W24 5:45:36
Blue Lake 92 228 41N14 85W19 5:41:16
Blue Lick 10 166 38N30'30 85W48'17 5:43:13
Blue Ridge 73 101 39N31'09 85W38'08 5:42:33
Blue River 88 165 38N31'48 85W56'22 5:43:45
Bluff Creek 41 97 39N33'27 86W13'15 5:44:53
Bluff Point 38 291 40N20'45 84W58'38 5:39:55
Bluffs 55 101 39N34'08 86W15'04 5:45:00
Bluffside 46 8 41N37 86W44 5:46:56
Bluffton 90 228 40N44'19 85W10'18 5:40:41
Bobtown 36 147 39N01'10 85W56'46 5:43:47
Bogard 14 85 38N47 87W04 5:48:16
Boggstown 73 101 39N33'47 85W54'59 5:43:40
Bogle Corner 11 89 39N10'39 87W11'05 5:48:44
Bolivar 4 148 40N31 87W09 5:48:36
Bolivar 85 269 40N57'51 85W47'15 5:43:09
Bonair 45 6 41N30 87W19 5:49:16
Bonds 59 160 38N40'52 86W37'46 5:46:31
Bonnell 15 33 39N10'06 84W58'27 5:39:54
Bonnenburger 10 166 38N18 85W45 5:43:00
Bonneyville Mills 20 259 41N43'05 85W45'55 5:43:04
Bono 47 344 38N43'53 86W19'16 5:45:17
Bono 83 73 39N45'37 87W29'38 5:49:59
Boon 87 53 38N04 87W16 5:49:04
Boone Grove 64 28 41N21'17 87W07'46 5:48:31
Boonville 87 54 38N02'57 87W16'27 5:49:06
Borden 10 166 38N28'00 85W56'45 5:43:47
Boston 89 315 39N44'28 84W51'07 5:39:24
Boston Corner 2 228 40N56'54 84W54'01 5:39:36
Boswell 4 135 40N31'16 87W22'42 5:49:31
Boundary City 38 291 40N20'40 84W55'19 5:39:41
Bourbon 50 326 41N17'44 86W06'59 5:44:28
Bowers 54 149 40N09'25 86W43'29 5:46:54
Bowerstown 35 287 40N53'19 85W26'33 5:41:46
Bowling Green 61 89 39N22'59 87W00'42 5:48:03
Bowman 63 59 38N29'47 87W20'49 5:49:23
Boxley 29 97 40N09'58 86W10'32 5:44:42
Boyd 70 101 39N43'07 85W33'04 5:42:12
Boyleston 12 181 40N17'11 86W23'41 5:45:35
Bracken 35 287 40N59'12 85W37'26 5:42:30
Bradfield Corner 61 73 39N43'56 87W17'56 5:49:12
Bradford 31 166 38N22'04 86W03'43 5:44:15
Bradford Park 18 254 40N11 85W26 5:41:44
Bradford Village 27 284 40N34 85W42 5:42:48
Bradley 74 61 38N01 87W02 5:48:08
Bramble 51 200 38N43 86W55 5:47:40
Branchville 62 69 38N09'49 86W34'47 5:46:19
Braxton 59 160 38N34 86W28 5:45:52
Braysville 15 33 39N17'17 84W52'11 5:39:29
Braysville 60 344 39N12'42 86W46'28 5:47:06
Braytown 78 35 38N43'50 85W09'31 5:40:38
Brazil 11 90 39N31'25 87W07'30 5:48:30
Breckenridge 31 166 38N13'04 86W01'59 5:44:08
Breezewood 27 284 40N34 85W42 5:42:48
Breezewood Park 18 254 40N11 85W23 5:41:32
Breezy Point 8 162 40N41'31 86W45'11 5:47:01
Bremen 50 218 41N26'47 86W08'53 5:44:36
Brems 75 221 41N20'21 86W41'51 5:46:47
Brendan Wood 6 247 40N04'02 86W28'08 5:45:53
Brendonwood 49 100 39N51'28 86W03'50 5:44:15
Brentwood 48 101 40N05'51 85W42'55 5:42:52
Brent Woods 73 101 39N32'18 85W45'25 5:43:02
Bretzville 19 67 38N17'58 86W52'23 5:47:30
Brewersville 40 128 39N05'04 85W36'42 5:42:27
Brewington Woods 18 254 40N11 85W23 5:41:32
Briarwood 55 101 39N33'03 86W30'24 5:46:02
Brice 38 291 40N25'05 84W53'47 5:39:35
Brick Chapel 67 128 39N42'42 86W52'09 5:47:29
Bridgeport 31 166 38N10'34 85W54'23 5:43:38
Bridgeport 49 100 39N43'56 86W19'02 5:45:16
Bridgeton 61 89 39N38'42 87W10'39 5:48:43
Brierwood Hills 2 233 41N03'19 85W14'03 5:40:56
Briggs 92 228 41N05'08 85W28'13 5:41:53
Bright 15 33 39N13'06 84W51'22 5:39:25
Brighton 44 30 41N43'20 85W18'40 5:41:15
Brightwood 49 100 39N48 86W06 5:44:24
Brimfield 57 32 41N27'15 85W23'53 5:41:36
Brinckley 68 307 40N15 85W10 5:40:40
Bringhurst 8 164 40N31'31 86W31'30 5:46:06

Brinker Heights 27 284 40N34 85w42 5:42:48
Brisco 86 129 40N24'40 87w21'30 5:49:26
Bristol 20 263 41N43'17 85w49'03 5:43:16
Bristow 62 69 38N08'24 86w43'18 5:46:53
Broadmoor 49 100 39N50'56 86w12'51 5:44:51
Broad Ripple 49 100 39N52 86w07 5:44:28
Broadview 27 284 40N34 85w42 5:42:48
Broadview 53 344 39N08'23 86w32'18 5:46:09
Broadview Park Plaza 47 344 38N51 86w30 5:46:00
Bromer 59 160 38N35'37 86w20'09 5:45:21
Brook 56 226 40N51'59 87w21'49 5:49:27
Brookfield 73 101 39N38'16 85w56'34 5:43:46
Brookhaven 27 284 40N31'11 85w36'57 5:42:28
Brook Knoll 47 344 38N51 86w30 5:46:00
Brooklyn 55 108 39N32'21 86w22'09 5:45:29
Brookmoor 55 97 39N34'03 86w22'29 5:45:30
Brooks 29 97 40N03 86w01 5:44:04
Brooksburg 39 97 38N44'11 85w14'37 5:40:58
Brookside Estates 2 233 41N08'48 85w04'45 5:40:19
Brookside Estates 84 77 39N26 87w24 5:49:36
Brookston 91 147 40N36'10 86w52'02 5:47:28
Brook Trails 71 208 41N43 86w15 5:45:00
Brookville 24 30 39N25'23 85w00'46 5:40:03
Brookville Heights 30 97 39N43'28 85w54'24 5:43:38
Brookwood 43 297 41N14 85w51 5:43:24
Brookwood 45 6 41N30 87w19 5:49:16
Broom Hill 10 166 38N26'56 85w52'39 5:43:31
Brown Jug Corner 84 82 39N17'17 87w15'32 5:49:02
Brown Landing 31 166 37N59'32 86w01'52 5:44:07
Brownsburg 32 97 39N50'36 86w23'52 5:45:35
Browns Corner 35 289 40N48'54 85w24'42 5:41:39
Browns Crossing 55 101 39N24'23 86w30'20 5:46:01
Brownstown 13 169 38N20 86w28 5:45:52
Brownstown 36 141 38N52'44 86w02'31 5:44:10
Browns Valley 54 149 39N54'11 86w59'31 5:47:58
Brownsville 81 313 39N39'52 85w00'17 5:40:01
Browntown 13 169 38N22'51 86w30'11 5:46:01
Bruce, Lake 25 328 41N04'13 86w27'52 5:45:51
Bruce Lake Station 25 327 41N04'10 86w24'53 5:45:40
Bruceville 42 87 38N45'34 87w24'56 5:49:40
Brummitt Acres 64 4 41N37'08 87w01'01 5:48:04
Brunerstown 67 128 39N39'09 86w59'54 5:48:00
Brunswick 11 89 39N11'49 87w07'12 5:48:29
Brunswick 45 2 41N22'40 87w30'29 5:50:02
Brushy Prairie 44 30 41N38'30 85w14'51 5:40:59
Bryant 38 288 40N32'00 84w57'50 5:39:51
Bryantsburg 39 97 38N53'09 85w22'28 5:41:30
Bryantsville 47 344 38N46'07 86w34'23 5:46:18
Buchanan Corner 11 89 39N11'33 87w12'12 5:48:49
Buck Creek 30 98 39N49 85w54 5:43:36
Buck Creek 79 152 40N29'16 86w45'41 5:47:03
Buckeye 35 287 40N41'28 85w21'14 5:41:25
Buckskin 26 59 38N13'42 87w24'43 5:49:39
Bucktown 77 80 38N59'41 87w15'36 5:49:02
Bud 41 97 39N26'49 86w10'33 5:44:42
Buddha 47 344 38N47'31 86w24'24 5:45:38
Buena Vista 24 275 39N26'20 85w16'21 5:41:05
Buena Vista 31 166 38N03'32 85w58'48 5:43:55
Buena Vista 68 307 40N07'14 85w04'23 5:40:18
Buffalo 58 38 39N01'14 84w53'02 5:39:32
Buffalo 91 181 40N52'57 86w44'43 5:46:59
Buffaloville 74 64 38N05'51 86w57'55 5:47:52
Buffington 45 6 41N38'14 87w25'33 5:49:42
Bufkin 65 58 37N59'16 87w50'45 5:51:23
Bugtown 65 58 38N10 87w47 5:51:08
Bullocktown 87 53 37N58'29 87w13'22 5:48:53
Bunker Hill 21 272 39N38'00 85w54'51 5:43:39
Bunker Hill 42 86 38N45 87w31 5:50:04
Bunker Hill 52 336 40N39'37 86w06'10 5:44:25
Bunker Hill 55 101 39N33'59 86w26'29 5:45:46
Bunker Hill 88 165 38N36 86w06 5:44:24
Burdick 64 4 41N36'04 86w58'22 5:47:53
Burge Terrace 49 100 39N44'36 85w59'47 5:43:59
Burglen Hills 62 69 37N57 86w46 5:47:04
Burket 43 296 41N09'19 85w58'07 5:43:52
Burlington 8 165 40N28'49 86w23'41 5:45:35
Burlington Beach 64 6 41N30'21 87w02'43 5:48:11
Burnett 84 82 39N32'34 87w17'44 5:49:11
Burnettsville 91 183 40N45'40 86w35'37 5:46:22
Burney 16 101 39N19'02 85w38'25 5:42:34
Burns City 51 323 38N49'21 86w53'13 5:47:33
Burns Harbor 64 4 41N37'05 87w08'00 5:48:32
Burnsville 3 147 39N10'22 85w44'25 5:42:58
Burr Oak 50 213 41N15'23 86w24'55 5:45:40
Burr Oak 67 30 41N19'23 85w25'59 5:41:44
Burrows 8 174 40N40'36 86w30'27 5:46:02
Bushrod 28 95 38N58'08 87w06'32 5:48:26
Busseron 42 86 38N50'08 87w26'57 5:49:48
Butler 17 235 41N25'47 84w52'17 5:39:29
Butler Center 17 228 41N18'30 85w08'12 5:40:33
Butlerville 40 128 39N02'04 85w30'46 5:42:03
Buttermilk Point 43 291 41N22'38 85w40'27 5:42:42
Byrneville 31 166 38N19'39 86w02'37 5:44:10
Byron 46 2 41N39'22 86w37'29 5:46:30
Byron 61 128 39N54'13 87w06'20 5:48:25
Caborn 65 58 37N58'14 87w47'31 5:51:10
Cadiz 33 253 39N57'05 85w29'12 5:41:57
Caesar Creek 15 33 38N58 85w05 5:40:20
Cagle Mill 67 344 39N29'14 86w56'23 5:47:46
Cain 23 156 40N05 87w10 5:48:40
Cairo 79 147 40N32'27 86w55'29 5:47:42
Cale 51 159 38N47'45 86w45'05 5:47:00
Caledonia 13 71 39N05'56 87w20'06 5:49:20
California 75 221 41N13 86w39 5:46:36
Calumet 45 6 41N33 87w24 5:49:36
Calvertville 28 193 39N06'59 86w54'14 5:47:37
Cambria 12 181 40N21'57 86w33'33 5:46:14
Cambridge City 89 317 39N48'45 85w10'18 5:40:41
Camby 49 98 38N45'25 86w00'33 5:44:02
Camden 8 164 40N36'31 86w32'24 5:46:10
Cammack 18 253 40N12'35 85w29'33 5:41:58
Campbell Corner 13 80 39N08'34 87w24'32 5:49:38
Campbellsburg 88 164 38N39'05 86w15'40 5:45:03
Campbelltown 63 59 38N25'17 87w14'24 5:48:58
Camp Brosend 87 53 37N57'52 87w23'45 5:49:35
Camp Roberts 7 145 39N10'42 86w11'37 5:44:46
Camp Shor 58 33 38N59'53 84w50'57 5:39:24
Canaan 39 97 38N52'00 85w17'45 5:41:11
C And C Beach 8 162 40N42'12 86w45'23 5:47:02
Candleglo Village 73 101 39N33'27 85w47'31 5:43:10
Candle Light Village 3 147 39N13 85w54 5:43:36
Cannelburg 14 85 38N40'11 86w59'54 5:48:00
Cannelton 62 68 37N54'41 86w44'40 5:46:59
Cantaloupe 42 86 38N31'53 87w31'10 5:50:05
Canton 88 165 37N37'03 86w07'58 5:44:32
Capehart 14 85 38N44'44 87w11'39 5:48:47
Cape Sandy 13 169 38N09'03 86w22'15 5:45:29
Carbon 11 89 39N35'52 87w07'07 5:48:28
Carbondale 86 156 40N21'36 87w20'52 5:49:23
Cardonia 11 89 39N33'42 87w07'08 5:48:29
Carey 29 97 40N03 86w01 5:44:04
Carlisle 77 72 38N58'06 87w24'20 5:49:37
Carlos 68 307 40N01'35 85w02'04 5:40:08
Carlos City 68 307 40N01 85w01 5:40:04
Carmel 29 244 39N58'42 86w07'05 5:44:28
Carp 60 344 39N23'06 86w45'39 5:47:03
Carpenter 37 224 40N47 87w11 5:48:44
Carpentersville 67 128 39N48'20 86w48'20 5:47:13
Carriage Estates 3 147 39N13 85w54 5:43:36
Carriage Estates 30 97 39N44'15 85w53'38 5:43:35
Carrollton 8 165 40N31'04 86w23'31 5:45:34
Carter 74 65 38N10 86w57 5:47:48
Cartersburg 32 248 39N41'55 86w27'49 5:45:51
Carthage 70 101 39N44'18 85w34'19 5:42:17
Carwood 10 166 38N26'54 85w51'50 5:43:27
Cascade 53 344 39N11'26 86w32'20 5:46:09
Cascade Heights 53 344 39N12 86w37 5:46:28
Cass 13 71 39N05'13 87w16'43 5:49:07
Cassville 34 331 40N33'36 86w07'22 5:44:29
Castleton 49 100 39N54'25 86w03'08 5:44:13
Cataract 60 344 39N25'39 86w48'59 5:47:16
Cates 23 156 39N59'48 87w20'16 5:49:21
Catlin 61 126 39N41'37 87w14'07 5:48:56
Cato 63 59 38N26'12 87w11'08 5:48:45
Cayuga 83 75 39N56'55 87w27'35 5:49:50
Cedar 17 228 41N18'46 85w09'22 5:40:37
Cedar Canyons 2 228 41N13'58 85w05'21 5:40:21
Cedar Creek 17 228 41N21 85w09 5:40:36
Cedar Farm Landing 31 166 37N58'23 86w03'44 5:44:15
Cedar Grove 24 30 39N21'23 84w42'48 5:38:51
Cedar Lake 45 15 41N21'53 87w26'28 5:49:46
Cedar Point 43 291 41N23'52 85w40'31 5:42:42
Cedar Point 91 162 40N42'32 86w45'37 5:47:02
Cedar Shores 2 228 41N13'39 85w04'20 5:40:17
Cedarville 2 228 41N12'13 85w01'19 5:40:05
Celestine 19 67 38N23'05 86w46'45 5:47:07
Celina 62 69 38N11'17 86w36'46 5:46:27
Cemar Estates 84 82 39N42 86w51 5:47:24
Cementville 10 166 38N20'59 85w44'46 5:42:59
Centenary 83 73 39N39'30 87w28'24 5:49:54
Centennial 23 156 39N58 87w17 5:49:08
Center 34 330 40N26'04 86w03'38 5:44:15
Center 38 291 40N26'42 85w04'37 5:40:18
Center 87 52 38N02'55 87w20'35 5:49:22
Center Point 61 89 39N25'01 87w04'38 5:48:19
Center Square 78 35 38N50'11 85w01'53 5:40:08
Centerton 55 108 39N30'54 86w23'42 5:45:35
Center Valley 55 97 39N30'49 86w24'32 5:45:38
Centerville 74 61 37N59'39 87w03'48 5:48:15
Centerville 89 316 39N49'04 84w59'47 5:39:59
Central 31 166 38N05'59 86w09'31 5:44:38
Central Barren 31 166 38N21'51 86w05'47 5:44:23
Ceylon 1 228 40N36'24 84w57'12 5:39:49
Chain-o-Lakes 71 202 41N42'30 86w22'48 5:45:31
Chalmers 91 147 40N39'47 86w52'10 5:47:29
Chambersburg 23 156 40N07'12 87w14'58 5:49:00
Chambersburg 59 160 38N31'05 86w23'32 5:45:34
Champion 84 77 39N28 87w26 5:49:44
Champlin Meadows 55 101 39N24'27 86w26'12 5:45:45
Chandler 63 59 38N25'17 87w21'08 5:49:25
Chandler 87 53 37N57'11 87w22'33 5:49:30
Chapel Bluff 3 147 39N13 85w54 5:43:36
Chapel Hill 49 100 39N46'30 86w16'55 5:45:08
Chapel Hill 53 344 38N59'54 86w26'57 5:45:48
Chapel Manor 45 6 41N28'34 87w19'54 5:49:20
Charlesmac Village 49 100 39N41'03 85w58'45 5:43:55
Charlestown 10 167 38N27'11 85w40'13 5:42:41
Charle Sumac Estates 49 100 39N40'43 85w58'28 5:43:54
Charlottesville 30 108 39N47'25 85w36'46 5:42:27
Charlottesville 81 30 39N32'10 84w51'11 5:39:25
Chase 4 147 40N31'10 87w20'31 5:49:22
Chatterton 86 129 40N24'13 87w14'23 5:48:58
Chelsea 39 113 38N39'02 85w31'30 5:42:06
Cherokee Terrace 10 166 38N18 85w45 5:43:00
Cherry Grove 54 147 40N08'08 86w54'16 5:47:37
Cherry Grove Tabernacle 68 307 40N01'10 84w58'44 5:39:55
Cherryvale 84 89 39N27'48 87w14'22 5:48:57
Chester 89 318 39N53'17 84w53'16 5:39:33
Chesterfield 48 108 40N06'45 85w35'49 5:42:23
Chesterton 29 100 39N55'44 86w07'15 5:44:29
Chesterton 64 4 41N36'38 87w03'51 5:48:15
Chesterville 15 33 39N04'04 85w03'08 5:40:13
Chestnut Hill 64 4 41N37 87w06 5:48:24
Chestnut Ridge 36 147 38N53'19 85w51'37 5:43:26
Chicago Avenue 45 6 41N38 87w28 5:49:52
Chili 52 338 40N51'36 86w01'35 5:44:06
China 39 97 38N49'33 85w20'18 5:41:21
Chippewa 71 208 41N38 86w14 5:44:56
Chrisney 74 62 38N00'53 87w02'11 5:48:09
Christiansburg 7 147 39N05'19 86w09'22 5:44:37
Churubusco 92 230 41N13'50 85w19'10 5:41:17
Cicero 29 97 40N07'26 86w00'48 5:44:03
Cicero Heights 80 121 40N18 86w03 5:44:12
Cincinnati 28 193 39N01'12 86w43'44 5:46:55
Circle Park 76 30 41N32'59 84w54'36 5:39:38
Circleville 70 101 39N36'01 85w26'21 5:41:45
Clanricarde 64 2 41N17'18 86w56'58 5:47:48
Clare 29 97 40N03 86w01 5:44:04
Clarke Junction 45 6 41N37'48 87w24'59 5:49:40
Clarksburg 16 101 39N26'00 85w20'52 5:41:23
Clarksdale 7 147 39N12'00 86w07'34 5:44:30
Clarks Hill 79 147 40N14'49 86w43'30 5:46:54
Clarks Landing 76 30 41N33'35 84w54'42 5:39:39
Clarksville 10 176 38N18 85w46 5:43:04
Clarksville 29 97 40N01'56 85w54'45 5:43:39
Clarkville 10 166 38N17'48 85w45'36 5:43:02
Clay City 11 89 39N16'36 87w06'46 5:48:27
Clay City 74 64 38N04'57 86w57'06 5:47:48
Claypool 43 292 41N07'45 85w52'50 5:43:31
Claysville 88 165 38N37'21 86w17'22 5:45:09
Clayton 32 252 39N41'21 86w31'21 5:46:05
Clear Creek 53 343 39N06'33 86w32'24 5:46:10
Clear Lake 76 30 41N45'05 84w50'21 5:39:21
Clear Spring 36 147 38N55'30 86w12'36 5:44:50
Clearspring 44 30 41N34 85w29 5:41:56
Clermont 49 100 39N48'35 86w19'21 5:45:17
Clermont Heights 32 98 39N49'36 86w20'39 5:45:23
Cleveland 30 108 39N47'25 85w38'41 5:42:35
Clifford 3 149 39N16'56 85w52'09 5:43:29
Clifton 81 313 39N41'25 84w57'21 5:39:49
Clifty 3 147 39N14 85w44 5:42:56
Clifty Village 3 147 39N13 85w54 5:43:36
Clinton 69 30 39N12'38 85w07'55 5:40:32
Clinton 83 76 39N39'25 87w23'53 5:49:36
Clinton Falls 67 128 39N43'09 86w57'50 5:47:51
Cloud Crest Hills 7 145 39N12 86w15 5:45:00
Cloverdale 67 128 39N30'53 86w47'38 5:47:11
Cloverland 11 89 39N30'05 87w13'53 5:48:56
Clover Village 73 101 39N36'27 85w51'33 5:43:26
Clunette 43 291 41N19'11 85w55'22 5:43:41
Clymers 9 164 40N42'27 86w26'56 5:45:48
Coal Bluff 84 82 39N34'58 87w13'12 5:48:53
Coal City 60 199 39N13'49 87w02'45 5:48:11
Coal Creek 23 187 40N02'11 87w22'50 5:49:31
Coalmont 11 89 39N11'36 87w13'52 5:48:55
Coatesville 32 115 39N41'16 86w40'13 5:46:41

Coats Spring 63 59 38N26'15 87W23'26 5:49:34
Cobb 84 82 39N34'52 87W13'24 5:48:54
Cobbs Corner 64 12 41N26'05 87W06'36 5:48:26
Coburg 64 2 41N31'08 86W56'58 5:47:48
Cochran 15 33 39N03'08 84W55'14 5:39:41
Coe 63 59 38N19 87W16 5:49:04
Coesse 92 228 41N07'40 85W23'43 5:41:35
Coesse Corners 92 228 41N08'24 85W23'45 5:41:35
Coffey 7 145 39N12 86W15 5:45:00
Cofield Corner 58 33 38N57'10 84W57'31 5:39:50
Colburn 71 205 41N32'56 86W16'06 5:45:04
Colburn 79 147 40N31'07 86W42'47 5:46:51
Colburn Acres 71 205 41N32 86W15 5:45:00
Cold Springs 15 33 39N04'17 85W04'23 5:40:18
Cold Springs 76 30 41N33'21 84W54'32 5:39:38
Cole 27 280 40N28'47 85W47'14 5:43:09
Colfax 12 183 40N11'42 86W40'02 5:46:40
Collamer 92 228 41N04'33 85W39'53 5:42:40
College Corner 38 291 40N24'39 84W58'38 5:39:55
College Corner 48 103 40N18'21 85W50'31 5:43:22
College Corner 85 264 40N41'55 85W53'08 5:43:33
College Corner 89 317 39N50'18 85W04'14 5:40:17
College Crest 49 100 39N55'30 86W09'02 5:44:36
College Hill 9 165 40N46 86W22 5:45:28
College Meadows 29 100 39N56'07 86W08'25 5:44:34
Collegeville 37 226 40N54'42 87W09'19 5:48:37
Collett 38 295 40N22'30 84W59'57 5:40:00
Collins 92 230 41N11'51 85W23'12 5:41:33
Coloma 61 128 39N47'18 87W17'31 5:49:10
Colonial Hills 87 53 37N57 87W24 5:49:36
Colonial Park 84 77 39N26 87W24 5:49:36
Colonial Village 30 101 39N56'15 85W50'06 5:43:20
Columbia 21 272 39N34'35 85W12'26 5:40:50
Columbia City 92 236 41N09'26 85W29'18 5:41:57
Columbus 3 130 39N12'05 85W55'17 5:43:41
Commercial Place 67 128 39N39 86W52 5:47:28
Commiskey 40 128 38N51'34 85W38'44 5:42:35
Como 38 291 40N23'07 85W05'13 5:40:21
Concord 17 228 41N19'34 84W56'43 5:39:47
Concord 79 147 40N17'36 86W50'15 5:47:21
Concordia Gardens 2 233 41N08'44 85W06'24 5:40:26
Connersville 21 273 39N38'25 85W15'44 5:41:03
Conrad 56 2 41N06'18 87W26'36 5:49:46
Converse 5 196 40N23'22 85W14'21 5:40:57
Converse 52 337 40N34'39 85W52'24 5:43:30
Cook 45 16 41N22'38 87W28'11 5:49:53
Cool Spring 46 9 41N39 86W51 5:47:24
Coolwood Acres 64 6 41N27'33 87W05'14 5:48:21
Cooper Corner 30 97 39N52'18 85W46'12 5:43:05
Cope 55 101 39N27'01 86W19'08 5:45:17
Coppess Corner 1 228 40N44'42 84W57'25 5:39:50
Cordry Lake 7 147 39N21 86W07 5:44:28
Corkwell 38 291 40N28'02 85W03'31 5:40:14
Corn Brook 3 147 39N14'40 85W56'21 5:43:45
Cornelius 7 147 39N17'59 86W17'53 5:45:12
Cornettsville 14 85 38N45'24 87W06'36 5:48:26
Corning 14 85 38N34'58 87W01'03 5:48:04
Correct 69 275 39N00'31 85W17'11 5:41:09
Cortland 36 147 38N58'23 85W57'51 5:43:51
Corunna 17 237 41N26'14 85W08'50 5:40:35
Cory 11 89 39N22'56 87W12'21 5:48:49
Corydon 31 168 38N12'43 86W07'19 5:44:29
Corydon Junction 31 166 38N18'12 86W06'01 5:44:24
Cosperville 57 47 41N28'51 85W28'27 5:41:54
Cottage Grove 81 313 39N35'47 84W51'42 5:39:27
Cotton 78 35 38N52 85W01 5:40:04
Country Club Gardens 2 233 41N02'59 85W13'21 5:40:53
Country Club Heights 48 101 40N07'22 85W41'14 5:42:45
Country Club Meadows 82 55 38N01'23 87W34'23 5:50:18
Countryside Estates 2 233 41N06 85W08 5:40:32
Country Terrace 18 254 40N11 85W23 5:41:32
Courter 52 335 40N50'13 86W03'47 5:44:15
Courtney Corner 76 30 41N37'46 84W50'19 5:39:21
Coveyville 47 344 38N58'24 86W28'21 5:45:53
Covington 23 163 40N08'30 87W23'41 5:49:35
Covington Dells 2 233 41N04'10 85W13'59 5:40:56
Cowan 18 253 40N06'21 85W23'19 5:41:33
Coxton 47 344 38N49'46 86W33'40 5:46:15
Coxville 61 73 39N39'07 87W17'40 5:49:11
Cradick Corner 67 344 39N32'38 86W48'21 5:47:13
Craig 16 106 39N19'56 85W31'10 5:42:05
Craig 78 35 38N45 85W09 5:40:36
Craig Highlands 29 97 40N03 86W01 5:44:04
Craigville 90 228 40N46'42 85W05'27 5:40:22
Crandall 31 166 38N17'15 86W03'59 5:44:16
Crane 51 323 38N53'28 86W54'14 5:47:37
Crawford 47 344 38N51 86W30 5:46:00
Crawfordsville 54 131 40N02'28 86W52'28 5:47:30
Crawleyville 26 59 38N17'00 87W50'00 5:51:20
Creekwood 49 100 39N52'38 86W07'08 5:44:29
Cree Lake 57 30 41N26 85W16 5:41:04
Cresco 92 228 41N14'09 85W29'30 5:41:58
Crestlawn 48 102 40N04'29 85W40'49 5:42:43
Crest Manor Addition 71 208 41N36'59 86W14'00 5:44:56
Crestmoor 73 101 39N30'50 85W45'50 5:43:03
Creston 18 254 40N12'40 85W22'27 5:41:30
Creston 45 2 41N20'16 87W25'53 5:49:44
Crestview 3 147 39N13 85W54 5:43:36
Crestview 64 12 41N27'07 87W03'29 5:48:14
Crestview Heights 55 97 39N35'06 86W18'59 5:45:16
Crestwood 2 233 41N08'24 85W07'23 5:40:30
Crete 68 307 40N02'36 84W51'42 5:39:27
Crisman 64 23 41N35'13 87W10'26 5:48:42
Critchfield 41 100 39N36'01 86W09'48 5:44:39
Crocker 64 4 41N35'17 87W07'20 5:48:29
Crompton Hill 83 73 39N39'21 87W25'09 5:49:41
Cromwell 57 34 41N24'02 85W36'57 5:42:28
Crooked Lake 76 30 41N41 85W02 5:40:08
Cross Plains 69 275 38N56'38 85W12'17 5:40:49
Cross Roads 18 253 40N05'30 85W29'59 5:42:00
Cross Roads 69 275 39N16'46 85W14'30 5:40:58
Crossroad Temple 49 100 39N45'09 86W04'00 5:44:16
Crothersville 36 139 38N48'02 85W50'30 5:43:22
Crown Center 55 101 39N34'46 86W35'23 5:46:22
Crown Colony 2 233 41N04 85W09 5:40:36
Crown Point 45 5 41N25'01 87W21'55 5:49:28
Crows Nest 49 100 39N51'29 86W10'07 5:44:40
Crumb Corner 79 147 40N27'14 86W55'40 5:47:43
Crumley Crossing 5 196 40N23 85W13 5:40:52
Crump Estates 3 147 39N13 85W54 5:43:36
Crumstown 71 204 41N37'27 86W24'29 5:45:38
Crystal 19 67 38N29'40 86W44'57 5:47:00
Cuba 2 228 41N11'08 84W56'19 5:39:45
Cuba 3 302 39N20'45 85W58'09 5:43:53
Cuba 60 344 39N22'41 86W47'53 5:47:12
Culver 50 215 41N13'08 86W25'23 5:45:42
Cumback 14 85 38N33'31 87W08'51 5:48:35
Cumberland 49 98 39N46'34 85W57'26 5:43:50
Cunot 60 344 39N31 86W48 5:47:12
Curby 13 169 38N17'15 86W22'38 5:45:31
Curry 77 80 39N13 87W24 5:49:36
Curryville 13 80 39N11'13 87W23'33 5:49:34
Curryville 90 228 40N47'11 85W04'19 5:40:17
Curtisville 80 119 40N19'06 85W53'55 5:43:36
Cutler 8 164 40N28'35 86W31'27 5:46:06
Cuzco 19 67 38N28'30 86W43'22 5:46:53
Cyclone 12 181 40N13'42 86W25'57 5:45:44
Cynthiana 65 58 38N11'15 87W42'37 5:50:50
Cypress 82 55 37N54'51 87W37'47 5:50:31
Dabney 69 275 39N05'24 85W20'49 5:41:23
Daggett 60 199 39N12'56 87W02'20 5:48:09
Daisy Hill 10 165 38N29'47 85W56'16 5:43:45
Dale 74 65 38N10'08 86W59'24 5:47:58
Dalecarlia 45 2 41N19'51 87W23'41 5:49:35
Daleville 18 253 40N07'16 85W33'29 5:42:14
Dallas 35 287 40N53 85W36 5:42:24
Dalton 89 317 39N58 85W10 5:40:40
Dana 83 82 39N48'28 87W29'42 5:49:59
Danville 32 250 39N45'38 86W31'35 5:46:06
Dark Hollow 47 344 38N53'20 86W32'22 5:46:09
Darlington 54 149 40N06'36 86W46'19 5:47:05
Darlington Woods 54 149 40N07'11 86W48'19 5:47:13
Darmstadt 82 55 38N05'57 87W34'44 5:50:19
Darrough Chapel 34 332 40N28'43 86W05'44 5:44:23
Davidson 31 166 37N58'03 86W02'50 5:44:11
Davis 46 9 41N42'53 86W49'34 5:47:18
Dawnbury 49 100 39N52'11 86W07'15 5:44:29
Daylight 82 55 38N03'33 87W29'26 5:49:58
Dayton 79 132 40N22'27 86W46'08 5:47:05
Dayville 87 53 37N57'15 87W19'20 5:49:17
Deacon 9 165 40N38'02 86W19'02 5:45:16
Dead Mans Crossing 65 58 37N57'30 87W54'30 5:51:38
Decatur 1 232 40N50 84W56 5:39:44
Decker 42 86 38N31'08 87W31'23 5:50:06
Deedsville 52 335 40N54'37 86W06'04 5:44:24
Deep River 45 6 41N28'32 87W13'24 5:48:54
Deer Corner 28 166 38N12'37 85W53'43 5:43:35
Deer Creek 8 165 40N36'51 86W23'28 5:45:34
Deer Creek 45 6 41N25'14 87W15'29 5:49:02
Deerfield 3 149 39N13 85W54 5:43:36
Deerfield 68 310 40N16'43 84W58'35 5:39:54
Deerfield 84 77 39N26 87W24 5:49:36
Deer Mill 54 147 39N56'51 87W03'20 5:48:13
Deer Park 37 2 41N09'32 87W11'57 5:48:48
Deers Mills 54 147 39N52 87W03 5:48:12
Defries Landing 43 291 41N21'57 85W46'05 5:43:04
De Gonia Springs 87 53 38N03'20 87W11'08 5:48:45
Delaware 69 275 39N08'52 85W12'26 5:40:50
Delaware Trails 49 100 39N52'48 86W10'53 5:44:44
Delong 25 327 41N08'18 86W24'59 5:45:40
Delp 79 147 40N29'22 86W48'33 5:47:14
Delphi 8 133 40N35'15 86W40'30 5:46:42
Deming 29 97 40N06'55 86W05'55 5:44:24
Deming Park 84 77 39N27'58 87W21'16 5:49:25
Deming Woods 84 77 39N27'36 87W21'28 5:49:26
Democrat 8 165 40N28 86W31 5:46:04
Demotte 37 2 41N11'42 87W11'55 5:48:48
Denham 66 183 41N09'07 86W42'49 5:46:51
Denmark 60 199 39N16'11 87W01'33 5:48:06
Denny Corner 30 101 39N53'08 85W49'20 5:43:17
Denver 52 338 40N51'58 86W04'39 5:44:19
Depauw 31 166 38N20'06 86W13'03 5:44:52
Deputy 39 114 38N47'39 85W39'12 5:42:37
Derby 62 69 38N01'49 86W31'38 5:46:07
Desoto 18 253 40N14'49 85W17'37 5:41:10
Deuchars 13 169 38N10'20 86W26'54 5:45:48
Devonshire 49 100 39N52'50 86W03'32 5:44:14
Devore 60 344 39N25'47 86W45'10 5:47:01
Dewberry 69 275 38N57'04 85W09'06 5:40:36
Dewey 46 29 41N19 86W52 5:47:28
Dewey 84 77 39N30'34 87W22'33 5:49:30
Dexter 62 69 38N03'33 86W28'43 5:45:55
Diamond 61 89 39N36'41 87W09'58 5:48:40
Diamond Lake 43 291 41N08 85W53 5:43:32
Diamond Lake 57 47 41N28 85W29 5:41:56
Dickeyville 87 53 38N09'22 87W13'11 5:48:53
Dick Johnson 11 89 39N34 87W10 5:48:40
Dike 26 59 38N24 87W35 5:50:20
Dillman 90 196 40N36'37 85W25'44 5:41:43
Dillsboro 15 38 39N01'04 85W03'32 5:40:14
Dinwiddie 45 2 41N17'22 87W18'04 5:49:12
Disko 85 242 41N00'08 85W56'40 5:43:47
Dixie 31 166 38N09'36 86W12'44 5:44:51
Dixon 2 228 40N58 84W52 5:39:28
Dixon 28 128 39N46'24 87W01'14 5:48:05
Doans 28 193 38N55'09 86W50'58 5:47:24
Dodd 62 69 37N54'44 86W39'07 5:46:36
Dodds Bridge 13 80 39N09'26 87W31'26 5:50:06
Dogwood 31 166 38N06'19 86W05'04 5:44:20
Dolan 53 344 39N14'25 86W29'57 5:46:00
Domestic 90 228 40N36'42 85W05'19 5:40:21
Donaldson 50 214 41N21'40 86W26'39 5:45:47
Dongola 26 59 38N22'19 87W20'25 5:49:22
Doolittle Mills 62 69 38N15'03 86W36'11 5:46:25
Door Village 46 8 41N34'29 86W46'08 5:47:05
Dooville 27 284 40N33'12 85W33'36 5:42:14
Douglas 26 59 38N19'50 87W30'06 5:50:00
Dover 6 247 40N03'16 86W37'12 5:46:29
Dover 15 33 39N14'29 84W56'52 5:39:47
Dover Hill 51 322 38N43'30 86W48'10 5:47:13
Dovers View 80 121 40N18 86W03 5:44:12
Dowden Acres 84 77 39N26 87W24 5:49:36
Downey Corner 58 33 38N56'19 85W00'37 5:40:02
Downeyville 16 101 39N25'39 85W33'16 5:42:13
Doyle 52 335 40N48'29 86W04'27 5:44:18
Doyle Ferguson 27 284 40N34'43 85W28'44 5:41:55
Dresden 28 193 38N56 86W44 5:46:56
Dresser 84 77 39N28 87W26 5:49:44
Drew 18 254 40N13'08 85W23'13 5:41:33
Drewersburg 24 30 39N20'25 84W50'14 5:39:21
Drexel Gardens 49 100 39N44'26 86W14'47 5:44:59
Driftwood 36 147 38N49 86W08 5:44:32
Driftwood Hills 49 100 39N55'01 86W07'20 5:44:29
Dublin 89 317 39N48'44 85W12'32 5:40:50
Dubois 19 67 38N26'43 86W48'16 5:47:13
Dubois Crossroads 19 67 38N28'52 86W48'43 5:47:15
Duck Creek 48 101 40N21 85W49 5:43:16
Dudley 33 253 39N50 85W16 5:41:04
Dudleytown 36 147 38N50'59 85W53'59 5:43:36
Duff 19 67 38N19'38 87W01'35 5:48:06
Dugger 13 72 39N04'10 87W15'36 5:49:02
Duncan 22 166 38N17'17 85W55'30 5:43:42
Dundee 48 101 40N16'20 85W45'22 5:43:01
Dune Acres 64 3 41N38'58 87W05'09 5:48:21
Duneland Beach 46 9 41N43 86W53 5:47:32
Dunfee 92 233 41N05'12 85W20'14 5:41:21
Dunkirk 9 165 40N45'23 86W23'37 5:45:34
Dunkirk 38 300 40N22'31 85W12'34 5:40:50
Dunlap 20 271 41N38'16 85W55'18 5:43:41
Dunlapsville 81 313 39N35'27 84W59'37 5:39:58
Dunn 4 147 40N33'50 87W27'50 5:49:51
Dunnington 4 147 40N33'51 87W29'27 5:49:58
Dunn Mill 2 233 41N09'44 85W14'09 5:40:57
Dunns Bridge 37 2 41N13'32 86W58'26 5:47:54
Dunreith 33 257 39N48'12 85W26'19 5:41:45
Dupont 39 161 38N53'24 85W30'51 5:42:03
Durbin 29 98 40N03'23 85W54'39 5:43:39
Durham 26 56 38N15'35 87W34'52 5:50:19
Durham 46 8 41N35'32 86W50'15 5:47:21
Dutch Town 17 228 41N21 85W09 5:40:36
Dyer 45 1 41N29'39 87W31'18 5:50:05
Eagle 6 97 39N58 86W17 5:45:08
Eagle Creek 45 2 41N17 87W17 5:49:08
Eagle Hollow 39 97 38N45 85W19 5:41:16
Eagle Point 43 291 41N19'39 85W40'40 5:42:43
Eagletown 29 98 40N02'32 86W11'37 5:44:46
Eagle Village 6 100 39N57'38 86W14'44 5:44:59
Eaglewood Estates 6 100 39N57'05 86W18'47 5:45:15
Eames 87 53 38N04'45 87W07'54 5:48:32
Earle 82 55 38N05'08 87W30'48 5:50:03
Earlham 89 318 39N52 84W52 5:39:28
Earl Park 4 147 40N40'58 87W24'42 5:49:39
East Cedar Lake 45 15 41N22 87W24 5:49:36

East Chicago 45 6 41N38'21 87W27'17 5:49:49
East Clifford 3 147 39N13 85W54 5:43:36
East Columbus 3 130 39N12'06 85W54'06 5:43:36
East Connersville 21 273 39N40 85W08 5:40:32
East Enterprise 78 35 38N52'22 84W59'17 5:39:57
Eastern Heights 48 101 40N06'32 85W39'26 5:42:38
Eastern Heights 53 344 39N10'29 86W28'49 5:45:55
East Gary 45 6 41N35 87W14 5:48:56
Eastgate 3 147 39N13 85W54 5:43:36
Eastgate 10 166 38N18 85W45 5:43:00
Eastgate 30 100 39N55'51 85W49'47 5:43:19
East Germantown 89 317 39N48'45 85W08'15 5:40:33
East Glenn 84 77 39N29'09 87W17'44 5:49:11
East Haven 89 318 39N50'21 84W55'51 5:39:43
East Lake Estates 20 271 41N41'52 85W55'47 5:43:43
Eastland Gardens 2 233 41N01'11 85W06'01 5:40:24
East Liberty 2 230 40N56'08 84W51'42 5:39:27
East Montcello 91 162 40N44'46 86W44'47 5:46:59
East Monticello 91 162 40N44'46 86W45'12 5:47:01
East Mount Carmel 26 59 38N23'36 87W44'41 5:50:59
East Oolitic 47 344 38N53'56 86W30'43 5:46:03
East Park 12 171 40N17'04 86W29'32 5:45:58
Eastridge Manor 3 147 39N13 85W54 5:43:36
East Shelburn 13 80 39N10'28 87W22'47 5:49:31
East Shoals 51 322 38N40 86W47 5:47:08
East Union 80 97 40N13'02 86W07'42 5:44:31
Eastwich 79 134 40N25'37 86W51'00 5:47:24
Easytown 83 82 39N36'38 87W30'01 5:50:00
Eaton 18 253 40N20'25 85W21'03 5:41:24
Eby 87 53 38N08'31 87W15'41 5:49:03
Echo Crest 29 100 39N57'02 86W07'46 5:44:31
Echo Heights 18 254 40N11 85W23 5:41:32
Eckerty 13 169 38N19'13 86W36'43 5:46:27
Economy 89 315 39N58'41 85W05'17 5:40:21
Eddy 44 30 41N32'11 85W26'18 5:41:45
Eden 30 97 39N54'22 85W46'12 5:43:05
Eden 44 30 41N34 85W36 5:42:24
Edgerton 2 228 41N04'36 84W48'22 5:39:13
Edgewater 64 6 41N30'58 87W02'48 5:48:11
Edgewood 3 147 39N13 85W54 5:43:36
Edgewood 46 9 41N43 86W53 5:47:32
Edgewood 47 344 38N51 86W30 5:46:00
Edgewood 48 101 40N06'12 85W44'03 5:42:56
Edgewood 49 100 39N41'05 86W08'03 5:44:32
Edgewood Lake 67 128 39N38'22 86W47'57 5:47:12
Edgewood Park 2 233 41N04 85W09 5:40:36
Edgewood Village 48 101 40N06'05 85W45'11 5:43:01
Edinburg 41 302 39N21'15 85W58'00 5:43:52
Edison Park 71 208 41N41 86W12 5:44:48
Edna Mills 12 147 40N25'03 86W40'04 5:46:40
Edwardsport 42 87 38N48'43 87W15'08 5:49:01
Edwardsville 22 166 38N17'03 85W54'34 5:43:38
Eel 9 165 40N45 86W20 5:45:20
Eel River 11 89 39N19'24 87W07'25 5:48:30
Effner 56 241 40N46 87W34 5:50:16
Egans Point 67 30 41N20'09 85W21'38 5:41:27
Ege 67 30 41N17'34 85W17'16 5:41:09
Egypt 37 224 40N51'33 87W12'14 5:48:49
Ehrmandale 84 82 39N32'06 87W14'20 5:48:57
Ekin 80 97 40N13'01 86W09'42 5:44:39
Elberfeld 87 59 38N09'35 87W26'54 5:49:48
El Dorado 41 100 39N35'28 86W09'45 5:44:39
Elizabeth 31 166 38N07'16 85W58'27 5:43:54
Elizabethtown 3 149 39N08'06 85W48'48 5:43:15
Elizaville 6 251 40N07'36 86W22'33 5:45:30
Elkhart 20 271 41N40'55 85W58'36 5:43:54
Elkinsville 7 145 39N04'34 86W15'53 5:45:04
Ellettsville 53 344 39N14'02 86W37'30 5:46:30
Elliott 82 55 38N07'07 87W28'26 5:49:54
Ellis 28 93 39N03'49 87W13'22 5:48:53
Ellis 76 30 41N37'57 84W54'55 5:39:40
Elliston 28 193 39N01'40 86W58'15 5:47:53
Ellisville 2 233 41N01'05 85W17'03 5:41:08
Ellsworth 19 67 38N25'40 86W43'06 5:46:52
Elmdale 54 147 40N08'12 87W01'03 5:48:04
Elmhurst 48 101 40N05'52 85W43'17 5:42:53
Elmira 44 30 41N35'31 85W12'16 5:40:49
Elmore 14 85 38N52 87W04 5:48:16
Elm Tree Crossroads 1 228 40N47'18 84W57'22 5:39:49
Elmwood 6 247 40N04'04 86W27'43 5:45:51
Elmwood 52 335 40N42 86W07 5:44:28
Elnora 14 85 38N52'42 87W05'09 5:48:21
Elon 59 67 38N25'25 86W39'29 5:46:38
Elrod 69 275 39N03'17 85W09'50 5:40:39
Elston 79 147 40N23'35 86W54'35 5:47:38
Elwood 48 103 40N16'37 85W50'31 5:43:22
Elwren 53 344 39N06'31 86W40'11 5:46:41
Eminence 55 113 39N31'17 86W38'29 5:46:34
Emison 42 86 38N48'18 87W27'29 5:49:50
Emma 44 30 41N36'40 85W32'28 5:42:10
Emporia 48 101 40N00'16 85W38'02 5:42:32
Enchanted Hills 43 291 41N24'07 85W40'00 5:42:40
Englewood 47 344 38N50'40 86W29'53 5:46:00
English 13 169 38N20'04 86W27'51 5:45:51
English Lake 75 29 41N15'57 86W49'25 5:47:18
Enochsburg 24 101 39N20'03 85W17'51 5:41:11
Enos 56 2 41N00'50 87W26'57 5:49:48
Enos Corner 63 59 38N17'21 87W15'40 5:49:03
Enosville 63 59 38N18 87W16 5:49:04
Enterprise 74 61 37N50'33 87W10'55 5:48:44
Epsom 14 85 38N47'07 87W03'47 5:48:15
Epworth Forest 43 291 41N19'59 85W41'10 5:42:45
Erie 47 344 38N52'57 86W22'53 5:45:32
Erie 52 335 40N48'04 85W59'29 5:43:58
Ervin 34 165 40N31 86W18 5:45:12
Erwin 65 58 37N58'48 87W55'09 5:51:41
Ethel 59 169 38N24'13 86W31'28 5:46:06
Etna 92 228 41N16'25 85W34'25 5:42:18
Etna Green 43 295 41N17 86W03 5:44:12
Eugene 83 73 39N57'59 87W28'22 5:49:53
Eureka 47 344 38N52'15 86W33'46 5:46:15
Eureka 74 61 37N52'50 87W12'54 5:48:52
Evans Landing 31 166 38N00'15 85W59'05 5:43:56
Evanston 74 64 38N02'22 86W50'30 5:47:22
Evansville 82 55 37N58'29 87W33'21 5:50:13
Evergreen Acres 10 166 38N18 85W45 5:43:00
Everroad Park 3 147 39N13'42 85W53'17 5:43:33
Everroad Park West 3 147 39N13 85W54 5:43:36
Everton 21 272 39N33'46 85W05'23 5:40:22
Ewing 36 141 38N53'05 86W03'19 5:44:13
Ewington 16 101 39N19'35 85W34'05 5:42:16
Exchange 55 101 39N30'06 86W19'20 5:45:17
Extension Heights 48 102 40N06'17 85W39'37 5:42:38
Fair Acres 88 165 38N01'05 86W13'54 5:44:56
Fairbanks 13 80 39N13'10 87W31'20 5:50:05
Fairdale 31 166 38N19'34 86W10'16 5:44:41
Fairfax 2 233 41N02'31 85W05'18 5:40:21
Fairfax 48 102 40N06'15 85W39'00 5:42:36
Fairfield 2 233 41N03 85W09 5:40:36
Fairfield Center 17 237 41N28'57 85W07'41 5:40:31
Fair Grounds 49 100 39N50 86W09 5:44:36
Fairland 73 101 39N35'09 85W51'49 5:43:27
Fairlawn 3 147 39N13 85W54 5:43:36
Fairmount 27 280 40N24'55 85W39'02 5:42:36
Fair Oaks 37 2 41N04'30 87W15'27 5:49:02
Fairplay 28 193 39N02 87W00 5:48:00
Fairview 68 307 40N17'53 85W11'43 5:40:47
Fairview 70 101 39N41'08 85W18'04 5:41:12
Fairview 78 35 38N52'24 85W04'51 5:40:19
Fairview 88 344 38N44'17 86W16'03 5:45:04
Fairview Park 83 73 39N40'49 87W25'03 5:49:40
Fairwood Hills 49 100 39N53'00 86W01'48 5:44:07
Fall Creek Highlands 49 100 39N53'48 85W59'28 5:43:58
Falmouth 70 101 39N42'03 85W18'04 5:41:12
Farabee 88 165 38N33'25 86W00'57 5:44:04
Fargo 4 123 40N31'08 87W16'46 5:49:07
Fargo 59 169 38N24'00 86W29'00 5:45:56
Farlen 14 91 38N51'02 86W55'22 5:47:41
Farleys Addition 49 100 39N47'00 86W16'44 5:45:07
Farmers 60 344 39N10'31 86W53'30 5:47:34
Farmers 70 101 39N41'56 85W32'14 5:42:09
Farmersburg 77 80 39N14'55 87W22'55 5:49:32
Farmers Retreat 15 33 38N58 85W06 5:40:24
Farmersville 65 58 37N58'49 87W53'46 5:51:35
Farmington 70 101 39N37'05 85W21'32 5:41:26
Farmland 68 307 40N11'16 85W07'39 5:40:31
Farnsworth 13 71 39N05'57 87W19'25 5:49:18
Farrabee 88 165 38N36 86W06 5:44:24
Farrville 27 284 40N34'52 85W27'59 5:41:52
Fayette 6 247 39N55'52 86W23'50 5:45:35
Fayette 84 82 39N34 87W28 5:49:52
Fayetteville 47 344 38N51'39 86W35'43 5:46:23
Federal Hill 29 97 40N03 86W01 5:44:04
Fenn Haven 62 69 37N55'53 86W45'24 5:47:02
Fenns 73 108 39N27'27 85W47'52 5:43:11
Ferdinand 19 67 38N13'26 86W51'44 5:47:27
Ferguson Hill 84 77 39N28'54 87W27'23 5:49:50
Fern 67 128 39N39 86W52 5:47:28
Ferndale 61 128 39N42'26 87W04'01 5:48:16
Fewell Rhoades 55 101 39N25'17 86W23'58 5:45:36
Fiat 38 291 40N33'12 85W09'00 5:40:36
Fickle 45 17 41N35 87W21 5:49:24
Fieldcrest 29 97 40N13 86W02 5:44:08
Fields 55 97 39N32'46 86W20'00 5:45:20
Fillmore 67 126 39N40'03 86W45'12 5:47:01
Fincastle 67 128 39N48'29 86W53'42 5:47:35
Finley 72 320 38N41 85W51 5:43:24
Finly 30 97 39N42'18 85W49'22 5:43:17
Fishers 29 97 39N57'20 86W00'50 5:44:03
Fishersburg 48 101 40N04'19 85W51'34 5:43:26
Fisher's Woodland 29 97 40N03 86W01 5:44:04
Fisherville 87 53 38N02'43 87W25'59 5:49:44
Fish Lake 44 30 41N39 85W25 5:41:40
Fish Lake 46 2 41N34'00 86W33'07 5:46:12
Fishtown 31 166 38N04'10 85W55'03 5:43:40
Fiskville 69 149 40N02'55 86W53'41 5:47:35
Five Points 2 228 41N07 84W51 5:39:24
Five Points 39 97 38N50'46 85W30'33 5:42:02
Five Points 42 86 38N36'37 87W20'53 5:49:24
Five Points 55 97 39N34'53 86W19'01 5:45:16
Five Points 78 35 38N44'48 85W10'30 5:40:42
Five Points 81 315 39N42'43 84W51'07 5:39:24
Five Points 86 129 40N19'00 87W19'12 5:49:17
Five Points 90 196 40N34'54 85W19'12 5:41:17
Five Points 92 228 41N11'34 85W29'30 5:41:58
Five Points Corner 64 19 41N19'58 87W02'09 5:48:09
Flackville 49 100 39N47 86W13 5:44:52
Flat Iron 83 73 40N03'12 87W29'24 5:49:58
Flat Rock 73 108 39N21'51 85W49'54 5:43:20
Flat Rock Park 3 147 39N15'10 85W54'56 5:43:40
Fleener 53 344 39N16'57 86W24'45 5:45:39
Fleming 36 147 38N58'25 85W48'23 5:43:14
Fletcher 25 165 40N54'43 86W19'58 5:45:20
Flint 76 30 41N39'00 85W07'38 5:40:31
Flintwood 3 147 39N13 85W54 5:43:36
Flora 8 170 40N32'50 86W31'28 5:46:06
Flora 52 335 40N44'02 86W06'00 5:44:24
Florence 78 35 38N47'03 84W55'28 5:39:42
Florida 48 101 40N09'37 85W42'37 5:42:50
Florida 61 72 39N38 87W25 5:49:40
Floyd 67 128 39N44 86W44 5:46:56
Floyds Knobs 22 166 38N19'28 85W52'25 5:43:30
Foley 33 253 39N57'55 85W22'40 5:41:31
Folsomville 87 53 38N07'45 87W09'51 5:48:39
Fontanet 84 82 39N34'34 87W14'37 5:48:58
Foraker 20 262 41N30'57 85W55'27 5:43:42
Ford 65 58 37N58'45 87W45'16 5:51:01
Foresman 4 148 40N29'59 87W09'02 5:48:36
Foresman 56 226 40N51'58 87W17'42 5:49:11
Forest 12 181 40N22'25 86W19'58 5:45:20
Forest City 37 2 41N11'41 87W16'00 5:49:04
Forest Glen 43 291 41N19'36 85W45'49 5:43:03
Forest Hill 16 101 39N15'25 85W36'48 5:42:27
Forest Hill 65 55 37N58'42 87W36'35 5:50:26
Forest Hills 45 6 41N30 87W19 5:49:16
Forest Hills 48 101 40N07'25 85W41'48 5:42:47
Forest Lake 32 97 39N42 86W23 5:45:32
Forest Manor 46 9 41N43 86W53 5:47:32
Forest Park 3 147 39N14'09 85W54'53 5:43:40
Forest Park 76 30 41N33'02 84W55'31 5:39:42
Forest Park Beach 76 30 41N32 84W55 5:39:40
Forest Park Heights 53 344 39N12'34 86W35'19 5:46:21
Forest Ridge 2 233 41N01'19 85W16'24 5:41:06
Forest Ridge 27 284 40N34 85W42 5:42:48
Forest Ridge Estates 2 233 41N04 85W10 5:40:40
Forrest Hills 48 101 40N21 85W44 5:42:56
Fort Benjamin Harrison 49 100 39N52 86W02 5:44:08
Fort Branch 26 56 38N15'04 87W34'52 5:50:19
Fort Ritner 47 344 38N46'23 86W16'52 5:45:07
Fortville 30 97 39N55'56 85W50'53 5:43:24
Fort Wayne 2 233 41N07'50 85W07'44 5:40:31
Foster 86 187 40N08'48 87W28'17 5:49:53
Fountain 23 129 40N13'20 87W20'07 5:49:20
Fountain City 89 282 39N57'20 84W55'03 5:39:40
Fountain Park 37 224 40N46'45 87W09'42 5:48:39
Fountain Park 76 30 41N32 84W55 5:39:40
Fountain Square 49 100 39N44 86W06 5:44:24
Fountaintown 73 101 39N41'41 85W46'59 5:43:08
Four Corners 40 128 38N57'15 85W44'25 5:42:58
Four Presidents Corners 2 228 41N00'29 84W51'14 5:39:25
Fowler 4 147 40N37'00 87W19'15 5:49:17
Fowlerton 27 280 40N24'34 85W34'25 5:42:18
Fox 27 284 40N38'23 85W41'42 5:42:47
Foxglen 29 97 40N03 86W01 5:44:04
Fox Hill 55 100 39N36'02 86W17'02 5:45:08
Fox Lake 76 30 41N38 85W00 5:40:00
Fox Ridge 67 128 39N37'57 86W50'55 5:47:24
Frances 41 100 39N36'21 86W10'08 5:44:41
Francesville 66 181 40N59'07 86W52'46 5:47:31
Francisco 26 59 38N19'56 87W26'43 5:49:47
Frankfort 12 171 40N16'46 86W30'39 5:46:03
Franklin 41 104 39N28'50 86W03'18 5:44:13
Franklin 89 317 39N58'26 85W11'28 5:40:46
Franklin Hills 62 69 37N57 86W46 5:47:04
Frankton 48 108 40N13'22 85W46'44 5:43:07
Fredericksburg 31 165 38N25'59 86W11'23 5:44:46
Fredonia 13 169 38N10'41 86W22'59 5:45:32
Free 4 147 40N37'18 87W27'26 5:49:50
Freedom 60 108 39N12'25 86W52'09 5:47:29
Freeland Park 4 147 40N36'52 87W29'28 5:49:58
Freelandville 42 86 38N51'53 87W18'21 5:49:13
Freeman 60 344 39N11'43 86W44'01 5:46:56
Freeport 73 101 39N39'31 85W43'33 5:42:54
Freetown 36 147 38N58'23 86W07'46 5:44:31
Fremont 76 32 41N43'51 84W55'58 5:39:44
French 1 228 40N42 85W02 5:40:08
French 58 38 39N02 84W53 5:39:32
French Lake 84 77 39N26 87W24 5:49:36
French Lick 59 142 38N32'56 86W37'12 5:46:29
Frenchtown 31 166 38N18'53 86W12'52 5:44:51
Friendly Corner 27 284 40N33'12 85W30'13 5:42:01
Friendship 69 275 38N58'13 85W08'52 5:40:35
Friendswood 32 100 39N38'47 86W19'58 5:45:20
Fritchton 42 86 38N40'49 87W25'23 5:49:42
Fritz Corner 63 59 38N17'51 87W09'32 5:48:38
Fruitdale 7 147 39N19'19 86W15'28 5:45:02

Fugit 16 101 39N24 85w22 5:41:28
Fulda 74 64 38N06'41 86w50'10 5:47:21
Fulton 25 328 40N56'50 86w15'46 5:45:03
Furnace 28 193 39N00'51 86w54'47 5:47:39
Furnessville 64 4 41N39'06 87w00'27 5:48:02
Gadsden 6 248 40N02'50 86w20'45 5:45:23
Galena 22 166 38N21'06 85w56'30 5:43:46
Galena 46 2 41N43 86w39 5:46:36
Galveston 9 164 40N34'44 86w11'25 5:44:46
Gambill 13 80 39N02'56 87w15'35 5:49:02
Gar Creek 2 233 41N04 85w03 5:40:12
Garden Acres 6 247 40N07 86w36 5:46:24
Garden Acres 53 344 39N07'28 86w34'41 5:46:19
Garden City 3 147 39N11'00 85w56'00 5:43:44
Garden Village 20 271 41N41'43 85w54'52 5:43:39
Garfield 49 100 39N44 86w06 5:44:24
Garfield 54 147 40N04'59 86w49'26 5:47:18
Garrett 17 238 41N20'58 85w08'08 5:40:33
Gary 45 17 41N35'36 87w20'47 5:49:23
Garyton 64 6 41N34'11 87w12'37 5:48:50
Gasburg 55 97 39N37 86w22 5:45:28
Gas City 27 282 40N29'14 85w36'47 5:42:27
Gaston 18 253 40N18'50 85w30'02 5:42:00
Gatchel 62 69 38N02'48 86w39'02 5:46:36
Gates Corner 18 253 40N06'22 85w15'10 5:41:01
Gates Corner 64 6 41N25'13 87w07'26 5:48:30
Gatesville 53 147 39N15'42 86w08'47 5:44:35
Gaynorsville 16 101 39N14'34 85w31'12 5:42:05
Geetingsville 12 181 40N17 86w31 5:46:04
Gem 30 97 39N46'46 85w53'48 5:43:35
Geneva 1 230 40N35'31 84w57'26 5:39:50
Geneva 73 101 39N23'30 85w43'12 5:42:53
Gentryville 74 64 38N06'15 87w01'59 5:48:08
Georgetown 2 228 41N13'55 84w51'56 5:39:28
Georgetown 9 165 40N44'26 86w30'17 5:46:01
Georgetown 22 166 38N17'40 85w58'32 5:43:54
Georgetown 68 307 40N15 85w10 5:40:40
Georgetown 88 165 38N38'53 86w00'33 5:44:02
Georgia 47 344 38N42'36 86w34'20 5:46:17
Georgia Heights 45 6 41N30 87w19 5:49:16
Gerald 62 69 38N00'27 86w34'23 5:46:18
Germantown 73 108 39N24'57 85w37'31 5:42:30
Gessie 83 73 40N04'57 87w29'59 5:50:00
Giberson 47 344 38N51 86w30 5:46:00
Gibson 45 6 41N36'19 87w27'41 5:49:51
Gibson 88 165 38N41 85w57 5:43:48
Gifford 37 2 41N04'15 87w03'09 5:48:13
Gilboa 4 147 40N42 87w09 5:48:36
Gilead 52 335 40N58'13 86w01'07 5:44:04
Gill 77 80 39N01 87w30 5:50:00
Gillam 37 226 41N04 86w58 5:47:52
Gilman 48 101 40N14'04 85w34'42 5:42:19
Gilmer Park 71 208 41N37'11 86w15'06 5:45:00
Gilmour 28 93 39N07'53 87w14'27 5:48:58
Gimco City 48 101 40N15'30 85w41'02 5:42:44
Gingrich 91 162 40N45 86w46 5:47:04
Gingrich Addition 8 162 40N40'26 86w45'15 5:47:01
Gings 70 101 39N40'15 85w22'15 5:41:29
Giro 26 59 38N30'47 87w28'05 5:49:52
Gladens Corner 79 147 40N15'31 86w49'42 5:47:19
Glenayr 84 77 39N29 87w22 5:49:28
Glen Cliff 86 129 40N18'59 87w14'56 5:49:00
Glendale 14 85 38N34 87w05 5:48:20
Glendale 49 100 39N52 86w07 5:44:28
Glendale Heights 49 100 39N53'09 86w06'39 5:44:27
Glendale Lake 27 284 40N34 85w42 5:42:48
Glendora 13 80 39N07'41 87w21'46 5:49:27
Glen Eden 76 30 41N41'28 85w01'02 5:40:04
Glenhall 79 147 40N21'15 87w02'27 5:48:10
Glen Haven Memorial Park 14 85 38N34'04 87w04'39 5:48:19
Glenn Ayr 84 77 39N28'19 87w17'43 5:49:11
Glenns Valley 49 100 39N38'31 86w11'47 5:44:47
Glen Park 45 6 41N32'30 87w20'10 5:49:21
Glenview 3 147 39N13 85w54 5:43:36
Glenwood 70 272 39N37'33 85w18'01 5:41:12
Glenwood Acres 65 58 37N56 87w54 5:51:36
Glenwood Park 2 233 41N06 85w08 5:40:32
Glezen 63 59 38N24'59 87w18'04 5:49:12
Glidas 31 166 38N03'24 86w11'04 5:44:44
Glyn Ellen 48 101 40N06'40 85w38'52 5:42:35
Gnaw Bone 7 145 39N12 86w15 5:45:00
Goblesville 35 287 40N59'24 85w30'37 5:42:02
Goff 27 284 40N34 85w42 5:42:48
Golden Acres 2 233 41N07'36 85w03'43 5:40:15
Golden Hill 91 162 40N42'37 86w45'38 5:47:03
Golden Lake 76 50 41N35 85w01 5:40:04
Goldsmith 80 120 40N17'22 86w08'57 5:44:36
Golfview Estates 10 166 38N18 85w45 5:43:00
Goodland 56 240 40N45'48 87w17'37 5:49:10
Goodwins Corner 81 97 39N38'57 84w50'01 5:39:20
Goose Lake 92 228 41N12 85w28 5:41:52
Goshen 20 258 41N34'56 85w50'04 5:43:20
Goshen 72 320 38N40'17 85w42'35 5:42:50
Gospel Grove 84 77 39N28'35 87w17'34 5:49:10
Gosport 60 342 39N21'03 86w40'01 5:46:40
Gowdy 70 101 39N31'08 85w33'47 5:42:15
Grabill 2 228 41N12'39 84w58'01 5:39:52
Graceland Heights 89 317 39N54 85w10 5:40:40
Grafton 65 58 38N48'42 85w38'55 5:42:36
Graham 14 85 38N43'18 87w11'47 5:48:47
Graham 23 129 40N09'25 87w11'42 5:48:47
Graham 39 114 38N47 85w38 5:42:32
Graham Valley 87 53 38N08'58 87w17'26 5:49:10
Graham Woods 64 4 41N37'03 87w01'38 5:48:07
Grammer 3 147 39N09'10 85w43'30 5:42:54
Grandview 48 101 40N07'06 85w42'30 5:42:50
Grandview 49 100 39N52'13 86w11'45 5:44:47
Grandview 53 344 39N12 86w37 5:46:28
Grandview 74 61 37N56'01 86w58'52 5:47:55
Grandview Lake 3 147 39N09'08 86w02'47 5:44:11
Grandview Village 22 166 38N18 85w49 5:43:16
Grange Corner 61 128 39N56'24 87w11'09 5:48:45
Grange Corner 84 82 39N26'45 87w15'29 5:49:02
Granger 71 203 41N45'12 86w06'39 5:44:27
Grant City 33 253 39N51'59 85w32'33 5:42:10
Grantsburg 13 169 38N17'17 86w28'10 5:45:53
Granville 18 253 40N19'02 85w19'07 5:41:16
Grass 74 61 38N00 87w06 5:48:24
Grass Creek 25 327 40N56'51 86w24'16 5:45:37
Grasselli 45 6 41N38 87w28 5:49:52
Grassy Fork 36 147 38N48 86w01 5:44:04
Gravel Beach 44 30 41N33'03 85w13'24 5:40:54
Gravel Hill 4 147 40N39'00 87w22'12 5:49:29
Gravelton 43 259 41N26'09 85w55'27 5:43:42
Grayford 40 126 38N57'46 85w34'27 5:42:18
Gray Junction 26 59 38N19'35 87w20'41 5:49:23
Graysville 13 80 39N07'03 87w33'22 5:50:13
Green Acres 45 6 41N29'02 87w17'50 5:49:11
Greenbriar 49 100 39N54'06 86w10'47 5:44:43
Greenbriar 67 128 39N39 86w52 5:47:28
Greenbrier 59 160 38N27'47 86w33'21 5:46:13
Greenbrier 87 53 38N07'14 87w17'01 5:49:08
Greencastle 67 122 39N38'40 86w51'53 5:47:28
Green Center 67 30 41N18'29 85w21'56 5:41:28
Greendale 2 233 41N06'48 85w05'20 5:40:21
Greendale 15 37 39N06'45 84w51'51 5:39:27
Greene 38 291 40N24'30 85w06'00 5:40:24
Greenfield 30 98 39N47'06 85w46'10 5:43:05
Greenfield Estates 27 284 40N34 85w42 5:42:48
Greenfield Mills 44 30 41N45'02 85w13'32 5:40:54
Green Hill 86 156 40N24'49 87w06'40 5:48:27
Greenleaf Manor 20 271 41N41'55 85w56'13 5:43:45
Green Meadows 73 101 39N37'51 85w53'31 5:43:34
Green Meadows 79 147 40N26'23 86w57'57 5:47:52
Green Oak 25 328 40N59'47 86w11'03 5:44:44
Greensboro 33 253 39N52'30 85w27'58 5:41:52
Greensburg 16 106 39N20'14 85w29'01 5:41:56
Greens Fork 89 315 39N53'33 85w02'30 5:40:10
Greentown 34 333 40N28'41 85w58'00 5:43:52
Green Valley 41 101 39N36'22 86w08'24 5:44:34
Greenville 13 80 39N08'27 87w18'07 5:49:12
Greenville 22 166 38N22'21 85w59'11 5:43:57
Greenville 90 228 40N39'16 85w13'35 5:40:54
Greenwood 41 100 39N36'49 86w06'24 5:44:26
Greenwood 44 30 41N33'00 85w13'58 5:40:56
Greenwood 90 231 40N50'40 85w10'37 5:40:42
Greer 87 53 38N10 87w25 5:49:40
Greetingville 12 183 40N24'59 86w28'07 5:45:52
Gregg 55 101 39N31 86w31 5:46:04
Greybrook Lake 60 344 39N27 86w57 5:47:48
Gridley 48 102 40N05'19 85w39'10 5:42:37
Griffin 65 58 38N12'15 87w54'53 5:51:40
Griffith 45 6 41N31'42 87w25'25 5:49:42
Groomsville 80 116 40N20'45 86w12'10 5:44:49
Grouseland 84 82 39N42 86w51 5:47:24
Groveland 67 128 39N45'38 86w43'12 5:46:53
Grovertown 75 223 41N22'23 86w30'25 5:46:02
Gudgel 26 59 38N18'17 87w21'52 5:49:27
Guernsey 91 162 40N48'01 86w48'46 5:47:15
Guilford 15 33 39N10'05 84w54'43 5:39:39
Guion 61 126 39N50'34 87w06'41 5:48:27
Gurley Corner 78 35 38N51'33 84w51'30 5:39:26
Gurley Landing 31 166 37N57'33 86w02'49 5:44:11
Guthrie 47 344 38N58'36 86w30'33 5:46:02
Guy 34 334 40N26'07 85w58'32 5:43:54
Gwynneville 73 101 39N39'39 85w38'53 5:42:36
Hacienda Village 2 233 41N07'02 85w01'48 5:40:07
Hackleman 27 280 40N25'18 85w44'53 5:43:00
Haddon 77 80 38N58 87w24 5:49:36
Hadley 32 115 39N43'53 86w36'10 5:46:25
Hagerstown 89 317 39N54'40 85w09'42 5:40:39
Haglund 64 4 41N36'45 87w06'57 5:48:28
Halbert 51 322 38N40 86w44 5:46:56
Haleysburg 88 165 38N44'31 86w09'03 5:44:36
Hall 19 67 38N23 86w45 5:47:00
Hall 55 113 39N33'00 86w32'09 5:46:09
Halls Corners 2 228 41N14'27 84w51'08 5:39:25
Hamblen 7 147 39N17 86w11 5:44:44
Hamburg 10 166 38N23'00 85w46'03 5:43:04
Hamburg 24 275 39N22'51 85w15'03 5:41:00
Hamilton 12 181 40N20'41 86w37'05 5:46:28
Hamilton 48 101 40N07'23 85w47'06 5:43:08
Hamilton 71 201 41N43'56 86w28'41 5:45:55
Hamilton 76 30 41N32'01 84w54'46 5:39:39
Hamilton Park 18 254 40N11 85w23 5:41:32
Hamlet 75 223 41N32'51 86w34'56 5:46:20
Hammond 45 6 41N35'00 87w30'00 5:50:00
Hamor Heights 3 147 39N13 85w54 5:43:36
Hancock 31 166 38N20 86w13 5:44:52
Hancock Corner 60 344 39N16'31 86w49'44 5:47:19
Handy 4 147 40N30'03 87w28'17 5:49:53
Handy 53 344 39N05'45 86w29'38 5:45:59
Haney Corner 69 275 38N56'20 85w18'21 5:41:13
Hanfield 27 284 40N36'16 85w34'49 5:42:19
Hanging Grove 37 226 40N56'03 86w59'01 5:47:56
Hangman Crossing 36 147 38N56'36 85w55'36 5:43:42
Hanna 46 29 41N24'43 86w46'48 5:47:07
Hanover 39 101 38N42'51 85w28'25 5:41:54
Happy Hollow 31 166 38N03'12 85w56'16 5:43:45
Happy Hollow Heights 79 147 40N26'34 86w54'01 5:47:36
Harbison 19 67 38N30 86w52 5:47:28
Harbor 45 6 41N38 87w28 5:49:52
Hardinsburg 15 37 39N07'19 84w50'51 5:39:23
Hardinsburg 88 165 38N27'39 86w16'43 5:45:07
Hardscrabble 48 101 40N01'11 85w50'36 5:43:22
Harlan 2 228 41N11'46 84w55'11 5:39:41
Harlansburg 35 287 40N48'52 85w33'52 5:42:15
Harmeson Heights 48 102 40N03'31 85w41'32 5:42:46
Harmony 11 89 39N32'12 87w06'21 5:48:25
Harper 16 101 39N08'48 85w35'37 5:42:22
Harris 50 211 41N24'53 86w18'13 5:45:13
Harrisburg 21 272 39N41'12 85w37'22 5:42:29
Harris City 16 101 39N16'53 85w31'38 5:42:07
Harrison Grange 31 168 38N12'55 86w06'08 5:44:25
Harrison Hills 3 147 39N13 85w54 5:43:36
Harrison Lake 3 147 39N13 85w54 5:43:36
Harristown 88 165 38N35'52 86w01'27 5:44:06
Harrisville 68 303 40N11'05 84w52'54 5:39:32
Harrodsburg 53 344 39N00'48 86w32'42 5:46:11
Hart 87 53 38N10 87w17 5:49:08
Hartford 1 228 40N37 85w03 5:40:12
Hartford 58 33 38N59'35 84w57'25 5:39:50
Hartford City 5 197 40N27'04 85w22'12 5:41:29
Hartford Place 3 147 39N13 85w54 5:43:36
Hartleyville 47 344 38N47'46 86w32'06 5:46:08
Hartsdale 45 6 41N30'28 87w28'17 5:49:53
Hartsville 3 147 39N16'03 85w41'53 5:42:48
Hartwell 63 59 38N19'21 87w10'47 5:48:43
Hartwell Junction 63 59 38N21'38 87w08'27 5:48:34
Hartzel 44 30 41N33'48 85w14'09 5:40:57
Hartz Lake 75 221 41N09 86w29 5:45:56
Harveysburg 23 156 39N58'56 87w17'41 5:49:11
Harwood 82 55 38N00'12 87w34'29 5:50:18
Hashtown 28 193 39N01'30 86w55'28 5:47:42
Haskell 46 2 41N29'02 86w54'07 5:47:36
Hastings 43 291 41N23'01 85w55'46 5:43:43
Hatfield 74 61 37N54'09 87w13'27 5:48:54
Haubstadt 26 59 38N12'18 87w34'27 5:50:18
Haw Creek 3 147 39N18 85w45 5:43:00
Hawthorne 47 344 38N51 86w30 5:46:00
Hawthorne Hills 45 5 41N23'41 87w22'45 5:49:31
Hawthorn Hills 29 97 39N56'40 85w58'49 5:43:55
Hayden 40 128 38N58'59 85w44'26 5:42:58
Haymond 24 275 39N18 85w13 5:40:52
Haysville 19 67 38N29'08 86w54'54 5:47:40
Haysville Corner 68 287 40N10'50 84w49'33 5:39:18
Hazelrigg 6 247 40N04'56 86w33'47 5:46:15
Hazelwood 2 233 41N06 85w08 5:40:32
Hazelwood 32 247 39N36'56 86w31'19 5:46:05
Hazelwood 73 101 39N33 85w48 5:43:12
Hazleton 26 59 38N29'20 87w32'30 5:50:10
Headlee 91 181 40N53'52 86w39'31 5:46:38
Heath 79 149 40N27'40 86w44'00 5:46:56
Heather Heights 3 147 39N13 85w54 5:43:36
Heaton Lake 20 271 41N41 85w59 5:43:56
Hebron 64 18 41N19'07 87w12'01 5:48:48
Hedrick 86 187 40N18'06 87w29'27 5:49:58
Heights Corner 60 344 39N17 86w46 5:47:04
Heilman 87 63 38N09'27 87w05'25 5:48:22
Helmcrest 30 101 39N56'26 85w50'26 5:43:22
Helmer 76 30 41N31'52 85w10'13 5:40:41
Helmsburg 7 151 39N15'55 86w17'34 5:45:10
Helt 83 73 39N45 87w28 5:49:52
Heltonville 47 344 38N55'40 86w22'32 5:45:30
Hemenway 87 53 38N12'14 87w08'04 5:48:32
Hemlock 34 330 40N25'12 86w02'29 5:44:10
Hemlock Lakes 23 187 39N58 87w17 5:49:08
Henderson 70 101 39N40'10 85w31'13 5:42:05
Hendricks 41 101 39N36'29 86w08'54 5:44:36
Hendricksville 28 193 39N08'10 86w42'14 5:46:49
Henryville 10 179 38N32'30 85w46'04 5:43:04
Hensley 41 101 39N23 86w11 5:44:44
Hepburn 65 58 38N04'13 87w48'04 5:51:12
Herbst 27 280 40N30'53 85w47'14 5:43:09
Herr 6 248 40N04 86w28 5:45:52
Hessen Cassel 2 233 40N58'40 85w04'45 5:40:19
Hesston 46 8 41N45'10 86w39'39 5:46:39

Hessville 45 6 41N35'44 87W27'42 5:49:51
Heth 31 166 38N04 86W10 5:44:40
Heusler 65 58 37N56'01 87W42'46 5:50:51
Hibbard 50 216 41N15'12 86W23'13 5:45:33
Hibernia 10 166 38N30'07 85W31'32 5:42:06
Hibernia 54 147 40N00'15 87W00'04 5:48:00
Hibernia Mills 54
147 40N00 86W56 5:47:44
Hickory Corner 60
96 39N18'18 87W02'40 5:48:11
Hickory Grove 4
147 40N32 87W29 5:49:56
Hickory Hills 27
284 40N34 85W42 5:42:48
Hickory Island 84
82 39N19'46 87W14'22 5:48:57
Hickory Ridge 26
59 38N15'30 87W49'36 5:51:18
Hicks 46 3 41N42'23 86W34'09 5:46:17
Hideaway Lake 23
156 39N58 87W17 5:49:08
Highbanks 43 291 41N19'24 85W40'16 5:42:41
Highets Corner 60
342 39N16'55 86W42'15 5:46:49
High Lake 57 30 41N24 85W26 5:41:44
Highland 45 6 41N33'13 87W27'07 5:49:48
Highland 82 55 38N02'23 87W34'23 5:50:18
Highland 83 73 39N47'40 87W23'45 5:49:35
Highland 88 165 38N38'58 86W07'39 5:44:31
Highland Center 24
30 39N19'18 85W00'14 5:40:01
Highland Meadows 27
284 40N34 85W42 5:42:48
Highlands Park 43
297 41N16'24 85W47'09 5:43:09
Highland Village 53
344 39N09'39 86W35'01 5:46:20
Highwoods 49 100 39N50'39 86W11'00 5:44:44
Hiker Trace 3 147 39N13 85W54 5:43:36
Hildebrand Village 73
101 39N32'48 85W47'10 5:43:09
Hill And Dale 10
166 38N19 85W44 5:42:56
Hillcrest 2 233 41N01'34 85W08'04 5:40:32
Hillcrest 3 147 39N13 85W54 5:43:36
Hillcrest 31 166 38N12'13 86W07'07 5:44:28
Hillcrest 48 102 40N06'28 85W39'54 5:42:40
Hillcrest 64 6 41N30'58 87W03'02 5:48:12
Hillcrest Circle 47
344 38N51 86W30 5:46:00
Hillcrest Terrace 87
53 37N56'56 87W23'47 5:49:35
Hillgrove 31 166 38N13 86W07 5:44:28
Hillham 19 67 38N30'50 86W42'02 5:46:48
Hillisburg 12 172 40N17'11 86W20'21 5:45:21
Hills And Dales 18
253 40N11 85W16 5:41:04
Hillsboro 23 129 40N06'32 87W11'08 5:48:45
Hillsboro 33 253 39N58'05 85W19'54 5:41:20
Hillsdale 82 53 38N04'58 87W33'02 5:50:12
Hillsdale 83 73 39N47'09 87W23'25 5:49:34
Hillside 46 2 41N42'37 86W37'03 5:46:28
Hilltown 40 128 38N50'13 85W39'44 5:42:39
Hillview Estates 3
147 39N13 85W54 5:43:36
Hindostan 59 160 38N39'56 86W36'16 5:46:25
Hindostan Falls 51
322 38N37'28 86W51'03 5:47:24
Hindustan 53 344 39N18'29 86W29'00 5:45:56
Hirt Corner 67 89 39N28'25 87W00'53 5:48:04
Hiser 89 317 39N48'54 85W04'40 5:40:19
Hitchcock 88 165 38N38'17 86W10'11 5:44:41
Hi-View Addition 71
208 41N36'30 86W10'42 5:44:43
Hoagland 2 230 40N56'53 84W59'42 5:39:59
Hobart 45 6 41N31'56 87W15'18 5:49:01
Hobbieville 28
193 38N59'57 86W42'23 5:46:50
Hobbs 80 117 40N17'01 85W56'51 5:43:47
Hoffman Crossing 11
344 39N21'33 86W56'59 5:47:48
Hoffman Lake 43
297 41N14 85W51 5:43:24
Hogan 15 33 39N04 84W58 5:39:52
Hogtown 13 169 38N21'30 86W19'04 5:45:16
Holaday Hills And Dales 29
100 39N56'11 86W07'10 5:44:29
Holida 49 100 39N53'11 86W11'24 5:44:46
Holiday 17 228 41N21 85W09 5:40:36
Holland 19 67 38N14'44 87W02'10 5:48:09
Hollandsburg 61
128 39N45'37 87W04'20 5:48:17
Hollybrook Lake 60
344 39N21 86W40 5:46:40
Holly Hills 84 77 39N26 87W24 5:49:36
Holmesville 46 21 41N35'59 86W52'52 5:47:31
Holton 69 275 39N04'30 85W23'14 5:41:33
Home Corner 27
284 40N31'25 85W38'26 5:42:34
Homecroft 49 100 39N40'12 86W07'53 5:44:32
Home Place 29 100 39N56'38 86W08'36 5:44:34
Homer 70 108 39N34'41 85W34'41 5:42:19
Homestead 15 33 39N07'27 84W51'09 5:39:25
Honduras 1 228 40N45'29 85W01'59 5:40:08
Honey Creek 33
108 40N02'02 85W29'08 5:41:57
Honeyville 44 32 41N34'54 85W36'06 5:42:24
Hooker Corner 86
129 40N27'17 87W18'59 5:49:16
Hoosier 28 92 39N04'00 87W11'09 5:48:45
Hoosier Acres 53
344 39N09'28 86W29'13 5:45:57
Hoosier Highlands 67
128 39N27 86W57 5:47:48
Hoosierville 61
89 39N28'30 87W06'30 5:48:26
Hoover 9 164 40N48'32 86W12'02 5:44:48
Hoover Crest 49
100 39N53'15 86W10'27 5:44:42
Hoover Mill 89
315 39N51'50 85W03'52 5:40:15
Hoover Park 5 197 40N27'15 85W21'40 5:41:27
Hope 3 148 39N18'14 85W46'17 5:43:05
Hopewell 17 228 41N16'52 85W01'14 5:40:05
Hopewell 41 97 39N29'31 86W07'02 5:44:28
Horace 16 101 39N15'45 85W33'51 5:42:15
Horton 29 97 40N08 86W13 5:44:52
Hortonville 29 98 40N05'10 86W09'39 5:44:39
Houston 36 147 39N00'59 86W11'27 5:44:46
Hovey 65 58 37N53'32 87W56'31 5:51:46
Howard 61 128 39N54'58 87W22'32 5:49:30
Howe 44 39 41N43'17 85W25'14 5:41:41
Howell 82 55 37N59 87W37 5:50:28
Howesville 11 89 39N10'37 87W08'49 5:48:35
Hubbard 71 202 41N41'47 86W25'08 5:45:41
Hubbell 60 199 39N10'59 87W00'44 5:48:03
Hubbells Corner 15
33 39N14'04 85W02'24 5:40:10
Huber 21 273 39N41'11 85W15'15 5:41:01
Hudnut 61 76 39N39'34 87W22'37 5:49:30
Hudson 76 30 41N31'58 85W04'52 5:40:19
Hudson Lake 46 3 41N42'37 86W32'03 5:46:08
Hudsonville 14 85 38N32'20 87W04'22 5:48:17
Huff 74 64 38N02 86W51 5:47:24
Huffman 74 64 38N06'07 86W46'37 5:47:06
Hull Addition 80
121 40N18 86W03 5:44:12
Hunter 49 100 39N43 86W01 5:44:04
Hunter Corner 23
144 40N10'17 87W14'35 5:48:58
Huntersville 24
275 39N18'13 85W13'59 5:40:56
Huntertown 2 239 41N13'42 85W10'21 5:40:41
Huntingburg 19 67 38N17'56 86W57'18 5:47:49
Huntington 35 290 40N52'59 85W29'51 5:41:59
Huntsville 48 101 40N00'31 85W43'49 5:42:55
Huntsville 68 307 40N04'16 85W04'20 5:40:17
Hurlburt 64 28 41N22'12 87W10'36 5:48:42
Huron 47 344 38N43'20 86W40'14 5:46:41
Hursh 2 228 41N14'53 84W58'27 5:39:54
Hurshtown 2 228 41N19 84W54 5:39:36
Hutton 84 82 39N19'03 87W32'02 5:50:08
Hyde Park 18 254 40N11'33 85W18'30 5:41:14
Hymera 13 80 39N11'11 87W18'06 5:49:12
Hyndsdale 55 101 39N24'57 86W29'05 5:45:56
Idaho 84 77 39N26 87W24 5:49:36
Idaville 91 182 40N45'25 86W38'58 5:46:36
Ijamsville 85 264 40N57'35 85W49'58 5:43:20
Ilene 28 194 38N56'15 87W06'45 5:48:27
Illinoi 45 2 41N11'23 87W31'34 5:50:06
Imperial Hills 41
100 39N37'54 86W08'30 5:44:34
Independence 86
129 40N20'15 87W10'08 5:48:41
Independence Hill 45
6 41N28'34 87W22'02 5:49:28
Indiana Beach 91
162 40N47'29 86W46'05 5:47:04
Indiana Girls School 49
100 39N48 86W15 5:45:00
Indiana Harbor 45
6 41N38'26 87W26'43 5:49:47
Indiana Lake 20
259 41N43 85W49 5:43:16
Indiana Oaks 10
166 38N19 85W44 5:42:56
Indianapolis 49
100 39N46'06 86W09'29 5:44:38
Indian Creek Estates 49
100 39N40'43 85W58'15 5:43:53
Indian Creek Settlement 42
86 38N43'45 87W20'44 5:49:23
Indianhead Lake 32
247 39N46 86W31 5:46:04
Indian Heights 34
331 40N25'38 86W07'32 5:44:30
Indian Hill 75
221 41N19'31 86W41'00 5:46:44
Indian Hills 3
147 39N13 85W54 5:43:36
Indian Lake 17
237 41N26 85W09 5:40:36
Indian Lake 49
100 39N53'07 85W59'13 5:43:57
Indianola 44 30 41N33'53 85W14'49 5:40:59
Indian Springs 51
159 38N47'47 86W45'54 5:47:04
Indian Village 2
233 41N02'54 85W10'21 5:40:41
Indian Village 67
30 41N21'57 85W38'22 5:42:33
Indian Village 71
208 41N42'50 86W14'08 5:44:57
Indian Village 79
147 40N27'59 86W54'03 5:47:36
Industry 18 254 40N11 85W23 5:41:32
Ingalls 48 101 39N57'25 85W48'19 5:43:13
Inglefield 82 53 38N06'29 87W33'32 5:50:14
Innisdale 48 101 40N16 85W41 5:42:44
Inverness 76 30 41N42'02 85W05'37 5:40:22
Inwood 50 327 41N19'03 86W12'11 5:44:49
Iona 42 59 38N32'55 87W28'18 5:49:53
Ireland 19 67 38N24'53 86W59'58 5:48:00
Irondale 48 102 40N05'55 85W39'27 5:42:38
Ironton 51 322 38N39'44 86W46'31 5:47:06
Iroquois 56 226 40N52 87W20 5:49:20
Irvington 18 254 40N10'35 85W20'48 5:41:23
Irvington 49 100 39N47 86W04 5:44:16
Irvington Plaza Shopping Cen 49
100 39N47 86W04 5:44:16
Island City 28 93 39N00'33 87W08'52 5:48:35
Island Park 43
297 41N17'13 85W48'01 5:43:12
Island Park 76 30 41N32'27 84W55'16 5:39:41
Iva 63 59 38N30'10 87W07'10 5:48:29
Ivanhoe 45 6 41N35'52 87W25'28 5:49:42
Ivanhoe 49 100 39N46'03 86W00'46 5:44:03
Ivy Hills 49 100 39N53'59 86W04'24 5:44:18
Jacksonburg 89
317 39N51'11 85W06'21 5:40:25
Jackson Hill 13
80 39N10'06 87W21'43 5:49:27
Jackson Park 18
254 40N11 85W23 5:41:32
Jacksons 80 121 40N19'45 86W03'38 5:44:15
Jacksonville 78
35 38N49'44 85W02'56 5:40:12
Jacksonville 83
73 39N40 87W24 5:49:36
Jadden 27 284 40N32'10 85W27'27 5:41:50
Jalapa 27 284 40N37'40 85W44'44 5:42:59
Jamestown 6 251 39N55'40 86W37'29 5:46:30
Jamestown 20 271 41N38'08 86W01'22 5:44:05
Jamestown 76 32 41N44'54 85W01'03 5:40:04
Janney 18 280 40N21'54 85W32'38 5:42:11
Jasonville 28 94 39N09'47 87W11'57 5:48:48
Jasper 19 66 38N23'29 86W55'52 5:47:43
Jay City 38 291 40N34'02 84W50'55 5:39:24
Jeff 90 196 40N36'19 85W21'11 5:41:25
Jefferson 12 183 40N16'46 86W35'24 5:46:22
Jefferson Proving Ground 39
97 38N45 85W19 5:41:16
Jeffersonville 10
176 38N17'24 85W45'06 5:43:00
Jericho 13 169 38N11'57 86W25'28 5:45:42
Jerome 34 334 40N27'19 85W55'51 5:43:43
Jessup 61 72 39N39'26 87W15'24 5:49:02
Jewell Village 3
147 39N11'55 85W50'59 5:43:24
Jimtown 20 271 41N41 85W59 5:43:56
Jimtown 26 59 38N16'23 87W51'11 5:51:25
Jockey 87 53 38N10'42 87W09'48 5:48:39
Johnsburg 19 67 38N13'04 86W57'20 5:47:49
Johnson 26 59 38N16'40 87W44'45 5:50:59
Johnsonville 86
156 40N13'39 87W29'11 5:49:57
Johnstown 28 193 39N10'00 87W00'32 5:48:02
Johnstown 42 86 38N45'52 87W19'24 5:49:18
Jolietville 29 98 40N02'31 86W13'52 5:44:55
Jonesboro 27 284 40N28'47 85W37'40 5:42:31
Jonestown 83 73 39N42'33 87W30'14 5:50:01
Jonesville 3 149 39N03'38 85W53'23 5:43:34
Joppa 32 97 39N37'56 86W25'56 5:45:44
Jordan 60 344 39N23'54 86W59'53 5:48:00
Jordon 14 85 38N41'19 87W12'25 5:48:50
Judah 47 344 38N57'39 86W32'14 5:46:09
Judson 34 330 40N30'14 86W16'17 5:45:05
Judson 61 128 39N48'47 87W08'04 5:48:32
Judyville 86 156 40N21'30 87W23'42 5:49:35
Julietta 49 100 39N44'15 85W57'26 5:43:50
Junction 52 335 40N42 86W07 5:44:28
Kalorama Park 43
291 41N20'04 85W45'39 5:43:03
Kanata Manayunk 43
291 41N24'37 85W41'30 5:42:46
Kankakee 46 2 41N30'30 86W32'22 5:46:09
Kappa Corner 34
330 40N31'58 86W16'15 5:45:05
Kasson 82 53 38N01'01 87W38'10 5:50:33
Keener 37 2 41N10 87W13 5:48:52
Keller 84 82 39N21'37 87W19'27 5:49:18
Kellerville 19 67 38N28'54 86W49'54 5:47:20
Kelso 15 33 39N15 84W58 5:39:52
Kempton 80 118 40N17'18 86W13'47 5:44:55
Kem Square 27 284 40N34 85W42 5:42:48
Kendallville 57
40 41N26'29 85W15'54 5:41:04
Kennard 33 253 39N54'14 85W31'10 5:42:05
Kennedy 74 64 38N04'53 86W55'21 5:47:41
Kenneth 9 165 40N45'40 86W28'23 5:45:54
Kent 39 97 38N44'16 85W32'24 5:42:10
Kent 86 187 40N12 87W29 5:49:56
Kentland 56 241 40N46'13 87W26'43 5:49:47
Kentwood 12 181 40N16'37 86W29'23 5:45:58
Kenwood 84 77 39N28 87W26 5:49:44
Kersey 37 2 41N11'39 87W09'23 5:48:38
Kewanna 25 325 41N01'07 86W24'48 5:45:39
Keyser 17 228 41N21 85W08 5:40:32
Keystone 90 196 40N35'44 85W15'34 5:41:02
Keystone Manor 49
100 39N45'48 86W16'35 5:45:06
Keytsville 67 128 39N39'05 87W00'44 5:48:03
Kiley 27 281 40N31'39 85W40'49 5:42:43
Kilmore 12 181 40N20'55 86W30'20 5:46:01
Kimmell 57 30 41N23'43 85W32'54 5:42:12
Kinder 41 97 39N32'38 86W11'50 5:44:47
King 26 56 38N18'15 87W34'34 5:50:18
Kingman 23 146 39N58'03 87W16'39 5:49:07
Kingsbury 46 7 41N31'39 86W42'00 5:46:48
Kings Cave 31 166 38N13 86W07 5:44:28
Kingsford Heights 46
2 41N28'50 86W41'30 5:46:46
Kingsland 90 231 40N49'48 85W10'38 5:40:43
Kingston 16 101 39N22'44 85W23'18 5:41:33
Kingswood Terrace 84
77 39N26 87W24 5:49:36
Kinsey 43 293 41N05'46 85W42'18 5:42:49
Kirby 53 344 39N08'12 86W36'36 5:46:26
Kirkland 1 228 40N47 85W02 5:40:08
Kirklin 12 182 40N11'36 86W21'38 5:45:27
Kirkpatrick 69
148 40N12'23 86W49'09 5:47:17
Kirksville 53 344 39N02'45 86W36'47 5:46:27
Kirkville 26 59 38N20 87W30 5:50:00
Kirschs Corner 15
33 39N07'19 84W56'12 5:39:45
Kitchell 81 97 39N40'59 84W51'41 5:39:27
Kitt 38 287 40N29'46 85W02'51 5:40:11
Kitterman Corners 62
69 38N13'21 86W41'51 5:46:47
Klaasville 45 2 41N21'21 87W31'03 5:50:04
Klemmes Corner 24
30 39N21'14 85W00'13 5:40:01
Klondike 79 147 40N28'03 86W57'44 5:47:51
Klondyke 61 73 39N47'28 87W20'21 5:49:21
Knapp Lake 57 30 41N24 85W37 5:42:28
Knarr Corner 16
106 39N18'15 85W25'43 5:41:43
Knight 82 55 37N58 87W28 5:49:52
Knighthood Grove 73
101 39N33'13 85W45'24 5:43:02
Knighthood Village 73
101 39N34'42 85W44'32 5:42:58
Knight Ridge 53
344 39N07'31 86W25'59 5:45:44
Knightstown 33
108 39N47'44 85W31'35 5:42:06

Knightstown Lake 33 108 39N48 85W31 5:42:04
Knightsville 11 88 39N31'33 87W06'45 5:48:27
Kniman 37 2 41N08'39 87W08'15 5:48:33
Knob Hill 82 55 38N01'56 87W31'07 5:50:04
Knollton Heights 49 100 39N50'28 86W12'07 5:44:48
Knox 33 108 39N49'23 85W32'31 5:42:10
Knox 75 220 41N17'45 86W37'30 5:46:30
Kokomo 34 332 40N29'11 86W08'01 5:44:32
Koleen 28 193 38N58'17 86W49'44 5:47:19
Koontz Lake 75 221 41N25'05 86W29'09 5:45:57
Kossuth 88 165 38N42'16 86W06'10 5:44:25
Kouts 64 19 41N19'00 87W01'33 5:48:06
Kramer 86 129 40N20'19 87W17'15 5:49:09
Kreitzburg 45 2 41N26'09 87W31'16 5:50:05
Kriete Corner 36 147 38N55'03 85W49'58 5:43:20
Kurtz 36 147 38N57'38 86W12'12 5:44:49
Kyana 19 67 38N18'18 86W56'56 5:47:08
Kyle 15 33 39N08'18 84W59'18 5:39:57
Laconia 31 166 38N01'54 86W05'08 5:44:21
La Crosse 46 29 41N19'03 86W53'29 5:47:34
Lacy 51 322 38N38'01 86W46'35 5:47:06
Ladoga 54 147 39N54'49 86W48'04 5:47:12
Lafayette 79 134 40N25'00 86W52'30 5:47:30
La Fontaine 85 268 40N40'26 85W43'17 5:42:53
Lagrange 44 31 41N38'30 85W25'00 5:41:40
Lagro 85 264 40N50'17 85W43'49 5:42:55
Lake Bodona 55 97 39N37 86W22 5:45:28
Lake Bruce 25 328 41N01 86W27 5:45:48
Lake Cicott 9 164 40N45'51 86W31'27 5:46:06
Lakecrest 29 97 40N03 86W01 5:44:04
Lake Dalecarlia 45 2 41N17 87W26 5:49:44
Lake Dilldear 15 33 39N01 85W04 5:40:16
Lake Edgewood 55 101 39N25 86W25 5:45:40
Lake Eliza 64 6 41N25'44 87W10'19 5:48:41
Lake Everett 2 233 41N06 85W10 5:40:40
Lake Front 45 6 41N39 87W30 5:50:00
Lake Geneva 78 35 38N45 85W04 5:40:16
Lake Hart 55 97 39N37 86W22 5:45:28
Lake Hills 45 23 41N27'51 87W26'46 5:49:47
Lake James 76 30 41N42'18 85W02'54 5:40:12
Lakeland 46 9 41N43 86W53 5:47:32
Lake Latonka 50 211 41N13 86W25 5:45:40
Lake Lincoln 74 64 38N07 87W00 5:48:00
Lake Manitou 25 328 41N03 86W11 5:44:44
Lake Maxine 55 113 39N27 86W43 5:46:52
Lake McCoy 16 101 39N21 85W33 5:42:12
Lake Mill 74 61 37N56'16 87W06'35 5:48:26
Lake Mohee 5 196 40N27 85W22 5:41:28
Lake Noji 84 77 39N26 87W24 5:49:36
Lake of the Four Seasons 45 6 41N29 87W23 5:49:32
Lake of the Woods 50 211 41N27 86W09 5:44:36
Lake Park 46 3 41N42'17 86W32'59 5:46:12
Lake Primrose 55 101 39N25 86W25 5:45:40
Lake Shore 64 9 41N43 86W53 5:47:32
Lake Shores 2 233 41N01'20 85W09'14 5:40:37
Lakeside 32 100 39N53'03 86W17'06 5:45:08
Lakeside 44 30 41N32'44 85W13'15 5:40:53
Lakeside 66 181 40N56'03 86W44'16 5:46:57
Lakeside Park 43 297 41N15'08 85W50'57 5:43:24
Lake Station 45 6 41N34'30 87W14'20 5:48:57
Lake Sullivan 77 71 39N06 87W25 5:49:40
Laketon 85 270 40N58'27 85W50'09 5:43:21
Lake View 24 275 39N29'08 85W14'54 5:41:00
Lakeview 44 30 41N32'45 85W13'15 5:40:53
Lake View 64 6 41N31'29 87W03'06 5:48:12
Lakeview Estates 84 77 39N26 87W24 5:49:36
Lakeview Spring 43 291 41N17'11 85W41'17 5:42:45
Lake Village 56 2 41N08'15 87W26'55 5:49:48
Lakeville 71 205 41N31'28 86W16'24 5:45:06
Lakewood 8 162 40N41'11 86W45'35 5:47:02
Lake Wood 27 284 40N33'11 85W34'05 5:42:16
Lakewood 84 77 39N26 87W24 5:49:36
Lakewood Hills 82 55 38N00'08 87W30'49 5:50:03
Lalimere 46 8 41N43'02 86W42'01 5:46:48
Lamar 74 64 38N04'09 86W54'20 5:47:37
Lamb 78 35 38N41'31 85W11'17 5:40:45
Lamb Lake 41 97 39N25 86W09 5:44:36
Lamong 29 97 40N08 86W13 5:44:52
Lamplighter 29 97 40N03 86W01 5:44:04
Lanam 7 145 39N14'01 86W19'39 5:45:19
Lancaster 35 287 40N44'56 85W30'25 5:42:02
Lancaster 39 97 38N49'53 85W31'07 5:42:04
Lancaster Park 53 344 39N12'37 86W33'39 5:46:15
Landersdale 55 100 39N37'10 86W15'47 5:45:03
Landess 27 280 40N36'39 85W33'40 5:42:15
Lane 87 53 38N12 87W11 5:48:44
Lanesville 31 188 38N14'13 85W59'09 5:43:57
Langenbaum Lake 66 181 41N09 86W29 5:45:56
Lantana Estate 73 101 39N30'15 85W45'45 5:43:03
Lantern Hills 27 284 40N34 85W42 5:42:48
Lantern Park 18 254 40N11 85W23 5:41:32
Laotto 67 48 41N17'25 85W11'53 5:40:48
LaPaz 50 217 41N27'35 86W18'30 5:45:14
LaPaz Junction 50 211 41N27'34 86W17'42 5:45:11
Lap Corner 61 89 39N25'51 87W04'18 5:48:17
Lapel 48 108 40N04'06 85W50'54 5:43:24
Lapland 54 147 39N54'18 86W54'10 5:47:37
La Porte 46 8 41N36'38 86W43'21 5:46:53
Larimer Hill 84 77 39N27'20 87W28'19 5:49:53
Larwill 92 230 41N10'50 85W37'32 5:42:30
Laud 92 228 41N02'58 85W27'08 5:41:49
Laughery 69 275 39N15 85W15 5:41:00
Lauramie 79 147 40N16 86W48 5:47:12
Laurel 24 275 39N30'03 85W11'11 5:40:45
Lawrence 49 100 39N50'19 86W01'31 5:44:06
Lawrenceburg 15 37 39N05'27 84W51'00 5:39:24
Lawrenceburg Junction 15 37 39N07'50 84W50'33 5:39:22
Lawrenceport 47 344 38N45'04 86W23'16 5:45:33
Lawrenceville 15 33 39N16'40 85W02'22 5:40:09
Lawton 66 181 41N05'59 86W31'30 5:46:06
Layton 23 156 40N07'41 87W20'00 5:49:20
Leases Corner 9 165 40N51'59 86W22'27 5:45:30
Leavenworth 13 169 38N11'59 86W20'39 5:45:23
Lebanon 6 250 40N02'54 86W28'09 5:45:53
Lee 91 147 40N53'47 86W58'05 5:47:52
Leesburg 2 233 41N03 85W08 5:40:32
Leesburg 43 294 41N19'55 85W51'00 5:43:24
Leesville 47 344 38N50'44 86W17'04 5:45:08
Legendary Hills 32 100 39N52'45 86W15'44 5:45:03
Leininger Acres 80 121 40N18 86W03 5:44:12
Leipsic 59 160 38N40'16 86W22'11 5:45:29
Leisure 48 109 40N21'51 85W50'35 5:43:22
Leiters Ford 25 328 41N07'18 86W23'09 5:45:33
Lena 61 89 39N36'18 87W06'26 5:48:26
Leo 2 228 41N13'24 85W00'40 5:40:03
Leonard Springs 53 344 39N08'26 86W34'38 5:46:19
Leopold 62 69 38N06'14 86W35'00 5:46:20
Leota 72 320 38N38'54 85W51'01 5:43:24
Leroy 45 29 41N21'36 87W16'19 5:49:05
Letts 16 101 39N14'06 85W33'54 5:42:16
Letts Corner 16 101 39N14'05 85W34'30 5:42:18
Lewis 84 83 39N16 87W16 5:49:04
Lewisburg 9 165 40N44'48 86W13'03 5:44:52
Lewis Creek 73 101 39N24'04 85W49'00 5:43:16
Lewisville 33 257 39N48'24 85W21'10 5:41:25
Lewisville 60 113 39N28'16 86W37'55 5:46:32
Lexington 8 165 40N27'32 86W29'20 5:45:57
Lexington 72 320 38N39'08 85W37'31 5:42:30
Liber 38 291 40N24'29 84W58'10 5:39:53
Liberal 74 64 38N02'45 86W56'35 5:47:46
Liberty 81 314 39N38'08 84W55'52 5:39:43
Liberty Center 90 228 40N41'57 85W16'50 5:41:07
Liberty Corners 18 254 40N11'36 85W19'48 5:41:19
Liberty Hills 2 233 41N02'00 85W15'59 5:41:04
Liberty Mills 85 269 41N02'01 85W44'09 5:42:57
Liberty Park 45 5 41N25'57 87W22'07 5:49:28
Libertyville 83 82 39N36'10 87W31'07 5:50:04
Licking 5 196 40N26 85W23 5:41:32
Liggett 84 77 39N28'45 87W29'01 5:49:56
Ligonier 57 49 41N27'57 85W35'15 5:42:21
Lilly Dale 62 69 38N00'42 86W39'05 5:46:36
Lima 44 30 41N44 85W26 5:41:44
Limberlost Hills 84 77 39N29 87W22 5:49:28
Limedale 67 126 39N37'09 86W52'45 5:47:31
Lincoln 9 164 40N36'56 86W12'36 5:44:50
Lincoln City 74 64 38N07'16 86W59'55 5:48:00
Lincoln Heights 10 166 38N18 85W45 5:43:00
Lincoln Heights 48 101 40N16 85W41 5:42:44
Lincoln Hills 64 12 41N28'06 87W06'28 5:48:26
Lincoln Park 10 166 38N18 85W45 5:43:00
Lincolnshire 2 233 41N01'39 85W08'25 5:40:34
Lincolnshire 20 265 41N27 86W00 5:44:00
Lincolnshire 27 284 40N34 85W42 5:42:48
Lincoln Village 45 6 41N28'27 87W22'55 5:49:32
Lincolnville 85 264 40N45'16 85W40'40 5:42:43
Linden 54 153 40N11'17 86W54'14 5:47:37
Lindenwood 49 100 39N39'31 86W09'15 5:44:37
Linkville 50 211 41N24'58 86W17'13 5:45:09
Linn Grove 1 228 40N38'42 85W01'59 5:40:08
Linnsburg 54 147 39N59'59 86W47'59 5:47:12
Linton 28 92 39N02'05 87W09'57 5:48:40
Linwood 48 101 40N11'37 85W40'54 5:42:44
Linwood 49 100 39N47 86W07 5:44:28
Lippe 65 58 38N00'55 87W45'14 5:51:01
Lisbon 57 30 41N24'40 85W15'35 5:41:02
Little 63 59 38N29 87W17 5:49:08
Little Acre 36 149 39N02'10 85W52'58 5:43:32
Little Acres 36 147 38N58 85W58 5:43:52
Little Point 55 113 39N33'54 86W37'55 5:46:32
Little Rock 42 86 38N29'41 87W40'45 5:50:43
Littles 63 59 38N24'04 87W17'14 5:49:09
Little Saint Louis 38 166 38N18'10 86W14'13 5:44:57
Little York 88 165 38N42'10 85W54'18 5:43:37
Liverpool 45 17 41N33'09 87W17'41 5:49:11
Livonia 88 165 38N33'25 86W16'39 5:45:07
Lizton 32 247 39N53'12 86W32'36 5:46:10
Loafers Station 87 63 38N07'32 87W07'05 5:48:28
Lochiel 4 147 40N39'51 87W16'26 5:49:06
Locke 20 264 41N28'18 86W00'44 5:44:03
Lockhart 63 59 38N17 87W09 5:48:36
Lockport 8 165 40N41'57 86W34'25 5:46:18
Locust Grove 89 315 39N46'10 84W51'07 5:39:24
Locust Point 31 166 38N10'16 85W54'28 5:43:38
Lodi 61 128 39N57'00 87W24'21 5:49:37
Logan 15 33 39N14'53 84W53'41 5:39:35
Logan 47 344 38N56'32 86W30'29 5:46:02
Logansport 9 173 40N45'16 86W21'24 5:45:26
Log Cabin Crossroads 54 147 40N01'31 86W42'01 5:46:48
Lomax 75 28 41N15'32 86W52'18 5:47:29
Lomong 29 98 40N05'08 86W12'12 5:44:49
London 73 101 39N37'32 85W55'13 5:43:41
London Heights 73 101 39N37'43 85W54'52 5:43:39
Lone Tree 28 93 39N07'33 87W07'44 5:48:31
Long Acres 73 101 39N33 85W48 5:43:12
Long Beach 46 9 41N44'44 86W51'03 5:47:24
Long Lake 76 32 41N44 84W53 5:39:32
Long Lake 85 264 41N00 85W46 5:43:04
Long Lake Island 64 6 41N31'18 87W02'54 5:48:12
Longnecker 15 33 39N16 84W52 5:39:28
Long Run 78 35 38N45'11 85W07'04 5:40:28
Longview Beach 10 166 38N18 85W45 5:43:00
Longwood Crossing 21 100 39N39'21 86W02'44 5:44:11
Loogootee 51 246 38N40'37 86W54'51 5:47:39
Lookout 69 275 39N11'43 85W12'27 5:40:50
Loon Lake 57 30 41N12 85W28 5:41:52
Lorane 92 228 41N12'25 85W33'31 5:42:14
Loree 52 335 40N38'44 86W03'29 5:44:14
Losantville 68 307 40N01'27 85W10'58 5:40:44
Lost Creek 84 82 39N29 87W18 5:49:12
Lost River 51 322 38N34 86W46 5:47:04
Lottaville 45 6 41N30'12 87W21'53 5:49:28
Lottick Corner 31 166 38N10'16 85W56'25 5:43:46
Lotus 81 313 39N36'47 84W53'24 5:39:34
Lovett 40 128 38N54'41 85W37'59 5:42:32
Lowell 3 147 39N15'11 85W56'47 5:43:47
Lowell 45 27 41N17'29 87W25'14 5:49:41
Lower Sunset Park 8 162 40N42'25 86W45'16 5:47:01
Lowman Corner 43 291 41N04'14 86W01'06 5:44:04
Lowmandale 48 102 40N04'41 85W39'48 5:42:39
Loyal 25 328 41N04 86W13 5:44:52
Luce 74 61 37N55 87W12 5:48:48
Lucerne 9 164 40N51'59 86W24'12 5:45:37
Ludwig Park 2 233 41N08'11 85W09'15 5:40:37
Lukens Lake 85 264 40N55 85W55 5:43:40
Luray 33 253 40N04'16 85W22'01 5:41:28
Luther 92 287 41N00'10 85W34'26 5:42:18
Lutheran Lake 3 147 38N58 85W58 5:43:52
Luxhaven 29 101 39N56'51 85W53'13 5:43:33
Lydick 71 202 41N41'35 86W22'19 5:45:29
Lyford 61 73 39N39'00 87W22'15 5:49:29
Lyles 26 59 38N22'13 87W39'33 5:50:38
Lynhurst 49 100 39N45'32 86W14'53 5:45:00
Lynn 68 312 40N02'59 84W56'23 5:39:46
Lynnville 87 53 38N11'46 87W17'48 5:49:11
Lyons 28 95 38N59'21 87W04'56 5:48:20
Lyonsville 21 272 39N39'09 85W03'14 5:40:13
Mace 54 147 40N00'37 86W47'47 5:47:11
Macedonia 31 166 38N03'14 85W57'36 5:43:50
Mac-Fair-Mar 9 165 40N46 86W22 5:45:28
Mackey 26 59 38N15'08 87W23'30 5:49:34
Macy 52 335 40N57'33 86W07'38 5:44:31
Madison 39 98 38N44'09 85W22'48 5:41:31
Magee 46 8 41N31'51 86W45'04 5:47:00
Magley 1 231 40N49'53 85W03'12 5:40:13
Magnet 62 69 38N05'48 86W27'48 5:45:51
Magnolia 13 169 38N14'57 86W23'35 5:45:34
Mahalasville 55 101 39N21'37 86W21'46 5:45:27
Mahan Crossing 59 160 38N33'26 86W21'52 5:45:27
Mahon 35 287 40N56'19 85W22'50 5:41:31
Mahoning 45 6 41N38 87W28 5:49:52
Majenica 35 287 40N46'12 85W27'12 5:41:49
Makin 35 289 40N57'57 85W35'08 5:42:21
Malden 64 2 41N22'34 87W01'37 5:48:06
Malott Park 49 100 39N50 86W09 5:44:36
Maltersville 19 67 38N20'47 86W53'23 5:47:34
Manchester 15 33 39N09'06 85W00'44 5:40:03
Manchester 69 147 40N05'52 86W54'15 5:47:37
Manhattan 67 128 39N39 86W52 5:47:28
Manhatten 67 128 39N33'18 86W55'39 5:47:43
Manilla 70 108 39N34'27 85W37'10 5:42:29
Manor Woods 2 233 41N01'31 85W15'44 5:41:03
Mansfield 61 128 39N40'35 87W06'08 5:48:25
Manson 12 183 40N14'24 86W35'25 5:46:22
Manville 39 97 38N47'16 85W17'08 5:41:09
Maple Lane 71 208 41N42'00 86W13'01 5:44:52
Maple Ridge 49 100 39N40'41 86W17'10 5:45:09
Maples 2 233 41N00'46 84W58'09 5:39:53
Mapleton 49 100 39N49 86W11 5:44:44
Mapleton Corner 16 101 39N11'27 85W32'46 5:42:11
Maple Valley 33 253 39N52'01 85W35'13 5:42:21
Maplewood 32 247 39N50'04 86W30'19 5:46:01
Maplewood 84 77 39N28 87W26 5:49:44
Maplewood Park 2 233 41N06'56 85W03'23 5:40:14

Marble Hill 26 101 38N35'33 85w27'02 5:41:48
Marco 28 194 38N56'09 87w08'32 5:48:34
Mardenis 35 287 40N54'15 85w24'49 5:41:39
Marengo 13 177 38N22'32 86w20'41 5:45:23
Mariah Hill 74 64 38N09'55 86w55'29 5:47:42
Marian Manor 64 6 41N28'01 87w05'15 5:48:21
Marietta 73 101 39N26'29 85w53'02 5:43:32
Marineland Gardens 43 291 41N22'41 85w41'04 5:42:44
Marion 27 281 40N33'30 85w39'33 5:42:38
Marion 73 101 39N35'30 85w45'18 5:43:01
Marion Heights 84 77 39N29'41 87w26'45 5:49:47
Marion Manor 64 6 41N29 87w23 5:49:32
Markland 78 35 38N46'55 84w59'12 5:39:57
Markle 90 288 40N49'45 85w20'08 5:41:21
Markles 84 77 39N31'37 87w21'07 5:49:24
Markleville 48 101 39N58'40 85w36'53 5:42:28
Marlin Hills 53 344 39N12'47 86w31'24 5:46:06
Marongo 13 177 38N22'09 86w20'37 5:45:22
Marquette Farm 84 82 39N42 86w51 5:47:24
Marrs Center 65 58 37N56'44 87w45'18 5:51:01
Marshall 61 128 39N50'53 87w11'16 5:48:45
Marshfield 86 190 40N14'57 87w27'10 5:49:49
Mars Hill 49 100 39N45 86w14 5:44:56
Marshtown 25 328 40N56'56 86w20'19 5:45:21
Martin 82 55 38N07'28 87w40'25 5:50:42
Martin Heights 88 165 38N01'38 86w15'37 5:45:02
Martinsburg 88 165 38N26'38 86w01'34 5:44:06
Martinsville 55 108 39N25'40 86w25'42 5:45:43
Martz 11 89 39N17 87w07 5:48:28
Maryland 84 77 39N26 87w25 5:49:40
Marysville 10 166 38N35'08 85w38'37 5:42:34
Marysville 63 59 38N21'07 87w16'42 5:49:07
Marywood 84 77 39N26 87w25 5:49:40
Matamoras 5 196 40N33'15 85w15'47 5:41:03
Matlock Heights 53 344 39N12 86w37 5:46:28
Matthews 27 280 40N23'19 85w29'58 5:42:00
Mattix Corner 12 181 40N20'39 86w34'01 5:46:16
Mauckport 31 166 38N01'29 86w12'07 5:44:48
Maumee 2 228 41N08 84w51 5:39:24
Maumee 36 147 39N01'16 86w15'42 5:45:03
Mauzy 70 101 39N37'26 85w20'18 5:41:21
Max 6 247 40N00'37 86w34'55 5:46:20
Maxinkuckee 50 211 41N12'30 86w22'53 5:45:32
Maxville 68 307 40N10'20 85w06'21 5:40:25
Maxville 74 69 38N00'00 86w48'48 5:47:15
Maxwell 30 97 39N51'27 85w46'12 5:43:05
Maxwell 55 101 39N23'14 86w27'20 5:45:49
Mayfield 18 254 40N11'42 85w21'00 5:41:24
Mayflower Meadows 49 100 39N53'00 86w05'04 5:44:20
Maynard 45 6 41N32'29 87w30'31 5:50:02
May Ridge 3 147 39N18 85w46 5:43:04
Mays 70 101 39N44'37 85w25'48 5:41:43
Maysville 14 85 38N38'52 87w13'42 5:48:55
Maysville Crossing 23 129 40N19'51 87w08'50 5:48:35
Maywood 49 100 39N43'34 86w12'57 5:44:52
McBride Heights 10 166 38N18 85w45 5:43:00
McCarthy Addition 48 101 40N16 85w41 5:42:44
McCarty 41 100 39N36'33 86w07'52 5:44:31
McClellan 56 2 41N02 87w27 5:49:48
McCol Place 88 165 38N04'50 86w17'26 5:45:10
McCool 64 23 41N34'48 87w08'37 5:48:34
McCordsville 30 97 39N53'38 85w55'12 5:43:41
McCoy 16 101 39N19'23 85w24'52 5:41:39
McCoysburg 37 226 40N54'52 87w01'19 5:48:05
McCutchanville 82 55 38N03'51 87w31'28 5:50:06
McDaniel 55 101 39N24'43 86w26'27 5:45:46
McGrawsville 52 338 40N37'49 86w00'50 5:44:03
McKinley 88 165 38N44'41 86w12'38 5:44:51
McKinley Town and Country Sh 71 208 41N40 86w10 5:44:40
McNatts 90 196 40N37'28 85w23'28 5:41:34
McQuinn Estates 79 147 40N26'15 86w57'32 5:47:50
McVille 28 193 39N09'11 86w44'19 5:46:57
Meadowbrook 2 233 41N03'37 85w02'21 5:40:09
Meadowbrook 48 102 40N04'43 85w40'41 5:42:43
Meadowbrook 64 4 41N36'56 87w07'19 5:48:29
Meadowbrook 79 147 40N25 86w53 5:47:32
Meadowdale 45 6 41N30 87w19 5:49:16
Meadowland Estates 45 6 41N30 87w19 5:49:16
Meadowland Manor 45 6 41N30 87w19 5:49:16
Meadowood 20 271 41N41 85w59 5:43:56
Meadowood 49 100 39N48 86w15 5:45:00
Meadowood Estates 48 101 40N21 85w44 5:42:56
Meadowview 9 165 40N46 86w22 5:45:28
Mead Village 3 147 39N13 85w54 5:43:36
Mecca 61 73 39N43'38 87w19'50 5:49:19
Mechanicsburg 6 251 40N09'35 86w28'52 5:45:55
Mechanicsburg 16 101 39N20'14 85w22'01 5:41:28
Mechanicsburg 33 253 41N17 87w26 5:49:44
Mechanicsburg 48 101 40N00'18 85w33'26 5:42:14
Medaryville 66 181 41N04'50 86w53'31 5:47:34
Medford 18 253 40N07'14 85w19'15 5:41:17
Medina 86 156 40N26 87w08 5:48:32
Medora 36 147 38N49'30 86w10'12 5:44:41
Meiks 73 101 39N33'11 85w45'00 5:43:00
Mellott 23 136 40N09'55 87w08'52 5:48:35
Melody Acres 43 297 41N14 85w51 5:43:24
Melody Hill 82 55 38N01'34 87w30'57 5:50:04
Meltzer 73 101 39N31'08 85w40'06 5:42:40
Memphis 10 179 38N29'00 85w45'41 5:43:03
Mentone 43 243 41N10'24 86w02'05 5:44:08
Mentor 19 67 38N18'59 86w43'08 5:46:53
Meridian Hills 49 100 39N53'24 86w09'26 5:44:38
Merom 13 80 39N01'49 87w32'23 5:50:10
Merriam 67 30 41N17'14 85w26'04 5:41:44
Merrillville 45 6 41N28'58 87w19'58 5:49:20
Messick 33 253 39N58'31 85w18'10 5:41:13
Metamora 24 275 39N26'59 85w08'22 5:40:33
Metea 9 165 40N52'09 86w18'34 5:45:14
Metz 76 30 41N36'58 84w50'22 5:39:21
Mexico 52 338 40N49'20 86w06'56 5:44:28
Miami 52 335 40N36'51 86w06'23 5:44:26
Miami Bend 9 165 40N45'03 86w17'53 5:45:12
Miami Trails 71 208 41N38 86w14 5:44:56
Miami Trails Addition 71 208 41N35'56 86w14'10 5:44:57
Michaels 27 284 40N34 85w42 5:42:48
Michaelsville 27 284 40N31'25 85w42'07 5:42:48
Michiana Shores 46 2 41N45 86w49 5:47:16
Michigan City 46 9 41N42'27 86w53'42 5:47:35
Michigantown 12 181 40N19'35 86w23'34 5:45:34
Mickleyville 49 100 39N44'51 86w15'41 5:45:03
Middle 32 247 39N51 86w28 5:45:52
Middleboro 89 318 39N53'38 84w49'55 5:39:20
Middle Branch 16 101 39N18'28 85w23'09 5:41:33
Middlebury 11 89 39N15'51 87w07'08 5:48:29
Middlebury 20 259 41N40'31 85w42'22 5:42:49
Middlefork 12 181 40N24'56 86w23'33 5:45:34
Middlefork 39 161 38N51'14 85w28'20 5:41:53
Middletown 33 108 40N03'26 85w32'14 5:42:09
Middletown 73 108 39N27'36 85w38'56 5:42:36
Middletown Park 18 254 40N09'44 85w25'29 5:41:42
Midland 28 93 39N07'19 87w11'30 5:48:46
Midland Junction 28 93 39N06'26 87w11'40 5:48:47
Midway 20 271 41N37'07 85w53'26 5:43:34
Midway 24 275 39N27'35 85w13'00 5:40:52
Midway 39 161 38N48'59 85w27'46 5:41:51
Midway 61 128 39N46'31 87w19'03 5:49:16
Midway 74 61 38N00'03 87w08'27 5:48:34
Mier 27 284 40N34'31 85w49'32 5:43:18
Mifflin 13 169 38N18'22 86w32'25 5:46:10
Milan 69 277 39N07'16 85w07'53 5:40:32
Milan Center 2 233 41N08'39 84w56'46 5:39:47
Milford 16 101 39N21'01 85w37'05 5:42:28
Milford 43 294 41N24'35 85w50'44 5:43:23
Milford Junction 43 294 41N25'42 85w50'31 5:43:22
Mill 27 285 40N29 85w38 5:42:32
Mill Creek 23 156 40N01 87w16 5:49:04
Mill Creek 29 97 40N03 86w01 5:44:04
Mill Creek 46 2 41N35 86w32 5:46:08
Milledgeville 6 247 39N58'27 86w29'49 5:45:59
Miller 15 33 39N11 84w52 5:39:28
Miller 45 20 41N36'08 87w15'30 5:49:02
Miller 55 100 39N37'14 86w16'55 5:45:08
Millersburg 20 261 41N31'40 85w41'40 5:42:47
Millersburg 29 97 40N11'41 86w01'26 5:44:06
Millersburg 59 160 38N33'26 86w20'08 5:45:21
Millersburg 87 53 38N04'12 87w23'34 5:49:34
Millersport 19 67 38N20'35 87w03'14 5:48:13
Millersville 49 100 39N51'11 86w05'30 5:44:22
Millgrove 5 198 40N24'30 85w16'30 5:41:06
Millhousen 16 101 39N12'38 85w25'57 5:41:44
Milligan 61 128 39N50'44 87w02'18 5:48:09
Millport 88 165 38N46'17 86w06'12 5:44:25
Milltown 13 178 38N20'32 86w16'34 5:45:06
Millville 33 257 39N55'29 85w15'07 5:41:00
Milners Corner 30 101 39N54'58 85w41'32 5:42:46
Milo 35 287 40N39'14 85w28'06 5:41:52
Milroy 70 101 39N29'49 85w28'11 5:41:53
Milton 58 33 38N58'42 85w00'52 5:40:03
Milton 89 317 39N47'17 85w09'19 5:40:37
Mineral 28 193 39N02 86w56 5:47:44
Mineral City 28 193 38N59'39 86w52'48 5:47:31
Mineral Springs 43 291 41N19'34 85w44'39 5:42:59
Miner City 13 80 39N14'53 87w22'40 5:49:31
Minshall 61 89 39N40'18 87w13'18 5:48:53
Mishawaka 71 207 41N39'43 86w09'31 5:44:38
Mitchell 47 341 38N43'58 76w23'38 5:05:35
Mitchellville 49 100 39N47 86w07 5:44:28
Mitcheltree 51 159 38N47 86w44 5:46:56
Mixersville 24 30 39N29'18 84w49'30 5:39:18
Moberly 31 166 38N16'11 86w12'34 5:44:50
Modesto 53 344 39N16'11 86w32'54 5:46:12
Modoc 68 307 40N02'43 85w07'35 5:40:30
Mohawk 30 97 39N50'37 85w50'27 5:43:22
Mongo 44 30 41N41'05 85w16'47 5:41:07
Monitor 79 147 40N25'11 86w45'23 5:47:02
Monmouth 1 228 40N52'04 84w56'40 5:39:47
Monon 91 154 40N52'04 86w52'44 5:47:31
Monoquet 43 297 41N17'22 85w51'42 5:43:27
Monroe 1 228 40N44'42 84w56'13 5:39:45
Monroe 79 147 40N17'11 86w44'07 5:46:56
Monroe City 42 86 38N36'55 87w21'16 5:49:25
Monroe Manor 46 8 41N36'04 86w41'18 5:46:45
Monroeville 2 230 40N58'29 84w52'06 5:39:28
Monrovia 55 101 39N34'44 86w28'56 5:45:56
Montclair 32 247 39N50'53 86w34'01 5:46:16
Monterey 66 182 41N09'25 86w28'58 5:45:56
Monterey Village 29 97 40N03'13 86w01'28 5:44:06
Montezuma 61 70 39N47'34 87w22'15 5:49:29
Montgomery 14 85 38N39'45 87w02'46 5:48:11
Monticello 91 162 40N44'43 86w45'53 5:47:04
Montmorenci 79 137 40N28'27 87w01'46 5:48:07
Montpelier 5 196 40N33'14 85w16'39 5:41:07
Moonlight 76 50 41N35'04 85w01'52 5:40:07
Moonville 48 101 40N11'38 85w36'05 5:42:24
Moore 17 230 41N23'49 84w57'09 5:39:49
Moorefield 49 100 39N47 86w13 5:44:52
Moorefield 78 35 38N48'20 85w10'13 5:40:41
Mooreland 33 253 39N59'51 85w15'04 5:41:00
Moores Hill 15 33 39N06'48 85w05'17 5:40:21
Moorestown 47 344 38N43'07 86w36'57 5:46:28
Mooresville 55 98 39N36'46 86w22'27 5:45:30
Moral 73 101 39N39 85w54 5:43:36
Moran 12 183 40N23'15 86w30'55 5:46:04
Morgan Park 64 4 41N36'30 87w02'45 5:48:11
Morgantown 55 110 39N22'17 86w15'40 5:45:03
Morningside 18 254 40N13'26 85w21'59 5:41:28
Morocco 56 2 40N56'46 87w27'12 5:49:49
Morris 69 278 39N16'56 85w10'39 5:40:43
Morristown 73 101 39N40'24 85w41'55 5:42:48
Morton 67 128 39N45'47 86w56'11 5:47:45
Morvins Landing 31 166 38N00'37 86w10'03 5:44:40
Moscow 70 101 39N29'07 85w33'24 5:42:14
Mott Station 31 166 38N17'53 86w05'26 5:44:22
Mound 86 187 40N09 87w28 5:49:52
Mound Haven 24 30 39N23'02 84w58'42 5:39:55
Mount Auburn 73 101 39N23'33 85w53'37 5:43:34
Mount Auburn 89 317 39N48'46 85w11'23 5:40:46
Mount Ayr 56 2 40N57'07 87w17'57 5:49:12
Mount Carmel 24 30 39N24'26 84w52'29 5:39:30
Mount Carmel 88 165 38N37 86w17 5:45:08
Mount Comfort 30 98 39N49'51 85w54'55 5:43:40
Mount Etna 35 287 40N44'33 85w33'43 5:42:15
Mount Healthy 3 147 39N04'50 86w02'16 5:44:09
Mount Jackson 49 100 39N45'55 86w12'24 5:44:50
Mount Lawn 33 253 39N54'42 85w27'41 5:41:51
Mount Liberty 7 147 39N11'03 86w07'49 5:44:31
Mount Meridian 67 128 39N36'07 86w45'27 5:47:02
Mount Olive 51 159 38N47'55 86w41'39 5:46:47
Mount Olympus 26 59 38N26'50 87w28'30 5:49:54
Mount Pisgah 44 30 41N39 85w25 5:41:40
Mount Pleasant 9 165 40N50'57 86w19'29 5:45:18
Mount Pleasant 18 253 40N05'20 85w18'21 5:41:13
Mount Pleasant 41 97 39N27'37 86w07'10 5:44:29
Mount Pleasant 51 200 38N39'07 86w53'32 5:47:34
Mount Pleasant 62 69 38N07'18 86w31'04 5:46:04
Mount Pleasant 84 77 39N25'35 87w22'11 5:49:29
Mounts 26 59 38N13'50 87w42'23 5:50:50
Mount Sinai 15 33 39N04'59 85w00'06 5:40:00
Mount Sterling 78 35 38N47'45 85w04'26 5:40:18
Mount Summit 33 253 40N00'16 85w23'05 5:41:32
Mount Tabor 53 344 39N18'41 86w38'00 5:46:32
Mount Vernon 65 58 37N55'56 87w53'42 5:51:35
Mount Vernon 85 264 40N40'10 85w49'27 5:43:18
Mount Zion 90 228 40N39'01 85w20'05 5:41:20
Mount Zion Corner 55 101 39N31'16 86w33'51 5:46:15
Mud Center 82 55 37N57'21 87w37'43 5:50:31
Mudlavia Springs 86 129 40N20'18 87w17'34 5:49:10
Mulberry 12 175 40N20'40 86w39'55 5:46:40
Mull 68 307 40N12'26 85w04'23 5:40:18
Muncie 18 254 40N11'36 85w23'11 5:41:33
Munster 45 24 41N33'52 87w30'45 5:50:03
Murdock 47 344 38N54'35 86w30'30 5:46:02
Muren 63 59 38N21'59 87w16'08 5:49:05
Murray 90 228 40N47'31 85w12'03 5:40:48
Musquabuck Park 43 291 41N22'07 85w46'53 5:43:08
Nabb 88 166 38N36'20 85w37'58 5:42:32
Napoleon 69 275 39N12'17 85w19'51 5:41:19
Nappanee 20 265 41N26'34 86w00'05 5:44:00
Nashville 7 145 39N12'26 86w15'04 5:45:00
Nashville 30 101 39N55'42 85w39'34 5:42:38
Natchez 51 322 38N37'02 86w42'39 5:46:51
Navilleton 37 166 38N22'54 85w56'19 5:43:45
Nead 52 335 40N42'26 86w07'39 5:44:31
Neavill Grove 39 97 38N47'00 85w30'42 5:42:03
Nebraska 40 128 39N03'49 85w27'34 5:41:50
Needham 41 101 39N31'48 85w58'16 5:43:53
Needmore 7 145 39N15'04 86w20'23 5:45:22
Needmore 47 344 38N55'38 86w31'48 5:46:07
Needmore 83 73 39N37'08 87w24'37 5:49:38

Neff Corner 16 101 39N09'55 85W31'56 5:42:08
Negangards Corner 69 275 39N11'28 85W05'41 5:40:23
Nevada 80 119 40N23'43 86W00'15 5:44:01
Nevada Mills 76 30 41N43'37 85W04'56 5:40:20
Nevins 84 82 39N34 87W15 5:49:00
New Albany 22 176 38N17'08 85W49'27 5:43:18
New Alsace 15 33 39N14'02 85W00'11 5:40:01
New Amsterdam 31 166 38N06'08 86W16'30 5:45:06
Newark 28 193 39N07'44 86W48'26 5:47:14
Newark Village 29 97 39N58'04 86W07'24 5:44:30
New Augusta 49 100 39N53'00 86W14'19 5:44:57
New Bellsville 7 147 39N13 85W54 5:43:36
Newbern 3 147 39N14'07 85W45'03 5:43:00
Newberry 28 191 38N55'30 87W01'10 5:48:05
New Boston 31 166 37N59'59 86W00'39 5:44:03
New Boston 74 64 38N03'31 86W48'37 5:47:14
New Britton 29 97 39N58'47 86W00'36 5:44:02
New Brunswick 6 247 39N56'39 86W31'22 5:46:05
Newburgh 87 53 37N56'40 87W24'19 5:49:37
New Burlington 18 254 40N07'12 85W17'52 5:41:11
New Carlisle 71 201 41N42'01 86W30'34 5:46:02
New Castle 33 256 39N55'44 85W22'13 5:41:29
New Chicago 45 6 41N33'30 87W16'28 5:49:06
New Columbus 48 101 40N01'08 85W39'21 5:42:37
New Corydon 38 287 40N34'07 84W50'24 5:39:22
New Durham 46 21 41N34 86W53 5:47:32
New Elizabethtown 36 147 38N55'02 85W59'13 5:43:57
New Elliot 45 6 41N29'35 87W25'03 5:49:40
New Era 17 228 41N17'38 85W07'17 5:40:29
New Fairfield 24 30 39N30'25 84W58'21 5:39:53
New Farmington 36 147 38N55'30 85W52'01 5:43:28
New Frankfort 72 320 38N44'12 85W42'40 5:42:51
New Garden 89 282 39N58 84W55 5:39:40
New Goshen 84 82 39N34'52 87W27'44 5:49:51
New Harmony 65 58 38N07'47 87W56'06 5:51:44
New Haven 2 233 41N04'14 85W00'52 5:40:03
New Haven Heights 2 233 41N04 85W03 5:40:12
New Hope 60 344 39N10'59 86W49'40 5:47:19
New Hope 87 53 37N59'23 87W13'21 5:48:53
New Lancaster 80 116 40N15'18 85W52'48 5:43:31
Newland 37 226 41N02'45 87W02'03 5:48:08
New Lebanon 13 80 39N02'27 87W28'16 5:49:53
New Liberty 10 165 38N34'05 85W52'02 5:43:28
New Lisbon 33 253 39N51'48 85W15'47 5:41:03
New Lisbon 68 311 40N14'37 84W49'28 5:39:18
New London 34 165 40N26'36 86W16'17 5:45:05
New Marion 69 275 39N00'27 85W21'32 5:41:26
New Market 10 166 38N32'08 85W37'01 5:42:28
New Market 54 149 39N57'09 86W55'17 5:47:41
New Maysville 67 128 39N47'26 86W43'45 5:46:55
New Middletown 31 189 38N09'50 86W03'03 5:44:12
New Mount Pleasant 38 291 40N21'21 85W03'54 5:40:16
New Palestine 30 101 39N43'19 85W53'21 5:43:33
New Paris 20 260 41N30'01 85W49'41 5:43:19
New Pekin 88 165 38N32'11 85W55'43 5:43:43
New Pennington 16 101 39N16'47 85W19'29 5:41:18
New Philadelphia 88 165 38N37'35 86W12'27 5:44:50
New Pittsburg 68 311 40N18'27 84W53'57 5:39:36
New Point 16 101 39N18'35 85W19'45 5:41:19
Newport 83 79 39N53'03 87W24'31 5:49:38
New Providence 10 166 38N28 85W57 5:43:48
New Richmond 54 147 40N11'44 86W58'44 5:47:55
New Ross 54 147 39N57'52 86W42'52 5:46:51
New Salem 70 101 39N32'32 85W21'29 5:41:26
New Salem 88 320 38N37'17 85W54'15 5:43:37
New Salisbury 31 166 38N18'49 86W05'42 5:44:23
New Santa Fe 52 335 40N40'25 85W59'16 5:43:57
Newton 37 227 40N58 87W14 5:48:56
Newton 85 264 40N58'02 85W49'17 5:43:17
Newton Stewart 59 169 38N24'17 86W37'25 5:46:30
Newtonville 74 64 38N00'07 86W56'36 5:47:46
Newtown 23 156 40N12'15 87W08'52 5:48:35
New Trenton 24 30 39N18'39 84W54'05 5:39:36
New Unionville 53 344 39N12'40 86W27'44 5:45:51
Newville 17 228 41N20'55 84W50'42 5:39:23
Newville Center 17 228 41N18'51 84W49'48 5:39:19
New Washington 10 166 38N33'47 85W32'23 5:42:10
New Waverly 9 174 40N45'51 86W11'33 5:44:46
New Whiteland 41 97 39N33'29 86W05'43 5:44:23
New Winchester 32 113 39N45'38 86W39'03 5:46:36
Nibbyville 20 259 41N42'50 85W51'39 5:43:27
Niles 18 253 40N21 85W16 5:41:04
Nine Mile 2 233 40N58'30 85W13'30 5:40:54
Nineveh 41 101 39N21'44 86W05'05 5:44:20
Nisbet 82 53 38N08'46 87W39'10 5:50:37
Noble 38 291 40N28'10 84W49'34 5:39:18
Noblesville 29 245 40N02'44 86W00'31 5:44:02
Noblitt Falls 3 147 39N13 85W54 5:43:36
Nora 49 100 39N54 86W08 5:44:32
Nora Plaza 49 100 39N54 86W08 5:44:32
Norland Park 17 234 41N22 85W04 5:40:16
Norma Jean Addition 79 147 40N22'35 86W52'59 5:47:32
Normal 27 280 40N27'54 85W49'31 5:43:18
Norman 36 147 38N57'09 86W16'30 5:45:06
Normanda 80 121 40N18'09 86W09'53 5:44:40
Normandy Addition 18 254 40N11 85W23 5:41:32
Norris 88 165 38N36 86W06 5:44:24
Norristown 73 101 39N21'55 85W45'38 5:43:03
North 50 211 41N26 86W17 5:45:08
North Anderson 48 101 40N08'07 85W40'41 5:42:43
North Augusta Addition 49 100 39N55'41 86W13'40 5:44:55
Northaven 10 166 38N18 85W45 5:43:00
North Bend 75 221 41N13 86W32 5:46:08
Northcliff 3 147 39N17'22 85W52'39 5:43:31
North Columbus 3 130 39N14'00 85W54'30 5:43:38
North Crane 79 147 40N20'19 86W48'37 5:47:14
Northcrest 2 233 41N07'23 85W08'06 5:40:32
North Crows Nest 49 100 39N51'57 86W09'48 5:44:39
North Delphi 8 133 40N35 86W40 5:46:40
Northeast 59 160 38N38 86W21 5:45:24
Northern Beach 29 97 39N57'20 86W04'14 5:44:17
Northern Meadows 6 100 39N58'00 86W15'32 5:45:02
Northfield 6 249 40N01'51 86W16'49 5:45:07
Northfield Village 6 247 40N03'42 86W28'40 5:45:55
North Gate 3 147 39N15'50 85W56'47 5:43:47
Northgate Village 27 284 40N34 85W42 5:42:48
North Grove 52 338 40N36'44 85W57'58 5:43:52
North Harbor 29 97 40N03 86W01 5:44:04
North Hayden 45 26 41N17'24 87W27'30 5:49:50
North Highland 2 233 41N05'20 85W09'58 5:40:40
North Judson 75 10 41N12'54 86W46'33 5:47:06
North Liberty 71 210 41N32'03 86W25'38 5:45:43
North Madison 39 98 38N46'04 85W23'48 5:41:35
North Manchester 85 269 41N00'02 85W46'07 5:43:04
North Oaks 90 228 40N46'36 85W10'26 5:40:42
North Ogilville 3 147 39N07'55 86W00'28 5:44:02
North Park 3 149 39N17'48 85W57'15 5:43:49
Northpine Estates 84 82 39N37 87W21 5:49:24
North Ridge Village 29 100 39N56'06 86W08'57 5:44:36
North Salem 32 251 39N51'35 86W38'33 5:46:34
Norths Landing 58 51 38N54'08 84W52'25 5:39:30
North Terre Haute 84 77 39N31'40 87W21'37 5:49:26
North Union 54 149 39N57'56 86W54'12 5:47:37
North Vernon 40 126 39N00'22 85W37'25 5:42:30
North Webster 43 291 41N19'32 85W41'52 5:42:47
Northwest 59 160 38N39 86W38 5:46:32
Northwest Manor 32 100 39N53'57 86W16'29 5:45:06
Northwood 20 265 41N27 86W00 5:44:00
Northwood 27 284 40N34 85W42 5:42:48
Northwood 67 128 39N39 86W52 5:47:28
Northwood Hills 29 97 39N57'41 86W03'42 5:44:15
Northwood Park 64 6 41N31'43 87W02'56 5:48:12
Norton 59 67 38N29'40 86W40'59 5:46:44
Nortonburg 3 147 39N16'06 85W49'24 5:43:18
Norway 91 181 40N46'42 86W45'34 5:47:02
Notre Dame 71 208 41N42 86W14 5:44:56
Nottingham 90 228 40N34'52 85W09'01 5:40:36
Nulltown 21 272 39N34'47 85W09'30 5:40:38
Numa 61 73 39N37'51 87W22'13 5:49:29
Nutwood 71 208 41N35'38 86W16'55 5:45:08
Nyesville 61 128 39N47'04 87W10'28 5:48:42
Nyona Lake 25 328 40N58 86W08 5:44:32
Oakcrest 3 147 39N13 85W54 5:43:36
Oakdale 52 335 40N46'06 86W03'13 5:44:13
Oakford 34 331 40N25'09 86W06'15 5:44:25
Oak Forest 24 30 39N23'05 85W05'07 5:40:20
Oak Grove 4 147 40N32 87W17 5:49:08
Oak Grove 65 58 37N50'10 88W01'18 5:52:05
Oak Grove 75 221 41N17'16 86W29'10 5:45:57
Oak Grove 84 77 39N26 87W24 5:49:36
Oak Hill 26 59 38N18'16 87W22'28 5:49:30
Oak Hills 3 147 39N18 85W46 5:43:04
Oakland City 26 59 38N20'19 87W20'42 5:49:23
Oakland City Junction 63 59 38N19'54 87W18'05 5:49:12
Oaklandon 49 100 39N52'22 85W57'25 5:43:50
Oaklawn Terrace 10 166 38N18 85W45 5:43:00
Oak Park 10 176 38N18'20 85W41'47 5:42:47
Oaktown 42 86 38N52'16 87W26'29 5:49:46
Oak Tree Crossroads 24 30 39N22'20 85W00'11 5:40:01
Oakville 18 253 40N04'45 85W23'26 5:41:34
Oakwood 46 8 41N40'42 86W47'11 5:47:09
Oakwood 76 30 41N32'59 84W54'49 5:39:39
Oakwood Commons 27 284 40N34 85W42 5:42:48
Oakwood Manor 46 9 41N43 86W53 5:47:32
Oakwood Park 43 291 41N24'41 85W44'18 5:42:57
Oakwood Shores 76 30 41N32 84W55 5:39:40
Oatsville 63 59 38N24'25 87W24'27 5:49:38
Ober 75 221 41N16'15 86W31'28 5:46:06
Occident 70 101 39N41'28 85W28'42 5:41:55
Ockley 8 128 40N29'18 86W38'02 5:46:32
Octagon 79 147 40N31'35 86W59'32 5:47:58
Odell 79 147 40N17'16 87W04'27 5:48:18
Odon 14 91 38N50'34 86W59'29 5:47:58
Ogden 33 108 39N47'57 85W28'08 5:41:53
Ogden Dunes 64 6 41N37'33 87W11'25 5:48:46
Ogilville 3 147 39N07'33 86W00'55 5:44:04
Ohio Falls 10 166 38N18 85W45 5:43:00
Oil 62 69 38N11 86W35 5:46:20
Old Bargersville 41 97 39N31'03 86W09'21 5:44:37
Old Bath 24 30 39N30'30 84W53'30 5:39:34
Oldenburg 24 275 39N20'23 85W12'16 5:40:49
Old Halfway 79 124 40N29'26 87W03'57 5:48:16
Old Hill 11 89 39N18'07 87W12'27 5:48:50
Old Milan 69 275 39N08'47 85W07'57 5:40:32
Old Otto 10 166 38N34 85W33 5:42:12
Old Pekin 88 165 38N29'47 86W00'22 5:44:01
Old Saint Louis 3 147 39N19'14 85W47'08 5:43:09
Old Stone 87 53 37N57 87W24 5:49:36
Old Tip Town 50 328 41N13'25 86W06'55 5:44:28
Oldtown 15 37 39N05'41 84W50'49 5:39:23
Old Town 86 146 40N15'29 87W23'12 5:49:33
Old Watson 10 166 38N18 85W45 5:43:00
Olean 69 275 38N59'25 85W13'07 5:40:52
Olin 86 163 40N08'57 87W25'50 5:49:43
Olive 71 201 41N42'00 86W26'53 5:45:48
Oliver 65 58 38N02'36 87W50'21 5:51:21
Omega 29 97 40N11'54 85W56'21 5:43:45
Ontario 44 30 41N42'08 85W22'57 5:41:32
Onward 9 164 40N41'41 86W11'42 5:44:47
Oolitic 47 344 38N54'03 86W31'31 5:46:06
Ora 75 222 41N10'26 86W33'11 5:46:13
Orange 21 272 39N35'03 85W17'57 5:41:12
Orangeville 17 228 41N20'09 84W51'25 5:39:26
Orangeville 59 160 38N37'53 86W33'24 5:46:14
Orchard Grove 45 2 41N17'23 87W21'13 5:49:25
Orchard Heights 71 208 41N40 86W14 5:44:56
Orchard Heights Addition 71 208 41N36'06 86W14'23 5:44:58
Orchard Highlands 46 9 41N40'58 86W50'09 5:47:21
Orchard Park 29 100 39N56'15 86W07'48 5:44:31
Oregon Heights 45 17 41N34 87W17 5:49:08
Orestes 48 112 40N16'10 85W43'41 5:42:55
Organ Springs 88 165 38N28'36 86W09'53 5:44:40
Oriole 62 69 38N10'08 86W30'17 5:46:01
Orland 76 30 41N43'50 85W10'18 5:40:41
Orleans 59 125 38N39'42 68W25'35 4:33:42
Ormas 92 30 41N17'42 85W32'46 5:42:11
Orrville 42 59 38N27'29 87W41'10 5:50:45
Osborn 45 6 41N35'33 87W28'08 5:49:53
Osborn Landing 43 297 41N16'52 85W47'49 5:43:11
Osceola 71 204 41N39'54 86W04'33 5:44:18
Osgood 69 279 39N07'29 85W17'21 5:41:09
Osolo 20 271 41N43 85W57 5:43:48
Ossian 90 228 40N52'50 85W09'59 5:40:40
Oswego 43 291 41N19'13 85W47'14 5:43:09
Otis 46 21 41N35'57 86W54'21 5:47:37
Otisco 10 166 38N32'32 85W40'02 5:42:40
Otsego Center 76 30 41N34'21 84W54'32 5:39:38
Otterbein 79 124 40N29'26 87W05'47 5:48:23
Otter Creek Junction 84 77 39N32'47 87W20'54 5:49:24
Otter Lake 76 30 41N38 85W00 5:40:00
Otter Village 69 275 39N07'07 85W19'53 5:41:20
Otto 10 166 38N34'15 85W28'01 5:41:52
Otwell 63 59 38N27'17 87W05'32 5:48:22
Owasco 8 128 40N27'39 86W37'41 5:46:31
Owen 10 166 38N27'29 85W32'31 5:42:10
Owensburg 28 193 38N55'23 86W43'47 5:46:55
Owensville 26 59 38N16'19 87W41'16 5:50:45
Oxford 4 123 40N31'11 87W14'52 5:48:59
Packerton 43 291 41N06'59 85W47'51 5:43:11
Paint Mill Lake 84 77 39N26 87W24 5:49:36
Palestine 24 30 39N25'02 84W55'40 5:39:43
Palestine 43 291 41N10'42 85W56'59 5:43:48
Palmer 45 6 41N23'29 87W14'20 5:48:57
Palmyra 31 166 38N24'28 86W06'36 5:44:26
Panama 76 30 41N42'23 85W06'27 5:40:26
Paoli 59 143 38N33'22 86W28'06 5:45:52
Papakeechie Lake 43 291 41N21 85W49 5:43:16
Paradise 87 53 37N59'44 87W22'46 5:49:31
Paradise Lakes 55 101 39N25 86W25 5:45:40
Paragon 55 115 39N23'42 86W33'45 5:46:15
Paris 40 58 38N49'27 85W38'02 5:42:32
Paris Crossing 40 128 38N49'46 85W38'53 5:42:36
Parish Grove 4 147 40N36 87W28 5:49:52
Park 28 193 39N00'58 86W50'58 5:47:24
Parker City 68 307 40N11'20 85W12'15 5:40:49

Parkersburg 54 147 39N52'24 86w54'10 5:47:37
Parkers Settlement 65 58 38N02'48 87w42'58 5:50:52
Park Fletcher 49 100 39N45 86w14 5:44:56
Park Forest Estates 3 147 39N13 85w54 5:43:36
Parkmor 20 271 41N41 85w59 5:43:56
Park Ridge 53 344 39N12 86w37 5:46:28
Parkside 3 147 39N14'18 85w54'41 5:43:39
Parkview 84 82 39N30'59 87w23'31 5:49:34
Park View Heights 52 335 40N44'29 86w02'59 5:44:12
Parkway Hills 2 233 41N01'42 85w15'52 5:41:03
Parkwood 10 166 38N18 85w45 5:43:00
Parr 37 2 41N01'38 87w13'07 5:48:52
Pate 58 33 38N57 84w51 5:39:24
Patoka 26 59 38N24'25 87w35'08 5:50:21
Patricksburg 60 344 39N18'56 86w57'33 5:47:50
Patriot 78 35 38N50'19 84w49'37 5:39:18
Patronville 74 61 37N51'30 87w06'38 5:48:27
Patton 8 162 40N42'29 86w44'26 5:46:58
Patton Hill 47 344 38N54'02 86w32'17 5:46:09
Patton Lake 55 101 39N25 86w25 5:45:40
Paw Paw 85 264 40N55 85w52 5:43:28
Paxton 13 80 39N01'16 87w23'19 5:49:33
Paynesville 26 101 38N37'16 85w29'36 5:41:58
Peabody 92 228 41N05'09 85w29'22 5:41:57
Pearsontown 59 160 38N25'15 86w23'31 5:45:34
Pecksburg 32 251 39N41'17 86w34'27 5:46:18
Peerless 47 344 38N55'28 86w30'12 5:46:01
Pekin 88 165 38N29'54 86w01'02 5:44:04
Pelzer 87 53 37N59'21 87w15'26 5:49:02
Pence 86 187 40N21'40 87w30'41 5:50:03
Pendleton 48 101 39N59'51 85w44'48 5:42:59
Penn Park 76 30 41N32'39 84w55'26 5:39:42
Penntown 69 275 39N16'12 85w05'51 5:40:23
Pennville 38 291 40N29'38 85w08'54 5:40:36
Pennville 89 317 39N48'50 85w06'41 5:40:27
Pennyville 14 85 38N33'14 87w00'29 5:48:02
Peoga 53 147 39N20'35 86w08'39 5:44:35
Peoria 52 335 40N43'07 85w57'38 5:43:51
Peppertown 24 275 39N23'56 85w10'27 5:40:42
Percy Junction 56 226 40N48'33 87w17'48 5:49:11
Perkins 56 240 40N45'54 87w21'47 5:49:27
Perkinsville 48 101 40N08'39 85w51'41 5:43:27
Perry Crossing 10 179 38N26'34 85w45'48 5:43:03
Perry Manor 49 100 39N40'31 86w06'25 5:44:26
Perrysburg 52 335 40N53'52 86w08'58 5:44:36
Perrysville 83 84 40N03'05 87w26'00 5:49:44
Perryville 1 287 40N35'28 85w02'26 5:40:10
Pershing 25 328 41N05'46 86w19'08 5:45:17
Pershing 36 139 39N00 86w09 5:44:36
Pershing 89 317 39N49 85w09 5:40:36
Perth 11 89 39N35'35 87w09'43 5:48:39
Peru 52 339 40N45'13 86w04'08 5:44:17
Petersburg 63 59 38N29'31 87w16'43 5:49:07
Peterson 1 228 40N48'47 85w00'53 5:40:04
Petersville 3 147 39N13'28 85w49'12 5:43:17
Petroleum 90 228 40N36'41 85w09'03 5:40:36
Pettit 79 147 40N25'03 86w42'33 5:46:50
Pettysville 52 335 40N52'53 85w58'54 5:43:56
Pheasant Run 2 233 41N04 85w09 5:40:36
Phenix 90 228 40N34'55 85w06'26 5:40:26
Philadelphia 30 97 39N46'53 85w50'44 5:43:23
Philomath 81 313 39N43'26 85w00'57 5:40:04
Phlox 34 334 40N25'16 85w55'07 5:43:40
Pickard 12 181 40N13'23 86w15'41 5:45:03
Pickwick Park 43 291 41N21 85w49 5:43:16
Pierce 88 165 38N31 86w04 5:44:16
Pierceton 43 295 41N12'01 85w42'20 5:42:49
Pierceville 69 275 39N08'00 85w10'47 5:40:43
Pierson 84 82 39N19 87w18 5:49:12
Pike 6 248 40N07'27 86w28'55 5:45:56
Pikes Peak 7 147 39N07'45 86w08'29 5:44:34
Pikeville 63 59 38N19'19 87w06'41 5:48:27
Pilot Knob 13 169 38N16'57 86w20'59 5:45:24
Pimento 84 82 39N18'34 87w22'45 5:49:31
Pinch 68 307 40N06'24 85w08'47 5:40:35
Pine 45 6 41N37'28 87w23'39 5:49:35
Pine Lake 46 8 41N38 86w46 5:47:04
Pine Ridge 84 77 39N28 87w26 5:49:44
Pine Valley 59 160 38N28'35 86w27'01 5:45:48
Pine Village 86 143 40N27'01 87w15'16 5:49:01
Pinhook 16 101 39N13'10 85w31'03 5:42:04
Pinhook 46 8 41N33'50 86w51'21 5:47:25
Pinhook 47 344 38N48'55 86w21'23 5:45:26
Pinhook 89 316 39N48'56 85w03'26 5:40:14
Pinola 46 8 41N35'56 86w47'52 5:47:11
Pioneer 85 264 40N44'16 85w53'44 5:43:35
Pittsboro 32 247 39N51'50 86w28'01 5:45:52
Pittsburg 8 128 40N35'34 86w42'06 5:46:48
Plain 43 291 41N18 85w49 5:43:16
Plainfield 32 98 39N42'15 86w23'58 5:45:36
Plainfield 46 201 41N42'29 86w28'36 5:45:54
Plainville 14 85 38N48'22 87w09'08 5:48:37
Plano 55 101 39N29'57 86w36'14 5:46:25
Plato 44 30 41N38'32 85w19'54 5:41:20
Plattsburg 88 165 38N43'10 86w05'23 5:44:22
Pleasant 78 35 38N52'15 85w11'02 5:40:44
Pleasant Acres 30 98 39N51'22 85w54'56 5:43:40
Pleasant Acres 49 100 39N53'28 86w06'10 5:44:25

Pleasant Gardens 67 128 39N33'05 86w57'52 5:47:51
Pleasant Lake 76 50 41N34'31 85w00'58 5:40:04
Pleasant Mills 1 228 40N46'40 84w50'32 5:39:22
Pleasant Plain 35 287 40N41'48 85w32'43 5:42:11
Pleasant Ridge 37 226 40N56'02 87w04'27 5:48:18
Pleasant Ridge 38 291 40N28'58 84w58'46 5:39:55
Pleasant Run 47 344 38N57 86w23 5:45:32
Pleasant Valley 51 322 38N37'55 86w48'05 5:47:12
Pleasant Valley 71 208 41N41'39 86w04'28 5:44:18
Pleasant View 73 101 39N39'48 85w56'30 5:43:46
Pleasant View Village 3 302 39N20'01 85w58'25 5:43:54
Pleasantville 77 80 38N58'01 87w15'01 5:49:00
Pleasure Valley 73 101 39N24'03 85w42'31 5:42:50
Plevna 34 331 40N32'09 85w58'34 5:43:54
Plummer 28 193 38N58'54 86w58'21 5:47:53
Plum Tree 35 287 40N44'32 85w23'33 5:41:34
Plymouth 50 219 41N20'37 86w18'35 5:45:14
Poe 2 233 40N56'09 85w05'13 5:40:21
Point 65 58 37N51 87w59 5:51:56
Point Commerce 28 193 39N07'31 86w57'55 5:47:52
Point Idalawn 7 147 39N15'38 86w22'08 5:45:29
Point Isabel 27 280 40N25'18 85w49'28 5:43:18
Poland 11 89 39N26'39 86w57'03 5:47:48
Poling 38 287 40N31'57 85w03'12 5:40:13
Poneto 90 228 40N39'25 85w13'18 5:40:53
Pontiac 11 89 39N35'25 87w07'07 5:48:28
Pony 38 291 40N26'41 85w05'41 5:40:23
Popcorn 47 344 38N58'33 86w39'25 5:46:38
Portage 64 6 41N34'33 87w10'34 5:48:42
Porter 64 11 41N36'56 87w04'27 5:48:18
Porter Crossroads 64 6 41N23'57 87w09'42 5:48:39
Portersville 19 67 38N29'58 86w58'42 5:47:55
Port Fulton 10 166 38N18 85w45 5:43:00
Portland 38 298 40N26'04 84w58'40 5:39:55
Portland Mills 67 128 39N46'41 87w00'33 5:48:02
Port Mitchell 67 30 41N21'43 85w26'20 5:41:45
Poseyville 65 58 38N10'12 87w46'59 5:51:08
Potawatomi Park 43 291 41N19'24 85w45'31 5:43:02
Potawatomi Point 9 165 40N44'52 86w18'30 5:45:14
Pottawattamie Park 46 9 41N43 86w52 5:47:28
Pottersville 60 344 39N12'26 86w48'51 5:47:15
Poundstone Corner 9 165 40N37'36 86w20'10 5:45:21
Powers 38 295 40N19'19 85w05'33 5:40:22
Prairie 65 58 37N55'17 87w58'55 5:51:56
Prairie City 61 89 39N26'44 87w06'48 5:48:27
Prairie Creek 84 82 39N18 87w31 5:50:04
Prairieton 84 82 39N22'12 87w28'28 5:49:54
Prairie Village 84 77 39N26 87w24 5:49:36
Prather 10 166 38N22'54 85w41'34 5:42:46
Prather 55 101 39N22'41 86w27'19 5:45:49
Preble 1 231 40N49'56 85w00'53 5:40:04
Prescott 73 101 39N28'45 85w42'30 5:42:50
Presidential Village 2 233 41N04 85w09 5:40:36
Preston 84 77 39N30'24 87w22'19 5:49:29
Pretty Lake 44 30 41N32 85w22 5:41:28
Prince Hall Plaza 27 284 40N34 85w42 5:42:48
Prince's Lakes 41 101 39N21 86w07 5:44:28
Princeton 26 60 38N21'19 87w34'03 5:50:16
Prince William 8 165 40N26'32 86w34'23 5:46:18
Progress 18 253 40N07'13 85w26'33 5:41:46
Progress Acres 84 82 39N42 86w51 5:47:24
Prospect 59 160 38N34'41 86w36'51 5:46:27
Prosperity 48 101 40N10'45 85w40'19 5:42:41
Providence 41 97 39N29'27 86w10'36 5:44:42
Prowsville 88 165 38N40'48 86w12'06 5:44:48
Publico 22 166 38N18 85w49 5:43:16
Puckett 27 284 40N31'27 85w34'20 5:42:17
Pueblo 74 61 37N49'34 87w06'37 5:48:26
Pulaski 66 181 40N58'31 86w39'30 5:46:38
Pumpkin Center 59 160 38N35'22 86w21'52 5:45:27
Purcell 42 86 38N35'44 87w31'09 5:50:05
Purdue University 79 147 40N26 86w56 5:47:44
Putnamville 67 128 39N34'27 86w51'55 5:47:28
Pyrmont 8 128 40N28'03 86w40'47 5:46:43
Quail Meadows Estates 24 275 39N18 85w13 5:40:52
Quaker 83 73 39N51'21 87w31'41 5:50:07
Quaker Haven Park 43 291 41N22'01 85w45'38 5:43:03
Queensville 40 126 39N03'04 85w40'38 5:42:43
Quercus Grove 78 35 38N51'12 84w55'22 5:39:41
Quincy 60 344 39N27'13 86w42'45 5:46:51
Raab Crossroads 67 344 39N29'16 86w59'31 5:47:58

Rabbitville 47 344 38N46'07 86w28'26 5:45:54
Raber 92 228 41N05'09 85w25'58 5:41:44
Raccoon 67 128 39N51'22 86w53'47 5:47:35
Radioville 66 181 41N09'35 86w53'28 5:47:34
Radley 27 284 40N26'11 85w44'01 5:42:56
Radnor 8 128 40N30'34 86w38'06 5:46:32
Raglesville 14 91 38N48'12 86w57'41 5:47:51
Ragsdale 42 86 38N44'45 87w19'30 5:49:18
Rahm 82 55 37N52'09 87w36'52 5:50:27
Railroad 75 2 41N13 86w52 5:47:28
Rainbow 49 100 39N47 86w13 5:44:52
Rainbow Highlands 49 100 39N53'24 85w58'54 5:43:56
Rainbow Ridge 49 100 39N47 86w13 5:44:52
Rainsville 86 129 40N24'57 87w18'56 5:49:16
Raintown 32 247 39N52'42 86w30'36 5:46:02
Raleigh 70 101 39N44'38 85w21'50 5:41:27
Ramsey 31 166 38N19'25 86w09'17 5:44:37
Ranburn Woods 45 6 41N32 87w22 5:49:28
Randall 83 73 39N42'29 87w31'21 5:50:05
Randolph 68 307 40N15'58 84w58'33 5:39:54
Ranger 62 69 38N05'45 86w41'08 5:46:45
Rapture 65 58 38N09'08 87w50'31 5:51:22
Raub 4 147 40N43'48 87w29'30 5:49:58
Ravenswood 49 100 39N53'17 86w07'52 5:44:31
Ravinamy 79 147 40N27'43 86w53'52 5:47:35
Ray 76 32 41N44 84w53 5:39:32
Raymond 24 30 39N28'18 84w50'58 5:39:24
Rays Crossing 73 101 39N33'16 85w40'09 5:42:41
Raysville 33 108 39N47'46 85w30'45 5:42:03
Reagan 12 181 40N11'31 86w30'34 5:46:02
Red Bank 82 55 37N58'17 87w37'33 5:50:30
Red Bridge 85 264 40N36 85w58 5:43:52
Red Bush 87 53 37N56'18 87w16'19 5:49:05
Redcuff Corner 28 89 39N09'18 87w08'50 5:48:35
Redding 36 147 39N01 85w56 5:43:44
Reddington 36 147 39N01'57 85w49'58 5:43:20
Redkey 38 301 40N20'56 85w09'00 5:40:36
Redmond Park 43 291 41N21 85w49 5:43:16
Reds Corner 41 101 39N36'04 85w58'18 5:43:53
Reed Station 18 254 40N12'54 85w31'05 5:42:04
Reedville Station 30 97 39N42'22 85w49'09 5:43:17
Reelsville 67 126 39N33'27 86w58'01 5:47:52
Reeve 14 85 38N33 86w59 5:47:56
Rego 59 160 38N29'06 86w19'04 5:45:16
Reiffsburg 90 228 40N39'21 85w09'07 5:40:36
Remington 37 225 40N45'39 87w09'03 5:48:36
Renner 5 196 40N28'20 85w25'53 5:41:44
Reno 32 113 39N42'37 86w40'13 5:46:41
Rensselaer 37 227 40N56'12 87w09'03 5:48:36
Reo 74 61 37N54'05 87w06'34 5:48:26
Republican 39 101 38N43 85w33 5:42:12
Reserve 61 73 39N49 87w25 5:49:40
Retreat 36 147 38N49'28 85w51'12 5:43:25
Rexville 45 6 41N30 87w19 5:49:16
Rexville 69 275 38N57'09 85w20'12 5:41:21
Reynolds 91 149 40N44'58 86w52'18 5:47:29
Rhodes 83 73 39N36'34 87w24'47 5:49:39
Riceville 13 169 38N19'28 86w39'56 5:46:40
Richey Park 91 162 40N45 86w46 5:47:04
Rich Grove 66 181 41N07 86w45 5:47:00
Richland 70 101 39N29'51 85w23'42 5:41:35
Richland 74 61 37N57 87w10 5:48:40
Richland Center 25 328 41N09'23 86w16'14 5:45:05
Richland City 74 61 37N56'43 87w10'04 5:48:40
Richmond 89 318 39N49'44 84w53'25 5:39:34
Richvalley 85 264 40N47'06 85w55'13 5:43:41
Riddle 13 169 38N15'02 86w25'50 5:45:43
Ridertown 38 196 40N26'08 85w12'23 5:40:50
Ridgemede 53 344 39N09'07 86w30'11 5:46:01
Ridgeport 28 193 39N02 86w56 5:47:44
Ridgeview 52 335 40N42 86w07 5:44:28
Ridgeview Heights 2 233 41N03 85w08 5:40:32
Ridgeville 68 309 40N17'21 85w01'44 5:40:07
Ridgeway 2 233 41N01 85w10 5:40:40
Ridgeway 34 330 40N29'21 86w17'44 5:45:11
Ridgewood 55 98 39N36'12 86w21'34 5:45:26
Ridgleville 42 59 38N34'00 87w25'39 5:49:43
Ridinger Lake 43 291 41N11 85w42 5:42:48
Rigdon 27 280 40N22'44 85w47'11 5:43:09
Riley 30 98 39N47'13 85w43'50 5:42:55
Riley 84 82 39N23'24 87w18'00 5:49:12
Rileysburg 83 73 40N06'15 87w31'33 5:50:06
Riley Village 73 101 39N30'23 85w46'05 5:43:04
Rincon 28 195 39N06'09 86w59'25 5:47:58
Ringwald 39 97 38N47'01 85w22'58 5:41:32
Ripley 66 183 41N06'02 86w39'37 5:46:38
Rising Sun 58 51 38N56'58 84w51'14 5:39:25
Risse 12 181 40N16'30 86w29'13 5:45:57
Rivare 1 231 40N48'44 84w50'29 5:39:22
River Forest 48 101 40N06'35 85w43'38 5:42:55
River Haven 2 233 41N04'39 85w03'15 5:40:13
River Ridge 10 166 38N22'43 85w38'44 5:42:35
Riverside 10 166 38N18 85w45 5:43:00
Riverside 23 129 40N19'30 87w09'58 5:48:40
Riverside 46 2 41N15'22 86w53'39 5:47:35
Riverside 90 228 40N41'47 85w05'07 5:40:20
Riverton 13 80 39N01'13 87w34'04 5:50:16
Rivervale 47 344 38N46'08 86w23'53 5:45:36
Riverview 13 80 39N12'01 87w35'01 5:50:20
Riverview Acres 3 147 39N14'32 85w55'16 5:43:41
Riverwood 29 97 40N06'02 85w58'05 5:43:52
Roachdale 67 128 39N50'56 86w48'08 5:47:13
Roadman Corner 61 89 39N28'27 87w02'02 5:48:08

Roann 85 269 40N54'42 85w55'28 5:43:42
Roanoke 35 287 40N57'45 85w22'24 5:41:30
Roanoke Station 35 287 40N57'07 85w21'51 5:41:27
Robb 65 58 38N10 87w49 5:51:16
Roberts 23 129 40N18'58 87w06'08 5:48:25
Robertsdale 45 6 41N40'59 87w30'29 5:50:02
Robinson 65 58 38N03 87w45 5:51:00
Robinwood 84 77 39N29 87w22 5:49:28
Roble Woods 64 6 41N31'20 87w03'16 5:48:13
Rob Roy 23 129 40N14'12 87w14'36 5:48:58
Rochester 25 329 41N03'53 86w12'57 5:44:52
Rockcreek 35 287 40N49 85w32 5:42:08
Rockdale 24 30 39N19'01 84w50'49 5:39:23
Rockfield 8 174 40N38'28 86w34'26 5:46:18
Rockford 36 139 38N59'14 85w53'29 5:43:34
Rockford 90 230 40N45'36 85w18'49 5:41:15
Rock Hill 74 61 37N56'42 87w02'24 5:48:10
Rock Island 49 100 39N52 86w14 5:44:56
Rock Lake 25 242 41N02 86w02 5:44:08
Rocklane 41 100 39N36'35 86w00'45 5:44:03
Rockport 74 57 37N52'59 87w02'58 5:48:12
Rockport Junction 74 64 38N06'26 87w00'24 5:48:02
Rockville 61 157 39N45'45 87w13'45 5:48:55
Rocky Ford 86 129 40N23'59 87w19'41 5:49:19
Rocky Fork Lake 61 89 39N31 87w08 5:48:32
Rocky Ripple 49 100 39N50'53 86w10'21 5:44:41
Rogers 63 59 38N32'18 87w13'26 5:48:54
Rogersville 33 253 40N02'08 85w19'46 5:41:19
Roland 59 160 38N35'43 86w40'55 5:46:44
Roll 5 196 40N33'08 85w23'25 5:41:34
Rolling Acres 87 53 38N03 87w16 5:49:04
Rolling Hill Estates 45 6 41N28'38 87w24'02 5:49:36
Rolling Hills 2 233 41N01'38 85w16'05 5:41:04
Rolling Hills 10 166 38N28'41 85w35'19 5:42:21
Rolling Hills 27 284 40N34 85w42 5:42:48
Rolling Prairie 46 22 41N40'15 86w36'57 5:46:28
Rolling Ridge 73 101 39N32'41 85w46'41 5:43:07
Rollins 51 322 38N40 86w47 5:47:08
Rome 62 69 37N55'24 86w31'25 5:46:06
Rome City 57 41 41N29'46 85w22'36 5:41:30
Romine Corner 86 163 40N08'31 87w25'59 5:49:44
Romney 79 147 40N14'58 86w54'15 5:47:37
Romona 60 342 39N19'38 86w43'48 5:46:55
Root 1 228 40N53 84w56 5:39:44
Rosebud 88 165 38N31'38 86w12'43 5:44:51
Roseburg 27 284 40N31'19 85w43'46 5:42:55
Roseburg 81 313 39N35'20 84w56'49 5:39:47
Rosedale 61 72 39N37'22 87w17'00 5:49:08
Rosedale Hills 49 100 39N41'37 86w07'53 5:44:32
Rose Hill Gardens 84 82 39N42 86w51 5:47:24
Roseland 71 208 41N42'58 86w15'09 5:45:01
Roselawn 56 2 41N08'30 87w18'53 5:49:16
Rosewood 31 166 38N02'17 85w55'45 5:43:43
Ross 45 6 41N31'36 87w22'29 5:49:30
Rossburg 16 101 39N19'33 85w19'34 5:41:18
Rosston 6 100 40N02'55 86w17'21 5:45:09
Rosstown 3 147 39N06'33 85w55'46 5:43:43
Rossville 12 147 40N25'01 86w35'41 5:46:23
Roth Park 8 162 40N41'11 86w44'57 5:47:00
Round Grove 91 147 40N35'25 87w01'49 5:48:07
Round Lake 57 30 41N26 85w16 5:41:04
Royal Center 9 170 40N51'52 86w29'59 5:46:00
Royal Oaks 2 233 41N07'36 85w04'29 5:40:18
Royalton 6 97 39N55'37 86w20'18 5:45:21
Royal View 3 147 39N13 85w54 5:43:36
Royer Lake 44 30 41N39 85w25 5:41:40
Royerton 18 254 40N15'49 85w21'56 5:41:28
Royville 2 239 41N11'59 85w07'59 5:40:32
Rugby 3 147 39N18'33 85w42'53 5:42:52
Rumble 63 59 38N26'09 87w20'34 5:49:22
Runyantown 10 166 38N29'22 85w36'53 5:42:28
Rural 68 307 40N06'24 84w57'58 5:39:52
Rush Creek Valley 88 165 38N41'43 86w10'14 5:44:41
Rushville 70 107 39N36'33 85w26'47 5:41:47
Rusk 51 322 38N33'26 86w45'25 5:47:02
Russell 67 128 39N50 86w58 5:47:52
Russell Lake 6 100 39N56'55 86w18'06 5:45:12
Russellville 67 128 39N51'30 86w59'02 5:47:56
Russels Point 76 30 41N33'14 84w55'27 5:39:42
Russiaville 34 165 40N25'03 86w16'17 5:45:05
Rustic Hills 87 53 37N57'20 87w22'03 5:49:28
Rutherford 51 200 38N34 86w53 5:47:32
Rutland 50 211 41N14'40 86w21'26 5:45:26
Ryan Place 65 58 37N56 87w54 5:51:36
Rykers Ridge 39 97 38N45 85w19 5:41:16
Saddle Lake 1 228 40N50 84w56 5:39:44
Sagers Lake 64 6 41N29 87w23 5:49:32
Sagunay Lake 46 2 41N40 86w37 5:46:28
Saint Anthony 19 67 38N18'52 86w49'36 5:47:18
Saint Bernice 83 73 39N42'33 87w31'17 5:50:05
Saint Croix 62 69 38N13'26 86w35'11 5:46:21
Saint Henry 19 67 38N13'03 86w55'43 5:47:43
Saint James 26 59 38N10'36 87w34'39 5:50:19
Saint Joe 17 228 41N18'55 84w54'05 5:39:36
Saint John 45 23 41N27'00 87w28'12 5:49:53
Saint John 87 53 38N10 87w27 5:49:48
Saint Johns 17 228 41N18'31 85w06'49 5:40:27
Saint Joseph 2 233 41N08 85w04 5:40:16
Saint Joseph 22 166 38N24'00 85w48'30 5:43:14
Saint Joseph 82 55 38N03'58 87w38'49 5:50:35
Saint Joseph Hill 10 166 38N19 85w44 5:42:56
Saint Leon 15 33 39N17'31 84w48'26 5:39:14
Saint Louis Crossing 3 149 39N19'08 85w50'48 5:43:23
Saint Marks 19 67 38N18'20 86w49'05 5:47:16
Saint Mary-of-the-Woods 84 77 39N30'39 87w28'02 5:49:52
Saint Marys 1 228 40N48 84w51 5:39:24
Saint Marys 22 166 38N21'21 85w51'53 5:43:28
Saint Marys 24 30 39N20'52 85w06'32 5:40:26
Saint Marys 71 208 41N42 86w14 5:44:56
Saint Maurice 16 101 39N21'58 85w20'04 5:41:20
Saint Meinrad 74 64 38N10'16 86w48'33 5:47:14
Saint Omer 16 101 39N26'08 85w35'45 5:42:23
Saint Paul 73 101 39N25'41 85w37'42 5:42:31
Saint Peter 24 30 39N19'18 85w01'54 5:40:08
Saint Phillip 65 58 37N59'13 87w42'57 5:50:52
Saint Thomas 42 86 38N45 87w31 5:50:04
Saint Wendell 82 55 38N06'20 87w41'50 5:50:47
Salamonia 38 287 40N22'55 84w51'55 5:39:28
Salamonie 35 287 40N42 85w23 5:41:32
Salem 1 228 40N43'01 84w51'12 5:39:25
Salem 38 287 40N18'37 84w50'36 5:39:22
Salem 81 313 39N35'47 84w53'25 5:39:34
Salem 88 180 38N03'16 86w15'33 5:45:02
Salem Center 76 30 41N35'06 85w08'23 5:40:34
Salem Heights 46 8 41N34'29 86w37'19 5:46:29
Saline City 11 89 39N21'55 87w07'56 5:48:32
Salt Creek Commons 64 6 41N29 87w23 5:49:32
Saltillo 88 165 38N39'54 86w17'21 5:45:09
Saluda 39 101 38N39'02 85w29'51 5:41:59
Samaria 41 97 39N24'14 86w11'11 5:44:45
Sandborn 42 86 38N53'47 87w11'12 5:48:45
Sandcut 84 82 39N33'53 87w19'25 5:49:18
Sanders 53 344 39N04'47 86w30'48 5:46:03
Sandford 84 82 39N32'43 87w31'50 5:50:07
Sand Pit 47 344 38N49'25 86w30'13 5:46:01
Sand Point 43 291 41N24'22 85w41'44 5:42:47
Sand Ridge 74 61 37N54'09 87w10'07 5:48:40
Sandusky 16 101 39N25'10 85w28'41 5:41:55
Sandy Beach 8 162 40N39'52 86w45'12 5:47:01
Sandy Hook 3 147 39N13 85w54 5:43:36
Sandy Hook 14 85 38N34'06 87w13'04 5:48:52
Sandytown 83 73 39N40'55 87w26'46 5:49:47
San Jacinto 40 128 38N57'23 85w29'50 5:41:59
San Pierre 75 2 41N12'13 86w53'31 5:47:34
Santa Claus 74 64 38N07'12 86w54'51 5:47:39
Santa Fe 52 335 40N39'11 85w59'10 5:43:57
Santa Fe 74 64 38N06'45 86w54'34 5:47:38
Saratoga 68 306 40N14'13 84w55'06 5:39:40
Sardinia 3 101 39N09'14 85w37'52 5:42:31
Sassafras 62 69 38N11'18 86w41'25 5:46:46
Savah 65 58 38N01'04 87w58'43 5:51:55
Scalesville 87 53 38N12'09 87w12'22 5:48:49
Scarlet 59 160 38N39'28 86w40'03 5:46:40
Scarlet Oaks 8 162 40N41'44 86w45'15 5:47:01
Scenic Heights 62 69 37N57 86w46 5:47:04
Scenic Hill 51 200 38N40'42 86w53'38 5:47:35
Schaefer Lake 3 147 39N18 85w46 5:43:04
Schererville 45 6 41N30'02 87w27'41 5:49:51
Schley 74 64 38N02'44 86w52'19 5:47:29
Schneider 45 2 41N11'13 87w26'54 5:49:48
Schnellville 19 67 38N20'28 86w45'22 5:47:01
Schooler Point Landing 13 169 38N09'29 86w20'29 5:45:22
Scipio 24 30 39N21 84w46 5:39:04
Scipio 40 126 39N04'45 85w43'03 5:42:52
Scircleville 12 184 40N17'15 86w18'00 5:45:12
Scotchtown 13 71 39N04'30 87w17'52 5:49:11
Scotland 28 193 38N54'46 86w54'14 5:47:37
Scott 44 30 41N44'01 85w33'25 5:42:14
Scott City 13 80 39N11'38 87w27'54 5:49:52
Scott Corner 68 307 40N05'31 85w07'37 5:40:30
Scottsburg 63 59 38N17'19 87w13'09 5:48:53
Scottsburg 72 321 38N41'08 85w46'13 5:43:05
Scottsville 22 166 38N24'07 85w54'33 5:43:38
Seafield 91 149 40N45'23 86w59'12 5:47:57
Searcy Crossroads 78 35 38N50'48 84w51'29 5:39:26
Sedalia 12 183 40N24'56 86w30'53 5:46:04
Sedan 17 237 41N26'11 85w05'58 5:40:24
Sedley 64 23 41N29'19 87w09'27 5:48:38
Seelyville 84 83 39N29'31 87w16'02 5:49:04
Sellersburg 10 179 38N23'53 85w45'18 5:43:01
Sellers Lake 43 291 41N11 85w42 5:42:48
Selma 18 253 40N11'30 85w16'08 5:41:05
Selvin 87 53 38N12'15 87w06'22 5:48:25
Servia 52 270 40N57'24 85w44'26 5:42:58
Sevastopol 43 291 41N07'45 86w01'08 5:44:05
Seven Springs 31 166 38N08'31 85w58'36 5:43:54
Seward 43 291 41N06 85w57 5:43:48
Sexton 70 101 39N42'00 85w26'05 5:41:44
Seyberts 44 30 41N42'01 85w30'48 5:42:03
Seymour 36 138 38N57'33 85w53'25 5:43:34
Shadeland 27 284 40N36'18 85w36'36 5:42:26
Shadeland 79 147 40N22'25 86w56'56 5:47:48
Shady Banks 43 294 41N23'32 85w49'49 5:43:19
Shady Hills 27 284 40N35'22 85w40'27 5:42:42
Shady Hills Estates 27 284 40N34 85w42 5:42:48
Shady Lane 11 89 39N32'44 87w08'01 5:48:32
Shady Lawn 45 6 41N23'35 87w21'17 5:49:25
Shady Nook 44 30 41N33'24 85w14'00 5:40:56
Shady Side 64 4 41N37 87w06 5:48:24
Shamrock Lakes 5 196 40N24 85w26 5:41:44
Shanghai 34 165 40N26'46 86w19'42 5:45:19
Shannondale 54 147 40N03'17 86w41'44 5:46:47
Sharon 8 170 40N33'13 86w23'29 5:45:34
Sharpsville 80 119 40N22'46 86w05'19 5:44:21
Sharptown 24 30 39N22'01 84w52'25 5:39:30
Shawnee 23 156 40N14 87w16 5:49:04
Shawswick 47 344 38N53'44 86w24'52 5:45:39
Shawville 84 82 39N42 86w51 5:47:24
Shedville 68 307 40N15'56 85w07'44 5:40:31
Sheff 4 147 40N42'20 87w26'57 5:49:48
Sheffield 79 147 40N21 86w46 5:47:04
Shelburn 13 81 39N10'42 87w23'37 5:49:34
Shelburne 55 101 39N26'07 86w23'34 5:45:34
Shelby 45 28 41N11'43 87w20'52 5:49:23
Shelbyville 73 111 39N31'17 85w46'37 5:43:06
Shepardsville 84 82 39N36'03 87w25'03 5:49:40
Shepherd 6 247 39N58'02 86w25'53 5:45:44
Sheridan 29 108 40N08'06 86w13'14 5:44:53
Sheridan 46 9 41N43 86w53 5:47:32
Sheridan Park 84 77 39N29'13 87w22'29 5:49:30
Sherwood Forest 49 100 39N55'08 86w07'47 5:44:31
Shideler 18 253 40N18'22 85w21'35 5:41:26
Shields 36 147 38N54'57 86w00'12 5:44:01
Shiloh 13 80 39N02'20 87w17'33 5:49:10
Shiloh Village 3 147 39N13 85w54 5:43:36
Shipshewana 44 30 41N40'22 85w34'49 5:42:19
Shirkieville 84 82 39N36'01 87w29'55 5:50:00
Shirley 33 97 39N53'31 85w34'37 5:42:18
Shoals 51 322 38N39'59 86w47'28 5:47:10
Shoe Lake 43 291 41N20 85w51 5:43:24
Shooters Hill 49 100 39N49'48 86w10'56 5:44:44
Shore Acres 49 100 39N52'35 86w08'12 5:44:33
Shoreland Hills 46 9 41N43 86w53 5:47:32
Shores Acres 49 100 39N52 86w07 5:44:28
Shorts Corner 88 165 38N29'59 86w06'01 5:44:24
Siberia 62 69 38N14'17 86w44'01 5:46:56
Sidney 43 293 41N06'20 85w44'37 5:42:58
Silex 60 342 39N21'38 86w39'35 5:46:38
Silver Creek 10 166 38N23 85w45 5:43:00
Silverdale 74 61 37N54'57 87w04'17 5:48:17
Silver Grove 22 166 38N18 85w49 5:43:16
Silver Hills 22 166 38N16'57 85w50'43 5:43:23
Silver Lake 43 291 41N04'20 85w53'30 5:43:34
Silver Lakes Estates 10 166 38N18 85w45 5:43:00
Silver Point 43 291 41N19'53 85w46'08 5:43:05
Silverville 47 344 38N51'27 86w39'55 5:46:40
Silverwood 23 156 39N57'20 87w24'12 5:49:37
Simonton Lake 20 271 41N41 85w59 5:43:56
Simpson 35 289 40N51'18 85w24'47 5:41:39
Simpson Corner 23 156 40N08'33 87w14'35 5:48:58
Sims 3 147 39N13 85w54 5:43:36
Sims 27 280 40N29'59 85w51'19 5:43:25
Sisson 42 86 38N31'50 87w33'41 5:50:15
Sitka 91 181 40N49'32 86w44'07 5:46:56
Six Points 32 100 39N43'34 86w20'09 5:45:21
Skelton 26 59 38N20'29 87w46'54 5:51:08
Skelton 87 53 38N05 87w09 5:48:36
Skinner Lake 57 30 41N24 85w26 5:41:44
Slabtown 16 101 39N16'42 85w24'05 5:41:36
Sleepy Hollow 73 101 39N23'48 85w43'03 5:42:52
Sleeth 8 128 40N38'57 86w43'03 5:46:52
Sloan 86 156 40N18'07 87w28'34 5:49:54
Smartsburg 54 147 40N02'49 86w49'43 5:47:19
Smedley 88 165 38N37'59 86w12'57 5:44:52
Smith 46 2 41N42'39 86w40'09 5:46:41
Smithfield 17 237 41N29 85w01 5:40:04
Smithfield 18 253 40N10'12 85w16'07 5:41:04
Smithland 73 101 39N27'37 85w50'48 5:43:23
Smithson 91 147 40N43'04 86w52'21 5:47:29
Smith Valley 41 97 39N36'19 86w11'49 5:44:47
Smithville 53 344 39N04'16 86w30'25 5:46:02
Smithville 60 199 39N19'15 87w01'33 5:48:06
Smockville 61 89 39N37'34 87w07'59 5:48:32
Smoke Corner 64 2 41N24'47 87w03'57 5:48:16
Smyrna 16 101 39N15'50 85w22'38 5:41:31
Smyrna 39 101 38N46'55 85w28'51 5:41:55
Smythe 65 55 37N59'29 87w29'33 5:49:58
Snacks 49 100 39N50 86w15 5:45:00
Snow Hill 61 89 39N39'20 87w10'12 5:48:41
Snow Hill 68 310 40N05'31 84w57'47 5:39:51
Solitude 65 58 38N00'53 87w53'56 5:51:36
Solsberry 28 193 39N05'00 86w45'22 5:47:01

Somerset 85 264 40N40'09 85W49'42 5:43:19
Somerville 26 59 38N16'35 87W22'40 5:49:31
South Bend 71 208 41N41'00 86W15'00 5:45:00
South Bethany 3 147 39N13 85W54 5:43:36
South Boston 88 165 38N34'58 85W58'45 5:43:55
South Center 46 2 41N28'35 86W38'24 5:46:34
Southeast 59 160 38N27 86W23 5:45:32
Southeast Grove 45 2 41N19'59 87W17'48 5:49:11
Southeast Manor 73 101 39N37'39 85W54'17 5:43:37
South Edgewood 48 101 40N05'50 85W43'58 5:42:56
South Elwood 48 103 40N15'45 85W50'32 5:43:22
South Gate 24 30 39N19'16 84W48'05 5:39:12
Southgate 46 9 41N43 86W53 5:47:32
South Harbor 29 97 40N03 86W01 5:44:04
South Haven 64 6 41N32'31 87W08'14 5:48:33
South Haven 85 264 40N47'01 85W49'45 5:43:19
South Hunt 49 100 39N45 86W14 5:44:56
South Kokomo 34 332 40N29 86W08 5:44:32
South Lake 84 77 39N28 87W26 5:49:44
South Marion 27 284 40N34 85W42 5:42:48
South Martin 51 67 38N32'40 86W52'27 5:47:30
South Milford 44 30 41N31'57 85W16'20 5:41:05
Southmoor 45 6 41N30 87W19 5:49:16
Southmoor Park 45 6 41N28'33 87W20'46 5:49:23
South Mud Lake 25 328 40N58 86W08 5:44:32
South Park 43 291 41N24'03 85W43'16 5:42:53
South Peru 52 335 40N44'44 86W03'25 5:44:14
Southport 49 100 39N39'54 86W07'40 5:44:31
Southport 60 342 39N16'37 86W45'42 5:47:03
South Raub 79 147 40N18'05 86W54'48 5:47:39
South Salem 68 287 40N09'04 84W50'28 5:39:22
South Wanatah 46 2 41N24'21 86W53'57 5:47:36
South Washington 14 85 38N38'05 87W10'43 5:48:43
Southwest 20 259 41N32'12 85W56'38 5:43:47
South Whitley 92 229 41N05'05 85W37'41 5:42:31
Southwick Village 2 233 41N04 85W09 5:40:36
Southwood 46 9 41N43 86W53 5:47:32
Southwood 84 77 39N24'11 87W24'06 5:49:36
Spades 69 275 39N15'14 85W07'22 5:40:29
Sparksville 36 147 38N46'40 86W14'14 5:44:57
Sparta 15 33 39N06'19 85W02'43 5:40:11
Spartanburg 68 307 40N03'58 84W51'06 5:39:24
Spearsville 53 147 39N19'50 86W11'47 5:44:47
Speed 10 185 38N24'44 85W45'09 5:43:01
Speedway 49 100 39N48'08 86W16'02 5:45:04
Speicherville 85 264 40N51'16 85W47'30 5:43:10
Spelterville 84 82 39N31'40 87W23'54 5:49:36
Spencer 60 342 39N17'12 86W45'45 5:47:03
Spencerville 17 228 41N16'59 84W55'19 5:39:41
Spiceland 33 253 39N50'18 85W26'20 5:41:45
Spice Valley 47 344 38N46 86W37 5:46:28
Spraytown 36 147 39N00'51 86W04'48 5:44:19
Springboro 91 147 40N35'40 86W46'33 5:47:06
Springersville 21 272 39N39'26 85W03'14 5:40:13
Springfield 46 9 41N42'55 86W46'39 5:47:07
Springfield 65 58 38N02'33 87W52'13 5:51:29
Spring Grove 89 318 39N50'54 84W53'39 5:39:35
Spring Grove Heights 89 318 39N50'36 84W53'33 5:39:34
Spring Hill 41 100 39N37'12 86W07'06 5:44:28
Spring Hill 84 77 39N24'45 87W22'38 5:49:31
Spring Hill Estates 84 77 39N26 87W24 5:49:36
Spring Hills 49 100 39N50'10 86W11'37 5:44:46
Spring Hollow 49 100 39N55'22 86W09'53 5:44:40
Spring Lake 30 97 39N46'36 85W51'11 5:43:25
Spring Lake Park 30 97 39N46 85W51 5:43:24
Spring Mill Estates 49 100 39N52'32 86W10'01 5:44:40
Spring Mill Woods 49 100 39N54'56 86W09'53 5:44:40
Springport 33 253 40N02'51 85W23'39 5:41:35
Springtown 32 247 39N42'08 86W36'22 5:46:25
Spring Valley Estates 84 77 39N26 87W24 5:49:36
Springville 46 8 41N41'07 86W44'12 5:46:57
Springville 47 344 38N56'10 86W37'10 5:46:29
Springwood 84 82 39N42 86W51 5:47:24
Spurgeon 63 59 38N15 87W16 5:49:04
Spurgeons Corner 7 147 39N04'15 86W08'42 5:44:35
Stacer 82 59 38N08'55 87W34'00 5:50:16
Stafford Center 17 235 41N24'30 84W49'55 5:39:20
Stalcup Corner 28 193 38N59'40 87W00'58 5:48:04
Stampers Creek 59 160 38N32 86W21 5:45:24
Standard 13 80 39N11'47 87W23'21 5:49:33
Stanford 53 344 39N05'23 86W40'00 5:46:40
Stanley 87 53 38N09'52 87W21'18 5:49:25
Star City 66 183 40N58'19 86W33'22 5:46:13
Stardust Village 29 97 40N03 86W01 5:44:04
Starlight 10 166 38N24'54 85W53'33 5:43:34
Star Mill 44 30 41N44'43 85W26'15 5:41:45
Starve Hollow Lake 36 147 38N51 86W06 5:44:24
State Line 45 6 41N39 87W30 5:50:00
State Line 84 77 39N26'13 87W31'46 5:50:07
State Line 86 187 40N11'50 87W31'37 5:50:06
State Line City 86 187 40N12 87W32 5:50:08
Staunton 11 88 39N29'15 87W11'20 5:48:45
Stavetown 24 30 39N24'39 85W00'36 5:40:02
Steam Corner 23 156 40N02'34 87W14'36 5:48:58
Stearleyville 61 89 39N26'42 87W03'41 5:48:15
Steele 1 228 40N45 84W57 5:39:48
Steele 14 85 38N46 87W10 5:48:40
Steen 42 86 38N39 87W18 5:49:12
Steinmeir Estates 49 100 39N53 86W04 5:44:16
Stendal 63 59 38N16'00 87W08'40 5:48:35
Stephens Crossing 23 136 40N09'39 87W10'51 5:48:43
Sterling 13 169 38N21 86W28 5:45:52
Sterling 23 156 40N06'51 87W14'59 5:49:00
Sterling Heights 49 100 39N44'33 86W17'03 5:45:08
Steubenville 76 30 41N31'56 85W01'22 5:40:05
Stevenson 87 53 38N01'00 87W26'00 5:49:44
Stewart 86 156 40N21'36 87W28'21 5:49:53
Stewartsville 65 58 38N11'05 87W49'58 5:51:20
Stilesville 32 113 39N38'18 86W38'01 5:46:32
Stillwell 46 2 41N33'21 86W36'10 5:46:25
Stines Mill Corner 55 101 39N28'33 86W22'22 5:45:29
Stinesville 53 344 39N17'55 86W39'08 5:46:37
Stockdale 85 335 40N54'54 85W56'39 5:43:47
Stockport 18 253 40N19'15 85W27'38 5:41:51
Stockton 60 93 39N14'20 87W01'20 5:48:05
Stockwell 79 147 40N17'10 86W46'15 5:47:05
Stone 68 310 40N14'12 85W00'16 5:40:01
Stone Bluff 23 144 40N10'12 87W15'10 5:49:01
Stoneburner Landing 43 297 41N17'06 85W46'36 5:43:06
Stonecrest 27 284 40N34 85W42 5:42:48
Stonegate Square 87 53 37N57 87W24 5:49:36
Stone Head 7 145 39N07'48 86W09'32 5:44:38
Stones Crossing 41 100 39N34'40 86W09'33 5:44:38
Stoney Creek 68 307 40N09 85W10 5:40:40
Stonington 47 344 38N43'54 86W22'03 5:45:28
Stony Lonesome 3 147 39N12'03 86W03'44 5:44:15
Stony Ridge 43 291 41N19'38 85W46'37 5:43:06
Story 7 145 39N05'56 86W12'50 5:44:51
Stoutsburg 37 147 40N43'57 87W09'59 5:48:40
Straughn 33 257 39N48'32 85W17'29 5:41:10
Strawtown 29 97 40N07'24 85W56'40 5:43:47
Stringtown 6 247 40N04'54 86W28'36 5:45:54
Stringtown 13 80 39N03'12 87W17'51 5:49:11
Stringtown 30 101 39N47'17 85W42'29 5:42:50
Stringtown 69 275 39N05'54 85W09'48 5:40:39
Stringtown 82 55 38N01'15 87W33'42 5:50:15
Stroh 44 30 41N34'53 85W11'58 5:40:48
Stumpke Corner 69 275 39N10'40 85W07'55 5:40:32
Suburban Gardens 45 6 41N31 87W28 5:49:52
Sugar Creek 73 101 39N38'26 85W54'47 5:43:39
Sugar Grove 31 166 38N07'04 85W54'40 5:43:39
Sugar Ridge 11 89 39N22 87W06 5:48:24
Sullivan 13 71 39N05'43 87W24'21 5:49:37
Sulphur 13 169 38N13'39 86W28'15 5:45:53
Sulphur Springs 13 169 38N12'43 86W28'30 5:45:54
Sulphur Springs 33 257 40N00'17 85W26'34 5:41:46
Suman 64 4 41N32'34 87W00'00 5:48:00
Sumava Resorts 56 2 41N10 87W26 5:49:44
Summit 17 237 41N30'47 85W01'34 5:40:06
Summit 28 93 39N01'52 87W11'58 5:48:48
Summit 32 252 39N41'17 86W32'12 5:46:09
Summit 46 8 41N38'35 86W47'51 5:47:11
Summit Grove 83 73 39N43'28 87W23'21 5:49:33
Summit Ridge 2 233 41N06 85W08 5:40:32
Summitville 48 101 40N20'19 85W38'40 5:42:35
Sun Down 49 100 39N43'33 85W59'23 5:43:58
Sundown Manor 55 97 39N35'02 86W22'41 5:45:31
Sunman 69 278 39N14'13 85W05'41 5:40:23
Sunnybrook Acres 2 233 41N09'22 85W04'19 5:40:17
Sunnycrest 27 284 40N34 85W42 5:42:48
Sunnymeadow 2 233 41N07'52 85W05'43 5:40:23
Sunnymede 2 233 41N04 85W09 5:40:36
Sunnymede 85 264 40N48'29 85W50'30 5:43:22
Sunnymede Woods 2 233 41N03'55 85W03'58 5:40:16
Sunny Slopes 53 344 39N07'55 86W31'52 5:46:07
Sunnyview 49 100 39N44'45 86W04'58 5:44:20
Sunrise Beach 43 291 41N24'10 85W41'12 5:42:45
Sunset Parkway 36 147 38N57'48 85W54'21 5:43:37
Sunset Village 10 166 38N27'25 85W32'04 5:42:08
Sunshine Gardens 49 100 39N41'17 86W12'40 5:44:51
Sunview 48 101 39N56'56 85W50'24 5:43:22
Surgeon 63 59 38N15'08 87W15'26 5:49:02
Surprise 36 147 38N58'14 86W03'32 5:44:14
Surrey 37 2 40N59'53 87W12'01 5:48:48
Survant 63 59 38N22'26 87W09'19 5:48:37
Sussex Woods 45 6 41N33 87W17 5:49:08
Swalls 84 77 39N27'37 87W17'20 5:49:09
Swan 67 30 41N18'57 85W12'45 5:40:51
Swanington 4 147 40N35'00 87W16'38 5:49:07
Swanville 39 113 38N41'11 85W33'31 5:42:14
Swayzee 27 284 40N30'30 85W49'32 5:43:18
Sweetser 27 284 40N34'19 85W46'09 5:43:05
Sweetwater Lake 7 147 39N21 86W07 5:44:28
Switz City 28 96 39N16'30 87W03'12 5:48:13
Switzer Crossroads 13 169 38N16'08 86W25'00 5:45:40
Sycamore 34 334 40N29'39 85W55'10 5:43:41
Sycamore Corner 86 156 40N21'36 87W26'04 5:49:44
Sycamore Ford 54 147 39N57'30 87W02'48 5:48:11
Sycamore Hills 48 101 40N21 85W44 5:42:56
Sycamore Knolls 84 77 39N26 87W24 5:49:36
Sycamore Park 84 77 39N29 87W27 5:49:48
Sylvan Hills 27 284 40N34 85W42 5:42:48
Sylvania 61 128 39N55'08 87W17'40 5:49:11
Sylvan Manor 64 6 41N27'32 87W06'27 5:48:26
Syndicate 83 73 39N37'02 87W24'51 5:49:39
Syracuse 43 299 41N25'40 85W45'09 5:43:01
Syria 59 160 38N35'10 86W24'06 5:45:36
Tab 86 156 40N24'40 87W28'22 5:49:53
Tabertown 84 82 39N29'41 87W15'11 5:49:01
Taggart 53 147 39N15'42 86W08'20 5:44:33
Taggart Crossing 55 101 39N22'45 86W24'02 5:45:36
Talbot 4 147 40N30'19 87W27'15 5:49:49
Tall Timbers 27 284 40N34 85W42 5:42:48
Talma 25 328 41N09'14 86W08'06 5:44:32
Tamarack 64 9 41N41 86W59 5:47:56
Tampico 36 147 38N53 86W05 5:44:20
Tangier 61 128 39N55'09 87W19'05 5:49:16
Tanglewood 2 233 41N04'24 85W00'16 5:40:01
Tarkeo Corner 16 101 39N15'46 85W29'02 5:41:56
Tarry Park 47 344 38N48'05 86W30'33 5:46:02
Taswell 13 169 38N20'03 86W33'40 5:46:15
Taylor 79 147 40N20'25 86W56'01 5:47:44
Taylor Corner 17 30 41N29'08 84W56'58 5:39:48
Taylor Corner 54 147 40N01'30 87W00'58 5:48:04
Taylorsville 3 149 39N17'45 85W57'03 5:43:48
Taylorville 84 77 39N27'45 87W25'25 5:49:42
Tecumseh 79 134 40N23'34 86W52'06 5:47:28
Tecumseh 84 77 39N33'47 87W25'18 5:49:41
Teegarden 50 211 41N27'54 86W22'39 5:45:31
Tee Lake 46 8 41N43'01 86W41'24 5:46:46
Tefft 37 25 41N11'55 86W58'26 5:47:54
Tell City 62 68 37N57'05 86W46'04 5:47:04
Temple 13 169 38N20'40 86W24'57 5:45:40
Templeton 4 147 40N30'46 87W12'28 5:48:50
Tennyson 87 53 38N04'56 87W07'06 5:48:28
Tera North 84 82 39N42 86W51 5:47:24
Terhune 6 108 40N09'55 86W16'49 5:45:07
Terrace Bay 8 162 40N42'54 86W44'46 5:46:59
Terrace Lake 3 147 39N13 85W54 5:43:36
Terre Coupee 71 201 41N42'08 86W28'38 5:45:55
Terre Haute 84 77 39N28'00 87W24'50 5:49:39
Terre Town 84 77 39N31'03 87W22'31 5:49:30
Terry 62 69 38N05'14 86W37'59 5:46:32
Tetersburg 80 116 40N16'31 86W09'04 5:44:36
Texas 15 33 39N02'51 84W53'37 5:39:34
Thales 19 67 38N30'37 86W47'55 5:47:12
Thayer 56 2 41N10'24 87W20'01 5:49:20
Thomas 14 85 38N36'46 87W13'54 5:48:56
Thomas Lake 67 128 39N39 86W52 5:47:28
Thomaston 46 2 41N22'42 86W48'51 5:47:15
Thorncreek 92 228 41N13 85W29 5:41:56
Thornhope 66 181 40N55'33 86W31'46 5:46:07
Thorntown 6 251 40N07'46 86W36'24 5:46:26
Thurman 2 233 41N07'12 85W00'15 5:40:01
Tilden 32 247 39N49'17 86W26'20 5:45:45
Tillman 2 228 41N01'27 84W53'36 5:39:34
Timbercrest 2 233 41N01'02 85W18'54 5:41:16
Timbercrest 9 165 40N46 86W22 5:45:28
Timberhurst 44 30 41N32'47 85W13'07 5:40:52
Times Corner 2 233 41N03'42 85W13'10 5:40:53
Tiosa 25 328 41N09'10 86W12'20 5:44:49
Tippecanoe 50 324 41N12'32 86W06'54 5:44:28
Tipton 80 121 40N16'56 86W02'28 5:44:10
Tipton Park 3 147 39N13 85W54 5:43:36
Titus 31 180 38N03'15 86W15'22 5:45:01
Toad Hop 84 77 39N27'32 87W27'49 5:49:51
Tobacco Landing 31 166 38N00'19 86W05'12 5:44:21
Tobin 62 69 37N57 86W35 5:46:20
Tobinsport 62 69 37N51'09 86W38'08 5:46:33
Tocsin 90 231 40N49'49 85W06'33 5:40:26
Toledo 35 287 40N49 85W32 5:42:08
Tolleston 45 17 41N35'35 87W21'58 5:49:28
Toll Gate Heights 90 228 40N45'26 85W09'57 5:40:40
Tomahawk Village 49 100 39N48 86W15 5:45:00
Topeka 44 42 41N32'21 85W32'23 5:42:10
Toto 75 221 41N15'34 86W41'53 5:46:48
Tower 13 169 38N14'31 86W21'36 5:45:26
Town Hill 7 145 39N11'53 86W14'48 5:44:59

Townley 2 228 41N01'05 84W51'50 5:39:27
Town of Pines 64 9 41N40'55 86W57'37 5:47:50
Tracy 46 2 41N29'07 86W40'57 5:46:44
Traders Point 49 100 39N53'19 86W17'49 5:45:11
Trafalgar 41 101 39N24'58 86W09'03 5:44:36
Trail Creek 46 9 41N41'54 86W51'33 5:47:26
Tratebas Mill 64 320 38N40'15 85W40'15 5:42:41
Travisville 90 228 40N41'31 85W12'29 5:40:50
Treaty 85 264 40N43'28 85W46'57 5:43:08
Tree Spring 83 84 40N05'48 87W25'59 5:49:44
Tremont 49 100 39N46'03 86W18'57 5:45:16
Tremont 64 4 41N38'55 87W02'37 5:48:10
Trenton 5 196 40N27'00 85W14'20 5:40:57
Trevlac 7 147 39N15'56 86W20'13 5:45:21
Trials End 29 97 39N57'15 86W03'57 5:44:16
Trier Ridge Park 2 233 41N03 85W08 5:40:32
Tri Lakes 92 228 41N14'45 85W26'31 5:41:46
Trilobi Hills 49 100 39N52'45 85W59'48 5:43:59
Trinity 38 287 40N32'33 84W50'55 5:39:24
Trinity Springs 51 159 38N45 86W46 5:47:04
Trotter Crossing 59 160 38N30'41 86W21'56 5:45:28
Troy 62 69 37N59'43 86W47'52 5:47:11
Tudor 3 147 39N13 85W54 5:43:36
Tulip 28 193 39N04'55 86W53'12 5:47:33
Tunker 92 228 41N02'55 85W33'27 5:42:14
Tunnelton 47 344 38N46'07 86W20'34 5:45:22
Turkey Creek 43 291 41N24 85W43 5:42:52
Turkey Creek 76 30 41N33'21 85W10'15 5:40:41
Turkey Creek Meadows 45 6 41N29'43 87W20'36 5:49:22
Turman 77 80 39N08 87W33 5:50:12
Turner 11 88 39N29'54 87W09'37 5:48:38
Turpin 87 53 38N03 87W16 5:49:04
Turpin Hill 87 53 38N08'32 87W17'25 5:49:10
Turtle Creek 27 284 40N34 85W42 5:42:48
Twelve Mile 9 165 40N51'59 86W13'31 5:44:54
Twelve Points 84 77 39N29'32 87W23'52 5:49:35
Twin Beach 11 89 39N31'05 87W12'18 5:48:49
Twin Branch 71 208 41N40 86W10 5:44:40
Twin Brooks 49 100 39N40'08 86W07'13 5:44:29
Twin Crest 3 147 39N13 85W54 5:43:36
Twin Lakes 50 211 41N18'15 86W21'26 5:45:26
Twin Oaks Lake 55 97 39N22 86W15 5:45:00
Tyner 50 211 41N24'35 86W24'09 5:45:37
Tyner Crossing 21 101 39N39'15 85W35'39 5:42:23
Ulen 6 247 40N03'47 86W27'52 5:45:51
Underwood 10 179 38N36'13 85W46'28 5:43:06
Underwood Meadows 48 101 40N21 85W44 5:42:56
Union 63 59 38N27'55 87W26'05 5:49:44
Union Center 46 2 41N29'03 86W38'23 5:46:34
Union City 68 304 40N12 84W49 5:39:16
Uniondale 90 231 40N49'50 85W14'30 5:40:58
Union Mills 46 2 41N29'35 86W46'39 5:47:07
Unionport 68 307 40N07'15 85W05'47 5:40:23
Uniontown 36 147 38N50'45 85W49'33 5:43:18
Uniontown 62 69 38N13'31 86W39'39 5:46:39
Unionville 53 344 39N13'48 86W24'58 5:45:40
Universal 83 73 39N37'18 87W27'05 5:49:48
University Heights 49 100 39N42'17 86W08'04 5:44:32
Upland 27 283 40N28'32 85W29'40 5:41:59
Upper Long Lake 57 30 41N24 85W26 5:41:44
Upper Sunset Park 8 162 40N43'30 86W45'16 5:47:01
Upton 65 58 37N57'52 87W57'42 5:51:51
Uptown 49 100 39N50 86W09 5:44:36
Urbana 85 264 40N53'54 85W47'34 5:43:10
Urmeyville 41 97 39N31'19 85W59'07 5:43:56
Utah 15 33 39N03'39 84W53'53 5:39:36
Utica 10 166 38N20'01 85W39'13 5:42:37
Valeene 59 160 38N26'20 86W23'50 5:45:35
Valentine 44 36 41N35'25 85W23'13 5:41:33
Valley Acres 27 284 40N34 85W42 5:42:48
Valley Brook 85 264 40N48'20 85W50'40 5:43:23
Valley City 31 166 38N05'38 86W13'22 5:44:53
Valley Mills 49 100 39N41'28 86W16'38 5:45:07
Valley View Hills 20 271 41N41 85W59 5:43:56
Vallonia 36 147 38N50'49 86W05'52 5:44:23
Vallyd Acres 2 233 41N04 85W09 5:40:36
Valparaiso 64 12 41N28'23 87W03'40 5:48:15
Van 9 165 40N46 86W22 5:45:28
Vanada 87 53 37N55'56 87W21'52 5:49:27
Vanada Camps 87 53 37N57 87W24 5:49:36
Van Bibber Lake 67 128 39N39 86W52 5:47:28
Van Buren 27 286 40N37'02 85W30'17 5:42:01
Van Buren Park 53 344 39N08'09 86W34'51 5:46:19
Vandalia 60 344 39N18'45 86W51'58 5:47:28
Van Loon 45 6 41N34'06 87W25'22 5:49:41
Vanmeter Park 66 181 41N05'09 86W34'05 5:46:16
Van Nuys 33 253 39N57'36 85W21'14 5:41:25
Vaughan 82 55 37N54'05 87W37'49 5:50:31
Vawter Park 43 291 41N23'15 85W41'33 5:42:46
Veale 14 85 38N35 87W10 5:48:40
Veedersburg 23 140 40N06'47 87W15'45 5:49:03
Velpen 63 59 38N21'19 87W06'07 5:48:24
Vera Cruz 90 228 40N42'04 85W04'45 5:40:19
Vermillion 83 73 39N53 87W27 5:49:48
Vermillion Acres 84 77 39N28 87W26 5:49:44
Vermont 34 331 40N29'57 86W01'55 5:44:08
Verne 42 86 38N38'12 87W25'46 5:49:43
Vernon 40 126 38N59'05 85W36'34 5:42:26
Versailles 69 275 39N04'19 85W15'07 5:41:00
Vesta 10 166 38N29'06 85W33'02 5:42:12
Vevay 78 35 38N44'52 85W04'02 5:40:16
Vicksburg 28 93 39N05'26 87W11'53 5:48:48
Victor 53 344 39N03'39 86W34'51 5:46:19
Victoria 28 93 39N02'47 87W13'22 5:48:53
Vienna 72 319 38N38'56 85W46'08 5:43:05
Vigo 42 86 38N48 87W15 5:49:00
Vigo 84 82 39N17'14 87W32'14 5:50:09
Vilas 60 344 39N10'12 86W50'24 5:47:22
Villa North 90 228 40N43 85W07 5:40:28
Vincennes 42 78 38N40'38 87W31'43 5:50:07
Vine 23 129 40N17'42 87W08'06 5:48:32
Virgie 37 2 41N06'55 87W10'48 5:48:43
Vistula 20 259 41N44'57 85W43'41 5:42:55
Vivalia 67 128 39N40'39 87W00'44 5:48:03
Volga 39 97 38N47'02 85W31'05 5:42:04
Vollmer 42 86 38N32'51 87W31'12 5:50:05
Wabash 85 267 40N47'52 85W49'14 5:43:17
Wabash Shores 79 147 40N26'57 86W54'39 5:47:39
Waco 14 85 38N32'07 87W02'25 5:48:10
Wadena 4 147 40N41'36 87W16'36 5:49:06
Wadesville 65 58 38N06'09 87W47'10 5:51:09
Wagoner 25 328 41N00'51 86W08'57 5:44:36
Wakarusa 20 266 41N57'14 86W03'53 5:44:16
Wakefield 39 101 38N47'14 85W33'36 5:42:14
Wakefield Village 57 30 41N26 85W16 5:41:04
Wakeland 55 113 39N28'09 86W34'31 5:46:18
Wake Robin Fields 64 4 41N36'54 87W01'34 5:48:06
Wakeville Village 57 30 41N27'47 85W15'25 5:41:02
Walden 2 233 41N06 85W08 5:40:32
Waldron 73 101 39N27'13 85W40'01 5:42:40
Waldron Lake 57 47 41N28 85W29 5:41:56
Wald View 45 6 41N24'01 87W21'17 5:49:25
Walesboro 3 149 39N08'43 85W54'52 5:43:39
Walford Manor 10 166 38N18 85W45 5:43:00
Walker Park 43 291 41N19'46 85W45'12 5:43:01
Walkerton 71 206 41N28'00 86W28'59 5:45:56
Walkerville 73 101 39N31'40 85W45'47 5:43:03
Wallace 23 156 39N59'11 87W08'54 5:48:36
Wallace Junction 60 113 39N27'49 86W43'37 5:46:54
Wallen 2 233 41N09'40 85W09'58 5:40:40
Wall Lake 44 30 41N44 85W10 5:40:40
Walnut 50 211 41N10'34 86W12'43 5:44:51
Walnut Gardens 8 162 40N41'56 86W45'16 5:47:01
Walnut Grove 29 97 40N09'43 85W56'23 5:43:46
Walnut Heights 47 344 38N51 86W30 5:46:00
Walnut Level 89 315 39N53 85W02 5:40:08
Walnut Ridge 10 166 38N18 85W45 5:43:00
Walnut Ridge 40 128 38N55'30 85W33'22 5:42:13
Walton 9 164 40N39'39 86W14'31 5:44:58
Waltz 85 264 40N42 85W51 5:43:24
Wanamaker 49 100 39N42'16 86W00'35 5:44:02
Wanatah 46 2 41N25'50 86W53'54 5:47:36
Wanda Lake 84 77 39N28 87W26 5:49:44
Ward 68 305 40N16 84W58 5:39:52
Warren 35 287 40N40'58 85W25'38 5:41:43
Warren Hills 49 100 39N46'55 85W59'51 5:43:59
Warren Park 49 100 39N46'55 86W03'01 5:44:12
Warrenton 26 59 38N10'23 87W31'58 5:50:08
Warrington 30 101 39N54'27 85W38'02 5:42:32
Warsaw 43 297 41N14'17 85W51'11 5:43:25
Washington 14 85 38N39'33 87W10'22 5:48:41
Washington Center 92 228 41N12 85W28 5:41:52
Washington Place 49 100 39N46'37 86W00'59 5:44:04
Waterford 46 9 41N40'17 86W50'42 5:47:23
Waterford Mills 20 259 41N32'35 85W49'50 5:43:19
Waterloo 17 237 41N25'55 85W01'12 5:40:05
Waterloo 21 272 39N42'13 85W06'11 5:40:25
Waterloo 41 97 39N33'45 86W11'51 5:44:47
Wathen Heights 10 166 38N18 85W45 5:43:00
Watson 10 166 38N20'55 85W42'00 5:42:48
Waugh 6 97 40N05'04 86W18'24 5:45:14
Wauhob Lake 64 6 41N29 87W23 5:49:32
Waveland 54 149 39N52'37 87W02'40 5:48:11
Waverly 55 101 39N33'25 86W16'17 5:45:05
Waverly Woods 55 101 39N33'05 86W16'11 5:45:05
Wawaka 57 47 41N27'25 85W28'56 5:41:56
Wawasee Village 43 291 41N24'52 85W44'51 5:42:59
Wa-Will-Away Park 43 297 41N17'24 85W46'41 5:43:07
Wawpecong 52 335 40N34'42 86W02'32 5:44:10
Waycross 7 147 39N18'13 86W20'39 5:45:23
Waymansville 3 147 39N03'47 86W02'35 5:44:10
Wayne 89 315 39N53'16 84W55'32 5:39:42
Wayne Center 57 30 41N28'54 85W15'03 5:41:00
Waynedale 2 233 41N01'19 85W10'32 5:40:42
Waynesburg 16 101 39N12'40 85W40'10 5:42:41
Waynesville 3 149 39N06'54 85W53'30 5:43:34
Waynetown 54 155 40N05'15 87W03'35 5:48:14
Wea 79 147 40N22 86W53 5:47:32
Weaver 27 284 40N27'55 85W43'45 5:42:55
Webers Landing 44 30 41N32'20 85W23'39 5:41:35
Webster 89 315 39N54'12 84W56'43 5:39:47
Weddleville 36 147 38N50'19 86W13'13 5:44:53
Wegan 36 147 38N49'37 86W01'09 5:44:05
Weisburg 15 33 39N13'05 85W02'46 5:40:11
Wellington Heights 73 101 39N31'03 85W45'48 5:43:03
Wells 52 335 40N43'56 86W06'40 5:44:27
Wellsboro 46 13 41N29'50 86W45'55 5:47:04
Wellsburg 90 228 40N39'58 85W13'18 5:40:53
Wenmeir 3 147 39N13 85W54 5:43:36
Wesley 54 147 40N04'04 87W00'24 5:48:02
Wesley Manor 12 171 40N17'47 86W30'43 5:46:03
West 50 211 41N20 86W24 5:45:36
Westacres 18 254 40N11 85W23 5:41:32
West Atherton 61 73 39N37 87W21 5:49:24
West Baden Springs 59 127 38N34'02 86W37'42 5:46:31
West Brook Acres 24 275 39N18 85W13 5:40:52
West Brook Downs 53 344 39N12'52 86W36'04 5:46:24
Westchester 2 233 41N01'36 85W07'43 5:40:31
Westchester 38 291 40N29'54 84W53'42 5:39:35
Westchester 64 4 41N38 87W03 5:48:12
Westchester Estates 49 100 39N53'50 86W12'28 5:44:50
West Clinton 83 73 39N41'40 87W31'31 5:50:06
West College Corner 81 313 39N34'03 84W48'58 5:39:16
West Creek 45 2 41N16 87W28 5:49:52
West Dana 83 73 39N45'22 87W31'28 5:50:06
West Elwood 80 116 40N16'47 85W51'38 5:43:27
Western Acres 64 4 41N35'57 87W05'01 5:48:20
Western Hills 65 58 37N56 87W54 5:51:36
Western Village 48 101 40N06'29 85W43'02 5:42:52
Westfield 29 98 40N02'34 86W07'39 5:44:31
Westfield 71 202 41N40'32 86W22'49 5:45:31
West Fork 13 169 38N14'01 86W31'35 5:46:06
West Franklin 65 58 37N53'42 87W42'46 5:50:51
West Glen Park 45 6 41N32 87W22 5:49:28
West Harrison 15 33 39N15'39 84W49'15 5:39:17
West Haven 43 297 41N14 85W51 5:43:24
Westhill 64 12 41N27'53 87W05'50 5:48:23
West Indianapolis 49 100 39N45 86W11 5:44:44
West Lafayette 79 134 40N25'33 86W54'29 5:47:38
Westland 30 101 40N53 81W35 5:26:20
Westlawn 2 233 41N04'49 85W13'39 5:40:55
Westlea 27 284 40N34 85W42 5:42:48
West Lebanon 86 146 40N16'12 87W23'12 5:49:33
West Liberty 34 334 40N25'50 85W53'26 5:43:34
West Liberty 38 287 40N32 84W58 5:39:52
West Linton 28 92 39N02 87W10 5:48:40
West Middleton 34 165 40N26'22 86W12'58 5:44:52
Westmoor 2 233 41N04'09 85W12'38 5:40:51
West Muncie 18 253 40N10'15 85W28'53 5:41:56
West Newton 49 100 39N39'11 86W16'58 5:45:08
West Noblesville 29 97 40N02'53 86W01'15 5:44:05
Westover 49 100 39N53'58 86W13'39 5:44:55
West Peru 52 335 40N42 86W07 5:44:28
West Petersburg 63 59 38N29'15 87W17'21 5:49:09
Westphalia 42 87 38N51'46 87W13'32 5:48:54
Westpoint 79 152 40N20'42 87W02'35 5:48:10
Westport 16 101 39N10'33 85W34'23 5:42:18
Westport Addition 18 254 40N11 85W23 5:41:32
Westside 15 33 39N03'50 84W54'26 5:39:38
West Terre Haute 84 77 39N27'54 87W27'00 5:49:48
West Union 61 128 39N50'37 87W20'12 5:49:21
Westville 46 9 41N32'29 86W54'02 5:47:36
Westwood 33 253 39N55'09 85W25'01 5:41:40
Westwood 49 100 39N47'12 86W19'35 5:45:18
Wey Lake 84 82 39N31 87W14 5:48:56
Wheatfield 37 26 40N33'52 87W06'25 5:48:26
Wheatland 42 86 38N39'49 87W18'34 5:49:14
Wheatonville 87 53 38N11'14 87W27'41 5:49:51
Wheeler 64 23 41N30'42 87W10'45 5:48:43
Wheeling 8 170 40N33'58 86W23'30 5:45:34
Wheeling 18 253 40N21'49 85W27'51 5:41:51
Wheeling 26 59 38N24'47 87W27'19 5:49:49
Whiskey Run 13 169 38N21 86W18 5:45:12
Whitaker 55 115 39N22'47 86W36'27 5:46:26
Whitcomb 24 30 39N26'54 84W56'13 5:39:45
Whitcomb Heights 84 77 39N29'18 87W27'17 5:49:49
White Cloud 31 166 38N13'41 86W13'28 5:44:54
Whitehall 60 344 39N10'27 86W41'04 5:46:44
Whiteland 41 98 39N33'00 86W04'47 5:44:19
Whiteoak 63 59 38N24'34 87W08'47 5:48:35
White Post 66 181 41N02 86W52 5:47:28

White Ridge 27 284 40N34 85w42 5:42:48
White River 26 59 38N23'39 87w45'11 5:51:01
White River Bluffs 47 344 38N51 86w30 5:46:00
White Rose 28 93 39N01'52 87w13'22 5:48:53
Whites Crossing 28 93 39N02 87w10 5:48:40
Whitestown 6 97 39N59'50 86w20'45 5:45:23
White Sulphur Springs 63 59 38N23'08 87w05'31 5:48:22
Whitesville 54 147 39N57'55 86w50'01 5:47:20
Whitewater 89 318 39N56'41 84w49'52 5:39:19
Whitfield 51 200 38N37'07 86w54'46 5:47:39
Whiting 45 14 41N40'47 87w29'40 5:49:59
Wickliffe 13 169 38N22'06 86w38'28 5:46:34
Widner 42 86 38N51 87w20 5:49:20
Wilbur 55 101 39N30'58 86w29'19 5:45:57
Wildcat 80 116 40N22 85w55 5:43:40
Wilders 46 28 41N16'00 86w53'46 5:47:35
Wildwood 27 284 40N34 85w42 5:42:48
Wildwood 76 30 41N35'41 85w11'22 5:40:45
Wildwood Lake 59 160 38N34 86w28 5:45:52
Wildwood Landing 76 30 41N35 85w12 5:40:48
Wilfred 13 80 39N11'12 87w21'09 5:49:25
Wilkinson 30 97 39N53'09 85w36'32 5:42:26
Williams 1 228 40N55'08 84w58'31 5:39:54
Williams 47 342 38N48'16 86w38'50 5:46:35
Williamsburg 89 315 39N57'03 84w59'47 5:39:59
Williams Creek 49 100 39N53'59 86w09'01 5:44:36
Williamsport 86 158 40N17'18 87w17'38 5:49:11
Williamstown 16 101 39N21 85w33 5:42:12
Willis 42 59 38N33'12 87w21'26 5:49:26
Willisville 63 59 38N27'03 87w17'44 5:49:11
Willow Branch 30 101 39N52'34 85w41'04 5:42:44
Willowbrook Estates 55 101 39N28'39 86w21'54 5:45:28
Willow Creek 64 23 41N35'11 87w11'00 5:48:44
Willow Valley 51 322 38N41'38 86w43'11 5:46:53
Wills 46 2 41N39 86w34 5:46:16
Wilmington 15 38 39N03'45 84w56'48 5:39:47
Wilmington 17 228 41N24 84w55 5:39:40
Wilmot 67 30 41N18'36 85w38'30 5:42:34
Wilshire 12 181 40N16'32 86w29'19 5:45:57
Wilson 10 166 38N26'40 85w49'47 5:43:19
Wilson 64 23 41N37'11 87w09'33 5:48:38
Wilson 73 101 39N33 85w48 5:43:12
Wilson Corner 73 101 39N26'18 85w45'19 5:43:01
Wilson Lake 92 228 41N12 85w28 5:41:52
Winamac 66 186 41N03'05 86w36'11 5:46:25
Winchester 68 308 40N10'19 84w58'53 5:39:56
Windemere Lake 84 77 39N28 87w26 5:49:44
Windfall 80 119 40N21'47 85w57'23 5:43:50
Windom 51 322 38N34'26 86w47'52 5:47:11
Windsor 68 307 40N09'16 85w12'46 5:40:51
Windsor Village 49 100 39N47 86w04 5:44:16
Winfield 45 29 41N24'19 87w16'43 5:49:07
Wingate 54 147 40N10'20 87w04'22 5:48:17
Winona 75 221 41N14'10 86w34'10 5:46:17
Winona Lake 43 297 41N13'38 85w49'19 5:43:17
Winslow 63 59 38N22'56 87w12'46 5:48:51
Winthrop 86 129 40N22'12 87w14'02 5:48:56
Wirt 39 161 38N48'34 85w27'13 5:41:49
Wiser 55 100 39N36'44 86w17'37 5:45:10
Witmer Manor 44 30 41N32'15 85w23'11 5:41:33
Witts 81 313 39N38 84w56 5:39:44
Witts Station 81 315 39N42'44 84w51'42 5:39:27
Wolcott 91 149 40N45'29 87w02'30 5:48:10
Wolcottville 57 43 41N31'33 85w22'00 5:41:28
Wolff 55 101 39N25'59 86w23'43 5:45:35
Wolfington 49 100 39N49'50 86w12'59 5:44:52
Wolflake 67 30 41N20'06 85w29'45 5:41:59
Wonder Lake 84 77 39N26 87w24 5:49:36
Wood 10 166 38N27 85w56 5:43:44
Woodburn 2 228 41N07'31 84w51'12 5:39:25
Woodbury 30 101 39N54'31 85w53'42 5:43:35
Woodcrest 55 101 39N26'15 86w23'41 5:45:35
Woodgate 84 77 39N23'05 87w23'07 5:49:32
Woodland 71 208 41N33'52 86w10'38 5:44:43
Woodland Heights 27 284 40N34 85w42 5:42:48
Woodland Lake 7 147 39N22 86w15 5:45:00
Woodland Park 18 254 40N11'48 85w18'29 5:41:14
Woodland Park 44 30 41N33'16 85w14'23 5:40:58
Woodland Trace 29 97 39N58 86w07 5:44:28
Woodlawn Grove 59 160 38N34'41 86w27'29 5:45:50
Woodlawn Heights 48 101 40N07'08 85w41'37 5:42:46
Woodmar 45 6 41N35'06 87w29'25 5:49:58
Woodridge 84 77 39N29 87w22 5:49:28
Woodruff 44 30 41N34'24 85w19'44 5:41:19
Woodruff Place 49 100 39N47 86w07 5:44:28
Woodside Park 12 171 40N17'26 86w31'37 5:46:06
Woodstock 36 147 38N58 85w58 5:43:52
Woodstock 49 100 39N49'39 86w11'05 5:44:44
Woodville 64 4 41N33'46 87w02'29 5:48:10
Woodville Hills 53 344 39N09'01 86w23'00 5:45:32
Wooley Corner 23 156 40N00'39 87w09'55 5:48:40
Wooster 43 291 41N12'33 85w44'34 5:42:58
Wooster 72 320 38N44'12 85w41'34 5:42:46
Worth 6 97 40N00 86w21 5:45:24
Worthington 28 195 39N07'30 86w58'46 5:47:55
Wright 28 93 39N07 87w11 5:48:44
Wright Manor 45 6 41N30 87w19 5:49:16
Wrights Corners 15 33 39N08'08 84w57'26 5:39:50
Wyandot 79 132 40N20'43 86w44'58 5:47:00
Wyandotte 13 169 38N13'43 86w17'41 5:45:11
Wyatt 71 209 41N31'33 86w10'10 5:44:41
Wynnedale 49 100 39N49'52 86w11'51 5:44:47
Yankee Town 81 313 39N41'44 84w59'08 5:39:57
Yankeetown 87 53 37N55'03 87w17'52 5:49:11
Yeagers Curve 4 147 40N41'55 87w26'21 5:49:45
Yeddo 23 156 40N00'41 87w15'36 5:49:02
Yellowbanks 43 291 41N19'18 85w40'44 5:42:43
Yellow Creek Lake 43 291 41N08 85w53 5:43:32
Yellowstone 53 344 38N59'56 86w20'33 5:45:22
Yenne 51 322 38N32'52 86w47'37 5:47:10
Yeoman 8 165 40N40'04 86w43'27 5:46:54
Yockey 47 344 38N47'17 86w29'35 5:45:58
Yoder 2 228 40N55'52 85w10'36 5:40:42
York 76 30 41N41'18 84w49'21 5:39:17
Yorktown 18 257 40N10'25 85w29'39 5:41:59
Yorkville 15 33 39N12'16 84w58'03 5:39:52
Young 55 101 39N36'37 86w20'15 5:45:21
Young America 9 165 40N34'07 86w20'48 5:45:23
Youngs Corner 24 30 39N21'15 85w03'27 5:40:14
Youngs Creek 59 160 38N28'36 86w29'44 5:45:59
Youngstown 84 77 39N21'44 87w22'56 5:49:32
Youngstown Acres 84 77 39N26 87w24 5:49:36
Youngstown Meadows 84 77 39N26 87w24 5:49:36
Yountsville 69 147 40N01'29 86w58'48 5:47:55
Yule Estates 48 101 40N16 85w41 5:42:44
Zanesville 90 228 40N55'02 85w16'50 5:41:07
Zeigler 71 202 41N41'54 86w26'01 5:45:44
Zelma 47 344 38N56'02 86w18'07 5:45:12
Zenas 40 128 39N07'12 85w28'30 5:41:54
Zionsville 6 97 39N57'03 86w15'43 5:45:03
Zoar 63 67 38N16'09 87w04'23 5:48:18
Zulu 2 228 41N02'13 85w00'00 5:40:00

TIME TABLES

Dates of daylight time observance are not completely reliable because of wide-spread local diversity, including varied observances within cities.

IA # 1
Before 11/18/1883 LMT
11/18/1883 12:00 CST
3/31/1918 02:00 CWT
10/27/1918 02:00 CST
3/30/1919 02:00 CWT
10/26/1919 02:00 CST
2/09/1942 02:00 CWT
9/30/1945 02:00 CST
4/26/1964 02:00 CDT
10/25/1964 02:00 CST
5/30/1965 02:00 CDT
9/06/1965 02:00 CST
4/24/1966 02:00 US#1

IA # 2
Before 11/18/1883 LMT
11/18/1883 12:00 CST
3/31/1918 02:00 CWT
10/27/1918 02:00 CST
3/30/1919 02:00 CWT
10/26/1919 02:00 CST
2/09/1942 02:00 CWT
9/30/1945 02:00 CST
5/30/1965 02:00 CDT
9/06/1965 02:00 CST
4/24/1966 02:00 US#1

IA # 3
Before 11/18/1883 LMT
11/18/1883 12:00 CST
3/31/1918 02:00 CWT
10/27/1918 02:00 CST
3/30/1919 02:00 CWT
10/26/1919 02:00 CST
2/09/1942 02:00 CWT
9/30/1945 02:00 CST
4/24/1960 02:00 CDT
10/30/1960 02:00 CST
4/26/1964 02:00 CDT
10/25/1964 02:00 CST
5/30/1965 02:00 CDT
9/06/1965 02:00 CST
4/24/1966 02:00 US#1

IA # 4
Before 11/18/1883 LMT
11/18/1883 12:00 CST
3/31/1918 02:00 CWT
10/27/1918 02:00 CST
3/30/1919 02:00 CWT
10/26/1919 02:00 CST
2/09/1942 02:00 CWT
9/30/1945 02:00 CST
4/24/1960 02:00 CDT
10/30/1960 02:00 CST
5/30/1965 02:00 CDT
9/06/1965 02:00 CST
4/24/1966 02:00 US#1

IA # 5
Before 11/18/1883 LMT
11/18/1883 12:00 CST
3/31/1918 02:00 CWT
10/27/1918 02:00 CST
3/30/1919 02:00 CWT
10/26/1919 02:00 CST
2/09/1942 02:00 CWT
9/30/1945 02:00 CST
4/28/1963 02:00 CDT
10/27/1963 02:00 CST
4/26/1964 02:00 CDT
10/25/1964 02:00 CST
5/30/1965 02:00 CDT
9/06/1965 02:00 CST
4/24/1966 02:00 US#1

IA # 6
Before 11/18/1883 LMT
11/18/1883 12:00 CST
3/31/1918 02:00 CWT
10/27/1918 02:00 CST
3/30/1919 02:00 CWT
10/26/1919 02:00 CST
2/09/1942 02:00 CWT
9/30/1945 02:00 CST
6/03/1963 02:00 CDT
8/26/1963 02:00 CST
4/26/1964 02:00 CDT
10/25/1964 02:00 CST
5/30/1965 02:00 CDT
9/06/1965 02:00 CST
4/24/1966 02:00 US#1

IA # 7
Before 11/18/1883 LMT
11/18/1883 12:00 CST
3/31/1918 02:00 CWT
10/27/1918 02:00 CST
3/30/1919 02:00 CWT
10/26/1919 02:00 CST
2/09/1942 02:00 CWT
9/30/1945 02:00 CST
4/26/1959 02:00 CDT
9/28/1959 02:00 CST
4/24/1960 02:00 CDT
10/30/1960 02:00 CST
4/30/1961 02:00 CDT
10/29/1961 02:00 CST
4/29/1962 02:00 CDT
10/28/1962 02:00 CST
4/28/1963 02:00 CDT
10/27/1963 02:00 CST
4/26/1964 02:00 CDT
10/25/1964 02:00 CST
5/30/1965 02:00 CDT
9/06/1965 02:00 CST
4/24/1966 02:00 US#1

IA # 8
Before 11/18/1883 LMT
11/18/1883 12:00 CST
3/31/1918 02:00 CWT
10/27/1918 02:00 CST
3/30/1919 02:00 CWT
10/26/1919 02:00 CST
2/09/1942 02:00 CWT
9/30/1945 02:00 CST
4/25/1954 02:00 CDT
9/26/1954 02:00 CST
4/24/1960 02:00 CDT
10/30/1960 02:00 CST
4/30/1961 02:00 CDT
10/29/1961 02:00 CST
4/29/1962 02:00 CDT
10/28/1962 02:00 CST
4/28/1963 02:00 CDT
10/27/1963 02:00 CST
4/26/1964 02:00 CDT
10/25/1964 02:00 CST
5/30/1965 02:00 CDT
9/06/1965 02:00 CST
4/24/1966 02:00 US#1

IA # 9
Before 11/18/1883 LMT
11/18/1883 12:00 CST
3/31/1918 02:00 CWT
10/27/1918 02:00 CST
3/30/1919 02:00 CWT
10/26/1919 02:00 CST
2/09/1942 02:00 CWT
9/30/1945 02:00 CST
4/28/1963 02:00 CDT
9/01/1963 02:00 CST
4/26/1964 02:00 CDT
10/25/1964 02:00 CST
5/30/1965 02:00 CDT
9/06/1965 02:00 CST
4/24/1966 02:00 US#1

IA # 10
Before 11/18/1883 LMT
11/18/1883 12:00 CST
3/31/1918 02:00 CWT
10/27/1918 02:00 CST
3/30/1919 02:00 CWT
10/26/1919 02:00 CST
2/09/1942 02:00 CWT
9/30/1945 02:00 CST
4/28/1946 02:00 CDT
9/29/1946 02:00 CST
4/27/1947 02:00 CDT
9/28/1947 02:00 CST
4/24/1960 02:00 CDT
10/23/1960 02:00 CST
4/30/1961 02:00 CDT
10/29/1961 02:00 CST
4/29/1962 02:00 CDT
9/15/1962 02:00 CST
4/28/1963 02:00 CDT
9/01/1963 02:00 CST
4/26/1964 02:00 CDT
9/27/1964 02:00 CST
5/30/1965 02:00 CDT
9/06/1965 02:00 CST
4/24/1966 02:00 US#1

IA # 11
Before 11/18/1883 LMT
11/18/1883 12:00 CST
3/31/1918 02:00 CWT
10/27/1918 02:00 CST
3/30/1919 02:00 CWT
10/26/1919 02:00 CST
2/09/1942 02:00 CWT
9/30/1945 02:00 CST
4/24/1960 02:00 CDT
10/30/1960 02:00 CST
4/30/1961 02:00 CDT
9/03/1961 02:00 CST
4/28/1963 02:00 CDT
8/25/1963 02:00 CST
4/26/1964 02:00 CDT
10/31/1964 02:00 CST
5/30/1965 02:00 CDT
9/06/1965 02:00 CST
4/24/1966 02:00 US#1

IA # 12
Before 11/18/1883 LMT
11/18/1883 12:00 CST
3/31/1918 02:00 CWT
10/27/1918 02:00 CST
3/30/1919 02:00 CWT
10/26/1919 02:00 CST
4/27/1941 02:00 CDT
9/28/1941 02:00 CST
2/09/1942 02:00 CWT
9/30/1945 02:00 CST
4/28/1957 02:00 CDT
10/29/1957 02:00 CST
4/27/1958 02:00 CDT
10/28/1958 02:00 CST
4/26/1959 02:00 CDT
10/27/1959 02:00 CST
4/24/1960 02:00 CDT
10/30/1960 02:00 CST
4/30/1961 02:00 CDT
10/29/1961 02:00 CST
4/29/1962 02:00 CDT
10/28/1962 02:00 CST
4/28/1963 02:00 CDT
10/27/1963 02:00 CST
4/26/1964 02:00 CDT
10/25/1964 02:00 CST
5/30/1965 02:00 CDT
9/06/1965 02:00 CST
4/24/1966 02:00 US#1

IA # 13
Before 11/18/1883 LMT
11/18/1883 12:00 CST
3/31/1918 02:00 CWT
10/27/1918 02:00 CST
3/30/1919 02:00 CWT
10/26/1919 02:00 CST
2/09/1942 02:00 CWT
9/30/1945 02:00 CST
6/01/1963 02:00 CDT
9/01/1963 02:00 CST
4/26/1964 02:00 CDT
10/25/1964 02:00 CST
5/30/1965 02:00 CDT
9/06/1965 02:00 CST
4/24/1966 02:00 US#1

IA # 14
Before 11/18/1883 LMT
11/18/1883 12:00 CST
3/31/1918 02:00 CWT
10/27/1918 02:00 CST
3/30/1919 02:00 CWT
10/26/1919 02:00 CST
2/09/1942 02:00 CWT
9/30/1945 02:00 CST
6/03/1962 02:00 CDT
8/26/1962 02:00 CST
4/26/1964 02:00 CDT
10/25/1964 02:00 CST
5/30/1965 02:00 CDT
9/06/1965 02:00 CST
4/24/1966 02:00 US#1

IA # 15
Before 11/18/1883 LMT
11/18/1883 12:00 CST
3/31/1918 02:00 CWT
10/27/1918 02:00 CST
3/30/1919 02:00 CWT
10/26/1919 02:00 CST
2/09/1942 02:00 CWT
9/30/1945 02:00 CST
4/28/1946 02:00 CDT
9/29/1946 02:00 CST
4/28/1957 02:00 CDT
9/29/1957 02:00 CST
4/29/1962 02:00 CDT
10/28/1962 02:00 CST
6/02/1963 02:00 CDT
9/01/1963 02:00 CST
4/26/1964 02:00 CDT
10/25/1964 02:00 CST
5/30/1965 02:00 CDT
9/06/1965 02:00 CST
4/24/1966 02:00 US#1

IA # 16
Before 11/18/1883 LMT
11/18/1883 12:00 CST
3/31/1918 02:00 CWT
10/27/1918 02:00 CST
3/30/1919 02:00 CWT
10/26/1919 02:00 CST
2/09/1942 02:00 CWT
9/30/1945 02:00 CST
4/24/1960 02:00 CDT
10/30/1960 02:00 CST
4/30/1961 02:00 CDT
10/29/1961 02:00 CST
4/29/1962 02:00 CDT
9/16/1962 02:00 CST
4/28/1963 02:00 CDT
9/29/1963 02:00 CST
4/26/1964 02:00 CDT
9/27/1964 02:00 CST
5/30/1965 02:00 CDT
9/06/1965 02:00 CST
4/24/1966 02:00 US#1

IA # 17
Before 11/18/1883 LMT
11/18/1883 12:00 CST
3/31/1918 02:00 CWT
10/27/1918 02:00 CST
3/30/1919 02:00 CWT
10/26/1919 02:00 CST
2/09/1942 02:00 CWT
9/30/1945 02:00 CST
4/24/1960 02:00 CDT
10/30/1960 02:00 CST
4/30/1961 02:00 CDT
10/29/1961 02:00 CST
4/29/1962 02:00 CDT
9/02/1962 02:00 CST
4/28/1963 02:00 CDT
9/01/1963 02:00 CST
4/26/1964 02:00 CDT
9/06/1964 02:00 CST
5/30/1965 02:00 CDT
9/06/1965 02:00 CST
4/24/1966 02:00 US#1

IA # 18
Before 11/18/1883 LMT
11/18/1883 12:00 CST
3/31/1918 02:00 CWT
10/27/1918 02:00 CST
3/30/1919 02:00 CWT
10/26/1919 02:00 CST
2/09/1942 02:00 CWT
9/30/1945 02:00 CST
4/24/1960 02:00 CDT
10/30/1960 02:00 CST
4/28/1963 02:00 CDT
10/27/1963 02:00 CST
4/26/1964 02:00 CDT
10/25/1964 02:00 CST
5/30/1965 02:00 CDT
9/06/1965 02:00 CST
4/24/1966 02:00 US#1

IA # 19
Before 11/18/1883 LMT
11/18/1883 12:00 CST
3/31/1918 02:00 CWT
10/27/1918 02:00 CST
3/30/1919 02:00 CWT
10/26/1919 02:00 CST
2/09/1942 02:00 CWT
9/30/1945 02:00 CST
5/26/1963 02:00 CDT
9/01/1963 02:00 CST
4/26/1964 02:00 CDT
10/25/1964 02:00 CST
5/30/1965 02:00 CDT
9/06/1965 02:00 CST
4/24/1966 02:00 US#1

IA # 20
Before 11/18/1883 LMT
11/18/1883 12:00 CST
3/31/1918 02:00 CWT
10/27/1918 02:00 CST
3/30/1919 02:00 CWT
10/26/1919 02:00 CST
2/09/1942 02:00 CWT
9/30/1945 02:00 CST
4/30/1961 02:00 CDT
10/29/1961 02:00 CST
4/29/1962 02:00 CDT
9/02/1962 02:00 CST
4/28/1963 02:00 CDT
9/01/1963 02:00 CST
4/26/1964 02:00 CDT
10/31/1964 02:00 CST
5/30/1965 02:00 CDT
9/06/1965 02:00 CST
4/24/1966 02:00 US#1

IA # 21
Before 11/18/1883 LMT
11/18/1883 12:00 CST
3/31/1918 02:00 CWT
10/27/1918 02:00 CST
3/30/1919 02:00 CWT
10/26/1919 02:00 CST
2/09/1942 02:00 CWT
9/30/1945 02:00 CST
4/24/1960 02:00 CDT
10/30/1960 02:00 CST
4/30/1961 02:00 CDT
9/03/1961 02:00 CST
4/29/1962 02:00 CDT
9/15/1962 02:00 CST
4/28/1963 02:00 CDT
9/29/1963 02:00 CST
4/26/1964 02:00 CDT
10/31/1964 02:00 CST
5/30/1965 02:00 CDT
9/06/1965 02:00 CST
4/24/1966 02:00 US#1

IA # 22
Before 11/18/1883 LMT
11/18/1883 12:00 CST
3/31/1918 02:00 CWT
10/27/1918 02:00 CST
3/30/1919 02:00 CWT
10/26/1919 02:00 CST
2/09/1942 02:00 CWT
9/30/1945 02:00 CST
4/24/1960 02:00 CDT
10/30/1960 02:00 CST
4/30/1961 02:00 CDT
9/03/1961 02:00 CST
4/26/1964 02:00 CDT
10/25/1964 02:00 CST
5/30/1965 02:00 CDT
9/06/1965 02:00 CST
4/24/1966 02:00 US#1

IA # 23
Before 11/18/1883 LMT
11/18/1883 12:00 CST
3/31/1918 02:00 CWT
10/27/1918 02:00 CST
3/30/1919 02:00 CWT
10/26/1919 02:00 CST
2/09/1942 02:00 CWT
9/30/1945 02:00 CST
5/26/1963 02:00 CDT
8/26/1963 02:00 CST
4/26/1964 02:00 CDT
10/25/1964 02:00 CST
5/30/1965 02:00 CDT
9/06/1965 02:00 CST
4/24/1966 02:00 US#1

IA # 24
Before 11/18/1883 LMT
11/18/1883 12:00 CST
3/31/1918 02:00 CWT
10/27/1918 02:00 CST
3/30/1919 02:00 CWT
10/26/1919 02:00 CST
2/09/1942 02:00 CWT
9/30/1945 02:00 CST
4/24/1960 02:00 CDT
10/30/1960 02:00 CST
4/29/1962 02:00 CDT
9/16/1962 02:00 CST
4/28/1963 02:00 CDT
9/15/1963 02:00 CST
4/26/1964 02:00 CDT
10/25/1964 02:00 CST
5/30/1965 02:00 CDT
9/06/1965 02:00 CST
4/24/1966 02:00 US#1

IA # 25
Before 11/18/1883 LMT
11/18/1883 12:00 CST
3/31/1918 02:00 CWT
10/27/1918 02:00 CST
3/30/1919 02:00 CWT
10/26/1919 02:00 CST
2/09/1942 02:00 CWT
9/30/1945 02:00 CST
4/29/1962 02:00 CDT
9/15/1962 02:00 CST
4/28/1963 02:00 CDT
9/29/1963 02:00 CST
4/26/1964 02:00 CDT
10/25/1964 02:00 CST
5/30/1965 02:00 CDT
9/06/1965 02:00 CST
4/24/1966 02:00 US#1

COUNTIES

1 Adair
2 Adams
3 Allamakee
4 Appanoose
5 Audubon
6 Benton
7 Black Hawk
8 Boone
9 Bremer
10 Buchanan
11 Buena Vista
12 Butler
13 Calhoun
14 Carroll
15 Cass
16 Cedar
17 Cerro Gordo
18 Cherokee
19 Chickasaw
20 Clarke
21 Clay
22 Clayton
23 Clinton
24 Crawford
25 Dallas
26 Davis
27 Decatur
28 Delaware
29 Des Moines
30 Dickinson
31 Dubuque
32 Emmet
33 Fayette
34 Floyd
35 Franklin
36 Fremont
37 Greene
38 Grundy
39 Guthrie
40 Hamilton
41 Hancock
42 Hardin
43 Harrison
44 Henry
45 Howard
46 Humboldt
47 Ida
48 Iowa
49 Jackson
50 Jasper
51 Jefferson
52 Johnson
53 Jones
54 Keokuk
55 Kossuth
56 Lee
57 Linn
58 Louisa
59 Lucas
60 Lyon
61 Madison
62 Mahaska
63 Marion
64 Marshall
65 Mills
66 Mitchell
67 Monona
68 Monroe
69 Montgomery
70 Muscatine
71 O'Brien
72 Osceola
73 Page
74 Palo Alto
75 Plymouth
76 Pocahontas
77 Polk
78 Pottawattamie
79 Poweshiek
80 Ringgold
81 Sac
82 Scott
83 Shelby
84 Sioux
85 Story
86 Tama
87 Taylor
88 Union
89 Van Buren
90 Wapello
91 Warren
92 Washington
93 Wayne
94 Webster
95 Winnebago
96 Winneshiek
97 Woodbury
98 Worth
99 Wright

Abingdon 51 2 41N04'56 92W08'20 6:08:33
Ackley 42 2 42N33'15 93W03'11 6:12:13
Ackworth 91 2 41N22'01 93W28'21 6:13:53
Adair 39 2 41N30'02 94W38'36 6:18:34
Adaville 75 2 42N45'03 96W24'15 6:25:37
Adaza 37 2 42N11'43 94W29'39 6:17:59
Adel 25 2 41N36'52 94W01'02 6:16:04
Adelphi 77 2 41N32'00 93W25'34 6:13:42
Afton 88 2 41N01'39 94W11'52 6:16:47
Agency (Agency City Sta) 90
4 40N59'42 92W18'24 6:09:14
Ainsworth 92 1 41N17'20 91W33'08 6:06:13
Akron 75 2 42N49'44 96W33'33 6:26:14
Albany 33 1 42N51'57 91W45'31 6:07:02
Albaton 67 2 42N11'08 96W17'26 6:25:10
Albert City 11 2 42N46'55 94W56'54 6:19:48
Albia 68 2 41N01'36 92W48'20 6:11:13
Albion 64 2 42N06'45 92W59'18 6:11:57
Alburnett 57 1 42N08'54 91W37'06 6:06:28
Alden 42 2 42N31'13 93W22'33 6:13:30
Alexander 35 2 42N48'21 93W28'35 6:13:54
Algona 55 2 43N04'12 94W13'58 6:16:56
Alice 57 1 42N11'51 91W41'44 6:06:47
Alleman 77 2 41N35'48 93W36'41 6:14:27
Allendorf 72 2 43N24'53 95W38'35 6:22:34
Allens Grove 82 1 41N43 90W45 6:03:00
Allerton 93 2 40N42'23 93W21'54 6:13:28
Allison 12 2 42N45'10 92W47'42 6:11:11
Almont 23 10 41N58'31 90W11'56 6:00:48
Almoral 28 1 42N32'08 91W17'23 6:05:10
Almoral Spring 28
1 42N30'59 91W16'21 6:05:05
Alpha 33 2 42N59'48 92W02'51 6:08:11
Alta 11 2 42N40'25 95W17'25 6:21:10
Alta Vista 19 2 43N11'55 92W25'01 6:09:40
Alton 84 2 42N59'15 96W00'37 6:24:02
Altoona 58 2 41N38'39 93W27'52 6:13:51
Alvord 60 2 43N20'32 96W18'03 6:25:12
Amana 48 1 41N48'00 91W52'14 6:07:29
Amaqua 8 2 42N04 94W06 6:16:24
Amber 53 1 42N07'41 91W10'48 6:04:43
Amboy 50 2 41N42 93W04 6:12:16
America 75 2 42N46 96W09 6:24:36
Ames 85 2 42N02'05 93W37'11 6:14:29
Amherst 18 2 42N47 95W48 6:23:12
Amish 52 1 41N32'09 91W47'11 6:07:09
Amity 73 2 40N37 95W05 6:20:20
Amsterdam 41 2 42N57 93W48 6:15:12
Anamosa 53 1 42N06'30 91W17'06 6:05:08
Anderson 36 2 40N48'05 95W36'14 6:22:25
Andover 23 1 41N58'45 90W15'06 6:01:00
Andrew 49 1 42N09'13 90W35'32 6:02:22
Andrews 77 2 41N45'12 93W45'25 6:15:02
Angus 8 2 41N53'00 94W09'26 6:16:38
Anita 15 2 41N26'43 94W45'52 6:19:03
Ankeny 77 2 41N43'47 93W36'20 6:14:25
Anthon 97 2 42N23'18 95W51'59 6:23:28
Aplington 12 2 42N35'03 92W53'03 6:11:32
Arbor Hill 1 2 41N22'00 94W19'05 6:17:16
Arcadia 14 2 42N01'54 95W02'45 6:20:11
Archer 71 2 43N06'55 95W44'44 6:22:59
Ardon 70 1 41N23'42 91W11'18 6:04:45
Aredale 12 2 42N49'59 93W00'19 6:12:01
Argo 82 7 41N37'33 90W25'57 6:01:44
Argyle 56 1 40N31'54 91W33'58 6:06:16
Arion 24 2 41N56'57 95W27'48 6:21:51
Arispe 88 2 40N56'58 94W13'08 6:16:53
Arlington 33 1 42N44'57 91W40'16 6:06:41
Armour 7 2 42N30'46 92W15'18 6:09:01
Armstrong 32 2 43N23'46 94W28'41 6:17:55
Armstrong Grove 32
2 43N23 94W30 6:18:00
Arnold 46 2 42N48'39 94W11'54 6:16:48
Arnold Park 30 2 43N22'22 95W07'25 6:20:30
Artesian 9 2 42N43'42 92W20'13 6:09:21
Arthur 47 2 42N20'05 95W20'50 6:21:23
Asbury 31 1 42N30'52 90W45'05 6:03:00
Ashawa 77 2 41N34'20 93W45'22 6:15:01
Ash Grove 26 2 40N52'15 92W33'10 6:10:13
Ashland 90 2 40N57'31 92W14'11 6:08:57
Ashton 72 2 43N18'41 95W47'27 6:23:10
Aspinwall 24 2 41N54'43 95W08'07 6:20:32
Astor 24 2 41N52'12 95W15'59 6:21:04
Atalissa 70 1 41N34'16 91W09'57 6:04:40
Athelstan 87 2 40N34'20 94W32'14 6:18:09
Athens 80 2 40N43 94W06 6:16:24
Atkins 6 1 41N59'49 91W51'43 6:07:27
Atlantic 15 2 41N24'13 95W00'49 6:20:03
Attica 63 2 41N13'47 93W00'57 6:12:04
Auburn 81 2 42N15'05 94W52'39 6:19:31
Audubon 5 2 41N43'05 94W55'56 6:19:44
Augusta 29 8 40N45'29 91W16'32 6:05:06
Aurelia 18 2 42N42'46 95W26'11 6:21:45
Aureola 34 2 42N58'06 92W52'40 6:11:31
Aurora 10 1 42N37'08 91W43'42 6:06:55
Austinville 12 2 42N35'09 92W57'25 6:11:50
Avery 68 2 41N03'55 92W42'51 6:10:51
Avoca 78 2 41N28'36 95W20'16 6:21:21
Avon 77 2 41N31'43 93W31'23 6:14:06
Avon Lake 77 2 41N31'19 93W30'03 6:14:00
Ayrshire 74 2 43N02'21 94W49'57 6:19:20
Badger 94 2 42N36'52 94W08'45 6:16:35
Bagley 39 2 41N50'46 94W25'47 6:17:43
Bailey 66 2 43N27'54 92W36'28 6:10:26
Baldwin 49 1 42N04'27 90W50'29 6:03:22
Balfour 65 2 41N02'56 95W40'03 6:22:40
Balltown 31 1 42N38'17 90W52'07 6:03:28
Ballyclough 31 1 42N25'33 90W43'05 6:02:52
Baltimore 44 22 40N53 91W26 6:05:44
Bancroft 55 2 43N17'34 94W13'04 6:16:52
Bangor 64 2 42N10'24 93W05'36 6:12:22
Banks 33 2 42N51 92W01 6:08:04
Bankston 31 1 42N31'07 90W57'40 6:03:51
Banner 97 2 42N31 96W09 6:24:36
Barclay 7 2 42N31 92W08 6:08:32
Barnes 11 2 42N52 95W13 6:20:52
Barnes City 62 2 41N30'30 92W28'05 6:09:52
Barney 61 2 41N10'00 94W00'13 6:16:01
Barnum 94 2 42N30'31 94W21'54 6:17:28
Barrett Superette 1
2 41N33 94W24 6:17:36
Bartlett 36 2 40N53'06 95W47'41 6:23:11
Barton 98 2 43N23 93W05 6:12:20
Bassett 19 2 43N03'47 92W30'55 6:10:04
Batavia 51 4 40N59'39 92W10'02 6:08:40
Bath 17 2 43N03 93W12 6:12:48
Battle 47 2 42N26 95W36 6:22:24
Battle Creek 47 2 42N18'56 95W35'54 6:22:24
Bauer 63 2 41N12'14 93W18'25 6:13:14
Baxter 50 2 41N49'34 93W09'05 6:12:36
Bayard 39 2 41N51'07 94W33'29 6:18:14
Beacon 62 2 41N16'37 92W40'46 6:10:43
Beaconsfield 80 2 40N48'28 94W03'01 6:16:12
Beaman 38 2 42N13'11 92W49'24 6:11:18
Bear Creek 79 2 41N44 92W29 6:09:56
Beaver 8 2 42N02'18 94W08'31 6:16:34
Beaverdale 29 8 40N50'48 91W12'30 6:04:50
Beaverdale 77 2 41N36 93W40 6:14:40
Beaverdale Heights 29
8 40N49 91W10 6:04:40
Beckwith 51 1 41N00'33 91W51'52 6:07:27
Bedford 87 2 40N40'01 94W43'16 6:18:53
Beebeetown 43 2 41N31'16 95W45'19 6:23:01
Beech 77 2 41N22'29 93W21'07 6:13:24
Bel Air Beach 11
2 42N38 95W11 6:20:44
Belinda 59 2 41N08'20 93W11'32 6:12:46
Belknap 26 2 40N49'14 92W25'34 6:09:42
Bellair 4 2 40N44 92W56 6:11:44
Belle Fountain 62
2 41N16'49 92W51'41 6:11:27
Belle Plaine 6 2 41N53'49 92W16'41 6:09:07
Bellevue 49 6 42N15'31 90W25'22 6:01:41
Bellville 76 2 42N37 94W38 6:18:32
Belmond 99 2 42N50'46 93W36'50 6:14:27
Belmont 91 2 41N17 93W23 6:13:32
Beloit 60 2 43N16'53 96W34'28 6:26:18
Belvidere 67 2 42N01 95W58 6:23:52
Bennett 16 1 41N44'25 90W58'25 6:03:54
Bennezette 12 2 42N52 92W58 6:11:52
Bennington 7 2 42N36 92W16 6:09:04
Benson 7 2 42N32'33 92W32'31 6:10:10
Bente Branch 22 1 42N48'48 91W20'15 6:05:21
Bentley 78 2 41N22'37 95W37'12 6:22:29
Benton 80 2 40N42'12 94W21'29 6:17:26
Bentonsport 89 1 40N43'32 91W51'13 6:07:25
Berea 1 2 41N22'27 94W40'48 6:18:43
Berkley 8 2 41N56'42 94W06'52 6:16:27
Bernard 31 1 42N18'44 90W49'54 6:03:20
Berne 24 2 42N04'52 95W39'09 6:22:37
Bertram 57 1 41N56'59 91W32'07 6:06:08
Berwick 77 2 41N39'54 93W32'41 6:14:11
Bethany Hall 19 2 43N10'38 92W14'23 6:08:58
Bethel 33 2 42N57 92W01 6:08:04
Bethelhem 93 2 40N50'29 93W12'43 6:12:51
Bethesda 73 2 40N50'35 95W05'58 6:20:24
Bethlehem 93 2 40N59 93W12 6:12:48
Bettendorf 82 7 41N31'28 90W30'56 6:02:04
Beulah 22 1 43N01'38 91W18'29 6:05:14
Bevington 61 2 41N21'38 93W47'26 6:15:10
Bidwell 90 2 41N01'08 92W32'18 6:10:09
Big Creek 7 2 42N19 92W13 6:08:52
Big Rock 82 1 41N46'13 90W49'34 6:03:18
Bingham 73 2 40N44'03 95W17'19 6:21:09
Birmingham 89 1 40N52'44 91W56'49 6:07:47
Black Corners 25
2 41N41'18 94W01'23 6:16:06
Black Oak 62 2 41N23 92W49 6:11:16
Bladensburg 90 2 41N02'46 92W14'13 6:08:57
Blairsburg 40 2 42N28'48 93W38'34 6:14:34
Blairstown 6 2 41N54'34 92W05'03 6:08:20
Blakesburg 90 2 40N57'44 92W38'02 6:10:32
Blanchard 73 2 40N34'45 95W13'17 6:20:53
Blencoe 67 2 41N55'49 96W04'50 6:24:19
Bliedorn 23 1 41N54'09 90W40'41 6:02:43
Blockton 87 2 40N36'56 94W28'37 6:17:54
Bloomfield 26 2 40N45'06 92W24'53 6:09:40
Bloomington 85 2 42N03'22 93W35'14 6:14:21
Blue Grass 82 5 41N30'32 90W45'57 6:03:04
Bluff Creek 68 2 41N07 92W48 6:11:12
Bluff Park 56 20 40N31'39 91W24'13 6:05:37
Bluffton 96 1 43N24'11 91W54'42 6:07:39
Boardman 22 1 42N52 91W26 6:05:44
Bode 46 2 42N52'06 94W17'22 6:17:09
Bolan 98 2 43N22'19 93W07'09 6:12:29
Bonair 45 2 43N25'19 92W11'33 6:08:46
Bonaparte 89 1 40N41'53 91W48'11 6:07:13
Bondurant 77 2 41N42'02 93W27'43 6:13:51
Boomer 78 2 41N28 95W46 6:23:04
Boone 8 2 42N03'35 93W52'48 6:15:31
Booneville 25 2 41N31'27 93W53'01 6:15:32
Booth 74 2 42N56 94W51 6:19:24
Border Plains 94
2 42N23'53 94W02'52 6:16:11
Botna 83 2 41N51'21 95W07'52 6:20:31
Boulder 57 1 42N15 91W26 6:05:44
Bouton 25 2 41N51'05 94W00'32 6:16:02
Bowsher 77 2 41N38'21 93W32'30 6:14:10
Boxholm 8 2 42N10'33 94W06'21 6:16:25
Boyd 19 2 43N00'45 92W15'28 6:09:02
Boyden 84 2 43N11'28 96W00'20 6:24:01
Boyer 24 2 42N10'55 95W14'06 6:20:56
Boyer River 24 2 42N11'21 95W12'16 6:20:49
Boyer Valley 81 2 42N26 95W09 6:20:36
Braddyville 73 2 40N35 95W02 6:20:08
Bradford 19 2 42N57 92W32 6:10:08
Bradford 35 2 42N37'59 93W14'41 6:12:59
Bradgate 46 2 42N48'11 94W25'04 6:17:40
Brainard 33 1 42N55'51 91W42'18 6:06:49
Brandon 7 1 42N18'52 92W00'07 6:08:00
Brayton 5 2 41N32'40 94W55'26 6:19:42
Brazil 4 2 40N45'29 92W57'15 6:11:49
Breda 14 2 42N10'54 94W58'36 6:19:54
Bremen 28 1 42N31 91W12 6:04:48
Bremer 9 2 42N46'24 92W23'41 6:09:35
Bridgeport 49 5 42N05'22 90W37'37 6:02:30
Bridgeport 93 2 40N45'12 93W13'53 6:12:56
Bridgewater 1 2 41N14'42 94W40'07 6:18:40
Brighton 92 1 41N10'29 91W49'10 6:07:17
Bristol 98 2 43N24'43 93W28'04 6:13:52
Bristow 12 2 42N46'26 92W54'26 6:11:38
Britt 41 2 43N05'52 93W48'06 6:15:12
Bromley 64 2 42N07'08 93W07'46 6:12:31
Brompton 68 2 40N55'53 92W44'04 6:10:56
Bronson 97 2 42N24'39 96W12'49 6:24:51
Brooke 11 2 42N52 95W21 6:21:24
Brooklyn 79 2 41N44'01 92W26'43 6:09:47
Brooks 2 2 40N57'55 94W48'17 6:19:13
Brookside 7 2 42N32 92W26 6:09:44
Brookville 51 2 41N03'20 92W05'20 6:08:21
Brown 57 1 42N05 91W25 6:05:40
Browns 23 1 42N01'50 90W29'57 6:02:00
Brownville 66 2 43N20'32 92W40'33 6:10:42
Bruce 6 2 42N15 92W14 6:08:56
Brunsville 75 2 42N48'35 96W16'08 6:25:05
Brushy 94 2 42N25'51 94W00'36 6:16:02
Bryant 23 1 41N57'48 90W19'48 6:01:19
Bryantsburg 10 1 42N34'29 91W54'19 6:07:37
Buchanan 16 7 41N45'54 91W14'48 6:04:59
Buck Creek 9 2 42N45'31 92W08'26 6:08:34
Buck Creek 28 1 42N20'14 91W20'31 6:05:22
Buckeye 42 2 42N25'02 93W22'29 6:13:30
Buck Grove 24 2 41N55'05 95W23'45 6:21:35
Buck Grove 38 2 42N30'51 92W50'58 6:11:24
Buckhorn 49 1 42N03'36 90W45'11 6:03:01
Buckingham 86 2 42N15'45 92W26'51 6:09:47
Bucknell 68 2 41N03'58 93W02'39 6:12:11
Budd 31 1 42N31'59 90W48'56 6:03:16
Buena Vista 23 1 41N44'31 90W44'25 6:02:58
Buffalo 82 5 41N27'23 90W43'24 6:02:54
Buffalo Center 95
2 43N23'09 93W56'47 6:15:47

Buffalo Heights 82 1 41N28'21 90W42'52 6:02:51
Bulgers Hollow 23 10 41N56'07 90W11'02 6:00:44
Buncombe 84 2 43N02 96W28 6:25:52
Burchinal 17 2 43N03'55 93W16'41 6:13:07
Burdette 35 2 42N34'19 93W21'36 6:13:26
Burlington 29 8 40N48'27 91W06'46 6:04:27
Burnside 94 2 42N20'45 94W06'24 6:16:26
Burrell 27 2 40N42 93W50 6:15:20
Burr Oak 65 2 40N56'09 95W47'15 6:23:09
Burr Oak 96 1 43N27'32 91W51'55 6:07:28
Burt 55 2 43N11'51 94W13'10 6:16:53
Bushville 87 2 40N51'24 94W44'17 6:18:57
Bussey 63 2 41N12'16 92W52'57 6:11:32
Butler Center 12 2 42N41'51 92W47'00 6:11:08
Buxton 68 2 41N09'30 92W49'16 6:11:17
Byron 10 1 42N31 91W47 6:07:08
Cairo 58 1 41N11'01 91W19'38 6:05:19
Calamus 23 1 41N49'33 90W45'29 6:03:02
Caldwell 4 2 40N38 92W48 6:11:12
Caledonia 71 2 42N58 95W48 6:23:12
Calhoun 43 2 41N37'54 95W53'42 6:23:35
California Junction 43 2 41N33'31 95W59'40 6:23:59
Callender 94 2 42N21'43 94W17'44 6:17:11
Call Terminal 97 2 42N30 96W23 6:25:32
Calmar 96 1 43N11'01 91W51'50 6:07:27
Caloma 63 2 41N16'38 93W18'33 6:13:14
Calumet 71 2 42N56'47 95W32'59 6:22:12
Camanche 23 9 41N47'17 90W15'22 6:01:01
Cambria 93 2 40N50'16 93W24'08 6:13:37
Cambridge 85 2 41N53'54 93W31'44 6:14:07
Cameron 5 2 41N49 94W55 6:19:40
Cameron 17 2 43N04'58 93W11'17 6:12:45
Cameron 31 1 42N39'58 90W51'57 6:03:28
Camp 77 2 41N33 93W23 6:13:32
Campbell 77 2 41N30'34 93W43'55 6:14:56
Camp Dodge 77 2 41N41'59 93W42'26 6:14:50
Canaan 44 1 41N03 91W26 6:05:44
Canby 1 2 41N25'02 94W33'59 6:18:16
Canoe 96 1 43N24 91W48 6:07:12
Canton 53 1 42N09'48 90W53'44 6:03:35
Cantril 89 2 40N38'39 92W04'11 6:08:17
Capel 84 2 43N07 96W03 6:24:12
Capitol Heights 77 2 41N38'00 93W31'12 6:14:05
Carbon 2 2 41N03'00 94W49'23 6:19:18
Carbon 26 2 40N53'47 92W25'18 6:09:41
Carbondale 77 2 41N34'56 93W30'11 6:14:01
Carl 2 2 41N07'12 94W39'46 6:18:39
Carlisle 91 2 41N30'03 93W29'27 6:13:58
Carlton 86 2 42N05 92W42 6:10:48
Carmel 84 2 43N07'40 96W14'06 6:24:56
Carnarvon 81 2 42N15'13 95W01'17 6:20:05
Carnes 84 2 42N55'38 96W03'24 6:24:14
Carney 77 2 41N41'18 93W36'01 6:14:24
Carnforth 79 2 41N43'20 92W20'58 6:09:24
Carpenter 66 2 43N24'54 93W00'53 6:12:04
Carroll 14 2 42N03'57 94W52'00 6:19:28
Carrollton 14 2 41N56'59 94W44'52 6:18:59
Carrville 34 2 43N00'32 92W34'29 6:10:18
Carson 78 2 41N14'12 95W25'04 6:21:40
Carter Lake 78 2 41N17'26 95W55'04 6:23:40
Cartersville 17 2 42N59'40 93W04'58 6:12:20
Cascade 31 1 42N17'55 91W00'53 6:04:04
Casey 39 2 41N30'18 94W31'09 6:18:05
Casino Beach 11 2 42N37'27 95W13'42 6:20:55
Castalia 96 1 43N06'43 91W40'34 6:06:42
Castana 67 2 42N04'28 95W54'30 6:23:38
Castle Grove 53 1 42N15 91W18 6:05:12
Cattese 31 1 42N27'40 90W37'52 6:02:31
Cedar 62 2 41N12'44 92W31'32 6:10:06
Cedar Bluff 16 7 41N47'09 91W18'29 6:05:14
Cedar City 7 2 42N32'26 92W26'27 6:09:46
Cedar Falls 7 2 42N31'40 92W26'43 6:09:47
Cedar Falls Junction 7 2 42N26'43 92W25'07 6:09:40
Cedar Hills 57 1 41N58'22 91W44'25 6:06:58
Cedar Rapids 57 1 42N00'30 91W38'38 6:06:35
Cedar Valley 16 1 41N43'35 91W14'47 6:04:59
Cedar View 34 2 43N04 92W41 6:10:44
Centennial 60 2 43N24 96W30 6:26:00
Centerdale 16 1 41N38'31 91W18'25 6:05:14
Center Grove 30 2 43N23 95W05 6:20:20
Center Grove 31 15 42N29'28 90W42'55 6:02:52
Center Junction 53 1 42N06'58 91W05'13 6:04:21
Center Point 57 1 42N11'27 91W47'06 6:07:08
Centerville 4 2 40N44'03 92W52'26 6:11:30
Centerville 8 2 42N05'34 93W56'07 6:15:44
Central City 57 1 42N12'14 91W31'26 6:06:06
Central College 63 2 41N24 92W55 6:11:40
Central Heights 17 2 43N08'06 93W14'30 6:12:58
Centralia 31 1 42N28'20 90W50'13 6:03:21
Ceres 22 1 42N49'14 91W11'10 6:04:45
Chapel Hill 82 12 41N29'32 90W38'50 6:02:35
Chapin 35 2 42N50'01 93W13'19 6:12:53
Chariton 59 2 41N00'50 93W18'23 6:13:14
Charles City 34 2 43N03'59 92W40'20 6:10:41
Charleston 56 1 40N35'27 91W31'52 6:06:07
Charlotte 23 1 41N57'37 90W27'54 6:01:52
Charter Oak 24 2 42N04'06 95W35'29 6:22:22
Chatsworth 84 2 42N54'58 96W30'58 6:26:04
Chautauqua 78 2 41N17'27 95W47'36 6:23:10
Chelsea 86 2 41N55'09 92W23'40 6:09:35
Cheney 6 1 42N15'15 91W55'38 6:07:43
Chequest 89 2 40N47 92W08 6:08:32
Cherokee 18 2 42N44'58 95W33'05 6:22:12
Chester 45 2 43N29'28 92W21'37 6:09:26
Chickasaw 19 2 43N02'02 92W29'42 6:09:59
Chillicothe 90 2 41N05'08 92W31'45 6:10:07
Church 3 1 43N21'08 91W20'20 6:05:21
Churchville 91 2 41N23'48 93W45'03 6:15:00
Churdan 37 2 42N09'07 94W28'27 6:17:54
Cincinnati 4 2 40N37'51 92W55'28 6:11:42
Clare 94 2 42N35'14 94W20'43 6:17:23
Clarence 16 1 41N53'20 91W03'23 6:04:14
Clarinda 73 2 40N44'31 95W02'17 6:20:09
Clarion 99 2 42N43'54 93W43'58 6:14:56
Clark 65 2 40N57'02 95W32'24 6:22:10
Clark 86 2 42N10 92W23 6:09:32
Clarkdale 4 2 40N47'07 92W54'17 6:11:37
Clarksville 12 2 42N47'05 92W40'03 6:10:40
Clay Mills 53 1 42N11'03 90W56'35 6:03:46
Clayton 22 1 42N54'14 91W08'50 6:04:35
Clayton Center 22 1 42N53'00 91W19'36 6:05:18
Clayworks 94 2 42N30 94W11 6:16:44
Clearfield 87 2 40N48'03 94W28'32 6:17:54
Clear Lake (Clear Lake City) 17 2 43N08'17 93W22'45 6:13:31
Cleghorn 18 2 42N48'44 95W42'45 6:22:51
Clemons 64 2 42N06'50 93W09'21 6:12:37
Clemons Grove 64 2 42N06'50 93W09'21 6:12:37
Cleona 82 5 41N38 90W51 6:03:24
Clermont 33 1 43N00'13 91W39'08 6:06:37
Cleves 42 2 42N28'22 93W02'42 6:12:11
Cliffland 90 2 40N57'57 92W19'34 6:09:18
Climax 65 2 40N55'50 95W21'56 6:21:28
Climbing Hill 97 2 42N20'30 96W04'39 6:24:19
Clinton 23 10 41N50'40 90W11'19 6:00:45
Clio 93 2 40N38'06 93W27'04 6:13:48
Clive 77 2 41N36'11 93W43'26 6:14:54
Cloverdale 72 2 43N20'49 95W41'08 6:22:45
Cloverhills 77 2 41N35 93W44 6:14:56
Clucas 61 2 41N29'48 94W03'06 6:16:12
Clutier 86 2 42N04'46 92W24'07 6:09:36
Clyde 50 2 41N50'31 93W15'54 6:13:04
Coal Creek 54 2 41N26'16 92W23'36 6:09:34
Coal Valley 8 2 42N01'54 93W57'02 6:15:48
Coalville 94 2 42N26'43 94W07'32 6:16:30
Coburg 65 2 40N55'03 95W15'51 6:21:03
Coffins Grove 28 1 42N29 91W21 6:05:24
Coggon 57 1 42N16'51 91W31'49 6:06:07
Coin 73 2 40N39'16 95W13'48 6:20:55
Coldwater 12 2 42N52 92W51 6:11:24
Colesburg 28 1 42N38'22 91W12'07 6:04:48
Colfax 50 2 41N40'40 93W14'42 6:12:59
College 57 1 41N54 91W39 6:06:36
College Springs 73 2 40N37'09 95W07'14 6:20:29
Collett 51 1 40N54'22 91W58'39 6:07:55
Collins 85 2 41N54'10 93W18'22 6:13:13
Colo 85 2 42N01'04 93W18'54 6:13:16
Colonial Village 77 2 41N35 93W44 6:14:56
Columbia 63 2 41N10'31 93W08'59 6:12:36
Columbus City 58 1 41N15'31 91W22'27 6:05:30
Columbus Junction 58 1 41N16'48 91W21'38 6:05:27
Colwell 34 2 43N09'21 92W35'38 6:10:23
Commerce 77 2 41N32'20 93W45'52 6:15:03
Communia 22 1 42N47'24 91W21'46 6:05:27
Competine 90 2 41N07'14 92W13'38 6:08:55
Concordia 29 1 40N45 91W07 6:04:28
Conesville 70 1 41N22'55 91W20'59 6:05:24
Confidence 93 2 40N51'46 93W07'31 6:12:30
Conger 91 2 41N21'07 93W45'29 6:15:02
Cono 10 1 42N20 91W47 6:07:08
Conover 96 1 43N12'59 91W53'50 6:07:35
Conrad 38 2 42N13'29 92W52'28 6:11:30
Conroy 48 1 41N43'45 91W59'51 6:07:59
Consol 68 2 41N04'17 93W00'06 6:12:00
Conway 87 2 40N44'55 94W37'07 6:18:28
Cook 81 2 42N26 95W16 6:21:04
Cool 91 1 41N13'24 93W34'38 6:14:19
Coon 11 2 42N42 94W57 6:19:48
Coon Rapids 37 2 41N52'15 94W40'38 6:18:43
Coon Valley 81 2 42N21 94W57 6:19:48
Cooper 37 2 41N55'13 94W20'40 6:17:23
Coppock 44 1 41N09'44 91W42'40 6:06:51
Coralville 52 1 41N40'35 91W34'49 6:06:19
Corinth 46 2 42N41 94W16 6:17:04
Corley 83 2 41N34'43 95W19'48 6:21:19
Cornelia 99 2 42N47'24 93W40'59 6:14:44
Cornell 21 2 42N56'40 95W08'23 6:20:34
Corning 2 2 40N59'24 94W44'26 6:18:58
Correctionville 97 2 42N28'30 95W47'07 6:23:08
Corwin 47 2 42N20 95W30 6:22:00
Corwith 41 2 42N59'34 93W57'26 6:15:50
Corydon 93 2 40N45'25 93W19'07 6:13:16
Cosgrove 52 1 41N38'34 91W44'08 6:06:57
Coster 12 2 42N40'18 92W42'41 6:10:51
Cottage Hill 31 1 42N35'07 90W54'49 6:03:39
Cotter 58 1 41N17'31 91W27'41 6:05:51
Cottonville 49 1 42N14'13 90W36'07 6:02:24
Cou Falls 52 1 41N49'02 91W40'21 6:06:41
Coulter 35 2 42N44'14 93W22'11 6:13:29
Council Bluffs 78 2 41N15'43 95W51'39 6:23:27
Covington 57 1 42N00'26 91W45'44 6:07:03
Cox Creek 22 1 42N47 91W26 6:05:44
Crab Town 49 1 42N10'24 90W48'21 6:03:13
Craig 75 2 42N53'45 96W18'34 6:25:14
Crandalls Lodge 30 2 43N26 95W06 6:20:24
Cranston 70 1 41N22'45 91W15'40 6:05:03
Crawfordsville 92 1 41N14'39 91W33'43 6:06:15
Crescent 78 2 41N21'54 95W51'28 6:23:26
Cresco 45 2 43N22'53 92W06'50 6:08:27
Creston 88 2 41N03'31 94W21'40 6:17:27
Crestwood 77 2 41N36'22 93W42'46 6:14:51
Cricket 62 2 41N11'02 92W48'25 6:11:14
Crocker 77 2 41N46'29 93W40'11 6:14:41
Cromwell 88 2 41N02'22 94W27'42 6:17:51
Crossroads Center 7 2 42N31 92W20 6:09:20
Crossroads Center 94 2 42N30 94W11 6:16:44
Crossroads School (Abandoned) 90 4 41N00'59 92W18'16 6:09:13
Croton 56 1 40N35'25 91W41'26 6:06:46
Crystal Lake 41 2 43N13'24 93W47'32 6:15:10
Culver 70 1 41N26 91W03 6:04:12
Cumberland 15 2 41N16'27 94W52'12 6:19:29
Cumberland Square 82 7 41N33 90W30 6:02:00
Cumming 91 2 41N29'00 93W45'44 6:15:03
Cummins 76 2 42N52 94W44 6:18:56
Curlew 74 2 42N58'44 94W44'27 6:18:58
Cushing 97 2 42N27'53 95W40'29 6:22:42
Cylinder 74 2 43N05'20 94W33'10 6:18:13
Dahlonega 90 2 41N03'31 92W22'11 6:09:29
Dakota City 46 2 42N43'12 94W12'00 6:16:48
Dakota Point 97 2 42N33'17 96W28'26 6:25:54
Dalby 3 1 43N15'51 91W16'26 6:05:06
Dale 39 2 41N35'45 94W20'30 6:17:22
Dales Ford 53 1 42N12'52 91W04'00 6:04:16
Dallas 63 2 41N13'59 93W14'30 6:12:58
Dallas Center 25 2 41N41'04 93W57'39 6:15:51
Dana 37 2 42N06'27 94W14'26 6:16:58
Danbury 97 2 42N14'03 95W43'19 6:22:53
Danville 29 11 40N51'52 91W18'52 6:05:15
Darbyville 4 2 40N48'58 92W52'23 6:11:30
Davenport 82 12 41N31'25 90W34'39 6:02:19
Davis City 27 2 40N38'21 93W48'41 6:15:15
Davis Corners 45 2 43N22'15 92W17'51 6:09:11
Dawson 25 2 41N50'34 94W13'20 6:16:53
Dayton 94 2 42N15'41 94W04'06 6:16:16
Daytonville 92 1 41N28'34 91W49'44 6:07:19
Dean 4 2 40N37'39 92W42'50 6:10:51
Decatur City 27 2 40N44'31 93W50'01 6:15:20
Decorah 96 1 43N18'12 91W47'08 6:07:09
Dedham 14 2 41N54'22 94W49'19 6:19:17
Deep Creek 23 1 42N00 90W22 6:01:28
Deep River 79 2 41N34'49 92W22'29 6:09:30
Deer Creek 98 2 43N29'58 93W07'36 6:12:30
Deerfield 19 2 43N09'49 92W29'43 6:09:59
Defiance 83 2 41N49'27 95W20'33 6:21:22
Delana 46 2 42N52 94W16 6:17:04
Delaware 28 1 42N28'31 91W20'43 6:05:23
Delhi 28 1 42N25'47 91W19'51 6:05:19
Delmar 23 1 42N00'08 90W36'25 6:02:26
Deloit 24 2 42N05'52 95W19'20 6:21:17
Delphos 80 2 40N39'49 94W20'21 6:17:21
Delta 54 2 41N19'22 92W19'48 6:09:19
Denhart 41 2 42N57'58 93W52'19 6:15:29
Denison 24 2 42N01'04 95W21'18 6:21:25
Denmark 56 1 40N44'30 91W20'14 6:05:21
Denver 9 2 42N40'17 92W20'14 6:09:21
Depew 74 2 43N11'03 94W32'32 6:18:10
Derby 59 2 40N55'54 93W27'22 6:13:49
Des Moines 77 2 41N36'02 93W36'32 6:14:26
De Soto 25 2 41N31'54 94W00'34 6:16:02
Devon 19 2 43N07'11 92W21'27 6:09:26
Dewar 7 2 42N31'32 92W13'08 6:08:53
De Witt 23 13 41N49'24 90W32'17 6:02:09
Dexter 25 2 41N31'06 94W13'34 6:16:54
Diagonal 80 2 40N48'34 94W20'31 6:17:22
Diamond 18 2 42N36 95W27 6:21:48
Diamond Center 18 2 42N43 95W26 6:21:44
Diamond Lake 30 2 43N28 95W13 6:20:52
Dickens 21 2 43N07'53 95W01'24 6:20:06
Dickierville 2 2 41N00'04 94W53'45 6:19:35
Dike 38 2 42N27'51 92W37'41 6:10:31
Dillon 64 2 41N58'37 92W49'26 6:11:18
Dinsdale 86 2 42N15'33 92W32'41 6:10:11
Dixon 82 5 41N44'34 90W46'56 6:03:08
Dodge Park 78 2 41N16 95W51 6:23:24
Dodgeville 29 1 40N56'35 91W10'50 6:04:43
Dolliver 32 2 43N27'52 94W37'30 6:18:30
Donahue 82 1 41N41'41 90W40'31 6:02:42
Donnan 33 1 42N53'46 91W52'40 6:07:31
Donnelley 63 2 41N20'06 93W10'36 6:12:42
Donnellson 56 14 40N38'34 91W33'52 6:06:15
Doon 60 2 43N16'46 96W13'57 6:24:56
Dorchester 3 1 43N28'11 91W30'39 6:06:03
Doris 10 1 42N29 91W53 6:07:32
Douds 89 2 40N50'22 92W05'11 6:08:21
Dougherty 17 2 42N55'20 93W02'31 6:12:10
Dow City 24 2 41N55'44 95W29'37 6:21:58
Downey 16 1 41N36'58 91W20'54 6:05:24
Dows 99 2 42N39'24 93W30'03 6:14:00
Doyle 20 2 40N57 93W56 6:15:44
Drakesville 26 2 40N47'54 92W28'53 6:09:56
Dresden 19 2 42N57 92W16 6:09:04
Dresden 79 2 41N34'40 92W21'20 6:09:25
Dubuque 31 15 42N30'02 90W39'52 6:02:39
Dudley 90 2 41N05'16 92W35'30 6:10:22
Dumfries 78 2 41N11'13 95W44'16 6:22:57
Dumont 12 2 42N45'07 92W58'31 6:11:54
Dunbar 64 2 41N56'27 92W47'47 6:11:11
Duncan 41 2 43N06'17 93W42'40 6:14:51
Duncombe 94 2 42N28'14 93W59'36 6:15:58
Dundee 28 1 42N34'45 91W32'47 6:06:11
Dunkerton 7 2 42N34'12 92W09'37 6:08:38
Dunlap 43 2 41N51'16 95W36'01 6:22:24
Durango 31 1 42N33'37 90W46'32 6:03:06
Durant 16 13 41N35'59 90W54'38 6:03:39
Durham 63 2 41N19'13 92W57'20 6:11:49
Dutch Creek 92 1 41N17 91W53 6:07:32
Dutchtown 28 1 42N33'08 91W24'39 6:05:39
Dyersville 31 1 42N29'04 91W07'22 6:04:29
Dysart 86 2 42N10'18 92W18'22 6:09:13
Eagle Center 7 2 42N20'27 92W21'26 6:09:26
Eagle City 42 2 42N28'18 93W08'42 6:12:35
Eagle Grove 99 2 42N39'51 93W54'15 6:15:37
Eagle Point 31 15 42N32'05 90W38'40 6:02:35
Earlham 61 2 41N29'31 94W07'26 6:16:30
Earling 83 2 41N46'32 95W25'02 6:21:40
Earlville 28 1 42N28'54 91W16'20 6:05:05
Early 81 2 42N27'41 95W09'06 6:20:36
East 69 2 40N56 95W00 6:20:00
East Amana 48 1 41N48'33 91W51'03 6:07:24
East Boyer 24 2 41N59 95W16 6:21:04
East Des Moines 77 2 41N35 93W37 6:14:28
East Lancaster 54 2 41N16 92W07 6:08:28
East Lincoln 66 2 43N14 92W38 6:10:32
East Lucas 52 1 41N38 91W32 6:06:08
East Orange 84 2 42N57 95W57 6:23:48
East Peru (Peru P O) 61 2 41N13'37 93W55'34 6:15:42

East Pleasant Plain 51
1 41n08'50 91w51'32 6:07:26
East Rickardsville 31
1 42n34'25 90w51'28 6:03:26
East River 73 2 40n41 94w59 6:19:56
East Waterloo 7 2 42n32 92w17 6:09:08
Eby's Mill 53 1 42n11'59 91w03'32 6:04:14
Eddyville 62 2 41n09'38 92w37'52 6:10:31
Edgewood 22 1 42n38'40 91w24'04 6:05:36
Edgewood Park 82
7 41n33 90w30 6:02:00
Edinburg 53 1 42n08'00 91w08'02 6:04:32
Edison 78 2 41n16 95w51 6:23:24
Edmore 31 1 42n33'22 90w40'43 6:02:43
Edna 60 2 43n23'06 96w05'39 6:24:23
Egan 3 1 43n09'24 91w17'22 6:05:09
Egralharve 30 2 43n24'08 95w10'22 6:20:41
Elberon 86 2 42n00'22 92w19'00 6:09:16
Eldergrove 3 1 43n14'23 91w13'11 6:04:53
Eldon 90 2 40n55'07 92w13'22 6:08:53
Eldora 42 2 42n21'39 93w05'58 6:12:24
Eldorado 33 1 43n03'02 91w50'07 6:07:20
Eldridge 82 5 41n39'29 90w35'04 6:02:20
Eleanor 12 2 42n36'51 92w50'57 6:11:24
Elgin 33 1 42n57'27 91w37'50 6:06:31
Eliot 58 1 41n06 91w00 6:04:00
Elkader 22 1 42n51'14 91w24'19 6:05:37
Elk Creek 50 2 41n33 92w56 6:11:44
Elkhart 77 2 41n27'25 93w31'19 6:14:05
Elk Horn 83 2 41n35'30 95w03'35 6:20:14
Elkport 22 1 42n44'23 91w16'40 6:05:07
Elk River 23 1 42n01 90w14 6:00:56
Elk River Junction 23
10 41n58'47 90w10'26 6:00:42
Elk Run Heights 7
2 42n28'01 92w15'23 6:09:02
Ell 41 2 43n02 93w34 6:14:16
Elliot 69 2 41n08'57 95w09'49 6:20:39
Ellis 42 2 42n26 93w18 6:13:12
Ellston 80 2 40n50'25 94w06'30 6:16:26
Ellsworth 40 2 42n18'46 93w34'43 6:14:19
Elma 45 2 43n14'48 92w26'09 6:09:45
Elmira 52 1 41n43'22 91w25'29 6:05:42
Elon 3 1 43n15'51 91w19'26 6:05:18
Elrick 58 23 41n11 91w11 6:04:44
Elrick Junction 58
1 41n05'55 91w07'03 6:04:28
Elvira 23 10 41n51'32 90w21'19 6:01:25
Elwood 23 1 41n59'30 90w44'20 6:02:57
Ely 57 1 41n52'25 91w35'06 6:06:20
Emeline 49 1 42n09'19 90w49'50 6:03:19
Emerson 65 2 41n01'02 95w24'07 6:21:36
Emery 17 2 43n08'01 93w16'48 6:13:07
Emmet 32 2 43n28 94w49 6:19:16
Emmetsburg 74 2 43n06'46 94w40'58 6:18:44
Emmons 98 2 43n29'58 93w29'17 6:13:57
Enterprise 77 2 41n43'55 93w31'48 6:14:07
Epworth 31 1 42n26'42 90w55'55 6:03:44
Ericson 8 2 42n01'43 93w47'46 6:15:11
Erin 41 2 43n02 93w48 6:15:12
Essex 73 2 40n50'01 95w18'29 6:21:14
Estherville 32 2 43n24'06 94w49'57 6:19:20
Etna 42 2 42n31 93w04 6:12:16
Euclid 43 2 41n32'38 95w51'38 6:23:27
Evans 62 2 41n18'10 92w43'37 6:10:54
Evansdale 7 2 42n28'09 92w16'51 6:09:07
Evans Junction 62
2 41n16 92w41 6:10:44
Evanston 94 2 42n26'03 94w03'27 6:16:14
Eveland 62 2 41n10'11 92w48'02 6:11:12
Evergreen 82 12 41n32 90w36 6:02:24
Everly 21 2 43n09'36 95w19'38 6:21:19
Ewart 79 2 41n38'28 92w36'37 6:10:26
Ewoldt 14 2 41n54 95w02 6:20:08
Excelsior 30 2 43n23 95w20 6:21:20
Exira 5 2 41n35'27 94w52'31 6:19:30
Exline 4 2 40n38'57 92w50'25 6:11:22
Fabius 26 2 40n39 92w35 6:10:20
Fairbank 10 2 42n38'21 92w02'49 6:08:11
Fairfax 57 1 41n55'10 91w46'51 6:07:07
Fairfield 51 3 41n00'31 91w57'45 6:07:51
Fair Ground 31 15 42n30 90w42 6:02:48
Fairmount Park 78
2 41n16 95w51 6:23:24
Fairport 70 1 41n26'09 90w54'16 6:03:37
Fairview 22 1 42n41'02 91w12'59 6:04:52
Fairview 53 1 42n04'41 91w19'47 6:05:19
Fairville 74 2 43n09'22 94w27'47 6:17:51
Falls 17 2 43n13 93w05 6:12:20
Famersburg 22 1 42n57'40 91w22'04 6:05:28
Fanslers 39 2 41n44'58 94w27'20 6:17:49
Farley 31 1 42n26'34 91w00'22 6:04:01
Farlin 37 2 42n04'35 94w26'54 6:17:48
Farmersburg 22 1 42n58 91w18 6:05:12
Farmers Creek 49
1 42n10 90w43 6:02:52
Farmington 89 1 40n38'25 91w44'34 6:06:58
Farnhamville 13 2 42n16'34 94w24'13 6:17:37
Farragut 36 2 40n43'19 95w28'50 6:21:55
Farrar 77 2 41n48'21 93w22'11 6:13:29
Farson 90 2 41n07'20 92w15'18 6:09:01
Faulkner 35 2 42n36'55 93w05'09 6:12:21
Fayette 33 1 42n50'31 91w48'07 6:07:12
Felix 38 2 42n15 92w57 6:11:48
Fenton 55 2 43n13'11 94w25'49 6:17:43
Ferguson 64 2 41n56'13 92w51'56 6:11:28
Fern 38 2 42n29'05 92w46'13 6:11:05
Fernald 85 2 42n04'15 93w23'41 6:13:35
Fern Valley 74 2 43n01 94w31 6:18:04
Fertile 98 2 43n15'52 93w25'05 6:13:40
Festina 96 1 43n07'10 91w52'01 6:07:28
Fielding 18 2 42n39'47 95w48'00 6:23:12
Fillmore 31 1 42n19'09 90w55'00 6:03:40
Fillmore 48 1 41n34 92w00 6:08:00
Finchford 7 2 42n37'38 92w32'37 6:10:10
Findley 43 2 41n31'43 95w52'44 6:23:31
Fiscus 83 2 41n44'20 95w05'34 6:20:22
Fisher 36 2 40n42 95w26 6:21:44
Fisk 1 2 41n12'04 94w31'40 6:18:07
Five Points 31 1 42n33'05 90w51'30 6:03:26
Flagler 63 2 41n19'29 93w01'18 6:12:05
Flint River 29 8 40n52 91w12 6:04:48
Florence 6 1 41n54 91w53 6:07:32
Florence 99 2 42n42'09 93w49'06 6:15:16
Florenceville 45
2 43n29'57 92w07'57 6:08:32
Floris 26 2 40n51'54 92w19'58 6:09:20
Floyd 34 2 43n07'40 92w44'10 6:10:57
Floyd Crossing 34
2 43n05'28 92w44'31 6:10:58
Floyd School 31 1 42n35'16 90w57'37 6:03:50
Flugstad 49 2 42n26'55 93w55'54 6:15:44
Folletts 82 1 41n44'55 90w21'17 6:01:25
Folsom 65 2 41n05'24 95w49'02 6:23:16
Fonda 76 2 42n34'53 94w50'45 6:19:23
Fontanelle 1 2 41n17'23 94w33'41 6:18:15
Forbush 4 2 40n46'08 92w52'37 6:11:30
Forest City 95 2 43n15'45 93w38'13 6:14:33
Forestville 28 1 42n35'48 91w31'42 6:06:07
Fort Atkinson 96
1 43n08'36 91w55'57 6:07:44
Fort Des Moines 77
2 41n31'13 93w36'56 6:14:28
Fort Dodge 94 2 42n29'51 94w10'04 6:16:40
Fort Madison 56
16 40n37'47 91w18'54 6:05:16
Foster 68 2 40n55'58 92w45'26 6:11:02
Fostoria 21 2 43n14'32 95w09'19 6:20:37
Four Corners 51 1 41n00 91w44 6:06:56
Four Mile 77 2 41n34 93w28 6:13:52
Fox 7 2 42n25 92w07 6:08:28
Fox River 26 2 40n47 92w35 6:10:20
Frankfort 69 2 41n02 95w06 6:20:24
Franklin 56 1 40n40'05 91w30'40 6:06:03
Franklin 78 2 41n16 95w51 6:23:24
Frankville 96 1 43n11'21 91w37'02 6:06:28
Fraser 8 2 42n07'38 93w57'53 6:15:52
Frederic 68 2 41n05'27 92w40'41 6:10:43
Fredericksburg 19
2 42n57'55 92w11'58 6:08:48
Frederika 9 2 42n52'54 92w18'29 6:09:14
Fredonia 58 1 41n17'05 91w20'19 6:05:21
Fredsville 38 2 42n29'03 92w34'26 6:10:18
Freeman 17 2 43n12'47 93w11'59 6:12:48
Freeman 21 2 43n08 94w58 6:19:52
Freeport 96 1 43n18'08 91w44'36 6:06:58
Fremont 62 2 41n12'45 92w26'07 6:09:44
French Creek 3 1 43n24 91w26 6:05:44
Frith Spur 31 1 42n32'59 90w42'06 6:02:48
Froelich 22 1 43n00'24 91w19'18 6:05:17
Fruitland 70 1 41n21'22 91w07'45 6:04:31
Fulton 49 1 42n09'13 90w40'41 6:02:43
Galbraith 55 2 42n58'50 94w09'32 6:16:38
Galesburg 50 2 41n33'32 92w56'46 6:11:47
Galland 56 20 40n30'02 91w22'28 6:05:30
Galt 99 2 42n41'37 93w36'19 6:14:25
Galva 47 2 42n30'25 95w25'01 6:21:40
Gambrill 82 1 41n45'07 90w32'08 6:02:09
Garber 22 1 42n44'31 91w15'43 6:05:03
Garden 8 2 41n54 93w45 6:15:00
Garden City 42 2 42n14'44 93w23'43 6:13:35
Garden Grove 93 2 40n49'38 93w36'25 6:14:26
Gardiner 25 2 41n49'28 94w01'40 6:16:07
Gardner 5 2 41n40'28 94w45'49 6:19:03
Garfield 4 2 40n46'07 93w00'06 6:12:00
Garland 29 1 41n03'33 91w13'03 6:04:52
Garnavillo 22 1 42n52'07 91w14'09 6:04:57
Garner 41 2 43n06'09 93w36'06 6:14:24
Garretville 25 2 41n31'03 94w04'47 6:16:19
Garrison 6 2 42n08'39 92w08'37 6:08:34
Garry Owen 49 1 42n17'00 90w49'54 6:03:20
Garwin 86 2 42n05'37 92w40'32 6:10:42
Gay 87 2 40n41 94w32 6:18:08
Gaza 71 2 43n01'13 95w34'47 6:22:19
Geneva 35 2 42n40'32 93w07'45 6:12:31
Genoa Bluff 48 2 41n47 92w04 6:08:16
George 60 2 43n20'38 96w00'07 6:24:00
Georgetown 68 2 41n00'46 92w57'18 6:11:49
Gerled 55 2 43n23'00 94w11'15 6:16:45
Germantown 71 2 42n57'12 95w46'50 6:23:07
German Valley 55
2 43n16'12 94w01'45 6:16:07
Germanville 51 1 41n06'15 91w46'09 6:07:05
Giard 22 1 43n00'20 91w17'21 6:05:09
Gibbsville 25 2 41n48'03 93w49'25 6:15:18
Gibson 54 2 41n28'52 92w23'36 6:09:34
Gifford 42 2 42n17'18 93w05'25 6:12:22
Gilbert 85 2 42n06'25 93w38'58 6:14:36
Gilbertville 7 2 42n24'58 92w12'53 6:08:52
Gillett Grove 21
2 43n00'57 95w02'14 6:20:09
Gilliatt 78 2 41n17'28 95w45'30 6:23:02
Gilman 64 2 41n52'44 92w47'21 6:11:09
Gilmore City 46 2 42n43'46 94w26'51 6:17:47
Gilt Edge 28 1 42n26'27 91w12'17 6:04:49
Givin 62 2 41n13'30 92w39'45 6:10:39
Gladbrook 86 2 42n11'16 92w42'54 6:10:52
Gladstone 86 2 41n57'50 92w29'50 6:09:59
Gladwin 58 1 41n21'35 91w27'03 6:05:48
Glasgow 51 1 40n56'27 91w46'49 6:07:07
Glendale Acres 78
2 41n16 95w51 6:23:24
Glendon 39 2 41n35'40 94w24'07 6:17:36
Glenwood 65 2 41n02'49 95w44'32 6:22:58
Glidden 14 2 42n03'25 94w43'43 6:18:55
Goddard 50 2 41n43'03 93w11'34 6:12:46
Godfield 99 2 42n44'14 93w55'12 6:15:41
Goewey 72 2 43n18 95w41 6:22:44
Goldfield 99 2 42n44 93w55 6:15:40
Gonoa Bluff 48 2 41n41'36 92w09'09 6:08:37
Goodell 41 2 42n55'23 93w36'58 6:14:28
Goodrich 24 2 42n05 95w22 6:21:28
Goose Lake 23 1 41n58'03 90w22'58 6:01:32
Goshen 70 1 41n33 91w11 6:04:44
Gosport 63 2 41n12'17 93w09'02 6:12:36
Gower 16 1 41n43 91w17 6:05:08
Gowrie 94 2 42n16'50 94w17'26 6:17:10
Grace Hill 92 1 41n15'49 91w49'47 6:07:19
Graettinger 74 2 43n14'16 94w45'04 6:19:00
Graf 31 1 42n29'35 90w52'16 6:03:29
Grafton 98 2 43n19'48 93w04'09 6:12:17
Graham 52 1 41n44 91w25 6:05:40
Grand 77 2 41n35 93w37 6:14:28
Grand Junction 37
2 42n01'54 94w14'26 6:16:58
Grand Mound 23 1 41n49'27 90w38'52 6:02:35
Grand River 27 2 40n49'10 93w57'44 6:15:51
Grandview 58 1 41n16'33 91w11'18 6:04:45
Grange 97 2 42n21 96w11 6:24:44
Granger 25 2 41n45'40 93w49'27 6:15:18
Granger Homesteads 25
2 41n45'52 93w50'20 6:15:21
Granite 60 2 43n28'08 96w33'22 6:26:13
Grant 69 2 41n08'34 94w59'04 6:19:56
Grant Center 67 2 42n10 96w00 6:24:00
Grant City 81 2 42n16'03 94w53'15 6:19:33
Grant Wood 82 7 41n33 90w30 6:02:00
Granville 84 2 42n59'08 95w52'24 6:23:30
Gravity 87 2 40n45'38 94w44'36 6:18:58
Gray 5 2 41n50'22 94w58'58 6:19:56
Great Oak 74 2 43n01 94w44 6:18:56
Greeley 28 1 42n35'09 91w20'29 6:05:22
Green Acres 82 12 41n34'12 90w36'36 6:02:26
Greenbrier 37 2 41n53 94w27 6:17:48
Greenbush 91 2 41n25'28 93w39'23 6:14:38
Green Castle 50 2 41n44'46 93w15'41 6:13:03
Greene 12 2 42n53'45 92w48'08 6:11:13
Greenfield 1 2 41n18'19 94w27'40 6:17:51
Greenfield Plaza 91
2 41n33 93w37 6:14:28
Green Island 49 1 42n09'13 90w19'19 6:01:17
Green Mountain 64
2 42n06'06 92w49'13 6:11:17
Greenville 21 2 43n01'00 95w08'45 6:20:35
Greenwood 55 2 43n18 94w16 6:17:04
Griggs 47 2 42n31 95w33 6:22:12
Grimes 77 2 41n41'18 93w47'27 6:15:10
Grinnell 79 2 41n44'35 92w43'20 6:10:53
Griswold 15 2 41n14'06 95w08'14 6:20:33
Grundy Center 38
2 42n21'42 92w46'06 6:11:04
Gruver 32 2 43n23'36 94w42'18 6:18:49
Guernsey 79 2 41n38'55 92w20'33 6:09:22
Guilford 68 2 41n01 92w56 6:11:44
Gunder 22 1 42n58'18 91w30'47 6:06:03
Gunwald 59 2 41n05'16 93w15'16 6:13:01
Guss 87 2 40n50'31 94w51'28 6:19:26
Guthrie Center 39
2 41n40'38 94w30'11 6:18:01
Guttenberg 22 1 42n47'09 91w05'58 6:04:24
Halbur 14 2 42n00'25 94w58'11 6:19:53
Hale 53 1 42n00'45 91w03'33 6:04:14
Halfa 32 2 43n21'07 94w32'30 6:18:10
Hamburg 36 2 40n36'16 95w39'27 6:22:38
Hamill 56 9 40n38 91w34 6:06:16
Hamilton 63 2 41n10'09 92w54'11 6:11:37
Hamlin 5 2 41n40'01 94w54'20 6:19:37
Hampshire 23 1 41n56 90w15 6:01:00
Hampton 35 2 42n44'31 93w12'08 6:12:49
Hancock 78 2 41n23'24 95w21'44 6:21:27
Hanford 17 2 43n04'27 93w08'29 6:12:34
Hanley 61 2 41n17'17 93w50'02 6:15:20
Hanlontown 98 2 43n16'49 93w22'43 6:13:31
Hanna 55 2 42n56'57 94w01'14 6:16:05
Hanover 3 1 43n21'39 91w31'14 6:06:05
Hanover 11 2 42n40 95w19 6:21:16
Hansell 35 2 42n45'28 93w06'14 6:12:25
Harcourt 94 2 42n15'46 94w10'32 6:16:42
Hardin 22 1 43n04'49 91w29'03 6:05:56
Hard Scratch 43 2 41n36'48 95w42'50 6:22:51
Hardy 46 2 42n48'38 94w03'04 6:16:12
Harlan 83 2 41n39'11 95w19'31 6:21:18
Harper 54 2 41n21'45 92w03'03 6:08:12
Harpers Ferry 3 1 43n12'02 91w09'11 6:04:37
Harris 72 2 43n26'43 95w26'02 6:21:44
Harrisburg 89 1 40n46'14 91w46'37 6:07:06
Hartford 91 2 41n27'34 93w24'17 6:13:37
Hartland 98 2 43n28 93w19 6:13:16
Hartley 71 2 43n10'48 95w28'36 6:21:54
Hartwick 79 2 41n47'05 92w20'36 6:09:22
Harvard 93 2 40n41'24 93w16'09 6:13:05
Harvey 63 2 41n18'57 92w55'26 6:11:42
Haskins 92 1 41n19'41 91w32'12 6:06:09
Hastie 77 2 41n33'46 93w29'22 6:13:57
Hastings 65 2 41n01'22 95w29'56 6:22:00
Hauntown 23 10 42n00'03 90w11'56 6:00:48
Havelock 76 2 42n50'10 94w42'01 6:18:48
Haven 86 2 41n53'30 92w28'44 6:09:55
Haverhill 64 2 41n56'42 92w57'38 6:11:51
Hawarden 84 2 42n59'45 96w29'06 6:25:56
Hawkeye 33 1 42n56'19 91w57'00 6:07:48
Hawleyville 73 2 40n46'36 94w56'10 6:19:45
Hawthorne 69 2 41n00'06 95w20'12 6:21:21
Hayesville 54 2 41n15'52 92w14'56 6:09:00
Hayfield 41 2 43n10'36 93w41'42 6:14:47
Hayfield Junction 41
2 43n08'02 93w35'57 6:14:24
Hazel Dell 78 2 41n24 95w46 6:23:04
Hazel Green 28 1 42n20 91w25 6:05:40
Hazleton 10 1 42n37'15 91w54'00 6:07:36
Hebron 1 2 41n15'17 94w17'06 6:17:08
Hebron 55 2 43n28 94w03 6:16:12
Hedrick 54 2 41n10'21 92w18'31 6:09:14
Helena 86 2 41n55'15 92w28'27 6:09:54
Henderson 69 2 41n08'26 95w25'51 6:21:43
Hepburn 73 2 40n50'57 95w01'01 6:20:04
Herdland 21 2 42n57 95w05 6:20:20
Herndon 39 2 41n50'44 94w20'57 6:17:24
Herrold 77 2 41n40 93w47 6:15:08
Hesper 96 1 43n29'11 91w46'06 6:07:04
Hiattsville 4 2 40n49'38 92w48'37 6:11:14
Hiawatha 57 1 42n02'09 91w40'55 6:06:44
Hicks 7 2 42n21'58 92w32'02 6:10:08
High 48 1 41n48 91w52 6:07:28
High Amana 48 1 41n48'12 91w56'17 6:07:45
High Lake 32 2 43n18 94w43 6:18:52
Highland 22 1 42n53'38 91w35'49 6:06:23
Highland Center 90
2 41n07'35 92w21'11 6:09:25
Highland Park 77
2 41n36 93w39 6:14:36
Highlandville 96
1 43n26'32 91w40'06 6:06:40
High Point 27 2 40n45'40 93w35'39 6:14:23
Highview 40 2 42n28'19 93w54'14 6:15:37
Hills 52 1 41n33'15 91w32'05 6:06:08
Hillsboro 44 1 40n50'12 91w42'56 6:06:52
Hillsdale 65 2 41n00'27 95w40'14 6:22:41
Hilltop 7 2 42n28'34 92w16'13 6:09:05

Hilton 48	1	41N44	92w00	6:08:00
Hinton 75	2	42N37'40	96w17'29	6:25:10
Hiteman 68	2	41N03'32	92w53'31	6:11:34
Hobarton 55	2	43N04	94w14	6:16:56
Hocking 68	2	40N59'27	92w49'13	6:11:17
Holbrook 48	1	41N35'27	92w02'18	6:08:09
Holiday Lake 79	2	41N44	92w27	6:09:48
Holland 38	2	42N23'56	92w48'01	6:11:12
Holly Springs 97	2	42N16'14	96w04'39	6:24:19
Holman 72	2	43N24	95w44	6:22:56
Holmes 99	2	42N44'21	93w50'01	6:15:20
Holstein 47	2	42N29'21	95w32'41	6:22:11
Holt 87	2	40N51	94w45	6:19:00
Holy Cross 31	1	42N36'02	90w59'44	6:03:59
Homer 40	2	42N22'26	93w55'24	6:15:42
Homestead 48	1	41N45'34	91w52'01	6:07:28
Honey Creek 78	2	41N25'50	95w51'58	6:23:28
Hopeville 20	2	40N56'34	93w59'47	6:15:59
Hopkinton 28	1	42N20'38	91w14'54	6:05:00
Hornick 97	2	42N13'50	96w05'50	6:24:23
Horton 9	2	42N50'51	92w28'31	6:09:54
Horton 72	2	43N28	95w34	6:22:16
Hospers 84	2	43N04'19	95w54'15	6:23:37
Houghton 56	9	40N47'01	91w36'10	6:06:25
Howard Center 45	2	43N23	92w15	6:09:00
Howardville 34	2	43N11'27	92w42'44	6:10:51
Howe 1	2	41N24'11	94w22'33	6:17:30
Hubbard 42	2	42N18'20	93w18'00	6:13:12
Hudson 7	2	42N24'24	92w27'19	6:09:49
Hull 84	2	43N11'19	96w08'00	6:24:32
Humboldt 46	2	42N43'15	94w12'54	6:16:52
Humeston 93	2	40N51'32	93w29'50	6:13:59
Hungerford 75	2	42N36	96w16	6:25:04
Huntington 32	2	43N29'30	94w47'30	6:19:10
Hurley 17	2	43N00'33	93w13'52	6:12:55
Huron 29	1	41N02'12	91w02'02	6:04:08
Hurstville 49	1	42N05'51	90w40'59	6:02:44
Hutchins 41	2	43N06	93w48	6:15:12
Huxley 85	2	41N54	93w36	6:14:24
Iconium 4	2	40N53'29	92w57'18	6:11:49
Ida Grove 47	2	42N20'42	95w28'17	6:21:53
Illyria 33	1	42N53'55	91w38'06	6:06:32
Imogene 36	2	40N52'46	95w25'36	6:21:42
Independence 10	1	42N28'07	91w53'21	6:07:33
Indiana 63	2	41N13	93w02	6:12:08
Indianapolis 62	2	41N23'49	92w26'00	6:09:44
Indian Creek 57	1	42N01	91w36	6:06:24
Indian Creek 78	2	41N16	95w51	6:23:24
Indianola 91	2	41N21'29	93w33'26	6:14:14
Indianola Junction 59	2	41N02'25	93w21'23	6:13:26
Indian Village 86	2	41N59	92w42	6:10:48
Industry 94	2	42N35	94w51	6:19:24
Ingham 35	2	42N47	93w04	6:12:16
Ingraham 65	2	41N07	95w35	6:22:20
Inland 16	1	41N43	90w58	6:03:52
Inwood 60	2	43N18'26	96w25'54	6:25:44
Ion 3	1	43N06'46	91w15'43	6:05:03
Ionia 19	2	43N02	92w27	6:09:48
Iowa Army Ammunition Plant 29	1	40N49	91w06	6:04:24
Iowa Center 85	2	41N55'43	93w24'18	6:13:37
Iowa City 52	1	41N39'40	91w31'48	6:06:07
Iowa Falls 42	2	42N31'21	93w15'04	6:13:00
Iowa Lake 32	2	43N28	94w30	6:18:00
Iowa State University Sta 85	2	42N03	93w35	6:14:20
Ira 50	2	41N46'40	93w12'20	6:12:49
Ireton 84	2	42N58'29	96w19'05	6:25:16
Ironhills 49	1	42N08'30	90w46'11	6:03:05
Irving 6	2	41N56'54	92w17'42	6:09:11
Irvington 55	2	43N00'27	94w11'43	6:16:47
Irwin 83	2	41N47'30	95w12'20	6:20:49
Ivester 38	2	42N20'23	92w56'38	6:11:47
Iveyville 2	2	40N54'03	94w47'44	6:19:11
Ivy 77	2	41N36'02	93w25'01	6:13:40
Jack Creek 32	2	43N18	94w37	6:18:28
Jackson Junction 96	2	43N06'54	92w01'56	6:08:08
Jacksonville 19	2	43N07'10	92w12'32	6:08:50
Jacksonville 83	2	41N38'43	95w08'59	6:20:36
Jamaica 39	2	41N50'46	94w18'34	6:17:14
James 75	2	42N34'37	96w19'02	6:25:16
James 78	2	41N23	95w26	6:21:44
Jamestown 45	2	43N23	92w30	6:10:00
Jamestown 82	1	41N29'40	90w42'29	6:02:50
Jamison 20	2	41N07'18	93w43'29	6:14:54
Janesville 9	2	42N38'46	92w27'46	6:09:51
Jay 20	2	41N06'24	93w35'11	6:14:21
Jefferson 37	2	42N00'55	94w22'38	6:17:31
Jenkins 66	2	43N23	92w37	6:10:28
Jerico 19	2	43N11'03	92w33'19	6:10:13
Jerome 4	2	40N43'08	93w01'41	6:12:07
Jesup 10	2	42N28'32	92w03'49	6:08:15
Jewell 40	2	42N18'25	93w38'24	6:14:34
Joetown 52	1	41N29	91w42	6:06:48
Johns 4	2	40N47	93w02	6:12:08
Johnston 77	2	41N40'23	93w41'51	6:14:47
Joice 98	2	43N21'46	93w27'13	6:13:49
Jolley 13	2	42N28'44	94w43'07	6:18:52
Jones 88	2	41N02	94w04	6:16:16
Jordan 8	2	42N02'57	93w47'02	6:15:08
Jordans Grove 57	1	42N09'21	91w29'54	6:06:00
Jubilee 7	2	42N23'03	92w06'13	6:08:25
Judd 94	2	42N28'20	94w02'58	6:16:12
Julien 31	15	42N28'52	90w46'46	6:03:07
Junction 37	2	42N04	94w14	6:16:56
Juniata 11	2	42N34'49	95w08'52	6:20:35
Kalo 94	2	42N25'52	94w07'54	6:16:32
Kalona 92	1	41N28'59	91w42'21	6:06:49
Kamrar 40	2	42N23'32	93w43'45	6:14:55
Kanawha 41	2	42N56'16	93w47'35	6:15:10
Kedron 97	2	42N26	95w50	6:23:20
Keg Creek 78	2	41N12	95w41	6:22:44
Kellerton 80	2	40N42'39	94w02'59	6:16:12
Kelley 85	2	41N57'02	93w39'54	6:14:40
Kellogg 50	2	41N43'05	92w54'26	6:11:38
Kendallville 96	2	43N26'22	92w02'10	6:08:09
Kendrick 37	2	42N05	94w34	6:18:16
Kenfield 5	2	41N34'35	94w43'10	6:18:53
Kennebec 67	2	42N05'51	96w00'45	6:24:03
Kennedy 25	2	41N36'24	94w07'29	6:16:30
Kensett 98	2	43N21'13	93w12'37	6:12:50
Kent 2	2	40N57'09	94w27'15	6:17:49
Kenwood 24	2	42N00'31	95w30'35	6:22:02
Keokuk 56	17	40N23'50	91w23'05	6:05:32
Keomah 62	2	41N17	92w38	6:10:32
Keosauqua 89	1	40N43'49	91w57'44	6:07:51
Keota 54	1	41N21'50	91w57'13	6:07:49
Kesley 12	2	42N39'45	92w54'36	6:11:38
Keswick 54	2	41N27'09	92w14'21	6:08:57
Keystone 6	2	41N59'54	92w11'50	6:08:47
Key West 31	15	42N26'56	90w41'02	6:02:44
Kilbourn 89	1	40N48'22	91w58'11	6:07:53
Killduff 50	2	41N36'29	92w54'16	6:11:37
Kimballton 5	2	41N37'43	95w04'22	6:20:17
King 31	1	42N24'19	90w35'30	6:02:22
Kingsley 75	2	42N35'18	95w58'02	6:23:52
Kingston 29	1	40N58'39	91w02'25	6:04:10
Kinross 54	1	41N27'39	91w59'12	6:07:57
Kirkman 83	2	41N43'43	95w15'54	6:21:04
Kirkville 90	2	41N08'44	92w30'14	6:10:01
Kiron 24	2	42N11'44	95w19'39	6:21:19
Klemme 41	2	43N00'25	93w36'10	6:14:25
Klinger 9	2	42N39'24	92w13'09	6:08:53
Klondike 60	2	43N23'16	96w31'14	6:26:05
Knierim 13	2	42N27'20	94w27'24	6:17:50
Kniest 14	2	42N10	94w56	6:19:44
Knittel 9	2	42N42	92w14	6:08:56
Knoke 13	2	42N31'01	94w45'46	6:19:03
Knowlton 80	2	40N49'35	94w19'55	6:17:20
Knoxville 63	2	41N19'15	93w06'33	6:12:26
Konigsmark 57	1	41N53'24	91w41'32	6:06:46
Kossuth 29	1	41N00'38	91w08'04	6:04:32
Koszta 48	2	41N49'38	92w12'19	6:08:49
Lacelle 20	2	41N02	93w46	6:15:04
Lacey 62	2	41N24'03	92w38'24	6:10:34
Lacona 91	2	41N11'23	93w22'58	6:13:32
Ladoga 87	2	40N44'30	94w47'42	6:19:11
Ladora 48	2	41N45'17	92w11'00	6:08:44
Lafayette 57	1	42N08'49	91w40'48	6:06:43
La Grange 43	2	41N33	95w46	6:23:04
Lainsville 49	19	42N07'47	90w12'16	6:00:49
Lake Canyada 82	12	41N32	90w36	6:02:24
Lake City 13	2	42N16'03	94w44'01	6:18:56
Lake Creek 13	2	42N21	94w42	6:18:48
Lake Mills 95	2	43N25'10	93w31'59	6:14:08
Lake Park 30	2	43N27'20	95w19'14	6:21:17
Lakeport 97	2	42N16	96w17	6:25:08
Lake Prairie 63	2	41N26	92w55	6:11:40
Lakeside 11	2	42N37'17	95w10'23	6:20:42
Lakeview 81	2	42N18'25	95w03'05	6:20:12
Lakeville 30	2	43N24	95w13	6:20:52
Lakewood 91	2	41N30'06	93w40'26	6:14:42
Lakewood Corner 60	2	43N20'46	96w10'33	6:24:42
Lakonta (Truax) 62	2	41N11'36	92w43'49	6:10:55
LaMoille 64	2	42N01'50	93w02'18	6:12:09
La Motte 49	1	42N17'45	90w37'15	6:02:29
La Porte City 7	2	42N18'54	92w11'31	6:08:46
Larrabee 18	2	42N51'39	95w32'42	6:22:11
Last Chance 59	2	40N57'23	93w33'12	6:14:13
Latimer 35	2	42N45'48	93w22'05	6:13:28
Lattnerville 31	1	42N29'08	90w52'58	6:03:32
Latty 29	1	40N54'12	91w07'18	6:04:29
Laurel 64	2	41N53'03	92w55'19	6:11:41
Laurens 76	2	42N50'48	94w51'06	6:19:24
Lavinia 13	2	42N24'28	94w44'47	6:18:59
Lawler 19	2	43N04'14	92w09'00	6:08:36
Lawn Hill 42	2	42N17'52	93w10'18	6:12:41
Lawton 97	2	42N28'43	96w11'01	6:24:44
Layton 78	2	41N28	95w11	6:20:44
Leando 89	2	40N50'01	92w05'19	6:08:21
Lebanon 84	2	43N05'55	96w21'23	6:25:26
Lebanon 89	1	40N43'33	92w04'56	6:08:20
Le Claire 82	18	41N35'52	90w20'47	6:01:23
Ledyard 55	2	43N25'18	94w09'43	6:16:39
Leeds 97	2	42N32'28	96w21'35	6:25:26
Le Grand 64	2	42N00'25	92w46'31	6:11:06
Lehigh 94	2	42N21'36	94w03'07	6:16:12
Leighton 62	2	41N20'14	92w47'13	6:11:09
Leland 95	2	43N20'14	93w38'06	6:14:32
Le Mars 75	2	42N47'39	96w09'55	6:24:40
Lena 94	2	42N13'14	94w17'15	6:17:09
Lenox 87	2	40N52'54	94w33'42	6:18:15
Leon 27	2	40N44'23	93w44'51	6:14:59
LeRoy 27	2	40N52'40	93w35'33	6:14:22
Leslie 20	2	40N56'34	93w47'52	6:15:11
Lester 60	2	43N26'41	96w19'58	6:25:20
Letts 58	1	41N19'42	91w14'13	6:04:57
Leverett 11	2	42N54'24	94w58'24	6:19:54
Levey 77	2	41N32'47	93w31'18	6:14:05
Levey 81	2	42N15	95w10	6:20:40
Lewis 15	2	41N18'21	95w04'59	6:20:20
Lexington 92	1	41N23'52	91w48'25	6:07:14
Liberal 60	2	43N24	96w02	6:24:08
Liberty 20	2	41N08'43	93w39'14	6:14:37
Liberty Center 91	2	41N12'17	93w29'55	6:14:00
Libertyville 51	2	40N57'27	92w03'04	6:08:12
Lidderdale 14	2	42N07'28	94w47'00	6:19:08
Lidtke Mill 45	2	43N27'52	92w16'41	6:09:07
Lima 33	1	42N52'06	91w44'34	6:06:58
Lime City 16	1	41N38'52	91w04'38	6:04:19
Lime Springs 45	2	43N25'48	92w18'00	6:09:12
Linby 51	2	41N09'02	92w08'28	6:08:34
Lincoln 86	2	42N15'46	92w41'30	6:10:46
Lincoln Center 2	2	41N06'57	94w52'19	6:19:29
Lincolnway Village 57	1	41N55'17	91w39'55	6:06:40
Linden 25	2	41N38'40	94w16'08	6:17:05
Lineville 93	2	40N34'53	93w31'25	6:14:06
Linn Grove 11	2	42N53'30	95w14'47	6:20:59
Linn Junction 57	1	42N01'08	91w43'14	6:06:53
Linton 3	1	43N09	91w18	6:05:12
Linwood 82	12	41N27'56	90w40'44	6:02:43
Lisbon 57	1	41N55'16	91w23'07	6:05:32
Liscomb 64	2	42N11'24	93w00'13	6:12:01
Liston 97	2	42N15	95w45	6:23:00
Little Cedar 66	2	43N22'49	92w43'32	6:10:54
Little Groves 82	12	41N32'15	90w41'19	6:02:45
Littleport 22	1	42N45'17	91w22'09	6:05:29
Little Rock 60	2	43N26'39	95w52'59	6:23:32
Little Sioux 43	2	41N48'34	96w01'15	6:24:05
Littleton 10	2	42N32'00	92w01'24	6:08:06
Little Turkey 19	2	43N07'47	92w06'03	6:08:24
Livermore 46	2	42N52'07	94w11'06	6:16:44
Livingston 4	2	40N38	92w55	6:11:40
Lizard 76	2	42N36	94w30	6:18:00
Lloyd 30	2	43N18	94w59	6:19:56
Loch Burns 90	2	41N01'32	92w21'00	6:09:24
Lockman 68	2	41N05'00	92w44'21	6:10:57
Lockridge 51	3	40N59'41	91w44'53	6:07:00
Locust 96	1	43N25'18	91w43'20	6:06:53
Lodomillo 22	1	42N42	91w26	6:05:44
Logan 43	2	41N38'35	95w47'19	6:23:09
Logansport 8	2	42N04'03	93w56'48	6:15:47
Lohrville 13	2	42N16'13	94w32'54	6:18:12
Lone Rock 55	2	43N13'07	94w19'36	6:17:18
Lone Tree 52	1	41N29'17	91w25'33	6:05:42
Long Creek 27	2	40N52	93w50	6:15:20
Longfellow 78	2	41N16	95w51	6:23:24
Long Grove 82	1	41N41'51	90w34'57	6:02:20
Long Point 86	2	41N56'43	92w29'01	6:09:56
Lonia 19	2	43N02'03	92w27'21	6:09:49
Lorah 15	2	41N28'13	94w57'18	6:19:49
Lore 31	15	42N31'05	90w47'59	6:03:12
Lorimor 88	2	41N07'42	94w03'11	6:16:13
Loring 77	2	41N50'05	93w26'06	6:13:44
Lost Grove 94	2	42N16	94w14	6:16:56
Lost Island 74	2	43N13	94w51	6:19:24
Lost Island Lake 21	2	43N07	94w53	6:19:32
Lost Nation 23	1	41N57'50	90w49'03	6:03:16
Lotts Creek 55	2	43N09'24	94w21'58	6:17:28
Louisa 57	1	42N01'53	91w40'02	6:06:40
Lourdes 45	2	43N15'44	92w17'55	6:09:12
Loveland 78	2	41N29'50	95w53'23	6:23:34
Lovell 53	1	42N16	91w11	6:04:44
Lovilia 68	2	41N08'09	92w54'14	6:11:37
Lovington 77	2	41N38'45	93w41'11	6:14:45
Lowden 16	1	41N51'27	90w55'41	6:03:43
Lowell 44	1	40N50'00	91w26'11	6:05:45
Low Moor 23	1	41N48'06	90w21'17	6:01:25
Luana 22	1	43N03'37	91w27'14	6:05:49
Lucas 59	2	41N01'42	93w27'35	6:13:50
Ludlow 3	1	43N13'35	91w34'00	6:06:16
Lundgren 94	2	42N22'07	94w10'28	6:16:42
Lundstrom Heights 77	2	41N39	93w37	6:14:28
Lunsford 26	2	40N36'10	92w26'07	6:09:44
Luray 64	2	41N59'26	93w00'00	6:12:00
Luther 8	2	41N58'04	93w49'07	6:15:16
Luton 97	2	42N20'23	96w13'34	6:24:54
Lu Verne 55	2	42N54'30	94w04'25	6:16:18
Luxemburg 31	1	42N36'10	91w04'26	6:04:18
Luzerne 6	2	41N53'53	92w10'47	6:08:43
Lycurgus 3	1	43N19'52	91w25'26	6:05:42
Lyman 15	2	41N13'52	94w59'03	6:19:56
Lyndale 3	1	43N17'56	91w17'00	6:05:08
Lynn 84	2	43N08	95w55	6:23:40
Lynn Grove 50	2	41N33	92w49	6:11:16
Lynnville 50	2	41N34'39	92w47'00	6:11:08
Lyons 23	10	41N52	90w12	6:00:48
Lyons 57	1	42N01	91w36	6:06:24
Lyons 65	2	40N57	95w44	6:22:56
Lytton 13	2	42N25'23	94w51'34	6:19:26
Macedonia 78	2	41N11'34	95w25'31	6:21:42
Mackey 8	2	42N09'59	93w45'24	6:15:02
Macksburg 61	2	41N12'53	94w11'06	6:16:44
Macy 42	2	42N33	93w02	6:12:08
Madison 78	2	41N16	95w51	6:23:24
Madrid 8	2	41N52'36	93w49'23	6:15:18
Magnolia 43	2	41N41'45	95w52'35	6:23:30
Magor 41	2	42N57	93w55	6:15:40
Maine 4	2	40N51'22	92w51'41	6:11:27
Maine 57	1	42N11	91w32	6:06:08
Makee 3	1	43N18	91w26	6:05:44
Malaka 50	2	41N49	93w04	6:12:16
Malcom 79	2	41N42'30	92w33'32	6:10:14
Mallard 74	2	42N56'11	94w40'55	6:18:44
Mallory 22	1	42N42	91w12	6:04:48
Malone 23	13	41N50	90w32	6:02:08
Maloy 80	2	40N40'28	94w24'43	6:17:39
Malvern 65	2	41N00'10	95w35'06	6:22:20
Manawa 78	2	41N16	95w51	6:23:24
Manchester 28	1	42N29'03	91w27'19	6:05:49
Manilla 24	2	41N53'23	95w13'55	6:20:56
Manly 98	2	43N17'14	93w12'07	6:12:48
Manning 14	2	41N54'33	95w03'53	6:20:16
Manson 13	2	42N32	94w32	6:18:08
Manteno 83	2	41N49'57	95w32'13	6:22:09
Mantua 68	2	41N02	92w42	6:10:48
Maple Heights 34	2	43N04	92w41	6:10:44
Maple Hill 32	2	43N23'32	94w37'30	6:18:30
Maple Leaf 45	2	43N19'15	92w22'44	6:09:31
Maple River 14	2	42N05	94w56	6:19:44
Maple River Junction 14	2	42N05'53	94w56'06	6:19:44
Mapleside 71	2	43N00'09	95w37'25	6:22:30
Mapleton 67	2	42N09'57	95w47'34	6:23:10
Maple Valley 11	2	42N36	95w21	6:21:24
Maquoketa 49	5	42N04'08	90w39'56	6:02:40
Marathon 11	2	42N51'42	94w58'56	6:19:56
Marble Rock 34	2	42N57'55	92w52'06	6:11:28
Marcus 18	2	42N49'33	95w48'26	6:23:14
Marcy 8	2	41N59	93w59	6:15:56
Marengo 48	2	41N47'53	92w04'14	6:08:17
Marietta 64	2	42N04'59	93w00'01	6:12:00
Marion 57	1	42N02'03	91w35'51	6:06:23
Mariposa 50	2	41N49	92w56	6:11:44
Mark 26	2	40N40	92w31	6:10:04
Marne 15	2	41N27'05	95w06'40	6:20:27
Marquette 22	1	43N02'40	91w10'41	6:04:43
Marquisville 77	2	41N39'24	93w36'02	6:14:24
Marsh 29	1	41N06'06	91w21'08	6:05:25
Marshall 58	1	41N10	91w19	6:05:16
Marshalltown 64	2	42N02'58	92w54'28	6:11:38

Martelle 53 1 42N01'18 91W21'35 6:05:26
Martensdale 91 2 41N22'23 93W44'08 6:14:57
Martinsburg 54 2 41N10'44 92W15'06 6:09:00
Martinstown 4 2 40N41'14 92W57'32 6:11:50
Mary Hill 18 2 42N44'08 95W41'18 6:22:45
Marysville 63 2 41N10'50 92W56'56 6:11:48
Maryville 33 1 42N41'16 91W38'43 6:06:35
Mason City 17 2 43N09'13 93W12'03 6:12:48
Masonville 28 1 42N28'46 91W35'28 6:06:22
Massena 15 2 41N15'15 94W46'05 6:19:04
Massey 31 15 42N25'49 90W35'06 6:02:20
Massillon 16 1 41N54'53 90W55'21 6:03:41
Matlock 84 2 43N14'38 95W56'06 6:23:44
Maud 3 1 43N13'35 91W22'13 6:05:29
Maurice 84 2 42N57'59 96W10'49 6:24:43
Maxfield 9 2 42N41 92W16 6:09:04
Maxon 68 2 41N02'27 92W46'33 6:11:06
Maxwell 85 2 41N53'31 93W23'58 6:13:36
May City 72 2 43N19'15 95W28'27 6:21:54
Maynard 33 1 42N46'26 91W52'56 6:07:32
Maysville 82 1 41N38'55 90W43'00 6:02:52
Mccallsburg 85 2 42N09'59 93W23'08 6:13:33
McCausland 82 5 41N44'46 90W26'35 6:01:46
McClelland 78 2 41N19'46 95W41'01 6:22:44
McGargels Ford 53 1 42N13'59 90W55'16 6:03:41
McGregor 22 1 43N01'06 91W10'57 6:04:44
McGregor Heights 22 1 43N02'02 91W10'38 6:04:43
McIntire 66 2 43N26'09 92W35'37 6:10:22
McNally 84 2 42N56'26 96W23'26 6:25:34
McPaul 36 2 40N49'19 95W48'09 6:23:13
McPherson 69 2 41N00'41 95W20'11 6:21:21
Mechanicsville 16 1 41N54'16 91W15'16 6:05:01
Mederville 22 1 42N45'47 91W25'22 6:05:41
Mediapolis 29 19 41N00'29 91W09'50 6:04:39
Medora 91 1 41N11'13 93W36'09 6:14:25
Mekee 31 1 42N29'33 91W02'44 6:04:11
Melbourne 64 2 41N56'29 93W06'11 6:12:25
Melcher 63 2 41N13'19 93W14'28 6:12:58
Melrose 68 2 40N58'34 93W03'01 6:12:12
Meltonville 98 2 43N26'50 93W01'34 6:12:06
Melville 5 2 41N44 94W48 6:19:12
Melvin 72 2 43N17'15 95W36'32 6:22:26
Mendon 22 1 43N01 91W13 6:04:52
Menlo 39 2 41N31'09 94W24'15 6:17:37
Mercer 2 2 40N56'36 94W38'56 6:18:36
Meriden 18 2 42N47'41 95W38'03 6:22:32
Merle Junction 87 2 40N46'54 94W35'33 6:18:22
Meroa 66 2 43N17 92W49 6:11:16
Merrill 75 2 42N43'11 96W14'54 6:25:00
Merrimac 51 1 41N05'14 91W43'07 6:06:52
Meservey 41 2 42N54'46 93W28'41 6:13:55
Mesquakie Indian Settlement 86 2 41N58'56 92W38'33 6:10:34
Methodist Camp 30 2 43N26 95W06 6:20:24
Metz 50 2 41N39'59 93W08'08 6:12:33
Meyer 66 2 43N27'28 92W41'33 6:10:46
Miami 68 2 41N08'50 92W50'23 6:11:22
Middle 48 1 41N59 91W39 6:06:36
Middle Amana 48 1 41N47'44 91W53'58 6:07:36
Middleburg 84 2 43N06'49 96W04'07 6:24:16
Middlefield 10 1 42N26 91W39 6:06:36
Middle Fork 80 2 40N36 94W18 6:17:12
Middle River 61 2 41N19'50 94W14'00 6:16:56
Middletown 29 8 40N49'42 91W15'32 6:05:02
Midland 60 2 43N28 96W01 6:24:04
Midvale 85 2 41N55'46 93W36'36 6:14:26
Midway 34 2 43N00'19 92W36'19 6:10:25
Midway 57 1 42N06'22 91W41'48 6:06:47
Midway Beach 70 1 41N27'33 90W49'42 6:03:19
Miles 49 1 42N02'54 90W18'56 6:01:16
Milford 30 2 43N19'29 95W08'59 6:20:36
Military 96 1 43N09 91W48 6:07:12
Miller 41 2 43N11'03 93W36'00 6:14:24
Millersburg 48 2 41N34'24 92W09'35 6:08:38
Millerton 93 2 40N50'58 93W18'19 6:13:13
Millman 77 2 41N32'28 93W40'38 6:14:43
Millnerville 75 2 42N41'55 96W29'17 6:25:57
Millville 22 1 42N42'00 91W04'27 6:04:18
Milo 91 2 41N17'30 93W26'32 6:13:46
Milton 89 2 40N40'24 92W09'43 6:08:39
Minburn 25 2 41N45'23 94W01'38 6:16:07
Minden 78 2 41N28'01 95W32'33 6:22:10
Mineola 65 2 41N08'35 95W41'43 6:22:47
Mineral Ridge 8 2 42N05 93W56 6:15:44
Minerva 64 2 42N06'59 93W05'16 6:12:21
Mingo 50 2 41N46'03 93W17'00 6:13:08
Missouri Valley 43 2 41N33'23 95W53'15 6:23:33
Mitchell 66 2 43N19'19 92W52'03 6:11:28
Mitchellville 77 2 41N40'07 93W21'27 6:13:26
Modale 43 2 41N37'11 96W00'42 6:24:03
Moingona 8 2 42N01'01 93W55'56 6:15:44
Mona 66 2 43N29'14 92W56'28 6:11:46
Mondamin 43 2 41N42'38 96W01'17 6:24:05
Moneta 71 2 43N07'45 95W23'25 6:21:34
Monette 88 2 41N05'05 94W04'19 6:16:17
Moningers 64 2 42N06'33 93W02'03 6:12:08
Monmouth 23 1 42N04'26 91W00'23 6:04:02
Monona 22 1 43N03'06 91W23'21 6:05:33
Monroe 50 2 41N31'20 93W06'06 6:12:24
Monteith 39 2 41N37'53 94W25'42 6:17:43
Monterey 26 2 40N39'08 92W35'16 6:10:21
Montezuma 79 2 41N35'09 92W31'38 6:10:07
Montgomery 30 2 43N26'27 95W12'09 6:20:49
Monti 10 1 42N22'37 91W38'14 6:06:33
Monticello 53 1 42N14'18 91W11'13 6:04:45
Montour 86 2 41N58'53 92W42'53 6:10:52
Montpelier 70 5 41N27'33 90W48'25 6:03:14
Montrose 56 20 40N31'56 91W24'53 6:05:40
Mooar 56 17 40N26'37 91W27'08 6:05:49
Moorhead 67 2 41N55'21 95W51'04 6:23:24
Moorland 94 2 42N26'30 94W17'41 6:17:11
Moran 25 2 41N48'39 93W54'27 6:15:38
Moravia 4 2 40N53'27 92W48'54 6:11:16
Morley 53 1 42N00'22 91W14'46 6:04:59
Morningside 97 2 42N28'08 96W21'32 6:25:26
Morning Sun 29 1 41N05'46 91W15'27 6:05:02
Morrison 38 2 42N20'39 92W40'25 6:10:42
Morse 52 1 41N44'58 91W26'04 6:05:44
Morton 73 2 40N41 95W19 6:21:16
Morton Mills 69 2 41N04'47 94W59'04 6:19:56
Mosalem 31 1 42N25 90W36 6:02:24
Moscow 70 1 41N34'30 91W04'57 6:04:20
Motor 22 1 42N48'25 91W21'04 6:05:24
Mott 35 2 42N47 93W12 6:12:48
Moulton 4 2 40N41'09 92W40'38 6:10:43
Mound Prairie 50 2 41N39 93W11 6:12:44
Mount Auburn 6 2 42N15'18 92W05'33 6:08:22
Mount Ayr 80 2 40N42'53 94W14'06 6:16:56
Mount Carmel 14 2 42N09'09 94W54'30 6:19:38
Mount Etna 2 2 41N07'14 94W44'06 6:18:56
Mount Hamill 56 1 40N45'02 91W36'47 6:06:27
Mount Joy 82 12 41N36'54 90W33'56 6:02:16
Mount Lucia 97 2 42N32'26 96W27'52 6:25:51
Mount Pleasant 44 21 40N57'49 91W33'28 6:06:14
Mount Sterling 89 1 40N37'04 91W55'55 6:07:44
Mount Union 44 1 41N03'28 91W23'25 6:05:34
Mount Valley 95 2 43N17 93W33 6:14:12
Mount Vernon 57 1 41N55'19 91W25'00 6:05:40
Mount Zion 89 1 40N47'19 91W56'01 6:07:44
Moville 97 2 42N29'20 96W04'20 6:24:17
Munterville 90 2 41N02'08 92W37'12 6:10:29
Murphy 9 2 42N44 92W29 6:09:56
Murray 20 2 41N02'30 93W56'57 6:15:48
Muscatine 70 5 41N25 91W03 6:04:12
Mystic 4 2 40N46'39 92W56'37 6:11:46
Nahant 82 12 41N29'15 90W38'16 6:02:33
Napier 53 2 41N58'47 93W43'04 6:14:52
Nashua 19 2 42N57'10 92W32'10 6:10:09
Nashville 49 1 42N03'45 90W47'01 6:03:08
Nassau 84 2 42N57 96W03 6:24:12
National 22 1 42N57 91W17 6:05:08
Nebraska 73 2 40N46 94W57 6:19:48
Neils 95 2 43N20 93W38 6:14:32
Nemaha 81 2 42N30'57 95W05'17 6:20:21
Neola 78 2 41N26'56 95W36'55 6:22:28
Neptune 75 2 42N39'49 96W09'21 6:24:37
Nevada 85 2 42N01'22 93W27'08 6:13:49
Nevinville 2 2 41N08'50 94W30'02 6:18:00
New Albany 85 2 42N01 93W16 6:13:04
New Albin 3 1 43N29'48 91W17'22 6:05:09
New Albion 12 2 42N38'34 92W43'53 6:10:56
Newark 94 2 42N36 94W03 6:16:12
Newbein 63 2 41N09'39 93W18'30 6:13:14
Newbern 59 2 41N11 93W23 6:13:32
New Boston 56 1 40N33'38 91W30'19 6:06:01
New Buda 27 2 40N37 93W50 6:15:20
Newburg 50 2 41N49'07 92W46'27 6:11:06
Newburg 66 2 43N24 92W58 6:11:52
New Dixon 82 1 41N44'05 90W46'16 6:03:05
Newell 11 2 42N36'20 95W00'09 6:20:01
New Era 70 1 41N27'58 90W53'31 6:03:34
Newhall 6 1 41N59'44 91W58'03 6:07:52
New Hampton 19 2 43N03'33 92W19'03 6:09:16
New Hartford 12 2 42N34'01 92W37'19 6:10:29
New Haven 66 2 43N17'04 92W38'31 6:10:34
New Hope 88 2 41N07 94W04 6:16:16
Newkirk 84 2 43N04'12 95W58'40 6:23:55
New Liberty 82 1 41N43'04 90W52'44 6:03:31
New London 44 22 40N55'37 91W23'58 6:05:36
New Market 87 2 40N43'52 94W53'58 6:19:36
New Oregon 45 2 43N17 92W08 6:08:32
Newport 52 1 41N44'19 91W28'26 6:05:54
Newport 53 1 42N02'43 91W12'02 6:04:48
Newport 58 1 41N05'20 91W10'58 6:04:44
New Providence 42 2 42N16'52 93W10'17 6:12:41
New Sharon 62 2 41N28'12 92W39'04 6:10:36
Newton 50 2 41N41'59 93W02'52 6:12:11
New Vienna 31 1 42N32'53 91W06'51 6:04:27
New Virginia 91 2 41N10'66 93W43'43 6:14:55
New Wine 31 1 42N31 91W04 6:04:16
New York 93 2 40N51'06 93W15'35 6:13:02
Nichols 70 1 41N28'52 91W18'27 6:05:14
Niles 34 2 43N08 92W37 6:10:28
Nira 92 1 41N27'15 91W55'56 6:07:44
Nishna 5 2 41N41'45 94W55'07 6:19:40
Nishnabotny 24 2 41N54 95W16 6:21:04
Noble 15 2 41N12 94W59 6:19:56
Noble 92 21 41N09'59 91W37'10 6:06:29
Nodaway 2 2 40N56'14 94W53'41 6:19:35
Nokomis 11 2 42N42 95W20 6:21:20
Nora Springs 34 2 43N08'34 93W00'15 6:12:01
Nordness 96 1 43N14'04 91W46'18 6:07:05
Northboro 73 2 40N36'28 95W17'29 6:21:10
North Branch 39 2 41N38'45 94W42'54 6:18:52
North Buena Vista 22 1 42N40'47 90W57'23 6:03:50
North Cedar 7 2 42N33'17 92W27'20 6:09:49
North English 48 2 41N30'50 92W04'34 6:08:18
Northfield 29 1 41N03'32 91W07'18 6:04:29
North Fork 28 1 42N26 91W12 6:04:48
North Liberty 52 1 41N44'57 91W35'52 6:06:23
North Side 97 2 42N31 96W24 6:25:36
North Washington 19 2 43N07'05 92W25'00 6:09:40
North Welton 23 1 41N54'49 90W36'16 6:02:25
Northwest 82 12 41N32 90W36 6:02:24
Northwood 98 2 43N26'39 93W13'15 6:12:53
Norwalk 91 2 41N28'32 93W40'43 6:14:43
Norway 6 1 41N54'10 91W55'17 6:07:41
Norway Center 15 2 41N20'45 94W52'20 6:19:29
Norwich 73 2 40N44'33 95W15'23 6:21:02
Norwood 59 2 41N07'00 93W28'43 6:13:55
Norwoodville 77 2 41N36 93W34 6:14:16
Norwoodville Norwood State 77 2 41N38'38 93W33'39 6:14:15
Numa 4 2 40N41'17 92W58'40 6:11:55
Nyman 73 2 40N52'51 95W12'13 6:20:49
Oak 65 2 41N07 95W42 6:22:48
Oak Dale 45 2 43N28 92W30 6:10:00
Oakdale 52 1 41N42'23 91W36'10 6:06:25
Oakfield 5 2 41N34 94W59 6:19:56
Oakland 35 2 42N34'52 93W26'35 6:13:46
Oakland 78 2 41N18'33 95W23'47 6:21:35
Oakland Acres 50 2 41N43'02 92W49'13 6:11:17
Oakland Mills 44 21 40N56'10 91W36'59 6:06:28
Oakley 59 2 41N06'04 93W21'54 6:13:28
Oakville 58 1 41N05'59 91W02'40 6:04:11
Oakwood 34 2 43N00'33 92W46'37 6:11:06
Oasis 52 1 41N42'22 91W23'07 6:05:32
Ocheyedan 72 2 43N24'58 95W32'04 6:22:08
Odebolt 81 2 42N18'44 95W15'01 6:21:00
Oelwein 33 1 42N40'24 91W54'48 6:07:39
Ogden 8 2 42N02'21 94W01'39 6:16:07
Ohio 61 2 41N15 93W55 6:15:40
Okoboji 30 2 43N23'11 95W08'53 6:20:36
Olaf 99 2 42N53'12 93W43'28 6:14:54
Old Balltown 31 1 42N37'54 90W51'30 6:03:26
Old Peru 61 2 41N14'09 93W56'42 6:15:47
Olds 44 1 41N08'03 91W32'41 6:06:11
Old Town 30 2 43N18'49 95W08'38 6:20:35
O'Leary 75 2 42N42'24 96W03'30 6:24:14
Olin 53 1 41N59'53 91W08'29 6:04:34
Olive 23 1 41N49 90W44 6:02:56
Olivet 62 2 41N18'49 92W49'48 6:11:19
Ollie 54 2 41N11'53 92W05'32 6:08:22
Olmitz 59 2 41N04'54 93W10'09 6:12:41
Omega 71 2 43N07 95W27 6:21:48
Onawa 67 2 42N01'36 96W05'49 6:24:23
Onawa Junction 18 2 42N43'30 95W33'27 6:22:14
Oneida 28 1 42N32'34 91W21'12 6:05:25
Onslow 53 1 42N06'25 91W00'54 6:04:04
Ontario 8 2 42N02'09 93W40'53 6:14:44
Oralabor 77 2 41N42'00 93W35'16 6:14:21
Oran 33 2 42N42'05 92W04'28 6:08:18
Orange 7 2 42N25'33 92W21'23 6:09:26
Orange City 84 2 43N00'26 96W03'29 6:24:14
Orchard 66 2 43N13'39 92W46'19 6:11:05
Oregon 92 1 41N18 91W32 6:06:08
Orient 1 2 41N12'11 94W24'52 6:17:39
Orillia 91 2 41N30'35 93W43'43 6:14:55
Orleans 4 2 40N43'32 92W39'26 6:10:38
Orleans 30 2 43N26'50 95W05'32 6:20:22
Ormanville 90 2 40N54'31 92W28'59 6:09:56
Orono 70 1 41N23 91W20 6:05:20
Orson 43 2 41N46'46 95W58'59 6:23:56
Orthel 41 2 43N07 93W54 6:15:36
Ortonville 25 2 41N36'54 93W57'34 6:15:50
Osage 66 2 43N17'03 92W48'39 6:11:15
Osborne 22 1 42N47'31 91W26'43 6:05:47
Osceola 20 2 41N02'02 93W45'55 6:15:04
Osgood 74 2 43N11'36 94W42'04 6:18:48
Oskaloosa 62 2 41N17'47 92W38'39 6:10:35
Ossian 96 1 43N08'47 91W45'52 6:07:03
Osterdock 22 1 42N44'01 91W09'28 6:04:38
Oswalt 50 2 41N41'45 93W17'51 6:13:11
Otho 94 2 42N25'29 94W09'00 6:16:36
Otley 63 2 41N28 93W02 6:12:08
Oto 97 2 42N17'02 95W53'34 6:23:34
Otranto 66 2 43N27'30 92W59'08 6:11:57
Ottawa 20 2 41N01'48 93W35'27 6:14:22
Otter 91 2 41N17 93W30 6:14:00
Otter Creek 49 1 42N14'26 90W40'57 6:02:44
Otterville 10 1 42N30'31 91W56'47 6:07:47
Ottosen 46 2 42N53'42 94W22'47 6:17:31
Ottumwa 90 4 41N00'15 92W22'25 6:09:30
Ottumwa Junction 90 2 41N02 92W25 6:09:40
Owasa 42 2 42N26'01 93W12'25 6:12:50
Owego 97 2 42N16'46 96W09'15 6:24:37
Owen 17 2 43N03 93W05 6:12:20
Oxford 52 1 41N43'24 91W47'25 6:07:10
Oxford Junction 53 1 41N59'01 90W57'22 6:03:49
Oxford Mills 53 1 41N58'13 90W57'35 6:03:50
Oyens 75 2 42N49'13 96W03'27 6:24:14
Ozark 49 1 42N11'43 90W52'31 6:03:30
Pacific City 65 2 41N02'52 95W48'00 6:23:12
Pacific Junction 65 2 41N01'07 95W47'56 6:23:12
Packard 12 2 42N51'03 92W43'55 6:10:56
Packwood 51 2 41N07'58 92W04'57 6:08:20
Page Center 73 2 40N42'44 95W07'46 6:20:31
Paint Creek 3 1 43N14 91W18 6:05:12
Painted Rocks 63 2 41N28 93W02 6:12:08
Palermo 38 2 42N20 92W50 6:11:20
Palestine 85 2 41N56 93W37 6:14:28
Palmer 76 2 42N37'50 94W36'01 6:18:24
Palm Grove 94 2 42N19'34 94W10'26 6:16:42
Palmyra 91 2 41N26'10 93W26'17 6:13:45
Palo 57 1 42N03'58 91W47'43 6:07:11
Palo Alto 50 2 41N39 93W03 6:12:12
Panama 83 2 41N43'35 95W28'19 6:21:53
Panora 39 2 41N41'30 94W21'46 6:17:27
Panorama Park 82 7 41N33 90W27 6:01:48
Panorania Park 82 7 41N33'20 90W27'11 6:01:49
Panther 25 2 41N41'18 94W06'22 6:16:25
Paradise 24 2 41N59 95W30 6:22:00
Paralta 57 1 42N01'53 91W26'33 6:05:46
Paris 26 2 40N47'19 92W35'32 6:10:22
Paris 57 1 42N14 91W35 6:06:20
Parkersburg 12 2 42N34'39 92W47'12 6:11:09
Park Hills 63 2 41N28 93W02 6:12:08
Parkview 82 1 41N41'39 90W32'44 6:02:11
Parnell 48 1 41N34'59 92W00'14 6:08:01
Paton 37 2 42N09'52 94W15'18 6:17:01
Patterson 61 2 41N20'54 93W52'49 6:15:31
Paullina 71 2 42N58'45 95W41'16 6:22:45
Payne 36 2 40N40'11 95W45'36 6:23:02
Pekin 51 2 41N09'46 92W09'34 6:08:38
Pella 63 2 41N24'29 92W54'58 6:11:40
Peoples 8 2 41N54 93W59 6:15:56
Peoria 62 2 41N27'43 92W48'04 6:11:12
Peosta 31 1 42N27'02 90W51'01 6:03:24
Percival 36 2 40N44'56 95W48'48 6:23:15
Perkins 84 2 43N11'17 96W11'07 6:24:44
Perlee 51 1 41N05'02 91W54'12 6:07:37
Perry 25 2 41N50'19 94W06'25 6:16:26
Pershing 63 2 41N15'47 93W00'22 6:12:01
Persia 43 2 41N34'48 95W34'04 6:22:16

Peru 31 1 42N36 90w44 6:02:56
Peru 61 2 41N15 93w55 6:15:40
Peter 78 2 42N21'17 95w39'14 6:22:37
Petersburg 28 1 42N33'18 91w12'47 6:04:51
Peterson 21 2 42N55'05 95w20'37 6:21:22
Petersville 23 1 41N58'03 90w32'01 6:02:08
Philby 71 2 43N04'11 95w48'05 6:23:12
Pickering 64 2 41N56'27 92w48'59 6:11:16
Pierce 73 2 40N51 95w20 6:21:20
Pierson 97 2 42N32'39 95w52'02 6:23:28
Pike 70 1 41N29 91w17 6:05:08
Pilot Grove 56 1 40N45'46 91w32'12 6:06:09
Pilot Grove 69 2 41N06 95w06 6:20:24
Pilot Mound 8 2 42N09'52 94w00'59 6:16:04
Pilot Rock 12 2 42N46'26 92w50'58 6:11:24
Pinehurst 78 2 41N16 95w51 6:23:24
Pioneer 46 2 42N39'14 94w23'32 6:17:34
Piper 13 2 42N21'54 94w33'12 6:18:13
Pisgah 43 2 41N49'53 95w55'31 6:23:42
Pitcher 18 2 42N42 95w27 6:21:48
Pittsburg 89 1 40N44'47 91w59'30 6:07:58
Pittsford 12 2 42N46 92w58 6:11:52
Pitzer 61 2 41N22'26 94w11'08 6:16:45
Plainfield 9 2 42N50'51 92w32'13 6:10:09
Plainview 82 1 41N40'06 90w46'57 6:03:08
Plank 54 2 41N21 92w07 6:08:28
Plano 4 2 40N45'20 93w02'47 6:12:11
Plato 84 2 43N07 96w16 6:25:04
Platteville 87 2 40N38'24 94w33'23 6:18:14
Plattville 65 2 41N02 95w47 6:23:08
Plaza Hills 77 2 41N36 93w41 6:14:44
Pleasant Grove 29 1 40N58'03 91w17'16 6:05:09
Pleasant Grove 31 1 42N23'23 90w55'34 6:03:42
Pleasant Hill 77 2 41N35'02 93w31'11 6:14:05
Pleasanton 27 2 40N34'50 93w44'37 6:14:58
Pleasant Plain 51 1 41N08'50 91w51'32 6:07:26
Pleasant Prairie 70 1 41N31'28 90w52'19 6:03:29
Pleasant Ridge 56 24 40N46 91w26 6:05:44
Pleasant Valley 82 1 41N34'11 90w25'23 6:01:42
Pleasantville 63 2 41N23'09 93w16'09 6:13:05
Plessis 71 2 43N14'01 95w32'52 6:22:11
Plover 76 2 42N52'42 94w37'13 6:18:29
Plum Creek 55 2 43N08 94w09 6:16:36
Plymouth 17 2 43N14'45 93w07'22 6:12:29
Pocahontas 76 2 42N44'08 94w40'08 6:18:41
Poe 80 2 40N41 94w11 6:16:44
Poland 11 2 42N53 94w58 6:19:52
Polk City 77 2 41N46'17 93w42'46 6:14:51
Polk City Junction 77 2 41N48'09 93w41'52 6:14:47
Pomeroy 13 2 42N33'04 94w41'01 6:18:44
Popejoy 35 2 42N35'38 93w25'33 6:13:42
Poplar 83 2 41N41'18 95w05'36 6:20:22
Portland 17 2 43N07'43 93w07'24 6:12:30
Port Louisa 58 1 41N14 91w08 6:04:32
Portsmouth 83 2 41N39'01 95w31'06 6:22:04
Pospect Park 78 2 41N16 95w51 6:23:24
Post 3 1 43N09 91w33 6:06:12
Postville 3 1 43N05'05 91w34'05 6:06:16
Powersville 34 2 42N56'11 92w41'13 6:10:45
Poweshiek 50 2 41N45 93w17 6:13:08
Powhatan 76 2 42N52 94w37 6:18:28
Poyner 7 2 42N31 92w13 6:08:52
Prairie 36 2 40N47 95w33 6:22:12
Prairieburg 57 1 42N14'18 91w25'20 6:05:41
Prairie City 50 2 41N35'58 93w14'06 6:12:56
Prairie Creek 31 1 42N20 90w51 6:03:24
Prairie Grove 29 8 40N52'45 91w15'08 6:05:01
Prairie Springs 49 1 42N20 90w37 6:02:28
Prescott 2 2 41N01'23 94w36'48 6:18:27
Preston 49 1 42N03'01 90w24'50 6:01:39
Primghar 71 2 43N05'13 95w37'37 6:22:30
Primrose 56 1 40N40'32 91w38'17 6:06:33
Princeton 82 5 41N40'29 90w20'25 6:01:22
Probstei 82 12 41N34'53 90w39'45 6:02:39
Prole 91 2 41N24'33 93w43'37 6:14:54
Promise City 93 2 40N44'51 93w08'49 6:12:35
Prospect Hill 29 1 40N49 91w06 6:04:24
Prospect Park 78 2 41N16 95w51 6:23:24
Protivin 45 2 43N12'58 92w05'27 6:08:22
Prussia 1 2 41N23 94w32 6:18:08
Pulaski 26 2 40N41'49 92w16'23 6:09:06
Purdy 59 2 41N09'38 93w13'59 6:12:56
Pymosa 15 2 41N27 94w59 6:19:56
Quandahl 3 1 43N27'00 91w36'23 6:06:26
Quarry 64 2 42N01'02 92w48'18 6:11:13
Quasqueton 10 1 42N23'40 91w45'39 6:07:03
Quick 78 2 41N17'24 95w40'12 6:22:41
Quimby 18 2 42N37'49 95w38'30 6:22:34
Quincy 2 2 41N02'25 94w47'24 6:19:10
Radcliffe 42 2 42N18'55 93w26'03 6:13:44
Raglan 43 2 41N44 95w58 6:23:52
Rake 95 2 43N29'02 93w55'07 6:15:40
Raleigh 32 2 43N20'22 94w52'07 6:19:28
Ralston 14 2 42N02'30 94w37'58 6:18:32
Ramsey 55 2 43N18 94w09 6:16:36
Randalia 33 1 42N51'47 91w53'08 6:07:33
Randall 40 2 42N14'18 93w36'02 6:14:24
Randolph 36 2 40N52'23 95w33'58 6:22:16
Rands 13 2 42N19'30 94w34'43 6:18:19
Rathbun 4 2 40N48'04 92w53'19 6:11:33
Rawles 65 2 40N57 95w38 6:22:32
Raymar 7 2 42N27'19 92w14'24 6:08:58
Raymond 7 2 42N28'08 92w13'10 6:08:53
Read 22 1 42N51 91w20 6:05:20
Readlyn 9 2 42N42'08 92w13'31 6:08:54
Reasnor 50 2 41N34'42 93w01'23 6:12:06
Redding 80 2 40N36'17 94w23'15 6:17:33
Redfield 25 2 41N35'22 94w11'45 6:16:47
Red Line 83 2 41N43'02 95w09'03 6:20:36
Red Oak 69 2 41N00'35 95w13'31 6:20:54
Red Rock 63 2 41N26 93w07 6:12:28
Reeceville 49 1 42N07'36 90w17'54 6:01:12
Reeve 35 2 42N41 93w12 6:12:48
Reilly Settlement 19 2 43N09'20 92w10'50 6:08:43
Reinbeck 38 2 42N19'25 92w35'57 6:10:24
Rembrandt 11 2 42N49'32 95w09'58 6:20:40
Remsen 75 2 42N48'53 95w58'23 6:23:54
Renwick 46 2 42N49'41 93w58'51 6:15:55
Republic 19 2 42N57'04 92w23'50 6:09:35
Rexfield 68 2 41N04'54 92w57'08 6:11:49
Rhodes 64 2 41N55'32 93w11'10 6:12:45
Rice 80 2 40N40 94w20 6:17:20
Riceville 45 2 43N21'50 92w33'14 6:10:13
Richards 13 2 42N25'40 94w31'46 6:18:07
Richfield 33 2 42N57'01 92w03'45 6:08:15
Richland 54 1 41N11'08 91w59'34 6:07:58
Richman 93 2 40N51 93w30 6:14:00
Richmond 92 1 41N26'59 91w41'50 6:06:47
Rickardsville 31 1 42N35'00 90w53'02 6:03:32
Ricketts 24 2 42N07'37 95w34'29 6:22:18
Rider 77 2 41N38'39 93w46'10 6:15:05
Ridgeport 8 2 42N10'37 93w55'02 6:15:40
Ridgeway 96 1 43N17'52 91w59'15 6:07:57
Ridotto 76 2 42N49'46 94w40'36 6:18:42
Riggs 23 1 42N00'18 90w31'48 6:02:07
Riley 80 2 40N37 94w05 6:16:20
Rinard 13 2 42N20'23 94w29'18 6:17:57
Ringsted 32 2 43N17'41 94w30'41 6:18:03
Ripley 12 2 42N42 92w51 6:11:24
Rippey 37 2 41N56'02 94w12'04 6:16:48
Rising Sun 77 2 41N35'36 93w28'53 6:13:56
Ritter 71 2 43N14'39 95w49'21 6:23:17
Riverdale 82 7 41N32'40 90w27'29 6:01:50
River Junction 52 1 41N29'26 91w29'48 6:05:59
Riverside 92 1 41N28'47 91w34'52 6:06:19
Riverside 97 2 42N31'08 96w28'55 6:25:56
River Sioux 43 2 41N48'21 96w02'46 6:24:11
Riverton 36 2 40N41'13 95w34'06 6:22:16
Roberts 94 2 42N25'37 94w10'27 6:16:42
Robertson 42 2 42N30'23 93w07'38 6:12:31
Roberts Park 78 2 41N16 95w51 6:23:24
Robins 57 1 42N04'16 91w40'00 6:06:40
Robinson 28 1 42N20'31 91w34'43 6:06:19
Robison-Whitaker Acres 85 2 41N55'33 93w26'06 6:13:44
Rochester 16 1 41N40'26 91w09'30 6:04:38
Rock Creek 50 2 41N44 92w49 6:11:16
Rock Creek 66 2 43N14'06 92w55'07 6:11:40
Rockdale 31 15 42N27'51 90w40'42 6:02:43
Rock Falls 17 2 43N12'27 93w05'04 6:12:20
Rockford 34 2 43N03'08 92w56'54 6:11:48
Rock Grove 34 2 43N10 92w58 6:11:52
Rock Rapids 60 2 43N25'38 96w10'32 6:24:42
Rock Valley 84 2 43N12'19 96w17'41 6:25:11
Rockville 28 1 42N25'07 91w08'31 6:04:34
Rockwell 17 2 42N59'07 93w11'30 6:12:46
Rockwell City 13 2 42N23'43 94w38'01 6:18:32
Rodman 74 2 43N01'43 94w31'51 6:18:07
Rodney 67 2 42N12'20 95w57'08 6:23:49
Roelyn 94 2 42N24'49 94w21'26 6:17:26
Rogers 57 1 42N11'48 91w34'43 6:06:19
Roland 85 2 42N09'59 93w30'06 6:14:00
Rolfe 76 2 42N48'46 94w31'36 6:18:06
Rome 44 4 40N58'53 91w40'56 6:06:44
Roosevelt 76 2 42N47 94w37 6:18:28
Roosevelt 78 2 41N16 95w51 6:23:24
Roscoe 26 2 40N39 92w15 6:09:00
Roscoe 29 1 41N01'25 91w15'35 6:05:02
Rose 31 1 42N34'55 90w41'57 6:02:48
Rose Grove 40 2 42N25 93w31 6:14:04
Rose Hill 62 2 41N19'19 92w27'43 6:09:51
Roselle 14 2 42N00'01 94w54'55 6:19:40
Roseville 34 2 43N00'33 92w48'35 6:11:14
Ross 5 2 41N46'27 94w55'07 6:19:40
Rosserdale 1 2 41N24'10 94w24'51 6:17:39
Rossie 21 2 43N00'48 95w11'18 6:20:45
Rossville 3 1 43N11'22 91w22'32 6:05:30
Rough Woods Hill 42 2 42N21'39 93w12'31 6:12:50
Round Prairie 51 1 40N57 91w47 6:07:08
Rowan 99 2 42N44'27 93w33'09 6:14:13
Rowley 10 1 42N22'12 91w50'38 6:07:23
Royal 21 2 43N03'56 95w17'01 6:21:08
Rubio 92 1 41N13'16 91w56'15 6:07:45
Ruble 75 2 42N48'29 96w24'34 6:25:38
Rudd 34 2 43N07'34 92w54'20 6:11:37
Runnells 77 2 41N30'40 93w21'26 6:13:26
Rush Lake 74 2 42N56 94w44 6:18:56
Russell 59 2 40N58'55 93w11'54 6:12:48
Ruthven 74 2 43N07'45 94w53'56 6:19:36
Rutland 46 2 42N45'33 94w17'51 6:17:11
Rutledge 90 2 41N03'40 92w25'16 6:09:41
Ryan 28 1 42N21'05 91w28'53 6:05:56
Sabula 49 19 42N04'16 90w10'26 6:00:42
Sac City 81 2 42N25'20 94w59'22 6:19:57
Sageville 31 1 42N33'10 90w42'32 6:02:50
Saint Ansgar 66 2 43N22'42 92w55'07 6:11:40
Saint Anthony 64 2 42N07'20 93w11'41 6:12:47
Saint Benedict 55 2 43N02'17 94w03'51 6:16:15
Saint Catherines 31 15 42N30 90w42 6:02:48
Saint Charles 61 2 41N17'18 93w48'33 6:15:14
Saint Donatus 49 1 42N21'39 90w32'21 6:02:09
Saint Johns 43 2 41N33 95w54 6:23:36
Saint Joseph 55 2 42N54'48 94w13'37 6:16:54
Saint Lucas 33 1 43N03'59 91w56'00 6:07:44
Saint Marys 91 2 41N18'29 93w43'46 6:14:55
Saint Olaf 22 1 42N55'43 91w23'10 6:05:33
Saint Paul 56 1 40N46'10 91w31'01 6:06:04
Saint Sebald 22 1 42N44'18 91w32'45 6:06:11
Salem 44 1 40N51'10 91w37'12 6:06:29
Salina 51 1 41N02'45 91w49'59 6:07:20
Salix 97 2 42N18'30 96w17'15 6:25:09
Sanborn 71 2 43N10'54 95w39'19 6:22:37
Sand Creek 88 2 40N57 94w12 6:16:48
Sand Prairie 56 1 40N32 91w34 6:06:16
Sand Springs 28 1 42N19'03 91w11'21 6:04:45
Sandusky 56 17 40N27'52 91w23'14 6:05:33
Sandyville 91 2 41N22'15 93w23'10 6:13:33
Santiago 77 2 41N42'36 93w22'29 6:13:30
Saratoga 45 2 43N22'17 92w24'21 6:09:37
Sattre 96 1 43N23'32 91w38'22 6:06:33
Saude 19 2 43N04 92w11 6:08:44
Savannah 26 2 40N37'27 92w27'15 6:09:49
Sawyer 56 1 40N41'47 91w21'18 6:05:25
Saydel 77 2 41N38 93w36 6:14:24
Saylor 77 2 41N39'58 93w35'47 6:14:23
Saylorville 77 2 41N40'43 93w37'46 6:14:31
Scarville 95 2 43N28'14 93w37'03 6:14:28
Schaller 81 2 42N30'00 95w17'34 6:21:10
Schleswig 24 2 42N09'55 95w26'12 6:21:45
Schley 45 2 43N18'12 92w13'08 6:08:53
Sciola 69 2 41N02'02 94w59'07 6:19:56
Scotch Grove 53 1 42N10'22 91w06'27 6:04:26
Scotch Ridge 91 2 41N28'21 93w33'30 6:14:14
Scranton 37 2 42N01'21 94w32'42 6:18:11
Sea City 55 2 43N23'04 94w18'53 6:17:16
Searsboro 79 2 41N34'50 92w42'12 6:10:49
Sedan 4 2 40N44 92w52 6:11:28
Seely 39 2 41N44 94w35 6:18:20
Selection 68 2 40N57'50 92w46'59 6:11:08
Selma 89 2 40N52'13 92w09'11 6:08:37
Seneca 55 2 43N17'57 94w23'02 6:17:32
Seney 75 2 42N51'10 96w07'50 6:24:31
Sergeant Bluff 97 2 42N24'14 96w21'30 6:25:26
Settlers 84 2 43N14 96w29 6:25:56
Sewal 93 2 40N38'39 93w15'31 6:13:02
Sexton 55 2 43N04'58 94w05'20 6:16:21
Seymour 93 2 40N40'57 93w07'15 6:12:29
Shady Grove 10 2 42N22'50 92w03'17 6:08:13
Shady Oak 94 2 42N27'42 94w09'24 6:16:38
Shaffton 23 10 41N45'22 90w19'55 6:01:20
Shambaugh 73 2 40N39'32 95w01'54 6:20:08
Shannon City 88 2 40N54'06 94w15'47 6:17:03
Sharon 5 2 41N40'27 94w59'43 6:19:59
Sharon 56 1 40N43'35 91w39'37 6:06:38
Sharon Center 52 1 41N34'09 91w39'40 6:06:39
Sharpsburg 87 2 40N48'09 94w38'32 6:18:34
Shawondasse 31 15 42N26'22 90w35'29 6:02:22
Sheffield 35 2 42N53'36 93w12'54 6:12:52
Shelby 83 2 41N30'58 95w27'00 6:21:48
Sheldahl 77 2 41N51'52 93w41'49 6:14:47
Sheldon 71 2 43N10'52 95w51'21 6:23:25
Shell Rock 12 2 42N42'37 92w34'58 6:10:20
Shellsburg 6 1 42N05'40 91w52'09 6:07:29
Shenandoah 73 2 40N45'56 95w22'19 6:21:29
Sheridan 79 2 41N50'02 92w35'28 6:10:22
Sherman 42 2 42N21'14 93w22'25 6:13:30
Sherrill 31 1 42N36'14 90w47'04 6:03:08
Sherwood 13 2 42N21'33 94w43'36 6:18:54
Shiloh 38 2 42N26 92w57 6:11:48
Shipley 85 2 41N58'48 93w30'41 6:14:03
Shueyville 52 1 41N51'02 91w38'47 6:06:35
Shunem 26 2 40N46'36 92w17'50 6:09:11
Siam 87 2 40N37'40 94w53'07 6:19:32
Sibley 72 2 43N23'57 95w45'06 6:23:00
Sidney 36 2 40N44'54 95w38'50 6:22:35
Sigourney 54 2 41N20'00 92w12'16 6:08:49
Silver 18 2 42N36 95w33 6:22:12
Silver City 65 2 41N06'48 95w38'13 6:22:33
Silver Creek 47 2 42N26 95w23 6:21:32
Silver Lake 98 2 43N28'51 93w21'59 6:13:28
Sinclair 12 2 42N30'00 92w43'54 6:10:56
Sioux Center 84 2 43N04'47 96w10'31 6:24:42
Sioux City 97 2 42N30'00 96w24'00 6:25:36
Sioux Rapids 11 2 42N53'36 95w09'03 6:20:36
Sixmile 23 1 41N54'35 90w17'43 6:01:11
Sixteen 3 1 43N07'36 91w18'57 6:05:16
Slater 85 2 41N52'40 93w40'42 6:14:43
Slifer 94 2 42N20'29 94w22'42 6:17:31
Sloan 97 2 42N13'58 96w13'40 6:24:55
Smithfield 33 1 42N46 91w47 6:07:08
Smithland 97 2 42N13'45 95w55'50 6:23:43
Smiths 49 6 42N19'21 90w15'21 6:01:43
Smyrna 20 2 40N56'32 93w36'34 6:14:26
Soap Creek 26 2 40N51 92w28 6:09:52
Soldier 67 2 41N59'07 95w46'45 6:23:07
Solomon 65 2 40N54'19 95w26'30 6:21:46
Solon 52 1 41N48'26 91w29'38 6:05:59
Somers 13 2 42N22'42 94w25'47 6:17:43
South 61 2 41N18 93w50 6:15:20
South Amana 48 1 41N46'34 91w58'02 6:07:52
South Augusta 56 8 40N45'08 91w16'38 6:05:07
South Des Moines 77 2 41N33 93w37 6:14:28
South English 54 2 41N27'08 92w05'25 6:08:22
South Garry Owen 49 1 42N13'50 90w48'25 6:03:14
South Muscatine 70 1 41N26 91w03 6:04:12
South Ottumwa 90 2 41N02 92w25 6:09:40
Spaulding 88 2 41N07 94w25 6:17:40
Spencer 21 2 43N08'29 95w08'39 6:20:35
Spencers Grove 6 1 42N17'04 91w52'08 6:07:29
Sperry 29 1 40N57'25 91w09'23 6:04:38
Spillville 96 1 43N12'18 91w57'03 6:07:48
Spirit Lake 30 2 43N25'20 95w06'07 6:20:24
Spragueville 49 1 42N04'21 90w26'06 6:01:44
Spring 18 2 42N52 95w27 6:21:48
Spring Branch 22 1 42N48'37 91w19'58 6:05:20
Springbrook 49 1 42N09'51 90w28'35 6:01:54
Spring Creek 7 2 42N21 92w07 6:08:28
Springdale 16 1 41N40'14 91w15'32 6:05:02
Springdale 97 2 42N31'24 96w22'11 6:25:29
Spring Fountain 9 2 42N49'58 92w10'49 6:08:43
Spring Grove 29 1 40N44'23 91w09'29 6:04:38
Spring Grove 57 5 42N15 91w40 6:06:40
Spring Hill 91 2 41N24'41 93w38'41 6:14:35

Place		Lat.	Long.	Time
Springhole 53	1	42N13'06	91W05'51	6:04:23
Spring Rock 23	1	41N49	90W51	6:03:24
Spring Valley 62	2	41N24'54	92W29'01	6:09:56
Springville 57	1	42N03'34	91W26'33	6:05:46
Squaw 91	2	41N12	93W36	6:14:24
Stacyville 66	2	43N26'10	92W46'56	6:11:08
Stacyville Junction 66	2	43N26'45	92W55'57	6:11:44
Stanhope 40	2	42N17'20	93W47'45	6:15:11
Stanley 10	1	42N38'34	91W48'45	6:07:15
Stanton 65	2	40N58'54	95W06'14	6:20:25
Stanwood 16	1	41N53'35	91W09'02	6:04:36
Stanzel 1	2	41N18'57	94W15'39	6:17:03
Stapleton 19	2	43N02	92W10	6:08:40
State Center 64	2	42N01'00	93W09'48	6:12:39
Steady Run 54	2	41N12	92W14	6:08:56
Steamboat Rock 42	2	42N24'34	93W03'56	6:12:16
Stennett 69	2	41N05'23	95W11'39	6:20:47
Sterling 49	1	42N04'36	90W15'10	6:01:01
Steuben 26	2	40N43'25	92W23'18	6:09:33
Stevens 55	2	43N25'54	94W00'14	6:16:01
Stiles 26	2	40N38'06	92W21'04	6:09:24
Stilson 41	2	43N02'18	93W53'06	6:15:32
Stockholm 24	2	42N10	95W16	6:21:04
Stockport 89	1	40N51'27	91W50'06	6:07:20
Stockton 70	5	41N35'29	90W51'31	6:03:26
Stock Yards 97	2	42N30	96W22	6:25:28
Stone City 53	1	42N06'50	91W20'57	6:05:24
Stonega 40	2	42N28'36	93W42'52	6:14:51
Storm Lake 11	2	42N38'28	95W12'34	6:20:50
Story City 85	2	42N11'14	93W35'44	6:14:23
Stout 38	2	42N30'00	92W42'42	6:10:51
Strahan 65	2	40N56'59	95W29'56	6:22:00
Stratford 40	2	42N16'17	93W55'37	6:15:42
Strawberry Point 22	1	42N41'01	91W32'02	6:06:08
Streepyville 4	2	40N41'46	92W54'57	6:11:40
Stringtown 2	2	40N58'44	94W33'27	6:18:14
Struble 75	2	42N53'43	96W11'42	6:24:47
Stuart 39	2	41N30'12	94W19'06	6:17:16
Sugar Grove 25	2	41N44	94W00	6:16:00
Sully 50	2	41N34'42	92W50'41	6:11:23
Sulphur Springs 11	2	42N37'19	95W05'49	6:20:23
Summerset 1	2	41N18	94W32	6:18:08
Summerset 91	1	41N25'53	93W32'41	6:14:11
Summitville 56	20	40N28'22	91W26'55	6:05:48
Sumner 9	2	42N50'51	92W05'29	6:08:22
Sunbury 16	1	41N40'12	90W55'51	6:03:43
Sunshine 4	2	40N44'23	92W55'30	6:11:42
Superior 30	2	43N25'49	94W56'46	6:19:47
Sutherland 71	2	42N58'27	95W29'50	6:21:59
Sutliff 52	1	41N50'21	91W23'29	6:05:34
Swaldale 17	2	42N58'43	93W26'17	6:13:45
Swaledale 17	2	42N59	93W19	6:13:16
Swan 63	2	41N27'55	93W18'40	6:13:15
Swanton 12	2	42N30'00	92W41'32	6:10:46
Swanwood 77	2	41N39'05	93W35'25	6:14:22
Swea City 55	2	43N23	94W19	6:17:16
Swedesburg 44	1	41N06'19	91W32'49	6:06:11
Sweetland 70	1	41N29	90W57	6:03:48
Sweetland Center 70	1	41N29'36	90W58'10	6:03:53
Swisher 52	1	41N50'44	91W41'34	6:06:46
Table Mound 31	1	42N26	90W43	6:02:52
Tabor 36	2	40N53'54	95W40'16	6:22:41
Taintor 62	2	41N30'04	92W44'18	6:10:57
Talleyrand 54	1	41N17'42	91W57'54	6:07:52
Talmage 88	2	41N01'37	94W06'42	6:16:27
Tama 86	2	41N58'00	92W34'36	6:10:18
Tara 94	2	42N30'01	94W17'44	6:17:11
Tarkio 73	2	40N46	95W12	6:20:48
Taylor 78	2	41N16'17	95W31'11	6:22:05
Taylorsville 33	1	42N46'02	91W38'48	6:06:35
Teeds Grove 23	1	42N00'42	90W14'51	6:00:59
Templar Park 30	2	43N26	95W06	6:20:24
Temple Hill 53	1	42N13'33	90W58'34	6:03:54
Templeton 14	2	41N55'06	94W56'33	6:19:46
Tenmile 23	1	41N56'44	90W20'02	6:01:20
Tennant 83	2	41N35'37	95W26'27	6:21:46
Tenville 69	2	41N00'31	94W59'31	6:19:58
Tenville Junction 69	2	40N56	94W59	6:19:56
Terre Haute 27	2	40N41'00	93W51'59	6:15:28
Terril 30	2	43N18'21	94W58'17	6:19:53
Tete Des Morts 49	1	42N20	90W30	6:02:00
Thayer 88	2	41N01'41	94W03'02	6:16:12
Thirty 4	2	40N41'46	92W52'03	6:11:28
Thomasville 22	1	42N45'14	91W34'51	6:06:19
Thompson 95	2	43N22'17	93W46'24	6:15:06
Thompson Corner 3	1	43N15'59	91W13'50	6:04:55
Thor 46	2	42N41'17	94W02'57	6:16:12
Thornburg 54	2	41N27'17	92W20'08	6:09:21
Thornton 17	2	42N56'41	93W23'04	6:13:32
Thorpe 28	1	42N33'58	91W26'57	6:05:48
Thurman 36	2	40N49'12	95W44'51	6:22:59
Ticonic 67	2	42N09'58	95W57'08	6:23:49
Tiffin 52	1	41N42'21	91W39'46	6:06:39
Tilden 18	2	42N42	95W48	6:23:12
Tilton 79	2	41N30'35	92W21'08	6:09:25
Timber Creek 64	2	41N59	92W56	6:11:44
Timberland Heights 85	2	42N03	93W35	6:14:20
Tingley 80	2	40N51'10	94W11'42	6:16:47
Tinley 78	2	41N16	95W51	6:23:24
Tippecanoe 44	1	40N58	91W38	6:06:32
Tipperary 59	2	41N06'49	93W09'15	6:12:37
Tipton 16	1	41N46'11	91W07'40	6:04:31
Titonka 55	2	43N14'13	94W02'28	6:16:10
Toddville 57	1	42N05'57	91W43'00	6:06:52
Toeterville 66	2	43N26'32	92W53'25	6:11:34
Toledo 86	2	41N59'44	92W34'36	6:10:18
Toolesboro 58	23	41N08'31	91W03'43	6:04:15
Toronto 23	1	41N54'18	90W51'50	6:03:27
Tracy 63	2	41N17	92W53	6:11:32
Traer 86	2	42N11'37	92W27'55	6:09:52
Trenton 44	1	41N03'42	91W38'14	6:06:33
Treynor 78	2	41N13'57	95W36'46	6:22:27
Triboji Beach 30	2	43N25'37	95W10'28	6:20:42
Tripoli 9	2	42N48'29	92W15'29	6:09:02
Troy 26	2	40N44'55	92W12'09	6:08:49
Troy Mills 57	1	42N17'24	91W40'56	6:06:44
Truax 62	2	41N11'36	92W43'49	6:10:55
Truesdale 11	2	42N43'45	95W10'57	6:20:44
Truro 61	2	41N14	93W50	6:15:20
Turin 67	2	42N01'10	95W57'58	6:23:52
Turkey River 22	1	42N42'22	91W01'33	6:04:06
Turro 61	2	41N12'29	93W50'45	6:15:23
Tuskeego 27	2	40N43	94W03	6:16:12
Twelve Mile Lake 32	2	43N18	94W50	6:19:20
Twin City Plaza Addition 78	2	41N16	95W51	6:23:24
Twin Lake 41	2	42N57	93W41	6:14:44
Twin Lakes 13	2	42N26	94W42	6:18:48
Twin Springs 31	1	42N30'55	90W50'25	6:03:22
Twin Springs 49	1	42N07'55	90W17'01	6:01:08
Twin View Heights 52	1	41N48'38	91W34'23	6:06:18
Tyrone 68	2	40N58'40	92W56'47	6:11:47
Udell 4	2	40N46'51	92W44'31	6:10:58
Ulmer 81	2	42N16'04	94W56'59	6:19:48
Ulster 34	2	43N04	92W51	6:11:24
Underwood 78	2	41N23'13	95W40'35	6:22:42
Union 42	2	42N14'44	93W03'52	6:12:15
Union Center 75	2	42N41'33	96W03'29	6:24:14
Union City 3	1	43N28	91W27	6:05:48
Union Mills 62	2	41N27'09	92W34'14	6:10:17
Union Prairie 3	1	43N18	91W33	6:06:12
Unionville 4	2	40N49'06	92W41'43	6:10:47
University Heights 52	1	41N40	91W34	6:06:16
University Heigts 52	1	41N39'18	91W33'24	6:06:14
University Park 62	2	41N17	92W37	6:10:28
Updegraff 22	1	42N41'02	91W14'13	6:04:57
Upper South Amana 48	1	41N45'57	91W58'04	6:07:52
Urbana 6	1	42N13'27	91W52'27	6:07:30
Urbandale 77	2	41N37'36	93W42'43	6:14:51
Ute 67	2	42N03'01	95W42'22	6:22:49
Utica 19	2	43N09	92W10	6:08:40
Utica 89	1	40N48'53	91W50'05	6:07:20
Vail 24	2	42N03'43	95W11'59	6:20:48
Valeria 50	2	41N43'48	93W19'30	6:13:18
Van Buren 49	1	42N05'04	90W21'53	6:01:28
Van Cleve 64	2	41N55'53	93W01'08	6:12:05
Vandalia 50	2	41N32'22	93W18'21	6:13:13
Van Horne 6	2	42N00'31	92W05'27	6:08:22
Van Meter 25	2	41N31'55	93W57'14	6:15:49
Van Wert 27	2	40N52'11	93W47'34	6:15:10
Varina 76	2	42N39'29	94W53'51	6:19:35
Ventura 17	2	43N07'35	93W28'39	6:13:55
Ventura Heights 17	2	43N07'04	93W28'26	6:13:54
Veo 51	1	41N11	92W00	6:08:00
Vermilion 4	2	40N43	92W52	6:11:28
Vernon 52	1	41N41'07	91W36'06	6:06:24
Vernon 89	1	40N43'21	91W51'18	6:07:25
Vernon Springs 45	2	43N21'00	92W08'17	6:08:33
Vernon View 57	1	41N58'32	91W34'22	6:06:17
Victor 48	2	41N43'54	92W17'52	6:09:11
Victoria 15	2	41N12	94W47	6:19:08
Victory 39	2	41N44	94W27	6:17:48
Viele 56	1	40N36'47	91W26'01	6:05:44
Vienna 64	2	42N10	92W50	6:11:20
Village 89	2	40N53	92W08	6:08:32
Village Creek 3	1	43N18'33	91W14'06	6:04:56
Villisca 69	2	40N55'47	94W58'33	6:19:54
Vincennes 56	1	40N29'47	91W34'11	6:06:17
Vincent 94	2	42N35'31	94W01'12	6:16:05
Vining 86	2	41N59'24	92W22'47	6:09:31
Vinje 95	2	43N28'24	93W40'36	6:14:42
Vinton 6	2	42N10'07	92W01'24	6:08:06
Viola 57	1	42N05'27	91W26'15	6:05:45
Viola Center 5	2	41N48'21	94W48'07	6:19:12
Virginia 91	2	41N12	93W43	6:14:52
Volga (Volga City) 22	1	42N48'17	91W32'27	6:06:10
Volney 3	1	43N07'50	91W22'25	6:05:30
Voorhies 7	2	42N20'09	92W28'57	6:09:56
Wacousta 46	2	42N52	94W23	6:17:32
Wadena 33	1	42N50'34	91W39'24	6:06:38
Wagner 22	1	42N58	91W26	6:05:44
Wahpeton 30	2	43N21'58	95W10'18	6:20:41
Walcott 82	5	41N35'05	90W46'19	6:03:05
Wald 16	1	41N50'16	91W07'56	6:04:32
Wales 69	2	41N07'01	95W19'37	6:21:18
Walford 6	1	41N52'42	91W50'04	6:07:20
Walker 57	1	42N17'12	91W46'50	6:07:07
Wallin 69	2	41N03'36	95W03'21	6:20:13
Wallingford 32	2	43N19'11	94W47'33	6:19:10
Wall Lake 81	2	42N16'16	95W05'34	6:20:22
Walnut 78	2	41N28'39	95W13'18	6:20:53
Walnut City 4	2	40N48'44	92W56'41	6:11:47
Walnut Grove 82	12	41N28'13	90W39'40	6:02:39
Wanetta Corner 26	2	40N37'28	92W16'09	6:09:05
Wapello 58	23	41N10'53	91W11'07	6:04:44
Wapsinonoc 70	1	41N33	91W17	6:05:08
Ward 20	2	41N02	93W51	6:15:24
Ward 68	2	41N01'46	92W53'11	6:11:33
Ware 76	2	42N47'25	94W45'32	6:19:02
Washburn 7	2	42N24'42	92W16'02	6:09:04
Washington 92	1	41N17'57	91W41'34	6:06:46
Washington Mills 31	1	42N18'02	90W46'56	6:03:08
Washta 18	2	42N34'32	95W43'02	6:22:52
Waterloo 7	2	42N29'34	92W20'34	6:09:22
Waterman 71	2	42N58	95W26	6:21:44
Waterville 3	1	43N12'28	91W17'51	6:05:11
Watkins 6	1	41N53'28	91W59'10	6:07:57
Watson 22	1	43N04'31	91W19'48	6:05:19
Waubeek 57	1	42N09'57	91W27'54	6:05:52
Waubonsie 80	2	40N43	94W22	6:17:28
Waucoma 33	2	43N03'22	92W01'59	6:08:08
Waukee 25	2	41N36'42	93W53'06	6:15:32
Waukon 3	1	43N16'10	91W28'32	6:05:54
Waukon Junction 3	1	43N09'12	91W11'17	6:04:45
Waupeton 31	1	42N40'04	90W52'56	6:03:32
Waveland 78	2	41N12	95W12	6:20:48
Waverly 9	2	42N43'33	92W28'31	6:09:54
Waverly Junction 9	2	42N40'04	92W31'41	6:10:07
Wayland 44	1	41N08'50	91W39'38	6:06:39
Weaver 46	2	42N41	94W23	6:17:32
Webb 21	2	42N56'55	95W00'42	6:20:03
Webster 54	2	41N26'18	92W10'08	6:08:41
Webster 61	2	41N21	94W00	6:16:00
Webster City 40	2	42N28'10	93W48'57	6:15:16
Welcome 84	2	43N07	96W09	6:24:36
Weldon 27	2	40N53'51	93W44'05	6:14:56
Weller 68	2	41N06'26	93W02'57	6:12:12
Wellman 92	1	41N27'51	91W50'17	6:07:21
Wells 4	2	40N38	92W42	6:10:48
Wellsburg 38	2	42N27'33	92W56'18	6:11:45
Welton 23	1	41N54'29	90W35'43	6:02:23
Wesley 55	2	43N05'18	93W59'24	6:15:58
West 48	1	41N48	91W58	6:07:52
West 69	2	40N57	95W19	6:21:16
West Amana 48	1	41N48'29	91W57'49	6:07:51
West Bend 74	2	42N57'25	94W26'27	6:17:46
West Branch 16	1	41N40'17	91W20'47	6:05:23
West Broadway 78	2	41N16	95W51	6:23:24
Westburg 10	2	42N25	92W01	6:08:04
West Burlington 29	18	40N49'30	91W09'23	6:04:38
West Chester 92	1	41N20'20	91W49'03	6:07:16
West Des Moines 77	2	41N34'38	93W42'40	6:14:51
Western 57	1	41N51'55	91W38'35	6:06:34
Western College 57	1	41N58	91W42	6:06:48
Westerville 27	2	40N50	93W56	6:15:44
Westfield 75	2	42N45'20	96W36'20	6:26:25
West Fort Dodge 94	2	42N30	94W11	6:16:44
Westgate 33	1	42N46'12	91W59'46	6:07:59
West Grove 26	2	40N43'29	92W33'36	6:10:14
West Lancaster 54	2	41N16	92W14	6:08:56
West Le Mars 75	2	42N47'35	96W13'33	6:24:54
West Liberty 70	1	41N34'12	91W15'49	6:05:03
West Lincoln 66	2	43N14	92W45	6:11:00
West Lucas 52	1	41N38	91W34	6:06:16
West Mitchell 66	2	43N19	92W52	6:11:28
West Okoboji 30	2	43N21'12	95W09'44	6:20:39
Weston 78	2	41N20'27	95W44'27	6:22:58
Westphalia 83	2	41N43'11	95W23'40	6:21:35
West Point 56	24	40N43'00	91W27'00	6:05:48
Westport 30	2	43N18	95W20	6:21:20
West Saint Marys 91	2	41N18'29	93W44'22	6:14:57
Westside 24	2	42N03'33	95W05'52	6:20:23
West Storm Lake 11	2	42N38	95W11	6:20:44
West Union 33	1	42N57'46	91W48'29	6:07:14
Wever 56	25	40N42'38	91W13'51	6:04:55
What Cheer 54	2	41N24'05	92W21'16	6:09:25
Wheatland 23	1	41N49'54	90W50'17	6:03:21
White Cloud 65	2	40N59'03	95W31'22	6:22:05
White Elm 26	2	40N51'05	92W12'23	6:08:50
White Oak 77	2	41N40'30	93W32'03	6:14:08
White Pigeon 54	2	41N31	92W04	6:08:16
Whitewater 31	1	42N20	90W58	6:03:52
Whiting 67	2	42N07'39	96W08'57	6:24:36
Whittemore 55	2	43N03'43	94W25'36	6:17:42
Whitten 42	2	42N15'39	93W00'19	6:12:01
Whittier 57	1	42N05'41	91W27'45	6:05:51
Wichita 39	2	41N44'00	94W36'14	6:18:25
Wick 91	2	41N20'41	93W44'19	6:14:57
Wieston 13	2	42N32	94W32	6:18:08
Wightman 13	2	42N13'57	94W36'34	6:18:26
Wildwood Camp 82	1	41N42	90W35	6:02:20
Wilke 42	2	42N29'48	93W28'09	6:13:53
Wilkins 31	1	42N24'34	90W32'28	6:02:10
Willey 14	2	41N58'45	94W49'19	6:19:17
William Penn College 62	2	41N17	92W38	6:10:32
Williams 40	2	42N29'18	93W32'41	6:14:11
Williamsburg 48	2	41N39'40	92W00'32	6:08:02
Williamson 2	2	41N08'37	94W33'57	6:18:16
Williamson 59	2	41N05'16	93W15'17	6:13:01
Williamstown 19	2	42N57'55	92W19'04	6:09:16
Williamstown 52	1	41N34'12	91W43'56	6:06:56
Wilmar 12	2	42N49'06	92W49'47	6:11:19
Wilson 72	2	43N28	95W41	6:22:44
Wilton 70	5	41N35'20	91W01'00	6:04:04
Winchester 89	1	40N51'01	91W53'59	6:07:36
Windham 52	1	41N36'32	91W45'43	6:07:03
Windsor 33	1	42N57	91W54	6:07:36
Windsor Heights 77	2	41N35'52	93W42'29	6:14:50
Winfield 44	1	41N07'23	91W26'28	6:05:46
Winkelmans 37	2	41N58'16	94W20'18	6:17:21
Winnebago Heights 17	2	43N09	93W13	6:12:52
Winterset 61	2	41N19'51	94W00'49	6:16:03
Winthrop 10	1	42N28'24	91W44'03	6:06:56
Wiota 15	2	41N24'01	94W53'12	6:19:33
Wiscotta 25	2	41N34'49	94W11'24	6:16:46
Wisner 35	2	42N52	93W26	6:13:44
Woden 41	2	43N13'59	93W54'32	6:15:38
Wolf 8	2	42N08'08	94W01'38	6:16:07
Wolf Creek 97	2	42N26	95W57	6:23:48
Wolf Lake Addition 64	2	41N59'43	92W53'08	6:11:33
Wood 22	1	42N39'27	91W19'57	6:05:20
Woodbine 43	2	41N44'18	95W42'09	6:22:49
Woodburn 20	2	41N00'43	93W35'56	6:14:24
Woodbury 97	2	42N26	96W18	6:25:12
Woodland 27	2	40N41'46	93W35'52	6:14:23
Woodland Hills 77	2	41N33'12	93W27'43	6:13:51
Woodward 25	2	41N51'25	93W55'18	6:15:41
Woolstock 99	2	42N34'00	93W50'37	6:15:22

Worth 8	2	42N00	93w51	6:15:24
Worthington 31	1	42N23'47	91w07'11	6:04:29
Worthington Acres 57	1	41N55'46	91w37'41	6:06:31
Wren 75	2	42N38'44	96w17'10	6:25:09
Wright 62	2	41N14'57	92w31'33	6:10:06
Wyacondah 26	2	40N40	92w28	6:09:52
Wyman 58	1	41N11'32	91w28'26	6:05:54
Wyoming 53	1	42N03'33	91w00'26	6:04:02
Yale 39	2	41N46'36	94w21'28	6:17:26
Yarmouth 29	1	41N01'35	91w19'24	6:05:18
Yellow Springs 29	1	41N02	91w11	6:04:44
Yetter 13	2	42N18'58	94w50'45	6:19:23
York Center 78	2	41N22'34	95w33'20	6:22:13
Yorkshire 43	2	41N31'14	95w34'47	6:22:19
Yorktown 73	2	40N44'00	95w09'24	6:20:38
Zaneta 38	2	42N23'37	92w33'07	6:10:12
Zearing 85	2	42N09'40	93w17'49	6:13:11
Zenorsville 85	2	42N06'26	93w43'04	6:14:52
Zion 1	2	41N12'02	94w17'55	6:17:12
Zook Spur 25	2	41N52	93w49	6:15:16
Zwingle 31	1	42N17'52	90w41'15	6:02:45

TIME TABLES

The time tables for western Kansas reflect the observed CST, rather than the MST mandated by the Interstate Commerce Commission. Zone shifts in the extreme western part of the state are sometimes estimated from incomplete information.

KS # 1

Before 11/18/1883		LMT
11/18/1883	12:00	CST
3/31/1918	02:00	CWT
10/27/1918	02:00	CST
3/30/1919	02:00	CWT
10/26/1919	02:00	CST
2/09/1942	02:00	CWT
9/30/1945	02:00	CST
4/30/1967	02:00	US#1

KS # 2

Before 11/18/1883		LMT
11/18/1883	12:00	MST
3/31/1918	02:00	MWT
10/27/1918	02:00	MST
3/30/1919	02:00	MWT
10/26/1919	02:00	MST
2/09/1942	02:00	MWT
9/30/1945	02:00	MST
4/24/1966	02:00	US#1

KS # 3

Before 11/18/1883		LMT
11/18/1883	12:00	MST
3/31/1918	02:00	MWT
10/27/1918	02:00	MST
3/30/1919	02:00	MWT
10/26/1919	02:00	MST
8/07/1927	02:00	CST
2/09/1942	02:00	CWT
9/30/1945	02:00	CST
4/30/1967	02:00	US#1

KS # 4

Before 11/18/1883		LMT
11/18/1883	12:00	MST
3/31/1918	02:00	MWT
10/27/1918	02:00	MST
3/30/1919	02:00	MWT
10/26/1919	02:00	MST
2/09/1942	02:00	MWT
9/30/1945	02:00	CST
4/30/1967	02:00	US#1

KS # 5

Before 11/18/1883		LMT
11/18/1883	12:00	MST
3/31/1918	02:00	MWT
10/27/1918	02:00	MST
3/30/1919	02:00	MWT
10/26/1919	02:00	MST
2/09/1942	02:00	MWT
9/30/1945	02:00	MST
4/28/1963	02:00	CST
4/30/1967	02:00	US#1

COUNTIES

1 Allen
2 Anderson
3 Atchison
4 Barber
5 Barton
6 Bourbon
7 Brown
8 Butler
9 Chase
10 Chautauqua
11 Cherokee
12 Cheyenne
13 Clark
14 Clay
15 Cloud
16 Coffey
17 Comanche
18 Cowley
19 Crawford
20 Decatur
21 Dickinson
22 Doniphan
23 Douglas
24 Edwards
25 Elk
26 Ellis
27 Ellsworth
28 Finney
29 Ford
30 Franklin
31 Geary
32 Gove
33 Graham
34 Grant
35 Gray
36 Greeley
37 Greenwood
38 Hamilton
39 Harper
40 Harvey
41 Haskell
42 Hodgeman
43 Jackson
44 Jefferson
45 Jewell
46 Johnson
47 Kearny
48 Kingman
49 Kiowa
50 Labette
51 Lane
52 Leavenworth
53 Lincoln
54 Linn
55 Logan
56 Lyon
57 McPherson
58 Marion
59 Marshall
60 Meade
61 Miami
62 Mitchell
63 Montgomery
64 Morris
65 Morton
66 Nemaha
67 Neosho
68 Ness
69 Norton
70 Osage
71 Osborne
72 Ottawa
73 Pawnee
74 Phillips
75 Pottawatomie
76 Pratt
77 Rawlins
78 Reno
79 Republic
80 Rice
81 Riley
82 Rooks
83 Rush
84 Russell
85 Saline
86 Scott
87 Sedgwick
88 Seward
89 Shawnee
90 Sheridan
91 Sherman
92 Smith
93 Stafford
94 Stanton
95 Stevens
96 Sumner
97 Thomas
98 Trego
99 Wabaunsee
100 Wallace
101 Washington
102 Wichita
103 Wilson
104 Woodson
105 Wyandotte

Place	Zone	Latitude	Longitude	Time
Abbyville 78	1	37N58'15	98w12'14	6:32:49
Abilene 21	1	38N55'02	97w12'49	6:28:51
Achilles 77	1	39N42'43	100w50'09	6:43:21
Acme 21	1	38N50'33	97w15'38	6:29:03
Ada 72	1	39N09'05	97w53'20	6:31:33
Adams 48	1	37N30'01	97w58'38	6:31:55
Adams 66	1	39N47	95w57	6:23:48
Adams Corner 78	1	38N03'27	98w05'13	6:32:21
Adamsville 96	1	37N10'24	97w10'34	6:28:42
Adell 90	1	39N31	100w14	6:40:56
Admire 56	1	38N38'28	96w06'10	6:24:25
Adrian 43	1	39N21	95w59	6:23:56
Aetna 4	1	37N05'02	98w57'45	6:35:51
Afton 87	1	37N36	97w38	6:30:32
Agency 70	1	38N34	95w33	6:22:12
Agenda 79	1	39N42'28	97w25'53	6:29:44
Agnes City 56	1	38N41	96w14	6:24:56
Agra 74	1	39N45'42	99w07'08	6:36:29
Agricola 16	1	38N25'10	95w32'05	6:22:08
Aikins 75	1	39N22'05	96w06'58	6:24:28
Aikman 8	1	37N59'23	96w40'50	6:26:43
Airbase Spur 5	1	38N22	98w46	6:35:04
Akron 18	1	37N21'06	97w00'53	6:28:04
Alameda 48	1	37N33'40	98w03'40	6:32:15
Alamota 51	1	38N27'40	100w18'35	6:41:14
Alanthus 32	1	38N42'00	100w10'00	6:40:40
Albano 93	1	37N53	98w52	6:35:28
Albert 5	1	38N27'10	99w00'40	6:36:03
Alcona 82	1	39N26	99w33	6:38:12
Alcove Spring 59	1	39N45'39	96w40'40	6:26:43
Alden 80	1	38N14'32	98w18'42	6:33:15
Aldine 69	1	39N57	99w54	6:39:36
Aleppo 87	1	37N41	97w41	6:30:44
Alexander 83	1	38N28'10	99w33'10	6:38:13
Alexandria 52	1	39N16	95w07	6:20:28
Alfmil 72	1	39N07'55	97w43'19	6:30:53
Aliceville 16	1	38N09'16	95w33'06	6:22:12
Alida 31	1	39N05'45	96w56'24	6:27:46
Allen 56	1	38N39'22	96w10'10	6:24:41
Allendorph 99	1	38N59'34	96w16'15	6:25:05
Allison 20	1	39N34'30	100w15'50	6:41:03
Allodium 33	1	39N30	100w06	6:40:24
Alma 99	1	39N01'00	96w17'20	6:25:09
Almelo 69	1	39N36	100w07	6:40:28
Almena 69	1	39N53'32	99w42'24	6:38:50
Alta 40	1	38N08	97w39	6:30:36
Alta Mills 40	1	38N07'04	97w35'30	6:30:22
Altamont 50	1	37N11'25	95w17'49	6:21:11
Alta Vista 99	1	38N51'50	96w29'20	6:25:57
Alton 71	1	39N28'15	98w56'52	6:35:47
Altoona 103	1	37N31'26	95w39'40	6:22:39
Altory 20	1	39N47	100w21	6:41:24
America City 66	1	39N34'25	96w01'54	6:24:08
Americus 56	1	38N30'25	96w15'42	6:25:03
Ames 15	1	39N34'10	97w26'30	6:29:46
Amiot 2	1	38N20'50	95w29'15	6:21:57
Amy 51	1	38N28'55	100w36'05	6:42:24
Andale 87	1	37N47'36	97w37'45	6:30:31
Andover 8	1	37N42'50	97w08'10	6:28:33
Angelus 90	1	39N11'28	100w41'02	6:42:44
Angola 50	1	37N06'20	95w26'57	6:21:48
Anna 6	1	37N42	94w47	6:19:08
Annelly 40	1	37N58'20	97w12'03	6:28:48
Anness 87	1	37N28'55	97w43'42	6:30:55
Anson 96	1	37N21'55	97w31'46	6:30:07
Antelope 58	1	38N26'10	96w58'25	6:27:54
Anthony 39	1	37N09'12	98w01'51	6:32:07
Antioch 61	1	38N43'24	94w56'43	6:19:47
Antonino 26	1	38N47'02	99w23'32	6:37:34
Appanoose 30	1	38N42	95w28	6:21:52
Appleton 13	1	37N24	100w05	6:40:20
Arbor 77	1	39N42	101w01	6:44:04
Arcade 74	1	39N47	99w14	6:36:56
Arcadia 19	1	37N38'31	94w37'25	6:18:30
Arcola 27	1	38N45'03	97w56'00	6:31:44
Ardell 24	1	37N54'06	99w29'46	6:37:59
Argentine 105	1	39N04'30	94w40'20	6:18:41
Argonia 96	1	37N15'57	97w45'55	6:31:04
Arion 15	1	39N29	97w46	6:31:04
Arkalon 88	1	37N08'35	100w48'25	6:43:14
Arkansas City 18	1	37N03'43	97w02'17	6:28:09
Arlington 78	1	37N53'48	98w10'42	6:32:43
Arma 19	1	37N32'38	94w42'00	6:18:48
Arnold 68	1	38N38'25	100w02'45	6:40:11
Arrington 3	1	39N27'46	95w32'10	6:22:09
Arthur Heights 87	1	37N46'11	97w15'53	6:29:04
Arvonia 70	1	38N28'50	95w52'10	6:23:29
Ash Creek 27	1	38N39	98w12	6:32:48
Asherville 62	1	39N24'21	97w58'36	6:31:54
Ash Grove 53	1	39N09'41	98w21'42	6:33:27
Ashland 13	1	37N11'19	99w45'55	6:39:04
Ashland 81	1	39N12	96w33	6:26:12
Ash Rock 82	1	39N31	99w06	6:36:24
Ashton 96	1	37N04'59	97w14'18	6:28:57
Ash Valley 73	1	38N18'18	99w12'58	6:36:52
Assaria 85	1	38N40'49	97w36'15	6:30:25
Astor 36	2	38N28'22	101w54'09	6:47:37
Atchison 3	1	39N33'47	95w07'17	6:20:29
Athelstane 14	1	39N11	97w12	6:28:48
Athens 45	1	39N37	98w20	6:33:20
Athens 104	1	37N54'25	95w36'49	6:22:27
Athol 92	1	39N45'54	98w55'09	6:35:41
Atlanta 18	1	37N26'11	96w45'52	6:27:03
Atlas 19	1	37N22'02	94w43'20	6:18:53
Attica 39	1	37N14'29	98w13'35	6:32:54
Atwood 77	1	39N48'24	101w02'30	6:44:10
Aubry 46	1	38N46'15	94w40'15	6:18:41
Auburn 89	1	38N54'22	95w48'57	6:23:16
Augusta 8	1	37N41'12	97w58'35	6:31:54
Augustine 55	4	38N45	101w22	6:45:28
Aulne 58	1	38N16'34	97w04'35	6:28:18
Aurora 15	1	39N27'07	97w31'37	6:30:06
Aurora Park 87	1	37N44	97w17	6:29:08
Avian 63	1	37N05'45	95w36'05	6:22:24
Avilla 17	1	37N05	99w18	6:37:12
Axtell 59	1	39N52'18	96w15'31	6:25:02
Bachelor 37	1	37N50	96w11	6:24:44
Badger 11	1	37N09'30	94w37'57	6:18:32
Baileyville 66	1	39N50'40	96w11'05	6:24:44
Bain City 52	1	39N17'02	94w54'13	6:19:37
Baker 7	1	39N45'15	95w33'46	6:22:15
Bala 81	1	39N18'35	96w56'58	6:27:48
Balderson 59	1	39N57	96w31	6:26:04
Baldwin City 23	1	38N46'30	95w11'10	6:20:45
Balta 84	1	38N53'05	98w54'55	6:35:40
Bancroft 66	1	39N36'30	95w54'00	6:23:36
Barber 19	1	37N34'04	94w38'54	6:18:36
Barclay 70	1	38N34'38	95w52'48	6:23:31
Barnard 53	1	39N11'26	98w02'30	6:32:10
Barnes 101	1	39N42'43	96w52'27	6:27:30
Barnesville 6	1	38N00'55	94w39'40	6:18:39
Barret 75	1	39N40'15	96w27'00	6:25:48
Barrett 97	1	39N31	101w17	6:45:08
Bartlett 50	1	37N03'17	95w12'38	6:20:51
Barton 53	1	38N59'38	98w04'38	6:32:19
Basehor 52	1	39N08'30	94w56'18	6:19:45
Basil 48	1	37N30'59	98w05'24	6:32:22
Bassett 1	1	37N54'10	95w24'14	6:21:37
Bassettville 20	1	39N42	100w41	6:42:44
Batesville 104	1	37N50'10	95w52'13	6:23:29
Battle Creek 53	1	39N11	98w13	6:32:52
Battle Hill 57	1	38N29	97w25	6:29:40
Bavaria 85	1	38N47'50	97w45'16	6:31:01
Baxter Junction 11	1	37N01'43	94w44'46	6:18:59
Baxter Springs 11	1	37N02	94w44	6:18:56
Bayard 1	1	38N05	95w12	6:20:48
Bayneville 87	1	37N33'15	97w26'37	6:29:46
Bazaar 9	1	38N16'19	96w32'06	6:26:08
Bazine 68	1	38N26'40	99w41'30	6:38:46
Beagle 61	1	38N25'05	94w57'17	6:19:49
Bear Creek 38	2	37N50	101w55	6:47:40
Beardsley 77	1	39N48'52	101w13'38	6:44:55
Beattie 59	1	39N51'40	96w25'10	6:25:41
Beaumont 8	1	37N39'29	96w31'57	6:26:08
Beaver 5	1	38N38'25	98w40'00	6:34:40
Beckerville 66	1	39N36'35	96w09'49	6:24:39
Beeler 68	1	38N26'40	100w11'40	6:40:47
Beeson 29	1	37N45	100w01	6:40:04
Bellaire 87	1	37N45'45	97w16'00	6:29:04
Bellaire 92	1	39N47'54	98w40'33	6:34:42
Bellefont 29	1	37N52'21	99w39'27	6:38:38
Belle Plain 69	1	39N47	99w48	6:39:12
Belle Plaine 96	1	37N23'38	97w16'51	6:29:07
Belle Prairie 83	1	38N25	99w32	6:38:08
Belleville 79	1	39N49'28	97w37'56	6:30:32
Bellview School 70	1	38N47'25	95w55'40	6:23:43
Belmont 48	1	37N31'25	97w59'20	6:31:57
Belmont 89	1	39N02'50	95w38'00	6:22:32
Beloit 62	1	39N27'22	98w06'21	6:32:25
Belpre 24	1	37N57'00	99w06'00	6:36:24
Belvidere 49	1	37N27'01	99w04'47	6:36:19
Belvue 75	1	39N13'00	96w10'40	6:24:43
Bendena 22	1	39N44'28	95w10'45	6:20:43
Benedict 103	1	37N37'35	95w44'37	6:22:58
Benedict Junction 103	1	37N36'37	95w46'15	6:23:05
Benkelman 12	4	39N40	101w55	6:47:40
Bennett 48	1	37N26	97w52	6:31:28
Bennington 72	1	39N01'50	97w35'38	6:30:23
Bentley 87	1	37N53'10	97w31'00	6:30:04
Benton 8	1	37N47'20	97w06'30	6:28:26
Berlin 6	1	37N55'17	94w53'45	6:19:35
Berlin 39	1	37N10	97w57	6:31:48
Bern 66	1	39N57'44	95w58'18	6:23:53
Berryton 89	1	38N56'27	95w37'53	6:22:32
Bert Wettar 73	1	38N11'29	99w22'05	6:37:28
Berwet 87	1	37N47'08	97w29'00	6:29:56
Berwick 66	1	39N56'00	95w50'40	6:23:23
Bestwall 59	1	39N42'40	96w38'50	6:26:35
Bethany 71	1	39N31	98w39	6:34:36
Bethel 105	1	39N08'40	94w45'30	6:19:02

Beto Junction 7 1 38N24'20 95w41'30 6:22:46
Beulah 19 1 37N26'25 94w49'41 6:19:19
Beverly 53 1 39N00'46 97w58'31 6:31:54
Beverly Hills 105 1 39N09'28 94w44'06 6:18:56
Big Bend 79 1 39N57 97w52 6:31:28
Big Bow 94 3 37N33'54 101w33'40 6:46:15
Bigelow 59 1 39N37 96w31 6:26:04
Big Springs 23 1 39N00'47 95w29'05 6:21:56
Big Timber 83 1 38N38 99w19 6:37:16
Bird City 12 4 39N45'03 101w31'57 6:46:08
Birmingham 43 1 39N24'33 95w40'56 6:22:44
Bisbee 37 1 38N03'12 96w06'20 6:24:25
Bismark Grove 23 1 38N59'05 95w12'35 6:20:50
Bison 83 1 38N31'22 99w11'49 6:36:47
Black Jack 23 1 38N46'04 95w06'56 6:20:28
Black Wolf 27 1 38N45'30 98w21'42 6:33:27
Blaine 75 1 39N29'48 96w24'10 6:25:37
Blair 22 1 39N47'02 95w00'09 6:20:01
Blake 63 1 37N10'03 95w45'25 6:23:02
Blakely 31 1 38N55 96w46 6:27:04
Blakeman 77 1 39N49'20 101w07'00 6:44:28
Block 61 1 38N30'18 94w48'28 6:19:14
Blodgett 37 1 37N37'32 96w27'46 6:25:51
Bloom 29 1 37N29'11 99w53'45 6:39:35
Bloomington 8 1 37N34'40 96w52'20 6:27:29
Bloomington 71 1 39N27'06 98w47'12 6:35:09
Blue 75 1 39N11 96w33 6:26:12
Blue Hill 62 1 39N18'25 98w21'48 6:33:27
Bluemont Hill 81 1 39N11'34 96w33'35 6:26:14
Blue Mound 54 1 38N05'24 95w00'22 6:20:01
Blue Rapids 59 1 39N40'55 96w39'34 6:26:38
Blue Valley 75 1 39N27 96w38 6:26:32
Bluff City 39 1 37N04'35 97w52'29 6:31:30
B N Junction 30 1 38N33'42 95w16'16 6:21:05
Bodaville 81 1 39N43 96w52 6:27:28
Bogue 33 1 39N21'45 99w41'13 6:38:45
Boicourt 54 1 38N16'15 94w43'12 6:18:53
Bois d'Arc 8 1 37N35'47 96w55'30 6:27:42
Bolton 18 1 37N02 97w02 6:28:08
Bolton 63 1 37N09'24 95w48'19 6:23:13
Bonaville 57 1 38N33 97w32 6:30:08
Bonita 46 1 38N48'40 94w48'52 6:19:15
Bonner Springs 105 1 39N03'35 94w53'00 6:19:32
Bonnie Brae 87 1 37N40'55 97w14'50 6:28:59
Bonnie Ridge 85 1 38N50 97w36 6:30:24
Bosse 42 1 38N05'13 99w50'00 6:39:20
Boyd 5 1 38N31'07 98w50'53 6:35:24
Boyle 44 1 39N20'25 95w21'09 6:21:25
Bradford 99 1 38N49'18 96w02'20 6:24:09
Brainerd 8 1 37N57'04 97w05'42 6:28:23
Brantford 101 1 39N42'44 97w21'34 6:29:26
Brazilton 19 1 37N33'35 94w57'26 6:19:50
Bremen 59 1 39N54'05 96w47'20 6:27:09
Brenham 49 1 37N36'35 99w12'28 6:36:50
Breton 97 1 39N27'09 100w48'49 6:43:15
Brewer 72 1 39N07'28 97w47'15 6:31:09
Brewster 97 1 39N22'00 101w22'35 6:45:30
Bridgeport 85 1 38N37'40 97w36'46 6:30:27
Broken Arrow Park 23 1 38N55'51 95w14'20 6:20:57
Bronson 1 1 37N53'45 95w04'23 6:20:18
Brookdale 83 1 38N32 99w25 6:37:40
Brookhaven 87 1 37N41'45 97w09'16 6:28:37
Brookhaven Estates 87 1 37N41 97w18 6:29:12
Brookridge 46 1 38N58 94w41 6:18:44
Brooks 103 1 37N23'05 95w36'09 6:22:25
Brookville 85 1 38N46'30 97w52'05 6:31:28
Broughton 14 1 39N19'17 97w03'11 6:28:13
Brown 13 1 37N23 99w48 6:39:12
Browndale 14 1 39N21'35 97w21'02 6:29:24
Brownell 68 1 38N38'25 99w44'45 6:38:59
Browns Creek 45 1 39N37 98w13 6:32:52
Browns Grove 73 1 38N13 99w31 6:38:04
Browns Spur 48 1 37N39 98w07 6:32:28
Brownstone 50 1 37N19'58 95w11'38 6:20:47
Brownville 97 1 39N11'10 101w21'11 6:45:25
Bruno 8 1 37N41 97w06 6:28:24
Bryant 33 1 39N12 100w04 6:40:16
Buck Creek 44 1 39N03'00 95w16'55 6:21:08
Buckeye 21 1 39N02'48 97w10'00 6:28:40
Bucklin 29 1 37N32'50 99w38'02 6:38:32
Bucyrus 61 1 38N43'35 94w43'05 6:18:52
Buffalo 103 1 37N42'35 95w41'50 6:22:47
Buffville 103 1 37N28'57 95w39'36 6:22:38
Buhler 78 1 38N08'04 97w46'11 6:31:05
Bunker Hill 84 1 38N52'33 98w42'13 6:34:49
Burden 18 1 37N18'46 96w45'14 6:27:01
Burdett 73 1 38N11'31 99w31'35 6:38:06
Burdick 64 1 38N33'49 96w50'43 6:27:23
Burkett 37 1 38N02'30 96w15'54 6:25:04
Burlingame 70 1 38N45'19 95w00'08 6:20:01
Burlington 16 1 38N11'40 95w44'33 6:22:58
Burns 58 1 38N05'25 96w53'10 6:27:33
Burntwood 77 1 39N56 101w16 6:45:04
Burr Oak 45 1 39N51'58 98w18'17 6:33:13
Burrton 40 1 38N01'26 97w40'10 6:30:41
Busby 25 1 37N28'10 96w02'39 6:24:11
Bush City 2 1 38N12'40 95w08'40 6:20:35
Bushnell 96 1 37N21'42 97w09'35 6:28:38
Bushong 56 1 38N38'35 96w15'25 6:25:02
Bushton 80 1 38N30'45 98w23'42 6:33:35
Butler 49 1 37N41 99w24 6:37:36
Buttermilk 17 1 37N06'10 99w19'30 6:37:18
Buxton 103 1 37N26'54 95w55'13 6:23:41
Byers 76 1 37N47'15 98w52'00 6:35:28
Byron 93 1 38N13 98w38 6:34:32
Cadmus 54 1 38N20'44 94w53'57 6:19:36
Cairo 76 1 37N39'00 98w33'15 6:34:13
Calderhead 101 1 39N40'59 97w19'51 6:29:19
Caldwell 96 1 37N01'56 97w36'24 6:30:26
Calhoun 12 4 39N56 101w41 6:46:44
California 16 1 38N18 95w53 6:23:32
Calista 48 1 37N38'23 98w16'56 6:33:08
Callahan 87 1 37N41 97w25 6:29:40
Calvert 69 1 39N50'59 99w45'27 6:39:02
Calvin 45 1 39N42 98w13 6:32:52
Cambria 85 1 38N55 97w33 6:30:12
Cambridge 18 1 37N18'58 96w39'51 6:26:39
Cameron 18 1 37N04'37 96w51'13 6:27:25
Camp Fifty 19 1 37N32'30 94w44'30 6:18:58
Camp Forsyth 31 1 39N11 96w52 6:27:28
Camp Funston 81 1 39N06 96w44 6:26:56
Camp Naish 105 1 39N05 94w45 6:19:00
Campus 32 1 39N08 100w52 6:43:28
Camp Whiteside 31 1 39N06 96w47 6:27:08
Canada 50 1 37N07 95w27 6:21:48
Canada 58 1 38N21'15 97w06'45 6:28:27
Caney 63 1 37N00'41 95w56'06 6:23:44
Caneyville 10 1 37N15 96w27 6:25:48
Canton 57 1 38N23'10 97w25'40 6:29:43
Canville 67 1 37N37 95w27 6:21:48
Capaldo 19 1 37N28'04 94w43'35 6:18:54
Capioma 66 1 39N46'36 95w49'12 6:23:17
Carbondale 70 1 38N49'07 95w41'20 6:22:45
Carden 59 1 39N49'40 96w34'50 6:26:19
Carlton 21 1 38N41'14 97w17'35 6:29:10
Carlyle 1 1 37N37'37 95w23'26 6:21:34
Carmi 76 1 37N47 98w38 6:34:32
Carneiro 27 1 38N44'20 98w01'50 6:32:07
Carona 11 1 37N16'49 94w52'06 6:19:28
Carr Creek 62 1 39N26 98w26 6:33:44
Caruso 91 2 39N20'19 101w48'54 6:47:16
Cassoday 8 1 38N02'20 96w38'20 6:26:33
Castle 57 1 38N23 97w52 6:31:28
Castleton 78 1 37N52'04 97w58'08 6:31:53
Catharine 26 1 38N55'38 99w12'59 6:36:52
Catlin 58 1 38N13 97w06 6:28:24
Cato 19 1 37N40'04 94w44'23 6:18:58
Cave 95 3 37N21'31 101w08'27 6:44:34
Cave Springs 25 1 37N32'00 96w07'20 6:24:29
Cawker City 62 1 39N30'45 98w26'00 6:33:44
Cedar 46 1 38N58'45 94w56'03 6:19:44
Cedar 92 1 39N39'26 98w56'24 6:35:46
Cedar Bluffs 20 1 39N58'44 100w33'41 6:42:15
Cedar Point 9 1 38N15'36 96w49'10 6:27:17
Cedar Vale 10 1 37N06'15 96w30'00 6:26:00
Cedron 53 1 39N11 98w26 6:33:44
Celia 77 1 39N48 101w18 6:45:12
Centerview 24 1 37N48'55 99w16'05 6:37:04
Centerville 54 1 38N13'15 95w00'50 6:20:03
Central 2 1 38N16'20 95w23'00 6:21:32
Centralia 66 1 39N43'33 96w07'37 6:24:30
Centropolis 30 1 38N42'58 95w21'00 6:21:24
Cessna 87 1 37N38'19 97w24'46 6:29:39
Chanute 67 1 37N40'45 95w27'25 6:21:50
Chapman 21 1 38N58'20 97w01'20 6:28:05
Chardon 77 1 39N39'17 101w03'24 6:44:14
Charleston 35 4 37N51'55 100w33'52 6:42:15
Charters Corner 78 1 38N03'27 98w10'44 6:32:43
Chase 80 1 38N21'18 98w20'57 6:33:24
Chautauqua 10 1 37N01'13 96w10'35 6:24:42
Cheever 21 1 39N05 97w12 6:28:48
Chelsea 8 1 37N54'14 96w46'28 6:27:06
Cheney 87 1 37N37'48 97w46'56 6:31:08
Chepstow 101 1 39N37'25 96w54'02 6:27:36
Cherokee 19 1 37N20'45 94w48'31 6:19:14
Cherry 63 1 37N19 95w33 6:22:12
Cherry Creek 12 4 39N47 101w57 6:47:48
Cherryvale 63 1 37N16'13 95w33'08 6:22:13
Chetopa 50 1 37N02'14 95w05'23 6:20:22
Chevron 86 4 38N18'45 100w54'35 6:43:38
Cheyenne 71 1 39N10'36 98w38'19 6:34:33
Cheyenne Gap 71 1 39N13'12 98w38'52 6:34:35
Chicaskia 39 1 37N21 97w52 6:31:28
Chicopee 19 1 37N22'55 94w44'30 6:18:58
Childs Acres 87 1 37N46'20 97w25'17 6:29:41
Chiles 61 1 38N40'47 94w45'41 6:19:03
Chisholm 87 1 37N38 97w21 6:29:24
Chouteau 46 1 39N02'50 94w49'48 6:19:19
Cicero 96 1 37N20'02 97w20'25 6:29:22
Cimarron 35 4 37N48'24 100w20'52 6:41:23
Circleville 43 1 39N30'30 95w51'30 6:23:26
Civic Center 105 1 39N06 94w40 6:18:40
Claflin 5 1 38N31'30 98w32'00 6:34:08
Clare 46 1 38N49'37 94w52'16 6:19:29
Clarence 5 1 38N24 98w59 6:35:56
Clark 58 1 38N29 97w06 6:28:24
Clarks Creek 64 1 38N44 96w53 6:27:32
Claudell 92 1 39N39'45 99w01'44 6:36:07
Clay Center 8 1 37N31'10 96w46'15 6:27:05
Clay Center 14 1 39N22'37 97w07'28 6:28:30
Clayton 69 1 39N44'15 100w10'38 6:40:43
Clearfield 23 1 38N49'34 95w05'36 6:20:22
Clear Fork 59 1 39N37 96w24 6:25:36
Clearview City 46 1 38N57 95w00 6:20:00
Clearwater 87 1 37N30'10 97w30'15 6:30:01
Clements 9 1 38N18'00 96w44'26 6:26:58
Cleveland 48 1 37N33'06 98w08'00 6:32:32
Cleveland Run 12 4 39N55 101w48 6:47:12
Clifford 8 1 38N03 96w59 6:27:56
Clifton 101 1 39N34'02 97w16'42 6:29:07
Climax 37 1 37N43'11 96w13'23 6:24:54
Clinton 23 1 38N54'42 95w23'25 6:21:34
Clonmel 87 1 37N33'46 97w33'13 6:30:13
Cloverdale 10 1 37N13'37 96w29'20 6:25:57
Cloverdale 78 1 38N04 97w57 6:31:48
Cloverdale 85 1 38N50 97w36 6:30:24
Clyde 15 1 39N35'28 97w23'55 6:29:36
Coalvale 19 1 37N36'56 94w38'55 6:18:36
Coats 76 1 37N30'43 98w49'26 6:35:18
Cochrane 52 1 39N16'00 94w52'43 6:19:31
Cockerill 19 1 37N33 94w37 6:18:28
Codell 82 1 39N11'36 99w10'37 6:36:42
Coffeyville 63 1 37N02'14 95w36'58 6:22:28
Cokedale 11 1 37N14'48 94w53'33 6:19:34
Colby 97 1 39N23'45 101w03'07 6:44:12
Coldspur 46 1 39N00'16 94w55'28 6:19:42
Coldwater 17 1 37N16'08 99w19'35 6:37:18
Coleman 87 1 37N51'51 97w27'49 6:29:51
Coleman 101 1 39N47 97w12 6:28:48
Collano 60 1 37N17'56 100w30'25 6:42:02
College 19 1 37N26 94w42 6:18:48
Collyer 98 1 39N02'08 100w07'03 6:40:28
Colony 2 1 38N04'15 95w21'55 6:21:28
Colorado 53 1 39N00 97w59 6:31:56
Columbia 27 1 38N49 98w19 6:33:16
Columbus 11 1 37N10'09 94w50'38 6:19:23
Colwich 87 1 37N46'45 97w32'10 6:30:09
Comanche 5 1 38N18 98w35 6:34:20
Commonwealth 11 1 37N00'04 94w44'25 6:18:58
Concordia 15 1 39N34'15 97w39'44 6:30:39
Conkling 73 1 38N19 99w19 6:37:16
Connell 87 1 37N37'10 97w17'41 6:29:11
Conway 57 1 38N22'10 96w47'10 6:27:09
Conway Springs 96 1 37N23'25 97w38'31 6:30:34
Cook 15 1 39N32'50 97w36'42 6:30:27
Cook 20 1 39N37 100w41 6:42:44
Cookville 104 1 37N49'13 95w35'31 6:22:22
Coolidge 38 2 38N02'30 102w00'30 6:48:02
Copeland 35 3 37N32'31 100w37'45 6:42:31
Cora 92 1 39N53'34 98w39'48 6:34:39
Corbin 63 1 37N15'07 95w33'15 6:22:13
Corbin 96 1 37N07'35 97w32'37 6:30:10
Corinth 71 1 39N24'58 98w32'42 6:34:11
Corinth Square Center 46 1 39N00 94w37 6:18:28
Cornell 19 1 37N27'48 94w37'50 6:18:31
Corning 66 1 39N39'26 96w01'45 6:24:07
Coronado 102 4 38N29'09 101w18'15 6:45:13
Corwin 39 1 37N05'03 98w18'15 6:33:13
Cottage Grove 1 1 37N45 95w20 6:21:20
Cottage Hill 59 1 39N35'50 96w44'58 6:27:00
Cottonwood 9 1 38N17 96w44 6:26:56
Cottonwood Falls 9 1 38N22'20 96w32'33 6:26:10
Council Grove 64 1 38N39'40 96w29'30 6:25:58
Countryside 46 1 39N01'00 94w39'15 6:18:37
County Acres 87 1 37N41'56 97w25'54 6:29:44
Coursens Grove 62 1 39N16'36 97w58'07 6:31:52
Courtland 79 1 39N46'53 97w53'33 6:31:34
Covert 71 1 39N16'49 98w48'38 6:35:15
Cow Town 87 1 37N41'38 97w21'26 6:29:26
Coyville 103 1 37N41'10 95w53'50 6:23:35
Craig 46 1 38N57'57 94w48'58 6:19:16
Crandall 16 1 38N05 95w38 6:22:32
Crane 63 1 37N16'46 95w47'48 6:23:11
Cravensville 11 1 37N01'55 94w50'40 6:19:23
Crawford 80 1 38N30'48 98w02'05 6:32:08
Creek 96 1 37N21 97w45 6:31:00
Crestline 11 1 37N10'15 94w42'15 6:18:49
Creswell 18 1 37N05 97w01 6:28:04
Crisfield 39 1 37N10'20 98w18'40 6:33:15
Critzer 54 1 38N08'24 94w54'45 6:19:39
Croft 76 1 37N30'12 98w59'40 6:35:59
Crooked Creek 60 1 37N24 100w20 6:41:20
Croweburg 19 1 37N33'25 94w39'57 6:18:40
Cruppers Corner 78 1 37N58'12 97w56'24 6:31:46
Crystal Plains 92 1 39N42 98w40 6:34:40
Crystal Springs 39 1 37N15'43 98w08'04 6:32:32
Cuba 79 1 39N48'10 97w27'20 6:29:49
Cullen Village 89 1 38N56'34 95w42'09 6:22:49
Cullison 76 1 37N37'50 98w54'18 6:35:37
Culver 72 1 38N58'15 97w45'31 6:31:02
Cummings 3 1 39N27'46 95w14'50 6:20:59
Cunningham 48 1 37N38'38 98w25'51 6:33:43
Cunningham Highlands 46 1 39N00 94w41 6:18:44
Curranville 19 1 37N30'49 94w37'53 6:18:32
Cutler 30 1 38N31 95w07 6:20:28
Daisy Hill 11 1 37N19'40 94w46'40 6:19:07
Dalbey 3 1 39N29'50 95w04'38 6:20:19
Dale 18 1 37N20'15 97w03'13 6:28:13
Dale 48 1 37N36 97w58 6:31:52
Dalton 96 1 37N16'09 97w16'20 6:29:05
Damar 82 1 39N19'08 99w34'56 6:38:20
Danville 39 1 37N17'10 97w53'30 6:31:34
Darlington 40 1 37N58 97w19 6:29:16
Darlow 78 1 37N56'27 97w56'59 6:31:48
Dartmouth 5 1 38N21'48 98w38'44 6:34:35
Dearing 63 1 37N03'31 95w42'47 6:22:51
Deerfield 47 5 37N58'47 101w07'58 6:44:32
Deerhead 4 1 37N14'18 98w54'41 6:35:39
De Graff 8 1 37N58'52 96w51'45 6:27:27
Delano 87 1 37N41 97w27 6:29:48
Delavan 64 1 38N39'22 96w48'47 6:27:15
Delhi 71 1 39N11 98w33 6:34:12
Delia 43 1 39N14'26 95w58'00 6:23:52
Dellvale 69 1 39N46'20 100w02'05 6:40:08
Delmore 57 1 38N29 97w32 6:30:08
Delphos 72 1 39N16'26 97w46'18 6:31:05
Denison 43 1 39N23'30 95w37'40 6:22:31
Denmark 53 1 39N05'21 98w17'12 6:33:09
Dennis 50 1 37N20'49 95w24'45 6:21:39
Densmore 69 1 39N38'18 99w44'20 6:38:57
Dent 12 4 39N42 101w45 6:47:00
Denton 22 1 39N43'58 95w16'09 6:21:05
Dentonia 45 1 39N41'02 98w28'02 6:33:52
Denton-McWorter Addition 87 1 37N46 97w28 6:29:52
Derby 87 1 37N32'44 97w16'07 6:29:04
Dermot 65 3 37N07 101w38 6:46:32
De Soto 46 1 38N58'45 94w58'06 6:19:52
Detroit 21 1 37N56'06 97w07'19 6:28:29

Devizes 69 1 39N59'28 100w03'25 6:40:14
Devon 6 1 37N55'20 94w49'08 6:19:17
Dexter 18 1 37N10'38 96w42'51 6:26:51
Diamond Creek 9 1 38N26 96w42 6:26:48
Diamond Springs 64 1 38N33'27 96w44'39 6:26:59
Diamond Valley 64 1 38N34 96w45 6:27:00
Dighton 51 1 38N28'55 100w28'00 6:41:52
Dillon 21 1 38N41'37 97w08'48 6:28:35
Dillwyn 93 1 37N58'15 98w52'46 6:35:31
Dispatch 92 1 39N35'47 98w30'17 6:34:01
Dixon 96 1 37N15 97w45 6:31:00
Dodge City 29 1 37N45'10 100w01'00 6:40:04
Doniphan 22 1 39N38'30 95w04'50 6:20:19
Dor 92 1 39N37 99w01 6:36:04
Dorrance 84 1 38N50'48 98w35'21 6:34:21
Doster 96 1 37N03'40 97w42'42 6:30:51
Douglass 8 1 37N31'10 97w00'45 6:28:03
Dover 89 1 38N57'53 95w56'14 6:23:45
Downing 64 1 38N44'25 96w34'25 6:26:18
Downs 71 1 39N30'08 98w32'47 6:34:11
Doyle 58 1 38N14 96w53 6:27:32
Dragoon 70 1 38N43 95w50 6:23:20
Dresden 20 1 39N37'27 100w25'19 6:41:41
Drexel Corner 61 1 38N28'35 94w40'35 6:18:42
Driftwood 77 1 39N57 101w04 6:44:16
Drum Creek 63 1 37N14 95w36 6:22:24
Drury 96 1 37N02'08 97w28'39 6:29:55
Dry Wood 19 1 37N39'35 94w42'45 6:18:51
Dubuque 5 1 38N41'45 98w36'31 6:34:26
Duck Creek 103 1 37N26 95w54 6:23:36
Dudley 41 3 37N34 101w01 6:44:04
Duluth 75 1 39N31'29 96w13'22 6:24:53
Dunavant 44 1 39N18'07 95w19'57 6:21:20
Dundee 5 1 38N18'31 98w53'25 6:35:34
Dungans Crossing 42 1 38N13'59 99w39'41 6:38:39
Dunkirk 19 1 37N29'04 94w44'30 6:18:58
Dunlap 64 1 38N34'35 96w21'56 6:25:28
Dunlay 54 1 38N15'30 94w59'50 6:19:59
Duquoin 39 1 37N22'58 98w04'24 6:32:18
Durand 104 1 37N53'23 95w41'34 6:22:46
Durham 58 1 38N29'10 97w13'40 6:28:55
Durham Park 58 1 38N29 97w12 6:28:48
Dwight 64 1 38N50'40 96w35'35 6:26:22
Earlton 67 1 37N35'17 95w28'08 6:21:53
Eastborough 87 1 37N41'17 97w15'48 6:29:03
East Branch 58 1 38N13 97w12 6:28:48
East Cooper 93 1 38N03 98w32 6:34:08
East El Dorado 8 1 37N49'15 96w50'07 6:27:20
East Fairmount 52 1 39N11'13 94w55'08 6:19:41
East Forbes 89 1 39N02 95w41 6:22:44
East Hale 97 1 39N23 101w13 6:44:52
East Hamilton 26 1 39N04 99w27 6:37:48
East Hess 35 3 37N36 100w16 6:41:04
East Hibbard 47 2 38N10 101w13 6:44:52
East Hutchinson 78 1 38N04 97w57 6:31:48
Easton 52 1 39N20'42 95w06'56 6:20:28
East Saline 90 1 39N14 100w13 6:40:52
Eastshore 58 1 38N22'55 97w04'25 6:28:18
East Washington 80 1 38N13 97w58 6:31:52
Eaton 18 1 37N13'47 96w46'12 6:27:05
Edalgo 53 1 38N58'18 98w02'48 6:32:11
Edgerton 46 1 38N45'53 95w00'28 6:20:02
Edison 19 1 37N30'50 94w44'47 6:18:59
Edmond 69 1 39N37'38 99w49'20 6:39:17
Edna 50 1 37N03'35 95w21'33 6:21:26
Edson 91 2 39N20'14 101w32'24 6:46:10
Edward 6 1 37N47'00 94w41'50 6:18:47
Edwards 102 4 38N37 101w14 6:44:56
Edwardsville 105 1 39N03'40 94w49'10 6:19:17
Effingham 3 1 39N31'20 95w24'02 6:21:36
Elbing 8 1 38N03'10 97w07'39 6:28:31
El Dorado 8 1 37N49'02 96w51'43 6:27:27
Eldred 4 1 37N03'02 98w46'03 6:35:04
Elgin 10 1 37N00'16 96w16'35 6:25:06
Elkader 55 4 38N47'36 100w51'30 6:43:26
Elk City 63 1 37N17'21 95w54'41 6:23:39
Elk Creek 79 1 39N42 97w25 6:29:40
Elk Falls 25 1 37N22'02 96w11'18 6:24:45
Elkhart 65 3 37N00'29 101w53'23 6:47:34
Elkhorn 53 1 39N00 98w06 6:32:24
Ellinor 9 1 38N23'36 96w25'40 6:25:43
Ellinwood 5 1 38N21'20 98w34'50 6:34:19
Ellis 26 1 38N56'17 99w33'37 6:38:14
Ellsworth 27 1 38N43'50 98w13'40 6:32:55
Elmdale 9 1 38N22'25 96w38'40 6:26:35
Elmer 78 1 37N58'10 97w55'48 6:31:43
Elmerdaro 56 1 38N15 96w03 6:24:12
Elm Grove 50 1 37N04 95w19 6:21:16
Elm Hollow Corner 81 1 39N11'22 96w42'43 6:26:51
Elmhurst 46 1 38N58'28 94w41'05 6:18:44
Elm Mills 4 1 37N26'02 98w41'12 6:34:45
Elmo 21 1 38N41'03 97w13'47 6:28:55
Elmont 89 1 39N09'55 95w42'10 6:22:49
Elsmore 1 1 37N47'40 95w09'00 6:20:36
Elwood 22 1 39N46'20 94w52'20 6:19:29
Elyria 57 1 38N17'26 97w37'36 6:30:30
Eminence 104 1 37N47 95w41 6:22:44
Emma 40 1 38N08 97w25 6:29:40
Emmeram 26 1 38N57'31 99w07'55 6:36:32
Emmett 75 1 39N18'26 96w03'21 6:24:13
Empire City 11 1 37N05 94w38 6:18:32
Emporia 56 1 38N24'14 96w10'53 6:24:44
Emporia Junction 56 1 38N24'10 96w09'40 6:24:39
Englevale 19 1 37N35'38 94w43'38 6:18:55
Englewood 13 1 37N02'18 99w58'59 6:39:56
Enosdale 101 1 39N46'16 97w09'40 6:28:39
Ensign 35 3 37N39'10 100w14'00 6:40:56
Enterprise 21 1 38N54'10 97w07'00 6:28:28
Erie 18 1 36N59'58 97w04'30 6:28:18
Erie 67 1 37N34'05 95w14'35 6:20:58
Erving 45 1 39N37 98w27 6:33:48
Esbon 45 1 39N49'20 98w26'08 6:33:45
Eskridge 99 1 38N51'32 96w06'32 6:24:26
Ettensan 52 1 39N13'33 94w51'46 6:19:27
Eudora 23 1 38N56'36 95w05'54 6:20:24
Eureka 37 1 37N49'26 96w17'20 6:25:09
Eureka Lake 81 1 39N09'07 96w38'20 6:26:33
Evan 48 1 37N41 97w52 6:31:28
Everest 7 1 39N40'38 95w25'28 6:21:42
Everett 104 1 37N59 95w39 6:22:36
Evergreen 12 4 39N52 101w28 6:45:52
Ewell 96 1 37N20'24 97w41'25 6:30:46
Exeter 14 1 39N16 97w12 6:28:48
Fairfax 15 1 39N08'30 94w36'45 6:18:27
Fairfax 70 1 38N43 95w40 6:22:40
Fairfield 84 1 38N44 98w46 6:35:04
Fairmont 81 1 39N10'37 96w32'55 6:26:12
Fairmont Addition 81 1 39N12 96w33 6:26:12
Fairmount 52 1 39N11'30 94w56'07 6:19:44
Fairplay 58 1 38N14 96w59 6:27:56
Fairport 84 1 39N02'45 99w01'46 6:36:07
Fairview 7 1 39N50'28 95w43'40 6:22:55
Fairway 46 1 39N01'20 94w37'54 6:18:32
Fall Leaf 2 1 38N58'27 95w06'37 6:20:26
Fall River 37 1 37N36'28 96w01'40 6:24:07
Falun 85 1 38N40'16 97w45'33 6:31:02
Fancy Creek 81 1 39N25 96w53 6:27:32
Fanning 22 1 39N50'05 95w09'40 6:20:39
Fargo 88 1 37N09 100w45 6:43:00
Farhman 5 1 38N34'46 98w29'56 6:34:00
Farlington 19 1 37N37'04 94w49'39 6:19:19
Farlinville 54 1 38N14'00 94w51'13 6:19:25
Farmington 3 1 39N31'07 95w18'34 6:21:14
Farmington 78 1 38N04 97w57 6:31:48
Faulkner 11 1 37N06'05 95w00'41 6:20:03
Fawn Creek 63 1 37N03 95w43 6:22:52
Fellsburg 24 1 37N48'43 99w10'30 6:36:42
Fern 50 1 37N20'49 95w22'34 6:21:30
Fiat 25 1 37N32'27 96w12'26 6:24:50
Fidelity 66 1 39N47'24 97w47'19 6:31:09
Filler 19 1 37N22'57 94w49'30 6:19:18
Finley 20 1 39N58 100w41 6:42:44
Five Creeks 14 1 39N21 97w19 6:29:16
Five Points 52 1 39N13'49 95w01'52 6:20:07
Fleming 19 1 37N22'05 94w46'58 6:19:08
Flora 21 1 39N05 97w18 6:29:12
Floral 18 1 37N21'10 96w55'14 6:27:41
Florence 58 1 38N14'40 96w55'40 6:27:43
Flush 75 1 39N17'40 96w26'25 6:25:46
Fontana 61 1 38N25'33 94w50'17 6:19:21
Foote 35 4 37N56 100w20 6:41:20
Ford 29 1 37N38'10 99w45'13 6:39:01
Forest City 4 1 37N19'21 98w43'49 6:34:55
Forest Hills 87 1 37N41'25 97w14'18 6:28:57
Formoso 45 1 39N46'48 97w59'31 6:31:58
Forney 71 1 39N24'56 98w37'11 6:34:29
Forrester 68 1 38N31 99w59 6:39:56
Fort Dodge 29 1 37N43'55 99w56'06 6:39:44
Fort Downer 98 1 38N50'27 99w58'40 6:39:55
Fort Riley 31 1 39N04 96w47 6:27:08
Fort Scott 6 1 37N50'23 94w42'29 6:18:50
Fostoria 75 1 39N26'23 96w30'27 6:26:02
Fountain 72 1 39N11 97w52 6:31:28
Four Corners 70 1 38N46'57 95w41'10 6:22:45
Four Mile 64 1 38N35 96w31 6:26:04
Fowler 60 1 37N23'08 100w11'43 6:40:47
Fox Town 19 1 37N30'49 94w38'55 6:18:36
Fragrant Hill 21 1 39N05 97w01 6:28:04
Frankfort 59 1 39N42'20 96w25'00 6:25:40
Franklin 19 1 37N31'35 94w42'20 6:18:49
Frantz 27 1 38N33'05 98w14'17 6:32:57
Frederick 80 1 38N30'48 98w16'05 6:33:04
Fredonia 103 1 37N32'02 95w49'35 6:23:18
Freemount 57 1 38N32'43 97w46'38 6:31:07
Freeport 39 1 37N11'55 97w51'24 6:31:26
Fremont 56 1 38N30 96w09 6:24:36
Friend 28 4 38N15'36 100w54'40 6:43:39
Frisbie 46 1 39N00'52 94w53'13 6:19:33
Frizell 73 1 38N09'58 99w12'50 6:36:51
Frontenac 19 1 37N27'20 94w41'20 6:18:45
Fruitland 63 1 37N12'14 95w42'38 6:22:51
Fuller 19 1 37N31'20 94w37'10 6:18:29
Fulton 6 1 38N00'36 94w43'10 6:18:53
Furley 87 1 37N52'45 97w12'45 6:28:51
Gaeland 32 1 38N56 100w44 6:42:56
Galatia 5 1 38N38'30 98w57'30 6:35:50
Gale 58 1 38N24 97w06 6:28:24
Galena 11 1 37N04'33 94w38'22 6:18:33
Galesburg 67 1 37N28'25 95w21'30 6:21:26
Galt 80 1 38N27'52 98w05'03 6:32:20
Galva 57 1 38N22'55 97w32'14 6:30:09
Gano 28 4 38N11'32 100w54'39 6:43:39
Garden City 28 4 37N58'18 100w52'20 6:43:29
Garden Plain 87 1 37N39'30 97w41'00 6:30:44
Gardner 46 1 38N48'39 94w55'37 6:19:42
Gardner Lake 46 1 38N49 94w55 6:19:40
Garfield 73 1 38N04'40 99w14'40 6:36:59
Garfield Center 14 1 39N31'25 97w07'40 6:28:31
Garland 6 1 37N43'54 94w37'20 6:18:29
Garnett 2 1 38N16'50 95w14'30 6:20:58
Garvin 50 1 37N14'31 95w11'38 6:20:47
Gas 1 1 37N55'25 95w20'45 6:21:23
Gaylord 92 1 39N38'38 98w50'50 6:35:23
Geary 22 1 39N46 94w57 6:19:48
Gem 97 1 39N25'40 100w53'50 6:43:35
Geneseo 80 1 38N30'58 98w09'23 6:32:38
Geneva 1 1 38N01'01 95w29'38 6:21:59
Georgia 48 1 37N37'40 98w00'30 6:32:02
Gerlane 4 1 37N09'09 98w32'58 6:34:12
German 92 1 39N58 99w01 6:36:04
Gettysburg 33 1 39N24 100w02 6:40:08
Geuda Springs 96 1 37N06'51 97w08'56 6:28:36
Gibbs 10 1 37N08'15 96w19'36 6:25:18
Gilbert 62 1 39N28'58 98w02'27 6:32:10
Gill 14 1 39N11 97w07 6:28:28
Gilman 66 1 39N52 95w57 6:23:48
Girard 19 1 37N30'40 94w50'16 6:19:21
Glade 74 1 39N41'05 99w18'34 6:37:14
Gladstone 9 1 38N20'35 96w29'39 6:25:59
Glasco 15 1 39N21'24 97w50'27 6:31:22
Glen Crouse 18 1 37N26'00 96w37'00 6:26:28
Glendale 85 1 38N53'54 97w52'29 6:31:30
Glen Elder 62 1 39N29'55 98w18'30 6:33:14
Glenlock 2 1 38N18'36 95w20'30 6:21:22
Glenville 87 1 37N36'45 97w20'50 6:29:23
Glenwood 74 1 39N58 99w14 6:36:56
Glick 49 1 37N28 99w05 6:36:20
Globe 23 1 38N46'56 95w23'58 6:21:36
Goddard 87 1 37N39'35 97w34'30 6:30:18
Godfrey 6 1 37N45'42 94w42'35 6:18:50
Goessel 58 1 38N14'47 97w20'55 6:29:24
Goff 66 1 39N39'50 95w55'55 6:23:44
Golden Belt 53 1 38N55 98w19 6:33:16
Golden Belt Spur 85 1 38N50 97w36 6:30:24
Goldenrod 53 1 39N03'36 98w14'39 6:32:59
Good Intent 3 1 39N36'00 95w13'00 6:20:52
Goodland 91 2 39N21'03 101w42'35 6:46:50
Goodman 46 1 39N01 94w42 6:18:48
Goodrich 54 1 38N17'05 94w59'30 6:19:58
Gordon 8 1 37N35'19 96w59'25 6:27:58
Gore 96 1 37N25 97w11 6:28:44
Gorham 84 1 38N52'54 99w01'22 6:36:05
Goshen 14 1 39N31 97w01 6:28:04
Gove 32 1 38N57'28 100w29'18 6:41:57
Grafton 10 1 37N12'01 96w08'58 6:24:36
Graham 33 1 39N30 99w48 6:39:12
Grainfield 32 1 39N06'49 100w27'53 6:41:52
Granada 66 1 39N43'12 95w47'36 6:23:10
Grand River 87 1 37N41 97w46 6:31:04
Grand Summit 18 1 37N22'05 96w32'47 6:26:11
Grandview 105 1 39N04'02 94w53'53 6:19:36
Grandview Plaza 31 1 39N10'45 98w47'20 6:35:09
Granite 74 1 39N58 99w28 6:37:52
Grant 53 1 39N07'07 98w20'00 6:33:20
Grantville 44 1 39N05'00 95w33'40 6:22:15
Grasshopper 3 1 39N37 95w29 6:21:56
Gray 42 1 38N09'30 99w38'30 6:38:34
Grays Park 105 1 39N03'00 94w38'00 6:18:32
Great Bend 5 1 38N21'52 98w45'52 6:35:03
Greeley 2 1 38N22'00 95w07'36 6:20:30
Green 14 1 39N25'40 97w00'06 6:28:00
Greenbush 19 1 37N30'52 94w59'16 6:19:57
Green Garden 27 1 38N34 98w19 6:33:16
Greenleaf 101 1 39N43'42 96w58'33 6:27:54
Greensburg 49 1 37N36'10 99w17'32 6:37:10
Greenwich 87 1 37N46'58 97w12'12 6:28:49
Greenwich Heights 87 1 37N39'12 97w12'18 6:28:49
Grenola 25 1 37N20'55 96w27'01 6:25:48
Gretna 74 1 39N45'55 99w12'45 6:36:51
Gridley 16 1 38N05'52 95w53'00 6:23:32
Grigston 86 4 38N29'05 100w43'00 6:42:52
Grinnell 55 1 39N07'38 100w37'43 6:42:31
Grinter Heights 105 1 39N04'26 94w45'50 6:19:03
Gross 19 1 37N36'03 94w38'58 6:18:36
Grove 50 1 37N19'30 95w25'50 6:21:43
Grove 89 1 39N10'03 95w51'32 6:23:26
Grove Center 105 1 39N03'45 94w48'05 6:19:12
Groveland 57 1 38N17'35 97w43'45 6:30:55
Grover 23 1 39N03'35 95w27'36 6:21:50
Guelph 96 1 37N04 97w18 6:29:12
Guilford 103 1 37N35'57 95w43'10 6:22:53
Guittard 59 1 39N52 96w24 6:25:36
Gypsum 85 1 38N42'20 97w25'40 6:29:43
Gypsum Creek 57 1 38N34 97w26 6:29:44
Hackberry 50 1 37N04 95w13 6:20:52
Hackney 18 1 37N09'58 97w08'50 6:28:35
Haddam 101 1 39N51'25 97w18'05 6:29:12
Haggard 35 4 37N38'04 100w19'12 6:41:17
Hale 10 1 37N14'05 96w03'17 6:24:13
Half Mound 44 1 39N24'21 95w29'50 6:21:59
Halford 97 1 39N22'23 100w52'10 6:43:29
Hallet 42 1 38N05 100w04 6:40:16
Hallowell 11 1 37N10'29 94w59'43 6:19:59
Halls Summit 16 1 38N20'50 95w40'30 6:22:42
Hallville 85 1 38N38'55 97w32'16 6:30:09
Halstead 40 1 38N00'05 97w30'30 6:30:02
Hamburg 73 1 38N07'32 99w10'12 6:36:41
Hamilton 37 1 37N58'46 96w09'50 6:24:39
Hamlin 7 1 39N54'58 95w37'40 6:22:31
Hammond 6 1 37N56'08 94w41'42 6:18:47
Hampden 16 1 38N12 95w42 6:22:48
Hampton 83 1 38N38 99w32 6:38:08
Hancock 71 1 39N21 98w40 6:34:40
Hanover 101 1 39N53'38 96w52'45 6:27:31
Hanston 42 1 38N07'19 99w42'45 6:38:51
Happy 33 1 39N12 99w53 6:39:32
Harbine 79 1 40N00'08 97w46'05 6:31:04
Harding 6 1 37N59'38 94w49'10 6:19:17
Hardtner 4 1 37N00'50 98w38'57 6:34:36
Hargrave 83 1 38N33'23 99w26'41 6:37:47
Harlan 92 1 39N36'20 98w46'00 6:35:04
Harmon 96 1 37N21 97w19 6:29:16
Harmony 95 3 37N19 101w27 6:45:48
Harold 68 1 38N16'21 99w55'59 6:39:44
Harper 39 1 37N17'12 98w01'32 6:32:06
Harris 2 1 38N19'10 95w26'10 6:21:45
Hartford 56 1 38N18'30 95w57'20 6:23:49
Hartland 47 2 37N53'14 101w22'18 6:45:29
Harveyville 99 1 38N47'24 95w57'41 6:23:51
Haskell 23 1 38N58 95w15 6:21:00
Haskell 41 3 37N33 100w51 6:43:24
Hasty 104 1 37N56'20 95w41'25 6:22:46
Hatton 38 2 37N59 101w45 6:47:00
Havana 63 1 37N05'30 95w56'30 6:23:46
Haven 78 1 37N53'56 97w46'57 6:31:08
Havensville 75 1 39N30'40 96w04'40 6:24:19
Haverhill 8 1 37N41'08 96w52'58 6:27:32
Haviland 49 1 37N37'10 99w06'22 6:36:25

Hawk 39	1	37N06'45	97w58'30	6:31:54
Hawkeye 71	1	39N32	98w53	6:35:32
Haworth 79	1	37N49'30	97w23'15	6:29:33
Hawthorne 3	1	39N28'35	95w12'50	6:20:51
Hayden 67	1	37N25'40	95w15'39	6:21:03
Hayne 88	1	37N06'02	100w48'13	6:43:13
Haynesville 76	1	37N46	98w31	6:34:04
Hays 26	1	38N52'45	99w19'35	6:37:18
Haysville 87	1	37N33'57	97w21'14	6:29:25
Hazelton 4	1	37N05'25	98w23'53	6:33:36
Healy 51	1	38N36'00	100w37'00	6:42:28
Hedville 85	1	38N51'46	97w45'40	6:31:03
Heizer 5	1	38N25'20	98w53'20	6:35:33
Helmick 64	1	38N37'40	96w36'00	6:26:24
Hendricks 10	1	37N03	96w18	6:25:12
Henry 72	1	39N05	97w52	6:31:28
Henson 61	1	38N30'20	94w51'56	6:19:28
Hepler 19	1	37N39'40	94w58'05	6:19:52
Herington 21	1	38N40'16	96w56'32	6:27:46
Herkimer 59	1	39N53'28	96w42'39	6:26:51
Hermansberg 59	1	39N56'02	96w46'05	6:27:04
Herndon 77	1	39N54'35	100w47'05	6:43:08
Herzog 26	1	38N54	99w09	6:36:36
Hesper 23	1	38N53'55	95w04'28	6:20:18
Hessdale 99	1	38N54'46	96w12'33	6:24:50
Hesston 40	1	38N08'18	97w25'52	6:29:43
Hewins 10	1	37N02'27	96w24'29	6:25:38
Hiatt 52	1	39N13'50	94w52'20	6:19:29
Hiattville 6	1	37N43'20	94w52'17	6:19:29
Hiawatha 7	1	39N51'09	95w32'08	6:22:09
Hickok 34	3	37N33'40	101w13'42	6:44:55
Hickory 8	1	37N36	96w38	6:26:32
Hidden Lakes 87	1	37N42	97w25	6:29:40
Highland 22	1	39N51'35	95w16'10	6:21:05
Highland 52	1	39N12'50	94w49'50	6:19:19
Highland Park 89	1	39N01'28	95w39'48	6:22:39
Highpoint 68	1	38N20	99w42	6:38:48
High Prairie 52	1	39N15	95w00	6:20:00
Hilford 103	1	37N26'59	95w40'35	6:22:42
Hill City 33	1	39N21'53	99w50'30	6:39:22
Hillcrest 78	1	38N04	97w57	6:31:48
Hilldale 44	1	39N10'55	95w28'33	6:21:54
Hilldale South 44	1	39N10'30	95w28'35	6:21:54
Hillsboro 58	1	38N21'07	97w12'15	6:28:49
Hillsdale 61	1	38N39'35	94w51'00	6:19:24
Hilltop 37	1	38N03'20	96w02'22	6:24:09
Hilton 57	1	38N26'32	97w40'31	6:30:42
Hitschmann 5	1	38N37'27	98w34'52	6:34:19
Hoag 11	1	37N09'53	95w02'40	6:20:11
Hobart 60	1	37N17'26	100w31'23	6:42:06
Hobart 82	1	39N21	99w19	6:37:16
Hocker Grove 46	1	39N01	94w42	6:18:48
Hodges 24	1	37N49'00	99w23'00	6:37:32
Hog Back 26	1	38N55'13	99w28'50	6:37:55
Hoge 52	1	39N10'20	94w59'41	6:19:59
Hoisington 5	1	38N31'05	98w46'40	6:35:07
Holcomb 28	4	37N59'10	100w59'20	6:43:57
Holland 21	1	38N45'43	97w16'45	6:29:07
Hollenberg 101	1	39N58'50	96w59'31	6:27:58
Holliday 46	1	39N02'18	94w48'28	6:19:14
Hollis 15	1	39N38	97w33	6:30:12
Hollister 6	1	37N45'46	94w50'08	6:19:21
Holmdel Gardens 78	1	38N04	97w58	6:31:52
Holmwood 45	1	39N52	98w13	6:32:52
Holton 43	1	39N27'55	95w44'10	6:22:57
Holyrood 27	1	38N35'13	98w24'39	6:33:39
Home 59	1	39N50'30	96w31'10	6:26:05
Homer 84	1	38N52'10	98w47'50	6:35:11
Homestead 9	1	38N10	96w41	6:26:44
Homewood 30	1	38N30'53	95w22'43	6:21:31
Hooser 18	1	37N08'18	96w37'47	6:26:31
Hoosier 48	1	37N41	98w12	6:32:48
Hope 21	1	38N41'25	97w04'35	6:28:18
Hopewell 76	1	37N48'17	98w59'43	6:35:59
Hopkins 8	1	37N53'50	96w55'55	6:27:44
Horace 36	2	38N28'35	101w47'25	6:47:10
Horton 7	1	39N39'38	95w31'34	6:22:06
Houston 92	1	39N37	98w53	6:35:32
Howard 25	1	37N28'13	96w15'48	6:25:03
Howell 29	1	37N47'00	100w10'44	6:40:43
Hoxie 97	1	39N21'27	100w26'29	6:41:46
Hoyt 43	1	39N14'52	95w42'22	6:22:49
Hudson 93	1	38N06'20	98w39'35	6:34:38
Hugoton 95	3	37N10'31	101w20'57	6:45:24
Humboldt 1	1	37N48'38	95w26'12	6:21:45
Hunnewell 96	1	37N00'18	97w24'16	6:29:37
Hunter 62	1	39N14'03	98w23'49	6:33:35
Huntsville 78	1	38N03'26	98w19'32	6:33:18
Huron 3	1	39N38'18	95w21'05	6:21:24
Huscher 15	1	39N31'27	97w35'20	6:30:21
Hutchins 86	4	38N26'23	100w54'54	6:43:40
Hutchinson 78	1	38N03'39	97w55'46	6:31:43
Hymer 9	1	38N29'10	96w41'20	6:26:45
Idana 14	1	39N21'27	97w15'50	6:29:03
Imes 30	1	38N34'25	95w09'29	6:20:38
Independence 63	1	37N13'27	95w42'29	6:22:50
Independent 5	1	38N34	98w32	6:34:08
Indian Creek 2	1	38N06	95w28	6:21:52
Indian Creek 46	1	38N58	94w38	6:18:32
Indian Ridge 44	1	39N13'05	95w28'30	6:21:54
Indian Valley 89	1	39N05	95w40	6:22:40
Indian Village 63	1	37N05	95w38	6:22:32
Industry 14	1	39N08'00	97w10'16	6:28:41
Ingalls 35	4	37N49'40	100w27'15	6:41:49
Inman 57	1	38N13'55	97w46'23	6:31:06
Iola 1	1	37N55'28	95w23'59	6:21:36
Ionia 45	1	39N39'50	98w20'50	6:33:23
Iowa Point 22	1	39N55'42	95w14'18	6:20:57
Irving 7	1	39N56	95w24	6:21:36
Isabel 4	1	37N28'00	98w33'00	6:34:12
Isbel 86	4	38N29	101w02	6:44:08
Itasca 91	2	39N19	101w40	6:46:40
Iuka 76	1	37N43'45	98w44'05	6:34:56
Ivanhoe 28	4	37N48	100w50	6:43:20
Ivanpah 37	1	37N53'53	96w28'56	6:25:56
Ivy 56	1	38N38	96w05	6:24:20
Jacobs 21	1	38N36'43	97w01'50	6:28:07
Jacobs Creek Landing 16	1	38N15'55	95w52'10	6:23:29
Jamestown 15	1	39N35'58	97w51'39	6:31:27
Janesville 37	1	37N59	96w11	6:24:44
Jaqua 12	4	39N40	102w01	6:48:04
Jarbalo 52	1	39N12'07	95w04'08	6:20:17
Jarrett 11	1	37N01	94w44	6:18:56
Jayhawk 23	1	38N58	95w15	6:21:00
Jefferson 63	1	37N06'44	95w45'40	6:23:03
Jenkins 57	1	38N33'00	97w43'18	6:30:53
Jennings 20	1	39N40'46	100w17'35	6:41:10
Jerome 32	1	38N47	100w29	6:41:56
Jetmore 42	1	38N05'04	99w53'35	6:39:34
Jewell 45	1	39N40'17	98w09'12	6:32:37
Jingo 61	1	38N24'14	94w41'45	6:18:47
Johnson 68	1	38N20	100w08	6:40:32
Johnson 94	3	37N34'14	101w45'02	6:47:00
Johnstown 57	1	38N29'34	97w40'31	6:30:42
Jones 65	3	37N04	101w59	6:47:56
Joy 49	1	37N35'43	99w23'40	6:37:35
Julian 94	3	37N33'43	101w37'34	6:46:30
Junction 70	1	38N41	95w34	6:22:16
Junction City 31	1	39N01'43	96w49'52	6:27:19
Juniata 53	1	38N54'55	97w57'52	6:31:51
Kackley 79	1	39N42'00	97w51'10	6:31:25
Kalloch 63	1	37N02	95w37	6:22:28
Kalvesta 28	4	38N03'34	100w17'09	6:41:09
Kanbrick 5	1	38N28'22	98w46'37	6:35:06
Kanco 36	2	38N28'20	102w03'32	6:48:14
Kanona 20	1	39N47'48	100w23'22	6:41:33
Kanopolis 27	1	38N42'40	98w09'25	6:32:38
Kanorado 91	2	39N19'59	102w02'15	6:48:09
Kansas City 105	1	39N06'51	94w37'38	6:18:31
Kansas Falls 31	1	38N59'00	96w54'48	6:27:39
Kanwaka 23	1	38N58'23	95w22'21	6:21:29
Kapioma 3	1	39N29	95w31	6:22:04
Keats 81	1	39N13'25	96w42'30	6:26:50
Kechi 87	1	37N47'45	97w16'45	6:29:07
Keeler 87	1	37N36'43	97w17'28	6:29:10
Keelville 11	1	37N01'52	94w55'21	6:19:41
Keene 99	1	38N57'27	96w02'20	6:24:09
Keighley 8	1	37N40'21	96w38'33	6:26:34
Kellogg 18	1	37N15'33	97w06'33	6:28:26
Kelly 66	1	39N44'16	96w00'11	6:24:01
Kelso 64	1	38N44'05	96w34'13	6:26:17
Kenbro 37	1	38N07'43	96w20'22	6:25:21
Kendall 38	2	37N56'05	101w32'44	6:46:11
Kennekuk 3	1	39N38'40	95w29'55	6:22:00
Kenneth 46	1	38N51'18	94w36'42	6:18:27
Kensington 92	1	39N46'01	99w01'53	6:36:08
Kentucky 44	1	39N07	95w25	6:21:40
Keystone 86	4	38N29	100w52	6:43:28
Keysville 73	1	38N08	99w24	6:37:36
Key West 16	1	38N23	95w45	6:23:00
Kickapoo 52	1	39N23'56	94w58'15	6:19:53
Kickapoo Indian Res 7	1	39N40	95w40	6:22:40
Kilbourns Corner 78	1	38N09'33	98w19'33	6:33:18
Kill Creek 71	1	39N21	98w53	6:35:32
Kimball 67	1	37N39'40	95w09'48	6:20:39
Kimeo 101	1	39N35'45	96w59'40	6:27:59
Kincaid 2	1	38N05'03	95w09'12	6:20:37
King City 57	1	38N18	97w39	6:30:36
Kingery 97	1	39N13	101w17	6:45:08
Kingman 48	1	37N38'45	98w06'48	6:32:27
Kingsdown 29	1	37N31'30	99w45'30	6:39:02
Kings Gardens 78	1	38N04	97w57	6:31:48
Kinsley 24	1	37N55'23	99w24'34	6:37:38
Kiowa 4	1	37N01'02	98w29'06	6:33:56
Kipp 85	1	38N47'02	97w27'15	6:29:49
Kirkwood 19	1	37N22'15	94w43'20	6:18:53
Kiro 89	1	39N05'49	95w47'51	6:23:11
Kirwin 74	1	39N40'23	99w07'19	6:36:29
Kismet 88	1	37N12'20	100w42'06	6:42:48
Klendike 19	1	37N22'04	94w45'34	6:19:02
Kniveton 19	1	37N20'18	94w38'35	6:18:34
Kramer 19	1	37N21'37	94w43'47	6:18:55
Labette 50	1	37N13'50	95w11'00	6:20:44
Lacey 97	1	39N27	100w53	6:43:32
Lackmans 46	1	38N55'28	94w45'50	6:19:03
Laclede 75	1	39N20'50	96w13'15	6:24:53
La Crosse 83	1	38N31'53	99w18'30	6:37:14
La Cygne 54	1	38N21'00	94w45'40	6:19:03
La Cygne Corner 54	1	38N20'44	94w40'40	6:18:43
Ladore 67	1	37N26	95w18	6:21:12
Ladysmith 14	1	39N16'17	97w11'03	6:28:44
Lafayette 10	1	37N15	96w09	6:24:36
Lafontaine 103	1	37N23'57	95w50'42	6:23:23
La Harpe 1	1	37N55'01	95w17'56	6:21:12
Laing 77	1	39N47	100w47	6:43:08
Laird 68	1	38N26'51	100w03'15	6:40:13
Lake City 4	1	37N21'12	98w49'14	6:35:17
Lake Kohola 9	1	38N35	96w22	6:25:28
Lake of the Forest 105	1	39N04'05	94w50'15	6:19:21
Lake Quivira 46	1	39N04	94w41	6:18:44
Lake Ridge 44	1	39N09'55	95w28'20	6:21:53
Lake Shore 27	1	38N43	98w09	6:32:36
Lake Shore 44	1	39N14'35	95w25'25	6:21:42
Lakeside Acres 87	1	37N43'08	97w11'25	6:28:46
Lakeside Acres Addition 87	1	37N42	97w17	6:29:08
Lakeside Village 44	1	39N10'31	95w25'16	6:21:41
Lakeview Heights 8	1	37N40'10	97w08'06	6:28:32
Lake Wabaunsee 99	1	39N01	96w17	6:25:08
Lakin 47	2	37N56'26	101w15'16	6:45:01
Lamar 72	1	39N15'22	97w34'28	6:30:18
Lamont 37	1	38N06'45	96w01'35	6:24:06
Lanark 82	1	39N31	99w13	6:36:52
Lancaster 3	1	39N34'22	95w18'09	6:21:13
Landergin 37	1	37N47'20	96w20'20	6:25:21
Lane 30	1	38N26'23	95w04'55	6:20:20
Laneville 50	1	37N19'58	95w07'35	6:20:30
Lang 56	1	38N27'36	96w05'00	6:24:20
Langdon 19	1	37N21'11	94w42'19	6:18:49
Langdon 78	1	37N51'14	98w19'27	6:33:18
Langley 27	1	38N32'48	97w57'45	6:31:51
Lanham 101	1	40N00'10	96w52'25	6:27:30
Lansdowne 48	1	37N37'06	97w51'45	6:31:27
Lansing 52	1	39N14'55	94w54'00	6:19:36
Lapland 37	1	37N59'05	96w23'35	6:25:34
Larkinburg 3	1	39N27'45	95w34'13	6:22:17
Larned 73	1	38N10'50	99w05'54	6:36:24
Larrabee 32	1	38N47	100w16	6:41:04
Lasita 81	1	39N24'32	96w56'32	6:27:46
Latham 8	1	37N32'10	96w38'30	6:26:34
Latimer 64	1	38N44'20	96w50'43	6:27:23
Laton 82	1	39N17'08	99w04'35	6:36:18
Lawn 39	1	37N15	98w18	6:33:12
Lawn Ridge 12	4	39N37	101w45	6:47:00
Lawrence 23	1	38N58'18	95w14'06	6:20:56
Lawton 11	1	37N13'19	94w38'09	6:18:33
Layton 10	1	37N04'56	96w24'28	6:25:38
Leanna 1	1	37N43'58	95w19'56	6:21:20
Leavenworth 52	1	39N18'40	94w55'20	6:19:41
Leawood 46	1	38N58'00	94w37'00	6:18:28
Lebanon 92	1	39N48'35	98w33'19	6:34:13
Lebo 16	1	38N25'00	95w51'10	6:23:25
Lecompton 23	1	39N02'40	95w23'40	6:21:35
Lees 55	4	38N44	100w55	6:43:40
Lehigh 58	1	38N22'22	97w18'10	6:29:13
Le Hunt 63	1	37N16'09	95w45'06	6:23:00
Le Loup 30	1	38N41'43	95w09'35	6:20:38
Lenape 52	1	38N59'50	94w57'02	6:19:48
Lenexa 46	1	38N57'13	94w44'00	6:18:56
Lenora 69	1	39N36'38	100w00'08	6:40:01
Lento 61	1	38N37'00	94w50'45	6:19:23
Leon 8	1	37N41'25	96w46'55	6:27:08
Leona 22	1	39N47'14	95w19'17	6:21:17
Leonardville 81	1	39N21'52	96w51'31	6:27:26
Leota 69	1	39N47	100w01	6:40:04
Leoti 102	4	38N28'47	101w21'30	6:45:26
Leoville 20	1	39N34'54	100w27'38	6:41:51
Lerado 78	1	37N46'35	98w16'56	6:33:08
Le Roy 16	1	38N05'02	95w38'03	6:22:32
Levant 97	1	39N23'08	101w11'40	6:44:47
Lewis 24	1	37N56'10	99w15'08	6:37:01
Lexington 13	1	37N17'38	99w35'57	6:38:24
Liberal 88	3	37N02'35	100w55'14	6:43:41
Liberty 63	1	37N09'20	95w35'40	6:22:23
Liebenthal 83	1	38N39'18	99w19'08	6:37:17
Lillis 59	1	39N36'35	96w17'45	6:25:11
Limestone 45	1	39N47	98w19	6:33:16
Lincoln 53	1	39N02'27	98w08'40	6:32:35
Lincoln Center 53	1	39N03	98w09	6:32:36
Lincolnville 58	1	38N29'36	96w57'35	6:27:50
Linda 77	1	39N48	101w02	6:44:08
Lindbloom Park 89	1	38N59'06	95w37'19	6:22:29
Lindsborg 57	1	38N34'25	97w40'27	6:30:42
Lindsey 72	1	39N05'37	97w40'40	6:30:43
Linn 101	1	39N40'48	97w05'02	6:28:20
Linwood 52	1	39N00'05	95w02'20	6:20:09
Linwood Acres 87	1	37N40'53	97w12'07	6:28:48
Litchfield 19	1	37N26'27	94w38'58	6:18:36
Little Blue 101	1	39N47	96w52	6:27:28
Little Caney 10	1	37N04	96w01	6:24:04
Little Kaw 52	1	39N02'12	94w55'16	6:19:41
Little River 80	1	38N23'53	98w00'42	6:32:03
Little Valley 57	1	38N13	97w52	6:31:28
Little Walnut 8	1	37N41	96w46	6:27:04
Llanos 91	2	39N28	101w27	6:45:48
Lockport 41	3	37N35	100w43	6:42:52
Loda Center 78	1	37N46'40	98w11'30	6:32:46
Logan 74	1	39N39'42	99w34'12	6:38:17
Logansport 55	4	38N53	101w03	6:44:12
Lola 11	1	37N10	95w01	6:20:04
Loma Vista 105	1	39N09'50	94w47'21	6:19:09
London 96	1	37N26	97w25	6:29:40
Lone Elm 2	1	38N04'48	95w14'35	6:20:58
Lone Elm 59	1	39N57'30	96w39'20	6:26:37
Lone Oak 19	1	37N26'13	94w44'30	6:18:58
Lone Star 23	1	38N52'00	95w21'18	6:21:25
Longford 14	1	39N10'12	97w19'52	6:29:19
Long Island 74	1	39N56'58	99w32'08	6:38:09
Longton 25	1	37N22'40	96w04'50	6:24:19
Lookout 26	1	38N45	99w22	6:37:28
Lorena 8	1	37N41'38	97w05'01	6:28:20
Loretta 83	1	38N39'13	99w10'49	6:36:43
Loring 52	1	39N00'50	94w54'30	6:19:38
Lorraine 27	1	38N34'08	98w18'59	6:33:16
Lost Springs 58	1	38N33'58	96w57'58	6:27:52
Louisburg 61	1	38N37'10	94w40'50	6:18:43
Louisville 75	1	39N15'01	96w18'52	6:25:15
Lovewell 45	1	39N51'55	97w58'53	6:31:56
Lowe 28	4	38N01'59	100w59'32	6:43:58
Lowe 101	1	39N57	97w12	6:28:48
Lowell 11	1	37N02'55	94w42'05	6:18:48
Lowemont 52	1	39N22'50	95w03'20	6:20:13
Lucas 84	1	39N03'22	98w32'10	6:34:09
Lucerne 90	1	39N29'48	100w12'00	6:40:48
Ludell 77	1	39N51'20	100w57'34	6:43:50
Lulu 62	1	39N31	97w59	6:31:56
Luray 84	1	39N06'38	98w41'19	6:34:45
Lydia 102	4	38N16'42	101w17'28	6:45:10
Lyle 20	1	39N57'28	100w12'58	6:40:52
Lyndon 70	1	38N36'36	95w41'03	6:22:44
Lyona 21	1	38N51'43	96w55'32	6:27:42
Lyons 80	1	38N20'42	98w12'05	6:32:48
Mackie 11	1	37N15'07	94w51'00	6:19:24

Mackie 67 1 38N35'45 97w48'16 6:31:13
Macksville 93 1 38N57'33 98w58'06 6:35:52
Macon 40 1 38N03 97w26 6:29:44
Macyville 15 1 39N28'54 97w48'58 6:31:16
Madison 37 1 38N08'08 96w08'08 6:24:33
Mahaska 101 1 39N59'15 97w21'14 6:29:25
Mahon 52 1 39N02'16 94w56'45 6:19:47
Maize 87 1 37N46'45 96w28'01 6:25:52
Maltby 52 1 39N13'10 94w50'10 6:19:21
Manchester 21 1 39N05'41 97w19'28 6:29:18
Manhattan 81 1 39N11'01 96w34'17 6:26:17
Mankato 45 1 39N47'14 98w12'35 6:32:50
Manning 86 4 38N33'19 100w43'23 6:42:54
Mansfield 28 4 37N55'22 100w46'00 6:43:04
Manter 94 4 37N31'23 101w53'04 6:47:32
Mantey 54 1 38N03'08 94w48'20 6:19:13
Maple 18 1 37N26 97w06 6:28:24
Maple City 18 1 37N03'21 96w46'05 6:27:04
Maple Hill 99 1 39N05'05 96w01'40 6:24:07
Mapleton 6 1 38N00'54 94w53'00 6:19:32
Marena 42 1 38N10 99w41 6:38:44
Marienthal 102 4 38N29'15 101w12'45 6:44:51
Marietta 59 1 39N56'35 96w36'30 6:26:26
Marion 58 1 38N20'54 97w01'01 6:28:04
Marion County Lake 58 1 38N21 97w01 6:28:04
Marketplace at Georgetown 46 1 39N00 94w41 6:18:44
Marmaton 6 1 37N49'55 94w49'28 6:19:18
Marquette 57 1 38N33'20 97w50'00 6:31:20
Marydel 85 1 38N56'40 97w43'20 6:30:53
Marysville 59 1 39N50'28 96w38'49 6:26:35
Matfield 9 1 38N09 96w31 6:26:04
Matfield Green 9 1 38N09'33 96w33'37 6:26:14
Mathews Park 89 1 38N59'55 95w39'20 6:22:37
May Day 81 1 39N32 96w53 6:27:32
Mayetta 43 1 39N20'20 95w43'20 6:22:53
Mayfield 96 1 37N15'30 97w32'40 6:30:11
Mayline 38 2 37N57'36 101w39'36 6:46:38
Maywood 52 1 39N13'34 94w50'40 6:19:23
McAdoo 4 1 37N26 98w49 6:35:16
McAllaster 55 4 39N00'22 101w23'28 6:45:34
McCamish 46 1 38N49 95w01 6:20:04
McClellan 76 1 37N41 98w57 6:35:48
McConnell Air Force Base 87 1 37N37'35 97w16'05 6:29:04
McCracken 83 1 38N34'50 99w34'15 6:38:17
Mc Cune 19 1 37N21'17 95w00'59 6:20:04
McDonald 77 1 39N47'09 101w22'31 6:45:30
McFarland 99 1 39N03'10 96w14'15 6:24:57
McGraw 40 1 38N00'43 97w22'05 6:29:28
Mclains 40 1 37N59'58 97w15'46 6:29:03
McLouth 44 1 39N11'45 95w12'29 6:20:50
McPherson 57 1 38N22'15 97w39'50 6:30:39
McVays Corner 78 1 38N09'32 98w15'07 6:33:00
Meade 60 1 37N17'08 100w20'23 6:41:22
Meadowview 87 1 37N41'23 97w25'38 6:29:43
Mecca Acres 8 1 37N40'32 97w08'46 6:28:35
Medford 78 1 38N07 98w12 6:32:48
Medicine 82 1 39N21 99w07 6:36:28
Medicine Lodge 4 1 37N16'52 98w34'48 6:34:19
Medina 44 1 39N04'40 95w25'15 6:21:41
Medora 78 1 38N08'56 97w50'43 6:31:23
Medway 38 2 38N00'49 101w52'55 6:47:32
Melrose 11 1 37N01'51 94w57'29 6:19:50
Melvern 70 1 38N30'25 95w38'15 6:22:33
Menlo 97 1 39N21'25 100w43'20 6:42:53
Menno 58 1 38N18 97w19 6:29:16
Menoken 89 1 39N05'27 95w45'20 6:23:01
Mentor 85 1 38N44'26 97w36'10 6:30:25
Mercier 7 1 39N42'30 95w36'05 6:22:24
Meredith 15 1 39N21 97w39 6:30:36
Meriden 44 1 39N11'20 95w34'10 6:22:17
Meridian 57 1 38N13 97w26 6:29:44
Merriam 46 1 39N01'25 94w41'36 6:18:46
Merrick 56 1 38N24'10 96w14'40 6:24:59
Mertilla 60 3 37N23 100w29 6:41:56
Mertz 19 1 37N35'05 94w38'53 6:18:36
Metcalf 96 1 37N04'02 97w47'02 6:31:08
Michigan 70 1 38N35 95w32 6:22:08
Michigan 86 4 38N38 100w54 6:43:36
Michigan Valley 70 1 38N40'54 95w31'35 6:22:06
Middle Creek 61 1 38N34 94w42 6:18:48
Middletown 103 1 37N43'11 95w49'59 6:23:20
Midian 26 1 37N48'37 96w57'10 6:27:49
Midland 23 1 39N01'42 95w14'31 6:20:58
Midland 87 1 37N36'50 97w20'06 6:29:20
Midland Park 87 1 37N35'20 97w20'15 6:29:21
Midland Tower 87 1 37N36'00 97w20'02 6:29:20
Midway 8 1 37N40'46 97w08'06 6:28:32
Midway 19 1 37N26'57 94w37'51 6:18:31
Midway 27 1 38N36'34 98w09'14 6:32:37
Midway 39 1 37N09'09 98w14'51 6:32:59
Midway 48 1 37N39'42 97w56'08 6:31:45
Midway 77 1 39N49'45 100w46'38 6:43:07
Mikesell 77 1 39N42 101w08 6:44:32
Milan 96 1 37N15'35 97w40'25 6:30:42
Milberger 84 1 38N42'43 98w54'43 6:35:39
Mildred 1 1 38N01'25 95w10'15 6:20:41
Milford 31 1 39N10'06 96w54'44 6:27:39
Millard 5 1 38N38'17 98w53'00 6:35:32
Millbrook 33 1 39N18 99w53 6:39:32
Millbrook 87 1 37N42 97w25 6:29:40
Miller 56 1 38N38'04 95w59'25 6:23:58
Millerton 96 1 37N26'12 97w33'22 6:30:13
Millwood 52 1 39N23'02 95w07'00 6:20:28
Milo 53 1 39N10'20 97w58'02 6:31:52
Milton 96 1 37N25'54 97w46'16 6:31:05
Miltonvale 15 1 39N20'54 97w26'45 6:29:47
Mineral 11 1 37N16 94w48 6:19:12
Mineral Springs 70 1 38N50'27 95w41'12 6:22:45
Mingo 97 1 39N16'42 100w57'43 6:43:51
Mingona 4 1 37N19'26 98w41'24 6:34:46
Minneapolis 72 1 39N07'19 97w42'23 6:30:50
Minneha 87 1 37N42'52 97w14'23 6:28:58
Minneola 13 1 37N26'36 100w00'53 6:40:04
Mirage 77 1 39N39 101w14 6:44:56
Mission 46 1 39N01'40 94w39'20 6:18:37
Mission Creek 99 1 38N56 96w02 6:24:08
Mission Highlands 46 1 39N02 94w38 6:18:32
Mission Hills 46 1 39N01'04 94w37'00 6:18:28
Mission Woods 46 1 39N02'06 94w36'30 6:18:26
Missler 60 1 37N19'04 100w26'05 6:41:44
Mitchell 80 1 38N23'02 98w05'58 6:32:24
Modell 69 1 39N37 99w55 6:39:40
Modoc 86 4 38N29'13 101w04'53 6:44:20
Moline 25 1 37N21'37 96w18'13 6:25:13
Mona Kay Heights 87 1 37N35'56 97w18'42 6:29:15
Monett 10 1 37N08'40 96w06'20 6:24:25
Monmouth 19 1 37N21'47 94w56'12 6:19:45
Monmouth 89 1 38N56 95w34 6:22:16
Monroe 2 1 38N18 95w12 6:20:48
Monrovia 3 1 39N31'27 95w20'45 6:21:23
Monrovia 46 1 39N01 94w42 6:18:48
Montana 50 1 37N16'31 95w07'26 6:20:30
Montezuma 35 3 37N35'45 100w26'34 6:41:46
Monticello 46 1 38N59'56 94w50'38 6:19:23
Mont Ida 2 1 38N13'00 95w22'05 6:21:28
Montrose 45 1 39N47'04 98w05'15 6:32:21
Monument 55 4 39N06'16 101w00'24 6:44:02
Moonlight 21 1 39N00'10 97w06'08 6:28:25
Moran 1 1 37N54'58 95w10'12 6:20:41
Moray 22 1 39N45'45 95w10'17 6:20:41
Morehead 67 1 37N23'03 95w30'27 6:22:02
Morgan 97 1 39N22 101w04 6:44:16
Morganville 14 1 39N27'59 97w12'06 6:28:48
Morlan 33 1 39N13 99w41 6:38:44
Morland 33 1 39N20'58 100w04'31 6:40:18
Morrill 7 1 39N55'42 95w41'30 6:22:46
Morris 105 1 39N03'43 94w45'05 6:19:00
Morrison Ridge 46 1 39N01 94w39 6:18:36
Morrowville 101 1 39N50'40 97w10'17 6:28:41
Morse 46 1 38N51'01 94w43'25 6:18:54
Moscow 95 3 37N19'25 101w12'19 6:44:49
Mound City 54 1 38N08'34 94w48'48 6:19:15
Moundridge 57 1 38N12'11 97w31'08 6:30:05
Mound Valley 50 1 37N12'19 95w24'17 6:21:37
Mount Ayr 71 1 39N21 98w59 6:35:56
Mount Hope 87 1 37N52'07 97w39'53 6:30:40
Mount Vernon 48 1 37N43'03 97w50'43 6:31:23
Moxham 18 1 37N06'52 97w02'47 6:28:11
Mulberry 19 1 37N33'25 94w37'18 6:18:29
Mullinville 49 1 37N35'10 99w28'31 6:37:54
Mulvane 96 1 37N28'28 97w14'37 6:28:58
Muncie 105 1 39N05'15 94w44'50 6:18:59
Munden 79 1 39N54'50 97w32'16 6:30:09
Munger 87 1 37N42 97w17 6:29:08
Munjor 26 1 38N48'40 99w15'52 6:37:03
Murdock 48 1 37N36'40 97w55'50 6:31:43
Murray 59 1 39N52 96w17 6:25:08
Murray Gill 87 1 37N35'35 97w24'25 6:29:38
Muscotah 3 1 39N33'10 95w31'17 6:22:05
Narka 79 1 39N57'38 97w25'32 6:29:42
Naron 76 1 37N47 98w57 6:35:48
Nashville 48 1 37N26'30 98w25'20 6:33:41
Natoma 71 1 39N11'27 99w01'42 6:36:07
Natrona 76 1 37N42'43 98w39'52 6:34:39
Navarre 21 1 38N47'49 97w06'20 6:28:25
Neal 37 1 37N50'03 96w04'48 6:24:19
Nearman 105 1 39N09'53 94w41'51 6:18:47
Nekoma 83 1 38N28'25 99w26'30 6:37:46
Nelson 15 1 39N31 97w32 6:30:08
Nemaha 66 1 39N57 96w04 6:24:16
Neodesha 103 1 37N25'06 95w40'48 6:22:43
Neola 93 1 37N52'10 98w30'31 6:34:02
Neosho Falls 104 1 38N00'20 95w33'25 6:22:14
Neosho Rapids 56 1 38N22'10 95w59'30 6:23:58
Nescatunga 17 1 37N14 99w13 6:36:52
Ness City 68 1 38N27'10 99w54'22 6:39:37
Netawaka 43 1 39N36'10 95w43'05 6:22:52
Nettleton 24 1 37N59'55 99w19'42 6:37:19
Neuchatel 66 1 39N34'05 96w12'06 6:24:48
Neutral 11 1 37N05'52 94w47'41 6:19:11
Neva 9 1 38N23'53 96w36'57 6:26:28
Nevada 68 1 38N38 99w55 6:39:40
New Albany 103 1 37N34'06 95w56'15 6:23:45
New Almelo 69 1 39N35'39 100w07'03 6:40:28
Newark 103 1 37N25 95w35 6:22:20
Newbern 21 1 38N50 97w12 6:28:48
Newbury 99 1 39N05'05 96w10'30 6:24:42
New Cambria 85 1 38N52'45 97w30'20 6:30:01
New Gottland 57 1 38N26'59 97w36'40 6:30:27
New Lancaster 61 1 38N27'45 94w43'58 6:18:56
Newman 44 1 39N04'50 95w27'52 6:21:51
New Salem 18 1 37N18'38 96w53'42 6:27:35
New Strawn 16 1 38N15'45 95w44'30 6:22:58
Newton 40 1 38N02'48 97w20'41 6:29:23
Nickerson 78 1 38N08'50 98w05'00 6:32:20
Nicodemus 33 1 39N23'40 99w37'00 6:38:28
Niles 72 1 38N58'10 97w27'45 6:29:51
Niotaze 10 1 37N04'25 96w00'48 6:24:03
Nippawalla 4 1 37N10 98w33 6:34:12
Nolan 59 1 39N34'00 96w16'40 6:25:07
Norcatur 20 1 39N50'13 100w11'15 6:40:45
Noria 23 1 38N56'58 95w10'37 6:20:42
Northampton 82 1 39N15 99w33 6:38:12
North Atwood 77 1 39N49'25 101w02'47 6:44:11
Northbranch 45 1 39N58'22 98w22'17 6:33:29
North Brown 24 1 37N52 99w19 6:37:16
Northern Hills 89 1 39N05 95w40 6:22:40
North Fort Riley 31 1 39N05 96w49 6:27:16
North Hayes 78 1 38N07 98w26 6:33:44
North Homestead 5 1 38N34 98w45 6:35:00
North Newton 40 1 38N04'20 97w20'43 6:29:23
North Osage City 70 1 38N38 95w49 6:23:16
North Randall 97 1 39N20 100w53 6:43:32
North Rich 2 1 38N08 95w08 6:20:32
North Roscoe 42 1 38N12 100w09 6:40:36
North Seward 93 1 38N13 98w45 6:35:00
North Topeka 89 1 39N04'20 95w40'00 6:22:40
North Wichita 87 1 37N42 97w19 6:29:16
Norton 69 1 39N50'02 99w53'28 6:39:34
Nortonville 44 1 39N25'00 95w20'00 6:21:20
Norway 79 1 39N41'46 97w46'25 6:31:06
Norwich 48 1 37N27'26 97w50'55 6:31:24
Norwood 30 1 38N42'35 95w14'48 6:20:59
Nutty Combe 12 4 39N58 101w57 6:47:48
Oak 92 1 39N48 98w33 6:34:12
Oak Hill 14 1 39N14'54 97w20'28 6:29:22
Oakland 89 1 39N04'00 95w38'10 6:22:33
Oaklawn 87 1 37N36'37 97w17'48 6:29:11
Oakley 55 4 39N08'00 100w51'48 6:43:27
Oak Mills 3 1 39N26'44 95w00'37 6:20:02
Oak Valley 25 1 37N20'36 96w00'35 6:24:02
Oatville 87 1 37N37'20 97w23'20 6:29:33
Obeeville 78 1 38N03'27 97w50'55 6:31:24
Oberlin 20 1 39N49'06 100w31'40 6:42:07
O'Brien 61 1 38N30'48 95w01'40 6:20:07
Ocheltree 46 1 38N46'07 94w48'57 6:19:16
Odee 60 1 37N05 100w21 6:41:24
Odell 39 1 37N15 97w51 6:31:24
Odense 67 1 37N42'11 95w15'06 6:21:00
Odin 5 1 38N33'58 98w36'30 6:34:26
Offerle 24 1 37N53'27 99w33'27 6:38:14
Ogallah 98 1 38N59'29 99w43'55 6:38:56
Ogden 81 1 39N06'40 96w42'21 6:26:49
Oketo 59 1 39N57'49 96w35'58 6:26:24
Olathe 46 1 38N52'53 94w49'08 6:19:17
Olcott 78 1 37N48 98w26 6:33:44
Olive 20 1 39N53 100w28 6:41:52
Olivet 16 1 38N28'50 95w45'05 6:23:00
Olmitz 5 1 38N31'00 98w56'10 6:35:45
Olpe 56 1 38N15'45 96w10'00 6:24:40
Olsburg 75 1 39N25'50 96w36'55 6:26:28
Omnia 18 1 37N26 96w47 6:27:08
Onaga 75 1 39N29'20 96w10'11 6:24:41
Oneida 66 1 39N51'50 95w56'20 6:23:45
Oneonta 15 1 39N39'00 97w53'00 6:31:32
Ontario 66 1 39N34'00 95w52'55 6:23:32
Opolis 19 1 37N20'40 94w37'15 6:18:29
Orchard Park 50 1 37N21'30 95w16'33 6:21:06
Orlando 12 4 39N47 101w42 6:46:48
Oronoque 69 1 39N47'20 100w01'30 6:40:06
Orsemus 41 1 37N29'52 98w56'11 6:35:45
Orwell 42 1 38N00'56 99w42'55 6:38:52
Osage City 70 1 38N38'02 95w49'32 6:23:18
Osawatomie 61 1 38N29'50 94w57'01 6:19:48
Osborn 96 1 37N16 97w32 6:30:08
Osborne 71 1 39N26'20 98w41'40 6:34:47
Osgood 68 1 38N39'28 99w50'38 6:39:23
Oskaloosa 44 1 39N12'55 95w18'45 6:21:15
Osro 10 1 37N03'57 96w26'09 6:25:45
Ost 78 1 37N52 97w40 6:30:40
Oswego 50 1 37N10'03 95w06'35 6:20:26
Otego 45 1 39N49'38 98w20'49 6:33:23
Otis 83 1 38N32'05 99w03'10 6:36:13
Ottawa 30 1 38N36'56 95w16'03 6:21:04
Ottawa Junction 30 1 38N38'03 95w16'10 6:21:05
Otter 18 1 37N10 96w33 6:26:12
Otter Creek 37 1 37N40 96w23 6:25:32
Ottumwa 16 1 38N16'40 95w47'55 6:23:12
Oursler 58 1 38N17'26 96w58'58 6:27:56
Overbrook 70 1 38N46'50 95w33'25 6:22:14
Overland 64 1 38N49 96w51 6:27:24
Overland Park 46 1 38N58'56 94w40'14 6:18:41
Owen 63 1 36N59'57 95w55'54 6:23:44
Owl Creek 104 1 37N52 95w35 6:22:20
Oxford 96 1 37N16'27 97w10'07 6:28:40
Ozark 2 1 38N05 95w21 6:21:24
Ozawkie 44 1 39N14'00 95w28'00 6:21:52
Packers 105 1 39N06 94w40 6:18:40
Padonia 7 1 39N55'24 95w33'45 6:22:15
Page City 55 4 39N05'23 101w08'45 6:44:35
Painterhood 25 1 37N29 96w03 6:24:12
Palacky 27 1 38N39 98w26 6:33:44
Palco 82 1 39N15'08 99w33'45 6:38:15
Palermo 22 1 39N43'57 94w58'35 6:19:54
Palestine 96 1 37N21 97w13 6:28:52
Palmer 101 1 37N37'55 97w08'24 6:28:34
Palmyra 23 1 38N49 95w10 6:20:40
Paola 61 1 38N34'20 94w52'44 6:19:31
Paradise 84 1 39N06'49 98w55'05 6:35:40
Paris 54 1 38N13 94w49 6:19:16
Park 32 1 39N06'45 100w21'30 6:41:26
Park City 87 1 37N48'00 97w19'05 6:29:16
Park East 87 1 37N41'03 97w10'10 6:28:41
Parker 54 1 38N19'42 94w59'30 6:19:58
Parkerville 64 1 38N45'50 96w39'40 6:26:39
Parnell 3 1 39N30'23 95w12'23 6:20:50
Parnell 90 1 39N26 100w30 6:42:00
Parsons 50 1 37N20'25 95w15'39 6:21:03
Partridge 78 1 37N58'02 98w05'32 6:32:22
Paton 96 1 37N12'58 97w10'37 6:28:42
Patterson 40 1 37N56'36 97w39'17 6:30:37
Pauline 89 1 38N57'48 95w41'25 6:22:46
Pawnee Rock 5 1 38N15'55 98w58'50 6:35:55
Pawnee Station 6 1 37N42'00 94w47'28 6:19:10
Paw Paw 25 1 37N34 96w14 6:24:56
Paxico 99 1 39N04'10 96w09'58 6:24:40
Paxon 76 1 37N31 98w38 6:34:32
Paxton 40 1 38N00'50 97w35'30 6:30:22
Paxton 55 4 38N45 101w09 6:44:36

Peabody 58 1 38N10'10 97W06'23 6:28:26
Pearl 21 1 38N51'06 97W02'38 6:28:11
Peck 96 1 37N28'39 97W22'19 6:29:29
Peck Addition 89 1 39N01 95W40 6:22:40
Penalosa 48 1 37N43'00 98W19'10 6:33:17
Pence 86 4 38N39'21 101W04'23 6:44:18
Pendennis 51 1 38N38'22 100W20'10 6:41:21
Penfield 50 1 37N09'46 95W24'28 6:21:38
Penn 71 1 39N26 98W41 6:34:44
Penokee 33 1 39N21'04 99W58'19 6:39:53
Peoria 30 1 38N35'05 95W08'55 6:20:36
Perry 44 1 39N04'33 95W23'35 6:21:34
Perth 96 1 37N10'29 97W30'18 6:30:01
Peru 10 1 37N05'19 96W05'40 6:24:23
Peters 48 1 37N31 98W18 6:33:12
Petersburg 6 1 37N46'33 94W58'45 6:19:55
Peterson 28 4 38N01'57 101W04'00 6:44:16
Peterton 70 1 38N40'25 95W49'00 6:23:16
Petrolia 1 1 37N44'45 95W28'17 6:21:53
Pfeifer 26 1 38N42'29 99W09'55 6:36:40
Phillipsburg 74 1 39N45'22 99W19'25 6:37:18
Phillips Village 85 1 38N45'40 97W41'50 6:30:47
Pickrell Corner 8 1 37N40'45 96W50'38 6:27:23
Piedmont 37 1 37N37'25 96W21'55 6:25:28
Pierceville 28 4 37N52'42 100W40'35 6:42:42
Pike 56 1 38N23 96W17 6:25:08
Pillsbury Crossing 81 1 39N07'47 96W26'25 6:25:46
Pilot Knob 39 1 37N15 97W58 6:31:52
Pilsen 58 1 38N28'17 97W02'24 6:28:10
Piper 105 1 39N08'35 94W51'40 6:19:27
Piqua 104 1 37N55'22 95W32'06 6:22:08
Pittsburg 19 1 37N24'39 94W42'17 6:18:49
Pixley 4 1 37N15'07 98W30'48 6:34:03
Plains 60 1 37N15'37 100W35'32 6:42:22
Plainview 74 1 39N37 99W28 6:37:52
Plainville 82 1 39N14'05 99W17'52 6:37:11
Pleasantdale 83 1 38N38 99W05 6:36:20
Pleasant Grove 23 1 38N51'20 95W16'10 6:21:05
Pleasant Hill 26 1 38N52 99W27 6:37:48
Pleasanton 54 1 38N10'40 94W42'40 6:18:51
Pleasant Ridge 73 1 38N08 99W18 6:37:12
Pleasant View 11 1 37N17 94W40 6:18:40
Pleasant View 46 1 38N53 94W49 6:19:16
Plevna 78 1 37N58'20 98W18'30 6:33:14
Plum 74 1 39N47 99W07 6:36:28
Plumb 99 1 38N48 96W00 6:24:00
Plum Creek 62 1 39N31 98W06 6:32:24
Plum Grove 8 1 37N57 96W59 6:27:56
Plymell 28 4 37N48'35 100W52'10 6:43:29
Plymouth 56 1 38N24'50 96W19'55 6:25:20
Polk 19 1 37N32'36 94W44'30 6:18:58
Pollard 80 1 38N26'59 98W12'37 6:32:50
Pomeroy 105 1 39N10'06 94W45'40 6:19:03
Pomona 30 1 38N36'30 95W27'05 6:21:48
Pontiac 8 1 37N49'03 96W42'57 6:26:52
Porter 12 4 39N56 101W33 6:46:12
Porterville 6 1 37N43'05 95W04'07 6:20:16
Portis 71 1 39N33'49 98W41'35 6:34:46
Portland 96 1 37N04'40 97W18'43 6:29:15
Port Williams 3 1 39N27'23 95W01'57 6:20:08
Potawatomi Indian Res 43 1 39N20 95W51 6:23:24
Potosi 54 1 38N11 94W41 6:18:44
Potter 3 1 39N25'33 95W08'30 6:20:34
Potwin 8 1 37N56'20 97W01'10 6:28:05
Powell 17 1 37N20 99W07 6:36:28
Powhattan 7 1 39N45'42 95W37'47 6:22:31
Prairie 45 1 39N37 98W06 6:32:24
Prairie Center 46 1 38N51'44 95W01'10 6:20:05
Prairie View 74 1 39N49'57 99W34'20 6:38:17
Prairie Village 8 1 37N41'58 97W08'16 6:28:33
Prairie Village 46 1 38N59'30 94W38'00 6:18:32
Pratt 76 1 37N38'38 98W44'14 6:34:57
Prescott 54 1 38N03'49 94W41'43 6:18:47
Preston 76 1 37N45'32 98W33'10 6:34:13
Pretty Prairie 78 1 37N46'48 98W01'10 6:32:05
Princeton 30 1 38N29'20 95W16'30 6:21:06
Prospect 8 1 37N48'25 96W47'20 6:27:09
Prospect 87 1 37N38'04 97W26'48 6:29:47
Prospect Park 87 1 37N37'40 97W25'15 6:29:41
Protection 17 1 37N12'05 99W29'01 6:37:56
Province Village 46 1 38N53 94W49 6:19:16
Punkin Center 78 1 38N00'50 97W46'30 6:31:06
Purcell 22 1 39N40'50 95W19'50 6:21:19
Purcell 87 1 37N36'40 97W21'25 6:29:26
Putnam 40 1 37N58'08 97W23'15 6:29:33
Quaker 11 1 37N07'54 94W45'30 6:19:02
Quartzite 53 1 39N01'16 98W05'40 6:32:23
Quenemo 70 1 38N34'47 95W31'36 6:22:06
Quinby 28 4 37N59'18 100W55'42 6:43:43
Quincy 37 1 37N52'55 95W59'33 6:23:58
Quindaro 105 1 39N09 94W45 6:19:00
Quinter 32 1 39N04'10 100W13'55 6:40:56
Quivira Lake 46 1 39N02'25 94W46'35 6:19:06
Radium 93 1 38N10'27 98W53'35 6:35:34
Radley 19 1 37N29'04 94W45'36 6:19:02
Rago 48 1 37N27'10 98W04'53 6:32:20
Rainbow Bend 18 1 37N10'30 97W07'50 6:28:31
Ramona 58 1 38N35'50 97W03'42 6:28:15
Randall 45 1 39N38'33 98W02'40 6:32:11
Randolph 81 1 39N25'50 96W45'35 6:27:02

Ransom 68 1 38N38'10 99W56'00 6:39:44
Ransomville 30 1 38N30'23 95W25'32 6:21:42
Rantoul 30 1 38N32'55 95W06'00 6:20:24
Ravanna 28 4 38N09'35 100W22'55 6:41:32
Ray 73 1 38N10'28 98W58'02 6:35:52
Raymond 80 1 38N16'37 98W24'56 6:33:40
Reading 56 1 38N31'10 95W57'30 6:23:50
Reager 69 1 39N49'37 100W05'45 6:40:23
Reamsville 92 1 39N55'48 98W52'00 6:35:28
Redel 46 1 38N49'50 94W38'00 6:18:32
Redfield 6 1 37N50'12 94W52'51 6:19:31
Red Onion 19 1 37N35'13 94W38'45 6:18:35
Red Vermillion 66 1 39N37 96W04 6:24:16
Redwing 5 1 38N31'19 98W39'51 6:34:39
Reece 37 1 37N47'56 96W26'46 6:25:47
Reedsville 59 1 39N46'09 96W32'19 6:26:09
Reilly 66 1 39N36 95W57 6:23:48
Renco 52 1 39N06 95W05 6:20:20
Reno 52 1 39N03'04 95W07'11 6:20:29
Republic 79 1 39N55'25 97W49'17 6:31:17
Republican 14 1 39N11 97W01 6:28:04
Reserve 7 1 39N58'38 95W33'42 6:22:15
Rest 103 1 37N39'11 95W39'37 6:22:38
Rexford 97 1 39N28'18 100W44'35 6:42:58
Rice 15 1 39N34'20 97W33'19 6:30:13
Rich 2 1 38N05 95W08 6:20:32
Richardson 52 1 39N16'00 94W54'00 6:19:36
Richfield 65 3 37N15'58 101W46'55 6:47:08
Richland 89 1 38N53'16 95W31'34 6:22:06
Richmond 30 1 38N24'10 94W15'13 6:17:01
Richter 30 1 38N36'42 95W22'42 6:21:31
Ridgeton 70 1 38N28'03 95W46'05 6:23:04
Ridgeway 70 1 38N49 95W40 6:22:40
Riga 98 1 38N57'02 99W39'00 6:38:36
Riley 81 1 39N17'56 96W49'50 6:27:19
Rinehart 21 1 38N55 96W59 6:27:56
Ringer 61 1 38N32'04 94W54'30 6:19:38
Ringer 87 1 37N42 97W25 6:29:40
Ringo 19 1 37N30'34 94W45'40 6:19:03
Rishel 21 1 38N37'47 97W00'50 6:28:03
Risley 58 1 38N23 97W12 6:28:48
Ritchal 28 4 38N01'57 101W01'40 6:44:07
River 73 1 38N13 98W58 6:35:52
Riverdale 96 1 37N23'24 97W22'20 6:29:29
Riverside 68 1 38N17'27 99W47'13 6:39:09
Riverside 87 1 37N36'54 97W19'19 6:29:17
Riverton 11 1 37N04'30 94W42'16 6:18:49
Riverview 26 1 39N05 99W19 6:37:16
Riverview 87 1 37N46'33 97W20'59 6:29:24
Robert L Roberts 105 1 39N08 94W41 6:18:44
Robinson 7 1 39N49'00 95W24'37 6:21:38
Rochester 48 1 37N26 98W18 6:33:12
Rock 18 1 37N26'25 97W00'22 6:28:01
Rock Branch 69 1 39N58 100W01 6:40:04
Rock Creek 44 1 39N14'45 95W32'13 6:22:09
Rockford 87 1 37N32 97W14 6:28:56
Rockland 9 1 38N25'43 96W38'37 6:26:34
Rockville 80 1 38N19 97W59 6:31:56
Rockwell 69 1 39N50'00 100W05'00 6:40:20
Rocky Ford 37 1 37N49'02 96W03'03 6:24:12
Rocky Ford 81 1 39N14'15 96W35'22 6:26:21
Rodkey 28 4 38N01'04 100W57'26 6:43:50
Roeland Park 46 1 39N02'15 94W37'55 6:18:32
Rogers 10 1 37N08'49 96W16'44 6:25:07
Roland 96 1 37N15'58 97W27'26 6:29:50
Rolla 65 3 37N07'12 101W07'54 6:44:32
Rollin 67 1 37N38'03 95W21'21 6:21:25
Rolling Hills 87 1 37N41'10 97W26'50 6:29:47
Rolling Prairie 64 1 38N50 96W46 6:27:04
Rome 96 1 37N09'41 97W08'33 6:28:34
Ronald 6 1 37N47'30 94W48'15 6:19:13
Roosevelt 20 1 39N53 100W21 6:41:24
Roper 103 1 37N39'40 95W43'57 6:22:56
Rosaco 15 1 39N34'44 97W37'40 6:30:31
Rosalia 8 1 37N48'55 96W37'10 6:26:29
Roscoe 33 1 39N28'51 99W46'09 6:39:05
Roscoe 78 1 37N47 98W05 6:32:20
Rose 104 1 37N47'35 95W41'10 6:22:45
Rose Creek 79 1 39N57 97W32 6:30:08
Rosedale 105 1 39N04 94W38 6:18:32
Rose Hill 8 1 37N33'30 97W08'05 6:28:32
Roseland 11 1 37N16'52 94W51'01 6:19:24
Rose Valley 93 1 37N53 98W45 6:35:00
Rosewood 50 1 37N20 95W16 6:21:04
Rossville 89 1 39N08'10 95W57'05 6:23:48
Rotate 77 1 39N39 101W21 6:45:24
Round Mound 71 1 39N16 99W00 6:36:00
Round Springs 62 1 39N15 98W12 6:32:48
Rovohl 97 1 39N31 101W03 6:44:12
Roxbury 57 1 38N33'03 97W25'48 6:29:43
Royal 29 1 37N52 100W07 6:40:28
Rozel 73 1 38N11'45 99W24'10 6:37:37
Ruella 39 1 37N04'50 98W11'00 6:32:44
Ruleton 91 2 39N20'22 101W53'20 6:47:33
Runnymede 39 1 37N21'23 97W55'46 6:31:43
Rush 82 1 39N21 99W26 6:37:44
Rush Center 83 1 38N27'55 99W18'35 6:37:14
Rushville 74 1 39N37 99W21 6:37:24
Russell 84 1 38N53'43 98W51'34 6:35:26
Russell Springs 55 4 38N54'48 101W10'52 6:44:43
Rutland 63 1 37N12 95W53 6:23:32
Ryan 96 1 37N16 97W38 6:30:32
Rydal 79 1 39N48'48 97W42'40 6:30:51
Ryus 34 3 37N29'52 101W06'28 6:44:26
Sabetha 66 1 39N54'08 95W48'02 6:23:12
Saffordville 9 1 38N24'00 96W23'33 6:25:34
Saint Benedict 66 1 39N53'14 96W05'55 6:24:24
Saint Bridget 59 1 39N57'58 96W15'49 6:25:03
Saint Clere 75 1 39N22'09 96W03'20 6:24:13
Saint Francis 12 4 39N46'20 101W47'58 6:47:12
Saint George 75 1 39N11'28 96W25'12 6:25:41
Saint Joe 78 1 37N44'56 97W43'54 6:30:56

Saint John 93 1 38N00'08 98W45'35 6:35:02
Saint Joseph 15 1 39N30'35 97W24'21 6:29:37
Saint Leo 48 1 37N31'45 98W24'36 6:33:38
Saint Mark 87 1 37N44'09 97W33'43 6:30:15
Saint Marys 75 1 39N11'39 96W04'15 6:24:17
Saint Marys 87 1 37N42'24 97W38'23 6:30:34
Saint Mary's College 52 1 39N19 94W55 6:19:40
Saint Pats 3 1 39N28'40 95W07'17 6:20:29
Saint Paul 67 1 37N31'08 95W10'23 6:20:42
Saint Paul 87 1 37N39'45 97W45'07 6:31:00
Saint Peter 33 1 39N11'23 100W05'20 6:40:21
Saint Theresa 102 4 38N29 101W21 6:45:24
Salamanca 11 1 37N10 94W53 6:19:32
Salem 77 1 39N52'18 98W29'03 6:33:56
Salemsborg 85 1 38N41'43 97W41'09 6:30:45
Salina 85 1 38N50'25 97W36'40 6:30:27
Saline 26 1 39N04 99W07 6:36:28
Sallyards 37 1 37N49'17 96W30'25 6:26:02
Salter 8 1 37N36'50 97W02'40 6:28:11
Salt Springs 37 1 37N39 96W02 6:24:08
Sand Burr Hill 87 1 37N34'14 97W18'45 6:29:15
Sand Creek 40 1 38N02'00 97W22'10 6:29:29
Sand Spring 21 1 38N54'25 97W17'01 6:29:08
Sanford 73 1 38N10'50 99W18'50 6:37:15
Santa Fe 73 1 38N08 99W11 6:36:44
Sappa 20 1 39N47 100W41 6:42:44
Saratoga 76 1 37N38 98W42 6:34:48
Sarcoxie 52 1 39N06 95W14 6:20:56
Satanta 41 3 37N26'14 101W58'18 6:47:53
Saunders 94 3 37N28'16 102W02'20 6:48:09
Savonburg 1 1 37N44'58 95W08'38 6:20:35
Sawlog 42 1 37N58 99W54 6:39:36
Sawmill 73 1 38N08 99W31 6:38:04
Sawyer 76 1 37N29'50 98W40'55 6:34:44
Saxman 80 1 38N16'50 98W07'32 6:32:30
Sayre 29 3 37N41'17 100W10'26 6:40:42
Scammon 11 1 37N16'39 94W49'29 6:19:18
Scandia 79 1 39N47'40 97W47'00 6:31:08
Schaffer 83 1 38N28'17 99W05'18 6:36:21
Schoenchen 26 1 38N42'48 99W19'55 6:37:20
Schulte 87 1 37N37'23 97W28'16 6:29:53
Scipio 2 1 38N22'06 95W13'03 6:20:52
Scott City 86 4 38N28'57 100W54'24 6:43:38
Scottsville 62 1 39N32'37 97W57'10 6:31:49
Scranton 70 1 38N46'54 95W44'18 6:22:57
Sears 29 1 37N45'45 100W06'20 6:40:25
Sedan 10 1 37N07'36 96W11'12 6:24:45
Sedgwick 87 1 37N55'00 97W25'20 6:29:41
Seguin 90 1 39N20'15 100W35'40 6:42:23
Selden 90 1 39N32'27 100W34'02 6:42:16
Selkirk 102 4 38N28'24 101W32'35 6:46:10
Selma 2 1 38N08'05 95W07'23 6:20:30
Seneca 66 1 39N50'03 96W03'50 6:24:15
Severance 22 1 39N46'02 95W14'59 6:21:00
Severy 37 1 37N37'20 96W13'40 6:24:55
Seward 93 1 38N10'40 98W47'40 6:35:11
Shady Bend 53 1 39N01'06 98W01'17 6:32:05
Shady Brook 21 1 38N44'22 96W58'58 6:27:56
Shaffer 83 1 38N27 99W01 6:36:04
Shallow Water 86 4 38N22'25 100W54'45 6:43:39
Shannon 3 1 39N33'55 95W14'35 6:20:58
Sharon 4 1 37N14'55 98W25'13 6:33:41
Sharon Springs 100 2 38N53'52 101W45'06 6:47:00
Sharpe 16 1 38N16'55 95W41'30 6:22:46
Shaw 67 1 37N36'08 95W19'02 6:21:16
Shawnee 46 1 39N02'30 94W43'12 6:18:53
Shawnee Mission 46 1 39N02 94W39 6:18:36
Shell Rock 37 1 38N07 96W01 6:24:04
Sherdahl 79 1 39N51'25 97W48'28 6:31:14
Sherlock 28 4 38N00 101W02 6:44:08
Sherman 11 1 37N15'26 95W03'25 6:20:14
Shermanville 91 2 39N29 101W34 6:46:16
Sherwin 11 1 37N10'48 94W56'51 6:19:47
Sherwood Estates 89 1 39N02 95W43 6:22:52
Shields 51 1 38N36'56 100W26'41 6:41:47
Shiley 73 1 38N18 99W32 6:38:08
Shiloh 67 1 37N26 95W28 6:21:52
Shimer 17 1 37N05 99W09 6:36:36
Shipton 85 1 38N54'50 97W40'55 6:30:44
Shirley 15 1 39N32 97W25 6:29:40
Shroyer 59 1 39N46'10 96W40'42 6:26:43
Sibley 15 1 39N37 97W40 6:30:40
Sibleyville 23 1 38N53'03 95W11'43 6:20:47
Silica 80 1 38N21'06 98W27'42 6:33:51
Silkville 30 1 38N27'00 95W29'20 6:21:57
Silverdale 18 1 37N02'31 96W54'11 6:27:37
Silver Lake 89 1 39N06'15 95W51'30 6:23:26
Simpson 62 1 39N23'07 97W55'52 6:31:43
Sinclair 45 1 39N52 97W59 6:31:56
Sitka 13 1 37N10'30 99W39'04 6:38:36
Skellyville 48 1 37N40'30 98W27'00 6:33:48
Skiddy 64 1 38N52'05 96W47'39 6:27:11
Skidmore 11 1 37N14'25 94W49'54 6:19:20
Smileyville 8 1 37N31'11 96W52'50 6:27:31
Smith 97 1 39N27 100W47 6:43:08
Smith Center 92 1 39N46'45 98W47'05 6:35:08
Smithfield 33 1 39N28'52 99W49'33 6:39:18
Smoky 91 2 39N12 101W43 6:46:52
Smoky Hill 31 1 39N01'27 96W50'25 6:27:22
Smoky View 85 1 38N39 97W39 6:30:36
Smolan 85 1 38N44'19 97W41'03 6:30:44
Sodville 29 1 37N31 99W45 6:39:00
Soldier 43 1 39N32'10 95W57'50 6:23:51
Solomon 21 1 38N55'10 97W22'15 6:29:29
Solomon Rapids 62 1 39N28'25 98W11'32 6:32:46
Somerset 61 1 38N36'18 94W46'07 6:19:04
South Basehor 52 1 39N07'44 94W56'18 6:19:45
South Bend 5 1 38N18 98W45 6:35:00
South Brown 24 1 37N47 99W20 6:37:20
South Dodge 29 1 37N44'32 100W01'10 6:40:05

Place		Lat.	Long.	Time
Southeast 87	1	37N41	97W17	6:29:08
South Haven 96	1	37N03'07	97W24'18	6:29:37
South Hoisington 5	1	38N30'20	98W46'30	6:35:06
South Homestead 5	1	38N29	98W46	6:35:04
South Hutchinson 78	1	38N01'41	97W56'24	6:31:46
South Mound 67	1	37N26'14	95W13'42	6:20:55
South Park 46	1	39N01	94W42	6:18:48
South Radley 19	1	37N28'17	94W45'36	6:19:02
South Randall 97	1	39N11	100W50	6:43:20
South Roscoe 42	1	37N58	100W07	6:40:28
South Salem 37	1	37N54	96W25	6:25:40
South Seneca Gardens 87	1	37N36'04	97W20'56	6:29:24
South Seward 93	1	38N08	98W45	6:35:00
South Sharps Creek 57	1	38N28	97W52	6:31:28
Southside 47	5	37N53	101W12	6:44:48
Southwest Gardens 46	1	39N01	94W42	6:18:48
Sparks 22	1	39N51'27	95W11'24	6:20:46
Spasticville 87	1	37N50'01	97W20'09	6:29:21
Spearville 29	1	37N51'00	99W45'23	6:39:02
Speed 74	1	39N40'38	99W25'14	6:37:41
Spence 101	1	39N55'57	96W56'10	6:27:45
Spencer 89	1	39N03'28	95W31'55	6:22:08
Spica 97	1	39N12'24	100W54'54	6:43:40
Spivey 48	1	37N26'45	98W09'47	6:32:39
Spring Brook 90	1	39N13	100W28	6:41:52
Springdale 52	1	39N15'34	95W07'27	6:20:30
Springdale 87	1	37N40'30	97W10'07	6:28:40
Spring Grove 11	1	37N05	94W38	6:18:32
Spring Hill 46	1	38N44'35	94W49'31	6:19:18
Springvale 76	1	37N30'43	98W56'45	6:35:47
Stafford 93	1	37N57'44	98W36'01	6:34:24
Stanley 46	1	38N51'16	94W39'56	6:18:40
Stano 34	3	37N31'14	101W29'22	6:45:57
Stanton 61	1	38N32'36	95W03'15	6:20:13
Star 16	1	38N13	95W36	6:22:24
Stark 67	1	37N41'24	95W08'34	6:20:34
Starr 15	1	39N21	97W25	6:29:40
State House 89	1	39N03	95W41	6:22:44
State Line 91	2	39N19	102W00	6:48:00
Sterling 80	1	38N12'36	98W12'24	6:32:50
Stickney 5	1	38N38'17	98W49'45	6:35:19
Stilwell 46	1	38N46'09	94W39'22	6:18:37
Stippville 11	1	37N13'20	94W50'15	6:19:21
Stockton 82	1	39N26'17	99W15'53	6:37:04
Stohrville 39	1	37N04	97W52	6:31:28
Stone 52	1	39N07'43	94W55'00	6:19:40
Stony Point 105	1	39N05'40	94W45'36	6:19:02
Stover 50	1	37N10'26	95W11'40	6:20:47
Straight Creek 43	1	39N31	95W38	6:22:32
Stranger 52	1	39N08	95W01	6:20:04
Strauss 50	1	37N20'25	95W05'08	6:20:21
Strawberry 101	1	39N42'43	97W15'18	6:29:01
Strawn 16	1	38N12	95W45	6:23:00
Strong 9	1	38N23'50	96W32'12	6:26:09
Strong City (Strong) 9	1	38N23'50	96W32'12	6:26:09
Stubbs 4	1	37N00'24	98W33'56	6:34:16
Studley 90	1	39N21'11	100W09'48	6:40:39
Stull 23	1	38N58'16	95W27'21	6:21:49
Stuttgart 74	1	39N47'58	99W27'18	6:37:49
Sublette 41	3	37N28'54	100W50'36	6:43:22
Suburban Heights 63	1	37N14	95W43	6:22:52
Sugar Creek 61	1	38N27	94W40	6:18:40
Sugar Loaf 82	1	39N31	99W27	6:37:48
Sullivan 34	3	37N26	101W19	6:45:16
Sullivan 59	1	39N39'55	96W21'20	6:25:25
Sullivans Track 34	3	37N35	101W22	6:45:28
Summerfield 59	1	39N59'50	96W21'00	6:25:24
Summers 97	1	39N14	101W03	6:44:12
Summit 8	1	37N49'16	96W33'50	6:26:15
Summit 59	1	39N53'50	96W20'50	6:25:23
Sumnerville 72	1	39N11'51	97W44'10	6:30:57
Sun City 4	1	37N22'43	98W54'56	6:35:40
Sunflower 46	1	38N56'45	95W00'10	6:20:01
Sunflower 105	1	39N03'55	94W51'50	6:19:27
Sunland 100	2	38N53'34	101W49'16	6:47:17
Sunnydale 87	1	37N52'06	97W17'57	6:29:12
Sunset Acres 8	1	37N43'30	97W07'42	6:28:31
Sunset Park 81	1	39N10'33	96W35'45	6:26:23
Sunset Park 87	1	37N34'38	97W20'20	6:29:21
Sun Springs 7	1	39N53'22	95W42'12	6:22:49
Suppesville 96	1	37N30'03	97W46'12	6:31:05
Susank 5	1	38N38'27	98W46'25	6:35:06
Sutphen 21	1	39N02'54	97W03'18	6:28:13
Sutton 47	2	37N54'21	101W27'54	6:45:52
Sutton 51	1	38N20	100W37	6:42:28
Swamp Angel 75	1	39N11'40	96W28'55	6:25:56
Swan 92	1	39N52	99W01	6:36:04
Swede Creek 81	1	39N32	96W43	6:26:52
Swissvale 70	1	38N50'01	95W34'48	6:22:19
Sycamore 63	1	37N19'37	95W42'55	6:22:52
Sylvan Grove 53	1	39N00'34	98W23'38	6:33:35
Sylvia 78	1	37N57'28	98W24'28	6:33:38
Syracuse 38	2	37N58'50	101W45'08	6:47:01
Tabor 79	1	39N51'25	97W31'00	6:30:04
Talleyrand 103	1	37N25	95W48	6:23:12
Talmage 21	1	39N01'30	97W15'37	6:29:02
Talmo 79	1	39N41'45	97W35'16	6:30:21
Taloga 65	3	37N04	101W53	6:47:32
Tampa 58	1	38N32'50	97W09'10	6:28:37
Tasco 90	1	39N21'15	100W17'27	6:41:10
Taussig 18	1	37N06'20	96W34'13	6:26:17
Tecumseh 89	1	39N02'53	95W34'44	6:22:19
Ten Mile 61	1	38N41	94W45	6:19:00
Tennis 28	4	38N09'48	101W54'38	6:47:39
Terra Cotta 27	1	38N44'30	97W57'25	6:31:50
Terra Heights 89	1	38N58'36	95W40'59	6:22:44
Terry 28	4	38N11	100W58	6:43:52
Tescott 72	1	39N00'29	97W52'31	6:31:30
Teterville 37	1	38N02'35	96W25'13	6:25:41
Thayer 67	1	37N29'35	95W28'12	6:21:53
The Dell 87	1	37N40'30	97W27'40	6:29:51
Thomas 27	1	38N34	98W12	6:32:48
Thompsonville 44	1	39N06'20	95W26'00	6:21:44
Thornburg 92	1	39N56'40	98W47'09	6:35:09
Thrall 37	1	38N00'36	96W19'15	6:25:17
Tice 41	3	37N30'58	100W43'35	6:42:54
Tilden 71	1	39N27	98W49	6:35:16
Timberhill 6	1	37N59	94W53	6:19:32
Timken 83	1	38N28'25	99W10'40	6:36:43
Tioga 67	1	37N41	95W28	6:21:52
Tipton 62	1	39N20'35	98W28'14	6:33:53
Tisdale 18	1	37N14'36	96W51'06	6:27:24
Togo 33	1	39N11'00	99W51'57	6:39:28
Toledo 9	1	38N25'20	96W22'15	6:25:29
Tolerville 87	1	37N45'10	97W16'08	6:29:05
Tonganoxie 52	1	39N06'35	95W05'15	6:20:21
Tonovay 37	1	37N51'08	96W10'40	6:24:43
Topeka 89	1	39N02'54	95W40'40	6:22:43
Toronto 104	1	37N47'56	95W56'56	6:23:48
Toulon 26	1	38N51'06	99W14'25	6:36:58
Towanda 8	1	37N47'51	96W59'58	6:28:00
Tower Grove 46	1	39N00	94W41	6:18:44
Trading Post 54	1	38N14'55	94W40'50	6:18:43
Traer 20	1	39N55'42	100W39'57	6:42:40
Travel Air 87	1	37N44	97W16	6:29:04
Treece 11	1	37N00'03	94W50'35	6:19:22
Trego Center 98	1	38N53'08	99W53'29	6:39:34
Trenton 24	1	37N51	99W31	6:38:04
Trenton 85	1	38N53'13	97W38'56	6:30:36
Tresham 18	1	37N10'12	97W02'58	6:28:12
Tribune 36	2	38N28'11	101W45'08	6:47:01
Trivoli 27	1	38N35	98W06	6:32:24
Trousdale 24	1	37N48'55	99W05'07	6:36:20
Troy 22	1	39N46'59	95W05'23	6:20:22
Turck 11	1	37N13'50	94W49'54	6:19:20
Turkville 26	1	39N06'12	99W14'43	6:36:59
Turner 105	1	39N05'00	94W42'15	6:18:49
Turon 78	1	37N48'26	98W25'35	6:33:42
Twin Grove 37	1	37N38	96W14	6:24:56
Twin Mound 82	1	39N16	99W13	6:36:52
Tyler 87	1	37N40'10	97W26'40	6:29:47
Tyro 63	1	37N02'16	95W49'16	6:23:17
Udall 18	1	37N23'15	97W06'50	6:28:27
Ulysses 34	3	37N34'53	101W21'17	6:45:25
Union Center 25	1	37N32	96W25	6:25:40
Uniontown 6	1	37N50'50	94W58'30	6:19:54
University 23	1	38N58	95W15	6:21:00
Upland 21	1	39N05'20	97W01'08	6:28:05
Upland 59	1	39N49'28	96W33'20	6:26:13
Upola 25	1	37N25'00	95W59'54	6:24:00
Urbana 67	1	37N33'29	95W23'57	6:21:36
Ursula 49	1	37N31	99W16	6:37:04
Utica 68	1	38N38'38	100W10'10	6:40:41
Utopia 37	1	37N53'52	96W13'26	6:24:54
V A Hospital 89	1	39N02	95W41	6:22:44
Valeda 50	1	37N02'50	95W26'50	6:21:47
Valencia 89	1	39N04'43	95W52'34	6:23:30
Valley Brook 70	1	38N37	95W40	6:22:40
Valley Center 87	1	37N50'05	97W22'23	6:29:30
Valley Falls 44	1	39N20'36	95W27'36	6:21:50
Valverde 96	1	37N11	97W12	6:28:48
Van Arsdale 40	1	37N59'57	97W25'36	6:29:42
Vance 2	1	38N09'28	95W04'36	6:20:18
Vanora 8	1	37N45'57	96W53'20	6:27:33
Varner 48	1	37N43'08	98W02'10	6:32:09
Vassar 70	1	38N38'50	95W37'20	6:22:29
Vaughn 73	1	38N20'28	99W17'09	6:37:09
Venango 27	1	38N38'20	97W59'10	6:31:57
Vera 99	1	39N04'01	96W05'41	6:24:23
Verdi 72	1	38N59'30	97W30'10	6:30:01
Verdigris 103	1	37N41	95W55	6:23:40
Vermillion 59	1	39N43'10	96W15'56	6:25:04
Vernon 18	1	37N15	97W06	6:28:24
Vernon 104	1	37N58'50	95W39'24	6:22:38
Vesper 53	1	39N01'55	98W16'47	6:33:07
Vesta 13	1	37N12	99W59	6:39:56
Vicksburg 45	1	39N42	97W59	6:31:56
Victor 62	1	39N14'53	98W17'01	6:33:08
Victor 71	1	39N16	98W53	6:35:32
Victoria 26	1	38N51'10	99W08'50	6:36:35
Victory Junction 105	1	39N07'44	94W54'04	6:19:36
Vienna 75	1	39N26	96W10	6:24:40
Vilas 103	1	37N39'15	95W35'10	6:22:21
Vincent 71	1	39N11'30	98W43'10	6:34:53
Vine Creek 72	1	39N07'05	97W24'56	6:29:40
Vinewood 105	1	39N10'18	94W47'36	6:19:10
Vining 101	1	39N34'01	97W17'42	6:29:11
Vinita 48	1	37N36	97W52	6:31:28
Vinland 23	1	38N50'22	95W10'55	6:20:44
Vinton 18	1	37N06'20	96W49'30	6:27:18
Viola 87	1	37N28'59	97W38'37	6:30:34
Virgil 37	1	37N58'51	96W00'36	6:24:02
Vliets 59	1	39N42'50	96W20'00	6:25:20
Voda 98	1	39N02'57	100W01'10	6:40:05
Volland 99	1	38N56'40	96W24'15	6:25:37
Voltaire 91	2	39N29	101W43	6:46:52
Voorhees 95	3	37N04	101W25	6:45:40
Wabaunsee 99	1	39N08'46	96W20'45	6:25:23
Waco 87	1	37N31'14	97W18'26	6:29:14
Wadsworth 52	1	39N16'42	94W54'00	6:19:36
Wagon Wheel Ranch 8	1	37N41	96W59	6:27:56
Wagstaff 61	1	38N39'54	94W47'46	6:19:11
Wakarusa 89	1	38N53'09	95W41'44	6:22:47
Wa Keeney 98	1	39N01'30	99W52'45	6:39:31
Wakefield 14	1	39N12'48	97W00'19	6:28:01
Waldeck 58	1	38N25'50	97W20'05	6:29:20
Waldeck 76	1	37N39'14	98W36'35	6:34:26
Waldo 84	1	39N07'06	98W47'52	6:35:11
Waldron 39	1	37N00'00	98W11'00	6:32:44
Walker 26	1	38N52'02	99W04'32	6:36:18
Walkinghood 36	2	38N28'20	101W58'20	6:47:53
Wallace 100	2	38N54'41	101W35'28	6:46:22
Wallula 105	1	39N10'21	94W54'01	6:19:36
Walnut 19	1	37N36'05	95W04'40	6:20:19
Walnut Creek 62	1	39N26	98W19	6:33:16
Walnut Grove 67	1	37N36	95W10	6:20:40
Walsburg 81	1	39N23'35	96W48'41	6:27:15
Walton 40	1	38N07'04	97W15'23	6:29:02
Wamego 75	1	39N12'07	96W18'17	6:25:13
Wano 12	4	39N47	101W48	6:47:12
Waring 68	1	38N37	99W42	6:38:48
Warren 64	1	38N45	96W25	6:25:40
Warwick 79	1	39N59'55	97W54'25	6:31:38
Washburn University 89	1	39N02	95W41	6:22:44
Washington 101	1	39N49'05	97W03'02	6:28:12
Washington Street 87	1	37N41	97W20	6:29:20
Waterloo 48	1	37N40'37	97W56'26	6:31:46
Waterloo 56	1	38N42	96W01	6:24:04
Waterville 59	1	39N41'28	96W44'50	6:26:59
Wathena 22	1	39N45'33	94W56'58	6:19:48
Watson 89	1	38N59'17	95W33'22	6:22:13
Wauneta 10	1	37N06'47	96W22'49	6:25:31
Waverly 16	1	38N23'38	95W36'10	6:22:25
Wayne 79	1	39N42'53	97W32'30	6:30:10
Wayside 63	1	37N07'29	95W52'23	6:23:30
Wea 61	1	38N42'55	94W40'00	6:18:40
Weaver 23	1	38N57'43	95W04'01	6:20:16
Webber 45	1	39N56'06	98W02'05	6:32:08
Webster 82	1	39N24'06	99W26'08	6:37:45
Wego-Waco 87	1	37N31'15	97W20'01	6:29:20
Weir 11	1	37N18'36	94W46'18	6:19:05
Welborn 105	1	39N08'36	94W42'00	6:18:48
Welda 2	1	38N10'10	95W17'40	6:21:11
Wellington 96	1	37N15'55	97W22'17	6:29:29
Wells 72	1	39N08'20	97W33'02	6:30:12
Wellsford 76	1	37N37'00	99W01'42	6:36:07
Wellsville 30	1	38N43'06	95W04'53	6:20:20
Wendell 97	1	39N31	100W49	6:43:16
Weskan 100	2	38N52'00	101W57'50	6:47:51
Wesleyan 85	1	38N50	97W36	6:30:24
Wesley Center 45	1	39N57'32	98W19'29	6:33:18
West Branch 58	1	38N13	97W19	6:29:16
West Center 95	3	37N11	101W27	6:45:48
West Cherry 63	1	37N19	95W38	6:22:32
West Coffeyville 63	1	37N02'20	95W40'11	6:22:41
West Cooper 93	1	38N03	98W38	6:34:32
Western 55	4	38N53	101W24	6:45:36
Westfall 53	1	38N55'48	98W00'40	6:32:03
West Hale 97	1	39N22	101W20	6:45:20
West Hamilton 26	1	39N04	99W32	6:38:08
West Hess 35	3	37N37	100W23	6:41:32
West Hibbard 47	2	38N10	101W26	6:45:44
Westland 49	1	37N31	99W30	6:38:00
Westlink Village 87	1	37N41'52	97W27'11	6:29:49
West Mineral 11	1	37N17'03	94W55'22	6:19:41
Westminster 78	1	37N57	98W12	6:32:48
Westmoreland 75	1	39N23'38	96W24'48	6:25:39
Westola 65	3	37N15	101W58	6:47:52
Westphalia 2	1	38N10'55	95W29'24	6:21:58
West Plains 60	1	37N15	100W32	6:42:08
West Saline 90	1	39N14	100W20	6:41:20
West Shore 44	1	39N11'20	95W20'37	6:21:54
West Union 69	1	39N37	99W42	6:38:48
West Washington 80	1	38N13	98W05	6:32:20
Westwood 46	1	39N02'26	94W37'00	6:18:28
Westwood Hills 46	1	39N02'20	94W36'35	6:18:26
Wetmore 66	1	39N38'00	95W48'40	6:23:15
Wettick 35	4	37N47'48	100W15'50	6:41:03
Wheaton 75	1	39N30'08	96W19'14	6:25:17
Wheatridge Addition 87	1	37N42	97W25	6:29:40
Wheeler 12	4	39N45'51	101W42'45	6:46:51
White 48	1	37N41	98W05	6:32:20
White City 64	1	38N47'44	96W44'08	6:26:57
White Cloud 22	1	39N58'35	95W17'48	6:21:11
Whitelaw 36	2	38N27'18	101W40'44	6:46:43
White Mound 45	1	39N52	98W27	6:33:48
White Rock 45	1	39N53'10	97W55'55	6:31:44
Whiteside 78	1	38N00'27	98W00'53	6:32:04
Whitewater 8	1	37N57'53	97W08'50	6:28:35
Whitewoman 102	4	38N21	101W21	6:45:24
Whiting 43	1	39N35'23	95W36'45	6:22:27
Whitman 96	1	37N19'57	97W11'14	6:28:45
Wichita 87	1	37N41'32	97W20'14	6:29:21
Wichita Heights 87	1	37N46'52	97W20'08	6:29:21
Wilburn 29	1	37N31	100W06	6:40:24
Wilburton 65	3	37N04'25	101W46'22	6:47:05
Wilder 46	1	39N02'35	94W52'10	6:19:29
Wild Horse 33	1	39N19	99W41	6:38:44
Willard 89	1	39N05'36	95W56'30	6:23:46
Willcox 98	1	38N47	99W52	6:39:28
Williams 24	1	37N49'00	99W20'00	6:37:20
Williamsburg 30	1	38N28'50	95W28'00	6:21:52
Williamsport 89	1	38N56	95W42	6:22:48
Williamstown 44	1	39N03'46	95W19'57	6:21:20
Willis 7	1	39N43'30	95W30'20	6:22:01
Willowbrook 78	1	38N06'07	97W59'30	6:31:58
Willowdale 48	1	37N30'55	98W18'05	6:33:12
Willow Springs 23	1	38N49	95W18	6:21:12
Wilmington 99	1	38N44'40	95W57'33	6:23:50
Wilmore 17	1	37N20'09	99W12'35	6:36:50

Wilmot 18	1	37N22'34	96W52'32	6:27:30
Wilroads 29	1	37N42'06	99W53'36	6:39:34
Wilroads Gardens 29	1	37N43'27	99W55'58	6:39:44
Wilsey 64	1	38N38'10	96W40'30	6:26:42
Wilson 27	1	38N49'30	98W28'30	6:33:54
Winchester 44	1	39N19'20	95W16'00	6:21:04
Windhorst 29	1	37N47'07	99W38'30	6:38:34
Windom 57	1	38N23'02	97W54'35	6:31:38
Windsor 18	1	37N19	96W38	6:26:32
Windsor Park 87	1	37N43	97W16	6:29:04
Windthorst 29	1	37N51	99W45	6:39:00
Winfield 18	1	37N14'23	96W59'43	6:27:59
Wingate 8	1	37N28'55	96W41'50	6:26:47
Wingfield 31	1	39N01	96W39	6:26:36
Winifred 59	1	39N46'10	97W28'50	6:29:55
Winkler 81	1	39N28'54	96W49'53	6:27:20
Winona 55	4	39N03'48	101W14'38	6:44:59
Winterset 84	1	38N45	98W59	6:35:56
Winway 50	1	37N20	95W16	6:21:04
Wolcott 105	1	39N11'20	94W48'05	6:19:12
Wolf 28	4	38N01'56	101W05'55	6:44:24
Wolf Creek 53	1	39N02'04	98W28'40	6:33:55
Wolf River 22	1	39N47	95W15	6:21:00
Womer 92	1	39N58'25	98W42'37	6:34:50
Wonsevu 9	1	38N09'03	96W46'19	6:27:05
Woodbine 21	1	38N47'46	96W57'30	6:27:50
Woodlawn 66	1	39N47'00	95W51'52	6:23:27
Woodruff 74	1	39N59'34	99W25'34	6:37:42
Woods 95	3	37N10'13	101W06'19	6:44:25
Woodston 82	1	39N27'19	99W05'43	6:36:23
Worden 23	1	38N46'56	95W20'03	6:21:20
Wreford 31	1	38N57'42	96W50'54	6:27:24
Wright 29	1	37N46'50	99W53'30	6:39:34
Wyandotte 105	1	39N05	94W46	6:19:04
Xavier 52	1	39N16'38	94W54'32	6:19:38
Xenia 6	1	37N59'43	94W59'10	6:19:57
Yaggy 78	1	38N05'49	98W00'31	6:32:02
Yale 19	1	37N29'02	94W38'30	6:18:34
Yankee Run 27	1	38N39'05	98W01'00	6:32:04
Yates Center 104	1	37N52'52	95W43'59	6:22:56
Yocemento 26	1	38N54'26	99W25'25	6:37:42
Yoder 78	1	37N56'25	97W52'05	6:31:28
York 93	1	37N52	98W32	6:34:08
Yuma 15	1	39N35'28	97W44'58	6:31:00
Zarah 46	1	39N00'26	94W49'25	6:19:18
Zeandale 81	1	39N09'34	96W25'35	6:25:42
Zenda 48	1	37N26'32	98W16'54	6:33:08
Zenith 93	1	37N57'26	98W29'30	6:33:58
Zimmerdale 40	1	38N06'10	97W23'23	6:29:34
Zook 73	1	38N03'28	99W05'12	6:36:21
Zurich 82	1	39N14'04	99W26'16	6:37:45
Zyba 96	1	37N26'05	97W23'20	6:29:33

TIME TABLES

Eastern Kentucky shows a gradual shift from Central to Eastern time. In order to comply with mandated CST, there was wide-spread observance of daylight time in central Kentucky during the late 1950's, including continuous observance of CDT in many cities after 1957. Since there was frequent local variation in starting and ending dates of daylight savings periods, caution must be advised.

KY # 1

Before 11/18/1883		LMT
11/18/1883	12:00	CST
3/31/1918	02:00	CWT
10/27/1918	02:00	CST
3/30/1919	02:00	CWT
10/26/1919	02:00	CST
2/09/1942	02:00	CWT
9/30/1945	02:00	CST
4/28/1968	02:00	US#1

KY # 2

Before 11/18/1883		LMT
11/18/1883	12:00	CST
3/31/1918	02:00	CWT
10/27/1918	02:00	CST
3/30/1919	02:00	CWT
10/26/1919	02:00	CST
2/09/1942	02:00	CWT
9/30/1945	02:00	CST
4/26/1953	02:00	CDT
9/27/1953	02:00	CST
4/28/1968	02:00	US#1

KY # 3

Before 11/18/1883		LMT
11/18/1883	12:00	CST
3/31/1918	02:00	CWT
10/27/1918	02:00	CST
3/30/1919	02:00	CWT
10/26/1919	02:00	CST
2/09/1942	02:00	CWT
9/30/1945	02:00	CST
4/29/1956	02:00	CDT
9/30/1956	02:00	CST
4/28/1968	02:00	US#1

KY # 4

Before 11/18/1883		LMT
11/18/1883	12:00	CST
3/31/1918	02:00	CWT
10/27/1918	02:00	CST
3/30/1919	02:00	CWT
10/26/1919	02:00	CST
2/09/1942	02:00	CWT
9/30/1945	02:00	CST
4/26/1964	02:00	CDT
10/25/1964	02:00	CST
4/28/1968	02:00	US#1

KY # 5

Before 11/18/1883		LMT
11/18/1883	12:00	CST
3/31/1918	02:00	CWT
10/27/1918	02:00	CST
3/30/1919	02:00	CWT
10/26/1919	02:00	CST
2/09/1942	02:00	CWT
9/30/1945	02:00	CST
4/26/1964	02:00	CDT
10/25/1964	02:00	CST
4/24/1966	02:00	US#1

KY # 6

Before 11/18/1883		LMT
11/18/1883	12:00	CST
3/31/1918	02:00	CWT
10/27/1918	02:00	CST
3/30/1919	02:00	CWT
10/26/1919	02:00	CST
4/27/1941	02:00	CDT
9/28/1941	02:00	CST
2/09/1942	02:00	CWT
9/30/1945	02:00	CST
4/28/1968	02:00	US#1

KY # 7

Before 11/18/1883		LMT
11/18/1883	12:00	CST
3/31/1918	02:00	CWT
10/27/1918	02:00	CST
3/30/1919	02:00	CWT
10/26/1919	02:00	CST
4/27/1941	02:00	CDT
9/28/1941	02:00	CST
2/09/1942	02:00	CWT
9/30/1945	02:00	CST
4/29/1956	02:00	CDT
9/30/1956	02:00	CST
4/28/1968	02:00	US#1

KY # 8

Before 11/18/1883		LMT
11/18/1883	12:00	CST
3/31/1918	02:00	CWT
10/27/1918	02:00	CST
3/30/1919	02:00	CWT
10/26/1919	02:00	CST
2/09/1942	02:00	CWT
9/30/1945	02:00	CST
4/24/1955	02:00	CDT
9/25/1955	02:00	CST
4/28/1957	02:00	CDT
9/29/1957	02:00	CST
4/28/1968	02:00	US#1

KY # 9

Before 11/18/1883		LMT
11/18/1883	12:00	CST
3/31/1918	02:00	CWT
10/27/1918	02:00	CST
3/30/1919	02:00	CWT
10/26/1919	02:00	CST
2/09/1942	02:00	CWT
9/30/1945	02:00	CST
4/29/1956	02:00	CDT
9/30/1956	02:00	CST
4/28/1957	02:00	CDT
9/29/1957	02:00	CST
4/28/1968	02:00	US#1

KY # 10

Before 11/18/1883		LMT
11/18/1883	12:00	CST
3/31/1918	02:00	CWT
10/27/1918	02:00	CST
3/30/1919	02:00	CWT
10/26/1919	02:00	CST
4/27/1941	02:00	CDT
9/28/1941	02:00	CST
2/09/1942	02:00	CWT
9/30/1945	02:00	CST
4/28/1946	02:00	CDT
6/02/1946	00:00	CST
4/29/1956	02:00	CDT
9/30/1956	02:00	CST
4/28/1968	02:00	US#1

KY # 11

Before 11/18/1883		LMT
11/18/1883	12:00	CST
3/31/1918	02:00	CWT
10/27/1918	02:00	CST
3/30/1919	02:00	CWT
10/26/1919	02:00	CST
4/03/1927	02:00	EST
2/09/1942	02:00	EWT
9/30/1945	02:00	EST
4/28/1968	02:00	US#1

KY # 12

Before 11/18/1883		LMT
11/18/1883	12:00	CST
3/31/1918	02:00	CWT
10/27/1918	02:00	CST
3/30/1919	02:00	CWT
10/26/1919	02:00	CST
4/03/1927	02:00	EST
2/09/1942	02:00	EWT
9/30/1945	02:00	EST
4/26/1953	02:00	EDT
9/27/1953	02:00	EST
4/28/1968	02:00	US#1

KY # 13

Before 11/18/1883		LMT
11/18/1883	12:00	CST
3/31/1918	02:00	CWT
10/27/1918	02:00	CST
3/30/1919	02:00	CWT
10/26/1919	02:00	CST
4/03/1927	02:00	EST
2/09/1942	02:00	EWT
9/30/1945	02:00	EST
4/26/1953	02:00	EDT
9/27/1953	02:00	EST
4/25/1954	02:00	EDT
9/06/1954	02:00	EST
4/28/1968	02:00	US#1

KY # 14

Before 11/18/1883		LMT
11/18/1883	12:00	CST
3/31/1918	02:00	CWT
10/27/1918	02:00	CST
3/30/1919	02:00	CWT
10/26/1919	02:00	CST
4/03/1927	02:00	EST
4/27/1941	02:00	EDT
9/28/1941	02:00	EST
2/09/1942	02:00	EWT
9/30/1945	02:00	EST
4/25/1954	02:00	EDT
9/26/1954	02:00	EST
4/28/1968	02:00	US#1

KY # 15

Before 11/18/1883		LMT
11/18/1883	12:00	CST
3/31/1918	02:00	CWT
10/27/1918	02:00	CST
3/30/1919	02:00	CWT
10/26/1919	02:00	CST
2/09/1942	02:00	CWT
9/30/1945	02:00	CST
9/28/1947	02:00	EST
4/28/1968	02:00	US#1

KY # 16

Before 11/18/1883		LMT
11/18/1883	12:00	CST
3/31/1918	02:00	CWT
10/27/1918	02:00	CST
3/30/1919	02:00	CWT
10/26/1919	02:00	CST
2/09/1942	02:00	CWT
9/30/1945	02:00	CST
4/03/1960	02:00	EST
4/28/1968	02:00	US#1

KY # 17

Before 11/18/1883		LMT
11/18/1883	12:00	CST
3/31/1918	02:00	CWT
10/27/1918	02:00	CST
3/30/1919	02:00	CWT
10/26/1919	02:00	CST
2/09/1942	02:00	CWT
9/30/1945	02:00	CST
4/29/1956	02:00	CDT
9/30/1956	02:00	CST
4/03/1960	02:00	EST
4/28/1968	02:00	US#1

KY # 18

Before 11/18/1883		LMT
11/18/1883	12:00	CST
3/31/1918	02:00	CWT
10/27/1918	02:00	CST
3/30/1919	02:00	CWT
10/26/1919	02:00	CST
2/09/1942	02:00	CWT
9/30/1945	02:00	CST
4/28/1957	02:00	CDT
9/29/1957	02:00	CST
4/03/1960	02:00	EST
4/28/1968	02:00	US#1

KY # 19

Before 11/18/1883		LMT
11/18/1883	12:00	CST
3/31/1918	02:00	CWT
10/27/1918	02:00	CST
3/30/1919	02:00	CWT
10/26/1919	02:00	CST
2/09/1942	02:00	CWT
9/30/1945	02:00	CST
4/30/1956	00:00	CDT
9/03/1956	00:00	CST
4/26/1959	02:00	CDT
4/03/1960	02:00	EST
4/28/1968	02:00	US#1

KY # 20

Before 11/18/1883		LMT
11/18/1883	12:00	CST
3/31/1918	02:00	CWT
10/27/1918	02:00	CST
3/30/1919	02:00	CWT
10/26/1919	02:00	CST
4/27/1941	02:00	CDT
9/28/1941	02:00	CST
2/09/1942	02:00	CWT
9/30/1945	02:00	CST
4/28/1946	02:00	CDT
6/02/1946	00:00	CST
4/30/1950	02:00	CDT
9/24/1950	02:00	CST
4/29/1951	02:00	CDT
9/30/1951	02:00	CST
4/25/1954	02:00	CDT
9/26/1954	02:00	CST
4/24/1955	02:00	CDT
9/25/1955	02:00	CST
4/29/1956	02:00	CDT
9/30/1956	02:00	CST
4/28/1957	02:00	CDT
4/03/1960	02:00	EST
4/28/1968	02:00	US#1

KY # 21

Before 11/18/1883		LMT
11/18/1883	12:00	CST
3/31/1918	02:00	CWT
10/27/1918	02:00	CST
3/30/1919	02:00	CWT
10/26/1919	02:00	CST
4/27/1941	02:00	CDT
9/28/1941	02:00	CST
2/09/1942	02:00	CWT
9/30/1945	02:00	CST
4/28/1946	02:00	CDT
6/02/1946	00:00	CST
4/26/1953	02:00	CDT
9/27/1953	02:00	CST
4/25/1954	02:00	CDT
9/26/1954	02:00	CST
4/24/1955	02:00	CDT
9/25/1955	02:00	CST
4/29/1956	02:00	CDT
9/30/1956	02:00	CST
4/28/1957	02:00	CDT
4/03/1960	02:00	EST
4/28/1968	02:00	US#1

KY # 22

Before 11/18/1883		LMT
11/18/1883	12:00	CST
3/31/1918	02:00	CWT
10/27/1918	02:00	CST
3/30/1919	02:00	CWT
10/26/1919	02:00	CST
2/09/1942	02:00	CWT
9/30/1945	02:00	CST
4/25/1954	02:00	CDT
9/26/1954	02:00	CST
4/24/1955	02:00	CDT
9/25/1955	02:00	CST
4/29/1956	02:00	CDT
9/30/1956	02:00	CST
4/28/1957	02:00	CDT
9/29/1957	02:00	CST
4/27/1958	02:00	CDT
10/26/1958	02:00	CST
4/26/1959	02:00	CDT
10/25/1959	02:00	CST
4/03/1960	02:00	EST
4/28/1968	02:00	US#1

KY # 23

Before 11/18/1883		LMT
11/18/1883	12:00	CST
3/31/1918	02:00	CWT
10/27/1918	02:00	CST
3/30/1919	02:00	CWT
10/26/1919	02:00	CST
2/09/1942	02:00	CWT
9/30/1945	02:00	CST
4/25/1954	02:00	CDT
9/26/1954	02:00	CST
4/24/1955	02:00	CDT
9/04/1955	02:00	CST
4/29/1956	02:00	CDT
9/30/1956	02:00	CST
4/28/1957	02:00	CDT
4/03/1960	02:00	EST
4/28/1968	02:00	US#1

KY # 24

Before 11/18/1883		LMT
11/18/1883	12:00	CST
3/31/1918	02:00	CWT
10/27/1918	02:00	CST
3/30/1919	02:00	CWT
10/26/1919	02:00	CST
4/27/1941	02:00	CDT
9/01/1941	02:00	CST
2/09/1942	02:00	CWT
9/30/1945	02:00	CST
4/03/1960	02:00	EST
4/28/1968	02:00	US#1

KY # 25

Before 11/18/1883		LMT
11/18/1883	12:00	CST
3/31/1918	02:00	CWT
10/27/1918	02:00	CST
3/30/1919	02:00	CWT
10/26/1919	02:00	CST
2/09/1942	02:00	CWT
9/30/1945	02:00	CST
4/30/1950	02:00	CDT
9/24/1950	02:00	CST
4/25/1954	02:00	CDT
9/06/1954	02:00	CST
4/24/1955	02:00	CDT
9/04/1955	02:00	CST
4/29/1956	02:00	CDT
9/04/1956	02:00	CST
4/28/1957	02:00	CDT
10/31/1959	02:00	CST
4/03/1960	02:00	EST
4/28/1968	02:00	US#1

KY # 26

Before 11/18/1883		LMT
11/18/1883	12:00	CST
3/31/1918	02:00	CWT
10/27/1918	02:00	CST
3/30/1919	02:00	CWT
10/26/1919	02:00	CST
2/09/1942	02:00	CWT
9/30/1945	02:00	CST
4/30/1950	02:00	CDT
9/30/1956	02:00	CST
4/28/1957	02:00	CDT
4/03/1960	02:00	EST
4/28/1968	02:00	US#1

KY # 27

Before 11/18/1883		LMT
11/18/1883	12:00	CST
3/31/1918	02:00	CWT
10/27/1918	02:00	CST
3/30/1919	02:00	CWT
10/26/1919	02:00	CST
4/27/1941	02:00	CDT
9/13/1941	02:00	CST
2/09/1942	02:00	CWT
9/30/1945	02:00	CST
4/28/1957	02:00	CDT
9/29/1957	02:00	CST
4/27/1958	02:00	CDT
10/26/1958	02:00	CST
4/03/1960	02:00	EST
4/28/1968	02:00	US#1

KY # 28

Before 11/18/1883		LMT
11/18/1883	12:00	CST
3/31/1918	02:00	CWT
10/27/1918	02:00	CST
3/30/1919	02:00	CWT
10/26/1919	02:00	CST
4/27/1941	02:00	CDT
10/01/1941	02:00	CST
2/09/1942	02:00	CWT
9/30/1945	02:00	CST
4/28/1946	02:00	CDT
6/02/1946	00:00	CST
4/30/1950	02:00	CDT
9/24/1950	02:00	CST
4/29/1951	02:00	CDT
9/30/1951	02:00	CST
4/27/1952	02:00	CDT
6/18/1952	02:00	CST
4/26/1953	02:00	CDT
9/27/1953	02:00	CST
4/25/1954	02:00	CDT
9/05/1954	02:00	CST
4/24/1955	02:00	CDT
9/05/1955	02:00	CST
4/29/1956	02:00	CDT
9/30/1956	02:00	CST
4/28/1957	02:00	CDT
4/03/1960	02:00	EST
4/28/1968	02:00	US#1

KY # 29

Before 11/18/1883		LMT
11/18/1883	12:00	CST
3/31/1918	02:00	CWT
10/27/1918	02:00	CST
3/30/1919	02:00	CWT
10/26/1919	02:00	CST
2/09/1942	02:00	CWT
9/30/1945	02:00	CST
4/25/1954	02:00	CDT
9/05/1954	02:00	CST
4/24/1955	02:00	CDT
9/05/1955	02:00	CST
4/29/1956	02:00	CDT
9/04/1956	02:00	CST
4/28/1957	02:00	CDT
4/03/1960	02:00	EST
4/28/1968	02:00	US#1

KY # 30

Before 11/18/1883		LMT
11/18/1883	12:00	CST
3/31/1918	02:00	CWT
10/27/1918	02:00	CST
3/30/1919	02:00	CWT
10/26/1919	02:00	CST
4/27/1941	02:00	CDT
10/01/1941	02:00	CST
2/09/1942	02:00	CWT
9/30/1945	02:00	CST
4/28/1946	02:00	CDT
5/19/1946	00:00	CST
4/30/1950	02:00	CDT
9/24/1950	02:00	CST
4/29/1951	02:00	CDT
9/30/1951	02:00	CST
4/26/1953	02:00	CDT
9/27/1953	02:00	CST
4/25/1954	02:00	CDT
9/05/1954	02:00	CST
4/24/1955	02:00	CDT
9/25/1955	02:00	CST
4/29/1956	02:00	CDT
9/30/1956	02:00	CST
4/28/1957	02:00	CDT
4/03/1960	02:00	EST
4/28/1968	02:00	US#1

KY # 31

Before 11/18/1883		LMT
11/18/1883	12:00	CST
3/31/1918	02:00	CWT
10/27/1918	02:00	CST
3/30/1919	02:00	CWT
10/26/1919	02:00	CST
4/27/1941	02:00	CDT
9/28/1941	02:00	CST
2/09/1942	02:00	CWT
9/30/1945	02:00	CST
4/28/1946	02:00	CDT
6/02/1946	00:00	CST
4/25/1954	02:00	CDT
9/26/1954	02:00	CST
4/24/1955	02:00	CDT
9/25/1955	02:00	CST
4/29/1956	02:00	CDT
9/03/1956	02:00	CST
4/28/1957	02:00	CDT
4/03/1960	02:00	EST
4/28/1968	02:00	US#1

KY # 32

Before 11/18/1883		LMT
11/18/1883	12:00	CST
3/31/1918	02:00	CWT
10/27/1918	02:00	CST
3/30/1919	02:00	CWT
10/26/1919	02:00	CST
2/09/1942	02:00	CWT
9/30/1945	02:00	CST
4/30/1956	00:00	CDT
9/03/1956	00:00	CST
5/29/1957	02:00	CDT
9/02/1957	00:00	CST
6/23/1958	00:00	CDT
9/02/1958	00:00	CST
4/26/1959	02:00	CDT

TIME TABLES

4/03/1960 02:00 EST
4/28/1968 02:00 US#1

KY # 33
Before 11/18/1883 LMT
11/18/1883 12:00 CST
3/31/1918 02:00 CWT
10/27/1918 02:00 CST
3/30/1919 02:00 CWT
10/26/1919 02:00 CST
4/27/1941 02:00 CDT
10/01/1941 02:00 CST
2/09/1942 02:00 CWT
9/30/1945 02:00 CST
4/28/1946 02:00 CDT
6/02/1946 00:00 CST
4/30/1950 02:00 CDT
9/24/1950 02:00 CST
4/26/1953 02:00 CDT
9/27/1953 02:00 CST
4/25/1954 02:00 CDT
9/06/1954 02:00 CST
4/24/1955 02:00 CDT
9/25/1955 02:00 CST
4/29/1956 02:00 CDT
9/01/1956 02:00 CST
4/28/1957 02:00 CDT
4/03/1960 02:00 EST
4/28/1968 02:00 US#1

KY # 34
Before 11/18/1883 LMT
11/18/1883 12:00 CST
3/31/1918 02:00 CWT
10/27/1918 02:00 CST
3/30/1919 02:00 CWT
10/26/1919 02:00 CST
2/09/1942 02:00 CWT
9/30/1945 02:00 CST
4/27/1958 02:00 CDT
10/26/1958 02:00 CST
4/03/1960 02:00 EST
4/28/1968 02:00 US#1

KY # 35
Before 11/18/1883 LMT
11/18/1883 12:00 CST
3/31/1918 02:00 CWT
10/27/1918 02:00 CST
3/30/1919 02:00 CWT
10/26/1919 02:00 CST
2/09/1942 02:00 CWT
9/30/1945 02:00 CST
4/29/1956 02:00 CDT
9/02/1956 00:00 CST
4/28/1957 02:00 CDT
4/03/1960 02:00 EST
4/28/1968 02:00 US#1

KY # 36
Before 11/18/1883 LMT
11/18/1883 12:00 CST
3/31/1918 02:00 CWT
10/27/1918 02:00 CST
3/30/1919 02:00 CWT
10/26/1919 02:00 CST
4/27/1941 02:00 CDT
9/28/1941 02:00 CST
2/09/1942 02:00 CWT
9/30/1945 02:00 CST
4/03/1960 02:00 EST
4/28/1968 02:00 US#1

KY # 37
Before 11/18/1883 LMT
11/18/1883 12:00 CST
3/31/1918 02:00 CWT
10/27/1918 02:00 CST
3/30/1919 02:00 CWT
10/26/1919 02:00 CST
4/27/1941 02:00 CDT
9/28/1941 02:00 CST
2/09/1942 02:00 CWT
9/30/1945 02:00 CST
4/29/1956 02:00 CDT
9/30/1956 02:00 CST
4/03/1960 02:00 EST
4/28/1968 02:00 US#1

KY # 38
Before 11/18/1883 LMT
11/18/1883 12:00 CST
3/31/1918 02:00 CWT
10/27/1918 02:00 CST
3/30/1919 02:00 CWT
10/26/1919 02:00 CST
4/27/1941 02:00 CDT
9/28/1941 02:00 CST
2/09/1942 02:00 CWT
9/30/1945 02:00 CST
4/25/1954 02:00 CDT
9/26/1954 02:00 CST
4/29/1956 02:00 CDT
9/30/1956 02:00 CST
4/28/1957 02:00 CDT
4/03/1960 02:00 EST
4/28/1968 02:00 US#1

KY # 39
Before 11/18/1883 LMT
11/18/1883 12:00 CST
3/31/1918 02:00 CWT
10/27/1918 02:00 CST
3/30/1919 02:00 CWT
10/26/1919 02:00 CST
2/09/1942 02:00 CWT
9/30/1945 02:00 CST
4/26/1953 02:00 CDT
9/27/1953 02:00 CST
4/25/1954 02:00 CDT
9/26/1954 02:00 CST
4/27/1958 02:00 CDT
10/26/1958 02:00 CST
4/03/1960 02:00 EST
4/28/1968 02:00 US#1

KY # 40
Before 11/18/1883 LMT
11/18/1883 12:00 CST
3/31/1918 02:00 CWT
10/27/1918 02:00 CST
3/30/1919 02:00 CWT
10/26/1919 02:00 CST
2/09/1942 02:00 CWT
9/30/1945 02:00 CST
4/25/1954 02:00 CDT
9/26/1954 02:00 CST
4/03/1960 02:00 EST
4/28/1968 02:00 US#1

KY # 41
Before 11/18/1883 LMT
11/18/1883 12:00 CST
3/31/1918 02:00 CWT
10/27/1918 02:00 CST
3/30/1919 02:00 CWT
10/26/1919 02:00 CST
2/09/1942 02:00 CWT
9/30/1945 02:00 CST
4/29/1956 02:00 CDT
9/30/1956 02:00 CST
4/28/1957 02:00 CDT
9/29/1957 02:00 CST
4/27/1958 02:00 CDT
10/26/1958 02:00 CST
4/26/1959 02:00 CDT
10/25/1959 02:00 CST
4/03/1960 02:00 EST
4/28/1968 02:00 US#1

KY # 42
Before 11/18/1883 LMT
11/18/1883 12:00 CST
3/31/1918 02:00 CWT
10/27/1918 02:00 CST
3/30/1919 02:00 CWT
10/26/1919 02:00 CST
2/09/1942 02:00 CWT
9/30/1945 02:00 CST
4/29/1956 02:00 CDT
9/30/1956 02:00 CST
4/28/1957 02:00 CDT
4/03/1960 02:00 EST
4/28/1968 02:00 US#1

KY # 43
Before 11/18/1883 LMT
11/18/1883 12:00 CST
3/31/1918 02:00 CWT
10/27/1918 02:00 CST
3/30/1919 02:00 CWT
10/26/1919 02:00 CST
4/27/1941 02:00 CDT
9/28/1941 02:00 CST
2/09/1942 02:00 CWT
9/30/1945 02:00 CST
4/24/1955 02:00 CDT
9/25/1955 02:00 CST
4/29/1956 02:00 CDT
9/30/1956 02:00 CST
4/28/1957 02:00 CDT
9/01/1957 02:00 CST
4/27/1958 02:00 CDT
10/26/1958 02:00 CST
4/26/1959 02:00 CDT
10/25/1959 02:00 CST
4/03/1960 02:00 EST
4/28/1968 02:00 US#1

KY # 44
Before 11/18/1883 LMT
11/18/1883 12:00 CST
3/31/1918 02:00 CWT
10/27/1918 02:00 CST
3/30/1919 02:00 CWT
10/26/1919 02:00 CST
2/09/1942 02:00 CWT
9/30/1945 02:00 CST
4/29/1951 02:00 CDT
9/30/1951 02:00 CST
4/25/1954 02:00 CDT
9/26/1954 02:00 CST
4/24/1955 02:00 CDT
9/25/1955 02:00 CST
4/29/1956 02:00 CDT
9/30/1956 02:00 CST
4/28/1957 02:00 CDT
4/03/1960 02:00 EST
4/28/1968 02:00 US#1

KY # 45
Before 11/18/1883 LMT
11/18/1883 12:00 CST
3/31/1918 02:00 CWT
10/27/1918 02:00 CST
3/30/1919 02:00 CWT
10/26/1919 02:00 CST
2/09/1942 02:00 CWT
9/30/1945 02:00 CST
4/30/1950 02:00 CDT
9/24/1950 02:00 CST
4/29/1951 02:00 CDT
9/30/1951 02:00 CST
4/25/1954 02:00 CDT
9/26/1954 02:00 CST
4/24/1955 02:00 CDT
9/25/1955 02:00 CST
4/29/1956 02:00 CDT
9/30/1956 02:00 CST
4/28/1957 02:00 CDT
4/03/1960 02:00 EST
4/28/1968 02:00 US#1

KY # 46
Before 11/18/1883 LMT
11/18/1883 12:00 CST
3/31/1918 02:00 CWT
10/27/1918 02:00 CST
3/30/1919 02:00 CWT
10/26/1919 02:00 CST
2/09/1942 02:00 CWT
9/30/1945 02:00 CST
4/28/1957 02:00 CDT
9/22/1957 02:00 CST
4/03/1960 02:00 EST
4/28/1968 02:00 US#1

KY # 47
Before 11/18/1883 LMT
11/18/1883 12:00 CST
3/31/1918 02:00 CWT
10/27/1918 02:00 CST
3/30/1919 02:00 CWT
10/26/1919 02:00 CST
2/09/1942 02:00 CWT
9/30/1945 02:00 CST
4/29/1957 02:00 CDT
9/29/1957 02:00 CST
4/27/1958 02:00 CDT
10/26/1958 02:00 CST
4/03/1960 02:00 EST
4/28/1968 02:00 US#1

KY # 48
Before 11/18/1883 LMT
11/18/1883 12:00 CST
3/31/1918 02:00 CWT
10/27/1918 02:00 CST
3/30/1919 02:00 CWT
10/26/1919 02:00 CST
4/27/1941 02:00 CDT
10/01/1941 02:00 CST
2/09/1942 02:00 CWT
9/30/1945 02:00 CST
4/28/1957 02:00 CDT
9/29/1957 02:00 CST
4/03/1960 02:00 EST
4/28/1968 02:00 US#1

KY # 49
Before 11/18/1883 LMT
11/18/1883 12:00 CST
3/31/1918 02:00 CWT
10/27/1918 02:00 CST
3/30/1919 02:00 CWT
10/26/1919 02:00 CST
2/09/1942 02:00 CWT
9/30/1945 02:00 CST
4/28/1946 02:00 CDT
5/19/1946 00:00 CST
4/28/1957 02:00 CDT
9/29/1957 02:00 CST
4/03/1960 02:00 EST
4/28/1968 02:00 US#1

KY # 50
Before 11/18/1883 LMT
11/18/1883 12:00 CST
3/31/1918 02:00 CWT
10/27/1918 02:00 CST
3/30/1919 02:00 CWT
10/26/1919 02:00 CST
2/09/1942 02:00 CWT
9/30/1945 02:00 CST
4/28/1946 02:00 CDT
6/02/1946 00:00 CST
4/29/1951 02:00 CDT
9/30/1951 02:00 CST
4/25/1954 02:00 CDT
9/26/1954 02:00 CST
4/24/1955 02:00 CDT
9/25/1955 02:00 CST
4/29/1956 02:00 CDT
9/30/1956 02:00 CST
4/28/1957 02:00 CDT
4/03/1960 02:00 EST
4/28/1968 02:00 US#1

KY # 51
Before 11/18/1883 LMT
11/18/1883 12:00 CST
3/31/1918 02:00 CWT
10/27/1918 02:00 CST
3/30/1919 02:00 CWT
10/26/1919 02:00 CST
2/09/1942 02:00 CWT
9/30/1945 02:00 CST
7/23/1961 02:00 EST
4/28/1968 02:00 US#1

KY # 52
Before 11/18/1883 LMT
11/18/1883 12:00 CST
3/31/1918 02:00 CWT
10/27/1918 02:00 CST
3/30/1919 02:00 CWT
10/26/1919 02:00 CST
2/09/1942 02:00 CWT
9/30/1945 02:00 CST
4/26/1953 02:00 CDT
9/27/1953 02:00 CST
4/24/1955 02:00 CDT
9/25/1955 02:00 CST
4/29/1956 02:00 CDT
9/30/1956 02:00 CST
4/28/1957 02:00 CDT
9/29/1957 02:00 CST
4/27/1958 02:00 CDT
10/26/1958 02:00 CST
4/26/1959 02:00 CDT
10/25/1959 02:00 CST
4/24/1960 02:00 CDT
10/30/1960 02:00 CST
4/30/1961 02:00 CDT
7/23/1961 02:00 EST
4/28/1968 02:00 US#1

KY # 53
Before 11/18/1883 LMT
11/18/1883 12:00 CST
3/31/1918 02:00 CWT
10/27/1918 02:00 CST
3/30/1919 02:00 CWT
10/26/1919 02:00 CST
4/27/1941 02:00 CDT
9/28/1941 02:00 CST
2/09/1942 02:00 CWT
9/30/1945 02:00 CST
4/26/1953 02:00 CDT
9/27/1953 02:00 CST
4/25/1954 02:00 CDT
9/26/1954 02:00 CST
4/24/1955 02:00 CDT
9/25/1955 02:00 CST
4/29/1956 02:00 CDT
9/30/1956 02:00 CST
4/27/1958 02:00 CDT
10/26/1958 02:00 CST
7/23/1961 02:00 EST
4/28/1968 02:00 US#1

KY # 54
Before 11/18/1883 LMT
11/18/1883 12:00 CST
3/31/1918 02:00 CWT
10/27/1918 02:00 CST
3/30/1919 02:00 CWT
10/26/1919 02:00 CST
2/09/1942 02:00 CWT
9/30/1945 02:00 CST
4/25/1954 02:00 CDT
9/26/1954 02:00 CST
4/24/1955 02:00 CDT
9/25/1955 02:00 CST
4/29/1956 02:00 CDT
9/30/1956 02:00 CST
4/28/1957 02:00 CDT
9/29/1957 02:00 CST
4/27/1958 02:00 CDT
10/26/1958 02:00 CST
4/26/1959 02:00 CDT
10/25/1959 02:00 CST
4/24/1960 02:00 CDT
10/30/1960 02:00 CST
4/30/1961 02:00 CDT
7/23/1961 02:00 EST
4/28/1968 02:00 US#1

KY # 55
Before 11/18/1883 LMT
11/18/1883 12:00 CST
3/31/1918 02:00 CWT
10/27/1918 02:00 CST
3/30/1919 02:00 CWT
10/26/1919 02:00 CST
4/27/1941 02:00 CDT
8/31/1941 02:00 CST
2/09/1942 02:00 CWT
9/30/1945 02:00 CST
4/28/1957 02:00 CDT
9/29/1957 02:00 CST
7/23/1961 02:00 EST
4/28/1968 02:00 US#1

KY # 56
Before 11/18/1883 LMT
11/18/1883 12:00 CST
3/31/1918 02:00 CWT
10/27/1918 02:00 CST
3/30/1919 02:00 CWT
10/26/1919 02:00 CST
2/09/1942 02:00 CWT
9/30/1945 02:00 CST
4/26/1953 02:00 CDT
9/27/1953 02:00 CST
4/27/1958 02:00 CDT
10/26/1958 02:00 CST
7/23/1961 02:00 EST
4/28/1968 02:00 US#1

KY # 57
Before 11/18/1883 LMT
11/18/1883 12:00 CST
3/31/1918 02:00 CWT
10/27/1918 02:00 CST
3/30/1919 02:00 CWT
10/26/1919 02:00 CST
2/09/1942 02:00 CWT
9/30/1945 02:00 CST
4/27/1958 02:00 CDT
10/26/1958 02:00 CST
7/23/1961 02:00 EST
4/28/1968 02:00 US#1

KY # 58
Before 11/18/1883 LMT
11/18/1883 12:00 CST
3/31/1918 02:00 CWT
10/27/1918 02:00 CST
3/30/1919 02:00 CWT
10/26/1919 02:00 CST
2/09/1942 02:00 CWT
9/30/1945 02:00 CST
4/26/1953 02:00 CDT
9/27/1953 02:00 CST
4/25/1954 02:00 CDT
9/26/1954 02:00 CST
7/23/1961 02:00 EST
4/28/1968 02:00 US#1

KY # 59
Before 11/18/1883 LMT
11/18/1883 12:00 CST
3/31/1918 02:00 CWT
10/27/1918 02:00 CST
3/30/1919 02:00 CWT
10/26/1919 02:00 CST
4/27/1941 02:00 CDT
9/28/1941 02:00 CST
2/09/1942 02:00 CWT
9/30/1945 02:00 CST
7/23/1961 02:00 EST
4/28/1968 02:00 US#1

KY # 60
Before 11/18/1883 LMT
11/18/1883 12:00 CST
3/31/1918 02:00 CWT
10/27/1918 02:00 CST
3/30/1919 02:00 CWT
10/26/1919 02:00 CST
4/27/1941 02:00 CDT
9/28/1941 02:00 CST
2/09/1942 02:00 CWT
9/30/1945 02:00 CST
4/26/1953 02:00 CDT
9/27/1953 02:00 CST
4/24/1955 02:00 CDT
9/25/1955 02:00 CST
4/29/1956 02:00 CDT
9/30/1956 02:00 CST
4/28/1957 02:00 CDT
9/29/1957 02:00 CST
4/27/1958 02:00 CDT
10/26/1958 02:00 CST
4/26/1959 02:00 CDT
10/25/1959 02:00 CST
4/24/1960 02:00 CDT
10/30/1960 02:00 CST
4/30/1961 02:00 CDT
7/23/1961 02:00 EST
4/28/1968 00:02 US#1

KY # 61
Before 11/18/1883 LMT
11/18/1883 12:00 CST
3/31/1918 02:00 CWT
10/27/1918 02:00 CST
3/30/1919 02:00 CWT
10/26/1919 02:00 CST
4/27/1941 02:00 CDT
9/28/1941 02:00 CST
2/09/1942 02:00 CWT
9/30/1945 02:00 CST
4/25/1954 02:00 CDT
9/26/1954 02:00 CST
4/24/1955 02:00 CDT
9/25/1955 02:00 CST
4/29/1956 02:00 CDT
9/30/1956 02:00 CST
4/28/1957 02:00 CDT
9/29/1957 02:00 CST
4/27/1958 02:00 CDT
10/26/1958 02:00 CST
4/26/1959 02:00 CDT
10/25/1959 02:00 CST
4/24/1960 02:00 CDT
10/30/1960 02:00 CST
4/30/1961 02:00 CDT
7/23/1961 02:00 EST
4/28/1968 02:00 US#1

KY # 62
Before 11/18/1883 LMT
11/18/1883 12:00 CST
3/31/1918 02:00 CWT
10/27/1918 02:00 CST
3/30/1919 02:00 CWT
10/26/1919 02:00 CST
4/27/1941 02:00 CDT
9/28/1941 02:00 CST
2/09/1942 02:00 CWT
9/30/1945 02:00 CST
4/26/1953 02:00 CDT
9/27/1953 02:00 CST
4/25/1954 02:00 CDT
9/06/1954 02:00 CST
4/24/1955 02:00 CDT
9/25/1955 02:00 CST
4/29/1956 02:00 CDT
9/30/1956 02:00 CST
4/28/1957 02:00 CDT
9/29/1957 02:00 CST
4/27/1958 02:00 CDT
10/26/1958 02:00 CST
4/26/1959 02:00 CDT
10/25/1959 02:00 CST
4/24/1960 02:00 CDT
10/30/1960 02:00 CST
4/30/1961 02:00 CDT
7/23/1961 02:00 EST
4/28/1968 02:00 US#1

KY # 63
Before 11/18/1883 LMT
11/18/1883 12:00 CST
3/31/1918 02:00 CWT
10/27/1918 02:00 CST
3/30/1919 02:00 CWT
10/26/1919 02:00 CST
2/09/1942 02:00 CWT
9/30/1945 02:00 CST
4/24/1955 02:00 CDT
9/25/1955 02:00 CST
4/29/1956 02:00 CDT
9/30/1956 02:00 CST
4/28/1957 02:00 CDT
9/29/1957 02:00 CST
4/27/1958 02:00 CDT
10/26/1958 02:00 CST

TIME TABLES

4/26/1959 02:00 CDT
10/25/1959 02:00 CST
4/24/1960 02:00 CDT
10/30/1960 02:00 CST
4/30/1961 02:00 CDT
7/23/1961 02:00 EST
4/28/1968 02:00 US#1

KY # 64
Before 11/18/1883 LMT
11/18/1883 12:00 CST
3/31/1918 02:00 CWT
10/27/1918 02:00 CST
3/30/1919 02:00 CWT
10/26/1919 02:00 CST
4/27/1941 02:00 CDT
9/28/1941 02:00 CST
2/09/1942 02:00 CWT
9/30/1945 02:00 CST
4/26/1953 02:00 CDT
9/27/1953 02:00 CST
4/27/1958 02:00 CDT
10/26/1958 02:00 CST
7/23/1961 02:00 EST
4/28/1968 02:00 US#1

KY # 65
Before 11/18/1883 LMT
11/18/1883 12:00 CST
3/31/1918 02:00 CWT
10/27/1918 02:00 CST
3/30/1919 02:00 CWT
10/26/1919 02:00 CST
2/09/1942 02:00 CWT
9/30/1945 02:00 CST
4/29/1956 02:00 CDT
9/30/1956 02:00 CST
4/28/1957 02:00 CDT
9/29/1957 02:00 CST
4/27/1958 02:00 CDT
10/26/1958 02:00 CST
4/26/1959 02:00 CDT
10/25/1959 02:00 CST
4/24/1960 02:00 CDT
10/30/1960 02:00 CST
4/30/1961 02:00 CDT
7/23/1961 02:00 EST
4/28/1968 02:00 US#1

KY # 66
Before 11/18/1883 LMT
11/18/1883 12:00 CST
3/31/1918 02:00 CWT
10/27/1918 02:00 CST
3/30/1919 02:00 CWT
10/26/1919 02:00 CST
4/27/1941 02:00 CDT
9/28/1941 02:00 CST
2/09/1942 02:00 CWT
9/30/1945 02:00 CST
5/02/1954 02:00 CDT
9/05/1954 02:00 CST
6/03/1956 02:00 CDT
9/02/1956 02:00 CST
4/28/1957 02:00 CDT
9/29/1957 02:00 CST
4/27/1958 02:00 CDT
10/26/1958 02:00 CST
4/26/1959 02:00 CDT
10/25/1959 02:00 CST
4/24/1960 02:00 CDT
10/30/1960 02:00 CST
4/30/1961 02:00 CDT
7/23/1961 02:00 EST
4/28/1968 02:00 US#1

KY # 67
Before 11/18/1883 LMT
11/18/1883 12:00 CST
3/31/1918 02:00 CWT
10/27/1918 02:00 CST
3/30/1919 02:00 CWT
10/26/1919 02:00 CST
2/09/1942 02:00 CWT
9/30/1945 02:00 CST
4/28/1957 02:00 CDT
9/29/1957 02:00 CST
4/27/1958 02:00 CDT
10/26/1958 02:00 CST
7/23/1961 02:00 EST
4/28/1968 02:00 US#1

KY # 68
Before 11/18/1883 LMT
11/18/1883 12:00 CST
3/31/1918 02:00 CWT
10/27/1918 02:00 CST
3/30/1919 02:00 CWT
10/26/1919 02:00 CST
2/09/1942 02:00 CWT
9/30/1945 02:00 CST
4/30/1950 02:00 CDT
9/24/1950 02:00 CST
4/29/1951 02:00 CDT
9/30/1951 02:00 CST
4/27/1952 02:00 CDT
9/28/1952 02:00 CST
4/26/1953 02:00 CDT
9/27/1953 02:00 CST
4/25/1954 02:00 CDT
9/26/1954 02:00 CST
4/24/1955 02:00 CDT
9/25/1955 02:00 CST
4/29/1956 02:00 CDT
10/28/1956 02:00 CST
4/28/1957 02:00 CDT
10/27/1957 02:00 CST
4/27/1958 02:00 CDT
10/26/1958 02:00 CST
4/26/1959 02:00 CDT
10/25/1959 02:00 CST
4/30/1960 02:00 CDT
10/29/1960 02:00 CST
4/30/1961 02:00 CDT
7/23/1961 02:00 EST
4/28/1968 02:00 EDT
10/27/1968 02:00 EST
4/27/1969 02:00 EDT
10/26/1969 02:00 EST
4/26/1970 02:00 EDT
10/25/1970 02:00 EST
4/25/1971 02:00 EDT
10/31/1971 02:00 EST
4/30/1972 02:00 EDT
10/29/1972 02:00 EST
4/29/1973 02:00 EDT
10/28/1973 02:00 EST
1/06/1974 02:00 CDT
10/27/1974 02:00 EST
10/27/1974 02:00 US#1

KY # 69
Before 11/18/1883 LMT
11/18/1883 12:00 CST
3/31/1918 02:00 CWT
10/27/1918 02:00 CST
3/30/1919 02:00 CWT
10/26/1919 02:00 CST
5/01/1921 02:00 CDT
9/01/1921 02:00 CST
4/27/1941 02:00 CDT
9/28/1941 02:00 CST
2/09/1942 02:00 CWT
9/30/1945 02:00 CST
4/28/1946 02:00 CDT
6/02/1946 00:00 CST
4/30/1950 02:00 CDT
9/24/1950 02:00 CST
4/29/1951 02:00 CDT
9/30/1951 02:00 CST
4/27/1952 02:00 CDT
9/28/1952 02:00 CST
4/26/1953 02:00 CDT
9/27/1953 02:00 CST
4/25/1954 02:00 CDT
9/26/1954 02:00 CST
4/24/1955 02:00 CDT
9/25/1955 02:00 CST
4/29/1956 02:00 CDT
10/28/1956 02:00 CST
4/28/1957 02:00 CDT
10/27/1957 02:00 CST
4/27/1958 02:00 CDT
10/26/1958 02:00 CST
4/26/1959 02:00 CDT
10/25/1959 02:00 CST
4/30/1960 02:00 CDT
10/29/1960 02:00 CST
4/30/1961 02:00 CDT
7/23/1961 02:00 EST
4/28/1968 02:00 EDT
10/27/1968 02:00 EST
4/27/1969 02:00 EDT
10/26/1969 02:00 EST
4/26/1970 02:00 EDT
10/25/1970 02:00 EST
4/25/1971 02:00 EDT
10/31/1971 02:00 EST
4/30/1972 02:00 EDT
10/29/1972 02:00 EST
4/29/1973 02:00 EDT
10/28/1973 02:00 EST
1/06/1974 02:00 CDT
10/27/1974 02:00 EST
10/27/1974 02:00 US#1

KY # 70
Before 11/18/1883 LMT
11/18/1883 12:00 CST
3/31/1918 02:00 CWT
10/27/1918 02:00 CST
3/30/1919 02:00 CWT
10/26/1919 02:00 CST
4/27/1941 02:00 CDT
9/28/1941 02:00 CST
2/09/1942 02:00 CWT
9/30/1945 02:00 CST
4/30/1950 02:00 CDT
9/24/1950 02:00 CST
4/29/1951 02:00 CDT
9/30/1951 02:00 CST
4/27/1952 02:00 CDT
9/28/1952 02:00 CST
4/26/1953 02:00 CDT
9/27/1953 02:00 CST
4/25/1954 02:00 CDT
9/26/1954 02:00 CST
4/24/1955 02:00 CDT
9/25/1955 02:00 CST
4/29/1956 02:00 CDT
10/28/1956 02:00 CST
4/28/1957 02:00 CDT
10/27/1957 02:00 CST
4/27/1958 02:00 CDT
10/26/1958 02:00 CST
4/26/1959 02:00 CDT
10/25/1959 02:00 CST
4/30/1960 02:00 CDT
10/29/1960 02:00 CST
4/30/1961 02:00 CDT
7/23/1961 02:00 EST
4/28/1968 02:00 EDT
10/27/1968 02:00 EST
4/27/1969 02:00 EDT
10/26/1969 02:00 EST
4/26/1970 02:00 EDT
10/25/1970 02:00 EST
4/25/1971 02:00 EDT
10/31/1971 02:00 EST
4/30/1972 02:00 EDT
10/29/1972 02:00 EST
4/29/1973 02:00 EDT
10/28/1973 02:00 EST
1/06/1974 02:00 CDT
10/27/1974 02:00 EST
10/27/1974 02:00 US#1

KY # 71
Before 11/18/1883 LMT
11/18/1883 12:00 CST
3/31/1918 02:00 CWT
10/27/1918 02:00 CST
3/30/1919 02:00 CWT
10/26/1919 02:00 CST
3/28/1920 02:00 CDT
10/31/1920 02:00 CST
4/02/1921 02:00 CDT
9/25/1921 02:00 CST
4/30/1922 02:00 CDT
9/24/1922 02:00 CST
4/29/1923 02:00 CDT
9/30/1923 02:00 CST
4/27/1924 02:00 CDT
9/28/1924 02:00 CST
4/26/1925 02:00 CDT
9/27/1925 02:00 CST
4/25/1926 02:00 CDT
8/05/1926 02:00 EST
2/09/1942 02:00 EWT
9/26/1943 02:00 CWT
4/30/1944 02:00 EWT
9/24/1944 02:00 CWT
9/30/1945 02:00 EST
4/30/1967 02:00 US#1

COUNTIES

1 Adair
2 Allen
3 Anderson
4 Ballard
5 Barren
6 Bath
7 Bell
8 Boone
9 Bourbon
10 Boyd
11 Boyle
12 Bracken
13 Breathitt
14 Breckinridge
15 Bullitt
16 Butler
17 Caldwell
18 Calloway
19 Campbell
20 Carlisle
21 Carroll
22 Carter
23 Casey
24 Christian
25 Clark
26 Clay
27 Clinton
28 Crittenden
29 Cumberland
30 Daviess
31 Edmonson
32 Elliott
33 Estill
34 Fayette
35 Fleming
36 Floyd
37 Franklin
38 Fulton
39 Gallatin
40 Garrard
41 Grant
42 Graves
43 Grayson
44 Green
45 Greenup
46 Hancock
47 Hardin
48 Harlan
49 Harrison
50 Hart
51 Henderson
52 Henry
53 Hickman
54 Hopkins
55 Jackson
56 Jefferson
57 Jessamine
58 Johnson
59 Kenton
60 Knott
61 Knox
62 Larue
63 Laurel
64 Lawrence
65 Lee
66 Leslie
67 Letcher
68 Lewis
69 Lincoln
70 Livingston
71 Logan
72 Lyon
73 McCracken
74 McCreary
75 McLean
76 Madison
77 Magoffin
78 Marion
79 Marshall
80 Martin
81 Mason
82 Meade
83 Menifee
84 Mercer
85 Metcalfe
86 Monroe
87 Montgomery
88 Morgan
89 Muhlenberg
90 Nelson
91 Nicholas
92 Ohio
93 Oldham
94 Owen
95 Owsley
96 Pendleton
97 Perry
98 Pike
99 Powell
100 Pulaski
101 Robertson
102 Rockcastle
103 Rowan
104 Russell
105 Scott
106 Shelby
107 Simpson
108 Spencer
109 Taylor
110 Todd
111 Trigg
112 Trimble
113 Union
114 Warren
115 Washington
116 Wayne
117 Webster
118 Whitley
119 Wolfe
120 Woodford

Aaron 27 1 36N48'45 85W10'51 5:40:43
Abbott 112 51 38N36 85W19 5:41:16
Abegall 101 11 38N39 83W58 5:35:52
Aberdeen 16 1 37N15'14 86W40'54 5:46:44
Abigail 101 11 38N34'36 83W58'56 5:35:56
Absher 1 1 37N10'07 85W15'33 5:41:02
Access 22 16 38N12'33 83W04'16 5:32:17
Acorn 100 19 37N07'59 84W22'40 5:37:31
Acton 109 51 37N20'49 85W14'53 5:41:00
Acup 97 46 37N12 83W08 5:32:32
Adaburg 92 1 37N35'30 86W50'52 5:47:23
Adair 46 1 37N57'02 86W49'36 5:47:18
Adairville 71 1 36N40'03 86W51'07 5:47:24
Adams 64 11 38N03'16 82W42'28 5:30:50
Adamson 67 16 37N12'06 82W34'45 5:30:19
Add 80 11 37N52 82W32 5:30:08
Addison 14 1 37N54'58 86W33'54 5:46:16
Adele (Insko P O) 88
16 37N45'26 83W18'04 5:33:12
Adeline 64 11 38N25 82W36 5:30:24
Aden 22 16 38N16'46 83W02'50 5:32:11
Adolphus 2 1 36N39'06 86W15'41 5:45:03
Advance 45 11 38N31 82W43 5:30:52
Aetnaville 92 1 37N40'22 86W47'26 5:47:10
Aflex 98 11 37N39'29 82W14'51 5:28:59
Agawam 25 33 37N54'52 84W05'17 5:36:21
Ages 48 15 36N51'28 83W14'47 5:32:59
Agnes 71 1 37N02'54 87W01'13 5:48:05
Airedale 65 16 37N36'09 83W38'22 5:34:33
Airport Gardens 97
46 37N17'13 83W12'11 5:32:49
Ajax 97 46 37N18 83W10 5:32:40
Akers 48 15 36N59 82W59 5:31:56
Akersville 86 1 36N38'51 85W56'16 5:43:45
Albany 27 1 36N41'27 85W08'05 5:40:32
Alberta 49 16 38N24'00 84W28'27 5:37:54
Albia 100 19 37N18'17 84W35'36 5:38:22
Albright 69 16 37N28 84W30 5:38:00
Alcalde 100 19 37N03'18 84W33'05 5:38:12
Alcorn 55 16 37N33'41 84W02'56 5:36:12
Alexandria 19 11 38N57'34 84W23'17 5:37:33
Alger 26 16 37N18'47 83W43'54 5:34:56
Alhambra 101 11 38N29'25 83W56'44 5:35:47
Aliceton 11 16 37N35'27 85W01'48 5:40:07
Allais 97 46 37N16'00 83W10'56 5:32:44
Allegheny Mine 98
11 37N16'40 82W28'48 5:29:55
Allegre 110 1 36N55'43 87W13'02 5:48:52
Allen City 36 11 37N36'34 82W43'40 5:30:55
Allendale 44 1 37N22'16 85W34'59 5:42:20
Allen Springs 2 1 36N49'54 86W18'54 5:45:16
Allensville 110 1 36N43'00 87W03'58 5:48:16
Allock 97 46 37N13'44 83W04'24 5:32:18
Almo 18 1 36N41'41 88W16'42 5:53:07
Almo Heights 18 1 36N41'34 88W17'45 5:53:11
Alonzo 2 1 36N41'35 86W20'41 5:45:23
Alpha 27 1 36N45'44 85W00'37 5:40:02
Alphoretta (Dinwood Station) 36
11 37N33'47 82W45'52 5:31:03
Alpine 100 19 36N55'30 84W31'15 5:38:05
Alta 92 1 37N34 86W44 5:46:56
Alton 3 44 38N05'20 84W56'06 5:39:44
Altona 79 1 37N03'08 88W23'46 5:53:35
Alton Station 3
44 38N04'41 84W56'32 5:39:46
Altro 13 16 37N22'51 83W22'56 5:33:32
Alumbaugh 33 27 37N35'51 83W55'48 5:35:43
Alum Springs 11
16 37N35'48 84W50'26 5:39:22
Alva 48 15 36N44'06 83W25'28 5:33:42
Alvaton 114 1 36N52'24 86W21'11 5:45:25
Alvin 36 11 37N38'12 82W41'42 5:30:47
Amandaville 29 1 36N53'48 85W18'40 5:41:15
Amba 36 11 37N31'47 82W38'35 5:30:34
Amburgey 60 16 37N15'41 82W59'55 5:32:00
Ammie 26 16 37N15'59 83W41'32 5:34:46
Ammons 14 1 37N57'04 86W29'38 5:45:59
Amos 2 1 36N39'09 86W05'18 5:44:21
Anchorage 56 70 38N16'00 85W31'59 5:42:08
Anco 60 16 37N14'59 83W03'16 5:32:13
Anderson 71 1 37N01'05 86W47'59 5:47:12
Anderson 110 1 36N41'45 87W10'13 5:48:41
Anderson City 3
44 38N00'26 85W01'33 5:40:06
Andyville 82 51 38N02'02 86W22'21 5:45:29
Anna 114 1 37N06'59 86W25'23 5:45:42

Anna Lynne 38 1 36N32'49 89w15'14 5:57:01
Anneta 43 1 37N22'15 86w14'43 5:44:59
Annville 55 16 37N19'09 83w58'14 5:35:53
Ano 100 19 37N06'48 84w20'11 5:37:21
Ansel 100 19 37N11'46 84w42'33 5:38:50
Antepast 26 16 37N16 83w39 5:34:36
Anthoston 51 1 37N45'34 87w32'18 5:50:09
Antioch 49 36 38N33'59 84w17'34 5:37:10
Antioch Mills 49
36 38N31 84w23 5:37:32
Anton 54 1 37N21'07 87w23'41 5:49:35
Apex 24 1 37N05'51 87w20'28 5:49:22
Apex 67 16 37N10 82w47 5:31:08
Apple Grove 5 1 37N03'19 86w04'22 5:44:17
Appliance Park 56
68 38N10 85w39 5:42:36
Arat 29 1 36N45'24 85w27'55 5:41:52
Arch 47 51 37N42 86w08 5:44:32
Argentum 45 11 38N33 82w58 5:31:52
Argillite 45 11 38N29'23 82w49'42 5:31:19
Argo 98 11 37N28'50 82w03'48 5:28:15
Argyle 23 51 37N13'33 84w48'27 5:39:14
Arista 109 51 37N22'07 85w18'17 5:41:13
Arjay 7 15 36N48'17 83w38'45 5:34:35
Ark 7 15 36N44 83w48 5:35:12
Arkansas 36 11 37N34'58 82w43'57 5:30:56
Arkansas Creek 36
11 37N34 82w45 5:31:00
Arkle 61 15 36N55'09 83w58'37 5:35:54
Arlington 20 1 36N47'25 89w00'46 5:56:03
Arlington 76 31 37N45'38 84w18'28 5:37:14
Arlington Heights 37
20 38N12 84w52 5:39:28
Arnett 95 16 37N24'37 83w34'07 5:34:16
Arnold 92 1 37N23'29 86w39'32 5:46:38
Arnold 113 1 37N34'52 87w55'05 5:51:40
Arrington Corner 46
1 37N46'29 86w44'55 5:47:00
Arrowood 13 16 37N27 83w27 5:33:48
Artemus 61 15 36N50'00 83w50'30 5:35:22
Arthur 31 1 37N10'32 86w12'24 5:44:50
Arthurmabel 77 11 37N35'42 82w56'51 5:31:47
Artville 83 16 37N55'25 83w27'46 5:33:51
Arvel 65 16 37N31'06 83w53'07 5:35:32
Ary 97 46 37N23 83w09 5:32:36
Asa 58 11 37N46'04 82w54'15 5:31:37
Ashbrook 3 44 37N55'55 85w02'45 5:40:11
Ashbyburg 54 1 37N32'07 87w22'08 5:49:29
Ashcamp 98 11 37N15'58 82w26'06 5:29:44
Asher 66 16 37N02'39 83w24'15 5:33:37
Ashers Fork 26 16 37N00'30 83w35'44 5:34:23
Ashland 10 11 38N28'42 82w38'17 5:30:33
Ashland Park 34
28 38N01'30 84w28'39 5:37:55
Ashlock 29 1 36N37'28 85w25'57 5:41:44
Ashville 56 68 38N08'05 85w34'50 5:42:19
Askin 92 1 37N38'18 86w38'24 5:46:34
Aspen Grove 19 11 38N53'47 84w23'09 5:37:33
Asphalt 31 1 37N11'27 86w21'00 5:45:24
Atchison 109 51 37N18'27 85w18'02 5:41:12
Athens 34 28 37N56'57 84w21'51 5:37:27
Athertonville 62
59 37N38'08 85w36'15 5:42:25
Athol 65 16 37N33'09 83w33'46 5:34:15
Atkinstown 55 16 37N22'59 83w57'46 5:35:51
Atlanta 63 37 37N13'57 84w02'58 5:36:12
Atoka 11 25 37N39'00 84w51'44 5:39:27
Atterson 23 1 37N20'18 85w04'41 5:40:19
Attilla 62 51 37N30'12 85w30'23 5:42:02
Atwood 59 11 38N52'20 84w32'18 5:38:09
Auburn 107 1 36N51'51 86w42'37 5:46:50
Auburndale 56 68 38N08'34 85w46'28 5:43:06
Audubon Park 56
69 38N12'14 85w43'31 5:42:54
Augusta 12 11 38N46'18 84w00'21 5:36:01
Ault 32 16 38N11'43 83w12'39 5:32:51
Aurora 79 1 36N46'36 88w08'39 5:52:35
Austerlitz 9 30 38N05'26 84w13'01 5:36:52
Austin 5 1 36N49'31 86w01'09 5:44:05
Auxier 36 11 37N44'13 82w45'30 5:31:02
Avawam 97 46 37N13'28 83w16'31 5:33:06
Avena 49 21 38N23 84w17 5:37:08
Avenstoke 3 20 38N06'30 85w00'02 5:40:00
Avoca 56 70 38N15'33 85w29'55 5:42:00
Avon 34 16 38N04'18 84w19'07 5:37:16
Avondale 73 1 37N03 88w37 5:54:28
Avondale Heights 73
1 37N04'20 88w39'00 5:54:36
Awe 68 11 38N25'17 83w20'38 5:33:23
Axtel 14 1 37N38'39 86w28'33 5:45:54
Ayers 118 15 36N37'51 84w13'43 5:36:55
Bachelors Rest 96
11 38N38'41 84w14'09 5:36:57
Backusburg 18 1 36N42'21 88w28'06 5:53:52
Badger 109 51 37N27'16 85w31'53 5:42:08
Bagdad 106 51 38N15'44 85w03'28 5:40:14
Bailey Creek 48
15 36N52'44 83w11'26 5:32:46
Bailey Mine 10 11 38N20 82w46 5:31:04
Baileys Branch 86
1 36N39 85w38 5:42:32
Baileys Switch 61
15 36N54 83w53 5:35:32
Bainbridge 24 1 36N59'44 87w39'40 5:50:39
Baizetown 92 1 37N22'14 86w42'39 5:46:51
Baker Branch 58
11 37N51 82w46 5:31:04
Bakers 17 1 37N11'02 88w02'08 5:52:09
Bakers Crossroads 18
1 36N33'08 88w21'25 5:53:26
Bakersport 24 1 37N12'28 87w20'41 5:49:23
Bakerton 29 1 36N50'54 85w20'01 5:41:20
Bald Eagle 6 16 38N12 83w56 5:35:44
Bald Hill 35 16 38N21'25 83w42'53 5:34:52
Bald Knob 37 16 38N16 84w56 5:39:44
Baldrock 63 37 36N59'25 84w17'01 5:37:08
Baldwin 76 31 37N47'48 84w25'31 5:37:42
Baldwin Ford 17 1 37N20'44 87w49'17 5:51:17
Balkan 7 15 36N45'33 83w32'40 5:34:11
Ballard 3 44 37N55'49 84w59'26 5:39:58
Ballardsville 56
60 38N19'04 85w32'22 5:42:09
Ballardsville 93
62 38N21'41 85w20'45 5:41:23
Balltown 90 51 37N44'19 85w30'23 5:42:02
Balltown 118 15 36N43'26 84w10'04 5:36:40
Baltimore 42 1 36N41'15 88w48'21 5:55:13
Bancroft 56 70 38N17 85w35 5:42:20
Bancroft 89 1 37N09'57 87w14'51 5:48:59
Bandana 4 1 37N08'46 88w56'45 5:55:47
Bandy 100 19 37N17 84w40 5:38:40
Bangor 103 16 38N02'36 83w26'20 5:33:45
Bank Lick 59 14 38N54'35 84w34'47 5:38:19
Banks 67 16 37N05'03 83w01'19 5:32:05
Banner 36 11 37N35'57 82w42'05 5:30:48
Banock 16 1 37N21'03 86w39'20 5:46:37
Baptist 119 16 37N43'53 83w28'45 5:33:55
Baralto 34 28 37N58'53 84w30'56 5:38:04
Barbourmeade 56
68 38N17'50 85w36'12 5:42:25
Barbourville 61
15 36N51'59 83w53'20 5:35:33
Barcreek 26 16 37N13'38 83w38'28 5:34:34
Bardo 48 15 36N45'35 83w20'40 5:33:23
Bardstown 90 65 37N48'33 85w28'01 5:41:52
Bardstown Junction 15
53 37N56'24 85w41'58 5:42:48
Bardwell 20 1 36N52'14 89w00'35 5:56:02
Bardwell West 20
1 36N51 89w03 5:56:12
Barefoot 91 38 38N25'25 84w07'01 5:36:28
Bark Camp 118 15 36N57 84w06 5:36:24
Barkers Mill 24 1 36N40'05 87w20'52 5:49:23
Barkley Shores 111
1 36N45'27 87w57'51 5:51:51
Barlow 4 1 37N03'06 89w02'48 5:56:11
Barnesburg 100 19 37N08'52 84w31'58 5:38:08
Barnes Store 17 1 37N07 87w53 5:51:32
Barnett Creek 1 1 37N16 85w03 5:40:12
Barnetts Creek 58
11 37N49'40 82w52'47 5:31:31
Barnett Springs 1
1 37N14'31 85w05'29 5:40:22
Barnrock 58 11 37N56 82w53 5:31:32
Barnsley 54 1 37N15'25 87w29'23 5:49:58
Barnyard 61 15 36N50 83w46 5:35:04
Barrallton 15 53 38N02'20 85w47'56 5:43:12
Barren River 114
10 37N02'57 86w31'00 5:46:04
Barridge 97 46 37N12 83w02 5:32:08
Barrier 116 1 36N46'08 84w46'02 5:39:04
Barterville 91 38 38N22'44 84w04'08 5:36:17
Barthell 74 16 36N41'11 84w31'31 5:38:06
Barwick 13 16 37N22'00 83w21'59 5:33:28
Bascom 32 16 38N02'24 83w09'41 5:32:39
Basil 1 1 37N04 85w25 5:41:40
Basin Spring 14 1 37N50'31 86w18'24 5:45:14
Baskett 51 1 37N52'15 87w27'45 5:49:51
Bass 23 51 37N20'19 85w08'41 5:40:35
Bath 60 16 37N14'33 82w54'41 5:31:39
Battle 115 51 37N46'43 85w01'43 5:40:07
Battle Run 35 16 38N20'59 83w50'39 5:35:23
Battletown 82 51 38N03'50 86w17'38 5:45:11
Bauer 74 19 36N55'56 84w26'50 5:37:47
Baughman 61 15 36N51'53 83w48'01 5:35:12
Baughman Heights 11
25 37N37'55 84w46'21 5:39:05
Baxter 48 15 36N51'35 83w19'51 5:33:19
Bayfork 114 1 36N53 86w21 5:45:24
Bayou 70 1 37N14'41 88w28'30 5:53:54
Bays 13 16 37N38'46 83w14'49 5:32:59
Bays Branch 36 11 37N43'22 82w46'05 5:31:04
Bealers Knob 75 1 37N32 87w16 5:49:04
Beals 51 1 37N52'00 87w24'10 5:49:37
Bear Branch 66 16 37N09'48 83w32'56 5:34:12
Beartown 32 16 38N11'10 83w11'19 5:32:45
Bearville 61 16 37N22'09 83w04'03 5:32:16
Bear Wallow 5 6 37N09'06 85w51'22 5:43:25
Bearwallow 115 51 37N42'13 85w19'03 5:41:16
Beattyville 65 16 37N34'18 83w42'25 5:34:50
Beaumont 85 1 36N52'32 85w39'07 5:42:36
Beaumont Park 34
28 38N01'57 84w33'37 5:38:14
Beauty 80 11 37N50'24 82w26'21 5:29:45
Beaver 36 11 37N23'48 82w39'16 5:30:37
Beaver Bottom 98
11 37N18'53 82w21'38 5:29:27
Beaver Dam 92 1 37N24'07 86w52'33 5:47:30
Beaver Junction 36
11 37N36'49 82w43'54 5:30:56
Beaverlick 8 11 38N52'44 84w41'40 5:38:47
Beckamridge 104 1 37N04 85w06 5:40:24
Beckley 56 70 38N15'03 85w28'35 5:41:54
Becknerville 25
33 37N57'59 84w16'46 5:37:07
Becks Store 29 1 36N58 85w26 5:41:44
Beckton 5 6 36N59'03 86w02'11 5:44:09
Beda 92 1 37N30'28 86w56'58 5:47:48
Bedford 112 57 38N35'33 85w19'04 5:41:16
Bee 50 1 37N16'08 86w05'05 5:44:20
Beech 13 16 37N22'11 83w25'44 5:33:43
Beech 48 15 36N47 83w20 5:33:20
Beech Bottom 23
51 37N22'13 84w56'07 5:39:44
Beechburg 35 16 38N26'48 83w38'25 5:34:34
Beech Creek 89 1 37N10'37 87w03'47 5:48:15
Beech Grove 15 51 37N56'02 85w45'21 5:43:01
Beech Grove 22 16 38N18'26 82w55'37 5:31:42
Beech Grove 75 1 37N36'58 87w23'47 5:49:35
Beechland 71 1 37N02'30 86w54'45 5:47:39
Beechland 82 51 38N04'59 86w21'39 5:45:27
Beechland Beach 56
68 38N21'14 85w38'02 5:42:32
Beechmont 56 69 38N10'54 85w45'44 5:43:03
Beechmont 89 1 37N10'28 87w01'57 5:48:08
Beechville 85 1 37N03'41 85w37'58 5:42:32
Beechwood 94 16 38N24'44 84w44'46 5:38:59
Beechwood Village 56
68 38N15'17 85w37'53 5:42:32
Beechy 45 11 38N37'28 82w57'15 5:31:49
Beefhide 67 11 37N14'23 82w37'39 5:30:31
Beelerton 53 1 36N35'39 88w52'56 5:55:32
Bee Lick 100 19 37N19'43 84w30'10 5:38:01
Bee Spring 31 1 37N17'22 86w17'05 5:45:08
Beetle 22 16 38N11'44 82w56'47 5:31:47
Bel Air 25 33 38N00'15 84w12'03 5:36:48
Belcher 98 11 37N20'30 82w22'25 5:29:30
Belcourt 117 1 37N29 87w30 5:50:00
Belfry 98 11 37N37'13 82w16'09 5:29:05
Belknap 119 16 37N43'16 83w17'39 5:33:11
Belknap Beach 93
52 38N22'58 85w37'24 5:42:30
Bell City 32 16 38N05'24 83w07'33 5:32:30
Bell City 42 1 36N32'15 88w30'02 5:54:00
Bellcraft 67 16 37N08'07 82w49'31 5:31:18
Bellefonte 45 11 38N29'33 82w41'25 5:30:46
Bellemeade 56 68 38N15'08 85w35'32 5:42:22
Bellepoint 37 20 38N12 84w52 5:39:28
Belle Point 65 16 37N33'45 83w44'53 5:35:00
Belleview (Grant P O) 8
11 38N59'10 84w49'32 5:39:18
Bellevue 19 71 39N06'23 84w28'44 5:37:55
Bellewood 56 68 38N15'27 85w39'35 5:42:38
Bell Farm 74 16 36N42 84w29 5:37:56
Bells Run 92 1 37N35'42 86w55'42 5:47:43
Belltown 78 66 37N32'01 85w18'19 5:41:13
Bellview 52 20 38N21'22 85w08'35 5:40:34
Bellville 117 1 37N22'54 87w47'57 5:51:12
Bellwood 90 51 37N47'40 85w32'51 5:42:11
Belmont 15 51 37N53'47 85w42'49 5:42:51
Belmont 49 21 38N23'22 84w18'31 5:37:14
Belton 89 1 37N10 87w02 5:48:08
Ben Bow 64 11 37N58'09 82w38'06 5:30:32
Bengal 109 51 37N21'33 85w27'26 5:41:50
Benge 26 16 37N13'42 83w55'23 5:35:42
Benham 48 15 36N57'53 82w56'55 5:31:48
Benito 48 15 36N54'00 83w07'42 5:32:31
Benleo 114 10 37N06'50 86w32'39 5:46:11
Bennettstown 24 1 36N41'44 87w36'41 5:50:27
Benson 37 20 38N12'25 84w57'34 5:39:50
Bent 100 19 37N06'43 84w26'41 5:37:47
Benton 79 3 36N51'26 88w21'01 5:53:24
Berea 76 43 37N34'07 84w17'47 5:37:11
Berkley 20 1 36N48'13 89w04'56 5:56:20
Berlin 12 11 38N41'41 84w09'45 5:36:39
Bernice 26 16 37N12'25 83w45'13 5:35:01
Bernstadt 63 16 37N09'22 84w11'41 5:36:47
Berry 49 36 38N31'14 84w23'04 5:37:32
Berrys Lick 16 1 37N03'37 86w45'36 5:47:02
Berry Store 5 6 36N57'12 86w08'27 5:44:34
Berrytown 56 70 38N16'09 85w31'09 5:42:05
Berry West 49 36 38N28 84w26 5:37:44
Bertha 61 15 36N57 84w00 5:36:00
Bethanna 77 11 37N46'31 83w11'01 5:32:44
Bethany 56 68 38N05'54 85w52'20 5:43:29
Bethany 119 16 37N39'01 83w28'25 5:33:54
Bethel 6 16 38N14'42 83w52'05 5:35:28
Bethel 57 29 37N53 84w34 5:38:16
Bethelridge 23 51 37N14'01 84w45'30 5:39:02
Bethesda 116 1 36N47'27 84w54'21 5:39:37
Bethlehem 52 51 38N24'02 85w04'10 5:40:17
Betsey 116 1 36N54'13 84w44'35 5:38:58
Betsy Layne 36 11 37N33'05 82w38'01 5:30:32
Betty 60 11 37N27'03 82w50'22 5:31:21
Beulah 53 1 36N46'04 88w52'05 5:55:28
Beulah 54 1 37N16'17 87w41'03 5:50:44
Beulah Heights 74
16 36N48'15 84w26'22 5:37:45
Beverly 24 1 36N45'24 87w31'32 5:50:06
Beverly 61 15 36N55'49 83w31'58 5:34:08
Beverly Hills 11
25 37N38'41 84w45'34 5:39:02
Bevier 89 1 37N14'40 87w04'55 5:48:20
Bevinsville 36 11 37N22 82w43 5:30:52
Bewleyville 14 1 37N50'24 86w14'40 5:44:59
Biddle 105 26 38N20'58 84w36'27 5:38:26
Big Bear Creek 79
1 37N10 87w02 5:48:08
Big Bone 8 11 38N53'19 84w45'07 5:39:00
Big Branch 98 11 37N18'22 82w28'32 5:29:54
Big Clifty 43 1 37N32'44 86w09'13 5:44:37
Big Creek 26 16 37N09'44 83w34'08 5:34:17
Big Eddy 37 20 38N10'12 84w51'30 5:39:26
Big Fork 66 16 37N03'00 83w14'56 5:33:00
Biggs 98 11 37N25'14 82w16'14 5:29:05
Bighill 76 16 37N33'16 84w12'30 5:36:50
Big Laurel 66 15 36N58'47 83w13'02 5:32:52
Big Ready 31 1 37N14 86w26 5:45:44
Big Reedy 31 1 37N16'09 86w26'08 5:45:45
Big Rock 66 16 37N02'35 83w12'26 5:32:50
Big Sandy Junction 10
11 38N24'57 82w35'59 5:30:24
Big Shoal 98 11 37N29 82w31 5:30:04
Big Spring 14 51 37N47'57 86w09'08 5:44:37
Bigstone 32 16 38N06'18 83w10'12 5:32:41
Big Windy 50 1 37N19'07 86w05'40 5:44:23
Big Woods 83 16 37N59'21 83w28'36 5:33:54
Billows 63 16 37N10'15 84w17'48 5:37:11
Bilvia 67 16 37N08 82w46 5:31:04
Bimble 61 15 36N52'30 83w49'50 5:35:19
Binghamtown 7 15 36N37'53 83w43'16 5:34:53
Binns Mill 24 1 36N45'09 87w39'35 5:50:38
Birdie 3 44 38N02'15 85w00'53 5:40:04
Birdsville 70 1 37N13'16 88w26'53 5:53:48
Birk City 30 1 37N47'07 87w17'04 5:49:08
Birmingham 79 1 36N54'23 88w13'25 5:52:54
Biscayne 67 16 37N14 82w46 5:31:04
Black Bottom 48
15 36N54'32 83w04'49 5:32:19
Blackburn 113 1 37N41'44 88w07'13 5:52:29
Black Diamond 89
1 37N13 87w03 5:48:12
Blackey 67 16 37N08'24 82w58'45 5:31:55
Blackford 117 1 37N26'54 87w56'05 5:51:44
Black Gnat 44 51 37N18'15 85w26'11 5:41:45
Black Gold 31 1 37N15'34 86w19'48 5:45:19
Black Hawk 111 1 36N57'36 87w52'38 5:51:31
Black Jack 107 1 36N46'04 86w30'46 5:46:03
Blackjoe 48 15 36N51'42 83w16'55 5:33:08
Blackmont (Hulen P O) 7
15 36N47'30 83w31'30 5:34:06
Black Mountain 48
15 36N50'55 83w08'45 5:32:35
Black Rock 43 1 37N27'38 86w21'18 5:45:25
Blacks Crossroads 9
30 38N15'03 84w08'18 5:36:33
Blacks Ferry 74
15 36N42 84w29 5:37:56

Black Snake 7 15 36N46'05 83W30'12 5:34:01
Blackwater 63 16 37N03'11 83W53'42 5:35:35
Blackwell 52 51 38N20 85W03 5:40:12
Bladeston 12 11 38N43'17 84W05'48 5:36:23
Blaine 64 11 38N01'39 82W50'36 5:31:22
Blair 48 15 36N59'25 82W57'11 5:31:49
Blair Mills 88 16 38N04'58 83W17'31 5:33:10
Blair Town 98 11 37N32'33 82W35'09 5:30:21
Blake 95 16 37N23'13 83W44'21 5:34:57
Blanche 7 15 36N49'05 83W39'19 5:34:37
Blanchet 41 11 38N31'11 84W34'18 5:38:17
Blandville 4 1 36N56'37 88W57'50 5:55:51
Blanton Flats 55
16 37N34'12 84W00'14 5:36:01
Blaze 88 16 38N01'18 83W19'59 5:33:20
Bledsoe 48 15 36N55'25 83W22'01 5:33:28
Blevins 64 11 38N04'26 82W54'14 5:31:37
Blincoe 115 59 37N38 85W24 5:41:36
Bliss 1 1 37N04'48 85W22'19 5:41:29
Bloomfield 90 59 37N54'37 85W19'00 5:41:16
Bloomingdale 25
33 37N53'13 84W07'37 5:36:30
Bloomington 43 1 37N29 86W18 5:45:12
Bloomington 77 11 37N49'01 83W08'39 5:32:35
Bloss 102 36 37N12'59 84W21'36 5:37:26
Blowing Spring 44
6 37N16 85W30 5:42:00
Blowing Springs 50
1 37N18 86W04 5:44:16
Bloyd 44 1 37N24'19 85W34'33 5:42:18
Bloyds Crossing 44
1 37N21'38 85W34'22 5:42:17
Bluebank 35 16 38N23'02 83W39'18 5:34:37
Blueberry Hill 34
28 37N58'54 84W31'21 5:38:05
Blue Diamond 97
46 37N18'28 83W12'57 5:32:52
Blue Gap 90 51 37N41'16 85W33'56 5:42:16
Blue Heron 74 16 36N40'17 84W32'44 5:38:11
Bluehole 26 16 37N06'01 83W45'23 5:35:02
Blue John 100 19 36N55'47 84W28'59 5:37:56
Blue Level 114 1 36N58'39 86W32'28 5:46:10
Blue Lick 69 16 37N29'27 84W42'27 5:38:50
Blue Lick Springs 91
38 38N19 84W02 5:36:08
Blue Moon 36 11 37N30'27 82W41'52 5:30:47
Blue Ridge Manor 56
70 38N14'35 85W33'47 5:42:15
Blue River 36 11 37N37'09 82W50'38 5:31:23
Blue Spring 111 1 36N49'44 87W56'15 5:51:45
Blue Spring Estates 111
1 36N50'13 87W57'23 5:51:50
Bluestone 103 16 38N08'59 83W30'41 5:34:03
Blue Water Estates 111
1 36N53'29 87W58'42 5:51:55
Bluff Boom 44 6 37N16'40 85W27'40 5:41:51
Bluff City 51 8 37N48'06 87W22'46 5:49:31
Bluff Spring 24 1 37N00'18 87W18'53 5:49:16
Blythe 86 1 36N40'35 85W32'56 5:42:12
Board Tree 98 11 37N32'19 82W09'44 5:28:39
Boat 97 46 37N15 83W11 5:32:44
Boatwright 18 1 36N38'39 88W07'25 5:52:30
Boaz 42 1 36N53'08 88W38'04 5:54:32
Bobbs 58 11 37N49 82W46 5:31:04
Bobs Creek 48 15 36N47'26 83W14'52 5:32:59
Bobtown 76 43 37N37'03 84W13'45 5:36:55
Bobtown 100 19 37N13'04 84W32'13 5:38:09
Bohon 84 16 37N48'42 84W55'11 5:39:41
Boiling Spring 114
10 37N00 86W25 5:45:40
Boldman 98 11 37N31'43 82W37'20 5:30:29
Boles 86 1 36N37'07 85W39'52 5:42:39
Boltsfork 10 11 38N15'47 82W41'59 5:30:48
Bolyn 60 16 37N26'37 82W54'22 5:31:37
Bon 118 15 36N43'24 84W11'30 5:36:46
Bon Air Estates 56
68 38N12'46 85W39'28 5:42:38
Bon Air Hills 37
20 38N11'34 84W49'31 5:39:18
Bonanza 36 11 37N41'31 82W51'50 5:31:27
Bon Ayr 5 1 37N01'28 86W03'32 5:44:14
Bond 55 16 37N18'57 83W59'10 5:35:57
Bondurant 38 1 36N31'24 89W19'11 5:57:17
Bondville 84 16 37N55'18 84W52'19 5:39:29
Boneyville 69 16 37N30'19 84W41'30 5:38:46
Bon Haven 25 33 38N00'17 84W11'45 5:36:47
Bonita 120 45 38N05'09 84W42'29 5:38:50
Bonnieville 50 1 37N22'43 85W54'11 5:43:37
Bonny 88 16 37N54'29 83W21'42 5:33:27
Bonnyman 97 46 37N17'23 83W14'11 5:32:57
Booker 115 51 37N46'55 85W18'00 5:41:12
Boone 102 16 37N31'03 84W19'00 5:37:16
Boone Furnace 22
16 38N28'06 83W07'32 5:32:30
Boone Heights 61
15 36N51'19 83W52'02 5:35:28
Boonesboro 76 33 37N54'30 84W16'19 5:37:05
Boonesborough 76
33 37N54'30 84W16'19 5:37:05
Booneville 95 16 37N28'34 83W40'30 5:34:42
Boons Camp 58 11 37N50 82W42 5:30:48
Booth 47 51 37N48'19 85W45'06 5:43:00
Booth 119 16 37N41'45 83W37'56 5:34:32
Bordley 113 1 37N33'33 87W52'11 5:51:29
Boreing 63 16 37N02'17 84W00'53 5:36:04
Bornes Ford 107 1 36N39'45 86W24'44 5:45:39
Bosco (Hueysville P O) 36
11 37N29'55 82W50'28 5:31:22
Boston 16 1 37N05'19 86W47'13 5:47:09
Boston 30 1 37N41'28 86W54'32 5:47:38
Boston 56 68 38N14'14 85W26'07 5:41:44
Boston 90 51 37N47'15 85W40'22 5:42:41
Boston 96 11 38N45'46 84W21'09 5:37:25
Botland 90 51 37N46'35 85W23'21 5:41:33
Botto 26 16 37N05'14 83W40'38 5:34:43
Boundary Oak 62
51 37N31'49 85W44'16 5:42:57
Bourbon 100 19 37N03'07 84W37'21 5:38:29
Bourbon Springs 90
51 37N51'04 85W28'59 5:41:56
Bourne 40 16 37N42'35 84W36'47 5:38:27
Bouty 118 15 36N44 84W10 5:36:40
Bow 29 1 36N45'45 85W20'42 5:41:23
Bowen 99 16 37N50'28 83W46'19 5:35:05
Bowling Green 114
10 36N59'25 86W26'37 5:45:46
Bowlingtown 97 46 37N18'34 83W27'10 5:33:49
Boxville 113 1 37N37'42 87W49'40 5:51:19
Boyce 114 1 36N49'55 86W22'46 5:45:31
Boyd 49 36 38N33'02 84W23'39 5:37:35
Boyds Crossing 44
1 37N20 85W33 5:42:12
Boydsville 42 1 36N30'07 88W31'24 5:54:06
Boydtown 105 16 38N17'03 84W30'10 5:38:01
Bracht 59 11 38N49'08 84W35'19 5:38:21
Bracktown 34 28 38N05'41 84W33'45 5:38:15
Bradford 12 11 38N47'06 84W08'44 5:36:35
Bradfordsville 78
51 37N29'39 85W08'56 5:40:36
Bradley 77 11 37N42'37 83W00'24 5:32:02
Bradshaw 55 16 37N25'30 83W57'48 5:35:51
Bradshaw 110 1 36N46'48 87W09'01 5:48:36
Brady 103 16 38N10'16 83W26'24 5:33:46
Brainard 36 11 37N39'50 82W53'47 5:31:35
Bramlett 44 6 37N09'43 85W27'43 5:41:51
Brandenburg 82 67 37N59'56 86W10'10 5:44:41
Brandenburg Station 82
67 37N58'08 86W08'26 5:44:34
Brandy Keg 36 11 37N41 82W46 5:31:04
Brannon 57 28 37N57'30 84W32'46 5:38:11
Brassfield 76 16 37N40'27 84W08'47 5:36:35
Bratton 101 11 38N34'06 84W05'43 5:36:23
Braxton 84 44 37N50'29 84W48'20 5:39:13
Brazil 55 16 37N31'29 84W02'30 5:36:10
Breck 94 16 38N29'45 84W44'08 5:38:57
Breckinridge 49
21 38N26'29 84W22'43 5:37:31
Breeding 1 1 36N57'33 85W26'04 5:41:44
Bremen 89 1 37N21'41 87W13'07 5:48:52
Brent 19 71 39N03'17 84W26'01 5:37:44
Brentsville 9 30 38N14'16 84W17'23 5:37:10
Brentwood 54 1 37N17'48 87W30'48 5:50:03
Breton 117 1 37N33'02 87W31'25 5:50:06
Brewers 79 1 36N46'17 88W26'20 5:53:45
Briartown 115 51 37N41'38 85W14'33 5:40:58
Briarwood 56 70 38N16'41 85W35'35 5:42:22
Briarwood Manor 114
10 36N59'10 86W24'41 5:45:39
Bridgeport 37 16 38N09'36 84W57'04 5:39:48
Bridge Street 73
1 37N03 88W37 5:54:28
Bridgeville 12 11 38N35'42 84W01'12 5:36:05
Brien 79 1 36N54'17 88W13'49 5:52:55
Briensburg 79 1 36N54'13 88W19'25 5:53:18
Brigadoon 34 28 37N59'12 84W31'05 5:38:04
Brighton 34 28 38N00'50 84W25'11 5:37:41
Brightshade 26 16 37N01'20 83W39'36 5:34:38
Brinegar 22 16 38N13'16 83W17'24 5:33:10
Brinkley 60 16 37N18'32 82W56'56 5:31:48
Bristletown 5 6 36N56'03 85W55'10 5:43:41
Bristow 114 1 37N01'07 86W21'36 5:45:26
Britmark 110 1 36N52'59 87W16'52 5:49:07
Broad Bottom 98
11 37N32'03 82W35'35 5:30:22
Broadfields 56 68 38N14 85W39 5:42:36
Broad Ford 43 1 37N22'53 86W04'46 5:44:19
Broadway 31 1 37N18'52 86W16'25 5:45:06
Broadwell 49 21 38N19'43 84W21'33 5:37:26
Brock 63 37 37N06'35 84W00'00 5:36:00
Brodhead 102 24 37N24'15 84W24'50 5:37:39
Bromley 59 71 39N04'55 84W33'37 5:38:14
Bromley 94 16 38N38'26 84W50'54 5:39:24
Bromo 102 36 37N21 84W20 5:37:20
Bronston 100 19 36N59'08 84W37'23 5:38:30
Brookhaven 34 28 38N00'06 84W30'50 5:38:03
Brooklyn 16 1 37N17'23 86W34'35 5:46:18
Brooks 15 51 38N03'40 85W42'35 5:42:50
Brookside 48 15 36N51'33 83W14'58 5:33:00
Brooksville 12 11 38N40'57 84W03'57 5:36:16
Broughtentown 69
16 37N23'02 84W32'36 5:38:10
Browder 89 1 37N11'50 87W02'11 5:48:09
Brownies Creek 7
15 36N46 83W35 5:34:20
Browning 114 1 36N56'49 86W36'35 5:46:26
Browning Corner 96
11 38N37'11 84W13'15 5:36:53
Brownings Corner 96
11 38N40 84W20 5:37:20
Brownington 15 51 37N56'54 85W35'07 5:42:20
Browningtown 15
53 38N00 85W43 5:42:52
Brownsboro 93 52 38N21'22 85W29'54 5:42:00
Brownsboro Farm 56
68 38N18'10 85W35'46 5:42:23
Brownsboro Village 56
68 38N15'47 85W39'57 5:42:40
Browns Crossroads 27
1 36N42'57 85W11'27 5:40:46
Browns Ford 2 1 36N43 85W58 5:43:52
Browns Fork 97 46 37N14'10 83W13'57 5:32:56
Browns Grove 42 1 36N37'26 88W29'14 5:53:57
Browns Valley 30
1 37N38'25 87W07'08 5:48:29
Brownsville 31 1 37N11'33 86W16'04 5:45:04
Brownsville 38 1 36N32'05 89W13'01 5:56:52
Brownwood Manor 30
1 37N45 87W07 5:48:28
Bruin 32 16 38N11'16 83W01'08 5:32:05
Brumfield 11 16 37N36'15 84W58'56 5:39:56
Brushart 45 11 38N31'08 83W04'58 5:32:20
Brush Grove 115
51 37N50'35 85W10'49 5:40:43
Brutus 26 16 37N14'50 83W34'37 5:34:18
Bryan 104 1 36N55'46 85W12'14 5:40:49
Bryant 37 20 38N14'21 84W57'04 5:39:48
Bryants 61 15 36N47 83W56 5:35:44
Bryantsville 40
16 37N42'52 84W38'57 5:38:36
Buchanan 64 11 38N14'38 82W36'39 5:30:27
Buck Creek 95 16 37N29 83W40 5:34:40
Buckettown 76 43 37N35 84W17 5:37:08
Buckeye 40 16 37N42'56 84W30'20 5:38:01
Buck Grove 82 51 37N55'08 86W07'40 5:44:31
Buckhorn 97 46 37N20'55 83W28'35 5:33:54
Buckingham 36 11 37N22'09 82W44'22 5:30:57
Buckner 93 62 38N23'01 85W26'24 5:41:46
Buechel 56 68 38N11'42 85W39'07 5:42:36
Buel 75 1 37N32'54 87W10'27 5:48:42
Buena Vista 40 16 37N45'01 84W39'55 5:38:40
Buena Vista 49 21 38N26'11 84W10'05 5:36:40
Buena Vista 68 11 38N36 83W19 5:33:16
Buena Vista 79 1 36N56'11 88W13'30 5:52:54
Buena Vista Estates 72
1 37N01'30 88W02'52 5:52:11
Buffalo 62 51 37N30'43 85W41'55 5:42:48
Buffalo 111 1 36N55'10 87W41'10 5:50:45
Buffalo Fork 71 1 36N59'58 86W40'24 5:46:42
Buford 92 1 37N33'51 86W59'02 5:47:56
Bug 27 1 36N39'17 85W06'33 5:40:26
Buggytown 76 43 37N38'08 84W22'09 5:37:29
Bugtussle 86 1 36N37'30 85W52'29 5:43:30
Bulan 97 46 37N18'05 83W09'54 5:32:40
Bull Creek 36 11 37N40'00 82W43'40 5:30:55
Bullittsville 8
11 39N04'31 84W44'19 5:38:57
Bummer 102 16 37N22 84W16 5:37:04
Bunker Hill 9 16 38N09'50 84W00'47 5:36:03
Bunnell Crossing 50
1 37N13'54 85W48'17 5:43:13
Buras 14 1 37N42'06 86W18'58 5:45:16
Burdick 109 51 37N16'25 85W22'34 5:41:30
Burdine 67 16 37N11'21 82W35'57 5:30:24
Burfield 116 1 36N43'35 84W47'24 5:39:10
Burg 88 16 37N46 83W18 5:33:12
Burgin 84 17 37N45'12 84W46'00 5:39:04
Burke 32 16 38N06'26 83W02'24 5:32:10
Burkes Spring 78
59 37N38'51 85W20'54 5:41:24
Burkesville 29 1 36N47'25 85W22'14 5:41:29
Burkhart 119 16 37N42'24 83W16'31 5:33:06
Burk Hollow 118
15 36N35 84W08 5:36:32
Burlington 8 11 39N01'39 84W43'27 5:38:54
Burna 70 1 37N14'44 88W21'38 5:53:27
Burnaugh 10 11 38N15'37 82W34'54 5:30:20
Burnetta 100 19 37N04'15 84W48'10 5:39:13
Burning Fork 77
11 37N44'00 83W01'24 5:32:06
Burning Springs 26
16 37N14'57 83W49'17 5:35:17
Burnside 100 32 36N59'20 84W36'00 5:38:24
Burnwell 98 11 37N37'44 82W13'24 5:28:54
Burr 102 36 37N20'31 84W18'18 5:37:13
Burton 36 11 37N21'34 82W43'26 5:30:54
Burtonville 68 11 38N29'45 83W34'24 5:34:18
Bush 63 16 37N05'33 83W52'13 5:35:29
Bushong 86 1 36N42 85W42 5:42:48
Bushtown 84 44 37N43'50 84W43'45 5:38:55
Buskirk 88 16 37N48'43 83W20'01 5:33:20
Buskirk 98 11 37N37'10 82W10'08 5:28:41
Busseyville 64 11 38N04'15 82W40'14 5:30:41
Busy 97 46 37N16'42 83W17'26 5:33:10
Butchertown 23 51 37N30'41 84W53'26 5:39:34
Butler 96 11 38N47'11 84W22'11 5:37:29
Butlersville 2 1 36N47'01 86W18'47 5:45:15
Buttenberry 75 1 37N26 87W09 5:48:36
Butterfly 97 46 37N17'18 83W16'21 5:33:05
Buttimer Hill 37
20 38N12 84W52 5:39:28
Buttonsberry 75 1 37N26'48 87W10'07 5:48:40
Bybee 76 16 37N43'59 84W07'29 5:36:30
Bypro 36 11 37N22 82W42 5:30:48
Cabell 116 1 36N49'52 85W00'25 5:40:02
Cabot 46 1 37N41'19 86W39'12 5:46:37
Caddo 96 11 38N44'51 84W14'42 5:36:59
Cadentown 34 28 38N00'44 84W25'36 5:37:42
Cadiz 111 1 36N51'54 87W50'07 5:51:20
Cains Store 100
19 37N08 84W50 5:39:20
Cairo 51 1 37N42'29 87W38'45 5:50:35
Caldwell 96 11 38N48'24 84W23'29 5:37:34
Caldwell Manor 11
25 37N39'29 84W46'55 5:39:08
Caleast 76 31 37N41'25 84W19'55 5:37:20
Caledonia 111 1 36N49'13 87W41'42 5:50:47
Calf Creek 80 11 37N52 82W32 5:30:08
Calhoun 75 4 37N32'20 87W15'30 5:49:02
California 19 11 38N55'07 84W15'49 5:37:03
Callaboose 119 16 37N45 83W33 5:34:12
Callaway 7 15 36N47'00 83W33'48 5:34:15
Calloway Crossing 33
27 37N43'27 84W00'20 5:36:01
Calvary 78 66 37N30'56 85W15'45 5:41:03
Calvert City 79 1 37N02'00 88W21'00 5:53:24
Calvin 7 15 36N43'20 83W37'20 5:34:29
Camargo 87 16 37N59'39 83W53'16 5:35:33
Cambridge 56 68 38N13'18 85W37'00 5:42:28
Cambridge Shores 79
1 36N56'24 88W13'42 5:52:55
Cambridge Village 56
68 38N13 85W37 5:42:28
Camelia 73 1 37N01'25 88W46'28 5:55:06
Camelot 56 70 38N17 85W35 5:42:20
Campbellsburg 52
51 38N31'25 85W12'10 5:40:49
Campbellsville 109
51 37N20'36 85W20'31 5:41:22
Camp Dick Robinson 40
16 37N37 84W35 5:38:20
Camp Dix 68 11 38N29 83W17 5:33:08
Camp Ground 63 16 36N58'19 84W04'20 5:36:17
Camp Kennedy 40
16 37N37 84W35 5:38:20
Camp Nelson 40 16 37N37 84W35 5:38:20
Camp Pleasant 37
16 38N16 84W41 5:38:44
Camp Springs 19
11 39N00'07 84W21'53 5:37:28
Camp Taylor 56 69 38N11'44 85W42'56 5:42:52
Campton 119 16 37N44'03 83W32'51 5:34:11
Canada 98 11 37N36'20 82W19'28 5:29:18
Canby 94 16 38N31'02 84W39'40 5:38:39
Cane Creek 13 16 37N33 83W22 5:33:28
Cane Creek 63 16 37N03'21 83W55'22 5:35:41
Cane Valley 1 1 37N10'49 85W19'11 5:41:17
Caney 88 16 37N48'05 83W15'33 5:33:02
Caneyville 43 1 37N25'27 86W29'18 5:45:57
Canmer 50 1 37N17'25 85W46'02 5:43:04

Cannel City 88 16 37N47'24 83w16'27 5:33:06
Cannon 61 15 36N54'52 83w51'30 5:35:26
Cannonsburg 10 11 38N23'19 82w42'10 5:30:49
Cannons Mill 27 1 36N41'20 85w05'24 5:40:22
Cannons Point 14 1 37N35'02 86w27'41 5:45:51
Canoe 13 16 37N26'56 83w26'55 5:33:48
Canton 111 1 36N47'56 87w57'39 5:51:51
Canton Heights Estates 111 1 36N48 87w58 5:51:52
Cantown 23 51 37N15'41 84w54'44 5:39:39
Canyon Falls 65 16 37N34'35 83w34'39 5:34:19
Capital Heights 37 20 38N12 84w52 5:39:28
Capito 7 15 36N36'51 83w49'50 5:35:19
Carbondale 54 1 37N10 87w41 5:50:44
Carbon Glow 67 16 37N10'47 82w57'12 5:31:49
Carcassonne 67 16 37N10'30 83w00'00 5:32:00
Carden 5 6 37N02'33 85w59'55 5:44:00
Cardinal 7 15 36N48'06 83w30'45 5:34:03
Cardinal Hill 34 28 38N02'34 84w32'20 5:38:09
Cardinal Valley 34 28 38N03'11 84w32'39 5:38:11
Cardwell 115 51 37N49'27 85w02'03 5:40:08
Carl 24 1 36N58'25 87w20'12 5:49:21
Carlinburg 51 1 37N53'00 87w19'24 5:49:18
Carlisle 91 38 38N18'43 84w01'39 5:36:07
Carmack 72 1 37N01'05 88w06'57 5:52:28
Carntown 96 11 38N50'17 84w14'28 5:36:58
Carpenter 118 15 36N42'57 83w58'17 5:35:53
Carr Creek 60 16 37N13'52 82w58'05 5:31:52
Carr Fork 60 16 37N15 82w58 5:31:52
Carrie 60 16 37N19'54 83w01'58 5:32:08
Carrollton 21 39 38N40'51 85w10'46 5:40:43
Carrs 68 11 38N39'27 83w25'10 5:33:41
Carrsville 70 1 37N23'51 88w22'29 5:53:30
Carson 21 16 38N40'48 84w57'46 5:39:51
Carter 22 16 38N25'44 83w07'15 5:32:29
Cartersville 40 16 37N32'17 84w24'29 5:37:38
Carthage 19 11 38N56'08 84w18'26 5:37:14
Cartwright 27 1 36N45'10 85w04'34 5:40:18
Carver 77 11 37N38'28 83w03'01 5:32:12
Cary 7 15 36N47'37 83w39'52 5:34:39
Casey 16 1 37N20'04 86w36'27 5:46:26
Casey Creek 1 1 37N16'20 85w09'27 5:40:38
Caseyville 113 1 37N32'16 88w03'51 5:52:15
Cash 50 1 37N28 85w54 5:43:36
Casky 24 1 36N49'01 87w25'56 5:49:44
Cassaday 114 10 37N00 86w25 5:45:40
Catalpa 64 11 38N25 82w36 5:30:24
Catawba 96 11 38N43'13 84w19'28 5:37:18
Catherine 104 1 37N08 84w55 5:39:40
Catlettsburg 10 11 38N24'17 82w36'02 5:30:24
Catron Creek 48 15 36N48 83w20 5:33:20
Caudell 67 16 37N07 82w49 5:31:16
Causey 66 16 37N03'26 83w16'51 5:33:07
Cave City 5 6 37N08'12 85w57'25 5:43:50
Cavehill 114 1 36N55 86w34 5:46:16
Cavelawn 37 20 38N12 84w52 5:39:28
Cave Ridge 85 1 36N59 85w37 5:42:28
Cave Spring 14 1 37N38'58 86w25'27 5:45:42
Cave Spring 71 1 36N51 86w53 5:47:32
Cave Springs 71 1 36N47'57 86w57'12 5:47:49
Cawood 48 15 36N47'02 83w13'42 5:32:55
Cayce 38 1 36N33'19 89w02'09 5:56:09
Cecil 73 1 37N06'09 88w40'01 5:54:40
Cecilia 47 51 37N39'57 85w57'24 5:43:50
Cedar Bluff 17 1 37N05'18 87w50'41 5:51:23
Cedarcrest 116 1 36N59 84w54 5:39:36
Cedar Flat 82 51 38N07'05 86w19'18 5:45:17
Cedar Flats 85 1 36N56'47 85w36'51 5:42:27
Cedar Grove 15 51 37N58'20 85w37'52 5:42:31
Cedar Grove 100 19 37N00'57 84w36'04 5:38:24
Cedar Grove 110 1 36N56'03 87w09'22 5:48:37
Cedar Knob 27 1 36N37'42 85w05'05 5:40:20
Cedar Point 93 52 38N24'28 85w28'40 5:41:55
Cedar Point 111 1 36N51'53 87w53'31 5:51:34
Cedar Spring 31 6 37N07'20 86w09'11 5:44:37
Cedar Springs 2 6 36N49'51 86w06'24 5:44:26
Cedarville 98 11 37N19 82w21 5:29:24
Center 85 1 37N08'32 85w41'35 5:42:46
Centerfield 93 60 38N21'00 85w24'27 5:41:38
Center Point 86 1 36N42 85w42 5:42:48
Centertown 92 1 37N25'02 86w59'46 5:47:59
Centerview 14 1 37N37'51 86w18'31 5:45:14
Centerville 9 30 38N13'26 84w23'29 5:37:34
Centerville 34 28 37N58'44 84w21'47 5:37:27
Central City 89 1 37N17'38 87w07'24 5:48:30
Ceralvo 92 1 37N21'54 87w01'53 5:48:08
Ceredo 4 1 37N02'28 88w52'01 5:55:28
Cerulean 111 1 36N57'34 87w42'36 5:50:50
Cerulean Springs 111 1 36N56 87w48 5:51:12
Chad 48 15 36N58'11 83w01'22 5:32:05
Chalybeate 31 1 37N07'37 86w14'10 5:44:57
Chambers 46 1 37N50'14 86w47'07 5:47:08
Chance 1 1 36N58'31 85w19'29 5:41:18
Chandlers Chapel 71 1 36N56'57 86w47'35 5:47:10
Chandlerville 58 11 37N56'05 82w48'49 5:31:15
Chapel Hill 2 1 36N43'11 86w17'34 5:45:10
Chaplin 90 51 37N53'52 85w13'17 5:40:53
Chapman 64 11 38N01'25 82w37'26 5:30:30
Chapman 113 1 37N42'58 87w54'55 5:51:40
Chappell 66 16 37N00'39 83w21'00 5:33:24
Charleston 54 1 37N13'29 87w40'19 5:50:41
Charley 64 11 37N58'29 82w42'28 5:30:50
Charlotte Furnace 22 16 38N24'42 83w02'00 5:32:08
Charters 68 11 38N34'25 83w26'00 5:33:44
Chatham 12 11 38N42'55 84w01'08 5:36:05
Chaumont 31 6 37N07'43 86w04'00 5:44:16
Chavies 97 46 37N20'52 83w21'23 5:33:26
Chenaultt 14 1 38N00'54 86w31'05 5:46:04
Chenoa 7 15 36N40'09 83w51'42 5:35:27
Chenowee 13 16 37N32'36 83w28'50 5:33:55
Cherokee 56 69 38N13 85w41 5:42:44
Cherokee 64 11 38N04'39 82w50'16 5:31:21
Cherokee Garden 56 68 38N14'44 85w40'39 5:42:43
Cherry 18 1 36N36 88w19 5:53:16
Cherry Grove 41 11 38N36'06 84w34'14 5:38:17
Cherrywood 56 68 38N16 85w39 5:42:36
Cherrywood Village 56 68 38N15'37 85w39'16 5:42:37
Chestnutburg 26 16 37N17'20 83w47'48 5:35:11
Chestnut Gap 95 16 37N27'31 83w39'32 5:34:38
Chestnut Grove 106 54 38N18'00 85w15'50 5:41:03
Chevrolet 48 15 36N49'02 83w16'29 5:33:06
Chevy Chase 34 28 38N01'13 84w29'15 5:37:57
Chicken Bristle 69 16 37N29'09 84w46'12 5:39:05
Chiles 73 1 37N06'49 88w44'57 5:55:00
Chilesburg 34 28 38N00'25 84w21'35 5:37:26
Chilton 23 51 37N27'18 84w59'15 5:39:57
Chloe 98 11 37N29 82w31 5:30:04
Choatville 37 20 38N12 84w52 5:39:28
Christianburg 106 51 38N16'41 85w05'58 5:40:24
Christine 1 1 37N08'32 85w12'25 5:40:50
Christopher 97 46 37N14'01 83w10'17 5:32:41
Christy 103 16 38N11'41 83w24'52 5:33:39
Church 43 1 37N29 86w18 5:45:12
Church Hill 24 1 36N48'08 87w34'20 5:50:17
Cimota City 73 1 37N05'32 88w51'22 5:55:25
Cinda 66 16 37N06'26 83w17'41 5:33:11
Cisco 77 11 37N51'09 83w08'07 5:32:32
Cisselville 115 51 37N41'36 85w16'37 5:41:06
Clare 2 1 36N42'54 86w23'41 5:45:35
Clarence 100 19 37N17'31 84w33'27 5:38:14
Clark 56 68 38N11 85w28 5:41:52
Clark Hill 22 16 38N17'42 83w11'27 5:32:46
Clark Landing 114 10 37N08'07 86w36'08 5:46:25
Clarksburg 68 11 38N35'06 83w21'58 5:33:28
Clarks Corner 85 1 37N02'31 85w39'40 5:42:39
Clarkson 43 1 37N29'43 86w13'17 5:44:53
Claryville 19 11 38N55'09 84w23'44 5:37:35
Claxton 17 1 37N06'15 87w45'58 5:51:04
Clay 117 1 37N28'36 87w49'12 5:51:17
Clay City 99 16 37N51'33 83w55'07 5:35:40
Clayhole 13 16 37N28'02 83w17'51 5:33:11
Claymour 110 1 36N53'12 87w06'41 5:48:27
Claypool 114 10 36N54'21 86w14'27 5:44:58
Claysville 49 16 38N31'09 84w11'07 5:36:44
Clay Village 106 51 38N11'33 85w06'26 5:40:26
Claywell 29 1 36N49'07 85w17'24 5:41:10
Clear Creek 7 15 36N46 83w42 5:34:48
Clear Creek Furnace 6 16 38N03'00 83w35'21 5:34:21
Clear Creek Springs 7 15 36N43'37 83w43'37 5:34:54
Clearfield 103 49 38N09'43 83w25'44 5:33:43
Clear Run 92 1 37N27 86w54 5:47:36
Clear Springs 42 1 36N49'40 88w32'19 5:54:09
Cleaton 89 1 37N15'16 87w05'20 5:48:21
Clementsville 23 51 37N17'24 85w05'35 5:40:22
Clemons 97 46 37N17'45 83w13'57 5:32:56
Cleopatra 75 1 37N37'20 87w17'34 5:49:10
Clermont 15 51 37N55'47 85w39'10 5:42:37
Cliff 36 11 37N40'53 82w46'50 5:31:07
Clifford 64 11 38N00'04 82w31'38 5:30:07
Clifton 11 25 37N38'58 84w41'17 5:38:45
Clifton 19 71 39N04'57 84w29'07 5:37:56
Clifton 120 45 38N05'10 84w49'34 5:39:18
Clifton Mills 14 1 37N52'02 86w23'17 5:45:33
Cliftons 56 69 38N15'19 85w42'57 5:42:52
Clifty 110 1 36N59'43 87w08'52 5:48:35
Climax 102 16 37N28'11 84w13'30 5:36:54
Clinton 53 1 36N40'02 88w59'36 5:55:58
Clintonville 34 16 38N05'06 84w16'06 5:37:04
Clio 118 15 36N49'04 84w11'58 5:36:48
Closplint 48 15 36N54'14 83w04'08 5:32:17
Cloud Crossing 79 1 37N01'58 88w23'18 5:53:33
Clover 48 15 36N55'41 82w57'56 5:31:52
Clover Bottom 55 16 37N29'56 84w09'05 5:36:36
Cloverdale 37 20 38N12 84w52 5:39:28
Clover-Darby 48 15 36N53'37 83w03'47 5:32:15
Cloverport 14 1 37N50'00 86w37'58 5:46:32
Clovertown 48 15 36N51'04 83w18'31 5:33:14
Cloyds Landing 29 1 36N45'15 85w29'28 5:41:58
Club House Heights 37 20 38N12 84w52 5:39:28
Clutts 48 15 36N58'19 82w58'14 5:31:53
Clyffeside 10 11 38N28 82w39 5:30:36
Coakley 44 1 37N22'34 85w32'08 5:42:09
Coalgood 48 15 36N48'46 83w15'18 5:33:01
Coal Run (P O) 98 11 37N30'27 82w32'57 5:30:12
Coalton 10 11 38N22'12 82w46'09 5:31:05
Cobb 17 1 36N59'25 87w46'44 5:51:07
Cobblers Knob 14 1 37N34'05 86w23'08 5:45:33
Cobhill 33 16 37N42'54 83w49'43 5:35:19
Coburg 1 6 37N12'05 85w20'09 5:41:21
Codyville 14 1 37N46'40 86w26'51 5:45:47
Coe 86 1 36N41'00 85w33'01 5:42:12
Cofer 85 1 36N57'35 85w29'25 5:41:58
Coffman 92 1 37N27'47 87w06'07 5:48:24
Cogswell 103 16 38N05'56 83w29'19 5:33:57
Coiltown 54 1 37N21'04 87w38'42 5:50:35
Coin 100 19 37N10'30 84w30'37 5:38:02
Colby 25 33 37N59'45 84w15'49 5:37:03
Colby Hills 25 33 37N59'20 84w11'52 5:36:47
Coldiron 48 15 36N49'36 83w27'13 5:33:49
Cold Spring 19 11 39N01'18 84w26'24 5:37:46
Cold Springs 82 51 38N03'14 86w17'22 5:45:09
Coldwater 18 1 36N39'03 88w27'19 5:53:49
Coleman 98 11 37N28'53 82w11'00 5:28:44
Colemansville 49 36 38N31'40 84w24'25 5:37:38
Coles Bend 5 1 37N03 86w13 5:44:52
Colesburg 47 51 37N47'05 85w46'26 5:43:06
Coletown 34 28 37N55'44 84w26'32 5:37:46
Colfax 35 16 38N12'45 83w38'03 5:34:32
Colitown Junction 54 1 37N20'09 87w37'58 5:50:32
College 76 43 37N35 84w17 5:37:08
College Campus 18 1 36N36 88w19 5:53:16
College Heights 114 10 37N00 86w25 5:45:40
College Hill 76 16 37N47'12 84w07'24 5:36:30
Collins 98 11 37N24'05 82w31'05 5:30:04
Collista 58 11 37N46'57 82w49'28 5:31:18
Colliver 36 11 37N35'46 82w44'12 5:30:57
Colly 67 16 37N07 82w47 5:31:08
Colmar 7 15 36N39'57 83w39'07 5:34:36
Colo 100 19 37N02'44 84w29'02 5:37:56
Colonial Terrace 56 70 38N17 85w35 5:42:20
Colony 34 28 38N02'36 84w33'43 5:38:15
Colony 63 16 37N08 84w11 5:36:44
Colson 67 16 37N13'26 82w51'23 5:31:26
Colts 48 15 36N52'49 83w08'48 5:32:35
Columbia 1 1 37N06'10 85w18'23 5:41:14
Columbus 34 28 38N02'13 84w21'56 5:37:28
Columbus 53 1 36N45'35 89w06'12 5:56:25
Colville 49 21 38N21'55 84w12'37 5:36:50
Comargo 74 16 36N40'39 84w32'29 5:38:10
Combs 97 46 37N16'01 83w12'46 5:32:51
Combs Ford 92 1 37N30'55 86w52'06 5:47:28
Comer 75 1 37N38'16 87w26'38 5:49:47
Commerce Landing 72 1 36N58'26 88w01'41 5:52:07
Commissary Corner 8 11 39N00'31 84w47'02 5:39:08
Concord 35 16 38N18'52 83w46'52 5:35:07
Concord 43 1 37N33'39 86w27'35 5:45:50
Concord 68 11 38N41'10 83w29'28 5:33:58
Concord 96 11 38N43'22 84w18'03 5:37:12
Concordia 82 51 38N03'32 86w25'41 5:45:43
Confederate 72 1 36N59'31 87w59'51 5:51:59
Confluence 66 16 37N16'11 83w23'03 5:33:32
Congleton 65 16 37N33'08 83w43'01 5:34:52
Congleton 75 1 37N36'33 87w26'58 5:49:48
Conkling 95 16 37N22'53 83w41'24 5:34:46
Conley 77 11 37N45'06 82w58'42 5:31:55
Conner 106 51 38N13'25 85w23'25 5:41:34
Connersville 49 21 38N22'48 84w24'46 5:37:39
Conoloway 43 1 37N22'05 86w12'56 5:44:52
Conrard 100 19 37N10'51 84w21'27 5:37:26
Consolation 106 51 38N15'24 85w02'34 5:40:10
Constance 8 11 39N04'26 84w38'15 5:38:33
Constantine 14 1 37N40'31 86w14'11 5:44:57
Conway 102 16 37N28'40 84w20'04 5:37:20
Cooksburg 102 16 37N23'20 84w11'07 5:36:44
Cooksville 42 1 36N36'44 88w31'24 5:54:06
Cooktown 5 1 36N50'05 85w56'27 5:43:46
Cool Springs 92 1 37N17'36 86w52'55 5:47:32
Coon 98 11 37N29 82w31 5:30:04
Cooper 116 1 36N46'16 84w51'41 5:39:27
Co-operative 74 16 36N41'34 84w36'28 5:38:26
Cooper Landing 70 1 37N03'43 88w20'01 5:53:20
Cooperstown 71 1 36N55'49 86w53'15 5:47:33
Coopersville 116 1 36N45'37 84w44'16 5:38:57
Copebranch 13 16 37N31'03 83w31'34 5:34:06
Copland 13 16 37N27'17 83w22'09 5:33:29
Coral Hill 5 6 37N03'05 85w51'23 5:43:26
Coral Ridge 56 68 38N06 85w45 5:43:00
Coraville 51 1 37N43'50 87w28'17 5:49:53
Corbin 118 15 36N56'55 84w05'49 5:36:23
Cordell 64 11 38N00'20 82w47'35 5:31:10
Cordia 60 16 37N16'44 83w06'39 5:32:27
Cordova 41 11 38N32'27 84w30'55 5:38:04
Corinth 41 11 38N29'48 84w33'51 5:38:15
Corinth 71 1 36N47'20 86w48'14 5:47:13
Cork 85 1 37N02'15 85w35'00 5:42:20
Corn Creek 112 51 38N36 85w19 5:41:16
Cornelius 55 16 37N18'50 84w00'32 5:36:02
Corners 14 1 37N47'41 86w13'49 5:44:55
Cornette 63 37 37N17'35 84w05'34 5:36:22
Cornettsville 97 46 37N08'02 83w04'37 5:32:18
Cornishville 84 16 37N48'01 84w59'37 5:39:58
Cornwell 83 16 37N57'24 83w42'40 5:34:51
Cory 22 16 38N17'02 83w06'47 5:32:27
Corydon 51 1 37N44'36 87w42'14 5:50:49
Costelow 71 1 36N59'27 86w46'04 5:47:04
Cote 48 15 36N52 83w12 5:32:48
Cottageville 68 11 38N36'16 83w36'10 5:34:25
Cottle 88 16 37N53'20 83w12'14 5:32:49
Cottonburg 76 31 37N43'50 84w27'43 5:37:51
Cottongim 26 16 37N03'53 83w48'09 5:35:13
Country Club Heights 81 11 38N38'17 83w47'24 5:35:10
Counts Crossroads 22 16 38N19'05 83w07'09 5:32:29
Covedale 68 11 38N39'34 83w31'16 5:34:05
Covington 95 71 39N05'01 84w30'31 5:38:02
Cowan 35 16 38N24'26 83w53'31 5:35:34
Cowcreek 95 16 37N26'19 83w36'38 5:34:27
Coxs Creek 90 51 37N53'55 85w28'25 5:41:54
Coxton 48 15 36N51'26 83w16'13 5:33:05
Crab Orchard 69 16 37N27'52 84w30'24 5:38:02
Cracker 36 11 37N34 82w45 5:31:00
Crailhope 44 1 37N09'35 85w39'57 5:42:40

Craintown 11 16 37N37'25 85W01'06 5:40:04
Craintown 35 16 38N23'16 83W47'10 5:35:09
Crane Nest 61 15 36N59'23 83W52'46 5:35:31
Cranetown 105 26 38N16'38 84W31'51 5:38:07
Craney 103 16 38N11 83W26 5:33:44
Cranks 48 15 36N45'53 83W10'20 5:32:41
Cranston 103 16 38N15'48 83W26'08 5:33:45
Cravens 90 51 37N48'31 85W32'34 5:42:10
Crawford 63 37 37N11'40 83W57'07 5:35:48
Crawford 97 46 37N18 83W13 5:32:52
Craycraft 1 1 37N05'38 85W12'10 5:40:49
Crayne 28 1 37N16'14 88W04'57 5:52:20
Craynor 36 11 37N26'13 82W40'08 5:30:41
Creal 44 1 37N27 85W40 5:42:40
Creech 48 15 36N46'02 83W23'42 5:33:35
Creekmore 74 16 36N37'22 84W21'42 5:37:27
Creekville 26 16 37N04'40 83W32'57 5:34:12
Creelsboro 104 1 36N53'06 85W11'51 5:40:47
Crenshaw 108 51 38N03'17 85W28'01 5:41:52
Crescent Hill 56 69 38N15 85W42 5:42:48
Crescent Park 59 71 39N02'36 84W34'27 5:38:18
Crescent Springs 59 71 39N03'05 84W34'54 5:38:20
Cressmont 65 16 37N31'51 83W47'42 5:35:11
Cressy 33 27 37N49'29 84W02'25 5:36:10
Crest 47 61 37N45'00 85W50'37 5:43:22
Crestmoor 114 10 36N58'18 86W28'06 5:45:52
Creston 23 51 37N16'00 85W02'32 5:40:10
Crestview 19 11 39N01'31 84W25'03 5:37:40
Crestview Hills 59 11 39N01'38 84W35'06 5:38:20
Crestwood 34 28 38N00'35 84W30'40 5:38:03
Crestwood 93 60 38N19'27 85W28'21 5:41:53
Creswell 17 1 37N16'07 87W54'44 5:51:39
Crider 17 1 37N09'26 87W58'28 5:51:54
Crittenden 41 11 38N46'58 84W36'19 5:38:25
Croakes 115 51 37N46'36 85W19'56 5:41:20
Crockett 88 16 37N59'08 83W05'27 5:32:22
Crockettsville 13 16 37N23'48 83W28'27 5:33:54
Crocus 1 1 36N58'50 85W12'39 5:40:51
Crofton 24 1 37N02'52 87W29'06 5:49:56
Croley 53 1 36N40 89W00 5:56:00
Cromona 67 16 37N11'11 82W41'50 5:30:47
Cromwell 92 1 37N20'25 86W47'17 5:47:09
Cropper 106 51 38N18'44 85W06'48 5:40:27
Crossgate 56 70 38N16'45 85W37'48 5:42:31
Crossland 18 1 36N30'02 88W22'49 5:53:31
Crossroad 71 1 36N52'00 87W01'19 5:48:05
Cross Road 72 1 37N00'48 88W05'32 5:52:22
Crowell Landing 70 1 37N03'19 88W29'43 5:53:59
Crown 67 16 37N09 82W50 5:31:20
Crowtown 17 1 37N07'40 87W53'37 5:51:34
Crow Valley 76 31 37N44'25 84W24'52 5:37:39
Cruise 63 16 37N19'06 84W07'23 5:36:30
Crum 68 11 38N27'35 83W27'02 5:33:48
Crummies 48 15 36N46'28 83W12'14 5:32:49
Crutchfield 38 1 36N34'36 88W56'07 5:55:44
Crystal 33 16 37N39'48 83W49'32 5:35:18
Crystal Lake 93 62 38N24 85W23 5:41:32
Cuba 42 1 36N35'06 88W37'45 5:54:31
Cubage 7 15 36N42'04 83W31'16 5:34:05
Cub Run 31 1 37N19'22 86W11'41 5:44:47
Culbertson 10 11 38N25 82W36 5:30:24
Cull 94 16 38N34'20 84W54'30 5:39:38
Cullen 113 1 37N35'22 87W52'41 5:51:31
Culver 32 16 38N05'02 82W59'28 5:31:58
Culvertown 90 59 37N42'36 85W32'02 5:42:08
Cumberland 48 15 36N58'41 82W59'19 5:31:57
Cumberland City 27 1 36N48'18 85W04'06 5:40:16
Cumberland College 118 15 36N44 84W10 5:36:40
Cumberland Falls 118 15 36N50 84W14 5:36:56
Cumberland Shores 111 1 36N45'08 87W56'52 5:51:47
Cumminsville 12 11 38N43'05 84W06'18 5:36:25
Cundiff 1 1 36N56'41 85W15'16 5:41:01
Cunningham 20 1 36N54'27 88W53'23 5:55:34
Cupio 15 64 38N00'22 85W52'42 5:43:31
Curdsville 30 1 37N44'06 87W19'54 5:49:20
Curlew 113 1 37N34'40 88W05'12 5:52:21
Currentsville 9 30 38N15'39 84W15'04 5:37:00
Curt 13 16 37N33 83W22 5:33:28
Curtis 85 1 36N55'59 85W34'35 5:42:18
Custer 14 1 37N44'18 86W15'17 5:45:01
Cutshin 66 16 37N05'20 83W15'18 5:33:01
Cutuno 77 11 37N43'05 83W14'36 5:32:58
Cuzick 76 31 37N50'03 84W27'13 5:37:49
Cyclone 86 1 36N50'15 85W40'46 5:42:43
Cynthiana 49 21 38N23'25 84W17'39 5:37:11
Cyrus 77 11 37N47'37 83W02'25 5:32:10
Dabney 100 19 37N11'02 84W33'00 5:38:12
Dabolt 55 16 37N20 84W01 5:36:04
Daffenville 79 1 36N55'11 88W20'19 5:53:21
Dahl 100 19 37N10'54 84W26'05 5:37:44
Daisy 97 46 37N06'49 83W05'42 5:32:23
Dal 118 15 36N43'05 84W05'44 5:36:23
Dale 77 11 37N41'29 83W14'03 5:32:56
Dalesburg 13 16 37N20'34 83W31'56 5:34:08
Dalesburg 35 16 38N27'50 83W40'41 5:34:43
Daley 66 16 37N08'09 83W13'56 5:32:56
Dallams Creek 71 1 36N59 86W57 5:47:48
Dalton 54 1 37N17'59 87W45'43 5:51:03
Dan 83 16 37N57'19 83W27'35 5:33:50
Dan 92 1 37N27 86W41 5:46:44
Dana 36 11 37N33'15 82W41'28 5:30:46
Danby 71 1 36N52'57 86W55'10 5:47:41
Daniel Boone 54 1 37N10'43 87W30'27 5:50:02
Daniels Creek 58 11 37N46 82W45 5:31:00
Danleytown 45 11 38N29'30 82W46'10 5:31:05
Dant (Dants Sta) 78 59 37N38'09 85W27'21 5:41:49
Dants 78 59 37N38 85W24 5:41:36
Danville 101 25 37N38'44 84W46'20 5:39:05
Darbyton 48 15 36N52 83W12 5:32:48
Darfork 97 46 37N17'02 83W11'15 5:32:45
Darkmont 48 15 36N52'22 83W10'46 5:32:43
Darnell 110 1 36N39'04 87W05'23 5:48:22
Dartmont 48 15 36N52 83W12 5:32:48
Datha 55 16 37N15'37 83W54'59 5:35:40
Davella 80 11 37N47'53 82W34'55 5:30:20
Davenport Landing 89 1 37N14'11 86W55'12 5:47:41
David 36 11 37N35'58 82W53'27 5:31:34
Davidson 92 1 37N32 86W41 5:46:44
Davis 105 16 38N22'27 84W28'20 5:37:53
Davis Branch 10 11 38N25 82W36 5:30:24
Davisburg 7 15 36N40'46 83W49'24 5:35:18
Davis Crossroads 16 1 37N03'05 86W44'29 5:46:58
Davis Hill 11 25 37N38'55 84W50'12 5:39:21
Davisport 80 11 37N49'19 82W37'57 5:30:32
Davistown 40 16 37N41'31 84W41'44 5:38:47
Davistown 120 48 38N08'29 84W39'06 5:38:36
Davisville 64 11 37N58'13 82W49'48 5:31:19
Dawkins 58 11 37N47'25 82W47'05 5:31:08
Dawson Springs 54 1 37N10'02 87W41'33 5:50:46
Day 67 16 37N04'17 82W50'48 5:31:23
Dayhoit 48 15 36N50'23 83W22'37 5:33:30
Daylight 54 1 37N10 87W41 5:50:44
Daysboro 119 16 37N47'36 83W22'34 5:33:30
Daysville 110 1 36N48'08 87W04'01 5:48:16
Dayton 19 71 39N06'46 84W28'22 5:37:53
Deane 67 16 37N14'19 82W46'24 5:31:06
Deanefield 92 1 37N39'34 86W48'25 5:47:14
Deanwood 28 1 37N21'41 87W55'35 5:51:42
Deatsville 90 51 37N53'49 85W33'33 5:42:14
Debord 80 11 37N49'35 82W33'05 5:30:12
Decatur 104 1 37N07'31 84W59'53 5:40:00
Decide 27 1 36N46'24 85W12'15 5:40:49
Decker 16 1 37N20'07 86W29'08 5:45:57
DeCoursey 59 71 39N00'28 84W29'15 5:37:57
Decoy 60 16 37N29'44 83W05'39 5:32:23
Dee Acres 30 1 37N44 86W59 5:47:56
Deep Creek 84 44 37N41'45 85W01'22 5:40:05
Deep Springs 34 28 38N03'47 84W26'41 5:37:47
Deerfield 34 28 38N00'41 84W31'18 5:38:05
Deer Lick 26 16 37N08'48 83W56'38 5:35:47
Deer Lick 71 1 37N00'57 87W02'12 5:48:09
Deese 55 16 37N20 84W01 5:36:04
Deevert 22 16 38N23'04 83W02'33 5:32:10
Defeated Creek 67 16 37N03'06 82W59'35 5:31:58
Defiance 97 46 37N12'12 83W05'31 5:32:22
Defoe 106 51 38N20'27 85W03'16 5:40:13
Defries 50 1 37N16'06 85W41'05 5:42:44
Dehart 88 40 37N57'52 83W20'14 5:33:21
Dekoven 113 1 37N34'29 88W04'20 5:52:17
Delafield 114 10 37N00'40 86W26'45 5:45:47
Delaplain 105 26 38N16'25 84W32'55 5:38:12
Delaware 30 1 37N41'02 87W24'15 5:49:37
Delia 41 11 38N39'32 84W40'19 5:38:41
Dellville 52 51 38N31 85W12 5:40:48
Delmer 100 19 37N01'44 84W44'05 5:38:56
Delphia 97 46 37N01'46 83W05'13 5:32:21
Delta 116 1 36N51'52 84W39'26 5:38:38
Delville 52 51 38N28'39 85W05'51 5:40:23
Delvinta 65 16 37N30'03 83W47'38 5:35:11
Dema 36 16 37N25'13 82W48'19 5:31:13
Demlytown 93 60 38N19 85W28 5:41:52
Democrat 67 16 37N14'00 82W48'12 5:31:13
Demond 88 16 37N49 83W26 5:33:44
DeMossville 96 11 38N48'18 84W25'01 5:37:40
Demplytown 93 62 38N23'04 85W28'28 5:41:54
Dempster 14 1 37N37'31 86W33'35 5:46:14
Demunbruns Store 31 1 37N11 86W06 5:44:24
Denison 50 1 37N18 86W04 5:44:16
Denmark 104 1 36N59 85W04 5:40:16
Denney 116 1 36N48'48 84W39'25 5:38:38
Dennis 71 1 36N50'34 86W47'14 5:47:09
Denniston 83 16 37N54'57 83W32'17 5:34:09
Denton 22 16 38N15'53 82W51'45 5:31:27
Denver 58 11 37N46'34 82W51'17 5:31:25
Depoy 89 1 37N12'57 87W14'25 5:48:58
Derby 117 1 37N27'33 87W54'09 5:51:37
Dermont 30 1 37N44'37 87W02'27 5:48:10
Desda 27 1 36N50'04 85W11'54 5:40:48
Devon 8 11 38N58'08 84W36'57 5:38:28
Devondale 56 68 38N16'30 85W36'54 5:42:28
Dewdrop 32 16 38N08'44 83W08'03 5:32:34
Dewitt 61 15 36N52'37 83W44'16 5:34:57
Dexter 18 1 36N44'34 88W17'47 5:53:11
Dexterville 16 1 37N19'03 86W39'22 5:46:37
Diablock 97 46 37N13'42 83W10'20 5:32:41
Diamond 117 1 37N25'00 87W48'08 5:51:13
Diamond Springs 71 1 37N02'08 86W58'33 5:47:54
Dice 97 46 37N21'46 83W13'39 5:32:55
Dietz Acres 47 51 37N51'56 85W57'00 5:43:48
Dillon 48 15 36N54'37 83W12'51 5:32:51
Dimple 16 1 37N06'10 86W43'13 5:46:53
Dingus 88 16 37N54'29 83W06'08 5:32:25
Dinwood 36 11 37N33'47 82W45'52 5:31:03
Dione 48 15 36N57'02 83W05'07 5:32:20
Dirigo 1 1 36N58 85W26 5:41:44
Dishman Springs 61 15 36N52'06 83W57'52 5:35:51
Disputanta 102 16 37N29'18 84W15'27 5:37:02
Divide 66 15 36N56'09 83W12'46 5:32:51
Dix Fork 98 11 37N37 82W21 5:29:24
Dixie 48 15 36N54 83W12 5:32:48
Dixie 51 1 37N40'47 87W41'09 5:50:45
Dixie 118 15 36N41'40 84W03'12 5:36:13
Dixie Heights 59 71 39N01 84W34 5:38:16
Dixie Plantation 34 28 38N03'07 84W26'26 5:37:46
Dixon 117 1 37N31'04 87W41'25 5:50:46
Dixon Town 57 28 37N56'14 84W39'31 5:38:38
Dixville 84 44 37N42'21 84W56'53 5:39:48
Dizney 48 15 36N51'10 83W07'00 5:32:28
Dobbins 32 16 38N09'25 82W55'47 5:31:43
Dobson 58 11 37N44'31 82W53'06 5:31:32
Dock 36 11 37N41 82W46 5:31:04
Doddy 2 6 36N45 86W11 5:44:44
Doe Creek 33 27 37N42 83W58 5:35:52
Doe Valley Estates 82 51 38N00 86W10 5:44:40
Dogcreek 50 1 37N19'14 86W07'31 5:44:30
Dogtown 79 1 36N50'16 88W19'24 5:53:18
Dog Walk 69 16 37N22'37 84W30'08 5:38:01
Dogwalk 92 1 37N24'17 86W37'49 5:46:31
Dogwood 24 1 36N56'57 87W24'38 5:49:39
Dogwood 42 1 36N53'03 88W34'33 5:54:18
Donaldson 111 1 36N45'05 87W53'41 5:51:35
Donansburg 44 1 37N14'14 85W37'34 5:42:30
Donerail 34 28 38N08'57 84W32'06 5:38:08
Dongola 67 16 37N05'50 82W50'38 5:31:23
Dony 36 11 37N27 82W43 5:30:52
Doorway 97 46 37N17'45 83W32'22 5:34:09
Dorena 100 1 37N02'49 84W54'08 5:39:37
Dorthae 63 16 36N59'36 84W06'17 5:36:25
Dorton 98 11 37N16'36 82W34'45 5:30:19
Dorton Branch 7 15 36N46'20 83W40'53 5:34:44
Do Stop 43 1 37N25'55 86W33'02 5:46:12
Dot 71 1 36N40'40 86W57'09 5:47:49
Dotson 36 11 37N38'49 82W51'29 5:31:26
Double Culvert 105 26 38N21'34 84W33'51 5:38:15
Dougan Town 29 1 36N48'01 85W21'50 5:41:27
Doughton 96 11 38N38'38 84W29'55 5:38:00
Douglas 98 11 37N22'46 82W32'33 5:30:10
Douglass Hills 56 68 38N15 85W32 5:42:08
Dover 81 11 38N45'29 83W52'59 5:35:32
Dow 97 46 37N09'25 83W09'47 5:32:39
Downingsville 41 11 38N38'30 84W42'48 5:38:51
Doylesville 76 31 37N50'39 84W09'39 5:36:39
Dozier Heights 54 1 37N17'47 87W30'28 5:50:02
Draffenville 79 1 36N51 88W21 5:53:24
Draffin 98 11 37N20'25 82W23'47 5:29:35
Drake 114 1 36N50'10 86W24'35 5:45:38
Drakesboro 89 1 37N13'03 87W02'56 5:48:12
Draper 48 15 36N51'38 83W12'14 5:32:49
Drennon Springs 52 51 38N30'28 85W03'14 5:40:13
Dressen 48 15 36N49'54 83W19'28 5:33:18
Dreyfus 76 16 37N37'02 84W10'36 5:36:42
Drift 36 11 37N28'49 82W44'52 5:30:59
Dripping Spring 31 1 37N03 86W13 5:44:52
Drip Rock 55 16 37N34'30 83W58'25 5:35:54
Druid Hills 56 68 38N15'49 85W39'42 5:42:39
Drum 100 19 37N05'37 84W28'49 5:37:55
Dry Creek 60 16 37N19'29 82W46'05 5:31:04
Dryden Estates 72 1 36N56'34 87W59'44 5:51:59
Drydock 3 44 37N59'19 85W01'21 5:40:05
Dry Fork 5 1 36N48'55 85W55'29 5:43:42
Dry Fork 98 11 37N19'50 82W25'55 5:29:44
Dryhill 66 16 37N13'19 83W22'39 5:33:31
Dry Ridge 41 13 38N40'55 84W35'24 5:38:22
Dublin 42 1 36N43'31 88W48'08 5:55:13
Dubre 29 1 36N50'20 85W33'31 5:42:14
Duckers 120 48 38N09'52 84W47'02 5:39:08
Duckrun 118 15 36N44'09 84W19'00 5:37:16
Duco 77 11 37N36'20 83W01'38 5:32:07
Duff 43 1 37N32'59 86W24'47 5:45:39
Dugansville 84 44 37N52'43 84W59'06 5:39:56
Dug Hill 43 1 37N21'11 86W08'55 5:44:36
Dukedom 42 1 36N34 88W49 5:55:16
Dukehurst 92 1 37N30'39 86W51'28 5:47:26
Dukes 46 1 37N49'29 86W41'54 5:46:48
Dulaney 17 1 37N05'49 87W58'50 5:51:55
Duluth 76 43 37N34'46 84W10'06 5:36:40
Dulworth 1 1 37N06 85W18 5:41:12
Dunbar 16 1 37N11'17 86W45'25 5:47:02
Dunbar Hill 1 1 37N12'57 85W10'18 5:40:41
Duncan 23 51 37N21'31 84W43'39 5:38:55
Duncan 84 44 37N50'57 84W59'25 5:39:58
Duncannon 76 31 37N39'34 84W20'53 5:37:24
Dundee 92 1 37N33'32 86W46'22 5:47:05
Dunham 67 16 37N11'24 82W38'52 5:30:35
Dunlap 98 11 37N25'41 82W14'33 5:28:58
Dunleary 98 11 37N19'05 82W21'59 5:29:28
Dunmor 89 1 37N04'25 86W59'46 5:47:59
Dunnville 23 51 37N12'00 85W00'36 5:40:02
Dunraven 97 46 37N18'21 83W18'11 5:33:13
Durbin 10 11 38N16'45 82W35'54 5:30:24
Durbintown 96 36 38N33'05 84W25'10 5:37:41
Durhamtown 109 51 37N23'59 85W24'50 5:41:39
Duval 105 26 38N14'47 84W38'29 5:38:34
Dwale 36 11 37N37'23 82W43'26 5:30:54
Dwarf 97 46 37N20'06 83W07'53 5:32:32
Dycusburg 28 1 37N09'34 88W11'04 5:52:44
Dyer 14 1 37N42'22 86W13'17 5:44:53
Dykes 100 19 37N04'05 84W26'09 5:37:45
Eadsville 116 1 36N53'17 84W53'20 5:39:33
Eagle Hill 94 16 38N42'11 84W47'19 5:39:09
Eagle Station 21 16 38N39 84W57 5:39:48
Earles 89 1 37N18'00 87W18'37 5:49:14
Earlington 54 1 37N16'27 87W30'43 5:50:03
Earnestville 65 16 37N29 83W40 5:34:40
East Bardstown 90 65 37N49'57 85W24'32 5:41:38
East Bernstadt 63 16 37N11'22 84W07'04 5:36:28
Easterday 21 39 38N40'32 85W04'28 5:40:18
Eastern 36 11 37N31'01 82W48'22 5:31:13
East Fayette 34 28 38N02 84W23 5:37:32
East Fork 85 1 36N59 85W37 5:42:28
East Frankfort 37 20 38N12 84W52 5:39:28
East Hickman 34 16 37N55'24 84W28'15 5:37:53
East Jenkins 67 16 37N11'16 82W36'15 5:30:25
Eastland 34 28 38N02'46 84W27'35 5:37:50
Eastland 81 11 38N35 83W52 5:35:28

Eastland Park 34 28 38N02'50 84w26'40 5:37:47
Eastland Park 114 10 36N57'34 86w26'18 5:45:45
East McDowell 36 11 37N26'51 82w43'31 5:30:54
Easton 46 1 37N42'22 86w40'54 5:46:44
East Pineville 7 15 36N44'05 83w40'16 5:34:41
East Point 58 11 37N44'46 82w47'27 5:31:10
East Somerset 100 32 37N06 84w36 5:38:24
East Union 91 38 38N14'24 83w58'50 5:35:55
Eastview 47 51 37N35'20 86w03'21 5:44:13
Eastwood 56 68 38N13'59 85w27'21 5:41:49
Eastwood Hills 82 67 37N59'56 86w09'56 5:44:40
Ebenezer 84 16 37N52'47 84w48'54 5:39:16
Ebenezer 86 1 36N42 85w42 5:42:48
Ebenezer 89 1 37N12'14 87w04'51 5:48:19
Eberle 55 16 37N17'58 84w04'49 5:36:19
Ebon 88 16 37N57'19 83w26'04 5:33:44
Eby 22 16 38N26'20 83w12'16 5:32:49
Echo 85 1 37N01'40 85w44'51 5:42:59
Echols 92 1 37N20'01 86w57'51 5:47:51
Eddy Bay 72 1 37N00'30 88w00'41 5:52:03
Eddyville 72 1 37N05'40 88w04'49 5:52:19
Eden 16 1 37N16'32 86w42'16 5:46:49
Eden Bay 72 1 37N01'48 88w02'25 5:52:10
Edenton 76 31 37N46'01 84w29'05 5:37:56
Edgewater 98 11 37N17'22 82w27'30 5:29:50
Edgewood 7 15 36N36'48 83w46'53 5:35:08
Edgewood 59 11 39N01'07 84w34'55 5:38:20
Edgington 45 11 38N40'48 82w52'57 5:31:32
Edgoten 24 1 36N38'30 87w25'26 5:49:42
Edmonton 85 1 36N58'48 85w36'44 5:42:27
Edna 77 11 37N47'36 83w09'02 5:32:36
Edsel 32 16 38N07'04 82w54'34 5:31:38
Edwards 71 1 36N57'33 86w56'27 5:47:46
Eglon 55 16 37N27'41 84w07'48 5:36:31
Egypt 55 16 37N18'47 83w53'46 5:35:35
Eighty Eight 5 1 36N55'06 85w47'11 5:43:09
Ekron 82 51 37N55'45 86w10'46 5:44:43
Elamton 88 16 37N55'39 83w08'51 5:32:35
Elba 75 1 37N39'12 87w21'46 5:49:27
Elcomb 48 15 36N49'16 83w19'58 5:33:20
Eldridge 32 16 38N02'10 83w03'26 5:32:14
Elfie 16 1 37N24 86w36 5:46:24
Eli 104 1 37N02'38 84w57'52 5:39:51
Elias 55 16 37N23'22 83w49'52 5:35:19
Elihu 100 19 37N02'47 84w35'32 5:38:22
Elimer 98 11 37N15'04 82w33'46 5:30:15
Elizabeth 9 30 38N13 84w15 5:37:00
Elizabethtown 47 61 37N41'38 85w51'33 5:43:26
Elizaville 35 16 38N25'10 83w49'32 5:35:18
Elkatawa 13 16 37N33'25 83w25'37 5:33:42
Elk Chester 34 45 38N04'19 84w37'05 5:38:28
Elk Creek 108 51 38N06'01 85w22'16 5:41:29
Elkfork 88 16 37N57'53 83w07'59 5:32:32
Elk Horn 109 51 37N18'59 85w17'07 5:41:08
Elkhorn City 98 11 37N18'14 82w21'04 5:29:24
Elkin 25 33 37N54'46 84w13'26 5:36:54
Elko 31 1 37N09'42 86w08'07 5:44:32
Elkton 110 1 36N48'36 87w09'15 5:48:37
Ella 1 1 37N09'24 85w08'23 5:40:34
Ellen 64 11 38N03'05 82w44'45 5:30:59
Eller 104 1 37N04 85w06 5:40:24
Ellington 29 1 36N45'26 85w25'23 5:41:42
Elliottville 103 16 38N10'58 83w16'33 5:33:06
Ellisburg 23 51 37N28'02 84w55'10 5:39:41
Elliston 41 11 38N44'04 84w44'48 5:38:59
Elliston 76 31 37N44'27 84w09'19 5:36:37
Ellisville 91 38 38N23'27 84w01'15 5:36:05
Ellmitch 92 1 37N37'46 86w41'59 5:46:48
Ellwood 98 11 37N19'28 82w34'43 5:30:19
Elmburg 106 51 38N19'16 85w04'17 5:40:17
Elmrock 60 11 37N27'08 83w01'33 5:32:06
Elmville 37 16 38N20'28 84w45'41 5:39:03
Elmwood 117 1 37N31'37 87w29'31 5:49:58
Elna 58 16 37N54'30 82w57'42 5:31:51
Elrod 100 19 37N13'09 84w28'10 5:37:53
Elsie 77 11 37N46'42 83w08'10 5:32:33
Elsinore 37 20 38N13'14 84w47'46 5:39:11
Elsmere 59 11 39N00'45 84w36'17 5:38:25
Elva 73 1 36N55'43 88w28'25 5:53:54
Elys 61 15 36N47 83w44 5:34:56
Emanuel 61 15 36N54'22 83w55'52 5:35:43
Emberton 86 1 36N42'47 85w48'23 5:43:14
Emerson 22 11 38N21'14 83w15'09 5:33:01
Eminence 52 63 38N22'12 85w10'50 5:40:43
Emlyn 118 15 36N42'16 84w08'36 5:36:34
Emma 36 11 37N38'07 82w42'01 5:30:48
Emmalena 60 16 37N20'03 83w04'28 5:32:18
Empire 24 1 37N05'11 87w29'50 5:49:59
Endee 95 16 37N25'47 83w45'15 5:35:01
Endicott 36 11 37N39'59 82w38'19 5:30:33
Engle 97 46 37N23'10 83w16'14 5:33:05
English 21 39 38N37'42 85w07'41 5:40:31
Ennis 89 1 37N11'54 86w58'27 5:47:54
Enoch 65 16 37N32'36 83w40'32 5:34:42
Enon 17 1 37N15'13 87w59'24 5:51:58
Ensor 30 1 37N47'21 86w58'50 5:47:55
Enterprise 22 16 38N15'35 83w15'17 5:33:01
Eolia 67 16 37N03'13 82w47'30 5:31:10
Epleys 71 1 36N55'37 86w56'19 5:47:45
Epperson 73 1 37N01'33 88w32'04 5:54:08
Epson 77 11 37N44'40 83w13'04 5:32:52
Epworth 68 11 38N30'40 83w35'34 5:34:22
Equality (Kronos Station) 92 1 37N23'45 87w03'57 5:48:16
Era 24 1 37N00'32 87w34'54 5:50:20
Eriline 26 16 37N11'19 83w35'35 5:34:22
Erlanger 59 11 39N01'00 84w36'03 5:38:24
Ermine 67 16 37N07'16 82w47'32 5:31:10
Erose 61 15 36N55'38 83w37'10 5:34:29
Esco 98 11 37N22'01 82w33'03 5:30:12
Escondida 9 30 38N07'34 84w13'41 5:36:55
Essie 66 16 37N03'42 83w27'07 5:33:48
Estesburg 100 19 37N15'27 84w35'37 5:38:22
Estill 36 11 37N27'25 82w49'08 5:31:17
Esto 104 1 37N00'15 85w06'39 5:40:27
Estrado 76 31 37N45 84w18 5:37:12
Ethridge 39 12 38N46'17 84w57'09 5:39:49
Etna 100 19 37N13'33 84w34'49 5:38:19
Etoile 5 1 36N50'08 85w54'00 5:43:36
Etty 98 11 37N15'08 82w40'38 5:30:43
Eubank 100 32 37N16'42 84w39'31 5:38:38
Eubanks Ford 2 1 36N41'33 86w24'49 5:45:39
Eunice 1 1 37N10'59 85w07'20 5:40:29
Euterpe 51 1 37N42'54 87w26'36 5:49:46
Evans Ford 23 51 37N13'52 84w59'08 5:39:57
Evanston 13 16 37N32'31 83w01'54 5:32:08
Evarts 48 15 36N51'57 83w11'26 5:32:46
Eve 44 1 37N18'40 85w40'43 5:42:43
Eveleigh 43 1 37N35'15 86w19'39 5:45:19
Evelyn 33 27 37N36'44 83w51'28 5:35:26
Ever 77 11 37N50'55 83w03'07 5:32:12
Everett 71 1 36N56'11 87w03'15 5:48:13
Evergreen 37 20 38N08'08 84w55'33 5:39:42
Evergreen 64 11 38N03'46 82w41'12 5:30:45
Eversole 95 16 37N26'51 83w38'34 5:34:34
Evona 23 51 37N11'39 84w54'38 5:39:39
Ewalt Crossroads 9 30 38N16'26 84w17'58 5:37:12
Ewing 35 16 38N25'38 83w51'48 5:35:27
Ewingford 112 51 38N36 85w19 5:41:16
Ewington 87 22 38N05'00 83w54'05 5:35:36
Exie 44 6 37N09'35 85w32'09 5:42:09
Ezel 88 16 37N53'28 83w26'40 5:33:47
Faber 118 15 36N52'25 84w07'49 5:36:31
Fagan 83 16 37N54'59 83w42'47 5:34:51
Fairbanks 42 1 36N31'26 88w32'51 5:54:11
Fairbanks 94 16 38N26'00 84w43'57 5:38:56
Fairdale 56 68 38N06'18 85w45'32 5:43:02
Fairdealing 79 1 36N50'48 88w14'21 5:52:57
Fairfield 14 1 37N40'17 86w17'14 5:45:09
Fairfield 90 59 37N56'01 85w23'01 5:41:32
Fair Grounds 81 11 38N35 83w52 5:35:28
Fairland 27 1 36N41 85w08 5:40:32
Fairmeade 56 68 38N14'56 85w38'02 5:42:32
Fairmont 56 68 38N10 85w36 5:42:24
Fairmont 117 1 37N27'36 87w51'00 5:51:24
Fairmount 56 68 38N06'59 85w34'15 5:42:17
Fairplay 1 1 37N00'44 85w18'14 5:41:13
Fairview 3 44 37N54'05 85w06'25 5:40:26
Fairview 10 11 38N28'14 82w41'03 5:30:44
Fairview 24 1 36N50'36 87w18'14 5:49:13
Fairview 31 1 37N11 86w19 5:45:16
Fairview 35 16 38N27'34 83w55'51 5:35:43
Fairview 59 71 39N03 84w32 5:38:08
Fairview 72 1 37N05'55 88w03'47 5:52:15
Fairview 118 15 36N36'00 84w06'42 5:36:27
Fairview Heights 37 20 38N12 84w52 5:39:28
Fairview Hill 22 16 38N17'04 82w55'12 5:31:41
Fairway 34 28 38N01'51 84w28'16 5:37:53
Falcon 77 11 37N47'23 83w00'07 5:32:00
Falling Branch 43 1 37N35'41 86w29'50 5:45:59
Fallis 52 51 38N25'48 84w56'07 5:39:44
Fall Rock 26 16 37N13'11 83w47'18 5:35:09
Fallsburg 64 11 38N10'30 82w40'25 5:30:42
Falls of Rough 14 1 37N35'24 86w32'56 5:46:12
Falmouth 96 11 38N40'36 84w19'49 5:37:19
Fancy Farm 42 1 36N47'58 88w47'29 5:55:10
Fannin 32 16 38N04'06 83w05'23 5:32:22
Fariston 63 37 37N04'12 84w03'24 5:36:14
Farler 97 46 37N09'17 83w11'32 5:32:46
Farmdale 37 20 38N06'34 84w55'00 5:39:40
Farmers 103 16 38N08'34 83w32'46 5:34:11
Farmers Mill 48 15 36N48'52 83w16'59 5:33:08
Farmersville 17 1 37N12'09 87w54'25 5:51:38
Farmington 42 1 36N40'10 88w31'33 5:54:06
Farraday 67 16 37N09'50 82w46'15 5:31:05
Farristown 76 16 37N37'21 84w18'01 5:37:12
Faubush 100 19 37N03'57 84w49'36 5:39:18
Faulconer 11 25 37N42'25 84w46'40 5:39:07
Faxon 18 1 36N40'43 88w08'51 5:52:35
Faye 32 16 38N04'07 83w09'44 5:32:39
Faywood 120 45 38N06'10 84w38'30 5:38:34
Fearisville 68 11 38N37'32 83w35'53 5:34:24
Fearsville 24 1 36N59'02 87w21'27 5:49:26
Feathersburg 1 1 37N18'41 85w10'09 5:40:41
Federal 98 11 37N18'41 82w21'40 5:29:27
Fedscreek 98 11 37N24'12 82w14'43 5:28:59
Fee 7 15 36N45 83w28 5:33:52
Feliciana 42 1 36N32'59 88w47'29 5:55:10
Felty 26 16 37N18'11 83w42'38 5:34:51
Fenton 111 1 36N46'37 88w06'10 5:52:25
Fentress McMahan 43 1 37N36'16 86w29'32 5:45:58
Fenwick 34 28 38N04'43 84w21'20 5:37:25
Fenwick 115 51 37N41 85w13 5:40:52
Ferguson 71 1 36N46'46 86w58'38 5:47:55
Ferguson 100 19 37N04'00 84w36'00 5:38:24
Ferguson Creek 98 11 37N29 82w31 5:30:04
Ferguson Spring 111 1 36N51'04 88w02'21 5:52:09
Fern Creek 56 68 38N09'35 85w35'16 5:42:21
Ferndale 7 15 36N41'46 83w41'05 5:34:44
Fernleaf 81 11 38N39'22 83w54'48 5:35:39
Fern View 56 68 38N10 85w36 5:42:24
Ferrells Creek 98 11 37N21 82w22 5:29:28
Fiddle Bow 54 1 37N16'18 87w39'29 5:50:38
Fidelio 24 1 36N43'58 87w27'31 5:49:50
Fidelity 74 16 36N39'49 84w36'36 5:38:26
Field (Crockett) 7 15 36N53'34 83w36'08 5:34:25
Fielden 32 16 38N06'10 82w56'52 5:31:47
Fies 54 1 37N19'20 87w22'26 5:49:30
Figgs 106 54 38N06'53 85w16'17 5:41:05
Fillmore 20 1 36N58'53 89w06'14 5:56:25
Fillmore 65 16 37N36'16 83w32'59 5:34:12
Fincastle 56 70 38N17 85w35 5:42:20
Fincastle 65 16 37N38'43 83w38'56 5:34:36
Finchville 106 51 38N09'13 85w18'46 5:41:15
Finley 109 51 37N27'41 85w20'22 5:41:21
Finley Addition 51 8 37N48'05 87w37'11 5:50:29
Finney 5 6 36N54'55 86w06'18 5:44:25
Firebrick 68 11 38N41'15 83w02'50 5:32:11
Firmantown 120 45 38N03'35 84w41'20 5:38:45
Fisher 14 1 37N34'35 86w22'06 5:45:28
Fisherville 56 68 38N11'23 85w27'47 5:41:51
Fishtrap 98 11 37N26 82w23 5:29:32
Fiskburg 59 11 38N48'38 84w30'25 5:38:02
Fisty 60 16 37N20'02 83w06'06 5:32:24
Fitch 22 16 38N19'12 83w20'15 5:33:21
Fitchburg 33 27 37N43'57 83w51'07 5:35:24
Five Forks 64 11 38N07'43 82w39'22 5:30:37
Fivemile 13 16 37N35'39 83w24'36 5:33:38
Five Points 18 1 36N37'00 88w19'45 5:53:19
Fixer 65 16 37N40'41 83w43'06 5:34:52
Flag Fork 37 16 38N19'17 84w56'54 5:39:48
Flagg Spring 19 11 38N53'08 84w15'53 5:37:04
Flag Spring 19 11 38N55 84w16 5:37:04
Flaherty 82 51 37N50'11 86w03'56 5:44:16
Flanagan 25 33 37N56'02 84w12'38 5:36:51
Flanary 98 11 37N23 82w15 5:29:00
Flat 119 16 37N39 83w33 5:34:12
Flat Fork 77 11 37N50'16 83w01'43 5:32:07
Flatgan 58 11 37N56'03 82w53'15 5:31:33
Flatgap 58 11 37N56 82w53 5:31:32
Flat Lick 61 15 36N49'44 83w46'13 5:35:05
Flat Rock 16 1 37N14 86w41 5:46:44
Flat Rock 17 1 37N14'01 87w57'57 5:51:52
Flat Rock 74 16 36N47'48 84w29'05 5:37:56
Flat Rock 102 16 37N21'39 84w16'16 5:37:05
Flat Rock 107 2 36N40'33 86w33'43 5:46:15
Flatwood 1 1 37N02'52 85w21'42 5:41:27
Flatwoods 45 11 38N31'21 82w43'02 5:30:52
Fleet 2 1 36N39'13 86w17'38 5:45:11
Fleming 67 16 37N11'44 82w41'57 5:30:48
Flemingsburg 35 35 38N25'20 83w44'02 5:34:56
Flemingsburg Junction 35 16 38N27'32 83w48'25 5:35:14
Flener 16 1 37N17'22 86w40'00 5:46:40
Fletcher 63 37 37N00'18 83w58'13 5:35:53
Flingsville 41 11 38N46'24 84w33'16 5:38:13
Flint 67 16 37N03'03 82w56'01 5:31:44
Flint Hill 47 1 37N29'54 85w59'26 5:43:58
Flint Springs 92 1 37N20'36 86w42'49 5:46:51
Flintville 13 16 37N29'05 83w18'02 5:33:12
Flippin 86 1 36N43'13 85w52'27 5:43:30
Flora 46 1 37N54 86w45 5:47:00
Floral 46 1 37N47'12 86w48'39 5:47:15
Florence 8 11 38N59'56 84w37'36 5:38:30
Florress 88 16 37N53'07 83w10'38 5:32:43
Flosie 116 1 36N52 84w39 5:38:36
Flournoy 113 1 37N41'44 87w51'41 5:51:27
Floyd 100 19 37N15'03 84w39'09 5:38:37
Floydsburg 93 60 36N43'15 87w59'00 5:51:56
Fogertown 26 16 37N13'10 83w54'04 5:35:36
Folsom 41 11 38N42'43 84w44'51 5:38:59
Folsomdale 42 1 36N53'01 88w40'28 5:54:42
Fonde 7 15 36N35'39 83w52'39 5:35:31
Fonthill 104 1 37N05'02 85w00'13 5:40:01
Foraker 77 11 37N39'36 83w08'14 5:32:33
Ford 25 16 37N52'54 84w15'37 5:37:02
Fords Branch 98 11 37N25'59 82w30'40 5:30:03
Fordsville 92 1 37N38'10 86w43'03 5:46:52
Forest Cottage 29 1 36N48 85w22 5:41:28
Forest Grove 25 33 37N56'44 84w13'28 5:36:54
Forest Hill 73 1 37N03'12 88w38'18 5:54:33
Forest Hills 56 68 38N12'55 85w35'09 5:42:21
Forest Hills 59 71 39N02'03 84w30'20 5:38:01
Forest Hills 98 11 37N37 82w14 5:28:56
Forest Springs 2 6 36N39'32 86w09'40 5:44:39
Forestville 50 1 37N16'06 85w59'48 5:43:59
Forkland 11 16 37N33'09 84w58'48 5:39:55
Forks 33 16 37N46 83w59 5:35:56
Forks of Elkhorn 37 20 38N12'56 84w47'52 5:39:11
Forkton 86 1 36N44'53 85w43'11 5:42:53
Forrestdale 73 1 37N05 88w53 5:55:32
Forrest Park 25 33 38N00'01 84w11'36 5:36:46
Fort Campbell 24 1 36N39 87w33 5:50:12
Fort Campbell North 24 1 36N38 87w28 5:49:52
Fort Heiman 18 1 36N30'07 88w03'21 5:52:13
Fort Knox 47 51 37N54 85w57 5:43:48
Fort Mitchell 59 71 39N03'34 84w32'51 5:38:11
Fort Spring 34 45 38N02'29 84w37'35 5:38:30
Fort Thomas 19 71 39N04'30 84w26'50 5:37:47
Fort Wright 59 71 39N03'06 84w32'03 5:38:08
Foster 12 11 38N47'57 84w12'47 5:36:51
Fount 61 15 36N59 83w50 5:35:20
Fountain Run 86 1 36N42'55 85w57'57 5:43:52
Four Corners 41 11 38N39'09 84w41'04 5:38:44
Four Corners 47 51 37N44'56 86w05'17 5:44:21
Fourmile 7 15 36N47'36 83w44'31 5:34:58
Four Oaks 96 11 38N38'02 84w19'05 5:37:16
Fourseam 97 46 37N13'14 83w10'43 5:32:43
Fox 33 27 37N45'33 84w04'01 5:36:16
Foxboro 56 70 38N15 85w34 5:42:16
Fox Creek 3 44 37N59'16 84w58'05 5:39:52
Foxport 35 16 38N28'29 83w35'33 5:34:22
Foxtown 55 16 37N30'15 83w59'37 5:35:58
Fragrant 43 1 37N27'15 86w10'11 5:44:41
Frakes 7 15 36N38'34 83w55'40 5:35:43
Frances 28 1 37N13'11 88w08'28 5:52:34
Francisville 8 11 39N06'18 84w43'28 5:38:54
Frankfort 37 20 38N12'03 84w52'24 5:39:30
Franklin 107 2 36N43'20 86w34'38 5:46:19

Franklin Acres 37 20 38N12 84w52 5:39:28
Franklin Cross Roads 47 51 37N40'12 86w00'54 5:44:04
Franklin Heights 37 20 38N12 84w52 5:39:28
Franklin Mines 28 1 37N20 88w04 5:52:16
Franklinton 52 51 38N27'09 85w03'20 5:40:13
Frazer 116 1 36N57'23 84w42'18 5:38:49
Frazertown 93 60 38N19 85w28 5:41:52
Fraziertown 93 60 38N18'50 85w30'16 5:42:01
Fredericktown 115 51 37N45'32 85w20'31 5:41:22
Fredonia 17 1 37N12'29 88w03'24 5:52:14
Fredville 77 11 37N36'19 82w57'53 5:31:52
Freeburn 98 11 37N33'52 82w08'31 5:28:34
Freedom 5 1 36N48 85w49 5:43:16
Freedom 104 1 36N55'22 85w06'20 5:40:25
Freemont 73 1 36N58'22 88w36'43 5:54:27
Freetown 86 1 36N40'49 85w47'50 5:43:11
Free Union 117 1 37N31'31 87w45'15 5:51:01
Fremont 73 1 36N58 88w37 5:54:28
Frenchburg 83 16 37N57'03 83w37'33 5:34:30
Fresh Meadows 48 15 36N50'35 83w22'25 5:33:30
Frew 66 16 37N10'57 83w14'45 5:32:59
Freys Hill 56 70 38N17'32 85w33'47 5:42:15
Friendly Hills 56 68 38N09 85w42 5:42:48
Friendship 17 1 37N03'25 87w45'59 5:51:04
Frisby 116 1 36N50'53 84w54'37 5:39:38
Fritz 77 11 37N42'05 83w09'06 5:32:36
Frogtown 34 45 38N01'59 84w38'59 5:38:36
Frogtown 78 59 37N35'25 85w22'21 5:41:29
Frogue 29 1 36N39'58 85w17'54 5:41:12
Frost 45 11 38N43'44 82w55'39 5:31:43
Frozen Creek 13 16 37N35'28 83w25'19 5:33:41
Fruit Hill 24 1 37N00'17 87w22'06 5:49:28
Fry 44 6 37N08'48 85w29'18 5:41:57
Fryer 17 1 37N15'44 87w49'11 5:51:17
Frymire 14 51 37N57'38 86w23'47 5:45:35
Fuget 58 11 37N53'18 82w55'25 5:31:42
Fulgham 53 1 36N39'10 88w52'13 5:55:29
Fullers 64 11 38N10'13 82w38'36 5:30:34
Fullerton 45 11 38N43'18 82w58'55 5:31:56
Fulton 38 1 36N30'15 88w52'27 5:55:30
Fultz 22 16 38N16'58 83w00'44 5:32:03
Funston 74 16 36N53'49 84w24'21 5:37:37
Furnace 33 16 37N45'43 83w49'54 5:35:20
Fusonia 97 46 37N10'26 83w05'26 5:32:22
Futrell 73 1 37N05'30 88w41'22 5:54:45
Future City 73 1 37N03'45 88w48'06 5:55:12
Gabbard 95 16 37N23 83w37 5:34:28
Gabe 44 6 37N18'28 85w34'27 5:42:18
Gadberry 1 1 37N02'37 85w18'34 5:41:14
Gaffey Heights 47 51 37N53'09 85w58'08 5:43:53
Gage 4 1 36N59'28 88w53'22 5:55:33
Gainesville 2 6 36N51'02 86w09'30 5:44:38
Gaithers 47 51 37N39'27 85w53'59 5:43:36
Galdia 77 11 37N37'59 82w59'19 5:31:57
Gallup 64 11 38N00'47 82w37'22 5:30:29
Galveston 36 11 37N25'31 82w36'45 5:30:27
Galveston PO 36 11 37N26'24 82w37'44 5:30:31
Gamaliel 86 1 36N38'23 85w47'48 5:43:11
Gamesway 34 28 37N59'16 84w29'02 5:37:56
Gandertown 78 59 37N40'59 85w23'24 5:41:34
Gano (Lejunior P O) 48 15 36N54'04 83w08'03 5:32:32
Gapcreek 116 1 36N44'36 85w00'08 5:40:01
Gap in Knob 15 53 38N01'00 85w42'11 5:42:49
Gapville 77 11 37N37'48 82w57'33 5:31:50
Gardenside 34 28 38N02'18 84w32'32 5:38:10
Garden Springs 34 28 38N01'44 84w32'55 5:38:12
Garden Village 98 11 37N25'15 82w27'55 5:29:52
Gardner 26 15 36N58'05 83w32'19 5:34:09
Gardnersville 96 11 38N46'00 84w30'16 5:38:01
Garfield 14 1 37N46'58 86w21'27 5:45:26
Garlin 1 1 37N06'50 85w15'08 5:41:01
Garmeada 7 15 36N37'30 83w50'33 5:35:22
Garner 10 11 38N17'41 82w44'09 5:30:57
Garner 60 16 37N21'29 82w55'31 5:31:42
Garnett 49 36 38N27'33 84w19'39 5:37:19
Garrard 26 16 37N07'25 83w44'47 5:34:59
Garrett 36 11 37N28'47 82w49'54 5:31:20
Garrett 82 51 37N53'52 86w06'47 5:44:27
Garrettsburg 24 1 36N40'07 87w32'34 5:50:10
Garrison 68 11 38N36'22 83w10'24 5:32:42
Garvin Ridge 22 16 38N18'00 83w12'33 5:32:50
Gascon 85 1 37N00'13 85w34'16 5:42:17
Gaskill 67 16 37N11'06 82w36'40 5:30:27
Gasper 71 1 36N57'00 86w44'31 5:46:58
Gasper River 114 1 37N00 86w33 5:46:12
Gassaway 5 6 37N00 85w55 5:43:40
Gates 103 16 38N14'02 83w22'00 5:33:28
Gatesville 117 1 37N31'01 87w36'29 5:50:26
Gatewood 30 1 37N49'59 86w51'58 5:47:28
Gatliff 118 15 36N40'54 84w01'35 5:36:06
Gatun 48 15 36N52'24 83w18'10 5:33:13
Gausdale 118 15 36N45'28 83w58'31 5:35:54
Gaybourn 120 45 38N02'34 84w40'00 5:38:40
Gays Creek 97 46 37N19'41 83w25'40 5:33:43
Geddes 107 1 36N39'24 86w32'59 5:46:12
Gee 3 44 38N02'42 85w03'47 5:40:15
Geneva 51 1 37N48'43 87w41'31 5:50:46
Geneva 69 16 37N26'22 84w44'47 5:38:59
Gentrys Mill 1 1 37N05'05 85w09'13 5:40:37
Georges Creek 64 11 37N58'40 82w39'24 5:30:38
Georgetown 48 15 36N53'21 83w03'19 5:32:13
Georgetown 105 26 38N12'35 84w33'32 5:38:14
Germantown 12 11 38N39'17 83w57'53 5:35:52
German Town 56 69 38N13'28 85w44'12 5:42:57
Gertrude 12 11 38N44'22 84w03'17 5:36:13
Gesling 22 16 38N25'23 83w05'33 5:32:22
Gest 52 51 38N25'03 84w52'58 5:39:32
Gethsemane 90 59 37N38'46 85w32'32 5:42:10
Ghent 21 16 38N44'15 85w03'30 5:40:14
Gibbs 61 15 37N01'15 83w54'09 5:35:37
Gifford 77 11 37N45'27 83w07'17 5:32:29
Gilbert 69 16 37N34'26 84w35'39 5:38:23
Gilbertsville 79 1 37N01'28 88w17'59 5:53:12
Gillem Branch 58 11 37N57 82w57 5:31:48
Gilley 67 16 36N58'27 83w06'44 5:32:27
Gillmore 119 16 37N44'14 83w22'10 5:33:29
Gilpin 23 51 37N15'24 84w52'55 5:39:32
Gilreath 74 16 36N40'50 84w23'59 5:37:36
Gilstrap 16 1 37N18'55 86w42'24 5:46:50
Gimlet 32 16 38N13'08 83w08'15 5:32:33
Ginseng 62 51 37N30'17 85w34'52 5:42:19
Girdler 61 15 36N56'23 83w50'36 5:35:22
Girkin 114 10 37N04'03 86w21'30 5:45:26
Gishton 89 1 37N19'31 87w13'04 5:48:52
Givens 113 1 37N36'40 87w46'20 5:51:05
Glade 79 1 36N49'08 88w18'42 5:53:15
Glasgow 5 6 36N59'45 85w54'43 5:43:39
Gleanings 62 51 37N33'30 85w32'02 5:42:08
Glenarm 93 60 38N21'13 85w27'47 5:41:51
Glencairn 119 16 37N45'49 83w40'12 5:34:41
Glencoe 39 12 38N42'52 84w49'22 5:39:17
Glendale 47 51 37N36'06 85w54'20 5:43:37
Glendale Junction 47 51 37N35'29 85w51'49 5:43:27
Glen Dean 14 1 37N39'12 86w32'28 5:46:10
Glengary 56 68 38N06 85w45 5:43:00
Glen Lily 50 1 37N18'28 85w47'40 5:43:11
Glenmore 114 1 37N10'06 86w23'56 5:45:36
Glensboro 3 44 38N00'17 85w03'36 5:40:14
Glens Fork 1 1 37N00'50 85w15'02 5:41:00
Glen Springs 68 11 38N30'39 83w29'07 5:33:56
Glenview 56 68 38N18'30 85w39'01 5:42:36
Glenview Acres 56 70 38N17'53 85w38'14 5:42:33
Glenview Heights 56 70 38N18'15 85w38'26 5:42:34
Glenview Hills 56 70 38N17 85w35 5:42:20
Glenview Manor 56 70 38N17'15 85w38'13 5:42:33
Glenville 75 1 37N35'41 87w11'30 5:48:46
Glenwood 64 16 38N13'20 82w47'10 5:31:09
Glo 36 11 37N26'52 82w48'34 5:31:14
Globe 22 16 38N17'15 83w14'42 5:32:59
Glomawr 97 46 37N13'36 83w09'26 5:32:38
Goddard 35 16 38N21'45 83w36'53 5:34:28
Goering 46 1 37N48'03 86w45'42 5:47:03
Goffs Corner 25 33 37N55'43 84w00'24 5:36:02
Goforth 96 11 38N39'53 84w26'56 5:37:48
Goins 118 15 36N42'00 83w56'22 5:35:45
Goldbug 118 15 36N47'33 84w10'05 5:36:40
Gold City 107 1 36N45'16 86w26'51 5:45:47
Golden Ash 48 15 36N51'38 83w17'28 5:33:10
Golden Pond 111 1 36N47'08 88w01'27 5:52:06
Gollihue 22 16 38N14'45 82w53'09 5:31:33
Golo 42 1 36N44'20 88w29'43 5:53:59
Goochland 102 16 37N26'09 84w11'13 5:36:45
Goochtown 100 19 37N19'18 84w35'13 5:38:21
Goodloe 36 11 37N36'13 82w51'46 5:31:27
Goodluck 85 1 36N55'31 85w38'30 5:42:34
Goodnight 5 6 37N05'36 85w52'49 5:43:31
Goodwater 100 19 37N04'31 84w22'24 5:37:30
Goody 98 11 37N39'43 82w16'11 5:29:05
Goose Creek 56 70 38N18'58 85w38'55 5:42:36
Goose Rock 26 16 37N05'25 83w41'40 5:34:47
Gordon 67 16 36N59'34 83w01'28 5:32:06
Gordon Ford 88 16 37N53'00 83w14'17 5:32:57
Gordonsville 71 1 36N50'24 87w01'08 5:48:05
Goshen 93 52 38N24'11 85w34'27 5:42:18
Gott 114 1 36N58'22 86w18'50 5:45:15
Grab 44 6 37N13'33 85w36'06 5:42:24
Grace 26 16 37N11'50 83w51'56 5:35:28
Gracey 24 1 36N52'41 87w39'44 5:50:39
Gradyville 1 1 37N03'48 85w25'21 5:41:41
Graefenburg 106 20 38N09'21 85w00'49 5:40:03
Graham 89 1 37N15'06 87w16'47 5:49:07
Graham Hill 51 8 37N49'24 87w31'48 5:50:07
Grahamton 82 51 37N54'10 86w01'32 5:44:06
Grahamville 73 1 37N06'27 88w46'48 5:55:07
Grahn 22 16 38N17'01 83w04'31 5:32:18
Grancer 16 1 37N18'32 86w32'46 5:46:11
Grand Rivers 70 1 37N00'11 88w14'04 5:52:56
Grandview 30 1 37N42'04 86w55'49 5:47:43
Grandview 86 1 36N43'10 85w41'14 5:42:45
Grandview Heights 37 20 38N12 84w52 5:39:28
Grange City 35 16 38N14'40 83w39'55 5:34:40
Grangertown 113 1 37N33'03 88w00'24 5:52:02
Grannie 119 16 37N41'48 83w34'58 5:34:20
Grant 8 11 38N59'10 84w49'32 5:39:18
Grant 59 71 38N57'49 84w27'05 5:37:48
Grants Lick 19 11 38N51'37 84w23'52 5:37:35
Grapevine 54 1 37N18'00 87w29'09 5:49:57
Grassland 31 1 37N11 86w19 5:45:16
Grassy Creek 88 16 37N52'01 83w20'43 5:33:23
Grassy Lick 87 22 38N04'53 84w01'13 5:36:05
Gratz 94 18 38N28'25 84w57'10 5:39:49
Gravel Switch 78 51 37N34'43 85w03'08 5:40:13
Gray 61 15 36N56'33 84w00'30 5:36:02
Grayfox 77 11 37N51'47 83w03'27 5:32:14
Gray Hawk 55 16 37N23'42 83w56'25 5:35:46
Graymoor 56 68 38N16'23 85w37'23 5:42:30
Grays Branch 45 11 38N39'12 82w52'31 5:31:30
Grays Knob 48 15 36N49 83w18 5:33:12
Grayson 22 47 38N19'57 82w56'55 5:31:48
Grayson Springs 43 1 37N27'33 86w13'28 5:44:54
Graysville 14 1 37N46'20 86w17'51 5:45:11
Greasy Creek 98 11 37N22'34 82w28'33 5:29:54
Great Crossing 105 26 38N12'52 84w36'19 5:38:25
Greear 88 40 37N52'38 83w17'53 5:33:12
Greeley 65 16 37N40'35 83w45'11 5:35:01
Green 32 16 38N08'26 83w04'31 5:32:18
Greenacres 72 1 37N01'29 88w00'58 5:52:04
Green Acres 78 25 37N39'15 84w45'38 5:39:03
Greenbriar 30 1 37N45 87w07 5:48:28
Greenbriar 78 66 37N29'40 85w13'53 5:40:56
Greenbrier 69 16 37N20 84w40 5:38:40
Greenbrier 90 51 37N43'46 85w27'33 5:41:50
Greencastle 114 1 37N05'30 86w29'44 5:45:59
Greendale 34 28 38N06'21 84w31'32 5:38:06
Green Fields Estates 25 33 37N59'34 84w12'31 5:36:50
Green Grove 29 1 36N44'02 85w16'11 5:41:05
Green Hall 95 16 37N24 83w50 5:35:20
Greenhaven 93 52 38N26'43 85w27'15 5:41:49
Green Hill 55 16 37N17'47 83w57'56 5:35:52
Greenhill 114 10 36N54'29 86w18'57 5:45:16
Greenmount 63 37 37N14'51 84w01'51 5:36:07
Greenough 98 11 37N17 82w28 5:29:52
Green Road 61 15 36N58 83w50 5:35:20
Greensburg 44 6 37N15'39 85w29'56 5:42:00
Green Spring 56 70 38N17 85w35 5:42:20
Greenup 45 11 38N34'23 82w49'49 5:31:19
Greenville 89 1 37N12'04 87w10'44 5:48:43
Greenwood 56 68 38N08'50 85w53'46 5:43:35
Greenwood 74 16 36N52'28 84w29'44 5:37:59
Greenwood 96 11 38N45'04 84w23'21 5:37:33
Greenwood 114 10 36N56'25 86w25'12 5:45:41
Grefco 22 16 38N18 83w11 5:32:44
Gregory 116 1 36N49'46 84w42'07 5:38:48
Gregoryville 22 16 38N19'37 83w01'17 5:32:05
Gresham 44 1 37N11'48 85w27'01 5:41:48
Grethel 36 11 37N29'28 82w38'52 5:30:35
Grethel PO 36 11 37N28'58 82w39'26 5:30:38
Grider 29 1 36N48'15 85w25'32 5:41:42
Griderville 5 6 37N06'46 85w52'13 5:43:29
Griffin 116 1 36N42'16 84w43'44 5:38:55
Griffith 30 1 37N48'55 87w12'46 5:48:51
Griffytown 56 70 38N15'13 85w32'43 5:42:11
Grigsby 97 16 37N17'09 83w08'16 5:32:33
Grove 118 16 36N55'57 84w13'25 5:36:54
Grove Center 113 1 37N38'23 88w00'47 5:52:03
Grundy 100 19 37N07'34 84w31'20 5:38:05
Guage 13 16 37N35'46 83w11'50 5:32:47
Gubser Mill 19 11 38N53'16 84w18'32 5:37:14
Gudgel 108 44 38N00'45 84w59'43 5:39:59
Guerrant 13 16 37N30'24 83w29'50 5:33:59
Guffey 48 15 36N52 83w12 5:32:48
Guffie 75 1 37N36'15 87w15'16 5:49:01
Gulfco 10 11 38N28 82w39 5:30:36
Gullett 77 11 37N44'14 83w07'37 5:32:30
Gulnare 98 11 37N37'49 82w32'49 5:30:11
Gulston 48 15 36N46'30 83w19'44 5:33:19
Guthrie Beach 56 68 38N19'48 85w38'39 5:42:35
Gum Sulphur 102 16 37N25'37 84w27'34 5:37:50
Gum Tree 86 1 36N43'27 85w49'10 5:43:17
Gunlock 77 11 37N32'51 82w55'34 5:31:42
Gunns Chapel 40 16 37N37 84w35 5:38:20
Gus 89 1 37N07'03 86w54'32 5:47:38
Guston 82 51 37N53'34 86w13'19 5:44:53
Guthrie 110 1 36N38'54 87w09'59 5:48:40
Guthrie's Ridge 29 1 36N42 85w22 5:41:28
Guy 114 10 37N07'26 86w36'47 5:46:27
Gwinn Island 11 25 37N39 84w46 5:39:04
Gypsy 77 11 37N39'45 82w57'50 5:31:51
Habit 30 1 37N41'52 86w59'47 5:47:59
Hackley 57 16 37N37'59 84w28'18 5:37:53
Haddix 13 16 37N29'14 83w20'54 5:33:24
Hadensville 110 1 36N40'13 87w07'52 5:48:31
Hadley 114 1 37N03'35 86w36'25 5:46:26
Hager 77 11 37N44'47 83w11'58 5:32:48
Hagerhill 58 11 37N47'10 82w47'37 5:31:10
Hail 100 19 36N59'39 84w27'49 5:37:51
Hailwell 53 1 36N40'35 89w06'21 5:56:25
Halcom 32 16 38N04'33 82w58'00 5:31:52
Haldeman 103 16 38N15'10 83w19'07 5:33:16
Haleys Mill 24 1 37N03'11 87w20'49 5:49:23
Halfway 2 1 36N47'44 86w17'46 5:45:11
Halfway 5 1 37N05'18 85w47'44 5:43:11
Halifax 2 6 36N49'42 86w14'32 5:44:58
Hall 57 29 37N47'02 84w37'01 5:38:28
Hall 60 16 37N17'57 82w46'13 5:31:05
Hallam 94 16 38N30'09 84w47'23 5:39:10
Hallie 67 16 37N06'08 83w01'17 5:32:05
Halls Gap 69 16 37N27'43 84w38'00 5:38:32
Halls Landing 93 52 38N27'06 85w31'51 5:42:07
Halls Store 71 1 36N45 86w53 5:47:32
Halo 36 11 37N18'56 82w44'22 5:30:57
Hamby 54 1 37N10'39 87w35'50 5:50:23
Hamilton 8 11 38N53'00 84w46'54 5:39:08
Hamim 103 16 38N07'39 83w18'50 5:33:15
Hamlin 18 1 36N35'54 88w04'35 5:52:18
Hammackville 110 1 36N43 87w16 5:49:04
Hammond 58 11 37N52 82w42 5:30:48
Hammond 61 15 36N57'25 83w43'39 5:34:55
Hammonville 50 1 37N24'53 85w47'51 5:43:11
Hamner 113 1 37N38'52 87w56'49 5:51:47
Hampton 70 1 37N16'59 88w22'17 5:53:29
Hampton Manor 25 33 37N58'58 84w11'32 5:36:46
Handshoe 60 16 37N28'12 82w54'24 5:31:38
Handyville 30 1 37N38'06 87w10'13 5:48:41
Hanging Rock 43 1 37N33'09 86w19'20 5:45:17
Hanly 57 29 37N50'13 84w35'27 5:38:22
Hannah 64 11 38N02'51 82w52'21 5:31:29
Hansbrough 47 51 37N38'04 85w59'37 5:43:58
Hansbrough 106 54 38N13 85w14 5:40:56
Hansford 102 36 37N16'11 84w22'12 5:37:29
Hanson 54 1 37N25'02 87w28'51 5:49:55
Happy 97 46 37N12'14 83w05'48 5:32:23

Happy Acre 104 1 37N04 85W06 5:40:24
Happy Landing 76
43 37N38'28 84W22'52 5:37:31
Harbell 7 15 36N43'55 83W40'24 5:34:42
Harcourt 47 51 37N33'21 86W00'44 5:44:03
Harcrow 48 15 36N52 83W12 5:32:48
Hardburly 97 46 37N18'06 83W07'27 5:32:30
Hardcastle 114 10 36N56'30 86W19'44 5:45:19
Hardesty 115 51 37N48'07 85W12'48 5:40:51
Hardin 79 1 36N45'53 88W17'43 5:53:11
Harding 113 1 37N38'53 87W59'08 5:51:57
Hardinsburg 14 1 37N46'48 86W27'38 5:45:51
Hardin Springs 47
51 37N36'34 86W15'23 5:45:02
Hardmoney 73 1 36N56'42 88W34'55 5:54:20
Hardshell 13 16 37N27'27 83W15'04 5:33:00
Hardwick 116 1 36N55'44 84W41'27 5:38:46
Hardy 98 11 37N37'17 82W14'39 5:28:59
Hardyville 50 1 37N15'15 85W47'10 5:43:09
Hare 63 16 37N11 84W07 5:36:28
Hargett 33 27 37N46'58 84W00'35 5:36:02
Hargis 58 11 37N50'29 82W58'38 5:31:55
Hargis 100 19 36N57'54 84W29'25 5:37:58
Harlan 48 15 36N50'35 83W19'19 5:33:17
Harlan Crossroads 86
1 36N39'11 85W42'14 5:42:49
Harlan Gas 48 15 36N51'02 83W18'18 5:33:13
Harmony 94 16 38N22'02 84W44'17 5:38:57
Harmony Lake Estates 93
52 38N24'30 85W34'43 5:42:19
Harmony Landing 93
52 38N24'41 85W37'03 5:42:28
Harmony Village 93
52 38N24'16 85W37'12 5:42:29
Harned 14 1 37N45'06 86W24'49 5:45:39
Harold 36 11 37N32'12 82W38'00 5:30:32
Harper 77 11 37N48'06 83W11'45 5:32:47
Harper Crossroads 16
1 37N05'25 86W53'07 5:47:32
Harper Ford 17 1 37N15'58 87W51'34 5:51:26
Harpers Ferry 52
51 38N20 85W03 5:40:12
Harreldsville 16
1 37N03'53 86W53'38 5:47:35
Harris 68 11 38N22'43 83W19'58 5:33:20
Harris Grove 18 1 36N34'12 88W25'40 5:53:43
Harris Hill Ford 79
1 36N56'50 88W27'03 5:53:48
Harrisonville 106
51 38N05'18 85W04'02 5:40:16
Harrodsburg 84 44 37N45'44 84W50'36 5:39:22
Harrods Creek 56
68 38N19'39 85W37'40 5:42:31
Hart 63 37 37N08 84W05 5:36:20
Hartford 92 1 37N27'04 86W54'33 5:47:38
Hartley 98 11 37N18'39 82W37'59 5:30:32
Harvey 79 1 36N48'30 88W25'04 5:53:40
Harveyton 97 46 37N18'44 83W12'06 5:32:48
Harvieland 37 20 38N15'15 84W54'46 5:39:39
Harvy 79 1 36N51 88W21 5:53:24
Haskingsville 44
6 37N11'13 85W23'43 5:41:35
Hatcher 109 51 37N17'41 85W21'59 5:41:28
Hatfield 98 11 37N43'28 82W22'07 5:29:28
Hatton 106 51 38N13'33 85W00'24 5:40:02
Hawesville 46 1 37N54'00 86W45'18 5:47:01
Hawkins 24 1 37N01'45 87W39'02 5:50:36
Hawthorne 19 11 38N58'50 84W25'13 5:37:41
Hayes 96 11 38N38'55 84W21'57 5:37:28
Haymond 67 16 37N10'50 82W41'15 5:30:45
Haynesville 92 1 37N41'06 86W45'24 5:47:02
Hays 114 1 37N01'53 86W08'20 5:44:33
Hays Crossing 103
16 38N14'39 83W20'40 5:33:23
Haysville 82 51 37N54'12 86W14'33 5:44:58
Hayward 22 16 38N15'22 83W17'09 5:33:09
Haywood 5 6 36N56'46 85W58'28 5:43:54
Hazard 97 46 37N14'58 83W11'36 5:32:46
Hazel 18 1 36N30'08 88W19'33 5:53:18
Hazel 113 1 37N30'44 87W59'22 5:51:57
Hazel Green 119
16 37N47'51 83W25'00 5:33:40
Hazel Patch 63 16 37N14'40 84W11'35 5:36:46
Hazelwood 56 69 38N10'40 85W46'53 5:43:08
Head of Cedar 105
16 38N16 84W41 5:38:44
Head of Grassy 68
11 38N24 83W16 5:33:04
Headquarters 91
21 38N21'30 84W06'52 5:36:27
Hearin 117 1 37N31'59 87W50'55 5:51:24
Heater 70 1 37N08'13 88W19'49 5:53:19
Heath 73 1 37N05'12 88W47'24 5:55:10
Heatherfield 56
69 38N12'11 85W49'36 5:43:18
Hebbardsville 51
1 37N46'34 87W22'31 5:49:30
Hebron 8 11 39N03'57 84W42'04 5:38:48
Hecla 54 1 37N17'06 87W31'37 5:50:06
Hector 26 16 37N09'11 83W39'14 5:34:37
Hedges 25 16 37N59'37 84W02'46 5:36:11
Hedgeville 11 16 37N38'00 84W41'01 5:38:44
Heekin 41 11 38N36'01 84W36'52 5:38:27
Heenon 98 11 37N40'00 82W29'24 5:29:58
Heflin 92 1 37N30'24 87W00'25 5:48:02
Hegira 29 1 36N42'24 85W16'34 5:41:06
Heidelberg 65 16 37N33'19 83W46'44 5:35:07
Heidrick 61 15 36N52'57 83W52'43 5:35:31
Heiner 97 46 37N18 83W10 5:32:40
Helechawa 119 16 37N45'57 83W20'22 5:33:21
Helena 81 11 38N29'36 83W46'31 5:35:06
Hellier 98 11 37N17'15 82W28'17 5:29:53
Helm 104 1 36N53'44 85W09'10 5:40:37
Helton 66 16 36N57'14 83W23'27 5:33:34
Hemphill (Jackhorn P O) 67
16 37N12'56 82W42'19 5:30:49
Hemp Ridge 106 51 38N08'54 85W07'08 5:40:29
Henderson 51 8 37N50'10 87W35'24 5:50:22
Hendricks 77 11 37N42'29 83W07'07 5:32:28
Hendron 73 1 37N02'22 88W37'45 5:54:31
Henrietta 58 11 37N53'24 82W40'49 5:30:43
Henry Clay 34 28 38N02 84W29 5:37:56
Henry Clay 98 11 37N18'41 82W28'36 5:29:54

Henryville 91 38 38N19 84W02 5:36:08
Henshaw 113 1 37N37'18 88W03'20 5:52:13
Hensley 14 1 37N47'31 86W20'06 5:45:20
Hensley 26 16 37N14'16 83W40'27 5:34:42
Hensley Ford 94
11 38N34'35 84W42'28 5:38:50
Hensleytown 24 1 36N39'31 87W24'46 5:49:39
Herbert 92 1 37N43'07 86W47'58 5:47:12
Herd 55 16 37N21'51 83W52'31 5:35:30
Herman 110 1 36N39 87W10 5:48:40
Hermitage Hills 34
28 38N03'59 84W26'57 5:37:48
Hermon 110 1 36N44'34 87W09'54 5:48:40
Herndon 24 1 36N44'01 87W33'55 5:50:16
Herron Hill 68 11 38N35'23 83W29'49 5:33:59
Heselton 68 11 38N36 83W19 5:33:16
Hesler 94 16 38N27'49 84W46'38 5:39:07
Hestand 86 1 36N39'15 85W37'46 5:42:31
Hi-Acres 34 28 38N03'36 84W26'49 5:37:47
Hiatt 102 16 37N24 84W25 5:37:40
Hibernia 109 51 37N27'32 85W33'36 5:42:14
Hickman 38 1 36N34'16 89W11'10 5:56:45
Hickory 42 1 36N49'21 88W38'51 5:54:35
Hickory Corner 43
1 37N35'14 86W32'01 5:46:08
Hickory Flat 107
1 36N42'28 86W27'43 5:45:51
Hickory Grove 3
44 37N58'02 84W59'36 5:39:58
Hickory Grove 29
1 36N42 85W22 5:41:28
Hickory Grove 42
1 36N50 88W42 5:54:48
Hickory Grove 74
16 36N40'30 84W29'11 5:37:57
Hicksville 42 1 36N47'46 88W30'10 5:54:01
Hico 18 1 36N43'46 88W11'00 5:52:44
Hidalgo 116 1 36N44'08 84W56'51 5:39:47
Higdon 43 1 37N25'46 86W10'28 5:44:42
High Bridge 57 29 37N49'27 84W43'06 5:38:52
High Falls 119 16 37N43'47 83W35'02 5:34:20
Highgate Springs 56
68 38N12'55 85W38'25 5:42:34
Highgrove 108 51 37N58'59 85W29'11 5:41:57
High Hickory 50 1 37N25'21 85W49'48 5:43:19
High Knob 55 16 37N17'10 83W54'26 5:35:38
Highland 69 16 37N25'41 84W39'14 5:38:37
Highland 107 1 36N42'24 86W26'21 5:45:45
Highland Heights 19
71 39N01'59 84W27'07 5:37:48
Highland Park 56
69 38N11'04 85W45'11 5:43:01
Highland Park 118
15 36N44'57 84W09'32 5:36:38
Highlands 34 28 38N05'23 84W30'30 5:38:02
Highlands 56 69 38N13'38 85W42'30 5:42:50
Highland Springs 5
6 37N07'53 86W01'33 5:44:06
High Plains 14 1 37N46'23 86W12'40 5:44:51
High Plains Corner 14
51 37N46'24 86W10'19 5:44:41
High Point 73 1 37N06'51 88W42'56 5:54:52
Highsplint 48 15 36N53'41 83W07'02 5:32:28
Hightop 63 16 37N01'58 84W11'16 5:36:45
Highview 56 68 38N08'34 85W37'27 5:42:30
Highview 92 1 37N18'21 86W50'40 5:47:23
Highway 27 1 36N44'18 85W12'32 5:40:50
Hi Hat 36 11 37N23'30 82W43'45 5:30:55
Hikes Point 56 68 38N13 85W37 5:42:28
Hilda 103 16 38N14'17 83W30'28 5:34:02
Hillcrest 76 31 37N45 84W18 5:37:12
Hillgrove 82 51 37N52'45 86W09'50 5:44:39
Hillsboro 35 16 38N17'36 83W39'32 5:34:38
Hillsdale 107 1 36N47'49 86W28'35 5:45:54
Hillside 89 1 37N14'54 87W09'48 5:48:39
Hill Top 35 16 38N21'37 83W50'21 5:35:21
Hilltop 41 11 38N36'19 84W34'24 5:38:18
Hilltop 43 1 37N23'42 86W06'26 5:44:26
Hilltop 71 1 36N39'51 86W46'45 5:47:07
Hill Top 74 16 36N43'21 84W32'00 5:38:08
Hillview 15 51 38N06 85W42 5:42:48
Hillview 31 1 37N17'57 86W13'43 5:44:55
Hilton 97 46 37N15 83W11 5:32:44
Hima 26 16 37N07'14 83W46'42 5:35:07
Himyar 61 15 36N49'58 83W47'59 5:35:12
Hinda Heights 34
28 38N00'23 84W30'10 5:38:01
Hindman 60 16 37N20'09 82W58'50 5:31:55
Hinesdale 50 1 37N19'03 85W49'25 5:43:18
Hinkle 61 15 36N54'45 83W49'08 5:35:17
Hinkleville 4 1 37N02'37 88W56'01 5:55:44
Hinton 49 16 38N27'26 84W31'46 5:38:07
Hinton Hills 14 1 37N37'24 86W27'40 5:45:51
Hippo 36 11 37N31'57 82W52'08 5:31:29
Hiram 48 15 36N57'59 83W02'50 5:32:11
Hisel 55 16 37N33'20 84W05'02 5:36:20
Hiseville 5 1 37N06'03 85W48'45 5:43:15
Hislope 100 19 37N01'18 84W44'00 5:38:56
Hitchins 22 16 38N16'51 82W55'13 5:31:41
Hite 36 11 37N33'25 82W45'13 5:31:01
Hites Falls 43 1 37N32'32 86W35'49 5:46:23
Hitesville 113 1 37N45'09 87W49'40 5:51:19
Hittville 101 11 38N34'59 84W03'50 5:36:15
Hobart 27 1 36N41'02 85W15'47 5:41:03
Hobbs 15 51 37N55'38 85W37'31 5:42:30
Hobson 109 51 37N25'32 85W22'08 5:41:29
Hode 80 11 37N53'08 82W25'33 5:29:42
Hodgenville 62 51 37N34'26 85W44'24 5:42:58
Hogue 100 19 37N09'48 84W42'35 5:38:50
Holbrook 41 11 38N35'26 84W42'51 5:38:51
Holiday Ford 94
11 38N33'50 84W43'34 5:38:54
Holiday Hills 34
28 38N03'06 84W33'24 5:38:14
Holifield 42 1 36N39'42 88W47'21 5:55:09
Holland 2 1 36N41'56 86W04'06 5:44:16
Holliday 88 16 37N48'39 83W13'23 5:32:54
Hollonville 119
16 37N40'06 83W28'06 5:33:52
Hollow Bill 71 1 37N03'22 86W59'18 5:47:57
Hollow Creek 56
68 38N11 85W39 5:42:36
Hollybush 60 16 37N20'15 82W51'07 5:31:24

Hollyhill 74 16 36N39'47 84W19'49 5:37:19
Hollyvilla 56 68 38N05'37 85W44'44 5:42:59
Hollywood 34 28 38N01'40 84W29'37 5:37:58
Holmes 1 1 37N12'27 85W16'11 5:41:05
Holmes Mill 48 15 36N52'06 83W00'09 5:32:01
Holt 14 1 37N54'39 86W34'52 5:46:19
Holt 64 11 38N05'05 82W35'54 5:30:24
Holt 89 1 37N15'21 87W05'45 5:48:23
Holy Cross 78 59 37N40'26 85W26'49 5:41:47
Homer 71 1 36N57'41 86W50'23 5:47:22
Honaker 36 11 37N31'25 82W40'48 5:30:43
Honey Acre 23 1 37N06'46 84W58'29 5:39:54
Honeybee 74 16 36N50'29 84W22'20 5:37:29
Honey Fork 98 11 37N20'50 82W21'15 5:29:25
Honey Grove 24 1 36N53'23 87W18'35 5:49:14
Hooker 26 16 37N08'10 83W50'08 5:35:21
Hooktown 91 21 38N21'16 84W09'06 5:36:36
Hooper 106 51 38N10'29 85W09'25 5:40:38
Hootentown 25 33 37N55'32 84W17'33 5:37:10
Hope 87 16 38N00'57 83W46'23 5:35:06
Hopeful Heights 8
11 39N00'04 84W39'28 5:38:38
Hopewell 45 16 38N24'22 82W54'39 5:31:39
Hopewell 56 68 38N10'28 85W30'27 5:42:02
Hopewell 63 16 36N59'33 84W05'31 5:36:22
Hopkinsville 24 1 36N51'56 87W29'19 5:49:57
Hopkinsville West 24
1 36N54 87W33 5:50:12
Hopson 17 1 36N59'24 87W50'49 5:51:23
Horn Back Mill 14
1 37N34'18 86W23'30 5:45:34
Horntown 43 1 37N28'36 86W07'35 5:44:30
Horntown 104 1 37N04'04 85W00'20 5:40:01
Horse Branch 92 1 37N27'21 86W40'36 5:46:42
Horse Cave 50 6 37N10'46 85W54'25 5:43:38
Horse Creek Junction 26
16 37N09 83W46 5:35:04
Horsemill 16 1 37N13'59 86W32'17 5:46:09
Horton 92 1 37N26'08 86W47'56 5:47:12
Hoskinston 66 16 37N04'38 83W23'30 5:33:34
Hosman 7 15 36N47 83W46 5:35:04
Hot Spot 67 16 37N07'39 82W55'00 5:31:40
Houckville 64 11 38N06'44 82W51'21 5:31:25
Houston 13 16 37N26'44 83W30'59 5:34:04
Houston Acres 56
68 38N12'51 85W36'50 5:42:27
Hovious 1 1 37N16 85W09 5:40:36
Howard 47 64 37N59'20 85W57'39 5:43:51
Howard Mills 87
22 38N03 83W57 5:35:48
Howards Creek 13
16 37N29 83W21 5:33:24
Howards Mill 87
16 38N03'50 83W50'51 5:35:23
Howardstown 90 51 37N34'20 85W35'31 5:42:22
Howel 24 1 36N41'57 87W32'08 5:50:09
Howe Valley 47 51 37N41'14 86W05'18 5:44:21
Hubble 69 16 37N35'49 84W39'17 5:38:37
Hubbs 61 15 36N47 83W55 5:35:40
Huddy 98 11 37N35'41 82W16'32 5:29:06
Hudgins 44 1 37N20'55 85W40'50 5:42:43
Hudson 14 1 37N39'04 86W16'36 5:45:06
Hudsonville 14 1 37N43 86W17 5:45:08
Hueys Corner 8 11 38N56'46 84W43'03 5:38:52
Hueysville 36 11 37N29'55 82W50'28 5:31:22
Huff 31 1 37N14'55 86W22'04 5:45:28
Huffman 43 1 37N23'24 86W13'09 5:44:53
Hughes Landing 82
51 37N57'53 86W01'48 5:44:07
Hughey 72 1 37N04 88W08 5:52:32
Huldeville 16 1 37N16'01 86W36'32 5:46:26
Hulen 7 15 36N47'30 83W31'30 5:34:06
Humble 104 1 37N05'19 85W04'00 5:40:16
Hume 8 11 38N50'38 84W43'25 5:38:54
Hummel 102 16 37N23'47 84W17'08 5:37:09
Hunnewell 45 11 38N24'48 82W50'44 5:31:23
Hunt 25 33 37N54'38 84W09'38 5:36:39
Hunter 36 11 37N30'22 82W45'23 5:31:02
Hunters 90 51 37N51'37 85W30'04 5:42:00
Hunters Trace 56
68 38N10'22 85W49'33 5:43:18
Huntersville 27 1 36N37'29 85W08'08 5:40:33
Hunterton 120 45 38N03 84W44 5:38:56
Hunter Town 120
45 38N02'06 84W41'59 5:38:48
Huntsville 16 1 37N10 86W53 5:47:32
Hurley 55 16 37N24'45 84W02'14 5:36:09
Hurricane Hills 90
51 37N47 85W40 5:42:40
Hurst 13 16 37N38'13 83W30'18 5:34:01
Hurstbourne Acres 56
68 38N13'16 85W35'21 5:42:21
Hustonville 69 16 37N28'23 84W48'57 5:39:16
Hutch 7 15 36N39'02 83W37'17 5:34:29
Hutchison 9 30 38N08'17 84W20'24 5:37:22
Hyattsville 40 16 37N36'18 84W31'21 5:38:05
Hyden 97 16 37N09'39 83W22'24 5:33:30
Hydro 114 1 36N58'32 86W09'23 5:44:38
Hylton 98 11 37N13'56 82W31'21 5:30:05
Iberia 43 1 37N22'23 86W09'58 5:44:40
Ibex 32 16 38N10'34 83W04'25 5:32:18
Ice 67 16 37N06'27 82W51'37 5:31:26
Ida 27 1 36N46'03 85W10'05 5:40:40
Ida May 65 16 37N31'16 83W45'59 5:35:04
Idle Hour 34 28 38N01'21 84W27'34 5:37:50
Idlewild 8 11 39N04'39 84W47'42 5:39:11
Ilsley 54 1 37N11'48 87W36'44 5:50:27
Independence 59
11 38N56'35 84W32'39 5:38:11
Index 88 40 37N53'53 83W17'06 5:33:08
Indiancreek 61 15 36N57 84W00 5:36:00
Indian Fields 25
16 37N56 84W00 5:36:00
Indian Hills 21
39 38N40'38 85W08'28 5:40:34
Indian Hills 34
28 38N00'33 84W33'12 5:38:13
Indian Hills 37
20 38N13'01 84W49'51 5:39:19
Indian Hills 47
61 37N42'32 85W50'46 5:43:23
Indian Hills 56
68 38N16'21 85W39'46 5:42:39

Indian Hills 72 1 37N02'04 88W03'28 5:52:14
Indian Hills 104 1 36N59'34 84W56'01 5:39:44
Indian Hills 105 26 38N12'11 84W34'07 5:38:16
Indian Hills 114 10 36N59'23 86W24'18 5:45:37
Indian Hills Cherokee Sect 56 68 38N16'46 85W39'00 5:42:36
Indian Lake 46 1 37N54 86W45 5:47:00
Indian Old Field 25 33 38N00 84W11 5:36:44
Indian Valley 43 1 37N34'29 86W26'25 5:45:46
Inez 80 11 37N51'59 82W32'20 5:30:09
Ingle 100 19 37N05'36 84W51'33 5:39:26
Ingleside 4 1 37N07'24 88W54'05 5:55:36
Ingram 7 15 36N43'49 83W47'54 5:35:12
Inroad 1 1 36N57'23 85W16'47 5:41:07
Insco 71 1 36N58'52 86W51'52 5:47:27
Insko 88 16 37N45'26 83W18'04 5:33:12
Insull 48 15 36N45'48 83W29'17 5:33:57
Iola 79 1 36N53'59 88W24'53 5:53:40
Irad 64 11 38N05'31 82W44'19 5:30:57
Irma 28 1 37N23'17 88W14'52 5:52:59
Iron Hill 22 16 38N24'22 83W02'17 5:32:09
Iron Mound 33 27 37N48'53 84W02'38 5:36:11
Ironville 10 11 38N27'23 82W41'33 5:30:46
Iroquois 56 69 38N10 85W47 5:43:08
Irvin Cobb Resort 18 1 36N38'44 88W07'57 5:52:32
Irvine 33 27 37N42'02 83W58'26 5:35:54
Irvington 14 1 37N52'49 86W17'02 5:45:08
Irvins Store 104 1 37N04 85W06 5:40:24
Irwin 68 11 38N40'58 83W34'10 5:34:17
Island 75 1 37N26'42 87W08'38 5:48:35
Island City 95 16 37N21'59 83W46'05 5:35:04
Isom 67 16 37N11'16 82W53'56 5:31:36
Isonville 32 16 38N03'54 83W03'10 5:32:13
Iuka 70 1 37N04'51 88W14'12 5:52:57
Ivel 36 11 37N35'28 82W40'06 5:30:40
Iverdale 7 15 36N46 83W42 5:34:48
Ivis 60 16 37N20 82W59 5:31:56
Ivor 96 11 38N51'35 84W14'27 5:36:58
Ivy Grove 7 15 36N49'20 83W41'45 5:34:47
Ivyton 77 11 37N42'32 82W58'43 5:31:55
Jabez 104 1 36N59'13 84W53'37 5:39:34
Jackhorn 67 16 37N12'56 82W42'19 5:30:49
Jacks Creek 26 16 37N12'25 83W33'24 5:34:14
Jacks Creek 36 11 37N21'57 82W43'59 5:30:56
Jackson 13 16 37N33'11 83W23'01 5:33:32
Jackson 84 44 37N49'30 84W52'15 5:39:29
Jacksonville 9 30 38N16'22 84W21'57 5:37:28
Jacksonville 106 51 38N16'27 85W00'47 5:40:03
Jackstown 91 16 38N14'41 84W03'31 5:36:14
Jacktown 23 51 37N26'38 85W00'56 5:40:04
Jacobs 22 16 38N13'51 83W14'29 5:32:58
Jacobs Addition 56 69 38N11'24 85W47'19 5:43:09
Jamboree 98 11 37N29'54 82W08'13 5:28:33
Jamestown 104 1 36N59'05 85W03'47 5:40:15
Jarvis 61 15 36N52 83W53 5:35:32
Jason 66 16 37N10'42 83W29'01 5:33:56
Jason 110 1 37N02'55 87W05'26 5:48:22
Jason Ridge 110 1 36N59 87W09 5:48:36
Jayem 7 15 36N46 83W42 5:34:48
Jeff 97 46 37N12 83W08 5:32:32
Jeffersontown 56 68 38N11'39 85W33'52 5:42:15
Jeffersonville 57 16 37N58'25 83W50'31 5:35:22
Jeffrey 86 1 36N45'04 85W50'26 5:43:22
Jellico 118 15 36N35 84W08 5:36:32
Jellicocreek 118 15 36N44 84W10 5:36:40
Jenkins 67 16 37N10'24 82W37'52 5:30:31
Jenkinsville 115 51 37N43'55 85W02'23 5:40:10
Jensenton 115 51 37N41 85W13 5:40:52
Jenson 7 15 36N46'37 83W37'48 5:34:31
Jeptha 88 40 37N56'32 83W06'00 5:32:24
Jeremiah 67 16 37N10'02 82W55'45 5:31:43
Jericho 41 11 38N43'51 84W40'25 5:38:42
Jericho 52 51 38N24'18 85W17'24 5:41:10
Jericho 62 51 37N31'07 85W38'54 5:42:36
Jericho 104 1 37N05'11 85W02'57 5:40:12
Jerico 71 1 36N59'48 86W58'39 5:47:55
Jeriel 22 16 38N13'33 82W51'17 5:31:25
Jessamine 57 29 37N52'33 84W37'17 5:38:29
Jessietown 78 51 37N28'51 85W19'30 5:41:18
Jetson 16 1 37N14'57 86W31'55 5:46:08
Jett 37 20 38N10'43 84W48'52 5:39:15
Jetts Creek 13 16 37N30'08 83W32'33 5:34:10
Jewell City 54 1 37N31'35 87W21'19 5:49:25
Jimtown 34 30 38N11'20 84W22'28 5:37:30
Jimtown 115 51 37N40'11 85W12'34 5:40:50
Jimtown 116 1 36N38'40 84W55'56 5:39:44
Jingo 92 1 37N29'55 86W48'30 5:47:14
Jinks 33 16 37N36'23 84W01'56 5:36:08
Job 80 11 37N55'04 82W32'38 5:30:11
Jock 31 1 37N17 86W17 5:45:08
Johnetta 102 16 37N24'56 84W11'31 5:36:46
Johns Creek 58 11 37N46 82W45 5:31:00
Johnson Bottom 98 11 37N34 82W09 5:28:36
Johnson Crossroads 43 1 37N23'55 86W12'06 5:44:48
Johnsontown 56 68 38N07'10 85W51'37 5:43:26
Johnsonville 3 44 37N56'06 85W06'25 5:40:26
Johns Run 22 16 38N14'18 82W54'42 5:31:39
Johnsville 12 11 38N45'12 84W08'54 5:36:36
Jolly 117 1 37N28'14 87W42'19 5:50:49
Jonancy 98 11 37N18'59 82W34'59 5:30:20
Jonesburg 51 1 37N43'15 87W44'39 5:50:59
Jones Mill 27 1 36N39'24 85W06'17 5:40:25
Jonestown 34 28 37N58'37 84W29'48 5:37:59
Jonesville 41 11 38N38'23 84W46'32 5:39:06
Jonesville 50 1 37N23'16 85W46'06 5:43:04
Jonican 98 11 37N26 82W23 5:29:32
Joppa 1 1 37N03'06 85W14'32 5:40:58
Jordan 38 1 36N30'12 89W02'13 5:56:09
Josephine 105 16 38N23'55 84W39'00 5:38:36
Joy 70 1 37N21'18 88W23'09 5:53:33
Joyes 106 54 38N12'35 85W17'28 5:41:10
Juan 13 16 37N33 83W22 5:33:28
Judio 29 1 36N41'45 85W28'51 5:41:55
Judson 40 16 37N41'11 84W34'09 5:38:17
Judy 87 22 38N07'47 83W57'31 5:35:50
Judyville 9 38 38N19 84W02 5:36:08
Jugville 43 1 37N27'47 86W35'56 5:46:24
Julien 24 1 36N50'12 87W38'23 5:50:34
Julip 118 15 36N44'34 84W03'57 5:36:16
Jumbo 69 16 37N27'29 84W41'21 5:38:45
Junction City 11 42 37N35'12 84W47'38 5:39:11
Juniper Beach 56 68 38N19'14 85W38'50 5:42:35
Junte 106 51 38N04'52 85W05'52 5:40:23
Justell 36 11 37N33'23 82W38'17 5:30:33
Justice 71 1 36N52'52 87W03'22 5:48:13
Justiceville 98 11 37N24'47 82W27'07 5:29:48
Kaler 42 1 36N53'08 88W32'47 5:54:11
Kaliopi 66 16 37N14'00 83W25'00 5:33:40
Kansas 42 1 36N54'06 88W43'42 5:54:55
Karlus 104 1 36N59'38 85W01'35 5:40:06
Katharyn 15 64 38N00'03 85W55'44 5:43:43
Kavanaugh 10 11 38N15'12 82W35'13 5:30:21
Kavito 104 1 37N04 84W50 5:39:20
Kayjay 61 15 36N44'39 83W50'57 5:35:24
Keaton 58 11 37N59 82W58 5:31:52
Keavy 63 16 37N00'13 84W09'40 5:36:39
Keck 13 16 37N36'16 83W21'33 5:33:26
Keefer 41 11 38N32'06 84W38'02 5:38:32
Keene 57 28 37N56'36 84W38'31 5:38:34
Keeneland 56 70 38N16'29 85W34'03 5:42:16
Kehoe 45 11 38N27'58 83W03'05 5:32:12
Keith 48 15 36N51'08 83W22'17 5:33:29
Kelat 49 36 38N31'34 84W18'44 5:37:15
Kellacey 88 40 37N57'43 83W23'30 5:33:34
Kelly 24 1 36N58'14 87W28'37 5:49:54
Kellyville 1 1 37N11'50 85W19'32 5:41:18
Keltner 1 1 37N05'42 85W30'37 5:42:02
Kemp 44 1 37N08'11 85W27'29 5:41:50
Kenawood 34 28 38N03'30 84W27'06 5:37:48
Kenmont 97 46 37N12 83W08 5:32:32
Kennebec 37 20 38N12'25 84W54'47 5:39:39
Kennedy 24 1 36N38'54 87W24'54 5:49:40
Keno 100 19 36N53'38 84W34'29 5:38:18
Kensee 118 15 36N35 84W08 5:36:32
Kensington 8 14 38N54'13 84W36'48 5:38:27
Kentenia 48 15 36N47'46 83W24'04 5:33:36
Kenton 59 11 38N52'06 84W27'22 5:37:49
Kenton Hills 59 71 39N05'02 84W31'54 5:38:08
Kentontown 101 11 38N29'34 84W07'10 5:36:29
Kenton Vale 59 71 39N03'03 84W31'09 5:38:05
Kentucky Ridge 7 15 36N42 83W45 5:35:00
Kenvir 48 15 36N51'13 83W09'26 5:32:38
Kenwood 56 69 38N09'52 85W46'09 5:43:05
Ken Wye 92 1 37N20'44 86W57'12 5:47:49
Kepler 114 1 36N58'29 86W12'02 5:44:48
Kerby Knob 55 16 37N31'18 84W06'48 5:36:27
Kernie 77 11 37N45'24 83W10'05 5:32:40
Kern Orchard 113 1 37N33 87W59 5:51:56
Kerz 58 11 37N55'00 82W50'23 5:31:22
Kessinger 50 1 37N18'21 85W57'34 5:43:50
Keswick 118 15 36N35 84W08 5:36:32
Kettle 29 1 36N42'08 85W21'40 5:41:27
Kettle Island 7 15 36N47'26 83W36'19 5:34:25
Kevil 4 1 37N05'06 88W53'12 5:55:33
Kewanee 98 11 37N26'37 82W30'58 5:30:04
Keysburg 71 1 36N39'04 87W00'29 5:48:02
Kidder 116 1 36N54'54 84W39'06 5:38:36
Kidds Crossing 116 1 36N45'23 84W40'48 5:38:43
Kidds Store 23 51 37N28 84W49 5:39:16
Kiddville 25 22 37N57'35 83W59'35 5:35:58
Kildav 48 15 36N51'30 83W12'21 5:32:49
Kilgore 22 16 38N20 82W46 5:31:04
Kimbrell 33 27 37N48'15 83W59'28 5:35:58
Kimper 98 11 37N29'49 82W21'02 5:29:24
Kinchloes Bluff 89 1 37N18 87W08 5:48:32
Kingbee 100 19 37N09'17 84W44'17 5:38:57
King Mills 113 1 37N44'12 87W45'08 5:51:01
Kings Creek 67 16 37N03'06 82W54'53 5:31:40
Kingsley 56 69 38N13'15 85W40'19 5:42:41
Kings Mountain 69 16 37N22'21 84W41'17 5:38:45
Kingston 34 28 38N05'11 84W27'12 5:37:49
Kingston 76 16 37N39'01 84W14'30 5:36:58
Kingswood 14 1 37N43'08 86W24'31 5:45:38
Kinniconick 68 11 38N31'16 83W20'17 5:33:21
Kino 5 6 36N56'52 85W46'39 5:43:07
Kirbyton 20 1 36N50'26 88W51'50 5:55:27
Kirk 14 1 37N43'26 86W28'43 5:45:55
Kirkland 115 44 37N46 84W51 5:39:24
Kirkmansville 110 1 37N00'36 87W14'33 5:48:58
Kirksey 18 1 36N41'55 88W23'43 5:53:35
Kirksville 76 31 37N39'55 84W24'33 5:37:38
Kirkville 68 11 38N41'51 83W02'29 5:32:10
Kirkwood 84 16 37N54'59 84W55'24 5:39:42
Kirkwood Springs 54 1 37N15'04 87W45'53 5:51:04
Kirtley 92 1 37N26'13 87W06'04 5:48:24
Kise 64 11 37N59'17 82W39'34 5:30:38
Kiserton 9 30 38N16'37 84W16'34 5:37:06
Kite 60 16 37N19'16 82W48'11 5:31:13
Kitts 48 15 36N51'21 83W17'43 5:33:11
Klondike 87 22 38N01'14 83W59'49 5:35:59
Klondyke 3 44 37N56'47 85W05'25 5:40:22
Knifley 1 1 37N14'34 85W11'22 5:40:45
Knightsburg 89 1 37N12'46 86W55'10 5:47:41
Knob Lick 85 1 37N04'42 85W41'40 5:42:47
Knopp 56 68 38N08'52 85W43'51 5:42:55
Knottsville 30 1 37N46'18 86W54'15 5:47:37
Knowlton 99 16 37N47'10 83W50'15 5:35:21
Knoxville 96 11 38N42'04 84W30'21 5:38:01
Kodak 97 46 37N12'19 83W01'53 5:32:08
Kohler 19 11 38N52'13 84W19'46 5:37:19
Kona 67 16 37N09'27 82W44'20 5:30:57
Koon 72 1 37N04 88W08 5:52:32
Korea 83 16 37N56'31 83W28'43 5:33:55
Kosmosdale 56 68 38N01'58 85W54'33 5:43:38
Kraft 47 51 37N43'01 85W58'15 5:43:53
Kragon 13 16 37N30'24 83W20'40 5:33:23
Krebs 73 1 36N59'40 88W36'21 5:54:25
Kronos 92 1 37N23'45 87W03'57 5:48:16
Krypton 97 46 37N18'40 83W20'22 5:33:21
Kuttawa 72 1 37N03'32 88W07'57 5:52:32
Kuttawa Springs 72 1 37N04 88W08 5:52:32
Kyrock 31 1 37N15'48 86W15'24 5:45:02
Labascus 23 51 37N13'35 84W55'09 5:39:41
La Center 4 1 37N04'36 88W58'25 5:55:54
Lacey 77 11 37N51'35 83W01'54 5:32:08
Lacie 52 57 38N31'37 85W07'46 5:40:31
Lackey 36 11 37N28'06 82W49'44 5:31:19
Lacon 43 1 37N29'32 86W05'03 5:44:20
Laden 48 15 36N54'59 83W11'36 5:32:46
La Fayette 24 1 36N39'30 87W39'30 5:50:38
La Grange 93 62 38N24'27 85W22'44 5:41:31
Lair 49 21 38N20'31 84W18'28 5:37:14
Lake 63 16 37N05'22 83W53'08 5:35:33
Lake City 70 1 37N01'39 88W14'54 5:53:00
Lake Dreamland 56 69 38N11 85W49 5:43:16
Lakeland 56 68 38N16'13 85W33'15 5:42:13
Lake Louisvilla 56 68 38N18'49 85W30'51 5:42:03
Lakeshore 17 1 37N08'03 87W41'58 5:50:48
Lakeside Park 59 71 39N02'08 84W34'09 5:38:17
Laketon 20 1 36N51'48 89W06'06 5:56:24
Lakeview 59 71 39N02'19 84W31'43 5:38:07
Lakeview Acres 34 28 38N00'29 84W28'57 5:37:56
Lakeview Heights 103 16 38N09'05 83W30'16 5:34:01
Lakeville 77 11 37N43'08 83W04'16 5:32:17
Lamasco 72 1 36N59'10 87W56'10 5:51:45
Lamb 59 71 38N57'22 84W26'53 5:37:48
Lamb 86 1 36N45'31 85W53'57 5:43:36
Lambert 36 11 37N23 82W44 5:30:56
Lambric 13 16 37N34'07 83W07'50 5:32:31
Lamero 63 16 37N18'03 84W09'38 5:36:39
Lamont 73 1 37N03'25 88W48'15 5:55:13
Lamont 97 46 37N20'59 83W18'49 5:33:15
Lancaster 40 35 37N37'10 84W34'41 5:38:19
Lancer 36 11 37N40'01 82W44'13 5:30:57
Landsaw 119 16 37N43'39 83W27'05 5:33:48
Lanes Mill 108 44 38N06'13 84W52'51 5:39:31
Langley (Maytown Station) 36 11 37N31'54 82W47'27 5:31:10
Langnau 63 37 37N08 84W05 5:36:20
Langstaff 21 39 38N38'29 85W06'48 5:40:27
Lanhamtown 23 51 37N20'10 84W52'57 5:39:32
Lansdowne 34 28 37N59'55 84W30'09 5:38:01
Larkslane 60 16 37N23'05 82W52'53 5:31:32
Larue 26 16 37N12'11 83W55'30 5:35:42
Latonia 59 71 39N02'53 84W30'32 5:38:02
Latonia Lakes 59 11 38N58'03 84W29'52 5:37:59
Laura 80 11 37N42'27 82W25'58 5:29:44
Laurel Creek 26 16 37N14'42 83W44'56 5:35:00
Laurel Ford 7 15 36N48'48 83W33'02 5:34:12
Laurel Fork 7 15 36N38 83W56 5:35:44
Laurel Gap 10 11 38N25 82W36 5:30:24
Lawhorn Hill 23 51 37N18'00 84W51'14 5:39:25
Lawrenceburg 3 50 38N02'14 84W53'48 5:39:35
Lawrenceville 41 11 38N34'05 84W39'00 5:38:36
Lawson 13 16 37N36'07 83W27'31 5:33:50
Lawton 22 16 38N16'00 83W13'15 5:32:53
Layman 48 15 36N49'43 83W27'48 5:33:51
Laynesville 36 11 37N32 82W38 5:30:32
Leach 10 11 36N38 83W56 5:35:44
Leafdale 62 51 37N33'48 85W39'53 5:42:40
Leander 58 11 37N45'11 82W52'18 5:31:29
Leatha 77 11 37N49'05 83W01'00 5:32:04
Leatherwood 97 46 37N01'58 83W10'21 5:32:41
Lebanon 78 66 37N34'11 85W15'10 5:41:01
Lebanon Junction 15 56 37N50'04 85W43'55 5:42:56
Leburn 60 16 37N20'53 82W57'19 5:31:49
Leckieville 98 11 37N39'32 82W16'21 5:29:05
Lecta 5 6 37N00'40 85W51'22 5:43:25
Ledbetter 70 1 37N02'51 88W28'37 5:53:54
Ledford 38 1 36N31'48 89W18'09 5:57:13
Ledocio 64 11 38N01'44 82W42'51 5:30:51
Lee 16 1 37N17'45 86W29'58 5:46:00
Lee City 119 16 37N44'21 83W19'59 5:33:20
Leeco 119 16 37N42'39 83W41'42 5:34:47
Leesburg 49 16 38N17'40 84W25'06 5:37:40
Lees Lick 49 21 38N20'09 84W25'07 5:37:40
Leestown 37 20 38N12 84W52 5:39:28
Leestown Terrace 37 20 38N12 84W52 5:39:28
Leetown 16 1 37N08'22 86W44'34 5:46:58
Legrand 50 6 37N11 85W54 5:43:36
LeGrande 50 6 37N10'41 85W46'56 5:43:08
Leighton 33 27 37N36'13 83W53'10 5:35:33
Leisure 88 40 38N02'41 83W18'15 5:33:13
Leitchfield 43 1 37N28'48 86W17'38 5:45:11
Leitchfield Crossing 50 1 37N18'05 85W54'45 5:43:39
L & E Junction 25 22 38N00'09 84W04'00 5:36:16
Lejunior 48 15 36N54'04 83W08'03 5:32:32
Lemen Landing 70 1 37N11'41 88W20'52 5:53:23
Lemon 75 1 37N34'52 87W22'42 5:49:31
Lenarue (Glidden Station) 48 15 36N48'22 83W16'03 5:33:04
Lennut 97 46 37N16 83W13 5:32:52
Lenore 90 51 37N56'18 85W30'34 5:42:02
Lenox 88 16 37N57'26 83W12'05 5:32:48
Lenoxburg 12 11 38N44'33 84W13'30 5:36:54
Leon 22 16 38N17'16 82W58'37 5:31:54
Lerose 95 16 37N28'56 83W36'56 5:34:28

Lesbas 63 37 37N04'44 83w59'44 5:35:59
Leslie 29 1 36N46'46 85w27'07 5:41:48
Letcher 67 16 37N08'42 82w57'33 5:31:50
Letitia 45 11 38N38'12 83w00'17 5:32:01
Levee 87 16 37N58'16 83w56'07 5:35:44
Level Green 102
36 37N16'52 84w25'34 5:37:42
Levi 95 16 37N28'49 83w43'15 5:34:53
Levias 28 1 37N18'28 88w10'51 5:52:43
Levisa Junction 98
11 37N24'21 82w26'32 5:29:46
Lewis 48 15 36N52 83w12 5:32:48
Lewisburg 71 16 36N59'11 86w56'50 5:47:47
Lewisburg 81 11 38N32'56 83w45'54 5:35:04
Lewis Creek 66 16 36N59'22 83w19'01 5:33:16
Lewisport 46 1 37N56'13 86w54'08 5:47:37
Lewistown 17 1 37N08'34 87w48'02 5:51:12
Lexie 119 16 37N43'44 83w24'14 5:33:37
Lexington 34 28 38N02'57 84w30'01 5:38:00
Lexington-Blue Grass Army De 9
28 38N04 84w29 5:37:56
Lexington Manor 34
28 38N02'35 84w28'11 5:37:53
Liberty 23 51 37N19'06 84w56'22 5:39:45
Liberty 82 51 38N01'41 86w19'09 5:45:17
Liberty 110 1 36N53'17 87w11'34 5:48:46
Liberty 117 1 37N31 87w41 5:50:44
Liberty 118 15 36N45'53 84w12'15 5:36:49
Liberty Heights 34
28 38N02'20 84w27'57 5:37:52
Liberty Road 88
40 37N54'20 83w17'34 5:33:10
Lick Branch 88 40 37N55 83w16 5:33:04
Lickburg 77 11 37N47'34 83w05'07 5:32:20
Lick Creek 98 11 37N22'49 82w17'50 5:29:11
Lick Fork 103 16 38N05'47 83w24'40 5:33:39
Licking River 88
40 37N56'14 83w18'23 5:33:14
Lickskillet 71 1 36N44'17 86w59'23 5:47:58
Lickskillet 82 51 37N56'02 86w03'26 5:44:14
Lida 63 16 37N04'56 83w56'05 5:35:44
Liggett 48 15 36N45'07 83w20'50 5:33:23
Ligon 36 11 37N22'13 82w40'22 5:30:41
Lilac 43 1 37N32'56 86w20'39 5:45:23
Liletown 44 6 37N08'38 85w35'00 5:42:20
Lily 63 16 37N01'28 84w04'31 5:36:18
Limaburg 8 11 39N01'12 84w41'14 5:38:45
Limestone 22 16 38N15'58 83w12'26 5:32:50
Limestone Springs 15
53 37N55'49 85w40'06 5:42:40
Limeville 45 11 38N42'27 82w52'52 5:31:31
Limp 47 51 37N35'32 86w11'51 5:44:47
Lincoln 26 16 37N03'28 83w44'21 5:34:57
Lincoln 31 1 37N16 86w15 5:45:00
Lincoln Ridge 106
51 38N13'06 85w22'31 5:41:30
Lincolnshire 56
68 38N13'23 85w37'17 5:42:29
Lindseyville 31 1 37N14'09 86w17'40 5:45:11
Linefork 67 16 37N01'11 82w57'35 5:31:50
Lines Mill 50 1 37N21'29 86w02'34 5:44:10
Linton 111 1 36N41'12 87w55'07 5:51:40
Linwood 43 1 37N20'31 86w10'34 5:44:42
Linwood 50 1 37N20'22 85w45'36 5:43:02
Linwood Park 43 1 37N21'02 86w08'34 5:44:34
Lionilli 98 11 37N15'38 82w36'41 5:30:27
Liro 93 62 38N24'04 85w20'19 5:41:21
Lisletown 25 33 37N55'09 84w16'25 5:37:06
Lisman 117 1 37N27'58 87w44'03 5:50:56
Litsey 115 51 37N46'10 85w11'34 5:40:46
Littcarr 60 16 37N14'27 82w56'56 5:31:48
Little 13 16 37N26'23 83w21'43 5:33:27
Little Barren 44
6 37N07'40 85w37'04 5:42:28
Little Bear Creek 79
1 36N57'20 88w14'30 5:52:58
Little Creek 7 15 36N48 83w39 5:34:36
Little Cypress 79
1 37N01'00 88w26'46 5:53:47
Little Dixie 98
11 37N27'41 82w33'34 5:30:14
Little Georgetown 34
45 38N01'35 84w36'57 5:38:28
Little Hickman 57
29 37N46'25 84w34'13 5:38:17
Little Mount 108
51 38N03'41 85w15'05 5:41:00
Little Muddy 16 1 37N14 86w41 5:46:44
Little Needmore 11
25 37N39'28 84w43'36 5:38:54
Little Rock 9 16 38N11'38 84w03'04 5:36:12
Little Sandy 32
16 38N03'40 83w10'55 5:32:44
Little Tar Springs 46
1 37N54 86w45 5:47:00
Little Texas 34
45 38N00'45 84w38'31 5:38:34
Littleton 26 16 37N09'45 83w45'17 5:35:01
Littleville 73 9 37N03'40 88w36'12 5:54:25
Little Zion 117 1 37N32'40 87w43'24 5:50:54
Littrell 29 1 36N41'09 85w23'47 5:41:35
Livermore 75 1 37N29'35 87w07'55 5:48:32
Livia 30 1 37N34'15 87w06'16 5:48:25
Livingston 102 16 37N17'52 84w12'54 5:36:52
Lloyd 45 11 38N37'12 82w51'53 5:31:28
Load 45 11 38N32'46 82w58'15 5:31:53
Loam 55 16 37N24'27 84w07'47 5:36:31
Lobb 44 1 37N20'45 85w38'42 5:42:35
Lockards Creek 26
16 37N07 83w45 5:35:00
Lockport 52 51 38N26'09 84w58'02 5:39:52
Lockwood 10 11 38N18'30 82w34'49 5:30:19
Locust 21 58 38N42'11 85w15'39 5:41:03
Locust 35 16 38N17'59 83w44'04 5:34:56
Locust Branch 33
16 37N35'10 84w04'11 5:36:17
Locust Grove 25
33 37N56'04 84w19'07 5:37:16
Locust Grove 96
11 38N38'14 84w29'17 5:37:57
Locust Hill 14 1 37N43'40 86w21'24 5:45:26
Lodale 82 51 38N02'35 86w16'51 5:45:07
Lodiburg 14 1 37N54'16 86w24'10 5:45:37
Logana 57 29 37N51'53 84w29'13 5:37:57
Logansport 16 1 37N17'06 86w46'05 5:47:04
Logantown 69 16 37N33'38 84w37'47 5:38:31
Log Lick 25 33 37N51'29 84w01'37 5:36:06
Logmont 7 15 36N37 83w44 5:34:56
Log Mountain 7 15 36N46 83w42 5:34:48
Logsdon Valley 50
1 37N15'58 85w57'43 5:43:51
Logville 77 11 37N52'22 83w06'36 5:32:26
Lola 70 1 37N19'07 88w18'28 5:53:14
Lombard 99 16 37N51 83w52 5:35:28
London 63 37 37N07'44 84w05'00 5:36:20
Lone 65 16 37N31'48 83w36'14 5:34:25
Lone Oak 43 1 37N25'32 86w04'18 5:44:17
Lone Oak 73 1 37N02'10 88w39'53 5:54:40
Lone Star 50 1 37N24'17 85w56'48 5:43:47
Long Bottom 104 1 36N52'56 85w07'47 5:40:31
Long Fork 98 11 37N18 82w39 5:30:36
Longlick 105 16 38N20'33 84w39'30 5:38:38
Long Ridge 29 1 36N44'40 85w17'46 5:41:11
Long Ridge 94 16 38N35'14 84w49'25 5:39:18
Long Run 56 68 38N13'54 85w25'27 5:41:42
Longstreet 104 1 37N04 85w06 5:40:24
Longton 48 15 36N50'08 83w24'37 5:33:38
Long View 47 61 37N47'22 85w54'47 5:43:39
Longview 56 68 38N17'57 85w39'32 5:42:38
Longview Beach 39
52 38N21'56 85w38'22 5:42:33
Lookout 98 11 37N18'48 82w28'01 5:29:52
Lookout Heights 59
71 39N04'02 84w32'36 5:38:10
Loradale 34 16 38N11'42 84w23'51 5:37:35
Loretto 78 59 37N38'07 85w24'03 5:41:36
Lost City 71 1 36N58'37 86w54'18 5:47:37
Lost Creek 13 16 37N28'54 83w19'31 5:33:18
Lost River 114 10 36N57'10 86w28'31 5:45:54
Lot 118 15 36N36'03 84w05'16 5:36:21
Lothair 97 46 37N14'31 83w10'51 5:32:43
Lotus 15 51 37N55'08 85w35'48 5:42:23
Louden 118 15 36N45'06 84w01'33 5:36:06
Louellen 48 15 36N54'46 83w05'39 5:32:23
Louisa 64 11 38N06'51 82w36'12 5:30:25
Louisville 56 69 38N15'15 85w45'34 5:43:02
Love 16 1 37N16'59 86w31'38 5:46:07
Lovelaceville 4 1 36N58'07 88w49'51 5:55:19
Lovely 80 11 37N49'33 82w24'05 5:29:36
Loving 114 1 37N01'13 86w17'28 5:45:10
Lowell 40 16 37N36'34 84w25'31 5:37:42
Lower Buffalo 65
16 37N31'40 83w41'16 5:34:45
Lower Gillmore 119
16 37N45'50 83w22'10 5:33:29
Lower Kings Addition 45
11 38N43 82w58 5:31:52
Lower Pompey 98
11 37N29 82w31 5:30:04
Lower Spencer 87
16 38N01'43 83w50'25 5:35:22
Lowes 20 1 36N53'08 88w46'26 5:55:06
Lowgap 1 1 36N58 85w26 5:41:44
Low Gap 116 1 36N38'42 84w57'32 5:39:50
Lowmansville 64
11 37N55'02 82w43'55 5:30:56
Loyall 48 15 36N51'07 83w21'15 5:33:25
L S Park 106 51 38N11'44 85w23'59 5:41:36
Lucas 5 1 36N53'30 86w02'15 5:44:09
Lucastown 67 16 37N12'23 82w47'48 5:31:11
Lucile 32 16 38N05 83w08 5:32:32
Lucky 118 15 36N44'13 84w04'20 5:36:17
Lucky Fork 95 16 37N22'03 83w34'12 5:34:17
Lucky Stop 57 16 37N57'53 83w48'53 5:35:16
Ludlow 59 71 39N05'33 84w32'51 5:38:11
Lunah 13 16 37N33'45 83w10'37 5:32:42
Luner 102 36 37N14'08 84w16'32 5:37:06
Lupton 48 15 36N52 83w12 5:32:48
Lusby's Mill 94
16 38N32 84w50 5:39:20
Luzerne 89 1 37N13'06 87w12'39 5:48:51
Luzon 117 1 37N31 87w41 5:50:44
Lykins 77 11 37N46'41 83w13'19 5:32:53
Lynch 48 15 36N57'58 82w55'21 5:31:41
Lyndale 25 33 37N58'09 84w12'19 5:36:49
Lyndon 56 68 38N15'24 85w36'06 5:42:24
Lynn 45 11 38N35'01 82w56'22 5:31:45
Lynncamp 63 16 36N57 84w06 5:36:24
Lynn City 89 1 37N22'18 87w15'03 5:49:00
Lynn Grove 18 1 36N35'21 88w26'17 5:53:45
Lynnview 56 69 38N10'42 85w42'35 5:42:50
Lynnville 42 1 36N33'37 88w34'09 5:54:17
Lyons 62 59 37N40'40 85w36'45 5:42:27
Lytten 32 16 38N06'16 83w13'16 5:32:53
Mac 109 51 37N24'00 85w30'38 5:42:03
Macedonia 24 1 37N03 87w29 5:49:56
Macedonia 55 16 37N27'31 83w57'57 5:35:52
Maceo 30 1 37N51'50 86w59'38 5:47:59
Mackville 115 51 37N44'12 85w04'03 5:40:16
Macon 50 1 37N19'51 86w01'11 5:44:05
Madisonville 54 4 37N19'41 87w29'56 5:50:00
Madrid 14 1 37N36'44 86w20'32 5:45:22
Magan 92 1 37N36'01 86w47'58 5:47:12
Magee Springs 20
1 36N55'21 88w56'15 5:55:45
Maggard 77 11 37N49'07 83w05'44 5:32:23
Maggie 111 1 36N52 87w50 5:51:20
Magnolia 62 51 37N26'38 85w44'37 5:42:58
Main Street 98 11 37N29 82w31 5:30:04
Majestic 98 11 37N32'02 82w06'00 5:28:24
Major 95 16 37N24'50 83w41'55 5:34:48
Malaga 119 16 37N42'42 83w25'39 5:33:43
Mallie 60 16 37N18 82w55 5:31:40
Malone 88 40 37N52'19 83w15'30 5:33:02
Maloneton 45 11 38N41'03 82w55'05 5:31:40
Maloney 65 16 37N34'57 83w40'29 5:34:42
Mammoth Cave 31 1 37N11'10 86w06'00 5:44:24
Manchester 26 16 37N09'13 83w45'43 5:35:03
Manco 98 11 37N17 82w28 5:29:52
Manda 92 1 37N20 86w47 5:47:08
Mangum 100 19 37N10'24 84w46'22 5:39:05
Manila 58 11 37N51 82w54 5:31:36
Manitou 54 1 37N22'16 87w34'47 5:50:19
Manning Crossing 14
1 37N59'45 86w28'52 5:45:55
Mannington 24 1 37N07'12 87w29'15 5:49:57
Mannsville 109 51 37N22'21 85w11'48 5:40:47
Manntown 104 1 36N52'42 85w09'39 5:40:39
Manor Creek 56 70 38N17 85w35 5:42:20
Manse 40 16 37N35'16 84w26'16 5:37:45
Manton 36 11 37N33 82w47 5:31:08
Manton 115 59 37N42'53 85w23'07 5:41:32
Manuel 97 46 37N21'02 83w18'17 5:33:13
Maple 109 51 37N27'51 85w30'08 5:42:01
Maple Grove 111 1 36N46'30 87w53'45 5:51:35
Maple Mount 30 1 37N42 87w26 5:49:44
Maples Corner 82
51 37N49'59 86w08'01 5:44:32
Maplesville 63 37 37N09'00 84w01'40 5:36:07
Marcellus 40 16 37N41'10 84w40'38 5:38:43
Marcum 26 16 37N06'38 83w33'35 5:34:14
Marcus 96 36 38N34'05 84w27'51 5:37:51
Mare Creek 36 11 37N35 82w39 5:30:36
Maretburg 102 36 37N21'19 84w23'14 5:37:33
Mariba 83 16 37N54'58 83w34'43 5:34:19
Marion 28 1 37N19'58 88w04'52 5:52:19
Mark 100 19 37N09'47 84w30'16 5:38:01
Marksbury 40 16 37N40'21 84w38'16 5:38:33
Marlow 27 1 36N46'38 85w05'33 5:40:22
Marlowe 67 16 37N07'52 82w49'51 5:31:19
Marne No 2 48 15 36N52 83w12 5:32:48
Marrowbone 29 1 36N49'40 85w30'24 5:42:02
Marrowbone 98 11 37N21'57 82w24'50 5:29:39
Marshall 79 1 36N56'45 88w14'05 5:52:56
Marshall 81 11 38N32'42 83w45'47 5:35:03
Marshallville 77
11 37N40'41 82w59'22 5:31:57
Marshes Siding 74
16 36N44'37 84w28'51 5:37:55
Martha 64 11 38N00'33 82w54'48 5:31:39
Martha Mills 35
16 38N25 83w47 5:35:08
Martin 36 11 37N34'22 82w45'10 5:31:01
Martinsburg 86 1 36N38'45 85w29'07 5:41:56
Martins Fork 48
15 36N42'58 83w19'20 5:33:17
Martinsville 114
1 36N55'28 86w12'53 5:44:52
Martwick 89 1 37N19'37 87w01'26 5:48:06
Mary 119 16 37N40'06 83w32'11 5:34:09
Mary Alice 48 15 36N47'03 83w19'48 5:33:19
Marydale 8 11 39N01'34 84w37'18 5:38:29
Marydell 63 16 37N06'33 83w54'32 5:35:38
Mary Helen (Coalgood P O) 48
15 36N48'46 83w15'18 5:33:01
Maryhill Estates 56
68 38N16'00 85w39'01 5:42:36
Mashfork 77 11 37N45'41 83w00'20 5:32:01
Mason 41 11 38N34'34 84w35'07 5:38:20
Mason 77 11 37N43'14 83w03'00 5:32:12
Masonic Home 56
69 38N13 85w45 5:43:00
Masonville 24 1 36N46'03 87w28'14 5:49:53
Masonville 30 1 37N40'30 87w02'05 5:48:08
Massac 73 1 37N01'00 88w43'50 5:54:55
Matanzas 92 1 37N27'02 87w03'31 5:48:14
Mathers Mill 62
51 37N32'25 85w46'09 5:43:05
Matlock 114 10 36N49'58 86w27'58 5:45:52
Matthew 88 16 37N51'22 83w09'31 5:32:38
Mattingly 14 1 37N45'46 86w36'07 5:46:24
Mattoon 28 1 37N24'12 88w01'23 5:52:06
Mattoxtown 34 28 38N07'38 84w27'01 5:37:48
Maud 115 51 37N49'17 85w17'48 5:41:11
Maulden 55 16 37N21'20 83w52'07 5:35:28
Maurice 59 71 39N00'46 84w32'01 5:38:08
Mavity 10 11 38N20'41 82w41'59 5:30:48
Mavo 84 44 37N52'21 84w55'34 5:39:42
Maxie 118 15 36N35 84w08 5:36:32
Maxine 62 51 37N27'54 85w47'44 5:43:11
Maxon 73 1 37N05'20 88w43'50 5:54:55
Maxon Crossing 73
1 37N04'59 88w45'04 5:55:00
Maxville 8 11 39N02 84w44 5:38:56
Maxwell 30 1 37N33'41 87w02'15 5:48:09
May 60 16 37N16'16 82w51'48 5:31:27
Mayfield 42 1 36N44'30 88w38'12 5:54:33
Mayflower 98 11 37N37 82w29 5:29:56
Mayhew 10 11 38N20 82w46 5:31:04
Mayking 67 16 37N08'00 82w45'58 5:31:04
Maynard 2 6 36N46'09 86w04'33 5:44:18
Mayo 84 16 37N52 84w56 5:39:44
Mayo Village 98
11 37N27'09 82w31'25 5:30:06
Mays Lick 81 11 38N31'03 83w50'31 5:35:22
Maysville 81 12 38N38'28 83w44'40 5:34:59
Maytown 88 16 37N50'56 83w28'19 5:33:53
Maywood 69 16 37N28'49 84w37'01 5:38:28
Mazie 64 11 38N01'37 82w58'21 5:31:53
McAfee 84 44 37N51'02 84w51'07 5:39:24
McAndrews 98 11 37N34'25 82w16'06 5:29:04
McBrayer 3 44 37N58'31 84w53'08 5:39:33
McCarr 98 11 37N36'39 82w10'12 5:28:41
McClure 80 11 37N45'53 82w29'14 5:29:57
McCombs 98 11 37N39'13 82w35'03 5:30:20
McCoy 14 1 37N37'07 86w22'54 5:45:32
McCreary 40 16 37N40'16 84w30'56 5:38:04
McCreight 26 16 37N01 83w49 5:35:16
McDaniels 14 1 37N36'24 86w25'30 5:45:42
McDavid 22 16 38N20 82w57 5:31:48
McDowell 36 11 37N27'21 82w44'11 5:30:57
McElroy Ford 2 1 36N44'02 86w24'36 5:45:38
McGaha 1 1 37N06 85w18 5:41:12
McGlone 22 16 38N17 83w05 5:32:20
McGowan 17 1 37N03'28 87w50'40 5:51:23
McHargue 63 15 37N00'19 84w01'03 5:36:04
McHenry 92 1 37N22'55 86w55'21 5:47:41
McKee 55 16 37N25'49 83w59'53 5:36:00
McKees Crossroads 120
16 38N07'15 84w46'34 5:39:06
McKinney 69 16 37N27'09 84w45'33 5:39:02
McKinneysburg 96
11 38N35'50 84w15'55 5:37:04
McNary 89 1 37N12'55 87w19'46 5:49:19
McQuady 14 1 37N42'30 86w31'08 5:46:05
McRoberts 67 16 37N12'27 82w40'19 5:30:41
McVeigh 98 11 37N32'18 82w15'22 5:29:01
McVille 8 11 38N58'39 84w49'27 5:39:18
McWhorter 63 37 37N14'03 84w00'00 5:36:00

Meador 2 6 36N53'28 86w10'34 5:44:42
Meadow Branch 119 16 37N45 83w33 5:34:12
Meadowbrook 25 33 38N00'08 84w12'16 5:36:49
Meadow Creek 118 15 36N50 84w07 5:36:28
Meadow Lawn 56 68 38N03'35 85w53'51 5:43:35
Meadowthorpe 34 28 38N04'12 84w31'24 5:38:06
Meadow Vale 56 70 38N17 85w35 5:42:20
Meadowview 76 31 37N45 84w18 5:37:12
Meadowview Estates 56 68 38N13'20 85w38'08 5:42:33
Meads 10 11 38N24'45 82w42'33 5:30:50
Meally 58 11 37N47'48 82w44'24 5:30:58
Means 83 16 37N56'57 83w46'21 5:35:05
Medora 56 68 38N03'11 85w52'12 5:43:29
Meece 100 19 37N01'42 84w30'32 5:38:02
Meeting Creek 47 51 37N35 86w03 5:44:12
Melber 73 1 36N56'47 88w43'31 5:54:54
Melbourne 19 11 39N01'47 84w21'59 5:37:28
Meldrum 7 15 36N40'01 83w41'39 5:34:47
Mell 44 6 37N06'44 85w31'43 5:42:07
Melrose 45 11 38N32'58 82w43'43 5:30:55
Melrose 47 1 37N29'21 85w59'32 5:43:58
Melvin 36 11 37N21'01 82w41'39 5:30:47
Memphis Junction 114 10 36N56'32 86w29'21 5:45:57
Mendola Village 58 11 37N47 82w48 5:31:12
Mentor 19 11 38N53'14 84w14'47 5:36:59
Menzie 96 11 38N44'23 84w20'24 5:37:22
Mercer 89 1 37N15'27 87w09'04 5:48:36
Meredith 43 1 37N24'09 86w14'13 5:44:57
Meridian 96 11 38N46'36 84w21'14 5:37:25
Merrifield 56 70 38N16'43 85w38'25 5:42:34
Merrimac 109 51 37N24'45 85w07'43 5:40:31
Merrittstown 24 1 36N50'47 87w34'17 5:50:17
Merry Oaks 5 1 37N01'20 86w06'22 5:44:25
Mershons 63 16 37N16'59 84w07'33 5:36:30
Meshack 86 1 36N43'57 85w32'56 5:42:12
Meta 98 11 37N34'13 82w26'15 5:29:45
Mexico 28 1 37N13'30 88w05'48 5:52:23
Midas 36 11 37N30'44 82w50'06 5:31:20
Middleburg 23 51 37N21'28 84w49'16 5:39:17
Middle Creek 62 51 37N34 85w44 5:42:56
Middlefork 55 16 37N26 84w00 5:36:00
Middlesboro 7 15 36N36'30 83w43'00 5:34:52
Middlesborough 7 15 36N36'30 83w43'00 5:34:52
Middleton 107 1 36N45'03 86w44'05 5:46:56
Middletown 56 68 38N14'43 85w32'20 5:42:09
Middletown 76 43 37N35'23 84w18'00 5:37:12
Middletown 104 1 37N01'14 85w04'34 5:40:18
Middletown Heights 106 54 38N12'57 85w14'32 5:40:58
Midland 6 16 38N07'59 83w34'40 5:34:19
Midland 89 1 37N18'21 87w13'50 5:48:55
Midway 17 1 37N08'16 87w46'52 5:51:07
Midway 18 1 36N33'05 88w19'26 5:53:18
Midway 28 1 37N18'20 88w10'33 5:52:42
Midway 82 51 37N57'07 86w14'19 5:44:57
Midway 120 48 38N09'03 84w41'02 5:38:44
Mikegrady 98 11 37N20'22 82w18'45 5:29:15
Milburn 20 1 36N47'55 88w53'59 5:55:36
Mildred 55 16 37N21'14 83w55'39 5:35:43
Milford 12 11 38N34'54 84w09'24 5:36:38
Millard 98 11 37N24'28 82w26'18 5:29:45
Mill Creek 81 11 38N31 83w50 5:35:20
Milledgeville 69 16 37N31'14 84w48'50 5:39:15
Miller 38 1 36N31'06 89w20'19 5:57:21
Miller Landing 70 1 37N11'02 88w22'45 5:53:31
Millersburg 9 30 38N18'07 84w08'51 5:36:35
Millers Creek 33 16 37N40'18 83w53'49 5:35:35
Millerstown 43 1 37N26'43 86w03'03 5:44:12
Million 76 31 37N46'47 84w23'15 5:37:33
Mill Pond 26 16 37N13'45 83w44'15 5:34:57
Millport 89 1 37N21'39 87w17'15 5:49:09
Mills 61 15 36N55 83w39 5:34:36
Millseat 10 11 38N29'26 82w40'15 5:30:41
Mill Springs 116 1 36N55'55 84w46'45 5:39:07
Millstone 67 16 37N10'02 82w45'06 5:31:00
Milltown 1 1 37N07'20 85w24'27 5:41:38
Milltown 91 16 38N20'00 83w50'46 5:35:23
Millville 120 16 38N08'13 84w49'19 5:39:17
Millwood 43 1 37N27'01 86w23'26 5:45:34
Milner 120 45 38N02'00 84w48'26 5:39:14
Milo 80 11 37N54'59 82w34'37 5:30:18
Milton 112 58 38N43'25 85w22'10 5:41:29
Mima 88 16 37N55'14 83w02'12 5:32:09
Mina 25 33 37N51'45 84w04'02 5:36:16
Minefork 77 11 37N51'48 83w00'43 5:32:03
Minerva 81 11 38N42'19 83w55'09 5:35:41
Miniard 97 46 37N05 83w06 5:32:24
Mining City 16 1 37N13'38 86w46'44 5:47:07
Minnie (Gibson Station) 36 11 37N28'20 82w45'15 5:31:01
Minor 103 16 38N07'56 83w15'55 5:33:04
Minor Lane Heights 56 68 38N07'25 85w43'11 5:42:53
Minorsville 105 16 38N19'46 84w42'13 5:38:49
Mintonville 23 51 37N10'38 84w48'39 5:39:15
Miracle 7 15 36N45'38 83w35'03 5:34:20
Miracle 69 16 37N28'00 84w40'57 5:38:44
Mistletoe 95 16 37N18'45 83w35'30 5:34:22
Mitchell Hill 54 1 37N21'11 87w32'15 5:50:09
Mitchell Landing 70 1 37N11'03 88w17'19 5:53:09
Mitchellsburg 11 16 37N36'02 84w56'59 5:39:48
Mize 88 16 37N51'34 83w22'25 5:33:30
Moberly 76 31 37N44'30 84w10'58 5:36:44
Mockingbird Valley 56 69 38N16'21 85w40'56 5:42:44
Moct 13 16 37N39'41 83w20'45 5:33:23
Modoc 29 1 36N44'09 85w18'10 5:41:13
Molus 48 15 36N48'47 83w29'26 5:33:58
Monford 16 1 37N16'02 86w38'29 5:46:34
Monica 65 16 37N35'03 83w36'06 5:34:24
Monitor 112 51 38N39'17 85w15'59 5:41:04
Monkeys Eyebrow 4 1 37N11'12 88w59'16 5:55:57
Monroe 50 1 37N13'56 85w41'52 5:42:47
Montclair 34 28 38N01'21 84w29'52 5:37:59
Montclair 106 54 38N13'12 85w19'44 5:41:19
Monterey 9 30 38N10'21 84w18'32 5:37:14
Monterey 94 18 38N25'19 84w52'21 5:39:29
Montgomery 111 1 36N52'41 87w44'26 5:50:58
Montgomerys Mill 44 6 37N16 85w30 5:42:00
Monticello 34 28 37N59'32 84w33'01 5:38:12
Monticello 116 1 36N49'47 84w50'57 5:39:24
Montpelier 1 1 37N01'08 85w11'08 5:40:45
Montrose 34 28 38N04'20 84w24'19 5:37:37
Montrose Park 37 20 38N12 84w52 5:39:28
Mook 14 1 37N40'24 86w21'08 5:45:25
Mooleyville 14 1 38N01'16 86w27'50 5:45:51
Moon 88 16 37N58'24 83w02'56 5:32:12
Moore 23 51 37N20'06 84w53'47 5:39:35
Moorefield 91 16 38N16'23 83w55'52 5:35:43
Moore Hill 61 15 36N56'08 84w04'53 5:36:20
Moores Creek 55 16 37N16'59 83w59'42 5:35:59
Moores Ferry 6 16 38N07 83w37 5:34:28
Moores Mill 86 1 36N42 85w42 5:42:48
Mooresville 115 51 37N47'56 85w15'55 5:41:04
Moorland 56 70 38N16'20 85w35'01 5:42:20
Moorman 89 1 37N23'00 87w08'39 5:48:35
Moranburg 81 11 38N40'16 83w48'47 5:35:15
Morcoal 98 11 37N34 82w15 5:29:00
Moree 80 11 37N43'08 82w30'16 5:30:01
Morehead 89 1 37N16'16 87w10'35 5:48:42
Morehead 103 49 38N11'02 83w25'58 5:33:44
Moreland 69 16 37N30'20 84w48'48 5:39:15
Morgan 96 11 38N36'10 84w23'56 5:37:36
Morganfield 113 1 37N41'00 87w55'00 5:51:40
Morgantown 16 1 37N13'32 86w41'01 5:46:44
Morning Glory 91 21 38N24'02 84w08'52 5:36:35
Morning View 59 11 38N49'55 84w27'23 5:37:50
Morrill 55 16 37N31'09 84w11'51 5:36:47
Morris Fork 13 16 37N22'57 83w30'58 5:34:04
Mortimer Station 71 1 36N40 86w51 5:47:24
Mortons Gap 54 1 37N14'12 87w28'31 5:49:54
Mortonsville 120 16 37N58'19 84w45'23 5:39:02
Moscow 38 1 36N36'25 89w02'10 5:56:09
Moseleyville 30 1 37N39'47 87w11'36 5:48:46
Mosley Bend 66 16 37N15 83w24 5:33:36
Mossy Bottom 98 11 37N31'48 82w34'46 5:30:19
Motley 114 10 36N54'27 86w17'17 5:45:09
Mount Aerial 2 1 36N45'12 86w23'34 5:45:34
Mountain Ash 118 15 36N39'27 84w07'44 5:36:31
Mountain Top 22 16 38N17'24 83w07'32 5:32:30
Mountain Valley 13 16 37N39'41 83w16'08 5:33:05
Mount Auburn 96 11 38N47'22 84w16'22 5:37:05
Mount Beulah 50 1 37N17'54 85w56'22 5:43:45
Mount Carmel 35 16 38N29'04 83w38'12 5:34:33
Mount Carmel 54 1 37N10'03 87w22'06 5:49:28
Mount Eden 108 51 38N03'22 85w09'04 5:40:36
Mount Gilead 44 6 37N10'23 85w23'03 5:41:32
Mount Gilead 81 16 38N30'39 83w42'11 5:34:49
Mount Gilead 86 1 36N42 85w42 5:42:48
Mount Herman 86 1 36N47 85w45 5:43:00
Mount Lebanon 57 29 37N49'36 84w30'16 5:38:01
Mount Olive 23 51 37N16'46 84w45'57 5:39:04
Mount Olive 65 16 37N37'38 83w43'51 5:34:55
Mount Olivet 101 11 38N31'53 84w02'13 5:36:09
Mount Pisgah 116 1 36N39'32 84w48'53 5:39:16
Mount Pleasant 92 1 37N24'40 86w45'04 5:47:00
Mount Pleasant 112 51 38N36'47 85w23'02 5:41:32
Mount Salem 69 16 37N25'02 84w47'58 5:39:12
Mount Savage 22 16 38N15'55 82w53'29 5:31:34
Mount Sherman 62 51 37N27'09 85w40'06 5:42:40
Mount Sterling 87 22 38N03'23 83w56'36 5:35:46
Mount Tabor 62 51 37N31 85w42 5:42:48
Mount Tabor 110 1 36N57'31 87w13'09 5:48:53
Mount Union 2 1 36N39 86w16 5:45:04
Mount Vernon 34 28 38N01'32 84w29'43 5:37:59
Mount Vernon 102 36 37N21'10 84w20'26 5:37:22
Mount Victor 114 10 36N58'45 86w23'42 5:45:35
Mount Victory 100 19 37N01'45 84w23'11 5:37:33
Mount Washington 15 51 38N03'00 85w32'45 5:42:11
Mount Zion 2 6 36N40'59 86w03'26 5:44:14
Mount Zion 25 33 38N01'51 84w05'46 5:36:23
Mount Zion 41 11 38N44'27 84w39'35 5:38:38
Mount Zion 100 19 37N11'03 84w40'35 5:38:42
Mousie 60 16 37N25'06 82w52'42 5:31:31
Moutardier 43 1 37N20'06 86w14'52 5:44:59
Mouthcard 98 11 37N23'03 82w15'19 5:29:01
Moxley 94 16 38N33'45 85w00'33 5:40:02
Moxley Landing 70 1 37N11'10 88w18'21 5:53:13
Mozelle 66 16 37N00'09 83w23'53 5:33:36
Mud Camp 29 1 36N48 85w22 5:41:28
Mud Creek 36 11 37N29 82w39 5:30:36
Muddy Ford 105 16 38N18'33 84w30'09 5:38:01
Mud Lick 86 1 36N45'10 85w46'50 5:43:07
Muir 34 28 38N06'21 84w22'38 5:37:31
Mulberry 106 54 38N15'54 85w08'03 5:40:32
Muldraugh 82 64 37N56'13 85w59'30 5:43:58
Mulfordtown 113 1 37N32'37 88w04'21 5:52:17
Mullikin Junction 70 1 37N13'33 88w19'31 5:53:18
Mullins 102 36 37N20'42 84w13'38 5:36:55
Mullins Addition 98 11 37N29 82w31 5:30:04
Mummie 55 16 37N23'37 83w52'16 5:35:29
Mundys Landing 120 45 37N51'15 84w46'15 5:39:05
Munfordville 50 1 37N16'20 85w53'28 5:43:34
Munk 39 11 38N46'32 84w41'48 5:38:47
Murl 116 1 36N48'48 84w57'29 5:39:50
Murphy Ford 54 1 37N08'50 87w39'00 5:50:36
Murphyfork 88 16 37N49'47 83w25'09 5:33:41
Murphysville 81 11 38N34'05 83w51'57 5:35:28
Murray 18 1 36N36'37 88w18'53 5:53:16
Muses Mills 35 16 38N21'00 83w31'38 5:34:07
Music 22 16 38N18'29 82w49'27 5:31:18
Myers 91 16 38N21'03 83w57'12 5:35:49
Myra 98 11 37N17'23 82w36'00 5:30:24
Mystic 14 1 37N53'49 86w26'34 5:45:46
Nada Lombard PO 99 16 37N48'54 83w43'10 5:34:53
Nampa 98 11 37N37 82w10 5:28:40
Nancy 100 19 37N04'18 84w44'53 5:39:00
Naomi 100 19 37N00'32 84w47'31 5:39:10
Napfor 97 46 37N18'48 83w18'44 5:33:15
Napier 66 16 36N59'04 83w17'08 5:33:09
Naples 45 11 38N26'09 82w46'11 5:31:05
Napoleon 39 12 38N45'37 84w47'20 5:39:09
Narrows 92 1 37N34'02 86w43'48 5:46:55
Narvel 27 1 36N47'05 85w02'44 5:40:11
Nash 31 1 37N19'13 86w25'51 5:45:43
Nashtown 68 11 38N30'33 83w31'58 5:34:08
Nathanton 55 16 37N21 83w54 5:35:36
Natlee 94 16 38N26'49 84w39'43 5:38:39
Natural Bridge 99 16 37N48 83w42 5:34:48
Nazareth 90 51 37N50'53 85w28'22 5:41:53
Neafus 16 1 37N23'42 86w36'43 5:46:27
Neatsville 1 1 37N11'50 85w07'32 5:40:30
Neave 12 11 38N38'51 84w12'08 5:36:49
Nebo 54 1 37N23'01 87w38'34 5:50:34
Nebo 89 1 37N14'30 87w11'39 5:48:47
Ned 13 16 37N24'30 83w16'15 5:33:05
Needmore 4 1 37N10'54 88w56'50 5:55:47
Needmore 11 25 37N39'06 84w52'40 5:39:31
Needmore 16 7 37N06'39 86w39'04 5:46:36
Needmore 17 1 37N13'18 87w50'43 5:51:23
Needmore 81 11 38N31 83w50 5:35:20
Needmore 94 11 38N34'28 84w44'03 5:38:56
Needmore 106 51 38N09 85w19 5:41:16
Nell 1 1 37N00'34 85w29'00 5:41:56
Nelse 98 11 37N24'14 82w26'25 5:29:46
Nelson 89 1 37N19'47 87w03'03 5:48:12
Nelsonville 90 51 37N43'51 85w38'23 5:42:34
Neon 67 16 37N11'29 82w42'49 5:30:51
Neon Junction 67 16 37N10'46 82w42'50 5:30:51
Neosheo 107 1 36N42'43 86w40'43 5:46:43
Nepton 35 16 38N26'07 83w50'03 5:35:20
Nerinx 78 59 37N39'51 85w23'58 5:41:36
Nero 58 11 37N44'54 82w44'37 5:30:58
Netty 77 11 37N44'49 83w14'19 5:32:57
Neubert 48 15 36N51 83w18 5:33:12
Nevada 84 16 37N41'47 84w54'35 5:39:38
Nevelsville 74 16 36N50'28 83w33'34 5:38:14
Nevin 3 44 37N56'46 84w53'00 5:39:32
Nevisdale 118 15 36N41'12 84w02'46 5:36:11
New 94 16 38N25'40 84w48'38 5:39:15
New Allen 36 11 37N36'53 82w43'18 5:30:53
Newbern 70 1 37N05'09 88w19'02 5:53:16
Newburg 56 68 38N09'36 85w39'35 5:42:38
Newby 76 31 37N45'47 84w24'54 5:37:40
New Camp 98 11 37N39'37 82w17'09 5:29:09
New Castle 52 57 38N26'00 85w10'11 5:40:41
New Columbus 94 16 38N27'27 84w38'43 5:38:35
Newcombe 32 16 38N05'04 83w03'15 5:32:13
New Concord 18 1 36N32'54 88w09'17 5:52:37
New Cypress 53 1 36N43'50 88w55'36 5:55:42
New Cypress 89 1 37N15'07 87w14'24 5:48:58
Newfound 26 16 37N16 83w39 5:34:36
Newfoundland 32 16 38N07'53 83w05'58 5:32:24
Newgarden 47 51 37N53 85w59 5:43:56
New Haven 90 59 37N39'28 85w35'28 5:42:22
New Hope 90 51 37N37'55 85w30'30 5:42:02
New Liberty 85 1 37N00'27 85w41'35 5:42:46
New Liberty 94 16 38N36'57 84w54'24 5:39:38
Newman 30 1 37N50'13 87w17'43 5:49:11
New Market 78 51 37N30'06 85w18'39 5:41:15
Newport 19 71 39N05'29 84w29'45 5:37:59
New Providence 18 1 36N31'44 88w14'13 5:52:57
New Roe 2 1 36N39'57 86w22'57 5:45:32
New Salem 28 1 37N17'00 88w11'39 5:52:47
New Salem 69 16 37N24'33 84w46'03 5:39:04
Newstead 24 1 36N47'57 87w37'49 5:50:31
New Stithton 47 51 37N53 85w59 5:43:56
Newt 44 6 37N10'45 85w33'53 5:42:16
Newtown 105 16 38N13'13 84w28'12 5:37:53
New York 4 1 36N59'20 88w57'09 5:55:49
New Zion 55 16 37N28'15 83w53'45 5:35:35
New Zion 105 28 38N10'45 84w29'19 5:37:57
Niagara 51 1 37N43'15 87w29'11 5:49:57
Nicholasville 57 29 37N52'50 84w34'23 5:38:18
Nichols 15 64 38N00 85w57 5:43:48
Nichols 53 1 36N41'37 88w52'11 5:55:29
Nicholson 59 11 38N54'20 84w32'39 5:38:11
Nick 31 1 37N07'47 86w18'40 5:45:15
Nickell 88 16 37N50'01 83w19'34 5:33:18
Nickolson 111 1 36N58 87w42 5:50:48

Nigh 98 11 37N25'50 82W16'12 5:29:05
Nihizertown 34 28 37N59'18 84W21'48 5:37:27
Nina 57 16 37N39'50 84W27'59 5:37:52
Nineteen 92 1 37N19'39 86W56'48 5:47:47
Ninevah 108 44 38N04'57 84W52'44 5:39:31
Nippa 58 11 37N51'57 82W47'15 5:31:09
Noble 13 16 37N27'03 83W11'20 5:32:45
Nobob 5 1 36N51'55 85W46'27 5:43:06
No Creek 92 1 37N28'50 86W57'30 5:47:50
Noctor 13 16 37N33'34 83W20'14 5:33:21
Node 85 1 37N07'45 85W38'38 5:42:35
Noetown 7 15 36N36'59 83W45'19 5:35:01
Noland 33 27 37N38'52 84W03'17 5:36:13
Nolansburg (Splint P O) 48 15 36N55'32 83W09'50 5:32:39
Nolin 47 51 37N33'40 85W54'10 5:43:37
Nolin Lake Estates 43 1 37N21'33 86W09'52 5:44:39
Nonesuch 120 45 37N54'22 84W45'20 5:39:01
Nonnell 89 1 37N14'14 87W03'34 5:48:14
Nora 27 1 36N45'38 85W02'34 5:40:10
Norbourne Estates 56 68 38N14'47 85W38'52 5:42:35
Norfleet 100 19 37N02'10 84W47'47 5:39:11
Noris 64 11 37N59'50 82W43'09 5:30:53
Normal 10 11 38N26'37 82W36'45 5:30:27
Normal Heights 37 20 38N12 84W52 5:39:28
Normandy 108 51 38N05'53 85W20'34 5:41:22
North 34 28 38N05 84W29 5:37:56
North Branch 22 11 38N19'49 82W48'22 5:31:13
North Corbin 63 16 36N57'38 84W05'36 5:36:22
Northcutt 41 11 38N43'38 84W33'24 5:38:14
Northern 36 11 37N30'28 82W48'56 5:31:16
North Fayette 34 28 38N08 84W28 5:37:52
Northfield 56 68 38N17'13 85W38'28 5:42:34
Northfield 100 19 37N00'22 84W30'29 5:38:02
North Hazard 97 46 37N15 83W11 5:32:44
North Irvine 33 27 37N42'51 83W58'47 5:35:55
Northland 34 28 38N03'56 84W28'46 5:37:55
North Lebanon 78 66 37N36 85W13 5:40:52
North Lyon 72 1 37N06 88W08 5:52:32
North Middletown 9 18 38N08'42 84W06'41 5:36:27
North Oldham 93 52 38N27 85W30 5:42:00
North Pleasureville 52 51 38N21'35 85W06'26 5:40:26
Northtown 50 6 37N12'51 86W00'03 5:44:00
Norton Branch 22 16 38N20 82W46 5:31:04
Nortonville 54 1 37N11'27 87W27'10 5:49:49
Norwood 56 70 38N17 85W35 5:42:20
Norwood 100 19 37N09'06 84W37'55 5:38:32
Nuckols 75 1 37N31'24 87W06'44 5:48:27
Nugent Crossroads 120 48 38N07'24 84W41'55 5:38:48
Nugym 7 15 36N48 83W39 5:34:36
Number One 116 16 36N48'39 84W52'06 5:39:28
Nunn 28 1 37N25'39 87W58'12 5:51:53
Oakdale 13 16 37N33'21 83W31'02 5:34:04
Oakdale 56 69 38N11'47 85W46'37 5:43:06
Oakdale 73 1 37N02'09 88W34'01 5:54:16
Oak Forest 2 6 36N42'57 86W05'54 5:44:24
Oak Grove (Thompsonville Sta 24 1 36N39'54 87W26'34 5:49:46
Oak Grove 92 1 37N20'39 86W45'17 5:47:01
Oak Hill 54 1 37N12'38 87W27'24 5:49:50
Oak Hill 100 19 37N03'29 84W38'47 5:38:35
Oakla 6 16 38N14'53 83W43'30 5:34:54
Oakland 114 1 37N02'31 86W14'54 5:45:00
Oakland Mills 91 38 38N19 84W02 5:36:08
Oak Level 79 1 36N52'01 88W27'56 5:53:52
Oakley 63 16 37N14'18 84W05'52 5:36:23
Oak Ridge 30 1 37N44'24 87W02'24 5:48:10
Oak Ridge 31 1 37N17'41 86W14'20 5:44:57
Oak Ridge 59 71 38N58'08 84W30'14 5:38:01
Oaks 7 15 36N43'21 83W33'23 5:34:14
Oaks 73 1 36N58'06 88W32'39 5:54:11
Oaks 92 1 37N38 86W43 5:46:52
Oakton 53 1 36N39'48 89W04'02 5:56:16
Oakville 71 1 36N44'56 86W52'32 5:47:30
O'Bannon 56 70 38N17'19 85W30'49 5:42:03
Odds 58 11 37N45'20 82W41'35 5:30:46
Oddville 49 21 38N27'20 84W14'20 5:36:57
Offutt 58 11 37N51 82W44 5:30:56
Ogle 26 16 37N01'48 83W42'42 5:34:51
Oil Center 100 19 37N06'21 84W42'25 5:38:50
Oil City 5 6 37N02'00 85W58'59 5:43:56
Oil Springs 58 11 37N48'36 82W56'33 5:31:46
Oilton 116 1 36N46'27 84W52'44 5:39:31
Oil Valley 116 1 36N46'28 84W47'54 5:39:12
O K 100 19 37N17 84W40 5:38:40
Oklahoma 30 1 37N39'42 86W52'38 5:47:31
Okolona 56 68 38N08'28 85W41'16 5:42:45
Olaton 92 1 37N31'33 86W41'15 5:46:45
Olcott 7 15 36N41'09 83W50'01 5:35:20
Old Allen 36 11 37N37 82W43 5:30:52
Old Christianburg 106 51 38N16'53 85W05'06 5:40:20
Old Cypress 53 1 36N43'24 88W53'59 5:55:36
Old Flat Lick 61 15 36N50'18 83W46'16 5:35:05
Oldham 93 52 38N29'51 85W25'16 5:41:41
Oldham Acres 93 52 38N23'52 85W37'13 5:42:29
Old Landing 65 16 37N38'11 83W48'25 5:35:14
Old Olga 104 1 36N55'32 85W10'07 5:40:40
Old Orchard 65 16 37N29 83W54 5:35:36
Old Pine Grove 25 16 38N01'35 84W16'19 5:37:05
Old Stephensburg 47 51 37N36'52 86W01'13 5:44:05
Oldtown 45 11 38N26'25 82W53'54 5:31:36
Old Volney 71 1 36N46'27 87W00'45 5:48:03
Olga 104 1 36N57'03 85W09'37 5:40:38
Olin 55 16 37N21'07 83W57'59 5:35:52
Olive 79 1 36N48'03 88W15'40 5:53:03
Olive Branch 35 16 38N19'21 83W49'20 5:35:17
Olive Branch 106 54 38N07'32 85W15'54 5:41:04
Olive Hill 22 34 38N18'00 83W10'27 5:32:42
Oliver 45 11 38N37 82W52 5:31:28
Oliver Station 45 11 38N37'29 82W51'45 5:31:27
Ollie 31 1 37N15'07 86W10'49 5:44:43
Olmstead 71 1 36N45'08 87W00'54 5:48:04
Olney 54 1 37N13'29 87W46'48 5:51:07
Olympia 6 16 38N05'53 83W41'45 5:34:47
Olympia Springs 6 16 38N03'43 83W40'23 5:34:42
Omaha 61 16 37N16'30 82W50'31 5:31:22
Omega 100 19 36N57'07 84W30'31 5:38:02
Oneida 26 16 37N16'10 83W38'57 5:34:36
Oneonta 19 11 38N59 84W18 5:37:12
Ono 104 1 36N59'19 84W58'00 5:39:52
Onton 117 1 37N33'18 87W26'13 5:49:45
Oolite 82 51 38N04'04 86W16'48 5:45:07
Open Gates 34 28 38N00'18 84W32'17 5:38:09
Ophir 88 16 37N54'26 83W00'52 5:32:03
Oppy 80 11 37N50 82W24 5:29:36
Orangeburg 81 11 38N34'03 83W41'20 5:34:45
Ordinary 32 16 38N09'17 83W11'41 5:32:47
Oregon 84 16 37N54'44 84W49'25 5:39:18
Orell 56 68 38N04'18 85W53'05 5:43:32
Orinoco 98 11 37N37 82W16 5:29:04
Oriole 54 1 37N17'52 87W34'13 5:50:17
Orkney 36 11 37N25'48 82W44'07 5:30:56
Orlando 102 16 37N22'22 84W16'05 5:37:04
Orr 64 11 38N08'08 82W53'31 5:31:34
Ortiz 117 1 37N33'23 87W36'33 5:50:26
Orville 52 51 38N23'54 84W54'56 5:39:40
Osborn 36 11 37N28'36 82W36'46 5:30:27
Oscaloosa 67 16 37N05'49 82W53'19 5:31:33
Oscar 4 1 37N08'11 89W01'37 5:56:06
Otas 118 15 36N57 84W06 5:36:24
Ote 44 6 37N16 85W30 5:42:00
Otia 86 1 36N41'16 85W34'09 5:42:17
Ottawa 102 16 37N21'42 84W27'22 5:37:49
Ottenheim 69 16 37N25'23 84W35'45 5:38:23
Otter Pond 17 1 37N01'40 87W49'23 5:51:18
Ottusville 37 20 38N19'22 84W53'44 5:39:35
Ova 77 11 37N43'31 83W10'18 5:32:41
Oven Fork 67 16 37N03'33 82W48'31 5:31:14
Overda 64 11 38N07'11 82W48'01 5:31:12
Overlook 72 1 37N05 88W05 5:52:20
Ovil 24 1 36N56'49 87W17'18 5:49:09
Owensboro 30 5 37N46'27 87W06'48 5:48:27
Owensby 104 1 36N59 85W04 5:40:16
Owenton 94 41 38N32'11 84W50'31 5:39:22
Owingsville 6 16 38N08'41 83W45'51 5:35:03
Owsley 98 11 37N30'05 82W35'19 5:30:21
Oxford 105 16 38N16'12 84W29'53 5:38:00
Oz 74 16 36N42'23 84W34'03 5:38:16
Ozark 1 1 37N04'45 85W13'53 5:40:56
Packard 118 15 36N40'03 84W03'21 5:36:13
Pactolus 22 16 38N21'55 82W56'06 5:31:44
Paducah 73 9 37N05'00 88W36'00 5:54:24
Paint Cliff 74 16 36N42 84W37 5:38:28
Paint Creek 88 16 37N56 83W05 5:32:20
Paint Lick 40 16 37N37'00 84W24'34 5:37:38
Paintsville 58 11 37N48'52 82W48'26 5:31:14
Palisades 72 1 37N01'18 88W01'38 5:52:07
Palma 79 1 36N57'45 88W22'42 5:53:31
Palmer 33 27 37N48'48 84W03'59 5:36:16
Panama 88 40 37N50'58 83W18'05 5:33:12
Panarama City 18 1 36N36 88W19 5:53:16
Panco 26 16 37N14'14 83W32'01 5:34:08
Panhandle 13 16 37N33'24 83W23'00 5:33:32
Panola 76 16 37N39'39 84W06'55 5:36:28
Pansy (Gulston P O) 48 15 36N46'30 83W19'44 5:33:19
Panther 30 1 37N38'24 87W13'30 5:48:54
Paradise 89 1 37N16'05 86W59'01 5:47:56
Paradise Hills 72 1 37N00'46 88W02'07 5:52:08
Paragon 103 16 38N02'53 83W23'58 5:33:36
Paris 9 30 38N12'35 84W15'11 5:37:01
Park 5 6 37N08'25 85W46'29 5:43:06
Park City 5 6 37N05'38 86W02'47 5:44:11
Parkers Lake 74 16 36N51 84W29 5:37:56
Park Hills 59 71 39N04'17 84W31'56 5:38:08
Parkland 56 69 38N14'32 85W48'57 5:43:16
Parkside 56 68 38N14'47 85W38'13 5:42:33
Parksville 11 16 37N35'52 84W53'29 5:39:34
Parkway Village 56 69 38N12'45 85W44'25 5:42:58
Parkwood 56 69 38N09'20 85W48'05 5:43:12
Parmleysville 116 1 36N41'03 84W45'14 5:39:01
Parnell 116 1 36N52'04 84W56'43 5:39:47
Parrot 55 16 37N19 84W03 5:36:12
Partridge 67 16 37N00'23 82W53'53 5:31:36
Parvin 33 27 37N42 83W58 5:35:52
Pascal 50 1 37N13'01 85W43'49 5:42:55
Patesville 46 1 37N46'55 86W43'08 5:46:53
Pathfork 48 15 36N45'21 83W27'53 5:33:52
Patrick 64 11 37N55'26 82W38'37 5:30:34
Patsey 33 16 37N42'42 83W47'52 5:35:11
Pauley 98 11 37N29'41 82W32'07 5:30:08
Paw Paw 98 11 37N26'15 82W06'39 5:28:27
Paxton 13 16 37N40'35 83W24'31 5:33:38
Payne 42 1 36N39'49 88W39'03 5:54:36
Payne Gap 67 16 37N09'19 82W39'34 5:30:38
Paynes 105 28 38N05 84W29 5:37:56
Paynes Depot 105 48 38N08'31 84W37'25 5:38:30
Payneville 82 51 37N59'22 86W18'47 5:45:15
Payton 88 16 37N48'08 83W17'57 5:33:12
Peabody 26 16 37N08'20 83W35'27 5:34:22
Peach Grove 96 11 38N49'51 84W17'27 5:37:10
Peach Orchard 64 11 37N56'31 82W36'55 5:30:28
Peaks Mill 37 16 38N17'54 84W48'45 5:39:15
Pea Ridge 105 16 38N16 84W41 5:38:44
Pea Ridge 110 1 36N48 87W09 5:48:36
Pearl 118 15 36N37'53 83W56'48 5:35:47
Pearman 43 1 37N22'28 86W06'31 5:44:26
Peasticks 6 16 38N09'22 83W41'56 5:34:48
Pebble 6 16 38N16'08 83W45'24 5:35:02
Pebworth 95 16 37N30'15 83W43'52 5:34:55
Peck Ford 78 66 37N29'53 85W13'26 5:40:54
Pecksridge 35 16 38N25 83W47 5:35:08
Peden Mill 107 1 36N40'52 86W31'32 5:46:06
Peedee 24 1 36N45'31 87W39'56 5:50:40
Peeled Oak 51 16 38N03'40 83W48'07 5:35:12
Pee Vee 54 1 37N18'25 87W32'26 5:50:10
Pekin 88 16 37N52'46 83W23'23 5:33:34
Pellville 46 1 37N45'08 86W48'49 5:47:15
Pellyton 1 1 37N12'42 85W05'03 5:40:20
Pembroke 24 1 36N46'33 87W21'20 5:49:25
Pence 68 11 38N41'47 83W31'58 5:34:08
Pence 119 16 37N38'02 83W28'27 5:33:54
Penchem 110 1 36N43 87W16 5:49:04
Pendleton 52 51 38N27'44 85W18'13 5:41:13
Penick 78 51 37N34'06 85W09'01 5:40:36
Penile 56 68 38N06'25 85W48'12 5:43:13
Penny 18 1 36N38'49 88W21'38 5:53:27
Penny 98 11 37N21'33 82W33'42 5:30:15
Pennyrile Mall 24 1 36N51 87W30 5:50:00
Penrod 89 1 37N06'51 86W59'57 5:48:00
Peonia 43 1 37N24'56 86W13'09 5:44:53
Peoples 55 16 37N17'22 84W03'12 5:36:13
Perkins 118 15 36N47'02 84W03'39 5:36:15
Permon 61 15 36N48'39 83W58'52 5:35:55
Perry Park 94 16 38N32'53 84W59'59 5:40:00
Perrytown 2 6 36N45 86W11 5:44:44
Perryville 11 42 37N39'01 84W57'06 5:39:48
Perryville 47 51 37N43'46 86W02'55 5:44:12
Perryville 50 1 37N17'06 85W53'54 5:43:36
Persimmon 86 1 36N48'11 85W38'33 5:42:34
Persimmon Grove 19 11 38N53'59 84W20'37 5:37:22
Persimon 86 1 36N42 85W42 5:42:48
Peter Creek 5 1 36N50'42 85W58'45 5:43:55
Petersburg 8 11 39N04'09 84W52'06 5:39:28
Petersburg 56 68 38N10'43 85W39'34 5:42:38
Petersville 68 11 38N26'39 83W29'26 5:33:58
Peth 43 1 37N24'25 86W26'12 5:45:45
Petra 12 11 38N37'27 84W08'02 5:36:32
Petrie 46 1 37N55'35 86W48'15 5:47:13
Petroleum 2 1 36N41'43 86W14'54 5:45:00
Petros 114 1 36N53'50 86W35'48 5:46:23
Pettit 30 1 37N41'20 87W07'55 5:48:32
Pewee Valley 93 60 38N18'38 85W29'15 5:41:57
Peytona 106 54 38N10'52 85W03'40 5:40:15
Peyton Creek 98 11 37N29 82W31 5:30:04
Peytonsburg 29 1 36N38'03 85W23'34 5:41:34
Peytons Store 23 51 37N27'50 84W58'14 5:39:53
Peytontown 76 31 37N40'10 84W19'53 5:37:20
Phelps 98 11 37N30'46 82W09'00 5:28:36
Phil 23 51 37N12'55 84W57'13 5:39:49
Phillipsburg 78 51 37N27'23 85W15'36 5:41:02
Philpot 30 1 37N43'59 86W59'20 5:47:57
Phyllis 98 11 37N26'33 82W20'10 5:29:21
Pickett 1 1 37N07'21 85W28'32 5:41:54
Picnic 1 1 36N58 85W26 5:41:44
Pierce 44 1 37N11'11 85W36'28 5:42:26
Pierce Mill 47 51 37N38'26 86W12'00 5:44:48
Pig 31 6 37N07'58 86W10'12 5:44:41
Pigeon 98 11 37N25'55 82W33'13 5:30:13
Pigeonroost 26 16 37N06'40 83W48'52 5:35:15
Pike View 50 1 37N22'46 85W45'11 5:43:01
Pikeville 98 11 37N28'45 82W31'08 5:30:05
Pilcher Landing 82 64 37N59'31 86W01'03 5:44:04
Pilgrim 80 11 37N47'57 82W25'17 5:29:41
Pilot 33 16 37N44'57 83W46'47 5:35:07
Pilot Oak 42 1 36N32'48 88W43'20 5:54:53
Pilot View 25 33 37N58'04 84W03'50 5:36:15
Pinchem 25 33 37N55'34 84W09'36 5:36:38
Pinchem 110 1 36N42'10 87W11'50 5:48:47
Pinckard 120 45 37N58'38 84W40'54 5:38:44
Pinckneyville 70 1 37N11'14 88W14'23 5:52:58
Pine Grove 23 51 37N21 84W50 5:39:20
Pine Grove 25 16 38N00'07 84W18'57 5:37:16
Pine Grove 63 16 37N03'56 84W06'08 5:36:25
Pine Hill 102 36 37N19'46 84W15'48 5:37:03
Pinehurst 34 28 38N04'20 84W27'26 5:37:50
Pine Knob 43 1 37N29'00 86W30'43 5:46:03
Pine Knot 74 16 36N39'03 84W26'19 5:37:45
Pine Meadows 34 28 38N02'36 84W31'58 5:38:08
Pine Mountain 66 51 37N42'49 85W28'51 5:41:55
Piner 59 11 38N49'53 84W32'09 5:38:09
Pine Ridge 119 16 37N45'50 83W36'50 5:34:27
Pine Springs 43 1 37N21'07 86W05'41 5:44:23
Pine Top 60 16 37N16'21 82W52'57 5:31:32
Pineville 7 15 36N45'43 83W41'42 5:34:47
Piney 28 1 37N23'47 87W54'14 5:51:37
Piney Fork 28 1 37N17'31 88W00'15 5:52:01
Piney Grove 100 19 37N06'01 84W29'11 5:37:57
Pink 57 29 37N46'46 84W33'04 5:38:12
Pinnacle 65 16 37N37'16 83W49'03 5:35:16
Pinsonfork 98 11 37N33'11 82W15'50 5:29:03
Pioneer Village 15 53 38N00 85W43 5:42:52
Pippa Passes 60 16 37N20 82W53 5:31:32
Piqua 101 11 38N27'58 84W02'43 5:36:11
Pisgah 120 45 38N03'24 84W39'18 5:38:37
Piso 98 11 37N38'09 82W28'03 5:29:52
Pitman 109 51 37N22'41 85W29'22 5:41:57
Pitts 33 27 37N42'33 83W53'02 5:35:32
Pittsburg 63 16 37N09'36 84W06'15 5:36:25
Pitts Point 15 51 37N55'00 85W49'34 5:43:18
Plank 26 16 37N04'34 83W38'49 5:34:35
Plano 114 10 36N52'49 86W25'06 5:45:40
Plantation 56 68 38N17'00 85W35'28 5:42:22
Plato 100 19 37N13'58 84W25'04 5:37:40

Pleasant Green Hill 24 1 36N55'45 87W31'38 5:50:07
Pleasant Grove 115 51 37N45'06 85W10'21 5:40:41
Pleasant Hill 16 1 37N10'49 86W51'55 5:47:28
Pleasant Hill 18 1 36N42'50 88W17'36 5:53:10
Pleasant Hill 24 1 36N54'26 87W22'07 5:49:28
Pleasant Hill 96 11 38N47 84W22 5:37:28
Pleasant Home 94 16 38N30'05 84W54'49 5:39:39
Pleasant Ridge 92 1 37N35'54 86W59'14 5:47:57
Pleasant Valley 91 16 38N22'45 83W56'17 5:35:45
Pleasant Valley 98 11 37N28'02 82W30'17 5:30:01
Pleasant View 118 15 36N40'40 84W07'43 5:36:31
Pleasure Ridge Park 56 68 38N09 85W49 5:43:16
Pleasureville 35 16 38N28'41 83W36'13 5:34:25
Pleasureville 106 51 38N20'45 85W06'55 5:40:28
Plum 9 16 38N10'44 84W01'53 5:36:08
Plummers Landing 35 16 38N19'08 83W33'40 5:34:15
Plummers Mill 35 16 38N18'02 83W34'11 5:34:17
Plum Springs 114 1 37N01'06 86W22'53 5:45:32
Plumville 81 11 38N36'05 83W40'28 5:34:42
Plutarch 77 11 37N50'23 83W05'17 5:32:21
Plymouth Village 56 68 38N14'19 85W38'53 5:42:36
Poindexter 49 21 38N26'13 84W18'30 5:37:14
Pointer 100 19 37N07'58 84W46'02 5:39:04
Point Leavell 40 16 37N35'36 84W29'46 5:37:59
Point Pleasant 92 1 37N27'04 87W06'02 5:48:24
Polin 115 51 37N49'09 85W12'32 5:40:50
Polksville 6 16 38N08'18 83W39'15 5:34:37
Polkville 114 1 36N58'21 86W16'15 5:45:05
Pollard 57 29 37N48'24 84W30'36 5:38:02
Polly 67 16 37N12'03 82W49'36 5:31:18
Polsgrove 37 20 38N20'53 84W53'06 5:39:32
Pomeroyton 83 16 37N52'16 83W31'18 5:34:05
Pomp 88 40 37N57'34 83W16'53 5:33:08
Pond Creek 55 16 37N19 83W58 5:35:52
Ponderosa 43 1 37N20'26 86W11'46 5:44:47
Pondsville 114 1 36N59'40 86W09'55 5:44:40
Pongo 102 36 37N13'21 84W19'23 5:37:18
Ponza 7 15 36N43'12 83W38'33 5:34:34
Poole 117 1 37N38'25 87W38'39 5:50:35
Poor Fork 48 15 36N55 83W12 5:32:48
Poortown 57 29 37N53 84W34 5:38:16
Pope 2 1 36N45'45 86W20'23 5:45:22
Poplar 22 16 38N26'31 83W09'11 5:32:37
Poplar Corner 78 51 37N36'30 85W08'55 5:40:36
Poplar Flat 68 11 38N35'40 83W31'25 5:34:06
Poplar Grove 35 16 38N30'13 83W40'39 5:34:43
Poplar Grove 75 1 37N28'09 87W18'26 5:49:14
Poplar Grove 94 16 38N39'29 84W50'28 5:39:22
Poplar Highlands 45 11 38N32'43 82W45'17 5:31:01
Poplar Level 15 51 37N55'12 85W38'21 5:42:33
Poplar Plains 35 16 38N21'39 83W40'28 5:34:42
Poplarville 100 19 37N01'27 84W26'16 5:37:45
Porter 105 16 38N22'55 84W36'19 5:38:25
Porter Junction 36 11 37N28'19 82W49'46 5:31:19
Portersburg 26 16 37N10'14 83W55'33 5:35:42
Portland 1 1 37N07'14 85W26'46 5:41:47
Portland 56 69 38N16'09 85W48'39 5:43:15
Portland 96 11 38N44'53 84W26'52 5:37:47
Port Oliver Ford 2 6 36N53'38 86W08'17 5:44:33
Port Royal 52 51 38N33'19 85W04'49 5:40:19
Portsmouth 13 16 37N31'53 83W18'55 5:33:16
Possum Trot 79 1 37N00'20 88W25'50 5:53:43
Post 43 1 37N28'23 86W28'32 5:45:54
Potters 64 11 38N07 82W36 5:30:24
Potters Fork 67 16 37N10'57 82W40'24 5:30:42
Pottertown 18 1 36N37'17 88W11'28 5:52:46
Pottsville 42 1 36N51'18 88W43'45 5:54:55
Pottsville 115 51 37N38'50 85W04'01 5:40:16
Poverty 75 1 37N34'15 87W19'16 5:49:17
Powderly 89 1 37N14'13 87W09'33 5:48:38
Powder Mill 50 1 37N20'49 85W42'48 5:42:51
Powell 33 27 37N42 83W58 5:35:52
Powell Valley 99 16 37N51'54 83W56'52 5:35:47
Powersburg 116 1 36N42'15 84W57'55 5:39:52
Powersville 12 11 38N39'24 84W06'44 5:36:27
Prairie Village 56 68 38N06'47 85W50'11 5:43:21
Prater 22 16 38N20'20 83W09'07 5:32:36
Pratt 117 1 37N36'54 87W34'08 5:50:17
Preachersville 69 16 37N31'38 84W32'02 5:38:08
Preece 80 11 37N46'54 82W31'41 5:30:07
Premier 7 15 36N35'44 83W45'50 5:35:03
Premium 67 16 37N04 82W58 5:31:52
Prentiss 92 1 37N20'05 86W50'26 5:47:22
Press 13 16 37N31'39 83W16'18 5:33:05
Preston 51 16 38N05'08 83W45'12 5:35:01
Prestonia 56 69 38N11'41 85W43'37 5:42:54
Prestonsburg 36 11 37N39'56 82W46'18 5:31:05
Prestonville 21 39 38N40'47 85W11'25 5:40:46
Prewitt 87 22 38N01'41 83W58'52 5:35:55
Price 36 11 37N24'09 82W44'32 5:30:58
Prices Mill 107 1 36N40'53 86W43'48 5:46:55
Pricetown 23 51 37N17'03 84W57'20 5:39:49
Pricetown 34 28 37N59'32 84W22'26 5:37:30
Priceville 50 1 37N22'27 85W59'14 5:43:57
Prichard Place 47 51 37N53'04 85W58'18 5:43:53
Pride 113 1 37N33'30 87W53'27 5:51:34
Primrose 65 16 37N36'08 83W36'31 5:34:26
Princess 10 11 38N23'15 82W44'45 5:30:59
Princeton 17 1 37N06'33 87W52'55 5:51:32
Printer 36 11 37N31'47 82W44'47 5:30:59
Pritchardsville 5 6 36N58'20 85W56'14 5:43:45
Privett 55 16 37N24'07 83W54'02 5:35:36
Proctor 65 16 37N34'12 83W42'50 5:34:51
Produce Place 56 68 38N12 85W39 5:42:36
Prospect 56 68 38N20'42 85W36'56 5:42:28
Prospect PO 56 68 38N21'23 85W36'41 5:42:27
Prosperity 31 1 37N19'18 86W19'03 5:45:16
Protemus 18 1 36N33'12 88W28'45 5:53:55
Providence 57 28 38N01 84W32 5:38:08
Providence 61 15 36N52'01 83W54'42 5:35:39
Providence 107 1 36N39'58 86W40'39 5:46:43
Providence 112 51 38N34'28 85W13'16 5:40:53
Providence 117 1 37N23'51 87W45'46 5:51:03
Provo 16 1 37N13'59 86W49'42 5:47:19
Pruden 7 15 36N35'26 83W53'29 5:35:34
Pryorsburg 42 1 36N41'12 88W42'51 5:54:51
Pryors Chapel 42 1 36N44 88W38 5:54:32
Pryse 33 16 37N39'31 83W52'32 5:35:30
Public 100 19 36N49 84W42 5:38:48
Pueblo 116 1 36N48'35 84W42'30 5:38:50
Pulaski 100 19 37N12'32 84W38'20 5:38:33
Pulliam 115 51 37N50'45 85W08'59 5:40:36
Pumpkin Center 17 1 37N07'27 87W50'52 5:51:23
Puncheon 60 16 37N18'06 82W47'22 5:31:09
Purdy 1 1 37N09'05 85W11'06 5:40:44
Putney 48 15 36N54'19 83W13'35 5:32:54
Pyramid 36 11 37N33'53 82W52'08 5:31:29
Pyrus 1 1 37N04 85W25 5:41:40
Quail 102 16 37N19'38 84W27'17 5:37:49
Quality 16 1 37N04'32 86W50'48 5:47:23
Queendale 26 16 37N00'40 83W31'52 5:34:07
Queens 68 11 38N38'01 83W26'20 5:33:45
Quicksand 13 16 37N31'44 83W20'42 5:33:23
Quincy 68 11 38N37'26 83W07'51 5:32:31
Quinn 17 1 37N17'36 87W50'11 5:51:21
Quinn Landing 75 1 37N38'30 87W29'48 5:49:59
Quinton 100 19 36N57'10 84W37'36 5:38:30
Rabbit Hash 8 11 38N56'29 84W50'50 5:39:23
Rabbit Ridge 54 1 37N17'31 87W41'35 5:50:46
Rabbit Town 25 33 37N54'21 84W00'55 5:36:04
Raccoon 98 11 37N29'25 82W26'24 5:29:46
Raceland 45 11 38N32'24 82W43'43 5:30:55
Raceland Junction 45 11 38N32'54 82W45'47 5:31:03
Radcliff 47 51 37N50'25 85W56'57 5:43:48
Ragland 73 1 37N09'49 88W53'18 5:55:33
Railton 5 6 36N58'54 86W07'14 5:44:29
Rain 118 15 36N43'14 83W56'42 5:35:47
Raleigh 113 1 37N43'40 88W03'34 5:52:14
Raley Ford 2 6 36N51'35 86W16'02 5:45:04
Ralph 92 1 37N37'05 86W50'15 5:47:21
Ramey 103 16 38N10'45 83W34'19 5:34:17
Ramsey Island 116 1 36N48'40 84W58'57 5:39:56
Randolph 85 1 36N58'15 85W42'38 5:42:51
Randy 100 19 37N17'37 84W30'13 5:38:01
Rangers Landing 75 1 37N40'03 87W27'29 5:49:50
Rankin 51 8 37N46'57 87W34'38 5:50:19
Rankin 116 1 36N55'03 84W50'16 5:39:21
Ransom 98 11 37N33'59 82W11'18 5:28:45
Rapids 107 1 36N43 86W35 5:46:20
Ratliff 83 16 37N59'46 83W34'30 5:34:18
Ratliff 98 11 37N20'29 82W25'36 5:29:42
Raven 60 16 37N24'10 82W48'23 5:31:14
Ravenna 33 27 37N41'04 83W57'11 5:35:49
Raydure 86 1 36N39'08 85W28'45 5:41:55
Raymond 14 1 37N56'20 86W21'55 5:45:28
Raymond Hill 106 54 38N17'29 85W16'00 5:41:04
Raywick 78 51 37N33'37 85W25'50 5:41:43
Ready 43 1 37N22'18 86W28'17 5:45:53
Rectorville 81 11 38N34'35 83W38'46 5:34:35
Red Ash 118 15 36N36'59 84W07'19 5:36:29
Red Bird 7 15 36N56 83W32 5:34:08
Redbird 118 15 36N45'43 84W13'12 5:36:53
Redbud 48 15 36N51'35 83W10'08 5:32:41
Redbush 58 11 37N56'23 82W56'57 5:31:48
Red Cross 5 6 36N58'43 86W05'09 5:44:21
Redfox 60 16 37N12'53 82W56'38 5:31:47
Red Hill 2 1 36N44'28 86W17'57 5:45:12
Red Hill 30 1 37N36'37 87W02'30 5:48:10
Red Hill 47 51 37N49'35 85W58'03 5:43:52
Redhouse 76 31 37N49'56 84W16'20 5:37:05
Red Lick 33 16 37N41 84W02 5:36:08
Redlick 85 1 36N59 85W37 5:42:28
Red River 71 1 36N40 86W51 5:47:24
Redwine 88 16 38N00'58 83W13'40 5:32:55
Reed 51 1 37N51'04 87W21'15 5:49:25
Reeds Crossing 76 31 37N44'21 84W13'21 5:36:53
Reedville 22 16 38N15'04 82W54'37 5:31:38
Reedyville 16 1 37N11'29 86W25'54 5:45:44
Regina 98 11 37N22 82W24 5:29:36
Region 16 1 37N14 86W26 5:45:44
Reidland 73 1 37N01'03 88W31'53 5:54:08
Reid Village 87 22 38N02'57 83W58'39 5:35:55
Relief 88 16 37N56'41 82W59'43 5:31:59
Rella 7 15 36N50'04 83W37'59 5:34:32
Renaker 49 36 38N27'46 84W25'32 5:37:42
Render 92 1 37N24 86W53 5:47:32
Renfro Valley 102 36 37N23'16 84W19'54 5:37:20
Renfrow 92 1 37N25'00 86W41'32 5:46:46
Renick 25 30 38N03'30 84W12'24 5:36:50
Repton 28 1 37N23'19 88W01'01 5:52:04
Republic 98 11 37N22'21 82W21'47 5:29:27
Revelo 74 16 36N41'00 84W28'14 5:37:53
Rex 48 15 36N51'06 83W18'01 5:33:12
Rex 50 1 37N13'22 85W47'08 5:43:09
Rexton 68 11 38N34'07 83W07'20 5:32:29
Rexville 88 16 37N49'25 83W22'16 5:33:29
Reynolds Station 92 1 37N40 86W46 5:47:04
Reynoldsville 6 16 38N11'25 83W49'25 5:35:18
Rhea 48 15 36N53'56 83W15'14 5:33:01
Rheber 23 51 37N15'33 85W01'19 5:40:05
Rhoda 31 1 37N09'21 86W13'31 5:44:54
Rhodelia 82 51 38N00'25 86W25'14 5:45:41
Ribbon 104 1 36N52'49 85W14'25 5:40:58
Ribolt 68 11 38N34'30 83W31'11 5:34:05
Ricedale 59 14 38N56'32 84W34'54 5:38:20
Rice Station 33 27 37N42 83W58 5:35:52
Ricetown 95 16 37N23'24 83W37'22 5:34:29
Riceville 38 1 36N30'51 88W53'35 5:55:34
Riceville 58 11 37N44'04 82W55'28 5:31:42
Richam 98 11 37N29 82W31 5:30:04
Richardson 64 11 37N56'38 82W38'33 5:30:34
Richardsville 114 1 37N06'17 86W28'15 5:45:53
Richelieu 16 1 37N00'21 86W41'34 5:46:46
Richland 54 1 37N16'38 87W35'41 5:50:23
Richlawn 56 68 38N15'17 85W38'22 5:42:33
Richmond 76 31 37N44'52 84W17'41 5:37:11
Rich Pond 114 1 36N53'39 86W30'34 5:46:02
Richwood 8 14 38N55'14 84W37'30 5:38:30
Riders Mill 50 1 37N24'38 85W59'57 5:44:00
Ridgedale 31 1 37N15'38 86W16'02 5:45:04
Ridgetop 15 51 37N54'25 85W37'16 5:42:29
Ridgeview Heights 59 11 38N59 84W35 5:38:20
Ridgeway 48 15 36N53'51 83W07'32 5:32:30
Rightangle 25 33 37N53'41 84W01'43 5:36:07
Riley 78 51 37N33'34 85W05'56 5:40:24
Rileyville 48 15 36N53'50 83W03'57 5:32:16
Rineltown 115 51 37N39'34 85W09'22 5:40:37
Rineyville 47 51 37N44'58 85W58'12 5:43:53
Ringgold 100 19 37N06'29 84W39'13 5:38:37
Ringos Mills 35 16 38N18 83W40 5:34:40
Rio 50 1 37N19'08 85W46'16 5:43:05
Rio Vista 48 15 36N50'38 83W21'34 5:33:26
Risner 36 11 37N35'12 82W50'25 5:31:22
Ritchie 60 16 37N18'41 83W05'01 5:32:20
Ritner 116 1 36N47'33 84W37'52 5:38:31
Rivals 108 51 38N05'51 85W18'16 5:41:13
River 58 11 37N52 82W44 5:30:56
Riverfront 56 69 38N14 85W49 5:43:16
River Ridge 48 15 36N52'37 83W10'18 5:32:41
Riverside 56 68 38N11 85W52 5:43:28
Riverside 114 1 37N09'32 86W32'37 5:46:10
Riverside Beach 56 68 38N19'38 85W38'43 5:42:35
Riverside Gardens 56 69 38N11'32 85W52'21 5:43:29
Riverton 45 11 38N34 82W50 5:31:20
Riverview 45 11 38N30'46 82W40'56 5:30:44
Riverview 73 1 37N01'46 88W32'04 5:54:08
Riverview Estates 84 44 37N45'24 84W52'10 5:39:29
Riverwood 56 70 38N17 85W35 5:42:20
Roachville 44 51 37N14'26 85W25'25 5:41:42
Road Creek Junction 98 11 37N19 82W21 5:29:24
Road Fork 98 11 37N38'17 82W17'38 5:29:11
Road Junction 98 11 37N21'15 82W23'09 5:29:33
Roanoke 62 59 37N40'37 85W42'21 5:42:49
Roaring Spring 111 1 36N43'32 87W42'25 5:50:50
Roark 66 16 37N01'21 83W30'55 5:34:04
Robards 51 1 37N40'26 87W32'48 5:50:11
Roberta 82 51 38N06'38 86W26'16 5:45:45
Robinson 49 36 38N29'28 84W20'54 5:37:24
Robinson Creek 98 11 37N23'13 82W32'15 5:30:09
Robinsville 76 31 37N45 84W18 5:37:12
Robinswood 56 68 38N17'04 85W39'01 5:42:36
Robridge 92 1 37N25 87W00 5:48:00
Rob Roy 92 1 37N23'13 86W47'54 5:47:12
Rochester 16 1 37N12'45 86W53'35 5:47:34
Rockbridge 86 1 36N47'02 85W41'03 5:42:44
Rockcastle 111 1 36N53'59 87W59'14 5:51:57
Rockcastle Shores 111 1 36N53'01 87W58'40 5:51:55
Rock Creek 43 1 37N25'55 86W09'29 5:44:38
Rockdale 10 11 38N25'08 82W41'53 5:30:48
Rockdale 94 16 38N24'33 84W41'05 5:38:44
Rockfield 114 1 36N54'37 86W33'52 5:46:15
Rock Haven 82 51 37N56'49 86W03'17 5:44:13
Rockholds 118 15 36N49'43 84W06'59 5:36:28
Rockhouse 98 11 37N19'37 82W27'09 5:29:49
Rockland 114 10 37N05'23 86W35'02 5:46:20
Rock Lick 13 16 37N39'08 83W18'43 5:33:15
Rockport 92 1 37N20'02 86W59'46 5:47:59
Rock Spring 117 1 37N29'42 87W52'39 5:51:31
Rock Springs 12 11 38N46'03 84W05'32 5:36:22
Rock Springs 51 1 37N43'33 87W39'17 5:50:37
Rockvale 14 1 37N37'57 86W34'36 5:46:18
Rockwood 34 28 38N03'20 84W27'23 5:37:50
Rockybranch 116 1 36N44'06 84W44'00 5:38:56
Rocky Hill 5 1 36N56'24 86W04'16 5:44:17
Rodburn 103 16 38N11'53 83W24'39 5:33:39
Rodemer 2 1 36N43'09 86W13'46 5:44:55
Roff 14 1 37N39'37 86W25'23 5:45:42
Rogers 119 16 37N44'38 83W38'08 5:34:33
Rogers Gap 105 26 38N18'16 84W32'10 5:38:09
Rogersville 47 61 37N49'13 85W55'44 5:43:43
Rolan 27 1 36N39'07 85W02'00 5:40:08
Roland Landing 117 1 37N35'27 87W26'06 5:49:44
Rolling Acres 56 68 38N15 85W39 5:42:36
Rollingburg 44 6 37N16 85W30 5:42:00

Rolling Fields 56 68 38N16'04 85w40'18 5:42:41
Rolling Hills 56 70 38N16'57 85w34'28 5:42:18
Rollington 93 60 38N19'10 85w29'51 5:41:59
Rome 30 1 37N43'16 87w10'51 5:48:43
Romine 109 51 37N14'08 85w21'01 5:41:24
Rooney 22 16 38N24'54 83w11'27 5:32:46
Roosevelt 13 16 37N24'22 83w22'01 5:33:28
Roper 42 1 36N36'53 88w48'22 5:55:13
Roscoe 32 16 38N02'02 83w05'41 5:32:23
Roseburg 50 1 37N19'48 86w04'46 5:44:19
Rose Crossroads 104 1 36N58'33 85w07'14 5:40:29
Rosefork 119 16 37N42'03 83w20'04 5:33:20
Rose Hill 22 11 38N20'09 83w14'04 5:32:56
Rose Hill 84 44 37N46 84w51 5:39:24
Rose Terrace 47 51 37N53'42 85w58'38 5:43:55
Rosetta 14 1 37N47'48 86w16'23 5:45:06
Roseville 5 6 36N53'14 85w55'32 5:43:42
Roseville 46 1 37N43'02 86w45'18 5:47:01
Rosewood 89 1 37N05'12 87w05'22 5:48:21
Rosine 92 1 37N27'01 86w44'29 5:46:58
Ross 19 11 39N01'13 84w19'59 5:37:20
Ross Crossing 4 1 36N57'41 88w53'24 5:55:34
Rossington 73 1 37N08'41 88w49'44 5:55:19
Rossland 61 15 36N55'34 83w59'19 5:35:57
Rosslyn 99 16 37N50'26 83w48'44 5:35:15
Rosspoint 48 15 36N52'56 83w17'22 5:33:09
Rothwell 83 16 37N57'32 83w41'46 5:34:47
Roundhill 31 1 37N14'13 86w25'51 5:45:43
Round Hill 76 31 37N40'44 84w24'58 5:37:40
Roundstone 102 36 37N26'18 84w18'53 5:37:16
Rouse 59 71 39N04 84w31 5:38:04
Rousseau 13 16 37N35'35 83w13'47 5:32:55
Routt 56 68 38N08'03 85w28'00 5:41:52
Rowdy 97 16 37N24'11 83w12'37 5:32:50
Rowena 104 1 36N52'40 85w06'23 5:40:26
Rowland 69 16 37N31'22 84w37'54 5:38:32
Rowland 73 1 37N03 88w37 5:54:28
Rowlandtown 73 1 37N05'30 88w38'00 5:54:32
Rowletts 50 6 37N14'27 85w53'39 5:43:35
Roxana 67 16 37N06'40 82w57'00 5:31:48
Royal 43 1 37N26'27 86w05'43 5:44:23
Royalton 77 11 37N40'30 83w01'19 5:32:05
Royrader 55 16 37N15'49 83w56'35 5:35:46
Royville 104 1 37N04'00 85w06'21 5:40:25
Rubert Ford 23 51 37N14'07 84w58'01 5:39:52
Ruckerville 25 33 37N56'01 84w05'40 5:36:23
Ruddels Mills 9 21 38N18'15 84w14'17 5:36:57
Rufus 17 1 37N14'04 87w53'02 5:51:32
Rugless 68 16 38N29'22 83w12'38 5:32:51
Ruin 32 16 38N05 83w08 5:32:32
Rumsey 75 1 37N31'55 87w15'29 5:49:02
Rural 98 11 37N42'16 82w21'27 5:29:26
Rush 10 11 38N20'07 82w46'54 5:31:08
Russell 45 11 38N31'02 82w41'52 5:30:47
Russell Corner 93 62 38N27'05 85w24'42 5:41:39
Russell Heights 45 11 38N31'58 82w42'21 5:30:49
Russell Springs 104 1 37N03'22 85w05'19 5:40:21
Russellville 71 1 36N50'43 86w53'14 5:47:33
Ruth 17 1 37N06'31 87w44'55 5:51:00
Ruth 100 19 37N04'30 84w31'27 5:38:06
Rutherford 48 15 36N53'05 83w02'13 5:32:09
Ruthton 76 31 37N43'58 84w26'01 5:37:44
Rutland 49 21 38N26'41 84w27'03 5:37:48
Ryan 35 16 38N22'12 83w28'58 5:33:56
Ryland 59 11 38N56'19 84w28'09 5:37:53
Ryland Heights 59 71 38N57'27 84w27'47 5:37:51
Ryle 39 11 38N47'43 84w43'00 5:38:52
Sackett 67 16 37N12'09 82w53'07 5:31:32
Sacramento 75 1 37N24'57 87w15'56 5:49:04
Sadieville 105 17 38N23'21 84w32'15 5:38:09
Sadler 43 1 37N21'28 86w20'03 5:45:20
Saint Catharine 115 51 37N42'24 85w15'42 5:41:03
Saint Charles 54 1 37N11'10 87w33'21 5:50:13
Saint Dennis 56 69 38N12'01 85w49'59 5:43:20
Saint Elmo 24 1 36N42'09 87w23'34 5:49:34
Saint Francis 78 59 37N37'35 85w25'40 5:41:43
Saint Helens 65 16 37N34'58 83w38'50 5:34:35
Saint John 47 51 37N41'54 85w57'59 5:43:52
Saint Johns 73 1 36N57'59 88w40'19 5:54:41
Saint Joseph 30 1 37N41'40 87w19'31 5:49:18
Saint Joseph 78 51 37N31'19 85w23'23 5:41:34
Saint Mary 78 59 37N34'50 85w20'47 5:41:23
Saint Matthews 56 68 38N15'10 85w39'21 5:42:37
Saint Paul 43 1 37N33'03 86w11'37 5:44:46
Saint Paul 68 11 38N40'15 83w05'14 5:32:21
Saint Regis Park 56 68 38N13'36 85w37'00 5:42:28
Saint Vincent 113 1 37N42'17 87w50'24 5:51:22
Saldee 13 16 37N27 83w22 5:33:28
Salem 70 1 37N15'52 88w14'39 5:52:59
Salem (Buskirk P O) 88 16 37N48'43 83w20'01 5:33:20
Salem 104 1 37N04'08 84w59'08 5:39:57
Salleetown 78 51 37N27'23 85w12'40 5:40:51
Salmon 107 1 36N46'42 86w33'47 5:46:15
Saloma 109 51 37N24'43 85w23'34 5:41:34
Salt Gum 61 15 36N57 83w42 5:34:48
Salt Lick 6 16 38N07'12 83w36'53 5:34:28
Salt River 15 53 37N58'45 85w42'45 5:42:51
Saltwell 91 38 38N19 84w02 5:36:08
Salvisa 84 16 37N55'00 84w51'28 5:39:26
Salyersville 77 11 37N45'09 83w04'08 5:32:17
Samaria 45 16 38N25'12 82w56'43 5:31:47
Sample 14 1 37N54'16 86w28'52 5:45:55
Sampson 48 15 36N43'35 83w16'46 5:33:07
Samuels 90 51 37N52'58 85w32'00 5:42:08
Sandclift 116 1 36N37'27 84w59'28 5:39:58
Sandefur Crossing 92 1 37N24'57 86w49'57 5:47:20
Sanders 21 16 38N39'19 84w56'50 5:39:47
Sanderville 34 28 38N05'15 84w31'11 5:38:05
Sandgap 55 16 37N29'10 84w05'26 5:36:22
Sand Hill 33 27 37N42 83w58 5:35:52
Sand Hill 48 15 36N58'29 83w00'24 5:32:02
Sand Hill 68 11 38N39'50 83w37'33 5:34:30
Sand Hill 114 10 37N06'18 86w23'09 5:45:33
Sand Lick 105 16 38N14'34 84w43'05 5:38:52
Sand Springs 55 16 37N31'34 84w00'00 5:36:00
Sand Springs 102 36 37N17'49 84w21'33 5:37:26
Sandy 89 1 37N18'28 87w16'06 5:49:04
Sandy City 10 11 38N25 82w36 5:30:24
Sandy Furnace 10 11 38N14'53 82w45'14 5:31:01
Sandy Gap 100 19 37N08'46 84w21'14 5:37:25
Sandy Hook 32 34 38N05'11 83w07'35 5:32:30
Sanfordtown 59 71 39N01'33 84w32'13 5:38:09
Sano 104 1 37N06'30 85w06'13 5:40:25
Santa Fe 12 11 38N34'16 84w07'18 5:36:29
Sarah 32 16 38N03'43 82w57'38 5:31:51
Saratoga 72 1 37N03'36 87w59'51 5:51:59
Sardis 81 11 38N31'54 83w57'21 5:35:49
Sardis 100 19 37N02'44 84w41'46 5:38:47
Sassafras 60 16 37N13'14 83w03'19 5:32:13
Sasser 63 16 37N04'17 83w53'28 5:35:34
Saul 97 46 37N16'21 83w29'44 5:33:59
Savage 27 1 36N41'34 85w02'52 5:40:11
Savage Branch 10 11 38N20'39 82w35'53 5:30:24
Savoy 118 15 36N43'21 84w09'24 5:36:38
Savoyard 85 6 37N06'43 85w44'28 5:42:58
Sawyer 74 16 36N54'00 84w21'06 5:37:24
Saxton 118 15 36N38'01 84w06'36 5:36:26
Saylor 66 16 36N53'57 83w27'44 5:33:51
Scale 79 1 36N54'20 88w21'35 5:53:26
Scalf 61 15 36N55'06 83w42'01 5:34:48
Schley 71 1 36N41'10 86w55'12 5:47:41
Schochoh 71 1 36N43'22 86w47'28 5:47:10
Schollsville 25 16 37N59'18 84w02'27 5:36:10
Schoolville 25 22 38N03 83w57 5:35:48
Schultztown 92 1 37N24 86w53 5:47:32
Schweizer 107 1 36N40'15 86w38'02 5:46:32
Science Hill 100 32 37N10'37 84w38'09 5:38:33
Scot 48 15 36N59 82w59 5:31:56
Scott 59 71 39N02 84w34 5:38:16
Scottown 92 1 37N19'23 86w57'55 5:47:52
Scottsburg 17 1 37N04'43 87w49'17 5:51:17
Scotts Ferry 29 1 36N48 85w22 5:41:28
Scotts Station 106 54 38N13 85w14 5:40:56
Scottsville 2 6 36N45'12 86w11'26 5:44:46
Scoville 95 16 37N27'14 83w43'12 5:34:53
Scranton 83 16 37N59'14 83w31'18 5:34:05
Scuddy 97 46 37N12'13 83w05'01 5:32:20
Scuffletown 15 51 37N52'21 85w38'55 5:42:36
Scuffletown 51 1 37N55'22 87w22'20 5:49:29
Scythia 30 1 37N49'19 86w54'19 5:47:37
Seatonville 56 68 38N07'51 85w31'04 5:42:04
Seaville 115 44 37N53'00 85w02'20 5:40:09
Sebastian 95 16 37N21'39 83w37'13 5:34:29
Sebastians Branch 13 16 37N26'09 83w28'24 5:33:54
Sebree 117 1 37N36'26 87w31'43 5:50:07
Seco 67 16 37N10'19 82w43'56 5:30:56
Sedalia 42 1 36N38'28 88w36'19 5:54:25
Segal 31 1 37N12'20 86w23'06 5:45:32
Seitz 77 11 37N41'45 83w10'11 5:32:41
Select 92 1 37N21'35 86w44'42 5:46:59
Sellars 88 16 37N47'30 83w20'17 5:33:21
Seminary 27 1 36N41 85w08 5:40:32
Seminary Village 56 68 38N15'20 85w40'09 5:42:41
Semiway 75 1 37N28'24 87w14'28 5:48:58
Seneca Gardens 56 69 38N13'44 85w40'39 5:42:43
Senterville 98 11 37N19 82w21 5:29:24
Se Ree 14 1 37N41'00 86w22'47 5:45:31
Sergent 67 16 37N08'51 82w46'11 5:31:05
Settle 2 1 36N52'10 86w12'52 5:44:51
Seven Corners 47 1 37N28'55 85w59'34 5:43:58
Seventy Six 27 1 36N47'11 85w08'38 5:40:35
Sewell 13 16 37N37'32 83w23'20 5:33:33
Sewell Shop 25 22 38N01'50 84w01'39 5:36:07
Sewellton 104 1 36N56'10 85w06'18 5:40:25
Sextons Creek 26 16 37N18'54 83w47'02 5:35:08
Seymour 50 6 37N09'57 85w48'12 5:43:13
Shade 33 16 37N38'30 83w51'53 5:35:28
Shadeland 34 28 38N00'44 84w29'51 5:37:59
Shady Grove 28 1 37N20'12 87w52'45 5:51:31
Shady Grove 73 1 36N58'35 88w30'28 5:54:02
Shady Grove 85 1 37N09'52 85w40'57 5:42:44
Shadynook 49 21 38N23 84w17 5:37:08
Shafter 100 19 37N00'50 84w41'30 5:38:46
Shakertown 84 29 37N49'08 84w44'24 5:38:58
Shannon 81 11 38N32'54 83w53'29 5:35:34
Sharer 16 1 37N02'12 86w40'15 5:46:41
Sharkey 103 16 38N13'51 83w33'36 5:34:14
Sharon 12 11 38N46 84w00 5:36:00
Sharondale 98 11 37N36'36 82w16'06 5:29:04
Sharon Grove 110 1 36N54'48 87w05'51 5:48:23
Sharpe 79 1 36N58'07 88w27'30 5:53:50
Sharpsburg 6 16 38N12'07 83w55'46 5:35:43
Sharpsville 115 44 37N51'19 85w04'03 5:40:16
Shaw 20 1 36N54'58 88w48'46 5:55:15
Shawhan 9 30 38N18'06 84w16'21 5:37:05
Shawnee Estates 114 10 36N57'10 86w27'26 5:45:50
Shawnee Hills 111 1 36N50'39 87w57'24 5:51:50
Shawneeland 56 69 38N15'12 85w49'09 5:43:17
Shawneetown 34 28 38N01'07 84w30'37 5:38:02
Shearer Valley 116 1 36N45'04 84w55'14 5:39:41
Shelbiana 98 11 37N25'31 82w29'35 5:29:58
Shelby 56 69 38N13 85w44 5:42:56
Shelby City 11 25 37N35'00 84w46'45 5:39:07
Shelby Gap 98 11 37N13 82w34 5:30:16
Shelbyville 106 54 38N12'43 85w13'25 5:40:54
Shelbyville Road Plaza 56 68 38N15 85w39 5:42:36
Shelton 117 1 37N34'07 87w47'46 5:51:11
Shepherdsville 15 53 37N59'18 85w42'57 5:42:52
Shepherdtown 26 16 37N17'13 83w51'54 5:35:28
Shepola 100 19 37N02'55 84w42'22 5:38:49
Sherburne 35 16 38N16'54 83w48'10 5:35:13
Sheridan 28 1 37N21'06 88w11'56 5:52:48
Sherman 41 11 38N43'57 84w35'48 5:38:23
Sherwood Shores 79 1 36N55'48 88w13'12 5:52:53
Shetland 120 45 38N02'50 84w42'19 5:38:49
Shields 48 15 36N53'47 83w08'31 5:32:34
Shiloh 18 1 36N41'09 88w12'49 5:52:51
Shipley 27 1 36N40'02 85w13'04 5:40:52
Shively 56 69 38N12'00 85w49'22 5:43:17
Shoal 66 16 37N16 83w26 5:33:44
Shop Branch 55 16 37N26 84w00 5:36:00
Shopville 100 19 37N09'31 84w28'48 5:37:55
Shore Acres 120 20 38N12 84w52 5:39:28
Short Creek 43 1 37N31'40 86w28'28 5:45:54
Short Mountain 116 1 36N50'30 84w53'44 5:39:35
Short Town 48 15 36N52'39 83w09'38 5:32:39
Shoulderblade 13 16 37N29'50 83w28'02 5:33:52
Shreve 92 1 37N34'43 86w37'44 5:46:31
Shrewsbury 43 1 37N22'44 86w23'05 5:45:32
Shultztown 92 1 37N17'32 86w50'16 5:47:21
Sibert 26 16 37N07'23 83w47'14 5:35:09
Sidell 26 16 37N11'33 83w49'30 5:35:18
Sideview 87 22 38N06'47 84w02'12 5:36:09
Sideway 32 16 38N11'04 83w13'33 5:32:54
Sidney 98 11 37N37'12 82w21'24 5:29:26
Sidville 9 30 38N07'41 84w15'35 5:37:02
Siler 61 15 36N56'28 84w02'23 5:36:10
Siler 118 15 36N41'40 83w57'32 5:35:50
Silerville (Strunk P O) 74 16 36N37'36 84w26'07 5:37:44
Siloam 45 11 38N44'07 82w53'41 5:31:35
Silver City 16 1 37N08'16 86w49'54 5:47:20
Silver Creek 76 43 37N39'26 84w21'58 5:37:28
Silver Grove 19 11 39N02'04 84w23'25 5:37:34
Silverhill 88 16 37N52'56 83w02'57 5:32:12
Simers 98 11 37N27'49 82w15'42 5:29:03
Simmons 92 1 37N21'27 86w56'32 5:47:46
Simpson 13 16 37N40'05 83w22'13 5:33:29
Simpsonville 106 51 38N13'21 85w21'19 5:41:25
Sims Fork 7 15 36N48 83w39 5:34:36
Simstown 78 66 37N38'02 85w10'40 5:40:43
Sinai 3 44 37N57'15 85w01'38 5:40:07
Sinking Fork 24 1 36N56'01 87w35'57 5:50:24
Sinking Valley 100 19 37N10'56 84w24'26 5:37:38
Sinks 102 36 37N20'04 84w14'01 5:36:56
Sip 58 11 37N55'30 82w49'40 5:31:19
Sirocco 82 51 37N59'21 86w16'20 5:45:05
Sitka 58 11 37N52'50 82w50'18 5:31:21
Sixth Vein 54 1 37N15'05 87w40'20 5:50:41
Sizerock 66 16 37N13'07 83w29'51 5:33:59
Skaggs 64 11 38N00'20 82w56'55 5:31:48
Skaggstown 43 1 37N26'01 86w11'12 5:44:45
Skate 63 37 37N08 84w05 5:36:20
Skibo 89 1 37N13 87w11 5:48:44
Skilesville 89 1 37N12'51 86w54'11 5:47:37
Skillman 46 1 37N53'34 86w40'18 5:46:41
Skinnersburg 105 16 38N18'22 84w38'32 5:38:34
Skullbuster 105 16 38N16 84w41 5:38:44
Skylight 93 52 38N25'57 85w31'18 5:42:05
Skyline 67 16 37N04'33 82w58'54 5:31:56
Slabtown 52 51 38N25'58 85w00'19 5:40:01
Slade 99 16 37N47'42 83w42'15 5:34:49
Slat 116 1 36N48'36 84w54'33 5:39:38
Slate Lick 76 43 37N32'47 84w18'40 5:37:15
Slater 4 1 37N00'59 88w59'21 5:55:57
Slate Valley 6 16 38N10'09 83w43'24 5:34:54
Slaughters 117 1 37N29'20 87w30'08 5:50:01
Slaughtersville 117 1 37N29 87w30 5:50:00
Slavans 74 16 36N45'13 84w39'56 5:38:40
Slemp 97 46 37N04'43 83w06'42 5:32:27
Slickford 116 1 36N41'44 84w53'40 5:39:35
Slick Rock 5 6 37N00'21 85w47'53 5:43:12
Slickway 37 20 38N11'13 84w47'57 5:39:12
Sligo 93 51 38N29'20 85w18'48 5:41:15
Sloan 36 11 37N37'11 82w45'28 5:31:02
Sloans Crossing 31 1 37N09'03 86w05'50 5:44:23
Sloans Valley 100 19 36N56'12 84w32'15 5:38:09
Smallhous 92 1 37N22'48 87w05'37 5:48:22
Smilax 66 16 37N08'08 83w16'56 5:33:08
Smile 103 16 38N15'27 83w29'25 5:33:58
Smith 48 15 36N44'09 83w15'34 5:33:02
Smithfield 52 51 38N23'12 85w15'25 5:41:02
Smith Ford 17 1 37N19'10 87w51'01 5:51:24
Smithland 70 1 37N08'20 88w24'12 5:53:37
Smith Mills 51 1 37N47'54 87w45'43 5:51:03
Smithsboro 60 16 37N13 83w03 5:32:12
Smiths Creek 22 16 38N27'31 83w11'10 5:32:45
Smiths Grove 114 1 37N03'09 86w12'28 5:44:50
Smith Town 74 16 36N42'12 84w30'20 5:38:01
Smithview 43 1 37N25'57 86w32'02 5:46:08
Smithville 15 51 38N00'47 85w30'51 5:42:03

Smoky Valley 22 16 38N21'31 83w12'19 5:32:49
Smyrna 56 68 38N07'57 85w39'07 5:42:36
Snap 43 1 37N24'11 86w09'22 5:44:37
Snell 100 19 37N05 84w26 5:37:44
Snow 27 1 36N45'01 85w08'13 5:40:33
Snow Hill 106 54 38N13 85w14 5:40:56
Soft Shell 60 16 37N24'08 82w56'32 5:31:46
Soldier 22 16 38N15'33 83w17'58 5:33:12
Solitude 15 51 37N58'23 85w32'25 5:42:10
Solway 47 51 37N37'16 86w10'36 5:44:42
Somerset 100 32 37N05'31 84w36'15 5:38:25
Somo 81 12 38N35'48 83w44'33 5:34:58
Sonora 47 51 37N31'27 85w53'35 5:43:34
Sophi 22 16 38N13'41 83w00'53 5:32:04
Sorgho 30 1 37N45'11 87w14'50 5:48:59
Sourwood 55 16 37N19'52 83w47'55 5:35:12
South 43 1 37N19'45 86w21'53 5:45:28
South 75 1 37N27 87w14 5:48:56
South Buffalo 62 51 37N30'15 85w42'09 5:42:49
South Campbellsville 109 51 37N20'00 85w19'32 5:41:18
South Carrollton 89 1 37N20'15 87w08'31 5:48:34
South Columbus 53 1 36N44'31 89w05'53 5:56:24
South Corbin 118 15 36N57 84w06 5:36:24
Southdown 67 16 37N09'30 82w47'50 5:31:11
Southeastern Hills 34 28 37N58'55 84w29'02 5:37:56
South Elkhorn 34 28 37N59'47 84w34'56 5:38:20
Southern Heights 56 69 38N10'59 85w46'26 5:43:06
South Fayette 34 28 37N57 84w27 5:37:48
South Fork 69 16 37N24'34 84w44'17 5:38:57
Southfork 95 16 37N24'51 83w39'43 5:34:39
South Fort Mitchell 59 71 39N02'28 84w33'22 5:38:13
Southgate 19 71 39N04'19 84w28'22 5:37:53
South Higginsport 12 11 38N46'40 83w58'00 5:35:52
South Highland 42 1 36N41'09 88w37'56 5:54:32
South Hill 16 1 37N10'33 86w48'17 5:47:13
South Irvine 33 27 37N41'00 83w58'37 5:35:54
Southland 34 28 38N01'10 84w31'51 5:38:07
South Lebanon 78 66 37N32 85w15 5:41:00
South Marshall 79 1 36N47'53 88w19'48 5:53:19
South Oldham 93 60 38N20 85w28 5:41:52
South Park 56 68 38N06'45 85w44'52 5:42:59
South Parkland 56 69 38N13'44 85w48'43 5:43:15
South Park View 56 68 38N07'06 85w43'18 5:42:53
South Portsmouth 45 11 38N43'28 83w00'48 5:32:03
South Ripley 81 11 38N44'28 83w51'15 5:35:25
South River 65 16 37N32 83w46 5:35:04
South Shore 45 11 38N43'15 82w57'30 5:31:50
South Union 71 1 36N52'35 86w39'23 5:46:38
Southville 106 54 38N06'36 85w10'55 5:40:44
South Wallins 48 15 36N48'54 83w24'39 5:33:39
South Williamson 98 11 37N40'19 82w17'03 5:29:08
Southwire 46 1 37N54 86w45 5:47:00
Spa 71 1 36N57'42 87w00'17 5:48:01
Spanglin 32 16 38N03'58 83w13'54 5:32:56
Spann 116 1 36N51'07 84w46'14 5:39:05
Sparksville 1 1 37N00'30 85w24'07 5:41:36
Sparrow 3 18 37N55'26 85w09'03 5:40:36
Sparta 39 12 38N40'37 84w54'25 5:39:38
Spears 34 28 37N52'21 84w26'16 5:37:45
Speck 109 1 37N18'24 85w11'16 5:40:45
Speedwell 76 31 37N40'27 84w10'31 5:36:42
Speight 98 11 37N16'30 82w41'15 5:30:45
Spence 19 71 39N05 84w29 5:37:56
Spencer 87 22 38N03 83w57 5:35:48
Spencer Ridge 65 16 37N35 83w43 5:34:52
Spice Knob 30 1 37N49'02 86w58'10 5:47:53
Spider 60 16 37N15'31 82w54'44 5:31:39
Spike 43 1 37N24'25 86w05'05 5:44:20
Spindletop Estates 34 28 38N08'04 84w31'23 5:38:06
Spiro 102 36 37N20'33 84w23'59 5:37:36
Splint 48 15 36N55'32 83w09'50 5:32:39
Sportsmens Paradise 43 1 37N21'18 86w05'22 5:44:21
Spottsville 51 1 37N51'27 87w24'49 5:49:39
Spout Springs 33 27 37N49'37 83w58'29 5:35:54
Spring Bayou 73 1 37N05 88w53 5:55:32
Spring Creek 26 16 37N03'46 83w32'34 5:34:10
Springdale 56 70 38N17'39 85w36'13 5:42:25
Springdale 59 71 38N59'45 84w27'47 5:37:51
Springdale 81 11 38N37'22 83w40'00 5:34:41
Springfield 115 51 37N41'07 85w13'20 5:40:53
Spring Grove 113 1 37N40'51 88w01'39 5:52:07
Spring Hill 53 1 36N44'14 88w58'18 5:55:53
Springhill 114 10 36N58'34 86w28'47 5:45:55
Spring Lake 59 11 39N00 84w28 5:37:52
Springlee 56 68 38N14'27 85w38'34 5:42:34
Spring Lick 43 1 37N26'41 86w33'24 5:46:14
Spring Station 120 48 38N09 84w41 5:38:44
Sprout 91 16 38N18'07 83w53'12 5:35:33
Spruce Pine 66 16 36N55'24 83w26'43 5:33:47
Sprule 61 15 37N00'58 83w50'59 5:35:24
Spurlington 109 51 37N24'44 85w16'29 5:41:06
Spurlock 26 16 37N12'42 83w38'05 5:34:32
Spurrier 47 1 37N28'28 86w03'15 5:44:13
Squib 100 19 37N09'19 84w19'36 5:37:18
Squiresville 94 16 38N32'32 84w57'17 5:39:49
Stab 100 19 37N09'05 84w26'13 5:37:45
Stacy (Rowdy P O) 97 16 37N24'11 83w12'37 5:32:50
Stacy Fork 88 16 37N50'29 83w15'27 5:33:02
Staffordsburg 59 11 38N54'49 84w30'04 5:38:00
Staffordsville 58 11 37N49'47 82w50'32 5:31:22
Stalcup 29 1 36N42'10 85w26'48 5:41:47
Stambaugh 58 11 37N53 82w48 5:31:12
Stamping Ground 105 17 38N16'18 84w41'11 5:38:45
Standing Rock 119 16 37N42'59 83w42'23 5:34:50
Stanfill 48 15 36N45'52 83w20'32 5:33:22
Stanford 69 41 37N31'52 84w39'43 5:38:39
Stanhope 117 1 37N26'42 87w40'07 5:50:40
Stanley 30 1 37N49'24 87w14'38 5:48:59
Stanley Addition 98 11 37N31'01 82w33'57 5:30:16
Stanley Landing 70 1 37N03'11 88w18'42 5:53:15
Stanton 99 17 37N50'44 83w51'30 5:35:26
Stanville 36 11 37N34'00 82w38'33 5:30:34
Stark 32 16 38N10'25 83w08'06 5:32:32
Star Mills 47 51 37N35'57 85w58'49 5:43:55
State Line 38 1 36N34 89w11 5:56:44
Static 27 1 36N37'19 85w05'06 5:40:20
Station Camp 33 16 37N38 83w56 5:35:44
Stay 95 16 37N30'37 83w39'08 5:34:37
Steamport Landing 117 1 37N36'12 87w29'05 5:49:56
Stearns 74 16 36N41'56 84w28'39 5:37:55
Steele 98 11 37N24'12 82w12'04 5:28:48
Steff 43 1 37N26 86w36 5:46:24
Stella 18 1 36N38'25 88w23'48 5:53:35
Stella 77 11 37N44'16 83w09'58 5:32:40
Stephens 32 16 38N08'07 82w57'32 5:31:50
Stephensburg 47 51 37N37'29 86w01'08 5:44:05
Stephensport 14 1 37N54'45 86w31'38 5:46:07
Stepstone 87 16 38N05'16 83w49'45 5:35:19
Steubenville 116 1 36N53'15 84w48'10 5:39:13
Stevenson 13 16 37N34'51 83w15'40 5:33:03
Stewart 84 44 37N41'28 85w00'30 5:40:02
Stewartsville 41 11 38N37'59 84w38'54 5:38:36
Stidham 80 11 37N52'57 82w35'07 5:30:20
Stiles 90 51 37N32'22 85w34'50 5:42:19
Stiles Crossing 73 1 37N01'07 88w30'10 5:54:01
Stillwater 119 16 37N45'23 83w29'04 5:33:56
Stinnett 66 16 37N05'25 83w23'44 5:33:35
Stinnettsville 14 1 37N46'51 86w18'31 5:45:14
Stinson 22 16 38N18'36 82w52'42 5:31:31
Stites 15 64 38N01'00 85w54'17 5:43:37
Stockholm 31 1 37N14 86w17 5:45:08
Stone 40 29 37N43'41 84w32'46 5:38:11
Stone 98 11 37N35'09 82w16'16 5:29:05
Stonewall 12 11 38N37'09 84w00'41 5:36:03
Stonewall 105 16 38N26'21 84w33'53 5:38:16
Stonewall Estates 34 28 38N00'10 84w32'59 5:38:12
Stoneybrook 34 28 37N59'01 84w30'59 5:38:04
Stoney Fork 7 15 36N49'56 83w32'05 5:34:08
Stoney Fork Junction 7 15 36N37 83w44 5:34:56
Stoney Point 12 11 38N45'55 83w55'23 5:35:42
Stony Fork Junction 7 15 36N36'06 83w45'08 5:35:01
Stony Point 9 30 38N07'14 84w11'38 5:36:47
Stoops 87 22 38N07'41 83w54'52 5:35:39
Stop 116 1 36N50 84w51 5:39:24
Stopover 98 11 37N30'57 82w05'29 5:28:22
Stormking 97 46 37N15 83w11 5:32:44
Stovall 5 6 37N03'23 86w00'37 5:44:02
Straight Creek 7 15 36N46'23 83w40'05 5:34:40
Straight Creek 22 16 38N16'04 82w52'39 5:31:31
Strait Creek 22 16 38N19 83w20 5:33:20
Strathmoor Gardens 56 68 38N13'08 85w40'25 5:42:42
Strathmoor Manor 56 69 38N13'05 85w41'01 5:42:44
Strathmoor Village 56 69 38N13'23 85w40'40 5:42:43
Straw 31 1 37N16'33 86w10'21 5:44:41
Stricklett 68 11 38N29'04 83w23'15 5:33:33
Stringtown 8 11 39N04'52 84w38'46 5:38:35
Stringtown 35 16 38N13'58 83w39'45 5:34:39
Stringtown 41 36 38N30'43 84w30'04 5:38:00
Stringtown 64 11 38N10'36 82w40'09 5:30:41
Stringtown 76 31 37N49'11 84w24'47 5:37:39
Stringtown 77 11 37N45'52 83w02'51 5:32:11
Stringtown 84 44 37N46'24 84w49'24 5:39:18
Stringtown 89 1 37N15'07 87w06'52 5:48:27
Stringtown 98 11 37N37'59 82w13'17 5:28:53
Stringtown 108 44 38N00'29 84w52'51 5:39:31
Stroud 89 1 37N24'32 87w09'09 5:48:37
Strunk 74 16 36N37'19 84w26'01 5:37:44
Stubblefield 42 1 36N38'14 88w40'47 5:54:43
Sturgeon 95 16 37N25'09 83w47'06 5:35:08
Sturgis 113 1 37N32'48 87w59'02 5:51:56
Sublett 77 11 37N40'39 83w02'15 5:32:09
Sublimity City 63 37 37N05'40 84w05'01 5:36:20
Subtle 85 1 36N59 85w37 5:42:28
Sudith 83 16 38N01'06 83w37'56 5:34:32
Sugar Bay 39 12 38N47 84w54 5:39:36
Sugar Grove 16 1 37N05'24 86w39'54 5:46:40
Sugar Grove 69 16 37N27'29 84w33'59 5:38:16
Sugar Hill 100 19 37N07'37 84w33'16 5:38:13
Sugartit 8 11 38N58'22 84w39'46 5:38:39
Sullivan 113 1 37N29'51 87w56'43 5:51:47
Sulphur 52 51 38N29'41 85w16'25 5:41:06
Sulphur Lick 86 1 36N48'19 85w44'19 5:42:57
Sulphur Springs 92 1 37N32'08 86w46'36 5:47:06
Sulphur Well 57 29 37N53 84w34 5:38:16
Sulphur Well 85 1 36N59 85w37 5:42:28
Summer Shade 85 1 36N53'03 85w42'09 5:42:49
Summersville 44 1 37N19'34 85w32'40 5:42:11
Summit 10 11 38N26'23 82w42'15 5:30:49
Summit 47 51 37N34'08 86w04'52 5:44:19
Summit 64 11 38N02'12 82w35'26 5:30:22
Summit Hills Heights 59 71 39N00'22 84w33'11 5:38:13
Sumpter 116 1 36N45'39 84w50'48 5:39:23
Sunfish 31 1 37N17'49 86w22'11 5:45:29
Sunny Acres 59 71 39N00'57 84w29'53 5:38:00
Sunnybrook 116 1 36N39'28 84w58'33 5:39:54
Sunny Corner 46 1 37N51'08 86w40'11 5:46:41
Sunnydale 92 1 37N32'10 86w49'10 5:47:17
Sunnyside 114 10 37N01'42 86w18'27 5:45:14
Sunrise 49 16 38N32'33 84w14'12 5:36:57
Sunset 35 16 38N17'04 83w41'26 5:34:46
Sunshine 45 11 38N42'27 82w56'55 5:31:48
Sunshine 48 15 36N50'14 83w19'43 5:33:19
Susie 116 1 36N46'35 84w57'23 5:39:50
Suterville 105 16 38N22'05 84w42'13 5:38:49
Sutherland 30 1 37N40'12 87w07'16 5:48:29
Sutton 35 16 38N25 83w47 5:35:08
Sutton 98 11 37N24'59 82w27'24 5:29:50
Suwanee 72 1 37N03'01 88w09'55 5:52:40
Swain 74 16 36N39 84w26 5:37:44
Swallowfield 37 20 38N20'21 84w50'55 5:39:24
Swamp Branch 58 11 37N44'09 82w53'42 5:31:35
Swampton 77 11 37N39'31 83w00'41 5:32:03
Swan Lake 61 15 36N49'34 83w55'38 5:35:43
Swanpond 61 15 36N49'51 83w54'11 5:35:37
Sweeden 31 1 37N15'13 86w16'44 5:45:07
Sweeneyville 109 51 37N21'08 85w23'57 5:41:36
Sweet Owen 94 11 38N33'21 84w45'38 5:39:03
Swifton 116 1 36N52'04 84w54'18 5:39:37
Switzer 37 16 38N16 84w41 5:38:44
Sycamore Estates 120 45 38N03 84w44 5:38:56
Sycamore Flat 104 1 37N07'26 85w02'36 5:40:10
Sylvandell 49 21 38N26'51 84w09'34 5:36:38
Sylvania 56 68 38N09'25 85w52'27 5:43:30
Symbol 63 16 37N16'26 84w08'20 5:36:33
Symsonia 42 1 36N55'13 88w31'12 5:54:05
Tabernacle 110 1 36N52'26 87w13'53 5:48:56
Tablow 115 44 37N51'53 85w00'51 5:40:03
Tacketts Mill 94 16 38N22'02 84w47'23 5:39:10
Tacky Town 48 15 36N51'02 83w28'31 5:33:54
Taffy 92 1 37N33'14 86w53'30 5:47:34
Taft 95 16 37N21'41 83w41'12 5:34:45
Talbert 13 16 37N25'17 83w27'31 5:33:50
Talcum 60 16 37N23 83w05 5:32:20
Tallega 65 16 37N33'37 83w35'25 5:34:22
Talley 62 51 37N27'02 85w50'38 5:43:23
Talmage 84 44 37N51'03 84w52'10 5:39:29
Tanbark 29 1 36N43'20 85w23'04 5:41:32
Tanglewood 37 20 38N12 84w52 5:39:28
Tanksley 26 16 37N13'00 83w42'37 5:34:50
Tanner 62 51 37N30'34 85w47'06 5:43:08
Tannery 22 11 38N32'38 83w12'57 5:32:52
Tarascon 52 51 38N24'41 85w18'33 5:41:14
Tar Fork 14 1 37N43'14 86w36'06 5:46:24
Tar Hill 43 1 37N33'56 86w13'06 5:44:52
Tarkiln 64 11 38N02 82w50 5:31:20
Tateville 100 19 36N57'52 84w34'53 5:38:20
Tatham Springs 115 51 37N51'57 85w07'26 5:40:30
Tatumsville 79 1 36N55'58 88w18'23 5:53:14
Taulbee 13 16 37N38'34 83w19'50 5:33:19
Taylor Mill 59 11 38N59'51 84w29'47 5:37:59
Taylor Mines 92 1 37N22'37 86w53'31 5:47:34
Taylorsport 8 11 39N05'59 84w41'36 5:38:46
Taylors Store 18 1 36N30 88w19 5:53:16
Taylorsville 108 55 38N01'54 85w20'33 5:41:22
Teaberry 36 11 37N25'36 82w38'35 5:30:34
Teatersville 40 16 37N41'20 84w30'25 5:38:02
Tebbs 25 33 37N59'52 84w16'57 5:37:08
Tedders 61 15 37N01'09 83w52'47 5:35:31
Teddy 23 51 37N10'47 84w56'31 5:39:46
Teetersville 48 15 36N48'47 83w20'10 5:33:21
Teges 26 16 37N17'40 83w40'03 5:34:40
Tejay 7 15 36N45'49 83w33'44 5:34:15
Temperance 107 1 36N46'37 86w25'52 5:45:43
Temple Hill 5 1 36N53'12 85w50'50 5:43:23
Ten Spot 48 15 36N50'37 83w13'02 5:32:52
Teresita 94 16 38N23'34 84w46'34 5:39:06
Terrapin 84 44 37N53'03 84w56'19 5:39:45
Terrill 76 31 37N41'10 84w15'33 5:37:02
Terry Manor 56 68 38N08 85w51 5:43:24
Terryville 64 11 37N59'23 82w59'14 5:31:57
Texas 115 51 37N39'20 85w06'37 5:40:26
Texola 33 16 37N39'13 83w52'17 5:35:29
Thealka 58 11 37N49'19 82w47'20 5:31:09
The Bluff 17 1 37N11'24 88w04'18 5:52:17
Thelma 58 11 37N49'09 82w45'56 5:31:04
The Moors 79 1 36N55'34 88w13'04 5:52:52
The Moors Camp 79 1 37N01 88w18 5:53:12
The Ridge 32 16 38N05'37 83w11'57 5:32:48
The Rocks 113 1 37N40'29 88w05'37 5:52:22
Thistleton 37 20 38N12 84w52 5:39:28
Thixton 56 68 38N06'02 85w33'56 5:42:16
Thomas 36 11 37N40'54 82w35'09 5:30:21
Thompson 25 22 38N03 83w57 5:35:48
Thompsonville 115 51 37N43'37 85w08'13 5:40:33
Thomson 25 22 38N00'21 84w01'34 5:36:06

Thorn Hill 37 20 38N12 84w52 5:39:28
Thorn Hill Heights 37
20 38N12 84w52 5:39:28
Thornton 67 16 37N10'24 82w46'43 5:31:07
Thoroughbred Acres 34
28 38N04'54 84w27'18 5:37:49
Thoroughbred Acres 56
70 38N17 85w35 5:42:20
Thousandsticks 66
16 37N11'06 83w25'44 5:33:43
Three Forks 40 16 37N41'27 84w34'30 5:38:18
Threeforks 80 11 37N45'40 82w27'33 5:29:50
Three Forks 114 1 36N57'11 86w12'14 5:44:49
Threelinks 55 36 37N28'04 84w11'22 5:36:45
Three Point 48 15 36N45'48 83w15'37 5:33:02
Three Springs 50
1 37N10'18 85w44'37 5:42:58
Three Springs 114
10 36N55'00 86w26'13 5:45:45
Thruston 30 1 37N48'04 87w01'41 5:48:07
Thurlow 44 6 37N12'45 85w32'11 5:42:09
Tidalwave 118 15 36N50 84w07 5:36:28
Tilden 117 1 37N36'15 87w42'37 5:50:50
Tilford 16 1 37N22'26 86w32'51 5:46:11
Tilford 97 46 37N01'50 83w03'58 5:32:16
Tiline 70 1 37N10'21 88w14'40 5:52:59
Tillie 67 16 37N10'51 82w51'50 5:31:27
Tilton 35 16 38N20'47 83w45'35 5:35:02
Timsley 7 15 36N47'03 83w46'06 5:35:04
Tina 60 16 37N21'40 83w01'11 5:32:05
Tinsley 7 15 36N47 83w46 5:35:04
Tiny Town 110 1 36N39 87w10 5:48:40
Tiptop 77 11 37N36'50 83w03'40 5:32:15
Titan Siding 98
11 37N27'46 82w31'34 5:30:06
Todds Point 106
51 38N17'03 85w20'45 5:41:23
Toddville 40 16 37N43'57 84w38'10 5:38:33
Toler 98 11 37N38'14 82w15'09 5:29:01
Toliver 119 16 37N48'49 83w27'28 5:33:50
Tollesboro 68 11 38N33'34 83w34'34 5:34:18
Tolliver Town 67
16 37N10'49 82w42'33 5:30:50
Tolu 28 1 37N25'59 88w14'43 5:52:59
Tomahawk 80 11 37N52'07 82w35'50 5:30:23
Tom Gray Ford 17
1 37N18'23 87w49'46 5:51:19
Tom Johns Crossing 50
6 37N14'59 86w01'28 5:44:06
Tompkinsville 86
1 36N42'08 85w41'30 5:42:46
Tonieville 62 51 37N36'34 85w47'46 5:43:11
Tooley Hill 89 1 37N13 87w11 5:48:44
Toonerville 98 11 37N22'12 82w13'51 5:28:55
Topmost 60 16 37N22 82w47 5:31:08
Topton 63 37 37N08 84w05 5:36:20
Torchlight 64 11 38N02'58 82w36'53 5:30:28
Toria 1 1 36N59'22 85w26'15 5:41:45
Torrent 119 16 37N42'57 83w39'47 5:34:39
Totz (Pine Mountain Station 48
15 36N56'41 83w07'04 5:32:28
Toulouse 66 16 37N17 83w17 5:33:08
Touristville 116
1 36N55'32 84w45'42 5:39:03
Tousey 43 1 37N30'52 86w32'52 5:46:11
Towers Chapel 75
1 37N25 87w16 5:49:04
Trace 68 11 38N36 83w19 5:33:16
Tracy 5 1 36N47'53 85w58'14 5:43:53
Tram 36 11 37N34'24 82w38'47 5:30:35
Trammel 2 6 36N47'07 86w21'12 5:45:25
Transylvania Beach 56
68 38N20'28 85w38'24 5:42:34
Trapp 25 33 37N53'00 84w03'18 5:36:13
Trappist 90 51 37N40 85w32 5:42:08
Travellers Rest 95
16 37N26'54 83w47'14 5:35:09
Tremont 48 15 36N50'38 83w23'50 5:33:35
Trent 119 16 37N46'19 83w27'41 5:33:51
Trenton 110 1 36N43'26 87w15'46 5:49:03
Tress Shop 110 1 36N49'44 87w13'06 5:48:52
Tribbey 97 46 37N18'16 83w08'40 5:32:35
Tribune 28 1 37N20'52 87w59'31 5:51:58
Tri City 42 1 36N35'23 88w31'55 5:54:08
Trigg Furnace 111
1 36N53'24 87w56'10 5:51:45
Trimble 100 19 37N00'43 84w44'09 5:38:57
Trinity 68 11 38N40'01 83w36'59 5:34:28
Triplett 103 16 38N17'36 83w23'47 5:33:35
Trisler 92 1 37N38 86w43 5:46:52
Tri-State 10 11 38N25 82w36 5:30:24
Trixie 26 16 37N20'07 83w40'12 5:34:41
Trosper 61 15 36N47'18 83w49'09 5:35:17
Trout 112 51 38N38'19 85w24'32 5:41:38
Troy 120 45 37N54'36 84w41'41 5:38:47
Truitt 45 11 38N34'30 83w00'31 5:32:02
Tuck 30 1 37N40'54 87w09'11 5:48:37
Tucker 56 68 38N06 85w42 5:42:48
Tuckertown 114 1 37N04'35 86w15'41 5:45:03
Tuggleville 7 15 36N46'20 83w30'16 5:34:01
Tunnel Hill 51 1 37N41'03 87w38'28 5:50:34
Tunnel Hills 47
61 37N43'58 85w49'53 5:43:20
Turin 95 16 37N29 83w40 5:34:40
Turkey 13 16 37N28'45 83w30'28 5:34:02
Turkey Creek 98
11 37N40'15 82w18'26 5:29:14
Turkey Foot 105
16 38N20'18 84w30'40 5:38:03
Turkeytown 69 16 37N25'14 84w29'13 5:37:57
Turner Landing 4
1 37N10'11 89w04'10 5:56:17
Turners Station 52
57 38N33'20 85w10'04 5:40:40
Turnersville 69
16 37N29'25 84w44'20 5:38:57
Turnertown (Berrys Lick P O) 16
1 37N03'37 86w45'36 5:47:02
Turnertown 107 1 36N46'29 86w39'19 5:46:37
Tutor Key 58 11 37N50'40 82w46'01 5:31:04
Tuttle 63 16 37N00'37 83w55'54 5:35:44
Tway 48 15 36N49'38 83w18'58 5:33:16
Twentysix 88 40 37N56'41 83w21'40 5:33:27

Twila 48 15 36N46'20 83w23'40 5:33:35
Twin Lakes 70 1 36N57'50 88w11'24 5:52:46
Twin Oaks 34 28 38N01'09 84w32'27 5:38:10
Tyewhoppety 110 1 37N01'56 87w07'22 5:48:29
Tygarts 45 11 38N36 83w00 5:32:00
Tygarts Valley 45
11 38N28'54 83w01'55 5:32:08
Tyler 38 1 36N30'27 89w21'05 5:57:24
Tyler 73 1 37N03'36 88w34'58 5:54:20
Tyner 55 16 37N20'43 83w54'15 5:35:37
Typo 97 46 37N16'48 83w15'18 5:33:01
Tyrone 3 44 38N01'58 84w50'11 5:39:21
Ula 100 19 37N05'54 84w25'50 5:37:43
Ulvah 67 16 37N07'40 83w03'08 5:32:13
Ulysses 64 11 37N56'45 82w40'25 5:30:42
Union 8 11 38N56'45 84w40'50 5:38:43
Union City 31 6 37N08'13 86w04'19 5:44:17
Union City 76 16 37N47'50 84w11'52 5:36:47
Union Hall 33 27 37N41 83w57 5:35:48
Union Mills 57 29 37N53'25 84w30'36 5:38:02
Union Ridge 89 1 37N08'13 87w00'07 5:48:00
Union Star 14 1 37N56'18 86w27'06 5:45:48
Uniontown 113 1 37N46'31 87w55'50 5:51:43
Unity 10 11 38N28 82w39 5:30:36
University 34 28 38N02 84w30 5:38:00
Uno 50 6 37N11'21 85w49'28 5:43:18
Upchurch 27 1 36N44'47 85w06'39 5:40:27
Upper Blue Licks 91
16 38N19'55 83w51'24 5:35:26
Upper Clover 48
15 36N53 83w04 5:32:16
Upper Elk 98 11 37N29 82w04 5:28:16
Upper Gillmore 119
16 37N43'25 83w21'46 5:33:27
Upper Hodge Landing 70
1 37N02'05 88w27'11 5:53:49
Upper Kings Addition 45
11 38N43 82w58 5:31:52
Upper Spencer 87
16 38N01'48 83w50'49 5:35:23
Upper Tygarts 22
16 38N17'45 83w16'46 5:33:07
Upton 47 51 37N27'54 85w53'36 5:43:34
Urban 26 16 37N09'26 83w50'49 5:35:23
Utica 30 1 37N36'08 87w06'47 5:48:27
Utility 46 1 37N54 86w45 5:47:00
Utley Ford 17 1 37N19'41 87w50'10 5:51:21
Uttingertown 34
28 38N02'23 84w22'10 5:37:29
Uz 67 16 37N07 82w49 5:31:16
Vada 65 16 37N37'21 83w35'27 5:34:22
Valeria 119 16 37N49'48 83w31'00 5:34:04
Valley 56 68 38N06'22 85w51'44 5:43:27
Valley Downs 56
68 38N06'50 85w52'23 5:43:30
Valley Gardens 56
68 38N07'04 85w52'21 5:43:29
Valley Hill 115
51 37N45'03 85w15'44 5:41:03
Valley Oak 100 19 37N11'21 84w28'20 5:37:53
Valley Station 56
68 38N06'40 85w52'13 5:43:29
Valley View 76 16 37N50'46 84w25'50 5:37:43
Van 67 16 37N09'05 82w52'25 5:31:30
Vanarsdell 84 44 37N53'33 84w52'50 5:39:31
Van Buren 3 18 37N58'28 85w09'55 5:40:40
Vanceburg 68 11 38N35'57 83w19'08 5:33:17
Vancleve 13 16 37N37'39 83w24'49 5:33:39
Van Cleve 18 1 36N39'16 88w14'20 5:52:57
Vanderburg 117 1 37N29'14 87w38'39 5:50:35
Vandetta 54 1 37N27'05 87w25'31 5:49:42
Vanhook 100 19 37N12'50 84w24'08 5:37:37
Van Lear 58 11 37N46'16 82w45'29 5:31:02
Van Voorhis Manor 82
51 37N54'19 85w59'21 5:43:57
Vanzant 14 1 37N38'35 86w36'45 5:46:27
Varilla 7 15 36N44'22 83w36'00 5:34:24
Varney 98 11 37N38'19 82w25'26 5:29:42
Vaughns Mill 99
16 37N48'47 83w55'00 5:35:40
Veachland 106 54 38N12'41 85w11'51 5:40:47
Vealsburg 42 1 36N36'10 88w32'24 5:54:10
Veazey 54 1 37N26'53 87w35'25 5:50:22
Veech 106 51 38N07'12 85w19'16 5:41:17
Veechdale 106 51 38N12'40 85w21'00 5:41:24
Venters 98 11 37N19'53 82w26'16 5:29:45
Vento 50 51 37N25'05 85w53'35 5:43:34
Venus 49 21 38N26'31 84w11'33 5:36:46
Verda 48 15 36N50'55 83w13'09 5:32:53
Verne 118 15 36N43'09 84w04'11 5:36:17
Vernon 86 1 36N38'13 85w30'33 5:42:02
Verona 8 11 38N49'06 84w39'39 5:38:39
Versailles 120 45 38N03'09 84w43'48 5:38:55
Vertrees 47 51 37N41'47 86w08'04 5:44:32
Vest 60 16 37N23'48 83w00'24 5:32:02
Vester 1 1 37N06 85w18 5:41:12
Vianna 25 27 37N50'10 84w02'18 5:36:09
Vicco 97 46 37N12'56 83w03'42 5:32:15
Vicksburg 70 1 37N11'07 88w19'58 5:53:20
Victoria 54 1 37N18'25 87w30'28 5:50:02
Victoria Crossroads 46
1 37N44'52 86w40'40 5:46:43
Victory 63 16 37N15'14 84w05'44 5:36:23
View 28 1 37N15'48 88w08'19 5:52:33
Viley 34 28 38N04'32 84w33'06 5:38:12
Villa Hills 59 71 39N03 84w35 5:38:20
Vincent 95 16 37N28'06 83w46'26 5:35:06
Vine 26 16 37N18'46 83w50'22 5:35:21
Vine Grove 47 51 37N48'36 85w58'53 5:43:56
Vine Grove Junction 47
51 37N49'55 85w56'05 5:43:44
Vineyard 16 1 37N14'45 86w29'18 5:45:57
Vineyard 57 29 37N50'38 84w35'16 5:38:21
Vinnie 104 1 37N00'39 84w52'09 5:39:29
Viola 42 1 36N51'20 88w38'29 5:54:34
Viper 97 46 37N10'58 83w08'54 5:32:36
Virden 99 16 37N52'55 83w57'18 5:35:49
Virgie 98 11 37N20'06 82w34'47 5:30:19
Virginia 117 1 37N27'50 87w53'30 5:51:34
Visalia 59 11 38N54'58 84w26'57 5:37:48
Volga 58 11 37N52'17 82w52'24 5:31:30
Vortex 119 16 37N41'50 83w31'38 5:34:07
Vox 63 16 36N59'11 84w11'57 5:36:48

Wabaco 97 46 37N15 83w11 5:32:44
Wabash 50 51 37N24'23 85w50'58 5:43:24
Wabd 102 36 37N18'48 84w23'23 5:37:34
Waco 76 16 37N44'33 84w08'39 5:36:35
Waddy 106 51 38N08'13 85w04'28 5:40:18
Wadesboro 18 1 36N44'53 88w19'17 5:53:17
Wagersville 33 27 37N37'35 83w57'14 5:35:49
Wagner 103 16 38N11 83w16 5:33:04
Wago 27 1 36N44'11 85w10'21 5:40:41
Waite 116 1 36N46'03 84w59'42 5:39:59
Waitman 46 1 37N54'29 86w57'03 5:47:48
Wakefield 108 51 37N58'18 85w18'29 5:41:14
Walbridge 64 11 38N04'39 82w36'10 5:30:25
Walche Cut 17 1 37N05'47 87w47'52 5:51:11
Walden 118 15 36N50'45 84w10'04 5:36:40
Waldo 77 11 37N34'33 82w58'40 5:31:55
Wales 98 11 37N20'10 82w38'17 5:30:33
Walker 61 15 36N52'59 83w42'54 5:34:52
Walkertown 97 46 37N15'49 83w11'26 5:32:46
Wallace 120 48 38N07'16 84w41'32 5:38:46
Wallaceton 76 16 37N34'05 84w21'44 5:37:27
Wallingford 35 16 38N24'18 83w36'44 5:34:27
Wallins Creek 48
15 36N49'52 83w25'01 5:33:40
Wallonia 111 1 36N56'40 87w47'00 5:51:08
Wallsend 7 15 36N45'58 83w42'36 5:34:50
Walltown 23 51 37N19'20 84w43'54 5:38:56
Walnut Flat 69 16 37N29'43 84w34'44 5:38:19
Walnut Grove 2 1 36N39 86w16 5:45:04
Walnut Grove 79 1 36N49'43 88w19'07 5:53:16
Walnut Grove 100
19 37N16'18 84w27'03 5:37:48
Walnut Hill 2 6 36N43'23 86w02'45 5:44:11
Walnut Hill 34 28 37N57'33 84w24'57 5:37:40
Walsh 45 11 38N40'52 82w57'54 5:31:52
Waltersville 99
16 37N51'53 83w56'04 5:35:44
Walton 8 14 38N52'12 84w36'48 5:38:27
Waltz 103 16 38N19'00 83w26'39 5:33:47
Wanamaker 117 1 37N36'00 87w39'27 5:50:38
Waneta 55 16 37N28'28 84w02'28 5:36:10
Warbranch 66 16 36N57'24 83w27'01 5:33:48
Warco 36 11 37N32'39 82w46'33 5:31:06
War Creek 13 16 37N35'47 83w29'12 5:33:57
Wards 44 51 37N27'34 85w36'37 5:42:26
Ware 23 51 37N12'31 84w46'08 5:39:05
Warfield 80 11 37N50'39 82w25'03 5:29:40
Warnock 45 11 38N29'33 82w58'43 5:31:55
Warren 61 15 36N45'12 83w50'39 5:35:23
Warrenton 34 28 38N03'59 84w28'01 5:37:52
Warsaw 39 12 38N47'00 84w54'06 5:39:36
Washington 81 11 38N36'57 83w48'31 5:35:14
Wasioto 7 15 36N44'51 83w41'20 5:34:45
Watauga 27 1 36N49'01 85w03'53 5:40:16
Waterford 108 51 38N02'20 85w26'14 5:41:45
Watergap 36 11 37N38'11 82w44'45 5:30:59
Waterloo 8 11 38N58'20 84w47'23 5:39:10
Water Valley 42 1 36N34 88w49 5:55:16
Waterview 29 1 36N49'01 85w27'30 5:41:50
Watkinsville 105
16 38N14'35 84w43'35 5:38:54
Watterfern Hills 56
68 38N10 85w36 5:42:24
Watts 13 16 37N26'40 83w18'50 5:33:15
Watts Creek 118
15 36N44 84w10 5:36:40
Waverly 113 1 37N42'35 87w48'46 5:51:15
Waverly Hills 56
68 38N07'26 85w50'27 5:43:22
Wax 43 1 37N21'15 86w07'20 5:44:29
Wayland 36 11 37N26'42 82w48'19 5:31:13
Waynesburg 69 16 37N19'58 84w40'18 5:38:41
Wayside 3 44 38N01'30 85w06'19 5:40:25
Weaverton 51 8 37N48'56 87w35'02 5:50:20
Webb Mills 47 51 37N33 86w02 5:44:08
Webbs 44 6 37N15'32 85w36'07 5:42:24
Webbs Cross Roads 104
1 37N06'33 85w03'13 5:40:13
Webbville 64 11 38N10'46 82w52'17 5:31:29
Weberstown 46 1 37N46'13 86w46'44 5:47:07
Webster 14 1 37N53'20 86w20'20 5:45:21
Wedonia 81 11 38N31 83w50 5:35:20
Weed 1 1 37N02'19 85w28'17 5:41:53
Weedonia 81 11 38N29'56 83w45'24 5:35:02
Weeksbury 36 11 37N19'40 82w41'18 5:30:45
Weir 89 1 37N07'23 87w12'45 5:48:51
Welborn 100 19 37N11'54 84w29'52 5:37:59
Welchburg 55 16 37N19'14 83w55'48 5:35:43
Welchs Creek 16 1 37N20'41 86w34'05 5:46:16
Welcome 16 1 37N18'13 86w39'05 5:46:36
Welco Station 36
11 37N29'12 82w50'10 5:31:21
Weldon 82 51 38N00 86w10 5:44:40
Wellhope 102 36 37N18'58 84w19'06 5:37:16
Wellington 56 68 38N12'59 85w40'09 5:42:41
Wellington 83 16 37N54'52 83w30'43 5:34:03
Wells 88 40 37N52 83w16 5:33:04
Wells 89 1 37N08'29 87w04'29 5:48:18
Wellsburg 12 11 38N46'17 84w06'13 5:36:25
Wells Fork 13 16 37N32'16 83w12'34 5:32:50
Wells Hill 88 40 37N55'36 83w16'19 5:33:05
Wells Landing 11
25 37N39 84w46 5:39:04
Wendover 66 16 37N07'35 83w21'46 5:33:27
Wentz 67 46 37N04'54 83w03'50 5:32:15
Wesco 54 1 37N17'33 87w30'42 5:50:03
Wesleyan Park 25
33 37N59'30 84w11'36 5:36:46
Wesleyville 22 16 38N23'41 83w10'18 5:32:41
Westbend 99 16 37N54'21 83w58'09 5:35:53
West Brook 24 1 36N48'17 87w30'41 5:50:03
West Buechel 56
68 38N11'49 85w39'48 5:42:39
West Clifty 43 1 37N30'48 86w11'18 5:44:45
West Covington 59
71 39N05'20 84w32'02 5:38:08
West Danville 11
25 37N38'41 84w47'25 5:39:10
Western 38 1 36N33 89w20 5:57:20
West Fairview 10
11 38N28'14 82w41'03 5:30:44
West Fayette 34
28 38N02 84w34 5:38:16

West Fork 2 1 36N46'58 86w16'50 5:45:07
West Frankfort 37 20 38N12 84w52 5:39:28
West Future City 73 1 37N03'47 88w48'36 5:55:14
West Garrett 36 11 37N29'04 82w50'06 5:31:20
West Irvine 33 27 37N42'05 83w59'27 5:35:58
West Liberty 88 40 37N55'17 83w15'35 5:33:02
West Louisville 30 1 37N41'48 87w17'13 5:49:09
Westmoreland 34 45 38N02'43 84w38'04 5:38:32
Weston 28 1 37N28'21 88w04'22 5:52:17
Weston 91 16 38N17'49 83w57'47 5:35:51
West Paducah 73 1 37N04'59 88w44'39 5:54:59
West Paris 9 30 38N13 84w15 5:37:00
Westplains 42 1 36N49'31 88w35'41 5:54:23
West Point 47 64 37N59'58 85w56'37 5:43:46
Westport 93 52 38N28'44 85w28'30 5:41:54
West Prestonsburg 36 11 37N40'16 82w46'55 5:31:08
West Royalton 77 11 37N41 83w02 5:32:08
West Russell 45 11 38N32'17 82w42'39 5:30:51
West Side Heights 54 1 37N16'38 87w31'23 5:50:06
West Van Lear 58 11 37N47'10 82w46'17 5:31:05
Westview 14 1 37N42'00 86w24'33 5:45:38
West Viola 42 1 36N51'19 88w39'46 5:54:39
West Wheatcroft 117 1 37N29'17 87w52'16 5:51:29
West Wind Park 56 68 38N08 85w51 5:43:24
Westwood 10 11 38N28'59 82w40'12 5:30:41
Westwood 56 68 38N16'48 85w34'58 5:42:20
Weymouth 42 1 36N30 88w53 5:55:32
Whaynes Corner 53 1 36N38'57 89w07'18 5:56:29
Wheatcroft 117 1 37N29'24 87w51'46 5:51:27
Wheatley 94 16 38N36'48 84w58'37 5:39:54
Wheel 42 1 36N51'20 88w48'13 5:55:13
Wheeler 61 15 36N43'31 83w50'35 5:35:22
Wheelersburg 77 11 37N49'36 83w00'40 5:32:03
Wheelers Mill 43 1 37N23'38 86w01'34 5:44:06
Wheel Rim 88 11 37N43'34 83w16'01 5:33:04
Wheelwright 36 11 37N19'57 82w43'16 5:30:53
Wheelwright Junction 36 11 37N21'11 82w43'01 5:30:52
Whetstone 100 19 37N05'13 84w23'28 5:37:34
Whick 13 16 37N25'18 83w22'34 5:33:30
Whickerville 50 1 37N12'01 85w41'26 5:42:46
Whipple 7 15 36N46 83w33 5:34:12
Whippoorwill 71 1 36N49'00 87w00'35 5:48:02
Whipps Millgate 56 70 38N16'24 85w34'20 5:42:17
Whipps Mill Village 56 70 38N17 85w35 5:42:20
Whispering Hills 56 68 38N09 85w42 5:42:48
Whitaker 36 11 37N43'24 82w50'49 5:31:23
Whitaker 67 16 37N10'20 82w43'18 5:30:53
Whitco 67 16 37N07'10 82w51'05 5:31:24
White Ash 65 16 37N33'23 83w44'12 5:34:57
White City 51 8 37N57'10 87w35'05 5:50:20
White City 54 1 37N11 87w23 5:49:32
White City 62 51 37N35'22 85w39'52 5:42:39
White Hall 76 31 37N45 84w18 5:37:12
Whitehouse 58 11 37N52'25 82w41'56 5:30:48
White Lily 100 19 37N04 84w31 5:38:04
White Mills 47 51 37N33'19 86w01'56 5:44:08
White Mills Junction 47 51 37N34'39 86w02'08 5:44:09
White Oak 40 16 37N44'16 84w38'35 5:38:34
White Oak 88 16 37N51'30 83w12'08 5:32:49
White Oak Junction 74 16 36N42'10 84w35'35 5:38:22
White Plains 2 6 36N45 86w11 5:44:44
White Plains 54 1 37N11'01 87w23'01 5:49:32
White Rose 109 51 37N25'16 85w27'40 5:41:51
White Run 92 1 37N26'41 86w38'31 5:46:34
Whites 76 43 37N37'50 84w17'58 5:37:12
Whitesburg 67 16 37N07'06 82w49'37 5:31:18
White Sulphur 17 1 37N08'44 87w56'24 5:51:46
White Sulphur 105 26 38N12'18 84w42'08 5:38:49
Whitesville 30 1 37N40'59 86w52'17 5:47:29
White Tower 59 11 38N55'30 84w30'48 5:38:03
White Villa 59 11 38N52'45 84w27'02 5:37:48
Whitewood 44 6 37N17'01 85w26'10 5:41:45
Whitfield 15 51 38N05'46 85w28'14 5:41:53
Whitley City 74 16 36N43'24 84w28'14 5:37:53
Whitner 56 69 38N11'19 85w41'30 5:42:46
Whittinghill 16 1 37N15'13 86w31'06 5:46:04
Whittle 104 1 37N01'19 84w57'42 5:39:51
Whoopflarea 95 16 37N17'52 83w34'05 5:34:16
Wiborg 74 16 36N48'33 84w29'27 5:37:58
Wickliffe 20 1 36N57'53 89w05'21 5:56:21
Wicks Well 54 1 37N20 87w30 5:50:00
Widecreek 13 16 37N36'40 83w31'53 5:34:08
Wilbur 64 11 37N59'10 82w47'05 5:31:08
Wild Cat 26 16 37N14'04 83w41'27 5:34:46
Wilder 19 71 39N02 84w27 5:37:48
Wilder Park 56 69 38N11'43 85w45'55 5:43:04
Wilders 19 71 39N03'35 84w28'49 5:37:55
Wildie 102 16 37N25'24 84w18'08 5:37:13
Wildwood 56 70 38N14'58 85w34'23 5:42:18
Wildwood Hills 72 1 37N00'32 88w02'23 5:52:10
Wilhelmina 110 1 36N50'35 87w09'28 5:48:38
Wilhoit (Dayhoit P O) 48 15 36N50'23 83w22'37 5:33:30
Wilhurst 13 16 37N37'58 83w24'53 5:33:40
Willailla 102 16 37N18'16 84w27'47 5:37:51
Willard 22 16 38N12'42 82w53'50 5:31:35
Williams 88 16 37N52 83w12 5:32:48
Williams 92 1 37N23 86w55 5:47:40
Williams 117 1 37N31'25 87w51'35 5:51:26
Williamsburg 118 15 36N44'36 84w09'35 5:36:38
Williams Creek 22 16 38N17'18 82w49'54 5:31:20
Williamsport 58 11 37N49'14 82w43'45 5:30:55
Williams Station 117 1 37N29 87w50 5:51:20
Williams Store 71 1 36N45 86w53 5:47:32
Williamstown 41 11 38N38'17 84w33'38 5:38:15
Williba 65 16 37N37'23 83w34'09 5:34:17
Willisburg 115 51 37N48'35 85w07'35 5:40:30
Willis Creek 27 1 36N48'51 85w13'19 5:40:53
Willow 12 11 38N39'56 84w09'09 5:36:37
Willow 65 16 37N35'28 83w48'49 5:35:15
Willow Crest 37 20 38N12 84w52 5:39:28
Willow Grove 12 11 38N47'18 84w10'19 5:36:41
Willow Shade 85 1 36N50'52 85w36'28 5:42:26
Willowtown 109 51 37N27'07 85w25'19 5:41:41
Willow Tree 33 27 37N41 83w57 5:35:48
Wilmore 57 23 37N51'43 84w39'42 5:38:39
Wilson 51 1 37N46'50 87w39'29 5:50:38
Wilsonville 11 25 37N35'39 84w52'39 5:39:31
Wilstacy 13 16 37N32'01 83w15'10 5:33:01
Wilton 61 15 36N53'25 84w02'51 5:36:11
Win 58 11 37N52'42 82w58'51 5:31:55
Winchester 25 33 37N59'24 84w10'47 5:36:43
Wind Cave 55 16 37N30'45 83w55'44 5:35:43
Winding Way 37 20 38N12 84w52 5:39:28
Windsor 23 51 37N07'40 84w54'44 5:39:39
Windy 116 1 36N44'47 84w58'52 5:39:55
Windy Hill 92 1 37N25'11 86w42'19 5:46:49
Windy Hills 56 68 38N16'26 85w38'04 5:42:32
Windyville 31 1 37N12'58 86w19'28 5:45:18
Windyville 43 1 37N21'37 86w25'08 5:45:41
Winesap 50 1 37N17'14 86w00'58 5:44:04
Winford 20 1 36N55'37 89w03'36 5:56:14
Wingo 42 1 36N38'32 88w44'20 5:54:57
Winifred 58 11 37N56'46 82w51'17 5:31:25
Winslow 10 11 38N27'13 82w40'55 5:30:44
Winslow Park 28 1 37N20 88w04 5:52:16
Winston 33 16 37N42'20 84w04'56 5:36:20
Winston Park 19 71 39N02'30 84w30'09 5:38:01
Wiscoal 60 16 37N14'14 83w03'22 5:32:13
Wisconsin 60 16 37N15 83w03 5:32:12
Wisdom 85 1 37N00'14 85w43'12 5:42:53
Wisemantown 33 27 37N40'43 84w00'23 5:36:02
Wises Landing 112 51 38N34'23 85w24'30 5:41:38
Wiswell 18 1 36N35'00 88w23'17 5:53:33
Withrow 90 65 37N50'06 85w28'21 5:41:53
Witt 33 27 37N40'23 84w01'36 5:36:06
Wittensville 58 11 37N51'46 82w47'59 5:31:12
Witt Springs 33 27 37N43'47 84w01'45 5:36:07
Wofford 118 15 36N46'57 84w08'07 5:36:32
Wolf 22 16 38N22'45 83w05'58 5:32:24
Wolf Coal 13 16 37N23'54 83w22'40 5:33:31
Wolf Creek 82 51 38N06'10 86w23'23 5:45:34
Wolf Lick 71 1 37N01'08 86w57'22 5:47:49
Wolfpit 98 11 37N21'10 82w25'23 5:29:42
Wolf River Dock 27 1 36N37'34 85w12'31 5:40:50
Wollingtown 43 1 37N22 86w15 5:45:00
Wolverine 13 16 37N34'51 83w24'30 5:33:38
Wonder 36 11 37N38'01 82w36'24 5:30:26
Wonnie 77 11 37N48'33 83w09'15 5:32:37
Woodbine 118 15 36N54'17 84w05'20 5:36:21
Woodburn 114 1 36N50'33 86w31'39 5:46:07
Woodbury 16 1 37N11'00 86w38'02 5:46:32
Woodford Village 120 45 38N02'32 84w43'31 5:38:54
Woodhill 56 68 38N09 85w42 5:42:48
Woodlake 37 20 38N12'38 84w45'13 5:39:01
Woodland Hills 56 70 38N14'25 85w31'27 5:42:06
Woodland Park 97 46 37N14'48 83w10'40 5:32:43
Woodlawn 19 71 39N05'33 84w28'31 5:37:54
Woodlawn 73 1 37N02'31 88w34'08 5:54:17
Woodlawn 90 51 37N48'47 85w21'55 5:41:28
Woodlawn Park 56 68 38N15'41 85w37'45 5:42:31
Woodman 98 11 37N31'16 82w02'41 5:28:11
Woodrow 14 1 37N44'29 86w19'11 5:45:17
Woods 36 11 37N38'08 82w39'10 5:30:37
Woods 48 15 36N51'39 83w10'44 5:32:43
Woodsbend 88 40 37N54'42 83w20'26 5:33:22
Woodside 31 1 37N15'12 86w15'54 5:45:04
Woodside 56 70 38N18'18 85w39'11 5:42:37
Woodside 98 11 37N24'27 82w20'03 5:29:20
Woodsonville 50 6 37N15'46 85w53'18 5:43:33
Woodstock 100 19 37N15'41 84w31'00 5:38:04
Woodville 73 1 37N05'48 88w52'24 5:55:30
Woolcott 12 11 38N43'58 84w06'01 5:36:24
Wooleyville 109 51 37N22'45 85w14'49 5:40:59
Woollum 61 15 37N01'11 83w49'03 5:35:16
Wooton 66 16 37N10'44 83w18'08 5:33:13
Worley 74 16 36N41'58 84w32'02 5:38:08
Worthington 45 11 38N32'54 82w43'28 5:30:54
Worthington 56 70 38N18'56 85w33'42 5:42:15
Worthville 21 17 38N36'35 85w04'03 5:40:16
Wray Gap 116 1 36N47'17 84w51'06 5:39:24
Wrights 109 51 37N18'45 85w24'00 5:41:36
Wrightsburg 75 1 37N35'29 87w24'11 5:49:37
Wrigley 88 16 38N01'06 83w16'17 5:33:05
Wurtland 45 11 38N33'01 82w46'41 5:31:07
Wyandotte 25 16 38N02'59 84w16'20 5:37:05
Wyett 32 16 38N06'35 83w15'13 5:33:01
Wyman 75 1 37N37'56 87w19'57 5:49:20
Wynns 24 1 37N11 87w23 5:49:32
Wyoming 6 16 38N13'11 83w41'55 5:34:48
Wysox 92 1 37N16'23 86w54'28 5:47:38
Yaden 118 15 36N44'25 84w06'08 5:36:25
Yamacraw 74 16 36N43'01 84w32'15 5:38:09
Yancey 48 15 36N46'07 83w19'15 5:33:17
Yarnallton 34 28 38N06'22 84w35'08 5:38:21
Yatesville 64 11 38N08'52 82w41'10 5:30:45
Yeaddiss 66 16 37N04'07 83w13'04 5:32:52
Yeager 61 15 36N52 83w48 5:35:12
Yeager 98 11 37N23'30 82w31'18 5:30:05
Yeaman 43 1 37N31'04 86w34'39 5:46:19
Yellow Creek 7 15 36N35'14 83w46'51 5:35:07
Yellow Rock 65 16 37N34'15 83w48'18 5:35:13
Yelvington 30 1 37N51'20 86w58'02 5:47:52
Yerkes 97 46 37N16'38 83w18'04 5:33:12
Yesse 2 6 36N51'11 86w11'50 5:44:47
Yocum 88 16 37N59'00 83w19'30 5:33:18
Yocum Creek 48 15 36N52 83w12 5:32:48
Yoder 108 51 38N03'38 85w20'42 5:41:23
York 45 11 38N33'56 83w02'47 5:32:11
Yorktown 98 11 37N26'34 82w31'30 5:30:06
Yosemite 23 51 37N20'48 84w49'29 5:39:18
Younger Creek 47 61 37N45'24 85w43'25 5:42:54
Youngs Creek 118 15 36N51'55 84w14'28 5:36:58
Youngtown 16 1 37N10'53 86w43'07 5:46:52
Yuba 113 1 37N34'34 87w50'19 5:51:21
Yuma 109 51 37N16'49 85w14'30 5:40:58
Zachariah 119 16 37N42'18 83w41'01 5:34:44
Zag 88 40 37N59'12 83w21'54 5:33:28
Zandale 34 28 38N00'19 84w30'44 5:38:03
Zebulon 98 11 37N32'00 82w28'00 5:29:52
Zekes Point 55 16 37N21'03 83w53'20 5:35:33
Zelda 64 11 38N11'42 82w36'17 5:30:25
Zilpo 6 16 38N04'28 83w29'36 5:33:58
Zion 41 11 38N44 84w45 5:39:00
Zion 51 1 37N48'53 87w29'01 5:49:56
Zion 110 1 36N40'40 87w17'45 5:49:11
Zion Hill 105 48 38N07'12 84w38'16 5:38:33
Zion Station 41 11 38N45'10 84w42'34 5:38:50
Zoe 65 16 37N40'49 83w41'03 5:34:44
Zoneton 15 53 38N03'48 85w40'14 5:42:41
Zula 116 1 36N46'02 84w58'46 5:39:55

TIME TABLES

LA # 1			LA # 2		
Before 11/18/1883		LMT	Before 11/18/1883		LMT
11/18/1883	12:00	CST	11/18/1883	12:00	CST
3/31/1918	02:00	CWT	3/31/1918	02:00	CWT
10/27/1918	02:00	CST	10/27/1918	02:00	CST
3/30/1919	02:00	CWT	3/30/1919	02:00	CWT
10/26/1919	02:00	CST	10/26/1919	02:00	CST
2/09/1942	02:00	CWT	2/09/1942	02:00	CWT
9/30/1945	02:00	CST	9/30/1945	02:00	CST
4/30/1967	02:00	US#1	4/29/1946	02:00	CDT
....			9/29/1946	02:00	CST
			4/30/1967	02:00	US#1

COUNTIES

1 Acadia
2 Allen
3 Ascension
4 Assumption
5 Avoyelles
6 Beauregard
7 Bienville
8 Bossier
9 Caddo
10 Calcasieu
11 Caldwell
12 Cameron
13 Catahoula
14 Claiborne
15 Concordia
16 De Soto
17 East Baton Rouge
18 East Carroll
19 East Feliciana
20 Evangeline
21 Franklin
22 Grant
23 Iberia
24 Iberville
25 Jackson
26 Jefferson
27 Jefferson Davis
28 Lafayette
29 Lafourche
30 La Salle
31 Lincoln
32 Livingston
33 Madison
34 Morehouse
35 Natchitoches
36 Orleans
37 Ouachita
38 Plaquemines
39 Pointe Coupee
40 Rapides
41 Red River
42 Richland
43 Sabine
44 St Bernard
45 St Charles
46 St Helena
47 St James
48 St John the Baptist
49 St Landry
50 St Martin
51 St Mary
52 St Tammany
53 Tangipahoa
54 Tensas
55 Terrebonne
56 Union
57 Vermilion
58 Vernon
59 Washington
60 Webster
61 West Baton Rouge
62 West Carroll
63 West Feliciana
64 Winn

Abbeville 57 1 29N58'28 92W08'03 6:08:32
Abby Plantation 29
1 29N48'42 90W50'27 6:03:22
Aben 3 1 30N06'28 90W56'34 6:03:46
Abington 41 1 32N06'41 93W28'43 6:13:55
Abita Springs 52
1 30N28'42 90W02'15 6:00:09
Acadia 29 1 29N46'07 90W48'05 6:03:12
Acadia Academy 1
1 30N29 92W25 6:09:40
Acme 15 1 31N17'08 91W49'13 6:07:17
Acy 3 1 30N13'07 90W49'13 6:03:17
Ada 7 1 32N32'45 93W08'25 6:12:34
Addis 61 1 30N21'13 91W15'55 6:05:04
Adeline 51 1 29N52'22 91W35'27 6:06:22
Adner 8 1 32N34'01 93W36'28 6:14:26
Advance 25 1 32N17 92W43 6:10:52
Afeman 40 1 31N06'09 92W49'06 6:11:16
Afton 33 1 32N14'41 91W11'29 6:04:46
Aimwell 13 1 31N47'00 91W59'36 6:07:58
Airview Terrace 40
1 31N17 92W29 6:09:56
Ajax 35 1 31N52'35 93W23'23 6:13:34
Akers 53 1 30N17 90W24 6:01:36
Alabama Landing 56
1 32N52'25 92W05'04 6:08:20
Albania 51 1 29N55 91W40 6:06:40
Albany 32 1 30N30'15 90W34'56 6:02:20
Albermarle 4 1 29N52'57 90W58'29 6:03:54
Alberta 7 1 32N13'58 93W09'13 6:12:37
Alco 58 1 31N20 93W08 6:12:32
Alden Bridge 8 1 32N46'30 93W43'12 6:14:53
Alexandria 40 1 31N18'40 92W26'42 6:09:47
Alexandria June 40
1 31N17'27 92W26'36 6:09:46
Alfalfa 40 1 31N22'10 92W37'06 6:10:28
Alfords 61 1 30N34'09 91W19'08 6:05:17
Algiers 36 2 29N56'41 90W02'48 6:00:11
Alhambra 24 1 30N10'35 91W07'23 6:04:30
Alice 63 1 30N55'11 91W17'51 6:05:11
Alice B 51 1 29N46'34 91W45'25 6:07:02
Allemand 55 1 29N39'36 90W45'56 6:03:04
Allemands 29 1 29N49 90W29 6:01:56
Allen 35 1 31N50'07 93W17'18 6:13:09
Allendale 61 1 30N29'47 91W16'22 6:05:05
Allen Landing 61
1 30N30'02 91W16'15 6:05:05
Alliance 38 1 29N41'18 89W58'54 5:59:56
Allon 39 1 30N38'28 91W29'38 6:05:59
Alluvial City 44
2 29N50'28 89W41'29 5:58:46
Alma 39 1 30N35'46 91W23'22 6:05:33
Almadane 58 1 30N56'30 93W30'17 6:14:01
Almedia 45 2 29N58'24 90W18'02 6:01:12
Aloha 22 1 31N34'59 92W46'20 6:11:05
Aloysia 24 1 30N10 91W09 6:04:36
Alpha 35 1 31N58'20 93W11'28 6:12:46
Alphenia Landing 54
1 31N49'10 91W34'14 6:06:17
Alsatia 18 1 32N36'46 91W10'56 6:04:44
Alsen 17 1 30N34'16 91W12'15 6:04:49
Alto 42 1 32N21'27 91W51'35 6:07:26
Alton 52 1 30N19'50 89W45'43 5:59:03
Altoona 33 1 32N27'16 91W27'13 6:05:49
Alvin Callender 38
2 29N45 90W00 6:00:00
Ama 45 2 29N57'07 90W17'47 6:01:11
Amelia 51 1 29N39'58 91W06'07 6:04:24
Amite 53 1 30N43'35 90W30'32 6:02:02
Amos 52 1 30N20'22 89W47'56 5:59:12
Anacoco 58 1 31N15'07 93W20'28 6:13:22
Anandale 40 1 31N15'18 92W27'14 6:09:49
Anchor 39 1 30N41'00 91W21'18 6:05:25
Anchorage 61 1 30N28'57 91W12'37 6:04:50
Anchor Landing 54
1 31N50'59 91W34'11 6:06:17
Andrepont 49 1 30N32 92W05 6:08:20
Andrew 57 1 30N05'05 92W14'34 6:08:58
Andrew Guillot 29
1 29N47 90W50 6:03:20
Angelina 48 1 30N03'28 90W38'04 6:02:32
Angie 59 1 30N57'59 89W48'34 5:59:14
Angola 63 1 30N57'01 91W34'09 6:06:17
Angola Landing 63
1 30N56'38 91W38'50 6:06:35
Annadale 24 1 30N07'55 91W07'52 6:04:31
Anse La Butte 50
1 30N15'34 91W58'05 6:07:52
Ansley 25 1 32N23'44 92W41'34 6:10:46
Antioch 14 1 32N51'52 92W55'28 6:11:42
Antonia 22 1 31N33'51 92W24'33 6:09:38
Antonio 61 1 30N24'22 91W13'29 6:04:54
Antrim 8 1 32N52'38 93W42'18 6:14:49
Arabi 44 2 29N57'15 90W00'19 6:00:01
Ararat 10 1 30N18'01 93W11'59 6:12:48
Arboth 61 1 30N34 91W21 6:05:24
Arbroth 61 1 30N36'37 91W19'08 6:05:17
Arcadia 7 1 32N32'56 92W55'12 6:11:41
Arceneaux 1 1 30N17'25 92W13'41 6:08:55
Archibald 42 1 32N20'56 91W46'38 6:07:07
Archie 13 1 31N34'47 91W58'02 6:07:52
Arcola 53 1 30N46'35 90W30'37 6:02:02
Ardoyne 55 1 29N38'47 90W49'18 6:03:17
Argo 13 1 31N22 91W54 6:07:36
Argyle 39 1 30N39'30 91W38'38 6:06:35
Argyle 55 1 29N34'19 90W44'49 6:02:59
Arizona 14 1 32N47'20 92W57'27 6:11:50
Arkana 8 1 33N01'06 93W40'28 6:14:42
Arlington 17 1 30N23'17 91W10'18 6:04:41
Armistead 41 1 32N00'19 93W22'49 6:13:31
Arnaudville 50 1 30N23'51 91W55'53 6:07:44
Ashland 35 1 32N08'30 93W05'53 6:12:24
Ashland 54 1 31N58'29 91W23'32 6:05:34
Ashland 55 1 29N31'46 90W40'32 6:02:42
Ashly 33 1 32N26'29 91W07'23 6:04:30
Ashton 51 1 29N50'09 91W36'29 6:06:26
Atchafalaya 50 1 30N20'45 91W43'23 6:06:54
Athens 14 1 32N39'01 93W01'32 6:12:06
Atherton 18 1 32N41'54 91W10'13 6:04:41
Atkins 8 1 32N18'34 93W30'53 6:14:04
Atlanta 64 1 31N48'18 92W44'17 6:10:57
Attakapas Canal 4
1 29N53'30 91W05'28 6:04:22
Attakapas Landing 4
1 29N51'03 91W06'11 6:04:25
Aubin 17 1 30N25'09 91W03'47 6:04:15
Audubon 17 1 30N27 91W08 6:04:32
Audubon Terrace 17
1 30N25 91W09 6:04:36
Augusta 24 1 30N11'23 91W12'55 6:04:52
Augusta 38 2 29N48'00 90W00'27 6:00:04
Augusta 49 1 30N50'01 92W12'17 6:08:49
Avalon 51 1 29N43'04 91W19'51 6:05:19
Avery Island 23 1 29N54'12 91W54'37 6:07:38
Avondale 26 2 29N54'46 90W12'13 6:00:49
Avondale 54 1 31N56'25 91W16'54 6:05:08
Aycock 14 1 32N42'29 92W55'03 6:11:40
Azucena 54 1 31N46'40 91W26'16 6:05:45
Bagdad 22 1 31N27'59 92W35'37 6:10:22
Bains 63 1 30N49'50 91W23'12 6:05:33
Baker 17 1 30N35'17 91W10'05 6:04:40
Bakers 21 1 32N20'28 91W31'16 6:06:05
Baldwin 51 1 29N50'16 91W32'39 6:06:11
Ball 40 1 31N24'55 92W24'42 6:09:39
Balmoral 54 1 32N06'53 91W13'26 6:04:54
Bancker 57 1 29N53'06 92W07'27 6:08:30
Bancroft 6 1 30N33'54 93W41'07 6:14:44
Banker Plantation 50
1 30N08'07 91W46'48 6:07:07
Bankers 50 1 30N08'21 91W44'33 6:06:58
Banks 17 1 30N33 91W10 6:04:40
Banks Springs 11
1 32N04'55 92W05'34 6:08:22
Baptist 53 1 30N30'17 90W31'59 6:02:08
Barataria 26 2 29N43'23 90W07'25 6:00:30
Barber 20 1 30N41'30 92W25'34 6:09:42
Barbreck 49 1 30N48'36 92W11'55 6:08:48
Barcelona 54 1 31N51'09 91W25'22 6:05:41
Bardel 42 1 32N33'03 91W45'27 6:07:02
Barksdale Air Force Base 8
1 32N30 93W38 6:14:32
Barmen 3 1 30N09'44 90W48'58 6:03:16
Barnes 33 1 32N22'45 91W07'23 6:04:30
Barnet Springs 31
1 32N30'27 92W40'33 6:10:42
Barnsdall 27 1 30N28'50 92W39'18 6:10:37
Barrett 40 1 31N22'01 92W30'48 6:10:03
Barron 40 1 31N20'12 92W14'58 6:09:00
Barso 8 1 32N44'41 93W43'39 6:14:55
Barton 3 1 30N05'10 91W03'16 6:04:13
Basile 20 1 30N29'06 92W35'45 6:10:23
Baskin 21 1 32N15'32 91W44'51 6:06:59
Baskinton 21 1 32N18'40 91W40'50 6:06:43
Bassa Bassa 26 1 29N21'49 89W59'40 5:59:59
Bastrop 34 1 32N46'43 91W54'51 6:07:39
Bat 49 1 30N43'00 91W53'53 6:07:36
Batchelor 39 1 30N50'25 91W39'41 6:06:39
Bates 1 1 30N25'17 92W23'54 6:09:36
Baton Rouge 17 1 30N27'02 91W09'16 6:04:37
Batree 47 1 30N00'00 90W47'11 6:03:09
Battle 19 1 30N49'35 91W04'53 6:04:20
Bawcomville 37 1 32N28'13 92W10'02 6:08:40
Bayou Barbary 32
1 30N30 90W45 6:03:00
Bayou Blue 29 1 29N36 90W43 6:02:52
Bayou Boeuf (Kraemer P O) 29
1 29N52'09 90W35'48 6:02:23
Bayou Cane 55 1 29N38 90W45 6:03:00
Bayou Chene 50 1 30N08'27 91W32'13 6:06:09
Bayou Chicot 20 1 30N49'01 92W21'03 6:09:24
Bayou Corne 4 1 30N00'52 91W09'18 6:04:37
Bayou Crab 4 1 29N52'02 91W04'34 6:04:18
Bayou Current 49
1 30N47'51 91W48'06 6:07:12
Bayou Gauche 45 1 29N47'14 90W24'47 6:01:39
Bayou Geneve 50 1 29N48'58 91W06'15 6:04:25
Bayou Goula 24 1 30N12'35 91W10'08 6:04:41
Bayou Jack 49 1 30N50'17 91W57'49 6:07:51
Bayou Paul 24 1 30N18'43 91W06'33 6:04:26
Bayou Pigeon 24 1 30N17 91W14 6:04:56
Bayou Sale 51 1 29N44'38 91W26'10 6:05:45
Bayou Sorrel 24 1 30N09'42 91W20'08 6:05:21
Bayou Vista 51 1 29N41'22 91W16'15 6:05:05
Baywood 17 1 30N41'27 90W52'59 6:03:32
Beachview 26 2 29N59 90W15 6:01:00
Beachwood 63 1 30N51'35 91W22'07 6:05:28
Beal Crossing 64
1 31N45'14 92W41'35 6:10:46
Bear Creek 25 1 32N18'52 92W45'31 6:11:02
Bear Skin 62 1 32N40'54 91W35'46 6:06:23
Beasley Crossing 35
1 31N34'02 93W07'51 6:12:31
Beaud 39 1 30N42'24 91W29'36 6:05:58
Beaulieu 61 1 30N25'26 91W12'58 6:04:52
Beaver 20 1 30N47'44 92W34'19 6:10:17
Bedford 33 1 32N14'27 91W00'54 6:04:04
Bee Bayou 42 1 32N28'23 91W41'44 6:06:47
Beech Springs 25
1 32N18'24 92W38'48 6:10:35
Beekman 34 1 32N55'25 91W53'03 6:07:32
Beggs 49 1 30N40'49 92W03'10 6:08:13
Bel 2 1 30N31'11 93W05'04 6:12:20
Belair 38 2 29N43'13 89W58'56 5:59:56
Belair Cove 20 1 30N38'54 92W13'35 6:08:54
Belcher 9 1 32N44'55 93W49'58 6:15:20
Belfield 10 1 30N20'20 93W12'02 6:12:48
Bell City 10 1 30N06'47 92W57'45 6:11:51
Belle Alliance 4
1 30N03'04 91W01'13 6:04:05
Belle Amie 29 1 29N29'38 90W19'40 6:01:19
Belle Chasse 38 2 29N51'17 89W59'26 5:59:58
Belle d'Eau 5 1 31N05'03 92W11'30 6:08:46
Belle Place 23 1 30N00'56 91W43'36 6:06:54
Belle Point 48 1 30N04 90W33 6:02:12
Belle River 4 1 29N42 91W14 6:04:56
Belle Rose 4 1 30N03'01 91W02'29 6:04:10
Belle Terre 4 1 30N04'10 91W00'57 6:04:04
Belleview 49 1 30N32 92W05 6:08:20
Bellevue 8 1 32N40'23 93W31'19 6:14:05
Bellevue 10 1 30N11'32 93W05'03 6:12:20
Bellevue 11 1 32N06'46 92W02'57 6:08:12
Bellevue 38 1 29N37'06 89W53'25 5:59:34
Bellewood 4 1 29N54'24 91W04'05 6:04:16
Bellfontaine 17 1 30N27 91W04 6:04:16
Bell Helene 3 1 30N12 91W01 6:04:04
Bellview 11 1 32N06 92W05 6:08:20
Bellview 26 2 29N54 90W03 6:00:12
Bellview 51 1 29N48 91W30 6:06:00
Bellwood 35 1 31N31'38 93W12'19 6:12:49
Belmont 43 1 31N42'58 93W30'32 6:14:02
Belmont (Hester P O) 47
1 30N01'08 90W46'45 6:03:07
Belmont 61 1 30N29'55 91W14'08 6:04:57
Belmont Landing 61
1 30N30'29 91W14'35 6:04:58

Bemis 56 1 32N57'25 92w10'42 6:08:43
Bend 47 1 30N01'15 90w45'09 6:03:01
Bennett Bay Landing 40
1 30N57'44 92w27'42 6:09:51
Benson 16 1 31N51'58 93w41'37 6:14:46
Bentley 22 1 31N30'56 92w29'17 6:09:57
Benton 8 1 32N41'41 93w44'30 6:14:58
Berard 23 1 29N59'20 91w47'18 6:07:09
Bermuda 35 1 31N39'44 93w00'13 6:12:01
Bernice 56 1 32N49'19 92w39'28 6:10:38
Bertie 4 1 29N55'09 90w59'16 6:03:57
Bertrandville 38
2 29N46'29 90w01'01 6:00:04
Berwick 51 1 29N41'40 91w13'08 6:04:53
Beshel 38 1 29N33'35 89w46'15 5:59:05
Bessie K 47 1 29N58'58 90w47'16 6:03:09
Bethany 9 1 32N22'23 94w02'33 6:16:10
Bethel 35 1 31N47'21 93w03'04 6:12:12
Bethlehem 64 1 32N00'19 92w46'24 6:11:06
Bickham 59 1 30N52'02 90w12'56 6:00:52
Bienville 7 1 32N21'24 92w58'49 6:11:55
Big A Plenty Landing 21
1 31N53'39 91w34'19 6:06:17
Big Bend 5 1 31N04'25 91w47'31 6:07:10
Big Branch 52 1 30N20'01 89w59'34 5:59:58
Big Cane 49 1 30N49'13 92w00'34 6:08:02
Big Creek 21 1 32N17'30 91w45'47 6:07:03
Big Island 40 1 31N20'13 92w09'55 6:08:40
Big Ridge 11 1 32N06 92w05 6:08:20
Big Woods 10 1 30N17'08 93w33'47 6:14:15
Bijou 40 1 31N06'28 92w14'33 6:08:58
Billeaud 28 1 30N08'08 91w56'44 6:07:47
Billy Goat Hill 58
1 31N05'19 93w16'14 6:13:05
Bird 17 1 30N28'27 91w07'23 6:04:30
Bissonet Plaza 26
2 30N00'48 90w12'59 6:00:52
Bivens 6 1 30N37'47 93w36'22 6:14:25
Blackburn 14 1 32N50'48 93w12'16 6:12:49
Black Hawk 15 1 31N09'20 91w38'09 6:06:33
Blade 30 1 31N39'15 92w03'10 6:08:13
Blairstown 19 1 30N45'09 90w57'45 6:03:51
Blanchard 9 1 32N34'51 93w53'33 6:15:34
Blanche 40 1 30N55'12 92w36'44 6:10:27
Blanks 39 1 30N33'11 91w36'01 6:06:24
Blankston 11 1 32N14'31 92w07'56 6:08:32
Blond 52 1 30N35'50 90w06'04 6:00:24
Blue Lake Landing 40
1 30N58'52 92w26'34 6:09:46
Bluff Creek 19 1 30N44'47 90w51'26 6:03:26
Blume 7 1 32N16'17 92w59'25 6:11:58
Blythwood 24 1 30N11'58 91w12'27 6:04:50
Bob Acres 23 1 29N56'54 91w57'55 6:07:52
Bodcau 8 1 32N32'03 93w35'44 6:14:23
Bodin 51 1 29N50'16 91w36'45 6:06:27
Bodoc 5 1 30N55'08 91w59'26 6:07:58
Boeuf 4 1 29N39'40 91w05'46 6:04:23
Bogalusa 59 1 30N47'27 89w50'55 5:59:24
Bohemian 38 1 29N32'37 89w45'20 5:59:01
Bolden 49 1 30N40'43 91w55'51 6:07:43
Boleyn 43 1 31N44 93w24 6:13:36
Bolinger 8 1 32N56'39 93w41'51 6:14:47
Bolivar 53 1 30N52'08 90w23'41 6:01:35
Bon Air 10 1 30N11'26 93w01'32 6:12:06
Bonaire 17 1 30N25 91w09 6:04:36
Bon Ami 6 1 30N48'27 93w17'42 6:13:11
Bond 2 1 30N41'27 92w36'46 6:10:27
Bonfouca 52 1 30N16'08 89w50'40 5:59:23
Bonham Landing 9
1 32N45'20 94w02'13 6:16:09
Bonita 34 1 32N55'09 91w40'37 6:06:42
Bonnabel Place 26
2 29N59'49 90w08'35 6:00:34
Bon Secour 47 1 29N59 90w50 6:03:20
Bon Secours Plantation 47
1 29N59'39 90w50'28 6:03:22
Bonvillain 51 1 29N48'00 91w40'07 6:06:40
Book 13 1 31N20'14 91w52'17 6:07:29
Boothville 38 1 29N20'36 89w25'11 5:57:41
Bordelonville 5 1 31N06'19 91w54'26 6:07:38
Bordenax 34 1 32N34'54 91w45'49 6:07:03
Borgne Mouth 44 2 29N54 89w54 5:59:36
Borodino 5 1 31N03'57 91w57'03 6:07:48
Bosco 37 1 32N17'24 92w05'20 6:08:21
Boscoville 49 1 30N31'45 92w01'29 6:08:06
Bossier City 8 1 32N30'57 93w43'55 6:14:56
Boston 57 1 29N52'59 92w03'20 6:08:13
Boudreaux 23 1 29N54'50 91w47'05 6:07:08
Boudreaux 55 1 29N24'53 90w42'00 6:02:48
Boudreaux Canal 55
1 29N27 90w36 6:02:24
Bougere 15 1 31N35 91w26 6:05:44
Bourg 55 1 29N33'12 90w36'08 6:02:25
Bourgeois Landing 23
1 29N58'32 91w38'21 6:06:33
Boutte 45 1 29N54'08 90w23'17 6:01:33
Bowie 18 1 32N45'29 91w16'05 6:05:04
Bowie 29 1 29N44'45 90w35'40 6:02:23
Boyce 40 1 31N23'25 92w40'09 6:10:41
Braithwaite 38 2 29N51'58 89w56'37 5:59:46
Brake 63 1 30N55'22 91w32'38 6:06:11
Branch 1 1 30N20'55 92w16'03 6:09:04
Brandon 63 1 30N54'15 91w31'08 6:06:05
Brannon 23 1 29N59'07 91w50'45 6:07:23
Brantley Landing 56
1 32N59'52 92w04'24 6:08:18
Breard 37 1 32N32'11 92w04'54 6:08:20
Breaux Bridge 50
1 30N16'24 91w53'57 6:07:36
Breezy Hill 22 1 31N39'37 92w26'12 6:09:45
Breton 38 1 29N29'38 89w10'26 5:56:42
Bridge City 26 2 29N55'59 90w10'12 6:00:41
Bridge Junction 10
1 30N15'49 93w11'49 6:12:47
Brignac 3 1 30N16'11 90w52'12 6:03:29
Brimstone 10 1 30N14'58 93w24'07 6:13:36
Bringhurst 40 1 31N04'29 92w31'13 6:10:05
Bristol 49 1 30N22'15 92w08'18 6:08:33
Brittany 3 1 30N12'43 90w52'53 6:03:32
Broadmoor 17 1 30N26'49 91w05'06 6:04:20
Broadmoor 36 2 29N57 90w06 6:00:24
Broadmoor 55 1 29N37'56 90w44'49 6:02:59
Bronson 23 1 30N04'10 91w44'09 6:06:57
Brooks 39 1 30N43'41 91w29'07 6:05:56
Brookstown 17 1 30N29'36 91w07'42 6:04:31
Brouillette 5 1 31N12'44 92w01'17 6:08:05
Broussard 28 1 30N08'49 91w57'40 6:07:51
Broussard Landing 24
1 30N19'19 91w11'55 6:04:48
Brousville 23 1 29N57'46 91w56'17 6:07:45
Brown 7 1 32N10'39 93w03'03 6:12:12
Brownell 21 1 32N06'59 91w44'31 6:06:58
Brownfields 17 1 30N33 91w10 6:04:40
Brown Heights 17
1 30N35'24 91w07'00 6:04:28
Brownlee 8 1 32N34'32 93w43'35 6:14:54
Browns 19 1 30N48'17 91w06'45 6:04:27
Brownsville 37 1 32N29'13 92w09'15 6:08:37
Brownview 39 1 30N43'36 91w35'09 6:06:21
Brownville 11 1 32N06 92w05 6:08:20
Brule 4 1 29N49'19 90w58'07 6:03:52
Brule Guillot 29
1 29N47 90w50 6:03:20
Brule Labadie 4 1 29N50 90w57 6:03:48
Brulie Maurin 4 1 30N02'44 90w59'18 6:03:57
Bruly La Croix 24
1 30N09'02 91w11'39 6:04:47
Bruly McCall 3 1 30N06'28 91w05'23 6:04:22
Bruly Saint Martin 4
1 30N02'45 91w05'50 6:04:23
Bruns 24 1 30N13'41 91w03'59 6:04:16
Brusle Saint Vincent 4
1 29N57'35 91w04'13 6:04:17
Brusly 61 1 30N23'39 91w15'13 6:05:01
Brusly Landing 61
1 30N23'00 91w13'59 6:04:56
Bryceland 7 1 32N27'03 92w58'45 6:11:55
Buckeye 40 1 31N21'58 92w11'20 6:08:45
Buckner 42 1 32N18'03 91w56'19 6:07:45
Bucktown 26 2 30N00'53 90w08'28 6:00:34
Bueche 61 1 30N34'15 91w20'54 6:05:24
Buhler 10 1 30N19'58 93w21'43 6:13:27
Buie 21 1 32N03'00 91w51'30 6:07:26
Buller 27 1 30N22'47 93w01'06 6:12:04
Bullion 3 1 30N19'40 90w59'50 6:03:59
Bull Run 55 1 29N39'12 90w52'25 6:03:30
Buncombe (historical) 9
1 32N27'29 93w50'44 6:15:23
Bunkie 5 1 30N57'11 92w10'57 6:08:44
Buras 38 1 29N21'06 89w31'27 5:58:06
Burke 23 1 30N03'39 91w52'55 6:07:32
Burkplace 7 1 32N15 93w10 6:12:40
Burns 51 1 29N34'24 91w31'58 6:06:08
Burnside 3 1 30N08'19 90w55'26 6:03:42
Burnstown 58 1 31N16'56 92w56'05 6:11:44
Burr Ferry 58 1 31N04 93w30 6:14:00
Burroughs 11 1 32N06 92w05 6:08:20
Burrwood 38 1 29N17 89w21 5:57:24
Burton Landing 10
1 30N06'07 93w19'45 6:13:19
Burton Lane 47 1 30N01'28 90w50'26 6:03:22
Burtville 17 1 30N19'56 91w08'04 6:04:32
Bush 52 1 30N36'31 89w54'00 5:59:36
Bushes 21 1 32N13'02 91w36'58 6:06:28
Bushville 50 1 30N22'16 91w53'49 6:07:35
Butte La Rose 50
1 30N16'39 91w41'12 6:06:45
Bywaters 36 2 29N58 90w04 6:00:16
Caddo 9 1 32N45 93w59 6:15:56
Cade 50 1 30N05'14 91w54'19 6:07:37
Cadeville 37 1 32N25'44 92w20'20 6:09:21
Caernarvon 44 2 29N51'49 89w54'23 5:59:38
Caffery 51 1 29N48'20 91w28'46 6:05:55
Caire 47 1 29N59'52 90w51'12 6:03:25
Caire Spur 47 1 29N59 90w50 6:03:20
Calcasieu 40 1 31N05'22 92w42'41 6:10:51
Calhoun 37 1 32N30'45 92w21'30 6:09:26
Calumet 51 1 29N41'58 91w21'48 6:05:27
Calvin 64 1 31N57'56 92w46'32 6:11:06
Camardelle 45 1 29N43'32 90w21'29 6:01:26
Camelia Gardens 40
1 31N17 92w29 6:09:56
Cameron 12 1 29N47'51 93w19'30 6:13:18
Camille 57 1 29N57'16 92w00'21 6:08:01
Campbell 40 1 31N24'06 92w47'40 6:11:11
Camperdown 51 1 29N50'44 91w29'02 6:05:56
Camp Hardtner 22
1 31N37'52 92w23'57 6:09:36
Camp Leroy Johnson 36
2 30N01'48 90w02'44 6:00:11
Campti 35 1 31N53'36 93w07'05 6:12:28
Canbeal 56 1 32N49'10 92w21'11 6:09:25
Cancienne 4 1 29N54'00 91w01'32 6:04:06
Canebrake 15 1 31N42 91w28 6:05:52
Caneland 51 1 29N49'47 91w36'59 6:06:28
Caney 58 1 31N07'12 93w23'15 6:13:33
Cankton 49 1 30N20'45 92w06'34 6:08:26
Cannonburg 24 1 30N11'47 91w06'12 6:04:25
Capitan 28 1 30N03'55 91w58'57 6:07:56
Capitol 17 1 30N28 91w11 6:04:44
Caplis 8 1 32N23'49 93w36'34 6:14:26
Carboco 5 1 30N55'19 92w13'52 6:08:55
Carencro 28 1 30N19'01 92w02'56 6:08:12
Carey 61 1 30N30'09 91w18'57 6:05:16
Cargas 37 1 32N41'38 92w00'52 6:08:03
Carla 64 1 31N56'24 92w41'05 6:10:44
Carlisle 38 1 29N41'12 89w57'44 5:59:51
Carlton 37 1 32N31 92w22 6:09:28
Carlyss 10 1 30N10'07 93w22'33 6:13:30
Carmel 16 1 32N05'14 93w37'14 6:14:29
Caroline 23 1 30N04'21 91w40'00 6:06:40
Carroll 41 1 32N04'43 93w23'29 6:13:34
Carrollton 36 2 29N57 90w07 6:00:28
Carrollwood 48 1 30N04'32 90w29'44 6:01:59
Carson 6 1 30N45'16 93w18'47 6:13:15
Carterville 8 1 32N58'11 93w35'17 6:14:21
Carthage Bluff Landing 32
1 30N18'28 90w35'16 6:02:21
Cartwright 25 1 32N32 92w31 6:10:04
Carville 24 1 30N13'02 91w05'46 6:04:23
Cash Point 9 1 32N37'04 93w46'16 6:15:05
Caspiana 9 1 32N17'20 93w33'22 6:14:13
Cassandra 5 1 31N11'20 92w10'08 6:08:41
Castille 1 1 30N18'07 92w13'24 6:08:54
Castle Village 40
1 31N17 92w29 6:09:56
Castlewood 17 1 30N27'17 91w05'12 6:04:21
Castor 7 1 32N15'11 93w09'56 6:12:40
Castor Plunge 40
1 31N12'30 92w35'38 6:10:23
Catahoula 50 1 30N12'52 91w42'32 6:06:50
Catahoula Cove 50
1 30N11'36 91w44'46 6:06:59
Catfish Landing 32
1 30N18'00 90w38'54 6:02:36
Catherine 24 1 30N09'55 91w10'22 6:04:41
Cat Island 11 1 32N06 92w05 6:08:20
Catuna 16 1 31N54'13 93w42'38 6:14:51
Cavett 9 1 32N47'33 93w50'16 6:15:21
Cecil 56 1 32N57'39 92w14'09 6:08:57
Cecile 9 1 32N19'10 93w35'31 6:14:22
Cecilia 50 1 30N20'13 91w51'11 6:07:25
Cedar Crest 17 1 30N26 91w04 6:04:16
Cedar Glen 17 1 30N31 91w09 6:04:36
Cedar Grove 9 1 32N26'31 93w44'33 6:14:58
Cedar Grove 24 1 30N10'32 91w09'47 6:04:39
Cedar Grove 38 2 29N47'41 90w01'20 6:00:05
Cedar Grove 40 1 31N14'57 92w16'45 6:09:07
Cedar Grove Plantation 4
1 29N51'30 90w57'50 6:03:51
Cedarton 31 1 32N37'48 92w31'39 6:10:07
Centenary 9 1 32N29 93w44 6:14:56
Center Point 5 1 31N14'53 92w12'35 6:08:50
Centerville 20 1 30N53'35 92w18'35 6:09:14
Centerville 51 1 29N45'34 91w25'42 6:05:43
Central 17 1 30N33'15 91w02'12 6:04:09
Central 47 1 30N04'06 90w53'14 6:03:33
Central 55 1 29N38'29 90w48'49 6:03:15
Chacahoula 55 1 29N42'21 90w54'40 6:03:39
Chackbay 29 1 29N47 90w50 6:03:20
Chalkley 10 1 30N09'07 93w05'50 6:12:23
Chalmette 44 2 29N56'33 89w57'48 5:59:51
Chalmette Vista 44
2 29N56'47 89w58'45 5:59:55
Chamberlin 61 1 30N32'06 91w18'12 6:05:13
Chambers 40 1 31N10'42 92w24'49 6:09:39
Chamblee 54 1 31N51'41 91w21'28 6:05:26
Champagne 50 1 30N18'07 91w50'54 6:07:24
Chandler Park 40
1 31N17 92w29 6:09:56
Charenton 51 1 29N52'53 91w31'30 6:06:06
Charles Park 40 1 31N17 92w29 6:09:56
Charlieville 42 1 32N18'24 91w55'09 6:07:41
Charlotte 23 1 29N59'44 91w54'46 6:07:39
Charon 57 1 30N01'17 92w01'23 6:08:06
Chase 21 1 32N05'49 91w41'56 6:06:48
Chataignier 20 1 30N34'06 92w19'19 6:09:17
Chatham 25 1 32N18'22 92w27'01 6:09:48
Chatman Town 47 1 30N02'07 90w50'37 6:03:22
Chaudiere Casse 45
1 29N43'48 90w19'57 6:01:20
Chauvin 55 1 29N26'18 90w35'43 6:02:23
Chef Menteur 36 2 30N04'10 89w48'07 5:59:12
Chegby 29 1 29N52'43 90w48'30 6:03:14
Chelly Landing 21
1 32N09'51 91w34'04 6:06:16
Chenal 39 1 30N36'44 91w22'47 6:05:31
Chenal Crossing 39
1 30N38'04 91w21'42 6:05:27
Chenango 61 1 30N19'56 91w15'22 6:05:01
Cheneyville 40 1 31N00'53 92w17'14 6:09:09
Cheniere 37 1 32N30'31 92w14'50 6:08:59
Cheniere au Tigre 57
1 29N34'05 92w12'11 6:08:49
Cherokee Court 26
2 29N58 90w13 6:00:52
Cherokee Village 40
1 31N17 92w29 6:09:56
Chesbrough 53 1 30N50'55 90w27'22 6:01:49
Chestnut 35 1 32N03'24 93w00'58 6:12:04
Chevey Chase 15 1 31N37'46 91w45'56 6:07:04
Chiasson 49 1 30N31'57 91w57'10 6:07:49
Chickama 40 1 31N05 92w24 6:09:36
Chickasaw 62 1 32N57'45 91w19'51 6:05:19
China 27 1 30N24'06 92w42'20 6:10:49
Chinchuba 52 1 30N23'13 90w04'47 6:00:19
Chipola 46 1 30N55'19 90w48'11 6:03:13
Chloe 10 1 30N14'23 93w06'51 6:12:27
Choctaw 24 1 30N07'34 91w16'35 6:05:06
Choctaw 29 1 29N47 90w50 6:03:20
Chopin 35 1 31N29'48 92w51'33 6:11:26
Chopique 20 1 30N34 92w19 6:09:16
Choudrant 31 1 32N31'48 92w30'51 6:10:03
Choupique 29 1 29N51'31 90w51'23 6:03:26
Choupique 51 1 29N50'02 91w34'48 6:06:19
Chula 4 1 29N50'33 90w57'19 6:03:49
Church Point 1 1 30N24'10 92w12'54 6:08:52
Church Spur 4 1 29N58'52 91w01'02 6:04:04
Cinclare 61 1 30N23'46 91w13'48 6:04:55
Cinclare Landing 61
1 30N23'31 91w13'28 6:04:54
Cindy Park 44 2 29N57 89w56 5:59:44
Claiborne 37 1 32N30'57 92w11'30 6:08:46
Claiborne 52 1 30N29 90w06 6:00:24
Claiborne Hill 52
1 30N28'37 90w05'10 6:00:21
Claibourne Gardens 26
2 29N54 90w09 6:00:36
Clare 43 1 31N19'31 93w36'16 6:14:25
Clarence 35 1 31N49'17 93w01'46 6:12:07
Clarks 11 1 32N01'35 92w08'20 6:08:33
Clarks Landing 20
1 30N57'33 92w27'07 6:09:48
Clay 25 1 32N25'58 92w40'37 6:10:42
Claybank 3 1 30N20'19 90w51'47 6:03:27
Clayton 15 1 31N43'21 91w32'35 6:06:10
Clearwater 20 1 30N59'25 92w23'38 6:09:35
Clifton 40 1 31N18'18 92w52'16 6:11:29
Clifton 59 1 30N55'31 90w10'47 6:00:43
Clifton Crossing 40
1 31N14'03 92w49'19 6:11:17
Clinton 19 1 30N51'56 91w00'56 6:04:04
Clio 32 1 30N18'34 90w36'35 6:02:26
Clotilda 29 1 29N40'19 90w32'05 6:02:08
Cloutierville 35
1 31N32'35 92w55'05 6:11:40
Clovelly Farms 29
1 29N32'25 90w17'35 6:01:10
Cloverdale 40 1 31N11'55 92w28'35 6:09:54

Clubhouse Landing 40 1 30N58'01 92w28'31 6:09:54
Cobb 37 1 32N24'03 92w07'07 6:08:28
Coburn 43 1 31N29'35 93w16'25 6:13:06
Coburn 53 1 30N30'44 90w23'54 6:01:36
Cocke 55 1 29N45 90w49 6:03:16
Cocodrie 55 1 29N14'48 90w39'41 6:02:39
Cocoville 5 1 31N06'10 92w03'50 6:08:15
Coldwater 64 1 31N58'55 92w51'50 6:11:27
Cole 19 1 30N46'16 91w14'10 6:04:57
Cole Central 58 1 30N52'55 93w05'10 6:12:21
Coleman 33 1 32N19'32 91w05'04 6:04:20
Coleman Town 46 1 30N53'21 90w49'12 6:03:17
Colfax 22 1 31N31'08 92w42'24 6:10:50
Colgrade 64 1 31N54'39 92w32'04 6:10:08
College 53 1 30N31 90w27 6:01:48
College Hills 17 1 30N23'32 91w09'00 6:04:36
Collegetown 17 1 30N24'12 91w09'55 6:04:40
Collinsburg 8 1 32N51'46 93w44'15 6:14:57
Collinston 34 1 32N41'27 91w52'18 6:07:29
Colonial Heights 9 1 32N28 93w49 6:15:16
Colony Park 26 2 29N59 90w15 6:01:00
Colquit 14 1 32N56'59 92w58'25 6:11:54
Colt 52 1 30N18'06 89w50'00 5:59:20
Columbia 11 1 32N06'18 92w04'40 6:08:19
Columbia 48 1 30N01'24 90w34'16 6:02:17
Columbia Heights 11 1 32N05'28 92w05'21 6:08:21
Comite 17 1 30N30'40 91w01'47 6:04:07
Como 21 1 32N05'55 91w36'09 6:06:25
Como Landing 63 1 30N54'22 91w31'41 6:06:07
Concession 38 2 29N49'51 90w00'14 6:00:01
Concord 62 1 32N52 91w23 6:05:32
Conn 9 1 32N35'25 93w46'18 6:15:05
Consuella 54 1 31N48 91w23 6:05:32
Contreras 44 2 29N50 89w52 5:59:28
Convent 47 1 30N01'14 90w49'47 6:03:19
Converse 43 1 31N46'53 93w41'37 6:14:46
Conway 56 1 32N53'18 92w23'49 6:09:35
Cooley 40 1 31N10'36 92w29'03 6:09:56
Coon 39 1 30N46'31 91w45'28 6:07:02
Cooper Road 9 1 32N33 93w49 6:15:16
Coopers 58 1 31N02'55 93w16'31 6:13:06
Cooters Landing 54 1 31N55'41 91w30'42 6:06:03
Cooters Point 54 1 31N48 91w23 6:05:32
Cooterville 8 1 32N16'27 93w29'11 6:13:57
Copeland Landing 13 1 31N50'06 91w34'15 6:06:17
Copenhague 11 1 32N01'25 92w02'20 6:08:09
Copley 56 1 32N52'40 92w38'07 6:10:32
Cora 24 1 30N10'35 91w07'49 6:04:31
Cora 58 1 31N06'32 92w52'06 6:11:28
Corbin 32 1 30N29'44 90w50'58 6:03:24
Corey 11 1 32N13'21 92w06'36 6:08:26
Corinth 31 1 32N42 92w39 6:10:36
Corleyville 43 1 31N29'56 93w21'42 6:13:27
Cornerview 3 1 30N14'27 90w58'00 6:03:52
Cornland 48 1 30N03'40 90w32'40 6:02:11
Cornor 63 1 31N06 91w18 6:05:12
Cortableau 49 1 30N33 91w58 6:07:52
Coteau 23 1 30N02'49 91w54'51 6:07:39
Coteau 55 1 29N36 90w43 6:02:52
Coteau Bourgeois 32 1 30N15'37 90w45'29 6:03:02
Coteau Holmes 50 1 30N07'47 91w43'34 6:06:54
Coteau Rodaire 50 1 30N23'28 91w53'57 6:07:36
Cote Blanche Landing 51 1 29N44'23 91w42'30 6:06:50
Cotile 40 1 31N22 92w45 6:11:00
Cotton Plant 11 1 32N03 92w07 6:08:28
Cottonport 5 1 30N59'02 92w03'12 6:08:13
Cotton Valley 60 1 32N49'09 93w25'03 6:13:40
Cottonwood 18 1 32N53'18 91w06'06 6:04:24
Couchwood 60 1 32N45'31 93w23'27 6:13:34
Coulon Plantation 29 1 29N48'52 90w49'46 6:03:19
Country Club 29 1 29N47 90w50 6:03:20
County Landing 33 1 32N24'00 91w29'08 6:05:57
Courtableau 49 1 30N32'57 91w52'53 6:07:32
Coushatta 41 1 32N00'53 93w20'31 6:13:22
Couters Neck 34 1 32N59'47 91w59'31 6:07:58
Coverdale 2 1 30N29'03 92w46'28 6:11:06
Covington 52 1 30N28'31 90w06'03 6:00:24
Covington Country Club Estat 52 1 30N29 90w06 6:00:24
Cow Island 12 1 29N50 92w46 6:11:04
Cow Island 57 1 29N58 92w07 6:08:28
Cox Crossing 7 1 32N17'28 92w52'32 6:11:30
Craig Landing 21 1 31N58'35 91w36'31 6:06:26
Cranky Corner 53 1 30N37'14 90w15'41 6:01:03
Cravens 58 1 30N58'00 93w02'06 6:12:08
Crawford Landing 52 1 30N18'09 89w42'25 5:58:50
Creedmoor 44 2 29N50 89w52 5:59:28
Creole 12 1 29N47'45 93w06'40 6:12:27
Crescent 24 1 30N14'51 91w17'14 6:05:09
Crescent 55 1 29N36'50 90w47'27 6:03:10
Crescent Landing 54 1 31N51'35 91w34'11 6:06:17
Creston 35 1 31N58'33 93w02'59 6:12:12
Crew Lake 42 1 32N29'17 91w53'13 6:07:33
Crews 64 1 31N43'04 92w55'40 6:11:43
Crichton 41 1 32N07'28 93w26'00 6:13:44
Crimea 54 1 31N58'37 91w20'11 6:05:21
Crosskeys 41 1 32N14'13 93w29'43 6:13:59
Cross Keys 54 1 31N53'02 91w21'28 6:05:26
Cross-road 11 1 32N03 92w07 6:08:28
Cross Roads 41 1 32N11'00 93w23'23 6:13:34
Crowley 1 1 30N12'50 92w22'28 6:09:30
Crown Point 26 2 29N46'19 90w05'07 6:00:20
Crowson 7 1 32N16'46 92w59'04 6:11:56
Crowville 21 1 32N14'26 91w35'24 6:06:22
Crozier 55 1 29N32'15 90w43'12 6:02:53
Cullen 60 1 32N58'08 93w27'02 6:13:48
Curry 64 1 31N51'44 92w26'24 6:09:46
Curtis 8 1 32N26'21 93w38'32 6:14:34
Custom House 36 2 29N58 90w04 6:00:16
Cut Off 29 1 29N32'33 90w20'17 6:01:21
Cutoff 36 2 29N55'04 89w58'40 5:59:55
Cut-Off Junction 9 1 32N26'15 93w48'45 6:15:15
Cut Off Landing 21 1 31N59'47 91w36'35 6:06:26
Cypremort 51 1 29N46'29 91w46'28 6:07:06
Cypress 35 1 31N36'19 93w02'19 6:12:09
Cypress 37 1 32N31 92w09 6:08:36
Cypress Creek 20 1 30N50'51 92w33'05 6:10:12
Cypress Gardens 44 2 29N55'58 89w55'36 5:59:42
Cypress Gardens 55 1 29N37'33 90w45'12 6:03:01
Cypress Island 50 1 30N10 91w50 6:07:20
Daigleville 55 1 29N36 90w43 6:02:52
Dalcour 38 2 29N48'26 89w59'55 6:00:00
Danks 49 1 30N43'01 91w52'41 6:07:31
Danville 7 1 32N13'44 92w50'52 6:11:23
Darbonne 49 1 30N36'19 91w52'46 6:07:31
D'Arbonne 56 1 32N40'29 92w28'27 6:09:54
Darby 50 1 30N23'03 91w55'12 6:07:41
Darley 14 1 32N36'39 93w03'14 6:12:13
Darlington 46 1 30N52'40 90w46'53 6:03:08
Darnell 62 1 32N40'39 91w27'11 6:05:49
Darrow 3 1 30N07'05 90w59'07 6:03:56
Daspit 23 1 30N02'26 91w48'01 6:07:12
Dauterive Landing 23 1 30N04'51 91w38'59 6:06:36
Davant 38 1 29N37 89w51 5:59:24
Davids 23 1 29N57'05 91w52'25 6:07:30
Davis Landing 52 1 30N19'30 89w42'30 5:58:50
Dawson Switch 39 1 30N43'05 91w34'12 6:06:17
Dayson 60 1 32N48'04 93w24'34 6:13:38
Dean 56 1 32N54'24 92w09'03 6:08:36
Dean Chapel 37 1 32N31 92w09 6:08:36
Dearborn 54 1 32N10'55 91w16'43 6:05:07
De Broeck Landing 9 1 32N19'21 93w42'34 6:14:50
Deerford 17 1 30N38'20 91w04'10 6:04:17
Deer Park 15 1 31N25'02 91w34'53 6:06:20
Deer Range 38 1 29N37 89w54 5:59:36
Degeneres 5 1 30N52'58 92w07'38 6:08:31
Dehlco 42 1 32N23'47 91w46'10 6:07:05
Delacroix 44 2 29N45'41 89w47'27 5:59:10
Delacroix 50 1 30N05'04 91w52'01 6:07:28
Delaware 23 1 29N53'31 91w45'04 6:07:00
Del Bueno Park 44 2 29N57 89w56 5:59:44
Delcambre 23 1 29N56'53 91w59'19 6:07:57
Delhi 42 1 32N27'27 91w29'35 6:05:58
Delhoste 15 1 31N16'02 91w49'47 6:07:19
Delmont Place 17 1 30N29'41 91w09'29 6:04:38
De Loach 37 1 32N26'54 92w06'17 6:08:25
Delombre 19 1 30N43'10 91w16'26 6:05:06
De Loutre 56 1 32N49'57 92w18'40 6:09:15
Delta (Delta Point Station) 33 1 32N19'32 90w55'37 6:03:42
Delta Farms 29 1 29N39 90w32 6:02:08
Denham Springs 32 1 30N29'12 90w57'22 6:03:49
Denhart 54 1 31N53'50 91w17'51 6:05:11
Denmark Landing 54 1 31N48'00 91w34'39 6:06:19
Dennis Mills 46 1 30N25 90w54 6:03:36
Dennison 23 1 29N56'57 91w50'10 6:07:21
Denson 32 1 30N15'52 90w38'02 6:02:32
Dent Terrace 17 1 30N25 91w09 6:04:36
De Quincy 10 1 30N27'01 93w25'59 6:13:44
De Ridder 6 1 30N50'46 93w17'20 6:13:09
Derouen 23 1 29N58'00 91w54'31 6:07:38
Derry 35 1 31N32'02 92w56'51 6:11:47
Des Allemands 45 1 29N49'25 90w28'30 6:01:54
De Selle 40 1 31N17 92w29 6:09:56
Des Glaise 24 1 30N22'38 91w36'07 6:06:24
Deshotel 1 1 30N18'42 92w12'34 6:08:50
De Siard (reduced usage) 37 1 32N42'29 92w03'45 6:08:15
Deslatte 23 1 29N53'04 91w42'44 6:06:51
Dess 43 1 31N26'19 93w31'49 6:14:07
Destrehan 45 1 29N56'34 90w21'06 6:01:24
Devalls 61 1 30N31'34 91w17'43 6:05:11
Deville 40 1 31N21'26 92w09'55 6:08:40
Dewdrop 34 1 32N47 91w55 6:07:40
Diamond 38 1 29N32'07 89w45'43 5:59:03
Dickey Landing 21 1 32N05'20 91w35'25 6:06:22
Dido 58 1 30N54'41 92w53'23 6:11:34
Dixie 9 1 32N41'33 93w50'05 6:15:20
Dixie Acres 37 1 32N42 92w04 6:08:16
Dixie Gardens 9 1 32N27'04 93w41'57 6:14:48
Dixie Inn 60 1 32N36 93w20 6:13:20
Dixie Landing 21 1 32N03'12 91w34'50 6:06:19
Dixie Plantation 29 1 29N50'14 90w53'31 6:03:34
Dobs Crossing 43 1 31N47'34 93w29'34 6:13:58
Dodson 64 1 32N04'49 92w39'37 6:10:38
Dolsen 48 1 30N03'32 90w35'53 6:02:24
Dona 16 1 32N05 93w49 6:15:16
Donaldsonville 3 1 30N06'03 90w59'34 6:03:58
Donner 55 1 29N41'44 90w56'39 6:03:47
Dora 5 1 30N59 92w03 6:08:12
Dorcheat 60 1 32N40'35 93w21'08 6:13:25
Dorcyville 24 1 30N10'45 91w09'34 6:04:38
Dossman 20 1 30N51'39 92w16'55 6:09:08
Douglas 31 1 32N34'53 92w31'36 6:10:06
Dove Landing 40 1 30N57'22 92w28'43 6:09:55
Downsville 56 1 32N37'36 92w24'51 6:09:39
Doyle 32 1 30N30 90w45 6:03:00
Doyline 60 1 32N32'08 93w24'39 6:13:39
Drew 10 1 30N13 93w12 6:12:48
Drew 37 1 32N32'42 92w14'28 6:08:58
Dry Creek 6 1 30N40'08 93w02'43 6:12:11
Dry Prong 22 1 31N34'52 92w31'58 6:10:08
Dubach 31 1 32N41'56 92w39'24 6:10:38
Dubberly 60 1 32N32'12 93w14'32 6:12:58
Duboin 23 1 29N55'24 91w49'14 6:07:17
Dubuisson 49 1 30N45'34 92w05'39 6:08:23
Duchamp 50 1 30N06'08 91w55'05 6:07:40
Duckroost 3 1 30N14'51 90w52'11 6:03:29
Dufresne 45 1 29N56'32 90w23'25 6:01:34
Dugan Landing 63 1 30N43'13 91w20'55 6:05:24
Dukedale 8 1 32N38'06 93w44'44 6:14:59
Dulac 55 1 29N23'19 90w42'50 6:02:51
Dumesnil 51 1 29N50'49 91w36'59 6:06:28
Dunbarton 13 1 31N43'36 91w39'31 6:06:38
Dunn 42 1 32N27'51 91w34'42 6:06:19
Duplessis 3 1 30N16'10 90w56'18 6:03:45
Dupont 5 1 30N55'45 91w56'52 6:07:47
Dupont 39 1 30N38'39 91w28'46 6:05:55
Dusenbury 58 1 31N19'17 93w08'04 6:12:32
Duson 28 1 30N14'08 92w11'07 6:08:44
Dutch Bayou 48 1 30N03'36 90w34'31 6:02:18
Dutch Town 3 1 30N15'15 90w59'19 6:03:57
Duty 13 1 31N54'54 91w55'26 6:07:42
Dwight Fields 4 1 29N51'17 91w03'04 6:04:12
Dykesville 14 1 32N54'55 93w14'01 6:12:56
East Hodge 25 1 32N17 92w43 6:10:52
East Krotz Springs 49 1 30N32 91w45 6:07:00
Easton 20 1 30N45'04 92w25'43 6:09:43
East Point 41 1 32N09'55 93w25'52 6:13:43
Eastside Columbia 11 1 32N06 92w05 6:08:20
Eastwood 8 1 32N33'22 93w34'01 6:14:16
Ebenezer 1 1 30N09'40 92w18'44 6:09:15
Ecco 60 1 32N46'45 93w24'00 6:13:36
Echo 40 1 31N06'36 92w14'30 6:08:58
Eden 30 1 31N39'14 92w12'54 6:08:52
Eden Park 17 1 30N27'29 91w09'18 6:04:37
Edgard 48 1 30N02'35 90w33'36 6:02:14
Edgefield 41 1 32N03'02 93w19'58 6:13:20
Edgerly 10 1 30N13'57 93w30'21 6:14:01
Edna 27 1 30N25'15 92w53'11 6:11:33
Edward Daigle 55 1 29N38'20 90w45'39 6:03:03
Effie 5 1 31N12'57 92w09'20 6:08:37
Egan 1 1 30N14'12 92w30'21 6:10:01
Egg Bend 5 1 31N08'01 92w11'24 6:08:46
Elam 21 1 31N57'17 91w39'24 6:06:38
Elba 49 1 30N45'19 91w45'50 6:07:03
Elder 2 1 30N34'04 92w47'49 6:11:11
Eliza 61 1 30N19'43 91w13'44 6:04:55
Elizabeth 2 1 30N52'06 92w47'34 6:11:10
Elks 28 1 30N10'57 91w59'21 6:07:57
Ellendale 55 1 29N37'55 90w48'33 6:03:14
Ellerslie 51 1 29N38'22 91w30'34 6:06:02
Ellington 45 1 29N54'20 90w22'50 6:01:31
Ellis 1 1 30N18'12 92w24'24 6:09:38
Ellsworth 55 1 29N40'23 90w48'54 6:03:16
Elmer 29 1 29N49'07 90w51'57 6:03:28
Elmer 40 1 31N07'56 92w40'51 6:10:43
Elmfield 4 1 29N56'12 90w59'43 6:03:59
Elm Grove 8 1 32N20'53 93w33'09 6:14:13
Elm Hall 4 1 29N56'02 91w03'02 6:04:12
Elm Hall Junction 4 1 29N55'12 91w02'31 6:04:10
Elm Park 63 1 30N49'34 91w20'03 6:05:20
Elmwood 58 1 31N02'11 93w18'22 6:13:13
Elton 27 1 30N28'52 92w41'44 6:10:47
Eltringham Landing 54 1 31N48'28 91w34'34 6:06:18
Emden 64 1 31N44'34 92w45'32 6:11:02
Emma 23 1 29N56'18 91w53'08 6:07:33
Emmett 41 1 32N04'18 93w26'33 6:13:46
Empire 38 1 29N23'15 89w35'50 5:58:23
Encalade 38 1 29N31'09 89w43'49 5:58:55
England 40 1 31N20 92w33 6:10:12
England Air Force Base 40 1 31N17 92w29 6:09:56
Englewood 33 1 32N23'06 91w12'25 6:04:50
Englewood 51 1 29N39'50 91w07'45 6:04:31
English 7 1 32N15'35 92w47'30 6:11:10
English Turn 38 2 29N53 89w58 5:59:52
Enoka 33 1 32N31'49 91w10'02 6:04:40
Enola 4 1 29N56'32 91w03'09 6:04:13
Enon 59 1 30N43'38 90w05'03 6:00:20
Enterprise 13 1 31N54'11 91w52'59 6:07:32
Enterprise 23 1 29N55 91w40 6:06:40
Eola 5 1 30N54'40 92w12'57 6:08:52
Epps 62 1 32N36'14 91w28'40 6:05:55
Erath 57 1 29N57'29 92w02'09 6:08:09
Eros 25 1 32N23'32 92w25'56 6:09:42
Erwinville 61 1 30N31'51 91w24'28 6:05:38
Esperance Landing 15 1 31N24'16 91w29'00 6:05:56
Essen 17 1 30N23'54 91w06'25 6:04:26
Essen Heights 17 1 30N25 91w09 6:04:36
Estelle 26 2 29N51 90w06 6:00:24
Esther 57 1 29N50'39 92w10'30 6:08:42
Estherwood 1 1 30N10'50 92w27'51 6:09:51
Esto 43 1 31N23'32 93w36'31 6:14:26
Ethel 19 1 30N47'28 91w07'50 6:04:31
Eunice 49 1 30N29'39 92w25'03 6:09:40
Eureka 37 1 31N54 92w15 6:09:00
Eva 15 1 31N25'44 91w47'15 6:07:09
Evangeline 1 1 30N15'44 92w34'14 6:10:17
Evans 58 1 30N59'20 93w30'07 6:14:00
Evelyn 16 1 31N59'16 93w26'35 6:13:46
Evergreen 5 1 30N57'09 92w06'31 6:08:26
Evergreen Plantation 24 1 30N16'11 91w11'57 6:04:48
Ewing 29 1 29N45'29 90w41'10 6:02:45
Extension 21 1 31N58'14 91w48'21 6:07:13
Fairbanks 37 1 32N38'39 92w02'11 6:08:09
Faircloth 22 1 31N36'51 92w36'17 6:10:25
Fairfax 51 1 29N48 91w30 6:06:00
Fair Grounds 9 1 32N28 93w49 6:15:16
Fairland 55 1 29N41'01 90w47'12 6:03:09
Fairlane 55 1 29N36 90w43 6:02:52
Fairmont 22 1 31N31 92w42 6:10:48

Fairview 15 1 31N19'30 91W31'56 6:06:08
Falgoust 47 1 29N59 90W50 6:03:20
Farmers 51 1 29N51'43 91W38'13 6:06:33
Farmerville 56 1 32N46'24 92W24'20 6:09:37
Fazendeville 44 2 29N57 90W01 6:00:04
Felixville 19 1 30N56'32 90W52'36 6:03:30
Fellowship 30 1 31N42 92W11 6:08:44
Felps 19 1 30N58'37 90W55'07 6:03:40
Fenton 27 1 30N22'01 92W55'05 6:11:40
Ferguson 8 1 32N33'02 93W40'31 6:14:42
Fern 35 1 31N30'39 92W53'43 6:11:35
Ferriday 15 1 31N37'48 91W33'16 6:06:13
Ferry Lake 9 1 32N44'22 94W00'27 6:16:02
Ferry Newlight Landing 54
1 32N06'14 91W25'45 6:05:43
Fields 6 1 30N31'34 93W34'29 6:14:18
Fifth Ward 5 1 31N07'48 92W10'22 6:08:41
Fillmore 8 1 32N33'46 93W30'54 6:14:04
Fisher 43 1 31N29'37 93W27'56 6:13:52
Fisherville 58 1 31N20'07 93W08'27 6:12:34
Fishville 22 1 31N31'17 92W21'43 6:09:27
Fiske 62 1 32N53'12 91W29'32 6:05:58
Five Forks 64 1 31N48'41 92W41'45 6:10:47
Fivemile Oaks 51
1 29N33'30 91W23'08 6:05:33
Flat Creek 64 1 31N58'16 92W23'27 6:09:34
Flatwoods 40 1 31N24'09 92W52'05 6:11:28
Flora Weaver Station 35
1 31N36'44 93W05'51 6:12:23
Florence 51 1 29N47'15 91W43'25 6:06:54
Florence Landing 57
1 29N55'10 92W30'47 6:10:03
Florenville 52 1 30N24'59 89W49'54 5:59:20
Florien 43 1 31N26'37 93W27'26 6:13:50
Florrissant 44 2 29N50 89W52 5:59:28
Flournoy 9 1 32N26'57 93W54'00 6:15:36
Flower Hill 63 1 30N52'54 91W25'00 6:05:40
Floyd 62 1 32N40'39 91W24'21 6:05:37
Floyd Landing 62
1 32N40'46 91W24'11 6:05:37
Fluker 53 1 30N49'17 90W30'39 6:02:03
Flynn 49 1 30N32 92W05 6:08:20
Foley 2 1 30N39'38 92W44'32 6:10:58
Foley 4 1 29N55'23 91W01'29 6:04:06
Folsom 52 1 30N37'48 90W11'14 6:00:45
Fondale 37 1 32N21'16 92W06'28 6:08:26
Fontenot 27 1 30N26'17 92W52'38 6:11:31
Forbing 9 1 32N23'33 93W43'38 6:14:55
Fordoche 39 1 30N35'45 91W36'59 6:06:28
Fords 7 1 32N32'53 92W59'43 6:11:59
Foreman 17 1 30N22'08 91W00'35 6:04:02
Foremans Hall 27
1 30N11'10 92W55'45 6:11:43
Forest 62 1 32N47'31 91W24'48 6:05:39
Forest Glen 52 1 30N19 89W56 5:59:44
Forest Hill 40 1 31N02'30 92W31'52 6:10:07
Forest Oaks 17 1 30N27 91W04 6:04:16
Forest Park 37 1 32N31 92W09 6:08:36
Forked Island 57
1 29N49'52 92W18'00 6:09:12
Forksville 37 1 32N30'27 92W19'25 6:09:18
Fort Buhlow 40 1 31N19'39 92W26'58 6:09:48
Fort de Russy 5 1 31N08 92W04 6:08:16
Fortier Heights 26
2 29N54 90W09 6:00:36
Fort Jackson 38 1 29N21'27 89W27'18 5:57:49
Fort Jesup 43 1 31N36'46 93W24'10 6:13:37
Fort Necessity 21
1 32N02'52 91W49'04 6:07:16
Fort Polk 58 1 31N04 93W11 6:12:44
Fort Randolph 40
1 31N19'24 92W26'55 6:09:48
Fort Saint Leon 38
2 29N45 90W00 6:00:00
Fort Saint Phillip 38
1 29N21'44 89W27'53 5:57:52
Fortune Fork 33 1 32N21'33 91W07'33 6:04:30
Fosters 8 1 32N31'35 93W40'14 6:14:41
Fosters Canal 38
1 29N31'42 89W45'00 5:59:00
Fouborge 49 1 30N42'50 92W10'08 6:08:41
Foules 13 1 31N49'20 91W35'42 6:06:23
Fountain Place 17
1 30N31 91W09 6:04:36
Fourborge 20 1 30N41 92W17 6:09:08
Four Corners 51 1 29N50'56 91W38'23 6:06:34
Four Forks 9 1 32N13'25 93W59'05 6:15:56
Fowler 37 1 32N39'24 92W01'58 6:08:08
Frances Place 44
2 29N55'03 89W54'35 5:59:38
Francis Place 44
2 29N57 89W56 5:59:44
Franklin 51 1 29N47'45 91W30'05 6:06:00
Franklinton 59 1 30N50'49 90W09'11 6:00:37
Fred 17 1 30N38'55 91W06'19 6:04:25
Freeland 63 1 30N46'41 91W16'01 6:05:04
Freetown 4 1 29N51'25 90W58'30 6:03:54
Freetown 51 1 29N47'02 91W39'58 6:06:40
Freilsen 45 2 29N58'13 90W17'24 6:01:10
French Settlement 32
1 30N17'42 90W47'42 6:03:11
Frenier 48 1 30N06'27 90W25'36 6:01:42
Frey 1 1 30N24'07 92W26'41 6:09:47
Friendship 7 1 32N14'22 92W52'57 6:11:32
Frierson 7 1 32N15'06 93W41'23 6:14:46
Frisco 39 1 30N35'08 91W31'32 6:06:06
Frogmore 15 1 31N36'11 91W40'13 6:06:41
Frogmore 39 1 30N31'09 91W31'27 6:06:06
Frost 32 1 30N24'14 90W44'21 6:02:57
Frost Town 37 1 31N54 92W15 6:09:00
Frozard 49 1 30N24'21 91W59'36 6:07:58
Fryeburg 7 1 32N24'46 93W14'03 6:12:56
Fullerton 58 1 30N59'35 92W58'55 6:11:56
Fulton 6 1 30N30'45 93W12'02 6:12:48
Funston 16 1 32N02'59 93W58'08 6:15:53
Gaars Mill 64 1 32N05 92W40 6:10:40
Gahagan 41 1 32N02'23 93W24'23 6:13:38
Gahn 51 1 29N51'39 91W39'20 6:06:37
Gajan 23 1 29N59'27 91W46'33 6:07:06
Galbraith 35 1 31N30 92W49 6:11:16
Galion 34 1 32N51'34 91W45'11 6:07:01
Gall 23 1 29N56'35 91W49'22 6:07:17
Galliano 29 1 29N26'31 90W17'57 6:01:12
Galva 48 1 30N16'47 90W23'56 6:01:36
Galvez 3 1 30N17'56 90W54'17 6:03:37
Gandy 43 1 31N24'09 93W26'51 6:13:47
Gandy Spur 43 1 31N27 93W27 6:13:48
Ganeyville 30 1 31N43'12 92W16'52 6:09:07
Gansville 64 1 32N08'07 92W44'03 6:10:56
Garden City 51 1 29N45'55 91W27'56 6:05:52
Gardere 17 1 30N20'44 91W08'24 6:04:34
Gardner 40 1 31N16'10 92W41'34 6:10:46
Garland 49 1 30N43'37 92W04'20 6:08:17
Garyville 48 1 30N03'21 90W37'09 6:02:29
Gassoway 18 1 32N59'23 91W13'29 6:04:54
Gatbraith 35 1 31N29'28 92W48'44 6:11:15
Gayles 9 1 32N20'52 93W37'33 6:14:30
Gaytine 6 1 30N26'52 93W12'04 6:12:48
Gecko 50 1 30N17'44 91W56'06 6:07:44
Ged 10 1 30N08'22 93W35'33 6:14:22
Geismar 3 1 30N12'15 91W01'21 6:04:05
Genessee 53 1 30N33'35 90W28'58 6:01:56
Gentilly 36 2 30N00 90W05 6:00:20
Georgetown 22 1 31N45'39 92W23'04 6:09:32
Georgeville 32 1 30N38'58 90W37'19 6:02:29
Georgia 4 1 29N50'24 90W59'18 6:03:57
Gheens 29 1 29N40'45 90W27'45 6:01:51
Gibbs 49 1 30N32'35 91W59'31 6:07:58
Gibbstown 12 1 29N49 93W07 6:12:28
Gibsland 7 1 32N32'38 93W03'10 6:12:13
Gibson 55 1 29N41'12 90W59'26 6:03:58
Gibson Landing 15
1 31N41'22 91W24'15 6:05:37
Gifford 60 1 32N35'36 93W20'05 6:13:20
Gilark 60 1 32N38'19 93W18'34 6:13:14
Gilbert 21 1 32N02'57 91W39'29 6:06:38
Gilead 19 1 30N47'39 90W51'43 6:03:27
Gilliam 9 1 32N49'37 93W50'42 6:15:23
Gillis 10 1 30N22'25 93W12'03 6:12:48
Gillyville 42 1 32N18'22 91W53'37 6:07:34
Girard 42 1 32N28'54 91W48'23 6:07:14
Glade Bayou Landing 54
1 32N06'10 91W23'35 6:05:34
Glencoe 51 1 29N48'20 91W40'04 6:06:40
Glen Dale 48 1 30N03 90W31 6:02:04
Glenmora 40 1 30N58'35 92W35'06 6:10:20
Glenmore 24 1 30N12'16 91W11'50 6:04:47
Glenwild 51 1 29N42'51 91W15'15 6:05:01
Glenwood 4 1 29N57'05 91W02'37 6:04:10
Gloria 28 1 30N17'52 92W02'20 6:08:09
Gloria 38 2 29N44'13 90W00'43 6:00:03
Gloster 16 1 32N11'27 93W48'53 6:15:16
Glynn 39 1 30N37'35 91W21'19 6:05:25
Godchaux 29 1 29N43 90W36 6:02:24
Godchaux Community 48
1 30N04 90W29 6:01:56
Gold Dust 5 1 30N51'26 92W11'58 6:08:48
Golden Meadow 29
1 29N22'44 90W15'36 6:01:02
Golden Star Plantation 48
1 29N55'45 90W39'45 6:02:39
Goldman 54 1 31N49'42 91W22'50 6:05:31
Goldman Landing 54
1 31N49'23 91W21'19 6:05:25
Gold Mine 51 1 29N50'10 91W35'59 6:06:24
Goldonna 35 1 32N01'00 92W54'33 6:11:38
Goldridge 24 1 30N06'56 91W11'25 6:04:46
Gonzales 3 1 30N14'18 90W55'12 6:03:41
Goodbee 52 1 30N29'44 90W11'51 6:00:47
Good Hope 45 1 29N59'28 90W24'02 6:01:36
Good Pine 30 1 31N41'35 92W09'43 6:08:39
Goodwill 60 1 32N35'19 93W25'57 6:13:44
Goodwill 62 1 32N46'44 91W33'42 6:06:15
Goodwood 17 1 30N26'40 91W06'39 6:04:27
Goodwood 49 1 30N43'50 91W45'50 6:07:03
Goosport 10 1 30N15'24 93W10'49 6:12:43
Gordon 6 1 30N29'03 93W19'23 6:13:18
Gordon 14 1 32N59'14 93W02'00 6:12:08
Gordon 49 1 30N49'46 91W48'36 6:07:14
Gordy 51 1 29N36'26 91W32'19 6:06:09
Gorhamtown 64 1 31N56 92W36 6:10:24
Gorum 35 1 31N25'58 92W56'36 6:11:46
Goss 10 1 30N18'24 93W08'59 6:12:36
Goss 16 1 32N03'40 93W33'28 6:14:14
Goudeau 5 1 30N52'18 92W00'51 6:08:03
Gouldsboro 26 2 29N54 90W03 6:00:12
Gowan 62 1 32N39'15 91W27'39 6:05:51
Gradney Island 49
1 30N32 92W05 6:08:20
Grambling 31 1 32N31'39 92W42'50 6:10:51
Grambling Corners 31
1 32N30'21 92W43'04 6:10:52
Gramercy 47 1 30N02'50 90W41'23 6:02:46
Grand Annse 50 1 30N20'34 91W47'47 6:07:11
Grand Bayou 4 1 30N00'54 91W07'50 6:04:31
Grand Bayou 38 1 29N30'40 89W45'55 5:59:04
Grand Bayou 41 1 32N05'12 93W28'23 6:13:54
Grandbois 29 1 29N33'09 90W32'17 6:02:09
Grand Caillou 55
1 29N36 90W43 6:02:52
Grand Cane 16 1 32N05'02 93W48'36 6:15:14
Grand Chenier 12
1 29N46'00 92W58'30 6:11:54
Grand Coteau 49 1 30N25'11 92W02'47 6:08:11
Grand Ecore 35 1 31N48'56 93W05'05 6:12:20
Grande Ecaille 38
1 29N22'44 89W46'50 5:59:07
Grand Isle 26 1 29N15'02 89W57'51 5:59:51
Grand Lake 12 1 30N01'50 93W16'19 6:13:05
Grand Point 47 1 30N03'40 90W46'12 6:03:01
Grand Prairie 49
1 30N40'59 92W08'51 6:08:35
Grand River 24 1 30N13'35 91W25'06 6:05:40
Grandstaff 22 1 31N46'28 92W21'46 6:09:27
Grangeville 46 1 30N44'32 90W50'01 6:03:20
Grant 2 1 30N47'18 92W56'54 6:11:48
Grappes Bluff 41
1 31N54'56 93W12'15 6:12:49
Gravel 56 1 32N55'56 92W09'06 6:08:36
Gray 55 1 29N41'51 90W47'11 6:03:09
Gray Point 20 1 30N42'49 92W25'41 6:09:43
Grays 19 1 30N50'54 91W03'01 6:04:12
Grayson 11 1 32N02'59 92W06'33 6:08:26
Greenacres 8 1 32N32 93W42 6:14:48
Green Acres 15 1 31N35 91W26 6:05:44
Green Acres 17 1 30N31 91W09 6:04:36
Green Acres 45 1 29N48'33 90W25'31 6:01:42
Greendale 17 1 30N30'25 91W06'55 6:04:28
Greenfield 18 1 32N45'29 91W13'42 6:04:55
Green Gables 40 1 31N23'00 92W20'15 6:09:21
Greenlaw 53 1 30N58'19 90W29'15 6:01:57
Green Lawn 26 2 29N59 90W15 6:01:00
Green Lawn Terrace 26
2 29N59 90W15 6:01:00
Greensburg 46 1 30N49'50 90W40'18 6:02:41
Greens Ditch 36 2 30N06'49 89W45'40 5:59:03
Greenville 13 1 31N47'34 91W34'45 6:06:19
Greenwell Springs 17
1 30N34'46 90W59'39 6:03:59
Greenwich Village 10
1 30N13 93W12 6:12:48
Greenwood 9 1 32N26'34 93W58'22 6:15:53
Greenwood 38 2 29N46'53 90W00'49 6:00:03
Greenwood 51 1 29N41'12 91W09'15 6:04:37
Greenwood 55 1 29N37'13 90W54'13 6:03:37
Greenwood Park 9
1 32N27 93W47 6:15:08
Greewood Plantation 29
1 29N48'50 90W52'08 6:03:29
Greig 23 1 29N56'55 91W49'47 6:07:19
Greinwich Terrace 10
1 30N13 93W12 6:12:48
Greinwich Village 10
1 30N11'40 93W10'59 6:12:44
Gretna 26 2 29N54'52 90W03'14 6:00:13
Gretna Green 54 1 31N52'45 91W27'48 6:05:51
Griffin 21 1 32N02'15 91W34'01 6:06:16
Grim 60 1 32N42'09 93W22'23 6:13:30
Grimes 18 1 32N39'21 91W10'54 6:04:44
Grosse Isle 57 1 29N57'54 92W05'27 6:08:22
Grosse Tete 24 1 30N24'39 91W26'01 6:05:44
Grove 60 1 32N44'15 93W19'52 6:13:19
Gueydan 57 1 30N01'33 92W30'30 6:10:02
Gulf Crossing 25
1 32N12'21 92W28'23 6:09:54
Gullett 53 1 30N42'52 90W30'23 6:02:02
Gum Bayou Landing 52
1 30N18'11 89W42'50 5:58:51
Gum Ridge 34 1 32N37'33 91W48'41 6:07:15
Gurley 19 1 30N52'09 91W08'02 6:04:32
Guthrie 37 1 32N40'52 92W01'12 6:08:05
Guy 2 1 30N37 92W46 6:11:04
Guynes 7 1 32N12'12 93W06'44 6:12:27
Guyton 37 1 32N24'47 92W22'38 6:09:31
Gypsy 48 1 30N01'54 90W28'03 6:01:52
Haas 5 1 30N56'53 92W15'33 6:09:02
Haaswood 52 1 30N19'43 89W44'40 5:58:59
Hackberry 12 1 29N59'45 93W20'31 6:13:22
Hackley 59 1 30N58'33 90W05'08 6:00:21
Haddens 58 1 31N11'10 93W31'59 6:14:08
Hagewood 35 1 31N43 93W13 6:12:52
Hahnville 45 1 29N58'35 90W24'32 6:01:38
Haile 56 1 32N49'51 92W08'46 6:08:35
Haire 57 1 30N00 92W17 6:09:08
Half Way 4 1 30N06 91W00 6:04:00
Halfway 41 1 32N06'35 93W22'03 6:13:28
Hall Summit 41 1 32N10'38 93W18'08 6:13:13
Hamburg 5 1 31N01'50 91W55'53 6:07:44
Hammet 15 1 31N35 91W26 6:05:44
Hammock (reduced usage) 37
1 32N38'11 92W02'16 6:08:09
Hammond 53 1 30N30'15 90W27'40 6:01:51
Hampton 2 1 30N35'24 92W40'18 6:10:41
Hancock 37 1 32N35'45 91W57'19 6:07:49
Hanna 41 1 31N57'40 93W20'51 6:13:23
Happy Jack 38 1 29N31'18 89W44'01 5:58:56
Harahan 26 2 29N56'25 90W12'11 6:00:49
Harahan Junction 26
2 29N58'23 90W11'36 6:00:46
Hardwood 63 1 30N48'22 91W23'02 6:05:32
Harelson 17 1 30N26'02 91W03'57 6:04:16
Hargis 22 1 31N41'03 92W49'47 6:11:19
Hargrove 10 1 30N28'41 93W27'37 6:13:50
Harlem 38 1 29N37'22 89W54'02 5:59:36
Harlem 57 1 29N58 92W07 6:08:28
Harmon 41 1 32N03'57 93W25'49 6:13:43
Harmony 2 1 30N35'45 92W54'49 6:11:39
Harold Park 26 2 29N59 90W15 6:01:00
Harris 35 1 31N54'44 93W24'53 6:13:40
Harris Landing 21
1 32N06'38 91W35'14 6:06:21
Harrisonburg 13 1 31N46'19 91W49'17 6:07:17
Harvey 26 2 29N54'12 90W04'38 6:00:19
Hatchersville 19
1 30N49'46 90W52'03 6:03:28
Hatches 43 1 31N47 93W42 6:14:48
Hatfield 64 1 31N54'42 92W38'48 6:10:35
Hathaway 27 1 30N20'58 92W40'17 6:10:41
Haughton 8 1 32N31'57 93W30'14 6:14:01
Hawthorne 58 1 31N11'03 93W17'18 6:13:09
Hayes 10 1 30N06'31 92W55'12 6:11:41
Haynes Landing 34
1 32N58'18 91W41'48 6:06:47
Haynesville 14 1 32N57'43 93W08'24 6:12:34
Hayti 9 1 32N42'43 93W50'07 6:15:20
Hazelwood 49 1 30N32'50 91W55'02 6:07:40
Head of Island 32
1 30N16'10 90W45'12 6:03:01
Hearn Island 11 1 32N06 92W05 6:08:20
Hebert 11 1 32N10'57 91W59'27 6:07:58
Hecker 10 1 30N21'18 93W05'17 6:12:21
Hedgeland Landing 13
1 31N52'11 91W34'51 6:06:19
Heflin 60 1 32N27'22 93W15'50 6:13:03
Helena 54 1 31N52'16 91W23'36 6:05:34
Helme 6 1 30N24'47 93W29'52 6:13:59
Helvetia 47 1 30N04'38 90W52'03 6:03:28
Hemphill 40 1 31N14'57 92W46'28 6:11:06
Henderson 50 1 30N18'47 91W47'25 6:07:10
Henfer Park 26 2 29N58 90W13 6:00:52
Henry 57 1 29N52'59 92W04'42 6:08:19
Hermitage 39 1 30N38'42 91W20'18 6:05:21
Hessmer 5 1 31N03'34 92W07'16 6:08:29
Hester 47 1 30N01 90W46 6:03:04
Hester Landing 40
1 30N57'28 92W29'22 6:09:57
Hewes 39 1 30N37 91W28 6:05:52
Hickory 5 1 30N57'05 92W01'15 6:08:05
Hickory 52 1 30N24'58 89W47'06 5:59:08

Hickory Grove 40 1 31N21 92W10 6:08:40
Hickory Valley 64 1 32N05 92W29 6:09:56
Hicks 58 1 31N11'05 93W00'57 6:12:04
Hicks Crossing 58 1 31N13'39 92W56'25 6:11:46
Hico 31 1 32N44'41 92W42'49 6:10:51
Higginbotham 1 1 30N20'44 92W11'36 6:08:46
High Island 8 1 32N16'11 93W26'06 6:13:44
Highland 18 1 32N51'22 91W13'06 6:04:52
Highland 54 1 31N50'16 91W29'08 6:05:57
Highland Acres 26 2 29N58 90W13 6:00:52
Highland Park 37 1 32N30 92W05 6:08:20
Highland Park 55 1 29N38'55 90W45'54 6:03:04
Highland Park Heights 17 1 30N25 91W09 6:04:36
High Mount 10 1 30N13 93W12 6:12:48
Highway Park 26 2 29N59 90W15 6:01:00
Hi-Land 44 2 29N54'31 89W54'13 5:59:37
Hillaryville 3 1 30N08'08 90W57'08 6:03:49
Hillsdale 46 1 30N44'40 90W37'15 6:02:29
Hillside 17 1 30N23'09 91W06'45 6:04:27
Hilltop 25 1 32N20'27 92W42'06 6:10:48
Hilly 31 1 32N38'54 92W40'42 6:10:43
Himalaya 4 1 29N50'57 90W59'50 6:03:59
Hineston 40 1 31N08'36 92W45'31 6:11:02
Hinkle 8 1 32N31'55 93W43'05 6:14:52
Hipple 10 1 30N13'40 93W08'49 6:12:35
Hite 6 1 30N49'21 93W19'25 6:13:18
Hobart 3 1 30N19'20 90W56'20 6:03:45
Hodge 25 1 32N16'36 92W43'24 6:10:54
Hohen Solms 3 1 30N11'56 91W02'38 6:04:11
Holden 32 1 30N30'15 90W40'09 6:02:41
Hollingsworth 41 1 31N58'39 93W21'45 6:13:27
Holloway 40 1 31N23'25 92W13'47 6:08:55
Holly 16 1 32N08'14 93W42'05 6:14:48
Holly Beach 12 1 29N46'14 93W27'33 6:13:50
Hollybrook 18 1 32N44'06 91W10'47 6:04:43
Holly Grove 21 1 31N55'40 91W42'12 6:06:49
Holly Ridge 42 1 32N28'03 91W37'36 6:06:30
Holly Ridge 54 1 31N53'44 91W28'18 6:05:53
Hollywood 10 1 30N13'39 93W19'33 6:13:18
Hollywood 55 1 29N36'00 90W45'29 6:03:02
Hollywood 63 1 30N56'59 91W24'32 6:05:38
Holmesville 5 1 30N54'12 92W11'40 6:08:47
Holmwood 10 1 30N07'33 93W04'47 6:12:19
Holsey 14 1 32N48 92W52 6:11:28
Holton 53 1 30N44'39 90W21'51 6:01:27
Holum 11 1 31N59'48 92W05'00 6:08:20
Home Place 38 1 29N27'45 89W41'00 5:58:44
Home Place 51 1 29N49'25 91W39'52 6:06:39
Homer 14 1 32N47'30 93W03'20 6:12:13
Honore 8 1 32N33'23 93W43'58 6:14:56
Hood 14 1 32N33 92W55 6:11:40
Hood Camp 40 1 31N23 92W57 6:11:48
Hope 23 1 29N56'41 91W42'29 6:06:50
Hopedale 44 1 29N49'13 89W39'24 5:58:38
Hope Villa 3 1 30N20'34 90W58'57 6:03:56
Hopewell Landing 54 1 32N07'39 91W23'34 6:05:34
Hornbeck 58 1 31N19'32 93W23'54 6:13:36
Horse Bluff Landing 32 1 30N21'57 90W37'38 6:02:31
Hortman 60 1 32N43'43 93W22'38 6:13:31
Hosston 9 1 32N53'15 93W52'42 6:15:31
Hot Wells 40 1 31N20'21 92W42'48 6:10:51
Houltonville 52 1 30N24'24 90W08'32 6:00:34
Houma 55 1 29N35'44 90W43'10 6:02:53
Houston River 10 1 30N15 93W15 6:13:00
Howard 41 1 32N13'35 93W28'57 6:13:56
Howcott 22 1 31N39'22 92W23'20 6:09:33
Howell 17 1 30N31'25 91W08'39 6:04:35
Howze Beach 52 1 30N12'34 89W47'24 5:59:10
Hubertville 23 1 29N55'38 91W40'46 6:06:43
Hudson 64 1 32N02'13 92W35'06 6:10:20
Hughes 8 1 32N47'16 93W42'35 6:14:50
Humphreys 34 1 32N59'48 91W57'58 6:07:52
Humphreys 55 1 29N36'31 90W51'24 6:03:26
Humphries 3 1 30N11'33 90W59'54 6:04:00
Hundley 1 1 30N26'27 92W21'58 6:09:28
Hunt 56 1 32N50'38 92W39'27 6:10:38
Hunter 16 1 31N53'49 93W51'04 6:15:24
Hunter Landing 15 1 31N45'11 91W34'59 6:06:20
Huron 50 1 30N24 91W56 6:07:44
Hurricane 14 1 32N37'03 92W56'24 6:11:46
Husser 53 1 30N40'45 90W20'14 6:01:21
Hutton 58 1 31N19'49 93W01'56 6:12:08
Hyams 35 1 31N50'13 93W07'13 6:12:29
Hyde 5 1 30N59 91W49 6:07:16
Hydell 24 1 30N18'03 91W06'51 6:04:27
Hydropolis 5 1 31N04 92W03 6:08:12
Hymel 47 1 30N02'41 90W50'48 6:03:23
Iberville (Bayou Paul Sta) 24 1 30N17'45 91W07'00 6:04:28
Ida 9 1 33N00'15 93W53'41 6:15:35
Idlewild 51 1 29N40'41 91W17'36 6:05:10
Idlewild 55 1 29N38'31 90W45'27 6:03:02
Ikes 6 1 30N52'26 93W13'03 6:12:52
Illinois Plant 12 1 30N02'21 92W54'41 6:11:39
Independence 53 1 30N38'07 90W30'03 6:02:00
Independent 23 1 30N01'56 91W51'02 6:07:24
Indian Bayou 57 1 30N07'33 92W14'33 6:08:58
Indian Beach 26 2 30N01'08 90W08'28 6:00:34
Indian Landing 33 1 32N16'48 91W31'24 6:06:06
Indian Mound 17 1 30N35 91W00 6:04:00
Indian Village 2 1 30N26'56 92W58'18 6:11:53
Indian Village 24 1 30N15'26 91W18'50 6:05:15
Indian Village 37 1 32N31 92W22 6:09:28
Industrial 9 1 32N33 93W47 6:15:08
Ingleside 4 1 29N53'53 90W59'15 6:03:57
Inglewood 40 1 31N13'47 92W25'16 6:09:41

Innis 39 1 30N52'40 91W40'50 6:06:43
Inniswold 17 1 30N24'17 91W05'00 6:04:20
Intracoastal City 57 1 29N47'03 92W09'22 6:08:37
Invincible 60 1 32N47'14 93W24'27 6:13:38
Iota 1 1 30N19'52 92W29'44 6:09:59
Iowa 10 1 30N14'12 93W00'49 6:12:03
Irene 17 1 30N36'44 91W13'48 6:04:55
Irish Bend 51 1 29N49'07 91W27'11 6:05:49
Irma 35 1 31N47'59 93W00'44 6:12:03
Ironton 38 1 29N38'55 89W57'41 5:59:51
Isabel 59 1 30N41'36 89W59'10 5:59:57
Island 39 1 30N40'35 91W23'27 6:05:34
Isle Labbe 50 1 30N09'55 91W46'35 6:07:06
Istrouma 17 1 30N28'44 91W09'35 6:04:38
Ithra 61 1 30N27'40 91W16'29 6:05:06
Ivan 8 1 32N47'39 93W32'07 6:14:08
Ivanhoe 51 1 29N46'57 91W44'23 6:06:58
Jack 46 1 30N44'17 90W42'44 6:02:51
Jackson 19 1 30N50'14 91W13'03 6:04:52
Jackson Landing 33 1 32N20'54 91W29'59 6:06:00
Jacoby 39 1 30N54'54 91W47'21 6:07:09
Jamestown 7 1 32N20'38 93W12'42 6:12:51
Janie 35 1 31N27'45 92W53'11 6:11:33
Jarreau 39 1 30N37'14 91W27'03 6:05:48
Jay 29 1 29N36 90W28 6:01:52
Jeanerette 23 1 29N54'39 91W39'48 6:06:39
Jean Lafitte 26 1 29N41 90W06 6:00:24
Jefferson 26 2 29N58 90W10 6:00:40
Jefferson Heights 26 2 29N57'49 90W09'54 6:00:40
Jefferson Island 23 1 29N58'21 91W58'32 6:07:54
Jefferson Terrace 17 1 30N25 91W09 6:04:36
Jena 30 1 31N40'59 92W08'01 6:08:32
Jenkins 59 1 30N48'43 90W08'13 6:00:33
Jennings 27 1 30N13'20 92W39'25 6:10:38
Jericho 58 1 31N16'02 92W51'59 6:11:28
Jesuit Bend 38 2 29N44'53 90W01'33 6:00:06
Jewella (historical) 9 1 32N28'07 93W48'22 6:15:13
Jigger 21 1 32N02'05 91W44'48 6:06:59
Johnson 48 1 30N00'59 90W38'05 6:02:32
Johnson 51 1 29N41'38 91W27'44 6:05:51
Johnson Bayou Landing 12 1 29N48'07 93W45'10 6:15:01
Johnson Landing 20 1 30N58'02 92W26'04 6:09:44
Johnson Ridge 55 1 29N45'56 90W48'58 6:03:16
Johnson's Bayou 12 1 29N48 93W37 6:14:28
Jones 34 1 32N58'03 91W38'53 6:06:36
Jonesboro 25 1 32N14'28 92W42'57 6:10:52
Jonesburg 42 1 32N31'30 91W45'24 6:07:02
Jones Creek 17 1 30N24'45 91W00'53 6:04:04
Jones Landing 21 1 31N52'57 91W46'42 6:07:07
Jones Park 26 2 29N59 90W15 6:01:00
Jonesville 13 1 31N37'35 91W49'05 6:07:16
Jordon Hill 64 1 31N51'14 92W31'21 6:10:05
Joyce 64 1 31N56'21 92W35'55 6:10:24
Juanita 6 1 30N37'06 93W25'30 6:13:42
Judd 1 1 30N21'46 92W24'14 6:09:37
Julien 51 1 29N51'26 91W37'56 6:06:32
Junction 6 1 30N50'16 93W30'32 6:14:02
Junction City 56 1 33N00'49 92W43'30 6:10:54
Jungle Gardens 23 1 29N54'30 91W54'42 6:07:39
Justina 54 1 31N58'38 91W25'46 6:05:43
Kadesh 22 1 31N42'15 92W54'40 6:11:39
Kahns 61 1 30N28'55 91W15'07 6:05:00
Kaplan 57 1 29N59'52 92W17'05 6:09:08
Karo 5 1 30N59'01 92W05'37 6:08:22
Kateland 22 1 31N27'22 92W40'32 6:10:42
Katy 51 1 29N49'38 91W30'39 6:06:03
Keatchie 16 1 32N11'18 93W54'19 6:15:37
Kedron 46 1 30N42 90W35 6:02:20
Keithville 9 1 32N19'59 93W50'10 6:15:21
Keller 39 1 30N56'30 91W43'19 6:06:53
Kelleys 25 1 32N28'33 92W33'30 6:10:14
Kelly 11 1 31N58'50 92W10'36 6:08:42
Kellys 25 1 32N32 92W38 6:10:32
Kemper 51 1 29N48'34 91W40'03 6:06:40
Kendale 26 2 29N59 90W15 6:01:00
Kendricks Ferry 21 1 32N03 91W39 6:06:36
Kenilworth 44 2 29N52'00 89W49'07 5:59:16
Kenmore 39 1 30N30'34 91W32'25 6:06:10
Kennedy Heights 26 2 29N54 90W09 6:00:36
Kenner 26 2 29N59'38 90W14'30 6:00:58
Kentwood 53 1 30N56'17 90W30'32 6:02:02
Kernan 6 1 30N30'25 93W15'44 6:13:03
Kessler 4 1 30N02'09 91W03'34 6:04:14
Keystone 1 1 30N20'53 92W29'00 6:09:56
Keystone 50 1 30N04'49 91W50'15 6:07:21
Kickapoo 16 1 32N11'36 93W50'13 6:15:21
Kilbourne 62 1 32N59'58 91W18'54 6:05:16
Kilgore Plantation 51 1 29N51'16 91W40'16 6:06:41
Killian 32 1 30N21'31 90W35'10 6:02:21
Killona 45 1 30N00'21 90W28'58 6:01:56
Kinder 2 1 30N29'07 92W51'02 6:11:24
King 33 1 32N14'26 91W07'17 6:04:29
King Hill 35 1 31N52'40 93W19'35 6:13:18
Kingston 16 1 32N11'03 93W42'39 6:14:51
Kingsville 40 1 31N21'44 92W24'41 6:09:39
Kirks Landing 54 1 31N51'52 91W34'25 6:06:18
Kiroli Woods 37 1 32N32'12 92W09'35 6:08:38
Kisatchie 35 1 31N24'56 93W10'27 6:12:42
Kleinpeter 17 1 30N20'59 91W01'33 6:04:06
Klondyke 55 1 29N32'47 90W35'11 6:02:21
Klotzville 4 1 30N00'55 91W02'48 6:04:11
Knapp 39 1 30N35'56 91W25'30 6:05:42
Knight 58 1 30N54'55 93W26'54 6:13:48
Knot Point 8 1 32N19'06 93W31'58 6:14:08
Kolin 40 1 31N16'59 92W19'21 6:09:17
Kolter 16 1 32N09'10 93W55'27 6:15:42

Koran 8 1 32N25'30 93W27'46 6:13:51
Kraemer 29 1 29N52'00 90W41'49 6:02:47
Krotz Springs 49 1 30N32'12 91W45'10 6:07:01
Kurthwood 58 1 31N20'14 93W09'56 6:12:40
Laark 34 1 32N59'31 91W30'36 6:06:02
Labadieville 4 1 29N50'14 90W57'22 6:03:49
Labarre 39 1 30N42'52 91W32'44 6:06:11
La Branche 45 1 30N03'05 90W22'07 6:01:28
Lacamp 58 1 31N09'49 92W54'52 6:11:39
Lacassine 27 1 30N14'07 92W55'17 6:11:41
Lachute 9 1 32N15'49 93W31'35 6:14:06
Lacombe 52 1 30N18'48 89W56'35 5:59:46
Lacour 39 1 30N49'41 91W36'50 6:06:27
Lafayette 28 1 30N13'26 92W01'11 6:08:05
Lafayette Square 36 2 29N56 90W05 6:00:20
Lafitte 26 1 29N40'00 90W06'30 6:00:26
Lafourche 29 1 29N46'01 90W45'57 6:03:04
Lagan 47 1 29N58'31 90W48'52 6:03:15
Lagonda 51 1 29N40'42 91W16'48 6:05:07
Lake 3 1 30N17'59 90W51'10 6:03:25
Lake Arthur 27 1 30N04'50 92W40'17 6:10:41
Lake Bruin 54 1 31N59'16 91W15'22 6:05:01
Lake Catherine 36 2 30N06'51 89W42'33 5:58:50
Lake Charles 10 1 30N13'35 93W13'02 6:12:52
Lake Cove 20 1 30N55'03 92W27'05 6:09:48
Lake End 41 1 31N55'17 93W18'17 6:13:13
Lakefield 25 1 32N16'46 92W45'17 6:11:01
Lake Hayes 9 1 32N25'53 93W54'28 6:15:38
Lake Judge Perez 38 1 29N33'30 89W53'10 5:59:33
Lakeland 39 1 30N36'02 91W23'50 6:05:35
Lake Providence 18 1 32N48'15 91W10'12 6:04:41
Lakeshore 37 1 32N30 92W05 6:08:20
Lakeside 12 1 30N05 92W40 6:10:40
Lakeside 40 1 31N19 92W25 6:09:40
Lake View 9 1 32N31'31 93W49'36 6:15:18
Lakeview 35 1 31N34'42 92W57'09 6:11:49
Lakeview 36 2 30N00 90W06 6:00:24
Lamar 21 1 32N18'38 91W32'25 6:06:10
Lamkin 37 1 32N34'57 92W04'22 6:08:17
Lamourie 40 1 31N08 92W25 6:09:40
Lampman 57 1 29N58 92W07 6:08:28
Landay Gautreaux 55 1 29N47 90W50 6:03:20
Landry 51 1 29N52'09 91W39'55 6:06:40
Langston 14 1 32N40'34 93W09'08 6:12:37
Lapeyrouse 55 1 29N23'51 90W35'08 6:02:21
Lapine 37 1 32N31 92W09 6:08:36
Laplace 48 1 30N03'59 90W28'48 6:01:55
Laran 56 1 32N58'25 92W29'07 6:09:56
La Reusitte 38 2 29N45 90W00 6:00:00
Larose 29 1 29N34'20 90W22'54 6:01:32
La Rosen 9 1 32N24'12 93W47'21 6:15:09
Larto 13 1 31N22'21 91W54'16 6:07:37
Lasalle 23 1 29N58'32 91W56'51 6:07:47
Latanier 40 1 31N12'07 92W21'22 6:09:25
Latex 9 1 32N36'16 94W02'34 6:16:10
Lauderdale 2 1 30N28'52 92W46'30 6:11:06
Lauderdale 47 1 30N05'10 90W54'52 6:03:39
Laurel Grove 29 1 29N49'25 90W52'44 6:03:31
Laurel Grove Plantation 29 1 29N49'38 90W52'43 6:03:31
Laurel Hill 63 1 30N57'12 91W20'25 6:05:22
Laurel Lea 17 1 30N25 91W09 6:04:36
Laurel Ridge 24 1 30N09'44 91W07'01 6:04:28
Laurel Ridge Plantation 47 1 29N59'22 90W47'25 6:03:10
Laurel Valley Plantation 29 1 29N48'44 90W46'18 6:03:05
Lawhon 7 1 32N22'35 93W13'13 6:12:53
Lawtell 49 1 30N31'06 92W11'05 6:08:44
Lazy Acres 55 1 29N40'03 90W46'38 6:03:07
Leander 58 1 31N08'54 92W50'47 6:11:23
Leavel 39 1 30N42'20 91W29'19 6:05:57
Lebeau 49 1 30N43'52 91W58'37 6:07:54
Le Blanc 2 1 30N30'32 92W56'56 6:11:48
LeBlanc 24 1 30N14'19 91W05'08 6:04:21
Le Bleu 10 1 30N16'33 93W04'52 6:12:19
Leche 4 1 29N51'42 90W57'56 6:03:52
Lecompte 40 1 31N05'40 92W24'01 6:09:36
Ledoux 49 1 30N37'08 92W11'24 6:08:46
Lee Bayou 13 1 31N45'47 91W33'37 6:06:14
Lee Heights 40 1 31N21'53 92W26'10 6:09:45
Lees Creek 59 1 30N44'31 89W52'29 5:59:30
Lees Landing 53 1 30N24'15 90W19'25 6:01:18
Leesville 58 1 31N08'36 93W15'39 6:13:03
Leeville 29 1 29N14'52 90W12'27 6:00:50
Lefleurs 20 1 30N38 92W25 6:09:40
Legonier 39 1 30N58'24 91W47'38 6:07:11
Leighton 29 1 29N47'47 90W51'28 6:03:26
Lejeune 61 1 30N28'58 91W16'54 6:05:08
Lela 8 1 32N58'27 93W40'54 6:14:44
Leland 13 1 31N49'23 91W43'17 6:06:53
Leleux 23 1 29N58'44 91W56'28 6:07:46
Leleux 57 1 30N04'06 92W21'39 6:09:27
Lemannville 3 1 30N06'33 90W55'13 6:03:41
Le Moyen 49 1 30N47'07 92W02'25 6:08:10
Lena 40 1 31N27'38 92W46'14 6:11:05
Lenwil 37 1 32N26'14 92W13'28 6:08:54
Leonville 49 1 30N28'13 91W58'42 6:07:55
Leroy 57 1 30N04'43 92W11'32 6:08:46
Leslie 8 1 32N35'19 93W28'59 6:13:56
Leton 60 1 32N51'36 93W15'09 6:13:01
Lettsworth 39 1 30N56'00 91W42'17 6:06:49
Levert 50 1 30N09'25 91W49'16 6:07:17
Levins 15 1 31N38 91W32 6:06:08
Lewisburg 49 1 30N26'57 92W10'08 6:08:41
Lewisburg 52 1 30N22'10 90W06'11 6:00:25
Lewiston 53 1 30N56 90W31 6:02:04
Lewistown 29 1 29N44'18 90W37'01 6:02:28
Liberty 41 1 32N04'21 93W11'50 6:12:47
Liberty Hill 7 1 32N20'15 92W53'31 6:11:34
Libuse 40 1 31N21'14 92W20'00 6:09:20
Liddieville 21 1 32N08'08 91W50'44 6:07:23
Lillie 56 1 32N55'55 92W39'24 6:10:38
Lincecum 22 1 31N41'14 92W23'33 6:09:34
Linda Lee 32 1 30N25 90W54 6:03:36
Lindsay 19 1 30N43'03 91W13'04 6:04:52
Link 1 1 30N21 92W16 6:09:04

Linton 8 1 32N41'16 93W38'11 6:14:33
Linville 56 1 32N50'31 92W11'34 6:08:46
Linwood 38 2 29N47'23 90W00'30 6:00:02
Linwood 51 1 29N52'09 91W31'32 6:06:06
Lions 48 1 30N03'15 90W35'21 6:02:21
Lisbon 14 1 32N47'45 92W51'54 6:11:28
Lismore 15 1 31N30'56 91W46'19 6:07:05
Litroe 56 1 32N59'36 92W11'46 6:08:47
Little Caillou 55
1 29N27 90W36 6:02:24
Little Creek 30 1 31N43'10 92W17'39 6:09:11
Little Farms 26 2 29N58 90W13 6:00:52
Little Prairie 3
1 30N19'24 90W55'20 6:03:41
Little Texas 4 1 29N52'50 91W01'09 6:04:05
Little Valley Plantation 23
1 29N55'13 91W46'03 6:07:04
Little Woods 36 2 30N04'30 89W56'39 5:59:47
Live Oak 38 2 29N45'17 90W01'43 6:00:07
Live Oak Manor 26
2 29N57'00 90W14'19 6:00:57
Liverpool 46 1 30N54'54 90W40'49 6:02:43
Livingston 32 1 30N30'07 90W44'52 6:02:59
Livonia 39 1 30N33'32 91W33'21 6:06:13
Lobdell 61 1 30N29'45 91W15'38 6:05:03
Loch Lomond 56 1 32N40'35 92W08'31 6:08:34
Lockhart 32 1 30N29'25 90W54'16 6:03:37
Lockhart 56 1 33N00'29 92W34'59 6:10:20
Lockmoor 10 1 30N14'12 93W17'30 6:13:10
Lockport 29 1 29N38'45 90W32'21 6:02:09
Lockport Heights 29
1 29N39'01 90W32'47 6:02:11
Loco 56 1 32N56'53 92W09'55 6:08:40
Locust Ridge 54 1 31N52'35 91W20'30 6:05:22
Lofton 64 1 31N43'36 92W45'26 6:11:02
Logansport 16 1 31N58'31 93W59'52 6:15:59
Log Cabin 34 1 32N49'58 91W52'39 6:07:31
Loggy Bayou 41 1 32N19 93W32 6:14:08
Logtown 37 1 32N20'06 92W05'19 6:08:21
Loisel 23 1 29N56'17 91W41'40 6:06:47
Lone Pine 12 1 29N59'45 93W37'50 6:14:31
Lone Pine 20 1 30N57'20 92W19'10 6:09:17
Lone Star 24 1 30N06'07 91W13'01 6:04:52
Lone Star 45 1 29N55'39 90W20'26 6:01:22
Long Bridge 5 1 31N00'50 92W01'06 6:08:04
Long Bridge 28 1 30N14'23 91W57'57 6:07:52
Longlake 11 1 32N06 92W05 6:08:20
Longleaf 40 1 31N00'23 92W33'09 6:10:13
Long Springs 60 1 32N40'26 93W20'11 6:13:21
Long Straw 25 1 32N32 92W31 6:10:04
Longstreet 16 1 32N05'51 93W57'07 6:15:48
Longview 21 1 32N15'43 91W34'41 6:06:19
Longville 6 1 30N36'18 93W13'54 6:12:56
Longwood 9 1 32N33'33 93W58'42 6:15:55
Longwood 17 1 30N20'24 91W08'13 6:04:33
Loranger 53 1 30N38'08 90W23'53 6:01:36
Loreauville 23 1 30N03'23 91W44'13 6:06:57
Lorelein 21 1 32N05'38 91W33'10 6:06:13
Loring 43 1 31N36'09 93W36'02 6:14:24
Lorraine 9 1 32N28'21 94W02'33 6:16:10
Lorraine 53 1 30N30'21 90W16'42 6:01:07
Lottie 39 1 30N33'22 91W38'30 6:06:34
Lotus 35 1 31N29'07 93W07'49 6:12:31
Louisiana and Arkansas Jct 64
1 31N55 92W38 6:10:32
Louisiana Junction 8
1 32N32 93W42 6:14:48
Louisville 3 1 30N13'29 91W00'03 6:04:00
Louisville 37 1 32N30 92W05 6:08:20
Lower Bonne Idee 34
1 32N38 91W46 6:07:04
Lower Texas 4 1 29N50'02 91W02'21 6:04:09
Lower Vacherie 47
1 29N56'10 90W40'43 6:02:43
Lowlands 29 1 29N46'09 90W53'56 6:03:36
Lowry 12 1 30N01'26 92W46'15 6:11:05
Loyds Bridge 40 1 31N01 92W17 6:09:08
Lozes 23 1 30N02'29 91W57'34 6:07:50
L T Plantation 29
1 29N50'05 90W53'15 6:03:33
Lucas 9 1 32N24'02 93W41'28 6:14:46
Lucas 10 1 30N22'26 93W33'44 6:14:15
Lucerne 15 1 31N35 91W26 6:05:44
Lucknow 42 1 32N28 91W45 6:07:00
Lucky 7 1 32N15'18 92W59'48 6:11:59
Lucy 48 1 30N02'48 90W30'27 6:02:02
Ludevine 29 1 29N35'07 90W25'39 6:01:43
Ludger 23 1 29N56'55 91W51'52 6:07:27
Ludington 6 1 30N52'26 93W17'06 6:13:08
Ludivine Plantation 29
1 29N35 90W25 6:01:40
Ludvine 29 1 29N39 90W32 6:02:08
Luella 35 1 31N46'32 92W59'42 6:11:59
Luke Landing 51 1 29N35'50 91W32'30 6:06:10
Lukeville 61 1 30N22'46 91W14'37 6:04:58
Lula 4 1 30N02'52 91W04'03 6:04:16
Lula 16 1 31N51'11 93W46'53 6:15:08
Luling 45 1 29N55'55 90W21'59 6:01:28
Lums 33 1 32N23'44 91W09'17 6:04:37
Luna 37 1 32N19'30 92W13'19 6:08:53
Lunita 10 1 30N21'30 93W35'40 6:14:23
Lutcher 47 1 30N02'25 90W41'56 6:02:48
Lydia 23 1 29N55'09 91W47'43 6:07:11
Lynch 61 1 30N23'52 91W21'23 6:05:26
Lyons 23 1 29N53'02 91W41'59 6:06:48
Lyons 25 1 32N09'35 92W29'02 6:09:56
Lyons Point 1 1 30N06'40 92W22'41 6:09:31
Mack 57 1 29N57'53 92W04'25 6:08:18
Macomb, Fort 36 2 30N03'53 89W48'14 5:59:13
Madewood 4 1 29N55'55 90W59'22 6:03:57
Madison Park 9 1 32N28 93W43 6:14:52
Madisonville 52 1 30N24'15 90W09'25 6:00:38
Magenta 8 1 32N22'25 93W34'42 6:14:19
Magenta 37 1 32N29'57 92W02'43 6:08:11
Magnolia 4 1 30N00'14 91W03'52 6:04:15
Magnolia 17 1 30N32'10 90W59'17 6:03:57
Magnolia 32 1 30N33'36 90W42'22 6:02:49
Magnolia 35 1 31N32'54 92W56'29 6:11:46
Magnolia 38 2 29N33'16 89W46'50 5:59:07
Magnolia 41 1 32N02'23 93W25'57 6:13:44
Magnolia 55 1 29N43'10 90W48'43 6:03:15
Magnolia Landing 32
1 30N18'13 90W37'49 6:02:31
Magnolia Plantation 55
1 29N42'51 90W49'02 6:03:16
Magnolia Woods 17
1 30N25 91W09 6:04:36
Mahan 14 1 32N53'28 93W02'43 6:12:11
Maidco 37 1 32N24'04 92W06'39 6:08:27
Maitland Landing 15
1 31N45'29 91W36'23 6:06:26
Majors 39 1 30N36'01 91W26'14 6:05:45
Mallard Junction 10
1 30N14'18 93W09'18 6:12:37
Mamou 20 1 30N38'01 92W25'09 6:09:41
Manchac 53 1 30N17'29 90W24'07 6:01:36
Manchester 10 1 30N11'39 93W05'49 6:12:23
Mandalay 55 1 29N33'57 90W46'16 6:03:05
Mandeville 52 1 30N21'29 90W03'56 6:00:16
Mangham 42 1 32N18'32 91W46'29 6:07:06
Manifest 13 1 31N42'36 91W57'43 6:07:51
Mansfield 16 1 32N02'15 93W42'00 6:14:48
Mansford 33 1 32N27'55 91W08'39 6:04:35
Mansura 5 1 31N03'28 92W02'56 6:08:12
Many 43 1 31N34'07 93W29'02 6:13:56
Maplewood 10 1 30N13'52 93W18'58 6:13:16
Marcarco 34 1 32N43'02 91W59'27 6:07:58
Marce 23 1 29N56'33 91W53'03 6:07:32
Marco 35 1 31N30'33 92W45'53 6:11:04
Marguerite 51 1 29N52'34 91W40'40 6:06:43
Maringouin 24 1 30N29'28 91W31'10 6:06:05
Marion 56 1 32N54'05 92W14'31 6:08:58
Mark 61 1 30N21'01 91W15'07 6:05:00
Markee 58 1 30N55'36 93W06'55 6:12:28
Marksville 5 1 31N07'40 92W03'58 6:08:16
Marrero 26 2 29N53'57 90W06'01 6:00:24
Marsalis 14 1 32N39'47 92W57'24 6:11:50
Mars Hill 64 1 31N48 92W45 6:11:00
Martello Castle 44
2 29N56'42 89W50'06 5:59:20
Marthaville 35 1 31N44'19 93W23'47 6:13:35
Martin 41 1 32N05'07 93W13'12 6:12:53
Martin Junction 60
1 32N28 93W16 6:13:04
Martin Park 40 1 31N17 92W29 6:09:56
Martins Landing 54
1 31N50'03 91W34'08 6:06:17
Maryland 17 1 30N32'45 91W10'33 6:04:42
Maryland 51 1 29N48 91W30 6:06:00
Maryland 54 1 31N55'21 91W22'07 6:05:28
Mason 21 1 32N10 91W43 6:06:52
Masters 23 1 29N52'59 91W41'26 6:06:46
Mathews 29 1 29N41'10 90W32'48 6:02:11
Matilda 51 1 29N53'04 91W36'14 6:06:25
Maude 52 1 30N22'22 89W48'45 5:59:15
Maurepas 32 1 30N17'48 90W39'50 6:02:39
Maurice 57 1 30N06'30 92W07'28 6:08:30
Maxie 1 1 30N19'30 92W24'28 6:09:38
Mayers 8 1 32N24'29 93W37'17 6:14:29
Mayfair 17 1 30N25 91W09 6:04:36
Mayflower 54 1 31N57'05 91W23'29 6:05:34
Mayhew Landing 13
1 31N45'39 91W35'22 6:06:21
Mayna 13 1 31N25'34 91W51'41 6:07:27
Mayo 58 1 31N11'57 93W02'00 6:12:08
McBride 55 1 29N39'47 90W49'11 6:03:17
McCall 3 1 30N06'57 91W02'36 6:04:10
McClane City 52 1 30N15'23 89W46'16 5:59:05
McClendon 59 1 30N51 90W09 6:00:36
McCrea 39 1 30N52'08 91W47'22 6:07:09
McDade 8 1 32N19'24 93W31'41 6:14:07
McDonoghville 26
2 29N55'32 90W02'46 6:00:11
McElroy 3 1 30N08'25 90W47'29 6:03:10
McGinty 34 1 33N00'06 91W37'44 6:06:31
McHugh 17 1 30N37'27 91W09'53 6:04:40
McIlhenny 23 1 29N55 91W55 6:07:40
McIntyre 60 1 32N35'13 93W22'06 6:13:28
McKenzie 14 1 32N50'40 93W05'50 6:12:23
McKneeley 39 1 30N36 91W37 6:06:28
McKnight Crossing 19
1 30N44'50 90W53'47 6:03:35
McLain 37 1 32N22'05 92W06'42 6:08:27
McLeod 29 1 29N38'47 90W31'04 6:02:04
McManus 19 1 30N50'03 91W08'10 6:04:33
McNary 40 1 30N59'14 92W34'34 6:10:18
McNeely 22 1 31N30'20 92W41'00 6:10:44
McNutt 40 1 31N18'50 92W38'51 6:10:35
McVeigh 50 1 30N24 91W56 6:07:44
Meadowbrook 26 2 29N54 90W03 6:00:12
Meadow Park Heights 9
1 32N27 93W47 6:15:08
Meadowview Park 8
1 32N32 93W42 6:14:48
Meaux 57 1 30N01'14 92W10'57 6:08:44
Mechanicsville 55
1 29N36 90W43 6:02:52
Meeker 40 1 31N03'23 92W22'50 6:09:31
Melder 40 1 31N06'18 92W38'11 6:10:33
Melodia Plantation 29
1 29N46'23 90W43'41 6:02:55
Melrose 35 1 31N35'55 92W58'01 6:11:52
Melville 39 1 30N41'34 91W44'38 6:06:59
Menefee Junction 64
1 31N57'08 92W33'57 6:10:16
Mengel Landing 17
1 30N30'45 91W11'41 6:04:47
Meraux 44 2 29N55'58 89W56'59 5:59:48
Meridian 20 1 30N55'31 92W24'19 6:09:37
Merlin 61 1 30N23'18 91W17'23 6:05:10
Mermentau 1 1 30N11'23 92W34'57 6:10:20
Mer Rouge 34 1 32N46'30 91W47'33 6:07:10
Merryville 6 1 30N45'15 93W32'25 6:14:10
Messick 35 1 31N58'13 93W11'10 6:12:45
Mestayer 23 1 30N04'00 91W41'33 6:06:46
Metairie 26 2 29N59'02 90W09'10 6:00:37
Methvin 41 1 32N09'40 93W14'36 6:12:58
Metropolis 21 1 31N57'48 91W41'28 6:06:46
Michoud 36 2 30N01'48 89W55'33 5:59:42
Mid City 36 2 29N59 90W05 6:00:20
Mid-city Annex 9
1 32N30 93W46 6:15:04
Midland 1 1 30N10'50 92W30'10 6:10:01
Midway 8 1 32N42'52 93W35'36 6:14:22
Midway 30 1 31N41'31 92W09'08 6:08:37
Midway 40 1 31N03'40 92W28'21 6:09:53
Midway 51 1 29N39'18 91W29'29 6:05:58
Midway 60 1 32N55'19 93W27'12 6:13:49
Migues 23 1 29N57'45 91W51'57 6:07:28
Milburn 5 1 30N52'03 92W12'42 6:08:51
Miles 3 1 30N08'21 91W05'07 6:04:20
Mill 64 1 32N07'21 92W50'34 6:11:22
Mill Creek 64 1 31N55 92W38 6:10:32
Milldale 17 1 30N40'03 91W01'39 6:04:07
Millerton 14 1 33N00'01 93W13'17 6:12:53
Millerville 1 1 30N19'58 92W36'59 6:10:28
Millerville 17 1 30N27'04 91W01'28 6:04:06
Mill Haven 37 1 32N29'43 91W59'25 6:07:58
Millikin 18 1 32N57'42 91W13'33 6:04:54
Milly Plantation 24
1 30N17 91W14 6:04:56
Milton 28 1 30N06'13 92W04'35 6:08:18
Mimosa Park 45 1 29N54'22 90W21'22 6:01:25
Minden 60 1 32N36'55 93W17'12 6:13:09
Mineral Springs 37
1 32N27'30 92W21'33 6:09:26
Minerva 55 1 29N36 90W43 6:02:52
Minerva Plantation 55
1 29N42'32 90W48'58 6:03:16
Mink 35 1 31N23'41 93W04'14 6:12:17
Minorca 15 1 31N34'45 91W28'54 6:05:56
Mira 9 1 32N56'31 93W53'20 6:15:33
Mire 1 1 30N17'59 92W11'37 6:08:46
Missionary 8 1 33N00'11 93W49'57 6:15:20
Mitchell 43 1 31N47'27 93W37'40 6:14:31
Mitchiner 42 1 32N34'53 91W29'10 6:05:57
Mittie 2 1 30N42'24 92W54'24 6:11:38
Mix 39 1 30N39'27 91W29'06 6:05:56
Modeste 3 1 30N10'15 91W00'53 6:04:04
Moncla 5 1 31N08 92W04 6:08:16
Monette Ferry 35
1 31N28 92W46 6:11:04
Monks Hammock 58
1 31N15'36 93W28'42 6:13:55
Monroe 37 1 32N30'33 92W07'09 6:08:29
Montcalm 7 1 32N32 92W47 6:11:08
Montcla 5 1 31N12'10 92W07'10 6:08:29
Montecello 54 1 31N48 91W23 6:05:32
Montegut 48 1 30N04'14 90W30'07 6:02:00
Montegut 55 1 29N28'27 90W33'25 6:02:14
Monterey 15 1 31N26'59 91W43'05 6:06:52
Montgomery 22 1 31N40'02 92W53'26 6:11:34
Monticello 18 1 32N35'47 91W23'38 6:05:35
Montpelier 46 1 30N40'51 90W38'56 6:02:36
Montrose 35 1 31N34'14 92W59'30 6:11:58
Montz 45 1 30N00'24 90W28'07 6:01:52
Moore 64 1 31N50'28 92W35'03 6:10:20
Mooringsport 9 1 32N41'15 93W57'39 6:15:51
Mora 35 1 31N22'23 92W56'52 6:11:47
Morameal 8 1 32N22'00 93W34'12 6:14:17
Morbihan 23 1 30N00'42 91W46'28 6:07:06
Moreauville 5 1 31N02'04 91W58'32 6:07:54
Moreland 40 1 31N11'48 92W25'23 6:09:42
Morgan Bluff 52 1 30N19'43 89W42'45 5:58:51
Morgan City 51 1 29N41'57 91W12'24 6:04:50
Morgan City Beach 51
1 29N41'37 91W06'07 6:04:24
Morganza 39 1 30N44'18 91W35'39 6:06:23
Morganza Landing 39
1 30N44'27 91W35'16 6:06:21
Morningside 9 1 32N27 93W47 6:15:08
Morrison 39 1 30N42'45 91W31'43 6:06:07
Morrisonville 24
1 30N19'19 91W13'29 6:04:54
Morrow 49 1 30N49'47 92W04'48 6:08:19
Morse 1 1 30N07'18 92W29'53 6:10:00
Morvant 29 1 29N48'45 90W53'49 6:03:35
Morville 15 1 31N35 91W26 6:05:44
Moss 9 1 32N18'52 93W35'03 6:14:20
Moss Bluff 10 1 30N18'09 93W11'26 6:12:46
Moss Lake 10 1 30N06'49 93W20'27 6:13:22
Mossville 10 1 30N14'51 93W18'32 6:13:14
Mot 8 1 32N54'24 93W34'16 6:14:17
Mound 33 1 32N20'21 91W01'26 6:04:06
Mount Airy 48 1 30N03'04 90W38'16 6:02:33
Mount Carmel 43 1 31N28'09 93W22'49 6:13:31
Mount Hermon 59 1 30N57'36 90W17'45 6:01:11
Mount Houmas 3 1 30N12'07 91W00'40 6:04:03
Mount Lawrence 4
1 29N51 91W00 6:04:00
Mount Lebanon 7 1 32N30'13 93W02'56 6:12:12
Mount Moriah 25 1 32N17'12 92W24'48 6:09:39
Mount Olive 7 1 32N19'52 92W48'14 6:11:13
Mount Pleasant 17
1 30N38'44 91W17'11 6:05:09
Mount Sinai 14 1 32N58 93W08 6:12:32
Mount Union 56 1 32N56 92W36 6:10:24
Mount Zion 41 1 32N02 93W20 6:13:20
Mount Zion 64 1 31N40 92W53 6:11:32
Mouton 28 1 30N16'26 92W01'59 6:08:08
Mowata 1 1 30N23'30 92W24'34 6:09:38
Mudville 22 1 31N42'46 92W23'46 6:09:35
Mulatto Bend Landing 61
1 30N30'39 91W13'56 6:04:56
Mulberry 55 1 29N33'16 90W43'10 6:02:53
Mulnix 14 1 32N41'40 93W02'20 6:12:09
Mulvey 57 1 30N00'22 92W24'14 6:09:37
Murray Junction 64
1 31N53'45 92W29'16 6:09:57
Musson 24 1 30N26'21 91W31'09 6:06:05
Myrtis 9 1 32N55'29 93W59'29 6:15:58
Myrtle Grove 38 1 29N38'14 89W56'57 5:59:48
Myrtle Grove Plantation 24
1 30N17'29 91W15'46 6:05:03
Naborton 16 1 32N02'30 93W34'59 6:14:20
Naff 34 1 32N56'06 91W55'06 6:07:40
Nairn 38 1 29N25'40 89W36'39 5:58:27
Naka 49 1 30N29'18 92W05'23 6:08:22
Naomi 38 2 29N42'36 89W59'32 5:59:58
Napoleonville 4 1 29N56'25 91W01'29 6:04:06
Napoleonville Junction 29
1 29N47 90W50 6:03:20
Naquin 29 1 29N47'23 90W50'29 6:03:22
Natalbany 53 1 30N32'46 90W29'05 6:01:56
Natchez 35 1 31N40'31 93W02'40 6:12:11
Natchitoches 35 1 31N45'38 93W05'10 6:12:21
Naylor 9 1 32N20'52 93W39'13 6:14:37
Neale 6 1 30N46'23 93W27'30 6:13:50
Neal Landing 32 1 30N22'22 90W38'50 6:02:35

Place		Latitude	Longitude	Time
Neame 58	1	30N58'28	93w16'54	6:13:08
Nebo 30	1	31N35'19	92w08'30	6:08:34
Negreet 43	1	31N28'09	93w34'29	6:14:18
Neita 49	1	30N50'08	91w48'39	6:07:15
Nero 38	1	29N36'41	89w52'06	5:59:28
Nesser 17	1	30N23'53	91w03'07	6:04:12
Nestor 38	1	29N29'49	89w41'46	5:58:47
New Belledeau 5	1	31N03	92w07	6:08:28
New California 39	1	30N50'54	91w44'42	6:06:59
Newellton 54	1	32N04'21	91w14'27	6:04:58
New Era 15	1	31N22'01	91w49'38	6:07:19
New Flanders 28	1	30N06'33	92w01'57	6:08:08
New Friendship 7	1	32N15'51	92w52'21	6:11:29
Newhlock 34	1	32N47'48	91w53'55	6:07:36
New Hope 41	1	32N08'40	93w25'29	6:13:42
Newhope 62	1	32N40'54	91w31'39	6:06:07
New Iberia 23	1	30N00'12	91w49'07	6:07:16
New Landgrove Landing 34	1	32N55'57	91w43'29	6:06:54
New Light 42	1	32N15'40	91w47'01	6:07:08
Newlight 54	1	32N06'12	91w26'00	6:05:44
Newllano 58	1	31N06'53	93w16'17	6:13:05
New Moore 64	1	31N51'10	92w35'18	6:10:21
New Orleans 36	2	29N57'16	90w04'30	6:00:18
New Quarters 54	1	32N09'13	91w25'31	6:05:42
New Roads 39	1	30N42'05	91w26'10	6:05:45
New Sarpy 45	1	29N58'40	90w23'16	6:01:33
Newton 10	1	30N18'41	93w12'01	6:12:48
New Verda 22	1	31N41'32	92w45'51	6:11:03
Niblett 27	1	30N06'10	92w51'13	6:11:25
Niblett Bluff 10	1	30N11'55	93w40'47	6:14:43
Nicholas 23	1	29N57'50	91w52'44	6:07:31
Nicholls University 29	1	29N47	90w50	6:03:20
Nichols (historical) 9	1	32N26'57	93w52'27	6:15:30
Nickel 30	1	31N48'33	92w03'14	6:08:13
Nina Station 50	1	30N18'18	91w50'28	6:07:22
Nine Forks 60	1	32N35'24	93w12'16	6:12:49
Ninock 8	1	32N14'48	93w27'25	6:13:50
Noble 43	1	31N41'22	93w41'02	6:14:44
Noble Manor 38	2	29N52'14	89w59'50	5:59:59
Nobrac 20	1	30N58'22	92w23'50	6:09:35
Noel 3	1	30N07'51	91w04'14	6:04:17
Noles Landing 60	1	32N27'49	93w20'56	6:13:24
Norah 29	1	29N36'50	90w29'28	6:01:58
Norbert 23	1	29N58'44	91w53'49	6:07:35
Norco 45	1	29N59'56	90w24'44	6:01:39
Norma 5	1	31N02'31	92w08'01	6:08:32
Normandy Park 26	2	29N54	90w09	6:00:36
North Bend 51	1	29N40'57	91w28'11	6:05:53
Northeast 37	1	32N30	92w05	6:08:20
North Fort Polk 58	1	31N06'52	93w10'04	6:12:40
North Highlands 9	1	32N34'09	93w47'23	6:15:10
North Highlands 17	1	30N29'36	91w08'25	6:04:34
North Hodge 25	1	32N17	92w43	6:10:52
North Island 12	1	29N42'48	92w44'04	6:10:56
North Maryland 17	1	30N33'13	91w11'55	6:04:48
North Merrydale 17	1	30N29	91w09	6:04:36
North Monroe 37	1	32N30	92w05	6:08:20
North Point 5	1	31N18'00	92w09'17	6:08:37
North Rodessa 9	1	32N58'51	94w00'05	6:16:00
North Shore 52	1	30N13'03	89w49'15	5:59:17
North Shore Beach 52	1	30N13'29	89w50'47	5:59:23
North Shreveport 9	1	32N33	93w48	6:15:12
North Side 52	1	30N09'33	89w36'00	5:58:24
North Slidell 52	1	30N18'16	89w46'41	5:59:07
Norton 9	1	32N19'59	93w41'47	6:14:47
Norton Corner 14	1	32N56'55	93w13'31	6:12:54
Norton Shop 14	1	32N56	93w18	6:13:12
Norwood 19	1	30N58'03	91w06'14	6:04:25
Notleyville 49	1	30N30'20	92w00'38	6:08:03
Notnac 54	1	32N06'11	91w12'08	6:04:49
Nuba 49	1	30N35'14	92w04'13	6:08:17
Nugent 5	1	30N51'47	91w57'22	6:07:49
Nugent 22	1	31N26'27	92w25'16	6:09:41
Numa 23	1	29N58'36	91w53'30	6:07:34
Nunez 57	1	29N59'28	92w13'43	6:08:55
Oak Alley 47	1	29N59'12	90w46'14	6:03:05
Oakbluff 51	1	29N48	91w30	6:06:00
Oakdale 2	1	30N48'57	92w39'37	6:10:38
Oakdale 26	2	29N53	90w05	6:00:20
Oak Dale Landing 54	1	31N49'43	91w34'05	6:06:16
Oak Forest 55	1	29N37'53	90w55'58	6:03:44
Oak Grove 3	1	30N19'04	90w58'29	6:03:54
Oak Grove 12	1	29N45'24	93w06'50	6:12:27
Oak Grove 22	1	31N35	92w32	6:10:08
Oak Grove 31	1	32N32	92w47	6:11:08
Oak Grove 43	1	31N47'14	93w38'41	6:14:35
Oak Grove 62	1	32N51'39	91w23'18	6:05:33
Oak Hills Place 17	1	30N25	91w09	6:04:36
Oakland 8	1	32N28'05	93w30'34	6:14:02
Oakland 39	1	30N35'40	91w24'32	6:05:38
Oakland 56	1	32N59'44	92w21'02	6:09:24
Oak Landing 34	1	32N57'41	91w43'02	6:06:52
Oaklawn 51	1	29N50'28	91w27'09	6:05:49
Oaklawn 52	1	30N17'55	89w55'16	5:59:41
Oakley 4	1	29N52'25	91w00'43	6:04:03
Oakley 21	1	31N59'53	91w37'11	6:06:29
Oakley 24	1	30N16'08	91w06'14	6:04:25
Oakley Landing 21	1	32N01'52	91w37'11	6:06:29
Oak Manor 17	1	30N27	91w04	6:04:16
Oaknolia 19	1	30N43'58	90w59'26	6:03:58
Oak Point 38	2	29N45	90w00	6:00:00
Oak Ridge 34	1	32N37'26	91w46'22	6:07:05
Oaks 14	1	32N55'12	93w07'07	6:12:28
Oakshire Manor 55	1	29N38'48	90w45'24	6:03:02
Oakville 38	2	29N46'58	90w01'35	6:00:06
Oakwood Landing 21	1	32N03'38	91w34'29	6:06:18
Oberlin 2	1	30N37'12	92w45'45	6:11:03
Odenburg 5	1	30N55'13	91w48'38	6:07:15
Odra 35	1	31N35'49	92w50'10	6:11:21
Oil Center 28	1	30N13	92w02	6:08:08
Oil City 9	1	32N44'38	93w58'17	6:15:53
Okaloosa 37	1	32N22'48	92w19'40	6:09:19
OK Landing 13	1	31N46'10	91w33'38	6:06:15
Old Athens 14	1	32N38'44	93w03'27	6:12:14
Oldfield 32	1	30N30	90w51	6:03:24
Old Lafitte 26	1	29N41	90w06	6:00:24
Old Shell Beach 44	1	29N51'59	89w40'42	5:58:43
Old Shongaloo 60	1	32N59'30	93w18'36	6:13:14
Olga 38	1	29N20	89w25	5:57:40
Olive Branch 19	1	30N44'38	91w03'43	6:04:15
Olivier 23	1	29N58'54	91w45'09	6:07:01
Olla 30	1	31N54'10	92w14'35	6:08:58
Ollie 38	2	29N44'34	90w01'03	6:00:04
Olympic Landing 54	1	31N45'28	91w33'02	6:06:12
Omega 15	1	31N34'18	91w48'12	6:07:13
Omega 33	1	32N30'59	91w08'22	6:04:33
Oneida 47	1	30N01'09	90w47'52	6:03:11
Opelousas 49	1	30N32'00	92w04'53	6:08:20
Orange Grove Plantation 29	1	29N50'56	90w48'41	6:03:15
Orchard 38	1	29N16'07	89w21'16	5:57:25
Oretta 6	1	30N31'33	93w26'14	6:13:45
Ormond 45	1	29N57	90w22	6:01:28
Oscar 39	1	30N36'54	91w27'40	6:05:51
Osceola 53	1	30N39'02	90w18'41	6:01:15
Osceola 54	1	31N58'10	91w15'10	6:05:01
Ossun 28	1	30N16'33	92w06'44	6:08:27
Ostrica 38	1	29N22'05	89w31'45	5:58:07
Otis 40	1	31N12'55	92w43'40	6:10:55
Ouachita 56	1	32N42	92w04	6:08:16
Oubre 23	1	30N03'44	91w44'12	6:06:57
Oxford 16	1	31N55'24	93w37'40	6:14:31
Oxford 51	1	29N51'14	91w28'43	6:05:55
Pace 60	1	32N36	93w19	6:13:16
Packton 64	1	31N47'51	92w34'36	6:10:18
Paincourtville 4	1	29N59	91w03	6:04:12
Palmer Landing 9	1	32N19'40	93w40'35	6:14:42
Palmetto 8	1	32N23'49	93w33'27	6:14:14
Palmetto 49	1	30N43'02	91w54'33	6:07:38
Palo Alto 3	1	30N05'30	91w02'17	6:04:09
Panchoville 27	1	30N21'54	92w39'04	6:10:36
Panola 15	1	31N38	91w32	6:06:08
Panola 18	1	32N54'27	91w13'33	6:04:54
Paradis 45	1	29N52'46	90w26'02	6:01:44
Paradise 40	1	31N23'02	92w24'25	6:09:38
Paradise Manor 26	2	29N58	90w13	6:00:52
Parhams 13	1	31N28'03	91w47'11	6:07:09
Park Manor 26	2	30N00	90w13	6:00:52
Parks 50	1	30N12'51	91w49'55	6:07:20
Parkside Manor 26	2	29N58	90w13	6:00:52
Parlange 39	1	30N37'41	91w29'15	6:05:57
Patin 39	1	30N41'23	91w24'22	6:05:37
Patin 50	1	30N17'25	91w50'15	6:07:21
Patoutville 23	1	29N54'12	91w44'01	6:06:56
Patterson 51	1	29N41'35	91w18'07	6:05:12
Paulina 47	1	30N01'34	90w42'47	6:02:51
Pawnee 2	1	30N53'25	92w37'37	6:10:30
Pearl 40	1	30N54'17	92w37'12	6:10:29
Pearl River 52	1	30N22'33	89w44'54	5:59:00
Peason 43	1	31N24'49	93w17'40	6:13:11
Pecan Grove 26	2	29N54	90w09	6:00:36
Pecaniere 49	1	30N29'03	91w56'17	6:07:45
Pecan Island 57	1	29N38'47	92w27'11	6:09:49
Pecan Landing 54	1	32N06'09	91w24'48	6:05:39
Pecan Place 24	1	30N17	91w14	6:04:56
Peck 13	1	31N55'30	91w39'40	6:06:39
Pelba 24	1	30N20'30	91w43'57	6:06:56
Pelican 16	1	31N52'56	93w35'09	6:14:21
Percle 4	1	29N52'06	91w00'42	6:04:03
Perkins 10	1	30N23'35	93w24'42	6:13:39
Perry 57	1	29N56'54	92w09'25	6:08:38
Perryville 34	1	32N42'28	92w00'19	6:08:01
Pertuits Store 47	1	29N59	90w50	6:03:20
Petetin 49	1	30N22'59	92w03'19	6:08:13
Peveto Beach 12	1	29N45'39	93w33'30	6:14:14
Philadelphia Point 3	1	30N09'27	91w00'46	6:04:03
Phoenix 38	1	29N38'45	89w56'23	5:59:46
Pickering 58	1	31N02'02	93w16'14	6:13:05
Pickett 9	1	32N38'23	93w47'19	6:15:09
Piermont 41	1	31N57'05	93w16'56	6:13:08
Pierre Part 4	1	29N57'54	91w12'11	6:04:49
Pigeon 24	1	30N04'36	91w17'58	6:05:12
Pikes Peak 47	1	29N58'49	90w48'29	6:03:14
Pilette 28	1	30N10'06	91w59'57	6:08:00
Pilottown 38	1	29N10'53	89w15'27	5:57:02
Pine 59	1	30N54'27	90w00'49	6:00:03
Pine Cliff 59	1	30N46'58	90w07'24	6:00:30
Pine Coupee 40	1	31N22'27	92w53'56	6:11:36
Pine Grove 37	1	32N27'12	92w03'04	6:08:12
Pine Grove 46	1	30N42'35	90w45'14	6:03:01
Pine Island 27	1	30N20'59	92w46'29	6:11:06
Pine Oak Terrace 9	1	32N27	93w47	6:15:08
Pine Prairie 20	1	30N47'01	92w25'31	6:09:42
Pineville 40	1	31N19'20	92w26'03	6:09:44
Pineville Junction 40	1	31N18'43	92w25'38	6:09:43
Pioneer 62	1	32N44'10	91w26'00	6:05:44
Pitkin 58	1	30N56'10	92w56'10	6:11:45
Pitreville 1	1	30N28'47	92w15'41	6:09:03
Plaincourtville 4	1	29N59'21	91w03'31	6:04:14
Plain Dealing 8	1	32N54'18	93w41'48	6:14:47
Plains 17	1	30N41'24	91w12'20	6:04:49
Plainview 32	1	30N32'23	90w58'12	6:03:53
Plainview 59	1	30N47	89w51	5:59:24
Plaisance 49	1	30N36'44	92w07'34	6:08:30
Plantation Acres 40	1	31N17	92w29	6:09:56
Plantation Park 8	1	32N32	93w42	6:14:48
Plaquemine 24	1	30N17'20	91w14'03	6:04:56
Plattenville 4	1	29N59'19	91w01'19	6:04:05
Plaucheville 5	1	30N57'55	91w58'54	6:07:56
Pleasant Hill 7	1	32N31	93w03	6:12:12
Pleasant Hill 43	1	31N49'11	93w30'51	6:14:03
Pleasant Hills 17	1	30N31	91w09	6:04:36
Pleasant Ridge 30	1	31N54	92w14	6:08:56
Plettenberg 63	1	30N52'40	91w29'32	6:05:58
Ploup 39	1	30N42'18	91w28'58	6:05:56
Plum Orchard Landing 60	1	32N24'51	93w22'34	6:13:30
Point 56	1	32N39'39	92w16'39	6:09:07
Point Au Chien 55	1	29N29	90w33	6:02:12
Point Barre 55	1	29N25'32	90w34'03	6:02:16
Point Blue 20	1	30N37'37	92w18'08	6:09:13
Point Breeze 15	1	31N03'17	91w34'25	6:06:18
Point Celeste 38	1	29N35'53	89w50'53	5:59:24
Pointe A La Hache 38	1	29N34'34	89w47'30	5:59:10
Pointe Claire 49	1	30N26'16	91w57'29	6:07:50
Pointe Coupee 39	1	30N44'03	91w25'59	6:05:44
Pointe Cypress 45	1	29N54'01	90w31'10	6:02:05
Point Pleasant 14	1	32N41'16	92w58'22	6:11:53
Point Pleasant 34	1	32N46'18	91w57'09	6:07:49
Poland 40	1	31N10'01	92w16'32	6:09:06
Pollock 22	1	31N31'32	92w24'25	6:09:38
Ponchatoula 53	1	30N26'19	90w26'29	6:01:46
Ponchatoula Beach 53	1	30N26	90w26	6:01:44
Pontchartrain Beach 36	2	30N01'59	90w03'43	6:00:15
Pont Des Mouton 28	1	30N16'19	91w59'00	6:07:56
Poole 8	1	32N17'11	93w29'31	6:13:58
Poplar Grove 49	1	30N32'10	91w59'55	6:08:00
Poplar Grove 61	1	30N28	91w13	6:04:52
Poplar Grove Plantation 61	1	30N29'23	91w12'26	6:04:50
Portage 50	1	30N24'44	91w51'41	6:07:27
Port Allen 61	1	30N27'07	91w12'36	6:04:50
Port Allen Landing 61	1	30N27'10	91w12'01	6:04:48
Port Barre 49	1	30N33'36	91w57'14	6:07:49
Port Barrow 3	1	30N06	91w00	6:04:00
Port Boliver 60	1	32N25'32	93w20'52	6:13:23
Port Eads 38	1	29N00'59	89w09'42	5:56:39
Porters Curve 59	1	30N57'32	90w19'01	6:01:16
Porters River Landing 52	1	30N21'43	89w43'55	5:58:56
Porterville 60	1	32N56'45	93w27'28	6:13:50
Port Hickey 17	1	30N39'39	91w17'25	6:05:10
Port Hickey Landing 17	1	30N39'25	91w17'32	6:05:10
Port Hudson 17	1	30N40'41	91w16'10	6:05:05
Port of New Iberia 23	1	29N56'31	91w50'30	6:07:22
Port Sulphur 38	1	29N28'49	89w41'38	5:58:47
Port Vincent 32	1	30N20'01	90w50'58	6:03:24
Post Trailer Park 58	1	31N08	93w16	6:13:04
Potash 38	1	29N29'34	89w42'20	5:58:49
Pot Cove 49	1	30N31	92w11	6:08:44
Poufette 23	1	29N56'35	91w55'51	6:07:43
Powell 63	1	30N44'21	91w19'47	6:05:19
Powhatan 35	1	31N52'22	93w12'04	6:12:48
Poydras 44	2	29N52'09	89w53'20	5:59:33
Prairie Laurent 49	1	30N29'06	92w02'28	6:08:10
Prairie Ronde 49	1	30N34'36	92w11'18	6:08:45
Prairieville 3	1	30N18'10	90w58'19	6:03:53
Pratt 7	1	32N29'29	92w59'21	6:11:57
Presquille 55	1	29N33'49	90w38'46	6:02:35
Preston 9	1	32N15'20	93w52'38	6:15:31
Prevost 51	1	29N50'29	91w36'05	6:06:24
Price Crossing 40	1	31N09'56	92w48'15	6:11:13
Pricetown 26	2	29N54'49	90w12'36	6:00:50
Pride 17	1	30N41'37	90w58'41	6:03:55
Prien 10	1	30N10'54	93w16'25	6:13:06
Princeton 8	1	32N35'21	93w30'54	6:14:04
Promised Land 38	2	29N47'43	90w00'16	6:00:01
Provencal 35	1	31N39'10	93w12'07	6:12:48
Providence 26	2	29N59	90w15	6:01:00
Prudhomme 1	1	30N28'20	92w19'30	6:09:18
Puckett 17	1	30N34'06	91w02'53	6:04:12
Pumpkin Center 53	1	30N27'17	90w32'31	6:02:10
Punkin Center 25	1	32N18'01	92w42'03	6:10:48
Quachita City 56	1	32N43'33	92w04'17	6:08:17
Quaid 13	1	31N37	91w49	6:07:16
Quarantine 38	1	29N12	89w16	5:57:04
Quebec 33	1	32N25'36	91w18'10	6:05:13
Quick 39	1	30N33'19	91w34'44	6:06:19
Quigley 56	1	32N51'17	92w18'17	6:09:13
Quimby 33	1	32N14'07	91w12'59	6:04:52
Quinton 39	1	30N49'20	91w42'18	6:06:49
Quitman 25	1	32N20'55	92w43'17	6:10:53
Raceland 29	1	29N43'38	90w35'56	6:02:24
Raceland Junction 29	1	29N44'52	90w34'23	6:02:18
Ragley 6	1	30N30'45	93w13'56	6:12:56

Ramah 24 1 30N24'08 91w30'26 6:06:02
Rambin 16 1 31N57'06 93w27'15 6:13:49
Ramos 51 1 29N40'37 91w08'19 6:04:33
Ramsay 52 1 30N31'32 90w07'33 6:00:30
Randall 49 1 30N32 92w05 6:08:20
Randolph 56 1 32N59'11 92w41'25 6:10:46
Rapides 40 1 31N21'48 92w35'12 6:10:21
Ratliff 4 1 29N56'39 91w01'25 6:04:06
Rattan 43 1 31N20'50 93w31'40 6:14:07
Ravenswood 39 1 30N40'19 91w41'22 6:06:45
Raymond 27 1 30N20'59 92w42'20 6:10:49
Rayne 1 1 30N14'05 92w16'06 6:09:04
Rayville 42 1 32N28'38 91w45'17 6:07:01
Readheimer 35 1 32N06'55 92w59'14 6:11:57
Readhimer 35 1 32N03 93w01 6:12:04
Rebecca 55 1 29N36 90w43 6:02:52
Rebecca Plantation 55 1 29N41'30 90w48'46 6:03:15
Red Chute 8 1 32N33'21 93w36'47 6:14:27
Reddell 20 1 30N40'26 92w25'34 6:09:42
Red Fish 5 1 30N59 91w49 6:07:16
Red Gum 15 1 31N45 91w32 6:06:08
Redich 1 1 30N24'58 92w33'52 6:10:15
Redland 8 1 32N57'22 93w36'54 6:14:28
Red Oak 17 1 30N27'56 91w04'03 6:04:16
Redoak 41 1 31N56'46 93w16'20 6:13:05
Red River Landing 39 1 30N57'33 91w39'54 6:06:40
Reedton 20 1 30N38 92w25 6:09:40
Reeves (Reaves School) 2 1 30N31'15 93w02'51 6:12:11
Reggio 44 1 29N49'52 89w45'16 5:59:01
Reids 2 1 30N56 92w56 6:11:44
Reiley 19 1 30N44'37 90w58'09 6:03:53
Reimer Crossing 19 1 30N44'35 90w55'18 6:03:41
Reisor 9 1 32N24'41 93w51'03 6:15:24
Remolina Landing 54 1 32N06'36 91w24'07 6:05:36
Remy 47 1 30N01'14 90w44'28 6:02:58
Reserve 48 1 30N03'13 90w33'06 6:02:12
Retreat 63 1 30N58'19 91w29'06 6:05:56
Reveille 24 1 30N16'17 91w11'15 6:04:45
Reynolds 5 1 31N13'00 92w13'40 6:08:55
Rhinehart 30 1 31N38'15 92w00'24 6:08:02
Rhodes 24 1 30N18'22 91w07'17 6:04:29
Rhymes 42 1 32N22'44 91w53'56 6:07:36
Riceville 57 1 30N04'34 92w30'51 6:10:03
Richard 1 1 30N25'18 92w18'46 6:09:15
Richard 51 1 29N49'41 91w35'49 6:06:23
Richardson 59 1 30N51'16 90w12'47 6:00:51
Richardson Landing 59 1 30N45'39 89w49'53 5:59:20
Richland 24 1 30N08'40 91w10'47 6:04:43
Richland 51 1 29N47'10 91w41'42 6:06:47
Richland 54 1 31N50'11 91w27'04 6:05:48
Richmond 33 1 32N25 91w11 6:04:44
Richwood 37 1 32N30 92w05 6:08:20
Ricohoc 51 1 29N42'27 91w23'00 6:05:32
Riddle 63 1 30N43'10 91w18'35 6:05:14
Rideau Settlement 49 1 30N41'01 91w54'12 6:07:37
Ridge 28 1 30N09'32 92w10'34 6:08:42
Ridgecrest 15 1 31N36 91w32 6:06:08
Ridgewood 17 1 30N35 91w00 6:04:00
Rienzi Plantation 29 1 29N48'50 90w48'37 6:03:14
Rigolets 36 2 30N08'55 89w38'32 5:58:34
Rigolette 40 1 31N23 92w24 6:09:36
Rilla 37 1 32N24'55 92w06'03 6:08:24
Ringgold 7 1 32N19'42 93w16'47 6:13:07
Ringwood 64 1 31N59'02 92w31'23 6:10:06
Rio 59 1 30N41'34 89w53'24 5:59:34
Risinger Woods 9 1 32N33 93w47 6:15:08
Rita 29 1 29N38'52 90w32'02 6:02:08
River Bend 44 2 29N52'53 89w53'34 5:59:34
Riverland Heights 48 1 30N04'28 90w29'25 6:01:58
Riverlands 48 1 30N04 90w29 6:01:56
River Ridge 26 2 29N58 90w13 6:00:52
Riverton 11 1 32N09'38 92w05'46 6:08:23
Riverwood 52 1 30N29 90w06 6:00:24
Roanoke 27 1 30N14'12 92w44'49 6:10:59
Robeline 35 1 31N41'25 93w18'16 6:13:13
Robert 53 1 30N30'22 90w20'27 6:01:22
Robinson 34 1 32N59'20 91w53'24 6:07:34
Robson 9 1 32N21'42 93w38'34 6:14:34
Rochelle 22 1 31N47'24 92w22'10 6:09:29
Rock (Rock Quarry) 40 1 31N26'13 92w44'04 6:10:56
Rockfield 25 1 32N17'27 92w43'30 6:10:54
Rock Hill 22 1 31N26'49 92w34'15 6:10:17
Rocky Branch 56 1 32N40'43 92w12'11 6:08:49
Rocky Mount 8 1 32N48'52 93w37'45 6:14:31
Rodessa 9 1 32N58'16 93w59'41 6:15:59
Rodriquez 51 1 29N49'57 91w34'04 6:06:16
Rogers 30 1 31N31'56 92w13'30 6:08:54
Rogers 34 1 32N55'53 91w58'33 6:07:54
Rogillioville 63 1 30N55'30 91w13'52 6:04:55
Romeville 47 1 30N03'44 90w50'48 6:03:23
Roosevelt 18 1 32N34'19 91w10'56 6:04:44
Rork 1 1 30N26'22 92w24'40 6:09:39
Rosa 49 1 30N45'18 92w00'26 6:08:02
Rosaryville 53 1 30N25'22 90w31'10 6:02:05
Rosebank 63 1 30N55'23 91w26'29 6:05:46
Rosedale 4 1 29N55'17 90w58'25 6:03:54
Rosedale 24 1 30N26'28 91w27'07 6:05:48
Rosefield 13 1 31N53'27 91w59'55 6:08:00
Rose Hill 57 1 29N55'01 92w07'41 6:08:31
Roseland 53 1 30N45'53 90w30'42 6:02:03
Rosepine 58 1 30N55'11 93w16'56 6:13:08
Rosewood 5 1 30N59'52 91w53'00 6:07:32
Rossignol 10 1 30N07'05 92w59'48 6:11:59
Rougon 39 1 30N36'32 91w22'27 6:05:30
Rousseau 29 1 29N45'48 90w43'21 6:02:53
Routon 30 1 31N41 92w07 6:08:28
Rowes Landing 63 1 30N55'24 91w33'41 6:06:15
Roxana 40 1 31N07'07 92w15'31 6:09:02
Roy 7 1 32N13'26 93w09'07 6:12:36
Ruby 40 1 31N11'21 92w14'55 6:09:00
Ruddock 48 1 30N12'15 90w25'30 6:01:42
Rum Center 56 1 32N59'24 92w39'06 6:10:36
Ruple 14 1 32N58 93w08 6:12:32
Rural Park 26 2 29N58 90w13 6:00:52
Ruston 31 1 32N31'23 92w38'16 6:10:33
Ruth 50 1 30N14'16 91w52'54 6:07:32
Rycade 50 1 30N15'45 91w36'11 6:06:25
Rynella 23 1 29N56'47 91w52'33 6:07:30
Sacksonia 42 1 32N27'59 91w36'07 6:06:24
Sadie 56 1 32N59'21 92w13'51 6:08:55
Sadou 28 1 30N14'14 92w08'34 6:08:34
Sailes 7 1 32N25'31 93w06'29 6:12:26
Saint Amant 3 1 30N13'28 90w52'08 6:03:29
Saint Benedict 52 1 30N31'36 90w06'45 6:00:27
Saint Bernard 44 2 29N52'01 89w51'31 5:59:26
Saint Bernard Grove 44 2 29N55'21 89w54'44 5:59:39
Saint Charles 29 1 29N43 90w36 6:02:24
Saint Clair 38 2 29N52'11 89w58'08 5:59:53
Saint Claude Heights 44 2 29N57'44 89w59'39 5:59:59
Saint Delphine 61 1 30N22 91w16 6:05:04
Saint Elmo 3 1 30N07'11 90w57'38 6:03:51
Saint Elmo 47 1 30N01'21 90w44'05 6:02:56
Saint Francisville 63 1 30N46'47 91w22'35 6:05:30
Saint Gabriel 24 1 30N15'27 91w05'57 6:04:24
Saint Genevieve 15 1 31N31'35 91w31'32 6:06:06
Saint James 47 1 29N58'54 90w49'54 6:03:20
Saint James Plantation 47 1 29N59'53 90w45'06 6:03:00
Saint Joe 52 1 30N20'40 89w45'22 5:59:01
Saint John 29 1 29N47 90w50 6:03:20
Saint John 50 1 30N09'31 91w48'31 6:07:14
Saint Joseph 54 1 31N55'06 91w14'00 6:04:56
Saint Landry 20 1 30N50'39 92w15'28 6:09:02
Saint Louis 24 1 30N15'23 91w13'51 6:04:55
Saint Louis 49 1 30N48'19 92w10'28 6:08:42
Saint Louis Plantation 24 1 30N15'57 91w12'56 6:04:52
Saint Martinville 50 1 30N07'30 91w50'00 6:07:20
Saint Maurice 64 1 31N45'34 92w57'32 6:11:50
Saint Rosalie 38 2 29N39'49 89w58'10 5:59:53
Saint Rose 45 1 29N56'48 90w19'23 6:01:18
Saint Rose Plantation 29 1 29N49'43 90w55'16 6:03:41
Saint Tammany 52 1 30N23'38 89w53'42 5:59:35
Saint Tammany Corner 52 1 30N25'37 89w53'08 5:59:33
Saint Thomas 4 1 29N53'36 91w00'24 6:04:02
Saline 7 1 32N09'52 92w58'27 6:11:54
Salix 45 1 29N55'34 90w18'33 6:01:14
Salsburg 47 1 30N05'29 90w54'57 6:03:40
Sambo 49 1 30N42'14 91w49'42 6:07:19
Sampusand 35 1 31N29'18 92w54'46 6:11:39
Samstown 24 1 30N08'06 91w09'33 6:04:38
Samtown 40 1 31N16'18 92w26'11 6:09:45
Sandager 23 1 29N57'26 91w43'20 6:06:53
Sandel 43 1 31N22'51 93w26'11 6:13:45
Sandra 9 1 33N00'12 94w00'46 6:16:03
Sand Spur 22 1 31N34'46 92w24'48 6:09:39
Sandy Hill 58 1 31N08 93w16 6:13:04
San Francisco Plantation 48 1 30N04 90w33 6:02:12
Santiague 23 1 29N59'05 91w54'15 6:07:37
Sarah 38 2 29N46'12 90w01'48 6:00:07
Sarah Plantation 55 1 29N28'55 90w34'43 6:02:19
Saranac 54 1 32N00'33 91w21'10 6:05:25
Sardis 43 1 31N45'03 93w38'41 6:14:35
Sarepta 60 1 32N53'34 93w26'54 6:13:48
Satsuma 32 1 30N30'09 90w48'01 6:03:12
Savage Fork 58 1 31N01'55 93w21'12 6:13:25
Savoie 55 1 29N38'43 90w41'14 6:02:45
Savoy 49 1 30N30'26 92w19'10 6:09:17
Scarsdale 38 2 29N50'42 89w58'40 5:59:55
Schriever 55 1 29N44'31 90w48'37 6:03:14
Scotlandville (Scotland Sta) 17 1 30N31'13 91w10'43 6:04:43
Scott 28 1 30N14'08 92w05'40 6:08:23
Scott Landing 33 1 32N26'03 91w29'14 6:05:57
Scottsville 14 1 32N56'14 92w46'00 6:11:04
Seale 6 1 30N33'42 93w26'09 6:13:45
Searcy 30 1 31N42'18 92w13'41 6:08:55
Sebastopol 44 2 29N52'03 89w52'22 5:59:29
Security 13 1 31N32'03 91w48'59 6:07:16
Segura 23 1 30N02'18 91w51'28 6:07:26
Sellers 45 1 29N59'56 90w25'36 6:01:42
Selma 22 1 31N44'28 92w23'13 6:09:33
Sentell 9 1 32N38'53 93w47'51 6:15:11
Serena 13 1 31N26 91w52 6:07:28
Seven Runs Crossing 11 1 32N11'52 92w16'01 6:09:04
Seymourville 24 1 30N16'38 91w13'25 6:04:54
Shady Grove 54 1 31N57'40 91w25'29 6:05:42
Shady Oaks 40 1 31N10'21 92w20'48 6:09:23
Shadyside 51 1 29N44'02 91w23'25 6:05:34
Shamrock 35 1 31N42'31 93w19'50 6:13:19
Sharkey 53 1 30N22'12 90w25'14 6:01:41
Sharon 14 1 32N46'18 92w45'50 6:11:03
Sharon Hills 17 1 30N31 91w09 6:04:36
Sharp 17 1 30N28'21 91w03'27 6:04:14
Sharp 40 1 31N24'12 92w46'41 6:11:07
Shaw 15 1 31N11'29 91w37'52 6:06:31
Shear 6 1 30N48'29 93w21'46 6:13:27
Shelburn 18 1 32N53'03 91w13'32 6:04:54
Shell Beach 44 1 29N51'11 89w40'46 5:58:43
Sheltons 34 1 32N49'45 91w54'26 6:07:38
Sherburne 39 1 30N30'53 91w43'08 6:06:53
Sheridan 59 1 30N52'06 90w00'11 6:00:01
Sherwood 13 1 31N51'01 91w56'52 6:07:47
Shexnayder 39 1 30N43'44 91w27'07 6:05:48
Shiloh 53 1 30N41'13 90w30'28 6:02:02
Shiloh 56 1 32N47'36 92w35'21 6:10:21
Shiloh Landing 56 1 32N57'58 92w05'17 6:08:21
Shongaloo 60 1 32N56'29 93w17'55 6:13:12
Shops 37 1 32N30 92w05 6:08:20
Shoreline 9 1 32N48'00 93w58'42 6:15:55
Shreve Island 9 1 32N28 93w43 6:14:52
Shreveport 9 1 32N31'30 93w45'00 6:15:00
Shrewsbury 26 2 29N58'15 90w08'32 6:00:34
Shuteston 49 1 30N25'41 92w06'01 6:08:24
Sibley 31 1 32N34'32 92w28'02 6:09:52
Sibley 60 1 32N32'21 93w17'46 6:13:11
Sicard 37 1 32N31'35 92w02'29 6:08:10
Sicily Island 13 1 31N50'47 91w39'22 6:06:37
Siegen 17 1 30N22'24 91w04'16 6:04:17
Siegle 37 1 32N29'22 92w10'30 6:08:42
Sieper 40 1 31N12'39 92w48'29 6:11:14
Sieps 40 1 31N19'18 92w27'41 6:09:51
Sikes 64 1 32N04'51 92w29'12 6:09:57
Silverwood 27 1 30N11'22 92w35'52 6:10:23
Simmesport 5 1 30N59'00 91w48'00 6:07:12
Simmons Settlement 2 1 30N40'34 92w53'31 6:11:34
Simms 22 1 31N27'40 92w25'24 6:09:42
Simpson 58 1 31N15'48 93w00'32 6:12:02
Simsboro 31 1 32N32'04 92w47'18 6:11:09
Singer 6 1 30N39'17 93w24'44 6:13:39
Siracusaville 51 1 29N41'13 91w08'53 6:04:36
Skidder 35 1 32N06'02 93w03'25 6:12:14
Slacks 24 1 30N27'56 91w29'36 6:05:58
Slagle 58 1 31N12'08 93w07'38 6:12:31
Slaughter 19 1 30N43'02 91w08'29 6:04:34
Slidell 52 1 30N16'30 89w46'52 5:59:07
Sligo 8 1 32N27'03 93w34'53 6:14:20
Slocum 15 1 31N16'58 91w38'19 6:06:33
Slone 16 1 32N07'20 93w39'37 6:14:38
Smiley Heights 17 1 30N28'14 91w07'49 6:04:31
Smithfield 61 1 30N32'43 91w17'40 6:05:11
Smithland 39 1 30N54'36 91w39'49 6:06:39
Smith Ridge 55 1 29N36 90w43 6:02:52
Smithville 40 1 31N19'28 92w24'36 6:09:38
Smoke Bend 3 1 30N06'30 91w01'13 6:04:05
Smurney 56 1 32N36'24 92w22'31 6:09:30
Socola 38 1 29N28 89w42 5:58:48
Soileau 49 1 30N39'04 92w07'00 6:08:28
Solitude 63 1 30N49'56 91w25'30 6:05:42
Solley Hill 9 1 32N52'02 94w02'10 6:16:09
Somerset 54 1 32N10'34 91w14'02 6:04:56
Sondheimer 18 1 32N33'00 91w10'33 6:04:42
Soniat 24 1 30N10 91w09 6:04:36
Sorrel 51 1 29N53'20 91w37'00 6:06:28
Sorrell 51 1 29N53 91w37 6:06:28
Sorrento 3 1 30N11'03 90w51'33 6:03:26
Soulouque 24 1 30N16'19 91w09'19 6:04:37
South Acres 10 1 30N13 93w21 6:13:24
South Bend 51 1 29N37'48 91w32'08 6:06:09
South Coast 51 1 29N48 91w30 6:06:00
Southdown 55 1 29N35'12 90w44'20 6:02:57
Southdown Plantation 47 1 29N58'58 90w43'42 6:02:55
Southeast 17 1 30N25 91w09 6:04:36
Southern 17 1 30N30 91w11 6:04:44
Southfield 9 1 32N28 93w43 6:14:52
South Fort Polk 58 1 31N03 93w12 6:12:48
South Kenner 26 2 29N57'31 90w16'14 6:01:05
South Lafourche 29 1 29N47 90w50 6:03:20
South Mansfield 16 1 32N01'18 93w42'51 6:14:51
South Park 40 1 31N17 92w29 6:09:56
South Park Trailer Court 58 1 31N08 93w16 6:13:04
South Pass 38 1 29N17 89w21 5:57:24
South Point 36 2 30N08'34 89w53'04 5:59:32
Southport 26 2 29N57'44 90w08'34 6:00:34
Southwestern 28 1 30N13 92w02 6:08:08
Southwood 3 1 30N13'08 91w02'57 6:04:12
Spanish Fort 36 2 30N01'15 90w04'57 6:00:20
Sparks 39 1 30N29'55 91w31'38 6:06:07
Sparta 7 1 32N22'02 93w04'46 6:12:19
Spaulding 11 1 31N56'51 92w10'57 6:08:44
Spearsville 56 1 32N56'09 92w36'18 6:10:25
Spencer 56 1 32N44'24 92w07'54 6:08:32
Spillman 63 1 30N55'47 91w17'01 6:05:08
Splane Place 37 1 32N31 92w09 6:08:36
Spokane 15 1 31N41'57 91w27'37 6:05:50
Spring Bayou Landing 5 1 31N08'28 92w02'11 6:08:09
Spring Creek 53 1 30N54'43 90w26'49 6:01:47
Springfield 32 1 30N25'44 90w32'55 6:02:12
Springhill 59 1 30N48'28 90w06'00 6:00:24
Springhill 60 1 33N00'21 93w28'00 6:13:52
Spring Lake 14 1 32N44'00 93w03'18 6:12:13
Spring Ridge 9 1 32N18'43 93w56'40 6:15:47
Spring Ridge 43 1 31N46'50 93w30'32 6:14:02
Springville 32 1 30N26'07 90w40'59 6:02:44
Springville 41 1 32N02 93w20 6:13:20
Spyker 34 1 32N44'32 91w57'13 6:07:49
Squealer Point Landing 20 1 30N58'31 92w24'59 6:09:40
Stacy 15 1 31N36'09 91w41'25 6:06:46
Stacy Landing 9 1 32N46'23 94w01'16 6:16:05
Stampley 34 1 32N49'18 91w46'47 6:07:07
Standard 30 1 31N55'03 92w13'12 6:08:53
Standard 58 1 31N09'20 93w21'39 6:13:27
Stanley 2 1 30N29'52 92w53'52 6:11:35
Stanley 16 1 31N57'39 93w53'52 6:15:35
Stanton 36 2 29N55'02 89w56'27 5:59:46
Staples 9 1 32N21'51 93w48'59 6:15:16
Star 38 2 29N45 90w00 6:00:00
Starhill 63 1 30N45'43 91w18'25 6:05:14
Starks 10 1 30N18'55 93w39'42 6:14:39
Starns 32 1 30N33'41 90w39'32 6:02:38
Start 42 1 32N29'11 91w51'33 6:07:26
State Line 59 1 30N51 90w09 6:00:36
Stay 22 1 31N28'20 92w29'31 6:09:58
Stegall 10 1 30N14'12 93w25'45 6:13:43
Stein 59 1 30N41'25 89w56'21 5:59:45

Stekey 28 1 30N19'12 92w00'33 6:08:02
Stella 38 2 29N49'09 89w59'45 5:59:59
Stephenville 50 1 29N46'41 91w09'57 6:04:40
Sterlington 37 1 32N41'46 92w05'09 6:08:21
Steven 37 1 32N29'46 92w10'02 6:08:40
Stevensdale 17 1 30N28'42 90w59'59 6:04:00
Stevenson 34 1 32N55'15 91w56'35 6:07:46
Stille 40 1 31N13'53 92w49'47 6:11:19
Stones Landing 21
1 32N05'05 91w34'01 6:06:16
Stonewall 16 1 32N16'54 93w49'26 6:15:18
Stonewell Plantation 39
1 30N43'31 91w30'14 6:06:01
Stoney Point 59 1 30N51 90w09 6:00:36
Stonypoint 17 1 30N35 91w00 6:04:00
Strader 53 1 30N19'24 90w24'27 6:01:38
Sugar Creek 14 1 32N40'05 92w53'12 6:11:33
Sugartown 6 1 30N50'23 93w00'53 6:12:04
Sugrue 58 1 30N57'43 93w02'39 6:12:11
Sulphur 10 1 30N14'11 93w22'38 6:13:31
Summerfield 14 1 32N54'45 92w49'45 6:11:19
Summerfield 22 1 31N34'47 92w43'17 6:10:53
Summer Grove 9 1 32N24'08 93w48'52 6:15:15
Summerville 30 1 31N45'19 92w09'44 6:08:39
Summit 37 1 32N23'53 92w10'36 6:08:42
Sun 52 1 30N38'56 89w53'33 5:59:34
Sunnybrook 17 1 30N29'34 91w05'13 6:04:21
Sunny Hill 59 1 30N55'27 90w19'38 6:01:19
Sunrise 61 1 30N28'38 91w12'08 6:04:49
Sunrise Landing 21
1 32N17'06 91w31'36 6:06:06
Sunset 49 1 30N24'40 92w04'06 6:08:16
Sunshine 24 1 30N16'43 91w07'50 6:04:31
Sun Spur 42 1 32N28 91w29 6:05:56
Superior 9 1 32N49'29 93w58'43 6:15:55
Supreme 4 1 29N51'33 90w58'52 6:03:55
Susan Park 26 2 29N59 90w15 6:01:00
Swampers 21 1 32N11'27 91w34'15 6:06:17
Swartz 37 1 32N34'07 91w59'06 6:07:56
Swayze Lake 49 1 30N38'24 91w49'36 6:07:18
Sweet Home 4 1 30N00'43 91w01'50 6:04:07
Sweet Lake 12 1 29N59'02 93w07'45 6:12:31
Swindleville 8 1 32N47'21 93w43'14 6:14:53
Swords 49 1 30N30'45 92w15'44 6:09:03
Tabatiere Perdue 45
1 29N43'37 90w20'23 6:01:22
Taconey 15 1 31N34'31 91w28'05 6:05:52
Taft 45 1 29N59'28 90w26'53 6:01:48
Talbot Landing 21
1 32N05'20 91w33'38 6:06:15
Talisheek 52 1 30N31'57 89w52'36 5:59:30
Talla Bena 33 1 32N29'30 91w09'12 6:04:37
Tallulah 33 1 32N24'30 91w11'12 6:04:45
Tally Ho 24 1 30N12'19 91w11'04 6:04:44
Tangipahoa 53 1 30N52'33 90w30'43 6:02:03
Tanglewood 17 1 30N32'16 91w04'30 6:04:18
Tanglewood 40 1 31N17 92w29 6:09:56
Tannehill 64 1 31N59'52 92w39'18 6:10:37
Tansey 64 1 31N49'35 92w22'55 6:09:32
Tate Cove 20 1 30N44'38 92w14'49 6:08:59
Taterville 49 1 30N48'25 91w57'14 6:07:49
Taylor 7 1 32N32'44 93w07'09 6:12:29
Taylor Hill 40 1 31N28 92w46 6:11:04
Taylortown 8 1 32N23'11 93w35'45 6:14:23
Taylorville 56 1 32N59'11 92w36'02 6:10:24
Tech 31 1 32N32 92w38 6:10:32
Teddy 19 1 30N59'03 90w58'36 6:03:54
Temple 58 1 31N16'41 92w57'19 6:11:49
Tendal 33 1 32N25'56 91w22'00 6:05:28
Tensas Bluff 54 1 32N09'42 91w24'20 6:05:37
Tensas Bluff Landing 54
1 32N09'53 91w24'15 6:05:37
Tepetate 1 1 30N24'51 92w33'09 6:10:13
Terry 62 1 32N55'46 91w20'55 6:05:24
Terrytown 26 2 29N54'36 90w01'57 6:00:08
Texas 24 1 30N10'18 91w08'17 6:04:33
Theall 57 1 29N52'36 92w13'01 6:08:52
The Parks 24 1 30N13'17 91w19'00 6:05:16
Theriot 29 1 29N45'01 90w37'55 6:02:32
Theriot 55 1 29N27'40 90w45'05 6:03:00
The Y 20 1 30N41 92w17 6:09:08
Thibodaux 29 1 29N47'44 90w49'22 6:03:17
Thibodaux Junction 29
1 29N45'10 90w47'58 6:03:12
Thirteen Points Landing 56
1 32N57'23 92w05'08 6:08:21
Thistlewaite 49 1 30N37 92w04 6:08:16
Thomas 59 1 30N58'04 90w01'43 6:00:07
Thomastown 33 1 32N21'26 91w04'11 6:04:17
Thornwell 27 1 30N05'54 92w47'50 6:11:11
Three Oaks 44 2 29N57 90w00 6:00:00
Three States 9 1 33N01'09 94w02'33 6:16:10
Thronwell 27 1 30N05 92w40 6:10:40
Tickfaw 53 1 30N34'38 90w28'59 6:01:56
Tiger Bluff Landing 32
1 30N18'19 90w39'34 6:02:38
Tigerville 48 1 30N02'33 90w32'36 6:02:10
Timberlane 26 2 29N54 90w03 6:00:12
Timber Trails 40
1 31N17 92w29 6:09:56
Timon 35 1 31N53'23 93w14'18 6:12:57
Tioga 40 1 31N23'13 92w25'32 6:09:42
Toca 44 1 29N51'59 89w50'11 5:59:21
Tony 23 1 30N02'29 91w44'00 6:06:56
Toomey 10 1 30N09'09 93w38'59 6:14:36
Topsy 27 1 30N24'33 93w07'20 6:12:29
Torbert 39 1 30N33'15 91w29'25 6:05:58
Toro 43 1 31N16'49 93w32'38 6:14:11
Torras 39 1 30N59'22 91w40'44 6:06:43
Torras Landing 39
1 30N58'10 91w40'01 6:06:40
Tortue 1 1 30N10'47 92w26'51 6:09:47
Tower Park 58 1 31N08 93w16 6:13:04
Town and Country 37
1 32N30 92w05 6:08:20
Traino Landing 53
1 30N24'21 90w15'45 6:01:03
Transylvania 18 1 32N40'42 91w10'57 6:04:44
Treat 60 1 32N47'36 93w24'31 6:13:38
Trees 9 1 32N47'15 94w01'51 6:16:07
Tremont 31 1 32N31'09 92w27'17 6:09:49
Trenton 16 1 31N57'00 93w43'09 6:14:53
Trinity 13 1 31N37'55 91w48'39 6:07:15
Trinity 24 1 30N26 91w27 6:05:48
Triumph 38 1 29N20'21 89w28'36 5:57:54
Tropical Bend 38
1 29N24'04 89w36'25 5:58:26
Trout 30 1 31N41'44 92w10'43 6:08:43
Troy 19 1 30N58 91w06 6:04:24
Troy 54 1 31N48'45 91w27'03 6:05:48
Truxno 56 1 32N56'51 92w24'21 6:09:37
Tulip 14 1 32N40'54 92w59'11 6:11:57
Tulla 6 1 30N44'25 93w15'01 6:13:00
Tullis 7 1 32N16'14 93w17'09 6:13:09
Tullos 30 1 31N49'09 92w19'47 6:09:19
Tunica 63 1 30N55'45 91w33'18 6:06:13
Tunica Landing 63
1 30N55'22 91w33'22 6:06:13
Turkey Creek 20 1 30N52'37 92w24'47 6:09:39
Turnbull 63 1 30N57'16 91w28'01 6:05:52
Turnerville 24 1 30N17'39 91w14'20 6:04:57
Turps 6 1 30N25'05 93w12'01 6:12:48
Turtle Lake 15 1 31N38 91w32 6:06:08
Twin Oaks 34 1 32N53'33 91w47'25 6:07:10
Tyrone 20 1 30N29'49 92w30'40 6:10:03
U and I Landing 13
1 31N46'10 91w33'40 6:06:15
Ulyssee 23 1 30N01'05 91w52'35 6:07:30
Unatex 20 1 30N29'38 92w31'33 6:10:06
Uncle Sam 47 1 30N35 91w11 6:04:44
Uneedus 53 1 30N37'02 90w15'40 6:01:03
Union 47 1 30N05'13 90w54'17 6:03:37
Union Church 7 1 32N21 92w43 6:10:52
Union Hill 40 1 30N59'40 92w43'52 6:10:55
Union Landing 32
1 30N19'16 90w41'40 6:02:47
Union Point 15 1 31N13'14 91w37'32 6:06:30
Union Springs 43
1 31N49'49 93w47'23 6:15:10
Unionville 31 1 32N40'09 92w38'29 6:10:34
University 17 1 30N25 91w11 6:04:44
University Place 10
1 30N10'19 93w13'15 6:12:53
Upco 56 1 32N45'52 92w08'08 6:08:33
Upland 34 1 32N43'52 91w52'59 6:07:32
Upper Texas 4 1 29N52'08 91w05'25 6:04:22
Upstream 26 2 29N58 90w13 6:00:52
Urania 30 1 31N51'49 92w17'45 6:09:11
Ursa 4 1 29N40'02 91w03'49 6:04:15
Uscarco 34 1 32N45'17 91w56'01 6:07:44
Utility 13 1 31N36'08 91w53'19 6:07:33
Vacherie 47 1 30N00'39 90w43'10 6:02:53
Valentine 29 1 29N35'40 90w28'02 6:01:52
Vallier 45 1 29N52'21 90w26'54 6:01:48
Valmar 44 2 29N57 89w56 5:59:44
Valverda 39 1 30N32'29 91w33'07 6:06:12
Vanceville 8 1 32N36'03 93w44'03 6:14:56
Varnado 59 1 30N53'37 89w49'46 5:59:19
Vatican 28 1 30N18'33 92w06'59 6:08:28
Vaughn 34 1 32N57'07 91w57'47 6:07:51
Veazie 49 1 30N31'46 92w08'20 6:08:33
Velma 53 1 30N42 90w35 6:02:20
Veltin 49 1 30N29'43 92w05'20 6:08:21
Venetian Isles 36
2 30N04'01 89w48'46 5:59:15
Venice 38 1 29N16'37 89w21'17 5:57:25
Ventress 39 1 30N40'54 91w24'29 6:05:38
Verda 22 1 31N41'59 92w46'22 6:11:05
Verdun 32 1 30N20'22 90w44'04 6:02:56
Verdunville 51 1 29N45'14 91w24'03 6:05:36
Vernon 25 1 32N23'19 92w34'17 6:10:17
Verret 10 1 30N09'23 92w55'44 6:11:43
Verret 44 1 29N51'42 89w46'47 5:59:07
Veterans Administration Hosp 9
1 32N30 93w45 6:15:00
Vick 5 1 31N13'48 92w06'20 6:08:25
Victoria 35 1 31N39'50 93w13'31 6:12:54
Vida 23 1 30N02'02 91w43'49 6:06:55
Vidalia 15 1 31N33'55 91w25'33 6:05:42
Vidrine 20 1 30N41'33 92w23'53 6:09:36
Vienna 31 1 32N35'27 92w38'52 6:10:35
Vieux Carre 36 2 29N57'37 90w03'53 6:00:16
Village de l'Est 36
2 30N02'13 89w55'43 5:59:43
Village St George 17
1 30N25 91w09 6:04:36
Ville Platte 20 1 30N41'16 92w16'17 6:09:05
Vincent 10 1 30N13 93w21 6:13:24
Vincent Landing 10
1 30N09'20 93w19'55 6:13:20
Vincent Park 44 2 29N57 89w56 5:59:44
Vinton 10 1 30N11'26 93w34'52 6:14:19
Violet 44 2 29N53'44 89w53'52 5:59:35
Viva 39 1 30N44'06 91w38'25 6:06:34
Vivian 9 1 32N52'17 93w59'14 6:15:57
Vixen 11 1 32N14'03 92w16'07 6:09:04
Voorhies 5 1 31N04'37 91w55'53 6:07:44
Vowells Mill 35 1 31N34'02 93w17'02 6:13:08
Wadely Landing 30
1 31N41 92w07 6:08:28
Wadesboro 53 1 30N25'27 90w29'07 6:01:56
Waggaman 26 2 29N55'06 90w12'39 6:00:51
Wakefield 63 1 30N53'21 91w21'00 6:05:24
Waldheim 52 1 30N33'22 90w00'43 6:00:03
Walding 40 1 31N12'14 92w46'04 6:11:04
Walet 23 1 30N06'09 91w43'35 6:06:54
Walker 25 1 32N11'24 92w35'01 6:10:20
Walker 32 1 30N29'16 90w51'41 6:03:27
Walkertown 26 2 29N53'24 90w06'49 6:00:27
Wallace 48 1 30N02'35 90w40'02 6:02:40
Wallace Ridge 13
1 31N42'34 91w49'38 6:07:19
Waller Landing 21
1 32N02'29 91w37'37 6:06:30
Wall Lake 37 1 32N31 92w09 6:08:36
Walls 61 1 30N35'13 91w19'34 6:05:18
Walnut Hill 58 1 31N12 93w08 6:12:32
Walroy 28 1 30N11'50 91w59'55 6:08:00
Walsh 7 1 32N22'15 92w54'48 6:11:39
Walters 13 1 31N32'50 91w59'45 6:07:59
Ward 2 1 30N44'25 92w42'08 6:10:49
Warden 42 1 32N32'15 91w29'49 6:05:59
Wardview 8 1 32N57'53 93w47'39 6:15:11
Wardville 34 1 32N52'29 91w54'18 6:07:37
Wardville 40 1 31N18'33 92w24'23 6:09:38
Warnerton 59 1 30N59'24 90w10'59 6:00:44
Warsaw Landing 21
1 32N17'42 91w31'46 6:06:07
Warsaw Landing 32
1 30N23'05 90w33'12 6:02:13
Washburn 16 1 32N11 93w55 6:15:40
Washington 49 1 30N36'58 92w03'25 6:08:14
Waterford 45 1 29N59'47 90w28'23 6:01:54
Waterloo 39 1 30N41'40 91w21'26 6:05:26
Waterproof 54 1 31N48'17 91w23'00 6:05:32
Waterproof 55 1 29N33'46 90w47'42 6:03:11
Watson 32 1 30N34'32 90w57'11 6:03:49
Waverly 33 1 32N26'46 91w24'41 6:05:39
Waxia 49 1 30N39'55 91w57'32 6:07:50
Webb Quarters 30
1 31N40'21 92w09'23 6:08:38
Weber City 3 1 30N13'45 90w53'20 6:03:33
Webre 24 1 30N25'06 91w26'49 6:05:47
Webre Steib Plantation 47
1 29N57'32 90w42'28 6:02:50
Weeks 23 1 29N48'27 91w48'25 6:07:14
Weil 40 1 31N18'42 92w33'38 6:10:15
Weiss 32 1 30N38'49 90w54'20 6:03:37
Welcome 47 1 30N03'33 90w52'06 6:03:28
Weldon 14 1 32N51'34 92w43'31 6:10:54
Welsh 27 1 30N14'09 92w49'21 6:11:17
Wemple 16 1 32N00'44 93w28'46 6:13:55
Westdale 41 1 32N09'53 93w28'47 6:13:55
West Erath 57 1 29N57'38 92w02'37 6:08:10
Westfield 4 1 29N59'03 91w04'46 6:04:19
Westgate 26 2 30N00'09 90w13'31 6:00:54
Westlake 10 1 30N14'31 93w15'02 6:13:00
Westminster 17 1 30N25 91w06 6:04:24
West Monroe 37 1 32N31'06 92w08'51 6:08:35
Weston 25 1 32N14'38 92w36'48 6:10:27
Westover 61 1 30N29'27 91w16'28 6:05:06
West Point 38 1 29N27'50 89w12'39 5:56:51
West Pointe A La Hache 38
1 29N34'10 89w48'02 5:59:12
Westport 40 1 30N56 92w56 6:11:44
Westwego 26 2 29N54'21 90w08'32 6:00:34
Westwood 54 1 32N11'06 91w19'12 6:05:17
Weyanoke 63 1 30N56'48 91w27'40 6:05:51
Wham 37 1 32N37'34 91w55'24 6:07:42
Whatley Landing 30
1 31N42 92w11 6:08:44
Wheeling 64 1 31N44'46 92w50'21 6:11:21
White 29 1 29N47 90w50 6:03:20
White Castle 24 1 30N10'11 91w08'49 6:04:35
Whitehall 30 1 31N37'27 92w02'30 6:08:10
Whitehall 32 1 30N17'18 90w42'01 6:02:48
White Hall 47 1 30N04'45 90w54'05 6:03:36
White Hills 17 1 30N35 91w10 6:04:40
White Kitchen 52
1 30N13'40 89w40'38 5:58:43
White Plantation 29
1 29N48'58 90w54'42 6:03:39
White Sulphur Springs 30
1 31N36'05 92w16'23 6:09:06
Whiteville 49 1 30N47'17 92w08'51 6:08:35
Whittington 40 1 31N17 92w29 6:09:56
Wickland Terrace 17
1 30N27 91w04 6:04:16
Wickliffe 39 1 30N41'11 91w23'51 6:05:35
Wilda 40 1 31N17'53 92w44'23 6:10:58
Wildcat 54 1 32N08'19 91w21'44 6:05:27
Wilds 37 1 32N25'55 92w10'30 6:08:42
Wildsville 15 1 31N36'56 91w47'02 6:07:08
Wildwood 4 1 29N54'43 91w03'23 6:04:14
Wildwood 13 1 31N47'09 91w34'35 6:06:18
Wildwood 17 1 30N25 91w09 6:04:36
Wilhite 56 1 32N37'00 92w16'49 6:09:07
Willetts 15 1 31N30'30 91w31'38 6:06:07
Willhite 56 1 31N54 92w15 6:09:00
Williams 1 1 30N27'56 92w27'58 6:09:52
Williams 41 1 32N11'38 93w28'51 6:13:55
Williamsport 39 1 30N53'42 91w40'02 6:06:40
Williana 22 1 31N40'12 92w33'58 6:10:16
Willis 59 1 30N44'11 90w04'00 6:00:16
Willow Chute 8 1 32N39'51 93w44'51 6:14:59
Willowdale 26 2 30N00'21 90w11'41 6:00:47
Willow Glen 40 1 31N14'47 92w25'56 6:09:44
Wills Point 38 2 29N44'48 90w00'21 6:00:01
Willswood 26 2 29N55'34 90w13'44 6:00:55
Wilmer 53 1 30N48'50 90w21'45 6:01:27
Wilshire Park 40
1 31N17 92w29 6:09:56
Wilson 19 1 30N55'12 91w06'56 6:04:28
Wilsona 54 1 31N55 91w14 6:04:56
Wilsonia 54 1 31N55'58 91w18'51 6:05:15
Wilson Point 40 1 31N08'44 92w15'16 6:09:01
Wilsons Landing 51
1 29N43'16 91w17'38 6:05:11
Wilton 9 1 32N33 93w47 6:15:08
Windsor 34 1 32N39'09 91w53'10 6:07:33
Winnfield 64 1 31N55'31 92w38'22 6:10:33
Winnsboro 21 1 32N09'47 91w43'14 6:06:53
Wisner 21 1 31N58'51 91w39'20 6:06:37
Womack 25 1 32N14'17 92w28'22 6:09:53
Womack 41 1 32N11'17 93w14'32 6:12:58
Woodardville 7 1 32N15'35 93w16'48 6:13:07
Woodchuck 9 1 32N19'45 93w36'12 6:14:25
Woodhaven 53 1 30N35 90w29 6:01:56
Wood Junction 25
1 32N20'31 92w24'41 6:09:39
Wood Lake 44 2 29N48'26 89w45'51 5:59:03
Woodland 19 1 30N56'50 90w56'10 6:03:45
Woodland 38 1 29N35'05 89w49'31 5:59:18
Woodlawn 4 1 29N54'47 90w58'27 6:03:54
Woodlawn 27 1 30N17'34 92w57'30 6:11:50
Woodlawn 38 2 29N52 89w57 5:59:48
Woodlawn 55 1 29N33'14 90w40'21 6:02:41
Woodside 40 1 31N17 92w29 6:09:56
Woodside 49 1 30N50'35 91w49'12 6:07:17
Woodville 31 1 32N27'27 92w41'54 6:10:48
Woodworth 40 1 31N08'47 92w29'50 6:09:59
Worsham Crossing 64
1 31N45'38 92w43'26 6:10:54
Wright (Haire Station) 57
1 30N00'26 92w25'43 6:09:43
Wyandotte 51 1 29N41'23 91w10'16 6:04:41
Wyatt 25 1 32N09'19 92w42'11 6:10:49
Yattan 61 1 30N36'04 91w19'16 6:05:17
Yellow Bayou 5 1 30N59'28 91w50'26 6:07:22

Yellow Pine 60 1 32N28'37 93w19'27 6:13:18
Young Landing 54 1 31N46'08 91w33'33 6:06:14
Youngs 57 1 29N58'03 92w06'58 6:08:28
Youngsville 28 1 30N05'58 91w59'24 6:07:58
Yscloskey 44 1 29N50'30 89w41'18 5:58:45
Yucatan Landing 54 1 32N04'47 91w09'14 6:04:37
Zachary 17 1 30N38'54 91w09'23 6:04:38
Zebedee 42 1 32N28 91w45 6:07:00
Zenora 30 1 31N44'46 92w20'12 6:09:21
Zenoria 30 1 31N42 92w11 6:08:44
Zimmerman 40 1 31N24'56 92w42'10 6:10:49
Zion 22 1 31N46'58 92w29'22 6:09:57
Zion City 17 1 30N31'04 91w08'11 6:04:33
Zona 59 1 30N44'53 90w04'52 6:00:19
Zwolle 43 1 31N37'53 93w38'38 6:14:35
Zylks 9 1 33N00'06 94w00'41 6:16:03

TIME TABLES

ME # 1
Before 1/01/1887 LMT
1/01/1887 12:00 EST
3/31/1918 02:00 EWT
10/27/1918 02:00 EST
3/30/1919 02:00 EWT
10/26/1919 02:00 EST
2/09/1942 02:00 EWT
9/30/1945 02:00 EST
4/24/1955 02:00 US#2

ME # 2
Before 1/01/1887 LMT
1/01/1887 12:00 ME#1
4/27/1941 02:00 US#2

ME # 3
Before 1/01/1887 LMT
1/01/1887 12:00 ME#1
4/24/1938 02:00 EDT
10/01/1938 02:00 EST
4/30/1939 02:00 EDT
9/24/1939 02:00 EST
4/28/1940 02:00 EDT
9/29/1940 02:00 EST
4/27/1941 02:00 EDT
9/28/1941 02:00 EST
2/09/1942 02:00 EWT
9/30/1945 02:00 EST
4/24/1955 02:00 US#2

ME # 4
Before 1/01/1887 LMT
1/01/1887 12:00 ME#1
4/24/1938 02:00 EDT
10/01/1938 02:00 EST
4/30/1939 02:00 US#2

ME # 5
Before 1/01/1887 LMT
1/01/1887 12:00 ME#1
4/24/1938 02:00 EDT
10/01/1938 02:00 EST
4/30/1939 02:00 EDT
9/24/1939 02:00 EST
4/28/1940 02:00 EDT
9/29/1940 02:00 EST
4/27/1941 02:00 EDT
9/28/1941 02:00 EST
2/09/1942 02:00 EWT
9/30/1945 02:00 EST
4/27/1947 02:00 US#2

ME # 6
Before 1/01/1887 LMT
1/01/1887 12:00 ME#1
4/24/1932 02:00 US#2

ME # 7
Before 1/01/1887 LMT
1/01/1887 12:00 ME#1
4/29/1934 02:00 EDT
9/30/1934 02:00 EST
4/28/1935 02:00 EDT
9/29/1935 02:00 EST
4/26/1936 02:00 EDT
9/27/1936 02:00 EST
4/25/1937 02:00 EDT
9/26/1937 02:00 EST
4/24/1938 02:00 EDT
10/01/1938 02:00 EST
4/30/1939 02:00 EDT
9/24/1939 02:00 EST
4/28/1940 02:00 EDT
9/24/1940 02:00 EST
4/27/1941 02:00 US#2

ME # 8
Before 1/01/1887 LMT
1/01/1887 12:00 ME#1
4/30/1933 02:00 US#2

ME # 9
Before 1/01/1887 LMT
1/01/1887 12:00 ME#1
4/24/1938 02:00 EDT
10/01/1938 02:00 EST
4/30/1939 02:00 EDT
9/24/1939 02:00 EST
2/09/1942 02:00 EWT
9/30/1945 02:00 EST
4/24/1955 02:00 US#2

ME # 10
Before 1/01/1887 LMT
1/01/1887 12:00 ME#1
4/24/1938 02:00 EDT
10/01/1938 02:00 EST
4/30/1939 02:00 EDT
9/24/1939 02:00 EST
2/09/1942 02:00 EWT
9/30/1945 02:00 EST
4/28/1946 02:00 US#2

ME # 11
Before 1/01/1887 LMT
1/01/1887 12:00 ME#1
4/24/1938 02:00 EDT
10/01/1938 02:00 EST
4/30/1939 02:00 EDT
9/24/1939 02:00 EST
2/09/1942 02:00 EWT
9/30/1945 02:00 EST
4/24/1949 02:00 US#2

ME # 12
Before 1/01/1887 LMT
1/01/1887 12:00 ME#1
4/29/1923 02:00 EDT
9/30/1923 02:00 EST
4/27/1924 02:00 EDT
9/28/1924 02:00 EST
4/26/1925 02:00 EDT
9/27/1925 02:00 EST
4/25/1926 02:00 EDT
9/26/1926 02:00 EST
4/24/1927 02:00 EDT
9/25/1927 02:00 EST
4/29/1928 02:00 EDT
9/30/1928 02:00 EST
4/28/1929 02:00 EDT
9/29/1929 02:00 EST
4/27/1930 02:00 EDT
9/28/1930 02:00 EST
4/26/1931 02:00 EDT
9/27/1931 02:00 EST
4/24/1932 02:00 EDT
9/25/1932 02:00 EST
4/30/1933 02:00 EDT
9/24/1933 02:00 EST
4/29/1934 02:00 EDT
9/30/1934 02:00 EST
4/28/1935 02:00 EDT
9/29/1935 02:00 EST
4/26/1936 02:00 EDT
9/27/1936 02:00 EST
4/25/1937 02:00 EDT
9/26/1937 02:00 EST
4/24/1938 02:00 EDT
10/01/1938 02:00 EST
4/30/1939 02:00 EDT
9/24/1939 02:00 EST
4/28/1940 02:00 EDT
9/29/1940 02:00 EST
4/27/1941 02:00 EDT
9/28/1941 02:00 EST
2/09/1942 02:00 EWT
9/30/1945 02:00 EST
4/24/1955 02:00 US#2

ME # 13
Before 1/01/1887 LMT
1/01/1887 12:00 ME#1
6/15/1923 02:00 EDT
9/15/1923 02:00 EST
6/15/1924 02:00 EDT
9/15/1924 02:00 EST
6/15/1925 02:00 EDT
9/15/1925 02:00 EST
6/15/1926 02:00 EDT
9/15/1926 02:00 EST
6/15/1927 02:00 EDT
9/15/1927 02:00 EST
6/15/1928 02:00 EDT
9/15/1928 02:00 EST
6/15/1929 02:00 EDT
9/15/1929 02:00 EST
6/15/1930 02:00 EDT
9/15/1930 02:00 EST
6/15/1931 02:00 EDT
9/15/1931 02:00 EST
6/15/1932 02:00 EDT
9/15/1932 02:00 EST
6/15/1933 02:00 EDT
9/15/1933 02:00 EST
6/15/1934 02:00 EDT
9/15/1934 02:00 EST
6/15/1935 02:00 EDT
9/15/1935 02:00 EST
4/26/1936 02:00 EDT
9/27/1936 02:00 EST
4/25/1937 02:00 EDT
9/26/1937 02:00 EST
4/24/1938 02:00 EDT
10/01/1938 02:00 EST
4/30/1939 02:00 EDT
9/24/1939 02:00 EST
4/28/1940 02:00 EDT
9/29/1940 02:00 EST
4/27/1941 02:00 EDT
9/28/1941 02:00 EST
2/09/1942 02:00 US#2

ME # 14
Before 1/01/1887 LMT
1/01/1887 12:00 ME#1
4/14/1920 02:00 EDT
9/26/1920 02:00 EST
4/03/1921 02:00 EDT
9/25/1921 02:00 EST
4/02/1922 02:00 EDT
9/24/1922 02:00 EST
4/29/1923 02:00 EDT
9/30/1923 02:00 EST
4/27/1924 02:00 EDT
9/28/1924 02:00 EST
4/26/1925 02:00 EDT
9/27/1925 02:00 EST
4/25/1926 02:00 EDT
9/26/1926 02:00 EST
4/24/1927 02:00 EDT
9/25/1927 02:00 EST
4/29/1928 02:00 EDT
9/30/1928 02:00 EST
4/28/1929 02:00 EDT
9/29/1929 02:00 EST
4/27/1930 02:00 EDT
9/28/1930 02:00 EST
4/26/1931 02:00 EDT
9/27/1931 02:00 EST
4/24/1932 02:00 EDT
9/25/1932 02:00 EST
4/30/1933 02:00 EDT
9/24/1933 02:00 EST
4/29/1934 02:00 EDT
9/30/1934 02:00 EST
4/28/1935 02:00 EDT
9/29/1935 02:00 EST
4/26/1936 02:00 EDT
9/27/1936 02:00 EST
4/25/1937 02:00 EDT
9/26/1937 02:00 EST
4/24/1938 02:00 EDT
10/01/1938 02:00 EST
4/30/1939 02:00 EDT
10/15/1939 02:00 EST
4/28/1940 02:00 US#2

ME # 15
Before 1/01/1887 LMT
1/01/1887 12:00 ME#1
4/26/1931 02:00 EDT
9/27/1931 02:00 EST
4/24/1932 02:00 EDT
9/25/1932 02:00 EST
4/30/1933 02:00 EDT
9/24/1933 02:00 EST
4/29/1934 02:00 EDT
10/30/1934 02:00 EST
4/28/1935 02:00 EDT
9/29/1935 02:00 EST
4/26/1936 02:00 EDT
9/27/1936 02:00 EST
4/25/1937 02:00 EDT
9/26/1937 02:00 EST
4/30/1938 02:00 EDT
9/25/1938 02:00 EST
4/30/1939 02:00 US#2

ME # 16
Before 1/01/1887 LMT
1/01/1887 12:00 ME#1
4/14/1920 02:00 EDT
9/26/1920 02:00 EST
4/03/1921 02:00 EDT
9/25/1921 02:00 EST
4/02/1922 02:00 EDT
9/24/1922 02:00 EST
4/29/1923 02:00 EDT
9/30/1923 02:00 EST
4/27/1924 02:00 EDT
9/28/1924 02:00 EST
4/26/1925 02:00 EDT
9/27/1925 02:00 EST
4/25/1926 02:00 EDT
9/26/1926 02:00 EST
4/24/1927 02:00 EDT
9/25/1927 02:00 EST
4/29/1928 02:00 EDT
9/30/1928 02:00 EST
4/28/1929 02:00 EDT
9/29/1929 02:00 EST
4/27/1930 02:00 EDT
9/28/1930 02:00 EST
4/26/1931 02:00 EDT
9/27/1931 02:00 EST
4/24/1932 02:00 EDT
9/25/1932 02:00 EST
4/30/1933 02:00 EDT
9/24/1933 02:00 EST
4/29/1934 02:00 EDT
9/30/1934 02:00 EST
4/28/1935 02:00 EDT
9/29/1935 02:00 EST
4/26/1936 02:00 EDT
9/27/1936 02:00 EST
4/25/1937 02:00 EDT
9/26/1937 02:00 EST
4/28/1938 02:00 EDT
10/01/1938 02:00 EST
4/30/1939 02:00 EDT
10/15/1939 02:00 EST
4/28/1940 02:00 US#2

ME # 17
Before 1/01/1887 LMT
1/01/1887 12:00 ME#1
4/29/1934 02:00 EDT
9/30/1934 02:00 EST
4/28/1935 02:00 EDT
9/29/1935 02:00 EST
4/26/1936 02:00 EDT
9/27/1936 02:00 EST
4/25/1937 02:00 EDT
9/26/1937 02:00 EST
6/01/1939 02:00 EDT
10/15/1939 02:00 EST
6/01/1940 02:00 EDT
10/15/1940 02:00 EST
6/01/1941 02:00 EDT
10/15/1941 02:00 EST
2/09/1942 02:00 US#2

ME # 18
Before 1/01/1887 LMT
1/01/1887 12:00 ME#1
4/24/1938 02:00 EDT
10/01/1938 02:00 EST
4/30/1939 02:00 EDT
10/15/1939 02:00 EST
4/28/1940 02:00 US#2

ME # 19
Before 1/01/1887 LMT
1/01/1887 12:00 ME#1
4/24/1938 02:00 EDT
10/01/1938 02:00 EST
4/30/1939 02:00 EDT
9/24/1939 02:00 EST
4/28/1940 02:00 EDT
9/29/1940 02:00 EST
4/27/1941 02:00 EDT
9/08/1941 02:00 EST
2/09/1942 02:00 EWT
9/30/1945 02:00 EST
4/24/1949 02:00 US#2

ME # 20
Before 1/01/1887 LMT
1/01/1887 12:00 ME#1
4/24/1932 02:00 EDT
9/25/1932 02:00 EST
4/29/1934 02:00 EDT
9/30/1934 02:00 EST
4/28/1935 02:00 EDT
9/29/1935 02:00 EST
4/26/1936 02:00 EDT
9/27/1936 02:00 EST
4/25/1937 02:00 EDT
9/26/1937 02:00 EST
4/24/1938 02:00 EDT
10/01/1938 02:00 EST
4/30/1939 02:00 EDT
10/01/1939 02:00 EST
4/28/1940 02:00 US#2

ME # 21
Before 1/01/1887 LMT
1/01/1887 12:00 ME#1
4/24/1938 02:00 EDT
10/01/1938 02:00 EST
4/30/1939 02:00 EDT
10/15/1939 02:00 EST
4/28/1940 02:00 EDT
9/29/1940 02:00 EST
2/09/1942 02:00 EWT
9/30/1945 02:00 EST
4/24/1949 02:00 US#2

ME # 22
Before 1/01/1887 LMT
1/01/1887 12:00 ME#1
4/27/1941 02:00 EDT
10/28/1941 02:00 EST
2/09/1942 02:00 US#2

ME # 23
Before 1/01/1887 LMT
1/01/1887 12:00 ME#1
4/24/1938 02:00 EDT
10/01/1938 02:00 EST
4/30/1939 02:00 EDT
9/24/1939 02:00 EST
4/28/1940 02:00 EDT
9/29/1940 02:00 EST
4/27/1941 02:00 EDT
9/07/1941 02:00 EST
2/09/1942 02:00 EWT
9/30/1945 02:00 EST
4/24/1955 02:00 US#2

ME # 24
Before 1/01/1887 LMT
1/01/1887 12:00 ME#1
4/25/1937 02:00 EDT
9/26/1937 02:00 EST
4/24/1938 02:00 EDT
10/01/1938 02:00 EST
4/30/1939 02:00 EDT
9/24/1939 02:00 EST
4/28/1940 02:00 EDT
9/29/1940 02:00 EST
4/27/1941 02:00 EDT
9/28/1941 02:00 EST
2/09/1942 02:00 EWT
9/30/1945 02:00 EST
4/27/1947 02:00 US#2

ME # 25
Before 1/01/1887 LMT
1/01/1887 12:00 ME#1
5/03/1936 02:00 EDT
9/27/1936 02:00 EST
4/25/1937 02:00 EDT
9/26/1937 02:00 EST
4/24/1938 02:00 EDT
10/01/1938 02:00 EST
4/30/1939 02:00 US#2

ME # 26
Before 1/01/1887 LMT
1/01/1887 12:00 ME#1
4/28/1935 02:00 EDT
9/29/1935 02:00 EST
4/26/1936 02:00 EDT
9/27/1936 02:00 EST
4/25/1937 02:00 EDT
9/26/1937 02:00 EST
4/24/1938 02:00 EDT
10/01/1938 02:00 EST
4/30/1939 02:00 EDT
9/24/1939 02:00 EST
4/28/1940 02:00 EDT
9/29/1940 02:00 EST
4/27/1941 02:00 EDT
9/28/1941 02:00 EST
2/09/1942 02:00 EWT
9/30/1945 02:00 EST
4/27/1947 02:00 US#2

ME # 27
Before 1/01/1887 LMT
1/01/1887 12:00 ME#1
4/26/1931 02:00 EDT
9/27/1931 02:00 EST
4/28/1935 02:00 EDT
9/29/1935 02:00 EST
4/26/1936 02:00 EDT
9/27/1936 02:00 EST
4/25/1937 02:00 EDT
9/26/1937 02:00 EST
4/24/1938 02:00 EDT
10/01/1938 02:00 EST
4/30/1939 02:00 US#2

ME # 28
Before 1/01/1887 LMT
1/01/1887 12:00 ME#1
4/29/1934 02:00 EDT
9/30/1934 02:00 EST
4/24/1938 02:00 EDT
10/01/1938 02:00 EST
4/30/1939 02:00 US#2

ME # 29
Before 1/01/1887 LMT
1/01/1887 12:00 ME#1
4/26/1931 02:00 EDT
9/27/1931 02:00 EST
4/24/1932 02:00 EDT
9/25/1932 02:00 EST
4/30/1933 02:00 EDT
9/24/1933 02:00 EST
4/29/1934 02:00 EDT
9/30/1934 02:00 EST
4/28/1935 02:00 EDT
9/29/1935 02:00 EST
4/26/1936 02:00 EDT
9/27/1936 02:00 EST
4/25/1937 02:00 EDT
9/26/1937 02:00 EST
4/24/1938 02:00 EDT
10/01/1938 02:00 EST
4/30/1939 02:00 EDT
9/24/1939 02:00 EST
4/28/1940 02:00 EDT
9/29/1940 02:00 EST
4/27/1941 02:00 EDT
9/28/1941 02:00 EST
2/09/1942 02:00 EWT
9/30/1945 02:00 EST
4/24/1955 02:00 US#2

ME # 30
Before 1/01/1887 LMT
1/01/1887 12:00 ME#1
4/26/1931 02:00 EDT
9/27/1931 02:00 EST
4/24/1932 02:00 EDT
9/25/1932 02:00 EST
4/30/1933 02:00 EDT
9/24/1933 02:00 EST
4/29/1934 02:00 EDT
9/30/1934 02:00 EST
4/28/1935 02:00 EDT
9/29/1935 02:00 EST
4/26/1936 02:00 EDT
9/27/1936 02:00 EST
4/25/1937 02:00 EDT
9/26/1937 02:00 EST
4/24/1938 02:00 EDT
10/01/1938 02:00 EST
4/30/1939 02:00 EDT
9/24/1939 02:00 EST
4/28/1940 02:00 EDT
9/29/1940 02:00 EST
4/27/1941 02:00 EDT
10/26/1941 02:00 EST
2/09/1942 02:00 US#2

ME # 31
Before 1/01/1887 LMT
1/01/1887 12:00 ME#1
4/29/1934 02:00 US#2

ME # 32
Before 1/01/1887 LMT
1/01/1887 12:00 ME#1
4/28/1935 02:00 US#2

ME # 33
Before 1/01/1887 LMT
1/01/1887 12:00 ME#1
4/26/1936 02:00 US#2

ME # 34
Before 1/01/1887 LMT
1/01/1887 12:00 ME#1
4/25/1937 02:00 US#2

ME # 35
Before 1/01/1887 LMT
1/01/1887 12:00 ME#1
4/28/1940 02:00 US#2

ME # 36
Before 1/01/1887 LMT
1/01/1887 12:00 ME#1
4/30/1933 02:00 EDT
9/24/1933 02:00 EST
4/24/1938 02:00 EDT
10/01/1938 02:00 EST
4/30/1939 02:00 US#2

ME # 37
Before 1/01/1887 LMT
1/01/1887 12:00 ME#1
4/30/1933 02:00 EDT
9/24/1933 02:00 EST
2/09/1942 02:00 US#2

ME # 38
Before 1/01/1887 LMT
1/01/1887 12:00 ME#1
4/24/1932 02:00 EDT
9/25/1932 02:00 EST
4/30/1933 02:00 EDT
9/24/1933 02:00 EST
4/28/1935 02:00 EDT
9/29/1935 02:00 EST
4/26/1936 02:00 EDT
9/27/1936 02:00 EST
4/25/1937 02:00 EDT
9/26/1937 02:00 EST
4/24/1938 02:00 EDT
10/01/1938 02:00 EST
4/30/1939 02:00 US#2

ME # 39
Before 1/01/1887 LMT

TIME TABLES

1/01/1887 12:00 ME#1
4/26/1931 02:00 EDT
9/27/1931 02:00 EST
4/24/1932 02:00 EDT
9/25/1932 02:00 EST
4/29/1934 02:00 EDT
9/30/1934 02:00 EST
4/28/1935 02:00 EDT
9/29/1935 02:00 EST
4/26/1936 02:00 EDT
9/27/1936 02:00 EST
4/25/1937 02:00 EDT
9/26/1937 02:00 EST
4/24/1938 02:00 EDT
10/01/1938 02:00 EST
4/30/1939 02:00 EDT
9/24/1939 02:00 EST
4/28/1940 02:00 EDT
9/29/1940 02:00 EST
4/27/1941 02:00 EDT
9/28/1941 02:00 EST
2/09/1942 02:00 EWT
9/30/1945 02:00 EST
4/24/1949 02:00 US#2

ME # 40
Before 1/01/1887 LMT
1/01/1887 12:00 ME#1
4/26/1931 02:00 EDT
9/27/1931 02:00 EST
4/24/1932 02:00 EDT
9/25/1932 02:00 EST
4/30/1933 02:00 EDT
9/24/1933 02:00 EST
4/26/1936 02:00 EDT
9/27/1936 02:00 EST
4/25/1937 02:00 EDT
9/26/1937 02:00 EST
4/24/1938 02:00 EDT
10/01/1938 02:00 EST
4/30/1939 02:00 US#2

ME # 41
Before 1/01/1887 LMT
1/01/1887 12:00 ME#1
4/24/1932 02:00 EDT
9/25/1932 02:00 EST
4/25/1937 02:00 EDT
9/26/1937 02:00 EST
4/24/1938 02:00 EDT
10/01/1938 02:00 EST
4/30/1939 02:00 US#2

ME # 42
Before 1/01/1887 LMT
1/01/1887 12:00 ME#1
4/30/1933 02:00 EDT
9/24/1933 02:00 EST
2/09/1942 02:00 EWT
9/30/1945 02:00 EST
4/24/1955 02:00 US#2

ME # 43
Before 1/01/1887 LMT
1/01/1887 12:00 ME#1
4/28/1946 02:00 EDT
9/29/1946 02:00 EST
4/25/1948 02:00 US#2

ME # 44
Before 1/01/1887 LMT
1/01/1887 12:00 ME#1
4/26/1931 02:00 US#2

ME # 45
Before 1/01/1887 LMT
1/01/1887 12:00 ME#1
4/28/1946 02:00 US#2

ME # 46
Before 1/01/1887 LMT
1/01/1887 12:00 ME#1
4/28/1940 02:00 EDT
9/29/1940 02:00 EST
4/27/1941 02:00 EDT
9/28/1941 02:00 EST
2/09/1942 02:00 EWT
9/30/1945 02:00 EST
4/27/1947 02:00 US#2

ME # 47
Before 1/01/1887 LMT
1/01/1887 12:00 ME#1
4/24/1949 02:00 US#2

ME # 48
Before 1/01/1887 LMT
1/01/1887 12:00 ME#1
4/26/1931 02:00 EDT
9/08/1931 02:00 EST
4/24/1932 02:00 EDT
9/25/1932 02:00 EST
4/30/1933 02:00 EDT
9/24/1933 02:00 EST
4/29/1934 02:00 EDT
9/30/1934 02:00 EST
4/28/1935 02:00 EDT
9/29/1935 02:00 EST
4/26/1936 02:00 EDT
9/27/1936 02:00 EST
4/25/1937 02:00 EDT
9/26/1937 02:00 EST
4/24/1938 02:00 EDT
10/01/1938 02:00 EST
4/30/1939 02:00 US#2

ME # 49
Before 1/01/1887 LMT
1/01/1887 12:00 ME#1
4/30/1939 02:00 EDT
9/24/1939 02:00 EST
4/28/1940 02:00 EDT
9/29/1940 02:00 EST
4/27/1941 02:00 EDT
9/28/1941 02:00 EST
2/09/1942 02:00 EWT
9/30/1945 02:00 EST
4/24/1955 02:00 US#2

COUNTIES

1 Androscoggin
2 Aroostook
3 Cumberland
4 Franklin
5 Hancock
6 Kennebec
7 Knox
8 Lincoln
9 Oxford
10 Penobscot
11 Piscataquis
12 Sagadahoc
13 Somerset
14 Waldo
15 Washington
16 York

Abbot 11 1 45N12 69W28 4:37:52
Abbotts Mill 9 44 44N28'33 70W37'57 4:42:32
Abbot Village 11 1 45N11'11 69W27'09 4:37:49
Acadia 2 1 46N59'10 68W01'56 4:32:08
Acadia Terrace 2 11 47N09 67W56 4:31:44
Acton 16 1 43N32'03 70W54'37 4:43:38
Adaline 2 1 46N45'43 68W07'28 4:32:30
Adams 11 1 45N19'39 68W54'04 4:35:36
Adams Corner 16 16 43N24'45 70W26'30 4:41:46
Addison 15 1 44N37'06 67W44'41 4:30:59
Admiralty Village 16 4 43N05'33 70W43'49 4:42:55
Agamenticus Station 16 44 43N14'38 70W46'32 4:43:06
Agamenticus Village 16 4 43N12'55 70W40'14 4:42:41
Albion 6 1 44N31'56 69W26'35 4:37:46
Alewife 16 48 43N27'10 70W36'37 4:42:26
Alexander 15 1 45N05'19 67W28'08 4:29:53
Alfred 16 14 43N28'35 70W43'08 4:42:53
Alfred Mills 16 14 43N27'50 70W42'09 4:42:49
Allagash Plantation 2 1 47N06 69W04 4:36:16
Allens Mills 4 8 44N42'58 70W04'54 4:40:20
Alna 8 1 44N06'22 69W36'15 4:38:25
Alna Center 8 1 44N04'51 69W37'07 4:38:28
Alton 10 47 45N02 68W44 4:34:56
Amherst 5 45 44N50'00 68W21'53 4:33:28
Amity 2 1 45N55 67W50 4:31:20
Andover 9 1 44N38'08 70W45'06 4:43:00
Anson 13 4 44N47'54 69W53'23 4:39:34
Appleton 7 1 44N17'21 69W15'05 4:37:00
Archers Corners 5 45 44N49'53 68W26'42 4:33:47
Arey 10 14 44N43'22 68W52'20 4:35:29
Arnold Corner 10 1 44N44'18 69W03'55 4:36:16
Arnolds Landing 13 23 44N57'24 69W52'12 4:39:29
Aroostook Farm 2 39 46N42 68W00 4:32:00
Arrowsic 12 1 43N50'59 69W46'43 4:39:07
Arundel 16 14 43N22'57 70W28'42 4:41:55
Ashdale 12 1 43N46'03 69W50'22 4:39:21
Ashland 2 47 46N37'52 68W24'24 4:33:38
Ash Point 7 7 44N03'20 69W05'14 4:36:21
Ashville 5 1 44N29'16 68W07'18 4:32:29
Asticou 5 1 44N18'14 68W16'56 4:33:08
Athearns Corner 7 1 44N16'23 69W09'59 4:36:40
Athens 13 31 44N55'23 69W40'24 4:38:42
Atkinson 11 1 45N10 69W04 4:36:16
Atkinson Corner 11 34 45N11 69W13 4:36:52
Atkinson Mills 11 1 45N09'35 69W04'58 4:36:20
Atlantic 5 1 44N10'18 68W25'29 4:33:42
Attean 13 4 45N34'29 70W19'07 4:41:16
Attean Landing 13 4 45N35'15 70W16'41 4:41:07
Auburn 1 13 44N05'52 70W13'54 4:40:56
Auburn Plains 1 13 44N10'33 70W13'56 4:40:56
Augusta 6 44 44N18'38 69W46'48 4:39:07
Aurora 5 45 44N51'15 68W19'43 4:33:19
Avon 4 1 44N48'22 70W16'18 4:41:05
Avon Corner 4 1 44N48'01 70W15'58 4:41:04
Ayers 15 1 44N59'04 67W14'19 4:28:57
Babb Corner 3 44 43N37'47 70W27'02 4:41:48
Back Narrows 8 1 43N53'34 69W35'33 4:38:22
Back Settlement 2 11 47N09'23 68W52'14 4:35:29
Back Settlement 10 32 45N32'19 68W19'09 4:33:17
Bailey Corner 6 6 44N10'20 69W44'42 4:38:59
Bailey Island 3 1 43N43'39 69W59'44 4:39:59
Baileyville 15 29 45N08 67W24 4:29:36
Baker Corner 3 31 43N49'29 70W23'20 4:41:33
Balch Pond 16 1 43N37 71W01 4:44:04
Bald Head 16 4 43N13'15 70W34'40 4:42:19
Bald Head Cliff 16 6 43N15 70W36 4:42:24
Bald Hill Crossing 16 33 43N20'33 70W40'24 4:42:42
Bald Mountain 9 45 44N57'17 70W47'28 4:43:10
Baldwin 3 34 43N50 70W42 4:42:48
Baldwin Corners 5 1 44N14'49 68W21'33 4:33:26
Bancroft 2 45 45N40'25 68W01'53 4:32:08
Bangor 10 14 44N48'04 68W46'42 4:35:07
Bangs Beach 6 35 44N28'21 69W46'31 4:39:06
Bar Harbor 5 12 44N23'15 68W12'16 4:32:49
Baring 15 1 45N08'10 67W19'02 4:29:16
Bar Mills 16 6 43N36'47 70W33'01 4:42:12
Barnard 11 1 45N21'59 69W12'27 4:36:50
Barnard Corner 11 22 45N18'26 69W07'25 4:36:30
Barnard Plantation 11 1 45N19 69W09 4:36:36
Barnjum 4 1 44N56'29 70W21'56 4:41:28
Barrett 2 1 46N52 68W01 4:32:04
Barretts 2 1 46N53'51 68W00'58 4:32:04
Barron Corner 13 4 44N49'15 69W50'42 4:39:23
Bartlett Mills 16 48 43N23'58 70W31'47 4:42:07
Basin 15 35 44N37 67W45 4:31:00
Basin Mills 10 31 44N52'28 68W40'01 4:34:40
Bass Harbor 5 1 44N14'24 68W20'40 4:33:23
Batchelders Crossing 6 6 44N11'23 69W56'25 4:39:46
Batesville 2 1 46N07'32 68W20'51 4:33:23
Bath 12 15 43N54'38 69W49'16 4:39:17
Bauneg Beg 16 14 43N26 70W46 4:43:04
Bay Point 12 1 43N45'23 69W46'31 4:39:06
Bayside 5 32 44N27'50 68W25'27 4:33:42
Bayside 14 36 44N22'47 68W58'09 4:35:53
Bay View 16 44 43N29'16 70W23'15 4:41:33
Bayville 8 1 43N51'35 69W36'12 4:38:25
Beacon Corner 16 16 43N25'45 70W27'16 4:41:49
Beals 15 1 44N31'11 67W36'56 4:30:28
Beans Corner 4 6 44N34'40 70W10'33 4:40:42
Beans Corner 14 1 44N27'25 69W15'45 4:37:03
Bear Frap Landing 15 1 45N14'37 67W47'36 4:31:10
Beaver Dam 16 44 43N16 70W52 4:43:28
Beddington 5 45 44N50'53 68W03'45 4:32:15
Bedell Crossing 16 4 43N06'10 70W40'34 4:42:42
Beech Ridge 16 4 43N08'58 70W43'12 4:42:53
Belfast 14 36 44N25'33 69W00'25 4:36:02
Belgrade 6 35 44N26'50 69W49'59 4:39:20
Belgrade Lakes 6 35 44N31'35 69W53'15 4:39:33
Belmont 14 1 44N23 69W07 4:36:28
Belmont Corner 14 36 44N23'50 69W08'10 4:36:33
Bemis 4 1 44N51'28 70W43'51 4:42:55
Benedicta 2 1 45N48'06 68W24'44 4:33:39
Benner Corner 8 7 44N09'23 69W19'10 4:37:17
Bennett 2 47 46N06'48 68W06'42 4:32:27
Benson 11 19 45N21'34 69W17'46 4:37:11
Benton 6 8 44N35'10 69W33'05 4:38:12
Benton Falls 6 8 44N34'38 69W33'13 4:38:13
Benton Station 6 8 44N35'21 69W35'08 4:38:21
Bernard 5 1 44N14'28 68W21'23 4:33:26
Bernier 16 14 43N26 70W46 4:43:04
Berry Mills 4 45 44N37'45 70W27'00 4:41:48
Berrys Corner 11 34 45N05'53 69W10'38 4:36:43
Berwick 16 44 43N15'57 70W51'54 4:43:28
Bethel 9 37 44N24'15 70W47'28 4:43:10
Bickfords Corner 14 1 44N21'46 69W08'57 4:36:36
Biddeford 16 16 43N29'33 70W27'14 4:41:49
Biddeford Pool 16 16 43N26'41 70W20'31 4:41:22
Bigelow 4 1 45N04'51 70W19'16 4:41:17
Billings Hill 10 6 44N50'10 69W11'54 4:36:48
Bingham 13 38 45N03'31 69W52'58 4:39:32
Bingo 15 1 45N20'56 67W40'37 4:30:42
Birch Harbor 5 1 44N23'19 68W02'16 4:32:09
Birch Island 3 1 43N55 69W58 4:39:52
Bishop 2 47 46N50'26 67W56'07 4:31:44
Black Corner 5 1 44N20'34 68W40'28 4:34:42
Blackinton Corners 7 7 44N07'24 69W07'04 4:36:28
Black Point 3 5 43N35 70W21 4:41:24
Blackstone 2 11 46N57'20 68W14'04 4:32:56
Blackstrap 3 44 43N46'07 70W19'52 4:41:19
Blackwater 2 47 46N25'38 68W18'30 4:33:14
Blackwell 13 20 44N48 69W53 4:39:32
Blackwell Corner 13 6 44N50'07 69W49'00 4:39:16
Blaine 2 1 46N30'17 67W52'09 4:31:29
Blair 13 4 45N37'59 70W10'33 4:40:42
Blaisdell Corners 16 45 43N20'52 70W55'41 4:43:43
Blake Corner 1 8 44N00'42 70W07'05 4:40:28
Blanchard 11 1 45N16'03 69W35'03 4:38:20
Blanchard Corner 15 1 45N00'20 67W16'31 4:29:06
Blanchard Plantation 11 1 45N15 69W37 4:38:28
Blue Hill 5 3 44N24'50 68W35'14 4:34:21
Blue Hill Falls 5 3 44N22'51 68W33'56 4:34:16
Blue Point 3 5 43N33'08 70W21'25 4:41:26
Boat Landing Camp 2 1 47N14'29 69W13'15 4:36:53
Bodfish 11 1 45N22'27 69W25'50 4:37:43
Bog Corner 13 1 44N50'34 69W19'25 4:37:18
Bogues Corner 8 26 44N10'04 69W22'44 4:37:31
Bolsters Mills 3 1 44N06'56 70W35'52 4:42:23
Bonny Eagle 16 1 43N41'23 70W36'54 4:42:28
Boothbay 8 3 43N52'35 69W38'03 4:38:32
Boothbay Harbor 8 3 43N51'08 69W37'43 4:38:31
Boothbay Park 16 44 43N34'01 70W26'57 4:41:48
Bowden 10 10 45N40'30 68W40'18 4:34:41
Bowdoin Center 12 31 44N02'12 69W58'24 4:39:54
Bowdoinham 12 31 44N00'36 69W53'56 4:39:36
Bowerbank 10 1 45N23'47 68W35'59 4:34:24
Bowerbank 11 1 45N16'22 69W12'45 4:36:51
Boyd Corner 16 44 43N17'47 70W42'51 4:42:51
Boyd Lake 11 45 45N11'14 68W53'31 4:35:34
Bradbury 2 11 47N11'40 68W50'40 4:35:23
Bradburys 2 11 47N14'16 68W34'42 4:34:19
Bradford 10 1 45N04'00 68W56'18 4:35:45
Bradford Center 10 1 45N04'20 68W53'48 4:35:35
Bradley 10 6 44N55'15 68W37'43 4:34:31
Bradleys Corner 3 44 43N39'33 70W17'51 4:41:11
Braeburn 16 4 43N13'29 70W34'52 4:42:19
Brannen 2 39 46N41 68W10 4:32:40
Brassua 13 1 45N37'36 69W54'46 4:39:39
Bremen 8 1 44N00 69W26 4:37:44
Brentwood Acres 3 44 43N38 70W16 4:41:04
Brewer 10 14 44N47'48 68W45'43 4:35:03
Brewer Lake 10 4 44N44 68W50 4:35:20
Brewster Corner 15 46 44N47'42 67W48'41 4:31:15
Brickett Place 9 1 44N16'03 71W00'17 4:44:01
Bridgewater 2 47 46N25'40 67W50'38 4:31:23
Bridgewater Corner 2 47 46N27'04 67W51'08 4:31:25
Bridgton 3 3 44N03'17 70W42'48 4:42:51
Briggs Corner 16 4 43N06'02 70W42'45 4:42:51
Brighams Cove 12 1 43N50'22 69W50'54 4:39:24
Brighton 13 1 45N02'43 69W41'43 4:38:47
Brighton Corner 3 44 43N39'59 70W17'47 4:41:11
Brighton Plantation 13 1 45N03 69W42 4:38:48
Brightwater 12 1 43N48'18 69W51'39 4:39:27

Brimstone Corner 9 30 44N12'27 70W29'50 4:41:59
Bristol 8 9 43N57'27 69W30'35 4:38:02
Brixham 16 4 43N11'09 70W44'41 4:42:59
Brixham Lower Corners 16 4 43N10'50 70W44'12 4:42:57
Brixham Upper Corners 16 4 43N09 70W39 4:42:36
Broad Cove 3 44 43N38 70W16 4:41:04
Broad Cove 8 26 44N02'16 69W24'55 4:37:40
Broadview Park 3 44 43N37'05 70W16'36 4:41:06
Brooklin 5 1 44N15'58 68W34'11 4:34:17
Brooks 14 1 44N33'01 69W07'17 4:36:29
Brooksville 5 1 44N20'48 68W41'03 4:34:44
Brookton 15 1 45N31'47 67W45'58 4:31:04
Brown Corner 2 11 46N53'54 67W55'42 4:31:43
Brown Corner 14 45 44N32'26 68W54'56 4:35:40
Brownfield 9 1 43N56'17 70W54'33 4:43:38
Browning 16 14 43N26 70W46 4:43:04
Browns Corner 6 6 44N13'33 69W53'54 4:39:36
Browns Corner 13 1 44N49'09 69W33'48 4:38:15
Brownville 11 47 45N18'25 69W02'02 4:36:08
Brownville Junction 11 47 45N21'00 69W03'10 4:36:13
Brunswick 3 14 43N54'52 69W57'57 4:39:52
Brunswick Naval Air Station 3 1 43N54 69W56 4:39:44
Bryant Pond 9 44 44N22'42 70W38'47 4:42:35
Bryants Corner 14 36 44N26'16 69W01'42 4:36:07
Buckfield 9 32 44N17'22 70W21'57 4:41:28
Bucks Harbor 15 41 44N38'31 67W23'20 4:29:33
Bucks Mills 5 44 44N37'36 68W43'48 4:34:55
Bucksport 5 44 44N34'25 68W47'46 4:35:11
Bucksport Center 5 4 44N37'52 68W50'04 4:35:20
Buffalo 2 47 46N49'37 68W29'11 4:33:57
Buffum Hill 16 6 43N17'47 70W35'17 4:42:21
Bugbee 2 47 46N46'44 68W09'20 4:32:37
Buggy Meetinghouse 3 5 43N35 70W21 4:41:24
Bullen Mills 4 8 44N41'45 70W04'09 4:40:17
Bunganuc Landing 3 1 43N51'50 70W01'21 4:40:05
Bunker Hill 8 35 44N02 69W33 4:38:12
Bunkers Harbor 5 1 44N23 68W03 4:32:12
Burdin Corner 11 1 45N05'37 69W31'53 4:38:08
Burkettville 7 1 44N17'53 69W19'06 4:37:16
Burlington 10 1 45N12'33 68W25'38 4:33:43
Burnham (Burnham Junction) 14 45 44N41'34 69W25'41 4:37:43
Burnt Landing 2 1 47N05'11 68W22'05 4:33:28
Burnt Meadow Ponp 9 1 43N56 70W55 4:43:40
Burnt Mill 2 47 47N08'29 68W42'15 4:34:49
Burton Corner 13 45 44N50'00 69W28'35 4:37:54
Bustins Island 3 8 43N47'56 70W04'13 4:40:17
Butlers Corner 14 1 44N24'27 69W06'06 4:36:24
Butterfield Landing 2 1 45N42'38 67W51'36 4:31:26
Buxton 16 45 43N38'16 70W31'10 4:42:05
Buxton Center 16 6 43N38'55 70W32'30 4:42:10
Byron 9 45 44N43'19 70W37'52 4:42:31
Calais 15 6 45N11'20 67W16'45 4:29:07
Caldwell Corner 9 1 44N10'19 70W27'32 4:41:50
California 2 11 47N04'09 68W06'23 4:32:26
Cambridge 13 1 45N01'27 69W28'28 4:37:54
Camden 7 9 44N12'35 69W03'55 4:36:16
Campbell 2 39 46N46'23 67W57'43 4:31:51
Campbells 15 47 45N10 67W16 4:29:04
Camp Ellis 16 44 43N27'49 70W22'51 4:41:31
Camp Wavus 8 1 44N11'09 69W29'29 4:37:58
Canaan 13 1 44N45'42 69W33'43 4:38:15
Canton 9 44 44N26'26 70W18'57 4:41:16
Canton Point 9 44 44N28'09 70W17'54 4:41:12
Cape Cottage 3 44 43N37'37 70W13'00 4:40:52
Cape Cottage Woods 3 44 43N38 70W16 4:41:04
Cape Elizabeth 3 44 43N33'49 70W12'02 4:40:48
Cape Junction 14 1 44N29 68W59 4:35:56
Cape Neddick 16 4 43N11'37 70W37'17 4:42:29
Cape Porpoise 16 44 43N22'21 70W26'19 4:41:45
Cape Rosier 5 1 44N19'53 68W47'58 4:35:12
Capitol Island 8 1 43N51 69W38 4:38:32
Caratunk 13 1 45N14'02 69W59'26 4:39:58
Caratunk Plantation 13 1 45N12 69W54 4:39:36
Cardville 10 1 45N03'21 68W35'58 4:34:24
Caribou 2 11 46N51'38 68W00'45 4:32:03
Carmel 10 45 44N47'51 69W03'06 4:36:12
Carrabassett 4 1 45N04'40 70W12'45 4:40:51
Carrabassett Valley 4 1 44N57 70W09 4:40:36
Carr Corner 10 40 45N01'42 69W14'15 4:36:57
Carriveau Mill 2 1 47N12'58 68W22'07 4:33:28
Carroll 10 1 45N24'52 68W02'19 4:32:09
Carrs Corner 14 1 44N26'24 69W24'34 4:37:38
Carson 2 47 46N50'37 68W08'05 4:32:32
Carthage 4 45 44N37'27 70W28'25 4:41:54
Carvers Corner 14 1 44N17'18 69W01'50 4:36:07
Cary 2 1 45N59'43 67W51'45 4:31:27
Carys Mills 2 11 46N06'07 67W52'22 4:31:29
Casco 3 1 44N00'24 70W31'24 4:42:06
Cash Corner 3 44 43N37'48 70W17'34 4:41:10
Cass Corner 13 31 44N54'13 69W41'58 4:38:48
Castine 5 9 44N23'16 68W48'01 4:35:12
Castle Harmony 13 31 44N56'28 69W30'32 4:38:02
Castle Hill 2 1 46N42 68W13 4:32:52
Caswell Plantation 2 1 47N00 67W50 4:31:20
Cathance 12 45 43N57'31 69W55'49 4:39:43
Cedar 15 1 45N03'29 67W27'52 4:29:51
Cedar Groves 8 8 44N06'58 69W45'49 4:39:03
Center Belmont 14 1 44N22'33 69W07'23 4:36:30
Center Lebanon 16 45 43N24'53 70W55'04 4:43:40
Center Lovell 9 1 44N10'46 70W53'33 4:43:34
Center Minot 1 13 44N08'01 70W18'59 4:41:16
Center Montville 14 1 44N26'48 69W14'48 4:36:59
Center Vassalboro 6 45 44N24'36 69W37'50 4:38:31
Centerville 15 1 44N42'20 67W40'46 4:30:43
Central Landing 3 1 43N44'10 70W06'29 4:40:26
Chamberlain 8 1 43N53'31 69W28'40 4:37:55
Chambers Corner 3 1 44N04'39 70W33'02 4:42:12
Chandler Cove Landing 3 1 43N42'57 70W07'36 4:40:30
Chapman 2 1 46N38'53 68W09'41 4:32:39
Charles Chase Corner 16 6 43N17'39 70W35'22 4:42:21
Charleston 10 1 45N05'06 69W02'28 4:36:10
Charlotte 15 1 45N01'16 67W14'45 4:28:59
Chase Corner 4 1 44N44'51 70W26'19 4:41:45
Chase Mills 1 1 44N15'35 70W17'31 4:41:10
Chase Mills 15 41 44N45'22 67W21'38 4:29:27
Chases Pond 16 4 43N11'17 70W39'09 4:42:37
Chebeague Island 3 1 43N44'27 70W06'31 4:40:26
Chelsea 6 6 44N15'01 69W43'04 4:38:52
Cherryfield 15 35 44N36'26 67W55'35 4:31:42
Chester 10 1 45N24'31 68W30'01 4:34:00
Chesterville 4 1 44N33'04 70W05'12 4:40:21
Chesuncook 11 1 46N03'37 69W24'36 4:37:38
Chicopee 16 44 43N42'02 70W33'14 4:42:13
China 6 1 44N28'43 69W31'04 4:38:04
Chisholm 4 44 44N28'53 70W12'00 4:40:48
Christmas Cove 8 1 43N50'49 69W33'15 4:38:13
Cider Hill 16 4 43N09'20 70W41'21 4:42:45
City Camp Landing 2 1 45N54'01 68W04'58 4:32:20
City Point 14 36 44N27'04 69W02'08 4:36:09
Clapboard Island 3 44 43N42 70W15 4:41:00
Clark Island 7 1 43N59'32 69W10'58 4:36:44
Clarks Corner 14 1 44N24'16 69W19'36 4:37:18
Clarks Mill 16 45 43N34'44 70W36'13 4:42:25
Clay Hill 16 4 43N10 70W36 4:42:24
Clayton Lake 2 1 46N36'39 69W31'22 4:38:05
Cleaves Landing 3 44 43N42'22 70W08'33 4:40:34
Cleveland 2 1 47N15'36 68W15'34 4:33:02
Cliff Island 3 44 43N41'46 70W06'30 4:40:26
Cliff Island Landing 3 44 43N41'42 70W06'38 4:40:27
Clifton 10 4 44N49'00 68W30'42 4:34:03
Clinton 6 32 44N38'16 69W30'13 4:38:01
Clock Farm Corner 16 44 43N24'18 70W25'39 4:41:43
Cobb Cove 3 1 44N04'16 70W30'12 4:42:01
Coburn 10 6 44N53'17 69W13'33 4:36:54
Coburn Gore 4 1 45N13 70W30 4:42:00
Codyville 15 1 45N26'23 67W41'41 4:30:47
Colby 2 1 46N54'01 68W08'11 4:32:33
Cold Brook 10 14 44N46'48 68W52'09 4:35:29
Cole Corner 11 1 45N10'21 69W30'58 4:38:04
Coles 6 1 44N27'13 69W29'49 4:37:59
Coles Corner 14 4 44N38 68W51 4:35:24
Columbia 15 46 44N39'29 67W46'30 4:31:06
Columbia Falls 15 46 44N39'13 67W43'41 4:30:55
Concordville 16 4 43N10'13 70W35'48 4:42:23
Connors Corner 14 36 44N22'27 69W16'55 4:37:08
Convene 3 2 43N53'16 70W43'44 4:42:55
Cook Mills 3 1 43N59'08 70W33'25 4:42:14
Cooks Corner 3 1 43N54'28 69W54'57 4:39:40
Cooks Corner 14 1 44N40'44 69W16'49 4:37:07
Coolidge Corner 10 40 45N02'24 69W14'55 4:37:00
Cooper 15 1 44N57'34 67W26'25 4:29:46
Coopers Corner 16 44 43N21'35 70W28'55 4:41:56
Coopers Mills 8 1 44N15'32 69W33'09 4:38:13
Coos Canyon 9 45 44N43'13 70W37'57 4:42:32
Coplin Plantation 4 1 45N06 70W28 4:41:52
Corea 5 1 44N24'03 67W58'32 4:31:54
Corinna 10 6 44N55'16 69W15'44 4:37:03
Corinna Center 10 6 44N57'05 69W14'50 4:36:59
Corinth 10 6 44N59 69W01 4:36:04
Cornish 16 5 43N48'17 70W48'06 4:43:12
Cornville 13 1 44N50'12 69W40'25 4:38:42
Corson Corner 13 31 44N53'58 69W36'10 4:38:25
Corsons Corner 13 1 44N58'47 69W40'56 4:38:44
Costigan 10 1 45N00'46 68W38'24 4:34:34
Costons Corner 13 1 44N53 69W27 4:37:48
Cote Corner 2 11 46N53'58 67W52'26 4:31:30
Cousins Island 3 8 43N45'32 70W08'39 4:40:35
Cozy Corners 16 33 43N20'38 70W33'44 4:42:15
Crams Corner 16 4 43N07'36 70W48'37 4:43:14
Cranberry Isles 5 1 44N14'54 68W15'39 4:33:03
Cranes Corners 5 44 44N32'57 68W44'31 4:34:58
Crawford 15 1 45N03'10 67W33'07 4:30:12
Crescent Beach 3 44 43N38 70W16 4:41:04
Crescent Beach 7 7 44N04'05 69W04'09 4:36:17
Crescent Lake 1 1 43N59'10 70W28'39 4:41:55
Criehaven 7 1 43N50'02 68W53'23 4:35:34
Crockertown 10 32 45N23'42 68W17'50 4:33:11
Crocker Turn 10 1 45N00'43 68W28'01 4:33:52
Crockett Corner 3 1 43N52'00 70W12'46 4:40:51
Crocketts Corner 3 44 43N37'48 70W18'44 4:41:15
Crocketts Neck 16 4 43N05 70W41 4:42:44
Croperly Turn 2 4 45N41'22 67W53'27 4:31:34
Crossman Corner 1 8 43N58'53 70W03'33 4:40:14
Crouseville 2 1 46N45'18 68W05'49 4:32:23
Crows Nest 14 36 44N18'32 68W57'48 4:35:51
Crystal 2 47 45N57'33 68W21'39 4:33:27
Cumberland Center 3 45 43N47'47 70W15'34 4:41:02
Cumberland Center Station 3 44 43N46'33 70W15'16 4:41:01
Cumberland Foreside 3 8 43N46'12 70W11'53 4:40:48
Cumberland Mills 3 44 43N40'53 70W20'37 4:41:22
Cummings 16 44 43N14'23 70W49'01 4:43:16
Cundys Harbor 3 1 43N47'49 69W53'37 4:39:34
Cupsuptie 9 45 44N58 70W47 4:43:08
Curtis Corner 1 46 44N15'58 70W05'35 4:40:22
Cushing 7 1 44N01'09 69W14'25 4:36:58
Cushing Briggs 3 8 43N49'51 70W06'06 4:40:24
Cushing Island 3 44 43N38'28 70W12'30 4:40:50
Cutler 15 41 44N39'27 67W12'16 4:28:49
Cutts Island 16 4 43N05'27 70W39'56 4:42:40
Cyr Plantation 2 1 47N06 67W58 4:31:52
Cyrs 13 1 44N56'59 69W28'25 4:37:54
Daaquam 2 1 46N35'54 70W00'42 4:40:03
Daggett 2 39 46N42 68W00 4:32:00
Daigle 2 1 47N11'22 68W27'41 4:33:51
Daigle Mill 2 11 47N14'11 68W07'29 4:32:30
Dallas 4 1 44N59'49 70W33'23 4:42:14
Damariscotta 8 4 44N01'58 69W31'09 4:38:05
Damariscotta Mills 8 4 44N03'43 69W31'27 4:38:06
Damascus 10 1 44N48'44 69W04'52 4:36:19
Dane Corner 13 20 44N48'56 69W58'17 4:39:53
Danforth 15 4 45N39'37 67W52'08 4:31:29
Danville (Danville Junction) 1 13 44N01'20 70W15'58 4:41:04
Danville Corner 1 13 44N02'10 70W15'23 4:41:02
Dark Harbor 14 1 44N15'38 68W54'51 4:35:39
Davenport Cove 2 4 45N40 67W52 4:31:28
Davidson 10 47 45N50'12 68W29'48 4:33:59
Davis Corner 8 26 44N08'51 69W22'29 4:37:30
Davis Island 8 27 43N59 69W39 4:38:36
Davis Town 4 45 45N05'14 70W47'10 4:43:09
Days Ferry 12 15 43N56'56 69W48'36 4:39:14
Days Mill 16 48 43N27'28 70W36'35 4:42:26
Dayton 16 45 43N33 70W35 4:42:20
Deadmans Corner 2 39 46N31'44 68W04'36 4:32:18
Deadwater 13 1 45N08'14 69W48'07 4:39:12
Deblois 15 45 44N44'29 68W00'55 4:32:04
Decker Corner 6 45 44N41'36 69W35'13 4:38:21
Dedham 5 45 44N41'30 68W39'45 4:34:39
Deep Cut 3 1 43N54'37 70W00'54 4:40:04
Deering 2 39 46N42 68W00 4:32:00
Deering 3 44 43N40'33 70W17'56 4:41:12
Deering Junction 3 44 43N41'13 70W17'27 4:41:10
Deer Isle 5 1 44N13'26 68W40'41 4:34:43
Delano Park 3 44 43N36'58 70W12'51 4:40:51
Denmark 9 2 43N58'13 70W48'14 4:43:13
Dennistown Plantation 13 1 45N40 70W20 4:41:20
Dennysville 15 24 44N54'13 67W13'45 4:28:55
Derby 11 4 45N14'11 68W58'51 4:35:55
Detroit 13 6 44N47'33 69W17'50 4:37:11
Dexter 10 40 45N01'26 69W17'25 4:37:10
Dickey 2 11 47N06'34 69W05'13 4:36:21
Dickvale 9 17 44N29'08 70W28'51 4:41:55
Dirigo Corner 6 1 44N24'33 69W31'16 4:38:05
Dixfield 9 17 44N32'02 70W27'23 4:41:50
Dixfield Center 9 17 44N32'27 70W22'58 4:41:32
Dixie Corner 13 6 44N56'59 69W19'23 4:37:18
Dixmont 10 1 44N40'49 69W09'48 4:36:39
Dixmont Center 10 1 44N41'22 69W07'15 4:36:29
Dixon Corner 6 1 44N42'42 69W29'38 4:37:59
Dodge Corner 14 45 44N32'40 68W58'40 4:35:55
Dog Corner 3 44 43N45'49 70W28'31 4:41:54
Dog Corners 5 45 44N47'18 68W12'03 4:32:48
Dog Island Corner 14 36 44N24'05 69W01'55 4:36:08
Dogtown 13 6 44N47'55 69W21'33 4:37:26
Dog Town 15 41 44N43'23 67W22'48 4:29:31
Dolby 10 9 45N38'00 68W36'17 4:34:25
Dolley Corner 3 31 43N50'02 70W24'34 4:41:38
Dorman 15 35 44N37'00 67W51'06 4:31:24
Double A Landing 10 14 44N54'01 68W48'11 4:35:13
Doughty Landing 3 44 43N41'55 70W09'06 4:40:36
Douglas Hill 3 34 43N52'47 70W41'59 4:42:48
Dover 8 3 43N55'23 69W38'18 4:38:33
Dover-Foxcroft 11 34 45N11'00 69W13'39 4:36:55
Dover South Mills 11 34 45N06'37 69W11'14 4:36:45
Dow Airport 10 14 44N49 68W45 4:35:00

Dow Corner 3 1 43N43'12 70W35'27 4:42:22
Dow Corner 13 1 44N54'22 69W21'06 4:37:24
Dow Pines 5 45 44N57'11 68W17'02 4:33:08
Drake Corner 14 1 44N17'20 69W05'55 4:36:24
Drake Place 10 1 45N22'06 68W07'55 4:32:32
Drakes Island 16 33 43N19'32 70W33'14 4:42:13
Dresden Mills 8 8 44N06'26 69W43'29 4:38:54
Drew Plantation 10 1 45N36 68W04 4:32:16
Drinkwater Corner 1 45 44N06'39 70W05'27 4:40:22
Dryden 4 6 44N35'12 70W12'37 4:40:50
Dry Mills 3 1 43N55'09 70W21'31 4:41:26
Ducktrap 14 1 44N17'43 69W00'30 4:36:02
Dudley 2 47 46N10'17 68W09'37 4:32:38
Dunham Corner 11 34 45N12'42 69W18'05 4:37:12
Dunkertown 3 1 44N02'43 70W30'56 4:42:04
Dunns 3 8 43N51'22 70W12'55 4:40:52
Dunns Corner 6 31 44N24'52 69W55'05 4:39:40
Durbin Corner 10 40 45N02'59 69W11'13 4:36:45
Durgintown 9 1 43N49'39 70W49'29 4:43:18
Durham 1 1 43N58 70W07 4:40:28
Dyer Brook 2 47 46N04'53 68W11'02 4:32:44
Dyer Corner 3 1 43N52'26 69W56'53 4:39:48
Dyer Cove 3 1 43N49'16 69W55'16 4:39:41
Dyerville 13 4 45N38'29 70W18'25 4:41:14
Eagle Island 5 1 44N12 68W42 4:34:48
Eagle Lake 2 11 47N02'24 68W35'24 4:34:22
Earley Landing 11 1 45N18'16 69W21'05 4:37:24
Earnest Corner 10 40 45N01'58 69W08'07 4:36:32
East Andover 9 1 44N36'58 70W42'55 4:42:52
East Auburn 1 13 44N08'34 70W13'39 4:40:55
East Baldwin 3 34 43N48 70W40 4:42:40
East Baldwin Mattocks Sta 3 34 43N48'11 70W40'43 4:42:43
East Bangor 10 14 44N51'10 68W48'46 4:35:15
East Benton 6 8 44N35'00 69W28'20 4:37:53
East Bethel 9 37 44N28'01 70W42'50 4:42:51
East Blue Hill 5 3 44N25'03 68W31'23 4:34:06
East Boothbay 8 3 43N51'54 69W35'13 4:38:21
Eastbrook 5 45 44N40'43 68W15'54 4:33:04
East Brownfield 9 1 43N56'41 70W53'20 4:43:33
East Buckfield 9 32 44N17'39 70W19'33 4:41:18
East Bucksport 5 45 44N40'28 68W42'09 4:34:49
East Corinth 10 6 45N00'09 69W01'27 4:36:06
East Deering 3 44 43N40'55 70W15'24 4:41:02
East Denmark 9 2 43N59'29 70W46'27 4:43:06
East Dixfield 4 6 44N34'24 70W18'15 4:41:13
East Dixmont 10 1 44N40'14 69W04'14 4:36:17
East Dover 11 34 45N11'12 69W10'14 4:36:41
East Eddington 10 4 44N47'31 68W35'00 4:34:20
East Edgecomb 8 27 43N56'38 69W36'01 4:38:24
East Eliot 16 4 43N09'02 70W45'46 4:43:03
East End 3 44 43N39'54 70W14'53 4:41:00
East Exeter 10 6 44N57'39 69W06'07 4:36:24
East Franklin 5 33 44N34'05 68W11'43 4:32:47
East Friendship 7 1 44N00'31 69W17'49 4:37:11
East Fryeburg 9 45 44N02'37 70W52'26 4:43:30
East Gray 3 1 43N53'20 70W17'39 4:41:11
East Hampden 10 14 44N46'14 68W47'44 4:35:11
East Harpswell 3 1 43N50'01 69W53'56 4:39:36
East Hebron 9 13 44N13'28 70W19'08 4:41:17
East Hiram 9 2 43N52'52 70W47'30 4:43:10
East Hodgdon 2 11 46N05'29 67W48'32 4:31:14
East Holden Station 10 4 44N44'15 68W38'01 4:34:32
East Knox 14 1 44N30'24 69W12'46 4:36:51
East Lamoine 5 32 44N27'53 68W19'01 4:33:16
East Lebanon 16 45 43N24'45 70W52'04 4:43:28
East Limington 16 34 43N44'02 70W39'30 4:42:38
East Livermore 1 44 44N24'47 70W08'40 4:40:35
East Lowell 10 45 45N12'18 68W27'13 4:33:49
East Lyndon 2 47 46N49'57 67W56'23 4:31:46
East Machias 15 41 44N44'21 67W23'26 4:29:34
East Madison 13 20 44N50'58 69W45'25 4:39:02
East Madrid 4 1 44N54'38 70W23'05 4:41:32
East Mercer 13 31 44N40'50 69W53'30 4:39:34
East Millinocket 10 9 45N37'39 68W34'30 4:34:18
East Milton 9 44 44N27'16 70W35'58 4:42:24
East Monmouth 6 31 44N14'34 69W58'44 4:39:55
East Newport 10 6 44N49'15 69W13'23 4:36:54
East New Portland 13 44 44N54'06 70W01'26 4:40:06
East Northport 14 36 44N22'55 68W58'50 4:35:55
Easton 2 9 46N38'28 67W54'36 4:31:38
Easton Center 2 18 46N38'38 67W52'02 4:31:28
Easton Station 2 1 46N39'40 67W54'37 4:31:38
East Orland 5 44 44N34'00 68W40'49 4:34:43
East Orrington 10 4 44N44'08 68W46'05 4:35:04
East Otisfield 3 1 44N05'40 70W31'34 4:42:06
East Palermo 14 1 44N22'13 69W23'32 4:37:34
East Parsonsfield 16 2 43N44'00 70W50'38 4:43:23
East Peru 9 17 44N29'18 70W22'46 4:41:31
East Pittston 6 6 44N10'27 69W40'25 4:38:42
East Poland (Empire Rd Sta) 1 44 44N04'14 70W19'43 4:41:19
Eastport 15 44 44N54'22 66W59'26 4:27:58
East Raymond 3 1 43N56'03 70W26'36 4:41:46
East Sangerville 11 22 45N09'09 69W17'31 4:37:10
East Sebago 3 35 43N51'19 70W38'24 4:42:34
East Steuben 15 1 44N30'10 67W55'34 4:31:42
East Stoneham 9 1 44N15'01 70W48'47 4:43:15
East Sullivan 5 33 44N30'13 68W09'10 4:32:37
East Sumner 9 32 44N21'24 70W22'37 4:41:30
East Surry 5 32 44N29'49 68W26'38 4:33:47
East Sweden 9 4 44N08'40 70W46'52 4:43:07
East Thorndike 14 1 44N35'30 69W12'06 4:36:48
East Troy 14 1 44N40'14 69W12'22 4:36:49
East Union 7 7 44N12'47 69W13'25 4:36:54
East Vassalboro 6 45 44N26'52 69W36'23 4:38:26
East Wales 1 1 44N09'27 70W02'28 4:40:10
East Warren 7 7 44N07'56 69W12'03 4:36:48
East Waterboro 16 45 43N34'17 70W40'46 4:42:43
East Waterford 9 4 44N12'42 70W40'57 4:42:44
East Wilton 4 6 44N36'57 70W11'36 4:40:46
East Windham 3 31 43N44 70W26 4:41:44
East Winn 10 32 45N25'33 68W18'25 4:33:14
East Winslow 6 8 44N32'39 69W32'19 4:38:09
East Winthrop 6 6 44N19'18 69W53'49 4:39:35
Eaton 15 4 45N36'19 67W48'22 4:31:13
Eddington 10 4 44N49'34 68W41'38 4:34:47
Eden 5 1 44N25'51 68W19'17 4:33:17
Edes Corner 11 3 45N12'41 69W23'17 4:37:33
Edes Falls 3 1 43N59'56 70W34'09 4:42:17
Edgecomb 8 27 43N57'30 69W37'52 4:38:31
Edinburg 10 1 45N11 68W40 4:34:40
Edmunds 15 24 44N52'19 67W09'53 4:28:40
Eggemoggin 5 1 44N18'22 68W44'03 4:34:56
Egypt 5 32 44N33'32 68W16'53 4:33:08
Eight Corners 3 5 43N37'07 70W20'42 4:41:23
Eliot 16 4 43N09'11 70W48'02 4:43:12
Elizabeth Park 3 44 43N35'38 70W14'09 4:40:57
Ellingswood Corner 14 4 44N38 68W51 4:35:24
Ellingwood Corner 14 4 44N40'30 68W55'08 4:35:41
Elliot Landing 10 14 44N53'37 68W46'22 4:35:05
Elliottsville Plantation 11 1 45N24 69W26 4:37:44
Ellis Corner 10 6 44N57'55 69W15'09 4:37:01
Ellis Corner 13 4 44N48'10 69W49'48 4:39:19
Ellis Pond 9 45 44N37 70W35 4:42:20
Ellsworth 5 32 44N32'36 68W25'12 4:33:41
Ellsworth Falls 5 32 44N33'44 68W26'21 4:33:45
Elmore 7 1 43N57'37 69W11'47 4:36:47
Elms 16 33 43N20'28 70W33'52 4:42:15
Elmwood 3 44 43N43'21 70W34'02 4:42:16
Elsemore Landing 15 1 45N10'52 67W53'55 4:31:36
Embden 13 1 44N55'05 69W52'02 4:39:28
Emerson Corner 13 6 44N47'55 69W28'29 4:37:54
Emery Mills 16 1 43N29'40 70W50'37 4:43:22
Emerys Bridge 16 44 43N14'47 70W43'39 4:42:55
Emerys Corner 16 1 43N43'32 70W45'45 4:43:03
Emory Corner 16 6 43N36'44 70W32'29 4:42:10
Empire 1 44 44N03'14 70W19'29 4:41:18
Enfield 10 34 45N14'56 68W34'08 4:34:17
English 2 39 46N42 68W00 4:32:00
E Plantation 2 1 46N29 67W56 4:31:44
Epping 15 46 44N40'55 67W46'00 4:31:04
Estabrook Settlement 2 1 45N55'13 67W53'06 4:31:32
Estcourt 2 11 47N27'34 69W13'31 4:36:54
Estes Hill 16 44 43N22'15 70W48'05 4:43:12
Estes Lake 16 14 43N26 70W46 4:43:04
Etna 10 45 44N49'15 69W06'42 4:36:27
Etna Center 10 1 44N47'12 69W06'23 4:36:26
Eugley Corner 8 26 44N04'00 69W24'04 4:37:36
Eustis 4 1 45N13'02 70W28'44 4:41:55
Evans Corner 14 1 44N29'26 69W06'01 4:36:24
Evergreen Landing 3 44 43N40'24 70W11'16 4:40:45
Exeter Center 10 6 44N58'12 69W08'26 4:36:34
Exeter Corners 10 6 44N59'11 69W08'39 4:36:35
Exeter Mills 10 6 44N58'12 69W04'45 4:36:19
Fairbanks 4 8 44N42'11 70W09'48 4:40:39
Fairfield 13 8 44N35'18 69W35'57 4:38:24
Fairfield Center 13 8 44N36'22 69W39'48 4:38:39
Fairmount 2 18 46N41'47 67W52'05 4:31:28
Falmouth 3 44 43N43'46 70W14'33 4:40:58
Falmouth Foreside 3 44 43N44'05 70W12'30 4:40:50
Farmingdale 6 6 44N14'40 69W46'19 4:39:05
Farmington 4 8 44N40'14 70W09'06 4:40:36
Farmington Falls 4 8 44N37'15 70W04'33 4:40:18
Farwells Corner 14 1 44N34'38 69W18'30 4:37:14
Fayette 6 44 44N24'32 70W02'03 4:40:08
Fayette Corner 6 44 44N25'14 70W04'21 4:40:17
Felch Corner 16 1 43N40'44 70W47'12 4:43:09
Fernald Shore 16 45 43N26'02 70W57'29 4:43:50
Ferry Beach 16 44 43N28'16 70W23'11 4:41:33
Feylers Corner 8 26 44N08'14 69W22'16 4:37:29
Five Corners 13 1 44N55 69W25 4:37:40
Five Corners 16 44 43N19'41 70W45'57 4:43:04
Five Islands 12 1 43N49'26 69W42'42 4:38:51
Five Mile Corners 5 44 44N33'32 68W42'11 4:34:49
Five Points 16 16 43N28'59 70W28'16 4:41:53
Flanders Corner 8 26 44N11'24 69W24'17 4:37:37
Flat Landing 5 1 44N21'31 68W46'12 4:35:05
Fletcher Field 15 1 45N02'06 67W53'27 4:31:34
Fletchers Landing 5 32 44N36'20 68W23'36 4:33:34
Foggs Corner 1 1 44N09'37 70W11'04 4:40:44
Foggs Corner 3 1 43N56'14 70W14'54 4:41:00
Forest 15 1 45N34'16 67W43'42 4:30:55
Forest City 15 1 45N39'35 67W43'49 4:30:55
Forest City Landing 15 1 45N39'33 67W42'15 4:30:49
Foristall Corners 16 4 43N12'47 70W39'53 4:42:40
Fort Baldwin 12 1 43N44'56 69W47'19 4:39:09
Fort Edgecomb 8 27 43N59'41 69W39'29 4:38:38
Fort Fairfield 2 18 46N46'20 67W50'04 4:31:20
Fort George 5 9 44N23'27 68W48'21 4:35:13
Fort Gorges 3 44 43N39'46 70W13'18 4:40:53
Fort Hill 16 16 43N29 70W27 4:41:48
Fort Kent 2 11 47N15'31 68W35'24 4:34:22
Fort Kent Mills 2 11 47N14'20 68W35'04 4:34:20
Fort Kent Village 2 11 47N14'44 68W36'29 4:34:26
Fort Levett 3 44 43N38'35 70W11'45 4:40:47
Fort Lyon 3 44 43N41'29 70W11'05 4:40:44
Fort Popham 12 1 43N45'18 69W47'02 4:39:08
Fort Preble 3 44 43N38'54 70W13'35 4:40:54
Fort Scammel 3 44 43N39'01 70W12'48 4:40:51
Fortunes Rocks 16 16 43N25'27 70W22'42 4:41:31
Fort Williams 3 44 43N38 70W16 4:41:04
Fosters Corner 3 31 43N48'13 70W24'27 4:41:38
Fosters Corner 14 1 44N29'51 69W11'20 4:36:45
Four Corners 2 11 46N52'41 67W49'31 4:31:18
Four Corners 16 48 43N21'16 70W30'21 4:42:01
Fournier 2 11 47N20'48 68W15'44 4:33:03
Fowler Landing 10 4 44N46'41 68W56'15 4:35:45
Frankfort 14 4 44N36'35 68W52'38 4:35:31
Franklin 5 33 44N35'13 68W13'58 4:32:56
Franklin Road 5 32 44N32'22 68W19'08 4:33:17
Freedom 14 9 44N31'49 69W17'54 4:37:12
Freeport 3 8 43N51'25 70W06'13 4:40:25
Frenchboro 5 1 44N07'05 68W21'47 4:33:27
French Mill 10 6 44N57'06 69W08'12 4:36:33
Frenchs Corner 6 6 44N14'11 69W53'16 4:39:33
French Settlement 10 6 44N58'11 68W43'36 4:34:54
Frenchville 2 11 46N40'52 68W20'01 4:33:20
Friendship 7 1 43N59'01 69W20'04 4:37:20
Frye 9 45 44N37'17 70W34'50 4:42:19
Fryeburg 9 45 44N00'59 70W58'52 4:43:55
Fryeburg Center 9 45 44N04'10 70W56'43 4:43:47
Fryeburg Harbor 9 45 44N01 70W59 4:43:56
Gag Corner 3 31 43N44'32 70W27'13 4:41:49
Gantners Landing 10 1 45N46'24 68W26'51 4:33:47
Gardiner 6 6 44N13'48 69W46'33 4:39:06
Garfield Plantation 2 1 46N37 68W28 4:33:52
Garland 10 40 45N02'18 69W09'39 4:36:39
Georges River 7 7 44N07 69W15 4:37:00
Georgetown 12 1 43N48'16 69W44'50 4:38:59
Gerrish Corner 14 1 44N38'15 69W16'43 4:37:07
Gerrishville 5 1 44N24'05 68W06'07 4:32:24
Gerry 10 6 45N01'01 68W49'08 4:35:17
Getchell Corner 6 45 44N27'33 69W39'55 4:38:40
Ghent 14 1 44N20'10 69W12'02 4:36:48
Gilbertville 9 44 44N27'25 70W18'26 4:41:14
Gilead 9 45 44N23'39 70W58'24 4:43:54
Gilford 10 1 45N21'51 68W40'08 4:34:41
Gilman Corner 11 34 45N05'47 69W16'11 4:37:05
Glantz Corner 3 1 43N50'34 70W24'01 4:41:36
Glenburn Center 10 14 44N54'38 68W50'52 4:35:23
Glen Cove 7 7 44N08'01 69W05'41 4:36:23
Glendon 8 26 44N06'04 69W27'04 4:37:48
Glenmere 7 1 43N57'05 69W15'30 4:37:02
Glenwood 2 1 45N46'28 68W07'07 4:32:28
Glenwood Plantation 2 1 45N48 68W06 4:32:24
Globe 7 1 44N13'37 69W23'20 4:37:33
Goffs Corner 11 34 45N12'50 69W14'25 4:36:58
Goodale Corner 10 4 44N42'01 68W45'05 4:35:00
Goodell Corner 11 1 45N16'58 69W25'35 4:37:42
Goodings 2 39 46N42 68W00 4:32:00
Goodrich 2 18 46N50'43 67W50'51 4:31:23
Goodrich Corner 4 8 44N43'16 70W03'27 4:40:14
Good Will Farm 13 1 44N41 69W38 4:38:32
Goodwin 2 18 46N48'49 67W53'22 4:31:33
Goodwin 5 1 44N32'36 68W04'01 4:32:16
Goodwin Corner 6 32 44N37'11 69W34'37 4:38:18
Goodwin Corner 13 6 44N49'08 69W18'30 4:37:14
Goodwins Mills 16 14 43N30'31 70W34'56 4:42:20
Goose Falls 5 1 44N21'12 68W48'36 4:35:14
Goose Rocks 7 1 44N08'07 68W49'56 4:35:20

Goose Rocks Beach 16 44 43N24'08 70W24'35 4:41:38
Gordon 10 32 45N31'48 68W17'05 4:33:08
Gordon Corner 10 40 45N01'59 69W12'06 4:36:48
Gorham 3 44 43N40'46 70W26'41 4:41:47
Gotts Island 5 1 44N16 68W19 4:33:16
Gould Corner 3 1 44N04'12 70W32'37 4:42:10
Gould Corner 13 1 44N50'47 69W36'40 4:38:27
Gould Corner 16 4 43N10'26 70W48'36 4:43:14
Gould Landing 10 14 44N53'50 68W47'19 4:35:09
Gould Landing 15 1 45N09'54 67W44'39 4:30:59
Gouldsboro 5 1 44N28'42 68W02'20 4:32:09
Grand Beach 3 44 43N32'16 70W21'05 4:41:24
Grand Falls Plantation 10 1 45N10 68W20 4:33:20
Grand Isle 2 9 47N18'19 68W09'09 4:32:37
Grand Lake Stream 15 1 45N10'46 67W46'30 4:31:06
Grange Corner 14 1 44N20'18 69W03'22 4:36:13
Granite Hill 6 6 44N16 69W47 4:39:08
Grants 4 1 45N06'12 70W45'01 4:43:00
Grants Camps 4 1 45N06'11 70W44'58 4:43:00
Grants Turn 7 1 44N15'40 69W08'01 4:36:32
Grass Corner 2 1 46N54'51 67W52'27 4:31:30
Grassy Landing 2 1 46N34'01 68W35'09 4:34:21
Gray 3 1 43N53'08 70W19'56 4:41:20
Grays Corner 5 1 44N22'49 68W39'37 4:34:38
Grays Corner 16 33 43N18'31 70W39'17 4:42:37
Great Diamond Island 3 45 44N51 68W20 4:33:20
Great Diamond Island Landing 3 44 43N40'14 70W12'01 4:40:48
Great Pond 5 45 44N56'25 68W16'57 4:33:08
Great Works 10 6 44N55'02 68W38'21 4:34:33
Great Works 16 44 43N13'11 70W47'52 4:43:11
Greeley Landing 11 34 45N15'04 69W14'14 4:36:57
Greely Corner 14 1 44N22'35 69W26'57 4:37:48
Green Acre 16 4 43N06'43 70W47'45 4:43:11
Greenbush 10 45 45N04'49 68W39'05 4:34:36
Greene 1 45 44N11'23 70W08'27 4:40:34
Greene Corner 1 1 44N10'41 70W10'06 4:40:40
Greenfield 10 1 45N02'50 68W28'55 4:33:56
Green Lake 5 45 44N40'16 68W33'19 4:34:13
Greenlaw Chopping Landing 15 1 45N09'57 67W43'30 4:30:54
Greenlaw Crossing 2 1 46N39'42 68W37'43 4:34:31
Greenlaws Corner 14 36 44N22'29 69W01'51 4:36:07
Greens Corner 14 1 44N39'31 69W17'43 4:37:11
Greenville 11 19 45N27'34 69W35'28 4:38:22
Greenville Junction 11 19 45N27'39 69W37'00 4:38:28
Greenwood 9 1 44N19'06 70W39'05 4:42:36
Greers Corner 14 1 44N22'28 69W07'50 4:36:31
Gregorys Corner 14 1 44N29'34 69W18'27 4:37:14
Grimes Mill 2 47 46N50'47 67W56'37 4:31:46
Grindstone 2 39 46N34'34 68W05'17 4:32:21
Grindstone 10 1 45N44'10 68W35'14 4:34:21
Grindstone Neck 5 1 44N24 68W05 4:32:20
Griswold 2 47 46N24'35 68W17'55 4:33:12
Grove 15 1 45N00'00 67W25'59 4:29:44
Groveville 16 44 43N39'49 70W31'14 4:42:05
Growstown 3 1 43N53'59 70W00'03 4:40:00
Guerette 2 1 47N07'46 68W19'04 4:33:16
Guilford 11 3 45N10'08 69W23'06 4:37:32
Guilford Center 11 22 45N11'34 69W20'56 4:37:24
Guillemette 16 14 43N26 70W46 4:43:04
Guinea Corner 16 16 43N27'19 70W25'46 4:41:43
Guiou 2 39 46N42 68W00 4:32:00
Gushees Corner 7 1 44N16'59 69W14'43 4:36:59
Hackett Mills 1 44 44N05'09 70W20'10 4:41:21
Haines Corner 1 44 44N25'20 70W08'41 4:40:35
Hale 9 44 44N35'24 70W33'43 4:42:15
Hales Corner 14 1 44N39'48 69W15'25 4:37:02
Hall Corner 6 1 44N16'09 69W34'22 4:38:17
Halldale 14 1 44N30'28 69W16'47 4:37:07
Hallowell 6 6 44N17'09 69W47'29 4:39:10
Hall Quarry 5 2 44N20'09 68W19'19 4:33:17
Halls Corner 2 1 46N07'26 68W23'48 4:33:35
Halls Corner 14 36 44N22'39 69W04'41 4:36:19
Halls Mills 15 41 44N46'13 67W15'55 4:29:04
Hamlin 2 11 47N03'57 67W47'40 4:31:11
Hammond Plantation 2 1 46N13 67W57 4:31:48
Hampden 10 4 44N44'40 68W50'15 4:35:21
Hampden Center 10 4 44N44'56 68W53'14 4:35:33
Hampden Highlands 10 14 44N43'56 68W50'30 4:35:22
Hampden Station 10 4 44N44'47 68W51'53 4:35:28
Hancock 5 33 44N31'45 68W15'15 4:33:01
Hancock Point 5 33 44N28'10 68W13'53 4:32:56
Hanford 2 47 46N54'48 68W15'34 4:33:02
Hanover 9 1 44N29'48 70W41'41 4:42:47
Happy Corner 11 1 45N10'08 69W34'28 4:38:18
Harborside 5 1 44N20'56 68W48'55 4:35:16
Harding 3 15 43N54'45 69W52'36 4:39:30
Hardy 11 1 45N19'52 68W49'13 4:35:17
Hardy Hill 10 4 44N45'20 68W49'12 4:35:17
Harmon Beach 3 1 43N48'16 70W32'59 4:42:12
Harmons Corner 1 13 44N02'23 70W13'23 4:40:54
Harmony 13 31 44N58'26 69W32'48 4:38:11
Harpswell Center 3 1 43N48'06 69W59'05 4:39:56
Harrimans Point 8 27 44N00 69W40 4:38:40
Harrington 15 35 44N37'09 67W48'39 4:31:15
Harrington Corner 8 4 44N04'24 69W29'43 4:37:59
Harrison 3 49 44N06'37 70W40'47 4:42:43
Hartford 9 45 44N22'22 70W20'50 4:41:23
Hartland 13 45 44N53'00 69W26'53 4:37:48
Harts Neck 7 1 43N58 69W12 4:36:48
Harvey 2 47 46N20'48 67W54'29 4:31:38
Harwards 12 8 44N02'03 69W49'38 4:39:19
Haseltine Corner 10 40 45N04'12 69W14'18 4:36:57
Haskell Corner 1 13 44N04'39 70W17'31 4:41:10
Hastings 9 45 44N21'17 70W59'26 4:43:58
Hasty Corner 10 6 44N49'27 69W15'28 4:37:02
Hatchs Corner 8 8 44N02'52 69W45'43 4:39:03
Haven 5 1 44N15'59 68W35'13 4:34:21
Hawkins 2 47 46N22'42 68W16'56 4:33:08
Hay Brook 10 1 45N45'56 68W34'27 4:34:18
Hayden Corner 6 45 44N31'29 69W37'10 4:38:29
Hayden Landing 13 1 45N18'27 70W10'44 4:40:43
Hayford Corner 14 36 44N24'40 69W04'20 4:36:17
Haynesville 2 1 45N49'34 67W59'30 4:31:58
Head of the Tide 14 36 44N26'55 69W03'16 4:36:13
Head of Tide 14 36 44N26 69W01 4:36:04
Heads Corner 9 2 43N58'41 70W47'04 4:43:08
Head Tide 8 1 44N06'52 69W37'19 4:38:29
Heals Corner 14 1 44N19'20 69W04'15 4:36:17
Hebron 9 45 44N11'53 70W24'25 4:41:38
Hendricks Harbor 8 1 43N49 69W41 4:38:44
Hermon 10 4 44N48'36 68W54'50 4:35:39
Hermon Center 10 14 44N47'47 68W53'18 4:35:33
Hermon Pond 10 4 44N46'58 68W57'20 4:35:49
Heron Island 8 1 43N49'49 69W34'03 4:38:16
Herricks 5 1 44N18'55 68W42'24 4:34:50
Herricks Corner 14 36 44N21'19 69W00'48 4:36:03
Hersey 2 1 46N04 68W23 4:33:32
Hibberts Corner 7 1 44N18'15 69W24'28 4:37:38
Hicks Corner 10 1 45N02'53 69W05'52 4:36:23
Higgins Beach 3 5 43N33'36 70W16'49 4:41:07
Higgins Corner 1 31 44N02'20 70W02'03 4:40:08
Higgins Corner 3 34 43N44'15 70W38'04 4:42:32
Higginsville 10 45 44N56'19 68W57'13 4:35:49
Highland 7 7 44N07 69W15 4:37:00
High Landing 2 47 46N50'11 68W41'49 4:34:47
High Landing 10 1 45N47'21 68W27'14 4:33:49
Highland Lake 3 44 43N44'37 70W21'19 4:41:25
Highland Lake Vista 3 31 43N44 70W26 4:41:44
Highland Park 9 45 44N02'35 70W56'31 4:43:46
Highland Plantation 13 1 45N03 70W05 4:40:20
Highlands 3 44 43N40'06 70W17'29 4:41:10
High Pasture 16 4 43N13'49 70W35'08 4:42:21
Highpine 16 33 43N21'21 70W39'16 4:42:37
Hildreths Mill 4 1 44N40'26 70W22'10 4:41:29
Hill 2 47 46N16'23 67W50'31 4:31:22
Hillman 2 47 46N12'17 68W09'38 4:32:39
Hills Beach 16 16 43N27'30 70W22'43 4:41:31
Hillside 3 45 43N56'45 70W42'58 4:42:52
Hinckley 13 45 44N41'08 69W37'59 4:38:32
Hiram 9 2 43N52'43 70W48'14 4:43:13
Hobbs Crossing 16 33 43N22'03 70W38'05 4:42:32
Hodgdon 2 1 46N03'14 67W52'02 4:31:28
Hodgdon Corners 2 1 46N02'32 67W51'35 4:31:26
Holden 10 4 44N45'10 68W40'46 4:34:43
Holeb 13 1 45N34'38 70W27'25 4:41:50
Holiday Beach 7 7 44N04'30 69W03'22 4:36:13
Hollandville 16 1 43N41 70W48 4:43:12
Hollis Center 16 6 43N36'18 70W35'37 4:42:22
Holmes Mill 14 36 44N26'41 69W03'42 4:36:15
Holway Corner 13 8 44N38'02 69W40'49 4:38:43
Hope 7 1 44N15'54 69W09'34 4:36:38
Houghton 9 45 44N45'54 70W39'00 4:42:36
Houghtonville 2 47 46N50'31 67W52'31 4:31:30
Houlton 2 11 46N07'34 67W50'27 4:31:22
Houston Corner 13 6 44N47'42 69W20'19 4:37:21
Howard Corner 11 22 45N09'58 69W18'21 4:37:13
Howe Brook 2 1 46N18'18 68W11'41 4:32:47
Howes Corner 1 1 44N19'55 70W13'07 4:40:52
Howes Corners 10 1 44N46 69W13 4:36:52
Howland 10 45 45N14'19 68W39'51 4:34:39
Hoxies 13 8 44N39'02 69W44'32 4:38:58
Hoyttown 15 41 44N43'22 67W26'42 4:29:47
Hudson 10 45 45N00'04 68W52'52 4:35:31
Huff Corner 11 1 45N04'31 69W36'28 4:38:26
Hulls Cove 5 1 44N25'09 68W15'04 4:33:00
Hunnewell Hill 3 5 43N35 70W21 4:41:24
Huntington Mill 10 1 45N06'24 68W55'49 4:35:43
Hunts Corner 9 37 44N18'07 70W44'59 4:43:00
Hurd 2 47 46N50'41 67W57'07 4:31:48
Hurd Corner 11 34 45N07'42 69W11'11 4:36:45
Hurd Corner 13 6 44N48'17 69W18'49 4:37:15
Hurds Corner 5 32 44N36'56 68W31'36 4:34:06
Hurds Corner 14 1 44N21'13 69W03'09 4:36:13
Huson Landing 2 1 46N30'45 68W11'39 4:32:47
Hutchins Corner 11 1 45N02'01 69W37'04 4:38:28
Hutchins Corner 14 1 44N29'05 69W22'40 4:37:31
Iceboro 12 8 44N06'44 69W46'45 4:39:07
Indian Island 10 6 44N56 68W40 4:34:40
Indian Landing 15 1 45N12'29 67W52'06 4:31:28
Indian Point 5 2 44N22'58 68W21'39 4:33:27
Indian Point 15 47 45N10 67W16 4:29:04
Indian River 15 35 44N34'19 67W38'36 4:30:34
Indian Township Passamaquodd 15 1 45N13 67W34 4:30:16
Industrial 2 39 46N42 68W00 4:32:00
Industry 4 1 44N45 70W03 4:40:12
Ingalls 3 3 43N59'07 70W43'34 4:42:54
Ingall's Hill 3 1 44N03 70W43 4:42:52
Intervale 3 1 43N57'07 70W15'48 4:41:03
Ireland Corner 3 31 43N48'42 70W22'36 4:41:30
Irish Settlement 15 4 45N39'28 67W54'44 4:31:39
Island Falls 2 45 46N00'33 68W16'19 4:33:05
Island Park 6 6 44N19'16 69W53'17 4:39:33
Isle Au Haut 7 1 44N04'31 68W38'02 4:34:32
Isle of Springs 8 1 43N51 69W38 4:38:32
Islesboro 14 1 44N18'30 68W54'14 4:35:37
Islesford 5 1 44N15'43 68W14'04 4:32:56
Jackins Settlement 2 1 46N00'59 67W49'16 4:31:17
Jackman 13 4 45N38'13 70W15'50 4:41:03
Jackman Mill 13 4 45N38'46 70W14'44 4:40:59
Jackman Station 13 4 45N37'22 70W15'11 4:41:01
Jackson 14 1 44N36'53 69W07'17 4:36:29
Jacksonville 15 45 44N45'38 67W23'45 4:29:35
Jay 4 44 44N30'14 70W13'00 4:40:52
Jefferson 8 1 44N12'24 69W27'11 4:37:49
Jemtland 2 11 47N00'26 68W08'40 4:32:35
Jenks Landing 3 1 43N43'02 70W06'57 4:40:28
Jewells Corner 2 47 46N20'26 67W50'35 4:31:22
Jewett 16 44 43N12'44 70W47'24 4:43:10
Johnson Corner 13 6 44N54'35 69W19'19 4:37:17
Jonesboro 15 1 44N39'45 67W34'23 4:30:18
Jones Corner 8 1 44N15'39 69W27'38 4:37:51
Jones Mill 2 1 47N06'02 68W50'52 4:35:23
Jonesport 15 1 44N31'58 67W35'56 4:30:24
Jones Wharf 3 44 43N39'21 70W12'01 4:40:48
Jordan Mills 10 32 45N33'12 68W22'47 4:33:31
Joyville 5 32 44N33'20 68W28'31 4:33:54
Jumbo Landing 15 1 45N12'52 67W52'35 4:31:30
Kalers Corner 8 26 44N05'45 69W23'06 4:37:32
Kamankeag 4 45 45N00'43 70W47'41 4:43:11
Katen Corner 10 40 44N59'06 69W16'49 4:37:07
Keegan 2 9 47N11'13 67W57'29 4:31:50
Keenes Corner 1 45 44N13'12 70W05'33 4:40:22
Kellyland 15 1 45N16'03 67W28'41 4:29:55
Kendalls Corner 14 36 44N27'06 69W05'12 4:36:21
Kenduskeag 10 45 44N55'10 68W55'56 4:35:44
Kennard Corner 16 4 43N07'36 70W47'49 4:43:11
Kennebago 4 1 45N06'27 70W46'19 4:43:05
Kennebago Lake 4 1 44N58 70W39 4:42:36
Kennebago Settlement 4 1 45N06'01 70W33'46 4:42:15
Kennebec 15 41 44N40'06 67W27'52 4:29:51
Kennebunk 16 48 43N23'02 70W32'43 4:42:11
Kennebunk Beach 16 48 43N20'42 70W30'10 4:42:01
Kennebunk Landing 16 48 43N22'40 70W30'33 4:42:02
Kennebunk Lower Village 16 44 43N22 70W29 4:41:56
Kennebunkport 16 44 43N21'42 70W28'38 4:41:55
Kennedy Corner 7 1 44N11'38 69W25'31 4:37:42
Kennedy Terrace 2 11 47N09 67W56 4:31:44
Kents Hill 6 1 44N24'18 70W00'05 4:40:00
Keough 4 4 45N33'22 70W33'43 4:42:15
Ketchum 9 37 44N30'10 70W54'56 4:43:40
Keyes Corner 8 1 44N14'57 69W38'08 4:38:33
Kezar Falls 9 1 43N48'28 70W53'22 4:43:33
Kimbles Corner 16 44 43N41'05 70W33'57 4:42:16
Kingfield 4 1 44N57'33 70W09'16 4:40:37
Kingman 10 35 45N32'58 68W12'00 4:32:48
Kingsbury 11 1 45N07'10 69W38'59 4:38:36
Kings Grant 3 44 43N38 70W16 4:41:04
Kinney Cove 15 4 45N40 67W52 4:31:28
Kinney Shores 16 44 43N29'35 70W23'17 4:41:33
Kittery 16 4 43N05'17 70W44'12 4:42:57
Kittery Foreside 16 4 43N05'10 70W44'38 4:42:59
Kittery Point 16 4 43N05'09 70W41'51 4:42:47
Knight Corner 10 40 45N02'11 69W10'24 4:36:42
Knights Corner 14 1 44N20'08 69W10'43 4:36:43
Knights Landing 11 1 45N21'39 68W57'05 4:35:48
Knightville 3 44 43N37'50 70W15'24 4:41:02

Knowles Corner 2 47 46N12'22 68w20'03 4:33:20
Knowlton Corner 8 26 44N02'53 69w29'11 4:37:57
Knowltons Corner 4 8 44N36'36 70w07'34 4:40:30
Knox Center 14 1 44N31'23 69w14'35 4:36:58
Knox Corner 14 1 44N31'57 69w16'16 4:37:05
Knox Hill Corner 10 40 44N59'19 69w15'30 4:37:02
Knox Ledge Corner 14 1 44N33'26 69w13'07 4:36:52
Kokadjo 11 1 45N40'16 69w26'51 4:37:47
Lac Frontiere 2 1 46N41'43 69w59'38 4:39:59
La Croix Depot 13 1 46N05'03 70w16'04 4:41:04
Lagrange 10 45 45N10'00 68w50'42 4:35:23
Lake City 7 1 44N14'42 69w05'47 4:36:23
Lake Moxie 13 45 45N21'04 69w53'05 4:39:32
Lake Parlin 13 1 45N31'07 70w05'39 4:40:23
Lakeside Landing 10 14 44N55'49 68w48'24 4:35:14
Lake View 11 1 45N19'24 68w55'35 4:35:42
Lakeville Plantation 10 1 45N21 68w04 4:32:16
Lakewood 5 32 44N37'48 68w26'06 4:33:44
Lakewood 13 6 44N49'53 69w46'43 4:39:07
Lambert Lake 15 1 45N33 67w32 4:30:08
Lamb Place 15 1 45N15'01 67w31'24 4:30:06
Lambs Corner 6 1 44N30'10 69w33'34 4:38:14
Lamoine 5 1 44N28'44 68w20'40 4:33:23
Lamoine Beach 5 32 44N27'02 68w17'34 4:33:10
Langtown Mill 4 1 45N03'59 70w34'38 4:42:19
Larone 13 8 44N40'53 69w43'32 4:38:54
Larrabee 15 41 44N40'05 67w23'36 4:29:34
Lawry 7 1 44N00'20 69w20'37 4:37:22
Leathers Corner 10 4 44N49'47 68w55'53 4:35:44
Lebanon 16 45 43N23'40 70w51'05 4:43:24
Lee 10 32 45N21'36 68w17'13 4:33:09
Leeds 1 46 44N18'12 70w07'12 4:40:29
Leeds Junction 1 1 44N12'23 70w04'46 4:40:19
Levant 10 45 44N52'09 68w56'07 4:35:44
Lewiston 1 14 44N06'01 70w12'55 4:40:52
Lewiston Junction 1 13 44N02'46 70w17'56 4:41:12
Libby Corner 10 6 45N19'17 68w29'09 4:33:57
Libby Hill 6 6 44N10'57 69w49'34 4:39:18
Libbytown 3 44 43N39'21 70w17'10 4:41:09
Liberty 14 1 44N23'21 69w18'12 4:37:13
Liberty Corner 9 2 44N01'09 70w51'34 4:43:26
Ligonia 3 44 43N38'15 70w17'34 4:41:10
Lille 2 11 47N16'48 68w06'37 4:32:26
Limerick 16 1 43N41'18 70w47'39 4:43:11
Limerick Mills 16 1 43N41'45 70w47'19 4:43:09
Limestone 2 11 46N54'31 67w49'35 4:31:18
Limington 16 34 43N43'54 70w42'41 4:42:51
Lincoln 10 6 45N21'44 68w30'20 4:34:01
Lincoln Center 10 6 45N23'13 68w28'13 4:33:53
Lincoln Compact 10 6 45N22 68w30 4:34:00
Lincoln Mills 10 6 44N57'18 69w16'36 4:37:06
Lincoln Plantation 9 1 44N56 71w02 4:44:08
Lincolnville 14 1 44N16'52 69w00'33 4:36:02
Lincolnville Center 14 1 44N17'52 69w06'29 4:36:26
Linekin 8 1 43N50'21 69w35'30 4:38:22
Linneus 2 1 46N02'19 67w57'38 4:31:51
Lisbon 1 8 44N01'53 70w06'18 4:40:25
Lisbon Center 1 8 44N01'11 70w05'38 4:40:23
Lisbon Falls 1 8 43N59'46 70w03'40 4:40:15
Litchfield Corners 6 6 44N07'59 69w57'56 4:39:52
Litchfield Plains 6 6 44N09'02 69w55'50 4:39:43
Little Canada 2 47 46N17'42 68w11'16 4:32:45
Little Deer Isle 5 1 44N17'11 68w41'47 4:34:47
Little Diamond Island Landin 3 44 43N39'46 70w12'38 4:40:51
Little Falls 3 31 43N43'53 70w25'41 4:41:43
Littlefield Corner 1 13 44N04'00 70w16'16 4:41:05
Littlejohn Island 3 1 43N45'18 70w08'06 4:40:32
Little Machias 15 41 44N38'50 67w14'31 4:28:58
Littleton 2 47 46N13'51 67w50'30 4:31:22
Livermore 1 44 44N23'02 70w14'59 4:41:00
Livermore Center 1 44 44N24'32 70w10'49 4:40:43
Livermore Falls 1 44 44N28'31 70w11'19 4:40:45
Locke Mills 9 37 44N24'00 70w42'09 4:42:49
Locks Corner 6 31 44N27'00 69w57'01 4:39:48
Long Beach 3 1 43N50'29 70w37'18 4:42:29
Long Beach 16 4 43N10'02 70w37'22 4:42:29
Longcove 7 1 44N01 69w12 4:36:48
Long Island 3 44 43N41'03 70w10'18 4:40:41
Long Island Plantation 5 1 44N11 68w21 4:33:24
Long Pond 13 47 45N37'17 70w05'13 4:40:21
Lookout 7 1 44N05 68w38 4:34:32
Loring Air Force Base 2 1 46N55 67w50 4:31:20
Loudville 8 1 43N55'43 69w25'53 4:37:44
Lovell 9 1 44N07'36 70w53'32 4:43:34
Lowell 10 1 45N11'16 68w28'06 4:33:52
Lowelltown 4 4 45N30'50 70w38'43 4:42:35
Lower Beddington 15 45 44N48'05 68w02'47 4:32:11
Lower Dennysville 15 24 44N55'47 67w13'39 4:28:55
Lower Landing 16 33 43N19'10 70w34'13 4:42:17
Lower Mill 13 20 44N51'10 69w44'26 4:38:58
Lower Shirley Corner 11 19 45N21'05 69w35'19 4:38:21
Lower Village 16 44 43N21'28 70w28'49 4:41:55
Lubec 15 42 44N51'38 66w59'05 4:27:56
Lucas Corner 7 1 44N17'00 69w20'04 4:37:20
Lucerne-in-Maine 5 45 44N41'59 68w36'04 4:34:24
Lucky Landing 10 14 44N54'38 68w48'14 4:35:13
Ludlow 2 47 46N08'26 68w02'26 4:32:10
Lunts Corner 3 44 43N41'09 70w16'08 4:41:05
Lyford Corner 13 6 44N55'29 69w19'50 4:37:19
Lyman 16 1 43N29 70w38 4:42:32
Lynchville 9 1 44N14'39 70w47'06 4:43:08
Machias 15 41 44N42'54 67w27'43 4:29:51
Machiasport 15 41 44N41'55 67w23'43 4:29:35
Mackamp 13 1 45N36'53 70w00'20 4:40:01
Mackworth Point 3 44 43N42 70w15 4:41:00
MacMahan 12 1 43N50'26 69w42'34 4:38:50
MacQuillis Corner 4 6 44N36'21 70w09'52 4:40:39
Macwahoc 2 1 45N37'42 68w15'48 4:33:03
Macy 4 45 44N53'43 70w45'12 4:43:01
Madawaska 2 11 46N53'03 67w56'52 4:31:47
Madawaska Lake 2 1 47N03 68w08 4:32:32
Maddocks Corner 7 1 44N20'40 69w17'32 4:37:10
Madison 13 20 44N47'51 69w52'49 4:39:31
Madrid 4 1 44N51'52 70w27'45 4:41:51
Madrid Junction 4 1 44N52'11 70w24'01 4:41:36
Magalloway Plantation 9 1 44N52 71w01 4:44:04
Maine 2 47 46N49'12 67w55'25 4:31:42
Maine Coast Mall 5 32 44N33 68w27 4:33:48
Maine Mall 3 44 43N38 70w16 4:41:04
Mainstream 13 31 44N58'10 69w30'27 4:38:02
Malbons Mills 13 1 44N47'46 69w41'09 4:38:45
Mallison Falls 3 31 43N44 70w26 4:41:44
Manchester 6 4 44N19'28 69w51'39 4:39:27
Manks Corner 8 26 44N10'26 69w20'02 4:37:20
Manset 5 1 44N16'05 68w18'48 4:33:15
Manson Corner 13 45 44N51'44 69w28'29 4:37:54
Maple Grove 2 18 46N43'44 67w51'50 4:31:27
Mapleton 2 39 46N40'55 68w09'48 4:32:39
Maplewood 16 1 43N40'27 70w54'41 4:43:39
Maranacook 6 31 44N20'49 69w57'31 4:39:50
Margison 2 1 46N55'01 68w08'20 4:32:33
Mariaville 5 45 44N43'14 68w24'58 4:33:40
Mariner 3 44 43N41'49 70w09'05 4:40:36
Marion 15 45 44N52'42 67w19'03 4:29:16
Marks Corner 5 1 44N29'45 68w38'44 4:34:35
Marlboro 5 32 44N28'32 68w16'14 4:33:05
Marrtown 12 1 43N47'40 69w46'55 4:39:08
Marsh Corner 13 6 44N52'53 69w19'03 4:37:16
Marshfield 15 41 44N43'59 67w28'41 4:29:55
Mars Hill 2 11 46N30'57 67w52'01 4:31:28
Marshville 15 35 44N36'58 67w47'06 4:31:08
Marston Corner 1 13 44N03'02 70w16'36 4:41:06
Martin 7 1 43N58'14 69w21'34 4:37:26
Martin Corner 13 6 44N48'25 69w48'26 4:39:14
Martins Corner 7 1 44N18'53 69w15'12 4:37:01
Martinsville 7 1 43N56'36 69w13'36 4:36:54
Masardis 2 47 46N30'13 68w21'42 4:33:27
Mason Bay 15 1 44N32 67w37 4:30:28
Mast Landing 3 8 43N51'27 70w05'03 4:40:20
Matinicus 7 1 43N51'54 68w53'15 4:35:33
Mattawamkeag 10 32 45N30'49 68w21'18 4:33:25
Mattimo Place 15 1 44N49'21 67w38'27 4:30:34
Maxfield 10 1 45N17 68w45 4:35:00
Mayberry Hill 3 1 44N00 70w32 4:42:08
Mayfield Corner 13 1 45N06'13 69w41'37 4:38:46
Maysville 2 39 46N46'41 67w58'13 4:31:53
Mayville 9 37 44N25'14 70w47'54 4:43:12
McCarty 11 1 46N04'16 69w00'49 4:36:03
McCoy Crossing 6 45 44N26'13 69w38'28 4:38:34
McFarlands Corner 14 1 44N24'58 69w19'23 4:37:18
McGray 2 47 46N48'56 67w59'02 4:31:56
McGregor Mill 10 6 44N59'11 69w03'16 4:36:13
McKeen Crossing 2 1 46N36'14 68w43'18 4:34:53
McNally 2 47 46N55'24 68w35'01 4:34:20
McShea 2 18 46N45'43 67w51'14 4:31:25
Meadowbrook 12 1 43N49'50 69w50'56 4:39:24
Meadowview 9 44 44N28'15 70w16'21 4:41:05
Meadowville 10 32 45N31'13 68w21'10 4:33:25
Mechanic Falls 1 6 44N06'42 70w23'32 4:41:34
Meddybemps 15 1 45N02'18 67w21'23 4:29:26
Medford 11 47 45N17'07 68w51'08 4:35:25
Medford Center 11 47 45N14'55 68w49'47 4:35:19
Medomak 8 1 44N00'02 69w24'21 4:37:37
Medway 10 1 45N36'32 68w31'53 4:34:08
Mee Corners 16 1 43N38'38 70w56'50 4:43:47
Melvin Heights 7 1 44N13'04 69w06'06 4:36:24
Mercer 13 31 44N40'41 69w56'13 4:39:45
Merepoint 3 8 43N49'29 70w01'33 4:40:06
Merrill 2 1 46N10 68w15 4:33:00
Merrill Corner 9 1 43N55'35 70w56'45 4:43:47
Merrow Landing 3 1 44N04'19 70w36'41 4:42:27
Mexico 9 44 44N33'39 70w32'45 4:42:11
Michigan Settlement 2 1 47N13'52 68w31'33 4:34:06
Middle Dam 9 1 44N46'48 70w55'22 4:43:41
Middle Intervale 9 37 44N27'46 70w47'16 4:43:09
Milbridge 15 1 44N32'07 67w52'53 4:31:32
Miles Corner 13 6 44N51'28 69w18'02 4:37:12
Milford 10 6 44N56'46 68w38'40 4:34:35
Mill Brook 11 47 45N22'19 69w01'20 4:36:05
Miller Corner 13 1 44N52'30 69w21'23 4:37:26
Miller Corner 16 1 43N28'44 70w56'47 4:43:47
Millers Crossing 16 14 43N24'21 70w29'21 4:41:57
Milliken Mills 16 44 43N32'40 70w23'34 4:41:34
Millinocket 10 10 45N39'26 68w42'37 4:34:50
Milltown 15 47 45N10'11 67w17'28 4:29:10
Millvale 5 44 44N37'43 68w46'14 4:35:05
Milo 11 4 45N15'13 68w59'11 4:35:57
Milton 9 44 44N26'52 70w39'13 4:42:37
Mingo Springs 4 45 44N57'19 70w42'53 4:42:52
Minot 1 34 44N05'08 70w19'14 4:41:17
Minturn 5 1 44N09 68w26 4:33:44
Minunn 5 1 44N08'33 68w26'13 4:33:45
Mitchell Corner 13 1 44N49'56 69w36'21 4:38:25
Mitchell Corner 14 1 44N40'26 69w16'02 4:37:04
Molunkus 2 35 45N36'55 68w18'14 4:33:13
Monarda 2 47 45N47'49 68w19'28 4:33:18
Monhegan 8 1 43N45'44 69w19'15 4:37:17
Monmouth 6 31 44N14'19 70w02'10 4:40:09
Monroe 14 1 44N36'54 69w01'07 4:36:04
Monroe Center 14 1 44N36'00 69w02'21 4:36:09
Monsapec 15 1 44N36'32 67w36'06 4:30:24
Monson 11 19 45N17'13 69w30'06 4:38:00
Monson Junction 11 1 45N12'55 69w28'19 4:37:53
Monticello 2 47 46N18'30 67w50'35 4:31:22
Montsweag 12 27 43N57'44 69w43'28 4:38:54
Montville 14 36 44N27 69w16 4:37:04
Moody 10 40 44N58'49 69w18'02 4:37:12
Moody 16 6 43N16'30 70w35'51 4:42:23
Moody Beach 16 6 43N16'32 70w35'00 4:42:20
Moody Corner 13 1 45N00'17 69w43'33 4:38:54
Moody Mountain 14 1 44N13 69w17 4:37:08
Moody Point 16 6 43N17'11 70w34'22 4:42:17
Mooresville 11 1 45N24'51 69w06'01 4:36:24
Moosehead 11 1 45N35'00 69w42'51 4:38:51
Moosehorn 4 4 45N23'08 70w47'41 4:43:11
Moosehorn 11 1 45N13'43 69w29'11 4:37:57
Moosehorn Crossing 10 1 46N19'53 68w46'54 4:35:08
Mooselookmeguntic 4 45 44N57'48 70w47'36 4:43:10
Moose River 13 4 45N39'10 70w16'00 4:41:04
Morang Corner 7 1 44N15'50 69w16'30 4:37:06
Morey Brow 2 47 46N17'36 67w57'29 4:31:50
Morgan Beach 10 34 45N16'14 68w33'20 4:34:13
Morkill 11 1 45N25'35 69w29'53 4:38:00
Moro Plantation 2 1 46N10 68w21 4:33:24
Morrill 14 36 44N26'35 69w08'59 4:36:36
Morrills Corner 3 44 43N41'15 70w17'37 4:41:10
Morris Corner 2 11 46N52'39 67w51'07 4:31:24
Morrison Corner 6 32 44N39'48 69w34'40 4:38:19
Morse Corners 10 6 44N55 69w16 4:37:04
Moscow (Wyman Dam P O) 13 38 45N04'14 69w53'30 4:39:34
Mosher Corner 3 5 43N41'27 70w24'10 4:41:37
Mosher Corner 13 6 44N46'57 69w25'11 4:37:41
Mountainview 4 45 44N58'02 70w45'44 4:43:03
Mountainview Park 3 44 43N37'47 70w13'35 4:40:54
Mountainville 5 1 44N12'43 68w37'46 4:34:31
Mount Chase Plantation 10 1 46N03 68w28 4:33:52
Mount Desert 5 2 44N22 68w20 4:33:20
Mount Pisgah 8 1 43N51'11 69w37'20 4:38:29
Mount Vernon 6 4 44N30'04 69w59'17 4:39:57
Mousam Lake 16 1 43N32 70w55 4:43:40
Moussam 1 44 44N04'49 70w20'29 4:41:22
Mud Landing 15 45 44N51'25 67w26'52 4:29:47
Munjoy Hill 3 44 43N40'02 70w14'58 4:41:00
Murphy Corner 1 13 44N02'27 70w14'02 4:40:56
Murphys Corner 12 15 43N55'36 69w44'04 4:38:56
Muscongus 8 1 43N58'10 69w26'38 4:37:47
Muscongus Bay 8 26 44N05 69w29 4:37:56
Myra 5 45 44N58'49 68w23'49 4:33:35
Naples 3 1 43N58'18 70w36'35 4:42:26
Nash Corner 13 6 44N44'57 69w26'50 4:37:47
Nashville Plantation 2 1 46N42 68w29 4:33:56
Naskeag 5 1 44N14'04 68w31'57 4:34:08
Nason Beach 1 1 44N09'16 70w06'56 4:40:28
Nasons Corner 3 44 43N40'30 70w18'53 4:41:16
Naval Base 16 4 43N04 70w47 4:43:08
Neadeauville 10 32 45N31 68w21 4:33:24
Nealeys Corner 10 4 44N41'54 68w56'42 4:35:47
Neals Corner 14 36 44N29'06 69w06'43 4:36:27
Nehumkeag 6 6 44N10'10 69w45'14 4:39:01
Nequasset 12 15 43N56'23 69w46'59 4:39:08
Newagen 8 1 43N47'21 69w39'24 4:38:38
New Auburn 1 13 44N05'00 70w13'24 4:40:54
New Boston 9 2 43N53'39 70w58'39 4:43:55

Newburgh Center 10 1 44N43'18 69W00'10 4:36:01
Newburgh Village 10 1 44N41'48 68W58'46 4:35:55
New Canada Plantation 2 1 47N11 68W32 4:34:08
Newcastle 8 35 44N02'06 69W32'14 4:38:09
New City 11 1 45N59'24 68W54'41 4:35:39
New Cloucester 3 1 43N57'46 70W16'59 4:41:08
Newfield 16 1 43N38'53 70W50'51 4:43:23
New Gloucester 3 31 43N49 70W21 4:41:24
Newhall 3 31 43N45'05 70W25'56 4:41:44
New Harbor 8 1 43N52'33 69W29'26 4:37:58
New Limerick 2 47 46N06'04 67W57'38 4:31:51
New Meadows 12 1 43N55 69W50 4:39:20
Newport 10 6 44N50'07 69W16'28 4:37:06
New Portland 13 44 44N53'03 70W05'50 4:40:23
Newry 9 1 44N29'14 70W47'15 4:43:09
New Sharon 4 31 44N38'20 70W00'58 4:40:04
New Sweden 2 10 46N56'30 68W07'16 4:32:29
New Sweden Station 2 10 46N57'13 68W06'04 4:32:24
Newtown 16 16 43N25'59 70W24'20 4:41:37
New Vineyard 4 1 44N48'15 70W07'19 4:40:29
Nickerson Mills 14 1 44N32'22 69W02'20 4:36:09
Nicohn 5 32 44N37'16 68W30'54 4:34:04
Nicolin 5 32 44N33 68W27 4:33:48
Nixon 2 47 46N52'47 68W31'21 4:34:05
Nobleboro 8 26 44N04'46 69W29'08 4:37:57
Nobles Corner 9 25 44N15'41 70W37'31 4:42:30
Norcross 10 45 45N37'46 68W48'11 4:35:13
Norridgewock 13 31 44N42'47 69W47'28 4:39:10
North Alfred 16 14 43N31'18 70W45'53 4:43:04
North Amity 2 1 45N56'30 67W49'51 4:31:19
North Anson 13 4 44N51'18 69W54'01 4:39:36
North Appleton 7 1 44N18'15 69W12'35 4:36:50
North Auburn 1 13 44N10'38 70W16'26 4:41:06
North Augusta 6 44 44N22'14 69W47'32 4:39:10
North Baldwin 3 34 43N50'44 70W41'22 4:42:45
North Bancroft 2 4 45N45'07 67W56'47 4:31:47
North Bangor 10 14 44N50'22 68W49'52 4:35:19
North Bath 12 15 43N56'05 69W48'59 4:39:16
North Belgrade 6 35 44N31'08 69W47'34 4:39:10
North Belgrade Station 6 35 44N30'21 69W46'44 4:39:07
North Berwick 16 44 43N18'13 70W44'02 4:42:56
North Bethel 9 37 44N25 70W48 4:43:12
North Blue Hill 5 3 44N25 68W36 4:34:24
North Bradford 10 1 45N07'05 68W57'44 4:35:51
North Brewer 10 14 44N49'06 68W42'12 4:34:49
North Bridgton 3 3 44N05'55 70W41'57 4:42:48
North Brooklin 5 1 44N18'19 68W34'14 4:34:17
North Brooksville 5 1 44N23'43 68W42'40 4:34:51
North Buckfield 9 32 44N18'37 70W24'18 4:41:37
North Bucksport 5 4 44N39'40 68W48'50 4:35:15
North Carmel 10 45 44N48 69W03 4:36:12
North Castine 5 44 44N25'08 68W46'21 4:35:05
North Chesterville 4 8 44N35'40 70W06'45 4:40:27
North Cushing 7 1 44N02'20 69W12'40 4:36:51
North Cutler 15 41 44N40'09 67W15'36 4:29:02
North Deering 3 44 43N41'59 70W17'18 4:41:09
North Deer Isle 5 1 44N15'58 68W40'24 4:34:42
North Dexter 10 40 45N04'34 69W20'05 4:37:20
North Dixmont 10 1 44N43'30 69W10'24 4:36:42
North East Carry 11 1 45N51'59 69W37'37 4:38:30
Northeast Harbor 5 1 44N17'39 68W17'25 4:33:10
North Edgecomb 8 27 43N59'20 69W38'27 4:38:34
North Ellsworth 5 32 44N35'31 68W30'38 4:34:03
Northern Maine Junction 10 14 44N47'33 68W51'35 4:35:26
North Fairfield 13 8 44N38'58 69W40'35 4:38:42
North Falmouth 3 44 43N46'53 70W20'12 4:41:21
North Fayette 6 44 44N27'00 70W04'10 4:40:17
Northfield 15 1 44N49'44 67W34'16 4:30:17
North Fryeburg 9 45 44N07'15 70W58'40 4:43:55
North Gorham 3 44 43N47'54 70W27'19 4:41:49
North Gray 3 1 43N55'01 70W19'11 4:41:17
North Guilford 11 3 45N14'05 69W25'17 4:37:41
North Harpswell 3 1 43N49'15 69W58'01 4:39:52
North Haven 7 1 44N07'41 68W52'29 4:35:30
North Hermon 10 4 44N50'56 68W52'34 4:35:30
North Hill 9 32 44N17 70W22 4:41:28
North Hollis 16 6 43N39'26 70W40'32 4:42:42
North Hope Corner 7 1 44N17'25 69W11'27 4:36:46
North Islesboro 14 1 44N20'13 68W54'01 4:35:36
North Jay 4 8 44N32'50 70W14'19 4:40:57
North Jefferson 8 1 44N12'49 69W26'16 4:37:45
North Lamoine 5 1 44N30'28 68W21'04 4:33:24
North Lebanon 16 45 43N26'16 70W53'05 4:43:32
North Leeds 1 46 44N20'36 70W07'54 4:40:32
North Limington 16 34 43N44'50 70W40'56 4:42:44
North Lincoln 10 1 45N25'37 68W27'45 4:33:51
North Litchfield 6 6 44N13 69W56 4:39:44
North Livermore 1 44 44N26'32 70W13'06 4:40:52
North Lovell 9 1 44N14'31 70W52'39 4:43:31
North Lubec 15 42 44N52'06 67W01'06 4:28:04
North Lyndon 2 1 46N56'22 68W01'27 4:32:06
North Mariaville 5 45 44N46'50 68W22'25 4:33:30
North Meadows 12 15 43N54'22 69W51'43 4:39:27
North Monmouth 6 31 44N16'40 70W01'53 4:40:08
North Monroe 14 1 44N37'28 69W05'48 4:36:23
North Newburgh 10 1 44N45'20 68W58'25 4:35:54
North Newcastle 8 35 44N05'09 69W34'29 4:38:18
North Newport 10 6 44N53'29 69W12'25 4:36:50
North New Portland 13 44 44N55'30 70W01'25 4:40:06
North Newry 9 1 44N32'45 70W50'01 4:43:20
North Nobleboro 8 26 44N06 69W23 4:37:32
North Norway 9 25 44N15'23 70W38'07 4:42:32
North Orland 5 44 44N38'19 68W38'28 4:34:34
North Orrington 10 4 44N44'54 68W48'26 4:35:14
North Palermo 14 1 44N27'05 69W23'42 4:37:35
North Paris 9 30 44N20'15 70W31'47 4:42:07
North Parsonsfield 16 2 43N45'26 70W55'23 4:43:42
North Penobscot 5 1 44N31'18 68W39'43 4:34:39
North Perry 15 44 45N01'49 67W06'31 4:28:26
North Pittston 6 6 44N13'25 69W41'35 4:38:46
Northport 14 36 44N20'16 68W57'43 4:35:51
North Pownal 3 1 43N56'15 70W11'36 4:40:46
North Raymond 3 1 43N58'49 70W24'18 4:41:37
North Scarborough 3 5 43N38'31 70W23'54 4:41:36
North Searsmont 14 36 44N24'32 69W13'01 4:36:52
North Searsport 14 45 44N33'14 68W57'24 4:35:50
North Sebago 3 35 43N53'17 70W37'57 4:42:32
North Sedgwick 5 1 44N20'26 68W35'22 4:34:21
North Shapleigh 16 1 43N36'06 70W53'18 4:43:33
North Sidney 6 45 44N28'01 69W41'31 4:38:46
North Sullivan 5 33 44N32'26 68W14'37 4:32:58
North Trescott 15 24 44N51'34 67W07'56 4:28:32
North Turner 1 1 44N20'35 70W15'25 4:41:02
North Union 7 1 44N16'37 69W18'36 4:37:14
North Vassalboro 6 45 44N29'10 69W37'23 4:38:30
North Wade 2 47 46N49'47 68W10'48 4:32:43
North Waldoboro 8 26 44N11'03 69W22'33 4:37:30
North Warren 7 7 44N07 69W15 4:37:00
North Waterboro 16 45 43N37'13 70W44'09 4:42:57
North Waterford 9 4 44N13'54 70W46'09 4:43:05
North Wayne 6 46 44N22'27 70W02'00 4:40:08
Northwest Bethel 9 37 44N25'22 70W50'42 4:43:23
North Whitefield 8 1 44N13'19 69W35'16 4:38:21
North Windham 3 31 43N50'03 70W26'20 4:41:45
North Windsor 6 1 44N20'54 69W34'53 4:38:20
North Woodstock 9 44 44N24'32 70W38'18 4:42:33
North Yarmouth 3 8 43N50 70W15 4:41:00
Norumbega 5 1 44N19'15 68W43'25 4:34:54
Norway 9 25 44N12'50 70W32'43 4:42:11
Norway Center 9 25 44N14'01 70W36'43 4:42:27
Norway Lake 9 25 44N12'48 70W34'49 4:42:19
Notre Dame 2 11 47N15'16 68W03'57 4:32:16
Number Four 9 1 44N08 70W53 4:43:32
Nutter Corner 13 1 44N55'15 69W21'20 4:37:25
Nyes Corner 13 45 44N39'12 69W37'07 4:38:28
Oakdale 3 44 43N39'39 70W16'54 4:41:08
Oakes Corner 7 1 44N17'14 69W16'12 4:37:05
Oakfield 2 47 46N05'56 68W09'02 4:32:36
Oak Hill 1 45 44N03'01 70W24'33 4:41:38
Oak Hill 3 5 43N35'23 70W20'04 4:41:20
Oak Hill 5 1 44N23'46 68W41'21 4:34:45
Oak Hill 8 15 43N53'42 69W40'50 4:38:43
Oakland 6 6 44N32'25 69W43'21 4:38:53
Oak Ridge 16 16 43N26'08 70W25'49 4:41:43
Oak Terrace 16 4 43N05'21 70W45'30 4:43:02
Oakwood 14 1 44N38'56 69W21'16 4:37:25
Ocean Park 16 44 43N30'02 70W23'12 4:41:33
Ocean Point 8 1 43N48'57 69W35'47 4:38:23
Oceanside 16 4 43N11 70W37 4:42:28
Oceanview Harbor 3 5 43N35 70W21 4:41:24
Oceanville 5 1 44N11'11 68W37'21 4:34:29
Ogontz 13 1 45N49'13 69W42'49 4:38:51
Ogren 2 1 46N54'39 68W03'23 4:32:14
Ogunquit 16 6 43N14'56 70W35'59 4:42:24
Olamon 10 45 45N07'15 68W36'40 4:34:27
Old City 11 1 46N00'44 68W52'01 4:35:28
Olde Mill Brook 3 5 43N35 70W21 4:41:24
Old Orchard Beach 16 44 43N31'02 70W22'41 4:41:31
Old Town 10 6 44N56'03 68W38'45 4:34:35
Old Town Landing 10 14 44N56'33 68W47'33 4:35:10
Oliver Hill Corner 10 40 45N03'57 69W10'24 4:36:42
Onawa 11 19 45N22'00 69W22'20 4:37:29
Oquossoc 4 45 44N57'59 70W46'27 4:43:06
Orffs Corner 8 26 44N09'49 69W24'55 4:37:40
Orient 2 1 45N49'01 67W50'26 4:31:22
Orland 5 44 44N34'13 68W44'11 4:34:57
Orono 10 31 44N52'59 68W40'21 4:34:41
Orrington 10 4 44N43'52 68W49'37 4:35:18
Orrington Center 10 4 44N43'16 68W47'21 4:35:09
Orrs Island 3 1 43N45'38 69W58'36 4:39:54
Osborn Plantation 5 45 44N47 68W16 4:33:04
Ossipee Mills 16 1 43N39'03 70W45'40 4:43:03
Otis 5 45 44N42'44 68W27'12 4:33:49
Otisfield 3 1 44N05 70W33 4:42:12
Otisfield Gore 3 1 44N08'54 70W33'52 4:42:15
Otter Creek 5 1 44N19'06 68W12'29 4:32:50
Ouellette 2 1 47N10'15 68W23'36 4:33:34
Overlake 4 1 44N44'31 70W05'24 4:40:22
Owls Head 7 7 44N04'56 69W03'28 4:36:14
Oxbow 2 1 46N25'07 68W29'26 4:33:58
Oxford 9 1 44N07'54 70W29'37 4:41:58
Oxford Station 9 1 44N08'41 70W27'46 4:41:51
Packard Landing 11 1 45N17'48 69W20'03 4:37:20
Packards 11 47 45N28'52 68W56'22 4:35:45
Paine Corner 9 6 44N09'29 70W25'53 4:41:44
Paines Corner 6 1 44N30'45 69W34'28 4:38:18
Palermo 14 1 44N24'28 69W28'28 4:37:54
Palmyra 13 1 44N50'47 69W21'33 4:37:26
Parent 2 11 47N14'01 68W01'46 4:32:07
Paris 9 30 44N15'35 70W30'04 4:42:00
Parker Head 12 1 43N47'04 69W48'11 4:39:13
Parkers 11 45 45N11'30 68W53'56 4:35:36
Parkhurst 2 39 46N44'54 67W57'26 4:31:50
Parkman 11 1 45N08'01 69W26'01 4:37:44
Parrot 11 1 45N15'18 69W33'16 4:38:13
Parsonage Corner 16 44 43N18'29 70W41'12 4:42:45
Parson Landing 11 1 45N15'41 69W11'18 4:36:45
Parsonsfield 16 1 43N43'37 70W55'45 4:43:43
Passadumkeag 10 45 45N11'07 68W37'02 4:34:28
Pattee Corner 14 1 44N35'13 69W04'58 4:36:20
Patten 10 47 45N59'47 68W26'48 4:33:47
Patten June 2 47 45N54'48 68W24'48 4:33:39
Pauls 2 1 46N50'43 68W02'46 4:32:11
Pauls Corner 14 1 44N22'48 69W13'04 4:36:52
Payneton 16 4 43N10'42 70W43'42 4:42:55
Payson Corner 7 1 44N15'05 69W09'18 4:36:37
Peabbles Cove 3 44 43N38 70W16 4:41:04
Pea Cove 10 6 44N59'09 68W41'39 4:34:47
Peaks Island 3 44 43N39'25 70W11'48 4:40:47
Pea Ridge 10 1 45N25'22 68W31'31 4:34:06
Pease Corner 7 1 44N16'30 69W17'15 4:37:09
Pejepscot 12 1 43N57'36 70W00'56 4:40:04
Pelton Hill 6 4 44N19'16 69W49'46 4:39:19
Pemaquid 8 1 43N54'24 69W30'56 4:38:04
Pemaquid Beach 8 1 43N52'28 69W31'19 4:38:05
Pemaquid Harbor 8 1 43N53'32 69W31'30 4:38:06
Pemaquid Point 8 1 43N50'26 69W30'37 4:38:02
Pembroke 15 24 44N57'13 67W09'45 4:28:39
Penley Corner 1 13 44N03'04 70W12'02 4:40:48
Pennellville 3 14 43N51'37 69W57'43 4:39:51
Penobscot 5 1 44N27'52 68W42'42 4:34:51
Penobscot Indian Reservation 10 1 46N21 68W34 4:34:16
Perham 2 47 46N50'39 68W11'52 4:32:47
Perham Junction 4 1 44N55'16 70W24'39 4:41:39
Perkins 10 45 45N36'46 68W49'03 4:35:16
Perkins Town 16 44 43N20'18 70W42'18 4:42:49
Perry 2 39 46N42 68W00 4:32:00
Perry 15 44 44N58'30 67W04'35 4:28:18
Perry Cove 12 1 43N50'23 69W50'41 4:39:23
Perrys Corner 16 1 43N42'01 70W49'18 4:43:17
Peru 9 17 44N30'24 70W24'21 4:41:37
Peter Dana Point 15 1 45N12'42 67W37'50 4:30:31
Phair 2 39 46N37'37 67W57'14 4:31:49
Phillips 4 1 44N49'23 70W20'24 4:41:22
Phillips Corner 13 6 44N48'45 69W26'34 4:37:46
Phippsburg 12 1 43N49'14 69W48'55 4:39:16
Pierre 2 11 47N13'57 68W40'26 4:34:42
Pigeon Hill 15 1 44N26'39 67W53'17 4:31:33
Pike Corner 3 1 43N58'58 70W31'03 4:42:04
Pine Cliff 8 1 43N49'51 69W39'03 4:38:36
Pine Corner 15 1 44N59'44 67W17'43 4:29:11
Pine Hill 16 4 43N13'53 70W35'52 4:42:23
Pine Knoll 11 1 46N10'56 69W01'30 4:36:06
Pine Park 16 44 43N31 70W23 4:41:32
Pine Point 3 5 43N32'28 70W20'41 4:41:23
Pingree Center 11 1 45N06'44 69W26'54 4:37:48
Pishon Ferry 6 45 44N41'13 69W37'43 4:38:31

Pitmans Corner 7 1 44N18'27 69w14'39 4:36:59
Pittsfield 13 6 44N46'57 69w23'02 4:37:32
Pittston 6 6 44N11 69w42 4:38:48
Pittston Farm 13 6 45N54 69w58 4:39:52
Plaisted 2 47 47N05'52 68w35'27 4:34:22
Plantation No 33 5 45 44N58 68w18 4:33:12
Plantation No 21 15 1 45N09 67w37 4:30:28
Pleasant Beach 7 1 44N00 69w07 4:36:28
Pleasantdale 3 44 43N37'59 70w16'09 4:41:05
Pleasant Hill 3 44 43N42'51 70w16'01 4:41:04
Pleasant Island 9 45 44N59'52 70w50'14 4:43:21
Pleasant Lake 15 1 45N08 67w19 4:29:16
Pleasant Point 7 1 43N58'20 69w17'03 4:37:08
Pleasant Point 15 44 44N57'26 67w02'34 4:28:10
Pleasant Point Indian Res 15 44 44N58 67w05 4:28:20
Pleasant Pond 13 1 45N15'24 69w56'32 4:39:46
Pleasant Ridge Plantation 13 38 45N05 69w59 4:39:56
Pleasant Vale Corner 10 6 44N55'43 69w18'14 4:37:13
Pleasantville 7 7 44N07 69w15 4:37:00
Plourde Mill 2 11 47N09'56 68w37'00 4:34:28
Plummer Corner 13 6 44N46'49 69w17'17 4:37:09
Plummer Island 3 5 43N35 70w21 4:41:24
Plummer Landing 3 3 44N03'34 70w41'01 4:42:44
Plummer Mill 1 8 43N59'01 70w06'05 4:40:24
Plymouth 10 1 44N46'02 69w12'39 4:36:51
Poland 1 44 44N03'38 70w23'39 4:41:35
Polands Corner 14 36 44N28'18 69w15'36 4:37:02
Poland Spring 1 1 44N01'40 70w21'36 4:41:26
Ponce Landing 3 44 43N41'22 70w10'07 4:40:40
Pond Cove 3 44 43N35'47 70w13'45 4:40:55
Pools Landing 8 27 43N56'28 69w35'25 4:38:22
Poors Mill 14 36 44N25'41 69w06'03 4:36:24
Popeville 3 31 43N47'04 70w25'11 4:41:41
Popham Beach 12 1 43N45'07 69w47'06 4:39:08
Poplar Ripps 13 1 45N41'56 69w52'14 4:39:29
Portage 2 47 46N45'47 68w28'35 4:33:54
Port Clyde 7 1 43N55'38 69w15'12 4:37:01
Porter 9 2 43N47'45 70w55'59 4:43:44
Porterfield 9 2 43N52'34 70w54'48 4:43:39
Porter Landing 3 8 43N50'40 70w06'00 4:40:24
Portland 3 44 43N39'41 70w15'21 4:41:01
Powers Corner 2 18 46N40'24 67w50'49 4:31:23
Pownal Center 3 1 43N53'32 70w11'09 4:40:45
Prairie 11 1 45N24'31 69w03'52 4:36:15
Pratt Corner 9 45 44N09'30 70w26'27 4:41:46
Preble Corner 10 40 45N02'44 69w12'51 4:36:51
Prentiss 10 1 45N29'30 68w04'56 4:32:20
Prentiss Plantation 10 1 45N30 68w07 4:32:28
Presque Isle 2 21 46N40'52 68w00'59 4:32:04
Presque Isle Junction 2 39 46N42'30 68w01'40 4:32:07
Pretty Marsh 5 1 44N20'25 68w23'59 4:33:36
Pride 2 47 46N21'02 68w16'23 4:33:06
Prides Corner 3 44 43N42'49 70w20'03 4:41:20
Princeton 15 1 45N13'24 67w34'22 4:30:17
Pripet 14 1 44N22'07 68w52'14 4:35:29
Proctors Corner 7 1 44N18'12 69w17'21 4:37:09
Promenade Mall 1 14 44N06 70w12 4:40:48
Promised Land 1 6 44N04'04 70w26'21 4:41:45
Prospect 14 4 44N33'11 68w51'55 4:35:28
Prospect Ferry 14 1 44N34'01 68w48'21 4:35:13
Prospect Harbor 5 1 44N24'32 68w01'36 4:32:06
Prouts Neck 3 5 43N32'00 70w18'54 4:41:16
Pulpit Harbor 7 1 44N09'31 68w53'03 4:35:32
Pumpkin Valley 3 1 44N03 70w43 4:42:52
Purgatory 6 6 44N12'56 69w56'04 4:39:44
Quimby 2 47 46N57'44 68w36'31 4:34:26
Quoddy 15 44 44N55'46 67w01'51 4:28:07
Rand Landing 2 1 46N34'42 68w41'22 4:34:45
Randolph 6 6 44N13'49 69w46'02 4:39:04
Rands 2 39 46N43'10 68w02'04 4:32:08
Rangeley 4 3 44N57'59 70w38'36 4:42:34
Rankins Mill 9 2 43N52'45 70w46'20 4:43:05
Ray Corner 14 1 44N30'44 69w10'58 4:36:44
Raymond 3 1 43N54'05 70w28'15 4:41:53
Rayville 3 1 44N06'11 70w33'15 4:42:13
Razorville 7 1 44N16'35 69w23'51 4:37:35
Reach 5 1 44N14'57 68w37'27 4:34:30
Readfield 6 31 44N23'16 69w58'02 4:39:52
Readfield Depot 6 31 44N22'45 69w56'25 4:39:46
Redbank Village 3 44 43N38 70w16 4:41:04
Red Beach 15 47 45N07'13 67w08'50 4:28:35
Red Beach Landing 15 1 45N07'56 67w41'47 4:30:47
Redding 9 1 44N24'40 70w30'40 4:42:03
Redington 4 1 44N59'04 70w26'09 4:41:45
Red Rock Corner 5 2 44N24'20 68w20'45 4:33:23
Reed 2 2 45N43'25 68w08'34 4:32:34
Reeds 4 1 44N53'12 70w24'39 4:41:39
Remick Corners 16 4 43N06'07 70w44'37 4:42:58
Reynolds Corner 14 1 44N39'35 69w21'38 4:37:27
Rice Corner 13 1 44N55'29 69w45'07 4:39:00
Richmond 12 8 44N05'14 69w47'58 4:39:12
Richmond Corner 12 31 44N06'12 69w53'28 4:39:34
Richmond Mill 6 46 44N23'27 70w04'11 4:40:17
Richville 3 1 43N47'07 70w33'58 4:42:16
Ridge 15 42 44N50'27 67w00'57 4:28:04
Ridlonville 9 44 44N33'19 70w32'24 4:42:10
Riley 4 44 44N30'18 70w14'50 4:40:59
Ring Hill 6 6 44N08'20 69w53'47 4:39:35
Ripley 13 40 44N59'28 69w22'20 4:37:29
Ripley 15 35 44N31'17 67w47'51 4:31:11
Rivers End 15 1 44N48'38 67w38'47 4:30:35
Riverside 6 35 44N23'53 69w42'37 4:38:50
Riverton 3 44 43N41'58 70w19'00 4:41:16
Riverview 2 39 46N42 68w00 4:32:00
Robbinston 15 1 45N04'41 67w06'36 4:28:26
Roberts 2 39 46N47'20 67w57'31 4:31:50
Roberts Corner 16 6 43N36'54 70w31'36 4:42:06
Robinhood 12 1 43N51'11 69w44'15 4:38:57
Robinson 2 11 46N31 67w52 4:31:28
Robinson Corner 1 14 44N04'33 70w06'56 4:40:28
Robinsons 2 47 46N28'24 67w50'27 4:31:22
Robyville 10 45 44N56'27 68w58'12 4:35:53
Rockland 7 7 44N06'13 69w06'34 4:36:26
Rockport 7 44 44N11'04 69w04'36 4:36:18
Rockville 7 7 44N09'17 69w07'01 4:36:28
Rockwood 13 1 45N40'40 69w44'29 4:38:58
Rogers Corners 14 1 44N40 69w14 4:36:56
Rollins Mill 10 1 45N03'07 69w01'49 4:36:07
Rollins Mills 10 1 44N43'46 69w08'46 4:36:35
Rome 6 1 44N35'06 69w52'11 4:39:29
Rome Corner 6 35 44N34'20 69w54'14 4:39:37
Roque Bluffs 15 1 44N36'46 67w28'49 4:29:55
Rosemary 16 4 43N09'28 70w47'23 4:43:10
Rosemont 3 44 43N40'15 70w18'05 4:41:12
Ross Corner 16 1 43N35'08 70w48'06 4:43:12
Round Mountain 2 1 46N35'40 68w47'42 4:35:11
Round Pond 8 1 43N56'52 69w27'42 4:37:51
Rowe Corner 1 13 44N03'12 70w13'38 4:40:55
Rowe Corner 10 6 44N51'37 69w17'08 4:37:09
Roxbury 9 45 44N40'11 70w35'38 4:42:23
Royal Corner 1 13 44N01'07 70w14'22 4:40:57
Royal Junction 3 44 43N47'58 70w13'21 4:40:53
Rumford 9 44 44N33'13 70w33'05 4:42:12
Rumford Center 9 44 44N30'47 70w37'09 4:42:29
Rumford Corner 9 44 44N29'41 70w40'25 4:42:42
Rumford Junction 1 13 44N03'15 70w15'01 4:41:00
Rumford Point 9 44 44N30'02 70w40'18 4:42:41
Russell Crossing 2 1 46N39'21 68w44'00 4:34:56
Sabattus 1 45 44N07'11 70w06'29 4:40:26
Sabbathday Lake 3 1 44N02 70w22 4:41:28
Sabino 12 1 43N51'17 69w51'49 4:39:27
Saco 16 13 43N30'03 70w26'36 4:41:46
Sagamore Village 3 44 43N40'37 70w19'18 4:41:17
Saint Agatha 2 1 47N14'35 68w18'51 4:33:15
Saint Albans 13 1 44N54'36 69w24'38 4:37:39
Saint Croix Junction 15 47 45N08'56 67w17'38 4:29:11
Saint David 2 11 47N20'22 68w13'55 4:32:56
Saint Francis 2 11 47N10'16 68w53'25 4:35:34
Saint Francis College 16 16 43N29 70w27 4:41:48
Saint George 7 1 44N00'59 69w11'58 4:36:48
Saint John 2 1 47N12'30 68w48'28 4:35:14
Saint John Plantation 2 1 47N13 68w46 4:35:04
Saint Josephs College 3 31 43N50 70w26 4:41:44
Salem 4 1 44N54'02 70w16'43 4:41:07
Salmon Falls 15 47 45N10 67w16 4:29:04
Salmon Falls 16 6 43N35'46 70w33'15 4:42:13
Salsbury Cove 5 1 44N25'50 68w17'03 4:33:08
Sanborn Corner 13 1 44N52'43 69w20'05 4:37:20
Sanderson Corners 6 44 44N25'44 70w03'11 4:40:13
Sandhill Corner 8 1 44N18'35 69w27'31 4:37:50
Sandy Beach 10 14 44N55'17 68w48'25 4:35:14
Sandy Brook 16 44 43N32'50 70w29'19 4:41:57
Sandy Creek 3 1 44N01'18 70w42'30 4:42:50
Sandy Point 14 1 44N30'53 68w48'48 4:35:15
Sandy River 13 4 44N43'34 69w53'10 4:39:33
Sandy River Beach 15 1 44N32 67w37 4:30:28
Sandy River Plantation 4 1 44N55 70w33 4:42:12
Sanford 16 14 43N26'21 70w46'29 4:43:06
Sangerville 11 22 45N09'53 69w21'25 4:37:26
Saponac 10 1 45N10'15 68w19'07 4:33:16
Sargentville 5 1 44N18'05 68w40'23 4:34:42
Saunders 2 39 46N42 68w00 4:32:00
Sawpit Corner 7 1 44N18'26 69w18'03 4:37:12
Sawyer Corner 2 39 46N46'05 67w56'27 4:31:46
Saywards Corner 16 33 43N21'44 70w40'09 4:42:41
Scarborough 3 5 43N34'41 70w19'20 4:41:17
Schoodic 5 33 44N33'47 68w08'42 4:32:35
Schoodic 11 1 45N26'08 68w57'34 4:35:50
Scituate 16 4 43N10'06 70w40'43 4:42:43
Scotland 3 44 43N47'26 70w21'22 4:41:25
Scotland 16 4 43N09'43 70w42'25 4:42:50
Scott 2 39 46N42 68w00 4:32:00
Scribners Mill 3 1 44N05'09 70w36'24 4:42:26
Seabury 16 4 43N07'24 70w39'06 4:42:36
Sealand 15 1 44N30'27 67w32'46 4:30:11
Seal Cove 5 1 44N17'09 68w23'57 4:33:36
Seal Harbor 5 1 44N18'11 68w14'27 4:32:58
Searsmont 14 1 44N21'42 69w11'44 4:36:47
Searsport 14 45 44N27'30 68w55'29 4:35:42
Seavey Island 16 4 43N04'51 70w44'06 4:42:56
Seaveys Corner 6 4 44N31'29 70w02'03 4:40:08
Seawall 5 1 44N15'10 68w17'44 4:33:11
Seaward Mills 6 45 44N24'09 69w38'13 4:38:33
Sebago Center 3 34 43N53'31 70w41'56 4:42:48
Sebago Lake 3 35 43N45'39 70w31'34 4:42:06
Sebasco 12 1 43N46'54 69w52'06 4:39:28
Sebasco Estates 12 1 43N46'00 69w51'36 4:39:26
Sebec 11 22 45N16'17 69w07'02 4:36:28
Sebec Corners 11 34 45N13'47 69w06'08 4:36:25
Sebec Lake 11 1 45N17'59 69w20'20 4:37:21
Seboeis 10 1 45N21'47 68w42'42 4:34:51
Seboomook 13 1 45N52'50 69w43'32 4:38:54
Sedgwick 5 1 44N18'13 68w37'00 4:34:28
Selden 2 1 45N46'21 67w54'27 4:31:38
Sennetts Corner 6 1 44N29'18 69w26'32 4:37:46
Shady Nook 16 1 43N36'48 70w55'33 4:43:42
Shaker Village 3 1 43N59'12 70w22'14 4:41:29
Shapleigh 16 1 43N32'26 70w50'55 4:43:24
Sharp 2 47 46N17'12 67w50'34 4:31:22
Shaw Mills 3 1 43N44'25 70w31'20 4:42:05
Shawmut 13 32 44N37'40 69w35'13 4:38:21
Sheepscot 8 35 44N02'58 69w36'24 4:38:26
Shepherds Hill 16 4 43N05'54 70w44'22 4:42:57
Sheridan 2 47 46N39'26 68w24'20 4:33:37
Sherman 2 47 45N52'16 68w25'06 4:33:40
Sherman Mills 2 47 45N52'23 68w23'07 4:33:32
Shermans Corner 14 36 44N27'29 69w00'25 4:36:02
Shermans Mill 7 1 44N16'46 69w14'07 4:36:56
Sherman Station 10 47 45N53'57 68w25'48 4:33:43
Sherwood Acres 3 44 43N38 70w16 4:41:04
Shiloh 1 8 43N58'34 70w02'49 4:40:11
Shin Pond 10 1 46N06'19 68w33'26 4:34:14
Shirley 11 19 45N22 69w37 4:38:28
Shirley Mills 11 19 45N21'56 69w37'07 4:38:28
Shore Acres 3 44 43N38 70w16 4:41:04
Shorey 2 47 46N13'37 68w09'00 4:32:36
Shy Corner 1 44 44N27'46 70w10'46 4:40:43
Siberia 10 47 45N52'33 68w27'50 4:33:51
Sibley Corner 14 9 44N30'20 69w21'18 4:37:25
Sidney 6 35 44N24'47 69w43'46 4:38:55
Silver Ridge 2 47 45N48'23 68w19'31 4:33:18
Silvers Mills 10 40 45N05'06 69w14'42 4:36:59
Simonton Corners 7 1 44N11'45 69w06'14 4:36:25
Simpsons Corner 14 36 44N25'03 69w02'35 4:36:10
Sinclair 2 1 47N10'00 68w16'12 4:33:05
Six Mile Falls 10 14 44N51'33 68w49'43 4:35:19
Skerry 2 1 46N41'51 68w29'05 4:33:56
Skillings Corner 1 13 44N11'56 70w16'26 4:41:06
Skinner 4 4 45N31'41 70w35'45 4:42:23
Skowhegan 13 6 44N45'54 69w43'11 4:38:53
Slab City 9 1 44N12'40 70w52'09 4:43:29
Slab City 14 1 44N18'14 69w03'22 4:36:13
Small Point 12 1 43N44'17 69w50'27 4:39:22
Small Point Beach 12 1 43N43'15 69w50'14 4:39:21
Smarts Corner 14 1 44N40'34 69w17'40 4:37:11
Smith Crossing 9 44 44N32'22 70w31'26 4:42:06
Smithfield 13 1 44N37'49 69w49'48 4:39:19
Smith Landing 15 1 44N48'06 67w36'03 4:30:24
Smiths Mills 3 1 43N46 70w32 4:42:08
Smithton 14 1 44N28'39 69w20'07 4:37:20
Smithville 15 1 44N32'13 67w57'28 4:31:50
Smyrna Center 2 47 46N09'36 68w06'07 4:32:24
Smyrna Mills 2 47 46N07'46 68w09'53 4:32:40
Snow Corner 10 14 44N49'29 68w53'29 4:35:34
Snow Settlement 2 47 46N24'44 67w48'42 4:31:15
Sodom 3 8 43N49'23 70w09'39 4:40:39
Sodom 9 4 44N11'07 70w38'01 4:42:32
Soldier Pond 2 11 47N09'22 68w34'35 4:34:18
Solon 13 23 44N56'58 69w51'32 4:39:26
Somers Corner 2 11 46N52'36 67w55'00 4:31:40
Somerset Junction 13 1 45N36'26 69w47'53 4:39:12
Somerville 8 1 44N18'33 69w29'22 4:37:57
Somerville Plantation 8 1 44N18 69w28 4:37:52
Somesville (Mount Desert PO) 5 2 44N21'44 68w20'05 4:33:20
Songo Lock 3 1 43N55'57 70w34'14 4:42:17
Sorrento 5 1 44N28'24 68w10'40 4:32:43
Soule Mill 4 1 44N56'36 70w13'38 4:40:55
Sound 5 2 44N22 68w20 4:33:20
South Acton 16 1 43N30'18 70w54'13 4:43:37
South Addison 15 35 44N30'48 67w43'02 4:30:52
South Albion 6 1 44N30'10 69w29'10 4:37:57

South Andover 9 1 44N35'38 70W44'14 4:42:57
South Arm 9 1 44N45'19 70W50'46 4:43:23
South Bancroft 2 4 45N43'15 67W59'09 4:31:57
South Berwick 16 44 43N14'04 70W48'36 4:43:14
South Blue Hill 5 3 44N21'14 68W32'57 4:34:12
South Brewer 10 14 44N46'13 68W46'50 4:35:07
South Bridgton 3 3 43N59'29 70W42'31 4:42:50
South Bristol 8 1 43N51'50 69W33'42 4:38:15
South Brooksville 5 1 44N20'30 68W44'23 4:34:58
South Buxton 3 44 43N37'14 70W28'45 4:41:55
South Casco 3 1 43N54'53 70W31'06 4:42:04
South China 6 1 44N23'44 69W34'18 4:38:17
South Corinth 10 45 44N58'08 68W58'28 4:35:54
South Cushing 7 1 43N59'40 69W16'52 4:37:07
South Deer Island 5 1 44N11'38 68W39'47 4:34:39
South Dover 11 34 45N08'36 69W08'18 4:36:33
South Dresden 8 8 44N02'57 69W46'21 4:39:05
South Durham 1 8 43N56'31 70W04'29 4:40:18
South Effingham 16 1 43N42'07 70W58'56 4:43:56
South Eliot 16 4 43N06'29 70W46'41 4:43:07
South Etna 10 45 44N49 69W07 4:36:28
South Exeter 10 6 44N56'38 69W08'20 4:36:33
South Freeport 3 8 43N49'11 70W06'36 4:40:26
South Gardiner 6 6 44N10'48 69W45'26 4:39:02
South Gorham 3 44 43N38'28 70W25'14 4:41:41
South Gouldsboro 5 1 44N25'47 68W06'29 4:32:26
South Gray 3 1 43N50'55 70W19'20 4:41:17
South Hancock 5 32 44N30'02 68W15'20 4:33:01
South Harpswell 3 1 43N44'30 70W00'54 4:40:04
South Hiram 9 2 43N48'46 70W52'41 4:43:31
South Hollis 16 6 43N34'11 70W38'00 4:42:32
South Hope 7 1 44N12'52 69W11'32 4:36:46
South Jefferson 8 35 44N09'50 69W32'51 4:38:11
South Lagrange 10 47 45N06'58 68W48'56 4:35:16
South Lebanon 16 45 43N20'15 70W56'34 4:43:46
South Leeds 1 46 44N15'12 70W07'53 4:40:32
South Levant 10 45 44N51'27 69W00'40 4:36:03
South Lewiston 1 14 44N03'56 70W08'35 4:40:34
South Liberty 14 36 44N19'24 69W21'34 4:37:26
South Limington 16 34 43N42'31 70W42'00 4:42:48
South Lincoln 10 6 45N20'04 68W34'56 4:34:20
South Livermore 1 44 44N22'06 70W12'20 4:40:49
South Lubec 15 42 44N49'27 66W59'36 4:27:58
South Monmouth 6 31 44N10'54 69W59'35 4:39:58
South Montville 14 36 44N22'28 69W16'03 4:37:04
South Naples 3 1 43N55'39 70W36'51 4:42:27
South Newburgh 10 1 44N41'23 69W00'44 4:36:03
South Newcastle 8 27 44N00'11 69W36'46 4:38:27
South Orland 5 44 44N30'24 68W45'34 4:35:02
South Orrington 10 4 44N41'36 68W49'04 4:35:16
South Paris 9 30 44N13'25 70W30'50 4:42:03
South Parsonsfield 16 1 43N41'45 70W54'01 4:43:36
South Penobscot 5 1 44N27'03 68W42'11 4:34:49
South Poland 1 1 44N01'22 70W21'55 4:41:28
Southport 8 9 43N50'27 69W39'33 4:38:38
South Portland 3 44 43N38'29 70W14'29 4:40:58
South Portland Gardens 3 44 43N38'20 70W18'57 4:41:16
South Portland Heights 3 44 43N38 70W16 4:41:04
South Princeton 15 1 45N08'58 67W30'03 4:30:00
South Rangeley 4 45 44N56'15 70W45'00 4:43:00
South Robbinston 15 44 45N03'26 67W07'14 4:28:29
South Rumford 9 44 44N31'33 70W32'05 4:42:08
South Sanford 16 14 43N24'40 70W44'35 4:42:58
South Sebec 11 34 45N12'29 69W05'03 4:36:20
South Side 16 4 43N08'04 70W40'50 4:42:43
South Solon 13 1 44N54'47 69W46'44 4:39:07
South Springfield 10 1 45N21'58 68W05'47 4:32:23
South Standish 3 1 43N40 70W36 4:42:24
South Strong 4 1 44N46'01 70W12'36 4:40:50
South Surry 5 32 44N24'45 68W27'46 4:33:51
South Thomaston 7 44 44N03'05 69W07'42 4:36:31
South Trescott 15 42 44N46'09 67W04'29 4:28:18
South Turner 1 13 44N12'45 70W14'09 4:40:57
South Union 7 7 44N11'49 69W15'51 4:37:03
South Vassalboro 6 45 44N23'06 69W36'56 4:38:28
South Waldoboro 8 26 44N02'29 69W19'49 4:37:19
South Warren 7 7 44N04'32 69W13'24 4:36:54
South Waterford 9 4 44N09'59 70W43'02 4:42:52
South West Bend 1 1 43N58'50 70W07'34 4:40:30
Southwest Harbor 5 1 44N16'47 68W19'32 4:33:18
South Windham 3 31 43N44'10 70W25'27 4:41:42
South Windsor 6 1 44N16'45 69W35'57 4:38:24
South Woodstock 9 44 44N21'17 70W33'28 4:42:14
South Woodville 10 1 45N29'05 68W29'00 4:33:56
Spang Mills 16 1 43N28'44 70W38'09 4:42:33
Spaulding 2 47 46N52'41 68W14'26 4:32:58
Spears Corner 6 6 44N12'16 69W53'02 4:39:32
Split Hill 15 42 44N49'37 67W02'36 4:28:10
Spooners Mill 10 40 45N00'27 69W16'03 4:37:04
Sprague City 16 1 43N37'34 70W50'24 4:43:22
Sprague Corner 8 26 44N04'06 69W26'30 4:37:46
Sprague Mill 1 45 44N11'38 70W06'58 4:40:28
Spragues Mill 10 6 44N54'43 69W14'56 4:37:00
Spragueville 2 39 46N37'38 68W00'47 4:32:03
Springfield 10 1 45N23'46 68W08'10 4:32:33
Spring Lake 13 1 45N13'48 70W17'06 4:41:08
Spring Lake Landing 13 1 45N15'03 70W13'25 4:40:54
Springvale 16 14 43N28'00 70W47'39 4:43:11
Spruce Head 7 1 44N00'41 69W08'00 4:36:32
Spruce Point 8 1 43N51 69W38 4:38:32
Spruce Shores 8 1 43N49'41 69W35'46 4:38:23
Spurrs Corner 3 1 44N03'23 70W33'24 4:42:14
Squa Pan 2 47 46N33'47 68W22'43 4:33:31
Squirrel Island 8 1 43N48 69W38 4:38:32
Stacyville 10 47 45N51'49 68W30'21 4:34:01
Standish 3 1 43N44'09 70W33'09 4:42:13
Stanwood Park 3 44 43N37'11 70W16'12 4:41:05
Starbird Corner 12 31 44N05'02 69W59'03 4:39:56
Starbirds 11 34 45N08'09 69W14'05 4:36:56
Starboard 15 41 44N36'39 67W23'50 4:29:35
Starks 13 1 44N43'50 69W58'00 4:39:52
State Road 2 39 46N43'52 68W09'10 4:32:37
Steadman Landing 11 1 45N15'34 69W12'19 4:36:49
Stebbins 2 18 46N46 67W50 4:31:20
Steep Falls 3 34 43N47'38 70W39'11 4:42:37
Steep Landing 5 45 44N47'17 68W10'03 4:32:40
Stephensons Landing 11 47 45N42'03 68W58'45 4:35:55
Stetson 10 1 44N53'30 69W08'36 4:36:34
Steuben 15 1 44N30'38 67W57'57 4:31:52
Stevens Corner 14 1 44N16'50 69W02'46 4:36:11
Stevens Corner 16 1 43N39'26 70W58'03 4:43:52
Stevens Mill 1 13 44N05'16 70W15'45 4:41:03
Stevensville 2 18 46N47'46 67W51'54 4:31:28
Stickney Corner 7 1 44N14'43 69W22'57 4:37:32
Stillwater 10 6 44N54'30 68W41'13 4:34:45
Stillwater Avenue 10 14 44N50'26 68W44'42 4:34:59
Stockholm 2 11 47N02'32 68W08'24 4:32:34
Stockton Springs 14 1 44N29'22 68W51'27 4:35:26
Stoneham 9 1 44N16 70W51 4:43:24
Stones Corner 4 44 44N30'09 70W10'44 4:40:43
Stonington 5 1 44N09'22 68W40'02 4:34:40
Stores Corner 10 45 45N07'53 68W53'29 4:35:34
Stover Corner 5 1 44N24'19 68W44'48 4:34:59
Stovers Corner 7 36 44N19'48 69W15'42 4:37:03
Stow 9 1 44N09'38 70W59'08 4:43:57
Stratton 4 9 45N08'28 70W26'28 4:41:46
Stricklands 1 46 44N22'24 70W08'36 4:40:34
Strong 4 1 44N48'27 70W13'17 4:40:53
Stronghold 13 1 44N55'00 69W28'16 4:37:53
Stroudwater 3 44 43N39'22 70W18'55 4:41:16
Stubbs Corner 10 6 44N57'51 69W10'55 4:36:44
Sturtevant Hill 6 6 44N20'22 69W59'30 4:39:58
Suckerville 3 1 43N55'34 70W23'39 4:41:35
Sugar Hill 2 47 46N26'09 67W48'10 4:31:13
Sullivan 5 33 44N31'13 68W11'50 4:32:47
Summer Harbor 5 1 44N24'56 68W06'23 4:32:26
Summerhaven 6 35 44N23'24 69W48'41 4:39:15
Sumner 9 32 44N23'31 70W26'20 4:41:45
Sunset 5 1 44N12'21 68W42'19 4:34:49
Sunset Landing 3 1 43N43'36 70W08'21 4:40:33
Sunset Park 3 44 43N37'02 70W18'48 4:41:15
Sunshine 5 1 44N11'50 68W34'54 4:34:20
Surfside 16 44 43N31'44 70W21'47 4:41:27
Surry 5 32 44N29'45 68W30'08 4:34:01
Sutton Island 5 1 44N18 68W17 4:33:08
Swans Island 5 1 44N08'42 68W27'08 4:33:49
Swanville 14 1 44N31'16 68W59'54 4:36:00
Sweden 2 10 46N56'30 68W08'24 4:32:34
Sweden 9 1 44N08'00 70W49'23 4:43:18
Tacoma 6 6 44N11'32 69W58'11 4:39:53
Tainter Corner 4 17 44N35'15 70W21'57 4:41:28
Tallwood 6 31 44N20'36 69W57'20 4:39:49
Talmadge 15 1 45N20 67W44 4:30:56
Tarratine 13 1 45N37'01 69W50'56 4:39:24
Tatnic 16 44 43N16'37 70W41'04 4:42:44
Tattle Corner 16 16 43N28'21 70W24'53 4:41:40
Tea Kettle Corner 16 16 43N26'34 70W26'29 4:41:46
Temple 4 1 44N41'06 70W13'37 4:40:54
Temple Heights 14 36 44N20'43 68W57'03 4:35:48
Temple Intervale 4 1 44N42'25 70W15'29 4:41:02
Tenants Harbor 7 1 43N58'02 69W12'31 4:36:50
Ten Degree 4 45 44N47'34 70W42'38 4:42:51
The Crossing 11 1 46N08'08 68W55'06 4:35:40
The Forks 13 1 45N20'10 69W58'04 4:39:52
The Highlands 11 19 45N28'52 69W35'06 4:38:20
The Landing 4 1 45N04'25 70W35'18 4:42:21
The Ledges 3 8 43N48 70W12 4:40:48
The Pines 15 1 45N11'39 67W59'34 4:31:58
The Ridge 3 1 44N03 70W43 4:42:52
Thomaston 7 7 44N04'44 69W10'56 4:36:44
Thompson 13 45 44N51'24 69W26'16 4:37:45
Thompson Corner 13 45 44N51'18 69W28'30 4:37:54
Thompson's Point 3 1 43N58 70W37 4:42:28
Thorndike 14 1 44N34'41 69W16'35 4:37:06
Thorndike Center 14 1 44N35 69W17 4:37:08
Thornton Heights 3 44 43N37'18 70W18'20 4:41:13
Three Streams 13 4 45N30'37 70W14'45 4:40:59
Thurstons Corner 14 36 44N28'01 69W20'18 4:37:21
Tibbettstown 15 46 44N39 67W44 4:30:56
Tilton Corner 13 1 44N47'32 69W29'32 4:37:58
Timoney 2 47 46N07'13 68W05'50 4:32:23
Tobeys Corner 16 4 43N07'06 70W47'33 4:43:10
Togus 6 6 44N16'28 69W42'13 4:38:49
Tomah 15 1 45N32'47 67W39'01 4:30:36
Topsfield 15 1 45N25'08 67W44'10 4:30:57
Topsham 12 1 43N55'39 69W58'35 4:39:54
Tory Hill 16 6 43N36'19 70W32'12 4:42:09
Toulouse Corner 13 8 44N36'25 69W41'49 4:38:47
Town Farm Hill 3 1 44N07 70W41 4:42:44
Town Hill 5 2 44N23'55 68W20'03 4:33:20
Townhouse Corner 14 1 44N18'46 69W05'18 4:36:21
Town House Corners 16 44 43N22'52 70W28'40 4:41:55
Town Landing 3 5 43N32'41 70W20'01 4:41:20
Tracy Corners 15 35 44N37 67W45 4:31:00
Trafton 2 47 46N38 68W24 4:33:36
Trainor Corner 8 6 44N13'11 69W39'32 4:38:38
Trap Corner 9 30 44N19'53 70W33'21 4:42:13
Trefethen 3 44 43N40'07 70W11'28 4:40:46
Tremont 5 1 44N16 68W23 4:33:32
Trenton 5 1 44N26'20 68W22'14 4:33:29
Trevett 8 15 43N53'05 69W40'24 4:38:42
Troutdale 13 45 45N17'34 69W50'11 4:39:21
Troy 14 1 44N39'53 69W14'29 4:36:58
Troy Center 14 1 44N40'57 69W15'26 4:37:02
Tunk Lake 5 33 44N32'56 68W06'51 4:32:27
Turbats Creek 16 44 43N21'16 70W27'02 4:41:48
Turner 1 1 44N15'23 70W15'24 4:41:02
Turner Center 1 1 44N16'17 70W13'10 4:40:53
Turners Corner 8 26 44N01'53 69W25'03 4:37:40
Twelve Corners 6 44 44N27'46 70W06'58 4:40:28
Twin Brook 10 1 45N01'32 69W06'22 4:36:25
Twitchell Corner 14 1 44N41'28 69W22'02 4:37:28
Two Lights 3 44 43N38 70W16 4:41:04
Two Trails 3 1 43N43'55 70W35'25 4:42:22
Tyler Corner 6 6 44N35'34 69W45'36 4:39:02
Tylers Corner 16 6 43N38'24 70W36'33 4:42:26
Union 7 7 44N12'41 69W16'29 4:37:06
Union Falls 16 45 43N34'15 70W33'37 4:42:14
Unionville 15 35 44N34'44 67W59'27 4:31:58
Unity 14 45 44N36'40 69W20'06 4:37:20
Unity College 14 45 44N40 69W14 4:36:56
Unity Plantation 6 6 44N32 69W43 4:38:52
Upper Abbot 11 1 45N12'18 69W27'51 4:37:51
Upper Dam 9 45 44N53'02 70W51'44 4:43:27
Upper Frenchville 2 11 47N16'48 68W25'30 4:33:42
Upper Gloucester 3 1 43N59'21 70W17'42 4:41:11
Upper Landing 16 33 43N19'46 70W34'02 4:42:16
Upper Shirley Corner 11 19 45N22'31 69W35'45 4:38:23
Upton 9 1 44N41'39 71W00'40 4:44:03
Van Buren 2 11 47N09'26 67W56'09 4:31:45
Vanceboro 15 43 45N33'48 67W25'49 4:29:43
Varney Corner 12 31 44N06'09 69W58'12 4:39:53
Varney Crossing 16 44 43N17'37 70W44'38 4:42:59
Vassalboro 6 45 44N27'33 69W40'41 4:38:43
Veazie 10 14 44N50'19 68W42'21 4:34:49
Verona 5 33 44N33'55 68W47'27 4:35:10
Verona Park 5 44 44N33'09 68W48'06 4:35:12
Vickerys Corner 14 1 44N24'06 69W06'48 4:36:27
Vienna 6 1 44N32'00 69W59'07 4:39:56
Viking Village 9 37 44N25 70W48 4:43:12
Villa Vaughn 10 14 44N53'50 68W45'45 4:35:03
Vinalhaven 7 1 44N02'53 68W49'56 4:35:20
Violette 2 11 47N09 67W56 4:31:44
Violette Settlement 2 11 47N13'10 68W38'59 4:34:36
Virginia 9 44 44N31'50 70W32'47 4:42:11
Wade 2 1 46N48 68W13 4:32:52
Waite 15 1 45N19'32 67W41'27 4:30:46
Waites Landing 3 44 43N42'22 70W13'04 4:40:52

Waldo 14 1 44N30'45 69w04'36 4:36:18
Waldoboro 8 26 44N05'43 69w22'34 4:37:30
Wales Corner 1 1 44N11'01 70w03'56 4:40:16
Walker 2 1 46N36'27 68w14'38 4:32:59
Walker Corner 14 1 44N33'58 69w13'10 4:36:53
Walker Settlement 2 45 46N01'56 68w12'41 4:32:51
Walkers Mill 9 37 44N25 70w48 4:43:12
Wallagrass 2 47 47N07'46 68w35'52 4:34:23
Walnut Hill 3 45 43N49'28 70w14'50 4:40:59
Walnut Hill 16 4 43N14'14 70w35'42 4:42:23
Walpole 8 1 43N57'21 69w33'33 4:38:14
Waltham 5 45 44N42'33 68w20'20 4:33:21
Waltons Mill 13 1 44N51'05 69w39'01 4:38:36
Wards Cove 3 1 43N49'53 70w36'28 4:42:26
Wardtown 3 8 43N52 70w06 4:40:24
Warren 7 7 44N07'13 69w14'26 4:36:58
Washburn 2 47 46N47'24 68w09'29 4:32:38
Washburn Junction 2 39 46N41'38 67w59'29 4:31:58
Washington 7 1 44N16'25 69w22'04 4:37:28
Washington Junction 5 32 44N33'12 68w22'52 4:33:31
Waterboro 16 45 43N32'08 70w42'56 4:42:52
Waterboro Center 16 45 43N35'21 70w42'37 4:42:50
Waterford 9 4 44N10'53 70w43'04 4:42:52
Waterman Beach 7 1 44N00 69w07 4:36:28
Waterville 6 14 44N33'07 69w37'56 4:38:32
Wattons Mill 7 7 44N10'23 69w14'04 4:36:56
Waukeag 5 33 44N31'24 68w14'21 4:32:57
Waverley 13 6 44N47'42 69w22'52 4:37:31
Wayne 6 46 44N20'55 70w04'00 4:40:16
Webb Hill 10 32 45N31'44 68w20'50 4:33:23
Webster 1 1 44N07 70w06 4:40:24
Webster 10 31 44N53'15 68w39'48 4:34:39
Webster Corner 1 8 44N03'36 70w05'11 4:40:21
Webster Plantation 10 1 45N28 68w09 4:32:36
Weeksboro 2 47 46N15'25 68w09'31 4:32:38
Weeks Corner 13 6 44N46'18 69w28'04 4:37:52
Weeks Mills 4 31 44N40'30 70w02'47 4:40:11
Weeks Mills 6 1 44N21'32 69w32'36 4:38:10
Welchville 9 1 44N08'01 70w27'52 4:41:51
Weld 4 1 44N41'55 70w25'19 4:41:41
Weld Corner 4 1 44N43'12 70w27'32 4:41:50
Wellington 11 1 45N02'23 69w35'52 4:38:23
Wells 16 33 43N19'19 70w34'53 4:42:20
Wells Beach 16 6 43N18'09 70w34'04 4:42:16
Wells Beach Station 16 33 43N19'26 70w35'31 4:42:22
Wells Branch 16 33 43N22'25 70w36'01 4:42:24
Wesley 15 1 44N57'08 67w39'41 4:30:39
West Appleton 7 36 44N21'04 69w15'40 4:37:03
West Athens 13 1 44N57'12 69w42'41 4:38:51
West Auburn 1 13 44N09'24 70w16'53 4:41:08
West Baldwin 3 34 43N49'59 70w46'42 4:43:07
West Bangor 10 14 44N47'42 68w50'02 4:35:20
West Bath 12 15 43N53 69w51 4:39:24
West Bethel 9 37 44N24'07 70w51'42 4:43:27
West Boothbay Harbor 8 3 43N50'56 69w38'38 4:38:35
West Bowdoin 12 31 44N02'50 70w01'31 4:40:06
West Bridgton 3 3 44N03'51 70w49'51 4:43:19
West Bristol 8 1 43N55'44 69w33'28 4:38:14
Westbrook 3 44 43N40'37 70w22'18 4:41:29
West Brooklin 5 1 44N17'31 68w36'59 4:34:28
West Brooksville 5 1 44N23'54 68w45'30 4:35:02
West Brownfield 9 1 43N55'03 70w58'45 4:43:55
West Buxton 16 1 43N40'01 70w36'13 4:42:25
West Castine 5 9 44N25'12 68w48'41 4:35:15
West Charleston 10 1 45N03'57 69w04'08 4:36:17
West Corinth 10 6 44N57'15 69w01'27 4:36:06
West Cumberland 3 44 43N48'56 70w18'53 4:41:16
West Denmark 9 2 43N59'33 70w52'16 4:43:29
West Dover 11 34 45N06'52 69w14'22 4:36:57
West Dresden 8 8 44N05'16 69w46'23 4:39:06
West Durham 1 8 43N56'57 70w08'52 4:40:35
West Ellsworth 5 32 44N33'26 68w32'49 4:34:11
West End 3 44 43N39'02 70w16'30 4:41:06
West Enfield 10 34 45N14'36 68w39'01 4:34:36
Western Landing 3 1 43N42'50 70w07'12 4:40:29
West Falmouth Corner 3 1 43N44'47 70w18'13 4:41:13
West Farmington 4 8 44N39'46 70w09'21 4:40:37
Westfield 2 47 46N34'13 67w55'23 4:31:42
West Forks 13 1 45N23'49 70w02'12 4:40:09
West Franklin 5 33 44N35'01 68w15'39 4:33:03
West Fryeburg 9 45 44N03'50 70w58'50 4:43:55
West Gardiner 6 6 44N13 69w52 4:39:28
West Georgetown 12 1 43N48'25 69w46'25 4:39:06
West Glenburn 10 45 44N52'31 68w52'47 4:35:31
West Gorham 3 44 43N41'37 70w29'33 4:41:58
West Gouldsboro 5 1 44N28'10 68w05'27 4:32:22
West Gray 3 1 43N51'33 70w22'33 4:41:30
West Hampden 10 4 44N44'57 68w55'39 4:35:43
West Harpswell 3 1 43N46'00 70w00'42 4:40:03
West Harrington 15 35 44N35'46 67w50'33 4:31:22
West Hollis 16 6 43N37'34 70w39'25 4:42:38
West Jonesport 15 1 44N31'44 67w37'18 4:30:29
West Kennebunk 16 48 43N24'31 70w34'55 4:42:20
West Lebanon 16 45 43N22'56 70w57'04 4:43:48
West Leeds 1 46 44N17'34 70w10'08 4:40:41
West Levant 10 45 44N54'09 69w00'41 4:36:03
West Lovell 9 1 44N08 70w53 4:43:32
West Lubec 15 42 44N48'53 67w04'14 4:28:17
West Mills 4 8 44N45'50 70w01'00 4:40:04
West Minot 1 34 44N10'16 70w21'59 4:41:28
West Montville 14 1 44N28'48 69w17'56 4:37:12
West Mount Vernon 6 4 44N27'11 70w00'57 4:40:04
West Newfield 16 1 43N38'38 70w55'27 4:43:42
West Old Town 10 6 44N59'05 68w46'50 4:35:07
Weston 2 1 45N43'59 67w52'43 4:31:31
West Palmyra 13 6 44N49'56 69w24'32 4:37:38
West Paris 9 30 44N19'27 70w34'28 4:42:18
West Pembroke 15 24 44N56'51 67w10'43 4:28:43
West Penobscot 5 1 44N28'27 68w46'47 4:35:07
West Peru 9 17 44N31'16 70w28'04 4:41:52
West Point 12 1 43N44'49 69w51'54 4:39:28
West Poland 1 44 44N02'08 70w26'21 4:41:45
Westport 8 27 43N53'57 69w42'32 4:38:50
Westport Island 8 15 43N56 69w42 4:38:48
West Pownal 3 1 43N54'02 70w14'15 4:40:57
West Princeton 15 1 45N11'19 67w35'24 4:30:22
West Ripley 13 1 44N59'10 69w25'31 4:37:42
West Rockport 7 1 44N10'55 69w08'09 4:36:33
West Scarborough 3 5 43N34'13 70w23'18 4:41:33
West Searsmont 14 1 44N23'59 69w14'46 4:36:59
West Sebago 3 35 43N56'55 70w44'06 4:42:56
West Seboeis 10 47 45N31'39 68w52'47 4:35:31
West Sidney 6 35 44N23'44 69w48'10 4:39:13
West Southport 8 1 43N49'23 69w40'45 4:38:43
West Stonington 5 1 44N09'59 68w41'31 4:34:46
West Sullivan 5 33 44N31'50 68w13'54 4:32:56
West Sumner 9 32 44N21'53 70w27'29 4:41:50
West Tremont 5 1 44N15'46 68w23'28 4:33:34
West Trenton 5 1 44N26'08 68w23'51 4:33:35
West Waldoboro 8 26 44N04'44 69w23'54 4:37:36
West Washington 7 1 44N15'39 69w26'29 4:37:46
West Windsor 6 1 44N20'18 69w36'24 4:38:26
West Winterport 14 4 44N37'15 68w57'11 4:35:49
Wheelock 2 1 47N13'29 68w44'38 4:34:59
Wheelock Mill 2 1 46N59'58 68w53'50 4:35:35
Whitcombs Corner 14 36 44N26'31 69w06'17 4:36:25
Whitefield 8 1 44N10'12 69w37'33 4:38:30
White Oak Corner 7 7 44N09'19 69w17'25 4:37:10
White Rock 3 44 43N45'09 70w28'06 4:41:52
White School Corner 13 6 44N48'53 69w45'51 4:39:03
Whites Corner 3 1 43N56'23 70w18'19 4:41:13
Whites Corner 14 36 44N26'49 69w18'14 4:37:13
Whiting 15 41 44N47'27 67w10'34 4:28:42
Whitlocks Mill 15 47 45N09'39 67w13'39 4:28:55
Whitney Corner 7 7 44N09'47 69w18'38 4:37:15
Whitneyville 15 45 44N43'19 67w31'26 4:30:06
Wildes Corner 16 44 43N21'25 70w28'12 4:41:53
Wildes District 16 44 43N21'45 70w27'13 4:41:49
Wildwood 13 1 44N54'21 69w27'53 4:37:52
Wildwood Park 3 1 43N45 70w18 4:41:12
Wiley Corner 7 1 44N01 69w12 4:36:48
Willard 3 44 43N38 70w16 4:41:04
Williamsburg 11 1 45N22'48 69w06'59 4:36:28
Willimantic 11 1 45N18'24 69w24'32 4:37:38
Willis Corners 7 7 44N06'09 69w10'28 4:36:42
Willis Mill 9 1 44N18'44 70w40'46 4:42:43
Wilson Corner 5 32 44N38'40 68w33'28 4:34:14
Wilsons Mills 9 1 44N56'17 71w02'09 4:44:09
Wilton 4 6 44N35'34 70w13'43 4:40:55
Wilton Intervale 4 6 44N38'01 70w17'34 4:41:10
Windemere 14 1 44N37'53 69w19'28 4:37:18
Windham Center 3 31 43N47'22 70w24'32 4:41:38
Windham Hill 3 44 43N47'52 70w25'34 4:41:42
Windsor 6 1 44N18'38 69w34'52 4:38:19
Windsorville 6 1 44N17'58 69w33'06 4:38:12
Wings Mills 6 35 44N25'57 69w54'19 4:39:37
Winkumpaugh Corners 5 32 44N37'35 68w37'44 4:34:31
Winn 10 32 45N29'08 68w22'22 4:33:29
Winnecook 14 1 44N39'16 69w23'18 4:37:33
Winnegance 12 1 43N52'20 69w49'11 4:39:17
Winslow 6 14 44N32'49 69w37'18 4:38:29
Winslow Hill 8 26 44N05'42 69w27'39 4:37:51
Winslows Mills 8 26 44N07'13 69w24'37 4:37:38
Winter Harbor 5 1 44N23'43 68w05'01 4:32:20
Winterport 14 4 44N38'16 68w50'44 4:35:23
Winterville 2 47 46N58'13 68w34'18 4:34:17
Winthrop 6 6 44N18'18 69w58'39 4:39:55
Winthrop Center 6 6 44N18'17 69w55'19 4:39:41
Wiscasset 8 27 44N00'10 69w39'58 4:38:40
Witham Corner 13 1 44N42'48 69w56'51 4:39:47
Wonderland 5 1 44N14'00 68w19'12 4:33:17
Wonsqueak Harbor 5 1 44N23 68w03 4:32:12
Woodard 10 1 45N24'25 68w35'05 4:34:20
Woodbridge Corner 2 47 45N52'13 68w19'49 4:33:19
Woodfords 3 44 43N40'24 70w16'55 4:41:08
Woodfords Corner 3 44 43N40'13 70w17'05 4:41:08
Woodland 15 29 45N09'25 67w24'19 4:29:37
Woodland Center 2 1 46N53'07 68w08'33 4:32:34
Woodland Junction 15 29 45N10'13 67w24'26 4:29:38
Woodmans Mills 14 1 44N21'56 69w15'13 4:37:01
Woodstock 9 44 44N23 70w35 4:42:20
Woodville 10 32 45N30 68w24 4:33:52
Woolwich 12 15 43N55'07 69w48'06 4:39:12
Worthley Pond 9 17 44N28'05 70w23'20 4:41:33
Wright Corner 3 1 44N05'29 70w32'12 4:42:09
Wrightville 2 47 46N39 68w24 4:33:36
Wyman 15 1 44N30'28 67w51'35 4:31:26
Wytopitlock 2 2 45N38'26 68w04'34 4:32:18
Yagger 9 25 44N12'39 70w38'07 4:42:32
Yarmouth 3 8 43N48'02 70w11'14 4:40:45
Yarmouth Junction 3 8 43N48'49 70w11'39 4:40:47
York 16 28 43N10 70w40 4:42:40
York Beach 16 28 43N10'17 70w36'34 4:42:26
York Center 16 28 43N09 70w38 4:42:32
York Cliffs 16 28 43N11'28 70w36'12 4:42:25
York Corner 16 28 43N09'03 70w40'00 4:42:40
York Harbor 16 28 43N08'12 70w38'46 4:42:35
York Heights 16 28 43N08'55 70w38'33 4:42:34
York Landing 3 44 43N43'43 70w12'34 4:40:50
Yorks Corner 14 1 44N29'57 69w00'24 4:36:02
York Village 16 28 43N08'37 70w39'05 4:42:36
Youngs Corner 1 13 44N07'38 70w16'18 4:41:05
Youngtown 14 1 44N16'07 69w05'53 4:36:24

TIME TABLES

Daylight time was unofficially observed in the greater Baltimore area various years during the 20's and 30's. Our tables reflect this informal usage of daylight time; however, caution must be advised during his period. Some reports indicate usage was infrequent during this period and seldom reflected in official records.

MD # 1

Date	Time	Type
Before 11/18/1883		LMT
11/18/1883	12:00	EST
3/31/1918	02:00	EWT
10/27/1918	02:00	EST
3/30/1919	02:00	EWT
10/26/1919	02:00	EST
3/28/1920	02:00	EDT
10/31/1920	02:00	EST
4/30/1922	02:00	EDT
9/24/1922	02:00	EST
4/27/1924	02:00	EDT
9/28/1924	02:00	EST
4/26/1925	02:00	EDT
9/27/1925	02:00	EST
4/25/1926	02:00	EDT
9/26/1926	02:00	EST
4/27/1930	02:00	EDT
9/28/1930	02:00	EST
2/09/1942	02:00	EWT
9/30/1945	02:00	EST
4/27/1947	02:00	EDT
9/28/1947	02:00	EST
4/25/1948	02:00	EDT
9/26/1948	02:00	EST
4/24/1949	02:00	EDT
9/25/1949	02:00	EST
4/30/1950	02:00	EDT
9/24/1950	02:00	EST
4/29/1951	02:00	EDT
9/30/1951	02:00	EST
4/27/1952	02:00	EDT
9/28/1952	02:00	EST
4/26/1953	02:00	EDT
9/27/1953	02:00	EST
4/25/1954	02:00	EDT
9/26/1954	02:00	EST
4/24/1955	02:00	EDT
9/25/1955	02:00	EST
4/29/1956	02:00	EDT
9/29/1956	02:00	EST
4/28/1957	02:00	US#4

MD # 2

Date	Time	Type
Before 11/18/1883		LMT
11/18/1883	12:00	EST
3/31/1918	02:00	EWT
10/27/1918	02:00	EST
3/30/1919	02:00	EWT
10/26/1919	02:00	EST
2/09/1942	02:00	EWT
9/30/1945	02:00	EST
4/24/1955	02:00	EDT
9/25/1955	02:00	EST
4/29/1956	02:00	EDT
9/30/1956	02:00	EST
4/30/1967	02:00	US#2

MD # 3

Date	Time	Type
Before 11/18/1883		LMT
11/18/1883	12:00	EST
3/31/1918	02:00	EWT
10/27/1918	02:00	EST
3/30/1919	02:00	EWT
10/26/1919	02:00	EST
2/09/1942	02:00	EWT
9/30/1945	02:00	EST
4/27/1947	02:00	US#4

MD # 4

Date	Time	Type
Before 11/18/1883		LMT
11/18/1883	12:00	EST
3/31/1918	02:00	EWT
10/27/1918	02:00	EST
3/30/1919	02:00	EWT
10/26/1919	02:00	EST
2/09/1942	02:00	EWT
9/30/1945	02:00	EST
5/19/1947	00:00	US#4

MD # 5

Date	Time	Type
Before 11/18/1883		LMT
11/18/1883	12:00	EST
3/31/1918	02:00	EWT
10/27/1918	02:00	EST
3/30/1919	02:00	EWT
10/26/1919	02:00	EST
2/09/1942	02:00	EWT
9/30/1945	02:00	EST
5/19/1947	02:00	EDT
9/02/1947	00:00	EST
4/25/1948	02:00	US#4

MD # 6

Date	Time	Type
Before 11/18/1883		LMT
11/18/1883	12:00	EST
3/31/1918	02:00	EWT
10/27/1918	02:00	EST
3/30/1919	02:00	EWT
10/26/1919	02:00	EST
2/09/1942	02:00	EWT
9/30/1945	02:00	EST
5/18/1947	02:00	EDT
9/28/1947	02:00	EST
5/02/1948	02:00	EDT
9/26/1948	02:00	US#4

MD # 7

Date	Time	Type
Before 11/18/1883		LMT
11/18/1883	12:00	EST
3/31/1918	02:00	EWT
10/27/1918	02:00	EST
3/30/1919	02:00	EWT
10/26/1919	02:00	EST
2/09/1942	02:00	EWT
9/30/1945	02:00	EST
4/25/1948	02:00	EDT
9/26/1948	02:00	EST
4/30/1950	02:00	US#4

MD # 8

Date	Time	Type
Before 11/18/1883		LMT
11/18/1883	12:00	EST
3/31/1918	02:00	EWT
10/27/1918	02:00	EST
3/30/1919	02:00	EWT
10/26/1919	02:00	EST
2/09/1942	02:00	EWT
9/30/1945	02:00	EST
4/25/1948	02:00	US#4

MD # 9

Date	Time	Type
Before 11/18/1883		LMT
11/18/1883	12:00	EST
3/31/1918	02:00	EWT
10/27/1918	02:00	EST
3/30/1919	02:00	EWT
10/26/1919	02:00	EST
2/09/1942	02:00	EWT
9/30/1945	02:00	EST
5/18/1947	02:00	US#4

MD # 10

Date	Time	Type
Before 11/18/1883		LMT
11/18/1883	12:00	EST
3/31/1918	02:00	EWT
10/27/1918	02:00	EST
3/30/1919	02:00	EWT
10/26/1919	02:00	EST
2/09/1942	02:00	EWT
9/30/1945	02:00	EST
5/11/1947	02:00	EDT
9/29/1947	02:00	US#4

MD # 11

Date	Time	Type
Before 11/18/1883		LMT
11/18/1883	12:00	EST
3/31/1918	02:00	EWT
10/27/1918	02:00	EST
3/30/1919	02:00	EWT
10/26/1919	02:00	EST
2/09/1942	02:00	EWT
9/30/1945	02:00	EST
5/19/1947	02:00	US#4

MD # 12

Date	Time	Type
Before 11/18/1883		LMT
11/18/1883	12:00	EST
3/31/1918	02:00	EWT
10/27/1918	02:00	EST
3/30/1919	02:00	EWT
10/26/1919	02:00	EST
2/09/1942	02:00	EWT
9/30/1945	02:00	EST
5/19/1947	02:00	EDT
9/02/1947	02:00	EST
4/25/1948	02:00	EDT
9/26/1948	02:00	EST
4/30/1950	02:00	US#4

MD # 13

Date	Time	Type
Before 11/18/1883		LMT
11/18/1883	12:00	EST
3/31/1918	02:00	EWT
10/27/1918	02:00	EST
3/30/1919	02:00	EWT
10/26/1919	02:00	EST
2/09/1942	02:00	EWT
9/30/1945	02:00	EST
4/29/1951	02:00	US#4

MD # 14

Date	Time	Type
Before 11/18/1883		LMT
11/18/1883	12:00	EST
3/31/1918	02:00	EWT
10/27/1918	02:00	EST
3/30/1919	02:00	EWT
10/26/1919	02:00	EST
2/09/1942	02:00	EWT
9/30/1945	02:00	EST
4/27/1947	02:00	EDT
9/28/1947	02:00	EST
5/11/1953	02:00	US#5

MD # 15

Date	Time	Type
Before 11/18/1883		LMT
11/18/1883	12:00	EST
3/31/1918	02:00	EWT
10/27/1918	02:00	EST
3/30/1919	02:00	EWT
10/26/1919	02:00	EST
2/09/1942	02:00	EWT
9/30/1945	02:00	EST
4/30/1950	02:00	US#4

MD # 16

Date	Time	Type
Before 11/18/1883		LMT
11/18/1883	12:00	EST
3/31/1918	02:00	EWT
10/27/1918	02:00	EST
3/30/1919	02:00	EWT
10/26/1919	02:00	EST
2/09/1942	02:00	EWT
9/30/1945	02:00	EST
5/11/1947	02:00	EDT
9/28/1947	02:00	EST
5/02/1948	02:00	EDT
9/26/1948	02:00	EST
4/24/1949	02:00	EDT
9/25/1949	02:00	EST
5/04/1950	02:00	EDT
9/24/1950	02:00	EST
4/29/1951	02:00	EDT
9/30/1951	02:00	EST
4/27/1952	02:00	EDT
9/28/1952	02:00	EST
4/30/1953	02:00	EDT
9/27/1953	02:00	EST
4/25/1954	02:00	US#3

MD # 17

Date	Time	Type
Before 11/18/1883		LMT
11/18/1883	12:00	EST
3/31/1918	02:00	EWT
10/27/1918	02:00	EST
3/30/1919	02:00	EWT
10/26/1919	02:00	EST
2/09/1942	02:00	EWT
9/30/1945	02:00	EST
4/25/1954	02:00	US#4

MD # 18

Date	Time	Type
Before 11/18/1883		LMT
11/18/1883	12:00	EST
3/31/1918	02:00	EWT
10/27/1918	02:00	EST
3/30/1919	02:00	EWT
10/26/1919	02:00	EST
2/09/1942	02:00	EWT
9/30/1945	02:00	EST
4/28/1957	02:00	US#4

MD # 19

Date	Time	Type
Before 11/18/1883		LMT
11/18/1883	12:00	EST
3/31/1918	02:00	EWT
10/27/1918	02:00	EST
3/30/1919	02:00	EWT
10/26/1919	02:00	EST
2/09/1942	02:00	EWT
9/30/1945	02:00	EST
4/25/1948	02:00	EDT
9/26/1948	02:00	EST
4/30/1950	02:00	US#5

MD # 20

Date	Time	Type
Before 11/18/1883		LMT
11/18/1883	12:00	EST
3/31/1918	02:00	EWT
10/27/1918	02:00	EST
3/30/1919	02:00	EWT
10/26/1919	02:00	EST
2/09/1942	02:00	EWT
9/30/1945	02:00	EST
4/27/1947	02:00	EDT
9/28/1947	02:00	EST
4/25/1948	02:00	EDT
9/26/1948	02:00	EST
4/24/1949	02:00	EDT
9/25/1949	02:00	EST
4/30/1950	02:00	EDT
9/24/1950	02:00	EST
4/29/1951	02:00	EDT
9/30/1951	02:00	EST
4/27/1952	02:00	EDT
9/28/1952	02:00	EST
4/26/1953	02:00	EDT
9/27/1953	02:00	EST
4/25/1954	02:00	EDT
9/26/1954	02:00	EST
4/24/1955	02:00	EDT
9/25/1955	02:00	EST
4/29/1956	02:00	EDT
9/29/1956	00:00	EST
4/28/1957	02:00	US#4

MD # 21

Date	Time	Type
Before 11/18/1883		LMT
11/18/1883	12:00	EST
3/31/1918	02:00	EWT
10/27/1918	02:00	EST
3/30/1919	02:00	EWT
10/26/1919	02:00	EST
2/09/1942	02:00	EWT
9/30/1945	02:00	EST
5/11/1947	02:00	EDT
9/28/1947	02:00	US#4

MD # 22

Date	Time	Type
Before 11/18/1883		LMT
11/18/1883	12:00	EST
3/31/1918	02:00	EWT
10/27/1918	02:00	EST
3/30/1919	02:00	EWT
10/26/1919	02:00	EST
2/09/1942	02:00	EWT
9/30/1945	02:00	EST
5/11/1947	02:00	EDT
9/02/1947	02:00	EST
4/25/1948	02:00	US#4

MD # 23

Date	Time	Type
Before 11/18/1883		LMT
11/18/1883	12:00	EST
3/31/1918	02:00	EWT
10/27/1918	02:00	EST
3/30/1919	02:00	EWT
10/26/1919	02:00	EST
2/09/1942	02:00	EWT
9/30/1945	02:00	EST
4/25/1948	02:00	US#5

MD # 24

Date	Time	Type
Before 11/18/1883		LMT
11/18/1883	12:00	EST
3/31/1918	02:00	EWT
10/27/1918	02:00	EST
3/30/1919	02:00	EWT
10/26/1919	02:00	EST
2/09/1942	02:00	EWT
9/30/1945	02:00	EST
4/27/1947	02:00	US#5

MD # 25

Date	Time	Type
Before 11/18/1893		LMT
11/18/1893	12:00	EST
3/31/1918	02:00	EWT
10/27/1918	02:00	EST
3/30/1919	02:00	EWT
10/26/1919	02:00	EST
2/09/1942	02:00	EWT
9/30/1945	02:00	EST
4/28/1946	02:00	US#4

MD # 26

Date	Time	Type
Before 11/18/1883		LMT
11/18/1883	12:00	EST
3/31/1918	02:00	EWT
10/27/1918	02:00	EST
3/30/1919	02:00	EWT
10/26/1919	02:00	EST
2/09/1942	02:00	EWT
9/30/1945	02:00	EST
5/19/1947	02:00	EDT
9/02/1947	02:00	EST
4/25/1948	02:00	US#5

MD # 27

Date	Time	Type
Before 11/18/1883		LMT
11/18/1883	12:00	EST
3/31/1918	02:00	EWT
10/27/1918	02:00	EST
3/30/1919	02:00	EWT
10/26/1919	02:00	EST
2/09/1942	02:00	EWT
9/30/1945	02:00	EST
5/19/1947	02:00	EDT
9/02/1947	02:00	EST
4/25/1948	02:00	US#4

MD # 28

Date	Time	Type
Before 11/18/1883		LMT
11/18/1883	12:00	EST
3/31/1918	02:00	EWT
10/27/1918	02:00	EST
3/30/1919	02:00	EWT
10/26/1919	02:00	EST
2/09/1942	02:00	EWT
9/30/1945	02:00	EST
5/19/1947	02:00	EDT
9/02/1947	02:00	EST
4/25/1948	02:00	EDT
9/26/1948	02:00	EST
4/30/1950	02:00	US#5

COUNTIES

1 Allegany
2 Anne Arundel
3 Baltimore
4 Calvert
5 Caroline
6 Carroll
7 Cecil
8 Charles
9 Dorchester
10 Frederick
11 Garrett
12 Harford
13 Howard
14 Kent
15 Montgomery
16 Prince George's
17 Queen Anne's
18 St Mary's
19 Somerset
20 Talbot
21 Washington
22 Wicomico
23 Worcester
24 Baltimore City

Place	Zone	Latitude	Longitude	Offset
Abell 18	4	38N15'15	76w44'38	5:06:59
Aberdeen 12	8	39N30'34	76w09'52	5:04:39
Aberdeen Proving Ground 12	8	39N28	76w08	5:04:32
Abingdon 12	8	39N27'44	76w16'46	5:05:07
Accident 11	2	39N37'43	79w19'12	5:17:17
Accokeek 16	16	38N40'03	77w01'43	5:08:07
Accokeek Acres 16	16	38N40'07	76w59'37	5:07:58
Accokeek Groves 16	16	38N40	77w02	5:08:08
Acco Park 16	16	38N40	77w02	5:08:08
Acredale 16	16	39N00'10	76w56'35	5:07:46
Adamstown 10	7	39N18'39	77w28'30	5:09:54
Adelina 4	9	38N28'50	76w37'18	5:06:29
Adelphi 16	16	39N00'11	76w58'20	5:07:53
Adelphi Manor 16	16	38N59	76w58	5:07:52
Adelphi Park 16	16	38N59'11	76w58'06	5:07:52
Admiral Heights 2	20	38N59'05	76w31'08	5:06:05
Ady 12	8	39N38'19	76w19'59	5:05:20
Aero Acres 3	3	39N19'56	76w27'12	5:05:49
Agner 5	15	38N45'20	75w47'23	5:03:10
Aikin 7	25	39N34'26	76w04'05	5:04:16
Airedele 18	4	38N07'06	76w20'54	5:05:24
Airey 9	8	38N31'22	75w59'35	5:03:58
Albantown 3	3	39N38'27	76w48'33	5:07:14
Albeth Heights 13	3	39N20	76w52	5:07:28
Aldino 12	8	39N33'50	76w11'46	5:04:47
Alesia 6	8	39N40'59	76w49'45	5:07:19
Allanwood 15	16	39N06'38	77w02'12	5:08:09
Allegany 1	24	39N39	78w55	5:15:40
Allegany Grove 1	3	39N38'24	78w49'42	5:15:19
Allen 22	7	38N17'14	75w41'18	5:02:45
Allenford 13	3	39N16	76w49	5:07:16
Allens Fresh 8	6	38N24'50	76w56'27	5:07:46
Allenwood 22	7	38N22	75w36	5:02:24
Allview 13	3	39N12	76w52	5:07:28
Allview Estates 13	3	39N16	76w49	5:07:16
Alpha 13	3	39N19'16	76w55'41	5:07:43
Alpine Beach 2	20	39N09	76w33	5:06:12
Altamont 11	2	39N25'39	79w16'56	5:17:08
Alta Vista 15	16	39N00'32	77w06'32	5:08:26
Alta Vista Gardens 15	16	39N01	77w08	5:08:32
Alta Vista Terrace 15	16	39N00'19	77w07'15	5:08:29

Amber Meadows 16
16 38N30 75w52 5:03:28
Amcelle 1 3 39N36'28 78w48'56 5:15:16
American Corner 5
15 38N46'02 75w49'10 5:03:17
American Square 16
16 38N47 76w58 5:07:52
Ammendale 16 16 39N03'03 76w53'49 5:07:35
Amos Mill 12 8 39N42'01 76w30'23 5:06:02
Anchorage 2 20 39N03 76w30 5:06:00
Ancient Oak Estates 15
16 39N08 77w12 5:08:48
Andersontown 5 15 38N50'16 75w47'01 5:03:08
Andora 7 7 39N41'05 75w51'40 5:03:27
Andover Estates 18
4 38N10'07 76w30'17 5:06:01
Andrews 9 8 38N21'24 76w06'37 5:04:26
Andrews 16 16 38N48 76w54 5:07:36
Andrews Air Force Base 16
16 38N48 76w52 5:07:28
Andrews Air Force Hospital 16
16 38N49 76w51 5:07:24
Andrews Estates 16
16 38N50 76w55 5:07:40
Andrews Hill 16
16 38N49 76w56 5:07:44
Andrews Manor 16
16 38N48'50 76w53'54 5:07:36
Annapolis 2 20 38N58'42 76w29'33 5:05:58
Annapolis Junction 13
3 39N08 76w47 5:07:08
Annapolis Roads 2
20 38N57'04 76w28'31 5:05:54
Annapolis Rock 13
3 39N16'54 77w07'55 5:08:32
Anneslie 3 3 39N22'33 76w36'17 5:06:25
Anthony 5 15 38N52'40 75w47'19 5:03:09
Antietam 21 8 39N24'58 77w44'33 5:10:58
Appeal 4 9 38N22'03 76w26'55 5:05:48
Apple Grove 16 16 38N47 76w58 5:07:52
Appleton 7 7 39N41'54 75w48'52 5:03:15
Appleton Acres 7
7 39N37 75w50 5:03:20
Appletown 21 7 39N31 77w39 5:10:36
Appolds 10 7 39N37'38 77w19'19 5:09:17
Aquasco 16 16 38N35'06 76w43'31 5:06:54
Arbutus 3 3 39N15'16 76w42'01 5:06:48
Arcola 15 16 39N02'52 77w03'07 5:08:12
Arden on the Severn 2
20 39N02 76w36 5:06:24
Ardmore 16 16 38N56'00 76w51'08 5:07:25
Ardwick 16 16 38N56'44 76w52'52 5:07:31
Argonne Hills 2
20 39N06'52 76w45'56 5:07:04
Arlington 24 1 39N20'22 76w41'03 5:06:44
Armacost 3 3 39N36'48 76w48'15 5:07:13
Armagh 3 3 39N22'52 76w37'13 5:06:29
Armiger 2 20 39N07'30 76w32'06 5:06:08
Armistead Gardens 24
3 39N18'06 76w32'59 5:06:12
Arnold 2 20 39N01'55 76w30'11 5:06:01
Arnold Heights 16
16 38N51'13 76w56'12 5:07:45
Arnoldtown 10 7 39N24'34 77w36'22 5:10:25
Arrowhead 13 3 39N16 76w49 5:07:16
Arrowood 15 16 39N00 77w08 5:08:32
Arters Mill 6 8 39N39'54 77w04'19 5:08:17
Arundel Beach 2
20 39N04'37 76w31'08 5:06:05
Arundel Gardens 2
20 39N12'45 76w37'09 5:06:29
Arundel on the Bay 2
20 38N57 76w29 5:05:56
Arundel Plaza 2
20 39N05 76w34 5:06:16
Arundel View 2 20 39N04 76w40 5:06:40
Arundel Village 2
20 39N13'20 76w36'16 5:06:25
Asbury 19 19 37N57 75w52 5:03:28
Ashbox 16 16 38N40'16 76w47'50 5:07:11
Ashburton 15 16 39N00'46 77w07'41 5:08:31
Asher Glade 11 2 39N42'14 79w26'51 5:17:47
Ashland 3 3 39N29'43 76w38'25 5:06:34
Ashland Landing 17
15 39N07'13 76w05'50 5:04:23
Ashleigh 15 16 39N01'01 77w09'39 5:08:39
Ashton 15 16 39N08'57 77w00'46 5:08:03
Ashton 21 7 39N37'48 77w54'55 5:11:40
Ashton Pond 15 16 39N09 77w01 5:08:04
Asleigh 15 16 39N00 77w08 5:08:32
Aspen Hill 15 16 39N04'46 77w04'24 5:08:18
Aspen Hill Park 15
16 39N04'19 77w05'41 5:08:23
Aspen Knolls 15
16 39N05'00 77w05'19 5:08:21
Athaloo Landing 22
7 38N25'34 75w49'16 5:03:17
Athel 22 7 38N25'34 75w47'19 5:03:09
Atholton 13 3 39N16 76w49 5:07:16
Atholton Manor 13
3 39N16 76w49 5:07:16
Atkinsons 23 19 38N12 75w30 5:02:00
Augusta 21 7 39N22'04 77w40'30 5:10:42
Aure Hill 15 16 39N00 77w08 5:08:32
Auth Village 16
16 38N49'15 76w54'09 5:07:37
Autumn Hill 13 3 39N16 76w49 5:07:16
Avalon 3 3 39N13'53 76w43'13 5:06:53
Avalon 20 13 38N42'33 76w20'19 5:05:21
Avalon Shores 2
20 38N50'15 76w31'05 5:06:04
Avenel 16 16 39N00'09 76w58'49 5:07:55
Avenue 18 4 38N15'22 76w46'05 5:07:04
Avery 15 16 39N06'34 77w07'19 5:08:29
Avilton 11 2 39N39'01 79w02'33 5:16:10
Avondale 6 8 39N33'33 77w01'52 5:08:07
Avondale 16 16 38N56'55 76w58'32 5:07:54
Avondale Terrace 16
16 38N57'12 76w58'35 5:07:54
Ayrlawn 15 16 39N01 77w08 5:08:32
Azundel Gardens 2
20 39N14 76w37 5:06:28
Bachman Mills 6 8 39N39'45 76w56'50 5:07:47

Back Bay Beach 2
20 38N49'53 76w32'08 5:06:09
Back River 3 3 39N18'02 76w29'37 5:05:58
Back River Highlands 3
3 39N19 76w28 5:05:52
Bacon Hall 3 3 39N34'17 76w40'56 5:06:44
Bacon Hill 7 7 39N36'14 75w53'34 5:03:34
Baden 16 16 38N39'33 76w46'41 5:07:07
Bagley 12 3 39N29'54 76w23'53 5:05:36
Bagtown 21 7 39N34'54 77w36'39 5:10:27
Baile 6 8 39N30'54 77w03'30 5:08:14
Bailes Mill 6 8 39N31'52 77w03'30 5:08:14
Bainbridge 7 7 39N36'08 76w06'20 5:04:25
Bakersville 21 7 39N30'53 77w45'28 5:11:02
Bald Eagle 16 16 38N40'35 76w43'22 5:06:53
Baldwin 3 3 39N29'41 76w28'14 5:05:53
Ballard 16 16 38N46'00 76w52'53 5:07:32
Ballard Gardens 3
3 39N20 76w27 5:05:48
Ballenger 10 7 39N23 77w29 5:09:56
Baltimore 24 1 39N17'25 76w36'45 5:06:27
Baltimore Corner 5
15 39N03'29 75w50'42 5:03:23
Baltimore Highlands 3
3 39N13'59 76w38'13 5:06:33
Banks o'Dee 8 6 38N23 76w57 5:07:48
Bannockburn 15 16 38N58'24 77w08'31 5:08:34
Bannockburn Estates 15
16 38N59'01 77w08'51 5:08:35
Bannockburn Heights 15
16 38N58'52 77w08'34 5:08:34
Barber 20 13 38N38'31 76w01'13 5:04:05
Barclay 17 15 39N08'39 75w51'52 5:03:27
Bare Hills 3 1 39N22'52 76w39'13 5:06:37
Bar Harbor 2 20 39N09'27 76w30'29 5:06:02
Bark Hill 6 8 39N35'12 77w09'10 5:08:37
Barksdale 7 7 39N40'08 75w48'54 5:03:16
Barnaby Manor Oaks 16
16 38N49'05 76w58'05 5:07:52
Barnaby Village 16
16 38N47 76w58 5:07:52
Bar Neck 20 13 38N43 76w20 5:05:20
Barnes Corner 7 7 39N40'30 76w03'57 5:04:16
Barnes Landing 9
8 38N23'25 76w06'19 5:04:25
Barnesville 15 16 39N13'14 77w22'40 5:09:31
Barrelville 1 24 39N42'06 78w50'34 5:15:22
Barren Creek 22 7 38N28 75w46 5:03:04
Barrett 6 8 39N24'27 77w01'00 5:08:04
Barstow 4 9 38N31'31 76w36'59 5:06:28
Bartholows 10 7 39N22'26 77w13'56 5:08:56
Barton 1 3 39N31'50 79w01'04 5:16:04
Bartonsville 10 7 39N23'33 77w21'30 5:09:26
Battery Park 15
16 38N59'22 77w06'28 5:08:26
Battle Grove 3 3 39N16'19 76w28'39 5:05:55
Bay 18 4 38N17 76w28 5:05:52
Bayberry 2 20 39N03'41 76w28'25 5:05:54
Bay City 17 15 38N59 76w19 5:05:16
Bay Hundred 20 13 38N45 76w19 5:05:16
Baynard 2 20 38N50'44 76w40'39 5:06:43
Baynesville 3 3 39N24'00 76w33'44 5:06:15
Bay Ridge 2 20 38N56'16 76w27'37 5:05:50
Bay Ridge Junction 2
20 38N58'43 76w30'17 5:06:01
Bay Shore Acres 23
19 38N20'34 75w06'14 5:00:25
Bayside Beach 2
20 39N08'11 76w26'37 5:05:46
Bay View 7 7 39N38'36 75w57'42 5:03:51
Bay View Estates 7
7 39N25 75w55 5:03:40
Beachville 18 4 38N08'55 76w24'58 5:05:40
Beachwood Forest 2
20 39N06'06 76w31'40 5:06:07
Beachwood Grove 2
20 39N06'21 76w31'57 5:06:08
Beacon Heights 16
16 38N58 76w55 5:07:40
Beacon Hill 2 20 39N02'32 76w25'13 5:05:41
Beallsville 15 16 39N10'44 77w24'47 5:09:39
Beantown 8 6 38N36'52 76w56'30 5:07:46
Beantown 15 16 39N05'43 77w08'25 5:08:34
Bear Creek Junction 3
3 39N14'41 76w28'02 5:05:52
Beaufort Park 13
3 39N10 76w54 5:07:36
Beaumont Park 24
1 39N21'20 76w36'36 5:06:26
Beauvue 18 4 38N15'10 76w37'37 5:06:30
Beaverbrook 13 3 39N16 76w49 5:07:16
Beaver Creek 21 7 39N35'02 77w38'32 5:10:34
Beaver Dam 23 19 38N04 75w34 5:02:16
Beaverdam Estates 16
16 38N56 76w53 5:07:32
Beaver Heights 16
16 38N54 76w54 5:07:36
Beckleysville 3 3 39N38'30 76w46'42 5:07:07
Becks Landing 14
15 39N09'54 76w08'34 5:04:34
Bedfordshire Estates 15
16 39N03 77w10 5:08:40
Beechwood on the Burley 2
20 38N59'56 76w26'58 5:05:48
Beelers Summit 21
7 39N24'45 77w40'13 5:10:41
Beetree 3 3 39N41'01 76w40'02 5:06:40
Bel Air 1 3 39N38 78w48 5:15:12
Bel Air 12 9 39N32'09 76w20'55 5:05:24
Belair 16 16 38N57 76w47 5:07:08
Bel Air Acres 8 6 38N37'51 76w55'32 5:07:42
Bel Air Acres 12
8 39N32 76w21 5:05:24
Belair Buckingham 16
16 38N57 76w47 5:07:08
Belair Chapel Forge 16
16 38N57 76w47 5:07:08
Belair Foxhill 16
16 38N57 76w47 5:07:08
Belair Heather Hills 16
16 38N57 76w47 5:07:08
Belair Idlewild 16
16 38N57 76w47 5:07:08

Belair Kenilworth 16
16 38N57 76w47 5:07:08
Belair Longridge 16
16 38N57 76w47 5:07:08
Belair Overbrook 16
16 38N57 76w47 5:07:08
Belair Rockledge 16
16 38N57 76w47 5:07:08
Belair Somerset 16
16 38N57 76w47 5:07:08
Belair Tulip Grove 16
16 38N57 76w47 5:07:08
Belair White Hall 16
16 38N57 76w47 5:07:08
Belair Yorktown 16
16 38N57 76w47 5:07:08
Bel Alton (Cox Station) 8
6 38N27'50 76w58'59 5:07:56
Belcamp 12 8 39N28'08 76w14'01 5:04:56
Belfast 3 3 39N32'52 76w40'44 5:06:43
Belgravia 24 3 39N21'03 76w32'04 5:06:08
Bell 16 16 38N58'12 76w48'06 5:07:12
Belle Farm Estates 3
3 39N22 76w43 5:06:52
Bellefonte 16 16 38N47 76w53 5:07:32
Bellegrove 1 3 39N42'24 78w20'18 5:13:21
Bellemead 16 16 38N56'31 76w53'11 5:07:33
Bellevue 20 13 38N42'12 76w11'05 5:04:44
Bellevue Estates 16
16 38N40 77w02 5:08:08
Bellhaven Beach 2
20 39N09 76w33 5:06:12
Bells Mill 10 7 39N19'58 77w34'40 5:10:19
Bells Mill 15 16 39N01'16 77w09'45 5:08:39
Belltown 3 3 39N25'37 76w48'19 5:07:13
Bellwood Park 8 6 38N38 76w53 5:07:32
Belmar 24 3 39N20'44 76w32'27 5:06:10
Belmont 3 3 39N18'26 76w45'15 5:07:01
Bel Pre Farms 15
16 39N05'28 77w03'45 5:08:15
Bel Pre Woods 15
16 39N05 77w07 5:08:28
Beltsville 16 16 39N02'05 76w54'28 5:07:38
Beltsville Heights 16
16 39N02 76w55 5:07:40
Belvedere 7 25 39N35'49 76w01'22 5:04:05
Belvedere Heights 2
20 39N03'21 76w30'09 5:06:01
Belvoir Manor 2
20 39N01'24 76w34'58 5:06:20
Bembe Beach 2 20 38N57'49 76w28'33 5:05:54
Benedict 8 6 38N30'33 76w40'48 5:06:43
Benevola 21 7 39N32'44 77w40'35 5:10:42
Benfield 2 20 39N05'19 76w37'21 5:06:29
Bengies 3 3 39N20'42 76w25'37 5:05:42
Bennsville 8 6 38N36'33 77w00'45 5:08:03
Ben Oaks 2 20 39N05 76w34 5:06:16
Benson 12 8 39N30'19 76w23'12 5:05:33
Bentley Springs 3
3 39N40'25 76w40'16 5:06:41
Bentons Pleasure 17
15 38N58 76w17 5:05:08
Benville 8 6 38N38 76w53 5:07:32
Berean 3 3 39N34'16 76w44'26 5:06:58
Berkley 12 8 39N39'41 76w12'33 5:04:50
Berkshire 16 16 38N51'02 76w53'39 5:07:35
Berlin 23 27 38N19'21 75w13'05 5:00:52
Berrett 6 8 39N25 77w01 5:08:04
Berry 16 6 38N38'55 76w57'26 5:07:50
Bertha 4 9 38N23'26 76w26'00 5:05:44
Berwyn 16 16 38N59'42 76w55'36 5:07:42
Berwyn Heights 16
16 38N59'38 76w54'39 5:07:39
Bessen Landing 23
19 38N01'17 75w22'55 5:01:32
Bestgate 2 20 38N59'30 76w32'49 5:06:11
Bestpitch 9 8 38N25'01 75w59'28 5:03:58
Bethany Manor 13
3 39N16 76w49 5:07:16
Bethel 6 8 39N32'46 76w55'10 5:07:41
Bethel 7 7 39N32'00 75w46'58 5:03:08
Bethel 10 7 39N34'12 77w12'35 5:08:50
Bethel 11 17 39N26'42 79w07'08 5:16:29
Bethesda 15 16 38N58'50 77w06'02 5:08:24
Bethgate 13 3 39N16 76w49 5:07:16
Bethlehem 5 15 38N44'46 75w56'40 5:03:47
Betterton 14 8 39N21'57 76w03'45 5:04:15
Beulah 9 8 38N40'40 75w53'58 5:03:36
Bevansville 11 2 39N39'15 79w11'35 5:16:46
Beverley Beach 2
20 38N52'50 76w30'33 5:06:02
Beverly Farms 15
16 39N03'13 77w10'51 5:08:43
Bier 1 3 39N32'31 78w52'34 5:15:30
Big Pines 15 16 39N05'04 77w13'36 5:08:54
Big Pool 21 7 39N37'25 78w00'58 5:12:04
Big Spring 3 3 39N29'43 76w44'25 5:06:58
Big Spring 21 7 39N37'45 77w56'23 5:11:46
Bigwoods 14 15 39N17'08 76w02'34 5:04:10
Birchwood City 16
16 38N49 76w59 5:07:56
Bird Hill 6 8 39N29'18 76w58'15 5:07:53
Bird River Beach 3
3 39N20 76w27 5:05:48
Birdsville 2 20 38N54'00 76w35'30 5:06:22
Birmingham Estates 16
16 39N02 76w55 5:07:40
Bishop 23 23 38N25'39 75w13'17 5:00:53
Bishops Head 9 8 38N16'05 76w04'05 5:04:16
Bishopville 23 23 38N26'33 75w11'38 5:00:47
Bittinger 11 2 39N36'08 79w13'25 5:16:54
Bivalve 22 7 38N18'22 75w53'22 5:03:33
Bixler 6 8 39N37'52 76w58'39 5:07:55
Black Bay Beach 2
20 38N51 76w36 5:06:24
Blackhorse 12 8 39N37'26 76w33'05 5:06:12
Black Oak 1 3 39N29'57 78w55'09 5:15:41
Black Rock Estates 15
16 39N10 77w16 5:09:04
Blackrock Mill 15
16 39N07'36 77w18'52 5:09:15
Blacks Corner 6 8 39N42'21 77w06'10 5:08:25
Blackwater 9 8 38N23'07 76w08'33 5:04:34

Bladensburg 16 16 38N56'21 76w56'03 5:07:44
Bladenwoods 16 16 38N57 76w56 5:07:44
Blair 15 16 39N00 77w02 5:08:08
Blair Portal 15 16 38N59'32 77w02'10 5:08:09
Blake 7 7 39N42'56 75w55'01 5:03:40
Blandford Village 16 16 38N43'03 76w53'26 5:07:34
Blenheim 3 3 39N29'22 76w32'47 5:06:11
Blocktown 15 16 39N11'42 77w19'36 5:09:18
Bloom 6 8 39N28'41 77w01'45 5:08:07
Bloomfield 10 7 39N28'32 77w25'18 5:09:41
Bloomfield 20 13 38N46'37 76w06'26 5:04:26
Blooming Rose Settlement 11 2 39N39 79w24 5:17:36
Bloomington 11 17 39N28'48 79w04'17 5:16:17
Bloomsbury 3 3 39N15'50 76w43'48 5:06:55
Blueball 7 7 39N42'00 75w55'54 5:03:44
Blueberry Hills 15 16 39N06 77w11 5:08:44
Blue Hill 21 8 39N41'53 78w11'38 5:12:47
Blue Mount 3 3 39N36'08 76w37'19 5:06:29
Blue Mountain 10 7 39N35'51 77w25'10 5:09:41
Blue Ridge Manor 15 16 39N03 77w03 5:08:12
Blue Ridge View 6 8 39N34 76w59 5:07:56
Blythedale 7 25 39N35'17 76w03'50 5:04:15
Bodt Corner 12 8 39N32'31 76w14'05 5:04:56
Bohemias Mills 7 7 39N27'58 75w46'43 5:03:07
Bolivar 10 7 39N27'59 77w35'31 5:10:22
Bolton 8 6 38N38'40 76w59'16 5:07:57
Bond Mill Woods 16 16 39N05 76w58 5:07:52
Bonds 16 16 38N40 77w02 5:08:08
Bon Haven 2 20 38N58'02 76w35'31 5:06:22
Bonnie Acres 13 3 39N16 76w49 5:07:16
Bonnie Brae 6 8 39N24 76w56 5:07:44
Bonnie Knob 10 7 39N32 77w19 5:09:16
Booker Heights 16 16 38N54 76w54 5:07:36
Boonsboro 5 15 38N57'00 75w51'37 5:03:26
Boonsboro 21 7 39N30'22 77w39'10 5:10:37
Bootjack 15 3 39N16'26 77w09'21 5:08:37
Borden Shaft 1 24 39N37'37 78w56'13 5:15:45
Borden Yard 1 24 39N39 78w55 5:15:40
Boring 3 3 39N31'54 76w49'23 5:07:18
Bostetter 21 7 39N39'52 77w45'14 5:11:01
Boulevard Heights 16 16 38N52'11 76w56'01 5:07:44
Bowens 4 9 38N29'43 76w37'21 5:06:29
Bowie 16 16 39N00'24 76w46'46 5:07:07
Bowleys Quarters 3 3 39N20'07 76w23'26 5:05:34
Bowling Alley 8 6 38N29 76w47 5:07:08
Bowling Green 1 3 39N37'25 78w48'17 5:15:13
Bowmans Mill 21 7 39N41'34 77w36'53 5:10:28
Boxiron 23 23 38N06'54 75w20'58 5:01:24
Boxwood Village 16 16 39N00'35 76w53'20 5:07:33
Boyds 15 16 39N11'01 77w18'47 5:09:15
Bozman 20 13 38N46'12 76w16'17 5:05:05
Bradbury Heights 16 16 38N51'49 76w55'53 5:07:44
Bradbury Park 16 16 38N51'28 76w55'28 5:07:42
Braddock 10 7 39N25'15 77w28'38 5:09:55
Braddock Estates 1 24 39N39 78w55 5:15:40
Braddock Heights 10 7 39N25'07 77w30'14 5:10:01
Bradley Farms 15 16 39N00'24 77w11'28 5:08:46
Bradley Hills 15 16 38N58'47 77w06'29 5:08:26
Bradley Hills Grove 15 16 39N00'11 77w08'06 5:08:32
Bradley Woods 15 16 38N59'32 77w07'16 5:08:29
Bradmoor 15 16 38N59'40 77w07'10 5:08:29
Bradshaw 3 8 39N25'23 76w22'53 5:05:32
Brady 1 3 39N35'32 78w49'19 5:15:17
Bramble Hills 6 8 39N34 76w59 5:07:56
Branchville 16 16 38N59'56 76w55'28 5:07:42
Brandywine 16 16 38N41'48 76w50'53 5:07:24
Brandywine Heights 16 16 38N41'22 76w51'19 5:07:25
Brandywine Woods 16 16 38N47 76w52 5:07:28
Breathedsville 21 7 39N32'37 77w43'06 5:10:52
Breezewood Farms 13 3 39N20 76w52 5:07:28
Breezy Point 4 9 38N37'19 76w30'58 5:06:04
Breezy Point Beach 3 3 39N16'39 76w23'05 5:05:32
Brentland 8 6 38N27'55 77w02'28 5:08:10
Brentwood 16 16 38N56'35 76w57'25 5:07:50
Breton Beach 18 4 38N14'14 76w41'14 5:06:45
Briarcrest Heights 10 7 39N22 77w32 5:10:08
Briarwood 16 16 39N05 76w58 5:07:52
Brice 8 6 38N33'31 76w56'36 5:07:46
Brick House Landing 9 8 38N25'42 75w57'30 5:03:50
Brick Wall Landing 5 11 38N55'46 75w50'03 5:03:20
Briddletown 23 27 38N20'05 75w11'43 5:00:47
Bridgeport 10 7 39N40'45 77w14'17 5:08:57
Bridgeport 11 7 39N38'32 77w40'42 5:10:43
Bridgetown 5 15 39N02'04 75w52'28 5:03:30
Bridlewood 3 3 39N25'25 76w36'46 5:06:27
Brighton 13 16 39N11'34 77w01'36 5:08:06
Brighton 24 1 39N21'08 76w42'25 5:06:50
Brightseat 16 16 38N54'49 76w51'40 5:07:27
Brightwood Acres 21 7 39N39 77w44 5:10:56
Brink 15 16 39N12'36 77w14'24 5:08:58
Brinkleigh 13 3 39N16 76w49 5:07:16
Brinkleigh Manor 13 3 39N16 76w49 5:07:16
Brinkley Manor 16 16 38N49 76w56 5:07:44
Brinkleys 19 23 38N02 75w43 5:02:52
Brinklow 15 16 39N09'57 77w00'57 5:08:04
Bristol 2 20 38N47'32 76w40'06 5:06:40
Bristol Landing 2 20 38N47'32 76w42'17 5:06:49
Britton 18 4 38N15'36 76w38'43 5:06:35
Broad Creek 12 8 39N43 76w21 5:05:24
Broadfording 21 7 39N41'09 77w48'11 5:11:13
Broadmoor 3 3 39N28'56 76w40'03 5:06:40
Broad Run 10 7 39N23'37 77w35'52 5:10:23
Broadview 16 16 38N48'45 76w55'37 5:07:42
Broadview Acres 10 7 39N26 77w27 5:09:48
Broadwater 2 20 38N47'34 76w32'05 5:06:08
Broadwater Estates 16 16 38N44'29 77w00'47 5:08:03
Broadwood Manor 15 16 39N04'43 77w07'09 5:08:29
Brock Bridge 16 16 39N05 76w58 5:07:52
Brock Hall 16 16 38N47 76w52 5:07:28
Brookdale 15 16 38N57'33 77w05'31 5:08:22
Brooke Manor 16 16 38N46'37 77w00'12 5:08:01
Brookeville 15 16 39N10'50 77w03'34 5:08:14
Brookfield 2 20 39N07'05 76w32'21 5:06:09
Brookhaven 15 16 39N05 77w07 5:08:28
Brook Hill 10 7 39N26 77w27 5:09:48
Brookland 16 16 38N59'28 76w49'13 5:07:17
Brooklandville 3 3 39N25'13 76w40'13 5:06:41
Brooklyn 24 20 39N13'49 76w36'09 5:06:25
Brooklyn Park 2 20 39N13'42 76w37'00 5:06:28
Brookmont 15 16 38N56'31 77w07'14 5:08:29
Brookside Forest 15 16 39N00'26 77w00'18 5:08:01
Brookside Manor 16 16 38N57'53 76w58'36 5:07:54
Brookview 9 8 38N34'31 75w47'47 5:03:11
Brookville Knolls 15 16 39N11 77w03 5:08:12
Brookwood 16 16 38N47 76w52 5:07:28
Broomes Island 4 9 38N25'05 76w32'40 5:06:11
Brown 15 16 39N08'45 77w13'05 5:08:52
Brown 16 16 38N51'10 76w48'09 5:07:13
Browningsville 15 16 39N18'26 77w14'36 5:08:58
Brown Landing 9 8 38N38'48 75w48'52 5:03:15
Browns Corner 15 16 39N07'20 76w59'21 5:07:57
Browns Corner 17 15 39N03 76w04 5:04:16
Brownstown 15 16 39N08'28 77w17'41 5:09:11
Brownsville 17 15 39N02'48 76w06'34 5:04:26
Brownsville 21 7 39N22'55 77w39'38 5:10:39
Browns Woods 2 20 39N00'21 76w28'06 5:05:52
Bruceville 6 8 39N36'35 77w14'07 5:08:56
Bruceville 20 13 38N40'16 75w59'03 5:03:56
Brummel 6 8 39N36'10 76w55'17 5:07:41
Brunswick 10 18 39N18'51 77w37'41 5:10:31
Bryans Road 8 6 38N37'37 77w04'24 5:08:18
Bryantown 8 6 38N33'18 76w50'32 5:07:22
Bryantown 17 15 38N56'30 76w10'13 5:04:41
Buckeystown 10 7 39N20'05 77w25'55 5:09:44
Buckeystown Station 10 7 39N19'54 77w26'55 5:09:48
Buckingham View 6 8 39N34 76w59 5:07:56
Bucklodge 15 16 39N11'33 77w20'08 5:09:21
Buck Lodge 16 16 39N00'30 76w57'47 5:07:51
Buck Neck Landing 14 15 39N16'28 76w10'06 5:04:40
Bucktown 9 8 38N27'33 76w01'52 5:04:07
Budd Landing 7 15 39N22'24 75w50'19 5:03:21
Budds Creek 18 4 38N26 76w44 5:06:56
Budds Landing 8 6 38N23'15 76w52'48 5:07:31
Buena Vista 4 9 38N31'40 76w39'07 5:06:36
Buena Vista 16 16 38N57'24 76w49'30 5:07:18
Buffalo Run 11 2 39N39 79w24 5:17:36
Bull Run 18 4 38N20'16 76w47'30 5:07:10
Burch 4 6 38N30'33 76w39'45 5:06:39
Burdette 15 16 39N11'58 77w18'19 5:09:13
Bureau 5 15 38N48'57 75w51'20 5:03:25
Burgundy Estates 15 16 39N05 77w07 5:08:28
Burgundy Knolls 15 16 39N05 77w10 5:08:40
Burgundy Village 15 16 39N05 77w10 5:08:40
Burkittsville 10 7 39N23'37 77w37'45 5:10:31
Burleytown 2 20 39N09'06 76w40'10 5:06:41
Burnbrae 3 3 39N23'56 76w37'11 5:06:29
Burning Tree Estates 15 16 39N00'28 77w09'22 5:08:37
Burning Tree Manor 15 16 39N00 77w08 5:08:32
Burns Corner 12 8 39N31'39 76w10'16 5:04:41
Burnt Hill 15 16 39N14 77w17 5:09:08
Burnt Mills 15 16 39N02'01 77w00'17 5:08:01
Burnt Mills Hills 15 16 39N01'58 76w59'40 5:07:59
Burnt Mills Knolls 15 16 39N01'53 76w59'17 5:07:57
Burnt Mills Manor 15 16 39N02'08 77w00'17 5:08:01
Burnt Mills Village 15 16 39N02'16 77w00'19 5:08:01
Burrisville 17 15 39N05'49 76w04'10 5:04:17
Burrsville 1 15 38N53'38 75w43'45 5:02:55
Burtner 21 7 39N31'26 77w43'13 5:10:53
Burtonsville 15 16 39N06'40 76w55'58 5:07:44
Bush 12 8 39N28'25 76w15'52 5:05:03
Bush River 12 8 39N26'28 76w14'16 5:04:57
Bushs Corner 12 8 39N40'19 76w24'34 5:05:38
Bushwood 18 4 38N17'47 76w46'46 5:07:07
Buteaux Crossing 8 6 38N35'29 77w06'41 5:08:27
Butler 3 3 39N32'07 76w43'42 5:06:55
Butlers Beach 9 8 38N27'25 75w50'11 5:03:21
Butlertown 14 15 39N16'57 76w06'17 5:04:25
Byeforde 15 16 39N00'41 77w05'04 5:08:20
Bynum 12 8 39N33'56 76w21'54 5:05:28
Bynum Ridge 12 8 39N35 76w23 5:05:32
Byrdtown 19 28 37N57'34 75w50'25 5:03:22
Cabin Creek 9 8 38N38 75w52 5:03:28
Cabin John 15 16 38N58'31 77w09'30 5:08:38
Cabin John Park 15 16 38N58'35 77w09'55 5:08:40
Cactus Hill 16 16 38N40 77w02 5:08:08
California 18 4 38N18'01 76w30'28 5:06:02
Callaway 18 4 38N14'18 76w31'10 5:06:05
Calloway Landing 18 4 38N10'07 76w27'40 5:05:51
Caltor Manor 16 16 38N47 76w58 5:07:52
Calvary 12 8 39N32'06 76w15'39 5:05:03
Calvert 7 7 39N42'01 75w58'58 5:03:56
Calvert 24 1 39N18 76w36 5:06:24
Calvert Beach 4 9 38N27'57 76w28'39 5:05:55
Calvert Hills 16 16 38N58'29 76w56'09 5:07:45
Calvert Manor 16 16 38N41'24 77w00'33 5:08:02
Calverton 16 16 39N03'27 76w56'10 5:07:45
Cambria 3 3 39N29'40 76w35'15 5:06:21
Cambridge 9 10 38N33'47 76w04'45 5:04:19
Camden 22 7 38N19 75w36 5:02:24
Camelback Village 15 16 39N09 77w05 5:08:20
Camelot 16 16 38N59 76w49 5:07:16
Camotop 15 16 39N03 77w10 5:08:40
Campbell 23 23 38N24'42 75w14'17 5:00:57
Campbell Corner 15 16 39N00'07 77w10'51 5:08:43
Campbelltown 23 23 38N27 75w11 5:00:44
Camp Springs 16 16 38N48'14 76w54'25 5:07:38
Campus Hills 3 3 39N24'23 76w34'59 5:06:20
Canada Hill 10 7 39N30 77w34 5:10:16
Canal 7 7 39N36 76w07 5:04:28
Candlewood Park 15 16 39N06 77w11 5:08:44
Canterbury Estates 3 3 39N23'43 76w42'57 5:06:52
Canton 24 1 39N16'49 76w34'01 5:06:16
Cape Anne 2 20 38N47'43 76w31'34 5:06:06
Cape Arthur 2 20 39N04'44 76w31'30 5:06:06
Cape Isle of Wight 23 19 38N21'10 75w07'06 5:00:28
Cape Loch Haven 2 20 38N55'25 76w31'26 5:06:06
Cape May Beach 3 3 39N18'09 76w25'05 5:05:40
Cape Saint Claire 2 20 39N02'35 76w26'43 5:05:47
Cape Saint John 2 20 38N57'40 76w34'13 5:06:17
Capital Estates 8 6 38N36 76w57 5:07:48
Capitola 22 7 38N17'19 75w48'24 5:03:14
Capitol Heights 16 16 38N53'06 76w54'58 5:07:40
Capitol Plaza 16 16 38N58 76w53 5:07:32
Capitol View Park 15 16 39N01'20 77w03'39 5:08:15
Captain Saint Claire 2 20 39N03 76w30 5:06:00
Captains Cove 16 16 38N47 76w58 5:07:52
Captains Hill 23 19 38N21'03 75w06'00 5:00:24
Carderock 15 16 38N58'39 77w11'41 5:08:47
Carderock Springs 15 16 38N59'20 77w10'04 5:08:40
Cardiff 12 8 39N43'02 76w20'17 5:05:21
Carea 12 8 39N42'01 76w30'23 5:06:02
Careytown 23 19 38N26'02 75w19'33 5:01:18
Carlos 1 24 39N37'23 78w57'26 5:15:50
Carlos Junction 1 24 39N36'20 78w56'36 5:15:46
Carmichael 17 15 38N56'32 76w08'02 5:04:32
Carmody Hills 16 16 38N53'47 76w53'43 5:07:35
Carney 3 3 39N23'39 76w31'26 5:06:06
Carney Grove 3 3 39N23'41 76w30'37 5:06:02
Carney Heights 3 3 39N23 76w33 5:06:12
Carole Acres 15 16 39N04'11 76w59'45 5:07:59
Carole Highlands 16 16 38N58'53 76w59'01 5:07:56
Carpenter Point 7 25 39N34 76w04 5:04:16
Carroll 24 1 39N16'51 76w40'20 5:06:41
Carroll Heights 21 7 39N39 77w44 5:10:56
Carroll Highlands 6 8 39N24 76w56 5:07:44
Carroll Island 3 3 39N20 76w27 5:05:48
Carroll Knolls 15 16 39N01'25 77w03'00 5:08:12
Carroll Manor 3 3 39N29'55 76w31'00 5:06:04
Carroll Manor 15 16 38N58'49 77w00'17 5:08:01
Carrollton 6 8 39N33'25 76w55'02 5:07:40
Carrollton Manor 2 20 39N04'35 76w35'02 5:06:20
Carrollwood 3 3 39N20 76w27 5:05:48
Carrs Mill 13 3 39N18'53 77w03'10 5:08:13
Carsins 12 8 39N32'14 76w12'46 5:04:51
Carsondale 16 16 38N56'30 76w51'14 5:07:25
Carter Hill 15 16 39N05 77w10 5:08:40
Carvel Beach 2 20 39N14 76w35 5:06:20
Carver Heights 18 4 38N15 76w27 5:05:48
Carville 17 15 39N02'57 76w00'15 5:04:01
Cascade 21 7 39N42'39 77w29'23 5:09:58

Cash Corner 19 28 37N59'27 75W48'36 5:03:14
Casselman 11 2 39N40'31 79W10'19 5:16:41
Castle Haven 9 8 38N37'35 76W10'23 5:04:42
Castle Manor 16
16 38N57'16 76W57'22 5:07:49
Castle Marina 17
15 38N58 76W17 5:05:08
Castleton 12 8 39N40'29 76W12'54 5:04:52
Catchpenny 22 7 38N21'18 75W42'38 5:02:51
Cathers Corner 7
7 39N39'09 76W03'02 5:04:12
Catoctin 10 7 39N34 77W33 5:10:12
Catoctin Furnace 10
7 39N34'45 77W25'58 5:09:44
Catoctin View 10
7 39N22 77W09 5:08:36
Catonsville 3 3 39N16'19 76W43'56 5:06:56
Catonsville Heights 3
3 39N17 76W43 5:06:52
Catonsville Manor 3
3 39N17'47 76W44'02 5:06:56
Caves Park 3 3 39N26'24 76W43'33 5:06:54
Cavetown 21 7 39N38'39 77W35'10 5:10:21
Cayots 7 7 39N29'09 75W50'53 5:03:24
Cearfoss 21 7 39N42'03 77W46'33 5:11:06
Cecilton 7 7 39N24'14 75W52'04 5:03:28
Cedar Acres 13 3 39N16 76W49 5:07:16
Cedar Beach 3 3 39N16'57 76W25'03 5:05:40
Cedar Cliff 1 3 39N36'30 78W48'27 5:15:14
Cedarcroft 24 3 39N22'01 76W36'36 5:06:26
Cedar Grove 15 16 39N14'48 77W14'03 5:08:56
Cedar Grove 21 7 39N31'54 77W49'21 5:11:17
Cedar Grove Beach 9
8 38N36 75W55 5:03:40
Cedar Hall 23 19 38N04 75W34 5:02:16
Cedarhaven 16 16 38N34'22 76W41'11 5:06:45
Cedar Heights 15
16 39N15'11 77W13'47 5:08:55
Cedar Heights 16
16 38N54'09 76W54'30 5:07:38
Cedar Hill 7 7 39N40'30 75W53'32 5:03:34
Cedarhurst 2 20 38N49'43 76W30'03 5:06:00
Cedarhurst 6 8 39N29'55 76W52'59 5:07:32
Cedarhurst-on-the-Bay 2
20 38N50 76W30 5:06:00
Cedar Landing 9 8 38N25'31 75W58'24 5:03:54
Cedar Landing 18
4 38N08'47 76W28'04 5:05:52
Cedar Lawn 21 7 39N38'58 77W45'52 5:11:03
Cedarmere 3 3 39N26 76W48 5:07:12
Cedar Park 2 20 39N03 76W30 5:06:00
Cedartown 23 27 38N11'45 75W18'14 5:01:13
Cedarville 16 16 38N39'46 76W48'09 5:07:13
Centennial 13 3 39N16 76W49 5:07:16
Centennial Estates 13
3 39N16 76W49 5:07:16
Center Court 15
16 39N08 77W12 5:08:48
Centerville 10 7 39N31'28 77W16'19 5:09:05
Centreville 17 11 39N02'30 76W04'00 5:04:16
Centreville Landing 17
11 39N03'17 76W04'26 5:04:18
Ceresville 10 7 39N27'13 77W22'01 5:09:28
Chadwick Manor 3
3 39N20 76W43 5:06:52
Chalk Point 2 20 38N51 76W36 5:06:24
Champ 19 26 38N09'37 75W48'29 5:03:14
Chance 19 26 38N10'19 75W56'29 5:03:46
Chaney 4 9 38N45'05 76W38'06 5:06:32
Chaneyville 4 9 38N41'30 76W38'25 5:06:34
Chapel 20 13 38N51 76W01 5:04:04
Chapel Hill 16 16 38N43'24 76W58'58 5:07:56
Chapel Oaks 16 16 38N54'29 76W55'05 5:07:40
Chapel View 13 3 39N16 76W49 5:07:16
Chapman Landing 8
6 38N37'17 77W07'10 5:08:29
Chapter Point 22
7 38N22'35 75W51'48 5:03:27
Chaptico 18 4 38N22'03 76W47'00 5:07:08
Charles Manor 12
8 39N31 76W25 5:05:40
Charlesmont 3 3 39N14 76W31 5:06:04
Charlestown 1 3 39N33'22 78W58'30 5:15:54
Charlestown 7 7 39N34'25 75W58'31 5:03:54
Charlestown Manor Beach 7
7 39N36 75W56 5:03:44
Charlesville 10 7 39N29'17 77W25'47 5:09:43
Charlotte Hall 18
4 38N28'51 76W46'42 5:07:07
Charlton 21 7 39N37'48 77W53'40 5:11:35
Charred Oak Estates 15
16 39N00'10 77W09'44 5:08:39
Chartley 3 3 39N27 76W49 5:07:16
Chase 3 3 39N21'48 76W22'17 5:05:29
Chatham 16 16 38N59'13 76W57'33 5:07:50
Chattolanee 3 3 39N24'30 76W44'35 5:06:58
Chelsea 12 8 39N25'10 76W13'23 5:04:54
Chelsea Beach 2
20 39N06'07 76W31'13 5:06:05
Chelsea Woods 16
16 39N00 76W53 5:07:32
Cheltenham 16 16 38N44'08 76W49'36 5:07:18
Cheltenham Forest 16
16 38N47 76W53 5:07:32
Cherry Hill 4 9 38N21'16 76W26'02 5:05:44
Cherry Hill 7 7 39N39'48 75W51'11 5:03:25
Cherry Hill 12 8 39N38'32 76W22'51 5:05:31
Cherry Hill 16 16 39N00'59 76W55'57 5:07:44
Cherry Hill 24 20 39N15'17 76W38'05 5:06:32
Cherrytown 6 8 39N41'15 77W01'30 5:08:06
Cherrywalk 22 7 38N25 75W41 5:02:44
Chesaco Park 3 3 39N18'48 76W29'46 5:05:59
Chesapeake Beach 4
9 38N41'10 76W32'06 5:06:08
Chesapeake City 7
7 39N31'51 75W48'28 5:03:14
Chesapeake Estates 17
15 38N59 76W19 5:05:16
Chesapeake Heights 22
7 38N22 75W36 5:02:24
Chesapeake Landing 14
15 39N13 76W04 5:04:16
Chesapeake Ranch Estates 4
9 38N25 76W27 5:05:48
Chesapeake Terrace 3
3 39N14 76W31 5:06:04
Cheshaven 7 7 39N25 75W55 5:03:40
Chester 17 15 38N58'31 76W17'23 5:05:10
Chesterfield 2 20 39N00'04 76W37'27 5:06:30
Chester Harbor 17
15 39N13 76W04 5:04:16
Chester River Beach 17
15 38N58 76W13 5:04:52
Chestertown 14 21 39N12'32 76W04'01 5:04:16
Chesterville 14
15 39N16'33 75W54'56 5:03:40
Chesterville Forest 14
15 39N16'06 75W53'37 5:03:34
Chestnut Grove 10
7 39N27'58 77W16'58 5:09:08
Chestnut Grove 21
7 39N24'34 77W41'45 5:10:47
Chestnut Hill 3 3 39N24'19 76W37'12 5:06:29
Chestnut Hill 12
8 39N36'46 76W21'13 5:05:25
Chestnut Hill Estates 13
3 39N16 76W49 5:07:16
Chestnut Hills 15
16 39N01'48 77W02'00 5:08:08
Chestnut Ridge 3
3 39N27'35 76W43'57 5:06:56
Chestnut Ridge 15
16 39N02'05 77W02'12 5:08:09
Cheswolde 24 1 39N21'50 76W41'22 5:06:45
Cheverly 16 16 38N55'41 76W54'58 5:07:40
Cheverly Manor 16
16 38N56 76W53 5:07:32
Chevy Chase 15 16 38N58'16 77W04'36 5:08:18
Chevy Chase Gardens 15
16 38N59 77W05 5:08:20
Chevy Chase Lake 15
16 38N59'31 77W04'15 5:08:17
Chevy Chase Manor 15
16 38N58'43 77W04'01 5:08:16
Chevy Chase Section 4 15
16 38N58'49 77W04'55 5:08:20
Chevy Chase Terrace 15
16 38N58'20 77W05'39 5:08:23
Chevy Chase View 15
16 39N01'11 77W04'58 5:08:20
Chewsville 11 8 39N38'34 77W38'07 5:10:32
Chicamuxen 8 6 38N32'14 77W12'45 5:08:51
Childs 7 7 39N38'46 75W52'19 5:03:29
Chillum 16 16 38N57'49 76W59'28 5:07:58
Chillum Gardens 16
16 38N57'33 76W59'22 5:07:57
Chillum Heights 16
16 38N57'35 76W58'54 5:07:56
Chillum Manor 16
16 38N58'14 76W59'18 5:07:57
Chingville 18 4 38N14'27 76W33'32 5:06:14
Choptank 5 15 38N40'51 75W56'55 5:03:48
Christs Rock 9 8 38N32'40 76W06'12 5:04:25
Chrome Hill 12 8 39N37'21 76W25'15 5:05:41
Church Creek 9 8 38N30'07 76W09'09 5:04:37
Church Hill 10 7 39N20'38 77W28'31 5:09:54
Church Hill 17 15 39N08'28 75W59'09 5:03:57
Churchill 15 16 39N10 77W16 5:09:04
Churchton 2 20 38N48'09 76W32'14 5:06:09
Churchville 12 8 39N33'40 76W14'45 5:04:59
Cissel Farms 13 3 39N11 76W57 5:07:48
Claggettsville 15
16 39N19'02 77W11'53 5:08:48
Claiborne 20 13 38N50'15 76W16'41 5:05:07
Clara 22 19 38N16'33 75W49'13 5:03:17
Clarksburg 15 16 39N14'19 77W16'47 5:09:07
Clarks Landing 18
4 38N20'32 76W30'16 5:06:01
Clarksville 13 3 39N12'23 76W56'36 5:07:46
Clarksville Ridge 13
3 39N12 76W57 5:07:48
Clarysville 1 24 39N38'33 78W53'19 5:15:33
Claysville 15 16 39N11'38 77W07'29 5:08:30
Clayton 12 8 39N27'01 76W21'18 5:05:25
Clayton Manor 12
8 39N25 76W22 5:05:28
Clearfield 6 8 39N32'58 76W57'12 5:07:49
Clear Ridge 6 8 39N34'58 77W07'29 5:08:30
Clear Spring 21 7 39N39'22 77W55'55 5:11:44
Clearview 12 8 39N23 76W15 5:05:00
Clearview Village 2
20 39N09 76W33 5:06:12
Clear Water Beach 2
20 39N09'59 76W31'39 5:06:07
Cleaves Fork 5 15 39N07'58 75W47'15 5:03:09
Clements 18 4 38N19'34 76W43'39 5:06:55
Clemsonville 10 7 39N31'18 77W10'46 5:08:43
Clevelandville 21
7 39N28'43 77W38'22 5:10:33
Clifford 24 20 39N14'49 76W38'00 5:06:32
Cliffs City 14 15 39N13 76W04 5:04:16
Clifton 8 6 38N23 76W57 5:07:48
Clifton 10 7 39N25'14 77W29'10 5:09:57
Clifton 24 1 39N19 76W35 5:06:20
Clifton Park Village 15
16 39N00'04 76W59'32 5:07:58
Clinton 16 16 38N45'54 76W53'55 5:07:36
Clinton Acres 16
16 38N42 76W51 5:07:24
Clinton Estates 16
16 38N47 76W53 5:07:32
Clinton Gardens 16
16 38N47 76W53 5:07:32
Clinton Heights 16
16 38N45'39 76W51'50 5:07:27
Clinton Vista 16
16 38N47 76W53 5:07:32
Clopper 15 16 39N08'59 77W14'36 5:08:58
Cloverfields 17
15 38N59 76W19 5:05:16
Clover Hill 10 7 39N26 77W27 5:09:48
Cloverlea 2 20 38N52'39 76W30'50 5:06:03
Cloverly 15 16 39N06'29 76W59'53 5:08:00
Club Hill 15 16 39N08 77W12 5:08:48
Cobb Island 8 6 38N16 76W51 5:07:24
Cobbler's Woods 16
16 38N58 76W51 5:07:24
Cockeysville 3 3 39N28'52 76W38'39 5:06:35
Coffee Hill 18 4 38N23'31 76W49'33 5:07:18
Cohasset 15 16 38N59'08 77W08'16 5:08:33
Cohill 21 8 39N38'47 78W15'15 5:13:01
Cokeland 9 8 38N24'18 75W52'40 5:03:31
Cokesbury 7 7 39N36 76W07 5:04:28
Cokesbury 19 5 38N07'37 75W34'46 5:02:19
Colbourne 23 27 38N15'41 75W27'16 5:01:49
Colebrooke 16 16 38N50'28 76W57'06 5:07:48
Coleman 14 15 39N20'29 76W04'42 5:04:19
Coles Corner 16
16 38N46'33 76W52'03 5:07:28
Colesville 15 16 39N04'32 77W00'08 5:08:01
Colesville Manor 15
16 39N05'09 77W00'14 5:08:01
Colesville Park 15
16 39N05'55 77W00'14 5:08:01
College 6 8 39N34 76W59 5:07:56
College Estates 10
7 39N26 77W27 5:09:48
College Gardens 15
16 39N05 77W10 5:08:40
College Heights 16
16 38N58'33 76W56'27 5:07:46
College Heights Estates 16
16 38N58'42 76W57'05 5:07:48
College Park 16
16 38N58'50 76W56'14 5:07:45
College Park Woods 16
16 39N00'31 76W57'05 5:07:48
College View 15
16 39N03 77W03 5:08:12
Collington 16 16 38N58'06 76W45'36 5:07:02
Collison Corner 2
20 38N54'54 76W33'08 5:06:13
Colmar Manor 16
16 38N55'59 76W56'46 5:07:47
Colonial Acres 7
7 39N37 75W50 5:03:20
Colonial Acres 12
8 39N32 76W21 5:05:24
Colonial Gardens 3
3 39N17 76W43 5:06:52
Colonial Heights 1
3 39N38 78W48 5:15:12
Colonial Park 3 3 39N20 76W43 5:06:52
Colonial Park 21
7 39N39 77W44 5:10:56
Colonial Village 24
3 39N21'35 76W42'38 5:06:51
Colora 7 7 39N40'19 76W05'56 5:04:24
Coltons Point 18
4 38N13'28 76W45'13 5:07:01
Columbia 13 3 39N14'25 76W50'23 5:07:22
Columbia Beach 2
20 38N49'04 76W30'03 5:06:00
Columbia Forest 15
16 38N59'24 77W05'10 5:08:21
Columbia Hills 13
3 39N16 76W49 5:07:16
Columbia Park 16
16 38N55'03 76W53'19 5:07:33
Colvilla 6 8 39N34 76W59 5:07:56
Compton 18 4 38N16'30 76W41'36 5:06:46
Comus 15 16 39N14'49 77W21'01 5:09:24
Conaways 2 20 39N01'23 76W41'35 5:06:46
Concord 5 15 38N48'09 75W47'22 5:03:09
Concord 7 7 39N32 75W49 5:03:16
Congressional Forest Estates 15
16 39N00 77W08 5:08:32
Congressional Manor 15
16 38N59'50 77W10'23 5:08:42
Connecticut Avenue Estates 15
16 39N03'14 77W04'08 5:08:17
Connecticut Avenue Hills 15
16 39N02'48 77W04'48 5:08:19
Connecticut Avenue Park 15
16 39N03'45 77W04'41 5:08:19
Connecticut Gardens 15
16 39N02'52 77W04'23 5:08:18
Conners Corner 19
23 38N00'34 75W44'13 5:02:57
Conococheague 21
7 39N39'26 77W50'42 5:11:23
Conowingo (P O) 7
7 39N40'40 76W09'34 5:04:38
Conowingo Village 12
8 39N39'08 76W10'49 5:04:43
Constant Friendship 12
8 39N28 76W17 5:05:08
Contee 16 16 39N04'44 76W51'57 5:07:28
Cooksville 13 3 39N19 77W01 5:08:04
Cooper 12 8 39N41'57 76W17'01 5:05:08
Coopersville 3 3 39N32'51 76W44'32 5:06:58
Coopstown 12 8 39N35'23 76W25'55 5:05:44
Copeland 14 15 39N18'05 76W10'24 5:04:42
Copenhaver 15 16 39N03 77W10 5:08:40
Copperville 6 8 39N38'02 77W09'14 5:08:37
Copperville 20 13 38N49'29 76W10'16 5:04:41
Coral Hills 16 16 38N52'13 76W55'17 5:07:41
Corbett 3 3 39N34'12 76W37'06 5:06:28
Corbett 21 7 39N39 77W44 5:10:56
Corbin 23 27 38N09'19 75W29'28 5:01:58
Cordova 20 8 38N52'32 75W59'47 5:03:59
Cornersville 9 8 38N35'47 76W12'34 5:04:50
Cornfield Harbor 18
4 38N05 76W21 5:05:24
Corriganville 1 3 39N41'34 78W47'35 5:15:10
Corsica Landing 17
15 39N04'33 76W06'43 5:04:27
Costen 19 19 38N06'17 75W37'02 5:02:28
Coster 4 9 38N21'26 76W28'16 5:05:53
Cottage City 16
16 38N56'17 76W56'55 5:07:48
Cottage Grove 19
23 38N06'07 75W40'16 5:02:41
Cottage Grove Beach 2
20 39N09'17 76W30'43 5:06:03
Country Club Acres 11
14 39N24 79W23 5:17:32

Country Club Park 3
3 39N25'34 76W37'57 5:06:32
Country Club Village 15
16 39N01 77W08 5:08:32
Courthouse 15 16 39N05 77W10 5:08:40
Courtleigh 3 3 39N22 76W45 5:07:00
Cove 11 2 39N37 79W19 5:17:16
Coventry 3 3 39N24'12 76W33'18 5:06:13
Cove Point 4 9 38N22'52 76W23'21 5:05:33
Covers Corner 6 8 39N27'44 77W06'56 5:08:28
Cowdensville 3 3 39N14'49 76W42'09 5:06:49
Cowentown 7 7 39N40'50 75W48'56 5:03:16
Cox 4 9 38N35'48 76W38'09 5:06:33
Cox Landing 22 7 38N19'56 75W43'45 5:02:55
Coxs Corner 22 7 38N20 75W52 5:03:28
Craigtown 7 7 39N36'01 76W04'25 5:04:18
Cranberry 6 8 39N37'46 76W56'02 5:07:44
Cranwood 3 3 39N23'38 76W42'33 5:06:50
Crapo 9 8 38N19'11 76W07'53 5:04:32
Creagerstown 10 7 39N34'38 77W21'55 5:09:28
Crellin 11 14 39N23'20 79W27'56 5:17:52
Cremona 18 4 38N27'23 76W39'25 5:06:38
Cresaptown 1 3 39N35'34 78W50'01 5:15:20
Crescendo 20 13 38N48 76W18 5:05:12
Cresthaven 15 16 39N01'30 76W59'29 5:07:58
Crest Leigh 13 3 39N16 76W49 5:07:16
Crestview 15 16 38N57'10 77W06'00 5:08:24
Crestview Manor 16
16 38N47 76W53 5:07:32
Crestwood 2 20 39N12 76W39 5:06:36
Crestwood 22 7 38N22 75W36 5:02:24
Crestwood Acres 12
8 39N23 76W15 5:05:00
Creswell 12 8 39N30'27 76W16'13 5:05:05
Crisfield 19 28 37N59'00 75W51'15 5:03:25
Criswood Manor 13
3 39N12 76W57 5:07:48
Crocheron 9 8 38N14'34 76W03'09 5:04:13
Crofton 2 20 39N00'06 76W41'16 5:06:45
Cromwood 3 3 39N24'05 76W33'14 5:06:13
Cronhardt 3 3 39N26'29 76W42'54 5:06:52
Croom 16 16 38N45'09 76W45'51 5:07:03
Cropley 15 16 38N58'48 77W13'13 5:08:53
Crosby 14 15 39N07'00 76W11'44 5:04:47
Crosier Gardens 16
16 38N50 76W55 5:07:40
Crossroads 9 8 38N23'02 76W11'30 5:04:46
Crouse Mill 6 8 39N37'01 77W12'19 5:08:49
Crowder 13 3 39N16 76W49 5:07:16
Crownsville 2 20 39N01'42 76W36'06 5:06:24
Crows Nest 22 7 38N18'41 75W38'53 5:02:36
Croydon Park 15
16 39N05'13 77W08'37 5:08:34
Crumpton 17 15 39N14'29 75W55'19 5:03:41
Crystal Beach 2
20 39N04'17 76W31'09 5:06:05
Crystal Beach 7 7 39N26'31 75W58'36 5:03:54
Crystal Beach Manor 7
7 39N25 75W55 5:03:40
Crystal Springs 16
16 39N00 76W55 5:07:40
Cub Hill 3 3 39N24'32 76W30'50 5:06:03
Cuckhold Creek 8
6 38N23 76W57 5:07:48
Cumberland 1 24 39N39'10 78W45'46 5:15:03
Cumberlandrive 1
3 39N38 78W48 5:15:12
Cumberstone 2 20 38N51'32 76W33'10 5:06:13
Curtis Bay 24 20 39N13'36 76W35'18 5:06:21
Dailsville 9 8 38N32'49 76W09'37 5:04:38
Daisy 13 3 39N17'37 77W04'08 5:08:17
Dalton 13 3 39N16 76W49 5:07:16
Dam 4 21 7 39N27 77W45 5:11:00
Damascus 15 16 39N17'18 77W12'15 5:08:49
Dameron 18 4 38N09'08 76W22'11 5:05:29
Dames Quarter 19
19 38N11'19 75W53'58 5:03:36
Daniel 6 8 39N26'06 77W03'14 5:08:13
Daniels 3 3 39N19'00 76W49'00 5:07:16
Daniels Park 16
16 39N00'23 76W55'31 5:07:42
Danville 1 3 39N30'20 78W55'42 5:15:43
Danville 16 16 38N41'07 76W55'19 5:07:41
Dar 3 24 39N41'40 76W42'02 5:06:48
Darcy Estates 16
16 38N49 76W56 5:07:44
Dares 4 9 38N33'31 76W32'25 5:06:10
Dares Beach 4 9 38N33'42 76W30'57 5:06:04
Dargan 21 7 39N22'38 77W44'00 5:10:56
Darleigh Manor 3
3 39N23 76W30 5:06:00
Darlington 12 8 39N38'21 76W12'11 5:04:49
Darnall 2 16 38N47'26 76W38'19 5:06:33
Darnestown 15 16 39N06'12 77W17'28 5:09:10
Darryl Gardens 3
3 39N23 76W26 5:05:44
Daugherty Town 19
28 37N59 75W51 5:03:24
Davidsonville 2
20 38N55'22 76W37'43 5:06:31
Dawson 1 3 39N28'39 78W56'38 5:15:47
Dawsonville 15 16 39N07'42 77W20'36 5:09:22
Day 6 8 39N23'14 77W03'20 5:08:13
Daysville 10 7 39N29'33 77W17'48 5:09:11
Dayton 13 3 39N14'21 76W59'13 5:07:57
Deale 2 20 38N46'35 76W33'20 5:06:13
Deale Beach 2 20 38N46'55 76W32'19 5:06:09
Deal Island 19 19 38N09'32 75W56'54 5:03:48
Deanwood Park 16
16 38N54'21 76W55'25 5:07:42
Decatur Heights 16
16 38N57 76W56 5:07:44
Deep Branch 22 7 38N18'52 75W49'33 5:03:18
Deep Creek 2 20 39N03 76W30 5:06:00
Deep Landing 4 16 38N35'46 76W40'09 5:06:41
Deep Landing 14
15 39N08'40 76W15'37 5:05:02
Deep Landing 17
15 39N14'25 75W57'37 5:03:50
Deep Run 6 8 39N41'06 76W59'24 5:07:58
Deerfield 12 8 39N38 76W12 5:04:48
Deerfield 15 16 39N00'54 77W09'50 5:08:39
Deer Park 3 3 39N23'56 76W49'49 5:07:19
Deerpark 6 8 39N30'52 76W57'48 5:07:51
Deer Park 11 14 39N25'25 79W19'31 5:17:18
Deer Park 15 16 39N04'03 76W57'02 5:07:48
Deer Park Heights 16
16 38N49'33 76W57'03 5:07:48
Deer Park Plaza 3
3 39N22 76W45 5:07:00
Deers Head 22 7 38N22 75W36 5:02:24
Defense Heights 16
16 38N56'43 76W54'15 5:07:37
Delight 3 3 39N26'26 76W48'23 5:07:14
Delmar 22 7 38N27'21 75W34'40 5:02:19
Delmont 2 20 39N09 76W40 5:06:40
Den Lee Acres 16
16 38N47 76W53 5:07:32
Denmore Park 24 1 39N20'42 76W40'17 5:06:41
Dennings 6 8 39N29'30 77W04'21 5:08:17
Dennis 22 7 38N19 75W24 5:01:36
Dennis Grove Apartments 16
16 38N48 76W59 5:07:56
Denton 5 11 38N53'04 75W49'39 5:03:19
Dentsville 8 6 38N28'54 76W53'34 5:07:34
Derwood 15 16 39N07'02 77W09'41 5:08:39
Detmold 1 3 39N33'15 78W59'23 5:15:58
Detour 6 8 39N36'14 77W16'06 5:09:04
Devonshire Forest 3
3 39N24'55 76W37'04 5:06:28
Dickens 1 3 39N42'26 78W41'36 5:14:46
Dickerson 15 16 39N13'12 77W25'28 5:09:42
Dickeyville 24 1 39N19'08 76W42'14 5:06:49
Dillon Park 16 16 38N51'57 76W56'15 5:07:45
Discovery 10 7 39N29 77W21 5:09:24
District Heights 16
16 38N51'27 76W53'23 5:07:34
Dixon 17 15 39N10 75W50 5:03:20
Dixon Hill 24 1 39N22'11 76W39'49 5:06:39
Dodge Park 16 16 38N56 76W53 5:07:32
Dodon 2 20 38N53'42 76W37'24 5:06:30
Dogtown 21 7 39N30'21 77W45'56 5:11:04
Dogwood Flats 1 3 39N31'29 79W01'01 5:16:04
Dogwood Hills 3 3 39N25'51 76W33'23 5:06:14
Dominion 17 15 38N56'49 76W16'53 5:05:08
Doncaster 8 6 38N29'52 77W12'39 5:08:51
Donleigh 13 3 39N11 76W52 5:07:28
Donnybrook 3 3 39N23'32 76W35'40 5:06:23
Donovans Pier 2
20 38N57'09 76W33'05 5:06:12
Dorceytown 6 8 39N23'15 77W08'38 5:08:35
Dorchester Estates 16
16 38N47 76W53 5:07:32
Dorchester Heights 24
20 39N15'13 76W39'05 5:06:36
Dorrs Corner 2 20 39N04'24 76W37'51 5:06:31
Dorsey 2 20 39N10'38 76W44'36 5:06:58
Dorsey Crossroads 6
8 39N25'45 77W00'29 5:08:02
Doubs 10 7 39N18'14 77W29'18 5:09:57
Doubs Mill 21 7 39N34'41 77W39'16 5:10:37
Dover 3 3 39N30'44 76W46'11 5:07:05
Dowell 4 9 38N20'46 76W27'33 5:05:50
Downes 5 15 38N55'16 75W53'34 5:03:34
Downsville 21 7 39N32'54 77W48'07 5:11:12
Drawbridge 9 8 38N26 75W53 5:03:32
Drayden 18 4 38N10'43 76W28'55 5:05:56
Dreams Landing 2
20 39N00'20 76W30'45 5:06:03
Dresden Green 16
16 38N58 76W51 5:07:24
Drexell Landing 23
27 38N08'47 75W27'02 5:01:48
Druid 24 1 39N19 76W38 5:06:32
Drumcliff 18 4 38N23'24 76W34'12 5:06:17
Drumeldra Hills 15
16 39N04'55 77W01'13 5:08:05
Drum Point 4 9 38N19'36 76W25'35 5:05:42
Drury 2 20 38N48'44 76W41'35 5:06:46
Drybranch 12 8 39N39'49 76W32'37 5:06:10
Dry Run 21 7 39N42'46 77W52'53 5:11:32
Dublin 12 8 39N39'03 76W16'01 5:05:04
Dubois 8 6 38N28'34 76W49'38 5:07:19
Ducat Town 16 16 38N57'14 76W55'12 5:07:41
Duckettsville 16
16 39N00'40 76W47'56 5:07:12
Dudley Corners 17
15 39N11'02 75W53'32 5:03:34
Duhamel Corners 17
15 39N11'30 75W49'49 5:03:19
Dulaney Village 3
3 39N24'56 76W36'19 5:06:25
Duley 16 16 38N44'55 76W47'54 5:07:12
Dulls Corner 2 20 39N00'06 76W28'40 5:05:55
Dumbarton 3 3 39N22'44 76W42'33 5:06:50
Dumbarton Heights 3
3 39N22 76W43 5:06:52
Dunbrook 2 20 39N09 76W33 5:06:12
Dundalk 3 3 39N15'02 76W31'15 5:06:05
Dundee Village 3
3 39N20 76W27 5:05:48
Dunkirk 4 9 38N43'18 76W39'39 5:06:39
Dunlaney Village 3
3 39N26 76W37 5:06:28
Dunloggin 13 3 39N16 76W49 5:07:16
Dunlops Hills 15
16 38N59'24 77W04'01 5:08:16
Dunwood 12 8 39N25 76W22 5:05:28
Dupont Heights 16
16 38N51'43 76W55'29 5:07:42
Dynard 18 4 38N18'34 76W44'21 5:06:57
Eagle Harbor 16
16 38N34'04 76W41'11 5:06:45
Eagle Hill 2 20 39N05'21 76W28'26 5:05:54
Eakles Mills 21 7 39N28'05 77W41'06 5:10:44
Earleigh Heights 2
20 39N05'33 76W34'33 5:06:18
Earle Landing 17
15 39N04'40 76W08'23 5:04:34
Earleville 7 7 39N24'55 75W55'04 5:03:40
Earlton 12 8 39N34'24 76W08'55 5:04:36
East Brooklyn 24
20 39N13'46 76W34'37 5:06:18
East Columbia Park 16
16 38N56 76W53 5:07:32
East End 24 1 39N18 76W35 5:06:20
Eastfield 3 3 39N14 76W31 5:06:04
East Meadow 16 16 38N48 76W59 5:07:56
East New Market 9
8 38N35'56 75W55'35 5:03:42
East Oakland 11
14 39N26 79W22 5:17:28
Easton 20 11 38N46'27 76W04'36 5:04:18
Easton Point 20
13 38N46 76W04 5:04:16
East Pines 16 16 38N57'35 76W54'35 5:07:38
Eastpoint 3 3 39N14 76W31 5:06:04
Eastport 2 20 38N58'17 76W28'43 5:05:55
East Princess Anne 20
26 38N13 75W38 5:02:32
East Riverdale 16
16 38N58 76W55 5:07:40
East Springbrook 15
16 39N03'30 76W59'16 5:07:57
Eastview 6 8 39N30'26 76W56'56 5:07:48
Eastview 10 7 39N26 77W27 5:09:48
East Vindex 11 2 39N25'04 79W11'15 5:16:45
Ebbvale 6 8 39N40'38 76W55'09 5:07:41
Eccleston 3 3 39N24'19 76W43'45 5:06:55
Eckhart Junction 1
24 39N40'15 78W47'19 5:15:09
Eckhart Mines 1
24 39N39'09 78W53'50 5:15:35
Eden 19 19 38N16'50 75W39'05 5:02:36
Eden Terrace 3 3 39N17 76W43 5:06:52
Eder 7 7 39N37'40 75W54'33 5:03:38
Edesville 14 15 39N09'18 76W12'28 5:04:50
Edgemere 3 3 39N14'31 76W26'54 5:05:48
Edgemont 10 7 39N25'24 77W29'39 5:09:59
Edgemont 21 7 39N40'41 77W32'30 5:10:10
Edgemoor 15 16 38N59'09 77W06'13 5:08:25
Edgewater 2 20 38N57'25 76W33'01 5:06:12
Edgewater Acres 23
19 38N27'01 75W04'05 5:00:16
Edgewater Beach 2
20 38N56'54 76W34'08 5:06:17
Edgewood 10 7 39N27'34 77W28'28 5:09:54
Edgewood 12 8 39N25'07 76W17'41 5:05:11
Edgewood 15 16 38N59'37 77W06'40 5:08:27
Edgewood 16 16 39N00'54 76W55'00 5:07:40
Edgewood Arsenal 12
8 39N28 76W08 5:04:32
Edgewood Heights 12
8 39N25'35 76W17'58 5:05:12
Edgewood Meadows 12
8 39N23 76W15 5:05:00
Edgewood Park 3 3 39N23 76W33 5:06:12
Editors Park 16
16 38N58 76W58 5:07:52
Edmondson Heights 3
3 39N20 76W43 5:06:52
Edmondson Ridge 3
3 39N17 76W43 5:06:52
Edmonston 16 16 38N56'48 76W55'53 5:07:44
Ednor 15 16 39N08'09 76W59'43 5:07:59
Ednor Acres 15 16 39N04 76W59 5:07:56
Egg Hill 7 7 39N37 75W50 5:03:20
Ehrmansville 2 20 39N11'55 76W42'09 5:06:49
Eklo 3 24 39N40'49 76W43'46 5:06:55
Elder Hill 11 2 39N39 79W24 5:17:36
Eldersburg 6 8 39N24'13 76W57'02 5:07:48
Eldorado 9 8 38N35'03 75W47'22 5:03:09
Elioak 13 3 39N14'05 76W53'13 5:07:33
Elk Mills 7 7 39N39'31 75W49'35 5:03:18
Elkmore 7 7 39N37 75W50 5:03:20
Elk Neck 7 7 39N30'46 75W57'06 5:03:48
Elk Ranch Park 7
7 39N37 75W50 5:03:20
Elkridge 13 3 39N12'45 76W42'50 5:06:51
Elkton 7 8 39N36'24 75W50'01 5:03:20
Elkton Heights 7
7 39N36'54 75W50'02 5:03:20
Elktonia 2 20 38N57'42 76W28'33 5:05:54
Elkton Landing 7
7 39N35'51 75W50'28 5:03:22
Elkwood Estates 7
7 39N37 75W50 5:03:20
Ellaville 16 16 38N57'33 76W56'36 5:07:46
Ellerslie 1 3 39N43'14 78W46'28 5:15:06
Ellerton 10 7 39N31'38 77W32'37 5:10:10
Ellicott City 13
3 39N16'02 76W47'55 5:07:12
Elliott 9 8 38N18'36 75W59'48 5:03:59
Ellwood 9 8 38N41'12 75W53'16 5:03:33
Elmer 15 16 39N08'10 77W29'02 5:09:56
Elmwood 3 3 39N21 76W32 5:06:08
Elvaton 2 20 39N07'12 76W35'20 5:06:21
Elvaton Acres 2
20 39N09 76W40 5:06:40
Elwood 9 8 38N38 75W52 5:03:28
Emery Corners 15
16 38N59'32 77W09'41 5:08:39
Emmertsville 21 7 39N32'14 77W44'00 5:10:56
Emmitsburg 10 3 39N42'16 77W19'38 5:09:19
Emmitsburg Junction 10
8 39N36'29 77W19'14 5:09:17
Emmorton 12 8 39N29'43 76W19'23 5:05:18
Emory Church 6 8 39N34 76W50 5:07:20
Emory Grove 3 24 39N28'55 76W49'01 5:07:16
Emory Grove 15 16 39N08'55 77W10'04 5:08:40
Englars Mill 6 8 39N30'39 77W07'36 5:08:30
Engles Mill 11 2 39N38'49 79W17'12 5:17:09
Englewood 16 16 38N56 76W53 5:07:32
English Consul 3
3 39N14'43 76W38'26 5:06:34
English Manor 15
16 39N05'16 77W05'12 5:08:21
English Village 15
16 38N59'17 77W06'56 5:08:28
Ennalls 9 8 38N36'02 75W50'51 5:03:23
Enterprise Estates 16
16 38N30 75W52 5:03:28
Epping Forest 2
20 39N00'51 76W31'55 5:06:08
Ernstville 21 7 39N37'58 78W01'37 5:12:06
Escena 16 16 38N47 76W58 5:07:52
Essex 3 3 39N18'33 76W28'31 5:05:54
Etchison 15 16 39N08 77W12 5:08:48

Etzler Estates 10 7 39N26 77w27 5:09:48
Evergreen 24 1 39N20'42 76w37'40 5:06:31
Evergreen Heights 12 8 39N32 76w21 5:05:24
Evergreen Park 3 3 39N15'22 76w26'10 5:05:45
Evergreen Valley Estates 13 3 39N16 76w49 5:07:16
Evitts Creek 1 3 39N37'27 78w44'03 5:14:56
Evna 3 3 39N35'23 76w41'49 5:06:47
Ewell 19 19 37N59'44 76w02'01 5:04:08
Ewingville 17 15 39N12'03 75w58'58 5:03:56
Exline 21 8 39N40'16 78w16'53 5:13:08
Fairbank 20 13 38N41'08 76w20'18 5:05:21
Fairfield 6 8 39N34 76w59 5:07:56
Fairfield 22 7 38N22 75w36 5:02:24
Fairfield 24 20 39N14'16 76w34'46 5:06:19
Fairfield Knolls 16 16 38N51 76w54 5:07:36
Fairgreen Acres 21 7 39N39 77w44 5:10:56
Fairhaven 2 20 38N44'39 76w33'29 5:06:14
Fairhaven-on-the-Bay 2 20 38N45'06 76w33'23 5:06:14
Fair Hill 7 7 39N42'08 75w52'06 5:03:28
Fairidge 15 16 39N08 77w12 5:08:48
Fairknoll 15 16 39N04'34 76w58'59 5:07:56
Fairland 15 16 39N04'34 76w57'29 5:07:50
Fairland Acres 15 16 39N07 76w56 5:07:44
Fairland Heights 15 16 39N05'05 76w57'42 5:07:51
Fairlee 14 15 39N13'21 76w10'20 5:04:41
Fairmont 12 8 39N32 76w21 5:05:24
Fairmount 19 23 38N05'25 75w49'04 5:03:16
Fairmount Heights 16 16 38N54'03 76w54'57 5:07:40
Fairplay 1 3 39N31'19 78w27'52 5:13:51
Fairplay 21 7 39N32'11 77w44'52 5:10:59
Fairtown 3 3 39N16'22 76w31'22 5:06:05
Fairview 2 20 39N09'13 76w29'45 5:05:59
Fairview 11 2 39N35'36 79w08'47 5:16:35
Fairview 21 7 39N42'13 78w10'41 5:12:43
Fairview Estates 15 16 39N03'54 76w59'12 5:07:57
Fairview Mill 21 7 39N42'02 77w49'50 5:11:19
Fairway 12 8 39N32 76w21 5:05:24
Fairway 15 16 39N01'08 77w01'09 5:08:05
Fairway Hills 15 16 38N58'14 77w08'18 5:08:33
Falls Orchard 15 16 39N03'56 77w10'19 5:08:41
Fallstaff 24 3 39N22'06 76w42'25 5:06:50
Fallston 12 8 39N30'52 76w24'41 5:05:39
Farmington 7 7 39N40'43 76w01'57 5:04:08
Farmington 15 16 38N59 77w05 5:08:20
Faulkner 8 6 38N26'20 76w58'43 5:07:55
Faulkner Ridge 13 3 39N16 76w49 5:07:16
Fawsett Farms 15 16 38N59'52 77w13'20 5:08:53
Feagaville 10 7 39N23'09 77w28'33 5:09:54
Federal Hill 12 8 39N38'27 76w28'18 5:05:53
Federalsburg 5 8 38N41'39 75w46'26 5:03:06
Feesersburg 6 8 39N35'36 77w12'10 5:08:49
Felicity Cove 2 20 38N50'50 76w29'39 5:05:59
Fellowship Forest 3 3 39N23'29 76w35'13 5:06:21
Fenby 6 8 39N31'38 76w59'34 5:07:58
Fenwick 8 6 38N38'34 77w06'30 5:08:26
Ferncliff 12 8 39N37'17 76w24'04 5:05:36
Ferndale 2 20 39N10'59 76w38'26 5:06:34
Fernglen Manor 2 20 39N10 76w37 5:06:28
Fernwood 15 16 39N01'05 77w08'15 5:08:33
Ferry Farms 2 20 38N59'39 76w28'45 5:05:55
Ferry Road 22 7 38N17'58 75w41'27 5:02:46
Fiddlesburg 11 7 39N39'27 77w41'20 5:10:45
Figgs Landing 23 27 38N07'15 75w17'47 5:01:11
Finchville 9 8 38N37'55 75w46'17 5:03:05
Finksburg 6 8 39N29'34 76w53'23 5:07:34
Finzel 11 2 39N42'52 78w56'44 5:15:47
Fishing Creek 9 8 38N20 76w14 5:04:56
Five Forks 3 3 39N40'44 76w39'30 5:06:38
Five Forks 10 7 39N32'56 77w30'05 5:10:00
Fleishman Village 16 16 38N50 76w55 5:07:40
Flickersville 21 7 39N27'01 77w42'09 5:10:49
Flint 10 7 39N39'28 77w26'38 5:09:47
Flint Hill 10 7 39N18'49 77w23'51 5:09:35
Flintstone 1 3 39N42'11 78w34'05 5:14:16
Flohrville 6 8 39N23'31 76w57'56 5:07:52
Florence 13 3 39N18'37 77w06'32 5:08:26
Flower Avenue Park 15 16 38N59 77w01 5:08:04
Flower Valley Estates 15 16 39N05 77w07 5:08:28
Floyd 11 24 39N30'15 79w09'21 5:16:37
Font Hill 13 3 39N16 76w49 5:07:16
Ford Landing 17 15 39N14'46 75w53'41 5:03:35
Foremans Corner 2 20 39N11'09 76w33'07 5:06:12
Forest Estates 15 16 39N01'16 77w02'24 5:08:10
Forest Glen 15 16 39N00'52 77w03'18 5:08:13
Forest Glen Park 15 16 39N00'41 77w03'34 5:08:14
Forest Greens 12 8 39N31 76w10 5:04:40
Forest Grove 22 7 38N22'22 75w28'28 5:01:54
Forest Heights 16 16 38N48'34 76w59'54 5:08:00
Forest Hill 12 8 39N35'06 76w23'17 5:05:33
Forest Knolls 15 16 39N01 77w00 5:08:00
Forest Lake 12 8 39N35 76w23 5:05:32
Forest Manor 16 16 38N50'22 76w53'00 5:07:32
Foreston 3 3 39N36'49 76w45'20 5:07:01
Forest Park 21 8 39N42'10 78w17'59 5:13:12
Forest Park 24 1 39N19'33 76w40'56 5:06:44
Forest Spring Park 3 3 39N17 76w43 5:06:52
Forest Villa 2 20 38N58'20 76w31'19 5:06:05
Forestville 16 16 38N50'42 76w52'31 5:07:30
Forestville Estates 16 16 38N51 76w54 5:07:36
Forestville Phelps Addition 16 16 38N51 76w54 5:07:36
Forge Acres 3 3 39N23 76w26 5:05:44
Forge Heights 3 3 39N24 76w29 5:05:56
Fork 3 3 39N28'05 76w26'32 5:05:46
Forrest Hall 18 4 38N26 76w44 5:06:56
Forsythe 21 7 39N40'35 77w59'17 5:11:57
Fort Carroll 3 3 39N12'50 76w31'09 5:06:05
Fort Deterick 10 3 39N26'07 77w25'44 5:09:43
Fort Detrick 10 7 39N26 77w27 5:09:48
Fort Foote 16 16 38N46'00 77w01'40 5:08:07
Fort Foote Estates 16 16 38N51 76w54 5:07:36
Fort Foote Village 16 16 38N46'11 77w01'04 5:08:04
Fort George G Meade 2 20 39N06'30 76w43'39 5:06:55
Fort Holabird 24 3 39N16'00 76w32'01 5:06:08
Fort Howard 3 3 39N12'26 76w26'43 5:05:47
Fort McHenry 24 20 39N15'47 76w34'48 5:06:19
Fort Meade 2 20 39N06'30 76w43'39 5:06:55
Fort Meade Junction 13 20 39N07'33 76w47'22 5:07:09
Fort Pendleton 11 2 39N17'43 79w22'28 5:17:30
Fort Ritchie 21 7 39N42 77w30 5:10:00
Fort Sumner 15 16 38N57 77w06 5:08:24
Fort Washington Estates 16 16 38N47 76w58 5:07:52
Fort Washington Forest 16 16 38N47 76w58 5:07:52
Foundry Siding 1 24 39N29 79w03 5:16:12
Fountaindale 10 7 39N26 77w33 5:10:12
Fountain Green 12 8 39N32'50 76w18'50 5:05:15
Fountain Green Heights 12 8 39N32 76w21 5:05:24
Fountain Head 21 8 39N42 77w43 5:10:52
Fountain Mills 10 7 39N20'29 77w16'06 5:09:04
Fountain Rock 10 7 39N28'29 77w22'20 5:09:29
Fountain Valley 6 8 39N35'49 77w02'48 5:08:11
Four Corners 5 11 38N57'48 75w45'55 5:03:04
Four Corners 15 16 39N01'13 77w00'47 5:08:03
Four Locks 21 7 39N36'56 77w56'51 5:11:47
Fourpoints 10 7 39N40'18 77w17'58 5:09:12
Four Winds 3 3 39N23'44 76w37'55 5:06:32
Fowblesburg 3 3 39N32'38 76w50'16 5:07:21
Fox Chapel 15 16 39N10 77w16 5:09:04
Foxhall 15 16 39N04'11 77w03'32 5:08:14
Fox Hills 15 16 39N02'25 77w10'17 5:08:41
Fox Hole Landing 14 15 39N22'26 75w49'47 5:03:19
Foxley Manor 14 15 39N13 76w04 5:04:16
Fox Rest Woods 16 16 39N05 76w58 5:07:52
Foxtown 11 2 39N37'57 79w14'19 5:16:57
Fox Trailer Village 3 3 39N20 76w27 5:05:48
Foxville 10 7 39N38'11 77w29'50 5:09:59
Franklin 1 24 39N29'53 79w02'47 5:16:11
Franklin 6 8 39N28 77w04 5:08:16
Franklin Knolls 15 3 39N00'53 76w59'53 5:08:00
Franklin Manor 2 20 38N48'05 76w30'54 5:06:04
Franklin Manor-on-the-Bay 2 20 38N48'05 76w30'54 5:06:04
Franklin Park 15 16 39N03'13 77w05'46 5:08:23
Franklintown 3 3 39N18'16 76w42'43 5:06:51
Franklinville 3 3 39N26'52 76w23'06 5:05:32
Franklinville 6 8 39N27'32 77w05'58 5:08:24
Frederick 10 3 39N24'51 77w24'39 5:09:39
Frederick Junction 10 7 39N22'18 77w23'19 5:09:33
Fredericktown 7 15 39N21'58 75w53'03 5:03:32
Freedom 6 8 39N24'34 76w58'21 5:07:53
Freeland 3 24 39N42'17 76w41'03 5:06:44
Frenchtown 7 25 39N34'31 76w04'55 5:04:20
Frenchtown 19 23 38N04'59 75w51'45 5:03:27
Fricks Crossing 11 14 39N24'41 79w20'01 5:17:20
Friendly 16 16 38N45'06 76w58'44 5:07:55
Friendly Farms 16 16 38N44'07 76w58'35 5:07:54
Friends Creek 10 7 39N42'52 77w24'13 5:09:37
Friendship 2 20 38N44'12 76w35'23 5:06:22
Friendship 15 16 39N18'25 77w11'51 5:08:47
Friendship 23 23 38N22'18 75w12'42 5:00:51
Friendship Heights 15 16 38N57'48 77w05'22 5:08:21
Friendship Park 21 7 39N39 77w44 5:10:56
Friendsville 11 2 39N39'49 79w24'20 5:17:37
Frizzellburg 6 8 39N36'18 77w03'46 5:08:15
Frogeye 19 19 38N01'39 75w41'26 5:02:46
Frogtown 12 8 39N33'29 76w22'14 5:05:29
Frostburg 1 24 39N39'29 78w55'43 5:15:43
Frostown 10 7 39N28'59 77w35'23 5:10:22
Fruitland 22 7 38N19'19 75w37'14 5:02:29
Fuller 10 7 39N24'49 77w28'14 5:09:53
Fullerton 3 3 39N22'18 76w30'41 5:06:03
Fulton 13 3 39N09'03 76w55'24 5:07:42
Funkstown 21 7 39N36'32 77w42'17 5:10:49
Furnace 12 8 39N35'00 76w29'44 5:05:59
Furnace 23 19 38N12'15 75w28'19 5:01:53
Furnace Branch 2 20 39N10'53 76w36'50 5:06:27
Furnace Ford 10 7 39N14'35 77w26'23 5:09:46
Gaither 6 8 39N21'41 76w59'36 5:07:58
Gaithersburg 15 16 39N08'36 77w12'06 5:08:48
Galena 14 15 39N20'26 75w52'45 5:03:31
Galestown 9 8 38N33'58 75w42'55 5:02:52
Galesville 2 20 38N50'35 76w32'38 5:06:11
Gallant Green 8 6 38N38 76w53 5:07:32
Galt 6 8 39N41'20 77w08'21 5:08:33
Gamber 6 8 39N27'53 76w56'03 5:07:44
Gambrills 2 20 39N04'01 76w39'56 5:06:40
Gannon 1 24 39N30'33 79w02'34 5:16:10
Gapland 21 7 39N24'10 77w39'38 5:10:39
Gardenville 24 1 39N19'51 76w33'41 5:06:15
Garfield 10 7 39N36'14 77w31'20 5:10:05
Garland 2 20 39N11'12 76w38'19 5:06:33
Garland 12 8 39N35'21 76w10'23 5:04:42
Garland Park 2 20 39N11'16 76w38'46 5:06:35
Garrett Forest 15 16 39N04 77w04 5:08:16
Garrett Park 15 16 39N02'17 77w05'36 5:08:22
Garrett Park Estates 15 16 39N02'13 77w06'11 5:08:25
Garretts Mill 21 7 39N21'08 77w41'05 5:10:44
Garrison 3 3 39N24'21 76w45'39 5:07:03
Gary 13 3 39N15'36 77w00'33 5:08:02
Gatts Corner 2 20 38N53'37 76w30'37 5:06:02
Gayfields 15 16 39N06'24 77w02'15 5:08:09
Gaywood 16 16 38N58 76w51 5:07:24
Gentsville 3 3 39N30'36 76w42'10 5:06:49
George Island Landing 23 19 38N02'34 75w21'43 5:01:27
Georges Creek 1 24 39N41'52 78w51'13 5:15:25
Georgetown 2 20 39N08'15 76w46'07 5:07:04
Georgetown 14 15 39N13'20 76w11'44 5:04:47
Georgetown Village 15 16 39N01'11 77w07'53 5:08:32
Georgian Forest 15 16 39N04'24 77w03'54 5:08:16
Germantown 2 20 38N53'33 76w31'24 5:06:06
Germantown 3 3 39N25'00 76w27'32 5:05:50
Germantown 15 16 39N10'23 77w16'19 5:09:05
Germantown 23 27 38N18'30 75w12'36 5:00:50
Germantown Estates 15 16 39N10 77w16 5:09:04
Gibson 12 8 39N35'35 76w19'27 5:05:18
Gibson Island 2 20 39N04'27 76w25'27 5:05:42
Gibson Manor 12 8 39N32 76w21 5:05:24
Gilmore 1 3 39N34'58 78w57'01 5:15:48
Gilpin 1 3 39N41'48 78w33'25 5:14:14
Gingerville 2 20 38N57'41 76w33'03 5:06:12
Ginns Corner 7 15 39N23'26 75w48'04 5:03:12
Girdletree 23 23 38N05'40 75w23'52 5:01:35
Gist 6 8 39N27'02 76w59'24 5:07:58
Gittings 3 3 39N28'10 76w29'26 5:05:58
Glade Town 10 7 39N29 77w21 5:09:24
Gladstone Acres 12 8 39N38 76w12 5:04:48
Glass Hill 22 7 38N23'22 75w26'22 5:01:45
Glassmanor 16 16 38N49'08 76w59'56 5:08:00
Glazewood Manor 16 16 38N59 77w01 5:08:04
Glebe Heights 2 20 38N55'38 76w32'34 5:06:10
Glee Mill 6 8 39N27'58 76w58'12 5:07:53
Glemont Forest 15 16 39N03'21 77w03'32 5:08:14
Glen 15 16 39N02'46 77w12'59 5:08:52
Glenallen 15 16 39N03'34 77w02'34 5:08:10
Glenarden 16 16 38N55'45 76w51'43 5:07:27
Glen Arm 3 3 39N27'12 76w29'41 5:05:59
Glenartney 3 20 39N13'49 76w43'44 5:06:55
Glenbrook 15 16 38N59'43 77w05'33 5:08:22
Glenbrook Knoll 15 16 38N59'30 77w06'09 5:08:25
Glenbrook Village 15 16 39N01 77w08 5:08:32
Glen Burnie 2 20 39N09'45 76w37'30 5:06:30
Glencoe 3 3 39N32'56 76w38'08 5:06:33
Glencoe 14 8 39N21'51 75w56'57 5:03:48
Glen Cove 15 16 38N57'26 77w05'51 5:08:23
Glendale 3 3 39N22'47 76w35'09 5:06:21
Glendale 22 7 38N22 75w36 5:02:24
Glendale Heights 16 16 38N58'29 76w49'01 5:07:16
Glen Echo 15 16 38N58'08 77w08'34 5:08:34
Glen Echo Heights 15 16 38N57'30 77w07'34 5:08:30
Glenelg 13 3 39N15'51 76w59'34 5:07:58
Glen Ellen 3 3 39N25'44 76w33'53 5:06:16
Glen Falls 3 8 39N29'15 76w51'51 5:07:27
Glen Farms 7 7 39N41 75w43 5:02:52
Glen Gardens 2 20 39N10 76w37 5:06:28
Glen Hills 15 16 39N04'23 77w12'06 5:08:48
Glen Isle 2 20 39N03 76w30 5:06:00
Glen Kyle 7 7 39N41 75w43 5:02:52
Glenmar 3 3 39N24'04 76w42'35 5:06:50
Glenmar Manor 3 3 39N20'40 76w26'43 5:05:47
Glen Mar Park 15 16 38N57'28 77w07'09 5:08:29
Glen Mary Heights 7 7 39N37 75w50 5:03:20
Glenmont 3 3 39N24 76w36 5:06:24
Glenmont 15 16 39N03'28 77w03'00 5:08:12
Glenmont Forest 15 16 39N04 77w04 5:08:16
Glenmont Heights 15 16 39N04 77w04 5:08:16
Glenmont Hills 15 16 39N03'53 77w03'39 5:08:15

Glenmont Village 15 16 39N03'35 77W03'20 5:08:13
Glenmore 2 20 39N10 76W37 5:06:28
Glenmore Park 24 1 39N20'51 76W41'06 5:06:44
Glen Morris 3 3 39N29'10 76W49'43 5:07:19
Glenndale 16 16 38N59'08 76W49'09 5:07:17
Glenn Heights 12 8 39N33 76W06 5:04:24
Glen Oaks 15 16 39N03 77W10 5:08:40
Glenora Hills 15 16 39N05'21 77W11'25 5:08:46
Glenside Park 3 3 39N23'13 76W31'14 5:06:05
Glenview 15 16 39N01'49 77W02'36 5:08:10
Glenville 12 8 39N36'36 76W12'58 5:04:52
Glenwaye Gardens 15 16 39N04 77W04 5:08:16
Glen Westover 7 7 39N41 75W43 5:02:52
Glenwood 12 8 39N32 76W21 5:05:24
Glenwood 13 3 39N17'15 77W01'42 5:08:07
Glenwood 15 16 38N59'44 77W06'27 5:08:26
Glenwood Park 16 16 38N58 76W51 5:07:24
Glover Acres 6 8 39N34 76W59 5:07:56
Gluckheim 9 8 38N34'47 75W58'08 5:03:53
Glymont 8 6 38N36'04 77W08'39 5:08:35
Glyndon 3 3 39N28'35 76W48'58 5:07:16
Glyn Mar 16 16 38N40 77W02 5:08:08
Golden Beach 18 4 38N29'23 76W40'57 5:06:44
Golden Hill 9 8 38N24'10 76W13'49 5:04:55
Golden Ring 3 3 39N20'04 76W29'41 5:05:59
Golden Ring Mall 3 3 39N20 76W31 5:06:04
Goldsboro 5 8 39N02'02 75W47'13 5:03:09
Golf Club Shores 23 27 38N19 75W13 5:00:52
Golts 14 15 39N20'12 75W46'30 5:03:06
Goodacre Knolls 15 16 38N59'54 77W00'26 5:08:02
Good Acres 21 7 39N39 77W44 5:10:56
Good Hope 15 16 39N05'47 76W59'14 5:07:57
Good Luck 16 16 39N00 76W48 5:07:12
Goodwill 23 19 38N04'14 75W29'31 5:01:58
Gordons Corner 16 16 38N49'57 76W56'25 5:07:46
Gores Mill 3 24 39N40'52 76W41'58 5:06:48
Gorman 11 2 39N17'43 79W20'48 5:17:23
Gortner 11 14 39N21'18 79W25'40 5:17:43
Goshen 15 16 39N12'12 77W11'16 5:08:45
Goshen Estates 15 16 39N08 77W12 5:08:48
Gosnell 6 8 39N24'07 77W05'49 5:08:23
Gotts 2 20 39N02 76W36 5:06:24
Govans 24 1 39N22 76W36 5:06:24
Govanstown 24 3 39N21'50 76W36'36 5:06:26
Governor Run 4 9 38N30'00 76W30'17 5:06:01
Graceham 10 7 39N36'51 77W22'55 5:09:32
Graceland 3 3 39N16'37 76W31'39 5:06:07
Graceland Park 3 3 39N14 76W31 5:06:04
Graceton 12 8 39N43'08 76W23'06 5:05:32
Grahamtown 1 24 39N38'46 78W55'20 5:15:41
Granby Woods 15 16 39N06 77W11 5:08:44
Grand Bel Manor 15 16 39N03 77W03 5:08:12
Granite 3 3 39N20'34 76W51'21 5:07:25
Grantsville 11 17 39N41'42 79W09'05 5:16:36
Grasonville 17 15 38N57'29 76W12'38 5:04:51
Gratitude 14 15 39N08'26 76W15'37 5:05:02
Gravel Hill 11 2 39N39'50 79W23'36 5:17:34
Gray 13 3 39N15'26 76W47'09 5:07:09
Gray Haven 3 3 39N16'09 76W29'11 5:05:57
Gray Manor 3 3 39N16'39 76W29'42 5:05:59
Gray Rock 13 3 39N16 76W49 5:07:16
Grays Corner 23 27 38N20'55 75W10'14 5:00:41
Graystone 3 8 39N37'37 76W38'07 5:06:32
Grayton 8 6 38N25'37 77W12'00 5:08:48
Greater Capitol Heights 16 16 38N52'41 76W55'16 5:07:41
Great Falls 15 16 39N00'08 77W14'47 5:08:59
Great Mills 18 4 38N14'12 76W29'51 5:05:59
Great Oak Manor 14 15 39N16'19 76W10'19 5:04:41
Green Acres 15 16 38N57'37 77W05'58 5:08:24
Green Acres 16 6 38N39'34 76W54'56 5:07:40
Greenbelt 16 16 39N00'16 76W52'33 5:07:30
Greenberry Hills 21 7 39N39 77W44 5:10:56
Greenbrier 3 3 39N23'45 76W35'26 5:06:22
Greenbrier 21 7 39N32'59 77W37'16 5:10:29
Greenfield 16 16 38N47 76W53 5:07:32
Greenfield Mills 10 7 39N15'50 77W26'21 5:09:45
Green Glade 11 2 39N28'26 79W15'54 5:17:04
Green Haven 2 20 39N08'22 76W32'53 5:06:12
Greenhill 19 23 38N07'07 75W39'40 5:02:39
Greenhill Acres 21 7 39N39 77W44 5:10:56
Green Landing 16 20 38N48'21 76W42'32 5:06:50
Green Manor 16 16 38N57'31 76W55'58 5:07:44
Green Meadows 8 6 38N37'14 77W05'20 5:08:21
Green Meadows 16 16 38N58'03 76W58'44 5:07:55
Greenmount 6 8 39N37'52 76W51'46 5:07:27
Greenock 2 20 38N48'55 76W38'00 5:06:32
Green Ridge 1 3 39N35'37 78W25'44 5:13:43
Green Ridge 3 3 39N25'09 76W36'46 5:06:27
Greensboro 5 11 38N58'25 75W48'19 5:03:13
Greensburg 21 7 39N39 77W34 5:10:16
Green Spring Furnace 21 7 39N37'21 77W58'29 5:11:54
Green Spring Hills 12 8 39N25 76W22 5:05:28
Green Spring Junction 3 3 39N24'32 76W46'18 5:07:05
Greentop Manor 3 3 39N28'19 76W37'58 5:06:32
Greentree 15 16 39N08 77W12 5:08:48
Green Tree Manor 15 16 39N00'31 77W07'51 5:08:31
Greenvale Village 21 7 39N39 77W34 5:10:16
Green Valley 10 7 39N18'33 77W17'51 5:09:11
Greenville 6 8 39N40 77W10 5:08:40
Greenwich Forest 15 16 38N59'31 77W06'53 5:08:28
Greenwood 3 3 39N26'02 76W41'53 5:06:48
Greenwood Acres 2 20 38N59'09 76W34'58 5:06:20
Greenwood Farms 13 3 39N11 76W57 5:07:48
Greenwood Forest 16 16 38N58 76W51 5:07:24
Green Wood Knolls 15 16 39N04'18 77W04'14 5:08:17
Grey Estates 15 16 39N02'55 77W01'03 5:08:04
Greystone Manor 21 7 39N39 77W44 5:10:56
Griffin 5 15 38N51'41 75W54'51 5:03:39
Grimes 21 7 39N31'16 77W46'17 5:11:05
Grimesville 3 24 39N41'35 76W42'32 5:06:50
Gross 1 3 39N41 78W40 5:14:40
Grosstown 8 6 38N30'23 76W52'19 5:07:29
Grove 5 15 38N44'57 75W52'38 5:03:31
Grove 10 3 39N24'02 77W23'36 5:09:34
Grove Hill 10 7 39N26 77W27 5:09:48
Guilford 13 3 39N10'11 76W49'51 5:07:19
Guilford 24 1 39N20'05 76W37'06 5:06:28
Guilford Downs 13 3 39N16 76W49 5:07:16
Gum Swamp 9 8 38N25'26 76W10'30 5:04:42
Gum Swamp 22 7 38N21'32 75W49'46 5:03:19
Gunpowder 3 8 39N24'53 76W23'17 5:05:33
Gunpowder Estates 3 3 39N24 76W29 5:05:56
Gwynn Acres 13 3 39N16 76W49 5:07:16
Gwynnbrook 3 3 39N26'38 76W46'55 5:07:08
Gwynn Oak 24 1 39N19'57 76W41'35 5:06:46
Hack Point 7 7 39N27'47 75W52'53 5:03:32
Hacks Point Acre 7 7 39N25 75W55 5:03:40
Hagerstown 11 25 39N38'30 77W43'13 5:10:53
Halethorpe 3 3 39N14'23 76W40'50 5:06:43
Haletown 3 3 39N35'48 76W45'23 5:07:02
Halfway 21 7 39N37'14 77W45'33 5:11:02
Hall 16 16 38N54'08 76W44'09 5:06:57
Hallett Heights 23 27 38N10 75W24 5:01:36
Halley Estates 8 6 38N36 76W57 5:07:48
Hall's Crossroad 12 8 39N32 76W10 5:04:40
Halpine 15 16 39N04 77W07 5:08:28
Halpine View 15 16 39N05 77W07 5:08:28
Halpine Village 15 16 39N03'45 77W07'11 5:08:29
Hambleton 2 20 38N57'24 76W35'21 5:06:21
Hambleton 20 11 38N41'42 76W03'53 5:04:16
Hambleton Estates 2 20 39N03 76W30 5:06:00
Hamilton 24 1 39N21'23 76W33'26 5:06:14
Hamilton Park 21 7 39N39 77W44 5:10:56
Hammond Park 13 3 39N05 76W58 5:07:52
Hammond Wood 15 16 39N03 77W03 5:08:12
Hampden 24 1 39N19'51 76W38'07 5:06:32
Hampshire Knolls 16 16 38N58'05 76W59'43 5:07:59
Hampstead 6 8 39N36'17 76W51'01 5:07:24
Hampton 3 3 39N25'22 76W35'06 5:06:20
Hampton Garden 3 3 39N24 76W36 5:06:24
Hampton Village 3 3 39N25'00 76W35'47 5:06:23
Hance Point 7 7 39N36 75W56 5:03:44
Hancock 21 8 39N41'56 78W10'48 5:12:43
Hanesville 14 15 39N16'33 76W08'09 5:04:33
Hanover 13 20 39N11'34 76W43'28 5:06:54
Hansonville 10 7 39N29'46 77W24'02 5:09:36
Harbor View 2 20 38N53'40 76W30'18 5:06:01
Harborview 3 3 39N16'56 76W31'34 5:06:06
Harewood 3 3 39N22'23 76W20'41 5:05:23
Harewood Park 3 3 39N22'31 76W22'05 5:05:28
Harford Estates 12 8 39N35 76W23 5:05:32
Harford Farms 3 3 39N23 76W33 5:06:12
Harford Furnace 12 8 39N29'42 76W15'42 5:05:03
Harford Hills 3 3 39N23'55 76W31'56 5:06:08
Harford Park 3 3 39N22'37 76W33'14 5:06:13
Harkins 12 8 39N41'49 76W27'04 5:05:48
Harman Gap 21 7 39N37'58 77W32'19 5:10:09
Harmans 2 20 39N09'26 76W41'49 5:06:47
Harmon Landing 23 27 38N11'48 75W15'39 5:01:03
Harmony 5 15 38N46'44 75W52'51 5:03:31
Harmony 10 7 39N29'34 77W31'49 5:10:07
Harmony Grove 10 7 39N27'13 77W23'58 5:09:36
Harmony Hall 16 16 38N44'44 77W00'08 5:08:01
Harmony Hills 15 16 39N04'27 77W04'36 5:08:18
Harney 6 8 39N42'50 77W12'25 5:08:50
Harper's Choice 13 3 39N16 76W49 5:07:16
Harpers Corner 18 4 38N26 76W44 5:06:56
Harrington Manor 3 3 39N25'13 76W31'42 5:06:07
Harrison Ferry 9 8 38N38 75W52 5:03:28
Harrisonville 3 3 39N23'09 76W50'01 5:07:20
Harristown 3 3 39N17'16 76W44'35 5:06:58
Harrisville 6 8 39N25'12 77W08'43 5:08:35
Harrisville 7 7 39N41'44 76W04'54 5:04:20
Harrisville 9 8 38N28'39 76W11'21 5:04:45
Harundale 2 20 39N09'10 76W36'54 5:06:28
Harwood 2 20 38N51'57 76W37'13 5:06:29
Harwood Park 13 3 39N11'37 76W44'17 5:06:57
Hauvers 10 7 39N40 77W28 5:09:52
Havenwood 3 3 39N25'45 76W37'09 5:06:29
Havenwood Hills 21 7 39N39 77W34 5:10:16
Haverford 3 3 39N26'31 76W37'20 5:06:29
Haver Hill 3 3 39N24'17 76W33'09 5:06:13
Havre de Grace 12 8 39N32'57 76W05'31 5:04:22
Havre de Grace Heights 12 8 39N33 76W06 5:04:24
Hawbottom 10 7 39N28'25 77W30'29 5:10:02
Hawkeye 9 8 38N33'34 75W55'09 5:03:41
Hawthorne 3 3 39N20 76W27 5:05:48
Hayden 17 15 39N04'41 75W58'37 5:03:54
Hayes Landing 23 27 38N16'07 75W11'52 5:00:47
Hazelhurst 11 2 39N28'13 79W16'18 5:17:05
Hazelmoor 7 7 39N25 75W55 5:03:40
Hazen 1 3 39N43'13 78W40'53 5:14:44
Head of the Creek 22 7 38N23 75W44 5:02:56
Heather Hill Apartments 16 16 38N49 76W56 5:07:44
Hebbville 3 3 39N20'29 76W45'47 5:07:03
Hebron 22 7 38N25'12 75W41'17 5:02:45
Helen 18 4 38N22'58 76W43'19 5:06:53
Henderson 5 15 39N04'27 75W45'59 5:03:04
Hendry Estates 15 16 39N01 77W08 5:08:32
Henekes Corner 2 20 39N02'10 76W29'36 5:05:58
Henrys Crossroads 9 8 38N25'16 75W52'05 5:03:28
Henryton 6 3 39N21'04 76W54'49 5:07:39
Hepbron 14 15 39N18'16 76W02'11 5:04:09
Herald Harbor 2 20 39N03'13 76W34'10 5:06:17
Hereford 3 3 39N35'20 76W39'49 5:06:39
Heritage Farm 15 16 39N03 77W10 5:08:40
Heritage Harbor 2 20 39N03 76W30 5:06:00
Hermanville 18 4 38N14'49 76W25'46 5:05:43
Hermitage Park 15 16 39N04'46 77W03'51 5:08:15
Hernwood 3 3 39N22'17 76W50'38 5:07:23
Hernwood Heights 3 3 39N22 76W45 5:07:00
Herrington Manor 11 14 39N27'10 79W27'12 5:17:49
Hess 12 3 39N33'21 76W31'33 5:06:06
Hickman 5 15 38N49'59 75W43'24 5:02:54
Hickory 12 8 39N34'43 76W20'44 5:05:23
Hickory Hills 12 8 39N32 76W21 5:05:24
Hickory Thicket 14 15 39N04'36 76W13'48 5:04:55
Hicksburg 9 8 38N33'11 75W57'28 5:03:50
Hidden Point 2 20 38N59'53 76W27'10 5:05:49
High Bridge 16 16 38N57 76W47 5:07:08
High Bridge Estates 16 16 38N58'49 76W46'38 5:07:07
Highfield 15 16 39N08 77W12 5:08:48
Highfield 21 7 39N43'05 77W28'53 5:09:56
Highland 10 7 39N31'15 77W31'06 5:10:04
Highland 13 3 39N10'44 76W57'28 5:07:50
Highland Beach 2 20 38N55'49 76W27'58 5:05:52
Highland Park 16 16 38N54'18 76W53'51 5:07:35
Highland Park 23 27 38N19'14 75W11'20 5:00:45
Highlands 15 16 39N09 77W05 5:08:20
Highland Stone 15 16 39N03 77W10 5:08:40
Highlandtown 24 1 39N17'11 76W34'09 5:06:17
Highland View 15 16 39N00'09 77W00'35 5:08:02
High Meadows 10 7 39N22 77W16 5:09:04
High Point 2 20 39N08'42 76W32'29 5:06:10
High Point 11 17 39N41'41 79W06'16 5:16:25
High Point 12 8 39N33'32 76W25'20 5:05:41
High Point 15 16 38N57'50 77W07'07 5:08:28
High Point Estates 15 16 39N02 76W55 5:07:40
High Ridge 13 3 39N07'05 76W51'32 5:07:26
High Ridge Park 13 3 39N05 76W58 5:07:52
Highview Estates 13 3 39N16 76W49 5:07:16
Highview on the Bay 2 20 38N47 76W36 5:06:24
Hillandale 15 16 39N01'35 76W58'28 5:07:54
Hillandale Forest 16 16 39N01'26 76W57'54 5:07:52
Hillandale Heights 15 16 39N01'15 76W59'19 5:07:57
Hill Crest 15 16 38N59 77W01 5:08:04
Hillcrest Heights 16 16 38N49'58 76W57'35 5:07:50
Hillendale 3 3 39N22'48 76W34'12 5:06:17
Hillendale Farms 3 3 39N23'20 76W33'20 5:06:13
Hillendale Park 3 3 39N23'01 76W33'43 5:06:15
Hillmead 15 16 38N59'52 77W07'39 5:08:31
Hillmeade 16 16 38N58'38 76W47'43 5:07:11
Hillmeade Manor 16 16 38N59'04 76W47'41 5:07:11
Hillsboro 5 15 38N55'00 75W56'21 5:03:45
Hillsborough 16 16 39N07'10 76W53'47 5:07:35
Hillsborough Estates 16 16 39N05 76W58 5:07:52
Hillside 6 8 39N34 76W59 5:07:56
Hillside 16 16 38N52'22 76W55'28 5:07:42
Hillsmere Shores 2 20 38N56'24 76W29'43 5:05:59
Hills Point 9 8 38N36'13 76W14'17 5:04:57
Hill Top 8 6 38N29'20 77W07'20 5:08:29
Hillville 18 4 38N22'21 76W36'10 5:06:25
Hi-Point 11 2 39N42'21 79W12'39 5:16:51

Hipsleys Mill 13 3 39N16'35 77w06'19 5:08:25
Hobbs 5 15 38N51'41 75w47'05 5:03:08
Hoffman 1 24 39N38'08 78w54'22 5:15:37
Hoffmans Mill 6 8 39N35'00 76w53'25 5:07:34
Hoffmanville 3 3 39N41'07 76w46'38 5:07:07
Hog Island 9 8 38N14'17 76w03'47 5:04:15
Holbrook 3 3 39N23'40 76w51'11 5:07:25
Holiday Acres 21 7 39N39 77w34 5:10:16
Holiday Beach 4 9 38N38'51 76w31'35 5:06:06
Holiday Park 15 16 39N03'03 77w04'57 5:08:20
Holland Cliff Shores 4 9 38N37 76w37 5:06:28
Hollands Crossroads 9 8 38N26'50 75w50'55 5:03:24
Hollingsworth Crossroads 5 15 39N02'37 75w49'34 5:03:18
Hollingsworth Manor 7 7 39N37 75w50 5:03:20
Hollinridge 15 16 39N03'17 77w12'41 5:08:51
Hollinsworth Manor 7 8 39N36'12 75w50'45 5:03:23
Hollofield 3 3 39N18'55 76w47'38 5:07:11
Holloway Estates 16 16 38N47 76w52 5:07:28
Holly Beach 3 3 39N17'10 76w23'18 5:05:33
Holly Grove 23 27 38N19'56 75w09'21 5:00:37
Holly Hill 15 16 39N00 77w08 5:08:32
Holly Hill Harbor 2 20 38N54'03 76w31'28 5:06:06
Holly Landing 2 20 38N49'50 76w32'52 5:06:11
Holly Spring 16 16 38N51 76w54 5:07:36
Hollywood 16 16 39N00'44 76w55'32 5:07:42
Hollywood 18 4 38N20'45 76w34'19 5:06:17
Hollywood Beach 7 7 39N32 75w49 5:03:16
Hollywood Estates 16 16 39N00 76w55 5:07:40
Hollywood Park 15 16 39N03'58 76w59'45 5:07:59
Hollywood Shores 18 4 38N23'29 76w34'48 5:06:19
Holmehurst 16 16 38N57'21 76w47'47 5:07:11
Home Acres 16 16 39N02'30 76w55'27 5:07:42
Homecrest 3 3 39N21 76w32 5:06:08
Homecrest 15 16 39N05'25 77w03'20 5:08:13
Homeland 24 1 39N21'29 76w37'29 5:06:30
Homestead Estates 15 16 39N03'11 76w59'13 5:07:57
Homewood 1 3 39N40'28 78w47'39 5:15:11
Homewood 15 16 39N01'31 77w03'47 5:08:15
Honga 9 8 38N20'40 76w13'48 5:04:55
Hood College 10 7 39N26 77w27 5:09:48
Hoods Mill 6 3 39N21'17 77w00'43 5:08:03
Hoopers Island 9 8 38N19 76w14 5:04:56
Hoopersville 9 8 38N15'40 76w10'49 5:04:43
Hope 17 15 39N02'31 75w58'11 5:03:53
Hope Hill 10 7 39N20'00 77w23'48 5:09:35
Hopeland 10 7 39N26 77w27 5:09:48
Hopewell 19 28 38N00'22 75w49'07 5:03:16
Hopkins Corner 12 8 39N39'06 76w13'04 5:04:52
Hopkins Mead 13 3 39N12 76w57 5:07:48
Horizon Run 15 16 39N08 77w12 5:08:48
Horsehead 16 16 38N38'59 76w46'18 5:07:05
Horse Landing 18 4 38N26'18 76w38'43 5:06:35
Horseshoe Curve 1 24 39N38'16 78w53'31 5:15:34
Houcks Mill 3 3 39N35'10 76w52'54 5:06:12
Houcksville 6 8 39N34'16 76w52'49 5:07:31
Howard Heights 13 3 39N16 76w49 5:07:16
Howard Park 24 1 39N19'52 76w41'42 5:06:47
Howardsville 3 3 39N21'41 76w43'26 5:06:54
Hoyes 11 2 39N35'25 79w22'11 5:17:29
Hoyes Run 11 2 39N31'41 79w24'39 5:17:39
Hubbard 9 8 38N36'24 75w54'13 5:03:37
Huckleberry 8 6 38N24'56 76w59'12 5:07:57
Hudson 9 8 38N35'31 76w15'17 5:05:01
Hudson Corner 19 23 38N03'11 75w42'32 5:02:50
Hudson Heights 24 3 39N17'04 76w32'00 5:06:08
Hudson Landing 23 23 38N05'00 75w21'05 5:01:24
Hughesville 8 6 38N31'57 76w47'03 5:07:08
Hungerford Towne 15 16 39N04'28 77w08'53 5:08:36
Hunt Club Estates 13 3 39N15 76w41 5:06:44
Hunters Hill 3 3 39N26'01 76w36'26 5:06:26
Hunters Mill 3 3 39N37'20 76w37'04 5:06:28
Huntersville 18 4 38N28'09 76w43'50 5:06:55
Hunting Hill 15 16 39N05'49 77w12'26 5:08:50
Hunting Hills 4 9 38N37 76w37 5:06:28
Hunting Lodge 3 3 39N25'09 76w31'31 5:06:06
Hunting Park 22 7 38N22 75w36 5:02:24
Hunting Ridge 24 3 39N17'33 76w42'08 5:06:49
Hunting Ridge Estates 12 8 39N30 76w28 5:05:52
Huntington 15 16 38N59'14 77w06'28 5:08:26
Huntington 16 16 39N00'11 76w46'44 5:07:07
Huntington Terrace 15 16 38N59'45 77w06'52 5:08:27
Huntingtown 4 9 38N36'57 76w36'48 5:06:27
Hunts Corner 16 16 38N48'06 76w59'57 5:08:00
Huntsmoor 3 3 39N15 76w41 5:06:44
Huntsville 16 16 38N52'36 76w55'36 5:07:42
Hunt Valley 3 3 39N29 76w39 5:06:36
Hurlock 9 8 38N37'27 75w51'17 5:03:25
Hurry 18 4 38N20'13 76w46'33 5:07:06
Hutchison 15 16 39N15'16 77w08'38 5:08:35
Hutton 11 14 39N24'51 79w28'47 5:17:55
Huyett 21 7 39N39'05 77w47'58 5:11:12
Hyattstown 15 16 39N16'58 77w18'54 5:09:16
Hyattsville 16 16 38N57'21 76w56'45 5:07:47
Hyattsville Hills 16 16 38N57'38 76w57'05 5:07:48
Hyde Park 3 3 39N17'15 76w26'28 5:05:46
Hydes 3 3 39N29'02 76w29'37 5:05:58
Hynesboro 16 16 38N58'18 76w51'37 5:07:26
Hynson 5 15 38N42'11 75w51'31 5:03:26
Idlewilde 2 20 38N51'00 76w29'47 5:05:59
Idlewylde 3 3 39N22'31 76w35'24 5:06:22
Iglehart 2 20 39N00'42 76w34'04 5:06:16
Ijamsville 10 7 39N21'37 77w19'23 5:09:18
Ilchester 13 3 39N15'03 76w45'54 5:07:04
Indianbone 9 8 38N29'24 76w00'46 5:04:03
Indian Hammock 19 28 37N59'47 75w46'12 5:03:05
Indian Head 8 6 38N36'00 77w09'45 5:08:39
Indian Head Manor 8 6 38N37'58 77w03'40 5:08:15
Indian Head Plant 8 6 38N35 77w12 5:08:48
Indian Queen East 16 16 38N47 76w58 5:07:52
Indian Queen Estates 16 16 38N47 76w58 5:07:52
Indian Springs 10 7 39N27'53 77w26'52 5:09:47
Indian Springs 21 7 39N38'47 78w00'07 5:12:00
Indian Spring Terrace 15 16 39N00'46 77w00'45 5:08:03
Indian Spring Village 15 3 39N01'08 77w00'13 5:08:01
Indian Town 17 15 39N07'08 76w05'43 5:04:23
Indiantown 18 4 38N21'54 76w50'06 5:07:20
Indiantown 23 27 38N11'19 75w24'28 5:01:38
Ingleside 17 15 39N05'32 75w52'38 5:03:31
Inverness 3 3 39N15'45 76w29'33 5:05:58
Inverness Forest 15 16 39N03 77w10 5:08:40
Inverness Village 15 16 39N03 77w10 5:08:40
Inwood 13 3 39N18'08 77w01'14 5:08:05
Iron Hill 7 7 39N38'44 75w47'27 5:03:10
Iron Pot Landing 16 20 38N47'35 76w43'15 5:06:53
Ironshire 23 27 38N17'02 75w13'53 5:00:56
Ironsides 8 6 38N29'30 77w09'36 5:08:38
Irvington 24 1 39N16'58 76w41'11 5:06:45
Island Creek 4 9 38N26'56 76w33'39 5:06:15
Island View Beach 3 3 39N16'00 76w23'49 5:05:35
Issue 8 6 38N17 76w53 5:07:32
Iverness 19 26 38N08'06 75w48'41 5:03:15
Ivory 13 3 39N16'57 76w58'44 5:07:55
Ivory Mill 12 8 39N40'27 76w32'12 5:06:09
Ivy Hills 13 3 39N16 76w49 5:07:16
Ivytown 20 13 38N46 76w04 5:04:16
Jackson 7 25 39N34'57 76w02'32 5:04:10
Jackson 10 7 39N31 77w33 5:10:12
Jackson Grove 2 20 39N06'14 76w42'31 5:06:50
Jackson Landing 16 20 38N46'22 76w42'37 5:06:50
Jacksonville 3 3 39N31'05 76w33'35 5:06:14
Jacksonville 19 28 37N59 75w51 5:03:24
Jacktown 9 8 38N34 76w05 5:04:20
Jacobsville 2 20 39N07'17 76w31'04 5:06:04
James 9 8 38N35'08 76w15'32 5:05:02
Jarrettsville 12 8 39N36'16 76w28'41 5:05:55
Jasontown 6 8 39N34'05 77w04'13 5:08:17
Jefferson 10 7 39N21'43 77w31'55 5:10:08
Jefferson Heights 10 7 39N22 77w32 5:10:08
Jefferson Heights 16 16 38N54 76w54 5:07:36
Jenkins 3 3 39N28'55 76w28'52 5:05:55
Jenkins Corner 16 16 38N47'11 76w53'51 5:07:35
Jenkins Landing 22 7 38N24'04 75w46'19 5:03:05
Jennings 11 2 39N38'47 79w10'58 5:16:44
Jericho Park 16 16 39N01'04 76w45'55 5:07:04
Jersey 19 19 37N58'27 75w51'40 5:03:27
Jerusalem 3 3 39N27'46 76w23'22 5:05:33
Jerusalem 10 7 39N31'27 77w34'49 5:10:19
Jerusalem 15 16 39N09'33 77w24'23 5:09:38
Jessup 2 20 39N08'57 76w46'32 5:07:06
Jesterville 22 7 38N17'12 75w53'46 5:03:35
Jewell 2 20 38N45'17 76w37'08 5:06:29
Jimtown 10 7 39N35'57 77w23'35 5:09:34
Johnny Landing 18 4 38N09'57 76w28'36 5:05:54
Johnsons 11 2 39N42 78w59 5:15:56
Johnsontown 14 15 39N08'15 76w07'01 5:04:28
Johnstown 4 9 38N19'44 76w27'50 5:05:51
Johnsville 6 8 39N24'59 76w57'27 5:07:50
Johnsville 10 7 39N32'02 77w13'52 5:08:55
Jones 2 20 39N03'22 76w31'46 5:06:07
Jones Landing 17 15 39N15'33 75w51'16 5:03:25
Jonestown 5 15 38N43'46 75w53'30 5:03:34
Jonestown 13 3 39N13'19 76w48'28 5:07:14
Jonestown 18 4 38N15'22 76w26'21 5:05:45
Jonesville 15 16 39N09'27 77w23'51 5:09:35
Joppa 12 8 39N26'01 76w21'29 5:05:26
Joppa Heights 3 3 39N24'07 76w32'47 5:06:11
Joppa Manor 3 3 39N23'48 76w31'55 5:06:08
Joppa Springs 3 3 39N23 76w33 5:06:12
Joppatowne 12 8 39N25 76w21 5:05:24
Josenhans 3 3 39N18'58 76w26'57 5:05:48
Joyce 2 20 39N01'29 76w31'13 5:06:05
Joyce Lane 2 20 39N03 76w30 5:06:00
Jugtown 21 7 39N36'45 77w35'39 5:10:23
Jumptown 5 15 38N57'40 75w55'08 5:03:41
Kaese Mill 11 2 39N39'01 79w17'47 5:17:11
Kalmia 12 8 39N36'19 76w18'16 5:05:13
Kalten Acres 6 8 39N34 76w59 5:07:56
Kane Crossroads 5 15 39N07'12 75w48'35 5:03:14
Kastle Acres 16 16 38N47 76w53 5:07:32
Kaywood Gardens 16 16 38N56'35 76w58'10 5:07:53
Kearney 11 2 39N20'35 79w19'21 5:17:17
Keedysville 21 7 39N29'10 77w42'00 5:10:48
Keeler Glade 11 2 39N39 79w24 5:17:36
Keifers 1 3 39N31'51 78w27'58 5:13:52
Keller 10 7 39N20'09 77w26'37 5:09:46
Kemp Mill 15 16 39N02 77w01 5:08:04
Kemp Mill Estates 15 16 39N02'32 77w01'20 5:08:05
Kemps 21 7 39N36'49 77w48'49 5:11:15
Kempton 11 2 39N12'24 79w29'08 5:17:57
Kemptown 10 7 39N20'11 77w13'41 5:08:55
Kendall 11 2 39N38'00 79w25'04 5:17:40
Ken Gar 15 16 39N01'53 77w04'42 5:08:19
Kenilworth Park 24 1 39N21'15 76w35'54 5:06:24
Kenmore 16 16 38N56 76w53 5:07:32
Kennedyville 14 8 39N18'19 75w59'43 5:03:59
Kensington 15 16 39N01'32 77w04'36 5:08:18
Kensington Estates 15 16 39N01'38 77w05'04 5:08:20
Kensington Heights 15 16 39N01'58 77w03'51 5:08:15
Kensington Knolls 15 16 39N02'36 77w04'25 5:08:18
Kensington View 15 16 39N02'23 77w03'36 5:08:14
Kent 16 16 38N55 76w51 5:07:24
Kent Island 17 15 38N57 76w19 5:05:16
Kent Island Estates 17 15 38N59 76w19 5:05:16
Kentland 16 16 38N55'25 76w52'49 5:07:31
Kentmore Park 14 15 39N21'59 75w58'04 5:03:52
Kentmorr 17 15 38N59 76w19 5:05:16
Kent Village 16 16 38N55'30 76w53'04 5:07:32
Kenwood 3 3 39N16'17 76w42'40 5:06:51
Kenwood 15 16 38N58'15 77w06'20 5:08:25
Kenwood Beach 4 9 38N29'52 76w30'13 5:06:01
Kenwood Park 15 16 38N58'39 77w07'06 5:08:28
Kerby Hill 16 16 38N46'49 77w00'09 5:08:01
Kerby Hills 16 16 38N48 76w59 5:07:56
Kettering 16 16 38N47 76w52 5:07:28
Keymar 6 8 39N35'58 77w14'14 5:08:57
Keysers Ridge 11 2 39N42 79w10 5:16:40
Keysville 6 8 39N38'02 77w15'32 5:09:02
Kidmore Lane 16 16 38N58 76w51 5:07:24
Kidwells Corner 16 16 38N53'45 76w43'08 5:06:53
Kifer 1 3 39N34 78w29 5:13:56
Kilby Corner 7 7 39N40'39 76w09'34 5:04:38
Kilmarock 15 16 38N59'18 76w59'55 5:08:00
Kimberley 15 16 38N58'50 77w09'01 5:08:36
Kings County 3 3 39N29 76w23 5:05:32
Kings Grove 1 3 39N43 78w44 5:14:56
Kingsley 15 16 39N15'53 77w16'44 5:09:07
Kings Manor 8 6 38N36 76w57 5:07:48
Kings Ridge 3 3 39N23'06 76w32'39 5:06:11
Kingston 19 23 38N04'28 75w43'42 5:02:55
Kingston Landing 20 15 38N46'54 75w57'56 5:03:52
Kingstown 17 15 39N12'17 76w03'06 5:04:12
Kings Valley 15 16 39N16'07 77w14'07 5:08:56
Kingsville 3 3 39N26'55 76w25'05 5:05:40
Kirby Landing 17 15 39N14'57 75w52'33 5:03:30
Kirkham 20 13 38N45'45 76w08'40 5:04:35
Kirkwood 16 16 38N57'34 76w58'07 5:07:52
Kitts Hill 23 27 38N19'56 75w11'14 5:00:45
Kittys Corner 20 8 38N50'46 75w59'03 5:03:56
Kitzmiller 11 2 39N23'16 79w10'57 5:16:44
Klej Grange 23 19 38N04 75w34 5:02:16
Kline Mill 21 7 39N33'02 77w40'44 5:10:43
Klondike 1 24 39N36'33 78w57'46 5:15:51
Knapps Meadow 1 3 39N34 78w59 5:15:56
Knettishall 3 3 39N23'34 76w34'12 5:06:17
Knoebel 3 3 39N29'23 76w31'23 5:06:06
Knoebels Corner 3 3 39N27 76w30 5:06:00
Knollview 13 3 39N16 76w49 5:07:16
Knollwood 3 3 39N23'15 76w35'42 5:06:23
Knollwood 13 16 39N15'49 77w01'34 5:08:06
Knollwood 16 16 39N01'33 76w57'30 5:07:50
Knotts Crossing 8 6 38N35'39 77w07'19 5:08:29
Knoxville 10 7 39N19'37 77w39'52 5:10:39
Kolbes Corner 16 16 38N54'01 76w47'34 5:07:10
Kraft Corner 3 3 39N19'59 76w49'20 5:07:17
Kreigbaum 11 3 39N41'32 78w47'10 5:15:09
Kump Station 6 8 39N40 77w10 5:08:40
Ladiesburg 10 7 39N34'35 77w15'55 5:09:04
Lake 3 3 39N23'29 76w38'28 5:06:34
Lake Ford 11 14 39N31'36 79w28'49 5:17:55
Lakeland 2 20 39N04'45 76w35'54 5:06:24
Lakeland 24 20 39N15'29 76w39'04 5:06:36
Lake Linganore 10 7 39N26 77w27 5:09:48
Lake Normandy Estates 15 16 39N02'36 77w11'19 5:08:45
Lake Roland 3 3 39N24 76w36 5:06:24
Lakes 9 8 38N22 76w08 5:04:32
Lake Shore 2 20 39N06'25 76w29'07 5:05:56
Lakeside Manor 15 16 39N05 77w07 5:08:28
Lakeside Vista 12 8 39N25 76w22 5:05:28
Lakesville 9 8 38N20'55 76w08'29 5:04:34
Lakeview 13 3 39N05 76w58 5:07:52
Lake Village 16 16 38N57 76w47 5:07:08
Lakewood 22 7 38N20'12 75w36'04 5:02:24
Lakewood Estates 4 9 38N43 76w40 5:06:40

Lakewood Estates 15
16 39N04'50 77w12'17 5:08:49
Lambson 14 15 39N18'39 75w53'24 5:03:34
Lancaster Corner 12
8 39N31'55 76w26'48 5:05:47
Landaff 20 11 38N43'32 76w04'55 5:04:20
Lander 10 7 39N18'32 77w33'34 5:10:14
Landon Village 15
16 38N59'11 77w07'18 5:08:29
Landonville 19 23 38N05'59 75w48'32 5:03:14
Landon Woods 15
16 39N01 77w08 5:08:32
Landover 16 16 38N56'02 76w53'49 5:07:35
Landover Estates 16
16 38N58 76w53 5:07:32
Landover Hills 16
16 38N56'35 76w53'33 5:07:34
Landover Knolls 16
16 38N56 76w53 5:07:32
Landover Park 16
16 38N55'30 76w54'46 5:07:39
Lands End 2 20 38N56'54 76w28'00 5:05:52
Lane Beach 18 4 38N18 76w39 5:06:36
Langford 14 15 39N11'18 76w08'28 5:04:34
Langley Park 16
16 38N59'19 76w58'54 5:07:56
Langmaid Landing 23
19 38N13'53 75w15'05 5:01:00
Lanham 16 16 38N58'01 76w51'44 5:07:27
Lanham Acres 16
16 38N58 76w51 5:07:24
Lanham Heights 16
16 38N58 76w51 5:07:24
Lansdowne 3 3 39N14'42 76w39'39 5:06:39
Lantz 10 7 39N41 77w27 5:09:48
Lap 1 24 39N41'41 78w50'49 5:15:23
Lapidum 12 8 39N35'52 76w07'45 5:04:31
LaPlata 8 6 38N31'45 76w58'32 5:07:54
Lappans 21 7 39N33'13 77w44'15 5:10:57
Larchmont Knolls 15
16 39N00'41 77w04'41 5:08:19
Largo 16 16 38N53'51 76w49'50 5:07:19
La-Rox Heights 6
8 39N34 76w59 5:07:56
Lauraville 24 1 39N20'41 76w33'28 5:06:14
Laurel 16 16 39N05'57 76w50'55 5:07:24
Laurel Acres 2 20 39N05'35 76w31'03 5:06:04
Laurel Brook 12 8 39N30'24 76w25'45 5:05:43
Laureldale 3 3 39N22'53 76w32'36 5:06:10
Laurel Grove 18 4 38N24'42 76w40'41 5:06:43
Laurel Shopping Center 16
16 39N05 76w58 5:07:52
Laurel Walk 16 16 39N05 76w58 5:07:52
LaVale 11 3 39N39'20 78w48'39 5:15:15
Lawndale 6 8 39N31'18 76w52'40 5:07:31
Lawsonia 19 28 37N58'29 75w50'03 5:03:20
Lawsons 19 19 38N00 75w48 5:03:12
Lawyer Heights 10
7 39N38 77w25 5:09:40
Layhill 15 16 39N05'32 77w02'41 5:08:11
Layhill Gardens 15
16 39N04 77w04 5:08:16
Layhill South 15
16 39N04'08 77w02'35 5:08:10
Layhill Village 15
16 39N05'03 77w03'06 5:08:12
Laytonia 15 16 39N08 77w12 5:08:48
Laytonsville 15
16 39N12'43 77w08'35 5:08:34
Leahigh 24 1 39N20'49 76w41'40 5:06:47
Leeds 7 7 39N39'09 75w52'50 5:03:31
Leeland 16 16 38N52'26 76w44'56 5:07:00
Lees Mill 6 8 39N30'54 77w01'27 5:08:06
Lees Woods 12 8 39N32 76w21 5:05:24
Le Gore 10 7 39N33'15 77w18'45 5:09:15
Lehmans Mill 11 8 39N42'42 77w40'31 5:10:42
Leisure World 15
16 39N04 77w04 5:08:16
Leitch 2 20 38N45'54 76w33'47 5:06:15
Leitersburg 21 7 39N41'33 77w37'23 5:10:30
Lelands Corner 15
16 39N00'43 77w09'37 5:08:38
Leon 2 20 38N47'34 76w42'06 5:06:48
Leonardtown 18 4 38N17'28 76w38'10 5:06:33
Lereley 3 3 39N24'20 76w24'10 5:05:37
Leslie 7 7 39N37'10 75w57'05 5:03:48
Level 12 8 39N34'49 76w11'37 5:04:46
Lewis Corner 23
27 38N17'24 75w09'05 5:00:36
Lewisdale 15 16 39N17'10 77w15'41 5:09:03
Lewisdale 16 16 38N58'24 76w58'27 5:07:54
Lewis Heights 16
16 38N59 76w58 5:07:52
Lewis Landing 9 8 38N24'50 75w51'05 5:03:24
Lewis Mill 10 7 39N22'21 77w33'35 5:10:14
Lewis Spring Manor 16
16 38N47 76w53 5:07:32
Lewistown 10 7 39N32'15 77w24'57 5:09:40
Lewistown 20 8 38N50'42 75w56'53 5:03:48
Lexington Park 18
4 38N16'00 76w27'15 5:05:49
Liberty 10 7 39N29 77w15 5:09:00
Liberty Grove 7 7 39N39'21 76w07'13 5:04:29
Liberty Manor 3 3 39N20 76w43 5:06:52
Libertytown 10 7 39N29'06 77w14'26 5:08:58
Libertytown 23 27 38N19'08 75w17'56 5:01:12
Lilypons 10 7 39N17'42 77w25'53 5:09:44
Lime Kiln 10 7 39N20'55 77w25'33 5:09:42
Linchester 5 15 38N42'03 75w53'47 5:03:35
Lincoln 16 16 38N57'47 76w49'11 5:07:17
Lincoln Avenue 21
7 39N39 77w44 5:10:56
Lincoln Heights 22
7 38N22 75w36 5:02:24
Lincoln Park 15
16 39N05 77w10 5:08:40
Linden 15 16 39N00'29 77w02'58 5:08:12
Linden Heights 3
3 39N23 76w33 5:06:12
Linden Springs 3
24 39N42'51 76w43'04 5:06:52
Lineboro 6 8 39N43'07 76w50'39 5:07:23
Linganore 10 7 39N26'25 77w12'30 5:08:50
Linhigh 3 3 39N21 76w32 5:06:08
Linkwood 9 8 38N32'23 75w56'47 5:03:47
Linstead-on-the-Severn 2
20 39N03'53 76w33'39 5:06:15
Linthicum 2 20 39N12 76w39 5:06:36
Linthicum Heights 2
20 39N12'12 76w39'45 5:06:39
Linwood 6 8 39N33'48 77w08'35 5:08:34
Lipins Corner 2
20 39N07'57 76w34'55 5:06:20
Lisbon 13 3 39N20'10 77w04'17 5:08:17
Little Georgetown 23
27 38N26'59 75w08'11 5:00:33
Little Orleans 1
3 39N37'33 78w23'12 5:13:33
Livingston Grove 16
16 38N40 77w02 5:08:08
Livingston Park 16
16 38N48 76w59 5:07:56
Llandaff 20 13 38N46 76w04 5:04:16
Lloyd Landing 20
13 38N41'54 75w59'57 5:04:00
Lloyds 9 8 38N35'23 76w11'00 5:04:44
Loartown 1 24 39N39 78w55 5:15:40
Loarville 1 24 39N37'15 78w53'41 5:15:35
Lochearn 3 3 39N20'26 76w43'21 5:06:53
Loch Glen 3 3 39N24 76w36 5:06:24
Loch Hill 3 3 39N22'36 76w34'56 5:06:20
Loch Lynn Heights 11
14 39N23'35 79w22'24 5:17:30
Loch Raven 3 3 39N25'08 76w32'08 5:06:09
Loch Raven Heights 3
3 39N23'18 76w33'45 5:06:15
Loch Raven Village 3
3 39N23'17 76w34'12 5:06:17
Locust Grove 11 2 39N39'12 79w27'35 5:17:50
Locust Grove 14 8 39N19'49 75w56'47 5:03:47
Locust Grove 21 7 39N26'54 77w39'54 5:10:40
Locust Grove Beach 4
9 38N39'09 76w31'42 5:06:07
Locust Hill Estates 15
16 39N00'39 77w05'45 5:08:23
Locust Valley 10
7 39N25'21 77w37'51 5:10:31
Lodgecliffe 9 8 38N34 76w05 5:04:20
Lodge Forest 3 3 39N14 76w31 5:06:04
Lombard 7 7 39N43'07 75w56'48 5:03:47
Lonaconing 1 24 39N33'57 78w58'50 5:15:55
Londontowne 2 20 38N56 76w33 5:06:12
Lone Holly 8 6 38N17'27 76w54'58 5:07:40
Lone Oak 15 16 39N01'11 77w07'06 5:08:28
Long 1 3 39N38 78w48 5:15:12
Long Bar Harbor 12
8 39N28 76w17 5:05:08
Long Beach 4 9 38N27'39 76w28'09 5:05:53
Long Corner 13 3 39N20'02 77w09'20 5:08:37
Longfellow 13 3 39N16 76w49 5:07:16
Longfield 9 8 38N26'10 76w01'29 5:04:06
Longford 3 3 39N26 76w37 5:06:28
Long Green 3 3 39N28'22 76w31'24 5:06:06
Long Green Station 3
3 39N27 76w30 5:06:00
Long Meadow 6 8 39N24 76w56 5:07:44
Long Meadow Estates 15
16 39N01 77w08 5:08:32
Long Meadows Estates 3
3 39N23'18 76w42'49 5:06:51
Longridge 23 23 38N23'26 75w16'51 5:01:07
Longview Beach 18
4 38N17'36 76w48'29 5:07:14
Longville 6 8 39N41'24 77w11'15 5:08:45
Longwood 15 16 39N00'37 77w08'43 5:08:35
Longwoods 20 8 38N51'29 76w04'45 5:04:19
Lord 1 24 39N39 78w55 5:15:40
Loreley 3 3 39N23 76w26 5:05:44
Loretta Heights 2
20 38N59'03 76w32'08 5:06:09
Loretto 19 7 38N15'37 75w40'55 5:02:44
Lothian 2 20 38N50 76w37 5:06:28
Louisville 6 8 39N26'55 76w55'27 5:07:42
Lou Mar Estates 12
8 39N28 76w17 5:05:08
Love Point 17 15 39N01'55 76w18'42 5:05:15
Loves 8 4 38N31'28 76w43'42 5:06:55
Loveville 18 4 38N21'43 76w41'00 5:06:44
Lower Magothy Beach 2
20 39N05 76w34 5:06:16
Lower Marlboro 4
9 38N39'21 76w40'56 5:06:44
Lowndes 1 3 39N32'56 78w51'38 5:15:27
Loyola 24 1 39N21 76w38 5:06:32
Loys 10 7 39N36'23 77w21'10 5:09:25
Luke 1 24 39N28'30 79w03'26 5:16:14
Lusby 4 9 38N24'38 76w27'20 5:05:49
Lusby Crossroads 2
20 38N59'16 76w35'06 5:06:20
Lutes 15 16 39N04'12 77w03'01 5:08:12
Lutherville 3 3 39N25'16 76w37'35 5:06:30
Lutz Hill 3 3 39N20 76w31 5:06:04
Luxmanor 15 16 39N02'33 77w07'19 5:08:29
Lyford Landing 5
15 38N50'39 75w52'02 5:03:28
Lynbrook 15 16 39N01 77w08 5:08:32
Lynch 14 8 39N17'43 76w03'47 5:04:15
Lynch Point 3 3 39N14 76w31 5:06:04
Lynchs Corner 12
3 39N29'31 76w23'39 5:05:35
Lynne Acres 3 3 39N20 76w43 5:06:52
Lyons Corner 8 6 38N34'07 76w58'50 5:07:55
Lyons Creek 2 20 38N51 76w36 5:06:24
Lyons Homes 3 3 39N14 76w31 5:06:04
Lystra Farms 3 3 39N25 76w43 5:06:52
Maceys Corner 2
20 39N04'49 76w32'42 5:06:11
Mackall 4 9 38N24'18 76w30'10 5:06:01
Macton 12 8 39N40'42 76w17'21 5:05:09
Maddox 18 4 38N19'57 76w48'43 5:07:15
Madison 9 8 38N30'41 76w13'14 5:04:53
Madonna 12 8 39N36'47 76w31'00 5:06:04
Magnolia 12 8 39N24'17 76w19'30 5:05:18
Magothy Beach 2
20 39N05'27 76w31'57 5:06:08
Magothy Park Beach 2
20 39N09 76w33 5:06:12
Mago Vista 2 20 39N03 76w30 5:06:00
Mago Vista Beach 2
20 39N03'55 76w30'33 5:06:02
Magruder Landing 16
9 38N38'38 76w41'39 5:06:47
Main Street 22 7 38N22 75w36 5:02:24
Mairs Mill 6 8 39N42'49 77w13'02 5:08:52
Malcolm 8 6 38N37'00 76w47'14 5:07:09
Malvern 3 3 39N24 76w36 5:06:24
Manadier 20 11 38N42'47 76w02'41 5:04:11
Manchester 6 3 39N39'40 76w53'07 5:07:32
Manchester Estates 16
16 38N48'49 76w54'32 5:07:38
Manhattan Beach 2
20 39N04'06 76w31'16 5:06:05
Manokin 19 23 38N06'55 75w45'22 5:03:01
Manor 3 3 39N33'26 76w33'54 5:06:16
Manor by the Lake 15
16 39N05 77w07 5:08:28
Manor Park 15 16 39N05'50 77w04'59 5:08:20
Manor View 3 3 39N27'36 76w31'36 5:06:06
Manor Woods 15 16 39N05 77w07 5:08:28
Manresa 2 20 39N00'23 76w29'26 5:05:58
Mantua 3 3 39N30'18 76w44'40 5:06:59
Maple Crest 3 3 39N20 76w27 5:05:48
Maplecrest 6 8 39N34 76w59 5:07:56
Maple Grove 6 8 39N38'57 76w51'38 5:07:27
Maple Plains 22 7 38N22 75w36 5:02:24
Mapleside 1 3 39N38 78w48 5:15:12
Maple View 6 8 39N34 76w59 5:07:56
Mapleville 10 7 39N22 77w09 5:08:36
Mapleville 21 7 39N32'20 77w38'52 5:10:35
Maplewood 15 16 39N00'27 77w06'13 5:08:25
Marble Hill 3 3 39N29'45 76w39'03 5:06:36
Marbury 8 6 38N34'31 77w09'21 5:08:37
Mardela Springs 22
7 38N27'35 75w45'33 5:03:02
Margate 2 20 39N10'03 76w35'44 5:06:23
Mariners 19 28 37N59'21 75w49'51 5:03:19
Marion 19 23 38N02'21 75w46'16 5:03:05
Marion Station 19
23 38N02 75w46 5:03:04
Marlboro 16 16 38N50 76w44 5:06:56
Marley 2 20 39N09'03 76w35'32 5:06:22
Marling Farms 17
15 38N58 76w17 5:05:08
Marlow Heights 16
16 38N50'00 76w57'07 5:07:48
Marlton 16 16 38N47 76w52 5:07:28
Marlywood 3 3 39N24'04 76w37'13 5:06:29
Marriott Hill 2
20 38N52'31 76w36'31 5:06:26
Marriottsville 13
3 39N21'00 76w53'59 5:07:36
Mars Estates 3 3 39N19'13 76w26'58 5:05:48
Marshall 12 8 39N37 76w29 5:05:56
Marshall Hall 8 6 38N41 77w06 5:08:24
Marshalls Corner 8
6 38N32'58 77w02'22 5:08:09
Marston 6 8 39N30'28 77w06'02 5:08:24
Martin Manor 6 8 39N34 76w59 5:07:56
Martinsburg 15 16 39N09'51 77w28'33 5:09:54
Martins Corner 22
7 38N17'49 75w47'49 5:03:11
Martins Crossroads 21
7 39N40'53 77w47'24 5:11:10
Martins Woods 16
16 38N58 76w51 5:07:24
Marumsco 19 19 38N00'28 75w41'06 5:02:44
Marydel 5 15 39N06'46 75w44'46 5:02:59
Maryland City 2
20 39N05'31 76w49'05 5:07:16
Maryland Line 3 3 39N42'51 76w39'15 5:06:37
Maryland Park 16
16 38N53'18 76w54'26 5:07:38
Maryland Point 8
6 38N23'51 77w12'19 5:08:49
Marymount 15 16 39N01'19 77w07'40 5:08:31
Maryvale 15 16 39N05'27 77w08'26 5:08:34
Mason Landing 23
19 38N14'14 75w15'28 5:01:02
Masons 8 6 38N33'33 76w48'02 5:07:12
Masons Beach 2 20 38N46'20 76w32'57 5:06:12
Mason Springs 8 6 38N36 77w10 5:08:40
Massey 14 15 39N18'35 75w49'32 5:03:18
Matapeake 17 15 38N57'32 76w20'45 5:05:23
Mattapex 17 15 38N54'06 76w21'00 5:05:24
Mattaponi Landing 23
27 38N07'45 75w28'04 5:01:52
Mattapony 16 16 38N57 76w56 5:07:44
Mattawoman 8 6 38N39'09 76w52'51 5:07:31
Matthews 20 13 38N48'58 75w57'11 5:03:49
Matthewstown 2 20 39N12 76w43 5:06:52
Maugansville 11 8 39N41'34 77w44'42 5:10:59
Mayberry 6 8 39N38'26 77w05'59 5:08:24
Mayberry Wells 16
16 39N05 76w58 5:07:52
Mayfield 2 20 39N05'45 76w41'49 5:06:47
Mayfield 13 3 39N17'37 76w55'07 5:07:40
Mayo 2 20 38N53'15 76w30'44 5:06:03
McAlpine 13 3 39N16 76w49 5:07:16
McAuley Park 15
16 39N01'09 77w10'48 5:08:43
McCahill Estates 16
16 39N05 76w58 5:07:52
McCanns Corner 12
8 39N37'34 76w16'35 5:05:06
McCleans Corner 14
15 39N11'53 76w11'23 5:04:46
McComas 12 8 39N26'10 76w18'27 5:05:14
McComas Beach 11
14 39N30'06 79w22'24 5:17:30
McConchie 8 6 38N30'07 77w03'17 5:08:14
McCoole 1 3 39N26'47 78w58'21 5:15:53
McDaniel 20 13 38N49'03 76w16'42 5:05:07
McDonald 10 8 39N26'00 77w09'52 5:08:39
McDonogh 3 3 39N23'28 76w45'53 5:07:04
Mcginnes 17 15 39N13'10 75w57'08 5:03:49
McHenry 11 2 39N33'30 79w21'11 5:17:25
McKaig 10 7 39N25'53 77w18'36 5:09:14
McKay Beach 18 4 38N11'13 76w33'06 5:06:12

McKendree 2 16 38N46'52 76w37'13 5:06:29
McKenney Hills 15 16 39N01'13 77w03'06 5:08:12
McKenzie 1 3 39N34'02 78w49'27 5:15:18
McKinleyville 14 15 39N06'52 76w10'56 5:04:44
McKinstrys Mill 6 8 39N32'03 77w09'34 5:08:38
McPherson 2 20 39N09'45 76w40'05 5:06:40
Meadedale 2 20 39N05'43 76w43'02 5:06:52
Meadowbrook 16 16 38N57 76w47 5:07:08
Meadowbrook Estates 15 16 39N10 77w16 5:09:04
Meadowcliff 3 3 39N27'04 76w31'55 5:06:08
Meadowood 15 16 39N03'51 77w00'22 5:08:01
Meadows 16 16 38N48'56 76w50'59 5:07:24
Meadowvale Manor 12 8 39N33 76w06 5:04:24
Meadowview 7 7 39N37 75w50 5:03:20
Meadowview Park 7 7 39N37 75w50 5:03:20
Mechanicsville 12 8 39N32 76w21 5:05:24
Mechanicsville 18 4 38N26'34 76w44'39 5:06:59
Mechanic Valley 7 7 39N37'54 75w55'12 5:03:41
Medford 6 8 39N32'53 77w03'15 5:08:13
Melitota 14 15 39N15'29 76w08'45 5:04:35
Mellwood 16 16 38N48'37 76w49'28 5:07:18
Melrose 6 8 39N41'23 76w53'53 5:07:36
Melson 22 7 38N26'30 75w28'35 5:01:54
Melvale 24 1 39N20'45 76w39'00 5:06:36
Melville Crossroads 5 15 39N04'37 75w47'18 5:03:09
Mercersville 21 7 39N29'57 77w46'00 5:11:04
Merchants 24 1 39N18 76w38 5:06:32
Merrill 11 2 39N35'56 79w05'00 5:16:20
Merrimack Park 15 16 38N58'29 77w07'40 5:08:31
Merritt Heights 22 7 38N22 75w36 5:02:24
Merrymount 3 3 39N20 76w43 5:06:52
Metropolitan Grove 15 16 39N08'54 77w13'28 5:08:54
Mexico 6 8 39N36'03 76w56'41 5:07:47
Meyer Manor 6 8 39N34 76w59 5:07:56
Miami Beach 3 3 39N18'25 76w22'13 5:05:29
Michaels Mill 10 7 39N19'44 77w25'05 5:09:40
Michaelsville 12 8 39N25'58 76w10'33 5:04:42
Michigan Park Hills 16 16 38N57'19 76w59'00 5:07:56
Middleborough 3 3 39N18'25 76w26'18 5:05:45
Middlebrook 15 16 39N10'38 77w14'20 5:08:57
Middle Brooke 6 8 39N34 76w59 5:07:56
Middleburg 6 8 39N35'38 77w12'47 5:08:51
Middlepoint 10 7 39N33'47 77w31'31 5:10:06
Middle River 3 3 39N20'03 76w26'23 5:05:46
Middlesex 3 3 39N19'39 76w27'18 5:05:49
Middleton Farm 16 16 38N48'42 76w55'06 5:07:40
Middletown 3 24 39N42 76w41 5:06:44
Middletown 8 6 38N18'27 76w53'05 5:07:32
Middletown 10 7 39N26'37 77w32'42 5:10:11
Middletown Heights 10 7 39N26 77w33 5:10:12
Midland 1 3 39N35'24 78w57'00 5:15:48
Midlothian 1 3 39N38'03 78w57'01 5:15:48
Milburn Landing 23 19 38N07'29 75w29'25 5:01:58
Milestown 18 4 38N17'14 76w46'26 5:07:06
Milford 3 3 39N20'52 76w44'29 5:06:58
Milford Ridge 3 3 39N20 76w43 5:06:52
Millards Mill 8 6 38N34'40 77w06'39 5:08:27
Millbrook 16 16 39N05 76w58 5:07:52
Mill Creek Towne 15 16 39N05 76w58 5:07:52
Miller 1 24 39N35'45 78w56'00 5:15:44
Millers 6 8 39N40'16 76w51'05 5:07:24
Millers Island 3 3 39N13 76w28 5:05:52
Millersville 2 20 39N03'34 76w38'54 5:06:36
Mill Green 12 8 39N39'47 76w19'31 5:05:18
Millhausens 2 20 39N04'56 76w35'08 5:06:21
Millington 14 15 39N15'29 75w50'15 5:03:21
Millpoint 21 7 39N31'43 77w41'09 5:10:45
Mill Run 1 24 39N29 79w03 5:16:12
Mill Swamp 2 20 38N53'04 76w34'08 5:06:17
Milltown Landing 16 9 38N37'59 76w41'33 5:06:46
Millwood 16 16 38N54 76w54 5:07:36
Milton 9 8 38N29'52 76w11'08 5:04:45
Mimosa Cove 2 20 38N47'02 76w32'39 5:06:11
Minefield 12 8 39N39'09 76w22'59 5:05:32
Mineral Spring 11 2 39N42'29 79w21'02 5:17:24
Mitchell Manor 11 2 39N11 76w52 5:07:28
Mitchellville 16 16 38N55'30 76w44'35 5:06:58
Mohican Hills 15 16 38N57'51 77w07'38 5:08:31
Mondell 21 7 39N29'39 77w45'44 5:11:03
Monie 19 26 38N11'13 75w49'15 5:03:17
Monkton 3 3 39N34'43 76w36'57 5:06:28
Monrovia 10 7 39N22'19 77w16'20 5:09:05
Montebello Park 24 1 39N20'33 76w34'08 5:06:17
Montel 1 24 39N37'35 78w53'54 5:15:36
Monterrey Village 15 16 39N02'36 77w03'28 5:08:14
Montevideo 2 3 39N09'45 76w46'02 5:07:04
Montgomery Hills 15 16 39N00'38 77w02'53 5:08:12
Montgomery Knolls 15 3 39N00'35 76w59'45 5:07:59
Montgomery Square 15 16 39N03'18 77w10'02 5:08:40
Montgomery Village 15 16 39N08 77w12 5:08:48
Montgomery White Oak 15 16 39N04 76w59 5:07:56
Montpelier 16 16 39N03'41 76w51'04 5:07:24
Montrose 15 16 39N03'25 77w07'54 5:08:32
Monumental 3 3 39N14'04 76w39'18 5:06:37
Mooresfield 13 3 39N10 76w54 5:07:36
Moores Mill 12 8 39N32'57 76w20'19 5:05:21
Morantown 1 24 39N40'43 78w53'28 5:15:34
Morgan 6 8 39N21'40 77w02'48 5:08:11
Morgantown 1 24 39N39 78w55 5:15:40
Morgantown 8 6 38N20'43 76w58'17 5:07:53
Morganza 18 4 38N22'31 76w41'45 5:06:47
Morgnec 14 8 39N15'13 76w00'03 5:04:00
Morningside 16 16 38N49'48 76w53'30 5:07:34
Morrell Park 24 1 39N15'52 76w39'40 5:06:39
Morrison 1 3 39N30'40 79w01'26 5:16:06
Moscow 1 3 39N32'37 79w00'19 5:16:01
Motters 10 7 39N39'32 77w19'50 5:09:19
Mount Aetna 21 7 39N36'08 77w37'28 5:10:30
Mountain 12 3 39N27'55 76w22'09 5:05:29
Mountaindale 10 7 39N31'10 77w27'03 5:09:48
Mountain Lake Park 11 14 39N23'54 79w22'55 5:17:32
Mountain Lake View 6 8 39N34 76w59 5:07:56
Mountain View Estates 15 16 39N08 77w12 5:08:48
Mount Airy 6 8 39N22'34 77w09'18 5:08:37
Mount Briar 21 7 39N26'33 77w41'10 5:10:45
Mount Calvert 16 20 38N47'07 76w42'54 5:06:52
Mount Carmel 2 20 39N06'25 76w27'45 5:05:51
Mount Carmel 3 3 39N35'19 76w44'27 5:06:58
Mount DeSales 3 3 39N16'58 76w43'32 5:06:54
Mount Ephraim 15 7 39N14'45 77w23'56 5:09:36
Mount Harmony 4 9 38N41'54 76w36'16 5:06:25
Mount Hebron 13 3 39N16 76w49 5:07:16
Mount Hermon 22 7 38N21'14 75w31'47 5:02:07
Mount Holly 9 8 38N33'09 76w00'12 5:04:01
Mount Hope 24 1 39N21'06 76w42'14 5:06:49
Mount Lena 21 7 39N33'33 77w37'42 5:10:31
Mount Olive 6 8 39N22 77w09 5:08:36
Mount Pisgah 8 6 38N32'01 77w06'47 5:08:27
Mount Pleasant 6 8 39N38'45 77w00'22 5:08:01
Mount Pleasant 10 7 39N27'13 77w19'34 5:09:18
Mount Pleasant 21 7 39N32'07 77w38'54 5:10:36
Mount Pleasant 22 7 38N21'10 75w20'06 5:01:20
Mount Pleasant Beach 2 20 39N08'59 76w31'56 5:06:08
Mount Rainier 16 16 38N56'29 76w57'55 5:07:52
Mount Savage 1 24 39N41'44 78w52'48 5:15:31
Mount Savage Junction 1 3 39N41'16 78w46'56 5:15:08
Mount Vernon 19 19 38N14'43 75w49'19 5:03:17
Mount Victoria 8 6 38N21'12 76w53'46 5:07:35
Mountview 13 3 39N19'05 76w56'27 5:07:46
Mount View Gardens 21 7 39N39 77w44 5:10:56
Mountville 10 7 39N20'38 77w31'04 5:10:04
Mountvista 3 3 39N27'37 76w27'25 5:05:50
Mount Washington 24 1 39N21'51 76w40'23 5:06:42
Mount Wesley 23 27 38N10'17 75w20'37 5:01:22
Mount Wilson 3 3 39N22'59 76w45'25 5:07:02
Mount Winans 24 20 39N15'49 76w38'22 5:06:33
Mount Zion (Lothian P O) 2 20 38N49'56 76w36'42 5:06:27
Mount Zion 5 15 39N05'58 75w47'09 5:03:09
Mount Zion 15 16 39N11'05 77w06'04 5:08:24
Mount Zoar 7 7 39N40'53 76w10'52 5:04:43
Mousetown 21 7 39N30'15 77w38'32 5:10:34
Muirkirk 16 16 39N03'42 76w53'08 5:07:33
Mullinix 13 3 39N17'40 77w08'46 5:08:35
Mumma Ford 10 7 39N37'26 77w17'57 5:09:12
Murray Hills 16 16 38N48 76w59 5:07:56
Mutual 4 9 38N28'15 76w32'54 5:06:12
Myers 6 8 39N41 77w02 5:08:08
Myersdale 21 8 39N42'12 78w11'28 5:12:46
Myersville 10 7 39N30'18 77w34'00 5:10:16
Nanjemoy 8 6 38N27'17 77w13'02 5:08:52
Nanticoke 22 7 38N16'20 75w54'21 5:03:37
Narrows 17 15 38N58'12 76w14'35 5:04:58
Narrows Park 11 3 39N40'00 78w48'02 5:15:12
National 1 24 39N36'32 78w56'26 5:15:46
National Naval Medical Ctr 15 16 39N01 77w08 5:08:32
Naval Academy 2 20 38N58 76w30 5:06:00
Naval Air Facility 16 16 38N52 77w00 5:08:00
Naylor 16 16 38N42'44 76w44'46 5:06:59
Neavitt 20 13 38N43'28 76w16'58 5:05:08
Neck 9 8 38N35 76w15 5:05:00
Necker 3 3 39N23'29 76w29'19 5:05:57
Needwood Estates 15 16 39N06 77w11 5:08:44
Neeld Estates 4 9 38N37 76w37 5:06:28
Neelsville 15 16 39N11'43 77w14'39 5:08:59
Neilwood 15 16 39N04 77w09 5:08:36
New Addition 10 7 39N19'06 77w38'48 5:10:35
Newark (Queponco Station) 23 19 38N15'02 75w17'29 5:01:10
New Birmingham Manor 15 16 39N06'21 76w54'54 5:07:40
Newburg 8 6 38N22'38 76w57'13 5:07:49
New Carrollton 16 16 38N58'11 76w52'49 5:07:31
Newcomb 20 13 38N45'13 76w10'35 5:04:42
New Germany 11 2 39N37'57 79w07'21 5:16:29
New Hampshire Estates 15 16 38N59'49 76w59'27 5:07:58
New Hampshire Gardens 16 16 38N59'13 76w59'31 5:07:58
Newhope 22 7 38N23'27 75w20'08 5:01:21
New London 10 7 39N25'19 77w15'12 5:09:01
Newmans Corner 17 15 39N09'58 75w58'01 5:03:52
New Market 10 7 39N22'57 77w16'11 5:09:05
Newmarket 18 4 38N28'25 76w46'29 5:07:06
New Midway 10 7 39N34'01 77w17'28 5:09:10
New Port 6 8 39N21'48 77w04'08 5:08:17
Newport 8 6 38N25'10 76w54'13 5:07:37
Newport Hills 15 16 39N02'26 77w04'20 5:08:17
New Road Landing 22 19 38N15'45 75w49'13 5:03:17
Newton 5 15 38N45'53 75w55'55 5:03:44
Newton Village 16 16 38N57 76w56 5:07:44
Newtown 4 9 38N21'01 76w27'29 5:05:50
Newtown 8 6 38N30'00 76w56'34 5:07:46
Newtown 14 15 39N18'15 76w08'54 5:04:36
New Town 22 7 38N18'15 75w50'45 5:03:23
New Valley 7 7 39N40 76w10 5:04:40
New Windsor 6 8 39N32'31 77w06'30 5:08:26
Nichols 5 15 38N43'23 75w48'44 5:03:15
Nikep 1 24 39N33'02 78w59'51 5:15:59
Nob Hill 13 3 39N16 76w49 5:07:16
Noble Mill 12 8 39N37'04 76w14'21 5:04:57
Norbeck 15 16 39N06'36 77w04'34 5:08:18
Normandy Heights 13 3 39N16 76w49 5:07:16
Normans 17 15 38N56'29 76w21'09 5:05:25
Normira 7 7 39N37 75w50 5:03:20
Norris Corner 12 8 39N28'33 76w17'48 5:05:11
Norrisville 12 8 39N42'17 76w32'06 5:06:08
Northampton 3 3 39N26'11 76w36'40 5:06:27
Northampton 16 16 38N47 76w52 5:07:28
North Barnaby 16 16 38N49'18 76w57'18 5:07:49
North Beach 4 9 38N42'26 76w31'53 5:06:08
North Beach Park 2 20 38N42 76w32 5:06:08
North Bend 24 3 39N16'50 76w42'17 5:06:49
North Branch 1 3 39N35'22 78w43'57 5:14:56
North Brentwood 16 16 38N56'43 76w57'07 5:07:48
Northbrook Estates 15 16 39N01'42 77w02'27 5:08:10
North Chevy Chase 15 16 39N00'02 77w04'23 5:08:18
North Deale 2 20 38N47'11 76w33'02 5:06:12
North East 7 7 39N36'00 75w56'30 5:03:46
Northeast Heights 7 7 39N34'23 75w57'03 5:03:48
North Englewood 16 16 38N56 76w53 5:07:32
Northern 21 7 39N39 77w44 5:10:56
North Forestville 16 16 38N51'15 76w52'41 5:07:31
North Glade 11 2 39N30'03 79w14'13 5:16:57
North Hampton 16 16 38N47 76w52 5:07:28
North Hills Sligo Park 15 16 39N00'50 77w01'18 5:08:05
North Indian Head Estates 8 6 38N38 77w04 5:08:16
North Junction 21 7 39N39 77w44 5:10:56
North Kenilworth 16 16 38N55'18 76w55'40 5:07:43
North Kensington 15 16 39N01'49 77w04'22 5:08:17
North Keys 16 16 38N42'28 76w46'03 5:07:04
North Laurel 13 3 39N05 76w58 5:07:52
North Laurel Park 13 3 39N05 76w58 5:07:52
North Linthicum 2 20 39N13'21 76w39'06 5:06:36
North Ocean City 23 19 38N22'26 75w04'13 5:00:17
North Point 3 3 39N16'38 76w28'38 5:05:55
North Point Village 3 3 39N16'00 76w28'19 5:05:53
North Potomac 15 16 39N03 77w10 5:08:40
Northridge Manor 21 7 39N39 77w44 5:10:56
North Sherwood Forest 15 16 39N05'34 77w00'54 5:08:04
Northshire 3 3 39N14 76w31 5:06:04
North Shore 2 20 39N09 76w33 5:06:12
North Springbrook 15 16 39N04'08 77w00'42 5:08:03
North Takoma Park 15 16 38N59'21 77w00'56 5:08:04
North Wellham 2 20 39N10 76w37 5:06:28
Northwest Park 15 16 38N59'33 77w05'54 5:08:24
Northwood 24 1 39N19 76w37 5:06:28
Northwood Forest 15 16 39N02'00 77w01'27 5:08:06
Northwood Park 15 16 39N01'40 77w00'58 5:08:04
North Woodridge 16 16 38N56'42 76w58'25 5:07:54
Northwood Village 15 16 39N03 77w03 5:08:12
Norwood 15 16 39N07'31 77w01'40 5:08:07
Norwood Estates 15 16 39N06'50 77w00'53 5:08:04
Notch Cliff 3 3 39N26'37 76w30'38 5:06:03
Nottingham 3 3 39N21'50 76w27'09 5:05:49
Nottingham 16 16 38N43 76w44 5:06:56
Nutters 22 7 38N19 75w33 5:02:12
Nutwell 2 20 38N46'47 76w34'35 5:06:18
Oak Acres 10 7 39N26 77w27 5:09:48
Oak Court 2 20 38N59'00 76w33'06 5:06:12
Oak Crest 16 16 39N05'08 76w51'42 5:07:27
Oakcrest Towers 16 16 38N51 76w54 5:07:36
Oakdale 15 16 39N07'49 77w04'17 5:08:17

Oak Forest 3 3 39N15'39 76w44'36 5:06:58
Oak Grove 16 16 38N52'27 76w46'37 5:07:06
Oakington 12 8 39N30'11 76w06'53 5:04:28
Oakland 2 20 38N48'51 76w32'39 5:06:11
Oakland 3 3 39N42'45 76w41'26 5:06:46
Oakland 5 15 38N59'19 75w52'35 5:03:30
Oakland 6 8 39N25'07 76w53'03 5:07:32
Oakland 11 14 39N24'28 79w24'25 5:17:38
Oakland 16 16 38N51'39 76w54'38 5:07:39
Oakland Mills 13 3 39N13'07 76w50'39 5:07:23
Oakland Park 3 3 39N22'18 76w46'04 5:07:04
Oakland Terrace 15 16 39N02 77w06 5:08:24
Oaklawn 16 16 38N46'22 76w57'04 5:07:48
Oakleigh 3 3 39N24'18 76w33'33 5:06:14
Oakleigh Forest 2 20 39N05 76w34 5:06:16
Oakleigh Manor 3 3 39N23'43 76w33'23 5:06:14
Oakley 18 4 38N16'22 76w44'24 5:06:58
Oaklyn Manor 12 8 39N25 76w22 5:05:28
Oakmont 15 16 39N00'13 77w06'49 5:08:27
Oak Orchard 10 7 39N29'30 77w09'15 5:08:37
Oak Orchard 16 16 38N47 76w53 5:07:32
Oak Park 3 3 39N15 76w41 5:06:44
Oak Park 11 14 39N24 79w23 5:17:32
Oak Ridge 21 7 39N39 77w44 5:10:56
Oaks 18 6 38N29'55 76w46'37 5:07:06
Oak Summit 3 3 39N23'41 76w30'54 5:06:04
Oakview 15 16 39N00'58 76w58'52 5:07:55
Oakville 18 4 38N23'28 76w38'38 5:06:35
Oakville 19 26 38N13'17 75w37'15 5:02:29
Oakwood 2 20 38N55'01 76w28'28 5:05:54
Oakwood 7 7 39N41'56 76w10'49 5:04:43
Oakwood Knolls 15 16 38N59'07 77w07'44 5:08:31
Ocean 1 24 39N36'09 78w56'39 5:15:47
Ocean City 23 12 38N20'11 75w05'07 5:00:20
Ocean City Harbor 23 19 38N23 75w05 5:00:20
Ocean Pines 23 27 38N23'43 75w09'22 5:00:37
Octoraro 7 7 39N39'31 76w09'18 5:04:37
Odenton 2 20 39N05'02 76w42'02 5:06:48
Odenton Gardens 2 20 39N02 76w41 5:06:44
Oella 3 3 39N16'26 76w47'13 5:07:09
Oklahoma 6 8 39N24'49 76w55'23 5:07:42
Old Baltimore 12 8 39N24'21 76w14'30 5:04:58
Old Bay Trail 16 16 38N47 76w52 5:07:28
Olde Colonial Woods 15 16 39N09 77w05 5:08:20
Olde Fort Village 16 16 38N47 76w58 5:07:52
Olde Towne Village 16 16 38N51 76w54 5:07:36
Old Farm 15 16 39N03'01 77w08'41 5:08:35
Old Field 9 8 38N30 76w09 5:04:36
Oldfield 10 7 39N29'46 77w11'35 5:08:46
Old Georgetown Estates 15 16 39N02'50 77w08'00 5:08:32
Old Germantown 15 16 39N09'43 77w16'54 5:09:08
Old Glory Beach 2 20 39N09'07 76w32'52 5:06:11
Old House Landing 9 8 38N21'15 76w03'02 5:04:12
Old Salem Village 15 16 39N05'37 77w00'22 5:08:01
Oldtown 1 3 39N32'29 78w36'42 5:14:27
Old Town 14 15 39N08'31 76w06'23 5:04:26
Olive 10 7 39N19'39 77w34'58 5:10:20
Oliver Beach 3 3 39N20 76w27 5:05:48
Olivet 4 9 38N20'16 76w26'35 5:05:46
Olivet Hill 14 15 39N20'17 75w51'59 5:03:28
Olney 15 16 39N09'11 77w04'02 5:08:16
Olney Mills 15 16 39N09 77w05 5:08:20
Olney Square 15 16 39N09 77w05 5:08:20
One Spot 13 3 39N09 76w47 5:07:08
Orangeville 24 3 39N17'55 76w33'00 5:06:12
Oraville 18 4 38N25'04 76w41'40 5:06:47
Orchard Beach 2 20 39N10'14 76w31'37 5:06:06
Orchard Hills 3 3 39N25'03 76w37'17 5:06:29
Orchard Hills 21 7 39N39 77w44 5:10:56
Oregon 3 3 39N29'50 76w41'12 5:06:45
Oriole 19 19 38N10'23 75w48'29 5:03:14
Orleans 1 3 39N40 78w25 5:13:40
Orme 16 16 38N38'33 76w45'57 5:07:04
Osborne 12 8 39N32'12 76w07'03 5:04:28
Otterdale Mill 6 8 39N36'58 77w10'02 5:08:40
Otter Point 12 8 39N28 76w17 5:05:08
Ottersdale 6 8 39N37'54 77w10'01 5:08:40
Overlea 3 3 39N21'48 76w31'15 5:06:05
Overton 14 15 39N01'58 76w12'37 5:04:50
Owings 4 20 39N43'03 76w36'06 5:06:24
Owings Beach 2 20 38N46'21 76w33'17 5:06:13
Owings Mills 3 3 39N25'10 76w46'50 5:07:07
Oxford 20 11 38N41'11 76w10'19 5:04:41
Oxon Hill 16 16 38N48'12 76w59'24 5:07:58
Oxon Run Hills 16 16 38N50'38 76w57'43 5:07:51
Oyster Harbor 2 20 38N55'28 76w27'56 5:05:52
Padonia 3 3 39N27'21 76w37'59 5:06:32
Pagetts Corner 16 16 38N47'35 76w55'43 5:07:43
Paint Branch Estates 15 16 39N04 76w59 5:07:56
Paint Branch Farm 15 16 39N04 76w59 5:07:56
Paint Branch Farms 15 16 39N04'50 76w59'39 5:07:59
Palmer Park 16 16 38N55'15 76w52'19 5:07:29
Palmers 18 4 38N14'01 76w45'28 5:07:02
Palmers Corner 16 16 38N46'32 76w57'29 5:07:50
Palmetto 19 26 38N13'26 75w38'46 5:02:35
Paradise 3 3 39N16'10 76w43'06 5:06:52
Paradise Beach 2 20 39N08'54 76w27'50 5:05:51
Paramount 11 7 39N40'59 77w41'47 5:10:47
Paramount Manor 21 7 39N39 77w44 5:10:56
Paris 4 9 38N42'09 76w34'59 5:06:20
Parker Creek 4 9 38N31'32 76w32'00 5:06:08
Parkertown 23 27 38N23'13 75w11'11 5:00:45
Parker Wharf 4 9 38N25'28 76w34'02 5:06:16
Park Hall 18 4 38N13 76w26 5:05:44
Park Hall 21 7 39N27'18 77w38'52 5:10:35
Park Head 21 7 39N39'47 78w03'46 5:12:15
Parkland 16 16 38N51'01 76w54'19 5:07:37
Parkland Apartments 16 16 38N51 76w54 5:07:36
Parkland Terrace 16 16 38N50'31 76w55'36 5:07:42
Park Mills 10 7 39N17'52 77w24'29 5:09:38
Park Overlook 15 16 39N06 77w11 5:08:44
Park Ridge 15 16 39N08 77w12 5:08:48
Parkside 15 16 39N01'39 77w06'15 5:08:25
Parkside Estates 15 16 39N06 77w11 5:08:44
Parkton 3 3 39N38'27 76w39'34 5:06:38
Parktowne 3 3 39N23 76w33 5:06:12
Parkview 16 16 38N47 76w53 5:07:32
Parkview Estates 15 16 39N00'19 77w04'00 5:08:16
Parkview Gardens 16 16 38N58 76w55 5:07:40
Parkville 3 3 39N22'38 76w32'24 5:06:10
Parkville Heights 3 3 39N22'50 76w33'06 5:06:12
Parkwood 15 16 39N01'11 77w05'30 5:08:22
Parole 2 20 38N58'46 76w31'51 5:06:07
Parran 4 9 38N36'10 76w34'14 5:06:17
Parrsville 6 8 39N21'46 77w09'15 5:08:37
Parsons 22 7 38N23 75w33 5:02:12
Parsonsburg 22 7 38N23'15 75w28'17 5:01:53
Parsonville 19 28 37N59'32 75w47'05 5:03:08
Partridge Place 15 16 39N08 77w12 5:08:48
Pasadena 2 20 39N06'26 76w34'17 5:06:17
Passapae Landing 5 11 38N55'27 75w49'33 5:03:18
Patapsco 2 20 39N12'49 76w41'17 5:06:45
Patapsco 6 8 39N32'19 76w53'32 5:07:34
Patricks Landing 22 7 38N20'42 75w39'43 5:02:39
Patterson 24 1 39N17 76w35 5:06:20
Patuxent 2 20 39N03'17 76w44'11 5:06:57
Patuxent 8 4 38N32'21 76w44'56 5:07:00
Patuxent Beach 18 4 38N18 76w31 5:06:04
Patuxent Palisades 4 9 38N43 76w40 5:06:40
Patuxent Park 18 4 38N15 76w27 5:05:48
Patuxent River 18 4 38N18 76w26 5:05:44
Pauls Corner 19 23 38N02'26 75w44'37 5:02:58
Peach Orchard Heights 15 16 39N06'08 76w57'29 5:07:50
Peachwood 15 16 39N04 76w59 5:07:56
Peacock Corners 14 15 39N15'18 75w48'45 5:03:15
Pea Hill 22 7 38N18'30 75w44'54 5:03:00
Pealiquor Landing 5 15 38N51'18 75w50'44 5:03:23
Pearl 10 7 39N26 77w27 5:09:48
Pearre 21 8 39N38'11 78w19'22 5:13:17
Pecktonville 21 7 39N40'11 78w02'40 5:12:11
Pekin 1 3 39N32 79w00 5:16:00
Pendennis Mount 2 20 38N59'54 76w28'35 5:05:54
Pen Mar 21 7 39N43'04 77w30'24 5:10:02
Pepper Mill Village 16 16 38N54 76w54 5:07:36
Perry Hall 3 3 39N24'45 76w27'50 5:05:51
Perry Hall Estates 3 3 39N23 76w30 5:06:00
Perry Hall Manor 3 3 39N24 76w29 5:05:56
Perryman 12 8 39N28'10 76w12'17 5:04:49
Perry Point 7 7 39N33'15 76w04'20 5:04:17
Perrys Corner 17 15 38N58 76w13 5:04:52
Perryville 7 8 39N33'36 76w04'18 5:04:17
Perrywood Estates 15 16 39N05'54 76w56'41 5:07:47
Perry Wright 8 6 38N35'48 77w09'08 5:08:37
Petersburg 9 8 38N36'13 75w51'25 5:03:26
Peters Corners 17 15 39N11'46 75w47'21 5:03:09
Petersville 10 7 39N20'47 77w36'40 5:10:27
Pfeiffer Corners 13 3 39N11'50 76w47'39 5:07:11
Phelps 16 16 38N50'59 76w52'17 5:07:29
Phelps Corner 16 16 38N48'20 76w58'24 5:07:54
Phoenix 3 3 39N30'59 76w36'59 5:06:28
Picketts Corner 6 8 39N24'29 77w03'13 5:08:13
Pigeon House Corner 2 20 38N59'29 76w42'13 5:06:49
Pike 15 16 39N04 77w09 5:08:36
Pikesville 3 3 39N22'27 76w43'22 5:06:53
Pilot 7 7 39N42'14 76w12'06 5:04:48
Pimlico Race Track 24 1 39N22 76w41 5:06:44
Pindell 2 20 38N46'32 76w41'00 5:06:44
Pine Cliff 10 7 39N26 77w27 5:09:48
Pinecrest 16 16 38N59 77w01 5:08:04
Pinefield 8 6 38N38 76w53 5:07:32
Pine Grove Village 2 20 39N09 76w33 5:06:12
Pine Hill 15 16 39N02'35 76w58'41 5:07:55
Pinehurst 2 20 39N07'03 76w26'02 5:05:44
Pinehurst 3 3 39N22'24 76w37'08 5:06:29
Pinehurst Estates 16 16 38N48 76w59 5:07:56
Pine Knoll 6 8 39N34 76w59 5:07:56
Pine Knolls 15 16 39N02'11 77w11'38 5:08:47
Pine Landing 18 4 38N09'53 76w28'42 5:05:55
Pine Orchard 13 3 39N16'39 76w51'41 5:07:27
Pine Ridge 3 3 39N24'57 76w31'28 5:06:06
Pinesburg 21 7 39N37'45 77w51'30 5:11:26
Pines-on-Severn 2 20 39N01'13 76w30'05 5:06:00
Pine Valley 3 3 39N26 76w37 5:06:28
Pine Whiff Beach 2 20 38N56'26 76w33'06 5:06:12
Pinewood Hill 16 16 38N47 76w58 5:07:52
Piney Glen Farms 15 16 39N03 77w10 5:08:40
Piney Grove 1 3 39N42'21 78w22'39 5:13:31
Piney Grove 11 2 39N41'05 79w04'24 5:16:18
Piney Grove 14 21 39N10'51 76w04'33 5:04:18
Piney Hill 3 3 39N34'11 76w39'31 5:06:38
Piney Point 18 4 38N08'32 76w30'28 5:06:02
Pinto 1 3 39N34'11 78w50'22 5:15:21
Pioneer City 2 20 39N09 76w40 5:06:40
Pipe Creek Mill 6 8 39N40'04 77w06'10 5:08:25
Piscataway 16 16 38N42'02 76w58'21 5:07:53
Piscataway Hills 16 16 38N42'27 76w59'52 5:07:59
Pisgah 8 6 38N32'46 77w08'06 5:08:32
Pittsville 22 7 38N23'43 75w24'48 5:01:39
Plainfield 22 7 38N22 75w36 5:02:24
Plane Number Four 10 7 39N22 77w09 5:08:36
Pleasant Grove 3 3 39N32'38 76w47'54 5:07:12
Pleasant Hill 3 3 39N26 76w48 5:07:12
Pleasant Hill 7 7 39N40'13 75w54'09 5:03:37
Pleasant Hills 12 8 39N29 76w23 5:05:32
Pleasant Springs 16 16 38N41'26 76w54'07 5:07:36
Pleasant Valley 1 3 39N42'35 78w38'27 5:14:34
Pleasant Valley 6 8 39N37'59 77w02'47 5:08:11
Pleasant Valley 21 7 39N38'11 77w32'10 5:10:09
Pleasant View 10 7 39N16'58 77w29'39 5:09:59
Pleasant View 13 3 39N16 76w49 5:07:16
Pleasantville 12 8 39N32'44 76w26'31 5:05:46
Pleasantville 21 7 39N20'23 77w44'17 5:10:57
Pleasant Walk 10 7 39N32'23 77w35'11 5:10:21
Plum Point 4 9 38N36'51 76w30'45 5:06:03
Plyers Mill Estates 15 16 39N01'39 77w03'04 5:08:12
Pocomoke 23 5 38N05 75w34 5:02:16
Pocomoke City 23 19 38N04'32 75w34'06 5:02:16
Pointer Ridge 16 16 38N30 75w52 5:03:28
Point Landing 8 6 38N32'41 77w13'50 5:08:55
Point Lookout 18 4 38N05 76w21 5:05:24
Point of Rocks 10 7 39N16'33 77w32'22 5:10:09
Point of Rocks Estates 10 7 39N17 77w32 5:10:08
Point Pleasant 2 20 39N10'43 76w35'16 5:06:21
Polk Landing 19 26 38N15'54 75w43'15 5:02:53
Polk Road 19 26 38N15'38 75w44'45 5:02:59
Pomfret 8 6 38N34'38 77w01'51 5:08:07
Pomona 14 15 39N09'44 76w06'35 5:04:26
Pomonkey 8 6 38N36'28 77w04'19 5:08:17
Pomonkey Landing 8 6 38N38'02 77w05'53 5:08:24
Ponder Cove 2 20 38N53'56 76w31'13 5:06:05
Pondsville 21 7 39N37'14 77w35'17 5:10:21
Pondtown 17 15 39N12'50 75w54'48 5:03:39
Pooks Hill 15 16 39N00'50 77w06'23 5:08:26
Poole 12 8 39N38'28 76w15'22 5:05:01
Poolesville 15 16 39N08'45 77w25'02 5:09:40
Popes Creek 8 6 38N23'56 76w59'29 5:07:58
Poplar 3 3 39N21'15 76w27'10 5:05:49
Poplar Grove 12 8 39N38'13 76w16'04 5:05:04
Poplar Hill 16 16 38N37'20 76w44'29 5:06:58
Poplar Hill Estates 16 16 38N47 76w53 5:07:32
Poplar Knob 10 7 39N38 77w25 5:09:40
Poplar Neck 22 7 38N24'30 75w23'15 5:01:33
Poplars 4 9 38N40'21 76w33'04 5:06:12
Poplar Springs 13 3 39N20'36 77w05'48 5:08:23
Port Deposit 7 7 39N36'17 76w06'56 5:04:28
Porters Crossing 23 27 38N13'22 75w21'49 5:01:27
Porters Park 3 3 39N15'18 76w24'23 5:05:38
Porterstown 21 7 39N27'57 77w42'48 5:10:51
Port Herman 7 7 39N30'07 75w54'09 5:03:37
Port Republic 4 9 38N30'03 76w31'47 5:06:07
Port Tobacco 8 6 38N30'49 77w01'07 5:08:04
Port Tobacco Riviera 8 6 38N30'39 77w01'48 5:08:07
Potomac 1 3 39N34'03 78w50'21 5:15:21
Potomac 15 16 39N01'05 77w12'32 5:08:50
Potomac Falls 15 16 39N00'48 77w13'51 5:08:55
Potomac Green 15 16 39N03 77w10 5:08:40
Potomac Heights 8 6 38N36'31 77w08'27 5:08:34
Potomac Heights 21 7 39N39 77w44 5:10:56
Potomac Hunt Acres 15 16 39N02'05 77w14'25 5:08:58

Potomac Manors 15 16 39N01'01 77w13'17 5:08:53
Potomac Park 1 3 39N36'42 78w48'22 5:15:13
Potomac Ranch 15 16 39N03 77w10 5:08:40
Potomac Shores 8 6 38N31 77w01 5:08:04
Potomac Valley 15 16 38N58 77w08 5:08:32
Potomac View 8 6 38N17'00 76w53'45 5:07:35
Potomac Woods 15 16 39N03'46 77w10'14 5:08:41
Pot Spring 3 3 39N26'50 76w35'53 5:06:24
Potters Landing 5 15 38N49'54 75w51'17 5:03:25
Powder Mill Estates 16 16 39N02'08 76w56'43 5:07:47
Powder Mill Village 16 16 39N02 76w55 5:07:40
Powellville 22 7 38N19'43 75w22'33 5:01:30
Powhatan Beach 2 20 39N08'17 76w33'54 5:06:16
Powhattan Mill 3 3 39N20 76w43 5:06:52
Prathertown 15 16 39N11'49 77w11'56 5:08:48
Pratt 1 3 39N41'26 78w30'24 5:14:02
Preston 5 15 38N42'42 75w54'31 5:03:38
Preston Manor 12 8 39N28 76w17 5:05:08
Prettyboy 3 3 39N36'21 76w43'14 5:06:53
Price 17 15 39N05'51 75w57'33 5:03:50
Priceville 3 3 39N32'42 76w40'10 5:06:41
Primrose Acres 2 20 38N57'31 76w30'15 5:06:01
Prince Frederick 4 9 38N32'25 76w35'05 5:06:20
Prince Georges Plaza 16 16 38N57 76w57 5:07:48
Princess Anne 19 26 38N12'10 75w41'34 5:02:46
Princeton 16 16 38N49 76w56 5:07:44
Principio Furnace 7 25 39N34'30 76w02'21 5:04:09
Prospect 12 8 39N41'25 76w18'11 5:05:13
Prospect Knolls 16 16 38N57 76w47 5:07:08
Providence 3 3 39N25'26 76w33'46 5:06:15
Providence 7 7 39N41'25 75w52'35 5:03:30
Providence 20 15 38N46'13 75w57'58 5:03:52
Providence Landing 20 15 38N45'49 75w58'34 5:03:54
Public Landing 23 27 38N08'56 75w17'16 5:01:09
Pumphrey 2 20 39N13'02 76w38'15 5:06:33
Pumpkin Center 1 3 39N37'18 78w33'56 5:14:16
Puncheon Landing 19 19 38N04'35 75w36'26 5:02:26
Purdum 15 16 39N17'04 77w14'26 5:08:58
Pusey Landing 17 15 39N04'25 76w05'46 5:04:23
Putnam 12 8 39N33'55 76w27'38 5:05:51
Putty Hill 3 3 39N22'36 76w30'23 5:06:02
Pylesville 12 8 39N41'23 76w22'24 5:05:30
Quail Run 15 16 39N08 77w12 5:08:48
Quaint Acres 15 16 39N02'46 76w59'50 5:07:59
Quaker Neck Landing 14 15 39N07'48 76w05'49 5:04:23
Quaker Ridge 16 16 38N47 76w52 5:07:28
Quantico 22 7 38N22'27 75w44'34 5:02:58
Queen Anne 17 13 38N55'15 75w57'20 5:03:49
Queen Anne Colony 17 15 38N59 76w19 5:05:16
Queens Chapel 16 16 38N58 76w58 5:07:52
Queens Chapel Manor 16 16 38N57'31 76w57'41 5:07:51
Queenstown 16 16 38N57'02 76w57'54 5:07:52
Queenstown 17 15 38N59'26 76w09'29 5:04:38
Queen Tree Landing 18 4 38N25'19 76w37'26 5:06:30
Quince Orchard 15 16 39N07'04 77w15'10 5:09:01
Quincy Manor 16 16 38N58 76w53 5:07:32
Rabbit Town 9 8 38N29'21 75w49'55 5:03:20
Radiant Valley 16 16 38N56'11 76w53'34 5:07:34
Ralph 9 8 38N30'25 75w49'50 5:03:19
Ralston 3 3 39N22'15 76w43'37 5:06:54
Ramblewood 24 3 39N21'46 76w35'14 5:06:21
Ramblewood Village 16 16 38N47 76w53 5:07:32
Ramgate 16 16 38N47 76w58 5:07:52
Ramona Beach 3 3 39N13'45 76w24'01 5:05:36
Ranchleigh 3 3 39N22'33 76w40'28 5:06:42
Randalia 7 7 39N31'10 75w52'20 5:03:29
Randallstown 3 3 39N22'02 76w47'44 5:07:11
Randle Cliff Beach 4 9 38N39'54 76w31'51 5:06:07
Randolph 15 16 39N02 77w06 5:08:24
Randolph Farms 15 16 39N05 77w07 5:08:28
Randolph Hills 15 16 39N03'02 77w05'42 5:08:23
Randolph Village 16 16 38N53'22 76w51'47 5:07:27
Random View 6 8 39N34 76w59 5:07:56
Raspeburg 24 1 39N21 76w32 5:06:08
Rawlings 1 3 39N32'04 78w53'01 5:15:32
Rawlings Heights 1 3 39N32 78w53 5:15:32
Raynor Heights 2 20 39N13'36 76w39'37 5:06:38
Rayville 3 3 39N38'57 76w42'04 5:06:48
Reckford 3 8 39N28'44 76w25'41 5:05:43
Reddings Corner 14 15 39N17 76w06 5:04:24
Redford Estates 16 16 38N47 76w58 5:07:52
Redgate 18 4 38N15'23 76w35'56 5:06:24
Red Hill 1 3 39N38'19 78w51'26 5:15:26
Redhill 8 6 38N33'58 77w07'45 5:08:31
Red Hill 21 7 39N28'05 77w41'51 5:10:47
Redhouse 11 14 39N18'31 79w27'15 5:17:49
Redland 15 16 39N08'43 77w08'40 5:08:35
Red Landing 23 27 38N09'08 75w26'27 5:01:46
Red Point 7 7 39N31'24 75w58'44 5:03:55
Reeder Development 10 7 39N26 77w27 5:09:48
Reels Mill 10 7 39N21'40 77w22'08 5:09:29
Reese 6 8 39N32'34 76w56'17 5:07:45
Regal Estates 4 9 38N43 76w40 5:06:40
Regency Estates 15 16 39N02'53 77w10'13 5:08:41
Regent Park 15 16 39N03 77w10 5:08:40
Regent Square 15 16 39N05 77w10 5:08:40
Rehobeth 19 19 38N02'20 75w39'48 5:02:39
Reid 11 8 39N42'44 77w40'46 5:10:43
Reids Grove 9 8 38N32'01 75w49'40 5:03:19
Reisterstown 3 3 39N28'10 76w49'47 5:07:19
Relay 3 3 39N13'40 76w42'12 5:06:49
Reliance 5 8 38N38'07 75w42'27 5:02:50
Remsburg Heights 10 7 39N26 77w27 5:09:48
Rest Haven 2 20 38N46'41 76w32'24 5:06:10
Revell 2 20 39N02'34 76w31'18 5:06:05
Rewastico 22 7 38N24'22 75w45'55 5:03:04
Reynolds 1 24 39N30'33 79w01'41 5:16:07
Rhodesdale 9 8 38N34'34 75w50'11 5:03:21
Rhodes Point 19 19 37N58'27 76w02'29 5:04:10
Richardsmere 7 7 39N41'21 76w07'36 5:04:30
Richards Oak 7 7 39N41'39 76w06'52 5:04:27
Riderwood 3 3 39N24'33 76w38'56 5:06:36
Riderwood Hills 3 3 39N24'42 76w37'20 5:06:29
Ridge 18 4 38N07'09 76w22'27 5:05:30
Ridge Grove 3 3 39N22'49 76w31'36 5:06:06
Ridgelake 13 3 39N16 76w49 5:07:16
Ridgeleigh 3 3 39N23'42 76w33'39 5:06:15
Ridgely 5 15 38N56'52 75w53'05 5:03:32
Ridgeview 2 20 39N09 76w42 5:06:48
Ridgeville 6 7 39N21'54 77w09'57 5:08:40
Ridgeway 2 20 39N06'53 76w41'02 5:06:44
Ridgeway 3 3 39N16'27 76w45'45 5:07:03
Ridgley Park 6 8 39N24 76w56 5:07:44
Riggins Corner 9 8 38N24'48 76w11'03 5:04:44
Ringgold 21 7 39N42'34 77w34'01 5:10:16
Rio Vista 20 13 38N47 76w13 5:04:52
Ripley 8 6 38N32'41 77w04'43 5:08:19
Rippling Estates 2 20 39N10 76w37 5:06:28
Rippling Ridge 2 20 39N10 76w37 5:06:28
Rising Sun 7 7 39N41'52 76w03'47 5:04:15
Rison 8 6 38N32'56 77w10'39 5:08:43
Ritchie 16 16 38N52'14 76w51'21 5:07:25
Ritchie Heights 16 16 38N51 76w54 5:07:36
Ritchie Manor 16 16 38N51 76w54 5:07:36
Riva 2 20 38N57'07 76w34'42 5:06:19
River Bend 16 16 38N47 76w58 5:07:52
River Bend Estates 16 16 38N51 76w54 5:07:36
River Club Estates 2 20 38N54'22 76w31'48 5:06:07
Riverdale 2 20 39N05'57 76w32'10 5:06:09
Riverdale 16 16 38N57'48 76w55'55 5:07:44
Riverdale Gardens 16 16 38N58'07 76w54'49 5:07:39
Riverdale Heights 16 16 38N57'50 76w54'55 5:07:40
Riverdale Hills 16 16 38N57'48 76w54'34 5:07:38
River Falls 15 16 39N03 77w10 5:08:40
River Forest 16 16 38N47 76w58 5:07:52
River Meadows 13 3 39N16 76w49 5:07:16
River Ridge Estates 16 16 38N47'11 77w00'11 5:08:01
Riverside 8 6 38N23'16 77w08'48 5:08:35
River Springs 18 4 38N14'46 76w46'40 5:07:07
Riverton 22 7 38N30'40 75w45'17 5:03:01
Riverview 16 16 38N43'26 77w01'41 5:08:07
Riverview 17 15 39N08'42 76w03'52 5:04:15
Riverview Village 8 6 38N36'20 77w09'58 5:08:40
Riviera Beach 2 20 39N10'00 76w30'30 5:06:02
Robbins 9 8 38N22'32 76w04'33 5:04:18
Robbins Landing 9 8 38N22'37 76w03'30 5:04:14
Roberts 1 3 39N37'52 78w48'14 5:15:13
Roberts 17 15 39N07'02 75w55'07 5:03:40
Roberts Glen 15 16 39N03 77w10 5:08:40
Robindale 15 16 39N03'48 77w05'37 5:08:22
Robinson 2 20 39N04'44 76w33'12 5:06:13
Robinwood 21 7 39N39 77w44 5:10:56
Rockaway Beach 3 3 39N17'41 76w23'58 5:05:36
Rock Creek Forest 15 16 38N59'27 77w03'24 5:08:14
Rock Creek Gardens 15 16 38N59'35 77w02'50 5:08:11
Rock Creek Hills 15 16 39N00'53 77w04'16 5:08:17
Rock Creek Knolls 15 16 38N59'50 77w03'57 5:08:16
Rock Creek Manor 15 16 39N05 77w07 5:08:28
Rock Creek Palisades 15 16 39N02'08 77w04'37 5:08:18
Rock Creek Village 15 16 39N04'52 77w06'10 5:08:25
Rockcrest 15 16 39N04'32 77w07'51 5:08:31
Rockdale 3 3 39N21'22 76w45'57 5:07:04
Rockdale 21 7 39N42'04 77w50'39 5:11:23
Rock Hall 10 7 39N16'07 77w31'35 5:10:06
Rock Hall 14 15 39N08'17 76w14'07 5:04:56
Rock Hill Beach 2 20 39N09'00 76w31'08 5:06:05
Rockland 3 3 39N24'05 76w40'05 5:06:40
Rockland 13 3 39N17'56 76w48'49 5:07:15
Rockland 15 16 39N04'21 77w07'36 5:08:30
Rock Point 8 6 38N16'19 76w50'28 5:07:22
Rock Run 12 8 39N36'29 76w08'36 5:04:34
Rocks 12 8 39N38 76w25 5:05:40
Rock Springs 7 7 39N42'54 76w09'32 5:04:38
Rockview Beach 2 20 39N08'35 76w30'55 5:06:04
Rockville 15 16 39N05'02 77w09'11 5:08:37
Rockwell 3 3 39N17 76w43 5:06:52
Rocky Acres 10 7 39N38 77w25 5:09:40
Rocky Brook Park 15 16 39N03'04 76w59'50 5:07:59
Rocky Forge 21 7 39N43'06 77w36'19 5:10:25
Rocky Gorge Estates 16 16 39N06'39 76w53'09 5:07:33
Rocky Hook 9 8 38N29'02 75w55'40 5:03:43
Rocky Ridge 10 8 39N36'18 77w19'04 5:09:16
Rocky Springs 10 7 39N26'52 77w27'13 5:09:49
Rodgers Forge 3 3 39N22'40 76w36'50 5:06:27
Rogers Heights 16 16 38N56'55 76w55'20 5:07:41
Rogers Mill 8 6 38N29'37 76w55'53 5:07:44
Rognel Heights 24 1 39N17'38 76w41'10 5:06:45
Rohrersville 21 7 39N26'00 77w39'47 5:10:39
Rohrersville Station 21 7 39N25'52 77w40'41 5:10:43
Roland Park 24 1 39N21'16 76w38'04 5:06:32
Roller 6 8 39N41'49 76w48'25 5:07:14
Rolling Acres 6 8 39N34 76w59 5:07:56
Rolling Acres 15 3 39N03'26 76w58'15 5:07:53
Rolling Ridge 16 16 38N54 76w54 5:07:36
Rolling Terrace 15 16 38N59 77w01 5:08:04
Rolling View 16 16 38N57'11 76w51'13 5:07:25
Rollingwood 15 16 38N59'00 77w04'08 5:08:17
Rollins Park 15 16 39N03'37 77w07'50 5:08:31
Rolph Landing 20 13 38N53'56 75w56'47 5:03:47
Rolphs 17 15 39N10'27 76w02'11 5:04:09
Romancoke 17 15 38N52'52 76w20'12 5:05:21
Romancoke on the Bay 17 15 38N59 76w19 5:05:16
Roop Mill 6 8 39N35'24 77w01'53 5:08:08
Rosaryville 16 16 38N45'24 76w48'36 5:07:14
Rosaryville Estates 16 16 38N47 76w52 5:07:28
Rosecroft Gardens 16 16 38N47 76w58 5:07:52
Rosecroft Park 16 16 38N47 76w58 5:07:52
Rosedale 3 3 39N19'12 76w30'57 5:06:04
Rosedale Estates 16 16 38N47 76w58 5:07:52
Rosedale Park 15 16 38N59'29 77w05'30 5:08:22
Rosedale Park 16 16 39N01'34 76w53'49 5:07:35
Rose Haven 2 20 38N43'32 76w32'21 5:06:09
Rose Hill Estates 15 16 39N00'39 77w09'27 5:08:38
Rosemary Hills 15 16 38N59'51 77w02'38 5:08:11
Rosemont 3 3 39N14'14 76w38'06 5:06:32
Rosemont 10 7 39N19'45 77w37'22 5:10:29
Rose Valley Estates 16 16 38N47 76w58 5:07:52
Rossville 3 3 39N20'18 76w28'48 5:05:55
Round Bay 2 20 39N03'43 76w32'15 5:06:09
Round Hill 10 7 39N26 77w27 5:09:48
Roundtop 21 8 39N42 78w11 5:12:44
Rowlandsville 7 7 39N39'40 76w08'50 5:04:35
Roxbury 21 7 39N33'16 77w42'14 5:10:49
Roxbury Mills 13 16 39N15'29 77w03'13 5:08:13
Royal Beach 2 20 39N06'23 76w32'34 5:06:10
Royal Oak 20 13 38N44'32 76w10'41 5:04:43
Royal Oak 22 7 38N20'59 75w47'35 5:03:10
Royal View 15 16 39N05 77w07 5:08:28
Rugby Hall 2 20 39N02'25 76w31'56 5:06:08
Ruhl 3 24 39N42'28 76w44'04 5:06:56
Rumbley 19 23 38N05'36 75w51'31 5:03:26
Rush 1 3 39N39'49 78w36'41 5:14:27
Rushville 15 16 39N04'13 77w19'40 5:09:19
Ruthsburg 17 15 39N00'11 75w57'30 5:03:50
Rutledge 12 8 39N33'25 76w29'47 5:05:59
Ruxton 3 3 39N24'00 76w38'42 5:06:35
Ryans Glade 11 2 39N18 79w26 5:17:44
Rycerville 8 6 38N26'08 76w49'51 5:07:19
Sabillasville 10 7 39N42'00 77w27'24 5:09:50
Sackertown 19 28 37N58'20 75w50'35 5:03:22
Saint Andrews Estates 18 4 38N18 76w31 5:06:04
Saint Anthony 10 7 39N40'35 77w21'23 5:09:26
Saint Aubins Heights 20 13 38N47'00 76w04'20 5:04:17
Saint Augustine 7 7 39N29'39 75w48'33 5:03:14
Saint Charles 8 6 38N36'11 76w56'20 5:07:45
Saint Clements Shores 18 4 38N16'48 76w42'18 5:06:49
Saint Denis 3 3 39N13'21 76w42'18 5:06:49
Saint George Island 18 4 38N07'12 76w29'02 5:05:56
Saint George Park 18 4 38N09'32 76w31'06 5:06:04
Saint Georges 3 3 39N27'58 76w48'29 5:07:14
Saint Helena 3 3 39N15'36 76w31'32 5:06:06
Saint Inigoes 18 4 38N09 76w23 5:05:32

Saint James 18 4 38N11'55 76w23'43 5:05:35
Saint James 21 7 39N33'45 77w45'30 5:11:02
Saint James 23 19 38N04 75w34 5:02:16
Saint Jeromes 18 4 38N09 76w22 5:05:28
Saint Johns Manor 13 3 39N16 76w49 5:07:16
Saint Johns Village 13 3 39N16 76w49 5:07:16
Saint Leonard 4 9 38N28'27 76w30'24 5:06:02
Saint Margarets 2 20 39N01'15 76w27'47 5:05:51
Saint Mark's 10 7 39N20 77w37 5:10:28
Saint Martin 23 23 38N22'19 75w14'54 5:01:00
Saint Marys City 18 4 38N11'13 76w26'05 5:05:44
Saint Michaels 20 11 38N47'06 76w13'29 5:04:54
Saint Peters 19 19 38N11 75w49 5:03:16
Saint Stephen 19 26 38N11'14 75w50'25 5:03:22
Salem 9 8 38N30'57 75w54'46 5:03:39
Salisbury 22 22 38N21'38 75w35'59 5:02:24
Samples Manor 21 7 39N22'19 77w43'13 5:10:53
Sams Creek 6 8 39N33 77w06 5:08:24
Sanders Park 2 20 39N08'51 76w30'07 5:06:00
Sandgates 18 4 38N24'46 76w36'56 5:06:28
Sand Spring 11 2 39N40'21 79w27'35 5:17:50
Sandy Acres 9 8 38N34 76w05 5:04:20
Sandy Bottom 14 15 39N11'35 76w11'04 5:04:44
Sandy Hook 21 7 39N19'33 77w42'39 5:10:51
Sandy Spring 15 16 39N08'58 77w01'38 5:08:07
Sandyville 6 8 39N31'29 76w55'32 5:07:42
Sanford 15 16 39N01'09 77w02'30 5:08:10
Sang Run 11 2 39N33 79w22 5:17:28
Sanmar 21 7 39N33'03 77w38'41 5:10:35
Sansbury Park 16 16 38N51 76w54 5:07:36
Santo Domingo 22 7 38N30'41 75w43'23 5:02:54
Sassafras 14 15 39N22'23 75w48'10 5:03:13
Satyr Hill 3 3 39N23 76w33 5:06:12
Saunders Point 2 20 38N53'15 76w29'33 5:05:58
Savage 13 3 39N08'16 76w49'27 5:07:18
Scaggsville 13 3 39N08'42 76w54'02 5:07:36
Scarboro 12 8 39N38'46 76w17'44 5:05:11
Scarboro 23 27 38N08'00 75w23'43 5:01:35
Scarboro Landing 23 23 38N04'09 75w22'01 5:01:28
Schell 11 2 39N20'31 79w15'36 5:17:02
Schultz 16 16 38N47 76w53 5:07:32
Scientists Cliffs 4 9 38N31'03 76w30'49 5:06:03
Scotland 15 16 39N02'26 77w09'34 5:08:38
Scotland 18 4 38N05'20 76w21'44 5:05:27
Scotland Beach 18 4 38N04'17 76w19'48 5:05:19
Scott Landing 23 27 38N05'56 75w18'56 5:01:16
Scotts Landing 23 27 38N05'01 75w12'58 5:00:52
Scotts Level 3 3 39N21'58 76w45'30 5:07:02
Scrabbletown 2 20 38N54 76w30 5:06:00
Seabrook 16 16 38N58'04 76w50'43 5:07:23
Seabrook Acres 16 16 38N58'33 76w50'29 5:07:22
Seabrook Park Estates 16 16 38N58 76w51 5:07:24
Seat Pleasant 16 16 38N53'46 76w54'25 5:07:38
Sebring 13 3 39N16 76w49 5:07:16
Secretary 9 8 38N36'33 75w56'52 5:03:47
Security 11 8 39N39'04 77w41'28 5:10:46
Selby Beach 2 20 38N54'25 76w30'59 5:06:04
Selby-on-the-Bay 2 20 38N55 76w31 5:06:04
Selbys Landing 16 20 38N45'04 76w41'58 5:06:48
Selbysport 11 2 39N41'11 79w22'50 5:17:31
Sellman 15 16 39N12'30 77w22'43 5:09:31
Seneca 15 16 39N04'43 77w20'22 5:09:21
Seneca Park 3 3 39N19'25 76w22'31 5:05:30
Seven Oaks 15 16 39N00'25 77w00'56 5:08:04
Severn 2 20 39N08'13 76w41'55 5:06:48
Severna Forest 2 20 39N05 76w34 5:06:16
Severna Park 2 20 39N04'13 76w32'44 5:06:11
Severn Crossroads 2 20 39N03'35 76w37'41 5:06:31
Severn Grove 2 20 39N00'24 76w32'01 5:06:08
Severn Heights 2 20 39N05 76w34 5:06:16
Severnside 2 20 39N00'06 76w29'12 5:05:57
Seward 9 8 38N26'49 76w04'52 5:04:19
Sewell Mills 5 8 38N59'47 75w46'46 5:03:07
Shad Landing 23 27 38N08'34 75w26'25 5:01:46
Shad Point 22 7 38N20'23 75w37'57 5:02:32
Shady Bower 21 7 39N39'32 77w53'50 5:11:35
Shady Oaks 2 20 38N49'36 76w33'00 5:06:12
Shady Side 2 20 38N50'30 76w30'45 5:06:03
Shaft 1 3 39N38 78w57 5:15:48
Shallmar 11 2 39N22'46 79w12'18 5:16:49
Shane 3 3 39N40'09 76w35'32 5:06:22
Sharewood Acres 13 3 39N09 76w47 5:07:08
Sharon 12 8 39N36'14 76w24'41 5:05:39
Sharonville 2 20 39N07'30 76w31'16 5:06:05
Sharperville 16 16 38N40'21 76w58'29 5:07:54
Sharpsburg 21 7 39N27'27 77w44'57 5:11:00
Sharpstown 14 15 39N08'11 76w13'08 5:04:53
Sharptown 22 7 38N32'33 75w43'11 5:02:53
Shavox 22 7 38N21'22 75w27'50 5:01:51
Shawan 3 3 39N29'44 76w42'31 5:06:50
Shawsville 12 8 39N38'16 76w33'19 5:06:13
Shawsville Acres 12 8 39N37 76w38 5:06:32
Shelltown 19 23 37N58'47 75w38'25 5:02:34
Shepperd 3 3 39N35'36 76w34'10 5:06:17
Shervettes Corner 6 8 39N23'48 76w53'44 5:07:35
Sherwood 20 13 38N45'41 76w19'09 5:05:17
Sherwood Forest 2 20 39N01'39 76w32'39 5:06:11
Sherwood Forest 15 16 39N04'43 77w00'46 5:08:03
Sherwood Manor 16 16 38N30 75w52 5:03:28
Shetland Hills 3 3 39N25'34 76w36'30 5:06:26
Shiloh 6 8 39N35'53 76w53'07 5:07:32
Shiloh 8 6 38N21'51 76w55'32 5:07:42
Shiloh 9 8 38N38 75w52 5:03:28
Shingle Landing 23 19 38N24'19 75w11'45 5:00:47
Shipley 2 20 39N11'55 76w39'24 5:06:38
Shipley Corner 2 20 39N09'32 76w42'50 5:06:51
Shipyard Landing 14 15 39N09'45 76w11'28 5:04:46
Shookstown 10 7 39N26'08 77w28'03 5:09:52
Shore Acres 2 20 39N03'20 76w27'35 5:05:50
Shoreham Beach 2 20 38N54'00 76w29'42 5:05:59
Shorewood Gardens 14 15 39N21 75w53 5:03:32
Shorewood Gardens Estates 14 15 39N20 75w47 5:03:08
Showell 23 19 38N23'52 75w12'55 5:00:52
Silesia 16 16 38N44'32 76w59'57 5:08:00
Siloam 22 7 38N19'40 75w41'00 5:02:44
Silver Grove 21 7 39N39 77w44 5:10:56
Silver Hill 16 16 38N50'30 76w56'46 5:07:47
Silver Hill Park 16 16 38N50'12 76w56'56 5:07:48
Silver Rock 15 16 39N04'52 77w07'40 5:08:31
Silver Run 6 8 39N40'58 77w02'40 5:08:11
Silver Spring 15 16 38N59'26 77w01'35 5:08:06
Silver Spring Heights 12 8 39N32 76w21 5:05:24
Silver Spring Park 15 16 38N59'36 77w01'12 5:08:05
Simms Landing 8 6 38N29'10 77w01'46 5:08:07
Simpsons Mill 6 8 39N35'03 77w13'30 5:08:54
Simpsonville 13 3 39N11'12 76w52'56 5:07:32
Sinepuxent 23 27 38N18'47 75w09'08 5:00:37
Singer 12 8 39N28'28 76w20'21 5:05:21
Singerly 7 7 39N38'56 75w50'39 5:03:23
Sixmile House 11 3 39N38'17 78w50'55 5:15:24
Skidmore 2 20 39N01'16 76w24'56 5:05:40
Skipton 20 8 38N53'43 76w03'33 5:04:14
Skyline 16 16 38N50 76w55 5:07:40
Skyline Estates 10 7 39N26 77w27 5:09:48
Slabtown 1 24 39N40'58 78w53'12 5:15:33
Slabtown 10 7 39N21'04 77w35'48 5:10:23
Slacks Corner 13 3 39N19'11 76w56'55 5:07:48
Slidell 15 16 39N13'10 77w19'56 5:09:20
Sligo Park Hills 15 16 38N59'31 77w00'39 5:08:03
Sligo Woods 15 16 39N01'35 77w01'32 5:08:06
Smallwood 6 8 39N30'46 76w58'29 5:07:54
Smith Island 19 19 38N02 76w00 5:04:00
Smith Landing 5 11 38N54'44 75w49'45 5:03:19
Smithsburg 21 8 39N39'17 77w34'23 5:10:18
Smithville 5 15 38N46'26 75w43'59 5:02:56
Smithville 9 8 38N28'18 76w16'21 5:05:05
Smithville 14 15 39N17'51 76w06'30 5:04:26
Smoketown 21 7 39N31 77w39 5:10:36
Sniders Estates 15 16 39N06'44 76w59'30 5:07:58
Snowden Manor 6 8 39N34 76w59 5:07:56
Snow Hill 23 27 38N10'37 75w23'35 5:01:34
Snow Hill Manor 16 16 39N05'00 76w50'58 5:07:24
Snug Harbor 2 20 38N50'11 76w29'46 5:05:59
Snug Harbor 23 27 38N19 75w13 5:00:52
Snydersburg 6 8 39N37'08 76w53'46 5:07:35
Snyders Landing 21 7 39N27'55 77w46'41 5:11:07
Society Hill 18 4 38N16'04 76w39'57 5:06:40
Sollers 4 4 38N23'18 76w29'34 5:05:58
Sollers Point 3 3 39N14 76w31 5:06:04
Solley 2 20 39N10'15 76w33'17 5:06:13
Solomons 4 9 38N19 76w27 5:05:48
Solomons Island 4 9 38N25 76w29 5:05:56
Somerset 15 16 38N57'57 77w05'47 5:08:23
Somerset Heights 15 16 38N58'08 77w05'42 5:08:23
Sonoma 15 16 39N00'04 77w06'50 5:08:27
Sotterley 18 4 38N22'42 76w32'00 5:06:08
South 24 1 39N16 76w38 5:06:32
South Baltimore 24 20 39N16'22 76w36'21 5:06:25
South Cheverly Forest 16 16 38N58 76w53 5:07:32
South Cumberland 1 24 39N37'57 78w45'22 5:15:01
South Down Shores 2 20 38N56'18 76w34'15 5:06:17
Southeast Landing 17 15 39N09'27 76w01'35 5:04:06
Southern Garden Apartments 16 16 38N50 77w00 5:08:00
South Gate 2 20 39N08 76w37 5:06:28
South Haven 2 20 38N57'47 76w34'58 5:06:20
South Kensington 15 16 39N01 77w05 5:08:20
Southland Hills 3 3 39N23'55 76w36'39 5:06:27
South Laurel 16 16 39N04 76w51 5:07:24
South Lawn 16 16 38N47'34 76w59'32 5:07:58
South Layhill 15 16 39N04 77w04 5:08:16
South Piscataway 16 16 38N41'09 76w58'50 5:07:55
South River 2 20 38N54'11 76w33'39 5:06:15
South River Manor 2 20 38N58'14 76w34'43 5:06:19
South River Park 2 20 38N56 76w33 5:06:12
South Salisbury 22 7 38N22 75w36 5:02:24
Southview Apartments 16 16 38N48 76w59 5:07:56
South Woodside Park 15 16 39N00'18 77w01'13 5:08:05
Sparks 3 3 39N31'51 76w38'46 5:06:35
Sparks Glencoe 3 3 39N32 76w39 5:06:36
Sparrows Point 3 3 39N13'09 76w28'35 5:05:54
Spaulding Heights 16 16 38N51 76w54 5:07:36
Spauldings 16 16 38N50 76w55 5:07:40
Spence 23 27 38N09'43 75w18'36 5:01:14
Spencerville 15 16 39N06'51 76w58'43 5:07:55
Spickler 21 7 39N39'29 77w52'13 5:11:29
Spielman 21 7 39N32'13 77w45'51 5:11:03
Spoolsville 10 7 39N27'00 77w33'42 5:10:15
Springbrook 15 16 39N03'13 76w59'42 5:07:59
Springbrook Forest 15 16 39N03'09 77w01'05 5:08:04
Springbrook Manor 15 16 39N02'59 76w59'18 5:07:57
Springbrook Terrace 16 16 38N57'19 76w55'04 5:07:40
Springbrook Village 15 16 39N04 76w59 5:07:56
Springdale Gardens 16 16 38N56'09 76w51'06 5:07:24
Springfield 15 16 38N58'02 77w06'54 5:08:28
Springfield 16 16 38N59'34 76w47'59 5:07:12
Spring Gap 1 3 39N33'55 78w43'00 5:14:52
Spring Garden Estates 10 7 39N29 77w21 5:09:24
Spring Grove 22 7 38N29'18 75w45'06 5:03:00
Springhill 8 6 38N30'16 76w59'06 5:07:56
Spring Hill 15 16 39N00'14 77w04'20 5:08:17
Spring Hill 22 7 38N25 75w41 5:02:44
Springhill Acres 22 7 38N22 75w36 5:02:24
Springhill Lake 16 16 39N00'07 76w54'12 5:07:37
Springlake 15 16 39N00 77w08 5:08:32
Spring Lake Park 15 16 39N03'33 77w06'55 5:08:28
Spring Mills 6 8 39N33'17 77w00'45 5:08:03
Spring Valley 21 7 39N39 77w44 5:10:56
Springwood 15 16 39N03'48 77w01'13 5:08:05
Spry Landing 14 15 39N14'38 75w57'11 5:03:49
Stablersville 3 3 39N39'02 76w36'58 5:06:28
Stafford 12 8 39N38 76w12 5:04:48
Stafford 16 16 38N58'18 76w53'16 5:07:33
Stanbrook 3 3 39N14 76w31 5:06:04
Standard 11 2 39N24'54 79w10'32 5:16:42
Stansbury Estates 3 3 39N19'11 76w25'11 5:05:41
Stansbury Manor 3 3 39N20 76w27 5:05:48
Starkeys Corner 17 15 39N07'14 76w00'53 5:04:04
Starr 17 15 38N58'41 76w00'38 5:04:03
Stemmers Run 3 3 39N19'50 76w28'20 5:05:53
Stephen Knolls 15 16 39N01'51 77w03'06 5:08:12
Stepney 12 8 39N31 76w10 5:04:40
Steuart Corner 2 20 38N56'01 76w34'10 5:06:17
Steuart Level 2 20 38N55'42 76w34'19 5:06:17
Stevens Corner 17 15 39N08'41 75w53'55 5:03:36
Stevenson 3 3 39N24'37 76w42'48 5:06:51
Stevensville 17 15 38N58'50 76w18'53 5:05:16
Stewart Corner 2 20 39N08'11 76w41'09 5:06:45
Stewart Town 15 16 39N10'45 77w11'24 5:08:46
Steyer 11 2 39N18'20 79w18'40 5:17:15
Stillmeadows 2 20 39N09 76w40 5:06:40
Still Pond 14 8 39N19'45 76w02'45 5:04:11
Stoakley 4 9 38N33'30 76w35'52 5:06:23
Stockton 12 3 39N28'29 76w22'50 5:05:31
Stockton 23 19 38N03'13 75w24'37 5:01:38
Stonecrest 13 3 39N16 76w49 5:07:16
Stone Cross 18 4 38N12'31 76w44'42 5:06:59
Stonegate 15 16 39N04 76w59 5:07:56
Stoneleigh 3 3 39N22'50 76w36'12 5:06:25
Stoney Brook 15 16 39N03'46 77w05'29 5:08:22
Stoney Brook Estates 15 16 39N03'56 77w04'56 5:08:20
Stony Beach 2 20 39N10'22 76w31'08 5:06:05
Stony Run 2 20 39N10'54 76w41'51 5:06:47
Straits 9 8 38N16 76w04 5:04:16
Stratford 3 3 39N26'53 76w37'10 5:06:29
Strathmore at Bel Pre 15 16 39N04 77w04 5:08:16
Stratton Woods 15 16 39N00'57 77w08'07 5:08:32
Strawberry Hills Estates 8 6 38N38 77w04 5:08:16
Strawleigh 10 7 39N26 77w27 5:09:48
Strawn 11 2 39N43'16 79w17'49 5:17:11
Strecker 11 2 39N28'30 79w11'28 5:16:46
Street 12 8 39N40'08 76w22'47 5:05:31
Stringtown 3 3 39N33'16 76w43'09 5:06:53
Stronghold 10 7 39N15'05 77w23'36 5:09:34
Stulls Ford 10 8 39N34'43 77w19'54 5:09:20

Stumptown 6 8 39N38'59 77w08'28 5:08:34
Stumptown 20 11 38N43'21 76w04'08 5:04:17
Sudbrook Park 3 3 39N22'02 76w43'42 5:06:55
Sudlersville 17 15 39N11'13 75w51'33 5:03:26
Sudley 2 20 38N49'00 76w34'43 5:06:19
Sugarland 15 16 39N05'58 77w23'29 5:09:34
Sugarloaf 9 8 38N20'53 76w02'02 5:04:08
Suitland 16 16 38N50'55 76w55'27 5:07:42
Suitland Manor 16 16 38N51'12 76w55'35 5:07:42
Sullivan Heights 6 8 39N34 76w59 5:07:56
Summerfield Farms 3 16 39N25'54 76w31'44 5:06:07
Summerhill 15 16 39N09 77w25 5:09:40
Summit Farms 3 3 39N20 76w31 5:06:04
Summit Knoll 2 20 39N06'13 76w32'11 5:06:09
Summit Park 3 3 39N22'44 76w40'54 5:06:44
Sumner 15 16 38N57'19 77w06'55 5:08:28
Sunderland 4 9 38N40'16 76w35'54 5:06:24
Sunny Acres 16 16 38N51 76w54 5:07:36
Sunnybrook 3 3 39N30'15 76w34'18 5:06:17
Sunnybrook Hills 3 3 39N31 76w37 5:06:28
Sunny Isle of Kent 17 15 38N59 76w19 5:05:16
Sunrise 6 8 39N34 76w59 5:07:56
Sunrise Beach 2 20 39N04'11 76w35'27 5:06:22
Sunset Acres 21 7 39N39 77w44 5:10:56
Sunset Beach 2 20 39N09'30 76w31'22 5:06:05
Sunset Hills 10 7 39N26 77w27 5:09:48
Sunset Knoll 2 20 39N09 76w33 5:06:12
Sunset Terrace 15 16 39N01'10 77w01'39 5:08:07
Sunset View 3 8 39N43'02 76w42'26 5:06:50
Sunshine 13 16 39N13'16 77w03'37 5:08:14
Sunyar 22 7 38N22 75w36 5:02:24
Surratts 16 16 38N46 76w53 5:07:32
Surratts Gardens 16 16 38N47 76w53 5:07:32
Susquehanna Hills 12 8 39N33 76w06 5:04:24
Sutton Acres 8 6 38N31 77w01 5:08:04
Swan Creek 12 8 39N31'23 76w08'16 5:04:33
Swan Point 3 3 39N14'00 76w24'11 5:05:37
Swanton 11 2 39N27'32 79w13'52 5:16:55
Sweet Air 3 3 39N30'44 76w32'15 5:06:09
Sycamore Acres 15 16 39N07'02 77w05'25 5:08:22
Sycamore Creek 15 16 39N05'32 77w05'46 5:08:23
Sykesville 6 8 39N22'25 76w58'05 5:07:52
Sylmar 7 7 39N43'17 76w01'41 5:04:07
Sylvan Grove 21 7 39N39'52 77w47'50 5:11:11
Sylvan Shores 2 20 38N57'10 76w34'53 5:06:20
Sylvan View 2 20 39N09 76w33 5:06:12
Table Rock 11 2 39N18 79w21 5:17:24
Takoma Park 15 16 38N58'40 77w00'28 5:08:02
Tall Timbers 18 4 38N10'08 76w32'43 5:06:11
Tammany Manor 21 7 39N36 77w49 5:11:16
Taneytown 6 8 39N39'28 77w10'29 5:08:42
Tangier 19 19 38N09 75w55 5:03:40
Tanglewood 2 20 38N59'57 76w26'14 5:05:45
Tannery 6 8 39N34'14 76w56'54 5:07:48
Tantallon 16 16 38N43'26 77w00'36 5:08:02
Tanterra 15 16 39N11 77w03 5:08:12
Tanyard 5 15 38N45'02 75w58'37 5:03:54
Tappers Corner 20 8 38N53'08 75w57'40 5:03:51
Taylor 12 8 39N34'34 76w31'03 5:06:04
Taylor Landing 23 23 38N04'31 75w21'57 5:01:28
Taylors Island 9 8 38N28'08 76w17'58 5:05:12
Taylors Landing 21 7 39N29'56 77w46'04 5:11:04
Taylorsville 6 8 39N27'28 77w05'13 5:08:21
Taylorville 23 27 38N21'30 75w10'07 5:00:40
TB 16 16 38N42'04 76w52'29 5:07:30
Temple Heights 16 16 38N49 76w56 5:07:44
Temple Hills 16 16 38N48'50 76w56'45 5:07:47
Temple Hills Park 16 16 38N48'34 76w56'40 5:07:47
Templeton Knolls 16 16 38N58 76w55 5:07:40
Templeton Manor 16 16 38N58 76w55 5:07:40
Templeville 5 15 39N08'10 75w45'59 5:03:04
Temple Woods 16 16 38N49 76w56 5:07:44
Ten Hills 24 3 39N17'03 76w42'05 5:06:48
Terrace Gardens 2 20 39N02'25 76w30'40 5:06:03
Texas 3 3 39N27'49 76w38'38 5:06:35
Thayerville 11 14 39N30'06 79w19'37 5:17:18
The Downs 2 20 39N03 76w30 5:06:00
The Elbow 11 2 39N35 79w03 5:16:12
The Glen 15 16 39N03 77w10 5:08:40
The Hamlet 15 16 38N59'12 77w04'26 5:08:18
The Oaks 13 3 39N16 76w49 5:07:16
Theodore 7 7 39N38'19 76w00'37 5:04:02
The Orchards 13 3 39N16 76w49 5:07:16
The Pines 16 16 38N47 76w52 5:07:28
Thistle 3 3 39N15'13 76w46'02 5:07:04
Thomas 9 8 38N34'17 76w16'38 5:05:07
Thomas Choice 15 16 39N08 77w12 5:08:48
Thomas Run 12 8 39N35'26 76w17'02 5:05:08
Thomas Town 5 15 38N55'01 75w55'43 5:03:43
Thompkinsville 8 6 38N19 76w53 5:07:32
Thompson 9 8 38N32'09 76w01'52 5:04:07
Thompson Corner 18 4 38N26'58 76w47'10 5:07:09
Thompsons Corner 15 16 39N14'32 77w19'35 5:09:18
Thompsontown 9 8 38N34'29 75w54'02 5:03:36
Thomson Estates 7 7 39N37 75w50 5:03:20
Thornleigh 3 3 39N23 76w38 5:06:32
Thorwood Park 3 3 39N23 76w33 5:06:12
Threemile Oak Corner 2 20 38N59'10 76w32'52 5:06:11
Thrift 16 16 38N43'09 76w55'58 5:07:44
Thurmont 10 8 39N37'25 77w24'40 5:09:39
Thurston 10 7 39N16'48 77w21'30 5:09:26
Tilden Woods 15 16 39N02'49 77w08'27 5:08:34
Tilghman 20 13 38N43'01 76w20'05 5:05:20
Tilghman Island Landing 20 13 38N42'31 76w19'49 5:05:19
Tilghmanton 21 7 39N32'00 77w44'28 5:10:58
Timber Grove 3 3 39N26 76w48 5:07:12
Timber Ridge 2 20 39N12 76w43 5:06:52
Timberview 13 3 39N15 76w41 5:06:44
Timmonstown 23 27 38N20'30 75w18'13 5:01:13
Timonium 3 3 39N26'13 76w37'12 5:06:29
Tintop Hill 18 4 38N19'20 76w37'08 5:06:29
Tippett 16 16 38N44'50 76w55'57 5:07:44
Tobytown 15 16 39N08 77w12 5:08:48
Toddville 9 8 38N17'59 76w04'15 5:04:17
Tolchester Beach 14 15 39N13'14 76w14'10 5:04:57
Tollgate 3 3 39N26 76w48 5:07:12
Tompkinsville 8 6 38N19'18 76w53'34 5:07:34
Tonytank 22 7 38N22 75w36 5:02:24
Tower Acres 13 3 39N05 76w58 5:07:52
Tower Garden on the Bay 17 15 38N59 76w19 5:05:16
Town Creek 1 3 39N31'32 78w32'21 5:14:09
Town Creek 18 4 38N19'18 76w28'47 5:05:55
Town Creek Manor 18 4 38N15 76w27 5:05:48
Town Point 7 7 39N29'44 75w53'48 5:03:35
Townshend 16 16 38N39'54 76w52'02 5:07:28
Towson 3 3 39N24'05 76w36'08 5:06:25
Towson Estates 3 3 39N23'51 76w34'45 5:06:19
Towson Park 3 3 39N24'26 76w36'20 5:06:25
Tracys Landing 2 20 38N46'48 76w35'46 5:06:23
Trappe 18 4 38N09 76w22 5:05:28
Trappe 20 11 38N39'30 76w03'30 5:04:14
Trappe 23 27 38N18'51 75w11'28 5:00:46
Trappe Landing 20 11 38N39'22 76w05'07 5:04:20
Trappe Station 20 13 38N41 76w10 5:04:40
Travilah 15 16 39N04'08 77w15'48 5:09:03
Treasure Cove 16 16 38N47 76w58 5:07:52
Trego 21 7 39N25'59 77w40'42 5:10:43
Trent Hall 18 4 38N26 76w44 5:06:56
Trenton 3 3 39N34'44 76w48'29 5:07:14
Trenton Mill 3 3 39N34'31 76w48'41 5:07:15
Trevanion 6 8 39N37'28 77w08'23 5:08:34
Trinity 22 7 38N17'37 75w44'48 5:02:59
Triple Lakes 1 3 39N34'52 78w50'49 5:15:23
Troupe Springs 21 7 39N40'27 77w47'35 5:11:10
Troutville 10 7 39N33'12 77w20'15 5:09:21
Troyer 3 3 39N36'18 76w34'42 5:06:19
Truitt 22 7 38N20'48 75w21'56 5:01:28
Truitt Landing 23 23 38N05'57 75w20'19 5:01:21
Truxton Heights 2 20 38N58'00 76w30'22 5:06:01
Tulip Hill 10 7 39N26 77w27 5:09:48
Tulip Hill 15 16 38N58'02 77w08'02 5:08:32
Tulls Corner 19 23 38N00'55 75w45'16 5:03:01
Tunis Mills 20 13 38N49'13 76w10'00 5:04:40
Turkey Point 2 20 38N54'22 76w29'48 5:05:59
Turner 3 3 39N14'41 76w30'54 5:06:04
Tuscarora 10 7 39N15'24 77w28'14 5:09:53
Tuxedo 16 16 38N55'15 76w55'10 5:07:41
Tuxedo Colony 16 16 38N54'44 76w54'40 5:07:39
Twiggs Corner 22 7 38N18'36 75w42'15 5:02:49
Twiggtown 1 3 39N38'22 78w39'21 5:14:37
Twin Brook 15 16 39N04'28 77w07'13 5:08:29
Twin Brook Forest 15 16 39N04'51 77w07'04 5:08:28
Twinkling Acres 16 16 38N47 76w53 5:07:32
Twin River Beach 3 3 39N20 76w27 5:05:48
Two Locks 21 7 39N36'54 77w55'27 5:11:42
Tyaskin 22 7 38N19'19 75w52'26 5:03:30
Tydings On The Bay 2 20 39N02'10 76w24'41 5:05:39
Tyler 3 3 39N25'39 76w51'13 5:07:25
Tyler Heights 2 20 38N57'34 76w29'54 5:06:00
Tylerton 19 19 37N58'04 76w01'24 5:04:06
Tyrone 6 8 39N37'07 77w05'38 5:08:23
Unicorn 17 15 39N14'53 75w51'48 5:03:27
Union Bridge 6 8 39N34'08 77w10'38 5:08:43
Union Corner 5 8 39N02 75w47 5:03:08
Union Mills 6 8 39N40'11 77w01'30 5:08:06
Union Street 1 24 39N39 78w43 5:14:52
Uniontown 6 8 39N35'36 77w06'59 5:08:28
Unionville 3 3 39N28 76w31 5:06:04
Unionville 10 7 39N28'29 77w11'09 5:08:45
Unionville 20 13 38N48'48 76w08'24 5:04:34
Unionville 23 19 38N03'38 75w35'58 5:02:24
Unity 15 16 39N11 77w03 5:08:12
University 13 16 39N13'34 77w04'11 5:08:17
University Gardens 16 16 38N58'53 76w58'13 5:07:53
University Hills 16 16 38N59 76w58 5:07:52
University Park 16 16 38N58'13 76w56'32 5:07:46
Upperco 3 3 39N33'46 76w50'08 5:07:21
Upper Crossroads 12 8 39N32'32 76w28'28 5:05:54
Upper Fairmount 19 23 38N06'14 75w47'30 5:03:10
Upper Falls 3 3 39N26'14 76w24'13 5:05:37
Upper Ferry Estates 22 7 38N22 75w36 5:02:24
Upper Hill 19 23 38N06'42 75w47'26 5:03:10
Upper Homewood 1 3 39N38 78w48 5:15:12
Upper Marlboro 16 16 38N48'57 76w45'00 5:07:00
Urbana 10 7 39N19'33 77w21'06 5:09:24
Utica 10 7 39N31'33 77w23'39 5:09:35
Utica Mills Estates 10 7 39N38 77w25 5:09:40
Vale 12 8 39N32'00 76w23'30 5:05:34
Vale Summit 1 3 39N37'07 78w54'23 5:15:38
Valley Crest 3 3 39N26'11 76w36'07 5:06:24
Valley Lee 18 4 38N11'45 76w30'47 5:06:03
Valley Mede 13 3 39N16 76w49 5:07:16
Valley Mill 3 3 39N40'24 76w41'34 5:06:46
Valley Stream 3 3 39N22'36 76w41'10 5:06:45
Valley Stream Estates 15 16 39N06'29 76w55'20 5:07:41
Valley View 13 3 39N16 76w49 5:07:16
Valley View 16 16 38N47 76w58 5:07:52
Valleywood 22 7 38N22 75w36 5:02:24
Van Bibber 12 8 39N26'37 76w18'08 5:05:13
Van Bibber Manor 12 8 39N23 76w15 5:05:00
Van Lear Manor 21 7 39N36 77w49 5:11:16
Vansville 16 16 39N02'36 76w53'45 5:07:35
Vardo 21 7 39N36'59 77w44'22 5:10:57
Venice on the Bay 2 20 39N09'19 76w28'46 5:05:55
Venton 19 26 38N11'48 75w46'46 5:03:07
Vernon 3 3 39N38'14 76w35'53 5:06:24
Verona 3 3 39N33'36 76w39'22 5:06:37
Victor Haven 2 20 38N57'14 76w29'35 5:05:58
Victory Villa 3 3 39N20'28 76w27'26 5:05:50
Vienna 9 8 38N29'05 75w49'30 5:03:18
Viers Mill Village 15 16 39N03'21 77w04'56 5:08:20
View More Acres 10 7 39N26 77w27 5:09:48
Villa Cresta 3 3 39N22'39 76w32'45 5:06:11
Village Square North 16 16 39N05 76w58 5:07:52
Villa Heights 16 16 38N56'14 76w55'08 5:07:41
Villa Maria 3 3 39N15 76w41 5:06:44
Villa Monticello 13 3 39N19 77w01 5:08:04
Villa Nova 3 3 39N21'05 76w44'02 5:06:56
Violetville 24 1 39N16'03 76w40'29 5:06:42
Vista Raceway 16 16 38N57'21 76w49'38 5:07:19
Waddells Corner 9 8 38N39'05 75w54'12 5:03:37
Waggaman Heights 16 16 38N48'25 76w56'33 5:07:46
Wagner Landing 19 26 38N16'33 75w43'48 5:02:55
Wagner Park 6 8 39N34 76w59 5:07:56
Wagners Crossroads 21 7 39N34'26 77w38'48 5:10:35
Wagners Mill 6 8 39N33'41 77w03'21 5:08:13
Wakefield 3 3 39N26'52 76w35'33 5:06:22
Wakefield 6 8 39N33'19 77w04'26 5:08:18
Wakefield Meadows 12 8 39N32 76w21 5:05:24
Wakefield Mill 6 8 39N34'01 77w03'56 5:08:16
Walbrook 24 1 39N18'32 76w40'18 5:06:41
Walden Farms 6 8 39N35'56 77w12'42 5:08:51
Waldon Woods 16 16 38N47 76w53 5:07:32
Waldorf 8 6 38N37'28 76w56'22 5:07:45
Walker 3 3 39N39'34 76w40'19 5:06:41
Walker Mill 16 16 38N52 76w55 5:07:40
Walkersville 10 7 39N29'10 77w21'08 5:09:25
Wallman 11 2 39N19'01 79w17'03 5:17:08
Wallville 4 9 38N24'55 76w30'20 5:06:01
Walnut 22 7 38N19'09 75w39'51 5:02:39
Walnut Grove Mills 6 8 39N30'31 76w55'47 5:07:43
Walnut Hill 15 16 39N08 77w12 5:08:48
Walnut Landing 9 8 38N25'14 76w14'47 5:04:59
Walnut Ridge 6 8 39N34 76w59 5:07:56
Walnut Woods 15 16 39N03'05 77w08'56 5:08:36
Walston 22 7 38N23'07 75w30'19 5:02:01
Walter Heights 16 16 38N49 76w56 5:07:44
Wango 22 7 38N19'17 75w27'01 5:01:48
Wardour 2 20 38N59'39 76w29'55 5:06:00
Wardour Bluffs 2 20 38N59'42 76w29'42 5:05:59
Wards Chapel 3 3 39N22 76w45 5:07:00
Warfieldsburg 6 8 39N31'35 77w01'59 5:08:08
Warington Hills 8 6 38N35'45 77w09'37 5:08:38
Warlinda 8 6 38N32 76w59 5:07:56
Warren 3 3 39N28'34 76w37'01 5:06:28
Warwick 7 7 39N25'00 75w46'43 5:03:07
Washington Grove 15 16 39N08'23 77w10'32 5:08:42
Washington Junction 10 7 39N16'21 77w31'35 5:10:08
Waterbury 2 20 39N02'51 76w37'37 5:06:30
Waterford 16 16 38N51 76w54 5:07:36
Waterloo 13 3 39N10'19 76w47'07 5:07:08
Wateroak Point 2 20 39N09 76w33 5:06:12
Watersville 13 8 39N22'03 77w06'14 5:08:25
Watervale 12 9 39N31'42 76w22'23 5:05:30
Waterview 22 7 38N14'49 75w54'12 5:03:37
Watkins Glen 15 16 39N03 77w10 5:08:40
Waverly 24 1 39N19'42 76w36'23 5:06:26
Wayside 8 6 38N23 76w57 5:07:48
Weaverton 21 7 39N19'58 77w40'55 5:10:44
Webster 12 8 39N34'24 76w09'24 5:04:38

Webster Village 12 8 39N33 76w06 5:04:24
Weems Creek 2 20 38N59'53 76w31'10 5:06:05
Weidman 17 15 39N09'03 75w54'35 5:03:38
Weisburg 3 3 39N37 76w38 5:06:32
Welbourne 23 19 38N01'12 75w27'17 5:01:49
Welcome 8 6 38N29 77w06 5:08:24
Weldon 6 8 39N28'43 77w07'05 5:08:28
Welhams 2 20 39N10 76w37 5:06:28
Wellington 19 19 38N09'23 75w36'35 5:02:26
Wellington Beach 8 6 38N21'58 77w11'45 5:08:47
Wellington Estates 13 3 39N05 76w58 5:07:52
Wells Corner 16 16 38N49'27 76w43'43 5:06:55
Wellwood 3 3 39N22'36 76w41'29 5:06:46
Wenona 19 19 38N08'20 75w57'02 5:03:48
Wentz 6 8 39N42'30 76w55'00 5:07:40
Wesley 9 8 38N20'49 76w05'01 5:04:20
Wesley 23 27 38N12'36 75w20'42 5:01:23
Wesley Grove 13 20 39N11'13 76w45'35 5:07:02
Wesmond 15 16 39N09 77w25 5:09:40
West 19 26 38N12 75w41 5:02:44
West Annapolis 2 20 38N59'27 76w30'00 5:06:00
West Arlington 24 1 39N20'12 76w41'43 5:06:47
West Baltimore 24 3 39N15'21 76w39'33 5:06:38
West Beach 4 9 38N41'42 76w32'02 5:06:08
West Bethesda 15 16 39N00 77w08 5:08:32
Westboro 15 16 38N59'21 77w05'30 5:08:22
West Bowie 16 16 38N57 76w47 5:07:08
Westchester 15 16 39N03 77w03 5:08:12
Westchester Estates 16 16 38N49 76w56 5:07:44
Westchester Park 16 16 39N00 76w55 5:07:40
West Chevy Chase Heights 15 16 38N59'33 77w05'15 5:08:21
West Denton 5 15 38N53'20 75w50'22 5:03:21
West Edmondale 3 3 39N17 76w41 5:06:44
West Elkridge 13 3 39N12'25 76w43'38 5:06:55
West End 2 20 39N03 76w30 5:06:00
West End Park 15 16 39N05'09 77w09'55 5:08:40
Westernport 1 24 39N29'07 79w02'42 5:16:11
Western Run 3 3 39N30'54 76w40'47 5:06:43
Western Shores Estates 4 9 38N30 76w32 5:06:08
West Forest Park 24 1 39N19'30 76w41'34 5:06:46
West Friendship 13 3 39N18'09 76w57'11 5:07:49
Westgate 15 16 38N57'18 77w06'08 5:08:25
Westgate 16 16 38N57'25 76w51'28 5:07:26
West Gate Woods 16 16 38N58 76w51 5:07:24
West Hills 3 3 39N17'44 76w42'49 5:06:51
West Hills 10 7 39N26 77w27 5:09:48
West Hyattsville 16 16 38N58 76w58 5:07:52
Westlake 22 7 38N22 75w36 5:02:24
West Lanham Hills 16 16 38N56'57 76w52'41 5:07:31
West Laurel 16 16 39N07 76w53 5:07:32
West Laurel Acres 16 16 39N06'30 76w54'07 5:07:36
West Liberty 3 3 39N41'04 76w35'51 5:06:23
Westminster 6 3 39N34'31 76w59'46 5:07:59
Westmore 15 16 39N05'47 77w09'13 5:08:37
Westmoreland Hills 15 16 38N56'56 77w06'21 5:08:25
West Nottingham 7 7 39N40'10 76w04'36 5:04:18
West Oakland 11 14 39N25 79w27 5:17:48
West Ocean City 23 19 38N19'53 75w06'26 5:00:26
Westover 19 23 38N07'26 75w42'24 5:02:50
Westowne 3 3 39N17'15 76w43'07 5:06:52
Westphalia 16 16 38N50'43 76w48'41 5:07:15
Westphalia Estates 16 16 38N47 76w52 5:07:28
Westphalia Woods 16 16 38N47 76w52 5:07:28
Westport 24 20 39N15'43 76w38'09 5:06:33
West Princess Anne 19 26 38N12 75w43 5:02:52
West River 2 20 38N51'01 76w35'47 5:06:23
West Riverdale 16 16 38N57'47 76w56'35 5:07:46
West Severna Park 2 20 39N04'26 76w33'34 5:06:14
West Shadyside 2 20 38N50'49 76w30'40 5:06:03
West Shoreham 2 20 38N53'56 76w29'51 5:05:59
West Springbrook 15 16 39N03 77w03 5:08:12
West Twin River 3 3 39N22'47 76w21'30 5:05:26
West Twin River Beach 3 3 39N20 76w27 5:05:48
Westview Park 3 3 39N17 76w43 5:06:52
West View Shores 7 7 39N25'45 75w59'48 5:03:59
West Vindex 11 2 39N25'03 79w12'21 5:16:49
Westwood 15 16 38N57'58 77w06'32 5:08:26
Westwood 16 16 38N39'23 76w44'24 5:06:58
Westwood Estates 16 16 38N47 76w52 5:07:28
Wetheredsville 24 1 39N18'55 76w42'13 5:06:49
Wetipquin 22 7 38N20'12 75w50'51 5:03:23
Weverton 21 7 39N20 77w37 5:10:28
Wexford 2 20 39N03 76w30 5:06:00
Whaleysville 23 19 38N23'48 75w18'09 5:01:13
Wheaton 15 16 39N02'23 77w03'20 5:08:13
Wheaton Crest 15 16 39N02'55 77w03'25 5:08:14
Wheaton Forest 15 16 39N02'17 77w02'51 5:08:11
Wheaton Hills 15 16 39N02'44 77w03'38 5:08:15
Wheaton View 15 16 39N03 77w03 5:08:12
Wheaton Woods 15 16 39N04'19 77w05'05 5:08:20
Whiskey Bottom 13 3 39N05 76w58 5:07:52
Whiteburg 23 27 38N11'06 75w32'17 5:02:09
White Crystal Beach 7 7 39N25 75w55 5:03:40
Whitefield Knolls 16 16 38N58 76w51 5:07:24
Whitefield Woods 16 16 38N58 76w51 5:07:24
Whiteford 12 8 39N42'32 76w20'45 5:05:23
White Hall 3 3 39N37'18 76w37'44 5:06:31
White Hall 16 16 38N41'10 76w59'21 5:07:57
Whitehall Manor 15 16 38N58'57 77w06'37 5:08:26
Whitehaven 22 7 38N16'09 75w47'29 5:03:10
Whitehouse 3 3 39N36'06 76w46'28 5:07:06
Whitehouse 16 16 39N01'25 76w55'27 5:07:42
White House Heights 16 16 38N54'48 76w53'26 5:07:34
White Landing 16 16 38N40'12 76w42'09 5:06:49
Whiteley 16 16 38N56'49 76w55'42 5:07:43
Whiteleysburg 5 15 38N57'24 75w43'58 5:02:56
White Marsh 3 3 39N23'01 76w25'57 5:05:44
White Marsh Station 3 3 39N22'48 76w25'40 5:05:43
White Oak 15 16 39N02'23 76w59'36 5:07:58
White Oak Manor 16 16 39N00'59 76w57'46 5:07:51
White Oak Shopping Center 15 16 39N04 76w59 5:07:56
White Plains 8 6 38N35'25 76w56'26 5:07:46
White Point Beach 18 4 38N13'25 76w37'14 5:06:29
White Rock 10 7 39N26 77w27 5:09:48
White Sands 4 9 38N25 76w27 5:05:48
Whitneys Landing 2 20 39N04'27 76w35'18 5:06:21
Whiton 22 27 38N17'22 75w22'38 5:01:31
Whittemore Park 3 3 39N15 76w41 5:06:44
Wickford 15 16 39N02'14 77w06'30 5:08:26
Wicomico 8 6 38N24'48 76w52'37 5:07:30
Wicomico Beach 8 6 38N23 76w57 5:07:48
Widgeon 19 26 38N15'04 75w46'10 5:03:05
Wilburn Estates 16 16 38N54 76w54 5:07:36
Wilde Lake 13 3 39N16 76w49 5:07:16
Wildercroft 16 16 38N58'09 76w53'41 5:07:35
Wild Rose Shores 2 20 38N57 76w29 5:05:56
Wild Wood Beach 3 3 39N19 76w28 5:05:52
Wildwood Estates 16 16 38N47 76w53 5:07:32
Wildwood Hills 15 16 39N01'09 77w09'00 5:08:36
Wildwood Manor 15 16 39N01'25 77w07'07 5:08:28
Wilelinor Estates 2 20 38N56 76w33 5:06:12
Wilhelm Park 24 1 39N16'29 76w39'51 5:06:39
Willards 22 7 38N23'28 75w20'56 5:01:24
Willerburn Acres 15 16 39N03'05 77w09'37 5:08:38
Williamsburg 9 8 38N39'28 75w49'46 5:03:19
Williamsburg Estates 15 16 39N00'30 77w12'02 5:08:48
Williamsburg Village 15 16 39N09 77w05 5:08:20
Williamsport 21 8 39N36'02 77w49'15 5:11:17
Williams Wharf 4 9 38N28 76w30 5:06:00
Williston 5 15 38N49'52 75w51'05 5:03:24
Willoughby 17 8 38N56'03 76w01'07 5:04:04
Willoughby Beach 12 8 39N23 76w15 5:05:00
Willow Beach Colony 4 9 38N37'43 76w31'04 5:06:04
Willowbrook 15 16 39N03 77w10 5:08:40
Willow Grove 23 19 38N05'33 75w30'11 5:02:01
Willows 4 9 38N37'39 76w32'17 5:06:09
Willows of Riverbend 16 16 38N47 76w58 5:07:52
Wills Creek 1 3 39N42 78w44 5:14:56
Willson Hills 15 16 39N05'43 77w02'29 5:08:10
Wilmers 17 15 39N09'18 76w02'57 5:04:12
Wilna 12 8 39N29'00 76w22'27 5:05:30
Wilson 4 9 38N36'11 76w31'20 5:06:05
Wilson 11 2 39N15'13 79w23'57 5:17:36
Wilson 21 7 39N39'29 77w50'56 5:11:24
Wilson Hills 15 16 39N04 77w04 5:08:16
Wilson Mill 12 8 39N37'00 76w12'08 5:04:49
Wilson Point 3 3 39N20 76w27 5:05:48
Wilsons 21 7 39N39 77w52 5:11:28
Wiltondale 3 3 39N23'11 76w36'05 5:06:24
Wilton Farm Acres 13 3 39N16 76w49 5:07:16
Winchester 2 20 39N00'49 76w29'37 5:05:58
Winchester 11 3 39N37'50 78w50'15 5:15:21
Winchester-on-the-Severn 2 20 39N00'54 76w30'40 5:06:03
Winchester Park 6 8 39N34 76w59 5:07:56
Windbrook 16 16 38N47 76w53 5:07:32
Windermere 15 16 39N04 77w09 5:08:36
Windham Manor 15 16 39N03'42 76w59'48 5:07:59
Winding Brook Village 7 7 39N37 75w50 5:03:20
Windmere Acres 13 3 39N08 76w49 5:07:16
Windsor Heights 6 8 39N34 76w59 5:07:56
Windsor Hills 24 1 39N18'50 76w40'53 5:06:44
Windsor Terrace 3 1 39N18'37 76w42'28 5:06:50
Windyhill 20 13 38N40'53 75w58'40 5:03:55
Winfield 6 8 39N26'50 77w03'19 5:08:13
Wingate 9 8 38N16'55 76w04'56 5:04:20
Wingates Point 9 8 38N18 76w06 5:04:24
Wings Landing 5 15 38N47'02 75w56'17 5:03:45
Wiseburg 3 3 39N37'19 76w39'29 5:06:38
Wittman 20 13 38N47'37 76w17'40 5:05:11
Wolf Acres 15 16 39N04'15 77w00'31 5:08:02
Wolfe Mill 1 24 39N40'24 78w43'30 5:14:54
Wolfs Mill 6 8 39N39'30 77w07'21 5:08:29
Wolfsville 10 7 39N34'27 77w33'03 5:10:12
Wolfsville Crossing 10 7 39N31'58 77w35'43 5:10:23
Wood Acres 15 16 38N58'05 77w07'26 5:08:30
Woodberry 24 1 39N19'54 76w38'59 5:06:36
Woodberry Beach 8 6 38N19'22 76w51'29 5:07:26
Woodberry Forest 16 16 38N49 76w56 5:07:44
Woodbine 6 8 39N21'35 77w03'46 5:08:15
Woodbrook 3 3 39N22'46 76w37'39 5:06:31
Woodburn 15 16 38N58'24 77w07'37 5:08:30
Woodcrest 2 20 39N11'59 76w37'10 5:06:29
Woodcroft 3 3 39N23'32 76w32'18 5:06:09
Woodensburg 3 3 39N30'20 76w50'04 5:07:20
Woodfield 15 16 39N14'48 77w11'27 5:08:46
Woodhaven 15 16 38N59'37 77w08'01 5:08:32
Woodhaven Park 8 6 38N32 76w59 5:07:56
Woodhome Heights 24 3 39N22'11 76w32'45 5:06:11
Woodland 1 24 39N36'30 78w57'04 5:15:48
Woodland 20 13 38N50'22 76w01'33 5:04:06
Woodland Acres 18 4 38N25 76w33 5:06:12
Woodland Beach 2 20 38N55'56 76w33'13 5:06:13
Woodland Point 8 6 38N16'34 76w52'55 5:07:32
Woodland Village 8 6 38N36 77w10 5:08:40
Wood Lane 16 16 38N58 76w51 5:07:24
Woodlark 16 16 38N58 76w51 5:07:24
Woodlawn 3 3 39N19'22 76w43'42 5:06:55
Woodlawn 7 7 39N38'03 76w04'34 5:04:18
Woodlawn 16 16 38N56'58 76w53'30 5:07:34
Woodlawn Heights 2 20 39N11'33 76w38'58 5:06:36
Woodley Gardens 15 16 39N05'54 77w10'23 5:08:42
Woodmont 15 16 38N59'23 77w05'56 5:08:24
Woodmont 21 8 39N37'54 78w18'16 5:13:13
Woodmoor 3 3 39N21 76w44 5:06:56
Woodmoor 15 16 39N01'26 77w00'41 5:08:03
Woodmore 16 16 38N55'16 76w48'12 5:07:13
Wood Point 11 7 39N39'38 77w44'20 5:10:57
Woodsboro 10 7 39N31'59 77w18'54 5:09:16
Woods Corner 16 16 38N49'18 76w55'16 5:07:41
Woodside 15 16 39N00'12 77w02'17 5:08:09
Woodside Forest 15 16 39N00'32 77w02'06 5:08:08
Woodside Park 15 16 39N00'23 77w01'50 5:08:07
Woodstock 13 3 39N19'43 76w52'20 5:07:29
Woodville 10 7 39N24'36 77w10'41 5:08:43
Woodyard 16 16 38N47'09 76w50'35 5:07:22
Woolerys 6 8 39N31 76w56 5:07:44
Woolford 9 8 38N30'09 76w11'01 5:04:44
Worthington 3 3 39N27'36 76w45'15 5:07:01
Worthington Valley 3 3 39N29 76w49 5:07:16
Worton 14 15 39N16'28 76w05'33 5:04:22
Worton Point Orchard 14 15 39N19'35 76w09'03 5:04:36
Wrights 9 8 38N34'56 76w14'05 5:04:56
Wrights Crossing 1 24 39N38'22 78w55'46 5:15:43
Wrights Landing 9 8 38N21'34 76w05'22 5:04:21
Wye Landing 17 8 38N53'32 76w06'11 5:04:25
Wye Mills 20 13 38N56'28 76w04'51 5:04:19
Wyngate 15 16 39N00'38 77w07'21 5:08:29
Wynne 18 4 38N06'35 76w24'20 5:05:37
Wynnewood 3 3 39N15 76w41 5:06:44
Yarrowsburg 21 7 39N22'28 77w41'02 5:10:44
Yellow Springs 10 7 39N28'46 77w27'37 5:09:50
Yeoho 3 3 39N34'17 76w43'19 5:06:53
Yonkers 1 3 39N41'42 78w38'57 5:14:36
Yorkleigh 3 3 39N23'12 76w36'23 5:06:26
Yorkshire Knolls 16 16 38N53'28 76w53'10 5:07:33
Yorktown 3 3 39N23'01 76w36'25 5:06:26
Yorktown Village 15 16 39N01 77w08 5:08:32
Zihlman 1 24 39N40'05 78w54'55 5:15:40
Zion 7 7 39N40'32 75w57'55 5:03:52
Zittlestown 21 7 39N29'07 77w37'27 5:10:30

TIME TABLES

MA # 1
Before 11/18/1883 LMT
11/18/1883 12:00 EST
3/31/1918 02:00 EWT
10/27/1918 02:00 EST
3/30/1919 02:00 EWT
10/26/1919 02:00 EST
4/25/1920 02:00 EDT
10/31/1920 02:00 EST
4/24/1921 02:00 EDT
9/25/1921 02:00 EST
4/30/1922 02:00 EDT
9/24/1922 02:00 EST
4/29/1923 02:00 EDT
9/30/1923 02:00 EST
4/27/1924 02:00 EDT
9/28/1924 02:00 EST
4/26/1925 02:00 EDT
9/27/1925 02:00 EST
4/25/1926 02:00 EDT
9/26/1926 02:00 EST
4/24/1927 02:00 EDT
9/25/1927 02:00 EST
4/29/1928 02:00 EDT
9/30/1928 02:00 EST
4/28/1929 02:00 EDT
9/29/1929 02:00 EST
4/27/1930 02:00 EDT
9/28/1930 02:00 EST
4/26/1931 02:00 EDT
9/27/1931 02:00 EST
4/24/1932 02:00 EDT
9/25/1932 02:00 EST
4/30/1933 02:00 EDT
9/24/1933 02:00 EST
4/29/1934 02:00 EDT
9/30/1934 02:00 EST
4/28/1935 02:00 EDT
9/29/1935 02:00 EST
4/26/1936 02:00 EDT
9/27/1936 02:00 EST
4/25/1937 02:00 EDT
9/26/1937 02:00 EST
4/24/1938 02:00 EDT
10/01/1938 02:00 EST
4/30/1939 02:00 EDT
9/24/1939 02:00 EST
4/28/1940 02:00 EDT
9/29/1940 02:00 EST
4/27/1941 02:00 EDT
9/28/1941 02:00 EST
2/09/1942 02:00 EWT
9/30/1945 02:00 EST
4/28/1946 02:00 EDT
9/29/1946 02:00 EST
4/27/1947 02:00 EDT
9/28/1947 02:00 EST
4/25/1948 02:00 EDT
9/26/1948 02:00 EST
4/24/1949 02:00 EDT
9/25/1949 02:00 EST
4/30/1950 02:00 EDT
9/24/1950 02:00 EST
4/29/1951 02:00 EDT
9/30/1951 02:00 EST
4/27/1952 02:00 EDT
9/28/1952 02:00 EST
4/26/1953 02:00 EDT
9/27/1953 02:00 EST
4/25/1954 02:00 EDT
10/31/1954 02:00 EST
4/24/1955 02:00 EDT
10/30/1955 02:00 EST
4/29/1956 02:00 EDT
10/28/1956 02:00 EST
4/28/1957 02:00 EDT
10/27/1957 02:00 EST
4/27/1958 02:00 EDT
10/26/1958 02:00 EST
4/26/1959 02:00 EDT
10/25/1959 02:00 EST
4/24/1960 02:00 EDT
10/30/1960 02:00 EST
4/30/1961 02:00 EDT
10/29/1961 02:00 EST
4/29/1962 02:00 EDT
10/28/1962 02:00 EST
4/28/1963 02:00 EDT
10/27/1963 02:00 EST
4/26/1964 02:00 EDT
10/25/1964 02:00 EST
4/25/1965 02:00 EDT
10/31/1965 02:00 EST
4/24/1966 02:00 EDT
10/30/1966 02:00 EST
4/30/1967 02:00 US#1
....
MA # 2
Before 11/18/1883 LMT
11/18/1883 12:00 EST
3/31/1918 02:00 EWT
10/27/1918 02:00 EST
3/30/1919 02:00 EWT
10/26/1919 02:00 EST
4/30/1922 02:00 EDT
9/24/1922 02:00 EST
4/29/1923 02:00 US#1

COUNTIES

1 Barnstable
2 Berkshire
3 Bristol
4 Dukes
5 Essex
6 Franklin
7 Hampden
8 Hampshire
9 Middlesex
10 Nantucket
11 Norfolk
12 Plymouth
13 Suffolk
14 Worcester

Aberdeen 13 1 42N20'40 71w09'00 4:44:36
Abington 12 1 42N06'17 70w56'45 4:43:47
Acapesket 1 1 41N33'00 70w34'35 4:42:18
Accord 12 1 42N10'28 70w53'03 4:43:32
Acoaxet 3 1 41N30'25 71w05'50 4:44:23
Acorn Terrace 11 1 42N05'40 71w22'20 4:45:29
Acton 9 1 42N29'06 71w26'00 4:45:44
Acushnet 3 1 41N40'50 70w54'30 4:43:38
Acushnet Station 3 1 41N40'30 70w56'24 4:43:46
Adams 2 1 42N37'27 73w07'05 4:52:28
Adamsdale 3 1 41N55'40 71w22'15 4:45:29
Adams Junction 2 1 42N27'30 73w12'30 4:52:50
Adams Shore 11 1 42N15'50 70w59'05 4:43:56
Adamsville 6 1 42N40'53 72w44'55 4:51:00
Agawam 7 1 42N04'10 72w36'55 4:50:28
Agawam Beach 12 1 41N46 70w43 4:42:52
Alander 2 1 42N03'22 73w28'00 4:53:52
Aldenville 7 1 42N10'22 72w35'55 4:50:24
Aldrich Mills 8 1 42N16'55 72w32'18 4:50:09
Alford 2 1 42N14'08 73w24'50 4:53:39
Algerie Four Corners 2 1 42N13'07 73w01'52 4:52:07
Algers Corner 3 1 42N00'38 71w04'00 4:44:16
Allendale 2 1 42N27 73w15 4:53:00
Allerton 12 1 42N18'15 70w53'02 4:43:32
Allston 13 1 42N21'30 71w07'45 4:44:30
Alms House 12 1 41N40'03 70w45'48 4:43:03
Amesbury 5 1 42N51'30 70w55'50 4:43:43
Amherst 8 1 42N22'25 72w31'15 4:50:05
Amostown 7 1 42N07'35 72w39'35 4:50:38
Amrita 1 1 41N39'35 70w37'10 4:42:29
Andover 5 1 42N39'30 71w08'15 4:44:33
Annisquam 5 1 42N39'30 70w40'40 4:42:43
Antassawamock 12 1 41N37'31 70w48'28 4:43:14
Antassawamock Beach 12 1 41N40 70w49 4:43:16
Apponagansett 3 1 41N36'05 70w57'45 4:43:51
Apponagansett Village 3 1 41N37 70w58 4:43:52
Arlington 9 1 42N24'55 71w09'25 4:44:38
Arlington Heights 9 1 42N25'13 71w10'50 4:44:43
Arnoldsville 2 1 42N35'17 73w08'03 4:52:32
Asbury Grove 5 1 42N37'20 70w53'05 4:43:32
Ashburnham 14 1 42N38'10 71w54'30 4:47:38
Ashby 9 1 42N40'40 71w49'15 4:47:17
Ashcroft 11 1 42N14'00 71w09'00 4:44:36
Ashdod 12 1 42N04'07 70w45'05 4:43:00
Ashfield 6 2 42N31'35 72w47'20 4:51:09
Ashland 9 1 42N15'40 71w27'50 4:45:51
Ashley Falls 2 1 42N03'22 73w20'08 4:53:21
Ashley Heights 3 1 41N46'45 70w55'15 4:43:41
Ashleyville 7 1 42N09'30 72w38'00 4:50:32
Ashmont 13 1 42N17'00 71w04'10 4:44:17
Assinippi 12 1 42N09'30 70w51'05 4:43:24
Assonet 3 1 41N47'45 71w04'06 4:44:16
Assonet Bay Shores 3 1 41N47'45 71w05'25 4:44:22
Assumption College 14 1 42N16 71w49 4:47:16
Astor 13 1 42N19 71w05 4:44:20
Athol 14 1 42N35'45 72w13'38 4:48:55
Athol Junction 7 1 42N07'40 72w33'45 4:50:15
Atlantic 11 1 42N16'50 71w01'45 4:44:07
Atlantic 12 1 42N16'01 70w50'54 4:43:24
Attitash 5 1 42N51 70w56 4:43:44
Attleboro 3 1 41N56'40 71w17'10 4:45:09
Attleboro Falls 3 1 41N58'15 71w19'00 4:45:16
Attleborough City 3 1 41N55'30 71w21'00 4:45:24
Auburn 14 1 42N11'40 71w50'10 4:47:21
Auburndale 9 1 42N20'50 71w15'00 4:45:00
Auburnville 12 1 42N04'10 70w57'50 4:43:51
Avon 11 1 42N07'50 71w02'30 4:44:10
Axtell Corner 14 1 42N13'55 71w41'03 4:46:44
Ayer 9 1 42N33'40 71w35'25 4:46:22
Ayers Village 5 1 42N47'13 71w10'10 4:44:41
Ayres City 9 1 42N37'30 71w18'45 4:45:15
Babbatasset Village 9 1 42N40'00 71w34'45 4:46:19
Babson Park 11 1 42N17'55 71w15'36 4:45:02
Back Bay 13 1 42N21'00 71w05'15 4:44:21
Back Bay Annex 13 1 42N19 71w05 4:44:20
Baconville 6 2 42N25'23 72w26'32 4:49:46
Baileys Corner 12 1 42N01'30 70w41'53 4:42:48
Baird Four Corners 7 1 42N07'15 72w55'55 4:51:44
Baker Bridge 9 1 42N25'40 71w20'13 4:45:21
Bakers Grove 14 1 42N32'07 71w53'00 4:47:32
Bakers Island 5 1 42N31 70w54 4:43:36
Baldwinville 14 1 42N36'30 72w04'35 4:48:18
Ballardvale 5 1 42N37'30 71w09'40 4:44:39
Bancroft 8 1 42N18'33 73w01'45 4:52:07
Baptist Corner 6 1 42N33'07 72w45'48 4:51:03
Baptist Corners 14 1 42N41'58 72w16'12 4:49:05
Baptist Village 7 1 42N02'50 72w28'15 4:49:53
Bardwell 6 1 42N33'24 72w40'43 4:50:43
Bardwell 8 1 42N13'06 72w22'10 4:49:29
Barkerville 2 1 42N25'21 73w18'33 4:53:14
Barlows Landing 1 1 41N41'27 70w37'32 4:42:30
Barneyville 3 1 41N46'18 71w17'10 4:45:09
Barnstable 1 1 41N42'00 70w18'00 4:41:12
Barre 14 1 42N25'22 72w06'20 4:48:25
Barre Falls 14 1 42N25'45 72w01'36 4:48:06
Barre Plains 14 1 42N22'40 72w06'35 4:48:26
Barrowsville 3 1 41N56'45 71w12'15 4:44:49
Bassets Corner 14 1 42N28'53 72w07'45 4:48:31
Bass Point 5 1 42N26 70w56 4:43:44
Bass River 1 1 41N39'10 70w12'15 4:40:49
Bass Rocks 5 1 42N36'51 70w38'09 4:42:33
Bayside 12 1 42N18'00 70w53'00 4:43:32
Bayside Beach 12 1 41N52'00 70w31'56 4:42:08
Bay State 8 1 42N19'20 72w39'50 4:50:39
Bayview 3 1 41N34'25 70w57'00 4:43:48
Bay View 5 1 42N40'12 70w39'55 4:42:40
Beach 13 1 42N25 71w00 4:44:00
Beach Bluff 5 1 42N28'45 70w53'10 4:43:33
Beachmont 13 1 42N23'45 70w59'15 4:43:57
Beach Park 12 1 41N56'25 70w37'14 4:42:29
Beach Point 1 1 42N02 70w06 4:40:24
Beachwood 2 1 42N19'30 73w19'15 4:53:17
Beacon Hill 13 1 42N21'31 71w04'06 4:44:16
Beaconsfield 11 1 42N20'12 71w08'30 4:44:34
Beaver Brook 5 1 42N34'45 70w57'30 4:43:50
Beaver Brook 14 1 42N15'50 71w49'45 4:47:19
Beaver Brook Station 9 1 42N22'45 71w13'15 4:44:53
Becket 2 1 42N19'55 73w05'00 4:52:20
Becket Center 2 1 42N17'00 73w03'50 4:52:15
Bedford 9 1 42N29'26 71w16'36 4:45:06
Bedford Springs 9 1 42N30'58 71w16'17 4:45:05
Beechwood 11 1 42N12'35 70w49'10 4:43:17
Belcher Square 2 1 42N12'00 73w20'50 4:53:23
Belchertown 8 1 42N16'37 72w24'05 4:49:36
Beldingville 6 2 42N32'15 72w46'13 4:51:05
Bellevue 13 1 42N17'15 71w08'45 4:44:35
Bellingham 11 1 42N05'12 71w28'30 4:45:54
Bell Rock 9 1 42N26 71w04 4:44:16
Belmont 9 1 42N23'45 71w10'45 4:44:43
Belmont Hill 14 1 42N16'15 71w47'50 4:47:11
Belvidere 9 1 42N38'20 71w17'25 4:45:10
Bemis 9 1 42N22'07 71w12'15 4:44:49
Bennetts Corner 12 1 42N01'07 71w00'53 4:44:04
Berkley 3 1 41N50'45 71w05'00 4:44:20
Berkley Bridge 3 1 41N50'00 71w06'24 4:44:26
Berkshire 2 1 42N30'45 73w11'36 4:52:46
Berkshire Christian College 2 1 42N21 73w17 4:53:08
Berkshire Heights 2 1 42N11'20 73w22'10 4:53:29
Berlin 14 1 42N22'52 71w38'15 4:46:33
Bernardston 6 1 42N40'15 72w33'00 4:50:12
Berryman Corner 3 1 41N39'00 71w04'00 4:44:16
Beulah Corners 3 1 41N39'40 71w05'05 4:44:20
Beverly 5 1 42N33'30 70w52'50 4:43:31
Beverly Cove 5 1 42N33'12 70w51'15 4:43:25
Beverly Farms 5 1 42N33'50 70w48'40 4:43:15
Beverly Road 14 1 42N17'55 71w47'00 4:47:08
Big Pond 2 1 42N10 73w02 4:52:08
Billerica 9 1 42N33'30 71w16'10 4:45:05
Birds Hill 11 1 42N16'30 71w12'45 4:44:51
Bisbee Corner 12 1 41N47'27 70w52'09 4:43:29
Bisbee Mill 8 1 42N22'28 72w49'10 4:51:17
Blackburn Village 14 1 42N37'37 71w52'52 4:47:31
Blackinton 2 1 42N42'15 73w10'00 4:52:40
Black Rock 11 1 42N14'37 70w49'45 4:43:19
Blackstone 14 1 42N01'04 71w32'30 4:46:10
Blanchardville 7 1 42N08'45 72w18'15 4:49:13
Blandford 7 1 42N10'50 72w55'40 4:51:43
Bleachery 9 1 42N37'40 71w18'15 4:45:13
Bliss Corner 3 1 41N36'42 70w56'20 4:43:45
Blissville 6 1 42N40'21 72w16'30 4:49:06
Bloomingdale 14 1 42N15'50 71w46'15 4:47:05
Blue Hills 11 1 42N14'35 71w05'55 4:44:24
Blush Hollow 8 1 42N21 73w01 4:52:04
Bolton 14 1 42N26'00 71w36'30 4:46:26
Bolton Station 14 1 42N25'08 71w39'36 4:46:38
Bondsville 7 1 42N12'45 72w20'45 4:49:23
Bonny Rigg Corners 2 1 42N15'50 73w03'05 4:52:12
Booth Corner 3 1 41N35'15 71w05'20 4:44:21
Boston 13 1 42N21'30 71w03'37 4:44:14
Boston College 9 1 42N19 71w10 4:44:40
Boston University 13 1 42N21 71w06 4:44:24
Bourne 1 1 41N44'28 70w35'58 4:42:24
Bourne Corners 1 1 41N45'04 70w36'30 4:42:26
Bournedale 1 1 41N46'31 70w33'46 4:42:15
Bowens Corners 2 1 42N36'57 73w06'27 4:52:26
Bowenville 3 1 41N43'30 71w08'48 4:44:35
Boxboro 9 1 42N29'30 71w31'40 4:46:07
Boxboro Station 9 1 42N30'15 71w29'36 4:45:58
Boxborough 9 1 42N29 71w31 4:46:04
Boxford 5 1 42N39'40 70w59'50 4:43:59
Boxford Station 5 1 42N38'44 71w03'30 4:44:14
Boylston 14 1 42N23'30 71w42'15 4:46:49
Boylston Center 14 1 42N21'10 71w44'08 4:46:57
Bradford 5 1 42N46'10 71w04'35 4:44:18
Bradstreet 8 2 42N24'38 72w35'32 4:50:22
Braggville 9 1 42N10'00 71w28'50 4:45:55
Braggville Station 9 1 42N09'45 71w28'30 4:45:54
Braintree 11 1 42N13'20 71w00'00 4:44:00
Braintree Highlands 11 1 42N10'45 71w00'45 4:44:03
Braleys 3 1 41N44'15 70w58'15 4:43:53
Bramanville 14 1 42N10'50 71w46'15 4:47:05
Brant Rock 12 1 42N05'10 70w38'30 4:42:34
Brattle 9 1 42N25'18 71w10'06 4:44:40
Brayton Point 3 1 41N42'50 71w11'00 4:44:44
Braytonville 2 1 42N41'54 73w07'50 4:52:31
Breezy Hill 12 1 42N01'55 70w50'40 4:43:23
Brewster 1 1 41N45'36 70w05'00 4:40:20
Briarwood Beach 12 1 41N44'15 70w44'30 4:42:58
Bridgewater 12 1 41N59'25 70w50'32 4:43:54
Brier 2 1 42N35'22 72w59'40 4:51:59
Brier Neck 5 1 42N37 70w40 4:42:40
Brigadoon Village 5 1 42N35'05 71w00'55 4:44:04
Briggs Corner 3 1 41N54'45 71w15'35 4:45:02
Briggsville 2 1 42N42'56 73w04'51 4:52:19
Brighton 13 1 42N21'00 71w09'25 4:44:38
Brightside 7 1 42N09'45 72w38'00 4:50:32
Brightwood 7 1 42N07'07 72w37'00 4:50:28
Brimfield 7 1 42N07'22 72w12'05 4:48:48
Brimstone Corner 12 1 42N03'32 70w47'02 4:43:08
Britanniaville 3 1 41N55'07 71w06'22 4:44:25
Brittan Square 14 1 42N17'10 71w47'15 4:47:09

Broadway 9 1 42N26 71W04 4:44:16
Brockton 12 1 42N05'00 71W01'08 4:44:05
Brockton Heights 12 1 42N05'20 71W03'55 4:44:16
Brockway Corner 14 1 42N26'34 71W33'40 4:46:15
Brookfield 14 1 42N12'50 72W06'10 4:48:25
Brookline 11 1 42N19'54 71W07'18 4:44:29
Brookline Hill 11 1 42N19'50 71W08'00 4:44:32
Brookline Village 11 1 42N19'58 71W07'00 4:44:28
Brooks 14 1 42N24'50 71W53'55 4:47:36
Brookside Station 9 1 42N36'30 71W24'42 4:45:39
Brooks Place 12 1 42N02'15 71W01'15 4:44:05
Brooks Village 14 1 42N33'45 72W06'28 4:48:26
Brookville 11 1 42N07'30 71W00'35 4:44:02
Brownell Corner 3 1 41N37'36 71W06'09 4:44:25
Browns Corner 9 1 42N24'00 71W35'40 4:46:23
Browns Point 5 1 42N50'20 70W49'50 4:43:19
Brush Hollow 8 1 42N20'30 73W02'00 4:52:08
Brushwood 11 1 42N06'10 71W25'47 4:45:43
Bryant Four Corners 8 1 42N28'07 72W55'57 4:51:44
Bryantville 12 1 42N02'38 70W50'35 4:43:22
Buckland 6 1 42N35'32 72W47'32 4:51:10
Buckland Four Corners 6 1 42N33'53 72W48'15 4:51:13
Buena Vista Shores 12 1 41N48'35 70W57'20 4:43:49
Buffington Corner 3 1 41N47'05 71W01'55 4:44:08
Buffumville 14 1 42N07'08 71W54'00 4:47:36
Bullardville 14 1 42N41'53 72W05'07 4:48:20
Burkville 6 1 42N30'23 72W42'45 4:50:51
Burleys Corner 5 1 42N34'38 70W59'25 4:43:58
Burlington 9 1 42N30'17 71W11'46 4:44:47
Burncoat 14 1 42N18'35 71W47'10 4:47:09
Burnt Swamp Corner 11 1 42N01'08 71W22'52 4:45:31
Burrage 12 1 42N01'45 70W51'22 4:43:25
Burrage Corner 14 1 42N31'15 72W13'30 4:48:54
Burtts Crossing 9 1 42N36'11 71W11'30 4:44:46
Butlerville 7 1 42N09'10 72W24'15 4:49:37
Buzzards Bay 1 1 41N44'43 70W37'07 4:42:28
Byfield 5 1 42N45'35 70W56'55 4:43:48
Cabot 9 1 42N21 71W12 4:44:48
Cadys Corners 7 1 42N10'05 72W30'20 4:50:01
Cahoon Hollow 1 1 41N56'40 69W59'10 4:39:57
Cambridge 9 1 42N22'00 71W06'00 4:44:24
Cambridge 14 1 42N14'40 71W48'45 4:47:15
Cambridgeport 9 1 42N21'30 71W06'15 4:44:25
Camp Ashmere 2 1 42N26'39 73W04'45 4:52:19
Camp Avoda 12 1 41N51'58 70W51'51 4:43:27
Camp Barton 14 1 42N09'15 71W53'45 4:47:35
Camp Becket 2 1 42N17'30 73W04'45 4:52:19
Campbells Station 11 1 42N07'50 71W17'55 4:45:12
Camp Bement 14 1 42N10'50 71W57'54 4:47:52
Camp Berkshire 7 1 42N01'53 72W45'40 4:51:03
Camp Bob White 9 1 42N13'35 71W28'08 4:45:53
Camp Breezy Meadow 11 1 42N10'26 71W26'37 4:45:46
Camp Burgess 1 1 41N41'52 70W27'20 4:41:49
Camp Cabot 9 1 42N24'00 71W13'57 4:44:56
Camp Caravan 14 1 42N38'34 72W09'17 4:48:37
Camp, Cedar Hill 9 1 42N23'24 71W13'07 4:44:52
Camp Chacalot 12 1 41N48'43 70W39'00 4:42:36
Camp Chappa Challa 12 1 42N03'00 70W40'00 4:42:40
Camp Chimney Corners 2 1 42N16'52 73W04'20 4:52:17
Camp Cielo Celeste 9 1 42N36'07 71W26'45 4:45:47
Camp Collier 14 1 42N37'08 71W57'52 4:47:51
Camp Danbee 2 1 42N26'34 73W04'33 4:52:18
Camp Edwards 1 1 41N39'25 70W32'40 4:42:11
Campello 12 1 42N03'15 71W01'15 4:44:05
Camp Emerson 2 1 42N25'57 73W08'00 4:52:32
Camp Glenmere 2 1 42N11'10 73W11'37 4:52:46
Camp Green Eyrie 14 1 42N29'50 71W35'50 4:46:23
Camp Greylock 2 1 42N18'00 73W04'05 4:52:16
Campground Landing 1 1 41N51'10 70W00'25 4:40:02
Camp Grounds 14 1 42N24 71W46 4:47:04
Camp Herbron 3 1 41N54'35 71W18'05 4:45:12
Camp Howe 8 1 42N27'07 72W47'35 4:51:10
Camp Immaculate Heart 9 1 42N38'45 71W29'42 4:45:59
Camp Jayson 2 1 42N11'15 73W11'53 4:52:48
Camp Kingsmont 2 1 42N18'05 73W24'52 4:53:39
Camp Kinneywood 14 1 42N17'50 71W51'45 4:47:27
Camp Kiwanis 9 1 42N41'46 71W22'38 4:45:31
Camp Kiwanis 12 1 42N03'30 70W51'00 4:43:24
Camp Lenore 2 1 42N26'23 73W05'35 4:52:22
Camp Lincoln Hill 11 1 42N04'15 71W12'55 4:44:52
Camp Mah-Kee-Nac 2 1 42N20'25 73W18'35 4:53:14
Camp Marion White 2 1 42N24'55 73W19'00 4:53:16
Camp Mar Vel 1 1 41N55'55 70W01'22 4:40:05
Camp Mary Day 9 1 42N19'38 71W19'35 4:45:18
Camp Massapoag 9 1 42N39'00 71W29'54 4:46:00
Camp Meadowlark 2 1 42N12'25 73W12'40 4:52:51
Camp Merrill 2 1 42N29'20 73W14'43 4:52:59
Camp Merriwood 3 1 41N47'35 71W06'15 4:44:25

Camp Mishannock 12 1 41N57'20 70W44'20 4:42:57
Camp Mohawk 2 1 42N32'01 73W12'03 4:52:48
Camp Muriel Flagg 2 1 42N44'28 73W11'08 4:52:45
Camp Nashoba 9 1 42N36'10 71W26'53 4:45:48
Camp Neyati 14 1 42N11'50 71W56'35 4:47:46
Camp Noquochoke 3 1 41N35'45 71W03'48 4:44:15
Camp Norse 12 1 41N56'12 70W44'45 4:42:59
Camp Ousamequin 12 1 42N00'25 70W51'02 4:43:24
Camp Resolute 14 1 42N25'20 71W35'15 4:46:21
Camp Rockne 12 1 41N51'09 70W40'38 4:42:43
Camp Romaca 2 1 42N25'37 73W07'59 4:52:32
Camp Rowe 6 2 42N41'22 72W53'53 4:51:36
Camp Russell 2 1 42N24'42 73W19'25 4:53:18
Camp Sayre 11 1 42N14'00 71W05'40 4:44:23
Camp Sea Haven 5 1 42N44'15 70W47'20 4:43:09
Camp Snipatuit 12 1 41N45'54 70W52'20 4:43:29
Camp Spruce Hill 7 1 42N02'37 73W01'30 4:52:06
Camp Squanto 12 1 41N49'51 70W38'15 4:42:33
Camp Stevenson 2 1 42N28'33 73W16'58 4:53:08
Camp Sumner 2 1 42N29'15 73W14'30 4:52:58
Camp Taconic 2 1 42N27'10 73W05'30 4:52:22
Camp Ted 9 1 42N23'50 71W13'43 4:44:55
Camp Titicut 12 1 41N56'00 70W59'58 4:44:00
Camp Virginia 14 1 42N25'30 71W34'50 4:46:19
Camp Wakitatina 9 1 42N36'01 71W27'03 4:45:48
Camp Wampatuck 12 1 42N03'50 70W51'47 4:43:27
Camp Warwick 6 1 42N41'55 72W19'05 4:49:16
Camp Welch 3 1 41N49'00 71W05'15 4:44:21
Camp Witawentin 2 1 42N28'30 73W17'11 4:53:09
Camp Woronoak 7 1 42N09'12 72W52'15 4:51:29
Camp Wyoma 2 1 42N25'42 73W07'33 4:52:30
Camp Yomechas 12 1 41N51'35 70W51'35 4:43:26
Canada Mills 14 1 42N22'23 71W49'40 4:47:19
Canedys Corner 12 1 41N48'05 70W58'35 4:43:54
Cannonville 12 1 41N39'35 70W47'55 4:43:12
Canterbury Estates 1 1 41N46 70W30 4:42:00
Canton 11 1 42N09'30 71W08'43 4:44:35
Canton Junction 11 1 42N09'45 71W09'45 4:44:39
Cape Cod Mall 1 1 41N39 70W17 4:41:08
Carey Corner 2 1 42N22'24 73W20'47 4:53:23
Carletonville 5 1 42N31 70W54 4:43:36
Carlisle 9 1 42N31'45 71W21'30 4:45:26
Carlisle Station 9 1 42N32'10 71W23'51 4:45:35
Carterville 14 1 42N23'18 71W38'45 4:46:35
Carver 12 1 41N53'00 70W45'47 4:43:03
Caryville 11 1 42N08'00 71W26'54 4:45:48
Castle Hill 5 1 42N31 70W54 4:43:36
Castleton Mall 11 1 42N08 71W06 4:44:24
Cataumet 1 1 41N39'58 70W37'13 4:42:29
Cataumet Station 1 1 41N39'56 70W36'50 4:42:27
Cathedral 13 1 42N20 71W04 4:44:16
Cayenne 7 1 42N07'50 72W38'15 4:50:33
Cedar 11 1 42N07'23 71W15'50 4:45:03
Cedar Bushes 12 1 41N53'50 70W33'00 4:42:12
Cedar Grove 13 1 42N16'50 71W03'30 4:44:14
Cedar Hill 11 1 42N08'00 71W17'00 4:45:08
Cedarville 12 1 41N48'37 70W33'21 4:42:13
Cedarville Landing 12 1 41N48'50 70W32'30 4:42:10
Cedarwood 9 1 42N22'15 71W15'47 4:45:03
Center 9 1 42N29 71W09 4:44:36
Centerville 1 1 41N38'55 70W20'55 4:41:24
Centerville 5 1 42N34'50 70W50'30 4:43:22
Centerville 14 1 42N04'23 71W36'47 4:46:27
Central Square 9 1 42N29'28 71W09'04 4:44:36
Central Village 3 1 41N34'25 71W05'30 4:44:22
Centralville 9 1 42N39'20 71W18'20 4:45:13
Centre Mills 3 1 41N58'30 71W11'07 4:44:44
Chadwicks Folly 10 1 41N19'11 69W59'25 4:39:58
Chadwick Square 14 1 42N17'25 71W48'35 4:47:14
Chaffin 14 1 42N21 71W51 4:47:24
Chaffinville 14 1 42N20'10 71W50'00 4:47:20
Chandler Hill 14 1 42N16'25 71W47'30 4:47:10
Chapel Hill Estates 12 1 42N04 70W49 4:43:16
Chapinville 14 1 42N20'13 71W37'30 4:46:30
Chappaquiddick 4 1 41N23'14 70W30'18 4:42:01
Chappaquiddick Island 4 1 41N23 70W31 4:42:04
Chappaquoit 1 1 41N36'15 70W39'00 4:42:36
Charlemont 6 1 42N37'40 72W52'13 4:51:29
Charles River 11 1 42N17 71W14 4:44:56
Charles River Grove 11 1 42N05'30 71W28'25 4:45:54
Charles River Station 11 1 42N15'44 71W15'47 4:45:03
Charles River Village 11 1 42N15'38 71W15'42 4:45:03
Charlestown 13 1 42N22'40 71W03'45 4:44:15
Charlton 14 1 42N08'08 71W58'14 4:47:53
Charlton City 14 1 42N08'45 71W59'20 4:47:57
Charlton Depot 14 1 42N10'23 71W58'45 4:47:55
Chartley 3 1 41N56'55 71W13'35 4:44:54
Chaseville 14 1 42N02'30 71W53'50 4:47:35

Chatham 1 1 41N40'55 69W57'37 4:39:50
Chatham Port 1 1 41N42'10 69W58'12 4:39:53
Cheapside 6 1 42N34'20 72W35'10 4:50:21
Chelmsford 9 1 42N36 71W21 4:45:24
Chelmsford Center 9 1 42N35'45 71W12'10 4:44:49
Chelsea 13 1 42N23'30 71W02'00 4:44:08
Cherry Brook 9 1 42N22 71W18 4:45:12
Cherry Valley 14 1 42N14'35 71W52'25 4:47:30
Cheshire 2 1 42N33'43 73W09'48 4:52:39
Cheshire Harbor 2 1 42N35'38 73W08'31 4:52:34
Chester 7 1 42N16'45 72W58'45 4:51:55
Chester Center 7 1 42N17'25 72W55'30 4:51:42
Chesterfield 8 1 42N23'30 72W50'25 4:51:22
Chestnut Hill 9 1 42N19'50 71W10'00 4:44:40
Chestnut Hill Meeting House 14 1 42N02'42 71W34'43 4:46:19
Chicopee 7 1 42N08'55 72W36'30 4:50:26
Chicopee Falls 7 1 42N09'07 72W34'35 4:50:18
Chilmark 4 1 41N20'35 70W44'43 4:42:59
Chiltonville 12 1 41N56'15 70W37'45 4:42:31
Churchill Landing 12 1 41N54'05 70W32'40 4:42:11
Churchill Shores 12 1 41N48'20 70W57'30 4:43:50
Cisco 10 1 41N15'15 70W09'15 4:40:37
City Mills 11 1 42N06'30 71W21'18 4:45:25
City Point 13 1 42N20'10 71W01'45 4:44:07
Clapps Corner 12 1 42N12'00 70W48'47 4:43:15
Clarendon Hill 13 1 42N16'30 71W07'30 4:44:30
Clarendon Hills 13 1 42N16'30 71W07'25 4:44:30
Clarksburg 2 1 42N43 73W05 4:52:20
Clayton 2 1 42N02'35 73W17'15 4:53:09
Cleghorn 14 1 42N35 71W48 4:47:12
Clematis Brook 9 1 42N23 71W14 4:44:56
Clematis Brook Station 9 1 42N22'54 71W12'40 4:44:51
Clevelandtown 4 1 41N23'00 70W31'10 4:42:05
Clicquot 11 1 42N10'17 71W21'10 4:45:25
Clifford 3 1 41N43'35 70W56'30 4:43:46
Clifton 5 1 42N29'00 70W52'50 4:43:31
Cliftondale 5 1 42N26'55 71W00'40 4:44:03
Clifton Heights 12 1 42N03'25 71W01'50 4:44:07
Clinton 14 1 42N25'00 71W41'00 4:46:44
Cobbs Village 1 1 41N42'30 70W17'30 4:41:10
Coburnville 9 1 42N16'22 71W26'10 4:45:45
Cochesett 12 1 42N01'00 71W02'20 4:44:09
Cochituate 9 1 42N19'15 71W21'53 4:45:28
Codfish Park 10 1 41N16'47 69W57'45 4:39:51
Cohasset 11 1 42N14'30 70W48'15 4:43:13
Coldbrook Springs 14 1 42N23'40 72W02'50 4:48:11
Cold Spring 2 1 42N09'15 73W04'30 4:52:18
Cold Spring 6 1 42N39'45 72W30'50 4:50:03
Cold Spring 8 1 42N14'48 72W21'22 4:49:25
Cole Corner 12 1 42N13'25 70W53'10 4:43:33
Cole Mill 12 1 41N55'35 70W47'57 4:43:12
College Hill 14 1 42N14'00 71W48'40 4:47:15
Collins Corner 3 1 41N42'40 71W06'25 4:44:26
Collinsville 9 1 42N41'00 71W21'10 4:45:25
Colonial Acres 1 1 41N38'52 70W15'22 4:41:01
Colonial Park 14 1 42N01'38 71W49'55 4:47:20
Colrain 6 1 42N40'23 72W41'50 4:50:47
Colton Hollow 7 1 42N06'35 72W21'15 4:49:25
Coltsville 2 1 42N28'03 73W12'15 4:52:49
Columbus Park 14 1 42N15'20 71W50'05 4:47:20
Cominsville 14 1 42N11'13 71W53'45 4:47:35
Community Park 14 1 42N06'55 71W54'30 4:47:38
Concord 9 1 42N27'37 71W20'58 4:45:24
Congamond 7 1 42N01'10 72W46'12 4:51:05
Conomo 5 1 42N38 70W47 4:43:08
Conway 6 1 42N30'35 72W42'00 4:50:48
Cooks Brook Beach 1 1 41N51'52 70W00'30 4:40:02
Cooks Corner 8 1 42N16'40 72W28'15 4:49:53
Cook Street 9 1 42N21 71W12 4:44:48
Cooleyville 6 1 42N27'47 72W22'23 4:49:30
Coolidge Corner 11 1 42N20'45 71W07'30 4:44:30
Copper Works 3 1 41N56'54 71W10'45 4:44:43
Cordage 12 1 41N58'45 70W41'30 4:42:46
Cordaville 14 1 42N16'08 71W31'28 4:46:06
Coskata 10 1 41N21'15 70W01'15 4:40:05
Cotley 3 1 41N54 71W06 4:44:24
Cottage Hill 13 1 42N22'05 70W58'10 4:43:53
Cottage Park 13 1 42N22'15 70W59'15 4:43:57
Cotuit 1 1 41N37'00 70W26'15 4:41:45
Cotuit Highlands 1 1 41N36'30 70W26'15 4:41:45
Countryside 9 1 42N26'31 71W11'40 4:44:47
Country View Estates 11 1 42N05'45 71W26'15 4:45:45
Court Park 13 1 42N22'22 70W59'43 4:43:59
Coury Heights 3 1 41N41'45 70W55'30 4:43:42
Cowen Corner 12 1 41N46'08 70W50'36 4:43:22
Cow Yard 3 1 41N31'55 70W58'00 4:43:52
Cox Corner 12 1 42N03'32 70W41'30 4:42:46
Coxs Corner 12 1 42N04'50 70W53'15 4:43:33
Craigville 1 1 41N38'22 70W20'08 4:41:21
Craigville Beach 1 1 41N38'12 70W20'45 4:41:23
Cranberry Bog Corner 3 1 41N33'45 70W59'10 4:43:57
Crane Lake Camp 2 1 42N20'17 73W22'45 4:53:31
Cranes Station 3 1 41N57'07 71W08'48 4:44:35
Crescent Beach 12 1 41N39'15 70W47'14 4:43:09

Crescent Beach 13
1 42N24'20 70W59'30 4:43:58
Crescent Mills 7
1 42N13'10 72W51'38 4:51:27
Crooks Corner 11
1 42N01'30 71W29'27 4:45:58
Crownridge Estates 11
1 42N11'18 71W19'17 4:45:17
Crow Point 12 1 42N15'42 70W53'45 4:43:35
Cummaquid 1 1 41N42'06 70W16'25 4:41:06
Cummingsville 9 1 42N28'52 71W10'30 4:44:42
Cummington 8 1 42N27'42 72W53'40 4:51:35
Curtis Crossing 12
1 42N06'10 70W49'25 4:43:18
Curzon Mill 5 1 42N49'15 70W56'15 4:43:45
Cushman 8 1 42N24'50 72W30'25 4:50:02
Cuttyhunk 4 1 41N25'15 70W55'47 4:43:43
Daley Corner 3 1 42N04'00 71W05'15 4:44:21
Dalton 2 1 42N28'25 73W10'00 4:52:40
Dana (historical) 14
1 42N26'00 72W16'00 4:49:04
Dana Center 14 1 42N25'20 72W13'30 4:48:54
Danvers 5 1 42N34'30 70W55'50 4:43:43
Danvers Center 5
1 42N34'20 70W57'40 4:43:51
Danversport 5 1 42N32'54 70W55'15 4:43:41
Dartmouth 3 1 41N37 70W58 4:43:52
Davisville 1 1 41N33'05 70W33'50 4:42:15
Dawson 14 1 42N20'23 71W51'05 4:47:24
Dayville 7 1 42N18'10 72W54'20 4:51:37
Dedham 11 1 42N14'30 71W10'00 4:44:40
Dedham Island 11
1 42N16'00 71W10'40 4:44:43
Deerfield 6 2 42N32'40 72W36'22 4:50:25
Dell 6 1 42N40'15 72W50'55 4:51:24
Dennis 1 1 41N44'07 70W11'40 4:40:47
Dennis Port 1 1 41N39'30 70W07'45 4:40:31
Derby Wharf 5 1 42N31'10 70W53'08 4:43:33
Devenscrest 9 1 42N33'00 71W34'00 4:46:16
Devereux 5 1 42N30 70W52 4:43:28
Dighton 3 1 41N48'50 71W07'15 4:44:29
Dingley Dell 7 1 42N07'08 72W15'30 4:49:02
Division Street 3
1 41N37 70W55 4:43:40
Dodge 14 1 42N09'43 71W56'00 4:47:44
Dodge Corner 6 1 42N36'00 72W50'35 4:51:22
Dodgeville 3 1 41N55'15 71W17'50 4:45:11
Dogtown Commons 5
1 42N38'10 70W39'55 4:42:40
Doles Corner 5 1 42N43'35 70W54'10 4:43:37
Dorchester 13 1 42N17'50 71W04'30 4:44:18
Dorchester Center 13
1 42N17'30 71W04'20 4:44:17
Dorchester Heights 13
1 42N20'00 71W02'40 4:44:11
Dorothy Manor 14
1 42N13'00 71W45'23 4:47:02
Dorothy Pond 14 1 42N13'14 71W45'37 4:47:02
Douglas 14 1 42N03'15 71W44'24 4:46:58
Douglas Corner 12
1 41N46'31 70W47'31 4:43:10
Dover 11 1 42N14'45 71W17'00 4:45:08
Downtown Crossing 13
1 42N21'16 71W03'30 4:44:14
Dracut 9 1 42N40'13 71W18'09 4:45:13
Drury 2 1 42N39'08 72W59'53 4:52:00
Drury Square 14 1 42N12'22 71W50'10 4:47:21
Dry Pond 11 1 42N08 71W06 4:44:24
Duckville 7 1 42N13'00 72W20'40 4:49:23
Dudley 14 1 42N02'42 71W55'50 4:47:43
Dudley Hill 14 1 42N03 71W54 4:47:36
Dudleyville 6 1 42N29'07 72W26'47 4:49:47
Duncan Knoll 7 1 42N12'20 72W33'15 4:50:13
Dunstable 9 1 42N40'30 71W29'00 4:45:56
Duxbury 12 1 42N02'30 70W40'22 4:42:41
Dwight 8 1 42N19'40 72W27'00 4:49:48
Eagle Hill 5 1 42N42 70W49 4:43:16
Eaglesville 14 1 42N33'00 72W16'15 4:49:05
East Acton 9 1 42N28'30 71W24'36 4:45:38
East Arlington 9
1 42N24'15 71W08'50 4:44:35
East Berlin 14 1 42N23'23 71W36'00 4:46:24
East Billerica 9
1 42N34'53 71W14'15 4:44:57
East Blackstone 14
1 42N02'30 71W30'45 4:46:03
East Bolton 14 1 42N26'45 71W33'45 4:46:15
East Boston 13 1 42N22'30 71W02'23 4:44:10
East Boxford 5 1 42N41'30 70W58'50 4:43:55
East Braintree 11
1 42N13'30 70W58'30 4:43:54
East Brewster 1 1 41N46'05 70W03'37 4:40:14
East Bridgewater 12
1 42N02'00 70W57'35 4:43:50
East Brimfield 7
1 42N06'40 72W08'56 4:48:36
East Brookfield 14
1 42N13'40 72W02'50 4:48:11
East Cambridge 9
1 42N22'00 71W04'50 4:44:19
East Carver 12 1 41N55'38 70W45'05 4:43:00
East Charlemont 6
1 42N37'20 72W47'25 4:51:10
East Chelmsford 9
1 42N37 71W22 4:45:28
East Chop 4 1 41N28'06 70W34'10 4:42:17
East Dedham 11 1 42N15'00 71W09'30 4:44:38
East Deerfield 6
1 42N34'00 72W33'57 4:50:16
East Dennis 1 1 41N44'33 70W09'45 4:40:39
East Douglas 14 1 42N04'20 71W42'50 4:46:51
East Douglas Station 14
1 42N03'40 71W42'38 4:46:51
East Everett 9 1 42N25 71W03 4:44:12
East Fairhaven 3
1 41N38'55 70W51'42 4:43:27
East Falmouth 1 1 41N34'42 70W33'33 4:42:14
East Farms 7 1 42N11'10 72W44'55 4:51:00
East Fitchburg 14
1 42N35 71W48 4:47:12
East Forest Park 7
1 42N05'50 72W32'15 4:50:09
East Foxboro 11 1 42N03'40 71W12'05 4:44:48
East Freetown 3 1 41N46'30 70W57'30 4:43:50
East Gardner 14 1 42N34'40 71W57'10 4:47:49
East Gloucester 5
1 42N36'40 70W38'55 4:42:36
East Greenfield 6
1 42N34'30 72W34'55 4:50:20
East Groton 9 1 42N38'30 71W30'00 4:46:00
East Hadley 8 1 42N19'43 72W33'36 4:50:14
Eastham 1 1 41N49'48 69W58'28 4:39:54
Easthampton 8 1 42N16'00 72W40'10 4:50:41
East Harwich 1 1 41N42'00 70W01'40 4:40:07
East Haverhill 5
1 42N47 71W05 4:44:20
East Holliston 9
1 42N12'45 71W25'15 4:45:41
East Junction 3 1 41N54'30 71W18'30 4:45:14
Eastland Heights 12
1 41N51'00 70W32'45 4:42:11
East Lee 2 1 42N17'50 73W13'30 4:52:54
East Leverett 6 2 42N26'23 72W28'50 4:49:55
East Lexington 9
1 42N25'38 71W12'15 4:44:49
East Littleton 9
1 42N33'36 71W27'15 4:45:49
East Longmeadow 7
1 42N03'52 72W30'47 4:50:03
East Lynn 5 1 42N28'10 70W55'40 4:43:43
East Mansfield 3
1 42N01'23 71W10'40 4:44:43
East Marion 12 1 41N42'45 70W44'45 4:42:59
East Middleboro 12
1 41N51 70W56 4:43:44
East Millbury 14
1 42N13'40 71W44'45 4:46:59
East Milton 11 1 42N15'30 71W02'35 4:44:10
East Natick 9 1 42N18'15 71W19'30 4:45:18
East Northfield 6
1 42N41'35 72W26'20 4:49:45
East Northfield Station 6
1 42N43'30 72W27'40 4:49:51
East Norton 3 1 41N58'30 71W10'15 4:44:41
Easton 3 1 42N01'28 71W07'45 4:44:31
Easton Center 3 1 42N02'10 71W05'50 4:44:23
Eastondale 3 1 42N02'10 71W04'10 4:44:17
Easton Green 3 1 42N02'30 71W04'43 4:44:19
Easton Station 3
1 42N02'18 71W05'42 4:44:23
East Orleans 1 1 41N47'06 69W58'15 4:39:53
East Otis 2 1 42N10'24 73W02'06 4:52:08
East Parish 5 1 42N39'50 71W01'00 4:44:04
East Pembroke 12
1 42N04'45 70W45'45 4:43:03
East Pepperell 9
1 42N39'55 71W34'25 4:46:18
East Princeton 14
1 42N28'22 71W50'22 4:47:21
East Sandwich 1 1 41N44'30 70W27'08 4:41:49
East Sharon 11 1 42N08'06 71W09'42 4:44:39
East Sheffield 2
1 42N02'52 73W18'05 4:53:12
East Shelburne 6
1 42N38'07 72W40'02 4:50:40
East Somerville 9
1 42N23'08 71W05'10 4:44:21
East Springfield 7
1 42N08'30 72W33'45 4:50:15
East Sudbury 9 1 42N23 71W25 4:45:40
East Sudbury Station 9
1 42N21'37 71W24'08 4:45:37
East Sutton 14 1 42N09'45 71W42'08 4:46:49
East Swansea 3 1 41N45 71W13 4:44:52
East Taunton 3 1 41N53'00 71W01'45 4:44:07
East Templeton 14
1 42N33'47 72W02'15 4:48:09
Eastview Park 9 1 42N24'03 71W12'55 4:44:52
East Village 8 1 42N22'38 72W29'53 4:50:00
East Village 14 1 42N03'40 71W51'52 4:47:27
Eastville 4 1 41N27'40 70W34'45 4:42:19
Eastville 12 1 42N02'16 70W55'20 4:43:41
East Walpole 11 1 42N09'43 71W12'40 4:44:51
East Wareham 12 1 41N45'29 70W40'27 4:42:42
East Watertown 9
1 42N22'10 71W09'45 4:44:39
East Weymouth 11
1 42N12'50 70W55'15 4:43:41
East Whately 6 2 42N26'45 72W36'55 4:50:28
East Wilbraham 7
1 42N09'15 72W23'45 4:49:35
East Windsor 2 1 42N28'40 72W59'10 4:51:57
East Woburn 9 1 42N29 71W09 4:44:36
Ebenville 14 1 42N26'15 71W42'10 4:46:49
Eddyville 12 1 41N55'27 70W50'52 4:43:23
Edgartown 4 1 41N23'20 70W30'50 4:42:03
Edgemere 14 1 42N14'55 71W44'30 4:46:58
Edgewater Estates 12
1 42N04 70W49 4:43:16
Edgeworth 9 1 42N25'08 71W04'50 4:44:19
Egremont 2 1 42N10 73W27 4:53:48
Egremont Plain 2
1 42N11'05 73W24'52 4:53:39
Egypt 12 1 42N12'45 70W45'32 4:43:02
Egypt Beach 13 1 42N13'12 70W44'43 4:42:59
Eliot 9 1 42N19'10 71W12'50 4:44:51
Ellis 11 1 42N12'50 71W11'30 4:44:46
Ellisville 12 1 41N50'40 70W32'32 4:42:10
Elmdale 14 1 42N05 71W38 4:46:32
Elm Grove 6 1 42N42'35 72W42'15 4:50:49
Elm Square 12 1 42N01'00 71W01'15 4:44:05
Elmwood 7 1 42N11'45 72W37'30 4:50:30
Elmwood 12 1 42N00'35 70W57'45 4:43:51
Elmwood Station 12
1 42N01'06 70W58'15 4:43:53
Endicott 11 1 42N13'54 71W09'30 4:44:38
Enfield (historical) 8
1 42N19'00 72W20'00 4:49:20
Englewood 1 1 41N38'45 70W14'50 4:40:59
Erving 6 1 42N36'00 72W23'55 4:49:36
Essex 5 1 42N37'55 70W47'00 4:43:08
Essex Falls 5 1 42N37'30 70W47'30 4:43:10
Everett 9 1 42N24'30 71W03'15 4:44:13
Factory Hollow 8
1 42N24'55 72W31'09 4:50:05
Fairhaven 3 1 41N38'15 70W54'15 4:43:37
Fairlawn 14 1 42N16'30 71W44'30 4:46:58
Fairmount 13 1 42N15'05 71W06'55 4:44:28
Fairview 7 1 42N12'15 72W34'30 4:50:18
Fall River 3 1 41N42'05 71W09'20 4:44:37
Fall River Station 3
1 41N42'50 71W09'15 4:44:37
Falls Mall Shopping Center 8
1 42N15 72W35 4:50:20
Falmouth 1 1 41N33'05 70W36'55 4:42:28
Falmouth Heights 1
1 41N32'45 70W35'45 4:42:23
Faneuil 13 1 42N21'20 71W09'50 4:44:39
Farley 6 1 42N36'00 72W26'22 4:49:45
Farmersville 1 1 41N41'25 70W26'39 4:41:47
Farm Hill 9 1 42N29 71W06 4:44:24
Farm Street Station 11
1 42N12'39 71W18'53 4:45:16
Farnams 2 1 42N32'30 73W11'10 4:52:45
Farnumsville 14 1 42N10'37 71W40'53 4:46:44
Faulkner 9 1 42N25'45 71W03'20 4:44:13
Faunce Corner 3 1 41N40'45 70W59'20 4:43:57
Fayville 14 1 42N17'40 71W30'22 4:46:01
Feeding Hills 7 1 42N04'05 72W40'45 4:50:43
Felchville 9 1 42N17'52 71W21'35 4:45:26
Fells 9 1 42N26'30 71W04'18 4:44:17
Fellsway 9 1 42N25 71W07 4:44:28
Fennerville 14 1 42N02'15 71W53'00 4:47:32
Fentonville 7 1 42N08'25 72W16'25 4:49:06
Ferncroft 5 1 42N34'45 70W57'30 4:43:50
Ferry Hill 12 1 42N08'22 70W41'59 4:42:48
Fiberloid 7 1 42N09'05 72W32'00 4:50:08
Fields Corner 13
1 42N18'00 71W03'30 4:44:14
Fieldston 12 1 42N06'26 70W39'52 4:42:39
Fighting Rock Corner 3
1 41N44'05 71W05'25 4:44:22
Findlen 11 1 42N14 71W10 4:44:40
Finnville 12 1 42N11'40 70W53'58 4:43:36
Fireworks 12 1 42N06'15 70W52'20 4:43:29
First Cliff 12 1 42N11'58 70W43'00 4:42:52
First Encounter 1
1 41N50 69W58 4:39:52
First Encounter Beach 1
1 41N49'22 70W00'15 4:40:01
Fishermans Landing 12
1 41N54'22 70W32'50 4:42:11
Fishers Landing 10
1 41N17'37 70W10'47 4:40:43
Fisherville 14 1 42N10'30 71W41'35 4:46:46
Fiskdale 14 1 42N06'58 72W06'50 4:48:27
Fitchburg 14 1 42N35'00 71W48'10 4:47:13
Five Corners 3 1 42N01'25 71W07'15 4:44:29
Five Corners 11 1 42N13'44 71W01'12 4:44:05
Five Corners 12 1 41N47'59 70W45'55 4:43:04
Five Corners 14 1 42N26'37 71W40'00 4:46:40
Five Pound Island 5
1 42N36'49 70W39'14 4:42:37
Flint 3 1 41N42 71W08 4:44:32
Flints Corner 9 1 42N39'18 71W26'00 4:45:44
Flint Village 3 1 41N41'20 71W07'50 4:44:31
Florence 8 1 42N20'08 72W40'20 4:50:41
Florida 2 1 42N40'00 73W00'42 4:52:03
Follen Heights 9
1 42N25'57 71W12'50 4:44:51
Fomer 8 1 42N14'42 72W47'40 4:51:11
Forbes Wharf 11 1 42N16'00 71W03'39 4:44:15
Fore River 11 1 42N15 71W00 4:44:00
Forestdale 1 1 41N41'30 70W30'00 4:42:00
Forestdale Estates 12
1 42N04 70W49 4:43:16
Forest Hills 13 1 42N17'48 71W06'15 4:44:25
Forest Lake 7 1 42N09 72W20 4:49:20
Forest Park 7 1 42N05'25 72W34'15 4:50:17
Forest Park 11 1 42N05'50 71W28'55 4:45:56
Forest River 5 1 42N31 70W54 4:43:36
Forge Village 9 1 42N34'48 71W29'15 4:45:57
Fort Andrews 12 1 42N17'59 70W55'44 4:43:43
Fort Bellingham 11
1 42N05 71W28 4:45:52
Fort Dawes 13 1 42N21'00 70W57'25 4:43:50
Fort Devens 9 1 42N33 71W36 4:46:24
Fort Duvall 12 1 42N18'00 70W53'47 4:43:35
Fort Heath 13 1 42N22 70W59 4:43:56
Fort Hill 12 1 42N14'15 70W54'15 4:43:37
Fort Independence 13
1 42N20'17 71W00'44 4:44:03
Fort Revere 12 1 42N18'22 70W54'30 4:43:38
Fort Standish 12
1 41N59'50 70W37'45 4:42:31
Fort Warren 13 1 42N19'10 70W55'45 4:43:43
Fort Winthrop 13
1 42N21'07 71W00'45 4:44:03
Foundry Village 6
1 42N40'25 72W43'08 4:50:53
Four Corners 7 1 42N11'09 72W20'55 4:49:24
Four Corners 9 1 42N40'28 71W34'40 4:46:19
Fourth Cliff 12 1 42N09'36 70W42'18 4:42:49
Foxboro 11 1 42N03'30 71W15'00 4:45:00
Foxvale 11 1 42N02'33 71W14'05 4:44:56
Framingham 9 1 42N16'45 71W25'00 4:45:40
Framingham Center 9
1 42N17'50 71W26'15 4:45:45
Franklin 11 1 42N05'00 71W23'50 4:45:35
Franklin Park 13
1 42N26'30 71W01'00 4:44:04
Frederick Corner 9
1 42N38'54 71W28'30 4:45:54
Freeman Knoll 7 1 42N11'53 72W33'00 4:50:12
Freetown 3 1 41N46 70W58 4:43:52
Fresh Brook 1 1 41N53'36 69W59'15 4:39:57
Fresh Pond 9 1 42N23 71W08 4:44:32
Freshwater Cove 5
1 42N37 70W40 4:42:40
Freshwater Cove Village 5
1 42N35'45 70W41'15 4:42:45
Fryeville 14 1 42N37'40 72W13'32 4:48:54
Fryville 14 1 42N24'30 71W37'13 4:46:29
Fuller Shores 12
1 41N49'05 70W56'25 4:43:46
Furnace 14 1 42N20'45 72W09'40 4:48:39
Furnace Pond Colony 12
1 42N04 70W49 4:43:16

Furnace Village 3
1 42N02 71W06 4:44:24
Further Creek 10
1 41N16'50 70W13'40 4:40:55
Gannett Corners 12
1 42N13'07 70W47'15 4:43:09
Gardner 14 1 42N34'30 71W59'55 4:48:00
Gates Crossing 14
1 42N29'45 71W44'15 4:46:57
Gay Head 4 1 41N20'37 70W48'55 4:43:16
Georgetown 5 1 42N43'30 70W59'30 4:43:58
Germantown 11 1 42N15'20 70W57'45 4:43:51
Germantown 13 1 42N15'45 71W09'17 4:44:37
Gibbs Crossing 8
1 42N14'14 72W17'20 4:49:09
Gibbs Grove 12 1 41N52'05 70W51'43 4:43:27
Gidleys Corner 3
1 41N34'55 71W02'25 4:44:10
Giffords Corner 3
1 41N37'20 71W04'50 4:44:19
Gilbertville 14 1 42N18'45 72W12'30 4:48:50
Gill 6 2 42N38'25 72W30'00 4:50:00
Gillett Corner 7
1 42N01'32 72W47'10 4:51:09
Gill Station 6 1 42N39'00 72W27'52 4:49:51
Ginty Corner 3 1 42N00'53 71W09'46 4:44:39
Gleasondale 9 1 42N24'22 71W31'38 4:46:07
Gleasondale Station 9
1 42N23'45 71W31'26 4:46:06
Glenallen 14 1 42N40'54 72W01'32 4:48:06
Glendale 2 1 42N17'00 73W20'40 4:53:23
Glendale 9 1 42N24'50 71W02'55 4:44:12
Glen Echo 11 1 42N08 71W06 4:44:24
Glen Grove 14 1 42N09'55 71W59'40 4:47:59
Glen Grove Annex 14
1 42N09'30 71W59'15 4:47:57
Glen Heights 14 1 42N09'25 71W59'35 4:47:58
Glen Mills 5 1 42N44'15 70W54'60 4:43:40
Glenridge 11 1 42N14'45 71W19'19 4:45:17
Glenwood 9 1 42N25 71W07 4:44:28
Globe Village 3 1 41N40'55 71W11'10 4:44:45
Globe Village 14
1 42N05'00 72W02'52 4:48:11
Gloucester 5 1 42N36'57 70W39'45 4:42:39
Golden Ring Camp 12
1 42N03'00 70W50'40 4:43:23
Gooch Corners 9 1 42N13'38 71W25'37 4:45:42
Goodrichville 14
1 42N35'52 71W42'10 4:46:49
Goshen 8 1 42N26'25 72W48'00 4:51:12
Gosnold 4 1 41N27 70W48 4:43:12
Goss Heights 8 1 42N15'45 72W52'25 4:51:30
Goulding Village 14
1 42N32'30 72W06'37 4:48:26
Gowards Corner 3
1 42N01'30 71W04'02 4:44:16
Graceland Park 5
1 42N46'20 71W09'37 4:44:38
Grafton 14 1 42N12'25 71W41'10 4:46:45
Granby 8 1 42N15'23 72W31'00 4:50:04
Graniteville 9 1 42N35'45 71W27'45 4:45:51
Grantville 11 1 42N18'45 71W16'30 4:45:06
Granville 7 1 42N04'00 72W51'43 4:51:27
Granville Center 7
1 42N04'02 72W52'45 4:51:31
Gray Gables 1 1 41N44'00 70W37'15 4:42:29
Great Barrington 2
1 42N11'45 73W21'45 4:53:27
Great Brook Valley 14
1 42N18'25 71W46'20 4:47:05
Great Neck 3 1 41N32'15 70W59'30 4:43:58
Great Swamp 8 1 42N14'40 72W36'50 4:50:27
Greenbush 12 1 42N10'45 70W45'00 4:43:00
Greendale 14 1 42N18'25 71W47'45 4:47:11
Greenfield 6 1 42N35'15 72W36'00 4:50:24
Green Harbor 12 1 42N04'40 70W39'00 4:42:36
Greenlodge 11 1 42N13'20 71W09'35 4:44:38
Green Ridge Park 2
1 42N27'06 73W11'18 4:52:45
Green, The 12 1 41N54'24 70W53'10 4:43:33
Greenville 14 1 42N12'15 71W55'00 4:47:40
Greenwich (historical) 14
1 42N21'30 72W17'48 4:49:11
Greenwich Village (historica 14
1 42N23'00 72W16'30 4:49:06
Greenwood 9 1 42N28'55 71W03'45 4:44:15
Greenwood Manor Estates 12
1 42N04 70W49 4:43:16
Greylock 2 1 42N41'47 73W09'07 4:52:36
Griswoldville 6 1 42N39'23 72W42'52 4:50:51
Grosvenor Corner 5
1 42N46'36 71W10'27 4:44:42
Groton 9 1 42N36'40 71W34'30 4:46:18
Grounts Corner 6
1 42N34'40 72W29'40 4:49:59
Grove Hall 13 1 42N18'40 71W04'30 4:44:18
Groveland 5 1 42N45'37 71W01'55 4:44:08
Gurneys Corner 12
1 42N02'35 70W51'18 4:43:25
Hadley 8 1 42N20'30 72W35'20 4:50:21
Haggetts 5 1 42N38'36 71W12'28 4:44:50
Hales Crossing 6
1 42N39'15 72W33'52 4:50:15
Halfway House 14
1 42N03'43 71W40'15 4:46:41
Halfway Pond 12 1 41N45 70W36 4:42:24
Halifax 12 1 41N59'28 70W51'45 4:43:27
Halifax Beach 12
1 42N00'00 70W51'10 4:43:25
Hallockville 6 1 42N33'09 72W56'32 4:51:46
Hamilton 5 1 42N37 70W51 4:43:24
Hamilton 14 1 42N15'22 71W46'05 4:47:04
Hamilton Beach 12
1 41N44'36 70W42'45 4:42:51
Hampden 7 1 42N03'50 72W24'50 4:49:39
Hampton Mills 8 1 42N16 72W39 4:50:36
Hancock 2 1 42N32'35 73W19'27 4:53:18
Hancock Village 11
1 42N18'00 71W09'15 4:44:37
Handy Four Corners 3
1 41N34'15 71W04'35 4:44:18
Hanleys Corner 12
1 42N02'30 71W03'30 4:44:14
Hanover 12 1 42N06'47 70W48'45 4:43:15
Hanover Center 12
1 42N07'00 70W50'30 4:43:22
Hanscom Air Force Base 9
1 42N29 71W17 4:45:08
Hanson 12 1 42N04'30 70W52'50 4:43:31
Happy Hills 11 1 42N06'57 71W28'29 4:45:54
Harbor Beach 12 1 41N40'08 70W45'45 4:43:03
Harbor View 3 1 41N37'45 70W53'35 4:43:34
Harding 11 1 42N12'13 71W19'28 4:45:18
Harding Estates 11
1 42N11 71W18 4:45:12
Hardwick 14 1 42N21'00 72W12'00 4:48:48
Harlows Landing 12
1 41N50'54 70W31'54 4:42:08
Harris 3 1 41N48'50 71W18'45 4:45:15
Harrisville 14 1 42N42'37 72W05'07 4:48:20
Harrubs Corner 12
1 41N59'17 70W48'11 4:43:13
Harthaven 4 1 41N26'35 70W33'25 4:42:14
Hartsville 2 1 42N09'35 73W15'32 4:53:02
Hartsville 4 1 41N26'29 70W33'19 4:42:13
Harvard 14 1 42N30'00 71W35'00 4:46:20
Harvard Station 14
1 42N31'20 71W36'00 4:46:24
Harwich 1 1 41N41'10 70W04'35 4:40:18
Harwich Port 1 1 41N40'00 70W04'45 4:40:19
Harwood 9 1 42N32 71W31 4:46:04
Hastings 9 1 42N23'15 71W17'23 4:45:10
Hatchville 1 1 41N37'45 70W33'50 4:42:15
Hatfield 8 2 42N22'15 72W35'55 4:50:24
Hatherly 12 1 42N09'24 70W55'30 4:43:42
Hatherly Beach 12
1 42N12'45 70W44'00 4:42:56
Hathorne 5 1 42N35'10 70W58'30 4:43:54
Havenville 9 1 42N30'08 71W12'40 4:44:51
Haverhill 5 1 42N46'34 71W04'40 4:44:19
Hawley 6 1 42N33'52 72W52'42 4:51:31
Hayden Row 9 1 42N12'15 71W30'40 4:46:03
Haydenville 8 1 42N22'30 72W42'05 4:50:48
Hayward Corner 9
1 42N38'54 71W27'08 4:45:49
Head of Plains 10
1 41N16'00 70W11'00 4:40:44
Head of Westport 3
1 41N37'15 71W03'45 4:44:15
Heald Village 14
1 42N25'30 72W05'45 4:48:23
Heard Street 14 1 42N13'50 71W50'35 4:47:22
Heath 6 1 42N40'24 72W49'20 4:51:17
Heaven Heights 3
1 41N47'10 70W57'00 4:43:48
Hemlocks 12 1 41N48'40 70W56'25 4:43:46
Hendersonville 9
1 42N24'15 71W04'00 4:44:16
Hephzibah Heights 2
1 42N10'00 73W11'25 4:52:46
Herbonville 3 1 41N54'10 71W19'15 4:45:17
Heywood 14 1 42N34 72W00 4:48:00
Hicksville 3 1 41N37 70W58 4:43:52
Highland 7 1 42N07 72W33 4:50:12
Highland 13 1 42N17'07 71W09'26 4:44:38
Highland Lake 11
1 42N07'35 71W18'37 4:45:14
Highland Park 8 1 42N13'20 72W37'15 4:50:29
Highlands 7 1 42N13'10 72W37'30 4:50:30
Highlands 9 1 42N37'50 71W20'15 4:45:21
Hillcrest 3 1 41N39'15 71W04'30 4:44:18
Hillcrest Acres 3
1 41N37 71W04 4:44:16
Hillsville 14 1 42N15'40 72W00'40 4:48:03
Hilltop Acres 12
1 41N47'55 70W57'25 4:43:50
Hingham 12 1 42N14'30 70W53'25 4:43:34
Hingham Center 12
1 42N14'00 70W52'50 4:43:31
Hinsdale 2 1 42N26'19 73W07'33 4:52:30
Hinsdale Estates 11
1 42N05 71W28 4:45:52
Hixville 3 1 41N40'54 71W01'55 4:44:08
Hockanum 8 1 42N17'35 72W36'15 4:50:25
Hodges Village 14
1 42N07'05 71W52'53 4:47:32
Hoicks Hollow 10
1 41N17'15 69W58'20 4:39:53
Holbrook 11 1 42N09'18 71W00'33 4:44:02
Holbrook Grove 11
1 42N09 71W01 4:44:04
Holden 14 1 42N21'06 71W51'50 4:47:27
Holden Center 14
1 42N21'00 71W51'30 4:47:26
Holland 7 1 42N03'50 72W09'28 4:48:38
Holliston 9 1 42N12'00 71W25'30 4:45:42
Holly Woods 12 1 41N39'32 70W45'32 4:43:02
Holyoke 7 1 42N12'15 72W37'00 4:50:28
Hoosac Tunnel 2 1 42N40'09 72W59'36 4:51:58
Hoosac Tunnel Station 6
1 42N40'06 72W59'15 4:51:57
Hopedale 14 1 42N07'50 71W32'30 4:46:10
Hopkinton 9 1 42N13'43 71W31'23 4:46:06
Horseneck Beach 3
1 41N37 71W04 4:44:16
Hortonville 3 1 41N46'30 71W12'00 4:44:48
Hosmer Corner 7 1 42N03'52 72W43'30 4:50:54
Houghs Neck 11 1 42N16'00 70W57'30 4:43:50
Houghtonville 2 1 42N42'46 73W04'30 4:52:18
Housatonic 2 1 42N15'15 73W22'00 4:53:28
Hovey Corner 9 1 42N40'46 71W36'05 4:46:24
Hovey's Corner 9
1 42N39 71W35 4:46:20
Howe 5 1 42N35'40 70W59'55 4:44:00
Howlands 12 1 41N47'50 70W50'45 4:43:23
Hubbard Corner 7
1 42N02'37 72W38'10 4:50:33
Hubbardston 14 1 42N28'25 72W00'24 4:48:02
Hubbardston Station 14
1 42N29'05 71W59'12 4:47:57
Huckleberry Corner 12
1 41N50'00 70W46'15 4:43:05
Huckleberry Shores 12
1 41N49'25 70W57'00 4:43:48
Huckleyberry Shores 12
1 41N51 70W56 4:43:44
Hudson 9 1 42N23'30 71W34'00 4:46:16
Hull 12 1 42N18'07 70W54'30 4:43:38
Humarock 12 1 42N08'10 70W41'26 4:42:46
Hundred Acre Lot 14
1 42N05'50 71W40'10 4:46:41
Huntington 8 1 42N14'10 72W52'35 4:51:30
Hyannis 1 1 41N39'10 70W17'00 4:41:08
Hyannis Park 1 1 41N38'45 70W16'10 4:41:05
Hyannis Port 1 1 41N38'08 70W18'00 4:41:12
Hyde Park 13 1 42N15'20 71W07'30 4:44:30
Hydeville 14 1 42N40'58 72W04'20 4:48:17
Idlewell 11 1 42N13'50 70W57'20 4:43:49
Idlewood 3 1 41N38'10 70W58'50 4:43:55
Indian Lands 4 1 41N20'00 70W49'00 4:43:16
Indian Mound Beach 12
1 41N45 70W36 4:42:24
Indian Orchard 7
1 42N09'30 72W30'00 4:50:00
Indian Shore 12 1 41N49'25 70W54'55 4:43:40
Ingleside 7 1 42N10'30 72W38'00 4:50:32
Inland Park 3 1 41N44'05 70W56'45 4:43:47
Inman Square 9 1 42N22 71W06 4:44:24
Interlaken 2 1 42N18'52 73W19'52 4:53:19
Ipswich 5 1 42N40'45 70W50'30 4:43:22
Ironstone 14 1 42N01'42 71W36'40 4:46:27
Island 14 1 42N14'50 71W48'15 4:47:13
Island Creek 12 1 42N00'45 70W43'30 4:42:54
Islington 11 1 42N13'25 71W11'25 4:44:46
Jabez Corner 12 1 41N56'45 70W38'48 4:42:35
Jamaica Plain 13
1 42N18'35 71W07'15 4:44:29
Jamesville 14 1 42N14'10 71W51'15 4:47:25
Jefferson 14 1 42N21'50 71W52'53 4:47:32
Jefferson Shores 12
1 41N45 70W36 4:42:24
Jeffries Point 13
1 42N21'55 71W02'00 4:44:08
Jerneganville 4 1 41N24'06 70W33'21 4:42:13
John Fitzgerald Kennedy 13
1 42N19 71W05 4:44:20
Johnson Corner 7
1 42N04'00 72W41'40 4:50:47
Joppa 5 1 42N48'20 70W51'30 4:43:26
Judson 3 1 41N55'00 71W00'18 4:44:01
June Street 14 1 42N16'07 71W50'08 4:47:21
Katama 4 1 41N21'30 70W30'27 4:42:02
Kearney Square 9
1 42N38 71W18 4:45:12
Kelly Corner 9 1 42N28'30 71W27'15 4:45:49
Kempton Croft 3 1 41N38'25 71W00'35 4:44:02
Kenberma 12 1 42N17'00 70W52'30 4:43:30
Kendal Green 9 1 42N22'47 71W16'56 4:45:08
Kendall Square 9
1 42N22 71W05 4:44:20
Kenmore 13 1 42N21 71W06 4:44:24
Kent Corner 5 1 42N42'20 70W54'35 4:43:38
Kent Park 12 1 42N06'30 70W41'25 4:42:46
Kenwood 9 1 42N39'40 71W15'50 4:45:03
Kettle Cove Village 5
1 42N34'48 70W43'48 4:42:55
King Corner 6 1 42N33'53 72W57'02 4:51:48
Kingdom Hall 1 1 41N34'40 70W32'46 4:42:11
Kingsbury Beach 1
1 41N50'15 70W00'15 4:40:01
Kings Forest 5 1 42N41'20 70W58'50 4:43:55
Kings Landing 12
1 42N09'30 70W46'02 4:43:04
Kingston 9 1 41N24'55 72W14'42 4:48:59
Kingston 12 1 41N59'40 70W43'30 4:42:54
Kingston Plaza 12
1 41N58 70W40 4:42:40
Kingston Shores 12
1 41N59'53 70W42'15 4:42:49
Kinsman Corner 5
1 42N38'15 70W58'30 4:43:54
Kirby Corner 3 1 41N36'10 71W05'10 4:44:21
Kittville 14 1 42N11'23 71W39'23 4:46:38
Knights Corner 8
1 42N21'07 72W24'13 4:49:37
Knights Crossing 5
1 42N46'30 70W53'20 4:43:33
Knightville 8 1 42N17'00 72W52'00 4:51:28
Knollmere 3 1 41N38'07 70W51'36 4:43:26
Konkapot 2 1 42N04'38 73W09'45 4:52:39
Lagoon Heights 4
1 41N27'00 70W34'47 4:42:19
Lake Forest Park 9
1 42N18'30 71W21'15 4:45:25
Lake Hiawatha 11
1 42N05 71W28 4:45:52
Lake Mattawa 6 1 42N35 72W19 4:49:16
Lake Pearl 11 1 42N04 71W20 4:45:20
Lake Pleasant 6 1 42N33'23 72W31'07 4:50:04
Lakeside 3 1 41N40'00 71W06'30 4:44:26
Lakeside 12 1 41N51'05 70W54'35 4:43:38
Lake Street 9 1 42N25 71W10 4:44:40
Lakeview 9 1 42N24'10 71W14'30 4:44:58
Lakeview 14 1 42N16'00 71W45'35 4:47:02
Lakeview Heights 12
1 41N48'05 70W57'25 4:43:50
Lakeview Terrace 2
1 42N29'30 73W14'26 4:52:58
Lakeville 12 1 41N50'45 70W57'00 4:43:48
Lakewood 2 1 42N26'58 73W13'35 4:52:54
Lakewood Hills 1
1 41N45 70W27 4:41:48
Lakewood Park 14
1 42N31'45 71W52'45 4:47:31
Lambs Grove 14 1 42N16'30 71W58'06 4:47:52
Lancaster 14 1 42N27'20 71W40'25 4:46:42
Lands End 5 1 42N38'25 70W36'00 4:42:24
Lanesborough 2 1 42N31'02 73W13'43 4:52:55
Lanesville 5 1 42N40'40 70W39'35 4:42:38
Lane Village 14 1 42N39'37 71W56'15 4:47:45
Larrywaug 2 1 42N18'00 73W20'05 4:53:20
Laurel Park 8 1 42N21'30 72W38'30 4:50:34
Lawrence 5 1 42N42'25 71W09'49 4:44:39
Le Count Hollow 1
1 41N55'25 69W58'40 4:39:55
Lee 2 1 42N18'15 73W14'55 4:53:00
Leeds 8 1 42N21'05 72W42'00 4:50:48
Leicester 14 1 42N14'45 71W54'33 4:47:38

Leightons Corner 5 1 42N43'25 70W56'10 4:43:45
Leino Park 14 1 42N31'30 71W52'40 4:47:31
Lenox 2 1 42N21'23 73W17'07 4:53:08
Lenox Dale 2 1 42N20'10 73W14'45 4:52:59
Lenox Station 2 1 42N21'00 73W14'42 4:52:59
Leominster 14 1 42N31'30 71W45'37 4:47:02
Leverett 6 2 42N27'07 72W30'07 4:50:00
Leverett Station 6 2 42N27'02 72W31'23 4:50:06
Lexington 9 1 42N26'50 71W13'30 4:44:54
Leyden 6 1 42N42'00 72W37'50 4:50:31
Liberty Heights 7 1 42N07'22 72W35'45 4:50:23
Liberty Plain 12 1 42N11'20 70W53'00 4:43:32
Lincoln 9 1 42N25'33 71W18'16 4:45:13
Lincoln Heights 11 1 42N13'25 70W55'10 4:43:41
Linden 9 1 42N26'00 71W01'55 4:44:08
Lindenwood 9 1 42N29'00 71W06'30 4:44:26
Linebrook 5 1 42N40'48 70W55'45 4:43:43
Linwood 14 1 42N05'50 71W38'43 4:46:35
Lithia 8 1 42N27'22 72W50'08 4:51:21
Little Acres 12 1 42N03 70W51 4:43:24
Little Bridge 12 1 42N09'36 70W44'37 4:42:58
Little Egypt 2 1 42N36'20 73W04'53 4:52:20
Little Harbor Beach 12 1 41N46 70W43 4:42:52
Little Nahant 5 1 42N26'10 70W56'00 4:43:44
Little Neck 3 1 41N45 71W13 4:44:52
Little Neck 5 1 42N41'45 70W47'35 4:43:10
Little Rest 7 1 42N08'26 72W11'15 4:48:45
Little River 7 1 42N06'00 72W43'12 4:50:53
Littleton 9 1 42N32'15 71W30'45 4:46:03
Littleton Common 9 1 42N32'45 71W28'30 4:45:54
Littleville 7 1 42N17'15 72W53'30 4:51:34
Lobsterville 4 1 41N21'00 70W47'53 4:43:12
Lockerville 9 1 42N17 71W21 4:45:24
Locks Village 6 1 42N30'00 72W26'05 4:49:44
Lokerville 9 1 42N17'20 71W23'50 4:45:35
Long Beach 5 1 42N37 70W40 4:42:40
Long Hill Acres 12 1 42N06 70W48 4:43:12
Long Island 13 1 42N15 71W00 4:44:00
Long Josephs Point 10 1 41N14'45 70W06'00 4:40:24
Longmeadow 7 1 42N03'00 72W35'00 4:50:20
Long Plain 3 1 41N44'15 70W53'45 4:43:35
Long Pond Park 9 1 42N41'45 71W21'50 4:45:27
Long Pond Village 12 1 41N45 70W36 4:42:24
Longwood 11 1 42N20'30 71W06'45 4:44:27
Loudville 8 1 42N17'15 72W44'17 4:50:57
Lovell Corners 11 1 42N11'48 70W55'37 4:43:42
Lovellville 14 1 42N22'15 71W51'04 4:47:24
Lowell 9 1 42N38'00 71W19'00 4:45:16
Lowell Junction 5 1 42N36'50 71W09'45 4:44:39
Lower Mills 13 1 42N16'30 71W04'15 4:44:17
Lower Village 9 1 42N26'00 71W29'06 4:45:56
Lower Wire Village 14 1 42N15'50 71W59'38 4:47:59
Ludlow 7 1 42N09'36 72W28'35 4:49:54
Ludlow 14 1 42N14'23 71W50'55 4:47:24
Ludlow Center 7 1 42N11'30 72W27'35 4:49:50
Ludlow City 7 1 42N13'13 72W29'58 4:50:00
Lunds Corner 3 1 41N41 70W56 4:43:44
Lunenburg 14 1 42N35'40 71W43'30 4:46:54
Lunenburg Station 14 1 42N32'10 71W42'15 4:46:49
Luther Corner 3 1 41N44'41 71W13'25 4:44:54
Luthers Corners 3 1 41N48'33 71W20'15 4:45:21
Lynn 5 1 42N28'00 70W57'00 4:43:48
Lynnfield 5 1 42N32'20 71W02'55 4:44:12
Lynnhurst 5 1 42N28'15 70W59'45 4:43:59
Lyonsville 6 1 42N40'20 72W42'57 4:50:52
Macomber Corner 3 1 41N35'35 70W58'50 4:43:55
Macombers Corner 3 1 41N34'10 71W06'25 4:44:26
Madaket 10 1 41N16'22 70W11'55 4:40:48
Maddequet 10 1 41N17'15 70W11'30 4:40:46
Magnolia 5 1 42N34'25 70W42'40 4:42:51
Mahkeenac Heights 2 1 42N19'35 73W18'45 4:53:15
Malden 9 1 42N25'30 71W04'00 4:44:16
Manchaug 14 1 42N05'40 71W44'53 4:47:00
Manchester 5 1 42N34'40 70W46'10 4:43:05
Manleys Corner 12 1 42N02'30 71W03'30 4:44:14
Mann Hill Beach 12 1 42N13'22 70W45'00 4:43:00
Manomet 12 1 41N55'07 70W34'00 4:42:16
Manomet Beach 12 1 41N53'32 70W32'05 4:42:08
Manomet Bluffs 12 1 41N54'45 70W32'55 4:42:12
Manomet Heights 12 1 41N55'30 70W33'15 4:42:13
Mansfield 3 1 42N02'00 71W13'10 4:44:53
Manson Corner 12 1 42N12'05 70W47'02 4:43:08
Mantyranta 14 1 42N32'20 71W52'57 4:47:32
Maple Grove 2 1 42N36'53 73W07'45 4:52:31
Maple Park 5 1 42N46'06 71W09'45 4:44:39
Maple Ridge 11 1 42N04'30 71W28'50 4:45:55
Maplewood 9 1 42N26'10 71W03'05 4:44:12
Maplewood 14 1 42N13'38 71W43'30 4:46:54
Mara Vista 1 1 41N32'50 70W35'14 4:42:21
Marblehead 5 1 42N30'00 70W51'30 4:43:26
Marblehead Lighthouse 5 1 42N30'22 70W50'04 4:43:20
Marblehead Neck 5 1 42N30'00 70W50'15 4:43:21
Marble Ridge Station 5 1 42N40'45 71W05'54 4:44:24
Marion 12 1 41N42'00 70W45'48 4:43:03
Marions Camp 14 1 42N09'20 71W46'22 4:47:05
Marks Garrison 14 1 42N14'05 72W09'35 4:48:38
Marlboro 5 1 42N43'00 70W58'25 4:43:54
Marlborough 9 1 42N20'45 71W33'10 4:46:13
Marlborough Junction 9 1 42N19'53 71W32'30 4:46:10
Marshall Corner 12 1 42N03'35 71W04'00 4:44:16
Marsh Corner 5 1 42N43'40 71W13'55 4:44:56
Marshfield 12 1 42N05'30 70W42'22 4:42:49
Marshfield Center 12 1 42N07'00 70W43'00 4:42:52
Marshfield Hills 12 1 42N08'45 70W44'25 4:42:58
Marston Corners 5 1 42N44'30 71W10'07 4:44:40
Marstons Mills 1 1 41N39'22 70W25'00 4:41:40
Martha's Vineyard 4 1 41N25 70W40 4:42:40
Mashpee 1 1 41N38'54 70W28'54 4:41:56
Masons Corner 3 1 41N46'00 70W56'35 4:43:46
Massasoit 14 1 42N14'22 71W46'58 4:47:08
Matfield 12 1 42N02'00 70W59'50 4:43:59
Matfield Corner 12 1 42N01'48 71W00'33 4:44:02
Matfield Junction 12 1 42N02'07 70W59'17 4:43:57
Mathies Manor 7 1 42N11'25 72W33'55 4:50:16
Mattapan 13 1 42N16'20 71W05'15 4:44:21
Mattapoisett 12 1 41N39'30 70W49'00 4:43:16
Maushop Village 1 1 41N33'50 70W28'18 4:41:53
Maxim Corner 12 1 41N52'38 70W48'19 4:43:13
Mayflower Grove 12 1 42N02'30 70W50'35 4:43:22
Mayflower Heights 1 1 42N03'50 70W09'10 4:40:37
Maynard 9 1 42N26'00 71W27'00 4:45:48
Mayo Beach 1 1 41N55'50 70W02'30 4:40:10
Mayo Corners 6 1 42N41'00 72W18'42 4:49:15
McKnight and Bay 7 1 42N07'00 72W34'00 4:50:16
Meadow Brook 3 1 41N56'15 71W10'05 4:44:40
Meads Corner 8 1 42N21'14 72W25'25 4:49:42
Medfield 11 1 42N11'15 71W18'25 4:45:14
Medfield Junction 11 1 42N11'50 71W19'35 4:45:18
Medford 9 1 42N25'06 71W06'24 4:44:26
Medford Hillside 9 1 42N24'45 71W07'33 4:44:30
Medway 11 1 42N08'30 71W23'50 4:45:35
Meeting House Hill 13 1 42N18'25 71W03'45 4:44:15
Megansett 1 1 41N39'10 70W37'15 4:42:29
Melrose 9 1 42N27'30 71W04'00 4:44:16
Melrose Highlands 9 1 42N28'15 71W03'43 4:44:15
Menauhant 1 1 41N33'15 70W33'02 4:42:12
Mendon 14 1 42N06'20 71W33'10 4:46:13
Menemsha 4 1 41N21'06 70W45'53 4:43:04
Mercer Square 12 1 42N07'55 70W51'33 4:43:26
Meriams Corner 9 1 42N27'35 71W19'30 4:45:18
Merino Village 14 1 42N03'00 71W53'25 4:47:34
Merrick 7 1 42N07'00 72W37'30 4:50:30
Merrimac 5 1 42N49'50 71W00'10 4:44:01
Merrimack College 5 1 42N42 71W08 4:44:32
Merrimacport 5 1 42N49'40 70W59'20 4:43:57
Merrimac Terrace 5 1 42N28'56 71W00'15 4:44:01
Merrymount 11 1 42N15'45 70W59'45 4:43:59
Metcalf 9 1 42N11'00 71W26'45 4:45:47
Methuen 5 1 42N43'34 71W11'29 4:44:46
Middleboro 12 1 41N53'35 70W54'42 4:43:39
Middlefield 8 1 42N20'54 73W00'56 4:52:04
Middle Pasture 10 1 41N16'15 70W01'00 4:40:04
Middlesex Village 9 1 42N38'05 71W20'50 4:45:23
Middleton 5 1 42N35'42 71W01'00 4:44:04
Middleton Colony 5 1 42N35'25 70W59'35 4:43:58
Midland 11 1 42N05'35 71W28'55 4:45:56
Mikas Pond 10 1 41N17'00 70W06'13 4:40:25
Mileoak Corner 7 1 42N06'28 72W26'14 4:49:45
Miles Bridge 3 1 41N46'20 71W17'00 4:45:08
Milford 14 1 42N08'23 71W31'00 4:46:04
Millbrook 12 1 42N02'55 70W41'15 4:42:45
Millbury 14 1 42N11'38 71W45'38 4:47:03
Millbury Junction 14 1 42N14'05 71W44'00 4:46:56
Millers Falls 6 1 42N34'55 72W29'35 4:49:58
Millerville 14 1 42N01'15 71W30'00 4:46:00
Millington (historical) 6 1 42N28'35 72W18'00 4:49:12
Millis 11 1 42N10'03 71W21'30 4:45:26
Mill River 2 1 42N06'50 73W16'05 4:53:04
Mill River 6 1 42N30'05 72W38'30 4:50:34
Mill Street 14 1 42N15'55 71W51'00 4:47:24
Mill Valley 8 1 42N21'20 72W31'15 4:50:05
Mill Village 14 1 42N26'00 72W06'10 4:48:25
Millville 14 1 42N01'40 71W34'53 4:46:20
Milton 8 1 42N15'00 71W04'00 4:44:16
Milton Center 11 1 42N15'15 71W04'50 4:44:19
Milton Hill 11 1 42N15'54 71W03'30 4:44:14
Milton Upper Mills 11 1 42N15'40 71W05'45 4:44:23
Milton Village 11 1 42N16'00 71W04'20 4:44:17
Minot 12 1 42N14'25 70W45'45 4:43:03
Miramar 12 1 42N00'23 70W43'15 4:42:53
Mishaum Point 3 1 41N37 70W58 4:43:52
Mishawum 9 1 42N30'09 71W08'30 4:44:34
M I T 9 1 42N22 71W06 4:44:24
Mittineague 7 1 42N06'15 72W38'45 4:50:35
Monomoy 10 1 41N16'40 70W04'54 4:40:20
Monponsett 12 1 42N01'06 70W50'50 4:43:23
Monroe 6 1 42N43 72W59 4:51:56
Monroe Bridge 6 1 42N43'20 72W56'30 4:51:46
Monroes 3 1 41N46'32 71W19'00 4:45:16
Monson 7 1 42N06'15 72W19'10 4:49:17
Montague 6 1 42N32'08 72W32'08 4:50:09
Montague City 6 1 42N35'12 72W34'30 4:50:18
Montague Station 6 1 42N32'38 72W32'08 4:50:09
Montclair 11 1 42N16'15 71W02'10 4:44:09
Montello 12 1 42N06'30 71W01'00 4:44:04
Monterey 2 1 42N10'45 73W12'45 4:52:51
Montgomery 7 1 42N12'24 72W48'20 4:51:13
Montrose 9 1 42N30'57 71W03'15 4:44:13
Montserrat 5 1 42N33'45 70W52'00 4:43:28
Montvale 9 1 42N28'40 71W07'30 4:44:30
Montville 2 1 42N07'07 73W07'35 4:52:30
Monument Beach 1 1 41N43'10 70W36'45 4:42:27
Moody Corner 8 1 42N16'50 72W33'33 4:50:14
Moores Corner 6 2 42N29'40 72W28'08 4:49:53
Moores Corners 14 1 42N26'00 71W48'45 4:47:15
Morningdale 14 1 42N18'50 71W45'30 4:47:02
Morrills 11 1 42N11 71W12 4:44:48
Morris Corner 3 1 42N02'25 71W05'27 4:44:22
Morse Corner 3 1 42N03'00 71W05'07 4:44:20
Morse Village 6 1 42N32'35 72W20'15 4:49:21
Morseville 9 1 42N15'30 71W20'30 4:45:22
Morseville 14 1 42N08'43 71W58'10 4:47:53
Mountain Farms Mall 8 1 42N21 72W35 4:50:20
Mountain Park 7 1 42N14'37 72W37'55 4:50:32
Mount Auburn 9 1 42N22'30 71W09'00 4:44:36
Mount Bowdoin 13 1 42N18'15 71W04'30 4:44:18
Mount Hermon 6 1 42N40'05 72W29'09 4:49:57
Mount Hermon Station 6 1 42N41'02 72W29'31 4:49:58
Mount Hope 13 1 42N17'00 71W07'30 4:44:30
Mount Ida 13 1 42N18'15 71W03'48 4:44:15
Mount Pleasant 3 1 41N39'45 70W57'10 4:43:49
Mount Saint James 14 1 42N15 71W49 4:47:16
Mount Tom 8 1 42N17'10 72W37'00 4:50:28
Mount Vernon Park 5 1 42N41'15 71W10'00 4:44:40
Mount Washington 2 1 42N06 73W28 4:53:52
Mundale 7 1 42N07'06 72W48'42 4:51:15
Mungo Corner 12 1 42N11'40 70W46'53 4:43:08
Munns Ferry 6 1 42N39'15 72W28'00 4:49:52
Munroe Station 9 1 42N26'26 71W12'47 4:44:51
Muschopauge 14 1 42N23'51 71W55'15 4:47:41
Myricks 3 1 41N49'50 71W01'40 4:44:07
Mystic Grove 14 1 42N10'55 72W00'10 4:48:01
Mystic Junction 9 1 42N23 71W06 4:44:24
Nabnasset 9 1 42N36'45 71W25'15 4:45:41
Nabs Corner 4 1 41N22'20 70W41'00 4:42:44
Nahant 5 1 42N25'35 70W55'10 4:43:41
Namasket Village 12 1 41N54'15 70W55'50 4:43:43
Nameloc Heights 12 1 41N49'18 70W32'52 4:42:11
Namskaket 1 1 41N47'30 70W01'00 4:40:04
Nancys Corner 5 1 42N38'55 70W52'20 4:43:29
Nantasket Beach 12 1 42N16'40 70W52'00 4:43:28
Nantasket Junction 12 1 42N14'42 70W52'14 4:43:29
Nantucket 10 1 41N17'00 70W06'00 4:40:24
Narrow Creek 10 1 41N16'50 70W13'05 4:40:52
Nashaquitsa 4 1 41N19'15 70W46'13 4:43:05
Nasketucket 3 1 41N38'39 70W52'30 4:43:30
Natick 9 1 42N17'00 71W21'00 4:45:24
Natick Laboratories 9 1 42N17 71W21 4:45:24
Nauset Heights 1 1 41N48'15 69W56'37 4:39:46
Naushon Station 4 1 41N29'30 70W44'40 4:42:59
Neale Place 14 1 42N39'24 72W08'13 4:48:33
Needham 11 1 42N17'00 71W14'00 4:44:56
Needham Corner 5 1 42N31'05 70W57'00 4:43:48
Needham Heights 11 1 42N17'40 71W14'00 4:44:56
Needham Junction 11 1 42N16'20 71W14'45 4:44:59
Nelsons Grove 12 1 41N50'55 70W55'55 4:43:44
Nelsons Shores 12 1 41N49'30 70W56'15 4:43:45
Nemasket 12 1 41N54'43 70W52'52 4:43:31
Neponset 13 1 42N17'10 71W02'45 4:44:11
New Ashford 2 1 42N36'18 73W14'24 4:52:58
New Bedford 3 1 41N38'10 70W56'05 4:43:44
New Boston 1 1 41N43'55 70W12'15 4:40:49
New Boston 2 1 42N05'37 73W04'35 4:52:18
New Boston 14 1 42N24'07 71W59'37 4:47:58
New Braintree 14 1 42N19'00 72W07'35 4:48:30
Newbury 5 1 42N46 70W53 4:43:32
Newbury Old Town 5 1 42N46'00 70W50'45 4:43:23
Newburyport 5 1 42N48'45 70W52'40 4:43:31
Newcomb Hollow 1 1 41N57'50 69W59'48 4:39:59
New Lenox 2 1 42N23'40 73W14'35 4:52:58
New Marlboro 2 1 42N12 73W22 4:53:28
New Marlborough 2 1 42N07'22 73W13'45 4:52:55
New Salem 6 1 42N30'15 72W19'57 4:49:20
Newstead Montegrade 13 1 42N18'40 71W05'45 4:44:23
Newton 9 1 42N20'13 71W12'35 4:44:50
Newton Center 9 1 42N19'50 71W12'00 4:44:48
Newton Corner 9 1 42N21'40 71W11'45 4:44:47
Newton Highlands 9 1 42N19'15 71W12'00 4:44:48

Newton Lower Falls 9 1 42N19'45 71w15'15 4:45:01
Newton Upper Falls 9 1 42N18'50 71w13'12 4:44:53
Newtonville 9 1 42N21'00 71w12'15 4:44:49
Newtown 1 1 41N40'18 70w26'21 4:41:45
New Village 14 1 42N06'53 71w41'00 4:46:44
Nichewaug 14 1 42N26'15 72w12'15 4:48:49
Nine Acre Corner 9 1 42N25'45 71w22'36 4:45:30
Nipmuck Pond 14 1 42N06 71w33 4:46:12
Nobscot 9 1 42N19'45 71w26'13 4:45:45
Nobska Beach 12 1 41N46 70w43 4:42:52
Nonantum 9 1 42N21'45 71w12'10 4:44:49
Nonquitt 3 1 41N33'45 70w56'35 4:43:46
Noquochoke 3 1 41N37 71w04 4:44:16
Norfolk 11 1 42N07'10 71w19'32 4:45:18
Norfolk Downs 11 1 42N16'20 71w01'15 4:44:05
Norris Corner 9 1 42N41'24 71w24'06 4:45:36
North 3 1 41N40 70w56 4:43:44
North Abington 12 1 42N07'45 70w57'00 4:43:48
North Acton 9 1 42N30'45 71w24'45 4:45:39
North Adams 2 1 42N42'03 73w06'33 4:52:26
North Agawam 7 1 42N05'52 72w38'10 4:50:33
North Amherst 8 1 42N24'37 72w31'53 4:50:08
Northampton 8 1 42N19'30 72w38'30 4:50:34
North Andover 5 1 42N41'55 71w08'08 4:44:33
North Andover Center 5 1 42N41'00 71w06'45 4:44:27
North Ashburnham 14 1 42N40'30 71w56'37 4:47:46
North Attleboro 3 1 41N59'00 71w20'00 4:45:20
North Bellingham 11 1 42N07'15 71w27'22 4:45:49
North Bernardston 6 1 42N43'10 72w34'25 4:50:18
North Beverly 5 1 42N34'50 70w53'15 4:43:33
North Billerica 9 1 42N35'00 71w17'06 4:45:08
North Blandford 7 1 42N12'37 72w58'55 4:51:56
Northborough 14 1 42N19'10 71w38'30 4:46:34
Northbridge 14 1 42N09'05 71w39'00 4:46:36
Northbridge Center 14 1 42N08'05 71w40'23 4:46:42
North Brighton 13 1 42N21'30 71w08'20 4:44:33
North Brookfield 14 1 42N16'00 72w05'00 4:48:20
North Cambridge 9 1 42N23'45 71w07'50 4:44:31
North Carver 12 1 41N55'13 70w48'00 4:43:12
North Chatham 1 1 41N42'05 69w57'15 4:39:49
North Chelmsford 9 1 42N38'20 71w23'00 4:45:32
North Chester 7 1 42N19'25 72w55'40 4:51:43
North Chicopee 7 1 42N11'00 72w36'00 4:50:24
North Cohasset 11 1 42N15'30 70w50'35 4:43:22
North Commons 11 1 42N14'50 71w01'00 4:44:04
North Dana (historical) 14 1 42N27'20 72w16'45 4:49:07
North Dartmouth 3 1 41N38'20 70w58'15 4:43:53
North Dennis 1 1 41N44'23 70w13'15 4:40:53
North Dighton 3 1 41N51'50 71w07'30 4:44:30
North Duxbury 12 1 42N04'17 70w43'15 4:42:53
North Eastham 1 1 41N51'54 69w59'30 4:39:58
North Easton 3 1 42N04'00 71w06'15 4:44:25
North Egremont 2 1 42N11'48 73w26'18 4:53:45
North End 7 1 42N06'48 72w36'15 4:50:25
North End 13 1 42N21'54 71w13'18 4:44:53
Northey Point 5 1 42N31 70w54 4:43:36
North Fairhaven 3 1 41N39'30 70w54'30 4:43:38
North Falmouth 1 1 41N38'45 70w37'08 4:42:29
North Falmouth Station 1 1 41N38'53 70w36'52 4:42:27
North Farms 8 1 42N21'55 72w40'18 4:50:41
Northfield 6 1 42N41'45 72w27'12 4:49:49
Northfield Farms 6 2 42N36'53 72w28'30 4:49:54
North Foxboro 11 1 42N04'36 71w15'30 4:45:02
North Grafton 14 1 42N14'00 71w42'30 4:46:50
North Hadley 8 1 42N23'10 72w34'55 4:50:20
North Hancock 2 1 42N36'40 73w17'17 4:53:09
North Hanover 12 1 42N08'45 70w52'05 4:43:28
North Hanson 12 1 42N03'30 70w54'00 4:43:36
North Harwich 1 1 41N41'45 70w07'15 4:40:29
North Hatfield 8 2 42N24'40 72w37'22 4:50:29
North Heath 6 1 42N42'23 72w49'35 4:51:18
North Lakeville 12 1 41N51 70w56 4:43:44
North Lancaster 14 1 42N28 71w41 4:46:44
North Leominster 14 1 42N32'30 71w44'15 4:46:57
North Leverett 6 2 42N30'30 72w29'35 4:49:58
North Lexington 9 1 42N27'48 71w14'15 4:44:57
North Littleton 9 1 42N32 71w31 4:46:04
North Marshfield 12 1 42N08'35 70w46'15 4:43:05
North Middleboro 12 1 41N56'00 70w58'30 4:43:54
North Milford 14 1 42N11'00 71w32'18 4:46:09
North Monson 7 1 42N07'20 72w18'30 4:49:14
North Natick 9 1 42N18'05 71w21'30 4:45:26
North New Salem 6 1 42N32'45 72w19'10 4:49:17
North Orange 6 1 42N38'07 72w15'45 4:49:03
North Otis 2 1 42N13'53 73w06'35 4:52:26
North Oxford 14 1 42N09'00 71w52'08 4:47:29
North Pasture 10 1 41N16'30 70w03'15 4:40:13
North Pembroke 12 1 42N05'35 70w47'35 4:43:10
North Pepperell 9 1 42N41'35 71w35'30 4:46:22
North Plymouth 12 1 41N58'15 70w41'00 4:42:44
North Plympton 12 1 41N59'18 70w48'28 4:43:14
North Pocasset 1 1 41N41'45 70w36'20 4:42:25
North Prescott 6 1 42N27'22 72w20'39 4:49:23
North Quincy 11 1 42N16'37 71w01'15 4:44:05
North Randolph 11 1 42N11'50 71w03'45 4:44:15
North Reading 9 1 42N34'30 71w04'45 4:44:19
North Rehoboth 3 1 41N54'10 71w13'10 4:44:53
North Rochester 12 1 41N46'55 70w53'25 4:43:34
North Rutland 14 1 42N25'50 71w58'35 4:47:54
North Salem 5 1 42N31'35 70w54'20 4:43:37
North Saugus 5 1 42N29'45 71w01'13 4:44:05
North Scituate 12 1 42N13'08 70w47'10 4:43:09
North Seekonk 3 1 41N52 71w19 4:45:16
North Shirley 9 1 42N35'05 71w38'50 4:46:35
Northside 14 1 42N09'53 71w57'13 4:47:49
North Sommerville 9 1 42N23 71w06 4:44:24
North Spencer 14 1 42N18'23 71w59'10 4:47:57
North Stoughton 11 1 42N09'05 71w04'30 4:44:18
North Sudbury 9 1 42N24'33 71w24'18 4:45:37
North Sunderland 6 2 42N30'15 72w33'30 4:50:14
North Swansea 3 1 41N46'05 71w15'50 4:45:03
North Tewksbury 9 1 42N38'04 71w14'47 4:44:59
North Tisbury 4 1 41N24'20 70w40'30 4:42:42
North Truro 1 1 42N02'00 70w05'45 4:40:23
North Uxbridge 14 1 42N05'15 71w38'30 4:46:34
North Village 14 1 42N03'40 71w52'45 4:47:31
Northville 12 1 42N03'37 70w55'40 4:43:43
North Waltham 9 1 42N23 71w14 4:44:56
Northwest Duxbury 12 1 42N03'30 70w44'30 4:42:58
North Weymouth 11 1 42N14'45 70w56'50 4:43:47
North Wilbraham 7 1 42N09'10 72w25'31 4:49:42
North Wilmington 9 1 42N34'10 71w09'25 4:44:38
North Woburn 9 1 42N30'30 71w09'30 4:44:38
North Woods 14 1 42N23'30 71w52'38 4:47:31
North Worcester 14 1 42N19'00 71w49'05 4:47:16
Norton 3 1 41N58'00 71w11'15 4:44:45
Norton Grove 3 1 41N59'30 71w11'45 4:44:47
Norwell 12 1 42N09'42 70w47'40 4:43:11
Norwich 8 1 42N17'20 72w50'20 4:51:21
Norwich Bridge 8 1 42N14'53 72w52'10 4:51:29
Norwood 11 1 42N11'40 71w12'00 4:44:48
Nutting Lake 9 1 42N32'16 71w16'10 4:45:05
Oak Bluffs 4 1 41N27'15 70w33'45 4:42:15
Oakdale 7 1 42N12'15 72w37'30 4:50:30
Oakdale 11 1 42N14'25 71w09'10 4:44:37
Oakdale 12 1 41N45'30 70w42'30 4:42:50
Oakdale 14 1 42N23'25 71w47'38 4:47:11
Oakdale Village 12 1 41N46 70w43 4:42:52
Oak Grove 9 1 42N26'05 71w04'30 4:44:18
Oakham 14 1 42N21'10 72w02'45 4:48:11
Oak Hill 14 1 42N15'30 71w47'25 4:47:10
Oak Hill Park 9 1 42N17'40 71w11'10 4:44:45
Oak Island 13 1 42N25'30 70w59'15 4:43:57
Oakland 3 1 41N54'40 71w08'20 4:44:33
Oakland 9 1 42N29 71w09 4:44:36
Oakland Heights 14 1 42N13'30 71w46'50 4:47:07
Oaklands 9 1 42N38'00 71w17'10 4:45:09
Oakland Square 12 1 42N02'10 70w48'02 4:43:12
Oakland Vale 5 1 42N28'18 71w01'55 4:44:08
O'Briens Corner 7 1 42N05'15 72w38'25 4:50:34
Ocean Bluff 12 1 42N05'50 70w39'15 4:42:37
Ocean Grove 3 1 41N43'45 71w12'35 4:44:50
Ocean Heights 4 1 41N24'23 70w33'08 4:42:13
Ocean Spray 13 1 42N22 70w59 4:43:56
Ocean View 5 1 42N41'05 70w37'30 4:42:30
Oklahoma Heights 4 1 41N26'20 70w36'33 4:42:26
Old Boat Point 11 1 42N14'18 70w58'24 4:43:54
Old Cambridge 9 1 42N22'40 71w07'00 4:44:28
Old City 9 1 42N38'15 71w43'48 4:46:55
Old Common 14 1 42N11'05 71w47'10 4:47:09
Old Furnace 14 1 42N18 72w12 4:48:48
Oldham Pines 12 1 42N04'20 70w49'45 4:43:19
Oldham Village 12 1 42N04'00 70w49'45 4:43:19
Old Harbor 1 1 41N36'00 69w59'00 4:39:56
Old Hill 7 1 42N06'15 72w34'05 4:50:16
Old Mouth North River 12 1 42N07'33 70w40'47 4:42:43
Old North Ashburnham Station 14 1 42N39'20 71w59'00 4:47:56
Old Oaken Bucket Homestead 12 1 42N10'40 70w45'23 4:43:02
Old Quaker Meetinghouse 1 1 41N44'47 70w27'32 4:41:50
Old Silver Beach 1 1 41N37'36 70w38'12 4:42:33
Old Spain 11 1 42N14'36 70w56'39 4:43:47
Old Sturbridge Village 14 1 42N06'25 72w05'57 4:48:24
Old Town Landing 3 1 41N48'15 71w07'17 4:44:29
Onset 12 1 41N44'30 70w39'30 4:42:38
Onset Station 12 1 41N45'22 70w40'39 4:42:43
Orange 6 1 42N35'25 72w18'37 4:49:14
Ordway 9 1 42N24 71w35 4:46:20
Orient Heights 13 1 42N23'15 71w00'15 4:44:01
Orleans 1 1 41N47'23 69w59'25 4:39:58
Osceola 2 1 42N23 73w22 4:53:28
Osterville 1 1 41N37'42 70w23'15 4:41:33
Otis 2 1 42N11'35 73w05'32 4:52:22
Otis Air Force Base 1 1 41N39 70w33 4:42:12
Otter River 14 1 42N35'52 72w03'05 4:48:12
Overbrook 11 1 42N18'18 71w19'30 4:45:18
Oxford 3 1 41N39'20 70w54'25 4:43:38
Oxford 14 1 42N07'00 71w51'55 4:47:28
Oxford Center 14 1 42N07 71w52 4:47:28
Oxford Heights 14 1 42N10'25 71w52'45 4:47:31
Oyster Harbors 1 1 41N37'15 70w24'57 4:41:40
Packard Heights 6 1 42N38'00 72w13'47 4:48:55
Packardville 8 1 42N20'45 72w23'05 4:49:32
Padanaram Village 3 1 41N37 70w58 4:43:52
Pages Beach 14 1 42N38 71w54 4:47:36
Pakachoag 14 1 42N13'30 71w48'50 4:47:15
Palmer 7 1 42N09'30 72w19'45 4:49:19
Palmer Center 7 1 42N10'52 72w18'55 4:49:16
Paper Mill Village 9 1 42N37'31 71w35'36 4:46:22
Paper Mill Village 12 1 41N59'25 70w56'33 4:43:46
Parkers Station 14 1 42N38'30 72w06'45 4:48:27
Parkerville 9 1 42N33'08 71w26'20 4:45:45
Park Street 9 1 42N25 71w07 4:44:28
Parkwood Beach 12 1 41N44'45 70w42'00 4:42:48
Partridgeville 14 1 42N32'52 72w02'52 4:48:11
Pattenville 9 1 42N34'45 71w13'36 4:44:54
Patuisset 1 1 41N41'00 70w37'37 4:42:30
Pawtucketville 9 1 42N39'30 71w19'50 4:45:19
Paxton 14 1 42N18'40 71w55'43 4:47:43
Payson Park 9 1 42N22'45 71w10'00 4:44:40
Peabody 5 1 42N31'40 70w55'45 4:43:43
Pelham 8 1 42N23'35 72w24'15 4:49:37
Pemberton 12 1 42N18'20 70w55'03 4:43:40
Pembroke 12 1 42N04'17 70w48'35 4:43:14
Pembroke Heights 12 1 42N06 70w48 4:43:12
Pembroke Pines 12 1 42N03 70w51 4:43:24
Pepperell 9 1 42N39'57 71w35'20 4:46:21
Pequoig 14 1 42N40'00 72w00'45 4:48:03
Perrins Crossing 3 1 41N53'10 71w19'20 4:45:17
Perry Manor 7 1 42N12'00 72w33'15 4:50:13
Perrys Corner 3 1 41N50'36 71w12'05 4:44:48
Perryville 3 1 41N51'45 71w15'30 4:45:02
Perryville 14 1 42N01'30 71w53'17 4:47:33
Peru 2 1 42N26'17 73w02'47 4:52:11
Petersham 14 1 42N29'15 72w11'15 4:48:45
Phelps Mills 5 1 42N32 70w57 4:43:48
Phillips Point 5 1 42N27'50 70w53'45 4:43:35
Phillipston 14 1 42N32'55 72w08'00 4:48:32
Phillipston Four Corners 14 1 42N34'10 72w08'00 4:48:32
Pierces Bridge 9 1 42N26 71w14 4:44:56
Pierceville 12 1 41N47 70w46 4:43:04
Piety Corner 9 1 42N23'25 71w14'23 4:44:58
Pigeon Cove 5 1 42N40'25 70w38'00 4:42:32
Pilgrim Heights 1 1 42N03'25 70w06'55 4:40:28
Pilgrim Pines Estates 12 1 42N03 70w51 4:43:24
Pilgrim Village 11 1 42N05 71w28 4:45:52
Pine Bluffs 12 1 41N49'30 70w55'25 4:43:42
Pinecrest 14 1 42N15'12 71w45'10 4:47:01
Pinedale 14 1 42N36'45 72w14'15 4:48:57
Pinefield 5 1 42N41'20 70w54'10 4:43:37
Pine Grove 8 1 42N18'05 72w42'25 4:50:50
Pine Grove 11 1 42N09'40 70w55'50 4:43:43
Pine Hill Acres 3 1 41N42'50 70w56'50 4:43:47
Pinehurst 9 1 42N31'45 71w13'43 4:44:55
Pinehurst Beach 12 1 41N44'48 70w42'37 4:42:50
Pine Island 5 1 42N46'33 70w49'40 4:43:19
Pine Island Lake 8 1 42N20 72w40 4:50:40
Pine Lake 9 1 42N23'45 71w27'15 4:45:49
Pine Point 7 1 42N07'15 72w31'45 4:50:07
Pine Rest 9 1 42N23'20 71w26'15 4:45:45
Pines, The 9 1 42N32'37 71w13'38 4:44:55
Pine Tree Corner 1 1 41N37'07 70w29'14 4:41:57
Piney Point Beach 12 1 41N41'45 70w43'20 4:42:53
Pingryville 9 1 42N33'06 71w32'13 4:46:09
Pitcherville 14 1 42N31'35 72w01'53 4:48:08
Pittsfield 2 1 42N27'00 73w14'45 4:52:59
Plainfield 8 1 42N30'55 72w55'00 4:51:40
Plainfield 10 1 41N16'30 69w59'00 4:39:56
Plainville 3 1 41N40'55 70w57'40 4:43:51
Plainville 8 1 42N22'39 72w33'00 4:50:12

Plainville 11 1 42N00'15 71w20'00 4:45:20
Pleasant Hills 5 1 42N27'20 71w00'50 4:44:03
Pleasant Lake 1 1 41N42'50 70w04'58 4:40:20
Pleasant Valley 14 1 42N21'20 71w46'10 4:47:05
Plimptonville 11 1 42N09'35 71w14'15 4:44:57
Plowed Neck 1 1 41N44'30 70w26'30 4:41:46
Plumbush 5 1 42N47'50 70w49'45 4:43:19
Plum Island 5 1 42N48'45 70w48'50 4:43:15
Plummer Corner 14 1 42N07'20 71w38'53 4:46:36
Plymouth 12 1 41N57'30 70w40'04 4:42:40
Plympton 12 1 41N57'10 70w48'54 4:43:16
Pocasset 1 1 41N41'10 70w37'00 4:42:28
Pocasset Station 1 1 41N41'36 70w36'57 4:42:28
Pocomo 10 1 41N18'50 70w01'15 4:40:05
Podunk 14 1 42N14 72w03 4:48:12
Point Allerton 12 1 42N17 70w53 4:43:32
Point Independence 12 1 41N44'30 70w39'00 4:42:36
Point of Pines 13 1 42N26'24 70w58'00 4:43:52
Point Pleasant 14 1 42N03 71w54 4:47:36
Point Shirley 13 1 42N21'35 70w58'15 4:43:53
Polpis 10 1 41N17'54 70w00'48 4:40:03
Ponakin Mill 14 1 42N28'52 71w41'15 4:46:45
Pondsville 1 1 41N41'06 70w25'15 4:41:41
Pond Village 1 1 42N01'50 70w05'40 4:40:23
Pondville 11 1 42N05'25 71w17'28 4:45:10
Pondville 12 1 41N48'00 70w35'57 4:42:24
Pondville 14 1 42N11'45 71w49'19 4:47:17
Ponkapoag 11 1 42N11'30 71w07'05 4:44:28
Pontoosuc 2 1 42N28'45 73w14'45 4:52:59
Pontoosuc Gardens 2 1 42N29'40 73w14'15 4:52:57
Pope Beach 3 1 41N37'55 70w52'45 4:43:31
Popponesset Beach 1 1 41N34'25 70w27'45 4:41:51
Post Island 11 1 42N15'45 70w58'28 4:43:54
Pottersville 3 1 41N45'00 71w08'30 4:44:34
Pratt Junction 14 1 42N28'07 71w44'30 4:46:58
Pratts Corner 3 1 42N01'02 71w05'42 4:44:23
Pratts Corner 6 1 42N25'03 72w28'30 4:49:54
Prattville 3 1 41N56'20 71w04'50 4:44:19
Precinct 12 1 41N51'20 70w58'50 4:43:55
Prentice Corner 14 1 42N06'34 71w41'46 4:46:47
Prentice Gardens 14 1 42N07 71w40 4:46:40
Prescott (historical) 6 1 42N23'30 72w20'45 4:49:23
Prides Crossing 5 1 42N33'35 70w49'30 4:43:18
Princeton 14 1 42N26'55 71w52'40 4:47:31
Princeton Station 14 1 42N26'53 71w55'30 4:47:42
Priscilla Beach 12 1 41N55'55 70w34'00 4:42:16
Proctor 5 1 42N32'05 70w57'10 4:43:49
Proctors corner 14 1 42N15'18 71w57'55 4:47:52
Prospect Hill 12 1 41N56'38 70w49'25 4:43:18
Prospectville 9 1 42N23'45 71w15'50 4:45:03
Provincetown 1 1 42N03'30 70w10'45 4:40:43
Prudential Center 13 1 42N19 71w05 4:44:20
Purdy Corner 3 1 42N00'23 71w14'57 4:45:00
Putnamville 5 1 42N35'10 70w56'15 4:43:45
Quaise 10 1 41N17'38 70w02'10 4:40:09
Quansoo 4 1 41N21'00 70w39'45 4:42:39
Quidnet 10 1 41N18'15 69w58'50 4:39:55
Quinapoxet 14 1 42N22'40 71w51'05 4:47:24
Quincy 11 1 42N15'10 71w00'10 4:44:01
Quincy Center 11 1 42N14'45 71w00'30 4:44:02
Quincy Neck 11 1 42N14'28 70w58'15 4:43:53
Quincy Point 11 1 42N14'45 70w59'00 4:43:56
Quinsigamond Village 14 1 42N13'45 71w47'50 4:47:11
Quissett 1 1 41N32'36 70w39'00 4:42:36
Quitnesset 1 1 41N39'23 69w57'45 4:39:51
Racing Beach 1 1 41N33'15 70w39'18 4:42:37
Raddin Station 5 1 42N27'35 70w58'45 4:43:55
Rakeville 11 1 42N01'32 71w27'55 4:45:52
Randolph 11 1 42N09'45 71w02'30 4:44:10
Raynham 3 1 41N56'55 71w04'25 4:44:18
Raynham Center 3 1 41N55'25 71w03'10 4:44:13
Reading 9 1 42N31'32 71w05'45 4:44:23
Reading Highlands 9 1 42N31'30 71w06'45 4:44:27
Readville 13 1 42N14'25 71w08'15 4:44:33
Readville Manor 11 1 42N13'45 71w08'40 4:44:35
Readyville Manor 11 1 42N14 71w10 4:44:40
Red Bridge 7 1 42N10'30 72w24'39 4:49:39
Redgate Corner 3 1 41N36'15 70w56'40 4:43:47
Redstone Shopping Center 9 1 42N29 71w06 4:44:24
Reeds Corner 11 1 42N13'18 70w48'30 4:43:14
Rehoboth 3 1 41N50'25 71w15'00 4:45:00
Renfrew 2 1 42N38'16 73w06'47 4:52:27
Reservoir 11 1 42N20'07 71w08'55 4:44:36
Revere 13 1 42N24'30 71w00'45 4:44:03
Revere Beach 13 1 42N25 71w00 4:44:00
Rexhame 12 1 42N06'50 70w40'30 4:42:42
Rial Side 5 1 42N33'00 70w53'45 4:43:35
Rice Square 14 1 42N14'45 71w47'20 4:47:09
Richardson Corners 14 1 42N09'04 71w55'32 4:47:42
Richmond 2 1 42N22'23 73w22'05 4:53:28
Richmond Furnace 2 1 42N21'40 73w22'52 4:53:31
Rings Island 5 1 42N49'00 70w52'00 4:43:28
Ringville 8 1 42N22'10 72w54'37 4:51:38
Rio Vista 9 1 42N32'35 71w18'20 4:45:13
Risingdale 2 1 42N14'55 73w21'20 4:53:25
Riverdale 5 1 42N38'00 70w40'30 4:42:42
Riverdale 7 1 42N07'00 72w37'30 4:50:30
Riverdale 11 1 42N16'20 71w10'40 4:44:43
Riverdale 14 1 42N08'18 71w38'23 4:46:34
Riverdale Station 5 1 42N38'30 70w40'20 4:42:41
Rivermoor 12 1 42N10'30 70w43'00 4:42:52
River Pines 9 1 42N33'50 71w17'20 4:45:09
Riverside 2 1 42N43 73w12 4:52:48
Riverside 5 1 42N45'50 71w03'00 4:44:12
Riverside 6 1 42N36'40 72w32'50 4:50:11
Riverside 9 1 42N32'10 71w18'15 4:45:13
Riverside 12 1 41N45'00 70w39'20 4:42:37
Riverview 5 1 42N37'55 70w40'55 4:42:44
Riverview 9 1 42N22'20 71w14'40 4:44:59
Riverview Landing 5 1 42N37'40 70w41'20 4:42:45
Roaring Brook Camp 6 1 42N28'53 72w40'08 4:50:41
Roberts 9 1 42N23 71w14 4:44:56
Robin Hill 9 1 42N21'38 71w35'47 4:46:23
Robinson Crusoe Camp 14 1 42N05'35 72w05'44 4:48:23
Robinsonville 3 1 42N00'45 71w16'00 4:45:04
Rochdale 14 1 42N11'40 71w54'23 4:47:38
Rochester 12 1 41N43'54 70w49'14 4:43:17
Rock 12 1 41N50'30 70w51'43 4:43:27
Rockdale 2 1 42N16 73w22 4:53:28
Rockdale 3 1 41N39'06 70w57'36 4:43:50
Rockdale Mills 2 1 42N17'28 73w22'36 4:53:30
Rock Harbor 1 1 41N47'50 70w00'15 4:40:01
Rock Island 11 1 42N15'44 70w57'45 4:43:51
Rockland 12 1 42N07'50 70w55'00 4:43:40
Rock Landing 1 1 41N33'54 70w28'10 4:41:53
Rockport 5 1 42N39'20 70w37'15 4:42:29
Rocks Village 5 1 42N48'35 71w00'10 4:44:01
Rock Valley 7 1 42N11'38 72w40'35 4:50:42
Rockville 11 1 42N08'26 71w21'35 4:45:26
Rocky Hill 14 1 42N09'08 71w29'16 4:45:57
Rocky Neck 5 1 42N36'20 70w39'30 4:42:38
Rocky Nook 12 1 41N59'15 70w42'03 4:42:48
Rocky Nook Park 12 1 41N59'37 70w42'05 4:42:48
Rocky Nook Point 12 1 41N59'55 70w42'27 4:42:50
Rolling Acres Estates 9 1 42N37 71w25 4:45:40
Roosterville 2 1 42N04'45 73w04'23 4:52:18
Rooty Plain 5 1 42N42'10 70w57'05 4:43:48
Rosemont 2 1 42N48'13 71w06'42 4:44:27
Roslindale 13 1 42N17'28 71w07'30 4:44:30
Rowe 6 2 42N41'36 72w54'00 4:51:36
Rowley 5 1 42N43'00 70w52'45 4:43:31
Roxbury 13 1 42N19'30 71w05'45 4:44:23
Roxbury Crossing 13 1 42N19'50 71w05'30 4:44:22
Royalston 14 1 42N40'39 72w11'18 4:48:45
Ruralville 14 1 42N23'24 71w52'36 4:47:30
Russell 7 1 42N11'23 72w51'35 4:51:26
Russells Mills 3 1 41N34'20 71w00'25 4:44:02
Russellville 8 1 42N12'07 72w46'07 4:51:04
Rust Craft 11 1 42N14 71w10 4:44:40
Rutland 14 1 42N22'10 71w56'55 4:47:48
Rye Hill 12 1 42N05'10 70w54'30 4:43:38
Saconesset Hills 1 1 41N34'40 70w38'25 4:42:34
Sagamore 1 1 41N46'12 70w31'44 4:42:07
Sagamore Beach 1 1 41N47'54 70w31'46 4:42:07
Sagamore Highlands 1 1 41N48'24 70w32'10 4:42:09
Saint Hyacinth College Semin 8 1 42N16 72w31 4:50:04
Salem 5 1 42N31'10 70w53'50 4:43:35
Salem Neck 5 1 42N32'00 70w52'05 4:43:28
Salem State College 5 1 42N31 70w54 4:43:36
Salisbury 5 1 42N50'30 70w51'40 4:43:27
Salisbury Beach 5 1 42N50'35 70w49'05 4:43:16
Salisbury Heights 14 1 42N17'38 71w50'45 4:47:23
Salisbury Plains 5 1 42N52'10 70w53'00 4:43:32
Salisbury Point 5 1 42N50'30 70w54'45 4:43:39
Salters Point 3 1 41N37 70w58 4:43:52
Sampsons Corner 12 1 41N51'00 70w56'45 4:43:47
Sandersdale 14 1 42N04'10 72w00'45 4:48:03
Sand Hill 12 1 42N12 70w44 4:42:56
Sand Hills 12 1 42N12'35 70w43'32 4:42:54
Sandisfield 2 1 42N06'45 73w08'37 4:52:34
Sandwich 1 1 41N45'32 70w29'40 4:41:59
Sandy Beach 11 1 42N14 70w48 4:43:12
Sandy Beach 14 1 42N20'20 71w56'40 4:47:47
Sandy Hill 7 1 42N09'15 72w36'25 4:50:26
Santuit 1 1 41N38'15 70w27'04 4:41:48
Satans Kingdom 6 1 42N42'45 72w28'50 4:49:55
Saugus 5 1 42N27'53 71w00'38 4:44:03
Saundersville 14 1 42N10'53 71w42'17 4:46:49
Savin Hill 13 1 42N18'45 71w03'30 4:44:14
Savoy 2 1 42N34'00 73w01'45 4:52:07
Savoy Center 2 1 42N36'25 73w02'35 4:52:10
Saxonville 9 1 42N19'35 71w24'00 4:45:36
Schoosett 12 1 42N06'15 70w47'55 4:43:12
Scituate 12 1 42N11'45 70w43'35 4:42:54
Scituate Center 12 1 42N12'15 70w45'40 4:43:03
Scituate Station 12 1 42N11'35 70w44'30 4:42:58
Scorton Shores 1 1 41N44'30 70w24'45 4:41:39
Scotland 12 1 41N58'20 71w00'25 4:44:02
Scott Corners 7 1 42N10'55 72w30'22 4:50:01
Scott Hill Acres 11 1 42N04'05 71w28'15 4:45:53
Searstown 14 1 42N32 71w46 4:47:04
Searsville 8 1 42N24'03 72w44'45 4:50:59
Sea View 12 1 42N08'22 70w42'50 4:42:51
Second Cliff 12 1 42N11'30 70w43'06 4:42:52
Seekonk 3 1 41N48'30 71w20'15 4:45:21
Segreganset 3 1 41N50'12 71w06'50 4:44:27
Sesachacha 10 1 41N17'00 69w59'00 4:39:56
Shakerhill 9 1 42N27'30 71w10'50 4:44:43
Shaker Village 2 1 42N25'53 73w20'15 4:53:21
Shaker Village 9 1 42N31'45 71w39'00 4:46:36
Shallow Pond 10 1 41N17'36 70w07'54 4:40:32
Sharon 11 1 42N07'25 71w10'45 4:44:43
Sharon Heights 11 1 42N06'30 71w11'50 4:44:47
Shattuckville 6 1 42N38'15 72w43'37 4:50:54
Shawkemo 10 1 41N17'40 70w03'30 4:40:14
Shawsheen Heights 5 1 42N40'32 71w09'35 4:44:38
Shawsheen Village 5 1 42N40'20 71w08'40 4:44:35
Shea Corner 7 1 42N02'30 72w42'05 4:50:48
Sheffield 2 1 42N06'37 73w21'20 4:53:25
Shelburne 6 1 42N35'23 72w41'20 4:50:45
Shelburne Falls 6 1 42N36'15 72w44'23 4:50:58
Sheldonville 11 1 42N02'05 71w23'15 4:45:33
Shell Beach 12 1 41N38'29 70w48'22 4:43:13
Shepardville 11 1 42N01'23 71w18'32 4:45:14
Sherborn 9 1 42N14'20 71w22'13 4:45:29
Sherman Corner 12 1 42N11'03 70w46'43 4:43:07
Sherwood Forest 2 1 42N20 73w05 4:52:20
Sherwood Forest 3 1 41N42'25 70w55'40 4:43:43
Sherwood Plaza 9 1 42N17 71w21 4:45:24
Shimmo 10 1 41N17'10 70w04'30 4:40:18
Shirkshire 6 1 42N33'05 72w43'37 4:50:54
Shirley 9 1 42N32'37 71w39'00 4:46:36
Shirley Center 9 1 42N34'20 71w39'05 4:46:36
Shooters Island 1 1 41N37'25 69w58'40 4:39:55
Shoppers' World 9 1 42N18 71w25 4:45:40
Shore Acres 3 1 41N33'25 70w56'25 4:43:46
Shore Acres 12 1 42N12'52 70w44'20 4:42:57
Shrewsbury 14 1 42N17'45 71w42'48 4:46:51
Shrewsbury Street 14 1 42N16'05 71w47'15 4:47:09
Shutesbury 6 1 42N27'23 72w24'37 4:49:38
Shutleff Corner 12 1 41N54'40 70w46'09 4:43:05
Siasconset 10 1 41N15'45 69w58'00 4:39:52
Sibleys Corner 14 1 42N15'06 71w58'38 4:47:55
Silver Beach 1 1 42N38'25 70w38'15 4:42:33
Silver Hill 9 1 42N23'45 71w18'10 4:45:13
Silver Lake 9 1 42N34'10 71w11'30 4:44:46
Silver Lake 12 1 42N00'15 70w47'37 4:43:10
Silver Shell Beach 3 1 41N36'30 70w51'55 4:43:28
Silver Spring Beach 1 1 41N52 69w59 4:39:56
Sippewisset 1 1 41N33'55 70w38'49 4:42:35
Sissons Corner 3 1 41N37'10 71w03'10 4:44:13
Sixteen Acres 7 1 42N07'00 72w30'05 4:50:00
Sky Farm 6 1 42N38'24 72w25'13 4:49:41
Skyland 7 1 42N04'17 73w02'51 4:52:11
Slades Corner 3 1 41N34'10 71w01'59 4:44:08
Slades Ferry 3 1 41N43'15 71w09'30 4:44:38
Slocums Corner 3 1 41N32'40 71w00'35 4:44:02
Smalltown 1 1 41N35'45 70w32'17 4:42:09
Smith Highlands 7 1 42N11'40 72w35'20 4:50:21
Smith Mills 3 1 41N38'20 70w59'30 4:43:58
Smiths (historical) 6 1 42N19'45 72w19'36 4:49:18
Smiths Ferry 7 1 42N15'30 72w36'53 4:50:28
Smithville 14 1 42N23'40 72w03'15 4:48:13
Smooth Hummocks 10 1 41N15'00 70w08'30 4:40:34
Snell Corner 3 1 41N35'10 71w04'55 4:44:20
Snug Harbor 12 1 42N02 70w40 4:42:40
Soldiers Field 13 1 42N22 71w08 4:44:32
Somerset 3 1 41N46'10 71w07'45 4:44:31
Somerville 9 1 42N23'15 71w06'00 4:44:24
South 3 1 41N41 71w10 4:44:40
South Acton 9 1 42N27'30 71w27'15 4:45:49
South Amherst 8 1 42N20'25 72w30'20 4:50:01
Southampton 8 2 42N13'45 72w43'50 4:50:55
South Ashburnham 14 1 42N36'37 71w56'22 4:47:45
South Ashfield 6 2 42N30'38 72w46'37 4:51:06
South Athol 14 1 42N31'53 72w15'45 4:49:03
South Attleboro 3 1 41N54'30 71w21'45 4:45:27
South Barre 14 1 42N23'07 72w05'45 4:48:23
South Bellingham 11 1 42N02'30 71w28'36 4:45:54
South Berlin 14 1 42N21'35 71w37'45 4:46:31
South Billerica 9 1 42N31'40 71w16'50 4:45:07
South Bolton 14 1 42N23'48 71w36'20 4:46:25
Southborough 14 1 42N18'20 71w31'30 4:46:06
South Boston 13 1 42N20'00 71w03'00 4:44:12
South Braintree 11 1 42N12'00 71w00'00 4:44:00
South Brewster 1 1 41N44'50 70w03'37 4:40:14
Southbridge 14 1 42N04'30 72w02'02 4:48:08

South Bridgewater 12 1 41N56'44 70w56'51 4:43:47
South Byfield 5 1 42N44'55 70w54'15 4:43:37
South Carver 12 1 41N50'26 70w44'50 4:42:59
South Charlton 14 1 42N05'53 71w55'30 4:47:42
South Chatham 1 1 41N40'45 70w01'30 4:40:06
South Chelmsford 9 1 42N34'15 71w22'35 4:45:30
South Commons 11 1 42N14'13 70w59'15 4:43:57
South Dartmouth 3 1 41N35'30 70w56'30 4:43:46
South Deerfield 6 1 42N28'38 72w36'30 4:50:26
South Dennis 1 1 41N41'22 70w09'25 4:40:38
South Duxbury 12 1 42N01'23 70w41'00 4:42:44
South Easton 3 1 42N02'50 71w04'55 4:44:20
Southeast Quarter 10 1 41N15'00 70w01'00 4:40:04
South Egremont 2 1 42N09'38 73w25'00 4:53:40
South End 7 1 42N05'45 72w35'00 4:50:20
South Essex 5 1 42N37'45 70w46'10 4:43:05
South Factory Village 7 1 42N04'20 72w19'40 4:49:19
Southfield 2 1 42N06'05 73w14'00 4:52:56
South Fitchburg 14 1 42N33'52 71w47'00 4:47:08
South Foxboro 11 1 42N02'12 71w16'15 4:45:05
South Framingham 9 1 42N18 71w25 4:45:40
South Gardner 14 1 42N33'30 71w58'45 4:47:55
South Georgetown 5 1 42N42'35 70w59'30 4:43:58
South Grafton 14 1 42N15 71w41 4:46:44
South Grafton Street 14 1 42N14'25 71w45'15 4:47:01
South Groveland 5 1 42N44'25 71w02'44 4:44:11
South Hadley 8 1 42N15'30 72w34'30 4:50:18
South Hadley Falls 8 1 42N13'00 72w36'00 4:50:24
South Halifax 12 1 41N57'20 70w52'00 4:43:28
South Hamilton 5 1 42N36'25 70w52'45 4:43:31
South Hanover 12 1 42N05'50 70w51'00 4:43:24
South Hanson 12 1 42N02'35 70w52'50 4:43:31
South Harwich 1 1 41N40'30 70w02'40 4:40:11
South Hawley 6 1 42N32'47 72w54'18 4:51:37
South Hingham 12 1 42N11'45 70w52'30 4:43:30
South Hyannis 1 1 41N39 70w17 4:41:08
South Lakeville 12 1 41N51 70w56 4:43:44
South Lancaster 14 1 42N26'40 71w41'15 4:46:45
Southlawn Cemetery 2 1 42N39'36 73w14'20 4:52:57
South Lawrence 5 1 42N41'45 71w09'15 4:44:37
South Lee 2 1 42N16'40 73w16'40 4:53:07
South Lincoln 9 1 42N24'50 71w19'35 4:45:18
South Lowell 9 1 42N37'10 71w17'15 4:45:09
South Lynnfield 5 1 42N31'00 71w00'07 4:44:00
South Mashpee 1 1 41N34'57 70w28'39 4:41:55
South Middleboro 12 1 41N49'27 70w49'41 4:43:19
South Middleton 5 1 42N34'15 71w01'45 4:44:07
South Milford 14 1 42N06'10 71w30'17 4:46:01
South Monson 7 1 42N05'30 72w18'40 4:49:15
South Natick 9 1 42N16'25 71w19'00 4:45:16
South Orleans 1 1 41N45'02 69w59'30 4:39:58
South Pasture 10 1 41N15'30 70w04'00 4:40:16
South Peabody 5 1 42N30'35 70w57'00 4:43:48
South Pocasset 1 1 41N40'30 70w36'33 4:42:26
South Pond 12 1 41N54'25 70w38'30 4:42:34
South Quarter 7 1 42N08'30 72w51'45 4:51:27
South Quincy 11 1 42N14'20 71w00'30 4:44:02
South Rehoboth 3 1 41N48'15 71w16'57 4:45:08
South Row 9 1 42N38'00 71w42'13 4:46:49
South Royalston 14 1 42N37'50 72w08'52 4:48:35
South Salem 5 1 42N30'40 70w53'35 4:43:34
South Sandisfield 2 1 42N04'06 73w09'36 4:52:38
South Sandwich 1 1 41N46 70w30 4:42:00
South Seekonk 3 1 41N47'20 71w19'10 4:45:17
South Sherborn 9 1 42N13'25 71w21'20 4:45:25
South Shrewsbury 14 1 42N16'35 71w43'00 4:46:52
South Spencer 14 1 42N13'07 72w00'55 4:48:04
South Stoughton 11 1 42N06'55 71w04'50 4:44:19
South Sudbury 9 1 42N21'45 71w24'50 4:45:39
South Sutton 14 1 42N06'00 71w42'45 4:46:51
South Swansea 3 1 41N43'05 71w12'15 4:44:49
South Truro 1 1 41N58'07 69w04'15 4:36:17
South Uxbridge 14 1 42N05 71w38 4:46:32
South Village 9 1 42N40'00 71w49'30 4:47:18
Southville 14 1 42N16'00 71w32'13 4:46:09
South Walpole 11 1 42N06'15 71w15'42 4:45:03
South Waltham 9 1 42N23 71w14 4:44:56
South Wareham 12 1 41N46'20 70w45'00 4:43:00
South Wellfleet 1 1 41N55'05 69w59'45 4:39:59
South Wendell 6 1 42N31'15 72w23'30 4:49:34
South Westport 3 1 41N34'15 71w03'30 4:44:14
South Weymouth 11 1 42N10'30 70w57'00 4:43:48
Southwick 7 1 42N03'17 72w46'15 4:51:05
South Williamstown 2 1 42N39'38 73w14'31 4:52:58
South Wilmington 9 1 42N30'55 71w09'25 4:44:38
South Worcester 14 1 42N14'45 71w50'40 4:47:23
South Worthington 8 1 42N20'37 72w53'25 4:51:34
South Yarmouth 1 1 41N40'00 70w11'07 4:40:44
Spencer 14 1 42N14'38 71w59'34 4:47:58
Spindleville 14 1 42N06'53 71w31'48 4:46:07
Springdale 7 1 42N11'30 72w37'15 4:50:29
Springdale 11 1 42N09'12 71w07'47 4:44:31
Springfield 7 1 42N06'05 72w35'25 4:50:22
Springfield Boys Camp 7 1 42N06'43 72w10'50 4:48:43
Springfield Girls Camp 7 1 42N04'35 72w10'10 4:48:41
Spring Hill 9 1 42N23'18 71w06'35 4:44:26
Springs, The 1 1 41N44'50 70w28'45 4:41:55
Spruce Corner 6 1 42N30'08 72w50'50 4:51:23
Squam 10 1 41N19'00 69w59'30 4:39:58
Squantum 11 1 42N17'45 71w00'45 4:44:03
Squibnocket 4 1 41N18'25 70w46'30 4:43:06
Standish 12 1 42N06'25 70w45'20 4:43:01
Stanley 12 1 42N00'12 70w58'55 4:43:56
Staples Corner 12 1 41N51'40 70w56'20 4:43:45
Staples Shore 12 1 41N51'10 70w55'30 4:43:42
State House 13 1 42N19 71w05 4:44:20
State Line 2 1 42N20'52 73w24'35 4:53:38
State Line 7 1 42N01'55 72w19'21 4:49:17
Stearnsville 2 1 42N26'25 73w18'00 4:53:12
Steep Brook 3 1 41N44'30 71w07'45 4:44:31
Sterling 14 1 42N26'15 71w45'40 4:47:03
Sterling Camp Grounds 14 1 42N24'25 71w45'45 4:47:03
Sterling Junction 14 1 42N24'15 71w46'15 4:47:05
Stetson Road 12 1 42N04 70w49 4:43:16
Stevens Corner 2 1 42N23'58 73w19'54 4:53:20
Stevens Crossing 5 1 42N41'32 71w06'40 4:44:27
Stewartville 6 1 42N42'40 72w40'25 4:50:42
Still River 14 1 42N29'30 71w37'05 4:46:28
Stockbridge 2 1 42N17'15 73w19'15 4:53:17
Stoneham 9 1 42N28'48 71w06'00 4:44:24
Stone Haven 11 1 42N14 71w10 4:44:40
Stoneville 6 1 42N35'45 72w23'00 4:49:32
Stoneville 14 1 42N13'00 71w50'47 4:47:23
Stony Beach 12 1 42N18'25 70w54'08 4:43:37
Stony Brook 9 1 42N22 71w18 4:45:12
Stonybrook Village 13 1 42N15'08 71w08'35 4:44:34
Stoughton 11 1 42N07'30 71w06'10 4:44:25
Stoughton Junction 11 1 42N05'50 71w05'47 4:44:23
Stow 9 1 42N26'13 71w30'22 4:46:01
Straits Pond 12 1 42N16'05 70w50'45 4:43:23
Sturbridge 14 1 42N06'30 72w04'45 4:48:19
Sturtevant Mill 12 1 41N42'22 70w50'26 4:43:22
Suburban Park 3 1 41N38'40 71w03'55 4:44:16
Sudbury 9 1 42N23'00 71w25'00 4:45:40
Suffield Corner 7 1 42N03'45 72w37'55 4:50:32
Suffolk Downs Station 13 1 42N23'23 70w59'54 4:44:00
Summer Heights 11 1 42N10'45 71w08'50 4:44:35
Summit 14 1 42N20'00 71w47'30 4:47:10
Summit Grove 3 1 41N38'15 70w59'50 4:43:59
Sunderland 6 2 42N28'00 72w34'45 4:50:19
Sunderland 14 1 42N14'40 71w46'20 4:47:05
Sunnyside 14 1 42N03'45 71w53'10 4:47:33
Surfside 10 1 41N14'40 70w05'18 4:40:21
Surfside 12 1 42N17 70w53 4:43:32
Sutton 14 1 42N09'00 71w45'48 4:47:03
Suttons Mills 4 1 42N42'25 71w08'00 4:44:32
Swampscott 5 1 42N28'15 70w55'05 4:43:40
Swan Avenue 14 1 42N15'30 71w50'55 4:47:24
Swan Corner 9 1 42N39'06 71w26'10 4:45:45
Swansea 3 1 41N44'53 71w11'25 4:44:46
Swansea Center 3 1 41N44'30 71w11'36 4:44:46
Swanson Corners 8 1 42N11'53 72w43'37 4:50:54
Sweets Corner 2 1 42N40'42 73w12'40 4:52:51
Swift River 8 1 42N26'50 72w51'30 4:51:26
Swifts Beach 12 1 41N44'30 70w43'15 4:42:53
Symmes Corner 9 1 42N26'35 71w08'00 4:44:32
Tafts Corner 14 1 42N15'23 71w57'36 4:47:50
Tahanto Beach 1 1 41N42'00 70w37'15 4:42:29
Tanglewood 2 1 42N20'50 73w18'35 4:53:14
Tapley Street Annex 7 1 42N07 72w33 4:50:12
Tapleyville 5 1 42N33'15 70w56'55 4:43:48
Tarkiln 12 1 42N02'00 70w44'20 4:42:57
Tasseltop 14 1 42N01'20 71w43'10 4:46:53
Tatham 7 1 42N06'15 72w40'48 4:50:43
Tatnuck 14 1 42N17'00 71w51'00 4:47:24
Taunton 3 1 41N54'00 71w05'25 4:44:22
Teaticket 1 1 41N33'52 70w35'47 4:42:23
Templeton 14 1 42N33'20 72w04'05 4:48:16
Templeton Station 14 1 42N33'33 72w04'55 4:48:20
Ten Hills 9 1 42N23'48 71w05'15 4:44:21
Tenneyville 7 1 42N09'05 72w18'50 4:49:15
Tennyville 7 1 42N09 72w20 4:49:20
Tewksbury 9 1 42N36'38 71w14'05 4:44:56
Tewksbury Junction 9 1 42N36'55 71w13'00 4:44:52
Texas 14 1 42N09'55 71w53'34 4:47:34
The Green 12 1 41N51 70w56 4:43:44
The Patten 6 1 42N37'29 72w42'33 4:50:50
The Pines 9 1 42N32 71w14 4:44:56
The Plains 10 1 41N16'30 70w09'30 4:40:38
Thermopylae 8 1 42N16'55 72w36'03 4:50:24
The Street 14 1 42N34'30 72w13'10 4:48:53
The X 7 1 42N05'10 72w33'30 4:50:14
Third Cliff 12 1 42N10'45 70w43'05 4:42:52
Thomastown 12 1 41N52'31 70w50'26 4:43:22
Thompsonville 9 1 42N18'55 71w11'05 4:44:44
Thorndike 7 1 42N11'15 72w20'10 4:49:21
Three Rivers 7 1 42N10'52 72w21'40 4:49:27
Thumpertown Beach 1 1 41N50'37 70w00'15 4:40:01
Tihonet 12 1 41N47'12 70w43'06 4:42:52
Tinkertown 12 1 42N01'25 70w43'15 4:42:53
Tinkhamtown 12 1 41N41'00 70w51'06 4:43:24
Tisbury 4 1 41N27 70w37 4:42:28
Tississa 4 1 41N21'30 70w39'10 4:42:37
Tobeys Island 1 1 41N43 70w37 4:42:28
Tolland 7 1 42N05 73w01 4:52:04
Tolland Center 7 1 42N04'52 73w00'45 4:52:03
Tonset 1 1 41N48'00 69w57'15 4:39:49
Topsfield 5 1 42N38'15 70w57'00 4:43:48
Touisset 3 1 41N43'15 71w13'40 4:44:55
Tower Hill 9 1 42N22'05 71w20'20 4:45:21
Town Crest Village 2 1 42N34'41 73w09'03 4:52:36
Town Hall 12 1 42N03'55 70w52'00 4:43:28
Town Pasture 10 1 41N17'00 70w07'00 4:40:28
Townsend 9 1 42N40'00 71w42'20 4:46:49
Townsend Harbor 9 1 42N39'10 71w40'20 4:46:41
Tozier Corner 5 1 42N45'30 71w10'17 4:44:41
Tracy Corner 3 1 41N56'20 71w03'15 4:44:13
Tree of Knowledge Corner 12 1 42N01'45 70w44'00 4:42:56
Tremont 12 1 41N47'25 70w46'15 4:43:05
Tremont 13 1 42N21 71w04 4:44:16
Trots Hills 10 1 41N17'15 70w09'30 4:40:38
Truro 1 1 41N59'36 70w03'01 4:40:12
Truro Station 1 1 41N59'30 70w04'15 4:40:17
Tufts University 9 1 42N25 71w07 4:44:28
Tully 6 1 42N38'15 72w14'55 4:49:00
Turkey Hill Shores 14 1 42N20'15 71w57'23 4:47:50
Turners Falls 6 1 42N36'15 72w33'25 4:50:14
Turnpike 14 1 42N17 71w43 4:46:52
Tuttleville 12 1 42N12'33 70w54'30 4:43:38
Tyngsboro 9 1 42N40'36 71w25'30 4:45:42
Tyringham 2 1 42N14'45 73w12'15 4:52:49
Union Chapel 14 1 42N11'03 72w02'02 4:48:08
Union Hill 14 1 42N15'05 71w47'30 4:47:10
Union Market 9 1 42N22 71w11 4:44:44
Union Point 14 1 42N03 71w54 4:47:36
Unionville 11 1 42N05'27 71w25'30 4:45:42
Unionville 14 1 42N21'30 71w50'20 4:47:21
University Park 14 1 42N15'00 71w49'00 4:47:16
Uphams Corner 13 1 42N19'00 71w03'40 4:44:15
Upper Four Corners 12 1 41N52'05 70w55'55 4:43:44
Upper Green 5 1 42N47'35 70w51'40 4:43:27
Upper Hill 7 1 42N06'35 72w33'15 4:50:13
Upper Wire Village 14 1 42N16'20 71w58'38 4:47:55
Upton 14 1 42N10'28 71w36'10 4:46:25
Uxbridge 14 1 42N04'38 71w37'48 4:46:31
Vallersville 12 1 41N52'12 70w32'10 4:42:09
Valley View 11 1 42N07'20 71w28'30 4:45:54
Van Deusenville 2 1 42N13'38 73w21'50 4:53:27
Varnumtown 9 1 42N42'15 71w22'00 4:45:28
Vernon Hill 14 1 42N14'40 71w48'00 4:47:12
Veterans Administration Hosp 13 1 42N19 71w07 4:44:28
Victory Hill 2 1 42N28'07 73w13'50 4:52:55
Village 11 1 42N08 71w24 4:45:36
Vineyard Haven 4 1 41N27'15 70w36'15 4:42:25
Vineyard Highlands 4 1 41N27'50 70w34'00 4:42:16
Vining Hill 7 1 42N01'52 72w48'20 4:51:13
Vose 9 1 42N36'45 71w38'00 4:46:32
Waban 9 1 42N19'40 71w13'40 4:44:55
Wachusett 14 1 42N32'20 71w52'16 4:47:29
Wachusett Station 14 1 42N33'30 71w50'45 4:47:23
Wades Corner 3 1 41N52'42 71w10'06 4:44:40
Wadsworth 11 1 42N03'30 71w26'15 4:45:45
Waites Corner 14 1 42N33'50 71w51'02 4:47:24
Wakeby 1 1 41N40'40 70w28'29 4:41:54
Wakefield 9 1 42N30'23 71w04'24 4:44:18
Wakefield Junction 9 1 42N29'45 71w04'15 4:44:17
Walden Pond 5 1 42N28 71w00 4:44:00
Wales 7 1 42N04'10 72w13'22 4:48:53
Walnut Hill 9 1 42N29'45 71w07'45 4:44:31
Walpole 11 1 42N08'30 71w15'00 4:45:00
Walpole Heights 11 1 42N08'30 71w13'30 4:44:54
Waltham 9 1 42N22'35 71w14'10 4:44:57
Waltham Highlands 9 1 42N23'03 71w14'50 4:44:59
Wamesit 9 1 42N37'30 71w15'50 4:45:03
Wampum Corner 11 1 42N03'00 71w20'47 4:45:23
Wampum Rock 11 1 42N02'25 71w19'55 4:45:20
Wapping 6 1 42N31'30 72w36'30 4:50:26
Waquoit 1 1 41N46 70w30 4:42:00
Waquoit Village 1 1 41N35'24 70w31'18 4:42:05
Ward Corner 9 1 42N34'42 71w23'47 4:45:35
Ward Hill 5 1 42N45'24 71w06'15 4:44:25
Ware 8 1 42N15'35 72w14'25 4:48:58
Ware Center 8 1 42N15'50 72w16'25 4:49:06
Wareham 12 1 41N45'45 70w43'20 4:42:53

Wareham Center 12 1 41N46'00 70w43'36 4:42:54
Warren 14 1 42N12'45 72w11'30 4:48:46
Warren Landing 10 1 41N17'10 71w11'33 4:44:46
Warren Terrace 12 1 42N04 70w49 4:43:16
Warrentown 12 1 41N55'19 70w55'03 4:43:40
Warwick 6 1 42N40'55 72w20'22 4:49:21
Washington 2 1 42N21'57 73w07'00 4:52:28
Watertown 9 1 42N22'15 71w11'00 4:44:44
Waterville 12 1 41N45'80 70w50'29 4:43:22
Waterville 14 1 42N40'30 72w04'05 4:48:16
Watson 6 1 42N32'15 72w51'24 4:51:26
Wauwinet 10 1 41N19'45 69w59'48 4:39:59
Waveland 12 1 42N17'30 70w52'50 4:43:31
Waverley 9 1 42N23'15 71w11'00 4:44:44
Wawela Park 14 1 42N02'38 71w50'15 4:47:21
Wayland 9 1 42N21'45 71w21'43 4:45:27
Wayside 12 1 41N49'45 70w55'55 4:43:44
Wayside Inn 9 1 42N23 71w25 4:45:40
Webster 14 1 42N03'00 71w52'50 4:47:31
Webster Square 14 1 42N14'35 71w49'55 4:47:20
Wedgemere 9 1 42N26'40 71w08'25 4:44:34
Weeset 1 1 41N48'20 69w57'25 4:39:50
Weir Village 3 1 41N53'00 71w05'10 4:44:21
Wellesley 11 1 42N17'47 71w17'35 4:45:10
Wellesley Farms 11 1 42N19'10 71w16'10 4:45:05
Wellesley Fells 11 1 42N18'30 71w19'00 4:45:16
Wellesley Hills 11 1 42N18'30 71w16'45 4:45:07
Wellfleet 1 1 41N56'15 70w02'00 4:40:08
Wellfleet by the Sea 1 1 41N55'47 69w58'45 4:39:55
Wellington 9 1 42N24'40 71w05'00 4:44:20
Wellville 14 1 42N39'37 71w54'22 4:47:37
Wendell 6 1 42N32'53 72w23'50 4:49:35
Wendell Depot 6 1 42N35'45 72w21'37 4:49:26
Wenham 5 1 42N36'15 70w53'30 4:43:34
Wenham 12 1 41N54'45 70w46'00 4:43:04
Wenham Neck 5 1 42N35'32 70w50'42 4:43:23
Wepua Point 4 1 41N20'45 70w28'12 4:41:53
Wessonville 14 1 42N17'10 71w37'38 4:46:31
West Abington 12 1 42N05'30 70w58'00 4:43:52
West Acton 9 1 42N28'30 71w28'30 4:45:54
West Agawam 7 1 42N04'45 72w39'00 4:50:36
West Andover 5 1 42N39'40 71w09'32 4:44:38
West Auburn 14 1 42N10'35 71w52'23 4:47:30
West Barnstable 1 1 41N42'20 70w22'30 4:41:30
West Becket 2 1 42N15'53 73w08'10 4:52:33
West Bedford 9 1 42N28'41 71w18'58 4:45:16
West Berlin 14 1 42N23'17 71w39'40 4:46:39
West Billerica 9 1 42N35 71w17 4:45:08
Westborough 14 1 42N16'10 71w37'00 4:46:28
West Boxford 5 1 42N42'25 71w03'52 4:44:15
West Boylston 14 1 42N22'00 71w47'10 4:47:09
West Brewster 1 1 41N44'40 70w06'37 4:40:26
West Bridgewater 12 1 42N01'08 71w00'30 4:44:02
West Brimfield 7 1 42N10'32 72w15'40 4:49:03
Westbrook 8 2 42N24'47 72w37'47 4:50:31
West Brookfield 14 1 42N14'07 72w08'30 4:48:34
West Cambridge 9 1 42N23 71w08 4:44:32
West Chatham 1 1 41N40'52 69w59'30 4:39:58
West Chelmsford 9 1 42N37'00 71w24'00 4:45:36
Westchester 14 1 42N18'00 71w49'45 4:47:19
West Chesterfield 8 1 42N24'10 72w52'35 4:51:30
West Chop 4 1 41N28'48 70w36'12 4:42:25
West Concord 9 1 42N27'30 71w23'45 4:45:35
West Cummington 8 1 42N29'30 72w58'05 4:51:52
Westdale 12 1 42N01'13 70w59'00 4:43:56
West Deerfield 6 1 42N31'58 72w37'52 4:50:31
West Dennis 1 1 41N39'52 70w10'24 4:40:42
West Dighton 3 1 41N50'36 71w11'45 4:44:47
West Dudley 14 1 42N02'55 71w59'00 4:47:56
West Duxbury 12 1 42N03'23 70w46'30 4:43:06
West Everett 9 1 42N24'40 71w03'50 4:44:15
West Falmouth 1 1 41N36'15 70w38'06 4:42:32
West Farms 7 1 42N11'07 72w46'40 4:51:07
Westfield 7 1 42N07'30 72w45'00 4:51:00
West Fitchburg 14 1 42N34'30 71w50'30 4:47:22
Westford 9 1 42N34'45 71w26'18 4:45:45
Westford Station 9 1 42N35'49 71w26'09 4:45:45
West Foxboro 11 1 42N04'30 71w16'15 4:45:05
Westgate Park 3 1 41N43'15 70w56'25 4:43:46
West Gloucester 5 1 42N36'48 70w42'40 4:42:51
West Granville 7 1 42N04'38 72w56'38 4:51:47
West Groton 9 1 42N36'15 71w37'40 4:46:31
Westhampton 8 1 42N18'10 72w46'30 4:51:06
West Hanover 12 1 42N07'10 70w53'00 4:43:32
West Harwich 1 1 41N40'00 70w07'00 4:40:28
West Hatfield 8 2 42N22'15 72w38'15 4:50:33
West Hawley 6 1 42N31'39 72w56'50 4:51:47
West Hingham 12 1 42N14'15 70w54'12 4:43:37
West Hyannisport 1 1 41N38'10 70w19'15 4:41:17
Westlands 9 1 42N36'55 71w20'30 4:45:22
West Leominster 14 1 42N32'40 71w45'50 4:47:03
West Leyden 6 1 42N42'05 72w39'55 4:50:40
West Lynn 5 1 42N27'55 70w58'55 4:43:56
West Manchester 5 1 42N34'00 70w47'00 4:43:08
West Mansfield 3 1 41N59'53 71w14'45 4:44:59
West Meadow 12 1 42N02'00 71w01'45 4:44:07
West Medford 9 1 42N25'20 71w08'00 4:44:32
West Medway 11 1 42N08'30 71w25'30 4:45:42
West Millbury 14 1 42N10'16 71w48'15 4:47:13
Westminster 14 1 42N32'45 71w54'40 4:47:39
West Natick 9 1 42N16'40 71w22'45 4:45:31
West New Boston 2 1 42N06'07 73w05'45 4:52:23
West Newbury 5 1 42N48'05 70w59'25 4:43:58
West Newton 9 1 42N21'00 71w14'00 4:44:56
West Northfield 6 1 42N43'35 72w27'53 4:49:52
Weston 9 1 42N22'00 71w18'13 4:45:13
Weston Station 9 1 42N22'15 71w17'37 4:45:10
West Opening 4 1 41N20'48 70w29'45 4:41:59
West Orange 6 1 42N35'55 72w20'33 4:49:22
West Otis 2 1 42N11'00 73w08'50 4:52:35
Westover Air Force Base 7 1 42N11 72w34 4:50:16
West Oxford 14 1 42N06'08 71w53'17 4:47:33
West Parish 5 1 42N47'15 71w08'24 4:44:34
West Peabody 5 1 42N32'45 70w59'40 4:43:59
West Pelham 8 1 42N22'40 72w28'15 4:49:53
West Pittsfield 2 1 42N25'51 73w18'37 4:53:14
Westport 3 1 41N38 71w05 4:44:20
Westport Factory 3 1 41N38'20 71w03'00 4:44:12
Westport Point 3 1 41N31'20 71w04'30 4:44:18
West Quincy 11 1 42N15'10 71w02'00 4:44:08
West Roxbury 13 1 42N16'45 71w09'00 4:44:36
West Royalston 14 1 42N41'40 72w14'50 4:48:59
West Rutland 14 1 42N21'30 71w59'18 4:47:57
West Side 14 1 42N16 71w50 4:47:20
West Somerville 9 1 42N23'45 71w07'23 4:44:30
West Springfield 7 1 42N06'25 72w37'15 4:50:29
West Sterling 14 1 42N27'00 71w49'10 4:47:17
West Stockbridge 2 1 42N20'45 73w22'00 4:53:28
West Stockbridge Center 2 1 42N18'20 73w24'10 4:53:37
West Stoughton 11 1 42N07'45 71w07'30 4:44:30
West Summit 2 1 42N41'47 73w04'00 4:52:16
West Sutton 14 1 42N06'50 71w48'00 4:47:12
West Tatnuck 14 1 42N16'55 71w52'20 4:47:29
West Tisbury 4 1 41N22'52 70w40'30 4:42:42
West Town Landing 5 1 42N30'24 70w52'24 4:43:30
West Townsend 9 1 42N40'39 71w44'27 4:46:58
West Upton 14 1 42N10'10 71w37'15 4:46:29
Westview 11 1 42N06'45 71w25'45 4:45:43
Westview Park 3 1 41N38'40 70w57'15 4:43:49
West Village 9 1 42N34'00 71w06'45 4:44:27
Westville 3 1 41N53'10 71w08'10 4:44:33
Westville 14 1 42N04'20 72w03'40 4:48:15
West Walpole 11 1 42N08 71w15 4:45:00
West Wapole 11 1 42N08'13 71w17'15 4:45:09
West Ware 8 1 42N16'23 72w19'50 4:49:19
West Wareham 12 1 41N47'23 70w45'39 4:43:03
West Warren 14 1 42N12'45 72w14'07 4:48:56
West Watertown 9 1 42N22 71w11 4:44:44
West Whately 6 1 42N16'18 72w40'53 4:50:44
West Wind Shores 12 1 41N45 70w36 4:42:24
West Woburn 9 1 42N29 71w09 4:44:36
Westwood 11 1 42N12'50 71w13'30 4:44:54
Westwood Hills 14 1 42N16'40 71w49'45 4:47:19
West Worthington 8 1 42N25'23 72w59'13 4:51:57
West Wrentham 11 1 42N01'30 71w24'43 4:45:39
West Yarmouth 1 1 41N39'00 70w14'30 4:40:58
Wethersfield 11 1 42N06'10 71w28'30 4:45:54
Weymouth 11 1 42N13'15 70w56'25 4:43:46
Weymouth Heights 11 1 42N13'48 70w56'45 4:43:47
Weymouth Landing 11 1 42N13'24 70w57'45 4:43:51
Whalom 14 1 42N34'30 71w44'50 4:46:59
Whately 6 2 42N26'23 72w38'07 4:50:32
Wheelockville 14 1 42N04'50 71w36'55 4:46:28
Wheelwright 14 1 42N21'07 72w08'25 4:48:34
Whidden Corner 9 1 42N37'35 71w25'15 4:45:41
Whipples 7 1 42N12'10 72w19'03 4:49:16
Whitcomb Summit 2 1 42N41'17 73w01'21 4:52:05
White City 14 1 42N07'13 71w32'30 4:46:10
White City Shopping Center 14 1 42N17 71w43 4:46:52
White Hall 14 1 42N22'26 71w59'55 4:48:00
Whitehead 12 1 42N17 70w53 4:43:32
White Horse Beach 12 1 41N55'51 70w33'30 4:42:14
White Island Shores 12 1 41N48'00 70w38'07 4:42:32
White Oaks 2 1 42N43'51 73w11'53 4:52:48
White Valley 14 1 42N23'25 72w04'50 4:48:19
Whiteville 3 1 42N02'15 71w11'15 4:44:45
Whitinsville 14 1 42N06'40 71w40'00 4:46:40
Whitman 12 1 42N04'50 70w56'10 4:43:45
Whitmanville 14 1 42N35'00 71w54'05 4:47:36
Whitneys 9 1 42N14'25 71w24'25 4:45:38
Whittenton 3 1 41N55'30 71w05'40 4:44:23
Whittenton Junction 3 1 41N55'00 71w06'52 4:44:27
Wianno 1 1 41N36'50 70w23'09 4:41:33
Wigwam Beach 3 1 41N37'23 70w51'35 4:43:26
Wilbraham 7 1 42N07'25 72w25'55 4:49:44
Wilburite Corner 3 1 41N35'35 70w58'50 4:43:55
Wilkins Four Corners 11 1 42N00'38 71w18'22 4:45:13
Wilkinsonville 14 1 42N10'30 71w43'15 4:46:53
Williamsburg 8 1 42N23'35 72w43'50 4:50:55
Williamsburg Station 8 1 42N23'15 72w43'03 4:50:52
Williamstown 2 1 42N42'43 73w12'15 4:52:49
Williamsville 2 1 42N15'55 73w22'50 4:53:31
Williamsville 14 1 42N28'30 72w04'46 4:48:19
Willimansett 7 1 42N10'45 72w37'15 4:50:29
Willowdale 9 1 42N40'19 71w23'05 4:45:32
Willows 9 1 42N33'30 71w32'24 4:46:10
Wilmington 9 1 42N32'47 71w10'27 4:44:42
Wilmington Junction 9 1 42N35'25 71w10'02 4:44:40
Wilson 5 1 42N37 70w40 4:42:40
Wimbledon 1 1 41N39 70w15 4:41:00
Winchendon 14 1 42N41'10 72w02'40 4:48:11
Winchendon Center 14 1 42N39'40 72w02'30 4:48:10
Winchendon Springs 14 1 42N41'40 72w00'55 4:48:04
Winchester 9 1 42N27'08 71w08'15 4:44:33
Winchester Highlands 9 1 42N28'00 71w07'35 4:44:30
Windemere 12 1 42N18'20 70w53'17 4:43:33
Windsor 2 1 42N30'42 73w03'30 4:52:14
Winmere 9 1 42N30 71w12 4:44:48
Winnecunnet 3 1 41N58'35 71w07'50 4:44:31
Winsegansett Heights 3 1 41N35'50 70w51'47 4:43:27
Winslows 11 1 42N10'15 71w12'40 4:44:51
Winslows Crossing 12 1 42N06'32 70w52'03 4:43:28
Winter Hill 9 1 42N23'45 71w05'58 4:44:24
Winters Corner 12 1 42N04'15 71w03'55 4:44:16
Winthrop 13 1 42N22'30 70w59'00 4:43:56
Winthrop Beach 13 1 42N22'40 70w58'25 4:43:54
Winthrop Highlands 13 1 42N23'15 70w58'20 4:43:53
Woburn 9 1 42N28'45 71w09'10 4:44:37
Woburn Highlands 9 1 42N28'25 71w08'37 4:44:34
Wolf Lake 12 1 41N42'15 70w51'00 4:43:24
Wollaston 11 1 42N15'50 71w01'20 4:44:05
Wood End 1 1 42N01'13 70w11'20 4:40:45
Woodland 9 1 42N20'10 71w14'33 4:44:58
Woodland Park 14 1 42N13'35 71w49'53 4:47:20
Woodlawn 8 1 42N15 72w35 4:50:20
Woods Corner 3 1 41N36'40 71w06'45 4:44:27
Woods Corner 9 1 42N28'32 71w12'52 4:44:51
Woods Hole 1 1 41N31'35 70w40'25 4:42:42
Woodside 14 1 42N19'48 71w37'47 4:46:31
Woodsville 9 1 42N34'24 71w37'30 4:46:30
Woodville 9 1 42N14'15 71w33'45 4:46:15
Worcester 14 1 42N15'45 71w48'10 4:47:13
Workmans Circle Camp 9 1 42N14'57 71w26'15 4:45:45
Woronoco 7 1 42N09'50 72w49'48 4:51:19
Woronoco Heights 7 1 42N09'35 72w52'30 4:51:30
Worthington Center 8 1 42N23'50 72w56'10 4:51:45
Worthington Corners 8 1 42N24'37 72w56'10 4:51:45
Wrentham 11 1 42N04'00 71w19'43 4:45:19
Wyben 7 1 42N10'20 72w46'40 4:51:07
Wynnmere 9 1 42N29'32 71w10'50 4:44:43
Wyoma 5 1 42N29'08 70w57'30 4:43:50
Wyoming 9 1 42N27'15 71w04'10 4:44:17
Yankee Orchards 2 1 42N27'04 73w11'55 4:52:48
Yarmouth 1 1 41N42'20 70w13'45 4:40:55
Yarmouth Port 1 1 41N42'07 70w15'00 4:41:00
Yarmouth Station 1 1 41N41'53 70w15'30 4:41:02
Zoar 6 1 42N39'09 72w55'55 4:51:44
Zylonite 2 1 42N39'07 73w06'30 4:52:26

TIME TABLES

Not all zone shifts have been documented: neither the lower peninsula shifts to Eastern time during the 20's and 30's, nor the upper peninsula shifts back and forth. Many dates for zone shifts given here are generalizations based on fragmentary information. The Eastern time zone portions of Michigan went on Daylight time in 1975 on April 27, rather than February 23 with the rest of the country. Most of the tables for the lower peninsula reflect a return to Central time beginning on February 15, 1943, for the duration of World War II, returning to Eastern time at the end of the War. The more industrial areas remained on EWT.

MI # 1		
Before	9/18/1885	LMT
9/18/1885	12:00	CST
3/31/1918	02:00	CWT
10/27/1918	02:00	CST
3/30/1919	02:00	CWT
10/26/1919	02:00	CST
4/26/1931	02:00	EST
2/09/1942	02:00	EWT
2/15/1943	02:00	CWT
9/30/1945	02:00	EST
6/14/1967	00:01	EDT
10/29/1967	00:01	EST
4/29/1973	02:00	EDT
10/28/1973	02:00	EST
1/06/1974	02:00	EDT
10/27/1974	02:00	EST
4/27/1975	02:00	EDT
10/26/1975	02:00	US#1

MI # 2		
Before	9/18/1885	LMT
9/18/1885	12:00	CST
5/15/1915	02:00	EST
2/09/1942	02:00	EWT
9/30/1945	02:00	EST
4/25/1948	02:00	EDT
9/26/1948	02:00	EST
6/14/1967	00:01	EDT
10/29/1967	00:01	EST
4/29/1973	02:00	EDT
10/28/1973	02:00	EST
1/06/1974	02:00	EDT
10/27/1974	02:00	EST
4/27/1975	02:00	EDT
10/26/1975	02:00	US#1

MI # 3		
Before	9/18/1885	LMT
9/18/1885	12:00	CST
3/31/1918	02:00	CWT
10/27/1918	02:00	CST
3/30/1919	02:00	CWT
10/26/1919	02:00	CST
6/13/1920	02:00	CDT
10/31/1920	02:00	CST
3/27/1921	02:00	CDT
10/31/1921	02:00	CST
4/30/1922	02:00	CDT
9/24/1922	02:00	CST
4/29/1923	02:00	CDT
9/30/1923	02:00	CST
4/27/1924	02:00	CDT
9/28/1924	02:00	CST
4/26/1925	02:00	CDT
9/27/1925	02:00	CST
4/25/1926	02:00	CDT
9/26/1926	02:00	CST
4/24/1927	02:00	CDT
9/25/1927	02:00	CST
4/29/1928	02:00	CDT
9/30/1928	02:00	CST
4/28/1929	02:00	CDT
9/29/1929	02:00	CST
4/27/1930	02:00	CDT
9/28/1930	02:00	CST
4/26/1931	02:00	EST
2/09/1942	02:00	EWT
2/15/1943	02:00	CWT
9/30/1945	02:00	EST
6/14/1967	00:01	EDT
10/29/1967	00:01	EST
4/29/1973	02:00	EDT
10/28/1973	02:00	EST
1/06/1974	02:00	EDT
10/27/1974	02:00	EST
4/27/1975	02:00	EDT
10/26/1975	02:00	US#1

MI # 4		
Before	9/18/1885	LMT
9/18/1885	12:00	CST
3/31/1918	02:00	CWT
10/27/1918	02:00	CST
3/30/1919	02:00	CWT
10/26/1919	02:00	CST
3/27/1921	02:00	CDT
10/31/1921	02:00	CST
4/30/1922	02:00	CDT
9/24/1922	02:00	CST
4/29/1923	02:00	CDT
9/30/1923	02:00	CST
4/27/1924	02:00	CDT
9/28/1924	02:00	CST
4/26/1925	02:00	CDT
9/27/1925	02:00	CST
4/25/1926	02:00	CDT
9/26/1926	02:00	CST
4/24/1927	02:00	CDT
9/25/1927	02:00	CST
4/29/1928	02:00	CDT
9/30/1928	02:00	CST
4/28/1929	02:00	CDT
9/29/1929	02:00	CST
4/27/1930	02:00	CDT
9/28/1930	02:00	CST
4/26/1931	02:00	EST
2/09/1942	02:00	EWT
2/15/1943	02:00	CWT
9/30/1945	02:00	EST
6/14/1967	00:01	EDT
10/29/1967	00:01	EST
4/29/1973	02:00	EDT
10/28/1973	02:00	EST
1/06/1974	02:00	EDT
10/27/1974	02:00	EST
4/27/1975	02:00	EDT
10/26/1975	02:00	US#1

MI # 5		
Before	9/18/1885	LMT
9/18/1885	12:00	CST
3/31/1918	02:00	CWT
10/27/1918	02:00	CST
3/30/1919	02:00	CWT
10/26/1919	02:00	CST
3/27/1921	02:00	CDT
10/31/1921	02:00	CST
4/30/1922	02:00	CDT
9/24/1922	02:00	CST
4/29/1923	02:00	CDT
9/30/1923	02:00	CST
4/27/1924	02:00	CDT
9/28/1924	02:00	CST
4/26/1925	02:00	CDT
9/27/1925	02:00	CST
4/25/1926	02:00	CDT
9/26/1926	02:00	CST
4/24/1927	02:00	CDT
9/25/1927	02:00	CST
4/29/1928	02:00	CDT
9/30/1928	02:00	CST
4/28/1929	02:00	CDT
9/29/1929	02:00	CST
4/27/1930	02:00	CDT
9/28/1930	02:00	CST
4/26/1931	02:00	EST
2/09/1942	02:00	EWT
2/15/1943	02:00	CWT
9/30/1945	02:00	EST
4/25/1948	02:00	EDT
9/26/1948	02:00	EST
6/14/1967	00:01	EDT
10/29/1967	00:01	EST
4/29/1973	02:00	EDT
10/28/1973	02:00	EST
1/06/1974	02:00	EDT
10/27/1974	02:00	EST
4/27/1975	02:00	EDT
10/26/1975	02:00	US#1

MI # 6		
Before	9/18/1885	LMT
9/18/1885	12:00	CST
3/31/1918	02:00	CWT
10/27/1918	02:00	CST
3/30/1919	02:00	CWT
10/26/1919	02:00	CST
4/26/1931	02:00	EST
2/09/1942	02:00	EWT
2/15/1943	02:00	CWT
9/30/1945	02:00	EST
4/28/1946	02:00	EDT
9/29/1946	02:00	EST
6/14/1967	00:01	EDT
10/29/1967	00:01	EST
4/29/1973	02:00	EDT
10/28/1973	02:00	EST
1/06/1974	02:00	EDT
10/27/1974	02:00	EST
4/27/1975	02:00	EDT
10/26/1975	02:00	US#1

MI # 7		
Before	9/18/1885	LMT
9/18/1885	12:00	CST
3/31/1918	02:00	CWT
10/27/1918	02:00	CST
3/30/1919	02:00	CWT
10/26/1919	02:00	CST
4/26/1931	02:00	EST
2/09/1942	02:00	EWT
2/15/1943	02:00	CWT
9/30/1945	02:00	EST
4/25/1948	02:00	EDT
9/26/1948	02:00	EST
6/14/1967	00:01	EDT
10/29/1967	00:01	EST
4/29/1973	02:00	EDT
10/28/1973	02:00	EST
1/06/1974	02:00	EDT
10/27/1974	02:00	EST
4/27/1975	02:00	EDT
10/26/1975	02:00	US#1

MI # 8		
Before	9/18/1885	LMT
9/18/1885	12:00	CST
3/31/1918	02:00	CWT
10/27/1918	02:00	CST
3/30/1919	02:00	CWT
10/26/1919	02:00	CST
4/10/1920	02:00	CDT
9/18/1920	02:00	CST
5/01/1921	02:00	CDT
10/02/1921	02:00	CST
5/01/1926	02:00	CDT
9/04/1926	02:00	CST
4/30/1927	02:00	CDT
9/03/1927	02:00	CST
4/29/1928	02:00	CDT
9/30/1928	02:00	CST
4/28/1929	02:00	CDT
9/29/1929	02:00	CST
4/27/1930	02:00	CDT
9/28/1930	02:00	CST
4/26/1931	02:00	EST
2/09/1942	02:00	EWT
2/15/1943	02:00	CWT
9/30/1945	02:00	EST
6/14/1967	00:01	EDT
10/29/1967	00:01	EST
4/29/1973	02:00	EDT
10/28/1973	02:00	EST
1/06/1974	02:00	EDT
10/27/1974	02:00	EST
4/27/1975	02:00	EDT
10/26/1975	02:00	US#1

MI # 9		
Before	9/18/1885	LMT
9/18/1885	12:00	CST
3/31/1918	02:00	CWT
10/27/1918	02:00	CST
3/30/1919	02:00	CWT
10/26/1919	02:00	CST
3/27/1921	02:00	CDT
10/31/1921	02:00	CST
4/30/1922	02:00	CDT
9/24/1922	02:00	CST
4/29/1923	02:00	CDT
9/30/1923	02:00	CST
4/27/1924	02:00	CDT
9/28/1924	02:00	CST
4/26/1925	02:00	CDT
9/27/1925	02:00	CST
4/25/1926	02:00	CDT
9/26/1926	02:00	CST
3/02/1927	02:00	CDT
11/05/1927	02:00	CST
4/26/1931	02:00	EST
2/09/1942	02:00	EWT
2/15/1943	02:00	CWT
9/30/1945	02:00	EST
6/14/1967	00:01	EDT
10/29/1967	00:01	EST
4/29/1973	02:00	EDT
10/28/1973	02:00	EST
1/06/1974	02:00	EDT
10/27/1974	02:00	EST
4/27/1975	02:00	EDT
10/26/1975	02:00	US#1

MI # 10		
Before	9/18/1885	LMT
9/18/1885	12:00	CST
3/31/1918	02:00	CWT
10/27/1918	02:00	CST
3/30/1919	02:00	CWT
10/26/1919	02:00	CST
4/26/1931	02:00	EST
2/09/1942	02:00	EWT
2/15/1943	02:00	CWT
9/30/1945	02:00	EST
4/25/1948	02:00	EDT
9/26/1948	02:00	EST
4/29/1973	02:00	EDT
10/28/1973	02:00	EST
1/06/1974	02:00	EDT
10/27/1974	02:00	EST
4/27/1975	02:00	EDT
10/26/1975	02:00	US#1

MI # 11		
Before	9/18/1885	LMT
9/18/1885	12:00	CST
3/31/1918	02:00	CWT
10/27/1918	02:00	CST
3/30/1919	02:00	CWT
10/26/1919	02:00	CST
2/09/1942	02:00	CWT
9/30/1945	02:00	EST
4/28/1946	02:00	EDT
9/29/1946	02:00	EST
4/25/1948	02:00	EDT
9/26/1948	02:00	EST
4/29/1973	02:00	EDT
10/28/1973	02:00	EST
1/06/1974	02:00	EDT
10/27/1974	02:00	EST
4/27/1975	02:00	EDT
10/26/1975	02:00	US#1

MI # 12		
Before	9/18/1885	LMT
9/18/1885	12:00	CST
3/31/1918	02:00	CWT
10/27/1918	02:00	CST
3/30/1919	02:00	CWT
10/26/1919	02:00	CST
2/09/1942	02:00	CWT
9/30/1945	02:00	EST
6/14/1967	00:01	EDT
10/29/1967	00:01	EST
4/29/1973	02:00	EDT
10/28/1973	02:00	EST
1/06/1974	02:00	EDT
10/27/1974	02:00	EST
4/27/1975	02:00	EDT
10/26/1975	02:00	US#1

MI # 13		
Before	9/18/1885	LMT
9/18/1885	12:00	CST
3/31/1918	02:00	CWT
10/27/1918	02:00	CST
3/30/1919	02:00	CWT
10/26/1919	02:00	CST
4/28/1929	02:00	CDT
9/29/1929	02:00	CST
4/27/1930	02:00	CDT
9/28/1930	02:00	CST
4/26/1931	02:00	CDT
9/27/1931	02:00	CST
4/24/1932	02:00	CDT
9/25/1932	02:00	CST
4/30/1933	02:00	CDT
9/24/1933	02:00	CST
4/29/1934	02:00	CDT
9/30/1934	02:00	CST
4/28/1935	02:00	CDT
9/29/1935	02:00	CST
4/26/1936	02:00	CDT
9/27/1936	02:00	CST
4/25/1937	02:00	CDT
9/26/1937	02:00	CST
4/24/1938	02:00	CDT
9/25/1938	02:00	CST
4/30/1939	02:00	CDT
9/24/1939	02:00	CST
4/28/1940	02:00	CDT
9/29/1940	02:00	CST
4/27/1941	02:00	CDT
10/26/1941	02:00	CST
2/09/1942	02:00	CWT
9/30/1945	02:00	EST
4/27/1947	02:00	EDT
9/28/1947	02:00	EST
4/25/1948	02:00	EDT
9/26/1948	02:00	EST
4/29/1973	02:00	EDT
10/28/1973	02:00	EST
1/06/1974	02:00	EDT
10/27/1974	02:00	EST
4/27/1975	02:00	EDT
10/26/1975	02:00	US#1

MI # 14		
Before	9/18/1885	LMT
9/18/1885	12:00	CST
3/31/1918	02:00	CWT
10/27/1918	02:00	CST
3/30/1919	02:00	CWT
10/26/1919	02:00	CST
4/26/1931	02:00	CDT
9/27/1931	02:00	CST
4/24/1932	02:00	CDT
9/25/1932	02:00	CST
4/30/1933	02:00	CDT
9/24/1933	02:00	CST
4/29/1934	02:00	CDT
9/30/1934	02:00	CST
4/28/1935	02:00	CDT
9/29/1935	02:00	CST
4/26/1936	02:00	CDT
9/27/1936	02:00	CST
4/25/1937	02:00	CDT
9/26/1937	02:00	CST
4/24/1938	02:00	CDT
9/25/1938	02:00	CST
4/30/1939	02:00	CDT
9/24/1939	02:00	CST
4/28/1940	02:00	CDT
9/29/1940	02:00	CST
4/27/1941	02:00	CDT
10/26/1941	02:00	CST
2/09/1942	02:00	CWT
9/30/1945	02:00	EST
4/25/1948	02:00	EDT
9/26/1948	02:00	EST
4/29/1973	02:00	EDT
10/28/1973	02:00	EST
1/06/1974	02:00	EDT
10/27/1974	02:00	EST
4/27/1975	02:00	EDT
10/26/1975	02:00	US#1

MI # 15		
Before	9/18/1885	LMT
9/18/1885	12:00	CST
3/31/1918	02:00	CWT
10/27/1918	02:00	CST
3/30/1919	02:00	CWT
10/26/1919	02:00	CST
2/09/1942	02:00	CWT
9/30/1945	02:00	EST
4/27/1947	02:00	EDT
9/28/1947	02:00	EST
4/25/1948	02:00	EDT
9/26/1948	02:00	EST
4/29/1973	02:00	EDT
10/28/1973	02:00	EST
1/06/1974	02:00	EDT
10/27/1974	02:00	EST
4/27/1975	02:00	EDT
10/26/1975	02:00	US#1

MI # 16		
Before	9/18/1885	LMT
9/18/1885	12:00	CST
3/31/1918	02:00	CWT
10/27/1918	02:00	CST
3/30/1919	02:00	CWT
10/26/1919	02:00	CST
4/27/1941	02:00	CDT
10/26/1941	02:00	CST
2/09/1942	02:00	CWT
9/30/1945	02:00	EST
4/28/1946	02:00	EDT
9/29/1946	02:00	EST
4/25/1948	02:00	EDT
9/26/1948	02:00	EST
4/29/1973	02:00	EDT
10/28/1973	02:00	EST
1/06/1974	02:00	EDT
10/27/1974	02:00	EST
4/27/1975	02:00	EDT
10/26/1975	02:00	US#1

MI # 17		
Before	9/18/1885	LMT
9/18/1885	12:00	CST
3/31/1918	02:00	CWT
10/27/1918	02:00	CST
3/30/1919	02:00	CWT
10/26/1919	02:00	CST
2/09/1942	02:00	CWT
9/30/1945	02:00	EST
4/28/1946	02:00	EDT
9/29/1946	02:00	EST
4/27/1947	02:00	EDT
9/28/1947	02:00	EST
4/25/1948	02:00	EDT
9/26/1948	02:00	EST
4/29/1973	02:00	EDT
10/28/1973	02:00	EST
1/06/1974	02:00	EDT
10/27/1974	02:00	EST
4/27/1975	02:00	EDT
10/26/1975	02:00	US#1

MI # 18		
Before	9/18/1885	LMT
9/18/1885	12:00	CST
3/31/1918	02:00	CWT
10/27/1918	02:00	CST
3/30/1919	02:00	CWT
10/26/1919	02:00	CST
2/09/1942	02:00	CWT
9/30/1945	02:00	EST
4/25/1948	02:00	EDT
9/26/1948	02:00	EST
4/24/1949	02:00	EDT
9/25/1949	02:00	EST
4/29/1973	02:00	EDT
10/28/1973	02:00	EST
1/06/1974	02:00	EDT
10/27/1974	02:00	EST
4/27/1975	02:00	EDT
10/26/1975	02:00	US#1

MI # 19		
Before	9/18/1885	LMT
9/18/1885	12:00	CST
3/31/1918	02:00	CWT
10/27/1918	02:00	CST
3/30/1919	02:00	CWT
10/26/1919	02:00	CST
4/29/1928	00:01	CDT
9/28/1928	00:01	CST
4/27/1930	00:01	CDT
9/28/1930	00:01	CST
4/26/1931	00:01	CDT
9/27/1931	00:01	CST
4/24/1932	00:01	CDT
9/25/1932	00:01	CST
4/30/1933	00:01	CDT
9/24/1933	00:01	CST
5/15/1934	00:01	CDT
10/01/1934	00:01	CST
4/28/1935	00:01	CDT
9/29/1935	00:01	CST
4/26/1936	00:01	CDT
9/27/1936	00:01	CST
4/25/1937	00:01	CDT

TIME TABLES

Date	Time	Zone
9/26/1937	00:01	CST
4/24/1938	00:01	CDT
9/25/1938	00:01	CST
4/30/1939	00:01	CDT
9/24/1939	00:01	CST
4/28/1940	00:01	CDT
9/29/1940	00:01	CST
4/27/1941	00:01	CDT
10/26/1941	00:01	CST
2/09/1942	02:00	CWT
9/30/1945	02:00	EST
4/28/1946	02:00	EDT
9/29/1946	02:00	EST
4/27/1947	02:00	EDT
9/28/1947	02:00	EST
4/25/1948	02:00	EDT
9/26/1948	02:00	EST
4/29/1973	02:00	EDT
10/28/1973	02:00	EST
1/06/1974	02:00	EDT
10/27/1974	02:00	EST
4/27/1975	02:00	EDT
10/26/1975	02:00	US#1

MI # 20

Date	Time	Zone
Before 9/18/1885		LMT
9/18/1885	12:00	CST
3/31/1918	02:00	CWT
10/27/1918	02:00	CST
3/30/1919	02:00	CWT
10/26/1919	02:00	CST
5/01/1932	02:00	CDT
10/02/1932	02:00	CST
4/30/1933	02:00	CDT
10/01/1933	02:00	CST
4/29/1934	02:00	CDT
9/30/1934	02:00	CST
5/01/1935	02:00	CDT
10/01/1935	02:00	CST
4/26/1936	02:00	CDT
9/27/1936	02:00	CST
4/25/1937	02:00	CDT
9/26/1937	02:00	CST
4/24/1938	02:00	CDT
9/25/1938	02:00	CST
4/30/1939	02:00	CDT
9/24/1939	02:00	CST
4/28/1940	02:00	CDT
9/29/1940	02:00	CST
4/27/1941	02:00	CDT
10/26/1941	02:00	CST
2/09/1942	02:00	CWT
9/30/1945	02:00	EST
4/28/1946	02:00	EDT
9/29/1946	02:00	EST
4/27/1947	02:00	EDT
9/28/1947	02:00	EST
4/25/1948	02:00	EDT
9/26/1948	02:00	EST
4/24/1949	02:00	EDT
9/25/1949	02:00	EST
4/29/1973	02:00	EDT
10/28/1973	02:00	EST
1/06/1974	02:00	EDT
10/27/1974	02:00	EST
4/27/1975	02:00	EDT
10/26/1975	02:00	US#1

MI # 21

Date	Time	Zone
Before 9/18/1885		LMT
9/18/1885	12:00	CST
3/31/1918	02:00	CWT
10/27/1918	02:00	CST
3/30/1919	02:00	CWT
10/26/1919	02:00	CST
5/04/1930	02:00	CDT
9/28/1930	02:00	CST
5/03/1931	02:00	CDT
9/27/1931	02:00	CST
6/01/1933	02:00	CDT
9/03/1933	02:00	CST
6/01/1934	02:00	CDT
9/02/1934	02:00	CST
5/01/1935	02:00	CDT
10/01/1935	02:00	CST
4/26/1936	02:00	CDT
9/27/1936	02:00	CST
4/25/1937	02:00	CDT
9/26/1937	02:00	CST
4/24/1938	02:00	CDT
9/25/1938	02:00	CST
4/30/1939	02:00	CDT
9/24/1939	02:00	CST
4/28/1940	02:00	CDT
9/29/1940	02:00	CST
4/27/1941	02:00	CDT
10/26/1941	02:00	CST
2/09/1942	02:00	CWT
9/30/1945	02:00	EST
4/28/1946	02:00	EDT
9/29/1946	02:00	EST
4/27/1947	02:00	EDT
9/28/1947	02:00	EST
4/25/1948	02:00	EDT
9/26/1948	02:00	EST
4/24/1949	02:00	EDT
9/25/1949	02:00	EST
4/29/1973	02:00	EDT
10/28/1973	02:00	EST
1/06/1974	02:00	EDT
10/27/1974	02:00	EST
4/27/1975	02:00	EDT
10/26/1975	02:00	US#1

MI # 22

Date	Time	Zone
Before 9/18/1885		LMT
9/18/1885	12:00	CST
3/31/1918	02:00	CWT
10/27/1918	02:00	CST
3/30/1919	02:00	CWT
10/26/1919	02:00	CST
5/04/1930	00:01	CDT
9/28/1930	00:01	CST
5/03/1931	00:01	CDT
9/27/1931	00:01	CST
5/01/1932	00:01	CDT
9/25/1932	00:01	CST
5/07/1933	00:01	CDT
10/01/1933	00:01	CST
5/06/1934	00:01	CDT
9/30/1934	00:01	CST
5/05/1935	00:01	CDT
9/29/1935	00:01	CST
4/26/1936	02:00	CDT
9/27/1936	02:00	CST
5/01/1937	02:00	CDT
10/01/1937	02:00	CST
4/24/1938	02:00	CDT
9/25/1938	02:00	CST
4/30/1939	02:00	CDT
9/24/1939	02:00	CST
5/05/1940	02:00	CDT
9/29/1940	02:00	CST
5/04/1941	02:00	CDT
9/28/1941	02:00	CST
2/09/1942	02:00	CWT
9/30/1945	02:00	EST
4/25/1948	02:00	EDT
9/26/1948	02:00	EST
4/29/1973	02:00	EDT
10/28/1973	02:00	EST
1/06/1974	02:00	EDT
10/27/1974	02:00	EST
4/27/1975	02:00	EDT
10/26/1975	02:00	US#1

MI # 23

Date	Time	Zone
Before 9/18/1885		LMT
9/18/1885	12:00	CST
3/31/1918	02:00	CWT
10/27/1918	02:00	CST
3/30/1919	02:00	CWT
10/26/1919	02:00	CST
5/04/1930	02:00	CDT
9/28/1930	02:00	CST
5/03/1931	02:00	CDT
9/27/1931	02:00	CST
5/01/1932	02:00	CDT
9/25/1932	02:00	CST
6/01/1933	02:00	CDT
9/03/1933	02:00	CST
6/01/1934	02:00	CDT
9/02/1934	02:00	CST
5/01/1935	02:00	CDT
10/01/1935	02:00	CST
4/26/1936	02:00	CDT
9/27/1936	02:00	CST
4/25/1937	02:00	CDT
9/26/1937	02:00	CST
4/24/1938	02:00	CDT
9/25/1938	02:00	CST
4/30/1939	02:00	CDT
9/24/1939	02:00	CST
4/28/1940	02:00	CDT
9/29/1940	02:00	CST
4/27/1941	02:00	CDT
10/26/1941	02:00	CST
2/09/1942	02:00	CWT
9/30/1945	02:00	EST
4/25/1948	02:00	EDT
9/26/1948	02:00	EST
4/24/1949	02:00	EDT
9/25/1949	02:00	EST
4/29/1973	02:00	EDT
10/28/1973	02:00	EST
1/06/1974	02:00	EDT
10/27/1974	02:00	EST
4/27/1975	02:00	EDT
10/26/1975	02:00	US#1

MI # 24

Date	Time	Zone
Before 9/18/1885		LMT
9/18/1885	12:00	CST
3/31/1918	02:00	CWT
10/27/1918	02:00	CST
3/30/1919	02:00	CWT
10/26/1919	02:00	CST
6/01/1928	02:00	CDT
10/01/1928	02:00	CST
6/01/1929	02:00	CDT
10/01/1929	02:00	CST
6/01/1930	02:00	CDT
10/01/1930	02:00	CST
2/09/1942	02:00	CWT
9/30/1945	02:00	EST
4/25/1948	02:00	EDT
9/26/1948	02:00	EST
4/29/1973	02:00	EDT
10/28/1973	02:00	EST
1/06/1974	02:00	EDT
10/27/1974	02:00	EST
4/27/1975	02:00	EDT
10/26/1975	02:00	US#1

MI # 25

Date	Time	Zone
Before 9/18/1885		LMT
9/18/1885	12:00	CST
3/31/1918	02:00	CWT
10/27/1918	02:00	CST
3/30/1919	02:00	CWT
10/26/1919	02:00	CST
2/09/1942	02:00	CWT
9/30/1945	02:00	EST
4/25/1948	02:00	EDT
9/26/1948	02:00	EST
4/29/1973	02:00	EDT
10/28/1973	02:00	EST
1/06/1974	02:00	EDT
10/27/1974	02:00	EST
4/27/1975	02:00	EDT
10/26/1975	02:00	US#1

MI # 26

Date	Time	Zone
Before 9/18/1885		LMT
9/18/1885	12:00	CST
3/31/1918	02:00	CWT
10/27/1918	02:00	CST
3/30/1919	02:00	CWT
10/26/1919	02:00	CST
5/01/1932	02:00	CDT
10/31/1932	02:00	CST
4/30/1933	02:00	CDT
9/24/1933	02:00	CST
4/29/1934	02:00	CDT
9/30/1934	02:00	CST
5/01/1935	02:00	CDT
10/01/1935	02:00	CST
5/01/1936	02:00	CDT
10/01/1936	02:00	CST
4/25/1937	02:00	CDT
9/26/1937	02:00	CST
2/09/1942	02:00	CWT
9/30/1945	02:00	EST
4/28/1946	02:00	EDT
9/29/1946	02:00	EST
4/25/1948	02:00	EDT
9/26/1948	02:00	EST
4/24/1949	02:00	EDT
9/25/1949	02:00	EST
6/14/1967	00:01	EDT
10/29/1967	00:01	EST
4/29/1973	02:00	EDT
10/28/1973	02:00	EST
1/06/1974	02:00	EDT
10/27/1974	02:00	EST
4/27/1975	02:00	EDT
10/26/1975	02:00	US#1

MI # 27

Date	Time	Zone
Before 9/18/1885		LMT
9/18/1885	12:00	CST
3/31/1918	02:00	CWT
10/27/1918	02:00	CST
3/30/1919	02:00	CWT
10/26/1919	02:00	CST
5/01/1932	02:00	CDT
10/31/1932	02:00	CST
2/09/1942	02:00	CWT
9/30/1945	02:00	EST
4/25/1948	02:00	EDT
9/26/1948	02:00	EST
4/29/1973	02:00	EDT
10/28/1973	02:00	EST
1/06/1974	02:00	EDT
10/27/1974	02:00	EST
4/27/1975	02:00	EDT
10/26/1975	02:00	US#1

MI # 28

Date	Time	Zone
Before 9/18/1885		LMT
9/18/1885	12:00	CST
3/31/1918	02:00	CWT
10/27/1918	02:00	CST
3/30/1919	02:00	CWT
10/26/1919	02:00	CST
5/01/1935	02:00	CDT
10/01/1935	02:00	CST
5/01/1937	02:00	CDT
9/01/1937	02:00	CST
2/09/1942	02:00	CWT
9/30/1945	02:00	EST
4/25/1948	02:00	EDT
9/26/1948	02:00	EST
4/24/1949	02:00	EDT
9/25/1949	02:00	EST
4/29/1973	02:00	EDT
10/28/1973	02:00	EST
1/06/1974	02:00	EDT
10/27/1974	02:00	EST
4/27/1975	02:00	EDT
10/26/1975	02:00	US#1

MI # 29

Date	Time	Zone
Before 9/18/1885		LMT
9/18/1885	12:00	CST
3/31/1918	02:00	CWT
10/27/1918	02:00	CST
3/30/1919	02:00	CWT
10/26/1919	02:00	CST
5/01/1935	02:00	CDT
10/01/1935	02:00	CST
2/09/1942	02:00	CWT
9/30/1945	02:00	EST
4/25/1948	02:00	EDT
9/26/1948	02:00	EST
4/24/1949	02:00	EDT
9/25/1949	02:00	EST
4/29/1973	02:00	EDT
10/28/1973	02:00	EST
1/06/1974	02:00	EDT
10/27/1974	02:00	EST
4/27/1975	02:00	EDT
10/26/1975	02:00	US#1

MI # 30

Date	Time	Zone
Before 9/18/1885		LMT
9/18/1885	12:00	CST
3/31/1918	02:00	CWT
10/27/1918	02:00	CST
3/30/1919	02:00	CWT
10/26/1919	02:00	CST
5/01/1935	02:00	CDT
10/01/1935	02:00	CST
5/01/1936	02:00	CDT
9/05/1936	02:00	CST
4/25/1937	02:00	CDT
9/26/1937	02:00	CST
2/09/1942	02:00	CWT
9/30/1945	02:00	EST
4/27/1947	02:00	EDT
9/28/1947	02:00	EST
4/25/1948	02:00	EDT
9/26/1948	02:00	EST
4/29/1973	02:00	EDT
10/28/1973	02:00	EST
1/06/1974	02:00	EDT
10/27/1974	02:00	EST
4/27/1975	02:00	EDT
10/26/1975	02:00	US#1

MI # 31

Date	Time	Zone
Before 9/18/1885		LMT
9/18/1885	12:00	CST
3/31/1918	02:00	CWT
10/27/1918	02:00	CST
3/30/1919	02:00	CWT
10/26/1919	02:00	CST
5/01/1937	02:00	CDT
10/01/1937	02:00	CST
2/09/1942	02:00	CWT
9/30/1945	02:00	EST
4/25/1948	02:00	EDT
9/26/1948	02:00	EST
4/29/1973	02:00	EDT
10/28/1973	02:00	EST
1/06/1974	02:00	EDT
10/27/1974	02:00	EST
4/27/1975	02:00	EDT
10/26/1975	02:00	US#1

MI # 32

Date	Time	Zone
Before 9/18/1885		LMT
9/18/1885	12:00	CST
3/31/1918	02:00	CWT
10/27/1918	02:00	CST
3/30/1919	02:00	CWT
10/26/1919	02:00	CST
5/01/1935	02:00	CDT
10/01/1935	02:00	CST
2/09/1942	02:00	CWT
9/30/1945	02:00	EST
4/25/1948	02:00	EDT
9/26/1948	02:00	EST
4/29/1973	02:00	EDT
10/28/1973	02:00	EST
1/06/1974	02:00	EDT
10/27/1974	02:00	EST
4/27/1975	02:00	EDT
10/26/1975	02:00	US#1

MI # 33

Date	Time	Zone
Before 9/18/1885		LMT
9/18/1885	12:00	CST
3/31/1918	02:00	CWT
10/27/1918	02:00	CST
3/30/1919	02:00	CWT
10/26/1919	02:00	CST
4/01/1937	02:00	CDT
10/11/1937	02:00	CST
2/09/1942	02:00	CWT
9/30/1945	02:00	EST
4/25/1948	02:00	EDT
9/26/1948	02:00	EST
4/29/1973	02:00	EDT
10/28/1973	02:00	EST
1/06/1974	02:00	EDT
10/27/1974	02:00	EST
4/27/1975	02:00	EDT
10/26/1975	02:00	US#1

MI # 34

Date	Time	Zone
Before 9/18/1885		LMT
9/18/1885	12:00	CST
3/31/1918	02:00	CWT
10/27/1918	02:00	CST
3/30/1919	02:00	CWT
10/26/1919	02:00	CST
5/01/1932	02:00	CDT
9/30/1932	02:00	CST
4/30/1933	02:00	CDT
9/24/1933	02:00	CST
4/29/1934	02:00	CDT
9/30/1934	02:00	CST
5/01/1935	02:00	CDT
10/01/1935	02:00	CST
5/01/1936	02:00	CDT
10/01/1936	02:00	CST
5/01/1937	02:00	CDT
10/01/1937	02:00	CST
2/09/1942	02:00	CWT
9/30/1945	02:00	EST
4/25/1948	02:00	EDT
9/26/1948	02:00	EST
4/29/1973	02:00	EDT
10/28/1973	02:00	EST
1/06/1974	02:00	EDT
10/27/1974	02:00	EST
4/27/1975	02:00	EDT
10/26/1975	02:00	US#1

MI # 35

Date	Time	Zone
Before 9/18/1885		LMT
9/18/1885	12:00	CST
3/31/1918	02:00	CWT
10/27/1918	02:00	CST
3/30/1919	02:00	CWT
10/26/1919	02:00	CST
5/01/1937	02:00	CDT
10/01/1937	02:00	CST
4/24/1938	02:00	CDT
9/25/1938	02:00	CST
4/30/1939	02:00	CDT
9/24/1939	02:00	CST
4/28/1940	02:00	CDT
9/29/1940	02:00	CST
4/27/1941	02:00	CDT
10/26/1941	02:00	CST
2/09/1942	02:00	CWT
9/30/1945	02:00	EST
4/27/1947	02:00	EDT
9/28/1947	02:00	EST
4/25/1948	02:00	EDT
9/26/1948	02:00	EST
4/29/1973	02:00	EDT
10/28/1973	02:00	EST
1/06/1974	02:00	EDT
10/27/1974	02:00	EST
4/27/1975	02:00	EDT
10/26/1975	02:00	US#1

MI # 36

Date	Time	Zone
Before 9/18/1885		LMT
9/18/1885	12:00	CST
3/31/1918	02:00	CWT
10/27/1918	02:00	CST
3/30/1919	02:00	CWT
10/26/1919	02:00	CST
4/15/1920	02:00	EST
2/09/1942	02:00	EWT
9/30/1945	02:00	EST
6/14/1967	00:01	EDT
10/29/1967	00:01	EST
4/29/1973	02:00	EDT
10/28/1973	02:00	EST
1/06/1974	02:00	EDT
10/27/1974	02:00	EST
4/27/1975	02:00	EDT
10/26/1975	02:00	US#1

MI # 37

Date	Time	Zone
Before 9/18/1885		LMT
9/18/1885	12:00	CST
3/31/1918	02:00	CWT
10/27/1918	02:00	CST
3/30/1919	02:00	CWT
10/26/1919	02:00	CST
4/15/1920	02:00	EST
2/09/1942	02:00	EWT
9/30/1945	02:00	EST
4/25/1948	02:00	EDT
9/26/1948	02:00	EST
6/14/1967	00:01	EDT
10/29/1967	00:01	EST
4/29/1973	02:00	EDT
10/28/1973	02:00	EST
1/06/1974	02:00	EDT
10/27/1974	02:00	EST
4/27/1975	02:00	EDT
10/26/1975	02:00	US#1

MI # 38

Date	Time	Zone
Before 9/18/1885		LMT
9/18/1885	12:00	CST
3/31/1918	02:00	CWT
10/27/1918	02:00	CST
3/30/1919	02:00	CWT
10/26/1919	02:00	CST
11/24/1921	02:00	EST
2/09/1942	02:00	EWT
9/30/1945	02:00	EST
6/14/1967	00:01	EDT
10/29/1967	00:01	EST
4/29/1973	02:00	EDT
10/28/1973	02:00	EST
1/06/1974	02:00	EDT
10/27/1974	02:00	EST
4/27/1975	02:00	EDT
10/26/1975	02:00	US#1

MI # 39

Date	Time	Zone
Before 9/18/1885		LMT
9/18/1885	12:00	CST
3/31/1918	02:00	CWT
10/27/1918	02:00	CST
3/30/1919	02:00	CWT
10/26/1919	02:00	CST
11/14/1922	02:00	EST
2/09/1942	02:00	EWT
9/30/1945	02:00	EST
6/14/1967	00:01	EDT
10/29/1967	00:01	EST
4/29/1973	02:00	EDT
10/28/1973	02:00	EST
1/06/1974	02:00	EDT
10/27/1974	02:00	EST
4/27/1975	02:00	EDT
10/26/1975	02:00	US#1

MI # 40

Date	Time	Zone
Before 9/18/1885		LMT
9/18/1885	12:00	CST
3/31/1918	02:00	CWT
10/27/1918	02:00	CST
3/30/1919	02:00	CWT
10/26/1919	02:00	CST
3/27/1921	02:00	CDT
10/31/1921	02:00	CST
4/30/1922	02:00	CDT
9/24/1922	02:00	CST
4/29/1923	02:00	CDT
9/30/1923	02:00	CST
4/01/1924	02:00	EST
2/09/1942	02:00	EWT
2/15/1943	02:00	CWT
9/30/1945	02:00	EST
6/14/1967	00:01	EDT
10/29/1967	00:01	EST
4/29/1973	02:00	EDT
10/28/1973	02:00	EST
1/06/1974	02:00	EDT
10/27/1974	02:00	EST
4/27/1975	02:00	EDT
10/26/1975	02:00	US#1

MI # 41

Date	Time	Zone
Before 9/18/1885		LMT
9/18/1885	12:00	CST
3/31/1918	02:00	CWT
10/27/1918	02:00	CST
3/30/1919	02:00	CWT

TIME TABLES

10/26/1919 02:00 CST
5/01/1923 02:00 CDT
5/01/1924 00:01 EST
2/09/1942 02:00 EWT
2/15/1943 02:00 CWT
9/30/1945 02:00 EST
6/14/1967 00:01 EDT
10/29/1967 00:01 EST
4/29/1973 02:00 EDT
10/28/1973 02:00 EST
1/06/1974 02:00 EDT
10/27/1974 02:00 EST
4/27/1975 02:00 EDT
10/26/1975 02:00 US#1

MI # 42
Before 9/18/1885 LMT
9/18/1885 12:00 CST
3/31/1918 02:00 CWT
10/27/1918 02:00 CST
3/30/1919 02:00 CWT
10/26/1919 02:00 CST
5/04/1925 02:00 EST
2/09/1942 02:00 EWT
2/15/1943 02:00 CWT
9/30/1945 02:00 EST
6/14/1967 00:01 EDT
10/29/1967 00:01 EST
4/29/1973 02:00 EDT
10/28/1973 02:00 EST
1/06/1974 02:00 EDT
10/27/1974 02:00 EST
4/27/1975 02:00 EDT
10/26/1975 02:00 US#1

MI # 43
Before 9/18/1885 LMT
9/18/1885 12:00 CST
3/31/1918 02:00 CWT
10/27/1918 02:00 CST
3/30/1919 02:00 CWT
10/26/1919 02:00 CST
3/27/1921 02:00 CDT
10/31/1921 02:00 CST
4/30/1922 02:00 CDT
9/24/1922 02:00 CST
4/29/1923 02:00 CDT
9/30/1923 02:00 CST
4/27/1924 02:00 CDT
9/28/1924 02:00 CST
4/26/1925 02:00 CDT
9/27/1925 02:00 CST
4/25/1926 02:00 CDT
9/26/1926 02:00 CST
4/01/1927 02:00 EST
2/09/1942 02:00 EWT
2/15/1943 02:00 CWT
9/30/1945 02:00 EST
6/14/1967 00:01 EDT
10/29/1967 00:01 EST
4/29/1973 02:00 EDT
10/28/1973 02:00 EST
1/06/1974 02:00 EDT
10/27/1974 02:00 EST
4/27/1975 02:00 EDT
10/26/1975 02:00 US#1

MI # 44
Before 9/18/1885 LMT
9/18/1885 12:00 CST
3/31/1918 02:00 CWT
10/27/1918 02:00 CST
3/30/1919 02:00 CWT
10/26/1919 02:00 CST
12/23/1928 02:00 EST
2/09/1942 02:00 EWT
2/15/1943 02:00 CWT
9/30/1945 02:00 EST
6/14/1967 00:01 EDT
10/29/1967 00:01 EST
4/29/1973 02:00 EDT
10/28/1973 02:00 EST
1/06/1974 02:00 EDT
10/27/1974 02:00 EST
4/27/1975 02:00 EDT
10/26/1975 02:00 US#1

MI # 45
Before 9/18/1885 LMT
9/18/1885 12:00 CST
3/31/1918 02:00 CWT
10/27/1918 02:00 CST
3/30/1919 02:00 CWT
10/26/1919 02:00 CST
12/23/1928 02:00 EST
2/09/1942 02:00 EWT
2/15/1943 02:00 CWT
9/30/1945 02:00 EST
5/15/1946 02:00 EDT
9/29/1946 02:00 EST
6/14/1967 00:01 EDT
10/29/1967 00:01 EST
4/29/1973 02:00 EDT
10/28/1973 02:00 EST
1/06/1974 02:00 EDT
10/27/1974 02:00 EST
4/27/1975 02:00 EDT
10/26/1975 02:00 US#1

MI # 46
Before 9/18/1885 LMT
9/18/1885 12:00 CST
3/31/1918 02:00 CWT
10/27/1918 02:00 CST
3/30/1919 02:00 CWT
10/26/1919 02:00 CST
2/28/1931 02:00 EST
2/09/1942 02:00 EWT
2/15/1943 02:00 CWT
9/30/1945 02:00 EST
6/14/1967 00:01 EDT
10/29/1967 00:01 EST
4/29/1973 02:00 EDT
10/28/1973 02:00 EST
1/06/1974 02:00 EDT
10/27/1974 02:00 EST
4/27/1975 02:00 EDT
10/26/1975 02:00 US#1

MI # 47
Before 9/18/1885 LMT
9/18/1885 12:00 CST
3/31/1918 02:00 CWT
10/27/1918 02:00 CST
3/30/1919 02:00 CWT
10/26/1919 02:00 CST
4/11/1920 02:00 CDT
10/10/1920 02:00 CST
4/17/1921 02:00 CDT
10/09/1921 02:00 CST
4/30/1922 02:00 CDT
10/01/1922 02:00 CST
4/15/1923 02:00 CDT
10/07/1923 02:00 CST
4/13/1924 02:00 CDT
10/05/1924 02:00 CST
4/12/1925 02:00 CDT
11/14/1926 02:00 CST
3/27/1927 00:01 CDT
10/31/1927 00:01 CST
3/18/1928 00:01 CDT
11/11/1928 00:01 CST
3/17/1929 00:01 CDT
11/10/1929 00:01 CST
3/16/1930 00:01 CDT
11/09/1930 00:01 CST
2/28/1931 02:00 EST
2/09/1942 02:00 EWT
2/15/1943 02:00 CWT
9/30/1945 02:00 EST
6/14/1967 00:01 EDT
10/29/1967 00:01 EST
4/29/1973 02:00 EDT
10/28/1973 02:00 EST
1/06/1974 02:00 EDT
10/27/1974 02:00 EST
4/27/1975 02:00 EDT
10/26/1975 02:00 US#1

MI # 48
Before 9/18/1885 LMT
9/18/1885 12:00 CST
3/31/1918 02:00 CWT
10/27/1918 02:00 CST
3/30/1919 02:00 CWT
10/26/1919 02:00 CST
3/29/1931 02:00 EST
2/09/1942 02:00 EWT
2/15/1943 02:00 CWT
9/30/1945 02:00 EST
6/14/1967 00:01 EDT
10/29/1967 00:01 EST
4/29/1973 02:00 EDT
10/28/1973 02:00 EST
1/06/1974 02:00 EDT
10/27/1974 02:00 EST
4/27/1975 02:00 EDT
10/26/1975 02:00 US#1

MI # 49
Before 9/18/1885 LMT
9/18/1885 12:00 CST
3/31/1918 02:00 CWT
10/27/1918 02:00 CST
3/30/1919 02:00 CWT
10/26/1919 02:00 CST
4/09/1922 00:01 CDT
9/24/1922 00:01 CST
4/08/1923 00:01 CDT
9/30/1923 00:01 CST
4/12/1924 00:01 CDT
9/28/1924 00:01 CST
4/12/1925 00:01 CDT
9/27/1925 00:01 CST
4/11/1926 00:01 CDT
9/26/1926 00:01 CST
4/10/1927 00:01 CDT
9/25/1927 00:01 CST
4/08/1928 00:01 CDT
9/30/1928 00:01 CST
4/14/1929 00:01 CDT
9/29/1929 00:01 CST
4/13/1930 00:01 CDT
9/28/1930 00:01 CST
4/11/1931 02:00 EST
2/09/1942 02:00 EWT
2/15/1943 02:00 CWT
9/30/1945 02:00 EST
6/14/1967 00:01 EDT
10/29/1967 00:01 EST
4/29/1973 02:00 EDT
10/28/1973 02:00 EST
1/06/1974 02:00 EDT
10/27/1974 02:00 EST
4/27/1975 02:00 EDT
10/26/1975 02:00 US#1

MI # 50
Before 9/18/1885 LMT
9/18/1885 12:00 CST
3/31/1918 02:00 CWT
10/27/1918 02:00 CST
3/30/1919 02:00 CWT
10/26/1919 02:00 CST
6/01/1928 02:00 CDT
10/01/1928 02:00 CST
6/01/1929 02:00 CDT
10/01/1929 02:00 CST
6/01/1930 02:00 CDT
10/01/1930 02:00 CST
6/01/1931 02:00 EST
2/09/1942 02:00 EWT
2/15/1943 02:00 CWT
9/30/1945 02:00 EST
4/25/1948 02:00 EDT
9/26/1948 02:00 EST
4/29/1973 02:00 EDT
10/28/1973 02:00 EST
1/06/1974 02:00 EDT
10/27/1974 02:00 EST
4/27/1975 02:00 EDT
10/26/1975 02:00 US#1

MI # 51
Before 9/18/1885 LMT
9/18/1885 12:00 CST
3/31/1918 02:00 CWT
10/27/1918 02:00 CST
3/30/1919 02:00 CWT
10/26/1919 02:00 CST
3/10/1932 02:00 EST
2/09/1942 02:00 EWT
2/15/1943 02:00 CWT
9/30/1945 02:00 EST
6/14/1967 00:01 EDT
10/29/1967 00:01 EST
4/29/1973 02:00 EDT
10/28/1973 02:00 EST
1/06/1974 02:00 EDT
10/27/1974 02:00 EST
4/27/1975 02:00 EDT
10/26/1975 02:00 US#1

MI # 52
Before 9/18/1885 LMT
9/18/1885 12:00 CST
3/31/1918 02:00 CWT
10/27/1918 02:00 CST
3/30/1919 02:00 CWT
10/26/1919 02:00 CST
3/10/1932 02:00 EST
2/09/1942 02:00 EWT
2/15/1943 02:00 CWT
9/30/1945 02:00 EST
4/28/1946 02:00 EDT
9/29/1946 02:00 EST
6/14/1967 00:01 EDT
10/29/1967 00:01 EST
4/29/1973 02:00 EDT
10/28/1973 02:00 EST
1/06/1974 02:00 EDT
10/27/1974 02:00 EST
4/27/1975 02:00 EDT
10/26/1975 02:00 US#1

MI # 53
Before 9/18/1885 LMT
9/18/1885 12:00 CST
3/31/1918 02:00 CWT
10/27/1918 02:00 CST
3/30/1919 02:00 CWT
10/26/1919 02:00 CST
3/17/1920 00:01 CDT
10/02/1920 00:01 CST
4/17/1921 00:01 CDT
10/02/1921 00:01 CST
4/16/1922 00:01 CDT
10/02/1922 00:01 CST
4/15/1923 00:01 CDT
9/03/1923 00:01 CST
5/04/1924 00:01 CDT
10/04/1924 00:01 CST
4/11/1925 00:01 CDT
10/11/1925 00:01 CST
4/10/1926 00:01 CDT
9/26/1926 00:01 CST
4/09/1927 00:01 CDT
9/25/1927 00:01 CST
3/21/1928 00:01 CDT
9/30/1928 00:01 CST
3/20/1929 00:01 CDT
9/29/1929 00:01 CST
4/12/1930 00:01 CDT
9/28/1930 00:01 CST
4/11/1931 00:01 CDT
9/27/1931 00:01 CST
3/10/1932 02:00 EST
2/09/1942 02:00 EWT
2/15/1943 02:00 CWT
9/30/1945 02:00 EST
6/14/1967 00:01 EDT
10/29/1967 00:01 EST
4/29/1973 02:00 EDT
10/28/1973 02:00 EST
1/06/1974 02:00 EDT
10/27/1974 02:00 EST
4/27/1975 02:00 EDT
10/26/1975 02:00 US#1

MI # 54
Before 9/18/1885 LMT
9/18/1885 12:00 CST
3/31/1918 02:00 CWT
10/27/1918 02:00 CST
3/30/1919 02:00 CWT
10/26/1919 02:00 CST
4/26/1931 02:00 CDT
9/27/1931 02:00 CST
3/10/1932 02:00 EST
2/09/1942 02:00 EWT
2/15/1943 02:00 CWT
9/30/1945 02:00 EST
6/14/1967 00:01 EDT
10/29/1967 00:01 EST
4/29/1973 02:00 EDT
10/28/1973 02:00 EST
1/06/1974 02:00 EDT
10/27/1974 02:00 EST
4/27/1975 02:00 EDT
10/26/1975 02:00 US#1

MI # 55
Before 9/18/1885 LMT
9/18/1885 12:00 CST
3/31/1918 02:00 CWT
10/27/1918 02:00 CST
3/30/1919 02:00 CWT
10/26/1919 02:00 CST
4/12/1931 02:00 CDT
10/11/1931 02:00 CST
3/10/1932 02:00 EST
2/09/1942 02:00 EWT
2/15/1943 02:00 CWT
9/30/1945 02:00 EST
6/14/1967 00:01 EDT
10/29/1967 00:01 EST
4/29/1973 02:00 EDT
10/28/1973 02:00 EST
1/06/1974 02:00 EDT
10/27/1974 02:00 EST
4/27/1975 02:00 EDT
10/26/1975 02:00 US#1

MI # 56
Before 9/18/1885 LMT
9/18/1885 12:00 CST
3/31/1918 02:00 CWT
10/27/1918 02:00 CST
3/30/1919 02:00 CWT
10/26/1919 02:00 CST
4/01/1931 02:00 CDT
10/01/1931 02:00 CST
3/10/1932 02:00 EST
2/09/1942 02:00 EWT
2/15/1943 02:00 CWT
9/30/1945 02:00 EST
6/14/1967 00:01 EDT
10/29/1967 00:01 EST
4/29/1973 02:00 EDT
10/28/1973 02:00 EST
1/06/1974 02:00 EDT
10/27/1974 02:00 EST
4/27/1975 02:00 EDT
10/26/1975 02:00 US#1

MI # 57
Before 9/18/1885 LMT
9/18/1885 12:00 CST
3/31/1918 02:00 CWT
10/27/1918 02:00 CST
3/30/1919 02:00 CWT
10/26/1919 02:00 CST
4/04/1932 02:00 EST
2/09/1942 02:00 EWT
2/15/1943 02:00 CWT
9/30/1945 02:00 EST
6/14/1967 00:01 EDT
10/29/1967 00:01 EST
4/29/1973 02:00 EDT
10/28/1973 02:00 EST
1/06/1974 02:00 EDT
10/27/1974 02:00 EST
4/27/1975 02:00 EDT
10/26/1975 02:00 US#1

MI # 58
Before 9/18/1885 LMT
9/18/1885 12:00 CST
3/31/1918 02:00 CWT
10/27/1918 02:00 CST
3/30/1919 02:00 CWT
10/26/1919 02:00 CST
3/27/1921 02:00 CDT
10/31/1921 02:00 CST
4/30/1922 02:00 CDT
9/24/1922 02:00 CST
4/29/1923 02:00 CDT
9/30/1923 02:00 CST
4/27/1924 02:00 CDT
9/28/1924 02:00 CST
4/26/1925 02:00 CDT
9/27/1925 02:00 CST
4/25/1926 02:00 CDT
9/26/1926 02:00 CST
4/24/1927 02:00 CDT
9/25/1927 02:00 CST
4/29/1928 02:00 CDT
9/30/1928 02:00 CST
4/28/1929 02:00 CDT
9/29/1929 02:00 CST
4/27/1930 02:00 CDT
9/28/1930 02:00 CST
4/26/1931 02:00 CDT
9/27/1931 02:00 CST
4/04/1932 02:00 EST
2/09/1942 02:00 EWT
2/15/1943 02:00 CWT
9/30/1945 02:00 EST
6/14/1967 00:01 EDT
10/29/1967 00:01 EST
4/29/1973 02:00 EDT
10/28/1973 02:00 EST
1/06/1974 02:00 EDT
10/27/1974 02:00 EST
4/27/1975 02:00 EDT
10/26/1975 02:00 US#1

MI # 59
Before 9/18/1885 LMT
9/18/1885 12:00 CST
3/31/1918 02:00 CWT
10/27/1918 02:00 CST
3/30/1919 02:00 CWT
10/26/1919 02:00 CST
4/04/1932 02:00 EST
2/09/1942 02:00 EWT
2/15/1943 02:00 CWT
9/30/1945 02:00 EST
4/28/1946 02:00 EDT
9/29/1946 02:00 EST
6/14/1967 00:01 EDT
10/29/1967 00:01 EST
4/29/1973 02:00 EDT
10/28/1973 02:00 EST
1/06/1974 02:00 EDT
10/27/1974 02:00 EST
4/27/1975 02:00 EDT
10/26/1975 02:00 US#1

MI # 60
Before 9/18/1885 LMT
9/18/1885 12:00 CST
3/31/1918 02:00 CWT
10/27/1918 02:00 CST
3/30/1919 02:00 CWT
10/26/1919 02:00 CST
4/04/1932 02:00 EST
2/09/1942 02:00 EWT
2/15/1943 02:00 CWT
9/30/1945 02:00 EST
4/25/1948 02:00 EDT
9/26/1948 02:00 EST
6/14/1967 00:01 EDT
10/29/1967 00:01 EST
4/29/1973 02:00 EDT
10/28/1973 02:00 EST
1/06/1974 02:00 EDT
10/27/1974 02:00 EST
4/27/1975 02:00 EDT
10/26/1975 02:00 US#1

MI # 61
Before 9/18/1885 LMT
9/18/1885 12:00 CST
3/31/1918 02:00 CWT
10/27/1918 02:00 CST
3/30/1919 02:00 CWT
10/26/1919 02:00 CST
4/04/1920 02:00 CDT
9/26/1920 02:00 CST
4/03/1921 02:00 CDT
9/25/1921 02:00 CST
4/02/1922 02:00 CDT
9/24/1922 02:00 CST
4/01/1923 02:00 CDT
9/30/1923 02:00 CST
4/06/1924 02:00 CDT
9/28/1924 02:00 CST
4/05/1925 02:00 CDT
9/27/1925 02:00 CST
4/04/1926 02:00 CDT
9/26/1926 02:00 CST
4/03/1927 02:00 CDT
9/25/1927 02:00 CST
4/01/1928 02:00 CDT
9/30/1928 02:00 CST
4/07/1929 02:00 CDT
9/29/1929 02:00 CST
4/06/1930 02:00 CDT
9/28/1930 02:00 CST
4/05/1931 02:00 CDT
9/27/1931 02:00 CST
4/04/1932 02:00 EST
2/09/1942 02:00 EWT
2/15/1943 02:00 CWT
9/30/1945 02:00 EST
4/28/1946 02:00 EDT
9/29/1946 02:00 EST
6/14/1967 00:01 EDT
10/29/1967 00:01 EST
4/29/1973 02:00 EDT
10/28/1973 02:00 EST
1/06/1974 02:00 EDT
10/27/1974 02:00 EST
4/27/1975 02:00 EDT
10/26/1975 02:00 US#1

MI # 62
Before 9/18/1885 LMT
9/18/1885 12:00 CST
3/31/1918 02:00 CWT
10/27/1918 02:00 CST
3/30/1919 02:00 CWT
10/26/1919 02:00 CST
4/12/1931 02:00 CDT
9/27/1931 02:00 CST
4/04/1932 02:00 EST
2/09/1942 02:00 EWT
2/15/1943 02:00 CWT
9/30/1945 02:00 EST
6/14/1967 00:01 EDT
10/29/1967 00:01 EST
4/29/1973 02:00 EDT
10/28/1973 02:00 EST
1/06/1974 02:00 EDT
10/27/1974 02:00 EST
4/27/1975 02:00 EDT
10/26/1975 02:00 US#1

MI # 63
Before 9/18/1885 LMT
9/18/1885 12:00 CST
3/31/1918 02:00 CWT
10/27/1918 02:00 CST
3/30/1919 02:00 CWT
10/26/1919 02:00 CST
5/01/1927 02:00 CDT
9/25/1927 02:00 CST
4/05/1931 02:00 CDT
10/04/1931 02:00 CST
4/04/1932 02:00 EST
2/09/1942 02:00 EWT
2/15/1943 02:00 CWT
9/30/1945 02:00 EST
6/14/1967 00:01 EDT
10/29/1967 00:01 EST
4/29/1973 02:00 EDT
10/28/1973 02:00 EST
1/06/1974 02:00 EDT
10/27/1974 02:00 EST

TIME TABLES

4/27/1975 02:00 EDT
10/26/1975 02:00 US#1

MI # 64
Before 9/18/1885 LMT
9/18/1885 12:00 CST
3/31/1918 02:00 CWT
10/27/1918 02:00 CST
3/30/1919 02:00 CWT
10/26/1919 02:00 CST
4/26/1931 02:00 CDT
9/27/1931 02:00 CST
4/04/1932 02:00 EST
2/09/1942 02:00 EWT
2/15/1943 02:00 CWT
9/30/1945 02:00 EST
6/14/1967 00:01 EDT
10/29/1967 00:01 EST
4/29/1973 02:00 EDT
10/28/1973 02:00 EST
1/06/1974 02:00 EDT
10/27/1974 02:00 EST
4/27/1975 02:00 EDT
10/26/1975 02:00 US#1

MI # 65
Before 9/18/1885 LMT
9/18/1885 12:00 CST
3/31/1918 02:00 CWT
10/27/1918 02:00 CST
3/30/1919 02:00 CWT
10/26/1919 02:00 CST
4/01/1931 02:00 CDT
11/01/1931 02:00 CST
4/04/1932 02:00 EST
2/09/1942 02:00 EWT
2/15/1943 02:00 CWT
9/30/1945 02:00 EST
6/14/1967 00:01 EDT
10/29/1967 00:01 EST
4/29/1973 02:00 EDT
10/28/1973 02:00 EST
1/06/1974 02:00 EDT
10/27/1974 02:00 EST
4/27/1975 02:00 EDT
10/26/1975 02:00 US#1

MI # 66
Before 9/18/1885 LMT
9/18/1885 12:00 CST
3/31/1918 02:00 CWT
10/27/1918 02:00 CST
3/30/1919 02:00 CWT
10/26/1919 02:00 CST
4/12/1931 02:00 CDT
9/12/1931 02:00 CST
4/04/1932 02:00 EST
2/09/1942 02:00 EWT
2/15/1943 02:00 CWT
9/30/1945 02:00 EST
6/14/1967 00:01 EDT
10/29/1967 00:01 EST
4/29/1973 02:00 EDT
10/28/1973 02:00 EST
1/06/1974 02:00 EDT
10/27/1974 02:00 EST
4/27/1975 02:00 EDT
10/26/1975 02:00 US#1

MI # 67
Before 9/18/1885 LMT
9/18/1885 12:00 CST
3/31/1918 02:00 CWT
10/27/1918 02:00 CST
3/30/1919 02:00 CWT
10/26/1919 02:00 CST
4/17/1932 02:00 EST
2/09/1942 02:00 EWT
2/15/1943 02:00 CWT
9/30/1945 02:00 EST
6/14/1967 00:01 EDT
10/29/1967 00:01 EST
4/29/1973 02:00 EDT
10/28/1973 02:00 EST
1/06/1974 02:00 EDT
10/27/1974 02:00 EST
4/27/1975 02:00 EDT
10/26/1975 02:00 US#1

MI # 68
Before 9/18/1885 LMT
9/18/1885 12:00 CST
3/31/1918 02:00 CWT
10/27/1918 02:00 CST
3/30/1919 02:00 CWT
10/26/1919 02:00 CST
4/12/1925 02:00 CDT
9/27/1925 02:00 CST
4/11/1926 02:00 CDT
9/26/1926 02:00 CST
4/10/1927 02:00 CDT
9/25/1927 02:00 CST
4/08/1928 02:00 CDT
9/30/1928 02:00 CST
4/14/1929 02:00 CDT
9/29/1929 02:00 CST
4/13/1930 02:00 CDT
9/28/1930 02:00 CST
4/12/1931 02:00 CDT
9/27/1931 02:00 CST
4/10/1932 02:00 CDT
9/25/1932 02:00 CST
11/10/1932 02:00 EST
2/09/1942 02:00 EWT
2/15/1943 02:00 CWT
9/30/1945 02:00 EST
6/14/1967 00:01 EDT
10/29/1967 00:01 EST
4/29/1973 02:00 EDT
10/28/1973 02:00 EST
1/06/1974 02:00 EDT
10/27/1974 02:00 EST
4/27/1975 02:00 EDT
10/26/1975 02:00 US#1

MI # 69
Before 9/18/1885 LMT
9/18/1885 12:00 CST
3/31/1918 02:00 CWT
10/27/1918 02:00 CST
3/30/1919 02:00 CWT
10/26/1919 02:00 CST
5/02/1932 02:00 CDT
11/22/1932 02:00 CST
4/30/1933 02:00 EST
2/09/1942 02:00 EWT
2/15/1943 02:00 CWT
9/30/1945 02:00 EST
4/25/1948 02:00 EDT
9/26/1948 02:00 EST
4/29/1973 02:00 EDT
10/28/1973 02:00 EST
1/06/1974 02:00 EDT
10/27/1974 02:00 EST
4/27/1975 02:00 EDT
10/26/1975 02:00 US#1

MI # 70
Before 9/18/1885 LMT
9/18/1885 12:00 CST
3/31/1918 02:00 CWT
10/27/1918 02:00 CST
3/30/1919 02:00 CWT
10/26/1919 02:00 CST
6/01/1931 02:00 CDT
9/01/1931 02:00 CST
6/01/1932 02:00 CDT
9/01/1932 02:00 CST
4/30/1933 02:00 EST
2/09/1942 02:00 EWT
2/15/1943 02:00 CWT
9/30/1945 02:00 EST
6/14/1967 00:01 EDT
10/29/1967 00:01 EST
4/29/1973 02:00 EDT
10/28/1973 02:00 EST
1/06/1974 02:00 EDT
10/27/1974 02:00 EST
4/27/1975 02:00 EDT
10/26/1975 02:00 US#1

MI # 71
Before 9/18/1885 LMT
9/18/1885 12:00 CST
3/31/1918 02:00 CWT
10/27/1918 02:00 CST
3/30/1919 02:00 CWT
10/26/1919 02:00 CST
4/02/1932 00:01 CDT
10/02/1932 00:01 CST
4/02/1933 00:01 CDT
10/02/1933 00:01 CST
4/02/1934 00:01 CDT
10/02/1934 00:01 CST
4/02/1935 00:01 EST
2/09/1942 02:00 EWT
2/15/1943 02:00 CWT
9/30/1945 02:00 EST
6/14/1967 00:01 EDT
10/29/1967 00:01 EST
4/29/1973 02:00 EDT
10/28/1973 02:00 EST
1/06/1974 02:00 EDT
10/27/1974 02:00 EST
4/27/1975 02:00 EDT
10/26/1975 02:00 US#1

MI # 72
Before 9/18/1885 LMT
9/18/1885 12:00 CST
3/31/1918 02:00 CWT
10/27/1918 02:00 CST
3/30/1919 02:00 CWT
10/26/1919 02:00 CST
4/07/1935 02:00 EST
2/09/1942 02:00 EWT
2/15/1943 02:00 CWT
9/30/1945 02:00 EST
6/14/1967 00:01 EDT
10/29/1967 00:01 EST
4/29/1973 02:00 EDT
10/28/1973 02:00 EST
1/06/1974 02:00 EDT
10/27/1974 02:00 EST
4/27/1975 02:00 EDT
10/26/1975 02:00 US#1

MI # 73
Before 9/18/1885 LMT
9/18/1885 12:00 CST
3/31/1918 02:00 CWT
10/27/1918 02:00 CST
3/30/1919 02:00 CWT
10/26/1919 02:00 CST
4/02/1933 02:00 CDT
10/15/1933 02:00 CST
4/08/1934 02:00 CDT
9/30/1934 02:00 CST
4/07/1935 02:00 EST
2/09/1942 02:00 EWT
2/15/1943 02:00 CWT
9/30/1945 02:00 EST
6/14/1967 00:01 EDT
10/29/1967 00:01 EST
4/29/1973 02:00 EDT
10/28/1973 02:00 EST
1/06/1974 02:00 EDT
10/27/1974 02:00 EST
4/27/1975 02:00 EDT
10/26/1975 02:00 US#1

MI # 74
Before 9/18/1885 LMT
9/18/1885 12:00 CST
3/31/1918 02:00 CWT
10/27/1918 02:00 CST
3/30/1919 02:00 CWT
10/26/1919 02:00 CST
4/26/1931 02:00 CDT
9/27/1931 02:00 CST
4/24/1932 02:00 CDT
9/25/1932 02:00 CST
4/30/1933 02:00 CDT
9/24/1933 02:00 CST
4/29/1934 02:00 CDT
9/30/1934 02:00 CST
4/07/1935 02:00 EST
2/09/1942 02:00 EWT
2/15/1943 02:00 CWT
9/30/1945 02:00 EST
6/14/1967 00:01 EDT
10/29/1967 00:01 EST
4/29/1973 02:00 EDT
10/28/1973 02:00 EST
1/06/1974 02:00 EDT
10/27/1974 02:00 EST
4/27/1975 02:00 EDT
10/26/1975 02:00 US#1

MI # 75
Before 9/18/1885 LMT
9/18/1885 12:00 CST
3/31/1918 02:00 CWT
10/27/1918 02:00 CST
3/30/1919 02:00 CWT
10/26/1919 02:00 CST
4/30/1933 02:00 CDT
9/24/1933 02:00 CST
4/29/1934 02:00 CDT
9/30/1934 02:00 CST
4/07/1935 02:00 EST
2/09/1942 02:00 EWT
2/15/1943 02:00 CWT
9/30/1945 02:00 EST
6/14/1967 00:01 EDT
10/29/1967 00:01 EST
4/29/1973 02:00 EDT
10/28/1973 02:00 EST
1/06/1974 02:00 EDT
10/27/1974 02:00 EST
4/27/1975 02:00 EDT
10/26/1975 02:00 US#1

MI # 76
Before 9/18/1885 LMT
9/18/1885 12:00 CST
3/31/1918 02:00 CWT
10/27/1918 02:00 CST
3/30/1919 02:00 CWT
10/26/1919 02:00 CST
4/03/1933 02:00 CDT
10/01/1933 02:00 CST
4/08/1934 02:00 CDT
10/01/1934 02:00 CST
4/07/1935 02:00 EST
2/09/1942 02:00 EWT
2/15/1943 02:00 CWT
9/30/1945 02:00 EST
6/14/1967 00:01 EDT
10/29/1967 00:01 EST
4/29/1973 02:00 EDT
10/28/1973 02:00 EST
1/06/1974 02:00 EDT
10/27/1974 02:00 EST
4/27/1975 02:00 EDT
10/26/1975 02:00 US#1

MI # 77
Before 9/18/1885 LMT
9/18/1885 12:00 CST
3/31/1918 02:00 CWT
10/27/1918 02:00 CST
3/30/1919 02:00 CWT
10/26/1919 02:00 CST
3/27/1921 02:00 CDT
10/31/1921 02:00 CST
4/30/1922 02:00 CDT
9/24/1922 02:00 CST
4/29/1923 02:00 CDT
9/30/1923 02:00 CST
4/27/1924 02:00 CDT
9/28/1924 02:00 CST
4/26/1925 02:00 CDT
9/27/1925 02:00 CST
4/25/1926 02:00 CDT
9/26/1926 02:00 CST
4/24/1927 02:00 CDT
9/25/1927 02:00 CST
4/29/1928 02:00 CDT
9/30/1928 02:00 CST
4/28/1929 02:00 CDT
9/29/1929 02:00 CST
4/27/1930 02:00 CDT
9/28/1930 02:00 CST
4/26/1931 02:00 CDT
9/27/1931 02:00 CST
4/24/1932 02:00 CDT
9/25/1932 02:00 CST
4/30/1933 02:00 CDT
9/24/1933 02:00 CST
4/29/1934 02:00 CDT
9/30/1934 02:00 CST
4/28/1935 02:00 EST
2/09/1942 02:00 EWT
2/15/1943 02:00 CWT
9/30/1945 02:00 EST
6/14/1967 00:01 EDT
10/29/1967 00:01 EST
4/29/1973 02:00 EDT
10/28/1973 02:00 EST
1/06/1974 02:00 EDT
10/27/1974 02:00 EST
4/27/1975 02:00 EDT
10/26/1975 02:00 US#1

MI # 78
Before 9/18/1885 LMT
9/18/1885 12:00 CST
3/31/1918 02:00 CWT
10/27/1918 02:00 CST
3/30/1919 02:00 CWT
10/26/1919 02:00 CST
4/28/1935 02:00 EST
2/09/1942 02:00 EWT
2/15/1943 02:00 CWT
9/30/1945 02:00 EST
4/25/1948 02:00 EDT
9/26/1948 02:00 EST
4/29/1973 02:00 EDT
10/28/1973 02:00 EST
1/06/1974 02:00 EDT
10/27/1974 02:00 EST
4/27/1975 02:00 EDT
10/26/1975 02:00 US#1

MI # 79
Before 9/18/1885 LMT
9/18/1885 12:00 CST
3/31/1918 02:00 CWT
10/27/1918 02:00 CST
3/30/1919 02:00 CWT
10/26/1919 02:00 CST
4/29/1925 02:00 CDT
9/30/1925 02:00 CST
4/24/1932 02:00 CDT
10/31/1932 02:00 CST
4/30/1933 02:00 CDT
9/24/1933 02:00 CST
4/29/1934 02:00 CDT
9/30/1934 02:00 CST
5/01/1935 02:00 CDT
10/01/1935 02:00 CST
5/01/1936 02:00 CDT
9/01/1936 02:00 CST
9/27/1936 02:00 EST
2/09/1942 02:00 EWT
2/15/1943 02:00 CWT
9/30/1945 02:00 EST
4/25/1948 02:00 EDT
9/26/1948 02:00 EST
4/24/1949 02:00 EDT
9/25/1949 02:00 EST
4/29/1973 02:00 EDT
10/28/1973 02:00 EST
1/06/1974 02:00 EDT
10/27/1974 02:00 EST
4/27/1975 02:00 EDT
10/26/1975 02:00 US#1

MI # 80
Before 9/18/1885 LMT
9/18/1885 12:00 CST
3/31/1918 02:00 CWT
10/27/1918 02:00 CST
3/30/1919 02:00 CWT
10/26/1919 02:00 CST
2/09/1942 02:00 CWT
9/30/1945 02:00 CST
4/25/1948 02:00 CDT
9/26/1948 02:00 CST
12/10/1967 02:00 EST
4/29/1973 02:00 EDT
10/28/1973 02:00 EST
1/06/1974 02:00 EDT
10/27/1974 02:00 EST
4/27/1975 02:00 EDT
10/26/1975 02:00 US#1

MI # 81
Before 9/18/1885 LMT
9/18/1885 12:00 CST
3/31/1918 02:00 CWT
10/27/1918 02:00 CST
3/30/1919 02:00 CWT
10/26/1919 02:00 CST
2/09/1942 02:00 CWT
9/30/1945 02:00 CST
4/24/1966 02:00 CDT
10/30/1966 02:00 CST
4/27/1969 02:00 EST
4/29/1973 02:00 CST
4/29/1973 02:00 US#1

MI # 82
Before 9/18/1885 LMT
9/18/1885 12:00 CST
3/31/1918 02:00 CWT
10/27/1918 02:00 CST
3/30/1919 02:00 CWT
10/26/1919 02:00 CST
5/15/1935 02:00 CDT
8/31/1935 02:00 CST
2/09/1942 02:00 CWT
9/30/1945 02:00 CST
4/28/1946 02:00 CDT
9/29/1946 02:00 CST
5/01/1950 02:00 CDT
10/01/1950 02:00 CST
4/27/1952 02:00 CDT
9/28/1952 02:00 CST
4/24/1966 02:00 CDT
10/30/1966 02:00 CST
4/27/1969 02:00 EST
4/29/1973 02:00 CST
4/29/1973 02:00 US#1

MI # 83
Before 9/18/1885 LMT
9/18/1885 12:00 CST
3/31/1918 02:00 CWT
10/27/1918 02:00 CST
3/30/1919 02:00 CWT
10/26/1919 02:00 CST
2/09/1942 02:00 CWT
9/30/1945 02:00 CST
5/05/1946 02:00 CDT
9/29/1946 02:00 CST
4/30/1950 02:00 CDT
9/24/1950 02:00 CST
4/24/1960 02:00 CDT
10/30/1960 02:00 CST
4/30/1961 02:00 CDT
9/24/1961 02:00 CST
4/29/1962 02:00 CDT
9/30/1962 02:00 CST
4/28/1963 02:00 CDT
9/29/1963 02:00 CST
4/26/1964 02:00 CDT
10/25/1964 02:00 CST
4/25/1965 02:00 CDT
10/31/1965 02:00 CST
4/24/1966 02:00 CDT
10/30/1966 02:00 CST
4/27/1969 02:00 EST
4/29/1973 02:00 CST
4/29/1973 02:00 US#1

MI # 84
Before 9/18/1885 LMT
9/18/1885 12:00 CST
3/31/1918 02:00 CWT
10/27/1918 02:00 CST
3/30/1919 02:00 CWT
10/26/1919 02:00 CST
5/15/1935 02:00 CDT
9/01/1935 02:00 CST
2/09/1942 02:00 CWT
9/30/1945 02:00 CST
5/01/1946 02:00 CDT
9/29/1946 02:00 CST
4/27/1947 02:00 CDT
9/28/1947 02:00 CST
5/01/1950 02:00 CDT
10/01/1950 02:00 CST
4/27/1952 02:00 CDT
9/28/1952 02:00 CST
4/24/1966 02:00 CDT
10/30/1966 02:00 CST
4/27/1969 02:00 EST
4/29/1973 02:00 CST
4/29/1973 02:00 US#1

MI # 85
Before 9/18/1885 LMT
9/18/1885 12:00 CST
3/31/1918 02:00 CWT
10/27/1918 02:00 CST
3/30/1919 02:00 CWT
10/26/1919 02:00 CST
2/09/1942 02:00 CWT
9/30/1945 02:00 CST
4/28/1946 02:00 CDT
9/29/1946 02:00 CST
4/27/1947 02:00 CDT
9/28/1947 02:00 CST
4/30/1961 02:00 CDT
9/24/1961 02:00 CST
4/29/1962 02:00 CDT
9/30/1962 02:00 CST
4/28/1963 02:00 CDT
9/29/1963 02:00 CST
4/26/1964 02:00 CDT
9/27/1964 02:00 CST
4/25/1965 02:00 CDT
10/31/1965 02:00 CST
4/24/1966 02:00 CDT
10/30/1966 02:00 CST
4/27/1969 02:00 EST
4/29/1973 02:00 CST
4/29/1973 02:00 US#1

MI # 86
Before 9/18/1885 LMT
9/18/1885 12:00 CST
3/31/1918 02:00 CWT
10/27/1918 02:00 CST
3/30/1919 02:00 CWT
10/26/1919 02:00 CST
2/09/1942 02:00 CWT
9/30/1945 02:00 CST
4/28/1946 02:00 CDT
9/29/1946 02:00 CST
4/24/1966 02:00 CDT
10/30/1966 02:00 CST
4/27/1969 02:00 EST
4/29/1973 02:00 CST
4/29/1973 02:00 US#1

MI # 87
Before 9/18/1885 LMT
9/18/1885 12:00 CST
3/31/1918 02:00 CWT
10/27/1918 02:00 CST
3/30/1919 02:00 CWT
10/26/1919 02:00 CST
2/09/1942 02:00 CWT
9/30/1945 02:00 CST
4/28/1946 02:00 CDT
9/29/1946 02:00 CST
4/25/1948 02:00 CDT
9/26/1948 02:00 CST
4/24/1960 02:00 CDT
10/30/1960 02:00 CST
4/30/1961 02:00 CDT
9/24/1961 02:00 CST
4/29/1962 02:00 CDT
9/30/1962 02:00 CST
4/28/1963 02:00 CDT
9/29/1963 02:00 CST
4/26/1964 02:00 CDT

TIME TABLES

10/25/1964 02:00 CST
4/25/1965 02:00 CDT
10/31/1965 02:00 CST
4/24/1966 02:00 CDT
10/30/1966 02:00 CST
4/27/1969 02:00 EST
4/29/1973 02:00 CST
4/29/1973 02:00 US#1

MI # 88

Before 9/18/1885 LMT
9/18/1885 12:00 CST
3/31/1918 02:00 CWT
10/27/1918 02:00 CST
3/30/1919 02:00 CWT
10/26/1919 02:00 CST
4/26/1931 02:00 EST
2/09/1942 02:00 EWT
9/30/1945 02:00 EST
6/14/1967 00:01 EDT
10/29/1967 00:01 EST
4/29/1973 02:00 EDT
10/28/1973 02:00 EST
1/06/1974 02:00 EDT
10/27/1974 02:00 EST
4/27/1975 02:00 EDT
10/26/1975 02:00 US#1

MI # 89

Before 9/18/1885 LMT
9/18/1885 12:00 CST
3/31/1918 02:00 CWT
10/27/1918 02:00 CST
3/30/1919 02:00 CWT
10/26/1919 02:00 CST
4/26/1931 02:00 EST
2/09/1942 02:00 EWT
9/30/1945 02:00 EST
4/25/1948 02:00 EDT
9/26/1948 02:00 EST
6/14/1967 00:01 EDT
10/29/1967 00:01 EST
4/29/1973 02:00 EDT
10/28/1973 02:00 EST
1/06/1974 02:00 EDT
10/27/1974 02:00 EST
4/27/1975 02:00 EDT
10/26/1975 02:00 US#1

MI # 90

Before 9/18/1885 LMT
9/18/1885 12:00 CST
3/31/1918 02:00 CWT
10/27/1918 02:00 CST
3/30/1919 02:00 CWT
10/26/1919 02:00 CST
12/01/1923 00:01 EST
2/09/1942 02:00 EWT
9/30/1945 02:00 EST
6/14/1967 00:01 EDT
10/29/1967 00:01 EST
4/29/1973 02:00 EDT
10/28/1973 02:00 EST
1/06/1974 02:00 EDT
10/27/1974 02:00 EST
4/27/1975 02:00 EDT
10/26/1975 02:00 US#1

MI # 91

Before 9/18/1885 LMT
9/18/1885 12:00 CST
3/31/1918 02:00 CWT
10/27/1918 02:00 CST
3/30/1919 02:00 CWT
10/26/1919 02:00 CST
11/14/1922 02:00 EST
2/09/1942 02:00 EWT
2/15/1943 02:00 CWT
9/30/1945 02:00 EST
6/14/1967 00:01 EDT
10/29/1967 00:01 EST
4/29/1973 02:00 EDT
10/28/1973 02:00 EST
1/06/1974 02:00 EDT
10/27/1974 02:00 EST
4/27/1975 02:00 EDT
10/26/1975 02:00 US#1

MI # 92

Before 9/18/1885 LMT
9/18/1885 12:00 CST
3/31/1918 02:00 CWT
10/27/1918 02:00 CST
3/30/1919 02:00 CWT
10/26/1919 02:00 CST
4/24/1932 02:00 EST
2/09/1942 02:00 EWT
2/15/1943 02:00 CWT
9/30/1945 02:00 EST
6/14/1967 00:01 EDT
10/29/1967 00:01 EST
4/29/1973 02:00 EDT
10/28/1973 02:00 EST
1/06/1974 02:00 EDT
10/27/1974 02:00 EST
4/27/1975 02:00 EDT
10/26/1975 02:00 US#1

MI # 93

Before 9/18/1885 LMT
9/18/1885 12:00 CST
3/31/1918 02:00 CWT
10/27/1918 02:00 CST
3/30/1919 02:00 CWT
10/26/1919 02:00 CST
6/13/1920 02:00 CDT
10/31/1920 02:00 CST
3/27/1921 02:00 CDT
10/31/1921 02:00 CST
4/30/1922 02:00 CDT
9/24/1922 02:00 CST
4/29/1923 02:00 CDT
9/30/1923 02:00 CST
4/27/1924 02:00 CDT
9/28/1924 02:00 CST
4/26/1925 02:00 CDT
9/27/1925 02:00 CST
4/25/1926 02:00 CDT
9/26/1926 02:00 CST
4/24/1927 02:00 CDT
9/25/1927 02:00 CST
4/29/1928 02:00 CDT
9/30/1928 02:00 CST
4/28/1929 02:00 CDT
9/29/1929 02:00 CST
4/27/1930 02:00 CDT
9/28/1930 02:00 CST
5/10/1931 02:00 CDT
9/19/1931 02:00 CST
4/24/1932 02:00 EST
2/09/1942 02:00 EWT
2/15/1943 02:00 CWT
9/30/1945 02:00 EST
6/14/1967 00:01 EDT
10/29/1967 00:01 EST
4/29/1973 02:00 EDT
10/28/1973 02:00 EST
1/06/1974 02:00 EDT
10/27/1974 02:00 EST
4/27/1975 02:00 EDT
10/26/1975 02:00 US#1

MI # 94

Before 9/18/1885 LMT
9/18/1885 12:00 CST
3/31/1918 02:00 CWT
10/27/1918 02:00 CST
3/30/1919 02:00 CWT
10/26/1919 02:00 CST
4/24/1932 02:00 EST
2/09/1942 02:00 EWT
2/15/1943 02:00 CWT
9/30/1945 02:00 EST
4/28/1946 02:00 EDT
9/29/1946 02:00 EST
6/14/1967 00:01 EDT
10/29/1967 00:01 EST
4/29/1973 02:00 EDT
10/28/1973 02:00 EST
1/06/1974 02:00 EDT
10/27/1974 02:00 EST
4/27/1975 02:00 EDT
10/26/1975 02:00 US#1

MI # 95

Before 9/18/1885 LMT
9/18/1885 12:00 CST
3/31/1918 02:00 CWT
10/27/1918 02:00 CST
3/30/1919 02:00 CWT
10/26/1919 02:00 CST
5/01/1931 00:00 CDT
10/01/1931 00:00 CST
4/24/1932 02:00 EST
2/09/1942 02:00 EWT
2/15/1943 02:00 CWT
9/30/1945 02:00 EST
4/25/1948 02:00 EDT
9/26/1948 02:00 EST
4/29/1973 02:00 EDT
10/28/1973 02:00 EST
1/06/1974 02:00 EDT
10/27/1974 02:00 EST
4/27/1975 02:00 EDT
10/26/1975 02:00 US#1

MI # 96

Before 9/18/1885 LMT
9/18/1885 12:00 CST
3/31/1918 02:00 CWT
10/27/1918 02:00 CST
3/30/1919 02:00 CWT
10/26/1919 02:00 CST
4/24/1932 02:00 EST
2/09/1942 02:00 EWT
2/15/1943 02:00 CWT
9/30/1945 02:00 EST
4/25/1948 02:00 EDT
9/26/1948 02:00 EST
4/29/1973 02:00 EDT
10/28/1973 02:00 EST
1/06/1974 02:00 EDT
10/27/1974 02:00 EST
4/27/1975 02:00 EDT
10/26/1975 02:00 US#1

MI # 97

Before 9/18/1885 LMT
9/18/1885 12:00 CST
3/31/1918 02:00 CWT
10/27/1918 02:00 CST
3/30/1919 02:00 CWT
10/26/1919 02:00 CST
4/26/1931 02:00 CDT
9/27/1931 02:00 CST
4/24/1932 02:00 EST
2/09/1942 02:00 EWT
2/15/1943 02:00 CWT
9/30/1945 02:00 EST
6/14/1967 00:01 EDT
10/29/1967 00:01 EST
4/29/1973 02:00 EDT
10/28/1973 02:00 EST
1/06/1974 02:00 EDT
10/27/1974 02:00 EST
4/27/1975 02:00 EDT
10/26/1975 02:00 US#1

MI # 98

Before 9/18/1885 LMT
9/18/1885 12:00 CST
3/31/1918 02:00 CWT
10/27/1918 02:00 CST
3/30/1919 02:00 CWT
10/26/1919 02:00 CST
6/01/1931 02:00 CDT
10/01/1931 02:00 CST
4/24/1932 02:00 EST
2/09/1942 02:00 EWT
2/15/1943 02:00 CWT
9/30/1945 02:00 EST
4/25/1948 02:00 EDT
9/26/1948 02:00 EST
4/29/1973 02:00 EDT
10/28/1973 02:00 EST
1/06/1974 02:00 EDT
10/27/1974 02:00 EST
4/27/1975 02:00 EDT
10/26/1975 02:00 US#1

MI # 99

Before 9/18/1885 LMT
9/18/1885 12:00 CST
3/31/1918 02:00 CWT
10/27/1918 02:00 CST
3/30/1919 02:00 CWT
10/26/1919 02:00 CST
3/29/1931 02:00 CDT
11/01/1931 02:00 CST
4/24/1932 02:00 EST
2/09/1942 02:00 EWT
2/15/1943 02:00 CWT
9/30/1945 02:00 EST
6/14/1967 00:01 EDT
10/29/1967 00:01 EST
4/29/1973 02:00 EDT
10/28/1973 02:00 EST
1/06/1974 02:00 EDT
10/27/1974 02:00 EST
4/27/1975 02:00 EDT
10/26/1975 02:00 US#1

MI # 100

Before 9/18/1885 LMT
9/18/1885 12:00 CST
3/31/1918 02:00 CWT
10/27/1918 02:00 CST
3/30/1919 02:00 CWT
10/26/1919 02:00 CST
2/29/1931 02:00 CDT
11/01/1931 02:00 CST
4/24/1932 02:00 EST
2/09/1942 02:00 EWT
2/15/1943 02:00 CWT
9/30/1945 02:00 EST
6/14/1967 00:01 EDT
10/29/1967 00:01 EST
4/29/1973 02:00 EDT
10/28/1973 02:00 EST
1/06/1974 02:00 EDT
10/27/1974 02:00 EST
4/27/1975 02:00 EDT
10/26/1975 02:00 US#1

MI # 101

Before 9/18/1885 LMT
9/18/1885 12:00 CST
3/31/1918 02:00 CWT
10/27/1918 02:00 CST
3/30/1919 02:00 CWT
10/26/1919 02:00 CST
3/08/1931 02:00 CDT
11/01/1931 02:00 CST
4/24/1932 02:00 EST
2/09/1942 02:00 EWT
2/15/1943 02:00 CWT
9/30/1945 02:00 EST
6/14/1967 00:01 EDT
10/29/1967 00:01 EST
4/29/1973 02:00 EDT
10/28/1973 02:00 EST
1/06/1974 02:00 EDT
10/27/1974 02:00 EST
4/27/1975 02:00 EDT
10/26/1975 02:00 US#1

MI # 102

Before 9/18/1885 LMT
9/18/1885 12:00 CST
3/31/1918 02:00 CWT
10/27/1918 02:00 CST
3/30/1919 02:00 CWT
10/26/1919 02:00 CST
3/01/1931 02:00 CDT
11/01/1931 02:00 CST
4/24/1932 02:00 EST
2/09/1942 02:00 EWT
2/15/1943 02:00 CWT
9/30/1945 02:00 EST
6/14/1967 00:01 EDT
10/29/1967 00:01 EST
4/29/1973 02:00 EDT
10/28/1973 02:00 EST
1/06/1974 02:00 EDT
10/27/1974 02:00 EST
4/27/1975 02:00 EDT
10/26/1975 02:00 US#1

MI # 103

Before 9/18/1885 LMT
9/18/1885 12:00 CST
3/31/1918 02:00 CWT
10/27/1918 02:00 CST
3/30/1919 02:00 CWT
10/26/1919 02:00 CST
4/27/1931 02:00 CDT
10/04/1931 02:00 CST
4/24/1932 02:00 EST
2/09/1942 02:00 EWT
2/15/1943 02:00 CWT
9/30/1945 02:00 EST
6/14/1967 00:01 EDT
10/29/1967 00:01 EST
4/29/1973 02:00 EDT
10/28/1973 02:00 EST
1/06/1974 02:00 EDT
10/27/1974 02:00 EST
4/27/1975 02:00 EDT
10/26/1975 02:00 US#1

MI # 104

Before 9/18/1885 LMT
9/18/1885 12:00 CST
3/31/1918 02:00 CWT
10/27/1918 02:00 CST
3/30/1919 02:00 CWT
10/26/1919 02:00 CST
4/01/1932 02:00 CDT
9/01/1932 02:00 CST
4/01/1933 02:00 EST
2/09/1942 02:00 EWT
2/15/1943 02:00 CWT
9/30/1945 02:00 EST
6/14/1967 00:01 EDT
10/29/1967 00:01 EST
4/29/1973 02:00 EDT
10/28/1973 02:00 EST
1/06/1974 02:00 EDT
10/27/1974 02:00 EST
4/27/1975 02:00 EDT
10/26/1975 02:00 US#1

MI # 105

Before 9/18/1885 LMT
9/18/1885 12:00 CST
3/31/1918 02:00 CWT
10/27/1918 02:00 CST
3/30/1919 02:00 CWT
10/26/1919 02:00 CST
4/30/1932 00:01 CDT
10/02/1932 00:01 CST
4/30/1933 01:00 CDT
9/24/1933 01:00 CST
4/29/1934 02:00 CDT
9/30/1934 02:00 CST
4/28/1935 02:00 CDT
9/29/1935 02:00 CST
3/01/1936 02:00 CDT
10/01/1936 02:00 CST
4/25/1937 02:00 EST
2/09/1942 02:00 EWT
2/15/1943 02:00 CWT
9/30/1945 02:00 EST
6/14/1967 00:01 EDT
10/29/1967 00:01 EST
4/29/1973 02:00 EDT
10/28/1973 02:00 EST
1/06/1974 02:00 EDT
10/27/1974 02:00 EST
4/27/1975 02:00 EDT
10/26/1975 02:00 US#1

MI # 106

Before 9/18/1885 LMT
9/18/1885 12:00 CST
3/31/1918 02:00 CWT
10/27/1918 02:00 CST
3/30/1919 02:00 CWT
10/26/1919 02:00 CST
4/30/1933 02:00 CDT
9/24/1933 02:00 CST
5/01/1934 02:00 CDT
10/01/1934 02:00 CST
5/01/1935 02:00 CDT
10/01/1935 02:00 CST
4/26/1936 02:00 CDT
9/27/1936 02:00 CST
4/25/1937 02:00 EST
2/09/1942 02:00 EWT
2/15/1943 02:00 CWT
9/30/1945 02:00 EST
6/14/1967 00:01 EDT
10/29/1967 00:01 EST
4/29/1973 02:00 EDT
10/28/1973 02:00 EST
1/06/1974 02:00 EDT
10/27/1974 02:00 EST
4/27/1975 02:00 EDT
10/26/1975 02:00 US#1

MI # 107

Before 9/18/1885 LMT
9/18/1885 12:00 CST
3/31/1918 02:00 CWT
10/27/1918 02:00 CST
3/30/1919 02:00 CWT
10/26/1919 02:00 CST
5/01/1932 02:00 CDT
10/01/1932 02:00 CST
4/30/1933 02:00 CDT
9/24/1933 02:00 CST
4/29/1934 02:00 CDT
9/30/1934 02:00 CST
4/28/1935 02:00 CDT
9/29/1935 02:00 CST
4/26/1936 02:00 CDT
9/27/1936 02:00 CST
4/25/1937 02:00 EST
2/09/1942 02:00 EWT
2/15/1943 02:00 CWT
9/30/1945 02:00 EST
6/14/1967 00:01 EDT
10/29/1967 00:01 EST
4/29/1973 02:00 EDT
10/28/1973 02:00 EST
1/06/1974 02:00 EDT
10/27/1974 02:00 EST
4/27/1975 02:00 EDT
10/26/1975 02:00 US#1

MI # 108

Before 9/18/1885 LMT
9/18/1885 12:00 CST
3/31/1918 02:00 CWT
10/27/1918 02:00 CST
3/30/1919 02:00 CWT
10/26/1919 02:00 CST
4/28/1935 02:00 CDT
9/29/1935 02:00 CST
5/01/1936 02:00 CDT
10/01/1936 02:00 CST
4/25/1937 02:00 EST
2/09/1942 02:00 EWT
2/15/1943 02:00 CWT
9/30/1945 02:00 EST
6/14/1967 00:01 EDT
10/29/1967 00:01 EST
4/29/1973 02:00 EDT
10/28/1973 02:00 EST
1/06/1974 02:00 EDT
10/27/1974 02:00 EST
4/27/1975 02:00 EDT
10/26/1975 02:00 US#1

MI # 109

Before 9/18/1885 LMT
9/18/1885 12:00 CST
3/31/1918 02:00 CWT
10/27/1918 02:00 CST
3/30/1919 02:00 CWT
10/26/1919 02:00 CST
4/27/1930 02:00 CDT
9/28/1930 02:00 CST
4/26/1931 02:00 CDT
9/27/1931 02:00 CST
4/24/1932 02:00 CDT
9/25/1932 02:00 CST
4/30/1933 02:00 CDT
9/24/1933 02:00 CST
4/29/1934 02:00 CDT
9/30/1934 02:00 CST
4/28/1935 02:00 CDT
9/29/1935 02:00 CST
3/01/1936 02:00 CDT
10/31/1936 02:00 CST
4/25/1937 02:00 CDT
9/26/1937 02:00 CST
4/24/1938 02:00 CDT
9/25/1938 02:00 CST
4/30/1939 02:00 CDT
9/24/1939 02:00 CST
4/28/1940 02:00 CDT
9/29/1940 02:00 CST
4/27/1941 02:00 CDT
10/26/1941 02:00 CST
2/09/1942 02:00 CWT
9/30/1945 02:00 EST
6/14/1967 00:01 EDT
10/29/1967 00:01 EST
4/29/1973 02:00 EDT
10/28/1973 02:00 EST
1/06/1974 02:00 EDT
10/27/1974 02:00 EST
4/27/1975 02:00 EDT
10/26/1975 02:00 US#1

MI # 110

Before 9/18/1885 LMT
9/18/1885 12:00 CST
3/31/1918 02:00 CWT
10/27/1918 02:00 CST
3/30/1919 02:00 CWT
10/26/1919 02:00 CST
4/26/1936 02:00 CDT
2/09/1942 02:00 EWT
2/15/1943 02:00 CWT
9/30/1945 02:00 EST
6/14/1967 00:01 EDT
10/29/1967 00:01 EST
4/29/1973 02:00 EDT
10/28/1973 02:00 EST
1/06/1974 02:00 EDT
10/27/1974 02:00 EST
4/27/1975 02:00 EDT
10/26/1975 02:00 US#1

MI # 111

Before 9/18/1885 LMT
9/18/1885 12:00 CST
3/31/1918 02:00 CWT
10/27/1918 02:00 CST
3/30/1919 02:00 CWT
10/26/1919 02:00 CST
4/26/1931 02:00 CDT
9/27/1931 02:00 CST
10/06/1931 02:00 EST
2/09/1942 02:00 EWT
2/15/1943 02:00 CWT
9/30/1945 02:00 EST
6/14/1967 00:01 EDT
10/29/1967 00:01 EST
4/29/1973 02:00 EDT
10/28/1973 02:00 EST
1/06/1974 02:00 EDT
10/27/1974 02:00 EST
4/27/1975 02:00 EDT
10/26/1975 02:00 US#1

COUNTIES

1 Alcona
2 Alger
3 Allegan
4 Alpena
5 Antrim
6 Arenac
7 Baraga
8 Barry
9 Bay
10 Benzie
11 Berrien
12 Branch
13 Calhoun
14 Cass
15 Charlevoix
16 Cheboygan
17 Chippewa
18 Clare
19 Clinton
20 Crawford
21 Delta
22 Dickinson
23 Eaton
24 Emmet
25 Genesee
26 Gladwin
27 Gogebic
28 Grand Traverse
29 Gratiot
30 Hillsdale
31 Houghton
32 Huron
33 Ingham
34 Ionia
35 Iosco
36 Iron
37 Isabella
38 Jackson
39 Kalamazoo
40 Kalkaska
41 Kent
42 Keweenaw
43 Lake
44 Lapeer
45 Leelanau
46 Lenawee
47 Livingston
48 Luce
49 Mackinac
50 Macomb
51 Manistee
52 Marquette
53 Mason
54 Mecosta
55 Menominee
56 Midland
57 Missaukee
58 Monroe
59 Montcalm
60 Montmorency
61 Muskegon
62 Newaygo
63 Oakland
64 Oceana
65 Ogemaw
66 Ontonagon
67 Osceola
68 Oscoda
69 Otsego
70 Ottawa
71 Presque Isle
72 Roscommon
73 Saginaw
74 St Clair
75 St Joseph
76 Sanilac
77 Schoolcraft
78 Shiawassee
79 Tuscola
80 Van Buren
81 Washtenaw
82 Wayne
83 Wexford

Abbottsford 74 1 43N01'12 82W38'00 5:30:32
Abscota 13 1 42N06 85W05 5:40:20
Ackerson Lake 38 90 42N15 84W24 5:37:36
Acme 28 1 44N46'19 85W30'05 5:42:00
Ada 41 64 42N57'15 85W29'20 5:41:57
Adair 74 1 42N47'53 82W38'02 5:30:32
Adams Park 39 100 42N09'14 85W28'22 5:41:53
Adamsville 14 72 41N47'07 85W59'38 5:43:59
Addison 46 1 41N59'11 84W20'50 5:37:23
Addison Junction 46 1 41N59'37 84W19'32 5:37:18
Adrian 46 5 41N53'51 84W02'14 5:36:09
Advance 15 1 45N13'17 85W04'39 5:40:19
Aetna 64 57 43N34'04 85W55'15 5:43:41
Afton 16 1 45N22'26 84W29'48 5:37:59
Agate 66 25 46N28'27 89W04'12 5:56:17
Agnew 70 51 42N57'54 86W10'36 5:44:42
Ahgosatown 45 1 45N04'52 85W35'30 5:42:22
Ahmeek 42 96 47N17'56 88W23'47 5:53:35
Ainger 23 1 42N28'58 84W56'04 5:39:44
Akron 79 1 43N34'05 83W30'51 5:34:03
Alabaster 35 1 44N11'11 83W33'29 5:34:14
Alabaster Junction 35 1 44N14'45 83W33'49 5:34:15
Alaiedon 33 1 42N38 84W25 5:37:40
Alamando 56 1 43N44'34 84W31'36 5:38:06
Alamo 39 92 42N22'31 85W42'28 5:42:50
Alanson 24 67 45N26'39 84W47'12 5:39:09
Alaska 41 57 42N50'24 85W28'41 5:41:55
Alba 5 1 44N58'29 84W58'07 5:39:52
Albee 73 1 43N16 83W59 5:35:56
Albert 60 1 44N53 84W17 5:37:08
Alberta 7 25 46N38'37 88W28'46 5:53:55
Albion 13 40 42N14'35 84W45'11 5:39:01
Albion 31 96 47N15 88W27 5:53:48
Albion Landing 13 1 42N22'55 84W47'03 5:39:08
Alcona 1 1 44N45'36 83W17'52 5:33:11
Alden 5 1 44N52'52 85W16'32 5:41:06
Alder 52 25 46N47'22 87W41'50 5:50:47
Alembic 37 1 43N35'51 84W40'06 5:38:40
Alfred 22 87 46N05'02 87W37'57 5:50:32
Algansee 12 1 41N49'57 84W52'51 5:39:31
Alger 6 1 44N07'32 84W07'16 5:36:29
Algoma 41 57 43N10 85W37 5:42:28
Algonac 74 1 42N37'06 82W31'52 5:30:07
Algonquin Lake 8 62 42N39 85W17 5:41:08
Alicia 73 1 43N16'15 84W01'57 5:36:08
Allegan 3 42 42N31'45 85W51'19 5:43:25
Allen 30 1 41N57'25 84W46'04 5:39:04
Allendale 18 1 44N00'14 84W47'06 5:39:08
Allendale 70 51 42N58'20 85W57'13 5:43:49
Allen Park 82 2 42N15'27 83W12'40 5:32:51
Allens Cove 58 1 41N48 83W27 5:33:48
Allenton 14 108 41N45'59 85W58'29 5:43:54
Allenton 74 1 42N55'10 82W56'44 5:31:47
Allenville 49 25 45N59'05 84W49'14 5:39:17
Allis 71 1 45N17 84W12 5:36:48
Allouez 42 96 47N17'14 88W24'34 5:53:38
Alma 29 44 43N22'44 84W39'35 5:38:38
Almeda Beach 9 1 43N49'03 83W55'23 5:35:42
Almeda Beach 72 1 44N30 84W36 5:38:24
Almena 80 72 42N15'53 85W49'31 5:43:18
Almer 79 1 43N31 83W24 5:33:36
Almira 10 1 44N44 85W53 5:43:32
Almont 44 1 42N55'14 83W02'42 5:32:11
Aloha 16 1 45N31'35 84W28'00 5:37:52
Alpena 4 1 45N03'42 83W25'58 5:33:44
Alpena Junction 4 1 45N03'31 83W27'22 5:33:49
Alpha 36 86 46N02'38 88W22'37 5:53:30
Alpine 41 61 43N04'22 85W41'06 5:42:44
Alston 31 25 46N46'06 88W45'11 5:55:01
Alto 41 64 42N51'24 85W22'49 5:41:31
Alton 21 25 45N52'59 86W53'03 5:47:32
Alton 41 57 43N00'59 85W21'06 5:41:24
Altona 54 1 43N32'23 85W18'49 5:41:15
Alverno 16 1 45N33'31 84W23'30 5:37:34
Alvin 1 1 44N31'28 83W26'33 5:33:46
Amadore 76 1 43N11'42 82W35'09 5:30:21
Amasa 36 81 46N13'58 88W26'55 5:53:48
Amber 53 57 43N58 86W21 5:45:24
Amble 59 57 43N25'53 85W23'19 5:41:33
Amboy 30 1 41N43 84W36 5:38:24
Amelith 9 36 43N36 83W54 5:35:36
Amsden 59 92 43N10'14 85W07'25 5:40:30
Anchor Bay Gardens 50 88 42N38'34 82W48'45 5:31:15
Anchor Bay Harbor 50 88 42N39'19 82W47'57 5:31:12
Anchor Bay Shores 50 88 42N38'08 82W49'00 5:31:16
Anchorville 74 1 42N41'28 82W41'19 5:30:45
Anderson 47 1 42N28'15 84W00'22 5:36:01
Anderson 56 1 43N37 84W12 5:36:48
Anderson Bayview 35 1 44N14'12 83W32'43 5:34:11
Andersonville 63 88 42N43'48 83W29'33 5:33:58
Andrews 11 72 41N57 86W20 5:45:20
Angling 40 1 44N40'12 85W00'33 5:40:02
Ann Arbor 81 38 42N17'00 83W44'45 5:34:59
Antioch 83 1 44N23 85W38 5:42:32
Antlers 52 25 46N45'16 87W39'21 5:50:37
Antoine 22 87 45N50'15 88W03'43 5:52:15
Antrim 5 1 44N53'24 85W04'26 5:40:18
Antrim Center 78 1 42N48'49 84W06'52 5:36:27
Antwerp 80 46 42N12 85W50 5:43:20
Anvil 27 81 46N28'13 90W01'06 6:00:04
Aplin Beach 9 36 43N39'03 83W52'15 5:35:29
Applegate 76 1 43N21'19 82W38'14 5:30:33
Arbela 79 1 43N15 83W38 5:34:32
Arbutus Beach 69 1 44N56'46 84W41'00 5:38:44
Arcada 29 1 43N20 84W40 5:38:40
Arcadia 51 1 44N29'35 86W13'54 5:44:56
Arden 11 72 41N59'09 86W23'31 5:45:34
Arenac 6 1 44N00'20 83W51'29 5:35:26
Argenta 3 102 42N27 85W39 5:42:36
Argentine 25 1 42N47'29 83W50'47 5:35:23
Argyle 76 1 43N33'51 82W56'10 5:31:45
Arlene 57 1 44N23'24 85W17'12 5:41:09
Arlington 80 74 42N18 86W03 5:44:12
Armada 50 1 42N50'39 82W53'04 5:31:32
Armstrong Corners 80 46 42N13 85W53 5:43:32
Arnheim 7 25 46N55'01 88W28'57 5:53:56
Arnold 52 25 46N03'03 87W29'31 5:49:58
Artesia Beach 72 1 44N21'23 84W29'30 5:37:58
Arthur 18 1 43N57 84W40 5:38:40
Arthur Bay 55 81 45N18'32 87W26'08 5:49:45
Arvon 7 25 46N50 88W12 5:52:48
Ash 58 1 42N03 83W21 5:33:24
Ash Acres 18 1 44N02'16 84W48'43 5:39:15
Ashland 4 1 45N12'11 83W27'04 5:33:48
Ashland 62 64 43N18'28 85W48'40 5:43:15
Ashland Center 62 64 43N20'11 85W51'06 5:43:24
Ashley 29 1 43N11'12 84W28'28 5:37:54
Ashmore 79 1 43N39 83W28 5:33:52
Ashton 67 97 43N58'23 85W30'13 5:42:01
Askel 31 25 46N49 88W38 5:54:32
Assinins 7 25 46N48'37 88W28'38 5:53:55
Assyria 8 57 42N27'52 85W07'53 5:40:32
Athens 13 1 42N05'19 85W14'05 5:40:56
Atkins 74 1 43N03'47 82W34'37 5:30:18
Atlanta 60 1 45N00'17 84W08'38 5:36:35
Atlantic Mine 31 96 47N05'50 88W37'39 5:54:31
Atlas 25 1 42N56'16 83W32'04 5:34:08
Attica 44 1 43N01'49 83W09'58 5:32:40
Atwood 5 1 45N10'45 85W20'43 5:41:23
Auburn 9 1 43N36'12 84W04'11 5:36:17
Auburn Heights 63 88 42N38'01 83W13'22 5:32:53
Au Gres 6 1 44N02'55 83W41'45 5:34:47
Augusta 39 92 42N20'11 85W21'08 5:41:25
Aura 7 25 46N51'46 88W19'07 5:53:16
Aurelius 33 1 42N31'27 84W31'20 5:38:05
Aurora 27 81 46N26'56 90W08'45 6:00:35
Au Sable 35 1 44N24'39 83W19'56 5:33:20
Au Sable River Park 72 1 44N24'12 84W27'37 5:37:50
Austin 30 1 41N44'14 84W41'39 5:38:47
Austin 52 25 46N17'04 87W27'25 5:49:50
Austin Center 76 1 43N37'21 82W56'15 5:31:45
Austin Corners 63 88 42N47'16 83W30'29 5:34:02
Austin Lake 39 47 42N13 85W35 5:42:20
Au Train 2 25 46N25'49 86W50'12 5:47:21
Auvinen Corner 27 81 46N31'13 90W05'46 6:00:23
Avalon Beach 58 36 41N51'26 83W23'34 5:33:34
Avalon Beach 74 1 42N41'20 82W30'30 5:30:02
Avalon Lake 60 1 45N04 83W54 5:35:36
Averill 56 1 43N39'56 84W20'31 5:37:22
Avery 11 74 41N48 86W37 5:46:28
Avery 60 1 44N57'27 84W01'53 5:36:08
Avoca 74 1 43N03'43 82W41'28 5:30:46
Avon 63 88 42N40 83W09 5:32:36
Avondale 61 49 43N12 86W14 5:44:56
Avondale 67 1 44N00'57 85W13'36 5:40:54
Ayr 24 67 45N29'32 84W51'12 5:39:25
Azalia 58 1 42N01'08 83W39'57 5:34:40
Babcock 13 1 42N13'02 84W48'00 5:39:12
Bach 32 1 43N40'59 83W21'21 5:33:25
Backus 72 1 44N18 84W33 5:38:12
Backus Beach 1 1 44N45'36 83W32'46 5:34:11
Bad Axe 32 1 43N48'07 83W00'03 5:32:00
Bagley 55 81 45N33'05 87W34'32 5:50:18
Bagley 69 6 44N59 84W41 5:38:44
Baie de Wasai 17 12 46N27'41 84W14'41 5:36:59
Bailey 61 64 43N16'40 85W48'37 5:43:14
Bainbridge Center 11 74 42N06'56 86W16'54 5:45:08
Bakersville 3 92 42N29'24 86W04'11 5:44:17
Bakertown 11 77 41N48'18 86W23'27 5:45:34
Baldwin 43 92 43N54'04 85W51'06 5:43:24
Baltimore 66 25 46N32'05 89W13'44 5:56:55
Ballards 41 64 43N10 85W42 5:42:48
Ballards Corners 41 64 43N07'01 85W42'36 5:42:50
Balsam 36 81 46N12'28 88W22'51 5:53:31
Baltic 31 96 47N04'03 88W38'00 5:54:32
Baltimore 8 57 42N33 85W15 5:41:00
Baltimore 66 25 46N31 89W11 5:56:44
Banat 55 81 45N31'04 87W41'51 5:50:47
Bancroft 78 1 42N52'43 84W03'50 5:36:15
Banfield 8 57 42N27'49 85W17'19 5:41:09
Bangor 80 74 42N18'45 86W06'47 5:44:27
Bankers 12 1 41N53'52 84W41'29 5:38:46
Banks 5 1 45N10 85W18 5:41:12
Banksons Lake 80 46 42N10 85W51 5:43:24
Bannister 29 1 43N07'57 84W25'18 5:37:41
Baraga 7 26 46N46'43 88W29'20 5:53:57
Barbeau 17 12 46N17'19 84W16'52 5:37:07
Barker Creek 40 1 44N46'49 85W18'48 5:41:15
Bark River 21 17 45N42'37 87W18'17 5:49:13
Bar Lake 51 111 44N17'51 86W18'25 5:45:14
Barnard 15 1 45N15'04 85W18'04 5:41:12
Barnum 52 25 46N30 87W40 5:50:40
Baroda 11 74 41N57'27 86W29'08 5:45:57
Barron Lake 14 105 41N51 86W12 5:44:48
Barry 8 57 42N28 85W23 5:41:32
Barryton 54 1 43N45'09 85W08'49 5:40:35
Barton 62 57 43N46 85W37 5:42:28
Barton City 1 1 44N41'03 83W36'20 5:34:25
Barton Hills 81 38 42N19'19 83W46'08 5:35:05
Barton Lake 39 100 42N05 85W34 5:42:16
Base Line Lake 3 92 42N22 85W53 5:43:32
Bass Lake 53 57 43N51 86W25 5:45:40
Basswood 36 81 46N11'19 88W50'42 5:55:23
Batavia 12 1 41N54'45 85W05'53 5:40:24
Batavia Center 12 1 41N56'26 85W07'06 5:40:28
Bates 28 1 44N46'22 85W26'39 5:41:47
Bates 36 81 46N09 88W36 5:54:24
Bates Junction 36 86 46N05'11 88W36'07 5:54:24
Bates Location 36 81 46N06'47 88W36'58 5:54:28
Bath 19 41 42N49'07 84W26'55 5:37:48
Battle Creek 13 43 42N19'16 85W10'47 5:40:43
Bauer 70 54 42N55'17 85W54'08 5:43:37
Baw Beese Lake 30 1 41N55 84W38 5:38:32
Baxter 83 1 44N30'14 85W31'37 5:42:06
Bay 15 1 45N18 85W03 5:40:12
Bay City 9 36 43N35'40 83W53'20 5:35:33
Bay de Noc 21 25 45N45 86W56 5:47:44
Bay Mills 17 110 46N26'14 84W35'02 5:38:20
Bay Park 79 1 43N39'17 83W35'21 5:34:21
Bay Port 32 1 43N50'58 83W22'24 5:33:30
Bayport Park 25 1 42N51'15 83W43'04 5:34:52
Bay Shore 15 1 45N21'30 85W05'50 5:40:23
Bay View 24 67 45N23'08 84W55'49 5:39:43
Beach Grove 55 81 45N17'58 87W26'15 5:49:45
Beachmont 3 92 42N38'47 86W13'25 5:44:54
Beachwood 65 1 44N25 84W07 5:36:28
Beacon 52 25 46N30'37 87W59'08 5:51:57
Beacon Hill 31 25 47N08'21 88W48'24 5:55:14
Beadle Lake 13 43 42N16'02 85W08'58 5:40:36
Beal City 37 1 43N40'09 84W54'31 5:39:38
Bear Creek 24 67 45N22 84W54 5:39:36
Bearinger 71 1 45N31 84W11 5:36:44
Bearinger Corners 58 1 41N46 83W45 5:35:00
Bear Lake 51 1 44N25'15 86W08'53 5:44:36
Bear Town 7 25 46N48'32 88W30'35 5:54:02
Beaton 27 81 46N17'45 89W20'21 5:57:21
Beaugrand 16 1 45N40 84W33 5:38:12
Beaver 9 1 43N42'42 84W04'04 5:36:16

Beaver 21 25 45N59'08 87w06'35 5:48:26
Beaver Creek 20 1 44N33 84w43 5:38:52
Beaverdam 70 54 42N50'54 85w57'36 5:43:50
Beaver Grove 52 25 46N33 87w24 5:49:36
Beaver Island 15 1 45N40 85w33 5:42:12
Beaverton 26 1 43N52'56 84w29'05 5:37:56
Bedford 13 43 42N23'43 85w13'56 5:40:56
Bedore 74 1 42N33'28 82w36'47 5:30:27
Beebe 29 1 43N20'07 84w32'53 5:38:12
Beech 82 36 42N22'40 83w17'44 5:33:11
Beecher 25 1 43N04 83w42 5:34:48
Beechwood 14 72 42N00'23 86w12'16 5:44:49
Beechwood 36 81 46N09'35 88w46'24 5:55:06
Beechwood 70 52 42N48 86w07 5:44:28
Belding 34 92 43N05'52 85w13'44 5:40:55
Belknap 71 1 45N19'55 83w50'36 5:35:22
Bellaire 5 1 44N58'49 85w12'40 5:40:51
Belle Isle 82 2 42N21 82w58 5:31:52
Belle River 74 1 42N49'25 82w42'01 5:30:48
Belleville 82 36 42N12'17 83w29'07 5:33:56
Belleville North 82 36 42N13'22 83w28'55 5:33:56
Bellevue 23 1 42N26'36 85w01'05 5:40:04
Bell Landing 71 1 45N29'22 84w04'27 5:36:18
Bell Oak 33 1 42N43'43 84w10'25 5:36:42
Belmont 41 61 43N04'32 85w36'33 5:42:26
Belsay 25 1 43N01'35 83w35'45 5:34:23
Belvedere 15 1 45N19 85w15 5:41:00
Belvidere 59 57 43N25 85w09 5:40:36
Bendon 10 1 44N37'59 85w50'16 5:43:21
Bengal 19 1 42N59 84w40 5:38:40
Bennington 78 1 42N56'07 84w14'31 5:36:58
Benona 64 57 43N34 86w30 5:46:00
Benson 83 1 44N12'31 85w29'49 5:41:59
Benson Park 35 1 44N12'13 83w33'16 5:34:13
Bentheim 3 97 42N42'34 85w55'08 5:43:41
Bentley 9 1 43N56'53 84w08'04 5:36:32
Bentleys Corners 13 1 42N06'08 84w52'00 5:39:28
Bently Corners 13 1 42N09 84w48 5:39:12
Benton 81 38 42N07'44 83w51'44 5:35:27
Benton Center 11 4 42N07'26 86w22'43 5:45:31
Benton Harbor 11 4 42N07'00 86w27'15 5:45:49
Benton Heights 11 4 42N07'52 86w24'26 5:45:38
Benzonia 10 1 44N37'17 86w05'57 5:44:24
Bergland 66 25 46N35'33 89w34'23 5:58:18
Berkley 63 2 42N30'11 83w11'01 5:32:44
Berlamont 80 72 42N23'24 85w59'38 5:43:59
Berlin Center 34 92 42N54'02 85w08'03 5:40:32
Berne 32 1 43N50'41 83w16'10 5:33:05
Berrien Center 11 72 41N57'24 86w16'36 5:45:06
Berrien Springs 11 72 41N56'47 86w20'20 5:45:21
Berry Junction 61 57 43N17'47 86w15'40 5:45:03
Berryville 38 1 42N24'19 84w29'14 5:37:57
Bertrand 11 105 41N46'28 86w15'44 5:45:03
Berville 74 1 42N54'30 82w52'59 5:31:32
Bessemer 27 86 46N28'53 90w03'10 6:00:13
Bete Grise 42 96 47N23'20 87w57'18 5:51:49
Bethany 29 1 43N25 84w33 5:38:12
Bethany Beach 11 74 41N53'29 86w37'05 5:46:28
Bethel 12 1 41N49'58 85w04'25 5:40:18
Betty B Landing 48 25 46N24'02 85w16'40 5:41:07
Betzer 30 1 41N45'11 84w28'33 5:37:54
Beulah 10 1 44N37'55 86w05'27 5:44:22
Beverly 41 61 42N55 85w42 5:42:48
Beverly Hills 52 25 46N30'49 87w36'24 5:50:26
Beverly Hills 63 88 42N31'26 83w13'24 5:32:54
Big Bay 52 25 46N48'57 87w43'42 5:50:55
Big Beaver 63 88 42N33'46 83w07'27 5:32:30
Big Bend Park 62 57 43N31'25 85w34'58 5:42:20
Big Creek 68 1 44N38 84w13 5:36:52
Big Cut 71 1 45N19'38 83w59'59 5:36:00
Bigelow 60 1 44N58'42 84w16'34 5:37:06
Biggs Settlement 68 1 44N42'37 84w07'48 5:36:31
Big Prairie 62 57 43N31'07 85w38'33 5:42:34
Big Rapids 54 1 43N41'53 85w29'01 5:41:56
Big Rock 60 1 45N00 84w09 5:36:36
Billings 26 1 43N50'59 84w20'50 5:37:23
Bingham 45 1 44N52'33 85w40'27 5:42:42
Bingham Farms 63 88 42N30'57 83w16'24 5:33:06
Birch 52 25 46N41'55 87w34'41 5:50:19
Birch Beach 76 1 43N12'07 82w30'45 5:30:03
Birch Creek 55 81 45N12'10 87w36'40 5:50:27
Birch Hill Park 82 36 42N18 83w23 5:33:32
Birch Hills 15 1 45N18'55 85w16'45 5:41:07
Birch Run 73 1 43N15'03 83w47'39 5:35:11
Birchwood 11 74 41N52'53 86w37'43 5:46:31
Birchwood 16 1 45N32'19 84w32'15 5:38:09
Birchwood Beach 60 1 44N52'21 84w19'19 5:37:17
Birchwood Shores 6 1 44N05'02 83w35'24 5:34:22
Birdsall 46 1 41N56'31 84w00'16 5:36:01
Birmingham 63 89 42N32'48 83w12'41 5:32:51
Birmingham Farms 63 88 43N15 83w48 5:35:12
Bishop 62 64 43N25'26 85w53'59 5:43:36
Bismarck 71 1 45N18 83w57 5:35:48
Bitely 64 57 43N44'49 85w51'42 5:43:27
Black Lake 71 1 45N25'53 84w14'55 5:37:00
Black Lake Bluffs 71 1 45N28'20 84w14'13 5:36:57
Blackman 38 90 42N17 84w25 5:37:40
Blackmar 73 1 43N15 83w48 5:35:12
Black River 1 1 44N49'02 83w18'12 5:33:13
Black River Harbor 27 81 46N27 90w09 6:00:36
Blaine 10 1 44N33 86w11 5:44:44
Blaine 74 1 43N06'57 82w34'51 5:30:19
Blair 28 1 44N38 85w39 5:42:36
Blanchard 37 57 43N31'11 85w04'48 5:40:19
Blaney Junction 77 25 46N01'29 85w54'40 5:43:39
Blaney Park 77 25 46N06'56 85w55'37 5:43:42
Blendon 70 51 42N54 85w58 5:43:52
Bliss 24 67 45N40'49 84w53'03 5:39:32
Blissfield 46 1 41N49'57 83w51'45 5:35:27
Blom 55 81 45N39'04 87w44'17 5:50:57
Bloomer 59 57 43N10 84w53 5:39:32
Bloomfield 63 88 42N32'16 83w13'59 5:32:56
Bloomfield Glens 63 88 42N32 83w17 5:33:08
Bloomfield Highlands 63 88 42N38 83w19 5:33:16
Bloomfield Hills 63 88 42N35'01 83w14'44 5:32:59
Bloomfield Village 63 88 42N33 83w12 5:32:48
Bloomingdale 80 72 42N22'58 85w57'25 5:43:50
Blue Creek 11 4 42N06 86w27 5:45:48
Blue Jacket 31 96 47N15 88w27 5:53:48
Blue Water Beach 76 1 43N12'26 82w30'56 5:30:04
Bluff Beach 75 1 41N48'54 85w32'14 5:42:09
Blumfield 73 1 43N26 83w45 5:35:00
Blumfield Corners 73 1 43N25'27 83w43'06 5:34:52
Boardman 40 1 44N39 85w17 5:41:08
Bodus 45 1 44N54'24 85w46'57 5:43:08
Bohemia 66 25 46N52 88w58 5:55:52
Boichott Acres 19 41 42N45 84w34 5:38:16
Bois Blanc 49 1 45N46 84w28 5:37:52
Bolles Harbor 58 36 41N52'03 83w23'10 5:33:33
Bolton 4 1 45N10'53 83w35'23 5:34:22
Bombay 56 1 43N44'30 84w15'59 5:37:04
Bonner Landing 15 1 45N42'15 85w34'46 5:42:19
Boon 83 1 44N17'23 85w36'07 5:42:24
Bootjack 31 96 47N12 88w24 5:53:36
Borculo 70 54 42N53'06 86w01'16 5:44:05
Borland 54 1 43N32'13 85w26'21 5:41:45
Boston 31 95 47N10'47 88w31'45 5:54:07
Boston 34 92 42N54 85w15 5:41:00
Bostwick Lake 41 65 43N05'06 85w27'02 5:41:48
Bourret 26 1 44N08 84w14 5:36:56
Bowens Mill 8 57 42N39'24 85w31'00 5:42:04
Bowmanville 26 1 44N05'00 84w14'48 5:36:59
Bowne Center 41 64 42N48'46 85w22'09 5:41:29
Boyd 3 74 42N43'37 86w05'23 5:44:22
Boyne City 15 1 45N13'00 85w00'50 5:40:03
Boyne Falls 15 1 45N10'05 84w54'58 5:39:40
Bradley 3 92 42N37'49 85w38'35 5:42:34
Bradleyville 79 1 43N35'00 83w37'25 5:34:30
Brady Center 73 1 43N10'21 84w13'38 5:36:55
Brampton 21 17 45N55'53 87w04'16 5:48:17
Branch 53 57 43N57 86w07 5:44:28
Brandon 63 88 42N50 83w23 5:33:32
Brandon Gardens 63 88 42N49'32 83w26'37 5:33:46
Brandywine Lake 80 72 42N22 85w53 5:43:32
Brant 73 1 43N15'33 84w13'47 5:36:55
Brassar 17 45 46N30'22 84w13'02 5:36:52
Bravo 3 92 42N30'47 86w05'31 5:44:22
Braywood 80 74 42N15'46 86w20'45 5:45:23
Breckenridge 29 1 43N24'29 84w28'30 5:37:54
Breedsville 80 74 42N20'47 86w04'23 5:44:18
Breen 22 87 45N59 87w42 5:50:48
Breezy Beach 75 1 41N48'09 85w33'34 5:42:14
Breitung 22 87 45N51 88w00 5:52:00
Brent Creek 25 1 43N07'04 83w53'12 5:35:33
Brentwood 61 49 43N12 86w16 5:45:04
Brest 58 1 41N58 83w15 5:33:00
Brethren 51 1 44N18'16 86w01'08 5:44:05
Bretton Woods 23 41 42N44 84w36 5:38:24
Brevort 49 25 46N01'08 85w02'30 5:40:10
Brice 29 1 43N09'42 84w45'30 5:39:02
Bridgehampton 76 1 43N28 82w42 5:30:48
Bridgeman 11 74 41N56'35 86w33'25 5:46:14
Bridgeport 73 91 43N21'34 83w52'54 5:35:32
Bridgeton 62 57 43N20'48 85w56'14 5:43:45
Bridgeville 59 1 43N08'09 84w35'34 5:38:22
Bridgewater 81 1 42N09'39 83w54'08 5:35:37
Bridgman 11 74 41N57 86w33 5:46:12
Brightmoor 82 2 42N24 83w14 5:32:56
Brighton 47 1 42N31'46 83w46'49 5:35:07
Briley 60 1 45N00 84w10 5:36:40
Brimley 17 110 46N24'19 84w34'20 5:38:17
Brinton 37 1 43N46'13 85w00'37 5:40:02
Brissette Beach 9 1 43N42'33 83w56'10 5:35:45
Bristol 41 61 42N59 85w42 5:42:48
Bristol 43 1 44N06'14 85w35'01 5:42:20
British Landing 49 25 45N52'39 84w38'42 5:38:35
Britton 46 1 41N59'12 83w49'52 5:35:19
Broad Acres 50 2 42N32'57 82w54'08 5:31:37
Broadbridge Station 74 1 42N40'43 82w30'43 5:30:03
Broadway Manor 61 49 43N12 86w14 5:44:56
Brockway 74 1 43N04'28 82w45'56 5:31:04
Brohman 64 57 43N41'07 85w48'11 5:43:16
Bronson 12 1 41N52'20 85w11'41 5:40:47
Brookfield 23 1 42N27'04 84w47'48 5:39:11
Brooklands 63 88 42N39 83w09 5:32:36
Brooklyn 38 1 42N06'21 84w14'54 5:37:00
Brook Park 61 49 43N12 86w16 5:45:04
Brooks 9 36 43N36 83w54 5:35:36
Brooks 62 64 43N25 85w45 5:43:00
Brookside 28 1 44N44'32 85w38'48 5:42:35
Brookside 61 49 43N12 86w16 5:45:04
Brookton Corners 52 25 46N32'58 87w27'21 5:49:49
Brookville 81 1 42N22'38 83w34'43 5:34:19
Brookwood 61 49 43N12 86w16 5:45:04
Broomfield Center 37 1 43N35'45 85w01'36 5:40:06
Brown 51 1 44N19 86w08 5:44:32
Brown City 76 1 43N12'44 82w59'23 5:31:58
Brownlee Park 13 43 42N19'08 85w08'33 5:40:34
Brownstown 82 36 42N07 83w15 5:33:00
Brownsville 14 73 41N52'41 85w57'15 5:43:49
Brownwood Lake 80 46 42N13 85w53 5:43:32
Bruce Crossing 66 32 46N32'06 89w10'43 5:56:43
Bruningville 71 1 45N23'07 83w49'28 5:35:18
Brunswick 61 57 43N25'59 86w02'25 5:44:10
Brutus 24 67 45N29'35 84w46'54 5:39:08
Bryant 1 1 44N31'30 83w39'57 5:34:40
Buchanan 11 77 41N49'38 86w21'40 5:45:27
Buckeye 26 1 43N57 84w26 5:37:44
Buckhorn 11 72 42N00'07 86w24'13 5:45:37
Buckley 83 1 44N30'16 85w40'37 5:42:42
Buckroe 52 25 46N40'20 87w31'27 5:50:06
Bucks 20 1 44N44'53 84w34'12 5:38:17
Bucks Corners 64 64 43N47 86w26 5:45:44
Buckshot Landing 66 25 46N48'59 89w47'42 5:59:11
Buck Trails 18 1 44N06'05 84w51'28 5:39:26
Buel 76 1 43N18 82w43 5:30:52
Buena Vista 73 91 43N25 83w54 5:35:36
Bullis Crossing 47 1 42N28'04 84w01'59 5:36:08
Bullock Creek 56 1 43N35'00 84w14'52 5:36:59
Bumbletown 42 96 47N17'20 88w25'10 5:53:41
Bunker Hill 33 1 42N28'32 84w19'03 5:37:16
Bunny Run 63 88 42N47 83w13 5:32:52
Burdell 67 1 44N07 85w30 5:42:00
Burdickville 45 1 44N50'56 85w56'53 5:43:48
Burgess 15 1 45N21'09 85w09'41 5:40:39
Burleigh 35 1 44N12 83w49 5:35:16
Burley Corner 13 43 42N20 85w10 5:40:40
Burlingame 41 61 42N55 85w42 5:42:48
Burlington 13 1 42N06'24 85w04'47 5:40:19
Burnips 3 92 42N43'55 85w50'22 5:43:21
Burns 78 1 42N49 83w59 5:35:56
Burnside 44 1 43N12'38 83w04'38 5:32:19
Burns Landing 52 25 46N49'39 87w43'44 5:50:55
Burnt 73 1 43N14'12 83w54'12 5:35:37
Burr Oak 75 1 41N50'50 85w19'07 5:41:16
Burt 73 1 43N14 83w54 5:35:36
Burtchville 74 1 43N07 82w30 5:30:00
Burt Lake 16 1 45N26'27 84w42'40 5:38:51
Burton 25 1 43N00 83w39 5:34:36
Burton 78 1 43N00'28 84w17'05 5:37:08
Bushnell 59 57 43N10 85w01 5:40:04
Butler 12 1 42N03'28 84w51'55 5:39:28
Butman 26 1 44N08'21 84w28'03 5:37:52
Butterfield 57 1 44N16'40 84w57'12 5:39:49
Butternut 59 57 43N11'00 84w54'56 5:39:40
Buttersville 53 63 43N56'42 86w27'20 5:45:49
Byron 78 1 42N49'22 83w56'40 5:35:47
Byron Center 41 57 42N48'44 85w43'22 5:42:53
Cableton 80 93 42N24 86w16 5:45:04
Cadillac 83 8 44N15'07 85w24'04 5:41:36
Cadmus 46 1 41N52'26 84w09'38 5:36:39
Cady 50 88 42N33'37 82w57'52 5:31:51
Caffey 49 25 46N10'08 85w11'07 5:40:44
Caffey Corner 49 25 46N09'43 85w11'07 5:40:44
Calcite 71 1 45N24'32 83w47'12 5:35:09
Calderwood 66 25 46N24'35 89w05'07 5:56:20
Caldwell 57 1 44N23 85w17 5:41:08
Caledonia 41 57 42N47'21 85w31'00 5:42:04
California 12 1 41N47'47 84w53'00 5:39:32
Calumet 31 10 47N14'48 88w27'14 5:53:49
Calvin Center 14 72 41N50'45 85w56'06 5:43:44
Cambria 30 1 41N49'19 84w39'54 5:38:40
Cambridge 46 1 42N02 84w11 5:36:44
Cambridge Junction 46 1 42N03'32 84w13'16 5:36:53
Camden 30 1 41N45'08 84w45'28 5:39:02
Campau 74 1 42N58 82w29 5:29:56
Campbell 21 25 46N01'02 87w07'52 5:48:31
Campbell 34 94 42N49 85w15 5:41:00
Campbell Corners 34 94 42N48'21 85w13'56 5:40:56
Campbells Corner 63 88 42N47'59 83w08'01 5:32:32
Campbells Corners 65 1 44N18'47 84w08'44 5:36:35
Camp Lake 41 64 43N10 85w42 5:42:48
Camp Lu Lay Lea 65 1 44N20'13 84w00'29 5:36:02
Canada Corners 61 64 43N14'07 85w50'57 5:43:24
Canada Creek Ranch 60 1 45N00 84w09 5:36:36
Canada Shores 12 1 41N48'28 84w57'45 5:39:51
Canal 17 45 46N29 84w21 5:37:24
Canandaigua 46 1 41N47'55 84w14'04 5:36:56
Canfield Beach 71 1 45N27'38 84w13'18 5:36:53
Cannon 41 57 43N04 85w30 5:42:00
Cannonburg 41 57 43N03'14 85w28'11 5:41:53
Cannonsburg 41 57 43N03 85w28 5:41:52
Canton 82 36 42N19 83w28 5:33:52
Capac 74 1 43N00'45 82w55'41 5:31:43
Carbondale 55 86 45N16'42 87w36'57 5:50:28
Caribou Lake 17 12 46N00 83w54 5:35:36
Carland 78 1 43N03'29 84w18'17 5:37:13
Carleton 58 7 42N03'33 83w23'27 5:33:34

Carlisle 23 1 42N33'11 84w57'59 5:39:52
Carlisle 41 61 42N49'35 85w41'00 5:42:44
Carlshend 52 25 46N18'39 87w13'15 5:48:53
Carlson 7 25 46N47 88w30 5:54:00
Carlton 8 60 42N43'36 85w15'05 5:41:00
Carmel 23 1 42N33 84w54 5:39:36
Carney 55 86 45N35'12 87w33'26 5:50:14
Caro 79 1 43N29'28 83w23'49 5:33:35
Carpenter Lake 30 1 41N50 84w45 5:39:00
Carpenter Landing 48 25 46N17'23 85w45'28 5:43:02
Carp Lake 24 67 45N41'50 84w45'00 5:39:00
Carp Lake Landing 66 25 46N49'49 89w42'59 5:58:52
Carr 53 92 43N52'25 86w02'18 5:44:09
Carrollton 73 91 43N27'31 83w55'49 5:35:43
Carrs 43 92 43N56 86w02 5:44:08
Carson City 59 57 43N10'37 84w50'47 5:39:23
Carsonville 76 1 43N25'37 82w40'17 5:30:41
Cascade 41 59 42N54'44 85w29'53 5:42:00
Cascade 52 11 46N26'49 87w29'07 5:49:56
Casco 74 1 42N45'09 82w40'18 5:30:41
Case 71 1 45N17 84w04 5:36:16
Caseville 32 1 43N56'28 83w16'17 5:33:05
Cash 76 1 43N20'54 82w47'11 5:31:09
Casnovia 61 64 43N14'05 85w47'26 5:43:10
Caspian 36 86 46N03'51 88w37'53 5:54:32
Cass City 79 1 43N36'03 83w10'29 5:32:42
Cassopolis 14 73 41N54'42 86w00'36 5:44:02
Castle 73 91 43N25 83w57 5:35:48
Castle Park 3 92 42N44'53 86w12'25 5:44:50
Castleton 8 57 42N38 85w08 5:40:32
Cathro 4 1 45N09'32 83w33'16 5:34:13
Cato 59 57 43N26 85w16 5:41:04
Cedar 45 1 44N50'52 85w47'44 5:43:11
Cedar 67 1 43N57 85w23 5:41:32
Cedar Bank 52 25 46N17'49 87w16'00 5:49:04
Cedar Bend 33 41 42N44 84w26 5:37:44
Cedar Bluff 3 92 42N29'08 86w14'46 5:44:59
Cedar Creek 8 57 42N31'13 85w19'39 5:41:19
Cedar Haven 35 1 44N10'34 83w33'45 5:34:15
Cedar Lake 59 57 43N24'22 84w58'30 5:39:54
Cedar Lake 80 72 42N01 85w49 5:43:16
Cedar River 55 81 45N24'40 87w21'16 5:49:25
Cedar Run 10 1 44N45'43 85w49'13 5:43:17
Cedar Springs 41 64 43N13'24 85w33'05 5:42:12
Cedarville 49 25 45N59'53 84w21'47 5:37:27
Cedarville 55 81 45N29 87w23 5:49:32
Cement City 46 1 42N04'12 84w19'50 5:37:19
Centennial 31 96 47N15'30 88w25'43 5:53:43
Centennial Heights 31 96 47N15'38 88w26'40 5:53:47
Center 24 67 45N36 84w54 5:39:36
Center Line 50 2 42N29'06 83w01'40 5:32:07
Centerville 45 1 44N54 85w45 5:43:00
Central 42 96 47N24'26 88w12'02 5:52:48
Central Lake 5 1 45N04'12 85w15'52 5:41:03
Central Park 70 51 42N47 86w07 5:44:28
Centreville 75 103 41N55'24 85w31'42 5:42:07
Ceresco 13 43 42N16'19 85w03'41 5:40:15
Chaison 21 17 45N52'37 87w03'53 5:48:16
Chalkerville 47 1 42N25'56 84w01'07 5:36:04
Chamberlain 75 1 42N03'57 85w44'34 5:42:58
Champion 52 29 46N30'50 87w57'48 5:51:51
Champion Mine 31 96 47N02'05 88w40'15 5:54:41
Chandler 21 25 45N52'12 87w09'21 5:48:37
Channing 22 87 46N08'30 88w05'38 5:52:23
Chapin 73 1 43N07'56 84w18'17 5:37:13
Charing Cross 63 88 42N34'18 83w13'17 5:32:53
Charing Cross Estates 63 88 42N34 83w16 5:33:04
Charles 49 25 46N00'52 84w41'33 5:38:46
Charleston 39 92 42N18 85w21 5:41:24
Charleston 76 1 43N39'33 82w41'10 5:30:45
Charlesworth 23 1 42N27'02 84w41'22 5:38:45
Charlevoix 15 1 45N19'05 85w15'30 5:41:02
Charlotte 23 1 42N33'49 84w50'09 5:39:21
Charlotte Landing 13 1 42N23'32 84w46'33 5:39:06
Charlton 69 1 44N59 84w26 5:37:44
Chase 43 1 43N53'21 85w38'08 5:42:33
Chassell 31 98 47N01'42 88w31'30 5:54:06
Chatham 2 25 46N20'52 86w55'44 5:47:43
Chauncey 41 61 43N03'01 85w33'01 5:42:12
Cheboygan 16 9 45N38'49 84w28'28 5:37:54
Chelsea 81 1 42N19'05 84w01'14 5:36:05
Cherry Beach 74 1 42N41'05 82w30'35 5:30:02
Cherry Bend 45 1 44N47'37 85w38'51 5:42:35
Cherry Grove 83 1 44N13 85w31 5:42:04
Cherry Hill 82 36 42N18'22 83w32'10 5:34:09
Cherry Island 82 36 42N04'50 83w11'41 5:32:47
Cherry Valley 43 92 43N57 85w45 5:43:00
Chesaning 73 1 43N11'05 84w06'54 5:36:28
Cheshire 3 92 42N28 85w57 5:43:48
Cheshire Center 3 42 42N27'06 85w56'04 5:43:44
Chester 23 1 42N36'21 84w54'53 5:39:40
Chesterfield 50 88 42N39'46 82w50'33 5:31:22
Chesterfield Shores 50 88 42N40'12 82w45'41 5:31:03
Chestonia 5 1 45N03'37 85w04'39 5:40:19
Cheviers 1 1 44N34'05 83w44'13 5:34:57
Chicagon 36 81 46N05'43 88w30'26 5:54:02
Chicagon Lake 36 81 46N06 88w20 5:53:20
Chicora 3 42 42N28'36 85w58'25 5:43:54
Chief Lake 51 1 44N22 86w01 5:44:04
Chikaming 11 74 41N51 86w38 5:46:32
Childsdale 41 65 43N06'17 85w34'49 5:42:19
Chilson 47 1 42N31'37 83w51'42 5:35:27
China 74 1 42N47 82w32 5:30:08
Chippewa Beach 16 1 45N26'25 84w38'21 5:38:33
Chippewa Lake 54 1 43N44'38 85w17'50 5:41:11
Chippewa Vista 54 1 43N44'18 85w05'58 5:40:24
Choate 66 11 46N32 89w17 5:57:08
Chocolay 52 25 46N28 87w18 5:49:12
Christie Lake 80 72 42N07 85w58 5:43:52
Christmas 2 22 46N26'13 86w42'05 5:46:48
Chums Corner 28 1 44N40'19 85w39'23 5:42:38
Churchill 61 49 43N12 86w16 5:45:04
Churchill 65 1 44N18 84w04 5:36:16
Church Street 25 1 43N01 83w42 5:34:48
Circle Pine Center 8 57 42N34'26 85w27'38 5:41:51
Cisco Lake 27 81 46N13 89w11 5:56:44
Clair Haven 50 88 42N36 82w49 5:31:16
Clam Lake 83 1 44N12 85w24 5:41:36
Clam River 5 1 44N56'43 85w16'49 5:41:07
Clam Union 57 1 44N13 85w02 5:40:08
Clare 18 1 43N49'10 84w46'07 5:39:04
Claremont 61 49 43N12 86w16 5:45:04
Clarence Center 13 1 42N22'52 84w46'05 5:39:04
Clarenceville 63 88 42N26'54 83w20'14 5:33:21
Clarendon 13 1 42N07'49 84w51'57 5:39:28
Clarion 15 1 45N16'42 84w55'24 5:39:42
Clark 49 25 46N01 84w22 5:37:28
Clark Bayshore 35 1 44N14'46 83w32'24 5:34:10
Clark Corners 70 51 43N01'22 86w08'42 5:44:35
Clarklake 38 1 42N07'17 84w20'42 5:37:23
Clarksburg 52 11 46N29'31 87w51'07 5:51:24
Clarkston 63 88 42N44'09 83w25'08 5:33:41
Clarksville 34 92 42N50'32 85w14'33 5:40:58
Clausedale 73 1 43N17'33 84w03'34 5:36:14
Clawson 63 2 42N32'00 83w08'47 5:32:35
Clay 74 1 42N38 82w35 5:30:20
Claybanks 64 57 43N31 86w26 5:45:44
Clays Landing 74 1 42N33'06 82w36'16 5:30:25
Clayton 46 1 41N51'48 84w14'11 5:36:57
Clear Lake 65 1 44N17 84w14 5:36:56
Clear Lake 75 97 41N57 85w38 5:42:32
Clearwater 40 1 44N49 85w16 5:41:04
Clement 26 1 44N08 84w20 5:37:20
Cleon 51 1 44N28 85w52 5:43:28
Cleveland 45 1 44N55 85w52 5:43:28
Clifford 44 1 43N18'53 83w10'45 5:32:43
Clifton Mill 50 88 42N47'06 83w05'10 5:32:21
Climax 39 101 42N14'18 85w20'06 5:41:20
Clinton 46 1 42N04'19 83w58'18 5:35:53
Clinton River Meadows 50 88 42N34 83w02 5:32:08
Clinton Village 19 41 42N47'45 84w31'53 5:38:08
Clintonville 63 88 42N41'25 83w21'22 5:33:25
Clio 25 1 43N10'39 83w44'03 5:34:56
Cloverdale 8 57 42N32 85w23 5:41:32
Cloverville 61 49 43N11'26 86w09'55 5:44:40
Clowry 52 25 46N31'24 87w53'53 5:51:36
Clyde 63 88 42N40'51 83w37'05 5:34:28
Coal Dock 52 25 46N33 87w24 5:49:36
Coalwood 2 25 46N20'26 86w43'54 5:46:56
Coats Grove 8 57 42N40'59 85w11'32 5:40:46
Coddes Beach 71 1 45N26'34 84w13'09 5:36:53
Cody 25 1 43N00 83w39 5:34:36
Coe 37 1 43N28'50 84w38'32 5:38:34
Cohoctah 47 1 42N45'35 83w56'55 5:35:48
Cohoctah Center 47 1 42N45'18 83w59'13 5:35:57
Colberry Park 63 88 42N34 83w16 5:33:04
Cold Springs 16 1 45N27'37 84w35'24 5:38:22
Cold Springs 40 1 44N49 85w02 5:40:08
Coldwater 12 4 41N56'25 85w00'02 5:40:00
Coleman 56 1 43N45'24 84w35'09 5:38:21
Colfax 64 57 43N44'36 86w04'45 5:44:19
College Park 82 2 42N25 83w09 5:32:36
College Town 9 36 43N36 83w54 5:35:36
Collens Landing 20 1 44N38'42 84w46'17 5:39:05
Colling 79 1 43N36'40 83w24'33 5:33:38
Collins 34 92 42N55'45 84w56'38 5:39:47
Collins Corner 39 92 42N12'30 85w28'56 5:41:56
Coloma 11 74 42N11'10 86w18'30 5:45:14
Colon 75 1 41N57'30 85w19'30 5:41:18
Colonville 18 1 43N50'39 84w42'21 5:38:49
Columbia 38 1 42N07 84w18 5:37:12
Columbiaville 44 1 43N09'24 83w24'38 5:33:39
Columbus 74 1 42N52'56 82w39'45 5:30:39
Columbus Grove 58 1 41N48 83w27 5:33:48
Colwood 79 1 43N36'42 83w21'08 5:33:25
Comins 68 1 44N44 84w02 5:36:08
Commerce 63 88 42N35'28 83w29'27 5:33:58
Comstock 39 47 42N17'12 85w30'48 5:42:03
Comstock Park 41 61 43N02'19 85w40'12 5:42:41
Concord 38 1 42N10'40 84w38'35 5:38:34
Condit 13 1 42N11'18 84w47'12 5:39:09
Cone 58 1 42N01'55 83w45'11 5:35:01
Conklin 61 51 43N07'44 85w52'53 5:43:32
Connorville 27 86 46N33'07 89w55'51 5:59:43
Constantine 75 92 41N50'28 85w40'07 5:42:40
Convis 13 1 42N23 85w00 5:40:00
Conway 24 67 45N25'00 84w52'01 5:39:28
Conway 47 1 42N44 84w06 5:36:24
Cooks 77 33 45N55'04 86w28'34 5:45:54
Cooks Corners 34 92 43N05'18 85w15'45 5:41:03
Cooks Mill 39 97 42N13'12 85w25'26 5:41:42
Cooper 39 92 42N22'35 85w36'37 5:42:26
Cooper Center 39 92 42N22 85w34 5:42:16
Coopersville 70 55 43N03'50 85w56'05 5:43:44
Cooperton 18 1 44N09'27 84w47'09 5:39:09
Copeland Corner 74 1 42N40'21 82w37'21 5:30:29
Copemish 51 1 44N28'54 85w55'21 5:43:41
Copenhagen 77 14 45N58 86w15 5:45:00
Copenhagen Beach 77 14 45N59'01 86w17'39 5:45:11
Copper City 31 96 47N17'01 88w23'13 5:53:33
Copper Falls 42 96 47N25'48 88w11'55 5:52:48
Copper Harbor 42 96 47N28'08 87w53'18 5:51:33
Coral 59 64 43N21'46 85w24'10 5:41:37
Cordell 17 12 46N11'23 84w50'52 5:39:23
Corey 14 97 41N54'10 85w45'39 5:43:03
Corey Lake 75 97 41N57 85w38 5:42:32
Corinne 49 25 46N05'12 85w43'19 5:42:53
Corinth 41 57 42N46'58 85w39'49 5:42:39
Cornell 21 25 45N54'05 87w13'20 5:48:53
Corning 3 92 42N43'29 85w36'03 5:42:24
Corunna 78 1 42N58'55 84w07'04 5:36:28
Corwith 69 1 45N09 84w39 5:38:36
Coryell Islands 49 25 46N00 84w22 5:37:28
Cottage Grove 72 1 44N30 84w36 5:38:24
Cottage Park 17 12 46N22 84w26 5:37:44
Cotton 40 1 44N41'57 85w03'12 5:40:13
Cottrellville 74 1 42N42 82w34 5:30:16
Court 39 47 42N17 85w35 5:42:20
Courtland 41 57 43N10 85w30 5:42:00
Covert 80 74 42N17'37 86w15'44 5:45:03
Covington 7 18 46N32'29 88w32'13 5:54:09
Craigsmere 66 25 46N25'17 89w14'27 5:56:58
Cranbrook 63 88 42N34 83w16 5:33:04
Crapo 54 97 43N51 85w27 5:41:48
Crawford 37 1 43N31'26 84w47'13 5:39:09
Creighton 77 25 46N20'48 86w16'40 5:45:07
Crescent Lake Estates 63 88 42N39 83w24 5:33:36
Cressey 8 57 42N25'41 85w28'17 5:41:53
Creswell 5 1 45N01'10 85w21'09 5:41:25
Crisp 70 51 42N53'07 86w04'49 5:44:19
Crockery 70 97 43N05 86w05 5:44:20
Crofton 40 1 44N40'24 85w14'12 5:40:57
Crooked Lake 8 57 42N30 85w24 5:41:36
Crooked Lake 47 1 42N32 83w47 5:35:08
Cross Village 24 67 45N38'32 85w02'15 5:40:09
Croswell 76 1 43N16'32 82w37'16 5:30:29
Crotch Lake 75 1 41N48 85w25 5:41:40
Croton 62 57 43N26'20 85w39'39 5:42:39
Croton Heights 62 64 43N27'23 85w38'05 5:42:32
Crow Island 73 91 43N28'11 83w54'14 5:35:37
Crump 9 1 43N45'14 84w05'14 5:36:21
Crystal 59 57 43N15'47 84w54'53 5:39:40
Crystal Beach 12 1 41N50'13 84w58'16 5:39:53
Crystal Beach 80 74 42N21'24 86w17'53 5:45:12
Crystal Falls 36 82 46N05'53 88w20'02 5:53:20
Crystal Lake 10 1 44N38 86w12 5:44:48
Crystall Falls 36 82 46N05 88w20 5:53:20
Crystallia 10 1 44N40'23 86w14'51 5:44:59
Crystal Spring 45 1 44N49'28 85w38'55 5:42:36
Crystal Valley 64 64 43N46'26 86w14'15 5:44:57
Cumber 76 1 43N37'17 82w58'39 5:31:55
Cumming 65 1 44N23 84w04 5:36:16
Cunard 55 81 45N44'17 87w40'00 5:50:40
Curran 1 1 44N42'53 83w48'28 5:35:14
Curtis 1 1 44N33 83w43 5:34:52
Curtis 49 25 46N12'21 85w44'43 5:42:59
Curtis 56 1 43N47'57 84w29'09 5:37:57
Curtisville 1 1 44N33'35 83w52'02 5:35:28
Cusino 77 25 46N26'42 86w21'31 5:45:26
Custer 53 64 43N57'07 86w13'10 5:44:53
Cutcheon 57 1 44N24'37 85w07'36 5:40:30
Cutlerville 41 61 42N50'27 85w39'49 5:42:39
Dafter 17 12 46N21'36 84w25'38 5:37:43
Daggett 55 86 45N27'49 87w36'23 5:50:26
Dailey 14 73 41N53'13 86w05'21 5:44:21
Dale 26 1 43N51'28 84w26'05 5:37:44
Dallas 19 1 42N59 84w47 5:39:08
Dalton 61 57 43N19'07 86w15'42 5:45:03
Damon 65 1 44N28'39 84w13'42 5:36:55
Danaher 48 25 46N20'37 85w46'51 5:43:07
Danak 9 36 43N36 83w54 5:35:36
Danby 34 92 42N49 84w54 5:39:36
Danish Landing 20 1 44N39'27 84w46'48 5:39:07
Dansville 33 1 42N33'21 84w18'12 5:37:13
Darragh 40 1 44N46'18 85w03'07 5:40:12
Daugherty Corners 39 47 42N17 85w34 5:42:16
Davis 50 88 42N43'51 82w57'37 5:31:50
Davisburg 63 88 42N45'08 83w32'29 5:34:10
Davison 25 1 43N02'05 83w31'05 5:34:04
Day 59 57 43N20 85w02 5:40:08
Dayton 11 106 41N47'54 86w26'22 5:45:45
Dayton 79 1 43N27'42 83w17'15 5:33:09
Daytona 79 1 43N29 83w24 5:33:36
Daytona Branch 79 1 43N27'33 83w17'28 5:33:10
Dayton Center 64 57 43N30'38 85w58'48 5:43:55
Dealno 6 1 44N03 83w41 5:34:44
Dean 56 1 43N35'33 84w12'50 5:36:51
Dearborn 82 2 42N19'20 83w10'35 5:32:42
Dearborn Heights 82 2 42N20'13 83w16'24 5:33:06
Decatur 80 72 42N06'29 85w58'28 5:43:54
Decker 76 1 43N27'32 83w03'03 5:32:12
Deckerville 76 1 43N31'36 82w44'07 5:30:56
Deep River 6 1 44N02 83w59 5:35:56

Deer Creek 47 1 42N45'36 83W54'26 5:35:38
Deerfield 46 1 41N53'20 83W46'44 5:35:07
Deerfield Center 37 1 43N35'51 84W54'28 5:39:38
Deerfield Center 47 1 42N44'01 83W51'44 5:35:27
Deerheart Valley 20 88 44N32'13 84W34'14 5:38:17
Deer Park 48 25 46N40'28 85W36'58 5:42:28
Deerton 2 25 46N28'28 87W02'31 5:48:10
Deford 79 1 43N30'48 83W11'33 5:32:46
Deibert 40 1 44N35'02 85W13'57 5:40:56
Delano 6 1 44N05'59 83W37'34 5:34:30
Delaware 42 96 47N25'16 88W05'45 5:52:23
Delaware 76 1 43N39 82W41 5:30:44
Delaware Mine 42 96 47N18 88W26 5:53:44
Delhi 33 41 42N38 84W32 5:38:08
Delhi 81 38 42N17 83W45 5:35:00
Delhi Mills 81 38 42N19'49 83W48'40 5:35:15
Delray 82 2 42N18 83W08 5:32:32
Delta Center 23 41 42N43'35 84W39'44 5:38:39
Delta Mills 23 41 42N45'54 84W38'51 5:38:35
Delton 8 57 42N29'59 85W24'29 5:41:38
Delwin 37 1 43N41'50 84W40'41 5:38:43
Denmark Junction 79 1 43N24'57 83W39'18 5:34:37
Dennison 70 55 43N04'24 85W59'14 5:43:57
Denton 81 36 42N15'28 83W31'27 5:34:06
Derby 11 74 42N00'53 86W28'55 5:45:56
De Tour Village 17 12 45N59'40 83W54'10 5:35:37
Detroit 82 2 42N19'53 83W02'45 5:32:11
Detroit Beach 58 1 41N55'52 83W19'37 5:33:18
Detroit River 82 2 42N22 83W04 5:32:16
Devereaux 38 1 42N19'12 84W42'31 5:38:50
Devils Corner 21 25 45N44'15 86W36'18 5:46:25
Devils Elbow 28 1 44N41'12 85W28'55 5:41:56
Devils Lake 38 1 42N00'28 84W17'33 5:37:10
Deward 20 1 44N50'26 84W49'36 5:39:18
DeWitt 19 41 42N50'32 84W34'09 5:38:17
Dexter 81 1 42N20'18 83W53'19 5:35:33
Diamond Lake 62 64 43N33 85W46 5:43:04
Diamond Shores 14 73 41N53'53 85W58'05 5:43:52
Diamond Springs 3 97 42N40'50 85W53'49 5:43:35
Diann 58 1 41N55'55 83W38'14 5:34:33
Dice 73 1 43N28'00 84W06'42 5:36:27
Dice Corners 56 1 43N36'45 84W22'10 5:37:29
Dick 17 12 46N11'27 84W49'53 5:39:20
Dickson 51 1 44N18 85W56 5:43:44
Diffin 2 25 46N12'36 87W02'02 5:48:08
Dighton 67 1 44N05'16 85W20'42 5:41:23
Dimondale 23 41 42N38'44 84W38'56 5:38:36
Dinca 57 1 44N16'44 85W03'15 5:40:13
Diorite 52 11 46N30'33 87W49'49 5:51:19
Disco 50 88 42N41'02 83W02'04 5:32:08
Dixboro 81 38 42N18'44 83W39'22 5:34:37
Dixon 2 25 46N19'57 86W51'11 5:47:25
Dodgeville 31 95 47N05'39 88W34'52 5:54:19
Dollar Bay 31 96 47N07'11 88W30'41 5:54:03
Dollar Settlement 17 12 46N27'42 84W44'21 5:38:57
Dollarville 48 24 46N21'05 85W32'31 5:42:10
Dolph 57 1 44N14'00 84W52'45 5:39:31
Dominican 46 1 41N54 84W02 5:36:08
Donahue Beach 9 36 43N39'24 83W52'47 5:35:31
Donaldson 17 45 46N29 84W21 5:37:24
Donken 31 25 46N56'30 88W47'40 5:55:11
Donnelly 60 1 44N59'37 84W18'46 5:37:15
Dorgans Crossing 17 110 46N23'47 84W36'50 5:38:27
Dorr 3 92 42N43'31 85W43'21 5:42:53
Dorrance 12 1 41N57 85W00 5:40:00
Dorsey 2 25 46N20'23 87W05'04 5:48:20
Doster 8 92 42N27'57 85W32'30 5:42:10
Doty 2 25 46N21'46 86W32'07 5:46:08
Doughertys Corners 39 92 42N17'44 85W42'59 5:42:52
Douglas 3 92 42N38'36 86W12'02 5:44:48
Douglas 51 111 44N19'20 86W13'24 5:44:54
Douglass 59 57 43N20 85W09 5:40:36
Dover 18 1 43N53'15 84W44'52 5:38:59
Dover 81 1 42N24'09 83W54'39 5:35:39
Dowagiac 14 71 41N59'03 86W06'31 5:44:26
Dowling 8 57 42N31'21 85W15'11 5:41:01
Downington 76 1 43N31 82W44 5:30:56
Doyle 77 25 46N10 86W03 5:44:12
Drayton Plains 63 88 42N41'03 83W22'38 5:33:31
Dreamland 31 96 47N05'52 88W24'47 5:53:39
Drenthe 70 54 42N46'58 85W56'24 5:43:46
Dresden Village 50 88 42N34 83W02 5:32:08
Drew 37 1 43N39'47 85W01'39 5:40:07
Drummond 17 12 45N59 83W43 5:34:52
Drummond Island 17 12 46N01 83W44 5:34:56
Dryburg 17 12 46N12'38 84W40'38 5:38:43
Dryden 44 1 42N56'46 83W07'26 5:32:30
Dublin 51 1 44N10'46 85W55'53 5:43:44
Duck Lake 3 92 42N22 85W53 5:43:32
Duck Lake 13 1 42N24'00 84W46'56 5:39:08
Duel 9 1 43N42'43 84W08'49 5:36:35
Duffield 25 1 42N55'41 83W54'36 5:35:38
Dukes 52 25 46N20'52 87W09'28 5:48:38
Dumont Lake 3 42 42N32 85W51 5:43:24
Duncan 16 1 44N48 82W55 5:31:40
Duncan 31 25 46N31 88W50 5:55:20
Dundee 58 1 41N57'26 83W39'35 5:34:38
Dunham 27 86 46N22'56 89W47'09 5:59:09
Dunningville 3 42 42N36'46 85W56'55 5:43:48
Dunn Location 36 86 46N04'05 88W22'29 5:53:30
Duplain 19 1 43N02'48 84W27'09 5:37:49
Durand 78 70 42N54'43 83W59'05 5:35:56
Dutton 41 61 42N50'28 85W35'06 5:42:20
Dwight 32 1 43N59 82W57 5:31:48
Eagle 19 1 42N48'28 84W47'19 5:39:09
Eagle Harbor 42 96 47N27'30 88W09'44 5:52:39
Eagle Lake 14 108 41N48 86W04 5:44:16
Eagle Mills 52 25 46N30'46 87W32'01 5:50:08
Eagle Nest 42 96 47N24'27 88W16'39 5:53:07
Eagle Point 14 73 41N53'43 85W58'59 5:43:56
Eagle River 42 10 47N24'50 88W17'44 5:53:11
Eagles Nest 55 81 45N11'26 87W36'41 5:50:27
Eames 63 88 42N41 83W20 5:33:20
East Bay 28 1 44N43 85W32 5:42:08
East China 74 1 42N46 82W29 5:29:56
East Comstock 39 92 42N17'10 85W29'23 5:41:58
East Cooper 39 92 42N20'58 85W33'06 5:42:12
East Dayton 79 1 43N24'39 83W17'07 5:33:08
East Detroit 50 2 42N28'06 82W57'20 5:31:49
East DeWitt 19 41 42N51'15 84W32'35 5:38:10
Eastern Heights 41 61 42N54 85W38 5:42:32
East Gilead 12 1 41N46'55 85W04'59 5:40:20
East Grand Rapids 41 61 42N56'28 85W36'36 5:42:26
East Highland 63 88 42N39'18 83W34'18 5:34:17
East Houghton 31 25 46N19 87W03 5:48:12
East Jordan 15 1 45N09'29 85W07'27 5:40:30
East Kingsford 22 87 45N47'42 88W03'52 5:52:15
East Lake 51 111 44N14'40 86W17'46 5:45:11
Eastland Center 82 2 42N25 82W54 5:31:36
East Lansing 33 41 42N44'13 84W29'02 5:37:56
Eastlawn 81 36 42N14'08 83W35'17 5:34:21
East Leroy 13 1 42N09'58 85W13'03 5:40:52
Eastmanville 70 55 43N01'01 85W57'23 5:43:50
East Melvindale 82 2 42N17 83W11 5:32:44
Eastmont 41 61 42N57'04 85W33'21 5:42:13
Easton 34 92 43N00 85W07 5:40:28
Easton 78 1 43N06'50 84W05'18 5:36:21
Eastover Farms 63 88 42N34 83W16 5:33:04
East Paris 41 61 42N54'36 85W34'06 5:42:16
Eastport 5 1 45N06'26 85W21'00 5:41:24
East Rockwood 82 36 42N02'54 83W12'39 5:32:51
East Saugatuck 3 74 42N40'54 86W05'35 5:44:22
East Sebwa 34 97 42N46 85W00 5:40:00
East Side 25 1 43N02 83W42 5:34:48
East Tawas 35 1 44N16'46 83W29'25 5:33:58
East Thetford 25 1 43N08 83W44 5:34:56
Eastview 50 1 42N48 83W01 5:32:04
Eastwood 39 47 42N18'11 85W33'01 5:42:12
Eaton 23 1 42N33 84W46 5:39:04
Eaton Rapids 23 1 42N30'33 84W39'21 5:38:37
Eau Claire 11 72 41N59'06 86W17'59 5:45:12
Eben Junction 2 25 46N21'18 86W58'12 5:47:53
Echo 5 1 45N04 85W09 5:40:36
Eckerman 17 12 46N21'55 85W02'07 5:40:08
Eckerman Corner 17 12 46N20'45 85W01'50 5:40:07
Eckerman Corner Lookout Towe 17 12 46N20'27 85W01'02 5:40:04
Eckford 13 1 42N12'07 84W51'59 5:39:28
Ecorse 82 2 42N14'40 83W08'45 5:32:35
Eden 33 1 42N31'26 84W25'42 5:37:43
Edenville 56 1 43N47'58 84W22'54 5:37:32
Edgemont Park 33 41 42N44 84W36 5:38:24
Edgerton 41 65 43N09'39 85W33'57 5:42:16
Edgewater 11 1 42N05 86W30 5:46:00
Edgewater Beach 16 1 45N46'07 84W43'30 5:38:54
Edgewater Heights 82 36 42N12'14 83W30'43 5:34:03
Edgewood 29 1 43N17'31 84W25'44 5:37:43
Edgewood 61 49 43N12 86W14 5:44:56
Edmore 59 57 43N24'29 85W02'19 5:40:09
Edwards 65 1 44N10'35 84W16'00 5:37:04
Edwardsburg 14 108 41N47'44 86W04'51 5:44:19
Edwards Corners 75 1 42N01 85W49 5:43:16
Egelston 61 57 43N14 86W06 5:44:24
Eightmile Corner 48 25 46N25'08 85W35'38 5:42:23
Eight Point Lake 18 1 43N51 85W00 5:40:00
Elba 44 1 43N02'11 83W26'24 5:33:46
Elberta 10 1 44N37'10 86W13'35 5:44:54
Elbow Lake 65 1 44N12'55 84W02'08 5:36:09
Elbridge 64 57 43N41'09 86W13'08 5:44:53
Eldorado 20 1 44N35'30 84W24'03 5:37:36
Elizabeth Lake Estates 63 88 42N39 83W24 5:33:36
Elkhorn 77 14 45N57'17 86W24'24 5:45:38
Elkland 79 1 43N38 83W11 5:32:44
Elk Rapids 5 1 44N53'44 85W24'59 5:41:40
Elkton 32 1 43N49'10 83W10'51 5:32:43
Ellington 79 1 43N33'14 83W19'17 5:33:17
Ellis 16 1 45N20 84W33 5:38:12
Ellsworth 5 1 45N09'56 85W14'46 5:40:59
Elm 82 36 42N22'36 83W19'53 5:33:20
Elmdale 34 47 42N51'13 85W18'40 5:41:15
Elmer 76 1 43N25'11 82W45'45 5:31:43
Elm Grove 18 1 43N50 84W46 5:39:04
Elm Hall 29 1 43N21'54 84W50'07 5:39:20
Elmhurst 16 1 45N29'46 84W41'19 5:38:45
Elmira 69 1 45N03'52 84W51'22 5:39:25
Elm River 31 25 46N54 88W51 5:55:24
Elmwood 36 81 46N13'20 88W54'35 5:55:38
Elmwood 79 1 43N35'05 83W17'00 5:33:08
Elo 31 25 46N52'24 88W38'13 5:54:33
Eloise 82 36 42N17'09 83W20'20 5:33:21
Elsie 19 1 43N05'19 84W23'13 5:37:33
Elwell 29 1 43N23'15 84W44'45 5:38:59
Ely 52 25 46N27 87W48 5:51:12
Emerald 54 1 43N54 85W16 5:41:04
Emerson 17 12 46N33'23 85W01'45 5:40:07
Emerson 29 1 43N20 84W33 5:38:12
Emerson Highlands 61 49 43N12 86W14 5:44:56
Emerson Station 4 1 45N03'51 83W39'15 5:34:37
Emery 81 38 42N21'36 83W40'59 5:34:44
Emmett 74 1 42N59'26 82W45'54 5:31:04
Empire 45 1 44N48'40 86W03'36 5:44:14
Engadine 49 25 46N07'00 85W34'15 5:42:17
Englishville 41 64 43N07'00 85W41'25 5:42:46
Ensign 21 25 45N53'51 86W52'08 5:47:29
Ensley Center 62 57 43N20'16 85W37'22 5:42:29
Enterprise 57 1 44N23 84W55 5:39:40
Entrican 59 57 43N21'01 85W09'13 5:40:37
Epoufette 49 25 46N03'20 85W10'06 5:40:40
Epsilon 24 67 45N21'46 84W48'07 5:39:12
Erickson Landing 36 81 46N08'30 88W24'15 5:53:37
Erie 58 1 41N47'39 83W29'47 5:33:59
Erwin 27 81 46N23 90W05 6:00:20
Escanaba 21 19 45N44'43 87W03'52 5:48:15
Essex 19 1 43N05 84W40 5:38:40
Essexville 9 1 43N36'55 83W50'31 5:35:22
Estey 26 1 43N52'12 84W12'20 5:36:49
Estral Beach 58 1 41N59'03 83W14'09 5:32:57
Ethelwood 27 86 46N29'14 89W43'28 5:58:54
Euclid Center 11 4 42N06 86W27 5:45:48
Eugene 29 1 43N17'32 84W42'25 5:38:50
Eureka 19 1 43N06'13 84W30'50 5:38:03
Eureka 59 57 43N10 85W16 5:41:04
Eureka Place 59 57 43N11'11 85W12'11 5:40:49
Eustis 55 11 45N45'31 87W20'07 5:49:20
Evangeline 15 1 45N15 85W01 5:40:04
Evans 41 64 43N11'43 85W27'19 5:41:49
Evans Lake 46 1 42N01 84W04 5:36:16
Evart 67 1 43N54'02 85W15'29 5:41:02
Eveline 15 1 45N14 85W09 5:40:36
Evelyn 2 25 46N22'01 86W32'03 5:46:08
Everett 62 64 43N31 85W45 5:43:00
Evergreen Acres 58 36 41N54'26 83W25'52 5:33:43
Evergreen Beach 71 1 45N29'37 83W58'43 5:35:55
Evergreen Park 70 68 43N04 86W11 5:44:44
Evergreen Shores 49 25 45N54'03 84W44'11 5:38:57
Evergreen Shores 77 14 45N58'26 86W18'39 5:45:15
Ewen 66 25 46N32'07 89W16'52 5:57:07
Ewing 52 25 46N05 87W18 5:49:12
Excelsior 40 1 44N44 85W02 5:40:08
Exeter 58 1 42N03 83W28 5:33:52
Eyedylwild Beach 69 1 44N57'43 84W42'15 5:38:49
Fabius 75 97 41N54'38 85W43'18 5:42:53
Factoryville 75 1 42N01 85W21 5:41:24
Fairbanks 21 25 45N40 86W40 5:46:40
Fairfax 75 1 41N57'19 85W21'58 5:41:28
Fairfield 46 1 41N48'46 84W02'28 5:36:10
Fairfield Addition 61 49 43N12 86W14 5:44:56
Fairgrove 79 1 43N31'25 83W32'36 5:34:10
Fairhaven 32 1 43N48 83W24 5:33:36
Fair Haven 74 1 42N40'45 82W39'14 5:30:37
Fairland 11 105 41N53'57 86W16'56 5:45:08
Fair Plain 11 4 42N05'13 86W27'21 5:45:49
Fairport 21 25 45N37'16 86W39'30 5:46:38
Fairview 68 1 44N43'30 84W03'04 5:36:12
Faithorn 55 81 45N40'47 87W45'07 5:51:00
Fallassburg 41 92 42N58'56 85W19'22 5:41:17
Falmouth 57 1 44N14'36 85W05'13 5:40:21
Fargo 74 1 43N06'11 82W39'33 5:30:38
Farmers Creek 44 1 42N57'46 83W20'24 5:33:22
Farmington 63 88 42N27'52 83W22'35 5:33:30
Farmington Acres 63 88 42N26'42 83W23'08 5:33:33
Farmington Hills 63 88 42N28 83W23 5:33:32
Farmwood 61 49 43N12 86W16 5:45:04
Farrandville 25 1 43N11'39 83W43'36 5:34:54
Farrar Landing 69 1 44N52'36 84W36'16 5:38:25
Farwell 18 1 43N50'06 84W52'01 5:39:28
Faunus 55 86 45N53'33 87W30'32 5:50:02
Fawn River 75 1 41N46'54 85W20'40 5:41:23
Fayette 21 25 45N43'03 86W40'04 5:46:40
Fayette 30 1 41N58 84W40 5:38:40
Fayettes Corner 65 1 44N24'25 84W05'46 5:36:23
Federal Station 63 88 42N38 83W17 5:33:08
Felch 22 87 45N59'50 87W49'32 5:51:18
Felch Mountain 22 87 46N00'04 87W49'55 5:51:20
Fenkell 82 2 42N24 83W08 5:32:32
Fenmore 73 1 43N10'22 84W20'43 5:37:23
Fennville 3 74 42N35'38 86W06'06 5:44:24
Fenton 25 1 42N47'52 83W42'18 5:34:49
Fenwick 59 57 43N08'57 85W04'49 5:40:19
Fern 53 64 43N50'47 86W13'05 5:44:52
Ferndale 61 49 43N12 86W14 5:44:56
Ferndale 63 2 42N27'38 83W08'05 5:32:32
Ferris 59 57 43N20 84W54 5:39:36
Ferry 64 57 43N35'03 86W13'29 5:44:54
Ferrysburg 70 68 43N05'04 86W13'13 5:44:53
Fibre 17 12 46N12'20 84W43'43 5:38:55
Fife Lake 28 1 44N34'37 85W21'02 5:41:24
Filer City 51 111 44N12'55 86W17'14 5:45:09
Filion 32 1 43N53'44 83W00'13 5:32:01
Fillmore 3 74 42N43'16 86W02'29 5:44:10
Findley 75 1 41N53'39 85W22'18 5:41:29

Fingerboard Corner 16 1 45N22'25 84w27'01 5:37:48
Firesteel 66 25 46N51'59 89w13'06 5:56:52
Fisher 12 1 41N53'04 84w52'59 5:39:32
Fisher 41 61 42N55 85w42 5:42:48
Fisher Building 82 2 42N22 83w04 5:32:16
Fishers Lake 75 97 41N57 85w38 5:42:32
Fisherville 9 1 43N36'15 84w06'32 5:36:26
Fish Lake 75 1 41N48 85w25 5:41:40
Fitchburg 33 1 42N26'21 84w16'40 5:37:07
Five Corners 20 1 44N38'13 84w31'42 5:38:07
Five Lakes 44 1 43N08'34 83w13'55 5:32:56
Fivemile Corner 28 1 44N44'48 85w31'22 5:42:05
Five Points 63 88 42N48'50 83w36'37 5:34:26
Five Points 78 1 42N59'52 84w13'33 5:36:54
Five Points 82 36 42N23 83w17 5:33:08
Five Points Corner 23 1 42N30'33 84w50'08 5:39:21
Five Points North 78 1 43N04'25 84w10'03 5:36:40
Flanders 4 1 45N03'36 83w44'48 5:34:59
Flat Rock 21 25 45N49'33 87w11'00 5:48:44
Flat Rock 82 37 42N05'47 83w17'31 5:33:10
Fleming 47 1 42N38'37 84w00'48 5:36:03
Fletcher 40 1 44N32'22 84w57'08 5:39:49
Flint 25 39 43N00'45 83w41'15 5:34:45
Floodwood 22 87 46N13'22 88w00'33 5:52:02
Florence 75 94 41N52 85w36 5:42:24
Florida 31 96 47N15 88w27 5:53:48
Flowerfield 75 92 42N03'57 85w39'29 5:42:38
Floyd 56 1 43N35'21 84w24'33 5:37:38
Flushing 25 1 43N03'47 83w51'04 5:35:24
Flynn 76 1 43N17 82w55 5:31:40
Foote Site Village 35 1 44N25'36 83w26'41 5:33:47
Forbes 36 81 46N06 88w39 5:54:36
Forbes Location 36 81 46N07'13 88w38'52 5:54:35
Forbush Corner 20 1 44N47'08 84w42'23 5:38:50
Ford Lake 53 57 44N03 86w11 5:44:44
Fordney 73 1 43N16'23 84w18'34 5:37:14
Ford River 21 11 45N40'46 87w08'24 5:48:34
Forest Beach 24 67 45N26 84w59 5:39:56
Forester 76 1 43N29'57 82w34'10 5:30:17
Forest Green Estates 78 1 42N48'54 84w16'13 5:37:05
Forest Grove 70 54 42N47'48 85w51'42 5:43:27
Forest Grove Station 70 54 42N48'40 85w52'54 5:43:32
Forest Hill 29 1 43N26'12 84w41'08 5:38:45
Forest Hills 33 1 42N42'41 84w24'12 5:37:37
Forest Hills 41 61 42N56 85w35 5:42:20
Forest Home 5 1 44N59 85w15 5:41:00
Forest Lake 2 25 46N20 86w51 5:47:24
Forestville 76 1 43N39'43 82w36'34 5:30:26
Fork 54 1 43N46 85w09 5:40:36
Forster 74 1 42N33'40 82w37'06 5:30:28
Forsyth 52 11 46N17 87w24 5:49:36
Fort Dearborn 82 2 42N18 83w15 5:33:00
Fort Gratiot 74 1 43N02 82w28 5:29:52
Fort Holmes 49 25 45N51'30 84w36'59 5:38:28
Fort Mackinac 49 25 45N51'11 84w37'04 5:38:28
Fort Shelby 82 2 42N22 83w04 5:32:16
Fortune Lake 36 81 46N05'41 88w24'58 5:53:40
Fort Wayne 82 2 42N17'58 83w05'46 5:32:23
Fort Wayne Junction 30 1 41N59 84w40 5:38:40
Foster 65 1 44N23 84w18 5:37:12
Foster 81 38 42N18'52 83w46'52 5:35:07
Foster City 22 87 45N57'48 87w44'38 5:50:59
Fosters 73 1 43N17'53 83w54'59 5:35:40
Fostoria 79 1 43N15'12 83w22'19 5:33:29
Fouch 45 1 44N50'02 85w43'16 5:42:53
Fountain 53 57 44N02'48 86w10'43 5:44:43
Fountain Park 30 1 41N49'53 84w31'45 5:38:07
Fountain Point 45 1 44N58'10 85w42'19 5:42:49
Fourmile Corner 48 25 46N25'09 85w30'38 5:42:03
Fourmile Lake 81 1 42N19'30 83w58'00 5:35:52
Four Towns 63 88 42N37'04 83w24'49 5:33:39
Fowler 19 1 43N00'06 84w44'23 5:38:58
Fowlerville 47 1 42N39'38 84w04'23 5:36:18
Fox 55 81 45N29'04 87w18'11 5:49:13
Frain Lake 81 38 42N19'45 83w37'01 5:34:28
Francisco 38 1 42N16'38 84w08'26 5:36:34
Francis Grove 56 1 43N43'15 84w23'24 5:37:34
Frandor 33 41 42N44 84w31 5:38:04
Frankenlust 9 1 43N33 83w59 5:35:56
Frankenmuth 73 1 43N19'54 83w44'17 5:34:57
Frankentrost 73 91 43N24'26 83w47'31 5:35:10
Frankfort 10 1 44N38'01 86w14'04 5:44:56
Franklin 63 88 42N31'20 83w18'22 5:33:13
Franklin Knolls 63 88 42N32 83w17 5:33:08
Franklin Mine 31 95 47N08'24 88w34'23 5:54:18
Fraser 50 88 42N32'21 82w56'58 5:31:48
Freda 31 96 47N08'07 88w49'07 5:55:16
Frederic 20 1 44N46'43 84w45'16 5:39:01
Fredonia 13 1 42N12 85w00 5:40:00
Freedom 16 1 45N44'10 84w38'28 5:38:34
Freedom 81 1 42N13 83w57 5:35:48
Freeland 73 1 43N31'30 84w07'22 5:36:29
Freeman 18 1 43N57 85w01 5:40:04
Freeman Landing 52 25 46N37'08 87w27'58 5:49:52
Freeport 8 64 42N45'58 85w18'48 5:41:15
Freesoil 53 57 44N06'25 86w13'00 5:44:52
Freiburgers 76 1 43N42 82w56 5:31:44
Freidberger 76 1 43N37'24 82w55'03 5:31:40
Fremont 62 58 43N28'03 85w56'31 5:43:46
French Landing 82 36 42N12'36 83w26'23 5:33:46
Frenchtown 52 25 46N28'24 87w40'44 5:50:43
Frenchtown 58 36 41N57 83w22 5:33:28
French Town 64 64 43N46'15 86w26'14 5:45:45
Friendship 24 67 45N31 85w02 5:40:08
Friendsville 80 74 42N18'28 86w13'25 5:44:54
Fritzburg 80 72 42N07'37 86w02'53 5:44:12
Frontier 30 1 41N46'54 84w36'17 5:38:25
Frost 18 1 44N06 84w47 5:39:08
Frost 31 25 46N36'18 88w52'23 5:55:30
Frost 73 1 43N27'10 84w07'17 5:36:29
Frost Corners 34 92 42N50'34 84w52'00 5:39:28
Fruitland 61 64 43N21 86w20 5:45:20
Fruitport 61 97 43N07'55 86w09'17 5:44:37
Fruit Ridge Center 41 64 43N07'05 85w46'09 5:43:05
Fuller 27 81 46N17'49 89w06'13 5:56:25
Fulton 29 1 43N10 84w40 5:38:40
Fulton 39 92 42N06'54 85w21'09 5:41:25
Fulton 42 96 47N17'56 88w21'36 5:53:26
Fulton Center 29 1 43N11 84w41 5:38:44
Gaastra 36 86 46N03'30 88w36'21 5:54:25
Gagetown 79 1 43N39'26 83w14'42 5:32:59
Gaines 25 1 42N52'21 83w54'51 5:35:39
Galesburg 39 92 42N17'19 85w25'05 5:41:40
Galewood 41 61 42N55 85w42 5:42:48
Galien 11 106 41N47'53 86w29'57 5:46:00
Galloway 73 1 43N19'54 84w22'10 5:37:29
Ganges 3 92 42N34'37 86w12'37 5:44:50
Garden 21 25 45N46'29 86w33'02 5:46:12
Garden City 82 36 42N19'32 83w19'52 5:33:19
Garden Corners 21 33 45N53'25 86w32'12 5:46:09
Gardendale 74 1 43N02'19 82w29'33 5:29:58
Gardenville 17 45 46N27'45 84w18'05 5:37:12
Gardner 55 81 45N32'11 87w42'28 5:50:50
Gardners Corners 39 92 42N07'45 85w21'11 5:41:25
Garfield 73 1 43N21'05 84w08'02 5:36:32
Garland Village 60 1 44N51'34 84w18'11 5:37:13
Garnet 49 25 46N09'30 85w18'24 5:41:14
Garth 21 25 45N54'00 86w56'57 5:47:48
Gay 42 96 47N13'39 88w09'49 5:52:39
Gaylord 69 1 45N01'39 84w40'29 5:38:42
Geddes 81 38 42N16'01 83w40'04 5:34:40
Geels 72 1 44N25'19 84w29'01 5:37:56
Genesee 25 1 43N06'45 83w37'04 5:34:28
Geneva 46 1 41N57'29 84w16'50 5:37:07
Genoa 47 1 42N34 83w50 5:35:20
Gentian 52 11 46N25'52 87w28'00 5:49:52
Georgetown 70 54 42N54 85w50 5:43:20
Gera 73 1 43N23'14 83w44'19 5:34:57
Germfask 77 25 46N14'58 85w55'33 5:43:42
Gerrish 72 1 44N28 84w41 5:38:44
Giauque Beach 16 1 45N29'01 84w35'39 5:38:23
Gibbs City 36 86 46N13'33 88w42'02 5:54:48
Gibbs Corners 67 1 43N51'26 85w08'50 5:40:35
Gibraltar 82 36 42N05'42 83w11'23 5:32:46
Gibson 9 1 43N57 84w06 5:36:24
Gibson Lake 36 81 46N12'11 88w25'48 5:53:43
Gidding 7 25 46N49 88w38 5:54:32
Giddings 40 1 44N35'04 85w11'46 5:40:47
Gilbert 83 1 44N22'32 85w25'07 5:41:40
Gilchrist 48 25 46N08'34 85w23'05 5:41:32
Gilead 12 1 41N48'03 85w09'20 5:40:37
Gilford 79 1 43N29'39 83w37'19 5:34:29
Gillet Landing 52 25 46N52'16 87w46'42 5:51:07
Gingell 63 88 42N41 83w20 5:33:20
Gingellville 63 88 42N43'18 83w18'28 5:33:14
Girard 12 1 42N01'46 85w00'05 5:40:00
Gitchel 70 54 42N46'56 85w50'30 5:43:22
Gladstone 21 13 45N51'10 87w01'18 5:48:05
Gladwin 26 1 43N58'51 84w29'11 5:37:57
Glen Arbor 45 1 44N53'51 85w59'07 5:43:56
Glencoe 32 1 43N57'51 82w53'09 5:31:33
Glendale 80 72 42N18'10 85w57'23 5:43:50
Glendora 11 74 41N53'06 86w29'13 5:45:57
Glengary 63 88 42N33'54 83w30'15 5:34:01
Glengary 83 1 44N25'23 85w43'16 5:42:53
Glen Haven 45 1 44N54'07 86w01'39 5:44:07
Glen Lord 11 74 42N02'28 86w30'22 5:46:01
Glenn 3 92 42N31'13 86w13'39 5:44:55
Glennie 1 1 44N33'38 83w43'33 5:34:54
Glenn Stores 3 92 42N29'54 86w14'08 5:44:57
Glenwood 14 71 42N03'18 86w01'59 5:44:08
Glenwood Beach 6 1 44N03'25 83w36'20 5:34:25
Glenwood Forest 41 61 42N54 85w38 5:42:32
Glovers Corner 7 25 46N53'42 88w06'30 5:52:26
Gobles 80 72 42N21'39 85w52'46 5:43:31
Goddyne 9 36 43N37 83w51 5:35:24
Godwin 41 61 42N55 85w42 5:42:48
Godwin Heights 41 61 42N55 85w42 5:42:48
Goetzville 17 12 46N03'29 84w05'32 5:36:22
Gogebic 27 86 46N21'09 89w30'09 5:58:01
Golden 22 87 46N08'34 88w01'14 5:52:05
Golden 56 1 43N36'36 84w10'06 5:36:40
Golden 64 64 43N41 86w27 5:45:48
Golfcrest 58 36 41N56'34 83w22'13 5:33:29
Golfside 81 38 42N16 83w43 5:34:52
Gomins 68 1 44N48'21 84w03'05 5:36:12
Goodar 65 1 44N30'04 83w53'47 5:35:35
Goodells 74 1 42N58'52 82w39'57 5:30:40
Good Hart 24 67 45N34'02 85w06'47 5:40:27
Gooding 41 64 43N10 85w42 5:42:48
Goodison 63 88 42N43'58 83w09'45 5:32:39
Goodland 44 1 43N05'41 83w04'21 5:32:17
Goodrich 25 1 42N55'01 83w30'23 5:34:02
Goodwell 62 57 43N36 85w37 5:42:28
Gordon 52 25 46N29'04 87w13'38 5:48:55
Gordon Beach 11 75 41N49'41 86w42'11 5:46:49
Gordonville 56 1 43N34'04 84w22'10 5:37:29
Gore 32 1 43N58 82w45 5:31:00
Gormer 67 1 44N06 85w09 5:40:36
Gotts 32 1 43N56 83w16 5:33:04
Gould City 49 25 46N05'43 85w41'48 5:42:47
Gourley 55 81 45N35'42 87w25'26 5:49:42
Gowen 59 57 43N15'06 85w18'07 5:41:12
Graafschap 3 92 42N45'15 86w08'11 5:44:33
Grace 71 1 45N33'05 84w07'46 5:36:31
Grafton 58 7 42N02'12 83w23'23 5:33:34
Graham Lake 13 43 42N20 85w11 5:40:44
Grandale Gardens 82 36 42N23 83w17 5:33:08
Grand Beach 11 109 41N46'24 86w47'51 5:47:11
Grand Blanc 25 1 42N55'39 83w37'48 5:34:31
Grand Circus Park 82 2 42N20 83w03 5:32:12
Grande Pointe 74 1 42N35'58 82w32'43 5:30:11
Grand Haven 70 68 43N03'47 86w13'42 5:44:55
Grand Island 2 25 46N30 86w40 5:46:40
Grand Junction 80 72 42N24'15 86w04'23 5:44:18
Grand Ledge 23 1 42N45'12 84w44'47 5:38:59
Grand Marais 2 80 46N40'15 85w59'06 5:43:56
Grand Rapids 41 61 42N57'48 85w40'05 5:42:40
Grand Rapids 66 25 46N45'57 89w16'32 5:57:06
Grand River 82 2 42N21 83w06 5:32:24
Grand Valley 70 51 42N58'28 85w52'11 5:43:29
Grand Valley State College 70 51 42N58 85w57 5:43:48
Grand View 16 1 45N24'01 84w39'51 5:38:39
Grand View 58 36 41N50'31 83w24'10 5:33:37
Grand View Acres 82 36 42N25'34 83w26'48 5:33:47
Grand View Beach 16 1 45N27'25 84w35'08 5:38:21
Grandview Beach 58 1 41N52 83w27 5:33:48
Grandville 41 61 42N54'35 85w45'47 5:43:03
Grange Corners 3 92 42N34'39 86w11'26 5:44:46
Granite Bluff 22 87 45N56'22 88w03'13 5:52:13
Grant 62 64 43N20'10 85w48'39 5:43:15
Grant Center 54 1 43N46'15 85w24'10 5:41:37
Grape 58 36 41N57'49 83w32'22 5:34:09
Grass Lake 38 1 42N15'03 84w12'47 5:36:51
Gratiot 82 2 42N21 83w01 5:32:04
Grattan 41 57 43N05'03 85w22'52 5:41:31
Gravel Lake 80 46 42N10 85w51 5:43:24
Grawn 28 1 44N39'45 85w41'37 5:42:46
Grayling 20 1 44N39'41 84w42'53 5:38:52
Great Lake Beach 76 1 43N16 82w32 5:30:08
Great Lakes Beach 76 1 43N13'01 82w31'20 5:30:05
Great Western 36 81 46N06 88w20 5:53:20
Greeley 4 1 45N05 83w43 5:34:52
Green 66 25 46N50'15 89w26'23 5:57:46
Greenbush 1 1 44N35'16 83w18'59 5:33:16
Greendale 56 1 43N36 84w32 5:38:08
Greenfield Park 13 43 42N20'06 85w08'14 5:40:33
Greenfield Village 82 2 42N18'19 83w13'29 5:32:54
Green Garden 52 25 46N26'19 87w16'45 5:49:07
Green Haven 2 80 46N32'20 86w00'56 5:44:04
Green Lake 3 92 42N47 85w31 5:42:04
Green Lake 28 1 44N39 85w45 5:43:00
Greenland 66 25 46N46'46 89w06'06 5:56:24
Greenleaf 76 1 43N38 83w04 5:32:16
Green Oak 47 1 42N29'33 83w41'53 5:34:48
Green River 5 1 44N59'21 85w03'19 5:40:13
Green Timbers 69 1 45N10'18 84w32'28 5:38:10
Greenville 59 57 43N10'39 85w15'10 5:41:01
Greenwood 52 25 46N29'14 87w45'21 5:51:01
Greenwood 65 1 44N10'34 84w09'24 5:36:38
Gregory 47 1 42N27'30 84w05'04 5:36:20
Greilickville (Rennies Sta) 45 1 44N46'59 85w38'19 5:42:33
Gresham 23 1 42N38'29 84w53'43 5:39:35
Grim 26 1 44N00 84w14 5:36:56
Grind Stone City 32 1 44N03'01 82w54'03 5:31:36
Groos 21 25 45N48'42 87w06'11 5:48:25
Gros Cap 49 25 45N53 84w49 5:39:16
Gros Gap 49 25 45N52'13 84w49'40 5:39:19
Grosse Ile 82 2 42N08 83w08 5:32:32
Grosse Pointe 82 2 42N23'10 82w54'43 5:31:39
Grosse Pointe Farms 82 2 42N24'33 82w53'31 5:31:34
Grosse Pointe Park 82 2 42N22'33 82w56'15 5:31:45
Grosse Pointe Shores 82 2 42N26'12 82w52'37 5:31:30
Grosse Pointe Woods 82 2 42N26'37 82w54'25 5:31:38
Grosvenor 46 1 41N50 83w52 5:35:28
Grout 26 1 43N57 84w33 5:38:12
Groveland 63 88 42N50 83w31 5:34:04
Groveland Corners 63 88 42N48'58 83w32'52 5:34:11
Groveton 73 1 43N14'33 84w07'45 5:36:31
Gulliver 77 25 45N59'35 86w00'43 5:44:03
Gull Lake 39 92 42N22'15 85w23'12 5:41:33
Gun Lake 53 57 44N06 86w13 5:44:52
Gunnisonville 19 41 42N48'47 84w31'23 5:38:06
Gunplain 3 102 42N27 85w36 5:42:24
Gustin 1 1 44N37'38 83w24'52 5:33:39

Guthrie 81 1 42N18'09 84w04'09 5:36:17
Gwinn 52 16 46N16'52 87w26'27 5:49:46
Haakwood 16 1 45N16 84w36 5:38:24
Hadley 44 1 42N57'16 83w24'12 5:33:37
Hagar 11 74 42N11 86w23 5:45:32
Hagar Shores 11 74 42N12 86w20 5:45:20
Hagensville 71 1 45N20'00 83w46'55 5:35:08
Hagerman Lake 36 81 46N06 88w39 5:54:36
Haight 66 25 46N24 89w11 5:56:44
Hale 35 1 44N22'40 83w48'17 5:35:13
Hallers Corners 47 1 42N41'41 83w42'13 5:34:49
Halls Corner 9 1 43N32'23 85w13'29 5:40:54
Hamar 7 25 46N47 88w30 5:54:00
Hamburg 47 1 42N26'55 83w48'06 5:35:12
Hamilton 3 97 42N40'38 86w00'22 5:44:01
Hamlin Lake 53 57 44N01'21 86w27'20 5:45:49
Hammell Beach 6 6 44N05'38 83w34'49 5:34:19
Hammond 71 1 45N29'50 84w02'13 5:36:09
Hammond Bay 71 1 45N24 84w05 5:36:20
Hampton 9 1 43N36 83w49 5:35:16
Hamtramck 82 2 42N23'34 83w02'59 5:32:12
Hancock 31 95 47N07'37 88w34'51 5:54:19
Hand 82 2 42N15'13 83w16'23 5:33:06
Handy 47 1 42N38 84w06 5:36:24
Hangore Heights 16 1 45N26'22 84w17'43 5:37:11
Hannah 28 1 44N35'05 85w38'08 5:42:33
Hannahville 55 86 45N39'09 87w20'46 5:49:23
Hanover 38 1 42N06'04 84w33'07 5:38:12
Hansen 55 81 45N14'22 87w36'47 5:50:27
Harbert 11 74 41N52'19 86w37'44 5:46:31
Harbor Beach 32 88 43N50'41 82w39'05 5:30:36
Harbor Haven 61 49 43N12 86w16 5:45:04
Harbor Hills 61 49 43N12 86w16 5:45:04
Harbor Park 61 49 43N12 86w16 5:45:04
Harbor Point 24 67 45N25'19 84w59'11 5:39:57
Harbor Springs 24 67 45N25'54 84w59'31 5:39:58
Harbor View 71 1 45N20'34 83w29'13 5:33:57
Hard Luck 26 1 44N04'18 84w11'35 5:36:46
Hardwood 22 87 45N57'42 87w41'28 5:50:46
Haring 83 1 44N17'55 85w24'47 5:41:39
Harlan 83 1 44N27'25 85w49'10 5:43:17
Harlem 70 51 42N52'14 86w06'49 5:44:27
Harmon City Heights 6 1 44N08'01 83w34'09 5:34:17
Harper 82 2 42N24 83w00 5:32:00
Harper Woods 82 2 42N25'59 82w55'27 5:31:42
Harrietta 83 1 44N18'36 85w41'52 5:42:47
Harris 55 86 45N42'13 87w20'43 5:49:23
Harrisburg 70 66 43N11'31 85w52'26 5:43:30
Harrison 18 1 44N01'09 84w47'58 5:39:12
Harrison Beach 77 14 45N58'50 86w18'05 5:45:12
Harrisville 1 1 44N39'23 83w17'41 5:33:11
Harsens Island 74 1 42N35 82w34 5:30:16
Hart 64 64 43N41'54 86w21'50 5:45:27
Hartford 80 74 42N12'24 86w10'00 5:44:40
Hartland 47 1 42N39'24 83w45'11 5:35:01
Hartley 27 86 46N23'28 89w48'57 5:59:16
Hartman 11 72 42N00'52 86w19'28 5:45:18
Hartwick 67 1 44N02 85w14 5:40:56
Harvard 41 64 43N11'40 85w25'00 5:41:40
Harvey 52 25 46N29'41 87w21'15 5:49:25
Harwood 22 87 45N57 87w42 5:50:48
Haslett 33 1 42N44'49 84w24'04 5:37:36
Hastings 8 62 42N38'45 85w17'27 5:41:10
Hatchs 45 1 44N49'35 85w40'56 5:42:44
Hatmaker 12 1 41N50'51 85w07'17 5:40:29
Hatton 18 1 43N55'22 84w49'07 5:39:16
Hautala Corner 27 81 46N31'15 90w09'20 6:00:37
Havana 73 1 43N08 84w10 5:36:40
Hawes 1 1 44N44 83w30 5:34:00
Hawkhead 3 93 42N28'10 86w12'26 5:44:50
Hawkins 62 97 43N48'02 85w36'11 5:42:25
Hawks 71 1 45N18'07 83w53'15 5:35:33
Hawthorne 74 1 42N46'24 82w28'22 5:29:53
Hay 26 1 43N58 84w19 5:37:16
Haynes 1 1 44N44 83w20 5:33:20
Hazel 36 81 46N08'53 88w44'40 5:54:59
Hazelhurst 11 74 41N52'42 86w37'43 5:46:31
Hazelhurst Camp 11 74 41N52 86w38 5:46:32
Hazel Park 63 2 42N27'45 83w06'15 5:32:25
Hazelton 78 1 43N05 83w59 5:35:56
Heath 3 97 42N39 85w57 5:43:48
Hebards 42 96 47N17'06 88w17'50 5:53:11
Hebron 16 1 45N41 84w40 5:38:40
Heimforth 45 1 44N51'27 85w42'32 5:42:50
Helena 5 1 44N54 85w15 5:41:00
Helena 32 1 43N46'29 82w41'27 5:30:46
Helena 52 11 46N13'06 87w16'20 5:49:05
Hell 47 1 42N26'05 83w59'06 5:35:56
Helmer 48 25 46N15'59 85w42'56 5:42:52
Helps 55 86 45N55'51 87w35'55 5:50:24
Hemans 76 1 43N27'42 83w05'22 5:32:21
Hematite 36 86 46N18 88w29 5:53:56
Hemlock 73 1 43N24'53 84w13'50 5:36:55
Henderson 78 1 43N05'11 84w11'43 5:36:47
Henderson 83 1 44N12 85w38 5:42:32
Hendricks 21 25 45N58'50 87w21'11 5:49:25
Hendricks 49 25 46N09 85w11 5:40:44
Henrietta 38 1 42N23 84w18 5:37:12
Herman 7 25 46N40'01 88w22'01 5:53:28
Hermansville 55 86 45N42'40 87w36'07 5:50:24
Herrick 37 1 43N48'02 84w42'24 5:38:50
Herrington 70 51 43N03'37 85w49'42 5:43:19
Herron 4 1 45N01'23 83w38'49 5:34:35
Hersey 67 97 43N50'55 85w26'40 5:41:47
Hesperia 64 57 43N34'08 86w02'22 5:44:09
Hessel 49 25 46N00'15 84w25'33 5:37:42
Hetherton 60 1 45N00'45 84w22'12 5:37:29
Hiawatha 36 81 46N06 88w39 5:54:36
Hiawatha 77 25 46N07'03 86w15'42 5:45:03
Hiawatha Location 36 86 46N04'26 88w38'41 5:54:35
Hickory Corners 8 57 42N26'29 85w22'32 5:41:30
Hickory Heights 63 88 42N34 83w16 5:33:04
Hickory Island 82 2 42N08 83w09 5:32:36
Hickory Ridge 63 88 42N40'47 83w39'54 5:34:40
Higbee Corner 54 1 43N32'32 85w23'33 5:41:34
Higgins 72 1 44N26 84w33 5:38:12
Higgins Lake 72 1 44N29'01 84w46'47 5:39:07
High Island 15 1 45N44 85w41 5:42:44
Highland 63 88 42N38'17 83w37'02 5:34:28
Highland 67 1 44N08'44 85w15'59 5:41:04
Highland Park 39 92 42N23'45 85w25'11 5:41:41
Highland Park 82 2 42N24'20 83w05'49 5:32:23
Highland View 61 49 43N12 86w16 5:45:04
Highway 31 96 47N15 88w27 5:53:48
Highwood 26 1 43N55'38 84w18'23 5:37:14
Higman Park 11 4 42N07'50 86w28'08 5:45:53
Hill 65 1 44N23 83w57 5:35:48
Hillcrest 27 81 46N29'32 90w09'22 6:00:37
Hillcrest 72 1 44N27'53 84w46'23 5:39:06
Hillcrest Orchard 58 1 41N50'58 83w28'36 5:33:54
Hilliards 3 92 42N40'29 85w43'42 5:42:55
Hillman 60 1 45N03'33 83w54'04 5:35:36
Hills and Dales 41 61 43N00 85w38 5:42:32
Hills Corners 11 74 41N53'06 86w28'31 5:45:54
Hillsdale 30 1 41N55'12 84w37'50 5:38:31
Hillside Gardens 38 90 42N15 84w24 5:37:36
Hilltop 28 1 44N36'42 85w39'22 5:42:37
Hinchman 11 72 41N58'20 86w25'38 5:45:43
Hinton 54 1 43N31 85w16 5:41:04
Hobart 83 1 44N10'58 85w26'54 5:41:48
Hockaday 26 1 44N05'16 84w25'38 5:37:43
Hodunk 12 1 42N00'53 85w03'42 5:40:15
Holland 70 53 42N47'15 86w06'32 5:44:26
Holloway 46 1 41N56'06 83w54'52 5:35:39
Holly 63 88 42N47'31 83w37'40 5:34:31
Hollywood 3 92 42N29'34 86w14'20 5:44:57
Hollywood 11 1 42N00'52 86w27'21 5:45:49
Holmes 55 81 45N32 87w44 5:50:56
Holt 33 41 42N38'26 84w30'55 5:38:04
Holton 61 57 43N24'48 86w04'46 5:44:19
Holy Corners 41 92 42N48'42 85w31'36 5:42:06
Home Acres 41 61 42N54 85w38 5:42:32
Home Acres 61 49 43N12 86w14 5:44:56
Homeier 52 25 46N46'21 87w40'47 5:50:43
Homer 13 1 42N08'45 84w48'32 5:39:14
Homer 36 81 46N06 88w39 5:54:36
Homer Location 36 81 46N07'00 88w39'30 5:54:38
Homestead 10 1 44N39 85w59 5:43:56
Homestead 17 45 46N20'17 84w07'21 5:36:29
Hongore Bay 16 1 45N21 84w13 5:36:52
Honor 10 1 44N39'50 86w01'05 5:44:04
Hooks Corner 11 75 41N49'40 86w40'06 5:46:40
Hooper 3 102 42N30'37 85w33'46 5:42:15
Hoovers Corners 78 1 43N06'01 84w18'20 5:37:13
Hope 56 1 43N45'52 84w20'17 5:37:21
Hopkins 3 92 42N37'25 85w45'37 5:43:02
Hopkinsburg 3 92 42N37'08 85w42'10 5:42:49
Hopwood Acres 33 41 42N44 84w31 5:38:04
Horr 37 1 43N41'01 85w02'51 5:40:11
Horton 38 1 42N09'01 84w31'02 5:38:04
Horton 65 1 44N12 84w11 5:36:44
Horton Bay 15 1 45N17'04 85w04'44 5:40:19
Houghton 31 95 47N07'19 88w34'08 5:54:17
Houghton Lake 72 1 44N18'53 84w45'53 5:39:04
Houghton Lake Heights 72 1 44N19'39 84w46'28 5:39:06
Houghton Point 72 1 44N22'20 84w45'33 5:39:02
Houle 55 81 45N42'20 87w23'48 5:49:35
Houseman 40 1 44N36'47 85w18'30 5:41:14
Houserville 29 1 43N23 84w39 5:38:36
Howard 14 105 41N51 86w11 5:44:44
Howard City 59 64 43N23'44 85w28'04 5:41:52
Howardsville 75 1 42N01'30 85w43'06 5:42:52
Howell 47 1 42N36'26 83w55'46 5:35:43
Howlandsburg 39 92 42N20'06 85w24'13 5:41:37
Hoxeyville 83 1 44N11'38 85w42'52 5:42:51
Hoytville 23 92 42N44'28 84w53'46 5:39:35
Hubbard Lake 4 1 44N52'25 83w35'14 5:34:21
Hubbardston 34 92 43N05'32 84w50'32 5:39:22
Hubbell 31 96 47N10'24 88w25'45 5:53:43
Huber 64 57 43N36'43 85w59'57 5:44:00
Hudson 46 1 41N51'18 84w21'14 5:37:25
Hudson Mills 81 1 42N23'14 83w55'01 5:35:40
Hudsonville 70 54 42N52'15 85w51'54 5:43:28
Hulbert 17 12 46N21'15 85w09'00 5:40:36
Humboldt 52 25 46N29'44 87w53'13 5:51:33
Humboldt Mine 52 25 46N29'02 87w53'52 5:51:35
Hume 32 1 43N58 83w03 5:32:12
Humphrey 51 1 44N28'19 86w03'37 5:44:14
Hunters Creek 44 1 42N59'08 83w17'38 5:33:11
Huntington Woods 63 2 42N28'50 83w10'01 5:32:40
Huntspur 49 25 46N02'31 85w51'15 5:43:25
Huron Beach 71 1 45N30 84w06 5:36:24
Huron City 32 1 44N01'45 82w49'58 5:31:20
Huron Gardens 63 88 42N39 83w24 5:33:36
Huron Heights 6 1 44N08'24 83w34'09 5:34:17
Huronia Heights 76 1 43N12'44 82w31'22 5:30:05
Huron Mountain 52 25 46N53'14 87w51'55 5:51:28
Huron Oaks 35 1 44N13'37 83w33'00 5:34:12
Hurontown 31 25 47N06'37 88w34'26 5:54:18
Hutula 7 25 46N32 88w36 5:54:24
Hyde 21 19 45N44'01 87w12'09 5:48:49
Hyde Park 35 1 44N13'01 83w33'10 5:34:13
Hylas 22 87 45N57'26 87w40'46 5:50:43
Ida 58 1 41N54'39 83w34'25 5:34:18
Ida Center 58 1 41N51'58 83w34'17 5:34:17
Idlewild 43 92 43N53'13 85w48'09 5:43:13
Imlay City 44 1 43N01'29 83w04'40 5:32:19
Imperial Heights 7 25 46N32'01 88w07'52 5:52:31
Ina 67 1 44N07'01 85w17'12 5:41:09
Independence 63 88 42N44 83w23 5:33:32
Indianfield 39 47 42N13 85w35 5:42:20
Indianfields 79 1 43N28 83w24 5:33:36
Indian Grove 80 93 42N23'19 86w16'58 5:45:08
Indian Lake 14 72 41N59 86w12 5:44:48
Indian River 16 1 45N24'45 84w36'45 5:38:27
Indian Town 2 22 46N24'32 86w33'47 5:46:15
Indiantown 55 86 45N42'10 87w21'58 5:49:28
Indiantown 73 91 43N28'20 83w50'12 5:35:21
Indian Village 61 49 43N12 86w16 5:45:04
Industrial Home 46 1 41N54 84w02 5:36:08
Ingalls 55 86 45N22'37 87w36'40 5:50:27
Ingallston 55 81 45N12'41 87w31'39 5:50:07
Ingersoll 56 1 43N31 84w14 5:36:56
Ingham 33 1 42N33 84w17 5:37:08
Ingleside 16 1 45N38 84w47 5:39:08
Inkster 82 2 42N17'39 83w18'36 5:33:14
Inland 10 1 44N39 85w53 5:43:32
Inland 77 25 46N02'17 85w52'08 5:43:29
Inland Corners 10 1 44N39 85w46 5:43:04
Interior 66 25 46N26 89w03 5:56:12
Interlaken 61 49 43N16 86w16 5:45:04
Interlochen 28 1 44N38'41 85w46'02 5:43:04
Inverness 16 1 45N35 84w31 5:38:04
Inwood 77 25 46N03 86w27 5:45:48
Ionia 34 92 42N59'14 85w04'16 5:40:17
Iosco 47 1 42N33 84w05 5:36:20
Ira 74 1 42N42 82w40 5:30:40
Iron Mountain 22 83 45N49'13 88w03'57 5:52:16
Iron River 36 84 46N05'34 88w38'32 5:54:34
Irons 43 1 44N08'24 85w54'57 5:43:40
Ironton 15 1 45N15'22 85w11'12 5:40:45
Ironwood 27 85 46N27'17 90w10'15 6:00:41
Irving 8 64 42N41'18 85w25'05 5:41:40
Isabella 21 25 45N53'51 86w36'20 5:46:25
Isabella 37 1 43N41 84w47 5:39:08
Isadore 45 1 44N52'40 85w46'25 5:43:06
Ishaward 20 1 44N48'48 84w50'22 5:39:21
Ishpeming 52 20 46N29'19 87w40'03 5:50:40
Island Lake 47 1 41N59 83w50 5:35:20
Island Park 39 92 42N23 85w27 5:41:48
Island View 21 25 45N38'22 87w11'51 5:48:47
Isle Royale 42 25 48N00 88w54 5:55:36
Isle Royale National Pk 42 25 48N00 88w54 5:55:36
Ithaca 29 1 43N17'30 84w36'27 5:38:26
Iva 73 1 43N27'48 84w16'10 5:37:05
Ivanhoe 32 1 43N42'20 83w05'39 5:32:23
Ivanrest 41 61 42N54 85w44 5:42:56
Jacks Landing 28 1 44N40'21 85w27'15 5:41:49
Jackson 38 90 42N14'45 84w24'05 5:37:36
Jacobsville 31 96 46N58'51 88w24'36 5:53:38
Jam 56 1 43N25 84w20 5:37:20
James 73 1 43N22 84w03 5:36:12
Jamestown 70 54 42N49'32 85w50'33 5:43:22
Jasper 46 1 41N47'36 84w02'26 5:36:10
Jeddo 74 1 43N09'06 82w35'00 5:30:20
Jefferson 38 1 42N06'32 84w17'24 5:37:10
Jefferson 82 2 42N22 82w59 5:31:56
Jenison 70 54 42N54'26 85w47'31 5:43:10
Jenison Park 70 51 42N47 86w07 5:44:28
Jennings 57 1 44N19'58 85w17'53 5:41:12
Jerico 11 74 41N58'19 86w32'00 5:46:08
Jerome 30 1 42N01'37 84w28'10 5:37:53
Jerome 56 1 43N41 84w25 5:37:40
Jerusalem 81 1 42N16'29 83w58'55 5:35:56
Jessieville 27 81 46N27'17 90w07'52 6:00:31
Johannesburg 69 1 44N59'08 84w27'21 5:37:49
Johnsons Landing 55 81 45N16'24 87w27'56 5:49:52
Johnstown 8 57 42N28 85w15 5:41:00
Johnswood 17 12 45N57'03 83w37'20 5:34:29
Jones 14 72 41N54'09 85w47'58 5:43:12
Jonesfield 73 1 43N26 84w20 5:37:20
Jonesville 12 1 41N59'03 84w39'43 5:38:39
Joppa 13 1 42N11'17 85w13'03 5:40:52
Jordan 5 1 45N05 85w02 5:40:08
Jordan 37 1 43N39'19 84w43'41 5:38:55
Jossman Acres 63 88 42N45'53 83w28'15 5:33:53
Joyfield 10 1 44N33 86w06 5:44:24
Joyfield 82 2 42N21 83w13 5:32:52
Juddville 78 1 43N03'31 83w59'15 5:35:57
Jugville 64 64 43N32'03 85w51'38 5:43:27
Juhl 76 1 43N21'35 82w56'47 5:31:47
Junet 27 81 46N30'34 90w11'52 6:00:47
Juniata 79 1 43N20'59 83w27'44 5:33:51
Juniper 2 22 46N21'29 86w35'25 5:46:22
Kaiserville 47 1 42N25'54 84w01'49 5:36:07
Kalamazoo 39 47 42N17'30 85w35'14 5:42:21
Kalamo 23 1 42N32'34 85w00'46 5:40:03
Kaleva 51 1 44N22'24 86w00'37 5:44:02
Kalkaska 40 1 44N44'03 85w10'33 5:40:42
Karlin 28 1 44N34'42 85w47'00 5:43:08
Karrs Corner 79 1 43N27'05 83w34'53 5:34:20
Kasson 45 1 44N49 85w53 5:43:32
Katakitckon Indian Village 27 81 46N09'05 89w05'27 5:56:22

Kawkawlin 9 1 43N39'07 83W56'35 5:35:46
Kearney 5 1 45N00 85W08 5:40:32
Kearsarge 31 25 47N16'30 88W24'58 5:53:40
Keego Harbor 63 88 42N36'29 83W20'38 5:33:23
Keelans Corner 57 1 44N20'16 85W04'32 5:40:18
Keeler 80 72 42N06'46 86W10'00 5:44:40
Keene 34 92 42N59 85W15 5:41:00
Keewahdin 74 1 43N02'23 82W26'40 5:29:47
Keewahdin Beach 74 1 42N58 82W29 5:29:56
Kegomic 24 67 45N22 84W57 5:39:48
Kelden 17 12 46N12'57 84W17'25 5:37:10
Kellogg 3 92 42N33 85W46 5:43:04
Kelloggsville 41 62 42N39 85W17 5:41:08
Kells 55 81 45N26'04 87W42'32 5:50:50
Kellys Corners 61 66 43N12 85W57 5:43:48
Kelso Junction 36 81 46N08'50 88W15'13 5:53:01
Kendall 80 72 42N21'42 85W48'48 5:43:15
Kenneth 49 25 46N05'55 84W55'52 5:39:43
Keno 72 1 44N28'20 84W24'38 5:37:39
Kenockee 74 1 43N02 82W41 5:30:44
Kensington 82 2 42N24 82W56 5:31:44
Kent City 41 64 43N13'12 85W45'04 5:43:00
Kenton 31 25 46N29'08 88W53'38 5:55:35
Kentucky 2 22 46N15'55 86W37'51 5:46:31
Kentwood 41 61 42N52'10 85W38'41 5:42:35
Kerby 78 1 42N59'58 84W04'09 5:36:17
Kercheval 82 2 42N23 82W57 5:31:48
Kerns Corner 40 1 44N44 85W11 5:40:44
Kerr Hill 44 1 42N53'46 83W23'46 5:33:35
Kessington 14 108 41N46'36 85W53'49 5:43:35
Keswick 45 1 44N55'44 85W39'13 5:42:37
Kew 55 81 45N09'31 87W36'57 5:50:28
Kewadin 5 1 44N55'43 85W22'23 5:41:30
Keweenaw Bay 7 27 46N51'37 88W28'54 5:53:56
Keystone 28 1 44N45 85W37 5:42:28
Kibbie 3 93 42N25'08 86W11'15 5:44:45
Kiernan 36 81 46N08'44 88W10'47 5:52:43
Killarney Beach 9 1 43N41'32 83W55'21 5:35:41
Killmaster 1 1 44N37'54 83W27'05 5:33:48
Kilmanagh 32 1 43N45'22 83W21'25 5:33:26
Kimball 74 1 42N56'53 82W33'45 5:30:15
Kimball Location 36 82 46N05'17 88W19'46 5:53:19
Kincheloe 17 12 46N16 84W29 5:37:56
Kincheloe Air Force Base 17 12 46N14 84W28 5:37:52
Kinde 32 1 43N56'22 82W59'49 5:31:59
Kinderhook 12 1 41N47'48 85W00'19 5:40:01
Kings Corner 59 57 43N14'57 85W04'24 5:40:18
Kingsford 22 87 45N47'42 88W04'19 5:52:17
Kingsland 23 1 42N35'20 84W39'06 5:38:36
Kings Landing 11 105 42N02'37 86W23'51 5:45:35
Kingsley 21 25 45N55'33 87W15'47 5:49:03
Kingsley 28 1 44N35'05 85W32'09 5:42:09
Kings Mill 44 1 43N08'32 83W10'22 5:32:41
Kingston 79 1 43N24'52 83W11'09 5:32:45
Kinneville 33 1 42N27'59 84W34'16 5:38:17
Kinney 41 61 43N00'57 85W46'06 5:43:04
Kinross 17 12 46N16'30 84W30'53 5:38:04
Kipling 21 13 45N52'24 87W00'42 5:48:03
K I Sawyer Air Force Base 52 25 46N20 87W22 5:49:28
Kissipee 60 1 44N59 84W27 5:37:48
Kisslers Corner 53 66 43N12 85W57 5:43:48
Kiva 2 25 46N15'14 87W05'04 5:48:20
Klacking 65 1 44N23 84W11 5:36:44
Klinger Lake 75 1 41N48 85W25 5:41:40
Klingers 75 1 41N47'35 85W31'34 5:42:06
Klingville 31 96 46N58'04 88W28'40 5:53:55
Kloman 55 81 45N41 87W32 5:50:08
Klondike 64 57 43N34 86W02 5:44:08
Kneeland 68 1 44N42'38 84W05'29 5:36:22
Knights Mill 6 1 44N07'12 83W57'04 5:35:48
Knollwood Park 38 90 42N14 84W24 5:37:36
Kochville 73 91 43N30'04 83W56'44 5:35:47
Koehler 16 1 45N25 84W31 5:38:04
Koss 55 81 45N23'26 87W42'23 5:50:50
Koylton 79 1 43N22 83W10 5:32:40
Krakow 71 1 45N17 83W35 5:34:20
Kurtz 1 1 44N33'40 83W38'44 5:34:35
Kyro 7 25 46N49 88W38 5:54:32
Labarge 41 57 42N48'43 85W29'15 5:41:57
La Branch 55 86 45N48 87W22 5:49:28
LaBranche 55 86 45N52'39 87W28'08 5:49:53
Lacey 8 57 42N29'35 85W11'28 5:40:46
Lachine 4 1 45N04'39 83W42'58 5:34:52
Lac La Belle 42 96 47N23'04 88W01'07 5:52:04
Lacota 80 72 42N24'49 86W07'47 5:44:31
Ladoga 2 25 46N16'55 87W03'17 5:48:13
Lafayette 29 1 43N20 84W26 5:37:44
LaFayette Landing 66 25 46N47'57 89W50'26 5:59:22
Lagoon Beach 9 36 43N39'40 83W53'24 5:35:34
La Grange 14 73 41N57'15 86W02'30 5:44:10
La Grange Park 43 92 43N54 85W51 5:43:24
Laing 76 1 43N31'14 82W56'02 5:31:44
Laingsburg 78 1 42N53'25 84W21'05 5:37:24
Laird 31 25 46N42 88W48 5:55:12
Lake 18 1 43N51'07 85W00'19 5:40:01
Lake Angeline 52 25 46N28'42 87W40'33 5:50:42
Lake Angelus 63 88 42N41'55 83W19'00 5:33:16
Lake Ann 10 1 44N43'26 85W50'35 5:43:22
Lake City 57 1 44N20'07 85W12'54 5:40:52
Lake Fenton 25 1 42N49 83W43 5:34:52
Lakefield 73 1 43N20'47 84W19'50 5:37:19
Lake George 18 1 43N57'48 84W56'49 5:39:47
Lake Gerald 31 25 46N56 88W49 5:55:16
Lake Harbor 61 49 43N12 86W16 5:45:04
Lake Harbor Estates 61 49 43N12 86W16 5:45:04
Lake Harbor Hills 61 49 43N12 86W16 5:45:04
Lake Harbor Point 61 49 43N12 86W16 5:45:04
Lake Huron Beach 35 1 44N13'59 83W32'51 5:34:11
Lakeland 47 1 42N27'48 83W50'39 5:35:23
Lake Lansing 33 1 42N45 84W24 5:37:36
Lake Leelanau 45 1 44N58'51 85W42'54 5:42:52
Lake Linden 31 96 47N11'39 88W24'26 5:53:38
Lake Margrethe 20 1 44N38'30 84W46'13 5:39:05
Lake Michigan Beach 11 74 42N13'15 86W22'10 5:45:29
Lake Michigan Estates 61 49 43N12 86W16 5:45:04
Lake Mine 66 25 46N46'31 89W02'45 5:56:11
Lake Nepessing 44 1 43N03 83W19 5:33:16
Lake Odessa 34 92 42N47'05 85W08'18 5:40:33
Lake of the Woods 12 1 41N57 85W00 5:40:00
Lake Orion 63 88 42N47'04 83W14'23 5:32:58
Lake Orion Heights 63 88 42N46'13 83W15'51 5:33:03
Lake Pleasant 44 1 43N02 83W10 5:32:40
Lakeport 74 1 43N06'54 82W29'25 5:29:58
Lake Roland 31 25 46N53'04 88W51'50 5:55:27
Lake Sherwood 63 88 42N36 83W29 5:33:56
Lake Shore 3 92 42N39 86W12 5:44:48
Lakeside 11 75 41N50'57 86W40'04 5:46:40
Lakeside 25 1 42N50'09 83W42'24 5:34:50
Lakeside 32 1 44N03 83W00 5:32:00
Lakeside 50 88 42N33'54 82W50'21 5:31:21
Laketon 48 25 46N20'34 85W44'54 5:43:00
Laketon 61 49 43N16 86W18 5:45:12
Laketown 3 92 42N44 86W10 5:44:40
Lakeview 11 75 41N50'00 86W41'34 5:46:46
Lakeview 13 43 42N17'54 85W12'40 5:40:51
Lakeview 59 57 43N26'47 85W16'27 5:41:06
Lakeville 63 88 42N49'17 83W09'01 5:32:36
Lakewood 4 1 45N11'27 83W26'02 5:33:44
Lakewood 39 47 42N16'43 85W32'27 5:42:10
Lakewood 52 25 46N29'49 87W20'42 5:49:23
Lakewood 58 1 41N48 83W27 5:33:48
Lakewood 61 57 43N22'36 86W14'11 5:44:57
Lakewood Club 61 57 43N22 86W15 5:45:00
Lakewood Point 11 74 42N11 86W19 5:45:16
Lamar 41 61 42N55 85W42 5:42:48
Lamb 74 1 42N59 82W40 5:30:40
Lambert 21 25 45N50'27 87W06'40 5:48:27
Lambertville 58 7 41N45'57 83W37'41 5:34:31
Lambs 74 1 42N55'58 82W42'30 5:30:50
Lamont 70 97 43N00'31 85W54'22 5:43:37
Lamotte 76 1 43N28 83W02 5:32:08
Lanewood 81 1 42N19'38 84W01'21 5:36:05
Langport 29 1 43N21'54 84W23'23 5:37:34
Langston 59 57 43N18'50 85W14'38 5:40:59
L'Anse 7 79 46N45'24 88W27'10 5:53:49
Lansing 33 41 42N43'57 84W33'20 5:38:13
Lapeer 44 1 43N03'05 83W19'08 5:33:17
Lapeer Heights 25 1 43N00'31 83W35'42 5:34:23
Laporte 56 1 43N29'47 84W11'20 5:36:45
Larch 21 19 45N47'23 87W03'52 5:48:15
Larkin 56 1 43N43'22 84W14'50 5:36:59
Larson Beach 1 1 44N48'03 83W31'25 5:34:06
La Salle 58 1 41N52'04 83W27'08 5:33:49
La Salle Gardens 63 88 42N39 83W24 5:33:36
Lathrop 21 11 46N08'53 87W13'19 5:48:53
Lathrup Village 63 2 42N29'47 83W13'22 5:32:53
Laurel 76 1 43N25 82W50 5:31:20
Laurium 31 96 47N14'15 88W26'35 5:53:46
Lavender Corner 77 78 46N30'06 85W56'23 5:43:46
Lawndale 39 47 42N17'11 85W27'44 5:41:51
Lawndale 73 91 43N28'51 84W02'04 5:36:08
Lawnel 61 49 43N12 86W16 5:45:04
Lawrence 80 72 42N13'09 86W03'05 5:44:12
Lawson 52 25 46N19'47 87W08'11 5:48:33
Lawton 39 104 42N10'02 85W50'49 5:43:23
Layton Corners 73 1 43N10'33 83W59'18 5:35:57
Leapers 55 81 45N47'14 87W41'40 5:50:47
Leaton 37 1 43N40'12 84W42'30 5:38:50
Leavitt 64 57 43N41 86W06 5:44:24
Lebanon 19 1 43N04 84W47 5:39:08
Lee 3 92 42N27'03 86W05'27 5:44:22
Lee Center 13 1 42N24'25 84W53'19 5:39:33
Leedys Gardens 58 36 41N55 83W23 5:33:32
Leelanau Schools 45 1 44N54'55 85W58'15 5:43:53
Leelanau Shores 45 1 44N53'32 85W41'36 5:42:46
Leer 4 1 45N11'52 83W44'22 5:34:57
Leetsville 40 1 44N47'36 85W08'41 5:40:35
Legrand 16 1 46N24'13 84W27'01 5:37:40
LeGraph 82 2 42N17 83W17 5:33:08
Leighton 3 92 42N44 85W36 5:42:24
Leisure 3 93 42N28'10 86W10'06 5:44:40
Leland 45 1 45N01'23 85W45'35 5:43:02
Lemon Park 39 100 42N09'08 85W29'55 5:42:00
Lenawee Junction 46 1 41N53'04 83W56'38 5:35:47
Lencel 48 25 46N21'01 85W25'46 5:41:43
Lennon 25 1 42N59'08 83W55'42 5:35:43
Lenox 50 88 42N46 82W48 5:31:12
Leo 7 18 46N32 88W32 5:54:08
Leonard 63 88 42N51'55 83W08'34 5:32:34
Leoni 38 90 42N14'38 84W16'09 5:37:05
Leonidas 75 1 42N01'22 85W21'07 5:41:24
Leota 18 1 44N08'22 84W53'22 5:39:33
Le Roy 67 1 44N02'17 85W27'14 5:41:49
Leroy 71 1 45N13'12 83W31'15 5:34:05
Les Cheneaux Club 49 25 45N59 84W22 5:37:28
Leslie 33 1 42N27'05 84W25'57 5:37:44
Lesterville 74 1 42N57'28 82W54'20 5:31:37
Level Park 39 43 42N21'37 85W16'21 5:41:05
Levering 24 67 45N38'09 84W47'13 5:39:09
Lewer Pewabic 31 95 47N09'06 88W33'37 5:54:14
Lewiston 60 1 44N53'02 84W18'20 5:37:13
Lewisville 32 1 43N56'40 82W50'06 5:31:20
Lexington 76 1 43N16'05 82W31'51 5:30:07
Lexington Heights 76 1 43N13'30 82W31'29 5:30:06
Liberty 38 1 42N06'08 84W24'02 5:37:36
Liberty Corners 58 1 41N44'59 83W35'14 5:34:21
Lickly Corners 30 1 41N47'47 84W27'30 5:37:50
Lidke's Corners 53 57 43N57 86W17 5:45:08
Lilley 62 57 43N46'15 85W51'02 5:43:24
Lima Center 81 1 42N17'45 83W57'27 5:35:50
Lime Creek 46 1 41N45'56 84W19'47 5:37:19
Lime Island 17 12 46N03 84W05 5:36:20
Limestone 2 25 46N15'39 86W55'45 5:47:43
Liminga 31 25 47N09'22 88W41'53 5:54:48
Lincoln 1 1 44N41'05 83W24'44 5:33:39
Lincoln 17 12 45N58'26 83W39'23 5:34:38
Lincoln 81 1 42N09'26 83W36'04 5:34:24
Lincoln Estates 61 49 43N12 86W16 5:45:04
Lincoln Junction 35 1 44N29'33 83W21'12 5:33:25
Lincoln Meadows 61 49 43N12 86W16 5:45:04
Lincoln Park 61 49 43N12 86W16 5:45:04
Lincoln Park 82 2 42N15'02 83W10'43 5:32:43
Linden 25 1 42N48'52 83W46'57 5:35:08
Linden Hills 80 74 42N18'15 86W19'29 5:45:18
Lindland's 61 49 43N12 86W16 5:45:04
Linkville 32 1 43N45'29 83W16'02 5:33:04
Linwood 9 1 43N44'21 83W57'44 5:35:51
Linwood 82 2 42N23 83W07 5:32:28
Linwood Beach 9 1 43N43'26 83W56'37 5:35:46
Lisbon 41 57 43N08 85W52 5:43:28
Liske 71 1 45N20'03 83W44'28 5:34:58
Litchfield 30 1 42N02'38 84W45'27 5:39:02
Littlefield 24 67 45N26 84W48 5:39:12
Little Killarney Beach 9 1 43N41'03 83W55'04 5:35:40
Little Lake 52 17 46N17'20 87W20'30 5:49:22
Little Manistee 43 1 44N05'44 85W54'33 5:43:38
Little Paw Paw Lake 11 74 42N13'10 86W17'02 5:45:08
Little Point Sable 64 64 43N38'05 86W32'15 5:46:09
Little Summer Island 21 25 45N37 86W41 5:46:44
Little Traverse 24 67 45N26 84W55 5:39:40
Little Venice 23 92 42N41'26 84W57'21 5:39:49
Livernois 82 2 42N20 83W08 5:32:32
Livingston 11 74 41N58'06 86W32'35 5:46:10
Livingston 69 1 45N04 84W41 5:38:44
Livonia 82 36 42N22'06 83W21'10 5:33:25
Loch Alpine 81 38 42N17 83W45 5:35:00
Locke 33 1 42N44 84W12 5:36:48
Lockport 56 1 43N31'29 84W14'58 5:37:00
Lockport 75 97 41N57 85W36 5:42:24
Lockwood 12 1 41N53'01 85W02'56 5:40:12
Lockwood Beach 26 1 43N50'34 84W20'08 5:37:21
Locust Corners 30 1 41N53'02 84W25'13 5:37:41
Lodi 40 1 44N38'26 85W10'31 5:40:42
Lodi 81 38 42N13 83W50 5:35:20
Loehme 9 1 43N41'25 84W04'04 5:36:16
London 58 1 42N01'12 83W36'48 5:34:27
Long Beach 61 49 43N12 86W16 5:45:04
Long Lake 18 1 44N01 84W48 5:39:12
Long Lake 28 1 44N44 85W45 5:43:00
Long Lake 30 1 41N50 84W45 5:39:00
Long Lake 34 92 43N04 85W08 5:40:32
Long Lake 35 1 44N25'11 83W52'19 5:35:29
Long Lake Heights 18 1 44N05'57 84W46'28 5:39:06
Long Point 16 1 45N31'17 84W32'53 5:38:12
Long Rapids 4 1 45N07'33 83W43'21 5:34:53
Longrie 55 81 45N24'21 87W43'30 5:50:54
Loomis 37 1 43N47'37 84W39'58 5:38:40
Loon Lake 63 88 42N33 83W30 5:34:00
Loretto 22 87 45N46'38 87W48'54 5:51:16
Lost Lake Woods 1 1 44N46'37 83W25'28 5:33:42
Lottivue 50 88 42N39'34 82W45'43 5:31:03
Loud 60 1 44N54 84W04 5:36:16
Louis Cabin Landing 20 1 44N39'54 84W38'12 5:38:33
Lovells 20 1 44N48'11 84W28'55 5:37:56
Lowell 41 57 42N56'01 85W20'31 5:41:22
Lower Chub Landing 69 1 44N53'27 84W35'04 5:38:20
Lower Pewabic 31 95 47N08 88W36 5:54:24
Lucas 57 1 44N13'06 85W17'06 5:41:08
Luce 73 1 43N14'03 84W01'48 5:36:07
Ludington 53 63 43N57'19 86W27'09 5:45:49
Lulu 58 1 41N52'47 83W36'39 5:34:27
Lum 44 1 43N05'58 83W09'04 5:32:36
Luna Pier 58 1 41N48'25 83W26'33 5:33:46
Lupton 65 1 44N25'52 84W01'33 5:36:06
Luther 43 1 44N02'25 85W40'57 5:42:44
Luzerne 68 1 44N36'57 84W16'16 5:37:05
Lyndon Center 81 1 42N22'53 84W04'59 5:36:20
Lynn 74 1 43N07 82W56 5:31:44
Lyon Lake 13 1 42N16 84W58 5:39:52
Lyon Manor 72 1 44N27'41 84W44'38 5:38:59

Lyons 34 92 42N58'55 84w56'49 5:39:47
Mable 28 1 44N46 85w24 5:41:36
Macatawa 70 51 42N46'11 86w12'22 5:44:49
Mackinac Island 49 25 45N50'57 84w37'08 5:38:29
Mackinaw 16 1 45N45 84w41 5:38:44
Mackinaw City 16 1 45N47'02 84w43'40 5:38:55
Macks Landing 3 92 42N37'53 86w09'16 5:44:37
Macomb 50 88 42N42'03 82w57'33 5:31:50
Macon 46 1 42N03'59 83w52'06 5:35:28
Madison Center 46 1 41N51'36 84w02'33 5:36:10
Madison Heights 63 2 42N29'09 83w06'19 5:32:25
Malcolm 51 1 44N29'33 86w09'21 5:44:37
Mancelona 5 1 44N54'08 85w03'39 5:40:15
Manchester 81 1 42N09'01 84w02'16 5:36:09
Mandan 42 96 47N25'30 88w00'56 5:52:04
Mangum 52 25 46N27'31 87w15'24 5:49:02
Manistee 51 111 44N14'40 86w19'27 5:45:18
Manistique 77 14 45N57'28 86w14'46 5:44:59
Manitou Beach 46 1 41N58'11 84w18'30 5:37:14
Manitou Beach 71 1 45N29'27 83w55'58 5:35:44
Manlius 3 74 42N38 86w05 5:44:20
Manning 16 1 45N30'54 84w21'04 5:37:24
Mansfield 36 86 46N05'15 88w08'55 5:52:36
Mansfield Location 36 86 46N07'09 88w13'10 5:52:53
Manton 83 1 44N24'39 85w23'56 5:41:36
Maple 82 2 42N19 83w10 5:32:40
Maple Beach 82 36 42N03'12 83w11'13 5:32:45
Maple City 45 1 44N51'20 85w51'21 5:43:25
Maple Forest 20 1 44N49 84w39 5:38:36
Maple Grove 52 25 46N18'15 87w09'26 5:48:38
Maple Grove 61 64 43N24'07 86w21'48 5:45:27
Maple Grove Downs 61 49 43N12 86w16 5:45:04
Maple Hill 59 57 43N19 85w30 5:42:00
Maplehurst 13 43 42N20'52 85w09'15 5:40:37
Maplehurst 61 49 43N12 86w16 5:45:04
Maple Island 14 72 42N03'48 86w10'38 5:44:43
Maple Lake 80 46 42N13 85w53 5:43:32
Maple Leaf 74 1 42N34'41 82w34'11 5:30:17
Maple Rapids 29 1 43N06'17 84w41'31 5:38:46
Maple Ridge 6 1 44N08'31 83w55'39 5:35:43
Maple River 24 67 45N31 84w47 5:39:08
Mapleton 28 1 44N53'43 85w30'24 5:42:02
Mapleton 36 86 46N06'24 88w33'46 5:54:15
Mapleton 56 1 43N34'00 84w10'58 5:36:44
Maple Valley 72 1 44N18'19 84w29'28 5:37:58
Maplewood 3 92 42N47 86w07 5:44:28
Maplewood 21 25 45N58'08 86w58'20 5:47:53
Marathon 44 1 43N12 83w24 5:33:36
Marble Lake 12 1 41N57 84w53 5:39:32
Marcellus 14 72 42N01'33 85w48'56 5:43:16
Marengo 13 1 42N16'17 84w50'55 5:39:24
Marenisco 27 86 46N22'35 89w41'46 5:58:47
Marilla 51 1 44N22'15 85w52'51 5:43:31
Marine City 74 1 42N43'10 82w29'32 5:29:58
Marion 67 1 44N06'09 85w08'49 5:40:35
Marion Springs 73 1 43N14'40 84w19'38 5:37:19
Markey 72 1 44N23 84w40 5:38:40
Marks 48 25 46N15'35 85w41'51 5:42:47
Marlborough 43 92 43N51'53 85w50'30 5:43:22
Marlette 76 1 43N19'37 83w04'49 5:32:19
Marne 70 51 43N02'10 85w49'40 5:43:19
Marquette 52 21 46N32'37 87w23'43 5:49:35
Marshall 13 1 42N16'20 84w57'48 5:39:51
Marsh Corner 24 67 45N34'46 84w56'06 5:39:44
Martin 3 92 42N32'13 85w38'30 5:42:34
Martindale Beach 74 1 42N41'29 82w30'27 5:30:02
Martins Landing 52 25 46N32'11 87w59'08 5:51:57
Martinsville 82 36 42N08'41 83w27'38 5:33:51
Martiny 54 1 43N41 85w16 5:41:04
Marysville 74 1 42N54'45 82w29'13 5:29:57
Mashek 52 25 46N02'52 87w28'17 5:49:53
Mason 31 96 47N08'28 88w27'56 5:53:52
Mason 33 1 42N34'45 84w26'37 5:37:46
Masonville 21 35 45N54'46 86w59'14 5:47:57
Mass City 66 25 46N45'50 89w05'10 5:56:21
Mastodon 36 86 46N01'06 88w20'55 5:53:24
Matchwood 66 25 46N33'23 89w23'46 5:57:35
Matherton 19 92 43N04'06 84w50'13 5:39:21
Mathias 2 25 46N12 86w54 5:47:36
Mattawan 80 72 42N12'34 85w47'04 5:43:08
Matteson 12 1 41N56'28 85w11'26 5:40:46
Matteson Lake 12 1 41N52 85w12 5:40:48
Maybee 58 7 42N00'14 83w30'56 5:34:04
Mayfield 28 1 44N37'34 85w31'43 5:42:07
Mayflower 31 96 47N15 88w27 5:53:48
Mayville 79 1 43N20'13 83w21'09 5:33:25
Maywood 21 25 45N50'12 86w59'12 5:47:57
Maywood 50 88 42N34 83w02 5:32:08
McBain 57 1 44N11'37 85w12'48 5:40:51
McBrides (McBride) 59 57 43N21'15 85w02'34 5:40:10
McCarron 17 12 46N19'55 84w16'51 5:37:07
McClean 62 57 43N28 85w56 5:43:44
McClure 26 1 44N02'16 84w25'38 5:37:43
McClures 73 91 43N27 83w57 5:35:48
McComb Corner 7 25 46N51'58 88w06'30 5:52:26
McCords 41 64 42N52'03 85w26'38 5:41:47
McDonald 80 74 42N15'55 86w09'25 5:44:38
McDonough 73 1 43N18 84w09 5:36:36
McFarland 52 11 46N10'49 87w14'41 5:48:59
McGregor 76 1 43N28'57 82w44'51 5:30:59
McGrew Junction 25 1 43N04'12 83w40'37 5:34:42
McHarg 4 1 45N02'08 83w36'50 5:34:27
McIntyre Landing 20 1 44N39'54 84w48'30 5:39:14
McIvor 35 1 44N14'04 83w40'59 5:34:44
McKain Corners 39 97 42N11 85w25 5:41:40
McKeever 66 25 46N44'44 89w03'09 5:56:13
McKinley 68 1 44N38'49 83w56'14 5:35:45
McLeods Corner 48 25 46N18'12 85w21'48 5:41:27
McManus Corner 28 1 44N32'27 85w27'22 5:41:49
McMillan 48 25 46N20'20 85w41'14 5:42:45
McMillan Corner 48 25 46N18'37 85w41'20 5:42:45
McPhees Landing 48 25 46N22'20 85w25'12 5:41:41
Meade 50 88 42N43'04 82w52'28 5:31:30
Meadowbrook 61 49 43N12 86w16 5:45:04
Meadow Lake Farms 63 88 43N15 83w48 5:35:12
Meads Landing 72 1 44N24'24 84w48'17 5:39:13
Mears 64 64 43N40'55 86w25'11 5:45:41
Meauwataka 83 1 44N21'11 85w32'23 5:42:10
Mecosta 9 1 43N37'13 85w13'35 5:40:54
Medina 46 1 41N48'29 84w15'50 5:37:03
Melita 6 1 44N06'46 84w00'26 5:36:02
Mellen 55 81 45N21 87w37 5:50:28
Melrose 15 1 45N15 84w55 5:39:40
Melstrand 2 25 46N27'47 86w24'54 5:45:40
Melvin 76 1 43N11'11 82w51'42 5:31:27
Melvindale 82 2 42N16'57 83w10'31 5:32:42
Memphis 50 1 42N53'47 82w46'08 5:31:05
Mendon 75 92 42N00'23 85w27'00 5:41:48
Menominee 55 86 45N06'28 87w36'51 5:50:27
Menonaqua Beach 24 67 45N24'55 84w54'47 5:39:39
Mentha 80 72 42N21'26 85w46'29 5:43:06
Meredith 18 1 44N07'50 84w36'26 5:38:26
Meridian 33 41 42N41'23 84w21'49 5:37:27
Merrill 73 1 43N24'35 84w19'44 5:37:19
Merriman 22 87 45N55'03 88w03'20 5:52:13
Merritt 9 1 43N31 83w45 5:35:00
Merritt 57 1 44N19'47 84w56'41 5:39:47
Merriweather 66 25 46N34'25 89w38'08 5:58:33
Merson 3 42 42N26'05 85w51'58 5:43:28
Mesick 83 1 44N24'19 85w42'48 5:42:51
Metamora 44 1 42N56'29 83w17'21 5:33:09
Metropolitan 22 87 45N59'41 87w53'38 5:51:35
Metz 71 1 45N17'23 83w48'05 5:35:12
Meyer 55 81 45N44 87w38 5:50:32
Meyers Beach 9 1 43N48'26 83w55'32 5:35:42
Miami Beach 16 1 45N27'05 84w33'23 5:38:14
Miami Park 3 93 42N27'55 86w15'00 5:45:00
Miami Park Beach 3 93 42N24 86w16 5:45:04
Michelson 72 1 44N22'44 84w50'34 5:39:22
Michiana 11 109 41N45'51 86w48'48 5:47:15
Michigamme 52 34 46N32'05 88w06'36 5:52:26
Michigan Center 38 90 42N13'59 84w19'38 5:37:19
Michigan State University 33 41 42N44 84w28 5:37:52
Michillinda 61 64 43N21'02 86w24'48 5:45:39
Michiwaukee Shores 77 14 45N57'04 86w21'18 5:45:25
Middlebelt 82 36 42N13 83w22 5:33:28
Middle Branch 67 1 44N02 85w09 5:40:36
Middlebury 78 1 43N00 84w20 5:37:20
Middle Island Point 52 25 46N33 87w24 5:49:36
Middleton 59 1 43N11'00 84w42'32 5:38:50
Middle Village 24 67 45N33'01 85w06'48 5:40:27
Middleville 8 57 42N42'47 85w27'43 5:41:51
Midland 56 88 43N36'56 84w14'50 5:36:59
Midland Park 39 92 42N23'27 85w23'08 5:41:33
Midway Gardens 58 1 41N47 83w34 5:34:16
Mikado 1 1 44N35'27 83w25'22 5:33:41
Milan 81 7 42N05'07 83w40'57 5:34:44
Milburg 11 4 42N06 86w27 5:45:48
Milford 63 88 42N35'37 83w35'58 5:34:24
Milham 39 47 42N15 85w34 5:42:16
Millbrook 54 57 43N30 85w09 5:40:36
Millbrool 37 57 43N32'55 85w05'08 5:40:21
Millburg 11 4 42N07'22 86w20'30 5:45:22
Millecoquins 49 25 46N08'07 85w30'27 5:42:02
Millecoquins Lake 49 25 46N07 85w34 5:42:16
Millen 1 1 44N38 83w37 5:34:28
Miller 74 1 42N32'57 82w39'32 5:30:38
Millersburg 71 1 45N20'04 84w03'39 5:36:15
Millers Park 5 1 44N54 85w25 5:41:40
Millersville 83 1 44N16'36 85w33'35 5:42:14
Millerton 53 92 44N02'23 86w03'01 5:44:12
Millett 23 41 42N42'00 84w37'17 5:38:29
Milleville Beach 82 36 42N02'58 83w11'13 5:32:45
Millgrove 3 42 42N34'00 85w53'35 5:43:34
Millington 79 1 43N16'53 83w31'47 5:34:07
MillIron Park 61 49 43N14 86w13 5:44:52
Mill Lake 80 72 42N22 85w53 5:43:32
Mill Mine Junction 31 96 47N05'05 88w39'07 5:54:36
Mills 31 96 47N10 88w26 5:53:44
Mills 76 1 43N31 82w44 5:30:56
Millville 33 1 42N31'45 84w11'28 5:36:46
Millville 44 1 43N03 83w19 5:33:16
Milnes 30 1 41N59 84w40 5:38:40
Milton 50 88 42N41'21 82w49'19 5:31:17
Milwaukee Junction 82 2 42N23 83w02 5:32:08
Milwood 39 47 42N15'33 85w33'56 5:42:16
Minard 38 1 42N15 84w36 5:38:24
Minards Mill 38 1 42N20'15 84w32'49 5:38:11
Minden City 76 1 43N40'17 82w46'42 5:31:07
Mineral Hills 36 81 46N06'48 88w38'52 5:54:35
Miner Lake 3 42 42N32 85w51 5:43:24
Miners Spur 21 25 45N56 86w58 5:47:52
Minor Beach 77 14 45N57'15 86w19'28 5:45:18
Mio 68 1 44N39'08 84w07'47 5:36:31
Missaukee Junction 83 1 44N18'32 85w24'52 5:41:39
Missaukee Park 57 1 44N20 85w12 5:40:48
Mission 17 110 46N26'50 84w35'51 5:38:23
Mitchell 1 1 44N44 83w48 5:35:12
Mizpah Park 11 4 42N09'45 86w26'10 5:45:45
Moddersville 57 1 44N13'13 84w57'09 5:39:49
Moffatt 6 1 44N08 84w07 5:36:28
Mohawk 42 96 47N18'14 88w21'53 5:53:28
Moline 3 92 42N44'21 85w39'50 5:42:39
Moltke 71 1 45N24'00 83w55'39 5:35:43
Mona Beach 61 49 43N12 86w14 5:44:56
Mona Shores 61 49 43N12 86w16 5:45:04
Mona View 61 49 43N12 86w14 5:44:56
Mona Vista 61 49 43N12 86w14 5:44:56
Monitor 9 36 43N36 83w58 5:35:52
Monongahela 36 81 46N06 88w20 5:53:20
Monongahela Location 36 81 46N05'13 88w22'17 5:53:29
Monroe 58 36 41N54'59 83w23'52 5:33:35
Monroe Center 28 1 44N36'49 85w41'48 5:42:47
Montague 61 64 43N25'00 86w21'25 5:45:26
Montcalm 59 57 43N15 85w16 5:41:04
Montello Park 70 51 42N47 86w07 5:44:28
Monterey 3 92 42N38 85w50 5:43:20
Monterey Center 3 92 42N38'18 85w50'23 5:43:22
Montgomery 30 1 41N46'38 84w48'15 5:39:13
Montmorency 60 1 45N09 84w02 5:36:08
Montrose 25 1 43N10'36 83w53'34 5:35:34
Moore 76 1 43N28 82w57 5:31:48
Moore Park 75 97 42N00'50 85w38'08 5:42:33
Moorestown 57 1 44N27'57 85w00'07 5:40:00
Mooreville 81 1 42N06'11 83w44'00 5:34:56
Moorland 61 66 43N13'42 85w59'16 5:43:57
Moran 49 25 45N59'39 84w49'51 5:39:19
Morenci 46 1 41N43'10 84w13'05 5:36:52
Morey 57 1 44N25'31 85w13'01 5:40:52
Morgan 8 57 42N37'21 85w10'35 5:40:42
Morgan Corners 13 43 42N13'52 85w12'09 5:40:49
Morley 54 1 43N29'27 85w26'38 5:41:47
Morres Junction 6 1 44N00'42 84w05'44 5:36:23
Morrice 78 1 42N50'19 84w10'42 5:36:43
Morseville 73 1 43N14'11 83w51'58 5:35:28
Morton 54 1 43N36 85w16 5:41:04
Moscow 30 1 42N02'58 84w30'36 5:38:02
Moseley 41 57 43N01'46 85w21'07 5:41:24
Mosherville 30 1 42N03'37 84w39'34 5:38:38
Motley 31 25 46N45 88w48 5:55:12
Mott Park 25 1 43N02 83w44 5:34:56
Mottville 75 1 41N47'58 85w45'25 5:43:02
Mountain Beach 70 51 42N55 86w09 5:44:36
Mount Clemens 50 88 42N35'50 82w52'41 5:31:31
Mount Elliott 82 2 42N26 83w03 5:32:12
Mount Forest 9 1 43N53'14 84w06'51 5:36:27
Mount Haley 56 1 43N32 84w20 5:37:20
Mount Morris 25 1 43N07'07 83w41'42 5:34:47
Mount Pleasant 3 93 42N27'26 86w14'50 5:44:59
Mount Pleasant 37 1 43N35'52 84w46'03 5:39:04
Mount Vernon 50 88 42N44'31 83w05'13 5:32:21
Mueller 77 25 46N04 85w55 5:43:40
Muir 34 92 42N59'45 84w56'33 5:39:46
Muirs 74 1 42N33'23 82w35'14 5:30:21
Mulberry 46 1 41N44'37 83w52'54 5:35:32
Mullet 16 1 45N30 84w35 5:38:20
Mullet Lake 16 1 45N34 84w32 5:38:08
Mulliken 23 92 42N45'44 84w53'47 5:39:35
Mundy 25 1 42N56 83w41 5:34:44
Munger 9 1 43N31'19 83w46'24 5:35:06
Munising 2 22 46N24'40 86w38'52 5:46:35
Munising Junction 2 22 46N22'45 86w42'36 5:46:50
Munith 38 1 42N23'26 84w15'02 5:37:00
Munro 16 1 45N36 84w39 5:38:36
Munson 46 1 41N42'41 84w19'45 5:37:19
Munuscong 17 12 46N14'43 84w11'06 5:36:44
Muskegon 61 49 43N14'03 86w14'54 5:45:00
Muskegon Heights 61 49 43N12'04 86w14'20 5:44:57
Mussey 74 1 43N02 82w56 5:31:44
Muttonville 74 1 42N47'47 82w44'07 5:30:56
Myren 2 25 46N25'34 86w25'38 5:45:43
Nadeau 55 86 45N36'32 87w33'10 5:50:13
Nagel Corner 71 1 45N18 83w53 5:35:32
Nahma 21 25 45N50'30 86w39'50 5:46:39
Nahma Junction 21 25 45N53'50 86w42'30 5:46:50
Nankin Mills 82 36 42N19 83w22 5:33:28
Naomi 11 72 42N02'34 86w16'16 5:45:05
Napier 11 74 42N05'37 86w16'49 5:45:07
Napoleon 38 1 42N09'38 84w14'46 5:36:59
Narenta 21 25 45N43'35 87w14'33 5:48:58
Nashville 8 57 42N36'10 85w05'35 5:40:22
Natalie 48 24 46N20'49 85w34'39 5:42:19
Nathan 55 81 45N34'45 87w42'25 5:50:50
National City 35 1 44N14'03 83w43'24 5:34:54
National Mine 52 25 46N27'31 87w40'53 5:50:44
Naubinway 49 25 46N05'33 85w26'51 5:41:47
Naults 36 86 45N59'30 88w23'38 5:53:35
Nazareth 39 47 42N19 85w33 5:42:12
Neebish Island 17 12 46N16 84w09 5:36:36
Needmore 23 1 42N41'00 84w51'22 5:39:25
Neeley 3 102 42N30'00 85w33'16 5:42:13
Negaunee 52 23 46N29'57 87w36'42 5:50:27

Nellsville 72 1 44N20'09 84w48'48 5:39:15
Nelson 41 57 43N15 85w30 5:42:00
Nelson 73 1 43N20'03 84w13'47 5:36:55
Nepco Camp No 7 42 96 47N24'12 88w08'40 5:52:35
Nessen City 10 1 44N31'12 85w52'41 5:43:31
Nester 72 1 44N12 84w29 5:37:56
Nestoria 7 25 46N34'13 88w15'49 5:53:03
New Allouez 42 96 47N18 88w24 5:53:36
Newark 59 1 43N14'55 84w42'35 5:38:50
Newark 63 88 42N51'36 83w37'31 5:34:30
Newaygo 62 64 43N25'11 85w48'00 5:43:12
New Baltimore 50 88 42N40'52 82w44'13 5:30:57
Newberg 14 72 41N56 85w49 5:43:16
Newberry 48 50 46N21'18 85w30'34 5:42:02
New Boston 82 36 42N09'45 83w24'11 5:33:37
New Bradford 50 88 42N34 83w02 5:32:08
New Bristol 36 82 46N06'16 88w23'11 5:53:33
New Buffalo 11 109 41N47'38 86w44'38 5:46:59
Newburg 46 1 42N02'32 83w58'06 5:35:52
Newburg 78 1 42N54'32 84w04'09 5:36:17
New Dalton 52 25 46N23'31 87w11'59 5:48:48
New Era 64 64 43N33'33 86w20'44 5:45:23
Newfield 64 57 43N35 86w06 5:44:24
New Greenleaf 76 1 43N39'42 83w04'42 5:32:19
New Groningen 70 51 42N47 86w07 5:44:28
New Haven 50 88 42N43'46 82w48'05 5:31:12
New Haven 78 1 43N05'37 84w09'12 5:36:37
New Haven Center 29 1 43N14'56 84w46'38 5:39:07
New Holland 70 51 42N51'22 86w04'44 5:44:19
New Hudson 63 88 42N30'39 83w36'56 5:34:28
Newkirk 43 1 44N04 85w44 5:42:56
Newland 51 111 44N15 86w19 5:45:16
New Lothrop 78 1 43N07'00 83w58'12 5:35:53
Newport 58 1 42N00'08 83w18'31 5:33:14
New Richmond 3 74 42N38'52 86w06'20 5:44:25
New Salem 3 92 42N45'14 85w48'07 5:43:12
New Swanzy 52 25 46N16'39 87w25'33 5:49:42
New Troy 11 74 41N52'35 86w32'59 5:46:12
Nicholson 47 1 42N46'37 84w07'26 5:36:30
Nicholsville 14 72 42N02'37 85w53'46 5:43:35
Nickel Plate 34 92 42N59 85w04 5:40:16
Niles 11 105 41N49'47 86w15'15 5:45:01
Nine Mile 9 1 43N52'36 84w03'55 5:36:16
Nirvana 43 1 43N54'09 85w42'43 5:42:51
Nisula 31 25 46N45'54 88w47'40 5:55:11
Noble 12 1 41N47 85w14 5:40:56
Nonesuch 66 25 46N45'19 89w37'10 5:58:29
Noordeloos 70 51 42N50'29 86w03'30 5:44:14
Norman 51 1 44N13 85w57 5:43:48
Norrie 27 85 46N26'47 90w09'46 6:00:39
North Adams 12 1 41N58'15 84w31'33 5:38:06
North Allis 71 1 45N24 84w12 5:36:48
North Arms 5 1 44N58'16 85w13'53 5:40:56
North Aurelius 33 1 42N34'55 84w32'35 5:38:10
North Bell 34 92 42N51 85w15 5:41:00
North Bessemer 27 81 46N30'34 90w03'58 6:00:16
North Blendon 70 54 42N55'44 85w57'44 5:43:51
North Bradley 56 1 43N42'41 84w29'24 5:37:58
North Branch 44 1 43N13'46 83w11'48 5:32:47
North Byron 41 57 42N50'42 85w43'58 5:42:56
North Dorr 41 92 42N46'07 85w45'43 5:43:03
Northeastern 82 2 42N20 83w11 5:32:44
North End 82 2 42N21 83w03 5:32:12
North Epworth 53 57 43N58'41 86w28'00 5:45:52
North Escanaba 21 19 45N45 87w04 5:48:16
North Farmington 63 88 42N31'40 83w22'47 5:33:31
Northfield 58 36 41N55 83w23 5:33:32
Northfield 81 38 42N20'38 83w43'35 5:34:54
Northfield Hills 63 88 42N34 83w09 5:32:36
North Fox Island 45 1 45N29 85w47 5:43:08
Northgate 41 61 43N00 85w38 5:42:32
North Ironwood 27 81 46N30'39 90w09'19 6:00:37
North Lake 44 1 43N13 83w28 5:33:52
North Lake 52 25 46N29'37 87w43'39 5:50:55
North Lake 80 72 42N22 85w53 5:43:32
North Lakeport 74 1 43N08'14 82w29'49 5:29:59
Northland 52 25 46N04'23 87w35'44 5:50:23
Northland Center 63 2 42N28 83w14 5:32:56
North Lansing 33 41 42N44 84w35 5:38:20
North Leslie 33 1 42N28'50 84w26'39 5:37:47
North Manitou 45 1 45N07'13 85w58'45 5:43:55
North Morenci 46 1 41N45'49 84w13'25 5:36:54
North Muskegon 61 49 43N15'22 86w16'03 5:45:04
North Niles 11 105 41N52 86w15 5:45:00
North Paynesville 66 25 46N33'51 89w06'56 5:56:28
North Plains 34 92 43N05 84w54 5:39:36
Northport 45 1 45N07'53 85w37'00 5:42:28
North Shade 29 1 43N10 84w47 5:39:08
North Shores 58 1 41N50'11 83w24'27 5:33:38
North Side 25 1 43N04 83w42 5:34:48
North Star 59 1 43N14'54 84w42'36 5:38:10
North Street 74 1 43N03 82w32 5:30:08
North Unity 45 1 44N51 85w51 5:43:24
Northville 41 61 43N00 85w38 5:42:32
Northville 82 36 42N25'52 83w29'00 5:33:56
Northwestern 82 2 42N22 83w08 5:32:32
North Wheeler 29 1 43N27'58 84w25'43 5:37:43
North Williams 9 1 43N38'23 84w05'20 5:36:21
Northwood 39 47 42N19'58 85w35'23 5:42:22
Norton 82 36 42N22'34 83w18'51 5:33:15
Nortondale 61 49 43N12 86w16 5:45:04
Norton Oaks 61 49 43N12 86w16 5:45:04
Norton Shores 61 49 43N10'08 86w15'50 5:45:03
Norvell 38 1 42N09'27 84w11'03 5:36:44
Norwalk 51 1 44N20'30 86w09'44 5:44:39
Norway 22 87 45N47'13 87w54'13 5:51:37
Norwayne 82 36 42N18 83w23 5:33:32
Norwood 15 1 45N13'00 85w22'53 5:41:32
Nottawa 75 1 41N55'08 85w26'56 5:41:48
Notten 81 1 42N16'43 84w07'24 5:36:30
Novesta 79 1 43N33 83w10 5:32:40
Novi 63 88 42N28'50 83w28'32 5:33:54
Nowesco 17 12 46N12 84w44 5:38:56
Nunda 16 1 45N15 84w29 5:37:56
Nunica 70 51 43N04'47 86w04'02 5:44:16
Oak 82 2 42N22'49 83w14'04 5:32:56
Oakdale 61 49 43N12 86w14 5:44:56
Oakfield 41 57 43N10 85w22 5:41:28
Oakfield Center 41 57 43N11 85w15 5:41:00
Oak Grove 47 1 42N42'01 83w55'55 5:35:44
Oak Grove 62 64 43N25 85w47 5:43:08
Oak Grove 63 88 42N37'13 83w14'21 5:32:57
Oak Grove 69 1 44N58'21 84w40'57 5:38:44
Oak Hill 51 111 44N13'28 86w18'14 5:45:13
Oakhurst 79 1 43N38'23 83w36'22 5:34:25
Oak Island 63 88 42N32 83w27 5:33:48
Oakland 3 97 42N41 86w00 5:44:00
Oakland 63 88 42N45 83w09 5:32:36
Oaklawn 70 51 42N47 86w07 5:44:28
Oaklawn Beechwood 70 51 42N48'18 86w06'52 5:44:27
Oakley 73 1 43N08'23 84w10'05 5:36:40
Oakley Park 63 88 42N34'08 83w29'48 5:33:59
Oak Park 39 43 42N21'30 85w15'25 5:41:02
Oak Park 63 2 42N27'34 83w10'58 5:32:44
Oak Point 38 1 42N11'34 84w15'21 5:37:01
Oak Ridge 17 12 46N17'19 84w12'36 5:36:50
Oak Ridge 63 2 42N31 83w09 5:32:36
Oak Shade Park 46 1 42N04'06 84w09'38 5:36:39
Oakville 58 1 42N04'53 83w34'51 5:34:19
Oakwood 39 47 42N15'23 85w37'12 5:42:29
Oakwood 63 88 42N50'03 83w20'12 5:33:21
Oakwood 75 1 41N47'44 85w33'07 5:42:12
Oakwood 82 2 42N17 83w11 5:32:44
Oakwood Junction 82 2 42N15 83w13 5:32:52
Oak Wood Shores 35 1 44N12'42 83w33'13 5:34:13
Oberlin 26 1 44N04'28 84w30'22 5:38:01
Oceola 47 1 42N39 83w51 5:35:24
Ocqueoc 71 1 45N24'30 84w05'24 5:36:22
Oden 24 67 45N25'25 84w49'41 5:39:19
Odessa 34 92 42N49 85w08 5:40:32
Odessac 71 1 45N26 84w04 5:36:16
Odgers 36 1 41N59 84w21 5:37:24
Odgers Location 36 82 46N05'51 88w20'56 5:53:24
Ogden 46 1 41N49'04 83w58'48 5:35:55
Ogden Center 46 1 41N46'19 83w57'35 5:35:50
Ogemaw 65 1 44N18 84w18 5:37:12
Ogemaw Springs 65 1 44N18'13 84w17'33 5:37:10
Ogontz 21 25 45N52'06 86w47'27 5:47:10
Oil City 56 1 43N36'39 84w35'18 5:38:21
Ojibway 42 96 47N20'22 88w19'40 5:53:19
Okemos 33 41 42N43'20 84w25'39 5:37:43
Ola 29 1 43N11 84w29 5:37:56
Old Mill Gardens 13 43 42N16'05 85w11'56 5:40:48
Old Mission 28 1 44N57'44 85w29'07 5:41:56
Oldport 58 1 41N59'41 83w17'12 5:33:09
Old Saugatuck 3 92 42N39'59 86w12'46 5:44:51
Old Squaw Skin Landing 3 74 42N38'29 86w04'09 5:44:17
Olive Center 70 51 42N54'51 86w04'53 5:44:20
Olive Hills 70 51 42N55 86w09 5:44:36
Olivers 43 1 43N52'57 85w34'56 5:42:20
Olivet 23 1 42N26'29 84w55'27 5:39:42
Olney Corners 78 1 43N07'41 84w20'41 5:37:23
Olson 56 1 43N37'32 84w25'45 5:37:43
Omena 45 1 45N03'20 85w35'20 5:42:21
Omer 6 1 44N02'51 83w51'16 5:35:25
Onaway 71 3 45N21'27 84w13'26 5:36:54
Oneida 23 1 42N44 84w46 5:39:04
O'Neil 40 1 44N38'29 85w04'26 5:40:18
Onekama 51 1 44N21'49 86w12'18 5:44:49
Onekama Junction 51 1 44N20'13 86w12'09 5:44:49
Onondaga 33 1 42N26'39 84w33'44 5:38:15
Onota 2 25 46N28'16 86w59'45 5:47:59
Onsted 46 1 42N00'22 84w11'24 5:36:46
Ontonagon 66 25 46N52'16 89w18'50 5:57:15
Ontwa 14 108 41N47 86w03 5:44:12
Orangeville 8 57 42N33'10 85w31'09 5:42:05
Orchard Beach 16 1 45N33'25 84w27'52 5:37:51
Orchard Lake 63 88 42N34'59 83w21'34 5:33:26
Orchard Lake Village 63 88 42N35 83w22 5:33:28
Orchard Park 13 43 42N20'27 85w11'08 5:40:45
Orchard Point 71 1 45N12'57 83w29'42 5:33:59
Oregon 44 1 43N06 83w24 5:33:36
Orient 67 1 43N52 85w09 5:40:36
Orion 63 88 42N44 83w17 5:33:08
Orlando Park 41 61 43N00 85w38 5:42:32
Orleans 34 92 43N04'07 85w08'06 5:40:32
Oronoko 11 72 41N57 86w23 5:45:32
Orr 73 1 43N22'49 84w10'13 5:36:41
Ortonville 63 88 42N51'08 83w26'35 5:33:46
Osceola 31 96 47N13'53 88w27'13 5:53:49
Oscoda 35 1 44N25'13 83w19'51 5:33:19
Oshtemo 39 92 42N15'32 85w40'39 5:42:43
Osier 21 25 45N56 86w58 5:47:52
Oskar 31 25 47N10'29 88w38'54 5:54:36
Ossawinamakee Beach 77 14 45N59'53 86w17'37 5:45:10
Osseo 30 1 41N53'09 84w32'39 5:38:11
Ossineke 4 1 44N54'08 83w26'33 5:33:46
Osterhout Lake 3 92 42N24 86w04 5:44:16
Otisco 34 92 43N04 85w16 5:41:04
Otisville 25 1 43N09'58 83w31'28 5:34:06
Otsego 3 102 42N27'38 85w41'47 5:42:47
Otsego Lake 69 1 44N55'01 84w41'33 5:38:46
Ottawa 58 1 41N46'02 83w31'17 5:34:05
Ottawa Beach 70 51 42N47 86w07 5:44:28
Ottawa Center 70 51 43N01'46 86w01'52 5:44:07
Ottawa Lake 58 1 41N46 83w45 5:35:00
Otterburn 25 1 42N59 83w47 5:35:08
Otter Lake 79 1 43N12'48 83w27'16 5:33:49
Otto 64 57 43N31 86w13 5:44:52
Overisel 3 97 42N43'42 86w00'35 5:44:02
Ovid 19 1 43N00'21 84w22'18 5:37:29
Owasippe 61 57 43N22 86w10 5:44:40
Owendale 32 1 43N43'45 83w16'05 5:33:04
Owosso 78 1 42N59'52 84w10'36 5:36:42
Oxbow 11 72 42N01'18 86w23'13 5:45:33
Oxbow 62 64 43N28'57 85w37'22 5:42:29
Oxbow 63 88 42N38'26 83w28'23 5:33:54
Oxbow Park 62 57 43N30'26 85w36'07 5:42:24
Oxford 63 88 42N49'29 83w15'53 5:33:04
Ozark 49 25 46N08'31 84w57'56 5:39:52
Paavola 31 95 47N09'01 88w32'39 5:54:11
Packard 33 41 42N40'56 84w36'11 5:38:25
Paines 73 1 43N23'59 84w02'20 5:36:09
Painesdale 31 96 47N02'36 88w40'20 5:54:41
Paint Creek 81 1 42N09'27 83w34'54 5:34:20
Palatka 36 81 46N02'59 88w37'26 5:54:30
Palestine 55 86 45N24'20 87w32'00 5:50:08
Palisades Park 80 74 42N18'45 86w19'16 5:45:17
Palmer 52 11 46N26'27 87w35'35 5:50:22
Palms 76 1 43N36'49 82w46'06 5:31:04
Palmyra 46 1 41N51'35 83w56'09 5:35:45
Palo 34 92 43N06'45 84w59'08 5:39:57
Panola 36 86 46N02'58 88w19'43 5:53:19
Papin 7 25 46N49 88w38 5:54:32
Paradise 17 12 46N37'39 85w02'15 5:40:09
Parchment 39 47 42N19'41 85w34'11 5:42:17
Paris 32 1 43N44 82w49 5:31:16
Paris 54 1 43N46'24 85w30'09 5:42:01
Parishfield 47 1 42N29'48 83w49'48 5:35:19
Parisville 32 1 43N42'50 82w47'58 5:31:12
Park 41 61 42N59 85w42 5:42:48
Parkdale 51 111 44N16'03 86w18'10 5:45:13
Parkers Corners 47 1 42N34'05 84w06'48 5:36:27
Park Grove 82 2 42N26 82w59 5:31:56
Parkington 77 25 46N00'40 85w56'50 5:43:47
Park Lake 19 41 42N49 84w27 5:37:48
Park Lake 67 1 44N08'45 85w12'22 5:40:49
Park Lake Corner 67 1 44N06 85w09 5:40:36
Park Plaza 82 2 42N14 83w11 5:32:44
Parks 62 57 43N46 85w30 5:42:00
Park Shore Resort 14 73 41N55 86w00 5:44:00
Parkview Terrace 61 49 43N12 86w14 5:44:56
Parkville 75 97 42N00'57 85w32'52 5:42:11
Parma 38 1 42N15'30 84w35'59 5:38:24
Parmelee 8 57 42N45'16 85w28'27 5:41:54
Parnell 41 64 43N02'36 85w24'41 5:41:39
Parshallburg (Havana) 73 1 43N08'47 84w08'10 5:36:33
Parshallville 47 1 42N41'31 83w46'56 5:35:08
Partello 13 1 42N24'16 84w50'52 5:39:23
Patons Corner 24 67 45N28'18 84w59'40 5:39:59
Patrick Landing 49 25 45N59'05 84w22'38 5:37:31
Patterson Gardens 58 36 41N55'06 83w25'50 5:33:43
Patterson Lake 47 1 42N27 83w57 5:35:48
Paulding 66 11 46N24'05 89w10'47 5:56:43
Pavilion 39 100 42N10'20 85w27'33 5:41:50
Pavilion Center 39 92 42N12'03 85w28'55 5:41:56
Pavlovic Corner 28 1 44N34'08 85w45'12 5:43:01
Paw Paw 80 46 42N13'04 85w53'28 5:43:34
Paw Paw Lake 11 74 42N12'44 86w16'19 5:45:05
Paxton 4 1 45N03'16 83w36'51 5:34:27
Payment 17 12 46N31'49 84w08'25 5:36:34
Paynesville 66 25 46N31'25 89w06'59 5:56:28
Peacock 43 92 44N02'46 85w53'19 5:43:33
Peaine 15 1 45N40 85w32 5:42:08
Pearl 3 74 42N32'31 86w05'34 5:44:22
Pearl Beach 12 1 41N49'27 84w59'11 5:39:57
Pearl Beach 74 1 42N37'36 82w35'52 5:30:23
Pearl Grange 11 4 42N05'28 86w21'32 5:45:26
Pearline 70 51 42N58'20 85w55'27 5:43:42
Pearl City 69 1 44N58'55 84w41'01 5:38:44
Peatville 76 1 43N38'16 82w49'03 5:31:16
Peck 76 1 43N15'31 82w49'03 5:31:16
Pelkie 7 25 46N48'48 88w38'11 5:54:33
Pellston 24 67 45N33'10 84w47'02 5:39:08
Pemberthy Crossing 40 1 44N37'58 84w54'30 5:39:38
Penford 82 2 42N14 83w16 5:33:04
Peninsula 28 1 44N52 85w32 5:42:08
Penn 14 76 41N56'49 85w56'09 5:43:45
Pennellwood 11 72 41N55'33 86w20'05 5:45:20
Pennfield 13 43 42N22'24 85w06'09 5:40:25

Penobscot 82 2 42N20 83w03 5:32:12
Pentland 48 25 46N18 85w28 5:41:52
Pentoga 36 81 46N00'11 88w29'40 5:53:59
Pentwater 64 64 43N46'54 86w25'59 5:45:44
Pequaming 7 25 46N51'07 88w24'01 5:53:36
Perch Point 74 1 42N39'54 82w37'13 5:30:29
Pere Cheney 20 1 44N34'39 84w38'16 5:38:33
Pere Marquette 53
57 43N57 86w25 5:45:40
Perkins 21 25 45N58'40 87w04'18 5:48:17
Perrinton 59 1 43N10'58 84w40'45 5:38:43
Perronville 55 81 45N47'55 87w21'11 5:49:25
Perry 78 1 42N49'35 84w13'10 5:36:53
Perry Lake Heights 63
88 42N49'40 83w24'04 5:33:36
Peshawbestown 45
1 45N01'27 85w36'03 5:42:24
Peters 74 1 42N44'40 82w37'54 5:30:32
Petersburg 58 7 41N54'04 83w42'54 5:34:52
Petersburg Junction 58
7 41N53'07 83w42'09 5:34:49
Petoskey 24 67 45N22'24 84w57'19 5:39:49
Petrieville 23 1 42N32'08 84w37'17 5:38:29
Pettysville 47 1 42N28'31 83w52'10 5:35:29
Pewabic 31 95 47N08'24 88w33'47 5:54:15
Pewamo 34 92 43N00'04 84w50'49 5:39:23
Phelps 15 1 45N13'15 85w15'40 5:41:03
Phelps 18 1 43N54'54 84w55'25 5:39:42
Phillipsville 31
25 47N16'47 88w24'48 5:53:39
Phoenix 42 96 47N23'20 88w16'39 5:53:07
Pickford 17 12 46N09'28 84w21'49 5:37:27
Pier Cove 3 92 42N35'09 86w13'34 5:44:54
Pierport 51 1 44N25'36 86w14'24 5:44:58
Pierson 59 57 43N19'11 85w29'52 5:41:59
Pigeon 32 1 43N49'48 83w16'12 5:33:05
Pike Lake 49 25 46N06 85w42 5:42:48
Pilgrim 10 1 44N39'54 86w14'45 5:44:59
Pilgrim 31 96 47N05'59 88w31'01 5:54:04
Pinckney 47 1 42N27'24 83w56'47 5:35:47
Pinconning 9 1 43N51'13 83w57'54 5:35:52
Pine 59 57 43N20 85w16 5:41:04
Pine Bluffs 72 1 44N30 84w36 5:38:24
Pine Creek 13 1 42N09'56 85w15'22 5:41:01
Pine Creek 70 52 42N49'40 86w08'15 5:44:33
Pine Grove 80 72 42N21'14 85w51'46 5:43:27
Pine Grove Beach 43
92 43N49'19 85w57'43 5:43:51
Pine Ridge 21 11 45N44'19 87w10'24 5:48:42
Pine Ridge 75 97 42N02'05 85w38'08 5:42:33
Pine River 6 1 43N59'00 83w53'19 5:35:33
Pine River 29 1 43N25 84w40 5:38:40
Pine Run 25 1 43N10'40 83w42'51 5:34:51
Pine Stump Junction 48
25 46N34'09 85w35'29 5:42:22
Pine Wood Park 6
1 44N09'40 83w34'05 5:34:16
Piney Ridge 53 57 44N00'55 86w28'18 5:45:53
Piney Woods 18 1 44N04'24 84w48'30 5:39:14
Pinnebog 32 1 43N56'07 83w06'14 5:32:25
Pinora 43 1 43N57 85w37 5:42:28
Pioneer 57 1 44N28'03 85w09'21 5:40:37
Pipestone 11 72 42N02 86w17 5:45:08
Pisgah Heights 67
1 44N05'40 85w13'34 5:40:54
Pittsburg 78 1 42N53'33 84w13'19 5:36:53
Pittsfield 81 38 42N12'37 83w43'27 5:34:54
Pittsford 30 1 41N51'44 84w28'37 5:37:54
Plainfield 47 1 42N29'49 84w06'27 5:36:26
Plainfield Heights 41
61 43N00 85w38 5:42:32
Plains 52 25 46N19'32 87w24'17 5:49:37
Plainwell 3 102 42N26'24 85w38'56 5:42:36
Planter 27 81 46N30'40 89w58'25 5:59:54
Platte 10 1 44N44 86w01 5:44:04
Plaza 13 43 42N16 85w12 5:40:48
Pleasant Lake 30
1 41N53 84w33 5:38:12
Pleasant Lake 38
1 42N22'48 84w20'57 5:37:24
Pleasanton 51 1 44N28'25 86w07'15 5:44:29
Pleasant Plains 43
92 43N52 85w51 5:43:24
Pleasant Ridge 63
2 42N28'16 83w08'32 5:32:34
Pleasant Valley 5
1 45N03'28 85w09'37 5:40:38
Pleasant Valley 56
1 43N30'35 84w35'17 5:38:21
Pleasant View 24
67 45N30'26 84w54'52 5:39:39
Plumbrook Estates 50
88 42N34 83w02 5:32:08
Plumbrook Farms 50
88 42N34 83w02 5:32:08
Plumbrook Village 50
88 42N34 83w02 5:32:08
Plymouth 27 81 46N27'53 89w58'46 5:59:55
Plymouth 82 36 42N22'17 83w28'13 5:33:53
Podunk 8 62 42N36'32 85w21'30 5:41:26
Podunk 26 1 44N03'10 84w33'57 5:38:16
Podunk 81 1 42N09 84w02 5:36:08
Pogy 54 97 43N47'56 85w20'40 5:41:23
Point au Gres 6 1 44N03 83w41 5:34:44
Pointe aux Barques 32
1 44N03'47 82w57'30 5:31:50
Pointe aux Chenes 74
1 42N36'39 82w32'22 5:30:09
Pointe aux Peaux Farms 58
1 41N58 83w15 5:33:00
Pointe aux Pins 49
1 45N43'57 84w28'40 5:37:55
Pointe aux Tremble 74
1 42N37'17 82w34'16 5:30:17
Point Lakeview 50
88 42N39'21 82w46'45 5:31:07
Point Mills 31 96 47N05'42 88w28'14 5:53:53
Point Nipigon 16
1 45N42'30 84w34'00 5:38:16
Pokagon 14 72 41N54'45 86w10'35 5:44:42
Polaski 71 1 45N14'01 83w39'30 5:34:38
Polkton 70 55 43N04 85w59 5:43:56
Pollok 33 1 42N36'54 84w20'21 5:37:21
Pomeroy 39 92 42N11'37 85w28'56 5:41:56
Pomona 51 1 44N28'15 85w52'47 5:43:31
Pompeii 59 1 43N11'02 84w36'03 5:38:24
Ponshewaing 24 67 45N25'16 84w48'12 5:39:13
Pontchartrain Shores 49
25 46N01'46 84w35'30 5:38:22
Pontiac 63 37 42N38'20 83w17'28 5:33:10
Pontiac Lake 63
88 42N39 83w24 5:33:36
Poplar Beach 8 57 42N27 85w14 5:40:56
Popple 32 1 43N46'16 83w05'46 5:32:23
Pori 31 25 46N40'47 88w57'36 5:55:50
Portage 39 92 42N12'04 85w34'48 5:42:19
Portage Entry 31
96 46N58'56 88w26'26 5:53:46
Portage Lake 75
92 42N00 85w27 5:41:48
Portage Point 51
1 44N22 86w14 5:44:56
Port Austin 32 1 44N02'46 82w59'39 5:31:59
Port Crescent 32
1 44N00'07 83w03'19 5:32:13
Port Dolomite 49
25 45N59'05 84w16'30 5:37:06
Porter 56 1 43N31'07 84w27'59 5:37:52
Port Gypsum 35 1 44N16 83w31 5:34:04
Port Hope 32 1 43N56'27 82w42'46 5:30:51
Port Huron 74 39 42N58'15 82w25'30 5:29:42
Port Inland 49 25 45N58'15 85w52'20 5:43:29
Portland 34 92 42N52'09 84w54'11 5:39:37
Port Oneida 45 1 44N56'52 85w56'44 5:43:47
Port Sanilac 76
88 43N25'51 82w32'33 5:30:10
Port Sheldon 70
51 42N53'58 86w11'59 5:44:48
Portsmouth 9 36 43N34 83w51 5:35:24
Posen 71 1 45N15'43 83w41'56 5:34:48
Poseyville 56 1 43N32'23 84w14'58 5:37:00
Potters Corners 34
92 42N56 85w13 5:40:52
Potters Lake 44 1 43N03 83w19 5:33:16
Potterville 23 1 42N37'45 84w44'20 5:38:57
Poverty Island 21
25 45N32 86w40 5:46:40
Powell 52 25 46N47 87w41 5:50:44
Powers 55 86 45N41'24 87w31'33 5:50:06
Prairie 34 92 42N59'05 85w02'03 5:40:08
Prairie Creek 34
92 42N59 85w04 5:40:16
Prairie Farm 73 1 43N18 84w09 5:36:36
Prairie Ronde 39
92 42N07 85w43 5:42:52
Prairie View 13
43 42N16 85w12 5:40:48
Prairieville 8 57 42N30'17 85w27'18 5:41:49
Prattville 30 1 41N46'56 84w23'59 5:37:36
Prescott 65 1 44N11'31 83w55'51 5:35:43
Presque Isle 71 1 45N18'15 83w28'37 5:33:54
Preston Corners 50
88 42N41'58 82w59'45 5:31:59
Price 19 1 42N55'44 84w29'01 5:37:56
Princeton 52 11 46N17'20 87w28'30 5:49:54
Prosper 57 1 44N14'34 85w01'59 5:40:08
Prudenville 72 1 44N17'54 84w39'07 5:38:36
Pulaski 38 1 42N06'54 84w38'33 5:38:34
Pulawski 71 1 45N20 83w43 5:34:52
Pullman 3 92 42N29'01 86w05'29 5:44:22
Pullman Corners 14
108 41N48 86w05 5:44:20
Putnam 47 1 42N28 83w58 5:35:52
Quakertown 63 88 42N29'10 83w22'40 5:33:31
Quanicassee 79 1 43N35'00 83w40'51 5:34:43
Quarry 32 1 43N51 83w23 5:33:32
Quincy 12 1 41N56'39 84w53'02 5:39:32
Quincy Mill 31 96 47N08'53 88w27'31 5:53:50
Quincy Mine 31 95 47N08 88w36 5:54:24
Quinnesec 22 87 45N48'23 87w59'18 5:51:57
Qumby 8 57 42N36'37 85w13'40 5:40:55
Rabbit Bay 31 96 47N03'49 88w21'19 5:53:25
Raber 17 12 46N05'21 84w04'17 5:36:17
Raco 17 12 46N22'32 84w43'22 5:38:53
Racy 73 1 43N11'42 84w18'22 5:37:13
Rainbow Bend 18 1 44N07'43 84w55'18 5:39:41
Rainy Beach 71 1 45N27'02 84w12'55 5:36:52
Raisin 46 1 41N57 83w58 5:35:52
Raisin Center 46
1 41N55'44 83w57'12 5:35:49
Raisinville 58 1 41N58 83w31 5:34:04
Ralph 22 87 46N06'31 87w47'01 5:51:08
Rambaultown 31 96 47N15 88w27 5:53:48
Ramona 64 64 43N36'15 85w48'07 5:43:12
Ramona Park 24 67 45N25'33 84w56'42 5:39:47
Ramona Park 39
100 42N11'23 85w32'28 5:42:10
Ramsay 27 81 46N28'13 89w59'47 5:59:59
Ranch Acres 70 68 43N04 86w11 5:44:44
Randall Beach 63
88 42N38 83w14 5:32:56
Randall Lake 12 1 41N57 85w00 5:40:00
Randville 22 87 45N59'30 88w03'25 5:52:14
Rankin 25 1 42N54'52 83w45'02 5:35:00
Ransom 30 1 41N46'31 84w32'03 5:38:08
Rapid City 40 1 44N50'04 85w16'57 5:41:08
Rapid River 21 35 45N55'37 86w58'01 5:47:52
Rapson 32 1 43N51'22 82w52'57 5:31:32
Rasmus 20 1 44N37'48 84w46'30 5:39:06
Rathbone 29 1 43N20'09 84w25'47 5:37:43
Rattle Run 74 1 42N51'59 82w35'59 5:30:24
Ravema 61 66 43N11'22 85w56'13 5:43:45
Ravenna 61 66 43N11 85w56 5:43:44
Ravenswood 33 41 42N44 84w36 5:38:24
Ravenswood Heights 39
47 42N17 85w34 5:42:16
Ravenwood 58 36 41N55 83w23 5:33:32
Rawsonville 81 36 42N12'55 83w33'06 5:34:12
Ray 12 1 41N45'35 84w52'19 5:39:29
Ray 50 88 42N45 82w55 5:31:40
Ray Center 50 88 42N45'42 82w54'05 5:31:36
Raymond Corners 43
1 44N02 85w41 5:42:44
Rea 58 1 41N57 83w40 5:34:40
Reade 52 25 46N03'35 87w33'42 5:50:15
Reading 30 1 41N50'22 84w44'53 5:39:00
Readmond 24 67 45N36 85w02 5:40:08
Recreation Park 39
47 42N14 85w35 5:42:20
Recreation Park 61
49 43N12 86w14 5:44:56
Redding 18 1 44N02 85w02 5:40:08
Redford 82 36 42N23 83w18 5:33:12
Redman 32 1 43N55'45 82w50'03 5:31:20
Red Oak 68 1 44N42'35 84w17'32 5:37:10
Red Park 51 111 44N21'07 86w14'34 5:44:58
Redridge 31 25 47N09'02 88w45'44 5:55:03
Redstone 56 1 43N28'53 84w28'08 5:37:53
Reed City 67 97 43N52'30 85w30'36 5:42:02
Reeder 57 1 44N18 85w10 5:40:40
Reeds Lake 41 61 42N56 85w37 5:42:28
Reeman 62 57 43N26'42 86w00'31 5:44:02
Reese 79 1 43N27'02 83w41'47 5:34:47
Remus 9 57 43N35'48 85w08'41 5:40:35
Reno 35 1 44N18 83w49 5:35:16
Reno 70 51 43N04'30 85w50'19 5:43:21
Republic 52 25 46N24'24 87w58'32 5:51:54
Rescue 32 1 43N39 83w15 5:33:00
Resort 24 67 45N20 85w01 5:40:04
Rexton 49 25 46N09'31 85w14'24 5:40:58
Reynolds 59 64 43N26 85w30 5:42:00
Rhodes 26 1 43N54'06 84w10'34 5:36:42
Rice Creek 13 1 42N20'04 84w49'43 5:39:19
Rich 44 1 43N17 83w17 5:33:08
Richfield Center 25
1 43N05'34 83w31'06 5:34:04
Richland 39 92 42N22'34 85w27'18 5:41:49
Richland Junction 39
92 42N24'04 85w29'49 5:41:59
Richmond 50 1 42N48'33 82w45'21 5:31:01
Richmondville 76
1 43N34'24 82w35'37 5:30:22
Richville 79 1 43N24'33 83w40'38 5:34:43
Ridgeville 46 1 41N45'26 84w01'18 5:36:05
Ridgeway 46 1 41N59'38 83w51'46 5:35:27
Riga 46 1 41N48'33 83w49'30 5:35:18
Riggsville 16 1 45N34'12 84w36'38 5:38:27
Riley 19 41 42N54'54 84w40'50 5:38:43
Riley Center 74 1 42N56'27 82w50'30 5:31:22
Ripley 31 95 47N07'36 88w33'13 5:54:13
Ritter Hills 61
49 43N12 86w16 5:45:04
River Bluff 11
105 41N50 86w15 5:45:00
Riverdale 29 1 43N23'08 84w50'08 5:39:21
Riverland 21 19 45N47'48 87w13'36 5:48:54
River Raisin 81 1 42N07'05 83w58'45 5:35:55
River Rouge 82 2 42N16'24 83w08'04 5:32:32
Riverside 11 74 42N11'00 86w22'58 5:45:32
Riverside 38 90 42N15 84w24 5:37:36
Riverside 57 1 44N13 85w09 5:40:36
Riverside 74 1 42N33'32 82w37'49 5:30:31
Riverton 53 57 43N52 86w20 5:45:20
Riverview 62 64 43N26'53 85w39'09 5:42:37
Riverview 82 2 42N10'27 83w10'46 5:32:43
Rives 38 1 42N23 84w25 5:37:40
Rives Junction 38
1 42N23'09 84w27'42 5:37:51
Roaring Brook 24
67 45N25'43 84w56'45 5:39:47
Robbins 66 25 46N22'55 89w13'32 5:56:54
Roberts Corner 48
25 46N18'12 85w29'19 5:41:57
Roberts Corners 48
25 46N21 85w30 5:42:00
Roberts Landing 74
1 42N39'35 82w30'57 5:30:04
Robinson 70 97 42N59'12 86w05'03 5:44:20
Rochester 63 88 42N40'50 83w08'02 5:32:32
Rock 21 15 46N04'08 87w09'57 5:48:40
Rockford 41 65 43N07'12 85w33'36 5:42:14
Rock Harbor Lodge 42
25 48N08'45 88w29'01 5:53:56
Rockland 66 25 46N44'17 89w10'46 5:56:43
Rockport 71 1 45N12'14 83w23'08 5:33:33
Rock River 2 25 46N27'50 86w54'47 5:47:39
Rockview 49 25 46N05'09 84w21'46 5:37:27
Rockwood 82 36 42N04'15 83w14'48 5:32:59
Rodney 54 1 43N40'25 85w19'42 5:41:19
Rogers 36 81 46N06 88w39 5:54:36
Rogers 71 1 45N27 83w52 5:35:28
Rogers City 71 1 45N25'17 83w49'06 5:35:16
Rogers Corner 81
1 42N14'20 83w58'27 5:35:54
Rogers Heights 41
61 42N55 85w42 5:42:48
Rogers Location 36
86 46N06'22 88w35'05 5:54:20
Rogersville 25 1 43N07'22 83w34'37 5:34:18
Rolland Center 37
1 43N31'27 84w59'46 5:39:59
Rollin 46 1 41N54'43 84w19'25 5:37:18
Rome Center 46 1 41N56'37 84w11'16 5:36:45
Romeo 50 1 42N48'10 83w00'47 5:32:03
Romulus 82 37 42N13'20 83w23'48 5:33:35
Ronald 34 92 43N05 85w01 5:40:04
Rondo 16 1 45N19'00 84w37'28 5:38:30
Roodmont 61 49 43N12 86w16 5:45:04
Roosevelt 73 1 43N20'57 84w11'25 5:36:46
Roosevelt Park 61
49 43N12 86w16 5:45:04
Roots 38 1 42N20'08 84w19'20 5:37:17
Roscommon 72 88 44N29'54 84w35'31 5:38:22
Roseburg 76 1 43N11'24 82w44'38 5:30:59
Rosebush 37 1 43N41'57 84w46'04 5:39:04
Rose Center 63 88 42N47 83w37 5:34:28
Rose City 65 1 44N25'17 84w07'00 5:36:28
Rose Corners 63
88 42N44'22 83w40'00 5:34:40
Rosedale 17 12 46N22'34 84w19'19 5:37:17
Rose Island 32 1 43N46'58 83w25'53 5:33:44
Rose Lake 67 1 44N01 85w24 5:41:36
Rosemary Beach 11
74 41N58'55 86w33'49 5:46:15
Roseville 50 2 42N29'50 82w56'14 5:31:45
Ross 41 57 42N46'57 85w41'40 5:42:47
Rosy Mound 70 68 43N01'48 86w13'22 5:44:53
Rothbury 64 64 43N30'26 86w20'51 5:45:23
Roulo 82 36 42N11'24 83w29'00 5:33:56

Round Lake 46 1 41N59 84w17 5:37:08
Round Lake 53 57 44N03 86w11 5:44:44
Rousseau 66 25 46N42'34 88w58'11 5:55:53
Rowes Corner 81 1 42N11'30 84w01'58 5:36:08
Roxand 23 92 42N43 84w54 5:39:36
Royal Oak 63 2 42N29'22 83w08'41 5:32:35
Royal Oak Beach 16 1 45N29'31 84w34'40 5:38:19
Royalton 11 1 42N01 86w26 5:45:44
Royalton Heights 11 1 42N05 86w30 5:46:00
Royston 60 1 45N09'34 83w53'35 5:35:34
Rubicon 32 1 43N54 82w43 5:30:52
Ruby 74 1 43N02'32 82w36'27 5:30:26
Rudds Mill 63 88 42N46'04 83w13'06 5:32:52
Rudyard 17 12 46N13'57 84w36'01 5:38:24
Rumely 2 25 46N20'54 87w01'59 5:48:08
Rush 78 1 43N05 84w14 5:36:56
Rushton 47 1 42N27'07 83w41'46 5:34:47
Rusk 70 54 42N57'27 86w00'45 5:44:03
Russell Island 74 1 42N37 82w32 5:30:08
Russellville 25 1 43N05'30 83w33'30 5:34:14
Rust 60 1 44N59'12 83w56'55 5:35:48
Rustford 54 1 43N30'45 85w20'34 5:41:22
Ruth 32 1 43N42'55 82w44'25 5:30:58
Rutland 8 57 42N39 85w22 5:41:28
Ryan 56 1 43N28'25 84w22'10 5:37:29
Sac Bay 21 25 45N39'00 86w41'30 5:46:46
Saddle Lake 80 72 42N24 86w04 5:44:16
Saganing 6 1 43N55'44 83w54'37 5:35:38
Sage 26 1 44N01 84w33 5:38:12
Saginaw 73 91 43N25'10 83w57'03 5:35:48
Sagola 22 87 46N05'25 88w04'39 5:52:19
Saint Anthony 58 7 41N47'57 83w39'21 5:34:37
Saint Charles 73 1 43N17'49 84w08'26 5:36:34
Saint Clair 74 1 42N49'15 82w29'10 5:29:57
Saint Clair Flats 74 1 42N35 82w34 5:30:16
Saint Clair Haven 50 88 42N35'00 82w47'25 5:31:10
Saint Clair Shores 50 2 42N29'49 82w53'20 5:31:33
Saint Elmo 56 1 43N35'01 84w28'12 5:37:53
Saint Helen 72 1 44N21'49 84w24'37 5:37:38
Saint Huberts 64 57 43N32'33 86w05'06 5:44:20
Saint Ignace 49 69 45N52'07 84w43'40 5:38:55
Saint Jacques 21 25 45N53'43 86w44'33 5:46:58
Saint James 15 1 45N45'04 85w30'56 5:42:04
Saint Johns 19 1 43N00'04 84w33'33 5:38:14
Saint Joseph 11 4 42N06'35 86w28'48 5:45:55
Saint Louis 29 1 43N24'30 84w36'24 5:38:26
Saint Martin Island 21 25 45N30 86w46 5:47:04
Saint Marys Junction 31 95 47N08 88w36 5:54:24
Saint Marys Lake 13 43 42N20 85w11 5:40:44
Saint Nicholas 21 25 45N59'08 87w13'36 5:48:54
Salem 81 1 42N24'22 83w34'48 5:34:19
Saline 81 38 42N10'00 83w46'54 5:35:08
Salisbury 52 25 46N28'30 87w40'37 5:50:42
Salmon Trout 31 25 47N06'38 88w44'25 5:54:58
Salva 21 25 45N53'16 87w12'16 5:48:49
Salzburg 9 36 43N36 83w54 5:35:36
Samaria 58 1 41N48'29 83w34'42 5:34:19
Sanborn 4 1 44N55 83w27 5:33:48
Sand Beach 32 1 43N49 82w41 5:30:44
Sand Creek 46 1 41N49'33 84w06'06 5:36:24
Sand Hill 73 91 43N26 84w00 5:36:00
Sand Lake 35 1 44N19'09 83w41'05 5:34:44
Sand Lake 41 57 43N18 85w31 5:42:04
Sand Lake Corners 46 1 42N00 84w11 5:36:44
Sand River 2 25 46N29'26 87w06'56 5:48:28
Sands 52 11 46N25'15 87w24'24 5:49:38
Sandstone 38 1 42N15'07 84w31'04 5:38:04
Sandusky 76 1 43N25'13 82w49'47 5:31:19
Sandy Beach 14 72 42N03'04 86w11'18 5:44:45
Sandy Beach 75 1 41N48'29 85w31'50 5:42:07
Sanford 56 1 43N40'22 84w22'50 5:37:31
Sanilac 76 1 43N24 82w35 5:30:20
Sans Souci 74 1 42N34'45 82w33'51 5:30:15
Sans Souci Beach 12 1 41N49'50 84w58'12 5:39:53
Santiago 6 1 44N06'46 83w42'02 5:34:48
Saranac 34 92 42N55'46 85w12'47 5:40:51
Sauble 43 92 44N02'03 85w59'57 5:44:00
Saugatuck 3 92 42N39'18 86w12'07 5:44:48
Sault Sainte Marie 17 45 46N29'43 84w20'43 5:37:23
Sawyer 11 74 41N53'07 86w35'22 5:46:21
Sawyer Air Force Base 52 25 46N20 87w22 5:49:28
Sawyer Lake 22 87 46N09 88w05 5:52:20
Schaffer 21 11 45N45'40 87w17'55 5:49:12
Schmidt Corner 31 25 47N09'21 88w38'34 5:54:34
Schomberg 45 1 44N55'17 85w46'26 5:43:06
Schoolcraft 39 99 42N06'51 85w38'16 5:42:33
Schultz 8 62 42N34'50 85w20'47 5:41:23
Scio 81 38 42N19'32 83w50'22 5:35:21
Sciota 78 1 42N54 84w19 5:37:16
Scipio 30 1 42N02 84w39 5:38:36
Scofield 58 7 42N01'17 83w28'55 5:33:56
Scottdale 11 1 42N02'31 86w26'07 5:45:44
Scott Lake 36 86 46N01'19 88w34'36 5:54:18
Scotts 39 97 42N11'45 85w24'47 5:41:39
Scottville 53 57 43N57'17 86w16'48 5:45:07
Sears 67 1 43N53'54 85w11'05 5:40:44
Sebewa 34 97 42N49 85w01 5:40:04
Sebewa Center 34 92 42N52 84w54 5:39:36
Sebewa Corners 34 92 42N47'58 84w57'21 5:39:49
Sebewaing 32 1 43N43'56 83w27'04 5:33:48
Sebille Manor 50 88 42N39'40 82w48'44 5:31:15
Secord 26 1 44N00'55 84w20'52 5:37:23
Seewhy 17 12 46N21'10 85w05'41 5:40:23
Segwun 41 57 42N55'26 85w20'34 5:41:22
Seidler Corners 9 1 43N36 84w05 5:36:20
Seidlers 9 1 43N40'58 84w05'16 5:36:21
Selfridge Air Force Base 50 88 42N37 82w49 5:31:16
Selkirk 65 1 44N18'47 84w04'02 5:36:16
Selma 52 25 46N21'44 87w10'55 5:48:44
Selma 83 1 44N17 85w32 5:42:08
Seminole Park 61 49 43N12 86w16 5:45:04
Seneca 42 96 47N18'50 88w21'42 5:53:27
Seneca 46 1 41N47'15 84w10'36 5:36:42
Seneca Location 42 96 47N18 88w26 5:53:44
Seney 77 78 46N20'44 85w56'43 5:43:47
Senter 31 96 47N06'20 88w26'08 5:53:45
Sethton 29 1 43N13'11 84w46'39 5:39:07
Seven Harbors 63 88 42N40'19 83w34'20 5:34:17
Seven Oaks 82 2 42N26 83w12 5:32:48
Seville 29 1 43N25 84w47 5:39:08
Seymour Square 41 61 42N58 85w40 5:42:40
Shabbona 76 1 43N31'53 83w03'15 5:32:13
Shady Shores 65 1 44N24'23 83w58'28 5:35:54
Shadyside 30 1 41N49'22 84w32'11 5:38:09
Shafer Location 36 81 46N05'06 88w21'26 5:53:26
Shaftsburg 78 1 42N48'17 84w17'35 5:37:10
Shallows 17 12 46N28'29 84w26'39 5:37:47
Shanghai Corners 11 72 42N02'00 86w19'42 5:45:19
Sharon 40 1 44N35'01 85w04'26 5:40:18
Sharon 81 1 42N12 84w04 5:36:16
Sharon Hollow 81 1 42N10'42 84w05'38 5:36:23
Sharps Corners 72 1 44N25'16 84w41'01 5:38:44
Shattuckville 73 91 43N27'07 84w03'05 5:36:12
Shaytown 23 92 42N42'15 84w58'34 5:39:54
Sheffield 41 64 43N11'38 85w29'27 5:41:58
Shelby 64 64 43N36'31 86w21'50 5:45:27
Shelby Village 50 88 42N37 83w02 5:32:08
Shelbyville 3 92 42N35'39 85w38'14 5:42:33
Sheldon 82 36 42N16'29 83w28'33 5:33:54
Shelldrake 17 12 46N40'40 85w02'01 5:40:08
Shepardsville 19 1 43N00'16 84w25'33 5:37:42
Shepherd 37 1 43N31'28 84w41'41 5:38:47
Sheridan 59 57 43N12'44 85w04'25 5:40:18
Sherman 83 1 44N25'26 85w41'48 5:42:47
Sherman City 37 1 43N43'36 85w04'38 5:40:19
Sherman Lake 39 92 42N20 85w21 5:41:24
Sherman Manor 61 49 43N12 86w16 5:45:04
Sherman Park 3 92 42N29'31 86w04'55 5:44:20
Sherman Woods 74 1 42N58 82w29 5:29:56
Sherwood 12 1 42N00'05 85w14'19 5:40:57
Sherwood Corners 68 1 44N39 84w08 5:36:32
Sherwood Park 39 47 42N17 85w34 5:42:16
Shiawassee 78 1 42N55'46 84w04'46 5:36:19
Shiawasseetown 78 1 42N55'46 84w04'46 5:36:19
Shields 73 1 43N24'55 84w03'23 5:36:14
Shiloh 34 92 43N06'17 85w05'06 5:40:20
Shingleton 2 30 46N20'54 86w28'12 5:45:53
Shorecrest 3 92 42N30'23 86w14'40 5:44:59
Shoreham 11 74 42N03'54 86w29'42 5:45:59
Shore Line Junction 31 95 47N08 88w36 5:54:24
Shorewood 3 92 42N39'02 86w13'19 5:44:53
Shorewood Hills 11 74 41N53'45 86w36'57 5:46:28
Sibley 82 36 42N08 83w13 5:32:52
Sickles 29 1 43N16'40 84w26'56 5:37:48
Sidnaw 31 25 46N30'17 88w42'30 5:54:50
Sidney 59 57 43N15'00 85w07'59 5:40:32
Siemens 27 81 46N28'30 90w06'12 6:00:25
Sigel 32 1 43N49 82w49 5:31:16
Sigma 40 1 44N40'12 85w03'12 5:40:13
Silver Beach 16 1 45N32'55 84w31'56 5:38:08
Silver City 66 25 46N49'49 89w34'13 5:58:17
Silver Creek 3 102 42N27 85w39 5:42:36
Silver Creek 14 72 42N02 86w10 5:44:40
Silver Lake 41 65 43N07 85w34 5:42:16
Silverwood 79 1 43N19'24 83w14'53 5:33:00
Simar 66 25 46N45 89w05 5:56:20
Simmons 49 12 46N05'46 84w35'47 5:38:23
Sims 6 1 44N04 83w38 5:34:32
Sister Lakes 80 72 42N04'20 86w11'59 5:44:48
Sitka 62 57 43N22'52 86w01'07 5:44:04
Six Lakes 59 57 43N25'30 85w09'00 5:40:36
Skandia 52 25 46N22'39 87w14'29 5:48:58
Skanee 7 25 46N52'24 88w12'50 5:52:51
Skeels 26 1 44N05'24 84w35'12 5:38:21
Skidmore 22 87 45N47'31 88w04'25 5:52:18
Skidway Lake 65 1 44N11'00 84w02'07 5:36:08
Skookum 43 1 44N04'50 85w38'37 5:42:34
Skyline Village 20 1 44N34'16 84w42'08 5:38:49
Slagle 83 1 44N18 85w46 5:43:04
Slapneck 2 25 46N20'34 86w53'11 5:47:33
Slaybaugh Corner 67 1 43N56'40 85w25'31 5:41:42
Sleepy Hollow 66 25 46N24'17 89w14'27 5:56:58
Slocum 61 66 43N13'20 85w54'35 5:43:38
Sly Farms 63 88 42N32 83w17 5:33:08
Smith Corners 64 64 43N42 86w22 5:45:28
Smith Crossing 78 1 43N01'35 84w13'23 5:36:54
Smiths Creek 74 1 42N54'50 82w36'14 5:30:25
Smithville 40 1 44N31'27 85w10'27 5:40:42
Smyrna 34 92 43N03'34 85w15'46 5:41:03
Snover 76 1 43N27'40 82w58'15 5:31:53
Snow 11 74 41N55'28 86w28'59 5:45:56
Snowshoe 42 96 47N13'50 88w14'29 5:52:58
Snowville 52 11 46N29'59 87w49'09 5:51:17
Snug Harbor 17 12 46N33'19 85w04'11 5:40:17
Snug Harbor 70 68 43N02'04 86w10'39 5:44:43
Snyderville 74 1 42N50'12 82w40'17 5:30:41
Sodus 11 1 42N02'37 86w22'09 5:45:29
Sokol Camp 11 75 41N48'56 86w43'18 5:46:53
Solon 45 1 44N48'34 85w45'40 5:43:03
Solon Center 41 57 43N14'55 85w36'41 5:42:27
Somerset 30 1 42N02'54 84w22'36 5:37:30
Somerset Center 30 1 42N03'04 84w24'49 5:37:39
Sonoma 13 43 42N13'58 85w13'41 5:40:55
Soo 17 45 46N30 84w21 5:37:24
Soo Corner 48 25 46N19 85w15 5:41:00
Soo Junction 48 25 46N20'08 85w15'34 5:41:02
South Arm 15 1 45N10 85w10 5:40:40
South Blendon 70 54 42N53'06 85w55'15 5:43:41
South Boardman 40 1 44N38'29 85w16'47 5:41:07
South Branch 65 1 44N28'00 83w53'20 5:35:33
South Butler 12 1 42N01'20 84w53'06 5:39:32
South Camden 30 1 41N47 84w48 5:39:12
South Fairfield 46 1 41N43'43 83w58'38 5:35:55
Southfield 63 88 42N28'24 83w13'19 5:32:53
South Fox Island 45 1 45N25 85w51 5:43:24
Southgate 82 2 42N12'50 83w11'38 5:32:47
South Greenwood 52 25 46N28'23 87w47'11 5:51:09
South Haven 80 93 42N24'11 86w16'25 5:45:06
South Haven Highlands 3 93 42N27'06 86w15'23 5:45:02
South Ionia 34 92 42N58'08 85w04'10 5:40:17
South Jackson 38 90 42N09'37 84w25'40 5:37:43
Southkent 41 61 42N54 85w38 5:42:32
Southland 38 90 42N14 84w24 5:37:36
Southland 46 1 41N43'51 83w46'59 5:35:08
South Lyon 63 88 42N27'38 83w39'06 5:34:36
South Manitou 45 1 45N01 85w45 5:43:00
South Monroe 58 36 41N54 83w25 5:33:40
South Monterey 3 92 42N36'09 85w50'37 5:43:22
South Park 74 1 42N56'34 82w27'23 5:29:50
South Range 31 96 47N04'12 88w38'35 5:54:34
South Riley 19 41 42N51'36 84w39'41 5:38:39
South Rockwood 58 1 42N03'50 83w15'40 5:33:03
South Whitehall 61 64 43N23'54 86w20'54 5:45:24
Spalding 55 81 45N41'45 87w30'39 5:50:03
Sparlingville 74 1 42N57'52 82w31'23 5:30:06
Sparr 69 1 45N02'29 84w34'21 5:38:17
Sparta 41 64 43N09'39 85w42'36 5:42:50
Spaulding 73 6 43N22 83w58 5:35:52
Speaker 76 1 43N12'18 82w48'15 5:31:13
Spencer 40 1 44N38'29 85w06'53 5:40:28
Spencer 41 57 43N15 85w22 5:41:28
Spinks Corners 11 4 42N05'38 86w19'15 5:45:17
Spratt 4 1 45N00'31 83w44'53 5:35:00
Spring Arbor 38 1 42N12'18 84w33'10 5:38:13
Spring Beach 14 73 41N54'26 85w57'30 5:43:50
Springdale 51 1 44N29 86w00 5:44:00
Springer 77 25 45N55'14 86w24'08 5:45:37
Springfield 13 43 42N19'35 85w14'21 5:40:57
Springfield 63 88 42N44'58 83w28'25 5:33:54
Springfield Place 13 43 42N18'30 85w13'09 5:40:53
Spring Grove 3 74 42N30'20 86w10'06 5:44:40
Spring Lake 70 56 43N04'37 86w11'49 5:44:47
Springport 38 1 42N22'42 84w41'55 5:38:48
Springvale 24 67 45N21 84w48 5:39:12
Springville 46 1 42N02'00 84w10'16 5:36:41
Springville 83 1 44N23 85w46 5:43:04
Springwell Heights 16 1 45N26'01 84w41'24 5:38:46
Springwells 82 2 42N19 83w07 5:32:28
Spruce 1 1 44N50'39 83w27'57 5:33:52
Spruce 22 87 45N59'09 87w46'38 5:51:07
Spurr 7 25 46N33 88w12 5:52:48
Stager 36 86 45N59'27 88w20'53 5:53:24
Stalls Corner 23 1 42N38'28 84w53'42 5:39:35
Stalwart 17 12 46N05'53 84w14'19 5:36:57
Stambaugh 36 86 46N04'52 88w37'37 5:54:30
Standale 41 61 42N58'21 85w46'35 5:43:06
Standish 6 1 43N58'59 83w57'32 5:35:50
Stanley 13 43 42N16 85w04 5:40:16
Stanley Corners 13 43 42N13'03 85w08'16 5:40:33
Stannard 66 25 46N36 89w10 5:56:40
Stanton 59 57 43N17'33 85w04'53 5:40:20
Stanwood 54 1 43N34'43 85w26'57 5:41:48
Star 2 30 46N20'50 86w23'32 5:45:34
Star 5 1 45N00 84w55 5:39:40
Star City 57 1 44N22'16 84w59'06 5:39:56
Star Corners 51 1 44N13 85w58 5:43:52
Stark 82 36 42N22'33 83w22'22 5:33:29
Starville 74 1 42N40'52 82w35'16 5:30:21
Steamburg 12 1 41N52'33 84w36'45 5:38:27
Steiner 58 36 41N59'20 83w23'15 5:33:33
Stephenson 55 86 45N24'55 87w36'27 5:50:26
Sterling 6 1 44N02'00 84w01'22 5:36:05

Sterling Heights 50 88 42N34'49 83W01'49 5:32:07
Steuben 77 25 46N11 86W27 5:45:48
Stevensville 11 74 42N00'52 86W31'10 5:46:05
Stickley 27 86 46N18'47 89W23'41 5:57:35
Stillman 2 25 46N20'33 86W45'04 5:47:00
Stirlingville 17 12 46N11'14 84W19'16 5:37:17
Stittsville 57 1 44N27'06 85W04'30 5:40:18
Stockbridge 33 1 42N27'04 84W10'50 5:36:43
Stoneport 71 1 45N17'46 83W25'27 5:33:42
Stoney Corners 57 1 44N11'37 85W17'05 5:41:08
Stoney Point 38 1 42N04'51 84W35'03 5:38:20
Stonington 21 25 45N43'23 86W58'35 5:47:54
Stonington 31 25 46N58'28 88W47'01 5:55:08
Stony Creek 58 36 41N57'51 83W20'03 5:33:20
Stony Creek 63 88 42N41'46 83W06'43 5:32:27
Stony Creek 81 1 42N09'21 83W39'10 5:34:37
Stony Lake 64 64 43N33'35 86W30'00 5:46:00
Stony Point 8 57 42N29'49 85W25'36 5:41:42
Stony Point 58 1 41N56'29 83W15'54 5:33:04
Stoughton Corners 80 74 42N13'46 86W09'59 5:44:40
Strasburg 58 36 41N54'51 83W30'09 5:34:01
Strathmoor 82 2 42N23 83W11 5:32:44
Strawberry Point 70 68 43N04 86W11 5:44:44
Strickland 37 1 43N29'42 84W50'07 5:39:20
Stringtown 12 1 41N53'01 84W50'05 5:39:20
Stronach 51 111 44N12'48 86W16'31 5:45:06
Strongs 17 12 46N21'28 84W58'10 5:39:53
Strongs Corner 17 12 46N20'46 84W58'09 5:39:53
Stuart Lake 13 1 42N16 84W58 5:39:52
Sturgeon Point 1 1 44N39 83W18 5:33:12
Sturgeon River 21 25 45N56 86W58 5:47:52
Sturgis 75 48 41N47'57 85W25'09 5:41:41
Stutsmanville 24 67 45N30'29 85W00'24 5:40:02
Sugar Grove 53 57 44N00'18 86W16'46 5:45:07
Sugar Island 17 12 46N28 84W12 5:36:48
Sugar Loaf 52 25 46N35'21 87W26'42 5:49:47
Sugar Rapids 26 1 44N05'17 84W24'28 5:37:38
Sullivan 61 57 43N11'01 86W03'11 5:44:13
Sullivans Landing 2 80 46N38'55 86W11'47 5:44:47
Sulphur Springs 80 93 42N24'58 86W14'06 5:44:56
Summer Haven 61 49 43N12 86W16 5:45:04
Summer Island 21 25 45N34 86W39 5:46:36
Summerton 29 1 43N27'59 84W43'34 5:38:54
Summit City 28 1 44N33'03 85W30'54 5:42:04
Summit Heights 72 1 44N18 84W45 5:39:00
Sumner 29 1 43N18'25 84W48'57 5:39:16
Sumnerville 14 72 41N54'42 86W12'27 5:44:50
Sumpter 82 36 42N09 83W29 5:33:56
Sun 62 64 43N20 85W49 5:43:16
Sundell 2 25 46N20'50 87W04'47 5:48:19
Sunfield 23 97 42N45'44 84W59'33 5:39:58
Sunnyside 74 1 42N59 82W40 5:30:40
Sunnyside 82 36 42N15'44 83W19'25 5:33:18
Sunrise Heights 13 43 42N18 85W10 5:40:40
Sunrise Landing 2 80 46N31'44 86W05'18 5:44:21
Sunset Beach 38 1 42N05'14 84W12'13 5:36:49
Sunset Beach 77 14 45N57'45 86W18'59 5:45:16
Sunshine Beach 31 96 47N05'20 88W30'56 5:54:04
Superior 31 95 47N04'31 88W35'52 5:54:23
Superior 81 36 42N15'47 83W38'16 5:34:33
Surrey 18 1 43N52 84W54 5:39:36
Suttons Bay 45 1 44N58'36 85W39'02 5:42:36
Swains Lake 38 1 42N10 84W39 5:38:36
Swan Creek 73 1 43N22'47 84W05'28 5:36:22
Swanson 55 81 45N28'29 87W42'31 5:50:50
Swanzy 52 17 46N18'10 87W22'26 5:49:30
Swartz Creek 25 1 42N57'26 83W49'50 5:35:19
Swedetown 31 96 47N14'11 88W27'53 5:53:52
Sweetwater 43 92 43N57 85W59 5:43:56
Sylvan 81 1 42N19 84W01 5:36:04
Sylvan Beach 61 64 43N22'19 86W25'25 5:45:42
Sylvan Center 81 1 42N17'10 84W04'40 5:36:19
Sylvan Lake 63 88 42N36'41 83W19'43 5:33:19
Sylvester 54 1 43N32'23 85W15'16 5:41:01
Tacoma Park 50 88 42N34 83W02 5:32:08
Taffeltown 40 1 44N32'26 85W10'30 5:40:42
Talbot 55 86 45N30'38 87W35'51 5:50:23
Tallmadge 70 51 42N59'33 85W50'03 5:43:20
Tallman 53 57 43N59'05 86W06'44 5:44:27
Tamarack 27 81 46N17'45 89W02'35 5:56:10
Tamarack 31 96 47N14'53 88W28'06 5:53:52
Tamarack Lake 27 81 46N09 88W46 5:55:04
Tapiola 31 96 46N55'29 88W37'35 5:54:30
Tappan 74 1 42N57'58 82W28'58 5:29:56
Tarryton 50 88 42N34 83W02 5:32:08
Tasmas Corners 70 51 42N48'17 86W09'25 5:44:38
Tawas 35 1 44N16'10 83W30'53 5:34:04
Tawas Center 35 1 44N17 83W34 5:34:16
Tawas City 35 1 44N16'10 83W30'53 5:34:04
Taylor 82 2 42N14'27 83W16'11 5:33:05
Taylor Park 39 47 42N18 85W37 5:42:28
Taylor Park 82 2 42N14 83W16 5:33:04
Taymouth 73 1 43N14'34 83W52'26 5:35:30
Teapot Dome 80 46 42N12'39 85W57'58 5:43:52
Tecumseh 46 1 42N00'14 83W56'42 5:35:47
Teeterville 56 1 43N29'42 84W24'59 5:37:40
Tekonsha 13 1 42N05'36 84W59'09 5:39:57
Teleford 82 2 42N19 83W16 5:33:04
Telreka 82 2 42N14 83W16 5:33:04
Temperance 58 1 41N46'45 83W34'08 5:34:17
Temple 18 1 44N01'51 85W01'42 5:40:07
Tent City 72 1 44N30'04 84W49'23 5:39:18
Tesch 21 25 45N45'04 87W17'03 5:49:08
Texas 39 92 42N12 85W42 5:42:48
Texas Corners 39 47 42N12'04 85W41'12 5:42:45
Thayer 27 86 46N19'45 89W27'43 5:57:51
The Finger Board Corner 16 1 45N22 84W30 5:38:00
The Heights 38 1 42N04'57 84W12'10 5:36:49
Theilers 27 86 46N27'49 89W41'55 5:58:48
The Jackpines 35 1 44N27'13 83W47'53 5:35:12
The Mission 17 110 46N24 84W34 5:38:16
Theodore 22 87 46N00'05 87W50'12 5:51:21
Thetford Center 25 1 43N10'45 83W38'25 5:34:34
Thomas 63 88 42N52'46 83W17'50 5:33:11
Thomas 73 1 43N25 84W05 5:36:20
Thomas 79 1 43N42'02 83W32'53 5:34:12
Thomaston 27 81 46N30'59 89W55'38 5:59:43
Thompson 77 25 45N54'18 86W19'49 5:45:19
Thompsonville 10 1 44N31'13 85W56'38 5:43:47
Thornapple 8 57 42N43 85W29 5:41:56
Thornton 74 1 42N55 82W36 5:30:24
Thornville 44 1 42N56'33 83W13'26 5:32:54
Thorton 74 1 42N58'07 82W37'03 5:30:28
Three Churches Corner 9 36 43N40'03 84W00'31 5:36:02
Three Lakes 7 25 46N33'16 88W12'04 5:52:48
Three Mile Lake 80 46 42N13 85W53 5:43:32
Three Oaks 11 107 41N47'55 86W36'38 5:46:27
Three Rivers 75 97 41N56'38 85W37'57 5:42:32
Tift Corner 62 64 43N23'45 85W37'22 5:42:29
Tilden 52 25 46N24 87W40 5:50:40
Timberlost 17 12 46N33'41 85W10'14 5:40:41
Tioga 7 25 46N33'30 88W20'55 5:53:24
Tipton 46 1 42N01'00 84W03'51 5:36:15
Tittabawassee 73 1 43N31 84W07 5:36:28
Titus 54 1 43N40'06 85W06'25 5:40:26
Tobacco 26 1 43N51 84W26 5:37:44
Tobico Beach 9 1 43N40'35 83W54'44 5:35:39
Tobin Location 36 81 46N05'33 88W21'22 5:53:25
Toivola 31 96 46N59'57 88W46'12 5:55:05
Tompkins 38 1 42N22'23 84W32'30 5:38:10
Tonquish 82 36 42N18 83W23 5:33:32
Topaz 66 25 46N34'16 89W28'08 5:57:53
Topinabee 16 1 45N29'02 84W35'43 5:38:23
Toquin 80 74 42N15'27 86W13'23 5:44:54
Torch Lake 5 1 45N04'31 85W21'31 5:41:26
Torch Lake Village 5 1 45N07 85W21 5:41:24
Torch River 40 1 44N51'04 85W19'26 5:41:18
Towar Gardens 33 41 42N44 84W28 5:37:52
Tower 16 1 45N21'19 84W18'02 5:37:12
Tower Hill 11 74 41N53 86W37 5:46:28
Tower Hill Shorelands 11 74 41N54'06 86W36'39 5:46:27
Town Corners 64 64 43N33 86W21 5:45:24
Traunik 2 25 46N15'39 86W58'10 5:47:53
Traverse 42 96 47N15'19 88W15'51 5:53:03
Traverse Bay 31 96 47N11'40 88W14'02 5:52:56
Traverse City 28 1 44N45'47 85W37'14 5:42:29
Tremaine Corners 34 92 42N54'02 85W04'29 5:40:18
Trenary 2 31 46N11'43 86W58'11 5:47:53
Trent 61 64 43N17 85W49 5:43:16
Trenton 82 37 42N08'22 83W10'42 5:32:43
Triangle Park 72 1 44N30 84W36 5:38:24
Trimountain 31 96 47N03'19 88W39'38 5:54:39
Trips 63 88 42N37 83W26 5:33:44
Trist 38 1 42N20'10 84W12'01 5:36:48
Trombly 21 25 46N02'35 87W08'53 5:48:36
Trout Creek 66 28 46N28'56 89W00'42 5:56:03
Trout Lake 17 92 46N11'37 85W01'08 5:40:05
Trowbridge 3 92 42N28 85W50 5:43:20
Trowbridge 16 1 45N13'46 84W35'11 5:38:21
Trowbridge 33 41 42N44 84W28 5:37:52
Trowbridge Park 52 25 46N33'24 87W26'14 5:49:45
Troy 62 57 43N44'35 86W01'09 5:44:05
Troy 63 88 42N36'20 83W09'00 5:32:36
Trufant 59 57 43N18'50 85W21'16 5:41:25
Tula 66 25 46N32'47 89W48'53 5:59:16
Tunis 7 25 46N26'36 88W37'03 5:54:28
Turin 52 11 46N12 87W15 5:49:00
Turk Lake 59 57 43N16'15 85W15'23 5:41:02
Turner 6 1 44N08'33 83W47'56 5:35:09
Turner 22 87 46N07'58 87W54'00 5:51:36
Turners Corner 8 57 42N25'38 85W25'32 5:41:42
Turner Shores 11 74 41N51'37 86W39'35 5:46:38
Turtle 35 1 44N11'27 83W44'33 5:34:58
Tuscarora 16 1 45N25 84W38 5:38:32
Tuscola 79 1 43N19'35 83W39'26 5:34:38
Tustin 67 1 44N06'09 85W27'32 5:41:50
Twelve Corners 11 4 42N08'41 86W22'43 5:45:31
Twin Beach 63 88 42N32 83W27 5:33:48
Twining 6 1 44N06'47 83W48'27 5:35:14
Twin Lake 61 57 43N21'46 86W09'53 5:44:40
Twin Lakes 14 71 41N59 86W07 5:44:28
Twin Lakes 31 25 46N53'50 88W51'03 5:55:24
Two Rivers 37 1 43N37'30 84W57'07 5:39:48
Tyre 76 1 43N40'30 82W53'28 5:31:34
Tyrone Lake 47 1 42N49 83W43 5:34:52
Ubly 32 1 43N42'36 82W55'54 5:31:44
Udell 51 1 44N14'01 86W05'29 5:44:22
Unadilla 47 1 42N25'43 84W03'24 5:36:14
Union 14 72 41N47'10 85W52'04 5:43:28
Union City 13 1 42N04'00 85W08'10 5:40:33
Union Lake 63 88 42N36'53 83W26'49 5:33:47
Union Pier 11 75 41N49'41 86W41'33 5:46:46
Union Plains 78 1 42N49'47 84W00'46 5:36:03
Unionville 79 1 43N39'13 83W27'58 5:33:52
University of Michigan 81 38 42N17 83W44 5:34:56
Updyke 61 57 43N11'10 86W06'23 5:44:26
Upjohn 39 47 42N13 85W35 5:42:20
Urbandale 13 43 42N21'08 85W14'39 5:40:59
Urbandale 33 41 42N41 84W33 5:38:12
Utica 50 88 42N37'34 83W02'01 5:32:08
Vail 2 25 46N20'12 86W46'22 5:47:05
Valley 3 92 42N33 85W58 5:43:52
Valley Center 76 1 43N11'06 82W55'07 5:31:40
Valley Farms 19 41 42N47'03 84W32'34 5:38:10
Valley Island 32 1 43N47'32 83W25'41 5:33:43
Van 24 67 45N35'38 84W46'57 5:39:08
Van Buren 82 36 42N13 83W29 5:33:56
Vandalia 14 76 41N55'01 85W54'53 5:43:40
Vanderbilt 69 1 45N08'34 84W39'37 5:38:38
Vandercook Lake 38 90 42N11'36 84W23'28 5:37:34
Van Dyke 50 2 42N28 83W00 5:32:00
Van Etten Lake 35 1 44N25 83W20 5:33:20
Van Meer 2 25 46N25'10 86W28'11 5:45:53
Van Pelham 82 2 42N17 83W17 5:33:08
Vantown 33 1 42N36'02 84W13'25 5:36:54
Vassar 79 1 43N22'19 83W35'00 5:34:20
Vega 55 81 45N47'09 87W36'11 5:50:25
Venice 78 1 43N00 83W59 5:35:56
Ventnor Manor 50 88 42N34 83W02 5:32:08
Vergennes 41 57 42N59 85W22 5:41:28
Vermilac 7 18 46N31'51 88W27'32 5:53:50
Vermilion 17 12 46N45'45 85W09'00 5:40:36
Vermontville 23 92 42N37'44 85W01'27 5:40:06
Vernon 78 70 42N56'21 84W01'46 5:36:07
Vernon City 37 1 43N50 84W46 5:39:04
Verona 13 43 42N19'49 85W09'20 5:40:37
Verona 27 81 46N28'39 89W59'20 5:59:57
Verona 32 6 43N48'21 82W52'52 5:31:31
Verona Park 13 43 42N21 85W09 5:40:36
Vestaburg 59 57 43N23'57 84W54'20 5:39:37
Veterans Administration Hosp 22 87 45N48 88W04 5:52:16
Vevay 33 1 42N33 84W25 5:37:40
Vick 52 25 46N19'29 87W09'28 5:48:38
Vickery Landing 8 57 42N30'14 85W16'17 5:41:05
Vickeryville 59 57 43N11'32 84W57'55 5:39:52
Vicksburg 39 100 42N07'12 85W31'58 5:42:08
Victor 19 1 42N54 84W25 5:37:40
Victoria 66 25 46N41'57 89W13'46 5:56:55
Victory 53 57 44N02 86W21 5:45:24
Vienna 58 1 41N47'13 83W28'41 5:33:55
Vienna Corners 69 1 44N58'13 84W22'15 5:37:29
Vienna Junction 58 1 41N45'00 83W30'18 5:34:01
Vienna Junction 60 1 44N52'47 84W19'25 5:37:18
Vineland 11 1 42N03'41 86W28'13 5:45:53
Virgil Location 36 84 46N06'28 88W38'11 5:54:33
Virginia Park 70 51 42N46'20 86W10'34 5:44:42
Vogel Center 57 1 44N11'33 85W03'09 5:40:13
Volinia 14 72 42N00'42 85W57'17 5:43:49
Volney 62 57 43N41'58 86W01'11 5:44:05
Vriesland 70 54 42N48'43 85W56'25 5:43:46
Vulcan 22 87 45N46'50 87W51'45 5:51:27
Wabaningo 61 64 43N22'14 86W25'18 5:45:41
Wacousta 19 1 42N49'40 84W42'03 5:38:48
Wadhams 74 1 42N59'14 82W32'19 5:30:09
Wagarville 26 1 44N01'51 84W28'03 5:37:52
Wagner Beach 6 1 44N06'53 83W34'02 5:34:16
Wahjamega 79 1 43N27'20 83W26'23 5:33:46
Wainola 66 25 46N43'49 89W01'53 5:56:08
Wakefield 27 86 46N28'31 89W56'23 5:59:46
Wakelee 14 72 41N59'02 85W52'44 5:43:31
Wakeshma 39 92 42N07 85W21 5:41:24
Waldenburg 50 88 42N39'26 82W56'15 5:31:45
Waldron 30 1 41N43'40 84W25'08 5:37:41
Wales Center 74 1 42N56'31 82W40'42 5:30:43
Walhalla 53 57 43N57'13 86W06'53 5:44:28
Walker 41 61 43N00'05 85W46'05 5:43:04
Walkers Point 49 1 44N48 82W55 5:31:40
Walkerville 64 57 43N42'52 86W07'28 5:44:30
Wallace 1 1 44N31'55 83W39'56 5:34:40
Wallace 55 81 45N19'34 87W36'50 5:50:27
Walled Lake 63 88 42N32'16 83W28'52 5:33:55
Wallin 10 1 44N34'15 85W53'20 5:43:33
Wall Lake 8 57 42N30 85W24 5:41:36
Walloon Lake 15 1 45N15'58 84W56'01 5:39:44
Walnut Lake 63 88 42N32 83W17 5:33:08
Walnut Point 13 1 42N21'01 84W59'07 5:39:56
Walsh 77 25 46N20'44 86W11'03 5:44:44
Walters 63 88 42N45'50 83W20'29 5:33:22
Walton 23 1 42N28 84W54 5:39:36
Walton 28 1 44N31'15 85W23'58 5:41:36
Walton Junction 28 1 44N31'39 85W24'07 5:41:36
Waltz 82 36 42N06'01 83W23'32 5:33:34
Wardcliff 33 41 42N44 84W28 5:37:52
Warner 5 1 45N04 84W54 5:39:36
Warren 50 2 42N28'39 83W01'40 5:32:07
Wasepi 75 103 41N56'27 85W27'42 5:41:51
Washington 50 88 42N43'28 83W02'10 5:32:09
Waterford 63 88 42N42'08 83W24'10 5:33:37
Waterloo 38 1 42N21'11 84W08'25 5:36:34
Watermill Lake 43 92 43N54 85W46 5:43:04
Waters 69 1 44N52'47 84W41'55 5:38:48
Watersmeet 27 86 46N16'04 89W10'40 5:56:43
Watertown 76 1 43N20'28 82W49'42 5:31:19

Watervale 10 1 44N33'13 86W12'52 5:44:51
Watervliet 11 74 42N11'12 86W15'38 5:45:03
Watrousville 79 1 43N27'08 83W31'23 5:34:06
Watson 3 92 42N32'13 85W42'06 5:42:48
Watson 52 25 46N01'09 87W24'52 5:49:39
Wattles Park 13
43 42N18'02 85W06'39 5:40:27
Watton 7 25 46N32'15 88W36'23 5:54:26
Wauban Beach 16 1 45N26'56 84W38'00 5:38:32
Waucedah 22 87 45N45'47 87W44'43 5:50:59
Waukuzoo 70 51 42N47 86W07 5:44:28
Waverland Beach 11
74 41N59'17 86W33'42 5:46:15
Waverly 23 41 42N44 84W36 5:38:24
Waverly 70 53 42N48'07 86W05'14 5:44:21
Wawatam Beach 16
1 45N47 84W44 5:38:56
Wayland 3 92 42N40'26 85W38'41 5:42:35
Wayne 82 36 42N16'53 83W23'11 5:33:33
Weadlock 16 1 45N38 84W47 5:39:08
Weadock 16 1 45N37'17 84W37'51 5:38:31
Weale 32 1 43N48'43 83W23'50 5:33:35
Weare 64 57 43N44'47 86W20'22 5:45:21
Webber 43 92 43N57 85W51 5:43:24
Webberville 33 1 42N40'01 84W10'27 5:36:42
Webster 81 1 42N23'43 83W48'17 5:35:13
Weesaw 11 74 41N52 86W32 5:46:08
Weidman 37 1 43N41'15 84W58'08 5:39:53
Weimer 53 57 44N00'59 86W27'22 5:45:49
Welcome Corner 8
62 42N41'49 85W17'29 5:41:10
Weldon 10 1 44N33'58 86W03'47 5:44:15
Wellington 4 6 45N09 83W49 5:35:16
Wellington 27 86 46N19'51 89W39'25 5:58:38
Wells 21 19 45N46'38 87W04'46 5:48:19
Wellston 51 1 44N13'01 85W57'28 5:43:50
Wellsville 46 1 41N53'04 83W53'08 5:35:33
Wequetonsing 24
67 45N25'41 84W58'03 5:39:52
West Acres 63 1 42N36 83W26 5:33:44
West Bangor 80 74 42N18'28 86W11'12 5:44:45
West Bloomfield 63
88 42N34 83W22 5:33:28
West Branch 65 1 44N16'35 84W14'19 5:36:57
Westchester Heights 19
1 42N55'09 84W22'52 5:37:31
Westchester Village 63
88 43N15 83W48 5:35:12
Western Location 36
82 46N06'05 88W18'51 5:53:15
Westgate 41 61 43N03 85W41 5:42:44
West Gladstone 21
25 45N50'26 87W03'45 5:48:15
West Highland 63
88 42N38'10 83W39'44 5:34:39
West Ishpeming 52
25 46N29'01 87W42'03 5:50:48
West Kinderhook 12
1 41N46'55 85W03'15 5:40:13
Westland 82 36 42N19'27 83W24'01 5:33:36
West Leroy 13 1 42N13'01 85W17'09 5:41:09
West Millbrook 54
57 43N31 85W05 5:40:20
West Novi 63 88 42N33 83W30 5:34:00
West Olive 70 51 42N55'17 86W08'47 5:44:35
Weston 46 1 41N46'13 84W05'52 5:36:23
Westons Iroquois Beach 17
110 46N29'09 84W40'21 5:38:41
Westphalia 19 1 42N55'46 84W47'55 5:39:12
West Plains 61 49 43N12 86W16 5:45:04
West Roodmont 61
49 43N12 86W16 5:45:04
West Sebewa 34 92 42N50'35 85W03'14 5:40:13
West Sumpter 82
36 42N07'21 83W30'34 5:34:02
West Tamarack 31
96 47N15'27 88W28'33 5:53:54
West Tappan 74 1 42N58'13 82W32'36 5:30:10
West Traverse 24
67 45N27 85W01 5:40:04
Westville 59 57 43N21'28 85W05'01 5:40:20
West Willow 81 36 42N15 83W37 5:34:28
West Windsor 23 1 42N38'50 84W41'50 5:38:47
Westwood 39 47 42N18'10 85W38'01 5:42:32
Westwood 40 1 44N51'06 85W06'07 5:40:24
Westwood 61 49 43N12 86W16 5:45:04
Wetmore 2 22 46N22'47 86W37'13 5:46:29
Wetmore Landing 52
25 46N37'00 87W27'54 5:49:52
Wetzel 5 1 44N55'53 85W01'49 5:40:07
Wexford 83 1 44N28 85W46 5:43:04
Wexford Corner 28
1 44N30'46 85W41'46 5:42:47
Whaley Drain 23 1 42N39'12 84W40'35 5:38:42
Wheatfield 33 1 42N39 84W18 5:37:12
Wheatland 30 1 41N58'16 84W24'04 5:37:36
Wheeler 29 1 43N24'46 84W26'16 5:37:45
White 31 25 46N46'01 88W49'37 5:55:18
White City 27 81 46N24'41 89W32'13 5:58:09
White City 31 96 46N58'56 88W25'30 5:53:42
White Cloud 64 64 43N33'01 85W46'19 5:43:05
Whitefish 17 12 46N35 85W07 5:40:28
Whitefish Point 17
12 46N45'57 84W57'55 5:39:52
Whiteford Center 58
1 41N46'36 83W40'59 5:34:44
Whitehall 61 64 43N24'36 86W20'55 5:45:24
Whitehouse Landing 17
12 46N33'07 85W10'18 5:40:41
White Lake 63 88 42N41'30 83W33'15 5:34:13
White Lake Center 63
88 42N37 83W26 5:33:44
White Oak 33 1 42N31'27 84W11'27 5:36:46
White Pigeon 75 1 41N47'53 85W38'36 5:42:34
White Pine 66 25 46N45'14 89W35'02 5:58:20
White River 61 57 43N26 86W25 5:45:40
White Rock 32 1 43N42'36 82W36'35 5:30:26
White Rock 35 1 44N15'09 83W41'02 5:34:44
Whites Beach 6 1 43N55'46 83W53'28 5:35:34
Whites Landing 69
1 44N54'26 84W34'21 5:38:17
White Star 26 1 43N58'50 84W21'57 5:37:28
Whitestone Point 6
1 44N06'31 83W33'57 5:34:16
Whitewater 28 1 44N47 85W23 5:41:32
Whitmore Lake 47
1 42N26'22 83W44'38 5:34:59
Whitney 6 6 44N07 83W37 5:34:28
Whitney 55 81 45N49'20 87W23'16 5:49:33
Whitneyville 41
64 42N52'18 85W27'32 5:41:50
Whittaker 81 1 42N07'41 83W35'59 5:34:24
Whittemore 35 1 44N14'01 83W48'11 5:35:13
Wic-a-te-wah 51 1 44N21'21 86W13'26 5:44:54
Wickware 76 1 43N36'18 83W02'14 5:32:09
Wico 27 81 46N27'57 89W57'48 5:59:51
Wilber 35 1 44N23'23 83W29'16 5:33:57
Wilcox 62 64 43N36 85W45 5:43:00
Wilder Center 41
61 43N01'47 85W43'50 5:42:55
Wildwood 15 1 45N15'55 85W00'08 5:40:01
Wildwood 16 67 45N21'47 84W42'39 5:38:51
Wildwood 20 1 44N41'05 84W32'47 5:38:11
Wildwood 51 1 44N25 86W11 5:44:44
Wildwood 61 49 43N12 86W16 5:45:04
Wildwood 80 93 42N21'59 86W17'41 5:45:11
Wiley 53 57 43N51'40 86W16'44 5:45:07
Willard 9 1 43N40'06 84W06'30 5:36:26
Williams 9 1 43N37 84W08 5:36:32
Williamsburg 28 1 44N46'25 85W24'14 5:41:37
Williams Crossing 2
25 46N26'25 86W26'21 5:45:45
Williams Landing 2
22 46N27'04 86W40'15 5:46:41
Williamston 33 1 42N41'20 84W16'59 5:37:08
Williamsville 14
76 41N52'00 85W51'51 5:43:27
Williamsville 47
1 42N26'20 84W05'48 5:36:23
Willis 81 36 42N09'30 83W33'29 5:34:14
Willow 82 36 42N06'55 83W23'44 5:33:35
Willow Run 81 36 42N15'15 83W34'50 5:34:19
Willwalk 17 45 46N29 84W21 5:37:24
Wilmot 16 1 45N15 84W40 5:38:40
Wilmot 79 1 43N27'50 83W11'25 5:32:46
Wilson 55 81 45N42'19 87W26'17 5:49:45
Winchester Village 25
1 42N59 83W47 5:35:08
Winde 21 25 45N58'07 87W05'49 5:48:23
Windemere 33 41 42N44 84W36 5:38:24
Windiate 63 88 42N42 83W24 5:33:36
Windigo 42 25 47N54'43 89W09'24 5:56:38
Windmill Island 70
51 42N47 86W07 5:44:28
Windsor 23 1 42N38 84W40 5:38:40
Winegars 26 1 43N56'41 84W21'57 5:37:28
Winfield 59 57 43N25 85W23 5:41:32
Wing Lake Shores 63
88 42N32 83W17 5:33:08
Winn 37 1 43N31'24 84W54'06 5:39:36
Winona 31 25 46N52'28 88W54'26 5:55:38
Winsor 32 1 43N48 83W18 5:33:12
Winterfield 18 1 44N07 85W02 5:40:08
Winters 2 25 46N10 86W58 5:47:52
Winthrop Junction 52
25 46N28'34 87W41'13 5:50:45
Wise 37 1 43N43'42 84W38'50 5:38:35
Wisner 79 1 43N36'59 83W35'03 5:34:20
Witbeck 52 25 46N18'55 88W00'15 5:52:01
Witch Lake 52 25 46N16'32 88W01'08 5:52:05
Wixom 63 88 42N31'29 83W32'11 5:34:09
Wobic 52 29 46N30'10 87W57'10 5:51:49
Wojciechowski 9
36 43N36 83W54 5:35:36
Wolcott Mills 50
88 42N46'08 82W55'37 5:31:42
Wolf Crossing 78
1 43N02'34 84W14'44 5:36:59
Wolf Lake 38 90 42N15 84W24 5:37:36
Wolf Lake 43 92 43N54 85W51 5:43:24
Wolf Lake 61 57 43N15'17 86W06'35 5:44:26
Wolverine 16 1 45N16'24 84W36'16 5:38:25
Wolverine 31 96 47N16'11 88W25'10 5:53:41
Wolverine Lake 63
88 42N33'24 83W28'26 5:33:54
Woodard Lake 34
92 43N09 85W05 5:40:20
Woodbridge 30 1 41N47 84W39 5:38:36
Woodbury 23 57 42N45'40 85W04'28 5:40:18
Wood Creek Farms 63
88 42N30'28 83W19'44 5:33:19
Wooden Shoe Village 26
1 43N58'44 84W21'22 5:37:25
Woodhaven 82 36 42N08'20 83W14'30 5:32:58
Woodhull 78 1 42N49 84W19 5:37:16
Woodland 8 57 42N43'36 85W08'01 5:40:32
Woodland Beach 58
1 41N56'24 83W18'48 5:33:15
Woodland Beach 80
72 42N04'55 86W11'30 5:44:46
Woodland Park 64
57 43N42'53 85W51'41 5:43:27
Woodlawn 21 25 45N56'40 87W18'01 5:49:12
Woodlawn Beach 8
92 42N25'19 85W25'03 5:41:40
Woods 37 1 43N45'20 84W53'18 5:39:33
Woods Corner 37 1 43N50 84W52 5:39:28
Woods Corners 34
92 43N04'34 85W04'30 5:40:18
Woodside 31 96 47N07 88W31 5:54:04
Wood Spur 66 25 46N52 89W18 5:57:12
Woodstock 46 1 42N02 84W18 5:37:12
Woodville 9 1 43N52'02 84W01'31 5:36:06
Woodville 38 90 42N15'31 84W29'01 5:37:56
Woodville 62 64 43N39'57 85W40'52 5:42:43
Wooster 64 57 43N30'38 85W52'26 5:43:30
Worden 81 38 42N23'16 83W38'42 5:34:35
Worth 6 1 43N55'31 83W57'56 5:35:52
Worth 76 1 43N13 82W33 5:30:12
Wright 70 51 43N06'39 85W48'31 5:43:14
Wrights Corners 13
1 42N12'13 84W57'43 5:39:51
Wurtsmith Air Force Base 35
1 44N27 83W24 5:33:36
Wyandotte 31 25 46N53'24 88W52'31 5:55:30
Wyandotte 82 2 42N12'51 83W09'00 5:32:36
Wyman 59 57 43N27'18 85W02'35 5:40:10
Wyoming 41 61 42N54'48 85W42'19 5:42:49
Wyoming Park 41
61 42N55 85W42 5:42:48
Yale 27 81 46N28'00 90W03'47 6:00:15
Yale 74 1 43N07'48 82W47'54 5:31:12
Yalmar 52 25 46N24'22 87W14'28 5:48:58
Yankee Springs 8
57 42N39 85W30 5:42:00
Yargerville 58 1 41N50'18 83W31'55 5:34:08
Yates 43 92 43N52 85W47 5:43:08
Yates 63 88 42N40'25 83W05'45 5:32:23
Yellow Jacket 31
96 47N15 88W27 5:53:48
York 81 1 42N08 83W43 5:34:52
Yorkville 39 92 42N22'31 85W24'06 5:41:36
Ypsilanti 81 36 42N14'28 83W36'47 5:34:27
Yuba 28 1 44N49'24 85W27'33 5:41:50
Yuma 83 1 44N20'48 85W45'17 5:43:01
Zeba 7 25 46N48'09 88W24'52 5:53:39
Zeeland 70 54 42N48'45 86W01'07 5:44:04
Zenith Heights 15
1 45N18'22 85W02'08 5:40:09
Zilwaukee 73 91 43N28'35 83W55'14 5:35:41
Zutphen 70 54 42N49'33 85W52'55 5:43:32

TIME TABLES

MN # 1

Date	Time	Zone
Before 2/26/1901		LMT
2/26/1901	12:00	CST
3/31/1918	02:00	CWT
10/27/1918	02:00	CST
3/30/1919	02:00	CWT
10/26/1919	02:00	CST
2/09/1942	02:00	CWT
9/30/1945	02:00	CST
4/28/1957	02:00	CDT
9/29/1957	02:00	CST
4/27/1958	02:00	CDT
9/02/1958	02:00	CST
5/24/1959	02:00	CDT
9/08/1959	02:00	CST
5/22/1960	02:00	CDT
9/06/1960	02:00	CST
5/28/1961	02:00	CDT
9/05/1961	02:00	CST
5/27/1962	02:00	CDT
9/04/1962	02:00	CST
5/26/1963	02:00	CDT
9/03/1963	02:00	CST
5/24/1964	02:00	CDT
9/08/1964	02:00	CST
5/23/1965	02:00	CDT
9/07/1965	02:00	CST
4/24/1966	02:00	US#1

MN # 2

Date	Time	Zone
Before 2/26/1901		LMT
2/26/1901	12:00	CST
3/31/1918	02:00	CWT
10/27/1918	02:00	CST
3/30/1919	02:00	CWT
10/26/1919	02:00	CST
4/24/1932	02:00	CDT
9/06/1932	02:00	CST
4/28/1946	02:00	CDT
9/29/1946	02:00	CST
4/28/1957	02:00	CDT
9/29/1957	02:00	CST
4/27/1958	02:00	CDT
9/02/1958	02:00	CST
4/26/1959	02:00	CDT
9/27/1959	02:00	CST
5/22/1960	02:00	CDT
9/06/1960	02:00	CST
5/28/1961	02:00	CDT
9/05/1961	02:00	CST
5/27/1962	02:00	CDT
9/04/1962	02:00	CST
5/26/1963	02:00	CDT
9/03/1963	02:00	CST
5/24/1964	02:00	CDT
9/08/1964	02:00	CST
4/25/1965	02:00	CDT
10/31/1965	02:00	CST
4/24/1966	02:00	US#1

MN # 3

Date	Time	Zone
Before 2/26/1901		LMT
2/26/1901	12:00	CST
3/31/1918	02:00	CWT
10/27/1918	02:00	CST
3/30/1919	02:00	CWT
10/26/1919	02:00	CST
2/09/1942	02:00	CWT
9/30/1945	02:00	CST
4/28/1957	02:00	CDT
9/29/1957	02:00	CST
4/27/1958	02:00	CDT
9/02/1958	02:00	CST
4/26/1959	02:00	CDT
9/27/1959	02:00	CST
5/22/1960	02:00	CDT
9/06/1960	02:00	CST
5/28/1961	02:00	CDT
9/05/1961	02:00	CST
5/27/1962	02:00	CDT
9/04/1962	02:00	CST
5/26/1963	02:00	CDT
9/03/1963	02:00	CST
5/24/1964	02:00	CDT
9/08/1964	02:00	CST
5/23/1965	02:00	CDT
9/07/1965	02:00	CST
4/24/1966	02:00	US#1

MN # 4

Date	Time	Zone
Before 2/26/1901		LMT
2/26/1901	12:00	CST
3/31/1918	02:00	CWT
10/27/1918	02:00	CST
3/30/1919	02:00	CWT
10/26/1919	02:00	CST
2/09/1942	02:00	CWT
9/30/1945	02:00	CST
4/28/1957	02:00	CDT
9/29/1957	02:00	CST
4/27/1958	02:00	CDT
9/02/1958	02:00	CST
4/26/1959	02:00	CDT
10/25/1959	02:00	CST
5/22/1960	02:00	CDT
9/06/1960	02:00	CST
5/28/1961	02:00	CDT
9/05/1961	02:00	CST
5/27/1962	02:00	CDT
9/04/1962	02:00	CST
5/26/1963	02:00	CDT
9/03/1963	02:00	CST
5/24/1964	02:00	CDT
9/08/1964	02:00	CST
5/23/1965	02:00	CDT
9/07/1965	02:00	CST
4/24/1966	02:00	US#1

MN # 5

Date	Time	Zone
Before 2/26/1901		LMT
2/26/1901	12:00	CST
3/31/1918	02:00	CWT
10/27/1918	02:00	CST
3/30/1919	02:00	CWT
10/26/1919	02:00	CST
2/09/1942	02:00	CWT
9/30/1945	02:00	CST
4/28/1957	02:00	CDT
9/29/1957	02:00	CST
4/27/1958	02:00	CDT
9/02/1958	02:00	CST
5/24/1959	02:00	CDT
9/08/1959	02:00	CST
5/22/1960	02:00	CDT
9/06/1960	02:00	CST
5/28/1961	02:00	CDT
9/05/1961	02:00	CST
5/27/1962	02:00	CDT
9/04/1962	02:00	CST
5/26/1963	02:00	CDT
9/03/1963	02:00	CST
5/24/1964	02:00	CDT
9/08/1964	02:00	CST
5/09/1965	02:00	CDT
10/31/1965	02:00	CST
4/24/1966	02:00	US#1

MN # 6

Date	Time	Zone
Before 2/26/1901		LMT
2/26/1901	12:00	CST
3/31/1918	02:00	CWT
10/27/1918	02:00	CST
3/30/1919	02:00	CWT
10/26/1919	02:00	CST
2/09/1942	02:00	CWT
9/30/1945	02:00	CST
4/28/1957	02:00	CDT
9/29/1957	02:00	CST
4/27/1958	02:00	CDT
9/02/1958	02:00	CST
5/24/1959	02:00	CDT
9/08/1959	02:00	CST
5/22/1960	02:00	CDT
9/06/1960	02:00	CST
5/28/1961	02:00	CDT
9/05/1961	02:00	CST
5/27/1962	02:00	CDT
9/04/1962	02:00	CST
5/26/1963	02:00	CDT
9/03/1963	02:00	CST
5/24/1964	02:00	CDT
9/08/1964	02:00	CST
4/25/1965	02:00	CDT
10/31/1965	02:00	CST
4/24/1966	02:00	US#1

MN # 7

Date	Time	Zone
Before 2/26/1901		LMT
2/26/1901	12:00	CST
3/31/1918	02:00	CWT
10/27/1918	02:00	CST
3/30/1919	02:00	CWT
10/26/1919	02:00	CST
2/09/1942	02:00	CWT
9/30/1945	02:00	CST
4/28/1957	02:00	CDT
9/29/1957	02:00	CST
4/27/1958	02:00	CDT
9/02/1958	02:00	CST
4/26/1959	02:00	CDT
9/27/1959	02:00	CST
5/22/1960	02:00	CDT
9/06/1960	02:00	CST
5/28/1961	02:00	CDT
9/05/1961	02:00	CST
5/27/1962	02:00	CDT
9/04/1962	02:00	CST
5/26/1963	02:00	CDT
9/03/1963	02:00	CST
5/24/1964	02:00	CDT
9/08/1964	02:00	CST
4/25/1965	02:00	CDT
10/31/1965	02:00	CST
4/24/1966	02:00	US#1

COUNTIES

1 Aitkin
2 Anoka
3 Becker
4 Beltrami
5 Benton
6 Big Stone
7 Blue Earth
8 Brown
9 Carlton
10 Carver
11 Cass
12 Chippewa
13 Chisago
14 Clay
15 Clearwater
16 Cook
17 Cottonwood
18 Crow Wing
19 Dakota
20 Dodge
21 Douglas
22 Faribault
23 Fillmore
24 Freeborn
25 Goodhue
26 Grant
27 Hennepin
28 Houston
29 Hubbard
30 Isanti
31 Itasca
32 Jackson
33 Kanabec
34 Kandiyohi
35 Kittson
36 Koochiching
37 Lac Qui Parle
38 Lake
39 Lake of the Woods
40 Le Sueur
41 Lincoln
42 Lyon
43 McLeod
44 Mahnomen
45 Marshall
46 Martin
47 Meeker
48 Mille Lacs
49 Morrison
50 Mower
51 Murray
52 Nicollet
53 Nobles
54 Norman
55 Olmsted
56 Otter Tail
57 Pennington
58 Pine
59 Pipestone
60 Polk
61 Pope
62 Ramsey
63 Red Lake
64 Redwood
65 Renville
66 Rice
67 Rock
68 Roseau
69 St Louis
70 Scott
71 Sherburne
72 Sibley
73 Stearns
74 Steele
75 Stevens
76 Swift
77 Todd
78 Traverse
79 Wabasha
80 Wadena
81 Waseca
82 Washington
83 Watonwan
84 Wilkin
85 Winona
86 Wright
87 Yellow Medicine

Place		Lat	Long	Time
Aastad 56	1	46N09	96W05	6:24:20
Acoma 43	1	44N56	94W26	6:17:44
Acton 47	1	45N05'03	94W39'38	6:18:39
Ada 9	1	47N17'59	96W30'54	6:26:04
Adams 50	1	43N33'55	92W43'09	6:10:53
Adolph 69	1	46N46'43	92W16'48	6:09:07
Adrian 53	1	43N38'06	95W55'57	6:23:44
Aetna 59	1	44N09	96W07	6:24:28
Afton 82	1	44N54'10	92W47'00	6:11:08
Agassiz 37	1	45N12	96W17	6:25:08
Agder 45	1	48N13	96W03	6:24:12
Agram 49	1	45N57	94W10	6:16:40
Airlie 59	1	44N01'12	96W26'16	6:25:45
Aitkin 1	1	46N31'59	93W42'36	6:14:50
Akeley 29	1	47N00'15	94W43'36	6:18:54
Alango 69	1	47N46	92W45	6:11:00
Alaska 4	1	47N47	95W04	6:20:16
Alba 32	1	43N43	95W24	6:21:36
Albany 73	1	45N37'48	94W34'11	6:18:17
Alberta 75	1	45N34'24	96W02'50	6:24:11
Albert Lea 24	1	43N38'53	93W22'05	6:13:28
Albertville 86	1	45N14'16	93W39'15	6:14:37
Albin 8	1	44N09	94W41	6:18:44
Albion Center 86	1	45N10'37	94W04'24	6:16:18
Alborn 69	1	46N58'23	92W34'33	6:10:18
Albright 86	1	45N07'46	94W06'51	6:16:27
Alden 24	1	43N40'13	93W34'33	6:14:18
Alder 31	1	47N33'42	93W42'13	6:14:49
Aldrich 80	1	46N22'35	94W56'11	6:19:45
Alexandria 21	1	45N53'07	95W22'38	6:21:31
Alford 9	1	46N37'55	92W23'00	6:09:32
Alfsborg 72	1	44N30	94W19	6:17:16
Alger 38	1	47N08'50	91W41'33	6:06:46
Alida 15	1	47N23'01	95W14'04	6:20:56
Allen (Allen Junction Sta) 69	1	47N30'59	92W05'55	6:08:24
Alliance 14	1	46N41	96W36	6:26:24
Alma 45	1	48N20	96W42	6:26:48
Alma City 81	1	44N01'21	93W43'40	6:14:55
Almelund 13	1	45N29'29	92W47'07	6:11:08
Almond 6	1	45N28	96W25	6:25:40
Almora 56	1	46N14'47	95W21'55	6:21:28
Alpha 32	1	43N38'20	94W52'14	6:19:29
Alta Vista 41	1	44N35	96W09	6:24:36
Alton 81	1	44N04	93W42	6:14:48
Altona 59	1	44N09	96W23	6:25:32
Altura 85	1	44N04'18	91W56'22	6:07:45
Alvarado 45	1	48N11'39	96W59'45	6:27:59
Alvwood 31	1	47N43'50	94W16'04	6:17:04
Amador 13	1	45N31	92W46	6:11:04
Amboy 7	1	43N53'17	94W09'23	6:16:38
Amherst 23	1	43N36'31	91W53'41	6:07:35
Amiret 42	1	44N19'00	95W41'48	6:22:47
Amo 17	1	43N59	95W16	6:21:04
Amor 56	1	46N24'45	95W44'42	6:22:59
Andersons Crossing Campgroun 80	1	46N41'57	94W52'55	6:19:32
Andover 2	3	45N14'00	93W17'28	6:13:10
Andover 60	1	47N44	96W41	6:26:44
Andrea 84	1	46N20	96W21	6:25:24
Andree 30	1	45N43'42	93W13'25	6:12:54
Andrusia 4	1	47N29'10	94W39'49	6:18:39
Andyville 50	1	43N43'26	92W59'22	6:11:57
Angle Inlet 39	1	49N20'43	95W03'45	6:20:15
Anglim 60	1	47N47'42	96W35'51	6:26:23
Angora 69	1	47N46'30	92W38'02	6:10:32
Angus 60	1	48N04'52	96W42'10	6:26:49
Ann 17	1	44N09	95W24	6:21:36
Annandale 86	1	45N15'46	94W07'27	6:16:30
Ann Lake 33	1	45N56	93W26	6:13:44
Anoka 2	1	45N11'52	93W23'13	6:13:33
Ansel 11	1	46N38	94W42	6:18:48
Anthony 54	1	47N20'46	96W39'57	6:26:40
Antlers Park 19	1	44N39'47	93W15'55	6:13:04
Antrim 83	1	43N53	94W26	6:17:44
Appleton 76	1	45N11'49	96W01'10	6:24:05
Apple Valley 19	1	44N43'55	93W13'03	6:12:52
Arago 29	1	47N03'04	95W09'41	6:20:39
Arbo 31	1	47N20	93W31	6:14:04
Arbutus 69	1	48N18'25	93W02'51	6:12:11
Arco 41	1	44N23'01	96W11'00	6:24:44
Arcola 82	5	45N07'24	92W45'59	6:11:04
Arctander 34	1	45N17	95W12	6:20:48
Arcturus 31	1	47N19	93W24	6:13:36
Arden Hills 62	3	45N03'01	93W09'23	6:12:38
Ardenhurst 31	1	47N48	94W13	6:16:52
Arena 37	1	45N01	96W17	6:25:08
Arendahl 23	1	43N49'31	91W54'34	6:07:38
Argonne 19	1	44N41'45	93W17'08	6:13:09
Argyle 45	1	48N19'58	96W49'14	6:27:17
Arlberg 69	1	46N55'24	92W36'50	6:10:27
Arlington 72	1	44N36'30	94W04'49	6:16:19
Arlone 58	1	45N56	92W45	6:11:00
Armour Number Two Mine 18	1	46N29'06	93W58'06	6:15:52
Armstrong 24	1	43N39'53	93W28'04	6:13:52
Armstrong 27	1	45N00'41	93W41'12	6:14:45
Arna 58	1	46N06	92W19	6:09:16
Arnesen 39	1	48N57'27	95W04'02	6:20:16
Arnold 69	1	46N52'49	92W05'25	6:08:22
Arrowhead 69	1	46N51	92W44	6:10:56
Arthyde 1	1	46N21'22	93W05'21	6:12:21
Artichoke 6	1	45N23'57	96W09'26	6:24:38
Artichoke Lake 6	1	45N14	96W10	6:24:40
Arveson 35	1	48N35	96W27	6:25:48
Asbury 12	1	44N52'44	95W32'01	6:22:08
Ashby 21	1	46N05'35	95W49'02	6:23:16
Ash Creek 67	1	43N32'18	96W11'38	6:24:47
Ash Lake 41	1	44N25	96W16	6:25:04
Ash Lake 69	1	48N13'08	92W54'57	6:11:40
Ashland 20	1	43N59	92W52	6:11:28
Ashley 73	1	45N43	95W05	6:20:20
Askov 58	1	46N11'12	92W46'56	6:11:08
Aspelund 25	1	44N16	92W59	6:11:56
Assumption 72	1	44N41'17	93W53'19	6:15:33
Athens 30	1	45N27	93W18	6:13:12
Atherton 84	1	46N35	96W28	6:25:52
Atkinson 9	1	46N36'44	92W33'55	6:10:16
Atlanta 3	1	47N01	96W08	6:24:32
Atwater 34	1	45N08'20	94W46'40	6:19:07
Atwood 27	3	44N51'47	93W21'49	6:13:27
Audubon 3	1	46N51'48	95W58'53	6:23:56
Augsburg 45	1	48N30	96W43	6:26:52
Augusta 10	1	44N48'18	93W41'16	6:14:45
Augusta 37	1	45N01	96W24	6:25:36
Ault 69	1	47N15	91W54	6:07:36
Aurdal 56	1	46N20	95W58	6:23:52
Aure 4	1	47N40'24	95W07'13	6:20:29
Aurora 69	1	47N31'48	92W14'13	6:08:57
Austin 50	1	43N40'00	92W58'28	6:11:54
Austin Acres 50	1	43N39'08	93W00'04	6:12:00
Auto Club 27	3	44N50	93W16	6:13:04
Automba 9	1	46N31'15	93W01'06	6:12:04
Averill 14	1	46N58'15	96W32'49	6:26:11
Avoca 51	1	43N56'55	95W38'43	6:22:35
Avon 73	1	45N36'33	94W27'05	6:17:48
Babbitt 69	1	47N42'31	91W56'40	6:07:47
Backus 11	1	46N49'13	94W30'58	6:18:04
Baden 69	1	47N00'37	92W35'18	6:10:21
Baden 70	1	44N42'51	93W35'17	6:14:21
Badger 68	1	48N46'57	96W00'51	6:24:03
Badoura 29	1	46N51'44	94W45'57	6:19:04
Bagley 15	1	47N31'18	95W23'53	6:21:36
Bailey 71	1	45N19'01	93W39'54	6:14:40
Bain 1	1	46N47'27	93W35'22	6:14:21
Baker 14	1	46N42'47	96W33'06	6:26:12
Balaton 42	1	44N14'00	95W52'19	6:23:29
Bald Eagle 62	1	45N06'07	93W00'49	6:12:03
Bald Eagle Center (Bemidji S 11	1	47N24'04	94W25'07	6:17:40
Baldwin 71	1	45N31	93W35	6:14:20

Balkan 69 1 47N32 92w52 6:11:28
Ball Bluff 1 1 46N57'17 93w16'23 6:13:06
Ball Club 31 1 47N19'33 93w56'09 6:15:45
Balmoral 56 1 46N17 95w43 6:22:52
Balsam 1 1 46N46'52 93w09'21 6:12:37
Bancroft 24 1 43N42'06 93w21'18 6:13:25
Bandon 65 1 44N35 94w48 6:19:12
Bangor 61 1 45N33 95w11 6:20:44
Banning 58 1 46N09'38 92w51'06 6:11:24
Baptism Crossing 38 1 47N31'47 91w20'28 6:05:22
Barber 22 1 43N43 93w57 6:15:48
Barclay 11 1 46N46 94w22 6:17:28
Barden 70 1 44N47'26 93w24'37 6:13:38
Barnesville 14 1 46N39'08 96w25'10 6:25:41
Barnett 68 1 48N40 96w04 6:24:16
Barnum 9 1 46N30'11 92w41'18 6:10:45
Baroda 22 1 43N43'15 93w40'29 6:14:42
Barr 25 1 44N18 92w40 6:10:40
Barrett 26 1 45N54'38 95w53'24 6:23:34
Barrows 18 1 46N18'04 94w15'13 6:17:01
Barry 6 1 45N33'29 96w33'32 6:26:14
Barsness 61 1 45N32 95w26 6:21:44
Bartlett 69 1 46N54'45 92w20'28 6:09:22
Bartlett 77 1 46N19 94w58 6:19:52
Barto 68 1 48N46 96w13 6:24:52
Bashaw 8 1 44N10 94w56 6:19:44
Bass Brook 31 1 47N14 93w39 6:14:36
Bassett 69 1 47N28 91w54 6:07:36
Basswood 56 1 46N27'20 95w41'35 6:22:46
Basswood Grove 82 1 44N49'38 92w47'57 6:11:12
Bath 24 1 43N49'32 93w23'23 6:13:34
Battle 4 1 47N59 94w42 6:18:48
Battle Lake 56 1 46N16'50 95w42'48 6:22:51
Battle Plain 67 1 43N48 96w07 6:24:28
Battle River 4 1 47N46 94w29 6:17:56
Baudette 39 1 48N42'45 94w35'59 6:18:24
Baxter 18 1 46N20'36 94w17'11 6:17:09
Bay Lake 18 1 46N24'34 93w52'25 6:15:30
Bayport 82 5 45N01'17 92w46'51 6:11:07
Baytown 82 1 45N01 92w48 6:11:12
Bayview 48 1 46N07'08 93w36'11 6:14:25
Bayview 69 2 46N44'50 92w11'43 6:08:47
Bear Creek 15 1 47N22 95w14 6:20:56
Beardsley 6 1 45N33'30 96w42'43 6:26:51
Bear Park 54 1 47N27 96w08 6:24:32
Bear River 69 1 47N46'40 93w04'58 6:12:20
Bear Valley 79 1 44N18'12 92w28'38 6:09:55
Bearville 31 1 47N44 93w09 6:12:36
Beatty 69 1 47N59 92w38 6:10:32
Beauford 7 1 44N00'27 93w57'30 6:15:50
Beaulieu 44 1 47N20'08 95w48'15 6:23:13
Beaver 85 1 44N09'12 92w00'44 6:08:03
Beaver Bay 38 1 47N15'28 91w18'01 6:05:12
Beaver Creek 67 1 43N36'51 96w21'51 6:25:27
Beaver Crossing 38 1 47N14'32 91w31'29 6:06:06
Beaver Falls 65 1 44N34'59 95w02'49 6:20:11
Bechyn 65 1 44N39'02 95w04'33 6:20:18
Becida 29 1 47N21'15 95w04'51 6:20:19
Becker 71 1 45N23'36 93w52'36 6:15:30
Beckville 47 1 45N02'40 94w33'49 6:18:15
Bee 28 1 43N30'04 91w34'14 6:06:17
Bejou 44 1 47N26'29 95w58'33 6:23:54
Belden 58 1 46N19'20 92w18'47 6:09:15
Belfast 51 1 43N54 95w31 6:22:04
Belgium 60 1 47N59 96w33 6:26:12
Belgrade 69 1 47N31'52 92w22'26 6:09:30
Belgrade 73 1 45N27'11 95w00'15 6:20:01
Bellaire 62 3 45N04'11 92w59'40 6:11:59
Bellechester 25 1 44N22'06 92w30'40 6:10:03
Belle Creek 25 1 44N26'18 92w46'14 6:11:05
Belle Plaine 70 1 44N37'22 93w46'06 6:15:04
Belle Prairie 49 1 46N02'02 94w20'14 6:17:21
Belle River 21 1 45N59'28 95w13'43 6:20:55
Bellevue 49 1 45N52 94w17 6:17:08
Bellingham 37 1 45N08'10 96w17'14 6:25:09
Belmont 32 1 43N43 95w05 6:20:20
Beltrami 60 1 47N32'33 96w31'48 6:26:07
Belvidere 25 1 44N25 92w28 6:09:52
Belvidere Mills 25 1 44N27'09 92w30'33 6:10:02
Belview 64 1 44N36'19 95w19'45 6:21:19
Bemidji 4 1 47N28'25 94w52'48 6:19:31
Bena 11 1 47N20'27 94w12'25 6:16:50
Benedict 29 1 47N09'29 94w41'25 6:18:46
Bengal 31 1 47N16'06 93w03'57 6:12:16
Ben Linn Landing 36 1 48N15'02 93w53'07 6:15:32
Bennett 31 1 47N24'58 93w05'05 6:12:20
Bennettville 1 1 46N24'07 93w44'55 6:15:00
Benning 7 1 44N12'12 93w59'41 6:15:59
Bennington 50 1 43N38 92w30 6:10:00
Benoit 60 1 47N42'06 96w23'40 6:25:35
Benson 76 1 45N18'54 95w35'59 6:22:24
Benton 10 1 44N46'34 93w46'51 6:15:07
Benville 4 1 48N19 95w33 6:22:12
Ben Wade 61 1 45N45 95w37 6:22:28
Bergen 32 1 43N47'24 94w59'40 6:19:59
Bergville 31 1 47N47'15 94w15'51 6:17:03
Berlin 74 1 43N54 93w21 6:13:24
Bernadotte 52 1 44N27'19 94w18'03 6:17:12
Berne 20 1 44N09'49 92w46'45 6:11:07
Berner 15 1 47N48'16 95w28'22 6:21:53
Berning Mill 27 1 45N12'25 93w37'27 6:14:30
Beroun 58 1 45N54'37 92w57'18 6:11:49
Bertha 77 1 46N16'00 95w03'45 6:20:15
Beseman 9 1 46N43 93w00 6:12:00
Bethany 85 1 44N01'27 91w54'41 6:07:39
Bethel 2 1 45N24'14 93w16'03 6:13:04
Beulah 11 1 46N50 93w52 6:15:28
Big Bear Landing 15 1 47N20'12 95w28'36 6:21:54
Big Bend City 12 1 45N08'35 95w46'18 6:23:05
Bigelow 53 1 43N30'19 95w41'23 6:22:46
Big Falls 36 1 48N11'28 93w48'23 6:15:14
Bigfork 31 1 47N44'40 93w39'14 6:14:37
Big Island 27 1 44N54 93w34 6:14:16
Big Lake 71 1 45N19'57 93w44'45 6:14:59
Big Lake Chapel 9 1 46N43'18 92w35'48 6:10:23
Big Spring 23 1 43N34'00 92w03'08 6:08:13
Big Stone 6 1 45N23 96w26 6:25:44
Big Stone City 6 1 45N17 96w26 6:25:44
Big Stone Colony 6 1 45N31'45 96w28'26 6:25:54
Big Woods 45 1 48N18'41 97w06'28 6:28:26
Bingham Lake 17 1 43N54'24 95w02'46 6:20:11
Birch 4 1 47N38 94w29 6:17:56
Birch 69 1 47N02'03 92w35'31 6:10:22
Birch Beach 39 1 48N57'09 94w55'54 6:19:44
Birch Cooley 65 1 44N35 94w56 6:19:44
Birch Creek 58 1 46N23 92w59 6:11:56
Birchdale 36 1 48N37'37 94w06'06 6:16:24
Birchdale 77 1 45N48 94w50 6:19:20
Birch Lake 11 1 46N56 94w29 6:17:56
Birchmont 4 1 47N32'47 94w51'37 6:19:26
Birchwood 82 3 45N03'40 92w58'33 6:11:54
Bird Island 65 1 44N46'03 94w53'43 6:19:35
Biscay 43 1 44N49'39 94w16'29 6:17:06
Bismarck 72 1 44N35 94w26 6:17:44
Biwabik 69 1 47N31'59 92w20'24 6:09:22
Bixby 74 1 43N56'40 93w05'49 6:12:23
Blackberry 31 1 47N10'51 93w23'25 6:13:34
Blackduck 4 1 47N43'59 94w32'54 6:18:12
Black Hammer 28 1 43N36'59 91w39'39 6:06:39
Blackhoof 9 1 46N31'58 92w27'43 6:09:51
Black River 36 1 48N31 93w48 6:15:12
Black River 57 1 48N00 96w17 6:25:08
Blaine 2 3 45N09'39 93w14'05 6:12:56
Blakeley 70 1 44N36'39 93w51'11 6:15:25
Blind Lake 11 1 46N51 94w18 6:17:12
Blomford 30 1 45N30'01 93w08'32 6:12:34
Blomkest 34 1 44N56'34 95w01'23 6:20:06
Bloom 53 1 43N48 95w45 6:23:00
Bloom Dale 27 3 44N50 93w19 6:13:16
Bloomer 45 1 48N19 96w57 6:27:48
Bloomfield 23 1 43N38 92w23 6:09:32
Blooming Grove 81 1 44N09 93w29 6:13:56
Blooming Prairie 20 1 43N52'00 93w03'03 6:12:12
Bloomington 27 3 44N50'27 93w17'53 6:13:12
Bloomington Ferry 27 1 44N47'59 93w23'03 6:13:32
Blooming Valley 68 1 48N57 96w21 6:25:24
Blowers 56 1 46N35 95w13 6:20:52
Blueberry 80 1 46N46 95w06 6:20:24
Blue Earth 22 1 43N38'15 94w06'07 6:16:24
Blue Grass 80 1 46N32'34 95w00'35 6:20:02
Blue Hill 71 1 45N31 93w42 6:14:48
Blue Mounds 61 1 45N33 95w34 6:22:16
Bluffton 56 1 46N28'09 95w13'58 6:20:56
Bock 48 1 45N47'06 93w33'24 6:14:14
Bodum 30 1 45N31'18 93w12'15 6:12:49
Bogus Brook 48 1 45N41 93w34 6:14:16
Boisberg 78 1 45N55'13 96w33'40 6:26:15
Bois Fort 36 1 48N03 92w50 6:11:20
Bombay 25 1 44N17'01 92w53'29 6:11:34
Bonanza Grove 6 1 45N26'44 96w42'33 6:26:50
Bondin 51 1 43N53 95w38 6:22:32
Bonga Landing 15 1 47N22'26 95w29'03 6:21:56
Bongards 10 1 44N45'45 93w50'54 6:15:24
Bonnie Glen 13 1 45N21'32 92w54'13 6:11:37
Boon Lake 65 1 44N51 94w33 6:18:12
Border 36 1 48N41'48 94w16'41 6:17:07
Borgholm 48 1 45N46 93w35 6:14:20
Borup 54 1 47N10'49 96w30'21 6:26:01
Bovey 31 1 47N17'44 93w25'07 6:13:40
Bowlus 49 1 45N49'10 94w24'33 6:17:38
Bowstring 31 1 47N32'35 93w47'47 6:15:11
Boxville 45 1 48N11 96w49 6:27:16
Boyd 37 1 44N50'55 95w54'10 6:23:37
Boy Lake 11 1 47N07 94w16 6:17:04
Boy River 11 1 47N10'05 94w07'19 6:16:29
Bradbury 48 1 46N02 93w45 6:15:00
Bradford 30 1 45N31'21 93w22'07 6:13:28
Braham 30 1 45N43'22 93w10'14 6:12:41
Brainerd 18 1 46N21'29 94w12'02 6:16:48
Branch 13 1 45N29'07 92w57'42 6:11:51
Brandon 21 1 45N57'55 95w35'54 6:22:24
Brandrup 84 1 46N09 96w29 6:25:56
Brandsvold 60 1 47N38 95w45 6:23:00
Brandt 60 1 48N04 96w35 6:26:20
Bratsberg 23 1 43N44'06 91w46'13 6:07:05
Bray 57 1 48N04 96w26 6:25:44
Breckenridge 84 1 46N15'49 96w35'16 6:26:21
Breda 69 1 47N18'43 91w53'08 6:07:33
Breezy Point 18 1 46N37'00 94w13'00 6:16:52
Breitung 69 1 47N49 92w14 6:08:56
Bremen 58 1 46N17 92w58 6:11:52
Bremen 79 1 44N12'31 92w18'38 6:09:15
Brennyville 5 1 45N48'31 93w54'20 6:15:37
Brevator 69 1 46N48 92w27 6:09:48
Brevik 11 1 47N04'59 94w17'18 6:17:09
Brewster 53 1 43N41'55 95w28'06 6:21:52
Bricelyn 22 1 43N33'44 93w48'42 6:15:15
Brickton 48 1 45N36'26 93w36'21 6:14:25
Bridgeman 11 1 46N23'02 94w34'49 6:18:19
Bridgewater 66 1 44N25 93w13 6:12:52
Briggs Lake 71 1 45N30'31 93w56'09 6:15:45
Brighton 52 1 44N21 94w19 6:17:16
Brimson 69 1 47N16'36 91w52'01 6:07:28
Brislet 60 1 48N08 96w42 6:26:48
Bristol 23 1 43N32'40 92w10'09 6:08:41
Britt 69 1 47N38'25 92w31'31 6:10:06
Brittmount 69 1 47N35'48 92w34'55 6:10:20
Brockway 73 1 45N43 94w20 6:17:20
Brookfield 65 1 44N51 94w42 6:18:48
Brooklyn 69 5 47N26'23 92w55'15 6:11:41
Brooklyn Center 27 3 45N04'34 93w19'57 6:13:20
Brooklyn Park 27 3 45N05'39 93w21'22 6:13:25
Brook Park 58 1 45N56'58 93w04'31 6:12:18
Brooks 63 1 47N48'52 96w00'07 6:24:00
Brookston 69 1 46N52'04 92w36'13 6:10:25
Brookville 64 1 44N20 94w55 6:19:40
Brooten 73 1 45N30'04 95w07'27 6:20:30
Browerville 77 1 46N05'09 94w51'56 6:19:28
Brownell 9 1 46N40'38 92w20'17 6:09:21
Browns Creek 63 1 47N57 96w17 6:25:08
Brownsdale 50 1 43N44'25 92w52'09 6:11:29
Browns Valley 78 1 45N35'43 96w49'59 6:27:20
Brownsville 28 1 43N41'39 91w16'47 6:05:07
Brownton 43 1 44N43'55 94w21'00 6:17:24
Bruce 67 1 43N31'20 96w23'53 6:25:36
Bruce 77 1 45N58 94w43 6:18:52
Bruno 58 1 46N16'45 92w39'51 6:10:39
Brunswick 33 1 45N47'20 93w16'32 6:13:06
Brush Creek 22 1 43N38'41 93w50'53 6:15:24
Brushvale 84 1 46N22'10 96w38'35 6:26:34
Buckman 49 1 45N53'51 94w05'36 6:16:22
Bucks Mill 3 1 46N43'23 95w54'53 6:23:40
Bucksnort 23 1 43N49'04 92w03'03 6:08:12
Buffalo 86 1 45N10'19 93w52'28 6:15:30
Buffalo Lake 65 1 44N44'14 94w37'00 6:18:28
Buh 49 1 46N02 94w08 6:16:32
Buhl 69 1 47N29'37 92w46'40 6:11:07
Bullard 80 1 46N30 94w50 6:19:20
Bull Moose 11 1 46N46 94w36 6:18:24
Bunde 12 1 44N56'05 95w18'36 6:21:14
Bungo 11 1 46N40 94w33 6:18:12
Burbank 34 1 45N22 94w57 6:19:48
Burchard 42 1 44N15'22 95w59'24 6:23:58
Burke 59 1 43N59 96w07 6:24:28
Burleene 77 1 46N04 95w05 6:20:20
Burlington 3 1 46N46 95w44 6:22:56
Burnett 69 1 46N54'03 92w31'27 6:10:06
Burnhamville 77 1 45N53 94w42 6:18:48
Burns 2 1 45N21 93w27 6:13:48
Burnside 25 1 44N35 92w37 6:10:28
Burnstown 8 1 44N14 94w56 6:19:44
Burnsville 19 1 44N46'04 93w16'39 6:13:07
Burntside 69 1 47N53'40 91w55'43 6:07:43
Burntside Lake 69 1 47N53'34 92w02'04 6:08:08
Burr 87 1 44N44'54 96w21'32 6:25:26
Burschville 27 1 45N07'30 93w38'10 6:14:33
Burton 87 1 44N40 96w02 6:24:08
Burtrum 77 1 45N52'03 94w41'05 6:18:44
Burwell 60 1 47N44'43 96w30'10 6:26:01
Buse 56 1 46N15 96w04 6:24:16
Bush Landing 15 1 47N19'54 95w28'23 6:21:54
Butler 56 1 46N41'17 95w21'10 6:21:25
Butterfield 83 1 43N57'30 94w47'40 6:19:11
Butterfly Lake 38 1 47N45'30 91w28'45 6:05:55
Butternut 7 1 44N08'16 94w19'44 6:17:19
Butternut Valley 7 1 44N09 94w18 6:17:12
Buyck 69 1 48N07'19 92w31'24 6:10:06
Buzzle 4 1 47N38 95w07 6:20:28
Bygland 60 1 47N48'42 96w55'55 6:27:44
Byron 55 1 44N01'58 92w38'43 6:10:35
Cable 71 1 45N30'42 94w04'26 6:16:18
Cairo 65 1 44N30 94w41 6:18:44
Caledonia 28 6 43N38'05 91w29'48 6:05:59
Calhoun Beach 27 3 44N56'59 93w18'55 6:13:16
Callaway 3 1 46N58'57 95w54'34 6:23:38
Calumet 31 1 47N19'19 93w16'36 6:13:06
Cambria 7 1 44N14'19 94w18'51 6:17:15
Cambridge 30 1 45N34'22 93w13'27 6:12:54
Camden 10 1 44N51 93w57 6:15:48
Camden 27 3 45N01 93w18 6:13:12
Cameron 51 1 44N04 96w00 6:24:00
Camp 65 1 44N31 94w48 6:19:12
Campbell 84 1 46N05'52 96w24'16 6:25:37
Camp Lake 76 1 45N22 95w27 6:21:48
Camp Release 37 1 44N56 95w49 6:23:16
Camp Ripley 49 1 46N04'13 94w19'41 6:17:19
Canby 87 1 44N42'32 96w16'34 6:25:06
Candor 56 1 46N40 95w51 6:23:24
Canisteo 20 1 43N59 92w44 6:10:56
Canisteo 31 1 47N17'16 93w27'14 6:13:49
Cannon 35 1 48N51 96w36 6:26:24
Cannon City 66 1 44N19'45 93w12'40 6:12:51
Cannon Falls 25 1 44N30'25 92w54'19 6:11:37
Cannon Lake 66 1 44N17 93w16 6:13:04
Canosia 69 1 46N54 92w14 6:08:56
Canton 23 1 43N31'47 91w55'47 6:07:43
Canyon 69 1 47N02'24 92w28'14 6:09:53
Cardigan Junction 62 3 45N03'10 93w06'33 6:12:26
Caribou 35 1 48N58'57 96w26'57 6:25:48
Carimona 23 1 43N39'37 92w09'27 6:08:38
Carlisle 56 1 46N22'06 96w11'22 6:24:45
Carlos 21 1 45N58'21 95w17'31 6:21:10
Carlston 24 1 43N43 93w35 6:14:20
Carlton 9 1 46N39'50 92w25'29 6:09:42
Carmel 4 1 48N16'54 95w26'39 6:21:47
Carmody 30 1 45N39'06 93w28'16 6:13:53
Carnelian Junction 82 1 45N07'29 92w49'48 6:11:19
Carp 39 1 48N30'19 94w38'49 6:18:35
Carpenter 31 1 47N51 93w16 6:13:04
Carpenters Corner 57 1 48N09'29 96w26'14 6:25:45
Carrolton 23 1 43N43 92w01 6:08:04
Carson 17 1 43N59 95w03 6:20:12
Carsonville 3 1 46N56 95w21 6:21:24
Carver 10 1 44N45'49 93w37'32 6:14:30
Carver Beach 10 1 44N52'41 93w32'15 6:14:09
Cascade 55 5 44N04 92w28 6:09:52
Casco 69 1 47N15'29 92w42'06 6:10:48
Casey 47 1 45N03'58 94w26'28 6:17:46
Cashel 76 1 45N12 95w32 6:22:08
Cashtown 6 1 45N17'55 96w26'20 6:25:45
Casino 11 1 46N25'37 94w32'24 6:18:10
Casperson 68 1 48N34'34 95w11'13 6:22:45
Cass Lake 11 1 47N22'46 94w36'14 6:18:25
Castle Danger 38 1 47N07'15 91w30'11 6:06:01
Castle Rock 19 1 44N32'38 93w09'08 6:12:37
Cazenovia 59 1 44N04'01 96w22'03 6:25:28
Cedar 2 1 45N19'11 93w17'09 6:13:09
Cedar Beach 55 1 44N09'42 92w27'53 6:09:52
Cedarbend 68 1 48N50 95w23 6:21:32
Cedar Grove 19 3 44N48'17 93w12'36 6:12:50
Cedar Lake 70 1 44N35'14 93w26'24 6:13:46

Cedar Mills 47 1 44N56'35 94w31'20 6:18:05
Cedar Valley 69 1 47N07 93w00 6:12:00
Cee Jefferson 28 1 43N30'51 91w16'49 6:05:07
Celina 69 1 47N51'57 93w03'42 6:12:15
Center 18 1 46N30 94w09 6:16:36
Center City 13 1 45N23'38 92w48'59 6:11:16
Center Creek 46 1 43N43 94w18 6:17:12
Centerville 2 1 45N09'47 93w03'20 6:12:13
Centerville 85 7 43N56'35 91w38'08 6:06:33
Central 36 1 48N41'58 94w20'34 6:17:22
Central Lakes 69 1 47N28 92w33 6:10:12
Central Point 25 1 44N28 92w17 6:09:08
Ceresco 7 1 43N59 94w18 6:17:12
Cerro Gordo 37 1 45N03'09 96w01'54 6:24:08
Ceylon 46 1 43N32'01 94w37'53 6:18:32
Chamberlain 29 1 46N54'19 94w43'17 6:18:53
Champion 84 1 46N04 96w20 6:25:20
Champlin 27 1 45N11'20 93w23'50 6:13:35
Chanarambie 51 1 43N59 96w00 6:24:00
Chandler 51 1 43N55'45 95w56'49 6:23:47
Chanhassen 10 1 44N51'44 93w31'50 6:14:07
Charlestown 64 1 44N14 95w09 6:20:36
Charlesville 78 1 45N56'57 96w16'06 6:25:04
Chaska 10 1 44N47'22 93w36'07 6:14:24
Chatfield 23 1 43N50'44 92w11'20 6:08:45
Chatham 86 1 45N10 93w57 6:15:48
Chemolite 82 1 44N50 92w56 6:11:44
Chengwatana 58 1 45N52 92w52 6:11:28
Cherry 69 1 47N24'03 92w42'25 6:10:50
Cherry Grove 23 1 43N35'15 92w17'19 6:09:09
Cherry Grove 25 1 44N14 92w52 6:11:28
Chester 55 5 44N00'25 92w20'42 6:09:23
Chicago Bay 16 1 47N50 89w58 5:59:52
Chicago Lake 27 3 44N56 93w15 6:13:00
Chickamaw Beach 11 1 46N44'37 94w23'06 6:17:32
Chief 44 1 47N22 95w52 6:23:28
Childs 84 1 46N03'56 96w32'03 6:26:08
Chippewa City 16 1 47N45'35 90w18'07 6:01:12
Chippewa Falls 61 1 45N32 95w20 6:21:20
Chisago City 13 1 45N22'25 92w53'23 6:11:34
Chisago Lake 13 1 45N22 92w51 6:11:24
Chisholm 69 1 47N29'21 92w53'01 6:11:32
Choice 23 1 43N39'35 91w47'26 6:07:10
Chokio 75 1 45N34'18 96w10'23 6:24:42
Chowens Corner 27 1 44N58 93w30 6:14:00
Christiania 32 1 43N48 95w05 6:20:20
Churchill 12 1 45N01'19 95w52'00 6:23:28
Churchill 65 1 44N49'06 94w40'14 6:18:41
Circle Pines 2 1 45N08'55 93w09'05 6:12:36
City 55 5 44N02 92w28 6:09:52
Civic Center 69 2 46N47 92w06 6:08:24
Clappers 69 1 47N26'08 91w57'53 6:07:52
Clara City 12 1 44N57'18 95w21'58 6:21:28
Claremont 20 1 44N02'40 92w59'51 6:11:59
Clarissa 77 1 46N07'49 94w56'54 6:19:48
Clarkfield 87 1 44N47'26 95w48'30 6:23:14
Clarks Grove 22 1 43N45'50 93w19'44 6:13:19
Claybank 25 1 44N26'30 92w37'54 6:10:32
Clayton 50 1 43N38 92w38 6:10:32
Clearbrook 15 1 47N41'31 95w25'51 6:21:43
Clear Lake 71 1 47N38'24 91w07'10 6:04:29
Clearwater 86 1 45N25'10 94w02'55 6:16:12
Clements 64 1 44N22'54 95w03'08 6:20:13
Clementson 39 1 48N41'27 94w26'10 6:17:45
Cleveland 40 1 44N19'32 93w50'15 6:15:21
Cliff 19 3 44N55 93w07 6:12:28
Clifton 69 1 46N52'53 91w55'13 6:07:41
Climax 60 1 47N36'28 96w49'00 6:27:16
Clinton 6 1 45N27'37 96w26'00 6:25:44
Clinton Falls 74 1 44N08'20 93w14'48 6:12:59
Clitherall 56 1 46N16'30 95w37'51 6:22:31
Clontarf 76 1 45N22'35 95w40'42 6:22:43
Cloquet 9 1 46N43'18 92w27'33 6:09:50
Clotho 77 1 46N01'11 95w02'33 6:20:10
Clough 49 1 46N09 94w30 6:18:00
Cloverdale 58 1 46N00'44 92w44'23 6:10:58
Clover Leaf 57 1 48N08 95w55 6:23:40
Cloverton 58 1 46N10'05 92w19'10 6:09:17
Clow 35 1 48N56 97w00 6:28:00
Clyde 85 1 43N53'41 91w58'45 6:07:55
Coates 19 1 44N43'02 93w02'04 6:12:08
Cobden 8 1 44N17'11 94w50'55 6:19:24
Coffee Pot Landing 15 1 47N20'58 95w10'58 6:20:44
Cohasset 31 1 47N15'49 93w37'12 6:14:29
Coin 33 1 45N44'06 93w18'23 6:13:14
Cokato 86 1 45N04'33 94w11'23 6:16:46
Colby 69 1 47N32'31 92w10'11 6:08:41
Cold Spring 73 1 45N27'21 94w25'43 6:17:43
Coleraine 31 1 47N17'20 93w25'39 6:13:43
Coleraine Junction 69 1 46N58'02 92w34'20 6:10:17
Colfax 34 1 45N22 95w04 6:20:16
Collegeville 73 1 45N35'40 94w21'46 6:17:27
Collins 43 1 44N46 94w26 6:17:44
Collinwood 47 1 45N02 94w18 6:17:12
Collis 78 1 45N38'48 96w25'31 6:25:42
Cologne 10 1 44N46'18 93w46'52 6:15:07
Columbia 60 1 47N33 95w37 6:22:28
Columbia Heights 2 3 45N02'27 93w15'46 6:13:03
Columbus 2 1 45N16 93w05 6:12:20
Colvin 69 1 47N20 92w13 6:08:52
Comfort 33 1 45N52 93w12 6:12:48
Comfrey 8 1 44N06'37 94w54'16 6:19:37
Commerce 27 3 44N58 93w16 6:13:04
Como 45 1 48N30 96w04 6:24:16
Como 62 3 45N00 93w11 6:12:44
Compton 56 1 46N25 95w13 6:20:52
Comstock 14 1 46N39'34 96w44'53 6:27:00
Comus 66 1 44N23'06 93w15'26 6:13:02
Conception 79 1 44N15'56 92w06'35 6:08:26
Concord 20 1 44N08'51 92w50'10 6:11:21
Conger 24 1 43N36'54 93w31'41 6:14:07
Connelly 84 1 46N20 96w34 6:26:16
Constance 2 3 45N15'19 93w17'07 6:13:08
Cook 69 1 47N51'09 92w41'22 6:10:45
Cooley 31 1 47N21'30 93w11'31 6:12:46
Coon Creek 2 3 45N09'06 93w18'03 6:13:12
Coon Creek 42 1 44N19 96w01 6:24:04
Coon Lake Beach 2 1 45N18'29 93w09'21 6:12:37
Coon Rapids 2 3 45N07'12 93w17'15 6:13:09
Coopers Corner 2 1 45N23'57 93w14'04 6:12:56
Copas 82 1 45N14'05 92w45'52 6:11:03
Copley 15 1 47N33 95w23 6:21:32
Corcoran 27 1 45N05'43 93w32'50 6:14:11
Cordova 40 1 44N20'11 93w40'17 6:14:41
Corinna 86 1 45N17 94w05 6:16:20
Cormant 4 1 47N52 94w37 6:18:28
Cormorant 3 1 46N43'50 96w03'55 6:24:16
Corning 24 1 43N45'40 93w02'57 6:12:12
Corona 9 1 46N40'14 92w45'58 6:11:04
Correll 6 1 45N13'51 96w09'33 6:24:38
Cort 31 1 47N19'58 93w14'49 6:12:59
Corvuso 47 1 44N56'10 94w36'16 6:18:25
Cosmos 47 1 44N56'10 94w41'47 6:18:47
Cottage Grove 82 1 44N49'40 92w56'37 6:11:46
Cottage Wood 27 1 44N54 93w34 6:14:16
Cotton 69 1 47N10'10 92w28'34 6:09:54
Cottonwood 42 1 44N36'32 95w40'26 6:22:42
Courtland 52 1 44N16'06 94w20'24 6:17:22
Cove 48 1 46N06'31 93w37'06 6:14:28
Craigville 36 1 47N54'11 93w36'46 6:14:27
Cramer 38 1 47N31'38 91w05'24 6:04:22
Crane Lake 69 1 48N16'00 92w29'18 6:09:57
Crate 12 1 45N00 95w26 6:21:44
Credit River 70 1 44N40'28 93w22'44 6:13:31
Crescent Beach 27 1 44N54'52 93w35'54 6:14:24
Cresson 59 1 44N06'40 96w26'06 6:25:44
Croftville 16 1 47N45'54 90w16'32 6:01:06
Croke 78 1 45N43 96w26 6:25:44
Cromwell 9 1 46N40'51 92w53'02 6:11:32
Crooked Creek 28 1 43N36 91w20 6:05:20
Crooked Lake 11 1 46N50 94w00 6:16:00
Crooks 65 1 44N51 95w11 6:20:44
Crookston 60 1 47N46'27 96w36'28 6:26:26
Crookston Junction 60 1 47N45'23 96w37'19 6:26:29
Crosby 18 1 46N28'56 93w57'27 6:15:50
Crosby Beach 18 1 46N28'18 93w56'58 6:15:48
Cross Lake 18 1 46N39'34 94w06'49 6:16:27
Crow Lake 73 1 45N27 95w04 6:20:16
Crown 30 1 45N26'41 93w27'36 6:13:50
Crow River 47 1 45N14'38 94w43'27 6:18:54
Crow Wing 18 1 46N16'48 94w17'32 6:17:10
Crow Wing Lake 29 1 46N51 94w52 6:19:28
Crystal 27 3 45N01'58 93w21'36 6:13:26
Crystal Bay 27 1 44N57'11 93w34'34 6:14:18
Crystal Bay 38 1 47N37 91w13 6:04:52
Crystal Spring 85 1 44N04'29 91w59'10 6:07:57
Cuba 3 1 46N56 96w07 6:24:28
Culdrum 49 1 45N59 94w34 6:18:16
Culver 69 1 46N55'33 92w33'30 6:10:14
Cummingsville 55 1 43N52'29 92w15'36 6:09:02
Current Lake 51 1 44N08'19 95w56'35 6:23:46
Currie 51 1 44N04'17 95w39'58 6:22:40
Cushing 49 1 46N08'23 94w34'36 6:18:18
Cusson 69 1 48N06'07 92w50'34 6:11:22
Custer 42 1 44N14 95w47 6:23:08
Cuyuna 18 1 46N31'01 93w55'22 6:15:41
Cyrus 61 1 45N36'53 95w44'16 6:22:57
Dads Corner 1 1 46N19'58 93w15'32 6:13:02
Dagget Brook 18 1 46N13 94w07 6:16:28
Dahlgren 10 1 44N46'36 93w41'00 6:14:44
Dailey 48 1 45N57 93w41 6:14:44
Dakomin 78 1 45N43'30 96w40'18 6:26:41
Dakota 85 6 43N54'49 91w21'35 6:05:26
Dakota Junction 57 1 48N09'32 96w11'39 6:24:47
Dalbo 30 1 45N39'32 93w23'55 6:13:36
Dale 14 1 46N54'19 96w13'10 6:24:53
Dale 17 1 43N59 95w09 6:20:36
Dalton 56 1 46N10'26 95w54'55 6:23:40
Dane Prairie 56 1 46N14 95w57 6:23:48
Danesville 55 1 44N05'38 92w40'43 6:10:43
Danforth 58 1 46N08 92w38 6:10:32
Danielson 47 1 45N01 94w41 6:18:44
Danube 65 1 44N47'31 95w05'49 6:20:23
Danvers 76 1 45N16'55 95w45'06 6:23:00
Danville 7 1 43N54 93w50 6:15:20
Darby Junction 38 1 47N21'34 91w37'55 6:06:32
Darfur 83 1 44N03'05 94w50'16 6:19:21
Darling 49 1 46N04 94w26 6:17:44
Darnen 75 1 45N33 95w56 6:23:44
Darwin 47 1 45N05'47 94w24'38 6:17:39
Dassel 47 1 45N04'54 94w18'24 6:17:14
Davidson 60 1 47N52'36 96w50'49 6:27:23
Davies 56 1 46N36'02 95w18'39 6:21:15
Davis 35 1 48N35 96w50 6:27:20
Dawson 37 1 44N55'58 96w03'15 6:24:13
Day 30 1 45N42'33 93w22'45 6:13:31
Days High Landing 11 1 47N15'08 93w48'20 6:15:13
Dayton 27 1 45N14'38 93w30'53 6:14:04
Daytons Bluff 62 3 44N58 93w04 6:12:16
Dead Lake 56 1 46N30 95w43 6:22:52
Dean Lake 18 1 46N36 93w48 6:15:12
Debs 4 1 47N43'53 95w07'40 6:20:31
Decoria 7 1 44N04 93w56 6:15:44
Deephaven 27 1 44N55'47 93w31'20 6:14:05
Deer 68 1 48N35 96w12 6:24:48
Deer Creek 56 1 46N23'28 95w19'16 6:21:17
Deerfield 74 1 44N10'03 93w21'34 6:13:26
Deerhorn 84 1 46N35 96w36 6:26:24
Deer Lane 29 1 47N02'24 94w58'40 6:19:55
Deer Park 19 1 44N42'07 93w19'03 6:13:16
Deer Park 57 1 48N00 95w47 6:23:08
Deer River 31 1 47N19'59 93w47'33 6:15:10
Deerwood 18 1 46N28'25 93w53'55 6:15:36
De Forest 69 1 47N27'36 92w34'45 6:10:19
De Graff 76 1 45N15'48 95w28'03 6:21:52
Delafield 32 1 43N49 95w12 6:20:48
Delano 86 1 45N02'31 93w47'20 6:15:09
Delavan 22 1 43N46'04 94w01'10 6:16:05
Delaware 26 1 45N53 96w04 6:24:16
Delft 17 1 43N59'11 95w05'19 6:20:21
Delhi 65 1 44N35'57 95w12'39 6:20:51
Dell 22 1 43N37'27 93w54'53 6:15:40
Dell Grove 58 1 46N12 92w55 6:11:40
Dellwood 82 1 45N05'24 92w58'20 6:11:53
Delorme 63 1 47N45'53 96w17'20 6:25:09
Delton 17 1 44N04 95w02 6:20:08
Denham 58 1 46N21'50 92w56'34 6:11:46
Denmark 82 1 44N45 92w51 6:11:24
Dennison 25 1 44N24'25 93w02'21 6:12:09
Dent 56 1 46N33'13 95w42'58 6:22:52
Denver 67 1 43N48 96w14 6:24:56
Derrynane 40 1 44N30 93w42 6:14:48
Des Moines 32 1 43N38 95w05 6:20:20
Des Moines River 51 1 43N59 95w31 6:22:04
Detroit 3 1 46N50 95w51 6:23:24
Detroit Lakes 3 1 46N49'02 95w50'42 6:23:23
Dewald 53 1 43N38 95w45 6:23:00
Dewey 68 1 48N41 96w18 6:25:12
Dexter 50 1 43N43'08 92w42'16 6:10:49
Diamond Corner 59 1 43N59'38 96w06'13 6:24:25
Diamond Lake 27 3 44N54 93w18 6:13:12
Diamond Lake 41 1 44N20 96w16 6:25:04
Dieter 68 1 48N56 95w58 6:23:52
Dilworth 14 1 46N52'36 96w42'11 6:26:49
Ditter 27 1 45N00'50 93w31'20 6:14:05
Dodge Center 20 1 44N01'41 92w51'16 6:11:25
Dollymount 78 1 45N43 96w20 6:25:20
Domaas 4 1 48N06'56 94w33'00 6:18:12
Donaldson 35 1 48N34'20 96w53'46 6:27:35
Donehower 85 6 43N57'40 91w24'23 6:05:38
Donnelly 75 1 45N41'26 96w00'44 6:24:03
Dora 56 1 46N35 95w51 6:23:24
Dora Lake 31 1 47N44'19 94w02'24 6:16:10
Doran 56 1 46N11'03 96w28'56 6:25:56
Dorothy 63 1 47N55'40 96w26'47 6:25:47
Dorset 29 1 46N57'23 94w57'08 6:19:49
Dotson 8 1 44N10'19 94w59'40 6:19:59
Douglas 55 1 44N06'29 92w34'25 6:10:18
Dover 55 1 43N58'25 92w08'20 6:08:33
Dovray 51 1 44N03'10 95w32'59 6:22:12
Dovre 34 1 45N12 95w04 6:20:16
Downer 14 1 46N45'15 96w29'12 6:25:57
Doyle 40 1 44N22'13 93w34'29 6:14:18
Drammen 41 1 44N20 96w23 6:25:32
Dresbach 85 1 43N53'44 91w20'35 6:05:22
Dryden 72 1 44N36 94w11 6:16:44
Dublin 76 1 45N12 95w26 6:21:44
Dudley 15 1 47N38 95w14 6:20:56
Dudley 42 1 44N25'30 95w41'28 6:22:46
Duelm 5 1 45N34'20 93w56'03 6:15:44
Duesler 9 1 46N30'43 92w30'30 6:10:02
Dugdale 60 1 47N42'06 96w15'58 6:25:04
Duluth 69 2 46N47'00 92w06'23 6:08:26
Duluth Heights 69 2 46N48'03 92w07'54 6:08:32
Duluth Junction 82 1 45N04'36 92w53'59 6:11:36
Dumblane 69 1 47N08'49 92w36'53 6:10:28
Dumfries 79 1 44N20'42 92w07'12 6:08:29
Dumont 78 1 45N42'57 96w25'32 6:25:42
Dunbar 22 1 43N48 93w46 6:15:04
Dunbar 31 1 47N39'30 94w13'28 6:16:54
Dundas 66 1 44N25'46 93w12'06 6:12:48
Dundee 53 1 43N50'49 95w28'00 6:21:52
Dunn 56 1 46N33 96w00 6:24:00
Dunnell 46 1 43N33'34 94w46'27 6:19:06
Dunvilla 56 1 46N39'47 96w00'57 6:24:04
Dunwoody Junction 69 5 47N27'07 92w52'02 6:11:28
Dupont 27 1 45N05'45 93w35'55 6:14:24
Duquette 58 1 46N22'11 92w33'11 6:10:13
Durand 4 1 47N41 94w53 6:19:32
Duxbury 58 1 46N07'40 92w30'31 6:10:02
Eagan 19 3 44N49 93w11 6:12:44
Eagle Bend 77 1 46N09'54 95w02'20 6:20:09
Eagle Creek 70 1 44N46 93w28 6:13:52
Eagle Lake 7 1 44N09'54 93w52'52 6:15:31
Eagle Point 45 1 48N30 97w07 6:28:28
Eagles Nest 69 1 47N50'24 92w05'47 6:08:23
Eagle Valley 77 1 46N09 94w57 6:19:48
East Beaver Bay 38 1 47N16'04 91w16'58 6:05:08
East Bethel 2 1 45N19'10 93w12'08 6:12:49
East Chain 46 1 43N33'32 94w21'54 6:17:28
East Cottage Grove 82 1 44N50'30 92w52'53 6:11:32
East End 69 2 46N47 92w06 6:08:24
Eastern 56 1 46N09 95w12 6:20:48
Eastern Heights 62 3 44N58 93w01 6:12:04
East Grand Forks 60 1 47N55'48 97w01'27 6:28:06
East Gull Lake 11 1 46N24'29 94w21'20 6:17:25
East Hastings 19 1 44N40 92w50 6:11:20
East Lake 1 1 46N32'18 93w17'00 6:13:08
East Lake Francis Shores 30 1 45N30'14 93w19'25 6:13:18
East Lake Lillian 34 1 44N56 94w49 6:19:16
Easton 22 1 43N45'57 93w54'03 6:15:36
East Park 45 1 48N30 96w19 6:25:16
East Prairieville 66 1 44N17 93w16 6:13:04
East Side 48 1 46N13 93w29 6:13:56
East Union 10 1 44N43'05 93w40'53 6:14:44
East Valley 45 1 48N20 96w05 6:24:20
Ebro 15 1 47N29'44 95w31'45 6:22:07
Echo 87 1 44N37'01 95w25'02 6:21:40
Echols 83 1 43N55'26 94w40'29 6:18:42
Eckles 4 1 47N33 94w59 6:19:56
Eckvoll 45 1 48N19 95w47 6:23:08

Eddsville 65 1 44N46 94w53 6:19:32
Eddy 15 1 47N38 95w30 6:22:00
Eden 20 1 44N05'17 92w53'05 6:11:32
Eden Lake 73 1 45N22 94w35 6:18:20
Eden Prairie 27 1 44N51'17 93w28'14 6:13:53
Eden Valley 47 1 45N19'34 94w32'45 6:18:11
Edgerton 59 1 43N52'21 96w07'42 6:24:31
Edgewood 30 1 45N32'11 93w13'50 6:12:55
Edina 27 3 44N53'23 93w20'59 6:13:24
Edison 76 1 45N11 95w54 6:23:36
Edna 56 1 46N35 95w44 6:22:56
Edwards 34 1 45N01 95w11 6:20:44
Edwards 56 1 46N26'56 95w59'19 6:23:57
Effie 31 1 47N50'25 93w38'34 6:14:34
Effington 56 1 46N14 95w27 6:21:48
Eggleston 25 1 44N37'12 92w40'19 6:10:41
Eglon 14 1 46N51 96w15 6:25:00
Eidsvold 42 1 44N35 96w02 6:24:08
Eidswold 70 1 44N33'43 93w17'01 6:13:08
Eitzen 28 1 43N30'29 91w27'41 6:05:51
Elba 85 1 44N05'19 92w01'07 6:08:04
Elbow Lake 26 1 45N59'39 95w58'35 6:23:54
Elbow Lake Village 3
1 47N08'48 95w33'06 6:22:12
Elcor 69 1 47N30'19 92w26'27 6:09:46
Eldes Corner 69 1 46N42'36 92w16'47 6:09:07
Eldorado 75 1 45N43 96w11 6:24:44
Eldred 60 1 47N40'58 96w46'48 6:27:07
Elevenmile Corner 11
1 47N11'45 93w57'22 6:15:49
Elgin 79 1 44N07'49 92w15'05 6:09:00
Elizabeth 56 1 46N22'47 96w07'44 6:24:31
Elk 53 1 43N43 95w38 6:22:32
Elk Lake 26 1 45N53 95w49 6:23:16
Elkland 66 1 44N17 93w16 6:13:04
Elko 70 1 44N33'53 93w19'36 6:13:18
Elk River 71 1 45N18'14 93w34'01 6:14:16
Elkton 50 1 43N39'46 92w42'30 6:10:50
Ellendale 81 1 43N52'22 93w18'04 6:13:12
Ellerth 45 1 48N21'18 96w28'38 6:25:55
Ellington 20 1 44N09 92w59 6:11:56
Ellis 11 1 46N30'51 94w41'48 6:18:47
Ellsborough 51 1 44N09 96w00 6:24:00
Ellsburg 69 1 47N15 92w25 6:09:40
Ellson 58 1 46N19'03 93w00'40 6:12:03
Ellsworth 53 1 43N31'05 96w01'05 6:24:04
Elm Creek 46 1 43N43 94w48 6:19:12
Elmdale 49 1 45N50'00 94w29'32 6:17:58
Elmer 69 1 47N06'13 92w46'37 6:11:06
Elmira 55 1 43N53 92w08 6:08:32
Elmo 56 1 46N14 95w20 6:21:20
Elmore 22 1 43N30'18 94w05'16 6:16:21
Elm Park 30 1 45N40'23 93w16'33 6:13:06
Elmwood 14 1 46N40 96w36 6:26:24
Elmwood 27 3 44N57 93w21 6:13:24
Elrosa 73 1 45N33'46 94w56'49 6:19:47
Elway 62 3 44N55 93w10 6:12:40
Ely 69 1 47N54'12 91w52'01 6:07:28
Elysian 40 1 44N11'55 93w40'25 6:14:42
Elysian, Lake 81
1 44N08'55 93w42'48 6:14:51
Emardville 63 1 47N53 96w02 6:24:08
Embarrass 69 1 47N39'33 92w11'52 6:08:47
Emco 69 1 47N31 92w09 6:08:36
Emerald 22 1 43N38 93w57 6:15:48
Emily 18 1 46N43'52 93w57'28 6:15:50
Emmaville 29 1 47N03'56 94w58'49 6:19:55
Emmet 65 1 44N45 95w10 6:20:40
Emmons 24 1 43N30'07 93w29'17 6:13:57
Empire 19 1 44N39'33 93w00'52 6:12:03
Enfield 86 1 45N21'27 93w55'52 6:15:43
Englund 45 1 48N29'09 96w37'40 6:26:31
Enok 35 1 48N39'14 96w45'29 6:27:02
Enstrom 68 1 48N51 95w33 6:22:12
Enterprise 32 1 43N43 94w55 6:19:40
Epsom 66 1 44N15'44 93w03'21 6:12:13
Equality 63 1 47N54 95w47 6:23:08
Erdahl 26 1 45N59'31 95w49'03 6:23:16
Erhard 56 1 46N29'08 96w05'54 6:24:24
Erhards Grove 56
1 46N30 96w06 6:24:24
Ericksonville 48
1 46N04 93w40 6:14:40
Ericsburg 36 1 48N29'16 93w19'52 6:13:19
Ericson 65 1 44N51 95w18 6:21:12
Erie 3 1 46N51 95w43 6:22:52
Erie 57 1 48N09 95w48 6:23:12
Erin 66 1 44N25 93w27 6:13:48
Erskine 60 1 47N40'03 96w00'35 6:24:02
Esko 9 1 46N42'21 92w21'47 6:09:27
Espelie 45 1 48N13'25 95w40'48 6:22:43
Essig 8 1 44N19'27 94w36'15 6:18:25
Esterdy 80 1 46N28'36 94w43'56 6:18:56
Estes Brook 48 1 45N38'56 93w44'13 6:14:57
Esther 60 1 48N04 97w03 6:28:12
Etna 23 1 43N36'08 92w20'48 6:09:23
Etter 19 1 44N39'42 92w44'37 6:10:58
Euclid 60 1 47N58'19 96w38'19 6:26:33
Eureka 27 1 44N54'04 93w36'15 6:14:25
Eureka Center 19
1 44N35'14 93w13'04 6:12:52
Evan 8 1 44N21'15 94w50'28 6:19:22
Evansville 21 1 46N00'15 95w40'57 6:22:44
Eveleth 69 1 47N27'45 92w32'23 6:10:10
Everdell 84 1 46N16'03 96w24'28 6:25:38
Everglade 75 1 45N38 96w11 6:24:44
Evergreen 3 1 46N45'36 95w27'02 6:21:48
Everts 56 1 46N20 95w43 6:22:52
Ewington 32 1 43N38 95w24 6:21:36
Excel 45 1 48N13 96w10 6:24:40
Excelsior 27 3 44N54'12 93w33'58 6:14:16
Eyota 55 1 43N59'18 92w13'42 6:08:55
Fahlun 34 1 45N01 94w56 6:19:44
Fairbanks 69 1 47N22'14 91w55'35 6:07:42
Fairfax 65 1 44N31'45 94w43'14 6:18:53
Fairfield 76 1 45N23'02 95w58'24 6:23:54
Fairhaven 73 1 45N19'18 94w12'40 6:16:51
Fairland 36 1 48N28'03 94w09'16 6:16:37
Fairmont 46 1 43N39'08 94w27'39 6:17:51
Faith 54 1 47N17'13 96w05'55 6:24:24
Falcon Heights 62
3 44N59'30 93w09'58 6:12:40
Falk 15 1 47N27 95w29 6:21:56
Fall Lake 38 1 48N00 91w39 6:06:36
Falls Junction 36
1 48N36'10 93w20'34 6:13:22
Falun 68 1 48N45 95w33 6:22:12
Fanny 60 1 47N54 96w40 6:26:40
Farden 29 1 47N22 94w45 6:19:00
Faribault 66 1 44N17'42 93w16'07 6:13:04
Farley 60 1 48N08 96w50 6:27:20
Farming 73 1 45N30'55 94w35'52 6:18:23
Farmington 19 1 44N38'25 93w08'36 6:12:34
Farm Island 1 1 46N28 93w44 6:14:56
Farris 29 1 47N22'36 94w42'09 6:18:49
Farwell 61 1 45N45'08 95w37'01 6:22:28
Faunce 39 1 48N35'35 94w57'08 6:19:49
Fawn Lake 77 1 46N14 94w43 6:18:52
Faxon 72 1 44N39 93w50 6:15:20
Fayal 69 1 47N26 92w29 6:09:56
Featherstone 25 1 44N30 92w36 6:10:24
Federal Dam 11 1 47N14'43 94w12'39 6:16:51
Feeley 31 1 47N10 93w17 6:13:08
Felton 14 1 47N04'43 96w30'22 6:26:01
Fenton 51 1 43N54 95w53 6:23:32
Fergus Falls 56 1 46N16'59 96w04'38 6:24:19
Fern 29 1 47N22 95w07 6:20:28
Fernando 43 1 44N39'06 94w27'27 6:17:50
Fertile 60 1 47N32'10 96w16'48 6:25:07
Field 69 1 47N51 92w45 6:11:00
Fieldon 83 1 43N59 94w26 6:17:44
Fifty Lakes 18 1 46N44'21 94w05'34 6:16:22
Fillmore 23 1 43N44'55 92w16'05 6:09:04
Fine Lakes 69 1 46N48 92w53 6:11:32
Finkle 14 1 46N48'50 96w44'49 6:26:59
Finland 38 1 47N24'53 91w14'56 6:05:00
Finlayson 58 1 46N12'06 92w54'57 6:11:40
Fisher 60 1 47N48'01 96w48'04 6:27:12
Fish Lake 13 1 45N35 93w05 6:12:20
Five Corners 69 1 46N48'28 92w16'47 6:09:07
Five Points 73 1 45N36'28 94w15'39 6:17:03
Flaming 54 1 47N27'24 96w16'13 6:25:05
Flensburg 49 1 45N57'19 94w32'05 6:18:08
Fletcher 27 1 45N10'21 93w32'28 6:14:10
Flom 54 1 47N09'58 96w07'50 6:24:31
Floodwood 69 1 46N55'45 92w55'10 6:11:41
Flora 65 1 44N40 95w10 6:20:40
Florence 42 1 44N14'14 96w03'06 6:24:12
Florenton 69 1 47N39'16 92w25'19 6:09:41
Florian 45 1 48N26'32 96w37'40 6:26:31
Florida 87 1 44N46 96w23 6:25:32
Flowing 14 1 47N01 96w31 6:26:04
Foldahl 45 1 48N20 96w34 6:26:16
Folden 56 1 46N21 95w26 6:21:44
Foley 5 1 45N39'53 93w54'34 6:15:38
Folsom 78 1 46N04 95w05 6:20:20
Fond du Lac 69 1 46N39'35 92w16'23 6:09:06
Fond Du Lac Indian Res 9
1 46N43 92w32 6:10:08
Forada 21 1 45N47'32 95w21'19 6:21:25
Forbes 69 1 47N22'18 92w36'14 6:10:25
Ford 33 1 46N07 93w14 6:12:56
Fordson 19 3 44N55 93w14 6:12:56
Forest 66 1 44N25 93w20 6:13:20
Forest Center 38
1 47N47'42 91w18'27 6:05:14
Forest City 47 1 45N12'23 94w27'58 6:17:52
Forest Grove 36 1 47N58'36 94w13'52 6:16:55
Forest Lake 82 1 45N16'44 92w59'06 6:11:56
Forest Mills 25 1 44N17'52 92w38'26 6:10:34
Foreston 48 1 45N44'04 93w42'37 6:14:50
Forest Prairie 47
1 45N17 94w27 6:17:48
Forestville 23 1 43N38'34 92w12'53 6:08:52
Fork 45 1 48N25 97w06 6:28:24
Forsman 69 1 47N42'29 92w34'43 6:10:19
Fortier 87 1 44N41 96w24 6:25:36
Fort Ripley 18 1 46N09'58 94w21'36 6:17:26
Fort Saint Charles 39
1 49N21'43 94w58'50 6:19:55
Fort Snelling 27
3 44N54 93w14 6:12:56
Fosston 60 1 47N34'35 95w45'04 6:23:00
Fossum 3 1 47N14'19 96w10'33 6:24:42
Foster 6 1 45N24'59 96w40'32 6:26:42
Fountain 23 1 43N44'24 92w08'10 6:08:33
Fountain Prairie 59
1 44N09 96w15 6:25:00
Four Corners 69 2 46N51'12 92w16'48 6:09:07
Four Town 4 1 48N16'52 95w20'07 6:21:20
Fox 68 1 48N50'20 95w53'55 6:23:36
Foxhome 84 1 46N16'38 96w18'35 6:25:14
Fox Lake 46 1 43N40'36 94w39'31 6:18:38
Frames Landing Campground 80
1 46N37'47 94w52'08 6:19:29
Framnas 75 1 45N37 95w49 6:23:16
Franconia 13 1 45N22'13 92w41'29 6:10:46
Frankford 50 1 43N44 92w31 6:10:04
Frankfort 86 1 45N13 93w41 6:14:44
Franklin 65 1 44N31'42 94w52'49 6:19:31
Franklin 69 1 47N32'16 92w31'08 6:10:05
Frazee 3 1 46N43'41 95w42'02 6:22:48
Fredenberg 69 1 46N58'26 92w13'01 6:08:52
Freeborn 24 1 43N45'57 93w33'50 6:14:15
Freeburg 28 6 43N36'40 91w21'51 6:05:27
Freedhem 49 1 46N03'23 94w12'30 6:16:50
Freedom 81 1 43N59 93w42 6:14:48
Freeland 37 1 44N51 96w16 6:25:04
Freeman 24 1 43N33 93w21 6:13:24
Freeman 60 1 47N49'10 96w45'38 6:27:03
Freeport 73 1 45N39'46 94w41'23 6:18:46
Freiheit Spring 23
1 43N42'21 92w19'02 6:09:16
Fremont 85 1 43N54'50 91w53'56 6:07:36
French 56 1 46N17'17 96w12'05 6:24:48
French 69 1 47N40 93w01 6:12:04
French Lake 86 1 45N12'00 94w11'07 6:16:44
French River 69 1 46N53'53 91w53'49 6:07:35
Friberg 56 1 46N25 95w58 6:23:52
Fridley 2 3 45N05'10 93w15'47 6:13:03
Friendship 87 1 44N46 95w48 6:23:12
Friesland 58 1 46N05'08 92w55'46 6:11:43
Frogner 9 1 46N33'15 92w18'23 6:09:14
Frohn 4 1 47N27 94w44 6:18:56
Frontenac 25 1 44N30'40 92w21'23 6:09:26
Frontier 36 1 48N39'23 94w15'23 6:17:02
Frost 22 1 43N35'11 93w55'35 6:15:42
Fruitville 5 1 45N42'47 94w04'45 6:16:19
Fulda 51 1 43N52'14 95w36'00 6:22:24
Funkley 4 1 47N47'01 94w25'52 6:17:43
Gail Lake 18 1 46N47 94w12 6:16:48
Galena 46 1 43N48 94w41 6:18:44
Gales 64 1 44N20 95w32 6:22:08
Gappas Landing Campground 69
1 48N26'22 93w01'21 6:12:05
Garden 60 1 47N33 96w08 6:24:32
Garden City 7 1 44N02'50 94w09'53 6:16:40
Garfield 21 1 45N56'27 95w29'30 6:21:58
Garnes 63 1 47N54'23 95w52'50 6:23:31
Garrison 18 1 46N17'40 93w49'36 6:15:18
Garvin 42 1 44N12'52 95w45'20 6:23:01
Gary 54 1 47N22'17 96w16'02 6:25:04
Gary 69 1 46N40'13 92w13'32 6:08:54
Gates Corner 4 1 48N27'10 95w19'08 6:21:17
Gates Corner 36 1 48N13'09 94w06'09 6:16:25
Gatzke 45 1 48N25'28 95w47'02 6:23:08
Gaylord 72 1 44N33'11 94w13'13 6:16:53
Gem Lake 62 3 45N03'27 93w01'56 6:12:08
Gemmell 36 1 47N58'24 94w07'25 6:16:30
Geneva 22 1 43N49'24 93w16'03 6:13:04
Gennessee 34 1 45N07 94w49 6:19:16
Genoa 55 1 44N06'36 92w36'26 6:10:26
Genoa 69 1 47N27'52 92w30'31 6:10:02
Genola 49 1 45N57'37 94w06'58 6:16:28
Gentilly 60 1 47N47'21 96w26'56 6:25:48
Georgetown 14 1 47N04'48 96w47'38 6:27:11
Georgeville 73 1 45N25'43 94w55'37 6:19:42
Germania 77 1 46N14 94w57 6:19:48
Germantown 17 1 44N09 95w10 6:20:40
Gervais 63 1 47N53 96w10 6:24:40
Getty 73 1 45N38 94w57 6:19:48
Gheen 69 1 47N58'05 92w48'29 6:11:14
Gheen Corner 69 1 47N57'51 92w49'44 6:11:19
Ghent 42 1 44N30'46 95w53'27 6:23:34
Gibbon 72 1 44N32'02 94w31'34 6:18:06
Giese 1 1 46N12'58 93w06'59 6:12:28
Gilbert 69 1 47N29'20 92w27'53 6:09:52
Gilchrist 61 1 45N27 95w19 6:21:16
Gilfillan 64 1 44N27'33 94w59'39 6:19:59
Gillford 79 1 44N20 92w22 6:09:28
Gilman 5 1 45N44'07 93w56'56 6:15:48
Gilmanton 5 1 45N42 93w58 6:15:52
Girard 56 1 46N22 95w35 6:22:20
Girard 60 1 47N43'43 96w40'26 6:26:42
Gladstone 62 3 45N00'06 93w01'49 6:12:07
Glasgow 79 1 44N20 92w08 6:08:32
Glen 1 1 46N25'07 93w30'54 6:14:04
Glencoe 43 1 44N46'09 94w09'05 6:16:36
Glendale 69 1 48N01'57 92w49'51 6:11:19
Glendorado 5 1 45N34'41 93w46'10 6:15:05
Glen Lake 27 3 44N54'12 93w28'02 6:13:52
Glenville 24 1 43N34'21 93w16'52 6:13:07
Glenwood 61 1 45N39'01 95w23'22 6:21:33
Glenwood Junction 27
3 44N59'14 93w19'57 6:13:20
Glory 1 1 46N25'03 93w36'01 6:14:24
Gloster 62 3 45N00'05 93w02'39 6:12:11
Gluek (Wesota Station) 12
1 44N59'07 95w28'23 6:21:54
Glyndon 14 1 46N52'31 96w34'43 6:26:19
Gnesen 69 1 47N00 92w07 6:08:28
Godahl 8 1 44N06'32 94w38'23 6:18:34
Godfrey 60 1 47N38 96w14 6:24:56
Golden Hill 55 5 43N59'18 92w28'05 6:09:52
Golden Hills 27 3 44N57 93w21 6:13:24
Goldenrod 3 1 47N05'40 95w14'02 6:20:56
Golden Valley 27
3 45N00'35 93w20'56 6:13:24
Gonvick 15 1 47N44'15 95w30'48 6:22:03
Goodhue 25 1 44N24'02 92w37'25 6:10:30
Goodland 31 1 47N09'43 93w08'08 6:12:33
Goodridge 57 1 48N08'36 95w48'33 6:23:14
Good Thunder 7 1 44N00'17 94w03'56 6:16:16
Goodview 85 6 44N03'45 91w41'44 6:06:47
Goose Prairie 14
1 47N01 96w16 6:25:04
Gordon 77 1 45N53 95w04 6:20:16
Gordonsville 24 1 43N30'46 93w15'12 6:13:01
Gorman 56 1 46N40 95w36 6:22:24
Gorton 26 1 45N53 96w11 6:24:44
Gotha 10 1 44N43'02 93w47'18 6:15:09
Gould 11 1 47N11 94w12 6:16:48
Gowan 69 1 46N51'51 92w50'49 6:11:23
Grace 12 1 45N07 95w33 6:22:12
Gracelock 12 1 45N03'02 95w34'49 6:22:19
Graceton 39 1 48N44'28 94w50'10 6:19:21
Graceville 6 1 45N34'09 96w26'03 6:25:44
Graff 11 1 46N34'21 94w32'48 6:18:11
Grafton 72 1 44N40 94w34 6:18:16
Graham 5 1 45N46 94w05 6:16:20
Graham Lakes 53 1 43N42 95w28 6:21:52
Grainwood 70 1 44N43'20 93w26'21 6:13:45
Granada 46 1 43N41'44 94w20'51 6:17:23
Granby 52 1 44N21 94w12 6:16:48
Grand Falls 36 1 48N11'55 93w47'33 6:15:10
Grand Forks 60 1 47N59 97w02 6:28:08
Grand Lake 69 1 46N52'00 92w28'04 6:09:52
Grand Marais 16 1 47N45'02 90w20'03 6:01:20
Grand Meadow 50 1 43N42'21 92w34'19 6:10:17
Grand Plain 45 1 48N13 95w55 6:23:40
Grand Portage 16
1 47N57'50 89w41'05 5:58:44
Grand Portage Indian Res 16
1 47N58 89w42 5:58:48
Grand Prairie 53
1 43N33 96w00 6:24:00
Grand Rapids 31 1 47N14'14 93w31'48 6:14:07
Grandview 42 1 44N30 95w55 6:23:40
Grand View Heights 56
1 46N36'48 95w31'22 6:22:05
Grandy 30 1 45N38'07 93w11'42 6:12:47
Grange 59 1 44N04 96w15 6:25:00
Granger 23 1 43N30'08 92w08'19 6:08:33
Granite 49 1 46N02 94w01 6:16:04
Granite Falls 87
1 44N48'36 95w32'43 6:22:11
Granite Ledge 5 1 45N46 93w49 6:15:16
Granite Rock 64 1 44N25 95w25 6:21:40
Grant 69 1 47N29'36 92w47'50 6:11:11

Place		Lat.	Long.	Time
Grant 82	1	45N05	92w54	6:11:36
Grant Valley 4	1	47N27	94w59	6:19:56
Granville 35	1	48N51	96w52	6:27:28
Grass Lake 33	1	45N46'41	93w10'03	6:12:40
Grasston 33	1	45N47'41	93w08'56	6:12:36
Grattan 31	1	47N48	94w06	6:16:24
Gray 59	1	43N59	96w14	6:24:56
Grayling 1	1	46N37'45	93w12'38	6:12:51
Greaney 69	1	47N58'02	93w01'15	6:12:05
Great Bend 17	1	43N54	95w09	6:20:36
Greater Leech Lake Indian Re 4	1	47N20	94w12	6:16:48
Great Scott 69	1	47N32	92w44	6:10:56
Greely 58	1	45N44'41	93w04'05	6:12:16
Greenbush 68	1	48N42'02	96w10'53	6:24:44
Greenfield 27	1	45N03	93w38	6:14:32
Green Isle 72	1	44N40'45	94w00'29	6:16:02
Green Lake 34	1	45N12	94w57	6:19:48
Greenland 40	1	44N12'24	93w43'38	6:14:55
Greenleaf 47	1	44N59'47	94w29'57	6:18:00
Greenleafton 23	1	43N34'49	92w12'33	6:08:50
Green Meadow 54	1	47N22	96w23	6:25:32
Green Prairie 49	1	46N03	94w22	6:17:28
Greenvale 19	1	44N30	93w13	6:12:52
Green Valley 42	1	44N31'37	95w45'25	6:23:02
Greenview 60	1	47N37'33	96w33'37	6:26:14
Greenwald 73	1	45N36'06	94w51'35	6:19:26
Greenway 31	1	47N19	93w17	6:13:08
Greenwood 27	1	44N54'54	93w33'11	6:14:13
Greenwood Junction 38	1	47N26'27	91w34'47	6:06:19
Gregory 44	1	47N27	95w52	6:23:28
Gregory 49	1	45N56'22	94w21'22	6:17:25
Grey Cloud Island 82	1	44N48	93w00	6:12:00
Grey Eagle 77	1	45N49'31	94w44'47	6:18:59
Grimstad 68	1	48N41	95w47	6:23:08
Grogan 83	1	44N00'59	94w10'56	6:16:44
Groningen 58	1	46N09'03	92w55'26	6:11:42
Grove 73	1	45N38	94w50	6:19:20
Grove City 47	1	45N09'02	94w40'58	6:18:44
Grove Lake 61	1	45N36'51	95w09'26	6:20:38
Groveland 27	1	44N56'30	93w29'09	6:13:57
Grove Park 60	1	47N42	96w10	6:24:40
Grow 2	1	45N15	93w20	6:13:20
Grygla 45	1	48N18'03	95w37'05	6:22:28
Guckeen 22	1	43N39'05	94w13'29	6:16:54
Gully 60	1	47N46'07	95w37'21	6:22:29
Gunn 31	1	47N12'58	93w28'30	6:13:54
Gutches Grove 77	1	45N56'39	94w57'33	6:19:50
Guthrie 29	1	47N18'01	94w47'27	6:19:10
Hackensack 11	1	46N55'51	94w31'13	6:18:05
Hackett 39	1	48N48'57	94w43'06	6:18:52
Hader 25	1	44N21'56	92w48'03	6:11:12
Hadler 54	1	47N22'07	96w32'06	6:26:08
Hadley 51	1	44N00'04	95w51'13	6:23:25
Hagali 4	1	47N43	94w44	6:18:56
Hagan 12	1	45N08'55	95w46'33	6:23:06
Hagen 14	1	47N06	96w22	6:25:28
Halden 69	1	46N54	92w59	6:11:56
Hale 43	1	44N56	94w12	6:16:48
Haley 69	1	47N55'16	92w43'57	6:10:56
Hallock 35	1	48N46'28	96w56'46	6:27:47
Halma 35	1	48N39'40	96w36'00	6:26:24
Halstad 54	1	47N21'06	96w49'42	6:27:19
Hamburg 10	3	44N44'00	93w58'01	6:15:52
Hamden 3	1	46N56	95w59	6:23:56
Hamel 27	1	45N02'28	93w31'31	6:14:06
Hamilton 23	1	43N45'42	92w26'54	6:09:48
Ham Lake 2	1	45N15'58	93w14'03	6:12:56
Hamlin 37	1	44N56	96w10	6:24:40
Hammer 87	1	44N46	96w17	6:25:08
Hammond 79	1	44N13'20	92w22'24	6:09:30
Hampden 35	1	48N51	97w00	6:28:00
Hampton 19	1	44N36'37	93w00'07	6:12:00
Hamre 4	1	48N15	95w25	6:21:40
Hancock 75	1	45N29'51	95w47'47	6:23:11
Hangaard 15	1	47N53	95w32	6:22:08
Hanley Falls 87	1	44N41'34	95w37'18	6:22:29
Hanover 86	1	45N09'21	93w39'58	6:14:40
Hanska 8	1	44N08'56	94w29'38	6:17:59
Hansonville 41	1	44N35	96w23	6:25:32
Hantho 37	1	45N07	96w04	6:24:16
Happyland 36	1	48N24	93w34	6:14:16
Harding 49	1	46N06'58	94w02'26	6:16:10
Hardwick 67	1	43N46'30	96w11'57	6:24:48
Harlis 58	1	46N24'44	92w18'45	6:09:15
Harliss 25	1	44N34'57	92w39'19	6:10:37
Harmony 23	1	43N33'19	92w00'36	6:08:02
Harnell Park 69	1	46N53'15	92w23'46	6:09:35
Harney 9	1	46N43'18	92w20'00	6:09:20
Harold 60	1	47N42'08	96w29'50	6:25:59
Harris 13	1	45N35'11	92w58'28	6:11:54
Harrison 34	1	45N12	94w49	6:19:16
Hart 85	1	43N54	91w47	6:07:08
Hartford 77	1	46N04	94w50	6:19:20
Hart Lake 29	1	47N17	94w45	6:19:00
Hartland 24	1	43N48'14	93w29'12	6:13:57
Hartley Spur 69	1	46N59'49	93w01'30	6:12:06
Harvey 47	1	45N12	94w34	6:18:16
Hassan 27	1	45N11	93w35	6:14:20
Hassan Valley 43	1	44N51	94w18	6:17:12
Hassman 1	1	46N36'07	93w36'46	6:14:27
Hastings 19	1	44N44'36	92w51'08	6:11:25
Hasty 86	1	45N22'16	93w58'22	6:15:53
Hatfield 59	1	43N57'27	96w11'42	6:24:47
Haug 68	1	48N49'11	96w11'03	6:24:44
Haugen 1	1	46N43	93w07	6:12:28
Havana 74	1	44N03'59	93w08'46	6:12:35
Havelock 12	1	45N01	95w33	6:22:12
Haven 71	1	45N31	94w04	6:16:16
Hawick 34	1	45N20'52	94w49'37	6:19:18
Hawk Creek 65	1	44N46	95w25	6:21:40
Hawley 14	1	46N52'51	96w18'59	6:25:16
Hay Brook 33	1	46N07	93w22	6:13:28
Hay Creek 25	1	44N29'31	92w32'37	6:10:10
Haydenville 37	1	45N00'34	96w18'34	6:25:14
Hayes 76	1	45N18	95w24	6:21:36
Hayfield 20	1	43N53'26	92w50'51	6:11:23
Hayland 48	1	45N51	93w35	6:14:20
Haypoint 1	1	46N53'59	93w36'49	6:14:27
Hayward 24	1	43N39'02	93w14'38	6:12:59
Hazel 57	1	48N01'12	96w06'54	6:24:28
Hazel Park 62	3	44N59'15	92w59'04	6:11:56
Hazel Run 87	1	44N45'07	95w42'53	6:22:52
Hazeltine 10	1	44N50'13	93w36'04	6:14:24
Hazelton 10	1	44N57'24	93w57'05	6:15:48
Hazelwood 66	1	44N31'21	93w17'09	6:13:09
Heatwole 43	1	44N50'03	94w23'58	6:17:36
Hector 65	1	44N44'38	94w42'55	6:18:52
Hegbert 76	1	45N22	96w04	6:24:16
Hegne 54	1	47N17	96w37	6:26:28
Heiberg 54	1	47N16'59	96w16'32	6:25:06
Heidelberg 40	1	44N29'29	93w37'34	6:14:30
Heier 44	1	47N27	95w44	6:22:56
Height of Land 3	1	46N52	95w36	6:22:24
Heinola 56	1	46N27'22	95w24'25	6:21:38
Helen 43	1	44N46	94w04	6:16:16
Helena 70	1	44N35	93w35	6:14:20
Helga 29	1	47N22	94w51	6:19:24
Helgeland 60	1	48N08	96w35	6:26:20
Henderson 72	1	44N31'42	93w54'27	6:15:38
Hendricks 41	1	44N30'26	96w25'26	6:25:42
Hendrickson 29	1	47N17	94w51	6:19:24
Hendrickson Landing 36	1	48N18'00	93w49'12	6:15:17
Hendrum 54	1	47N15'52	96w48'40	6:27:15
Henning 56	1	46N19'18	95w26'42	6:21:47
Henrietta 29	1	46N56	94w59	6:19:56
Henriette 58	1	45N52'18	93w07'02	6:12:28
Henrytown 23	1	43N35'40	91w55'45	6:07:43
Henryville 65	1	44N40	95w03	6:20:12
Hereim 68	1	48N41	96w12	6:24:48
Herman 26	1	45N48'31	96w08'35	6:24:34
Hermantown 69	2	46N48	92w08	6:08:32
Heron Lake 32	1	43N47'42	95w19'12	6:21:17
Hersey 53	1	43N43	95w31	6:22:04
Hewitt 77	1	46N19'32	95w05'11	6:20:21
Hiawatha Spur 19	3	44N54	93w14	6:12:56
Hibbing 69	5	47N25'00	92w55'47	6:11:43
Hickory 57	1	47N59	95w39	6:22:36
Hidden Valley 82	1	45N16	92w59	6:11:56
Higdem 60	1	48N08	97w06	6:28:24
High Forest 55	1	43N50'42	92w32'59	6:10:12
Highland 23	1	43N40'51	91w52'12	6:07:29
Highland 27	3	45N00	93w18	6:13:12
Highland 38	1	47N12'18	91w43'09	6:06:53
Highland 86	1	45N07'23	94w01'57	6:16:08
Highland Grove 14	1	46N55	96w14	6:24:56
High Landing 57	1	48N02'58	95w48'30	6:23:14
Highland Park 62	3	44N55	93w10	6:12:40
Highwater 17	1	44N09	95w16	6:21:04
Highwood 62	3	44N54'53	93w00'51	6:12:03
Hill 35	1	48N51	97w07	6:28:28
Hill City 1	1	46N59'36	93w35'54	6:14:24
Hill Lake 1	1	46N59	93w37	6:14:28
Hillman 49	1	46N00'15	93w53'37	6:15:34
Hill River 60	1	47N43	95w46	6:23:04
Hills 67	1	43N31'41	96w21'30	6:25:26
Hillsdale 85	1	44N03	91w47	6:07:08
Hillside 69	2	46N48	92w06	6:08:24
Hilltop 2	3	45N03'12	93w14'50	6:12:59
Hillview 56	1	46N40'49	95w15'27	6:21:02
Hinckley 58	1	46N00'41	92w56'39	6:11:47
Hines 4	1	47N41'10	94w37'57	6:18:32
Hinsdale 69	1	47N36'04	92w08'52	6:08:35
Hiram 11	1	46N57	94w34	6:18:16
Hitterdal 14	1	46N58'39	96w15'32	6:25:02
Hixon 60	1	47N49'03	96w40'31	6:26:42
Hobart 56	1	46N09	95w50	6:23:20
Hodges 75	1	45N33	95w48	6:23:12
Hoff 61	1	45N33	95w41	6:22:44
Hoffman 26	1	45N49'46	95w47'30	6:23:10
Hoffmans Corner 62	3	45N03'01	93w01'54	6:12:08
Hokah 28	6	43N45'34	91w20'47	6:05:23
Holden 25	1	44N20	92w59	6:11:56
Holding 73	1	45N43	94w27	6:17:48
Holdingford 73	1	45N43'52	94w28'11	6:17:53
Holland 59	1	44N05'30	96w11'18	6:24:45
Hollandale 22	1	43N45'39	93w12'14	6:12:49
Hollandale Junction 24	1	43N39'49	93w11'21	6:12:45
Holloway 76	1	45N14'55	95w54'28	6:23:38
Holly 51	1	44N09	95w31	6:22:04
Hollywood 10	1	44N54'21	93w58'16	6:15:53
Holman 31	1	47N18'36	93w22'17	6:13:29
Holmes City 21	1	45N50'01	95w32'27	6:22:10
Holmesville 3	1	46N56	95w44	6:22:56
Holst 15	1	47N38	95w30	6:22:00
Holt 45	1	48N17'31	96w11'32	6:24:46
Holy Cross 14	1	46N40	96w43	6:26:52
Holyoke 9	1	46N28'03	92w23'18	6:09:33
Home 8	1	44N21	94w42	6:18:48
Home Brook 11	1	46N28	94w27	6:17:48
Home Lake 54	1	47N11	96w15	6:25:00
Homer 85	1	44N01'17	91w33'23	6:06:14
Homestead 56	1	46N35	95w20	6:21:20
Honner 64	1	44N33	95w04	6:20:16
Hoot Lake 56	1	46N18	96w06	6:24:24
Hope 74	1	43N57'43	93w16'33	6:13:06
Hopkins 27	3	44N55'30	93w27'45	6:13:51
Hopper 69	1	47N30'36	92w34'51	6:10:19
Hornby 69	1	47N20'36	91w54'07	6:07:36
Hornet 4	1	47N48	94w30	6:18:00
Horton 29	1	46N48'40	95w05'49	6:20:23
Horton 75	1	45N29	95w56	6:23:44
Houpt 31	1	47N48'02	94w23'28	6:17:34
Houston 28	6	43N45'48	91w34'06	6:06:16
Hovland 16	1	47N50'20	89w58'19	5:59:53
Howard Lake 86	1	45N03'39	94w04'23	6:16:18
Hoyt Lakes 69	1	47N31'11	92w08'18	6:08:33
Hubbard 29	1	46N50'12	95w00'36	6:20:02
Hudson 21	1	45N49	95w20	6:21:20
Hugo 82	1	45N09'36	92w59'35	6:11:58
Hull 69	1	47N11'51	92w55'23	6:11:42
Humboldt 35	1	48N55'16	97w05'35	6:28:22
Hunter 32	1	43N38	95w12	6:20:48
Hunters Park 69	2	46N49'45	92w04'23	6:08:18
Huntersville 80	1	46N46'33	94w53'33	6:19:34
Huntley 22	1	43N43'54	94w14'14	6:16:57
Huntly 45	1	48N30	96w12	6:24:48
Huntsville 60	1	47N53	96w57	6:27:48
Huot 63	1	47N51'55	96w25'23	6:25:42
Husby Spur 62	3	45N04	93w10	6:12:40
Huss 68	1	48N35	96w04	6:24:16
Hutchinson 43	1	44N53'16	94w22'10	6:17:29
Hutton 23	1	43N36'58	92w02'41	6:08:11
Hyde Park 79	1	44N16	92w21	6:09:24
Hydes Lake 10	1	44N49'08	93w50'57	6:15:24
Iberia 8	1	44N14'21	94w41'42	6:18:47
Ida 21	1	45N59	95w28	6:21:52
Ideal 18	1	46N40	94w09	6:16:36
Ideal Corners 18	1	46N36	94w11	6:16:44
Idington 69	1	47N44'00	92w39'06	6:10:36
Idun 1	1	46N13	93w22	6:13:28
Ihlen 59	1	43N54'26	96w22'01	6:25:28
Illgen City 38	1	47N20'49	91w11'22	6:04:45
Imogene 46	1	43N39'37	94w20'43	6:17:23
Independence 27	1	45N01'31	93w42'26	6:14:50
Independence 69	1	46N57'30	92w27'37	6:09:50
Indian Lake 53	1	43N33	95w31	6:22:04
Indus 36	1	48N37'31	93w50'15	6:15:21
Industrial 62	3	44N57	93w10	6:12:40
Industrial 69	1	46N53	92w29	6:09:56
Inez 4	1	47N51'37	94w34'48	6:18:19
Inger 31	1	47N33'15	93w59'06	6:15:56
Inguadona 11	1	46N59	94w08	6:16:32
Inman 56	1	46N20	95w19	6:21:16
Interlachen 27	3	44N56	93w25	6:13:40
International Falls 36	1	48N36'04	93w24'39	6:13:39
Inver Grove Heights 19	3	44N50'53	93w02'33	6:12:10
Iona (Iona Lake Station) 51	1	43N54'56	95w47'02	6:23:08
Iosco 81	1	44N09	93w36	6:14:24
Iron 69	1	47N25	92w36	6:10:24
Irondale 18	1	46N28	94w01	6:16:04
Ironhub 18	1	46N32	93w42	6:14:48
Iron Junction 69	1	47N25'08	92w36'12	6:10:25
Iron Range 31	1	47N21	93w24	6:13:36
Ironton 18	1	46N28'39	93w58'39	6:15:55
Irving 34	1	45N17	94w49	6:19:16
Isabella 38	1	47N37'02	91w21'17	6:05:25
Isanti 30	1	45N29'25	93w14'51	6:12:59
Isinours 23	1	43N42'37	92w03'20	6:08:13
Island 69	1	46N59'10	93w00'48	6:12:03
Island Lake 4	1	47N47'20	95w01'04	6:20:04
Island Park 27	1	44N55'29	93w38'17	6:14:33
Island View 36	1	48N35'43	93w10'00	6:12:40
Isle 48	1	46N08'17	93w28'14	6:13:53
Isle Harbor 48	1	46N06	93w30	6:14:00
Itasca 15	1	47N17	95w14	6:20:56
Ivanhoe 41	1	44N27'48	96w14'49	6:24:59
Iverson 9	1	46N39'59	92w31'45	6:10:07
Jack Pine 15	1	47N23'00	95w31'13	6:22:05
Jackson 32	1	43N37'15	94w59'18	6:19:57
Jacobson 1	1	47N00'03	93w16'02	6:13:04
Jacobs Prairie 73	1	45N29'13	94w23'34	6:17:34
Jadis 68	1	48N52	95w48	6:23:12
Jakeville 5	1	45N45'01	93w59'11	6:15:57
Jameson 36	1	48N36'14	93w21'57	6:13:28
Jamestown 7	1	44N13	93w50	6:15:20
Janesville 81	1	44N06'58	93w42'28	6:14:50
Jarrett 79	1	44N14'10	92w20'20	6:09:21
Jasper 59	1	43N51'00	96w23'54	6:25:36
Jay 46	1	43N38	94w48	6:19:12
Jay See Landing 38	1	47N32'45	91w28'40	6:05:55
Jeffers 17	1	44N03'21	95w11'47	6:20:47
Jefferson 28	1	43N32	91w20	6:05:20
Jelle 4	1	48N14'17	95w24'00	6:21:36
Jenkins 18	1	46N38'46	94w20'04	6:17:20
Jennie 47	1	45N00'28	94w20'52	6:17:23
Jessenland 72	1	44N34'19	93w55'23	6:15:42
Jessie Lake 31	1	47N36'04	93w49'01	6:15:16
Jevne 1	1	46N37	93w22	6:13:28
Jo Daviess 22	1	43N38	94w11	6:16:44
Johnsburg 50	1	43N30'20	92w46'08	6:11:05
Johnsdale 48	1	46N01'58	93w47'18	6:15:09
Johnson 6	1	45N34'22	96w17'42	6:25:11
Johnsonville 64	1	44N20	95w25	6:21:40
Johnsville 2	3	45N11'50	93w14'03	6:12:56
Jonathan 10	1	44N48	93w37	6:14:28
Jones 4	1	47N28	95w07	6:20:28
Jordan 38	1	47N22'35	91w37'48	6:06:31
Jordan 70	1	44N40'01	93w37'36	6:14:30
Judge 55	1	43N53'57	92w28'33	6:09:54
Judson 7	1	44N11'47	94w11'42	6:16:47
Jupiter 35	1	48N40	96w43	6:26:52
Jurgenson 31	1	47N19'56	93w13'46	6:12:55
Kabekona Corner 29	1	47N14'05	94w52'35	6:19:30
Kabetogama 69	1	48N26'16	93w01'38	6:12:07
Kalevala 9	1	46N33	92w53	6:11:32
Kalmar 55	1	44N04	92w37	6:10:28
Kanabec 33	1	45N52	93w26	6:13:44
Kanaranzi 67	1	43N34'33	96w05'39	6:24:23
Kandiyohi 34	1	45N07'56	94w55'51	6:19:43
Kandota 77	1	45N49	94w58	6:19:52
Karlstad 35	1	48N34'39	96w31'13	6:26:05
Kasota 52	1	44N17'33	93w57'53	6:15:52
Kasson 20	1	44N01'48	92w45'02	6:11:00
Kathio 48	1	46N09	93w47	6:15:08
Keenan 69	1	47N23'00	92w36'15	6:10:25
Keene 14	1	46N56	96w21	6:25:24
Keewatin 31	1	47N23'59	93w04'20	6:12:17
Kego 11	1	47N01	94w15	6:17:00
Kelliher 4	1	47N56'30	94w26'53	6:17:48
Kellogg 79	1	44N18'31	91w59'44	6:07:59
Kelly Lake 69	1	47N25'03	93w00'23	6:12:02
Kelly Landing 38	1	47N40'36	91w20'09	6:05:21
Kelsey 69	1	47N09'14	92w35'57	6:10:24
Kelso 72	1	44N30	94w04	6:16:16
Kennedy 35	1	48N38'31	96w54'31	6:27:38

Kennedy Landing 38 1 47N22'46 91W09'02 6:04:36
Kenneth 67 1 43N45'13 96W04'20 6:24:17
Kensington 21 1 45N46'41 95W41'45 6:22:47
Kent 84 1 46N26'11 96W41'04 6:26:44
Kenyon 25 1 44N16'20 92W59'07 6:11:56
Kerkhoven 76 1 45N11'35 95W19'13 6:21:17
Kerns 52 1 44N12'40 94W06'35 6:16:26
Kerr 69 1 47N25'25 92W58'47 6:11:55
Kerrick 58 1 46N20'20 92W35'08 6:10:21
Kertsonville 60 1 47N43 96W25 6:25:40
Kettle Falls 69 1 48N30'10 92W38'22 6:10:33
Kettle River 9 1 46N29'30 92W52'40 6:11:31
Kevin 31 1 47N20'55 93W11'37 6:12:46
Keystone 60 1 47N59 96W49 6:27:16
Key West 60 1 47N56'05 96W46'59 6:27:08
Kiester 22 1 43N32'11 93W42'43 6:14:51
Kildare 76 1 45N17 95W27 6:21:48
Kilkenny 40 1 44N18'48 93W34'26 6:14:18
Kimball 32 1 43N48 94W58 6:19:52
Kimball 73 1 45N18'45 94W18'00 6:17:12
Kimball Prairie 73 1 45N19 94W18 6:17:12
Kimberly 1 1 46N33'39 93W27'58 6:13:52
Kinbrae 53 1 43N49'33 95W29'13 6:21:57
King 60 1 47N37 95W53 6:23:32
Kinghurst 31 1 47N43 94W06 6:16:24
Kingman 65 1 44N51 94W57 6:19:48
Kingsdale 58 1 46N14'18 92W18'41 6:09:15
Kingsley Corner 55 1 44N04'42 92W06'51 6:08:27
Kings Park 55 1 44N10 92W32 6:10:08
Kingston 47 1 45N11'49 94W18'47 6:17:15
Kinmount 69 1 48N03 92W50 6:11:20
Kinney 69 1 47N30'51 92W43'50 6:10:55
Kintire 64 1 44N35 95W18 6:21:12
Kirk 69 1 47N24'55 92W39'45 6:10:39
Kitzville 69 5 47N27'08 92W53'51 6:11:35
Klondyke 18 1 46N26'30 93W57'57 6:15:52
Klossner 52 1 44N21'57 94W25'32 6:17:42
Knapp 86 1 45N09'08 94W13'34 6:16:54
Knife Falls 9 1 46N43 92W30 6:10:00
Knife Lake 33 1 45N56 93W19 6:13:16
Knife River 38 1 46N56'58 91W46'44 6:07:07
Knute 60 1 47N38 96W00 6:24:00
Komensky 43 1 44N54'26 94W16'36 6:17:06
Kost 13 1 45N29'31 92W52'04 6:11:28
Kragero 12 1 45N06 95W55 6:23:40
Kragnes 14 1 46N59'18 96W45'05 6:27:00
Krain 73 1 45N44 94W34 6:18:16
Kratka 57 1 48N04 95W55 6:23:40
Kroschel 33 1 46N04'18 93W04'33 6:12:18
Kugler 69 1 47N45 92W15 6:09:00
Kurtz 14 1 46N45 96W44 6:26:56
LaBelle 3 1 46N52'58 96W03'44 6:24:15
Lac qui Parle 37 1 45N00'02 95W54'21 6:23:37
LaCrescent 28 6 43N49'41 91W18'14 6:05:13
La Crosse 32 1 43N48 95W24 6:21:36
Lafayette 52 1 44N26'48 94W23'42 6:17:35
La Garde 44 1 47N16 95W44 6:22:56
Lagoona Beach 6 1 45N21'59 96W29'07 6:25:56
La Grand 21 1 45N54 95W26 6:21:44
Lake Alice 29 1 47N12 95W06 6:20:24
Lake Andrew 34 1 45N18 95W04 6:20:16
Lake Belt 46 1 43N33 94W40 6:18:40
Lake Benton 41 1 44N15'40 96W17'14 6:25:09
Lake Bronson 35 1 48N44'08 96W39'45 6:26:39
Lake Center 3 1 46N52 95W59 6:23:56
Lake City 79 1 44N26'58 92W16'00 6:09:04
Lake Crystal 7 1 44N06'21 94W13'07 6:16:52
Lake Edwards 18 1 46N30 94W12 6:16:48
Lake Elizabeth 34 1 45N01 94W49 6:19:16
Lake Elmo 82 1 44N59'45 92W52'45 6:11:31
Lake Emma 29 1 47N01 94W59 6:19:56
Lake Eunice 3 1 46N44'46 95W58'08 6:23:53
Lakefield 32 1 43N40'39 95W10'17 6:20:41
Lake Five State Wildlife Man 33 1 46N08'23 93W08'18 6:12:33
Lake Fremont 46 1 43N33 94W49 6:19:16
Lake Fremont 71 1 45N26'36 93W35'23 6:14:22
Lake George 29 1 47N12'02 94W59'36 6:19:58
Lake Grove 44 1 47N11 95W52 6:23:28
Lake Hanska 8 1 44N09 94W33 6:18:12
Lake Hattie 29 1 47N17 95W06 6:20:24
Lake Henry 73 1 45N27'38 94W47'46 6:19:11
Lake Hubert 18 1 46N30'08 94W15'26 6:17:02
Lake Ida 54 1 47N17 96W22 6:25:28
Lake Itasca 15 1 47N15'14 95W12'44 6:20:51
Lake Jessie 31 1 47N38 93W51 6:15:24
Lake Johanna 61 1 45N28 95W10 6:20:40
Lakeland 82 1 44N57'23 92W45'56 6:11:04
Lakeland Shores 82 1 44N56'53 92W45'50 6:11:03
Lake Lillian 34 1 44N56'37 94W52'47 6:19:31
Lake Marshall 42 1 44N25 95W47 6:23:08
Lake Mary 21 1 45N48 95W27 6:21:48
Lake Netta 2 3 45N16'48 93W11'30 6:12:46
Lake Nichols 69 1 47N02 92W28 6:09:52
Lake Park 3 1 46N53'11 96W05'39 6:24:23
Lake Pleasant 63 1 47N48 96W17 6:25:08
Lakeport 29 1 47N12 94W44 6:18:56
Lake Prairie 52 1 44N25 94W04 6:16:16
Lake Saint Croix Beach 82 1 44N55'15 92W46'00 6:11:04
Lake Sarah 27 1 45N04'19 93W41'24 6:14:46
Lake Sarah 51 1 44N08 95W46 6:23:04
Lake Shore 11 1 46N29'08 94W21'37 6:17:26
Lake Shore Park 62 3 45N04'18 93W00'40 6:12:03
Lakeside 65 1 44N50'03 94W33'32 6:18:14
Lakeside 69 2 46N50 92W04 6:08:16
Lake Stay 41 1 44N25 96W08 6:24:32
Laketown 10 1 44N51 93W42 6:14:48
Lake Valley 78 1 45N48 96W28 6:25:52
Lakeville 19 1 44N38'59 93W14'33 6:12:58
Lake Wilson 51 1 43N59'48 95W57'09 6:23:49
Lakewood 69 1 46N51'50 91W57'45 6:07:51
Lakin 49 1 45N52 93W51 6:15:24
Lambert 63 1 47N48 95W54 6:23:36
Lamberton 64 1 44N13'52 95W15'50 6:21:03
Lammers 4 1 47N33 95W07 6:20:28
Lamoille 85 1 44N00'08 91W28'20 6:05:53
Lamson 47 1 44N59'25 94W16'28 6:17:06
Lancaster 35 1 48N51'30 96W48'14 6:27:13
Land 26 1 45N48 95W49 6:23:16
Landfall 82 3 44N57'03 92W58'35 6:11:54
Lanesboro 23 1 43N43'15 91W58'36 6:07:54
Lanesburgh 40 1 44N30 93W34 6:14:16
Langdon 82 1 44N48'36 92W55'43 6:11:43
Langhei 61 1 45N27 95W34 6:22:16
Langola 5 1 45N47 94W12 6:16:48
Langor 4 1 47N46'51 94W35'29 6:18:22
Lansing 50 1 43N44'43 92W58'12 6:11:53
Laona 68 1 48N51 95W10 6:20:40
Laporte 29 1 47N12'50 94W45'14 6:19:01
La Prairie 31 1 47N13'42 93W29'20 6:13:57
Largo 69 1 47N28'49 92W34'13 6:10:17
Larkin 53 1 43N43 95W52 6:23:28
Larsmont 38 1 46N58'45 91W44'44 6:06:59
La Salle 83 1 44N04'15 94W34'10 6:18:17
Lastrup 49 1 46N02'22 94W03'47 6:16:15
Lauderdale 62 3 44N59'55 93W12'20 6:12:49
Laurel 36 1 48N30'54 93W40'28 6:14:42
Lauren 38 1 47N11'05 91W41'51 6:06:47
Lavell 69 1 47N16 92W49 6:11:16
Lavinia 4 1 47N30'54 94W48'41 6:19:15
Lavinia 69 5 47N28'21 92W56'46 6:11:47
Lawler 1 1 46N32'10 93W10'13 6:12:41
Lawndale 84 1 46N33'25 96W21'36 6:25:26
Lawrence 70 1 44N39'29 93W41'04 6:14:44
Lax Lake 38 1 47N20'39 91W18'31 6:05:14
Leader 11 1 46N31'43 94W39'17 6:18:37
Leaf Lake 56 1 46N25 95W28 6:21:52
Leaf Mountain 56 1 46N09 95W35 6:22:20
Leaf River 79 1 46N29'19 95W04'53 6:20:20
Leaf Valley 21 1 46N02'58 95W27'28 6:21:50
Leander 69 1 47N48'11 92W39'01 6:10:36
Leavenworth 8 1 44N13'21 94W48'06 6:19:12
Le Center 40 1 44N23'22 93W43'48 6:14:55
Leech Lake 11 1 47N11 94W36 6:18:24
Leeds 51 1 43N59 95W53 6:23:32
Leenthrop 12 1 44N56 95W33 6:22:12
Leetonia 69 5 47N25'45 92W59'06 6:11:56
Legionville 18 1 46N26'50 94W11'57 6:16:48
LeHillier 7 1 44N09'07 94W02'06 6:16:08
Leiding 69 1 48N02 92W50 6:11:20
Leigh 49 1 46N02 93W54 6:15:36
Leighton 27 1 45N03'55 93W37'12 6:14:29
Lemond 74 1 43N58'57 93W22'48 6:13:31
Lengby 60 1 47N30'57 95W38'08 6:22:33
Lennox 18 1 46N14'37 94W20'34 6:17:22
Lenora 23 1 43N34'21 91W52'56 6:07:32
Lent 13 1 45N31 92W57 6:11:48
Leo 68 1 48N45'39 96W15'01 6:25:00
Leonard 15 1 47N39'07 95W16'19 6:21:05
Leonardsville 78 1 45N37 96W19 6:25:16
Leonidas 69 1 47N27'42 92W34'18 6:10:17
Leota 53 1 43N50'02 96W00'48 6:24:03
Le Ray 7 1 44N12 93W49 6:15:16
Lerdal 24 1 43N43'26 93W16'08 6:13:05
Le Roy 50 1 43N30'35 92W30'13 6:10:01
Le Sauk 73 1 45N38 94W14 6:16:56
Leslie 77 1 45N58 95W04 6:20:16
Lessor 60 1 47N43 95W54 6:23:36
Lester Park 69 1 46N50'15 92W01'10 6:08:05
Lester Prairie 43 1 44N53'02 94W02'29 6:16:10
Le Sueur 40 1 44N30'07 93W52'46 6:15:31
Leven 61 1 45N43 95W20 6:21:20
Lewis 48 1 46N01 93W30 6:14:00
Lewis Lake 33 1 45N46'00 93W22'07 6:13:28
Lewiston 85 1 43N59'04 91W52'09 6:07:29
Lewisville 83 1 43N55'24 94W26'14 6:17:45
Lexington 2 3 45N08'33 93W09'47 6:12:39
Lexington 40 1 44N26'33 93W42'08 6:14:49
Libby 1 1 46N47'03 93W19'30 6:13:18
Lien 26 1 45N53 95W56 6:23:44
Lilydale 19 3 44N54'58 93W07'33 6:12:30
Lima 11 1 47N02 93W56 6:15:44
Lime 7 1 44N13 93W57 6:15:48
Lime Creek 51 1 43N53'23 95W33'42 6:22:15
Lime Lake 51 1 43N59 95W38 6:22:32
Limestone 41 1 44N30 96W08 6:24:32
Lincoln 77 1 46N12'37 94W38'26 6:18:34
Lind 68 1 48N35 96W20 6:25:20
Linden 8 1 44N10'53 94W24'33 6:17:38
Linden Grove 69 1 47N51'47 92W52'13 6:11:29
Linden Hills 27 3 44N55 93W19 6:13:16
Lindford 36 1 48N24'39 93W46'54 6:15:08
Lindstrom 13 1 45N23'22 92W50'52 6:11:23
Lino Lakes 2 1 45N09'37 93W05'19 6:12:21
Linsell 45 1 48N31 95W40 6:22:40
Linwood 2 1 45N21'25 93W06'41 6:12:27
Lisbon 87 1 44N51 95W48 6:23:12
Lismore 53 1 43N44'52 95W56'49 6:23:47
Litchfield 47 1 45N07'38 94W31'40 6:18:07
Litomysl 74 1 43N56'50 93W11'09 6:12:45
Little Canada 62 3 45N01'37 93W05'15 6:12:21
Little Chicago 66 1 44N28'45 93W19'19 6:13:17
Little Elk 77 1 46N04 94W43 6:18:52
Little Falls 49 1 45N58'35 94W21'44 6:17:27
Littlefork 36 1 48N23'56 93W33'20 6:14:13
Little Marais 38 1 47N24'39 91W06'36 6:04:26
Little Pine 18 1 46N44'44 93W51'40 6:15:27
Little Rock 49 1 45N49'57 94W05'33 6:16:22
Little Rock 53 1 43N33 95W52 6:23:28
Little Sauk 77 1 45N51'50 94W55'05 6:19:40
Little Swan 69 5 47N17'50 92W49'51 6:11:19
Livonia 71 1 45N26 93W34 6:14:16
Lockhart 54 1 47N26'24 96W33'03 6:26:12
Lodi 50 1 43N33 92W38 6:10:32
Loerch 18 1 46N24'12 94W04'20 6:16:17
Loman 36 1 48N30'46 93W48'10 6:15:13
London 24 1 43N31'34 93W03'45 6:12:15
London 38 1 47N12'10 91W34'10 6:06:17
Lone Pine 31 1 47N19 93W08 6:12:32
Lone Tree 12 1 45N01 95W18 6:21:12
Long Beach 61 1 45N39'17 95W25'02 6:21:40
Long Lake 27 1 44N59'12 93W34'17 6:14:17
Long Point 39 1 48N58'38 94W57'35 6:19:50
Long Prairie 77 1 45N58'29 94W51'55 6:19:28
Long Siding 48 1 45N34 93W35 6:14:20
Longville 11 1 46N59'11 94W12'40 6:16:51
Longworth 68 1 48N58'57 95W21'53 6:21:28
Lonsdale 66 1 44N28'49 93W25'42 6:13:43
Loon Lake 11 1 46N34 94W21 6:17:24
Loop 27 3 44N59 93W16 6:13:04
Lorain 53 1 43N38 95W31 6:22:04
Loretto 27 1 45N03'17 93W38'07 6:14:32
Loring 27 3 44N58 93W17 6:13:08
Loring Park 27 3 44N58 93W18 6:13:12
Lorne 87 1 44N44'46 95W34'27 6:22:18
Louisburg 37 1 45N09'58 96W10'15 6:24:41
Louriston 12 1 45N06 95W26 6:21:44
Lowell 60 1 47N48 96W48 6:27:12
Lower Sioux Indian Res 64 1 44N31 94W59 6:19:56
Lowry 61 1 45N42'18 95W31'04 6:22:04
Lowry Hill 27 3 44N58 93W18 6:13:12
Lowville 51 1 44N04 95W53 6:23:32
Lucan 64 1 44N24'35 95W24'37 6:21:38
Lucas 42 1 44N35 95W40 6:22:40
Luce 56 1 46N39'28 95W39'09 6:22:37
Lucknow 69 1 47N30'04 92W44'10 6:10:57
Lude 39 1 48N46 94W57 6:19:48
Luna 45 1 48N15'13 96W47'36 6:27:10
Lund 21 1 46N03 95W41 6:22:44
Lura 22 1 43N48 93W57 6:15:48
Lutsen 16 1 47N38'50 90W40'29 6:02:42
Luverne 67 1 43N39'15 96W12'45 6:24:51
Luxemburg 73 1 45N27'10 94W14'46 6:16:59
Lydia 70 1 44N39'10 93W30'03 6:14:00
Lyle 50 1 43N30'19 92W56'38 6:11:47
Lyman 56 1 46N20'24 95W14'54 6:21:00
Lynd 42 1 44N23'10 95W53'24 6:23:34
Lyndale 27 1 44N58'57 93W43'54 6:14:56
Lynden 73 1 45N24 94W05 6:16:20
Lynn 43 1 44N51 94W26 6:17:44
Lynwood 69 5 47N25 92W55 6:11:40
Lyra 7 1 43N59 94W04 6:16:16
Mabel 23 1 43N31'14 91W46'10 6:07:05
Macsville 26 1 45N49 96W04 6:24:16
Macville 1 1 46N54 93W38 6:14:32
Madelia 83 1 44N03'03 94W25'05 6:17:40
Madison 37 1 45N00'35 96W11'44 6:24:47
Madison Lake 7 1 44N12'16 93W48'55 6:15:16
Mae 11 1 46N49'56 93W51'55 6:15:28
Magnolia 67 1 43N38'43 96W04'44 6:24:19
Mahkonce 44 1 47N19'28 95W36'55 6:22:28
Mahnomen 44 1 47N18'55 95W58'06 6:23:52
Mahoning 69 5 47N26'57 92W58'19 6:11:53
Mahtomedi 82 3 45N04'11 92W57'05 6:11:48
Mahtowa 9 1 46N34'26 92W37'54 6:10:32
Maine 56 1 46N24'44 95W49'01 6:23:16
Maine Prairie 73 1 45N22 94W19 6:17:16
Makinen 69 1 47N21'26 92W22'03 6:09:28
Malcolm 4 1 48N19'28 95W20'07 6:21:20
Mallory 60 1 47N52'36 96W54'41 6:27:39
Malmo 1 1 46N20'02 93W31'09 6:14:05
Malta 6 1 45N27 96W18 6:25:12
Malung 68 1 48N46'21 95W43'26 6:22:54
Mamre 34 1 45N12 95W11 6:20:44
Manannah 47 1 45N15'13 94W37'02 6:18:28
Manchester 24 1 43N43'32 93W27'06 6:13:48
Mandt 12 1 45N06 95W41 6:22:44
Maney 69 1 46N59'25 92W36'28 6:10:26
Manfred 37 1 44N51 96W24 6:25:36
Manganese 18 1 46N31'39 94W00'34 6:16:02
Manhattan Beach 18 1 46N43'42 94W08'04 6:16:32
Manitoba Junction 14 1 46N54'24 96W14'50 6:24:59
Manitou 27 1 44N54 93W34 6:14:16
Manitou 36 1 48N37'42 93W59'34 6:15:58
Manitou Junction 38 1 47N34'07 91W15'30 6:05:02
Mankato 7 1 44N09'49 93W59'57 6:16:00
Manley 67 1 43N35'25 96W25'51 6:25:43
Mansfield 24 1 43N34'21 93W36'31 6:14:26
Manston 84 1 46N30 96W28 6:25:52
Mantorville 20 1 44N04'09 92W45'20 6:11:01
Mantrap 29 1 47N01 94W51 6:19:24
Manyaska 46 1 43N38 94W40 6:18:40
Maple 10 3 44N52'54 93W48'56 6:15:16
Maple 11 1 46N35 94W26 6:17:44
Maple 38 1 47N27'29 91W09'06 6:04:36
Maple Bay 60 1 47N38'09 96W13'29 6:24:54
Maple Grove 27 1 45N04'21 93W27'20 6:13:49
Maple Hill 16 1 47N48'28 90W18'17 6:01:13
Maple Island 24 1 43N45'42 93W09'49 6:12:39
Maple Island 82 1 45N10'27 92W51'18 6:11:25
Maple Lake 86 1 45N13'45 94W00'06 6:16:00
Maple Plain 27 1 45N00'26 93W39'20 6:14:37
Maple Springs 79 1 44N24'35 92W09'42 6:08:39
Mapleton 7 1 43N55'44 93W57'21 6:15:49
Mapleview 50 1 43N41'20 92W58'45 6:11:55
Maplewood 62 3 44N57'11 92W59'42 6:11:59
Marble 31 1 47N19'14 93W17'54 6:13:12
Marcell 31 1 47N35'35 93W41'26 6:14:46
March 45 1 48N11'42 96W53'49 6:27:35
Margie 36 1 48N05'43 93W56'23 6:15:46
Marietta 37 1 45N00'30 96W25'02 6:25:40
Marine on Saint Croix 82 1 45N22'00 92W46'15 6:11:05
Marion 55 1 43N56'37 92W20'53 6:09:24
Markham 69 1 47N17'57 92W13'06 6:08:52
Markville 58 1 46N05'31 92W19'50 6:09:19
Marna 22 1 43N36'21 94W00'27 6:16:02
Marshall 42 1 44N26'49 95W47'17 6:23:09
Marshan 19 1 44N40 92W51 6:11:24
Marsh Creek 44 1 47N22 95W59 6:23:56
Marshfield 41 1 44N20 96W08 6:24:32
Marsh Grove 45 1 48N20 96W26 6:25:44
Martin 67 1 43N33 96W24 6:25:36
Martin Lake 2 1 45N22'52 93W05'41 6:12:23
Martin Landing 38 1 47N44'42 91W18'13 6:05:13
Martinsburg 65 1 44N40 94W41 6:18:44

Place		Lat	Long	Time
Marty 73	1	45N23'59	94w19'57	6:17:20
Mary 54	1	47N12	96w37	6:26:28
Marysburg 40	1	44N14'25	93w49'00	6:15:16
Marysland 76	1	45N17	95w49	6:23:16
Marystown 70	1	44N43'15	93w32'28	6:14:10
Marysville 86	1	45N06	93w57	6:15:48
Mason 51	1	44N04	95w46	6:23:04
Matawan 81	1	43N51'29	93w38'09	6:14:33
Mattson 35	1	48N41'22	97w04'24	6:28:18
Mavie 57	1	48N08'41	95w56'19	6:23:45
Max 31	1	47N36'53	94w04'04	6:16:16
Maxwell 37	1	44N51	96w02	6:24:08
Mayer 10	1	44N53'06	93w53'15	6:15:33
Mayfield 57	1	48N00	95w54	6:23:36
Mayhew 5	1	45N42'48	94w06'38	6:16:27
Mayhew Lake 5	1	45N41	94w04	6:16:16
Maynard 12	1	44N54'25	95w28'07	6:21:52
Mayville 28	1	43N38	91w26	6:05:44
Mayville 50	1	43N45'50	92w54'33	6:11:38
Maywood 5	1	45N42	93w49	6:15:16
Mazeppa 79	1	44N16'23	92w32'41	6:10:11
McCauleyville 84	1	46N26'30	96w42'27	6:26:50
McComber 69	1	47N50'56	92w03'55	6:08:16
McCrea 45	1	48N14	96w42	6:26:48
McDavitt 69	1	47N19	92w37	6:10:28
McDonaldsville 54	1	47N17	96w30	6:26:00
McGrath 1	1	46N14'24	93w16'20	6:13:05
McGregor 1	1	46N36'24	93w18'49	6:13:15
McIntosh 60	1	47N38'13	95w53'10	6:23:33
McKee 19	3	44N55	93w14	6:12:56
McKinley 69	1	47N30'46	92w24'39	6:09:39
McNair 38	1	47N19'12	91w40'21	6:06:41
McPherson 7	1	44N04	93w50	6:15:20
Meadow 80	1	46N41	94w58	6:19:52
Meadow Brook 11	1	46N29	94w38	6:18:32
Meadow Brook 69	1	47N51'46	92w57'16	6:11:49
Meadowlands 69	1	47N04'19	92w43'56	6:10:56
Meadows 84	1	46N25	96w28	6:25:52
Medford 74	1	44N10'27	93w14'46	6:12:59
Medicine Lake 27	3	44N59'43	93w24'55	6:13:40
Medina 27	1	45N02	93w35	6:14:20
Medo 7	1	43N59	93w50	6:15:20
Mehurin 37	1	44N56	96w24	6:25:36
Meire Grove 73	1	45N37'47	94w52'08	6:19:29
Melby 21	1	46N03'50	95w44'08	6:22:57
Melrose 73	1	45N40'29	94w48'26	6:19:14
Melrude 69	1	47N14'44	92w25'01	6:09:40
Melville 65	1	44N46	94w49	6:19:16
Melvin 60	1	47N37'15	96w23'20	6:25:33
Menahga 79	1	46N45'14	95w05'52	6:20:23
Mendota 19	3	44N53'14	93w09'51	6:12:39
Mendota Heights 19	3	44N53'01	93w08'17	6:12:33
Mentor 60	1	47N41'54	96w08'27	6:24:34
Meriden 74	1	44N04'27	93w23'12	6:13:33
Merriam 70	1	44N44'16	93w35'39	6:14:23
Merrifield 18	1	46N27'54	94w10'21	6:16:41
Merton 74	1	44N08'46	93w08'47	6:12:35
Mesaba 69	1	47N34'08	92w07'54	6:08:32
Meyhew Lake 5	1	45N35	94w10	6:16:40
Mickinock 68	1	48N40	95w41	6:22:44
Middle River 45	1	48N26'03	96w09'50	6:24:39
Middletown 32	1	43N33	95w05	6:20:20
Middleville 86	1	45N07	94w04	6:16:16
Midland Junction 79	1	44N19'16	92w00'05	6:08:00
Midvale 62	3	44N58'18	92w59'41	6:11:59
Midway 3	1	46N46'55	95w15'36	6:21:02
Midway 62	3	44N57	93w10	6:12:40
Midway 69	1	47N29'28	92w31'32	6:10:06
Miesville 19	1	44N36'02	92w48'46	6:11:15
Milaca 48	1	45N45'21	93w39'15	6:14:37
Milan 12	1	45N06'31	95w54'47	6:23:39
Mildred 11	1	46N45'18	94w27'52	6:17:51
Milford 8	1	44N20	94w53	6:19:32
Mille Lacs Indian Res 58	1	46N03	92w28	6:09:52
Millersburg 66	1	44N25'40	93w19'54	6:13:20
Millerville 21	1	46N04'03	95w33'44	6:22:15
Millstone Landing 28	1	43N32'21	91w16'32	6:05:06
Millville 79	1	44N14'41	92w17'44	6:09:11
Millwood 73	1	45N43	94w42	6:18:48
Milo 48	1	45N41	93w42	6:14:48
Miloma 32	1	43N45'46	95w22'05	6:21:28
Milroy 64	1	44N25'04	95w33'11	6:22:13
Milton 20	1	44N09	92w44	6:10:56
Miltona 21	1	46N02'39	95w17'28	6:21:10
Minden 5	1	45N36	94w05	6:16:20
Minerva 15	1	47N22'09	95w22'55	6:21:32
Minneapolis 27	3	44N58'48	93w15'49	6:13:03
Minnehaha 27	3	44N57	93w14	6:12:56
Minneiska 85	6	44N11'42	91w52'18	6:07:29
Minneola 25	1	44N19	92w44	6:10:56
Minneota 42	1	44N34	95w59	6:23:56
Minnesota 42	1	44N33'32	95w59'07	6:23:56
Minnesota Boys Town 30	1	45N33'24	93w10'35	6:12:42
Minnesota City 85	1	44N05'38	91w44'58	6:07:00
Minnesota Falls 87	1	44N46	95w32	6:22:08
Minnesota Lake 22	1	43N50'31	93w49'54	6:15:20
Minnesota Transfer 62	3	44N57	93w11	6:12:44
Minnetonka 27	3	44N54'48	93w30'11	6:14:01
Minnetonka Beach 27	1	44N56'23	93w34'35	6:14:18
Minnetonka Mills 27	3	44N56'28	93w26'30	6:13:46
Minnetrista 27	1	44N56	93w42	6:14:48
Minnewana 1	1	46N36	93w19	6:13:16
Minnewaska 61	1	45N39	95w29	6:21:56
Minnewawa 1	1	46N41'55	93w16'29	6:13:06
Minnie 4	1	48N19	95w16	6:21:04
Missabe Junction 69	2	46N45'34	92w07'42	6:08:31
Missabe Mountain 69	1	47N30	92w29	6:09:56
Mission 18	1	46N35'17	94w03'03	6:16:12
Mission Creek 58	1	45N58'13	92w56'59	6:11:48
Mission Farms 27	3	45N01'06	93w25'26	6:13:42
Mitchell 69	5	47N26'44	92w53'42	6:11:35
Mitchell 84	1	46N30	96w35	6:26:20
Mizpah 36	1	47N55'27	94w12'13	6:16:49
Moe 21	1	45N53	95w35	6:22:20
Moland 14	1	46N56	96w37	6:26:28
Moland 74	1	44N11'48	93w03'41	6:12:15
Moltke 72	1	44N35	94w34	6:18:16
Money Creek 28	1	43N49'17	91w36'48	6:06:27
Monroe 42	1	44N14	95w40	6:22:40
Monson 78	1	45N53	96w30	6:26:00
Monterey 46	1	43N45	94w43	6:18:52
Montevideo 12	1	44N56'33	95w43'24	6:22:54
Montgomery 40	1	44N26'20	93w34'52	6:14:19
Monticello 86	1	45N18'20	93w47'38	6:15:11
Montrose 86	1	45N03'54	93w54'39	6:15:39
Moonshine 6	1	45N32	96w18	6:25:12
Moore 75	1	45N28	95w48	6:23:12
Moorhead 14	1	46N52'26	96w46'02	6:27:04
Moose 68	1	48N51	96w04	6:24:16
Moose Creek 15	1	47N28	95w14	6:20:56
Moose Lake 9	1	46N27'15	92w45'42	6:11:03
Moose Park 31	1	47N43	94w21	6:17:24
Moose River 45	1	48N30	95w49	6:23:16
Mora 33	1	45N52'37	93w17'37	6:13:10
Moran 77	1	46N14	94w50	6:19:20
Moranville 68	1	48N51	95w18	6:21:12
Morcom 69	1	47N46	93w01	6:12:04
Morgan 64	1	44N25'01	94w55'31	6:19:42
Morgan Park 69	1	46N41'18	92w12'36	6:08:50
Morken 14	1	47N01	96w38	6:26:32
Morningside 27	3	44N55	93w20	6:13:20
Morrill 49	1	45N50'20	93w58'10	6:15:53
Morris 75	1	45N35'10	95w54'49	6:23:39
Morrison 1	1	46N37	93w37	6:14:28
Morristown 40	1	44N13'38	93w26'40	6:13:47
Mort 2	1	45N21'38	93w11'07	6:12:44
Morton 65	1	44N33'05	94w59'03	6:19:56
Moscow 24	1	43N42'26	93w05'53	6:12:24
Motley 49	1	46N20'12	94w38'45	6:18:35
Moulton 51	1	43N54	95w59	6:23:56
Mound 27	1	44N56'12	93w39'57	6:14:40
Mound Prairie 28	1	43N47	91w26	6:05:44
Mounds View 62	3	45N06'18	93w12'30	6:12:50
Mountain Iron 69	1	47N31'57	92w37'24	6:10:30
Mountain Lake 17	1	43N56'20	94w55'46	6:19:43
Mount Morris 49	1	45N57	93w52	6:15:28
Mount Pleasant 79	1	44N25	92w22	6:09:28
Mount Royal 69	2	46N50	92w06	6:08:24
Mount Vernon 85	1	44N09	91w54	6:07:36
Moyer 76	1	45N17	95w55	6:23:40
Moylan 45	1	48N14	95w47	6:23:08
Muckland 24	1	43N44'41	93w11'20	6:12:45
Mudbaden 70	1	44N41'30	93w37'03	6:14:28
Mudgett 48	1	45N56	93w35	6:14:20
Mulligan 8	1	44N10	94w48	6:19:12
Munch 58	1	45N56	92w50	6:11:20
Munger 69	2	46N48'03	92w20'37	6:09:22
Munson 73	1	45N27	94w35	6:18:20
Murdock 76	1	45N13'26	95w23'35	6:21:34
Murphy City 38	1	47N30'35	91w19'28	6:05:18
Murray 51	1	44N04	95w39	6:22:36
Murray 69	1	47N48'58	92w10'49	6:08:43
Murtaugh 24	1	43N36'00	93w19'41	6:13:19
Muskoda 14	1	46N51'42	96w24'23	6:25:38
Myrtle 24	1	43N33'52	93w09'48	6:12:39
Nakoda 36	1	48N30'54	93w27'29	6:13:50
Nansen 25	1	44N21'01	92w55'54	6:11:44
Nary 29	1	47N22'01	94w49'23	6:19:18
Nashua 84	1	46N02'15	96w18'28	6:25:14
Nashville Center 46	1	43N50'03	94w18'27	6:17:14
Nashwauk 31	1	47N22'49	93w10'05	6:12:40
Nassau 37	1	45N03'59	96w26'22	6:25:45
Navarre 27	1	44N58	93w36	6:14:24
Naytahwaush 44	1	47N15'46	95w37'33	6:22:30
Nebish 4	1	47N46'17	94w50'50	6:19:23
Nelson 21	1	45N53'22	95w15'50	6:21:03
Nelson Park 45	1	48N30	96w35	6:26:20
Nemadji 9	1	46N28'46	92w35'40	6:10:23
Nereson 68	1	48N41	95w57	6:23:48
Nerstrand 66	1	44N20'31	93w04'04	6:12:16
Nesbit 60	1	47N53	96w48	6:27:12
Ness 69	1	46N59	92w45	6:11:00
Nessel 13	1	45N41	93w04	6:12:16
Nett Lake 69	1	48N06'40	93w05'38	6:12:23
Nett Lake Indian Reservation 36	1	48N06'40	93w05'38	6:12:23
Nett River 36	1	48N12	93w22	6:13:28
Nevada 50	1	43N33	92w52	6:11:28
Nevis 29	1	46N57'55	94w50'21	6:19:21
New Auburn 72	1	44N40'25	94w13'46	6:16:55
New Avon 64	1	44N25	95w10	6:20:40
New Brighton 62	3	45N03'56	93w12'06	6:12:48
Newburg 23	1	43N34'02	91w48'52	6:07:15
New Dosey 58	1	46N11	92w22	6:09:28
New Duluth 69	1	46N39'36	92w13'34	6:08:54
Newfolden 45	1	48N21'20	96w19'47	6:25:19
New Germany 10	1	44N53'03	93w58'13	6:15:53
New Hartford 85	1	43N52'43	91w28'32	6:05:54
New Haven 55	1	44N09	92w37	6:10:28
New Hope 27	3	45N02'17	93w23'11	6:13:33
Newhouse 28	1	43N31'30	91w42'00	6:06:48
New Independence 69	1	46N58	92w29	6:09:56
New London 34	1	45N18'04	94w56'38	6:19:47
New Maine 45	1	48N25	96w19	6:25:16
New Market 70	1	44N34'23	93w21'12	6:13:25
New Munich 73	1	45N37'49	94w45'12	6:19:01
Newport 82	3	44N51'59	93w00'01	6:12:00
New Prague 40	1	44N32'36	93w34'33	6:14:18
New Prairie 61	1	45N38	95w42	6:22:48
New Richland 81	1	43N53'38	93w29'37	6:13:58
New Rome 72	1	44N32'36	94w05'32	6:16:22
Newry 24	1	43N48	93w05	6:12:20
New Scandia 82	1	45N15	92w50	6:11:20
New Solum 45	1	48N14	96w18	6:25:12
New Sweden 52	1	44N24'27	94w11'23	6:16:46
Newton 56	1	46N30	95w20	6:21:20
New Trier 19	1	44N36'05	92w56'02	6:11:44
New Ulm 8	1	44N18'45	94w27'37	6:17:50
New York Mills 56	1	46N31'05	95w22'33	6:21:30
Nichols 1	1	46N19'37	93w47'05	6:15:08
Nichols 69	1	47N30	92w36	6:10:24
Nickerson 58	1	46N24'39	92w29'57	6:10:00
Nicollet 52	1	44N16'34	94w11'14	6:16:45
Nicollet Landing 52	1	44N16'58	94w12'58	6:16:52
Nicols 19	3	44N49'20	93w13'13	6:12:53
Nicolville 50	1	43N40'29	92w52'41	6:11:31
Nidaros 56	1	46N14	95w35	6:22:20
Nielsville 60	1	47N31'39	96w48'53	6:27:16
Nilsen 84	1	46N20	96w28	6:25:52
Nimrod 80	1	46N38'20	94w52'50	6:19:31
Nininger 19	1	44N46'09	92w54'07	6:11:36
Nisswa 18	1	46N31'14	94w17'18	6:17:09
Nodine 85	1	43N54'18	91w26'10	6:05:45
Nokay Lake 18	1	46N23	94w00	6:16:00
Nokomis 27	3	44N54	93w15	6:13:00
Nopeming 69	1	46N42	92w16	6:09:04
Norcross 26	1	45N52'09	96w11'50	6:24:47
Norden 57	1	48N08	96w18	6:25:12
Nordick 84	1	46N25	96w35	6:26:20
Nore 31	1	47N49	94w21	6:17:24
Norfolk 65	1	44N40	94w55	6:19:40
Normandale 27	3	44N53	93w21	6:13:24
Normania 87	1	44N38'48	95w48'30	6:23:14
Normanna 69	1	47N01	91w59	6:07:56
Norseland 52	1	44N24'46	94w06'59	6:16:28
Norshor Junction 38	1	47N22'00	91w37'32	6:06:30
North 57	1	48N08	96w10	6:24:40
North Benton 5	1	45N46'46	93w56'45	6:15:47
North Branch 13	1	45N30'41	92w58'48	6:11:55
Northcote 35	1	48N50'43	97w00'03	6:28:00
North Cross Lake 18	1	46N41	94w08	6:16:32
Northdale 2	3	45N10'43	93w16'48	6:13:07
North Douglas 27	3	45N01	93w21	6:13:24
Northern 4	1	47N33	94w51	6:19:24
Northfield 66	1	44N27'30	93w09'41	6:12:39
North Fork 73	1	45N33	95w04	6:20:16
North Germany 80	1	46N35	94w58	6:19:52
North Hero 64	1	44N14	95w25	6:21:40
North Hibbing 69	5	47N25	92w55	6:11:40
North Mankato 52	1	44N10'24	94w02'01	6:16:08
North Oaks 62	3	45N06'10	93w04'44	6:12:19
Northome 36	1	47N52'21	94w16'49	6:17:07
North Ottawa 26	1	45N59	96w12	6:24:48
North Prairie 49	1	45N48'03	94w20'57	6:17:24
North Red River 35	1	48N46	97w06	6:28:24
North Redwood 64	1	44N33'48	95w05'39	6:20:23
Northrop 46	1	43N44'11	94w26'10	6:17:45
North Saint Paul 62	3	45N00'45	92w59'30	6:11:58
North Shore 77	1	45N48'10	94w44'16	6:18:57
Northside 24	1	43N39	93w22	6:13:28
North Star 8	1	44N14	95w03	6:20:12
North Star 52	1	44N17'26	94w04'45	6:16:19
Northwest Terminal 27	3	45N01	93w15	6:13:00
Norton 85	1	44N04	91w54	6:07:36
Norway Lake 34	1	45N17'01	95w08'05	6:20:32
Norwegian Grove 56	1	46N36'33	96w13'13	6:24:53
Norwood 10	3	44N46'05	93w55'38	6:15:43
Nowthen 2	3	45N19'41	93w28'12	6:13:53
Noyes 35	1	48N59'51	97w12'15	6:28:49
Noyes Junction 60	1	47N47'41	96w36'19	6:26:25
Numedal 57	1	48N09	96w26	6:25:44
Nunda 24	1	43N33	93w29	6:13:56
Nymore 4	1	47N32	94w49	6:19:16
Oak 73	1	45N38	94w42	6:18:48
Oakbury 82	3	44N56'56	92w56'01	6:11:44
Oak Center 79	1	44N21'14	92w24'01	6:09:36
Oakdale 82	3	44N59	92w58	6:11:52
Oak Grove 2	1	45N20	93w20	6:13:20
Oakhill 77	1	45N59	94w51	6:19:24
Oak Island 39	1	49N19	94w51	6:19:24
Oak Knoll 27	3	44N58'17	93w25'40	6:13:43
Oakland 24	1	43N40'26	93w05'19	6:12:21
Oak Lawn 18	1	46N22	93w20	6:13:20
Oak Park 2	3	45N10'05	93w15'56	6:13:04
Oak Park 5	1	45N41'52	93w49'04	6:15:16
Oak Park Heights 82	1	45N01'53	92w47'34	6:11:10
Oakport 14	1	46N56	96w45	6:27:00
Oakridge 85	1	44N07'15	91w55'11	6:07:41
Oaks Corner 39	1	48N25'28	94w56'59	6:19:48
Oak Terrace 27	3	44N53'46	93w28'13	6:13:53
Oak Valley 56	1	46N20	95w13	6:20:52
Oakwood 79	1	44N14	92w15	6:09:00
O'Brien 4	1	47N48	94w43	6:18:52
Odessa 6	1	45N15'35	96w19'43	6:25:19
Odin 83	1	43N51'59	94w44'33	6:18:58
Ogema 3	1	47N06'10	95w55'29	6:23:42
Ogilvie 33	1	45N49'56	93w25'34	6:13:42
Okabena 32	1	43N44'22	95w18'56	6:21:16
Oklee 63	1	47N50'21	95w51'15	6:23:25
Old Frontenac 25	1	44N31'34	92w19'55	6:09:20
Old Mesaba 69	1	47N34'56	92w07'56	6:08:32
Olga 60	1	47N41'14	95w39'48	6:22:39
Olivia 65	1	44N46'35	94w59'22	6:19:57
Olney 53	1	43N38	95w52	6:23:28
Omro 87	1	44N46	96w02	6:24:08
Onamia 48	1	46N04'14	93w40'03	6:14:40
Onega 69	5	47N19'07	92w49'38	6:11:19
Oneka 82	1	45N10	92w57	6:11:48

Oneota 69 2 46N44'47 92W09'57 6:08:40
Onigum 11 1 47N06'34 94W32'40 6:18:11
Onstad 60 1 47N38 96W23 6:25:32
Opole 73 1 45N44'48 94W22'07 6:17:28
Opstead 48 1 46N14'02 93W28'19 6:13:53
Orange 21 1 45N48 95W12 6:20:48
Orchard Garden 19
1 44N43'32 93W17'45 6:13:11
Orchard Lake 19 1 44N41 93W15 6:13:00
Oreland 18 1 46N27'03 93W55'07 6:15:40
Org 53 1 43N34'53 95W39'05 6:22:36
Orion 55 1 43N53 92W15 6:09:00
Orleans 35 1 48N55'34 96W56'11 6:27:45
Ormsby 46 1 43N50'54 94W41'51 6:18:47
Orono 27 1 44N58'17 93W36'15 6:14:25
Oronoco 55 1 44N09'58 92W32'05 6:10:08
Orr 69 1 48N03'13 92W49'51 6:11:19
Orrock 71 1 45N26'38 93W44'10 6:14:57
Orth 31 1 47N50'21 94W18'54 6:17:16
Orton 80 1 46N40 94W51 6:19:24
Ortonville 6 1 45N18'17 96W26'40 6:25:47
Orwell 56 1 46N14 96W12 6:24:48
Osage 3 1 46N55'13 95W15'24 6:21:02
Osakis 21 1 45N52'01 95W09'07 6:20:36
Osborne 59 1 43N53 96W07 6:24:28
Oscar 56 1 46N25 96W13 6:24:52
Osceola 65 1 44N51 94W49 6:19:16
Oshawa 11 1 46N48'14 94W38'19 6:18:33
Oshawa 52 1 44N18'01 94W06'18 6:16:25
Oshkosh 87 1 44N46 96W09 6:24:36
Oslo 20 1 43N53'32 92W44'18 6:10:57
Oslo 45 1 48N11'43 97W07'54 6:28:32
Oslund 31 1 47N39'20 94W01'59 6:16:08
Osseo 27 3 45N07'10 93W24'08 6:13:37
Oster 86 1 44N58'48 93W58'55 6:15:56
Ostrander 23 1 43N36'49 92W25'40 6:09:43
Oteneagen 31 1 47N28 94W07 6:16:28
Otisco 81 1 43N58'43 93W30'07 6:14:00
Otisville 82 1 45N14'49 92W45'53 6:11:04
Otrey 6 1 45N22 96W18 6:25:12
Otsego 86 1 45N17'23 93W36'48 6:14:27
Ottawa 40 1 44N22'56 93W56'44 6:15:47
Otter Creek 9 1 46N37'31 92W32'19 6:10:09
Ottertail 56 1 46N25'32 95W33'25 6:22:14
Otto 4 1 48N05'17 94W36'26 6:18:26
Otto 56 1 46N30 95W28 6:21:52
Outing 11 1 46N49'14 93W56'52 6:15:47
Owanka 51 1 44N07'34 95W40'32 6:22:42
Owatonna 74 1 44N05'02 93W13'33 6:12:54
Owens 69 1 47N50 92W37 6:10:28
Oxboro 27 3 44N49'35 93W17'30 6:13:10
Oxford 30 1 45N27 93W10 6:12:40
Oxlip 30 1 45N30'01 93W23'19 6:13:33
Oylen 80 1 46N34'29 94W47'54 6:19:12
Paddock 56 1 46N40 95W13 6:20:52
Padua 73 1 45N36'51 95W03'24 6:20:14
Page 48 1 45N53'15 93W39'48 6:14:39
Palisade 1 1 46N42'48 93W29'18 6:13:57
Palmdale 13 1 45N27'20 92W44'00 6:10:56
Palmer 71 1 45N31 93W56 6:15:44
Palmer 81 1 44N09'11 93W32'30 6:14:10
Palmers 69 2 46N55'29 91W51'02 6:07:24
Palmville 68 1 48N36 95W46 6:23:04
Palmyra 65 1 44N40 94W48 6:19:12
Palo 69 1 47N24'55 92W15'34 6:09:02
Parent 5 1 45N37'57 93W59'10 6:15:57
Park 58 1 46N18 92W29 6:09:56
Parkdale 56 1 46N14'00 96W00'45 6:24:03
Parke 14 1 46N46 96W15 6:25:00
Parkers Prairie 56
1 46N09'11 95W19'43 6:21:19
Park Rapids 29 1 46N55'20 95W03'30 6:20:14
Parkville 69 1 47N31'52 92W34'44 6:10:19
Partridge 58 1 46N12 92W44 6:10:56
Paupores 69 1 46N52'21 92W45'51 6:11:03
Paxton 64 1 44N30 95W03 6:20:12
Payne 69 1 47N05'46 92W35'57 6:10:24
Paynesville 73 1 45N22'50 94W42'42 6:18:51
Peace 33 1 46N01 93W15 6:13:00
Pearl Lake 73 1 45N19 94W18 6:17:12
Peary 69 1 47N22'19 92W33'22 6:10:13
Pease 48 1 45N41'53 93W38'52 6:14:35
Pelan 35 1 48N38'37 96W23'35 6:25:34
Pelican Lake 26 1 46N05 95W51 6:23:24
Pelican Lakes 18
1 46N37 94W12 6:16:48
Pelican Rapids 56
1 46N34'15 96W04'58 6:24:20
Pelland 36 1 48N31'22 93W34'30 6:14:18
Pemberton 7 1 44N00'31 93W46'59 6:15:08
Pembina 44 1 47N17 96W00 6:24:00
Penasse 39 1 49N22'04 94W57'31 6:19:50
Pencer 68 1 48N41'57 95W38'15 6:22:33
Pengilly 31 1 47N19'58 93W11'49 6:12:47
Penn 43 1 44N40 94W19 6:17:16
Pennington 4 1 47N29'01 94W28'47 6:17:55
Pennock 34 1 45N08'56 95W10'34 6:20:42
Pepin 79 1 44N23 92W08 6:08:32
Pepperton 75 1 45N38 96W04 6:24:16
Pequaywan Lake 69
2 46N50 92W06 6:08:24
Pequot Lakes 18 1 46N36'11 94W18'33 6:17:14
Perault 63 1 47N48'45 96W17'23 6:25:10
Percy 35 1 48N46 96W36 6:26:24
Perham 56 1 46N35'40 95W34'20 6:22:17
Perkins 28 1 43N46'59 91W38'39 6:06:35
Perley 54 1 47N10'40 96W48'18 6:27:13
Perry 37 1 45N07 96W17 6:25:08
Perry Lake 18 1 46N35 93W58 6:15:52
Perth 7 1 44N04'47 94W21'31 6:17:26
Petersburg 32 1 43N31'49 94W55'07 6:19:40
Peterson 23 1 43N47'11 91W50'05 6:07:20
Petran 24 1 43N39'24 93W12'32 6:12:50
Peyla 69 1 47N47'07 92W21'47 6:09:27
Pfingsten 53 1 43N48'20 95W40'24 6:22:42
Phelps 56 1 46N22'49 95W49'13 6:23:17
Philbin 31 1 47N09'36 93W20'28 6:13:22
Philbrook 77 1 46N17'00 94W43'00 6:18:52
Pickerel Lake 24
1 43N38 93W29 6:13:56
Pickwick 85 7 43N58'54 91W29'40 6:05:59
Pierz 49 1 45N58'54 94W06'16 6:16:25
Pigeon River 16 1 48N01 89W42 5:58:48
Pike 69 1 47N40 92W22 6:09:28
Pike Bay 11 1 47N22 94W37 6:18:28
Pike Creek 49 1 45N59 94W27 6:17:48
Pike Lake 69 2 46N48 92W08 6:08:32
Pillager 11 1 46N19'48 94W28'26 6:17:54
Pillsbury 76 1 45N12 95W18 6:21:12
Pillsbury 77 1 45N56'00 94W41'00 6:18:44
Pilot Grove 22 1 43N31'45 94W13'39 6:16:55
Pilotmound 23 1 43N49 92W01 6:08:04
Pine Bend 19 1 44N46'45 93W02'05 6:12:08
Pine Bend 44 1 47N25'35 95W35'27 6:22:22
Pine Brook 30 1 45N35'13 93W23'18 6:13:33
Pine Center 18 1 46N12'52 93W54'51 6:15:39
Pine City 58 1 45N49'34 92W58'06 6:11:52
Pine Creek 28 1 43N50'43 91W24'12 6:05:37
Pinecreek 68 1 48N58'42 95W56'33 6:23:46
Pine Island 25 1 44N12'05 92W38'46 6:10:35
Pine Knoll 1 1 46N34'38 93W45'27 6:15:02
Pine Point 3 1 46N58'40 95W23'00 6:21:32
Pine River 11 1 46N43'05 94W24'14 6:17:37
Pine Springs 82 1 45N02'09 92W57'15 6:11:49
Pinetop 36 1 47N54'21 94W06'06 6:16:24
Pineville 69 1 47N32'10 92W17'38 6:09:11
Pinewood 4 1 47N35'50 95W07'39 6:20:31
Pioneer 62 3 44N58 93W05 6:12:20
Pipestone 59 1 44N00'02 96W19'02 6:25:16
Pitt 39 1 48N43'03 94W44'09 6:18:57
Plainview 79 1 44N09'54 92W10'17 6:08:41
Plato 43 1 44N46'28 94W02'23 6:16:10
Platte 49 1 46N06'20 94W04'55 6:16:20
Platte Lake 18 1 46N13 94W00 6:16:00
Pleasant Beach 77
1 45N46'41 94W44'06 6:18:56
Pleasant Grove 55
1 43N52'09 92W23'08 6:09:33
Pleasant Hill 85
1 43N54 91W32 6:06:08
Pleasant Lake 73
1 45N29'52 94W17'11 6:17:09
Pleasant Mound 7
1 43N53 94W18 6:17:12
Pleasant Prairie 46
1 43N38 94W18 6:17:12
Pleasant Valley 9
1 46N32'18 92W23'05 6:09:32
Pleasant Valley 50
1 43N48 92W38 6:10:32
Pleasant View 54
1 47N22 96W32 6:26:08
Pliny 1 1 46N17 93W15 6:13:00
Plummer 63 1 47N54'41 96W02'29 6:24:10
Plymouth 27 3 45N00'38 93W27'19 6:13:49
Pohlitz 68 1 48N56 96W04 6:24:16
Point Douglas 82
1 44N45'04 92W49'04 6:11:16
Pokegama 58 1 45N52 93W02 6:12:08
Polk Centre 57 1 48N00 96W25 6:25:40
Polonia 68 1 48N46 96W19 6:25:16
Pomme de Terre 26
1 46N04 95W57 6:23:48
Pomroy 31 1 47N49'03 93W59'34 6:15:58
Ponemah 4 1 48N01'14 94W54'49 6:19:39
Ponsford 3 1 46N58'12 95W23'01 6:21:32
Ponsford Landing 15
1 47N19'53 95W27'17 6:21:49
Ponto Lake 11 1 46N50 94W21 6:17:24
Pontoria 11 1 46N51'48 94W20'11 6:17:21
Poor Farm Landing 52
1 44N19'44 94W14'27 6:16:58
Poplar 11 1 46N35'12 94W41'47 6:18:47
Poplar Grove 68 1 48N35 95W56 6:23:44
Poplar River 63 1 47N48 96W02 6:24:08
Popple 15 1 47N33 95W30 6:22:00
Popple Creek 5 1 45N39'43 94W01'27 6:16:06
Popple Grove 44 1 47N12 96W00 6:24:00
Poppleton 35 1 48N51 96W44 6:26:56
Portage 69 1 48N08 92W35 6:10:20
Port Cargill 70 1 44N47'18 93W19'51 6:13:19
Porter 87 1 44N38'11 96W09'55 6:24:40
Port Hope 4 1 47N38 94W45 6:19:00
Posen 87 1 44N35 95W32 6:22:08
Post Town 55 1 44N05'26 92W38'19 6:10:33
Potsdam 55 1 44N09'56 92W20'20 6:09:21
Powderhorn 27 3 44N56 93W15 6:13:00
Powers 11 1 46N50 94W28 6:17:52
Prairie Island Indian Res 25
1 44N39 92W38 6:10:32
Prairie Lake 69 1 46N48 92W58 6:11:52
Prairie Portage 38
1 48N03'03 91W26'19 6:05:45
Prairie View 84 1 46N35 96W21 6:25:24
Prairieville 8 1 44N20 94W48 6:19:12
Prairieville 66 1 44N17'02 93W11'31 6:12:46
Pratt 74 1 44N01'21 93W09'33 6:12:38
Preble 23 1 43N38 91W47 6:07:08
Predmore 55 1 43N56'17 92W19'43 6:09:19
Prescott 22 1 43N43 94W04 6:16:16
Preston 23 1 43N40'13 92W04'59 6:08:20
Preston Lake 65 1 44N45 94W34 6:18:16
Priam 34 1 45N04'06 95W08'26 6:20:34
Princeton 48 1 45N34'12 93W34'53 6:14:20
Prinsburg 34 1 44N56'02 95W11'14 6:20:45
Prior 6 1 45N27 96W33 6:26:12
Prior Lake 70 1 44N42'48 93W25'21 6:13:41
Prior Lake Indian Res 27
1 47N32 94W49 6:19:16
Proctor 69 1 46N44'50 92W13'31 6:08:54
Prosit 69 1 46N59'53 92W37'03 6:10:28
Prosper 23 1 43N30'28 91W52'10 6:07:29
Providence 37 1 44N50'04 96W06'46 6:24:27
Pulaski 49 1 46N07 94W00 6:16:00
Puposky 4 1 47N40'40 94W54'25 6:19:38
Quamba 33 1 45N54'56 93W10'23 6:12:42
Queen 60 1 47N38 95W37 6:22:28
Quincy 55 1 44N03 92W08 6:08:32
Quiring 4 1 47N52'57 94W41'58 6:18:48
Rabbit Lake 18 1 46N32 93W51 6:15:24
Racine 50 1 43N46'34 92W28'58 6:09:56
Radium 45 1 48N13'46 96W36'48 6:26:27
Rail Prairie 49 1 46N16 94W24 6:17:36
Rainy Junction 69
1 47N29'55 92W32'42 6:10:11
Ramey 49 1 45N50'07 93W56'15 6:15:45
Ramsey 2 1 45N16 93W26 6:13:44
Ramsey 50 1 43N42'35 92W58'10 6:11:53
Ramshaw 69 1 47N25'39 92W34'52 6:10:19
Randall 49 1 46N05'28 94W30'12 6:18:01
Randolph 19 1 44N31'34 93W01'11 6:12:05
Ranier 36 1 48N36'47 93W20'55 6:13:24
Ransom 53 1 43N32'38 95W47'38 6:23:11
Ranum 54 1 47N27'20 96W07'53 6:24:32
Rapidan 7 1 44N05'40 94W04'06 6:16:16
Rasset 86 1 45N09'08 93W59'30 6:15:58
Rauch 36 1 47N57'32 93W08'44 6:12:35
Ravenna 19 1 44N41 92W45 6:11:00
Ray 36 1 48N24'39 93W12'37 6:12:50
Raymond 34 1 45N00'57 95W14'18 6:20:57
Reading 53 1 43N42'13 95W42'46 6:22:51
Reads Landing 79
1 44N24'08 92W04'44 6:08:19
Redby 4 1 47N52'43 94W54'46 6:19:39
Red Eye 80 1 46N41 95W06 6:20:24
Red Lake 4 1 47N52'35 95W01'00 6:20:04
Red Lake Falls 63
1 47N52'56 96W16'26 6:25:06
Red Lake Indian Reservation 4
1 47N53 95W01 6:20:04
Redore 69 5 47N26'37 92W53'56 6:11:36
Redpath 78 1 45N54 96W19 6:25:16
Red Rock 16 1 47N55'15 89W44'18 5:58:57
Red Rock 50 1 43N43 92W52 6:11:28
Redtop 1 1 46N10'34 93W23'50 6:13:35
Red Wing 25 1 44N33'45 92W32'01 6:10:08
Redwood Falls 64
1 44N32'22 95W07'00 6:20:28
Reformatory 71 1 45N32 94W13 6:16:52
Regal 34 1 45N24'26 94W50'43 6:19:23
Reine 68 1 48N34 95W32 6:22:08
Reiner 57 1 48N08 95W40 6:22:40
Reis 60 1 47N33 96W31 6:26:04
Remer 11 1 47N03'22 93W54'57 6:15:40
Rendsville 75 1 45N43 95W56 6:23:44
Reno 28 1 43N36'04 91W16'30 6:05:06
Reno 69 1 47N25'05 91W57'01 6:07:48
Renova 50 1 43N44'19 92W45'56 6:11:04
Renville 65 1 44N47'21 95W12'41 6:20:51
Revere 64 1 44N13'26 95W21'51 6:21:27
Reynolds 77 1 45N59 94W58 6:19:52
Rheiderland 12 1 44N56 95W18 6:21:12
Rhinehart 60 1 47N54 97W01 6:28:04
Rice 5 1 45N45'07 94W13'12 6:16:53
Riceford 28 1 43N34'34 91W43'36 6:06:54
Rice Junction 73
1 45N32 94W13 6:16:52
Rice Lake 69 2 46N52 92W07 6:08:28
Rice Lake 74 1 44N06'38 93W02'45 6:12:11
Rice Lake 86 1 45N00'51 94W08'39 6:16:35
Riceland 24 1 43N43 93W12 6:12:48
Rice River 1 1 46N29 93W14 6:12:56
Riceville 3 1 47N01 96W00 6:24:00
Richards 3 1 46N50'10 95W54'43 6:23:39
Richardson 49 1 46N07 93W53 6:15:32
Richardville 35 1 48N56 96W52 6:27:28
Richdale 56 1 46N33'17 95W28'29 6:21:54
Richfield 27 3 44N53'00 93W16'58 6:13:08
Richland 66 1 44N14 93W06 6:12:24
Richmond 73 1 45N27'15 94W31'05 6:18:04
Rich Valley 19 3 44N44'46 93W02'37 6:12:10
Rich Valley 43 1 44N51 94W11 6:16:44
Richville 56 1 46N30'24 95W37'31 6:22:30
Richwood 3 1 46N58'29 95W49'21 6:23:17
Ridge 69 1 47N37'21 92W02'09 6:08:09
Ridgely 52 1 44N26 94W40 6:18:40
Ridgeway 85 6 43N54'43 91W33'36 6:06:14
Riley 69 5 47N21'47 92W55'47 6:11:43
Rindal 54 1 47N29'58 96W07'52 6:24:31
Ringe 55 5 44N06'29 92W23'57 6:09:36
River 63 1 47N57 96W10 6:24:40
Riverdale 83 1 44N04 94W34 6:18:16
River Falls 57 1 48N00 96W09 6:24:36
River Junction 28
6 43N50'46 91W17'50 6:05:11
River Point 74 1 43N56'21 93W14'42 6:12:59
Riverside 27 3 44N58 93W16 6:13:04
Riverside 37 1 44N56 96W02 6:24:08
Riverside 69 2 46N42'36 92W12'14 6:08:49
Riverside Heights 22
1 43N39'53 94W06'37 6:16:26
Riverton 18 1 46N27'36 94W03'06 6:16:12
River Valley 57 1 48N01'13 95W46'55 6:23:08
Riverview 62 3 44N55 93W05 6:12:20
Roan 60 1 48N09'00 96W44'35 6:26:58
Robbin 35 1 48N34'22 97W08'32 6:28:34
Robbinsdale 27 3 45N01'56 93W20'18 6:13:21
Roberts 84 1 46N30 96W41 6:26:44
Robinson 69 1 47N51'34 92W02'30 6:08:10
Rochert 3 1 46N51'36 95W41'15 6:22:45
Rochester 55 5 44N01'18 92W28'11 6:09:53
Rock 59 1 44N04 96W07 6:24:28
Rock Creek 58 1 45N45'27 92W57'44 6:11:51
Rock Dell 55 1 43N55'15 92W38'18 6:10:33
Rockford 27 1 45N05'18 93W44'03 6:14:56
Rock Lake 42 1 44N14 95W54 6:23:36
Rocksbury 57 1 48N04 96W09 6:24:36
Rockville 73 1 45N28'19 94W20'26 6:17:22
Rockwell 54 1 47N11 96W23 6:25:32
Rogers 27 1 45N11'20 93W33'10 6:14:13
Rogers 40 1 44N15'38 93W34'42 6:14:19
Roland 63 1 47N56'39 95W46'43 6:23:07
Rollag 14 1 46N44'24 96W14'16 6:24:57
Rolling Forks 61
1 45N27 95W26 6:21:44
Rolling Green 46
1 43N38 94W33 6:18:12
Rollingstone 85 6 44N05'52 91W49'00 6:07:16
Rollins 69 1 47N15'24 91W50'42 6:07:23
Rollis 45 1 48N25 95W48 6:23:12
Rome 22 1 43N33 93W56 6:15:44
Ronald 1 1 46N26'50 93W03'18 6:12:13
Ronneby 5 1 45N40'53 93W51'52 6:15:27
Roome 60 1 47N42 96W48 6:27:12
Roosevelt 68 1 48N48'13 95W05'48 6:20:23
Rosby 4 1 47N24'36 94W48'23 6:19:14
Roscoe 25 1 44N13'31 92W46'17 6:11:05
Roscoe 73 1 45N26'02 94W38'22 6:18:33

Roscoe Center 25 1 44N15'40 92W43'37 6:10:54
Roseau 68 1 48N50'46 95W45'45 6:23:03
Rosebud 60 1 47N33 95W44 6:22:56
Rose City 21 1 46N04'39 95W09'59 6:20:40
Rose Creek 50 1 43N36'13 92W49'54 6:11:20
Rosedale 44 1 47N19 95W58 6:23:52
Rose Dell 67 1 43N48 96W22 6:25:28
Rose Hill 17 1 43N58 95W24 6:21:36
Roseland 34 1 44N56'07 95W06'18 6:20:25
Rosemount 19 1 44N44'22 93W07'32 6:12:30
Rosen 37 1 45N09'13 96W24'04 6:25:36
Rosendale 47 1 45N02'26 94W42'23 6:18:50
Roseport 19 3 44N46'33 93W02'58 6:12:12
Roseville 62 3 45N00'22 93W09'23 6:12:38
Rosewood 45 1 48N11'22 96W17'24 6:25:10
Rosing 49 1 46N18 94W26 6:17:44
Ross 60 1 47N47'51 96W44'22 6:26:57
Ross 68 1 48N54'22 95W55'12 6:23:41
Rossburg 1 1 46N32'07 93W34'47 6:14:19
Ross Lake 18 1 46N40 93W51 6:15:24
Rost 32 1 43N38'43 95W17'40 6:21:11
Rosy 31 1 47N39'29 94W18'21 6:17:13
Rothman 69 1 47N45'58 91W57'51 6:07:51
Rothsay 84 1 46N28'30 96W16'49 6:25:07
Round Grove 43 1 44N41 94W26 6:17:44
Round Lake 53 1 43N32'26 95W28'05 6:21:52
Round Prairie 77 1 45N54'16 94W53'07 6:19:32
Rowena 64 1 44N23'23 95W09'07 6:20:36
Rowland 27 1 44N51'37 93W25'31 6:13:42
Royal 41 1 44N30 96W15 6:25:00
Royalton 49 1 45N49'48 94W17'36 6:17:10
Roy Lake 15 1 47N19'31 95W33'05 6:22:12
Ruby Junction 69 5 47N26'06 92W55'09 6:11:41
Runeberg 3 1 46N46 95W13 6:20:52
Rush City 13 1 45N41'08 92W57'55 6:11:52
Rushford 23 1 43N48'30 91W45'10 6:07:01
Rushford Village 23 1 43N48'24 91W47'29 6:07:10
Rush Lake 56 1 46N31 95W37 6:22:28
Rushmore 53 1 43N37'10 95W48'01 6:23:12
Rush Point 13 1 45N39'31 93W06'14 6:12:25
Rush River 72 1 44N28'02 94W03'02 6:16:12
Rushseba 13 1 45N41 92W56 6:11:44
Ruskin 66 1 44N16'03 93W09'42 6:12:39
Russell 42 1 44N19'09 95W57'05 6:23:48
Russia 60 1 47N38 96W31 6:26:04
Rustad 14 1 46N44'00 96W44'40 6:26:59
Ruthton 59 1 44N10'36 96W06'13 6:24:25
Rutland 46 1 43N43 94W25 6:17:40
Rutledge 58 1 46N15'52 92W52'02 6:11:28
Ryan 25 1 44N25'26 92W42'55 6:10:52
Ryan Village 11 1 47N21'32 94W17'20 6:17:09
Sabin 14 1 46N46'47 96W39'10 6:26:37
Saco 74 1 44N00'16 93W15'58 6:13:04
Sacred Heart 65 1 44N47'13 95W21'05 6:21:24
Saga Hill 27 1 44N57'17 93W38'23 6:14:34
Saginaw 69 1 46N51'33 92W26'39 6:09:47
Sago 31 1 47N04 93W17 6:13:08
Saint Anna 73 1 45N39'42 94W28'30 6:17:54
Saint Anthony 27 3 45N01'14 93W13'04 6:12:52
Saint Anthony 73 1 45N41'12 94W36'43 6:18:27
Saint Anthony Falls 27 3 44N59 93W14 6:12:56
Saint Augusta 73 1 45N28'43 94W09'14 6:16:37
Saint Benedict 70 1 44N35'17 93W36'49 6:14:27
Saint Bonifacius 27 1 44N54'20 93W44'50 6:14:59
Saint Charles 85 1 43N58'10 92W03'51 6:08:15
Saint Clair 7 1 44N04'55 93W51'27 6:15:26
Saint Clair 62 3 44N56 93W10 6:12:40
Saint Clair Junction 69 1 47N28'14 92W50'40 6:11:23
Saint Cloud 73 1 45N33'39 94W09'44 6:16:39
Saint Croix Junction 82 1 44N40 92W50 6:11:20
Saint Francis 2 1 45N23'13 93W21'33 6:13:26
Saint Francis 73 1 45N45'36 94W35'05 6:18:20
Saint George 52 1 44N23'22 94W31'56 6:18:08
Saint Henry 40 1 44N23'03 93W47'18 6:15:09
Saint Hilaire 57 1 48N00'50 96W12'52 6:24:51
Saint James 83 1 43N58'57 94W37'36 6:18:30
Saint Johns 34 1 45N07 95W11 6:20:44
Saint Johns Landing Camp 58 1 45N59'15 92W31'36 6:10:06
Saint Joseph 73 1 45N33'54 94W19'05 6:17:16
Saint Killian 53 1 43N47'25 95W52'15 6:23:29
Saint Lawrence 70 1 44N39 93W41 6:14:44
Saint Leo 87 1 44N43'02 96W03'07 6:24:12
Saint Louis Park 27 3 44N56'54 93W20'52 6:13:23
Saint Martin 73 1 45N30'07 94W40'07 6:18:40
Saint Mary 81 1 44N01'42 93W36'06 6:14:24
Saint Marys Point 82 1 44N54'52 92W45'56 6:11:04
Saint Mathias 18 1 46N13'22 94W15'03 6:17:00
Saint Michael 86 1 45N12'36 93W39'53 6:14:40
Saint Nicholas 73 1 45N22'51 94W26'11 6:17:45
Saint Olaf 56 1 46N14 95W50 6:23:20
Saint Patrick 70 1 44N35'41 93W30'07 6:14:00
Saint Paul 62 3 44N56'40 93W05'35 6:12:22
Saint Paul Church 69 1 46N47'06 92W12'41 6:08:51
Saint Paul Park 82 3 44N50'32 92W59'28 6:11:58
Saint Peter 52 1 44N19'25 93W57'28 6:15:50
Saint Rosa 73 1 45N43'50 94W42'56 6:18:52
Saint Stephen 73 1 45N42'10 94W16'27 6:17:06
Saint Stephens 73 1 45N42 94W16 6:17:04
Saint Thomas 40 1 44N29'52 93W45'26 6:15:02
Saint Vincent 35 1 48N58'04 97W13'29 6:28:54
Saint Vincent Junction 35 1 48N58'25 97W11'55 6:28:48
Saint Wendel 73 1 45N39'58 94W22'39 6:17:31
Salem Corners 55 1 43N59'09 92W36'28 6:10:26
Salida 71 1 45N21'24 93W49'09 6:15:17
Salo 1 1 46N33 93W07 6:12:28
Salo Corner 69 1 47N39'40 92W16'40 6:09:07
Salol 68 1 48N51'58 95W34'14 6:22:17
Sanborn 64 1 44N12'35 95W07'42 6:20:31
Sand Creek 70 1 44N41 93W35 6:14:20
Sanders 57 1 48N04 96W18 6:25:12
Sand Lake 31 1 47N38 93W58 6:15:52
Sandnes 87 1 44N40 95W39 6:22:36
Sandstone 58 1 46N07'52 92W52'02 6:11:28
Sandsville 60 1 48N08 96W57 6:27:48
Sandy 69 1 47N40 92W30 6:10:00
Sanford 26 1 45N58 95W57 6:23:48
San Francisco 10 1 44N42 93W43 6:14:52
Santiago 71 1 45N32'21 93W49'11 6:15:17
Saratoga 85 1 43N53'31 92W04'11 6:08:17
Sargeant 50 1 43N48'19 92W48'07 6:11:12
Sartell 73 1 45N37'18 94W12'24 6:16:50
Sauk Centre 73 1 45N44'15 94W57'08 6:19:49
Sauk Rapids 5 1 45N35'31 94W09'57 6:16:40
Saum 4 1 47N58'29 94W40'36 6:18:42
Savage 70 1 44N46'45 93W20'10 6:13:21
Savannah 3 1 47N06 95W14 6:20:56
Savannah 31 1 47N19 93W24 6:13:36
Sawbill Landing 38 1 47N42'55 91W16'04 6:05:04
Sawyer 9 1 46N40'17 92W37'59 6:10:32
Sax 69 1 47N12'42 92W36'10 6:10:25
Scambler 56 1 46N40 96W07 6:24:28
Scandia 60 1 47N32 96W38 6:26:32
Scandia 82 1 45N15'13 92W48'20 6:11:13
Scandia Valley 49 1 46N15 94W34 6:18:16
Scanlon 9 1 46N42'24 92W25'41 6:09:43
Schechs Mill 28 1 43N40'03 91W34'51 6:06:19
Schley 11 1 47N22'08 94W24'57 6:17:40
Schoolcraft 29 1 47N17 94W59 6:19:56
Schroeder 16 1 47N32'40 90W53'30 6:03:34
Sciota 19 1 44N31 93W04 6:12:16
Scott 69 1 47N26'59 92W46'10 6:11:05
Scott 75 1 45N33 96W03 6:24:12
Scott Junction 38 1 47N24'30 91W36'37 6:06:26
Scotts Corner 9 1 46N35'53 92W25'43 6:09:43
Scranton 69 5 47N25'33 92W56'56 6:11:48
Scribner 4 1 47N32'04 95W00'44 6:20:03
Seaforth 64 1 44N28'38 95W19'34 6:21:18
Searles 8 1 44N13'43 94W26'04 6:17:44
Seavey 1 1 46N17 93W22 6:13:28
Sebeka 80 1 46N37'48 95W05'19 6:20:21
Section Thirty 38 1 47N54'37 91W46'49 6:07:07
Sedan 61 1 45N34'32 95W14'52 6:20:59
Sedil 19 1 44N45'12 92W58'23 6:11:54
Seely 22 1 43N33 93W53 6:15:32
Selma 17 1 44N04 94W55 6:19:40
Severance 72 1 44N30 94W33 6:18:12
Seward 53 1 43N49 95W39 6:22:36
Shafer 13 1 45N23'13 92W44'51 6:10:59
Shakopee 70 1 44N47'53 93W31'36 6:14:06
Shamrock 1 1 46N43 93W13 6:12:52
Shanty Town 55 1 43N58'27 92W38'23 6:10:34
Shaokatan 41 1 44N25 96W23 6:25:32
Sharon 40 1 44N25 93W49 6:15:16
Shaw 69 1 47N06'48 92W21'10 6:09:25
Sheffield Mill 66 1 44N17 93W16 6:13:04
Shelburne 42 1 44N15 96W02 6:24:08
Shelby 7 1 43N53 94W11 6:16:44
Sheldon 28 1 43N40'42 91W35'35 6:06:22
Shell Lake 3 1 46N56 95W29 6:21:56
Shell River 80 1 46N46 94W59 6:19:56
Shell Rock 24 1 43N33 93W13 6:12:52
Shelly 54 1 47N27'29 96W49'05 6:27:16
Shephard 18 1 46N12'50 94W06'14 6:16:25
Sherack 60 1 48N01'15 96W46'53 6:27:08
Sherburn 46 1 43N39'08 94W43'36 6:18:54
Sheridan 64 1 44N30 95W17 6:21:08
Sherman 43 1 44N56'52 94W08'00 6:16:32
Sherman 64 1 44N29 94W56 6:19:44
Shermans Corner 69 1 47N46'45 92W39'22 6:10:37
Sherwood 69 1 47N27'06 92W44'27 6:10:58
Sheshebee 1 1 46N42'17 93W14'32 6:12:58
Shetek 51 1 44N10 95W38 6:22:32
Shevlin 15 1 47N31'49 95W15'30 6:21:02
Shible 76 1 45N17 96W03 6:24:12
Shieldsville 66 1 44N21'58 93W24'31 6:13:38
Shingobee 11 1 47N03 94W36 6:18:24
Shirley 60 1 47N52'08 96W36'51 6:26:27
Shooks 4 1 47N52'27 94W26'17 6:17:45
Shoreham 3 1 46N45'27 95W53'55 6:23:36
Shoreview 62 3 45N04'45 93W08'49 6:12:35
Shorewood 27 1 44N54'03 93W35'20 6:14:21
Shotley 4 1 48N02'56 94W38'19 6:18:33
Shovel Lake 1 1 46N57'27 93W45'12 6:15:01
Side Lake 69 1 47N39'55 93W00'56 6:12:04
Siegel 82 5 45N00'56 92W48'24 6:11:14
Sigel 8 1 44N15 94W33 6:18:12
Sigsbee 24 1 43N41'36 93W12'31 6:12:50
Silica 69 5 47N15'53 93W01'14 6:12:05
Silo 85 1 43N59 91W52 6:07:28
Silver 9 1 46N27 92W52 6:11:28
Silver Bay 38 1 47N17'40 91W15'26 6:05:02
Silver Brook 9 1 46N37 92W26 6:09:44
Silver Creek 38 1 47N06'45 91W36'04 6:06:24
Silver Creek 86 1 45N18'54 93W58'46 6:15:55
Silverdale 36 1 47N59'10 93W06'34 6:12:26
Silver Lake 43 1 44N54'12 94W11'43 6:16:47
Silver Leaf 3 1 46N45 95W36 6:22:24
Silver Rapids 38 1 47N54'14 91W45'19 6:07:01
Silverton 57 1 48N08 96W03 6:24:12
Silverwood 31 1 47N19'04 93W18'34 6:13:14
Simar 69 2 46N48'47 92W20'37 6:09:22
Simpson 55 1 43N55'26 92W24'35 6:09:38
Sinclair 15 1 47N43 95W16 6:21:04
Sinnott 45 1 48N30 96W51 6:27:24
Sioux Agency 87 1 44N41 95W25 6:21:40
Sioux Valley 32 1 43N32'38 95W18'16 6:21:13
Six Mile Grove 76 1 45N17 95W41 6:22:44
Skagen 68 1 48N45 96W05 6:24:20
Skandia 51 1 44N09 95W53 6:23:32
Skane 35 1 48N40 96W58 6:27:52
Skelton 9 1 46N32 92W43 6:10:52
Skibo 69 1 47N29'08 91W59'39 6:07:59
Skime 68 1 48N32'49 95W36'09 6:22:25
Skree 14 1 46N45 96W20 6:25:20
Skyberg 25 1 44N12'41 92W55'55 6:11:44
Skyburg 25 1 44N16 92W59 6:11:56
Skyline 7 1 44N08'32 94W01'50 6:16:07
Slater 11 1 47N05 93W59 6:15:56
Slayton 51 1 43N59'16 95W45'20 6:23:01
Sleepy Eye 8 1 44N17'50 94W43'26 6:18:54
Sletten 60 1 47N32 95W53 6:23:32
Smiley 57 1 48N04 96W03 6:24:12
Smith Lake 86 1 45N04'59 94W06'53 6:16:28
Smiths Mill 81 1 44N08'16 93W46'04 6:15:04
Smithville 69 1 46N42'13 92W12'58 6:08:52
Smoky Hollow 11 1 46N57 93W49 6:15:16
Snellman 3 1 46N53'22 95W24'46 6:21:39
Snowden 69 1 47N27'19 92W33'01 6:10:12
Sobieski 49 1 45N55'28 94W27'32 6:17:50
Soderville 2 1 45N17'17 93W14'05 6:12:56
Sodus 42 1 44N20 95W47 6:23:08
Sogn 25 1 44N24'23 92W55'40 6:11:43
Solana 1 1 46N19'04 93W09'11 6:12:37
Solem 21 1 45N48 95W42 6:22:48
Soler 68 1 48N50 96W11 6:24:44
Solway 4 1 47N31'12 95W07'44 6:20:31
Somerset 74 1 43N59 93W14 6:12:56
Soudan 69 1 47N48'57 92W14'15 6:08:57
South Bend 7 1 44N08 94W05 6:16:20
South Branch 83 1 43N53'02 94W32'57 6:18:12
Southbrook 17 1 43N54 95W24 6:21:36
Southdale 27 3 44N53 93W21 6:13:24
South Fork 33 1 45N47 93W28 6:13:52
South Grove 19 3 44N53 93W03 6:12:12
South Harbor 48 1 46N06 93W38 6:14:32
South Haven 86 1 45N17'33 94W12'42 6:16:51
South Hollandale 24 1 43N43'15 93W11'22 6:12:45
South International Falls 36 1 48N35'12 93W23'56 6:13:36
South Red River 35 1 48N40 97W04 6:28:16
South Ridge 28 1 43N49'31 91W25'37 6:05:42
South Rushford 23 1 43N47'46 91W45'18 6:07:01
South Saint Paul 19 3 44N53'34 93W02'05 6:12:08
Southside 86 1 45N17 94W12 6:16:48
South Silver Lake 43 1 44N53'06 94W11'56 6:16:48
South Troy 79 1 44N12'20 92W25'57 6:09:44
Spafford 32 1 43N36'58 95W22'18 6:21:29
Spalding 1 1 46N33 93W15 6:13:00
Spang 31 1 47N04 93W39 6:14:36
Sparta 12 1 44N57 95W42 6:22:48
Sparta 69 1 47N28'03 92W28'38 6:09:55
Spaulding 77 1 45N46'34 94W51'09 6:19:25
Spectacle Lake 30 1 45N34 93W13 6:12:52
Spencer 1 1 46N32 93W38 6:14:32
Spencer Brook 30 1 45N31'19 93W26'25 6:13:46
Spicer 34 1 45N13'59 94W56'23 6:19:46
Split Rock 9 1 46N28 92W59 6:11:56
Spooner 39 1 48N43 94W36 6:18:24
Spring Brook 35 1 48N35 96W43 6:26:52
Spring Creek 87 1 44N43'05 95W50'54 6:23:24
Springdale 64 1 44N15 95W32 6:22:08
Springfield 8 1 44N14'20 94W58'32 6:19:54
Spring Grove 28 1 43N33'40 91W38'09 6:06:33
Spring Hill 73 1 45N31'29 94W49'45 6:19:19
Spring Lake 30 1 45N32'32 93W03'56 6:12:16
Spring Lake 31 1 47N38'33 93W52'04 6:15:28
Spring Lake 70 1 44N42'23 93W27'47 6:13:51
Spring Lake Park 62 3 45N06'28 93W14'16 6:12:57
Spring Park 27 1 44N56'07 93W37'55 6:14:32
Spring Prairie 14 1 46N50 96W30 6:26:00
Springsteel Island 68 1 48N54 95W19 6:21:16
Springvale 30 1 45N37'50 93W18'24 6:13:14
Spring Valley 23 1 43N41'13 92W23'20 6:09:33
Springwater 67 1 43N43 96W22 6:25:28
Spruce 68 1 48N50 95W41 6:22:44
Spruce 69 1 47N25'39 92W33'46 6:10:15
Spruce Center 21 1 46N04'14 95W13'24 6:20:54
Spruce Hill 21 1 46N04 95W14 6:20:56
Spruce Valley 45 1 48N25 96W11 6:24:44
Squaw Lake 31 1 47N37'57 94W08'10 6:16:33
Squier 56 1 46N08'15 96W04'53 6:24:20
Stacy 13 1 45N23'53 92W59'14 6:11:57
Stafford 68 1 48N46 95W49 6:23:16
Stanchfield 30 1 45N40'24 93W10'59 6:12:44
Stanchfield Corner 30 1 45N40'25 93W11'34 6:12:46
Stanford 30 1 45N26 93W24 6:13:36
Stanley 30 1 45N33'02 93W09'09 6:12:37
Stanley 42 1 44N30 95W40 6:22:40
Stanton 25 1 44N28'19 93W01'22 6:12:05
Staples 77 1 46N21'20 94W47'31 6:19:10
Star 57 1 48N04 95W40 6:22:40
Starbuck 61 1 45N36'52 95W31'51 6:22:07
Stark 8 1 44N14'22 94W38'58 6:18:36
Stark 13 1 45N34'50 93W03'37 6:12:14

Star Lake 56 1 46N35 95w51 6:23:24
Stately 8 1 44N09 95w02 6:20:08
Steele Center 74
1 43N59'22 93w13'34 6:12:54
Steelton 69 1 46N40'13 92w13'13 6:08:53
Steen 67 1 43N30'53 96w15'46 6:25:03
Steenerson 4 1 48N14 95w17 6:21:08
Stephen 45 1 48N27'00 96w52'20 6:27:29
Sterling Center 7
1 43N54'22 94w04'37 6:16:18
Stevens 75 1 45N28 96w11 6:24:44
Stevenson 69 1 47N26'12 93w03'28 6:12:14
Stewart 38 1 47N06'12 91w42'33 6:06:50
Stewart 43 1 44N43'29 94w29'08 6:17:57
Stewartville 55 1 43N51'20 92w29'18 6:09:57
Stillwater 82 5 45N03'23 92w48'21 6:11:13
Stockholm 86 1 45N02'11 94w13'15 6:16:53
Stockton 85 1 44N01'39 91w46'11 6:07:05
Stoneham 12 1 44N56 95w26 6:21:44
Stoney Brook 69 1 46N49 92w36 6:10:24
Stony Brook 26 1 46N04 96w05 6:24:20
Stony Run 87 1 44N51 95w39 6:22:36
Storden 17 1 44N04 95w17 6:21:08
Stowe Prairie 77
1 46N18 95w05 6:20:20
Straight River 29
1 46N51 95w06 6:20:24
Strand 54 1 47N22 96w15 6:25:00
Strandquist 45 1 48N29'25 96w26'49 6:25:47
Strathcona 68 1 48N33'14 96w10'07 6:24:40
Stroden 17 1 44N02'16 95w19'05 6:21:16
Stroms 25 1 44N37'46 92w39'41 6:10:39
Strout 47 1 45N01'48 94w35'39 6:18:23
Stubbs Bay 27 1 44N58'30 93w36'52 6:14:27
Stuntz 69 5 47N24 92w57 6:11:48
Sturgeon 69 1 47N46'36 92w52'07 6:11:28
Sturgeon Lake 58
1 46N22'52 92w49'25 6:11:18
Sturgeon River Landing 36
1 48N12'45 93w53'10 6:15:33
Sugarloaf 85 7 44N01'36 91w37'23 6:06:30
Sullivan 60 1 47N59 96w56 6:27:44
Sultan 35 1 48N59'27 97w10'39 6:28:43
Summit 74 1 43N55'15 93w11'07 6:12:44
Summit Lake 53 1 43N43 95w44 6:22:56
Sumner 23 1 43N48 92w23 6:09:32
Sumter 43 1 44N44'22 94w15'47 6:17:03
Sunburg 34 1 45N20'52 95w14'17 6:20:57
Sundal 54 1 47N27'23 96w11'53 6:24:48
Sundown 64 1 44N20 95w03 6:20:12
Sunfish Lake 19 3 44N52'15 93w05'54 6:12:24
Sunnyside 84 1 46N14 96w27 6:25:48
Sunrise 13 1 45N32'49 92w51'17 6:11:25
Suomi 31 1 47N29'00 93w44'28 6:14:58
Svea 34 1 45N00'12 95w01'16 6:20:05
Sveadahl 83 1 44N04'27 94w44'21 6:18:57
Sverdrup 56 1 46N20 95w50 6:23:20
Swanburg 18 1 46N44'25 94w10'31 6:16:42
Swan Lake 75 1 45N43 95w49 6:23:16
Swan River 31 1 47N05'12 93w11'41 6:12:47
Swanville 49 1 45N54'37 94w38'36 6:18:34
Swatara 1 1 46N53'44 93w40'26 6:14:42
Swede Grove 47 1 45N12 94w42 6:18:48
Swede Prairie 87
1 44N40 95w55 6:23:40
Swedes Forest 64
1 44N39 95w19 6:21:16
Sweet 59 1 43N59 96w22 6:25:28
Swenoda 76 1 45N12 95w41 6:22:44
Swift 68 1 48N51'12 95w13'16 6:20:53
Swift Falls 76 1 45N23'56 95w25'25 6:21:42
Sylvan 11 1 46N20'06 94w24'23 6:17:38
Synnes 75 1 45N28 96w03 6:24:12
Syre 54 1 47N10'49 96w15'30 6:25:02
Tabor 60 1 48N04'45 96w51'45 6:27:27
Taconite 31 1 47N18'46 93w22'55 6:13:32
Taconite Harbor 16
1 47N31'21 90w55'43 6:03:43
Taft 69 1 46N59'40 92w19'57 6:09:20
Talmoon 31 1 47N36'00 93w46'25 6:15:06
Tamarac 45 1 48N25 96w50 6:27:20
Tamarack 1 1 46N38'40 93w07'37 6:12:30
Tanberg 84 1 46N30 96w21 6:25:24
Tansem 14 1 46N40'31 96w14'09 6:24:57
Taopi 50 1 43N33'29 92w38'33 6:10:34
Taunton 42 1 44N35'37 96w03'56 6:24:16
Tawney 23 1 43N36'59 91w47'23 6:07:10
Taylor 78 1 45N59 96w30 6:26:00
Taylors Falls 13
1 45N24'07 92w39'08 6:10:37
Tegner 35 1 48N40 96w51 6:27:24
Telen 35 1 48N35 97w05 6:28:20
Tenhassen 46 1 43N33 94w32 6:18:08
Ten Lake 4 1 47N27 94w37 6:18:28
Tenmile Corner 83
1 43N58'43 94w25'44 6:17:43
Ten Mile Lake 37
1 44N51 95w54 6:23:36
Tenney 84 1 46N02'40 96w27'11 6:25:49
Tenstrike 4 1 47N39'24 94w40'28 6:18:42
Terrace 61 1 45N30'36 95w19'11 6:21:17
Terrebonne 63 1 47N49'57 96w07'59 6:24:32
The Arches 85 1 43N59 91w52 6:07:28
Theilman 79 1 44N17'21 92w11'31 6:08:46
Thief Lake 45 1 48N30 95w57 6:23:48
Thief River Falls 57
1 48N07'09 96w10'51 6:24:43
Third Crow Wing Lake 29
1 46N58 94w51 6:19:24
Third River 31 1 47N38 94w21 6:17:24
Thomastown 80 1 46N25 94w51 6:19:24
Thompson 35 1 48N46 96w52 6:27:28
Thompson Grove 82
1 44N50 92w56 6:11:44
Thompson Heights 2
3 45N10'59 93w20'15 6:13:21
Thompson Park 2 3 45N10 93w16 6:13:04
Thompson Riverview Terrace 2
3 45N09'27 93w19'54 6:13:20
Thomson 9 1 46N39'49 92w23'52 6:09:35
Thor 1 1 46N28'34 93w25'14 6:13:41
Thorhult 4 1 48N13'49 95w14'52 6:20:59
Thorpe 29 1 47N06 94w52 6:19:28

Three Lakes 64 1 44N24 95w03 6:20:12
Thunder Lake 11 1 46N56 94w01 6:16:04
Tilden 60 1 47N33 96w23 6:25:32
Tilden Junction 60
1 47N42'08 96w17'19 6:25:09
Timothy 18 1 46N44 94w07 6:16:28
Tintah 78 1 46N00'35 96w19'20 6:25:17
Toad Lake 3 1 46N51 95w28 6:21:52
Tobique 11 1 47N06'56 94w02'22 6:16:09
Todd 29 1 46N57 95w06 6:20:24
Tofte 16 1 47N34'26 90w50'10 6:03:21
Togo 31 1 47N49'17 93w09'21 6:12:37
Toimi 38 1 47N24'02 91w46'03 6:07:04
Toivola 69 1 47N10'01 92w48'39 6:11:15
Tonka Bay 27 1 44N54'31 93w35'34 6:14:22
Toqua 6 1 45N33 96w33 6:26:12
Tordenskjold 56 1 46N14 95w50 6:23:20
Torfin 68 1 48N35'52 95w44'00 6:22:56
Torning 76 1 45N18 95w34 6:22:16
Torrey 11 1 47N11 93w51 6:15:24
Tower 69 1 47N48'20 92w16'28 6:09:06
Tower Junction 69
1 47N48'18 92w15'22 6:09:01
Tracy 42 1 44N14'00 95w37'08 6:22:29
Traffic 27 3 44N58 93w17 6:13:08
Trail 60 1 47N46'48 95w41'31 6:22:46
Trails End 16 1 47N45 90w20 6:01:20
Transit 72 1 44N35 94w19 6:17:16
Traverse 52 1 44N20'55 94w01'02 6:16:04
Trelipe 11 1 46N58 94w07 6:16:28
Trimont 46 1 43N45'44 94w42'25 6:18:50
Triumph 46 1 43N45 94w43 6:18:52
Trommald 18 1 46N30'19 94w01'05 6:16:04
Trondhjem 56 1 46N30 96w13 6:24:52
Trondjem 66 1 44N28'45 93w23'34 6:13:34
Trosky 59 1 43N53'21 96w15'24 6:25:02
Trout Brook 25 1 44N33 92w32 6:10:08
Trout Lake 31 1 47N14 93w24 6:13:36
Troy 85 1 43N52'15 92w04'04 6:08:16
Truman 46 1 43N49'40 94w26'13 6:17:45
Tumuli 56 1 46N09 95w57 6:23:48
Tunsberg 12 1 45N02 95w47 6:23:08
Turner 1 1 46N48 93w15 6:13:00
Turtle Creek 77 1 46N09 94w43 6:18:52
Turtle River 4 1 47N35'15 94w45'05 6:19:00
Twig 69 1 46N53'40 92w21'52 6:09:27
Twig Station 69 1 46N52'40 92w20'46 6:09:23
Twin Cities 27 3 44N54 93w14 6:12:56
Twin Grove 24 1 43N42'10 93w11'17 6:12:45
Twin Lakes 24 1 43N33'35 93w25'22 6:13:41
Twin Valley 54 1 47N15'37 96w15'31 6:25:02
Two Harbors 38 6 47N01'22 91w40'14 6:06:41
Two Inlets 3 1 47N03'10 95w13'02 6:20:52
Two Rivers 49 1 45N49 94w23 6:17:32
Tyler 41 1 44N16'42 96w08'04 6:24:32
Tynsid 60 1 47N43 96w54 6:27:36
Tyro 87 1 44N46 95w55 6:23:40
Tyrone 40 1 44N30 93w49 6:15:16
Udolpho 50 1 43N48 92w59 6:11:56
Ulen 14 1 47N04'44 96w15'31 6:25:02
Underwood 56 1 46N17'07 95w52'14 6:23:29
Union 28 1 43N42 91w25 6:05:40
Union 74 1 43N53'31 93w07'31 6:12:30
Union Grove 47 1 45N17 94w42 6:18:48
Union Hill 40 1 44N32'37 93w40'01 6:14:40
University 27 3 44N59 93w14 6:12:56
Upper Nicollet 27
3 44N58 93w17 6:13:08
Upper Sioux Indian Res 65
1 44N46 95w30 6:22:00
Upsala 49 1 45N48'39 94w34'16 6:18:17
Uptown 27 3 44N57 93w17 6:13:08
Urbank 56 1 46N07'22 95w30'42 6:22:03
Urness 21 1 45N53 95w42 6:22:48
Utica 85 1 43N58'32 91w57'17 6:07:49
Vadnais Heights 62
3 45N03'27 93w04'25 6:12:18
Vail 64 1 44N25 95w17 6:21:08
Vallers 42 1 44N35 95w47 6:23:08
Valley 45 1 48N19 95w40 6:22:40
Valley Ridge 19 1 44N47 93w15 6:13:00
Van Buren 69 1 46N58 92w53 6:11:32
Varco 50 1 43N36'21 92w57'23 6:11:50
Vasa 25 1 44N30'12 92w43'20 6:10:53
Vawter 49 1 45N54'44 94w14'41 6:16:59
Vega 45 1 48N14 96w57 6:27:48
Veldt 45 1 48N25 95w41 6:22:44
Verdi 41 1 44N12'31 96w21'07 6:25:24
Verdon 1 1 46N54 93w22 6:13:28
Vergas 56 1 46N39'24 95w48'18 6:23:13
Vermillion Lake 69
1 47N45 92w22 6:09:28
Vermillion 19 1 44N40'25 92w58'01 6:11:52
Vermillion Dam 69
1 48N03 92w50 6:11:20
Vermillion Lake Indian Res 69
1 47N50 92w18 6:09:12
Vern 15 1 47N18'14 95w12'51 6:20:51
Verndale 79 1 46N23'54 95w00'52 6:20:03
Vernon 20 1 43N54'12 92w44'17 6:10:57
Vernon Center 7 1 43N57'43 94w10'08 6:16:41
Verona 22 1 43N43 94w11 6:16:44
Veseli 66 1 44N30'54 93w27'35 6:13:50
Vesta 64 1 44N30'28 95w24'58 6:21:40
Victor 86 1 45N01 94w04 6:16:16
Victoria 10 3 44N51'31 93w39'41 6:14:39
Viding 14 1 47N06 96w38 6:26:32
Vienna 67 1 43N43 96w07 6:24:28
Viking 45 1 48N13'07 96w24'20 6:25:37
Villard 61 1 45N42'56 95w16'08 6:21:05
Vineland 48 1 46N09'49 93w45'26 6:15:02
Vineland 60 1 47N38 96w49 6:27:16
Vining 56 1 46N15'47 95w32'12 6:22:09
Viola 55 1 44N03'48 92w16'05 6:09:04
Virginia 69 5 47N31'24 92w32'11 6:10:09
Visgers Landing Public Acces 28
1 43N31'28 91w16'48 6:05:07
Vista 81 1 43N57'26 93w27'59 6:13:52
Vivian 81 1 43N53 93w40 6:14:40
Vlasaty 20 1 43N57'53 92w50'56 6:11:24
Waasa 69 1 47N40 92w07 6:08:28
Wabana 31 1 47N24 93w31 6:14:04
Wabasha 79 1 44N23'02 92w01'58 6:08:08

Wabasso 64 1 44N24'07 95w15'20 6:21:01
Wabedo 11 1 46N55'14 94w11'16 6:16:45
Waconia 10 3 44N51'03 93w47'12 6:15:09
Wacouta 25 1 44N32'42 92w26'05 6:09:44
Wacouta Beach 25
1 44N32'45 92w24'37 6:09:38
Wadena 80 1 46N26'33 95w08'09 6:20:33
Wagner 1 1 46N13 93w06 6:12:24
Wahkon 48 1 46N07'06 93w31'15 6:14:05
Wahlsten 69 1 47N44'09 92w17'00 6:09:08
Wahnena 11 1 47N15 93w54 6:15:36
Waite Park 73 1 45N33'26 94w13'26 6:16:54
Wakefield 73 1 45N28 94w27 6:17:48
Wakemup 69 1 47N55'27 92w38'42 6:10:35
Walbo 30 1 45N35'14 93w19'36 6:13:18
Walcott 66 1 44N15 93w13 6:12:52
Waldeck 1 1 46N40'28 93w36'27 6:14:26
Waldo 38 1 47N03'58 91w41'56 6:06:48
Waldorf 81 1 43N56'06 93w41'50 6:14:47
Wales 38 1 47N02 91w41 6:06:44
Walker 11 1 47N06'05 94w35'13 6:18:21
Wall Lake 56 1 46N17'27 95w57'52 6:23:51
Walls 78 1 45N43 96w34 6:26:16
Walnut Grove 64 1 44N13'23 95w28'09 6:21:53
Walnut Lake 22 1 43N43 93w53 6:15:32
Walter 37 1 45N07 96w24 6:25:36
Walters 22 1 43N36'21 93w40'23 6:14:42
Waltham 50 1 43N49'18 92w52'37 6:11:30
Walworth 3 1 47N06 96w08 6:24:32
Wanamingo 25 1 44N18'16 92w47'25 6:11:10
Wanda 64 1 44N18'59 95w12'41 6:20:51
Wang 65 1 44N51 95w25 6:21:40
Wanger 45 1 48N25 96w43 6:26:52
Wangs 25 1 44N24'24 92w58'46 6:11:55
Wannaska 68 1 48N39'30 95w44'04 6:22:56
Warba 81 1 47N07'44 93w15'59 6:13:04
Ward 77 1 46N09 94w50 6:19:20
Ward Springs 77 1 45N47'31 94w48'17 6:19:13
Warman 33 1 46N03'30 93w17'03 6:13:08
Warren 45 1 48N11'48 96w46'21 6:27:05
Warrenton 45 1 48N14 96w49 6:27:16
Warroad 68 1 48N54'19 95w18'51 6:21:15
Warsaw 40 1 44N14'58 93w23'37 6:13:34
Waseca 81 1 44N04'40 93w30'26 6:14:02
Washington 23 1 43N46'33 92w20'19 6:09:21
Washington 40 1 44N15 93w48 6:15:12
Washington Lake 72
1 44N40 93w57 6:15:48
Wasioja 20 1 44N04'49 92w49'09 6:11:17
Waskish 36 1 48N09'41 94w30'44 6:18:03
Wastedo 25 1 44N24'17 92w51'04 6:11:24
Watab 5 1 45N40'35 94w10'51 6:16:43
Waterbury 64 1 44N20 95w17 6:21:08
Waterford 20 1 44N29'02 93w08'34 6:12:34
Watertown 10 1 44N57'49 93w50'49 6:15:23
Waterville 40 1 44N13'08 93w34'04 6:14:16
Watkins 47 1 45N18'55 94w24'30 6:17:38
Watopa 79 1 44N14 92w00 6:08:00
Watson 12 1 45N00'35 95w48'04 6:23:12
Waubun 44 1 47N10'50 95w56'20 6:23:45
Waukenabo 1 1 46N44'24 93w36'00 6:14:24
Waukon 54 1 47N22'08 96w07'51 6:24:31
Waverly 86 1 45N04'00 93w57'58 6:15:52
Wawina 31 1 47N03'11 93w07'08 6:12:29
Wayland 36 1 48N28'06 94w19'13 6:17:17
Wayzata 27 4 44N58'10 93w30'50 6:14:03
Wealthwood 1 1 46N21'47 93w39'14 6:14:37
Weaver 79 1 44N12'54 91w55'43 6:07:43
Weber 30 1 45N28'30 93w07'26 6:12:30
Webster 66 1 44N31'47 93w21'09 6:13:25
Wegdahl 12 1 44N53'24 95w38'42 6:22:35
Weimer 32 1 43N49 95w16 6:21:04
Welch 25 1 44N34'06 92w44'18 6:10:57
Welcome 46 1 43N40'01 94w37'09 6:18:29
Wellington 65 1 44N35 94w41 6:18:44
Wells 22 1 43N44'46 93w43'43 6:14:55
Weme 15 1 47N38'39 95w32'16 6:22:09
Wendell 26 1 46N02'08 96w06'03 6:24:24
Wergeland 87 1 44N41 96w09 6:24:36
Werner 4 1 47N36'59 94w55'21 6:19:41
Wescott 19 3 44N49'11 93w06'20 6:12:25
West Albany 79 1 44N18'05 92w17'07 6:09:08
West Albion 86 1 45N11'45 94w08'05 6:16:32
West Bank 76 1 45N12 95w48 6:23:12
Westbrook 17 1 44N02'32 95w26'09 6:21:45
Westbury 3 1 46N55'02 95w54'34 6:23:38
West Concord 20 1 44N09'13 92w53'58 6:11:36
West Coon Rapids 27
3 45N09'35 93w20'58 6:13:24
West Duluth 69 2 46N44'08 92w11'10 6:08:45
West End 62 3 44N56 93w07 6:12:28
Westerheim 42 1 44N35 95w55 6:23:40
Western 56 1 46N09'07 96w10'58 6:24:44
Westfield 20 1 43N54 92w59 6:11:56
Westford 46 1 43N48 94w26 6:17:44
West Heron Lake 32
1 43N43 95w19 6:21:16
West Lake Francis Shores 30
1 45N30'28 93w20'14 6:13:21
West Lakeland 82
1 44N58 92w49 6:11:16
Westline 64 1 44N25 95w32 6:22:08
West Newton 52 1 44N25 94w33 6:18:12
West Newton 79 1 44N15'54 91w54'02 6:07:36
Weston 82 1 45N11'20 92w59'04 6:11:56
West Point 30 1 45N33'28 93w23'20 6:13:33
Westport 61 1 45N42'54 95w10'01 6:20:40
West Red Wing 25
1 44N33 92w32 6:10:08
West Rock 58 1 45N50 92w58 6:11:52
West Saint Paul 19
3 44N54'58 93w06'05 6:12:24
Westside 53 1 43N38 96w00 6:24:00
West Union 77 1 45N48'03 95w04'59 6:20:20
West Valley 45 1 48N25 96w27 6:25:48
West Virginia 69
1 47N30'56 92w34'12 6:10:17
Whalan 23 1 43N43'56 91w55'35 6:07:42
Wheatland 66 1 44N27'53 93w29'00 6:13:56
Wheaton 78 1 45N48'16 96w29'56 6:26:00
Wheeler Landing 38
1 47N43'33 91w17'24 6:05:10

Wheelers Point 39	1	48N50'16	94w41'51	6:18:47
Wheeling 66	1	44N20	93w06	6:12:24
Whipholt 11	1	47N02'56	94w21'54	6:17:28
White 69	1	47N28	92w15	6:09:00
White Bear 62	3	45N05	93w01	6:12:04
White Bear Beach 62	1	45N05'59	92w59'20	6:11:57
White Bear Lake 62	3	45N05'05	93w00'35	6:12:02
Whited 33	1	45N56	93w12	6:12:48
White Earth 3	1	47N05'48	95w50'35	6:23:22
White Earth Indian Res 3	1	47N06	95w51	6:23:24
Whiteface 69	1	47N11'12	92w21'58	6:09:28
Whitefield 34	1	45N08	95w02	6:20:08
Whiteford 45	1	48N25	95w54	6:23:36
White Hawk 18	1	46N23'53	93w49'31	6:15:18
White Iron 38	1	47N54'12	91w46'36	6:07:06
White Oak 29	1	46N56	94w43	6:18:52
White Pine 1	1	46N22	93w15	6:13:00
White Rock 25	1	44N27'23	92w46'01	6:11:04
Whitewater 85	1	44N09	92w01	6:08:04
White Willow 25	1	44N21'51	92w39'04	6:10:36
Whitman 85	6	44N09'12	91w48'21	6:07:13
Whyte 38	1	47N27'06	91w33'43	6:06:15
Wig Wam Bay 48	1	46N04	93w40	6:14:40
Wilbert 46	1	43N32'38	94w32'21	6:18:09
Wildcat Landing Public Acces 28	1	43N41'13	91w16'22	6:05:05
Wilder 32	1	43N49'36	95w11'50	6:20:47
Wild Rice 54	1	47N17	96w15	6:25:00
Wilds 60	1	47N44'44	96w38'09	6:26:33
Wildwood 36	1	47N53'26	93w58'00	6:15:52
Wilkinson 11	1	47N15'03	94w37'39	6:18:31
Willernie 82	3	45N03'15	92w57'23	6:11:50
Williams 39	1	48N46'06	94w57'18	6:19:49
Willington Grove 28	1	43N34'42	91w34'44	6:06:19
Willmar 34	1	45N07'19	95w02'35	6:20:10
Willow Creek 7	1	43N53'41	94w16'06	6:17:04
Willow Lake 64	1	44N20	95w10	6:20:40
Willow River 58	1	46N19'06	92w50'28	6:11:22
Willow Valley 69	1	47N56	92w53	6:11:32
Wilma 58	1	46N08	92w28	6:09:52
Wilmington 28	1	43N32'49	91w32'32	6:06:10
Wilmont 53	1	43N45'53	95w49'37	6:23:18
Wilno 41	1	44N29'59	96w13'52	6:24:55
Wilpen 69	5	47N26'26	92w49'40	6:11:19
Wilson 85	1	43N57'36	91w41'04	6:06:44
Wilton 4	1	47N30'13	95w00'03	6:20:00
Wilton 81	1	44N00'50	93w32'03	6:14:08
Winchester 54	1	47N12	96w30	6:26:00
Windemere 58	1	46N23	92w44	6:10:56
Windom 17	1	43N51'59	95w07'00	6:20:28
Windsor 78	1	45N41	96w41	6:26:44
Winfield 65	1	44N51	95w03	6:20:12
Winger 60	1	47N32'10	95w59'17	6:23:57
Wing River 80	1	46N30	94w58	6:19:52
Winnebago 22	1	43N46'04	94w09'56	6:16:40
Winnebago 28	6	43N38	91w29	6:05:56
Winner 68	1	48N35'52	95w26'23	6:21:46
Winnipeg Junction 14	1	46N53'45	96w14'47	6:24:59
Winona 85	7	44N03'00	91w38'21	6:06:33
Winsor 15	1	47N48	95w30	6:22:00
Winsted 43	1	44N57'50	94w02'50	6:16:11
Winter 38	1	47N31'38	91w29'25	6:05:58
Winthrop 72	1	44N32'35	94w21'58	6:17:28
Winton 38	1	47N55'35	91w48'02	6:07:12
Wirock 51	1	43N53'13	95w42'12	6:22:49
Wirt 31	1	47N43'50	93w57'35	6:15:50
Wisconsin 32	1	43N38	94w55	6:19:40
Wiscoy 85	1	43N54	91w39	6:06:36
Wisner 36	1	48N18'25	93w40'34	6:14:42
Withrow 82	1	45N07'27	92w53'50	6:11:35
Witoka 85	1	43N56'00	91w37'12	6:06:29
Wolf 69	1	47N27'02	92w36'31	6:10:26
Wolf Lake 3	1	46N48'11	95w21'08	6:21:25
Wolford 18	1	46N32'44	93w58'44	6:15:55
Wolverton 84	1	46N33'48	96w44'00	6:26:56
Woodbury 9	1	46N40'45	92w57'35	6:11:50
Woodbury 82	3	44N55'26	92w57'33	6:11:50
Wood Lake 87	1	44N39'10	95w32'17	6:22:09
Woodland 27	1	44N56'49	93w30'14	6:14:01
Woodland 33	1	46N06'57	93w17'02	6:13:08
Woodland 69	2	46N50'46	92w04'56	6:08:20
Woodland Park 56	1	46N19	95w26	6:21:44
Woodrow 18	1	46N23'18	94w04'27	6:16:18
Woods 12	1	45N06	95w18	6:21:12
Woodstock 59	1	44N00'33	96w06'01	6:24:24
Woodville 81	1	44N04	93w28	6:13:52
Woodward Brook 48	1	45N40'34	93w35'06	6:14:20
Workman 1	1	46N43	93w23	6:13:32
Worthington 53	1	43N37'12	95w35'46	6:22:23
Wouri 69	1	47N36	92w29	6:09:56
Wrenshall 9	1	46N37'01	92w22'56	6:09:32
Wright 9	1	46N40'09	93w00'24	6:12:02
Wrightstown 56	1	46N16'26	95w11'09	6:20:45
Wyandotte 57	1	48N00	96w03	6:24:12
Wyanett 30	1	45N35'13	93w27'02	6:13:48
Wyattville 85	1	43N56'27	91w47'24	6:07:10
Wykeham 77	1	46N09	95w05	6:20:20
Wykoff 23	1	43N42'26	92w16'05	6:09:04
Wylie 63	1	47N57'43	96w21'10	6:25:25
Wyman 69	1	47N31'57	92w06'27	6:08:26
Wyoming 13	1	45N20'11	92w59'49	6:11:59
Yankeetown 6	1	45N29'28	96w44'23	6:26:58
Yellow Bank 37	1	45N12	96w24	6:25:36
Yola 29	1	47N13'56	95w00'43	6:20:03
York 23	1	43N31'59	92w16'08	6:09:05
York 38	1	47N07'37	91w42'12	6:06:49
Yorktown 27	3	44N53	93w21	6:13:24
Young America 10	3	44N46'58	93w54'48	6:15:39
Yucatan 28	1	43N40'50	91w41'19	6:06:45
Zemple 31	1	47N19'23	93w47'07	6:15:08
Zerkel 15	1	47N18'39	95w22'53	6:21:32
Zim 69	1	47N18'25	92w36'11	6:10:25
Zimmerman 71	1	45N27	93w35	6:14:20
Zion 73	1	45N27	94w42	6:18:48
Zumbra Heights 10	1	44N54	93w34	6:14:16
Zumbro 79	1	44N14	92w24	6:09:36
Zumbro Falls 79	1	44N17'00	92w25'19	6:09:41
Zumbrota 25	1	44N17'39	92w40'08	6:10:41

TIME TABLES

MS # 1			MS # 2		
Before 11/18/1883		LMT	Before 11/18/1883		LMT
11/18/1883	12:00	CST	11/18/1883	12:00	CST
3/31/1918	02:00	CWT	3/31/1918	02:00	CWT
10/27/1918	02:00	CST	10/27/1918	02:00	CST
3/30/1919	02:00	CWT	3/30/1919	02:00	CWT
10/26/1919	02:00	CST	10/26/1919	02:00	CST
2/09/1942	02:00	CWT	4/28/1935	02:00	CDT
9/30/1945	02:00	CST	9/29/1935	02:00	CST
4/30/1967	02:00	US#1	2/09/1942	02:00	CWT
....			9/30/1945	02:00	CST
			4/30/1967	02:00	US#1

COUNTIES

1 Adams	22 Grenada	43 Lincoln	64 Simpson
2 Alcorn	23 Hancock	44 Lowndes	65 Smith
3 Amite	24 Harrison	45 Madison	66 Stone
4 Attala	25 Hinds	46 Marion	67 Sunflower
5 Benton	26 Holmes	47 Marshall	68 Tallahatchie
6 Bolivar	27 Humphreys	48 Monroe	69 Tate
7 Calhoun	28 Issaquena	49 Montgomery	70 Tippah
8 Carroll	29 Itawamba	50 Neshoba	71 Tishomingo
9 Chickasaw	30 Jackson	51 Newton	72 Tunica
10 Choctaw	31 Jasper	52 Noxubee	73 Union
11 Claiborne	32 Jefferson	53 Oktibbeha	74 Walthall
12 Clarke	33 Jefferson Davis	54 Panola	75 Warren
13 Clay	34 Jones	55 Pearl River	76 Washington
14 Coahoma	35 Kemper	56 Perry	77 Wayne
15 Copiah	36 Lafayette	57 Pike	78 Webster
16 Covington	37 Lamar	58 Pontotoc	79 Wilkinson
17 De Soto	38 Lauderdale	59 Prentiss	80 Winston
18 Forrest	39 Lawrence	60 Quitman	81 Yalobusha
19 Franklin	40 Leake	61 Rankin	82 Yazoo
20 George	41 Lee	62 Scott	
21 Greene	42 Leflore	63 Sharkey	

Place		Latitude	Longitude	Time
Abbeville 36	1	34N30'11	89w30'11	5:58:01
Abbott 13	1	33N40'48	88w46'28	5:55:06
Aberdeen 48	1	33N49'30	88w32'37	5:54:10
Abney 29	1	34N12'48	88w29'13	5:53:57
Ackerman 10	1	33N18'36	89w10'22	5:56:41
Acme 31	1	31N58'03	89w10'24	5:56:42
Acona 26	1	33N16'18	90w00'58	6:00:04
Adair 8	1	33N18'49	90w05'26	6:00:22
Adams 25	1	32N09'35	90w33'38	6:02:15
Adams Landing 28	1	32N34'13	90w43'36	6:02:54
Adaton 53	1	33N28'38	88w55'17	5:55:41
Addie 28	1	32N59'14	91w04'33	6:04:18
Aderdeen Junction 26	1	33N01'57	89w52'39	5:59:31
Agricola 20	1	30N48'27	88w31'12	5:54:05
Aiken 69	1	34N37'51	89w44'23	5:58:58
Airey 24	1	30N38'54	89w04'38	5:56:19
Akron 35	1	32N44'27	88w31'29	5:54:06
Alamucha 38	1	32N21'31	88w28'07	5:53:52
Albin 68	1	33N54'48	90w19'47	6:01:19
Alcorn 11	1	31N52'40	91w08'21	6:04:33
Alcorn State University 11	1	31N49	91w03	6:04:12
Aldens 17	1	34N56'00	90w01'29	6:00:06
Alesville 36	1	34N22	89w31	5:58:04
Algoma 58	1	34N10'34	89w01'52	5:56:07
Alice 50	1	32N54'39	89w16'48	5:57:07
Allen 15	1	31N44'54	90w39'30	6:02:38
Allen 60	1	34N08'45	90w14'02	6:00:56
Allen (nanachehaw) 75	1	32N06'28	90w57'29	6:03:50
Allentown 2	1	34N51'26	88w36'18	5:54:25
Alligator 6	1	34N05'22	90w43'10	6:02:53
Alma 41	1	34N26	88w40	5:54:40
Alonzo 61	1	32N03'01	90w12'55	6:00:52
Alphaba 17	1	34N46'26	89w52'25	5:59:30
Alpine 73	1	34N29'43	88w47'52	5:55:11
Altitude 59	1	34N40'06	88w26'35	5:53:46
Altus 36	1	34N20'27	89w23'46	5:57:35
Alva 49	1	33N38'16	89w30'26	5:58:02
Amistead 14	1	34N22	90w38	6:02:32
Amory 48	1	33N59'03	88w29'17	5:53:57
Anchor 9	1	33N49'36	89w02'17	5:56:09
Anchorage 27	1	32N55'53	90w36'51	6:02:27
Anderson Landing 14	1	34N08'23	90w52'00	6:03:28
Anding 82	1	32N41'31	90w23'52	6:01:35
Anguilla 63	1	32N58'26	90w49'28	6:03:18
Anna 1	1	31N41'48	91w21'05	6:05:24
Annandale 45	1	32N30'53	90w11'18	6:00:45
Anse 61	1	32N07'08	90w06'03	6:00:24
Ansley 23	1	30N13'30	89w29'01	5:57:56
Antioch 34	1	31N38'01	89w03'29	5:56:14
Antioch 69	1	34N41'57	89w52'16	5:59:29
Anvil 70	1	34N54	88w54	5:55:36
Apple Ridge 25	2	32N19	90w11	6:00:44
Arbo 16	1	31N43'36	89w38'02	5:58:32
Arcola 76	1	33N16'11	90w52'47	6:03:31
Ariel 3	1	31N06'02	90w59'14	6:03:57
Arkabutla 69	1	34N41'56	90w07'20	6:00:29
Arlington 43	1	31N25'06	90w33'24	6:02:14
Arlington 50	1	32N52'36	89w10'38	5:56:43
Arm 39	1	31N30'10	90w00'58	6:00:04
Armistead 14	1	34N21'51	90w36'44	6:02:27
Arnold Line 37	1	31N20'06	89w22'24	5:57:30
Artesia 44	1	33N24'55	88w38'38	5:54:35
Artonish 79	1	31N11'23	91w35'01	6:06:20
Arunde 38	1	32N18'11	88w45'44	5:55:03
Asa 54	1	34N16'08	90w04'16	6:00:17
Ashland 5	1	34N49'58	89w10'33	5:56:42
Ashland 32	1	31N48'00	91w20'53	6:05:24
Ashley 15	1	31N48'07	90w15'47	6:01:03
Ashley Crossing 76	1	33N25'03	90w59'20	6:03:57
Ashwood 79	1	31N02'41	91w17'49	6:05:11
Askew 54	1	34N32'13	90w11'36	6:00:46
Athens 48	1	33N52'20	88w26'30	5:53:46
Atlanta 9	1	33N47'54	89w08'51	5:56:35
Atway 47	1	34N51'57	89w24'46	5:57:39
Aubrey 52	1	33N08'51	88w19'56	5:53:20
Auburn 41	1	34N17'05	88w37'54	5:54:32
Auburn 43	1	31N21'33	90w36'28	6:02:26
Austin 72	1	34N38'26	90w26'57	6:01:48
Australia Landing 6	1	34N03'56	90w52'40	6:03:31
Avalon 8	1	33N39'18	90w05'08	6:00:21
Avent 20	1	30N58'53	88w46'45	5:55:07
Avent Station 21	1	31N00'06	88w46'23	5:55:06
Avera 21	1	31N17'45	88w44'29	5:54:58
Avon 76	1	33N13'48	91w02'50	6:04:11
Bacots 57	1	31N14	90w28	6:01:52
Bailey 38	1	32N28'03	88w43'22	5:54:53
Baird 67	1	33N26	90w35	6:02:20
Baker 73	1	34N30'09	88w56'50	5:55:47
Bald Hill 73	1	34N24'47	89w05'07	5:56:20
Baldwyn 41	1	34N30'34	88w38'07	5:54:32
Ballard 45	1	32N36'10	90w04'43	6:00:19
Ballardsville 29	1	34N14'33	88w32'17	5:54:09
Ballentine 54	1	34N23'39	90w05'47	6:00:23
Ballground 75	1	32N32'15	90w44'48	6:02:59
Baltzer 67	1	33N58'55	90w35'41	6:02:23
Banks 72	1	34N49'33	90w13'47	6:00:55
Bankston 10	1	33N16	89w17	5:57:08
Banner 7	1	34N05'19	89w23'05	5:57:32
Barbara 56	1	30N59'31	88w58'42	5:55:55
Barfoot 50	1	32N34'51	89w10'48	5:56:43
Barksdale 60	1	34N13'26	90w23'41	6:01:35
Barland 11	1	31N53'15	90w48'38	6:03:15
Barlow 15	1	31N49'21	90w38'57	6:02:36
Barnes 40	1	32N54'08	89w30'06	5:58:00
Barnes Prairie 61	1	32N25'17	90w00'51	6:00:03
Barnett 12	1	31N59'12	88w54'18	5:55:37
Barr 69	1	34N37'28	89w46'48	5:59:07
Barron 18	1	31N08'53	89w09'53	5:56:40
Barrontown 18	1	31N22'31	89w13'03	5:56:52
Bartahatchie 48	1	33N41	88w19	5:53:16
Barth 55	1	30N50	89w32	5:58:08
Bartlett 51	1	32N15'30	89w19'00	5:57:16
Barto 57	1	31N10'32	90w18'41	6:01:15
Barton 47	1	34N57'50	89w41'21	5:58:45
Basic 12	1	32N13'06	88w46'09	5:55:05
Basin 20	1	30N55	88w35	5:54:20
Bassfield 32	1	31N29'47	89w44'22	5:58:57
Batesville 54	1	34N18'41	89w56'39	5:59:47
Batson 18	1	31N16'08	89w11'45	5:56:47
Battlefield 25	2	32N19	90w11	6:00:44
Battle Field 51	1	32N30	88w51	5:55:24
Battles 77	1	31N30'06	88w30'34	5:54:02
Batt Place 56	1	30N58'31	88w58'45	5:55:55
Baugh 14	1	34N13	90w43	6:02:52
Baxter 31	1	32N11'28	89w10'11	5:56:41
Baxterville 37	1	31N05'02	89w35'25	5:58:22
Bayland 82	1	32N53'14	90w39'30	6:02:38
Bay Saint Louis 23	1	30N18'31	89w19'48	5:57:19
Bayside Park 23	1	30N16'57	89w26'12	5:57:45
Bay Springs 31	1	31N58'44	89w17'14	5:57:09
Bay View Plaza 24	1	30N25	88w55	5:55:40
Beacon Hill 73	1	34N27'25	88w58'33	5:55:54
Beans Ferry 29	1	34N12'35	88w23'06	5:53:32
Bear Creek 25	1	32N03'49	90w31'10	6:02:05
Beardens 57	1	31N10'58	90w19'48	6:01:19
Bear Garden 76	1	33N11	90w51	6:03:24
Bear Town 57	1	31N13'22	90w27'37	6:01:50
Beasley 13	1	33N35	88w57	5:55:48
Beatline 50	1	32N40'23	89w04'30	5:56:18
Beatrice 12	1	32N04'16	88w52'51	5:55:31
Beatrice 66	1	30N44'20	88w56'49	5:55:47
Beatty 8	1	33N16'11	89w44'20	5:58:57
Beaumont 56	1	31N10'09	88w55'12	5:55:41
Beauregard 15	1	31N43'18	90w22'56	6:01:32
Beauvoir 24	1	30N23'37	88w58'02	5:55:52
Becker 48	1	33N55'59	88w28'52	5:53:55
Beech Grove 15	1	31N59'36	90w15'26	6:01:02
Beech Springs 41	1	34N19'17	88w42'22	5:54:49
Beechwood 3	1	31N07'13	90w51'44	6:03:27
Beechwood 75	1	32N19'39	90w49'36	6:03:18
Bee Lake 26	1	33N02'49	90w19'31	6:01:18
Belden 41	1	34N18'37	88w47'18	5:55:09
Belen 60	1	34N16'23	90w21'15	6:01:25
Bellefontaine 78	1	33N38'55	89w18'36	5:57:14
Belle Isle 23	1	30N15	89w37	5:58:28
Belle Prairie 82	1	33N00'18	90w23'10	6:01:33
Belleville 56	1	31N12'44	89w07'35	5:56:30
Bellewood 27	1	33N13'54	90w33'33	6:02:14
Bells School 53	1	33N28	88w49	5:55:16
Belmont 71	1	34N30'35	88w12'33	5:52:50
Belmont 77	1	31N34'07	88w29'02	5:53:56
Belzoni 27	1	33N11'03	90w29'21	6:01:57
Benndale 20	1	30N48'39	88w45'16	5:55:01
Benoit 6	1	33N39'05	91w00'34	6:04:02
Benson 34	1	31N32'54	89w13'08	5:56:53
Bentley 7	1	33N44	89w04	5:56:16
Bent Oak 44	1	33N26'19	88w32'34	5:54:10
Benton 82	1	32N49'35	90w15'34	6:01:02
Bentonia 82	1	32N38'27	90w21'53	6:01:28
Benwood 81	1	33N56'26	89w30'57	5:58:04
Berclair 42	1	33N28'18	90w21'54	6:01:28
Bernard 25	2	32N06'47	90w15'31	6:01:02
Berryville 82	1	32N44'55	90w09'58	6:00:40
Bertice 40	1	32N36	89w35	5:58:20
Berwick 3	1	31N06'35	90w55'46	6:03:43
Bet 69	1	34N41	89w59	5:59:56
Bethany 41	1	34N30'19	88w43'45	5:54:55
Betheden 80	1	33N13'11	88w56'27	5:55:46
Bethel 5	1	34N43'22	89w08'09	5:56:33
Bethel 51	1	32N19	89w10	5:56:40
Bethesda 25	2	32N08'13	90w22'13	6:01:29
Bethlehem 47	1	34N34'42	89w19'39	5:57:19
Bethsaida 50	1	32N40'34	89w02'05	5:56:08
Bett 69	1	34N41'32	89w45'27	5:59:02
Beulah 6	1	33N47'12	90w58'47	6:03:55
Beulah 51	1	32N30'30	89w01'48	5:56:07
Beverly (Davenport Station) 14	1	34N10'26	90w38'31	6:02:34
Bewelcome 3	1	31N13'07	90w56'19	6:03:45
Bew Springs 22	1	33N47'10	89w53'41	5:59:35
Bexley 20	1	30N57'59	88w40'27	5:54:42
Bigbee 48	1	34N00'58	88w31'09	5:54:05
Bigbee Valley 52	1	33N14'53	88w20'59	5:53:24
Big Black 75	1	32N12'56	90w50'23	6:03:22
Big Creek 7	1	33N51'09	89w24'40	5:57:39
Big Eddy Landing 63	1	32N56'22	90w46'13	6:03:05
Biggersville 2	1	34N50'08	88w33'31	5:54:14
Big Level 66	1	30N48'41	89w03'05	5:56:12
Big Point 30	1	30N35'12	88w28'55	5:53:56
Billups 44	1	33N25'50	88w35'06	5:54:20
Biloxi 24	1	30N23'45	88w53'07	5:55:32
Binford 48	1	33N45'11	88w34'51	5:54:19
Binnsville 35	1	32N54'47	88w22'58	5:53:32
Birdie 60	1	34N23'31	90w22'55	6:01:32
Birmingham 41	1	34N24'30	88w46'09	5:55:05
Bissell 41	1	34N14'46	88w46'58	5:55:08
Black Bayou Junction 42	1	33N47'56	90w16'09	6:01:05
Black Hawk 8	1	33N19'34	90w00'42	6:00:03
Blackjack 53	1	33N28	88w49	5:55:16
Blackland 59	1	34N38'24	88w39'57	5:54:40
Blackmonton 8	1	33N20	89w45	5:59:00
Blackwater 35	1	32N37'08	88w40'57	5:54:44
Blackwater 47	1	34N33'19	89w35'48	5:58:23
Blaine 67	1	33N36'28	90w31'21	6:02:05
Blair 41	1	34N27'04	88w44'13	5:54:57
Blakely 75	1	32N26'37	90w49'20	6:03:17
Blanton 63	1	32N44'55	90w55'50	6:03:43
Blissdale 26	1	33N05'13	90w13'15	6:00:53
Blodgett 34	1	31N27'41	88w59'11	5:55:57
Bloody Springs 71	1	34N35'18	88w08'27	5:52:34

Bloomfield 35 1 32N47'41 88W44'19 5:54:57
Bloomfield 50 1 32N44'01 89W01'05 5:56:04
Blueberry Hill 43 1 31N24'09 90W26'39 6:01:47
Blue Hill 32 1 31N45'46 90W51'27 6:03:26
Blue Hills 11 1 31N53 90W53 6:03:32
Blue Lake 68 1 33N49 90W32 6:02:08
Blue Mountain 70 1 34N40'15 89W01'35 5:56:06
Blue Springs 73 1 34N24'06 88W52'22 5:55:29
Bluff 70 1 34N36'48 88W57'21 5:55:49
Bluff Springs 35 1 32N46'51 88W48'55 5:55:16
Blythe Crossing 71 1 34N47'39 88W10'06 5:52:40
Bobo 14 1 34N07'55 90W40'32 6:02:42
Bobo 60 1 34N17'03 90W10'33 6:00:42
Boggan Bend 41 1 34N27'05 88W45'14 5:55:01
Bogue Chitto 43 1 31N26'19 90W27'08 6:01:49
Boice 77 1 31N44'51 88W39'17 5:54:37
Bolatusha 40 1 32N55'22 89W42'08 5:58:49
Bolivar 6 1 33N39'35 91W03'11 6:04:13
Bolivar Landing 6 1 33N39'59 91W03'16 6:04:13
Bolton 25 1 32N20'57 90W27'36 6:01:50
Bond 50 1 32N51'31 88W59'14 5:55:57
Bond 66 1 30N53'39 89W10'07 5:56:40
Bonhomie 18 1 31N17'20 89W18'35 5:57:14
Bonita 38 1 32N21'55 88W39'57 5:54:40
Bonner 34 1 31N48'49 89W02'56 5:56:12
Boon 80 1 33N06'02 88W57'23 5:55:50
Boone 14 1 34N12 90W34 6:02:16
Booneville 59 1 34N39'29 88W34'00 5:54:16
Booth 28 1 32N57'38 90W55'54 6:03:44
Bothwell 21 1 31N19'39 88W44'36 5:54:58
Bounds 7 1 33N53'57 89W27'25 5:57:50
Bounds Crossroads 29 1 34N19'45 88W12'44 5:52:51
Bourbon 76 1 33N19'27 90W47'55 6:03:12
Bovina 75 1 32N21'07 90W44'05 6:02:56
Bowdre 72 1 34N47'48 90W19'56 6:01:20
Bowerton 15 1 31N45'22 90W34'10 6:02:17
Bowie 18 1 31N23'34 89W22'18 5:57:29
Bowles 67 1 33N20'11 90W35'23 6:02:22
Bowling Green 26 1 33N09'45 89W54'47 5:59:39
Bowman 69 1 34N41'58 89W50'44 5:59:23
Boyer 67 1 33N32'12 90W38'16 6:02:33
Boyette 4 1 33N01'19 89W49'59 5:59:20
Boyle 6 1 33N42'14 90W43'35 6:02:54
Bradie 25 2 32N16'54 90W15'11 6:01:01
Bradley 21 1 31N10'30 88W40'17 5:54:41
Bradley 53 1 33N22'28 88W58'48 5:55:55
Branch 62 1 32N28 89W44 5:58:56
Brandon 61 1 32N16'23 89W59'09 5:59:57
Branyan 73 1 34N27'05 88W48'04 5:55:12
Brasfield 32 1 31N49 91W03 6:04:12
Braxton 64 1 32N01'30 89W58'13 5:59:53
Brazil 68 1 34N01'35 90W16'50 6:01:07
Brewer 12 1 31N58'29 88W36'22 5:54:25
Brewer 41 1 34N08'52 88W41'01 5:54:44
Brewer 56 1 31N22'21 88W51'59 5:55:28
Bridgeport 64 1 31N49'25 90W05'27 6:00:22
Bright 17 1 34N50'49 89W55'13 5:59:41
Bright Corner (reduced Usage 42 1 33N33'17 90W07'02 6:00:28
Bristers Store 39 1 31N22 90W12 6:00:48
Brody 5 1 34N55'55 89W04'12 5:56:17
Brookhaven 43 1 31N34'44 90W26'26 6:01:46
Brook Hollow 25 2 32N19 90W11 6:00:44
Brooklyn 18 1 31N03'22 89W11'10 5:56:45
Brooklyn 27 1 33N10'21 90W29'11 6:01:57
Brooks 67 1 33N47'46 90W27'38 6:01:51
Brookside 3 1 31N17'59 90W45'09 6:03:01
Brooksville 52 1 33N14'04 88W34'56 5:54:20
Brownfield 70 1 34N59'24 88W53'33 5:55:34
Browning 42 1 33N31'05 90W07'11 6:00:29
Brownsville 25 1 32N26'55 90W26'13 6:01:45
Browntown 21 1 31N04'16 88W26'12 5:53:45
Brozville 26 1 33N01'59 90W06'44 6:00:27
Bruce 7 1 33N59'31 89W20'56 5:57:24
Bruce Junction 81 1 33N57'52 89W41'05 5:58:44
Bruinsburg 11 1 31N56'32 91W09'26 6:04:38
Brunswick 75 1 32N33'16 91W03'42 6:04:15
Bryant 81 1 33N55'32 89W42'12 5:58:49
Buchannan 58 1 34N20'20 89W05'58 5:56:24
Buckatunna 77 1 31N32'20 88W31'44 5:54:07
Buckhorn 58 1 34N05'33 89W09'27 5:56:38
Buckleytown 62 1 32N18'13 89W21'39 5:57:27
Bude 19 1 31N27'46 90W51'00 6:03:24
Buena Vista 9 1 33N53'04 88W50'17 5:55:21
Buena Vista 70 1 34N40'00 88W54'54 5:55:40
Bugh 53 1 33N21'58 89W00'06 5:56:00
Bunker Hill 46 1 31N23'15 89W48'12 5:59:13
Bunkley 19 1 31N21'44 90W59'27 6:03:58
Burdette 76 1 33N20'54 90W54'53 6:03:40
Burgess 36 1 34N22 89W31 5:58:04
Burke Landing 14 1 34N16'13 90W47'18 6:03:09
Burnell 11 1 31N48'32 90W44'51 6:02:59
Burns 65 1 32N08'07 89W32'52 5:58:11
Burnside 50 1 32N51'12 89W06'12 5:56:25
Burnsville 71 1 34N50'26 88W18'53 5:53:16
Burrow 2 1 34N54 88W54 5:55:36
Burt 36 1 34N29'44 89W20'00 5:57:20
Burton 59 1 34N38'17 88W20'22 5:53:21
Busey 6 1 33N33'31 90W51'48 6:03:27
Bush 64 1 31N51'43 89W59'12 5:59:57
Busy Corner 3 1 31N16'43 90W51'48 6:03:27
Butler 26 1 33N13'39 90W17'56 6:01:12
Buxton 54 1 34N32'52 90W11'52 6:00:47
Byhalia 47 1 34N52'20 89W41'26 5:58:46
Bynum 37 1 31N23'39 89W32'31 5:58:10
Byram 25 1 32N10'45 90W14'43 6:00:59
Byrd 21 1 31N13'12 88W44'23 5:54:58
Bywy 10 1 33N26'14 89W14'28 5:56:58
Cadamy 29 1 34N10'53 88W15'33 5:53:02
Cadaretta 78 1 33N42'22 89W27'04 5:57:48
Cadillac 32 1 31N39'05 91W06'37 6:04:26
Caesar 55 1 30N35'03 89W32'48 5:58:11
Caile 67 1 33N18'00 90W35'24 6:02:22
Cairo 59 1 34N43'36 88W20'53 5:53:24
Caledonia 44 1 33N40'58 88W19'28 5:53:18
Calhoun 34 1 31N41'45 89W12'19 5:56:49
Calhoun 51 1 32N19 89W10 5:56:40
Calhoun City 7 1 33N51'19 89W18'41 5:57:15
Calyx 52 1 32N57'01 88W29'42 5:53:59
Cambridge 36 1 34N25 89W37 5:58:28
Camden 45 1 32N46'56 89W50'19 5:59:21
Cameron 45 1 32N50'08 89W53'02 5:59:32
Cameta 63 1 33N00'28 90W50'28 6:03:22
Campbell 70 1 34N44 88W57 5:55:48
Campbellville 82 1 32N48'44 90W41'43 6:02:47
Camphill 70 1 34N57 88W54 5:55:36
Canaan 5 1 34N55'49 89W07'36 5:56:30
Candlestick 25 2 32N19 90W11 6:00:44
Cannonsburg 32 1 31N38'01 91W12'40 6:04:51
Canton 45 1 32N36'45 90W02'12 6:00:09
Cantwell Mill 33 1 31N30'32 89W41'24 5:58:46
Capell 3 1 31N01'29 90W59'16 6:03:57
Cardsville 29 1 34N09'20 88W24'09 5:53:37
Carlisle 11 1 32N00'09 90W47'04 6:03:08
Carlos 43 1 31N37'05 90W22'45 6:01:31
Carmack 4 1 33N20 89W45 5:59:00
Carmich 46 1 31N23'02 89W59'06 5:59:56
Carmichael 12 1 31N57'05 88W35'05 5:54:20
Carmichael 25 1 32N04'11 90W31'53 6:02:08
Carmichael 56 1 31N10 88W55 5:55:40
Carnes 18 1 30N59'36 89W15'35 5:57:02
Carolina 29 1 34N07'06 88W28'55 5:53:56
Carpenter 15 1 32N02'02 90W40'49 6:02:43
Carriere 55 1 30N37'00 89W39'09 5:58:37
Carrollton 8 1 33N30'29 89W55'13 5:59:41
Carson 33 1 31N32'16 89W47'42 5:59:11
Carter 82 1 32N59'20 90W26'57 6:01:48
Carter Branch 71 1 34N39'46 88W09'52 5:52:39
Carters 35 1 32N45'39 88W33'43 5:54:15
Carterville 18 1 31N19'11 89W14'46 5:56:59
Carthage 1 1 31N31'35 91W26'45 6:05:47
Carthage 40 1 32N43'57 89W32'10 5:58:09
Carto 74 1 31N07'16 90W04'41 6:00:19
Cary 63 1 32N48'21 90W55'36 6:03:42
Cascilla 68 1 33N51'24 90W00'15 6:00:01
Caseyville 43 1 31N40'22 90W39'20 6:02:37
Cassels 3 1 31N12 91W01 6:04:04
Castleman 27 1 33N12'13 90W31'07 6:02:04
Catfish Point Landing 6 1 33N42'08 91W09'48 6:04:39
Cato 61 1 32N05'24 89W52'41 5:59:31
Cayce 47 1 34N57'19 89W37'05 5:58:28
Cayuga 25 1 32N09'33 90W41'38 6:02:47
Cecil 4 1 33N12 89W47 5:59:08
Cedar Bluff 13 1 33N35'12 88W49'56 5:55:20
Cedar Hill 45 1 32N28'59 90W10'33 6:00:42
Cedar Hill 49 1 33N33'54 89W35'12 5:58:21
Cedar Lake 24 1 30N28'05 88W56'17 5:55:45
Cedars 75 1 32N15'02 90W55'31 6:03:42
Cedarview 17 1 34N54'49 89W49'55 5:59:20
Center 4 1 32N56'43 89W25'51 5:57:43
Center 73 1 34N27'57 88W55'37 5:55:42
Center Hill 38 1 32N31'20 88W45'52 5:55:03
Center Point 43 1 31N23'58 90W36'57 6:02:28
Center Ridge 65 1 31N56'49 89W28'37 5:57:54
Center Ridge 80 1 33N04'20 89W03'54 5:56:16
Centerville 29 1 34N21'51 88W30'33 5:54:02
Centralgrove 48 1 33N50 88W33 5:54:12
Centreville 79 1 31N05'22 91W04'06 6:04:16
Cessions Landing 6 1 34N05'49 90W52'49 6:03:31
Chalybeate 70 1 34N55'49 88W52'05 5:55:28
Champion Hill 25 1 32N21'00 90W32'14 6:02:09
Chancy 60 1 34N07'15 90W16'52 6:01:07
Chapel Hill 25 1 32N06'51 90W30'49 6:02:03
Chapel Landing 63 1 32N56'20 90W47'13 6:03:09
Chapeltown 54 1 34N15'42 90W01'42 6:00:07
Chapelville 41 1 34N26'24 88W35'27 5:54:22
Charleston 68 1 34N00'24 90W03'24 6:00:14
Charlton 45 1 32N34'54 90W07'42 6:00:31
Chatawa 57 1 31N03'37 90W28'20 6:01:53
Chatham 76 1 33N06'02 91W05'52 6:04:23
Cheraw 46 1 31N09'20 89W50'36 5:59:22
Cherry Creek 58 1 34N21'02 88W59'15 5:55:57
Chester 10 1 33N21'31 89W14'18 5:56:57
Chesterville 58 1 34N17'11 88W49'32 5:55:18
Chicora 77 1 31N33'49 88W34'31 5:54:18
Chipwood 24 1 30N25 88W55 5:55:40
Chiwapa 58 1 34N10'53 88W55'51 5:55:43
Choctaw 6 1 33N33'28 90W48'47 6:03:15
Choctaw 22 1 33N49'49 89W38'47 5:58:35
Choctaw 26 1 33N10'22 90W18'16 6:01:13
Choctaw 34 1 31N42 89W08 5:56:32
Choctaw Indian Reservation 50 1 32N48 89W14 5:56:56
Choctaw Landing 63 1 32N52'11 90W48'32 6:03:14
Christmas 6 1 33N46'35 90W58'42 6:03:55
Chulahoma 47 1 34N39'13 89W37'49 5:58:31
Chunky 51 1 32N19'32 88W55'41 5:55:43
Church Hill 32 1 31N43 91W14 6:04:56
Clack 72 1 34N50'45 90W17'35 6:01:10
Clara 77 1 31N34'49 88W41'47 5:54:47
Claremont 14 1 34N07'14 90W31'26 6:02:06
Clark 21 1 31N17'17 88W34'26 5:54:18
Clark 32 1 31N53 90W53 6:03:32
Clarksburg 62 1 32N19'48 89W43'46 5:58:55
Clarksdale 14 1 34N12'00 90W34'15 6:02:17
Clarkson 78 1 33N38'07 89W08'58 5:56:36
Clarmont 14 1 34N12 90W34 6:02:16
Clarysville 70 1 34N38'38 88W54'42 5:55:39
Clay 29 1 34N16'12 88W20'14 5:53:21
Clayton 72 1 34N36'00 90W24'59 6:01:40
Clayton Village 53 1 33N28'26 88W45'21 5:55:01
Claytown 80 1 32N58'35 88W57'59 5:55:52
Clear Springs 65 1 32N08'38 89W20'38 5:57:23
Cleary 61 1 32N09'55 90W10'50 6:00:43
Clem 33 1 31N42'39 89W47'16 5:59:09
Cleo 34 1 31N42'01 89W02'12 5:56:09
Clermont Harbor 23 1 30N15'41 89W24'58 5:57:40
Cleveland 6 1 33N44'38 90W43'29 6:02:54
Cleveland 35 1 32N45'04 88W49'48 5:55:19
Cleveland Crossing 6 1 33N44'50 90W47'51 6:03:11
Clifton 62 1 32N27'58 89W33'59 5:58:16
Cliftonville 52 1 33N14'08 88W25'30 5:53:42
Clinton 25 1 32N20'29 90W19'18 6:01:17
Clove Hill 14 1 34N13 90W32 6:02:08
Cloverdale 1 1 31N29'52 91W25'14 6:05:41
Clover Hill 14 1 34N16'30 90W32'39 6:02:11
Clyde 37 1 31N21'00 89W28'04 5:57:52
Coahoma 14 1 34N22'00 90W31'23 6:02:06
Coal Oil Corner 47 1 34N52'06 89W40'14 5:58:41
Coats 64 1 31N50'45 89W42'17 5:58:49
Cobbs 43 1 31N33'35 90W34'28 6:02:18
Cobbville 45 1 32N40'19 90W00'24 6:00:02
Cockrum 17 1 34N48'10 89W48'43 5:59:15
Coffeeville 81 1 33N58'36 89W40'32 5:58:42
Cohay 65 1 31N55'41 89W35'49 5:58:23
Coila 8 1 33N23'43 89W58'16 5:59:53
Colby 82 1 32N52'42 90W41'09 6:02:45
Coldwater 50 1 32N42'53 89W12'51 5:56:51
Coldwater 69 1 34N41'30 89W58'38 5:59:55
Coles 3 1 31N16'38 91W01'54 6:04:08
Coles Creek 7 1 33N51 89W25 5:57:40
College 44 1 33N34 88W25 5:53:40
College Hill 36 1 34N25'18 89W34'14 5:58:17
Collins 16 1 31N38'43 89W33'19 5:58:13
Collins Crossing 2 1 34N48'27 88W43'27 5:54:54
Collinstown 2 1 34N48'27 88W43'58 5:54:56
Collinsville 38 1 32N29'52 88W50'45 5:55:23
Coll Town 30 1 30N30'43 88W33'02 5:54:12
Colonial 25 2 32N19 90W11 6:00:44
Colony Town 42 1 33N30 90W20 6:01:20
Colsub 48 1 33N59 88W29 5:53:56
Columbia 46 1 31N15'06 89W50'15 5:59:21
Columbus 44 1 33N29'44 88W25'38 5:53:43
Columbus Air Force Base 44 1 33N39 88W27 5:53:48
Commerce 72 1 34N49'04 90W22'15 6:01:29
Commerce Landing 72 1 34N49'55 90W23'05 6:01:32
Como 54 1 34N30'38 89W56'23 5:59:46
Compromise 3 1 31N12'02 90W53'11 6:03:33
Concord 73 1 34N33'13 88W58'57 5:55:56
Concordia 6 1 33N58'39 90W57'02 6:03:48
Conehatta 51 1 32N27'04 89W17'07 5:57:08
Conerly 57 1 31N10'29 90W17'22 6:01:09
Conn 15 1 31N53'52 90W42'36 6:02:50
Conway 40 1 32N51'22 89W35'24 5:58:22
Cooks Landing 71 1 34N55'52 88W10'00 5:52:40
Cooksville 52 1 32N59'01 88W21'32 5:53:26
Cooperville 62 1 32N14'26 89W42'47 5:58:51
Coosa 40 1 32N50'32 89W25'20 5:57:41
Coral 37 1 31N23'10 89W31'47 5:58:07
Corinth 2 1 34N56'03 88W31'20 5:54:05
Corinth 56 1 31N20'37 89W08'23 5:56:34
Cormorant, Lake 17 1 34N54'15 90W12'52 6:00:51
Cornersville 47 1 34N32'20 89W15'20 5:57:01
Corrona 41 1 34N28'12 88W46'02 5:55:04
Cottondale 67 1 33N41'24 90W32'34 6:02:10
Cotton Plant 70 1 34N36'01 89W00'16 5:56:01
Cottonville 69 1 34N41 89W59 5:59:56
Counts 14 1 34N04'10 90W33'35 6:02:14
County Line 21 1 31N26 88W28 5:53:52
Courtland 54 1 34N14'27 89W56'34 5:59:46
Cowart 68 1 34N00 90W03 6:00:12
Coxburg 26 1 32N59'54 90W12'36 6:00:50
Coxs Ferry 25 1 32N21 90W28 6:01:52
Coy 35 1 32N54'12 88W54'53 5:55:40
Craig 27 1 32N55'48 90W35'45 6:02:23
Craigside 42 1 33N35'19 90W11'37 6:00:46
Craig Springs 53 1 33N18'54 88W55'22 5:55:41
Crandall 12 1 31N58'28 88W31'56 5:54:08
Crane Creek 23 1 30N47 89W08 5:56:32
Cranfield 1 1 31N32'38 91W12'21 6:04:49
Crawford 44 1 33N18'05 88W36'53 5:54:28
Crenfree 42 1 33N34'51 90W06'42 6:00:27
Crenshaw 60 1 34N30'09 90W11'55 6:00:48
Crockett 69 1 34N37 89W58 5:59:52
Crosby 3 1 31N17'01 91W03'47 6:04:15
Crossroad 40 1 32N53'02 89W29'40 5:57:59
Crossroad 69 1 34N36'43 89W50'13 5:59:21
Crossroads 20 1 30N53'06 88W42'38 5:54:51
Crossroads 50 1 32N45'32 88W56'54 5:55:48
Crossroads 55 1 30N46'57 89W46'29 5:59:06
Cross Roads 61 1 32N19 89W47 5:59:08
Cross Roads 71 1 34N55'27 88W15'21 5:53:01
Crossroads 76 1 33N25 91W00 6:04:00
Crotts 34 1 31N36 89W12 5:56:48
Crowder 60 1 34N10'24 90W08'15 6:00:33
Cruger 26 1 33N19'15 90W13'56 6:00:56
Crumtown 2 1 34N50'21 88W44'00 5:54:56
Crupp 82 1 32N47'07 90W27'59 6:01:52
Crystal Springs 15 1 31N59'14 90W21'25 6:01:26
Cub Lake 17 1 34N47'11 90W08'57 6:00:36
Cuevas 24 1 30N19 89W14 5:56:56
Cullum 35 1 32N38'26 88W36'29 5:54:26
Cumberland 78 1 33N37'13 89W04'45 5:56:19
Currie 34 1 31N37'53 89W08'49 5:56:35
Curtis Station 54 1 34N20'24 90W08'21 6:00:33
Cybur 55 1 30N37'40 89W46'15 5:59:05
Cynthia 25 2 32N24'10 90W14'56 6:01:00
Cypress Corner 54 1 34N33'15 90W05'35 6:00:22
Dabney Crossroads 25 1 32N05'10 90W25'40 6:01:43
Dahomey 6 1 33N39 91W01 6:04:04
Daisy-Vestry 30 1 30N47 89W08 5:56:32
Dale 20 1 30N50'05 88W40'59 5:55:08
Daleville 38 1 32N34'11 88W40'34 5:54:42
Dallas Jones Crossing 36 1 34N13'19 89W38'34 5:58:34
Damascus 35 1 32N39'27 88W50'02 5:55:20

Damascus 62 1 32N33'19 89w23'18 5:57:33
Dancy 78 1 33N40'10 89w03'32 5:56:14
Danforth 14 1 34N27'50 90w30'14 6:02:01
Daniel 65 1 32N07'41 89w43'15 5:58:53
Dantzler 30 1 30N42'46 88w52'32 5:55:30
Darbun 74 1 31N16'34 90w02'49 6:00:11
Darden 73 1 34N30'11 89w11'37 5:56:46
Darling 60 1 34N21'32 90w16'27 6:01:06
Darlove 76 1 33N13'55 90w47'04 6:03:08
Darracott 48 1 33N50 88w33 5:54:12
Darrington 79 1 31N18'24 91w14'08 6:04:57
Davenport 14 1 34N12 90w34 6:02:16
Davis 45 1 32N41'30 90w01'23 6:00:06
Davo 74 1 31N06'21 90w06'40 6:00:27
Days 17 1 34N54'40 90w04'40 6:00:19
Dean Landing 20 1 30N46'52 88w28'21 5:53:53
Deasonville 82 1 32N47'32 90w05'34 6:00:22
Decatur 51 1 32N26'20 89w06'30 5:56:26
Deemer 50 1 32N44'43 89w07'05 5:56:28
Deen 33 1 31N33'12 89w40'41 5:58:43
Deep Creek 56 1 30N55'11 88w54'59 5:55:40
Deerbrook 52 1 33N14'07 88w29'12 5:53:57
Dees Landing 30 1 30N31'25 88w40'51 5:54:43
Deeson 6 1 34N01'23 90w51'34 6:03:26
De Kalb 35 1 32N46'03 88w39'03 5:54:36
Delay 36 1 34N14'56 89w24'14 5:57:37
De Lisle 24 1 30N22'45 89w15'52 5:57:03
Delta 14 1 34N24'16 90w34'20 6:02:17
Delta 54 1 34N25'23 90w07'44 6:00:31
Delta City 63 1 33N04'26 90w47'42 6:03:11
Delta Drive 25 2 32N19 90w11 6:00:44
Delta State College 6
1 33N44 90w43 6:02:52
Denham 77 1 31N39'13 88w31'32 5:54:06
Denmark 36 1 34N18'39 89w20'48 5:57:23
Dennis 71 1 34N33'31 88w13'34 5:52:54
Dennis Crossroads 32
1 31N45'29 90w57'34 6:03:50
Dennis Landing 6
1 34N01'07 90w55'41 6:03:43
Dennis Settlement 62
1 32N21'39 89w20'57 5:57:24
Denton 60 1 34N08'46 90w18'45 6:01:15
Dentontown 7 1 33N44'27 89w26'34 5:57:46
Dentville 15 1 31N57'35 90w33'19 6:02:13
Deovolente 27 1 33N13'09 90w27'00 6:01:48
Derby 55 1 30N45'34 89w34'59 5:58:20
Derma 7 1 33N51'20 89w17'04 5:57:08
De Soto 12 1 31N58'25 88w42'48 5:54:51
DeWeese 50 1 32N42'36 88w56'15 5:55:45
Dexter 74 1 31N04'27 89w59'34 5:59:58
Diamondhead 23 1 30N19 89w20 5:57:20
D'Iberville 24 1 30N25'34 88w53'27 5:55:34
Dickerson 14 1 34N19'16 90w38'11 6:02:33
Dillon 74 1 31N01'20 90w13'24 6:00:54
Dinan 74 1 31N13'02 90w11'33 6:00:46
Dinsmore 52 1 33N05'20 88w21'11 5:53:25
Distall 68 1 33N51'30 90w10'53 6:00:44
Dixie 6 1 34N06'27 90w50'45 6:03:23
Dixie 18 1 31N01'26 89w12'08 5:56:49
Dixie Pine 18 1 31N17'41 89w16'12 5:57:05
Dixon 25 2 32N19'32 90w15'09 6:01:01
Dixon 50 1 32N39'55 89w13'14 5:56:53
D'Lo 64 1 31N59'08 89w54'04 5:59:36
Dockery 67 1 33N43'43 90w37'00 6:02:28
Doddsville 67 1 33N39'27 90w31'29 6:02:06
Dogtown 36 1 34N15'53 89w17'09 5:57:09
Dogwood Landing 63
1 32N57'10 90w47'06 6:03:08
Doloroso 79 1 31N18'18 91w21'34 6:05:26
Domascus 35 1 32N46 88w39 5:54:36
Donegal 79 1 31N03'21 91w22'37 6:05:30
Donohoe 62 1 32N21'05 89w22'57 5:57:32
Dooley 72 1 34N40'14 90w14'13 6:00:57
Doolittle 51 1 32N19 89w10 5:56:40
Dorsey 29 1 34N15'07 88w30'35 5:54:02
Doskie 71 1 34N54'21 88w17'42 5:53:11
Dossville 40 1 32N55'50 89w32'59 5:58:12
Double Springs 53
1 33N28'53 89w03'39 5:56:15
Dover 50 1 32N35'03 89w12'51 5:56:51
Dover 82 1 32N41'54 90w19'26 6:01:18
Dowdville 50 1 32N41'09 89w18'13 5:57:13
Dowell 40 1 32N54'04 89w33'48 5:58:15
Dragon 18 1 31N22'39 89w15'59 5:57:04
Drew 67 1 33N48'34 90w31'35 6:02:06
Dry Creek 16 1 31N38 89w33 5:58:12
Dry Grove 25 2 32N07'44 90w26'11 6:01:45
Dubard 22 1 33N46'35 89w55'07 5:59:40
Dubbs 72 1 34N34'06 90w22'25 6:01:30
Dublin 14 1 34N04'20 90w29'26 6:01:58
Duck Hill 49 1 33N37'59 89w42'40 5:58:51
Dueitt 21 1 31N09'02 88w32'04 5:54:08
Duffee 51 1 32N29'21 88w55'37 5:55:42
Duke 25 1 32N06'46 90w43'02 6:02:52
Dulweber 26 1 33N20'30 90w14'14 6:00:57
Dumas 70 1 34N38'25 88w50'38 5:55:23
Duncan 6 1 34N02'40 90w44'41 6:02:59
Dundee 72 1 34N31'27 90w27'20 6:01:49
Dunkirk 76 1 33N27'26 90w52'54 6:03:32
Dunleith 76 1 33N26'09 90w49'14 6:03:17
Durant 26 1 33N04'30 89w51'16 5:59:25
Dwiggins 67 1 33N50'44 90w34'53 6:02:20
Dwyer 67 1 33N33'51 90w31'43 6:02:07
Dykes Crossing 57
1 31N05'52 90w17'07 6:01:08
Eagle Bend 75 1 32N31'13 91w00'24 6:04:02
Eagle Lake 75 1 32N20 90w52 6:03:28
Eagle Landing 72
1 34N32'04 90w32'41 6:02:11
Eagles Nest 14 1 34N17'31 90w28'02 6:01:52
Early Grove 47 1 34N58'33 89w23'05 5:57:32
East Aberdeen 48
1 33N49'18 88w30'59 5:54:04
Eastabuchie 18 1 31N26'07 89w17'00 5:57:08
East Fork 3 1 31N12'11 90w40'06 6:02:40
Eastland 67 1 33N39'02 90w31'19 6:02:05
Eastlawn 30 1 30N23 88w32 5:54:08
East Lincoln 43 1 31N29'06 90w17'31 6:01:10
Eastman 29 1 34N20'18 88w14'10 5:52:57
East Moss Point 30
1 30N24 88w31 5:54:04
Eastport 71 1 34N53'08 88w06'02 5:52:24
Eastside 30 1 30N24 88w31 5:54:04
East Side 56 1 31N21'17 88w54'40 5:55:39
East Tupelo 41 1 34N15 88w43 5:54:52
Eastview 34 1 31N41'49 89w05'28 5:56:22
Eatonville 18 1 31N24'50 89w19'45 5:57:19
Ebenezer 26 1 32N58'14 90w05'27 6:00:22
Ecru 58 1 34N21'11 89w01'23 5:56:06
Eddiceton 19 1 31N30'07 90w47'29 6:03:10
Eden 82 1 32N59'05 90w19'24 6:01:18
Edgewater Park 24
1 30N23'36 88w59'13 5:55:57
Edinburg 40 1 32N47'57 89w20'10 5:57:21
Edwards 25 1 32N19'48 90w36'20 6:02:25
Effie 68 1 33N56'05 90w10'38 6:00:43
Eggville 41 1 34N19'51 88w34'06 5:54:16
Egremont 63 1 32N51'38 90w54'12 6:03:37
Egypt 9 1 33N53'54 88w43'47 5:54:55
Egypt 26 1 33N20'28 90w16'38 6:01:07
Egypt Hill 15 1 32N00'36 90w15'44 6:01:03
Eldorado 75 1 32N34'46 90w39'34 6:02:38
Eldridge 6 1 34N06'41 90w50'28 6:03:22
Electric Mills 35
1 32N46'09 88w27'50 5:53:51
Elizabeth 76 1 33N25'25 90w52'52 6:03:31
Ellard 7 1 34N00'57 89w24'53 5:57:40
Elliott 22 1 33N41'00 89w44'57 5:59:00
Ellis Cliffs 1 1 31N24'05 91w27'07 6:05:48
Ellistown 73 1 34N26'41 88w50'27 5:55:22
Ellisville 34 1 31N36'14 89w11'44 5:56:47
Ellwood Landing 82
1 32N42'20 90w41'14 6:02:45
Elsie 7 1 33N53 89w11 5:56:44
Elton 25 1 32N13'15 90w13'09 6:00:53
Elwood 12 1 32N01'05 88w48'06 5:55:12
Embry 78 1 33N39'22 89w22'08 5:57:29
Emerald 57 1 31N04'37 90w21'49 6:01:27
Eminence 16 1 31N36'46 89w26'02 5:57:44
Emory 26 1 33N15'09 89w55'26 5:59:42
Empire 76 1 33N13'08 90w49'53 6:03:20
Endville 58 1 34N19'20 88w52'59 5:55:32
Energy 12 1 32N10'46 88w32'59 5:54:12
Enid 68 1 34N06'59 89w56'23 5:59:46
Enola 82 1 32N43'38 90w35'05 6:02:20
Enola Landing 82
1 32N43'38 90w35'20 6:02:21
Enon 74 1 31N18'13 90w13'23 6:00:54
Enondale 35 1 32N38'07 88w28'06 5:53:52
Enterprise 3 1 31N09'53 90w52'41 6:03:31
Enterprise 12 1 32N10'27 88w49'53 5:55:20
Enterprise 43 1 31N28'24 90w23'07 6:01:32
Enterprise 73 1 34N28'01 89w09'26 5:56:38
Enzor 38 1 32N28 88w40 5:54:40
Epley 37 1 31N22'35 89w30'40 5:58:03
Epps 18 1 31N07'51 89w11'45 5:56:47
Eret 77 1 31N28'12 88w28'56 5:53:56
Errata 34 1 31N45'31 89w03'36 5:56:14
Erwin 76 1 33N06'14 91w02'37 6:04:10
Escatawpa 30 1 30N26'25 88w32'37 5:54:10
Eset 77 1 31N26 88w28 5:53:52
Eskridge 49 1 33N34'31 89w42'03 5:58:48
Esperanza 58 1 34N21'28 89w09'39 5:56:39
Essex 60 1 34N19'47 90w16'29 6:01:06
Estes 80 1 33N03'40 89w02'57 5:56:12
Estesmill 40 1 32N39'02 89w28'12 5:57:53
Estill 76 1 33N13'05 90w52'15 6:03:29
Ethel 4 1 33N07'13 89w27'57 5:57:52
Etta 73 1 34N28'13 89w13'39 5:56:55
Eucutta 77 1 31N48'18 88w52'20 5:55:29
Eudora 17 1 34N49'49 90w08'57 6:00:36
Eulogy 26 1 33N02'01 90w10'29 6:00:42
Eunice 3 1 31N17'21 90w58'28 6:03:54
Eupora 78 1 33N32'26 89w16'01 5:57:04
Eureka Springs 54
1 34N14'37 89w51'52 5:59:27
Eutaw 6 1 33N39'31 91w09'02 6:04:36
Eutaw Landing 6 1 33N39'06 91w10'12 6:04:41
Evans 82 1 32N51'11 90w10'29 6:00:42
Evanston 20 1 30N54'26 88w33'49 5:54:15
Evansville 72 1 34N38'25 90w23'19 6:01:33
Everett 64 1 32N01'39 89w49'20 5:59:17
Evergreen 24 1 30N24 89w05 5:56:20
Evergreen 29 1 34N09'43 88w30'41 5:54:03
Expose 46 1 31N19'22 89w51'48 5:59:27
Fairchilds Crossroads 25
1 32N12'17 90w28'22 6:01:53
Fairfield 73 1 34N25'19 88w50'30 5:55:22
Fairground 50 1 32N46 89w07 5:56:28
Fairhaven 17 1 34N57 89w49 5:59:16
Fairhill 52 1 32N56'39 88w39'54 5:54:40
Fair Oak Springs 43
1 31N33'16 90w19'13 6:01:17
Fair River 43 1 31N32'45 90w16'09 6:01:05
Fairview 29 1 34N21'52 88w19'02 5:53:16
Fairview 50 1 32N45'14 89w10'32 5:56:42
Fairview 67 1 33N30'33 90w44'48 6:02:59
Fairview Landing 82
1 32N44'54 90w42'06 6:02:48
Falcon 60 1 34N23'35 90w15'23 6:01:02
Falkner 70 1 34N50'31 88w56'03 5:55:44
Fame 78 1 33N33 89w16 5:57:04
Famosla 27 1 33N14'19 90w23'24 6:01:34
Fannin 61 1 32N25'02 89w57'24 5:59:50
Farmhaven 45 1 32N38'51 89w48'38 5:59:15
Farmington 2 1 34N55'48 88w27'08 5:53:49
Farrell 14 1 34N15'51 90w40'20 6:02:41
Fayette 32 1 31N42'41 91w03'38 6:04:15
Fearns Springs 80
1 33N00'25 88w50'45 5:55:23
Fenton 23 1 30N24'53 89w22'51 5:57:31
Fentress 10 1 33N17'48 89w13'20 5:56:53
Fenwick 1 1 31N33'21 91w14'56 6:05:00
Ferguson 39 1 31N37'56 90w04'54 6:00:20
Ferguson 56 1 31N11'38 88w58'32 5:55:54
Fernwood 57 1 31N11'07 90w26'56 6:01:48
Fikestown 62 1 32N18'12 89w24'13 5:57:37
Fitler 28 1 32N43'31 91w02'01 6:04:08
Fitzhugh 67 1 33N53'18 90w30'31 6:02:02
Flatwood 73 1 34N23'20 89w07'43 5:56:31
Flora 45 1 32N32'35 90w18'33 6:01:14
Florence 61 1 32N09'12 90w07'52 6:00:31
Flowerdale 41 1 34N17'06 88w44'15 5:54:57
Floweree 75 1 32N32'39 90w51'00 6:03:24
Flowers 74 1 31N03'24 90w00'49 6:00:03
Flowers 75 1 32N23'21 90w40'26 6:02:42
Flowood 61 2 32N18'34 90w08'20 6:00:33
Floyd 5 1 34N50 89w11 5:56:44
Fondren 25 2 32N19 90w11 6:00:44
Fontainbleau 30 1 30N24'07 88w43'11 5:54:53
Fontainebleau 30
1 30N26 88w49 5:55:16
Foote 76 1 33N05'29 91w01'58 6:04:08
Ford 30 1 30N25'30 88w31'23 5:54:06
Fords Creek 55 1 30N56'54 89w41'23 5:58:46
Fordyke 82 1 32N54'18 90w07'39 6:00:31
Forest 62 1 32N21'52 89w28'27 5:57:54
Forestdale 50 1 32N46'44 88w56'56 5:55:48
Forest Hill 25 2 32N15'55 90w16'51 6:01:07
Forkland 76 1 33N31'35 91w00'51 6:04:03
Forkville 62 1 32N27'38 89w39'39 5:58:39
Forreston 44 1 33N20'14 88w18'49 5:53:15
Fort Adams 79 1 31N05'11 91w32'53 6:06:12
Fortenberry 46 1 31N18'26 89w51'19 5:59:25
Fort Loring Landing 42
1 33N29'21 90w14'48 6:00:59
Fort Stephens 35
1 32N28 88w43 5:54:52
Foster 1 1 31N36'01 91w19'44 6:05:19
Fouke 31 1 32N01'44 89w06'58 5:56:28
Four Corners 4 1 33N03 89w35 5:58:20
Four Forks 32 1 31N37'41 91w07'39 6:04:31
Four Mile 27 1 33N17'14 90w28'20 6:01:53
Four Points 18 1 31N15'04 89w11'10 5:56:45
Fox 49 1 33N31'01 89w39'54 5:58:40
Foxworth 46 1 31N14'17 89w52'07 5:59:28
Francis 6 1 34N04'54 90w51'17 6:03:25
Franklin 19 1 31N25'17 91w05'53 6:04:24
Franklin 26 1 33N02'09 90w00'07 6:00:00
Frankstown 59 1 34N34'35 88w37'47 5:54:31
Frazier 67 1 33N34'01 90w43'55 6:02:56
Freeny 40 1 32N42'03 89w28'53 5:57:56
Freerun 82 1 32N51 90w24 6:01:36
Free Trade 40 1 32N41'46 89w24'54 5:57:40
Freewoods 19 1 31N20'44 91w04'29 6:04:18
Freeze Corner 17
1 34N50 89w59 5:59:56
French Camp 10 1 33N17'35 89w23'58 5:57:36
Friars Point 14 1 34N22'10 90w38'20 6:02:33
Friendship 43 1 31N35 90w27 6:01:48
Friendship 58 1 34N19'26 89w02'15 5:56:09
Frog Island 41 1 34N21'55 88w45'23 5:55:02
Frostbridge 77 1 31N41 88w39 5:54:36
Fruitland Park 18
1 30N54'57 89w10'16 5:56:41
Fugate 82 1 32N44'56 90w12'07 6:00:48
Fulcher 10 1 33N20'17 89w07'23 5:56:30
Fulton 29 1 34N16'26 88w24'33 5:53:38
Furrs 58 1 34N14'06 88w51'36 5:55:26
Furry 67 1 33N31'13 90w31'47 6:02:07
Futheyville 22 1 33N46'52 89w46'34 5:59:06
Gainesville 23 1 30N21'03 89w38'23 5:58:34
Galena 47 1 34N39'25 89w33'08 5:58:13
Gallatin 15 1 31N51'02 90w27'13 6:01:49
Gallman 15 1 31N55'55 90w23'21 6:01:33
Galloway 11 1 32N03'59 90w58'00 6:03:52
Gandsi 16 1 31N34'14 89w29'56 5:58:00
Garden City 19 1 31N22'01 91w07'40 6:04:31
Garlandville 31 1 32N13'10 89w07'21 5:56:29
Gaston 59 1 34N42'15 88w35'53 5:54:24
Gatesville 15 1 31N59'52 90w14'36 6:00:58
Gatewood 81 1 33N58'29 89w45'52 5:59:03
Gattman 48 1 33N53'07 88w14'07 5:52:56
Gautier 30 1 30N23'08 88w36'42 5:54:27
Geeslin Corner 22
1 33N49'26 89w50'20 5:59:21
Geeville 59 1 34N34'34 88w41'27 5:54:46
Geneill 76 1 33N23'20 90w47'58 6:03:12
George 82 1 32N51'00 90w42'06 6:02:48
Georgetown 15 1 31N52'17 90w09'52 6:00:39
Gerlach Mill 72 1 34N30'10 90w19'58 6:01:20
Germania 82 1 32N36'22 90w35'32 6:02:22
Gershorn 58 1 34N05'19 89w01'36 5:56:06
Gholson 52 1 32N56'11 88w44'02 5:54:56
Gibbons 63 1 32N48 90w56 6:03:44
Gibson 48 1 33N50'24 88w41'04 5:54:44
Gibson Landing 20
1 30N46'02 88w40'13 5:54:41
Gift 2 1 34N56'44 88w38'28 5:54:34
Giles 35 1 32N49'51 88w22'48 5:53:31
Gill 6 1 33N48'20 90w58'35 6:03:54
Gill 40 1 32N40'46 89w31'54 5:58:08
Gillsburg 3 1 31N01'30 90w39'21 6:02:37
Gilmore 16 1 31N46'47 89w29'30 5:57:58
Gilton 47 1 34N43'10 89w26'53 5:57:48
Gitano 34 1 31N46'41 89w19'28 5:57:18
Glade 34 1 31N39'18 89w06'26 5:56:26
Gladhurst 57 1 31N01'46 90w22'27 6:01:30
Glading 3 1 31N08'33 90w38'25 6:02:34
Glancy 15 1 31N49'06 90w29'47 6:01:59
Glen 2 1 34N52 88w31 5:54:04
Glen Allan 76 1 33N01'26 91w01'48 6:04:07
Glen Aubin 14 1 34N20'28 90w36'38 6:02:27
Glendale 18 1 31N21'52 89w18'22 5:57:13
Glendora 68 1 33N49'45 90w17'35 6:01:10
Glenfield 73 1 34N30'40 89w02'01 5:56:08
Glens Glen (P O) 2
1 34N51'58 88w24'50 5:53:39
Glenville 54 1 34N31'42 89w44'24 5:58:58
Glenwild 22 1 33N43'15 89w46'55 5:59:08
Gloster 3 1 31N11'50 91w01'18 6:04:05
Glover 17 1 34N55'57 90w10'48 6:00:43
Gluckstadt 45 1 32N30'59 90w06'03 6:00:24
Golden 71 1 34N29'18 88w11'19 5:52:45
Golden Grove 50 1 32N37'51 89w05'23 5:56:22
Goldfield 67 1 33N49 90w32 6:02:08
Gooden Lake 27 1 33N08'17 90w36'25 6:02:26
Goodfood 58 1 34N15 89w01 5:56:04
Goodford 58 1 34N06'31 88w56'33 5:55:46
Good Hope 26 1 33N06'06 90w18'01 6:01:12
Good Hope 40 1 32N37'41 89w37'44 5:58:31
Good Hope 50 1 32N43'40 89w09'25 5:56:38
Good Hope 56 1 31N24'15 88w56'56 5:55:48
Goodluck 18 1 31N19'36 89w09'23 5:56:38
Goodman 26 1 32N58'12 89w54'44 5:59:39
Goodwater 12 1 31N54'58 88w51'36 5:55:26
Goodyear 55 1 30N32 89w40 5:58:40
Gordon 11 1 31N53'48 90w58'20 6:03:53

Gore Springs 22 1 33N45'15 89w36'59 5:58:28
Goshen Springs 61
1 32N28'14 89w54'57 5:59:40
Goss 46 1 31N21'19 89w53'19 5:59:33
Grace 28 1 32N59'58 90w57'23 6:03:50
Grady 78 1 33N30'46 89w18'31 5:57:14
Graham 38 1 32N20'33 88w50'57 5:55:24
Graham 73 1 34N32'58 88w47'36 5:55:10
Grand Gulf 11 1 32N01'59 91w03'09 6:04:13
Grange 39 1 31N44 89w59 5:59:56
Grange Hall 75 1 32N20 90w52 6:03:28
Grapeland 6 1 33N37'01 90w59'15 6:03:57
Grass Lake 27 1 33N10'14 90w23'00 6:01:32
Gravel Hill 8 1 33N24'05 90w02'46 6:00:11
Gravel Siding 71
1 34N49 88w11 5:52:44
Graves 41 1 34N27'05 88w46'37 5:55:06
Gravestown 70 1 34N44'55 89w05'00 5:56:20
Gray 40 1 32N54'40 89w26'49 5:57:47
Graysport Crossing 22
1 33N48'59 89w36'49 5:58:27
Greenbrier Park 55
1 30N32 89w40 5:58:40
Green Crossing 25
2 32N26'15 90w15'55 6:01:04
Greenfield 51 1 32N27 89w17 5:57:08
Greenfield 61 1 32N14'57 90w03'10 6:00:13
Greenfield Addition 76
1 33N25 91w00 6:04:00
Green Grove 14 1 34N09'46 90w45'39 6:03:03
Greenland 51 1 32N33'04 89w03'10 5:56:13
Greenville 76 1 33N24'36 91w03'42 6:04:15
Greenwood 29 1 34N13'04 88w30'36 5:54:02
Greenwood 42 1 33N30'58 90w10'46 6:00:43
Greenwood Springs 48
1 33N53'13 88w18'32 5:53:14
Grenada 22 1 33N46'08 89w48'30 5:59:14
Grenada Junction 42
1 33N32'21 90w09'53 6:00:40
Grenada Landing 22
1 33N48'14 89w46'02 5:59:04
Gretna 77 1 31N45'34 88w30'07 5:54:00
Gridley 31 1 32N03'35 89w06'45 5:56:27
Griffith 13 1 33N38'06 88w49'41 5:55:19
Guide 61 1 32N17'55 89w51'48 5:59:27
Gulf Hills 30 1 30N25'49 88w50'32 5:55:22
Gulf Hills Country Club 30
1 30N26 88w49 5:55:16
Gulf Park Estates 30
1 30N26 88w49 5:55:16
Gulfport 24 1 30N22'02 89w05'34 5:56:22
Gum Grove 26 1 33N04'39 90w25'37 6:01:42
Gums 81 1 33N55'39 89w37'44 5:58:31
Gums Crossing 81
1 33N54'38 89w37'45 5:58:31
Gum Springs 62 1 32N27'34 89w27'03 5:57:48
Gum Springs 80 1 33N14'01 89w03'08 5:56:13
Gunn 65 1 32N04 89w41 5:58:44
Gunnison 6 1 33N56'39 90w56'42 6:03:47
Guntown 41 1 34N26'35 88w39'35 5:54:38
Gwin 26 1 33N10'25 90w13'24 6:00:54
Gwinville 33 1 31N45'05 89w53'57 5:59:36
Hale 12 1 31N57'49 88w46'32 5:55:06
Hall 9 1 33N53'19 89w04'06 5:56:16
Halltown 73 1 34N31'27 88w48'45 5:55:15
Halstead 67 1 33N42'14 90w38'29 6:02:34
Hamage 46 1 31N13'32 89w56'39 5:59:47
Hamburg 19 1 31N34'43 91w04'00 6:04:16
Hamilton 48 1 33N44'25 88w24'40 5:53:39
Hamlin 72 1 34N30'11 90w27'26 6:01:50
Hampton 76 1 33N01'51 91w00'07 6:04:00
Hand 35 1 32N28 88w43 5:54:52
Handle 80 1 32N57'39 88w52'28 5:55:30
Handsboro 24 1 30N23'54 89w01'37 5:56:06
Handy Corner 17 1 34N57'44 89w44'31 5:58:58
Haney 34 1 31N48'57 89w00'34 5:56:02
Hankinson 11 1 32N06'23 90w52'46 6:03:31
Hannah 6 1 33N38'13 91w01'32 6:04:06
Harbert Landing 72
1 34N39'13 90w33'26 6:02:14
Hard Cash 27 1 33N11 90w29 6:01:56
Hardee 28 1 32N35'35 90w51'18 6:03:25
Hardy 22 1 33N52'55 89w49'46 5:59:19
Harleston 30 1 30N43'21 88w30'32 5:54:02
Harmontown 36 1 34N32'25 89w38'54 5:58:36
Harmony 12 1 31N59'07 88w48'58 5:55:16
Harmony 43 1 31N31'20 90w16'05 6:01:04
Harperville 62 1 32N29'39 89w29'22 5:57:57
Harriston 32 1 31N43'30 91w01'56 6:04:08
Harrisville 64 1 31N58'20 90w04'40 6:00:19
Hartman 43 1 31N30'49 90w26'12 6:01:45
Harvey 18 1 31N19'52 89w15'44 5:57:03
Hathorn 33 1 31N23'35 89w55'09 5:59:41
Hatley 48 1 33N58'36 88w25'14 5:53:41
Hattiesburg 18 1 31N19'37 89w17'25 5:57:10
Hawkes 34 1 31N45'17 89w04'34 5:56:18
Hawthorne 55 1 30N38'59 89w38'33 5:58:34
Hayes Crossing 54
1 34N26'58 89w45'41 5:59:03
Haynes Bluff 75 1 32N30'58 90w47'07 6:03:08
Hays 62 1 32N32'14 89w21'40 5:57:27
Hazel 51 1 32N22'52 89w18'05 5:57:12
Hazlehurst 15 1 31N51'37 90w23'45 6:01:35
Heads 76 1 33N28'14 90w50'47 6:03:23
Heater 65 1 32N03'31 89w38'22 5:58:33
Heathman 67 1 33N26'24 90w43'13 6:02:53
Hebron 33 1 31N43'24 89w57'08 5:59:49
Hebron 34 1 31N42'22 89w22'15 5:57:29
Heidelberg 31 1 31N53'12 88w59'02 5:55:56
Helena 30 1 30N29'40 88w29'45 5:53:59
Helm 76 1 33N30'03 90w50'04 6:03:20
Henderson Point 24
1 30N18'31 89w17'13 5:57:09
Hendrix 49 1 33N27'59 89w37'41 5:58:31
Henley 35 1 32N50 88w29 5:53:56
Henleyfield 55 1 30N41'49 89w45'50 5:59:03
Herbert Springs 50
1 32N36'12 88w55'43 5:55:43
Hermanville 11 1 31N57'33 90w50'24 6:03:22
Hernando 17 1 34N49'26 89w59'37 5:59:58
Hero 31 1 32N19 89w10 5:56:40
Hesterville 4 1 33N09'38 89w39'15 5:58:37
Heucks 43 1 31N35 90w27 6:01:48

Hickman Landing 63
1 32N56'06 90w46'44 6:03:07
Hickory 51 1 32N19'03 89w01'32 5:56:06
Hickory Flat 5 1 34N36'57 89w11'18 5:56:45
Hickory Grove 37
1 31N23'40 89w38'46 5:58:35
Hickory Grove 53
1 33N28 88w49 5:55:16
Hickory Grove 55
1 30N59'51 89w24'27 5:57:38
Hicks 32 1 31N43 91w04 6:04:16
Hidi 27 1 33N01'28 90w23'07 6:01:32
Higdon 47 1 34N46'05 89w23'13 5:57:33
Higgins 37 1 31N25'23 89w35'51 5:58:23
High Hill 40 1 32N46 89w07 5:56:28
Highlandale 42 1 33N40'50 90w20'38 6:01:23
Highpoint 10 1 33N11'17 89w08'46 5:56:35
High Point 71 1 34N57'41 88w14'21 5:52:57
Hightown 2 1 34N49'18 88w40'22 5:54:41
Highway Village 79
1 31N06 91w18 6:05:12
Hillhouse 14 1 34N07'32 90w49'05 6:03:16
Hillman 21 1 31N08'00 88w37'58 5:54:32
Hillsboro 62 1 32N27'33 89w30'41 5:58:03
Hillsdale 55 1 30N55'40 89w29'50 5:57:59
Hinchcliff 60 1 34N18'35 90w16'25 6:01:06
Hinkle 2 1 34N46 88w32 5:54:08
Hintonville 56 1 31N15'39 88w55'19 5:55:41
Hinze 80 1 33N01'58 89w16'13 5:57:05
Hiram 68 1 34N03'48 90w16'52 6:01:07
Hiram 79 1 31N13'42 91w07'34 6:04:30
Hiwannee 77 1 31N48'36 88w41'26 5:54:46
Hobo Station 59 1 34N33'39 88w27'58 5:53:52
Hoffman 26 1 33N08'45 89w48'32 5:59:14
Hohenlinden 78 1 33N43'44 89w09'49 5:56:39
Holcomb 22 1 33N45'40 89w58'33 5:59:54
Holcut 71 1 34N43'47 88w18'21 5:53:13
Hollandale 76 1 33N10'08 90w51'14 6:03:25
Holland Landing 63
1 32N57'53 90w46'50 6:03:07
Hollis 7 1 33N53 89w11 5:56:44
Hollis Creek 77 1 31N31'51 88w50'01 5:55:20
Holly Bluff 82 1 32N49'17 90w42'32 6:02:50
Holly Grove 8 1 33N24'39 90w10'12 6:00:41
Hollyknowe 76 1 33N24'05 90w49'49 6:03:19
Holly Landing 30
1 30N42'53 88w42'40 5:54:51
Holly Ridge 67 1 33N26'44 90w45'12 6:03:01
Holly Springs 46
1 31N18'56 89w58'40 5:59:55
Holly Springs 47
1 34N46'03 89w26'55 5:57:48
Hollywood 72 1 34N44'43 90w21'29 6:01:26
Holmesville 57 1 31N12'12 90w18'31 6:01:14
Holts 71 1 34N50 88w19 5:53:16
Home Landing 6 1 33N39'51 91w06'48 6:04:27
Homewood 62 1 32N14'24 89w30'22 5:58:01
Homochitto 3 1 31N19'11 90w59'02 6:03:56
Honey Island 27 1 33N11 90w13 6:00:52
Hoodtown 15 1 31N58'40 90w36'17 6:02:25
Hookston 38 1 32N25'54 88w47'26 5:55:10
Hoover Lake and Park 61
1 32N09 90w08 6:00:32
Hope 50 1 32N44'50 89w14'43 5:56:59
Hopedale 28 1 32N57'25 91w00'45 6:04:03
Hopewell 5 1 34N58'05 89w02'53 5:56:12
Hopewell 15 1 31N56'50 90w12'55 6:00:52
Hopoca 40 1 32N50'03 89w30'23 5:58:02
Hopson 14 1 34N09'31 90w32'47 6:02:11
Horatio 54 1 34N26'16 90w03'20 6:00:13
Horn 12 1 31N55'54 88w32'23 5:54:10
Horn Lake 17 1 34N58 90w02 6:00:08
Horn Place Landing 82
1 32N44'58 90w42'01 6:02:48
Horseshoe 26 1 33N15'03 90w17'02 6:01:08
Horseshoe 62 1 32N33'11 89w24'43 5:57:39
Hortontown 58 1 34N21'07 89w04'44 5:56:19
Hot Coffee 16 1 31N44 89w27 5:57:48
Houlka 9 1 34N02'17 89w01'19 5:56:05
House 50 1 32N37'43 88w59'41 5:55:59
Houston 9 1 33N53'54 88w59'57 5:56:00
Hovey 24 1 30N36'52 89w08'00 5:56:32
Howard 26 1 33N07'22 90w11'27 6:00:46
Howison 24 1 30N39'55 89w08'18 5:56:33
Hoy 34 1 31N45'53 89w07'57 5:56:32
Hub 46 1 31N08'43 89w45'00 5:59:00
Hubbard 25 1 32N12'45 90w39'36 6:02:38
Hubbard Creek 81
1 34N09'43 89w52'46 5:59:31
Hudsonville 47 1 34N51'40 89w22'30 5:57:30
Humber 14 1 34N12 90w34 6:02:16
Humphreys 11 1 32N04'49 90w50'27 6:03:22
Huntsville 49 1 33N20'53 89w27'40 5:57:51
Hurley 30 1 30N39'39 88w29'39 5:53:59
Huron 3 1 31N06'00 90w38'29 6:02:34
Hurricane 58 1 34N21'04 89w08'52 5:56:35
Hurricane Branch 22
1 33N47'58 89w42'06 5:58:48
Hurricane Creek 12
1 32N12'39 88w27'16 5:53:49
Hushpuckena 6 1 34N00'17 90w45'11 6:03:01
Hustler 3 1 31N16'55 90w41'51 6:02:47
Hutchins Landing 1
1 31N23'30 91w27'29 6:05:50
Improve 46 1 31N20'34 89w42'01 5:58:48
Increase 38 1 32N15'25 88w33'32 5:54:14
Inda 66 1 30N47 89w08 5:56:32
Independence 62 1 32N21 89w39 5:58:36
Independence 69 1 34N42'18 89w48'32 5:59:14
Indian Hills 41 1 34N19'03 88w41'04 5:54:44
Indianola 67 1 33N27'03 90w39'18 6:02:37
Indian Springs 2
1 34N50'25 88w24'53 5:53:40
Indian Springs 56
1 31N17'51 89w08'16 5:56:33
Industrial 55 1 30N34'34 89w45'48 5:59:03
Ingleside 11 1 32N02'08 90w58'58 6:03:56
Ingomar 73 1 34N24'33 89w02'12 5:56:09
Ingrams Mill 17 1 34N49'27 89w46'06 5:59:04
Insmore 11 1 32N00'50 90w43'55 6:02:56
Inverness 67 1 33N21'13 90w35'33 6:02:22
Inwood 67 1 33N30'21 90w31'29 6:02:06
Iowana 30 1 30N24 88w38 5:54:32

Ireland 79 1 31N20'49 91w13'21 6:04:53
Irene 57 1 31N17 90w28 6:01:52
Isola 27 1 33N15'43 90w35'32 6:02:22
Issaquena 63 1 32N46'39 90w56'02 6:03:44
Itta Bena 42 1 33N29'42 90w19'11 6:01:17
Iuka 71 1 34N48'42 88w11'24 5:52:46
Jacinto 2 1 34N45'35 88w25'42 5:53:43
Jack 15 1 32N01'02 90w34'12 6:02:17
Jackson 25 2 32N17'55 90w11'05 6:00:44
Jackson Landing 23
1 30N12'22 89w34'24 5:58:18
Jago 17 1 34N56'10 89w58'36 5:59:54
Jaketown 27 1 33N15'01 90w28'46 6:01:55
James 76 1 33N12'13 91w03'26 6:04:14
Jamestown 46 1 31N11'00 89w51'19 5:59:25
Janice 56 1 31N01'31 89w02'12 5:56:09
Jaquith 67 1 33N46'05 90w32'09 6:02:09
Jayess 39 1 31N21'53 90w12'21 6:00:49
Jeannette 1 1 31N29'11 91w14'41 6:04:59
Jeff 51 1 32N25'16 89w07'40 5:56:31
Jeff Davis 75 1 32N11'34 90w52'45 6:03:31
Jefferson 8 1 33N37'57 89w53'42 5:59:35
Jeffries 14 1 34N30'17 90w32'19 6:02:09
Jenkins 34 1 31N35'38 89w09'19 5:56:37
Jennings 57 1 31N09 90w27 6:01:48
Jericho 73 1 34N30'40 88w45'16 5:55:01
Jobes 2 1 34N51'41 88w29'59 5:54:00
Johns 61 1 32N07'51 89w50'17 5:59:21
Johnson 34 1 31N32'20 89w08'36 5:56:34
Johnstons Station 57
1 31N20'54 90w27'15 6:01:49
Johnsville 1 1 31N33'01 91w20'57 6:05:24
Jonathan 21 1 31N13'21 88w38'15 5:54:33
Jones Crossing 26
1 33N07'10 90w08'10 6:00:33
Jones Mill 24 1 30N23'52 89w11'04 5:56:44
Jonestown 2 1 34N52'15 88w40'00 5:54:40
Jonestown 14 1 34N19'10 90w27'20 6:01:49
Jonestown 82 1 32N50'30 90w25'50 6:01:43
Joseph 4 1 32N58'32 89w43'40 5:58:55
Jug Fork 41 1 34N25'35 88w47'21 5:55:09
Jumpertown 59 1 34N42'39 88w39'50 5:54:39
Junction City 12
1 31N57'39 88w34'23 5:54:18
Kalem 62 1 32N21 89w39 5:58:36
Kansas Landing 82
1 32N44'50 90w42'45 6:02:51
Katzenmeyer 75 1 32N31'14 90w49'32 6:03:18
Kearney 82 1 32N45'11 90w43'44 6:02:55
Kearney Park 45 1 32N35'20 90w18'55 6:01:16
Keel 36 1 34N24'46 89w22'04 5:57:28
Keesler Air Force Base 24
1 30N25 88w55 5:55:40
Keirn 26 1 33N16'28 90w13'27 6:00:54
Kelley's Crossing 69
1 34N43'40 90w06'18 6:00:25
Kellis Store 35 1 32N56 88w44 5:54:56
Kelona 31 1 31N56 88w56 5:55:44
Kelso 63 1 32N40'09 90w54'13 6:03:37
Kendrick 2 1 34N58'13 88w22'54 5:53:32
Keownville 73 1 34N32'29 88w54'43 5:55:39
Kerin 26 1 33N19 90w14 6:00:56
Kerr 10 1 33N07'38 89w16'11 5:57:05
Kewanee 38 1 32N25'26 88w26'18 5:53:45
Key Field 38 1 32N28 88w40 5:54:40
Kienstra 1 1 31N13'33 91w36'21 6:06:25
Kilmichael 49 1 33N26'36 89w34'18 5:58:17
Kiln 23 1 30N24'32 89w26'06 5:57:44
Kimball Lake 6 1 33N45'55 90w48'00 6:03:12
Kimberly 75 1 32N09'29 90w56'36 6:03:46
Kincaid 22 1 33N45'02 89w39'19 5:58:37
King 61 1 32N05'14 90w07'49 6:00:31
King And Anderson 14
1 34N17'42 90w36'18 6:02:25
Kings 75 1 32N23'49 90w51'23 6:03:26
Kings Corner 54 1 34N29'47 90w03'26 6:00:14
Kingston 1 1 31N24'19 91w16'39 6:05:07
Kinlock 67 1 33N18'34 90w42'27 6:02:50
Kioto 74 1 31N09'50 90w14'44 6:00:59
Kirby 19 1 31N30'41 90w58'51 6:03:55
Kirklin 74 1 31N02'52 90w06'57 6:00:28
Kirkman Landing 22
1 33N51'02 89w45'41 5:59:03
Kirkville 29 1 34N27'05 88w29'23 5:53:58
Kirkville 57 1 31N12'47 90w29'49 6:01:59
Kitchener 50 1 32N34'55 89w17'06 5:57:08
Kittrell 21 1 31N25'49 88w33'47 5:54:15
Kittrell 56 1 31N12'25 88w54'48 5:55:39
Klondike 35 1 32N37'20 88w45'22 5:55:01
Knobtown 21 1 31N22'41 88w31'24 5:54:06
Knoxo 74 1 31N08'07 90w02'46 6:00:11
Knoxville 19 1 31N22'43 91w07'15 6:04:29
Koch 61 1 32N29'44 89w53'11 5:59:33
Kokomo 46 1 31N11'50 90w00'10 6:00:01
Kola 16 1 31N37'30 89w31'38 5:58:07
Kolola Springs 44
1 33N39'14 88w24'32 5:53:38
Kosciusko 4 1 33N03'27 89w35'15 5:58:21
Kossuth 2 1 34N52'19 88w38'45 5:54:35
Kreole 30 1 30N24'21 88w29'41 5:53:59
Lackey 48 1 33N48'11 88w27'44 5:53:51
Lafayette Springs 36
1 34N19'02 89w15'40 5:57:03
Lake 62 1 32N20'35 89w19'43 5:57:19
Lake Charles Landing 14
1 34N08'34 90w52'21 6:03:29
Lake City 27 1 32N55'23 90w29'35 6:01:58
Lake City 59 1 34N38'31 88w32'59 5:54:12
Lake Como 31 1 31N57'44 89w12'45 5:56:51
Lake Cormorant 17
1 34N54 90w13 6:00:52
Lakeland 61 2 32N13'22 90w09'24 6:00:38
Lake of Hills 17
1 34N50 89w59 5:59:56
Lakeshore 23 1 30N14'47 89w26'09 5:57:45
Lakeside 81 1 34N09'40 89w48'31 5:59:14
Lake View 17 1 34N59'20 90w08'23 6:00:34
Lake Vista 6 1 33N36'32 91w03'46 6:04:15
Lamar 5 1 34N55'02 89w19'04 5:57:16
Lamar Park 37 1 31N19'09 89w21'37 5:57:26
Lambert 60 1 34N12'06 90w17'00 6:01:08
Lamkin 27 1 33N02'33 90w27'56 6:01:52
Lamont 6 1 33N32'07 91w04'34 6:04:18

Lampton 46 1 31N11'35 89W47'53 5:59:12
Landon 24 1 30N26'16 89W06'10 5:56:25
Laneheart 79 1 31N11'36 91W22'06 6:05:28
Langford 61 1 32N20'47 89W58'20 5:59:53
Langsdale 12 1 31N53'20 88W35'04 5:54:20
Lanham 34 1 31N34'59 89W05'49 5:56:23
Lantrip 7 1 34N00 89W21 5:57:24
Larue 30 1 30N37'27 88W50'54 5:55:24
Latimer 30 1 30N26 88W49 5:55:16
Latonia 20 1 30N55 88W35 5:54:20
Lauderdale 38 1 32N31'14 88W30'42 5:54:03
Laughlin 6 1 33N43'06 90W47'52 6:03:11
Laughter Flat Landing 30
1 30N34'19 88W25'01 5:53:40
Laurel 34 1 31N41'38 89W07'50 5:56:31
Laurel Hill 50 1 32N43'52 89W18'59 5:57:16
Lawrence 51 1 32N19'30 89W13'58 5:56:56
Laws Hill 47 1 34N34'46 89W34'26 5:58:18
Leaf 21 1 31N01'32 88W47'44 5:55:11
Leakesville 21 1 31N09'20 88W33'28 5:54:14
Learned 25 1 32N11'48 90W32'50 6:02:11
Leavell Woods 25
2 32N19 90W11 6:00:44
Lebanon 25 1 32N10'00 90W30'46 6:02:03
Lebanon 47 1 34N39 89W18 5:57:12
Leedy 71 1 34N47'43 88W21'40 5:53:27
Leesburg 61 1 32N26'25 89W45'37 5:59:02
Leesdale 1 1 31N32'48 91W09'28 6:04:38
Leeville 18 1 31N23'38 89W15'23 5:57:02
Leflore 22 1 33N41'37 90W03'17 6:00:13
Leggett 57 1 31N08'07 90W18'14 6:01:13
Lehr 74 1 31N02'02 90W10'51 6:00:43
Leland 76 1 33N24'19 90W53'51 6:03:35
Lemon 65 1 32N08'09 89W30'05 5:58:00
Lena 40 1 32N35'39 89W36'43 5:58:27
Leotis 9 1 34N04'02 88W44'36 5:54:58
Lessley 79 1 31N09'40 91W25'46 6:05:43
Le Tourneau 75 1 32N12'51 90W56'18 6:03:45
Leverett 68 1 33N52'58 90W04'32 6:00:18
Lewisburg 17 1 34N51'43 89W50'00 5:59:20
Lexie 74 1 31N04'43 90W10'15 6:00:41
Lexington 26 1 33N06'47 90W03'11 6:00:13
Liberty 3 1 31N09'29 90W48'44 6:03:15
Liberty 35 1 32N39'40 88W45'32 5:55:02
Lightsey 77 1 31N44'08 88W56'09 5:55:45
Lilac 49 1 33N40'10 89W35'18 5:58:21
Lillian 62 1 32N30'18 89W32'43 5:58:11
Limbert 34 1 31N42 89W08 5:56:32
Limerick 82 1 32N45'18 90W33'44 6:02:15
Lines 80 1 32N56 88W44 5:54:56
Lingle 65 1 32N11'44 89W34'38 5:58:19
Linn 67 1 33N39'35 90W36'59 6:02:28
Linton 12 1 32N02'03 88W35'15 5:54:21
Linwood 1 1 31N30'39 91W24'50 6:05:39
Linwood 50 1 32N39'37 89W09'03 5:56:36
Linwood 82 1 32N47'32 90W08'42 6:00:35
Little Creek 56 1 31N10 88W55 5:55:40
Little Rock 51 1 32N31'33 89W01'31 5:56:06
Little Springs 19
1 31N24'08 90W43'36 6:02:54
Little Texas 72 1 34N37'38 90W16'55 6:01:08
Little Yazoo 82 1 32N42'28 90W22'21 6:01:29
Litton 6 1 33N38'45 90W50'14 6:03:21
Livingston 45 1 32N33'10 90W12'58 6:00:52
Lizana 24 1 30N32'15 89W15'08 5:57:01
Lizelia 38 1 32N32'08 88W39'36 5:54:38
Lobdell 6 1 33N43'06 90W58'56 6:03:56
Lobutcha 80 1 33N12 89W20 5:57:20
Loch Leven 79 1 31N12'31 91W34'30 6:06:18
Loch Lomond 82 1 32N52'09 90W41'46 6:02:47
Locke Station 54
1 34N19 89W57 5:59:48
Lockhart 38 1 32N29'22 88W35'09 5:54:21
Locum 73 1 34N35'35 88W50'37 5:55:22
Lodi 27 1 33N02'47 90W24'36 6:01:38
Lodi 49 1 33N33'01 89W31'15 5:58:05
Logtown 23 1 30N16'58 89W37'16 5:58:29
Lombardy 67 1 33N54'20 90W36'25 6:02:26
Lone Pine 2 1 34N58'16 88W44'33 5:54:58
Lone Star 16 1 31N38'19 89W44'16 5:58:57
Long 76 1 33N26'35 90W47'40 6:03:11
Long Beach 24 1 30N21'01 89W09'10 5:56:37
Long Branch 81 1 34N08'05 89W50'48 5:59:23
Longino 50 1 32N48'18 89W06'14 5:56:25
Long Lake 14 1 34N22'05 90W34'40 6:02:19
Long Lake 75 1 32N24'31 90W53'00 6:03:32
Longshot 6 1 33N38'43 90W54'09 6:03:37
Longstreet 60 1 34N06'48 90W19'47 6:01:19
Longtown 54 1 34N30'39 90W07'27 6:00:30
Longview 53 1 33N24'14 88W55'16 5:55:41
Longview 58 1 34N16'52 88W53'43 5:55:35
Longwood 76 1 33N08'49 91W03'58 6:04:16
Looxahoma 69 1 34N35'50 89W50'13 5:59:21
Lorena 65 1 32N10'58 89W30'34 5:58:02
Lorenzen 63 1 32N56'55 90W54'23 6:03:38
Loring 45 1 32N46'49 89W56'16 5:59:45
Lorman 32 1 31N49'13 91W03'00 6:04:12
Lorraine 24 1 30N27'19 89W01'31 5:56:06
Lost Gap 38 1 32N20'30 88W48'25 5:55:14
Lost Lake 72 1 34N47'01 90W14'38 6:00:59
Louin 31 1 32N04'16 89W15'39 5:57:03
Louise 27 1 32N58'56 90W35'19 6:02:21
Louisville 80 1 33N07'25 89W03'18 5:56:13
Love 17 1 34N45'12 89W58'12 5:59:53
Lovelace 46 1 31N12'44 89W51'33 5:59:26
Lowrey 70 1 34N40'45 89W01'39 5:56:07
Loyd 7 1 33N57'29 89W13'19 5:56:53
Loyd Star 43 1 31N37'35 90W33'00 6:02:12
Lucas 33 1 31N35'16 89W57'30 5:59:50
Lucedale 20 1 30N55'30 88W35'24 5:54:22
Lucern 51 1 32N31'00 89W13'45 5:56:55
Lucien 19 1 31N31'00 90W39'50 6:02:39
Luckney 61 2 32N20'29 90W04'32 6:00:18
Ludlow 62 1 32N34'18 89W42'46 5:58:51
Lula 14 1 34N27'11 90W28'43 6:01:55
Lumberton 37 1 31N00'04 89W27'08 5:57:49
Lurand 14 1 34N08'09 90W31'40 6:02:07
Lurline 69 1 34N44'35 89W50'45 5:59:23
Luther 40 1 32N44 89W32 5:58:08
Lux 16 1 31N26'42 89W24'03 5:57:36
Lyman 24 1 30N29'50 89W06'39 5:56:27
Lynchburg 17 1 34N57'44 90W05'45 6:00:23
Lynchburg 25 1 32N26'24 90W32'56 6:02:12
Lynn Creek 52 1 33N14'00 88W43'50 5:54:55
Lynville 35 1 32N51'18 88W48'56 5:55:16
Lyon 14 1 34N13'04 90W32'31 6:02:10
Maben 53 1 33N33'19 89W05'05 5:56:20
Macedonia 18 1 31N22'55 89W10'07 5:56:40
Macedonia 41 1 34N21'45 88W47'44 5:55:11
Macedonia 52 1 33N01'17 88W40'22 5:54:41
Macedonia 73 1 34N30'10 89W12'31 5:56:50
Macel 68 1 33N49'20 90W09'47 6:00:39
Mack 47 1 34N50'18 89W28'48 5:57:55
Macon 52 1 33N06'19 88W33'39 5:54:15
Madden 40 1 32N40'44 89W20'53 5:57:24
Maddox 64 1 31N53'19 89W40'10 5:58:41
Madison 45 1 32N27'42 90W06'55 6:00:28
Madisonville 45 1 32N31'36 89W58'39 5:59:55
Magee 64 1 31N52'25 89W44'01 5:58:56
Magenta 76 1 33N25'52 90W57'48 6:03:51
Magna Vista 28 1 32N39'29 91W03'42 6:04:15
Magnolia 57 1 31N08'35 90W27'31 6:01:50
Mahned 56 1 31N12'32 89W04'51 5:56:19
Mahon 47 1 34N48'53 89W30'55 5:58:04
Malmaison 8 1 33N31'20 90W00'26 6:00:02
Malone 47 1 34N34'34 89W28'40 5:57:55
Malone Landing 14
1 34N08'01 90W50'28 6:03:22
Malvina 6 1 33N50'58 90W55'02 6:03:40
Mannassa 12 1 31N59'50 88W34'35 5:54:18
Mannsdale 45 1 32N31'24 90W11'30 6:00:46
Mantachie 29 1 34N19'27 88W29'28 5:53:58
Mantee 78 1 33N43'53 89W03'19 5:56:13
Marathon 76 1 33N03'55 91W01'09 6:04:05
Marcella 26 1 33N07'46 90W17'51 6:01:11
Marianna 47 1 34N43'03 89W35'56 5:58:24
Marie 67 1 33N27 90W39 6:02:36
Marienette 17 1 34N52'19 90W13'05 6:00:52
Marietta 59 1 34N30'07 88W28'08 5:53:53
Marion 38 1 32N25'02 88W38'52 5:54:35
Maris Town 45 1 32N37 90W02 6:00:08
Marks 60 1 34N15'23 90W16'19 6:01:05
Marksville 26 1 33N18'33 90W16'49 6:01:07
Markwald 31 1 31N49'34 89W00'09 5:56:01
Mars Hill 3 1 31N18'11 90W37'41 6:02:31
Martin 38 1 32N32'58 88W50'42 5:55:23
Martinsville 15 1 31N47'27 90W24'25 6:01:38
Martintown 73 1 34N27'30 89W03'16 5:56:13
Martinville 64 1 31N58'24 89W45'14 5:59:01
Marydell 40 1 32N53'07 89W23'01 5:57:32
Mashulaville 52 1 33N05'12 88W44'39 5:54:59
Mason Landing 6 1 34N01'19 90W53'45 6:03:35
Matagorda 14 1 34N20'17 90W27'25 6:01:50
Matherville 12 1 31N52'38 88W34'08 5:54:17
Mathews Crossing 42
1 33N20'11 90W23'40 6:01:35
Mathiston 78 1 33N32'24 89W07'27 5:56:30
Matthews 58 1 34N05'33 89W13'06 5:56:52
Mattoon 67 1 33N27'04 90W28'16 6:01:53
Mattson 14 1 34N05'52 90W30'36 6:02:02
Maud 72 1 34N33'43 90W26'13 6:01:45
Maxie 18 1 30N58'40 89W11'45 5:56:47
Maybank 18 1 31N24'27 89W22'11 5:57:29
Maybell 34 1 31N36 89W12 5:56:48
Mayday 42 1 33N21'39 90W18'50 6:01:15
Mayersville 28 1 32N54'07 91W03'04 6:04:12
Mayhew 44 1 33N29'05 88W38'04 5:54:32
Mayton 61 1 32N06'24 89W44'50 5:58:59
Maywood 17 1 34N57 89W49 5:59:16
McAdams 4 1 33N01'16 89W41'18 5:58:45
McAfee 40 1 32N44'33 89W29'46 5:57:59
McBride 32 1 31N45'56 90W46'56 6:03:08
McCall Creek 19 1 31N30'45 90W41'55 6:02:48
McCall Landing 30
1 30N31'28 88W40'45 5:54:43
McCallum 18 1 31N14'15 89W12'39 5:56:51
McCarley 8 1 33N31'23 89W50'02 5:59:20
McComb 57 1 31N14'37 90W27'11 6:01:49
McCondy 9 1 33N49'20 88W50'33 5:55:22
McCool 4 1 33N12'07 89W20'42 5:57:23
McCrary 44 1 33N27'50 88W17'01 5:53:08
McCutcheon 76 1 33N21 90W56 6:03:44
McDonald 50 1 32N39'37 89W07'58 5:56:32
McElveen 3 1 31N12'03 90W35'44 6:02:23
McGhee 54 1 34N32'21 89W56'58 5:59:48
McHenry 66 1 30N42'27 89W08'18 5:56:33
McLain 21 1 31N06'31 88W49'38 5:55:19
McLaurin 18 1 31N10'04 89W13'02 5:56:52
McLaurin Heights 61
2 32N16'59 90W06'32 6:00:26
McLaurlin Heights 61
2 32N19 90W09 6:00:36
McLeod 52 1 33N05'32 88W27'06 5:53:48
McMillan 26 1 33N06'09 89W56'33 5:59:46
McMillan 80 1 33N10'12 89W06'33 5:56:26
McNair 32 1 31N38'18 91W02'31 6:04:10
McNeal 31 1 32N02'29 89W09'13 5:56:37
McNeill 55 1 30N40'07 89W38'18 5:58:33
McRaney 16 1 31N36'34 89W43'02 5:58:52
McRaven 25 1 32N18'13 90W19'37 6:01:18
McSwain 56 1 31N18'52 88W58'37 5:55:54
McVille 4 1 32N55'53 89W37'19 5:58:29
McWillie 4 2 32N19 90W11 6:00:44
Meadville 19 1 31N28'20 90W53'48 6:03:35
Mechanicsburg 82
1 32N37'57 90W30'10 6:02:01
Meehan 38 1 32N19'41 88W51'59 5:55:28
Meeks 26 1 33N17'58 90W11'21 6:00:45
Mehr 68 1 33N48'13 90W08'57 6:00:36
Melba 32 1 31N26'41 89W38'44 5:58:35
Melis 74 1 31N13'47 90W06'45 6:00:27
Melton 32 1 31N47'11 91W03'25 6:04:14
Meltonia 6 1 33N36'09 90W53'10 6:03:33
Meltonville 45 1 32N30'59 90W02'16 6:00:09
Memphis Junction 22
1 33N48'02 89W47'48 5:59:11
Mendenhall 64 1 31N57'42 89W52'12 5:59:29
Meridian 38 1 32N21'51 88W42'13 5:54:49
Merigold 6 1 33N50'20 90W43'34 6:02:54
Merit 64 1 31N55'40 89W54'31 5:59:38
Merrill 20 1 30N58'44 88W43'14 5:54:53
Mesa 74 1 31N08'50 90W12'01 6:00:48
Metcalfe 76 1 33N27'14 91W00'26 6:04:02
Meyers 18 1 31N18 89W18 5:57:12
Mhoon Landing 72
1 34N44'30 90W26'31 6:01:46
Mhoons Valley 13
1 33N34'47 88W45'15 5:55:01
Michigan City 5 1 34N58'51 89W15'02 5:57:00
Middleton 12 1 32N09'49 88W36'44 5:54:27
Midnight 27 1 33N02'58 90W34'24 6:02:18
Midway 15 1 31N43'00 90W33'23 6:02:14
Midway 25 2 32N10'08 90W22'32 6:01:30
Midway 40 1 32N48'27 89W26'27 5:57:46
Midway 62 1 32N32'46 89W31'54 5:58:08
Midway 71 1 34N43'52 88W13'29 5:52:54
Midway 82 1 32N53'11 90W11'32 6:00:46
Mikoma 68 1 33N57'01 90W17'02 6:01:08
Mildred 46 1 31N08'52 89W50'31 5:59:22
Mile Branch 19 1 31N28 90W54 6:03:36
Mileston 26 1 33N06'37 90W16'24 6:01:06
Millard 55 1 30N43'20 89W35'54 5:58:24
Mill Creek 34 1 31N41'36 88W57'39 5:55:51
Mill Creek 55 1 30N40'14 89W42'09 5:58:49
Millcreek 80 1 33N09'24 88W56'56 5:55:48
Mill Creek Cabin Area 71
1 34N49 88W11 5:52:44
Miller 17 1 34N55'03 89W46'07 5:59:04
Miller Landing 82
1 32N42'29 90W41'35 6:02:46
Millers Landing 28
1 32N55'01 91W03'39 6:04:15
Millington 35 1 32N52'52 88W24'57 5:53:40
Mill Town 45 1 32N37 90W02 6:00:08
Mimms 54 1 34N19 89W57 5:59:48
Mims 54 1 34N13'45 90W07'44 6:00:31
Mineral Wells 17
1 34N59'26 89W51'56 5:59:28
Minerva 49 1 33N31'42 89W34'45 5:58:19
Mingo 71 1 34N37'55 88W09'01 5:52:36
Minot 67 1 33N56'31 90W29'23 6:01:58
Minter City 42 1 33N45'12 90W17'40 6:01:11
Missala 30 1 30N27'28 88W24'00 5:53:36
Missionary 31 1 32N09 89W00 5:56:00
Mississippi City 24
1 30N22'54 89W02'38 5:56:11
Mississippi College 25
1 32N51 89W36 5:58:24
Mississippi Valley State Col 42
1 33N30 90W20 6:01:20
Misterton 22 1 33N42'28 89W34'56 5:58:20
Mitchell 70 1 34N42'34 88W50'35 5:55:22
Mixon 3 1 31N07'38 90W34'30 6:02:18
Mize 65 1 31N52'06 89W33'21 5:58:13
Mocarter 72 1 34N49 90W19 6:01:16
Molino 73 1 34N34'31 88W53'33 5:55:34
Moncure 25 2 32N03'19 90W15'34 6:01:02
Money 42 1 33N39'04 90W12'33 6:00:50
Monroe 19 1 31N28'17 90W49'36 6:03:18
Monterey 61 1 32N11'05 90W04'51 6:00:19
Montevista 78 1 33N42'18 89W14'08 5:56:57
Montgomery 26 1 33N17'50 90W19'36 6:01:18
Montgomery 43 1 31N38'30 90W25'10 6:01:41
Mont Helena 63 1 32N56'44 90W51'50 6:03:27
Monticello 39 1 31N33'13 90W06'26 6:00:26
Montpelier 13 1 33N43'04 88W56'52 5:55:47
Montrose 31 1 32N07'27 89W14'08 5:56:57
Moon 14 1 34N25'19 90W29'18 6:01:57
Moores Mill 71 1 34N28'55 88W19'35 5:53:18
Mooreville 41 1 34N16'03 88W34'36 5:54:18
Moorhead 67 1 33N27'00 90W30'20 6:02:01
Morgan City 42 1 33N22'50 90W21'01 6:01:24
Morgans Store 25
1 32N05'36 90W22'20 6:01:29
Morgantown 1 1 31N34'21 91W20'51 6:05:23
Morgantown 46 1 31N18'44 89W54'57 5:59:40
Morgantown 53 1 33N18'20 88W59'49 5:55:59
Morning Star 25 1 32N13'11 90W34'25 6:02:18
Morris 32 1 31N27'44 89W39'41 5:58:39
Morriston 18 1 31N24'56 89W11'46 5:56:47
Morton 62 1 32N21'13 89W39'16 5:58:37
Moscow 35 1 32N42'36 88W48'00 5:55:12
Moselle 34 1 31N30'08 89W16'44 5:57:07
Moss (Mossville Station) 31
1 31N48'54 89W10'40 5:56:43
Moss Point 30 1 30N24'41 88W32'04 5:54:08
Mound Bayou 6 1 33N52'41 90W43'38 6:02:55
Mound City 6 1 33N46'45 90W54'55 6:03:40
Mound City 73 1 34N27'08 88W55'08 5:55:41
Mound Landing 6 1 33N36'26 91W07'37 6:04:30
Mount Carmel 33 1 31N38'42 89W47'23 5:59:10
Mount Olive 3 1 31N20'37 90W42'36 6:02:50
Mount Olive 16 1 31N45'40 89W39'18 5:58:37
Mount Olive 19 1 31N21'18 90W56'07 6:03:44
Mount Olive 34 1 31N44'39 89W03'08 5:56:13
Mount Pleasant 29
1 34N14 88W16 5:53:04
Mount Pleasant 47
1 34N57'21 89W30'57 5:58:04
Mount Vernon 41 1 34N19'48 88W45'13 5:55:01
Mount Zion 34 1 31N38'43 89W14'52 5:56:59
Mount Zion 64 1 31N52 89W44 5:58:56
Movella 20 1 30N45'50 88W30'23 5:54:02
Mulberry 77 1 31N28'37 88W50'52 5:55:23
Muldon 48 1 33N43'56 88W39'14 5:54:37
Muldrow 53 1 33N32'48 88W42'16 5:54:49
Mullins Store 36
1 34N22 89W31 5:58:04
Murdock Crossing 42
1 33N25'01 90W18'23 6:01:14
Murphreesboro 68
1 33N59 89W54 5:59:36
Murphy 76 1 33N07'15 90W42'05 6:02:48
Murry 70 1 34N44 88W57 5:55:48
Muskedine 76 1 33N13'28 90W59'01 6:03:56
Muskegon 62 1 32N20'53 89W21'08 5:57:25
Myles 15 1 32N01'11 90W42'23 6:02:50
Myrick 34 1 31N39'39 89W59'39 5:55:59
Myrleville 82 1 32N42'47 90W16'39 6:01:07
Myrtle 73 1 34N33'30 89W07'09 5:56:29
Nancy 12 1 31N56'36 88W50'33 5:55:22
Nanih Waiya 80 1 32N55'17 88W56'55 5:55:48
Napanee 76 1 33N30'22 90W52'15 6:03:29
Napoleon 23 1 30N19'34 89W37'39 5:58:31
Nason 22 1 33N43'23 89W53'55 5:59:36
Natchez 1 1 31N33'37 91W24'11 6:05:37
Natcole 46 1 31N10'26 89W50'59 5:59:24
National Cemetery 75
1 32N20 90W52 6:03:28

Naval Air Station 38
1 32N28 88W40 5:54:40
Necaise 23 1 30N36'06 89W24'51 5:57:39
Neely 21 1 31N09'53 88W45'17 5:55:01
Negro Crossroads 25
1 31N59 90W22 6:01:28
Neil 71 1 34N35'46 88W13'49 5:52:55
Nellieburg 38 1 32N24'24 88W46'38 5:55:07
Nesbit 17 1 34N52'54 90W00'31 6:00:02
Neshoba 50 1 32N37'24 89W08'17 5:56:33
Nettleton 41 1 34N05'20 88W37'20 5:54:29
Nevada 25 1 32N31'26 90W28'05 6:01:52
Neville 50 1 32N35'01 89W14'52 5:56:59
New Albany 73 1 34N29'39 89W00'28 5:56:02
New Augusta 56 1 31N12'08 89W02'05 5:56:08
New Byram 25 2 32N11'07 90W15'34 6:01:02
New Canaan 5 1 34N56'51 89W07'04 5:56:28
New Fitler 28 1 32N37 91W01 6:04:04
New Hamilton 48 1 33N44'16 88W26'41 5:53:47
New Harmony 73 1 34N23'38 88W55'11 5:55:41
New Hebron 39 1 31N43'51 89W58'43 5:59:55
New Hope 19 1 31N33'12 90W49'58 6:03:20
New Hope 24 1 30N26'17 89W08'11 5:56:33
New Hope 44 1 33N28'05 88W19'36 5:53:18
New Hope 59 1 34N37'34 88W23'32 5:53:34
Newman 25 1 32N14'08 90W41'50 6:02:47
Newmans 75 1 32N21'03 90W45'10 6:03:01
Newmans Grove 75
1 32N20'45 90W46'15 6:03:05
Newport 4 1 32N56'13 89W45'52 5:59:03
New Salem 29 1 34N08'22 88W21'31 5:53:26
New Sight 43 1 31N39'15 90W26'54 6:01:48
New Site 59 1 34N33'33 88W24'34 5:53:38
Newsom 46 1 31N19'34 89W56'03 5:59:44
Newton 51 1 32N19'16 89W09'48 5:56:39
Newtonia 79 1 31N02'25 91W12'21 6:04:49
New Town 69 1 34N36'43 89W54'54 5:59:40
New Wren 48 1 33N58'18 88W36'48 5:54:27
Niblett Landing 6
1 33N42'11 91W02'16 6:04:09
Nichols 42 1 33N19'04 90W24'46 6:01:39
Nicholson 55 1 30N28'37 89W41'37 5:58:46
Nida 26 1 33N05 90W26 6:01:44
Niles 6 1 33N51'19 90W57'26 6:03:50
Nitta Yuma 63 1 33N01'27 90W50'57 6:03:24
Nixon 27 1 33N03 90W34 6:02:16
Nixon 58 1 34N17'12 88W58'20 5:55:53
Nod 82 1 32N45'23 90W13'50 6:00:55
Nogan 25 2 32N14'52 90W12'46 6:00:51
Nola 39 1 31N36'51 90W14'17 6:00:57
Norfield 43 1 31N24'27 90W28'02 6:01:52
Norfolk 17 1 34N57'05 90W13'50 6:00:55
Norris 62 1 32N17'38 89W26'09 5:57:45
North 25 2 32N19 90W11 6:00:44
North 38 1 32N28 88W40 5:54:40
North Bend 50 1 32N46 89W07 5:56:28
North Carrollton 8
1 33N31'05 89W55'14 5:59:41
North Crossroads 71
1 34N49 88W11 5:52:44
North Gulfport 24
1 30N24 89W05 5:56:20
North Haven 73 1 34N29 89W01 5:56:04
North Junction 58
1 34N15'25 89W00'55 5:56:04
North Tunica 72 1 34N42 90W23 6:01:32
Northwest Junior College 69
1 34N37 89W58 5:59:52
Northwood Hills 24
1 30N24 89W05 5:56:20
Norway 82 1 32N54'14 90W23'53 6:01:36
Noxapater 80 1 32N59'32 89W03'58 5:56:16
Nugent 24 1 30N28'13 89W06'13 5:56:25
Oak Bowery 34 1 31N37'09 89W23'21 5:57:33
Oak Grove 26 1 33N15'03 90W18'33 6:01:14
Oak Grove 34 1 31N32'10 89W12'28 5:56:50
Oak Grove 35 1 32N40'27 88W33'52 5:54:15
Oak Grove 37 1 31N17'09 89W24'52 5:57:39
Oak Grove 56 1 31N02'10 88W58'27 5:55:54
Oakland 29 1 34N16'58 88W13'57 5:52:56
Oakland 57 1 31N15'41 90W30'02 6:02:00
Oakland 81 1 34N03'20 89W54'59 5:59:40
Oaklawn 11 1 32N00'18 90W59'52 6:03:59
Oakley 25 1 32N13'03 90W30'11 6:02:01
Oak Ridge 75 1 32N28'52 90W42'23 6:02:50
Oaks 45 1 32N47'59 89W58'37 5:59:54
Oak Vale 39 1 31N26'18 89W57'52 5:59:51
Obadiah 38 1 32N30'44 88W43'36 5:54:54
Ocean Springs 30
1 30N24'40 88W49'40 5:55:19
Ocobla 50 1 32N45'17 89W01'31 5:56:06
Ofahoma 40 1 32N42'26 89W42'02 5:58:48
Oil City 82 1 32N41'28 90W26'02 6:01:44
Okahola 37 1 31N12'25 89W23'11 5:57:33
Oklahoma 8 1 33N20'01 90W10'06 6:00:40
Okolona 9 1 34N00'06 88W45'19 5:55:01
Oktibbeha 53 1 33N33 89W05 5:56:20
Oktoc 53 1 33N19'56 88W45'28 5:55:02
Old Americus 30 1 30N42'33 88W35'45 5:54:23
Old Avera 21 1 31N21'39 88W34'01 5:54:16
Old Cairo 59 1 34N40 88W34 5:54:16
Old Dominion 42 1 33N23'40 90W23'11 6:01:33
Oldenburg 19 1 31N34'26 90W58'28 6:03:54
Oldham 71 1 34N46'23 88W07'42 5:52:31
Old Hamilton 48 1 33N44 88W27 5:53:48
Old Houlka 9 1 34N02'17 88W59'39 5:55:59
Old Myrtle 73 1 34N31'39 89W07'21 5:56:29
Old Union 41 1 34N08'51 88W44'12 5:54:57
Olio 3 1 31N03'16 90W55'16 6:03:41
Olive Branch 17 1 34N57'42 89W49'46 5:59:19
Oloh 37 1 31N17'48 89W35'24 5:58:22
Oma 39 1 31N43'36 90W08'41 6:00:35
Omega 26 1 33N07'24 90W18'47 6:01:15
O'Neil 3 1 31N18'13 90W53'04 6:03:32
Onward 63 1 32N43'31 90W56'31 6:03:46
Ora 16 1 31N39'27 89W34'28 5:58:18
Orange 19 1 31N31'39 91W04'21 6:04:17
Orange 31 1 32N05'42 88W55'14 5:55:41
Orange Grove 24 1 30N27'16 89W05'18 5:56:21
Orange Grove 30 1 30N25'14 88W27'31 5:53:50
Orange Hill 25 1 32N21 90W28 6:01:52
O'Reilly 6 1 33N40'02 90W43'45 6:02:55
Orion 47 1 34N42'55 89W39'07 5:58:36
Orvisburg 55 1 30N54'46 89W31'31 5:58:06
Orwood 36 1 34N22 89W31 5:58:04
Osborn 53 1 33N31'17 88W43'20 5:54:53
Osborne Creek 59
1 34N40 88W34 5:54:16
Osyka 57 1 31N00'24 90W28'20 6:01:53
Overby 76 1 33N08'37 90W51'12 6:03:25
Ovett 34 1 31N29'07 89W01'58 5:56:08
Owens Wells 26 1 33N05'42 89W58'04 5:59:52
Oxberry 22 1 33N47'06 90W02'08 6:00:09
Oxford 3 1 31N16'04 90W53'53 6:03:36
Oxford 36 1 34N21'59 89W31'09 5:58:05
Ozona 55 1 30N35'04 89W39'49 5:58:39
Pace 6 1 33N47'29 90W51'25 6:03:26
Pachuta 12 1 32N02'25 88W53'05 5:55:32
Paden 71 1 34N39'35 88W15'57 5:53:04
Palestine 25 2 32N10'51 90W25'01 6:01:40
Palmers Crossing 18
1 31N16'56 89W16'32 5:57:06
Palmetto 41 1 34N11'30 88W46'51 5:55:07
Pannell 58 1 34N09'18 89W06'46 5:56:27
Panther Burn 63 1 33N03'58 90W52'06 6:03:28
Parchman 67 1 33N55'04 90W29'47 6:01:59
Parham 48 1 34N00'35 88W20'26 5:53:22
Paris 36 1 34N10'43 89W27'35 5:57:50
Parkersburg 9 1 33N57'56 88W57'10 5:55:49
Parkplace 54 1 34N31 89W56 5:59:44
Parks 73 1 34N29'26 88W52'33 5:55:30
Parsons 22 1 33N44'00 90W01'54 6:00:08
Pascagoula 30 1 30N21'56 88W33'22 5:54:13
Pass Christian 24
1 30N18'56 89W14'51 5:56:59
Pat 61 1 32N10'42 90W00'36 6:00:02
Patmos 63 1 32N48'47 90W43'42 6:02:55
Patosi 82 1 32N54'59 90W37'10 6:02:29
Patrick 53 1 33N29'16 88W46'18 5:55:05
Patterson 4 1 32N58'39 89W25'55 5:57:44
Pattison 11 1 31N53'18 90W53'14 6:03:33
Paul 68 1 33N51 90W00 6:00:00
Paulding 31 1 32N01'50 89W02'15 5:56:09
Paulette 52 1 32N59'47 88W25'47 5:53:43
Paynes 68 1 33N55'15 90W04'10 6:00:17
Pearl 61 2 32N16'28 90W07'55 6:00:32
Pearl 64 1 32N00'07 90W11'56 6:00:48
Pearl City 61 2 32N19 90W09 6:00:36
Pearlhaven 43 1 31N35 90W27 6:01:48
Pearlington 23 1 30N14'47 89W36'40 5:58:27
Pearl River 50 1 32N47'00 89W13'40 5:56:55
Pearson 61 2 32N14'48 90W07'23 6:00:30
Pecan 30 1 30N26'36 88W25'45 5:53:43
Pecan Grove 34 1 31N35'52 89W08'14 5:56:33
Peck 73 1 34N29 89W01 5:56:04
Peelers 75 1 32N29'29 91W02'48 6:04:11
Peetsville 15 1 31N46 90W22 6:01:28
Pelahatchie 61 1 32N18'46 89W47'54 5:59:12
Pellez 78 1 33N28'37 89W22'54 5:57:32
Penantly 31 1 32N09 89W00 5:56:00
Pendorff 34 1 31N39'11 89W10'35 5:56:42
Penns 44 1 33N21'08 88W38'09 5:54:33
Pentecost 67 1 33N35'05 90W31'43 6:02:07
Penton 17 1 34N51'57 90W16'47 6:01:07
Peoples 70 1 34N44 88W57 5:55:48
Peoria 3 1 31N08'29 90W40'51 6:02:43
Percy 76 1 33N06'32 90W52'46 6:03:31
Perdue 51 1 32N30'52 88W58'56 5:55:56
Perkinston 66 1 30N46'55 89W08'17 5:56:33
Perry 66 1 30N43'14 89W08'29 5:56:34
Perrytown 79 1 31N19'48 91W09'58 6:04:40
Perth 32 1 31N39'33 90W52'04 6:03:28
Perthshire 6 1 33N58'38 90W54'44 6:03:39
Petal 18 1 31N20'47 89W15'36 5:57:02
Peteet 42 1 33N20'35 90W23'16 6:01:33
Petertown 71 1 34N39'34 88W07'57 5:52:32
Peyton 11 1 31N50'15 90W48'08 6:03:13
Pheba 13 1 33N35'03 88W56'59 5:55:48
Philadelphia 50 1 32N46'17 89W07'00 5:56:28
Philipp 68 1 33N45'27 90W12'15 6:00:49
Phillipstown 42 1 33N23'21 90W16'44 6:01:07
Phoenix 82 1 32N34'52 90W33'46 6:02:15
Piave 21 1 31N23'39 88W44'41 5:54:59
Picayune 55 1 30N31'31 89W40'46 5:58:43
Pickens 26 1 32N53'01 89W58'17 5:59:53
Pickwick 46 1 31N08'08 89W50'15 5:59:21
Pierce Crossroads 82
1 32N53'39 90W14'44 6:00:59
Piggtown 40 1 32N38'59 89W36'57 5:58:28
Pinchback 26 1 33N16'38 90W11'35 6:00:46
Pinckneyville 79
1 31N00'57 91W28'51 6:05:55
Pine Bluff 8 1 33N20'54 90W09'14 6:00:37
Pinebluff 13 1 33N44 89W04 5:56:16
Pinebur 46 1 31N08'09 89W42'07 5:58:48
Pinedale 73 1 34N24'18 89W11'33 5:56:46
Pine Flat 36 1 34N09 89W38 5:58:32
Pine Flat 71 1 34N58'27 88W16'48 5:53:07
Pine Grove 5 1 34N42'21 89W10'29 5:56:42
Pine Grove 18 1 31N16'41 89W10'50 5:56:43
Pine Grove 25 2 32N07'46 90W22'16 6:01:29
Pine Grove 26 1 33N01'35 90W08'45 6:00:35
Pine Grove 37 1 31N11'15 89W28'56 5:57:56
Pine Grove 41 1 34N05'21 88W42'32 5:54:50
Pine Grove 70 1 34N39'51 88W48'04 5:55:12
Pine Ridge 1 1 31N37'43 91W20'42 6:05:23
Pine Ridge 12 1 32N03'59 88W28'32 5:53:54
Pine Ridge 37 1 31N12'11 89W26'43 5:57:47
Pine Springs 38 1 32N28'02 88W46'17 5:55:05
Pine Valley 81 1 34N04'06 89W31'13 5:58:05
Pineview 77 1 31N43'34 88W56'34 5:55:46
Pineville 65 1 32N08'06 89W24'10 5:57:37
Piney Woods 61 1 32N03'45 89W59'34 5:59:58
Pinola 64 1 31N52'37 89W57'43 5:59:51
Pisgah 21 1 31N06'15 88W29'19 5:53:57
Pisgah 59 1 34N44'27 88W37'55 5:54:32
Pisgah 61 1 32N28'11 89W52'12 5:59:29
Pistol Ridge 18 1 31N00'11 89W19'05 5:57:16
Pittman 7 1 33N56'58 89W29'26 5:57:58
Pittman 46 1 31N10 89W50 5:59:20
Pittsboro 7 1 33N56'25 89W20'15 5:57:21
Plain 61 2 32N13'54 90W09'42 6:00:39
Plainview 61 2 32N12'15 90W09'15 6:00:37
Plantersville 41
1 34N12'48 88W39'52 5:54:39
Plattsburg 80 1 32N56'29 89W11'33 5:56:46
Pleasant Grove 54
1 34N26'21 90W05'22 6:00:21
Pleasant Hill 15
1 31N43'27 90W44'12 6:02:57
Pleasant Hill 17
1 34N54'52 89W53'40 5:59:35
Pleasant Hill 73
1 34N29 89W01 5:56:04
Pleasant Home Landing 82
1 32N42'25 90W41'30 6:02:46
Pleasant Ridge 34
1 31N39'49 89W14'23 5:56:58
Pleasant Ridge 73
1 34N34'08 88W50'12 5:55:21
Plum Point 17 1 34N58'46 89W57'17 5:59:49
Pluto 26 1 33N03'12 90W22'52 6:01:31
Plymouth 58 1 34N15 89W01 5:56:04
Poagville 69 1 34N40'58 89W51'45 5:59:27
Pocahontas 25 1 32N28'27 90W17'10 6:01:09
Pokal 64 1 31N44 89W59 5:59:56
Polfry 30 1 30N26 88W49 5:55:16
Polkville 65 1 32N11'37 89W41'33 5:58:46
Pollock 67 1 33N27 90W39 6:02:36
Pontotoc 58 1 34N14'52 88W59'55 5:56:00
Poolville 73 1 34N28'03 89W07'12 5:56:29
Pope 54 1 34N12'54 89W56'52 5:59:47
Poplar Corners 17
1 34N58 90W16 6:01:04
Poplar Creek 49 1 33N21'07 89W33'20 5:58:13
Poplar Springs 9
1 34N04'08 88W43'08 5:54:53
Poplar Springs 26
1 33N13'36 89W58'34 5:59:54
Poplar Springs 49
1 33N22'47 89W33'59 5:58:16
Poplar Springs 51
1 32N19 89W10 5:56:40
Poplarville 55 1 30N50'24 89W32'03 5:58:08
Porterville 35 1 32N41'16 88W28'20 5:53:53
Port Gibson 11 1 31N57'39 90W59'02 6:03:56
Porticaw Landing 30
1 30N30'42 88W37'04 5:54:28
Possum Corner 79
1 31N21'06 91W17'59 6:05:12
Possumneck 4 1 33N08'28 89W44'30 5:58:58
Possum Trot 58 1 34N18'08 89W05'04 5:56:20
Post 38 1 32N30 88W51 5:55:24
Potts Camp 47 1 34N38'46 89W18'19 5:57:13
Powell 14 1 34N29'06 90W31'35 6:02:06
Powers 34 1 31N41'52 89W04'07 5:56:16
Prairie 48 1 33N47'48 88W40'03 5:54:40
Prairie Point 52
1 33N08'50 88W23'37 5:53:34
Pratts 41 1 34N28'48 88W35'07 5:54:20
Prentiss 33 1 31N35'54 89W52'01 5:59:28
Presidential Hills 25
2 32N19 90W11 6:00:44
Preston 35 1 32N52'57 88W49'44 5:55:19
Pricedale 57 1 31N17'25 90W17'41 6:01:11
Prichard 72 1 34N41'58 90W14'39 6:00:59
Prince Chapel 35
1 32N53 88W50 5:55:20
Priscilla 76 1 33N30'57 90W58'59 6:03:56
Prismatic 35 1 32N35'30 88W44'18 5:54:57
Progress 33 1 31N32'06 89W56'16 5:59:45
Progress 56 1 31N04'34 88W51'22 5:55:25
Progress 57 1 31N02'46 90W19'36 6:01:18
Prospect 51 1 32N33'08 89W16'08 5:57:05
Puckett 61 1 32N04'51 89W46'33 5:59:06
Pulaski 62 1 32N16'19 89W36'08 5:58:25
Pumpkin Center 73
1 34N31'53 89W02'04 5:56:08
Purnell 42 1 33N27'11 90W26'16 6:01:45
Purvis 37 1 31N08'35 89W24'35 5:57:38
Pushmataha Landing 14
1 34N08'12 90W51'36 6:03:26
Pyland 9 1 33N53'02 89W06'27 5:56:26
Quentin 19 1 31N30'22 90W44'47 6:02:59
Quincy 48 1 33N54'35 88W22'01 5:53:28
Quitman 12 1 32N02'24 88W43'41 5:54:55
Quito 42 1 33N26'19 90W18'04 6:01:12
Quofaloma 26 1 33N06'17 90W20'46 6:01:23
Rafn 43 1 31N37'32 90W17'28 6:01:10
Rainey 34 1 31N31'16 89W21'02 5:57:24
Raleigh 65 1 32N02'00 89W31'20 5:58:05
Ralston 18 1 31N14'19 89W14'30 5:56:58
Ramsey Springs 66
1 30N46'14 88W54'53 5:55:40
Randolph 58 1 34N10'53 89W10'06 5:56:40
Rankin 61 1 32N17'11 89W54'25 5:59:38
Ras 31 1 32N05 89W15 5:57:00
Ratliff 29 1 34N23'36 88W32'01 5:54:08
Ratliff Landing 63
1 32N55'57 90W45'45 6:03:03
Ravine 52 1 33N12'49 88W22'01 5:53:28
Rawhide 75 1 32N27'58 90W37'40 6:02:31
Rawls Springs 18
1 31N22'50 89W22'17 5:57:29
Raworth 62 1 32N21'47 89W33'52 5:58:15
Raymond 25 1 32N15'33 90W25'21 6:01:41
Raytown 45 1 32N41'21 89W47'55 5:59:12
Red Banks 47 1 34N49'41 89W33'52 5:58:15
Redbone 75 1 32N13'03 90W53'27 6:03:34
Redding 22 1 33N43'21 89W30'47 5:58:03
Reddoch 16 1 31N50 89W26 5:57:44
Redhill 56 1 31N07'47 89W03'51 5:56:15
Red Lick 32 1 31N47'32 90W58'45 6:03:55
Redstar 43 1 31N35 90W27 6:01:48
Red Top 55 1 30N58'09 89W28'38 5:57:55
Redwater 40 1 32N46'00 89W32'12 5:58:09
Redwood 75 1 32N28'39 90W48'13 6:03:13
Reedtown 25 1 32N04'33 90W38'34 6:02:34
Reese 73 1 34N24'57 88W53'39 5:55:35
Reese Landing 14
1 34N13'09 90W53'16 6:03:33
Reform 10 1 33N25'50 89W09'17 5:56:37
Refuge 27 1 33N08'13 90W20'04 6:01:20
Refuge 76 1 33N18'13 91W08'11 6:04:33
Reganton 11 1 32N08'30 90W44'55 6:03:00
Reid 7 1 34N00'08 89W11'43 5:56:47
Remus 40 1 32N52'07 89W20'37 5:57:22
Rena Lara 14 1 34N08'59 90W46'49 6:03:07
Renfroe 40 1 32N51'34 89W27'04 5:57:48

Renova 6 1 33N46'43 90w43'17 6:02:53
Renshaw 82 1 32N55'14 90w22'45 6:01:31
Rescue Landing 14
1 34N14'10 90w49'45 6:03:19
Retreat 7 1 33N51'53 89w27'29 5:57:50
Revive 45 1 32N45'34 89w45'51 5:59:03
Rexburg 76 1 33N25'52 90w50'38 6:03:23
Rexford 64 1 32N02'33 90w04'29 6:00:18
Rhodes 56 1 31N25'55 88w57'56 5:55:52
Riceville 24 1 30N36'22 89w17'45 5:57:11
Rich 14 1 34N24'58 90w26'41 6:01:47
Richardson 55 1 30N33'36 89w40'02 5:58:40
Richburg 37 1 31N16'27 89w21'11 5:57:25
Richey 63 1 33N01'48 90w43'58 6:02:56
Richland 26 1 32N58'27 89w59'11 5:59:57
Richland 27 1 33N03'51 90w29'19 6:01:57
Richmond 41 1 34N11'29 88w33'24 5:54:14
Richton 45 1 32N34'44 90w08'58 6:00:36
Richton 56 1 31N20'57 88w56'24 5:55:46
Ridgeland 45 1 32N25'42 90w07'56 6:00:32
Rienzi 2 1 34N45'57 88w31'36 5:54:06
Rio 35 1 32N36'50 88w52'32 5:55:30
Ripley 70 1 34N43'47 88w57'02 5:55:48
Rising Sun 42 1 33N27'31 90w12'31 6:00:50
Riverdale 22 1 33N50'03 89w49'29 5:59:18
River Oakes 1 1 31N34 91w22 6:05:28
Riverside 18 1 31N21'14 89w19'54 5:57:20
Riverside Junction 63
1 32N55'53 90w52'22 6:03:29
Riverton 14 1 34N12 90w34 6:02:16
Riverton Landing 6
1 33N49'11 91w01'15 6:04:05
Riverview 60 1 34N17'01 90w14'56 6:01:00
Robbs 58 1 34N06'05 89w12'25 5:56:50
Roberts 51 1 32N13'45 89w13'46 5:56:55
Robinson Gin 17 1 34N47'12 90w01'29 6:00:06
Robinsons Junction 77
1 31N34'28 88w33'33 5:54:14
Robinsonville 72
1 34N49'02 90w18'58 6:01:16
Robinwood 39 1 31N28'55 90w05'18 6:00:21
Rochdale 6 1 34N05'58 90w51'01 6:03:24
Rock Creek 51 1 32N33'43 89w01'37 5:56:06
Rock Hill 2 1 34N54 88w34 5:54:16
Rock Hill 18 1 31N05'06 89w18'34 5:57:14
Rock Hill 61 1 32N16 89w59 5:59:56
Rockhill 69 1 34N42'51 89w44'21 5:58:57
Rockport 15 1 31N47'41 90w09'24 6:00:38
Rocky Hill 53 1 33N28 88w49 5:55:16
Rocky Springs 11
1 32N05'19 90w48'54 6:03:16
Rodney 32 1 31N51'40 91w11'59 6:04:48
Roebuck 42 1 33N26'41 90w14'04 6:00:56
Rogerslacy 31 1 31N47 89w02 5:56:08
Rolling Fork 63 1 32N54'23 90w52'41 6:03:31
Rome 67 1 33N57'47 90w28'42 6:01:55
Roseacres 14 1 34N23'44 90w27'00 6:01:48
Rosebloom 68 1 33N52'34 89w57'07 5:59:48
Rosebud 40 1 32N38'57 89w23'31 5:57:34
Rosedale 6 1 33N51'12 91w01'40 6:04:07
Rose Hill 31 1 32N08'40 88w59'45 5:55:59
Rose Hill 75 1 32N21'32 90w48'25 6:03:14
Rose Hill Center 45
1 32N44'45 90w00'32 6:00:02
Rosella 39 1 31N36'26 90w07'42 6:00:31
Rosemary 25 2 32N05'17 90w15'35 6:01:02
Roseneath 26 1 33N04'04 90w25'42 6:01:43
Rosetta 79 1 31N18'59 91w06'03 6:04:24
Ross Crossing 2 1 34N49'05 88w43'43 5:54:55
Rough Edge 58 1 34N15'21 88w58'32 5:55:54
Roundaway 14 1 34N00'51 90w35'53 6:02:24
Round Lake 6 1 34N03'12 90w51'10 6:03:25
Rounsaville 21 1 31N10'07 88w27'25 5:53:50
Rowlands 55 1 30N41'40 89w28'19 5:57:53
Roxie 19 1 31N30'16 91w04'08 6:04:17
Roy 12 1 32N10'50 88w42'32 5:54:50
Royce 21 1 31N03'44 88w48'19 5:55:13
Ruby 42 1 33N41'41 90w13'40 6:00:55
Rudyard 14 1 34N20'06 90w32'12 6:02:09
Rufus 61 1 32N10'41 89w46'50 5:59:07
Ruleville 67 1 33N43'33 90w33'05 6:02:12
Runnelstown 56 1 31N22'32 89w06'42 5:56:27
Runnymede 42 1 33N29'48 90w18'38 6:01:15
Rural Hill 80 1 33N04'34 89w17'56 5:57:12
Rushing 74 1 31N07'50 90w10'37 6:00:42
Ruslor Junction 2
1 34N57'27 88w31'40 5:54:07
Russell 38 1 32N24'13 88w35'38 5:54:23
Russellville 75 1 32N32'27 90w39'10 6:02:37
Russum 11 1 31N52'38 91w00'41 6:04:03
Ruth 43 1 31N22'53 90w18'59 6:01:16
Ryans l'Argent Landing 82
1 32N40'18 90w39'57 6:02:40
Sabino 60 1 34N12'15 90w24'26 6:01:38
Sable 12 1 32N12'04 88w41'16 5:54:45
Sabougla 7 1 33N46'33 89w27'51 5:57:51
Sago 63 1 33N01'55 90w54'43 6:03:39
Saint Ann 40 1 32N46'58 89w39'37 5:58:38
Saint Elmo 11 1 31N59'42 90w48'37 6:03:14
Saint Francis Island Landing 72
1 34N41'12 90w32'28 6:02:10
Saint Martin 30 1 30N26 88w54 5:55:36
Saints Rest 67 1 33N27 90w39 6:02:36
Salem 16 1 31N40'49 89w31'49 5:58:07
Salem 25 1 32N10'05 90w32'28 6:02:10
Salem 40 1 32N35'50 89w20'56 5:57:24
Salem 74 1 31N13'47 90w07'02 6:00:28
Sallis 4 1 33N01'20 89w45'55 5:59:04
Saltillo 41 1 34N22'35 88w40'54 5:54:44
Sanatorium 64 1 31N53'55 89w46'39 5:59:07
Sandersville 34 1 31N47'11 89w01'56 5:56:08
Sand Hill 15 1 31N44'00 90w18'21 6:01:13
Sand Hill 21 1 31N20'48 88w45'49 5:55:03
Sand Hill 34 1 31N37'14 89w16'54 5:57:08
Sand Hill 61 1 32N29'15 89w52'49 5:59:31
Sandpoint 65 1 32N01 89w27 5:57:48
Sandtown 50 1 32N47'41 89w00'06 5:56:00
Sandy Creek 71 1 34N59'32 88w15'26 5:53:02
Sandy Hook 46 1 31N02'10 89w48'17 5:59:13
Sandy Ridge 42 1 33N42'54 90w13'08 6:00:53
Sandy Springs 29
1 34N25'58 88w22'30 5:53:30
Sanford 16 1 31N29'12 89w25'37 5:57:42
Santa Rosa 23 1 30N25'46 89w38'52 5:58:35
Sapa 78 1 33N32'51 89w12'07 5:56:48
Sarah 72 1 34N34'10 90w12'37 6:00:50
Saratoga 64 1 31N47'49 89w40'39 5:58:43
Sardis 15 1 31N48'03 90w19'27 6:01:18
Sardis 54 1 34N26'13 89w54'57 5:59:40
Sarepta 7 1 34N07'28 89w17'15 5:57:09
Sartinsville 74 1 31N19'37 90w06'58 6:00:28
Satartia 82 1 32N40'15 90w32'39 6:02:11
Saucier 24 1 30N38'08 89w08'06 5:56:32
Saukum 79 1 31N13'52 91w11'05 6:04:44
Sauls 39 1 31N23 90w19 6:01:16
Savage 69 1 34N37'47 90w13'23 6:00:54
Savannah 55 1 30N44'22 89w29'27 5:57:58
Savannah Grove 38
1 32N20'42 88w44'40 5:54:59
Savoy 38 1 32N16'14 88w46'11 5:55:05
Sawyer 49 1 33N31'31 89w44'11 5:58:57
Schamberville 38
1 32N28'27 88w51'49 5:55:27
Schlater 42 1 33N38'26 90w20'53 6:01:24
Schley 64 1 31N47'14 90w05'39 6:00:23
Sciples Mill 35 1 32N52'01 88w43'34 5:54:54
Scobey 81 1 33N56'29 89w51'57 5:59:28
Scooba 35 1 32N49'41 88w28'35 5:53:54
Scotland 82 1 32N42'19 90w13'16 6:00:53
Scotland Fork 82
1 32N42'47 90w13'26 6:00:54
Scott 6 1 33N35'30 91w04'27 6:04:18
Searcy Town 2 1 34N49'03 88w29'37 5:53:58
Sebastopol 62 1 32N34'22 89w20'06 5:57:20
Sellers 55 1 30N35'29 89w21'27 5:57:26
Selma 1 1 31N36'05 91w16'44 6:05:07
Sels Prairie 12 1 31N56'17 88w37'51 5:54:31
Seminary 16 1 31N33'44 89w29'51 5:57:59
Senatobia 69 1 34N37'03 89w58'07 5:59:52
Seneca 37 1 31N02'21 89w26'22 5:57:45
Service 34 1 31N44'08 89w13'24 5:56:54
Sessions 14 1 34N20'29 90w37'53 6:02:32
Sessums 53 1 33N24'58 88w42'51 5:54:51
Seven Pines 8 1 33N22'13 90w05'41 6:00:23
Seven Springs 25
1 32N12'57 90w22'25 6:01:30
Shackleford 26 1 33N08'50 90w14'11 6:00:57
Shady Grove 15 1 31N51'55 90w21'00 6:01:24
Shady Grove 34 1 31N45'09 89w09'14 5:56:37
Shannon 41 1 34N06'58 88w42'42 5:54:51
Shari 73 1 34N30'58 89w02'44 5:56:11
Sharkey 68 1 34N00 90w03 6:00:12
Sharon 34 1 31N47'22 89w05'55 5:56:24
Sharon 45 1 32N39'30 89w56'10 5:59:45
Sharpsburg 45 1 32N45'21 89w59'22 5:59:57
Shaw 6 1 33N36'06 90w46'25 6:03:06
Shelby 6 1 33N57'03 90w46'04 6:03:04
Shellmound 42 1 33N36'23 90w16'47 6:01:07
Shelton 34 1 31N29'32 89w20'57 5:57:24
Shepherd 7 1 33N58'09 89w23'58 5:57:36
Sheppardtown 42 1 33N23'29 90w18'48 6:01:15
Sherard 14 1 34N12'56 90w42'22 6:02:49
Sherman 58 1 34N21'33 88w50'28 5:55:22
Sherwood 10 1 33N29'16 89w08'02 5:56:32
Sherwood Forest 61
1 32N12'30 89w58'01 5:59:52
Shiloh 12 1 32N00'37 88w29'49 5:53:59
Shiloh 29 1 34N19'24 88w31'38 5:54:07
Shiloh 61 1 32N19 89w47 5:59:08
Shipman 20 1 30N52'38 88w28'30 5:53:54
Shivers 64 1 31N47'47 89w59'15 5:59:57
Shoccoe 45 1 32N36'35 89w54'04 5:59:36
Shongelo 65 1 32N06'10 89w30'47 5:58:03
Shrock 4 1 32N58 89w55 5:59:40
Shubuta 12 1 31N51'36 88w41'58 5:54:48
Shucktown 19 1 31N35'33 90w39'46 6:02:39
Shucktown 38 1 32N32'39 88w46'13 5:55:05
Shuford 54 1 34N13'20 89w48'25 5:59:14
Shuqualak 52 1 32N58'42 88w34'12 5:54:17
Sibleton 49 1 33N26 89w34 5:58:16
Sibley 1 1 31N22'45 91w23'55 6:05:36
Sibleyton 49 1 33N26'17 89w31'30 5:58:06
Sidon 42 1 33N24'29 90w12'14 6:00:49
Signal 75 1 32N24'03 90w51'14 6:03:25
Siloam 13 1 33N38'12 88w45'27 5:55:02
Silver City 27 1 33N05'47 90w29'48 6:01:59
Silver Creek 39 1 31N36'18 89w59'54 6:00:00
Silver Run 55 1 30N44'00 89w20'44 5:57:23
Simonds 74 1 31N00'35 90w10'49 6:00:43
Simrall 75 1 32N12'06 90w56'43 6:03:47
Sinai 61 1 32N07'21 90w11'13 6:00:45
Singleton 40 1 32N53'10 89w32'12 5:58:09
Singleton Settlement 62
1 32N23'00 89w24'32 5:57:38
Sipsey Fork 48 1 33N56'57 88w14'37 5:52:58
Sisloff Junction 42
1 33N45'55 90w13'36 6:00:54
Siwell 25 2 32N14'49 90w18'10 6:01:13
Skene 6 1 33N42'13 90w47'39 6:03:11
Skuna 7 1 33N57'29 89w27'19 5:57:49
Skyline 41 1 34N15'49 88w38'28 5:54:34
Slate Spring 7 1 33N44'26 89w22'16 5:57:29
Slayden 47 1 34N56'49 89w26'27 5:57:46
Sledge 60 1 34N25'55 90w13'15 6:00:53
Sloan 45 1 32N33'36 90w03'35 6:00:14
Smalco 73 1 34N31'56 89w04'45 5:56:19
Smedes 63 1 32N41'37 90w55'14 6:03:41
Smith 16 1 31N45'25 89w34'11 5:58:17
Smith 38 1 32N25'27 88w28'30 5:53:54
Smithburg 57 1 31N01'42 90w17'25 6:01:10
Smithdale 3 1 31N20'22 90w40'58 6:02:44
Smiths 25 1 32N20'21 90w40'23 6:02:42
Smithtown 77 1 31N26'14 88w42'57 5:54:52
Smithville 48 1 34N04'12 88w23'28 5:53:34
Smyrna 4 1 32N59'19 89w29'07 5:57:56
Smyrna 15 1 31N52'12 90w30'33 6:02:02
Snave 28 1 32N37 91w01 6:04:04
Snell 12 1 32N11'30 88w30'06 5:54:00
Snow Lake Shores 5
1 34N50 89w11 5:56:44
Society Hill 33 1 31N24'31 89w53'20 5:59:33
Somerville 42 1 33N47'31 90w15'56 6:01:04
Sonora 9 1 33N56 89w00 5:56:00
Sontag 39 1 31N39'08 90w12'15 6:00:49
Sorghum Lake 27 1 33N42'35 90w07'40 6:00:31
Soso 34 1 31N45'24 89w16'27 5:57:06
South Amory 48 1 33N59 88w29 5:53:56
Southaven 17 1 34N59 90w01 6:00:04
Southern 18 1 31N18 89w18 5:57:12
South McComb 57 1 31N14 90w28 6:01:52
Spanish Fort 63 1 32N45'34 90w44'05 6:02:56
Sparta 9 1 33N46'07 88w58'45 5:55:55
Spay 10 1 33N12 89w20 5:57:20
Spearman 81 1 33N55'38 89w35'36 5:58:22
Splunge 48 1 33N58'08 88w16'07 5:53:04
Spraggins 47 1 34N33'17 89w29'08 5:57:57
Spring Cottage 46
1 31N05'22 89w45'59 5:59:04
Spring Creek 50 1 32N49'56 89w02'23 5:56:10
Springdale 36 1 34N13'18 89w36'33 5:58:26
Spring Hill 5 1 34N55'58 89w12'40 5:56:51
Springhill 34 1 31N44'40 89w12'51 5:56:51
Spring Hill 36 1 34N15 89w14 5:56:56
Spring Hill 50 1 32N43'12 89w06'09 5:56:25
Spring Ridge 25 1 32N11'15 90w19'47 6:01:19
Springville 58 1 34N13'54 89w06'13 5:56:25
Stafford Springs 31
1 31N54'17 88w56'00 5:55:44
Stage 62 1 32N16'57 89w38'06 5:58:32
Stallo 50 1 32N55'12 89w06'02 5:56:24
Stampley 32 1 31N38'13 91w07'52 6:04:31
Standing Pine 40
1 32N44 89w32 5:58:08
Stanton 1 1 31N36'57 91w14'25 6:04:58
Star 61 1 32N05'38 90w02'46 6:00:11
Starkville 53 1 33N27'01 88w49'06 5:55:16
State College 53
1 33N27 88w47 5:55:08
State Line 21 1 31N26'10 88w28'28 5:53:54
Steel 62 1 32N22 89w28 5:57:52
Steens 44 1 33N33'48 88w18'58 5:53:16
Steiner 67 1 33N36'58 90w37'04 6:02:28
Stella 57 1 31N11'02 90w20'41 6:01:23
Stephen 13 1 33N33'45 88w32'41 5:54:11
Stewart 78 1 33N27'02 89w26'10 5:57:45
Stokes 45 1 32N35'42 90w12'14 6:00:49
Stoneville 76 1 33N25'26 90w54'54 6:03:40
Stonewall 12 1 32N07'54 88w47'36 5:55:10
Stonewall 17 1 34N51'34 89w45'43 5:59:03
Stonewall 26 1 33N05'00 90w22'13 6:01:29
Stonington 32 1 31N45'32 91w01'02 6:04:04
Stout 75 1 32N18'01 90w53'57 6:03:36
Stovall 14 1 34N17'48 90w38'41 6:02:35
Stover 68 1 34N02'52 90w16'43 6:01:07
Straight Bayou 63
1 32N58 90w50 6:03:20
Stratton 51 1 32N29'58 89w08'03 5:56:32
Strayhorn 69 1 34N36'44 90w08'38 6:00:35
Strengthford 77 1 31N36'49 88w53'05 5:55:32
Strickland 2 1 34N52'42 88w26'29 5:53:46
Stringer 31 1 31N52'00 89w15'48 5:57:03
Stringtown 6 1 33N34'29 90w59'04 6:03:56
Strong 48 1 33N41'43 88w36'16 5:54:25
Stronghope 15 1 31N44'38 90w15'48 6:01:03
Strongs 48 1 33N50 88w33 5:54:12
Sturgis 53 1 33N20'40 89w02'43 5:56:11
Sucarnoochee 35 1 32N43'52 88w28'23 5:53:54
Success 24 1 30N36'38 89w00'35 5:56:12
Sumbax 46 1 31N14'07 89w55'23 5:59:42
Summerland 34 1 31N47'57 89w21'37 5:57:26
Summit 57 1 31N17'01 90w28'06 6:01:52
Sumner 68 1 33N58'15 90w22'07 6:01:28
Sumrall 37 1 31N25'02 89w32'32 5:58:10
Sunflower 59 1 34N39'50 88w33'05 5:54:12
Sunflower 67 1 33N32'34 90w32'13 6:02:09
Sunflower Landing 14
1 34N09'58 90w48'07 6:03:12
Sunnycrest 22 1 33N47 89w48 5:59:12
Sunnyside 42 1 33N41'47 90w17'42 6:01:11
Sunrise 18 1 31N18'44 89w12'50 5:56:51
Sunrise 40 1 32N46'14 89w26'20 5:57:45
Suqualena 38 1 32N26'36 88w49'35 5:55:18
Swan Lake 68 1 33N52'29 90w17'00 6:01:08
Sweatman 49 1 33N38'03 89w34'47 5:58:19
Swiftown 42 1 33N18'20 90w25'30 6:01:42
Swiftwater 76 1 33N20'15 91w03'35 6:04:14
Sykes 12 1 32N05'38 88w35'32 5:54:22
Sylvarena 65 1 32N00'39 89w22'50 5:57:31
Symonds 6 1 33N50'02 90w53'25 6:03:34
Tabbville 9 1 33N50'50 89w05'12 5:56:21
Tallahala 56 1 31N23'11 89w07'23 5:56:30
Tallula 28 1 32N46'46 91w06'52 6:04:27
Talowah 37 1 31N04'33 89w25'49 5:57:43
Tamola 35 1 32N35'12 88w28'37 5:53:54
Tanglewood 51 1 32N16'32 89w18'17 5:57:13
Taska 47 1 34N55'08 89w33'55 5:58:16
Tatum 3 1 31N08'56 91w02'37 6:04:10
Tawanta 34 1 31N32'51 89w14'58 5:57:00
Taylor 36 1 34N16'20 89w35'19 5:58:21
Taylorsville 25 2 32N13'33 90w14'19 6:00:57
Taylorsville 65 1 31N49'46 89w25'41 5:57:43
Tchula 26 1 33N10'58 90w13'22 6:00:53
Teasdale 68 1 34N07 89w56 5:59:44
Teckville 36 1 34N30'23 89w39'46 5:58:39
Ted 65 1 32N05 89w15 5:57:00
Ten Mile 66 1 30N45'55 89w08'37 5:56:34
Teoc 8 1 33N34'45 90w03'19 6:00:13
Terrell 33 1 31N35'57 89w43'54 5:58:56
Terrene Landing 6
1 33N53'26 91w02'25 6:04:10
Terry 25 1 32N05'46 90w17'39 6:01:11
Terrys Creek 3 1 31N04'07 90w31'41 6:02:07
Terza 54 1 34N19 89w57 5:59:48
Texas 66 1 30N53'09 89w16'19 5:57:05
Thaxton 58 1 34N18'27 89w10'41 5:56:43
Thayer 43 1 31N29'24 90w26'52 6:01:47
Theadville 12 1 32N03 88w43 5:54:52
Thelma 9 1 33N59'15 89w01'35 5:56:06
The Mall 75 1 32N20 90w52 6:03:28
Theo 2 1 34N55'51 88w41'51 5:54:47
Thomastown 40 1 32N51'50 89w40'10 5:58:41
Thomasville 61 1 32N09'23 90w00'46 6:00:03
Thompson 3 1 31N15'24 90w38'17 6:02:33
Thompson 25 1 32N17'52 90w21'59 6:01:28
Thompsonville 25
1 32N03'33 90w27'33 6:01:50
Thorn 9 1 33N56'33 89w06'09 5:56:25
Thornton 26 1 33N04'45 90w19'21 6:01:17
Thrashers 59 1 34N43'10 88w32'02 5:54:08

Threadville 12	1	31N58'27	88w30'41	5:54:03
Three Rivers 30	1	30N35'12	88w33'45	5:54:15
Thyatira 69	1	34N38'01	89w45'16	5:59:01
Tibbee 13	1	33N31'42	88w37'53	5:54:32
Tibbs 72	1	34N28'02	90w18'36	6:01:14
Tie Plant 22	1	33N44'29	89w47'24	5:59:10
Tilden 29	1	34N11'12	88w21'07	5:53:24
Tillatoba 81	1	33N59'05	89w53'48	5:59:35
Tillman 11	1	31N51'16	90w54'58	6:03:40
Tillman 15	1	31N53'33	90w26'47	6:01:47
Tilton 39	1	31N24'53	90w01'15	6:00:05
Tinnin 25	1	32N25'27	90w20'43	6:01:23
Tinsley 82	1	32N43'55	90w27'37	6:01:50
Tiplersville 70	1	34N53'44	88w54'27	5:55:38
Tippah 5	1	34N50	89w11	5:56:44
Tippo 68	1	33N54'43	90w10'50	6:00:43
Tisdell Landing 63	1	32N55'56	90w45'24	6:03:02
Tishomingo 71	1	34N38'12	88w13'54	5:52:56
Toccopola 58	1	34N15'23	89w14'08	5:56:57
Tocowa 54	1	34N15	89w56	5:59:44
Tolarville 26	1	33N02'50	90w13'07	6:00:52
Tollison 10	1	33N15'12	89w11'29	5:56:46
Tomnolen 10	1	33N29'05	89w21'38	5:57:27
Toomsuba 38	1	32N25'06	88w30'25	5:54:02
Topeka 39	1	31N24'54	90w11'18	6:00:45
Topisaw 57	1	31N17'23	90w16'23	6:01:06
Topton 38	1	32N28'02	88w36'08	5:54:25
Touchstone 64	1	31N59'54	90w02'04	6:00:08
Tougaloo 25	1	32N23'51	90w09'32	6:00:38
Townsend 35	1	32N45'19	88w32'56	5:54:12
Tralake 76	1	33N16'13	90w47'41	6:03:11
Trapp 50	1	32N44'22	89w12'49	5:56:51
Traxler 65	1	32N00'35	89w38'58	5:58:36
Trebloc 9	1	33N50'28	88w49'49	5:55:19
Tremont 29	1	34N14'05	88w15'31	5:53:02
Trenton 65	1	32N10'09	89w36'39	5:58:27
Triangle-Hospital 24	1	30N26	88w54	5:55:36
Tribbett 76	1	33N21'05	90w47'54	6:03:12
Trinity 17	1	34N48'33	90w10'31	6:00:42
Trinity 44	1	33N20'45	88w27'44	5:53:51
Trotter Landing 72	1	34N32'37	90w31'59	6:02:08
Troy 58	1	34N07'08	88w53'06	5:55:32
Truitt 45	1	32N48'25	89w54'32	5:59:38
Tryus 39	1	31N41'29	90w11'57	6:00:48
Tucker 34	1	31N38	89w06	5:56:24
Tucker 50	1	32N42'23	89w03'14	5:56:13
Tuckers Crossing 34	1	31N37'38	89w05'24	5:56:22
Tuckers Crossing 40	1	32N39'14	89w34'26	5:58:18
Tula 36	1	34N13'58	89w21'44	5:57:27
Tunica 72	1	34N41'04	90w22'58	6:01:32
Tupelo 41	1	34N15'27	88w42'12	5:54:49
Turkey Creek 81	1	33N53'15	89w40'55	5:58:44
Turnbull 79	1	31N01'20	91w17'31	6:05:10
Turnerville 31	1	32N01'32	89w12'12	5:56:49
Turon 29	1	34N06'15	88w19'30	5:53:18
Tuscan 10	1	33N18'44	89w09'16	5:56:37
Tuscola 40	1	32N37'12	89w31'40	5:58:07
Tutwiler 68	1	34N00'53	90w25'54	6:01:44
Twin 46	1	30N58	89w49	5:59:16
Twin Lake 75	1	32N29'20	90w49'12	6:03:17
Tyler 55	1	30N42'26	89w36'22	5:58:25
Tylertown 74	1	31N06'57	90w08'31	6:00:34
Tyro 69	1	34N35'01	89w42'19	5:58:49
Tyson 81	1	33N56'02	89w32'00	5:58:08
Una 13	1	33N47'49	88w48'25	5:55:14
Union 34	1	31N28'45	89w12'04	5:56:48
Union 41	1	34N09'39	88w37'54	5:54:32
Union 51	1	32N34'17	89w07'17	5:56:29
Union 64	1	31N52'50	90w05'02	6:00:20
Union Church 32	1	31N41	90w47	6:03:08
Union Hall 43	1	31N35	90w27	6:01:48
Union Hill 73	1	34N29'11	88w57'07	5:55:48
Unity 41	1	34N23'24	88w34'08	5:54:17
University of Mississippi 36	1	34N21	89w32	5:58:08
Updike 63	1	33N03'34	90w46'07	6:03:04
Upton 64	1	31N59'24	89w42'14	5:58:49
U S Naval Construction Batt 24	1	30N24	89w05	5:56:20
Usrytown 62	1	32N23'11	89w22'52	5:57:31
Ustane 3	1	31N17'12	90w49'53	6:03:20
Utica 25	1	32N06'34	90w37'24	6:02:30
Utica Junior College 15	1	32N06	90w37	6:02:28
Vaiden 8	1	33N19'55	89w44'28	5:58:58
Valewood 28	1	33N02	91w02	6:04:08
Valley 82	1	32N45'35	90w28'49	6:01:55
Valley Hill 8	1	33N30	89w55	5:59:40
Valley Park 28	1	32N38'00	90w52'00	6:03:28
Value 61	1	32N17'15	89w59'44	5:59:59
Van Buren 29	1	34N11'30	88w24'41	5:53:39
Vance 60	1	34N04'22	90w21'03	6:01:24
Vancleave 30	1	30N32	88w42	5:54:48
Van Vleet 9	1	33N59'13	88w54'01	5:55:36
Van Winkle 25	2	32N17'55	90w15'49	6:01:03
Vardaman 7	1	33N52'32	89w10'38	5:56:43
Varnado 37	1	31N20'19	89w21'28	5:57:26
Vaughan 20	1	30N51'32	88w30'56	5:54:04
Vaughan 82	1	32N48'23	90w02'30	6:00:10
Vaughn 43	1	31N34'37	90w34'24	6:02:18
Vaughts 57	1	31N10'09	90w15'46	6:01:03
Velma 81	1	34N03'37	89w38'40	5:58:35
Verna 39	1	31N22'23	90w14'33	6:00:58
Vernal 21	1	31N02'18	88w36'39	5:54:27
Vernon 31	1	31N54'36	89w09'12	5:56:37
Vernon 45	1	32N35'22	90w19'47	6:01:19
Vernon 80	1	32N59'08	88w55'53	5:55:44
Verona 41	1	34N11'39	88w43'11	5:54:53
Vestry 30	1	30N43'36	88w46'33	5:55:06
Vickland 63	1	33N02'34	90w50'52	6:03:23
Vicksburg 75	1	32N21'09	90w52'40	6:03:31
Victor 6	1	33N46'37	90w49'30	6:03:18
Victoria 47	1	34N50'46	89w37'05	5:58:28
Vidalia 24	1	30N29'55	89w20'22	5:57:21
Villanova 75	1	32N26'01	90w46'22	6:03:05
Villa Ridge 55	1	31N00	89w27	5:57:48
Vimville 38	1	32N19'48	88w53'22	5:54:17
Vinton 13	1	33N39'30	88w31'24	5:54:06
Violet 32	1	31N49'14	90w51'10	6:03:25
Virlilia 45	1	32N37'34	90w07'53	6:00:32
Virlilia 45	1	32N37	90w02	6:00:08
Vossburg 31	1	31N55'43	88w56'27	5:55:46
Vowell 80	1	32N58'58	89w18'27	5:57:14
Waco 67	1	33N21	90w35	6:02:20
Waddell 13	1	33N34'49	88w52'16	5:55:29
Wade 30	1	30N38'32	88w34'11	5:54:17
Wade 67	1	33N49	90w32	6:02:08
Wahalak 35	1	32N54'20	88w31'47	5:54:07
Waites 47	1	34N42'02	89w22'08	5:57:29
Wakefield 69	1	34N44'35	89w44'27	5:58:58
Wakeland 42	1	33N37'07	90w11'58	6:00:48
Waldo 50	1	32N44'14	89w16'37	5:57:06
Waldrup 31	1	31N57'54	89w06'28	5:56:26
Walker Siding 71	1	34N49'55	88w17'20	5:53:09
Wallace Creek 81	1	34N09'37	89w53'32	5:59:34
Wallerville 73	1	34N26'30	88w56'45	5:55:47
Wallfield 58	1	34N06'33	89w01'37	5:56:06
Wallhill 47	1	34N42'52	89w42'14	5:58:49
Wallis (reduced Usage) 18	1	31N09'19	89w14'18	5:56:57
Walls 17	1	34N57'28	90w09'06	6:00:36
Walnut 60	1	34N08'56	90w23'56	6:01:36
Walnut 70	1	34N56'46	88w53'59	5:55:36
Walnut Grove 14	1	34N08'25	90w46'10	6:03:05
Walnut Grove 40	1	32N35'25	89w27'30	5:57:50
Walsh 75	1	32N34'16	90w50'22	6:03:21
Walters 34	1	31N38'36	89w10'41	5:56:43
Waltersville 75	1	32N22'46	90w52'04	6:03:28
Walthall 78	1	33N36'26	89w16'38	5:57:07
Wanilla 39	1	31N38'34	90w07'54	6:00:32
Wardwell 7	1	33N53	89w11	5:56:44
Wardwell 37	1	31N20'34	89w22'32	5:57:30
Warrenton 75	1	32N14'50	90w55'42	6:03:43
Warsaw 47	1	34N49'51	89w41'10	5:58:45
Warsaw 76	1	33N11'39	90w51'54	6:03:28
Washington 1	1	31N34'43	91w17'57	6:05:12
Waterford 47	1	34N38'51	89w27'26	5:57:50
Water Oak 77	1	31N41	88w39	5:54:36
Waters Landing 20	1	30N47'26	88w27'53	5:53:52
Water Valley 81	1	34N09'05	89w37'53	5:58:32
Water Valley Landing 81	1	34N08'57	89w46'24	5:59:06
Watson 47	1	34N47'15	89w41'19	5:58:45
Watson Center 47	1	34N47'15	89w40'15	5:58:41
Wautubbee 12	1	32N06'58	88w51'30	5:55:26
Waveland 23	1	30N17'12	89w22'34	5:57:30
Waverly 13	1	33N34'03	88w30'14	5:54:01
Waxhaw 6	1	33N55'03	90w58'09	6:03:53
Way 45	1	32N44'38	90w01'59	6:00:08
Waynesboro 77	1	31N40'29	88w38'46	5:54:35
Wayside 76	1	33N16'08	91w02'01	6:04:08
Weathersby 64	1	31N56'21	89w49'54	5:59:20
Webb 68	1	33N56'50	90w20'39	6:01:23
Webster 80	1	33N13'03	88w59'01	5:55:56
Weir 10	1	33N16'00	89w17'27	5:57:10
Wellman 43	1	31N27'30	90w21'38	6:01:27
Wells 44	1	33N35'52	88w23'40	5:53:35
Wells 61	2	32N19'15	90w06'28	6:00:26
Wells Town 37	1	31N01'22	89w28'29	5:57:54
Wenasoga 2	1	34N59'13	88w35'26	5:54:22
Wesson 15	1	31N42'04	90w23'51	6:01:35
West 26	1	33N11'49	89w46'38	5:59:07
West 38	1	32N28	88w40	5:54:40
West Biloxi 24	1	30N25	88w55	5:55:40
West Days 17	1	34N54'41	90w05'45	6:00:23
Westfield 26	1	33N07'33	90w15'39	6:01:03
West Gulfport 24	1	30N24'14	89w05'39	5:56:23
West Hill 26	1	33N06'08	89w54'53	5:59:40
West Jackson 25	2	32N19	90w11	6:00:44
West King 77	1	31N45'02	88w42'03	5:54:48
Westland 25	2	32N19	90w11	6:00:44
West Lincoln 43	1	31N29'34	90w34'09	6:02:17
West Marks 60	1	34N15'53	90w18'19	6:01:13
West Point 13	1	33N36'27	88w39'01	5:54:36
West Poplarville 55	1	30N50'03	89w34'17	5:58:17
Westside 11	1	31N54'18	91w07'43	6:04:31
West Union 73	1	34N33	89w07	5:56:28
Whaley 8	1	33N37'25	90w06'22	6:00:25
Wheeler 59	1	34N34'49	88w36'27	5:54:26
Whistle 77	1	31N41'49	88w48'16	5:55:13
White Apple 19	1	31N27'25	91w04'27	6:04:18
White Bluff 46	1	31N21'53	89w57'57	5:59:52
Whitebury 44	1	33N25'46	88w22'35	5:53:30
White Cap 3	1	31N12'55	90w58'28	6:03:54
Whitehead 68	1	33N50'55	90w17'55	6:01:12
White House Landing 63	1	32N56'01	90w45'37	6:03:02
White Oak 65	1	32N04'14	89w41'16	5:58:45
Whites 13	1	33N39'37	88w37'15	5:54:29
Whites 61	1	32N05'11	90w11'33	6:00:46
Whitesand 33	1	31N36'04	89w55'06	5:59:40
White Sand 55	1	30N47'57	89w39'29	5:58:38
Whites Crossing 66	1	30N50'53	89w02'25	5:56:10
Whitfield 34	1	31N26'42	89w04'28	5:56:18
Whitfield 61	1	32N14'07	90w04'19	6:00:17
Whitney 67	1	33N50'52	90w30'58	6:02:04
Whittaker 79	1	31N01'31	91w06'13	6:04:25
Whitten Town 70	1	34N46'37	89w03'33	5:56:14
Whynot 38	1	32N28	88w40	5:54:40
Wickware 51	1	32N19	89w10	5:56:40
Wiggins 40	1	32N42'07	89w38'12	5:58:33
Wiggins 66	1	30N51'29	89w08'07	5:56:32
Wildwood 42	1	33N37'09	90w14'28	6:00:58
Wilkinson 43	1	31N23'25	90w24'34	6:01:38
Wilkinson 79	1	31N13'20	91w14'20	6:04:57
Willet 76	1	33N07'13	90w45'03	6:03:00
Williams 10	1	33N23'40	89w10'11	5:56:41
Williams 43	1	31N33'11	90w36'56	6:02:28
Williamsburg 16	1	31N37'09	89w36'38	5:58:27
Williamsville 4	1	33N01'36	89w34'01	5:58:16
Williamsville 50	1	32N45'32	89w08'37	5:56:34
Willing 15	1	31N57'39	90w36'15	6:02:25
Willis Heights 41	1	34N15	88w43	5:54:52
Willowood 25	2	32N19	90w11	6:00:44
Willows 11	1	32N02'10	90w53'46	6:03:35
Wilmot 76	1	33N18'18	90w53'33	6:03:34
Wiltshire 8	1	33N20	89w45	5:59:00
Winborn 5	1	34N37'52	89w16'23	5:57:06
Winchester 77	1	31N37'03	88w35'26	5:54:22
Windsor Park 30	1	30N26	88w49	5:55:16
Wingate 56	1	31N12'09	89w00'05	5:56:00
Winona 49	1	33N28'55	89w43'41	5:58:55
Winstonville 6	1	33N54'36	90w45'05	6:03:00
Winterville 76	1	33N30'06	91w03'30	6:04:14
Wise Gap 48	1	33N53'56	88w19'54	5:53:20
Wisner 65	1	31N50'30	89w28'14	5:57:53
Wolf Springs 38	1	32N28	88w40	5:54:40
Woodburn 67	1	33N27	90w39	6:02:36
Woodland 9	1	33N46'43	89w03'05	5:56:12
Woodland 58	1	34N09'36	88w53'53	5:55:36
Woodland Lake 17	1	34N50	89w59	5:59:56
Woodlawn 75	1	32N22'35	90w48'38	6:03:15
Woodlawn 82	1	32N51'39	90w16'50	6:01:07
Woodside 76	1	33N00'55	90w58'28	6:03:54
Wood Springs 10	1	33N26'17	89w21'34	5:57:26
Woodville 79	1	31N06'16	91w17'58	6:05:12
Woodwards 77	1	31N41'37	88w39'50	5:54:39
Wool Market 24	1	30N29	89w01	5:56:04
Woolworth 43	1	31N37'59	90w16'24	6:01:06
Wortham 24	1	30N33'16	89w07'57	5:56:32
Wren 48	1	33N58'18	88w35'59	5:54:24
Wright 6	1	33N53'04	90w59'55	6:04:00
Wyatt 26	1	33N13'59	90w13'13	6:00:53
Wyatte 69	1	34N38'30	89w41'39	5:58:47
X-Prairie 52	1	33N08'49	88w27'53	5:53:52
Yazoo City 82	1	32N51'18	90w24'20	6:01:37
Yazoo Junction 82	1	32N53'17	90w23'22	6:01:33
Yocona 36	1	34N16'41	89w24'53	5:57:40
Yokena 75	1	32N10'30	90w56'31	6:03:46
Young 55	1	30N59'52	89w22'09	5:57:29
Youngs 22	1	33N51'11	89w32'04	5:58:08
Youngton 75	1	32N26'51	90w37'13	6:02:29
Zama 4	1	32N58'30	89w22'48	5:57:31
Zeiglerville 82	1	32N57'01	90w10'12	6:00:41
Zelleria 82	1	32N57'49	90w20'58	6:01:24
Zemuly 4	1	32N56'57	89w43'18	5:58:53
Zero 38	1	32N18'00	88w39'02	5:54:36
Zetus 43	1	31N33'49	90w31'46	6:02:07
Zieglerville 82	1	32N50	90w15	6:01:00
Zion 58	1	34N12'21	88w53'10	5:55:33
Zion Hill 3	1	31N18'53	90w49'36	6:03:18
Zumbro 6	1	33N46'46	90w40'34	6:02:42

TIME TABLES

MO # 1

Before 11/18/1883		LMT
11/18/1883	12:00	CST
3/31/1918	02:00	CWT
10/27/1918	02:00	CST
3/30/1919	02:00	CWT
10/26/1919	02:00	CST
2/09/1942	02:00	CWT
9/30/1945	02:00	CST
4/28/1946	02:00	CDT
9/29/1946	02:00	CST
4/27/1947	02:00	CDT
9/28/1947	02:00	CST
4/25/1948	02:00	CDT
9/26/1948	02:00	CST
4/24/1949	02:00	CDT
9/25/1949	02:00	CST
4/30/1950	02:00	CDT
9/24/1950	02:00	CST
4/29/1951	02:00	CDT
9/30/1951	02:00	CST
4/27/1952	02:00	CDT
9/28/1952	02:00	CST
4/26/1953	02:00	CDT
9/27/1953	02:00	CST
4/25/1954	02:00	CDT
9/26/1954	02:00	CST
4/24/1955	02:00	CDT
9/25/1955	02:00	CST
4/29/1956	02:00	CDT
10/28/1956	02:00	CST
4/28/1957	02:00	CDT
10/27/1957	02:00	CST
4/27/1958	02:00	CDT
10/26/1958	02:00	CST
4/26/1959	02:00	CDT
10/25/1959	02:00	CST
4/24/1960	02:00	CDT
10/30/1960	02:00	CST
4/30/1961	02:00	CDT
10/29/1961	02:00	CST
4/29/1962	02:00	CDT
10/28/1962	02:00	CST
4/28/1963	02:00	CDT
10/27/1963	02:00	CST
4/26/1964	02:00	CDT
10/25/1964	02:00	CST
4/25/1965	02:00	CDT
10/31/1965	02:00	CST
4/24/1966	02:00	CDT
10/30/1966	02:00	CST
4/30/1967	02:00	US#1

MO # 2

Before 11/18/1883		LMT
11/18/1883	12:00	CST
3/31/1918	02:00	CWT
10/27/1918	02:00	CST
3/30/1919	02:00	CWT
10/26/1919	02:00	CST
2/09/1942	02:00	CWT
9/30/1945	02:00	CST
4/27/1947	02:00	CDT
9/28/1947	02:00	CST
4/25/1948	02:00	CDT
9/26/1948	02:00	CST
4/24/1949	02:00	CDT
9/25/1949	02:00	CST
4/30/1950	02:00	CDT
9/24/1950	02:00	CST
4/29/1951	02:00	CDT
9/30/1951	02:00	CST
4/27/1952	02:00	CDT
9/28/1952	02:00	CST
4/26/1953	02:00	CDT
9/27/1953	02:00	CST
4/25/1954	02:00	CDT
9/26/1954	02:00	CST
4/24/1955	02:00	CDT
9/25/1955	02:00	CST
4/29/1956	02:00	CDT
9/30/1956	02:00	CST
4/28/1957	02:00	MO#1
4/30/1967	02:00	US#1

MO # 3

Before 11/18/1883		LMT
11/18/1883	12:00	CST
3/31/1918	02:00	CWT
10/27/1918	02:00	CST
3/30/1919	02:00	CWT
10/26/1919	02:00	CST
2/09/1942	02:00	CWT
9/30/1945	02:00	CST
4/30/1967	02:00	US#1

MO # 4

Before 11/18/1883		LMT
11/18/1883	12:00	CST
3/31/1918	02:00	CWT
10/27/1918	02:00	CST
3/30/1919	02:00	CWT
10/26/1919	02:00	CST
2/09/1942	02:00	CWT
9/30/1945	02:00	CST
4/24/1949	02:00	CDT
9/25/1949	02:00	CST
4/26/1953	02:00	CDT
9/27/1953	02:00	CST
4/27/1958	02:00	CDT
10/26/1958	02:00	CST
4/29/1962	02:00	MO#1
4/30/1967	02:00	US#1

MO # 5

Before 11/18/1883		LMT
11/18/1883	12:00	CST
3/31/1918	02:00	CWT
10/27/1918	02:00	CST
3/30/1919	02:00	CWT
10/26/1919	02:00	CST
2/09/1942	02:00	CWT
9/30/1945	02:00	CST
4/25/1954	02:00	CDT
9/26/1954	02:00	CST
4/24/1955	02:00	CDT
9/25/1955	02:00	CST
4/29/1956	02:00	CDT
9/30/1956	02:00	CST
4/28/1957	02:00	CDT
10/27/1957	02:00	CST
4/27/1958	02:00	CDT
10/26/1958	02:00	CST
4/26/1959	02:00	CDT
10/25/1959	02:00	CST
4/30/1967	02:00	US#1

MO # 6

Before 11/18/1883		LMT
11/18/1883	12:00	CST
3/31/1918	02:00	CWT
10/27/1918	02:00	CST
3/30/1919	02:00	CWT
10/26/1919	02:00	CST
2/09/1942	02:00	CWT
9/30/1945	02:00	CST
4/25/1954	02:00	CDT
9/26/1954	02:00	CST
4/29/1956	02:00	MO#1
4/30/1967	02:00	US#1

MO # 7

Before 11/18/1883		LMT
11/18/1883	12:00	CST
3/31/1918	02:00	CWT
10/27/1918	02:00	CST
3/30/1919	02:00	CWT
10/26/1919	02:00	CST
2/09/1942	02:00	CWT
9/30/1945	02:00	CST
4/25/1954	02:00	CDT
9/26/1954	02:00	CST
4/26/1964	02:00	MO#1
4/30/1967	02:00	US#1

MO # 8

Before 11/18/1883		LMT
11/18/1883	12:00	CST
3/31/1918	02:00	CWT
10/27/1918	02:00	CST
3/30/1919	02:00	CWT
10/26/1919	02:00	CST
2/09/1942	02:00	CWT
9/30/1945	02:00	CST
4/24/1955	02:00	MO#2
4/30/1967	02:00	US#1

MO # 9

Before 11/18/1883		LMT
11/18/1883	12:00	CST
3/31/1918	02:00	CWT
10/27/1918	02:00	CST
3/30/1919	02:00	CWT
10/26/1919	02:00	CST
2/09/1942	02:00	CWT
9/30/1945	02:00	CST
4/29/1956	02:00	CDT
9/30/1956	02:00	CST
4/30/1967	02:00	US#1

MO # 10

Before 11/18/1883		LMT
11/18/1883	12:00	CST
3/31/1918	02:00	CWT
10/27/1918	02:00	CST
3/30/1919	02:00	CWT
10/26/1919	02:00	CST
2/09/1942	02:00	CWT
9/30/1945	02:00	CST
4/29/1956	02:00	CDT
9/30/1956	02:00	CST
4/28/1957	02:00	CDT
10/27/1957	02:00	CST
4/24/1966	02:00	CDT
10/30/1966	02:00	CST
4/30/1967	02:00	US#1

MO # 11

Before 11/18/1883		LMT
11/18/1883	12:00	CST
3/31/1918	02:00	CWT
10/27/1918	02:00	CST
3/30/1919	02:00	CWT
10/26/1919	02:00	CST
2/09/1942	02:00	CWT
9/30/1945	02:00	CST
4/29/1956	02:00	CDT
9/30/1956	02:00	CST
4/27/1958	02:00	CDT
10/26/1958	02:00	CST
4/30/1967	02:00	US#1

MO # 12

Before 11/18/1883		LMT
11/18/1883	12:00	CST
3/31/1918	02:00	CWT
10/27/1918	02:00	CST
3/30/1919	02:00	CWT
10/26/1919	02:00	CST
2/09/1942	02:00	CWT
9/30/1945	02:00	CST
4/29/1956	02:00	MO#2
4/30/1967	02:00	US#1

MO # 13

Before 11/18/1883		LMT
11/18/1883	12:00	CST
3/31/1918	02:00	CWT
10/27/1918	02:00	CST
3/30/1919	02:00	CWT
10/26/1919	02:00	CST
2/09/1942	02:00	CWT
9/30/1945	02:00	CST
4/27/1958	02:00	CDT
10/26/1958	02:00	CST
4/30/1967	02:00	US#1

MO # 14

Before 11/18/1883		LMT
11/18/1883	12:00	CST
3/31/1918	02:00	CWT
10/27/1918	02:00	CST
3/30/1919	02:00	CWT
10/26/1919	02:00	CST
2/09/1942	02:00	CWT
9/30/1945	02:00	CST
4/26/1959	02:00	CDT
10/25/1959	02:00	CST
4/24/1960	02:00	CDT
10/30/1960	02:00	CST
4/29/1962	02:00	CDT
10/28/1962	02:00	CST
4/28/1963	02:00	CDT
10/27/1963	02:00	CST
4/26/1964	02:00	CDT
10/25/1964	02:00	CST
4/24/1966	02:00	US#1

MO # 15

Before 11/18/1883		LMT
11/18/1883	12:00	CST
3/31/1918	02:00	CWT
10/27/1918	02:00	CST
3/30/1919	02:00	CWT
10/26/1919	02:00	CST
2/09/1942	02:00	CWT
9/30/1945	02:00	CST
4/26/1959	02:00	CDT
10/25/1959	02:00	CST
4/28/1963	02:00	MO#1
4/30/1967	02:00	US#1

MO # 16

Before 11/18/1883		LMT
11/18/1883	12:00	CST
3/31/1918	02:00	CWT
10/27/1918	02:00	CST
3/30/1919	02:00	CWT
10/26/1919	02:00	CST
2/09/1942	02:00	CWT
9/30/1945	02:00	CST
4/26/1959	02:00	MO#1
4/30/1967	02:00	US#1

MO # 17

Before 11/18/1883		LMT
11/18/1883	12:00	CST
3/31/1918	02:00	CWT
10/27/1918	02:00	CST
3/30/1919	02:00	CWT
10/26/1919	02:00	CST
2/09/1942	02:00	CWT
9/30/1945	02:00	CST
4/24/1960	02:00	MO#1
4/30/1967	02:00	US#1

MO # 18

Before 11/18/1883		LMT
11/18/1883	12:00	CST
3/31/1918	02:00	CWT
10/27/1918	02:00	CST
3/30/1919	02:00	CWT
10/26/1919	02:00	CST
2/09/1942	02:00	CWT
9/30/1945	02:00	CST
4/24/1960	02:00	CDT
10/30/1960	02:00	CST
4/28/1963	02:00	CDT
10/27/1963	02:00	CST
4/30/1967	02:00	US#1

MO # 19

Before 11/18/1883		LMT
11/18/1883	12:00	CST
3/31/1918	02:00	CWT
10/27/1918	02:00	CST
3/30/1919	02:00	CWT
10/26/1919	02:00	CST
2/09/1942	02:00	CWT
9/30/1945	02:00	CST
4/25/1965	02:00	CDT
10/31/1965	02:00	CST
4/30/1967	02:00	US#1

MO # 20

Before 11/18/1883		LMT
11/18/1883	12:00	CST
3/31/1918	02:00	CWT
10/27/1918	02:00	CST
3/30/1919	02:00	CWT
10/26/1919	02:00	CST
2/09/1942	02:00	CWT
9/30/1945	02:00	CST
4/25/1965	02:00	CDT
9/05/1965	02:00	CST
4/24/1966	02:00	US#1

MO # 21

Before 11/18/1883		LMT
11/18/1883	12:00	CST
3/31/1918	02:00	CWT
10/27/1918	02:00	CST
3/30/1919	02:00	CWT
10/26/1919	02:00	CST
2/09/1942	02:00	CWT
9/30/1945	02:00	CST
4/29/1962	02:00	CDT
9/30/1962	02:00	CST
4/28/1963	02:00	CDT
9/08/1963	02:00	CST
4/26/1964	02:00	CDT
9/06/1964	02:00	CST
4/25/1965	02:00	CDT
10/03/1965	02:00	CST
4/24/1966	02:00	US#1

MO # 22

Before 11/18/1883		LMT
11/18/1883	12:00	CST
3/31/1918	02:00	CWT
10/27/1918	02:00	CST
3/30/1919	02:00	CWT
10/26/1919	02:00	CST
2/09/1942	02:00	CWT
9/30/1945	02:00	CST
4/28/1963	02:00	CDT
9/08/1963	02:00	CST
4/26/1964	02:00	CDT
9/28/1964	02:00	CST
4/30/1967	02:00	US#1

MO # 23

Before 11/18/1883		LMT
11/18/1883	12:00	CST
3/31/1918	02:00	CWT
10/27/1918	02:00	CST
3/30/1919	02:00	CWT
10/26/1919	02:00	CST
2/09/1942	02:00	CWT
9/30/1945	02:00	CST
4/30/1961	02:00	CDT
10/29/1961	02:00	CST
4/29/1962	02:00	CDT
10/28/1962	02:00	CST
4/28/1963	02:00	CDT
8/31/1963	02:00	CST
4/26/1964	02:00	CDT
8/29/1964	02:00	CST
4/30/1967	02:00	US#1

MO # 24

Before 11/18/1883		LMT
11/18/1883	12:00	CST
3/31/1918	02:00	CWT
10/27/1918	02:00	CST
3/30/1919	02:00	CWT
10/26/1919	02:00	CST
2/09/1942	02:00	CWT
9/30/1945	02:00	CST
4/24/1960	02:00	CDT
10/30/1960	02:00	CST
4/29/1962	02:00	CDT
9/30/1962	02:00	CST
4/28/1963	02:00	CDT
9/08/1963	02:00	CST
4/26/1964	02:00	CDT
9/06/1964	02:00	CST
4/25/1965	02:00	CDT
10/03/1965	02:00	CST
4/24/1966	02:00	US#1

MO # 25

Before 11/18/1883		LMT
11/18/1883	12:00	CST
3/31/1918	02:00	CWT
10/27/1918	02:00	CST
3/30/1919	02:00	CWT
10/26/1919	02:00	CST
2/09/1942	02:00	CWT
9/30/1945	02:00	CST
4/24/1960	02:00	CDT
10/30/1960	02:00	CST
4/29/1962	02:00	CDT
9/30/1962	02:00	CST
4/28/1963	02:00	CDT
10/26/1963	02:00	CST
4/26/1964	02:00	MO#1
4/30/1967	02:00	US#1

MO # 26

Before 11/18/1883		LMT
11/18/1883	12:00	CST
3/31/1918	02:00	CWT
10/27/1918	02:00	CST
3/30/1919	02:00	CWT
10/26/1919	02:00	CST
2/09/1942	02:00	CWT
9/30/1945	02:00	CST
4/28/1963	02:00	CDT
9/01/1963	02:00	CST
5/01/1964	02:00	CDT
9/01/1964	02:00	CST
5/07/1965	02:00	CDT
9/05/1965	02:00	CST
4/24/1966	02:00	US#1

MO # 27

Before 11/18/1883		LMT
11/18/1883	12:00	CST
3/31/1918	02:00	CWT
10/27/1918	02:00	CST
3/30/1919	02:00	CWT
10/26/1919	02:00	CST
2/09/1942	02:00	CWT
9/30/1945	02:00	CST
4/24/1960	02:00	CDT
10/30/1960	02:00	CST
4/30/1961	02:00	CDT
9/10/1961	02:00	CST
4/29/1962	02:00	CDT
9/09/1962	02:00	CST
4/28/1963	02:00	CDT
9/08/1963	02:00	CST
4/26/1964	02:00	CDT
9/13/1964	02:00	CST
4/25/1965	02:00	CDT
9/12/1965	02:00	CST
4/24/1966	02:00	CDT
9/11/1966	02:00	CST
4/30/1967	02:00	US#1

MO # 28

Before 11/18/1883		LMT
11/18/1883	12:00	CST
3/31/1918	02:00	CWT
10/27/1918	02:00	CST
3/30/1919	02:00	CWT
10/26/1919	02:00	CST
2/09/1942	02:00	CWT
9/30/1945	02:00	CST
4/26/1964	02:00	CDT
10/31/1964	02:00	CST
4/25/1965	02:00	MO#1
4/30/1967	02:00	US#1

MO # 29

Before 11/18/1883		LMT
11/18/1883	12:00	CST
3/31/1918	02:00	CWT
10/27/1918	02:00	CST
3/30/1919	02:00	CWT
10/26/1919	02:00	CST
2/09/1942	02:00	CWT
9/30/1945	02:00	CST
4/26/1964	02:00	CDT
9/06/1964	02:00	CST
4/30/1967	02:00	US#1

MO # 30

Before 11/18/1883		LMT
11/18/1883	12:00	CST
3/31/1918	02:00	CWT
10/27/1918	02:00	CST
3/30/1919	02:00	CWT
10/26/1919	02:00	CST
2/09/1942	02:00	CWT
9/30/1945	02:00	CST
4/30/1961	02:00	CDT
10/29/1961	02:00	CST
5/20/1962	02:00	CDT
8/25/1962	02:00	CST
5/19/1963	02:00	CDT
8/25/1963	02:00	CST
5/17/1964	02:00	CDT
9/01/1964	02:00	CST
5/23/1965	02:00	CDT
9/04/1965	02:00	CST
4/24/1966	02:00	US#1

MO # 31

Before 11/18/1883		LMT
11/18/1883	12:00	CST
3/31/1918	02:00	CWT
10/27/1918	02:00	CST
3/30/1919	02:00	CWT
10/26/1919	02:00	CST
2/09/1942	02:00	CWT
9/30/1945	02:00	CST
4/25/1954	02:00	CDT
9/26/1954	02:00	CST
4/28/1963	02:00	MO#1
4/30/1967	02:00	US#1

MO # 32

Before 11/18/1883		LMT
11/18/1883	12:00	CST
3/31/1918	02:00	CWT
10/27/1918	02:00	CST
3/30/1919	02:00	CWT
10/26/1919	02:00	CST
2/09/1942	02:00	CWT
9/30/1945	02:00	CST
5/17/1964	02:00	CDT
9/01/1964	02:00	CST
5/23/1965	02:00	CDT
8/22/1965	02:00	CST
5/22/1966	02:00	CDT
8/27/1966	02:00	CST
4/30/1967	02:00	US#1

MO # 33

Before 11/18/1883		LMT
11/18/1883	12:00	CST
3/31/1918	02:00	CWT
10/27/1918	02:00	CST
3/30/1919	02:00	CWT
10/26/1919	02:00	CST
2/09/1942	02:00	CWT
9/30/1945	02:00	CST
4/29/1962	02:00	CDT
9/09/1962	02:00	CST
4/28/1963	02:00	CDT
9/29/1963	02:00	CST
5/17/1964	02:00	CDT
9/01/1964	02:00	CST
4/25/1965	02:00	CDT
10/31/1965	02:00	CST
4/24/1966	02:00	CDT
9/24/1966	02:00	CST
4/30/1967	02:00	US#1

MO # 34

Before 11/18/1883		LMT
11/18/1883	12:00	CST
3/31/1918	02:00	CWT
10/27/1918	02:00	CST
3/30/1919	02:00	CWT
10/26/1919	02:00	CST
2/09/1942	02:00	CWT
9/30/1945	02:00	CST
4/28/1963	02:00	CDT
10/27/1963	02:00	CST
5/18/1964	02:00	CDT
9/01/1964	02:00	CST
5/22/1965	02:00	CDT
8/28/1965	02:00	CST
4/24/1966	02:00	CDT
10/30/1966	02:00	CST
4/30/1967	02:00	US#1

TIME TABLES

MO # 35		
Before 11/18/1883		LMT
11/18/1883	12:00	CST
3/31/1918	02:00	CWT
10/27/1918	02:00	CST
3/30/1919	02:00	CWT
10/26/1919	02:00	CST
2/09/1942	02:00	CWT
9/30/1945	02:00	CST
4/30/1961	02:00	CDT
9/09/1961	02:00	CST
4/29/1962	02:00	CDT
9/30/1962	02:00	CST
4/28/1963	02:00	CDT
9/08/1963	02:00	CST
4/26/1964	02:00	CDT
9/28/1964	02:00	CST
4/25/1965	02:00	MO#1
4/30/1967	02:00	US#1

MO # 36		
Before 11/18/1883		LMT
11/18/1883	12:00	CST
3/31/1918	02:00	CWT
10/27/1918	02:00	CST
3/30/1919	02:00	CWT
10/26/1919	02:00	CST
2/09/1942	02:00	CWT
9/30/1945	02:00	CST
4/25/1965	02:00	CDT
9/05/1965	02:00	CST
4/24/1966	02:00	CDT
10/30/1966	02:00	CST
4/30/1967	02:00	US#1

MO # 37		
Before 11/18/1883		LMT
11/18/1883	12:00	CST
3/31/1918	02:00	CWT
10/27/1918	02:00	CST
3/30/1919	02:00	CWT
10/26/1919	02:00	CST
2/09/1942	02:00	CWT
9/30/1945	02:00	CST
4/24/1960	02:00	CDT
10/30/1960	02:00	CST
4/29/1962	02:00	CDT
9/02/1962	02:00	CST
4/26/1964	02:00	CDT
9/06/1964	02:00	CST
4/25/1965	02:00	CDT
9/05/1965	02:00	CST
4/24/1966	02:00	CDT
9/04/1966	02:00	CST
4/30/1967	02:00	US#1

MO # 38		
Before 11/18/1883		LMT
11/18/1883	12:00	CST
3/31/1918	02:00	CWT
10/27/1918	02:00	CST
3/30/1919	02:00	CWT
10/26/1919	02:00	CST
2/09/1942	02:00	CWT
9/30/1945	02:00	CST
4/28/1963	02:00	CDT
9/29/1963	02:00	CST
4/26/1964	02:00	CDT
9/27/1964	02:00	CST
4/30/1965	02:00	CDT
10/31/1965	02:00	CST
4/24/1966	02:00	US#1

MO # 39		
Before 11/18/1883		LMT
11/18/1883	12:00	CST
3/31/1918	02:00	CWT
10/27/1918	02:00	CST
3/30/1919	02:00	CWT
10/26/1919	02:00	CST
2/09/1942	02:00	CWT
9/30/1945	02:00	CST
4/24/1960	02:00	CDT
10/30/1960	02:00	CST
4/29/1962	02:00	CDT
9/09/1962	02:00	CST
4/28/1963	02:00	CDT
9/08/1963	02:00	CST
4/26/1964	02:00	CDT
9/13/1964	02:00	CST
4/25/1965	02:00	CDT
9/05/1965	02:00	CST
4/24/1966	02:00	CDT
9/11/1966	02:00	CST
4/30/1967	02:00	US#1

MO # 40		
Before 11/18/1883		LMT
11/18/1883	12:00	CST
3/31/1918	02:00	CWT
10/27/1918	02:00	CST
3/30/1919	02:00	CWT
10/26/1919	02:00	CST
2/09/1942	02:00	CWT
9/30/1945	02:00	CST
4/28/1963	02:00	MO#1
4/30/1967	02:00	US#1

MO # 41		
Before 11/18/1883		LMT
11/18/1883	12:00	CST
3/31/1918	02:00	CWT
10/27/1918	02:00	CST
3/30/1919	02:00	CWT
10/26/1919	02:00	CST
2/09/1942	02:00	CWT
9/30/1945	02:00	CST
4/28/1963	02:00	CDT
9/08/1963	02:00	CST
4/26/1964	02:00	CDT
9/13/1964	02:00	CST
4/30/1967	02:00	US#1

MO # 42		
Before 11/18/1883		LMT
11/18/1883	12:00	CST
3/31/1918	02:00	CWT
10/27/1918	02:00	CST
3/30/1919	02:00	CWT
10/26/1919	02:00	CST
2/09/1942	02:00	CWT
9/30/1945	02:00	CST
4/28/1963	02:00	CDT
9/29/1963	02:00	CST
4/30/1965	02:00	CDT
10/31/1965	02:00	CST
4/24/1966	02:00	US#1

MO # 43		
Before 11/18/1883		LMT
11/18/1883	12:00	CST
3/31/1918	02:00	CWT
10/27/1918	02:00	CST
3/30/1919	02:00	CWT
10/26/1919	02:00	CST
2/09/1942	02:00	CWT
9/30/1945	02:00	CST
5/20/1962	02:00	CDT
8/25/1962	02:00	CST
5/15/1964	02:00	CDT
9/01/1964	02:00	CST
4/25/1965	02:00	CDT
9/05/1965	02:00	CST
4/24/1966	02:00	US#1

MO # 44		
Before 11/18/1883		LMT
11/18/1883	12:00	CST
3/31/1918	02:00	CWT
10/27/1918	02:00	CST
3/30/1919	02:00	CWT
10/26/1919	02:00	CST
2/09/1942	02:00	CWT
9/30/1945	02:00	CST
4/24/1966	02:00	US#1

MO # 45		
Before 11/18/1883		LMT
11/18/1883	12:00	CST
3/31/1918	02:00	CWT
10/27/1918	02:00	CST
3/30/1919	02:00	CWT
10/26/1919	02:00	CST
2/09/1942	02:00	CWT
9/30/1945	02:00	CST
4/24/1966	02:00	CDT
9/05/1966	02:00	CST
4/30/1967	02:00	US#1

MO # 46		
Before 11/18/1883		LMT
11/18/1883	12:00	CST
3/31/1918	02:00	CWT
10/27/1918	02:00	CST
3/30/1919	02:00	CWT
10/26/1919	02:00	CST
2/09/1942	02:00	CWT
9/30/1945	02:00	CST
4/26/1965	02:00	MO#1
4/30/1967	02:00	US#1

MO # 47		
Before 11/18/1883		LMT
11/18/1883	12:00	CST
3/31/1918	02:00	CWT
10/27/1918	02:00	CST
3/30/1919	02:00	CWT
10/26/1919	02:00	CST
2/09/1942	02:00	CWT
9/30/1945	02:00	CST
4/29/1956	02:00	CDT
9/30/1956	02:00	CST
4/24/1966	02:00	US#1

MO # 48		
Before 11/18/1883		LMT
11/18/1883	12:00	CST
3/31/1918	02:00	CWT
10/27/1918	02:00	CST
3/30/1919	02:00	CWT
10/26/1919	02:00	CST
2/09/1942	02:00	CWT
9/30/1945	02:00	CST
5/08/1956	02:00	CDT
9/30/1956	02:00	CST
4/30/1967	02:00	US#1

MO # 49		
Before 11/18/1883		LMT
11/18/1883	12:00	CST
3/31/1918	02:00	CWT
10/27/1918	02:00	CST
3/30/1919	02:00	CWT
10/26/1919	02:00	CST
2/09/1942	02:00	CWT
9/30/1945	02:00	CST
4/26/1964	02:00	CDT
10/25/1964	02:00	CST
4/30/1967	02:00	US#1

COUNTIES

1 Adair
2 Andrew
3 Atchison
4 Audrain
5 Barry
6 Barton
7 Bates
8 Benton
9 Bollinger
10 Boone
11 Buchanan
12 Butler
13 Caldwell
14 Callaway
15 Camden
16 Cape Girardeau
17 Carroll
18 Carter
19 Cass
20 Cedar
21 Chariton
22 Christian
23 Clark
24 Clay
25 Clinton
26 Cole
27 Cooper
28 Crawford
29 Dade
30 Dallas
31 Daviess
32 Dekalb
33 Dent
34 Douglas
35 Dunklin
36 Franklin
37 Gasconade
38 Gentry
39 Greene
40 Grundy
41 Harrison
42 Henry
43 Hickory
44 Holt
45 Howard
46 Howell
47 Iron
48 Jackson
49 Jasper
50 Jefferson
51 Johnson
52 Knox
53 Laclede
54 Lafayette
55 Lawrence
56 Lewis
57 Lincoln
58 Linn
59 Livingston
60 McDonald
61 Macon
62 Madison
63 Maries
64 Marion
65 Mercer
66 Miller
67 Mississippi
68 Moniteau
69 Monroe
70 Montgomery
71 Morgan
72 New Madrid
73 Newton
74 Nodaway
75 Oregon
76 Osage
77 Ozark
78 Pemiscot
79 Perry
80 Pettis
81 Phelps
82 Pike
83 Platte
84 Polk
85 Pulaski
86 Putnam
87 Ralls
88 Randolph
89 Ray
90 Reynolds
91 Ripley
92 St Charles
93 St Clair
94 St Francois
95 St Louis
96 Ste Genevieve
97 Saline
98 Schuyler
99 Scotland
100 Scott
101 Shannon
102 Shelby
103 Stoddard
104 Stone
105 Sullivan
106 Taney
107 Texas
108 Vernon
109 Warren
110 Washington
111 Wayne
112 Webster
113 Worth
114 Wright
115 St Louis City

Place		Latitude	Longitude	Time
Aaron 7	3	38N25'23	94W09'13	6:16:37
Abadyl 22	3	37N02'18	92W56'49	6:11:47
Abesville 104	3	36N50'23	93W22'14	6:13:29
Abo 53	47	37N41'52	92W27'54	6:09:52
Acorn Corner 78	3	36N05'18	89W46'14	5:59:05
Acorn Ridge 103	3	36N54'48	90W03'29	6:00:14
Adair 1	3	40N15'08	92W22'35	6:09:30
Adair 15	3	38N09	92W59	6:11:56
Adam Ford 53	3	37N37'42	92W19'43	6:09:19
Adonis 84	3	37N47'47	93W21'47	6:13:27
Adrian 7	3	38N23'51	94W21'05	6:17:24
Advance 103	3	37N06'16	89W54'38	5:59:39
Aeiker Ford 36	3	38N22'44	91W04'22	6:04:17
Affton 95	40	38N33'02	90W19'59	6:01:20
Agency 11	3	39N38'41	94W44'23	6:18:58
Agnes 53	47	37N30'44	92W29'54	6:10:00
Aholt 21	3	39N15'52	92W54'17	6:11:37
Aid 103	3	36N52'37	90W02'28	6:00:10
Aikinsville 71	3	38N33'29	92W50'10	6:11:21
Airline Acres 67	3	36N48'12	89W21'29	5:57:26
Air Line Junction 48	3	39N07'19	94W29'51	6:17:59
Airport 95	40	38N46	90W24	6:01:36
Airport Drive 49	3	37N08'33	94W30'38	6:18:03
Akers 101	3	37N22'34	91W33'13	6:06:13
Akron 41	3	40N31'10	93W49'02	6:15:16
Alanthus 38	3	40N13	94W32	6:18:08
Alanthus Grove 38	3	40N18'25	94W32'38	6:18:11
Alba 49	3	37N14'18	94W25'02	6:17:40
Albany 38	3	40N14'55	94W19'51	6:17:19
Albany 89	3	39N13'24	94W06'47	6:16:27
Albany Junction 38	3	40N13'37	94W22'08	6:17:29
Albatross 55	3	37N11'21	93W50'20	6:15:21
Alberta 42	3	38N21'50	93W40'10	6:14:41
Aldrich 84	3	37N32'51	93W33'16	6:14:13
Alexander 8	3	38N08	93W26	6:13:44
Alexandria 23	20	40N21'34	91W27'19	6:05:49
Alfalfa Center 67	3	36N57'47	89W12'26	5:56:50
Algonquin 95	40	38N36	90W20	6:01:20
Allbright 62	3	37N19'44	90W13'36	6:00:54
Allen 113	3	40N26	94W17	6:17:08
Allendale 113	3	40N29'08	94W17'18	6:17:09
Allen Ford 75	3	36N32'14	91W31'04	6:06:04
Allenton 95	40	38N30'13	90W40'33	6:02:42
Allenville 16	3	37N13'18	89W45'27	5:59:02
Alley Spring 101	3	37N08'39	91W26'38	6:05:47
Alliance 9	3	37N33'44	89W59'48	5:59:59
All Saints Village 92	2	38N45'38	90W39'41	6:02:39
Alma 54	3	39N05'43	93W32'42	6:14:11
Almartha 77	3	36N45'51	92W31'01	6:10:04
Almon 43	3	37N57	93W13	6:12:52
Alpha 40	3	39N59'07	93W25'15	6:13:41
Alpine 104	3	36N38	93W33	6:14:12
Altamont 31	3	39N53'19	94W05'20	6:16:21
Altenburg 79	3	37N37'51	89W35'07	5:58:20
Altheim 95	40	38N37'53	90W29'16	6:01:57
Alton 75	3	36N41'39	91W23'57	6:05:36
Altona 7	3	38N23'59	94W14'05	6:16:56
Amazonia 2	3	39N53'10	94W53'30	6:19:34
Americus 70	3	38N46'49	91W33'50	6:06:15
Amity 32	3	39N52'15	94W26'08	6:17:45
Amoret 7	3	38N15'19	94W35'15	6:18:21
Amos 108	3	38N00'57	94W34'48	6:18:19
Amsterdam 7	3	38N20'59	94W35'20	6:18:21
Amy 46	3	36N36'20	92W00'13	6:08:01
Anabel 61	45	39N44'45	92W19'59	6:09:20
Anaconda 36	17	38N18'06	91W02'26	6:04:10
Ancell 100	3	37N13	89W31	5:58:04
Anderson 60	3	36N39'02	94W26'36	6:17:46
Andover 41	3	40N33'54	93W53'42	6:15:35
Angus 12	3	36N38'04	90W29'01	6:01:56
Ann 34	3	37N01'51	92W11'50	6:08:47
Annada 82	21	39N15'40	90W49'39	6:03:19
Annapolis 47	3	37N21'37	90W41'51	6:02:47
Anniston 67	3	36N49'33	89W19'40	5:57:19
Anson 23	3	40N34'38	91W45'57	6:07:04
Anthonies Mill 110	46	38N04'47	91W05'10	6:04:21
Antioch 23	30	40N19'29	91W41'35	6:06:46
Antioch 24	3	39N12	94W32	6:18:08
Antonia 50	3	38N21'45	90W27'56	6:01:52
Anutt 33	3	37N42'57	91W43'11	6:06:53
Apache Flats 26	3	38N35'01	92W17'58	6:09:12
Apex 57	3	39N06'39	90W45'18	6:03:01
Apple Creek 16	3	37N32	89W46	5:59:04
Appleton (Old Appleton PO) 81	3	37N35'50	89W42'46	5:58:51
Appleton City 93	3	38N11'26	94W01'45	6:16:07
Aptus 110	3	38N02'25	90W50'54	6:03:24
Aquilla 103	3	36N56'49	89W54'53	5:59:40
Arab 9	3	37N05'37	90W04'36	6:00:18
Arbela 99	3	40N27'45	92W01'00	6:08:04
Arbor 16	3	37N09'33	89W48'08	5:59:13
Arbor Terrace 95	40	38N41'54	90W17'03	6:01:08
Arbyrd 35	3	36N03'03	90W14'19	6:00:57
Arcadia 47	3	37N35'17	90W37'44	6:02:31
Archie 19	3	38N28'54	94W21'15	6:17:25
Arcola 29	3	37N32'57	93W52'30	6:15:30
Ardath 6	3	37N36'36	94W36'18	6:18:25
Arden 34	3	36N59'07	92W48'16	6:11:13
Ardeola 103	3	37N00'04	89W51'10	5:59:25
Arditta 46	3	36N36'59	92W03'45	6:08:15
Ardmore 61	3	39N38'35	92W32'08	6:10:09
Argentville 57	16	39N00'58	90W47'53	6:03:12
Argo 37	46	38N11'02	91W19'49	6:05:19
Argyle 76	3	38N17'40	92W01'25	6:08:06
Arkmo 35	3	36N03	90W15	6:01:00
Arkoe 74	3	40N15'29	94W49'39	6:19:19

Arley 24 3 39N24'16 94W26'42 6:17:47
Arlington 81 3 37N55'13 91W58'15 6:07:53
Armour 11 3 39N32'55 95W02'46 6:20:11
Armstrong 45 3 39N16'11 92W42'04 6:10:48
Arnica 20 3 37N45'06 93W42'30 6:14:50
Arno 34 3 36N56'23 92W44'49 6:10:59
Arnold 50 3 38N25'58 90W22'39 6:01:31
Arnsberg 16 3 37N34'11 89W46'39 5:59:07
Aroma 73 44 36N51'49 94W15'52 6:17:03
Arroll 107 3 37N06'27 91W43'35 6:06:54
Arrowhead Beach 66 3 38N10'48 92W37'46 6:10:31
Arrow Rock 97 3 39N04'11 92W56'47 6:11:47
Arthur 108 3 38N00'47 94W22'09 6:17:29
Arthur Spring Ford 37 3 38N12'21 91W34'04 6:06:16
Asbury 49 3 37N16'28 94W36'19 6:18:25
Ascalon 95 40 38N42'03 90W24'34 6:01:38
Ash 5 3 36N33 94W02 6:16:08
Ash 69 3 39N30'54 92W17'23 6:09:10
Ashburn 82 22 39N32'41 91W10'07 6:04:40
Asherville 103 3 36N53'55 90W11'14 6:00:45
Ash Grove 39 3 37N18'55 93W35'06 6:14:20
Ash Hill 12 3 36N46'32 90W13'59 6:00:56
Ashland 10 3 38N46'28 92W15'25 6:09:02
Ashley 82 3 39N15'04 91W13'13 6:04:53
Ashley Creek 107 3 37N24'11 91W41'18 6:06:45
Ashton 23 3 40N26'46 91W48'27 6:07:14
Aspenhoff 109 3 38N42'05 91W09'05 6:04:36
Athens 23 3 40N34'57 91W41'54 6:06:48
Athens 38 3 40N14 94W18 6:17:12
Atherton 48 3 39N11'10 94W18'19 6:17:13
Athol 7 3 38N10'21 94W22'43 6:17:31
Athol 48 3 39N06'26 94W28'59 6:17:56
Atlanta 61 3 39N53'55 92W28'51 6:09:55
Atlas 49 3 37N05'42 94W23'09 6:17:33
Atwell 66 47 38N02'18 92W12'45 6:08:51
Auburn 57 25 39N07'36 90W58'26 6:03:54
Aud 76 3 38N34'49 91W43'14 6:06:53
Augusta 109 3 38N34'21 90W52'55 6:03:32
Aullville 54 3 39N01'04 93W40'40 6:14:43
Aurora 55 3 36N58'15 93W43'04 6:14:52
Aurora Springs 66 3 38N19'29 92W35'06 6:10:20
Austin 19 3 38N30'10 94W17'59 6:17:12
Austin 35 3 36N09'39 90W09'33 6:00:38
Auxvasse 14 3 39N01'05 91W53'49 6:07:35
Ava 34 3 36N57'07 92W39'37 6:10:38
Avalon 59 3 39N39'33 93W26'29 6:13:46
Avenue City 2 3 39N51'48 94W45'25 6:19:02
Avert 103 3 36N55'46 89W50'52 5:59:23
Avery 8 3 38N04'04 93W21'36 6:13:26
Avilla 49 3 37N11'43 94W07'46 6:16:31
Avon 19 3 38N49'49 94W18'56 6:17:16
Avon 96 3 37N45'05 90W13'24 6:00:54
Avondale 24 3 39N09'15 94W32'48 6:18:11
Axtell 61 3 39N49'28 92W28'22 6:09:53
Azen 99 3 40N33'35 92W02'17 6:08:09
Babbtown 76 3 38N20'20 92W08'18 6:08:33
Bachelor 14 3 38N59'36 91W46'19 6:07:05
Bacon 68 3 38N42'31 92W27'12 6:09:49
Bacon 108 3 37N59 94W07 6:16:28
Baden 115 1 38N42'20 90W13'48 6:00:55
Baderville 72 3 36N33'16 89W44'13 5:58:57
Badger 108 3 37N48 94W14 6:16:56
Bado 107 3 37N16'09 92W07'24 6:08:30
Bagnell 66 3 38N13'36 92W36'05 6:10:24
Bahner 80 3 38N34'10 93W07'42 6:12:31
Bainbridge 16 3 37N24'38 89W26'13 5:57:45
Baird 35 3 36N26'51 90W00'13 6:00:01
Baker 93 3 38N11'53 93W35'23 6:14:22
Baker 103 3 36N46'22 89W45'51 5:59:03
Bakersfield 77 3 36N31'21 92W08'31 6:08:34
Bakerville 78 3 36N14'02 89W55'04 5:59:40
Baldwin Lake 19 3 38N48 94W16 6:17:04
Baldwin Park 19 3 38N48 94W16 6:17:04
Ballard 7 3 38N21'41 94W08'35 6:16:34
Ballwin 95 40 38N35'42 90W32'46 6:02:11
Bancroft 31 3 40N07'09 93W51'30 6:15:26
Bangert 33 3 37N46'16 91W30'57 6:06:04
Banner 47 3 37N41'49 90W50'04 6:03:20
Bannister 15 3 38N02'06 92W59'17 6:11:57
Bannister Ford 15 3 38N02'30 92W59'05 6:11:56
Bardley 91 3 36N41'39 91W07'18 6:04:29
Baring 52 3 40N14'39 92W12'20 6:08:49
Barnard 74 3 40N10'28 94W49'25 6:19:18
Barnesville 25 3 39N30'15 94W13'52 6:16:55
Barnesville 61 3 39N53'58 92W35'23 6:10:22
Barnett 71 3 38N22'42 92W40'28 6:10:42
Barnhart 50 3 38N20'39 90W23'36 6:01:34
Barnumton 15 3 38N06'36 92W56'11 6:11:45
Barren Fork 77 3 36N44 92W30 6:10:00
Barretts 95 40 38N34'18 90W27'36 6:01:50
Barron 12 3 36N46'17 90W15'47 6:01:03
Barry 24 3 39N14'47 94W36'02 6:18:24
Bartlett 101 3 37N00'17 91W24'51 6:05:39
Barton City 6 3 37N36 94W26 6:17:44
Barwick 13 3 39N47 94W06 6:16:24
Basher 34 3 36N59'48 92W36'21 6:10:25
Bassinger Corner 4 3 39N16'51 91W38'39 6:06:35
Bassville 39 3 37N20'40 93W07'56 6:12:32
Bates City 54 3 39N00'22 94W04'20 6:16:17
Bates Corner 5 3 36N39'15 93W48'31 6:15:14
Bates Creek Camp 110 3 37N54'22 90W49'17 6:03:17
Batesville 12 3 36N41'56 90W14'46 6:00:59
Battlefield 39 3 37N06'56 93W22'12 6:13:29
Baxter 104 3 36N34 93W30 6:14:00
Bay 37 3 38N30'30 91W33'30 6:06:14
Bayfield 32 3 39N46'55 94W35'45 6:18:23
Bayou 77 3 36N34 92W11 6:08:44
Bayouville 72 3 36N39'04 89W21'51 5:57:27
Bayshore 50 3 38N26 90W23 6:01:32
Beach 112 3 37N25'52 92W57'32 6:11:50
Beal 101 3 37N06'49 91W05'45 6:04:23
Beaman 80 3 38N45'26 93W08'00 6:12:32
Bean Lake 83 3 39N35 95W01 6:20:04
Bearcreek 20 3 37N39'26 93W39'29 6:14:38
Beaufort 36 3 38N25'15 91W11'20 6:04:45
Beauvais 96 3 37N51 90W04 6:00:16

Beaver 106 3 36N44 92W53 6:11:32
Beaver Dam 12 3 36N42 90W32 6:02:08
Beck 50 3 38N24'42 90W22'58 6:01:32
Beckville 111 3 37N08'38 90W42'01 6:02:48
Bedford 57 3 39N00 91W00 6:04:00
Bedford 59 3 39N41'46 93W22'22 6:13:29
Bedison 74 3 40N17'36 94W46'27 6:19:06
Bee Branch 21 3 39N39 92W47 6:11:08
Beemont 36 3 38N28'50 91W21'33 6:05:26
Bee Ridge 52 3 40N05 92W07 6:08:28
Belew Creek 50 3 38N17'53 90W34'01 6:02:16
Belfast 73 44 36N51'59 94W27'15 6:17:49
Belgique 79 3 37N50'15 89W46'52 5:59:07
Belgrade 110 3 37N47'12 90W50'57 6:03:24
Bellair 27 3 38N49'59 92W50'39 6:11:23
Bellamy 108 3 37N41'06 94W10'49 6:16:43
Bella Villa 95 1 38N32'28 90W16'48 6:01:07
Bell City 103 3 37N01'25 89W49'11 5:59:17
Belle 63 3 38N17'09 91W43'13 6:06:53
Belle Center 49 3 37N06'04 94W34'57 6:18:20
Bellefontaine 95 40 38N39'25 90W33'16 6:02:13
Bellefontaine 110 3 37N59 90W41 6:02:44
Bellefontaine Neighbors 95 40 38N44'25 90W13'35 6:00:54
Bellerive 95 40 38N42'41 90W18'54 6:01:16
Bellerive Estates 95 40 38N40 90W26 6:01:44
Belleview 47 3 37N41'15 90W44'25 6:02:58
Belleville 49 3 37N07'28 94W35'25 6:18:22
Bellflower 70 3 39N00'24 91W21'18 6:05:25
Bell Ridge 95 40 38N42'33 90W19'33 6:01:18
Belmont Landing 67 3 36N45'59 89W07'18 5:56:29
Bel-Nor 95 40 38N42'07 90W19'01 6:01:16
Belton 19 3 38N48'43 94W31'54 6:18:08
Belvidere 48 3 38N51'29 94W31'26 6:18:06
Bem 37 3 38N15'57 91W28'11 6:05:53
Ben Avis 95 1 38N41 90W16 6:01:04
Benbow 64 3 39N54'54 91W44'38 6:06:59
Benbush 95 40 38N41'27 90W29'42 6:01:59
Bend 63 3 38N11'40 91W50'47 6:07:23
Bendavis 107 3 37N17'54 92W12'26 6:08:50
Benjamin 56 23 40N09'43 91W38'03 6:06:32
Bennett 91 3 36N44'01 91W00'16 6:04:01
Bennett Springs 53 3 37N43'37 92W51'20 6:11:25
Benton 100 3 37N05'52 89W33'45 5:58:15
Benton 115 1 38N37'07 90W18'12 6:01:13
Benton City 4 3 39N08'04 91W45'54 6:07:04
Benton Park 115 1 38N38 90W15 6:01:00
Bentonville 8 3 38N06'02 93W26'56 6:13:48
Berdell Hills 95 40 38N43'04 90W17'44 6:01:11
Berger 36 3 38N40'27 91W20'19 6:05:21
Berkeley 95 40 38N45'16 90W19'52 6:01:19
Berlin 38 3 40N03'13 94W21'03 6:17:24
Bernheimer 109 3 38N40'05 91W15'17 6:05:01
Bernie 103 3 36N40'08 89W58'07 5:59:52
Berry Ford 30 3 37N51'51 92W52'45 6:11:31
Berryman 28 3 37N55'08 91W05'43 6:04:23
Bertha 34 3 36N50'16 92W23'04 6:09:32
Bertrand 67 3 36N54'34 89W27'09 5:57:49
Berwick 73 3 36N55'59 94W05'40 6:16:23
Bessville 9 3 37N22'17 90W05'20 6:00:21
Bethany 35 3 36N36'42 90W04'09 6:00:17
Bethany 41 3 40N16'06 94W01'41 6:16:07
Bethel 102 3 39N52'36 92W01'26 6:08:06
Bethlehem 42 3 38N19 93W41 6:14:44
Bethlehem 60 3 36N43'15 94W07'56 6:16:32
Bethpage 60 3 36N41'24 94W14'10 6:16:57
Beulah 62 3 37N19'44 90W30'08 6:02:01
Beulah 81 3 37N37'27 91W55'01 6:07:40
Beverly 83 3 39N22'05 94W52'01 6:19:28
Beverly Hills 95 40 38N42'00 90W17'32 6:01:10
Bevier 61 44 39N44'49 92W33'50 6:10:15
Bible Grove 99 3 40N21'10 92W18'15 6:09:13
Bidwell 53 3 37N52'18 92W42'34 6:10:50
Biehle 79 3 37N36'19 89W50'28 5:59:22
Big Apple 75 3 36N37 91W37 6:06:28
Big Bend 63 47 38N03'15 92W01'56 6:08:08
Bigelow 44 3 40N06'38 95W17'22 6:21:09
Big Piney 85 3 37N40'19 92W05'52 6:08:23
Big Prairie 72 3 36N46 89W33 5:58:12
Big Ridge 72 3 36N46 89W35 5:58:20
Big Spring 70 3 38N48'09 91W28'39 6:05:55
Billings 22 3 37N04'03 93W33'07 6:14:12
Billingsville 27 3 38N54'11 92W47'39 6:11:11
Billmore 75 3 36N33'46 91W12'54 6:04:52
Binkley 61 3 39N38'36 92W32'52 6:10:11
Birch Tree 101 3 36N59'28 91W29'33 6:05:58
Birds Corner 103 3 36N53'23 89W45'49 5:59:03
Birds Corners 103 3 36N48 89W49 5:59:16
Birds Nest 28 3 37N59'51 91W21'33 6:05:26
Birdsong 93 3 37N51'58 93W43'51 6:14:55
Birds Point 67 3 36N57'57 89W09'23 5:56:38
Bird Springs 77 3 36N44'53 92W14'06 6:08:56
Birdtown 77 3 36N47 92W13 6:08:52
Birmingham 24 3 39N09'57 94W27'04 6:17:48
Bismarck 94 3 37N46'09 90W37'29 6:02:30
Bixby 47 3 37N39'37 91W06'54 6:04:28
Black 90 3 37N31'53 90W55'59 6:03:44
Blackburn 97 3 39N06'23 93W29'00 6:13:56
Black Creek 102 3 39N49 92W04 6:08:16
Blackjack 93 3 37N42 93W48 6:15:12
Black Jack 95 40 38N47'36 90W16'02 6:01:04
Black Oak 13 3 39N32'50 93W50'18 6:15:21
Black Pond 75 3 36N51 91W33 6:06:12
Black Walnut 92 18 38N52'24 90W22'16 6:01:29
Blackwater 27 3 38N58'49 92W59'26 6:11:58
Blackwell 94 3 38N02'37 90W37'26 6:02:30
Blairstown 42 49 38N33'21 93W57'38 6:15:51
Blake 31 3 39N56'49 93W52'15 6:15:29
Blanche 34 3 36N49'12 92W18'11 6:09:13
Bland 37 3 38N18'06 91W37'58 6:06:32
Blase 92 15 38N52'21 90W28'38 6:01:55
Blendville 49 3 37N04 94W30 6:18:00

Bliss 110 3 38N05'35 90W44'25 6:02:58
Blodgett 100 3 37N00'15 89W31'37 5:58:06
Blomeyer 16 3 37N13'26 89W39'35 5:58:38
Bloodland 85 3 37N41'14 92W09'07 6:08:36
Bloomfield 103 3 36N53'09 89W55'45 5:59:43
Blooming Rose 81 3 37N36'46 91W58'21 6:07:53
Bloomington 11 3 39N35 94W56 6:19:44
Bloomington 61 44 39N47'49 92W33'36 6:10:14
Bloomsdale 96 3 38N00'34 90W13'04 6:00:52
Blue Branch 8 3 38N14'08 93W21'25 6:13:26
Blue Eye 104 3 36N29'55 93W23'48 6:13:35
Blue Lick 97 3 39N00'48 93W12'36 6:12:50
Blue Mills 48 3 39N08'58 94W18'10 6:17:13
Blue Mound 59 3 39N37'40 93W33'28 6:14:14
Blue Ridge 41 3 40N11'32 93W56'07 6:15:44
Blue Springs 48 3 39N01'01 94W16'53 6:17:08
Blue Summit 48 3 39N05 94W29 6:17:56
Blue Vue 48 3 39N00 94W28 6:17:52
Bluffton 70 3 38N42'27 91W37'28 6:06:30
Blythedale 41 3 40N28'31 93W55'36 6:15:42
Boaz 22 3 37N01'07 93W24'01 6:13:36
Boekerton 72 3 36N24'14 89W45'43 5:59:03
Bogard 17 3 39N27'27 93W31'24 6:14:06
Bogle 38 3 40N21 94W24 6:17:36
Bois Brule 79 3 37N49 89W47 5:59:08
Bois d'Arc 39 3 37N15'26 93W30'26 6:14:02
Bolckow 2 3 40N06'47 94W49'19 6:19:17
Boles 36 3 38N31'51 90W53'24 6:03:34
Bolivar 84 3 37N36'52 93W24'37 6:13:38
Bollinger Mill 9 3 37N32'41 89W57'03 5:59:48
Bona 29 3 37N32'41 93W40'17 6:14:41
Bonanza 13 3 39N38'39 93W58'21 6:15:53
Bonfils 95 40 38N46'09 90W26'24 6:01:46
Bonham 55 3 36N56'32 93W38'04 6:14:32
Bonhomme 95 40 38N38 90W30 6:02:00
Bonne Femme 45 3 39N13 92W31 6:10:04
Bonne Terre 94 3 37N55'23 90W33'19 6:02:13
Bonnots Mill 76 3 38N34'41 91W57'56 6:07:52
Boonesboro 45 3 39N04'37 92W50'29 6:11:22
Boons Lick 45 3 39N04 92W52 6:11:28
Boonville 27 3 38N58'25 92W44'35 6:10:58
Boschertown 92 2 38N50'00 90W28'12 6:01:53
Bosky Dell 60 3 36N36'05 94W26'46 6:17:47
Boss 33 3 37N38'35 91W11'21 6:04:45
Boston 6 3 37N24'46 94W16'54 6:17:08
Bosworth 17 3 39N28'11 93W20'04 6:13:20
Boulder City 73 44 36N47'38 94W14'57 6:17:00
Boulware 37 3 38N30 91W33 6:06:12
Bounds 111 3 37N12'38 90W27'45 6:01:51
Bourbois 37 3 38N12 91W35 6:06:20
Bourbon 28 46 38N09'17 91W14'38 6:04:59
Bowdry 17 3 39N16'56 93W30'40 6:14:03
Bowen 42 3 38N33'29 93W35'27 6:14:22
Bowers Mill 49 3 37N08'59 94W03'22 6:16:13
Bowie Corner 35 3 36N07'57 90W00'17 6:00:01
Bowlan 101 3 37N10 91W08 6:04:32
Bowling Green 82 3 39N20'31 91W11'42 6:04:47
Bowman 105 3 40N10 93W16 6:13:04
Bowmansville 51 3 38N42'33 93W44'01 6:14:56
Box 20 3 37N49 94W00 6:16:00
Boydsville 14 3 38N48'57 92W06'37 6:08:26
Boyer 114 3 37N18'58 92W33'05 6:10:12
Boylers Mill 71 3 38N20'50 93W04'14 6:12:17
Boynton 105 3 40N17'02 93W05'03 6:12:20
Boys Ranch 84 3 37N28 93W21 6:13:24
Boys Town 81 10 38N00 91W37 6:06:28
Boze Mill 75 3 36N39'47 91W11'38 6:04:47
Braddy Ford 62 3 37N30'05 90W27'28 6:01:50
Bradfield 104 3 37N00 93W38 6:14:32
Bradleyville 106 3 36N47'01 92W54'29 6:11:38
Braggadocio 78 3 36N10'31 89W49'46 5:59:19
Bragg City 78 3 36N16'05 89W54'39 5:59:39
Braley 25 3 39N40'51 94W25'35 6:17:42
Branch 15 3 37N54'39 93W00'18 6:12:01
Brandon 8 3 38N30'29 93W25'22 6:13:41
Brandsville 46 3 36N39'01 91W41'24 6:06:46
Branson 106 3 36N38'37 93W13'06 6:12:52
Brashear 1 3 40N08'56 92W22'44 6:09:31
Brasher 78 3 36N04 89W42 5:58:48
Braymer 13 3 39N35'13 93W47'45 6:15:11
Brays 66 3 38N07'13 92W14'40 6:08:59
Brazeau 79 3 37N39'40 89W39'10 5:58:37
Brazil 110 3 37N50'46 91W03'48 6:04:15
Brazito 26 3 38N26'44 92W18'09 6:09:13
Breckenridge 13 3 39N45'44 93W48'15 6:15:13
Breckenridge Hills 95 40 38N42'52 90W22'02 6:01:28
Breen Acres 83 3 39N11'29 94W36'24 6:18:26
Bremen 115 1 38N38 90W15 6:01:00
Brentwood 95 40 38N37'03 90W20'57 6:01:24
Breton 110 3 37N55 90W45 6:03:00
Brevator 57 14 38N57'29 90W44'35 6:02:58
Brewer 79 3 37N46'51 89W55'31 5:59:42
Brian 35 3 36N36'24 90W05'35 6:00:22
Briar 91 3 36N38'54 90W58'18 6:03:53
Brickeys 96 3 38N05'04 90W12'38 6:00:51
Bridgeport 109 3 38N46 91W21 6:05:24
Bridges 77 3 36N36 92W26 6:09:44
Bridgeton 95 40 38N44'38 90W24'49 6:01:39
Bridgeton Terrace 95 40 38N44'47 90W23'11 6:01:33
Brighton 84 3 37N27'28 93W20'52 6:13:23
Brimson 40 3 40N08'37 93W44'19 6:14:57
Brinktown 63 3 38N07'36 92W05'04 6:08:20
Briscoe 57 3 39N04'55 91W00'43 6:04:03
Bristle Ridge 51 3 38N42'50 93W39'28 6:14:38
Bristow 108 3 37N48'18 94W15'51 6:17:03
Brixey 77 3 36N45'02 92W24'17 6:09:37
Broadwater 72 3 36N34'55 89W55'16 5:59:41
Broadway 115 1 38N32'35 90W15'45 6:01:03
Brock 99 3 40N33'04 92W09'06 6:08:36
Bronaugh 108 3 37N41'39 94W28'07 6:17:52
Brookdale 95 40 38N40 90W26 6:01:44
Brookfield 58 44 39N47'04 93W04'24 6:12:18
Brookline (Brookline Sta) 39 3 37N09'48 93W25'12 6:13:41
Brooklyn 41 3 40N23'54 94W02'26 6:16:10

Brooklyn Heights 49
3 37n10'24 94w22'59 6:17:32
Brookside 16 3 37n27'33 89w41'46 5:58:47
Brooks Junction 100
3 37n01'27 89w38'33 5:58:34
Broseley 12 3 36n40'30 90w14'30 6:00:58
Brown 34 3 36n52 92w29 6:09:56
Brownbranch 106 3 36n47'40 92w49'50 6:11:19
Brownfield 53 3 37n40'01 92w20'41 6:09:23
Browning 58 3 40n02'07 93w09'44 6:12:39
Brownington 42 3 38n14'45 93w43'22 6:14:53
Browns 10 3 39n03'00 92w15'40 6:09:03
Browns 72 3 36n51'45 89w37'58 5:58:32
Browns Crossing 111
3 36n58'19 90w35'41 6:02:23
Browns Ford 14 3 38n42'18 91w57'32 6:07:50
Browns Ford 93 3 38n08'16 93w37'00 6:14:28
Brown Shanty 37 3 38n33'04 91w34'28 6:06:18
Browns Spring 104
3 36n58'26 93w30'38 6:14:03
Brownwood 103 3 37n04'51 89w57'16 5:59:49
Brumley 66 3 38n05'11 92w29'12 6:09:57
Bruner 22 3 37n00'53 92w59'09 6:11:57
Brunot 111 3 37n17 90w38 6:02:32
Brunswick 21 3 39n25'24 93w07'49 6:12:31
Brush Arbor 12 3 36n54'27 90w38'53 6:02:36
Brush Creek 53 47 37n36'58 92w42'48 6:10:51
Brushyknob 34 3 36n57'53 92w29'09 6:09:57
Brussells 57 3 39n03'03 90w52'44 6:03:31
Bryan 34 3 36n56 92w15 6:09:00
Bryant 34 3 37n02'20 92w36'38 6:10:27
Bryant 48 3 38n57'35 94w30'42 6:18:03
Bryson 80 3 38n34'49 93w28'43 6:13:55
Buchanan 9 3 37n12'40 90w11'32 6:00:46
Buck Donic 35 3 36n02'23 90w19'33 6:01:18
Buckeye 101 3 37n07 91w15 6:05:00
Buckhart 34 3 36n53'38 92w19'08 6:09:17
Buckhorn 62 3 37n20'17 90w17'22 6:01:09
Buckhorn 85 3 37n46'59 92w16'09 6:09:05
Bucklin 58 3 39n46'54 92w53'24 6:11:34
Buckner 48 3 39n07'57 94w11'54 6:16:48
Buck Prairie 55 3 37n00 93w39 6:14:36
Bucoda 35 3 36n05'24 90w12'51 6:00:51
Bucyrus 107 3 37n20'39 92w01'00 6:08:04
Budapest 91 3 36n46'08 90w42'39 6:02:51
Buell 70 3 39n02'03 91w26'20 6:05:45
Buffalo 30 3 37n38'38 93w05'32 6:12:22
Buffington 103 3 36n49'50 89w44'35 5:58:58
Buick 47 3 37n36'25 91w07'36 6:04:30
Bullion 1 3 40n10'17 92w29'17 6:09:57
Bumgarden Ford 112
3 37n16'06 92w58'43 6:11:55
Bunceton 27 3 38n47'17 92w47'57 6:11:12
Bunker 90 3 37n27'20 91w12'34 6:04:50
Bunker Camp 90 3 37n30'23 91w15'12 6:05:01
Bunker Hill 45 3 39n13'05 92w31'50 6:10:07
Bunker Hill 98 44 40n34'36 92w23'06 6:09:32
Bunnville 108 3 37n50'36 94w34'59 6:18:20
Burbank 111 3 37n08'49 90w22'13 6:01:29
Burch 111 3 37n16'06 90w21'16 6:01:25
Burdett 7 3 38n26'01 94w28'57 6:17:56
Burdine 107 3 37n07 92w05 6:08:20
Burfordville 16 3 37n22'03 89w48'25 5:59:14
Burgess 6 3 37n33'22 94w36'53 6:18:28
Burke City 95 1 38n41 90w16 6:01:04
Burksville 102 3 39n51'43 91w55'02 6:07:40
Burlington Junction 74
3 40n26'44 95w03'57 6:20:16
Burney Ford 114 3 37n25'39 92w23'56 6:09:36
Burnham 46 3 36n55'36 91w57'27 6:07:50
Burns 84 3 37n36'17 93w18'32 6:13:14
Burr 91 3 36n30'07 90w59'10 6:03:57
Burris Fork 68 3 38n30 92w31 6:10:04
Burr Oak 57 3 39n04 90w46 6:03:04
Burton 45 3 39n12'53 92w36'43 6:10:27
Burtonville 5 3 36n45'06 93w58'13 6:15:53
Burtville 51 3 38n40'35 93w37'06 6:14:28
Busch 82 22 39n34'47 91w11'33 6:04:46
Bushburg 50 12 38n18'19 90w22'35 6:01:30
Butcher 43 3 37n53 93w33 6:14:12
Bute 105 3 40n05'40 92w56'58 6:11:48
Butler 7 3 38n15'31 94w19'49 6:17:19
Butler Hill Estates 95
40 38n31 90w22 6:01:28
Butterfield 5 3 36n45'00 93w54'27 6:15:38
Butts 28 46 37n59'45 91w09'22 6:04:37
Buxton 83 3 39n19'08 94w52'23 6:19:30
Buzzards Roost 69
3 39n28'16 91w47'39 6:07:11
Byers 50 3 38n23'44 90w22'27 6:01:30
Bynumville 21 3 39n37'00 92w46'33 6:11:06
Byrd 16 3 37n23 89w41 5:58:44
Byrnes Mill 50 3 38n26'16 90w34'54 6:02:20
Byrnesville 50 3 38n23'34 90w38'23 6:02:34
Byron 76 3 38n20'07 91w42'38 6:06:51
Cabanne 115 1 38n38 90w15 6:01:00
Cabool 107 3 37n07'26 92w06'04 6:08:24
Caddo 112 3 37n20'31 93w02'49 6:12:11
Cadet 110 3 37n59'15 90w41'18 6:02:45
Caffeyville 53 3 37n36'07 92w42'44 6:10:51
Cainsville 41 3 40n26'18 93w46'34 6:15:06
Cairo 88 3 39n30'43 92w26'25 6:09:46
Caldwell 14 3 38n43 92w00 6:08:00
Caledonia 110 3 37n45'48 90w46'22 6:03:05
Calhoun 42 3 38n28'02 93w37'34 6:14:30
California 68 3 38n37'39 92w33'59 6:10:16
Caligoa 35 3 36n36'05 90w09'01 6:00:36
Callao 61 44 39n45'39 92w37'23 6:10:30
Callaway 92 3 38n45 90w52 6:03:28
Calm 75 3 36n33'06 91w09'42 6:04:39
Calumet 82 24 39n19'37 91w00'43 6:04:03
Calverton Park 95
40 38n45'53 90w18'49 6:01:15
Calvey 36 3 38n24 90w47 6:03:08
Calwood 14 3 38n55'13 91w51'09 6:07:25
Cambridge 97 3 39n15'28 92w56'55 6:11:48
Camden 89 3 39n11'50 94w01'22 6:16:05
Camden Junction 89
3 39n11'30 94w02'19 6:16:09
Camden Point 83 3 39n27'10 94w44'29 6:18:58
Camdenton 15 3 38n00'29 92w44'40 6:10:59
Cameron 25 3 39n44'25 94w14'27 6:16:58
Campbell 35 3 36n29'36 90w04'30 6:00:18
Campbellton 36 3 38n32'24 91w09'38 6:04:39
Camp Clark 108 3 37n51 94w21 6:17:24
Camp Lakewood 110
3 37n56'54 90w55'49 6:03:43
Camp Wyman 95 40 38n31'26 90w40'05 6:02:40
Canaan 37 3 38n18'44 91w33'32 6:06:14
Canalou 72 3 36n45'18 89w41'13 5:58:45
Cane Creek 12 3 36n53 90w35 6:02:20
Cane Hill 20 3 37n34'44 93w43'53 6:14:56
Caney Creek 100 3 37n07'46 89w41'15 5:58:45
Cannon Mines 110
3 38n03'12 90w41'53 6:02:48
Canton 56 23 40n07'30 91w37'30 6:06:30
Cantwell 94 3 37n52'21 90w30'42 6:02:03
Cap au Gris 57 16 38n59'56 90w41'30 6:02:46
Cape Fair 104 3 36n43'48 93w30'36 6:14:02
Cape Girardeau 16
3 37n18'21 89w31'05 5:58:04
Caplinger Mills 20
3 37n47'39 93w48'15 6:15:13
Cappeln 92 17 38n41'03 90w56'20 6:03:45
Capps 66 3 38n14'32 92w19'15 6:09:17
Capps Creek 5 44 36n54 94w01 6:16:04
Carbon Center 108
3 38n02'46 94w19'18 6:17:17
Cardinal Acres 107
3 37n03'19 91w40'06 6:06:40
Cardwell 35 3 36n02'49 90w17'34 6:01:10
Cardy 61 3 40n00'06 92w35'43 6:10:23
Carl Junction 49
3 37n10'36 94w33'55 6:18:16
Carlow 31 3 39n52'51 93w49'56 6:15:20
Carmack 38 3 40n14'27 94w25'33 6:17:42
Carns Ford 29 3 37n33'49 93w41'54 6:14:48
Carola 12 3 36n33'06 90w20'09 6:01:21
Carondelet 115 1 38n33'22 90w15'57 6:01:04
Carr 95 40 38n48 90w20 6:01:20
Carrington 14 3 38n48'29 92w03'34 6:08:14
Carr Lane 104 3 36n30'28 93w33'56 6:14:16
Carrol Junction 53
3 37n44'19 92w36'06 6:10:24
Carrollton 17 3 39n21'30 93w29'44 6:13:59
Carsonville 95 40 38n43 90w18 6:01:12
Carter 18 3 36n59 91w01 6:04:04
Carterville 49 3 37n08'57 94w26'34 6:17:46
Carthage 49 3 37n10'35 94w18'36 6:17:14
Caruth 35 3 36n08'03 90w05'12 6:00:21
Caruthersville 78
3 36n11'35 89w39'20 5:58:37
Carytown 49 3 37n15'58 94w18'33 6:17:14
Cascade 111 3 37n17'58 90w16'09 6:01:05
Case 109 3 38n44'06 91w22'26 6:05:30
Casey Ford 53 3 37n35'39 92w21'35 6:09:26
Caseyville 36 3 38n12'19 91w04'47 6:04:19
Cash 61 44 39n51'32 92w38'02 6:10:32
Cassidy 22 3 37n04'03 93w14'46 6:12:59
Cassville 5 3 36n40'37 93w52'07 6:15:28
Castle Point 95
40 38n44 90w15 6:01:00
Castle Rock 49 3 37n04 94w30 6:18:00
Castlewood 95 40 38n33'00 90w33'13 6:02:13
Catawissa 36 3 38n25'29 90w46'57 6:03:08
Catherine 62 3 37n33 90w17 6:01:08
Cato 5 3 36n43'15 93w40'48 6:14:43
Catron 72 3 36n36'41 89w42'11 5:58:49
Caulfield 46 3 36n36'52 92w06'17 6:08:25
Caverna 60 3 36n29'57 94w15'58 6:17:04
Cave Spring 39 3 37n21'05 93w27'48 6:13:51
Cawood 2 3 40n06'46 94w44'58 6:19:00
Cazzell 21 3 39n18'25 92w56'31 6:11:46
Cedar Bluff 75 3 36n33 91w09 6:04:36
Cedar Bluff 95 40 38n32'28 90w34'17 6:02:17
Cedar City 14 3 38n35'50 92w10'46 6:08:43
Cedar Creek 106 3 36n34'44 92w59'51 6:11:59
Cedar Ford 28 3 37n53'41 91w28'47 6:05:55
Cedar Gap 114 3 37n06'20 92w40'10 6:10:41
Cedargrove 101 3 37n25'07 91w36'25 6:06:26
Cedar Hill 50 3 38n21 90w39 6:02:36
Cedar Hill Lakes 50
3 38n21 90w39 6:02:36
Cedar Ridge 30 3 37n36 92w59 6:11:56
Cedar Springs 20
3 37n52'25 93w53'36 6:15:34
Cedar Valley 12 3 36n46'01 90w27'11 6:01:49
Cedarville 29 3 37n34'28 93w59'03 6:15:56
Cedar Vista 84 3 37n31'33 93w22'12 6:13:29
Celt 30 3 37n52'33 92w54'05 6:11:36
Cement City 48 3 39n08'41 94w25'00 6:17:40
Centaur 95 40 38n38'40 90w41'56 6:02:48
Center 87 3 39n30'29 91w31'43 6:06:07
Centertown 26 3 38n37'07 92w24'44 6:09:39
Centerview 51 3 38n44'39 93w50'42 6:15:23
Centerville 90 3 37n26'06 90w57'30 6:03:50
Central 48 3 39n03 94w31 6:18:04
Central 115 1 38n38 90w15 6:01:00
Central City 49 3 37n05'08 94w35'00 6:18:20
Centralia 10 3 39n12'37 92w08'16 6:08:33
Centropolis 48 3 39n05'23 94w29'39 6:17:59
Chadwick 22 3 36n56 93w03 6:12:12
Chaffee 100 3 37n10'48 89w39'18 5:58:37
Chain of Rocks 57
14 38n54'54 90w48'05 6:03:12
Chalk Level 93 3 38n05'36 93w48'34 6:15:14
Chambersburg 23
30 40n31'26 91w47'57 6:07:12
Chamois 76 3 38n40'31 91w46'10 6:07:05
Champ 95 2 38n44'29 90w26'42 6:01:47
Champion 34 3 36n55'53 92w23'27 6:09:34
Champion City 36
3 38n19'10 91w16'13 6:05:05
Chandler 24 3 39n18'01 94w22'57 6:17:32
Channel 78 3 36n03'35 89w56'27 5:59:46
Chaonia Landing Recreation A 111
3 36n58'23 90w21'36 6:01:26
Chapel 46 3 36n56 91w43 6:06:52
Chapel 86 3 40n32'26 92w43'46 6:10:55
Chapel Hill 54 3 38n55'03 94w03'29 6:16:14
Chapin 46 3 36n41'26 91w46'17 6:07:05
Chariton 86 3 40n34'13 92w46'52 6:11:07
Charity 30 3 37n30'55 93w00'58 6:12:04
Charlack 95 40 38n42'09 90w20'36 6:01:22
Charles Nagel 115
1 38n40 90w15 6:01:00
Charleston 67 3 36n55'15 89w21'02 5:57:24
Charlotte 7 3 38n16 94w28 6:17:52
Charrette 109 3 38n39 91w05 6:04:20
Charter Oak 103 3 36n42'55 89w43'11 5:58:53
Cherokee Pass 62
3 37n32 90w19 6:01:16
Cherry Box 102 3 39n55'29 92w14'06 6:08:56
Cherry Valley 17
3 39n15 93w43 6:14:52
Cherry Valley Estates 39
44 37n11 93w17 6:13:08
Cherryville 28 3 37n51'07 91w16'36 6:05:06
Chesapeake 55 3 37n07'01 93w40'53 6:14:44
Chesterfield 95
40 38n39'47 90w34'37 6:02:18
Chestnutridge 22
3 36n50'12 93w15'06 6:13:00
Chicopee 18 3 36n59'06 91w00'20 6:04:01
Chilhowee 51 3 38n35'20 93w51'15 6:15:25
Chillicothe 59 3 39n47'43 93w33'08 6:14:13
Chilton 18 3 36n55'59 90w55'17 6:03:41
Chitwood 49 3 37n05'20 94w32'55 6:18:12
Chloe 93 3 38n11'03 93w43'59 6:14:56
Chloride 47 3 37n27'38 90w41'13 6:02:45
Chouteau 24 3 39n12 94w28 6:17:52
Chouteau 115 1 38n37 90w16 6:01:04
Chouteau Springs 27
3 38n55'30 92w53'41 6:11:35
Christian Bechtold 115
1 38n36 90w14 6:00:56
Christian Center 22
3 36n56'27 93w10'00 6:12:40
Christopher 73 44 36n47'55 94w17'22 6:17:09
Chula 59 3 39n55'18 93w28'27 6:13:54
Cincinnati 87 3 39n33'48 91w35'39 6:06:23
Cinque Hommes 79
3 37n39 89w51 5:59:24
Circle City 103 3 36n51'24 89w48'08 5:59:13
Civic Center 48 3 39n06 94w34 6:18:16
Civil Bend 31 3 39n59'50 94w06'00 6:16:24
Clair 11 3 39n46'43 94w43'35 6:18:54
Clapper 69 37 39n35'24 91w50'42 6:07:23
Clara 107 3 37n17'59 92w01'16 6:08:05
Clarence 102 45 39n44'31 92w15'30 6:09:02
Clark 88 3 39n16'52 92w20'33 6:09:22
Clark City 23 30 40n25'15 91w40'53 6:06:44
Clark Ford 53 3 37n31'17 92w23'28 6:09:34
Clark Fork 27 3 38n51 92w42 6:10:48
Clarksburg 68 3 38n39'33 92w39'48 6:10:39
Clarksdale 32 3 39n48'49 94w33'01 6:18:12
Clarks Fork 27 3 38n53'13 92w39'09 6:10:37
Clarkson Valley 95
40 38n37'06 90w35'21 6:02:21
Clarksville 82 24 39n22'14 90w54'18 6:03:37
Clarkton 35 3 36n27'06 89w58'01 5:59:52
Claryville 79 3 37n53'32 89w49'44 5:59:19
Claud 20 3 37n48'48 93w42'42 6:14:51
Clay 1 3 40n13'39 92w27'08 6:09:49
Claycomo 24 3 39n12'09 94w29'32 6:17:58
Claysville 10 3 38n39'41 92w15'33 6:09:02
Clayton 95 40 38n38'33 90w19'25 6:01:18
Clear Creek 27 3 38n50 92w56 6:11:44
Clearmont 74 3 40n30'35 95w01'55 6:20:08
Clear Spring 18 3 37n00 91w01 6:04:04
Clear Springs 107
3 37n05'46 91w51'11 6:07:25
Clearwater 96 3 37n46 90w08 6:00:32
Cleavesville 37 3 38n16'22 91w36'06 6:06:24
Clement 96 3 38n03'25 90w09'55 6:00:40
Clementine 81 3 37n52'35 92w01'02 6:08:04
Cleopatra 65 3 40n32'55 93w24'15 6:13:37
Cleveland 19 3 38n40'45 94w35'36 6:18:22
Clever 22 3 37n01'49 93w28'22 6:13:53
Cliff 16 3 37n10'07 89w47'18 5:59:09
Cliff Cave 95 40 38n27'42 90w17'15 6:01:09
Cliff Village 73
3 37n01'24 94w30'54 6:18:04
Clifton 88 3 39n28 92w40 6:10:40
Clifton City 27 3 38n45'53 93w02'28 6:12:10
Clifton Heights 115
1 38n36'33 90w17'10 6:01:09
Clifton Hill 88 3 39n26'17 92w39'58 6:10:40
Climax Springs 15
3 38n06'15 93w03'00 6:12:12
Clines Island 103
3 36n54'14 89w47'37 5:59:10
Clinton 42 3 38n22'07 93w46'41 6:15:07
Clinton 81 3 37n48'49 91w33'34 6:06:14
Cliquot 84 3 37n41'38 93w28'39 6:13:55
Clover Bottom 109
49 38n30'13 91w07'10 6:04:29
Cloverdale 30 3 37n36 92w59 6:11:56
Clubb 111 3 37n12'52 90w20'44 6:01:23
Clyde 74 3 40n16'09 94w40'06 6:18:40
Coal 42 3 38n19'33 93w36'54 6:14:28
Coal Hill 20 3 37n52'42 93w56'00 6:15:44
Coatsville 86 3 40n35'21 92w38'00 6:10:32
Cobalt City 62 3 37n32 90w17 6:01:08
Cobb 93 3 37n53'40 93w45'16 6:15:01
Cobb 103 3 36n55'03 90w12'48 6:00:51
Cobbler 48 3 39n09'49 94w19'41 6:17:19
Cockrell 21 3 39n34 92w49 6:11:16
Cockrell 48 3 38n53'08 94w14'15 6:16:57
Cody 39 3 37n07'07 93w07'09 6:12:29
Coffey 31 3 40n06 94w00 6:16:00
Coffeyton 28 46 38n07'00 91w16'22 6:05:05
Coffman 96 3 37n47'04 90w11'39 6:00:47
Coldspring 34 3 36n58'18 92w25'49 6:09:43
Cold Spring 81 3 37n50 91w45 6:07:00
Cold Springs 8 3 38n13'53 93w22'59 6:13:32
Coldwater 111 3 37n18'12 90w24'35 6:01:38
Cole 8 3 38n19 93w12 6:12:48
Cole Camp 8 3 38n27'36 93w12'09 6:12:49
Cole Camp Junction 8
3 38n27'46 93w16'31 6:13:06
Cole Junction 26
3 38n36'51 92w13'27 6:08:54
Coleman 19 3 38n45'05 94w23'40 6:17:35
College Mound 61
3 39n37'23 92w34'21 6:10:17
Collins 93 3 37n53'28 93w37'22 6:14:29
Coloma 17 3 39n31'53 93w31'23 6:14:06
Colony 52 3 40n15'14 91w59'26 6:07:58

Columbia 10 3 38N57'06 92w20'02 6:09:20
Columbus 51 3 38N51'31 93w53'26 6:15:34
Combs 17 3 39N24 93w22 6:13:28
Comet 29 3 37N23'50 93w37'56 6:14:32
Commerce 100 3 37N09'32 89w26'34 5:57:46
Commerce Tower 48 3 39N03 94w31 6:18:04
Commercial 39 44 37N14 93w18 6:13:12
Como 72 3 36N37'12 89w45'19 5:59:01
Competition 53 3 37N29'01 92w25'44 6:09:43
Conception 74 3 40N14'34 94w41'12 6:18:45
Conception Junction 74 3 40N16'11 94w41'30 6:18:46
Conclay 95 40 38N38 90w22 6:01:28
Concord 14 3 39N01'59 91w58'03 6:07:52
Concord 78 3 36N17'36 89w42'03 5:58:48
Concord 115 40 38N31'28 90w21'26 6:01:26
Concord Hill 109 3 38N39'01 91w08'10 6:04:33
Concordia 54 3 38N59'00 93w34'06 6:14:16
Conklin 112 3 37N23'07 93w01'08 6:12:05
Connelsville 1 3 40N16'39 92w42'00 6:10:48
Conrads Mill 9 3 37N30'23 89w51'38 5:59:27
Conran 72 3 36N29'00 89w38'48 5:58:35
Converse 25 3 39N29'56 94w16'34 6:17:06
Conway 53 3 37N30'07 92w49'15 6:11:17
Cook Station 28 3 37N48'46 91w26'16 6:05:45
Cookville 85 3 37N38'56 92w12'35 6:08:50
Cool Valley 95 40 38N43'39 90w18'39 6:01:15
Coon Island 12 3 36N33 90w24 6:01:36
Cooper 38 3 40N13 94w31 6:18:04
Cooper Hill 76 3 38N25'38 91w39'41 6:06:39
Cooter 78 3 36N02'48 89w48'36 5:59:14
Copper Mine 96 3 37N54'13 90w08'47 6:00:35
Cora 105 3 40N06'35 93w07'49 6:12:31
Corbin 93 3 38N03'57 93w35'47 6:14:23
Corder 54 3 39N05'54 93w38'26 6:14:34
Corkery 30 3 37N47'43 92w51'40 6:11:27
Cornelia 51 3 38N38'37 93w44'21 6:14:57
Corner Campbell School (Aban 59 3 39N42'21 93w28'57 6:13:56
Cornertown 46 3 36N29'57 91w45'30 6:07:02
Corning 44 3 40N14'54 95w27'14 6:21:49
Cornwall 62 3 37N30'44 90w12'10 6:00:49
Corridon 90 3 37N22'55 91w04'20 6:04:17
Corry 29 3 37N29'15 93w43'30 6:14:54
Corsicana 5 3 36N47'56 93w59'41 6:15:59
Corso 57 3 39N07'38 91w11'09 6:04:45
Corticelli 68 3 38N31 92w26 6:09:44
Cosby 2 3 39N51'51 94w40'41 6:18:43
Cossville 49 3 37N19'33 94w26'53 6:17:48
Cote Sans Dessein 14 3 38N38 91w59 6:07:56
Cottage Farm 50 3 38N14'22 90w40'07 6:02:40
Cottleville 92 2 38N44'46 90w39'14 6:02:37
Cotton Hill 35 3 36N34 90w00 6:00:00
Cotton Plant 35 3 36N05'24 90w05'28 6:00:22
Cottonwood Point 78 3 36N03'50 89w41'57 5:58:48
Couch 75 3 36N36'22 91w22'59 6:05:32
Coulstone 33 3 37N31'22 91w45'04 6:07:00
Country Club 48 3 39N01 94w35 6:18:20
Country Club Hills 95 40 38N43'15 90w16'29 6:01:06
Country Club Village 2 44 39N49'56 94w49'17 6:19:17
Country Life Acres 95 40 38N37'26 90w27'22 6:01:49
Courtney 48 3 39N09'20 94w23'36 6:17:34
Courtois 110 3 37N45'53 91w04'19 6:04:17
Cove 60 3 36N34'50 94w06'09 6:16:25
Covington 78 3 36N06'26 89w52'40 5:59:31
Cowan 111 3 37N12 90w19 6:01:16
Cowgill 13 3 39N33'33 93w55'36 6:15:42
Cox 61 3 39N38'14 92w22'58 6:09:32
Coy 60 3 36N39'40 94w31'55 6:18:08
Crabbs 112 3 37N09 92w46 6:11:04
Craddock 81 3 37N38'22 91w50'45 6:07:23
Crag O Lea 60 3 36N36'33 94w21'08 6:17:25
Craig 44 3 40N11'41 95w22'15 6:21:29
Crane 104 3 36N54'19 93w34'17 6:14:17
Crane Creek 5 3 36N52 93w39 6:14:36
Crawford 99 3 40N28'29 92w16'31 6:09:06
Cream Ridge 59 3 39N47'07 93w27'45 6:13:51
Creek Nation 62 3 37N30'50 90w23'17 6:01:33
Creighton 19 3 38N29'41 94w04'23 6:16:18
Crescent 95 40 38N31'16 90w36'22 6:02:25
Crescent Hill 7 3 38N25'56 94w20'50 6:17:23
Crescent Lake 24 3 39N19'32 94w14'25 6:16:58
Crest 8 3 38N27'01 93w08'05 6:12:32
Crestwood 95 40 38N33'25 90w22'54 6:01:32
Cretcher 97 3 39N01'53 93w19'26 6:13:18
Creve Coeur 95 40 38N39'39 90w25'21 6:01:41
Crider 46 3 36N43'05 92w04'41 6:08:19
Crisp 29 3 37N34'11 93w47'16 6:15:09
Crites Corner 18 3 36N57'01 90w49'21 6:03:17
Crocker 85 47 37N56'56 92w15'49 6:09:03
Crockerville 8 3 38N26'34 93w06'15 6:12:25
Crook 76 3 38N33'02 91w46'39 6:07:07
Crooked Creek 9 3 37N25 90w04 6:00:16
Crooked River 89 3 39N17 93w50 6:15:20
Crooks Springs 93 3 37N55'01 93w50'28 6:15:22
Crosno 67 3 36N47'51 89w10'38 5:56:43
Cross Boards 34 3 36N51'01 92w51'15 6:11:25
Cross Keys 95 40 38N48'32 90w17'55 6:01:12
Cross Roads 34 3 36N58 92w40 6:10:40
Cross Roads 77 3 36N43'55 92w13'40 6:08:55
Cross Roads 104 3 36N49'19 93w31'58 6:14:08
Crossroads School (Abandoned 19 3 38N48'00 94w19'12 6:17:17
Crossroads Store 114 3 37N11'22 92w23'33 6:09:34
Cross Timbers 43 3 38N01'29 93w13'36 6:12:54
Crosstown 79 3 37N44'47 89w43'40 5:58:55
Cross Way 112 3 37N22'17 93w03'20 6:12:13
Crowder 100 3 36N57'45 89w41'00 5:58:44
Crown 112 3 37N15'52 92w57'04 6:11:48
Cruise Mill 110 3 38N04'57 90w43'58 6:02:56
Crump 16 3 37N16'43 89w49'45 5:59:19
Crystal City 50 12 38N13'16 90w22'44 6:01:31
Crystal Lake Park 95 40 38N37'20 90w26'03 6:01:44
Cuba 28 3 38N03'46 91w24'12 6:05:37
Cull 46 3 36N43'38 91w41'03 6:06:44
Cullen 85 3 37N50 92w09 6:08:36
Culp Ford 75 3 36N38'40 91w36'06 6:06:24
Cunningham 21 3 39N38'30 93w14'24 6:12:58
Curdton 103 3 36N57'52 90w03'19 6:00:13
Cureall 46 3 36N40'02 92w04'14 6:08:17
Current River 91 3 36N32 90w50 6:03:20
Current View 91 3 36N29'56 90w46'41 6:03:07
Curryville 82 3 39N20'44 91w20'41 6:05:23
Custer 33 3 37N32'11 91w31'10 6:06:05
Cyclone 60 3 36N37'06 94w15'22 6:17:01
Cypress 41 3 40N10 94w03 6:16:12
Cyrene 82 3 39N17'11 91w06'23 6:04:26
Dadeville 29 3 37N28'49 93w40'25 6:14:42
Daggetts Ford 76 3 38N19'29 91w50'52 6:07:23
Daisy 16 3 37N31'25 89w47'35 5:59:10
Dale 3 3 40N20 95w16 6:21:04
Dale 103 3 36N52'48 90w14'33 6:00:58
Dallas 48 3 38N56'23 94w36'10 6:18:25
Dallion Ford 30 3 37N41'10 92w59'19 6:11:57
Dalton 21 3 39N23'51 92w59'23 6:11:58
Damascus 93 3 38N00 93w38 6:14:32
Dameron 57 25 39N13'05 90w48'01 6:03:12
Damsel 15 3 38N06'35 92w41'24 6:10:46
Danby 50 3 38N06'33 90w18'27 6:01:14
Danforth 1 3 40N14'29 92w44'02 6:10:56
Danville 70 3 38N54'38 91w32'05 6:06:08
Dardenne 92 2 38N45'57 90w45'22 6:03:01
Darien 33 3 37N31'12 91w35'32 6:06:22
Daris Crossing 94 3 37N52 90w31 6:02:04
Darksville 88 3 39N33'09 92w34'56 6:10:20
Darlington 38 3 40N11'54 94w23'45 6:17:35
Date 107 3 37N06 91w43 6:06:52
Daugherty 19 3 38N36'13 94w16'53 6:17:08
Davis 57 3 39N03'29 91w01'10 6:04:05
Davis 94 3 37N49'18 90w35'28 6:02:22
Davis Ford 63 3 38N04'17 91w49'28 6:07:18
Davis Store 12 3 36N40 90w15 6:01:00
Davisville 28 3 37N48'28 91w11'06 6:04:44
Dawn 59 3 39N40'06 93w38'07 6:14:32
Dawson 114 3 37N15'25 92w18'28 6:09:14
Dawsonville 74 3 40N27'52 95w05'57 6:20:24
Dawt 77 3 36N36'36 92w16'36 6:09:06
Dawt Mill 77 3 36N36'35 92w16'41 6:09:07
Day 106 3 36N48'47 93w14'37 6:12:58
Dayton 19 3 38N29'07 94w11'37 6:16:46
Daytown 94 3 37N51'33 90w34'53 6:02:20
Dean 2 44 39N52'16 94w49'54 6:19:20
Dean Ford 81 10 37N55'17 91w38'27 6:06:34
Dean Ford 108 3 37N52'52 94w23'17 6:17:33
Dearborn 83 3 39N31'19 94w46'11 6:19:05
Decatur 26 3 38N27'09 92w25'11 6:09:41
Decaturville 15 3 37N54'27 92w41'59 6:10:48
Dederick 108 3 37N51'26 94w07'39 6:16:31
Deep Ford 60 3 36N36'35 94w21'04 6:17:24
Deepwater 42 3 38N15'38 93w46'22 6:15:05
Deer 76 3 38N37'19 91w47'48 6:07:11
Deerfield 108 3 37N50'19 94w30'21 6:18:01
Deering 78 3 36N11'27 89w52'58 5:59:32
Deering Junction 78 3 36N11'24 89w54'19 5:59:37
Deer Land 35 3 36N09'41 90w00'15 6:00:01
Deer Park 10 3 38N51'41 92w15'00 6:09:00
Deer Ridge 56 34 40N12'46 91w53'44 6:07:35
Defiance 92 3 38N37'56 90w46'42 6:03:07
Deicke 95 40 38N31 90w39 6:02:36
Delmar 42 3 38N21'24 93w56'31 6:15:46
De Kalb 11 3 39N35'13 94w55'30 6:19:42
Delaney 25 3 39N38'30 94w27'05 6:17:48
De Lassus 94 3 37N45'52 90w27'20 6:01:49
Delaware 101 3 37N06'12 91w24'29 6:05:38
Delbridge 110 3 37N47'41 90w59'12 6:03:57
Dell 8 3 38N10'19 93w18'31 6:13:14
Dell Junction 8 3 38N10'28 93w19'05 6:13:16
Dellwood 95 40 38N44'58 90w17'08 6:01:09
Delmar 42 3 38N23 93w46 6:15:04
Delmar 53 3 37N46'57 92w33'00 6:10:12
Delmo 72 3 36N48'37 89w40'52 5:58:43
Delta 16 3 37N11'48 89w44'10 5:58:57
Denlow 34 3 36N58'51 92w22'24 6:09:30
Dennis Acres 73 3 37N02'48 94w30'19 6:18:01
Dent 47 3 37N40 91w04 6:04:16
Dent Ford 33 3 37N42'03 91w26'47 6:05:47
Denton 51 3 38N36'48 93w55'44 6:15:43
Denton 78 3 36N05'23 89w53'29 5:59:34
Denver 113 3 40N23'50 94w19'21 6:17:17
Derby 94 3 37N49'30 90w32'19 6:02:09
Derrahs 56 23 40N13'23 91w39'50 6:06:39
Des Arc 47 3 37N16'57 90w38'14 6:02:33
Desloge 94 3 37N52'22 90w31'40 6:02:07
Des Moines 23 43 40N25 91w33 6:06:12
DeSoto 50 4 38N08'22 90w33'18 6:02:13
Des Peres 95 40 38N36'03 90w25'58 6:01:44
Dessa 73 44 36N48'25 94w31'17 6:18:05
Detmold 36 3 38N32'34 91w17'25 6:05:10
Deventer 67 3 36N49'20 89w12'42 5:56:51
Devils Elbow 85 3 37N50'45 92w03'49 6:08:15
DeWitt 17 3 39N23'04 93w13'15 6:12:53
Dexter 103 3 36N47'45 89w57'28 5:59:50
Diamond 73 3 36N59'43 94w18'57 6:17:16
Dickens 106 3 36N43'39 93w02'50 6:12:11
Dickerson 56 26 40N06 91w39 6:06:36
Diehlstadt 100 3 36N57'30 89w25'51 5:57:43
Diggins 112 3 37N10'21 92w51'15 6:11:25
Dilday Mill 29 3 37N19'31 93w46'50 6:15:07
Dillard 28 3 37N44'12 91w12'15 6:04:49
Dillman 35 3 36N11'05 90w06'17 6:00:25
Dillon 81 10 37N58'19 91w41'52 6:06:47
Dissen 36 3 38N33'35 91w16'33 6:05:06
Dittmer 50 3 38N20'08 90w41'17 6:02:45
Dixie 14 3 38N43'08 92w00'33 6:08:02
Dixon 85 47 37N59'30 92w05'37 6:08:22
Dockery 89 3 39N21'40 93w59'18 6:15:57
Dodds 72 3 36N36'07 89w40'26 5:58:42
Dodson 48 3 38N58'30 94w33'10 6:18:13
Doe Run 94 3 37N44'34 90w29'51 6:01:59
Dogwood 34 3 37N02'16 92w49'51 6:11:19
Dogwood 67 3 36N49'31 89w27'13 5:57:49
Dolan 19 3 38N37 94w30 6:18:00
Dongola 9 3 37N10'05 89w57'35 5:59:50
Doniphan 91 3 36N37'15 90w49'24 6:03:18
Doolittle 81 3 37N56'25 91w52'51 6:07:31
Dora 77 3 36N46'37 92w13'02 6:08:52
Dorena 67 3 36N36'58 89w14'14 5:56:57
Dorena Landing 67 3 36N35'03 89w13'02 5:56:52
Doss 33 3 37N34'34 91w29'05 6:05:56
Dove 53 47 37N47'27 92w40'57 6:10:44
Dover 54 3 39N11'36 93w41'15 6:14:45
Dover 56 3 40N00'44 91w35'46 6:06:23
Dover Station 54 3 39N12'29 93w41'56 6:14:48
Downing 98 44 40N29'15 92w22'09 6:09:29
Doyal 93 3 37N58 93w41 6:14:44
Doylesport 6 3 37N36 94w13 6:16:52
Drake 37 3 38N28'06 91w27'52 6:05:51
Dresden 80 3 38N45'04 93w20'05 6:13:20
Drew 53 47 37N32'53 92w28'05 6:09:52
Drewel Ford 37 3 38N23'57 91w38'18 6:06:33
Drexel 19 3 38N28'46 94w36'30 6:18:26
Dripping Spring 10 3 38N58 92w13 6:08:52
Drum 9 3 37N11'19 89w53'37 5:59:34
Drury 34 3 36N55'48 92w19'21 6:09:17
Drynob 53 3 37N38'30 92w27'01 6:09:48
Dry Valley 55 3 37N01'30 94w02'29 6:16:10
Drywood 108 3 37N42 94w20 6:17:20
Duck Creek 103 3 36N53 90w09 6:00:36
Dudenville 49 3 37N18'20 94w04'59 6:16:20
Dudley 103 3 36N47'19 90w05'35 6:00:22
Duenweg 49 3 37N05'01 94w24'48 6:17:39
Dugginsville 77 3 36N30'35 92w41'43 6:10:47
Duke 81 3 37N39'37 92w00'38 6:08:03
Dun (Impo P O) 107 3 37N08'28 92w11'25 6:08:46
Duncan 105 3 40N05 93w11 6:12:44
Duncan 112 3 37N16'54 92w41'30 6:10:46
Duncans Bridge 69 45 39N34'32 92w15'49 6:09:03
Dundee 36 49 38N35'36 91w07'28 6:04:30
Dunksburg 51 3 38N53'57 93w29'51 6:13:59
Dunlap 40 3 40N06'30 93w28'56 6:13:56
Dunn 107 3 37N08 92w16 6:09:04
Dunnegan 84 3 37N42'29 93w34'36 6:14:18
Duquesne 49 3 37N04'36 94w27'33 6:17:50
Durbin 114 3 37N22'33 92w30'05 6:10:00
Durham 56 26 39N58'34 91w40'04 6:06:40
Durnell 103 3 37N01 89w49 5:59:16
Dutchtown 16 3 37N15'10 89w39'35 5:58:38
Dutzow 109 49 38N36'20 90w59'40 6:03:59
Duval 49 3 37N18 94w27 6:17:48
Dye 83 3 39N29'06 94w55'43 6:19:43
Dykes 107 3 37N20'01 92w06'56 6:08:28
Eagle 61 3 39N49 92w27 6:09:48
Eagle Rock 5 3 36N32'53 93w45'15 6:15:01
Eaglette 103 3 37N02'08 90w02'22 6:00:09
Eagleville 41 3 40N28'09 93w59'13 6:15:57
Earl 14 3 38N55'52 92w03'40 6:08:15
Earnestville 30 3 37N33'37 92w53'31 6:11:34
Easley 10 3 38N48'06 92w22'33 6:09:30
Easley 61 3 40N00 92w41 6:10:44
East Benton 22 3 37N04 92w57 6:11:48
East Bonne Terre 94 3 37N55'16 90w31'39 6:02:07
East Boone 7 3 38N26 94w27 6:17:48
East Dallas 112 3 37N12 92w54 6:11:36
East End 47 3 37N40'31 91w02'01 6:04:08
East Fulton 14 3 38N50 91w54 6:07:36
East Independence 48 3 39N05'44 94w21'18 6:17:25
East James 104 3 36N37 93w22 6:13:28
East Kansas City 24 3 39N10 94w30 6:18:00
East Kirkwood 95 40 38N37 90w21 6:01:24
East Leavenworth 83 3 39N18'52 94w51'06 6:19:24
East Lynne 19 3 38N40'06 94w13'45 6:16:55
East Mexico 4 3 39N10 91w52 6:07:28
Easton 11 3 39N43'20 94w38'29 6:18:34
East Prairie 67 19 36N46'47 89w23'08 5:57:33
East Purdy 5 3 36N48'55 93w52'42 6:15:31
East Trenton Lake 40 3 40N07 93w35 6:14:20
Eastville 14 3 38N57'09 92w01'55 6:08:08
Eastwood 18 3 36N53'27 91w01'58 6:04:08
Ebenezer 39 44 37N20'25 93w18'25 6:13:14
Eccles 21 3 39N29'21 92w52'07 6:11:28
Echo Lake Ranch 50 3 38N27'16 90w34'46 6:02:19
Economy 61 3 39N53'21 92w25'14 6:09:41
Ectonville 24 3 39N22'04 94w28'40 6:17:55
Edgar Springs 81 3 37N42'16 91w51'59 6:07:28
Edgehill 90 3 37N35'18 90w56'00 6:03:44
Edgerton 83 3 39N30'18 94w37'59 6:18:32
Edgerton Junction 83 3 39N28'39 94w40'29 6:18:42
Edgewater Beach 106 3 36N39'41 93w08'30 6:12:34
Edgewood 82 3 39N16'18 91w04'29 6:04:18
Edina 52 3 40N10'03 92w10'21 6:08:41
Edinburg 40 3 40N04'53 93w41'37 6:14:46
Edmonson 8 3 38N18'34 93w13'26 6:12:54
Edmundson 95 40 38N44'09 90w21'50 6:01:27
Edwards 8 3 38N08'12 93w10'10 6:12:41
Egypt 17 3 39N18 93w42 6:14:48
Egypt Grove 46 3 36N36'51 92w01'51 6:08:07
Egypt Mills 16 3 37N24'18 89w27'49 5:57:51
Elaver 28 3 37N58'07 91w16'42 6:05:07
Eldon 66 3 38N20'54 92w34'53 6:10:20
Eldorado Springs 20 3 37N52'37 94w01'16 6:16:05
Eldridge 53 3 37N49'47 92w44'56 6:11:00
Elijah 77 3 36N36'42 92w08'56 6:08:36
Elk 103 3 36N42 89w49 5:59:16

Place		Lat.	Long.	Time
Elk Creek 107	3	37N11'20	91w59'49	6:07:59
Elk Creek 114	3	37N25	92w28	6:09:52
Elk Fork 80	3	38N41	93w27	6:13:48
Elkhart 7	3	38N21	94w27	6:17:48
Elkhead 22	3	37N00'49	92w55'49	6:11:43
Elkhorn 89	3	39N18'33	94w06'45	6:16:27
Elkhurst 10	3	38N49'57	92w15'07	6:09:00
Elkland 112	3	37N26'35	93w01'51	6:12:07
Elko 86	3	40N24'54	92w51'53	6:11:28
Elk River 60	3	36N33	94w30	6:18:00
Elk Springs 60	3	36N35'01	94w27'22	6:17:49
Elkton 43	3	37N51'09	93w25'33	6:13:42
Ellendale 115	31	38N36'47	90w18'44	6:01:15
Ellenorah 38	3	40N20'19	94w19'54	6:17:20
Elliff 60	3	36N41'52	94w25'56	6:17:44
Ellington 90	3	37N14'30	90w58'07	6:03:52
Elliot Ford 75	3	36N39'45	91w37'20	6:06:29
Elliott 55	3	37N02'34	93w44'51	6:14:59
Ellis 108	3	37N49'29	94w26'54	6:17:48
Ellis Prairie 107	3	37N24'48	92w02'22	6:08:09
Ellisville 95	40	38N35'33	90w35'13	6:02:21
Ellsinore 18	3	36N56'03	90w44'48	6:02:59
Elm 51	3	38N51'12	94w02'32	6:16:10
Elm 86	3	40N25	92w46	6:11:04
Elmdale Village 95	40	38N42	90w22	6:01:28
Elmer 61	3	39N57'25	92w39'01	6:10:36
Elmira 89	3	39N30'26	94w09'16	6:16:37
Elmira Camp 89	3	39N29'47	94w09'27	6:16:38
Elmo 74	3	40N31'06	95w06'55	6:20:28
Elmont 36	44	38N14'08	91w14'33	6:04:58
Elm Point 92	2	38N49'05	90w29'13	6:01:57
Elmwood 82	35	39N25'58	91w04'06	6:04:16
Elmwood 97	3	39N04'07	93w25'58	6:13:44
Elsberry 57	25	39N10'00	90w46'51	6:03:07
Elsey 104	3	36N51'15	93w32'26	6:14:10
Elston 26	3	38N36'46	92w19'30	6:09:18
Elvins 94	3	37N50'12	90w31'58	6:02:08
Elwood 39	44	37N13'41	93w25'52	6:13:43
Ely 64	39	39N41'30	91w37'59	6:06:32
Embree 114	3	37N24'44	92w15'24	6:09:02
Emden 102	3	39N47'47	91w51'46	6:07:27
Emerson 64	3	39N53'22	91w41'51	6:06:47
Eminence 101	3	37N09'02	91w21'27	6:05:26
Emma 97	3	38N58'18	93w29'40	6:13:59
Empire 2	3	40N00	94w41	6:18:44
Empire Prairie 2	3	40N04'59	94w38'20	6:18:33
Englewood 10	3	38N49'18	92w11'03	6:08:44
Englewood 48	3	39N05'13	94w27'21	6:17:49
Enon 68	3	38N27'25	92w29'22	6:09:57
Enon 92	8	38N51'47	90w49'52	6:03:19
Enough 47	3	37N42'26	90w55'00	6:03:40
Enterprise 58	3	40N01'28	93w05'06	6:12:20
Enterprise 102	45	39N38'56	92w15'36	6:09:02
Enyart 38	3	40N21'44	94w32'52	6:18:11
Eolia 82	3	39N14'09	91w00'29	6:04:02
Epps 12	3	36N49	90w33	6:02:12
Epworth 102	3	39N53'39	92w05'39	6:08:23
Equality 66	3	38N15	92w30	6:10:00
Erie 60	3	36N43'40	94w21'47	6:17:27
Ernest 29	3	37N29	93w56	6:15:44
Ernestville 54	3	38N55'56	93w37'48	6:14:31
Essex 103	3	36N48'45	89w51'41	5:59:27
Estes 82	3	39N14'12	91w22'34	6:05:30
Esther 94	3	37N51'01	90w29'55	6:02:00
Estill 45	3	39N02'54	92w44'39	6:10:59
Ethel 61	3	39N53'41	92w44'16	6:10:57
Ethlyn 57	14	38N56'27	90w49'33	6:03:18
Etlah 36	3	38N38'21	91w16'35	6:05:06
Etna 99	3	40N25'03	91w58'45	6:07:55
Eton 48	3	39N10'15	94w20'50	6:17:23
Etterville 66	3	38N22'03	92w28'12	6:09:53
Eudora 84	3	37N28'57	93w32'15	6:14:09
Eugene 26	3	38N21'10	92w24'13	6:09:37
Eunice 107	3	37N14'42	91w46'46	6:07:07
Eureka 95	40	38N30'09	90w37'40	6:02:31
Europa 35	3	36N05'24	90w10'39	6:00:43
Evans 34	3	36N53'45	92w26'26	6:09:46
Evansville 11	3	39N41'46	94w43'13	6:18:53
Evansville 69	3	39N26'59	92w18'08	6:09:13
Eve 108	3	37N50'23	94w35'00	6:18:20
Evening Shade 107	3	37N34'32	92w08'29	6:08:34
Everett 19	3	38N30'16	94w25'37	6:17:42
Eversonville 58	3	39N54'32	93w21'35	6:13:26
Everton 29	3	37N20'33	93w42'08	6:14:49
Evona 38	3	40N11'52	94w19'44	6:17:19
Ewing 56	26	40N00'22	91w42'49	6:06:51
Excello 61	3	39N38'10	92w28'31	6:09:54
Excelsior 71	3	38N28'39	92w43'19	6:10:53
Excelsior Springs 24	3	39N20'21	94w13'33	6:16:54
Excelsior Springs Junction 24	3	39N14'16	94w14'25	6:16:58
Exeter 5	3	36N40'20	93w56'27	6:15:46
Fabius 52	3	40N17'19	92w08'16	6:08:33
Fagus 12	3	36N30'41	90w16'01	6:01:04
Fairdealing 91	3	36N39'46	90w37'00	6:02:28
Fairfax 3	3	40N20'19	95w23'35	6:21:34
Fairfield 8	3	38N09'05	93w23'39	6:13:35
Fair Grounds 115	1	38N40	90w13	6:00:52
Fair Grove 39	3	37N23'02	93w09'04	6:12:36
Fair Haven 108	3	37N58'35	94w10'23	6:16:42
Fairleigh 11	3	39N47	94w48	6:19:12
Fairmont 23	3	40N19'53	91w54'35	6:07:38
Fairmount 48	3	39N06'38	94w27'46	6:17:51
Fair Play 84	3	37N37'48	93w34'23	6:14:18
Fairport 32	3	39N59'16	94w20'45	6:17:23
Fairview 73	3	36N49'03	94w05'17	6:16:21
Fairview 95	40	38N44	90w15	6:01:00
Fairview 106	3	36N38'16	92w51'31	6:11:26
Fairview Acres 94	3	37N51'28	90w32'00	6:02:08
Fairville 97	3	39N13'55	93w13'05	6:12:52
Faith 66	3	38N03'16	92w23'51	6:09:35
Falcon 53	3	37N36'18	92w22'43	6:09:31
Falling Spring 75	3	36N51	91w17	6:05:08
Fanchon 46	3	36N47'42	91w42'01	6:06:48
Fanning 28	3	38N02'14	91w28'11	6:05:53
Farber 4	3	39N16'21	91w34'28	6:06:18
Farewell 75	3	36N30'04	91w21'41	6:05:27
Farley 83	3	39N16'56	94w49'52	6:19:19
Farmer 82	3	39N15'26	91w18'33	6:05:14
Farmers City 3	3	40N33'11	95w26'56	6:21:48
Farmersville 59	3	39N57'39	93w32'30	6:14:10
Farmington 96	3	37N46'51	90w25'18	6:01:41
Faro 62	3	37N26'50	90w26'15	6:01:45
Farrar 79	3	37N42'08	89w41'19	5:58:45
Farrenburg 72	3	36N41'17	89w30'02	5:58:00
Faucett 11	3	39N36'00	94w47'50	6:19:11
Fayette 45	3	39N08'45	92w41'01	6:10:44
Fayetteville 51	3	38N52'52	93w45'22	6:15:01
Federal 94	3	37N50'31	90w30'17	6:02:01
Federal Reserve 48	3	39N03	94w31	6:18:04
Fegley 1	3	40N17'10	92w38'57	6:10:36
Feigler Ferry 37	3	38N33'50	91w36'39	6:06:27
Femme Osage 92	3	38N38'12	90w56'30	6:03:46
Fenton 95	40	38N30'47	90w26'09	6:01:45
Fenwick 51	3	38N40'11	94w06'18	6:16:25
Ferguson 95	40	38N44'39	90w18'22	6:01:13
Fern Glen 95	40	38N33'07	90w31'53	6:02:08
Fernridge 95	40	38N40'51	90w28'39	6:01:55
Fernview Estates 95	40	38N40	90w26	6:01:44
Ferrelview 83	3	39N18'40	94w39'53	6:18:40
Fertile 110	3	38N04'26	90w41'08	6:02:45
Festus 50	12	38N13'14	90w23'45	6:01:35
Fiddlers Ford 29	3	37N23'02	93w47'56	6:15:12
Fidelity 49	3	37N04'05	94w18'47	6:17:15
Field 115	1	38N38	90w15	6:01:00
Fields Creek 42	3	38N25	93w47	6:15:08
Filley 20	3	37N45'32	93w56'56	6:15:48
Fillmore 2	3	40N01'31	94w58'24	6:19:54
Findley 34	3	37N01	92w41	6:10:44
Finey 42	3	38N14'02	93w32'44	6:14:11
Finley Falls 112	3	37N08'19	92w50'24	6:11:22
Firma 92	2	38N53'21	90w40'33	6:02:42
Fishertown 101	3	37N00	91w20	6:05:20
Fisk 12	3	36N46'55	90w12'31	6:00:50
Five Mile 73	3	36N58	94w33	6:18:12
Flag Spring 81	10	38N01'30	91w36'13	6:06:25
Flag Springs 2	3	40N01'30	94w40'00	6:18:40
Flamm City 50	3	38N25'01	90w21'24	6:01:26
Flat 81	3	37N44'43	91w55'44	6:07:43
Flat River 94	3	37N51'04	90w31'14	6:02:05
Flatwood 101	3	37N13'16	91w26'51	6:05:47
Flatwoods 91	3	36N40'50	90w42'01	6:02:48
Fleming 89	3	39N11'57	94w03'55	6:16:16
Flemington 84	3	37N48'17	93w30'04	6:14:00
Fletchall 113	3	40N31	94w24	6:17:36
Fletcher 50	3	38N09'57	90w44'00	6:02:56
Flinn 48	3	38N57'29	94w32'57	6:18:12
Flint Hill 87	3	39N37'26	91w22'59	6:05:32
Flint Hill 92	8	38N51'18	90w51'40	6:03:27
Flordell Hills 95	40	38N43'03	90w15'56	6:01:04
Florence 71	3	38N35'20	92w58'44	6:11:55
Florida 69	3	39N29'35	91w47'13	6:07:09
Florissant 95	40	38N47'21	90w19'21	6:01:17
Floyd 89	3	39N11'33	94w06'38	6:16:27
Flucom 50	4	38N06'04	90w26'33	6:01:46
Foil 77	3	36N45'22	92w38'07	6:10:32
Foley 57	16	39N02'47	90w44'32	6:02:58
Folk 76	3	38N25'17	92w05'52	6:08:23
Folker 23	3	40N32	91w53	6:07:32
Foose 30	3	37N33'41	93w08'47	6:12:35
Forbes 44	3	39N54'10	95w04'57	6:20:20
Ford City 38	3	40N06'42	94w27'52	6:17:51
Fordham 32	3	39N49'48	94w16'13	6:17:05
Fordland 112	3	37N09'27	92w56'26	6:11:46
Forest City 44	3	39N58'57	95w11'30	6:20:46
Forest Green 21	3	39N18'54	92w50'15	6:11:21
Forest Mills 49	3	37N10'36	94w12'55	6:16:52
Forest Park 55	3	36N56	93w55	6:15:40
Forest Springs 52	3	40N11'10	91w57'18	6:07:49
Foristell 92	17	38N48'54	90w57'21	6:03:49
Forker 58	3	39N43'09	93w11'08	6:12:45
Forkners Hill 112	3	37N28'22	92w54'32	6:11:38
Fornfelt 100	3	37N13	89w31	5:58:04
Forrest Mill 49	3	37N07	94w10	6:16:40
Forsyth 106	3	36N41'06	93w07'11	6:12:29
Fort Bellefontaine 95	40	38N50'10	90w14'31	6:00:58
Fortescue 44	3	40N03'08	95w19'05	6:21:16
Fort Henry 88	3	39N27'49	92w36'27	6:10:26
Fort Leonard Wood 85	11	37N50	92w12	6:08:48
Fort Osage 48	3	39N09	94w14	6:16:56
Fortuna 68	3	38N34'00	92w47'52	6:11:11
Fort Wyman Heights 81	10	37N57	91w48	6:07:12
Fort Zumwalt 92	2	38N49	90w42	6:02:48
Foster 7	3	38N09'58	94w30'26	6:18:02
Fountain Grove 58	3	39N42'39	93w18'56	6:13:16
Fourmile Corner 109	49	38N30'40	91w02'46	6:04:11
Four Points 28	3	37N57'10	91w05'44	6:04:23
Fowkes 69	3	39N28'59	92w04'17	6:08:17
Fowler 107	3	37N14'00	92w12'59	6:08:52
Fox Creek 41	3	40N15	93w49	6:15:16
Fox Creek 95	6	38N34'16	90w41'20	6:02:45
Fox Springs 28	3	38N00'31	91w27'33	6:05:50
Fraile 72	3	36N25'05	89w49'02	5:59:16
Frankclay 94	3	37N51'42	90w36'54	6:02:28
Frankenstein 76	3	38N34'27	91w52'56	6:07:32
Frankford 82	3	39N29	91w19	6:05:16
Franklin 45	3	39N00'42	92w45'11	6:11:01
Franks 85	47	37N57'10	92w02'12	6:08:09
Frazier 11	3	39N37'44	94w40'03	6:18:40
Fredericksburg 37	3	38N36'27	91w38'29	6:06:34
Fredericktown 62	3	37N33'35	90w17'38	6:01:11
Fredville 73	44	36N54'34	94w24'45	6:17:39
Freeborn 35	3	36N26	89w59	5:59:56
Freeburg 76	3	38N18'54	91w55'21	6:07:41
Freedom 54	3	38N59	93w37	6:14:28
Freedom 76	3	38N27'49	91w41'26	6:06:46
Freeman 19	3	38N37'06	94w30'18	6:18:01
Freistatt 55	3	37N01'06	93w53'51	6:15:35
Fremont 18	3	36N57'08	91w09'51	6:04:39
French Mills 62	3	37N27'21	90w29'21	6:01:57
French Village 94	3	37N58'21	90w23'23	6:01:34
Friedenburg 79	3	37N42'03	89w47'38	5:59:11
Friedheim 16	3	37N34'12	89w49'12	5:59:17
Frisbee 35	3	36N21'00	90w01'43	6:00:07
Frisco 103	3	36N45'32	89w51'44	5:59:27
Fristoe 8	3	38N07'00	93w16'32	6:13:06
Frohna 79	3	37N38'19	89w37'17	5:58:29
Frontenac 95	40	38N38'08	90w24'54	6:01:40
Fruitland 16	3	37N26'55	89w38'19	5:58:33
Fruitland 39	3	37N23'21	93w14'00	6:12:56
Frumet 50	4	38N09'34	90w41'35	6:02:46
Fuersville 76	3	38N23'37	91w40'29	6:06:42
Fulton 14	3	38N50'48	91w56'52	6:07:47
Furner 10	3	38N55'03	92w24'00	6:09:36
Fuson 114	3	37N19'56	92w29'54	6:10:00
Gads Hill 111	3	37N14'18	90w41'48	6:02:47
Gaines 42	3	38N17'14	93w39'41	6:14:39
Gaines Ford 63	3	38N03'36	91w53'33	6:07:34
Gainesville 77	3	36N36'11	92w25'41	6:09:43
Galena 104	3	36N48'19	93w27'59	6:13:52
Galesburg 49	3	37N16'10	94w30'55	6:18:04
Gallatin 31	3	39N54'52	93w57'43	6:15:51
Galloway 39	44	37N08'12	93w14'16	6:12:57
Galmey 43	3	37N53'39	93w21'43	6:13:27
Galt 40	3	40N07'43	93w23'12	6:13:33
Gamburg 91	3	36N38'14	90w38'24	6:02:34
Game 78	3	36N11	89w40	5:58:40
Gamma 70	3	39N04'02	91w20'29	6:05:22
Gara 38	3	40N22'15	94w15'48	6:17:03
Garber 106	3	36N41'30	93w17'56	6:13:12
Garden City 19	3	38N33'40	94w11'28	6:16:46
Gardenview 95	40	38N48	90w20	6:01:20
Gardner 41	3	40N18'43	93w58'31	6:15:54
Gardnerville 92	2	38N48'41	90w31'34	6:02:06
Garfield 75	3	36N35'07	91w19'33	6:05:18
Garland 42	3	38N23	93w46	6:15:04
Garnsey 53	3	37N49'25	92w27'25	6:09:50
Garrettsburg 11	3	39N41'15	94w42'03	6:18:48
Garrison 22	3	36N50'20	93w01'10	6:12:05
Garwood 90	3	37N03'59	90w52'40	6:03:31
Gasconade 37	3	38N40'10	91w33'36	6:06:14
Gascondy 76	3	38N17'58	91w51'33	6:07:26
Gashland 24	3	39N14'47	94w34'32	6:18:18
Gateway Drive 73	3	37N03'07	94w28'42	6:17:55
Gatewood 91	3	36N34'37	91w05'23	6:04:22
Gaunt Ford 30	3	37N35'59	92w59'14	6:11:57
Gaynor 74	3	40N29'16	94w42'28	6:18:50
Gazette 82	3	39N12'16	91w23'45	6:05:35
Gentry 38	3	40N19'54	94w25'12	6:17:41
Gentryville 34	3	36N51'50	92w21'38	6:09:27
Gentryville 38	3	40N07'59	94w20'38	6:17:23
Georgetown 80	3	38N45'31	93w14'16	6:12:57
Georgeville 89	3	39N29'46	93w54'29	6:15:38
Gerald 36	3	38N23'59	91w19'50	6:05:19
Germantown (Noah) 42	3	38N17'24	94w01'07	6:16:04
Gerster 93	3	37N57'12	93w34'32	6:14:18
Gibbs 1	3	40N05'52	92w25'00	6:09:40
Giboney 79	3	37N48'17	89w59'26	5:59:58
Gibson 35	3	36N26'28	90w01'51	6:00:07
Gibson 78	3	36N07'04	89w50'42	5:59:23
Gideon 72	3	36N27'07	89w55'09	5:59:41
Gifford (South Gifford) 61	3	40N01'32	92w40'53	6:10:44
Gilbert 35	3	36N01'59	90w02'34	6:00:10
Gilbertson Ford 53	3	37N47'28	92w50'26	6:11:22
Gildehouse 36	3	38N29'05	90w56'18	6:03:45
Gill 78	3	36N13'09	89w47'22	5:59:09
Gilliam 97	3	39N14'00	93w00'16	6:12:01
Gillis Bluff 12	3	36N33	90w17	6:01:08
Gilman City 41	3	40N08'37	93w52'18	6:15:29
Gilmore 92	8	38N48'37	90w48'22	6:03:13
Ginger Blue 60	3	36N35'19	94w27'38	6:17:51
Gipsy 9	3	37N08'49	90w10'46	6:00:43
Girdner 34	3	36N51'14	92w35'13	6:10:21
Gladden 33	3	37N29'55	91w27'23	6:05:50
Gladstone 24	3	39N12'14	94w33'16	6:18:13
Glaser Ford 37	3	38N13'57	91w31'11	6:06:05
Glasgow 45	3	39N13'38	92w50'47	6:11:23
Glasgow Village 95	40	38N45'13	90w11'54	6:00:48
Glaze 66	3	38N06	92w31	6:10:04
Glenaire 24	3	39N13'17	94w27'04	6:17:48
Glenallen 9	3	37N19'04	90w01'40	6:00:07
Glencoe 95	40	38N32'40	90w37'25	6:02:30
Glendale 86	3	40N29'12	92w45'48	6:11:03
Glendale 95	40	38N35'45	90w22'37	6:01:30
Glen Echo 95	40	38N43	90w18	6:01:12
Glen Echo Park 95	40	38N42'04	90w17'52	6:01:11
Glenn 91	3	36N31'49	90w41'03	6:02:44
Glennon 9	3	37N11'20	89w55'06	5:59:40
Glennonville 35	3	36N34'51	90w09'20	6:00:37
Glen Park 50	12	38N17	90w24	6:01:36
Glensted 71	3	38N30'56	92w51'19	6:11:25
Glenstone 39	44	37N11	93w17	6:13:08
Glen Town 29	3	37N30'44	93w48'24	6:15:14
Glenwood 98	44	40N31'03	92w34'34	6:10:18
Glenwood Junction 98	44	40N31'53	92w35'10	6:10:21
Glidewell 39	44	37N18'16	93w19'37	6:13:18
Globe 55	3	36N55'51	93w50'43	6:15:23
Glover 47	3	37N29'11	90w41'28	6:02:46
Gobler 35	3	36N09'22	89w57'33	5:59:50
Godair 78	3	36N22	89w43	5:58:52
Goebel 75	3	36N43	91w18	6:05:12
Golden 5	3	36N31'27	93w39'13	6:14:37
Golden City 6	3	37N23'35	94w05'37	6:16:22
Goldman 50	3	38N17'50	90w31'17	6:02:05
Goldsberry 46	3	37N00	91w43	6:06:52
Goldsberry 61	3	39N57'44	92w46'09	6:11:05
Gomer 13	3	39N45	93w56	6:15:44
Gooch Mill 27	3	38N49	92w35	6:10:20

Goodfellow Terrace 95
40 38N41'50 90w16'14 6:01:05
Goodhope 34 3 36N54'32 92w48'27 6:11:14
Goodland 47 3 37N38'10 91w00'06 6:04:00
Goodland 52 3 39N58'48 92w18'05 6:09:12
Goodman 60 3 36N44'30 94w23'56 6:17:36
Goodman Heights 60
3 36N44 94w23 6:17:32
Goodson 84 3 37N42'07 93w15'05 6:13:00
Good Water 47 3 37N42'48 91w02'46 6:04:11
Gordonville 16 3 37N18'40 89w40'45 5:58:43
Gore 109 3 38N42'52 91w19'20 6:05:17
Gorin (South Gorin) 99
3 40N21'36 92w01'27 6:08:06
Goshen 65 5 40N22'58 93w40'46 6:14:43
Gospel Ridge 85 3 37N49'17 92w09'32 6:08:38
Goss 69 3 39N30'50 91w56'32 6:07:46
Gowdy 19 3 38N45'56 94w17'49 6:17:11
Gower 25 3 39N36'39 94w35'57 6:18:24
Grace 53 3 37N51'27 92w44'40 6:10:59
Graff 114 3 37N19'03 92w16'57 6:09:08
Graham 74 3 40N12'03 95w02'11 6:20:09
Grain Valley 48 3 39N00'54 94w11'54 6:16:48
Granby 73 44 36N55'09 94w15'18 6:17:01
Grand Center 88
44 39N46 92w37 6:10:28
Grand Falls 73 3 37N04 94w30 6:18:00
Grandin 18 3 36N49'45 90w49'22 6:03:17
Grand Pass 97 3 39N12'23 93w26'33 6:13:46
Grandview 48 3 38N53'09 94w31'58 6:18:08
Granger 99 3 40N28'04 91w58'32 6:07:54
Graniteville 47 3 37N39'01 90w40'47 6:02:43
Grant 95 40 38N34 90w20 6:01:20
Grant City 113 3 40N29'15 94w24'39 6:17:39
Grantsville 58 3 39N56 93w04 6:12:16
Grantwood 95 40 38N33'15 90w20'42 6:01:23
Granville 69 3 39N33'45 92w05'51 6:08:23
Grape Grove 89 3 39N26 93w51 6:15:24
Grassy 9 3 37N15'39 90w07'25 6:00:30
Gratiot 115 1 38N37'20 90w16'53 6:01:08
Gravel Hill 16 3 37N21'27 89w50'24 5:59:22
Gravelton 111 3 37N17'54 90w15'14 6:01:01
Gravois 115 1 38N35 90w19 6:01:16
Gravois Mills 71
3 38N18'30 92w49'31 6:11:18
Graydon Springs 84
3 37N27'24 93w30'35 6:14:02
Grayridge (Gray Ridge Sta) 103
3 36N49'27 89w46'51 5:59:07
Grayson 25 3 39N32'00 94w33'51 6:18:15
Grays Point 55 3 37N14'46 93w58'38 6:15:55
Gray Summit 36 6 38N29'23 90w49'00 6:03:16
Graysville 86 3 40N26'45 92w46'44 6:11:07
Greeley 90 3 37N30'54 91w11'13 6:04:45
Green Bay Terrace 15
3 38N05'34 92w45'42 6:11:03
Greenbrier 9 3 37N06'38 90w01'32 6:00:06
Green Castle 105
3 40N15'43 92w52'44 6:11:31
Green City 105 3 40N16'07 92w57'11 6:11:49
Green Cox 16 3 37N08'26 89w50'20 5:59:21
Greendale 95 40 38N41'43 90w18'50 6:01:15
Greenfield 29 3 37N24'55 93w50'27 6:15:22
Green Forest 12 3 36N46'01 90w27'54 6:01:52
Green Grove 1 3 40N18'50 92w43'13 6:10:53
Greenlawn 87 3 39N28'39 91w41'10 6:06:45
Green Mound Ridge 22
3 36N56 93w17 6:13:08
Green Mountain 114
3 37N20'09 92w19'29 6:09:18
Green Oaks 103 3 36N47'17 90w09'51 6:00:39
Green Ridge 80 3 38N37'13 93w24'33 6:13:38
Greensburg 52 3 40N17'47 92w13'00 6:08:52
Greenstreet 36 3 38N24'23 91w12'11 6:04:49
Greentop 98 3 40N20'49 92w34'08 6:10:17
Green Town 75 3 36N30'51 91w32'32 6:06:10
Greenview 85 3 37N39'22 92w15'28 6:09:02
Greenville 24 3 39N23'06 94w15'45 6:17:03
Greenville 111 3 37N07'38 90w27'00 6:01:48
Greenville Ford 91
3 36N44'44 90w44'08 6:02:57
Greenwood 48 3 38N51'06 94w20'37 6:17:22
Greer 75 3 36N46'10 91w21'12 6:05:25
Gregory 23 23 40N08 91w30 6:06:00
Gregory Landing 23
3 40N16'53 91w29'46 6:05:59
Gretna 106 3 36N39'37 93w16'04 6:13:04
Griffin Ford 60 3 36N34'00 94w18'17 6:17:13
Grimes Mill 114 3 37N19'18 92w23'34 6:09:34
Grimmet 46 3 36N46'53 92w00'23 6:08:02
Grisham 9 3 37N22'47 90w06'03 6:00:24
Grogan 107 3 37N09'17 91w53'10 6:07:33
Grover 51 3 38N52 93w33 6:14:12
Grover 95 40 38N34'34 90w38'14 6:02:33
Grovespring 114 3 37N23'59 92w36'34 6:10:26
Grubville 50 3 38N17'18 90w45'17 6:03:01
Guam 103 3 36N54'07 89w49'25 5:59:18
Guilford 74 3 40N10'13 94w44'10 6:18:57
Guinn 86 3 40N34'54 92w39'17 6:10:37
Gulfton 49 3 37N11'01 94w32'41 6:18:11
Gumbo 94 3 37N51'45 90w33'45 6:02:15
Gumbo 95 40 38N40'05 90w37'04 6:02:28
Gunn City 19 3 38N40'02 94w09'43 6:16:39
Guthrie 14 3 38N45'25 92w05'47 6:08:23
Guyton 25 3 39N30'52 94w19'25 6:17:18
Hackleman Corner 20
3 37N51'04 93w52'29 6:15:30
Hackler Ford 30 3 37N41'34 92w58'28 6:11:54
Hadley 90 3 37N04'22 90w47'53 6:03:12
Hadley 95 40 38N39 90w19 6:01:16
Hadsell 19 3 38N41'54 94w08'12 6:16:33
Hagers Grove 102
45 39N49'52 92w13'23 6:08:54
Hahatonka 15 3 37N58'22 92w46'06 6:11:04
Hahn 9 3 37N12'19 90w04'11 6:00:17
Hahns Mill 62 3 37N33'31 90w09'18 6:00:37
Hailey 5 3 36N42'39 93w42'26 6:14:50
Hale 17 3 39N36'13 93w20'32 6:13:22
Hale Crossing 34
3 36N52'56 92w11'14 6:08:45
Half Rock 65 3 40N16'23 93w26'08 6:13:45
Half Way 84 3 37N36'59 93w14'40 6:12:59
Halifax 94 3 38N00'43 90w29'23 6:01:58
Halls 11 3 39N38'00 94w58'23 6:19:54
Hallsville 10 3 39N07'01 92w13'14 6:08:53
Halltown 55 3 37N11'36 93w37'31 6:14:30
Halston Mill 29 3 37N27'16 93w43'54 6:14:56
Hamburg 92 3 38N40'11 90w43'54 6:02:56
Hamden 21 3 39N34'38 92w49'23 6:11:18
Hamilton 13 3 39N44'37 93w59'53 6:16:00
Hamlin Farm 78 3 36N14 89w45 5:59:00
Hammond 77 3 36N40'32 92w38'39 6:10:35
Hampton 83 3 39N16'53 94w43'59 6:18:56
Hams Prairie 14 3 38N46'02 91w55'08 6:07:41
Hancock 85 47 37N59'11 92w10'54 6:08:44
Handley 30 3 37N31'42 92w55'46 6:11:43
Handley 108 3 37N52'56 94w11'50 6:16:47
Handy 91 3 36N48'33 91w06'25 6:04:26
Hanley Hills 95
40 38N41'09 90w19'26 6:01:18
Hanleyville 12 3 36N41'19 90w17'24 6:01:10
Hanna 85 3 37N44'06 92w14'48 6:08:59
Hannibal 64 27 39N42'30 91w21'30 6:05:26
Hannon 6 3 37N37'21 94w29'38 6:17:59
Happy Hollow 110
3 38N00'05 90w43'30 6:02:54
Hardeman 97 3 39N05'22 93w00'37 6:12:02
Hardenville 77 3 36N35'21 92w22'16 6:09:29
Hardin 89 3 39N16'15 93w50'03 6:15:20
Hardyville 93 3 37N53'40 93w45'36 6:15:02
Harg 10 3 38N55'36 92w13'52 6:08:55
Hargrove 35 3 36N03'57 90w19'13 6:01:17
Harkes 88 3 39N20'54 92w28'50 6:09:55
Harlem 24 3 39N07'04 94w35'12 6:18:21
Harlow Ford 107 3 37N04'20 91w42'18 6:06:49
Harmony 110 3 37N49 91w00 6:04:00
Harold 39 3 37N22'40 93w30'55 6:14:04
Harper 93 3 38N03'45 93w31'06 6:14:04
Harrelson 19 3 38N46'08 94w29'28 6:17:58
Harrill Ford 53
47 37N43'37 92w27'51 6:09:51
Harris 105 3 40N18'21 93w21'00 6:13:24
Harrisburg 10 3 39N08'30 92w27'45 6:09:51
Harrisonville 19
3 38N39'12 94w20'55 6:17:24
Harry S Truman 48
3 39N04 94w25 6:17:40
Hart 60 44 36N44'14 94w36'20 6:18:25
Hart 61 3 39N50'11 92w49'23 6:11:18
Hart 114 3 37N12 92w28 6:09:52
Hartford 82 3 39N11 91w17 6:05:08
Hartford 86 3 40N28'11 92w50'08 6:11:21
Hartle Ford 16 3 37N25'59 89w51'11 5:59:25
Hartsburg 10 3 38N41'42 92w18'31 6:09:14
Hartshorn 107 3 37N15'53 91w40'13 6:06:41
Hartville 114 3 37N15'03 92w30'37 6:10:02
Hartwell 42 3 38N26'07 93w56'04 6:15:44
Hartzell 72 3 36N29'07 89w51'21 5:59:25
Harvester 92 2 38N44'45 90w34'50 6:02:19
Harvey 42 3 38N26'36 93w51'14 6:15:25
Harviell 12 3 36N39'53 90w28'20 6:01:53
Harwood 108 3 37N57'22 94w09'15 6:16:37
Haseltine 39 44 37N12'34 93w23'09 6:13:33
Hassard 87 37 39N39'25 91w39'34 6:06:38
Hastain 8 3 38N12'07 93w10'34 6:12:42
Hatch 87 3 39N35'20 91w37'04 6:06:28
Hatfield 41 3 40N31'44 94w09'17 6:16:37
Hattie 107 3 37N04'47 91w46'24 6:07:06
Hatton 14 3 39N01'27 92w01'34 6:08:06
Havenhurst 60 3 36N35'00 94w22'27 6:17:30
Haw Creek 71 3 38N27 92w58 6:11:52
Hawkeye 85 47 38N00'20 92w23'34 6:09:34
Hawk Point 57 28 38N58'15 91w07'52 6:04:31
Hayden 63 47 38N04'30 91w58'36 6:07:54
Haydite 83 3 39N29'51 94w48'06 6:19:12
Hayes Park 48 3 39N11 94w12 6:16:48
Haynesville 25 3 39N27'41 94w18'56 6:17:16
Hayti 78 3 36N14'01 89w44'58 5:59:00
Hayti Heights 78
3 36N14'02 89w46'10 5:59:05
Hayward 78 3 36N23'55 89w40'12 5:58:41
Hayward City 100
3 37N00'29 89w36'04 5:58:24
Haywood City 100
3 37N02 89w38 5:58:32
Hazelgreen 53 3 37N46'04 92w25'40 6:09:43
Hazel Hill 51 3 38N53 93w47 6:15:08
Hazel Run 94 3 37N56'49 90w27'56 6:01:52
Hazelwood 95 40 38N46'17 90w22'15 6:01:29
Hazleton 107 3 37N31'30 92w01'29 6:08:06
Head Ford 111 3 37N18'22 90w27'57 6:01:52
Heagy 103 3 37N02'18 89w48'10 5:59:13
Heaths Creek 80 3 38N52 93w07 6:12:28
Heatonville 55 3 37N11'18 93w47'57 6:15:12
Hebron 34 3 36N44 91w52 6:07:28
Hecla 58 3 39N56'23 93w18'14 6:13:13
Hedge City 52 3 40N01'48 92w08'12 6:08:33
Helena 2 3 39N54'46 94w38'57 6:18:36
Helm 85 47 37N59'03 92w09'15 6:08:37
Helton 64 27 39N46'29 91w25'16 6:05:41
Heman Park 95 40 38N40 90w18 6:01:12
Hematite 50 3 38N12'07 90w28'51 6:01:55
Hemenway 91 3 36N32'54 90w39'06 6:02:36
Hemple 25 3 39N43'32 94w33'41 6:18:15
Henderson 112 3 37N08'28 93w03'35 6:12:14
Henderson Ford 63
3 38N10'40 91w51'52 6:07:27
Henderson Mound 72
3 36N46 89w35 5:58:20
Hendrickson 12 3 36N54'16 90w28'08 6:01:53
Henley 26 3 38N20'40 92w19'20 6:09:17
Henrietta 89 3 39N14'03 93w56'07 6:15:44
Henry 108 3 38N00 94w33 6:18:12
Henson 67 3 36N51'22 89w15'09 5:57:01
Herculaneum 50 12 38N16'06 90w22'48 6:01:31
Hercules 106 3 36N42'27 92w52'22 6:11:29
Hereford 14 3 38N59'30 92w05'37 6:08:22
Hermann 37 19 38N42'15 91w26'14 6:05:45
Hermitage 43 3 37N56'29 93w18'58 6:13:16
Hermondale 78 3 36N00'58 89w54'53 5:59:40
Herndon 97 3 39N00'15 93w16'12 6:13:05
Herrick Ford 30 3 37N51'39 92w54'45 6:11:39
Hester 64 3 39N54'39 91w37'36 6:06:30
Hickman 103 3 36N59'26 90w07'01 6:00:28
Hickman Mills 48
3 38N55'10 94w31'06 6:18:04
Hickory 44 3 40N05 95w06 6:20:24
Hickory Barren 39
3 37N20'52 93w13'16 6:12:53
Hickory Creek 40
3 39N59'59 93w39'56 6:14:40
Hickory Grove 109
17 38N48 91w00 6:04:00
Hickory Hill 26 3 38N24'02 92w21'34 6:09:26
Higbee 88 3 39N18'17 92w30'45 6:10:03
Higdon 62 3 37N35'34 90w10'04 6:00:40
Higginsville 54 3 39N04'21 93w43'01 6:14:52
High Gate 63 10 38N09'28 91w40'29 6:06:42
High Hill 70 3 38N52'42 91w23'00 6:05:32
Highland 79 3 37N39'52 89w53'29 5:59:34
Highlandville 22
3 36N55'58 93w16'49 6:13:07
Highley Heights 94
3 37N52'55 90w31'20 6:02:05
High Place Lookout Tower 77
3 36N42'54 92w10'01 6:08:40
High Point 68 3 38N29'04 92w35'26 6:10:22
High Prairie 112
3 37N18 92w45 6:11:00
High Ridge 50 3 38N27'32 90w32'11 6:02:09
Hilda 106 3 36N39'49 92w58'55 6:11:56
Hilderorand 16 3 37N34'32 89w51'14 5:59:25
Hill 17 3 39N34 93w35 6:14:20
Hill City 5 3 36N39'58 93w40'18 6:14:41
Hilldale 45 3 39N03'47 92w33'40 6:10:15
Hillhouse Addition 15
3 37N52 92w24 6:09:36
Hilliard 12 3 36N49'31 90w25'00 6:01:40
Hillsboro 50 3 38N13'56 90w33'46 6:02:15
Hillsdale 95 40 38N41'00 90w17'02 6:01:08
Hills Store 103 3 36N43'11 89w48'32 5:59:14
Hilltop 5 3 36N39'15 93w51'21 6:15:25
Hill Top 91 3 36N38'27 90w48'06 6:03:12
Himmel 103 3 36N58'34 89w45'10 5:59:01
Hinch 28 46 38N03'46 91w09'19 6:04:37
Hine 95 40 38N40'59 90w31'24 6:02:06
Hines Landing 16
3 37N33'28 89w31'35 5:58:06
Hinton 10 3 39N03'13 92w20'25 6:09:22
Hiram 111 3 37N10'44 90w18'53 6:01:16
Hitt 99 3 40N33'49 92w15'20 6:09:01
Hobart 57 3 39N12'39 91w05'56 6:04:24
Hoberg 55 3 37N04'11 93w50'55 6:15:24
Hobson 33 3 37N45'20 91w37'55 6:06:32
Hocomo 46 3 36N36'53 92w00'14 6:08:01
Hodge 54 3 39N13'25 93w37'36 6:14:30
Hoecker 66 3 38N19'55 92w17'25 6:09:10
Hoene Spring 50 3 38N27'05 90w36'52 6:02:27
Hoffins 28 3 38N05'45 91w21'38 6:05:27
Hoffman 27 3 38N50'37 92w56'42 6:11:47
Hoffman Junction 94
3 37N54'36 90w33'23 6:02:14
Hogan 47 3 37N30'40 90w41'45 6:02:47
Holcomb 35 3 36N23'57 90w01'25 6:00:06
Holden 51 3 38N42'51 93w59'28 6:15:58
Holiday Shores 110
3 37N44'21 90w40'28 6:02:42
Holland 78 3 36N03'21 89w52'15 5:59:29
Holliday 69 3 39N29'40 92w07'43 6:08:31
Holliday Landing 111
3 37N02'10 90w25'22 6:01:41
Hollister 106 3 36N37'16 93w12'55 6:12:52
Hollow 95 6 38N33'00 90w42'29 6:02:50
Hollywood 35 3 36N03'15 90w11'10 6:00:45
Holman 112 3 37N16'23 93w03'11 6:12:13
Holmes Park 48 3 38N57'09 94w32'08 6:18:09
Holmes Place 35 3 36N32'19 90w11'36 6:00:46
Holstein 109 3 38N39'19 91w10'16 6:04:41
Holt 24 3 39N27'10 94w20'31 6:17:22
Holts Summit 14 3 38N38'25 92w07'20 6:08:29
Homer 7 3 38N16 94w34 6:18:16
Homestead Village 89
3 39N20 94w13 6:16:52
Homestown 78 3 36N19'55 89w49'33 5:59:18
Honey Creek 26 3 38N32 92w10 6:08:40
Honey Creek 42 3 38N26 93w51 6:15:24
Hooker 53 3 37N46 92w46 6:11:04
Hooker 85 3 37N51'36 92w03'38 6:08:15
Hoover 83 3 39N22'08 94w40'00 6:18:40
Hope 76 3 38N31'42 91w40'16 6:06:41
Hope 82 22 39N35'44 91w12'07 6:04:48
Hopewell 109 3 38N41'19 91w08'26 6:04:34
Hopewell 110 3 37N53'15 90w42'10 6:02:49
Hopkins 74 3 40N33'03 94w49'09 6:19:17
Hopkinsville 57 3 39N10'27 91w06'20 6:04:25
Horine 50 12 38N16'00 90w25'28 6:01:42
Hornersville 35 3 36N02'30 90w06'50 6:00:27
Hornersville Junction 35
3 36N02'23 90w05'01 6:00:20
Hornet 73 44 36N57'43 94w33'25 6:18:14
Hortense 42 3 38N23 93w46 6:15:04
Horton 108 3 37N58'29 94w21'54 6:17:28
Hough 72 3 36N44 89w28 5:57:52
House Creek 18 3 37N01'03 91w03'45 6:04:15
House Springs 50
3 38N24'32 90w34'12 6:02:17
Houston 107 3 37N19'34 91w57'21 6:07:49
Houstonia 80 3 38N53'56 93w21'29 6:13:26
Houston Lake 83 3 39N11'34 94w37'12 6:18:29
Howards Ridge 77
3 36N31'44 92w19'55 6:09:20
Howardville 72 3 36N34'05 89w36'02 5:58:24
Howell 46 3 36N43 91w50 6:07:20
Howell 92 2 38N44'35 90w36'39 6:02:27
Howes 33 3 37N42'34 91w30'52 6:06:03
Howes Mill 33 3 37N38'04 91w15'32 6:05:02
Howland 86 3 40N32'05 92w57'26 6:11:50
H S Jewell 39 44 37N12 93w18 6:13:12
Hubbard 88 3 39N34'57 92w41'34 6:10:46
Hubbells 12 3 36N34'03 90w33'26 6:02:14
Hubble 16 3 37N17 89w43 5:58:52
Huben 53 3 37N35'14 92w45'05 6:11:00
Huber 19 3 38N41'18 94w20'12 6:17:21
Huckaby 84 3 37N47'22 93w14'59 6:13:00
Hudson 7 3 38N12'13 94w05'24 6:16:22
Huggins 38 3 40N16 94w26 6:17:44
Huggins 107 3 37N19'12 92w11'54 6:08:48
Hughes 74 3 40N12 95w00 6:20:00
Hughesville 80 3 38N50'19 93w17'43 6:13:11

Hugo 15 3 37N59'43 92w39'32 6:10:38
Huiskamp 64 41 39N48'58 91w26'26 6:05:46
Humansville 84 3 37N47'40 93w34'40 6:14:19
Hume 7 3 38N05'24 94w35'01 6:18:20
Humphreys 105 3 40N07'32 93w19'08 6:13:17
Hunnewell 102 29 39N40'05 91w51'42 6:07:27
Hunter 18 3 36N53'26 90w50'56 6:03:24
Hunter Crossing 75 3 36N40'43 91w40'02 6:06:40
Hunterville 103 3 36N49'14 89w48'27 5:59:14
Huntingdale 42 3 38N28'36 93w49'01 6:15:16
Huntington 87 3 39N39'41 91w35'55 6:06:24
Huntleigh 95 40 38N36'57 90w24'38 6:01:39
Huntsdale 10 3 38N54'42 92w28'20 6:09:53
Huntsville 88 3 39N26'26 92w32'42 6:10:11
Hurdland 52 3 40N09'00 92w18'07 6:09:12
Hurley 104 3 36N55'53 93w29'56 6:14:00
Hurlingen 11 3 39N47'54 94w38'11 6:18:33
Huron 84 3 37N42'57 93w21'11 6:13:25
Hurricane 9 3 37N24'58 90w00'43 6:00:03
Hurricane Deck 15 3 38N07'54 92w47'37 6:11:10
Hurryville 94 3 37N50'24 90w27'29 6:01:50
Hutchison 87 3 39N20'45 91w38'33 6:06:34
Hutton Valley 46 3 36N57'42 91w52'59 6:07:32
Huzzah 28 3 37N54'15 91w09'26 6:04:38
Iantha 6 3 37N31'01 94w23'51 6:17:35
Iatan 83 3 39N28'31 94w58'57 6:19:56
Iberia 66 3 38N05'25 92w17'33 6:09:10
Iconium 93 3 38N06'21 93w32'40 6:14:11
Idalia 103 3 36N51'50 89w51'39 5:59:27
Idlewild 28 3 38N00'46 91w23'49 6:05:35
Idlewild 103 3 37N00'13 90w06'14 6:00:25
Ike 106 3 36N45 93w23 6:13:32
Ilasco 87 3 39N40'17 91w18'38 6:05:15
Illmo 100 19 37N13'11 89w30'32 5:58:02
Imperial 50 3 38N22'11 90w22'42 6:01:31
Independence 48 3 39N05'28 94w24'55 6:17:40
Index 19 3 38N37 94w09 6:16:36
Indian 82 3 39N16 91w21 6:05:24
Indian Creek 69 3 39N35'40 91w46'36 6:07:06
Indian Grove 21 3 39N30'38 93w02'05 6:12:08
Indian Lake 28 3 38N04 91w24 6:05:36
Indian Village 48 3 38N57'54 94w35'17 6:18:21
Ink 101 3 37N15'29 91w29'01 6:05:56
Inza 11 3 39N43 94w52 6:19:28
Ionia 8 3 38N30'15 93w19'26 6:13:18
Ipley 35 3 36N17'41 90w01'43 6:00:07
Ira 53 3 37N52'22 92w50'58 6:11:24
Irena 113 3 40N32'59 94w23'28 6:17:34
Irondale 110 3 37N49'55 90w40'41 6:02:43
Iron Gates 49 3 37N04'01 94w33'15 6:18:13
Iron Mountain 94 3 37N41'43 90w38'25 6:02:34
Iron Mountain Lake 94 3 37N41'35 90w37'21 6:02:29
Ironton 47 3 37N35'50 90w37'38 6:02:31
Irwin 6 3 37N35'19 94w17'07 6:17:08
Isabella 77 3 36N34'51 92w36'45 6:10:27
Isadora 113 3 40N31'33 94w31'03 6:18:04
Island City 38 3 40N08'44 94w34'15 6:18:17
Iuka Springs 93 3 38N05'51 93w55'16 6:15:41
Ives 103 3 36N47'07 90w09'51 6:00:39
Ivory 115 1 38N31'36 90w16'37 6:01:06
Jack 33 3 37N34'34 91w37'16 6:06:29
Jacket 60 3 36N30'37 94w06'28 6:16:26
Jackson 16 3 37N22'56 89w39'58 5:58:40
Jackson Mill 34 3 36N53'50 92w46'24 6:11:06
Jacksonville 53 3 37N33'30 92w25'21 6:09:41
Jacksonville 88 3 39N35'18 92w28'16 6:09:53
Jacobs 92 2 38N42'23 90w36'09 6:02:25
Jadwin 33 3 37N29'12 91w34'15 6:06:17
Jake Prairie 28 3 38N09'48 91w30'40 6:06:03
James 104 3 36N38 93w25 6:13:40
James Bayou 67 3 36N38 89w16 5:57:04
James Crews 48 3 39N05 94w33 6:18:12
Jameson 31 3 40N00'19 93w58'45 6:15:55
Jamesport 31 3 39N58'29 93w48'03 6:15:12
Jamestown 68 3 38N45'56 92w28'50 6:09:55
Jamesville 104 3 36N57'36 93w22'15 6:13:29
Jane 60 3 36N32'50 94w18'18 6:17:13
Japan 36 44 38N14'21 91w18'21 6:05:13
Jarvis 50 3 38N16'05 90w29'39 6:01:59
Jasper 49 3 37N20'10 94w18'04 6:17:12
Jaudon 19 3 38N45'34 94w35'21 6:18:21
Jaywye 72 3 36N28'57 89w42'04 5:58:48
Jedburgh 95 40 38N32'17 90w34'55 6:02:20
Jeddo 52 3 40N05 92w00 6:08:00
Jeff 75 3 36N30'27 91w23'17 6:05:33
Jefferson 2 44 39N51 94w50 6:19:20
Jefferson Barracks 95 1 38N29'39 90w16'49 6:01:07
Jefferson City 26 3 38N34'36 92w10'24 6:08:42
Jefferson Memorial 95 1 38N38 90w12 6:00:48
Jeffreys 48 3 38N55'41 94w31'52 6:18:07
Jeffriesburg 36 3 38N26'25 91w05'17 6:04:21
Jenkins 5 3 36N46'43 93w41'09 6:14:45
Jennings 95 40 38N43'09 90w15'37 6:01:02
Jerico 114 3 37N10'29 92w40'22 6:10:41
Jerico Springs 20 3 37N37'27 94w00'35 6:16:02
Jerktail 114 3 37N25'27 92w26'12 6:09:45
Jerome 81 3 37N55'34 91w58'39 6:07:55
Jesse M Donaldson 83 3 38N45 92w26 6:09:44
Jewett 62 3 37N22'49 90w30'05 6:02:00
J & G Junction 49 3 37N04 94w30 6:18:00
Jim Henry 66 3 38N18 92w18 6:09:12
Joachim 50 12 38N15 90w26 6:01:44
Joanna 87 3 39N32'27 91w40'09 6:06:41
Jobe 75 3 36N35'01 91w15'05 6:05:00
Johnson City 93 3 38N07'01 93w55'40 6:15:43
Johnson Ford 63 3 38N07'56 91w53'22 6:07:33
Johnson Mill 35 3 36N11'08 90w07'53 6:00:32
Johnston 61 3 40N00 92w22 6:09:28
Johnston Ford 112 3 37N21'38 92w47'45 6:11:11
Johnstown 7 3 38N18'36 94w04'56 6:16:20
Johnstown 49 3 37N09 94w26 6:17:44
Johnstown 58 3 39N54'12 92w58'27 6:11:54
Jolly 73 3 36N53'45 94w04'12 6:16:17
Jonesburg 70 3 38N51'12 91w18'21 6:05:13
Joplin 49 3 37N05'03 94w30'47 6:18:03
Jordan 43 3 38N01'17 93w08'28 6:12:34
Jordan W Chambers 95 1 38N39 90w12 6:00:48
Josephville 92 8 38N50'34 90w47'47 6:03:11
Joy 33 3 37N30'52 91w40'27 6:06:42
Judge 76 3 38N25'14 91w46'50 6:07:07
Junction City 62 3 37N34 90w17 6:01:08
Junction Ferry 101 3 37N11'24 91w16'04 6:05:04
Junction Lookout 33 3 37N37'06 91w21'28 6:05:26
Junland 12 3 36N46'07 90w16'51 6:01:07
Kahoka 23 30 40N25'13 91w43'10 6:06:53
Kaiser 66 3 38N08'01 92w35'23 6:10:22
Kampville 92 2 38N51'09 90w32'45 6:02:11
Kampville Beach 92 2 38N47 90w30 6:02:00
Kampville Court 92 2 38N47 90w30 6:02:00
Kansas City 48 3 39N05'59 94w34'42 6:18:19
Kaolin 47 3 37N40 90w53 6:03:32
Karlin 84 3 37N33'15 93w24'50 6:13:39
Kaseyville 61 44 39N37'28 92w39'47 6:10:39
Kearney 24 3 39N22'04 94w21'43 6:17:27
Keener 111 3 36N55'49 90w31'43 6:02:07
Keeners 12 3 36N55'23 90w30'20 6:02:01
Keethtown 66 3 38N02'35 92w25'26 6:09:42
Kellerville 102 3 39N49'19 92w08'05 6:08:32
Kelley 91 3 36N46 90w58 6:03:52
Kelley Springs 60 3 36N42'55 94w25'11 6:17:41
Kellogg 61 3 39N47'46 92w26'32 6:09:46
Kelso 100 3 37N11'26 89w32'58 5:58:12
Keltner 22 3 36N58'08 92w56'53 6:11:48
Kendall 102 3 39N43'00 91w55'01 6:07:40
Kendricktown 49 3 37N11'41 94w18'35 6:17:14
Kenmoor 11 3 39N39'03 94w56'22 6:19:45
Kennett 35 3 36N14'10 90w03'20 6:00:13
Kenoma 6 3 37N26'22 94w11'50 6:16:47
Kenwood 52 3 40N11'44 92w17'13 6:09:09
Keota 61 44 39N42'27 92w34'35 6:10:18
Kern 61 3 39N46'32 92w42'03 6:10:48
Kerr 13 3 39N45 94w14 6:16:56
Kerrville 83 3 39N22'42 94w41'42 6:18:47
Kersey Coates 48 3 39N03 94w34 6:18:16
Kewanee 72 3 36N40'16 89w34'26 5:58:18
Keyes Summit 95 40 38N34'02 90w27'46 6:01:51
Keystone 25 3 39N41'30 94w18'57 6:17:16
Keysville 28 3 37N52'31 91w23'20 6:05:33
Keytesville 21 3 39N26'04 92w56'17 6:11:45
Kidder 13 3 39N46'49 94w06'08 6:16:25
Kiddoo 73 44 36N52 94w22 6:17:28
Kiel 36 3 38N31'18 91w14'37 6:04:58
Killarney Shores 47 3 37N35'42 90w33'55 6:02:16
Kilwinning 99 3 40N31'37 92w20'13 6:09:21
Kimberling City 104 3 36N45 93w23 6:13:32
Kimberling Hills 104 3 36N45 93w23 6:13:32
Kimberly 88 3 39N25'54 92w29'20 6:09:57
Kimble 107 3 37N34'37 91w50'28 6:07:22
Kime 111 3 37N03'04 90w23'59 6:01:36
Kimmswick 50 3 38N21'55 90w21'46 6:01:27
Kinder 103 3 37N00'57 90w04'41 6:00:19
Kinderpost 107 3 37N34'23 91w56'41 6:07:47
Kinfolks Ridge 78 3 36N07'27 89w38'42 5:58:35
King 75 3 36N47 91w12 6:04:48
King City 38 3 40N03'05 94w31'26 6:18:06
Kingdom City 14 3 38N57'35 91w55'55 6:07:44
King Prairie 5 3 36N53 93w52 6:15:28
Kings Lake 57 16 39N04'06 90w44'37 6:02:58
Kings Point 29 3 37N19'16 93w56'04 6:15:44
Kingston 13 3 39N38'39 94w02'18 6:16:09
Kingsville 51 3 38N44'35 94w04'11 6:16:17
Kinloch 95 40 38N44'24 90w19'35 6:01:18
Kinsey 96 3 38N01'52 90w18'00 6:01:12
Kirby 102 3 39N50'44 92w06'52 6:08:27
Kirbyville 106 3 36N37'23 93w09'50 6:12:39
Kirk 35 3 36N15'15 89w58'15 5:59:53
Kirksville 1 3 40N11'41 92w34'59 6:10:20
Kirkwood 95 31 38N35'00 90w24'24 6:01:38
Kirschner 11 3 39N42'51 94w53'00 6:19:32
Kissee Mills 106 3 36N41'01 93w02'59 6:12:12
Kissenger 82 21 39N18'18 90w51'30 6:03:26
Kissick 39 3 37N06'28 93w15'26 6:13:02
Klein Ford 28 3 37N53'29 91w27'14 6:05:49
Klendike 62 3 37N26'26 90w13'29 6:00:54
Kliever 68 3 38N41'50 92w30'12 6:10:01
Klondike 49 3 37N08'42 94w35'57 6:18:24
Klondike 92 3 38N34'42 90w50'33 6:03:22
Knights 49 3 37N08'25 94w15'04 6:17:00
Knobby 8 3 38N09'09 93w05'43 6:12:23
Knob Lick 94 3 37N40'31 90w22'02 6:01:28
Knob Noster 51 3 38N45'54 93w33'23 6:14:14
Knobtown 48 3 38N57'56 94w25'44 6:17:43
Knobview 28 3 38N04 91w29 6:05:56
Knorpp 50 4 38N05'18 90w27'46 6:01:51
Knox 84 3 37N28'28 93w36'37 6:14:26
Knox City (Knox Station) 52 3 40N08'37 92w00'33 6:08:02
Knoxville 89 3 39N26'46 94w01'00 6:16:04
Kodiak 2 3 39N57'07 94w45'25 6:19:02
Koeltztown 76 3 38N19'29 92w02'31 6:08:10
Koenig 76 3 38N21'22 91w46'05 6:07:04
Koester 94 3 38N01'20 90w24'34 6:01:38
Kohl City 36 3 38N35'54 91w21'52 6:05:27
Koshkonong 75 3 36N35'45 91w38'44 6:06:35
Krakow 36 49 38N29'51 91w02'44 6:04:11
Krueger Ford 37 3 38N30'17 91w36'31 6:06:26
Kurreville 16 3 37N28'31 89w49'17 5:59:17
Kyle 11 3 39N41'11 94w49'56 6:19:20
Labadie 36 3 38N31'44 90w51'00 6:03:24
LaBelle 56 32 40N07'01 91w54'45 6:07:39
Laclede 58 3 39N47'08 93w09'59 6:12:40
Lacyville 7 3 38N23'50 94w28'56 6:17:56
Laddonia 4 3 39N14'33 91w38'43 6:06:35
La Due 42 3 38N18'45 93w52'36 6:15:30
Ladue 95 40 38N38'59 90w22'50 6:01:31
Lafayette 25 3 39N42 94w32 6:18:08
Laflin 9 3 37N16'37 89w53'18 5:59:33
La Font 72 3 36N30 89w39 5:58:36
La Forge 72 3 36N40'17 89w31'32 5:58:06
Lagonda 21 3 39N39'25 92w43'58 6:10:56
La Grange 56 33 40N02'34 91w29'51 6:05:59
Laguna Beach 15 3 38N07'49 92w39'05 6:10:36
Lake 95 40 38N40'46 90w31'12 6:02:05
Lake Adelle 50 3 38N21 90w39 6:02:36
Lake Arrowhead 36 3 38N18 90w50 6:03:20
Lake City 48 3 39N06'37 94w15'18 6:17:01
Lake City Arsenal 48 3 39N06 94w26 6:17:44
Lake Contrary 11 3 39N46 94w51 6:19:24
Lake Creek 8 3 38N30'41 93w08'00 6:12:32
Lake Fork 76 3 38N24'32 91w44'21 6:06:57
Lake Junction 95 40 38N36'20 90w19'58 6:01:20
Lakeland 66 3 38N11 92w38 6:10:32
Lake Lotawana 48 3 38N55'23 94w14'38 6:16:59
Lakenan 102 3 39N40'20 91w57'03 6:07:48
Lake-of-the-Woods 40 3 40N07 93w35 6:14:20
Lake Ozark 66 3 38N11'55 92w38'19 6:10:33
Lake Sherwood 109 3 38N38 91w03 6:04:12
Lakeshire 95 40 38N32'19 90w20'06 6:01:20
Lakeside 49 3 37N09'32 94w24'53 6:17:40
Lakeside 50 3 38N26 90w23 6:01:32
Lakeside 66 3 38N13 92w36 6:10:24
Lake Spring 33 3 37N46'57 91w40'43 6:06:43
Lake Tapawingo 48 3 39N01 94w19 6:17:16
Lake Tekakwitha 50 6 38N29 90w44 6:02:56
Lakeview 66 3 38N16 92w36 6:10:24
Lakeview 104 3 36N45 93w23 6:13:32
Lakeview Heights 8 3 38N15'32 93w09'22 6:12:37
Lake Viking 31 3 39N55 93w58 6:15:52
Lake Waukomis 83 3 39N14 94w38 6:18:32
Lake Winnebago 19 3 38N49 94w22 6:17:28
Lake Wittona 40 3 40N07 93w35 6:14:20
Lamar 6 3 37N29'42 94w16'35 6:17:06
Lamar Heights 6 3 37N29'37 94w17'51 6:17:11
Lambert 100 3 37N06 89w33 5:58:12
Lamine 27 3 38N56'48 92w52'28 6:11:30
LaMonte (Lamonte Station) 80 3 38N46'27 93w25'28 6:13:42
LaMotte 82 22 39N33'38 91w10'46 6:04:43
Lampe 104 3 36N33'49 93w26'16 6:13:45
Lanagan 60 3 36N36'29 94w26'51 6:17:47
Lancaster 98 44 40N31'15 92w31'40 6:10:07
Lanes Prairie 63 3 38N11'10 91w43'44 6:06:55
Langdon 3 3 40N21'23 95w34'46 6:22:19
Langston 39 44 37N10'52 93w14'38 6:12:59
Lanton 46 3 36N31'02 91w48'05 6:07:12
LaPlata 61 3 40N01'24 92w29'29 6:09:58
Laquey 85 3 37N46'13 92w18'12 6:09:13
Laredo 40 3 40N01'32 93w26'47 6:13:47
Larimore 95 40 38N46'24 90w12'25 6:00:50
La Russell 49 3 37N08'29 94w03'41 6:16:15
Latham 68 3 38N33'39 92w40'56 6:10:44
Latham Mill 114 3 37N17'06 92w22'20 6:09:33
Lathrop 25 3 39N32'54 94w19'47 6:17:19
Latour 51 3 38N38'04 94w06'07 6:16:24
Latty 110 3 37N59'16 90w51'02 6:03:24
Laubinger Ford 36 3 38N20'29 91w14'43 6:04:59
Laurel Heights 48 3 39N00 94w28 6:17:52
Laurie 71 3 38N12 92w50 6:11:20
LaValle 103 3 36N40'31 89w46'25 5:59:06
Lawrenceburg 55 3 37N14'40 93w39'36 6:14:38
Lawrenceton 96 3 37N57'54 90w18'18 6:01:13
Lawson 89 3 39N26'18 94w12'14 6:16:49
Layneville 6 3 37N29'41 94w05'43 6:16:23
Leachville Junction 35 3 36N02'47 90w06'35 6:00:26
Lead Branch Junction 28 3 37N54'13 91w22'32 6:05:30
Lead Hill 22 3 36N56 92w56 6:11:44
Leadington 94 3 37N50'25 90w29'30 6:01:58
Leadmine 30 3 37N50'12 92w57'43 6:11:51
Leadwood 94 3 37N52'02 90w35'35 6:02:22
Leann 5 3 36N48'46 93w41'21 6:14:46
Leasburg 28 3 38N05'31 91w17'47 6:05:11
Leawood 73 3 37N02'13 94w29'48 6:17:59
Lebanon 53 47 37N40'50 92w39'49 6:10:39
Lebeck 20 3 37N53'23 93w54'47 6:15:39
Lebo 46 3 36N31'13 91w54'31 6:07:38
Lecoma 33 3 37N46'34 91w43'51 6:06:55
Lee 83 3 39N19 94w51 6:19:24
Leeds 48 3 39N03'21 94w30'30 6:18:02
Leemon 16 3 37N27'51 89w35'18 5:58:21
Leeper 111 3 37N04'30 90w42'28 6:02:50
Lees Summit 48 3 38N54'39 94w22'55 6:17:32
Leesville 42 3 38N20'54 93w32'43 6:14:11
Leeton 51 3 38N34'59 93w41'40 6:14:47
Leibig 91 3 36N32'55 90w57'05 6:03:48
Leich Ford 69 3 39N30'33 91w50'02 6:07:20
Lemay 115 40 38N32'00 90w17'13 6:01:09
Lemons 86 3 40N24'20 93w02'58 6:12:12
Lenox 33 3 37N39'11 91w45'40 6:07:03
Lentner 102 3 39N43'07 92w08'52 6:08:35
Leonard 102 3 39N53'47 92w10'42 6:08:43
Leopold 9 3 37N15'28 89w55'35 5:59:42
Leora 103 3 37N00'01 90w01'05 6:00:04
Leota 46 3 36N31'53 92w02'15 6:08:09
Leroy 6 3 37N36 94w33 6:18:12
Le Sieur 72 3 36N26 89w37 5:58:28

Leslie 36 3 38N25'04 91w13'55 6:04:56
Lesterville 90 3 37N27'14 90w50'36 6:03:22
Leta 17 3 39N22'14 93w19'42 6:13:19
Levasy 48 3 39N08'08 94w07'58 6:16:32
Levick Mill 88 3 39N34'34 92w20'47 6:09:23
Lewis 42 3 38N26'07 93w41'29 6:14:46
Lewis and Clark Village 11 3 39N32'35 95w03'09 6:20:13
Lewis Mill 21 3 39N15'27 92w51'10 6:11:25
Lewistown 56 34 40N05'10 91w48'47 6:07:15
Lexington 54 3 39N11'05 93w52'47 6:15:31
Liberal 6 3 37N33'29 94w31'11 6:18:05
Liberty 14 3 38N41'21 91w57'33 6:07:50
Liberty 24 3 39N14'46 94w25'08 6:17:41
Libertyville 94 3 37N42'13 90w17'17 6:01:09
Lick 27 3 38N58 92w45 6:11:00
Lick Creek 77 3 36N32 92w20 6:09:20
Licking 107 3 37N29'58 91w51'25 6:07:26
Liege 70 3 39N00 91w21 6:05:24
Light 63 10 38N00 91w37 6:06:28
Liguori 50 3 38N21 90w24 6:01:36
Lilbourn 72 3 36N35'32 89w36'55 5:58:28
Lilly 25 3 39N28'12 94w26'39 6:17:47
Limberlost 28 3 37N48'25 91w21'33 6:05:26
Limekiln Ford 30 3 37N30'04 92w58'06 6:11:52
Lincoln 8 3 38N23'27 93w20'04 6:13:20
Lincoln Beach 95 40 38N32'47 90w32'22 6:02:09
Linda 72 3 36N24'39 89w32'49 5:58:11
Lindale 93 3 38N09'12 94w02'37 6:16:10
Lindbergh 14 3 38N57'21 92w07'41 6:08:31
Linden 3 3 40N29'11 95w32'14 6:22:09
Linden 22 3 37N02'47 93w08'02 6:12:32
Lindenlure Lake 22 3 37N07 93w04 6:12:16
Lindley 65 3 40N31 93w42 6:14:48
Lindley 105 3 40N04'55 93w22'05 6:13:28
Lindsey 8 3 38N19 93w24 6:13:36
Lindstrew Ford 112 3 37N15'55 92w55'18 6:11:41
Lingo 61 3 39N46'05 92w49'13 6:11:17
Linkville 83 3 39N18'40 94w38'56 6:18:36
Linn 76 3 38N29'09 91w51'01 6:07:24
Linn Creek 15 3 38N02'17 92w42'41 6:10:51
LinNeus 58 3 39N52'43 93w11'19 6:12:45
Lisbon 45 3 39N06'23 92w54'22 6:11:37
Lisle 19 3 38N32'58 94w35'40 6:18:23
Lithium 79 3 37N50'00 89w53'09 5:59:33
Little Blue 48 3 38N59'27 94w24'44 6:17:39
Little Prairie 78 3 36N09 89w43 5:58:52
Little River 78 3 36N21 89w50 5:59:20
Little Rock Landing 96 3 38N00'18 90w03'36 6:00:14
Lively 8 3 38N12'37 93w06'28 6:12:26
Livingston 42 3 38N24'28 93w48'38 6:15:15
Livonia 86 3 40N29'29 92w42'00 6:10:48
Lixville 9 3 37N34'37 89w54'42 5:59:39
Locale 50 3 38N22'25 90w37'22 6:02:29
Lockspring 31 3 39N50'56 93w46'38 6:15:07
Lockwood 29 3 37N23'08 93w57'11 6:15:49
Locust 77 3 36N33'49 92w32'32 6:10:10
Locust Creek 58 3 39N53 93w10 6:12:40
Locust Hill 52 3 40N01'33 92w16'32 6:09:06
Lodi 111 3 37N15'23 90w27'10 6:01:49
Loehr 95 40 38N36'54 90w32'28 6:02:10
Logan 55 3 37N00'52 93w36'57 6:14:28
Log Cabin Station 89 3 39N18 93w41 6:14:44
Lohman 26 3 38N32'35 92w21'51 6:09:27
Lohmer 5 3 36N39'59 93w42'31 6:14:50
Loimbach Landing 79 3 37N42'01 89w33'02 5:58:12
Lois 63 3 38N08'53 91w45'20 6:07:01
Loma Linda 12 3 36N47'36 90w26'13 6:01:45
Lonedell 36 3 38N18'29 90w49'39 6:03:19
Lone Elm 27 3 38N49'30 92w44'12 6:10:57
Lone Elm 49 3 37N06'51 94w31'31 6:18:06
Lone Hill 12 3 36N42'04 90w32'14 6:02:09
Lone Jack 48 3 38N52'20 94w10'22 6:16:41
Lone Oak 7 3 38N12 94w19 6:17:16
Lone Star 38 3 40N20'29 94w15'11 6:17:01
Lone Star 72 3 36N30'55 89w44'12 5:58:57
Lone Tree 19 3 38N34'20 94w21'39 6:17:27
Long Beach 106 3 36N42'26 93w07'47 6:12:31
Long Lane 30 3 37N36'41 92w54'33 6:11:38
Long Prairie 67 3 36N52 89w27 5:57:48
Longrun 77 3 36N38'57 92w43'23 6:10:54
Longtown 79 3 37N40'10 89w46'20 5:59:05
Longview 48 3 38N54'15 94w24'16 6:17:37
Longview 60 3 36N43'23 94w12'10 6:16:49
Longwood 80 3 38N53'57 93w10'11 6:12:41
Looney 84 3 37N28 93w23 6:13:32
Loose Creek 76 3 38N30'29 91w57'26 6:07:50
Lopez 94 3 37N39'07 90w38'47 6:02:35
Lorance 9 3 37N18 89w59 5:59:56
Loring 114 3 37N20'41 92w34'28 6:10:18
Lorwood 72 3 36N36'34 89w51'21 5:59:25
Lost Creek 111 3 37N02 90w17 6:01:08
Lost Creek Landing 111 3 37N01'20 90w18'23 6:01:14
Loughboro 94 3 37N46'42 90w31'19 6:02:05
Louisburg 30 3 37N45'28 93w08'21 6:12:33
Louisiana 82 35 39N26'56 91w03'05 6:04:12
Louisville 57 3 39N11'59 91w10'28 6:04:42
Low Gap 22 3 36N52'01 93w06'17 6:12:25
Lowground 86 3 40N22'26 92w44'07 6:10:56
Lowndes 111 3 37N08'56 90w15'48 6:01:03
Lowry City 93 3 38N08'24 93w43'36 6:14:54
Low Wassie 101 3 36N59'19 91w15'29 6:05:02
Lucas 42 3 38N24'59 94w01'43 6:16:07
Lucas and Hunt Village 95 40 38N43 90w18 6:01:12
Lucerne 86 3 40N27'50 93w17'31 6:13:10
Ludlow 59 3 39N39'18 93w42'07 6:14:48
Ludwig 50 12 38N14'06 90w25'13 6:01:41
Luebbering 36 3 38N16'13 90w49'09 6:03:17
Lulu 75 3 36N42 91w24 6:05:36
Luna 77 3 36N39'07 92w18'20 6:09:13
Lupus 68 3 38N50'46 92w27'11 6:09:49
Luray 23 3 40N27'11 91w52'54 6:07:32
Lusk 100 3 37N01'56 89w22'54 5:57:32
Lutesville 9 3 37N18'01 89w58'52 5:59:55
Luystown 76 3 38N33'29 91w50'02 6:07:20
Lyda 61 3 39N55 92w27 6:09:48
Lynch 107 3 37N26 92w01 6:08:04
Lynchburg 53 3 37N29'35 92w17'39 6:09:11
Lyon 36 3 38N30'42 91w10'26 6:04:42
Mabel 31 3 39N49'18 94w11'59 6:16:48
Macedonia 81 10 37N57 91w48 6:07:12
Machens 92 18 38N54'11 90w19'56 6:01:20
Mackenzie 95 40 38N34'45 90w19'01 6:01:16
Macks Creek 15 3 37N57'59 92w58'09 6:11:53
Macomb 114 3 37N05'39 92w29'30 6:09:58
Macon 61 44 39N44'32 92w28'21 6:09:53
Macy 96 3 37N58'14 90w04'36 6:00:18
Madison 69 3 39N28'25 92w12'35 6:08:50
Madisonville 87 3 39N27'26 91w29'47 6:05:59
Madry 5 3 36N52'10 93w43'12 6:14:53
Magill 31 3 39N52'41 93w53'23 6:15:34
Magnolia 51 3 38N38'21 93w54'50 6:15:39
Main City 19 3 38N29'22 94w29'31 6:17:58
Maines 114 3 37N22'47 92w21'48 6:09:27
Maitland 44 3 40N12'03 95w04'27 6:20:18
Majorville 8 3 38N10'55 93w16'11 6:13:05
Malden 35 3 36N33'25 89w57'59 5:59:52
Malta Bend 97 3 39N11'36 93w21'46 6:13:27
Mammoth 77 3 36N36 92w26 6:09:44
Manchester 95 40 38N35'49 90w30'33 6:02:02
Mandeville 17 3 39N29'47 93w37'15 6:14:29
Manes 114 3 37N23 92w22 6:09:28
Manila 80 3 38N33'04 93w20'10 6:13:21
Mano 5 3 36N34'37 93w41'51 6:14:47
Mansfield 114 3 37N06'24 92w34'50 6:10:19
Many Springs 75 3 36N42 91w24 6:05:36
Mapaville 50 3 38N14'56 90w29'01 6:01:56
Maple Grove 49 3 37N15'13 94w07'32 6:16:30
Maple Hill 25 3 39N42'06 94w24'27 6:17:38
Maple Park 24 3 39N11'23 94w30'29 6:18:02
Maples 107 3 37N35'03 91w47'00 6:07:08
Maplewood 95 31 38N36'45 90w19'28 6:01:18
Marais Croche 92 18 38N50'52 90w24'05 6:01:36
Marble Hill 9 3 37N18'21 89w58'13 5:59:53
Marceline 58 3 39N42'43 92w56'53 6:11:48
March 30 3 37N31'21 93w05'21 6:12:21
Marco 103 3 36N44'52 89w48'29 5:59:14
Marcoot 90 3 37N33'16 91w15'30 6:05:02
Margona Village 95 40 38N42 90w20 6:01:20
Marion 68 3 38N41'27 92w21'58 6:09:28
Marionville 55 3 37N00'11 93w38'14 6:14:33
Mark 64 41 39N53'17 91w27'48 6:05:51
Marlborough 48 3 38N58'36 94w33'43 6:18:15
Marlborough 95 40 38N34'13 90w20'13 6:01:21
Marling 70 3 39N08'02 91w18'35 6:05:14
Marquand 62 3 37N25'45 90w10'05 6:00:40
Marshall 97 3 39N07'23 93w11'48 6:12:47
Marshall Junction 97 3 38N57'29 93w12'23 6:12:50
Marsh Creek 62 3 37N25'02 90w27'52 6:01:51
Marshfield 112 3 37N20'19 92w54'25 6:11:38
Marston 72 3 36N31'08 89w36'45 5:58:27
Marthasville 109 3 38N37'42 91w03'27 6:04:14
Martin City 48 3 38N53'10 94w35'24 6:18:22
Martinsburg 4 3 39N06'08 91w38'51 6:06:35
Martinstown 86 3 40N24'38 92w46'13 6:11:05
Martinsville 41 3 40N20'19 94w09'41 6:16:39
Marvel Cave 104 3 36N41'59 93w20'12 6:13:21
Marvin 71 3 38N24'59 92w46'14 6:11:05
Marvin Terrace 95 40 38N42 90w22 6:01:28
Maryden 110 3 37N46 90w37 6:02:28
Maryknoll 57 14 38N56'07 90w46'41 6:03:07
Maryland Heights 95 40 38N42'47 90w25'47 6:01:43
Mary Ridge 95 40 38N43'14 90w22'24 6:01:30
Marys Home 66 3 38N18'20 92w21'18 6:09:25
Maryville 74 3 40N20'46 94w52'20 6:19:29
Mason 64 27 39N44 91w24 6:05:36
Masters 20 3 37N36'20 93w39'41 6:14:39
Matson 92 3 38N36'29 90w47'49 6:03:11
Mattese 95 40 38N29'08 90w20'55 6:01:24
Matthews 72 3 36N45'33 89w35'12 5:58:21
Maud 102 45 39N38'00 92w11'43 6:08:47
Maulsby 103 3 36N38'47 89w48'36 5:59:14
Maupin 36 3 38N16 90w49 6:03:16
Maurine 42 49 38N29'27 93w54'44 6:15:39
Mauser Mill 101 3 37N18'46 91w18'54 6:05:16
Max 33 3 37N34'29 91w23'00 6:05:32
Maxey 11 3 39N40'21 94w49'22 6:19:17
Maxville 49 3 37N11'53 94w16'05 6:17:04
Maxville 50 3 38N26'11 90w23'19 6:01:33
May 60 3 36N45'04 94w31'19 6:18:05
May 83 3 39N15 94w41 6:18:44
Mayesburg 7 3 38N24'09 94w05'09 6:16:21
Mayfield 9 3 37N27'15 89w56'57 5:59:48
Mayfield 53 3 37N49 92w28 6:09:52
Maysville 32 3 39N53'21 94w21'42 6:17:27
Mayview 54 3 39N03'11 93w49'49 6:15:19
Maywood 48 3 39N05'42 94w26'43 6:17:47
Maywood 56 3 39N57'15 91w36'11 6:06:25
McBaine 10 3 38N53'13 92w26'47 6:09:47
McBride 79 3 37N49'58 89w50'24 5:59:22
McCann Landing 92 2 38N51'53 90w35'50 6:02:23
McCarty 78 3 36N07'04 89w41'56 5:58:48
McClurg 34 3 36N47'04 92w46'29 6:11:06
McCracken 22 3 37N01'03 93w09'28 6:12:38
McCredie 14 3 38N57 91w58 6:07:52
McCullough Ford 60 3 36N37'45 94w15'10 6:17:01
McCune 82 3 39N24'33 91w15'16 6:05:01
McCurry 38 3 40N12'27 94w25'31 6:17:42
McDowell 5 3 36N49'27 93w47'35 6:15:10
McElhany 73 3 36N47'17 94w23'55 6:17:36
McElyea Place 35 3 36N30'03 90w08'21 6:00:33
McFall 38 3 40N06'39 94w13'23 6:16:54
McFry Ford 75 3 36N45'16 91w15'34 6:05:02
McGee 111 3 37N04'28 90w11'44 6:00:47
McGirk 68 3 38N36'40 92w28'34 6:09:54
McGuire 35 3 36N29'53 89w58'14 5:59:53
McIntosh 82 35 39N24'15 90w58'24 6:03:54
McKinley 55 3 37N03'40 93w37'38 6:14:31
McKittrick 70 3 38N44'06 91w26'37 6:05:46
McMillen 60 3 36N40 94w33 6:18:12
McMullin 100 3 36N57'15 89w37'13 5:58:29
McMurtrey 34 3 36N56 92w28 6:09:52
McNatt 60 3 36N44'08 94w18'45 6:17:15
McPheters Ford 30 3 37N49'19 92w52'20 6:11:29
Meacham Park 95 40 38N33'45 90w24'08 6:01:37
Meadors Ford 60 3 36N37'09 94w17'45 6:17:11
Meadowbrook Downs 95 40 38N42 90w22 6:01:28
Meadville 58 3 39N47'03 93w18'07 6:13:12
Mecca 25 3 39N29'03 94w31'22 6:18:05
Medford 51 3 38N39'06 94w00'25 6:16:02
Medill 23 30 40N26'04 91w46'33 6:07:06
Medoc 49 3 37N18'26 94w31'36 6:18:06
Mehlville 115 40 38N30'30 90w19'22 6:01:17
Meinert 29 3 37N20'07 93w59'26 6:15:58
Melbourne 41 3 40N08'30 93w47'15 6:15:09
Melrose 95 6 38N34'22 90w43'23 6:02:54
Melva 106 3 36N34'37 93w12'43 6:12:51
Melville 48 3 38N59'25 94w32'41 6:18:11
Melzo 50 4 38N00'36 90w34'10 6:02:17
Memphis 99 36 40N27'28 92w10'16 6:08:41
Mendon 21 3 39N35'23 93w08'04 6:12:32
Mendota 86 3 40N34'02 92w53'40 6:11:35
Menfro 79 3 37N46'37 89w43'24 5:58:54
Mentor 39 3 37N06'22 93w11'56 6:12:48
Mercer 65 3 40N30'41 93w31'55 6:14:08
Mercyville 61 3 39N58'18 92w38'35 6:10:34
Merna 27 3 38N58'16 92w38'58 6:10:36
Merritt 34 3 36N53'55 92w52'09 6:11:29
Merwin 7 3 38N24'17 94w35'27 6:18:22
Mesler 103 3 37N05 89w48 5:59:12
Messler 103 3 37N03'58 89w48'12 5:59:13
Meta 76 3 38N18'45 92w09'57 6:08:40
Metz 108 3 37N59'51 94w26'35 6:17:46
Mexico 4 3 39N10'11 91w52'58 6:07:32
Meyerstown 63 47 38N09'41 92w09'41 6:08:39
Miami 97 3 39N19'17 93w13'40 6:12:55
Michelles Corner 107 3 37N21 92w01 6:08:04
Micola 78 3 36N07'54 89w47'09 5:59:09
Middlebrook 47 3 37N39'44 90w38'49 6:02:35
Middle Grove 69 3 39N23'42 92w16'13 6:09:05
Middleton 54 3 39N09 93w33 6:14:12
Middletown 70 3 39N07'37 91w24'50 6:05:39
Midland 95 40 38N43 90w24 6:01:36
Midridge 101 3 37N20'07 91w13'18 6:04:53
Midvale 107 3 37N12'40 91w43'47 6:06:55
Midway 10 3 38N59'06 92w26'57 6:09:48
Midway 34 3 37N01'46 92w35'42 6:10:23
Midway 73 3 37N03'17 94w30'09 6:18:01
Midway 86 3 40N28'31 93w09'43 6:12:39
Mike 21 3 39N35'47 92w57'26 6:11:50
Milan 105 3 40N12'08 93w07'30 6:12:30
Mildred 106 3 36N38'13 93w05'57 6:12:24
Miles Point 17 3 39N13'52 93w41'57 6:14:48
Milford 6 3 37N35'05 94w09'25 6:16:38
Millard 1 3 40N06'26 92w32'45 6:10:11
Millbrook 26 3 38N29'57 92w21'23 6:09:26
Millcreek 62 3 37N31'36 90w18'35 6:01:14
Mill Creek 71 3 38N36 92w53 6:11:32
Miller 55 3 37N12'53 93w50'23 6:15:22
Miller Ford 30 3 37N52'38 92w53'17 6:11:33
Millers 96 3 37N51'38 90w16'13 6:01:05
Millersburg 14 3 38N53'55 92w07'24 6:08:30
Millersville 16 3 37N25'58 89w47'58 5:59:12
Mill Grove 65 3 40N18'33 93w35'36 6:14:22
Millheim 79 3 37N37'03 89w53'14 5:59:33
Millport 52 3 40N16'02 92w05'35 6:08:22
Millrock Ford 36 44 38N19'52 91w18'12 6:05:13
Mill Spring 111 3 37N03'43 90w41'02 6:02:44
Milltown 12 3 36N46'39 90w36'18 6:02:25
Millville 89 3 39N24'19 93w55'04 6:15:40
Millwood 57 3 39N06'10 91w06'22 6:04:25
Milo 108 3 37N45'22 94w18'21 6:17:13
Milton 3 3 40N17'05 95w25'01 6:21:40
Milton 88 3 39N28'12 92w19'44 6:09:19
Miltondale 24 3 39N15'30 94w13'19 6:16:53
Minaville 24 3 39N09'48 94w27'44 6:17:51
Mincy 106 3 36N33'51 93w06'36 6:12:26
Mindenmines 6 3 37N28'17 94w35'23 6:18:22
Mine La Motte 62 3 37N36'56 90w17'23 6:01:10
Mineola 70 3 38N53'17 91w34'17 6:06:17
Miner 100 3 36N53'29 89w32'18 5:58:09
Mineral City 94 3 37N42'59 90w32'01 6:02:08
Mineral Point 110 3 37N56'41 90w43'27 6:02:54
Mineral Spring 5 3 36N40'14 93w46'22 6:15:05
Mingo 7 3 38N25 94w07 6:16:28
Mingo 103 3 36N56'14 90w12'00 6:00:48
Mingsville 114 3 37N27'06 92w20'22 6:09:21
Minimum 47 3 37N22'34 90w35'15 6:02:21
Minnie 10 3 39N11'20 92w27'24 6:09:50
Minnith 96 3 37N47'53 90w03'00 6:00:12
Mint Hill 76 3 38N32'57 91w44'49 6:06:59
Minton 44 3 40N03 95w19 6:21:16
Mirabile 13 3 39N36'58 94w08'30 6:16:34
Missionary Acres 111 3 37N12'15 90w25'15 6:01:41
Mississippi 67 3 36N49 89w13 5:56:52
Missouri City 24 3 39N14'27 94w17'16 6:17:09
Mitchell 94 3 37N50'48 90w34'47 6:02:19
Mitchells Corner 107 3 37N24'32 92w04'19 6:08:17
Moah 85 3 37N47'29 92w03'57 6:08:16
Moberly 88 3 39N25'06 92w26'17 6:09:45
Moccasin Springs 16 3 37N27'06 89w27'30 5:57:50
Mock Corner 11 3 39N32'01 94w53'27 6:19:34
Modena 65 3 40N18'01 93w48'03 6:14:43
Mohawk Corner 84 3 37N45'28 93w18'19 6:13:13
Mokane 14 3 38N40'30 91w52'27 6:07:30
Moline Acres 95 40 38N44'49 90w14'24 6:00:58

Molino 4 3 39N18'06 91w52'41 6:07:31
Monarch 95 40 38N38'36 90w40'17 6:02:41
Monark Springs 73
44 36N51'52 94w17'29 6:17:10
Monegaw 93 3 38N09 93w53 6:15:32
Monegaw Springs 93
3 38N01'49 93w50'26 6:15:22
Monett 5 3 36N55'44 93w55'39 6:15:43
Monkey Run 87 3 39N40'20 91w18'04 6:05:12
Monroe City 87 37 39N39'13 91w44'04 6:06:56
Montague 22 3 36N55'41 93w19'40 6:13:19
Montague Hill 97
3 39N07'42 93w09'08 6:12:37
Montauk 33 3 37N26'52 91w41'44 6:06:47
Monteith Junction 7
3 38N12'51 94w22'00 6:17:28
Monterey 47 3 37N34'19 90w51'11 6:03:25
Montevallo 108 3 37N43'34 94w06'29 6:16:26
Montgomery 114 3 37N25 92w20 6:09:20
Montgomery City 70
3 38N58'39 91w30'17 6:06:01
Monticello 56 3 40N07'06 91w42'43 6:06:51
Montier 101 3 36N59'13 91w34'31 6:06:18
Montreal 15 3 37N58'08 92w35'31 6:10:22
Montrose 42 3 38N15'28 93w58'52 6:15:55
Montserrat 51 3 38N46'29 93w37'18 6:14:29
Moody 46 3 36N31'46 91w59'21 6:07:57
Mooney 84 3 37N29 93w15 6:13:00
Mooresville 59 3 39N44'43 93w43'03 6:14:52
Moors 25 3 39N43'10 94w23'31 6:17:34
Mora 8 3 38N31'25 93w12'56 6:12:52
Morehouse 72 3 36N50'50 89w41'07 5:58:44
Moreland 100 3 37N07 89w33 5:58:12
Morgan 53 3 37N30'37 92w40'35 6:10:42
Morgan Heights 49
3 37N09'57 94w21'18 6:17:25
Morgan Heights 85
3 37N50'28 92w05'40 6:08:23
Morley 100 3 37N02'37 89w36'37 5:58:26
Morrison 37 3 38N40'22 91w38'10 6:06:33
Morrisville 84 3 37N28'52 93w25'38 6:13:43
Morschels 95 40 38N32'22 90w32'09 6:02:09
Morse Mill 50 3 38N16'36 90w39'11 6:02:37
Morton 89 3 39N19'10 93w51'38 6:15:27
Mosby 24 3 39N18'56 94w17'37 6:17:10
Moscow Mills 57
38 38N56'52 90w55'05 6:03:40
Moselle 36 3 38N23'12 90w53'52 6:03:35
Moss Creek 17 3 39N19 93w35 6:14:20
Motley 49 3 37N03'37 94w11'09 6:16:45
Mound 7 3 38N21 94w22 6:17:28
Mound City 44 3 40N07'52 95w13'53 6:20:56
Moundville 108 3 37N45'51 94w27'07 6:17:48
Mountain Grove 114
3 37N07'50 92w15'48 6:09:03
Mountain Ridge 95
40 38N33'00 90w32'27 6:02:10
Mountain View 46
3 36N59'43 91w42'13 6:06:49
Mount Airy 88 3 39N22'37 92w38'05 6:10:32
Mount Hope 36 17 38N17'54 90w52'25 6:03:30
Mount Hulda 8 3 38N28 93w12 6:12:48
Mount Leonard 97
3 39N07'27 93w23'34 6:13:34
Mount Moriah 41 3 40N19'47 93w47'40 6:15:11
Mount Olive 51 3 38N54'02 93w41'41 6:14:47
Mount Pleasant 66
3 38N22'05 92w31'24 6:10:06
Mount Pleasant Ford 37
3 38N10'06 91w32'38 6:06:11
Mount Shira 60 3 36N34'54 94w27'51 6:17:51
Mount Sterling 37
3 38N27'54 91w37'37 6:06:30
Mount Vernon 55 3 37N06'13 93w49'06 6:15:16
Mount Washington 48
3 39N05'58 94w27'58 6:17:52
Mount Zion 34 3 37N00'48 92w39'39 6:10:39
Mount Zion 42 3 38N13'03 93w38'16 6:14:33
Mud Town 110 3 38N01'10 90w44'22 6:02:57
Muffittville 12 3 36N36 90w15 6:01:00
Muirfield 95 40 38N40 90w26 6:01:44
Mulberry 6 3 37N33 94w37 6:18:28
Mulberry 7 3 38N15 94w35 6:18:20
Mundy Landing 82
22 39N33'06 91w09'39 6:04:39
Munger 90 3 37N35'51 90w47'47 6:03:11
Mungers 64 27 39N45'20 91w24'08 6:05:37
Munsell 101 3 37N05'53 91w19'39 6:05:19
Munsons 50 12 38N15'05 90w25'34 6:01:42
Murphy 50 40 38N29'25 90w29'13 6:01:57
Murray 39 3 37N19 93w28 6:13:52
Murry 10 3 39N02'34 92w10'36 6:08:42
Musicks Ferry 95
40 38N51'41 90w20'18 6:01:21
Musselfork 21 3 39N33'05 92w52'31 6:11:30
Myatt 46 3 36N33 91w44 6:06:56
Myers 40 3 40N14 93w21 6:13:24
Myrick 54 3 39N10'32 93w54'10 6:15:37
Myrtle 75 3 36N30'31 91w16'01 6:05:04
Mystic 105 3 40N09'23 92w55'54 6:11:44
Nadine 87 3 39N18 91w29 6:05:56
Nance 106 3 36N36'39 92w48'00 6:11:12
Naomi 64 3 39N55'35 91w41'44 6:06:47
Napier 44 3 40N02'56 95w15'27 6:21:02
Napoleon 54 3 39N07'53 94w04'14 6:16:17
Napton 97 3 39N03'10 93w05'01 6:12:20
Narrows 61 3 39N39 92w28 6:09:52
Nash 16 3 37N14'17 89w37'10 5:58:29
Nashua 24 3 39N18'02 94w34'47 6:18:19
Nashville 6 3 37N22'28 94w29'26 6:17:58
Nassau Junction 108
3 37N49'13 94w19'18 6:17:17
Natural Bridge Junction 95
40 38N45'27 90w25'59 6:01:44
Nauvoo 104 3 36N30'14 93w30'43 6:14:03
Naylor 91 3 36N34'31 90w36'14 6:02:25
Nebo 53 3 37N34'16 92w20'06 6:09:20
Neck City 49 3 37N15'25 94w26'39 6:17:47
Needmore 96 3 38N04'18 90w14'18 6:00:57
Neely 12 3 36N34 90w32 6:02:08
Neelys Landing 16
3 37N30'07 89w30'06 5:58:00
Neelyville 12 3 36N33'42 90w30'22 6:02:01
Neeper 23 30 40N19'57 91w47'29 6:07:10
Neier 36 3 38N23'28 91w06'37 6:04:26
Nelson 97 3 38N59'41 93w01'57 6:12:08
Nelsonville 64 3 39N55'34 91w47'47 6:07:11
Nemo 43 3 37N52'36 93w15'42 6:13:03
Neola 29 3 37N30'20 93w52'10 6:15:29
Neongwah 15 3 38N01'58 92w47'33 6:11:10
Neosho 73 44 36N52'08 94w22'04 6:17:28
Netherlands 78 3 36N17'57 89w45'04 5:59:00
Nettleton 13 3 39N45'29 93w54'16 6:15:37
Nevada 108 3 37N50'21 94w21'16 6:17:25
Newark 52 3 39N59'35 91w58'22 6:07:53
New Bloomfield 14
3 38N43'13 92w05'28 6:08:22
New Boston 58 3 39N57'07 92w51'34 6:11:26
New Bourbon 96 3 37N56'59 90w01'15 6:00:05
Newburg 81 48 37N54'51 91w54'09 6:07:37
New Cambria 61 3 39N46'31 92w45'01 6:11:00
New Castle 51 3 38N34'14 93w38'11 6:14:33
New Court Village 56
26 40N06 91w45 6:07:00
New Florence 70 3 38N54'37 91w26'53 6:05:48
New Frankfort 97
3 39N18'20 93w00'21 6:12:01
New Franklin 45 3 39N01'02 92w44'14 6:10:57
New Grove 114 3 37N14'41 92w39'48 6:10:39
Newhall 21 3 39N34'38 93w01'55 6:12:08
New Hamburg 100 3 37N07'35 89w35'36 5:58:22
New Hampton 41 3 40N15'49 94w11'45 6:16:47
New Harmony 82 3 39N17'39 91w22'29 6:05:30
New Hartford 82 3 39N11'58 91w16'12 6:05:05
New Haven 36 3 38N36'30 91w13'08 6:04:53
New Home 7 3 38N08'37 94w28'20 6:17:53
New Hope 57 3 39N08'12 90w51'51 6:03:27
Newland 80 3 38N48'34 93w10'23 6:12:42
New Lebanon 27 3 38N45'50 92w56'21 6:11:45
New Liberty 75 3 36N51'52 91w16'50 6:05:07
New Lisbon 103 3 36N58 90w01 6:00:04
New London 87 3 39N35'07 91w24'03 6:05:36
New Madrid 72 3 36N35'11 89w31'40 5:58:07
New Market 83 3 39N30'09 94w47'57 6:19:12
New Melle 92 3 38N42'35 90w52'46 6:03:31
New Offenburg 96
3 37N54'31 90w11'50 6:00:47
New Piper 42 3 38N21'28 94w00'49 6:16:03
New Point 44 3 40N03'17 95w04'44 6:20:19
Newport 6 3 37N31'40 94w06'15 6:16:25
New Santa Fe 48 3 38N54'24 94w36'16 6:18:25
New Survey 78 3 36N06'12 89w54'50 5:59:39
Newton 101 3 37N21 91w25 6:05:40
Newtonia 73 3 36N52'36 94w11'07 6:16:44
Newtown 105 3 40N22'35 93w20'05 6:13:20
New Truxton 109 3 38N58'42 91w14'16 6:04:57
New Wells 16 3 37N33'22 89w37'28 5:58:30
New Woollam 37 3 38N22'37 91w34'22 6:06:17
New York 13 3 39N40 93w55 6:15:40
Niangua 112 3 37N23'14 92w49'57 6:11:20
Nichols 39 44 37N13'04 93w21'43 6:13:27
Nickellton 61 3 39N55'36 92w18'26 6:09:14
Nickelville 55 3 37N14'24 93w42'02 6:14:48
Nind 1 3 40N04'14 92w46'04 6:11:04
Nine Mile Prairie 14
3 38N55 91w43 6:06:52
Ninnescah 93 3 38N15 93w46 6:15:04
Ninnescah Park 93
3 38N11'18 93w36'53 6:14:28
Nishnabotna 3 3 40N17'46 95w30'29 6:22:02
Nixa 22 3 37N02'36 93w17'39 6:13:11
Noble 77 3 36N44'51 92w34'11 6:10:17
Nodaway 2 3 39N54'34 94w58'03 6:19:52
Noel 60 3 36N32'44 94w29'06 6:17:56
Nona 109 3 38N33'58 90w56'25 6:03:46
Norborne 17 3 39N18'09 93w40'38 6:14:43
Norman 33 3 37N45 91w35 6:06:20
Normandy 95 40 38N43'31 90w17'48 6:01:11
Norris 42 49 38N31'14 93w53'43 6:15:35
North 29 3 37N31 93w53 6:15:32
North Benton 30 3 37N41 93w06 6:12:24
North Boonville 45
3 39N01 92w44 6:10:56
North Campbell 39
44 37N15 93w18 6:13:12
North County 95
40 38N46 90w12 6:00:48
Northeast 48 3 39N07 94w31 6:18:04
Northern Heights 83
3 39N12'48 94w36'08 6:18:25
North Fork 6 3 37N25 94w21 6:17:24
North Fork 69 3 39N36'40 91w55'08 6:07:41
North Galloway 22
3 36N56 93w17 6:13:08
North Jefferson 14
3 38N36'21 92w09'49 6:08:39
North Kansas City 24
3 39N07'48 94w33'43 6:18:15
Northland Shopping Center 95
40 38N44 90w15 6:01:00
North Lilbourn 72
3 36N36'06 89w37'12 5:58:29
North Moniteau 27
3 38N45 92w39 6:10:36
Northmoor 24 3 39N10'59 94w35'33 6:18:22
North Morgan 29 3 37N33 93w40 6:14:40
North Noel 60 3 36N33 94w30 6:18:00
North Patton 9 3 37N31'49 90w00'54 6:00:04
North River 64 41 39N50'38 91w29'22 6:05:57
North Salem 58 3 40N01'53 92w59'18 6:11:57
North Sugar Creek 88
3 39N27 92w28 6:09:52
Northview 112 3 37N17'12 92w59'47 6:11:59
North Wardell 78
3 36N21'31 89w48'52 5:59:15
Northwood Acres 83
3 39N13 94w40 6:18:40
Northwoods 95 40 38N42'15 90w16'54 6:01:08
Northwye 81 10 37N58'30 91w45'20 6:07:01
Norton 97 3 39N11'46 93w08'05 6:12:32
Norville 59 3 39N45'16 93w28'20 6:13:53
Norwood 114 3 37N06'30 92w24'53 6:09:40
Norwood Court 95
40 38N43'06 90w17'32 6:01:10
Noser Mill 36 3 38N23'35 91w11'32 6:04:46
Nottinghill 77 3 36N40'06 92w34'28 6:10:18
Novelty 52 3 40N00'45 92w12'29 6:08:50
Novinger 1 3 40N13'55 92w42'30 6:10:50
Noxall 72 3 36N43'21 89w34'40 5:58:19
Number Eight 61
44 39N43'54 92w33'40 6:10:15
Nyhart 7 3 38N12'15 94w26'00 6:17:44
Nyssa 12 3 36N38'23 90w14'33 6:00:58
Oak 32 3 39N53'37 94w31'46 6:18:07
Oak Grove 36 44 38N13'32 91w09'04 6:04:36
Oak Grove 48 3 39N00'18 94w07'45 6:16:31
Oak Grove 62 3 37N34'22 90w23'41 6:01:35
Oak Grove Heights 39
44 37N10'26 93w07'06 6:12:28
Oakhill 5 3 36N30'03 93w42'36 6:14:50
Oak Hill 28 44 38N12'21 91w25'14 6:05:41
Oakland 49 3 37N09 94w28 6:17:52
Oakland 53 47 37N38'11 92w33'33 6:10:14
Oakland 95 40 38N34'35 90w23'08 6:01:33
Oakland Park 49 3 37N06'46 94w28'33 6:17:54
Oak Ridge 5 3 36N42'44 93w47'32 6:15:10
Oak Ridge 16 3 37N30'04 89w43'47 5:58:55
Oak Ridge 108 3 37N51'33 94w08'55 6:16:36
Oaks 24 3 39N11'47 94w34'10 6:18:17
Oakside 101 3 37N06'26 91w39'08 6:06:37
Oakton 6 3 37N27'29 94w21'14 6:17:25
Oakvale 50 4 38N05'30 90w27'36 6:01:50
Oakview 24 3 39N12'31 94w34'05 6:18:16
Oakville 78 3 36N09'13 89w53'47 5:59:35
Oakville 95 40 38N28'12 90w18'16 6:01:13
Oakwood 24 3 39N12'07 94w34'12 6:18:17
Oakwood 87 3 39N41'07 91w23'48 6:05:35
Oakwood Manor 24
3 39N11'49 94w33'51 6:18:15
Oakwood Park 24 3 39N12'12 94w34'25 6:18:18
Oasis 57 16 39N03 90w45 6:03:00
Oasis 106 3 36N32'19 93w17'58 6:13:12
Oates 90 3 37N33'46 91w03'23 6:04:14
Ocie 77 3 36N33'31 92w45'32 6:11:02
Octa 35 3 36N10'16 90w07'23 6:00:30
Odessa 54 3 38N59'57 93w57'12 6:15:49
Odin 114 3 37N16'06 92w37'06 6:10:28
Oermann 50 3 38N18'29 90w43'24 6:02:54
Oetters 36 3 38N33'19 90w47'37 6:03:10
O'Fallon 92 2 38N48'38 90w41'59 6:02:48
Ogborn 96 3 37N49'52 90w25'18 6:01:41
Oglesville 12 3 36N34'49 90w18'37 6:01:14
Ohio 67 3 36N56 89w11 5:56:44
Ohio 93 3 38N09'20 93w51'06 6:15:24
Oil City 21 3 39N20'40 92w50'57 6:11:24
Okete 57 3 39N05'52 90w55'49 6:03:43
Olathia 34 3 37N01'38 92w31'10 6:10:05
Old Appleton 16 3 37N36 89w43 5:58:52
Old Bland 37 3 38N18'54 91w37'22 6:06:29
Old Chilhowee 51
3 38N36'23 93w51'02 6:15:24
Olden 46 3 36N50'02 91w54'37 6:07:38
Old Farm Estates 95
40 38N40 90w26 6:01:44
Oldfield 22 3 36N58'42 93w02'24 6:12:10
Old Fredonia 8 3 38N15 93w23 6:13:32
Oldham 10 3 38N43'51 92w15'46 6:09:03
Old Linn Creek 15
3 38N04'21 92w44'11 6:10:57
Old Merritt 34 3 36N53'59 92w53'14 6:11:33
Old Mines 110 3 38N00'55 90w45'21 6:03:01
Old Monroe 57 14 38N55'54 90w44'48 6:02:59
Old Orchard 95 40 38N36 90w20 6:01:20
Old Peculiar 19 3 38N43'09 94w26'29 6:17:46
Old Success 107 3 37N27'27 92w05'13 6:08:21
Old Town 75 3 36N30'14 91w32'36 6:06:10
Old Van Cleve 63
3 38N19 92w10 6:08:40
Old Westport Landing 57
25 39N10'32 90w44'00 6:02:56
Old Woollam 37 3 38N23'34 91w33'12 6:06:13
Olean 66 3 38N24'39 92w31'45 6:10:07
Olga 112 3 37N05'19 92w54'24 6:11:38
Olinger 55 3 37N16'36 93w50'13 6:15:21
Olive 30 3 37N27'33 93w06'31 6:12:26
Olive 95 1 38N38 90w12 6:00:48
Oliver 106 3 36N36 93w13 6:12:52
Olivette 95 40 38N39'55 90w22'33 6:01:30
Olney 57 3 39N05'02 91w14'35 6:04:58
Olympia 20 3 37N43'34 94w01'42 6:16:07
Olympia Village 50
3 36N50 89w20 5:57:20
Omaha 86 3 40N31'57 92w48'02 6:11:12
One Hundred and One Ranch 50
3 38N21'02 90w39'56 6:02:40
Ongo 34 3 36N59'26 92w53'38 6:11:35
Opal 55 3 37N01'16 93w46'12 6:15:05
Oran 100 3 37N05'06 89w39'19 5:58:37
Orange 55 3 37N02'42 93w43'00 6:14:52
Orchard Farm 45
15 38N52'43 90w26'46 6:01:47
Orchard Lakes 95
40 38N40 90w26 6:01:44
Orchid 32 3 39N57'06 94w31'46 6:18:07
Ore 19 3 38N43'40 94w20'02 6:17:20
Orearville 97 3 39N10'18 93w04'27 6:12:18
Oregon 44 3 39N59'13 95w08'41 6:20:35
Origanna 53 3 37N28'42 92w30'41 6:10:03
Oriole 16 3 37N26'32 89w32'07 5:58:08
Orla 53 47 37N41 92w40 6:10:40
Oronogo 49 3 37N11'18 94w28'12 6:17:53
Orrick 89 3 39N12'46 94w07'21 6:16:29
Orrsburg 74 3 40N25'51 94w43'16 6:18:53
Orrville 95 40 38N38'13 90w39'36 6:02:38
Osa 5 3 36N54'16 93w38'03 6:14:32
Osage Beach 15 3 38N09'01 92w37'04 6:10:28
Osage Bend 26 3 38N32 92w10 6:08:40
Osage Bluff 26 3 38N26'15 92w13'02 6:08:52
Osage City 26 3 38N33'09 92w01'56 6:08:08
Osage Heights 93
3 37N58'59 93w48'36 6:15:14
Osage Hills 95 40 38N34'06 90w26'52 6:01:47
Osborn 12 3 36N34'50 90w12'41 6:00:51
Osborn 25 3 39N44'50 94w21'18 6:17:25
Osborn Crossing 34
3 36N54'23 92w11'32 6:08:46
Oscar 107 3 37N24'51 91w49'49 6:07:19
Osceola 93 3 38N02'48 93w42'15 6:14:49
Osgood 105 3 40N11'58 93w20'49 6:13:23

Place		Lat.	Long.	Time
Osiris 20	3	37N37	94w01	6:16:04
Oskaloosa 6	3	37N38'21	94w35'32	6:18:22
Ott 46	3	36N29'55	92w04'43	6:08:19
Otterville 27	3	38N41'59	93w00'07	6:12:00
Otto 50	3	38N22'15	90w30'01	6:02:00
Ottoville 50	3	38N25	90w34	6:02:16
Overland 95	40	38N42'04	90w21'44	6:01:27
Overton 68	3	38N56'52	92w34'34	6:10:18
Owasco 105	3	40N08'17	92w58'40	6:11:55
Owenmont 91	3	36N37'12	90w47'01	6:03:08
Owens 114	3	37N13'08	92w24'10	6:09:37
Owensville 37	3	38N20'44	91w30'05	6:06:00
Owsley 51	3	38N38'43	93w30'55	6:14:04
Oxford 113	3	40N25'16	94w32'25	6:18:10
Oxly 91	3	36N35'42	90w41'15	6:02:45
Oyer 93	3	37N57'38	93w52'15	6:15:29
Ozark 22	3	37N01'15	93w12'21	6:12:49
Ozark Beach 106	3	36N39'32	93w08'19	6:12:33
Ozark Springs 85	3	37N50'23	92w20'16	6:09:21
Ozark View 95	40	38N34'35	90w27'45	6:01:51
Ozora 96	3	37N51'52	90w02'04	6:00:08
Pacetown 20	3	37N45'12	93w59'43	6:15:59
Pacific 36	6	38N28'55	90w44'29	6:02:58
Pack 60	3	36N33	94w30	6:18:00
Page City 54	3	39N07'37	93w43'51	6:14:55
Pagedale 95	40	38N41'00	90w18'28	6:01:14
Painton 103	3	37N04'56	89w47'41	5:59:11
Palace 85	3	37N37'13	92w08'23	6:08:34
Palemon 17	3	39N19'05	93w36'37	6:14:26
Palestine 27	3	38N51	92w50	6:11:20
Palisades 95	40	38N32	90w35	6:02:20
Palmer 110	3	37N50'22	90w59'45	6:03:59
Palmetto 39	3	37N08'32	93w05'43	6:12:23
Palmyra 64	39	39N47'39	91w31'23	6:06:06
Palo Pinto 8	3	38N22'54	93w27'19	6:13:49
Panama 108	3	38N02'49	94w21'17	6:17:25
Papin 50	4	38N04'04	90w28'14	6:01:53
Papinsville 7	3	38N04	94w05	6:16:20
Paradise 24	3	39N25'39	94w30'56	6:18:04
Paris 69	3	39N28'51	92w00'04	6:08:00
Paris Springs 55	3	37N11'39	93w40'45	6:14:43
Parkdale 50	3	38N29	90w32	6:02:08
Parkdale 83	3	39N11'24	94w38'51	6:18:35
Parker Lake 79	3	37N41'12	90w04'39	6:00:19
Parkers Landing 57	16	39N03'21	90w43'09	6:02:53
Parkers Park 57	16	39N02'37	90w43'15	6:02:53
Parks 12	3	36N36'50	90w33'55	6:02:16
Parkville 83	3	39N11'42	94w40'55	6:18:44
Parkway 36	17	38N20'17	90w58'11	6:03:53
Parkway 48	3	39N01	94w32	6:18:08
Parma 72	3	36N36'49	89w48'59	5:59:16
Parnell 74	3	40N26'24	94w37'23	6:18:30
Parshley 49	3	37N04'27	94w14'22	6:16:57
Parson Creek 58	3	39N46	93w18	6:13:12
Pasadena Hills 95	40	38N42'30	90w17'34	6:01:10
Pasadena Park 95	40	38N42'38	90w17'53	6:01:12
Pascola 78	3	36N16'00	89w49'36	5:59:18
Pasley 5	3	36N37'41	93w53'18	6:15:33
Passaic 7	3	38N19'19	94w20'53	6:17:24
Passo 8	3	38N15	93w23	6:13:32
Passover 15	3	38N04'51	92w35'56	6:10:24
Paterson Ford 91	3	36N44'00	90w44'00	6:02:56
Patsy 28	3	37N57'43	91w16'20	6:05:05
Patterson 111	3	37N11'18	90w33'02	6:02:12
Patton 9	3	37N30'08	90w00'48	6:00:03
Patton Junction 9	3	37N31'08	90w00'55	6:00:04
Pattonsburg 31	3	40N02'48	94w08'08	6:16:33
Pattonville 95	40	38N44'11	90w24'24	6:01:38
Paulding 35	3	36N00'49	90w14'10	6:00:57
Pauldingville 92	17	38N46'29	90w57'19	6:03:49
Paulina Hills 50	3	38N27'39	90w25'42	6:01:43
Pawnee 41	3	40N31'19	94w03'02	6:16:12
Paw Paw 105	3	40N05'28	93w05'15	6:12:21
Paydown 63	3	38N13'44	91w48'13	6:07:13
Paydown Ford 63	3	38N13'56	91w48'42	6:07:15
Payne Ford 26	3	38N27'38	92w27'09	6:09:49
Paynesville 82	21	39N15'45	90w54'01	6:03:36
Peace Valley 46	3	36N52'28	91w43'52	6:06:55
Peach Orchard 78	3	36N21'56	89w56'02	5:59:44
Peaksville 23	3	40N30'25	91w41'49	6:06:47
Pea Ridge 110	44	38N07'33	91w02'31	6:04:10
Pearl 39	3	37N21'06	93w29'11	6:13:57
Pease 53	3	37N29'41	92w37'57	6:10:32
Pebble Acres 95	40	38N40	90w26	6:01:44
Peculiar 19	3	38N43'09	94w27'30	6:17:50
Peerless Park 95	40	38N32'36	90w29'42	6:01:59
Peers 109	3	38N38'03	91w07'18	6:04:29
Pemiscot 78	3	36N04	89w44	5:58:56
Pendleton 94	3	37N44	90w29	6:01:56
Pendleton 109	17	38N49'38	91w14'06	6:04:56
Penermon 103	3	36N48	89w49	5:59:16
Penn 105	3	40N16	92w57	6:11:48
Pennsboro 29	3	37N19'38	93w50'02	6:15:20
Pennville 105	3	40N21'46	92w56'48	6:11:47
Peno 82	3	39N29	91w17	6:05:08
Peoria 110	3	37N45'22	90w53'03	6:03:32
Pepsin 73	44	37N01'25	94w14'30	6:16:58
Perche 10	3	39N06	92w25	6:09:40
Perkins 100	3	37N05'41	89w46'31	5:59:06
Perrin 25	3	39N39'37	94w24'08	6:17:37
Perry 87	3	39N25'52	91w40'30	6:06:42
Perryville 79	3	37N43'27	89w51'40	5:59:27
Pershing 37	3	38N34'38	91w36'51	6:06:27
Peru 7	3	38N16	94w20	6:17:20
Peruque 92	2	38N52'06	90w36'29	6:02:26
Petersburg 42	3	38N31'09	93w50'47	6:15:23
Petersburg 45	3	39N03'30	92w53'35	6:11:34
Peters Ford 36	3	38N22'28	91w12'27	6:04:50
Petersville 36	3	38N35'14	90w44'48	6:02:59
Pettys Hill 95	40	38N32'53	90w30'19	6:02:01
Pevely 50	12	38N17'00	90w23'42	6:01:35
Phelps 55	3	37N11'23	93w54'08	6:15:37
Phelps City 3	3	40N24'12	95w35'54	6:22:24
Phenix 39	3	37N22'43	93w32'44	6:14:11
Philadelphia 64	3	39N50'19	91w44'20	6:06:57
Phillipsburg 53	3	37N33'14	92w47'05	6:11:08
Phillips Ford 43	3	38N03'41	93w19'23	6:13:18
Pickering 74	3	40N27'03	94w50'31	6:19:22
Piedmont 111	3	37N09'16	90w41'44	6:02:47
Pierce City 55	44	36N56'40	94w00'15	6:16:01
Pierpont 10	3	38N51'44	92w18'53	6:09:16
Pierre Laclede 115	1	38N38	90w15	6:01:00
Pilgrim 29	3	37N21'27	93w46'31	6:15:06
Pilot Grove 27	3	38N52'29	92w54'41	6:11:39
Pilot Knob 47	3	37N37'16	90w38'25	6:02:34
Pinckney 109	3	38N40'43	91w13'58	6:04:56
Pine 91	3	36N37	90w49	6:03:16
Pine City 35	3	36N22'57	90w01'26	6:00:06
Pine Creek 77	3	36N41	92w19	6:09:16
Pine Crest 107	3	37N05'31	91w39'31	6:06:38
Pine Lawn 95	40	38N41'41	90w16'42	6:01:07
Pine Ridge 22	3	36N50'14	93w06'47	6:12:27
Pineville 60	3	36N35'40	94w23'02	6:17:32
Piney Park 36	17	38N18'04	90w56'34	6:03:46
Pinhook 67	3	36N44'20	89w18'36	5:57:14
Pinkston 11	3	39N38'49	94w48'16	6:19:13
Pioneer 5	3	36N50'09	94w03'17	6:16:13
Piper 42	3	38N20'37	94w00'52	6:16:03
Pippin Place 85	11	37N50'43	92w15'00	6:09:00
Pisgah 27	3	38N46'35	92w38'57	6:10:36
Pitcher 14	3	38N45'01	91w57'57	6:07:52
Pittsburg 43	3	37N50'02	93w18'01	6:13:12
Pittsville 51	3	38N51'02	93w59'24	6:15:58
Plad 30	3	37N44'55	92w58'31	6:11:54
Plainview 60	3	36N39'54	94w17'45	6:17:11
Plainview 61	3	39N55'38	92w33'02	6:10:12
Plano 39	3	37N11'34	93w33'03	6:14:12
Plato 107	3	37N30'13	92w13'29	6:08:54
Platte City 83	3	39N22'13	94w46'56	6:19:08
Platte Gardens 83	3	39N18'10	94w41'09	6:18:45
Platte Woods 83	3	39N13'45	94w38'52	6:18:35
Plattin 50	3	38N07'52	90w24'41	6:01:39
Plattsburg 25	3	39N33'56	94w26'52	6:17:47
Plaza 48	3	39N03	94w36	6:18:24
Plaza 115	1	38N38	90w15	6:01:00
Pleasant Gap 7	3	38N10'22	94w10'55	6:16:44
Pleasant Green 27	3	38N48'22	92w57'45	6:11:51
Pleasant Grove 27	3	38N52'07	92w33'06	6:10:12
Pleasant Hill 19	3	38N47'15	94w16'09	6:17:05
Pleasant Hope 84	3	37N27'47	93w16'21	6:13:05
Pleasant Ridge 5	3	36N53'47	93w47'29	6:15:10
Pleasant Ridge 7	3	38N11	94w02	6:16:08
Pleasant Valley 24	3	39N12'59	94w29'02	6:17:56
Pleasant Valley 49	3	37N09'17	94w20'32	6:17:22
Plevna 52	3	39N58'25	92w05'10	6:08:21
Plew 55	3	37N11'34	94w02'12	6:16:09
Plum Ford 36	17	38N16'39	90w59'50	6:03:59
Plummer 26	3	38N33'41	92w19'21	6:09:17
Plum Valley 107	3	37N21'36	92w04'57	6:08:20
Plymouth 17	3	39N35'48	93w42'06	6:14:48
Pocahontas 16	3	37N30'04	89w38'20	5:58:33
Pocohontas Crossing 46	3	36N41'07	91w41'12	6:06:45
Point Lookout 106	3	36N37	93w14	6:12:56
Point Pleasant 72	3	36N27'09	89w34'28	5:58:18
Point Rest 79	3	37N48'58	89w42'45	5:58:51
Polk 84	3	37N43'45	93w17'57	6:13:12
Pollock 105	3	40N21'33	93w05'05	6:12:20
Polo 13	3	39N33'08	94w02'26	6:16:10
Pomona 46	3	36N52'02	91w54'51	6:07:39
Pom-o-sa Heights 8	3	38N10'28	93w23'45	6:13:35
Ponce deLeon 104	3	36N52'33	93w21'05	6:13:24
Pond 95	40	38N34'49	90w39'22	6:02:37
Pond Creek 39	3	37N08	93w34	6:14:16
Ponder 91	3	36N35'02	90w59'20	6:03:57
Pondfork 77	3	36N42'00	92w42'35	6:10:50
Pontiac 77	3	36N30'56	92w36'13	6:10:25
Poole Ford 60	3	36N34'25	94w25'01	6:17:40
Poplar Bluff 12	13	36N45'25	90w23'34	6:01:34
Portage 72	3	36N27	89w47	5:59:08
Portage Des Sioux 92	18	38N55'30	90w20'39	6:01:23
Portageville 72	3	36N25'31	89w41'58	5:58:48
Porter 22	3	37N03	93w19	6:13:16
Port Hudson 36	3	38N27'14	91w15'14	6:05:01
Portia 108	3	37N54'30	94w04'29	6:16:18
Portland 14	3	38N42'39	91w43'03	6:06:52
Possum Trot 104	3	36N58'43	93w25'44	6:13:43
Possum Walk 74	3	40N29'40	95w05'03	6:20:20
Postal 80	3	38N53'51	93w04'59	6:12:20
Post Oak 51	3	38N34'08	93w45'03	6:15:00
Potosi 110	3	37N56'11	90w47'16	6:03:09
Pottersville 46	3	36N41'45	92w01'52	6:08:07
Potts 76	3	38N28'27	91w47'01	6:07:08
Powe 103	3	36N39'33	90w05'48	6:00:23
Powell 60	3	36N37'22	94w10'50	6:16:43
Powellville 81	3	37N53'22	92w00'52	6:08:03
Powersite 106	3	36N39'20	93w07'16	6:12:29
Powersville 86	3	40N32'57	93w18'00	6:13:12
Poynor 91	3	36N31'13	90w54'25	6:03:38
Prairie City 7	3	38N04'44	94w10'28	6:16:42
Prairie Hill 21	3	39N31'07	92w44'16	6:10:57
Prairie Home 27	3	38N48'47	92w35'25	6:10:22
Prairieville 82	3	39N16	91w00	6:04:00
Prankford 82	3	39N29'35	91w19'08	6:05:17
Prater 36	3	38N26'58	90w45'35	6:03:02
Prathersville 10	3	39N01'05	92w19'18	6:09:17
Prathersville 24	3	39N18'45	94w16'20	6:17:05
Pratt 91	3	36N31'48	90w49'52	6:03:19
Prescott 107	3	37N26'13	91w55'17	6:07:41
Preston 43	3	37N56'27	93w12'27	6:12:50
Preston 49	3	37N16'45	94w23'20	6:17:33
Prettyman 19	3	38N37'36	94w25'53	6:17:44
Price Landing 100	3	37N02'13	89w22'42	5:57:31
Prices Branch 70	3	38N57'04	91w20'15	6:05:21
Princeton 65	5	40N24'03	93w34'49	6:14:19
Principia 95	40	38N37	90w26	6:01:44
Progress 115	1	38N38	90w15	6:01:00
Prospect 112	3	37N23	92w50	6:11:20
Prospect Grove 99	3	40N31'35	91w58'55	6:07:56
Prospect Hill 95	40	38N44'15	90w13'09	6:00:53
Prosperine 53	3	37N47'34	92w45'58	6:11:04
Prosperity 49	3	37N07'35	94w25'14	6:17:41
Protem 106	3	36N31'44	92w51'31	6:11:26
Providence 10	3	38N50'15	92w24'19	6:09:37
Providence 35	3	36N30'59	89w58'18	5:59:53
Pulaski 91	3	36N36'50	90w44'48	6:02:59
Pulaskifield 5	3	36N56	93w55	6:15:40
Pumpkin Center 30	3	37N44'42	93w04'14	6:12:17
Pumpkin Center 74	3	40N12'01	94w52'03	6:19:28
Punkin Center 45	3	39N12'03	92w30'32	6:10:02
Purcell 49	3	37N14'32	94w26'06	6:17:44
Purdin 58	3	39N57'07	93w09'56	6:12:40
Purdy 5	3	36N49'02	93w55'14	6:15:41
Pure Air 1	3	40N14	92w43	6:10:52
Purina Farm 36	6	38N29	90w49	6:03:16
Purman 91	3	36N31'22	90w44'48	6:02:59
Purvis 15	3	38N09'50	92w49'02	6:11:16
Puxico 103	3	36N56'59	90w09'30	6:00:38
Pyletown 103	3	36N43'29	90w01'07	6:00:04
Pyrmont 71	3	38N30'32	93w01'10	6:12:05
Quail 104	3	36N53'42	93w30'55	6:14:04
Quaker 110	3	37N46'52	91w00'07	6:04:00
Quarles 42	3	38N28'15	93w45'13	6:15:01
Queen City 98	3	40N24'33	92w34'03	6:10:16
Quick City 51	3	38N34'52	94w01'43	6:16:07
Quincy 43	19	38N00'30	93w28'20	6:13:53
Quitman 74	3	40N22'24	95w04'35	6:20:18
Qulin 12	3	36N35'45	90w14'50	6:00:59
Quote 17	3	39N32'21	93w40'59	6:14:44
Racine 73	3	36N53'46	94w31'38	6:18:07
Racket 8	3	38N17'36	93w29'31	6:13:58
Racola 110	3	38N01'57	90w45'24	6:03:02
Radar 63	3	38N11	91w57	6:07:48
Rader 112	3	37N27'37	92w43'08	6:10:53
Ralls 87	3	39N41'01	91w24'05	6:05:36
Ralphwhite Ford 30	3	37N50'00	92w51'59	6:11:28
Randles 16	3	37N08'16	89w46'03	5:59:04
Randol 16	3	37N24	89w32	5:58:08
Randolph 24	3	39N09'28	94w29'43	6:17:59
Randolph Springs 88	3	39N25'26	92w36'18	6:10:25
Raney 93	3	37N57'07	93w43'43	6:14:55
Ranken 95	40	38N32'05	90w30'43	6:02:03
Rapinsville 7	3	38N04'02	94w13'36	6:16:54
Rat 101	3	37N22'21	91w13'39	6:04:55
Ratcliff Ford 107	3	37N03'22	91w41'03	6:06:44
Ravanna 65	3	40N27'18	93w27'55	6:13:52
Ravena 24	3	39N13	94w28	6:17:52
Ravena Gardens 24	3	39N13	94w28	6:17:52
Ravenwood 74	3	40N21'08	94w40'25	6:18:42
Rayborn 114	3	37N18'16	92w21'27	6:09:26
Raymondville 107	3	37N20'23	91w50'02	6:07:20
Raymore 19	3	38N48'07	94w27'09	6:17:49
Raytown 48	3	39N00'31	94w27'48	6:17:51
Rayville 89	3	39N20'54	94w03'46	6:16:15
Rea 2	3	40N03'43	94w45'52	6:19:03
Reading 82	3	39N29'29	91w07'56	6:04:32
Readsville 14	3	38N48'16	91w43'08	6:06:53
Rector 101	3	37N24'25	91w30'34	6:06:02
Red Bank 34	3	36N56'18	92w48'38	6:11:15
Redbird 37	3	38N10'54	91w34'13	6:06:17
Red Bridge 48	3	38N55'37	94w34'32	6:18:18
Redd 103	3	36N50'52	90w03'38	6:00:15
Reddish 56	3	40N14	91w46	6:07:04
Redford 90	3	37N19'12	90w53'54	6:03:36
Redings Mill 73	3	37N01'18	94w31'19	6:18:05
Redman 61	45	39N51'56	92w20'12	6:09:21
Redmondville 47	3	37N37'32	90w58'09	6:03:53
Red Oak 55	3	37N13'43	94w00'40	6:16:03
Red Onion 35	3	35N59'46	90w20'32	6:01:22
Redtop 30	3	37N30'13	93w08'38	6:12:35
Red Top 112	3	37N17'59	93w00'37	6:12:02
Reeds 49	3	37N06'58	94w09'56	6:16:40
Reeds Spring 104	3	36N44'59	93w22'40	6:13:31
Reform 14	3	38N45'55	91w46'44	6:07:07
Regal 89	3	39N28'03	93w48'52	6:15:15
Reger 105	3	40N08'38	93w11'33	6:12:46
Regina 60	3	38N19'36	90w35'31	6:02:22
Renick 88	3	39N20'34	92w24'49	6:09:39
Rensselaer 87	3	39N40'14	91w32'52	6:06:11
Republic 39	3	37N07'12	93w28'48	6:13:55
Rescue 55	3	37N11'30	93w58'43	6:15:55
Revere 23	3	40N29'42	91w40'39	6:06:43
Revisville 5	3	36N52'59	93w38'52	6:14:35
Reynolds 90	3	37N24'03	91w04'24	6:04:18
Reynolds Ford 16	3	37N25'40	89w50'10	5:59:21
Rhineland 70	3	38N43'03	91w31'02	6:06:04
Rhyse 33	3	37N34'09	91w41'10	6:06:45
Rices Corner 4	3	39N12'05	91w33'53	6:06:16
Richards 108	3	37N54'26	94w33'25	6:18:14
Richards-Gebaur A F B 48	3	38N54	94w32	6:18:08

Rich Fountain 76
3 38N23'45 91w52'47 6:07:31
Rich Hill 7 3 38N05'47 94w21'39 6:17:27
Richie 11 3 39N39'39 94w48'49 6:19:15
Richland 85 9 37N51'24 92w24'18 6:09:37
Richmond 89 3 39N16'43 93w58'36 6:15:54
Richmond Heights 95
40 38N37'43 90w19'10 6:01:17
Richville 34 3 36N50'25 92w14'21 6:08:57
Richville 44 3 39N59'23 95w02'51 6:20:11
Richwood 60 3 36N42 94w07 6:16:28
Richwoods 110 3 38N09'37 90w49'41 6:03:19
Ridge 17 3 39N29 93w22 6:13:28
Ridgedale 106 3 36N30'14 93w13'25 6:12:54
Ridgeley 83 3 39N27'21 94w38'17 6:18:33
Ridge Prairie 97
3 38N57'20 93w04'05 6:12:16
Ridgeway 41 3 40N22'41 93w56'12 6:15:45
Ridgley 5 3 36N41'50 94w01'12 6:16:05
Riggs 10 3 39N10'16 92w20'43 6:09:23
Rimby 84 3 37N45'36 93w14'11 6:12:57
Rinehart 108 3 37N57'22 94w29'54 6:18:00
Rington 35 3 35N59'52 90w11'07 6:00:44
Ripley 48 3 39N08'03 94w18'52 6:17:15
Risco 72 3 36N33'12 89w49'04 5:59:16
Ristine 72 3 36N38'56 89w32'53 5:58:12
Ritchey 73 3 36N56'39 94w11'05 6:16:44
Ritter 39 44 37N15'49 93w23'01 6:13:32
River aux Vases 96
3 37N52'20 90w06'46 6:00:27
River Bend Estates 95
40 38N37 90w35 6:02:20
Riverdale 22 3 36N59'43 93w17'23 6:13:10
Rivermines 94 3 37N50'54 90w31'52 6:02:07
Riverside 35 3 36N02'33 90w20'14 6:01:21
Riverside 50 12 38N17'12 90w22'48 6:01:31
Riverside 83 3 39N10'39 94w36'46 6:18:27
Riverside Inn 60
3 36N34'02 94w25'42 6:17:43
Riverton 75 3 36N38'54 91w12'05 6:04:48
Riverview 71 3 38N16'33 93w04'10 6:12:17
Riverview 95 40 38N44'52 90w12'41 6:00:51
Rives 35 3 36N05'37 90w00'48 6:00:03
Roach 15 3 37N59'38 92w50'10 6:11:21
Roads 17 3 39N28'00 93w42'04 6:14:48
Roanoke 45 3 39N19'01 92w41'19 6:10:45
Roaring River 5 3 36N33 93w45 6:15:00
Roark 37 3 38N39 91w28 6:05:52
Robberson 39 3 37N21 93w20 6:13:20
Robbins 51 3 38N54'23 93w48'28 6:15:14
Robertson 95 40 38N45'51 90w22'55 6:01:32
Robertsville 36 3 38N24'53 90w48'50 6:03:15
Roblee 82 24 39N22'46 90w56'29 6:03:46
Roby 107 3 37N30'56 92w08'20 6:08:33
Rocheport 10 3 38N58'48 92w33'50 6:10:15
Rochester 2 3 39N54'44 94w41'04 6:18:44
Rock 50 3 38N26 90w25 6:01:40
Rockaway Beach 106
3 36N41'57 93w09'35 6:12:38
Rockbridge 77 3 36N47'22 92w24'32 6:09:38
Rock Creek 50 3 38N26'23 90w29'51 6:01:59
Rock Creek Junction 48
3 39N06'49 94w28'46 6:17:55
Rockford 21 3 39N20'47 92w54'51 6:11:39
Rock Ford 36 3 38N19'23 91w15'23 6:05:02
Rockford Beach 50
3 38N25'19 90w35'24 6:02:22
Rock Hill 95 40 38N36'27 90w22'42 6:01:31
Rockingham 89 3 39N21'24 93w46'56 6:15:08
Rockport 3 3 40N24'36 95w30'52 6:22:03
Rock Prairie 29 3 37N20 93w41 6:14:44
Rock Prairie 84 3 37N28'59 93w12'09 6:12:49
Rock Springs 94 3 37N45'23 90w29'00 6:01:56
Rockview 100 3 37N12'08 89w38'22 5:58:33
Rockville 7 3 38N04'17 94w04'46 6:16:19
Rocky Comfort 60
3 36N44'47 94w05'25 6:16:22
Rocky Ford 108 3 38N02'09 94w11'40 6:16:47
Rocky Fork 10 3 39N05 92w15 6:09:00
Rocky Mount 71 3 38N17'41 92w41'51 6:10:47
Rocky Ridge 96 3 37N53 90w13 6:00:52
Rodger Ford 15 3 37N57'34 92w49'56 6:11:20
Rogersville 112 3 37N07'01 93w03'20 6:12:13
Rolla 81 10 37N57'05 91w46'16 6:07:05
Romance 77 3 36N43'01 92w30'09 6:10:01
Rombauer 12 3 36N50'35 90w16'48 6:01:07
Rome 34 3 36N50'29 92w46'24 6:11:06
Rondo 84 3 37N45'58 93w26'59 6:13:48
Roosevelt 34 3 36N49'50 92w07'24 6:08:30
Roosterville 24 3 39N17'43 94w26'11 6:17:45
Rosati 81 10 38N01'37 91w31'51 6:06:07
Roscoe 93 3 37N58'22 93w48'43 6:15:15
Rosebud 37 3 38N23'14 91w24'03 6:05:36
Rose Hill 51 3 38N37'58 94w04'08 6:16:17
Roseland 42 3 38N23'36 93w32'32 6:14:10
Roselle 62 3 37N35'58 90w31'33 6:02:06
Rosendale 2 3 40N02'40 94w49'14 6:19:17
Rosewood 86 3 40N25'30 92w55'22 6:11:41
Ross Bridge 85 3 37N39'57 92w02'54 6:08:12
Rossville 12 3 36N43'59 90w14'47 6:00:59
Rothville 21 3 39N39'12 93w03'50 6:12:15
Roubidoux 107 3 37N25'21 92w08'52 6:08:35
Round Bottom Ford 43
3 38N01'48 93w20'16 6:13:21
Round Grove 55 3 37N16'00 93w54'18 6:15:37
Round Prairie 14
3 38N49 92w05 6:08:20
Round Spring 101
3 37N16'50 91w24'40 6:05:39
Rousertown 108 3 37N42'11 94w14'05 6:16:56
Rover 75 3 36N43'18 91w37'15 6:06:29
Rowena 4 3 39N19'33 92w03'27 6:08:14
Roy 34 3 36N53'25 92w48'13 6:11:13
Royal 81 10 38N07'41 91w34'47 6:06:19
Royal Heights 49
3 37N04 94w30 6:18:00
Ruble 90 3 37N08'54 90w53'46 6:03:35
Rucker 7 3 38N10'26 94w31'49 6:18:07
Rucker 10 3 39N13'53 92w24'48 6:09:39
Rueter 106 3 36N36'30 92w52'08 6:11:29
Rum Branch 16 3 37N09'27 89w51'09 5:59:25
Rush 11 3 39N34 95w02 6:20:08
Rush Hill 4 3 39N12'36 91w43'17 6:06:53
Rush Tower 50 12 38N13 90w24 6:01:36
Rushville 11 3 39N35'12 95w01'33 6:20:06
Ruskin 48 3 38N55'22 94w30'49 6:18:03
Ruskin Heights 48
3 38N55'17 94w30'18 6:18:01
Russ 53 47 37N35'02 92w35'09 6:10:21
Russellville 26 3 38N30'42 92w26'24 6:09:46
Russellville 89 3 39N24'24 93w49'48 6:15:19
Ruth 104 3 36N45 93w22 6:13:28
Rutledge 99 3 40N18'49 92w05'17 6:08:21
Ryder 88 3 39N18'17 92w26'15 6:09:45
Ryors 76 3 38N28'57 91w41'53 6:06:48
Sabula 47 3 37N24'17 90w41'46 6:02:47
Sac 29 3 37N31 93w46 6:15:04
Saco 62 3 37N21'56 90w26'21 6:01:45
Sac-o-Sage Heights 93
3 37N59 93w49 6:15:16
Sacville 39 3 37N23'38 93w25'44 6:13:43
Sadler 83 3 39N26'19 94w56'30 6:19:46
Safe 63 10 38N05'18 91w39'07 6:06:36
Sage Hill 55 3 36N55'29 93w41'01 6:14:44
Saginaw 73 3 37N01'26 94w28'05 6:17:52
Sagrada 15 3 38N13'18 93w03'11 6:12:13
Saint Albans 92 3 38N34'48 90w46'22 6:03:05
Saint Ann 95 40 38N43'38 90w22'59 6:01:32
Saint Anthony 66
3 38N09'20 92w16'26 6:09:06
Saint Aubert 76 3 38N39'00 91w51'23 6:07:26
Saint Catharine 58
3 39N47'45 92w59'37 6:11:58
Saint Charles 92
2 38N47'02 90w28'52 6:01:55
Saint Clair 36 17 38N20'43 90w58'51 6:03:55
Saint Clement 82
3 39N17'00 91w12'33 6:04:50
Saint Cloud 28 46 38N10'07 91w13'03 6:04:52
Saint Cloud 89 3 39N17'34 94w01'05 6:16:04
Sainte Genevieve 96
3 37N59 90w03 6:00:12
Saint Elizabeth 66
3 38N15'21 92w16'04 6:09:04
Saint Ferdinand 95
40 38N45 90w14 6:00:56
Saint Francisville 23
3 40N27'30 91w34'08 6:06:17
Saint Francois 94
3 37N52 90w31 6:02:04
Saint George 95
40 38N32'12 90w18'53 6:01:16
Saint George 114
3 37N22'51 92w26'31 6:09:46
Saint James 81 10 37N59'50 91w36'51 6:06:27
Saint John 85 3 37N53'21 92w22'46 6:09:31
Saint John 86 3 40N32'24 93w11'20 6:12:45
Saint Johns 95 40 38N42'55 90w20'42 6:01:23
Saint Joseph 11 3 39N46'07 94w50'47 6:19:23
Saint Jude Acres 96
3 37N58 90w03 6:00:12
Saint Louis 115 1 38N37'38 90w11'52 6:00:47
Saint Martins 26
3 38N35'39 92w20'13 6:09:21
Saint Marys 96 3 37N52'44 89w56'57 5:59:48
Saint Michael 62
3 37N33 90w17 6:01:08
Saint Patrick 23
3 40N15'52 91w37'39 6:06:31
Saint Paul 92 2 38N51'41 90w44'30 6:02:58
Saint Peters 92 2 38N48'01 90w37'35 6:02:30
Saint Robert 85 3 37N49'41 92w10'39 6:08:43
Saint Thomas 26 3 38N22'06 92w13'00 6:08:52
Salcedo 100 3 36N53'20 89w41'00 5:58:44
Salem (Coffey P O and Sta) 31
3 40N06'17 94w00'23 6:16:02
Salem 33 3 37N38'44 91w32'09 6:06:09
Saline 65 3 40N31'37 93w43'40 6:14:55
Saline City 97 3 39N08'25 92w56'35 6:11:46
Saline Junction 79
3 37N47'20 89w53'12 5:59:33
Saling 4 3 39N18'48 92w09'30 6:08:38
Salisbury 21 3 39N25'26 92w48'05 6:11:12
Salt Creek 21 3 39N34 93w02 6:12:08
Salt Fork 97 3 39N01 93w09 6:12:36
Salt Pond 97 3 39N00 93w26 6:13:44
Salt River 87 3 39N34'58 91w18'19 6:05:13
Salt Spring 88 3 39N26 92w33 6:10:12
Salt Springs 97 3 39N06'44 93w20'50 6:13:23
Samford 78 3 36N04'27 89w54'51 5:59:39
Samos 67 3 36N52'05 89w16'35 5:57:06
Sampsell 59 3 39N48'50 93w42'30 6:14:50
Sampson 112 3 37N26'30 92w50'32 6:11:22
Samtown 66 3 38N02'12 92w25'26 6:09:42
San Antonio 11 3 39N46'37 94w41'00 6:18:44
Sand Hill 99 3 40N18'41 92w07'40 6:08:31
Sandy Hook 68 3 38N44'54 92w24'30 6:09:38
Sandywoods 100 3 36N59 89w31 5:58:04
Sank 9 3 37N10'18 90w00'49 6:00:03
Sankey 28 3 37N58'37 91w20'37 6:05:22
Santa Fe 69 3 39N22'08 91w49'08 6:07:17
Santa Rosa 32 3 39N58'47 94w12'19 6:16:49
Santiago 8 3 38N25'37 93w27'24 6:13:50
Sapp 10 3 38N49'30 92w21'06 6:09:24
Sappington 95 40 38N32'13 90w22'47 6:01:31
Saratoga 60 3 36N32'29 94w33'23 6:18:14
Sarcoxie 49 3 37N04'09 94w06'59 6:16:28
Sargent 100 3 36N54'03 89w30'21 5:58:01
Sargent 107 3 37N05'12 92w01'37 6:08:06
Savannah 2 3 39N56'30 94w49'48 6:19:19
Saverton 87 41 39N38'47 91w16'05 6:05:04
Saxton 11 3 39N43'21 94w45'32 6:19:02
Scearces 25 3 39N34'53 94w30'30 6:18:02
Schell City 108 3 38N01'12 94w06'56 6:16:28
Schlatitz 9 3 37N06 89w55 5:59:40
Schluersburg 92 3 38N37'50 90w51'35 6:03:26
Schmitt Ford 36 3 38N21'49 91w10'42 6:04:43
Schnurbusch 79 3 37N36'43 89w45'06 5:59:00
Schofield 84 3 37N33'08 93w12'23 6:12:50
Scholten 5 3 36N50'59 93w37'46 6:14:31
Schubert 26 3 38N31'03 92w02'58 6:08:12
Schuermann Heights 95
40 38N43'23 90w21'57 6:01:28
Schundler 81 10 38N00'23 91w35'47 6:06:23
Scobeville 35 3 36N11'07 90w04'28 6:00:18
Scopus 9 3 37N26 89w56 5:59:44
Scotia 28 46 38N01'40 91w12'49 6:04:51
Scotland 49 3 37N04'59 94w22'37 6:17:30
Scott 26 3 38N37'08 92w16'37 6:09:06
Scott 106 3 36N33 93w06 6:12:24
Scott City 100 3 37N13'00 89w31'28 5:58:06
Scott Ford 28 3 37N58'41 91w27'20 6:05:49
Scotts Corner 4 3 39N09'46 91w38'52 6:06:35
Scrivner 26 3 38N27'17 92w22'46 6:09:31
Scruggs 26 3 38N33'44 92w16'56 6:09:08
Seaton 81 3 37N48'28 91w36'08 6:06:25
Sebree 45 3 39N07'37 92w31'51 6:10:07
Seckman 50 3 38N24'08 90w26'00 6:01:44
Sedalia 80 3 38N42'16 93w13'41 6:12:55
Sedgewickville 9
3 37N30'58 89w54'25 5:59:38
Seeburger 92 15 38N51'55 90w30'38 6:02:03
Seligman 5 3 36N31'21 93w56'22 6:15:45
Sellers 56 26 40N03'59 91w40'24 6:06:42
Selma 50 12 38N08'59 90w20'29 6:01:22
Selmore 22 3 36N58'05 93w13'48 6:12:55
Selsa 48 3 39N03'05 94w20'31 6:17:22
Senate Grove 36 3 38N36 91w13 6:04:52
Senath 35 3 36N08'03 90w09'35 6:00:38
Seneca 73 44 36N50'29 94w36'39 6:18:27
Sentinel 84 3 37N47'37 93w17'44 6:13:11
Seopus 9 3 37N23'56 89w55'14 5:59:41
Sequiota 39 44 37N08'51 93w14'20 6:12:57
Sereno 79 3 37N47'52 89w51'04 5:59:24
Seven Pines 95 40 38N40 90w26 6:01:44
Seventysix 79 3 37N43'12 89w36'44 5:58:27
Sewell Ford 37 3 38N11'19 91w33'50 6:06:15
Seybert 29 3 37N31'07 93w46'25 6:15:06
Seymour 112 3 37N08'47 92w46'07 6:11:04
Shackleford 97 3 39N06'37 93w17'44 6:13:11
Shackleford Crossing 27
3 38N53'31 93w02'00 6:12:08
Shade 78 3 36N10'32 89w46'00 5:59:04
Shady Dell 12 3 36N46'04 90w26'31 6:01:46
Shady Dell 103 3 36N57'50 89w49'21 5:59:17
Shady Grove 22 3 37N00 93w05 6:12:20
Shady Grove 85 3 37N51'31 92w16'40 6:09:07
Shafter 58 3 39N59'02 93w17'05 6:13:08
Shamrock 14 3 39N00'10 91w41'39 6:06:47
Shannondale 21 3 39N21'33 92w50'59 6:11:24
Shannondale 101 3 37N23'24 91w26'15 6:05:45
Sharon 97 3 39N18'02 93w07'59 6:12:32
Shaver Ford 87 3 39N31'18 91w41'22 6:06:45
Shaw 10 3 38N58'25 92w12'11 6:08:49
Shawan 103 3 36N57'50 89w46'47 5:59:07
Shawnee Mound 42
3 38N31'47 93w45'42 6:15:03
Shawneetown 16 3 37N33'04 89w39'07 5:58:36
Shearwood 59 3 39N59 93w48 6:15:12
Sheil 87 3 39N38'02 91w35'54 6:06:24
Shelbina 102 3 39N41'38 92w02'34 6:08:10
Shelby 58 3 39N58'07 93w01'05 6:12:04
Shelby 75 3 36N30'13 91w31'20 6:06:05
Shelbyville 102 3 39N48'21 92w02'29 6:08:10
Sheldon 108 3 37N39'29 94w17'33 6:17:10
Shell Knob 5 3 36N37'56 93w38'03 6:14:32
Shelton 52 3 40N05 92w16 6:09:04
Shelton Ford 62 3 37N21'05 90w28'45 6:01:55
Sheridan 113 3 40N31'05 94w36'43 6:18:27
Sherley 91 3 36N38 90w56 6:03:44
Sherman 95 40 38N32'16 90w35'31 6:02:22
Sherrill 107 3 37N35'19 91w52'34 6:07:30
Shibboleth 110 3 38N00'20 90w42'19 6:02:49
Shibleys Point 1
3 40N18'48 92w45'39 6:11:03
Shirley 110 3 37N54'54 90w55'09 6:03:41
Shoal 25 3 39N42 94w16 6:17:04
Shoal Creek 73 3 37N01 94w30 6:18:00
Shoal Creek Drive 73
3 37N02'27 94w31'09 6:18:05
Shook 111 3 37N02'34 90w18'32 6:01:14
Short Bend 33 3 37N44'47 91w26'02 6:05:44
Shoveltown 95 40 38N48'56 90w16'50 6:01:07
Shrewsbury 95 40 38N35'25 90w20'12 6:01:21
Shrum 9 3 37N23'02 90w00'54 6:00:04
Sibley 48 3 39N10'43 94w11'35 6:16:46
Sidney 86 3 40N21'15 92w49'08 6:11:17
Sigsbee 102 3 39N54'27 91w52'07 6:07:28
Sikeston 100 3 36N52'36 89w35'16 5:58:21
Silex 57 3 39N07'24 91w03'15 6:04:13
Silica 50 12 38N14'05 90w25'39 6:01:43
Siloam Springs 34
3 36N47'44 92w04'31 6:08:18
Silva 111 3 37N10'34 90w27'49 6:01:51
Silver Creek 73 3 37N02'26 94w28'21 6:17:53
Silver Dollar City 104
3 36N39 93w13 6:12:52
Silver Lake 79 3 37N41'01 89w59'24 5:59:58
Silver Mine 62 3 37N33 90w17 6:01:08
Silver Springs 94
3 37N59'57 90w31'28 6:02:06
Simcoe 60 3 36N43'18 94w10'02 6:16:40
Simmons 107 3 37N13'50 92w00'55 6:08:04
Simpson 51 3 38N53 93w40 6:14:40
Sinking 33 3 37N28 91w17 6:05:08
Sinsabaugh 91 3 36N30'16 90w42'07 6:02:48
Sisson 46 3 36N51 91w46 6:07:04
Sitze Store 9 3 37N16 90w07 6:00:28
Six Flags Over Mid-America 115
1 38N30 90w37 6:02:28
Skidmore 74 3 40N17'20 95w04'52 6:20:19
Skinner 4 3 39N15'59 91w59'20 6:07:57
Slabtown 62 3 37N34'35 90w19'28 6:01:18
Slabtown 107 3 37N33'47 92w01'10 6:08:05
Slagle 84 3 37N31'56 93w22'30 6:13:30
Slater 97 3 39N13'05 93w04'08 6:12:17
Sledd 82 21 39N13'53 90w53'26 6:03:34
Sleeper 53 3 37N45'38 92w35'34 6:10:22
Sligo 33 3 37N46'26 91w22'39 6:05:31
Sloan Ford 75 3 36N34'51 91w32'59 6:06:12
Smallett 34 3 36N50'55 92w42'50 6:10:51
Smileyville 64 3 39N52'01 91w33'46 6:06:15
Smithfield 49 3 37N10'08 94w36'10 6:18:25
Smith Ford 53 3 37N49'56 92w50'53 6:11:24
Smithton 80 3 38N40'48 93w05'34 6:12:22
Smithville 24 3 39N23'13 94w34'51 6:18:19
Smoky Hollow 33 3 37N37'20 91w41'34 6:06:46
Snadon Ford 29 3 37N20'26 93w47'21 6:15:09
Sni Mills 48 3 38N56'27 94w07'56 6:16:32

Snow Hill 57 3 39N03 90w53 6:03:32
Snow Hollow Lake 47 3 37N37'44 90w41'07 6:02:44
Snyder 21 3 39N30'59 93w14'24 6:12:58
Solo 107 3 37N14'00 91w57'11 6:07:49
Somerset 65 3 40N31 93w26 6:13:44
Sorrell 105 3 40N12'54 93w01'13 6:12:05
Souder 77 3 36N47'20 92w27'30 6:09:50
Soulard 115 1 38N38 90w15 6:01:00
South 29 3 37N19 93w47 6:15:08
Southard 53 3 37N32'21 92w20'15 6:09:21
South Benton 30 3 37N37 93w06 6:12:24
South Carrollton 17 3 39N20'28 93w29'43 6:13:59
South Cedar City 14 3 38N36 92w10 6:08:40
Southeast 48 3 38N58 94w32 6:18:08
Southern Aire 50 3 38N26 90w23 6:01:32
South Fork 46 3 36N37'40 91w57'45 6:07:51
South Galloway 22 3 36N52 93w17 6:13:08
South Gifford 61 3 40N02 92w41 6:10:44
South Gorin 99 3 40N22 92w01 6:08:04
South Greenfield 29 3 37N22'34 93w50'27 6:15:22
Southhampton 115 1 38N35'36 90w17'43 6:01:11
South Lee 48 3 38N53'20 94w22'40 6:17:31
South Liberty 24 3 39N12'04 94w23'20 6:17:33
South Lineville 65 3 40N34'44 93w31'25 6:14:06
South Moniteau 27 3 38N43 92w40 6:10:40
South Morgan 29 3 37N29 93w40 6:14:40
South Point 36 49 38N33 91w01 6:04:04
South River 64 41 39N49'57 91w26'52 6:05:47
South Shore 92 15 38N51'55 90w31'23 6:02:06
South Side 39 44 37N12 93w18 6:13:12
South Sugar Creek 88 3 39N25 92w24 6:09:36
South Troost 48 3 38N58 94w35 6:18:20
South Troy 57 3 38N57'26 90w59'39 6:03:59
South Van Buren 18 3 36N59'17 91w00'49 6:04:03
South West 6 3 37N25 94w33 6:18:12
Southwest 115 1 38N36 90w17 6:01:08
South West City 60 3 36N30'53 94w36'40 6:18:27
Spalding 87 3 39N37'07 91w31'35 6:06:06
Spanish Lake 95 40 38N47'16 90w12'57 6:00:52
Sparta 22 3 37N00'04 93w04'53 6:12:20
Speed 27 3 38N50'53 92w48'11 6:11:13
Speedwell 93 3 37N57 93w58 6:15:52
Spencer 55 3 37N11'04 93w42'08 6:14:49
Spencerburg 82 3 39N25'18 91w23'15 6:05:33
Sperry 1 3 40N16'47 92w29'18 6:09:57
Spickard 40 3 40N14'38 93w35'39 6:14:23
Splitlog 60 3 36N42'28 94w27'31 6:17:50
Spokane 22 3 36N52'05 93w17'48 6:13:11
Sprague 7 3 38N05'44 94w27'34 6:17:50
Spring Bluff 36 44 38N17'44 91w14'16 6:04:57
Spring Branch 48 3 39N06 94w26 6:17:44
Spring City 73 3 36N59'12 94w32'02 6:18:08
Spring Creek 81 3 37N45'45 92w01'26 6:08:06
Springfield 39 44 37N12'55 93w17'53 6:13:12
Spring Forest 50 3 38N24'19 90w25'01 6:01:40
Spring Fork 80 3 38N34'43 93w14'18 6:12:57
Spring Garden 66 3 38N23'07 92w25'21 6:09:41
Spring Grove 30 3 37N33'07 93w02'15 6:12:09
Spring Hill 59 3 39N52'25 93w38'37 6:14:34
Spring Hollow 53 3 37N40 92w48 6:11:12
Spring River 55 3 36N58 93w49 6:15:16
Springtown 110 3 37N55'25 90w45'38 6:03:03
Spring Valley 60 3 36N33 94w30 6:18:00
Sprott 96 3 37N51'50 90w19'42 6:01:19
Spruce 7 3 38N15'59 94w07'59 6:16:32
Spurgeon 73 44 36N56'04 94w28'17 6:17:53
Squires 34 3 36N51'05 92w37'29 6:10:30
Stahl 1 3 40N17'29 92w47'20 6:11:09
Stanberry 38 3 40N13'04 94w32'17 6:18:09
Standish 17 3 39N23'04 93w25'45 6:13:43
Stanhope 97 3 39N11'15 93w15'37 6:13:02
Stanley 78 3 36N20'14 89w42'04 5:58:48
Stanton 36 3 38N16'28 91w06'20 6:04:25
Star 103 3 36N53'52 90w13'43 6:00:55
Star City 5 3 36N46'13 93w48'49 6:15:15
Starfield 25 3 39N38'43 94w31'03 6:18:04
Stark 43 3 37N56 93w10 6:12:40
Stark 82 35 39N22'21 91w01'29 6:04:06
Stark City 73 3 36N51'44 94w11'08 6:16:45
Starkenburg 70 3 38N44'09 91w33'07 6:06:12
Starland 79 3 37N42'33 89w35'07 5:58:20
Steedman 14 3 38N42'17 91w49'04 6:07:16
Steele 78 3 36N05'02 89w49'45 5:59:19
Steeles 91 3 36N40'50 90w47'29 6:03:10
Steelville 28 3 37N58'05 91w21'17 6:05:25
Steffenville 56 3 39N58'14 91w52'55 6:07:32
Ste Genevieve 96 3 37N58'53 90w02'30 6:00:10
Steinmetz 45 3 39N14'06 92w45'27 6:11:02
Stella 73 3 36N45'41 94w11'28 6:16:46
Stepanek Crossing 57 3 39N01'14 91w03'55 6:04:16
Stephens 10 3 39N01'44 92w15'58 6:09:04
Sterling 46 3 37N02'38 92w00'29 6:08:02
Sterling Landing 57 16 39N06'47 90w41'39 6:02:47
Stet 17 3 39N25'23 93w45'31 6:15:02
Stewart 78 3 36N22'21 89w36'59 5:58:28
Stewartsville 32 3 39N45'03 94w29'47 6:17:59
Sticklerville 105 3 40N09'38 92w53'37 6:11:34
Stickney 63 47 38N04'03 91w56'07 6:07:44
Stillhouse Ford 57 3 39N04'21 91w15'35 6:05:02
Stillhouse Springs 85 3 37N48'04 92w20'04 6:09:20
Stillings 83 3 39N19'11 94w53'16 6:19:33
Stinson 55 3 37N14'47 93w45'08 6:15:01
Stockbridge 11 3 39N45'05 94w39'59 6:18:40
Stockdale 24 3 39N17'27 94w20'32 6:17:22
Stockton 20 3 37N41'56 93w47'45 6:15:11
Stockyards 11 3 39N43 94w51 6:19:24
Stockyards 48 3 39N06 94w36 6:18:24
Stoddard 103 3 36N47'29 90w02'03 6:00:08
Stokes Mound 17 3 39N34 93w29 6:13:56
Stokley 80 3 38N50'22 93w28'10 6:13:53
Stone Hill 33 3 37N36'06 91w20'31 6:05:22
Stones Corner 49 3 37N04 94w30 6:18:00
Stony Hill 37 3 38N32'34 91w22'25 6:05:30
Stotesbury 108 3 37N58'19 94w33'48 6:18:15
Stotts City 55 3 37N06'13 93w56'58 6:15:48
Stoutland 15 3 37N48'51 92w30'50 6:10:03
Stoutsville 69 3 39N32'50 91w51'30 6:07:26
Stover 71 3 38N26'27 92w59'30 6:11:58
Strafford 39 3 37N16'06 93w07'01 6:12:28
Strain 36 44 38N17'30 91w18'10 6:05:13
Strasburg 19 3 38N45'36 94w09'58 6:16:40
Stringtown 12 3 36N45'10 90w34'58 6:02:20
Stringtown 26 3 38N31'22 92w21'14 6:09:25
Stringtown 49 3 37N10'13 94w34'47 6:18:19
Stringtown 62 3 37N34'24 90w17'16 6:01:09
Strother 69 3 39N25'32 91w53'18 6:07:33
Stubbs 83 3 39N25'30 94w45'03 6:19:00
Stubtown 78 3 36N10'34 89w41'57 5:58:48
Stults 104 3 36N45 93w23 6:13:32
Sturdivant 9 3 37N02'58 90w00'50 6:00:03
Sturgeon 10 3 39N14'03 92w16'50 6:09:07
Sturges 59 3 39N52'38 93w30'03 6:14:00
Stutts 104 3 36N45'55 93w20'50 6:13:23
Sublette 1 3 40N18'02 92w34'17 6:10:17
Success 107 3 37N26'37 92w05'15 6:08:21
Sudheimer 63 47 38N07'59 92w10'43 6:08:43
Sue City 61 3 39N58'02 92w21'54 6:09:28
Suelthaus Ford 37 3 38N24'27 91w35'45 6:06:23
Sugar Beach 60 3 36N36'13 94w22'00 6:17:28
Sugar Creek 48 3 39N06'35 94w26'40 6:17:47
Sugar Lake 11 3 39N35 95w01 6:20:04
Sugartree 17 3 39N16'19 93w35'51 6:14:23
Sugartree 81 3 37N58'04 91w58'14 6:07:53
Sullivan 36 44 38N12'29 91w09'37 6:04:38
Sulphur Springs 50 3 38N20'10 90w22'26 6:01:30
Sumach 35 3 36N24 90w01 6:00:04
Summerfield 63 3 38N17'01 91w48'17 6:07:13
Summersville 107 3 37N10'45 91w39'24 6:06:38
Summit 110 3 37N54'43 90w42'29 6:02:50
Summit City 77 3 36N44'21 92w36'49 6:10:27
Sumner 21 3 39N39'09 93w14'40 6:12:59
Sunland Hills 95 40 38N48 90w20 6:01:20
Sunlight 110 3 37N46'54 90w54'18 6:03:37
Sunnyside 50 3 38N20'54 90w22'10 6:01:29
Sunny Slope 48 3 39N02 94w34 6:18:16
Sunnyvale 73 3 37N03'03 94w29'42 6:17:59
Sunrise 35 3 36N03'37 90w01'50 6:00:07
Sunrise Beach 15 3 38N10'33 92w47'03 6:11:08
Sunset Hills 95 40 38N32'20 90w24'26 6:01:38
Sutherland 51 3 38N35'06 93w35'33 6:14:22
Svenite 94 3 37N40'36 90w23'30 6:01:34
Swan 106 3 36N47'43 93w03'45 6:12:15
Swanwick 89 3 39N18'51 94w01'51 6:16:07
Swart 108 3 37N45'04 94w35'00 6:18:20
Swedeborg 85 3 37N54'50 92w19'54 6:09:20
Sweden 34 3 36N52'39 92w30'03 6:10:00
Sweet Hollow Ford 53 3 37N50'03 92w50'25 6:11:22
Sweet Home 23 3 40N31 91w40 6:06:40
Sweet Springs 97 3 38N57'49 93w24'53 6:13:40
Sweetwater 73 44 36N49'36 94w15'56 6:17:04
Sweetwater 90 3 37N41 90w12 6:00:48
Swift 78 3 36N19'40 89w45'06 5:59:00
Swinton 103 3 37N01'40 89w56'41 5:59:47
Swiss 37 3 38N33'46 91w28'16 6:05:53
Switzler 10 3 39N00'06 92w16'32 6:09:06
Sycamore 77 3 36N42'12 92w16'27 6:09:06
Sycamore Hills 95 40 38N42'03 90w20'59 6:01:24
Syenite 94 3 37N41 90w22 6:01:28
Sylvania 29 3 37N30'28 94w01'21 6:16:05
Sylvania 100 3 37N06 89w42 5:58:48
Syracuse 71 3 38N40'12 92w52'23 6:11:30
Taber 93 3 38N03 94w00 6:16:00
Taberville 93 3 38N00'30 93w59'40 6:15:59
Table Rock 81 3 37N57'49 91w59'47 6:07:59
Table Rock Townsite 106 3 36N39 93w13 6:12:52
Tackner 8 3 38N14'09 93w25'47 6:13:43
Taft 12 3 36N38'06 90w32'16 6:02:09
Taitsville 89 3 39N29'04 93w57'28 6:15:50
Tallapoosa 72 3 36N30'29 89w49'09 5:59:17
Tallent 9 3 37N27'55 90w04'06 6:00:16
Taneyville 106 3 36N44'29 93w02'03 6:12:08
Tanner 100 3 36N55'05 89w41'00 5:58:44
Tanyard 73 3 37N04 94w30 6:18:00
Taos 11 3 39N34'39 94w50'05 6:19:20
Taos 26 3 38N30'23 92w04'15 6:08:17
Tapawingo, Lake 48 3 39N01'17 94w18'41 6:17:15
Tara 95 40 38N34 90w20 6:01:20
Tarkio 3 3 40N26'25 95w22'39 6:21:31
Tarrant 82 3 39N21'24 91w10'58 6:04:44
Tarrytown 83 3 39N17'04 94w40'40 6:18:43
Tarsney 48 3 38N56'29 94w12'56 6:16:52
Tarsney Lakes 48 3 38N56'59 94w12'13 6:16:49
Tauria 104 3 36N45 93w23 6:13:32
Tavern 63 47 38N09'45 92w07'46 6:08:31
Taylor 64 3 39N56'17 91w31'25 6:06:06
Tea 37 3 38N18'00 91w23'47 6:05:35
Tebbetts 14 3 38N37'14 91w57'44 6:07:51
Tebo 42 3 38N30 93w40 6:14:40
Tecamseh 77 3 36N35'12 92w17'11 6:09:09
Tecumseh 77 3 36N35 92w17 6:09:08
Temples Corner 78 3 36N01'50 89w57'32 5:59:50
Templeton 3 3 40N23 95w37 6:22:28
Tempo 95 40 38N40 90w26 6:01:44
Ten Brook 50 3 38N26'01 90w21'00 6:01:24
Ten Mile 61 3 39N48'30 92w22'35 6:09:30
Teresita 101 3 36N59'05 91w37'43 6:06:31
Terre DuLac 94 3 37N55 90w33 6:02:12
Terre Haute 86 3 40N26'22 93w14'02 6:12:56
Terrell 22 3 37N04'58 93w25'08 6:13:41
Texas 33 3 37N34 91w41 6:06:44
Thayer 75 3 36N31'28 91w32'17 6:06:09
Theodosia 77 3 36N34'58 92w40'33 6:10:42
Theodosia Hills 77 3 36N35 92w40 6:10:40
Third Creek 37 3 38N24 91w34 6:06:16
Thirtyfour Corner 67 3 36N46'36 89w12'39 5:56:51
Thomas 91 3 36N33 90w38 6:02:32
Thomas Hill 88 3 39N31'15 92w39'20 6:10:37
Thomasville 75 3 36N47'21 91w31'55 6:06:08
Thompson 4 3 39N11'19 91w58'58 6:07:56
Thoms 49 3 37N08'39 94w33'21 6:18:13
Thomson 99 3 40N28 92w01 6:08:04
Thomure 96 3 38N00'14 90w03'34 6:00:14
Thornfield 77 3 36N42'31 92w39'33 6:10:38
Thorpe 30 3 37N29'09 92w59'53 6:12:00
Thrush 42 3 38N23 93w46 6:15:04
Tiff 110 3 38N01'09 90w39'10 6:02:37
Tiffany Springs 83 3 39N15'41 94w41'46 6:18:47
Tiff City 60 3 36N40'06 94w37'01 6:18:28
Tiffin 93 3 37N57'18 93w56'17 6:15:45
Tiger Fork 102 3 39N53 91w54 6:07:36
Tightwad 42 3 38N18'34 93w32'49 6:14:11
Tigris 34 3 37N01'22 92w46'16 6:11:05
Tillman 103 3 37N03'19 89w51'51 5:59:27
Tilsit 16 3 37N19'49 89w44'31 5:58:58
Timber 101 3 37N21'47 91w25'35 6:05:42
Times Beach 95 40 38N30'31 90w36'09 6:02:25
Tina 17 3 39N32'10 93w26'24 6:13:46
Tindall 40 3 40N09'40 93w36'29 6:14:26
Tinkerville 78 3 36N11'26 89w57'35 5:59:50
Tinney Grove 89 3 39N30'15 93w48'19 6:15:13
Tin Town 84 3 37N27'14 93w11'35 6:12:46
Tipperary 1 3 40N11'30 92w42'35 6:10:50
Tipton 68 3 38N39'20 92w46'47 6:11:07
Tipton Ford 73 3 36N58'36 94w25'33 6:17:42
Tip Top 47 3 37N35 90w38 6:02:32
Tobin 99 3 40N21 92w12 6:08:48
Toga 103 3 37N06'58 89w53'05 5:59:32
Toledo 14 3 38N50'26 91w49'05 6:07:16
Toledo 77 3 36N46'28 92w41'07 6:10:44
Tolona 56 34 40N02'35 91w44'54 6:07:00
Tom 8 3 38N15 93w26 6:13:44
Tom Hollow Ford 53 3 37N50'46 92w51'05 6:11:24
Topaz 34 3 36N56'44 92w12'10 6:08:49
Toppertown 103 3 36N57'47 89w50'28 5:59:22
Torch 91 3 36N32'11 90w40'34 6:02:42
Toronto 15 3 38N00'13 92w31'31 6:10:06
.Tower Grove 115 1 38N37'21 90w15'58 6:01:04
Town and Country 95 40 38N36'44 90w27'48 6:01:51
Townley 35 3 36N37'00 89w58'11 5:59:53
Town N Four Village 95 40 38N40 90w26 6:01:44
Tracy 83 3 39N22'37 94w47'34 6:19:10
Tracy 93 3 37N58'48 93w39'18 6:14:37
Trail 77 3 36N46'05 92w17'44 6:09:11
Trail Creek 41 3 40N20 93w49 6:15:16
Trask 46 3 36N58'39 91w48'05 6:07:12
Treloar 109 3 38N38'40 91w11'16 6:04:45
Tremont 11 3 39N40 94w39 6:18:36
Trenton 40 3 40N04'44 93w36'59 6:14:28
Trimble 25 3 39N28'16 94w33'52 6:18:15
Triplett 21 3 39N29'53 93w11'37 6:12:46
Trotter 17 3 39N24 93w35 6:14:20
Troutt 110 3 37N56 90w47 6:03:08
Troy 57 42 38N58'46 90w58'50 6:03:55
Truesdale 109 17 38N48'42 91w07'49 6:04:31
Truman Corners 48 3 38N54'29 94w31'10 6:18:05
Truxton 57 3 39N00'07 91w14'23 6:04:58
Tuckahoe 49 3 37N07'43 94w31'45 6:18:07
Tucker 91 3 36N32'41 91w04'16 6:04:17
Tuckers Corner 49 3 37N19'50 94w29'04 6:17:56
Tulip 4 3 39N20'34 92w09'25 6:08:38
Tunas 30 3 37N50'59 93w01'39 6:12:07
Turkey Ridge 85 3 37N49'18 92w19'36 6:09:18
Turley 107 3 37N26'48 92w10'55 6:08:44
Turnback 55 3 37N07 93w39 6:14:36
Turner Ford 30 3 37N50'50 92w52'25 6:11:30
Turners (Turners Station) 39 3 37N10'51 93w09'19 6:12:37
Turners Mill 75 3 36N45'59 91w15'59 6:05:04
Turnerville 46 3 37N02'26 91w44'21 6:06:57
Turney 25 3 39N38'09 94w19'16 6:17:17
Turtle 33 3 37N31'24 91w24'44 6:05:39
Tuscumbia 66 3 38N13'59 92w27'30 6:09:50
Tuxedo Park 95 40 38N36 90w20 6:01:20
Twelve Mile 62 3 37N22 90w25 6:01:40
Twin Groves 49 3 37N13 94w34 6:18:16
Twin Oaks 95 40 38N33'53 90w29'47 6:01:59
Twin Springs 36 3 38N16'19 91w04'25 6:04:18
Tyler 43 3 37N51 93w25 6:13:40
Tyler 78 3 36N02'02 89w44'14 5:58:57
Tyrone 107 3 37N12'12 91w52'35 6:07:30
Tyson 95 40 38N32'13 90w33'42 6:02:15
Udall 77 3 36N32'38 92w15'31 6:09:02
Udall Landing 77 3 36N32'35 92w17'20 6:09:09
Ulman 66 3 38N09'11 92w26'38 6:09:47
Umber 20 3 37N37'29 93w45'19 6:15:01
Union 36 3 38N26'44 91w00'20 6:04:01
Union 89 3 39N26 94w10 6:16:40
Union City 104 3 36N58'44 93w27'56 6:13:52

Union Star 32 3 39N58'50 94W35'39 6:18:23
Uniontown 81 3 37N36'53 89W42'50 5:58:51
Unionville 86 3 40N28'37 93W00'11 6:12:01
Unity Village (Unity) 48
3 38N57'05 94W24'05 6:17:36
University City 95
40 38N40 90W20 6:01:20
University Park 95
40 38N39'21 90W18'33 6:01:14
Upalika 111 3 36N56'12 90W38'21 6:02:33
Uplands Park 95
40 38N41'35 90W16'56 6:01:08
Upper Loutre 70 3 39N06 91W32 6:06:08
Upton 107 3 37N22'08 92W09'50 6:08:39
Urbana 30 3 37N50'32 93W10'00 6:12:40
Urbandale 88 3 39N23'42 92W26'38 6:09:47
Urich 42 3 38N27'35 94W00'02 6:16:00
Utica 59 3 39N44'37 93W37'35 6:14:30
Vada 107 3 37N28'18 92W03'03 6:08:12
Vale 48 3 38N56'37 94W26'15 6:17:45
Valentine Ford 37
3 38N24'41 91W38'17 6:06:33
Valle 50 4 38N06 90W33 6:02:12
Valles Mines 50 3 38N02'31 90W29'59 6:02:00
Valley 61 3 39N50 92W41 6:10:44
Valley City 51 3 38N51'56 93W36'42 6:14:27
Valley Park 95 40 38N32'57 90W29'33 6:01:58
Valley Plaza 12 3 36N46 90W24 6:01:36
Valley Ridge 35 3 36N33'53 90W05'01 6:00:20
Valley View 8 3 38N12'22 93W25'41 6:13:43
Valley View 96 3 38N01 90W13 6:00:52
Valley Water Mills 39
44 37N15'57 93W14'52 6:12:59
Van 84 3 37N33'41 93W17'13 6:13:09
Van Buren 18 3 36N59'44 91W00'52 6:04:03
Vance 112 3 37N26'22 92W46'47 6:11:07
Van Cleve 63 3 38N14'06 92W09'26 6:08:38
Vandalia 4 3 39N18'39 91W29'18 6:05:57
Vandiver 4 3 39N09'47 91W50'36 6:07:22
Vanduser 100 3 36N59'26 89W41'08 5:58:45
Van Horn 17 3 39N29 93W28 6:13:52
Vanzant 34 3 36N58'11 92W18'10 6:09:13
Varner 91 3 36N36 90W41 6:02:44
Varsh Ford 62 3 37N22'26 90W27'15 6:01:49
Vastus 12 3 36N33'04 90W24'29 6:01:38
Velda 95 40 38N41'24 90W17'40 6:01:11
Velda Village Hills 95
40 38N41'26 90W17'14 6:01:09
Venice 101 3 37N12'28 91W23'59 6:05:36
Venus 63 3 38N10'49 92W02'02 6:08:08
Vera 82 3 39N22'42 91W08'42 6:04:35
Vera Cruz 34 3 36N54'50 92W29'36 6:09:58
Verdella 6 3 37N36'23 94W26'18 6:17:45
Vernon 23 3 40N21 91W29 6:05:56
Verona 55 3 36N57'50 93W47'44 6:15:11
Versailles 71 3 38N25'53 92W50'27 6:11:22
Vest 99 3 40N28 92W17 6:09:08
Veterans Hospital 24
3 39N04 94W33 6:18:12
Vibbard 89 3 39N22'50 94W08'46 6:16:35
Viburnum 47 3 37N42'55 91W08'06 6:04:32
Vichy 63 3 38N06'41 91W45'37 6:07:02
Victor 69 3 39N27'15 91W49'45 6:07:19
Victoria 50 4 38N10'40 90W31'33 6:02:06
Vida 81 3 37N51'25 91W47'58 6:07:12
Vienna 63 3 38N11'12 91W56'49 6:07:47
Vigus 95 2 38N44'08 90W27'53 6:01:52
Vilander 28 46 38N05'47 91W07'53 6:04:32
Villa Heights 49
3 37N04 94W30 6:18:00
Villa Ridge 36 3 38N28'21 90W53'12 6:03:33
Vincit 35 3 36N09'57 90W04'09 6:00:17
Vineland 50 4 38N05'43 90W36'46 6:02:27
Vineyard 55 3 37N07 93W59 6:15:56
Vinita Park 95 40 38N41'24 90W20'33 6:01:22
Vinita Terrace 95
40 38N41'08 90W19'45 6:01:19
Vinson 103 3 36N48 89W58 5:59:52
Viola 104 3 36N34'23 93W34'55 6:14:20
Violet 84 3 37N40'03 93W19'10 6:13:17
Virgil City 108 3 37N45'59 94W04'21 6:16:17
Virginia 7 3 38N16'01 94W29'44 6:17:59
Virginia 78 3 36N06 89W54 5:59:36
Vista 93 3 37N59'18 93W39'50 6:14:39
Vulcan 47 3 37N18'34 90W39'45 6:02:39
Wabash Crossing 31
3 39N55'42 93W56'16 6:15:45
Waco 49 3 37N14'49 94W35'57 6:18:24
Wagoner 20 3 37N40'14 93W55'31 6:15:42
Wainwright 14 3 38N35'01 92W04'05 6:08:16
Wakenda 17 3 39N18'51 93W22'37 6:13:30
Waldo 48 3 38N59'38 94W35'30 6:18:22
Waldo 112 3 37N11'21 92W44'40 6:10:59
Waldron 83 3 39N13'20 94W47'35 6:19:10
Walker 108 3 37N53'55 94W13'55 6:16:56
Walkers Corner 8
3 38N10'57 93W05'47 6:12:23
Walkersville 102
3 39N44'26 92W04'06 6:08:16
Wallace 11 3 39N33'19 94W50'48 6:19:23
Walls 34 3 36N51 92W35 6:10:20
Wall Street 30 3 37N36'45 92W57'17 6:11:49
Walnut 61 3 39N59'25 92W43'05 6:10:52
Walnut Creek 61 3 39N55 92W41 6:10:44
Walnut Grove 39 3 37N24'40 93W32'58 6:14:12
Walnut Shade 106
3 36N43'57 93W11'36 6:12:46
Wanamaker 97 3 39N07 93W12 6:12:48
Wanda 73 3 36N48'38 94W11'58 6:16:48
Wappapello 111 3 36N56'08 90W16'15 6:01:05
Wardell 78 3 36N21'05 89W49'04 5:59:16
Wardsville 26 3 38N29'20 92W10'27 6:08:42
Ware 50 3 38N12'49 90W39'45 6:02:39
Warren 64 37 39N46'25 91W45'23 6:07:02
Warrensburg 51 3 38N45'46 93W44'09 6:14:57
Warrenton 109 17 38N48'41 91W08'29 6:04:34
Warsaw 8 3 38N14'35 93W22'54 6:13:32
Warson Woods 95
40 38N36'26 90W23'00 6:01:32
Washburn 5 3 36N35'13 93W57'57 6:15:52
Washington 109 49 38N33'29 91W00'43 6:04:03
Washington Center 41
3 40N25'37 94W09'24 6:16:38

Wasola 77 3 36N47'37 92W34'32 6:10:18
Waterloo 54 3 39N07'59 94W02'03 6:16:08
Watkins 33 3 37N43 91W44 6:06:56
Watkins 66 3 38N07'25 92W22'52 6:09:31
Watson 3 3 40N28'37 95W37'13 6:22:29
Waukomis Lake 83
3 39N14'00 94W38'13 6:18:33
Waverly 54 3 39N12'34 93W31'03 6:14:04
Wayland 23 43 40N23'40 91W34'59 6:06:20
Wayne 5 3 36N38'15 93W57'43 6:15:51
Waynesville 85 9 37N49'43 92W12'02 6:08:48
W B Junction 17 3 39N20'06 93W31'48 6:14:07
Weatherby 32 3 39N54'34 94W14'39 6:16:59
Weatherby Lake 83
3 39N14'16 94W41'45 6:18:47
Weaubleau 43 3 37N53'26 93W32'30 6:14:10
Webb 90 3 37N10 90W49 6:03:16
Webb City 49 3 37N08'47 94W27'46 6:17:51
Weber Hill 50 3 38N26'01 90W33'09 6:02:13
Webster Groves 95
31 38N35'33 90W21'26 6:01:26
Webster Park 95
40 38N36 90W20 6:01:20
Wedgewood 95 40 38N48 90W20 6:01:20
Wedgewood Green 95
40 38N48 90W20 6:01:20
Weingarten 96 3 37N53'15 90W12'52 6:00:51
Wela 73 44 36N50 94W37 6:18:28
Wela Park 73 3 36N52'28 94W33'19 6:18:13
Welch 16 3 37N11 89W46 5:59:04
Weldon 92 2 38N41'27 90W39'52 6:02:39
Weldon Spring 92
2 38N42'48 90W41'21 6:02:45
Weldon Spring Heights 92
2 38N42'18 90W41'14 6:02:45
Wellington 54 3 39N08'03 93W58'57 6:15:56
Wellston 95 40 38N40'22 90W17'57 6:01:12
Wellsville 70 3 39N04'19 91W34'12 6:06:17
Wentworth 73 3 36N59'36 94W04'27 6:16:18
Wentzville 92 8 38N48'41 90W51'10 6:03:25
Wesco 28 3 37N51'34 91W25'55 6:05:44
West 72 3 36N48 89W39 5:58:36
West Alton 92 7 38N51'54 90W13'21 6:00:53
West Aurora 66 3 38N18'52 92W35'44 6:10:23
West Boone 7 3 38N26 94W34 6:18:16
Westboro 3 3 40N32'05 95W19'08 6:21:17
Westbridge 25 3 39N32'22 94W30'02 6:18:00
West County 95 40 38N40 90W26 6:01:44
West County Center 115
1 38N37 90W26 6:01:44
West Dallas 112 3 37N12 93W00 6:12:00
West Dolan 19 3 38N37 94W35 6:18:20
West Doniphan 91
3 36N36 90W52 6:03:28
West Ely 64 3 39N42'39 91W33'45 6:06:15
West Eminence 101
3 37N08'25 91W22'28 6:05:30
West Fork 90 3 37N29'30 91W06'32 6:04:26
West Fulton 14 3 38N50 92W00 6:08:00
West Glasgow 97 3 39N12'58 92W52'35 6:11:30
West Hermondale 78
3 36N01'50 89W55'55 5:59:44
West Keystone 25
3 39N41'25 94W20'09 6:17:21
Westland Estates 95
40 38N40 90W26 6:01:44
West Lebanon 53
47 37N40'10 92W40'35 6:10:42
West Line 19 3 38N37'56 94W35'02 6:18:20
Weston 83 3 39N24'40 94W54'05 6:19:36
Westover 28 3 37N55'21 91W13'40 6:04:55
West Peculiar 19
3 38N43 94W28 6:17:52
Westphalia 76 3 38N26'31 91W59'57 6:08:00
West Plains 46 3 36N43'41 91W51'08 6:07:25
West Platte 83 3 39N23'25 94W50'23 6:19:22
West Point 7 3 38N21 94W33 6:18:12
Westport 48 3 39N03 94W35 6:18:20
West Quincy 64 3 39N55'43 91W26'12 6:05:45
Westview 73 44 36N50'13 94W31'12 6:18:05
Westville 21 3 39N38'34 92W54'28 6:11:38
Westwood 95 40 38N38'37 90W26'23 6:01:46
Wet Glaize 15 3 37N55'20 92W32'01 6:10:08
Wexford 25 3 39N32'35 94W23'42 6:17:35
Wheatland 43 3 37N56'46 93W24'03 6:13:36
Wheaton 5 3 36N45'46 94W03'21 6:16:13
Wheelers Mill 85
47 37N54'30 92W10'33 6:08:42
Wheelerville 5 3 36N50'11 93W37'49 6:14:31
Wheeling 59 3 39N47'12 93W23'07 6:13:32
Whispering Hills 95
40 38N40 90W26 6:01:44
Whitakerville 8 3 38N12'50 93W22'15 6:13:29
White Bear 64 3 39N41'54 91W27'38 6:05:51
White Branch 8 3 38N14'04 93W21'16 6:13:25
White Church 46 3 36N51'01 91W47'10 6:07:09
White City 15 3 37N56'09 92W50'43 6:11:23
White City 104 3 36N52'49 93W23'52 6:13:35
White Cloud 43 3 38N01'16 93W22'23 6:13:30
White Cloud 74 3 40N12 94W53 6:19:32
Whitecorn 92 18 38N53'53 90W21'27 6:01:26
White Hall Fields 24
3 39N13 94W28 6:17:52
White House 95 3 38N25'05 90W19'32 6:01:18
Whiteman 51 3 38N44 93W33 6:14:12
Whiteman Air Force Base 51
3 38N43 93W23 6:13:32
White Oak 35 3 36N19'49 90W01'40 6:00:07
White River 5 3 36N32 93W38 6:14:32
White Rock 17 3 39N20'04 93W17'04 6:13:08
White Rock 60 3 36N32 94W16 6:17:04
Whiteside 57 3 39N11'07 91W01'00 6:04:04
Whitesville 2 3 40N03'40 94W43'09 6:18:53
Whitewater 16 3 37N14'13 89W47'47 5:59:11
Whitham 21 3 39N33'04 93W11'52 6:12:47
Whiting 67 3 36N47'20 89W22'26 5:57:30
Whitten 38 3 40N10'38 94W16'23 6:17:06
Wickes 50 3 38N23'35 90W21'13 6:01:25
Wide Ford 62 3 37N25'53 90W27'19 6:01:49
Wien 21 3 39N39'39 92W47'03 6:11:08
Wilbur Park 115
40 38N33'11 90W18'34 6:01:14
Wilby 12 3 36N52'15 90W26'23 6:01:46

Wilcox 74 3 40N23'56 94W58'01 6:19:52
Wilderness 28 3 37N47 91W12 6:04:48
Wilderness 75 3 36N47'20 91W11'31 6:04:46
Wildwood 41 3 40N16 94W02 6:16:08
Wildwood Estates 39
44 37N11 93W17 6:13:08
Wildwood Lake 48
3 39N00 94W28 6:17:52
Wilhelmina 35 3 36N30'53 90W10'57 6:00:44
Wilkie 45 18 38N53'22 90W23'55 6:01:36
Willard 39 3 37N18'18 93W25'42 6:13:43
Willhoit 77 3 36N41'00 92W30'24 6:10:02
William M Chick 48
3 39N06 94W32 6:18:08
Williamsburg 14 3 38N55'13 91W42'05 6:06:48
Williamstown 56 3 40N14'27 91W47'49 6:07:11
Williamsville 111
3 36N58'16 90W32'58 6:02:12
Willmathsville 1
3 40N19'35 92W24'32 6:09:38
Willow Brook 11 3 39N37'55 94W47'44 6:19:11
Willow Fork 68 3 38N37 92W47 6:11:08
Willow Springs 46
3 36N59'32 91W58'11 6:07:53
Willowville 20 3 37N49'05 93W58'39 6:15:55
Wilson City 67 3 36N55'21 89W13'26 5:56:54
Wilsons Creek 39
3 37N05'51 93W24'14 6:13:37
Wilton 10 3 38N44'06 92W21'32 6:09:26
Wilton Springs 97
3 39N04'31 93W07'12 6:12:29
Wimmer 6 3 37N31'49 94W28'46 6:17:55
Winchester 23 23 40N19'04 91W36'40 6:06:27
Winchester 95 40 38N35'25 90W31'40 6:02:07
Winchester Gap 53
47 37N41 92W40 6:10:40
Windsor 42 3 38N31'56 93W31'19 6:14:05
Windsor Junction 8
3 38N32'05 93W16'19 6:13:05
Windsor Springs 95
40 38N34'00 90W24'42 6:01:39
Windyville 30 3 37N42'24 92W55'37 6:11:42
Winfield 57 16 38N59'50 90W44'18 6:02:57
Wingate 19 3 38N43'52 94W12'16 6:16:49
Winigan 105 3 40N02'44 92W54'12 6:11:37
Winkler 81 3 37N50'09 91W33'25 6:06:14
Winner 24 3 39N19'57 94W29'30 6:17:58
Winnipeg 53 3 37N36'16 92W18'07 6:09:12
Winnwood Gardens 24
3 39N10'50 94W30'43 6:18:03
Winona 101 3 37N00'35 91W19'24 6:05:18
Winslow 32 3 40N00'37 94W27'44 6:17:51
Winston 31 3 39N52'12 94W08'23 6:16:34
Wintersville 105
3 40N16'06 93W19'36 6:13:18
Winthrop 11 3 39N33'35 95W06'26 6:20:26
Wisdom 8 3 38N10'01 93W28'36 6:13:54
Wishart 84 3 37N30'32 93W27'34 6:13:50
Withers Mill 64 3 39N42'52 91W28'53 6:05:56
Witte Ford 37 3 38N24'39 91W34'36 6:06:18
Wittenberg 79 3 37N39'09 89W31'28 5:58:06
Wolf Island 67 3 36N44'21 89W12'37 5:56:50
Womack 96 3 37N40'52 90W11'47 6:00:47
Woodbine Heights 95
40 38N37 90W21 6:01:24
Woodcliffe 39 44 37N11 93W17 6:13:08
Wood Heights 24 3 39N20'22 94W09'45 6:16:39
Woodhill 24 3 39N10'37 94W32'16 6:18:09
Wood Hill 30 3 37N44'38 93W02'19 6:12:09
Woodhine Heights 95
40 38N34'10 90W26'02 6:01:44
Woodland 64 39 39N45'10 91W35'37 6:06:22
Woodland Park 66
3 38N16 92W36 6:10:24
Woodlandville 10
3 39N03'44 92W29'01 6:09:56
Woodlawn 69 3 39N34'42 92W12'45 6:08:51
Woodridge 95 40 38N48 90W20 6:01:20
Woodruff 83 3 39N26'38 94W48'59 6:19:16
Woods Heights 89
3 39N20 94W10 6:16:40
Woodside 75 3 36N45 91W23 6:05:32
Woodson Terrace 95
40 38N43'35 90W21'31 6:01:26
Woodstock 95 40 38N43'52 90W17'34 6:01:10
Woodville 61 3 39N37'13 92W20'10 6:09:21
Woolam 37 3 38N18 91W38 6:06:32
Woolridge 68 3 38N54'22 92W31'23 6:10:06
Worcester 4 3 39N16'25 91W45'14 6:07:01
Worland 7 3 38N11'16 94W35'30 6:18:22
Wornall 48 3 38N58 94W16 6:17:04
Worth 113 3 40N24'18 94W26'38 6:17:47
Wortham 94 3 37N50'40 90W36'31 6:02:26
Worthington 86 3 40N24'30 92W41'19 6:10:45
Wright City 109
17 38N49'39 91W01'12 6:04:05
Wyaconda 23 3 40N23'23 91W55'37 6:07:42
Wyatt 67 3 36N54'33 89W13'21 5:56:53
Wyatt Park 11 3 39N45 94W48 6:19:12
Wyeth 2 3 40N01'30 94W48'07 6:19:12
Yama 78 3 36N15'36 89W56'35 5:59:46
Yancy Mills 81 3 37N47'28 91W50'02 6:07:20
Yarrow 1 3 40N05'38 92W40'49 6:10:43
Yates 88 3 39N18'37 92W35'57 6:10:24
Yeatman 95 40 38N32'36 90W36'43 6:02:27
Yonkerville 5 44 36N54'58 94W00'33 6:16:02
York 86 3 40N32 93W17 6:13:08
Youngers 14 3 39N03'04 92W07'28 6:08:30
Youngstown 1 3 40N10'29 92W40'55 6:10:44
Yount 79 3 37N36'19 90W02'20 6:00:09
Yucatan 14 3 38N51'16 91W45'01 6:07:00
Yukon 107 3 37N16'23 91W50'53 6:07:24
Zadock 103 3 36N59'20 89W56'14 5:59:45
Zalma 9 3 37N08'41 90W04'34 6:00:18
Zanoni 77 3 36N41'10 92W19'54 6:09:20
Zell 96 3 37N57'09 90W08'34 6:00:34
Zenar 112 3 37N05'42 92W58'13 6:11:53
Zion 62 3 37N33 90W17 6:01:08
Zion Hill 81 10 38N00 91W37 6:06:28
Zora 8 3 38N17'11 93W05'47 6:12:23

TIME TABLES

MT # 1
Before 11/18/1883 LMT
11/18/1883 12:00 MST
3/31/1918 02:00 MWT
10/27/1918 02:00 MST
3/30/1919 02:00 MWT
10/26/1919 02:00 MST
2/09/1942 02:00 MWT
9/30/1945 02:00 MST
4/30/1967 02:00 US#1

MT # 2
Before 11/18/1883 LMT
11/18/1883 12:00 MST
3/31/1918 02:00 MWT
10/27/1918 02:00 MST
3/30/1919 02:00 MWT
10/26/1919 02:00 MST
2/09/1942 02:00 MWT
9/30/1945 02:00 MST
5/15/1946 02:00 MDT
9/28/1946 02:00 MST
5/31/1947 02:00 MDT
8/31/1947 02:00 MST
5/02/1948 02:00 MDT
9/06/1948 02:00 MST
5/01/1949 02:00 MDT
9/04/1949 02:00 MST
4/30/1950 02:00 MDT
9/04/1950 02:00 MST
5/06/1951 02:00 MDT
9/30/1951 02:00 MST
4/25/1954 02:00 MDT
9/07/1954 02:00 MST
4/24/1955 02:00 MDT
9/04/1955 02:00 MST
5/06/1956 02:00 MDT
9/03/1956 02:00 MST
4/28/1957 02:00 MDT
9/29/1957 02:00 MST
4/27/1958 02:00 MDT
9/28/1958 02:00 MST
5/31/1959 02:00 MDT
9/13/1959 02:00 MST
5/29/1960 02:00 MDT
9/06/1960 02:00 MST
5/30/1961 02:00 MDT
9/04/1961 02:00 MST
5/30/1962 02:00 MDT
9/05/1962 02:00 MST
5/30/1963 02:00 MDT
9/02/1963 02:00 MST
5/30/1964 02:00 MDT
9/08/1964 02:00 MST
5/30/1965 02:00 MDT
9/06/1965 02:00 MST
4/24/1966 02:00 US#1

MT # 3
Before 11/18/1883 LMT
11/18/1883 12:00 MST
3/31/1918 02:00 MWT
10/27/1918 02:00 MST
3/30/1919 02:00 MWT
10/26/1919 02:00 MST
4/28/1935 02:00 MDT
9/29/1935 02:00 MST
4/26/1936 02:00 MDT
9/27/1936 02:00 MST
5/30/1963 02:00 MDT
9/02/1963 02:00 MST
4/30/1967 02:00 US#1

MT # 4
Before 11/18/1883 LMT
11/18/1883 12:00 MST
3/31/1918 02:00 MWT
10/27/1918 02:00 MST
3/30/1919 02:00 MWT
10/26/1919 02:00 MST
2/09/1942 02:00 MWT
9/30/1945 02:00 MST
5/30/1964 02:00 MDT
9/08/1964 02:00 MST
4/30/1967 02:00 US#1

MT # 5
Before 11/18/1883 LMT
11/18/1883 12:00 MST
3/31/1918 02:00 MWT
10/27/1918 02:00 MST
3/30/1919 02:00 MWT
10/26/1919 02:00 MST
2/09/1942 02:00 MWT
9/30/1945 02:00 MST
5/15/1946 02:00 MDT
9/28/1946 02:00 MST
5/12/1947 02:00 MDT
8/31/1947 02:00 MST
5/02/1948 02:00 MDT
9/06/1948 02:00 MST
4/24/1949 02:00 MDT
9/05/1949 02:00 MST
5/01/1950 02:00 MDT
9/04/1950 02:00 MST
5/06/1951 02:00 MDT
9/03/1951 02:00 MST
4/27/1952 02:00 MDT
9/01/1952 02:00 MST
4/26/1953 02:00 MDT
9/07/1953 02:00 MST
4/25/1954 02:00 MDT
9/06/1954 02:00 MST
4/24/1955 02:00 MDT
9/04/1955 02:00 MST
5/06/1956 02:00 MDT
9/03/1956 02:00 MST
4/28/1957 02:00 MDT
9/29/1957 02:00 MST
4/27/1958 02:00 MDT
9/28/1958 02:00 MST
5/31/1959 02:00 MDT
9/13/1959 02:00 MST
5/29/1960 02:00 MDT
9/06/1960 02:00 MST
5/30/1961 02:00 MDT
9/04/1961 02:00 MST
5/30/1962 02:00 MDT
9/05/1962 02:00 MST
5/30/1963 02:00 MDT
9/02/1963 02:00 MST
5/30/1964 02:00 MDT
9/08/1964 02:00 MST
5/30/1965 02:00 MDT
9/06/1965 02:00 MST
4/24/1966 02:00 US#1

MT # 6
Before 11/18/1883 LMT
11/18/1883 12:00 MST
3/31/1918 02:00 MWT
10/27/1918 02:00 MST
3/30/1919 02:00 MWT
10/26/1919 02:00 MST
2/09/1942 02:00 MWT
9/30/1945 02:00 MST
4/25/1955 02:00 MDT
9/25/1955 02:00 MST
4/29/1956 02:00 MDT
9/03/1956 02:00 MST
4/30/1967 02:00 US#1

MT # 7
Before 11/18/1883 LMT
11/18/1883 12:00 MST
3/31/1918 02:00 MWT
10/27/1918 02:00 MST
3/30/1919 02:00 MWT
10/26/1919 02:00 MST
2/09/1942 02:00 MWT
9/30/1945 02:00 MST
5/01/1949 02:00 MDT
9/05/1949 02:00 MST
5/31/1953 02:00 MDT
9/06/1953 02:00 MST
4/25/1954 02:00 MDT
9/07/1954 02:00 MST
4/30/1967 02:00 US#1

MT # 8
Before 11/18/1883 LMT
11/18/1883 12:00 MST
3/31/1918 02:00 MWT
10/27/1918 02:00 MST
3/30/1919 02:00 MWT
10/26/1919 02:00 MST
2/09/1942 02:00 MWT
9/30/1945 02:00 MST
4/27/1952 02:00 MDT
9/28/1952 02:00 MST
4/30/1967 02:00 US#1

MT # 9
Before 11/18/1883 LMT
11/18/1883 12:00 PST
1/01/1895 00:00 MST
3/31/1918 02:00 MWT
10/27/1918 02:00 MST
3/30/1919 02:00 MWT
10/26/1919 02:00 MST
2/09/1942 02:00 MWT
9/30/1945 02:00 MST
4/30/1967 02:00 US#1

MT # 10
Before 11/18/1883 LMT
11/18/1883 12:00 PST
1/01/1895 00:00 MST
3/31/1918 02:00 MWT
10/27/1918 02:00 MST
3/30/1919 02:00 MWT
10/26/1919 02:00 MST
2/09/1942 02:00 MWT
9/30/1945 02:00 MST
5/15/1946 02:00 MDT
9/28/1946 02:00 MST
5/31/1947 02:00 MDT
8/31/1947 02:00 MST
5/02/1948 02:00 MDT
9/06/1948 02:00 MST
4/26/1953 02:00 MDT
9/07/1953 02:00 MST
4/30/1967 02:00 US#1

COUNTIES

1 Beaverhead
2 Big Horn
3 Blaine
4 Broadwater
5 Carbon
6 Carter
7 Cascade
8 Chouteau
9 Custer
10 Daniels
11 Dawson
12 Deer Lodge
13 Fallon
14 Fergus
15 Flathead
16 Gallatin
17 Garfield
18 Glacier
19 Golden Valley
20 Granite
21 Hill
22 Jefferson
23 Judith Basin
24 Lake
25 Lewis and Clark
26 Liberty
27 Lincoln
28 McCone
29 Madison
30 Meagher
31 Mineral
32 Missoula
33 Musselshell
34 Park
35 Petroleum
36 Phillips
37 Pondera
38 Powder River
39 Powell
40 Prairie
41 Ravalli
42 Richland
43 Roosevelt
44 Rosebud
45 Sanders
46 Sheridan
47 Silver Bow
48 Stillwater
49 Sweet Grass
50 Teton
51 Toole
52 Treasure
53 Valley
54 Wheatland
55 Wibaux
56 Yellowstone

Aberdeen 5	1	45N03'16	107w21'23	7:09:26
Absarokee 48	1	45N31'14	109w26'32	7:17:46
Accola 16	1	45N56'59	111w11'04	7:24:44
Acton 56	1	45N55'50	108w40'48	7:14:43
Adel 7	1	47N01'40	111w37'23	7:26:30
Agawam 50	1	48N00'00	112w10'00	7:28:40
Agency 45	9	47N19'41	114w17'33	7:37:10
Ahles 44	1	46N28'44	107w09'50	7:08:39
Alberton 31	9	47N00'06	114w28'21	7:37:53
Albion 6	1	45N11'14	104w16'35	6:57:06
Alder 29	1	45N19'26	112w06'23	7:28:26
Aldridge 34	1	45N05'13	110w49'15	7:23:17
Alex Boggio Place 5	1	45N18'57	109w26'13	7:17:45
Alhambra 22	1	46N27'05	111w59'15	7:27:57
Allard 11	1	47N02'20	104w34'00	6:58:16
Allentown 24	9	47N26'26	114w05'44	7:36:23
Aloe 51	1	48N39'26	112w00'18	7:28:01
Alpine 5	1	45N12'05	109w38'26	7:18:34
Alta 41	9	45N37'08	114w17'56	7:37:12
Alzada 6	1	45N01'23	104w24'43	6:57:39
Amazon 22	1	46N19'13	112w06'23	7:28:26
Amherst 14	1	47N08'59	109w37'27	7:18:30
Amsterdam 16	1	45N45'29	111w19'09	7:25:17
Anaconda 12	2	46N07'43	112w56'29	7:31:46
Anceney 16	1	45N38'55	111w21'14	7:25:25
Andes 42	1	47N57'20	104w32'54	6:58:12
Angela 44	1	46N43'48	106w12'02	7:04:48
Anita 56	1	45N56'39	108w01'17	7:12:05
Antelope 46	1	48N41'23	104w27'28	6:57:50
Ant Flat 27	9	48N43'27	114w52'32	7:39:30
Apex 1	9	45N22'55	112w42'23	7:30:50
Apgar 15	9	48N31'40	113w59'32	7:35:58
Archer 46	1	48N47'34	104w48'37	6:59:14
Argenta 1	9	45N16'47	112w51'40	7:31:27
Arlee 24	9	47N09'43	114w05'03	7:36:20
Armington 7	1	47N21'59	110w54'10	7:23:37
Armington Junction 7	1	47N20'53	110w53'37	7:23:34
Arnold 16	1	45N42'52	111w21'15	7:25:25
Arrow Creek 23	1	47N20'40	110w10'28	7:20:42
Ashfield 36	1	48N25'38	107w31'12	7:10:05
Ashland 44	1	45N35'40	106w16'13	7:05:05
Ashuelot 7	1	47N33'26	111w48'38	7:27:15
Atkins 16	1	45N37'17	111w11'47	7:24:47
Aubrey Crossing 37	1	48N20'16	112w24'37	7:29:38
Augusta 25	1	47N29'34	112w23'29	7:29:34
Austin 25	1	46N38'21	112w14'40	7:28:59
Avon 39	9	46N35'50	112w36'04	7:30:24
Babb 18	9	48N51'37	113w26'09	7:33:45
Bainville 43	1	48N08'24	104w13'20	6:56:53
Baker 13	1	46N22'01	104w17'03	6:57:08
Bald Butte 25	1	46N43'27	112w20'44	7:29:23
Ballantine 56	1	45N56'56	108w08'40	7:12:35
Ball Place 29	1	45N08'29	112w09'04	7:28:36
Balmont 16	4	45N37'41	111w06'16	7:24:25
Bannack 1	9	45N09'40	112w59'41	7:31:59
Barber 19	1	46N18'48	109w23'04	7:17:32
Barite 32	9	46N56'43	113w26'16	7:33:45
Barker 23	1	47N04'17	110w38'23	7:22:34
Barretts 1	9	45N07'53	112w44'23	7:30:58
Bascom 44	1	46N37'34	107w45'10	7:11:01
Baseline 56	3	45N47'02	108w42'09	7:14:49
Basin 22	1	46N16	112w16	7:29:04
Baxter 14	1	47N09'02	109w26'20	7:17:45
Bay Horse 38	1	45N02'36	105w33'59	7:02:16
Baylor 53	1	48N39'48	106w28'44	7:05:55
Beacon Point 29	1	45N23'20	111w21'30	7:25:26
Beals 29	1	45N44'39	111w48'59	7:27:16
Bearcreek 5	1	45N09'39	109w09'23	7:16:38
Bearmouth 20	9	46N42'37	113w19'50	7:33:19
Bear Spring 14	1	47N19	109w57	7:19:48
Beartown 20	9	46N47'36	113w20'21	7:33:21
Beaverton 53	1	48N25'25	107w15'12	7:09:01
Becket 14	1	46N59'31	108w55'22	7:15:41
Bedford 4	1	46N21'47	111w32'59	7:26:12
Beebe 9	1	46N03'19	105w34'08	7:02:17
Beehive 48	1	45N28'45	109w43'12	7:18:53
Belfry 5	1	45N08'31	109w00'17	7:16:01
Belgrade 16	1	45N46'34	111w10'34	7:24:42
Belgrade Junction 16	1	45N46'47	111w16'45	7:25:07
Belknap 45	9	47N39'44	115w24'28	7:41:38
Bell Crossing 41	9	46N26'36	114w07'23	7:36:30
Belle Creek 38	1	45N08'21	105w06'37	7:00:26
Belltower 6	1	45N38'18	104w22'36	6:57:30
Belmont 19	1	46N13'53	108w59'17	7:15:57
Belt 7	1	47N23'10	110w55'29	7:23:42
Belt Creek 7	1	47N33'11	110w57'24	7:23:50
Benchland 23	1	47N04'46	110w01'03	7:20:04
Bend 45	9	47N54'34	115w02'55	7:40:12
Benteen 2	1	45N27'23	107w23'45	7:09:35
Benz 40	1	46N39'35	105w30'03	7:02:00
Benzien 17	1	47N15'20	107w40'46	7:10:43
Bernice 22	1	46N15'28	112w20'11	7:29:21
Biddle 38	1	45N05'58	105w20'16	7:01:21
Biem 43	1	48N09	104w55	6:59:40
Big Arm 24	9	47N47'53	114w17'38	7:37:11
Bigfork 15	9	48N03'48	114w04'18	7:36:17
Bighorn 52	1	46N09'42	107w26'53	7:09:48
Big Sag 8	1	47N35'52	110w42'46	7:22:51
Big Sandy 8	1	48N10'43	110w06'41	7:20:27
Big Sky 16	4	45N41	111w03	7:24:12
Big Timber 49	1	45N50'06	109w57'17	7:19:49
Bill Bracket Place 30	1	46N15'50	110w35'26	7:22:22
Billings 56	3	45N47'00	108w30'00	7:14:00
Billings Heights 56	3	45N47	108w30	7:14:00
Bing 41	9	46N26'36	114w05'00	7:36:20
Birdseye 25	1	46N39'56	112w08'58	7:28:36
Birney 44	1	45N19'18	106w30'52	7:06:03
Birney Day School 44	1	45N24'58	106w27'53	7:05:52
Bisel 16	4	45N42'21	111w05'03	7:24:20
Bishop Place 1	9	45N13'30	112w29'09	7:29:57
Bison 18	9	48N23'14	113w15'55	7:33:04
Black Eagle 7	1	47N31'29	111w16'39	7:25:07
Blackfeet Indian Reservation 18	9	48N33	113w01	7:32:04
Blackfoot 18	9	48N34'31	112w52'33	7:31:30
Blackleaf 50	1	48N00'45	112w36'19	7:30:25
Blacktail 15	9	48N16'37	113w26'50	7:33:47
Blackwood 16	1	45N38'31	111w08'41	7:24:35
Blair 43	1	48N08'48	104w37'32	6:58:30
Blair Crossing 37	1	48N24'12	112w17'26	7:29:10
Blanchards Corner 45	9	47N33'24	114w52'14	7:39:29
Blatchford 40	1	46N42'37	105w26'56	7:01:48
Bloomfield 11	1	47N24'46	104w55'00	6:59:40
Blossburg 39	1	46N37'58	112w19'16	7:29:17
Bluffport 40	1	46N48'52	105w09'56	7:00:40
Blythe 7	1	47N18'05	110w49'40	7:23:19
Bole 50	1	47N42'39	112w00'36	7:28:02
Bond 1	9	45N18'21	112w39'53	7:30:40
Bone Crossing 36	1	48N31'16	107w19'44	7:09:19
Bonfield 9	1	46N37'58	105w34'15	7:02:17
Bonner 32	9	46N52'24	113w51'49	7:35:27
Bonner Junction 32	9	46N51'36	113w52'51	7:35:31
Borax 31	9	47N25'59	115w40'06	7:42:40
Boulder 22	1	46N14'12	112w07'12	7:28:29
Bowdoin 36	1	48N22'40	107w40'58	7:10:44
Bowler 5	1	45N12'18	108w43'06	7:14:52
Bowman Place 29	1	45N06'47	112w02'56	7:28:12
Box Elder 21	1	48N19'02	110w00'45	7:20:03
Boyd 5	1	45N27'28	109w03'57	7:16:16
Boyes 6	1	46N16'05	105w01'50	7:00:07
Bozeman 16	4	45N40'47	111w02'16	7:24:09
Bozeman Hot Springs 16	4	45N41	111w03	7:24:12
Bradman 20	9	46N41'53	113w13'26	7:32:54
Brady 37	1	48N02'08	111w50'21	7:27:21
Brandenberg 44	1	45N48'58	106w13'57	7:04:56
Brandon 29	1	45N28'06	112w08'20	7:28:33
Bredette 43	1	48N30'20	105w17'57	7:01:12
Brewer 4	1	46N08'17	111w24'00	7:25:36
Bridger 5	1	45N17'45	108w54'47	7:15:39
Brisbin 34	1	45N31'23	110w36'28	7:22:26
Broadus 38	1	45N26'38	105w24'25	7:01:38
Broadview 56	1	46N05'52	108w52'35	7:15:30
Broadwater 25	1	46N36'13	112w05'09	7:28:21
Brock Creek 39	9	46N36'13	112w51'17	7:31:25
Brockton 43	1	48N09'05	104w54'59	6:59:40
Brockway 28	1	47N17'52	105w45'43	7:03:03

Place		Lat.	Long.	Time
Brooks 14	1	47N12'15	109w25'14	7:17:41
Brown Addition 7	1	47N24	111w10	7:24:40
Browning 18	9	48N33'25	113w00'45	7:32:03
Bruce Place 30	1	46N17'18	110w51'30	7:23:26
Bruno 30	1	46N22'20	110w37'38	7:22:31
Brusett 17	1	47N25'31	107w15'58	7:09:04
Bryson 31	9	47N24'55	115w34'33	7:42:18
Buell 16	1	45N47'16	111w19'15	7:25:17
Buelow 26	1	48N33'35	110w50'11	7:23:21
Buffalo 14	1	46N49'16	109w49'40	7:19:19
Buffalo Creek 56	1	46N13	107w51	7:11:24
Bull Mountain 56	1	46N01'21	107w51'25	7:11:26
Bundy 33	1	46N17'34	108w46'41	7:15:07
Burdick Place 29	1	45N10'30	112w12'45	7:28:51
Burnham 21	1	48N33'38	109w51'52	7:19:27
Burns 42	1	47N22'41	104w24'17	6:57:37
Busby 2	1	45N32'14	106w57'18	7:07:49
Busch 16	1	45N48'13	111w04'56	7:24:20
Busteed 48	1	45N56'30	109w20'54	7:17:24
Butte 47	5	46N00'14	112w32'02	7:30:08
Butte Creek 10	1	48N52'55	105w50'52	7:03:23
Buxton 47	10	45N56'36	112w42'42	7:30:51
Bynum 50	1	47N58'45	112w18'39	7:29:15
Byrne 20	9	46N42'14	113w27'09	7:33:49
Cabin City 31	9	47N21'59	115w15'48	7:41:03
Cabin Creek 13	1	46N36'48	104w25'16	6:57:41
Calais 43	1	48N08'52	104w48'55	6:59:16
Caldwell 36	1	48N58'18	108w10'19	7:12:41
Calvert 7	1	47N09'55	111w08'01	7:24:32
Calypso 40	1	46N46'23	105w25'20	7:01:41
Camas 45	9	47N37'05	114w39'25	7:38:38
Camas Prairie 45	9	47N27'46	114w36'22	7:38:25
Cameron 29	1	45N12'12	111w40'40	7:26:43
Cameron Crossing 38	1	45N45'42	105w49'29	7:03:18
Cameron Park 56	3	45N47'59	108w34'52	7:14:19
Camona 16	4	45N45'57	111w04'50	7:24:19
Campbell Place 29	1	45N09'01	112w11'45	7:28:47
Canton 4	1	46N24'50	111w30'09	7:26:01
Canyon Creek 25	1	46N48'20	112w15'49	7:29:03
Canyon Creek Boat Landing 15	9	48N12'50	113w46'02	7:35:04
Canyon Ferry 25	1	46N39'20	111w43'03	7:26:52
Capitol 6	1	45N26'10	104w03'54	6:56:16
Carbella 34	1	45N12'28	110w54'14	7:23:37
Carbert 10	1	48N58'33	105w48'36	7:03:14
Cardwell 22	1	45N51'36	111w57'06	7:27:48
Carlton 32	9	46N40'33	114w04'40	7:36:19
Carlyle 55	1	46N39'18	104w04'32	6:56:18
Carney 49	1	45N45'55	110w07'23	7:20:30
Carpenter 16	1	45N53'29	111w27'49	7:25:51
Carter 8	1	47N46'52	110w57'20	7:23:49
Cartersville 44	1	46N17'58	106w28'01	7:05:52
Cascade 7	1	47N16'16	111w41'59	7:26:48
Cassidy Curve 18	9	48N49'39	113w32'59	7:34:12
Castle Rock 44	1	46N16	106w41	7:06:44
Castle Town 30	1	46N26'29	110w40'16	7:22:41
Castner Falls 7	1	47N18'24	111w29'41	7:25:59
Cat Creek 35	1	47N04	108w00	7:12:00
Catron 16	4	45N42'03	111w03'40	7:24:15
Cedric 22	1	45N49'30	112w15'56	7:29:04
Centerville 7	1	47N23'23	111w08'31	7:24:34
Centerville 47	5	46N01'22	112w32'55	7:30:12
Central Park 16	1	45N47	111w11	7:24:44
Chadborn 34	1	45N48'42	110w32'16	7:22:09
Chance 5	1	45N00'43	109w03'45	7:16:15
Chapman 36	1	48N52'07	108w07'57	7:12:32
Chappell 8	1	47N56'05	110w29'54	7:22:00
Charlo 24	9	47N26'19	114w10'17	7:36:41
Charlos Heights 41	9	46N07'35	114w10'37	7:36:42
Checkerboard 30	1	46N34'21	110w32'46	7:22:11
Chelsea 43	1	48N07'59	105w20'16	7:01:21
Cherry Ridge 3	1	48N54'52	108w59'54	7:16:00
Chester 26	1	48N30'38	110w58'00	7:23:52
Chestnut 16	4	45N38'52	110w53'17	7:23:33
Chico 34	1	45N19'16	110w42'16	7:22:49
Chico Hot Springs 34	1	45N20'16	110w41'29	7:22:46
Chicory 34	1	45N24'20	110w42'03	7:22:48
Childs 45	9	47N46'43	115w29'09	7:41:57
Chimney Crossing 17	1	47N00'56	107w37'06	7:10:28
Chimney Rock 34	1	45N33'00	110w44'17	7:22:57
Chinatown 1	9	44N52'58	113w11'41	7:32:47
Chinook 3	1	48N35'24	109w13'50	7:16:55
Choteau 50	1	47N48'50	112w40'45	7:30:43
Choteau Junction 50	1	47N48'18	112w10'34	7:28:42
Christina 14	1	47N22'55	109w19'24	7:17:18
Church Hill 16	1	45N45'03	111w18'13	7:25:13
Circle 28	1	47N20'45	105w35'30	7:02:22
Clancy 22	1	46N28'00	111w58'00	7:27:52
Clarkston 16	1	46N01'48	111w24'46	7:25:39
Clasoil 22	1	46N33'47	111w47'34	7:27:10
Clearwater 32	9	47N00'01	113w22'37	7:33:30
Clear Water Crossing Ranger 31	9	46N54'32	114w48'10	7:39:13
Cleiv 50	1	47N41'39	111w53'46	7:27:35
Cleveland 3	1	48N16'10	109w09'07	7:16:36
Cliff Lake 29	1	44N49'47	111w31'08	7:26:05
Cline 56	1	45N52'56	108w24'30	7:13:38
Clinton 32	9	46N46'09	113w42'42	7:34:51
Clyde Park 34	1	45N53'13	110w36'11	7:22:25
Coal Banks Landing 8	1	48N02'02	110w13'38	7:20:55
Coalridge 46	1	48N41'54	104w11'19	6:56:45
Coalwood 38	1	45N43'41	105w35'24	7:02:22
Cobb 41	9	46N20'43	114w06'06	7:36:24
Cobden 31	9	47N12	114w53	7:39:32
Coburg 3	1	48N27'05	108w26'19	7:13:45
Coffee Creek 14	1	47N20'52	110w04'51	7:20:19
Cohagen 17	1	47N03'16	106w37'01	7:06:28
Cold Spring 44	1	46N16'58	106w45'27	7:07:02
Cole 36	1	48N32'28	107w28'05	7:09:52
Colgate 11	1	47N00'38	104w45'18	6:59:01
Collins 50	1	47N55'42	111w48'34	7:27:14
Coloma 32	9	46N50'35	113w22'47	7:33:31
Colorado Gulch 25	1	46N35	112w02	7:28:08
Colstrip 44	1	45N53'03	106w37'23	7:06:30
Columbia Falls 15	9	48N22'21	114w10'50	7:36:43
Columbia Gardens 47	5	46N00'24	112w27'48	7:29:51
Columbia Heights 15	9	48N22	114w11	7:36:44
Columbus 48	1	45N38'12	109w15'05	7:17:00
Comanche 56	1	45N59'52	108w46'22	7:15:05
Comertown 46	1	48N53'49	104w14'54	6:57:00
Comet 22	1	46N18'39	112w10'09	7:28:41
Como 41	9	46N05'23	114w10'28	7:36:42
Condon 32	9	47N31'40	113w42'35	7:34:50
Conkelley 15	9	48N23'22	114w07'55	7:36:32
Conner 41	9	45N55'51	114w07'25	7:36:30
Conrad 37	1	48N10'13	111w56'43	7:27:47
Contact 34	1	45N30'30	110w13'31	7:20:54
Content 36	1	48N02'49	107w32'26	7:10:10
Cooke City 34	1	45N01'00	109w56'00	7:19:44
Cooper 7	1	47N31'20	111w08'10	7:24:33
Copper City 4	1	45N58'52	111w32'55	7:26:12
Copper Cliff 32	9	46N48'32	113w27'14	7:33:49
Coram 15	9	48N25'05	114w02'43	7:36:11
Corbin 22	1	46N22'50	112w03'40	7:28:15
Cordova 50	1	47N43'18	111w46'58	7:27:08
Corinth 2	1	45N51'21	107w57'51	7:11:51
Corvallis 41	9	46N18'51	114w06'43	7:36:27
Corwin Springs 34	1	45N06'47	110w47'21	7:23:09
Cottonwood 14	1	47N00'21	109w30'46	7:18:03
Cottonwood 39	6	46N23	112w40	7:30:40
Cowan 16	1	45N43'25	111w11'04	7:24:44
Cowboys Heaven 29	1	45N28'23	111w35'12	7:26:21
Crackerville 12	9	46N03'53	112w48'15	7:31:13
Craig 25	1	47N04'28	111w57'45	7:27:51
Crain Place 44	1	46N02'38	106w18'34	7:05:14
Crane 42	1	47N34'33	104w15'43	6:57:03
Craver 48	1	45N41'49	109w22'49	7:17:31
Cree Crossing 36	1	48N32'26	107w31'07	7:10:04
Creston 15	9	48N11'22	114w08'11	7:36:33
Crow Agency 2	1	45N36'06	107w27'38	7:09:51
Crow Indian Reservation 2	1	45N36	107w27	7:09:48
Crow Rock 40	1	46N54'41	106w04'13	7:04:17
Crystal Ford 15	9	48N36'32	113w50'52	7:35:23
Crystal Point 15	9	48N45'06	113w47'12	7:35:09
Culbertson 43	1	48N08'40	104w30'59	6:58:04
Curry 11	1	47N05'25	104w37'35	6:58:30
Cushman 19	1	46N17'18	109w02'31	7:16:10
Custer 56	1	46N07'45	107w33'16	7:10:13
Cut Bank 18	1	48N37'59	112w19'31	7:29:18
Cyr 31	9	47N00'37	114w35'02	7:38:20
Dagmar 46	1	48N35'00	104w01'52	6:56:47
Dahl Place 34	1	45N38'09	110w25'33	7:21:42
Dailey 34	1	45N17'27	110w50'27	7:23:22
Daleview 46	1	48N54'48	104w56'00	6:59:44
Dalys 1	9	45N05'07	112w46'45	7:31:07
Danielsville 39	2	46N17'32	113w00'52	7:32:03
Danvers 14	1	47N13'31	109w42'59	7:18:52
Darby 41	9	46N01'22	114w10'38	7:36:43
Dayton 24	9	47N51'57	114w16'41	7:37:07
Dean 48	1	45N24'17	109w41'23	7:18:46
Dearborn 25	1	47N00	112w04	7:28:16
De Borgia 31	9	47N22'33	115w20'42	7:41:23
Decker 2	1	45N00'43	106w51'46	7:07:27
Deerfield Colony 14	1	47N15'35	109w40'36	7:18:42
Deer Lodge 39	6	46N23'45	112w43'45	7:30:55
Deer Lodge Valley 12	9	46N09	112w50	7:31:20
Deer Park 16	1	46N07'50	111w16'13	7:25:05
Delano Place 47	10	45N53'56	112w51'14	7:31:25
Del Bonita 18	1	48N59'53	112w47'14	7:31:09
Dell 1	9	44N43'23	112w41'47	7:30:47
Delphia 33	1	46N30'17	108w13'07	7:12:52
Delpine 30	1	46N38	110w19	7:21:16
Dempsey 39	6	46N16'44	112w44'52	7:30:59
Denton 14	1	47N19'11	109w56'48	7:19:47
Dentons Point 12	2	46N08	112w57	7:31:48
De Smet 32	9	46N56'00	114w06'08	7:36:25
Devon 51	1	48N28'00	111w28'40	7:25:55
Dewey 1	9	45N46'38	112w51'15	7:31:25
Diamond City 4	1	46N35'50	111w25'23	7:25:42
Dillon 1	9	45N12'59	112w38'12	7:30:33
Divide 47	10	45N45'04	112w44'47	7:30:59
Dixon 45	9	47N19'00	114w18'47	7:37:15
Dodge Summit 27	9	48N55'09	115w21'25	7:41:26
Dodson 36	1	48N23'44	108w14'37	7:12:58
Donald 22	5	45N50'42	112w25'36	7:29:42
Donlan 45	9	47N19'49	114w56'04	7:39:44
Dooley 46	1	48N52'52	104w23'20	6:57:33
Dover 23	1	47N13'14	110w16'03	7:21:04
Dovetail 35	1	47N00	108w21	7:13:24
Drexel 31	9	47N19'36	115w15'06	7:41:00
Drummond 20	9	46N40'03	113w08'47	7:32:35
Dryer Place 36	1	47N44'35	107w33'53	7:10:16
Dublin Gulch 47	5	46N00	112w31	7:30:04
Dunham 24	9	47N36'43	114w07'12	7:36:29
Dunkirk 51	1	48N28'41	111w39'48	7:26:39
Dunmore 2	1	45N40'43	107w30'14	7:10:01
Dupuyer 37	1	48N11'33	112w29'55	7:30:00
Durant 47	10	46N01'17	112w47'24	7:31:10
Durham 18	9	48N31'08	113w06'58	7:32:28
Dutton 50	1	47N50'34	111w42'39	7:26:51
DY Junction 36	1	47N47'44	108w37'58	7:14:32
Eagleton 8	1	48N11	110w06	7:20:24
East Butte 47	5	46N00'41	112w29'45	7:29:59
East Glacier Park 18	9	48N26'29	113w13'02	7:32:52
Eastham Junction 50	1	47N43'45	112w05'36	7:28:22
East Helena 25	1	46N35'23	111w54'53	7:27:40
East Missoula 32	9	46N52'15	113w56'37	7:35:46
East Portal 31	9	47N23'50	115w38'03	7:42:32
East Powder River 38	1	45N20	105w16	7:01:04
Eddies Corner 14	1	46N59'00	109w44'41	7:18:59
Eddy 45	9	47N33'30	115w07'56	7:40:32
Eden 7	1	47N16'12	111w16'17	7:25:05
Edgar 5	1	45N27'53	108w51'06	7:15:24
Edilou 16	1	45N52'44	111w11'45	7:24:47
Edwards 17	1	47N08'25	107w19'59	7:09:20
Edwards Crossing 37	1	48N28'01	112w27'04	7:29:48
Ekalaka 6	1	45N53'20	104w33'08	6:58:13
Electric 34	1	45N04'43	110w46'52	7:23:07
Elkhorn 1	9	45N29'22	113w02'08	7:32:09
Elkhorn 22	1	46N16'29	111w56'42	7:27:47
Elkhorn Hot Springs 1	9	45N27'20	113w06'32	7:32:26
Elk Park 22	5	46N09'54	112w22'17	7:29:29
Elliston 39	1	46N33'44	112w25'48	7:29:43
Elmdale 42	1	48N09	104w55	6:59:40
Elmo 24	9	47N49'50	114w20'55	7:37:24
Elso 33	1	46N20'55	108w40'36	7:14:42
Elton 34	1	45N41'45	110w18'26	7:21:14
Emerson Junction 7	1	47N31'12	111w22'08	7:25:29
Emigrant 34	1	45N22'13	110w43'58	7:22:56
Enid 42	1	47N41'44	104w46'45	6:59:07
Ennis 29	1	45N20'56	111w43'44	7:26:55
Epsie 38	1	45N29'30	105w39'02	7:02:36
Ermont Mill 1	9	45N16'01	112w54'53	7:31:40
Eskay 8	1	48N11	110w06	7:20:24
Essex 15	9	48N16'41	113w36'42	7:34:27
Ethridge 51	1	48N33'28	112w07'11	7:28:29
Eureka 27	9	48N52'48	115w03'09	7:40:13
Eustis 4	1	45N59'23	111w27'57	7:25:52
Eustis 22	1	45N59	111w58	7:27:52
Evans 7	1	47N10'25	111w05'30	7:24:22
Evaro 32	9	47N01'56	114w05'26	7:36:22
Evergreen 15	9	48N13'33	114w16'31	7:37:06
Everson 14	1	47N19	109w57	7:19:48
Fairfield 50	1	47N36'53	111w58'46	7:27:55
Fairview 42	1	47N51'23	104w02'40	6:56:11
Fallon 40	1	46N50'08	105w07'08	7:00:29
False Summit 18	9	48N22'19	113w16'43	7:33:07
Farmington 50	1	47N53'13	112w10'05	7:28:40
Farralltown 33	1	46N23'47	108w32'53	7:14:12
Fee 56	1	46N05'16	107w40'44	7:10:43
Feely 47	10	45N52'36	112w41'18	7:30:45
Ferdig 51	1	48N45'15	111w46'27	7:27:06
Fergus 14	1	47N19'51	109w03'59	7:16:16
Ferndale 24	9	48N03'06	114w00'23	7:36:02
Fields 7	1	47N27'02	111w14'20	7:24:57
Fife 7	1	47N27'21	111w01'20	7:24:05
Finch 44	1	46N17'01	106w58'32	7:07:54
Findon 30	1	46N38	110w19	7:21:16
Finlen 47	10	46N02'18	112w47'25	7:31:10
Finn 39	9	46N45'58	112w42'10	7:30:49
First Creek 36	1	47N56	107w59	7:11:56
Fishtail 48	1	45N27'13	109w30'13	7:18:01
Fishtrap 12	2	45N52'20	113w13'43	7:32:55
Five Mile Creek 5	1	45N22	108w49	7:15:16
Flathead Indian Reservation 15	9	47N32	114w06	7:36:24
Flatwillow 35	1	46N49'55	108w23'58	7:13:36
Flaxville 10	1	48N48'14	105w10'20	7:00:41
Floral Park 47	5	45N59'10	112w29'34	7:29:58
Florence 41	9	46N37'54	114w04'41	7:36:19
Floweree 8	1	47N43'47	111w01'36	7:24:06
Flynn 44	1	46N17'38	106w32'29	7:06:10
Foraker 31	9	47N18'02	115w11'46	7:40:47
Ford Place 30	1	46N15'11	110w48'11	7:23:13
Forest Green 30	1	46N45'41	110w44'23	7:22:58
Forestgrove 14	1	46N59'29	109w04'46	7:16:19
Forest Heights 25	1	46N34'42	112w17'44	7:29:11
Forest Park 11	1	47N06'17	104w45'28	6:59:02
Forsyth 44	1	46N15'59	106w40'38	7:06:43
Fort Belknap 3	1	48N14	108w38	7:14:32
Fort Belknap Agency 3	1	48N28'57	108w45'53	7:15:04
Fort Belknap Indian Res 3	1	48N29	108w46	7:15:04
Fort Benton 8	1	47N49'12	110w40'20	7:22:41
Fort Connah 24	9	47N24'20	114w05'14	7:36:21
Fortine 27	9	48N45'52	114w54'08	7:39:37
Fort Keogh 9	1	46N24	105w50	7:03:20
Fort Kipp 43	1	48N08'48	104w42'55	6:58:52
Fort Logan 30	1	46N40'43	111w10'19	7:24:41
Fort Missoula 32	9	46N50'34	114w03'29	7:36:14
Fort Peck 53	1	48N00'37	106w26'49	7:05:47
Fort Peck Indian Reservation 43	1	48N05	105w38	7:02:32
Fort Piegan 18	9	48N37'50	112w38'48	7:30:35
Fort Shaw 7	1	47N30'20	111w48'34	7:27:14
Fort Smith 2	1	45N18'46	107w56'11	7:11:45
Foster 2	1	45N55'30	107w35'25	7:10:22
Four Buttes 10	1	48N48'35	105w36'21	7:02:25
Fourchette 36	1	47N56	107w59	7:11:56
Four Corners 51	1	48N44	111w51	7:27:24
Four Range 25	1	46N34'59	111w55'37	7:27:42
Fowler 37	1	48N18'57	111w47'03	7:27:08
Fox 5	1	45N16'37	109w12'59	7:16:52

Fox Crossing 21 1 48N57'38 110W39'03 7:22:36
Francis 16 1 46N08'45 111W05'18 7:24:21
Franklin 19 1 46N22'18 109W16'01 7:17:04
Frazer 53 1 48N03'33 106W02'30 7:04:10
Frenchie Place 1 9 45N06'41 112W52'45 7:31:31
French Town 12 2 45N56'14 112W59'27 7:31:58
Frenchtown 32 9 47N00'54 114W13'44 7:36:55
Fresno 21 1 48N34'04 109W59'09 7:19:57
Fries Place 29 1 45N03'39 112W14'56 7:29:00
Froid 43 1 48N20'04 104W29'44 6:57:59
Fromberg 5 1 45N23'32 108W54'21 7:15:37
Frontier Town 25 1 46N34'10 112W18'20 7:29:13
Fuller 22 1 46N15'43 112W12'10 7:28:49
Gage 33 1 46N28'36 108W23'33 7:13:34
Galata 51 1 48N28'32 111W21'05 7:25:24
Galbraith 44 1 46N35'55 107W28'32 7:09:54
Galen 12 8 46N14'08 112W46'31 7:31:06
Gallatin Gateway 16 1 45N35'30 111W11'49 7:24:47
Gallup City 37 1 48N05'38 112W06'44 7:28:27
Gardiner 34 1 45N01'55 110W42'18 7:22:49
Garland 9 1 46N24 105W50 7:03:20
Garneill 14 1 46N45'09 109W45'07 7:19:00
Garnet 20 9 46N49'31 113W20'17 7:33:21
Garrison 39 9 46N31'24 112W48'39 7:31:15
Garryowen 2 1 45N31'36 107W25'08 7:09:41
Gateway 27 9 48N59'57 115W10'20 7:40:41
Gearing 25 1 46N42'52 112W07'59 7:28:32
Genevieve 36 1 48N43'36 107W09'45 7:08:39
George Place 5 1 45N21'33 109W30'58 7:18:04
Georgetown 12 2 46N11'58 113W14'44 7:32:59
Geraldine 8 1 47N36'13 110W15'54 7:21:04
Gerber 7 1 47N27'04 111W09'51 7:24:39
Geyser 23 1 47N15'33 110W29'33 7:21:58
Gibbtown 33 1 46N24'49 108W33'18 7:14:13
Gibson Flats 7 1 47N28'11 111W14'46 7:24:59
Giffen 7 1 47N18'50 111W11'09 7:24:45
Gildford 21 1 48N34'10 110W17'56 7:21:12
Gilman 25 1 47N30'33 112W21'52 7:29:27
Gilroy 16 1 45N39'36 111W09'51 7:24:39
Giltedge 14 1 47N07'37 109W12'05 7:16:48
Girard 42 1 47N52'04 104W25'16 6:57:41
Gird Point 41 9 46N12'27 113W54'38 7:35:39
Glacier 15 9 48N43 113W57 7:35:48
Glacier Colony 18 1 48N49'58 112W13'05 7:28:52
Glacier National Park 18 9 48N45 113W37 7:34:28
Glasgow 53 1 48N11'49 106W38'10 7:06:33
Glasgow Air Base 53 1 48N12 106W38 7:06:32
Gleason Resort 50 1 47N49 112W11 7:28:44
Glen 1 9 45N28'36 112W41'23 7:30:46
Glendale 1 10 45N38'31 112W46'20 7:31:05
Glendive 11 1 47N06'19 104W42'43 6:58:51
Glengarry 14 1 47N01'37 109W32'50 7:18:11
Glentana 53 1 48N50'53 106W14'56 7:05:00
Gloss Place 1 9 45N21'39 113W16'25 7:33:06
Gloster 25 1 46N45'46 112W20'19 7:29:21
Gold Butte 51 1 48N52'25 111W23'06 7:25:32
Goldcreek 39 9 46N35'12 112W55'40 7:31:43
Golden Ridge 50 1 47N34'04 112W13'34 7:28:54
Goldstone 21 1 48N53'59 110W31'54 7:22:08
Gordon 7 1 47N37'46 111W38'45 7:26:35
Gorus 41 9 46N03'46 114W10'16 7:36:41
Grace 47 1 45N48'24 112W19'46 7:29:19
Grahams Place 29 1 44N51'32 111W35'00 7:26:20
Granite 20 7 46N19'03 113W14'37 7:32:58
Grannis 34 1 45N45'24 110W29'44 7:21:59
Grant 1 9 45N00'31 113W03'58 7:32:16
Grantsdale 41 9 46N12'13 114W08'27 7:36:34
Grassrange 14 1 47N01'16 108W48'21 7:15:13
Grass Valley 32 9 46N56'09 114W08'22 7:36:33
Graying 1 9 45N02'48 112W49'12 7:31:17
Grayling 16 1 44N48'20 111W11'37 7:24:46
Great Falls 7 1 47N30'00 111W18'00 7:25:12
Greenfield 50 1 47N38'24 111W51'31 7:27:26
Greenough 32 9 46N55'00 113W26'09 7:33:45
Greenwood 16 1 45N40'38 111W12'41 7:24:51
Gregson 47 10 46N02'53 112W48'31 7:31:14
Gregson Hot Springs 47 10 46N02'35 112W48'33 7:31:14
Greycliff 49 1 45N45'48 109W47'02 7:19:08
Groveland 30 1 46N26'13 110W23'48 7:21:35
Gunsight 18 1 48N38'14 112W27'40 7:29:51
Guntner Place 1 9 45N11'34 112W27'55 7:29:52
Hackney 47 10 46N01'53 112W47'30 7:31:10
Hagans Crossing 37 1 48N27'30 112W30'48 7:30:03
Hale Place 29 1 45N06'33 112W07'03 7:28:28
Halfmoon 15 9 48N23'16 114W14'20 7:36:57
Hall 20 9 46N35'07 113W11'45 7:32:47
Hamen 30 1 46N18'35 110W42'00 7:22:48
Hamilton 41 9 46N14'49 114W09'34 7:36:38
Hammond 6 1 45N13'32 104W55'03 6:59:40
Hammond Valley 44 1 46N16 106W41 7:06:44
Hanover 14 1 47N07'17 109W33'14 7:18:13
Happys Inn 27 9 48N05'00 115W08'22 7:40:33
Happy Valley 15 9 48N24 114W20 7:37:20
Hardin 2 1 45N43'57 107W36'41 7:10:27
Hardy 7 1 47N16 111W42 7:26:48
Harlem 3 1 48N32'00 108W47'00 7:15:08
Harlowton 54 1 46N26'08 109W50'01 7:19:20
Harrison 29 1 45N42'03 111W47'08 7:27:09
Harrison Mill 29 1 45N43'08 111W45'29 7:27:02
Haskell 20 9 46N36'47 113W02'36 7:32:10
Hassel 4 1 46N18'19 111W39'52 7:26:39
Hathaway 44 1 46N16'34 106W11'46 7:04:47
Hauck 23 1 46N57'34 109W49'48 7:19:19
Haugan 31 9 47N23'00 115W23'55 7:41:36
Havre 21 1 48N33'00 109W41'00 7:18:44
Hays 3 1 47N59'21 108W41'37 7:14:46

Heart Butte 37 9 48N17'00 112W50'09 7:31:21
Heath 14 1 46N59'45 109W15'59 7:17:04
Hedgesville 54 1 46N27'24 109W30'07 7:18:00
Helena 25 1 46N35'34 112W02'07 7:28:08
Hellgate 32 9 46N51 114W01 7:36:04
Helmville 39 9 46N52'00 112W57'37 7:31:50
Henderson 31 9 47N21'30 115W18'32 7:41:14
Heron 45 9 48N03'32 115W57'22 7:43:49
Herron Park 21 1 48N33 109W41 7:18:44
Hesper 56 3 45N44'31 108W42'32 7:14:50
Higgins 30 1 46N17'27 110W44'28 7:22:58
Highview 47 5 45N55'15 112W25'30 7:29:42
Highwood 8 1 47N35'01 110W47'22 7:23:09
Hilger 14 1 47N15'14 109W21'33 7:17:26
Hillman 16 1 45N53'21 111W11'48 7:24:47
Hillsboro 5 1 45N06'00 108W13'56 7:12:56
Hillside 17 1 46N54'40 106W23'58 7:05:36
Hillside Colony 51 1 48N58'45 112W04'03 7:28:16
Hingham 21 1 48N33'18 110W25'17 7:21:41
Hinsdale 53 1 48N23'39 107W05'03 7:08:20
Hirsch 56 3 45N49'04 108W24'47 7:13:39
Hobson 23 1 47N00'02 109W52'27 7:19:30
Hodges 11 1 46N59'01 104W23'14 6:57:33
Hoffman 34 1 45N34'21 110W47'02 7:23:08
Hoffman Place 29 9 45N10'30 112W24'57 7:29:40
Hoffmanville 42 1 47N30'39 104W18'07 6:57:12
Hogeland 3 1 48N51'09 108W39'29 7:14:38
Holden Place 29 9 45N12'55 112W24'54 7:29:40
Holker 4 1 46N15'16 111W28'38 7:25:55
Holland 16 1 45N44'39 111W14'40 7:24:59
Holt 15 9 48N04'56 114W06'32 7:36:26
Holter Dam 25 1 47N00 112W04 7:28:16
Homestake 22 5 45N55'24 112W24'36 7:29:38
Homestead 46 1 48N25'16 104W32'18 6:58:09
Hoosac 14 1 47N16'33 109W50'22 7:19:21
Hopp 8 1 48N11 110W06 7:20:24
Hoppers 34 1 45N39'56 110W43'03 7:22:52
Horton 9 1 46N20'29 106W03'41 7:04:15
Hot Springs 45 9 47N36'33 114W40'04 7:38:40
Howard 44 1 46N16 106W41 7:06:44
Hoyt 11 1 46N55'47 104W51'15 6:59:25
Hughesville 23 1 47N05'00 110W37'54 7:22:32
Hungry Horse 15 9 48N23'09 114W03'36 7:36:14
Hungry Joe 11 1 47N05'46 104W41'56 6:58:48
Hunters Hot Springs 34 1 45N45'29 110W15'21 7:21:01
Huntley 56 1 45N53'58 108W18'03 7:13:12
Huson 32 9 47N01'53 114W19'35 7:37:18
Hysham 52 1 46N17'34 107W14'01 7:08:56
Iliad 8 1 47N47'55 109W47'07 7:19:08
Independence 34 1 45N12'45 110W14'44 7:20:59
Indian Arrow 56 1 45N47'01 108W10'27 7:12:42
Ingomar 44 1 46N34'36 107W22'18 7:09:29
Intake 11 1 47N17'38 104W31'17 6:58:05
Inverness 21 1 48N33 110W41 7:22:44
Iris 32 9 46N43'32 113W38'11 7:34:33
Iron 25 1 46N41'12 112W03'35 7:28:14
Ismay 9 1 46N29'50 104W47'37 6:59:10
Iverness 21 1 48N33'23 110W41'18 7:22:45
Jackson 1 9 45N22'05 113W24'29 7:33:38
Janney 47 5 45N54'34 112W29'40 7:29:59
Jardine 34 1 45N04'12 110W38'01 7:22:32
Jeffers 29 1 45N20'56 111W42'17 7:26:49
Jefferson City 22 1 46N23'18 112W01'36 7:28:06
Jefferson Island 29 1 45N51'03 111W56'23 7:27:46
Jellison Place 54 1 46N40'24 110W04'17 7:20:17
Jennings 27 9 48N21'56 115W20'37 7:41:22
Jens 39 9 46N36'15 113W00'19 7:32:01
Jimtown 44 1 45N40'44 106W41'15 7:06:45
Joliet 5 1 45N29'07 108W58'11 7:15:53
Joplin 26 1 48N33'39 110W46'18 7:23:05
Joppa 44 1 46N16'34 106W19'53 7:05:20
Jordan 17 1 47N19'15 106W54'34 7:07:38
Jordan Crossing 36 1 48N30'26 107W17'12 7:09:09
Judith Gap 54 1 46N40'38 109W45'04 7:19:00
Kalispell 15 9 48N11'45 114W18'43 7:37:15
Kelley 35 1 46N45'51 108W10'39 7:12:43
Kenilworth 8 1 48N10'32 110W26'23 7:21:46
Kenspur 41 9 46N35'37 114W05'28 7:36:22
Kerns 16 1 45N42'42 111W08'38 7:24:35
Kershaw 8 1 47N48'48 110W44'19 7:22:57
Kevin 51 1 48N44'43 111W57'52 7:27:51
Keystone 31 9 47N16'06 114W56'05 7:39:44
Kidd 1 9 44N48'04 112W45'07 7:31:00
Kila 15 9 48N07'13 114W27'21 7:37:49
Kingley 2 1 45N53'55 107W36'04 7:10:24
Kingrey Place 29 1 45N13'36 112W08'42 7:28:35
Kingston 14 1 47N07'47 109W35'48 7:18:23
Kinsey 9 1 46N34'15 105W39'23 7:02:38
Kintyre 53 1 48N04'23 106W09'05 7:04:36
Kiowa 18 9 48N32'52 113W16'12 7:33:05
Kirby 2 1 45N19'57 106W58'52 7:07:55
Klein 33 1 46N24'15 108W32'55 7:14:12
Knowles 45 9 47N20'50 114W42'44 7:38:51
Knowlton 9 1 46N20'37 105W05'15 7:00:21
Knox 56 1 45N56'38 108W11'51 7:12:47
Kolin 23 1 47N06'24 109W46'20 7:19:05
Kootenai Falls 27 9 48N26'53 115W46'54 7:43:08
Kotke 34 1 45N20'19 110W53'49 7:23:35
Koyl 50 1 47N54'01 112W15'43 7:29:03
Kremlin 21 1 48N34'11 110W05'09 7:20:21
Kuehn 2 1 46N17 107W14 7:08:56
Kuka Crossing 37 1 48N18'50 112W23'32 7:29:34
La Chapelle Place 25 1 47N20'26 112W17'24 7:29:10
La Hood Park 22 1 45N51'11 111W55'17 7:27:41
Lake Mary Ronan 24 9 47N56'35 114W23'37 7:37:34

Lake McDonald 15 9 48N37'15 113W52'15 7:35:29
Lakeside 15 9 48N01'10 114W13'25 7:36:54
Lakeside 25 1 46N40'41 111W50'07 7:27:20
Lakeside 43 1 48N04'31 104W10'38 6:56:43
Lakeview 1 1 44N35'58 111W48'35 7:27:14
Lakeview 16 1 44N48'17 111W14'24 7:24:58
Lambert 42 1 47N41'01 104W37'13 6:58:29
Lame Deer 44 1 45N37'23 106W39'58 7:06:40
Lanark 43 1 48N08'05 104W21'42 6:57:27
Lander Crossing 8 1 47N38'35 110W55'57 7:23:44
Landusky 36 1 47N53'52 108W37'18 7:14:29
Larchwood 45 9 47N51'01 115W37'37 7:42:30
Laredo 21 1 48N25'53 109W52'57 7:19:32
Larslan 53 1 48N35 106W12 7:04:48
La Salle 15 9 48N18'47 114W14'35 7:36:58
Laurel 56 1 45N40'09 108W46'15 7:15:05
Laurin 29 1 45N21'10 112W07'02 7:28:28
Lavina 19 1 46N17'41 108W56'14 7:15:45
Lavon 29 9 45N28 112W43 7:30:52
Leadville 22 6 46N18'52 112W32'32 7:30:10
Leary Place 29 1 45N01'23 112W03'49 7:28:15
Lebo 30 1 46N20'40 110W23'36 7:21:34
Ledger 37 1 48N15'37 111W49'20 7:27:17
Lehigh 23 1 47N02'36 110W12'23 7:20:50
Leiterville 29 1 45N33'18 112W07'19 7:28:29
Lennep 30 1 46N24'58 110W32'33 7:22:10
Leonard Place 29 1 45N13'53 112W10'14 7:28:41
Leroy 3 1 47N52'27 109W19'04 7:17:16
Lewistown 14 1 47N03'45 109W25'39 7:17:43
Lewistown Junction 14 1 47N03'13 109W24'57 7:17:40
Libby 27 9 48N23'18 115W33'18 7:42:13
Lima 1 9 44N38'13 112W35'28 7:30:22
Limestone 48 1 45N28'40 109W54'06 7:19:36
Lincoln 25 9 46N57'18 112W40'51 7:30:43
Lindisfarne (Camp Marshall) 24 9 47N48'32 114W13'39 7:36:55
Lindsay 11 1 47N13'08 105W09'12 7:00:37
Lingshire 30 1 46N50'28 111W24'24 7:25:38
Lippard 8 1 47N57'06 110W23'25 7:21:34
Little Missouri 6 1 45N21 104W36 6:58:24
Living Springs 54 1 46N35'32 109W32'08 7:18:09
Livingston 34 4 45N39'45 110W33'37 7:22:14
Lloyd 3 1 48N17'25 109W21'41 7:17:27
Locate 9 1 46N26 105W18 7:01:12
Lockwood 56 3 45N47 108W30 7:14:00
Lodge Grass 2 1 45N18'52 107W21'45 7:09:27
Lodge Pole 3 1 48N02'05 108W31'57 7:14:08
Logan 16 1 45N53'04 111W25'36 7:25:42
Lohman 3 1 48N35'23 109W24'16 7:17:37
Lolo 32 9 46N45'32 114W04'48 7:36:19
Lolo Hot Springs 32 9 46N43'40 114W31'47 7:38:07
Loma 8 1 47N56'13 110W30'10 7:22:01
Lombard 4 1 46N06'27 111W23'53 7:25:36
Lonepine 45 9 47N42'11 114W38'09 7:38:33
Loring 36 1 48N47'32 107W51'40 7:11:27
Lost Creek 12 2 46N10'33 112W56'54 7:31:48
Lothair 26 1 48N28'18 111W13'53 7:24:56
Lothrop 32 9 46N59'27 114W26'46 7:37:47
Louisville 22 1 46N33'46 111W47'42 7:27:11
Lower Ellis Place 25 1 47N17'00 112W17'30 7:29:10
Lower Sun River 7 1 47N30 111W17 7:25:08
Loweth 30 1 46N22'08 110W42'25 7:22:50
Lowry 50 1 47N30'45 112W00'32 7:28:02
Lozeau 31 9 47N07'03 114W46'45 7:39:07
Ludington 42 1 47N49'34 104W03'40 6:56:15
Lupfer 15 9 48N29'01 114W30'37 7:38:02
Lustre 53 1 48N24 105W53 7:03:32
Luther 5 1 45N17'04 109W25'41 7:17:43
Macless 16 1 45N51'38 111W16'16 7:25:05
Macon 43 1 48N06'35 105W31'04 7:02:04
Maddux 3 1 48N08'26 109W25'02 7:17:40
Madison Valley 29 1 45N16 111W40 7:26:40
Madoc 10 1 48N48'39 105W17'07 7:01:08
Maiden 14 1 47N10'40 109W13'46 7:16:55
Maiden Rock 47 10 45N41'48 112W44'09 7:30:57
Malmstrom 7 1 47N31 111W12 7:24:48
Malmstrom Air Force Base 7 1 47N31 111W12 7:24:48
Malone 50 1 47N56'30 112W10'00 7:28:40
Malta 36 1 48N21'35 107W52'25 7:11:30
Mammoth 29 1 45N40'11 112W00'57 7:28:04
Manchester 7 1 47N32'27 111W27'41 7:25:51
Manhattan 16 1 45N51'24 111W19'54 7:25:20
Mann 56 1 45N58'15 108W06'47 7:12:27
Manson 37 1 48N14'15 112W00'20 7:28:01
Many Glacier Hotel 18 9 48N51 113W26 7:33:44
Marion 15 9 48N06'20 114W39'44 7:38:39
Marsh 11 1 46N53 104W56 6:59:44
Martin City 15 9 48N23'30 114W02'14 7:36:09
Martinsdale 30 1 46N27'30 110W18'45 7:21:15
Martinsdale Colony 54 1 46N29'22 110W16'00 7:21:04
Marysville 25 1 46N45'02 112W17'58 7:29:12
Matthews 16 4 46N37'40 111W05'01 7:24:20
Maudlow 16 1 46N06'28 111W10'20 7:24:41
Maxville 20 9 46N27'53 113W14'00 7:32:56
Mc Allister 29 1 45N26'40 111W43'53 7:26:56
McCabe 43 1 48N14'37 104W22'38 6:57:31
McClain 32 9 46N42'22 114W04'37 7:36:18
Mc Clave 14 1 46N48'31 109W46'24 7:19:06
McClellans Creek 25 1 46N36 111W55 7:27:40
McCloud 40 1 46N54'03 105W35'59 7:02:24
McDonald 45 9 47N19'24 114W27'40 7:37:51
McElroy 46 1 48N52'49 104W40'71 6:58:45
McGlone Heights 47 5 46N00 112W31 7:30:04
Mc Leod 49 1 45N39'46 110W06'55 7:20:28
McNamara 32 9 46N54'41 113W40'36 7:34:42
McQueen 47 5 46N01'13 112W29'40 7:29:59
Meaderville 47 5 46N01'20 112W30'16 7:30:01

Medicine Hot Springs 41
9 45N50'46 114w02'04 7:36:08
Medicine Lake 46
1 48N30'05 104w30'15 6:58:01
Medicine Springs 41
9 45N56 114w07 7:36:28
Melrose 47 10 45N37'55 112w41'01 7:30:44
Melstone 33 1 46N35'55 107w52'17 7:11:29
Melville 49 1 46N06'11 109w57'11 7:19:49
Menard 16 1 45N58'26 111w10'24 7:24:42
Menard Wye 16 1 45N58'02 111w10'53 7:24:44
Merino 23 1 47N14'38 110w21'55 7:21:28
Meriwether 18 9 48N36'23 112w45'36 7:31:02
Merriman 34 1 45N20'20 110w46'04 7:23:04
Meyers Creek 48
1 45N29'40 109w55'52 7:19:43
Midale 36 1 47N54'15 108w09'41 7:12:39
Midby 46 1 48N46'04 104w41'08 6:58:45
Mid Canon 7 1 47N07'56 111w53'13 7:27:33
Midway 42 1 47N30'54 104w19'12 6:57:17
Mildred 40 1 46N40'33 104w57'34 6:59:50
Miles City 9 1 46N24'30 105w50'24 7:03:22
Miles Crossing 47
10 46N00'45 112w43'31 7:30:54
Miles Crossing 53
1 48N28'54 107w09'04 7:08:36
Milford Colony 25
1 47N19'47 112w12'32 7:28:50
Mill Creek 12 2 46N08 112w57 7:31:48
Millegan 7 1 47N01'14 111w22'08 7:25:29
Miller 32 9 46N53'39 113w46'37 7:35:06
Miller Colony 50
1 47N55'35 112w17'21 7:29:09
Mill Iron 6 1 45N51'13 104w13'08 6:56:53
Milltown 32 9 46N52'17 113w52'51 7:35:31
Miner 34 1 45N11'57 110w54'28 7:23:38
Minnie Rahn Place 34
1 45N38'02 110w26'10 7:21:45
Missoula 32 9 46N52'20 113w59'35 7:35:58
Missoula West 32
9 46N51 114w04 7:36:16
Mizpah 9 1 46N14'41 105w16'01 7:01:04
Moccasin 23 1 47N03'12 109w54'35 7:19:38
Moffit Canyon 16
4 45N41 111w03 7:24:12
Moiese 24 9 47N22'14 114w15'54 7:37:04
Molt 48 1 45N51'41 108w55'38 7:15:43
Mona 42 1 48N09 104w55 6:59:40
Monarch 7 1 47N05'54 110w50'16 7:23:21
Monida 1 1 44N33'43 112w18'46 7:29:15
Montague 8 1 47N40'45 110w27'12 7:21:49
Montana City 22
1 46N32'16 111w55'55 7:27:44
Montanapolis Springs 34
1 45N25 110w38 7:22:32
Montaqua 5 1 45N30'33 108w54'02 7:15:36
Moon Creek 9 1 46N09 105w59 7:03:56
Moore 14 1 46N58'32 109w41'46 7:18:47
Moorhead 38 1 45N03'54 105w52'14 7:03:29
Moose Town 47 5 45N46'34 112w34'02 7:30:16
Morel 12 8 46N09'02 112w46'01 7:31:04
Morgan 36 1 49N00 107w50 7:11:20
Mosby 17 1 46N59'32 107w52'59 7:11:32
Moss Agate 30 1 46N21'57 110w49'39 7:23:19
Mossmain 56 1 45N41'05 108w42'37 7:14:50
Moulton 14 1 47N20'45 109w21'14 7:17:25
Mount Ellis 16 4 45N41 111w03 7:24:12
Moyne 30 1 46N15'23 110w52'28 7:23:30
Muir 34 1 45N39'47 110w47'34 7:23:10
Murray Place 53
1 47N48'24 107w03'55 7:08:16
Musselshell 33 1 46N31'07 108w05'26 7:12:22
Myers 52 1 46N15'03 107w20'23 7:09:22
Nagos 32 9 46N59'30 114w06'43 7:36:27
Naismith 51 1 48N23'11 111w46'25 7:27:06
Nashua 53 1 48N07'56 106w21'21 7:05:25
Navajo 10 1 48N47'32 105w03'35 7:00:14
Neihart 7 1 46N56'00 110w44'06 7:22:56
Nelson 25 1 46N49'01 111w48'30 7:27:14
New Chicago 20 9 46N37'37 113w08'29 7:32:34
Newcomb 47 5 45N55'12 112w31'08 7:30:05
Newlon Junction 42
1 47N39'31 104w11'48 6:56:47
New Rockport Colony 50
1 47N51'49 112w01'22 7:28:05
Newton 56 1 45N58'44 108w03'28 7:12:14
New Year 14 1 47N10'19 109w17'23 7:17:10
Niarada 15 9 47N48'51 114w36'13 7:38:25
Nibbe 56 1 45N59'02 108w01'36 7:12:06
Nichols 44 1 46N15'50 106w48'58 7:07:16
Nickwall 28 1 48N02'57 105w18'23 7:01:14
Nimrod 15 9 48N14'20 113w34'03 7:34:16
Nimrod 20 9 46N42'01 113w28'35 7:33:54
Ninemile 32 9 47N01'12 114w24'30 7:37:38
Nine-mile 47 5 45N54'19 112w27'56 7:29:52
Nissler 47 5 46N00'17 112w38'29 7:30:34
Nohly 42 1 47N59'44 104w05'29 6:56:22
Norris 29 1 45N34'05 111w41'24 7:26:46
North Country 19
1 46N34 109w12 7:16:48
North Custer 9 1 46N38 105w49 7:03:16
Northern Cheyenne Indian Res 2
1 45N37 106w40 7:06:40
North Fork 3 1 48N35'10 109w06'37 7:16:26
North Garfield 17
1 47N25 107w13 7:08:52
North Havre 21 1 48N33 109w41 7:18:44
North of The Yellowstone 49
1 46N02 109w54 7:19:36
Northridge Heights 15
9 48N13'05 114w19'55 7:37:20
North Treasure 52
1 46N17 107w19 7:09:16
Noxon 45 9 47N59'46 115w46'50 7:43:07
Number Seven 7 1 47N24'13 111w09'04 7:24:36
Nyack 15 9 48N26'22 113w48'17 7:35:13
Nye 48 1 45N26'38 109w48'19 7:19:13
Ohio Camp 51 1 48N49'59 111w50'45 7:27:23
Oilmont 51 1 48N44'24 111w50'24 7:27:22
Old Banks Place 26
1 48N55'13 111w06'58 7:24:28
Old Ford Place 2
1 45N54'14 107w27'24 7:09:50
Old Weiss And French Place 25
1 46N48'25 111w55'25 7:27:42
Old Whitcomb Place 36
1 47N59'07 107w58'40 7:11:55
Olive 38 1 45N33'02 105w31'39 7:02:07
Ollie 13 1 46N35'05 104w05'03 6:56:20
Olney 15 9 48N32'55 114w34'38 7:38:19
Olson Place 7 1 47N28'17 112w00'33 7:28:02
Opheim 53 1 48N51'24 106w24'24 7:05:38
Opportunity 12 9 46N06'26 112w49'38 7:31:19
Orchard Homes 32
9 46N51'48 114w02'51 7:36:11
Orinoco 44 1 46N17'46 106w35'29 7:06:22
Ossette 10 1 48N35 106w12 7:04:48
Oswego 53 1 48N03'31 105w52'50 7:03:31
Otter 38 1 45N12'28 106w12'04 7:04:48
Outlook 46 1 48N53'15 104w46'38 6:59:07
Ovando 39 9 47N01'13 113w07'56 7:32:32
Ozan 20 9 46N42'03 113w14'32 7:32:58
Pablo 24 9 47N36'01 114w07'05 7:36:28
Pacific Junction 21
1 48N33'23 109w45'33 7:19:02
Pack and Lacey Crossing 8
1 47N32'41 110w53'57 7:23:36
Packers Roost 15
9 48N44'45 113w46'45 7:35:07
Paisley 53 1 48N13'55 106w43'26 7:06:54
Pappas Place 22
5 45N58'17 112w21'29 7:29:26
Paradise 45 9 47N23'22 114w48'04 7:39:12
Paragon 9 1 46N21'55 106w00'10 7:04:01
Park City 25 1 46N32'29 112w06'31 7:28:26
Park City 48 1 45N37'58 108w55'02 7:15:40
Parker 4 1 46N10'47 111w36'25 7:26:26
Park Grove 53 1 48N01'49 106w26'41 7:05:47
Patterson 16 4 45N37'41 111w03'05 7:24:12
Patterson Corner 1
9 45N47'15 112w53'29 7:31:34
Peerless 10 1 48N46'57 105w49'50 7:03:19
Pendroy 50 1 48N04'25 112w17'53 7:29:12
Perma 45 9 47N21'50 114w35'02 7:38:20
Peterson Place 5
1 45N22'26 109w27'19 7:17:49
Petrolia 35 1 47N00 108w21 7:13:24
Philipsburg 20 7 46N19'56 113w17'36 7:33:10
Phillips 36 1 48N05'37 108w09'48 7:12:39
Piche 42 1 47N36'31 104w13'49 6:56:55
Piedmont 22 1 45N50'09 112w08'00 7:28:32
Piegan 18 9 48N26'05 112w41'37 7:30:46
Pierce Crossing 37
1 48N20'51 112w29'20 7:29:57
Piltzville 32 9 46N51'41 113w51'42 7:35:27
Pine Creek 34 1 45N30'27 110w33'48 7:22:15
Pinegrove 32 9 46N52'49 113w54'08 7:35:37
Pinnacle 15 9 48N21'22 113w39'08 7:34:37
Pioneer 39 9 46N30'45 112w57'55 7:31:52
Pioneer 56 3 45N47 108w34 7:14:16
Pioneer Junction 27
9 48N20'10 115w31'03 7:42:04
Piper 14 1 46N59'24 109w11'59 7:16:48
Pipestone 22 1 45N54'19 112w13'10 7:28:53
Pipestone Hot Springs 22
1 45N53'39 112w13'48 7:28:55
Plains 45 9 47N27'37 114w52'55 7:39:32
Pleasant Prairie 10
1 48N35'32 105w04'55 7:00:20
Pleasant Valley 15
9 48N06 114w40 7:38:40
Pleasant View 11
1 47N02'10 104w55'46 6:59:43
Plentywood 46 1 48N46'29 104w33'43 6:58:15
Plevna 13 1 46N25'05 104w31'12 6:58:05
Plum Creek 14 1 47N14 109w43 7:18:52
Polaris 1 9 45N22'11 113w07'07 7:32:28
Polebridge 15 9 48N45'55 114w17'03 7:37:08
Polson 24 9 47N41'37 114w09'44 7:36:39
Pompeys Pillar 56
1 45N59'29 107w57'05 7:11:48
Pony 29 1 45N39'31 111w53'37 7:27:34
Poplar 43 1 48N06'47 105w11'52 7:00:47
Portage 7 1 47N39'10 111w07'26 7:24:30
Portal 22 1 46N20'15 112w07'03 7:28:28
Porters Corner 20
7 46N15'07 113w19'52 7:33:19
Post Creek 24 9 47N23'57 114w05'45 7:36:23
Potomac 32 9 46N52'54 113w34'43 7:34:19
Powderville 38 1 45N45'32 105w06'53 7:00:28
Power 50 1 47N42'57 111w41'10 7:26:45
Powers 16 1 45N47'48 111w09'29 7:24:38
Pownal 14 1 47N24'45 110w11'38 7:20:47
Pray 34 1 45N22'49 110w40'51 7:22:43
Primrose 32 9 46N55'38 114w09'57 7:36:40
Princeton 20 9 46N25'01 113w09'53 7:32:40
Proctor 24 9 47N53'33 114w18'16 7:37:13
Pryor 2 1 45N25'47 108w31'57 7:14:08
Quartz 31 9 47N03'07 114w46'06 7:39:04
Quast 41 9 46N19'39 114w06'10 7:36:25
Quebec 49 1 45N43'36 109w39'31 7:18:38
Queen 22 1 46N15'05 111w57'51 7:27:51
Queens Point 33
1 46N34'08 107w58'34 7:11:54
Quietus 2 1 45N05'47 106w16'57 7:05:08
Quigley 20 9 46N36'44 113w38'51 7:34:35
Quinn 47 10 45N41'39 112w44'27 7:30:58
Quinns 45 9 47N19'29 114w48'03 7:39:12
Quintonkon 15 9 48N01'35 113w42'22 7:34:49
Racetrack 39 6 46N24 112w44 7:30:56
Radersburg 4 1 46N11'45 111w37'52 7:26:31
Radnor 15 9 48N36'36 114w39'35 7:38:38
Rainbow 7 1 47N32'18 111w11'57 7:24:48
Ramsay 47 10 46N00'21 112w41'07 7:30:44
Rankin Place 5 1 45N15'42 109w29'30 7:17:58
Rapelje 48 1 45N58'19 109w15'16 7:17:01
Rattlesnake 3 1 48N05'53 109w02'53 7:16:12
Rattlesnake 32 9 46N53 113w58 7:35:52
Ravalli 24 9 47N16'38 114w10'47 7:36:43
Ravenna 20 9 46N42'52 113w31'50 7:34:07
Raymond 46 1 48N52'35 104w34'47 6:58:19
Raynesford 23 1 47N16'12 110w43'45 7:22:55
Red Bluff 29 1 45N35'19 111w38'50 7:26:35
Red Lodge 5 1 45N11'09 109w14'46 7:16:59
Red Rock 1 9 44N54'02 112w49'05 7:31:16
Red Rock Point 15
9 48N41'43 113w48'55 7:35:16
Redstone 46 1 48N49'18 104w56'37 6:59:46
Red Top 11 1 47N24'45 104w48'40 6:59:15
Reeder Place 29
1 45N02'59 112w00'04 7:28:00
Reed Point (Reedpoint P O) 48
1 45N42'34 109w32'29 7:18:10
Regina 36 1 47N54'24 107w55'16 7:11:41
Renova 22 1 45N48'56 112w07'37 7:28:30
Reserve 46 1 48N36'20 104w27'33 6:57:50
Rexford 27 9 48N52'22 115w13'22 7:40:53
Reynolds City 39
9 46N49'16 113w17'10 7:33:09
Rhodes 15 9 48N16'45 114w28'24 7:37:54
Riceville 7 1 47N12'53 110w55'58 7:23:44
Richel Lodge 5 1 45N04'55 109w22'29 7:17:30
Richey 11 1 47N38'38 105w04'28 7:00:18
Richland 53 1 48N49'15 106w03'02 7:04:12
Ridge 6 1 45N02'49 105w01'11 7:00:05
Ridgelawn 42 1 47N47'31 104w05'09 6:56:21
Ridgeway 6 1 45N29'07 104w30'41 6:58:03
Riebeling 25 1 47N30'16 112w08'53 7:28:36
Rimini 25 1 46N29'17 112w14'45 7:28:59
Rimrock 56 3 45N48'08 108w42'08 7:14:49
Rim Rock Colony 51
1 48N53'45 112w05'40 7:28:23
Ringling 30 1 46N16'18 110w48'23 7:23:14
Ripley 27 9 48N23'05 115w27'04 7:41:48
Rising Sun 18 9 48N41'47 113w31'01 7:34:04
Riverdale 7 1 47N20'48 111w35'31 7:26:22
Riverside 33 1 46N25'54 108w34'19 7:14:17
Riverside 41 9 46N16'29 114w09'26 7:36:38
Riverside (The Barns) 16
1 44N39'35 111w04'15 7:24:17
Riverview 42 1 47N40'27 104w10'28 6:56:42
Rivulet 31 9 47N00 114w29 7:37:56
Roanwood 53 1 48N56'29 106w29'50 7:05:59
Robere 37 1 48N19'32 112w33'04 7:30:12
Roberts 5 1 45N21'35 109w10'01 7:16:40
Robinson 30 1 46N28'26 110w40'03 7:22:40
Rochester 29 1 45N36'46 112w30'18 7:30:01
Rock Crossing 46
1 48N29'33 104w20'49 6:57:23
Rocker 47 5 46N00'12 112w36'19 7:30:25
Rock Springs 44
1 46N49'01 106w14'47 7:04:59
Rockvale 5 1 45N31'21 108w51'40 7:15:27
Rocky Boy 21 1 48N15'22 109w47'15 7:19:09
Rocky Boys Indian Res 8
1 48N19 110w01 7:20:04
Rocky Crossing 8
1 48N15'58 110w04'09 7:20:17
Rodgers Hill 28
1 47N33'55 106w01'09 7:04:05
Rogers 7 1 47N32'36 110w59'44 7:23:59
Rollins 24 9 47N54'22 114w11'51 7:36:47
Ronan 24 9 47N31'44 114w06'02 7:36:24
Roosville 27 9 48N59'57 115w03'20 7:40:13
Roscoe 5 1 45N20'59 109w29'45 7:17:59
Rosebud 44 1 46N16'28 106w26'39 7:05:47
Rose Crossing 15
9 48N15'18 114w16'32 7:37:06
Ross Fork 14 1 47N04'38 109w41'32 7:18:46
Ross Hall 17 1 47N12'34 107w56'13 7:11:45
Round Butte 24 9 47N31'47 114w15'42 7:37:03
Round Prairie 15
9 48N24'04 114w25'51 7:37:43
Roundup 33 1 46N26'43 108w32'28 7:14:10
Rowley 2 1 45N43'35 107w46'29 7:11:06
Roy 14 1 47N19'53 108w57'33 7:15:50
Roy-Winifred Junction 14
1 47N05'20 109w26'02 7:17:44
Ruby 29 1 45N19'42 112w05'08 7:28:21
Rudyard 21 1 48N33'36 110w33'12 7:22:13
Rumsey 20 7 46N17'31 113w15'04 7:33:00
Ryegate 19 1 46N17'50 109w15'29 7:17:02
Saco 36 1 48N27'26 107w20'31 7:09:22
Sage Creek Colony 26
1 48N55'46 110w58'25 7:23:54
Saint Ignatius 24
9 47N19'12 114w05'35 7:36:22
Saint Johns 21 1 48N47'57 110w00'23 7:20:02
Saint Labre Mission 44
1 45N27 106w05 7:04:20
Saint Mary 18 9 48N44'38 113w25'43 7:33:43
Saint Peter 7 1 47N16 111w42 7:26:48
Saint Regis 31 9 47N17'58 115w06'06 7:40:24
Saint Xavier 2 1 45N27'40 107w43'16 7:10:53
Salem 7 1 47N32'14 111w02'22 7:24:09
Salmon Prairie 24
9 47N37'48 113w47'04 7:35:08
Saltese 31 9 47N24'37 115w30'31 7:42:02
Samples Crossing 14
1 47N16'25 109w43'10 7:18:53
Sand Coulee 7 1 47N23'58 111w10'01 7:24:40
Sand Creek 28 1 48N06 105w39 7:02:36
Sanders 52 1 46N17'29 107w05'46 7:08:23
Sand Springs 17
1 47N06'03 107w29'06 7:09:56
Santa Rita 18 1 48N42'02 112w19'09 7:29:17
Sapphire Village 23
1 46N53'21 110w15'02 7:21:00
Sappington 16 1 45N47'42 111w46'00 7:27:04
Sarpy 2 1 45N48 107w17 7:09:08
Saugus 40 1 46N41'30 105w29'30 7:01:58
Savage 42 1 47N27'13 104w20'32 6:57:22
Savoy 3 1 48N28'27 108w32'35 7:14:10
Sayle 38 1 45N13'37 105w59'42 7:03:59
Saypo 50 1 47N48'32 112w33'55 7:30:16
Schilling 32 9 46N57'51 114w12'03 7:36:48
Schley 32 9 47N06'12 114w03'11 7:36:13
Scholtztown 23 1 47N02'16 110w13'34 7:20:54
Schusters Place 29
1 44N52'27 111w32'40 7:26:11
Sciuchetti Place 47
10 45N56'35 112w46'21 7:31:05
Scobey 10 1 48N47'33 105w25'13 7:01:41
Seaver Park 25 1 46N35 112w02 7:28:08
Sedan 16 1 45N57'32 110w51'01 7:23:24
Seeley Lake 32 9 47N10'46 113w29'01 7:33:56
Selmes 5 1 45N23'31 109w07'53 7:16:32

Shambo Springs 21 1 48N17'35 109w39'54 7:18:40
Shawmut 54 1 46N20'33 109w31'27 7:18:06
Shaw Place 34 1 45N38'45 110w27'27 7:21:50
Shaws 29 1 45N39'46 111w46'43 7:27:07
Sheffels 7 1 47N35'41 111w08'58 7:24:36
Sheffield 9 1 46N19'58 106w08'20 7:04:33
Shelby 51 1 48N30'19 111w51'22 7:27:25
Shepherd 56 1 45N56'37 108w20'30 7:13:22
Shepherd Crossing 8 1 47N36'25 110w53'31 7:23:34
Sheridan 29 1 45N27'20 112w11'46 7:28:47
Sherry One 20 9 46N33'10 113w13'02 7:32:52
Shields 34 1 45N57'25 110w38'24 7:22:34
Shields Crossing 37 1 48N28'20 112w21'27 7:29:26
Shields Valley 34 1 45N55 110w39 7:22:36
Shirley 9 1 46N35'29 105w34'46 7:02:19
Shonkin 8 1 47N37'44 110w34'19 7:22:17
Sidney 42 1 47N43'00 104w09'21 6:56:37
Sieben 25 1 46N53'55 112w07'35 7:28:30
Silca 12 9 46N06'19 112w52'58 7:31:32
Silesia 5 1 45N33'24 108w50'27 7:15:22
Silver Bow 47 10 46N00'13 112w40'01 7:30:40
Silver Bow Park 47 5 46N00'02 112w29'47 7:29:59
Silver City 25 1 46N45'20 112w10'08 7:28:41
Silver Gate 34 1 45N00'25 109w59'20 7:19:57
Silver Star 29 1 45N41'25 112w16'56 7:29:08
Simms 7 1 47N29'30 111w55'38 7:27:43
Simpkins Place 5 1 45N18'48 109w24'26 7:17:38
Simpson 21 1 48N55'43 110w12'19 7:20:49
Sinclair 39 6 46N24 112w44 7:30:56
Singleshot 15 9 48N14'50 113w28'47 7:33:55
Sioux Crossing 49 1 45N52'17 110w14'37 7:20:58
Sioux Pass 42 1 47N55'21 104w19'31 6:57:18
Sipple 23 1 46N55'25 109w45'42 7:19:03
Sixmile Crossing 38 1 45N41'26 105w11'37 7:00:46
Sixteen 30 1 46N12'55 110w59'49 7:23:59
Siyeh Bend 18 9 48N42'06 113w40'00 7:34:40
Skones 47 5 45N57'48 112w27'41 7:29:51
Skyline 25 1 46N39'04 112w17'04 7:29:08
Slab Crossing 43 1 48N17'16 104w41'52 6:58:47
Slayton Junction 19 1 46N17'53 109w03'39 7:16:15
Sloan 45 9 47N29'34 114w19'42 7:37:19
Smelter Hill 7 1 47N32 111w17 7:25:08
Snider 45 9 47N36'14 115w13'03 7:40:52
Snowden 43 1 48N01'37 104w05'01 6:56:20
Snowslip 15 9 48N15'34 113w27'16 7:33:49
Sodak Mill 1 9 45N25'42 112w36'00 7:30:24
Soda Springs 56 1 45N33'56 108w16'18 7:13:05
Sohon 31 9 47N26'34 115w42'07 7:42:48
Somers 15 9 48N04'49 114w13'14 7:36:53
Sonnette 38 1 45N24'47 105w49'51 7:03:19
Soudan 32 9 47N01'35 114w24'00 7:37:36
Sourdough 49 1 45N54'07 109w48'49 7:19:15
South Butte 47 5 45N56 112w29 7:29:56
Southern Cross 12 2 46N08 112w57 7:31:48
South Fork 15 9 48N23 114w00 7:36:00
South Garfield 17 1 47N04 106w45 7:07:00
South of The Yellowstone 49 1 45N40 110w02 7:20:08
South Toole 51 1 48N30 111w45 7:27:00
South Treasure 52 1 46N05 107w09 7:08:36
South Yellowstone 56 1 45N43 108w29 7:13:56
Spear 2 1 45N11'59 107w22'43 7:09:31
Sperry Chalets 15 9 48N36'18 113w47'05 7:35:08
Sphinx 34 1 45N10'16 110w52'38 7:23:31
Spion Kop 23 1 47N17'06 110w36'59 7:22:28
Split Rock Junction 25 1 47N30'55 112w27'27 7:29:50
Spring Creek Colony 14 1 47N04 109w26 7:17:44
Spring Creek Junction 14 1 47N07'38 109w34'24 7:18:18
Springdale 34 1 45N44'18 110w13'35 7:20:54
Springdale Colony 30 1 46N27'43 111w00'56 7:24:04
Spring Gulch 31 9 47N13'49 114w58'47 7:39:55
Springhill 16 1 45N49'34 111w06'57 7:24:28
Springtime 48 1 45N41'54 109w23'12 7:17:33
Springtown 20 9 46N47'59 113w16'43 7:33:07
Sprole 43 1 48N06'26 105w03'46 7:00:15
Spurling 56 1 45N39'02 108w50'41 7:15:23
Square Butte 8 1 47N30'54 110w11'51 7:20:47
Stacey 38 1 45N43'12 105w53'26 7:03:34
Staley Place 30 1 46N14'37 110w39'21 7:22:37
Stanford 23 1 47N09'13 110w13'03 7:20:52
Stark 32 9 47N07'32 114w30'15 7:38:01
Starr School 18 9 48N35'21 113w08'23 7:32:34
State Capitol 25 1 46N35 112w02 7:28:08
Staton 12 9 46N05'24 112w52'26 7:31:30
Stemple 25 1 46N49 112w16 7:29:04
Sterling 29 1 45N33'55 111w45'31 7:27:02
Stevensville 41 9 46N30'36 114w05'32 7:36:22
Steves Fork 17 1 47N16'23 107w20'11 7:09:21
Stipek 11 1 47N12'44 104w39'52 6:58:39
Stockett 7 1 47N21'24 111w09'52 7:24:39
Stone 20 9 46N30'19 113w13'31 7:32:54
Stonehill 27 9 48N44'46 115w17'58 7:41:12
Stoner Place 25 1 47N30'52 112w43'45 7:30:55
Story 16 4 45N43'37 111w04'53 7:24:20
Stranahan 8 1 47N59'44 110w19'14 7:21:17
Straw 14 1 46N49 109w50 7:19:20
Stryker 27 9 48N40'27 114w46'09 7:39:05
Stuart 12 9 46N05'09 112w47'49 7:31:11
Stump Town 12 9 46N09'03 113w02'24 7:32:10
Suffolk 14 1 47N28'01 109w21'18 7:17:25
Sula 41 9 45N50'12 113w58'51 7:35:55
Sumatra 44 1 46N37'06 107w33'02 7:10:12
Summit 18 9 48N19'10 113w21'09 7:33:25
Summit 29 1 45N13'08 111w55'48 7:27:43
Summit Valley 29 1 45N46'14 111w53'30 7:27:34
Sumner 36 1 48N46'47 108w06'13 7:12:25
Sunburst 51 1 48N52'58 111w54'38 7:27:39
Sundance 18 1 48N38'02 112w31'58 7:30:08
Sunlight 22 1 45N54'00 112w01'00 7:28:04
Sunnyside 12 2 46N06'56 112w59'34 7:31:58
Sun Prairie 36 1 47N50'44 107w44'45 7:10:59
Sun River 7 1 47N32'00 111w43'14 7:26:53
Sunset 32 9 46N56'17 113w27'57 7:33:52
Superior 31 9 47N11'30 114w53'27 7:39:34
Swan Lake 24 9 47N55'45 113w50'38 7:35:23
Sweetgrass 51 1 48N59'46 111w57'35 7:27:50
Swiftcurrent 18 9 48N47'51 113w40'05 7:34:40
Sylvanite 27 9 48N42'59 115w52'24 7:43:30
Taft 31 9 47N25'09 115w35'50 7:42:23
Talc 45 9 47N43'13 115w26'04 7:41:44
Tampico 53 1 48N18'17 106w49'35 7:07:18
Tarkio 31 9 47N01'17 114w44'17 7:38:57
Tate Place 29 1 45N03'14 112w00'58 7:28:04
Tattnall 36 1 48N37'38 107w32'32 7:10:10
Teigen 35 1 47N02'12 108w35'46 7:14:23
Terminal Annex 56 3 45N47 108w30 7:14:00
Terry 40 1 46N47'35 105w18'42 7:01:15
Thebes 44 1 46N31'45 107w14'43 7:08:59
Theony 53 1 48N52'37 106w55'01 7:07:40
The Pines 45 9 47N28 114w53 7:39:32
Thompson Falls 45 9 47N35'50 115w20'36 7:41:22
Three Forks 7 1 47N16'54 111w05'22 7:24:21
Three Forks 15 9 48N06'49 113w18'28 7:33:14
Three Forks 16 1 45N53'33 111w33'05 7:26:12
Three Forks Junction 4 1 45N53'55 111w35'56 7:26:24
Thurlow 44 1 46N17'16 106w18'20 7:05:13
Tiber 26 1 48N30'32 111w04'48 7:24:19
Tiber Dam Camp 26 1 48N18'37 111w05'12 7:24:21
Tippet Place 22 1 45N55'33 112w10'56 7:28:44
Tobacco 27 9 48N49'52 114w58'34 7:39:54
Tobin 25 1 46N38'17 112w06'13 7:28:25
Toluca 2 1 45N44'50 107w52'17 7:11:29
Toole 31 9 47N19'34 115w01'19 7:40:05
Top O'Deep 20 9 46N49'28 113w15'30 7:33:02
Toston 4 1 46N10'22 111w26'25 7:25:46
Townsend 4 1 46N19'09 111w31'12 7:26:05
Tracy 7 1 47N24'47 111w09'12 7:24:37
Trailcreek 15 9 48N55'09 114w24'23 7:37:38
Trask 22 5 46N06'10 112w24'59 7:29:40
Trego 27 9 48N42'19 114w52'06 7:39:28
Trident 16 1 45N56'51 111w28'33 7:25:54
Trout Creek 45 9 47N50'13 115w35'50 7:42:23
Troy 27 9 48N27'48 115w53'19 7:43:33
Truchot Hill 50 1 47N50'11 112w11'29 7:28:46
Truly 7 1 47N21'21 111w26'26 7:25:46
Tucker 41 9 46N22'15 114w08'30 7:36:34
Tunis 8 1 47N48'25 110w50'31 7:23:22
Turah 32 9 46N50'10 113w49'45 7:35:19
Turner 3 1 48N50'37 108w24'23 7:13:38
Tuscor 45 9 47N54'12 115w41'24 7:42:46
Tusler 9 1 46N30'21 105w43'31 7:02:54
Twin Bridges 29 1 45N32'40 112w19'49 7:29:19
Twin Creeks 32 9 46N54'46 113w42'47 7:34:51
Twodot 54 1 46N25'28 110w04'20 7:20:17
Tyman Place 30 1 46N13'18 110w38'19 7:22:33
Ulm 7 1 47N25'50 111w30'23 7:26:02
Ulmer 9 1 46N21'16 105w55'44 7:03:43
Unionville 25 1 46N32'29 112w05'03 7:28:20
University Heights 41 9 46N02'01 114w12'53 7:36:52
Upper Ellis Place 25 1 47N18'55 112w20'14 7:29:21
Upper Yellowstone Valley 34 1 45N31 110w36 7:22:24
Ural 27 9 48N36'35 115w15'12 7:41:01
Urback Place 34 1 45N40'28 110w27'03 7:21:48
Utica 23 1 46N58'06 110w05'30 7:20:22
Valentine 14 1 47N18'42 108w25'17 7:13:41
Valier 37 1 48N18'28 112w14'56 7:29:00
Valleytown 36 1 48N42'20 107w14'21 7:08:57
Vananda 44 1 46N23'31 107w00'06 7:08:00
Vandalia 53 1 48N21'17 106w54'33 7:07:38
Van Norman 17 1 47N21 106w23 7:05:32
Varney 29 1 45N13'57 111w45'39 7:27:03
Vaughn 7 1 47N33'38 111w32'42 7:26:11
Vendome 22 1 45N49'04 112w14'30 7:28:58
Verona 8 1 48N07'22 110w11'22 7:20:45
Victor 41 9 46N25'00 114w08'57 7:36:36
Victor Crossing 41 9 46N24'52 114w07'13 7:36:29
Vida 28 1 47N49'55 105w29'33 7:01:58
Vincent 16 1 45N41'45 111w21'33 7:25:26
Virden 51 1 48N31'28 111w54'25 7:27:38
Virgelle 8 1 48N00'55 110w14'59 7:21:00
Virginia City 29 1 45N17'38 111w56'43 7:27:47
Vista 15 9 48N27'48 114w23'37 7:37:34
Volborg 9 1 45N50'34 105w40'50 7:02:43
Volcour 27 9 48N32'55 115w13'00 7:40:52
Volt 43 1 48N06 105w39 7:02:36
Waco 56 1 46N04'26 107w42'23 7:10:50
Wade 5 1 45N09'31 108w49'07 7:15:16
Wagner 36 1 48N22'14 108w04'37 7:12:18
Walkerville 47 5 46N02'03 112w32'06 7:30:08
Wall City 39 9 46N32'38 112w56'16 7:31:45
Waltham 8 1 47N34'11 110w53'24 7:23:34
Wan-i-gan 34 1 45N25 110w38 7:22:32
Ward 41 9 46N09'13 114w10'41 7:36:43
Ware 14 1 47N11'04 109w40'02 7:18:40
Warland 27 9 48N30'03 115w17'11 7:41:09
Warm Spring Creek 36 1 48N08 108w12 7:12:48
Warm Springs 12 8 46N10'53 112w47'02 7:31:08
Warren 5 1 45N03'36 108w39'28 7:14:38
Warrick 8 1 48N04'18 109w36'19 7:18:25
Washoe 5 1 45N09'50 109w12'45 7:16:51
Waterloo 29 1 45N43'19 112w11'29 7:28:46
Watkins 28 1 47N14'34 105w52'22 7:03:29
Watkins 29 1 45N25'18 111w39'25 7:26:38
Watson 30 1 46N40'09 111w22'06 7:25:28
Wayne 7 1 47N26'31 110w57'30 7:23:50
Webster 13 1 46N22 104w16 6:57:04
Weed 25 1 46N38'56 112w15'15 7:29:01
Weeksville 45 9 47N31'23 114w59'35 7:39:58
Welch 22 5 45N55'52 112w18'51 7:29:15
Weldon 28 1 47N25 105w35 7:02:20
Westby 46 1 48N52'13 104w03'05 6:56:12
West End 16 4 45N39'57 110w49'29 7:23:18
West End 31 9 47N19 115w10 7:40:40
Westfall 31 9 47N07'16 114w47'13 7:39:09
West Fork 10 1 48N41'13 105w54'40 7:03:39
West Gallatin 16 1 45N42'10 111w13'05 7:24:52
West Glacier 15 9 48N30'00 113w58'40 7:35:55
Westlake 16 1 45N43'46 111w20'24 7:25:22
West Lewistown 14 1 47N05'54 109w27'51 7:17:51
Westmore 13 1 46N28'27 104w38'40 6:58:35
West Park Plaza 56 3 45N47 108w34 7:14:16
West Riverside 32 9 46N52'38 113w53'20 7:35:33
West Shore 24 9 47N51 114w21 7:37:24
West Valley 12 9 46N09'07 113w01'18 7:32:05
West Yellowstone 16 1 44N39'44 111w06'12 7:24:25
Wetzel 18 9 48N45'12 113w09'50 7:32:39
Whately 53 1 48N09'46 106w30'39 7:06:03
Wheeler 53 1 48N00'34 106w30'20 7:06:01
White 16 1 45N48'39 111w19'22 7:25:17
White City 34 1 45N18'14 110w41'08 7:22:45
Whitefish 15 9 48N24'40 114w20'12 7:37:21
Whitefish Lake 15 9 48N24 114w25 7:37:40
Whitehall 22 1 45N52'15 112w05'48 7:28:23
White Haven 27 9 48N20'42 115w30'59 7:42:04
White Pine 45 9 47N44'37 115w28'53 7:41:56
Whites City 4 1 46N38'03 111w26'32 7:25:46
White Sulphur Springs 30 1 46N32'54 110w54'05 7:23:36
Whitetail 10 1 48N53'42 105w09'46 7:00:39
Whitewater 36 1 48N45'34 107w37'37 7:10:30
Whitlash 26 1 48N54'30 111w15'08 7:25:01
Wibaux 55 1 46N59'06 104w11'16 6:56:45
Wickes 22 1 46N20'59 112w06'09 7:28:25
Wilborn 25 1 46N53'01 112w20'32 7:29:22
Willard 13 1 46N11'38 104w22'10 6:57:29
Williams 37 1 48N16'31 112w07'46 7:28:31
Williamsburg 47 5 45N59'31 112w33'23 7:30:14
Willow Creek 16 1 45N49'31 111w38'38 7:26:35
Willow Crossing 38 1 45N31'38 106w11'13 7:04:45
Wilsall 34 1 45N59'38 110w39'34 7:22:38
Windham 23 1 47N04'43 110w08'23 7:20:34
Winifred 14 1 47N33'28 109w22'27 7:17:30
Winnett 35 1 47N00'10 108w21'05 7:13:24
Winston 4 1 46N28'36 111w39'29 7:26:38
Wisdom 1 9 45N37'05 113w27'00 7:33:48
Wise River 1 9 45N47'29 112w56'55 7:31:48
Wisner Crossing 16 4 45N46'37 111w04'53 7:24:20
Wolf Creek 25 1 47N00'22 112w04'06 7:28:16
Wolf Point 43 1 48N05'26 105w38'24 7:02:34
Woodin 47 10 45N48'41 112w42'29 7:30:50
Wood Place 44 1 45N43'22 106w25'25 7:05:42
Woods Bay 24 9 48N00'06 114w02'58 7:36:12
Woods Crossing 8 1 47N52'40 111w16'02 7:25:04
Woodside 41 9 46N18'48 114w09'15 7:36:37
Woodside Crossing 41 9 46N18'46 114w08'39 7:36:35
Woods Place 34 1 45N41'39 110w15'38 7:21:03
Woods Place 35 1 47N30'09 108w08'42 7:12:35
Woodville 12 5 46N03'08 112w26'43 7:29:47
Woodward Place 29 1 45N07'58 111w45'46 7:27:03
Woodworth 39 9 47N06'23 113w18'06 7:33:12
Wooley 42 1 47N45'54 104w06'19 6:56:25
Worden 56 1 45N57'36 108w09'37 7:12:38
Wurtz Hill 15 9 48N54'14 114w23'22 7:37:33
Wyola 2 1 45N07'46 107w23'33 7:09:34
X Crossing 36 1 47N42'12 107w46'55 7:11:08
Yaak 27 9 48N49'59 115w42'28 7:42:50
Yakt 27 9 48N32'44 115w58'04 7:43:52
Yarnell 27 9 48N28'15 115w17'29 7:41:10
Yates 55 1 46N57'04 104w07'48 6:56:31
Yegen 56 3 45N43'25 108w37'19 7:14:29
Yellowtail 2 1 45N44 107w37 7:10:28
Yogo Crossing 23 1 46N51'20 110w18'57 7:21:16
York 25 1 46N43'18 111w45'04 7:27:00
Yreka 32 9 46N51'41 113w19'48 7:33:19
Zero 40 1 46N40'09 105w29'17 7:01:57
Zortman 36 1 47N55'04 108w31'32 7:14:06
Zurich 3 1 48N35'04 109w01'47 7:16:07

TIME TABLES

NE # 1

Before 11/18/1883		LMT
11/18/1883	12:00	CST
3/31/1918	02:00	CWT
10/27/1918	02:00	CST
3/30/1919	02:00	CWT
10/26/1919	02:00	CST
2/09/1942	02:00	CWT
9/30/1945	02:00	CST
4/30/1967	02:00	US#1

NE # 2

Before 11/18/1883		LMT
11/18/1883	12:00	MST
3/31/1918	02:00	MWT
10/27/1918	02:00	MST
3/30/1919	02:00	MWT
10/26/1919	02:00	MST
2/09/1942	02:00	MWT
9/30/1945	02:00	MST
4/30/1967	02:00	US#1

NE # 3

Before 11/18/1883		LMT
11/18/1883	12:00	MST
3/31/1918	02:00	MWT
10/27/1918	02:00	MST
3/30/1919	02:00	MWT
10/26/1919	02:00	MST
2/09/1942	02:00	MWT
9/30/1945	02:00	MST
4/30/1967	02:00	MDT
10/29/1967	02:00	MST
1/01/1968	02:00	CST
4/28/1968	02:00	CDT
4/28/1968	02:00	US#1

NE # 4

Before 11/18/1883		LMT
11/18/1883	12:00	MST
3/31/1918	02:00	MWT
10/27/1918	02:00	MST
3/30/1919	02:00	MWT
10/26/1919	02:00	MST
2/09/1942	02:00	MWT
9/30/1945	02:00	MST
1/01/1955	00:00	MDT
12/31/1955	24:00	MST
4/29/1956	02:00	MDT
9/29/1956	02:00	MST
4/30/1967	02:00	MDT
10/29/1967	02:00	MST
1/01/1968	02:00	CST
4/28/1968	02:00	CDT
4/28/1968	02:00	US#1

NE # 5

Before 11/18/1883		LMT
11/18/1883	12:00	MST
3/31/1918	02:00	MWT
10/27/1918	02:00	MST
3/30/1919	02:00	MWT
10/26/1919	02:00	MST
2/09/1942	02:00	MWT
9/30/1945	02:00	MST
4/30/1967	02:00	MDT
10/29/1967	02:00	MST
4/28/1968	02:00	MDT
10/27/1968	02:00	MST
4/27/1969	02:00	MDT
6/29/1969	02:00	CDT
10/26/1969	02:00	CST
10/26/1969	02:00	US#1

NE # 6

Before 11/18/1883		LMT
11/18/1883	12:00	MST
3/31/1918	02:00	MWT
10/27/1918	02:00	MST
3/30/1919	02:00	MWT
10/26/1919	02:00	MST
2/09/1942	02:00	MWT
9/30/1945	02:00	MST
1/01/1955	00:00	MDT
12/31/1955	24:00	MST
4/29/1956	02:00	MDT
9/29/1956	02:00	MST
4/30/1967	02:00	MDT
10/29/1967	02:00	MST
4/28/1968	02:00	MDT
10/27/1968	02:00	MST
4/27/1969	02:00	MDT
6/29/1969	02:00	CDT
10/26/1969	02:00	CST
10/26/1969	02:00	US#1

COUNTIES

1 Adams
2 Antelope
3 Arthur
4 Banner
5 Blaine
6 Boone
7 Box Butte
8 Boyd
9 Brown
10 Buffalo
11 Burt
12 Butler
13 Cass
14 Cedar
15 Chase
16 Cherry
17 Cheyenne
18 Clay
19 Colfax
20 Cuming
21 Custer
22 Dakota
23 Dawes
24 Dawson
25 Deuel
26 Dixon
27 Dodge
28 Douglas
29 Dundy
30 Fillmore
31 Franklin
32 Frontier
33 Furnas
34 Gage
35 Garden
36 Garfield
37 Gosper
38 Grant
39 Greeley
40 Hall
41 Hamilton
42 Harlan
43 Hayes
44 Hitchcock
45 Holt
46 Hooker
47 Howard
48 Jefferson
49 Johnson
50 Kearney
51 Keith
52 Keya Paha
53 Kimball
54 Knox
55 Lancaster
56 Lincoln
57 Logan
58 Loup
59 McPherson
60 Madison
61 Merrick
62 Morrill
63 Nance
64 Nemaha
65 Nuckolls
66 Otoe
67 Pawnee
68 Perkins
69 Phelps
70 Pierce
71 Platte
72 Polk
73 Red Willow
74 Richardson
75 Rock
76 Saline
77 Sarpy
78 Saunders
79 Scotts Bluff
80 Seward
81 Sheridan
82 Sherman
83 Sioux
84 Stanton
85 Thayer
86 Thomas
87 Thurston
88 Valley
89 Washington
90 Wayne
91 Webster
92 Wheeler
93 York

Place	Table	Latitude	Longitude	Time
Abbott 40	1	40N58'29	98w28'52	6:33:55
Abby 46	2	41N52	101w16	6:45:04
Abel 78	1	41N04'27	96w21'18	6:25:25
Abie 12	1	41N20'03	96w56'55	6:27:48
Adams 34	1	40N27'34	96w30'35	6:26:02
Addison 54	1	42N45	97w40	6:30:40
Agate 83	2	42N25	103w48	6:55:12
Agnew 55	1	41N01'01	96w48'52	6:27:15
Ainsworth 9	4	42N33'00	99w51'44	6:39:27
Air Park West 55	1	40N51	96w47	6:27:08
Akron 6	1	41N44'29	98w14'31	6:32:58
Alban 65	1	40N08	98w13	6:32:52
Albany 42	1	40N18	99w28	6:37:52
Albion 6	1	41N41'27	98w00'12	6:32:01
Alda 40	1	40N52'16	98w28'04	6:33:52
Alden 62	2	41N33'41	103w02'09	6:52:09
Alexandria 85	1	40N14'43	97w23'20	6:29:33
Alexis 12	1	41N21	97w19	6:29:16
Alfalfa Center 10	1	40N41'32	99w10'44	6:36:43
Algernon 21	1	41N14	99w19	6:37:16
Alkali 35	2	41N51	102w22	6:49:28
Allen 26	1	42N24'59	96w50'42	6:27:23
Alliance 7	2	42N06	102w52	6:51:28
Allston 29	2	40N11	101w43	6:46:52
Alma 42	1	40N05'51	99w21'42	6:37:27
Almeria 58	1	41N49'33	99w31'18	6:38:05
Aloys 20	1	41N49'46	96w54'11	6:27:37
Altona 90	1	42N06'18	96w59'31	6:27:58
Alvo 13	1	40N52'19	96w23'14	6:25:33
Amboy 91	1	40N05'25	98w26'18	6:33:45
Amelia 45	1	42N14'08	98w54'42	6:35:39
Ames 27	1	41N27'13	96w37'33	6:26:30
Amherst 10	1	40N46'08	99w16'10	6:37:05
Anan 18	1	40N28'00	98w11'02	6:32:44
Andrews 83	2	42N37'53	103w44'00	6:54:56
Angora 62	2	41N51'07	103w07'29	6:52:30
Angus 65	1	40N16'56	97w58'45	6:31:55
Anncar 45	1	42N48'26	98w44'35	6:34:58
Anoka 8	1	42N56'49	98w49'50	6:35:19
Anselmo 21	3	41N37'07	99w51'53	6:39:28
Ansley 21	1	41N17'16	99w22'53	6:37:32
Antioch 81	2	42N04	102w35	6:50:20
Arabia 16	5	42N43'52	100w22'20	6:41:29
Arago 74	1	40N08	95w30	6:22:00
Arapahoe 33	1	40N18'15	99w54'00	6:39:36
Arbor 55	1	40N53'44	96w40'22	6:26:41
Arborville 93	1	41N01'22	97w46'27	6:31:06
Arcadia 88	1	41N25'24	99w07'33	6:36:30
Archer 61	1	41N09'55	98w08'08	6:32:33
Arizona 11	1	41N48'52	96w08'00	6:24:32
Arlington 89	1	41N27'09	96w21'03	6:25:24
Armada 10	1	40N55	99w22	6:37:28
Arnold 21	1	41N25'21	100w11'35	6:40:46
Arthur 3	2	41N34'18	101w41'28	6:46:46
Ashby 38	2	42N01'19	101w55'38	6:47:43
Ash Grove 31	1	40N14	99w07	6:36:28
Ashland 78	1	41N02'21	96w22'05	6:25:28
Ashton 82	1	41N14'53	98w47'38	6:35:11
Assumption 1	1	40N30'36	98w34'19	6:34:17
Aten 14	1	42N50'24	97w26'26	6:29:46
Atkins 62	2	41N43'26	103w12'53	6:52:52
Atkinson 45	1	42N31'53	98w58'40	6:35:55
Atlanta 69	1	40N22'00	99w28'22	6:37:53
Auburn 64	1	40N23'34	95w50'19	6:23:21
Aurora 41	1	40N52'02	98w00'14	6:32:01
Autumn Hills 28	1	41N18	96w02	6:24:08
Avery 77	1	41N09'49	95w55'20	6:23:41
Avoca 13	1	40N47'46	96w07'02	6:24:28
Axtell 50	1	40N28'42	99w07'35	6:36:30
Ayr 1	1	40N26'15	98w26'24	6:33:46
Ayr Junction 1	1	40N27'28	98w25'53	6:33:44
Badger 34	1	40N05'18	96w35'43	6:26:23
Baker 93	1	40N50	97w39	6:30:36
Bancroft 20	1	42N00'46	96w34'21	6:26:17
Barada 74	1	40N13'07	95w34'39	6:22:19
Barley 16	2	42N41	101w22	6:45:28
Barneston 34	1	40N02'54	96w34'36	6:26:18
Bartlett 92	1	41N53'07	98w33'07	6:34:12
Bartley 73	1	40N14'57	100w18'42	6:41:15
Barton 25	2	41N02'02	102w10'26	6:48:42
Basin 8	1	42N57	99w08	6:36:32
Bassett 75	1	42N35'09	99w32'15	6:38:09
Batin 91	1	40N13	98w33	6:34:12
Battle Creek 60	1	41N59'58	97w35'53	6:30:24
Baxter 79	2	41N51'34	103w28'16	6:53:53
Bayard 62	2	41N45'18	103w19'25	6:53:18
Bayonne 16	2	42N47'08	101w58'38	6:47:55
Bazile 2	1	42N24	97w54	6:31:36
Bazile Mills 54	1	42N30'46	97w54'17	6:31:37
Beacon View 77	1	41N04'02	96w19'34	6:25:18
Beatrice 34	1	40N16'05	96w44'48	6:26:59
Beaver City 33	3	40N08'15	99w49'45	6:39:19
Beaver Creek 91	1	40N08	98w20	6:33:20
Beaver Crossing 80	1	40N46'43	97w16'55	6:29:08
Beck 56	1	41N08'17	100w41'36	6:42:46
Bedford 64	1	40N19	95w51	6:23:24
Bee 80	1	41N00'23	97w03'25	6:28:14
Beechwood 28	1	41N19'25	95w56'32	6:23:46
Beemer 20	1	41N55'48	96w48'41	6:27:15
Belden 14	1	42N24'47	97w12'23	6:28:50
Belfast 39	1	41N38'15	98w36'59	6:34:28
Belgrade 63	1	41N28'23	98w04'05	6:32:16
Bell Creek 11	1	41N52	96w24	6:25:36
Belle 45	1	42N39	98w50	6:35:20
Belle Prairie 30	1	40N24	97w32	6:30:08
Bellevue 77	1	41N08'12	95w53'26	6:23:34
Bellwood 12	1	41N20'34	97w14'17	6:28:57
Belmar 51	2	41N17'56	101w54'58	6:47:40
Belmont 23	2	42N32'59	103w21'22	6:53:25
Belmont 66	1	40N39	95w57	6:23:48
Belvidere 85	1	40N15'07	97w33'27	6:30:14
Benedict 93	1	41N00'21	97w36'22	6:30:25
Benkelman 29	2	40N02'57	101w31'57	6:46:08
Bennet 55	1	40N40'48	96w30'22	6:26:01
Bennett 30	1	40N34	97w47	6:31:08
Bennington 28	1	41N21'53	96w09'27	6:24:38
Benson 28	1	41N18	96w01	6:24:04
Benton 64	1	40N18	95w59	6:23:56
Berea 7	2	42N12'51	102w58'47	6:51:55
Berks 76	1	40N39'31	96w54'48	6:27:39
Berlin 66	1	40N45	96w04	6:24:16
Bertha 11	1	41N53'13	96w20'49	6:25:23
Bertrand 69	1	40N31'36	99w38'00	6:38:32
Berwyn 21	1	41N21'04	99w29'57	6:38:00
Bethany 55	1	40N49'57	96w37'59	6:26:32
Beverly 44	3	40N16'51	100w58'25	6:43:54
Big Blue 76	1	40N34	96w58	6:27:52
Bignell 56	1	41N03'48	100w36'38	6:42:27
Big Springs 25	2	41N03'41	102w04'26	6:48:18
Bingham 81	2	42N01'16	102w05'17	6:48:21
Birdwood 56	3	41N09'13	100w53'04	6:43:32
Bismarck 20	1	41N52	96w57	6:27:48
Bismark 71	1	41N31	97w18	6:29:12
Bixby 30	1	40N39'18	97w47'08	6:31:09
Blackbird 87	1	42N08	96w22	6:25:28
Bladen 91	1	40N19'20	98w35'40	6:34:23
Blaine 1	1	40N36'42	98w20'00	6:33:20
Blair 89	1	41N32'40	96w07'29	6:24:30
Blakely 34	1	40N18	96w52	6:27:28
Bloomfield 54	1	42N35'56	97w38'43	6:30:35
Bloomington 31	1	40N05'39	99w02'12	6:36:09
Blue Creek 35	2	41N32	102w06	6:48:24
Blue Hill 91	1	40N19'57	98w26'54	6:33:48
Blue River Lodge 76	1	40N37	96w57	6:27:48
Blue Springs 34	1	40N08'22	96w39'32	6:26:38
Bluff 41	1	41N05	97w53	6:31:32
Boelus 47	1	41N04'26	98w42'55	6:34:52
Bonanza 6	1	41N45	98w14	6:32:56
Bondville 73	3	40N08	100w29	6:41:56
Bone Creek 12	1	41N21	97w05	6:28:20
Bonner 62	2	41N56'23	103w01'12	6:52:05
Bookwalter 67	1	40N03'42	96w22'09	6:25:29
Boone 6	1	41N37'35	97w55'02	6:31:40
Bordeaux 23	2	42N46'05	102w48'49	6:51:15
Bostwick 65	1	40N02'54	98w11'02	6:32:44
Bowen 83	2	42N39	103w57	6:55:48
Bow Valley 14	1	42N42'53	97w14'57	6:29:00
Bow Valley Mills 14	1	42N45'42	97w10'00	6:28:40
Box Butte 7	2	42N16	102w51	6:51:24
Box Elder 56	1	40N54	100w36	6:42:24
Boys Town 28	1	41N15'40	96w07'54	6:24:32
Brace 37	1	40N39	99w55	6:39:40
Braden 3	2	41N30	101w52	6:47:28
Bradley 79	2	41N46'13	103w22'54	6:53:32
Bradshaw 93	1	40N53'02	97w44'48	6:30:59
Brady 56	1	41N01'20	100w22'02	6:41:28
Brainard 12	1	41N11'02	97w00'13	6:28:01
Branard 12	1	41N10'52	96w59'50	6:27:59
Brandon 68	2	40N48'12	101w54'43	6:47:39
Brayton 39	1	41N27'48	98w28'38	6:33:55
Brenna 90	1	42N08	97w04	6:28:16
Breslau 70	1	42N21'01	97w41'55	6:30:48
Brewster 5	3	41N56'20	99w51'52	6:39:27
Bridgeport 62	2	41N39'55	103w05'55	6:52:24
Briggs 28	1	41N21'01	96w00'27	6:24:02
Brinkerhoff 75	1	42N41	99w38	6:38:32
Bristol 82	1	41N05	98w52	6:35:28
Bristow 8	1	42N50'31	98w35'04	6:34:20
Broadwater 62	2	41N35'46	102w51'08	6:51:25
Brock 64	1	40N28'48	95w57'33	6:23:50
Brocksburg 52	1	42N55'49	99w19'55	6:37:20
Broganville 51	2	41N12'26	101w30'58	6:46:04
Broken Bow 21	1	41N24'07	99w38'20	6:38:33
Brown 93	1	40N50	97w46	6:31:04
Brownlee 16	5	42N17'17	100w37'31	6:42:30
Brownson 17	2	41N11'15	103w06'45	6:52:27
Brownville 64	1	40N23'52	95w39'28	6:22:38
Brule 51	2	41N05'39	101w53'15	6:47:33
Bruning 85	1	40N20'10	97w33'56	6:30:16
Bruno 12	1	41N17'02	96w57'30	6:27:50
Brunswick 2	1	42N20'16	97w58'13	6:31:53
Brush Creek 76	1	40N29	97w05	6:28:20
Bryant 30	1	40N24	97w46	6:31:04
Buchanan 56	1	40N45	100w37	6:42:28
Buckeye 21	1	41N11'26	99w34'05	6:38:16
Buckley 48	1	40N04	97w18	6:29:12
Bucktail 3	3	41N34	101w26	6:45:44
Buda 10	1	40N42'51	98w59'37	6:35:58
Buda 55	1	40N34	96w45	6:27:00

Buffalo 24 1 40N59'21 99w50'06 6:39:20
Bunker Hill 17 2 41N17 103w07 6:52:28
Burchard 67 1 40N08'51 96w21'00 6:25:24
Burge 16 5 42N44'30 100w48'31 6:43:14
Burnett 2 1 42N03 97w53 6:31:32
Burr 66 1 40N32'08 96w17'59 6:25:12
Burress 30 1 40N34'53 97w30'05 6:30:00
Burr Oak 21 1 41N07'32 99w33'33 6:38:14
Burrows 71 1 41N37 97w32 6:30:08
Burt 57 3 41N39 100w20 6:41:20
Burton 52 1 42N54'42 99w35'29 6:38:22
Burtons Bend 33
1 40N19 100w01 6:40:04
Burwell 36 1 41N46'54 99w07'58 6:36:32
Bush 8 1 42N51 98w23 6:33:32
Bushnell 53 2 41N13'56 103w53'29 6:55:34
Bussell 15 2 40N27 101w51 6:47:24
Butler 71 1 41N23 97w28 6:29:52
Butte 8 1 42N54'41 98w50'56 6:35:24
Butterfly 84 1 41N52 97w12 6:28:48
Byron 85 1 40N00'14 97w46'07 6:31:04
Cadams 65 1 40N06'14 98w00'35 6:32:02
Cairo 40 1 41N00'04 98w36'26 6:34:26
Calamus 9 3 42N11 99w45 6:39:00
Caldwell 92 1 41N57 98w22 6:33:28
Calf Creek 16 2 42N11 101w22 6:45:28
Callaway 21 1 41N17'31 99w55'20 6:39:41
Calora 3 3 41N38'25 101w26'50 6:45:47
Calvert 29 2 40N18 101w23 6:45:32
Cambridge 33 1 40N16'55 100w09'55 6:40:40
Cameron 40 1 40N55'02 98w38'06 6:34:32
Campbell 91 1 40N17'54 98w43'54 6:34:56
Camp Clark 62 2 41N42 103w05 6:52:20
Canada 72 1 41N13 97w26 6:29:44
Canby 15 2 40N35 101w44 6:46:56
Capehart 77 1 41N07'33 95w57'24 6:23:50
Carleton 85 1 40N18'02 97w40'42 6:30:43
Carlisle 30 1 40N21'02 97w45'53 6:31:04
Carlson 79 2 41N52'23 103w30'52 6:54:03
Carns 52 1 42N44'05 99w28'55 6:37:56
Carroll 90 1 42N16'34 97w11'20 6:28:45
Cascade 16 3 42N10'53 100w23'07 6:41:32
Castle Rock 79 2 41N45 103w29 6:53:56
Catalpa 45 1 42N46'34 98w52'06 6:35:28
Catherton 91 1 40N13 98w40 6:34:40
Cedar Bluffs 78
1 41N23'49 96w36'40 6:26:27
Cedar Creek 13 1 41N02'12 96w05'57 6:24:24
Cedar Rapids 6 1 41N34 98w09 6:32:36
Center 54 1 42N36'34 97w52'35 6:31:30
Centerville 55 1 40N39'14 96w44'34 6:26:58
Central City 61
1 41N06'57 98w00'05 6:32:00
Ceresco 78 1 41N03'26 96w38'40 6:26:35
Chadron 23 2 42N49'46 103w00'00 6:52:00
Chalco 77 1 41N11'02 96w09'00 6:24:36
Chambers 45 1 42N12'18 98w44'55 6:35:00
Champion 15 2 40N28'09 101w44'53 6:47:00
Chapin 90 1 42N13 97w12 6:28:48
Chapman 61 1 41N01'27 98w09'32 6:32:38
Chappell 25 2 41N05'34 102w28'13 6:49:53
Chase 15 2 40N34 101w49 6:47:16
Chelsea 30 1 40N29 97w32 6:30:08
Cheney 55 1 40N43'32 96w35'45 6:26:23
Cherry Creek 10
1 41N00 98w47 6:35:08
Chester 85 1 40N00'37 97w37'05 6:30:28
Chicago 28 1 41N15 96w14 6:24:56
Clark 26 1 42N29 96w57 6:27:48
Clarks 61 1 41N12'55 97w50'08 6:31:21
Clarkson 19 1 41N43'36 97w07'19 6:28:29
Clatonia 34 1 40N27'55 96w50'58 6:27:24
Clay Center 18 1 40N31'18 98w03'18 6:32:13
Clearwater 2 1 42N10'12 98w11'17 6:32:45
Cliff 21 3 41N30 99w59 6:39:56
Clinton 81 2 42N45'36 102w20'56 6:49:24
Closter 6 1 41N53'13 97w53'20 6:31:33
Clover Valley 70
1 42N13 97w40 6:30:40
Clyde 69 1 40N24'48 99w25'04 6:37:40
Cody 16 2 42N56'09 101w14'39 6:44:59
Cody Lake 57 3 41N39 100w29 6:41:56
Coker 56 3 41N11'02 101w07'00 6:44:28
Coleman 45 1 42N45 98w44 6:34:56
Coleridge 14 1 42N30'22 97w12'12 6:28:49
Colfax 19 1 41N32 96w58 6:27:52
College View 55
1 40N46'20 96w39'07 6:26:36
Collins 10 1 40N41 99w08 6:36:32
Colon 78 1 41N17'51 96w36'20 6:26:25
Colton 17 2 41N09'12 102w51'24 6:51:26
Columbia 54 1 42N29 97w40 6:30:40
Columbus 71 1 41N25'47 97w22'05 6:29:28
Comstock 21 1 41N33'38 99w15'00 6:37:00
Concord 26 1 42N23'01 96w59'17 6:27:57
Conley 45 1 42N08 98w45 6:35:00
Constance 14 1 42N42'25 97w26'08 6:29:45
Conterra 16 5 42N26'51 100w37'45 6:42:31
Cook 49 1 40N30'35 96w09'48 6:24:39
Copenhagen 2 1 42N21 97w47 6:31:08
Cordova 80 1 40N43'02 97w21'10 6:29:25
Cornell 44 3 40N03 100w56 6:43:44
Corner 21 1 41N42 99w17 6:37:08
Cornlea 71 1 41N40'48 97w33'58 6:30:16
Cortland 34 1 40N30'20 96w42'20 6:26:49
Cosmo 50 1 40N24 98w53 6:35:32
Costin 79 2 41N51'52 103w43'51 6:54:55
Cotesfield 47 1 41N21'26 98w37'56 6:34:32
Cotterell 27 1 41N31 96w44 6:26:56
Council Creek 63
1 41N26 97w53 6:31:32
Court House Rock 62
2 41N36 103w01 6:52:04
Covert 79 2 41N53'49 103w42'54 6:54:52
Covington 22 1 42N28 96w28 6:25:52
Cowles 91 1 40N10'18 98w26'43 6:33:47
Cox 56 1 41N14 100w29 6:41:56
Coyote 24 1 40N52 99w51 6:39:24
Cozad 24 1 40N51'35 99w59'13 6:39:57
Crab Orchard 49
1 40N20'06 96w25'17 6:25:41
Craft 62 2 41N48'57 103w20'45 6:53:23
Craig 11 1 41N47'08 96w21'49 6:25:27
Crawford 23 2 42N40'59 103w24'44 6:53:39
Creighton 54 1 42N28'00 97w54'21 6:31:37
Creston 71 1 41N42'24 97w21'44 6:29:27
Crete 15 2 40N26'57 101w51'17 6:47:25
Crete 76 1 40N37'48 96w57'40 6:27:51
Crofton 54 1 42N43'44 97w29'43 6:29:59
Crookston 16 5 42N55'42 100w45'07 6:43:00
Crowell 27 1 41N43'41 96w42'27 6:26:50
Crown Point 28 1 41N19 96w02 6:24:08
Cub Creek 48 1 40N13 97w05 6:28:20
Culbertson 44 3 40N13'47 100w50'17 6:43:21
Cullom 13 1 41N03'21 96w01'24 6:24:06
Cuming City 89 1 41N36 96w09 6:24:36
Cumminsville 92
1 41N59'13 98w32'53 6:34:12
Cumro 21 1 41N06'19 99w29'32 6:37:58
Curtis 32 1 40N37'48 100w30'55 6:42:04
Cushing 47 1 41N17'50 98w22'05 6:33:28
Cushman 55 1 40N48'30 96w46'46 6:27:07
Daily 26 1 42N34 96w57 6:27:48
Dakota City 22 1 42N24'56 96w25'05 6:25:40
Dakota Junction 23
2 42N51'35 103w05'37 6:52:22
Dalton 17 2 41N24'26 102w58'24 6:51:54
Danbury 73 3 40N02'22 100w24'14 6:41:37
Dannebrog 47 1 41N07'06 98w32'44 6:34:11
Dannevirke 47 1 41N19'21 98w42'29 6:34:50
Darr 24 1 40N49'15 99w53'00 6:39:32
Davenport 85 1 40N18'46 97w48'42 6:31:15
Davey 55 1 40N59'15 96w39'57 6:26:40
David City 12 1 41N15'10 97w07'47 6:28:31
Davis Creek 88 1 41N27 98w55 6:35:40
Davison 17 2 41N23 103w07 6:52:28
Dawes 87 1 42N04 96w28 6:25:52
Dawson 74 1 40N07'52 95w49'49 6:23:19
Daykin 48 1 40N19'20 97w17'54 6:29:12
Day Ranch 92 1 41N56'39 98w24'24 6:33:38
Debolt 28 1 41N19'25 96w00'41 6:24:03
Decatur 11 1 42N00'27 96w14'58 6:25:00
Deep Well 41 1 40N50 98w14 6:32:56
Deerfield 43 3 40N39 101w17 6:45:08
Deerfield Corner 33
3 40N07'52 99w53'37 6:39:34
DeGraw 62 2 41N42'54 103w09'19 6:52:37
Delaware 66 1 40N39 96w04 6:24:16
Delight 21 1 41N16 99w58 6:39:52
Deloit 45 1 42N07'05 98w19'11 6:33:17
Denman 10 1 40N41'58 98w43'27 6:34:54
Denton 55 1 40N44'16 96w50'39 6:27:23
Denver 1 1 40N34 98w26 6:33:44
Deshler 85 1 40N08'27 97w43'21 6:30:53
De Soto 89 1 41N29'55 96w03'26 6:24:14
Deverre 36 1 41N53'33 99w05'12 6:36:21
Devils Gap 37 1 40N34'46 99w52'18 6:39:29
Deweese 18 1 40N21'17 98w08'18 6:32:33
De Witt 76 1 40N23'37 96w55'21 6:27:41
Dickens 56 3 40N49'34 100w59'33 6:43:58
Diller 48 1 40N06'34 96w56'05 6:27:44
Dimick 84 1 41N47 97w19 6:29:16
Dix 53 2 41N14'07 103w29'09 6:53:57
Dixon 26 1 42N24'58 96w59'49 6:27:59
Dodge 27 1 41N43'16 96w52'57 6:27:32
Dolphin 54 1 42N39 97w33 6:30:12
Doniphan 40 1 40N46'19 98w22'09 6:33:29
Dorchester 76 1 40N38'50 97w06'47 6:28:27
Dorp 57 3 41N29 100w40 6:42:40
Dorsey 7 2 42N22 103w05 6:52:20
Dorsey 45 1 42N40'54 98w20'39 6:33:23
Doughboy 16 2 42N36'47 101w16'36 6:45:06
Douglas 66 1 40N35'44 96w23'14 6:25:33
Douglas Grove 21
1 41N33 99w21 6:37:24
Dowling 54 1 42N34 97w32 6:30:08
Downtown 28 1 41N17 95w57 6:23:48
Doyle 79 2 41N59'22 103w49'58 6:55:20
Driftwood 44 3 40N03 100w49 6:43:16
Dry Cedar 36 1 41N47 98w52 6:35:28
Dublin 6 1 41N39 98w14 6:32:56
DuBois 67 1 40N02'05 96w02'53 6:24:12
Duff 75 1 42N12'09 99w36'14 6:38:25
Dukerville 54 1 42N41'33 98w08'02 6:32:32
Duluth 38 2 42N01'04 101w38'07 6:46:32
Dumas 36 1 42N12 98w45 6:35:00
Dunbar 66 1 40N40'05 96w01'47 6:24:07
Duncan 71 1 41N23'22 97w29'40 6:29:59
Dunning 5 3 41N49'43 100w06'15 6:40:25
Durant 72 1 41N05'32 97w39'49 6:30:39
Dustin 45 1 42N49'37 99w04'11 6:36:17
Dwight 12 1 41N05'01 97w01'11 6:28:05
Dyer 75 1 42N48'12 99w29'53 6:38:00
Eagle 13 1 40N49'00 96w25'48 6:25:43
Earl 32 1 40N29 100w09 6:40:36
East Chadron 23
2 42N51 102w53 6:51:32
East Custer 21 1 41N16 99w38 6:38:32
East Gordon 81 2 42N44 102w08 6:48:32
East Hinman 56 1 41N08 100w44 6:42:56
East Mirage 81 2 42N30 102w36 6:50:24
East Newman 63 1 41N21 97w53 6:31:32
East Ogallala 51
2 41N06 101w40 6:46:40
East Omaha 28 1 41N17'06 95w54'00 6:23:36
East Rock Bluffs 13
1 40N55 95w51 6:23:24
East Valley 73 1 40N13 100w16 6:41:04
East Winters Creek 79
2 41N53 103w37 6:54:28
Eastwood 62 2 41N38 102w43 6:50:52
Eaton 50 1 40N34 98w48 6:35:12
Eckery 68 2 40N56 101w45 6:47:00
Eddyville 24 1 41N00'41 99w37'26 6:38:30
Edgar 18 1 40N22'20 97w58'16 6:31:53
Edholm 12 1 41N23'39 97w02'19 6:28:09
Edison 33 1 40N16'38 99w46'36 6:39:06
Edward 3 2 41N38 101w52 6:47:28
Eight Mile Grove 13
1 41N01 96w04 6:24:16
Elba 47 1 41N17'08 98w34'03 6:34:16
Elberon 66 1 40N38'42 95w56'17 6:23:45
Eldorado 18 1 40N41'03 97w59'43 6:31:59
Elgin 2 1 41N59'00 98w05'00 6:32:20
Eli 16 2 42N56'37 101w29'27 6:45:58
Elim 21 1 41N15 100w08 6:40:32
Elk City 28 1 41N22'18 96w16'03 6:25:04
Elk Creek 49 1 40N17'10 96w07'45 6:24:31
Elkhorn 28 1 41N17'11 96w14'03 6:24:56
Ellis 48 1 40N13'06 96w52'32 6:27:30
Ellsworth 81 2 42N03'31 102w16'49 6:49:07
Elm Creek 10 1 40N43'10 99w22'18 6:37:29
Elmwood 13 1 40N50'30 96w17'36 6:25:10
Elmwood Park 28
1 41N15 96w00 6:24:00
Elsie 68 2 40N50'51 101w23'17 6:45:33
Elsmere 16 5 42N09'55 100w11'06 6:40:44
Elwood 37 1 40N35'25 99w51'38 6:39:27
Elyria 88 1 41N40'51 99w00'21 6:36:01
Emerald 55 1 40N48'50 96w50'05 6:27:20
Emerick 60 1 41N54'07 97w44'11 6:30:57
Emerson 26 1 42N16'43 96w43'35 6:26:54
Emmet 45 1 42N28'32 98w48'21 6:35:13
Enders 15 2 40N27'19 101w32'00 6:46:08
Endicott 48 1 40N05'00 97w05'53 6:28:24
Enola 60 1 41N54'14 97w27'45 6:29:51
Epworth 4 2 41N29 104w00 6:56:00
Ericson 92 1 41N46'48 98w40'37 6:34:42
Erina 36 1 42N02 98w53 6:35:32
Essen 11 1 41N47'00 96w29'17 6:25:57
Etna 21 1 41N08'26 100w09'25 6:40:38
Eustis 32 1 40N39'37 100w09'20 6:40:37
Evergreen 23 2 42N34 103w22 6:53:28
Ewing 45 1 42N15'28 98w20'46 6:33:23
Exeter 30 1 40N38'39 97w27'00 6:29:48
Extension 81 2 42N57 102w33 6:50:12
Fairbury 48 1 40N08'14 97w10'49 6:28:43
Fairfield 18 1 40N25'54 98w06'20 6:32:25
Fairmont 30 1 40N38'13 97w35'06 6:30:20
Falls City 74 1 40N03'39 95w36'06 6:22:24
Falter Place 16
5 42N08'38 100w16'14 6:41:05
Fanning 79 2 41N58 103w45 6:55:00
Farmers 31 1 40N08 99w08 6:36:32
Farmers Valley 41
1 40N45 97w53 6:31:32
Farnam 24 1 40N42'21 100w12'52 6:40:51
Farwell 47 1 41N12'56 98w37'40 6:34:31
Ferry 22 1 42N28 96w24 6:25:36
Filley 34 1 40N17'10 96w32'06 6:26:08
Finchville 21 1 41N22'16 100w04'59 6:40:20
First Lafayette 64
1 40N28 96w01 6:24:04
Firth 55 1 40N31'57 96w36'21 6:26:25
Five Points 83 2 42N46'50 103w41'21 6:54:45
Flats 59 3 41N34'08 101w21'05 6:45:24
Florence 28 1 41N21 95w59 6:23:56
Flournoy 87 1 42N12 96w43 6:26:52
Flowerfield 4 2 41N29 103w53 6:55:32
Flynn Junction 42
1 40N07'53 99w30'57 6:38:04
Fontanelle 89 1 41N32'19 96w25'40 6:25:43
Ford 79 2 41N59 103w55 6:55:40
Fordyce 14 1 42N41'55 97w21'43 6:29:27
Fort Calhoun 89
1 41N27'21 96w01'34 6:24:06
Fort Crook 77 1 41N07'32 95w55'39 6:23:43
Fort Robinson 23
2 42N40 103w28 6:53:52
Foster 70 1 42N16'26 97w39'51 6:30:39
Four Mile 66 1 40N39 95w51 6:23:24
Fox Creek 56 1 40N47 100w30 6:42:00
Frankfort 54 1 42N49 97w32 6:30:08
Franklin 31 1 40N05'46 98w57'08 6:35:49
Freedom 32 1 40N25'28 100w22'08 6:41:29
Freedom 44 3 40N03 101w10 6:44:40
Fremont 27 1 41N26'00 96w29'52 6:25:59
Frenchtown 2 1 42N14 98w14 6:32:56
Friend 76 1 40N39'13 97w17'09 6:29:09
Fritsch 73 1 40N18 100w28 6:41:52
Fullerton 63 1 41N21'48 97w58'08 6:31:53
Funk 69 1 40N27'45 99w14'56 6:37:00
Funston 79 2 41N57 103w38 6:54:32
Gables 36 1 41N56'18 98w50'59 6:35:24
Gage Valley 47 1 41N12 98w20 6:33:20
Galena 26 1 42N29 96w50 6:27:20
Gandy 57 3 41N28'11 100w27'29 6:41:50
Gardiner 71 1 41N21'27 97w33'52 6:30:15
Gardner 10 1 40N55 98w47 6:35:08
Garland 80 1 40N56'41 96w59'07 6:27:56
Garrison 12 1 41N10'38 97w10'01 6:28:40
Gaslin 56 1 40N58 100w23 6:41:32
Gates 21 1 41N38'25 99w38'08 6:38:33
Geneva 30 1 40N31'37 97w35'44 6:30:23
Genoa 63 1 41N26'55 97w43'49 6:30:55
Georgia 16 2 42N53 100w58 6:43:52
Geranium 88 1 41N37 99w09 6:36:36
Gering 79 2 41N49'33 103w39'36 6:54:38
Germanville 43 3 40N34 100w50 6:43:20
Gibbon 10 1 40N44'54 98w50'40 6:35:23
Gibson 48 1 40N18 97w05 6:28:20
Gilchrist 62 2 41N56 102w49 6:51:16
Gilead 85 1 40N08'47 97w24'46 6:29:39
Gillan 24 1 40N56 99w57 6:39:48
Gillaspie 16 2 42N32 101w23 6:45:32
Gilmore 77 1 41N08'40 95w57'04 6:23:48
Gilmore Junction 77
1 41N09'00 95w56'05 6:23:44
Giltner 41 1 40N46'26 98w09'12 6:32:37
Gladstone 48 1 40N09'35 97w18'28 6:29:14
Glen 83 2 42N41 103w25 6:53:40
Glengary 30 1 40N29 97w25 6:29:40
Glenover 34 1 40N16'52 96w45'24 6:27:02
Glenrock 64 1 40N26'37 95w53'27 6:23:34
Glenville 18 1 40N30'25 98w15'20 6:33:01
Glenwood Park 10
1 40N44'59 99w04'59 6:36:20
Goehner 80 1 40N49'56 97w13'15 6:28:53
Golden 45 1 42N19 98w23 6:33:32
Good Luck 77 1 41N11 95w58 6:23:52
Good Samaritan Village 1
1 40N34'44 98w22'03 6:33:28
Good Streak 62 2 41N58 103w16 6:53:04
Goodwin 22 1 42N27'19 96w39'18 6:26:37
Goose Creek 16 5 42N20 100w18 6:41:12
Gordon 81 2 42N48'17 102w12'10 6:48:49
Gothenburg 24 1 40N55'46 100w09'37 6:40:38
Government 43 3 40N34 101w00 6:44:00
Grace 68 2 40N47 102w00 6:48:00

Gracy 75	1	42N09	99w21	6:37:24
Graf 49	1	40N22	96w11	6:24:44
Grafton 30	1	40N37'41	97w42'49	6:30:51
Grainton 68	3	40N49'23	101w17'13	6:45:09
Grand Island 40	1	40N55'30	98w20'30	6:33:22
Grand Prairie 71	1	41N37	97w25	6:29:40
Grant 68	2	40N50'31	101w43'29	6:46:54
Granville 71	1	41N42	97w33	6:30:12
Grattan 45	1	42N29	98w39	6:34:36
Greeley 39	1	41N32'55	98w31'51	6:34:07
Green 78	1	41N06	96w31	6:26:04
Green Garden 60	1	41N47	97w32	6:30:08
Green Meadows 28	1	41N16'44	96w07'43	6:24:31
Green Valley 45	1	42N26	99w07	6:36:28
Greenwood 13	1	40N57'46	96w26'27	6:25:46
Gresham 93	1	41N01'42	97w24'07	6:29:36
Gretna 77	1	41N08'27	96w14'22	6:24:57
Gross 8	1	42N56'45	98w34'19	6:34:17
Grove 60	1	41N57	97w46	6:31:04
Grover 80	1	40N46'47	97w02'15	6:28:09
Guide Rock 91	1	40N04'29	98w19'49	6:33:19
Gurley 17	2	41N19'20	102w58'13	6:51:53
Hackberry 72	1	41N06	97w26	6:29:44
Hadar 70	1	42N06'18	97w26'56	6:29:48
Haig 79	2	41N52'46	103w45'31	6:55:02
Haigler 29	2	40N00'50	101w56'20	6:47:45
Hallam 55	1	40N32'16	96w47'13	6:27:09
Halloran 1	1	40N35'15	98w17'47	6:33:11
Halsey 86	3	41N54'12	100w16'07	6:41:04
Hamlet 43	3	40N23'06	101w14'03	6:44:56
Hammond 65	1	40N19	97w53	6:31:32
Hampton 41	1	40N52'44	97w53'08	6:31:33
Hancock 90	1	42N08	97w12	6:28:48
Hanlon 55	1	40N39'30	96w40'15	6:26:41
Hansen 40	1	40N41'47	98w22'12	6:33:29
Harbine 48	1	40N11'32	96w58'20	6:27:53
Hardy 65	1	40N00'32	97w55'36	6:31:42
Harmony 91	1	40N19	98w40	6:34:40
Harrisburg 4	2	41N33'23	103w44'17	6:54:57
Harrison 83	2	42N41'14	703w52'56	6:55:32
Hartgraves Place 16	5	42N19'12	100w16'04	6:41:04
Hartington 14	1	42N37'21	97w15'51	6:29:03
Hartman 79	2	41N52'36	103w59'05	6:55:56
Harvard 18	1	40N37'08	98w05'49	6:32:23
Hastings 1	1	40N35'10	98w23'17	6:33:33
Hat Creek 83	2	42N48	103w44	6:54:56
Havelock 5	1	40N51'44	96w37'20	6:26:29
Havens 61	1	41N15'55	97w44'58	6:31:00
Hawley 5	3	42N00	100w02	6:40:08
Hayes Center 43	3	40N30'39	101w01'09	6:44:05
Hayland 1	1	40N39'53	98w35'13	6:34:21
Haymow 84	1	41N53	97w04	6:28:16
Haynes 62	2	41N51	103w08	6:52:32
Hays 93	1	40N45	97w39	6:30:36
Hay Springs 81	2	42N41'02	102w41'22	6:50:45
Hazard 82	1	41N05'26	99w04'44	6:36:19
Heartwell 50	1	40N34'14	98w47'15	6:35:09
Heber 61	1	41N06'40	97w58'29	6:31:54
Hebron 85	1	40N09'59	97w35'08	6:30:21
Hecla 46	2	42N02'21	101w14'14	6:44:57
Hedrix 48	1	40N12'17	97w14'28	6:28:58
Heldt 79	2	41N53'16	103w42'18	6:54:49
Helena 49	1	40N27	96w17	6:25:08
Helvey 48	1	40N16'00	97w15'17	6:29:01
Hemingford 7	2	42N19'18	103w04'21	6:52:17
Henderson 93	1	40N46'47	97w48'43	6:31:15
Hendley 33	3	40N07'49	99w58'10	6:39:53
Hendricks 66	1	40N34	96w24	6:25:36
Henry 79	2	41N59'55	104w02'49	6:56:11
Herman 89	1	41N40'24	96w12'53	6:24:52
Herrick 54	1	42N49	97w40	6:30:40
Hershey 56	3	41N09'31	101w00'08	6:44:01
Heun 19	1	41N37'48	97w02'25	6:28:10
Hickman 55	1	40N37'12	96w37'44	6:26:31
High Ridge 43	3	40N34	101w11	6:44:44
Hildreth 31	1	40N20'14	99w02'36	6:36:10
Hill 54	1	42N44	97w47	6:31:08
Hillerage 79	2	41N51'42	103w36'11	6:54:25
Hillside 24	1	40N55	99w44	6:38:56
Hinman 56	1	41N09	100w50	6:43:20
Hire 16	2	42N10'28	101w25'04	6:45:40
Hoag 34	1	40N19'03	96w49'57	6:27:20
Hoagland 57	3	41N29'25	100w21'58	6:41:28
Hoffland 81	2	42N04'31	102w39'27	6:50:38
Holbrook 33	1	40N18'17	100w00'35	6:40:02
Holdrege 69	1	40N26'25	99w22'10	6:37:29
Holland 55	1	40N35'47	96w35'29	6:26:22
Hollinger 33	1	40N09'33	99w42'27	6:38:50
Holmes 24	1	40N44	100w03	6:40:12
Holmesville 34	1	40N12'03	96w39'27	6:26:38
Holstein 1	1	40N27'55	98w39'06	6:34:36
Holt 34	1	40N24	96w45	6:27:00
Holt Creek 45	1	42N20	99w10	6:36:40
Homer 22	1	42N19'18	96w29'21	6:25:57
Hooper 27	1	41N36'38	96w32'52	6:26:11
Hoover 29	2	40N13	101w36	6:46:24
Hopewell 43	3	40N24	101w04	6:44:16
Horace 39	1	41N32'35	98w40'23	6:34:42
Hord 61	1	41N09'00	98w04'01	6:32:16
Hordville 41	1	41N04'32	97w53'06	6:31:32
Horn 23	2	42N45'46	103w26'36	6:53:46
Horrell 32	1	40N34	100w16	6:41:04
Hoskins 90	1	42N06'44	97w18'21	6:29:13
Houston 93	1	40N54'57	97w32'23	6:30:10
Howard City 47	1	41N04	98w43	6:34:52
Howe 64	1	40N19'19	95w49'08	6:23:17
Howells 19	1	41N43'30	97w00'09	6:28:01
Hubbard 22	1	42N23'12	96w35'21	6:26:21
Hubbard Corner 79	2	41N52'20	103w48'46	6:55:15
Hubbell 85	1	40N00'33	97w29'50	6:29:59
Hull 4	2	41N38	103w57	6:55:48
Humboldt 74	1	40N09'50	95w56'41	6:23:47
Humphrey 71	1	41N41'30	97w29'03	6:29:56
Hunter 90	1	42N13	96w57	6:27:48
Huntley 42	1	40N12'36	99w17'31	6:37:10
Huntsman 17	2	41N13'15	102w58'24	6:51:54
Huskerville 55	1	40N51'35	96w47'37	6:27:10
Hyannis 38	2	42N00'02	101w45'41	6:47:03
Imperial 15	2	40N31'01	101w38'34	6:46:34
Inavale 91	1	40N05'29	98w38'57	6:34:36
Independent 88	1	41N27	98w48	6:35:12
Indian Creek 29	2	40N08	101w30	6:46:00
Indianola 73	1	40N14'04	100w25'01	6:41:40
Industry 69	1	40N24	99w29	6:37:56
Inez 45	1	42N17'28	99w00'04	6:36:00
Ingleside 1	1	40N34'48	98w26'38	6:33:47
Inglewood 27	1	41N24'59	96w30'04	6:26:00
Inland 18	1	40N35'49	98w13'20	6:32:53
Inman 45	1	42N22'55	98w31'40	6:34:07
Iowa 45	1	42N28	98w22	6:33:28
Irvington 28	1	41N19'16	96w03'16	6:24:13
Irwin 16	2	42N52'38	101w57'16	6:47:49
Island Grove 34	1	40N08	96w31	6:26:04
Ithaca 78	1	41N09'46	96w32'22	6:26:09
Jacinto 53	2	41N13'33	103w24'13	6:53:37
Jackson 22	1	42N26'55	96w33'52	6:26:15
Jamaica 55	1	40N41'56	96w41'22	6:26:45
James 79	2	41N55'55	103w34'42	6:54:19
Jamison 52	1	42N59'52	99w18'27	6:37:14
Jane 79	2	41N55'29	103w46'24	6:55:06
Janise 79	2	41N51'11	104w00'11	6:56:01
Jansen 48	1	40N11'07	97w05'00	6:28:20
Jeffrey 56	1	40N52	100w23	6:41:32
Jelen 54	1	42N37'41	98w08'44	6:32:35
Joder 83	2	42N51'30	103w33'04	6:54:12
Johnson 64	1	40N24'39	95w59'52	6:23:59
Johnson Lake 37	1	40N35	99w52	6:39:28
Johnsons Corner 9	3	42N12'59	99w44'24	6:38:58
Johnstown 9	3	42N34'18	100w03'28	6:40:14
Joliet 71	1	41N37	97w39	6:30:36
Josie 45	1	42N08	99w11	6:36:44
Josselyn 24	1	40N44'59	99w37'26	6:38:30
Joyce 79	2	41N55'41	103w58'05	6:55:52
Julian 64	1	40N31'22	95w52'03	6:23:28
Juniata 1	1	40N35'24	98w30'21	6:34:01
Kalamazoo 60	1	41N47	97w40	6:30:40
Karkaw 63	1	41N23'41	97w45'08	6:31:01
Kearney 10	1	40N41'58	99w04'52	6:36:19
Keene 50	1	40N25'31	99w03'56	6:36:16
Keith 56	1	41N05'26	100w33'49	6:42:15
Kelso 46	3	42N02'37	100w55'33	6:43:42
Kelso 47	1	41N10	98w40	6:34:40
Kem 56	1	40N54	100w50	6:43:20
Kemp 62	2	41N42'47	103w06'28	6:52:26
Kenesaw 1	1	40N37'16	98w39'26	6:34:38
Kennard 89	1	41N28'23	96w12'11	6:24:49
Kennebec 24	1	41N01	99w40	6:38:40
Kennedy 16	2	42N32'50	100w48'59	6:43:16
Kent 58	1	41N48	99w17	6:37:08
Kewanee 16	5	42N55	100w22	6:41:28
Keystone 51	2	41N12'58	101w34'59	6:46:20
Kilfoil 21	3	41N29	99w48	6:39:12
Kilgore 16	2	42N56'18	100w57'19	6:43:49
Kimball 53	2	41N14'09	103w39'45	6:54:39
Kincaid 35	2	41N55	102w09	6:48:36
King Lake 28	1	41N18'49	96w18'03	6:25:12
Kingsburg 84	1	41N57	97w04	6:28:16
Kiowa 79	2	41N52	103w58	6:55:52
Kirkwood 75	1	42N43	99w19	6:37:16
Knievels Corner 45	1	42N07'05	98w20'21	6:33:21
Knowles 32	1	40N24	100w23	6:41:32
Knox 93	1	40N48'50	97w35'22	6:30:21
Knoxville 54	1	42N40'07	98w17'46	6:33:11
Koinzan Ranch 92	1	41N58'20	98w24'34	6:33:38
Koller 50	1	40N32'17	98w51'37	6:35:26
Koshopan 9	3	42N06'04	100w06'14	6:40:25
Kowanda 35	2	41N24	102w21	6:49:24
Kramer 55	1	40N35'18	96w52'30	6:27:30
Krider 34	1	40N04'15	96w44'45	6:26:59
Kronborg 41	1	41N00'10	97w56'23	6:31:46
Kuesters Lake 40	1	40N56	98w21	6:33:24
Lackey 16	2	42N22	101w32	6:46:08
Lake Forest Estates 28	1	41N18	96w02	6:24:08
Lakeland 9	3	42N17	100w04	6:40:16
Lake Platte View 28	1	41N14'40	96w21'07	6:25:24
Lakeside 81	2	42N03'21	102w25'28	6:49:42
Lamar 15	2	40N34'19	101w58'41	6:47:55
Lamont 29	2	40N19'15	101w52'22	6:47:29
Lancaster 55	1	40N50	96w36	6:26:24
Lane 28	1	41N14'31	96w09'38	6:24:39
Lanham 34	1	40N00'06	96w52'24	6:27:30
LaPlatte 77	1	41N04'29	95w55'24	6:23:42
Laurel 14	1	42N25'46	97w05'22	6:28:21
Lavaca 16	2	42N42	101w58	6:47:52
LaVista 77	1	41N11'02	96w01'51	6:24:07
Lawn 7	2	42N18	103w19	6:53:16
Lawrence 65	1	40N17'31	98w15'35	6:33:02
Laws 32	1	40N34	100w37	6:42:28
Lay 75	1	42N29	99w20	6:37:20
Leat 16	2	42N54'18	101w48'31	6:47:14
Lebanon 73	3	40N03'02	100w16'33	6:41:06
Lee Valley 28	1	41N18	96w02	6:24:08
Leicester 18	1	40N39	98w13	6:32:52
Leigh 19	1	41N42'19	97w14'16	6:28:57
Lembke Landing 54	1	42N40'02	96w48'05	6:27:12
Lemley 59	3	41N30	100w49	6:43:16
Lemon 56	1	41N17	100w45	6:43:00
Lemoyne 51	2	41N16'21	101w48'46	6:47:15
Lena 3	2	41N42'04	101w29'53	6:46:00
Leonard 23	2	42N29	103w18	6:53:12
Leroy 93	1	40N50	97w33	6:30:12
Leshara 78	1	41N19'47	96w25'41	6:25:43
Leslie 90	1	42N08	96w52	6:27:28
Lester Junction 91	1	40N05'08	98w26'36	6:33:46
Letan 7	2	42N00'53	102w56'25	6:51:46
Level 1	1	40N32'20	98w18'11	6:33:13
Lewellen 35	2	41N19'53	102w08'36	6:48:34
Lewis 18	1	40N34	97w59	6:31:56
Lewiston 34	1	40N14'36	96w24'12	6:25:37
Lexington 24	1	40N46'51	99w44'28	6:38:58
Liberty 34	1	40N05'05	96w28'57	6:25:56
Lillian 21	1	41N35'23	99w38'38	6:38:35
Lime Grove 26	1	42N39'49	96w59'57	6:28:00
Lincoln 55	1	40N48'00	96w40'00	6:26:40
Lindsay 71	1	41N42'00	97w41'37	6:30:46
Lindy 54	1	42N44'03	97w44'23	6:30:58
Line 91	1	40N02	98w33	6:34:12
Linoma Beach 77	1	41N03'50	96w19'07	6:25:16
Linscott 5	3	41N44'34	100w00'48	6:40:03
Linwood 12	1	41N24'44	96w55'52	6:27:43
Lisbon 68	2	40N48	101w54	6:47:36
Lisco 35	2	41N29'50	102w37'11	6:50:29
Litchfield 82	1	41N09'27	99w09'19	6:36:37
Little Blue 1	1	40N24	98w20	6:33:20
Little Salt 55	1	41N00	96w44	6:26:56
Little York 58	1	41N59	99w21	6:37:24
Lockridge 93	1	40N55	97w39	6:30:36
Lockwood 61	1	40N58'12	98w14'39	6:32:59
Lodgepole 17	2	41N08'59	102w38'09	6:50:33
Lodi 21	1	41N12'56	99w51'09	6:39:25
Logan 57	1	41N29'41	100w18'00	6:41:12
Loma 12	1	41N07'41	96w56'30	6:27:46
Lone Pine 4	2	41N29	103w29	6:53:56
Lonergan 51	2	41N19	101w54	6:47:36
Lone Valley 57	3	41N39	100w38	6:42:32
Long Pine 9	1	42N32'11	99w42'01	6:38:48
Long Springs 4	2	41N32	103w43	6:54:52
Loomis 69	1	40N28'42	99w30'24	6:38:02
Lorenzo 17	2	41N02'51	103w04'03	6:52:16
Loretto 6	1	41N45'53	98w04'49	6:32:19
Lorton 66	1	40N35'44	96w01'27	6:24:06
Louisville 13	1	40N59'52	96w09'43	6:24:39
Loup City 82	1	41N16'32	98w57'59	6:35:52
Loup Ferry 63	1	41N21	98w07	6:32:28
Loup Fork 47	1	41N05	98w41	6:34:44
Lowell 50	1	40N38'51	98w50'49	6:35:23
Lushton 93	1	40N43'29	97w43'29	6:30:54
Lutz 29	2	40N18	101w39	6:46:36
Lyman 79	2	41N55'02	104w02'19	6:56:09
Lynch 8	1	42N49'49	98w27'57	6:33:52
Lynden 33	3	40N07	100w02	6:40:08
Lynn 18	1	40N35	98w04	6:32:16
Lynn 62	2	41N24'10	102w58'33	6:51:54
Lyons 11	1	41N56'15	96w28'37	6:25:54
Lyons Place 3	2	41N33'05	101w36'27	6:46:26
Macedonia 15	2	40N36	101w51	6:47:24
Macon 31	1	40N12'18	98w57'08	6:35:49
Macy 87	1	42N06'47	96w21'22	6:25:25
Madison 60	1	41N49'42	97w27'17	6:29:49
Madison Square 58	1	41N46	99w33	6:38:12
Madrid 68	2	40N51'00	101w32'35	6:46:10
Magnet 14	1	42N27'18	97w28'11	6:29:53
Malcolm 55	1	40N54'24	96w51'45	6:27:27
Malmo 78	1	41N15'58	96w43'19	6:26:53
Manchester 6	1	41N42	98w00	6:32:00
Manley 13	1	40N55'11	96w09'56	6:24:40
Maple 27	1	41N31	96w37	6:26:28
Maple Grove 49	1	40N18	96w17	6:25:08
Maple Hill 28	1	41N18	96w02	6:24:08
Mapps 93	1	40N56'41	97w36'24	6:30:26
Marble 78	1	41N11	96w23	6:25:32
Marengo 43	3	40N38'19	100w54'36	6:43:38
Marian Center 55	1	40N52'57	96w34'08	6:26:17
Mariaville 75	1	42N46'31	99w20'06	6:37:20
Marietta 78	1	41N16	96w31	6:26:04
Marion 73	3	40N00'57	100w28'48	6:41:55
Mariposa 78	1	41N16	96w44	6:26:56
Marquette 41	1	41N00'11	98w00'33	6:32:02
Marshall 18	1	40N29	97w59	6:31:56
Marsland 23	2	42N26'38	103w17'53	6:53:12
Martell 55	1	40N38'15	96w45'30	6:27:02
Martin 40	1	40N43	98w34	6:34:16
Martin 51	2	41N15'22	101w41'26	6:46:46
Martinsburg 26	1	42N30'30	96w49'50	6:27:19
Martland 30	1	40N27'07	97w40'16	6:30:41
Marvin 68	2	40N47	101w17	6:45:08
Mascot 42	1	40N15'52	99w32'45	6:38:11
Maskell 26	1	42N41'24	96w58'56	6:27:56
Mason City 21	1	41N13'23	99w18'00	6:37:12
Max 29	2	40N06'50	101w24'08	6:45:37
Maxwell 56	1	41N04'44	100w31'28	6:42:06
May 50	1	40N29	98w47	6:35:08
Mayberry 67	1	40N13'23	96w18'42	6:25:15
Mayfield 40	1	41N00	98w33	6:34:12
Maywood 32	1	40N39'27	100w37'18	6:42:29
McArdle 28	1	41N17	96w05	6:24:20
McClure 45	1	42N13	98w34	6:34:16
McCook 73	1	40N12'07	100w37'31	6:42:30
McCool Junction 93	1	40N44'39	97w35'50	6:30:23
McCulley 8	1	42N57	98w57	6:35:48
McFadden 93	1	40N45	97w32	6:30:08
McGrew 79	2	41N44'48	103w25'04	6:53:40
McKeag 3	2	41N27'00	101w45'43	6:47:03
McLean 70	1	42N23'08	97w28'06	6:29:52
Mead 78	1	41N13'40	96w29'15	6:25:57
Meadow 77	1	41N00'58	96w09'23	6:24:38
Meadow Grove 60	1	42N01'44	97w44'01	6:30:56
Meadville 52	3	42N45'32	99w50'55	6:39:24
Medicine 56	1	40N46	100w45	6:43:00
Meek 45	1	42N41'49	98w37'38	6:34:31
Megeath 51	2	41N04'47	101w59'07	6:47:56
Melbeta 79	2	41N46'54	103w31'02	6:54:04
Melia 77	1	41N05'46	96w16'31	6:25:06
Memphis 78	1	41N05'42	96w25'52	6:25:43
Menominee 14	1	42N47'13	97w22'27	6:29:30
Mercer 28	1	41N22'28	96w25'32	6:25:42
Merchiston 63	1	41N23'25	97w53'04	6:31:32
Meridian 48	1	40N13	97w18	6:29:12
Merna 21	3	41N29'02	99w45'35	6:39:02
Merriman 16	2	42N55'11	101w42'01	6:46:48
Merry 87	1	42N13	96w35	6:26:20
Michigan 88	1	41N37	99w03	6:36:12
Middle Creek 55	1	40N49	96w52	6:27:28
Midland 54	1	42N28'02	97w42'01	6:30:48

NEBRASKA

Midvale 36 1 41N47 98w59 6:35:56
Midway 45 1 42N41'49 98w39'26 6:34:38
Midway 47 1 41N12'53 98w33'24 6:34:14
Mignery Ranch 92 1 41N56'58 98w26'26 6:33:46
Milan 81 2 42N52 102w25 6:49:40
Milburn 21 3 41N43'10 99w43'51 6:38:55
Milerton 12 1 41N11'09 97w12'52 6:28:51
Miles 67 1 40N08 96w17 6:25:08
Milford 80 1 40N46'28 97w03'01 6:28:12
Mill 55 1 41N00 96w31 6:26:04
Millard 28 1 41N12'30 96w07'15 6:24:29
Miller 10 1 40N55'40 99w23'34 6:37:34
Milligan 30 1 40N30'01 97w23'14 6:29:33
Millis Beach 22 1 42N26'05 96w26'53 6:25:48
Mills 52 1 42N56'26 99w26'37 6:37:46
Milton 21 1 40N56 99w24 6:37:36
Minatare 79 2 41N48'34 103w30'12 6:54:01
Minden 50 1 40N29'55 98w56'51 6:35:47
Minersville 66 1 40N35'49 95w47'20 6:23:09
Minnetonka 81 2 42N32 102w25 6:49:40
Mintle 79 2 41N56'45 103w40'48 6:54:43
Mirage 50 1 40N29 99w06 6:36:24
Mission Creek 67 1 40N03 96w24 6:25:36
Mitchell 79 2 41N56'25 103w48'29 6:55:14
Mohler 62 2 41N42'53 103w14'04 6:52:56
Momence 30 1 40N29 97w46 6:31:04
Monowi 8 1 42N49'43 98w19'46 6:33:19
Monroe 71 1 41N28'27 97w35'57 6:30:24
Monterey 20 1 41N47'34 96w48'17 6:27:13
Montrose 83 2 42N55'21 103w43'42 6:54:55
Moomaw Corner 62 2 41N49'00 103w19'24 6:53:18
Moon Lake 9 3 42N24 100w05 6:40:20
Moorefield 32 1 40N41'24 100w23'56 6:41:36
Morrill 79 2 41N57'48 103w55'33 6:55:42
Morse Bluff 78 1 41N25'55 96w45'58 6:27:04
Mother Lake 16 2 42N11 101w48 6:47:12
Mount Clare 65 1 40N10'58 98w13'04 6:32:52
Mount Pleasant 13 1 40N55 96w03 6:24:12
Mud Creek 92 1 41N47 98w23 6:33:32
Mullally 42 1 40N08 99w14 6:36:56
Mullen 46 2 42N02'34 101w02'32 6:44:10
Mumper 35 2 41N45'41 102w26'23 6:49:46
Murdock 13 1 40N55'32 96w16'47 6:25:07
Muriel 1 1 40N30'36 98w21'13 6:33:25
Murphy 41 1 40N52'45 98w06'42 6:32:27
Murray 13 1 40N54'55 95w55'48 6:23:43
Mynard 13 1 40N58'25 95w55'25 6:23:42
Nacora 22 1 42N19'07 96w39'38 6:26:39
Naper 8 1 42N57'49 99w05'47 6:36:23
Naponee 31 1 40N04'36 99w08'28 6:36:34
Nashville 89 1 41N24'23 95w59'47 6:23:59
Natick 86 3 41N57'21 100w26'21 6:41:45
Nebraska City 66 1 40N40'36 95w51'32 6:23:26
Nehawka 13 1 40N49'46 95w59'29 6:23:58
Neligh 2 1 42N07'43 98w01'46 6:32:07
Nelson 65 1 40N12'06 98w04'03 6:32:16
Nemaha 64 1 40N20'18 95w40'22 6:22:41
Nenzel 16 2 42N55'40 101w06'09 6:44:25
Nevens 51 2 41N11'06 101w25'26 6:45:42
Newark 50 1 40N38'28 98w57'46 6:35:51
Newcastle 54 1 42N39'05 96w52'24 6:27:30
New Era 33 1 40N18 99w41 6:38:44
New Helena 21 3 41N36'41 99w45'03 6:39:00
Newman 78 1 41N11 96w51 6:27:24
Newman Grove 60 1 41N45'00 97w46'30 6:31:06
Newport 75 1 42N36'05 99w19'37 6:37:18
Newton 48 1 40N03 96w58 6:27:52
New York 93 1 40N55 97w32 6:30:08
Nickerson 89 1 41N32'04 96w28'12 6:25:53
Nimburg 12 1 41N21'55 96w56'49 6:27:47
Nim City 74 1 40N02'38 95w52'10 6:23:29
Niobrara 54 1 42N45'17 98w01'42 6:32:07
Noble 88 1 41N42 98w51 6:35:24
Nonpareil 7 2 42N22'20 103w10'51 6:52:43
Nora 65 1 40N09'42 97w58'12 6:31:53
Norden 52 1 42N52'07 100w04'25 6:40:18
Norfolk 60 1 42N02 97w25 6:29:40
Norman 50 1 40N28'47 98w47'31 6:35:10
North Auburn 64 1 40N23 95w51 6:23:24
North Bend 27 1 41N27'43 96w46'46 6:27:07
North Bluff 55 1 40N55 96w37 6:26:28
North Cedar 78 1 41N25 96w37 6:26:28
North Crawford 23 2 42N47 103w26 6:53:44
North Deer Creek 60 1 42N04 97w39 6:30:36
North Dry Creek 70 1 42N24 97w47 6:31:08
North Fork 76 1 40N29 97w12 6:28:48
North Franklin 31 1 40N18 98w47 6:35:08
North Loup 88 1 41N29'43 98w46'22 6:35:05
North Mc Williams 66 1 40N35 96w04 6:24:16
North Oaks 28 1 41N19 96w02 6:24:08
North Omaha 28 1 41N19 95w57 6:23:48
North Palmyra 66 1 40N44 96w24 6:25:36
North Platte 56 1 41N07'26 100w45'54 6:43:04
Northport 62 2 41N40'56 103w05'13 6:52:21
North Rosedale 56 3 41N20 100w55 6:43:40
North Russell 66 1 40N44 96w17 6:25:08
North Shore 22 1 42N26'26 96w26'29 6:25:46
North Star 32 1 40N29 100w30 6:42:00
North Star 63 1 41N22'24 98w08'04 6:32:32
North Syracuse 66 1 40N40 96w11 6:24:44
North Valley 73 1 40N18 100w14 6:40:56
Northwest 28 1 41N18 96w02 6:24:08
Norway 86 3 41N59'56 100w43'04 6:42:52
Nowell 56 3 41N05 100w59 6:43:56
Nysted 47 1 41N08'04 98w36'51 6:34:27
Oak 65 1 40N14'13 97w54'11 6:31:37
Oakdale 2 1 42N04'11 97w58'08 6:31:53
Oak Grove 31 1 40N03 99w01 6:36:04
Oakland 11 1 41N50'09 96w28'00 6:25:52
Oak Mill 65 1 40N13'33 97w52'32 6:31:30
Obert 14 1 42N41'23 97w01'40 6:28:07
Oconee 71 1 41N28'12 97w31'07 6:30:04
O'Connor 39 1 41N30'38 98w28'25 6:33:54
Oconto 21 1 41N08'28 99w45'46 6:39:03
Octavia 12 1 41N20'53 97w03'31 6:28:14
Odell 34 1 40N03'00 96w48'11 6:27:13
Odessa 10 1 40N42'06 99w15'23 6:37:02
O'Fallons 56 3 41N09'37 101w04'36 6:44:18
Offutt Air Force Base 77 1 41N09 95w57 6:23:48
Ogallala 51 2 41N07'41 101w43'09 6:46:53
Ohio 74 1 40N08 95w37 6:22:28
Ohiowa 30 1 40N24'52 97w27'09 6:29:49
Old Mill 28 1 41N18 96w02 6:24:08
Olean 19 1 41N44'10 96w56'42 6:27:47
Olean 88 1 41N33'39 98w48'26 6:35:14
Olive Branch 55 1 40N34 96w51 6:27:24
Oliver 53 2 41N13'46 103w47'15 6:55:09
Omadi 22 1 42N24 96w29 6:25:56
Omaha 28 1 41N15'31 95w56'15 6:23:45
Omaha Indian Reservation 87 1 42N07 96w28 6:25:52
Oneida 50 1 40N24 99w06 6:36:24
O'Neill 45 1 42N27'28 98w38'50 6:34:35
Ong 18 1 40N23'55 97w50'08 6:31:21
Opportunity 45 1 42N35'46 98w30'03 6:34:00
Orafino 32 1 40N29'50 100w13'43 6:40:55
Orange 23 2 42N39 103w23 6:53:32
Orchard 2 1 42N20'08 98w14'33 6:32:58
Ord 88 1 41N36'12 98w55'33 6:35:42
Ordville 17 2 41N15 103w03 6:52:12
Oreapolis 13 1 41N02'51 95w55'05 6:23:40
Orella 83 2 42N53'36 103w30'00 6:54:00
Orleans 42 1 40N07'45 99w27'18 6:37:49
Orum 89 1 41N32'45 96w16'13 6:25:05
Orville 41 1 40N44 98w00 6:32:00
Osage 66 1 40N34 96w11 6:24:44
Osborn 32 1 40N24 100w44 6:42:56
Osceola 72 1 41N10'47 97w32'50 6:30:11
Osgood 56 1 41N05 100w46 6:43:04
Oshkosh 35 2 41N24'18 102w20'38 6:49:23
Osmond 70 1 42N21'36 97w35'47 6:30:23
Otis 41 1 41N00 97w53 6:31:32
Otoe 66 1 40N43'25 96w07'00 6:24:28
Otter Creek 26 1 42N27 96w45 6:27:00
Ough 29 2 40N19'20 101w30'44 6:46:03
Overland 41 1 40N39'39 97w59'09 6:31:57
Overton 24 1 40N44'19 99w32'14 6:38:09
Ovina 40 1 40N58'07 98w27'18 6:33:49
Owasco 53 2 41N14'22 103w34'28 6:54:18
Oxford 42 1 40N14'54 99w37'59 6:38:32
Oxford Junction 42 1 40N14'06 99w35'55 6:38:24
Paddock 45 1 42N46'41 98w37'07 6:34:28
Paddock 61 1 41N04'54 98w03'37 6:32:14
Page 45 1 42N24'03 98w25'01 6:33:40
Palisade 44 3 40N20'57 101w06'26 6:44:26
Palmer 61 1 41N13'20 98w15'25 6:33:02
Palmyra 66 1 40N42'16 96w23'14 6:25:33
Panama 55 1 40N35'52 96w30'38 6:26:03
Panhandle 83 2 42N26 103w57 6:55:48
Papillion 77 1 41N09'16 96w02'31 6:24:10
Park 35 2 41N17 102w09 6:48:36
Parks 29 2 40N02'30 101w43'29 6:46:54
Parkview 40 1 40N54'10 98w20'50 6:33:23
Paul 66 1 40N35'43 95w53'47 6:23:35
Pauline 1 1 40N24'59 98w20'43 6:33:23
Pawnee City 67 1 40N06'30 96w09'15 6:24:37
Pawnee Village 91 1 40N03'31 98w24'14 6:33:37
Paxton 51 2 41N07'27 101w21'21 6:45:25
Payne 56 1 41N03 100w36 6:42:24
Pearl 15 2 40N40 101w38 6:46:32
Pebble 27 1 41N42 96w44 6:26:56
Peckham 56 1 40N56 100w17 6:41:08
Pelton 79 2 41N55'15 103w49'58 6:55:20
Pender 87 1 42N06'51 96w42'25 6:26:50
Penn 35 2 41N24 102w21 6:49:24
Peoria 54 1 42N39 97w40 6:30:40
Perrin 62 2 41N48'45 103w14'45 6:52:59
Perry 73 1 40N12'37 100w43'21 6:42:53
Pershing 11 1 41N47 96w30 6:26:00
Peru 64 1 40N28'27 95w44'00 6:22:56
Petersburg 6 1 41N51'12 98w04'42 6:32:19
Pewaukee 75 1 42N11 99w34 6:38:16
Phillips 41 1 40N53'50 98w12'52 6:32:51
Pickrell 34 1 40N22'43 96w43'42 6:26:55
Pierce 70 1 42N11'57 97w31'35 6:30:06
Pigeon Creek 22 1 42N24 96w41 6:26:44
Pilger 84 1 42N00'31 97w03'13 6:28:13
Pine 9 3 42N33 99w42 6:38:48
Pine Creek 81 2 42N20 102w24 6:49:36
Pine Glen 9 3 42N41 99w45 6:39:00
Pine Lake 55 1 40N44'40 96w36'42 6:26:27
Pine Ridge 23 2 42N29'40 103w28'18 6:53:53
Piper 62 2 41N45'35 103w15'29 6:53:02
Pishelville 54 1 42N43'37 98w12'43 6:32:51
Plainview 70 1 42N20'59 97w47'30 6:31:10
Plant 56 1 41N00 100w41 6:42:44
Platte Center 71 1 41N32'15 97w29'17 6:29:57
Platte Valley 28 1 41N21 96w21 6:25:24
Plattsmouth 13 1 41N00'41 95w52'55 6:23:32
Pleasant 48 1 40N08 96w58 6:27:52
Pleasant Dale 80 1 40N47'32 96w55'45 6:27:43
Pleasant Hill 21 3 41N28'49 100w04'41 6:40:19
Pleasant Hill 76 1 40N35'12 97w04'53 6:28:20
Pleasant Home 72 1 41N06 97w45 6:31:00
Pleasanton 10 1 40N58'03 99w05'10 6:36:21
Pleasant Valley 14 1 42N36'46 97w25'35 6:29:42
Pleasant Valley 27 1 41N37 96w51 6:27:24
Plum Grove 70 1 42N24 97w33 6:30:12
Plymouth 48 1 40N18'11 96w59'19 6:27:57
Pohocco 78 1 41N22 96w31 6:26:04
Point of Rocks 17 2 41N12'37 103w14'44 6:52:59
Polk 72 1 41N04'36 97w47'01 6:31:08
Ponca 26 1 42N33'45 96w42'19 6:26:49
Ponca 54 1 42N42'43 98w04'27 6:32:18
Ponce Indian Reservation 54 1 42N43 98w04 6:32:16
Poole 10 1 40N58'47 98w58'10 6:35:53
Portal 77 1 41N10'35 96w04'50 6:24:19
Porter 74 1 40N13 95w51 6:23:24
Posen 47 1 41N13 98w40 6:34:40
Potsdam 91 1 40N18 98w27 6:33:48
Potter 17 2 41N13'03 103w18'55 6:53:16
Powell 48 1 40N13'15 97w17'04 6:29:08
Prague 78 1 41N18'37 96w48'29 6:27:14
Prairie 69 1 40N24 99w22 6:37:28
Prairie Center 10 1 40N51'32 99w03'17 6:36:13
Prairie Dog 42 3 40N02 99w22 6:37:28
Prairie Home 55 1 40N51'53 96w31'14 6:26:05
Prairie Island 61 1 41N09 97w52 6:31:28
Precept 33 3 40N04'04 99w43'58 6:38:56
Preston 74 1 40N02'04 95w31'01 6:22:04
Primrose 6 1 41N37'23 98w14'16 6:32:57
Princeton 55 1 40N34'25 96w42'16 6:26:49
Prosser 1 1 40N41'14 98w34'35 6:34:18
Purdum 5 3 42N03'54 100w15'29 6:41:02
Quick 32 1 40N26'21 100w38'50 6:42:35
Quinnebaugh 11 1 41N57 96w12 6:24:48
Rackett 35 2 41N40'00 102w12'20 6:48:49
Raeville 6 1 41N53'47 98w03'13 6:32:13
Ragan 42 1 40N18'37 99w17'22 6:37:09
Ralston 28 1 41N12'19 96w02'32 6:24:10
Ramshorn 84 1 41N47 97w12 6:28:48
Randolph 14 1 42N22'43 97w21'24 6:29:26
Ravenna 10 1 41N01'34 98w54'44 6:35:39
Raymond 55 1 40N57'25 96w46'57 6:27:08
Read 12 1 41N05 97w19 6:29:16
Reading 12 1 41N11 97w19 6:29:16
Redbird 45 1 42N45'42 98w26'32 6:33:46
Red Cloud 91 1 40N05'20 98w31'09 6:34:05
Redington 4 2 41N35'02 103w16'21 6:53:05
Redus 79 2 41N59'58 103w52'15 6:55:29
Red Willow 73 3 40N13'31 100w29'49 6:41:59
Regency 28 1 41N16 96w03 6:24:12
Rellers Park 28 1 41N22'57 96w18'00 6:25:12
Reno 81 2 42N10 102w37 6:50:28
Republican City 42 1 40N05'59 99w13'12 6:36:53
Reuben 42 1 40N13 99w28 6:37:52
Reynolds 30 1 40N03'35 97w20'07 6:29:20
Richardson 12 1 41N05 96w58 6:27:52
Richfield 77 1 41N06'30 96w04'30 6:24:18
Richland 19 1 41N26'08 97w12'44 6:28:51
Richmond 33 3 40N03 99w48 6:39:12
Ridgeley 27 1 41N37 96w44 6:26:56
Ridnour 44 3 40N13 101w02 6:44:08
Ringgold 59 3 41N30'31 100w47'28 6:43:10
Rising City 12 1 41N11'58 97w17'45 6:29:11
Riverdale 10 1 40N47'04 99w09'43 6:36:39
Riverside 78 1 41N05'58 96w21'19 6:25:25
Riverside Lakes 28 1 41N17 96w17 6:25:08
Riverside Park 61 1 41N05'47 97w58'21 6:31:53
Riverside Park 80 1 40N47'15 97w03'03 6:28:12
Riverton 31 1 40N05'22 98w45'31 6:35:02
Riverview 52 1 42N43'45 99w35'21 6:38:21
Roach 33 2 42N01'20 103w56'01 6:55:44
Roanoke 28 1 41N18 96w02 6:24:08
Robb 37 1 40N40 99w42 6:38:48
Roca 55 1 40N39'27 96w39'28 6:26:38
Rockford 34 1 40N15'06 96w36'00 6:26:24
Rockton 33 3 40N03 100w01 6:40:04
Rockville 82 1 41N07'06 98w49'53 6:35:20
Rogers 19 1 41N27'55 96w54'53 6:27:40
Rohrs 64 1 40N23'34 95w55'56 6:23:44
Rokeby 55 1 40N42'43 96w44'09 6:26:57
Rosalie 87 1 42N03'23 96w30'44 6:26:03
Roscoe 51 2 41N07'50 101w35'07 6:46:20
Rose 75 1 42N10'50 99w31'31 6:38:06
Rosedale 40 1 40N42'47 98w28'23 6:33:54
Rosedale 56 3 41N14 100w54 6:43:36
Roseland 1 1 40N28'13 98w33'32 6:34:14
Roselma 6 1 41N40 98w07 6:32:28
Rosemont 91 1 40N17'13 98w21'50 6:33:27
Rosenburg 71 1 41N37'55 97w45'13 6:31:01
Roubadeau 79 2 41N47 103w46 6:55:04
Rounds Place 3 2 41N36'04 101w36'20 6:46:25
Round Valley 21 1 41N34'06 99w31'09 6:38:05
Royal 2 1 42N19'56 98w07'32 6:32:30
Ruby 80 1 40N49'53 97w04'36 6:28:18
Rudy 48 1 40N03'52 97w03'16 6:28:13
Rulo 74 1 40N03'07 95w25'36 6:21:42
Rumsey 77 1 41N08'48 95w59'36 6:23:58
Running Water 83 2 42N25 103w47 6:55:08
Rusco 10 1 40N55 99w07 6:36:28
Rush Creek 35 2 41N18 102w29 6:49:56
Rushville 81 2 42N43'06 102w27'49 6:49:51
Ruskin 65 1 40N08'38 97w52'08 6:31:29
Ruthton 51 2 41N18'40 102w00'37 6:48:02
Ryno 21 1 41N21 99w48 6:39:12
Sacramento 69 1 40N24'32 99w16'29 6:37:06
Saint Bernard 71 1 41N43'19 97w37'43 6:30:31
Saint Charles 20 1 41N47'36 96w44'55 6:27:00
Saint Columbans 77 1 41N05 95w52 6:23:28

Place		Lat.	Long.	Time
Saint Edward 71	1	41N34'12	97w51'56	6:31:28
Saint Helena 14	1	42N48'35	97w14'55	6:29:00
Saint James 14	1	42N44'17	97w09'02	6:28:36
Saint Johns 22	1	42N28	96w35	6:26:20
Saint Libory 47	1	41N04'55	98w21'18	6:33:25
Saint Mary 49	1	40N25'27	96w17'23	6:25:10
Saint Michael 10	1	41N01'25	98w44'51	6:34:59
Saint Paul 47	1	41N12'53	98w27'28	6:33:50
Saint Stephens 65	1	40N15'13	98w15'21	6:33:01
Salem 74	1	40N04'32	95w43'14	6:22:53
Salt Creek 13	1	40N59	96w24	6:25:36
Saltillo 55	1	40N42'00	96w40'56	6:26:44
Sanborn 29	2	40N03'13	102w01'11	6:48:05
Sand Creek 45	1	42N43	98w59	6:35:56
Sandridge 9	3	42N33'23	99w56'57	6:39:48
Santee 54	1	42N50'28	97w51'02	6:31:24
Santee Indian Reservation 54	1	42N50	97w51	6:31:24
Sappa 42	3	40N08	99w34	6:38:16
Saratoga 45	1	42N45	98w50	6:35:20
Sarben 51	2	41N10	101w18	6:45:12
Sargent 21	1	41N38'26	99w22'15	6:37:29
Saronville 18	1	40N36'04	97w56'17	6:31:45
Sartoria 10	1	40N58'42	99w12'49	6:36:51
Saunders 88	1	41N35'10	98w53'17	6:35:33
Savannah 12	1	41N21	97w12	6:28:48
Scandinavia 42	1	40N19	99w20	6:37:20
Schaupps 82	1	41N15	98w48	6:35:12
Schneider 10	1	40N55	98w53	6:35:32
Schoolcraft 60	1	41N52	97w39	6:30:36
School Creek 18	1	40N39	97w53	6:31:32
Schuyler 19	1	41N26'50	97w03'33	6:28:14
Scotia 39	1	41N27'59	98w42'10	6:34:49
Scotia Junction 39	1	41N27'19	98w43'02	6:34:52
Scottsbluff 79	2	41N52'00	103w40'00	6:54:40
Scovill 41	1	40N45	98w13	6:32:52
Scoville 33	2	42N00'56	103w55'03	6:55:40
Scribner 27	1	41N40'00	96w39'56	6:26:40
Sears 79	2	41N53'36	104w00'18	6:56:01
Second Lafayette 64	1	40N29	95w56	6:23:44
Sedan 65	1	40N20'33	97w53'49	6:31:35
Selden 75	1	42N20	99w34	6:38:16
Sellers 56	3	41N00	100w50	6:43:20
Seneca 86	3	42N02'36	100w49'57	6:43:20
Seward 80	1	40N54'25	97w05'55	6:28:24
Seymour Park 28	1	41N13	96w03	6:24:12
Shamrock 45	1	42N18	98w44	6:34:56
Sharon 10	1	40N50	98w47	6:35:08
Sheep Creek 83	2	42N12	103w51	6:55:24
Shelby 72	1	41N11'32	97w25'30	6:29:42
Sheldonville 71	1	41N27'50	97w25'32	6:29:42
Shelton 10	1	40N47	98w44	6:34:56
Shelton 40	1	41N32'55	98w43'50	6:34:55
Shestak 76	1	40N34'05	96w57'47	6:27:51
Shickley 30	1	40N25'00	97w43'20	6:30:53
Shields 45	1	42N34	98w39	6:34:36
Shippee 73	3	40N03'33	100w12'07	6:40:48
Sholes 90	1	42N19'58	97w17'39	6:29:11
Shubert 74	1	40N14'11	95w40'55	6:22:44
Sicily 34	1	40N08	96w45	6:27:00
Sidney 17	2	41N08'34	102w58'39	6:51:55
Silver Creek 61	1	41N18'32	97w39'27	6:30:38
Silver Lake 1	1	40N23	98w33	6:34:12
Simeon 16	6	42N36'48	100w43'10	6:42:53
Skull Creek 12	1	41N16	96w58	6:27:52
Slough 70	1	42N13	97w25	6:29:40
Smith 9	3	42N21	99w45	6:39:00
Smithfield 37	1	40N34'21	99w44'31	6:38:58
Smyrna 65	1	40N07'07	98w04'01	6:32:16
Snake Creek 83	2	42N15	103w36	6:54:24
Snyder 27	1	41N42'14	96w47'18	6:27:09
Somerset 56	3	40N49'31	100w51'38	6:43:27
South 53	2	41N03	103w40	6:54:40
South Bayard 62	2	41N42'57	103w19'16	6:53:17
South Bend 13	1	41N00'06	96w14'42	6:24:59
South Cedar 78	1	41N21	96w37	6:26:28
South Crawford 23	2	42N39	103w23	6:53:32
South Deer Creek 60	1	42N01	97w39	6:30:36
South Dry Creek 70	1	42N19	97w46	6:31:04
South Loup 40	1	41N00	98w39	6:34:36
South Mc Williams 66	1	40N33	96w04	6:24:16
South Minden 50	1	40N30	98w57	6:35:48
South Mitchell 79	2	41N54'40	103w48'46	6:55:15
South Morrill 79	2	41N55'47	103w55'40	6:55:43
South Omaha 28	1	41N12'38	95w57'44	6:23:51
South Palmyra 66	1	40N40	96w24	6:25:36
South Pass 55	1	40N34	96w38	6:26:32
South Russell 66	1	40N39	96w18	6:25:12
South Sioux City 22	1	42N28'26	96w24'48	6:25:39
South Syracuse 66	1	40N38	96w11	6:24:44
South Yankton 14	1	42N50'58	97w23'53	6:29:36
Spade 54	1	42N39	97w54	6:31:36
Spalding 39	1	41N41'20	98w21'47	6:33:27
Sparks 16	5	42N56'28	100w15'20	6:41:01
Sparta 54	1	42N39'19	97w58'24	6:31:54
Speiser 74	1	40N03	95w57	6:23:48
Spelts 88	1	41N35'48	98w50'49	6:35:23
Spencer 8	1	42N52'26	98w42'04	6:34:48
Spencer Park 1	1	40N35	98w24	6:33:36
Spotted Horse 3	2	41N28	101w34	6:46:16
Spotted Tail 83	2	42N02	103w45	6:55:00
Sprague 55	1	40N37'33	96w44'40	6:26:59
Spring Bank 26	1	42N24	96w50	6:27:20
Spring Branch 84	1	42N03	97w19	6:29:16
Spring Creek 21	1	41N28	99w17	6:37:08
Springfield 77	1	41N04'55	96w08'03	6:24:32
Spring Green 33	3	40N03	99w55	6:39:40
Spring Grove 42	1	40N19	99w34	6:38:16
Spring Ranch 18	1	40N24	98w13	6:32:52
Springview 52	1	42N49'28	99w44'55	6:39:00
Spurlor Place 83	2	42N08'41	103w54'18	6:55:37
Spurville 84	1	42N01'08	97w12'50	6:28:51
Stafford 45	1	42N19'42	98w26'48	6:33:47
Stamford 42	3	40N07'59	99w35'33	6:38:22
Stanton 84	1	41N57'01	97w13'25	6:28:54
Staplehurst 80	1	40N58'30	97w10'20	6:28:41
Stapleton 57	1	41N28'49	100w30'45	6:42:03
Star 45	1	42N36'41	98w20'24	6:33:22
Starkey 44	3	40N13	101w09	6:44:36
State House 55	1	40N49	96w40	6:26:40
Steel Creek 45	1	42N41	98w21	6:33:24
Steele City 48	1	40N02'16	97w01'28	6:28:06
Stegall 79	2	41N52'17	103w56'49	6:55:47
Steinauer 67	1	40N12'28	96w14'02	6:24:56
Stella 74	1	40N13'59	95w46'23	6:23:06
Sterling 49	1	40N27'33	96w22'38	6:25:31
Stevens Creek 55	1	40N50	96w31	6:26:04
Stewart 93	1	41N00	97w26	6:29:44
Still Meadow 28	1	41N19	96w02	6:24:08
Stillwater 91	1	40N13	98w20	6:33:20
Stockham 41	1	40N42'58	97w56'22	6:31:45
Stocking 78	1	41N11	96w37	6:26:28
Stockton 55	1	40N44	96w31	6:26:04
Stockville 32	1	40N31'58	100w22'59	6:41:32
Stock Yards 28	1	41N13	95w58	6:23:52
Stokes Ranch 92	1	41N58'39	98w28'59	6:33:56
Storm Lake 62	2	41N48	102w44	6:50:56
Story 83	2	42N55'48	103w56'17	6:55:45
Stove Creek 13	1	40N49	96w18	6:25:12
Strahan 90	1	42N13	97w05	6:28:20
Strang 30	1	40N24'56	97w35'12	6:30:21
Stratton 44	3	40N08'53	101w13'35	6:44:54
Straussville 74	1	40N06'30	95w38'01	6:22:32
Strohl 58	1	41N50	99w31	6:38:04
Stromsburg 72	1	41N06'51	97w35'55	6:30:24
Stuart 45	1	42N35'57	99w08'32	6:36:34
Sugar Loaf 83	2	42N54	103w35	6:54:20
Sughrue 35	2	41N17	102w20	6:49:20
Sumner 24	1	40N57'00	99w30'28	6:38:02
Sumter 88	1	41N35'22	98w47'17	6:35:09
Sunnyslope 28	1	41N18	96w02	6:24:08
Sunol 17	2	41N09'19	102w45'47	6:51:03
Sunshine 56	3	41N04	101w12	6:44:48
Superior 65	1	40N01'15	98w04'11	6:32:17
Surprise 12	1	41N06'31	97w18'39	6:29:15
Survey 16	2	42N01	101w56	6:47:44
Sutherland 56	3	41N09'25	101w07'33	6:44:30
Sutton 18	1	40N36'20	97w51'32	6:31:26
Swan Creek 76	1	40N23	97w05	6:28:20
Swan Lake 43	3	40N29	101w10	6:44:40
Swan Lake 45	1	42N10'12	99w01'17	6:36:05
Swanton 76	1	40N22'43	97w04'46	6:28:19
Swedeburg 78	1	41N08'09	96w37'16	6:26:29
Swedehome 72	1	41N09'46	97w39'48	6:30:39
Sweetwater 10	1	41N02'40	99w00'26	6:36:02
Syracuse 66	1	40N39'26	96w11'10	6:24:45
Table Rock 67	1	40N10'42	96w05'47	6:24:23
Tabor 79	2	41N50	103w31	6:54:04
Talmage 66	1	40N31'50	96w01'17	6:24:05
Tamora 80	1	40N53'38	97w13'29	6:28:54
Tangeman 66	1	40N33'31	96w05'10	6:24:21
Tarnov 71	1	41N36'57	97w30'07	6:30:00
Taylor 58	1	41N46'13	99w22'42	6:37:31
Tecumseh 49	1	40N22'00	96w11'45	6:24:47
Tekamah 11	1	41N46'42	96w13'15	6:24:53
Telbasta 89	1	41N34'54	96w23'09	6:25:33
Terrytown 79	2	41N50'51	103w39'40	6:54:39
Tewsville 54	1	42N45'25	97w44'22	6:30:57
Thatcher 16	5	42N48'22	100w27'57	6:41:52
Thayer 93	1	41N12'35	97w29'51	6:29:59
Thedford 86	3	41N58'42	100w34'33	6:42:18
The Mall 56	1	41N08	100w46	6:43:04
Thomas Place 16	5	42N20'56	100w19'57	6:41:20
Thompson 30	1	40N04'06	97w15'30	6:29:02
Thompson 70	1	42N23	97w39	6:30:36
Thornburg 43	3	40N29	100w50	6:43:20
Thornton 10	1	40N50	99w00	6:36:00
Thune 3	2	41N29	101w27	6:45:48
Thurman 75	1	42N29	99w32	6:38:08
Thurston 87	1	42N10'38	96w42'02	6:26:48
Tilden 60	1	42N02'50	97w50'01	6:31:20
Timber Creek 63	1	41N26'53	98w11'44	6:32:47
Tipton 13	1	40N50	96w24	6:25:36
Tobias 76	1	40N25'05	97w20'09	6:29:21
Todd 13	1	40N52'52	95w55'48	6:23:43
Todd Creek 49	1	40N19	96w08	6:24:32
Tony 79	2	41N49'50	103w23'43	6:53:35
Touhy 78	1	41N07'59	96w49'22	6:27:17
Townhall 30	1	40N32'47	97w25'32	6:29:42
Townsend 83	2	42N05	104w01	6:56:04
Trenton 44	3	40N10'32	101w00'45	6:44:03
Triumph 21	1	41N23	100w00	6:40:00
Trognitz 17	2	41N22	103w18	6:53:12
Trout 79	2	41N53'47	103w36'10	6:54:25
Trued 24	1	40N43'40	99w27'50	6:37:51
Trumbull 18	1	40N40'46	98w16'23	6:33:06
Tryon 59	3	41N33'10	100w57'26	6:43:50
Tyrone 73	3	40N08	100w15	6:41:00
Uehling 27	1	41N44'03	96w30'17	6:26:01
Ulysses 12	1	41N04'19	97w12'06	6:28:48
Unadilla 66	1	40N41'00	96w16'10	6:25:05
Union 13	1	40N48'48	95w55'21	6:23:41
Union Creek 84	1	41N52	97w18	6:29:12
Union Valley 17	2	41N24	102w54	6:51:36
University Place 55	1	40N50'27	96w39'18	6:26:37
Upland 31	1	40N19'07	98w54'03	6:35:36
Upper Driftwood 44	3	40N03	101w03	6:44:12
Utica 93	1	40N53'58	97w23'57	6:29:36
Valentine 16	6	42N52'22	100w33'02	6:42:12
Valley 28	1	41N18'46	96w20'45	6:25:23
Valley Grange 73	3	40N09	100w36	6:42:24
Valparaiso 78	1	41N04'53	96w49'53	6:27:20
Vance 62	2	41N46'38	103w06'46	6:52:27
Velma 3	2	41N37'53	101w56'29	6:47:46
Venango 68	2	40N45'49	102w02'25	6:48:10
Venice 28	1	41N14'02	96w21'12	6:25:25
Venus 2	1	42N27'26	98w16'03	6:33:04
Verdel 54	1	42N48'40	98w11'32	6:32:46
Verdigre 54	1	42N35'49	98w02'00	6:32:08
Verdon 74	1	40N08'54	95w42'45	6:22:51
Vernon, Mount 17	2	41N06'24	103w11'57	6:52:48
Verona 1	1	40N39	98w33	6:34:12
Verona 18	1	40N33'13	97w57'57	6:31:52
Vesta 49	1	40N21'23	96w20'14	6:25:21
Veterans Administration Hosp 28	1	41N15	95w58	6:23:52
Victor 65	1	40N18	98w13	6:32:52
Victoria 21	3	41N37	99w48	6:39:12
Vieregg 61	1	40N57	98w15	6:33:00
Vincent 33	3	40N13	100w01	6:40:04
Vinton 88	1	41N31	99w02	6:36:08
Virginia 34	1	40N14'45	96w29'48	6:25:59
Vothees 6	1	41N38'54	97w53'20	6:31:33
Vroman 56	1	40N58'01	100w15'25	6:41:02
Wabash 13	1	40N53'11	96w15'15	6:25:01
Waco 93	1	41N43'59	97w27'47	6:29:51
Wagners Lake 71	1	41N25'19	97w23'07	6:29:32
Wahoo 78	1	41N12'41	96w37'12	6:26:29
Wakefield 26	1	42N16'09	96w51'53	6:27:28
Wallace 56	3	40N50'18	101w09'52	6:44:39
Walnut 54	1	42N32'58	98w12'31	6:32:50
Walnut Creek 91	1	40N03	98w40	6:34:40
Walnut Grove 54	1	42N31	98w15	6:33:00
Walthill 87	1	42N08'54	96w29'17	6:25:57
Walton 55	1	40N47'55	96w33'42	6:26:15
Walworth 21	1	41N39'10	99w34'38	6:38:19
Wanda 1	1	40N34	98w40	6:34:40
Wann 78	1	41N08'48	96w21'20	6:25:25
Warbonnet 83	2	42N49	103w55	6:55:40
Ware 8	1	42N59	98w46	6:35:04
Warnerville 60	1	41N57'36	97w26'45	6:29:47
Warsaw 47	1	41N12	98w34	6:34:16
Washington 89	1	41N23'51	96w12'28	6:24:50
Waterbury 26	1	42N27'28	96w44'04	6:26:56
Waterloo 28	1	41N17'13	96w17'07	6:25:08
Wauneta 15	2	40N25'06	101w22'15	6:45:29
Wausa 54	1	42N29'58	97w32'30	6:30:10
Waverly 55	1	40N55'03	96w31'41	6:26:07
Wayne 90	1	42N13'50	97w01'03	6:28:04
Wayside 23	2	42N57	103w20	6:53:20
Webster 27	1	41N35'50	96w47'23	6:27:10
Weeping Water 13	1	40N52'12	96w08'25	6:24:34
Wee Town 70	1	42N12'24	97w25'33	6:29:42
Weir 46	2	42N02'17	101w21'59	6:45:28
Weissert 21	1	41N28'02	99w26'34	6:37:46
Weitzel 6	1	41N42	97w53	6:31:32
Well 56	1	40N53	100w42	6:42:48
Wellfleet 56	1	40N45'08	100w43'46	6:42:55
Wells 16	2	42N17	101w02	6:44:08
Wescott 21	1	41N32'20	99w16'11	6:37:05
West Branch 67	1	40N03	96w17	6:25:08
West Chadron 23	2	42N51	103w04	6:52:16
West Dodge 28	1	41N16	95w58	6:23:52
Western 76	1	40N23'37	97w11'52	6:28:47
Westerville 21	1	41N23'46	99w22'50	6:37:31
West Gordon 81	2	42N49	102w16	6:49:04
West Lincoln 55	1	40N50'16	96w43'51	6:26:55
Westmark 69	1	40N35'52	99w31'47	6:38:07
West Mirage 81	2	42N27	102w42	6:50:48
West Newman 63	1	41N18	98w02	6:32:08
West Oak 55	1	41N00	96w51	6:27:24
West Ogallala 51	2	41N07	101w47	6:47:08
West Omaha 28	1	41N16	96w03	6:24:12
Weston 78	1	41N11'39	96w44'33	6:26:58
West Point 20	1	41N50'30	96w42'30	6:26:50
West Rock Bluffs 13	1	40N55	95w57	6:23:48
Westside 69	1	40N38	99w35	6:38:20
West Union 21	1	41N41	99w30	6:38:00
West Winters Creek 79	2	41N53	103w42	6:54:48
Weyerts 17	2	41N09	102w38	6:50:32
Whistle Creek 83	2	42N25	103w34	6:54:16
Whiteclay 81	2	42N59'49	102w33'15	6:50:13
White River 83	2	42N37	103w32	6:54:08
Whitetail 51	2	41N16	101w36	6:46:24
Whitewater 59	3	41N39	101w17	6:45:08
Whitman 38	2	42N02'31	101w31'22	6:46:05
Whitney 23	2	42N46'58	103w15'20	6:53:01
Whittier 56	1	41N22	100w31	6:42:04
Wilber 76	1	40N28'53	96w57'37	6:27:50
Wilbur 90	1	42N18	97w05	6:28:20
Wilcox 50	1	40N21'54	99w10'11	6:36:41
Williamsburg 69	1	40N39	99w27	6:37:48
Willis 22	1	42N28'31	96w37'43	6:26:31
Willow Creek 70	1	42N14	97w46	6:31:04

Willowdale 45 1 42N34 98w25 6:33:40
Willow Grove 73
3 40N14 100w35 6:42:20
Willow Island 24
1 40N53'19 100w04'16 6:40:17
Willow Springs 36
1 41N51 99w05 6:36:20
Wilson Ranch 45
1 42N41'42 99w04'37 6:36:18
Wilsonville 33 3 40N06'43 100w06'24 6:40:26
Winnebago 87 1 42N14'09 96w28'20 6:25:53
Winnebago Indian Reservation 87
1 42N14 96w28 6:25:52
Winnetoon 54 1 42N30'45 97w57'38 6:31:51
Winside 90 1 42N10'35 97w10'29 6:28:42
Winslow 89 1 41N36'33 96w30'15 6:26:01
Wisner 20 1 41N59'14 96w54'50 6:27:39
Wolbach 47 1 41N23'49 98w23'38 6:33:35
Woodcliff 78 1 41N22'54 96w28'17 6:25:53
Wood Lake 16 5 42N38'19 100w14'16 6:40:57
Woodlawn 55 1 40N52'48 96w46'44 6:27:07
Wood River 40 1 40N49'14 98w35'59 6:34:24
Woodson 68 2 40N57 101w22 6:45:28
Woodville 71 1 41N34 97w46 6:31:04
Worden 59 3 41N39 101w04 6:44:16
Worms 61 1 41N05'50 98w16'07 6:33:04
Wounded Knee 81
2 42N57 102w14 6:48:56
Wright 7 2 42N06 103w03 6:52:12
Wrights 4 2 41N37 103w29 6:53:56
Wymore 34 1 40N07'20 96w39'44 6:26:39
Wynot 14 1 42N44'25 97w10'08 6:28:41
Wyoming 66 1 40N44'08 95w55'09 6:23:41
Yale 88 1 41N26 99w02 6:36:08
Yankee 68 2 40N47 101w24 6:45:36
Yankee Hill 55 1 40N46 96w44 6:26:56
Yockey 62 2 41N45 103w11 6:52:44
York 93 1 40N52'05 97w35'30 6:30:22
Yossem's Paradise Valley 28
1 41N18 96w02 6:24:08
Yutan 78 1 41N14'42 96w23'49 6:25:35
Zero 1 1 40N24 98w27 6:33:48
Zimmer 32 1 40N29 100w43 6:42:52

TIME TABLES

There is uncertainty about the time zone boundary in the sparsely populated eastern part of the state. Changes from Mountain time to Pacific time or the reverse in rural areas are undocumented.

NV # 1

Before 11/18/1883		LMT
11/18/1883	12:00	PST
3/31/1918	02:00	PWT
10/27/1918	02:00	PST
3/30/1919	02:00	PWT
10/26/1919	02:00	PST
2/09/1942	02:00	PWT
9/30/1945	02:00	PST
3/14/1948	02:00	PDT
1/01/1949	02:00	PST
4/30/1950	02:00	PDT
9/24/1950	02:00	PST
4/29/1951	02:00	PDT
9/30/1951	02:00	PST
4/27/1952	02:00	PDT
9/28/1952	02:00	PST
4/26/1953	02:00	PDT
9/27/1953	02:00	PST
4/25/1954	02:00	PDT
9/26/1954	02:00	PST
4/24/1955	02:00	PDT
9/25/1955	02:00	PST
4/29/1956	02:00	PDT
9/30/1956	02:00	PST
4/28/1957	02:00	PDT
9/29/1957	02:00	PST
4/27/1958	02:00	PDT
9/28/1958	02:00	PST
4/26/1959	02:00	PDT
9/27/1959	02:00	PST
4/24/1960	02:00	PDT
9/25/1960	02:00	PST
4/30/1961	02:00	PDT
9/24/1961	02:00	PST
4/29/1962	02:00	PDT
10/28/1962	02:00	PST
4/28/1963	02:00	PDT
10/27/1963	02:00	PST
4/26/1964	02:00	PDT
10/25/1964	02:00	PST
4/25/1965	02:00	PDT
10/31/1965	02:00	PST
4/24/1966	02:00	PDT
10/30/1966	02:00	PST
4/30/1967	02:00	US#1

NV # 2

Before 11/18/1883		LMT
11/18/1883	12:00	PST
3/31/1918	02:00	PWT
10/27/1918	02:00	PST
3/30/1919	02:00	PWT
10/26/1919	02:00	PST
1/01/1930	00:00	MST
2/09/1942	02:00	MWT
9/30/1945	02:00	MST
4/30/1967	02:00	US#1

NV # 3

Before 11/18/1883		LMT
11/18/1883	12:00	MST
3/31/1918	02:00	MWT
10/27/1918	02:00	MST
3/30/1919	02:00	MWT
10/26/1919	02:00	MST
2/09/1942	02:00	MWT
9/30/1945	02:00	MST
9/24/1965	00:00	PST
4/24/1966	02:00	US#1

NV # 4

Before 11/18/1883		LMT
11/18/1883	12:00	PST
3/31/1918	02:00	PWT
10/27/1918	02:00	PST
3/30/1919	02:00	PWT
10/26/1919	02:00	PST
1/01/1930	00:00	MST
2/09/1942	02:00	MWT
9/30/1945	02:00	MST
9/24/1965	00:00	PST
4/24/1966	02:00	US#1

COUNTIES

1 Churchill
2 Clark
3 Douglas
4 Elko
5 Esmeralda
6 Eureka
7 Humboldt
8 Lander
9 Lincoln
10 Lyon
11 Mineral
12 Nye
13 Pershing
14 Storey
15 Washoe
16 White Pine
17 Carson City

Place	TT	Latitude	Longitude	Time
Abbotts Fork 9	3	37N59'03	114w36'40	7:38:27
Acoma 9	3	37N32'54	114w10'18	7:36:41
Adaven 12	1	38N07'56	115w35'58	7:42:24
Adelaide 7	1	40N49'00	117w31'29	7:50:06
Adits Mill 8	1	39N13'39	117w08'08	7:48:33
Adverse 16	4	39N22'53	114w46'29	7:39:06
Alamo 9	3	37N21'54	115w09'49	7:40:39
Alazon 4	1	41N08'01	115w01'45	7:40:07
Alkali 5	1	37N49'33	117w20'12	7:49:21
Alpha 6	1	40N00'37	116w11'32	7:44:46
Alunite 2	1	35N59	114w55	7:39:40
Amador 8	1	39N33'35	117w04'51	7:48:19
Amber 2	1	36N36'29	114w29'36	7:37:58
Anderson 15	1	39N37'03	119w54'38	7:59:39
Andys Place 15	1	41N47'40	119w23'04	7:57:32
Apex 2	1	36N19'45	114w55'37	7:39:42
Appian 10	1	39N23'15	119w12'54	7:56:52
Arabia 13	1	40N21'49	118w23'30	7:53:34
Arden 2	1	36N01'05	115w13'48	7:40:55
Arena Rock 8	1	39N23'56	117w02'18	7:48:09
Argenta 8	1	40N40'28	116w42'17	7:46:49
Argo 10	1	39N35'51	119w09'46	7:56:39
Arrolime 2	1	36N21'05	114w54'30	7:39:38
Arrowhead 2	1	36N39'32	114w34'30	7:38:18
Arthur 4	1	40N47'48	115w11'24	7:40:46
Ash Springs 9	3	37N27'38	115w11'32	7:40:46
Ashton 12	1	36N43'13	116w40'18	7:46:41
Atlanta 9	3	37N57'25	114w29'03	7:37:56
Austin 8	1	39N29'36	117w04'07	7:48:16
Awakening 7	1	41N16'32	117w57'09	7:51:49
Babbitt 11	1	38N32'22	118w38'12	7:54:33
Baker 16	2	39N00'48	114w07'19	7:36:29
Bald Mountain 15	1	41N44	119w41	7:58:44
Baltimore Mill 16	4	39N17'04	114w52'05	7:39:28
Bango 1	1	39N30'02	119w02'24	7:56:10
Bannock 8	1	40N31'00	117w06'01	7:48:24
Barclay 9	3	37N30'49	114w15'35	7:37:02
Bard 2	1	35N59'16	115w14'12	7:40:57
Barth 6	1	40N34'54	116w16'06	7:45:04
Basalt 11	1	38N00'27	118w16'20	7:53:05
Battle Mountain 8	1	40N38	116w56	7:47:44
Beatty 12	1	36N54'31	116w45'30	7:47:02
Bellehelen 12	1	38N04'06	116w27'54	7:45:52
Belmont 12	1	38N35'46	116w52'24	7:47:30
Belmont Mill 16	4	39N16'35	115w30'49	7:42:03
Beowawe 6	1	40N35'34	116w28'35	7:45:54
Berlin 12	1	38N52'55	117w36'24	7:50:26
Bernard Place 15	1	41N23'06	119w22'46	7:57:31
Big Trees 9	3	37N54'10	114w33'35	7:38:14
Blackburn 6	1	40N13'42	116w10'01	7:44:40
Black Horse 16	2	39N08'46	114w16'53	7:37:08
Black Springs 15	1	39N36'35	119w51'18	7:59:25
Blair 5	1	37N47'35	117w38'54	7:50:36
Blair Junction 5	1	38N01'07	117w46'34	7:51:06
Bliss 7	1	41N01'45	117w36'29	7:50:26
Blue Diamond 2	1	36N02'47	115w24'11	7:41:37
Bolivia 1	1	39N59'33	117w54'44	7:51:39
Bonanza 2	1	36N12	115w10	7:40:40
Bonnie Claire 12	1	37N13'36	117w07'12	7:48:29
Bonnie Springs 2	1	36N03'33	115w27'09	7:41:49
Borax 2	1	35N42'52	115w20'23	7:41:22
Border Town 15	1	39N40'33	119w59'25	7:59:58
Boulder City 2	1	35N58'43	114w49'54	7:39:20
Boulder Junction 2	1	36N04'52	115w11'50	7:40:47
Boyd 9	3	37N26'16	114w33'59	7:38:16
Bracken 2	1	36N06'27	115w11'25	7:40:46
Bradys Hot Springs 1	1	39N47	119w02	7:56:08
Brown 9	3	37N36'26	114w07'55	7:36:32
Brucite 12	1	38N51'46	117w54'04	7:51:36
Brunswick 17	1	39N10'35	119w41'15	7:58:45
Buckeye 3	1	38N57'38	119w43'24	7:58:54
Buckingham Camp 8	1	40N36'47	117w04'18	7:48:17
Bull Fork 12	1	39N04'25	115w45'59	7:43:04
Bullfrog 12	1	36N53'25	116w49'58	7:47:20
Bullion 4	1	40N31'26	115w59'44	7:43:59
Bullion 7	1	41N34'27	117w28'41	7:49:55
Bunkerville 2	1	36N46'23	114w07'38	7:36:31
Cactus Springs 2	1	36N34'40	115w43'36	7:42:54
Caliente 9	3	37N36'54	114w30'40	7:38:03
Calumet 16	4	39N15'47	114w52'33	7:39:30
Camp Desert Rock 12	1	36N37'38	116w01'09	7:44:05
Canal 10	1	39N35	119w15	7:57:00
Candelaria Junction (Site) 11	1	38N10'33	118w10'54	7:52:44
Carlin 4	1	40N42'50	116w06'11	7:44:25
Carlton Square 2	1	36N12	115w08	7:40:32
Carp 9	3	37N06'43	114w29'31	7:37:58
Carrara 12	1	36N48'03	116w42'41	7:46:51
Carroll Station 8	1	39N27	118w45	7:55:00
Carson City 17	1	39N09'50	119w45'59	7:59:04
Carson Hot Springs 15	1	39N11'38	119w45'06	7:59:00
Carson Meadows 17	1	39N09	119w47	7:59:08
Carver Park 2	1	36N02'47	114w58'36	7:39:54
Carvers 12	1	38N47'12	117w10'42	7:48:43
Caselton 9	3	37N55'09	114w29'04	7:37:56
Caselton Heights 9	3	37N54'50	114w28'42	7:37:55
Castle Place 4	1	41N26'01	116w54'26	7:47:38
Cathcart 4	2	41N59'15	116w59'32	7:47:58
Cavin Place 15	1	41N11'54	119w34'16	7:58:17
Centerville 3	1	38N54'38	119w46'42	7:59:07
Charleston 4	2	41N40'15	115w30'35	7:42:02
Charleston Park 2	1	36N15'32	115w38'31	7:42:34
Cherry Creek 16	2	39N54'02	114w53'06	7:39:32
Chinatown 7	1	41N31'54	119w12'18	7:56:49
Churchill 10	1	39N16'18	119w16'48	7:57:07
Cibola Park 2	1	36N12	115w08	7:40:32
Clan Alpine 1	1	39N32'13	117w50'04	7:51:20
Clark 14	1	39N33'51	119w28'50	7:57:55
Clifside 4	2	40N54'58	114w16'35	7:37:06
Cluro 6	1	40N34'51	116w19'21	7:45:17
Coaldale 5	1	38N01'39	117w52'56	7:51:32
Coaldale Junction 5	1	38N01'54	117w53'10	7:51:33
Cobre 4	2	41N06'43	114w24'00	7:37:36
Coin 4	1	40N52'59	115w42'53	7:42:52
Colado 13	1	40N14'44	118w23'31	7:53:34
Cold Spring 9	3	37N45'05	114w25'26	7:37:42
Cold Springs 1	1	39N24'44	117w50'18	7:51:21
Columbus 5	1	38N06'37	118w01'06	7:52:04
Como 10	1	39N10'21	119w28'32	7:57:54
Comus 7	1	41N00'02	117w19'34	7:49:18
Conradts Landing 1	1	39N38'33	118w24'20	7:53:37
Contact 4	2	41N46'10	114w45'06	7:39:00
Copper Basin 8	1	40N36'11	117w02'44	7:48:11
Coppereid 1	1	39N50'56	118w13'05	7:52:52
Copperfield 15	1	39N37'54	119w56'38	7:59:47
Cordero 7	2	41N59	117w46	7:51:04
Cortez 8	1	40N08'28	116w36'09	7:46:25
Cosgrave 13	1	40N47'48	118w00'53	7:52:04
Cottonwood Cove 2	1	35N28	114w55	7:39:40
Cover City 4	1	41N06	114w58	7:39:52
Coyote Hole 5	1	37N45'48	117w43'30	7:50:54
Crescent Valley 6	1	40N35	116w29	7:45:56
Crestline 9	3	37N39'49	114w07'31	7:36:30
Crossroads 9	3	37N33'57	114w15'19	7:37:01
Crows Nest 12	1	38N21'06	115w39'45	7:42:39
Crystal 2	1	36N30'05	114w45'43	7:39:03
Crystal Bay 15	1	39N13'34	120w00'11	8:00:01
Currant 12	1	38N44'32	115w28'26	7:41:54
Currie 4	2	40N16'00	114w44'32	7:38:58
Danville 12	1	38N46'10	116w31'03	7:46:04
Darroughs Hot Springs 12	1	38N49'13	117w10'47	7:48:43
Darwin 10	1	39N35'22	119w06'04	7:56:24
Daveytown 7	1	41N17'42	117w54'08	7:51:37
Dayton 10	1	39N14'14	119w35'31	7:58:22
Decoy 4	2	40N40'18	114w29'13	7:37:57
Deep Creek 4	2	41N33'59	116w08'36	7:44:34
Deeth 4	1	41N03'56	115w16'26	7:41:06
Delamar 9	3	37N27'29	114w46'09	7:39:05
Delaplain 4	2	41N55'54	114w39'18	7:38:37
Del Monte 11	1	38N17'40	118w55'45	7:55:43
Denio 7	1	41N59'24	118w38'00	7:54:32
Denio Junction 7	1	41N57'06	118w37'26	7:54:30
Desert Inn Country Club 2	1	36N07	115w08	7:40:32
Desert View Point 2	1	36N18'44	115w35'07	7:42:20
Dewitt Mill 8	1	40N38'03	117w06'26	7:48:26
Dike 2	1	36N18'05	115w00'45	7:40:03
Dinner Station 4	1	41N06'00	115w51'55	7:43:28
Dixie 1	1	39N52'26	118w00'54	7:52:04
Dixie Valley 1	1	39N41'16	118w04'47	7:52:19
Dodge 15	1	39N40'15	119w18'40	7:57:15
Dolly Varden 4	2	40N32'41	114w32'04	7:38:08
Douglas 16	4	38N51'16	115w08'37	7:40:34
Downtown 2	1	36N11	115w07	7:40:28
Dresslerville 3	1	38N53'53	119w42'57	7:58:52
Dry Lake 2	1	36N27'24	114w50'32	7:39:22
Duck Valley 4	1	41N57	116w06	7:44:24
Duckwater 12	1	38N54	115w41	7:42:44
Duckwater Indian Reservation 12	1	38N54	115w41	7:42:44
Dun Glen 13	1	40N44'31	117w55'16	7:51:41
Dunphy 6	1	40N42'32	116w31'45	7:46:07
Dyer 5	1	37N40'42	118w05'01	7:52:20
Dyke 7	1	41N34'29	118w34'17	7:54:17
East Ely 16	4	39N15'18	114w52'06	7:39:28
East Fork 3	1	38N58	119w45	7:59:00
Eastgate 1	1	39N18'20	117w52'41	7:51:31
East Las Vegas 2	1	36N05'40	115w02'28	7:40:10
East Line 4	2	40N31	114w17	7:37:08
Eberhardt 16	1	39N11'42	115w28'47	7:41:55
Eccles 9	3	37N36'55	114w25'51	7:37:43
Echo Bay 2	1	36N33	114w27	7:37:48
Edgewood 3	1	38N57'39	119w56'27	7:59:46
Elburz 4	1	40N55'45	115w30'15	7:42:01
Elgin 9	3	37N21'07	114w32'06	7:38:08
Elko 4	1	40N49'57	115w45'44	7:43:03
Elks Point 3	1	39N00	119w57	7:59:48
Ellison 7	1	40N50'56	117w05'51	7:48:23
Ely 16	4	39N14'51	114w53'16	7:39:33
Empire 15	1	40N34'33	119w20'28	7:57:22
Empire 17	1	39N11'06	119w42'44	7:58:51
Erie 2	1	35N52'14	115w14'10	7:40:57
Esmeralda 5	1	38N51	117w07	7:48:28
Etna 9	3	37N33'19	114w34'14	7:38:17
Eunice Place 6	4	39N33'51	115w54'16	7:43:37
Eureka 6	4	39N30'46	115w57'35	7:43:50
Fallon 1	1	39N28'25	118w46'35	7:55:06
Fallon Indian Reservation 1	1	39N32	118w37	7:54:28
Fallon Station 1	1	39N26	118w43	7:54:52
Farrier 2	1	36N48'46	114w39'11	7:38:37
Fay 9	3	37N54'29	114w04'09	7:36:17
Federal 2	1	36N11	115w07	7:40:28
Fenelon 4	2	41N12'08	114w39'44	7:38:39
Fernley 10	1	39N36'29	119w15'03	7:57:00
Flanigan 15	1	40N10'15	119w53'08	7:59:33
Fleish 15	1	39N28'53	119w59'34	7:59:58
Fletcher 11	1	38N21'25	118w53'51	7:55:35
Florence Hill 5	1	37N42'28	117w13'04	7:48:52
Fort McDermitt Indian Reserv 7	2	42N00	117w43	7:50:52
Franktown 15	1	39N16'18	119w50'23	7:59:22
Frenchman 1	1	39N16'46	118w16'09	7:53:05
Gaar Place 4	2	41N56'15	115w16'01	7:41:04
Gabbs 12	1	38N52'08	117w55'16	7:51:41
Galena 8	1	40N33'52	117w07'45	7:48:31
Galena 15	1	39N31	119w49	7:59:16
Galt 9	3	37N01'03	114w36'18	7:38:25
Gardnerville 3	1	38N56'29	119w44'55	7:59:00
Gardnerville Ranchos 3	1	38N49	119w41	7:58:44
Garnet 2	1	36N23'19	114w52'13	7:39:29
Garside 2	1	36N10	115w12	7:40:48
Gemfield 5	1	37N44'23	117w17'39	7:49:11
Genoa 3	1	39N00'16	119w50'46	7:59:23
Gerald 6	1	40N35'01	116w14'55	7:45:00
Gerlach 15	1	40N39'06	119w21'15	7:57:25
Gilbert 5	1	38N11'46	117w41'45	7:50:47

Gilpin 14 1 39N35'53 119w20'05 7:57:20
Glassand 2 1 36N33'25 114w27'50 7:37:51
Glenbrook 3 1 39N05'22 119w56'17 7:59:45
Glendale 2 1 36N39'55 114w34'06 7:38:16
Glendale 15 1 39N31'14 119w44'22 7:58:57
Glenn 16 4 39N29'11 114w49'46 7:39:19
Golconda 7 1 40N57'12 117w29'18 7:49:57
Gold Acres 8 1 40N15'44 116w43'54 7:46:56
Gold Bar 12 1 36N56'17 116w53'33 7:47:34
Gold Butte 2 1 36N16'49 114w11'59 7:36:48
Gold Center 12 1 36N52'06 116w45'59 7:47:04
Golden 12 1 38N38'45 117w33'18 7:50:13
Golden Arrow 12 1 37N59'52 116w36'19 7:46:25
Goldfield 5 1 37N42'31 117w14'05 7:48:56
Gold Hill 14 1 39N17'26 119w39'23 7:58:38
Gold Hit 5 1 37N56'01 118w16'45 7:53:07
Gold Point 5 1 37N21'17 117w21'51 7:49:27
Goldquartz 8 1 40N18'39 116w41'58 7:46:48
Gold Run 7 1 41N03 117w15 7:49:00
Goldyke 12 1 38N44'13 117w52'07 7:51:28
Goodsprings 2 1 35N49'57 115w26'00 7:41:44
Goose Landing 1 1 39N37'16 118w25'43 7:53:43
Goshute 4 2 40N10'15 114w42'31 7:38:50
Goshute Indian Reservation 16 2 39N53 114w00 7:36:00
Gouge Eye 7 1 41N34'17 117w28'11 7:49:53
Granite Point 13 1 40N05'47 118w34'45 7:54:19
Grantsville 12 1 38N50'44 117w34'20 7:50:17
Greenbrae 15 1 39N36 119w45 7:59:00
Greenbrae School 15 1 39N32'55 119w44'48 7:58:59
Greens 16 2 40N02'10 114w44'48 7:38:59
Hafed 15 1 39N30'53 119w37'46 7:58:31
Halleck 4 1 40N57'03 115w27'07 7:41:48
Hamilton 16 4 39N15'11 115w29'08 7:41:57
Harney 6 1 40N34'39 116w19'26 7:45:18
Hawthorne 11 1 38N31'29 118w37'25 7:54:30
Hazen 1 1 39N33'55 119w02'43 7:56:11
Helene 9 3 37N28'52 114w46'33 7:39:06
Henderson 2 1 36N02'23 114w58'52 7:39:55
Henry 4 2 41N41'49 114w49'32 7:39:18
Herrin 7 1 40N53'16 117w13'09 7:48:53
Hidden Valley 15 1 39N31 119w48 7:59:12
Hiko 9 3 37N35'49 115w13'24 7:40:54
Hilltop 8 1 40N24'53 116w47'58 7:47:12
Hogan 4 2 40N44'39 114w35'53 7:38:24
Hogum 16 2 39N03'23 114w24'38 7:37:39
Holborn 4 2 41N10'28 114w42'29 7:38:50
Holbrook Junction 3 1 38N44'02 119w33'14 7:58:13
Horseshoe Bend 9 3 37N41'03 114w07'43 7:36:31
Hoya 9 3 36N56'49 114w39'05 7:38:36
Huffakers 15 1 39N31 119w48 7:59:12
Humboldt 13 1 40N36'11 118w15'03 7:53:00
Humboldt City 13 1 40N35'04 118w12'39 7:52:51
Hunter 4 1 40N45'10 115w54'09 7:43:37
Huntridge 2 1 36N09 115w08 7:40:32
Huxley 1 1 39N52'14 118w46'17 7:55:05
Imlay 13 1 40N39'39 118w08'58 7:52:36
Incline Village 15 1 39N15'05 119w58'19 7:59:53
Indian Cove 9 3 37N39'19 114w29'40 7:37:59
Indian Springs 2 1 36N34'11 115w40'11 7:42:41
Ione 12 1 38N56'54 117w35'12 7:50:21
Iron Point 7 1 40N56'52 117w16'33 7:49:06
Islen 9 3 37N31'47 114w19'15 7:37:17
Jackman 2 1 36N38'32 114w32'22 7:38:09
Jackpot 4 2 41N59'00 114w40'26 7:38:42
Jarbidge 4 2 41N52'25 115w25'52 7:41:43
Jean 2 1 35N46'44 115w19'23 7:41:18
Jefferson 12 1 38N42'48 116w50'54 7:47:56
Jenkins 8 1 40N41'03 116w51'31 7:47:26
Jessup 1 1 39N56'55 118w52'26 7:55:30
Jiggs 4 1 40N25'33 115w39'52 7:42:39
Johnnie 12 1 36N25'11 116w04'15 7:44:17
Joseco 9 3 37N30'07 114w13'42 7:36:55
Jungo 7 1 40N55'02 118w22'58 7:53:32
Kampos 8 1 40N41'45 116w42'03 7:46:48
Keystone 12 1 38N26'42 116w22'57 7:45:32
Keystone 16 4 39N16'55 114w58'03 7:39:52
Keystone Junction 16 4 39N16'59 114w57'47 7:39:51
Kimberly 16 4 39N15'48 115w01'18 7:40:05
Kingston 8 1 39N30 117w04 7:48:16
Kinkaid 11 1 38N32'42 118w23'38 7:53:35
Knight 7 1 40N54'20 117w09'14 7:48:37
Kodak 13 1 40N13'39 118w25'10 7:53:41
Kogan Place 16 4 39N28'03 114w59'42 7:39:59
Kyle 9 3 37N18'52 114w29'23 7:37:58
Kyle Hot Springs 13 1 40N24'23 117w52'57 7:51:32
Lake 13 1 40N24 118w20 7:53:20
Lake Mead Base 2 1 36N12 115w05 7:40:20
Lakeridge 3 1 39N02'11 119w56'50 7:59:47
Lake Tahoe 3 1 39N01 119w57 7:59:48
Lakeview 15 1 39N12'30 119w48'16 7:59:13
Lamoille 4 1 40N43'41 115w28'39 7:41:55
Lane 16 4 39N15'47 114w56'26 7:39:46
Lane City 16 4 39N15'38 114w55'50 7:39:43
Las Vegas 2 1 36N10'30 115w08'11 7:40:33
Las Vegas Highlands 2 1 36N12 115w08 7:40:32
Lathrop Wells 12 1 36N38'38 116w23'58 7:45:36
Laughlin 2 1 35N10'04 114w34'20 7:38:17
Lavon 16 4 39N19'40 114w47'45 7:39:11
Lawton 15 1 39N30'44 119w54'20 7:59:37
Lee 4 1 40N34 115w36 7:42:24
Lee Canyon Camp 2 1 36N18'38 115w40'27 7:42:42
Leeland 12 1 36N35'10 116w35'07 7:46:20
Lemmon Valley 15 1 39N31 119w49 7:59:16
Lida 5 1 37N27'30 117w29'50 7:49:59
Lincoln Park 3 1 39N02'23 119w56'50 7:59:47

Lockes 12 1 38N33'18 115w46'27 7:43:06
Lockwood 14 1 39N30'26 119w38'44 7:58:35
Logan 2 1 36N37 114w26 7:37:44
Logandale 2 1 36N35'48 114w29'00 7:37:56
Longacres Park 2 1 36N11 115w07 7:40:28
Loray 4 2 41N08'32 114w19'02 7:37:16
Lovell 2 1 36N17'29 115w02'32 7:40:10
Lovelock 13 1 40N10'46 118w28'21 7:53:53
Lower Rochester 13 1 40N17'09 118w12'00 7:52:48
Lucky Boy 11 1 38N27'37 118w40'41 7:54:43
Lund 16 4 38N51'24 115w00'25 7:40:02
Luning 11 1 38N30'23 118w10'50 7:52:43
Lux 10 1 39N07'38 119w06'46 7:56:27
Lyman Crossing 9 3 37N09'32 114w28'22 7:37:53
Majors Place 16 4 39N01'30 114w34'52 7:38:19
Manhattan 12 1 38N32'20 117w04'21 7:48:17
Marietta 11 1 38N14'36 118w20'16 7:53:21
Martin 15 1 39N36'15 119w52'15 7:59:29
Mason 10 1 38N57'00 119w11'21 7:56:45
Mason Valley 10 1 38N59 119w08 7:56:32
Massie 1 1 39N35'49 118w58'30 7:55:54
McCoy 8 1 40N19'13 117w13'27 7:48:54
McDermitt 7 2 41N59'51 117w43'02 7:50:52
McGill 16 4 39N24'18 114w46'40 7:39:07
McGill Junction 16 4 39N22'20 114w48'01 7:39:12
McLeans 5 1 38N02'52 117w39'04 7:50:36
Melandco 4 1 41N17'00 114w50'08 7:39:21
Mellan 12 1 37N42'45 116w35'38 7:46:23
Mendha 9 3 37N57'22 114w30'49 7:38:03
Mercury 12 1 36N39'38 115w59'37 7:43:58
Mesquite 2 1 36N48'20 114w03'59 7:36:16
Metropolis 4 1 41N06 114w58 7:39:52
Midas 4 1 41N14'39 116w47'45 7:47:11
Middlegate 1 1 39N17'16 118w01'32 7:52:06
Midway 11 1 38N43'25 118w18'01 7:53:12
Mill City 13 1 40N41'01 118w04'10 7:52:17
Millens Landing 1 1 39N37'36 118w31'19 7:54:05
Millers 5 1 38N08'12 117w27'24 7:49:50
Mina 11 1 38N23'26 118w06'28 7:52:26
Minden 3 1 38N57'15 119w45'53 7:59:04
Mine Mountain Junction 12 1 36N58'24 116w10'21 7:44:41
Mineral 6 1 40N10'25 116w11'09 7:44:45
Minerva 16 4 38N49'42 114w23'29 7:37:34
Miriam 1 1 39N57'31 118w41'13 7:54:45
Mizpah 4 2 40N23'45 114w39'45 7:38:39
Moapa 2 1 36N40'33 114w37'12 7:38:29
Moapa River 2 1 39N09 119w47 7:59:08
Mogul 15 1 39N30'50 119w55'30 7:59:42
Moleen 4 1 40N44'19 115w56'48 7:43:47
Montello 4 2 41N15'41 114w11'36 7:36:46
Montezuma 5 1 37N42'14 117w22'05 7:49:28
Montezuma Wells 5 1 38N10'19 117w24'56 7:49:40
Moor 4 1 41N07'02 114w48'51 7:39:15
Morey 12 1 38N40'00 116w15'22 7:45:01
Mosel 8 1 40N40'26 116w38'54 7:46:36
Mosier 16 4 39N15'38 114w49'34 7:39:18
Mote 7 1 40N44'33 117w03'35 7:48:14
Mottsville 3 1 38N55'43 119w50'12 7:59:21
Mountain City 4 2 41N50'19 115w57'52 7:43:51
Mountain Springs 2 1 36N01'15 115w30'29 7:42:02
Mount Airy 8 1 39N30'13 117w22'43 7:49:31
Mount Montgomery 11 1 37N58'47 118w19'14 7:53:17
Mud Springs 9 3 38N16'48 114w08'05 7:36:32
Mustang 15 1 39N31'19 119w37'39 7:58:31
Narrow Landing 1 1 39N38'05 118w29'45 7:53:59
Nellis 2 1 36N14 115w03 7:40:12
Nellis Air Force Base 2 1 36N12 115w05 7:40:20
Nelson 2 1 35N42'29 114w49'26 7:39:18
Nelsons Landing 2 1 35N42'28 114w42'45 7:38:51
New Empire 17 1 39N10'47 119w43'27 7:58:54
New River 1 1 39N30 118w46 7:55:04
New Washoe City 15 1 39N17'47 119w46'29 7:59:06
Nightingale 13 1 40N00'39 119w13'30 7:56:54
Ninemile Rocks 9 3 37N46'57 114w13'29 7:36:54
Nixon 15 1 39N49'55 119w21'25 7:57:26
Nordyke 10 1 38N53'29 119w11'10 7:56:45
North Battle Mountain 8 1 40N43 116w54 7:47:36
North Fork 4 1 40N50 115w46 7:43:04
North Las Vegas 2 1 36N11'56 115w07'00 7:40:28
Oasis 4 2 41N02 114w29 7:37:56
Ocala 1 1 39N54'37 118w44'04 7:54:56
Ola 4 2 40N43'17 114w08'45 7:36:35
Old Page Place 12 1 38N32'25 116w26'40 7:45:47
Olinghouse 15 1 39N39'30 119w25'41 7:57:43
Oreana 13 1 40N20'04 118w19'17 7:53:17
Orovada 7 1 41N34'12 117w47'04 7:51:08
Osceola 16 2 39N05'26 114w23'05 7:37:32
Osino 4 1 40N55'56 115w39'35 7:42:38
Overton 2 1 36N32'36 114w26'46 7:37:47
Owyhee 4 2 41N56'52 116w05'52 7:44:23
Pactolus 12 1 38N40'09 117w48'05 7:51:12
Pahrump 12 1 36N12'30 115w58'59 7:43:56
Palisade 6 1 40N36'37 116w11'52 7:44:47
Panaca 9 3 37N47'26 114w23'19 7:37:33
Panther 15 1 39N35'44 119w50'06 7:59:20
Paradise 2 1 36N07 115w08 7:40:32
Paradise Hill 7 1 40N59 117w44 7:50:56
Paradise Palms 2 1 36N07 115w08 7:40:32
Paradise Valley 2 1 36N07 115w08 7:40:32

Paradise Valley 7 1 41N29'37 117w32'01 7:50:08
Park Terrace 17 1 39N09 119w47 7:59:08
Parran 1 1 39N48'05 118w46'20 7:55:05
Patrick 15 1 39N32'50 119w34'42 7:58:19
Patsville 4 2 41N48'37 115w57'24 7:43:50
Peavine 15 1 39N31 119w48 7:59:12
Peers Landing 1 1 39N37'34 118w29'27 7:53:58
Pequop 4 2 41N13'02 114w35'19 7:38:21
Perth 13 1 40N07'44 118w30'51 7:54:03
Petersons Mill 8 1 39N33'28 117w25'54 7:49:44
Phil 15 1 40N38'34 119w28'06 7:57:52
Pilot 4 2 40N49'06 114w14'01 7:36:56
Pine Grove 10 1 38N40'42 119w07'33 7:56:30
Pioche 9 3 37N55'47 114w27'05 7:37:48
Pittman 2 1 36N03 114w59 7:39:56
Piute 8 1 40N41'47 117w00'06 7:48:00
Pleasant Valley 15 1 39N21'09 119w46'30 7:59:06
Point of Rocks 4 2 41N46'38 115w47'39 7:43:11
Poker Brown 13 1 40N32'09 118w25'09 7:53:41
Poker Brown Crossing 13 1 40N34'44 118w18'15 7:53:13
Pony Springs 9 3 38N19'08 114w36'21 7:38:25
Preble 7 1 40N58'36 117w23'50 7:49:35
Preston 16 4 38N54'49 115w03'35 7:40:14
Primeaux 6 1 40N38'56 116w18'03 7:45:12
Prince 9 3 37N54 114w28 7:37:52
Proctor 4 2 40N54 114w17 7:37:08
Pyramid 15 1 40N04'30 119w42'03 7:58:48
Pyramid Lake Indian Res 15 1 39N50 119w21 7:57:24
Quinn River Crossing 7 1 41N34'36 118w26'03 7:53:44
Raglan 7 1 40N54'34 117w58'09 7:51:53
Raleigh Heights 15 1 39N35'25 119w50'23 7:59:22
Ralston 12 1 37N33'22 117w09'07 7:48:36
Rawhide 1 1 39N01'15 118w23'35 7:53:34
Red House 7 1 40N59'49 117w14'50 7:48:59
Red House 15 1 39N12'21 119w52'22 7:59:29
Reese River 12 1 39N30 117w04 7:48:16
Reipetown 16 4 39N17 114w59 7:39:56
Rennox 8 1 40N41'53 116w52'45 7:47:31
Reno 15 1 39N31'47 119w48'46 7:59:15
Reynard 15 1 40N29'48 119w38'27 7:58:34
Rhyolite 12 1 36N54'14 116w49'42 7:47:19
Rice Landing 1 1 39N37'27 118w26'04 7:53:44
Riepetown 16 4 39N15'52 115w00'39 7:40:03
Ripley 2 1 35N47'53 115w36'03 7:42:24
Riverside 2 1 36N44'10 114w13'11 7:36:53
Rixies 6 1 40N41'52 116w33'02 7:46:12
Roach 2 1 35N38'27 115w21'30 7:41:26
Rochester 13 1 40N17'20 118w09'59 7:52:40
Rock House 4 2 41N59'03 115w39'41 7:42:39
Rockland 10 1 38N39'08 119w05'36 7:56:22
Rose Creek 7 1 40N53'24 117w53'39 7:51:35
Rose Valley 9 3 37N56'17 114w15'06 7:37:00
Rosny 8 1 40N36'45 116w50'15 7:47:21
Round Mountain 12 1 38N42'40 117w04'00 7:48:16
Rowland 4 2 41N56'12 115w40'40 7:42:43
Rox 9 3 36N52'51 114w39'59 7:38:40
Ruby 4 1 40N57'38 114w56'57 7:39:48
Ruby Valley 4 2 40N30 115w21 7:41:24
Ruppes Place 16 4 38N45'15 115w03'35 7:40:14
Russells 8 1 40N46'36 116w59'37 7:47:58
Ruth 16 4 39N16'42 114w59'18 7:39:57
Rye Patch 13 1 40N26'51 118w17'19 7:53:09
Ryndon 4 1 40N56'31 115w35'41 7:42:23
Sage 4 2 40N46'13 114w32'45 7:38:11
Salt Wells 1 1 39N23 118w35 7:54:20
Sand Pass 15 1 40N15'42 119w46'42 7:59:07
Sandy 2 1 35N48'15 115w36'15 7:42:25
San Jacinto 4 2 41N52'07 114w40'32 7:38:42
Sano 15 1 40N20'30 119w40'58 7:58:44
Schoer Place 4 2 41N28'54 114w55'38 7:39:43
Schurz 11 1 38N57'03 118w48'37 7:55:14
Scossa 13 1 40N44'24 118w35'44 7:54:23
Scottys Junction 12 1 37N17'56 117w03'07 7:48:12
Scraper Springs 4 1 41N20'16 116w40'49 7:46:43
Searchlight 2 1 35N27'55 114w55'08 7:39:41
Seven Troughs 13 1 40N27'45 118w49'00 7:55:16
Shafter 4 2 40N51'17 114w26'38 7:37:47
Shannon 6 1 40N06'01 116w12'03 7:44:48
Shanty Town 4 1 40N09'43 115w30'07 7:42:00
Sheridan 3 1 38N53'53 119w49'18 7:59:17
Shermantown 16 4 39N12'10 115w30'13 7:42:01
Shores 4 2 41N32'25 114w47'55 7:39:12
Shoshone 6 1 40N41'51 116w33'22 7:46:13
Sierra 15 1 39N36 119w54 7:59:36
Silverbow 12 1 37N53'17 116w29'28 7:45:58
Silver City 10 1 39N15'49 119w38'22 7:58:33
Silverpeak 5 1 37N45'18 117w38'02 7:50:32
Silver Springs 10 1 39N24'56 119w13'25 7:56:54
Silver Zone 4 2 40N55'13 114w21'09 7:37:25
Simpson 10 1 38N52'10 119w23'54 7:57:36
Skyland 3 1 39N01'21 119w56'50 7:59:47
Sloan 2 1 35N56'37 115w12'59 7:40:52
Smith 10 1 38N48'02 119w19'35 7:57:18
Smith Valley 10 1 38N46 119w17 7:57:08
Smoke Creek 15 1 40N26'51 119w39'57 7:58:40
Sodaville 11 1 38N20'28 118w06'07 7:52:24
South Swan Landing 1 1 39N39'10 118w27'30 7:53:50
Sparks 15 1 39N32'06 119w45'06 7:59:00
Spooner Junction 3 1 39N06'03 119w54'34 7:59:38
Springdale 12 1 37N01'48 116w45'15 7:47:01
Spruce 4 2 40N47'54 114w39'27 7:38:38
Sprucemont 4 2 40N33'02 114w52'17 7:39:29
Stagecoach 10 1 39N25 119w14 7:56:56
Stateline 2 1 35N47 115w20 7:41:20

Stateline 3	1	39N01	119w57	7:59:48
Steamboat 15	1	39N23	119w44	7:58:56
Steigmeyer Mill 12	1	38N44'03	117w03'24	7:48:14
Steptoe 16	4	39N24'25	114w45'47	7:39:03
Stewart 17	1	39N06'59	119w45'27	7:59:02
Stewarts Point 2	1	36N33	114w27	7:37:48
Stillwater 1	1	39N31'18	118w32'46	7:54:11
Stine 9	3	37N29'43	114w35'17	7:38:21
Sugar Bunker 12	1	36N50'22	115w57'37	7:43:50
Sulfur 10	1	38N37'11	119w15'10	7:57:01
Sulphur 7	1	40N52'29	118w44'08	7:54:57
Summit Lake 7	1	41N35	119w05	7:56:20
Sunnyside 12	4	38N25'24	115w01'13	7:40:05
Sunrise Manor 2	1	36N11	115w03	7:40:12
Sun Valley 15	1	39N36	119w47	7:59:08
Sutcliffe 15	1	39N57'01	119w35'58	7:58:24
Sutro 10	1	39N16'48	119w34'59	7:58:20
Swedes Place 15	1	41N13'01	119w29'43	7:57:59
Tahoe 3	1	39N01	119w57	7:59:48
Tahoe Village 3	1	38N58'13	119w56'06	7:59:44
Talapoosa 10	1	39N27'15	119w16'30	7:57:06
Tecoma 4	2	41N19'13	114w04'50	7:36:19
Tempiute 9	3	37N39'09	115w38'06	7:42:32
Tenabo 8	1	40N18'52	116w40'33	7:46:42
The Crossing 5	1	37N52'11	117w58'14	7:51:53
Thisbe 15	1	39N35'18	119w25'13	7:57:41
Thomas Place 6	1	40N30'04	116w13'37	7:44:54
Thorne 11	1	38N36'07	118w35'26	7:54:22
Thousand Springs 4	1	41N06	114w58	7:39:52
Tippett 16	2	39N52'07	114w20'56	7:37:24
Tokop 5	1	37N18'06	117w15'37	7:49:02
Tonka 4	1	40N43'02	116w00'33	7:44:02
Tonopah 12	1	38N04'02	117w13'45	7:48:55
Tonopah Junction 11	1	38N15'52	118w05'42	7:52:23
Topaz Lake 3	1	38N49	119w41	7:58:44
Topaz Ranch Estates 3	1	38N45	119w23	7:57:32
Toulon 13	1	40N03'46	118w38'38	7:54:35
Toy 13	1	40N01'01	118w40'20	7:54:41
Tracy-Clark 15	1	39N36	119w45	7:59:00
Trego 13	1	40N45'53	119w08'34	7:56:34
Tulasco 4	1	41N07'47	115w07'18	7:40:29
Tule 7	1	41N01'27	117w38'57	7:50:36
Tule Lake Landing 1	1	39N37'56	118w29'30	7:53:58
Tungsten 13	1	40N46'45	118w07'27	7:52:30
Tuscarora 4	1	41N18'51	116w13'15	7:44:53
Tybo 12	1	38N22'12	116w24'01	7:45:36
Tyrol 4	1	40N40'42	116w09'11	7:44:37
Union 6	1	40N10'03	116w01'25	7:44:06
Union 7	1	41N04	117w53	7:51:32
Unionville 13	1	40N26'44	118w07'11	7:52:29
University 15	1	39N33	119w50	7:59:20
Ursine 9	3	37N59'05	114w12'52	7:36:51
Ute 2	1	36N33'58	114w42'53	7:38:52
Valley 2	1	36N16'27	115w04'14	7:40:17
Valley View 12	1	38N04'06	117w13'25	7:48:54
Valmy 7	1	40N47'34	117w07'33	7:48:30
Van Riper Place 15	1	41N24'15	119w22'54	7:57:32
Vegas Creek 2	1	36N09	115w05	7:40:20
Vegas View 2	1	36N12	115w08	7:40:32
Ventosa 4	1	40N51'26	114w48'12	7:39:13
Verdi 15	1	39N31'06	119w59'16	7:59:57
Vernon 13	1	40N25'34	118w47'19	7:55:09
Victory Village 2	1	36N03	114w59	7:39:56
Virginia City 14	1	39N18'35	119w38'55	7:58:36
Vista 15	1	39N31'35	119w41'59	7:58:48
Vivian 4	1	40N43'30	116w03'20	7:44:13
Vya 15	1	41N35'32	119w51'34	7:59:26
Wabuska 10	1	39N08'38	119w10'56	7:56:44
Wadsworth 15	1	39N38'02	119w17'04	7:57:08
Walker River Indian Res 1	1	38N57	118w49	7:55:16
Walleys Hot Springs 3	1	38N58'52	119w50'00	7:59:20
Wann 2	1	36N14'00	115w06'45	7:40:27
Warm Springs 12	1	38N11'26	116w22'09	7:45:29
Warm Springs 16	4	39N39'12	114w48'06	7:39:12
Washington 15	1	39N32	119w50	7:59:20
Washoe City 15	1	39N19'13	119w48'31	7:59:14
Washoe-Dresslerville Indian 3	1	38N55	119w45	7:59:00
Weed Heights 10	1	38N59'14	119w12'29	7:56:50
Weepah 5	1	37N55'49	117w33'31	7:50:14
Welcome 4	1	41N06'01	115w06'13	7:40:25
Wellington 10	1	38N45'23	119w22'30	7:57:30
Wells 4	1	41N06'42	114w57'49	7:39:51
Wendover 4	2	40N44	114w02	7:36:08
Weso 7	1	41N00'41	117w41'26	7:50:46
West Reno 15	1	39N30'55	119w51'00	7:59:24
West Spring 5	1	37N43'20	117w16'11	7:49:05
Whitney 2	1	36N06	115w03	7:40:12
Wild Horse Crossing 4	2	41N43'34	115w53'47	7:43:35
Wilkins 4	2	41N25'31	114w45'03	7:39:00
Williams Cabin 4	2	41N43'02	115w40'13	7:42:41
Willow Beach 2	1	35N58	114w50	7:39:20
Willow Grove 16	4	39N01'21	115w16'03	7:41:04
Wimer Place 15	1	41N47'54	119w43'31	7:58:54
Winchester 2	1	36N08	115w07	7:40:28
Winnemucca 7	1	40N58'23	117w44'05	7:50:56
Woolsey 13	1	40N16'52	118w21'49	7:53:27
Yankee Blade 8	1	39N31'55	117w03'01	7:48:12
Yerington 10	1	38N59'09	119w09'43	7:56:39
Yerington Indian Reservation 10	1	39N03	119w11	7:56:44
Yomba Indian Reservation 12	1	39N08	117w25	7:49:40
Youngs Crossing 3	1	38N47'37	119w41'34	7:58:46
Zenobia 15	1	40N09'23	119w44'21	7:58:57
Zephyr Cove 3	1	39N00'08	119w57'18	7:59:49

TIME TABLES

NH # 1

Before 11/18/1883		LMT
11/18/1883	12:00	EST
3/31/1918	02:00	EWT
10/27/1918	02:00	EST
3/30/1919	02:00	EWT
10/26/1919	02:00	EST
5/11/1937	02:00	EDT
9/26/1937	02:00	EST
4/24/1938	02:00	EDT
10/02/1938	02:00	EST
4/30/1939	02:00	EDT
9/24/1939	02:00	EST
4/28/1940	02:00	EDT
9/29/1940	02:00	EST
4/27/1941	02:00	EDT
9/28/1941	02:00	EST
2/09/1942	02:00	EWT
9/30/1945	02:00	EST
4/28/1946	02:00	EDT
9/29/1946	02:00	EST
4/27/1947	02:00	EDT
9/28/1947	02:00	EST
4/25/1948	02:00	EDT
9/26/1948	02:00	EST
4/24/1949	02:00	EDT
9/25/1949	02:00	EST
4/30/1950	02:00	EDT
9/24/1950	02:00	EST
4/29/1951	02:00	EDT
9/30/1951	02:00	EST
4/27/1952	02:00	EDT
9/28/1952	02:00	EST
4/26/1953	02:00	EDT
9/27/1953	02:00	EST
4/25/1954	02:00	EDT
10/27/1954	02:00	EST
4/24/1955	02:00	US#2

NH # 2

Before 11/18/1883		LMT
11/18/1883	12:00	EST
3/31/1918	02:00	EWT
10/27/1918	02:00	EST
3/30/1919	02:00	EWT
10/26/1919	02:00	EST
4/26/1931	02:00	EDT
9/27/1931	02:00	EST
4/24/1932	02:00	EDT
9/25/1932	02:00	EST
4/30/1933	02:00	EDT
9/24/1933	02:00	EST
4/29/1934	02:00	EDT
9/30/1934	02:00	EST
4/28/1935	02:00	EDT
9/29/1935	02:00	EST
4/26/1936	02:00	EDT
9/27/1936	02:00	EST
4/25/1937	02:00	EDT
9/26/1937	02:00	EST
4/24/1938	02:00	NH#1
4/24/1955	02:00	US#1

NH # 3

Before 11/18/1883		LMT
11/18/1883	12:00	EST
3/31/1918	02:00	EWT
10/27/1918	02:00	EST
3/30/1919	02:00	EWT
10/26/1919	02:00	EST
4/24/1932	02:00	EDT
9/25/1932	02:00	EST
4/30/1933	02:00	EDT
9/24/1933	02:00	EST
4/29/1934	02:00	EDT
9/30/1934	02:00	EST
4/28/1935	02:00	EDT
9/29/1935	02:00	EST
4/26/1936	02:00	EDT
9/27/1936	02:00	EST
4/25/1937	02:00	EDT
9/26/1937	02:00	EST
4/24/1938	02:00	NH#1
4/24/1955	02:00	US#1

NH # 4

Before 11/18/1883		LMT
11/18/1883	12:00	EST
3/31/1918	02:00	EWT
10/27/1918	02:00	EST
3/30/1919	02:00	EWT
10/26/1919	02:00	EST
4/30/1933	02:00	EDT
9/24/1933	02:00	EST
4/29/1934	02:00	EDT
9/30/1934	02:00	EST
4/28/1935	02:00	EDT
9/29/1935	02:00	EST
4/26/1936	02:00	EDT
9/27/1936	02:00	EST
4/25/1937	02:00	EDT
9/26/1937	02:00	EST
4/24/1938	02:00	NH#1
4/24/1955	02:00	US#1

NH # 5

Before 11/18/1883		LMT
11/18/1883	12:00	EST
3/31/1918	02:00	EWT
10/27/1918	02:00	EST
3/30/1919	02:00	EWT
10/26/1919	02:00	EST
4/29/1934	02:00	EDT
9/30/1934	02:00	EST
4/28/1935	02:00	EDT
9/29/1935	02:00	EST
4/26/1936	02:00	EDT
9/27/1936	02:00	EST
4/25/1937	02:00	EDT
9/26/1937	02:00	EST
4/24/1938	02:00	NH#1
4/24/1955	02:00	US#1

NH # 6

Before 11/18/1883		LMT
11/18/1883	12:00	EST
3/31/1918	02:00	EWT
10/27/1918	02:00	EST
3/30/1919	02:00	EWT
10/26/1919	02:00	EST
4/28/1935	02:00	EDT
9/29/1935	02:00	EST
4/26/1936	02:00	EDT
9/27/1936	02:00	EST
4/25/1937	02:00	EDT
9/26/1937	02:00	EST
4/24/1938	02:00	NH#1
4/24/1955	02:00	US#1

NH # 7

Before 11/18/1883		LMT
11/18/1883	12:00	EST
3/31/1918	02:00	EWT
10/27/1918	02:00	EST
3/30/1919	02:00	EWT
10/26/1919	02:00	EST
4/26/1936	02:00	EDT
9/27/1936	02:00	EST
5/11/1937	02:00	NH#1
4/24/1955	02:00	US#1

NH # 8

Before 11/18/1883		LMT
11/18/1883	12:00	EST
3/31/1918	02:00	EWT
10/27/1918	02:00	EST
3/30/1919	02:00	EWT
10/26/1919	02:00	EST
4/24/1932	02:00	EDT
9/25/1932	02:00	EST
4/30/1933	02:00	EDT
9/24/1933	02:00	EST
5/11/1937	02:00	NH#1
4/24/1955	02:00	US#1

NH # 9

Before 11/18/1883		LMT
11/18/1883	12:00	EST
3/31/1918	02:00	EWT
10/27/1918	02:00	EST
3/30/1919	02:00	EWT
10/26/1919	02:00	EST
4/30/1933	02:00	EDT
9/24/1933	02:00	EST
4/28/1935	02:00	EDT
9/29/1935	02:00	EST
5/11/1937	02:00	NH#1
4/24/1955	02:00	US#1

NH # 10

Before 11/18/1883		LMT
11/18/1883	12:00	EST
3/31/1918	02:00	EWT
10/27/1918	02:00	EST
3/30/1919	02:00	EWT
10/26/1919	02:00	EST
4/24/1932	02:00	EDT
9/25/1932	02:00	EST
4/30/1933	02:00	EDT
9/24/1933	02:00	EST
4/29/1934	02:00	EDT
9/30/1934	02:00	EST
5/11/1937	02:00	NH#1
4/24/1955	02:00	US#1

NH # 11

Before 11/18/1883		LMT
11/18/1883	12:00	EST
3/31/1918	02:00	EWT
10/27/1918	02:00	EST
3/30/1919	02:00	EWT
10/26/1919	02:00	EST
4/26/1931	02:00	EDT
9/27/1931	02:00	EST
4/28/1935	02:00	EDT
9/29/1935	02:00	EST
4/26/1936	02:00	EDT
9/27/1936	02:00	EST
4/25/1937	02:00	EDT
9/26/1937	02:00	EST
4/24/1938	02:00	NH#1
4/24/1955	02:00	US#1

NH # 12

Before 11/18/1883		LMT
11/18/1883	12:00	EST
3/31/1918	02:00	EWT
10/27/1918	02:00	EST
3/30/1919	02:00	EWT
10/26/1919	02:00	EST
4/30/1933	02:00	EDT
9/24/1933	02:00	EST
4/29/1934	02:00	EDT
9/30/1934	02:00	EST
5/11/1937	02:00	NH#1
4/24/1955	02:00	US#1

NH # 13

Before 11/18/1883		LMT
11/18/1883	12:00	EST
3/31/1918	02:00	EWT
10/27/1918	02:00	EST
3/30/1919	02:00	EWT
10/26/1919	02:00	EST
4/29/1934	02:00	EDT
9/30/1934	02:00	EST
5/11/1937	02:00	NH#1
4/24/1955	02:00	US#1

NH # 14

Before 11/18/1883		LMT
11/18/1883	12:00	EST
3/31/1918	02:00	EWT
10/27/1918	02:00	EST
3/30/1919	02:00	EWT
10/26/1919	02:00	EST
4/24/1932	02:00	EDT
9/25/1932	02:00	EST
4/30/1933	02:00	EDT
9/24/1933	02:00	EST
4/29/1934	02:00	EDT
9/30/1934	02:00	EST
5/11/1937	02:00	NH#1
4/24/1955	02:00	US#1

NH # 15

Before 11/18/1883		LMT
11/18/1883	12:00	EST
3/31/1918	02:00	EWT
10/27/1918	02:00	EST
3/30/1919	02:00	EWT
10/26/1919	02:00	EST
4/26/1931	02:00	EDT
9/27/1931	02:00	EST
4/29/1934	02:00	EDT
9/30/1934	02:00	EST
4/26/1936	02:00	EDT
9/27/1936	02:00	EST
5/11/1937	02:00	NH#1
4/24/1955	02:00	US#1

NH # 16

Before 11/18/1883		LMT
11/18/1883	12:00	EST
3/31/1918	02:00	EWT
10/27/1918	02:00	EST
3/30/1919	02:00	EWT
10/26/1919	02:00	EST
4/29/1934	02:00	EDT
9/30/1934	02:00	EST
4/28/1935	02:00	EDT
9/29/1935	02:00	EST
5/11/1937	02:00	NH#1
4/24/1955	02:00	US#1

NH # 17

Before 11/18/1883		LMT
11/18/1883	12:00	EST
3/31/1918	02:00	EWT
10/27/1918	02:00	EST
3/30/1919	02:00	EWT
10/26/1919	02:00	EST
4/30/1933	02:00	EDT
9/24/1933	02:00	EST
5/11/1937	02:00	NH#1
4/24/1955	02:00	US#1

NH # 18

Before 11/18/1883		LMT
11/18/1883	12:00	EST
3/31/1918	02:00	EWT
10/27/1918	02:00	EST
3/30/1919	02:00	EWT
10/26/1919	02:00	EST
4/29/1934	02:00	EDT
9/30/1934	02:00	EST
5/11/1937	02:00	NH#1
4/24/1955	02:00	US#1

COUNTIES

1 Belknap
2 Carroll
3 Cheshire
4 Coos
5 Grafton
6 Hillsborough
7 Merrimack
8 Rockingham
9 Strafford
10 Sullivan

Ackerman's Trailer Park 8	2	42N47	71w12	4:44:48
Acworth 10	1	43N13'04	72w17'33	4:49:10
Albany 2	1	43N57'28	71w10'05	4:44:40
Alderbrook 5	1	44N19'36	71w41'49	4:46:47
Alexandria 5	1	43N38	71w50	4:47:20
Allens Mills 1	1	43N24'30	71w27'07	4:45:48
Allenstown 7	1	43N09'28	71w24'22	4:45:37
Alstead 3	1	43N08'56	72w21'40	4:49:27
Alstead Center 3	1	43N07'07	72w19'35	4:49:18
Alton 1	1	43N27'08	71w13'05	4:44:52
Alton Bay 1	1	43N28'07	71w13'57	4:44:56
Ames 1	3	43N33'45	71w20'07	4:45:20
Amherst 6	14	42N51'41	71w37'33	4:46:30
Andover 7	1	43N26'13	71w49'26	4:47:18
Antrim 6	1	43N01'51	71w56'22	4:47:45
Antrim Center 6	1	43N03'01	71w57'58	4:47:52
Appalachia 4	1	44N22'16	71w17'23	4:45:10
Apthorp 5	13	44N18'28	71w44'34	4:46:58
Arlington Park 8	2	42N49'49	71w13'28	4:44:54
Ashland 5	1	43N41'43	71w37'52	4:46:31
Ashuelot 3	7	42N46'39	72w25'27	4:49:42
Atkinson 8	2	42N50'18	71w08'51	4:44:35
Atkinson Heights 8	2	42N49'24	71w09'57	4:44:40
Atlantic 8	2	42N52'16	70w51'42	4:43:27
Atlantic Heights 8	2	43N05'32	70w46'23	4:43:06
Auburn 8	1	43N00'16	71w20'56	4:45:24
Austin Corners 8	5	42N54'40	70w57'53	4:43:52
Baboosic Lake 6	14	42N52	71w38	4:46:32
Baglett Grove 8	2	42N52'59	71w10'47	4:44:43
Bagley 7	6	43N16'00	71w46'45	4:47:07
Baileys 4	1	44N24'26	71w30'20	4:46:01
Baileys Corner 7	1	43N06'20	71w34'54	4:46:20
Baker Corner 3	1	43N08'15	72w14'58	4:49:00
Ballock 10	1	43N25'56	72w23'33	4:49:34
Bank 6	1	42N45'01	71w50'15	4:47:21
Bank Village 6	1	42N42	71w51	4:47:24
Barnstead 1	1	43N20'02	71w17'36	4:45:10
Barrett 5	1	44N15'29	71w49'45	4:47:19
Barrington 9	1	43N13'22	71w02'51	4:44:11
Barryvilla 9	17	43N18	70w59	4:43:56
Bartlett 2	8	44N04'41	71w17'00	4:45:08
Base 4	1	44N16	71w33	4:46:12
Bath 5	1	44N10'01	71w58'00	4:47:52
Bayside 8	2	43N03'05	70w52'05	4:43:28
Bean Island 8	1	43N03'47	71w14'36	4:44:58
Bear Island 1	3	43N39'26	71w25'04	4:45:40
Beatties 4	1	44N42'28	71w35'43	4:46:23
Beaver Lake 8	2	42N54	71w19	4:45:16
Bedford 6	7	42N56'47	71w30'59	4:46:04
Beebe River 5	9	43N49'43	71w39'05	4:46:36
Belmont 1	1	43N26'43	71w28'42	4:45:55
Bennett Corners 2	1	43N49'39	71w19'42	4:45:19
Bennington 6	1	43N00'11	71w55'30	4:47:42
Benton 5	1	44N06'11	71w54'08	4:47:37
Berlin 4	10	44N28'07	71w11'08	4:44:45
Berrys Corner 9	1	43N16'30	71w04'10	4:44:17
Bersum Gardens 8	2	43N04'59	70w46'14	4:43:05
Bethlehem 5	1	44N16'49	71w41'19	4:46:45
Big Rock Corner 2	1	43N46'52	71w26'59	4:45:48
Birch Hill 9	1	43N27	71w13	4:44:52
Black Mountain Cabin 2	8	44N11'51	71w10'20	4:44:41
Blackwater 9	17	43N14'44	70w54'51	4:43:39
Blair 5	16	43N48'36	71w39'56	4:46:40
Blais Park 4	10	44N27	71w11	4:44:44
Blodgett Landing 7	1	43N22'25	72w02'33	4:48:10
Bonds Corner 3	1	42N54'06	72w01'30	4:48:06
Boscawen 7	1	43N18'54	71w37'17	4:46:29
Boutin Corner 5	1	44N05'53	71w52'35	4:47:30
Bow Bog 7	2	43N07'14	71w30'43	4:46:03
Bow Center 7	2	43N07'55	71w32'59	4:46:12
Bow Junction 7	2	43N10'35	71w31'35	4:46:06
Bowkerville 3	1	42N48'21	72w09'53	4:48:40
Bow Lake Village (Strafford) 9	1	43N14'29	71w09'04	4:44:36
Bowman 4	1	44N21'31	71w21'10	4:45:25
Bow Mills 7	2	43N10'01	71w32'01	4:46:08
Box Corner 7	1	43N15'39	72w01'46	4:48:07
Boyce 7	1	43N17'43	71w34'38	4:46:19
Bradford 7	4	43N16'12	71w57'38	4:47:51
Bradford Center 7	4	43N14'14	71w58'19	4:47:53
Breakfast Hill 8	2	43N00'38	70w48'58	4:43:16
Breezy Point 5	1	43N57'58	71w50'07	4:47:20
Brentwood 8	1	42N58'43	71w04'24	4:44:18
Brentwood Corners 8	1	43N00'30	71w04'36	4:44:18
Bretton Woods 4	1	44N15'29	71w26'30	4:45:46
Brick School Corner 8	5	42N56'21	70w57'01	4:43:48
Bridgewater 5	1	43N38'18	71w44'13	4:46:57
Bristol 5	1	43N35'28	71w44'14	4:46:57
Broad Acres 6	2	42N46'08	71w30'26	4:46:02
Brookfield 2	1	43N33'32	71w03'57	4:44:16
Brookhurst 1	1	43N30'29	71w15'52	4:45:03
Brookline 6	1	42N44'05	71w39'31	4:46:38
Browns Corner 6	1	42N58'44	71w36'41	4:46:27
Bucks Corner 5	1	43N44'16	71w56'55	4:47:48
Bungy 4	1	44N50'38	71w23'36	4:45:34
Burkehaven 10	1	43N22'32	72w04'17	4:48:17
Cable Road 8	2	42N59'29	70w45'54	4:43:04
Cambridge 4	1	44N40	71w08	4:44:32
Camp Forest Lake 3	1	42N47'19	72w21'36	4:49:26
Camp Gundalow 8	2	43N01'48	70w50'52	4:43:23
Camp Hedding 8	1	43N02'34	71w01'56	4:44:08
Camp Notre Dame 3	18	42N55'12	72w26'16	4:49:45
Campton 5	9	43N50	71w39	4:46:36
Campton Hollow 5	16	43N49'24	71w38'29	4:46:34
Campton Lower Village 5	9	43N51'32	71w38'00	4:46:32
Campton Station 5	9	43N51'13	71w39'05	4:46:36
Campton Upper Village 5	9	43N51'57	71w38'19	4:46:33
Canaan 5	1	43N38'51	72w00'44	4:48:03
Canaan Center 5	1	43N40'49	72w03'11	4:48:13
Canaan Street 5	1	43N39'55	72w02'34	4:48:10
Candia 8	1	43N04'40	71w16'38	4:45:07
Candia Four Corners 8	1	43N03'41	71w17'20	4:45:09
Candia Village 8	2	42N48	71w15	4:45:00
Canobie Lake 8	2	42N48'20	71w14'44	4:44:59
Canterbury 7	1	43N20'13	71w33'57	4:46:16
Canterbury Station 7	1	43N19'43	71w36'33	4:46:26
Carroll 4	1	44N17'54	71w32'28	4:46:10
Cascade 4	10	44N26'58	71w11'35	4:44:46
Cedre Pond 4	1	44N34	71w11	4:44:44
Cemetery Corners 8	2	42N57'47	70w50'27	4:43:22
Center Barnstead 1	1	43N20'21	71w15'36	4:45:02
Center Conway 2	1	43N59'41	71w03'41	4:44:15

Center Effingham 2 1 43N44'22 71w00'34 4:44:02
Center Harbor 2 1 43N42'35 71w27'39 4:45:51
Center Haverhill 5 1 44N04'37 71w59'10 4:47:57
Center Ossipee 2 1 43N45'18 71w09'09 4:44:37
Center Sandwich 2 1 43N48'27 71w26'23 4:45:46
Center Strafford 9 1 43N16'12 71w07'33 4:44:30
Center Tuftonboro 2 1 43N39'15 71w14'52 4:44:59
Central Park 9 7 43N14'00 70w52'57 4:43:32
Chandlers Mills 10 15 43N21'29 72w14'54 4:49:00
Charlestown 10 1 43N14'19 72w25'30 4:49:42
Chases Grove 8 2 42N51'42 71w13'02 4:44:52
Chases Mill 2 1 43N43'16 71w00'11 4:44:01
Chase Village 6 1 43N06'38 71w45'05 4:47:00
Chateau Richelieu 6 2 42N45 71w29 4:45:56
Chatham 2 1 44N09'52 71w00'42 4:44:03
Cheever 5 1 43N47'56 71w54'39 4:47:39
Chesham 3 1 42N55'50 72w08'57 4:48:36
Chester 8 1 42N57'24 71w15'28 4:45:02
Chesterfield 3 1 42N53'14 72w28'15 4:49:53
Chichester 7 1 43N14'57 71w24'01 4:45:36
Chicks Corner 2 1 43N48'10 71w28'24 4:45:54
Chickville 2 1 43N43'48 71w09'24 4:44:38
Chocorua 2 1 43N52'44 71w13'13 4:44:53
Christian Hollow 3 1 43N02'12 72w23'24 4:49:34
Christian Shore 8 2 43N05'11 70w46'14 4:43:05
Cilleyville 7 1 43N25'50 71w52'00 4:47:28
Claremont 10 7 43N22'36 72w20'50 4:49:23
Claremont Junction 10 7 43N22'06 72w22'42 4:49:31
Clark Hill 8 5 43N02'47 70w57'19 4:43:49
Clark Landing 2 1 43N42'29 71w20'57 4:45:24
Clarks Landing 2 1 43N43 71w28 4:45:52
Clarksville 4 1 45N01 71w21 4:45:24
Clinton Grove 6 1 43N04'41 71w45'32 4:47:02
Clinton Village 6 1 43N02'27 71w57'53 4:47:52
Clovelly 6 2 42N45 71w29 4:45:56
Cluffs Crossing 8 2 42N45'55 71w13'05 4:44:52
Coburn 9 1 43N27'32 71w07'57 4:44:32
Coburn Woods 6 2 42N45 71w29 4:45:56
Cocheco 9 17 43N13'47 70w56'21 4:43:45
Coffins Mill 8 2 42N56'35 70w52'33 4:43:30
Colby 7 1 43N08'58 71w46'09 4:47:05
Cold River 3 1 43N07'20 72w25'40 4:49:43
Colebrook 4 1 44N53'40 71w29'47 4:45:59
Collettes Grove 8 2 42N52'37 71w12'53 4:44:52
Columbia 4 1 44N50 71w29 4:45:56
Columbia Valley 4 1 44N54 71w30 4:46:00
Concord 7 2 43N12'29 71w32'17 4:46:09
Concord Heights 7 2 43N12'45 71w30'37 4:46:02
Cones 4 1 44N49'11 71w33'59 4:46:16
Conleys Grove 8 2 42N51'27 71w12'31 4:44:50
Contoocook 7 1 43N13'19 71w42'52 4:46:51
Converseville 3 5 42N44'21 71w58'51 4:47:55
Conway 2 1 43N58'45 71w07'15 4:44:29
Cooks Crossing 2 8 44N05'23 71w12'22 4:44:49
Coos Junction 4 1 44N30'22 71w34'06 4:46:16
Copperville 4 1 44N32'04 71w14'23 4:44:58
Cornish Center 10 1 43N28'58 72w19'12 4:49:17
Cornish City 10 1 43N28'00 72w21'02 4:49:24
Cornish Flat 10 1 43N29'50 72w16'48 4:49:07
Cornish Mills 10 1 43N27'52 72w22'10 4:49:29
Cotoocook Lake 3 5 42N49 72w01 4:48:04
Cowbell Corners 8 2 42N50'57 71w12'57 4:44:52
Crane Crossing 8 2 42N51'29 71w04'41 4:44:19
Crawford Notch 4 1 44N16 71w33 4:46:12
Creek Area 8 2 43N04'33 70w46'32 4:43:06
Crescent Lake 10 1 43N15'58 72w15'22 4:49:01
Cricket Corner 6 14 42N50'31 71w35'46 4:46:23
Crockett Corner 7 1 43N23'57 71w57'42 4:47:51
Crocketts Crossing 9 7 43N14'26 70w50'56 4:43:24
Croydon 10 15 43N27'02 72w09'49 4:48:39
Croydon Flat 10 15 43N24'54 72w11'15 4:48:45
Crystal 4 10 44N37'08 71w19'49 4:45:19
Curits Corner 3 1 42N44'33 72w23'18 4:49:33
Curtis Corner 6 3 42N52'28 71w44'47 4:46:59
Cushman 4 1 44N24'21 71w43'23 4:46:54
Cutter Hill 3 5 42N44'55 71w59'24 4:47:58
Dalton 4 1 44N24'57 71w41'43 4:46:47
Danbury 7 1 43N31'32 71w51'44 4:47:27
Danville 8 1 42N54'45 71w07'30 4:44:30
Davis 6 1 42N45'20 71w52'20 4:47:29
Davis 9 1 43N24'48 71w08'26 4:44:34
Davisville 6 3 42N51'21 71w47'18 4:47:09
Davisville 7 1 43N15'07 71w43'58 4:46:56
Deephaven 5 1 43N46'11 71w32'21 4:46:09
Deerfield 5 1 44N13'50 71w37'03 4:46:28
Deerfield 8 1 43N08'46 71w13'01 4:44:52
Deerfield Center 8 1 43N07'57 71w14'30 4:44:58
Deerfield Parade 8 1 43N08'38 71w14'04 4:44:56
Deering 6 1 43N04'23 71w50'42 4:47:23
Derry 8 2 42N52'50 71w19'40 4:45:19
Derry Village 8 2 42N53'30 71w18'45 4:45:15
Dexter Corner 9 1 43N22'09 71w09'32 4:44:38
Dimond 7 1 43N14'44 71w45'14 4:47:01
Dingit Corner 7 1 43N17'48 71w41'26 4:46:46
Dixville 4 1 44N53 71w16 4:45:04
Dixville Notch 4 1 44N52'15 71w18'23 4:45:14
Dockham Shore 1 3 43N35'41 71w25'10 4:45:41
Dodge Hollow 10 1 43N12'10 72w13'05 4:48:52
Dodge Tavern 3 1 43N06'14 72w23'22 4:49:33
Dole Junction 3 7 42N45'16 72w28'10 4:49:53
Dorchester 5 1 43N45'24 71w56'57 4:47:48
Dorrs Corner 2 1 43N45'09 71w10'46 4:44:43
Dover 9 7 43N11'52 70w52'27 4:43:30
Dover Point 9 7 43N12 70w53 4:43:32
Dows Corner 8 5 42N58'13 70w53'55 4:43:36
Drewsville 3 1 43N07'41 72w23'33 4:49:34
Drury 6 1 42N50'40 71w57'54 4:47:52
Dublin 3 1 42N54'27 72w03'47 4:48:15
Ducks Head 2 8 44N08'27 71w11'18 4:44:45
Dummer 4 1 44N40 71w15 4:45:00
Dunbarton 7 1 43N06'09 71w37'01 4:46:28
Dunbarton Center 7 1 43N06'09 71w37'01 4:46:28
Dundee 2 1 44N08'23 71w07'56 4:44:32
Durham 9 1 43N08'02 70w55'37 4:43:42
East Acworth 10 1 43N13'14 72w14'14 4:48:57
East Alstead 3 1 43N07'26 72w16'46 4:49:07
East Alton 1 1 43N31'05 71w12'01 4:44:48
East Andover (Halcyon Sta) 7 1 43N27'34 71w44'53 4:47:00
East Barrington 9 1 43N12'56 71w00'26 4:44:02
East Bear Island 1 3 43N38'35 71w23'39 4:45:35
East Candia 8 1 43N02'53 71w14'57 4:45:00
East Concord 7 2 43N14'31 71w32'19 4:46:09
East Conway 2 1 44N01'21 71w00'21 4:44:01
East Deering 6 1 43N04'26 71w48'49 4:47:15
East Derry 8 2 42N53'40 71w17'30 4:45:10
East Dummer 4 1 44N34 71w11 4:44:44
East Freedom 2 1 43N47'35 70w59'34 4:43:58
East Grafton 5 1 43N34'07 71w55'41 4:47:43
East Grantham 10 1 43N29'12 72w07'06 4:48:28
East Hampstead 8 2 42N53'28 71w08'37 4:44:34
East Haverhill 5 1 44N01'36 71w58'18 4:47:53
East Hebron 5 1 43N41'36 71w46'12 4:47:05
East Holderness 5 1 43N43'00 71w31'53 4:46:08
East Kingston 8 1 42N55'32 71w01'02 4:44:04
East Lempster 10 1 43N13'30 72w10'44 4:48:43
East Madison 2 1 43N51'38 71w05'19 4:44:21
Eastman 10 1 43N29 72w08 4:48:32
Eastman Corners 8 5 42N54'25 70w55'37 4:43:42
Eastman Point 8 2 42N55'00 70w49'20 4:43:17
East Milford 6 14 42N49'24 71w37'34 4:46:30
Easton 5 1 44N08'46 71w47'26 4:47:10
East Plainfield 10 1 43N34'35 72w13'34 4:48:54
East Rindge 3 5 42N44'15 71w57'59 4:47:52
East Rochester 9 17 43N19'59 70w56'31 4:43:46
East Sandwich 2 1 43N43 71w28 4:45:52
East Springfield 10 1 43N29'11 71w58'44 4:47:55
East Sullivan 3 1 42N59'38 72w11'46 4:48:47
East Sutton 7 6 43N18'04 71w51'22 4:47:25
East Swanzey 3 1 42N51'05 72w15'32 4:49:02
East Tilton 1 1 43N28'47 71w32'27 4:46:10
East Unity 10 15 43N17'52 72w11'47 4:48:47
Eastview 3 1 42N55'55 72w02'15 4:48:09
East Wakefield 2 1 43N36'51 71w00'20 4:44:01
East Washington 10 1 43N11'28 72w01'08 4:48:05
East Westmoreland 3 1 42N59'25 72w23'27 4:49:34
East Wilder 5 1 43N40'55 72w17'43 4:49:11
East Wolfeboro 2 1 43N36'36 71w06'31 4:44:26
Eaton Center 2 1 43N54'33 71w05'03 4:44:20
Edgemont 7 1 43N20'25 72w03'37 4:48:14
Effingham 2 1 43N45'40 70w59'49 4:43:59
Effingham Falls 2 1 43N47'45 71w03'19 4:44:13
Elkins 7 1 43N25'15 71w56'16 4:47:45
Ellisville 3 1 43N01'09 72w12'00 4:48:48
Ellsworth 5 1 43N52'26 71w44'13 4:46:57
Elmwood 6 1 42N58'19 71w57'20 4:47:49
Elmwood 7 1 43N31'04 71w50'30 4:47:22
Elmwood Corners 8 2 42N55'51 70w49'43 4:43:19
Elwyn Park 8 1 43N02'17 70w46'27 4:43:06
Enfield 5 1 43N38'26 72w08'40 4:48:35
Enfield Center 5 1 43N35'24 72w06'41 4:48:27
Epping 8 1 43N02'00 71w04'29 4:44:18
Epsom 7 1 43N13'22 71w19'57 4:45:20
Epsom Circle 7 1 43N13'40 71w21'39 4:45:27
Errol 4 1 44N46'53 71w08'18 4:44:33
Etna 5 1 43N41'34 72w13'20 4:48:53
Exeter 8 5 42N58'53 70w56'54 4:43:48
Fabyan 4 1 44N15'48 71w27'32 4:45:50
Fairhill Manor 8 1 43N01'53 70w43'33 4:42:54
Fairview 5 3 44N00'55 71w40'40 4:46:43
Farmington 9 1 43N23'23 71w03'56 4:44:16
Federal Corner 2 1 43N39'44 71w13'46 4:44:55
Fernald 2 1 43N36'48 71w10'11 4:44:41
Ferncroft 2 1 43N54'44 71w21'37 4:45:26
Fernwood 10 1 43N24'29 72w03'54 4:48:16
Fitzwilliam 3 1 42N46'50 72w08'32 4:48:34
Fitzwilliam Depot 3 1 42N45'53 72w09'05 4:48:36
Five Corners 5 1 44N14'39 71w38'03 4:46:32
Five Corners 8 5 42N56'19 70w55'31 4:43:42
Fogg Corner 8 2 42N57'42 70w49'39 4:43:19
Fogg Corners 8 2 42N54'11 70w52'37 4:43:30
Fords Crossing 7 1 43N32'52 71w53'27 4:47:34
Fords Mill 7 1 43N32'29 71w54'01 4:47:36
Forest Lake 3 1 42N46 72w23 4:49:32
Forest Ridge 6 2 42N45 71w29 4:45:56
Foster Corners 8 2 42N46'09 71w12'17 4:44:49
Foundry 9 7 43N15'06 70w51'19 4:43:25
Four Corners 8 5 43N03'48 70w58'11 4:43:53
Foyes Corner 8 1 43N02'45 70w44'50 4:42:59
Francestown 6 1 42N59'15 71w48'47 4:47:15
Franconia 5 1 44N13'37 71w44'54 4:47:00
Franklin 7 11 43N26'39 71w38'52 4:46:35
Franklin Pierce College 3 5 42N46 72w02 4:48:08
Freedom 2 1 43N48'44 71w02'10 4:44:09
Fremont 8 1 42N59'27 71w08'35 4:44:34
Fremont Station 8 1 42N58'47 71w07'27 4:44:30
Gardners Grove 1 1 43N27'30 71w31'55 4:46:08
Gates Corner 9 7 43N13'18 70w53'12 4:43:33
Gaza 1 6 43N31'19 71w35'42 4:46:23
Gee Mill 3 1 43N09'08 72w12'14 4:48:49
Georges Mills 10 1 43N25'54 72w04'04 4:48:16
Gerrish 7 1 43N21'41 71w39'04 4:46:36
Gerrish Corner 7 1 43N15'57 71w41'54 4:46:48
Gibson Four Corners 6 1 42N43'42 71w51'02 4:47:24
Gilboa 3 1 42N59'43 72w23'26 4:49:34
Gilford 1 3 43N32'51 71w24'26 4:45:38
Gilmans Corner 5 1 43N54'09 71w59'25 4:47:58
Gilmanton 1 1 43N25'27 71w24'54 4:45:40
Gilmanton Ironworks 1 1 43N25'02 71w17'52 4:45:11
Gilsum 3 1 43N02'54 72w15'48 4:49:03
Glen 2 8 44N06'36 71w10'59 4:44:44
Glencliff 5 1 43N58'58 71w53'38 4:47:35
Glendale 1 3 43N34'57 71w23'15 4:45:33
Glen House 4 1 44N17'18 71w13'33 4:44:54
Glenmere 9 5 43N05'58 71w00'23 4:44:02
Goffs Falls 6 7 42N55'55 71w27'11 4:45:49
Goffstown 6 1 43N01'13 71w36'03 4:46:24
Gonic 9 17 43N16'28 70w58'43 4:43:55
Gooch Corner 8 5 42N58'08 70w59'09 4:43:57
Goodrich Falls 2 8 44N07'41 71w11'24 4:44:46
Goose Hollow 5 9 43N52'52 71w35'54 4:46:24
Gorham 4 12 44N23'16 71w10'25 4:44:42
Goshen 10 1 43N18'04 72w08'54 4:48:36
Goshen Four Corners 10 1 43N16'42 72w07'53 4:48:32
Gosport 8 2 42N58'39 70w36'55 4:42:28
Gossville 7 1 43N13'35 71w21'05 4:45:24
Grafton 5 1 43N33'31 71w56'40 4:47:47
Grafton Center 5 1 43N34'26 71w58'26 4:47:54
Grandliden 10 1 43N24'08 72w04'27 4:48:18
Grange 4 1 44N29'10 71w31'31 4:46:06
Granite 2 1 43N41'28 71w03'33 4:44:14
Grantham 10 1 43N29'22 72w08'17 4:48:33
Grape Corner 2 1 43N41'12 71w01'20 4:44:05
Grasmere 6 7 43N01'20 71w32'37 4:46:10
Great Boars Head 8 2 42N55'13 70w47'59 4:43:12
Greenfield 6 1 42N57'02 71w52'22 4:47:29
Greenland 8 2 43N02'10 70w50'00 4:43:20
Greenland Station 8 2 43N02'38 70w49'27 4:43:18
Greenville 6 1 42N46'02 71w48'46 4:47:15
Groton 5 1 43N42'06 71w50'10 4:47:21
Groveton 4 1 44N35'55 71w30'42 4:46:03
Guild 10 15 43N22'36 72w08'19 4:48:33
Hadley 3 5 42N50'05 71w59'18 4:47:57
Hampshire Road 8 2 42N44'35 71w12'06 4:44:48
Hampstead 8 2 42N52'28 71w10'54 4:44:44
Hampton 8 2 42N56'15 70w50'22 4:43:21
Hampton Beach 8 2 42N54'26 70w48'45 4:43:15
Hampton Falls 8 2 42N54'58 70w51'51 4:43:27
Hampton Landing 8 2 42N55'28 70w50'11 4:43:21
Hancock 6 1 42N58'21 71w59'05 4:47:56
Hanover 5 1 43N42'08 72w17'24 4:49:10
Hanover Center 5 1 43N43'32 72w11'36 4:48:46
Happy Corner 4 1 45N05'11 71w18'48 4:45:15
Happy Valley 6 1 42N55'03 71w55'01 4:47:40
Hardscrabble 5 1 43N49'54 72w07'04 4:48:28
Harrisville 3 1 42N56'42 72w05'49 4:48:23
Harts Location 2 1 44N08 71w22 4:45:28
Hastings 7 1 43N24'04 72w01'55 4:48:08
Hatfield Corner 7 1 43N10'50 71w44'31 4:46:58
Haven Hill 9 17 43N18 70w59 4:43:56
Haverhill 5 1 44N02'04 72w03'52 4:48:15
Hayes 9 17 43N18 70w59 4:43:56
Hayes Corner 9 1 43N24'30 71w01'30 4:44:06
Haynes Corner 8 5 42N58'37 70w55'19 4:43:41
Hays 8 5 42N59 70w57 4:43:48
Hazens 4 1 44N22'08 71w33'43 4:46:15
Hebron 5 1 43N41'38 71w48'22 4:47:13
Hedding 8 1 43N02 71w04 4:44:16
Hell Hollow 10 1 43N31'23 72w19'31 4:49:18
Hemlock Center 10 1 43N14'08 72w23'09 4:49:33
Henniker 7 1 43N10'47 71w49'22 4:47:17
Henniker Junction 7 1 43N10'28 71w48'15 4:47:13
High Bridge 6 1 42N45'03 71w49'39 4:47:19
Highlands 4 1 44N22'22 71w26'20 4:45:45
Hill 7 1 43N31'27 71w42'05 4:46:48
Hill Center 7 1 43N31'25 71w44'24 4:46:58
Hillsboro 6 1 43N06'50 71w53'45 4:47:35
Hillsboro Center 6 1 43N08'42 71w56'03 4:47:44
Hillsboro Lower Village 6 1 43N06'44 71w56'41 4:47:47

NEW HAMPSHIRE

Hillsboro Upper Village 6
1 43N07'50 71w58'35 4:47:54
Hills Corner 7 1 43N23'33 71w29'51 4:45:59
Hills Corner 9 1 43N20'02 71w08'43 4:44:35
Hinsdale 3 7 42N47'10 72w29'13 4:49:57
Holderness 5 1 43N43'55 71w35'20 4:46:21
Hollis 6 1 42N44'35 71w35'32 4:46:22
Hollis Depot 6 1 42N42'46 71w32'57 4:46:12
Holton 6 1 43N04'52 71w54'30 4:47:38
Hooks Crossing 8
1 43N01'30 71w19'51 4:45:19
Hooksett 7 3 43N05'48 71w27'56 4:45:52
Hopkinton 7 1 43N11'29 71w40'33 4:46:42
Hornetown 9 1 43N22'02 71w06'57 4:44:28
Horse Corner 7 1 43N14'01 71w26'32 4:45:46
Howards Grove 8 2 42N52'21 71w13'17 4:44:53
Hoyts Corner 7 4 43N16 71w57 4:47:48
Hubbard 8 2 42N52'56 71w14'44 4:44:59
Hudson 6 2 42N45'53 71w26'25 4:45:46
Hudson Center 6 2 42N46'18 71w24'30 4:45:38
Idlewilde 4 1 45N09'05 71w10'46 4:44:43
Interlaken Park 1
3 43N36'10 71w27'19 4:45:49
Intervale 2 1 44N04'27 71w08'26 4:44:34
Ireland 5 1 44N09'34 71w53'38 4:47:35
Jackson 2 8 44N08'39 71w10'53 4:44:44
Jackson Falls 2 8 44N08'53 71w10'54 4:44:44
Jady Hill 8 5 42N59'09 70w56'38 4:43:47
Jaffrey 3 5 42N48'50 72w01'25 4:48:06
Jaffrey Center 3
5 42N49'40 72w03'20 4:48:13
Jefferson 4 1 44N25'08 71w28'30 4:45:54
Jefferson Highland 4
1 44N23'06 71w25'21 4:45:41
Jenness Beach 8 2 42N59 70w46 4:43:04
Jericho 2 8 44N06'28 71w12'16 4:44:49
Jericho 5 1 44N08'38 71w50'58 4:47:24
Jockey Hill 5 1 44N11'11 71w54'22 4:47:37
Johnson Corner 6
3 42N53'19 71w44'05 4:46:56
Jones Corner 3 5 42N44'14 72w01'22 4:48:05
Joslin 3 1 42N54'33 72w15'22 4:49:01
Kearsarge 2 1 44N04'31 71w07'05 4:44:28
Keene 3 1 42N56'01 72w16'43 4:49:07
Keewayden 2 1 43N36'06 71w15'06 4:45:00
Kelleys Corner 1
1 43N22'06 71w21'17 4:45:25
Kellyville 10 15 43N21'36 72w13'27 4:48:54
Kelwyn Park 9 7 43N13'30 70w52'51 4:43:31
Kensington 8 5 42N55'37 70w56'40 4:43:47
Keyes Hollow 10 1 43N15'01 72w13'41 4:48:55
Kezer Seminary 7
1 43N20'41 71w30'40 4:46:03
Kidderville 4 1 44N52'35 71w22'37 4:45:30
Kingston 8 2 42N56'11 71w03'14 4:44:13
Klondike Corner 6
1 42N57'20 71w37'17 4:46:29
Laconia 1 3 43N31'40 71w28'15 4:45:53
Lakeport 1 3 43N32'50 71w27'47 4:45:51
Lake Shore Park 1
3 43N34'30 71w20'54 4:45:24
Lakeside 7 1 43N24'37 72w01'54 4:48:08
Lamprey Corners 8
5 42N55'06 70w55'49 4:43:43
Lancaster 4 1 44N29'20 71w34'11 4:46:17
Landaff Center 5
1 44N10'30 71w53'15 4:47:33
Langdon 10 1 43N10'01 72w22'48 4:49:31
Langs Corner 8 1 43N01'33 70w45'17 4:43:01
Laskey Corner 9 1 43N28'51 70w59'45 4:43:59
Laurel Lake 3 1 42N47 72w09 4:48:36
Lawrence Corner 6
1 42N50'50 71w31'26 4:46:06
Leavitt Park 1 1 43N40'40 71w27'15 4:45:49
Leavitts Hill 8 2 43N07'11 71w17'27 4:45:10
Lebanon 5 1 43N38'32 72w15'08 4:49:01
Lee 9 1 43N07'23 71w00'43 4:44:03
Lee Five Corners 9
1 43N09'02 70w58'37 4:43:54
Lee's 8 5 42N59 70w57 4:43:48
Lees Mill 2 1 43N44'21 71w23'25 4:45:34
Leighton Corners 9
1 43N18'31 71w11'28 4:44:46
Lempster 10 1 43N14'18 72w12'40 4:48:51
Leominster Corner 3
1 43N04'09 72w11'24 4:48:46
Lincoln 5 3 44N02'44 71w40'14 4:46:41
Lincoln Park 6 2 42N45'26 71w30'31 4:46:02
Lisbon 5 1 44N12'48 71w54'41 4:47:39
Litchfield 6 1 42N50'39 71w28'49 4:45:55
Little Boars Head 8
2 42N57'29 70w46'36 4:43:06
Littlefield 8 1 43N02'19 70w59'52 4:43:59
Little Island Pond 6
1 42N44 71w19 4:45:16
Littleton 5 13 44N18'22 71w46'14 4:47:05
Livermore 2 1 44N04'31 71w22'32 4:45:30
Livermore Falls 5
16 43N45 71w41 4:46:44
Lochmere 1 1 43N28'16 71w31'50 4:46:07
Lockehaven 5 1 43N39 72w09 4:48:36
Lockes Corner 1 1 43N21'41 71w10'57 4:44:44
Lockhaven 5 1 43N36'38 72w05'18 4:48:21
Londonderry 8 2 42N51'54 71w22'28 4:45:30
Long Sands 2 1 43N46'58 71w06'48 4:44:27
Loon Cove 1 1 43N29'49 71w15'35 4:45:02
Lost Nation 4 1 44N30'34 71w29'31 4:45:58
Lost River 5 3 44N02'13 71w47'05 4:47:08
Loudon 7 1 43N17'08 71w28'04 4:45:52
Loudon Center 7 1 43N20'09 71w24'08 4:45:37
Louisburg Square 6
2 42N45 71w29 4:45:56
Lovejoy Sands 1 3 43N38'56 71w25'38 4:45:43
Loverens Mill 6 1 43N04'22 72w01'08 4:48:05
Lower Bartlett 2
1 44N06'08 71w09'02 4:44:36
Lower Gilmanton 1
1 43N22'51 71w21'16 4:45:25
Lower Shaker Village 5
1 43N37'12 72w08'48 4:48:35
Lower Village 3 1 43N02'17 72w16'13 4:49:05
Lower Village 7 6 43N16'27 71w47'38 4:47:11
Lyford Crossing 8
1 43N00'40 71w05'58 4:44:24
Lyman 5 1 44N16 71w56 4:47:44
Lyme 5 1 43N48'34 72w09'23 4:48:38
Lyme Center 5 1 43N47'57 72w07'24 4:48:30
Lyndeborough 6 3 42N54'27 71w46'01 4:47:04
Lynn 10 1 43N13'10 72w16'48 4:49:07
MacDowell Colony 6
1 42N53'24 71w57'16 4:47:49
Madbury 9 1 43N10'09 70w55'28 4:43:42
Madison 2 1 43N53'57 71w08'56 4:44:36
Manchester 6 7 42N59'44 71w27'19 4:45:49
Mapleton 4 1 44N38'55 71w33'10 4:46:13
Maplewood 5 1 44N16'55 71w39'28 4:46:38
Maplewood 6 1 43N04 71w38 4:46:32
Marlborough 3 1 42N54'15 72w12'30 4:48:50
Marlow 3 1 43N06'57 72w11'51 4:48:47
Marlow Junction 3
1 43N10'02 72w13'13 4:48:53
Marshall Corner 8
5 42N59'33 71w00'53 4:44:04
Marshfield Station 4
1 44N16'09 71w21'26 4:45:26
Martin 7 3 43N02'36 71w27'17 4:45:49
Martin Crossing 8
1 43N01'15 71w05'11 4:44:21
Martins Corner 7
3 43N02'53 71w25'58 4:45:44
Mascoma 5 1 43N39'04 72w10'58 4:48:44
Mason 6 1 42N44'37 71w46'10 4:47:05
Masons 4 1 44N41'10 71w35'21 4:46:21
Massabesic 6 7 43N00'13 71w23'35 4:45:34
Meaderboro Corner 9
17 43N17'55 71w01'47 4:44:07
Meadowbrook 8 2 43N04'07 70w46'42 4:43:07
Meadows 4 1 44N22 71w28 4:45:52
Melrose Beach 8 1 43N10'36 71w10'13 4:44:41
Melrose Corner 9
17 43N20'53 70w58'33 4:43:54
Melvin Mills 7 6 43N16'08 71w54'50 4:47:39
Melvin Village 2
1 43N41'20 71w18'17 4:45:13
Meredith 1 1 43N39'27 71w30'03 4:46:00
Meredith Center 1
1 43N36'51 71w31'47 4:46:07
Meriden 10 1 43N32'38 72w15'11 4:49:01
Merrill Corners 9
17 43N19'28 71w04'19 4:44:17
Merrimack 6 1 42N51'54 71w29'38 4:45:59
Merriwood Camp 5
1 43N54'12 71w59'30 4:47:58
Middleton Corners 9
1 43N28'34 71w04'12 4:44:17
Milan 4 1 44N34'24 71w11'08 4:44:45
Milford 6 14 42N50'07 71w38'58 4:46:36
Mill Hollow 3 1 43N07'22 72w17'56 4:49:12
Mill Hollow 10 1 43N33'12 72w15'57 4:49:04
Millsfield 4 1 44N47 71w15 4:45:00
Mill Village 3 1 43N04'39 72w05'35 4:48:22
Mill Village 10 1 43N32'03 72w20'11 4:49:21
Millville 8 2 42N48'09 71w12'54 4:44:52
Millville Lake 8
2 42N47 71w12 4:44:48
Milton 9 1 43N24'35 70w59'20 4:43:57
Milton Mills 9 1 43N30'04 70w57'51 4:43:51
Mirror Lake 2 1 43N37'21 71w16'36 4:45:06
Monahan Corner 8
1 42N55'17 70w59'32 4:43:58
Monroe 4 1 44N15'37 72w03'19 4:48:13
Mont Vernon 6 1 42N53'40 71w40'29 4:46:42
Moultonboro 2 1 43N45'17 71w23'50 4:45:35
Moultonborough Falls 2
1 43N44'38 71w24'40 4:45:39
Moultonville 2 1 43N45'16 71w10'13 4:44:41
Mountain Base 6 1 42N59'11 71w34'45 4:46:19
Mountain View Estates 6
2 42N45 71w29 4:45:56
Mount Major 1 1 43N31'20 71w16'18 4:45:05
Mount Saint Mary College 7
3 43N03 71w27 4:45:48
Mount Sunapee 7 1 43N20'26 72w04'17 4:48:17
Mount Washington 4
1 44N16 71w18 4:45:12
Munsonville 3 1 43N00'51 72w08'57 4:48:36
Murray Hill 7 1 43N32'32 71w47'45 4:47:11
Nashua 6 2 42N45'55 71w28'05 4:45:52
Nason Corners 8 5 42N55'12 70w54'32 4:43:38
Nelson 3 1 42N59'26 72w07'53 4:48:32
New Boston 6 1 42N58'34 71w41'40 4:46:47
Newbury 7 1 43N19'17 72w02'11 4:48:09
New Castle 8 2 43N04'20 70w43'00 4:42:52
New Durham 9 1 43N26'12 71w10'22 4:44:41
New Durham Corner 9
1 43N25'19 71w07'30 4:44:30
Newfields 8 5 43N02'13 70w56'20 4:43:45
New Hampton 1 1 43N36'20 71w39'17 4:46:37
Newington 8 1 43N06'00 70w50'03 4:43:20
Newington Station 8
1 43N06'44 70w49'19 4:43:17
New Ipswich 6 1 42N44'53 71w51'17 4:47:25
New Ipswich Center 6
1 42N45'29 71w51'08 4:47:25
New London 7 1 43N24'50 71w59'08 4:47:57
Newmarket 7 6 43N16'40 71w52'26 4:47:30
Newmarket 8 5 43N04'58 70w56'08 4:43:45
Newport 10 15 43N21'55 72w10'26 4:48:42
New Portsmouth 9
1 43N30'18 71w03'15 4:44:13
New Rye 7 1 43N11'02 71w21'50 4:45:27
Newton 8 2 42N52'10 71w02'06 4:44:08
Newton Junction 8
2 42N52'02 71w03'59 4:44:16
Noone 6 1 42N51'35 71w57'54 4:47:52
North Barnstead 1
1 43N21 71w16 4:45:04
North Beach 8 2 42N56'02 70w47'56 4:43:12
North Branch 6 1 43N04'50 71w58'40 4:47:55
North Brookline 6
14 42N45'33 71w40'32 4:46:42
North Charleston 10
1 43N18'30 72w23'15 4:49:33
North Charlestown 10
1 43N14 72w25 4:49:40
North Chatham 2 1 44N14'32 71w01'02 4:44:04
North Chester 8 1 43N00'14 71w16'33 4:45:06
North Chichester 7
1 43N15'27 71w22'23 4:45:30
North Conway 2 1 44N03'13 71w07'44 4:44:31
North Danville 8
3 42N56'44 71w06'50 4:44:27
North Dorchester 5
1 43N48'09 71w58'17 4:47:53
North Epping 8 1 43N04'17 71w03'39 4:44:15
Northfield 7 6 43N25'59 71w35'34 4:46:22
North Grantham 10
1 43N31'44 72w07'53 4:48:32
North Groton 5 1 43N45'35 71w52'13 4:47:29
North Hampton 8 2 42N58'21 70w49'49 4:43:19
North Hampton Center 8
2 42N58'35 70w50'54 4:43:24
North Haverhill 5
1 44N05'25 72w01'37 4:48:06
North Hinsdale 3
7 42N49'30 72w31'09 4:50:05
North Holderness 5
16 43N45 71w41 4:46:44
North Littleton 5
13 44N21'35 71w48'09 4:47:13
North Londonderry 8
2 42N55'05 71w23'58 4:45:36
North Newport 10
15 43N23'19 72w12'54 4:48:52
North Nottingham 8
1 43N10'01 71w06'22 4:44:25
North Pelham 6 1 42N46'25 71w21'11 4:45:25
North Pembroke 7
1 43N12'10 71w25'43 4:45:43
North Richmond 3
1 42N47'35 72w16'21 4:49:05
North Rochester (Hayes Sta) 9
17 43N22'22 70w59'10 4:43:57
North Salem 8 2 42N50'13 71w13'16 4:44:53
North Sanbornton 1
6 43N33'07 71w36'36 4:46:26
North Sandwich 2
1 43N50'26 71w23'51 4:45:35
North Stratford 4
1 44N45'06 71w37'45 4:46:31
North Sutton 7 1 43N21'50 71w56'24 4:47:46
North Swanzey 3 1 42N56 72w17 4:49:08
Northumberland 4
1 44N33'48 71w33'33 4:46:14
North Village 6 1 42N53'56 71w56'22 4:47:45
North Wakefield 2
1 43N38'10 71w03'19 4:44:13
North Walpole 3 1 43N08'20 72w26'55 4:49:48
North Weare 6 1 43N06'52 71w44'18 4:46:57
North Wilmot 7 1 43N29'47 71w56'04 4:47:44
North Wolfeboro 2
1 43N39'13 71w08'05 4:44:32
Northwood 8 1 43N11'39 71w09'05 4:44:36
Northwood Center 8
1 43N13'02 71w12'26 4:44:50
Northwood Narrows 8
1 43N13'33 71w14'40 4:44:59
Northwood Ridge 8
1 43N12'34 71w10'50 4:44:43
North Woodstock 5
3 44N01'49 71w41'11 4:46:45
Notchland 2 1 44N06'56 71w21'20 4:45:25
Nottingham 8 1 43N06'52 71w06'01 4:44:24
Nottingham Square 8
1 43N06'11 71w06'40 4:44:27
Noyes Terrace 8 2 42N45'16 71w12'12 4:44:49
Nutter 5 1 44N08'41 71w56'43 4:47:47
Nuttings Beach 5
1 43N39'45 71w47'26 4:47:10
Odell 4 1 44N44 71w23 4:45:32
Old Millstream Estates 8
5 42N59 70w57 4:43:48
Old Northwood 8 1 43N12 71w06 4:44:24
Onway Lake 8 3 43N02'03 71w13'00 4:44:52
Orange 5 1 43N39'16 71w58'19 4:47:53
Orford 5 1 43N54'19 72w08'26 4:48:34
Orfordville 5 1 43N53'00 72w06'10 4:48:25
Ossipee 2 1 43N41'07 71w07'02 4:44:28
Ossipee Lake Shores 2
1 43N48'09 71w05'39 4:44:23
Ossipee Valley 2
1 43N47'31 71w10'41 4:44:43
Otterville 7 1 43N25'46 72w02'46 4:48:11
Pages Corner 7 1 43N08'59 71w37'49 4:46:31
Pannaway Manor 8
2 43N03'52 70w48'06 4:43:12
Panno Place 2 8 44N08'50 71w08'16 4:44:33
Paris 4 10 44N39'04 71w19'17 4:45:17
Parker 6 7 43N01'33 71w37'41 4:46:31
Parker Hill 5 1 44N15'15 71w57'02 4:47:48
Parkman Corner 8
5 42N59'40 70w55'41 4:43:43
Partridge Lake 5
13 44N18 71w46 4:47:04
Passaconaway 2 1 43N59'42 71w20'26 4:45:22
Paugus Mill 2 1 43N55'26 71w18'17 4:45:13
Pearls Corner 7 1 43N20'32 71w28'08 4:45:53
Pease Air Force Base 8
2 43N04 70w47 4:43:08
Pelham 6 1 42N44'04 71w19'30 4:45:18
Pembroke 7 1 43N08'48 71w27'29 4:45:50
Penacook 7 1 43N16'49 71w36'02 4:46:24
Pendleton Beach 1
3 43N36'32 71w26'41 4:45:47
Peppermint Corner 8
2 42N52'03 71w19'33 4:45:18
Pequawket 2 1 43N55'12 71w13'42 4:44:55
Percy 4 1 44N37'29 71w23'18 4:45:33
Perham Corner 6 3 42N51'44 71w43'00 4:46:52
Perkins Hill 8 5 42N57'46 70w59'28 4:43:58
Peterborough 6 1 42N52'14 71w57'08 4:47:49
Pettyboro 5 1 44N12'15 71w57'43 4:47:51
Pickering 9 17 43N15'09 70w57'11 4:43:49
Pickpocket Woods 8
5 42N59 70w57 4:43:48
Pierce Bridge 5 1 44N16'21 71w37'54 4:46:32
Piermont 5 1 43N58'11 72w04'52 4:48:19
Pike 5 1 44N01'51 72w00'31 4:48:02

Pinardville 6	7	42N59'39	71W30'28	4:46:02
Pine Brook Estates 8	5	42N59	70W57	4:43:48
Pine Cliff 7	1	43N20'28	72W02'30	4:48:10
Pinecrest 8	5	42N59	70W57	4:43:48
Pine Grove Park 8	2	42N47'55	71W11'52	4:44:47
Pine River 2	1	43N43'55	71W04'27	4:44:18
Pine Valley 6	3	42N51	71W44	4:46:56
Pinkhams Grant 4	1	44N16	71W15	4:45:00
Piscataqua 8	2	43N06'02	70W47'36	4:43:10
Pittsburg 4	1	45N03'04	71W23'31	4:45:34
Pittsfield 7	1	43N18'21	71W19'29	4:45:18
Place 9	17	43N21'09	71W01'34	4:44:06
Plaice Cove 8	2	42N56'49	70W47'21	4:43:09
Plainfield 10	1	43N32'03	72W21'24	4:49:26
Plaistow 8	2	42N50'11	71W05'43	4:44:23
Plymouth 5	16	43N45'25	71W41'19	4:46:45
Pollys Crossing 2	1	43N42'29	71W07'50	4:44:31
Ponemah 6	14	42N49'01	71W36'20	4:46:25
Poocham 3	1	42N57'02	72W28'40	4:49:55
Portsmouth 8	2	43N04'18	70W45'47	4:43:03
Portsmouth Plains 8	2	43N03'25	70W46'49	4:43:07
Potash Corner 6	2	42N48'50	71W24'31	4:45:38
Potter Place 7	1	43N26'07	71W51'29	4:47:26
Powwow River 8	1	42N54'33	71W00'58	4:44:04
Pratt 6	1	42N47'01	71W45'49	4:47:03
Prescott Corner 8	5	42N56'40	70W56'06	4:43:44
Puckershire 10	1	43N21'22	72W18'58	4:49:16
Quaker City 10	1	43N16'17	72W19'58	4:49:20
Quebec Junction 4	1	44N20'57	71W33'09	4:46:13
Quincy 5	1	43N47'15	71W46'30	4:47:06
Quint 2	1	43N59'50	71W07'59	4:44:32
Quinttown 5	1	43N51'57	72W03'21	4:48:13
Rand 3	5	42N44'10	72W02'33	4:48:10
Randolph 4	1	44N22'31	71W16'49	4:45:07
Randolph Hill 4	1	44N23'17	71W16'44	4:45:07
Raymond 8	3	43N02'10	71W11'02	4:44:44
Redstone 2	1	44N00'53	71W06'06	4:44:24
Reeds Ferry 6	1	42N52'59	71W28'35	4:45:54
Richardson 6	14	42N50	71W39	4:46:36
Richmond 3	1	42N45'17	72W16'20	4:49:05
Rim Junction 4	1	44N16'59	71W03'00	4:44:12
Rindge 3	5	42N45'04	72W00'37	4:48:02
Rings Corner 7	1	43N18'50	71W21'42	4:45:27
Rivercrest 5	1	43N43'35	72W16'17	4:49:05
Riverdale 6	7	43N01'55	71W38'44	4:46:35
Riverhill 7	1	43N14'57	71W37'12	4:46:29
Riverside 8	2	42N52'57	70W49'26	4:43:18
Riverton 4	1	44N26'44	71W31'46	4:46:07
Robinson Corner 5	1	43N32'03	71W58'23	4:47:54
Roby 7	6	43N17'19	71W53'11	4:47:33
Rochester 9	17	43N18'16	70W58'34	4:43:54
Rockingham 8	5	43N03'00	70W56'00	4:43:44
Rockwood 3	1	42N47'39	72W10'54	4:48:44
Rockywold 5	1	43N46'27	71W32'38	4:46:11
Rogers Crossing 2	8	44N04'54	71W14'39	4:44:59
Roland Park 2	1	43N43'56	71W12'00	4:44:48
Rollinsford 9	1	43N14'10	70W49'15	4:43:17
Rollinsford Station 9	7	43N13'46	70W50'36	4:43:22
Roundys Corner 3	1	43N03'08	72W17'46	4:49:11
Rowes Corner 7	3	43N04'11	71W22'58	4:45:32
Rowes Corner 8	2	42N52'32	71W01'33	4:44:06
Roxbury Center 3	1	42N57'20	72W12'24	4:48:50
Royal Crest Estates 6	2	42N45	71W29	4:45:56
Rumney 5	1	43N48'19	71W48'47	4:47:15
Rumney Depot 5	1	43N47'36	71W48'19	4:47:13
Russell 6	1	42N55'02	71W50'43	4:47:23
Ryder Corner 10	15	43N24'19	72W07'42	4:48:31
Rye 8	1	43N00'48	70W46'17	4:43:05
Rye Beach 8	2	42N58'36	70W45'58	4:43:04
Rye North Beach 8	1	43N00'46	70W44'09	4:42:57
Sabattus Heights 7	1	43N21'54	71W24'09	4:45:37
Sachem Village 5	1	43N40'59	72W17'10	4:49:09
Salem 8	2	42N47'18	71W12'05	4:44:48
Salem Depot 8	2	42N47'12	71W13'37	4:44:54
Salisbury 7	1	43N22'48	71W43'03	4:46:52
Salisbury Heights 7	1	43N23'28	71W44'41	4:46:59
Sanborn Corners 8	2	42N56'06	70W53'30	4:43:34
Sanbornton 1	1	43N29'21	71W34'58	4:46:20
Sanbornville 2	1	43N33'15	71W01'53	4:44:08
Sandown 8	1	42N55'43	71W11'15	4:44:45
Sandwich 2	1	43N47'25	71W24'42	4:45:39
Sandwich Landing 2	1	43N47'06	71W28'17	4:45:53
Sargent Corners 8	2	42N51'41	71W02'36	4:44:10
Savageville 5	1	44N12'42	71W53'39	4:47:35
Sawyers 9	7	43N10'51	70W53'23	4:43:34
Sawyers River 2	1	44N05'23	71W21'04	4:45:24
Scotland 3	1	42N45'26	72W21'29	4:49:26
Scott 4	1	44N24'44	71W38'15	4:46:33
Scribners Corner 7	1	43N22'06	71W47'46	4:47:11
Seabrook 8	2	42N53'41	70W52'18	4:43:29
Seabrook Beach 8	2	42N53'12	70W48'58	4:43:16
Seabrook Station 8	2	42N53'15	70W51'38	4:43:27
Seacrest Village 8	2	43N04	70W47	4:43:08
Severance 8	7	43N00'38	71W22'51	4:45:31
Shaker Village 7	1	43N21'31	71W29'26	4:45:58
Sharon 6	5	42N48'47	71W54'58	4:47:40
Shaws Corner 3	1	43N03'09	72W20'01	4:49:20
Shaws Hill 8	2	43N04'17	70W43'39	4:42:55
Shelburne 4	1	44N24'04	71W04'31	4:44:18
Sherwood Forest 8	5	42N59	70W57	4:43:48
Shingle Mill Corner 7	1	43N21'13	71W54'55	4:47:40
Shirley Hill 6	7	43N00	71W31	4:46:04
Short Falls 7	1	43N11'54	71W22'12	4:45:29
Silver Lake (Madison Sta) 2	1	43N53'17	71W10'33	4:44:42
Slab City 6	1	43N05'55	71W45'42	4:47:03
Smith Colony 8	2	42N56'54	70W47'43	4:43:11
Smith Corner 8	1	42N53'36	70W59'21	4:43:57
Smiths Corner 7	1	43N21'06	71W47'27	4:47:10
Smiths Point 1	3	43N33	71W29	4:45:56
Smithtown 8	2	42N52'35	70W52'14	4:43:29
Smithville 6	1	42N44'15	71W52'18	4:47:29
Snowville 2	1	43N54'45	71W03'30	4:44:14
Snumshire 10	1	43N14'54	72W24'57	4:49:40
Snyders Hill 7	1	43N17'16	71W42'44	4:46:51
Somersworth 9	7	43N15'42	70W51'57	4:43:28
Sonth Lancaster 4	1	44N27'31	71W38'45	4:46:35
Soo Nipi 7	1	43N25	71W58	4:47:52
South Acworth 10	1	43N11'27	72W17'09	4:49:09
South Alexandria 7	1	43N33'27	71W47'43	4:47:11
South Barnstead 1	1	43N18'54	71W13'44	4:44:55
South Barrington 9	1	43N10'56	71W02'05	4:44:08
South Bow 7	3	43N05'24	71W31'08	4:46:05
South Brookline 6	1	42N42'56	71W39'42	4:46:39
South Charlestown 10	1	43N10'46	72W26'16	4:49:45
South Chatham 2	1	44N06'04	71W00'27	4:44:02
South Conway 2	1	43N57'47	71W01'23	4:44:06
South Cornish 10	1	43N27'01	72W18'36	4:49:14
South Danbury (Converse Sta) 7	1	43N29'02	71W53'15	4:47:33
South Danville 8	1	42N54'04	71W07'36	4:44:30
South Deerfield 8	1	43N05'45	71W16'06	4:45:04
South Effingham 2	1	43N42'04	70W59'02	4:43:56
South Hampton 8	1	42N52'51	70W57'47	4:43:51
South Hemlock 10	1	43N12'11	72W22'05	4:49:28
South Hooksett 7	3	43N01'35	71W26'09	4:45:45
South Keene 3	1	42N55'01	72W14'44	4:48:59
South Kingston 8	2	42N52'50	71W04'55	4:44:20
South Lee 9	5	43N05'55	71W02'32	4:44:10
South Lyndeboro 6	3	42N53	71W47	4:47:08
South Lyndeborough 6	3	42N52'48	71W47'03	4:47:08
South Merrimack 6	2	42N48'17	71W33'20	4:46:13
South Milford 6	14	42N49'28	71W39'39	4:46:39
South Newbury 7	1	43N17'44	71W59'50	4:47:59
South Pittsfield 7	1	43N18	71W20	4:45:20
South Seabrook 8	2	42N52'17	70W51'25	4:43:26
South Stoddard 3	1	43N02'24	72W04'20	4:48:17
South Sutton 7	1	43N19'12	71W56'05	4:47:44
South Tamworth 2	1	43N49'29	71W18'13	4:45:13
South Weare 6	1	43N03'22	71W42'53	4:46:52
South Wolfeboro 2	1	43N33'41	71W10'40	4:44:43
Spofford 3	18	42N54'25	72W25'12	4:49:41
Spragueville 3	1	42N53'47	72W15'50	4:49:03
Springfield 10	1	43N29'42	72W02'02	4:48:08
Springfield Junction 10	1	43N15'01	72W25'32	4:49:42
Spring Haven 1	3	43N33'19	71W19'06	4:45:16
Squag City 10	1	43N30'58	72W22'19	4:49:29
Squantum 3	5	42N47'26	71W59'10	4:47:57
Stark 4	1	44N36	71W24	4:45:36
Starr King 4	1	44N24'05	71W26'35	4:45:46
State Landing 2	1	43N43'34	71W22'28	4:45:30
State Line 3	5	42N43'05	72W05'02	4:48:20
Stewartstown 4	1	44N58	71W25	4:45:40
Stewartstown Hollow 4	1	44N56'55	71W27'11	4:45:49
Stillwater 5	1	44N07'07	71W28'12	4:45:53
Stinson Lake 5	1	43N51'40	71W48'32	4:47:14
Stockbridge Corner 2	1	43N38'09	71W12'12	4:44:49
Stockbridge Corners 1	1	43N24'51	71W12'11	4:44:49
Stoddard 3	1	43N04'43	72W06'54	4:48:28
Strafford 9	1	43N19'37	71W11'05	4:44:44
Strafford Corner 9	1	43N17'39	71W04'39	4:44:19
Stratford 4	1	44N39'18	71W33'22	4:46:13
Stratham 8	5	43N01'26	70W54'51	4:43:39
Stratham Station 8	2	43N03'10	70W53'45	4:43:35
Strawberry Banke 8	2	43N04	70W47	4:43:08
Success 4	1	44N32	71W05	4:44:20
Sugar Hill 5	1	44N13	71W47	4:47:08
Sullivan 3	1	43N00'47	72W13'17	4:48:53
Sunapee 10	1	43N23'15	72W05'18	4:48:21
Suncook 7	1	43N07'50	71W27'13	4:45:49
Surry 3	1	43N01'04	72W19'18	4:49:17
Sutton 7	1	43N20'03	71W57'07	4:47:48
Swanzey 3	18	42N52'11	72W16'56	4:49:08
Swanzey Factory 3	1	42N54'30	72W15'55	4:49:04
Swanzey Station 3	18	42N53'12	72W17'15	4:49:09
Swetts Mills 7	1	43N18'53	71W43'16	4:46:53
Swiftwater 5	1	44N07'58	71W57'07	4:47:48
Tamworth 2	1	43N51'35	71W15'49	4:45:03
Tappan Corners 8	1	42N54'38	70W59'25	4:43:58
Tavern Village 6	1	43N02'21	71W42'14	4:46:49
Temple 6	1	42N49'05	71W51'07	4:47:24
The Five Corners 8	2	42N56'17	70W49'12	4:43:17
The Glen 4	1	45N06'15	71W15'30	4:45:02
The Plains 1	1	43N27'48	71W32'58	4:46:12
The Plantation 8	2	42N55'45	70W48'24	4:43:14
The Willows 8	2	42N54'41	70W49'29	4:43:18
Thomas 3	5	42N44'58	72W02'38	4:48:11
Thompson Corner 7	1	43N23'49	71W43'05	4:46:52
Thornton 5	1	43N53'34	71W40'35	4:46:42
Thorntons Ferry 6	1	42N50'31	71W29'35	4:45:58
Tilton 1	6	43N26'32	71W35'22	4:46:21
Tinkerville 4	1	44N46'50	71W35'02	4:46:20
Tinkerville 5	1	44N16'20	71W56'08	4:47:45
Towles Corner 8	5	42N53'42	70W55'42	4:43:43
Town Hall Corner 8	2	42N55'17	70W52'24	4:43:30
Town House 9	1	43N26'28	70W59'07	4:43:56
Trapshire 10	1	43N11'42	72W26'20	4:49:45
Tripoli Mill 5	3	43N59'53	71W34'40	4:46:19
Troy 3	1	42N49'26	72W10'54	4:48:44
Tuftonboro 2	1	43N41'47	71W13'21	4:44:53
Twin Lakes Village 10	1	43N26'28	72W00'41	4:48:03
Twin Mountain 4	1	44N16'20	71W32'22	4:46:09
Tyler 7	1	43N14'04	71W41'24	4:46:46
Union 2	1	43N29'29	71W01'25	4:44:06
Union Wharf 2	1	43N39'07	71W16'58	4:45:08
Unity 10	1	43N17'38	72W15'39	4:49:03
Upper Kidderville 4	1	44N52'57	71W21'54	4:45:28
Upper Shaker Village 5	1	43N36'42	72W08'19	4:48:33
Upper Village 4	12	44N23'53	71W11'44	4:44:47
Upper Village 5	1	44N10'38	71W56'41	4:47:47
Wadley Falls 9	5	43N05'31	71W00'30	4:44:02
Wakefield 2	1	43N34'05	71W01'50	4:44:07
Wallis Sands 8	1	43N01'26	70W43'58	4:42:56
Walpole 3	1	43N04'46	72W25'35	4:49:42
Walton Landing 8	2	42N53'14	70W50'30	4:43:22
Warner 7	6	43N16'50	71W49'02	4:47:16
Warren 5	1	43N55'23	71W53'33	4:47:34
Washburn Corner 10	1	43N31'28	72W04'51	4:48:19
Washington 10	1	43N10'33	72W05'50	4:48:23
Waterloo 7	6	43N17'22	71W51'19	4:47:25
Water Village 2	1	43N40'57	71W11'06	4:44:44
Waterville Estates 5	9	43N52	71W38	4:46:32
Waterville Valley 5	1	43N57'00	71W30'00	4:46:00
Waumbeck Junction 4	1	44N22'26	71W31'13	4:46:05
Wawbeek 2	1	43N40'19	71W17'52	4:45:11
Weare 6	1	43N05'41	71W43'52	4:46:55
Weare Corner 8	5	42N53'53	70W54'42	4:43:39
Weares Mill 8	2	42N54'09	70W54'06	4:43:36
Webb 3	1	42N52'27	72W12'47	4:48:51
Webster 7	1	43N19'44	71W43'06	4:46:52
Webster Lake 7	11	43N27'36	71W40'58	4:46:44
Webster Place 7	11	43N24'23	71W39'19	4:46:37
Websters Mill 7	1	43N16'42	71W20'45	4:45:23
Weirs Beach 1	3	43N36'32	71W27'40	4:45:51
Welshs Corner 9	1	43N20'04	71W07'54	4:44:32
Wendell 10	15	43N22'25	72W15'01	4:49:00
Wentworth 5	1	43N52'18	71W54'53	4:47:40
Wentworth Acres 8	2	43N05'21	70W47'04	4:43:08
Wentworth By The Sea 8	2	43N04	70W43	4:42:52
Wentworth Hill 2	1	43N47'29	71W24'49	4:45:39
Wentworth Location 4	1	44N51'29	71W03'21	4:44:13
Wentworth Terrace 9	1	43N07'26	70W49'54	4:43:20
West Alton 1	3	43N33'04	71W18'42	4:45:15
West Andover 7	1	43N26'39	71W52'38	4:47:31
West Barrington 9	1	43N12'17	71W06'18	4:44:25
West Bath 5	1	44N10'27	71W59'16	4:47:57
West Brentwood 8	2	42N56	71W03	4:44:12
West Brookline 6	1	42N44'10	71W40'47	4:46:43
West Campton 5	9	43N50'50	71W39'59	4:46:40
West Canaan 5	1	43N38'58	72W05'48	4:48:23
West Center Harbor 1	1	43N42	71W38	4:46:32
West Chesterfield 3	1	42N54'15	72W30'58	4:50:04
West Claremont 10	1	43N23'46	72W22'11	4:49:29
West Concord 7	2	43N14'37	71W34'24	4:46:18
West Deering 6	1	43N03'53	71W54'19	4:47:37
West Derry 8	2	42N52'24	71W20'17	4:45:21
West Drummer 4	10	44N27	71W11	4:44:44
West Epping 8	1	43N02'14	71W07'23	4:44:30
West Franklin 7	11	43N27	71W39	4:46:36
West Gonic 9	17	43N16'43	70W58'59	4:43:56
West Hampstead 8	2	42N54'13	71W13'02	4:44:52
West Henniker 7	1	43N11	71W49	4:47:16
West Henniker Emerson Sta 7	1	43N10'12	71W50'37	4:47:22
West Hollis 6	1	42N42'20	71W37'17	4:46:29
West Hopkinton 7	1	43N11'31	71W44'55	4:47:00
West Kingston 8	2	42N54'36	71W04'08	4:44:17
West Lebanon 5	1	43N38'57	72W18'39	4:49:15

NEW HAMPSHIRE

West Milan 4	10	44N35'55	71w18'17	4:45:13
Westmoreland 3	1	42N57'43	72w26'34	4:49:46
Westmoreland Depot 3	1	43N00'07	72w26'02	4:49:44
West Nottingham 8	1	43N10'25	71w08'27	4:44:34
West Ossipee 2	1	43N49'29	71w12'19	4:44:49
West Peterborough 6	1	42N53'14	71w59'09	4:47:57
West Plymouth 5	16	43N46'13	71w45'46	4:47:03
Westport 3	1	42N50'30	72w20'53	4:49:24
West Rindge 3	5	42N45'48	72w01'55	4:48:08
West Rumney 5	1	43N48'49	71w52'16	4:47:29
West Rye 8	1	43N00'04	70w47'54	4:43:12
West Salisbury 7	1	43N23'56	71w46'51	4:47:07
West Springfield 10	1	43N29'55	72w03'30	4:48:14
West Stewartstown 4	1	44N59'43	71w31'54	4:46:08
West Swanzey 3	18	42N52'12	72w19'20	4:49:17
West Thornton 5	9	43N56'09	71w41'17	4:46:45
West Unity 10	1	43N17'17	72w19'01	4:49:16
Westville 8	2	42N49'39	71w07'03	4:44:28
West Wilton 6	3	42N49'49	71w48'23	4:47:14
West Windham 8	3	42N48'09	71w21'09	4:45:25
Whiteface 2	1	43N52'00	71w23'55	4:45:36
Whitefield 4	1	44N22'23	71w36'38	4:46:27
Whittier 2	1	43N49'55	71w16'02	4:45:04
Wilder 6	5	42N47'14	71w55'45	4:47:43
Wildwood 5	1	44N04'42	71w48'03	4:47:12
Willey House 2	1	44N05	71w17	4:45:08
Wilmot 7	1	43N27'06	71w54'51	4:47:39
Wilmot Flat 7	1	43N25'04	71w53'44	4:47:35
Wilson 8	2	42N55'01	71w22'06	4:45:28
Wilson Corners 8	2	42N47'32	71w11'12	4:44:45
Wilton 6	3	42N50'36	71w44'08	4:46:57
Wilton Center 6	3	42N49'58	71w46'39	4:47:07
Winchester 3	1	42N46'24	72w23'01	4:49:32
Windham 8	3	42N48'02	71w18'17	4:45:13
Windham Depot 8	3	42N50'29	71w18'01	4:45:12
Windsor 6	1	43N08	72w01	4:48:04
Winniconic 8	5	43N01'20	70w52'35	4:43:30
Winnicut Mills 8	2	43N00'39	70w52'28	4:43:30
Winnipesaukee 2	1	43N40'27	71w20'08	4:45:21
Winnisquam 1	1	43N30'05	71w30'45	4:46:03
Winona 1	1	43N39'58	71w33'31	4:46:14
Wolfeboro 2	1	43N35'02	71w12'28	4:44:50
Wolfeboro Center 2	1	43N37'10	71w10'20	4:44:41
Wolfeboro Falls 2	1	43N35'31	71w12'22	4:44:49
Wonalancet 2	1	43N54'26	71w21'04	4:45:24
Woodland Park 6	1	42N52'15	71w30'45	4:46:03
Woodlands 1	3	43N31'52	71w16'10	4:45:05
Woodman 2	1	43N38'05	70w59'00	4:43:56
Woodmere 3	5	42N47'00	72w00'31	4:48:02
Woods Mill 3	1	43N02'30	72w09'17	4:48:37
Woodstock 5	3	43N58'39	71w41'08	4:46:45
Woodsville 5	1	44N09'08	72w02'16	4:48:09

TIME TABLES

NJ # 1

Date	Time	Zone
Before 11/18/1883		LMT
11/18/1883	12:00	EST
3/31/1918	02:00	EWT
10/27/1918	02:00	EST
3/30/1919	02:00	EWT
10/26/1919	02:00	EST
3/28/1920	02:00	EDT
10/31/1920	02:00	EST
4/24/1921	02:00	EDT
9/25/1921	02:00	EST
4/30/1922	02:00	EDT
9/24/1922	02:00	EST
4/29/1923	02:00	EDT
9/30/1923	02:00	EST
4/27/1924	02:00	EDT
9/28/1924	02:00	EST
4/26/1925	02:00	EDT
9/27/1925	02:00	EST
4/25/1926	02:00	EDT
9/26/1926	02:00	EST
4/24/1927	02:00	EDT
9/25/1927	02:00	EST
4/29/1928	02:00	EDT
9/30/1928	02:00	EST
4/28/1929	02:00	EDT
9/29/1929	02:00	EST
4/27/1930	02:00	EDT
9/28/1930	02:00	EST
4/26/1931	02:00	EDT
9/27/1931	02:00	EST
4/24/1932	02:00	EDT
9/25/1932	02:00	EST
4/30/1933	02:00	EDT
9/24/1933	02:00	EST
4/29/1934	02:00	EDT
9/30/1934	02:00	EST
4/28/1935	02:00	EDT
9/29/1935	02:00	EST
4/26/1936	02:00	EDT
9/27/1936	02:00	EST
4/25/1937	02:00	EDT
9/26/1937	02:00	EST
4/24/1938	02:00	EDT
9/25/1938	02:00	EST
4/30/1939	02:00	EDT
9/24/1939	02:00	EST
4/28/1940	02:00	EDT
9/29/1940	02:00	EST
4/27/1941	02:00	EDT
9/28/1941	02:00	EST
2/09/1942	02:00	EWT
9/30/1945	02:00	EST
4/28/1946	02:00	EDT
9/29/1946	02:00	EST
4/27/1947	02:00	EDT
9/28/1947	02:00	EST
4/25/1948	02:00	EDT
9/26/1948	02:00	EST
4/24/1949	02:00	EDT
9/25/1949	02:00	EST
4/30/1950	02:00	EDT
9/24/1950	02:00	EST
4/29/1951	02:00	EDT
9/30/1951	02:00	EST
4/27/1952	02:00	EDT
9/28/1952	02:00	EST
4/26/1953	02:00	EDT
9/27/1953	02:00	EST
4/25/1954	02:00	EDT
9/26/1954	02:00	EST
4/24/1955	02:00	EDT
10/30/1955	02:00	EST
4/29/1956	02:00	EDT
10/28/1956	02:00	EST
4/28/1957	02:00	EDT
10/27/1957	02:00	EST
4/27/1958	02:00	EDT
10/26/1958	02:00	EST
4/26/1959	02:00	EDT
10/25/1959	02:00	EST
4/24/1960	02:00	EDT
10/30/1960	02:00	EST
4/30/1961	02:00	EDT
10/29/1961	02:00	EST
4/29/1962	02:00	EDT
10/28/1962	02:00	EST
4/28/1963	02:00	EDT
10/27/1963	02:00	EST
4/26/1964	02:00	EDT
10/25/1964	02:00	EST
4/25/1965	02:00	EDT
10/31/1965	02:00	EST
4/24/1966	02:00	EDT
10/30/1966	02:00	EST
4/30/1967	02:00	US#1

NJ # 2

Date	Time	Zone
Before 11/18/1883		LMT
11/18/1883	12:00	EST
3/31/1918	02:00	EWT
10/27/1918	02:00	EST
3/30/1919	02:00	EWT
10/26/1919	02:00	EST
4/24/1921	02:00	US#2

NJ # 3

Date	Time	Zone
Before 11/18/1883		LMT
11/18/1883	12:00	EST
3/31/1918	02:00	EWT
10/27/1918	02:00	EST
3/30/1919	02:00	EWT
10/26/1919	02:00	EST
4/30/1922	02:00	US#2

NJ # 4

Date	Time	Zone
Before 11/18/1883		LMT
11/18/1883	12:00	EST
3/31/1918	02:00	EWT
10/27/1918	02:00	EST
3/30/1919	02:00	EWT
10/26/1919	02:00	EST
4/29/1928	02:00	US#2

NJ # 5

Date	Time	Zone
Before 11/18/1883		LMT
11/18/1883	12:00	EST
3/31/1918	02:00	EWT
10/27/1918	02:00	EST
3/30/1919	02:00	EWT
10/26/1919	02:00	EST
4/27/1930	02:00	US#2

NJ # 6

Date	Time	Zone
Before 11/18/1883		LMT
11/18/1883	12:00	EST
3/31/1918	02:00	EWT
10/27/1918	02:00	EST
3/30/1919	02:00	EWT
10/26/1919	02:00	EST
3/28/1920	02:00	EDT
10/31/1920	02:00	EST
4/24/1921	02:00	EDT
9/25/1921	02:00	EST
4/30/1922	02:00	EDT
9/24/1922	02:00	EST
4/29/1923	02:00	EDT
9/30/1923	02:00	EST
4/27/1924	02:00	EDT
9/28/1924	02:00	EST
4/26/1925	02:00	EDT
9/27/1925	02:00	EST
4/25/1926	02:00	EDT
9/26/1926	02:00	EST
4/24/1927	02:00	EDT
9/25/1927	02:00	EST
4/29/1928	02:00	EDT
9/30/1928	02:00	EST
4/28/1929	02:00	EDT
9/29/1929	02:00	EST
4/27/1930	02:00	EDT
9/28/1930	02:00	EST
4/26/1931	02:00	EDT
9/27/1931	02:00	EST
4/24/1932	02:00	EDT
9/25/1932	02:00	EST
4/30/1933	02:00	EDT
9/24/1933	02:00	EST
4/29/1934	02:00	EDT
9/30/1934	02:00	EST
4/28/1935	02:00	EDT
9/29/1935	02:00	EST
4/26/1936	02:00	EDT
9/27/1936	02:00	EST
4/25/1937	00:01	EDT
9/26/1937	00:01	EST
4/24/1938	00:01	EDT
9/25/1938	00:01	EST
4/30/1939	00:01	EDT
9/24/1939	00:01	EST
4/28/1940	00:01	EDT
9/29/1940	00:01	EST
4/27/1941	00:01	EDT
9/28/1941	00:01	EST
2/09/1942	02:00	EWT
9/30/1945	02:00	EST
4/28/1946	00:01	EDT
9/29/1946	00:01	EST
4/27/1947	00:01	EDT
9/28/1947	00:01	EST
4/25/1948	00:01	EDT
9/26/1948	00:01	EST
4/24/1949	00:01	EDT
9/25/1949	00:01	EST
4/30/1950	00:01	EDT
9/24/1950	00:01	EST
4/29/1951	00:01	EDT
9/30/1951	00:01	EST
4/27/1952	00:01	EDT
9/28/1952	00:01	EST
4/26/1953	00:01	EDT
9/27/1953	00:01	EST
4/25/1954	00:01	EDT
9/26/1954	00:01	EST
4/24/1955	00:01	EDT
10/30/1955	00:01	EST
4/29/1956	00:01	EDT
10/28/1956	00:01	EST
4/28/1957	00:01	EDT
10/27/1957	00:01	EST
4/27/1958	00:01	EDT
10/26/1958	00:01	EST
4/26/1959	00:01	EDT
10/25/1959	00:01	EST
4/24/1960	00:01	EDT
10/30/1960	00:01	EST
4/30/1961	00:01	EDT
10/29/1961	00:01	EST
4/29/1962	00:01	EDT
10/28/1962	00:01	EST
4/28/1963	00:01	EDT
10/27/1963	00:01	EST
4/26/1964	00:01	EDT
10/25/1964	00:01	EST
4/25/1965	00:01	EDT
10/31/1965	00:01	EST
4/24/1966	00:01	EDT
10/30/1966	00:01	EST
4/30/1967	02:00	US#1

NJ # 7

Date	Time	Zone
Before 11/18/1883		LMT
11/18/1883	12:00	EST
3/31/1918	02:00	EWT
10/27/1918	02:00	EST
3/30/1919	02:00	EWT
10/26/1919	02:00	EST
6/05/1921	02:00	EDT
9/25/1921	02:00	EST
4/30/1922	02:00	US#2

NJ # 8

Date	Time	Zone
Before 11/18/1883		LMT
11/18/1883	12:00	EST
3/31/1918	02:00	EWT
10/27/1918	02:00	EST
3/30/1919	02:00	EWT
10/26/1919	02:00	EST
6/05/1921	02:00	EDT
9/25/1921	02:00	EST
6/04/1922	02:00	EDT
9/24/1922	02:00	EST
6/03/1923	02:00	EDT
9/23/1923	02:00	EST
6/01/1924	02:00	EDT
9/28/1924	02:00	EST
4/26/1925	02:00	EDT
9/27/1925	02:00	EST
4/25/1926	02:00	EDT
9/26/1926	02:00	EST
4/24/1927	02:00	EDT
9/25/1927	02:00	EST
4/29/1928	02:00	EDT
9/30/1928	02:00	EST
4/28/1929	02:00	EDT
9/29/1929	02:00	EST
4/27/1930	02:00	EDT
9/28/1930	02:00	EST
4/26/1931	02:00	EDT
9/27/1931	02:00	EST
6/26/1932	02:00	EDT
9/25/1932	02:00	EST
4/30/1933	02:00	US#2

NJ # 9

Date	Time	Zone
Before 11/18/1883		LMT
11/18/1883	12:00	EST
3/31/1918	02:00	EWT
10/27/1918	02:00	EST
3/30/1919	02:00	EWT
10/26/1919	02:00	EST
4/18/1920	02:00	EDT
10/31/1920	02:00	US#2

NJ # 10

Date	Time	Zone
Before 4/02/1902		LMT
4/02/1902	12:00	EST
3/31/1918	02:00	EWT
10/27/1918	02:00	EST
3/30/1919	02:00	EWT
10/26/1919	02:00	EST
6/10/1922	02:00	EDT
9/24/1922	02:00	EST
6/03/1923	02:00	EDT
9/30/1923	02:00	EST
6/01/1924	02:00	EDT
9/28/1924	02:00	EST
6/07/1925	02:00	EDT
9/27/1925	02:00	EST
6/06/1926	02:00	EDT
9/26/1926	02:00	EST
6/05/1927	02:00	EDT
9/25/1927	02:00	EST
6/03/1928	02:00	EDT
9/30/1928	02:00	EST
6/02/1929	02:00	EDT
9/29/1929	02:00	EST
6/01/1930	02:00	EDT
9/28/1930	02:00	EST
6/06/1931	02:00	EDT
9/26/1931	02:00	EST
6/03/1932	02:00	EDT
9/25/1932	02:00	EST
6/04/1933	02:00	EDT
9/24/1933	02:00	EST
6/05/1934	02:00	EDT
9/30/1934	02:00	EST
6/06/1935	02:00	EDT
9/29/1935	02:00	EST
4/26/1936	02:00	US#2

NJ # 11

Date	Time	Zone
Before 11/18/1883		LMT
11/18/1883	12:00	EST
3/31/1918	02:00	EWT
10/27/1918	02:00	EST
3/30/1919	02:00	EWT
10/26/1919	02:00	EST
3/28/1920	00:01	EDT
10/31/1920	00:01	EST
4/24/1921	00:01	EDT
9/25/1921	00:01	EST
4/30/1922	00:01	EDT
9/24/1922	00:01	EST
4/29/1923	00:01	EDT
9/30/1923	00:01	EST
4/27/1924	00:01	EDT
9/28/1924	00:01	EST
4/26/1925	00:01	EDT
9/27/1925	00:01	EST
4/25/1926	00:01	EDT
9/26/1926	00:01	EST
4/24/1927	00:01	EDT
9/25/1927	00:01	EST
4/29/1928	00:01	EDT
9/30/1928	00:01	EST
4/28/1929	00:01	EDT
9/29/1929	00:01	EST
4/27/1930	00:01	EDT
9/28/1930	00:01	EST
4/26/1931	00:01	EDT
9/27/1931	00:01	EST
4/24/1932	00:01	EDT
9/25/1932	00:01	EST
4/30/1933	00:01	EDT
9/24/1933	00:01	EST
4/29/1934	00:01	EDT
9/30/1934	00:01	EST
4/28/1935	00:01	EDT
9/29/1935	00:01	EST
4/26/1936	00:01	EDT
9/27/1936	00:01	EST
4/25/1937	00:01	EDT
9/26/1937	00:01	EST
4/24/1938	00:01	EDT
9/25/1938	00:01	EST
4/30/1939	00:01	EDT
9/24/1939	00:01	EST
4/28/1940	00:01	EDT
9/29/1940	00:01	EST
4/27/1941	00:01	EDT
9/28/1941	00:01	EST
2/09/1942	02:00	EWT
9/30/1945	02:00	EST
4/28/1946	00:01	EDT
9/29/1946	00:01	EST
4/27/1947	00:01	EDT
9/28/1947	00:01	EST
4/25/1948	00:01	EDT
9/26/1948	00:01	EST
4/24/1949	00:01	EDT
9/25/1949	00:01	EST
4/30/1950	00:01	EDT
9/24/1950	00:01	EST
4/29/1951	00:01	EDT
9/30/1951	00:01	EST
4/27/1952	00:01	EDT
9/28/1952	00:01	EST
4/26/1953	00:01	EDT
9/27/1953	00:01	EST
4/25/1954	00:01	EDT
9/26/1954	00:01	EST
4/24/1955	00:01	EDT
10/30/1955	00:01	EST
4/29/1956	00:01	EDT
10/28/1956	00:01	EST
4/28/1957	00:01	EDT
10/27/1957	00:01	EST
4/27/1958	00:01	EDT
10/26/1958	00:01	EST
4/26/1959	00:01	EDT
10/25/1959	00:01	EST
4/24/1960	00:01	EDT
10/30/1960	00:01	EST
4/30/1961	00:01	EDT
10/29/1961	00:01	EST
4/29/1962	00:01	EDT
10/28/1962	00:01	EST
4/28/1963	00:01	EDT
10/27/1963	00:01	EST
4/26/1964	00:01	EDT
10/25/1964	00:01	EST
4/25/1965	00:01	EDT
10/31/1965	00:01	EST
4/24/1966	00:01	EDT
10/30/1966	00:01	EST
4/30/1967	02:00	US#1

NJ # 12

Date	Time	Zone
Before 11/18/1883		LMT
11/18/1883	12:00	EST
3/31/1918	02:00	EWT
10/27/1918	02:00	EST
3/30/1919	02:00	EWT
10/26/1919	02:00	EST
4/25/1937	02:00	US#2

NJ # 13

Date	Time	Zone
Before 11/18/1883		LMT
11/18/1883	12:00	EST
3/31/1918	02:00	EWT
10/27/1918	02:00	EST
3/30/1919	02:00	EWT
10/26/1919	02:00	EST
4/26/1931	02:00	EDT
9/27/1931	02:00	EST
4/25/1937	02:00	US#2

NJ # 14

Date	Time	Zone
Before 11/18/1883		LMT
11/18/1883	12:00	EST
3/31/1918	02:00	EWT
10/27/1918	02:00	EST
3/30/1919	02:00	EWT
10/26/1919	02:00	EST
4/24/1932	02:00	US#2

NJ # 15

Date	Time	Zone
Before 11/18/1883		LMT
11/18/1883	12:00	EST
3/31/1918	02:00	EWT
10/27/1918	02:00	EST
3/30/1919	02:00	EWT
10/26/1919	02:00	EST
4/30/1933	02:00	US#2

NJ # 16

Date	Time	Zone
Before 11/18/1883		LMT
11/18/1883	12:00	EST
3/31/1918	02:00	EWT
10/27/1918	02:00	EST
3/30/1919	02:00	EWT
10/26/1919	02:00	EST
4/29/1934	02:00	US#2

NJ # 17

Date	Time	Zone
Before 11/18/1883		LMT
11/18/1883	12:00	EST
3/31/1918	02:00	EWT
10/27/1918	02:00	EST
3/30/1919	02:00	EWT
10/26/1919	02:00	EST
4/26/1931	02:00	US#2

NJ # 18

Date	Time	Zone
Before 11/18/1883		LMT
11/18/1883	12:00	EST
3/31/1918	02:00	EWT
10/27/1918	02:00	EST
3/30/1919	02:00	EWT
10/26/1919	02:00	EST
4/26/1936	02:00	US#2

COUNTIES

1 Atlantic	7 Essex	13 Monmouth	19 Sussex
2 Bergen	8 Gloucester	14 Morris	20 Union
3 Burlington	9 Hudson	15 Ocean	21 Warren
4 Camden	10 Hunterdon	16 Passaic	
5 Cape May	11 Mercer	17 Salem	
6 Cumberland	12 Middlesex	18 Somerset	

Place	Table	Latitude	Longitude	Offset
Abertown 19	17	41N15'03	74W47'06	4:59:08
Ablett Village 4	2	39N56'55	75W06'10	5:00:25
Absecon 1	2	39N25'42	74W29'46	4:57:59
Absecon Highlands 1	2	39N26'48	74W28'28	4:57:54
Academy 7	1	40N44	74W11	4:56:44
Academy Estates 14	1	40N49	74W25	4:57:40
Ackermans Mills 2	17	41N01'38	74W10'09	4:56:41
Ackerson 19	17	41N04'56	74W40'06	4:58:40
Ackors Corner 11	12	40N20'05	74W50'58	4:59:24
Acton 17	17	39N35'03	75W24'49	5:01:39
Adams 12	1	40N27'03	74W29'37	4:57:58
Adamston 15	12	40N02'43	74W05'44	4:56:23
Adelphia 13	1	40N13'05	74W15'24	4:57:02
Afton 14	1	40N46'21	74W23'24	4:57:34
Agasote 11	1	40N14	74W47	4:59:08
Ajax Park 11	1	40N14	74W47	4:59:08
Albion 4	17	39N46'43	74W57'19	4:59:49
Albion Place 16	1	40N53'28	74W10'34	4:56:42
Aldene 20	1	40N39'48	74W16'24	4:57:06
Aldine 17	1	39N34'08	75W16'31	5:01:06
Aldrich Estates 13	12	40N14	74W13	4:56:52
Alexandria 10	13	40N36	75W01	5:00:04
Alexauken 10	1	40N23'22	74W56'22	4:59:45
Algers Mills 13	1	40N09'55	74W04'30	4:56:18
Allaire 13	12	40N09'30	74W07'33	4:56:30
Allamuchy 21	15	40N55'18	74W48'38	4:59:15
Allendale 2	2	41N02'29	74W07'46	4:56:31

Allenhurst 13 1 40N14'10 74w00'04 4:56:00
Allens Corner 10
13 40N32'48 74w56'20 4:59:45
Allens Mills 21
17 40N44'24 75w07'08 5:00:29
Allentown 13 12 40N10'40 74w35'02 4:58:20
Allenwood 13 1 40N08'29 74w06'01 4:56:24
Allerton 10 13 40N36'40 74w52'44 4:59:31
Alliance 17 1 39N31'07 75w05'32 5:00:22
Alloway 17 17 39N33'39 75w21'46 5:01:27
Alloway Junction 17
17 39N34'53 75w21'48 5:01:27
Alluvium 4 17 39N50'06 74w56'32 4:59:46
Allwood 16 1 40N50'33 74w09'33 4:56:38
Almolind 8 1 39N49 75w08 5:00:32
Almonesson 8 1 39N49'08 75w05'56 5:00:24
Alpha 21 17 40N40'01 75w09'28 5:00:38
Alphano 21 12 40N54'08 74w51'43 4:59:27
Alpine 2 1 40N57'21 73w55'54 4:55:44
Altura 11 1 40N16'03 74w49'00 4:59:16
Alvater Corner 10
13 40N33'57 74w58'13 4:59:53
Amber Terrace 4 1 39N48 75w00 5:00:00
Amon Heights 4 2 39N58 75w03 5:00:12
Ampere 7 1 40N46'00 74w11'43 4:56:47
Amsterdam 10 13 40N35'15 75w09'32 5:00:38
Amwell 10 12 40N25'53 74w45'09 4:59:01
Anchorage 15 1 40N00'05 74w08'35 4:56:34
Ancora 4 2 39N41'40 74w50'30 4:59:22
Anderson 21 13 40N46'14 74w55'10 4:59:41
Andover 19 12 40N59'09 74w44'33 4:58:58
Andover Junction 19
12 40N59'49 74w44'46 4:58:59
Andrews 4 1 39N43'26 74w57'34 4:59:50
Anglesea 5 11 39N01'07 74w47'43 4:59:11
Annandale 10 13 40N38'27 74w52'54 4:59:32
Anthony 10 13 40N44'54 74w52'54 4:59:32
Applegarth 12 1 40N16'42 74w28'23 4:57:54
Apple Hill 4 2 39N54 75w00 5:00:00
Apshawa 16 16 41N01'03 74w21'48 4:57:27
Arbor 12 1 40N34 74w27 4:57:48
Archers Corner 15
12 40N05'18 74w27'21 4:57:49
Archertown 15 12 40N03'55 74w30'01 4:58:00
Arcola 2 1 40N55'33 74w05'23 4:56:22
Ardena 13 1 40N12'41 74w13'59 4:56:56
Ardmore Estates 13
1 40N12'22 74w13'30 4:56:54
Arlington 9 1 40N46'39 74w08'19 4:56:33
Armstrong 19 17 41N08'58 74w41'25 4:58:46
Arneys Mount 3 3 40N00'35 74w41'49 4:58:47
Arneytown 13 12 40N06'05 74w33'59 4:58:16
Arrowhead Park 15
12 40N02 74w07 4:56:28
Arrowhead Village 15
12 40N04'35 74w06'15 4:56:25
Asbury 8 10 39N46'21 75w17'03 5:01:08
Asbury 21 13 40N41'45 75w00'38 5:00:03
Asbury Gardens 13
1 40N12 74w02 4:56:08
Asbury Park 13 6 40N13'13 74w00'45 4:56:03
Aserdaten 15 1 39N51'23 74w20'18 4:57:21
Ashland 4 2 39N51'47 75w00'23 5:00:02
Atco 4 17 39N46'11 74w53'16 4:59:33
Athenia 16 3 40N52'00 74w09'17 4:56:37
Atlantic City 1 7 39N21'51 74w25'24 4:57:42
Atlantic Highlands 13
1 40N24'28 74w02'05 4:56:08
Atsion 3 12 39N44'33 74w43'35 4:58:54
Auburn 17 10 39N42'39 75w22'05 5:01:28
Audubon 4 2 39N53'27 75w04'24 5:00:18
Augusta 19 17 41N07'44 74w43'43 4:58:55
Aura 8 1 39N40'22 75w08'16 5:00:33
Avalon 5 2 39N06'04 74w43'05 4:58:52
Avenel 12 2 40N34'49 74w17'08 4:57:09
Avis Mills 8 17 39N39'57 75w14'55 5:01:00
Avon-by-the-Sea 13
1 40N11'32 74w00'59 4:56:04
Avondale 7 1 40N48'53 74w09'02 4:56:36
Avon Park 12 17 40N35'35 74w24'00 4:57:36
Awosting 16 12 41N09'16 74w20'13 4:57:21
Babbitt 9 1 40N48'35 74w01'13 4:56:05
Bacons Neck 6 1 39N28 75w15 5:01:00
Baileys Corner 13
1 40N09'10 74w04'21 4:56:17
Baileytown 6 12 39N19'10 75w04'24 5:00:18
Bairdsville 13 12 40N14'31 74w23'03 4:57:32
Bakersville 1 2 39N22 74w34 4:58:16
Bakersville 11 1 40N16'29 74w42'24 4:58:50
Baldwins Corner 11
12 40N18'50 74w47'11 4:59:09
Baleville 19 12 41N06'15 74w45'36 4:59:02
Ballingers Mill 17
1 39N34'35 75w16'10 5:01:05
Baltusrol 20 1 40N43'28 74w19'42 4:57:19
Bamber Lake 15 14 39N50 74w11 4:56:44
Bamberry Estates 15
1 39N59'37 74w13'05 4:56:52
Baptistown 10 12 40N31'18 75w00'23 5:00:02
Barber 12 1 40N31'50 74w15'30 4:57:02
Barbertown 10 12 40N29'07 75w01'39 5:00:07
Barclay Farm 4 2 39N54'21 74w59'39 4:59:59
Bargaintown 1 1 39N21'45 74w34'53 4:58:20
Barkers Corner 21
12 40N52 74w55 4:59:40
Barley Sheaf 10 1 40N31 74w52 4:59:28
Barlow 4 2 39N49 75w06 5:00:24
Barnard 1 2 39N37'15 74w47'05 4:59:08
Barnegat 15 1 39N45'11 74w13'24 4:56:54
Barnegat Bay 15 1 39N45'29 74w11'31 4:56:46
Barnegat Bay Estates 15
12 39N58'15 74w07'48 4:56:31
Barnegat Beach 15
1 39N46'43 74w11'28 4:56:46
Barnegat Estates 15
1 39N45'40 74w15'34 4:57:02
Barnegat Light 15
12 39N45'27 74w06'24 4:56:26
Barnegat Pier 15
12 39N56 74w08 4:56:32
Barnegat Pines 15
14 39N53'46 74w12'37 4:56:50
Barnsboro 8 2 39N45'42 75w09'37 5:00:38

Barrington 4 2 39N51'53 75w03'20 5:00:13
Barrington Manor 4
2 39N54 75w02 5:00:08
Bartles Corners 10
1 40N32'12 74w51'28 4:59:26
Bartley 14 12 40N49'21 74w43'07 4:58:52
Basking Ridge 18
1 40N42'22 74w32'59 4:58:12
Bass River 3 17 39N35'33 74w26'35 4:57:46
Bates Mill 4 2 39N42'25 74w51'56 4:59:28
Batesville 4 2 39N49 75w06 5:00:24
Batsto 3 2 39N38'30 74w38'53 4:58:36
Battentown 8 10 39N45 75w19 5:01:16
Bay Harbor Estates 15
12 40N01'15 74w08'00 4:56:32
Bay Head 15 2 40N04'18 74w03'17 4:56:13
Bay Head Junction 15
2 40N04'40 74w02'47 4:56:11
Bayonne 9 1 40N40'07 74w06'53 4:56:28
Bay Shore 15 1 39N57'03 74w06'49 4:56:27
Bay Shore West 5
1 38N56 74w55 4:59:40
Bay Side 6 1 39N22'57 75w24'25 5:01:38
Bay Side 15 1 39N40'07 74w12'49 4:56:51
Bayside Beach 15
14 39N49'13 74w10'52 4:56:43
Bayview Harbors 15
1 39N57'49 74w07'15 4:56:29
Bayview Shores 15
2 40N03 74w03 4:56:12
Bayville 15 12 39N54'33 74w09'19 4:56:37
Bayway 20 1 40N38'20 74w12'46 4:56:51
Baywood 15 12 40N02 74w07 4:56:28
Beach Creek 5 11 39N00 74w49 4:59:16
Beach Glen 14 12 40N55'47 74w29'12 4:57:57
Beach Haven 15 17 39N33'33 74w14'37 4:56:58
Beach Haven Crest 15
17 39N36'45 74w12'12 4:56:49
Beach Haven Gardens 15
17 39N34'56 74w13'39 4:56:55
Beach Haven Heights 15
17 39N32'04 74w15'39 4:57:03
Beach Haven Park 15
17 39N35'51 74w12'47 4:56:51
Beach Haven Terrace 15
17 39N35'10 74w13'26 4:56:54
Beach Haven West 15
1 39N40'11 74w13'56 4:56:56
Beach View 15 1 39N43'29 74w14'35 4:56:58
Beachwood 15 1 39N56'20 74w11'36 4:56:46
Beals Mill 6 12 39N31'43 75w15'58 5:01:04
Bear Tavern 11 12 40N18'32 74w50'56 4:59:24
Beattystown 21 1 40N48'47 74w50'36 4:59:22
Beaufort 7 1 40N49'04 74w19'48 4:57:19
Beaver Dam 17 12 39N39'01 75w29'33 5:01:58
Beaver Lake 19 17 41N06'27 74w33'14 4:58:13
Beaver Run 19 17 41N09'12 74w37'12 4:58:29
Beaverville 3 12 39N54'06 74w44'32 4:58:58
Beckerville 15 1 40N01 74w19 4:57:16
Bedminster 18 12 40N40'50 74w38'45 4:58:35
Beechwood Heights 14
14 40N52 74w38 4:58:32
Beemerville 19 1 41N12'38 74w41'31 4:58:46
Beesleys Point 5
17 39N16'36 74w38'12 4:58:33
Belcoville 1 17 39N26'14 74w44'11 4:58:57
Belford 13 2 40N25'33 74w05'14 4:56:21
Bellcrest Park 15
1 39N58'30 74w08'15 4:56:33
Belle Mead 18 2 40N28'00 74w39'40 4:58:39
Belleplain 5 12 39N16'07 74w52'01 4:59:28
Belleville 7 1 40N47'37 74w09'02 4:56:36
Bellmawr 4 2 39N52'03 75w05'42 5:00:23
Bells Crossing 10
13 40N42'16 74w56'37 4:59:46
Bells Lake 8 2 39N45'13 75w02'57 5:00:12
Bellview 3 2 40N01'15 74w59'42 4:59:59
Bellwood Park 4 2 39N53 75w06 5:00:24
Belmar 13 1 40N10'42 74w01'20 4:56:05
Belvidere 21 17 40N49'47 75w04'41 5:00:19
Belwood Park 7 1 40N48 74w10 4:56:40
Benders Corner 20
1 40N40'49 74w24'42 4:57:39
Bennett 5 1 38N59'00 74w54'06 4:59:36
Bennetts Mill 6 2 39N25'28 74w54'42 4:59:39
Bennetts Mills 15
1 40N07'44 74w16'32 4:57:06
Bennys Landing 5
13 39N04'02 74w48'47 4:59:15
Berdines Corners 12
1 40N28'02 74w27'14 4:57:49
Bergen 9 1 40N43'45 74w03'58 4:56:16
Bergenfield 2 1 40N55'39 73w59'52 4:55:59
Bergenline 9 1 40N46 74w02 4:56:08
Bergen Mills 13
12 40N15'46 74w25'11 4:57:41
Bergen Point 9 1 40N38'51 74w08'30 4:56:34
Bergerville 13 1 40N12'07 74w15'43 4:57:03
Berkeley 15 1 39N55 74w10 4:56:40
Berkeley Heights 20
17 40N41'00 74w26'35 4:57:46
Berkeley Shores 15
12 39N54'45 74w08'00 4:56:32
Berkshire Valley 14
1 40N55'48 74w35'28 4:58:22
Berlin 4 17 39N47'28 74w55'46 4:59:43
Berlin Heights 3
17 39N48'47 74w53'27 4:59:34
Bernardsville 18
1 40N43'07 74w34'11 4:58:17
Berryland 8 1 39N36'40 74w54'22 4:59:37
Bertrand Island 14
1 40N55 74w38 4:58:32
Bethlehem 10 13 40N40 75w01 5:00:04
Betsytown 20 1 40N40 74w12 4:56:48
Bevans 19 12 41N11'47 74w51'04 4:59:24
Beverly 3 1 40N03'55 74w55'10 4:59:41
Biddles Landing 17
1 39N40'32 75w27'57 5:01:52
Big Oak 6 1 39N29'10 75w12'32 5:00:50
Big Springs 19 17 41N07'40 74w37'20 4:58:29
Billingsport 8 2 39N50'54 75w14'32 5:00:58
Birchfield 3 17 39N56'10 74w55'30 4:59:42

Birch Hills 14 1 40N48'34 74w25'55 4:57:44
Birchwood Lakes 3
17 39N51'58 74w48'46 4:59:15
Birchwood Park 15
12 40N02 74w07 4:56:28
Birmingham 3 12 39N58'33 74w42'38 4:58:51
Bishops 4 17 39N47'07 74w54'24 4:59:38
Bishop Wood 4 1 39N45'15 75w00'52 5:00:03
Bissell 10 13 40N40'00 74w47'32 4:59:10
Bivalve 6 12 39N14'03 75w02'03 5:00:08
Black Horse 12 1 40N25'05 74w30'09 4:58:01
Black Horse Pike 4
2 39N53 75w04 5:00:16
Blackwells Mills 18
12 40N28'32 74w34'18 4:58:17
Blackwood 4 2 39N48'08 75w03'52 5:00:15
Blackwood Terrace 8
1 39N48'18 75w05'10 5:00:21
Blairstown 21 14 40N58'58 74w57'39 4:59:51
Blansingburg 13 1 40N08'12 74w03'27 4:56:14
Blawenburg 18 12 40N24'27 74w42'11 4:58:49
Blenheim 4 2 39N48'33 75w04'40 5:00:19
Bloomfield 7 1 40N48'24 74w11'09 4:56:45
Bloomfield Terrace 12
12 40N24 74w21 4:57:24
Bloomingdale 16
16 41N00'07 74w19'37 4:57:18
Bloomingdale 18 2 40N29'51 74w38'52 4:58:35
Bloomsbury 10 13 40N39'14 75w05'13 5:00:21
Blue Anchor 4 17 39N41'22 74w52'59 4:59:32
Blue Bell 8 17 39N34'19 74w58'28 4:59:54
Blue Star 18 2 40N37 74w25 4:57:40
Bogota 2 1 40N52'34 74w01'49 4:56:07
Bon Air 4 2 39N58'09 75w01'24 5:00:06
Bonaparte Landing 19
12 40N57'13 74w38'24 4:58:34
Bonhamptown 12 17 40N32 74w22 4:57:28
Bonhamtown 12 17 40N31'24 74w21'29 4:57:26
Boonton 14 1 40N54'09 74w24'27 4:57:38
Bordentown 3 1 40N08'46 74w42'44 4:58:51
Borton Landing 3
17 40N00'10 74w53'20 4:59:33
Bossert Estates 3
1 40N08'50 74w41'30 4:58:46
Bougher 3 17 39N59'36 74w52'48 4:59:31
Bound Brook 4 2 39N49 75w06 5:00:24
Bound Brook 18 17 40N34'06 74w32'20 4:58:09
Bound Brook Heights 12
1 40N34 74w27 4:57:48
Bound Brook Junction 18
2 40N33'32 74w33'57 4:58:16
Bowentown 6 1 39N25'28 75w16'36 5:01:06
Bowman Manor 5 12 39N00'58 74w56'04 4:59:44
Bowne 10 1 40N25'11 74w54'47 4:59:39
Boynton Beach 12
1 40N32'50 74w15'18 4:57:01
Bozuretown 3 12 39N49'36 74w41'22 4:58:45
Braddock 4 17 39N42'03 74w53'24 4:59:34
Braddocks Mill 3
17 39N49'20 74w50'57 4:59:24
Bradevelt 13 1 40N20'04 74w14'23 4:56:58
Bradley Beach 13
1 40N12'08 74w00'45 4:56:03
Bradley Gardens 18
2 40N33'46 74w39'18 4:58:37
Bradley Park 13 1 40N12'18 74w01'29 4:56:06
Brady Park 14 12 40N57'38 74w37'08 4:58:29
Braeburn Heights 11
1 40N15'24 74w46'07 4:59:04
Braeburn Park 11
1 40N16 74w46 4:59:04
Brainards 21 17 40N46'25 75w10'12 5:00:41
Brainy Boro 12 17 40N32 74w22 4:57:28
Branchburg 18 2 40N34 74w42 4:58:48
Branchburg Park 18
2 40N34'20 74w41'07 4:58:44
Branchport 13 1 40N18'32 73w59'54 4:56:00
Branchville 19 17 41N08'47 74w45'10 4:59:01
Branchville Junction 19
17 41N04'25 74w42'06 4:58:48
Brant Beach 15 17 39N37'15 74w11'51 4:56:47
Brantwood 7 1 40N43'45 74w20'25 4:57:22
Brass Castle 21
13 40N45'53 75w00'41 5:00:03
Breton Woods 15
12 40N02'44 74w06'33 4:56:26
Briar Manor 11 12 40N12'42 74w39'32 4:58:38
Brick 15 12 40N04 74w07 4:56:28
Brick Church 7 1 40N45 74w13 4:56:52
Bricksboro 6 2 39N18'07 74w58'44 4:59:55
Brick Town 15 12 40N02 74w07 4:56:28
Bridgeboro 3 17 40N01'19 74w55'58 4:59:44
Bridgepoint 18 2 40N25'57 74w38'56 4:58:36
Bridgeport 8 10 39N48'03 75w20'52 5:01:23
Bridgeton 6 1 39N25'38 75w14'04 5:00:56
Bridgeton Junction 6
1 39N27'10 75w12'47 5:00:51
Bridgeville 21 17 40N50'12 75w01'35 5:00:06
Bridgewater 18 2 40N36 74w37 4:58:28
Brielle 13 2 40N06'28 74w03'25 4:56:14
Brigadoon 8 1 39N49 75w08 5:00:32
Brigantine 1 17 39N24'36 74w21'54 4:57:28
Brighton 19 12 40N59'06 74w45'50 4:59:03
Brighton Beach 15
17 39N36'23 74w12'30 4:56:50
Brights 12 2 40N28 74w20 4:57:20
Brimfield Crossing 1
17 39N34'15 74w54'29 4:59:38
Brindletown 15 12 40N02'50 74w30'20 4:58:01
Broad Lane 8 1 39N40'13 74w55'36 4:59:42
Broadway 21 13 40N43'55 75w03'07 5:00:12
Bromley Place 11
1 40N13 74w44 4:58:56
Brookdale 4 2 39N49 75w06 5:00:24
Brookdale 7 1 40N50'01 74w11'00 4:56:44
Brookfield 4 2 39N52'57 75w00'58 5:00:04
Brookfields 4 2 39N49 75w06 5:00:24
Brooklawn 4 2 39N52'41 75w07'16 5:00:29
Brookside 14 12 40N47'39 74w34'06 4:58:16
Brookside Heights 15
12 39N57'42 74w09'37 4:56:38
Brook Valley 14
16 40N57'52 74w22'06 4:57:28

Brookview 12 1 40N25'14 74w28'28 4:57:54
Brookville 10 1 40N24'02 74w57'59 4:59:52
Brookville 15 1 39N46'54 74w18'28 4:57:14
Brookwood 15 12 40N08 74w20 4:57:20
Brotmanville 17 1 39N31'14 75w04'58 5:00:20
Brownings 21 12 40N57'09 75w06'49 5:00:27
Browns 16 12 41N09'24 74w20'55 4:57:24
Browns Mills 3 3 39N58'21 74w35'00 4:58:20
Browns Mills Junction 3 3 39N56'54 74w35'25 4:58:22
Brownsville 4 1 39N48'43 75w01'08 5:00:05
Browntown 12 12 40N24'06 74w18'25 4:57:14
Brunswick 12 1 40N29 74w27 4:57:48
Brunswick Gardens 12 12 40N23'26 74w20'12 4:57:21
Buckingham 15 12 39N55'52 74w26'52 4:57:47
Buckingham Park 3 17 40N02'37 74w53'10 4:59:33
Buckingham Village 8 17 39N45'37 75w08'15 5:00:33
Buck Landing 5 1 38N56'57 74w54'45 4:59:39
Buckshutem 6 2 39N19'08 75w00'47 5:00:03
Bucks Mill 13 12 40N17'04 74w11'53 4:56:48
Budd Lake 14 1 40N52'16 74w44'04 4:58:56
Buddtown 3 12 39N56'21 74w42'12 4:58:49
Buena 1 17 39N30'49 74w55'30 4:59:42
Bullock 15 12 39N52'54 74w27'00 4:57:48
Bulltown 3 8 39N38'17 74w35'40 4:58:23
Bunker Hill 8 17 39N45 75w04 5:00:16
Bunnvale 10 12 40N42'06 74w53'01 4:59:32
Burcliff Farms 11 1 40N16 74w46 4:59:04
Burkesville 15 2 40N09'38 74w25'17 4:57:41
Burleigh 5 13 39N02'44 74w51'07 4:59:24
Burlington 3 1 40N04'16 74w51'55 4:59:28
Burlington Heights 13 12 40N16'18 74w14'10 4:56:57
Burnt Mills 18 2 40N38'09 74w41'14 4:58:45
Burrs Mill 3 3 39N53'18 74w39'01 4:58:36
Bustleton 3 1 40N05'17 74w46'59 4:59:08
Butler 14 16 41N00'13 74w20'31 4:57:22
Butler Park 21 13 40N45'06 74w55'53 4:59:44
Butlers Place 3 14 39N51'15 74w30'30 4:58:02
Butterworth Farms 14 17 40N49'17 74w31'25 4:58:06
Buttzville 21 17 40N49'56 75w00'24 5:00:02
Byram 10 1 40N25'25 75w03'36 5:00:14
Byram 19 1 40N57 74w43 4:58:52
Byram Cove 19 1 40N57'20 74w39'37 4:58:38
Caldwell 7 1 40N50'23 74w16'37 4:57:06
Califon 10 12 40N43'10 74w50'10 4:59:21
Callahans 14 1 40N55 74w39 4:58:36
Calno 21 12 41N03'22 75w00'20 5:00:01
Cambridge 3 17 40N01'44 74w58'23 4:59:54
Camden 4 2 39N55'33 75w07'12 5:00:29
Camelot 15 1 39N57'38 74w12'55 4:56:52
Campbells Corner 6 1 39N29'09 75w19'09 5:01:17
Camp Columbus 15 12 39N53'45 74w19'18 4:57:17
Campgaw 2 17 41N01'26 74w12'05 4:56:48
Camp Osborne 15 12 40N00'30 74w03'33 4:56:14
Camp Tecumseh 10 13 40N35 74w58 4:59:52
Candlewood 13 1 40N09'00 74w12'50 4:56:51
Candlewyck 4 17 39N53'31 74w56'45 4:59:47
Canton 17 17 39N28'15 75w24'55 5:01:40
Cape Breton 15 12 40N02 74w07 4:56:28
Cape May 5 1 38N56'06 74w54'23 4:59:38
Cape May Court House 5 13 39N04'57 74w49'27 4:59:18
Cape May Point 5 1 38N56 74w58 4:59:52
Capitol Hill 3 17 40N03'19 74w54'14 4:59:37
Cardiff 1 2 39N24'36 74w35'15 4:58:21
Carey 14 1 40N51'20 74w40'44 4:58:43
Carlls Corner 6 1 39N27'46 75w12'20 5:00:49
Carlstadt 2 1 40N50'25 74w05'28 4:56:22
Carlton Hill 2 1 40N50'47 74w06'40 4:56:27
Carmantown 1 17 39N30'33 74w41'40 4:58:47
Carmel 6 2 39N26'03 75w07'18 5:00:29
Carmerville 13 1 40N10'37 74w07'46 4:56:31
Carneys Point 17 1 39N42'40 75w28'14 5:01:53
Carpentersville 21 17 40N38'09 75w11'20 5:00:45
Carrs Corner 13 12 40N13'59 74w22'15 4:57:29
Carrs Tavern 13 2 40N10'17 74w25'19 4:57:41
Carsons Mills 13 12 40N13'01 74w33'37 4:58:14
Carteret 12 1 40N34'38 74w13'43 4:56:55
Cassville 15 12 40N06'16 74w23'13 4:57:33
Castle Point 9 1 40N45 74w02 4:56:08
Catawba 1 17 39N24'25 74w42'52 4:58:51
Cecil 8 1 39N38'54 74w56'51 4:59:47
Cedar Beach 13 17 40N26 74w07 4:56:28
Cedar Beach 15 12 39N52'24 74w08'59 4:56:36
Cedar Bonnet Island 15 1 39N42 74w15 4:57:00
Cedar Bridge 15 12 40N03'21 74w07'43 4:56:31
Cedar Bridge Manor 15 12 40N02 74w07 4:56:28
Cedar Brook 4 17 39N42'55 74w54'04 4:59:36
Cedar Crest 15 12 39N54'09 74w19'21 4:57:17
Cedar Crest Manor 17 1 39N40'38 75w28'34 5:01:54
Cedar Croft 15 12 40N02 74w07 4:56:28
Cedar Glen Lakes 15 12 39N57 74w23 4:57:32
Cedar Glen West 15 1 40N02'31 74w17'35 4:57:10
Cedar Grove 5 13 39N09'45 74w46'01 4:59:04
Cedar Grove 7 1 40N51'06 74w13'46 4:56:55
Cedar Grove 8 17 39N42'07 75w13'52 5:00:55
Cedar Grove 11 12 40N22'05 74w41'43 4:58:47
Cedar Grove 15 12 39N58'24 74w10'08 4:56:41
Cedar Heights 10 13 40N39'38 74w52'38 4:59:31
Cedar Knolls 14 1 40N49'19 74w26'57 4:57:48
Cedar Lake 1 1 39N35'01 74w54'02 4:59:36
Cedar Lake 14 12 40N53 74w29 4:57:56
Cedar Run 15 2 39N41'05 74w16'03 4:57:04
Cedar Springs 5 2 39N14'43 74w42'26 4:58:50
Cedarville 6 12 39N19'57 75w12'00 5:00:48
Cedarville 17 17 39N37'28 75w20'30 5:01:22
Cedarwood Park 15 12 40N02'59 74w07'50 4:56:31
Centennial Lake 3 17 39N54 74w55 4:59:40
Center 11 1 40N13 74w46 4:59:04
Center Square 8 10 39N45 75w19 5:01:16
Centerton 3 17 39N59'44 74w52'24 4:59:30
Centerton 17 1 39N31'31 75w10'05 5:00:40
Centerville 10 12 40N32'18 74w45'16 4:59:01
Centerville 11 12 40N20'47 74w45'52 4:59:03
Centerville 13 2 40N24'53 74w09'29 4:56:38
Central 7 1 40N45 74w13 4:56:52
Central Park 12 1 40N29 74w17 4:57:08
Central Park 17 12 39N39'35 75w30'54 5:02:04
Centre City 8 2 39N46'33 75w10'52 5:00:43
Centre Grove 6 2 39N21'23 75w07'20 5:00:29
Ceramics 12 17 40N32 74w22 4:57:28
Chadwick 15 12 39N59'35 74w03'51 4:56:15
Chadwick Beach 15 12 39N59'35 74w03'51 4:56:15
Chairville 3 17 39N53'54 74w47'22 4:59:09
Chambersburg 11 1 40N13 74w45 4:59:00
Chambers Corner 3 1 40N01'04 74w43'59 4:58:56
Changewater 21 12 40N44'17 74w56'40 4:59:47
Chapel Heights 8 17 39N45 75w04 5:00:16
Chapel Hill 13 1 40N23'50 74w04'15 4:56:17
Charcoal Landing 3 8 39N38'30 74w30'44 4:58:03
Charleston 3 17 40N02'20 74w53'30 4:59:34
Charleston East 4 2 39N53'22 74w58'44 4:59:55
Charleston Springs 13 1 40N12'02 74w22'25 4:57:30
Charlestown 10 13 40N41'21 74w58'22 4:59:53
Charlotteburg 14 12 41N01'49 74w25'27 4:57:42
Chatham 14 1 40N44'27 74w23'03 4:57:32
Chatsworth 3 14 39N49'03 74w32'07 4:58:08
Cheesequake 12 12 40N25'29 74w17'17 4:57:09
Chelsea Heights 1 7 39N21'20 74w27'47 4:57:51
Cherry Downs 4 2 39N53'21 74w57'22 4:59:49
Cherry Hill 2 1 40N55'15 74w02'20 4:56:09
Cherry Hill 4 2 39N56'05 75w01'52 5:00:07
Cherry Hill Estates 4 2 39N56'00 75w01'10 5:00:05
Cherry Quay 15 12 40N01'35 74w07'24 4:56:30
Cherry Ridge 4 2 39N49 75w06 5:00:24
Cherry Ridge 19 12 41N09'38 74w26'45 4:57:47
Cherry Valley 4 2 39N56'13 74w59'28 4:59:58
Cherryville 10 1 40N33'40 74w54'13 4:59:37
Cherrywood 4 1 39N47'54 75w01'32 5:00:06
Chesilhurst 4 17 39N43'56 74w52'53 4:59:32
Chester 14 12 40N47'03 74w41'50 4:58:47
Chesterfield 3 12 40N06'54 74w38'23 4:58:34
Chestnut 20 1 40N42 74w16 4:57:04
Chestnut Estates 15 1 40N03'14 74w12'53 4:56:52
Chestnut Ridge 2 1 41N03'25 74w04'05 4:56:16
Chewalla Park 11 1 40N13'53 74w42'46 4:58:51
Chews Landing 4 2 39N50'00 75w03'48 5:00:15
Chimney Rock 18 17 40N34'47 74w33'26 4:58:14
Christopher Mills 3 17 39N52'41 74w51'33 4:59:26
Chrome 12 12 40N34'35 74w13'00 4:56:52
Church Landing 17 12 39N40'33 75w30'40 5:02:03
Churchtown 17 12 39N40'19 75w30'37 5:02:02
Cinnaminson 3 2 39N59'48 74w59'35 4:59:58
Clara Barton 12 17 40N32'03 74w20'23 4:57:22
Clark 20 1 40N38'27 74w18'40 4:57:15
Clarksboro 8 2 39N47'59 75w13'27 5:00:54
Clarksburg 13 2 40N11'19 74w26'28 4:57:46
Clarks Landing 1 8 39N34'25 74w32'26 4:58:10
Clarks Landing 15 2 40N05'26 74w03'40 4:56:15
Clarks Mill 1 2 39N31'03 74w30'23 4:58:02
Clarks Mill 6 2 39N21'35 75w01'03 5:00:04
Clarks Mills 12 12 40N19'01 74w21'02 4:57:24
Clarkstown 1 17 39N26'06 74w42'56 4:58:52
Clarksville 10 13 40N42'05 74w56'37 4:59:46
Clarksville 11 2 40N17'47 74w40'50 4:58:43
Clarktown 1 17 39N27 74w44 4:58:56
Clayton 8 1 39N39'36 75w05'33 5:00:22
Claytons Corner 13 12 40N19'43 74w17'13 4:57:09
Clayville 6 1 39N26'00 75w01'52 5:00:07
Clearwater 19 12 41N01'40 74w42'45 4:58:51
Clementon 4 1 39N48'41 74w59'00 4:59:56
Clements Bridge 4 2 39N50'27 75w05'01 5:00:20
Clermont 3 1 39N59'26 74w48'00 4:59:12
Clermont 5 13 39N05 74w50 4:59:20
Cliffdale Park 14 12 40N47 74w55 4:59:40
Cliffside Park 2 1 40N49'17 73w59'17 4:55:57
Cliffwood 13 2 40N26'12 74w14'24 4:56:58
Cliffwood Beach 13 2 40N26'31 74w13'02 4:56:52
Cliffwood Lake 19 17 41N05 74w31 4:58:04
Clifton 16 3 40N51'30 74w09'51 4:56:39
Clinton 7 1 40N52'45 74w18'55 4:57:16
Clinton 10 13 40N38'12 74w54'37 4:59:38
Clinton 16 12 41N04'17 74w27'03 4:57:48
Clinton Hill 7 1 40N43 74w12 4:56:48
Closter 2 1 40N58'23 73w57'43 4:55:51
Closter Plaza 2 1 40N58 73w58 4:55:52
Cloverdale 4 2 39N53 75w06 5:00:24
Cloverhill 10 1 40N29'17 74w46'57 4:59:08
Clover Leaf Lakes 1 17 39N28'13 74w42'39 4:58:51
Clyde 18 1 40N29'11 74w30'39 4:58:03
Cobbs Corner 14 1 40N52'14 74w25'09 4:57:41
Cobbs Mill 17 17 39N31'45 75w19'17 5:01:17
Coffins Corner 4 2 39N51'36 74w59'21 4:59:57
Cohansey 17 1 39N30'41 75w17'43 5:01:11
Cokesbury 10 13 40N41'00 74w50'12 4:59:21
Cold Indian Springs 13 1 40N14'32 74w04'00 4:56:16
Cold Spring 5 1 38N58'00 74w55'00 4:59:40
Coleman Hollow 14 14 40N48'44 74w36'28 4:58:26
Colemantown 3 17 39N55'47 74w53'15 4:59:33
Colestown 4 2 39N56'00 74w59'21 4:59:57
Colesville 19 12 41N16'30 74w39'01 4:58:36
College Town 8 1 39N42 75w07 5:00:28
Colliers Mills 15 12 40N04'03 74w26'59 4:57:48
Collings Lakes 1 1 39N35'44 74w52'55 4:59:32
Collingswood 4 1 39N55'05 75w04'18 5:00:17
Collingwood Park 13 12 40N13'20 74w08'03 4:56:32
Collinsville 14 17 40N48 74w29 4:57:56
Cologne 1 8 39N30'17 74w36'49 4:58:27
Colonia 12 2 40N34'28 74w18'09 4:57:13
Colonial Gardens 12 1 40N29 74w27 4:57:48
Colonial Gardens 15 1 39N58'40 74w12'37 4:56:50
Colonial Manor 8 1 39N51'18 75w09'06 5:00:36
Colonial Terrace 13 1 40N14 74w01 4:56:04
Colts Neck 13 12 40N17'15 74w10'22 4:56:41
Columbia 21 12 40N55'34 75w05'35 5:00:22
Columbia Lakes 4 2 39N56'05 75w00'19 5:00:01
Columbus 3 1 40N04'21 74w43'16 4:58:53
Colwick 4 2 39N57'07 75w01'24 5:00:06
Comical Corners 3 3 39N59'00 74w41'01 4:58:44
Commercial 6 12 39N17 75w02 5:00:08
Communipaw 9 1 40N42'31 74w03'41 4:56:15
Congressional Estates 4 2 39N49 75w06 5:00:24
Conklintown 16 1 41N02 74w18 4:57:12
Conovertown 1 2 39N26'23 74w28'44 4:57:55
Constable Hook 9 1 40N40 74w07 4:56:28
Convent Station 14 1 40N47 74w27 4:57:48
Cooks Mills 13 1 40N17'21 74w06'50 4:56:27
Cookstown 3 3 40N02'56 74w33'46 4:58:15
Cooleys Corner 13 1 40N12'53 74w31'00 4:58:04
Coontown 18 2 40N37'07 74w31'07 4:58:04
Cooper 8 10 39N47'57 75w19'59 5:01:20
Cooper 16 12 41N09'46 74w19'57 4:57:20
Cooper Park Village 4 2 39N49 75w06 5:00:24
Coopers Corner 11 12 40N22'19 74w50'54 4:59:24
Cooperstown 3 17 40N02'48 74w54'13 4:59:37
Coopersville 21 13 40N42'25 75w06'34 5:00:26
Cooper Village 8 1 39N49'12 75w07'04 5:00:28
Copper Hill 10 12 40N28'30 74w51'50 4:59:27
Corbin City 1 12 39N18'12 74w45'22 4:59:01
Cornish 21 17 40N47'51 75w02'06 5:00:08
Cottageville 12 1 40N24'37 74w29'05 4:57:56
Cottrell Corners 12 12 40N24'11 74w17'47 4:57:11
Country Club Ridge 3 1 40N01'00 74w53'45 4:59:35
Country Lake Estates 3 12 39N56'33 74w32'40 4:58:11
Country Place 15 1 40N05'18 74w13'45 4:56:55
Courses Landing 17 1 39N39'40 75w24'34 5:01:38
Coventry Square 15 1 40N06'28 74w12'28 4:56:50
Coxs Corner 3 17 39N55'14 74w52'45 4:59:31
Coxs Corner 11 2 40N19'34 74w41'40 4:58:47
Coxstown 15 2 39N38'55 74w17'48 4:57:11
Coytesville 2 1 40N51'51 73w57'45 4:55:51
Cozy Lake 14 12 41N03 74w29 4:57:56
Cragmere Park 2 12 41N05'40 74w08'11 4:56:33
Cramer Hill 4 1 39N57'27 75w05'07 5:00:20
Cranberry Lake 19 1 40N57'15 74w44'49 4:58:59
Cranbury 12 1 40N18'58 74w30'51 4:58:03
Cranbury Station 12 1 40N18'07 74w29'32 4:57:58
Crandon Lakes 19 12 41N03 74w45 4:59:00
Crane Square 20 1 40N40'55 74w12'31 4:56:50
Cranford 20 1 40N39'30 74w18'00 4:57:12
Cranford Junction 20 1 40N39'43 74w17'30 4:57:10
Cranmoor Manor 15 12 39N57'03 74w10'18 4:56:41
Crawford Corners 13 12 40N23'05 74w11'21 4:56:45
Cream Ridge 13 12 40N08'06 74w31'28 4:58:06
Creesville 8 17 39N45'23 75w04'52 5:00:19
Crescent Heights 3 3 39N58'07 74w43'01 4:58:52
Crescent Park 4 2 39N53 75w06 5:00:24
Cresskill 2 1 40N56'29 73w57'35 4:55:50
Crestmoor 14 12 40N47 74w46 4:59:04
Crestmoore 14 12 40N44'54 74w49'37 4:59:18

Creston 11 1 40N13'53 74w41'36 4:58:46
Crestview 14 1 40N44'42 74w24'30 4:57:38
Crestwood Village 15 12 39N56'53 74w21'40 4:57:27
Cropwell 3 17 39N53'37 74w56'09 4:59:45
Cross Keys 8 1 39N42'48 75w01'48 5:00:07
Crossmans 12 1 40N29'06 74w19'18 4:57:17
Crossroads 3 17 39N54'55 74w49'35 4:59:18
Crosswicks 3 1 40N09'12 74w38'53 4:58:36
Croton 10 1 40N30'39 74w55'50 4:59:43
Crowfoot 3 17 39N47'40 74w53'58 4:59:36
Crowleytown 3 8 39N37'42 74w37'05 4:58:28
Croxton 9 1 40N44'23 74w03'48 4:56:15
Crystal Lake 2 17 41N01'08 74w12'46 4:56:51
Crystal Lake 15 12 39N53'39 74w11'20 4:56:45
Culvers Inlet 19 17 41N10'07 74w47'33 4:59:10
Culvers Lake 19 17 41N09 74w45 4:59:00
Cumberland 6 2 39N22'11 74w56'28 4:59:46
Cushetunk 10 12 40N37'20 74w47'28 4:59:10
Cuthbert Manor 4 1 39N55 75w04 5:00:16
Cyn-Wyd 3 1 40N05 74w51 4:59:24
Da Costa 1 2 39N37'00 74w46'30 4:59:06
Danceys Corner 17 1 39N42'05 75w26'21 5:01:45
Daretown 17 1 39N36'15 75w15'28 5:01:02
Darlington 2 12 41N04'49 74w10'57 4:56:44
Darlington Heights 3 12 39N56 74w45 4:59:00
Darts Mills 10 1 40N32'20 74w50'03 4:59:20
Davis 13 12 40N08 74w32 4:58:08
Davis Bridge 14 12 40N40'49 74w31'38 4:58:07
Davis Mill 6 1 39N25'29 75w22'01 5:01:28
Davisville 3 12 40N06'35 74w37'06 4:58:28
Davisville 4 2 39N47'35 75w02'48 5:00:11
Dayton 12 1 40N22'21 74w30'38 4:58:03
Deacons 3 1 40N02'16 74w49'40 4:59:19
Deal 15 1 40N14'35 74w00'04 4:56:00
Deal Park 13 1 40N15'05 74w00'33 4:56:02
Deans 12 12 40N24'15 74w30'59 4:58:04
Deauville Beach 15 12 40N00 74w04 4:56:16
De Cou Village 11 1 40N12 74w44 4:58:56
Deepwater 17 1 39N41'00 75w29'27 5:01:58
Deer Chase Manor 15 1 39N58'05 74w13'25 4:56:54
Deerfield 6 12 39N31'25 75w14'11 5:00:57
Deerhaven 15 2 39N41'25 74w16'40 4:57:07
Deer Lake Park 15 1 39N42'05 74w15'36 4:57:02
Deer Park 4 2 39N54'22 74w58'35 4:59:54
Deer Trail Lake 19 17 41N05 74w31 4:58:04
Deerwoods 4 2 39N55'15 74w59'06 4:59:56
DeKays 19 12 41N13'49 74w26'27 4:57:46
Delair 4 2 39N58'53 75w03'07 5:00:12
Delair Junction 4 2 39N58'27 75w03'54 5:00:16
Delanco 3 17 40N03'02 74w57'14 4:59:49
Delawanna 16 1 40N49'44 74w08'29 4:56:34
Delaware 21 15 40N53'34 75w03'54 5:00:16
Delaware Gardens 4 2 39N57'38 75w04'03 5:00:16
Delaware Park 21 17 40N41 75w10 5:00:40
Delcrest 3 17 40N02 74w57 4:59:48
Del Haven 5 12 39N02'48 74w55'12 4:59:41
Dellette 3 12 39N47'27 74w46'28 4:59:06
Delmont 8 12 39N12'51 74w57'01 4:59:48
Delran 3 2 40N01 74w58 4:59:52
Delwood 4 2 39N49 75w06 5:00:24
Demarest 2 1 40N57'26 73w57'50 4:55:51
Dennis 5 12 39N11 74w48 4:59:12
Dennisville 5 12 39N11'35 74w49'32 4:59:18
Denville 14 12 40N53'32 74w28'40 4:57:55
Deptford 8 1 39N49 75w08 5:00:32
Devonshire 1 8 39N32'33 74w40'04 4:58:40
Dias Creek 5 13 39N05'20 74w52'51 4:59:31
Dickerson Corner 6 1 39N27'27 75w19'19 5:01:17
Dicktown 4 1 39N45'22 74w58'54 4:59:56
Dilkesboro 8 17 39N44'21 75w04'50 5:00:19
Dilkes Mills 8 12 39N44'05 75w16'55 5:01:08
Dilts Corner 10 1 40N24'45 74w56'06 4:59:44
Dividing Creek 6 12 39N16'13 75w06'05 5:00:24
Doddtown 7 1 40N46 74w12 4:56:48
Dogs Corners 13 1 40N15'53 74w02'33 4:56:10
Dolphin 1 2 39N22 74w34 4:58:16
Donaldson Park 12 1 40N29'22 74w25'32 4:57:42
Donlontown 3 17 39N54'36 74w55'58 4:59:44
Dorchester 6 17 39N16'22 74w58'38 4:59:55
Dorothy 1 12 39N24'02 74w49'27 4:59:18
Double Trouble 15 14 39N53'52 74w13'16 4:56:53
Doughty 1 12 39N26'43 74w51'43 4:59:27
Dover 14 1 40N53'02 74w33'45 4:58:15
Dover Forge 15 1 39N54'40 74w16'55 4:57:08
Dover Hills 14 1 40N53 74w34 4:58:16
Dover Shores 15 1 39N56 74w13 4:56:52
Downe 6 12 39N16 75w07 5:00:28
Downer 8 1 39N41'40 75w03'08 5:00:13
Downs Farm 4 2 39N52'04 75w00'06 5:00:00
Downstown 8 17 39N32'23 74w57'22 4:59:49
Dragston 6 12 39N15'56 75w04'21 5:00:17
Drakestown 14 1 40N50'37 74w46'58 4:59:08
Dreahook 10 12 40N36'00 74w46'54 4:59:08
Drew University 14 1 40N45 74w25 4:57:40
Dukes Bridge 3 14 39N47'41 74w31'29 4:58:06
Dumont 2 1 40N56'26 73w59'50 4:55:59
Dunbarton 4 17 39N44'57 74w52'31 4:59:30
Dundee 16 1 40N52 74w08 4:56:32
Dunellen 12 2 40N35'21 74w28'20 4:57:53
Dunhams Corners 12 12 40N25'26 74w25'20 4:57:41
Dunham Siding 2 1 40N47 74w01 4:56:04
Dunnfield 21 12 40N58'16 75w07'27 5:00:30
Dunns Mills 3 1 40N07'45 74w41'38 4:58:47
Durham 12 17 40N32 74w22 4:57:28
Durham Park 12 1 40N34 74w27 4:57:48
Dutch Neck 11 12 40N16'56 74w36'51 4:58:27
Dutchtown 3 12 39N43'14 74w44'15 4:58:57
Dutchtown 18 2 40N26'52 74w41'25 4:58:46
Duttonville 19 1 41N21'05 74w41'11 4:58:45
Eagle 3 14 39N46'02 74w34'05 4:58:16
Eagleswood 15 2 39N39 74w18 4:57:12
Earle 13 12 40N13'31 74w08'26 4:56:34
Earlys Crossing 3 3 39N54'31 74w36'22 4:58:25
East 16 4 40N55 74w09 4:56:36
Eastampton 3 1 40N00 74w45 4:59:00
East Amwell 10 12 40N26 74w49 4:59:16
East Berlin 4 17 39N47'50 74w54'56 4:59:40
East Bound Brook 12 17 40N35 74w30 4:58:00
East Bridgeton 6 1 39N28 75w15 5:01:00
East Brunswick 12 12 40N26 74w25 4:57:40
East Burlington 3 1 40N04'44 74w50'18 4:59:21
East Camden 4 2 39N57'10 75w06'07 5:00:24
East Freehold 13 1 40N16'51 74w15'06 4:57:00
East Greenwich 8 2 39N48 75w14 5:00:56
East Hanover 14 17 40N49 74w21 4:57:24
East Keansburg 13 17 40N26'20 74w07'02 4:56:28
East Lake 17 17 39N38'40 75w18'52 5:01:15
East Long Branch 13 1 40N18'48 73w58'42 4:55:55
East Millstone 18 12 40N30'05 74w34'52 4:58:19
East Newark 13 1 40N44'54 74w09'44 4:56:39
East Orange 7 1 40N46'02 74w12'19 4:56:49
East Paterson 2 1 40N54 74w08 4:56:32
East Pennsauken 4 2 39N58'16 75w01'22 5:00:05
East Riverton 3 2 40N01'03 74w59'43 4:59:59
East Rutherford 2 1 40N50'02 74w05'51 4:56:23
East Side 6 1 39N28 75w15 5:01:00
East Spotswood 12 12 40N24'41 74w21'53 4:57:28
East Trenton Heights 11 1 40N15'31 74w42'37 4:58:50
East Vineland 1 1 39N28'51 74w55'11 4:59:41
East Wenonah 8 2 39N48 75w08 5:00:32
East Windsor 11 1 40N16 74w33 4:58:12
East Woodbury 8 1 39N49 75w08 5:00:32
Eatontown 13 1 40N17'46 74w03'05 4:56:12
Eayrestown 3 1 39N56'42 74w47'26 4:59:10
Ebenezer 21 16 40N57'17 74w55'48 4:59:43
Echelon 4 2 39N50 75w01 5:00:04
Echo Lake 16 12 41N03'31 74w23'42 4:57:35
Edgar 12 2 40N34'03 74w16'34 4:57:06
Edgebrook 11 12 40N11'34 74w38'46 4:58:35
Edgebrook 12 1 40N29'05 74w24'13 4:57:37
Edgemere Estates 15 1 40N01'13 74w14'13 4:56:57
Edgewater 9 1 40N49'37 73w58'34 4:55:54
Edgewater Park 3 1 40N04'05 74w54'04 4:59:36
Edgewater Park Estates 3 1 40N05 74w51 4:59:24
Edgewood 5 13 39N05 74w50 4:59:20
Edgewood Park 15 12 40N08'47 74w15'45 4:57:03
Edinburg 11 12 40N15'29 74w36'59 4:58:28
Edinburg Park 11 12 40N16'07 74w37'02 4:58:28
Edison 12 1 39N31'07 74w24'45 4:57:39
Edison 19 17 41N03'50 74w34'05 4:58:16
Egg Harbor City 1 8 39N31'43 74w38'54 4:58:36
Eilers Corner 13 1 40N14'00 74w31'53 4:58:08
Elberon 13 1 40N16'09 73w59'32 4:55:58
Elberon Park 13 1 40N15'41 74w00'23 4:56:02
Eldora 5 12 39N12'55 74w54'23 4:59:38
Eldridge Hill 17 17 39N39'52 75w18'14 5:01:13
Eldridge Park 11 1 40N15'55 74w44'43 4:58:59
Elizabeth 20 1 40N39'50 74w12'40 4:56:51
Elizabethport 20 1 40N39'00 74w11'15 4:56:45
Elk 8 1 39N40 75w08 5:00:32
Elks Terrace 17 17 39N33'32 75w26'29 5:01:46
Ellisburg 4 2 39N54'49 75w00'39 5:00:03
Ellisdale 3 12 40N07'54 74w35'04 4:58:20
Elm 4 2 39N40'45 74w49'46 4:59:19
Elmer 17 1 39N35'42 75w10'14 5:00:41
Elmora 20 1 40N39'44 74w13'40 4:56:55
Elmwood Park 2 1 40N54'14 74w07'08 4:56:29
Elsinboro 17 17 39N33 75w29 5:01:56
Elsmere 8 1 39N41'47 75w08'15 5:00:33
Elton 13 12 40N13'01 74w20'30 4:57:22
Elwood 1 12 39N34'35 74w43'02 4:58:52
Ely 13 1 40N12'11 74w23'15 4:57:33
Elys Corner 13 1 40N14'11 74w28'40 4:57:55
Emerson 2 1 40N58'34 74w01'36 4:56:06
Emmelsville 1 17 39N29'16 74w46'04 4:59:04
Englewood 2 9 40N53'34 73w58'23 4:55:54
Englewood Cliffs 2 1 40N53'07 73w57'10 4:55:49
English Creek 1 17 39N20'57 74w40'16 4:58:41
English Creek Landing 1 17 39N20'05 74w40'42 4:58:43
Englishtown 13 12 40N17'50 74w21'31 4:57:26
Erial 4 1 39N46'24 75w00'24 5:00:02
Erlton 4 2 39N55'01 75w01'06 5:00:04
Erma 5 1 38N58'50 74w54'30 4:59:38
Erma Park 5 1 39N00'21 74w53'02 4:59:32
Ernston 12 2 40N27'22 74w18'39 4:57:15
Erskine 16 12 41N05'27 74w15'31 4:57:02
Erskine Lakes 16 12 41N06'20 74w15'05 4:57:00
Esponong 14 12 40N57 74w37 4:58:28
Essex Fells 7 1 40N49'28 74w17'06 4:57:08
Estell Manor 1 12 39N24'43 74w44'34 4:58:58
Estellville 1 12 39N23'45 74w44'51 4:58:59
Estelville 1 12 39N22 74w47 4:59:08
Estling Lake 14 12 40N53 74w29 4:57:56
Etra 11 1 40N15'09 74w30'26 4:58:02
Evans Corner 3 17 39N52'41 74w54'13 4:59:37
Everett 13 12 40N21'15 74w08'49 4:56:35
Evergreen Shores 15 12 40N00'17 74w08'16 4:56:33
Everittstown 10 13 40N33'57 75w01'45 5:00:07
Evesboro 3 17 39N54'48 74w55'26 4:59:42
Evesham 3 17 39N51 74w53 4:59:32
Ewan 8 1 39N41'55 75w11'11 5:00:45
Ewansville 3 1 39N58'42 74w44'08 4:58:57
Ewing 11 1 40N16'11 74w48'01 4:59:12
Ewingville 11 1 40N16'37 74w46'52 4:59:07
Extonville 3 12 40N08'36 74w35'57 4:58:24
Fairfield 7 1 40N53 74w17 4:57:08
Fairfield 13 1 40N12'19 74w12'51 4:56:51
Fair Haven 13 1 40N21'38 74w02'19 4:56:09
Fair Lawn 2 2 40N56'25 74w07'56 4:56:32
Fairmount 10 12 40N43'37 74w46'36 4:59:06
Fair Play 13 2 40N14'12 74w27'54 4:57:52
Fairton 6 1 39N22'54 75w13'13 5:00:53
Fairview 2 1 40N48'45 73w59'58 4:56:00
Fairview 3 17 40N01'03 74w57'01 4:59:48
Fairview 4 1 39N54'24 75w06'10 5:00:25
Fairview 13 2 40N22'23 74w05'14 4:56:21
Fairview 18 12 40N26'00 74w43'04 4:58:52
Fairview Estates 15 12 39N59'00 74w08'45 4:56:35
Fairview Knolls 12 12 40N25'45 74w25'35 4:57:42
Fairwoods 14 1 40N46'07 74w25'44 4:57:43
Falcon Courts North 3 3 40N01 74w38 4:58:32
Fanwood 20 2 40N38'27 74w23'02 4:57:32
Fardale 2 17 41N02'27 74w10'37 4:56:42
Far Hills 18 12 40N41'03 74w38'10 4:58:33
Farmersville 10 12 40N43'34 74w48'26 4:59:14
Farmingdale 6 2 39N22'34 75w06'36 5:00:26
Farmingdale 13 12 40N11'47 74w10'08 4:56:41
Farmington 1 2 39N23 74w33 4:58:12
Farnerville 3 1 40N04'10 74w51'53 4:59:28
Farrington Lake Heights 12 1 40N26'08 74w27'25 4:57:50
Fayson Lakes 14 16 40N58'33 74w21'27 4:57:26
Feaster Park 12 1 40N29'04 74w26'35 4:57:46
Febletown 21 12 40N55'54 74w57'45 4:59:51
Fellowship 3 17 39N55'39 74w58'01 4:59:52
Fenwick 17 17 39N37'03 75w20'14 5:01:21
Ferdinands Mills 2 17 41N01'32 74w11'35 4:56:46
Fernwood 11 1 40N15'32 74w47'47 4:59:11
Fernwood Terrace 11 1 40N14 74w47 4:59:08
Ferrell 8 1 39N40'31 75w11'57 5:00:48
Ferry Road Manor 11 1 40N15'12 74w48'17 4:59:13
Fieldsboro 3 1 40N08'11 74w43'45 4:58:55
Fieldstone 18 1 40N42 74w33 4:58:12
Fieldville 12 1 40N32'50 74w30'25 4:58:02
Finderne 18 2 40N33'47 74w34'41 4:58:19
Finesville 10 17 40N36'30 75w10'17 5:00:41
Finley 6 1 39N28'38 75w12'09 5:00:49
Firthtown 21 17 40N41 75w10 5:00:40
Fish House 4 2 39N58 75w03 5:00:12
Fishing Creek 5 1 39N01'22 74w56'03 4:59:44
Fithians Corner 6 1 39N25'37 75w17'31 5:01:10
Five Corners 9 1 40N43 74w04 4:56:16
Five Points 1 1 39N28'47 74w53'38 4:59:35
Five Points 17 17 39N45'23 75w24'54 5:01:40
Five Points 19 12 41N05'10 74w51'29 4:59:26
Flagtown 18 2 40N31'01 74w41'05 4:58:44
Flanders 14 1 40N50'44 74w41'43 4:58:47
Flatbrookville 19 12 41N06'01 74w57'50 4:59:51
Flemington 10 1 40N30'44 74w51'35 4:59:26
Flemington Junction 10 1 40N31'54 74w50'24 4:59:22
Floral Hill 14 1 40N43'46 74w24'23 4:57:38
Florence 3 1 40N07'10 74w48'21 4:59:13
Florence 4 17 39N44'03 74w55'07 4:59:40
Florence Station 3 12 40N06'30 74w47'04 4:59:08
Florham Park 14 1 40N47'16 74w23'19 4:57:33
Flyat 3 12 39N49'22 74w45'27 4:59:02
Folsom 1 12 39N36'07 74w50'35 4:59:22
Folwell 3 1 40N02'38 74w42'33 4:58:50
Ford Estates 8 1 39N49 75w08 5:00:32
Ford Landing 3 2 40N00 75w01 5:00:04
Fords 12 1 40N31'45 74w18'59 4:57:16
Fordville 6 1 39N25'31 75w10'13 5:00:41
Forest Acres 15 12 39N57'41 74w10'25 4:56:42
Forest Grove 6 1 39N31'36 75w02'35 5:00:10
Forest Hill 4 2 39N49 75w06 5:00:24
Forest Hill 15 12 39N55 74w09 4:56:36
Forked River 15 14 39N50'23 74w11'26 4:56:46
Forked River Beach 15 14 39N49'01 74w10'14 4:56:41
Forked River Point 15 14 39N49'34 74w11'52 4:56:47
Fork Landing 3 2 39N58'40 75w00'47 5:00:03
Forrest Lake Estates 8 17 39N34 75w02 5:00:08
Fort Dix 3 3 40N01'47 74w37'08 4:58:29
Fort Elfsborg 17 17 39N32'54 75w31'33 5:02:06
Fortescue 6 12 39N14'15 75w10'19 5:00:41
Fort Hancock 13 1 40N24 73w59 4:55:56
Fort Lee 2 1 40N51'03 73w58'14 4:55:53

Fort Mercer 8 1 39N51 75w10 5:00:40
Fort Monmouth 13 1 40N19 74w02 4:56:08
Fort Mott 17 17 39N34 75w28 5:01:52
Fort Plains 13 1 40N11'00 74w15'17 4:57:01
Fostertown 3 1 39N56'34 74w49'04 4:59:16
Foster Village 2 1 40N55 74w04 4:56:16
Foul Rift 21 17 40N48'08 75w05'53 5:00:24
Four Corners 19 12 41N17'17 74w45'47 4:59:03
Four Mile 3 14 39N53'29 74w34'53 4:58:20
Four Mile Circle 3 3 39N53'53 74w35'45 4:58:23
Fox Chase 3 12 39N51'23 74w43'36 4:58:54
Fox Hill 14 1 40N52'39 74w26'40 4:57:47
Fox Hollow Woods 4 2 39N52'44 74w57'23 4:59:50
Foxs Mill 17 1 39N36'48 75w15'15 5:01:01
Frames Corner 6 12 39N18'12 75w09'51 5:00:39
Francis Mills 15 12 40N08'05 74w23'52 4:57:35
Frankford 19 17 41N10 74w44 4:58:56
Frankfort 18 2 40N30'31 74w41'01 4:58:44
Franklin 7 1 40N51'05 74w17'42 4:57:11
Franklin 10 13 40N37'31 74w55'32 4:59:42
Franklin 14 17 40N52'27 74w30'43 4:58:03
Franklin 19 17 41N07'19 74w34'51 4:58:19
Franklin Corner 11 1 40N16'49 74w43'01 4:58:52
Franklin Grove 21 16 41N01'52 74w57'26 4:59:50
Franklin Lakes 2 17 41N01'00 74w12'22 4:56:49
Franklin Park 3 17 40N01'30 74w54'30 4:59:38
Franklin Park 12 12 40N26'20 74w32'08 4:58:09
Franklinville 8 12 39N37'05 75w04'34 5:00:18
Frazier Park 15 17 39N40'45 74w09'06 4:56:36
Fredon 19 15 41N02'21 74w48'33 4:59:14
Free Acres 20 17 40N39'38 74w26'39 4:57:47
Freehold 13 1 40N15'36 74w16'27 4:57:06
Freewood Acres 13 12 40N10'08 74w14'18 4:56:57
Frelinghuysen 21 18 40N58 74w53 4:59:32
Frenchtown 10 12 40N31'34 75w03'43 5:00:15
Freneau 13 2 40N24'06 74w14'17 4:56:57
Fresh Ponds 12 1 40N24'19 74w27'58 4:57:52
Friars Landing 8 2 39N49'45 75w13'40 5:00:55
Friendship 3 14 39N45'03 74w35'08 4:58:21
Friendship 6 1 39N29'00 75w11'39 5:00:47
Friendship Station 17 1 39N44'03 75w27'33 5:01:50
Friesburg 17 1 39N32'41 75w17'22 5:01:09
Fries Mill 8 1 39N39'22 75w02'44 5:00:11
Furmans Corner 10 1 40N27'35 74w47'13 4:59:09
Galilee 13 1 40N20'11 73w58'29 4:55:54
Galloping Hill 18 1 40N42 74w33 4:58:12
Galloway 1 2 39N29 74w32 4:58:08
Gandys Beach 6 12 39N16'19 75w14'07 5:00:56
Garden City 8 1 39N47'50 75w05'22 5:00:21
Garden Lake 4 1 39N48 75w00 5:00:00
Gardens 5 1 39N16 74w35 4:58:20
Garden State 2 1 40N57 74w04 4:56:16
Gardenville 8 1 39N49'21 75w07'16 5:00:29
Gardenville Center 8 1 39N49'48 75w07'22 5:00:29
Gardiners Landing 3 2 39N37'30 74w38'25 4:58:34
Garfield 2 1 40N52'53 74w06'49 4:56:27
Garfield Park 3 1 40N01'15 74w52'47 4:59:31
Garfield Park East 3 1 40N01'23 74w52'03 4:59:28
Garfield Park North 3 1 40N01'52 74w51'44 4:59:27
Garrison Corner 6 12 39N26'45 75w23'26 5:01:34
Garton 6 1 39N28'07 75w10'10 5:00:41
Garwood 20 1 40N39'34 74w19'24 4:57:18
Gary Corner 10 1 40N31'50 74w55'16 4:59:41
General Lafayette 9 1 40N43 74w04 4:56:16
Genoa 12 2 40N25 74w14 4:56:56
Georgetown 3 12 40N04'46 74w39'13 4:58:37
Georgia 13 1 40N11'14 74w17'06 4:57:08
Germania 1 8 39N30'42 74w35'59 4:58:24
Germania Gardens 1 8 39N30'12 74w36'34 4:58:26
Gibbsboro 4 17 39N50'17 74w57'55 4:59:52
Gibbstown 8 2 39N49'30 75w17'02 5:01:08
Gibson Landing 1 12 39N21'22 74w43'36 4:58:54
Giffordtown 15 2 39N36'01 74w22'20 4:57:29
Gigantic City 1 12 39N29'47 74w49'26 4:59:18
Gilford Park 15 12 39N56'55 74w08'15 4:56:33
Gillespie 12 2 40N27'07 74w21'23 4:57:26
Gillette 14 17 40N40'26 74w27'59 4:57:52
Gilliandtown 12 12 40N23'49 74w25'12 4:57:41
Gilman Lake 8 1 39N38 75w10 5:00:40
Glacier Hills 14 17 40N50 74w29 4:57:56
Gladstone 18 12 40N43'21 74w39'57 4:58:40
Glassboro 8 1 39N42'10 75w06'44 5:00:27
Glasser 19 1 40N56 74w40 4:58:40
Glen Alpin 14 12 40N45'15 74w31'36 4:58:06
Glen Cove 15 12 39N53'00 74w08'35 4:56:34
Glendale 4 2 39N51'13 74w58'58 4:59:56
Glendale 11 1 40N14'47 74w46'58 4:59:08
Glendola 13 1 40N11'27 74w04'38 4:56:19
Glendora 4 2 39N50'22 75w04'26 5:00:18
Glenfield 14 1 40N44'35 74w24'20 4:57:37
Glen Gardner 10 13 40N41'48 74w56'28 4:59:46
Glenmoore 11 12 40N22'05 74w47'04 4:59:08
Glen Ridge 7 2 40N48'19 74w12'15 4:56:49
Glen Rock 2 4 40N57'46 74w08'00 4:56:32
Glenside 17 12 39N39'59 75w29'19 5:01:57
Glenview 4 2 39N49 75w06 5:00:24
Glenwood 19 12 41N15'04 74w29'24 4:57:58
Gloucester City 4 2 39N53'30 75w07'00 5:00:28
Gloucester Heights 4 2 39N53'52 75w06'17 5:00:25
Glouster Landing 1 8 39N35'05 74w34'01 4:58:16
Godfrey Manor 15 12 40N02 74w07 4:56:28
Golden Crest 11 12 40N12'30 74w39'53 4:58:40
Golf Hill 14 14 40N52 74w38 4:58:32
Golf Manor 17 1 39N41'48 75w28'16 5:01:53
Golf View 17 1 39N42'02 75w28'11 5:01:53
Golf View Manor 11 12 40N16'50 74w35'30 4:58:22
Good Intent 8 1 39N48'15 75w04'41 5:00:19
Goodmans Crossing 20 2 40N36'55 74w20'24 4:57:22
Gordon Lakes 16 16 41N00 74w21 4:57:24
Gordons Corner 13 12 40N19'04 74w18'21 4:57:13
Goshen 5 13 39N08'29 74w51'12 4:59:25
Goshen Crossing 5 13 39N07'41 74w49'31 4:59:18
Gouldtown 6 1 39N25'14 75w11'05 5:00:44
Grandin 10 13 40N37'03 74w56'03 4:59:44
Grand Spruce 8 10 39N45'41 75w20'17 5:01:21
Granton Junction 9 1 40N47 74w01 4:56:04
Grantwood 9 1 40N49'36 73w59'15 4:55:57
Grasselli 20 1 40N36'54 74w12'33 4:56:50
Grassy Sound 5 11 39N00'48 74w48'59 4:59:16
Gravel Hill 12 12 40N17'59 74w25'11 4:57:41
Gravelly Run 1 17 39N25'33 74w42'06 4:58:48
Great Eastern Mills 16 4 40N54 74w12 4:56:48
Greater Cross Roads 18 12 40N40'08 74w40'49 4:58:43
Great Meadows 21 12 40N52'15 74w54'45 4:59:39
Great Notch 16 4 40N52'28 74w12'29 4:56:50
Green 19 15 40N59 74w48 4:59:12
Green Acres 11 1 40N14 74w47 4:59:08
Green Bank 3 8 39N36'46 74w35'18 4:58:21
Green Brook 18 17 40N36 74w29 4:57:56
Green Creek 5 12 39N02'46 74w54'06 4:59:36
Green Curve Heights 11 1 40N15'58 74w47'06 4:59:08
Greendell 19 15 40N58'26 74w49'17 4:59:17
Greenfield 5 2 39N13'42 74w42'22 4:58:49
Greenfield Heights 8 1 39N48'35 75w10'07 5:00:40
Green-Fields 8 1 39N49'01 75w10'00 5:00:40
Green Grove 13 12 40N14'03 74w04'40 4:56:19
Greenhaven 4 2 39N55'00 74w59'45 4:59:59
Green Hut Park 14 1 40N53 74w34 4:58:16
Green Knoll 18 2 40N36'00 74w36'45 4:58:27
Greenland 4 2 39N51'32 75w01'48 5:00:07
Green Pond 14 12 41N01'02 74w28'41 4:57:55
Green Pond Junction 14 12 41N01'38 74w25'01 4:57:40
Greensand 12 17 40N29'30 74w23'15 4:57:33
Greens Bridge 21 17 40N41 75w10 5:00:40
Green Tree 8 17 39N45'03 75w04'35 5:00:18
Greentree Village 3 17 39N54'45 74w56'20 4:59:45
Green Village 14 1 40N44'21 74w27'14 4:57:49
Greenville 9 1 40N42'01 74w05'41 4:56:23
Greenville 15 1 40N06'06 74w10'20 4:56:41
Greenville 17 1 39N34'00 75w11'33 5:00:46
Greenwich 6 12 39N23'23 75w20'20 5:01:21
Greenwood Manor 15 1 39N58'45 74w14'50 4:56:59
Greenwood Village 11 1 40N13 74w44 4:58:56
Grenloch 4 2 39N47'08 75w03'22 5:00:13
Grenloch Terrace 8 2 39N46'49 75w03'47 5:00:15
Griggstown 18 12 40N26'16 74w36'49 4:58:27
Grove 7 1 40N48 74w11 4:56:44
Grove Chapel 6 17 39N33 75w01 5:00:04
Grovers Mill 11 2 40N19'00 74w36'35 4:58:26
Groveville 11 1 40N10'11 74w40'19 4:58:41
Gum Tree Corner 6 1 39N26'15 75w23'07 5:01:32
Guttenberg 9 1 40N47'31 74w00'15 4:56:01
Hackensack 2 1 40N53'09 74w02'38 4:56:11
Hackettstown 21 1 40N51'14 74w49'46 4:59:19
Hacklebarney 14 12 40N46'01 74w43'15 4:58:53
Haddon 4 1 39N53'51 75w05'47 5:00:23
Haddonfield 4 2 39N53'29 75w02'17 5:00:09
Haddon Heights 4 2 39N52'38 75w03'54 5:00:16
Haddon Hills 4 2 39N54'00 75w03'10 5:00:13
Haddon Leigh 4 2 39N53'23 75w02'50 5:00:11
Haddon Towne 4 2 39N53'11 75w00'42 5:00:03
Hagerville 17 17 39N32'00 75w28'00 5:01:52
Hainesburg 21 12 40N57'18 75w03'42 5:00:15
Haines Corner 4 2 39N52'07 74w56'41 4:59:47
Haines Corner 11 12 40N12'21 74w39'04 4:58:36
Hainesport 3 1 39N59'01 74w49'39 4:59:19
Hainesville 19 17 41N15'07 74w48'12 4:59:13
Halberton 6 2 39N17'44 74w54'34 4:59:38
Haledon 16 4 40N56'08 74w11'12 4:56:45
Haleyville 6 12 39N17'22 75w01'02 5:00:04
Half Acre 12 1 40N19'14 74w27'10 4:57:49
Halls Corners 12 12 40N25 74w23 4:57:32
Halltown 17 12 39N38'17 75w24'47 5:01:39
Halsey 19 12 41N05'49 74w44'56 4:59:00
Hamburg 19 17 41N09'12 74w34'36 4:58:18
Hamden 10 13 40N36'12 74w54'03 4:59:36
Hamilton 13 1 40N12'25 74w04'54 4:56:20
Hamilton 18 2 40N30'22 74w37'14 4:58:29
Hamilton Square 11 1 40N13'38 74w39'13 4:58:37
Hammond Heights 8 2 39N48 75w08 5:00:32
Hammonton 1 2 39N38'11 74w48'10 4:59:13
Hampton 10 13 40N42'25 74w57'23 4:59:50
Hampton Furnace 3 12 39N46'10 74w40'51 4:58:43
Hampton Gate 3 12 39N48'15 74w40'44 4:58:43
Hampton Junction 10 13 40N42'40 74w57'11 4:59:49
Hampton Lakes 3 12 39N53'30 74w42'44 4:58:51
Hancocks Bridge 17 17 39N30'19 75w27'44 5:01:51
Haneys Mill 19 12 41N07'44 74w54'39 4:59:39
Hanford 19 1 41N17'43 74w33'48 4:58:15
Hanover 14 1 40N48'16 74w22'02 4:57:28
Hanover Furnace 3 12 39N58'53 74w31'36 4:58:06
Hanover Neck 14 17 40N49'54 74w21'12 4:57:25
Harbourton 11 12 40N21'08 74w51'09 4:59:25
Harding 8 1 39N38'36 75w07'20 5:00:29
Harding 14 12 40N45 74w30 4:58:00
Harding Lakes 1 17 39N27'09 74w45'09 4:59:01
Hardingville 8 1 39N39'36 75w10'28 5:00:42
Hardistonville 19 17 41N08'20 74w34'11 4:58:17
Hardwick 21 16 41N03'16 74w55'57 4:59:44
Hardwick Center 21 16 41N00'30 74w56'56 4:59:48
Hardyston 19 17 41N07 74w34 4:58:16
Harfield 15 12 40N08 74w20 4:57:20
Harker Village 8 1 39N49 75w08 5:00:32
Harlingen 18 2 40N26'51 74w39'46 4:58:39
Harmersville 17 17 39N29'56 75w26'05 5:01:44
Harmony 6 1 39N29'57 75w17'17 5:01:09
Harmony 13 2 40N25'08 74w07'29 4:56:30
Harmony 15 12 40N09'07 74w18'04 4:57:12
Harmony 21 17 40N44'48 75w08'16 5:00:33
Harmony Park 13 2 40N26 74w13 4:56:52
Harmonyvale 19 17 41N08'48 74w38'13 4:58:33
Harneys Corner 11 1 40N14'57 74w44'35 4:58:58
Harrington Park 2 1 40N59'01 73w58'49 4:55:55
Harrison 9 1 40N44'47 74w09'24 4:56:38
Harrison Mountain Lake 16 12 41N06 74w16 4:57:04
Harrisonville 8 12 39N41'06 75w15'59 5:01:04
Harrisonville 17 17 39N36'06 75w29'50 5:01:59
Harrisville 3 14 39N39'41 74w31'20 4:58:05
Hartford 3 17 39N58'34 74w53'40 4:59:35
Harts Corner 11 12 40N18'32 74w48'47 4:59:15
Harvey Cedars 15 12 39N42'22 74w08'04 4:56:32
Hasbrouck Heights 2 1 40N51'29 74w04'52 4:56:19
Haskell 16 1 41N01'42 74w17'47 4:57:11
Haven Beach 15 17 39N35'36 74w12'58 4:56:52
Haven Homes 12 17 40N30'34 74w24'24 4:57:38
Haworth 2 1 40N57'39 73w59'26 4:55:58
Hawthorne 16 1 40N56'57 74w09'15 4:56:37
Hawthorne Park 3 1 40N02'18 74w52'23 4:59:30
Hazelton 12 2 40N35'18 74w17'28 4:57:10
Hazen 21 17 40N48'51 75w02'36 5:00:10
Hazlet 13 2 40N24'56 74w11'29 4:56:46
Head of River 1 12 39N16 74w47 4:59:08
Heatherwood 12 12 40N24 74w21 4:57:24
Heath Manor 11 1 40N15'32 74w45'47 4:59:03
Hedding 3 1 40N06'28 74w44'39 4:58:59
Heislerville 6 12 39N13'23 74w59'34 4:59:58
Helmetta 12 12 40N22'36 74w25'30 4:57:42
Hemlock Glen 21 12 40N58'50 75w02'27 5:00:10
Hendrickson Corners 13 2 40N24'39 74w08'13 4:56:33
Henningers Mill 13 2 40N23'44 74w15'13 4:57:01
Hensfoot 10 13 40N37'46 74w58'10 4:59:53
Herberts 12 12 40N26'09 74w25'24 4:57:42
Herberts Corner 13 12 40N19'51 74w15'40 4:57:03
Herbertsville 15 12 40N06'43 74w06'34 4:56:26
Heritage Village 3 17 39N53'27 74w54'19 4:59:37
Herman 3 8 39N37'03 74w35'41 4:58:23
Herwood 4 2 39N56'16 75w00'20 5:00:01
Hesstown 6 2 39N21'49 74w55'51 4:59:43
Hewitt 16 12 41N08'30 74w18'40 4:57:15
Hibernia 14 12 40N56'38 74w29'35 4:57:58
Hickory Corner 11 1 40N16'19 74w33'25 4:58:14
Hickory Tree 14 1 40N44'47 74w25'57 4:57:44
Hickstown 4 2 39N46'45 75w00'45 5:00:03
Higbeeville 1 2 39N30'55 74w27'25 4:57:50
Higginsville 10 1 40N30'36 74w47'20 4:59:09
High Bank Landing 1 17 39N26'05 74w43'30 4:58:54
High Bridge 10 13 40N40'01 74w53'46 4:59:35
High Crossing 3 12 39N46'09 74w38'40 4:58:35
Highland Beach 13 1 40N22 73w59 4:55:56
Highland Lakes 19 12 41N10'38 74w28'09 4:57:53
Highland Park 4 2 39N53'19 75w06'30 5:00:26

Highland Park 12 1 40N29'45 74w25'29 4:57:42
Highlands 13 1 40N24'13 73w59'31 4:55:58
High Point 15 17 39N42'35 74w07'58 4:56:32
High Point Manor 12 12 40N24 74w21 4:57:24
Highs Beach 5 13 39N04'45 74w54'32 4:59:38
Hightstown 11 1 40N16'10 74w31'25 4:58:06
Highview Park 13 1 40N07 74w03 4:56:12
Hillcrest 11 1 40N14'33 74w47'03 4:59:08
Hillcrest 16 4 40N55 74w12 4:56:48
Hillcrest 21 17 40N41 75w10 5:00:40
Hilliard 15 1 39N42 74w15 4:57:00
Hillsborough 18 2 40N28'39 74w37'38 4:58:31
Hillsdale 2 1 41N00'09 74w02'27 4:56:10
Hillsdale 13 1 40N20'21 74w13'32 4:56:54
Hillsdale Manor 2 1 41N00'42 74w02'33 4:56:10
Hillside 20 1 40N42'04 74w13'50 4:56:55
Hillside Terrace 11 12 40N12'03 74w36'35 4:58:26
Hilltop 4 2 39N49'28 75w04'04 5:00:16
Hilltop Estates 15 1 39N58'33 74w14'30 4:56:58
Hilltop Terrace 12 12 40N25 74w23 4:57:32
Hilltown 14 1 40N55'16 74w33'04 4:58:12
Hillwood Lakes 11 1 40N16 74w46 4:59:04
Hilton 13 1 40N24'43 74w01'21 4:56:05
Hinchman 4 2 39N49 75w06 5:00:24
Hi-Nella 4 2 39N50 75w01 5:00:04
Hoboken 9 1 40N44'38 74w01'58 4:56:08
Hockamik 3 3 40N02'11 74w32'49 4:58:11
Hoffman 12 12 40N19'04 74w24'44 4:57:39
Hoffmans 10 12 40N42'21 74w51'38 4:59:27
Hoffmans Mill 6 12 39N15'32 74w54'36 4:59:38
Ho-ho-kus 2 2 40N59'47 74w06'06 4:56:24
Holcomb Mills 10 1 40N31'33 74w49'49 4:59:19
Holgate 15 17 39N32'24 74w15'26 4:57:02
Holiday City 15 1 40N01'20 74w10'00 4:56:40
Holiday Estates 15 12 39N58'17 74w08'43 4:56:35
Holland 10 13 40N34'19 75w09'57 5:00:40
Holland 13 17 40N23'27 74w08'44 4:56:35
Holland 19 17 41N03'59 74w31'36 4:58:06
Holly Brook 3 1 40N00 74w47 4:59:08
Holly Crest 15 12 40N02 74w07 4:56:28
Holly Park 15 12 39N53'43 74w08'36 4:56:34
Holmansville 15 12 40N06'03 74w19'06 4:57:16
Holmdel 13 12 40N20'42 74w11'04 4:56:44
Holmeson 13 2 40N09'56 74w25'02 4:57:40
Homes Mills 13 12 40N08'04 74w32'34 4:58:10
Homestead 9 1 40N47 74w01 4:56:04
Homestead Park 14 17 40N41'24 74w27'02 4:57:48
Homestead Village 18 1 40N42 74w33 4:58:12
Hootens Hollow 4 2 39N49 75w06 5:00:24
Hoot Owl Estates 3 17 39N52'58 74w50'51 4:59:23
Hoover Village 6 1 39N28 75w15 5:01:00
Hopatcong 19 1 40N55'58 74w39'35 4:58:38
Hopatcong Heights 19 1 40N55'14 74w40'43 4:58:43
Hopatcong Hills 19 1 40N56'38 74w40'16 4:58:41
Hope 21 12 40N54'40 74w58'04 4:59:52
Hopelawn 12 1 40N31'37 74w17'36 4:57:10
Hopewell 11 12 40N23'21 74w45'44 4:59:03
Hopewell 19 12 41N02'57 74w33'00 4:58:12
Hopkins Corner 19 17 41N08'08 74w38'37 4:58:34
Hornerstown 13 12 40N06'22 74w30'52 4:58:03
Houses Corner 19 12 41N04'15 74w39'15 4:58:37
Howardsville 15 1 39N48'46 74w21'55 4:57:28
Howell 13 12 40N10 74w12 4:56:48
Hudson City 9 1 40N45 74w04 4:56:16
Hudson Heights 9 1 40N48'25 74w00'15 4:56:01
Hughesville 10 12 40N37'19 75w09'22 5:00:37
Hunters Mill 1 12 39N19'25 74w51'39 4:59:27
Huntington 21 17 40N41 75w10 5:00:40
Huntsburg 19 12 40N59'50 74w50'17 4:59:21
Huntsville 19 12 40N58'49 74w46'33 4:59:06
Hunt Tract 4 2 39N49 75w06 5:00:24
Hurdtown 14 12 40N58'12 74w35'58 4:58:24
Hurffville 8 17 39N45'45 75w06'31 5:00:26
Husted 6 1 39N31'31 75w11'22 5:00:45
Husted Landing 6 12 39N21'05 75w15'27 5:01:02
Hutchinson 21 17 40N46'25 75w07'54 5:00:32
Hutchinson Mills 11 1 40N14'44 74w42'32 4:58:50
Hutton Park 7 1 40N46'45 74w15'03 4:57:00
Huyler Landing 2 1 40N55'35 73w55'31 4:55:42
Hyson 15 12 40N08'27 74w16'01 4:57:04
Ideal Beach 13 17 40N27 74w08 4:56:32
Idell 10 12 40N27'30 75w01'42 5:00:07
Imlaystown 13 12 40N10'03 74w30'56 4:58:04
Imperial Manor 4 2 39N49 75w06 5:00:24
Independence 21 1 40N53 74w53 4:59:32
Independence Corner 19 1 41N12'36 74w33'06 4:58:12
Indian Cabin 1 8 39N33 74w37 4:58:28
Indian Lake 14 12 40N53 74w29 4:57:56
Indian Mills 3 12 39N47'38 74w44'41 4:58:59
Interlaken 13 1 40N14'00 74w00'58 4:56:04
Iona 8 12 39N36'05 75w04'03 5:00:16
Ironbound 7 1 40N43 74w10 4:56:40
Ironia 14 14 40N49'22 74w37'34 4:58:30
Iron Rock 4 2 39N57'34 75w01'31 5:00:06
Irven Heights 11 1 40N16 74w46 4:59:04
Irvington 7 2 40N44 74w14 4:56:56
Iselin 12 2 40N34'31 74w19'22 4:57:17
Island Beach 15 12 39N56 74w05 4:56:20
Island Beach Heights 15 12 39N57'15 74w09'23 4:56:38
Island Heights 15 1 39N56'31 74w09'01 4:56:36
Ivystone Farms 4 17 39N46'02 74w54'20 4:59:37
Ivywood 3 2 39N58'55 74w59'23 4:59:58
Jackson 4 17 39N46'35 74w51'46 4:59:27
Jackson 15 12 40N06 74w19 4:57:16
Jacksonburg 21 16 40N59'30 74w58'51 4:59:55
Jacksons Mills 15 12 40N08'52 74w19'28 4:57:18
Jacksonville 3 1 40N03'01 74w45'50 4:59:03
Jacksonville 14 17 40N57'09 74w19'49 4:57:19
Jacobstown 3 3 40N04'33 74w35'01 4:58:20
Jamesburg 12 12 40N21'09 74w26'26 4:57:46
Jamesburg Gardens 12 12 40N20'35 74w25'15 4:57:41
Jamesburg Park 12 12 40N22'47 74w26'21 4:57:45
Janvier 8 12 39N37'37 75w01'04 5:00:04
Jeffers Landing 13 17 39N19'05 74w39'08 4:58:37
Jefferson 13 17 39N45'13 75w12'44 5:00:51
Jeffrey Lane Estates 15 12 39N55 74w09 4:56:36
Jenkins 3 14 39N41'53 74w31'37 4:58:06
Jericho 6 12 39N28'12 75w21'07 5:01:24
Jericho 8 1 39N48'20 75w08'25 5:00:34
Jersey City 9 1 40N43'41 74w04'41 4:56:19
Jerseyville 13 1 40N14'21 74w13'47 4:56:55
Jessups Mill 17 17 39N39'42 75w13'51 5:00:55
Jobstown 3 3 40N02'13 74w41'36 4:58:46
Johnsonburg 21 18 40N57'52 74w52'44 4:59:31
Johnson Place 3 14 39N51'46 74w37'06 4:58:28
Johnsontown 1 2 39N31'25 74w27'37 4:57:50
Jones Island 6 12 39N20 75w12 5:00:48
Jones Mill 3 14 39N47'47 74w31'38 4:58:07
Jones Mill 6 2 39N19'16 74w56'29 4:59:46
Jordantown 4 2 39N57'51 75w02'16 5:00:09
Journal Square 9 1 40N44 74w04 4:56:16
Juliustown 3 3 40N00'48 74w40'09 4:58:41
Jumbo 17 10 39N46'23 75w23'57 5:01:36
Jutland 10 13 40N37'22 74w57'53 4:59:52
Kalarama 21 12 40N57'57 74w59'33 4:59:58
Kampe 19 12 41N10'01 74w27'24 4:57:50
Kampfe Lake 16 16 41N01 74w20 4:57:20
Karrsville 21 12 40N48'33 74w55'57 4:59:44
Kay Gardens 17 17 39N44'38 75w25'12 5:01:41
Keansburg 13 17 40N26'30 74w07'49 4:56:31
Kearny 9 2 40N46'06 74w08'45 4:56:35
Keasbey 12 1 40N31'00 74w18'20 4:57:13
Kendall Park 12 12 40N25'15 74w33'40 4:58:15
Kenilworth 20 1 40N40'35 74w17'28 4:57:10
Kennedy Mills 21 17 40N39'39 75w06'49 5:00:27
Kennedys 21 17 40N38'53 75w07'40 5:00:31
Kenvil 14 14 40N52'47 74w37'08 4:58:29
Kenwood 4 2 39N49 75w06 5:00:24
Kernan Corner 6 1 39N27'12 75w20'00 5:01:20
Keswick Grove 15 12 39N57'02 74w20'40 4:57:23
Keyport 13 2 40N25'59 74w12'00 4:56:48
Kimbles Beach 5 13 39N06'16 74w53'39 4:59:35
Kimseytown 5 1 39N00'04 74w56'06 4:59:44
King Crab Landing 5 13 39N04'37 74w54'38 4:59:39
Kingfisher Cove 15 12 40N02 74w07 4:56:28
Kings Hill 4 2 39N49 75w06 5:00:24
Kingsland 2 1 40N48'23 74w06'41 4:56:27
Kingston 18 2 40N22'31 74w36'50 4:58:27
Kingston Estates 4 2 39N55'25 74w59'18 4:59:57
Kingsway Village 4 2 39N49 75w06 5:00:24
Kingswood 4 2 39N49 75w06 5:00:24
Kings Woods 2 1 40N57'06 73w55'33 4:55:42
Kingtown 10 13 40N35'37 74w56'48 4:59:47
Kingwood 10 12 40N28'11 75w01'10 5:00:05
Kinkora 3 1 40N07'03 74w45'20 4:59:01
Kinnelon 14 16 41N00'06 74w22'03 4:57:28
Kirbys Mill 3 17 39N55'00 74w48'17 4:59:13
Kirbys Mills 13 12 40N07'43 74w32'22 4:58:09
Kirkwood 4 2 39N49'52 74w59'30 4:59:58
Kitchell 14 12 41N00'25 74w27'54 4:57:52
Kittatinny Lake 19 17 41N09 74w45 4:59:00
Klinesville 10 1 40N32'29 74w52'53 4:59:32
Knollwood 4 2 39N49 75w06 5:00:24
Knollwood 14 1 40N45'37 74w24'16 4:57:37
Knowlton 21 15 40N55'49 75w01'42 5:00:07
Kresson 4 17 39N51'27 74w55'18 4:59:41
Lacey 15 1 39N52'21 74w17'44 4:57:11
Lafayette 19 17 41N05'54 74w41'20 4:58:45
Lafayette Mills 13 1 40N18'27 74w18'16 4:57:13
Lahiere 12 17 40N31'08 74w24'10 4:57:37
Lake 8 17 39N33 75w01 5:00:04
Lake Arrowhead 14 12 40N53 74w29 4:57:56
Lake Club 13 12 40N08'46 74w14'55 4:57:00
Lake Como 13 1 40N09'35 74w01'43 4:56:07
Lake Denmark 14 1 40N53 74w34 4:58:16
Lake Forest 14 1 40N55 74w39 4:58:36
Lake Grinnell 19 17 41N06 74w38 4:58:32
Lake Hiawatha 14 1 40N52'57 74w22'55 4:57:32
Lake Hopatcong 14 12 40N56'54 74w37'03 4:58:28
Lakehurst 15 1 40N00'52 74w18'42 4:57:15
Lakehurst Naval Air Station 15 1 40N01 74w19 4:57:16
Lake Iliff 19 12 41N03 74w45 4:59:00
Lake Intervale 14 1 40N54 74w25 4:57:40
Lake Junction 14 1 40N54'19 74w36'04 4:58:24
Lake Lackawanna 19 1 40N55 74w42 4:58:48
Lakeland 4 1 39N47'07 75w04'33 5:00:18
Lake Lenape 19 12 41N00 74w44 4:58:56
Lake Lookover 16 12 41N08 74w18 4:57:12
Lake Mohawk 19 12 41N01 74w39 4:58:36
Lake Nelson 12 1 40N34 74w27 4:57:48
Lake Owassa 19 12 41N03 74w45 4:59:00
Lake Parsippany 14 1 40N51'00 74w25'45 4:57:43
Lake Pine 3 17 39N51'57 74w50'59 4:59:24
Lake Ridge 12 2 40N25 74w14 4:56:56
Lake Riviera 15 12 40N02 74w07 4:56:28
Lake Shawnee 14 1 40N54 74w35 4:58:20
Lakeside 16 12 41N10'54 74w20'11 4:57:21
Lakeside Park 11 1 40N11'34 74w41'15 4:58:45
Lake Stockholm 14 17 41N04 74w32 4:58:08
Lake Swannanoa 14 12 41N03 74w29 4:57:56
Lake Tamarack 19 17 41N05 74w31 4:58:04
Lake Telemark 14 12 40N57'24 74w29'54 4:58:00
Lakeview 13 12 40N11 74w35 4:58:20
Lake View 16 1 40N53'31 74w08'49 4:56:35
Lakeview Terrace 15 12 39N42'18 74w16'40 4:57:07
Lake Villa Estates 4 17 39N49 74w58 4:59:52
Lakewood 15 1 40N05'52 74w13'05 4:56:52
Lakewood Corner Estates 15 1 40N01'52 74w13'47 4:56:55
Lambertville 10 1 40N21'57 74w56'36 4:59:46
Lambs Terrace 4 1 39N46'14 75w02'35 5:00:10
Lamington 18 12 40N39'39 74w43'04 4:58:52
Landing 14 1 40N54'18 74w39'56 4:58:40
Landisville 1 17 39N31'29 74w56'19 4:59:45
Land of Pines 13 1 40N09'29 74w13'45 4:56:55
Landsdown 10 13 40N39 74w53 4:59:32
Lanes Mills 15 1 40N05'28 74w09'11 4:56:37
Lanoka Harbor 15 14 39N52'00 74w10'06 4:56:40
Lansdowne 10 13 40N36'30 74w54'24 4:59:38
Larisons Corner 10 12 40N26'29 74w51'24 4:59:26
Larrabees 13 1 40N06'52 74w11'48 4:56:47
Laurel Acres 15 12 40N02 74w07 4:56:28
Laureldale 1 17 39N29'57 74w41'08 4:58:45
Laurel Farms 10 12 40N41'35 74w46'52 4:59:07
Laurel Harbor 15 14 39N51'37 74w08'04 4:56:32
Laurel Homes 12 1 40N31 74w17 4:57:08
Laurelhurst 15 12 40N02 74w07 4:56:28
Laurel Lake 6 2 39N20'22 75w01'49 5:00:07
Laurel Manor 4 1 39N48 75w00 5:00:00
Laurel Manor 15 12 40N02 74w07 4:56:28
Laurel Park 12 2 40N27'25 74w18'50 4:57:15
Laurel Springs 4 1 39N49'12 75w00'24 5:00:02
Laurelton 15 12 40N04'07 74w07'51 4:56:31
Laurelton Acres 15 12 40N02 74w07 4:56:28
Laurelton Heights 15 12 40N02 74w07 4:56:28
Laurelton Park 15 12 40N02 74w07 4:56:28
Laurence Harbor 12 2 40N27'24 74w14'49 4:56:59
Lavallette 15 12 39N58'13 74w04'09 4:56:17
Lawnside 4 2 39N51'59 75w01'43 5:00:07
Lawrence 11 1 40N16'26 74w40'48 4:58:43
Lawrence Brook 12 12 40N25 74w23 4:57:32
Lawrence Brook Manor 12 12 40N28'20 74w24'58 4:57:40
Lawrence Corner 17 1 39N32'58 75w08'08 5:00:33
Lawrenceville 11 1 40N17'50 74w43'48 4:58:55
Layton 19 12 41N12'58 74w49'24 4:59:18
Leamings Mill 6 2 39N24'10 74w58'47 4:59:55
Lebanon 10 13 40N38'30 74w50'11 4:59:21
Lebanon Lake Estates 3 12 39N54'25 74w33'54 4:58:16
Lebanon Lakes 3 12 39N58 74w34 4:58:16
Lebanon Park 3 12 39N56 74w45 4:59:00
Ledgewood 14 14 40N52'52 74w39'23 4:58:38
Leeds Point 1 17 39N29'31 74w25'46 4:57:43
Leektown 3 8 39N37'28 74w28'03 4:57:52
Leesburg 6 17 39N15'24 74w59'16 4:59:57
Leesville 15 12 40N08'01 74w22'58 4:57:32
Legler 15 1 40N03'02 74w20'07 4:57:20
Leisuretowne 3 12 39N53'32 74w42'09 4:58:49
Leisure Village 15 1 40N02'33 74w11'07 4:56:44
Leisure World 12 12 40N21 74w26 4:57:44
Lenola 3 17 39N57'44 74w58'58 4:59:56
Leonardo 13 1 40N25'02 74w03'45 4:56:15
Leonards 8 2 39N50'32 75w12'23 5:00:50
Leonardville 13 1 40N24'22 74w02'32 4:56:10
Leonia 2 1 40N51'41 73w59'19 4:55:57
Levittown 3 1 40N03 74w53 4:59:32
Lewisburg 19 1 41N11'48 74w36'45 4:58:27
Lewistown 3 3 40N00'22 74w38'55 4:58:36
Lewisville 11 1 40N17'20 74w43'35 4:58:54
Liberty 21 12 40N52 74w57 4:59:48

Liberty Corner 18
1 40N39'53 74W34'40 4:58:19
Liberty Square 20
1 40N39'00 74W11'39 4:56:47
Libertyville 19 1 41N14'23 74W39'17 4:58:37
Lincoln 8 17 39N40'10 75W14'28 5:00:58
Lincoln Park 12
17 40N31'12 74W23'09 4:57:33
Lincroft 13 1 40N19'50 74W07'17 4:56:29
Linden 20 1 40N37'19 74W14'42 4:56:59
Lindeneau 12 17 40N32 74W22 4:57:28
Lindenwold 4 1 39N49'27 74W59'53 5:00:00
Lindy Lake 16 16 41N00 74W21 4:57:24
Linvale 10 12 40N23'35 74W50'10 4:59:21
Linwood 1 1 39N20'23 74W34'32 4:58:18
Linwood 2 1 40N51'47 73W58'05 4:55:52
Lippincotts Corner 3
1 39N55'45 74W46'39 4:59:07
Little Brook 10
12 40N44'28 74W51'41 4:59:27
Little Egg Harbor 15
2 39N37 74W21 4:57:24
Little Falls 16
17 40N52'08 74W12'31 4:56:50
Little Ferry 2 1 40N51'10 74W02'33 4:56:10
Little Rocky Hill 12
12 40N23'51 74W35'21 4:58:21
Little Silver 13
1 40N20'12 74W02'51 4:56:11
Little Silver Point 13
1 40N20'08 74W01'45 4:56:07
Littleton 14 17 40N50'36 74W27'47 4:57:51
Littletown 10 13 40N34'30 74W57'50 4:59:51
Little York 10 13 40N36'40 75W04'35 5:00:18
Livingston 7 1 40N47'45 74W18'55 4:57:16
Livingston Park 12
1 40N29 74W27 4:57:48
Llewellyn Park 7
1 40N47'15 74W14'30 4:56:58
Loantaka Estates 14
1 40N46'20 74W26'26 4:57:46
Loch Arbour 13 1 40N13'58 74W00'05 4:56:00
Locktown 10 1 40N29'05 74W58'13 4:59:53
Lockwood 19 1 40N55'14 74W43'11 4:58:53
Locust 13 2 40N23'40 74W01'36 4:56:06
Locust Corner 11
1 40N17'04 74W33'43 4:58:15
Locust Grove 4 17 39N53'31 74W57'19 4:59:49
Locust Manor 15 1 40N03'00 74W13'58 4:56:56
Locustwood 4 2 39N55'27 75W01'43 5:00:07
Lodi 2 1 40N52'56 74W05'01 4:56:20
Logan 8 10 39N48 75W21 5:01:24
Logansville 14 1 40N43'33 74W31'20 4:58:05
Lommasons Glen 21
17 40N47'39 75W05'00 5:00:20
Long Beach 15 12 39N41'08 74W08'43 4:56:35
Long Beach Park 15
17 39N42'55 74W07'49 4:56:31
Long Branch 13 1 40N18'15 73W59'34 4:55:58
Long Bridge 21 12 40N55'12 74W50'26 4:59:22
Long Hill 14 17 40N42'28 74W25'48 4:57:43
Longport 1 7 39N18'51 74W31'31 4:58:06
Long Valley 14 12 40N47'09 74W46'50 4:59:07
Longwood Lake 14
12 41N03 74W29 4:57:56
Lopatcong 21 17 40N42 75W10 5:00:40
Lores Mill 6 12 39N17'02 75W03'57 5:00:16
Lorillard Beach 13
2 40N26 74W11 4:56:44
Lorraine 20 1 40N40 74W16 4:57:04
Louden 4 17 39N46'32 74W52'30 4:59:30
Loveladies 15 17 39N43'25 74W08'03 4:56:32
Lower 5 1 38N59 74W55 4:59:40
Lower Alloways Creek 17
12 39N29 75W25 5:01:40
Lower Bank 3 8 39N36'12 74W32'54 4:58:12
Lower Berkshire Valley 14
1 40N54 74W35 4:58:20
Lower Fairmount 10
12 40N42'21 74W46'31 4:59:06
Lower Forge 3 2 39N43'29 74W40'24 4:58:42
Lower Harmony 21
17 40N44'11 75W08'28 5:00:34
Lower Longwood 14
12 40N57'53 74W33'54 4:58:16
Lower Mill 3 3 39N56'40 74W36'33 4:58:26
Lower Montville 14
1 40N54'02 74W21'54 4:57:28
Lower Squankum 13
12 40N09'31 74W09'26 4:56:38
Lower Valley 10
12 40N43'36 74W50'39 4:59:23
Low Moor 13 1 40N20'59 73W58'26 4:55:54
Lows Hollow 21 13 40N42'50 75W06'52 5:00:27
Loyds Corner 6 12 39N21'38 75W18'04 5:01:12
Lozier Park 2 1 40N57 74W02 4:56:08
Lucaston 4 17 39N49'06 74W58'04 4:59:52
Lumberton 3 1 39N57'57 74W48'20 4:59:13
Lummistown 6 12 39N21'03 75W10'46 5:00:43
Lyndhurst 2 1 40N48'43 74W07'29 4:56:30
Lynn Oaks 12 2 40N35 74W19 4:57:16
Lynn Woodoaks 12
1 40N35'20 74W20'01 4:57:20
Lyons 18 1 40N41'07 74W32'51 4:58:11
Lyonsville 14 1 40N57'24 74W26'24 4:57:46
MacArthur Manor 12
17 40N27'30 74W22'10 4:57:29
Macedonia 13 1 40N17'10 74W05'49 4:56:23
Macopin 16 16 41N03'08 74W23'21 4:57:33
Madison 14 1 40N45'35 74W25'03 4:57:40
Madison Heights 14
1 40N45'13 74W25'56 4:57:44
Madison Hill 20 1 40N36'40 74W18'33 4:57:14
Madison Park 12 2 40N27'05 74W18'30 4:57:14
Madisonville 18 1 40N43'10 74W32'27 4:58:10
Magnolia 1 12 39N35'20 74W43'27 4:58:54
Magnolia 3 3 39N56'59 74W39'40 4:58:39
Magnolia 4 2 39N51'16 75W02'22 5:00:09
Mahoneyville 17
12 39N37'56 75W30'36 5:02:02
Mahwah 2 12 41N05'19 74W08'39 4:56:35
Malaga 8 17 39N34'11 75W02'53 5:00:12
Malapardis 14 1 40N49'46 74W25'56 4:57:44
Mall 7 1 40N44 74W19 4:57:16
Manahawkin 15 1 39N41'43 74W15'33 4:57:02
Manahawkin Terrace 15
1 39N42'07 74W14'52 4:56:59
Manalapan 13 12 40N15'26 74W23'46 4:57:35
Manasquan 13 1 40N07'34 74W02'59 4:56:12
Manasquan Park 13
1 40N06'00 74W04'30 4:56:18
Manasquan Shores 13
1 40N07 74W03 4:56:12
Manchester 15 12 39N57 74W24 4:57:36
Mandalay 15 12 40N00'55 74W05'26 4:56:22
Manitou Park 15 1 39N58'20 74W11'03 4:56:44
Mannington 17 12 39N37 75W25 5:01:40
Mannington Mills 17
17 39N35'13 75W27'17 5:01:49
Manor Park 15 12 40N02 74W07 4:56:28
Mansfield 3 1 40N05'28 74W42'51 4:58:51
Mansfield Square 3
12 40N06'58 74W42'22 4:58:49
Mantoloking 13 2 40N02'21 74W03'01 4:56:12
Mantoloking Estates 15
12 40N00'25 74W03'47 4:56:15
Mantoloking Shores 15
12 40N01'05 74W03'30 4:56:14
Mantua 8 2 39N47'38 75W10'21 5:00:41
Mantua Grove 8 2 39N49'03 75W11'39 5:00:47
Mantua Heights 8
2 39N46 75W10 5:00:40
Manumuskin 6 17 39N20'06 74W57'41 4:59:51
Manunka Chunk 21
12 40N51'41 75W02'55 5:00:12
Manville 18 2 40N32'27 74W35'17 4:58:21
Maplecrest 7 1 40N44 74W16 4:57:04
Maple Grove 17 1 39N37'28 75W12'04 5:00:48
Maple Meade 12 1 40N26'37 74W28'33 4:57:54
Maple Shade 3 2 39N57'09 74W59'34 4:59:58
Maple Shade 15 1 39N58'47 74W12'27 4:56:50
Maplewood 7 1 40N46'26 74W16'26 4:57:06
Marble Hill 21 12 40N53'09 74W56'07 4:59:44
Marcella 14 12 40N59'13 74W28'29 4:57:54
Margate City 1 7 39N19'40 74W30'14 4:58:01
Mariannes Corner 10
13 40N39'11 74W54'45 4:59:39
Marion 9 1 40N44'07 74W04'28 4:56:18
Marksboro 21 16 40N59'18 74W54'28 4:59:38
Marlboro 3 17 39N54'10 74W55'20 4:59:41
Marlboro 6 1 39N29'06 75W19'42 5:01:19
Marlboro 13 1 40N18'55 74W14'48 4:56:59
Marlton 3 17 39N53'28 74W55'20 4:59:41
Marlton Heights 17
17 39N39'50 75W21'28 5:01:26
Marlton Hills 3
17 39N54 74W55 4:59:40
Marlton Lakes 3
17 39N48'32 74W53'55 4:59:36
Marlyn Manor 5 1 39N01'01 74W52'26 4:59:30
Marmora 5 17 39N16'00 74W38'43 4:58:35
Marshalls Corner 11
12 40N21'41 74W47'47 4:59:11
Marshalltown 17
12 39N38'15 75W27'13 5:01:49
Marshallville 5
12 39N17'47 74W46'08 4:59:05
Martha 3 14 39N40'55 74W30'39 4:58:03
Martins 19 1 41N11'37 74W35'40 4:58:23
Martins Beach 3 1 40N00'30 74W53'16 4:59:33
Martins Landing 12
17 40N29'35 74W24'00 4:57:36
Martinsville 18
17 40N36'04 74W33'34 4:58:14
Maryland 15 12 40N09'10 74W22'41 4:57:31
Maskells Mill 17
17 39N29'11 75W24'05 5:01:36
Masonicus 2 12 41N04'58 74W07'36 4:56:30
Masonville 3 17 39N58'42 74W52'14 4:59:29
Matawan 13 2 40N24'53 74W13'48 4:56:55
Matchaponix 12 12 40N20'18 74W22'46 4:57:31
Matthews 13 12 40N09'25 74W15'28 4:57:02
Maurer 12 1 40N32'13 74W16'10 4:57:05
Maurice River 6
17 39N13'54 75W01'45 5:00:07
Mauricetown 6 17 39N17'09 74W59'37 4:59:58
Maxim 13 1 40N09'10 74W10'55 4:56:44
Maxwell 3 14 39N40'09 74W32'47 4:58:11
Mayetta 15 2 39N40'40 74W16'24 4:57:06
Mayfair At Marlton 3
17 39N54 74W55 4:59:40
Mayfair Gardens 8
17 39N45 75W04 5:00:16
Mays Landing 1 17 39N27'08 74W43'41 4:58:55
Mayville 5 13 39N04'02 74W49'55 4:59:20
Maywood 2 1 40N54'09 74W03'44 4:56:15
McAfee 19 17 41N10'42 74W32'27 4:58:10
McCoys Corner 19
1 41N11'52 74W37'50 4:58:31
McCrea Mills 10
12 40N39'42 74W46'00 4:59:04
McDonald 3 12 39N54'24 74W32'43 4:58:11
McDonoughs 12 1 40N29 74W17 4:57:08
McGuire 3 3 40N02 74W35 4:58:20
McGuire Air Force Base 3
3 40N01 74W36 4:58:24
McKee City 1 2 39N27'01 74W38'28 4:58:34
McPherson 10 13 40N36'24 74W50'53 4:59:24
Meadford Farms 3
12 39N51'49 74W44'34 4:58:58
Meadowbrook 3 2 39N58'43 74W47'47 4:59:11
Meadowbrook 4 2 39N58'04 75W02'25 5:00:10
Meadowbrook Village 15
12 40N08 74W20 4:57:20
Meadows Terrace 11
12 40N14'32 74W36'07 4:58:24
Meadowview 9 1 40N47 74W01 4:56:04
Meadow Village 7
1 40N52'07 74W14'08 4:56:57
Mechanicsville 4
2 39N48'40 75W04'07 5:00:16
Mechanicsville 12
1 40N29'14 74W17'43 4:57:11
Mechlings Corner 10
13 40N36'37 74W59'18 4:59:57
Medford 3 17 39N54'03 74W49'26 4:59:18
Medford Farms 3
12 39N52 74W45 4:59:00
Medford Lakes 3
17 39N51'30 74W48'12 4:59:13
Melrose 3 17 39N53'55 74W51'11 4:59:25
Melrose 12 1 40N29'27 74W17'50 4:57:11
Menantico 6 2 39N21'39 74W59'31 4:59:58
Mendham 14 14 40N46'33 74W36'04 4:58:24
Menlo Park 12 17 40N33'54 74W20'16 4:57:21
Menlo Park Mall 12
17 40N32 74W22 4:57:28
Menlo Park Terrace 12
17 40N33'09 74W19'26 4:57:18
Mercerville 11 1 40N14'13 74W41'13 4:58:45
Merchantville 4 2 39N56'50 75W04'01 5:00:16
Meriden 14 1 40N56'50 74W27'29 4:57:50
Merrygold 3 17 39N36'22 74W27'03 4:57:48
Metedeconk 15 12 40N03'24 74W05'02 4:56:20
Metedeconk Park 15
12 40N02 74W07 4:56:28
Metedeconk Pines 15
12 40N02 74W07 4:56:28
Mettler 18 1 40N29'57 74W32'32 4:58:10
Metuchen 12 17 40N32'35 74W21'49 4:57:27
Meyersville 14 17 40N41'23 74W28'15 4:57:53
Miami Beach 5 12 39N02'04 74W56'14 4:59:45
Mickles Mill 17 1 39N29'36 75W20'35 5:01:22
Mickleton 8 2 39N47'24 75W14'17 5:00:57
Middle 5 13 39N04 74W51 4:59:24
Middlebush 18 1 40N29'51 74W31'47 4:58:07
Middlesex 12 17 40N34'21 74W29'35 4:57:58
Middlesex Downs 12
12 40N17'15 74W24'15 4:57:37
Middletown 5 12 39N16'16 74W44'38 4:58:59
Middletown 13 12 40N23'39 74W07'03 4:56:28
Middletown 14 1 40N54'57 74W30'50 4:58:03
Middle Valley 14
12 40N45'38 74W49'15 4:59:17
Middleville 19 12 41N03'21 74W51'48 4:59:27
Midland Park 2 2 40N59'21 74W08'28 4:56:34
Midstreams 15 12 40N02 74W07 4:56:28
Midtown 7 1 40N44 74W11 4:56:44
Midvale 16 1 41N02 74W18 4:57:12
Midwood 15 12 40N05'50 74W25'07 4:57:40
Mile Hollow 3 1 40N09'39 74W42'01 4:58:48
Milford 10 12 40N34'07 75W05'42 5:00:23
Military Ocean Terminal 9
1 40N40 74W07 4:56:28
Millbridge 4 1 39N48'25 75W02'04 5:00:08
Mill Brook 14 1 40N51'52 74W33'28 4:58:14
Millbrook 21 12 41N04'24 74W57'48 4:59:51
Millbrook Park 3
1 40N01'30 74W53'22 4:59:33
Millburn 7 1 40N44'22 74W18'16 4:57:13
Millhurst 13 12 40N15'13 74W20'31 4:57:22
Millington 14 12 40N40'38 74W31'05 4:58:04
Millside Heights 3
17 40N00'26 74W57'12 4:59:49
Millstone 12 12 40N17'17 74W31'55 4:58:08
Millstone 18 12 40N29'57 74W35'21 4:58:21
Milltown 10 12 40N27'12 75W01'30 5:00:06
Milltown 12 1 40N27'22 74W26'37 4:57:46
Milltown 14 12 40N46'47 74W43'15 4:58:53
Milltown 17 17 39N38'09 75W17'11 5:01:09
Milltown 18 2 40N34'07 74W41'00 4:58:44
Milltown 20 1 40N42'07 74W19'01 4:57:16
Millville 6 2 39N24'07 75W02'23 5:00:10
Millville 19 12 41N18'47 74W46'49 4:59:07
Milmay 1 12 39N26'21 74W51'26 4:59:26
Milton 14 12 41N01'17 74W32'10 4:58:09
Mimosa Lake 3 17 39N54 74W55 4:59:40
Mine Brook 18 12 40N41'35 74W36'27 4:68:26
Mine Hill 14 14 40N52'40 74W35'39 4:58:23
Minotola 1 17 39N31'07 74W56'55 4:59:48
Miramar 5 17 39N16 74W39 4:58:36
Mizpah 1 12 39N29'12 74W50'10 4:59:21
Moe 16 12 41N09'44 74W23'13 4:57:33
Moerls Corner 12
12 40N21'38 74W19'04 4:57:16
Money Island 15 1 39N56 74W13 4:56:52
Monitor 9 1 40N47 74W01 4:56:04
Monks 16 12 41N07'22 74W18'00 4:57:12
Monksville 16 1 41N02 74W18 4:57:12
Monmouth 13 1 40N19 74W04 4:56:16
Monmouth Beach 13
2 40N19'49 73W58'55 4:55:56
Monmouth Heights at Manalapa 13
1 40N18'03 74W17'38 4:57:11
Monmouth Heights at Marlboro 13
1 40N19'40 74W14'37 4:56:58
Monmouth Hills 13
1 40N24'11 74W00'08 4:56:01
Monmouth Junction 12
12 40N22'44 74W32'49 4:58:11
Monmouth Park 13
1 40N19 74W01 4:56:04
Monroe 14 1 40N48'46 74W26'34 4:57:46
Monroe 19 17 41N06'52 74W38'04 4:58:32
Monroeville 17 1 39N37'44 75W09'35 5:00:38
Montague 19 12 41N18'11 74W47'38 4:59:11
Montana 21 17 40N45'54 75W04'04 5:00:16
Montclair 7 1 40N49'33 74W12'34 4:56:50
Montclair Heights 7
1 40N51'27 74W12'10 4:56:49
Monterey Beach 15
12 39N59'05 74W04'04 4:56:16
Montgomery 18 12 40N28'42 74W45'15 4:59:01
Montrose 13 1 40N18'06 74W13'18 4:56:53
Montvale 2 1 41N02'48 74W01'24 4:56:06
Montville 14 1 40N54'53 74W23'03 4:57:32
Moonachie 2 1 40N50'28 74W02'44 4:56:11
Moore 11 12 40N19'27 74W54'54 4:59:40
Moores Corner 17
17 39N33'16 75W28'00 5:01:52
Moores Meadows 3
12 39N56 74W45 4:59:00
Moores Mill 3 12 39N51'41 74W43'32 4:58:54
Moorestown 3 17 39N58'01 74W56'35 4:59:46
Morehousetown 7 1 40N47'48 74W20'29 4:57:22
Morgan 12 1 40N28'00 74W16'07 4:57:04
Morgan Heights 12
1 40N27'45 74W15'49 4:57:03

Morgan Village 4
2 39N54'45 75W06'46 5:00:27
Morganville 13 2 40N22'35 74W14'41 4:56:59
Morrell Corners 13
2 40N24'40 74W11'27 4:56:46
Morris 4 2 39N59'14 75W02'41 5:00:11
Morris 14 17 40N48 74W29 4:57:56
Morris Beach 1 17 39N18'30 74W38'13 4:58:33
Morris Park 21 17 40N41 75W10 5:00:40
Morris Plains 14
17 40N49'18 74W28'53 4:57:56
Morristown 12 2 40N25'30 74W15'15 4:57:01
Morristown 14 17 40N47'48 74W28'55 4:57:56
Morrisville 4 2 39N58'20 75W02'57 5:00:12
Morsemere 2 1 40N50'34 74W00'18 4:56:01
Morses Creek 20 1 40N38 74W15 4:57:00
Mount 3 8 39N41'07 74W36'22 4:58:25
Mountain Lake 21
17 40N50 75W05 5:00:20
Mountain Lakes 14
1 40N53'41 74W26'00 4:57:44
Mountainside 20 1 40N40'20 74W21'28 4:57:26
Mountain Spring 16
16 41N02 74W23 4:57:32
Mountain Spring Lakes 16
16 41N00 74W21 4:57:24
Mountain Station 7
2 40N45 74W16 4:57:04
Mountain View 16
17 40N55'04 74W15'59 4:57:04
Mountainville 10
13 40N41'26 74W48'43 4:59:15
Mount Airy 10 12 40N23'55 74W54'27 4:59:38
Mount Arlington 14
12 40N55'33 74W38'07 4:58:32
Mount Bethel 18
12 40N38'15 74W30'54 4:58:04
Mount Bethel 21 1 40N49'34 74W54'06 4:59:36
Mount Ephraim 4 2 39N52'42 75W05'35 5:00:22
Mount Fern 14 14 40N51'56 74W34'44 4:58:19
Mount Freedom 14
14 40N49'34 74W34'14 4:58:17
Mount Hermon 21
16 40N55'29 74W59'39 4:59:59
Mount Holly 3 1 39N59'34 74W47'17 4:59:09
Mount Hope 14 1 40N55'34 74W32'35 4:58:10
Mount Hope Mineral Junction 14
1 40N54 74W35 4:58:20
Mount Horeb 18 17 40N37'06 74W33'43 4:58:15
Mount Joy 10 13 40N35'13 75W11'14 5:00:45
Mount Laurel 3 17 39N56'02 74W53'29 4:59:34
Mount Lebanon 10
13 40N45'25 74W52'05 4:59:28
Mount Misery 3 12 39N55'11 74W31'24 4:58:06
Mount Olive 14 1 40N51'05 74W44'00 4:58:56
Mount Pisgah 19
17 41N09'03 74W45'56 4:59:04
Mount Pleasant 1
12 39N24'05 74W30'48 4:58:03
Mount Pleasant 2
1 41N01'40 74W05'08 4:56:21
Mount Pleasant 5
12 39N13'15 74W46'46 4:59:07
Mount Pleasant 10
12 40N34'48 75W03'01 5:00:12
Mount Pleasant 13
12 40N22'27 74W13'03 4:56:52
Mount Pleasant 21
12 40N58'00 75W04'35 5:00:18
Mount Rose 11 12 40N22'09 74W44'22 4:58:57
Mount Royal 8 2 39N48'36 75W12'42 5:00:51
Mount Salem 10 13 40N36'29 74W59'06 4:59:56
Mount Salem 19 1 41N18'52 74W36'59 4:58:28
Mounts Mills 12
12 40N19'32 74W21'41 4:57:27
Mount Tabor 14 12 40N53 74W29 4:57:56
Mount Vernon 21
12 40N59'43 75W01'59 5:00:08
Mowers 17 17 39N35'12 75W21'47 5:01:27
Muhlenberg 20 2 40N37 74W25 4:57:40
Muirhead 10 12 40N27'05 74W51'34 4:59:26
Mullica 1 12 39N36 74W42 4:58:48
Mullica Hill 8 17 39N44'21 75W13'28 5:00:54
Munion Field 15 2 39N39'52 74W23'32 4:57:34
Murphy 4 2 39N39'16 74W49'57 4:59:20
Murray Grove 15
14 39N51'25 74W10'41 4:56:43
Murray Hill 20 1 40N41'43 74W24'05 4:57:36
Myrtle Grove 19
12 41N06'26 74W47'23 4:59:10
Mystic Islands 15
2 39N32'39 74W22'58 4:57:32
Natco 13 2 40N26'23 74W09'35 4:56:38
National Park 8 2 39N51'57 75W10'45 5:00:43
Naughright 14 12 40N47'48 74W44'46 4:58:59
Navesink 13 1 40N23'58 74W02'09 4:56:09
Navesink Beach 13
1 40N23'22 73W58'33 4:55:54
Necombtown 6 2 39N23'55 75W03'05 5:00:12
Nejecho Beach 15
12 40N02 74W07 4:56:28
Nelsonville 13 12 40N10'13 74W32'07 4:58:08
Neptune 13 1 40N13 74W02 4:56:08
Neptune City 15 1 40N12'00 74W01'42 4:56:07
Nesco 1 2 39N38'17 74W41'49 4:58:47
Neshanic 18 2 40N29'52 74W43'13 4:58:53
Neshanic Station 18
2 40N30'29 74W43'50 4:58:55
Netcong 14 1 40N53'56 74W42'25 4:58:50
Netherwood 20 2 40N37'50 74W24'45 4:57:39
New Albany 3 2 40N00'05 74W58'18 4:59:53
Newark 7 1 40N44'08 74W10'22 4:56:41
Newark Heights 7
1 40N44'03 74W15'30 4:57:02
Newbakers Corners 21
16 40N59 74W57 4:59:48
New Bedford 13 1 40N10'45 74W03'45 4:56:15
Newbolds Corner 3
1 39N57'47 74W46'48 4:59:07
New Bridge 2 1 40N55'00 74W01'43 4:56:07
New Brooklyn 8 1 39N41'35 74W56'35 4:59:46
New Brunswick 12
1 40N29'10 74W27'08 4:57:49
New Brunswick Heights 12
1 40N34 74W27 4:57:48
New Canton 13 12 40N11'13 74W34'01 4:58:16
New Dover 12 1 40N35'06 74W20'37 4:57:22
New Durham 9 1 40N47'05 74W02'00 4:56:08
New Durham 12 1 40N32'37 74W24'23 4:57:38
New Egypt 15 12 40N04'03 74W31'52 4:58:07
New England Crossroads 6
1 39N21'40 75W13'32 5:00:54
Newfield 8 17 39N32'47 75W01'31 5:00:06
Newfoundland 16
12 41N02'47 74W26'08 4:57:45
New Freedom 4 17 39N45'31 74W55'37 4:59:42
New Freedom 17 1 39N39'19 75W11'25 5:00:46
New Gretna 3 17 39N35'32 74W27'05 4:57:48
New Hampton 10 13 40N43'19 74W57'38 4:59:51
New Hanover 3 3 40N03 74W34 4:58:16
New Italy 6 1 39N27'35 74W56'14 4:59:45
New Jersey & New York Jct 2
1 40N50 74W06 4:56:24
New Lisbon 3 3 39N57'29 74W37'42 4:58:31
New Market 12 1 40N34'27 74W27'10 4:57:49
New Milford 2 1 40N56'06 74W01'10 4:56:05
New Monmouth 13 1 40N24'43 74W06'13 4:56:25
Newport 6 12 39N17'48 75W10'37 5:00:42
Newport 10 13 40N43'30 74W54'34 4:59:38
Newport Landing 6
12 39N17'23 75W11'52 5:00:47
New Providence 20
1 40N41'54 74W24'07 4:57:36
New Sharon 8 17 39N48'30 75W07'45 5:00:31
New Sharon 13 12 40N12'22 74W33'03 4:58:12
New Shrewsbury 13
1 40N19'50 74W05'25 4:56:22
Newstead 7 1 40N45'09 74W16'42 4:57:07
Newstead North 7
1 40N45'34 74W16'22 4:57:05
Newton 19 12 41N03'29 74W45'11 4:59:01
Newton Heights 12
12 40N25'58 74W23'54 4:57:36
Newtonville 1 17 39N33'32 74W51'59 4:59:28
Newtown 12 1 40N33'07 74W27'39 4:57:51
New Vernon 14 12 40N44'43 74W29'52 4:57:59
New Village 21 13 40N43'02 75W04'58 5:00:20
New York & Greenwood Lake Jc 9
1 40N46 74W09 4:56:36
Nixon 12 17 40N30'51 74W22'04 4:57:28
Norburys Landing 5
12 39N03'01 74W55'41 4:59:43
Norma 17 1 39N29'46 75W05'18 5:00:21
Normandie 13 1 40N22'47 73W58'32 4:55:54
Normandy Beach 15
12 40N00'09 74W03'39 4:56:15
Normandy Harbor 15
12 40N00 74W04 4:56:16
Normanook 19 17 41N11'12 74W48'10 4:59:13
North 7 1 40N46 74W10 4:56:40
North Arlington 2
1 40N47'18 74W08'01 4:56:32
North Asbury Park 13
1 40N14 74W01 4:56:04
North Beach 15 17 39N37 74W12 4:56:48
North Beach Haven 15
17 39N34'23 74W13'55 4:56:56
North Bergen 9 1 40N48'15 74W00'45 4:56:03
North Branch 18 2 40N36'07 74W40'40 4:58:43
North Brunswick 12
1 40N29 74W27 4:57:48
North Caldwell 7
1 40N52 74W16 4:57:04
North Cape May 5
1 38N58'55 74W57'30 4:59:50
North Cedarville 6
12 39N20 75W12 5:00:48
North Center 7 1 40N48 74W11 4:56:44
North Centerville 13
2 40N25'30 74W09'40 4:56:39
North Church 19
17 41N06 74W35 4:58:20
North Church Estates 19
17 41N09 74W35 4:58:20
North Crosswicks 11
1 40N09'32 74W38'53 4:58:36
North Dennis 5 12 39N12'04 74W51'16 4:59:25
North Edison 12
17 40N36'00 74W22'40 4:57:31
North Elizabeth 20
1 40N40 74W13 4:56:52
Northfield 1 2 39N22'13 74W33'02 4:58:12
Northfield 7 1 40N46'27 74W19'30 4:57:18
North Hackensack 2
1 40N54'53 74W02'20 4:56:09
North Haledon 16
4 40N57'18 74W11'11 4:56:45
North Hanover 3
12 40N04 74W24 4:57:36
North Hawthorne 16
4 40N55 74W10 4:56:40
North Highlands Beach 5
12 39N00'54 74W56'41 4:59:47
North Long Branch 13
1 40N18'47 73W59'04 4:55:56
North Merchantville 4
2 39N57 75W03 5:00:12
Northmont 4 2 39N53'00 75W05'43 5:00:23
North Plainfield 18
2 40N37'48 74W25'40 4:57:43
North Port Norris 6
12 39N16'07 75W01'38 5:00:07
North Princeton 11
2 40N21'50 74W39'41 4:58:39
Northrup 19 17 41N08'10 74W43'03 4:58:52
North Stelton 12
1 40N32'13 74W25'17 4:57:41
Northvale 2 12 41N00'23 73W56'58 4:55:48
Northville 6 1 39N30'40 75W12'17 5:00:49
North Vineland 6
1 39N31'34 75W01'22 5:00:05
North Wildwood 5
1 39N00'02 74W47'59 4:59:12
Northwood 4 2 39N54'57 74W59'03 4:59:56
Northwood 19 12 40N58'19 74W38'10 4:58:33
North Woodbury 8
1 39N51'15 75W08'11 5:00:33
Norton 10 13 40N39'26 74W58'53 4:59:55
Nortonville 8 10 39N47'07 75W24'23 5:01:38
Norwood 2 17 40N59'53 73W57'44 4:55:51
Nottingham 11 1 40N13'57 74W40'56 4:58:44
Nugentown 15 2 39N36'41 74W21'21 4:57:25
Nummytown 5 12 39N01'30 74W53'48 4:59:35
Nutley 7 5 40N49'20 74W09'37 4:56:38
Oakdale 3 1 40N00 74W47 4:59:08
Oak Glen 13 12 40N10'09 74W11'52 4:56:47
Oak Glen 15 12 39N59'10 74W09'00 4:56:36
Oak Grove 10 1 40N32'03 74W57'17 4:59:49
Oak Hill 13 12 40N22'00 74W08'05 4:56:32
Oak Hill 15 1 40N00'47 74W08'33 4:56:34
Oakhurst 13 1 40N16'15 74W01'00 4:56:04
Oakhurst Manor 13
1 40N15'37 74W00'45 4:56:03
Oak Island Junction 7
1 40N42'44 74W08'47 4:56:35
Oakland 2 17 41N00'47 74W15'53 4:57:04
Oakland 17 17 39N35'55 75W20'30 5:01:22
Oakland Mills 13
12 40N13'59 74W20'41 4:57:23
Oaklyn 4 2 39N54'03 75W05'06 5:00:20
Oak Ridge 15 1 39N58'23 74W13'30 4:56:54
Oak Ridge 16 12 41N02'46 74W29'11 4:57:57
Oak Ridge Lake 14
12 41N03 74W29 4:57:56
Oak Shade 3 12 39N52'09 74W44'00 4:58:56
Oak Shades 13 2 40N25 74W14 4:56:56
Oak Tree 12 17 40N34'40 74W22'37 4:57:30
Oak Valley 8 2 39N48'04 75W09'46 5:00:39
Oakville 1 12 39N21'43 74W45'25 4:59:02
Oakwood 3 17 39N53 74W49 4:59:16
Oakwood 15 12 40N08'28 74W15'29 4:57:02
Oakwood Beach 17
17 39N33'18 75W31'08 5:02:05
Oakwood Lakes 3
17 39N52'22 74W49'55 4:59:20
Oakwood Park 20 1 40N42'34 74W24'26 4:57:38
Ocean 13 1 40N14 74W01 4:56:04
Ocean Beach 15 12 39N58'53 74W04'00 4:56:16
Ocean City 5 1 39N16'39 74W34'30 4:58:18
Ocean Gate 15 12 39N55'36 74W08'03 4:56:32
Ocean Grove 13 1 40N12'43 74W00'25 4:56:02
Ocean Heights 1 1 39N19'45 74W35'16 4:58:21
Oceanic 13 1 40N22'40 74W00'40 4:56:03
Oceanport 13 1 40N19'05 74W00'56 4:56:04
Ocean View 5 2 39N10'35 74W44'02 4:58:56
Oceanville 1 2 39N28'16 74W27'39 4:57:51
Ogden 8 2 39N48'42 75W12'09 5:00:49
Ogdensburg 19 17 41N04'54 74W35'34 4:58:22
Old Bridge 12 12 40N24'53 74W21'57 4:57:28
Old Charleston Woods 4
2 39N49 75W06 5:00:24
Old Forge Village 14
17 40N48 74W29 4:57:56
Old Manor 13 2 40N26 74W13 4:56:52
Oldmans 17 1 39N45'24 75W25'50 5:01:43
Old Mill Farms 11
2 40N18'54 74W36'15 4:58:25
Old Orchard 4 2 39N49 75W06 5:00:24
Old Tappan 2 1 41N00'38 73W59'30 4:55:58
Oldwick 10 12 40N40'21 74W44'52 4:58:59
Oliphants Mills 3
17 39N53'06 74W50'00 4:59:20
Olivet 17 1 39N32'53 75W09'18 5:00:37
Ong 3 3 39N54'39 74W37'16 4:58:29
Oradell 2 1 40N57'31 74W02'14 4:56:09
Orange 7 1 40N46'14 74W13'59 4:56:56
Orchard Center 6
1 39N28'37 75W13'04 5:00:52
Orchard Estates 13
1 40N17'00 74W14'50 4:56:59
Orchard Heights 12
12 40N26'13 74W24'12 4:57:37
Orchard View 3 1 40N03'57 74W52'28 4:59:30
Ordmont 17 1 39N44'27 75W27'32 5:01:50
Oriental 3 12 39N48'56 74W43'39 4:58:55
Ormond 6 2 39N19'42 74W57'12 4:59:49
Orston 4 2 39N53 75W04 5:00:16
Ortley Beach 15
12 39N57'14 74W04'19 4:56:17
Ortley Terrace 15
12 39N57'28 74W04'09 4:56:17
Osage 4 2 39N51'01 75W00'26 5:00:02
Osbornes Mills 13
1 40N09'13 74W03'33 4:56:14
Osborn Mills 14 1 40N43'18 74W31'52 4:58:07
Osbornsville 15
12 40N02'18 74W06'29 4:56:26
Othello 6 1 39N24'45 75W20'50 5:01:23
Outcalt 12 12 40N22'38 74W24'28 4:57:38
Outwater 2 1 40N53 74W06 4:56:24
Overbrook 4 1 39N49'04 74W59'18 4:59:57
Overbrook 7 1 40N51 74W14 4:56:56
Overlook 20 1 40N42'45 74W21'07 4:57:24
Owens 19 1 41N15'49 74W31'42 4:58:07
Oxford 21 17 40N48'11 74W59'24 4:59:58
Oyster Creek 1 17 39N30'15 74W25'01 4:57:40
Packanack Lake 16
17 40N56'33 74W15'24 4:57:02
Pages Corner 13
12 40N12'48 74W35'01 4:58:20
Pahaquarry 21 16 41N59'06 75W07'53 5:00:32
Palatine 17 1 39N33'12 75W10'53 5:00:44
Palermo 5 17 39N14'24 74W40'22 4:58:41
Palisade 2 1 40N51 73W58 4:55:52
Palisades Park 2
1 40N50'53 73W59'53 4:56:00
Palmyra 3 2 40N00'25 75W01'43 5:00:07
Palmyra 10 13 40N33'41 75W00'56 5:00:04
Pamrapo 9 1 40N40 74W07 4:56:28
Pancoast 1 17 39N31'21 74W52'16 4:59:29
Panther Lake 19
12 40N59 74W45 4:59:00
Papakating 19 1 41N11'38 74W35'20 4:58:21
Paradise 8 2 39N50'21 75W13'21 5:00:53
Paradise Lakes 17
17 39N31'35 75W20'21 5:01:21
Paramus 2 1 40N56'40 74W04'33 4:56:18
Park 16 4 40N55 74W09 4:56:36

Parkdale 4 12 39N43'16 74w45'37 4:59:02
Parker 14 12 40N45'30 74w45'31 4:59:02
Parkers Landing 8
2 39N48'45 75w12'35 5:00:50
Parkers Landing 15
2 39N35'23 74w20'23 4:57:22
Parkertown 15 2 39N37'37 74w18'55 4:57:16
Park Ridge 2 1 41N02'15 74w02'28 4:56:10
Park Ridge Farms 3
1 40N09 74w42 4:58:48
Parkside 4 2 39N55'42 75w05'49 5:00:23
Parkside 21 17 40N41 75w10 5:00:40
Park Village 20 1 40N39'05 74w17'28 4:57:10
Parkville 8 1 39N48'53 75w10'57 5:00:44
Parkway Manor 15
1 39N57'25 74w12'55 4:56:52
Parkway Pines 13
1 40N06'10 74w09'00 4:56:36
Parkway Village 11
1 40N15'33 74w47'20 4:59:09
Parlin 12 2 40N27'43 74w20'19 4:57:21
Parry 3 2 39N59'15 75w00'37 5:00:02
Parsippany 14 1 40N51'28 74w25'35 4:57:42
Parsonville 3 1 40N10'11 74w41'50 4:58:47
Pasadena 15 12 39N57 74w23 4:57:32
Passaic 16 1 40N51'24 74w07'44 4:56:31
Passaic Junction 2
1 40N54'08 74w06'16 4:56:25
Passaic Park 16 1 40N52 74w08 4:56:32
Paterson 16 4 40N55'00 74w10'20 4:56:41
Patricks Corners 12
1 40N25'26 74w28'38 4:57:55
Pattenburg 10 13 40N38'10 75w01'00 5:00:04
Paulas Corners 12
1 40N24'54 74w27'53 4:57:52
Paulding 17 17 39N36'33 75w17'02 5:01:08
Paulina 21 16 40N56'35 74w56'39 4:59:47
Paulins Kill 19
12 41N03'29 74w49'25 4:59:18
Paulsboro 8 2 39N49'49 75w14'27 5:00:58
Pavonia 4 1 39N57'03 75w05'15 5:00:21
Paynters Crossing 6
12 39N18'23 75w07'19 5:00:29
Peahala Park 15
17 39N36'07 74w12'43 4:56:51
Peapack 18 12 40N43'00 74w39'25 4:58:38
Pebble Beach 15 1 39N45'55 74w11'50 4:56:47
Pecks Corner 17 1 39N30'24 75w20'56 5:01:24
Pedricktown 17 17 39N46'02 75w24'54 5:01:40
Peermont 5 2 39N06 74w44 4:58:56
Pelican Island 15
12 39N57 74w05 4:56:20
Pellettown 19 17 41N09'41 74w40'30 4:58:42
Pemberton 3 3 39N58'19 74w41'00 4:58:44
Pemberton Heights 3
3 39N57'45 74w40'45 4:58:43
Penbryn 4 17 39N45'45 74w56'35 4:59:46
Pennington 11 12 40N19'42 74w47'28 4:59:10
Penn Place 3 1 39N44'33 74w28'09 4:57:53
Pennsauken 4 2 39N57 75w03 5:00:12
Penns Beach 17 12 39N38'31 75w31'40 5:02:07
Penns Grove 17 1 39N43'46 75w28'06 5:01:52
Penns Neck 11 2 40N19'56 74w38'14 4:58:33
Pennsville 17 12 39N39'12 75w31'01 5:02:04
Pennypacker Park 3
17 40N01'54 74w53'59 4:59:36
Penny Pot 1 2 39N34'19 74w49'21 4:59:17
Penton 17 17 39N34'42 75w24'07 5:01:36
Penwell 10 12 40N46'41 74w54'10 4:59:37
Peppermill Farms 4
2 39N49 75w06 5:00:24
Pequannock 14 17 40N57'08 74w17'57 4:57:12
Pequest 21 17 40N49'47 74w58'37 4:59:54
Perkintown 17 17 39N44'00 75w25'23 5:01:42
Perrineville 13 2 40N13'42 74w26'28 4:57:46
Perryville 10 13 40N38'09 74w58'11 4:59:53
Perth Amboy 12 1 40N30'24 74w15'57 4:57:04
Perth Amboy Junction 20
2 40N35'53 74w17'09 4:57:09
Pestletown 4 2 39N42'15 74w49'09 4:59:17
Petersburg 5 17 39N15'13 74w43'37 4:58:54
Petersburg 14 12 41N00'29 74w31'28 4:58:06
Petersburg 21 1 40N52'46 74w51'29 4:59:26
Pettys Island 4 2 39N58 75w03 5:00:12
Phalanx 13 12 40N19'03 74w08'18 4:56:33
Pheasant Run 3 2 39N59'35 74w57'50 4:59:51
Philips Mills 13
2 40N25'22 74w08'03 4:56:32
Phillipsburg 21
17 40N41'37 75w11'26 5:00:46
Phoenix 12 17 40N28'40 74w18'48 4:57:15
Picatinny 14 1 40N53 74w34 4:58:16
Pierce Heights 10
13 40N39'47 74w53'05 4:59:32
Pierces 5 12 39N03'55 74w53'55 4:59:36
Pierces Point 5
13 39N05'02 74w54'21 4:59:37
Piersonville 3 12 40N12 74w40 4:58:40
Pilesgrove 17 17 39N39 75w19 5:01:16
Pill Hill 18 1 40N42'02 74w35'28 4:58:22
Pine Acres 8 2 39N48 75w08 5:00:32
Pine Acres 15 1 40N02'31 74w11'38 4:56:47
Pine Beach 15 1 39N56'09 74w10'17 4:56:41
Pine Brook 13 1 40N16'50 74w05'45 4:56:23
Pine Brook 14 1 40N51'37 74w20'27 4:57:22
Pine Cliff Lake 16
12 41N08 74w22 4:57:28
Pine Crest 3 14 39N47'47 74w34'53 4:58:20
Pine Grove 3 17 39N53'01 74w52'49 4:59:31
Pine Hill 4 17 39N47'03 74w59'33 4:59:58
Pinehurst 1 2 39N28'42 74w33'00 4:58:12
Pine Island 17 17 39N25'13 75w25'32 5:01:42
Pine Lake Park 15
1 40N00'11 74w15'25 4:57:02
Pine Lane 3 3 40N01'50 74w41'18 4:58:45
Pines Lake 16 17 40N59'30 74w15'45 4:57:03
Pine Tavern 17 17 39N39'42 75w12'37 5:00:50
Pine Terrace 15 1 40N00'29 74w07'15 4:56:29
Pine Valley 4 1 39N47'08 74w58'32 4:59:54
Pinewald 15 12 39N53'44 74w10'24 4:56:42
Piney Hollow 8 17 39N35'16 74w55'40 4:59:43
Pinkneyville 19
12 41N02'47 74w41'34 4:58:46
Pipers Corner 3
17 39N49'58 74w47'01 4:59:08
Piscataway 12 17 40N29'57 74w23'58 4:57:36
Pitman 8 2 39N43'58 75w07'55 5:00:32
Pittsgrove 17 12 39N32 75w08 5:00:32
Pittstown 10 13 40N34'55 74w57'34 4:59:50
Plainfield 20 2 40N38'01 74w24'28 4:57:38
Plains 19 17 41N08'26 74w42'08 4:58:49
Plainsboro 12 2 40N20'00 74w36'03 4:58:24
Plainville 8 12 39N35'33 75w00'57 5:00:04
Plainville 18 2 40N27'58 74w40'57 4:58:44
Plauderville 2 1 40N53 74w06 4:56:24
Plaza Park 3 1 40N04'04 74w52'33 4:59:30
Pleasantdale 7 1 40N48'37 74w15'39 4:57:03
Pleasant Grove 14
12 40N46'47 74w51'04 4:59:24
Pleasant Grove 15
12 40N07'28 74w20'36 4:57:22
Pleasant Hill 14
12 40N48'39 74w41'46 4:58:47
Pleasant Mills 3
2 39N38'23 74w39'42 4:58:39
Pleasant Plains 12
12 40N26'52 74w33'30 4:58:14
Pleasant Plains 14
12 40N41'51 74w29'51 4:57:59
Pleasant Plains 15
1 40N00'12 74w12'50 4:56:51
Pleasant Run 3 2 40N00 75w00 5:00:00
Pleasant Run 10 1 40N33'41 74w47'36 4:59:10
Pleasant Terrace 6
12 39N13 74w57 4:59:48
Pleasant Valley 13
12 40N22'00 74w12'48 4:56:51
Pleasant Valley 14
14 40N44'55 74w37'54 4:58:32
Pleasant Valley 21
13 40N45'05 75w00'31 5:00:02
Pleasant Valley Crossroads 13
12 40N20'43 74w11'43 4:56:47
Pleasantview 18 2 40N28'39 74w39'21 4:58:37
Pleasantville 1 2 39N23'23 74w31'28 4:58:06
Pleasantville 6 1 39N32'40 75w02'58 5:00:12
Pleasantville 14
12 40N43'59 74w29'17 4:57:57
Pleasure Bay 13 1 40N18 74w00 4:56:00
Pluckemin 18 12 40N38'44 74w38'22 4:58:33
Plumbsock 19 1 41N13'07 74w40'16 4:58:41
Plumsted 15 12 40N05 74w30 4:58:00
Pohatcong 21 17 40N40 75w10 5:00:40
Point Airy 17 17 39N40'35 75w19'11 5:01:17
Point Breeze 10 1 40N30'22 74w57'53 4:59:52
Pointers 17 17 39N35'38 75w26'44 5:01:47
Point of Woods 4
17 39N54'34 74w57'28 4:59:50
Point Pleasant 15
2 40N04'59 74w04'07 4:56:16
Point Pleasant 19
1 40N55'22 74w39'29 4:58:38
Point Pleasant Beach 15
2 40N05'28 74w02'54 4:56:12
Pointville 3 12 40N00'13 74w36'12 4:58:25
Pole Tavern 17 1 39N37'00 75w13'46 5:00:55
Polhemustown 13
12 40N09'02 74w32'53 4:58:12
Polktown 10 13 40N40'17 74w56'45 4:59:47
Polkville 21 12 40N56'19 75w03'06 5:00:12
Pomona 1 17 39N28'42 74w34'32 4:58:18
Pompton 16 1 40N59'29 74w16'48 4:57:07
Pompton Junction 16
1 41N00'13 74w18'02 4:57:12
Pompton Lakes 16
1 41N00'19 74w17'28 4:57:10
Pompton Plains 14
1 40N58'05 74w17'46 4:57:11
Porches Mill 8 17 39N42'01 75w19'59 5:01:20
Porchtown 8 17 39N35'40 75w05'00 5:00:20
Port-au-Peck 13 1 40N18'54 74w00'30 4:56:02
Port Colden 21 13 40N45'47 74w57'15 4:59:49
Port Elizabeth 6
17 39N18'48 74w58'53 4:59:56
Portertown 17 17 39N36'49 75w21'12 5:01:25
Port Johnson 9 1 40N39'08 74w07'00 4:56:28
Port Mercer 11 2 40N18'15 74w41'07 4:58:44
Port Monmouth 13
17 40N25'48 74w05'56 4:56:24
Port Morris 14 1 40N54'18 74w41'07 4:58:44
Port Murray 21 12 40N47'08 74w54'59 4:59:40
Port Norris 6 12 39N14'45 75w02'08 5:00:09
Port Reading 12 1 40N33'55 74w15'39 4:57:03
Port Republic 1 2 39N31'14 74w29'10 4:57:57
Port Warren 21 13 40N41'41 75w08'27 5:00:34
Possumtown 12 1 40N33'16 74w29'31 4:57:58
Post Corner 11 12 40N16'58 74w38'15 4:58:33
Postville 16 12 41N05'18 74w24'57 4:57:40
Potato Island 5
13 39N05'00 74w51'45 4:59:27
Potters 12 17 40N35'37 74w21'42 4:57:27
Potterstown 10 13 40N38'32 74w47'56 4:59:12
Pottersville 18
12 40N42'49 74w43'20 4:58:53
Powerville 14 1 40N55'17 74w25'38 4:57:43
Prallsville 10 12 40N24'42 74w59'13 4:59:57
Preakness 16 17 40N55'49 74w13'41 4:56:55
Presidential Lake Estates 3
12 39N54'59 74w33'55 4:58:16
Presidential Lakes 3
12 39N58 74w34 4:58:16
Princessville 11
2 40N17'33 74w42'29 4:58:50
Princeton 11 2 40N20'55 74w39'34 4:58:38
Princeton Colonial Park 11
12 40N18'07 74w37'10 4:58:29
Princeton Estates 11
12 40N17'53 74w36'46 4:58:27
Princeton Ivy East 11
12 40N18'00 74w36'24 4:58:26
Princeton Junction 11
2 40N19'02 74w37'13 4:58:29
Prospect 8 10 39N47'37 75w22'08 5:01:29
Prospect Heights 11
1 40N14'53 74w45'52 4:59:03
Prospect Highlands 11
1 40N16 74w46 4:59:04
Prospect Park 11
1 40N14'25 74w46'00 4:59:04
Prospect Park 16
4 40N56'13 74w10'29 4:56:42
Prospect Plains 12
1 40N19'26 74w28'17 4:57:53
Prospect Point 14
1 40N57'47 74w37'39 4:58:31
Prospertown 15 12 40N07'43 74w28'12 4:57:53
Prossers Mills 8
2 39N45'15 75w03'30 5:00:14
Pulis Mills 2 17 41N01'49 74w10'36 4:56:42
Pullentown 13 12 40N10'20 74w32'53 4:58:12
Pumptown 12 17 40N33'47 74w22'25 4:57:30
Quaker Gardens 11
1 40N15'05 74w41'02 4:58:44
Quakertown 10 13 40N33'56 74w56'31 4:59:46
Quarryville 19 1 41N15'23 74w34'48 4:58:19
Quinton 17 17 39N32'45 75w24'46 5:01:39
Radburn 2 1 40N56'33 74w07'01 4:56:28
Rahway 20 2 40N36'29 74w16'41 4:57:07
Rainbow Lakes 14
12 40N53 74w29 4:57:56
Raines Corner 17
1 39N42'43 75w27'00 5:01:48
Ralston 14 14 40N46'16 74w37'32 4:58:30
Ramblewood 3 17 39N55'43 74w56'39 4:59:47
Rammel Mill 6 1 39N28'09 75w14'33 5:00:58
Ramsey 2 12 41N03'26 74w08'29 4:56:34
Ramseyburg 21 15 40N53'00 75w03'35 5:00:14
Ramtown 13 1 40N07'15 74w08'39 4:56:35
Rancocas 3 1 40N00'38 74w52'02 4:59:28
Rancocas Heights 3
1 39N58'56 74w50'53 4:59:24
Rancocas Woods 3
1 39N59'20 74w51'38 4:59:27
Randolph 14 14 40N51 74w35 4:58:20
Randolphville 12
1 40N32'22 74w27'08 4:57:49
Raritan 18 2 40N34'10 74w38'00 4:58:32
Raritan Gardens 12
1 40N29'11 74w25'09 4:57:41
Raritan Manor 12
17 40N32'11 74w20'13 4:57:21
Raritan River RR Junction 12
1 40N29 74w17 4:57:08
Raven Rock 10 1 40N24'39 75w02'01 5:00:08
Readingsburg 10
12 40N40'55 74w52'38 4:59:31
Readington 10 12 40N34'07 74w44'17 4:58:57
Reaville 10 1 40N28'42 74w49'01 4:59:16
Rebel Hill 18 1 40N42 74w33 4:58:12
Red Bank 8 1 39N52'22 75w10'23 5:00:42
Red Bank 13 2 40N20'49 74w03'53 4:56:16
Red Hill 13 12 40N23'03 74w07'54 4:56:32
Red Lion 3 12 39N53'22 74w44'42 4:58:59
Red Lion 12 1 40N26'37 74w28'15 4:57:53
Red Mill 10 13 40N43'09 74w55'16 4:59:41
Red Oak Grove 15
1 39N50'07 74w24'35 4:57:38
Redshaw Corner 12
12 40N21'24 74w21'19 4:57:25
Red Valley 13 12 40N09'42 74w28'15 4:57:53
Reed Crossing 4
17 39N47'53 74w55'58 4:59:44
Reeds Beach 5 13 39N07'01 74w53'29 4:59:34
Reega 1 2 39N25'57 74w39'40 4:58:39
Reevytown 13 1 40N14'26 74w06'19 4:56:25
Remsen Mill 13 1 40N11'53 74w04'13 4:56:17
Remsterville 17
17 39N33'35 75w20'16 5:01:21
Repaupo 8 10 39N47'59 75w17'57 5:01:12
Retreat 3 12 39N54'59 74w42'47 4:58:51
Revere Run 4 2 39N46'32 75w02'19 5:00:09
Richard Mine 14 1 40N55'02 74w33'30 4:58:14
Richfield 16 3 40N52'08 74w10'23 4:56:42
Richland 1 17 39N29'30 74w52'16 4:59:29
Richmantown 17 17 39N37'38 75w17'38 5:01:11
Richwood 8 1 39N43'21 75w09'57 5:00:40
Riddleton 17 17 39N35'40 75w21'11 5:01:25
Ridge Acres 18 1 40N42 74w33 4:58:12
Ridgedale Park 14
1 40N46'00 74w24'44 4:57:39
Ridgefield 2 1 40N50'03 74w00'33 4:56:02
Ridgefield Park 2
1 40N51'25 74w01'19 4:56:05
Ridgeway 15 1 40N01'53 74w17'04 4:57:08
Ridgewood 2 2 40N58'45 74w07'01 4:56:28
Ridgewood Junction 2
4 40N58'10 74w07'37 4:56:30
Riegel Ridge 10
13 40N36'35 75w07'13 5:00:29
Riegelsville 10
12 40N35'37 75w11'44 5:00:47
Rileyville 10 12 40N25'30 74w47'32 4:59:10
Ringoes 10 12 40N25'44 74w52'05 4:59:28
Ringwood 16 12 41N06'48 74w14'45 4:56:59
Rio Grande 5 1 39N00'52 74w52'55 4:59:32
Ritz 2 1 40N53 74w06 4:56:24
River Bank 15 1 39N56'01 74w09'27 4:56:38
Rivercrest Manor 15
1 39N59'00 74w12'15 4:56:49
Riverdale 14 1 40N59'38 74w18'14 4:57:13
River Edge 2 1 40N55'43 74w02'25 4:56:10
River Edge Manor 2
1 40N56 74w01 4:56:04
Riverside 3 2 40N01'56 74w57'28 4:59:50
Riverside 10 1 40N30'35 74w47'04 4:59:08
Riverside 16 4 40N56'08 74w09'07 4:56:36
Riverside Park 3
2 40N02'15 74w58'30 4:59:54
Riverton 3 2 40N00'41 75w00'55 5:00:04
River Vale 2 1 40N59'43 74w00'45 4:56:03
Riverview Estates 15
1 39N57'37 74w13'24 4:56:54
Riverview Manor 12
1 40N30'55 74w28'30 4:57:54
Riviera Beach 15
1 40N05'52 74w06'02 4:56:24
Riviera on the Barnegat 15
14 39N50'57 74w10'30 4:56:42

Riviera on the Bay 15 12 40N00'08 74w07'45 4:56:31
Roadstown 6 1 39N26'27 75w19'07 5:01:16
Robanna 8 1 39N41'07 75w01'06 5:00:04
Robbinsville 13 12 40N12'52 74w37'11 4:58:29
Robert Barry Apartments 8 1 39N50 75w09 5:00:36
Robertsville 13 12 40N20'46 74w17'18 4:57:09
Robin Estates 15 12 40N08 74w20 4:57:20
Robin Hood Homes 3 17 40N03 74w56 4:59:44
Robinsville 13 2 40N12'23 74w28'42 4:57:55
Robinvale 12 17 40N32'35 74w21'08 4:57:25
Rochelle Park 2 1 40N54'26 74w04'32 4:56:18
Rockaway 14 12 40N54'04 74w30'53 4:58:04
Rockaway Neck 14 1 40N52 74w25 4:57:40
Rockaway Valley 14 1 40N55'41 74w26'41 4:57:47
Rockefellows Mills 10 1 40N31'11 74w49'16 4:59:17
Rockingham 12 2 40N23'52 74w37'10 4:58:29
Rockleigh 2 12 41N00'01 73w55'51 4:55:43
Rock Mill 18 12 40N26'15 74w44'36 4:58:58
Rockport 19 1 41N18'33 74w35'55 4:58:24
Rockport 21 1 40N49'25 74w52'38 4:59:31
Rock Ridge Lake 14 12 40N53 74w29 4:57:56
Rocktown 10 12 40N24'21 74w51'42 4:59:27
Rockwood 1 12 39N41'40 74w41'30 4:58:46
Rocky Hill 11 2 40N23'59 74w38'05 4:58:32
Roebling 3 12 40N06'57 74w47'12 4:59:09
Roosevelt 13 2 40N13'12 74w28'25 4:57:54
Roosevelt City 15 12 39N56'17 74w23'22 4:57:33
Roosevelt Park 6 2 39N22'41 75w01'31 5:00:06
Rosedale 1 2 39N39'00 74w49'36 4:59:18
Rosedale 11 2 40N20'17 74w43'20 4:58:53
Rosedale Village 14 1 40N46'05 74w23'45 4:57:35
Rose Hill Heights 21 17 40N41 75w10 5:00:40
Roseland 7 1 40N49'14 74w17'39 4:57:11
Roselle 20 1 40N39'51 74w15'49 4:57:03
Roselle Park 20 1 40N39'52 74w15'53 4:57:04
Rosemont 10 12 40N25'38 74w59'25 4:59:58
Rosemont 11 1 40N14'21 74w41'40 4:58:47
Rosenhayn 6 12 39N28'41 75w07'54 5:00:32
Roseville 7 1 40N45'18 74w11'28 4:56:46
Roseville 19 12 40N57'27 74w41'31 4:58:46
Ross Corner 19 17 41N07'12 74w42'47 4:58:51
Round Top 18 17 40N37'11 74w32'43 4:58:11
Rowland Mills 10 1 40N33'24 74w51'15 4:59:25
Roxburg 21 17 40N46'48 75w06'00 5:00:24
Roxbury 14 14 40N52 74w39 4:58:36
Royal Estates 12 12 40N25 74w23 4:57:32
Royce Valley 18 2 40N32'07 74w36'44 4:58:27
Roys 19 17 41N10'14 74w39'29 4:58:38
Rudeville 19 17 41N08'58 74w32'42 4:58:11
Rulon Road 8 10 39N45'35 75w17'49 5:01:11
Rumson 13 1 40N22'19 73w59'58 4:56:00
Runnemede 4 2 39N51'08 75w04'06 5:00:16
Runyon 12 2 40N26'03 74w19'57 4:57:20
Russia 14 12 41N02'26 74w31'59 4:58:08
Rutgers 12 1 40N29'17 74w24'40 4:57:39
Rutherford 2 2 40N49'35 74w06'26 4:56:26
Saddle Brook 2 1 40N53'56 74w05'35 4:56:22
Saddle River 2 1 41N01'54 74w06'09 4:56:25
Saint Cloud 7 1 40N46'30 74w16'27 4:57:06
Saint Josephs Village 2 1 41N00'21 73w56'07 4:55:44
Saint Vladimirs 15 12 40N06'53 74w23'28 4:57:34
Salem 17 17 39N34'18 75w28'03 5:01:52
Salem Hill 13 1 40N09'30 74w12'44 4:56:51
Salina 8 17 39N46'23 75w07'28 5:00:30
Sally Marshall Crossing 5 1 39N00'05 74w53'32 4:59:34
Samptown 12 2 40N34'53 74w25'50 4:57:43
Sand Brook 10 1 40N28'09 74w55'02 4:59:40
Sand Hills 12 1 40N31'30 74w19'11 4:57:17
Sand Hills 19 17 41N11'31 74w30'33 4:58:02
Sands Point 13 1 40N19'35 74w00'13 4:56:01
Sandtown 3 17 39N54'25 74w47'19 4:59:09
Sandy Point 15 12 40N02 74w07 4:56:28
Sandy Ridge 10 1 40N25'23 74w57'10 4:59:49
Sandyston 19 12 41N13 74w49 4:59:16
Sarepta 21 17 40N51'24 75w01'48 5:00:07
Saxton Falls 21 1 40N53'23 74w47'47 4:59:11
Sayerwood South 12 12 40N23'50 74w19'30 4:57:18
Sayres Neck 6 12 39N20 75w12 5:00:48
Sayreville 12 17 40N27'33 74w21'41 4:57:27
Sayreville Junction 12 2 40N27'55 74w19'51 4:57:19
Sayreville Station 12 2 40N28'22 74w21'15 4:57:25
Sayre Woods 12 2 40N27'40 74w17'30 4:57:10
Schalks 12 2 40N20'33 74w35'32 4:58:22
Schellenger Landing 5 1 38N56'55 74w54'20 4:59:37
Schepps Valley 17 12 39N28'43 75w21'32 5:01:26
Schooleys Mountain 14 1 40N47'57 74w48'51 4:59:15
Scobeyville 13 12 40N17'49 74w08'37 4:56:34
Scotch Bonnet 5 13 39N04'06 74w47'18 4:59:09
Scotch Plains 20 2 40N39'19 74w23'25 4:57:34
Scow Landing 15 2 39N35'53 74w20'24 4:57:22
Scrapetown 3 12 39N56'52 74w41'33 4:58:46
Scrappy Corner 10 12 40N45'43 74w50'55 4:59:24
Scratch Ridge 3 3 39N58'09 74w44'00 4:58:56
Scudders Falls 11 1 40N15'33 74w50'14 4:59:21
Scull Landing 1 17 39N21'56 74w42'51 4:58:51
Scullville 1 17 39N20'06 74w38'36 4:58:34
Seaboard 9 1 40N46 74w09 4:56:36
Sea Breeze 6 1 39N19'16 75w19'14 5:01:17
Sea Bright 13 2 40N21'41 73w58'28 4:55:54
Seabrook 6 1 39N30'06 75w13'10 5:00:53
Seabrook Farms 6 12 39N30 75w13 5:00:52
Sea Girt 13 1 40N07'55 74w02'06 4:56:08
Sea Isle City 5 2 39N09'12 74w41'36 4:58:46
Seaside Heights 15 12 39N56'39 74w04'24 4:56:18
Seaside Heights Harbor 15 12 39N57'53 74w07'42 4:56:31
Seaside Park 15 12 39N55'36 74w04'39 4:56:19
Seaview Park 1 2 39N26'32 74w28'40 4:57:55
Seaville 5 2 39N12'30 74w42'16 4:58:49
Secaucus 9 2 40N47'22 74w03'25 4:56:14
Sedgefield 14 17 40N50 74w29 4:57:56
Seeley 6 1 39N28'55 75w15'29 5:01:02
Sergeantsville 10 12 40N26'45 74w56'38 4:59:47
Serviss Acres 12 12 40N25 74w23 4:57:32
Seven Stars 15 1 40N03'26 74w13'13 4:56:53
Seven Stars 17 17 39N41'08 75w20'21 5:01:21
Sewaren 12 1 40N33'07 74w15'33 4:57:02
Sewell 8 2 39N45'59 75w08'41 5:00:35
Shacks Corner 13 1 40N13'37 74w11'42 4:56:47
Shady Lawn Manor 14 1 40N46'19 74w26'11 4:57:45
Shafto Corners 13 12 40N14 74w13 4:56:52
Shamong 3 12 39N47 74w45 4:59:00
Shark River Hills 13 1 40N11'38 74w02'57 4:56:12
Sharon 13 1 40N12'23 74w32'11 4:58:09
Sharp 3 1 40N05'32 74w44'34 4:58:58
Sharps Corner 4 17 39N47'59 74w57'59 4:59:52
Sharptown 17 17 39N39'20 75w21'56 5:01:28
Shawcrest 5 11 38N59'15 74w50'18 4:59:21
Shaws Mill 6 12 39N18'38 75w09'24 5:00:38
Shaytown 19 17 41N15'30 74w47'30 4:59:10
Shellbed Landing 5 13 39N03'45 74w49'10 4:59:17
Shell Pile 6 12 39N14'25 75w01'29 5:00:06
Shelter Cove 15 1 39N56 74w13 4:56:52
Sheppards Mill 6 1 39N24'37 75w19'06 5:01:16
Sherbrook Estates 11 2 40N18'52 74w36'54 4:58:28
Sherwood Green 8 1 39N49 75w08 5:00:32
Shiloh 6 12 39N27'32 75w17'58 5:01:12
Shiloh 21 12 40N55'03 74w55'52 4:59:43
Shiloh Crossing 6 1 39N28 75w15 5:01:00
Shimer Manor 21 17 40N41 75w10 5:00:40
Shinntown 3 17 39N54'00 74w50'40 4:59:23
Ship Bottom 15 12 39N38'34 74w10'51 4:56:43
Shippenport 14 1 40N53'54 74w40'10 4:58:41
Shirley 17 1 39N34'10 75w14'19 5:00:57
Shongum 14 14 40N50'39 74w32'00 4:58:08
Shore Acres 15 12 40N01'31 74w06'07 4:56:24
Shore Crest 12 2 40N35 74w19 4:57:16
Shore Hills 14 1 40N54'39 74w39'24 4:58:38
Shore Road Estates 12 12 40N21'40 74w23'35 4:57:34
Shore View 12 1 40N35'25 74w19'42 4:57:19
Short Hills 7 1 40N44'52 74w19'33 4:57:18
Shrewsbury 13 1 40N19'46 74w03'43 4:56:15
Sicklerville 4 1 39N43'02 74w58'11 4:59:53
Sidney 10 13 40N36'15 74w55'21 4:59:41
Siloam 13 1 40N11'10 74w20'54 4:57:24
Silver Bay 15 1 40N00'12 74w07'24 4:56:30
Silver Beach 15 12 39N59'45 74w03'45 4:56:15
Silver Lake 7 1 40N48 74w10 4:56:40
Silver Lake 21 16 40N59 74w57 4:59:48
Silver Ridge 15 1 39N57'33 74w13'08 4:56:53
Silver Springs 14 1 40N54'56 74w39'14 4:58:37
Silverton 15 1 40N00'57 74w08'43 4:56:35
Silverton Estates 15 1 40N00'38 74w08'57 4:56:36
Silverton Pine Terrace 15 12 40N00'34 74w07'48 4:56:31
Sim Place 3 1 39N44'09 74w25'16 4:57:41
Singac 16 4 40N53'12 74w14'29 4:56:58
Sinnickson Landing 2 17 39N34'11 75w29'46 5:01:59
Sixmile Run 18 1 40N27'27 74w30'43 4:58:03
Six Points 17 1 39N31'53 75w06'28 5:00:26
Skillman 18 12 40N25'12 74w42'54 4:58:52
Skin Corner 3 17 40N00'46 74w56'07 4:59:44
Skylands 16 12 41N07'37 74w14'14 4:56:57
Sky Line Lake 16 1 41N02 74w18 4:57:12
Sky View Manor 15 12 39N58'40 74w08'45 4:56:35
Slackwood 11 1 40N15'11 74w44'06 4:58:56
Slapes Corner 17 12 39N38'23 75w26'10 5:01:45
Sloop Creek Estates 15 12 39N55 74w09 4:56:36
Sloping Hills 18 1 40N42 74w33 4:58:12
Smalleytown 18 17 40N39'21 74w28'43 4:57:55
Smithburg 13 12 40N12'32 74w21'12 4:57:25
Smiths Mills 16 16 41N00'52 74w22'24 4:57:30
Smithtown 10 12 40N28'19 75w04'10 5:00:17
Smith Tract 15 17 39N37 74w12 4:56:48
Smithville 1 2 39N29'38 74w27'27 4:57:50
Smithville 3 1 39N59'09 74w44'56 4:59:00
Smocks Corners 13 1 40N21'23 74w14'10 4:56:57
Smoke Rise 14 16 40N59'43 74w24'10 4:57:37
Snow Hill 4 2 39N52'12 75w01'59 5:00:08
Snug Harbor 15 1 39N59'30 74w08'40 4:56:35
Snydertown 10 12 40N23'55 74w50'03 4:59:20
Soho 7 1 40N48 74w10 4:56:40
Somerdale 4 2 39N50'38 75w01'23 5:00:06
Somerset 11 1 40N16'34 74w50'58 4:59:24
Somersetin 18 1 40N44'24 74w34'36 4:58:18
Somerset Park 3 17 40N02'52 74w53'30 4:59:34
Somers Point 1 1 39N19'03 74w35'42 4:58:23
Somerville 18 3 40N34'27 74w36'37 4:58:26
Sooy Place 3 12 39N52'03 74w39'09 4:58:37
South 7 1 40N43 74w11 4:56:44
South Amboy 12 2 40N28'40 74w17'28 4:57:10
South Amboy Junction 12 1 40N29'30 74w17'01 4:57:08
Southampton 3 12 39N55 74w43 4:58:52
Southard 13 1 40N08'18 74w13'31 4:56:54
South Belmar 15 1 40N10'15 74w01'40 4:56:07
South Bound Brook 13 17 40N33'12 74w31'55 4:58:08
South Branch 18 2 40N32'38 74w41'50 4:58:47
South Brunswick 12 12 40N23 74w32 4:58:08
South Brunswick Terrace 12 12 40N22'45 74w34'00 4:58:16
South Camden 4 2 39N55 75w06 5:00:24
South Dennis 5 12 39N10'42 74w49'13 4:59:17
South Egg Harbor 1 8 39N31'16 74w39'07 4:58:36
South Glassboro 8 1 39N42 75w07 5:00:28
South Hackensack 2 1 40N51'45 74w02'54 4:56:12
South Harrison 8 12 39N42 75w16 5:01:04
South Kearny 9 1 40N46 74w09 4:56:36
South Lakewood 15 1 40N04'18 74w14'45 4:56:59
South Livingston 7 1 40N47 74w19 4:57:16
South Mantoloking 15 2 40N03 74w03 4:56:12
South Mantoloking Beach 15 2 40N01'22 74w03'19 4:56:13
South Merchantville 4 2 39N57 75w03 5:00:12
South Ogdensburg 19 17 41N04'29 74w35'48 4:58:23
South Old Bridge 12 12 40N24'29 74w21'17 4:57:25
South Orange 7 1 40N45 74w15 4:57:00
South Orange Village, Townsh 7 1 40N47'26 74w15'35 4:57:02
South Park 3 14 39N49'34 74w36'17 4:58:25
South Paterson 16 1 40N54 74w09 4:56:36
South Pemberton 3 3 39N58'03 74w41'07 4:58:44
South Penns Grove 17 1 39N43'18 75w27'35 5:01:50
South Plainfield 12 2 40N34'45 74w24'43 4:57:39
South River 12 12 40N26'47 74w23'11 4:57:33
South Seaside Park 15 12 39N54'38 74w04'49 4:56:19
South Seaville 5 12 39N10'44 74w45'37 4:59:02
South Toms River 15 1 39N56'31 74w12'17 4:56:49
Southtown 21 1 40N56'16 74w53'42 4:59:35
South Vineland 6 1 39N26'45 75w01'45 5:00:07
South Westville 8 1 39N51'38 75w07'55 5:00:32
Southwest Vineland 6 1 39N29 75w01 5:00:04
South Woodstown 17 17 39N39 75w20 5:01:20
Sparta 19 17 41N02'00 74w38'20 4:58:33
Sparta Junction 19 12 41N03'51 74w40'18 4:58:41
Sparta Lake 19 17 41N03 74w34 4:58:16
Speedwell 3 14 39N45'47 74w32'45 4:58:11
Sperry Springs 19 1 40N57'20 74w38'56 4:58:36
Spotswood 12 12 40N23'30 74w23'56 4:57:36
Spotswood Manor 12 12 40N22'40 74w23'00 4:57:32
Spraguetown 15 2 39N39'00 74w18'21 4:57:13
Spray Beach 15 17 39N34'42 74w13'48 4:56:55
Springdale 4 2 39N54'09 74w58'00 4:59:52
Springdale 18 17 40N36'25 74w30'33 4:58:02
Springdale 19 12 41N01'13 74w46'10 4:59:05
Springfield 3 3 40N02'35 74w38'45 4:58:35
Springfield 20 1 40N43'23 74w18'40 4:57:15
Spring Gardens 11 1 40N14 74w47 4:59:08
Spring Lake 13 1 40N09'12 74w01'43 4:56:07
Spring Lake Heights 13 1 40N09'01 74w01'53 4:56:08
Spring Mill 13 12 40N10'27 74w36'11 4:58:25
Spring Mills 10 12 40N35'39 75w07'01 5:00:28
Springside 3 1 40N03'37 74w51'03 4:59:24
Springtown 6 1 39N24'51 75w19'55 5:01:20
Springtown 14 12 40N47'33 74w47'34 4:59:10
Springtown 21 17 40N38'55 75w08'53 5:00:36
Spring Valley 13 12 40N22'15 74w16'41 4:57:07
Spring Valley 21 16 41N00'21 74w56'24 4:59:46
Springville 3 17 39N56'14 74w52'06 4:59:28
Spruce Gardens 15 1 40N04'09 74w12'34 4:56:50
Spruce Run 10 13 40N42'31 74w55'21 4:59:41
Squankum 13 12 40N09'58 74w09'15 4:56:37
Stafford 15 12 39N41 74w16 4:57:04
Stafford Forge 15 2 39N40'01 74w19'11 4:57:17
Staffordville 15 2 39N39'58 74w16'52 4:57:07

Staffordville Public Landing 15
2 39N39'21 74W16'14 4:57:05
Stanhope 19 1 40N54'10 74W42'34 4:58:50
Stanton 10 13 40N34'30 74W50'17 4:59:21
Stanwick 3 17 39N58'23 74W56'13 4:59:45
Stanwick Glen 3
17 39N58'45 74W56'22 4:59:45
Star Cross 8 1 39N38'47 75W00'56 5:00:04
State Hospital 11
1 40N13 74W46 4:59:04
Staten Island Junction 20
1 40N39'32 74W17'15 4:57:09
Steelman Landing 1
12 39N22'40 74W43'56 4:58:56
Steelmantown 5 12 39N16'00 74W48'07 4:59:12
Steelmanville 1 1 39N20'03 74W35'41 4:58:23
Steels Corner 17
1 39N34'53 75W11'33 5:00:46
Stelton 12 17 40N30'51 74W24'14 4:57:37
Stephensburg 14
12 40N47'35 74W52'24 4:59:30
Stephenville 12
17 40N32 74W22 4:57:28
Sterling Woods 13
1 40N06'20 74W05'06 4:56:20
Stevens 3 1 40N05'19 74W49'31 4:59:18
Stewartsville 21
13 40N41'37 75W06'41 5:00:27
Still Valley 21
17 40N40'26 75W08'20 5:00:33
Stillwater 19 12 41N02'09 74W52'43 4:59:31
Stirling 14 12 40N40'19 74W29'43 4:57:59
Stockholm 19 17 41N05'22 74W31'03 4:58:04
Stockington 17 1 39N33'54 75W19'10 5:01:17
Stockton 10 1 40N24'28 74W58'43 4:59:55
Stone Church 13 1 40N23'53 74W01'13 4:56:05
Stone Harbor 5 17 39N03'03 74W45'30 4:59:02
Stone Harbor Manor 5
13 39N03'35 74W46'12 4:59:05
Stonehurst East 13
1 40N13'48 74W17'15 4:57:09
Stonehurst West 13
1 40N13'48 74W18'15 4:57:13
Stone Mill 10 12 40N40'53 74W52'48 4:59:31
Stone Tavern 13
12 40N11'20 74W28'18 4:57:53
Stonetown 16 1 41N05'42 74W18'14 4:57:13
Stoney Brook Estates 8
1 39N49 75W08 5:00:32
Stony Hill 20 17 40N40'13 74W25'40 4:57:43
Stoutsburg 11 12 40N23'55 74W44'09 4:58:57
Stow Acres 3 17 39N54'37 74W54'52 4:59:39
Stow Creek 6 12 39N27 75W21 5:01:24
Stow Creek Landing 6
1 39N26'33 75W24'32 5:01:38
Stoys Landing 4 2 39N54'59 75W02'05 5:00:08
Stratford 4 2 39N49'36 75W00'57 5:00:04
Strathmere 5 17 39N11'44 74W39'30 4:58:38
Strathmore 13 2 40N23'45 74W12'50 4:56:51
Sturwood Hamlet 11
1 40N16'24 74W44'33 4:58:58
Styertowne 16 1 40N51 74W09 4:56:36
Suburban 13 1 40N21 74W03 4:56:12
Suburban Park 15
1 39N57'58 74W13'55 4:56:56
Succasunna 14 14 40N52'06 74W38'27 4:58:34
Summerfield 21 17 40N47'15 75W02'36 5:00:10
Summit 20 1 40N44'29 74W21'36 4:57:26
Summit Avenue 9 1 40N46 74W02 4:56:08
Summit East 15 1 39N58'40 74W14'40 4:56:59
Sunbury 3 3 39N58 74W41 4:58:44
Sunnyside 10 13 40N34'54 74W52'48 4:59:31
Sunrise Beach 15
14 39N50 74W11 4:56:44
Sunrise Park 14
14 40N52 74W38 4:58:32
Sunset Beach 5 1 38N56'45 74W58'15 4:59:53
Sunset Beach 8 1 39N48'50 75W05'46 5:00:23
Sunset Hill 18 2 40N21 74W39 4:58:36
Sunset Hill Garden 18
12 40N26'12 74W35'15 4:58:21
Surf City 15 12 39N39'43 74W09'56 4:56:40
Surrey Place 4 2 39N55'56 74W59'46 4:59:59
Sussex 19 1 41N12'35 74W36'29 4:58:26
Sussex Mills 19
12 41N03'05 74W40'51 4:58:43
Sutton Park 14 1 40N49'30 74W42'20 4:58:49
Swain 5 13 39N07'31 74W48'02 4:59:12
Swainton 5 13 39N07'53 74W46'40 4:59:07
Swartswood 19 12 41N05'13 74W49'39 4:59:19
Swartswood Lake 19
12 41N03 74W45 4:59:00
Swayzes Mills 21
16 40N53'48 74W59'51 4:59:59
Swedesboro 8 10 39N44'51 75W18'39 5:01:15
Sweetman 13 12 40N13'10 74W23'17 4:57:33
Sweetwater 1 2 39N37'35 74W38'59 4:58:36
Swinesburg 10 12 40N38'19 75W03'28 5:00:14
Sykesville 3 3 40N03'49 74W37'08 4:58:29
Sylvan Glen 3 1 40N10'42 74W42'18 4:58:49
Sylvan Lake 3 1 40N05 74W51 4:59:24
Tabernacle 3 12 39N50'38 74W42'38 4:58:51
Tabor 14 12 40N52'16 74W28'49 4:57:55
Tanners Corner 12
12 40N26'17 74W23'35 4:57:34
Tansboro 4 17 39N46'08 74W55'12 4:59:41
Taunton Lake 3 17 39N51'02 74W50'57 4:59:24
Taurus 9 1 40N47 74W01 4:56:04
Tavistock 4 2 39N52'34 75W01'48 5:00:07
Taylor Mills 13 1 40N17'48 74W20'26 4:57:22
Taylortown 14 1 40N56'16 74W23'42 4:57:35
Teabo 14 1 40N54 74W35 4:58:20
Teaneck 2 1 40N53'51 74W00'59 4:56:04
Tenafly 2 1 40N55'31 73W57'48 4:55:51
Ten Mile Run 12
12 40N24'50 74W34'25 4:58:18
Tennent 13 1 40N16'46 74W20'05 4:57:20
Terrestria 4 1 39N45'48 75W02'00 5:00:08
Teterboro 2 1 40N51'35 74W03'35 4:56:14
Tewksbury 10 12 40N42 74W47 4:59:08
Texas 3 17 39N56'33 74W56'04 4:59:44
Texas 12 12 40N21'38 74W22'11 4:57:29

Thachers Hill 10
1 40N31'33 74W52'42 4:59:31
The Acres 8 1 39N42 75W07 5:00:28
The Dunes 15 17 39N37 74W12 4:56:48
Thelma 1 2 39N24'54 74W39'23 4:58:38
The Maples 3 17 39N54'27 74W55'30 4:59:42
The Orchards 11 1 40N14'20 74W41'51 4:58:47
Thompson Beach 6
12 39N15 75W07 5:00:28
Thompsontown 1 17 39N24'59 74W42'33 4:58:50
Thorofare 8 2 39N50'32 75W11'48 5:00:47
Three Bridges 10
1 40N31'11 74W47'59 4:59:12
Tierneys Corner 14
12 40N57'32 74W35'52 4:58:23
Tilghmans Corner 3
3 40N03'38 74W37'57 4:58:32
Timber Lakes 8 1 39N41 75W00 5:00:00
Timbuctoo 3 1 40N00'11 74W48'52 4:59:15
Tindells Landing 6
1 39N22'35 75W14'45 5:00:59
Tinton Falls 13 1 40N18'15 74W06'03 4:56:24
Titusville 11 12 40N18'34 74W52'51 4:59:31
Tomlin 8 2 39N46'41 75W16'22 5:01:05
Tomlinsons Mill 3
17 39N52'02 74W53'42 4:59:35
Toms River 15 1 39N57'13 74W11'54 4:56:48
Totowa 16 4 40N54'18 74W12'37 4:56:50
Towaco 14 16 40N55'19 74W20'45 4:57:23
Town Bank 5 1 38N59'15 74W57'13 4:59:49
Town Brook 13 2 40N23'32 74W06'00 4:56:24
Town Estates 3 1 40N03'31 74W52'04 4:59:28
Townley 20 1 40N42 74W16 4:57:04
Townsbury 21 17 40N51'03 74W56'02 4:59:44
Townsends Inlet 5
2 39N07'35 74W42'42 4:58:51
Tracy 12 12 40N18'10 74W23'02 4:57:32
Tranquility 19 15 40N57'22 74W48'32 4:59:14
Tremley 20 1 40N36'47 74W13'49 4:56:55
Tremley Point 20
1 40N36'06 74W12'19 4:56:49
Tremont Park 20 1 40N42'18 74W21'14 4:57:25
Trenton 11 1 40N13'01 74W44'36 4:58:58
Trenton East 11 1 40N13 74W45 4:59:00
Trenton Gardens 11
1 40N11'50 74W41'59 4:58:48
Trenton Highlands 11
1 40N14 74W42 4:58:48
Trenton Naval Air Propulsion 11
1 40N15 74W48 4:59:12
Troy Hills 14 1 40N51'10 74W23'33 4:57:34
Tuckahoe 5 12 39N17'24 74W45'15 4:59:01
Tuckerton 15 2 39N36'11 74W20'26 4:57:22
Tumble Falls 10 1 40N27'13 75W03'45 5:00:15
Turkey Point Corner 6
12 39N16'58 75W07'58 5:00:32
Turnersville 8 1 39N46'23 75W03'06 5:00:12
Tuttles Corner 19
17 41N11'53 74W48'11 4:59:13
Twin Hill Park 3
1 40N00'30 74W52'40 4:59:31
Twin Rivers 11 1 40N15'50 74W29'30 4:57:58
Two Bridges 7 1 40N53'44 74W16'39 4:57:07
Twombly Landing 2
1 40N57'45 73W54'48 4:55:39
Tyler Park 9 1 40N47 74W01 4:56:04
Tylertown 3 8 39N39'17 74W36'34 4:58:26
Tyndall Village 4
2 39N53'32 75W01'17 5:00:05
Ukrainian Village 18
1 40N31'40 74W30'48 4:58:03
Undercliff 2 1 40N53'17 73W56'28 4:55:46
Undercliff Junction 2
1 40N49'43 74W01'28 4:56:06
Union 10 13 40N40'10 74W55'28 4:59:42
Union 20 1 40N41'51 74W15'49 4:57:03
Union Beach 13 2 40N26'47 74W10'43 4:56:43
Unionburg 20 1 40N42'19 74W16'54 4:57:08
Union Center 20 1 40N42 74W16 4:57:04
Union City 9 1 40N46'46 74W01'27 4:56:06
Union Grove 17 17 39N38'27 75W16'57 5:01:08
Union Hill 14 1 40N52'02 74W31'21 4:58:05
Union Landing 3 2 40N01'19 74W59'48 4:59:59
Union Mills 3 1 39N58'20 74W51'23 4:59:26
Union Square 20 1 40N39'31 74W12'10 4:56:49
Uniontown 21 17 40N43'14 75W08'27 5:00:34
Union Valley 12 1 40N18'13 74W27'23 4:57:50
Union Village 20
17 40N40'00 74W27'21 4:57:49
Unionville 1 2 39N31'37 74W30'06 4:58:00
Unionville 3 1 40N00'19 74W45'54 4:59:04
Unionville 10 12 40N25'43 74W50'24 4:59:22
Upper 5 17 39N15 74W41 4:58:44
Upper Berkshire Valley 14
1 40N54 74W35 4:58:20
Upper Deerfield 6
1 39N29 75W12 5:00:48
Upper Freehold 13
1 40N12 74W31 4:58:04
Upper Greenwood Lake 16
12 41N10'54 74W22'57 4:57:32
Upper Harmony 21
17 40N41 75W10 5:00:40
Upper Longwood 14
12 40N58'38 74W32'45 4:58:11
Upper Macopin 16
12 41N05'06 74W23'10 4:57:33
Upper Mill 3 12 39N54'45 74W34'26 4:58:18
Upper Mohawk 19
17 41N01'52 74W39'49 4:58:39
Upper Montclair 7
1 40N50'46 74W12'06 4:56:48
Upper Montvale 2
1 41N03'38 74W03'09 4:56:13
Upper Penns Neck 17
1 39N43 75W28 5:01:52
Upper Pittsgrove 17
1 39N37 75W12 5:00:48
Upper Saddle River 2
12 41N03'30 74W05'56 4:56:24
Upton 3 12 39N56'05 74W31'28 4:58:06
Uptown 9 1 40N45 74W02 4:56:08
Uttertown 16 12 41N07'36 74W25'00 4:57:40

V A Hospital 7 1 40N45 74W13 4:56:52
Vail 21 12 40N57'46 75W01'14 5:00:05
Vail Homes 13 1 40N19 74W04 4:56:16
Vails 21 12 40N56 75W06 5:00:24
Vailsburg 7 1 40N45 74W14 4:56:56
Valentine 12 17 40N31'51 74W19'33 4:57:18
Valley 10 13 40N40'02 75W01'57 5:00:08
Valley 12 17 40N32 74W22 4:57:28
Vanada Woods 15
12 40N02 74W07 4:56:28
Vanderburg 13 12 40N18'51 74W11'22 4:56:45
Van Dorans Mills 18
1 40N43'53 74W32'28 4:58:10
Van Hiseville 15
12 40N06'42 74W20'35 4:57:22
Van Marters Corner 13
2 40N26'15 74W10'50 4:56:43
Van Syckel 10 13 40N38'59 74W58'15 4:59:53
Van Syckles 19 1 41N16'15 74W34'42 4:58:19
Vasa Home 14 1 40N52 74W50 4:59:20
Vauxhall 20 1 40N43'53 74W17'00 4:57:08
Venice Park 1 2 39N22'35 74W26'44 4:57:47
Ventnor City 1 7 39N20'25 74W28'40 4:57:55
Ventnor Heights 1
7 39N20'58 74W29'06 4:57:56
Verga 8 1 39N51'40 75W09'33 5:00:38
Vernon 4 2 39N53'50 75W01'56 5:00:08
Vernon 19 12 41N11'54 74W29'01 4:57:56
Vernoy 10 12 40N44'07 74W49'37 4:59:18
Verona 7 1 40N49'47 74W14'26 4:56:58
Victoria 8 17 39N33 75W01 5:00:04
Victory Gardens 14
1 40N52'33 74W32'34 4:58:10
Victory Lakes 8 1 39N41 75W00 5:00:00
Vienna 21 12 40N52'07 74W53'22 4:59:33
Vienna Gardens 1
8 39N30'40 74W37'22 4:58:29
Village of Glen Oaks 4
1 39N49'24 75W02'17 5:00:09
Villa Madonna 21
15 40N54'52 74W48'46 4:59:15
Villa Marie Claire 2
1 41N00'49 74W06'07 4:56:24
Villa Park 13 1 40N08'37 74W02'33 4:56:10
Villas 5 12 39N01'43 74W56'20 4:59:45
Vincentown 3 12 39N56'02 74W44'56 4:59:00
Vineland 6 1 39N29'10 75W01'34 5:00:06
Vineyard Homes 12
17 40N32 74W22 4:57:28
Vliettown 18 12 40N40'56 74W43'02 4:58:52
Voken Tract 4 2 39N49 75W06 5:00:24
Voorhees 4 17 39N51 74W59 4:59:56
Voorhees 18 1 40N28'52 74W29'01 4:57:56
Voorhees Corner 10
1 40N30'09 74W48'33 4:59:14
Vulcanite 21 17 40N41 75W10 5:00:40
Wading River 3 8 39N36'55 74W30'16 4:58:01
Waldwick 2 2 41N00'38 74W07'06 4:56:28
Walkers Forge 1
17 39N26'26 74W45'22 4:59:01
Wall 13 1 40N10 74W05 4:56:20
Wallace Mill 3 12 40N06'26 74W37'52 4:58:31
Wallington 2 1 40N51'11 74W06'51 4:56:27
Wallkill Lake 19
1 41N13 74W36 4:58:24
Wallpack Center 19
12 41N09'32 74W52'50 4:59:31
Wallworth Park 4
2 39N49 75W06 5:00:24
Walnford 13 12 40N08'04 74W33'37 4:58:14
Walnut Valley 21
12 40N58'33 75W01'23 5:00:06
Walt Whitman Homes 8
2 39N51 75W12 5:00:48
Wanamassa 13 12 40N13'54 74W01'33 4:56:06
Wanaque 16 1 41N02'17 74W17'40 4:57:11
Wantage 19 1 41N14'39 74W33'04 4:58:12
Warbasse 19 17 41N05'01 74W42'00 4:58:48
Waretown 15 1 39N47'29 74W11'44 4:56:47
Waretown Junction 15
1 39N46'44 74W12'18 4:56:49
Warners 20 1 40N38 74W15 4:57:00
Warners Mill 1 12 39N18'50 74W48'24 4:59:14
Warner Village 11
1 40N14'01 74W43'34 4:58:54
Warren 18 12 40N38 74W30 4:58:00
Warren Glen 21 13 40N37'58 75W08'07 5:00:32
Warren Grove 15 1 39N44'47 74W22'15 4:57:29
Warren Point 2 1 40N55'37 74W06'30 4:56:26
Warrenville 18 17 40N36'54 74W29'47 4:57:59
Warrington 21 12 40N55'53 75W05'04 5:00:20
Washington 3 8 39N41'02 74W34'35 4:58:18
Washington 21 12 40N45'30 74W58'47 4:59:55
Washington Corner 14
12 40N46'05 74W33'48 4:58:15
Washington Crossing 11
12 40N17'48 74W52'02 4:59:28
Washington Heights 12
12 40N27'18 74W24'36 4:57:38
Washington Park 12
1 40N30'50 74W23'55 4:57:36
Washington Valley 14
17 40N48'20 74W31'39 4:58:07
Washingtonville 18
2 40N37 74W25 4:57:40
Washingtonville 19
12 41N05'52 74W45'05 4:59:00
Watchung 18 2 40N38'16 74W27'05 4:57:48
Waterford 4 17 39N46 74W51 4:59:24
Waterford Works 4
17 39N43'23 74W50'58 4:59:24
Waterloo 13 1 40N21'22 73W59'15 4:55:57
Waterloo 19 1 40N54'54 74W45'17 4:59:01
Waterwitch 13 1 40N24'23 73W59'52 4:55:59
Watsessing 7 1 40N48 74W11 4:56:44
Watson Corner 17
1 39N34'07 75W17'24 5:01:10
Watsons Corner 6
12 39N17'40 75W09'54 5:00:40
Watsontown 4 1 39N48 75W00 5:00:00
Wawayanda 19 12 41N00'41 74W44'19 4:58:57
Wayne 16 17 40N55'31 74W16'37 4:57:06
Wayside 13 1 40N15'24 74W04'30 4:56:18

Webbs Mill 15 12 39N53'23 74w22'49 4:57:31
Weber Park 11 1 40N14'42 74w46'25 4:59:06
Weehawken 9 1 40N46'10 74w01'15 4:56:05
Weeks Landing 5 1 38N59'23 74w53'00 4:59:32
Weekstown 1 8 39N35'31 74w36'12 4:58:25
Weequahic 7 1 40N43 74w12 4:56:48
Weirtown 21 15 40N54'17 74w49'21 4:59:17
Welchville 17 17 39N36'03 75w25'21 5:01:41
Weldon 14 12 40N59'31 74w35'18 4:58:21
Wellington Park 3 2 39N59'43 74w58'51 4:59:55
Wells Mills 15 1 39N47'39 74w16'34 4:57:06
Wellwood 4 2 39N57'10 75w02'58 5:00:12
Wenonah 8 1 39N47'40 75w08'57 5:00:36
Wertheins Corner 13 1 40N15'06 74w02'25 4:56:10
Wertsville 10 12 40N26'59 74w47'53 4:59:12
Wescoatville 1 12 39N38'23 74w43'13 4:58:53
West 7 1 40N44 74w12 4:56:48
West Allenhurst 13 1 40N14'18 74w00'44 4:56:03
Westampton 3 1 40N01 74w50 4:59:20
West Amwell 10 12 40N23 74w53 4:59:32
West Arlington 9 1 40N46 74w09 4:56:36
West Atco 4 17 39N44'45 74w53'29 4:59:34
West Atlantic City 1 2 39N22'40 74w29'23 4:57:58
West Belmar 15 1 40N10'09 74w02'09 4:56:09
West Bergen 9 1 40N42'45 74w05'01 4:56:20
West Berlin 4 17 39N48'31 74w56'30 4:59:46
Westboro 13 1 40N21 74w03 4:56:12
West Brunswick 18 1 40N29 74w29 4:57:56
West Caldwell 7 1 40N50'27 74w18'08 4:57:13
West Cape May 5 1 38N56'19 74w56'32 4:59:46
West Carteret 12 12 40N35'40 74w14'48 4:56:59
West Collingswood 4 2 39N54'22 75w05'36 5:00:22
West Collingswood Heights 4 2 39N53'39 75w05'49 5:00:23
Westcotville 8 2 39N49'34 75w06'57 5:00:28
West Creek 15 2 39N38'04 74w18'27 4:57:14
West Deal 13 1 40N14'30 74w01'45 4:56:07
West Deptford 8 1 39N50 75w10 5:00:40
West Egg Harbor 1 8 39N30'58 74w40'01 4:58:40
West End 8 1 39N50'05 75w09'57 5:00:40
West End 13 1 40N17'10 73w59'56 4:56:00
West Englewood 2 1 40N54'07 74w00'13 4:56:01
West Essex 7 1 40N51 74w16 4:57:04
West Farms 13 12 40N11'31 74w12'06 4:56:48
Westfield 20 1 40N39'32 74w20'52 4:57:23
West Fort Lee 2 1 40N51 73w58 4:55:52
West Freehold 13 1 40N14'31 74w18'06 4:57:12
West Grove 13 1 40N12'40 74w02'11 4:56:09
West Haddonfield 4 2 39N54'06 75w02'28 5:00:10
West Hoboken 9 1 40N46 74w02 4:56:08
West Hudson 9 1 40N46 74w09 4:56:36
West Keansburg 13 17 40N27 74w08 4:56:32
West Long Branch 13 1 40N17'25 74w01'05 4:56:04
West Mahwah 2 12 41N06'10 74w09'07 4:56:36
West Mantoloking 15 12 40N02'39 74w04'25 4:56:18
West Merchantville 4 2 39N57 75w03 5:00:12
West Milford 16 12 41N07'52 74w22'04 4:57:28
Westmont 4 2 39N54'35 75w02'54 5:00:12
West Moorestown 3 17 39N57'37 74w57'21 4:59:49
West New York 9 1 40N47'16 74w00'53 4:56:04
West Norwood 2 17 41N00 73w58 4:55:52
West Ocean City 5 17 39N16 74w39 4:58:36
West Ocean Grove 13 1 40N12 74w02 4:56:08
Weston 18 2 40N32'06 74w35'28 4:58:22
Westons Mills 12 1 40N29'07 74w24'46 4:57:39
West Orange 7 1 40N47'55 74w14'22 4:56:57
West Paterson 16 4 40N53'23 74w11'43 4:56:47
West Point Island 15 12 39N58 74w04 4:56:16
West Point Pleasant 15 2 40N05 74w03 4:56:12
West Portal 10 13 40N39'44 75w02'01 5:00:08
West Shrewsbury 13 1 40N18'57 74w05'08 4:56:21
West Side 9 1 40N45 74w02 4:56:08
West Trenton 11 1 40N15'50 74w49'08 4:59:17
West Tuckerton 15 2 39N36'05 74w21'14 4:57:25
West Tuckerton Landing 15 2 39N35'45 74w20'33 4:57:22
West View 2 1 40N51'54 74w01'41 4:56:07
West Village 6 1 39N30'07 75w13'37 5:00:54
Westville 7 1 40N50'40 74w18'00 4:57:12
Westville 8 2 39N52'04 75w07'55 5:00:32
Westville Grove 8 1 39N51'23 75w07'05 5:00:28
Westville Oaks 8 1 39N50 75w09 5:00:36
West Wildwood 5 11 39N00'08 74w49'29 4:59:18
West Windsor 11 2 40N18 74w37 4:58:28
Westwood 2 1 40N59'28 74w01'59 4:56:08
Wexford East 4 2 39N53'50 74w57'46 4:59:51
Weymouth 1 17 39N30'54 74w46'45 4:59:07
Whale Beach 5 17 39N12 74w39 4:58:36
Wharton 14 1 40N53'35 74w34'56 4:58:20
Wheatland 15 12 39N53'42 74w26'03 4:57:44
Wheat Road 1 17 39N30'42 74w58'27 4:59:54
Whig Lane 17 1 39N38'22 75w13'45 5:00:55
Whippany 14 1 40N49'28 74w25'03 4:57:40
White 21 17 40N49 75w03 5:00:12
Whitehall 19 1 40N57'52 74w44'23 4:58:58
White Horse 11 1 40N11'26 74w42'10 4:58:49
Whitehouse 10 12 40N37'06 74w44'41 4:58:59
Whitehouse Station 10 12 40N36'55 74w46'15 4:59:05
White Meadow Lake 14 12 40N55 74w31 4:58:04
White Oak Bottom 15 1 40N01'14 74w11'58 4:56:48
White Oak Ridge 7 1 40N44'45 74w20'05 4:57:20
Whitesbog 3 12 39N57'33 74w30'35 4:58:02
Whitesboro 5 13 39N02'20 74w51'26 4:59:26
Whitesville 13 1 40N13'15 74w02'09 4:56:09
Whitesville 15 13 40N04'05 74w16'20 4:57:05
Whiting 15 12 39N57'16 74w22'44 4:57:31
Whitings 15 12 39N57 74w23 4:57:32
Whitman Park 4 2 39N55'55 75w06'57 5:00:28
Whitman Square 8 1 39N44'45 75w02'05 5:00:08
Whittier Oaks 13 1 40N19'25 74w19'18 4:57:17
Wickatunk 13 12 40N21'00 74w14'54 4:57:00
Wilburtha 11 1 40N15'07 74w49'58 4:59:20
Wilburtha Manor 11 1 40N15 74w48 4:59:12
Wilderness Acres 4 2 39N49 75w06 5:00:24
Wildwood 5 11 38N59'30 74w48'55 4:59:16
Wildwood Crest 5 11 38N58'29 74w50'02 4:59:20
Wildwood Gables 5 11 38N57'56 74w50'47 4:59:23
Wildwood Gardens 5 1 39N01'36 74w51'59 4:59:28
Wildwood Highlands Beach 5 12 39N00'47 74w56'48 4:59:47
Wildwood Junction 5 1 39N01'47 74w51'57 4:59:28
Wileys Corners 13 1 40N15'25 74w05'34 4:56:22
Williamstown 8 1 39N41'10 74w59'44 4:59:59
Williamstown Junction 4 17 39N44'48 74w55'44 4:59:43
Willingboro 3 1 40N01'40 74w52'10 4:59:29
Willis Corner 6 1 39N26'05 75w22'34 5:01:30
Willow Brook 19 12 41N12'38 74w23'03 4:57:32
Willowdale 4 2 39N52'50 74w58'56 4:59:56
Willow Grove 17 17 39N33'15 75w04'45 5:00:19
Willow Grove 21 13 40N41'56 75w05'11 5:00:21
Willow Ridge 3 17 39N52'12 74w54'30 4:59:38
Wilsons Landing 1 17 39N25'42 74w42'47 4:58:51
Windor Park 15 1 39N57'27 74w07'05 4:56:28
Windsor 13 12 40N14'32 74w34'54 4:58:20
Windsor Park 4 2 39N55'42 75w00'33 5:00:02
Windsor Park 15 12 39N57'12 74w09'00 4:56:36
Winfield 20 1 40N38'33 74w17'09 4:57:09
Winslow 4 2 39N39'26 74w51'46 4:59:27
Winslow Junction 4 2 39N39'54 74w50'52 4:59:23
Winston Park 13 12 40N09'27 74w14'23 4:56:58
Wintringham Park -15 1 39N58'18 74w12'28 4:56:50
Wolfert 8 2 39N47'02 75w15'41 5:01:03
Wood Acres 12 17 40N32 74w22 4:57:28
Woodair Estates 15 12 40N05'18 74w24'00 4:57:36
Woodbine 5 12 39N14'30 74w48'56 4:59:16
Woodbine Junction 5 12 39N14'05 74w47'35 4:59:10
Woodbourne 19 1 41N12'16 74w38'36 4:58:34
Woodbridge 12 1 40N33'27 74w17'06 4:57:08
Woodbridge Oaks 12 1 40N34'57 74w20'02 4:57:20
Woodbury 8 1 39N50'17 75w09'11 5:00:37
Woodbury Gardens 8 1 39N50'30 75w08'15 5:00:33
Woodbury Heights 8 1 39N49'01 75w09'20 5:00:37
Woodcliff 9 1 40N47 74w01 4:56:04
Woodcliff Lake 2 1 41N01'24 74w04'01 4:56:16
Woodcrest 4 2 39N52'20 74w59'56 5:00:00
Woodcrest Acres 4 2 39N51'33 74w58'55 4:59:56
Woodfern 18 12 40N30'31 74w45'29 4:59:02
Woodglen 10 13 40N43'09 74w53'17 4:59:33
Woodland 3 14 39N50 74w32 4:58:08
Woodland Park 20 1 40N42'10 74w22'45 4:57:31
Woodlane 3 1 40N00'42 74w48'07 4:59:12
Woodlawn Estates 15 1 39N58'25 74w12'18 4:56:49
Wood-Lynne 4 1 39N55'02 75w05'48 5:00:23
Woodmansie 3 14 39N52'04 74w28'01 4:57:52
Woodmere 15 12 40N05'17 74w19'16 4:57:17
Woodmere 17 17 39N30'36 75w23'16 5:01:33
Woodport 14 12 40N59'07 74w36'39 4:58:27
Wood-Ridge 2 1 40N50'44 74w05'18 4:56:21
Woodruff 6 1 39N28'07 75w11'10 5:00:45
Woodruff 15 12 40N03'37 74w27'45 4:57:51
Woodruffs 6 1 39N28 75w15 5:01:00
Woodruffs Gap 19 12 41N04'17 74w39'20 4:58:37
Woods Mills 17 1 39N37'17 75w15'32 5:01:02
Woods Tavern 18 2 40N30'08 74w38'42 4:58:35
Woodstock 14 12 40N59'43 74w31'35 4:58:06
Woodstown 17 17 39N39'05 75w19'43 5:01:19
Woodstream 3 17 39N54'07 74w56'52 4:59:47
Woods Upper Mill 17 17 39N30'00 75w22'42 5:01:31
Woodsville 11 12 40N22'49 74w49'45 4:59:19
Woodville 15 12 39N59'18 74w08'52 4:56:35
Woolwich 8 10 39N45 75w19 5:01:16
Wortendyke 2 2 40N59'51 74w09'02 4:56:36
Wrangell Brook Park 15 1 39N57'36 74w17'03 4:57:08
Wrights 12 1 40N27 74w25 4:57:40
Wrights Mill 8 1 39N41'05 75w10'35 5:00:42
Wrightstown 3 1 40N02'10 74w37'06 4:58:28
Wrightsville 3 2 39N59'06 74w59'56 5:00:00
Wrightsville 13 2 40N10'53 74w30'35 4:58:02
Wyckoff 2 17 41N00'34 74w10'24 4:56:42
Wyckoff Mills 13 1 40N12'12 74w15'22 4:57:01
Wyckoffs Mills 12 1 40N16'47 74w29'10 4:57:57
Wykertown 19 17 41N10'26 74w42'02 4:58:48
Wynnewood 12 1 40N34 74w27 4:57:48
Wyoming 7 1 40N43'45 74w17'30 4:57:10
Yardley Village 14 1 40N46'11 74w24'48 4:57:39
Yardville 11 1 40N10'52 74w39'53 4:58:40
Yardville Heights 11 1 40N11'00 74w41'10 4:58:45
Yellow Frame 19 12 41N03 74w45 4:59:00
York Estates 11 1 40N16 74w32 4:58:08
Yorktown 17 17 39N36'45 75w18'19 5:01:13
Zarephath 18 17 40N32'11 74w34'30 4:58:18
Zion 18 12 40N26'26 74w44'20 4:58:57

TIME TABLES

NM # 1
Before 11/18/1883 LMT
11/18/1883 12:00 MST
3/31/1918 02:00 MWT
10/27/1918 02:00 MST
3/30/1919 02:00 MWT
10/26/1919 02:00 MST
2/09/1942 02:00 MWT
9/30/1945 02:00 MST
4/30/1967 02:00 US#1

NM # 2
Before 11/18/1883 LMT
11/18/1883 12:00 MST
3/31/1918 02:00 MWT
10/27/1918 02:00 MST
3/30/1919 02:00 MWT
10/26/1919 02:00 MST
2/09/1942 02:00 MWT
9/30/1945 02:00 MST
4/24/1966 02:00 US#1

NM # 3
Before 11/18/1883 LMT
11/18/1883 12:00 MST
3/31/1918 02:00 MWT
10/27/1918 02:00 MST
3/30/1919 02:00 MWT
10/26/1919 02:00 MST
2/09/1942 02:00 MWT
9/30/1945 02:00 MST
4/26/1953 02:00 MDT
9/27/1953 02:00 MST
4/25/1954 02:00 MDT
9/26/1954 02:00 MST
4/24/1955 02:00 MDT
9/25/1955 02:00 MST
4/29/1956 02:00 MDT
9/30/1956 02:00 MST
4/28/1957 02:00 MDT
9/29/1957 02:00 MST
4/27/1958 02:00 MDT
9/28/1958 02:00 MST
4/26/1959 02:00 MDT
9/27/1959 02:00 MST
4/24/1960 02:00 MDT
9/25/1960 02:00 MST
4/30/1961 02:00 MDT
9/24/1961 02:00 MST
4/29/1962 02:00 MDT
9/30/1962 02:00 MST
4/28/1963 02:00 MDT
9/29/1963 02:00 MST
4/26/1964 02:00 MDT
9/27/1964 02:00 MST
4/25/1965 02:00 MDT
9/26/1965 02:00 MST
4/24/1966 02:00 US#1

NM # 4
Before 11/18/1883 LMT
11/18/1883 12:00 MST
3/31/1918 02:00 MWT
10/27/1918 02:00 MST
3/30/1919 02:00 MWT
10/26/1919 02:00 MST
2/09/1942 02:00 MWT
9/30/1945 02:00 MST
4/24/1955 02:00 MDT
5/08/1955 02:00 MST
4/30/1967 02:00 US#1

COUNTIES

1 Bernalillo
2 Catron
3 Chaves
4 Cibola
5 Colfax
6 Curry
7 De Baca
8 Dona Ana
9 Eddy
10 Grant
11 Guadalupe
12 Harding
13 Hidalgo
14 Lea
15 Lincoln
16 Los Alamos
17 Luna
18 McKinley
19 Mora
20 Otero
21 Quay
22 Rio Arriba
23 Roosevelt
24 Sandoval
25 San Juan
26 San Miguel
27 Santa Fe
28 Sierra
29 Socorro
30 Taos
31 Torrance
32 Union
33 Valencia

Place		Lat	Long	Time
Abbott 5	1	36N18	104w16	6:57:04
Abe Yarbrough 13	1	31N39'07	108w50'42	7:15:23
Abeytas 29	1	34N28'03	106w48'39	7:07:15
Abiquiu 22	1	36N12'26	106w19'05	7:05:16
Abo 31	1	34N27'21	106w19'57	7:05:20
Abuelo 19	1	35N56'42	105w21'37	7:01:26
Acme 3	1	33N35'32	104w19'41	6:57:19
Acoma 4	1	35N05	107w36	7:10:24
Acoma Indian Reservation 4	1	35N05	107w36	7:10:24
Acoma Pueblo 4	1	34N53'47	107w34'52	7:10:19
Acoma Village 4	1	34N53'55	107w35'11	7:10:21
Acomita 4	1	35N03'19	107w34'16	7:10:17
Adelino 33	1	34N42'57	106w43'50	7:06:55
Aden 8	1	32N09'10	107w07'37	7:08:30
Adero Az 26	1	35N21'13	104w27'31	6:57:50
Adobe 29	1	33N51'44	106w18'16	7:05:13
Adobe Acres 1	1	35N04	106w41	7:06:44
Afton 8	1	32N04'22	106w56'37	7:07:46
Agua Fria 5	1	36N25'48	105w17'54	7:01:12
Agua Fria 27	1	35N39'16	106w01'18	7:04:05
Agua Zarca 26	1	35N33'48	105w16'17	7:01:05
Agudo 7	1	34N24'19	104w18'11	6:57:13
Air Base City 14	1	32N46'11	103w11'41	6:52:47
Akela 17	1	34N28'25	107w24'18	7:09:37
Akers Place Windmill 20	1	32N00'51	105w04'52	7:00:19
Alameda 1	1	35N11'12	106w37'03	7:06:28
Alamillo 29	1	34N15'17	106w54'56	7:07:40
Alamito 19	1	35N49'21	104w26'13	6:57:45
Alamo 29	1	34N07	107w14	7:08:56
Alamogordo 20	1	32N53'58	105w57'35	7:03:50
Alamo Hueco 13	1	31N26'26	108w25'37	7:13:42
Alaska 4	1	35N03'10	107w35'44	7:10:23
Albert 12	1	35N56'04	103w51'53	6:55:28
Albuquerque 1	1	35N05'04	106w39'02	7:06:36
Alcalde 22	1	36N05'20	106w03'11	7:04:13
Alexander Place 31	1	34N41'10	106w15'13	7:05:01
Algodones 24	1	35N22'50	106w28'43	7:05:55
Alire 22	1	36N28'35	106w34'49	7:06:19
Alivio 28	1	32N50'12	107w01'13	7:08:05
Alley Place 1	1	34N58'21	106w14'59	7:05:00
Allison 18	1	35N31'27	108w47'04	7:15:08
Alma 2	1	33N22'46	108w54'10	7:15:37
Alpine Village 15	1	33N20	105w40	7:02:40
Alto 15	1	33N23'55	105w40'49	7:02:43
Alto Crest 15	1	33N20	105w40	7:02:40
Alvarado 20	1	32N08'11	106w14'12	7:04:57
Amalia 30	1	36N56'31	105w27'14	7:01:49
Amargo 22	1	36N56'16	106w53'28	7:07:34
Ambrosia Lake 18	1	35N25'08	107w49'16	7:11:17
Amistad 32	1	35N55'08	103w09'12	6:52:37
Anaconda 4	1	35N10	107w52	7:11:28
Anapra 8	1	31N47'03	106w33'48	7:06:15
Ancho 15	1	33N56'16	105w44'21	7:02:57
Ancon 26	1	35N42'55	104w25'30	6:57:42
Ancones 22	1	36N25'26	106w03'45	7:04:15
Anderson Place 31	1	34N40'50	106w20'56	7:05:24
Andrews Place 14	1	32N01'57	103w23'51	6:53:35
Angel Fire 5	1	36N33	105w16	7:01:04
Angostura 8	1	32N39'07	107w05'33	7:08:22
Angostura 24	1	35N22'27	106w29'34	7:05:58
Angostura 30	1	36N06'06	105w29'09	7:01:57
Animas 13	1	31N56'56	108w48'24	7:15:14
Antelope 13	1	31N57'25	108w42'48	7:14:51
Antelope Springs 31	1	34N49'56	106w04'03	7:04:16
Antelope Wells 13	1	31N20'56	108w30'30	7:14:02
Anthony 8	1	32N00'14	106w36'19	7:06:25
Anton Chico 11	1	35N12'00	105w08'30	7:00:34
Anzac 4	1	35N04'07	107w43'34	7:10:54
Apache 20	1	33N19'31	105w54'08	7:03:37
Apache Creek 2	1	33N49'59	108w37'28	7:14:30
Apache Park 15	1	33N20	105w40	7:02:40
Apache Springs 26	1	35N22'20	105w11'33	7:00:46
Apodaca 22	1	36N11'55	105w51'42	7:03:27
Arabela 15	1	33N35'13	105w10'22	7:00:41
Arabella 11	1	34N51'49	104w47'01	6:59:08
Aragon 2	1	33N52'52	108w32'18	7:14:09
Aragon 4	1	35N06'33	108w07'54	7:12:32
Arch 23	1	34N06'48	103w08'31	6:52:34
Archuleta (Navajo Dam P O) 25	1	36N47'39	107w42'30	7:10:50
Arena 17	1	31N48'07	107w24'54	7:09:40
Arenal 1	1	35N03'12	106w42'13	7:06:49
Arenas Valley 10	1	32N47'38	108w11'01	7:12:44
Arkansas Junction 14	1	32N41'48	103w21'02	6:53:24
Armijo 1	1	35N03'13	106w40'36	7:06:42
Arrey 28	1	32N50'55	107w19'07	7:09:16
Arriba 26	1	35N37'36	105w11'54	7:00:48
Arroyo del Agua 22	1	36N09'34	106w39'06	7:06:36
Arroyo Hondo 30	1	36N32'09	105w40'09	7:02:41
Arroyo Seco 30	1	36N30'58	105w34'09	7:02:17
Arsco 17	1	32N17'02	107w47'14	7:11:09
Artesia 9	1	32N50'32	104w24'10	6:57:37
Artesia Camp 20	1	32N48	105w34	7:02:16
Aspen Mountain 2	1	33N41'53	108w57'54	7:15:52
Atarque 4	1	34N44'11	108w42'09	7:14:49
Atencio 32	1	36N46'17	103w07'31	6:52:30
Atoka 9	1	32N46'10	104w23'18	6:57:33
Atrisco 1	1	35N04'52	106w41'13	7:06:45
Augustine 1	1	34N56'13	106w11'37	7:04:46
Aurora 19	1	36N10	105w03	7:00:12
Aurora 26	1	35N08'48	105w26'55	7:01:48
Avalon 9	1	32N29'51	104w14'10	6:56:57
Avis 20	1	32N42'01	105w27'15	7:01:49
Aztec 25	1	36N49'20	107w59'32	7:11:58
Azul 33	1	34N41'38	106w45'28	7:07:02
Bacaville 33	1	34N38'32	106w46'48	7:07:07
Baird Place 14	1	32N09'39	103w25'39	6:53:43
Banning Place 5	1	36N55'20	105w07'43	7:00:31
Barber Crossing 9	1	32N29'07	104w23'46	6:57:35
Bard 21	2	35N08	103w15	6:53:00
Barelas 1	1	35N04'23	106w39'22	7:06:37
Barr 1	1	34N58'39	106w40'01	7:06:40
Barranca 22	1	36N12'13	106w20'43	7:05:23
Barranca 30	1	36N15'43	105w52'02	7:03:28
Barranco 26	1	35N19'25	105w24'53	7:01:40
Barton 1	1	35N04'59	106w14'47	7:04:59
Basgal Place 18	1	35N21'59	108w28'22	7:13:53
Bates Place 12	2	35N29'40	103w24'46	6:53:39
Bayard 10	1	32N45'42	108w07'48	7:12:31
Beatty Wells 3	1	33N43'33	103w56'59	6:55:48
Becenti 18	1	35N41	108w09	7:12:36
Becker 33	1	34N29'46	106w36'54	7:06:28
Beenham 32	1	36N12'52	103w38'02	6:54:32
Belen 33	1	34N39'46	106w46'33	7:07:06
Bell Ranch 26	1	35N32	104w06	6:56:24
Bellview 6	1	34N49'16	103w06'26	6:52:26
Bene Dunagan 13	1	31N42'50	108w49'20	7:15:17
Bennett 14	1	32N04'04	103w12'38	6:52:51
Benson Place 31	1	34N41'44	106w18'38	7:05:15
Bent 20	1	33N09'31	105w51'23	7:03:26
Berino 8	1	32N04'05	106w37'23	7:06:30
Bermadez Place 31	1	34N40'34	106w19'02	7:05:16
Bernal 26	1	35N23'34	105w19'01	7:01:16
Bernalillo 24	1	35N18'00	106w33'02	7:06:12
Bernardo 29	1	34N25'07	106w49'59	7:07:20
Bethel 23	1	34N13'43	103w28'27	6:53:54
Beulah 26	1	35N46	105w15	7:01:00
Bibo 4	1	35N10'27	107w23'17	7:09:33
Big Horn 22	1	36N59'21	106w10'54	7:04:44
Big Mill 10	1	32N39'32	107w59'28	7:11:58
Biklabito 25	1	36N50	109w01	7:16:04
Bingham 29	1	33N54'39	106w20'56	7:05:24
Birchfield 13	1	31N37'51	108w51'05	7:15:24
Bisti 25	1	36N46	108w10	7:12:40
Bitlabito 25	1	36N50'29	109w01'08	7:16:05
Black Forest 15	1	33N20	105w40	7:02:40
Black Lake 5	1	36N17'54	105w15'29	7:01:02
Black River Village 9	1	32N12'06	104w15'09	6:57:01
Black Rock 18	1	35N05'18	108w47'26	7:15:10
Blackwell Place 27	1	35N05'58	106w08'34	7:04:34
Blanchard 26	1	35N23'19	105w21'25	7:01:26
Blanco 25	1	36N43'27	107w49'29	7:11:18
Bland 24	1	35N45'27	106w27'53	7:05:52
Blazers Mill 20	1	33N09'23	105w47'13	7:03:09
Bloodgood Place 10	1	33N03'05	107w58'09	7:11:53
Bloomfield 25	1	36N42'40	107w59'02	7:11:56
Bluewater 4	1	35N15'18	107w59'06	7:11:56
Bluewater 15	1	33N33'28	105w11'08	7:00:45
Bluit 23	1	33N37'45	103w10'59	6:52:44
Boaz 3	1	33N44'12	103w58'15	6:55:53
Bodega 33	1	34N33'07	106w40'31	7:06:42
Boles 20	1	32N55	105w57	7:03:48
Bonito 15	1	33N27'02	105w42'30	7:02:50
Boon Place 4	1	35N16'38	108w23'32	7:13:34
Borica 11	1	34N40'31	104w38'50	6:58:35
Bosque 33	1	34N33'36	106w47'19	7:07:09
Bosquecito 29	1	33N58'38	106w51'01	7:07:24
Bosque Farms 33	1	35N04	106w41	7:06:44
Box Bar Place 2	1	34N25'27	107w47'26	7:11:10
Boyd 8	1	32N19'21	106w34'23	7:06:18
Boys Ranch 29	1	34N40	106w46	7:07:04
Bramlett 29	1	31N20'03	108w50'36	7:15:22
Brazos 22	1	36N45'05	106w33'39	7:06:15
Bread Springs 18	1	35N23'54	108w39'59	7:14:40
Briggs Place 27	1	35N06'48	106w10'26	7:04:42
Brilliant 5	1	36N57'22	104w32'02	6:58:08
Brimhall 18	1	35N47	108w37	7:14:28
Brizendine Place 31	1	34N40'11	106w17'22	7:05:09
Broadmoor 3	1	33N23	104w32	6:58:08
Broadmoor Shopping Center 14	1	32N42	103w09	6:52:36
Broadview 6	1	34N49'10	103w12'47	6:52:51
Broadview Acres 4	1	35N10	107w52	7:11:28
Brockman 10	1	32N07'23	108w29'03	7:13:56
Broncho 31	1	34N33'32	106w08'09	7:04:33
Brown Place 12	1	35N32'08	103w25'07	6:53:40
Brown Place 31	1	34N44'21	106w19'42	7:05:19
Bruce Place 24	1	35N47'10	106w29'04	7:05:56
Buchanan 7	1	34N25'55	104w47'31	6:59:10
Buckeye 14	1	32N48'07	103w30'19	6:54:01
Buckhorn 10	1	33N02'13	108w42'28	7:14:50
Buckman 27	1	35N49'55	106w09'22	7:04:37
Budville 4	1	35N04'12	107w31'31	7:10:06
Buena Ventura 1	1	35N04'35	106w32'14	7:06:09
Buena Vista 19	1	35N54'49	105w14'55	7:01:00
Buena Vista 22	1	36N12'10	106w20'17	7:05:21
Buena Vista 30	1	36N47'02	105w36'12	7:02:25
Bueyeros 12	1	35N58'46	103w41'12	6:54:45
Buffalo Springs 18	1	35N56'05	108w39'12	7:14:37
Bunk Clay Place 15	2	35N24'48	103w19'53	6:53:20
Burnham 25	1	36N46	108w10	7:12:40
Butterfield Park 8	1	32N20	106w43	7:06:52
Caballo 28	1	32N58'32	107w18'26	7:09:14
Cabezon 24	1	35N37'35	107w05'50	7:08:23
Cambray 17	1	32N13'31	107w19'01	7:09:16
Cameo 23	1	34N17'15	103w13'22	6:52:53
Cameron 21	2	34N49	103w19	6:53:16
Campana 26	1	35N34'31	103w53'36	6:55:34
Campbell 3	1	33N36'29	104w11'47	6:56:47
Campus 29	1	34N03	106w54	7:07:36
Canada de los Alamos 27	1	35N35'35	105w51'38	7:03:27
Canada Village 1	1	35N03'59	106w30'10	7:06:01
Candelaria Place 31	1	34N40'20	106w21'07	7:05:24
Canjilon 22	1	36N28'46	106w26'14	7:05:45
Cannon 6	1	34N25	103w19	6:53:16
Cannon Air Force Base 6	1	34N24	103w16	6:53:04
Canon 30	1	36N23'27	105w33'46	7:02:15
Canoncito 1	1	35N08'13	106w22'22	7:05:29
Canoncito 22	1	36N10'51	105w49'54	7:03:20
Canoncito 26	1	35N47'56	105w19'19	7:01:17
Canoncito 27	1	35N40	105w57	7:03:48
Canoncito Indian Reservation 1	1	35N05	107w00	7:08:00
Canones 22	1	36N11'17	106w26'20	7:05:45
Canon Landing 24	1	35N40'05	106w44'38	7:06:59

Canon Plaza 22 1 36N33 106w09 7:04:36
Canova 22 1 36N09'33 105w59'04 7:03:56
Cantara 23 1 34N25'28 103w44'33 6:54:58
Canyon 24 1 35N37 106w44 7:06:56
Canyoncito 27 1 35N35 105w46 7:03:04
Canyon Mill 29 1 34N18'52 106w42'53 7:06:52
Capitan 15 1 33N32'43 105w34'18 7:02:17
Capitan Hill 5 1 36N40'13 104w46'26 6:59:06
Caprock 14 1 33N23'31 103w42'43 6:54:51
Capulin 32 1 36N44'28 103w59'35 6:55:58
Cardenas 7 1 34N29'28 104w50'47 6:59:23
Carisbrook 5 1 36N55'01 104w22'15 6:57:29
Carlsbad 9 1 32N25'14 104w13'42 6:56:55
Carne 17 1 32N17'17 107w34'15 7:10:17
Carnero 31 1 34N37'27 105w23'11 7:01:33
Carnuel 1 1 35N03'50 106w27'24 7:05:50
Carracas 22 1 36N59'55 107w14'40 7:08:59
Carrizo 20 1 33N17'01 105w42'23 7:02:50
Carrizozo 15 1 33N38'30 105w52'36 7:03:30
Carson 30 1 36N21'52 105w45'53 7:03:04
Carthage 29 1 33N53'01 106w39'31 7:06:38
Casa Blanca 4 1 35N02'44 107w28'15 7:09:53
Casa Fria 4 1 35N15'49 107w27'59 7:09:52
Casa Grande 5 1 36N53'18 104w58'42 6:59:55
Casa Loma 1 1 35N06'39 106w23'07 7:05:32
Casa Salazar 24
1 35N29'00 107w06'56 7:08:28
Causey 23 1 33N52'45 103w07'34 6:52:30
Cavasos Place 31
1 35N05'05 106w01'34 7:04:06
C Davis Place 31
1 34N57'43 106w06'36 7:04:26
Cebolla 22 1 36N32'18 106w29'09 7:05:57
Cedar Creek 15 1 33N20 105w40 7:02:40
Cedar Crest 1 1 35N06'27 106w22'20 7:05:29
Cedar Grove 27 1 35N10'15 106w11'22 7:04:45
Cedar Hill 25 1 36N56'13 107w53'23 7:11:34
Cedarvale 31 1 34N22 105w42 7:02:48
Cedarville 31 1 34N22'14 105w42'05 7:02:48
Cedro 1 1 35N01'20 106w21'11 7:05:25
Cedro Village 1
1 35N05 106w23 7:05:32
Center Mill 3 1 33N16'30 104w46'27 6:59:06
Centerville 32 1 35N47'51 103w05'22 6:52:21
Centerville Corner 32
1 35N47'48 103w07'35 6:52:30
Central 10 1 32N46'46 108w08'59 7:12:36
Cerrillos 27 1 35N26'15 106w07'28 7:04:30
Cerrito Colorado 30
1 36N33'51 105w34'04 7:02:16
Cerritos 26 1 35N18 105w22 7:01:28
Cerro 30 1 36N45'14 105w36'44 7:02:27
Chacon 19 1 36N08'39 105w22'02 7:01:28
Chama 22 1 36N54'11 106w34'44 7:06:19
Chamberino 8 1 32N02'59 106w40'29 7:06:42
Chamisal 30 1 36N09'57 105w44'14 7:02:57
Chamita 22 1 36N04'13 106w05'47 7:04:23
Chamizal 29 1 34N13'03 106w54'47 7:07:39
Chaparral 20 1 32N00 106w36 7:06:24
Chapelle 26 1 35N23'21 105w17'35 7:01:10
Chaperito 26 1 35N21'57 104w56'41 6:59:47
Chapman Place 10
1 32N53'27 108w59'32 7:15:58
Chappel 8 1 32N11'30 107w11'03 7:08:44
Chato 31 1 34N37'51 106w20'54 7:05:24
Chaves Place 28
1 33N24'03 107w30'19 7:10:01
Chaves Place 31
1 34N44'30 106w22'27 7:05:30
Chelwood Park 1
1 35N05'46 106w30'23 7:06:02
Chical 24 1 35N20'24 106w31'18 7:06:05
Chical 33 1 34N52'06 106w40'04 7:06:40
Chi Chil Tah 18
1 35N14'54 108w54'26 7:15:38
Chico 5 1 36N29'12 104w11'32 6:56:46
Childres Place 27
1 35N19'40 105w43'11 7:02:53
Chili 22 1 36N06'18 106w08'57 7:04:36
Chilili 1 1 34N53'22 106w13'56 7:04:56
Chimayo 22 1 36N00'09 105w55'47 7:03:43
Chippeway Park 20
1 32N54'34 105w42'17 7:02:49
Chise 28 1 33N16'20 107w35'49 7:10:23
Chisum 3 1 33N15'43 104w25'06 6:57:40
Chloride 28 1 33N20'19 107w40'38 7:10:43
Christopher Place 25
1 36N55'15 107w30'49 7:10:03
Chupadera 31 1 34N16'14 106w21'36 7:05:26
Chupadero 27 1 35N49'21 105w54'58 7:03:40
Church Rock 18 1 35N32'02 108w35'57 7:14:24
Cimarron 5 1 36N30'39 104w54'55 6:59:40
Ciruela 19 1 35N57'16 104w49'05 6:59:16
Clapham 32 1 36N28 103w11 6:52:44
Clara Peak 22 1 36N02'08 106w14'23 7:04:58
Claud 6 1 34N35'39 103w10'43 6:52:43
Claunch 29 1 34N08'31 105w59'38 7:03:59
Clayton 32 1 36N27'06 103w11'01 6:52:44
Cleveland 19 1 35N59'36 105w22'12 7:01:29
Cliff 10 1 32N57'44 108w36'38 7:14:27
Clines Corners 31
1 35N00'34 105w40'07 7:02:40
Cloud Country Estates 20
1 32N57 105w45 7:03:00
Cloudcroft 20 1 32N57'26 105w44'31 7:02:58
Cloverdale 13 1 31N57 108w48 7:15:12
Cloverdale 29 1 31N25'01 108w55'45 7:15:43
Clovis 6 1 34N24'17 103w12'17 6:52:49
Coalora 15 1 33N34'04 105w35'48 7:02:23
Coane 29 1 33N48'03 106w19'36 7:05:18
Cobre 10 1 32N46'50 108w06'41 7:12:27
Cochiti 24 1 35N37 106w21 7:05:24
Cochiti Indian Reservation 24
1 35N37 106w21 7:05:24
Cochiti Lake 24
1 35N34 106w20 7:05:20
Cochiti Pueblo 24
1 35N36'34 106w20'37 7:05:22
Cole Place 9 1 32N49'13 104w44'35 6:58:58
Colfax 5 1 36N35'48 104w44'16 6:58:57
Colmor 5 1 36N13'14 104w38'56 6:58:36
Colonias 11 1 35N06'35 104w50'48 6:59:23
Columbine 30 1 36N42 105w36 7:02:24
Columbus 17 1 31N49'39 107w38'22 7:10:33
Community Center 16
3 35N51 106w16 7:05:04
Conchas 26 1 35N22 104w11 6:56:44
Conchas Dam 26 1 35N28 104w05 6:56:20
Continental Divide 18
1 35N25 108w19 7:13:16
Contreras 29 1 34N22'58 106w48'47 7:07:15
Coolidge 18 1 35N26'49 108w21'46 7:13:27
Cooney 2 1 33N25'22 108w48'26 7:15:14
Cooper 15 1 33N55'48 105w47'07 7:03:08
Copperas Vista 10
1 33N07'06 108w11'49 7:12:47
Copperton 4 1 35N08'46 108w08'58 7:12:36
Cora Crew 15 1 33N28'57 106w01'28 7:04:06
Corazon 26 1 35N36 105w13 7:00:52
Cordillera 19 1 35N58'56 105w21'32 7:01:26
Cordova 22 1 36N00'26 105w51'36 7:03:26
Corner Ranch 13
1 31N21'22 108w12'38 7:12:51
Corner Well 3 1 33N38'32 103w37'50 6:54:31
Corner Well 20 1 32N29'53 105w04'17 7:00:17
Corner Windmill 7
1 34N24'45 104w20'20 6:57:21
Corner Windmill 11
1 35N05'07 104w27'39 6:57:51
Corner Windmill 28
1 33N06'23 107w04'01 7:08:16
Corona 31 1 34N15'03 105w35'46 7:02:23
Coronado 27 1 35N40 105w57 7:03:48
Corrales (Sandoval P O) 24
1 35N14'16 106w36'22 7:06:25
Correo 33 1 34N57'18 107w11'03 7:08:44
Coruco 26 1 35N22 105w27 7:01:48
Corugo 26 1 35N21'58 105w26'17 7:01:45
Costilla 30 1 36N58'33 105w31'50 7:02:07
Cotton City 13 1 32N05'18 108w52'43 7:15:31
Cotton Place 14
1 32N13'29 103w39'46 6:54:39
Cottonwood 25 1 36N52'26 108w23'33 7:13:34
Counselor 24 1 36N12'33 107w27'26 7:09:50
Country Club Estates 1
1 35N10 106w39 7:06:36
Country Club Heights 15
1 33N20 105w40 7:02:40
Cowles 26 1 35N48'43 105w39'33 7:02:38
Coyote 15 1 33N48'45 105w49'23 7:03:18
Coyote 22 1 36N10'03 106w36'57 7:06:28
Coyote Canyon (Brimhall P O) 18
1 35N46'29 108w37'13 7:14:29
Crane Place 4 1 34N48'54 107w23'02 7:09:32
Crocker 28 1 33N20'32 107w01'48 7:08:07
Crossroads 14 1 33N30'44 103w20'21 6:53:21
Crownpoint 18 1 35N40'41 108w09'02 7:12:36
Cruzville 2 1 33N48'26 108w39'53 7:14:40
Crystal 25 1 36N02'45 108w57'56 7:15:52
Cuba 24 1 36N01'20 106w57'28 7:07:50
Cubero 4 1 35N05'09 107w31'03 7:10:04
Cuchillo 28 1 33N14'09 107w21'36 7:09:26
Cudai 25 1 36N51'45 108w47'29 7:15:10
Cuervo 11 1 35N01'52 104w24'29 6:57:38
Cuervo Crossing 24
1 35N20'03 107w01'02 7:08:04
Cueva de los Novios 23
1 35N18'06 107w18'19 7:09:13
Culebra 31 1 34N40'57 105w46'04 7:03:04
Cummings Place 15
2 35N18'00 103w22'54 6:53:32
Cundiyo 27 1 35N57'33 105w53'45 7:03:35
Cutter 28 1 33N03'37 107w01'19 7:08:05
Cuyamungue 27 1 35N52'11 106w00'13 7:04:01
Dahlia 11 1 35N07'17 105w16'35 7:01:06
Dalies 33 1 34N46'19 106w51'36 7:07:26
Dalton Pass 18 1 35N41 108w09 7:12:36
Danvik Place 31
1 34N57'48 106w13'20 7:04:53
Datil 2 1 34N08'42 107w50'35 7:11:22
Davies Place 2 1 34N13'03 108w46'57 7:15:08
Dawson 5 1 36N39'51 104w46'27 6:59:06
Dayton 9 1 32N43'53 104w23'05 6:57:32
D Candelaria Place 31
1 34N36'53 106w21'41 7:05:27
Deer 13 1 31N22'56 108w37'48 7:14:31
Deer Creek Landing 24
1 35N44'39 106w46'27 7:07:06
Deer Creek Wells 13
1 31N26'04 108w41'26 7:14:46
Deering Place 3
1 33N57'16 104w17'23 6:57:10
Deer Lake 24 1 35N59'46 106w51'31 7:07:26
Defiance 18 1 35N29'26 108w53'45 7:15:35
Del Norte 15 1 33N20 105w40 7:02:40
Delphos 23 1 34N04'31 103w29'31 6:53:58
Deming 17 1 32N16'07 107w45'29 7:11:02
Dennison Place 27
1 35N15'18 106w02'59 7:04:12
Derramadero 31 1 34N49'41 105w20'03 7:01:20
Derry 28 1 32N47'17 107w16'54 7:09:08
Des Moines 32 1 36N45'40 103w50'01 6:55:20
De Vargas Shopping Center 27
1 35N40 105w57 7:03:48
Dexter 3 1 33N11'50 104w22'21 6:57:29
Diamante Mill 3
1 33N19'42 104w50'18 6:59:21
Diener 4 1 35N10'29 108w07'36 7:12:30
Dilia 11 1 35N11'35 105w03'47 7:00:15
Dillon 6 1 36N51'56 104w27'21 6:57:49
Dixon 22 1 36N11'55 105w53'17 7:03:33
Dog Canyon Estates 20
1 32N55 105w57 7:03:48
Domingo 24 1 35N30'39 106w19'15 7:05:17
Dona 8 1 32N12'38 107w15'38 7:09:03
Dona Ana 8 1 32N23'22 106w48'48 7:07:15
Dora 23 1 33N56'19 103w20'10 6:53:21
Dos Tristes 18 1 35N15'19 107w14'11 7:08:57
Double Adobes 13
1 31N38'42 108w45'19 7:15:01
Double Crossing 15
1 33N31'34 105w26'23 7:01:46
Double Mills 11
1 35N03'56 104w31'21 6:58:05
Douthit Place 26
1 35N15'50 105w39'28 7:02:38
Downtown 1 1 35N05 106w39 7:06:36
Dulce 22 1 36N56'01 106w59'54 7:08:00
Dummoor 31 1 34N37'47 105w42'16 7:02:49
Dunken 3 1 32N48'46 105w12'07 7:00:48
Dunlap 7 1 34N05'05 104w31'41 6:58:07
Dunn Place 28 1 33N03'30 107w43'32 7:10:54
Dunn Place 31 1 34N59'36 106w09'15 7:04:37
Duran 31 1 34N28'02 105w23'47 7:01:35
Duranes 22 1 36N16'08 106w03'06 7:04:12
Dusty 29 1 33N38 107w39 7:10:36
Dwyer (Faywood P O) 10
1 32N37'42 107w51'59 7:11:28
Eagle Nest 5 1 36N33'17 105w15'47 7:01:03
Eagle Nest 18 1 35N26'18 107w19'26 7:09:18
Eakins 13 1 31N43'15 108w49'27 7:15:18
East De Baca 7 1 34N21 104w10 6:56:40
East Grand Plains 3
1 33N20'08 104w26'13 6:57:45
East Pecos 26 1 35N34'25 105w39'48 7:02:39
East Vaughn 11 1 34N36 105w13 7:00:52
Eaton Place 13 1 31N40'50 108w56'10 7:15:45
E Davis Place 31
1 34N54'47 106w05'22 7:04:21
Edgal Place 10 1 32N40'51 108w34'52 7:14:19
Edgewood 27 1 35N03'41 106w11'27 7:04:46
El Alto 19 1 35N58'44 105w18'27 7:01:14
El Ancon 26 1 35N23'22 105w27'30 7:01:50
El Cerrito 26 1 35N18 105w22 7:01:28
El Cerro 33 1 34N43'37 106w42'37 7:06:50
El Curuco 22 1 36N12'25 106w19'21 7:05:17
El Dado 18 1 35N30'56 107w31'00 7:10:04
El Duende 22 1 36N04'27 106w07'10 7:04:29
Elephant Butte 28
1 33N08'55 107w11'03 7:08:44
El Guacho 22 1 36N00'24 106w05'11 7:04:21
El Huerfano 25 1 36N43 107w59 7:11:56
Elida 23 1 33N56'48 103w39'22 6:54:37
Elizaabethtown 5
1 36N37'09 105w17'02 7:01:08
Elk 3 1 32N56'35 105w20'02 7:01:20
Elkins 3 1 33N41'40 104w03'16 6:56:13
Eller Place 17 1 32N01'21 107w58'22 7:11:53
El Llanito 24 1 35N19'48 106w31'51 7:06:07
El Llano 22 1 36N00'56 106w02'38 7:04:11
El Llano 26 1 35N38'46 105w16'11 7:01:05
El Macho 26 1 35N40'29 105w41'23 7:02:46
El Monte Rojo 22
1 36N20'03 106w29'38 7:05:59
El Morro 4 1 35N02'40 108w19'11 7:13:17
El Ojito 8 1 32N00'19 106w40'39 7:06:43
El Padro 30 1 36N25'54 105w34'27 7:02:18
El Portero 27 1 36N00 105w56 7:03:44
El Porvenir 26 1 35N41'48 105w22'56 7:01:32
El Prado 30 1 36N26 105w35 7:02:20
El Pueblo 26 1 35N22 105w27 7:01:48
El Rancho 27 1 35N53'21 106w04'45 7:04:19
El Rancho Loma Linda 30
1 36N11 105w40 7:02:40
El Refugio 1 1 35N07'03 106w20'15 7:05:21
El Renz-O-Ranch 5
1 36N33 105w16 7:01:04
El Rincon de los Trujillos 22
1 36N00 105w56 7:03:44
El Rito 4 1 34N59'57 107w17'58 7:09:12
El Rito 22 1 36N20'36 106w11'17 7:04:45
El Rito 30 1 36N48'00 105w34'02 7:02:16
El Turquillo 19
1 36N04'47 105w15'02 7:01:00
El Vado 22 1 36N35'38 106w43'41 7:06:55
El Valle 30 1 36N06'37 105w43'34 7:02:54
Elwood 20 1 32N17'37 106w08'12 7:04:33
Embudo 22 1 36N12'27 105w57'38 7:03:51
Emplazado 26 1 35N44'22 105w11'20 7:00:45
Enchanted Hills 15
1 33N20 105w40 7:02:40
Encinal 4 1 35N07'02 107w27'51 7:09:51
Encino 31 1 34N39'04 105w27'40 7:01:51
Encinoso 15 1 33N41'08 105w28'58 7:01:56
Endee 21 2 35N08'16 103w06'26 6:52:26
Engle 28 1 33N10'37 107w01'51 7:08:07
En Medio 27 1 35N49'33 105w54'14 7:03:37
Ensenada 22 1 36N43'38 106w31'58 7:06:08
Escabosa 1 1 34N55'30 106w17'22 7:05:09
Escondida 29 1 34N06'05 106w53'45 7:07:35
Espanola 22 1 35N59'28 106w04'48 7:04:19
Espuela 9 1 32N55'47 104w23'14 6:57:33
Estaca 22 1 36N06'43 106w03'29 7:04:14
Estancia 31 1 34N45'30 106w03'19 7:04:13
Estes City 15 1 33N34'36 106w16'01 7:05:04
Estes Place 10 1 32N53'07 108w55'14 7:15:41
Eunice 14 1 32N26'14 103w09'31 6:52:38
Evanola 7 1 34N24'57 104w29'37 6:57:58
Fairacres 8 1 32N18'14 106w50'46 7:07:23
Fairbanks 3 1 33N21'11 104w29'06 6:57:56
Fairview 22 1 36N00'35 106w03'50 7:04:15
Farley 5 1 36N21'10 104w02'19 6:56:09
Farmington 25 1 36N43'41 108w13'05 7:12:52
Faywood 10 1 32N30 108w00 7:12:00
Faywood Hot Springs 17
1 32N33'15 107w59'37 7:11:58
Fence Lake 4 1 34N39'12 108w40'38 7:14:43
Field 6 1 34N37'43 103w33'54 6:54:16
Fierro 10 1 32N50'43 108w04'39 7:12:19
Fivemile Crossing 25
1 36N41'31 107w45'10 7:11:01
Five Points 1 1 35N03'58 106w39'58 7:06:40
Flora Vista 25 1 36N47'40 108w04'47 7:12:19
Florida 17 1 32N24'57 107w34'34 7:10:18
Florida 29 1 34N05'28 106w53'52 7:07:35
Floyd 28 1 34N12'51 103w34'48 6:54:19
Flume Canyon 15
1 33N20 105w40 7:02:40
Flying H 3 1 33N02 105w08 7:00:32
Folsom 32 1 36N50'42 103w55'02 6:55:40
Forest Heights 15
1 33N20 105w40 7:02:40
Forest Park 1 1 35N06'59 106w22'19 7:05:29
Forrest 21 2 34N47'41 103w36'03 6:54:24
Fort Bayard 10 1 32N47'46 108w08'59 7:12:36
Fort Selden 8 1 32N29'01 106w54'45 7:07:39
Fort Stanton 15
1 33N29'45 105w31'21 7:02:05
Fort Sumner 7 1 34N28'18 104w14'42 6:56:59

Fort Wingate 18 1 35N28'04 108w32'26 7:14:10
Fort Wingate Army Depot 18 1 35N31 108w44 7:14:56
Four Forks 9 1 32N23'25 104w21'35 6:57:26
Four Points 8 1 32N15'54 106w47'08 7:07:09
Four Wells 9 1 32N22'23 104w43'00 6:58:52
Francisco Rascon Place 28 1 33N00'42 107w37'20 7:10:29
Franks Place 28 1 33N24'23 107w48'11 7:11:13
French 5 1 36N28'27 104w33'28 6:58:14
French Corners 5 1 36N22 104w35 6:58:20
Frijoles (Monument Hdq) 24 1 35N46'44 106w16'14 7:05:05
Frijoles Spring 22 1 36N09'40 106w22'12 7:05:29
Frontier Post 9 1 32N41'19 104w23'41 6:57:35
Fruitland 25 1 36N44'21 108w23'42 7:13:35
Gabaldon 26 1 35N28'32 105w17'28 7:01:10
Gage 17 1 32N13'46 108w05'08 7:12:21
Galisteo 27 1 35N23'44 105w56'45 7:03:47
Gallaher 6 1 34N24'10 103w17'47 6:53:11
Gallegos 12 1 35N36'35 103w42'24 6:54:50
Gallegos (Ojo Caliente P O) 22 1 36N17'19 106w03'00 7:04:12
Gallina 22 1 36N14 106w51 7:07:24
Gallinas 15 1 34N08'49 105w39'13 7:02:37
Gallinas 26 1 35N40'48 105w21'10 7:01:25
Gallup 18 1 35N31'41 108w44'31 7:14:58
Gamerco 18 1 35N34'20 108w45'53 7:15:04
Garanbuio 26 1 35N18'57 105w24'48 7:01:39
Garcia 29 1 31N20'02 108w51'45 7:15:27
Garcia Place 25 1 36N58'34 107w36'13 7:10:25
Garcia Place 28 1 33N10'16 107w29'12 7:09:57
Gardiner 5 1 36N53'07 104w28'55 6:57:56
Garfield 8 1 32N45'25 107w15'50 7:09:03
Garita 26 1 35N16 104w29 6:57:56
Garrison 23 1 33N51'02 103w12'46 6:52:51
Gary 13 1 32N19'27 108w49'04 7:15:16
Gascon 19 1 35N53'12 105w26'44 7:01:47
Gavilan 22 1 36N18 107w03 7:08:12
Gibbs Place 29 1 34N16'04 106w43'46 7:06:55
Gibson 13 1 31N38'12 108w56'19 7:15:45
Gibson Place 13 1 31N45'51 108w47'39 7:15:11
Gila 10 1 32N57'57 108w34'34 7:14:18
Gila Hot Springs 10 1 33N11'43 108w12'24 7:12:50
Gilman 24 1 35N42'58 106w45'34 7:07:02
Gise 26 1 35N26'35 105w36'58 7:02:28
Gladiola 14 1 33N15'26 103w10'46 6:52:43
Gladstone 32 1 36N18'17 103w58'21 6:55:53
Glencoe 15 1 33N24'33 105w26'54 7:01:48
Glen Grove 15 1 33N20 105w40 7:02:40
Glenrio 21 2 35N10'44 103w02'30 6:52:10
Glenwood 2 1 33N19'00 108w52'57 7:15:32
Glorieta 27 1 35N34'59 105w46'10 7:03:05
Glover Place 31 1 34N48'03 106w17'42 7:05:11
Gobernador 22 1 36N43 107w50 7:11:20
Golden 27 1 35N16'01 106w12'48 7:04:51
Golondrinas 19 1 35N53'28 105w11'07 7:00:44
Gonzales 18 1 35N25'42 108w19'13 7:13:17
Gonzales Ranch 26 1 35N14'45 105w27'36 7:01:50
Grady 6 1 34N49'17 103w19'01 6:53:16
Grafton 28 1 33N25'50 107w44'44 7:10:59
Grama 8 1 32N44'34 107w01'54 7:08:08
Grande 32 1 36N40'14 103w46'26 6:55:06
Gran Quivira 31 1 34N15'49 106w06'05 7:04:24
Grants 4 1 35N09'08 107w50'33 7:11:22
Grassie Place 4 1 34N41'12 108w21'23 7:13:26
Greenfield 3 1 33N09'55 104w20'55 6:57:24
Green Meadows 15 1 33N20 105w40 7:02:40
Green Tree 15 1 33N20 105w35 7:02:20
Grenville 32 1 36N36 103w37 6:54:28
Gribble Place 2 1 33N57'47 108w52'31 7:15:30
Grier 6 1 34N24'38 103w23'53 6:53:36
Grubisich Place 18 1 35N19'15 108w25'37 7:13:42
Guachupangue 22 1 35N58'58 106w05'01 7:04:20
Guadalupe 7 1 34N32'46 104w25'39 6:57:43
Guadalupe 24 1 35N32'29 107w09'03 7:08:36
Guadalupita 19 1 36N08'15 105w14'17 7:00:57
Guagolotes 26 1 35N18 105w22 7:01:28
Guess Place 10 1 32N10'27 108w15'49 7:13:03
Guique 22 1 36N05'16 106w04'25 7:04:18
Gunn Place Abandoned) 10 1 32N51'23 108w50'14 7:15:21
Gutierrezville 2 1 34N03'36 107w55'25 7:11:42
Guy 32 1 36N48'52 103w25'55 6:53:44
Hachita 10 1 31N55'05 108w19'11 7:13:17
Hacienda Acres 8 1 32N20 106w43 7:06:52
Hagerman 3 1 33N06'54 104w19'35 6:57:18
Hagerman Heights 9 1 32N24'58 104w13'15 6:56:53
Hahn 1 1 35N07'50 106w38'03 7:06:32
Halfway 14 1 32N33'06 103w44'06 6:54:56
Hamilton Terrace 15 1 33N20 105w40 7:02:40
Hanover 10 1 32N48'48 108w05'26 7:12:22
Hanover Junction 10 1 32N46'42 108w06'53 7:12:28
Happy Valley 9 1 32N25 104w14 6:56:56
Harden Cienega 10 1 33N10'24 109w02'18 7:16:09
Hard Luck Crossing 29 1 33N32'50 106w58'54 7:07:56
Hargis 21 2 35N08'46 103w48'57 6:55:16
Harkey Crossing 9 1 32N14'11 104w11'49 6:56:47
Harrisburg 4 1 35N02'53 107w30'07 7:10:00
Harroun Crossing 9 1 32N14'26 104w02'53 6:56:12
Hassell 21 2 34N42'24 104w01'23 6:56:06
Hatch 8 1 32N39'55 107w09'09 7:08:37
Hayden 32 1 35N58'06 103w16'16 6:53:05
Hebron 5 1 36N44'19 104w27'55 6:57:52
Hendricks Place 15 2 35N20'16 103w29'54 6:54:00
Hermanas 17 1 31N51'03 107w57'05 7:11:48
Hermosa 28 1 33N09'27 107w43'46 7:10:55
Hernandez 22 1 36N03'46 106w07'08 7:04:29
Herrera 1 1 35N11'32 107w06'51 7:08:27
Hersey Place 8 1 32N30'46 107w04'42 7:08:19
Hewitt Place 31 1 34N33'55 106w20'41 7:05:23
Hext Place (site) 10 1 32N48'57 108w55'41 7:15:43
Higgins Place (abandoned) 3 1 33N10'46 104w31'28 6:58:06
High Lonesome Wells 13 1 31N25'04 108w33'27 7:14:14
High Rolls 20 1 32N57'03 105w50'06 7:03:20
Highway Mill 3 1 33N21'58 104w50'52 6:59:23
Hill 8 1 32N25'38 106w51'11 7:07:25
Hillburn City 14 1 33N05'08 103w18'57 6:53:16
Hillsboro 28 1 32N55'15 107w33'59 7:10:16
Hobbies 1 1 35N05 106w23 7:05:32
Hobbs 14 1 32N42'09 103w08'08 6:52:33
Hockett 8 1 32N36'09 107w17'05 7:09:08
Hoffman Town 1 1 35N06'48 106w32'14 7:06:09
Hogg Place 4 1 34N41'21 108w15'06 7:13:00
Holiday Acres 15 1 33N20 105w40 7:02:40
Hollene 6 1 34N46'39 103w05'25 6:52:22
Holloman 20 1 32N52 106w06 7:04:24
Holloman Air Force Base 20 1 32N52 106w06 7:04:24
Hollywood 15 1 33N19'24 105w38'04 7:02:32
Holman 19 1 36N02'18 105w22'59 7:01:32
Holy Ghost 26 1 35N45'36 105w41'31 7:02:46
Home Place Well 23 1 33N45'15 103w42'34 6:54:50
Hondo 15 1 33N23'15 105w16'13 7:01:05
Hooverville 26 1 35N22'34 104w13'02 6:56:52
Hope 9 1 32N48'37 104w43'56 6:58:56
Horse Springs 2 1 34N09 107w51 7:11:24
Horton Place 27 1 35N08'31 106w12'31 7:04:50
Hospah 18 1 35N44'07 107w44'45 7:10:59
Hot Springs 26 1 35N39'14 105w17'28 7:01:10
Hot Springs Landing 28 1 33N12'26 107w12'36 7:08:50
House 21 2 34N39 103w54 6:55:36
Hudson 21 2 35N15'51 103w31'57 6:54:08
Hughes Place 4 1 34N40'41 107w46'49 7:11:07
Humble City 14 1 32N47'42 103w13'07 6:52:52
Hunter Place 9 1 32N51'45 104w44'18 6:58:57
Hurley 10 1 32N41'57 108w07'53 7:12:32
Hyde Park Estates 27 1 35N40 105w57 7:03:48
Hyde Place 31 1 34N42'50 106w22'12 7:05:29
Hyer 27 1 35N12'52 106w07'07 7:04:28
Idlewild 5 1 36N32'58 105w18'17 7:01:13
Ilfeld 26 1 35N25'16 105w33'30 7:02:14
Inca 25 1 36N53'34 107w55'36 7:11:42
Indian Hills 15 1 33N20 105w40 7:02:40
Inez 23 1 33N58'00 103w08'36 6:52:34
Isleta 1 1 34N54'26 106w41'19 7:06:45
Isleta Indian Reservation 1 1 34N54 106w40 7:06:40
Isleta Pueblo 1 1 34N54'25 106w40'49 7:06:43
Iyanbito 18 1 35N31'20 108w28'37 7:13:54
Jack Canon Place 26 1 35N17'20 105w37'37 7:02:30
Jacona 27 1 35N53'26 106w02'30 7:04:10
Jaconita 27 1 35N53'10 106w03'34 7:04:14
Jal 14 1 32N06'47 103w11'35 6:52:46
Jarales 33 1 34N36'47 106w45'47 7:07:03
Jarett Place 31 1 35N02'19 106w07'56 7:04:32
Jarosa 22 1 36N02'48 106w41'04 7:06:44
Jeffers Place 2 1 34N11'44 107w46'26 7:11:06
Jemez 24 1 35N43 106w43 7:06:52
Jemez Indian Reservation 24 1 35N40 106w43 7:06:52
Jemez Pueblo 24 1 35N36'50 106w43'31 7:06:54
Jemez Springs 24 1 35N44'56 106w42'34 7:06:50
Jewkes Place 28 1 33N25'01 107w33'01 7:10:12
Jicarilla 15 1 33N52'08 105w39'45 7:02:39
Jicarilla 22 1 36N49 107w10 7:08:40
Jicarilla Indian Reservation 22 1 36N56 107w00 7:08:00
Jim Robinson 13 1 31N46'14 108w48'09 7:15:13
Joe Yarbrough 13 1 31N39'58 108w49'54 7:15:20
Joffre 11 1 34N29'14 105w02'38 7:00:11
Johnson 20 1 32N18'03 103w11'22 6:52:45
Johns Place 31 1 35N00'46 106w05'18 7:04:21
Jones City 14 1 32N28'14 103w07'31 6:52:30
Jordan 21 2 34N47'40 103w50'52 6:55:23
Jornada 28 1 33N07'23 107w02'00 7:08:08
Juan Tomas 1 1 35N01'37 106w17'52 7:05:11
Julian Place 4 1 34N39'17 108w14'33 7:12:58
Junta 22 1 36N13 105w56 7:03:44
Kearney 20 1 32N58'54 105w59'29 7:03:58
Kelly 29 1 34N04'59 107w12'17 7:08:49
Kelso Place 28 1 33N03'13 107w45'11 7:11:01
Kenna 23 1 33N50'32 103w46'17 6:55:05
Kennedy 27 1 35N24'15 105w59'08 7:03:57
Kenzin 8 1 32N06'23 107w00'57 7:08:04
Keota 5 1 36N57'16 104w28'33 6:57:54
Kermit 23 1 34N00'04 103w35'32 6:54:22
Kimball Place 8 1 32N30'53 107w02'40 7:08:11
Kimbeto 25 1 36N11'01 107w50'27 7:11:22
Kimmons 15 1 33N29'27 106w01'08 7:04:05
Kinebeto 25 1 36N46 108w10 7:12:40
King Place 31 1 34N46'51 106w18'47 7:05:15
Kingston 28 1 32N55'01 107w42'20 7:10:49
Kingswood 15 1 33N20 105w40 7:02:40
Kinney 1 1 35N00'37 106w39'37 7:06:38
Kinney Wells 29 1 33N52'16 106w44'58 7:07:00
Kiowa 5 1 36N39'14 104w06'26 6:56:26
Kiowa Village 30 1 36N34'45 105w35'47 7:02:23
Kirtland 25 1 36N44'03 108w21'33 7:13:26
Kirtland Addition 1 1 35N03'19 106w37'49 7:06:31
Kirtland Air Force Base 1 1 35N02 106w37 7:06:28
Kline Place 28 1 33N26'57 107w51'26 7:11:26
Knowles 14 1 32N50'25 103w07'38 6:52:31
Knowles Place 9 1 32N33'32 104w34'45 6:58:19
Koehler 5 1 36N44'27 104w37'04 6:58:28
Krider 23 1 34N26'02 103w50'37 6:55:22
Kroenigs 26 1 35N44'07 105w02'16 7:00:09
La Bajada 27 1 35N33'22 106w14'25 7:04:58
La Bolsa 22 1 36N12'56 105w54'15 7:03:37
La Borcita 29 1 33N59'24 106w53'00 7:07:32
La Careda 22 1 36N12'06 106w19'16 7:05:17
La Chuachia 22 1 36N05'42 106w08'15 7:04:33
La Cienaga 22 1 36N12'49 105w55'23 7:03:42
La Cienega 27 1 35N33'46 106w07'49 7:04:31
La Constancia 33 1 34N40'42 106w44'04 7:06:56
La Cuesta 1 1 35N04'42 106w30'23 7:06:02
La Cuestecita 22 1 36N09'51 105w48'12 7:03:13
La Cueva 19 1 35N56'30 105w14'55 7:01:00
La Cueva 27 1 35N35'28 105w43'57 7:02:56
Lacy Place 27 1 35N04'53 106w08'21 7:04:33
La Fragua 26 1 35N18'53 105w24'22 7:01:37
La Gotera 24 1 35N18'34 107w11'25 7:08:46
Laguna 4 1 35N02'12 107w22'56 7:09:32
Laguna Indian Reservation 4 1 35N02 107w23 7:09:32
Lagunas 26 1 35N31'45 105w20'15 7:01:21
Lagunita 26 1 35N22'02 105w14'39 7:00:59
Lagunitas 24 1 35N59'33 106w59'11 7:07:57
La Huerta 9 1 32N26'34 104w13'14 6:56:53
La Jara 19 1 36N02'59 105w10'58 7:00:44
La Jara 24 1 36N05'16 106w58'27 7:07:54
La Joya 27 1 35N35 105w46 7:03:04
La Joya 29 1 34N20'46 106w50'42 7:07:23
La Junta 22 1 36N12'41 105w54'59 7:03:40
Lake Arthur 3 1 32N59'53 104w21'58 6:57:28
Lake Valley 25 1 36N05'30 108w09'24 7:12:38
Lake Valley 28 1 32N43'04 107w34'02 7:10:16
Lakeview Pines 5 1 36N30'31 105w18'11 7:01:13
Lakewood 9 1 32N38 104w23 6:57:32
La Ladera 33 1 34N49'36 106w39'58 7:06:40
La Lande 7 1 34N26'53 104w08'01 6:56:32
La Liendre 26 1 35N25'20 105w03'00 7:00:12
La Loma 11 1 35N11 105w07 7:00:28
La Loma 27 1 35N37'10 105w55'48 7:03:43
La Luz 20 1 32N58'40 105w56'29 7:03:46
Lama 30 1 36N38'59 105w37'04 7:02:28
LaMadera 22 1 36N23'13 106w02'27 7:04:10
La Madera 24 1 35N13'22 106w22'12 7:05:29
La Manga 26 1 35N30'34 105w15'48 7:01:03
La Mesa 8 1 32N07'19 106w42'26 7:06:50
La Mesilla 8 1 32N18 106w47 7:07:08
La Mesilla 22 1 35N56'54 106w04'12 7:04:17
Lamy 27 1 35N28'53 105w52'45 7:03:31
Lanark 8 1 31N58'12 106w48'57 7:07:16
La Petra 28 1 33N25'59 107w25'14 7:09:41
La Placita 24 1 36N02'07 106w57'29 7:07:50
LaPlata 25 1 36N55'43 108w11'23 7:12:46
Laplata PO 25 1 36N54'00 108w11'23 7:12:46
La Puebla 27 1 35N59'21 105w59'45 7:03:59
La Puente 22 1 36N42'00 106w36'01 7:06:24
Largo 7 1 34N26'49 104w42'40 6:58:51
Largo 15 1 33N54'07 105w47'21 7:03:09
Las Colonias 24 1 35N22'28 106w29'06 7:05:56
Las Cruces 8 1 32N18'44 106w46'40 7:07:07
Las Dispensas 26 1 35N44'43 105w21'33 7:01:26
Las Dos 27 1 35N45'42 106w01'48 7:04:07
Las Nutrias 29 1 34N28'36 106w46'12 7:07:05
Las Palomas 28 1 33N03'45 107w17'52 7:09:11
Las Placitas 22 1 36N19'23 106w09'43 7:04:39
Las Tablas 22 1 36N33'20 106w01'43 7:04:07
Las Tusas 26 1 35N45'55 105w16'57 7:01:08
Las Vegas 26 1 35N35'38 105w13'00 7:00:52
Las Vegas City 26 1 35N35'38 105w13'00 7:00:52
Las Vegas Town (W Las Vegas) 26 1 35N35'27 105w13'48 7:00:55
La Union 8 1 31N57'02 106w39'40 7:06:39
Lava 22 1 36N58'48 106w05'39 7:04:23
LaVentana 24 1 35N49'38 106w58'15 7:07:53
La Villita 22 1 36N06'12 106w02'51 7:04:11
Lea 14 1 32N31'20 103w31'58 6:54:08
Lea North Central 14 1 32N57 103w22 6:53:28
Leasburg 8 1 32N27'14 106w52'57 7:07:32
Lea South Central 14 1 32N44 103w14 6:52:56
Ledoux 19 1 35N55'25 105w21'39 7:01:27
Lee Acres 1 1 35N08'55 106w38'47 7:06:35
Lehew 2 1 34N27'27 108w02'09 7:12:09
Lemitar 29 1 34N09'35 106w54'35 7:07:38
Leon 18 1 35N34'16 107w35'58 7:10:24
Leoncito 11 1 34N40'18 105w08'17 7:00:33
Lesbia 21 2 35N09'43 103w34'41 6:54:19
Levy 19 1 36N05'17 104w41'10 6:58:45
Leyba 26 1 35N13 105w34 7:02:16
Limitar 29 1 34N09'20 106w53'47 7:07:35
Lincoln 15 1 33N29'31 105w23'00 7:01:32
Linda Vista 3 1 33N23 104w32 6:58:08

Lindrith 22 1 36N18'16 107W02'40 7:08:11
Lingo 23 1 33N47'18 103W06'51 6:52:27
Lisbon 13 1 32N16'40 108W32'49 7:14:11
Little Walnut Village 10
1 32N46 108W16 7:13:04
Little Water 25
1 36N26'47 108W43'27 7:14:54
Lizard 8 1 31N49'18 106W37'42 7:06:31
Llano 30 1 36N08'24 105W40'52 7:02:43
Llano Del Medio 11
1 35N11'23 105W06'33 7:00:26
Llano Largo 30 1 36N08'26 105W39'31 7:02:38
Llano Quemado 30
1 36N20'56 105W36'44 7:02:27
Llano Viejo (La Loma P O) 11
1 35N11'15 105W07'17 7:00:29
Llaves 22 1 36N22'22 106W51'58 7:07:28
Lobato 22 1 36N57'15 106W32'27 7:06:10
Loco Hills 9 1 32N49'08 103W58'38 6:55:55
Logan 15 2 35N21'55 103W24'37 6:53:38
Loma Parda 19 1 35N50'48 105W04'31 7:00:18
Lon 15 1 34N08'51 105W07'23 7:00:30
Lone Wolf 3 1 33N41'33 103W50'24 6:55:22
Long Place Windmill 21
2 35N22'14 103W14'33 6:52:58
Lookout Crossing 9
1 32N13'31 104W07'07 6:56:28
Lordsburg 13 1 32N21'01 108W42'29 7:14:50
Los Alamos 16 3 35N53 106W19 7:05:16
Los Alamos 26 1 35N43'55 105W09'04 7:00:36
Los Canderlarias 1
1 35N07'24 106W39'48 7:06:39
Los Chavez 33 1 34N43'36 106W45'11 7:07:01
Los Cisneros 19
1 36N04'25 105W13'45 7:00:55
Los Cocas 19 1 36N06'46 105W12'48 7:00:51
Los Cordovas 30
1 36N23'14 105W38'13 7:02:33
Los Duranes 1 1 35N06'31 106W40'37 7:06:42
Los Febres 19 1 36N10 105W03 7:00:12
Los Griegos 1 1 35N08'22 106W39'01 7:06:36
Los Huerros 19 1 36N09'46 105W07'05 7:00:28
Los LeFebres 19
1 36N11'58 105W06'50 7:00:27
Los Lentes 33 1 34N49'24 106W43'54 7:06:56
Los Luceros 22 1 36N05 106W03 7:04:12
Los Lunas 33 1 34N48'22 106W43'58 7:06:56
Los Marias 27 1 35N24'49 105W56'33 7:03:46
Los Medinas 19 1 36N02'39 105W13'20 7:00:53
Los Montoyas 26
1 35N25'10 105W12'26 7:00:50
Los Ojitos 11 1 34N41'07 104W27'38 6:57:51
Los Ojos 22 1 36N44 106W34 7:06:16
Los Pachecos 22
1 36N00'33 105W56'01 7:03:44
Los Padillas 1 1 34N58'09 106W41'43 7:06:47
Los Pinos 1 1 35N06'57 106W18'58 7:05:16
Los Pinos 22 1 36N59'18 106W03'50 7:04:15
Los Ranchos 1 1 35N05 106W39 7:06:36
Los Ranchos de Albuquerque 1
1 35N09'43 106W38'32 7:06:34
Los Tanos 11 1 34N59'43 104W32'32 6:58:10
Lost Lodge 20 1 32N57 105W45 7:03:00
Los Trujillos 33
1 34N38'48 106W45'37 7:07:02
Los Vigiles 26 1 35N38'58 105W15'47 7:01:03
Lourdes 26 1 35N36 105W13 7:00:52
Lovato 26 1 35N17'14 105W23'29 7:01:34
Lovelace 15 1 33N46'05 106W02'27 7:04:10
Lovett 13 1 31N38'37 108W56'00 7:15:44
Loving 9 1 32N17'10 104W05'43 6:56:23
Loving Place (abandoned) 3
1 33N11'12 104W30'36 6:58:02
Lovington 14 1 32N56'38 103W20'53 6:53:24
Lower Colonias 26
1 35N32'30 105W34'59 7:02:20
Lower La Posada 26
1 35N38'17 105W40'43 7:02:43
Lower Lovett Place 13
1 31N39'23 108W56'32 7:15:46
Lower Nutria 18
1 35N15'24 108W35'20 7:14:21
Lower Pueblo 26
1 35N19'35 105W25'46 7:01:43
Lower Ranchito 30
1 36N30 106W01 7:04:04
Lower Rociada 26
1 35N51 105W26 7:01:44
Lower San Francisco Plaza 2
1 33N39'46 108W47'12 7:15:09
Lucero 19 1 36N00'59 105W13'40 7:00:55
Lucero 26 1 35N23'28 105W27'40 7:01:51
Lucero Place 25
1 36N54'07 107W35'22 7:10:21
Lucy 31 1 34N39'07 105W50'11 7:03:21
Luis Lopez 29 1 33N59 106W53 7:07:32
Lumberton 22 1 36N55'48 106W56'11 7:07:45
Luna 2 1 33N49'08 108W57'14 7:15:49
Luna 15 1 33N58'07 105W41'56 7:02:48
Lybrook 22 1 36N14'00 107W33'42 7:10:15
Lyden 22 1 36N08'46 106W00'18 7:04:01
Mace 13 1 31N37'38 108W54'42 7:15:39
MacImiliano 26 1 35N36 105W13 7:00:52
Mackey Place 25
1 36N59'05 107W32'07 7:10:08
Madrid 27 1 35N24'24 106W09'07 7:04:36
Madrone 33 1 34N35'38 106W43'57 7:06:56
Maes 26 1 35N36 105W13 7:00:52
Maez Place 31 1 34N39'47 106W17'13 7:05:09
Magdalena 29 1 34N07'00 107W14'36 7:08:58
Malaga 9 1 32N13'26 104W04'19 6:56:17
Maljamar 14 1 32N51'22 103W45'44 6:55:03
Malpais 8 1 31N47'54 107W15'09 7:09:01
Mangas 2 1 34N09'31 108W19'06 7:13:16
Mangas Springs 10
1 32N50'33 108W30'40 7:14:03
Manuelitas 26 1 35N48'02 105W16'41 7:01:07
Manuelito 18 1 35N25'19 108W59'36 7:15:58
Manuelito Place 2
1 34N08'37 108W46'34 7:15:06
Manzano 31 1 34N38'48 106W20'40 7:05:23
Marcia 20 1 32N49'43 105W46'02 7:03:04
Mariano Lake 18
1 35N34'41 108W19'17 7:13:17
Marmon 4 1 35N01'02 107W18'00 7:09:12
Martinez 31 1 34N59'57 106W11'26 7:04:46
Martinez Town 1
1 35N05'21 106W38'29 7:06:34
Martin Place 31
1 34N32'11 106W19'48 7:05:19
Masons Mill 10 1 32N56'25 108W11'24 7:12:46
Mastodon 8 1 31N49'19 106W41'43 7:06:47
Mater 15 2 35N17'22 103W28'02 6:53:52
Matthew Place (abandoned) 10
1 32N50'57 108W50'07 7:15:20
Maxwell 5 1 36N32'24 104W32'34 6:58:10
Mayhill 20 1 32N53'22 105W28'39 7:01:55
Maypens 20 1 32N21'37 103W09'08 6:52:37
McAlister 21 2 34N41'32 103W46'33 6:55:06
McCartys 4 1 35N03'46 107W40'08 7:10:41
McCartys 12 1 35N37 103W06 6:52:24
McCord Place 2 1 34N25'26 107W48'51 7:11:15
McCord Place 4 1 34N41'55 107W40'26 7:10:42
McCrystal Place 5
1 36N48'38 105W08'41 7:00:35
McCune 18 1 35N31'40 108W35'25 7:14:22
McDaniel Cimarron Place 5
1 36N28'06 104W50'46 6:59:23
McDermott Wells 3
1 33N46'20 104W27'13 6:57:49
McDonald 14 1 33N08'26 103W19'01 6:53:16
McFarlands 13 1 31N28'19 108W19'31 7:13:18
McGaffey 18 1 35N22'31 108W30'54 7:14:04
McGhee Wells 13
1 32N10'49 108W55'54 7:15:44
McGreggor Place 30
1 36N49'51 105W50'42 7:03:23
McIntosh 31 1 34N51'53 106W03'04 7:04:12
McKelvey Place (abandoned) 10
1 32N49'24 108W53'23 7:15:34
McKinley Place 31
1 34N38'18 106W22'53 7:05:32
McNess Crossing 32
1 36N41'30 103W03'44 6:52:15
McNierney 29 1 34N11'37 106W54'20 7:07:37
Meadow Lake 33 1 34N49 106W44 7:06:56
Meadow Vista 8 1 31N48 106W35 7:06:20
Medanales 22 1 36N10'32 106W10'58 7:04:44
Medlin Place 14
1 32N07'22 103W22'20 6:53:29
Melena 3 1 33N32'34 104W23'51 6:57:35
Melrose 6 1 34N25'49 103W37'55 6:54:32
Mentmore 18 1 35N30'51 108W50'42 7:15:23
Merrill Place 18
1 35N20'44 108W29'03 7:13:56
Mesa 3 1 33N59'03 104W40'38 6:58:43
Mesa Poleo 22 1 36N10 106W37 7:06:28
Mesa Village 1 1 35N05'23 106W32'33 7:06:10
Mescalero 20 1 33N09'27 105W46'25 7:03:06
Mescalero Indian Reservation 20
1 33N09 105W46 7:03:04
Mesilla 8 1 32N16'12 106W48'01 7:07:12
Mesilla Park 8 1 32N16'33 106W45'58 7:07:04
Mesita 4 1 35N01'06 107W18'44 7:09:15
Mesquite 8 1 32N09'52 106W41'46 7:06:47
Mexican Springs 18
1 35N47'34 108W49'35 7:15:18
Miami 5 1 36N21'00 104W47'33 6:59:10
Middle Place Windmills 17
1 32N27'29 107W29'39 7:09:59
Middle Wells 13
1 31N40'11 108W50'01 7:15:20
Midway 3 1 33N17'41 104W27'00 6:57:48
Midway 23 1 34N15'22 103W14'35 6:52:58
Miera 32 1 36N05'28 103W33'06 6:54:12
Milagro 11 1 34N56'18 105W14'19 7:00:57
Milan 4 1 35N10'11 107W53'25 7:11:34
Mill Place 29 1 33N56'25 107W14'51 7:08:59
Mills 12 1 36N05'07 104W15'17 6:57:01
Milnesand 23 1 33N38'34 103W20'21 6:53:21
Mimbres 10 1 32N51'22 107W58'45 7:11:55
Mimbres 17 1 31N48'02 107W45'14 7:11:01
Mineral Hill 26
1 35N36'35 105W24'03 7:01:36
Minero 10 1 31N56'06 108W22'33 7:13:30
Mirage 17 1 32N19'48 107W39'36 7:10:38
Mission Park 33
1 34N49 106W44 7:06:56
Mitchell Place 13
1 32N14'48 108W36'48 7:14:27
Mogollon 2 1 33N23'48 108W47'37 7:15:10
Moly 30 1 36N41'49 105W29'32 7:01:58
Mondel 13 1 32N15'42 108W54'50 7:15:39
Monero 22 1 36N54'07 106W51'17 7:07:25
Monte Aplanado 19
1 35N57'19 105W23'40 7:01:35
Montecito 22 1 36N11'24 105W51'16 7:03:25
Monte Verde 5 1 36N33 105W16 7:01:04
Montezuma 26 1 35N39'08 105W16'33 7:01:06
Monticello 28 1 33N23'49 107W27'01 7:09:48
Montoya 21 2 35N05'59 104W03'48 6:56:15
Monument 14 1 32N37'26 103W15'50 6:53:03
Moorehead Place 31
1 34N37'50 106W16'15 7:05:05
Moore Place 10 1 32N53'29 108W59'13 7:15:57
Moquino 4 1 35N10'21 107W22'06 7:09:28
Mora 19 1 35N58'27 105W19'46 7:01:19
Moriarty 31 1 34N59'24 106W02'55 7:04:12
Morine Place 29
1 33N55'10 107W35'22 7:10:21
Moses 32 1 36N42'44 103W03'35 6:52:14
Mosley Place 27
1 35N04'57 106W09'43 7:04:39
Mosquero 12 1 35N46'37 103W57'22 6:55:49
Mossman 3 1 33N03'14 104W21'11 6:57:25
Mountainair 31 1 34N31'13 106W14'26 7:04:58
Mountain Park 20
1 32N57'02 105W49'27 7:03:18
Mountainview 1 1 34N59'42 106W39'50 7:06:39
Mountain View 3
1 33N20'24 104W31'22 6:58:05
Mount Dora 32 1 36N31 103W29 6:53:56
Mouser Place 13
1 31N47'58 108W55'18 7:15:41
Mule Creek 10 1 33N07'19 108W57'20 7:15:49
Mullen Place 25
1 36N55'16 107W31'32 7:10:06
Murphy Place 28
1 33N02'30 107W47'22 7:11:09
Myers 26 1 35N26'24 105W12'48 7:00:51
Myndus 17 1 32N15'36 107W27'24 7:09:50
Nadine 14 1 32N37'26 103W07'37 6:52:30
Nageezi 25 1 36N16'00 107W44'29 7:10:58
Nambe 27 1 35N53'36 105W58'55 7:03:56
Nambe Indian Reservation 27
1 35N53 105W58 7:03:52
Nambe Pueblo 27
1 35N53'15 105W57'52 7:03:51
Naranjos 19 1 36N09'42 104W58'57 6:59:56
Nara Visa 21 2 35N36'27 103W05'57 6:52:24
Naschitti 25 1 36N03'54 108W40'53 7:14:44
Navajo 15 1 33N20 105W40 7:02:40
Navajo 18 1 35N04 108W51 7:15:24
Navajo 22 1 36N56'46 107W03'45 7:08:15
Navajo City 22 1 36N45'07 107W36'06 7:10:24
Navajo Dam 25 1 36N56 107W56 7:11:44
Navajo Indian Reservation 18
1 35N41 109W03 7:16:12
Navajo Wingate Village 18
1 35N46 108W35 7:14:20
Navarre Place 18
1 35N19'25 108W27'17 7:13:49
Negra 31 1 34N39'50 105W32'12 7:02:09
Nelson Place 31
1 34N46'36 106W20'03 7:05:20
Newcomb 25 1 36N17'05 108W42'19 7:14:49
Newkirk 11 1 35N04'06 104W15'51 6:57:03
New Laguna 4 1 35N02'27 107W25'17 7:09:41
Newman 20 1 32N00'12 106W19'21 7:05:17
New York 4 1 35N03'31 107W31'36 7:10:06
No Agua 30 1 36N43'14 105W58'07 7:03:52
Nogal 15 1 33N33'29 105W42'26 7:02:50
Noria 8 1 31N48'17 106W51'46 7:07:27
North Carmen 19
1 35N54'24 105W19'33 7:01:18
North Chaves 18
1 35N23'31 108W09'27 7:12:38
North Guam 18 1 35N29'19 108W22'22 7:13:29
North Harding 12
1 36N01 104W04 6:56:16
North Hidalgo 13
1 32N18 108W53 7:15:32
North Hurley 10
1 32N42 108W08 7:12:32
North Lucy 31 1 34N51'26 105W34'50 7:02:19
North San Ysidro 26
1 35N28'09 105W33'11 7:02:13
North Valley 1 1 35N10 106W38 7:06:32
Norton 21 2 34N59'54 103W31'29 6:54:06
Nutrias 22 1 36N42 106W33 7:06:12
Nutt 17 1 32N34'22 107W26'56 7:09:48
Oak Grove 10 1 32N37'51 108W20'39 7:13:23
Oasis 28 1 32N55'28 107W19'00 7:09:16
Obar 32 2 35N32'06 103W12'03 6:52:48
Ocate 19 1 36N10'32 105W02'51 7:00:11
Ochoa 14 1 32N11'30 103W26'23 6:53:46
Oil Center 14 1 32N29'57 103W15'39 6:53:03
Oil City 9 1 32N42'34 104W12'45 6:56:51
Ojita 26 1 35N29'55 105W14'42 7:00:59
Ojito 22 1 36N25'47 107W05'14 7:08:21
Ojito 30 1 36N08'26 105W42'51 7:02:51
Ojitos Frios (Gabaldon PO) 26
1 35N31'00 105W19'01 7:01:16
Ojo Caliente 4 1 34N55'00 108W58'04 7:15:52
Ojo Caliente 30
1 36N18'11 106W02'46 7:04:11
Ojo Feliz 19 1 36N03'28 105W07'04 7:00:28
Ojo Sarco 22 1 36N07'21 105W46'58 7:03:08
Old Albuquerque 1
1 35N06 106W40 7:06:40
Old Campbell Place 2
1 33N50'40 108W53'31 7:15:34
Old Chilili 1 1 34N54'23 106W11'48 7:04:47
Old Hachita 10 1 31N54'50 108W25'56 7:13:44
Old Horner Place 9
1 32N47'56 104W30'25 6:58:02
Old Horse Springs 2
1 33N55'28 108W13'38 7:12:55
Old Isaacs Place 13
1 31N41'41 108W53'50 7:15:35
Old Longbotbam Place 3
1 32N56'00 105W10'16 7:00:41
Old Moses 32 1 36N41'02 103W04'38 6:52:19
Old Picacho 8 1 32N18 106W50 7:07:20
Old Place Windmill 7
1 34N26'04 104W29'19 6:57:57
Old Place Windmill 11
1 34N47'35 104W47'10 6:59:09
Old Town 1 1 35N05'42 106W40'13 7:06:41
Old Waterman Place 2
1 33N25'53 108W44'16 7:14:57
Old Wright Place 20
1 32N28'50 105W53'58 7:03:36
Olive 3 1 33N57'03 104W02'15 6:56:09
Omega 2 1 34N19'23 108W22'26 7:13:30
Omlee 20 1 32N50'13 105W58'16 7:03:53
Onava 26 1 35N41'48 105W05'38 7:00:23
O'Neil Landing 24
1 35N51'59 106W47'42 7:07:11
Optimo 19 1 35N53'25 104W48'11 6:59:13
Orange 8 1 31N51'39 106W38'08 7:06:33
Orchard Place 4
1 34N41'34 107W28'35 7:09:54
Organ 8 1 32N25'32 106W35'46 7:06:23
Orogrande 20 1 32N22'16 106W05'02 7:04:20
Oscura 15 1 33N29'10 106W03'06 7:04:12
Otis 9 1 32N21'04 104W10'05 6:56:40
Otowi 27 1 35N52'33 106W08'31 7:04:34
Otto 31 1 35N04'23 106W00'30 7:04:02
Pacheco Village 19
1 35N57'47 105W22'59 7:01:32
Page 18 1 35N19'16 108W26'24 7:13:46
Paguate 4 1 35N08'19 107W22'42 7:09:31
Pajarita 26 1 35N28'19 105W38'40 7:02:35
Pajarito 1 1 34N59'11 106W41'46 7:06:47
Pajarito 27 1 35N54'19 106W07'36 7:04:30
Pajarito Acres 16
3 35N51 106W16 7:05:04

Palma 31 1 34N58'43 105w27'55 7:01:52
Palmer Plaza 25
1 36N46 108w10 7:12:40
Palomas 21 2 35N07'42 103w55'02 6:55:40
Paquita 33 1 34N51'55 106w46'35 7:07:06
Paradise Hills 1
1 35N12'02 106w42'02 7:06:48
Paraje (Casa Blanca P O) 4
1 35N03'19 107w28'30 7:09:54
Park Springs 26
1 35N15'43 104w55'41 6:59:43
Park View 22 1 36N43'46 106w34'14 7:06:17
Pastura 11 1 34N46'58 104w56'39 6:59:47
Paxton Springs 4
1 35N02'21 108w03'58 7:12:16
Payne Place 29 1 34N34'00 107w23'40 7:09:35
Pecos 26 1 35N34'27 105w40'28 7:02:42
Pedernal 31 1 34N38'35 105w37'14 7:02:29
Pena Blanca 24 1 35N34'22 106w20'11 7:05:21
Penasco 30 1 36N10'10 105w41'09 7:02:45
Penasco Blanco 26
1 35N52'02 105w20'54 7:01:24
Pendaries 26 1 35N51 105w26 7:01:44
Penistaja 24 1 35N58'07 107w13'13 7:08:53
Pennington 32 1 36N18'19 103w37'58 6:54:32
Pen Place Windmill 14
1 32N46'16 103w39'14 6:54:37
Pep 23 1 33N50'10 103w20'06 6:53:20
Peralta 33 1 34N50'13 106w41'24 7:06:46
Perea 18 1 35N30'16 108w31'06 7:14:04
Peruhill 17 1 32N18'11 107w48'23 7:11:14
Pescado 18 1 35N06'21 108w34'47 7:14:19
Petaca 22 1 36N30'30 106w00'36 7:04:02
Peveler Place 14
1 33N08'42 103w25'50 6:53:43
Philadelphia 4 1 35N02'22 107w30'40 7:10:03
Philmont 5 1 36N31 104w55 6:59:40
Picacho 8 1 32N19'29 106w50'57 7:07:24
Picacho 15 1 33N21'06 105w08'40 7:00:35
Picuris 30 1 36N11 105w43 7:02:52
Picuris Indian Reservation 30
1 36N12 105w43 7:02:52
Picuris Pueblo 30
1 36N12'03 105w42'34 7:02:50
Piedra de la Aguila 18
1 35N35'04 107w44'36 7:10:58
Piedra Lumbre 4
1 35N09'21 107w14'25 7:08:58
Pierce 13 1 31N27'22 108w20'23 7:13:22
Pierce Canyon Crossing 9
1 32N11'21 103w58'39 6:55:55
Pie Town 2 1 34N17'54 108w08'03 7:12:32
Pilar 30 1 36N16'11 105w47'15 7:03:09
Pine 26 1 35N34 105w40 7:02:40
Pinedale 18 1 35N36'14 108w26'47 7:13:47
Pinehaven 18 1 35N19'58 108w40'11 7:14:41
Pine Lodge 15 1 33N37'23 105w14'40 7:00:59
Pines 24 1 35N46'49 106w26'11 7:05:45
Pine Springs 31
1 34N57'56 106w13'59 7:04:56
Pine View 30 1 36N11 105w40 7:02:40
Pineywoods Estates 20
1 32N57 105w45 7:03:00
Pinon 20 1 32N37'05 105w23'38 7:01:35
Pino Place 29 1 34N34'13 107w26'42 7:09:47
Pinos Altos 10 1 32N51'48 108w13'15 7:12:53
Pinos Altos 26 1 35N09'47 105w23'27 7:01:34
Pinoswells 31 1 34N22 105w42 7:02:48
Pintada 11 1 34N52'56 105w04'18 7:00:17
Place Windmill 33
1 34N49'01 107w14'53 7:09:00
Placita 30 1 36N11 105w40 7:02:40
Placitas 8 1 32N39'54 107w10'05 7:08:40
Placitas 22 1 36N26'45 106w26'28 7:05:46
Placitas 24 1 35N18'25 106w25'27 7:05:42
Placitas 28 1 33N22'38 107w25'57 7:09:44
Playas 13 1 31N58'08 108w36'29 7:14:26
Plaza Blanca 22
1 36N42'14 106w36'28 7:06:26
Pleasant Hill 6
1 34N31'13 103w04'24 6:52:18
Pleasanton 2 1 33N16'20 108w52'20 7:15:29
Point of Sands 20
1 32N44'49 106w11'43 7:04:47
Pojoaque 27 1 35N53'34 106w01'21 7:04:05
Pojoaque Indian Reservation 27
1 35N54 106w01 7:04:04
Pojoaque Valley 27
1 35N40 105w57 7:03:48
Polich Place 18
1 35N21'37 108w29'28 7:13:58
Polly 15 1 33N34'31 105w57'26 7:03:50
Polvadera 29 1 34N12'17 106w55'16 7:07:41
Ponderosa 24 1 35N39'36 106w40'01 7:06:40
Ponderosa Heights 15
1 33N20'40 105w40'59 7:02:44
Ponderosa Pines 1
1 34N58'37 106w19'25 7:05:18
Portair 6 1 34N24'19 103w18'05 6:53:12
Portales 23 1 34N11'10 103w20'02 6:53:20
Porter 21 2 35N12'56 103w18'46 6:53:15
Porter 24 1 35N49'08 106w47'11 7:07:09
Potato Patch 2 1 33N45'19 108w54'28 7:15:38
Pot Creek 30 1 36N25 105w34 7:02:16
Pothook 10 1 31N58'29 108w29'40 7:13:59
Potrillo 8 1 31N48'06 106w59'32 7:07:58
Prairieview 14 1 33N05'48 103w11'49 6:52:47
Prewitt 18 1 35N21'46 108w02'36 7:12:10
Progreso 31 1 34N28'40 105w52'50 7:03:31
Pronto 8 1 32N07'27 107w03'45 7:08:15
P Simmons Place 27
1 35N13'55 106w07'04 7:04:28
Pueblito 22 1 36N04'29 106w04'36 7:04:18
Pueblito 29 1 34N07'19 106w52'41 7:07:31
Pueblitos 33 1 34N37'23 106w46'38 7:07:07
Pueblo Pintado 18
1 35N58'38 107w40'22 7:10:41
Puertecito 24 1 35N16'31 106w17'47 7:05:11
Puertecito 29 1 34N26'53 107w23'32 7:09:34
Puertocito 19 1 35N55'02 105w18'05 7:01:12
Puertocito Indian Res 29
1 34N27 107w24 7:09:36

Puerto De Luna 11
1 34N49'55 104w37'15 6:58:29
Punta de Agua 31
1 34N36'00 106w17'00 7:05:08
Puye 22 3 35N58'18 106w13'47 7:04:55
Quarris Acres 20
1 32N57 105w45 7:03:00
Quarteles 27 1 35N59'31 106w00'47 7:04:03
Quay 21 2 34N56'02 103w45'36 6:55:02
Queen 9 1 32N11'27 104w44'43 6:58:59
Quemado 2 1 34N20'38 108w29'42 7:13:59
Querinda Park 30
1 36N42 105w24 7:01:36
Questa 30 1 36N42'14 105w35'40 7:02:23
Radium Springs 8
1 32N30'04 106w55'39 7:07:43
Ragland 21 2 34N49'21 103w44'30 6:54:58
Rain Place 21 2 35N16'49 103w03'57 6:52:16
Rainsville 19 1 35N58'43 105w12'31 7:00:50
Ramah 18 1 35N07'59 108w29'28 7:13:58
Ramah Indian Reservation 4
1 35N00 108w20 7:13:20
Ramon 15 1 34N13'58 104w53'58 6:59:36
Ramsdale Place 15
1 33N48'08 105w43'22 7:02:53
Ranches of Taos 30
1 36N21'31 105w36'32 7:02:26
Ranchito 24 1 35N20'55 106w31'34 7:06:06
Ranchito 30 1 36N24'15 105w35'50 7:02:23
Ranchitos 22 1 36N01'41 106w03'48 7:04:15
Rancho del Monte 27
1 35N47'59 105w55'17 7:03:41
Ranchos De Taos 30
1 36N21'31 105w36'32 7:02:26
Ranchos Lake Conchas 26
1 35N22 104w11 6:56:44
Rancho Valle 27
1 35N59'08 106w00'31 7:04:02
Ranchvale 6 1 34N29'33 103w19'06 6:53:16
Rastus Place 10
1 33N00'45 108w25'22 7:13:41
Raton 5 1 36N54'12 104w26'19 6:57:45
Rattlesnake 25 1 36N45'19 108w48'05 7:15:12
Rayado 5 1 36N22'07 104w55'35 6:59:42
Recheulos 22 1 36N03'10 106w20'18 7:05:21
Red Bluff 9 1 32N04'26 104w02'23 6:56:10
Red Hill 2 1 34N13'07 108w52'18 7:15:29
Red Mill 29 1 34N17'43 106w44'58 7:07:00
Red River 30 1 36N42'29 105w24'20 7:01:37
Redrock 10 1 32N41'10 108w44'15 7:14:57
Red Rock 18 1 35N27'15 108w45'19 7:15:01
Redstone 10 1 32N56'21 108w11'49 7:12:47
Regina 24 1 36N11'03 106w57'22 7:07:49
Rehoboth 18 1 35N31'44 108w39'15 7:14:37
Rencona 26 1 35N18'09 105w39'46 7:02:39
Reservation 18 1 35N49 108w44 7:14:56
Reserve 2 1 33N42'47 108w45'26 7:15:02
Reventon 15 1 33N47'42 105w38'22 7:02:33
Ribera 26 1 35N22'25 105w26'53 7:01:48
Ricardo 7 1 34N23'26 104w23'05 6:57:32
Richland 23 1 33N49'18 103w15'55 6:53:04
Riley 29 1 34N22'50 107w13'45 7:08:55
Riley Place 31 1 34N48'40 106w20'09 7:05:21
Rincon 8 1 32N40'22 107w03'51 7:08:15
Rinconado 22 1 36N13'06 105w52'22 7:03:29
Rincon Montoso 26
1 35N46 105w15 7:01:00
Ring Place 5 1 36N46'20 105w07'14 7:00:29
Rio Chama 22 1 36N13 106w13 7:04:52
Rio Chiquito 22
1 36N00'09 105w54'15 7:03:37
Rio Grande 29 1 34N09 106w52 7:07:28
Rio Grande Estates 33
1 34N40 106w46 7:07:04
Rio Lucio 30 1 36N11'44 105w43'30 7:02:54
Rio Pueblo 30 1 36N11'07 105w38'17 7:02:33
Rio Puerco 22 1 36N12'39 106w35'02 7:06:20
Rio Puerco 33 1 34N47'35 106w59'35 7:07:58
Rio Rancho 24 1 35N20 106w35 7:06:20
Rio Rancho Estates 24
1 35N14'19 106w40'00 7:06:40
Rito de las Sillas 22
1 36N11 106w34 7:06:16
Rivajana 24 1 35N20'17 106w32'07 7:06:08
River Mill 3 1 33N17'36 104w45'17 6:59:01
Riverside 9 1 32N50 104w25 6:57:40
Riverside 10 1 32N55'54 108w35'43 7:14:23
Riverside 15 1 33N19'58 105w03'35 7:00:14
Riverside 22 1 35N59'32 106w03'59 7:04:16
Riverside 25 1 36N58'57 107w52'29 7:11:30
Roberson Place 15
1 33N28'39 106w09'04 7:04:36
Robertson Wells 3
1 33N41'58 103w55'18 6:55:41
Robin Hood Park 20
1 32N57 105w45 7:03:00
Robsart 15 1 33N44'11 105w49'57 7:03:20
Rociada 26 1 35N49'56 105w25'13 7:01:41
Rock Cabin (Freeman) 13
1 31N43'23 108w52'10 7:15:29
Rock Canyon 28 1 33N13'25 107w12'32 7:08:50
Rock Springs 18
1 35N31 108w44 7:14:56
Rock Wall 30 1 36N10'36 105w37'13 7:02:29
Rodarte 30 1 36N09'07 105w40'20 7:02:41
Rodeo 13 1 31N50'07 109w01'50 7:16:07
Rodey 8 1 32N39'24 107w08'07 7:08:32
Rogers 23 1 33N58'54 103w13'48 6:52:55
Romero 26 1 35N32'10 105w13'26 7:00:54
Romero Place 4 1 34N52'12 107w23'57 7:09:36
Romero Place 31
1 34N38'37 106w17'46 7:05:11
Romeroville 26 1 35N31'22 105w14'39 7:00:59
Rosario 27 1 35N28'49 106w13'37 7:04:54
Rosebud 12 1 35N50'28 103w26'42 6:53:47
Rosebud Farms 12
1 35N48'46 103w25'27 6:53:42
Rose Place 9 1 32N04'19 103w43'33 6:54:54
Roswell 3 1 33N23'39 104w31'21 6:58:05
Rouse Place 28 1 33N26'48 107w37'08 7:10:29
Rowe 26 1 35N29'30 105w40'29 7:02:42
Roy 12 1 35N56'38 104w11'44 6:56:47
Royce 32 1 36N29'13 103w18'46 6:53:15

Ruidoso 15 1 33N19'54 105w40'21 7:02:41
Ruidoso Downs 15
1 33N19'44 105w36'14 7:02:25
Rutheron 22 1 36N43'07 106w36'40 7:06:27
Rutter 8 1 32N01'17 106w52'28 7:07:30
Ruyle Place 2 1 33N50'59 108w55'13 7:15:41
Sabinal 29 1 34N29'37 106w48'25 7:07:14
Sabino 12 1 35N59'26 103w57'32 6:55:50
Sabinoso 26 1 35N41'56 104w24'27 6:57:38
Sacramento 20 1 32N47'33 105w33'36 7:02:14
Saint Vrain 6 1 34N24'58 103w29'21 6:53:57
Sais 33 1 34N27'55 106w30'44 7:06:03
Saiz Place 31 1 34N39'08 106w19'35 7:05:18
Salado 7 1 34N35'16 104w24'40 6:57:39
Salem 8 1 32N42'27 107w12'45 7:08:51
Salinas 20 1 33N14'06 106w03'35 7:04:14
Salt Lake 2 1 34N27'12 108w46'09 7:15:05
San Acacia 29 1 34N15'19 106w53'56 7:07:36
San Antonio 1 1 35N06'07 106w22'38 7:05:31
San Antonio 26 1 35N37'43 105w14'41 7:00:59
San Antonio 29 1 33N55'04 106w51'55 7:07:28
San Antonio de Padua del Ran 27
1 35N40 105w57 7:03:48
San Antonito 1 1 35N09'47 106w20'49 7:05:23
San Antonito 29
1 33N53'34 106w52'26 7:07:30
San Augustin (Lourdes P O) 26
1 35N27'28 105w08'43 7:00:35
Sanchez 26 1 35N37'38 104w25'22 6:57:41
Sanchez Place 18
1 35N18'46 108w23'10 7:13:33
Sanchez Place 31
1 34N37'32 106w17'31 7:05:10
San Cristobal 30
1 36N35'47 105w38'20 7:02:33
San Cristoval 27
1 35N16 106w01 7:04:04
Sanctuario 27 1 35N59'23 105w55'59 7:03:44
Sand Corner 4 1 35N05'53 108w19'42 7:13:19
Sandia 33 1 34N49'31 106w50'17 7:07:21
Sandia Indian Reservation 24
1 35N15 106w34 7:06:16
Sandia Knoll 1 1 35N10 106w22 7:05:28
Sandia Park 1 1 35N10'04 106w21'54 7:05:28
Sandia Pueblo 24
1 35N15'21 106w34'17 7:06:17
Sandia Vista 1 1 35N05'05 106w31'22 7:06:05
Sands 26 1 35N24'18 105w29'27 7:01:58
Sand Springs 15
2 35N28'20 103w16'58 6:53:08
San Felipe Indian Res 24
1 35N26 106w27 7:05:48
San Felipe Pueblo 24
1 35N26'02 106w26'46 7:05:47
San Fidel 4 1 35N04'56 107w35'55 7:10:24
San Francisco 29
1 34N23'45 106w50'19 7:07:21
San Francisco Plaza 2
1 33N41'36 108w45'56 7:15:04
San Geronimo 26
1 35N34'48 105w23'41 7:01:35
San Geronimo 29
1 34N20'03 106w52'21 7:07:29
San Ignacio 11 1 34N54'48 104w56'43 6:59:47
San Ignacio 26 1 35N46'16 105w21'14 7:01:25
San Ildefonso 27
1 35N53 106w07 7:04:28
San Ildefonso Indian Res 27
1 35N53 106w07 7:04:28
San Ildefonso Pueblo 27
1 35N53'31 106w07'04 7:04:28
San Jon 21 2 35N06'27 103w19'41 6:53:19
San Jose 9 1 32N24'29 104w13'52 6:56:55
San Jose 22 1 36N02'21 106w05'51 7:04:23
San Jose 26 1 35N23'50 105w28'28 7:01:54
San Juan 10 1 32N45'39 107w54'17 7:11:37
San Juan 26 1 35N08'44 105w21'54 7:01:28
San Juan Indian Reservation 22
1 36N03 106w04 7:04:16
San Juan Pueblo 22
1 36N03'10 106w04'12 7:04:17
San Lorenzo 10 1 32N48'36 107w55'10 7:11:41
San Lorenzo 22 1 36N02'55 106w17'05 7:05:08
San Luis 24 1 35N40'57 107w03'00 7:08:12
San Marcial 29 1 33N42'00 106w59'12 7:07:57
San Mateo 4 1 35N19'53 107w38'33 7:10:34
San Mateo Springs 4
1 35N20 107w39 7:10:36
San Miguel 8 1 32N09'19 106w44'04 7:06:56
San Miguel 22 1 36N57'41 106w09'36 7:04:38
San Miguel 24 1 35N54'47 106w54'47 7:07:39
San Miguel 26 1 35N22 105w27 7:01:48
Sanostee 25 1 36N25'29 108w52'25 7:15:30
San Pablo 8 1 32N14'58 106w46'20 7:07:05
San Pablo 24 1 35N56'42 106w54'38 7:07:39
San Pablo 26 1 35N32'49 105w23'55 7:01:36
San Patricio 15
1 33N24'32 105w19'35 7:01:18
San Pedro 22 1 35N59'07 106w03'50 7:04:15
San Pedro 27 1 35N14'23 106w12'32 7:04:50
San Pedro 29 1 33N54'37 106w50'30 7:07:22
San Rafael 4 1 35N06'45 107w52'55 7:11:32
San Rafael 26 1 35N28 104w25 6:57:40
San Ramon 26 1 35N32'47 104w25'01 6:57:40
San Sebastian 27
1 35N35 105w59 7:03:56
Santa Ana 26 1 35N28'45 105w17'42 7:01:11
Santa Ana Indian Reservation 24
1 35N26 106w37 7:06:28
Santa Ana Pueblo 24
1 35N25'44 106w37'06 7:06:28
Santa Clara 22 1 35N58'11 106w05'11 7:04:21
Santa Clara Indian Res 22
1 35N58 106w05 7:04:20
Santa Clara Pueblo 22
1 35N57'56 106w05'17 7:04:21
Santa Cruz 27 1 35N59'32 106w02'48 7:04:11
Santa Fe 27 4 35N41'13 105w56'14 7:03:45
Santana Place 28
1 33N25'58 107w48'05 7:11:12
Santa Rita 10 1 32N48'13 108w03'37 7:12:14
Santa Rosa 11 1 34N56'19 104w40'55 6:58:44

Santo Domingo 24 1 35N34 106W26 7:05:44
Santo Domingo Indian Res 24 1 35N31 106W22 7:05:28
Santo Domingo Pueblo 24 1 35N30'53 106W21'55 7:05:28
Santo Nino 22 1 36N00'10 106W03'46 7:04:15
Santo Tomas 8 1 32N10'54 106W44'44 7:06:59
San Vincente 10 1 32N38'28 108W12'27 7:12:50
San Ysidro 24 1 35N33'48 106W46'12 7:07:05
Sapello 26 1 35N46'22 105W15'10 7:01:01
Satathite Place 2 1 33N54'29 107W43'58 7:10:56
Sawyer 4 1 35N10'45 108W14'52 7:12:59
Scholle 31 1 34N25'39 106W24'58 7:05:40
Schomberg 5 1 36N38'20 104W29'56 6:58:00
Seama 4 1 35N02'23 107W31'27 7:10:06
Seboyeta 4 1 35N12'04 107W23'19 7:09:33
Seboyetita 4 1 35N12 107W23 7:09:32
Sedan 32 1 36N08'40 103W07'48 6:52:31
Sedillo 1 1 35N05'59 106W17'42 7:05:11
Sedillo Hill 1 1 35N05 106W23 7:05:32
Self Place 25 1 36N58'26 107W30'31 7:10:02
Sena 26 1 35N17'54 105W23'32 7:01:34
Seneca 32 1 36N37'42 103W07'34 6:52:30
Senorito 24 1 35N58'41 106W54'51 7:07:39
Separ 10 1 32N12'03 108W25'18 7:13:41
Serafina 26 1 35N23'51 105W19'23 7:01:18
Servilleta Plaza 22 1 36N23 106W02 7:04:08
Seton Village 27 1 35N35'57 105W55'55 7:03:44
Seven Lakes 18 1 35N47'05 107W56'06 7:11:44
Seven Rivers 9 1 32N35'42 104W25'16 6:57:41
Seven Springs 24 1 35N54'07 106W42'41 7:06:51
Shady Brook 30 1 36N22'12 105W28'02 7:01:52
Shakespeare 13 1 32N19'33 108W44'16 7:14:57
Sheep Crossing Campground 30 1 36N45'07 105W40'17 7:02:41
Sheep Springs 25 1 36N08'36 108W42'24 7:14:50
Sheridan 26 1 35N29'45 105W14'37 7:00:58
Sherman 10 1 32N44'48 107W53'09 7:11:33
Sherman Place 3 1 33N17'14 104W37'46 6:58:31
Shiprock 25 1 36N47'08 108W41'11 7:14:45
Shoemaker 19 1 35N48'59 104W52'33 6:59:30
Sid Place 10 1 32N56'13 108W58'09 7:15:53
Sierra Vista 15 1 33N24'32 105W41'33 7:02:46
Sierra Vista Estates 1 1 35N04 106W31 7:06:04
Sile 24 1 35N33'52 106W22'20 7:05:29
Silio 31 1 34N35'21 105W56'01 7:03:44
Silver City 10 1 32N46'12 108W16'47 7:13:07
Smith Lake 18 1 35N31'20 108W08'21 7:12:33
Smith Place Windmill 11 1 34N57'35 104W32'49 6:58:11
Smiths Lake 18 1 35N24 108W13 7:12:52
Socorro 29 1 34N03'30 106W53'27 7:07:34
Sofia 32 1 36N27'06 103W49'43 6:55:19
Soham 26 1 35N24'56 105W29'37 7:01:58
Solano 12 1 35N50'54 104W04'01 6:56:16
Solo 30 1 36N20'21 105W57'02 7:03:48
Sombrillo 27 1 35N58'48 106W02'22 7:04:09
South Carmen 19 1 35N53'37 105W20'09 7:01:21
South Chaves 18 1 35N23'18 108W09'05 7:12:36
South Garcia 33 1 34N52'51 107W04'49 7:08:19
South Guam 18 1 35N28'30 108W22'43 7:13:31
South Harding 12 1 35N45 103W34 6:54:16
South Hidalgo 13 1 31N41 108W43 7:14:52
South Mill 3 1 33N10'02 104W08'38 6:56:35
South Petaca 22 1 36N29'50 106W00'35 7:04:02
South San Ysidro 26 1 35N27'00 105W34'37 7:02:18
South Spring 3 1 33N20'08 104W28'20 6:57:53
South Spring Acres 3 1 33N20'40 104W29'06 6:57:56
South Springs Acres 3 1 33N23 104W32 6:58:08
South Valley 1 1 35N03 106W40 7:06:40
Spalding 17 1 32N26'57 107W58'01 7:11:52
Spears 13 1 31N43'47 108W49'01 7:15:16
Spencerville 25 1 36N49'12 108W03'27 7:12:14
Spiess 27 1 35N27'33 105W54'22 7:03:37
Spindle 15 1 33N33 105W34 7:02:16
Springer 5 1 36N21'40 104W35'41 6:58:23
Springstead 18 1 35N46 108W35 7:14:20
Spur Lake 2 1 33N59'35 108W52'31 7:15:30
Standing Rock 18 1 35N48'11 108W21'37 7:13:26
Stanley 27 1 35N08'51 105W58'35 7:03:54
Star Lake 18 1 36N01 107W04 7:08:16
Stead 32 1 36N06 103W12 6:52:48
Steins 13 1 32N13'45 108W59'20 7:15:57
Stockton Place 31 1 34N51'20 105W46'47 7:03:07
Strauss 8 1 31N51'51 106W41'54 7:06:48
Sublette 22 1 36N59'20 106W13'46 7:04:55
Sugarite 5 1 36N56'38 104W22'53 6:57:32
Sulphur Springs 24 1 35N54'27 106W36'55 7:06:28
Sunland Park 8 1 31N48 106W35 7:06:20
Sunny Side 5 1 36N21'49 104W54'05 6:59:36
Sunset 15 1 33N20'22 105W04'29 7:00:18
Sunshine 17 1 32N15 107W45 7:11:00
Sunshine 30 1 36N50'38 105W38'22 7:02:33
Sunspot 20 1 32N39 105W42 7:02:48
Sun Valley 15 1 33N24'44 105W40'55 7:02:44
Suwanee 33 1 34N56'06 107W08'12 7:08:33
Taiban 7 1 34N26'24 104W00'31 6:56:02
Tajique 31 1 34N45'06 106W17'14 7:05:09
Talpa 30 1 36N20'29 105W35'47 7:02:23
Taos 30 1 36N24'26 105W34'21 7:02:17
Taos Indian Reservation 30 1 36N26 105W33 7:02:12
Taos Junction 30 1 36N21'45 105W53'46 7:03:35
Taos Pueblo 30 1 36N26'19 105W32'38 7:02:11
Taos Ski Valley 30 1 36N25 105W34 7:02:16
Tapicitoes 22 1 36N27'33 107W00'48 7:08:03
Tatum 14 1 33N15'25 103W19'02 6:53:16
Taylor Springs 5 1 36N19'38 104W29'30 6:57:58
Teague 20 1 32N16'51 103W11'08 6:52:45
Techado 4 1 34N35'07 108W23'11 7:13:33
Tecolote 15 1 34N00'04 105W40'00 7:02:40
Tecolote 24 1 35N19'10 106W24'18 7:05:37
Tecolote 26 1 35N27'37 105W16'48 7:01:07
Tecolotito 26 1 35N14'04 105W09'32 7:00:38
Tejon 11 1 34N35'23 105W17'08 7:01:09
Tekapo 18 1 35N01'19 108W56'32 7:15:46
Tererro 26 1 35N46 105W40 7:02:40
Tesuque 27 1 35N45'49 105W55'55 7:03:44
Tesuque Indian Reservation 27 1 35N40 105W57 7:03:48
Tesuque Pueblo 27 1 35N40 105W57 7:03:48
Texico 6 1 34N23'19 103W03'03 6:52:12
Thomas 32 1 36N14'44 103W17'31 6:53:10
Thompson Place 31 1 34N56'38 106W08'10 7:04:33
Thoreau 18 1 35N24'09 108W13'22 7:12:53
Three Forks 9 1 32N21'05 104W46'54 6:59:08
Three Rivers 20 1 33N19'17 106W04'28 7:04:18
Tierra Amarilla 22 1 36N42'01 106W32'57 7:06:12
Tierra Monte 26 1 35N51'33 105W20'49 7:01:23
Tiffany 29 1 33N43'23 106W56'34 7:07:46
Tijeras 1 1 35N04'51 106W23'15 7:05:33
Timberon 20 1 32N37 105W24 7:01:36
Tinaja 4 1 35N04'57 108W15'50 7:13:03
Tinaja 5 1 36N39'11 104W23'23 6:57:34
Tinen Place 27 1 35N15'33 106W00'46 7:04:03
Tingle 4 1 34N40'19 108W32'26 7:14:10
Tinian 18 1 35N50'24 107W19'32 7:09:18
Tinnie 15 1 33N22'14 105W13'33 7:00:54
Tinsley Crossing 23 1 34N07'37 103W25'15 6:53:41
Tiptonville 19 1 35N49'14 104W59'49 6:59:59
Toadlena 25 1 36N14'13 108W53'31 7:15:34
Tocito 25 1 36N23'58 108W46'50 7:15:07
Tohatchi 18 1 35N51'32 108W45'39 7:15:03
Tohlakai 18 1 35N31 108W44 7:14:56
Tokay 29 1 33N52'25 106W44'19 7:06:57
Tolar 23 1 34N27'03 103W55'52 6:55:43
Toltec 4 1 35N12'52 107W54'35 7:11:38
Toltec 22 1 36N58'58 106W16'18 7:05:05
Tomasino Mill 29 1 34N15'09 106W40'22 7:06:41
Tome 33 1 34N44'27 106W43'40 7:06:55
Tonuco 8 1 32N35'27 106W59'46 7:07:59
Tony 11 1 34N36'54 105W10'54 7:00:44
T-O Ranch 5 1 36N54 104W26 6:57:44
Toril 5 1 36N23'15 104W35'08 6:58:21
Tornero 23 1 33N53'04 103W42'48 6:54:51
Torrence 31 1 34N20'28 105W31'39 7:02:07
Torreon 24 1 36N01 107W04 7:08:16
Torreon 31 1 34N43'20 106W17'53 7:05:12
Tortugas 8 1 32N16'12 106W45'08 7:07:01
Totavi 27 1 35N52'28 106W10'45 7:04:43
Trampas 30 1 36N07'52 105W45'30 7:03:02
Trechado 4 1 34N39 108W41 7:14:44
Trementina 26 1 35N28'11 104W31'38 6:58:07
Tres Lagunas 2 1 34N22'56 108W05'39 7:12:23
Tres Lagunas 26 1 35N43'16 105W40'39 7:02:43
Tres Piedras 30 1 36N38'49 105W58'00 7:03:52
Tres Ritos 30 1 36N07'50 105W30'55 7:02:04
Trout Springs 26 1 35N39'35 105W20'24 7:01:22
Truchas 22 1 36N02'37 105W48'40 7:03:15
Trujillo 26 1 35N32'05 104W41'27 6:58:46
Truth Or Consequences 28 1 33N07'42 107W15'08 7:09:01
Tsaya 25 1 36N07'59 108W10'25 7:12:42
Tucumcari 21 2 35N10'18 103W43'28 6:54:54
Tularosa 20 1 33N04'26 106W01'05 7:04:04
Tunis 17 1 32N15'05 107W55'02 7:11:40
Turley 25 1 36N45'09 107W45'52 7:11:03
Turn 33 1 34N34'26 106W44'55 7:07:00
Turnerville 10 1 32N48'07 108W05'03 7:12:20
Turquillo 19 1 36N08 105W14 7:00:56
Turquoise 20 1 32N26'42 106W01'56 7:04:08
Twin Buttes 18 1 35N30'16 108W50'48 7:15:23
Twin Forks Estates 20 1 32N57 105W45 7:03:00
Twining 30 1 36N35'41 105W26'59 7:01:48
Twin Lakes 18 1 35N42'33 108W46'27 7:15:06
Two Grey Hills 25 1 36N14'15 108W48'07 7:15:12
Tyrone 10 1 32N39'29 108W21'34 7:13:26
Ulibarri Place 25 1 36N57'25 107W31'27 7:10:06
Ulmoris 13 1 32N19'44 108W37'54 7:14:32
Union Hill 10 1 32N50'04 108W04'42 7:12:19
University 23 1 34N11 103W20 6:53:20
Upham 28 1 32N53'11 107W00'06 7:08:00
Upper Anton Chico 11 1 35N12'30 105W10'06 7:00:40
Upper Colonias 26 1 35N34'35 105W35'02 7:02:20
Upper Dilia 11 1 35N11'05 105W04'49 7:00:19
Upper Frijoles Crossing 16 3 35N48'55 106W21'39 7:05:27
Upper La Jara 24 1 36N07'14 106W55'20 7:07:41
Upper La Posada 26 1 35N38'57 105W40'52 7:02:43
Upper Lovett Place 13 1 31N39'14 108W56'56 7:15:48
Upper Nutria 18 1 35N16'11 108W34'13 7:14:17
Upper Pueblo 26 1 35N20'03 105W25'47 7:01:43
Upper Rociada 26 1 35N51'18 105W25'35 7:01:42
Upshaw Place 13 1 31N41'55 108W42'22 7:14:49
Upton 23 1 34N09'19 103W39'09 6:54:37
Urraca Place 5 1 36N24'36 104W50'36 6:59:22
Ute Mountain Indian Res 25 1 36N55 108W20 7:13:20
Ute Park 5 1 36N33'29 105W06'52 7:00:27
Vadito 30 1 36N11'28 105W40'13 7:02:41
Vado 8 1 32N06'42 106W39'43 7:06:39
Valdez 30 1 36N32'04 105W35'00 7:02:20
Valdez Place 5 1 36N16'27 104W51'14 6:59:25
Valedon 13 1 32N19'03 108W44'40 7:14:59
Valencia 33 1 34N47'58 106W41'59 7:06:48
Vallecito 30 1 36N09'27 105W47'02 7:03:08
Vallecitos 19 1 35N59'39 105W24'31 7:01:38
Vallecitos 22 1 36N29'42 106W06'58 7:04:28
Vallecitos 30 1 36N15'24 105W36'29 7:02:26
Vallecitos Corrales 22 1 36N04'00 106W21'20 7:05:25
Vallecitos de los Indios 24 1 35N46 106W41 7:06:44
Valle Escondido 30 1 36N21'59 105W22'49 7:01:31
Valmont 20 1 32N44'48 105W59'13 7:03:57
Valmora 19 1 35N48'59 104W55'21 6:59:41
Val Verde 5 1 36N33 105W16 7:01:04
Val Verde 29 1 33N42'11 106W55'49 7:07:43
Vanadium 10 1 32N46'45 108W07'01 7:12:28
Vander Wagen 18 1 35N16'26 108W45'15 7:15:01
Van Houten 5 1 36N47'32 104W33'55 6:58:16
Variadero (Garita P O) 26 1 35N23'17 104W27'32 6:57:50
Varney 31 1 34N18'17 105W33'50 7:02:15
Vaughn 11 1 34N36'06 105W12'28 7:00:50
Vegas Junction 11 1 34N58'35 104W59'26 6:59:58
Veguita 29 1 34N30'58 106W46'00 7:07:04
Velarde 22 1 36N09'32 105W58'27 7:03:54
Ventero 30 1 36N59'01 105W24'19 7:01:37
Vermejo Park 5 1 36N54 104W26 6:57:44
Vest Wells 3 1 33N38'07 103W41'58 6:54:48
Vevay 8 1 31N55'07 106W45'34 7:07:02
Villa de Cubero 4 1 35N05'05 107W32'30 7:10:10
Villa Madonna 15 1 33N25'21 105W43'23 7:02:54
Villanueva 26 1 35N16'00 105W21'37 7:01:26
Virden 13 1 32N41'13 109W00'05 7:16:00
Vista 10 1 31N57'55 108W26'18 7:13:45
Vista Encantada 1 1 35N06'39 106W34'03 7:06:16
Voght Place 18 1 35N36'24 107W42'58 7:10:52
Volcano Cliffs 1 1 35N11 106W42 7:06:48
Wagon Mound 19 1 36N00'32 104W42'22 6:58:49
Waldo 27 1 35N27'02 106W08'50 7:04:35
Walker 3 1 33N23 104W32 6:58:08
Warren 14 1 32N36'33 103W08'49 6:52:35
Water Canyon 29 1 34N05 107W05 7:08:20
Waterfall 20 1 32N57 105W45 7:03:00
Waterflow 25 1 36N45 108W27 7:13:48
Waterloo 17 1 31N59'06 107W43'18 7:10:53
Watrous 19 1 35N47'26 104W58'52 6:59:55
Weber City 6 1 34N38'01 103W38'09 6:54:33
Weed 20 1 32N48'09 105W31'01 7:02:04
West Carlsbad 9 1 32N25'34 104W15'15 6:57:01
West De Baca 7 1 34N26 104W36 6:58:24
West Las Vegas 26 1 35N36 105W13 7:00:52
West Village 4 1 35N03'09 107W34'54 7:10:20
Wheatland 21 2 34N54'31 103W21'13 6:53:25
Whitehorse 18 1 35N48'40 107W44'50 7:10:59
White Lakes 27 1 35N12'06 105W47'11 7:03:09
White Oaks 15 1 33N44'51 105W44'09 7:02:57
White Rock 16 1 35N49'39 106W12'12 7:04:49
White Rock 25 1 36N05'19 108W16'12 7:13:05
Whites 9 1 32N11 104W22 6:57:28
White Sands 8 1 32N22'51 106W28'44 7:05:55
White Sands Missile Range 8 1 32N22 106W37 7:06:28
Whites City 9 1 32N10'32 104W22'34 6:57:30
White Signal 10 1 32N33'21 108W21'56 7:13:28
Whitetail 20 1 33N13'44 105W33'19 7:02:13
Whitewater 10 1 32N34'53 108W08'00 7:12:32
Wilcox Peak 2 1 33N16'51 108W48'57 7:15:16
Willard 31 1 34N35'45 106W01'59 7:04:08
Williams Acres 18 1 35N31 108W44 7:14:56
Williamsburg 28 1 33N06'58 107W17'34 7:09:10
Willow Creek 22 1 36N53'22 106W39'01 7:06:36
Willow Mountain 2 1 33N21'03 108W40'36 7:14:42
Wilna 10 1 32N12'25 108W14'03 7:12:56
Wimsatt 20 1 32N57'29 105W38'31 7:02:34
Wimsattville 10 1 32N48'20 108W05'02 7:12:20
Window Rock Junction 18 1 35N31 108W44 7:14:56
Windy Point 2 1 33N16'39 108W42'32 7:14:50
Wingate 18 1 35N30'52 108W32'39 7:14:11
Winston 28 1 33N20'48 107W38'48 7:10:35
Witt 31 1 34N50'26 106W03'09 7:04:13
Woods Place 21 2 35N21'42 103W21'35 6:53:26
Wright Place 22 1 36N30'07 106W40'32 7:06:42
Yah-ta-hey 18 1 35N37'41 108W46'47 7:15:07
Yankee 5 1 36N56'42 104W19'39 6:57:19
Yarbrough Place 13 1 31N40'56 108W43'02 7:14:52
Yates 12 1 36N07'49 103W54'03 6:55:36
Yerba 23 1 34N09'24 103W22'45 6:53:31
Yeso 7 1 34N26'21 104W36'34 6:58:26
Young Place 25 1 36N59'40 107W31'03 7:10:04

Young Place 27 1 35N16'10 105W45'41 7:03:03
Youngsville 22 1 36N11'15 106W33'21 7:06:13
Yrisarri 1 1 34N57'59 106W17'27 7:05:10
Zamora 1 1 35N06'08 106W21'18 7:05:25
Zia Indian Reservation 24
1 35N30 106W43 7:06:52
Zia Pueblo 24 1 35N30'25 106W43'11 7:06:53
Zuni 18 1 35N04'10 108W50'52 7:15:23
Zuni Indian Reservation 18
1 35N04 108W51 7:15:24
Zuni Pueblo 18 1 35N04 108W51 7:15:24

TIME TABLES

NY # 1

Before 11/18/1883		LMT
11/18/1883	12:00	EST
3/31/1918	02:00	EWT
10/27/1918	02:00	EST
3/30/1919	02:00	EWT
10/26/1919	02:00	EST
3/28/1920	02:00	EDT
10/31/1920	02:00	EST
4/24/1921	02:00	EDT
9/25/1921	02:00	EST
4/30/1922	02:00	EDT
9/24/1922	02:00	EST
4/29/1923	02:00	EDT
9/30/1923	02:00	EST
4/27/1924	02:00	EDT
9/28/1924	02:00	EST
4/26/1925	02:00	EDT
9/27/1925	02:00	EST
4/25/1926	02:00	EDT
9/26/1926	02:00	EST
4/24/1927	02:00	EDT
9/25/1927	02:00	EST
4/29/1928	02:00	EDT
9/30/1928	02:00	EST
4/28/1929	02:00	EDT
9/29/1929	02:00	EST
4/27/1930	02:00	EDT
9/28/1930	02:00	EST
4/26/1931	02:00	EDT
9/27/1931	02:00	EST
4/24/1932	02:00	EDT
9/25/1932	02:00	EST
4/30/1933	02:00	EDT
9/24/1933	02:00	EST
4/29/1934	02:00	EDT
9/30/1934	02:00	EST
4/28/1935	02:00	EDT
9/29/1935	02:00	EST
4/26/1936	02:00	EDT
9/27/1936	02:00	EST
4/25/1937	02:00	EDT
9/26/1937	02:00	EST
4/24/1938	02:00	EDT
9/25/1938	02:00	EST
4/30/1939	02:00	EDT
9/24/1939	02:00	EST
4/28/1940	02:00	EDT
9/29/1940	02:00	EST
4/27/1941	02:00	EDT
9/28/1941	02:00	EST
2/09/1942	02:00	EWT
9/30/1945	02:00	EST
4/28/1946	02:00	EDT
9/29/1946	02:00	EST
4/27/1947	02:00	EDT
9/28/1947	02:00	EST
4/25/1948	02:00	EDT
9/26/1948	02:00	EST
4/24/1949	02:00	EDT
9/25/1949	02:00	EST
4/30/1950	02:00	EDT
9/24/1950	02:00	EST
4/29/1951	02:00	EDT
9/30/1951	02:00	EST
4/27/1952	02:00	EDT
9/28/1952	02:00	EST
4/26/1953	02:00	EDT
9/27/1953	02:00	EST
4/25/1954	02:00	EDT
9/26/1954	02:00	EST
4/24/1955	02:00	EDT
10/30/1955	02:00	EST
4/29/1956	02:00	EDT
10/28/1956	02:00	EST
4/28/1957	02:00	EDT
10/27/1957	02:00	EST
4/27/1958	02:00	EDT
10/26/1958	02:00	EST
4/26/1959	02:00	EDT
10/25/1959	02:00	EST
4/24/1960	02:00	EDT
10/30/1960	02:00	EST
4/30/1961	02:00	EDT
10/29/1961	02:00	EST
4/29/1962	02:00	EDT
10/28/1962	02:00	EST
4/28/1963	02:00	EDT
10/27/1963	02:00	EST
4/26/1964	02:00	EDT
10/25/1964	02:00	EST
4/25/1965	02:00	EDT
10/31/1965	02:00	EST
4/24/1966	02:00	EDT
10/30/1966	02:00	EST
4/30/1967	02:00	US#1

NY # 2

Before 11/18/1883		LMT
11/18/1883	12:00	EST
3/31/1918	02:00	EWT
10/27/1918	02:00	EST
3/30/1919	02:00	EWT
10/26/1919	02:00	EST
3/28/1920	02:00	EDT
10/31/1920	02:00	EST
4/24/1921	02:00	EDT
9/25/1921	02:00	EST
4/30/1922	02:00	EDT
9/24/1922	02:00	EST
4/29/1923	02:00	EDT
9/30/1923	02:00	EST
4/27/1924	02:00	EDT
9/28/1924	02:00	EST
4/26/1925	02:00	EDT
9/27/1925	02:00	EST
4/25/1926	02:00	EDT
9/26/1926	02:00	EST
4/24/1927	02:00	EDT
9/25/1927	02:00	EST
4/29/1928	02:00	EDT
9/30/1928	02:00	EST
4/28/1929	02:00	EDT
9/29/1929	02:00	EST
4/27/1930	02:00	EDT
9/28/1930	02:00	EST
4/26/1931	02:00	EDT
9/27/1931	02:00	EST
4/24/1932	02:00	EDT
9/25/1932	02:00	EST
4/30/1933	02:00	EDT
9/24/1933	02:00	EST
4/29/1934	02:00	EDT
9/30/1934	02:00	EST
4/28/1935	02:00	EDT
9/29/1935	02:00	EST
4/26/1936	02:00	EDT
9/27/1936	02:00	EST
4/25/1937	02:00	EDT
9/26/1937	02:00	EST
4/24/1938	02:00	EDT
9/25/1938	02:00	EST
4/30/1939	02:00	EDT
9/24/1939	02:00	EST
4/28/1940	02:00	EDT
9/29/1940	02:00	EST
4/27/1941	02:00	EDT
9/28/1941	02:00	EST
2/09/1942	02:00	EWT
9/30/1945	02:00	EST
4/24/1955	02:00	US#2

NY # 3

Before 11/18/1883		LMT
11/18/1883	12:00	EST
3/31/1918	02:00	EWT
10/27/1918	02:00	EST
3/30/1919	02:00	EWT
10/26/1919	02:00	EST
3/28/1920	02:00	EDT
10/31/1920	02:00	EST
4/29/1928	02:00	EDT
9/30/1928	02:00	EST
4/28/1929	02:00	EDT
9/29/1929	02:00	EST
4/27/1930	02:00	EDT
9/28/1930	02:00	EST
4/26/1931	02:00	EDT
9/27/1931	02:00	EST
4/24/1932	02:00	EDT
9/25/1932	02:00	EST
4/30/1933	02:00	EDT
9/24/1933	02:00	EST
4/29/1934	02:00	EDT
9/30/1934	02:00	EST
4/28/1935	02:00	EDT
9/29/1935	02:00	EST
4/26/1936	02:00	EDT
9/27/1936	02:00	EST
4/25/1937	02:00	EDT
9/26/1937	02:00	EST
4/24/1938	02:00	EDT
9/25/1938	02:00	EST
4/30/1939	02:00	EDT
9/24/1939	02:00	EST
4/28/1940	02:00	EDT
9/29/1940	02:00	EST
4/27/1941	02:00	EDT
9/28/1941	02:00	EST
2/09/1942	02:00	EWT
9/30/1945	02:00	EST
4/24/1955	02:00	US#2

NY # 4

Before 11/18/1883		LMT
11/18/1883	12:00	EST
3/31/1918	02:00	EWT
10/27/1918	02:00	EST
3/30/1919	02:00	EWT
10/26/1919	02:00	EST
3/28/1920	02:00	EDT
10/31/1920	02:00	EST
2/09/1942	02:00	US#2

NY # 5

Before 11/18/1883		LMT
11/18/1883	12:00	EST
3/31/1918	02:00	EWT
10/27/1918	02:00	EST
3/30/1919	02:00	EWT
10/26/1919	02:00	EST
3/28/1920	02:00	EDT
10/31/1920	02:00	EST
4/24/1938	02:00	EDT
9/25/1938	02:00	EST
4/30/1939	02:00	EDT
9/24/1939	02:00	EST
2/09/1942	02:00	EWT
9/30/1945	02:00	EST
4/24/1955	02:00	US#2

NY # 6

Before 11/18/1883		LMT
11/18/1883	12:00	EST
3/31/1918	02:00	EWT
10/27/1918	02:00	EST
3/30/1919	02:00	EWT
10/26/1919	02:00	EST
3/28/1920	02:00	EDT
10/31/1920	02:00	EST
4/29/1923	02:00	US#2

NY # 7

Before 11/18/1883		LMT
11/18/1883	12:00	EST
3/31/1918	02:00	EWT
10/27/1918	02:00	EST
3/30/1919	02:00	EWT
10/26/1919	02:00	EST
3/28/1920	02:00	EDT
10/31/1920	02:00	EST
4/26/1925	02:00	US#2

NY # 8

Before 11/18/1883		LMT
11/18/1883	12:00	NY#4
4/29/1928	02:00	NY#1
4/30/1967	02:00	US#1

NY # 9

Before 11/18/1883		LMT
11/18/1883	12:00	NY#4
4/28/1929	02:00	NY#1
4/30/1967	02:00	US#1

NY # 10

Before 11/18/1883		LMT
11/18/1883	12:00	NY#4
4/27/1930	02:00	NY#1
4/30/1967	02:00	US#1

NY # 11

Before 11/18/1883		LMT
11/18/1883	12:00	NY#4
4/26/1931	02:00	NY#1
4/30/1967	02:00	US#1

NY # 12

Before 11/18/1883		LMT
11/18/1883	12:00	NY#4
4/24/1938	02:00	NY#1
4/30/1967	02:00	US#1

NY # 13

Before 11/18/1883		LMT
11/18/1883	12:00	NY#4
4/30/1939	02:00	NY#1
4/30/1967	02:00	US#1

NY # 14

Before 11/18/1883		LMT
11/18/1883	12:00	NY#4
4/28/1940	02:00	NY#1
4/30/1967	02:00	US#1

NY # 15

Before 11/18/1883		LMT
11/18/1883	12:00	NY#4
4/27/1941	02:00	NY#1
4/30/1967	02:00	US#1

NY # 16

Before 11/18/1883		LMT
11/18/1883	12:00	EST
3/31/1918	02:00	EWT
10/27/1918	02:00	EST
3/30/1919	02:00	EWT
10/26/1919	02:00	EST
3/28/1920	02:00	EDT
10/31/1920	02:00	EST
2/09/1942	02:00	EWT
9/30/1945	02:00	EST
4/27/1947	02:00	NY#1
4/30/1967	02:00	US#1

NY # 17

Before 11/18/1883		LMT
11/18/1883	12:00	EST
3/31/1918	02:00	EWT
10/27/1918	02:00	EST
3/30/1919	02:00	EWT
10/26/1919	02:00	EST
3/28/1920	02:00	EDT
10/31/1920	02:00	EST
2/09/1942	02:00	EWT
9/30/1945	02:00	EST
4/25/1948	02:00	NY#1
4/30/1967	02:00	US#1

NY # 18

Before 11/18/1883		LMT
11/18/1883	12:00	EST
3/31/1918	02:00	EWT
10/27/1918	02:00	EST
3/30/1919	02:00	EWT
10/26/1919	02:00	EST
3/28/1920	02:00	EDT
10/31/1920	02:00	EST
2/09/1942	02:00	EWT
9/30/1945	02:00	EST
4/24/1949	02:00	NY#1
4/30/1967	02:00	US#1

NY # 19

Before 11/18/1883		LMT
11/18/1883	12:00	EST
3/31/1918	02:00	EWT
10/27/1918	02:00	EST
3/30/1919	02:00	EWT
10/26/1919	02:00	EST
3/28/1920	02:00	EDT
10/31/1920	02:00	EST
2/09/1942	02:00	EWT
9/30/1945	02:00	EST
4/30/1950	02:00	NY#1
4/30/1967	02:00	US#1

NY # 20

Before 11/18/1883		LMT
11/18/1883	12:00	EST
3/31/1918	02:00	EWT
10/27/1918	02:00	EST
3/30/1919	02:00	EWT
10/26/1919	02:00	EST
3/28/1920	02:00	EDT
10/31/1920	02:00	EST
2/09/1942	02:00	EWT
9/30/1945	02:00	EST
4/29/1951	02:00	NY#1
4/30/1967	02:00	US#1

NY # 21

Before 11/18/1883		LMT
11/18/1883	12:00	NY#4
4/30/1933	02:00	NY#1
4/30/1967	02:00	US#1

NY # 22

Before 11/18/1883		LMT
11/18/1883	12:00	EST
3/31/1918	02:00	EWT
10/27/1918	02:00	EST
3/30/1919	02:00	EWT
10/26/1919	02:00	EST
3/28/1920	02:00	EDT
10/31/1920	02:00	EST
2/09/1942	02:00	EWT
9/30/1945	02:00	EST
4/26/1953	02:00	NY#1
4/30/1967	02:00	US#1

NY # 23

Before 11/18/1883		LMT
11/18/1883	12:00	NY#4
4/26/1931	02:00	NY#2
4/24/1955	02:00	US#2

NY # 24

Before 11/18/1883		LMT
11/18/1883	12:00	NY#4
4/28/1940	02:00	NY#2
4/24/1955	02:00	US#2

NY # 25

Before 11/18/1883		LMT
11/18/1883	12:00	EST
3/31/1918	02:00	EWT
10/27/1918	02:00	EST
3/30/1919	02:00	EWT
10/26/1919	02:00	EST
3/28/1920	02:00	EDT
10/31/1920	02:00	EST
4/27/1941	02:00	EDT
9/28/1941	02:00	EST
2/09/1942	02:00	EWT
9/30/1945	02:00	EST
4/24/1955	02:00	NY#1
4/30/1967	02:00	US#1

NY # 26

Before 11/18/1883		LMT
11/18/1883	12:00	EST
3/31/1918	02:00	EWT
10/27/1918	02:00	EST
3/30/1919	02:00	EWT
10/26/1919	02:00	EST
3/28/1920	02:00	EDT
10/31/1920	02:00	EST
4/28/1940	02:00	EDT
9/29/1940	02:00	EST
2/09/1942	02:00	EWT
9/30/1945	02:00	EST
4/24/1955	02:00	NY#1
4/30/1967	02:00	US#1

NY # 27

Before 11/18/1883		LMT
11/18/1883	12:00	NY#4
9/29/1946	02:00	EST
4/24/1955	02:00	NY#1
4/30/1967	02:00	US#1

NY # 28

Before 11/18/1883		LMT
11/18/1883	12:00	EST
3/31/1918	02:00	EWT
10/27/1918	02:00	EST
3/30/1919	02:00	EWT
10/26/1919	02:00	EST
3/28/1920	02:00	EDT
10/31/1920	02:00	EST
2/09/1942	02:00	EWT
9/30/1945	02:00	EST
4/27/1947	02:00	EDT
9/28/1947	02:00	EST
4/24/1955	02:00	NY#1
4/30/1967	02:00	US#1

NY # 29

Before 11/18/1883		LMT
11/18/1883	12:00	EST
3/31/1918	02:00	EWT
10/27/1918	02:00	EST
3/30/1919	02:00	EWT
10/26/1919	02:00	EST
3/28/1920	02:00	EDT
10/31/1920	02:00	EST
2/09/1942	02:00	EWT
9/30/1945	02:00	EST
4/25/1948	02:00	EDT
9/26/1948	02:00	EST
4/24/1955	02:00	NY#1
4/30/1967	02:00	US#1

NY # 30

Before 11/18/1883		LMT
11/18/1883	12:00	EST
3/31/1918	02:00	EWT
10/27/1918	02:00	EST
3/30/1919	02:00	EWT
10/26/1919	02:00	EST
3/28/1920	02:00	EDT
10/31/1920	02:00	EST
2/09/1942	02:00	EWT
9/30/1945	02:00	EST
4/24/1949	02:00	EDT
9/25/1949	02:00	EST
4/24/1955	02:00	NY#1
4/30/1967	02:00	US#1

NY # 31

Before 11/18/1883		LMT
11/18/1883	12:00	EST
3/31/1918	02:00	EWT
10/27/1918	02:00	EST
3/30/1919	02:00	EWT
10/26/1919	02:00	EST
3/28/1920	02:00	EDT
10/31/1920	02:00	EST
2/09/1942	02:00	EWT
9/30/1945	02:00	EST
4/29/1951	02:00	EDT
9/30/1951	02:00	EST
4/24/1955	02:00	NY#1
4/30/1967	02:00	US#1

NY # 32

Before 11/18/1883		LMT
11/18/1883	12:00	EST
3/31/1918	02:00	EWT
10/27/1918	02:00	EST
3/30/1919	02:00	EWT
10/26/1919	02:00	EST
3/28/1920	02:00	EDT
10/31/1920	02:00	EST
2/09/1942	02:00	EWT
9/30/1945	02:00	EST
4/26/1953	02:00	EDT
9/27/1953	02:00	EST
4/24/1955	02:00	NY#1
4/30/1967	02:00	US#1

NY # 33

Before 11/18/1883		LMT
11/18/1883	12:00	EST
3/31/1918	02:00	EWT
10/27/1918	02:00	EST
3/30/1919	02:00	EWT
10/26/1919	02:00	EST
3/28/1920	02:00	EDT
10/31/1920	02:00	EST
2/09/1942	02:00	EWT
9/30/1945	02:00	EST
4/27/1947	02:00	EDT
9/28/1947	02:00	EST
4/25/1948	02:00	EDT
9/26/1948	02:00	EST
4/24/1955	02:00	NY#1
4/30/1967	02:00	US#1

NY # 34

Before 11/18/1883		LMT
11/18/1883	12:00	EST
3/31/1918	02:00	EWT
10/27/1918	02:00	EST
3/30/1919	02:00	EWT
10/26/1919	02:00	EST
3/28/1920	02:00	EDT
10/31/1920	02:00	EST
2/09/1942	02:00	EWT
9/30/1945	02:00	EST
4/25/1948	02:00	EDT
9/26/1948	02:00	EST
4/24/1949	02:00	EDT
9/25/1949	02:00	EST
4/24/1955	02:00	NY#1
4/30/1967	02:00	US#1

NY # 35

Before 11/18/1883		LMT
11/18/1883	12:00	EST
3/31/1918	02:00	EWT
10/27/1918	02:00	EST
3/30/1919	02:00	EWT
10/26/1919	02:00	EST
3/28/1920	02:00	EDT
10/31/1920	02:00	EST
2/09/1942	02:00	EWT
9/30/1945	02:00	EST
4/25/1948	02:00	EDT
9/26/1948	02:00	EST
4/24/1949	02:00	EDT
9/25/1949	02:00	EST
4/30/1950	02:00	EDT
9/24/1950	02:00	EST
4/24/1955	02:00	NY#1
4/30/1967	02:00	US#1

NY # 36

Before 11/18/1883		LMT
11/18/1883	12:00	EST
3/31/1918	02:00	EWT
10/27/1918	02:00	EST
3/30/1919	02:00	EWT
10/26/1919	02:00	EST
3/28/1920	02:00	EDT
10/31/1920	02:00	EST
2/09/1942	02:00	EWT
9/30/1945	02:00	EST
4/27/1947	02:00	EDT
9/28/1947	02:00	EST
4/25/1948	02:00	EDT
9/26/1948	02:00	EST
4/24/1949	02:00	EDT
9/25/1949	02:00	EST
4/30/1950	02:00	EDT
9/24/1950	02:00	EST
4/24/1955	02:00	NY#1
4/30/1967	02:00	US#1

NY # 37

Before 11/18/1883		LMT
11/18/1883	12:00	NY#4
4/28/1935	02:00	NY#1
4/30/1967	02:00	US#1

NY # 38

Before 11/18/1883		LMT
11/18/1883	12:00	NY#1
9/29/1946	02:00	EST

TIME TABLES

4/24/1955 02:00 NY#1
4/30/1967 02:00 US#1
....
NY # 39
Before 11/18/1883 LMT
11/18/1883 12:00 NY#2
4/25/1948 02:00 EDT
9/26/1948 02:00 EST
4/24/1955 02:00 NY#1
4/30/1967 02:00 US#1
....
NY # 40
Before 11/18/1883 LMT
11/18/1883 12:00 NY#4
4/29/1934 02:00 NY#1
4/30/1967 02:00 US#1
....
NY # 41
Before 11/18/1883 LMT
11/18/1883 12:00 NY#1
9/25/1921 02:00 EST
4/30/1939 02:00 NY#1
4/30/1967 02:00 US#1
....
NY # 42
Before 11/18/1883 LMT
11/18/1883 12:00 NY#4
4/24/1932 02:00 NY#1
4/30/1967 02:00 US#1
....
NY # 43
Before 11/18/1883 LMT
11/18/1883 12:00 NY#2
4/29/1951 02:00 NY#1
4/30/1967 02:00 US#1
....
NY # 44
Before 11/18/1883 LMT
11/18/1883 12:00 EST
3/31/1918 02:00 EWT
10/27/1918 02:00 EST
3/30/1919 02:00 EWT
10/26/1919 02:00 EST
3/28/1920 02:00 EDT
10/31/1920 02:00 EST
4/28/1940 02:00 EDT
9/29/1940 02:00 EST
4/27/1941 02:00 EDT
9/28/1941 02:00 EST
2/09/1942 02:00 EWT
9/30/1945 02:00 EST
4/28/1946 02:00 EDT
9/29/1946 02:00 EST
4/24/1955 02:00 NY#1
4/30/1967 02:00 US#1
....
NY # 45
Before 11/18/1883 LMT
11/18/1883 12:00 EST
3/31/1918 02:00 EWT
10/27/1918 02:00 EST
3/30/1919 02:00 EWT
10/26/1919 02:00 EST
3/28/1920 02:00 EDT
10/31/1920 02:00 EST
4/24/1921 02:00 EDT
9/25/1921 02:00 EST
4/25/1937 02:00 NY#1
4/30/1967 02:00 US#1
....
NY # 46
Before 11/18/1883 LMT
11/18/1883 12:00 NY#2
4/29/1951 02:00 EDT
9/30/1951 02:00 EST
4/26/1953 02:00 NY#1
4/30/1967 02:00 US#1
....
NY # 47
Before 11/18/1883 LMT
11/18/1883 12:00 NY#4
4/25/1937 02:00 EDT
9/26/1937 02:00 EST
2/09/1942 02:00 EWT
9/30/1945 02:00 EST
4/24/1955 02:00 NY#1
4/30/1967 02:00 US#1
....
NY # 48
Before 11/18/1883 LMT
11/18/1883 12:00 EST
3/31/1918 02:00 EWT
10/27/1918 02:00 EST
3/30/1919 02:00 EWT
10/26/1919 02:00 EST
3/28/1920 02:00 EDT
10/31/1920 02:00 EST
4/29/1923 02:00 EDT
9/30/1923 02:00 EST
4/27/1924 02:00 EDT
9/28/1924 02:00 EST
4/26/1925 02:00 EDT
9/27/1925 02:00 EST
4/25/1926 02:00 EDT
9/26/1926 02:00 EST
4/24/1927 02:00 EDT
9/25/1927 02:00 EST
4/29/1928 02:00 EDT
9/30/1928 02:00 EST
4/28/1929 02:00 EDT
9/29/1929 02:00 EST
4/27/1930 02:00 EDT
9/28/1930 02:00 EST
4/26/1931 02:00 EDT
9/27/1931 02:00 EST
4/24/1932 02:00 EDT
9/25/1932 02:00 EST
4/30/1933 02:00 EDT
9/24/1933 02:00 EST
4/29/1934 02:00 EDT
9/30/1934 02:00 EST
4/28/1935 02:00 EDT
9/29/1935 02:00 EST
4/26/1936 02:00 EDT
9/27/1936 02:00 EST
4/25/1937 02:00 EDT
9/26/1937 02:00 EST
4/24/1938 02:00 EDT
9/25/1938 02:00 EST
4/30/1939 02:00 EDT
9/24/1939 02:00 EST
4/28/1940 02:00 EDT
9/29/1940 02:00 EST
4/27/1941 02:00 EDT
9/28/1941 02:00 EST
2/09/1942 02:00 EWT
9/30/1945 02:00 EST
4/25/1948 02:00 EDT
9/26/1948 02:00 EST
4/24/1955 02:00 NY#1
4/30/1967 02:00 US#1
....
NY # 49
Before 11/18/1883 LMT
11/18/1883 12:00 NY#4
4/25/1937 02:00 NY#1
4/30/1967 02:00 US#1
....
NY # 50
Before 11/18/1883 LMT
11/18/1883 12:00 NY#4
4/28/1935 02:00 EDT
9/29/1935 02:00 EST
4/26/1936 02:00 EDT
9/27/1936 02:00 EST
4/25/1937 02:00 EDT
9/26/1937 02:00 EST
4/24/1938 02:00 EDT
9/25/1938 02:00 EST
4/30/1939 02:00 EDT
9/24/1939 02:00 EST
2/09/1942 02:00 EWT
9/30/1945 02:00 EST
4/24/1955 02:00 NY#1
4/30/1967 02:00 US#1
....
NY # 51
Before 11/18/1883 LMT
11/18/1883 12:00 NY#1
4/30/1939 02:00 EDT
10/01/1939 02:00 NY#1
4/30/1967 02:00 US#1
....
NY # 52
Before 11/18/1883 LMT
11/18/1883 12:00 EST
3/31/1918 02:00 EWT
10/27/1918 02:00 EST
3/30/1919 02:00 EWT
10/26/1919 02:00 EST
3/28/1920 02:00 EDT
10/31/1920 02:00 EST
4/24/1932 02:00 EDT
9/25/1932 02:00 EST
4/30/1933 02:00 EDT
9/24/1933 02:00 EST
4/29/1934 02:00 EDT
9/30/1934 02:00 EST
4/28/1935 02:00 EDT
9/29/1935 02:00 EST
4/26/1936 02:00 EDT
9/27/1936 02:00 EST
4/25/1937 02:00 EDT
9/26/1937 02:00 EST
4/24/1938 02:00 EDT
9/25/1938 02:00 EST
4/30/1939 02:00 EDT
9/24/1939 02:00 EST
4/28/1940 02:00 EDT
9/29/1940 02:00 EST
4/27/1941 02:00 EDT
9/28/1941 02:00 EST
2/09/1942 02:00 EWT
9/30/1945 02:00 EST
4/24/1955 02:00 NY#1
4/30/1967 02:00 US#1
....
NY # 53
Before 11/18/1883 LMT
11/18/1883 12:00 EST
3/31/1918 02:00 EWT
10/27/1918 02:00 EST
3/30/1919 02:00 EWT
10/26/1919 02:00 EST
3/28/1920 02:00 EDT
10/31/1920 02:00 EST
4/29/1934 02:00 EDT
9/30/1934 02:00 EST
4/28/1935 02:00 EDT
9/29/1935 02:00 EST
4/26/1936 02:00 EDT
9/27/1936 02:00 EST
4/25/1937 02:00 EDT
9/26/1937 02:00 EST
4/24/1938 02:00 EDT
9/25/1938 02:00 EST
4/30/1939 02:00 EDT
9/24/1939 02:00 EST
4/28/1940 02:00 EDT
9/29/1940 02:00 EST
4/27/1941 02:00 EDT
9/28/1941 02:00 EST
2/09/1942 02:00 EWT
9/30/1945 02:00 EST
4/24/1955 02:00 NY#1
4/30/1967 02:00 US#1
....
NY # 54
Before 11/18/1883 LMT
11/18/1883 12:00 NY#4
4/26/1936 02:00 NY#1
4/30/1967 02:00 US#1
....
NY # 55
Before 11/18/1883 LMT
11/18/1883 12:00 NY#4
4/29/1923 02:00 EDT
9/30/1923 02:00 EST
4/27/1924 02:00 EDT
9/28/1924 02:00 EST
4/26/1925 02:00 EDT
9/27/1925 02:00 EST
4/25/1926 02:00 EDT
9/26/1926 02:00 EST
4/24/1927 02:00 EDT
9/25/1927 02:00 EST
4/29/1928 02:00 EDT
9/30/1928 02:00 EST
4/28/1929 02:00 EDT
9/29/1929 02:00 EST
4/27/1930 02:00 EDT
9/28/1930 02:00 EST
4/26/1931 02:00 EDT
9/27/1931 02:00 EST
4/24/1932 02:00 EDT
9/25/1932 02:00 EST
4/30/1933 02:00 EDT
9/24/1933 02:00 EST
4/29/1934 02:00 EDT
9/30/1934 02:00 EST
4/28/1935 02:00 EDT
9/29/1935 02:00 EST
4/26/1936 02:00 EDT
9/27/1936 02:00 EST
4/25/1937 02:00 EDT
9/26/1937 02:00 EST
4/24/1938 02:00 EDT
9/25/1938 02:00 EST
4/30/1939 02:00 EDT
9/24/1939 02:00 EST
4/28/1940 02:00 EDT
9/29/1940 02:00 EST
4/27/1941 02:00 EDT
9/28/1941 02:00 EST
2/09/1942 02:00 EWT
9/30/1945 02:00 EST
4/28/1946 02:00 EDT
9/29/1946 02:00 EST
4/27/1947 02:00 EDT
9/28/1947 02:00 EST
4/25/1948 02:00 EDT
9/26/1948 02:00 EST
4/30/1950 02:00 NY#1
4/30/1967 02:00 US#1
....
NY # 56
Before 11/18/1883 LMT
11/18/1883 12:00 EST
3/31/1918 02:00 EWT
10/27/1918 02:00 EST
3/30/1919 02:00 EWT
10/26/1919 02:00 EST
3/28/1920 02:00 EDT
10/31/1920 02:00 EST
4/28/1935 02:00 EDT
9/29/1935 02:00 EST
6/07/1936 02:00 EDT
9/01/1936 02:00 EST
5/30/1937 02:00 EDT
9/07/1937 02:00 EST
6/05/1938 02:00 EDT
9/10/1938 02:00 EST
4/30/1939 02:00 EDT
9/24/1939 02:00 EST
6/02/1940 02:00 NY#1
4/30/1967 02:00 US#1
....
NY # 57
Before 11/18/1883 LMT
11/18/1883 12:00 EST
3/31/1918 02:00 EWT
10/27/1918 02:00 EST
3/30/1919 02:00 EWT
10/26/1919 02:00 EST
3/28/1920 02:00 EDT
10/31/1920 02:00 EST
4/26/1925 02:00 EDT
9/27/1925 02:00 EST
4/25/1926 02:00 EDT
9/26/1926 02:00 EST
4/24/1927 02:00 EDT
9/25/1927 02:00 EST
4/29/1928 02:00 EDT
9/30/1928 02:00 EST
4/28/1929 02:00 EDT
9/29/1929 02:00 EST
4/27/1930 02:00 EDT
9/28/1930 02:00 EST
4/26/1931 02:00 EDT
9/27/1931 02:00 EST
4/24/1932 02:00 EDT
9/25/1932 02:00 EST
4/30/1933 02:00 EDT
9/24/1933 02:00 EST
4/29/1934 02:00 EDT
9/30/1934 02:00 EST
4/28/1935 02:00 EDT
9/29/1935 02:00 EST
4/26/1936 02:00 EDT
9/27/1936 02:00 EST
4/25/1937 02:00 EDT
9/26/1937 02:00 EST
4/24/1938 02:00 EDT
9/25/1938 02:00 EST
4/30/1939 02:00 EDT
9/24/1939 02:00 EST
4/28/1940 02:00 EDT
9/29/1940 02:00 EST
4/27/1941 02:00 EDT
9/28/1941 02:00 EST
2/09/1942 02:00 EWT
9/30/1945 02:00 EST
4/27/1947 02:00 NY#1
4/30/1967 02:00 US#1
....
NY # 58
Before 11/18/1883 LMT
11/18/1883 12:00 NY#4
6/13/1937 02:00 EDT
9/07/1937 02:00 EST
4/24/1938 02:00 NY#1
4/30/1967 02:00 US#1
....
NY # 59
Before 11/18/1883 LMT
11/18/1883 12:00 NY#4
6/25/1940 02:00 EDT
9/10/1940 02:00 EST
2/09/1942 02:00 EWT
9/30/1945 02:00 EST
4/24/1949 02:00 NY#1
4/30/1967 02:00 US#1
....
NY # 60
Before 11/18/1883 LMT
11/18/1883 12:00 NY#4
4/26/1925 02:00 EDT
9/27/1925 02:00 EST
4/30/1939 02:00 NY#1
4/30/1967 02:00 US#1
....
NY # 61
Before 11/18/1883 LMT
11/18/1883 12:00 EST
3/31/1918 02:00 EWT
10/27/1918 02:00 EST
3/30/1919 02:00 EWT
10/26/1919 02:00 EST
3/28/1920 02:00 EDT
10/31/1920 02:00 EST
4/26/1925 02:00 EDT
9/27/1925 02:00 EST
4/25/1926 02:00 EDT
9/26/1926 02:00 EST
4/24/1927 02:00 EDT
9/25/1927 02:00 EST
4/29/1928 02:00 EDT
9/30/1928 02:00 EST
4/28/1929 02:00 EDT
9/29/1929 02:00 EST
4/27/1930 02:00 EDT
9/28/1930 02:00 EST
4/26/1931 02:00 EDT
9/27/1931 02:00 EST
4/24/1932 02:00 EDT
9/25/1932 02:00 EST
4/30/1933 02:00 EDT
9/24/1933 02:00 EST
4/29/1934 02:00 EDT
9/30/1934 02:00 EST
4/28/1935 02:00 EDT
9/29/1935 02:00 EST
4/26/1936 02:00 EDT
9/27/1936 02:00 EST
4/25/1937 02:00 EDT
9/26/1937 02:00 EST
4/24/1938 02:00 EDT
9/25/1938 02:00 EST
4/30/1939 02:00 EDT
9/24/1939 02:00 EST
4/28/1940 02:00 EDT
9/29/1940 02:00 EST
4/27/1941 02:00 EDT
9/28/1941 02:00 EST
2/09/1942 02:00 EWT
9/30/1945 02:00 EST
4/28/1946 02:00 EDT
9/29/1946 02:00 EST
4/24/1949 02:00 NY#1
4/30/1967 02:00 US#1
....
NY # 62
Before 11/18/1883 LMT
11/18/1883 12:00 EST
3/31/1918 02:00 EWT
10/27/1918 02:00 EST
3/30/1919 02:00 EWT
10/26/1919 02:00 EST
3/28/1920 02:00 EDT
10/31/1920 02:00 EST
4/26/1925 02:00 EDT
9/27/1925 02:00 EST
4/25/1926 02:00 EDT
9/26/1926 02:00 EST
4/24/1927 02:00 EDT
9/25/1927 02:00 EST
4/29/1928 02:00 EDT
9/30/1928 02:00 EST
4/28/1929 02:00 EDT
9/29/1929 02:00 EST
4/27/1930 02:00 EDT
9/28/1930 02:00 EST
4/26/1931 02:00 EDT
9/27/1931 02:00 EST
4/24/1932 02:00 EDT
9/25/1932 02:00 EST
4/30/1933 02:00 EDT
10/01/1933 02:00 NY#1
4/30/1967 02:00 US#1
....
NY # 63
Before 11/18/1883 LMT
11/18/1883 12:00 EST
3/31/1918 02:00 EWT
10/27/1918 02:00 EST
3/30/1919 02:00 EWT
10/26/1919 02:00 EST
3/28/1920 02:00 EDT
10/31/1920 02:00 EST
4/26/1931 02:00 EDT
9/27/1931 02:00 EST
4/24/1932 02:00 EDT
9/25/1932 02:00 EST
4/30/1933 02:00 EDT
9/24/1933 02:00 EST
4/29/1934 02:00 EDT
9/30/1934 02:00 EST
4/28/1935 02:00 EDT
9/02/1935 02:00 EST
4/26/1936 02:00 EDT
9/07/1936 02:00 EST
4/25/1937 02:00 NY#1
4/30/1967 02:00 US#1
....
NY # 64
Before 11/18/1883 LMT
11/18/1883 12:00 EST
3/31/1918 02:00 EWT
10/27/1918 02:00 EST
3/30/1919 02:00 EWT
10/26/1919 02:00 EST
3/28/1920 02:00 EDT
10/31/1920 02:00 EST
4/26/1925 02:00 EDT
9/27/1925 02:00 EST
4/25/1926 02:00 EDT
9/26/1926 02:00 EST
4/24/1927 02:00 EDT
9/25/1927 02:00 EST
4/29/1928 02:00 EDT
9/30/1928 02:00 EST
4/28/1929 02:00 EDT
9/29/1929 02:00 EST
4/27/1930 02:00 EDT
9/28/1930 02:00 EST
4/26/1931 02:00 EDT
9/27/1931 02:00 EST
4/24/1932 02:00 EDT
9/25/1932 02:00 EST
4/30/1933 02:00 EDT
9/24/1933 02:00 EST
4/29/1934 02:00 EDT
9/30/1934 02:00 EST
4/28/1935 02:00 EDT
9/29/1935 02:00 EST
4/26/1936 02:00 EDT
9/27/1936 02:00 EST
4/25/1937 02:00 EDT
9/26/1937 02:00 EST
4/24/1938 02:00 EDT
9/25/1938 02:00 EST
4/30/1939 02:00 EDT
9/24/1939 02:00 EST
4/28/1940 02:00 EDT
9/29/1940 02:00 EST
4/27/1941 02:00 EDT
9/28/1941 02:00 EST
2/09/1942 02:00 EWT
9/30/1945 02:00 EST
4/27/1947 02:00 EDT
9/28/1947 02:00 EST
4/25/1948 02:00 EDT
9/26/1948 02:00 EST
4/26/1953 02:00 NY#1
4/30/1967 02:00 US#1
....
NY # 65
Before 11/18/1883 LMT
11/18/1883 12:00 EST
3/31/1918 02:00 EWT
10/27/1918 02:00 EST
3/30/1919 02:00 EWT
10/26/1919 02:00 EST
3/28/1920 02:00 EDT
10/31/1920 02:00 EST
4/26/1931 02:00 EDT
9/27/1931 02:00 EST
2/09/1942 02:00 EWT
9/30/1945 02:00 EST
4/25/1948 02:00 NY#1
4/30/1967 02:00 US#1
....
NY # 66
Before 11/18/1883 LMT
11/18/1883 12:00 EST
3/31/1918 02:00 EWT
10/27/1918 02:00 EST
3/30/1919 02:00 EWT
10/26/1919 02:00 EST
3/28/1920 02:00 EDT
10/31/1920 02:00 EST
4/26/1931 02:00 EDT
9/27/1931 02:00 EST
4/24/1932 02:00 EDT
9/25/1932 02:00 EST
4/30/1933 02:00 EDT
9/24/1933 02:00 EST
4/29/1934 02:00 EDT
9/30/1934 02:00 EST
4/28/1935 02:00 EDT
9/29/1935 02:00 EST
4/26/1936 02:00 EDT
9/27/1936 02:00 EST
4/25/1937 02:00 EDT
9/26/1937 02:00 EST
4/24/1938 02:00 EDT
10/02/1938 02:00 NY#1
4/30/1967 02:00 US#1
....
NY # 67
Before 11/18/1883 LMT
11/18/1883 12:00 NY#4
5/12/1940 02:00 EDT
9/02/1940 02:00 EST
4/27/1941 02:00 NY#1
4/30/1967 02:00 US#1
....
NY # 68
Before 11/18/1883 LMT
11/18/1883 12:00 EST

TIME TABLES

3/31/1918 02:00 EWT
10/27/1918 02:00 EST
3/30/1919 02:00 EWT
10/26/1919 02:00 EST
3/28/1920 02:00 EDT
10/31/1920 02:00 EST
4/24/1932 02:00 EDT
9/25/1932 02:00 EST
4/30/1933 02:00 EDT
9/24/1933 02:00 EST
4/29/1934 02:00 EDT
9/30/1934 02:00 EST
4/28/1935 02:00 EDT
9/29/1935 02:00 EST
4/26/1936 02:00 EDT
9/27/1936 02:00 EST
4/25/1937 02:00 EDT
9/26/1937 02:00 EST
4/24/1938 02:00 EDT
10/02/1938 02:00 NY#1
4/30/1967 02:00 US#1

NY # 69
Before 11/18/1883 LMT
11/18/1883 12:00 EST
3/31/1918 02:00 EWT
10/27/1918 02:00 EST
3/30/1919 02:00 EWT
10/26/1919 02:00 EST
3/28/1920 02:00 EDT
10/31/1920 02:00 EST
4/26/1931 02:00 EDT
9/27/1931 02:00 EST
4/24/1932 02:00 EDT
9/25/1932 02:00 EST
4/30/1933 02:00 EDT
9/24/1933 02:00 EST
4/29/1934 02:00 EDT
9/30/1934 02:00 EST
4/28/1935 02:00 EDT
9/29/1935 02:00 EST
4/26/1936 02:00 EDT
9/27/1936 02:00 EST
4/25/1937 02:00 EDT
9/26/1937 02:00 EST
4/24/1938 02:00 EDT
9/25/1938 02:00 EST
4/30/1939 02:00 EDT
9/24/1939 02:00 EST
4/28/1940 02:00 EDT
9/29/1940 02:00 EST
4/27/1941 02:00 EDT
9/28/1941 02:00 EST
2/09/1942 02:00 EWT
9/30/1945 02:00 EST
4/27/1947 02:00 NY#1
4/30/1967 02:00 US#1

NY # 70
Before 11/18/1883 LMT
11/18/1883 12:00 NY#4
4/26/1931 02:00 EDT
9/16/1931 02:00 EST
4/24/1932 02:00 NY#1
4/30/1967 02:00 US#1

NY # 71
Before 11/18/1883 LMT
11/18/1883 12:00 EST
3/31/1918 02:00 EWT
10/27/1918 02:00 EST
3/30/1919 02:00 EWT
10/26/1919 02:00 EST
3/28/1920 02:00 EDT
10/31/1920 02:00 EST
4/24/1938 02:00 EDT
9/25/1938 02:00 EST
4/30/1939 02:00 EDT
9/24/1939 02:00 EST
4/28/1940 02:00 EDT
9/29/1940 02:00 EST
4/27/1941 02:00 EDT
9/28/1941 02:00 EST
2/09/1942 02:00 EWT
9/30/1945 02:00 EST
4/29/1951 02:00 NY#1
4/30/1967 02:00 US#1

NY # 72
Before 11/18/1883 LMT
11/18/1883 12:00 EST
3/31/1918 02:00 EWT
10/27/1918 02:00 EST
3/30/1919 02:00 EWT
10/26/1919 02:00 EST
3/28/1920 02:00 EDT
10/31/1920 02:00 EST
4/30/1933 02:00 EDT
9/24/1933 02:00 EST
4/29/1934 02:00 EDT
9/30/1934 02:00 EST
4/28/1935 02:00 EDT
9/29/1935 02:00 EST
4/26/1936 02:00 EDT
9/27/1936 02:00 EST
4/25/1937 02:00 EDT
9/26/1937 02:00 EST
4/24/1938 02:00 EDT
9/25/1938 02:00 EST
4/30/1939 02:00 EDT
9/24/1939 02:00 EST
4/28/1940 02:00 EDT
9/29/1940 02:00 EST
4/27/1941 02:00 EDT
9/28/1941 02:00 EST
2/09/1942 02:00 EWT
9/30/1945 02:00 EST
4/25/1948 02:00 EDT
9/26/1948 02:00 EST
4/24/1955 02:00 NY#1
4/30/1967 02:00 US#1

NY # 73
Before 11/18/1883 LMT
11/18/1883 12:00 NY#5
9/25/1938 02:00 EST
2/09/1942 02:00 EWT
9/30/1945 02:00 EST
4/24/1949 02:00 EDT
9/25/1949 02:00 EST
4/24/1955 02:00 NY#1
4/30/1967 02:00 US#1

NY # 74
Before 11/18/1883 LMT
11/18/1883 12:00 EST
3/31/1918 02:00 EWT
10/27/1918 02:00 EST
3/30/1919 02:00 EWT
10/26/1919 02:00 EST
3/28/1920 02:00 EDT
10/31/1920 02:00 EST
4/26/1931 02:00 EDT
9/27/1931 02:00 EST
4/24/1932 02:00 EDT
9/25/1932 02:00 EST
4/30/1933 02:00 EDT
9/24/1933 02:00 EST
4/29/1934 02:00 EDT
9/30/1934 02:00 EST
4/28/1935 02:00 EDT
9/29/1935 02:00 EST
4/26/1936 02:00 EDT
9/27/1936 02:00 EST
4/25/1937 02:00 EDT
9/26/1937 02:00 EST
4/24/1938 02:00 EDT
9/25/1938 02:00 EST
4/30/1939 02:00 EDT
9/24/1939 02:00 EST
4/28/1940 02:00 EDT
9/29/1940 02:00 EST
4/27/1941 02:00 EDT
9/28/1941 02:00 EST
2/09/1942 02:00 EWT
9/30/1945 02:00 EST
4/25/1948 02:00 EDT
9/26/1948 02:00 EST
4/24/1955 02:00 NY#1
4/30/1967 02:00 US#1

NY # 75
Before 11/18/1883 LMT
11/18/1883 12:00 NY#4
4/24/1938 02:00 EDT
9/25/1938 02:00 EST
4/30/1939 02:00 EDT
9/24/1939 02:00 EST
4/28/1940 02:00 EDT
9/29/1940 02:00 EST
4/27/1941 02:00 EDT
9/28/1941 02:00 EST
2/09/1942 02:00 EWT
9/30/1945 02:00 EST
4/25/1948 02:00 EDT
9/26/1948 02:00 EST
4/24/1955 02:00 NY#1
4/30/1967 02:00 US#1

NY # 76
Before 11/18/1883 LMT
11/18/1883 12:00 EST
3/31/1918 02:00 EWT
10/27/1918 02:00 EST
3/30/1919 02:00 EWT
10/26/1919 02:00 EST
3/28/1920 02:00 EDT
10/31/1920 02:00 EST
4/28/1935 02:00 EDT
9/29/1935 02:00 EST
4/26/1936 02:00 EDT
9/27/1936 02:00 EST
4/25/1937 02:00 EDT
9/26/1937 02:00 EST
4/24/1938 02:00 EDT
9/25/1938 02:00 EST
4/30/1939 02:00 EDT
9/24/1939 02:00 EST
4/28/1940 02:00 EDT
9/29/1940 02:00 EST
4/27/1941 02:00 EDT
9/28/1941 02:00 EST
2/09/1942 02:00 EWT
9/30/1945 02:00 EST
4/25/1948 02:00 EDT
9/26/1948 02:00 EST
4/24/1955 02:00 NY#1
4/30/1967 02:00 US#1

NY # 77
Before 11/18/1883 LMT
11/18/1883 12:00 EST
3/31/1918 02:00 EWT
10/27/1918 02:00 EST
3/30/1919 02:00 EWT
10/26/1919 02:00 EST
3/28/1920 02:00 EDT
10/31/1920 02:00 EST
4/28/1940 02:00 EDT
9/29/1940 02:00 EST
4/27/1941 02:00 EDT
9/28/1941 02:00 EST
2/09/1942 02:00 EWT
9/30/1945 02:00 EST
4/25/1948 02:00 NY#1
4/30/1967 02:00 US#1

NY # 78
Before 11/18/1883 LMT
11/18/1883 12:00 EST
3/31/1918 02:00 EWT
10/27/1918 02:00 EST
3/30/1919 02:00 EWT
10/26/1919 02:00 EST
3/28/1920 02:00 EDT
10/31/1920 02:00 EST
4/30/1939 02:00 EDT
9/24/1939 02:00 EST
2/09/1942 02:00 EWT
9/30/1945 02:00 EST
4/27/1947 02:00 EDT
9/28/1947 02:00 EST
4/25/1948 02:00 EDT
9/26/1948 02:00 EST
4/24/1955 02:00 NY#1
4/30/1967 02:00 US#1

NY # 79
Before 11/18/1883 LMT
11/18/1883 12:00 EST
3/31/1918 02:00 EWT
10/27/1918 02:00 EST
3/30/1919 02:00 EWT
10/26/1919 02:00 EST
3/28/1920 02:00 EDT
10/31/1920 02:00 EST
4/26/1931 02:00 EDT
9/27/1931 02:00 EST
4/24/1932 02:00 EDT
9/25/1932 02:00 EST
4/30/1933 02:00 EDT
9/24/1933 02:00 EST
4/29/1934 02:00 EDT
9/30/1934 02:00 EST
4/28/1935 02:00 EDT
9/29/1935 02:00 EST
4/26/1936 02:00 EDT
9/27/1936 02:00 EST
4/25/1937 02:00 EDT
9/26/1937 02:00 EST
4/24/1938 02:00 EDT
9/25/1938 02:00 EST
4/30/1939 02:00 EDT
9/24/1939 02:00 EST
4/28/1940 02:00 EDT
9/29/1940 02:00 EST
4/27/1941 02:00 EDT
9/28/1941 02:00 EST
2/09/1942 02:00 EWT
9/30/1945 02:00 EST
4/24/1949 02:00 NY#1
4/30/1967 02:00 US#1

NY # 80
Before 11/18/1883 LMT
11/18/1883 12:00 EST
3/31/1918 02:00 EWT
10/27/1918 02:00 EST
3/30/1919 02:00 EWT
10/26/1919 02:00 EST
3/28/1920 02:00 EDT
10/31/1920 02:00 EST
4/30/1933 02:00 EDT
9/24/1933 02:00 EST
4/29/1934 02:00 EDT
9/30/1934 02:00 EST
4/24/1938 02:00 NY#2
4/24/1955 02:00 US#2

NY # 81
Before 11/18/1883 LMT
11/18/1883 12:00 EST
3/31/1918 02:00 EWT
10/27/1918 02:00 EST
3/30/1919 02:00 EWT
10/26/1919 02:00 EST
3/28/1920 02:00 EDT
10/31/1920 02:00 EST
4/26/1925 02:00 EDT
9/27/1925 02:00 EST
4/25/1926 02:00 EDT
9/26/1926 02:00 EST
4/24/1927 02:00 EDT
9/25/1927 02:00 EST
4/29/1928 02:00 EDT
9/30/1928 02:00 EST
4/28/1929 02:00 EDT
9/29/1929 02:00 EST
4/27/1930 02:00 EDT
9/28/1930 02:00 EST
4/26/1931 02:00 EDT
9/27/1931 02:00 EST
4/24/1932 02:00 EDT
9/25/1932 02:00 EST
4/30/1933 02:00 EDT
9/24/1933 02:00 EST
4/29/1934 02:00 EDT
9/30/1934 02:00 EST
4/28/1935 02:00 EDT
9/29/1935 02:00 EST
5/03/1936 02:00 EDT
9/27/1936 02:00 EST
4/25/1937 02:00 EDT
9/26/1937 02:00 EST
4/24/1938 02:00 EDT
9/11/1938 02:00 EST
4/30/1939 02:00 NY#1
4/30/1967 02:00 US#1

NY # 82
Before 11/18/1883 LMT
11/18/1883 12:00 NY#4
5/18/1940 02:00 EDT
9/08/1940 02:00 EST
4/27/1941 02:00 NY#1
4/30/1967 02:00 US#1

NY # 83
Before 11/18/1883 LMT
11/18/1883 12:00 NY#4
5/03/1936 02:00 EDT
9/27/1936 02:00 NY#1
4/30/1967 02:00 US#1

NY # 84
Before 11/18/1883 LMT
11/18/1883 12:00 EST
3/31/1918 02:00 EWT
10/27/1918 02:00 EST
3/30/1919 02:00 EWT
10/26/1919 02:00 EST
3/28/1920 02:00 EDT
10/31/1920 02:00 EST
4/24/1932 02:00 EDT
9/25/1932 02:00 EST
2/09/1942 02:00 EWT
9/30/1945 02:00 EST
4/29/1951 02:00 NY#1
4/30/1967 02:00 US#1

NY # 85
Before 11/18/1883 LMT
11/18/1883 12:00 EST
3/31/1918 02:00 EWT
10/27/1918 02:00 EST
3/30/1919 02:00 EWT
10/26/1919 02:00 EST
3/28/1920 02:00 EDT
10/31/1920 02:00 EST
4/24/1938 02:00 EDT
9/25/1938 02:00 EST
4/30/1939 02:00 EDT
9/24/1939 02:00 EST
2/09/1942 02:00 EWT
9/30/1945 02:00 EST
4/27/1947 02:00 EDT
9/28/1947 02:00 EST
4/25/1948 02:00 EDT
9/26/1948 02:00 EST
4/24/1949 02:00 EDT
9/25/1949 02:00 EST
4/30/1950 02:00 EDT
9/24/1950 02:00 EST
4/29/1951 02:00 EDT
9/30/1951 02:00 EST
4/25/1954 02:00 NY#1
4/30/1967 02:00 US#1

NY # 86
Before 11/18/1883 LMT
11/18/1883 12:00 NY#1
9/25/1921 02:00 EST
7/01/1931 02:00 EDT
9/01/1931 02:00 EST
4/24/1932 02:00 EDT
9/25/1932 02:00 EST
4/30/1933 02:00 EDT
9/24/1933 02:00 EST
4/29/1934 02:00 EDT
9/30/1934 02:00 EST
6/01/1935 02:00 EDT
9/08/1935 02:00 EST
5/31/1936 02:00 EDT
9/06/1936 02:00 EST
5/30/1937 02:00 EDT
9/07/1937 02:00 EST
6/05/1938 02:00 EDT
9/11/1938 02:00 EST
4/30/1939 02:00 NY#1
4/30/1967 02:00 US#1

NY # 87
Before 11/18/1883 LMT
11/18/1883 12:00 NY#4
6/01/1932 02:00 EDT
10/01/1932 02:00 EST
2/09/1942 02:00 EWT
9/30/1945 02:00 EST
4/24/1949 02:00 EDT
9/25/1949 02:00 EST
4/24/1955 02:00 NY#1
4/30/1967 02:00 US#1

NY # 88
Before 11/18/1883 LMT
11/18/1883 12:00 EST
3/31/1918 02:00 EWT
10/27/1918 02:00 EST
3/30/1919 02:00 EWT
10/26/1919 02:00 EST
3/28/1920 02:00 EDT
10/31/1920 02:00 EST
4/30/1933 02:00 EDT
9/24/1933 02:00 EST
4/29/1934 02:00 EDT
9/30/1934 02:00 EST
4/28/1935 02:00 EDT
9/29/1935 02:00 EST
4/26/1936 02:00 EDT
9/27/1936 02:00 EST
4/25/1937 02:00 EDT
9/26/1937 02:00 EST
4/24/1938 02:00 EDT
9/25/1938 02:00 EST
4/30/1939 02:00 EDT
9/24/1939 02:00 EST
4/28/1940 02:00 EDT
9/29/1940 02:00 EST
4/27/1941 02:00 EDT
9/28/1941 02:00 EST
2/09/1942 02:00 EWT
9/30/1945 02:00 EST
4/24/1949 02:00 NY#1
4/30/1967 02:00 US#1

NY # 89
Before 11/18/1883 LMT
11/18/1883 12:00 NY#4
4/30/1939 02:00 EDT
10/01/1939 02:00 EST
4/28/1940 02:00 EDT
9/29/1940 02:00 EST
4/27/1941 02:00 EDT
9/28/1941 02:00 EST
2/09/1942 02:00 EWT
9/30/1945 02:00 EST
4/27/1947 02:00 NY#1
4/30/1967 02:00 US#1

NY # 90
Before 11/18/1883 LMT
11/18/1883 12:00 NY#4
6/01/1931 02:00 EDT
9/01/1931 02:00 EST
4/28/1935 02:00 NY#1
4/30/1967 02:00 US#1

NY # 91
Before 11/18/1883 LMT
11/18/1883 12:00 EST
3/31/1918 02:00 EWT
10/27/1918 02:00 EST
3/30/1919 02:00 EWT
10/26/1919 02:00 EST
3/28/1920 02:00 EDT
10/31/1920 02:00 EST
4/30/1939 02:00 EDT
9/24/1939 02:00 EST
4/28/1940 02:00 EDT
9/29/1940 02:00 EST
4/27/1941 02:00 EDT
9/28/1941 02:00 EST
2/09/1942 02:00 EWT
9/30/1945 02:00 EST
4/27/1947 02:00 NY#1
4/30/1967 02:00 US#1

NY # 92
Before 11/18/1883 LMT
11/18/1883 12:00 EST
3/31/1918 02:00 EWT
10/27/1918 02:00 EST
3/30/1919 02:00 EWT
10/26/1919 02:00 EST
3/28/1920 02:00 EDT
10/31/1920 02:00 EST
4/30/1939 02:00 EDT
9/24/1939 02:00 EST
4/28/1940 02:00 EDT
9/29/1940 02:00 EST
4/27/1941 02:00 EDT
9/28/1941 02:00 EST
2/09/1942 02:00 EWT
9/30/1945 02:00 EST
4/30/1950 02:00 NY#1
4/30/1967 02:00 US#1

NY # 93
Before 11/18/1883 LMT
11/18/1883 12:00 EST
3/31/1918 02:00 EWT
10/27/1918 02:00 EST
3/30/1919 02:00 EWT
10/26/1919 02:00 EST
3/28/1920 02:00 EDT
10/31/1920 02:00 EST
4/30/1939 02:00 EDT
9/24/1939 02:00 EST
4/28/1940 02:00 EDT
9/29/1940 02:00 EST
4/27/1941 02:00 EDT
9/28/1941 02:00 EST
2/09/1942 02:00 EWT
9/30/1945 02:00 EST
4/29/1951 02:00 NY#1
4/30/1967 02:00 US#1

NY # 94
Before 11/18/1883 LMT
11/18/1883 12:00 NY#4
6/01/1931 02:00 EDT
10/01/1931 02:00 NY#1
4/30/1967 02:00 US#1

NY # 95
Before 11/18/1883 LMT
11/18/1883 12:00 EST
3/31/1918 02:00 EWT
10/27/1918 02:00 EST
3/30/1919 02:00 EWT
10/26/1919 02:00 EST
3/28/1920 02:00 EDT
10/31/1920 02:00 EST
4/28/1940 02:00 EDT
9/29/1940 02:00 EST
2/09/1942 02:00 EWT
9/30/1945 02:00 EST
4/28/1946 02:00 NY#1
4/30/1967 02:00 US#1

NY # 96
Before 11/18/1883 LMT
11/18/1883 12:00 EST
3/31/1918 02:00 EWT
10/27/1918 02:00 EST
3/30/1919 02:00 EWT
10/26/1919 02:00 EST
3/28/1920 02:00 EDT
10/31/1920 02:00 EST
4/28/1940 02:00 EDT
9/29/1940 02:00 EST
2/09/1942 02:00 EWT
9/30/1945 02:00 EST
4/25/1948 02:00 EDT
9/26/1948 02:00 EST
4/24/1955 02:00 NY#1
4/30/1967 02:00 US#1

NY # 97
Before 11/18/1883 LMT

TIME TABLES

11/18/1883 12:00 EST
3/31/1918 02:00 EWT
10/27/1918 02:00 EST
3/30/1919 02:00 EWT
10/26/1919 02:00 EST
3/28/1920 02:00 EDT
10/31/1920 02:00 EST
4/28/1940 02:00 EDT
9/29/1940 02:00 EST
5/25/1941 02:00 EDT
9/01/1941 02:00 EST
2/09/1942 02:00 EWT
9/30/1945 02:00 EST
4/25/1948 02:00 NY#1
4/30/1967 02:00 US#1

NY # 98
Before 11/18/1883 LMT
11/18/1883 12:00 EST
3/31/1918 02:00 EWT
10/27/1918 02:00 EST
3/30/1919 02:00 EWT
10/26/1919 02:00 EST
3/28/1920 02:00 EDT
10/31/1920 02:00 EST
4/28/1940 02:00 EDT
9/29/1940 02:00 EST
4/27/1941 02:00 EDT
9/28/1941 02:00 EST
2/09/1942 02:00 EWT
9/30/1945 02:00 EST
4/27/1947 02:00 EDT
9/28/1947 02:00 EST
4/25/1948 02:00 EDT
9/26/1948 02:00 EST
4/24/1955 02:00 NY#1
4/30/1967 02:00 US#1

NY # 99
Before 11/18/1883 LMT
11/18/1883 12:00 EST
3/31/1918 02:00 EWT
10/27/1918 02:00 EST
3/30/1919 02:00 EWT
10/26/1919 02:00 EST
3/28/1920 02:00 EDT
10/31/1920 02:00 EST
4/28/1940 02:00 EDT
9/29/1940 02:00 EST
4/27/1941 02:00 EDT
9/28/1941 02:00 EST
2/09/1942 02:00 EWT
9/30/1945 02:00 EST
4/27/1947 02:00 NY#1
4/30/1967 02:00 US#1

NY # 100
Before 11/18/1883 LMT
11/18/1883 12:00 EST
3/31/1918 02:00 EWT
10/27/1918 02:00 EST
3/30/1919 02:00 EWT
10/26/1919 02:00 EST
3/28/1920 02:00 EDT
10/31/1920 02:00 EST
4/28/1940 02:00 EDT
9/29/1940 02:00 EST
4/27/1941 02:00 EDT
9/28/1941 02:00 EST
2/09/1942 02:00 EWT
9/30/1945 02:00 EST
4/29/1951 02:00 NY#1
4/30/1967 02:00 US#1

NY # 101
Before 11/18/1883 LMT
11/18/1883 12:00 EST
3/31/1918 02:00 EWT
10/27/1918 02:00 EST
3/30/1919 02:00 EWT
10/26/1919 02:00 EST
3/28/1920 02:00 EDT
10/31/1920 02:00 EST
4/28/1940 02:00 EDT
9/29/1940 02:00 EST
4/27/1941 02:00 EDT
9/28/1941 02:00 EST
2/09/1942 02:00 EWT
9/30/1945 02:00 EST
4/28/1946 02:00 EDT
9/29/1946 02:00 EST
4/27/1947 02:00 EDT
9/28/1947 02:00 EST
4/25/1948 02:00 EDT
9/26/1948 02:00 EST
4/29/1951 02:00 NY#1
4/30/1967 02:00 US#1

NY # 102
Before 11/18/1883 LMT
11/18/1883 12:00 EST
3/31/1918 02:00 EWT
10/27/1918 02:00 EST
3/30/1919 02:00 EWT
10/26/1919 02:00 EST
3/28/1920 02:00 EDT
10/31/1920 02:00 EST
4/30/1939 02:00 EDT
9/24/1939 02:00 EST
4/28/1940 02:00 EDT
9/29/1940 02:00 EST
4/27/1941 02:00 EDT
9/28/1941 02:00 EST
2/09/1942 02:00 EWT
9/30/1945 02:00 EST
4/28/1946 02:00 EDT
9/29/1946 02:00 EST
4/29/1951 02:00 NY#1
4/30/1967 02:00 US#1

NY # 103
Before 11/18/1883 LMT
11/18/1883 12:00 EST
3/31/1918 02:00 EWT
10/27/1918 02:00 EST
3/30/1919 02:00 EWT
10/26/1919 02:00 EST
3/28/1920 02:00 EDT
10/31/1920 02:00 EST
4/27/1941 02:00 EDT
9/28/1941 02:00 EST
2/09/1942 02:00 EWT
9/30/1945 02:00 EST
4/27/1947 02:00 EDT
9/28/1947 02:00 EST
4/24/1955 02:00 NY#1
4/30/1967 02:00 US#1

NY # 104
Before 11/18/1883 LMT
11/18/1883 12:00 NY#4
4/30/1939 02:00 EDT
9/03/1939 02:00 EST
6/02/1940 02:00 EDT
9/01/1940 02:00 EST
5/25/1941 02:00 EDT
9/07/1941 02:00 EST
2/09/1942 02:00 NY#1
4/30/1967 02:00 US#1

NY # 105
Before 11/18/1883 LMT
11/18/1883 12:00 EST
3/31/1918 02:00 EWT
10/27/1918 02:00 EST
3/30/1919 02:00 EWT
10/26/1919 02:00 EST
3/28/1920 02:00 EDT
10/31/1920 02:00 EST
4/27/1941 02:00 EDT
9/28/1941 02:00 EST
2/09/1942 02:00 EWT
9/30/1945 02:00 EST
4/27/1947 02:00 NY#1
4/30/1967 02:00 US#1

NY # 106
Before 11/18/1883 LMT
11/18/1883 12:00 EST
3/31/1918 02:00 EWT
10/27/1918 02:00 EST
3/30/1919 02:00 EWT
10/26/1919 02:00 EST
3/28/1920 02:00 EDT
10/31/1920 02:00 EST
4/27/1941 02:00 EDT
9/28/1941 02:00 EST
2/09/1942 02:00 EWT
9/30/1945 02:00 EST
4/25/1948 02:00 NY#1
4/30/1967 02:00 US#1

NY # 107
Before 11/18/1883 LMT
11/18/1883 12:00 EST
3/31/1918 02:00 EWT
10/27/1918 02:00 EST
3/30/1919 02:00 EWT
10/26/1919 02:00 EST
3/28/1920 02:00 EDT
10/31/1920 02:00 EST
4/27/1941 02:00 EDT
9/28/1941 02:00 EST
2/09/1942 02:00 EWT
9/30/1945 02:00 EST
4/29/1951 02:00 NY#1
4/30/1967 02:00 US#1

NY # 108
Before 11/18/1883 LMT
11/18/1883 12:00 EST
3/31/1918 02:00 EWT
10/27/1918 02:00 EST
3/30/1919 02:00 EWT
10/26/1919 02:00 EST
3/28/1920 02:00 EDT
10/31/1920 02:00 EST
4/27/1941 02:00 EDT
9/28/1941 02:00 EST
2/09/1942 02:00 EWT
9/30/1945 02:00 EST
4/26/1953 02:00 NY#1
4/30/1967 02:00 US#1

NY # 109
Before 11/18/1883 LMT
11/18/1883 12:00 EST
3/31/1918 02:00 EWT
10/27/1918 02:00 EST
3/30/1919 02:00 EWT
10/26/1919 02:00 EST
3/28/1920 02:00 EDT
10/31/1920 02:00 EST
4/30/1939 02:00 EDT
9/24/1939 02:00 EST
4/28/1940 02:00 EDT
9/29/1940 02:00 EST
4/27/1941 02:00 EDT
9/28/1941 02:00 EST
2/09/1942 02:00 EWT
9/30/1945 02:00 EST
4/28/1946 02:00 EDT
9/29/1946 02:00 EST
4/29/1951 02:00 NY#1
4/30/1967 02:00 US#1

NY # 110
Before 11/18/1883 LMT
11/18/1883 12:00 EST
3/31/1918 02:00 EWT
10/27/1918 02:00 EST
3/30/1919 02:00 EWT
10/26/1919 02:00 EST
3/28/1920 02:00 EDT
10/31/1920 02:00 EST
4/27/1941 02:00 EDT
9/28/1941 02:00 EST
2/09/1942 02:00 EWT
9/30/1945 02:00 EST
4/27/1947 02:00 EDT
9/28/1947 02:00 EST
4/25/1948 02:00 EDT
9/26/1948 02:00 EST
4/30/1950 02:00 EDT
9/24/1950 02:00 EST
4/29/1951 02:00 EDT
9/30/1951 02:00 EST
4/27/1952 02:00 EDT
9/28/1952 02:00 EST
4/24/1955 02:00 NY#1
4/30/1967 02:00 US#1

NY # 111
Before 11/18/1883 LMT
11/18/1883 12:00 EST
3/31/1918 02:00 EWT
10/27/1918 02:00 EST
3/30/1919 02:00 EWT
10/26/1919 02:00 EST
3/28/1920 02:00 EDT
10/31/1920 02:00 EST
4/26/1931 02:00 EDT
9/27/1931 02:00 EST
4/24/1932 02:00 EDT
9/25/1932 02:00 EST
4/30/1933 02:00 EDT
10/29/1933 02:00 NY#1
4/30/1967 02:00 US#1

NY # 112
Before 11/18/1883 LMT
11/18/1883 12:00 EST
3/31/1918 02:00 EWT
10/27/1918 02:00 EST
3/30/1919 02:00 EWT
10/26/1919 02:00 EST
3/28/1920 02:00 EDT
10/31/1920 02:00 EST
6/01/1931 02:00 EDT
9/01/1931 02:00 EST
4/24/1932 02:00 NY#1
4/30/1967 02:00 US#1

NY # 113
Before 11/18/1883 LMT
11/18/1883 12:00 NY#4
5/16/1937 02:00 EDT
9/26/1937 02:00 EST
5/01/1938 02:00 EDT
10/02/1938 02:00 EST
4/30/1939 02:00 EDT
9/24/1939 02:00 EST
5/15/1940 02:00 EDT
9/15/1940 02:00 EST
4/27/1941 02:00 EDT
9/28/1941 02:00 EST
2/09/1942 02:00 EWT
9/30/1945 02:00 EST
4/27/1947 02:00 EDT
9/28/1947 02:00 EST
5/17/1948 02:00 EDT
9/26/1948 02:00 NY#1
4/30/1967 02:00 US#1

NY # 114
Before 11/18/1883 LMT
11/18/1883 12:00 EST
3/31/1918 02:00 EWT
10/27/1918 02:00 EST
3/30/1919 02:00 EWT
10/26/1919 02:00 EST
3/28/1920 02:00 EDT
10/31/1920 02:00 EST
4/24/1932 02:00 EDT
9/25/1932 02:00 EST
4/30/1933 02:00 EDT
10/01/1933 02:00 NY#1
4/30/1967 02:00 US#1

NY # 115
Before 11/18/1883 LMT
11/18/1883 12:00 NY#4
5/26/1940 02:00 NY#1
4/30/1967 02:00 US#1

NY # 116
Before 11/18/1883 LMT
11/18/1883 12:00 EST
3/31/1918 02:00 EWT
10/27/1918 02:00 EST
3/30/1919 02:00 EWT
10/26/1919 02:00 EST
3/28/1920 02:00 EDT
10/31/1920 02:00 EST
6/15/1930 02:00 EDT
8/30/1930 02:00 EST
6/28/1931 02:00 EDT
9/06/1931 02:00 EST
5/07/1939 02:00 EDT
9/24/1939 02:00 EST
4/28/1940 02:00 EDT
10/06/1940 02:00 NY#1
4/30/1967 02:00 US#1

NY # 117
Before 11/18/1883 LMT
11/18/1883 12:00 EST
3/31/1918 02:00 EWT
10/27/1918 02:00 EST
3/30/1919 02:00 EWT
10/26/1919 02:00 EST
3/28/1920 02:00 EDT
10/31/1920 02:00 EST
2/09/1942 02:00 EWT
9/30/1945 02:00 EST
4/28/1946 02:00 EDT
9/29/1946 02:00 EST
4/27/1947 02:00 EDT
9/28/1947 02:00 EST
4/25/1948 02:00 EDT
9/26/1948 02:00 EST
4/30/1950 02:00 EDT
9/24/1950 02:00 EST
4/29/1951 02:00 EDT
9/30/1951 02:00 EST
4/24/1955 02:00 NY#1
4/30/1967 02:00 US#1

NY # 118
Before 11/18/1883 LMT
11/18/1883 12:00 NY#4
6/21/1941 02:00 EDT
9/01/1941 02:00 EST
2/09/1942 02:00 EWT
9/30/1945 02:00 EST
4/24/1955 02:00 NY#1
4/30/1967 02:00 US#1

NY # 119
Before 11/18/1883 LMT
11/18/1883 12:00 EST
3/31/1918 02:00 EWT
10/27/1918 02:00 EST
3/30/1919 02:00 EWT
10/26/1919 02:00 EST
3/28/1920 02:00 EDT
10/31/1920 02:00 EST
4/24/1938 02:00 EDT
9/25/1938 02:00 EST
4/30/1939 02:00 EDT
9/24/1939 02:00 EST
5/12/1940 02:00 EDT
9/03/1940 02:00 EST
4/27/1941 02:00 NY#1
4/30/1967 02:00 US#1

NY # 120
Before 11/18/1883 LMT
11/18/1883 12:00 NY#4
6/02/1940 02:00 EDT
9/02/1940 02:00 EST
4/27/1941 02:00 NY#1
4/30/1967 02:00 US#1

NY # 121
Before 11/18/1883 LMT
11/18/1883 12:00 NY#4
6/01/1931 02:00 EDT
9/01/1931 02:00 EST
5/29/1932 02:00 EDT
9/05/1932 02:00 EST
5/21/1933 02:00 EDT
9/24/1933 02:00 EST
4/29/1934 02:00 NY#1
4/30/1967 02:00 US#1

NY # 122
Before 11/18/1883 LMT
11/18/1883 12:00 EST
3/31/1918 02:00 EWT
10/27/1918 02:00 EST
3/30/1919 02:00 EWT
10/26/1919 02:00 EST
3/28/1920 02:00 EDT
10/31/1920 02:00 EST
4/26/1931 02:00 EDT
9/27/1931 02:00 EST
5/01/1932 02:00 NY#1
4/30/1967 02:00 US#1

NY # 123
Before 11/18/1883 LMT
11/18/1883 12:00 NY#4
4/30/1933 02:00 EDT
9/24/1933 02:00 EST
6/01/1936 02:00 EDT
9/27/1936 02:00 EST
4/24/1938 02:00 NY#1
4/30/1967 02:00 US#1

NY # 124
Before 11/18/1883 LMT
11/18/1883 12:00 EST
3/31/1918 02:00 EWT
10/27/1918 02:00 EST
3/30/1919 02:00 EWT
10/26/1919 02:00 EST
3/28/1920 02:00 EDT
10/31/1920 02:00 EST
2/09/1942 02:00 EWT
9/30/1945 02:00 EST
4/27/1947 02:00 EDT
9/28/1947 02:00 EST
4/24/1949 02:00 NY#1
4/30/1967 02:00 US#1

NY # 125
Before 11/18/1883 LMT
11/18/1883 12:00 EST
3/31/1918 02:00 EWT
10/27/1918 02:00 EST
3/30/1919 02:00 EWT
10/26/1919 02:00 EST
3/28/1920 02:00 EDT
10/31/1920 02:00 EST
2/09/1942 02:00 EWT
9/30/1945 02:00 EST
4/27/1947 02:00 EDT
9/28/1947 02:00 EST
4/30/1950 02:00 NY#1
4/30/1967 02:00 US#1

NY # 126
Before 11/18/1883 LMT
11/18/1883 12:00 EST
3/31/1918 02:00 EWT
10/27/1918 02:00 EST
3/30/1919 02:00 EWT
10/26/1919 02:00 EST
3/28/1920 02:00 EDT
10/31/1920 02:00 EST
2/09/1942 02:00 EWT
9/30/1945 02:00 EST
4/27/1947 02:00 EDT
9/28/1947 02:00 EST
4/29/1951 02:00 NY#1
4/30/1967 02:00 US#1

NY # 127
Before 11/18/1883 LMT
11/18/1883 12:00 EST
3/31/1918 02:00 EWT
10/27/1918 02:00 EST
3/30/1919 02:00 EWT
10/26/1919 02:00 EST
3/28/1920 02:00 EDT
10/31/1920 02:00 EST
2/09/1942 02:00 EWT
9/30/1945 02:00 EST
4/27/1947 02:00 EDT
9/28/1947 02:00 EST
4/26/1953 02:00 NY#1
4/30/1967 02:00 US#1

NY # 128
Before 11/18/1883 LMT
11/18/1883 12:00 NY#4
6/02/1935 02:00 EDT
9/02/1935 02:00 EST
6/07/1936 02:00 EDT
9/07/1936 02:00 EST
5/31/1937 02:00 EDT
9/06/1937 02:00 EST
6/05/1938 02:00 EDT
9/04/1938 02:00 EST
6/04/1939 02:00 EDT
9/03/1939 02:00 EST
6/02/1940 02:00 EDT
9/01/1940 02:00 EST
4/27/1941 02:00 EDT
9/28/1941 02:00 EST
2/09/1942 02:00 EWT
9/30/1945 02:00 EST
4/28/1946 02:00 EDT
9/29/1946 02:00 EST
4/27/1947 02:00 EDT
9/28/1947 02:00 EST
4/25/1948 02:00 EDT
9/26/1948 02:00 EST
4/24/1949 02:00 EDT
9/25/1949 02:00 EST
4/29/1951 02:00 NY#1
4/30/1967 02:00 US#1

NY # 129
Before 11/18/1883 LMT
11/18/1883 12:00 NY#4
4/25/1937 02:00 EDT
9/01/1937 02:00 EST
4/24/1938 02:00 EDT
9/25/1938 02:00 EST
5/01/1939 02:00 EDT
9/16/1939 02:00 EST
4/28/1940 02:00 EDT
9/01/1940 02:00 EST
4/27/1941 02:00 NY#1
4/30/1967 02:00 US#1

NY # 130
Before 11/18/1883 LMT
11/18/1883 12:00 EST
3/31/1918 02:00 EWT
10/27/1918 02:00 EST
3/30/1919 02:00 EWT
10/26/1919 02:00 EST
3/28/1920 02:00 EDT
10/31/1920 02:00 EST
2/09/1942 02:00 EWT
9/30/1945 02:00 EST
4/27/1947 02:00 EDT
9/28/1947 02:00 EST
4/25/1948 02:00 EDT
9/26/1948 02:00 EST
4/29/1951 02:00 NY#1
4/30/1967 02:00 US#1

NY # 131
Before 11/18/1883 LMT
11/18/1883 12:00 EST
3/31/1918 02:00 EWT
10/27/1918 02:00 EST
3/30/1919 02:00 EWT
10/26/1919 02:00 EST
3/28/1920 02:00 EDT
10/31/1920 02:00 EST
2/09/1942 02:00 EWT
9/30/1945 02:00 EST
4/27/1947 02:00 EDT
9/28/1947 02:00 EST
4/25/1948 02:00 EDT
9/26/1948 02:00 EST
4/24/1949 02:00 EDT
9/25/1949 02:00 EST
4/30/1950 02:00 EDT
9/24/1950 02:00 EST
4/26/1953 02:00 EDT
9/27/1953 02:00 EST
4/24/1955 02:00 NY#1
4/30/1967 02:00 US#1

TIME TABLES

NY # 132
Before 11/18/1833 LMT
11/18/1833 12:00 EST
3/31/1918 02:00 EWT
10/27/1918 02:00 EST
3/30/1919 02:00 EWT
10/26/1919 02:00 EST
3/28/1920 02:00 EDT
10/31/1920 02:00 EST
2/09/1942 02:00 EWT
9/30/1945 02:00 EST
4/27/1947 02:00 EDT
9/28/1947 02:00 EST
4/24/1949 02:00 EDT
9/25/1949 02:00 EST
4/29/1951 02:00 NY#1
4/30/1967 02:00 US#1

NY # 133
Before 11/18/1883 LMT
11/18/1883 12:00 EST
3/31/1918 02:00 EWT
10/27/1918 02:00 EST
3/30/1919 02:00 EWT
10/26/1919 02:00 EST
3/28/1920 02:00 EDT
10/31/1920 02:00 EST
2/09/1942 02:00 EWT
9/30/1945 02:00 EST
4/27/1947 02:00 EDT
9/28/1947 02:00 EST
4/25/1948 02:00 EDT
9/26/1948 02:00 EST
4/29/1951 02:00 EDT
9/30/1951 02:00 EST
4/26/1953 02:00 NY#1
4/30/1967 02:00 US#1

NY # 134
Before 11/18/1883 LMT
11/18/1883 12:00 NY#4
6/14/1936 02:00 EDT
9/13/1936 02:00 EST
4/28/1940 02:00 NY#1
4/30/1967 02:00 US#1

NY # 135
Before 11/18/1883 LMT
11/18/1883 12:00 EST
3/31/1918 02:00 EWT
10/27/1918 02:00 EST
3/30/1919 02:00 EWT
10/26/1919 02:00 EST
3/28/1920 02:00 EDT
10/31/1920 02:00 EST
2/09/1942 02:00 EWT
9/30/1945 02:00 EST
4/25/1948 02:00 EDT
9/26/1948 02:00 EST
4/29/1951 02:00 EDT
9/30/1951 02:00 EST
4/24/1955 02:00 NY#1
4/30/1967 02:00 US#1

NY # 136
Before 11/18/1883 LMT
11/18/1883 12:00 NY#4
5/25/1936 02:00 NY#1
4/30/1967 02:00 US#1

NY # 137
Before 11/18/1883 LMT
11/18/1883 12:00 EST
3/31/1918 02:00 EWT
10/27/1918 02:00 EST
3/30/1919 02:00 EWT
10/26/1919 02:00 EST
3/28/1920 02:00 EDT
10/31/1920 02:00 EST
4/28/1940 02:00 EDT
9/29/1940 02:00 EST
2/09/1942 02:00 EWT
9/30/1945 02:00 EST
4/25/1948 02:00 NY#1
4/30/1967 02:00 US#1

NY # 138
Before 11/18/1883 LMT
11/18/1883 12:00 NY#4
5/08/1935 02:00 EDT
9/29/1935 02:00 EST
4/26/1936 02:00 NY#1
4/30/1967 02:00 US#1

NY # 139
Before 11/18/1883 LMT
11/18/1883 12:00 NY#4
6/15/1939 02:00 EDT
9/04/1939 02:00 EST
4/28/1940 02:00 NY#1
4/30/1967 02:00 US#1

NY # 140
Before 11/18/1883 LMT
11/18/1883 12:00 NY#4
4/28/1940 02:00 EDT
9/02/1940 02:00 EST
2/09/1942 02:00 EWT
9/30/1945 02:00 EST
4/27/1947 02:00 NY#1
4/30/1967 02:00 US#1

NY # 141
Before 11/18/1883 LMT
11/18/1883 12:00 EST
3/31/1918 02:00 EWT
10/27/1918 02:00 EST
3/30/1919 02:00 EWT
10/26/1919 02:00 EST
3/28/1920 02:00 EDT
10/31/1920 02:00 EST
2/09/1942 02:00 EWT
9/30/1945 02:00 EST
4/25/1948 02:00 EDT
9/26/1948 02:00 EST
4/24/1949 02:00 EDT
9/25/1949 02:00 EST
4/29/1951 02:00 NY#1
4/30/1967 02:00 US#1

NY # 142
Before 11/18/1883 LMT
11/18/1883 12:00 NY#4
5/31/1931 02:00 EDT
10/01/1931 02:00 EST
4/30/1939 02:00 NY#1
4/30/1967 02:00 US#1

NY # 143
Before 11/18/1883 LMT
11/18/1883 12:00 NY#4
6/02/1940 02:00 EDT
9/02/1940 02:00 EST
4/27/1941 02:00 EDT
9/28/1941 02:00 EST
2/09/1942 02:00 EWT
9/30/1945 02:00 EST
4/25/1948 02:00 EDT
9/26/1948 02:00 EST
4/24/1955 02:00 NY#1
4/30/1967 02:00 US#1

NY # 144
Before 11/18/1883 LMT
11/18/1883 12:00 NY#4
6/20/1941 02:00 EDT
9/01/1941 02:00 EST
2/09/1942 02:00 NY#1
4/30/1967 02:00 US#1

NY # 145
Before 11/18/1883 LMT
11/18/1883 12:00 NY#4
6/27/1937 02:00 EDT
8/29/1937 02:00 EST
6/04/1939 02:00 EDT
9/10/1939 02:00 EST
4/28/1940 02:00 EDT
9/29/1940 02:00 EST
2/09/1942 02:00 EWT
9/30/1945 02:00 EST
4/24/1955 02:00 NY#1
4/30/1967 02:00 US#1

NY # 146
Before 11/18/1883 LMT
11/18/1883 02:00 NY#4
5/06/1939 02:00 EDT
9/30/1939 02:00 EST
4/28/1940 02:00 EDT
9/29/1940 02:00 EST
4/27/1941 02:00 EDT
9/28/1941 02:00 EST
2/09/1942 02:00 EWT
9/30/1945 02:00 EST
4/28/1946 02:00 EDT
9/20/1946 02:00 EST
4/27/1947 02:00 NY#1
4/30/1967 02:00 US#1

NY # 147
Before 11/18/1883 LMT
11/18/1883 12:00 NY#4
6/23/1940 02:00 EDT
9/02/1940 02:00 EST
4/27/1941 02:00 EDT
9/28/1941 02:00 EST
2/09/1942 02:00 EWT
9/30/1945 02:00 EST
4/26/1953 02:00 NY#1
4/30/1967 02:00 US#1

NY # 148
Before 11/18/1883 LMT
11/18/1883 12:00 EST
3/31/1918 02:00 EWT
10/27/1918 02:00 EST
3/30/1919 02:00 EWT
10/26/1919 02:00 EST
3/28/1920 02:00 EDT
10/31/1920 02:00 EST
4/30/1939 02:00 EDT
9/24/1939 02:00 EST
4/28/1940 02:00 EDT
9/02/1940 02:00 EST
4/27/1941 02:00 EDT
9/28/1941 02:00 EST
2/09/1942 02:00 EWT
9/30/1945 02:00 EST
4/29/1951 02:00 NY#1
4/30/1967 02:00 US#1

NY # 149
Before 11/18/1883 LMT
11/18/1883 12:00 NY#4
6/23/1940 02:00 EDT
9/01/1940 02:00 EST
6/20/1941 02:00 EDT
9/01/1941 02:00 EST
2/09/1942 02:00 NY#1
4/30/1967 02:00 US#1

NY # 150
Before 11/18/1883 LMT
11/18/1883 12:00 NY#4
5/14/1940 02:00 EDT
9/02/1940 02:00 EST
4/27/1941 02:00 EDT
9/28/1941 02:00 EST
2/09/1942 02:00 EWT
9/30/1945 02:00 EST
4/28/1946 02:00 EDT
9/29/1946 02:00 EST
4/27/1947 02:00 EDT
9/28/1947 02:00 EST
4/25/1948 02:00 EDT
9/26/1948 02:00 EST
4/24/1955 02:00 NY#1
4/30/1967 02:00 US#1

NY # 151
Before 11/18/1883 LMT
11/18/1883 12:00 NY#4
6/15/1930 02:00 EDT
8/30/1930 02:00 EST
6/28/1931 02:00 EDT
9/06/1931 02:00 EST
5/07/1939 02:00 EDT
9/24/1939 02:00 EST
5/05/1940 02:00 EDT
9/29/1940 02:00 NY#1
4/30/1967 02:00 US#1

NY # 152
Before 11/18/1883 LMT
11/18/1883 12:00 NY#4
6/20/1941 02:00 EDT
9/08/1941 02:00 EST
2/09/1942 02:00 EWT
9/30/1945 02:00 EST
4/27/1947 02:00 EDT
9/28/1947 02:00 EST
4/24/1949 02:00 EDT
9/25/1949 02:00 EST
4/30/1950 02:00 EDT
9/24/1950 02:00 EST
4/26/1953 02:00 NY#1
4/30/1967 02:00 US#1

NY # 153
Before 11/18/1883 LMT
11/18/1883 12:00 NY#1
9/23/1951 02:00 EST
4/27/1952 02:00 NY#1
4/30/1967 02:00 US#1

NY # 154
Before 11/18/1883 LMT
11/18/1883 12:00 NY#4
5/04/1941 02:00 EDT
9/28/1941 02:00 EST
2/09/1942 02:00 EWT
9/30/1945 02:00 EST
4/27/1947 02:00 EDT
9/28/1947 02:00 EST
4/25/1948 02:00 EDT
9/26/1948 02:00 EST
4/24/1949 02:00 EDT
9/25/1949 02:00 EST
4/30/1950 02:00 EDT
9/24/1950 02:00 EST
4/24/1955 02:00 NY#1
4/30/1967 02:00 US#1

NY # 155
Before 11/18/1883 LMT
11/18/1883 12:00 EST
3/31/1918 02:00 EWT
10/27/1918 02:00 EST
3/30/1919 02:00 EWT
10/26/1919 02:00 EST
3/28/1920 02:00 EDT
10/31/1920 02:00 EST
6/23/1940 02:00 EDT
9/01/1940 02:00 EST
6/01/1941 02:00 EDT
8/31/1941 02:00 EST
2/09/1942 02:00 EWT
9/30/1945 02:00 EST
4/27/1947 02:00 NY#1
4/30/1967 02:00 US#1

NY # 156
Before 11/18/1883 LMT
11/18/1883 12:00 NY#4
5/16/1937 02:00 EDT
9/05/1937 02:00 EST
5/12/1940 02:00 EDT
9/03/1940 02:00 EST
4/27/1941 02:00 EDT
9/28/1941 02:00 EST
2/09/1942 02:00 EWT
9/30/1945 02:00 EST
4/25/1948 02:00 NY#1
4/30/1967 02:00 US#1

NY # 157
Before 11/18/1883 LMT
11/18/1883 12:00 NY#4
4/24/1938 02:00 EDT
9/06/1938 02:00 EST
4/30/1939 02:00 EDT
9/24/1939 02:00 EST
4/28/1940 02:00 EDT
9/29/1940 02:00 EST
6/20/1941 02:00 EDT
9/08/1941 02:00 EST
2/09/1942 02:00 EWT
9/30/1945 02:00 EST
4/27/1947 02:00 EDT
9/28/1947 02:00 EST
4/30/1950 02:00 NY#1
4/30/1967 02:00 US#1

NY # 158
Before 11/18/1883 LMT
11/18/1883 12:00 NY#4
6/09/1935 02:00 EDT
9/02/1935 02:00 EST
6/07/1936 02:00 EDT
9/12/1936 02:00 EST
6/06/1937 02:00 EDT
9/06/1937 02:00 EST
6/05/1938 02:00 EDT
9/05/1938 02:00 EST
4/30/1939 02:00 EDT
9/24/1939 02:00 EST
4/28/1940 02:00 EDT
9/29/1940 02:00 EST
2/09/1942 02:00 EWT
9/30/1945 02:00 EST
4/27/1947 02:00 EDT
9/28/1947 02:00 EST
4/26/1953 02:00 NY#1
4/30/1967 02:00 US#1

NY # 159
Before 11/18/1883 LMT
11/18/1883 12:00 NY#4
6/01/1927 02:00 EDT
10/01/1927 02:00 EST
6/01/1928 02:00 EDT
10/01/1928 02:00 EST
6/01/1929 02:00 EDT
10/01/1929 02:00 EST
4/27/1930 02:00 NY#1
4/30/1967 02:00 US#1

NY # 160
Before 11/18/1883 LMT
11/18/1883 12:00 NY#4
4/30/1939 02:00 EDT
10/01/1939 02:00 EST
4/28/1940 02:00 EDT
9/03/1940 02:00 EST
4/27/1941 02:00 NY#1
4/30/1967 02:00 US#1

NY # 161
Before 11/18/1883 LMT
11/18/1883 12:00 NY#4
6/01/1941 02:00 EDT
9/26/1941 02:00 EST
2/09/1942 02:00 EWT
9/30/1945 02:00 EST
4/28/1946 02:00 EDT
9/29/1946 02:00 EST
4/27/1947 02:00 EDT
9/28/1947 02:00 EST
4/25/1948 02:00 EDT
9/26/1948 02:00 EST
4/30/1950 02:00 EDT
9/24/1950 02:00 EST
4/29/1951 02:00 EDT
9/30/1951 02:00 EST
4/24/1955 02:00 NY#1
4/30/1967 02:00 US#1

NY # 162
Before 11/18/1883 LMT
11/18/1883 12:00 NY#1
4/30/1939 02:00 EDT
10/01/1939 02:00 NY#1
4/30/1967 02:00 US#1

NY # 163
Before 11/18/1883 LMT
11/18/1883 12:00 NY#4
6/23/1940 02:00 EDT
9/03/1940 02:00 EST
6/22/1941 02:00 EDT
9/01/1941 02:00 EST
2/09/1942 02:00 EWT
9/30/1945 02:00 EST
4/27/1947 02:00 NY#1
4/30/1967 02:00 US#1

NY # 164
Before 11/18/1883 LMT
11/18/1883 12:00 NY#4
4/28/1940 02:00 EDT
9/02/1940 02:00 EST
4/27/1941 02:00 EDT
9/07/1941 02:00 EST
2/09/1942 02:00 EWT
9/30/1945 02:00 EST
4/24/1955 02:00 NY#1
4/30/1967 02:00 US#1

NY # 165
Before 11/18/1883 LMT
11/18/1883 12:00 EST
3/31/1918 02:00 EWT
10/27/1918 02:00 EST
3/30/1919 02:00 EWT
10/26/1919 02:00 EST
3/28/1920 02:00 EDT
10/31/1920 02:00 EST
4/26/1925 02:00 EDT
9/27/1925 02:00 EST
4/25/1926 02:00 EDT
9/26/1926 02:00 EST
4/24/1927 02:00 EDT
9/25/1927 02:00 EST
4/29/1928 02:00 EDT
9/30/1928 02:00 EST
4/28/1929 02:00 EDT
9/29/1929 02:00 EST
4/27/1930 02:00 EDT
9/28/1930 02:00 EST
4/26/1931 02:00 EDT
9/27/1931 02:00 EST
4/30/1932 00:01 EDT
10/01/1932 00:01 EST
4/29/1933 00:01 EDT
9/30/1933 00:01 EST
4/29/1934 00:01 EDT
9/30/1934 00:01 EST
4/28/1935 00:01 EDT
9/29/1935 00:01 EST
4/26/1936 00:01 EDT
9/27/1936 00:01 EST
4/25/1937 00:01 EDT
9/26/1937 00:01 EST
4/24/1938 00:01 EDT
9/25/1938 00:01 EST
4/30/1939 00:01 EDT
9/24/1939 00:01 EST
4/28/1940 00:01 EDT
9/29/1940 00:01 EST
4/27/1941 00:01 EDT
9/28/1941 00:01 EST
2/09/1942 02:00 NY#1
4/30/1967 02:00 US#1

NY # 166
Before 11/18/1883 LMT
11/18/1883 12:00 EST
3/31/1918 02:00 EWT
10/27/1918 02:00 EST
3/30/1919 02:00 EWT
10/26/1919 02:00 EST
3/28/1920 02:00 EDT
10/31/1920 02:00 EST
4/26/1925 02:00 EDT
9/27/1925 02:00 EST
4/25/1926 02:00 EDT
9/26/1926 02:00 EST
4/24/1927 02:00 EDT
9/25/1927 02:00 EST
4/29/1928 02:00 EDT
9/30/1928 02:00 EST
4/28/1929 02:00 EDT
9/29/1929 02:00 EST
4/27/1930 02:00 EDT
9/28/1930 02:00 EST
4/26/1931 02:00 EDT
9/27/1931 02:00 EST
4/03/1932 02:00 EDT
9/25/1932 02:00 EST
4/02/1933 02:00 EDT
9/24/1933 02:00 EST
4/01/1934 02:00 EDT
9/30/1934 02:00 EST
4/07/1935 02:00 EDT
9/29/1935 02:00 EST
4/26/1936 02:00 NY#1
4/30/1967 02:00 US#1

NY # 167
Before 11/18/1883 LMT
11/18/1883 12:00 NY#4
6/01/1941 02:00 EDT
8/31/1941 02:00 EST
2/09/1942 02:00 EWT
9/30/1945 02:00 EST
6/02/1946 02:00 EDT
9/01/1946 02:00 EST
4/29/1951 02:00 NY#1
4/30/1967 02:00 US#1

NY # 168
Before 11/18/1883 LMT
11/18/1883 12:00 NY#4
5/06/1923 02:00 EDT
9/30/1923 02:00 EST
5/04/1924 02:00 EDT
9/28/1924 02:00 EST
5/03/1925 02:00 EDT
9/27/1925 02:00 EST
5/02/1926 02:00 EDT
9/26/1926 02:00 EST
5/08/1927 02:00 EDT
9/25/1927 02:00 EST
5/06/1928 02:00 EDT
9/30/1928 02:00 EST
5/05/1929 02:00 EDT
9/29/1929 02:00 EST
4/30/1933 02:00 EDT
9/30/1933 02:00 EST
2/09/1942 02:00 EWT
9/30/1945 02:00 EST
4/24/1955 02:00 NY#1
4/30/1967 02:00 US#1

NY # 169
Before 11/18/1883 LMT
11/18/1883 12:00 NY#4
5/19/1940 02:00 EDT
9/22/1940 02:00 EST
4/27/1941 02:00 EDT
9/28/1941 02:00 EST
2/09/1942 02:00 EWT
9/30/1945 02:00 EST
4/24/1955 02:00 NY#1
4/30/1967 02:00 US#1

NY # 170
Before 11/18/1883 LMT
11/18/1883 12:00 NY#4
6/15/1930 02:00 EDT
8/30/1930 02:00 EST
4/28/1935 02:00 EDT
9/29/1935 02:00 EST
4/26/1936 02:00 EDT
9/27/1936 02:00 EST
5/07/1939 02:00 EDT
9/24/1939 02:00 EST
5/05/1940 02:00 EDT
9/29/1940 02:00 EST
4/27/1941 02:00 NY#1
4/30/1967 02:00 US#1

NY # 171
Before 11/18/1883 LMT
11/18/1883 12:00 NY#4
6/01/1941 02:00 EDT
9/07/1941 02:00 EST
2/09/1942 02:00 NY#1
4/30/1967 02:00 US#1

TIME TABLES

NY # 172

Before 11/18/1883		LMT
11/18/1883	12:00	NY#4
6/04/1939	02:00	EDT
9/04/1939	02:00	EST
2/09/1942	02:00	EWT
9/30/1945	02:00	EST
4/24/1955	02:00	NY#1
4/30/1967	02:00	US#1

NY # 173

Before 11/18/1883		LMT
11/18/1883	12:00	EST
3/31/1918	02:00	EWT
10/27/1918	02:00	EST
3/30/1919	02:00	EWT
10/26/1919	02:00	EST
3/28/1920	02:00	EDT
10/31/1920	02:00	EST
6/04/1939	02:00	EDT
9/04/1939	02:00	EST
4/28/1940	02:00	EDT
9/29/1940	02:00	EST
4/27/1941	02:00	EDT
9/28/1941	02:00	EST
2/09/1942	02:00	EWT
9/30/1945	02:00	EST
4/29/1951	02:00	NY#1
4/30/1967	02:00	US#1

NY # 174

Before 11/18/1883		LMT
11/18/1883	12:00	EST
3/31/1918	02:00	EWT
10/27/1918	02:00	EST
3/30/1919	02:00	EWT
10/26/1919	02:00	EST
3/28/1920	02:00	EDT
10/31/1920	02:00	EST
5/06/1923	02:00	EDT
9/30/1923	02:00	EST
5/04/1924	02:00	EDT
9/28/1924	02:00	EST
5/03/1925	02:00	EDT
9/27/1925	02:00	EST
5/02/1926	02:00	EDT
9/26/1926	02:00	EST
5/08/1927	02:00	EDT
9/25/1927	02:00	EST
5/06/1928	02:00	EDT
9/30/1928	02:00	EST
5/05/1929	02:00	EDT
9/29/1929	02:00	EST
4/26/1931	02:00	EDT
9/27/1931	02:00	EST
4/24/1932	02:00	EDT
9/25/1932	02:00	EST
4/30/1933	02:00	EDT
9/24/1933	02:00	EST
4/29/1934	02:00	EDT
9/30/1934	02:00	EST
4/28/1935	02:00	EDT
9/29/1935	02:00	EST
4/26/1936	02:00	EDT
9/27/1936	02:00	EST
4/25/1937	02:00	EDT
9/26/1937	02:00	EST
4/24/1938	02:00	EDT
9/25/1938	02:00	EST
4/30/1939	02:00	EDT
9/24/1939	02:00	EST
4/28/1940	02:00	EDT
9/29/1940	02:00	EST
4/27/1941	02:00	EDT
9/28/1941	02:00	EST
2/09/1942	02:00	EWT
9/30/1945	02:00	EST
4/30/1950	02:00	NY#1
4/30/1967	02:00	US#1

NY # 175

Before 11/18/1883		LMT
11/18/1883	12:00	NY#1
4/24/1932	02:00	EDT
10/30/1932	02:00	EST
4/30/1933	02:00	NY#1
4/30/1967	02:00	US#1

NY # 176

Before 11/18/1883		LMT
11/18/1883	12:00	NY#4
4/30/1939	02:00	EDT
10/01/1939	02:00	EST
4/28/1940	02:00	EDT
9/29/1940	02:00	EST
4/27/1941	02:00	EDT
9/28/1941	02:00	EST
2/09/1942	02:00	EWT
9/30/1945	02:00	EST
4/27/1947	02:00	EDT
9/28/1947	02:00	EST
5/17/1948	02:00	EDT
9/26/1948	02:00	NY#1
4/30/1967	02:00	US#1

NY # 177

Before 11/18/1883		LMT
11/18/1883	12:00	NY#4
4/24/1921	00:01	EDT
9/25/1921	00:01	EST
4/30/1922	00:01	EDT
9/24/1922	00:01	EST
4/29/1923	00:01	EDT
9/30/1923	00:01	EST
4/27/1924	00:01	EDT
9/28/1924	00:01	EST
4/26/1925	00:01	EDT
9/27/1925	00:01	EST
4/25/1926	00:01	EDT
9/26/1926	00:01	EST
4/24/1927	00:01	EDT
9/25/1927	00:01	EST
4/29/1928	00:01	EDT
9/30/1928	00:01	EST
4/28/1929	00:01	EDT
9/29/1929	00:01	EST
4/27/1930	00:01	EDT
9/28/1930	00:01	EST
4/26/1931	00:01	EDT
9/27/1931	00:01	EST
4/24/1932	00:01	EDT
9/25/1932	00:01	EST
4/30/1933	00:01	EDT
9/24/1933	00:01	EST
4/29/1934	00:01	EDT
9/30/1934	00:01	EST
4/28/1935	00:01	EDT
9/29/1935	00:01	EST
4/26/1936	00:01	EDT
9/27/1936	00:01	EST
4/25/1937	00:01	EDT
9/26/1937	00:01	EST
4/24/1938	00:01	EDT
9/25/1938	00:01	EST
4/30/1939	00:01	EDT
9/24/1939	00:01	EST
4/28/1940	00:01	EDT
9/29/1940	00:01	EST
4/27/1941	00:01	EDT
9/28/1941	00:01	EST
2/09/1942	02:00	EWT
9/30/1945	02:00	EST
4/24/1955	02:00	NY#1
4/30/1967	02:00	US#1

NY # 178

Before 11/18/1883		LMT
11/18/1883	12:00	NY#4
5/05/1941	02:00	EDT
9/11/1941	02:00	EST
2/09/1942	02:00	EWT
9/30/1945	02:00	EST
4/25/1948	02:00	NY#1
4/30/1967	02:00	US#1

NY # 179

Before 11/18/1883		LMT
11/18/1883	12:00	EST
3/31/1918	02:00	EWT
10/27/1918	02:00	EST
3/30/1919	02:00	EWT
10/26/1919	02:00	EST
3/28/1920	02:00	EDT
10/31/1920	02:00	EST
4/24/1921	02:00	EDT
9/25/1921	02:00	EST
4/02/1932	02:00	EDT
9/24/1932	02:00	EST
4/02/1933	02:00	EDT
9/24/1933	02:00	EST
4/02/1934	02:00	EDT
9/24/1934	02:00	EST
4/02/1935	02:00	EDT
9/24/1935	02:00	EST
4/02/1936	02:00	EDT
9/24/1936	02:00	EST
4/02/1937	02:00	EDT
9/24/1937	02:00	EST
4/02/1938	02:00	EDT
9/24/1938	02:00	EST
4/02/1939	02:00	EDT
9/24/1939	02:00	EST
4/02/1940	02:00	EDT
9/24/1940	02:00	EST
4/02/1941	02:00	EDT
9/24/1941	02:00	EST
2/09/1942	02:00	NY#1
4/30/1967	02:00	US#1

NY # 180

Before 11/18/1883		LMT
11/18/1883	12:00	NY#4
6/25/1939	02:00	EDT
9/03/1939	02:00	EST
4/28/1940	02:00	NY#1
4/30/1967	02:00	US#1

NY # 181

Before 11/18/1883		LMT
11/18/1883	12:00	NY#4
5/12/1940	02:00	EDT
10/20/1940	02:00	EST
4/26/1941	02:00	EDT
9/01/1941	02:00	EST
2/09/1942	02:00	EWT
9/30/1945	02:00	EST
4/24/1955	02:00	NY#1
4/30/1967	02:00	US#1

NY # 182

Before 11/18/1883		LMT
11/18/1883	12:00	NY#4
4/28/1940	02:00	EDT
9/03/1940	02:00	EST
4/27/1941	02:00	NY#1
4/30/1967	02:00	US#1

NY # 183

Before 11/18/1883		LMT
11/18/1883	12:00	EST
3/31/1918	02:00	EWT
10/27/1918	02:00	EST
3/30/1919	02:00	EWT
10/26/1919	02:00	EST
3/28/1920	02:00	EDT
10/31/1920	02:00	EST
5/06/1923	02:00	EDT
9/30/1923	02:00	EST
5/04/1924	02:00	EDT
9/28/1924	02:00	EST
5/03/1925	02:00	EDT
9/27/1925	02:00	EST
5/02/1926	02:00	EDT
9/26/1926	02:00	EST
5/08/1927	02:00	EDT
9/25/1927	02:00	EST
5/06/1928	02:00	EDT
9/30/1928	02:00	EST
5/05/1929	02:00	EDT
9/29/1929	02:00	EST
4/26/1931	02:00	EDT
9/27/1931	02:00	EST
4/24/1932	02:00	EDT
9/25/1932	02:00	EST
4/30/1933	02:00	EDT
9/30/1933	02:00	EST
4/29/1934	02:00	EDT
9/30/1934	02:00	EST
4/28/1935	02:00	EDT
9/29/1935	02:00	EST
4/26/1936	02:00	EDT
9/27/1936	02:00	EST
4/25/1937	02:00	EDT
9/26/1937	02:00	EST
4/24/1938	02:00	EDT
9/25/1938	02:00	EST
4/30/1939	02:00	EDT
9/24/1939	02:00	EST
4/28/1940	02:00	EDT
9/29/1940	02:00	EST
4/27/1941	02:00	EDT
9/28/1941	02:00	EST
2/09/1942	02:00	EWT
9/30/1945	02:00	EST
4/28/1946	02:00	EDT
9/29/1946	02:00	EST
4/25/1948	02:00	NY#1
4/30/1967	02:00	US#1

NY # 184

Before 11/18/1883		LMT
11/18/1883	12:00	NY#1
4/23/1922	02:00	EDT
9/24/1922	02:00	EST
4/29/1923	02:00	EDT
9/02/1923	02:00	EST
5/30/1924	02:00	EDT
9/01/1924	02:00	EST
5/30/1925	02:00	EDT
9/05/1925	02:00	EST
5/30/1926	02:00	EDT
9/06/1926	02:00	EST
5/08/1927	00:01	EDT
9/25/1927	00:01	EST
4/29/1928	00:01	EDT
9/30/1928	00:01	EST
4/28/1929	00:01	EDT
9/29/1929	00:01	EST
4/27/1930	00:01	EDT
9/28/1930	00:01	EST
4/26/1931	00:01	EDT
9/27/1931	00:01	EST
5/02/1932	00:01	EDT
9/27/1932	00:01	EST
4/30/1933	02:00	EDT
9/24/1933	02:00	EST
4/29/1934	02:00	EDT
9/30/1934	02:00	EST
4/28/1935	02:00	EDT
9/29/1935	02:00	EST
4/26/1936	02:00	EDT
9/27/1936	02:00	EST
4/25/1937	02:00	EDT
9/26/1937	02:00	EST
4/24/1938	02:00	EDT
9/25/1938	02:00	EST
4/30/1939	02:00	EDT
9/24/1939	02:00	EST
4/28/1940	02:00	EDT
9/29/1940	02:00	EST
4/27/1941	02:00	EDT
9/28/1941	02:00	EST
2/09/1942	02:00	EWT
9/30/1945	02:00	EST
4/25/1948	02:00	EDT
9/26/1948	02:00	EST
4/26/1953	02:00	NY#1
4/30/1967	02:00	US#1

NY # 185

Before 11/18/1883		LMT
11/18/1883	12:00	EST
3/31/1918	02:00	EWT
10/27/1918	02:00	EST
3/30/1919	02:00	EWT
10/26/1919	02:00	EST
3/28/1920	02:00	EDT
10/31/1920	02:00	EST
4/28/1940	02:00	EDT
9/29/1940	02:00	EST
4/27/1941	02:00	EDT
10/04/1941	02:00	EST
2/09/1942	02:00	EWT
9/30/1945	02:00	EST
4/28/1946	02:00	EDT
9/29/1946	02:00	EST
4/27/1947	02:00	EDT
9/28/1947	02:00	EST
4/25/1948	02:00	EDT
9/26/1948	02:00	EST
4/24/1949	02:00	EDT
9/25/1949	02:00	EST
4/30/1950	02:00	EDT
9/24/1950	02:00	EST
4/29/1951	02:00	EDT
9/23/1951	02:00	EST
4/27/1952	02:00	NY#1
4/30/1967	02:00	US#1

NY # 186

Before 11/18/1883		LMT
11/18/1883	12:00	NY#4
5/08/1921	02:00	EDT
9/11/1921	02:00	EST
5/14/1922	02:00	EDT
9/10/1922	02:00	EST
5/13/1923	02:00	EDT
9/09/1923	02:00	EST
5/11/1924	02:00	EDT
9/14/1924	02:00	EST
4/30/1939	02:00	NY#1
4/30/1967	02:00	US#1

NY # 187

Before 11/18/1883		LMT
11/18/1883	12:00	NY#4
6/25/1932	02:00	EDT
9/25/1932	02:00	EST
4/30/1933	02:00	EDT
9/24/1933	02:00	EST
6/02/1935	02:00	EDT
9/02/1935	02:00	EST
6/07/1936	02:00	EDT
9/07/1936	02:00	EST
6/06/1937	02:00	EDT
9/06/1937	02:00	EST
6/05/1938	02:00	EDT
9/04/1938	02:00	EST
6/04/1939	02:00	EDT
9/03/1939	02:00	EST
4/28/1940	02:00	EDT
9/29/1940	02:00	EST
4/27/1941	02:00	EDT
9/28/1941	02:00	EST
2/09/1942	02:00	EWT
9/30/1945	02:00	EST
4/28/1946	02:00	EDT
9/29/1946	02:00	EST
4/27/1947	02:00	EDT
9/28/1947	02:00	EST
4/25/1948	02:00	EDT
9/26/1948	02:00	EST
4/24/1949	02:00	EDT
9/25/1949	02:00	EST
4/29/1951	02:00	NY#1
4/30/1967	02:00	US#1

NY # 188

Before 11/18/1883		LMT
11/18/1883	12:00	NY#4
6/16/1940	02:00	EDT
9/01/1940	02:00	EST
6/20/1941	02:00	EDT
9/08/1941	02:00	EST
2/09/1942	02:00	EWT
9/30/1945	02:00	EST
4/27/1947	02:00	NY#1
4/30/1967	02:00	US#1

NY # 189

Before 11/18/1883		LMT
11/18/1883	12:00	NY#4
5/22/1921	02:00	EDT
9/25/1921	02:00	EST
5/21/1922	02:00	EDT
9/30/1922	02:00	EST
5/06/1923	02:00	EDT
9/30/1923	02:00	EST
5/17/1925	02:00	EDT
9/13/1925	02:00	EST
5/16/1926	02:00	EDT
9/12/1926	02:00	EST
5/15/1927	02:00	EDT
9/10/1927	02:00	EST
4/29/1928	02:00	EDT
9/30/1928	02:00	EST
4/28/1929	02:00	EDT
9/29/1929	02:00	EST
4/27/1930	02:00	EDT
9/28/1930	02:00	EST
4/26/1931	02:00	EDT
9/27/1931	02:00	EST
4/24/1932	02:00	EDT
9/25/1932	02:00	EST
4/30/1933	02:00	EDT
9/24/1933	02:00	EST
4/29/1934	02:00	EDT
9/30/1934	02:00	EST
4/28/1935	02:00	EDT
9/29/1935	02:00	EST
4/26/1936	02:00	EDT
9/27/1936	02:00	EST
4/25/1937	02:00	EDT
9/26/1937	02:00	EST
4/24/1938	02:00	EDT
9/25/1938	02:00	EST
4/30/1939	02:00	EDT
9/24/1939	02:00	EST
4/28/1940	02:00	EDT
9/29/1940	02:00	EST
4/27/1941	02:00	EDT
9/28/1941	02:00	EST
2/09/1942	02:00	EWT
9/30/1945	02:00	EST
4/25/1948	02:00	EDT
9/26/1948	02:00	EST
4/24/1955	02:00	NY#1
4/30/1967	02:00	US#1

NY # 190

Before 11/18/1883		LMT
11/18/1883	12:00	NY#4
6/01/1927	02:00	EDT
8/31/1927	02:00	EST
5/23/1929	02:00	EDT
9/03/1929	02:00	EST
5/25/1930	02:00	EDT
9/02/1930	02:00	EST
4/26/1931	02:00	EDT
9/27/1931	02:00	EST
5/29/1932	02:00	EDT
9/06/1932	02:00	EST
4/30/1933	02:00	NY#1
4/30/1967	02:00	US#1

NY # 191

Before 11/18/1883		LMT
11/18/1883	12:00	NY#4
5/26/1940	02:00	EDT
9/29/1940	02:00	EST
4/27/1941	02:00	EDT
9/28/1941	02:00	EST
2/09/1942	02:00	EWT
9/30/1945	02:00	EST
4/25/1948	02:00	NY#1
4/30/1967	02:00	US#1

NY # 192

Before 11/18/1883		LMT
11/18/1883	12:00	EST
3/31/1918	02:00	EWT
10/27/1918	02:00	EST
3/30/1919	02:00	EWT
10/26/1919	02:00	EST
3/28/1920	02:00	EDT
10/31/1920	02:00	EST
4/26/1931	02:00	EDT
9/27/1931	02:00	EST
4/24/1932	02:00	EDT
9/25/1932	02:00	EST
4/30/1933	02:00	EDT
9/24/1933	02:00	EST
4/29/1934	02:00	EDT
9/30/1934	02:00	EST
4/28/1935	02:00	EDT
9/29/1935	02:00	EST
4/26/1936	02:00	EDT
9/27/1936	02:00	EST
4/25/1937	02:00	EDT
9/26/1937	02:00	EST
4/24/1938	02:00	EDT
9/25/1938	02:00	EST
4/30/1939	02:00	EDT
9/24/1939	02:00	EST
4/28/1940	02:00	EDT
9/29/1940	02:00	EST
4/27/1941	02:00	EDT
9/28/1941	02:00	EST
2/09/1942	02:00	EWT
9/30/1945	02:00	EST
4/28/1946	02:00	EDT
9/29/1946	02:00	EST
4/27/1947	02:00	EDT
9/28/1947	02:00	EST
4/25/1948	02:00	EDT
9/26/1948	02:00	EST
4/24/1949	02:00	EDT
10/01/1949	00:01	EST
4/30/1950	02:00	NY#1
4/30/1967	02:00	US#1

NY # 193

Before 11/18/1883		LMT
11/18/1883	12:00	EST
3/31/1918	02:00	EWT
10/27/1918	02:00	EST
3/30/1919	02:00	EWT
10/26/1919	02:00	EST
3/28/1920	02:00	EDT
10/31/1920	02:00	EST
4/26/1925	02:00	EDT
9/27/1925	02:00	EST
4/25/1926	02:00	EDT
9/26/1926	02:00	EST
4/24/1927	02:00	EDT
9/25/1927	02:00	EST
4/29/1928	02:00	EDT
9/30/1928	02:00	EST
4/28/1929	02:00	EDT
9/29/1929	02:00	EST
4/27/1930	02:00	EDT
9/28/1930	02:00	EST
4/26/1931	02:00	EDT
9/27/1931	02:00	EST
4/24/1932	02:00	EDT
9/25/1932	02:00	EST
4/30/1933	02:00	EDT
9/24/1933	02:00	EST
4/29/1934	02:00	EDT
9/30/1934	02:00	EST
6/23/1935	02:00	EDT
9/29/1935	02:00	EST
6/04/1936	02:00	EDT
9/05/1936	02:00	EST
6/20/1937	02:00	EDT
9/05/1937	02:00	EST
6/19/1938	02:00	EDT
9/03/1938	02:00	EST
6/18/1939	02:00	EDT
9/03/1939	02:00	EST
6/16/1940	02:00	EDT
9/01/1940	02:00	EST
6/15/1941	02:00	EDT
9/07/1941	02:00	EST
2/09/1942	02:00	EWT
9/30/1945	02:00	EST
4/27/1947	02:00	NY#1
4/30/1967	02:00	US#1

NY # 194

Before 11/18/1883		LMT
11/18/1883	12:00	EST
3/31/1918	02:00	EWT
10/27/1918	02:00	EST
3/30/1919	02:00	EWT
10/26/1919	02:00	EST
3/28/1920	02:00	EDT
10/31/1920	02:00	EST
4/26/1931	02:00	EDT

TIME TABLES

9/27/1931 02:00 EST
4/24/1932 02:00 EDT
9/25/1932 02:00 EST
4/30/1933 02:00 EDT
10/01/1933 02:00 EST
4/29/1934 02:00 NY#1
4/30/1967 02:00 US#1

NY # 195
Before 11/18/1883 LMT
11/18/1883 12:00 NY#4
6/02/1940 02:00 EDT
9/01/1940 02:00 EST
4/27/1941 02:00 EDT
9/28/1941 02:00 EST
2/09/1942 02:00 EWT
9/30/1945 02:00 EST
4/25/1948 02:00 NY#1
4/30/1967 02:00 US#1

NY # 196
Before 11/18/1883 LMT
11/18/1883 12:00 EST
3/31/1918 02:00 EWT
10/27/1918 02:00 EST
3/30/1919 02:00 EWT
10/26/1919 02:00 EST
3/28/1920 02:00 EDT
10/31/1920 02:00 EST
5/06/1923 02:00 EDT
9/30/1923 02:00 EST
5/04/1924 02:00 EDT
9/28/1924 02:00 EST
5/03/1925 02:00 EDT
9/27/1925 02:00 EST
5/02/1926 02:00 EDT
9/26/1926 02:00 EST
5/08/1927 02:00 EDT
9/25/1927 02:00 EST
5/06/1928 02:00 EDT
9/30/1928 02:00 EST
5/05/1929 02:00 EDT
9/29/1929 02:00 EST
4/27/1930 02:00 EDT
9/28/1930 02:00 EST
4/26/1931 02:00 EDT
9/27/1931 02:00 EST
4/24/1932 02:00 EDT
9/25/1932 02:00 EST
4/30/1933 02:00 EDT
9/24/1933 02:00 EST
4/29/1934 02:00 EDT
9/30/1934 02:00 EST
4/28/1935 02:00 EDT
9/29/1935 02:00 EST
4/26/1936 02:00 EDT
9/27/1936 02:00 EST
4/25/1937 02:00 EDT
9/26/1937 02:00 EST
4/24/1938 02:00 EDT
9/25/1938 02:00 EST
4/30/1939 02:00 EDT
9/24/1939 02:00 EST
4/28/1940 02:00 EDT
9/29/1940 02:00 EST
4/27/1941 02:00 EDT
9/28/1941 02:00 EST
2/09/1942 02:00 EWT
9/30/1945 02:00 EST
4/25/1948 02:00 EDT
9/26/1948 02:00 EST
4/24/1955 02:00 NY#1
4/30/1967 02:00 US#1

NY # 197
Before 11/18/1883 LMT
11/18/1883 12:00 NY#4
5/15/1927 02:00 EDT
9/12/1927 02:00 EST
4/26/1931 02:00 EDT
9/27/1931 02:00 EST
4/24/1932 02:00 EDT
9/25/1932 02:00 EST
5/07/1933 02:00 EDT
9/24/1933 02:00 EST
4/22/1934 02:00 EDT
9/23/1934 02:00 EST
4/28/1935 02:00 NY#1
4/30/1967 02:00 US#1

NY # 198
Before 11/18/1883 LMT
11/18/1883 12:00 NY#4
5/15/1939 02:00 EDT
9/15/1939 02:00 EST
6/15/1940 02:00 EDT
9/01/1940 02:00 EST
5/01/1941 02:00 EDT
9/01/1941 02:00 EST
2/09/1942 02:00 EWT
9/30/1945 02:00 EST
4/25/1948 02:00 NY#1
4/30/1967 02:00 US#1

NY # 199
Before 11/18/1883 LMT
11/18/1883 12:00 NY#1
3/24/1921 02:00 EDT
9/25/1921 02:00 EST
4/29/1923 02:00 EDT
9/30/1923 02:00 EST
5/30/1926 02:00 EDT
9/26/1926 02:00 EST
6/09/1929 02:00 EDT
9/01/1929 02:00 EST
6/08/1930 02:00 EDT
9/07/1930 02:00 EST
6/14/1931 02:00 EDT
9/04/1931 02:00 EST
5/14/1932 02:00 EDT
9/05/1932 02:00 EST
5/21/1933 02:00 EDT
9/24/1933 02:00 EST
4/29/1934 02:00 NY#1
4/30/1967 02:00 US#1

NY # 200
Before 11/18/1883 LMT
11/18/1883 12:00 EST
3/31/1918 02:00 EWT
10/27/1918 02:00 EST
3/30/1919 02:00 EWT
10/26/1919 02:00 EST
3/28/1920 02:00 EDT
10/31/1920 02:00 EST
4/30/1939 02:00 EDT
9/24/1939 02:00 EST
5/11/1940 02:00 EDT
9/14/1940 02:00 EST
4/27/1941 02:00 NY#1
4/30/1967 02:00 US#1

NY # 201
Before 11/18/1883 LMT
11/18/1883 12:00 NY#4
4/26/1925 02:00 EDT
9/27/1925 02:00 EST
5/31/1936 02:00 EDT
9/01/1936 02:00 EST
5/26/1937 02:00 EDT
9/08/1937 02:00 EST
5/29/1938 02:00 EDT
9/04/1938 02:00 EST
5/28/1939 02:00 EDT
9/03/1939 02:00 EST
5/26/1940 02:00 EDT
9/01/1940 02:00 EST
4/27/1941 02:00 NY#1
4/30/1967 02:00 US#1

NY # 202
Before 11/18/1883 LMT
11/18/1883 12:00 NY#1
9/26/1926 02:00 EST
6/05/1927 02:00 EDT
8/28/1927 02:00 EST
4/29/1928 02:00 NY#1
4/30/1967 02:00 US#1

NY # 203
Before 11/18/1883 LMT
11/18/1883 12:00 NY#4
6/02/1940 02:00 EDT
9/01/1940 02:00 EST
5/18/1941 02:00 EDT
9/07/1941 02:00 EST
2/09/1942 02:00 NY#1
4/30/1967 02:00 US#1

NY # 204
Before 11/18/1883 LMT
11/18/1883 12:00 EST
3/31/1918 02:00 EWT
10/27/1918 02:00 EST
3/30/1919 02:00 EWT
10/26/1919 02:00 EST
3/28/1920 02:00 EDT
10/31/1920 02:00 EST
4/24/1921 02:00 EDT
9/25/1921 02:00 EST
6/12/1927 02:00 EDT
9/11/1927 02:00 EST
4/29/1928 02:00 NY#1
4/30/1967 02:00 US#1

NY # 205
Before 11/18/1883 LMT
11/18/1883 12:00 NY#1
9/29/1940 02:00 EST
5/04/1941 02:00 EDT
9/28/1941 02:00 NY#1
4/30/1967 02:00 US#1

NY # 206
Before 11/18/1883 LMT
11/18/1883 12:00 NY#4
5/05/1940 02:00 EDT
9/01/1940 02:00 EST
4/27/1941 02:00 EDT
9/28/1941 02:00 EST
2/09/1942 02:00 EWT
9/30/1945 02:00 EST
4/24/1955 02:00 NY#1
4/30/1967 02:00 US#1

NY # 207
Before 11/18/1883 LMT
11/18/1883 12:00 NY#4
4/25/1937 02:00 EDT
9/26/1937 02:00 EST
6/16/1940 02:00 EDT
9/01/1940 02:00 EST
4/27/1941 02:00 EDT
9/28/1941 02:00 EST
2/09/1942 02:00 EWT
9/30/1945 02:00 EST
4/27/1947 02:00 NY#1
4/30/1967 02:00 US#1

NY # 208
Before 11/18/1883 LMT
11/18/1883 12:00 EST
3/31/1918 02:00 EWT
10/27/1918 02:00 EST
3/30/1919 02:00 EWT
10/26/1919 02:00 EST
3/28/1920 02:00 EDT
10/31/1920 02:00 EST
4/24/1921 02:00 EDT
9/25/1921 02:00 EST
4/06/1930 02:00 EDT
9/28/1930 02:00 EST
4/26/1931 02:00 NY#1
4/30/1967 02:00 US#1

NY # 209
Before 11/18/1883 LMT
11/18/1883 12:00 EST
3/31/1918 02:00 EWT
10/27/1918 02:00 EST
3/30/1919 02:00 EWT
10/26/1919 02:00 EST
3/28/1920 02:00 EDT
10/31/1920 02:00 EST
4/24/1921 02:00 EDT
9/25/1921 02:00 EST
5/30/1926 02:00 EDT
9/12/1926 02:00 EST
5/29/1927 02:00 EDT
9/11/1927 02:00 EST
5/18/1930 02:00 EDT
9/28/1930 02:00 EST
4/30/1939 02:00 EDT
10/01/1939 02:00 EST
4/28/1940 02:00 EDT
9/29/1940 02:00 EST
4/27/1941 02:00 EDT
9/28/1941 02:00 EST
2/09/1942 02:00 EWT
9/30/1945 02:00 EST
4/28/1946 02:00 EDT
9/29/1946 02:00 EST
4/27/1947 02:00 EDT
9/28/1947 02:00 EST
4/25/1948 02:00 EDT
9/26/1948 02:00 EST
4/24/1949 02:00 EDT
9/25/1949 02:00 EST
4/30/1950 02:00 EDT
9/24/1950 02:00 EST
4/29/1951 02:00 EDT
9/23/1951 02:00 EST
4/27/1952 02:00 NY#1
4/30/1967 02:00 US#1

NY # 210
Before 11/18/1883 LMT
11/18/1883 12:00 NY#4
5/01/1921 02:00 EDT
9/02/1921 02:00 EST
4/30/1922 02:00 NY#1
4/30/1967 02:00 US#1

NY # 211
Before 11/18/1883 LMT
11/18/1883 12:00 NY#4
5/15/1927 02:00 EDT
9/01/1927 02:00 EST
4/26/1931 02:00 NY#1
4/30/1967 02:00 US#1

NY # 212
Before 11/18/1883 LMT
11/18/1883 12:00 NY#1
4/24/1921 00:01 EDT
9/25/1921 00:01 EST
4/30/1922 00:01 EDT
9/24/1922 00:01 EST
4/29/1923 00:01 EDT
9/30/1923 00:01 EST
4/27/1924 00:01 EDT
9/28/1924 00:01 EST
4/26/1925 00:01 EDT
9/27/1925 00:01 EST
4/25/1926 00:01 EDT
9/26/1926 00:01 EST
4/24/1927 00:01 EDT
9/25/1927 00:01 EST
4/29/1928 00:01 EDT
9/30/1928 00:01 EST
4/28/1929 00:01 EDT
9/29/1929 00:01 EST
4/27/1930 00:01 EDT
9/28/1930 00:01 EST
4/26/1931 00:01 EDT
9/27/1931 00:01 EST
4/24/1932 00:01 EDT
9/25/1932 00:01 EST
4/30/1933 00:01 EDT
9/24/1933 00:01 EST
4/29/1934 00:01 EDT
9/30/1934 00:01 EST
4/28/1935 00:01 EDT
9/29/1935 00:01 EST
4/26/1936 00:01 EDT
9/27/1936 00:01 EST
4/25/1937 00:01 EDT
9/26/1937 00:01 EST
4/24/1938 00:01 EDT
9/25/1938 00:01 EST
4/30/1939 00:01 EDT
9/24/1939 00:01 EST
4/28/1940 00:01 EDT
9/29/1940 00:01 EST
4/27/1941 00:01 EDT
9/28/1941 00:01 EST
2/09/1942 02:00 EWT
9/30/1945 02:00 EST
4/24/1955 02:00 NY#1
4/30/1967 02:00 US#1

NY # 213
Before 11/18/1883 LMT
11/18/1883 12:00 EST
3/31/1918 02:00 EWT
10/27/1918 02:00 EST
3/30/1919 02:00 EWT
10/26/1919 02:00 EST
3/28/1920 02:00 EDT
10/31/1920 02:00 EST
4/26/1931 02:00 EDT
9/27/1931 02:00 EST
4/24/1932 02:00 EDT
9/25/1932 02:00 EST
4/30/1933 02:00 EDT
9/24/1933 02:00 EST
4/29/1934 02:00 EDT
9/30/1934 02:00 EST
4/28/1935 02:00 EDT
9/29/1935 02:00 EST
4/26/1936 02:00 EDT
9/27/1936 02:00 EST
4/25/1937 02:00 EDT
9/26/1937 02:00 EST
4/24/1938 02:00 EDT
9/25/1938 02:00 EST
4/30/1939 02:00 EDT
9/24/1939 02:00 EST
4/28/1940 02:00 EDT
9/29/1940 02:00 EST
4/27/1941 02:00 EDT
9/28/1941 02:00 EST
2/09/1942 02:00 EWT
9/30/1945 02:00 EST
4/28/1946 02:00 EDT
10/31/1946 02:00 EST
4/27/1947 02:00 NY#1
4/30/1967 02:00 US#1

NY # 214
Before 11/18/1883 LMT
11/18/1883 12:00 NY#4
4/28/1941 02:00 EDT
9/17/1941 02:00 EST
2/09/1942 02:00 EWT
9/30/1945 02:00 EST
4/24/1955 02:00 NY#1
4/30/1967 02:00 US#1

NY # 215
Before 11/18/1883 LMT
11/18/1883 12:00 EST
3/31/1918 02:00 EWT
10/27/1918 02:00 EST
3/30/1919 02:00 EWT
10/26/1919 02:00 EST
3/28/1920 02:00 EDT
10/31/1920 02:00 EST
4/26/1925 02:00 EDT
9/27/1925 02:00 EST
4/25/1926 02:00 EDT
9/26/1926 02:00 EST
4/24/1927 02:00 EDT
9/25/1927 02:00 EST
4/29/1928 02:00 EDT
9/30/1928 02:00 EST
4/28/1929 02:00 EDT
9/29/1929 02:00 EST
4/27/1930 02:00 EDT
9/28/1930 02:00 EST
4/26/1931 02:00 EDT
9/27/1931 02:00 EST
4/24/1932 02:00 EDT
9/25/1932 02:00 EST
4/30/1933 02:00 EDT
9/24/1933 02:00 EST
4/29/1934 02:00 EDT
9/30/1934 02:00 EST
4/28/1935 02:00 EDT
9/29/1935 02:00 EST
4/26/1936 02:00 EDT
9/27/1936 02:00 EST
4/25/1937 02:00 EDT
9/26/1937 02:00 EST
4/24/1938 02:00 EDT
9/25/1938 02:00 EST
4/30/1939 02:00 EDT
10/01/1939 02:00 EST
4/28/1940 02:00 EDT
9/29/1940 02:00 EST
4/27/1941 02:00 EDT
9/28/1941 02:00 EST
2/09/1942 02:00 EWT
9/30/1945 02:00 EST
4/28/1946 02:00 EDT
9/30/1946 02:00 EST
4/27/1947 02:00 NY#1
4/30/1967 02:00 US#1

NY # 216
Before 11/18/1883 LMT
11/18/1883 12:00 NY#4
6/11/1936 02:00 EDT
9/09/1936 02:00 EST
6/11/1937 02:00 EDT
9/10/1937 02:00 EST
6/12/1938 02:00 EDT
9/11/1938 02:00 EST
5/12/1940 02:00 EDT
9/01/1940 02:00 EST
5/12/1941 02:00 EDT
9/08/1941 02:00 NY#4
4/24/1955 02:00 US#2

NY # 217
Before 11/18/1883 LMT
11/18/1883 12:00 NY#4
4/28/1941 02:00 EDT
9/02/1941 02:00 EST
2/09/1942 02:00 EWT
9/30/1945 02:00 EST
4/29/1951 02:00 NY#1
4/30/1967 02:00 US#1

NY # 218
Before 11/18/1883 LMT
11/18/1883 12:00 NY#4
4/26/1931 02:00 EDT
9/27/1931 02:00 EST
4/24/1932 02:00 EDT
9/25/1932 02:00 EST
6/01/1939 02:00 EDT
8/31/1939 02:00 EST
6/01/1940 02:00 EDT
8/31/1940 02:00 EST
4/27/1941 02:00 EDT
9/28/1941 02:00 EST
2/09/1942 02:00 EWT
9/30/1945 02:00 EST
4/24/1955 02:00 NY#1
4/30/1967 02:00 US#1

NY # 219
Before 11/18/1883 LMT
11/18/1883 12:00 EST
3/31/1918 02:00 EWT
10/27/1918 02:00 EST
3/30/1919 02:00 EWT
10/26/1919 02:00 EST
3/28/1920 02:00 EDT
10/31/1920 02:00 EST
4/26/1931 02:00 EDT
9/27/1931 02:00 EST
4/24/1932 02:00 EDT
9/25/1932 02:00 EST
4/30/1933 02:00 EDT
9/24/1933 02:00 EST
4/29/1934 02:00 EDT
9/30/1934 02:00 EST
4/28/1935 02:00 EDT
9/29/1935 02:00 EST
4/26/1936 02:00 EDT
9/27/1936 02:00 EST
4/25/1937 02:00 EDT
9/26/1937 02:00 EST
4/24/1938 02:00 EDT
9/25/1938 02:00 EST
4/30/1939 02:00 EDT
9/24/1939 02:00 EST
4/28/1940 02:00 EDT
9/29/1940 02:00 EST
4/27/1941 02:00 EDT
9/28/1941 02:00 EST
2/09/1942 02:00 EWT
9/30/1945 02:00 EST
4/28/1946 02:00 EDT
10/27/1946 02:00 EST
4/27/1947 02:00 NY#1
4/30/1967 02:00 US#1

NY # 220
Before 11/18/1883 LMT
11/18/1883 12:00 EST
3/31/1918 02:00 EWT
10/27/1918 02:00 EST
3/30/1919 02:00 EWT
10/26/1919 02:00 EST
3/28/1920 02:00 EDT
10/31/1920 02:00 EST
4/26/1931 02:00 EDT
9/27/1931 02:00 EST
4/02/1932 02:00 EDT
9/24/1932 02:00 EST
4/01/1933 02:00 EDT
9/30/1933 02:00 EST
4/07/1934 02:00 EDT
9/29/1934 02:00 EST
4/06/1935 02:00 EDT
9/28/1935 02:00 EST
4/26/1936 02:00 NY#1
4/30/1967 02:00 US#1

NY # 221
Before 11/18/1883 LMT
11/18/1883 12:00 NY#4
6/22/1936 02:00 EDT
9/14/1936 02:00 EST
5/30/1937 02:00 EDT
9/12/1937 02:00 EST
4/24/1938 02:00 EDT
9/25/1938 02:00 EST
6/11/1939 02:00 EDT
9/10/1939 02:00 EST
4/28/1940 02:00 NY#1
4/30/1967 02:00 US#1

NY # 222
Before 11/18/1883 LMT
11/18/1883 12:00 NY#1
9/26/1926 02:00 EST
6/05/1927 02:00 EDT
8/28/1927 02:00 EST
4/29/1928 02:00 NY#1
4/30/1967 02:00 US#1

NY # 223
Before 11/18/1883 LMT
11/18/1883 12:00 NY#4
4/15/1930 02:00 EDT
10/15/1930 02:00 EST
4/26/1931 02:00 EDT
9/27/1931 02:00 EST
4/24/1932 02:00 EDT
9/25/1932 02:00 EST
4/30/1933 02:00 EDT
9/24/1933 02:00 EST
4/29/1934 02:00 EDT
9/30/1934 02:00 EST
4/28/1935 02:00 EDT
9/29/1935 02:00 EST
4/26/1936 02:00 EDT
9/27/1936 02:00 EST
4/25/1937 02:00 EDT
9/26/1937 02:00 EST
4/24/1938 02:00 EDT
9/25/1938 02:00 EST
4/30/1939 02:00 EDT
9/24/1939 02:00 EST
4/28/1940 02:00 EDT
9/29/1940 02:00 EST

TIME TABLES

4/27/1941 02:00 EDT
9/28/1941 02:00 EST
2/09/1942 02:00 EWT
9/30/1945 02:00 EST
4/28/1946 02:00 EDT
10/31/1946 02:00 EST
4/27/1947 02:00 NY#1
4/30/1967 02:00 US#1
....
NY # 224
Before 11/18/1883 LMT
11/18/1883 12:00 EST
3/31/1918 02:00 EWT
10/27/1918 02:00 EST
3/30/1919 02:00 EWT
10/26/1919 02:00 EST
3/28/1920 02:00 EDT
10/31/1920 02:00 EST
4/30/1939 02:00 EDT
9/24/1939 02:00 EST
4/28/1940 02:00 EDT
9/29/1940 02:00 EST
4/27/1941 02:00 EDT
9/28/1941 02:00 EST
2/09/1942 02:00 EWT
9/30/1945 02:00 EST
4/28/1946 02:00 EDT
9/29/1946 02:00 EST
5/04/1947 02:00 EDT
9/28/1947 02:00 EST
4/25/1948 02:00 NY#1
4/30/1967 02:00 US#1
....

NY # 225
Before 11/18/1883 LMT
11/18/1883 12:00 NY#4
4/28/1929 02:00 EDT
9/29/1929 02:00 EST
7/03/1938 02:00 EDT
9/04/1938 02:00 EST
7/02/1939 02:00 EDT
9/03/1939 02:00 EST
6/02/1940 02:00 EDT
9/01/1940 02:00 EST
4/27/1941 02:00 NY#1
4/30/1967 02:00 US#1
....

NY # 226
Before 11/18/1883 LMT
11/18/1883 12:00 NY#4
2/09/1942 02:00 EWT
9/30/1945 02:00 EST
4/24/1955 02:00 NY#1
4/30/1967 02:00 US#1

COUNTIES

1 Albany
2 Allegany
3 Bronx
4 Broome
5 Cattaraugus
6 Cayuga
7 Chautauqua
8 Chemung
9 Chenango
10 Clinton
11 Columbia
12 Cortland
13 Delaware
14 Dutchess
15 Erie
16 Essex
17 Franklin
18 Fulton
19 Genesee
20 Greene
21 Hamilton
22 Herkimer
23 Jefferson
24 Kings
25 Lewis
26 Livingston
27 Madison
28 Monroe
29 Montgomery
30 Nassau
31 New York
32 Niagara
33 Oneida
34 Onondaga
35 Ontario
36 Orange
37 Orleans
38 Oswego
39 Otsego
40 Putnam
41 Queens
42 Rensselaer
43 Richmond
44 Rockland
45 St Lawrence
46 Saratoga
47 Schenectady
48 Schoharie
49 Schuyler
50 Seneca
51 Steuben
52 Suffolk
53 Sullivan
54 Tioga
55 Tompkins
56 Ulster
57 Warren
58 Washington
59 Wayne
60 Westchester
61 Wyoming
62 Yates

Abbotts 5 226 42n15'25 78w19'08 5:13:17
Abell Corners 27 14 42n53'54 75w49'43 5:03:19
Abrams Landing 52 1 40n59'33 72w06'22 4:48:25
Academy 1 1 42n39 73w47 4:55:08
Academy 35 14 42n53 77w17 5:09:08
Accord 56 76 41n47'08 74w13'46 4:56:55
Acidalia 53 226 41n53'58 75w02'01 5:00:08
Ack 44 4 41n05 73w55 4:55:40
Acra 20 226 42n18'39 74w03'21 4:56:13
Adams 23 143 43n48'33 76w01'28 5:04:06
Adams Basin 28 226 43n11'51 77w51'15 5:11:25
Adams Center 23 143 43n51'36 76w00'21 5:04:01
Adams Corner 9 226 42n25'36 75w43'43 5:02:55
Adams Corners 40 6 41n21'12 73w50'24 4:55:22
Adams Cove 23 49 44n00'23 76w09'32 5:04:38
Adamsville 58 123 43n19'15 73w28'25 4:53:54
Addison 51 13 42n06'10 77w14'02 5:08:56
Addison Hill 51 13 41n59 77w19 5:09:16
Adelphi 24 1 40n40'51 73w57'54 4:55:52
Aden 53 189 41n51'38 74w40'25 4:58:42
Adirondack 57 226 43n45'50 73w45'32 4:55:02
Adrian 51 20 42n15'16 77w31'16 5:10:05
Afton 9 144 42n13'41 75w31'37 5:02:06
Afton Lake 9 144 42n14 75w31 5:02:04
Agnes Corners 33 13 43n10'33 75w36'24 5:02:26
Aiden Lair 16 49 43n52'18 74w00'11 4:56:01
Air City 33 211 43n13'12 75w25'22 5:01:41
Airmont 44 4 41n06'03 74w07'00 4:56:28
Airmont Heights 44 4 41n08 74w06 4:56:24
Akins Corners 40 7 41n31 73w36 4:54:24
Akron 15 145 43n01'15 78w29'44 5:13:59
Akron Junction 15 145 43n00'17 78w32'05 5:14:08
Alabama 19 226 43n05'47 78w23'28 5:13:34
Albany 1 1 42n39'09 73w45'24 4:55:02
Alberts Landing 52 11 41n00'12 72w07'12 4:48:29
Albertson 30 11 40n46'24 73w38'37 4:54:34
Albia 42 220 42n42'12 73w39'08 4:54:37
Albion 37 146 43n14'47 78w11'38 5:12:47
Albion Center 38 25 43n29'19 76w02'31 5:04:10
Alburg 17 125 44n46'38 74w34'55 4:58:20
Alcove 1 11 42n28'07 73w55'34 4:55:42
Alden 15 38 42n54'00 78w29'32 5:13:58
Alden Bend 10 16 44n53 73w39 4:54:36
Alden Center 15 38 42n54'40 78w31'25 5:14:06
Alden Manor 30 11 40n41'39 73w43'05 4:54:52
Alder Bend 10 16 44n50'53 73w43'17 4:54:53
Alder Brook 17 113 44n30'48 73w56'38 4:55:47
Alder Creek 33 14 43n25'24 75w13'42 5:00:55
Aldrich 45 25 44n08'55 75w06'42 5:00:27
Alene 27 226 43n00'44 75w44'14 5:02:57
Alewife Brook Landing 52 11 41n01'56 72w14'24 4:48:58
Alexander 19 25 42n54'04 78w15'25 5:13:02
Alexandria 23 17 44n18 75w52 5:03:28
Alexandria Bay 23 17 44n20'09 75w55'05 5:03:40
Alexandria Center 23 17 44n18'27 75w52'35 5:03:30
Alfred 2 27 42n15'15 77w47'27 5:11:10
Alfred Station 2 226 42n16'11 77w45'34 5:11:02
Alice 51 226 42n01'15 77w36'51 5:10:27
Allaben 56 88 42n07'00 74w22'15 4:57:29
Allard Corners 36 11 41n34 74w11 4:56:44
Allegany 5 20 42n05'24 78w29'40 5:13:59
Allegany Indian Reservation 5 226 42n07 78w44 5:14:56
Allen 2 226 42n24 78w01 5:12:04
Allen Center 2 226 42n23'10 78w00'56 5:12:04
Allen Corners 40 226 41n28'14 73w44'57 4:55:00
Allendale 23 143 43n46'50 76w01'01 5:04:04
Allens Hill 35 47 42n50'27 77w30'55 5:10:04
Allentown 2 226 42n05'01 78w03'53 5:12:16
Allentown 46 40 43n19'30 73w57'19 4:55:49
Allenwood 30 1 40n48 73w44 4:54:56
Allerton 3 1 40n53 73w52 4:55:28
Alligerville 56 11 41n47'45 74w10'46 4:56:43
Alloway 59 99 43n01'25 76w59'20 5:07:57
Alma 2 109 42n00'45 78w03'29 5:12:14
Almond 2 71 42n19'20 77w44'19 5:10:57
Aloquin 35 14 42n51'39 77w08'43 5:08:35
Alpina 25 226 44n10'09 75w25'37 5:01:42
Alpine 49 226 42n18'47 76w43'28 5:06:54
Alpine Junction 49 226 42n17'37 76w42'38 5:06:51
Alplaus 47 4 42n51'19 73w53'58 4:55:36
Alps 42 226 42n38 73w33 4:54:12
Alsen 20 11 42n09'29 73w55'11 4:55:41
Altamont 1 40 42n42'02 74w02'03 4:56:08
Altay 49 13 42n26'22 77w01'13 5:08:05
Altmar 38 25 43n30'36 76w00'09 5:04:01
Alton 59 226 43n12'40 76w58'51 5:07:55
Altona 17 124 44n53'18 73w39'22 4:54:37
Alverson 23 45 43n56'52 76w01'28 5:04:06
Amagansett 52 11 40n58'25 72w08'39 4:48:35
Amawalk 60 16 41n17 73w46 4:55:04
Amber 34 13 42n53'14 76w17'49 5:05:11
Amberville 9 226 42n32 75w23 5:01:32
Amblers Crossing 39 226 42n40'24 75w15'47 5:01:03
Amblerville 9 226 42n32'28 75w24'01 5:01:36
Amboy 34 25 43n04'10 76w16'22 5:05:05
Amboy Center 38 25 43n22'08 75w56'32 5:03:46
Amchir 36 1 41n28 74w24 4:57:36
Amenia 14 11 41n50'57 73w33'26 4:54:14
Amenia Union 14 11 41n49'28 73w30'20 4:54:01
Ames 29 7 42n50'15 74w36'07 4:58:24
Amherst 15 1 42n59 78w48 5:15:12
Amity 36 11 41n16'05 74w27'19 4:57:49
Amity Harbor 52 11 40n39'48 73w23'55 4:53:36
Amityville 52 6 40n40'44 73w25'03 4:53:40
Amsdell Heights 15 153 42n45 78w51 5:15:24
Amsterdam 29 1 42n56'19 74w11'19 4:56:45
Anaquassacook 58 213 43n04'29 73w18'46 4:53:15
Ancram 11 11 42n03'02 73w38'12 4:54:33
Ancramdale 11 226 42n01'05 73w35'30 4:54:22
Anderson 53 75 41n54'11 74w42'26 4:58:50
Andes 13 226 42n11'19 74w47'10 4:59:09
Andover 2 107 42n09'23 77w47'45 5:11:11
Andrea Park Estates 60 16 41n17 73w46 4:55:04
Angelica 2 226 42n18'24 78w00'58 5:12:04
Angells Corner 59 99 43n01'39 76w51'45 5:07:27
Angola 15 11 42n38'18 79w01'41 5:16:07
Angola Lake Shore Addition 15 22 42n37'05 79w05'55 5:16:24
Angola-on-the-Lake 15 11 42n39'01 79w03'18 5:16:13
Angus 62 12 42n44'05 76w58'23 5:07:54
Annadale 43 11 40n32'40 74w10'37 4:56:42
Annandale-on-Hudson 14 7 42n00'46 73w54'31 4:55:38
Annsville 60 6 41n18'27 73w55'42 4:55:43
Ansonia 31 1 40n48 74w06 4:56:24
Antrim 44 7 41n07'26 74w08'30 4:56:34
Antwerp 23 106 44n11'57 75w36'26 5:02:26
Apalachin 54 36 42n04'10 76w09'18 5:04:37
Apaquogue 52 11 40n56'34 72w12'45 4:48:51
Apex 13 97 42n04'02 75w14'58 5:01:00
Applegate Corner 55 186 42n27'05 76w36'42 5:06:27
Appleton 32 150 43n19'39 78w38'54 5:14:36
Apulia 34 91 42n49'26 76w03'14 5:04:13
Apulia Station 34 91 42n49'07 76w04'22 5:04:17
Aquebogue 52 11 40n56'40 72w37'39 4:50:31
Aqueduct 47 6 42n50'53 73w53'22 4:55:33
Aquetuck 1 1 42n27'38 73w50'20 4:55:21
Arabia 13 226 42n17'59 75w03'20 5:00:13
Arabia 48 226 42n32'02 74w38'10 4:58:33
Arcade 61 147 42n32'02 78w25'24 5:13:42
Arcadia 59 226 43n06 77w04 5:08:16
Archdale 58 226 43n01'59 73w28'53 4:53:56
Archville 60 6 41n07'18 73w51'42 4:55:27
Arctic 13 167 42n11'08 75w24'53 5:01:40
Arden 36 4 41n16'28 74w09'12 4:56:37
Ardonia 56 11 41n40'33 74w04'23 4:56:18
Ardsley 60 7 41n00'38 73w50'39 4:55:23
Ardsley-on-Hudson 60 7 41n01'30 73w52'15 4:55:29
Arena 13 226 42n06'56 74w44'16 4:58:57
Argo Village 30 11 40n42 73w42 4:54:48
Argusville 48 11 42n47'26 74w31'10 4:58:05
Argyle 58 226 43n14'16 73w29'31 4:53:58
Arietta 21 226 43n14'46 74w31'05 4:58:04
Aristotle 2 226 42n20'59 78w00'51 5:12:03
Arkport 51 20 42n23'40 77w41'49 5:10:47
Arkville 13 42 42n08'52 74w37'13 4:58:29
Arkwright 7 15 42n24'25 79w14'12 5:16:57
Arlington 14 1 41n41'45 73w53'50 4:55:35
Arlington 43 1 40n37'56 74w09'56 4:56:40
Arlyn Oaks 30 11 40n41 73w28 4:53:52
Armawalk 60 16 41n17'16 73w46'17 4:55:05
Armonk 60 1 41n07'35 73w42'52 4:54:51
Armor 15 153 42n44'26 78w47'57 5:15:12
Arnett 28 209 43n08'38 77w38'27 5:10:34
Arnolds Mill 11 10 42n20'29 73w35'44 4:54:23
Arrochar 43 1 40n35'54 74w04'23 4:56:18
Arsenal Hill 35 14 42n53'00 77w17'48 5:09:11
Arshamonaque 52 1 41n05'22 72w23'28 4:49:34
Arthur 38 14 43n29'42 76w14'54 5:05:00
Arthur Manor 60 1 40n58'36 73w47'36 4:55:10
Arthursburg 14 226 41n37'42 73w46'19 4:55:05
Art Village 52 11 40n53'02 72w25'25 4:49:42
Arverne 41 1 40n35'28 73w47'47 4:55:11
Asbury 55 13 42n31'36 76w29'32 5:05:58
Asbury 56 215 42n08'28 73w57'30 4:55:50
Ashantee 26 226 42n53'49 77w45'54 5:11:04
Asharoken 52 11 40n55'40 73w21'37 4:53:26
Ashford 5 226 42n19'13 78w36'30 5:14:26
Ashford Hollow 5 226 42n24'12 78w41'08 5:14:45
Ash Grove 58 11 43n01'55 73w19'54 4:53:20
Ashland 6 13 42n45'46 76w28'42 5:05:55
Ashland 20 226 42n18'13 74w20'02 4:57:20
Ashokan 56 11 41n58'32 74w11'50 4:56:47
Ashville 7 20 42n05'47 79w22'33 5:17:30
Ashville Bay 7 20 42n06 79w23 5:17:32
Ashwood 37 15 43n19'40 78w18'37 5:13:14
Assembly Park 34 91 42n46'47 76w07'50 5:04:31
Assembly Point 41 1 40n47 73w47 4:55:08
Association Island 23 65 43n52 76w12 5:04:48
Astoria 41 1 40n46'19 73w55'50 4:55:43
Athens 20 11 42n15'37 73w48'36 4:55:14
Athol 57 226 43n29'33 73w50'36 4:55:22
Athol Springs 15 11 42n46'11 78w52'00 5:15:28
Atlanta 51 14 42n33'15 77w28'22 5:09:53
Atlantic 43 11 40n31 74w15 4:57:00
Atlantic Beach 30 11 40n35'20 73w43'46 4:54:55
Atlantique 52 11 40n38'30 73w10'16 4:52:41
Attica 61 148 42n51'51 78w16'50 5:13:07
Attica Center 61 148 42n48'56 78w14'05 5:12:56
Attlebury 14 226 41n55'02 73w40'08 4:54:41
Atwaters 6 226 42n37'51 76w39'00 5:06:36
Atwell 22 226 43n31'26 74w56'41 4:59:47
Atwell Corners 27 14 42n55'29 75w54'24 5:03:38
Atwood 56 11 41n53'34 74w09'37 4:56:38
Auburn 6 13 42n55'54 76w33'59 5:06:16
Audubon 31 1 40n50 73w56 4:55:44
Augusta 33 13 42n58'29 75w30'06 5:02:00
Aurelius 6 14 42n56 76w40 5:06:40
Auriesville 29 22 42n55'46 74w19'01 4:57:16
Aurora 6 13 42n45'14 76w42'10 5:06:49

Aurora Tract 34 13 43N07 76w12 5:04:48
Ausable 10 27 44N31 73w36 4:54:24
Ausable Chasm 10 27 44N31'21 73w27'56 4:53:52
Au Sable Forks 16 44 44N26'26 73w40'30 4:54:42
Austerlitz 11 11 42N18'42 73w28'25 4:53:54
Austin 6 13 42N48'39 76w28'16 5:05:53
Ava 33 226 43N25'08 75w28'47 5:01:55
Averill Park 42 226 42N38'02 73w33'15 4:54:13
Averys Place 21 226 43N17'39 74w33'18 4:58:13
Averyville 16 83 44N14'38 74w03'07 4:56:12
Avoca 51 14 42N24'34 77w25'18 5:09:41
Avon 26 20 42N54'43 77w44'45 5:10:59
Awosting 56 226 41N40'09 74w17'30 4:57:10
Axeville 5 20 42N14'57 78w57'34 5:15:50
Axton Landing 17 221 44N12'10 74w19'45 4:57:19
Babbitt Corner 23 12 43N52'25 76w07'05 5:04:28
Babbitt Corner 35 14 42N50'10 77w11'05 5:08:44
Babcock Hill 33 13 42N55'54 75w13'16 5:00:53
Babcock Lake 42 11 42N48'48 73w24'18 4:53:37
Babylon 52 1 40N41'44 73w19'34 4:53:18
Backus 45 118 44N10'10 75w16'53 5:01:08
Bacon Hill 46 226 43N08'00 73w36'22 4:54:25
Bagdad 15 42 42N28'58 78w55'13 5:15:41
Baggs Corner 23 45 43N57'25 76w03'29 5:04:14
Bailey 28 20 43N04'21 77w39'37 5:10:38
Baileys Gap 56 51 41N41'31 74w00'02 4:56:00
Baileys Settlement 34 16 42N53'13 76w09'23 5:04:38
Baileyville 36 4 41N28'20 74w29'02 4:57:56
Bainbridge 9 149 42N17'36 75w28'47 5:01:55
Bains Corner 14 11 41N44'20 73w33'45 4:54:15
Baird Corners 34 226 43N13'20 76w27'38 5:05:51
Baiting Hollow 52 11 40N57'22 72w44'41 4:50:59
Baker 26 226 42N58'38 77w47'32 5:11:10
Baker Corner 14 7 41N35'15 73w33'48 4:54:15
Baker Corners 22 222 43N06'34 75w08'33 5:00:34
Bakers Mills 57 49 43N36'53 74w01'31 4:56:06
Bakerstand 5 226 42N21'02 78w32'56 5:14:12
Bakertown 57 226 43N23'57 74w07'53 4:56:32
Balcom 7 217 42N22'11 79w05'48 5:16:23
Balcom Beach 2 226 42N23'11 78w12'06 5:12:48
Balcom Corners 7 217 42N22'11 79w05'26 5:16:22
Bald Mountain 58 226 43N07'46 73w32'19 4:54:09
Baldwin 16 6 43N48'33 73w26'47 4:53:47
Baldwin 30 7 40N39'23 73w36'35 4:54:26
Baldwin Corner 37 146 43N20'19 78w11'28 5:12:46
Baldwin Corner 58 123 43N23'15 73w29'38 4:53:59
Baldwin Harbor 30 11 40N38'22 73w36'32 4:54:26
Baldwin Heights 5 226 42N05'57 78w25'22 5:13:41
Baldwin Place 40 29 41N20'51 73w45'45 4:55:03
Baldwinsville 34 91 43N09'31 76w19'59 5:05:20
Ballard Corners 46 226 43N09'11 73w40'55 4:54:44
Ballina 27 14 42N53'52 75w50'51 5:03:23
Ballston 46 8 42N56 73w53 4:55:32
Ballston Center 46 8 42N57'21 73w51'57 4:55:28
Ballston Lake 46 8 42N54'42 73w52'07 4:55:28
Ballston Spa 46 8 43N00'03 73w50'58 4:55:24
Balltown 7 226 42N29'26 79w04'36 5:16:18
Balmat 45 226 44N14'54 75w23'43 5:01:35
Balmville 36 1 41N32'05 74w00'55 4:56:04
Baltimore 12 91 42N44'07 76w07'34 5:04:30
Bangall 14 226 41N52'32 73w41'30 4:54:46
Bangall 34 41 43N06'44 76w23'00 5:05:32
Bangor 17 16 44N48'44 74w23'52 4:57:35
Bangor Station 17 16 44N50 74w26 4:57:44
Bank Plaza 30 11 40N40 73w34 4:54:16
Banksville 60 1 41N08'28 73w38'24 4:54:34
Baptist Corners 6 13 42N54'13 76w28'07 5:05:52
Barberville 42 226 42N41'00 73w32'28 4:54:10
Barbourville 13 167 42N08'14 75w21'24 5:01:26
Barcelona 7 225 42N20'25 79w35'46 5:18:23
Barclay Heights 56 215 42N04 73w57 4:55:48
Bardeen Corners 38 182 43N20'43 76w09'08 5:04:37
Bardonia 44 4 41N06'34 73w59'48 4:55:59
Bar Harbour Shopping Center 30 11 40N51 73w27 4:53:48
Barker 32 150 43N19'48 78w33'18 5:14:13
Barkers Grove 58 11 42N59'16 73w33'08 4:54:13
Barkersville 46 226 43N05'18 74w02'24 4:56:10
Barkertown 26 226 43N23'05 77w54'01 5:11:36
Barleytown 36 4 41N18'29 74w04'54 4:56:20
Barnard 28 209 43N12'45 77w38'35 5:10:34
Barnegat 14 1 41N37'55 73w56'50 4:55:47
Barnerville 48 12 42N41'15 74w25'37 4:57:42
Barnes Corners 25 226 43N49'01 75w49'05 5:03:16
Barnes Hole 52 11 40N59'57 72w07'59 4:48:32
Barnes Landing 52 11 41N00'16 72w07'32 4:48:30
Barneveld 33 82 43N16'20 75w11'25 5:00:46
Barney Mills 51 226 42N05'32 77w42'21 5:10:49
Barnum 5 226 42N00'08 78w24'43 5:13:39
Barnum Corners 40 226 41N27'32 73w33'22 4:54:13
Barnum Island 30 11 40N36 73w39 4:54:36
Barre 37 146 43N10 78w13 5:12:52
Barre Center 37 146 43N11'10 78w11'40 5:12:47
Barrett Corners 39 226 42N43'07 75w10'24 5:00:42
Barrington 62 14 42N32'49 77w03'23 5:08:14
Barrytown 14 7 41N59'54 73w55'28 4:55:42
Barryville 53 20 41N28'39 74w54'41 4:59:39
Bartlett 33 211 43N08'04 75w26'32 5:01:46
Bartlett Corners 28 13 43N18'37 77w47'41 5:11:11
Bartlett Hollow 13 104 42N19'11 75w10'56 5:00:44
Bartletts Corner 23 17 44N15'36 75w43'30 5:02:54
Barton 54 224 42N02'34 76w26'56 5:05:48
Basket 53 226 41N50'56 75w06'37 5:00:26
Basom 19 226 43N04'02 78w23'30 5:13:34
Batavia 19 142 42N59'53 78w11'16 5:12:45
Batchellerville 46 7 43N12'42 74w04'56 4:56:20
Bates 7 226 42N15'11 79w09'16 5:16:37
Bates 48 226 42N26'47 74w16'29 4:57:06
Bath 51 14 42N20'13 77w19'05 5:09:16
Bath Beach 24 1 40N36'16 74w00'17 4:56:01
Battenville 58 226 43N06'33 73w25'28 4:53:42
Baxter Estates 30 11 40N50'05 73w41'45 4:54:47
Bay 24 1 40N35 73w57 4:55:48
Bayberry 34 13 43N07 76w12 5:04:48
Bayberry Dunes 52 11 40N41'23 72w59'23 4:51:58
Bayberry Park 60 1 40N56'48 73w46'28 4:55:06
Baychester 3 1 40N51'40 73w50'30 4:55:22
Bay Colony 30 11 40N37'46 73w35'45 4:54:23
Bay Park 30 11 40N37'59 73w40'15 4:54:41
Bay Point 52 11 41N00'12 72w18'56 4:49:16
Bay Pond 17 221 44N25'53 74w24'44 4:57:39
Bayport 52 11 40N44'18 73w03'04 4:52:12
Bay Ridge 24 1 40N38'02 74w00'54 4:56:04
Bay Shore 52 1 40N43'30 73w14'45 4:52:59
Bay Shores 34 13 42N51'44 76w16'28 5:05:06
Bayside 41 1 40N46'06 73w46'39 4:55:07
Bay Terrace 41 1 40N46 73w47 4:55:08
Bayview 7 226 42N10'36 79w23'53 5:17:36
Bay View 15 11 42N46'45 78w51'29 5:15:26
Bay View 24 1 40N38 73w54 4:55:36
Bay View 28 185 43N11'50 77w31'59 5:10:08
Bayview 52 11 41N04 72w26 4:49:44
Bayville 30 7 40N54'38 73w33'45 4:54:15
Beach Hampton 52 1 40N58'41 72w06'29 4:48:26
Beach Ridge 32 1 43N05'05 78w49'24 5:15:18
Beachville 51 226 42N27'21 77w37'59 5:10:32
Beachwood 7 20 42N06 79w19 5:17:16
Beacon 14 57 41N30'17 73w58'12 4:55:53
Beacon Hills 14 6 41N30'34 73w55'44 4:55:43
Bean Hill Crossing 23 17 44N19'50 75w47'18 5:03:09
Beantown 8 226 42N07 76w33 5:06:12
Bear Creek 59 226 43N16'35 77w16'40 5:09:07
Beards Hollow 48 13 42N36'23 74w33'16 4:58:13
Bear Mountain 44 6 41N19 73w59 4:55:56
Bearsville 56 11 42N02'26 74w09'20 4:56:37
Beartown 10 86 44N45'29 73w34'51 4:54:19
Beartown 33 226 43N21'03 75w27'16 5:01:49
Beartown 57 40 43N19'43 73w45'56 4:55:04
Beaver Brook 53 226 41N36 75w04 5:00:16
Beaver Dam Lake 36 1 41N31 74w03 4:56:12
Beaver Dams 49 14 42N17'28 76w57'36 5:07:50
Beaver Falls 25 226 43N53'13 75w25'40 5:01:43
Beaverkill 53 75 41N58'53 74w50'09 4:59:21
Beaver Meadow 9 226 42N39'34 75w40'50 5:02:43
Beaver River 22 226 43N54'13 74w54'37 4:59:38
Beckers Corners 1 11 42N32'54 73w48'41 4:55:15
Becks Grove 33 211 43N15'19 75w36'15 5:02:25
Bedell 13 42 42N11'42 74w33'02 4:58:12
Bedford 24 1 40N41'19 73w57'20 4:55:49
Bedford 60 7 41N12'15 73w38'39 4:54:35
Bedford Center 60 7 41N13'12 73w39'31 4:54:38
Bedford Corners 5 226 42N03'16 78w18'42 5:13:15
Bedford Hills 60 6 41N14'12 73w41'42 4:54:47
Bedford Park 3 1 40N52'12 73w53'10 4:55:33
Bedford-Stuyvesant 24 1 40N41 73w55 4:55:40
Beechertown 45 105 44N42'07 74w47'20 4:59:09
Beecherville 38 226 43N34'43 75w54'31 5:03:38
Beechford 56 37 42N01'16 74w16'15 4:57:05
Beech Hill 60 1 40N59'11 73w49'01 4:55:16
Beechhurst 41 1 40N47'29 73w48'18 4:55:13
Beechmont 60 1 40N55'51 73w47'05 4:55:08
Beechmont Woods 60 1 40N56'04 73w46'28 4:55:06
Beechurst 41 1 40N47 73w49 4:55:16
Beechwood 28 13 43N10 77w34 5:10:16
Beehive Crossing 42 11 42N54 73w21 4:53:24
Beehive Crossing 61 20 42N47'38 78w09'10 5:12:37
Beekman 14 226 41N36'39 73w42'48 4:54:51
Beekman Corners 48 11 42N48 74w37 4:58:28
Beekmantown 10 86 44N46'15 73w29'33 4:53:58
Beerston 13 226 42N07'31 75w09'47 5:00:39
Beixedon Estates 52 11 41N04'06 72w24'41 4:49:39
Belair Road 43 1 40N36 74w05 4:56:20
Belcher 58 213 43N16'49 73w23'18 4:53:33
Belcoda 28 226 43N01'29 77w50'47 5:11:23
Belden 4 17 42N12'13 75w40'31 5:02:42
Belfast 2 20 42N20'34 78w06'42 5:12:27
Belfort 25 226 43N55'41 75w19'57 5:01:20
Belgium 34 226 43N10'35 76w16'30 5:05:06
Belknap Crossing 61 142 42N51'51 78w09'46 5:12:39
Bellaire 41 1 40N42'50 73w45'16 4:55:01
Belle Ayr 56 226 42N04'19 74w36'35 4:58:26
Belle Harbor 41 1 40N34'33 73w50'55 4:55:24
Belle Isle 34 41 43N05 76w20 5:05:20
Bellerose 30 1 40N43'27 73w42'56 4:54:52
Bellerose Terrace 30 1 40N43'14 73w43'35 4:54:54
Belle Terre 52 11 40N57'35 73w04'06 4:52:16
Belleview 7 20 42N07'45 79w20'20 5:17:21
Belleville 23 226 43N47'00 76w07'11 5:04:29
Bellevue 15 7 42N53'36 78w44'03 5:14:56
Bellevue 47 1 42N47'39 73w58'12 4:55:53
Bellmont 17 226 44N49 74w09 4:56:36
Bellmont Center 17 226 44N50'53 74w08'10 4:56:33
Bellmore 30 7 40N40'07 73w31'39 4:54:07
Bellona 62 14 42N45'25 77w00'54 5:08:04
Bellport 52 7 40N45'25 72w56'23 4:51:46
Belltown 6 13 42N38'13 76w35'43 5:06:23
Bellvale 36 6 41N15'01 74w18'40 4:57:15
Bellview Beach 52 11 40N47'01 72w47'11 4:51:09
Bellville 2 226 42N20'22 78w15'12 5:13:01
Bellwood 25 226 43N48'10 75w40'55 5:02:44
Belmont 2 107 42N13'23 78w02'05 5:12:08
Belvidere 2 20 42N15'15 78w03'34 5:12:14
Bemis Heights 46 11 42N58'16 73w38'02 4:54:32
Bemus Point 7 226 42N09'42 79w23'31 5:17:34
Benedict 18 226 43N07'06 74w08'37 4:56:34
Benedict Beach 28 105 43N20'55 77w52'21 5:11:29
Bennett Bridge 38 25 43N31 76w00 5:04:00
Bennetts 2 226 42N19'16 77w56'31 5:11:46
Bennetts 51 226 42N11'20 77w37'16 5:10:29
Bennettsburg 49 14 42N25'31 76w48'41 5:07:15
Bennetts Corners 27 60 43N02'36 75w36'13 5:02:25
Bennetts Corners 34 24 43N02'05 76w21'55 5:05:28
Bennetts Corners 37 117 43N11'42 78w01'03 5:12:04
Bennettsville 9 149 42N15'20 75w26'49 5:01:47
Bennington 61 226 42N50'13 78w23'52 5:13:35
Benson 21 226 43N15'07 74w16'44 4:57:07
Bensonhurst 24 1 40N36'06 73w59'40 4:55:59
Benson Mines 45 25 44N10'11 75w00'57 5:00:04
Bentleys Corners 23 77 44N13'44 75w41'39 5:02:47
Benton 62 14 42N43'03 77w02'38 5:08:11
Benton Center 62 14 42N43'02 77w04'01 5:08:16
Benton Corners 56 122 41N41'54 74w11'33 4:56:46
Berea 36 11 41N31'27 74w10'48 4:56:43
Bergen 19 110 43N05'07 77w56'33 5:11:46
Bergen Beach 24 1 40N37'13 73w54'26 4:55:38
Bergen Beach 50 226 42N36'53 76w40'59 5:06:44
Bergen Park 52 11 40N51 73w24 4:53:36
Bergholtz 32 1 43N06'11 78w54'25 5:15:38
Berkshire 18 226 43N02'57 74w19'10 4:57:17
Berkshire 34 13 43N02 76w01 5:04:04
Berkshire 54 226 42N18'15 76w11'13 5:04:45
Berkshire Terrace 40 226 41N29'45 73w42'09 4:54:49
Berlin 42 11 42N41'35 73w22'21 4:53:29
Berne 1 40 42N37'31 74w08'02 4:56:32
Bernhards Bay 38 15 43N14'40 75w56'02 5:03:44
Berryville 29 174 42N57'42 74w24'56 4:57:40
Berwyn 34 16 42N51'58 76w02'28 5:04:10
Besemer 55 186 42N23'46 76w24'37 5:05:38
Best 42 226 42N36'56 73w38'16 4:54:33
Bethany 19 13 42N55 78w08 5:12:32
Bethany Center 19 13 42N54'14 78w08'01 5:12:32
Bethel 14 226 41N57'16 73w38'03 4:54:32
Bethel 53 226 41N41'00 74w52'18 4:59:29
Bethel Corners 6 226 43N14'57 76w34'59 5:06:20
Bethel Corners 38 226 43N34'19 76w11'15 5:04:45
Bethel Grove 55 186 42N24'19 76w25'47 5:05:43
Bethford 15 153 42N48 78w49 5:15:16
Bethlehem 1 226 42N36 73w50 4:55:20
Bethlehem Center 1 11 42N36'07 73w47'31 4:55:10
Bethlehem Heights 1 11 42N32'03 73w49'59 4:55:20
Bethpage 30 11 40N44'39 73w28'57 4:53:56
Bettsburg 9 17 42N12'06 75w32'51 5:02:11
Beukendaal 47 1 42N51'18 73w58'51 4:55:55
Beulah 28 226 43N01'07 77w53'31 5:11:34
Beverly Inn Corners 39 226 42N45 75w11 5:00:44
Beyers Corners 18 1 42N59'53 74w06'55 4:56:28
Bible School Park 4 151 42N06 75w58 5:03:52

Bidwell 15 153 42N55 78w53 5:15:32
Big Bay 38 14 43N14'46 76w07'14 5:04:29
Big Bend 34 16 42N52'39 76w05'24 5:04:22
Big Brook 33 226 43N19'20 75w19'38 5:01:19
Big Creek 51 226 42N22'08 77w34'31 5:10:18
Bigelow 45 226 44N25'18 75w21'59 5:01:28
Big Flats 8 13 42N08'14 76w56'14 5:07:45
Big Hollow 57 1 43N26'00 73w45'22 4:55:01
Big H Shopping Center 52 11 40N51 73w23 4:53:32
Big Indian 56 30 42N06'09 74w26'39 4:57:47
Big Island 36 7 41N19'14 74w24'17 4:57:37
Big Moose 22 73 43N49'06 74w54'56 4:59:40
Big Tree 15 11 42N46'11 78w48'42 5:15:15
Big Wolf Lake 17 221 44N14 74w28 4:57:52
Billings 14 226 41N40'16 73w45'49 4:55:03
Billington Bay 27 14 43N12 76w02 5:04:08
Billington Heights 15 170 42N47 78w37 5:14:28
Billsboro 35 41 42N48'06 76w58'43 5:07:55
Billsboro Corners 35 41 42N48'38 77w00'29 5:08:02
Biltmore Shores 30 11 40N39'49 73w28'00 4:53:52
Bingham Mills 11 226 42N06'34 73w49'55 4:55:20
Binghamton 4 151 42N05'55 75w55'06 5:03:40
Bingley 27 14 42N57'42 75w49'52 5:03:19
Binnewater 56 11 41N51'23 74w05'09 4:56:21
Birchton 46 11 43N00'03 73w58'07 4:55:52
Bird 5 226 42N21'58 78w32'41 5:14:11
Birdsall 2 226 42N23'29 77w55'14 5:11:41
Birmingham Corners 22 13 42N53'19 75w08'17 5:00:33
Bishas Mill 23 226 44N00'20 75w15'24 5:01:02
Bishopville 2 226 42N22'07 77w44'51 5:10:59
Blackbridge 21 226 43N22'14 74w19'26 4:57:18
Black Brook 10 226 44N27'30 73w44'34 4:54:58
Black Corners 7 15 42N23'39 79w11'54 5:16:48
Black Creek 2 20 42N16'32 78w13'36 5:12:54
Blackesley Corner 9 149 42N15'57 75w36'04 5:02:24
Black Lake 53 226 41N38'43 74w51'44 4:59:27
Blackmans Corners 10 198 44N58 73w39 4:54:36
Blackmans Corners 33 211 43N09'32 75w32'52 5:02:11
Black River 23 12 44N00'45 75w47'41 5:03:11
Black Rock 6 13 42N42'13 76w39'36 5:06:38
Blackwatch Hills 28 13 43N05 77w28 5:09:52
Blairville 32 226 43N14'02 79w01'02 5:16:04
Blakeley 15 170 42N44'08 78w35'44 5:14:23
Blakeslee 27 226 43N00'25 75w48'54 5:03:16
Blasdell 15 153 42N47'50 78w49'25 5:15:18
Blatchley 4 20 42N01'17 75w44'04 5:02:56
Blauvelt 44 28 41N03'48 73w57'29 4:55:50
Bleecker 18 226 43N07'11 74w22'05 4:57:28
Bleecker Center 18 226 43N09'02 74w23'41 4:57:35
Blenheim 48 226 42N29 74w30 4:58:00
Blennes Corner 33 226 43N18'41 75w40'53 5:02:44
Bliss 61 226 42N34'37 78w15'11 5:13:01
Bliss Corner 18 226 43N09'27 74w40'07 4:58:40
Blockville 7 226 42N04'54 79w24'45 5:17:39
Blodgett Mills 12 41 42N34'06 76w07'34 5:04:30
Bloomerville 51 14 42N25'51 77w27'36 5:09:50
Bloomfield 43 1 40N36'45 74w10'43 4:56:43
Bloomfield Park 33 211 43N12'53 75w26'24 5:01:46
Bloomingburg 53 11 41N33'15 74w26'24 4:57:46
Bloomingdale 16 81 44N24'28 74w05'15 4:56:21
Blooming Grove 36 20 41N24'33 74w11'44 4:56:47
Bloomington 56 11 41N52'44 74w02'40 4:56:11
Bloomville 13 31 42N20'00 74w48'29 4:59:14
Blossom 15 153 42N51'22 78w41'36 5:14:46
Blossvale 33 211 43N16'47 75w38'38 5:02:35
Blue Mountain 56 215 42N06'30 74w01'13 4:56:05
Blue Mountain Lake 21 226 43N51'19 74w26'38 4:57:47
Blue Point 52 11 40N44'38 73w02'06 4:52:08
Blue Ridge 16 226 43N57'26 73w47'06 4:55:08
Blue Store 11 226 42N06'32 73w49'05 4:55:16
Bluff Point 62 14 42N36'51 77w06'14 5:08:25
Blythebourne 24 1 40N38 74w00 4:56:00
Boardmanville 5 226 42N05'26 78w25'36 5:13:42
Boght Corners 1 1 42N46'59 73w44'41 4:54:59
Bohemia 52 11 40N46'09 73w06'56 4:52:28
Boiceville 56 37 42N00'18 74w15'59 4:57:04
Bolivar 2 24 42N04'00 78w10'05 5:12:40
Bolivar 27 226 43N04'16 75w53'21 5:03:33
Bolton 57 23 43N32'11 73w40'05 4:54:40
Bolton Landing 57 226 43N33'26 73w39'19 4:54:37
Bolts Corners 6 13 42N47 76w34 5:06:16
Bombay 17 226 44N56'20 74w34'05 4:58:16
Bonita 7 187 42N06'55 79w16'55 5:17:08
Bonney 9 15 42N43'17 75w40'17 5:02:41
Bonni Castle 59 226 43N14'17 76w56'04 5:07:44
Bonnie Crest 60 1 40N57'35 73w47'11 4:55:09
Bonny Hill 51 14 42N16'14 77w20'02 5:09:20
Boomertown 7 226 42N04'47 79w22'11 5:17:29
Boonville 33 137 43N29'01 75w20'13 5:01:21
Borden 51 13 42N02'30 77w19'40 5:09:19
Borden Estate 56 11 41N35'38 74w10'18 4:56:41
Border City 50 41 42N52'43 76w57'39 5:07:51
Boreas River 16 49 43N56'29 73w57'49 4:55:51
Borodino 34 13 42N51'32 76w20'18 5:05:21
Borodino Landing 34 13 42N51'25 76w21'12 5:05:25
Borough Hall 41 1 40N43 73w50 4:55:20
Borough Park 24 1 40N38'02 73w59'50 4:55:59
Bosley Corner 26 20 42N49'17 77w36'38 5:10:27
Boston 15 226 42N37'44 78w44'16 5:14:57
Boston Corner 11 11 42N03'10 73w31'18 4:54:05
Bostwick Corners 55 186 42N25'17 76w37'46 5:06:31
Boswell Corners 35 226 42N43'07 77w25'29 5:09:42
Botanical 3 1 40N52 73w53 4:55:32
Bouckville 27 180 42N53'21 75w33'06 5:02:12
Boughton Hill 35 19 42N57'40 77w24'43 5:09:39
Boulevard 3 1 40N49 73w54 4:55:36
Boulevard Mall 15 7 42N58 78w48 5:15:12
Boultons Beach 23 12 43N56'08 76w08'05 5:04:32
Bouquet 16 129 44N18'13 73w24'10 4:53:37
Bournes Beach 7 225 42N21'35 79w33'04 5:18:12
Boutonville 60 16 41N15'25 73w33'54 4:54:16
Bovina 13 226 42N16'10 74w43'38 4:58:55
Bovina Center 13 226 42N15'43 74w47'06 4:59:08
Bowen 5 20 42N07'46 79w00'56 5:16:04
Bowen Corners 38 182 43N18'24 76w15'06 5:05:00
Bowens Corners 38 226 43N16'31 76w27'50 5:05:51
Bowers Corner 6 13 42N39'03 76w35'46 5:06:23
Bowerstown 39 13 42N41'09 74w55'05 4:59:40
Bowler 2 22 42N00'11 78w14'47 5:12:59
Bowling Green 31 1 40N43 74w01 4:56:04
Bowmansville 15 7 42N56'18 78w41'06 5:14:44
Boylston 38 226 43N39 75w57 5:03:48
Boylston Center 38 226 43N39'37 75w57'54 5:03:52
Boyntonville 42 11 42N50'42 73w27'23 4:53:50
Boysen Bay 34 14 43N12 76w02 5:04:08
Braddock Heights 28 226 43N18'25 77w41'59 5:10:48
Bradford 51 226 42N22'16 77w06'33 5:08:26
Bradford Junction 5 20 42N05'49 78w37'35 5:14:30
Bradley 53 189 41N49'26 74w40'36 4:58:42
Bradtville 18 43 43N04'21 74w30'26 4:58:02
Braeside 42 11 42N32'13 73w36'33 4:54:26
Brainard 42 11 42N29'45 73w30'45 4:54:03
Brainards Corners 39 226 42N45 75w11 5:00:44
Brainardsville 17 188 44N51'28 74w02'02 4:56:08
Braman Corners 47 226 42N48'31 74w13'09 4:56:53
Bramanville 48 12 42N41'10 74w24'06 4:57:36
Branch 56 226 41N59'39 74w28'14 4:57:53
Branchport 62 226 42N35'55 77w09'15 5:08:37
Brandon 17 226 44N44 74w25 4:57:40
Brandon Center 17 226 44N46'26 74w24'45 4:57:39
Brandreth 22 226 43N56'15 74w51'11 4:59:25
Brandy Brook 45 226 44N14'49 74w46'34 4:59:06
Brandywine 47 6 42N47 73w54 4:55:36
Brant 15 11 42N35'18 79w01'05 5:16:04
Brantingham 25 226 43N41'19 75w17'33 5:01:10
Brant Lake 57 11 43N40'35 73w45'00 4:55:00
Brasher 45 105 44N53 74w45 4:59:00
Brasher Center 45 105 44N52'02 74w47'03 4:59:08
Brasher Falls 45 105 44N48'27 74w46'27 4:59:06
Brasher Iron Works 45 105 44N53'24 74w41'54 4:58:48
Brasie Corners 45 178 44N24'30 75w35'38 5:02:23
Brayton 57 226 43N27'04 73w37'33 4:54:30
Brayton Hollow 17 188 44N56'30 74w07'38 4:56:31
Breakabeen 48 226 42N31'27 74w24'36 4:57:38
Breesport 8 13 42N10'24 76w44'03 5:06:56
Breezy Point 41 1 40N33'23 73w55'36 4:55:42
Brentwood 52 11 40N46'52 73w14'48 4:52:59
Breukelen 24 1 40N38 73w54 4:55:36
Brevoort 24 1 40N41 73w57 4:55:48
Brewers Corner 33 13 43N06'41 75w32'04 5:02:08
Brewerton 34 14 43N14'17 76w08'28 5:04:34
Brewster 40 85 41N23'50 73w37'03 4:54:28
Brewster Heights 40 85 41N24'22 73w37'59 4:54:32
Brewster Hills 40 85 41N25 73w36 4:54:24
Briarcliff Manor 60 1 41N08'44 73w49'27 4:55:18
Briar Park 30 11 41N04 73w30 4:54:00
Brick House Corners 19 164 42N59'35 78w24'22 5:13:37
Brick Tavern 11 11 42N16'21 73w43'26 4:54:54
Bridge 32 199 43N07 79w02 5:16:08
Bridgehampton 52 11 40N56'16 72w18'05 4:49:12
Bridgeport 27 14 43N09'19 75w58'11 5:03:53
Bridgeport 50 14 42N54'57 76w45'10 5:07:01
Bridgeville 53 197 41N38'03 74w37'10 4:58:29
Bridgewater 33 13 42N52'45 75w15'05 5:01:00
Brier Hill 45 20 44N31'53 75w39'47 5:02:39
Briggs 45 25 44N09'54 75w08'15 5:00:33
Briggs Corner 25 226 43N52'28 75w32'10 5:02:09
Briggs Hollow 54 36 42N01'03 76w18'23 5:05:14
Brighton 15 7 42N59'28 78w50'14 5:15:21
Brighton 24 1 40N35 73w57 4:55:48
Brighton 28 13 43N08'51 77w33'03 5:10:12
Brighton 39 78 42N52'04 75w01'45 5:00:07
Brighton Beach 24 1 40N34'40 73w57'36 4:55:50
Brightside 21 226 43N49 74w40 4:58:40
Brightwaters 52 11 40N43'15 73w61'04 4:56:04
Brinckerhoff 14 6 41N32'38 73w52'07 4:55:28
Brisben 9 130 42N21'54 75w40'55 5:02:44
Briscoe 53 189 41N45'51 74w52'44 4:59:31
Bristol 35 47 42N50'43 77w25'28 5:09:42
Bristol Center 35 14 42N48'32 77w23'27 5:09:34
Bristol Springs 35 226 42N42'22 77w22'49 5:09:31
Broadacres 4 151 42N07 75w56 5:03:44
Broadalbin 18 226 43N03'31 74w11'49 4:56:47
Broadalbin Junction 18 226 43N05'06 74w17'40 4:57:11
Broad Channel 41 1 40N36'11 73w49'15 4:55:17
Broadway 41 1 40N45 73w56 4:55:44
Broadway Junction 24 1 40N40'36 73w54'02 4:55:36
Brockport 28 13 43N12'49 77w56'22 5:11:45
Brockville 37 146 43N15'40 78w05'27 5:12:22
Brockway 14 7 41N31'50 73w58'41 4:55:55
Brocton 7 160 42N23'19 79w26'29 5:17:46
Brodhead 56 37 41N56'37 74w15'28 4:57:02
Bromley 34 91 42N46'57 76w11'00 5:04:44
Bronck House 20 11 42N20'43 73w50'49 4:55:23
Bronx 3 1 40N51 73w54 4:55:36
Bronxdale 3 1 40N51'02 73w52'01 4:55:28
Bronxville 60 7 40N56'17 73w49'57 4:55:20
Bronxville Heights 60 1 40N57'58 73w50'36 4:55:22
Brookdale 28 15 43N04'46 77w43'04 5:10:52
Brookdale 45 207 44N48'30 74w53'31 4:59:34
Brookfield 27 16 42N48'46 75w19'05 5:01:16
Brookfield 33 226 43N18'00 75w34'11 5:02:17
Brookhaven 52 11 40N46'45 72w54'57 4:51:40
Brooklyn 5 226 42N25'59 78w44'55 5:15:00
Brooklyn 13 104 42N20'39 75w10'15 5:00:41
Brooklyn 24 1 40N38 73w56 4:55:44
Brooklyn Heights 24 1 40N41'43 73w59'39 4:55:59
Brooklyn Manor 41 1 40N41'41 73w50'53 4:55:24
Brooklyn Naval Station 24 1 40N42 73w58 4:55:52
Brookman Corners 29 62 42N55'02 74w43'36 4:58:54
Brooksburg 20 226 42N18'10 74w12'26 4:56:50
Brooks Corner 27 130 42N45'58 75w29'50 5:01:59
Brooks Grove 26 13 42N37'50 77w55'42 5:11:43
Brooktondale 55 226 42N22'50 76w23'42 5:05:35
Brookvale 4 4 42N07'32 75w47'12 5:03:09
Brookview 42 11 42N32'28 73w43'13 4:54:53
Brookville 19 226 42N55'16 78w12'46 5:12:51
Brookville 30 11 40N48'47 73w34'04 4:54:16
Brookville Park 52 11 40N44 73w13 4:52:52
Broome 48 226 42N30 74w18 4:57:12
Broome Center 48 226 42N27'47 74w21'06 4:57:24
Brothertown 33 11 42N56'55 75w25'18 5:01:41
Brown Center 34 13 43N10'10 76w02'20 5:04:09
Browns Bridge 45 226 44N33 74w56 4:59:44
Browns Corners 23 17 44N17'57 75w51'28 5:03:26
Browns Crossing 51 13 42N14'57 77w27'04 5:09:48
Brownsell Corner 44 4 41N09'49 73w59'19 4:55:57
Browns Hollow 29 162 42N48'27 74w30'26 4:58:02
Brownsville 24 1 40N39'39 73w55'14 4:55:41
Brownsville 35 19 43N00'42 77w22'00 5:09:28
Browntown 51 13 42N01'37 77w03'10 5:08:13
Brownville 23 45 44N00'25 75w59'04 5:03:56
Brownville 56 48 41N47'59 74w22'52 4:57:31
Bruceville 56 11 41N49'53 74w07'19 4:56:29
Brunswick 42 11 42N44'09 73w33'43 4:54:15
Brunswick Center 42 220 42N45'25 73w37'00 4:54:28
Brushton 17 152 44N49'49 74w30'50 4:58:03
Brutus 6 24 43N03 76w32 5:06:08
Bruynswick 56 11 41N39'27 74w13'36 4:56:54
Bryant 31 1 40N46 73w59 4:55:56
Bryants Mill 17 30 44N41'11 74w07'04 4:56:28
Bryn Mawr Park 60 1 40N56'46 73w51'54 4:55:28
Buchanan 60 11 41N15'43 73w56'19 4:55:45
Buckhout Corners 60 1 41N07'59 73w49'09 4:55:17
Buckingham Estates 44 4 41N08 73w56 4:55:44
Buckley Hollow 9 226 42N24'03 75w39'38 5:02:39
Buckleyville 11 10 42N20'45 73w36'19 4:54:25
Bucks Bridge 45 226 44N42'18 75w09'34 5:00:38
Bucks Corner 42 226 42N41'18 73w26'14 4:53:45
Buck Settlement 51 14 42N17'28 77w24'01 5:09:36
Buckton 45 105 44N44'18 74w47'15 4:59:09
Bucyrus Heights 15 11 43N01'48 78w47'57 5:15:12

Buel 29 162 42N50'57 74w39'34 4:58:38
Buellville 34 13 42N59'12 75w57'00 5:03:48
Buena Vista 51 226 42N18'02 77w30'33 5:10:02
Buffalo 15 153 42N53'11 78w52'43 5:15:31
Buffalo Corners 61 226 42N46'41 78w00'29 5:12:02
Bullet Hole 40 17 41N23'25 73w47'23 4:55:10
Bull Hill 22 84 43N15'50 74w54'37 4:59:38
Bull Mine 36 226 41N21'58 74w11'46 4:56:47
Bull Run 56 226 41N54'50 74w26'45 4:57:47
Bulls Head 14 226 41N54'17 73w47'18 4:55:09
Bulls Head 28 209 43N09 77w38 5:10:32
Bulls Head 43 1 40N36'25 74w09'45 4:56:39
Bullville 36 11 41N32'39 74w21'43 4:57:27
Bulsontown 44 6 41N15'37 74w01'01 4:56:04
Bundy Crossing 38 204 43N22'59 76w26'44 5:05:47
Bundys 38 204 43N27 76w30 5:06:00
Bunker 6 13 42N48'22 76w38'49 5:06:35
Burden 11 11 42N09'32 73w49'40 4:55:19
Burden Lake 42 226 42N38 73w33 4:54:12
Burdett 49 14 42N25'12 76w50'57 5:07:24
Burdick Crossing 16 138 43N59'08 73w25'32 4:53:42
Burgoyne 46 226 43N05'23 73w39'47 4:54:39
Burke 17 141 44N54'17 74w10'11 4:56:41
Burke Center 17 141 44N55'08 74w10'48 4:56:43
Burk Hill 61 226 42N46'41 78w01'35 5:12:06
Burlingham 53 11 41N35'24 74w22'57 4:57:32
Burlington 39 226 42N43'22 75w07'33 5:00:30
Burlington Flats 39 226 42N44'43 75w11'00 5:00:44
Burma Woods 37 146 43N10'55 78w15'16 5:13:01
Burnhams 7 173 42N20'08 79w19'24 5:17:18
Burns 2 20 42N25'47 77w43'31 5:10:54
Burnside 36 11 41N27'24 74w12'33 4:56:50
Burns-Whitney Estates 1 1 42N44 73w45 4:55:00
Burnt Hills 46 226 42N54'35 73w53'44 4:55:35
Burnwood 13 226 41N56'48 75w03'39 5:00:15
Burr Mills 23 45 43N55'58 75w51'33 5:03:26
Burrs Mills 23 45 43N59 75w56 5:03:44
Burt 32 11 43N18'59 78w42'51 5:14:51
Burtonsville 29 12 42N48'18 74w15'35 4:57:02
Bush Corner 35 226 42N54'16 77w31'14 5:10:05
Bushes Landing 25 226 43N46'39 75w24'34 5:01:38
Bushnell Basin 28 13 43N03'34 77w28'28 5:09:54
Bushnellsville 56 88 42N09'12 74w24'55 4:57:40
Bush Terminal 24 1 40N39 74w00 4:56:00
Bushville 19 142 43N00'07 78w15'31 5:13:02
Bushville 36 197 41N22'21 74w34'13 4:58:17
Bushville 53 72 41N42'54 74w44'47 4:58:59
Bushwick 24 1 40N41'39 73w55'09 4:55:41
Bushwick Junction 41 1 40N42'55 73w54'31 4:55:38
Buskirk 42 11 42N57'13 73w26'05 4:53:44
Busti 7 226 42N02'17 79w17'01 5:17:08
Butcher Corner 51 226 42N21'01 77w34'39 5:10:19
Butler 59 226 43N11 76w46 5:07:04
Butler Center 59 25 43N10'07 76w46'18 5:07:05
Butlerville 60 16 41N20'57 73w40'22 4:54:41
Butterfield 33 222 43N06 75w15 5:01:00
Butternut Grove 13 80 41N57'26 74w59'27 4:59:58
Butternuts 39 226 42N28 75w20 5:01:20
Butterville 23 12 43N50'33 76w06'16 5:04:25
Butterville 56 11 41N45'40 74w07'09 4:56:29
Button City 9 226 42N43'18 75w19'31 5:01:18
Butts Corner 13 13 42N28'32 74w49'18 4:59:17
Byersville 26 226 42N35'00 77w47'28 5:11:10
Byrdcliffe 56 11 42N03'09 74w08'49 4:56:35
Byron 19 17 43N04'47 78w03'51 5:12:15
Cabinhill 13 226 42N12 74w58 4:59:52
Cadiz 5 226 42N19'14 78w28'03 5:13:52
Cadosia 13 97 41N58'33 75w16'02 5:01:04
Cadyville 10 14 44N41'53 73w37'55 4:54:32
Cagwin Corners 33 13 43N08'59 75w34'33 5:02:18
Cahoonzie 36 1 41N27'00 74w42'45 4:58:51
Cains Corners 38 226 43N18'19 76w35'50 5:06:23
Cairo 20 3 42N17'56 73w59'56 4:56:00
Cairo Junction 20 3 42N15'11 73w58'01 4:55:52
Calcium 23 45 44N01'18 75w50'47 5:03:23
Calcutta 39 14 42N37'58 74w40'36 4:58:42
Caledonia 26 4 42N58'23 77w51'11 5:11:25
Calico Colony 46 11 42N51 73w48 4:55:12
Callanans Corners 1 1 42N28 73w48 4:55:12
Callicoon 53 20 41N46'02 75w03'24 5:00:14
Callicoon Center 53 226 41N50'12 74w56'49 4:59:47
Calverton 52 11 40N54'23 72w44'38 4:50:59
Cambria 31 226 43N12 78w49 5:15:16
Cambria Center 32 226 43N10'40 78w49'11 5:15:17
Cambria Heights 41 1 40N41'40 73w44'20 4:54:57
Cambridge 58 11 43N01'41 73w22'54 4:53:32
Camby 14 226 41N43'33 73w39'52 4:54:39
Camden 33 14 43N20'04 75w44'54 5:03:00
Cameron 51 20 42N11'57 77w24'24 5:09:38
Cameron Mills 51 20 42N10'49 77w21'50 5:09:27
Camillus 34 13 43N02'21 76w18'16 5:05:13
Campbell 27 13 42N48'20 75w37'03 5:02:28
Campbell 51 126 42N13'59 77w11'52 5:08:47
Campbell Hall 36 11 41N27'19 74w15'47 4:57:03
Campbell Hall Junction 36 11 41N27'37 74w15'41 4:57:03
Camp Hemlock 53 11 41N33 74w26 4:57:44
Camp Hill 44 4 41N11'11 74w03'15 4:56:13
Camp Lakeland 15 11 42N40'04 79w03'37 5:16:14
Camp Pioneer 15 11 42N37'59 79w04'52 5:16:19
Camps Mills 23 45 43N56'12 76w04'18 5:04:17
Campville 54 13 42N05'15 76w08'57 5:04:36
Camroden 33 211 43N15'10 75w21'20 5:01:25
Canaan 11 13 42N24'43 73w26'51 4:53:47
Canaan Center 11 11 42N23'11 73w27'20 4:53:49
Canada Lake 18 226 43N10'27 74w30'43 4:58:03
Canadice 35 226 42N44'13 77w32'31 5:10:10
Canajoharie 29 162 42N54'20 74w34'20 4:58:17
Canal Street 31 1 40N43 74w00 4:56:00
Canandaigua 35 14 42N52'07 77w20'09 5:09:21
Canarsie 24 1 40N38'37 73w54'04 4:55:36
Canaseraga 2 20 42N27'41 77w46'38 5:11:07
Canastota 27 92 43N04'46 75w45'04 5:03:00
Canawaugus 26 226 42N55'37 77w46'47 5:11:07
Candor 54 154 42N13'58 76w20'34 5:05:22
Caneadea 2 226 42N23'11 78w09'14 5:12:37
Canisteo 51 100 42N16'13 77w36'22 5:10:25
Canisteo Center 51 100 42N15'56 77w34'45 5:10:19
Cannon Corners 10 198 44N58 73w39 4:54:36
Canoe Place 52 11 40N53'20 72w30'16 4:50:01
Canoga 50 13 42N51'12 76w44'56 5:07:00
Canoga Springs 50 13 42N51'04 76w46'01 5:07:04
Canterbury Hill 33 211 43N15'24 75w24'57 5:01:40
Canton 45 155 44N35'44 75w10'10 5:00:41
Cape Vincent 23 29 44N07'40 76w20'00 5:05:20
Capitol 1 1 42N40 73w47 4:55:08
Capitol Hills 36 226 41N21 74w11 4:56:44
Captain Kidd Estates 52 11 40N59 72w32 4:50:08
Cardiff 34 16 42N53'23 76w08'37 5:04:34
Cards Corners 34 13 42N59'21 76w15'03 5:05:00
Cardtown 39 226 42N38'39 75w14'46 5:00:59
Careys Corners 33 14 43N08'50 75w17'45 5:01:11
Carle Place 30 11 40N45'09 73w36'39 4:54:27
Carle Terrace 56 114 41N59 74w00 4:56:00
Carley Mills 38 14 43N22'43 76w07'18 5:04:29
Carlisle 48 226 42N45'25 74w26'46 4:57:47
Carlisle Center 48 12 42N43'29 74w25'42 4:57:43
Carlisle Gardens 32 190 43N10'45 78w39'22 5:14:37
Carlton 37 146 43N19'40 78w11'28 5:12:46
Carman 47 6 42N46'14 73w56'02 4:55:44
Carmel 40 135 41N25'48 73w40'50 4:54:43
Carmel Hills 40 85 41N24'16 73w40'16 4:54:41
Carmel Park Estates 40 226 41N29'31 73w44'07 4:54:56
Carmen 1 6 42N46 73w56 4:55:44
Carmichael Hill 33 226 43N20'21 75w20'18 5:01:21
Carnegie 15 153 42N44'50 78w50'44 5:15:23
Caroga 18 226 43N08 74w29 4:57:56
Caroga Lake 18 226 43N08'16 74w28'54 4:57:56
Caroline 55 226 42N22'16 76w24'00 5:05:36
Caroline Center 55 226 42N21'07 76w19'08 5:05:17
Caroline Depot 55 226 42N22'12 76w24'14 5:05:37
Carpenters Corners 18 7 43N13'07 74w09'16 4:56:37
Carroll 5 226 42N00'23 78w19'41 5:13:19
Carroll 7 128 42N03 79w06 5:16:24
Carrollton 5 20 42N06'30 78w39'07 5:14:36
Carson 51 226 42N16 77w37 5:10:28
Carterville 38 15 43N20'22 75w53'35 5:03:34
Carthage 23 156 43N58'41 75w36'35 5:02:26
Cascade 6 13 42N45'19 76w28'25 5:05:54
Cascade Valley 4 226 42N00'08 75w34'46 5:02:19
Case 34 16 42N54 76w06 5:04:24
Casowasco 6 13 42N47'00 76w29'39 5:05:59
Cass 15 7 42N53 78w49 5:15:16
Cassadaga 7 173 42N20'39 79w18'35 5:17:14
Cassville 33 13 42N56'45 75w15'17 5:01:01
Castile 61 24 42N37'44 78w03'17 5:12:13
Castle 60 1 40N55 73w47 4:55:08
Castle Creek 4 13 42N13'39 75w55'07 5:03:40
Castle Hill 3 1 40N51 73w52 4:55:28
Castle Point 14 6 41N32'46 73w57'36 4:55:50
Castleton Corners 43 1 40N36'47 74w07'22 4:56:29
Castleton-on-Hudson 1 11 42N31'06 73w45'06 4:55:00
Castorland 25 191 43N53'18 75w30'42 5:02:03
Catatonk 54 205 42N09'25 76w18'28 5:05:14
Catawba 51 181 42N29'44 77w09'37 5:08:38
Cat Elbow Corner 50 226 42N32'39 76w50'56 5:07:24
Catfish Corners 38 182 43N22'12 76w12'26 5:04:50
Catharine 49 226 42N18'46 76w47'06 5:07:08
Cathedral 31 1 40N48 73w58 4:55:52
Catherineville 45 226 44N37'46 74w46'03 4:59:04
Catlin 8 14 42N15 76w55 5:07:40
Catlin Hill 54 226 42N06'17 76w20'17 5:05:21
Cato 6 24 43N10'05 76w34'24 5:06:18
Caton 51 13 42N03'22 77w01'41 5:08:07
Cator Corners 59 226 43N05'38 77w18'08 5:09:13
Catskill 20 1 42N13'02 73w51'54 4:55:28
Cattaraugus 5 20 42N19'45 78w52'06 5:15:28
Cattaraugus Indian Res 5 42 42N29 78w59 5:15:56
Cattown 39 13 42N43'49 75w00'12 5:00:01
Caughdenoy 38 182 43N16'21 76w12'27 5:04:50
Cauterskill 20 1 42N13'12 73w53'30 4:55:34
Cayuga 6 14 42N55'08 76w43'36 5:06:54
Cayuga Heights 55 186 42N27'34 76w29'13 5:05:57
Cayuga Junction 6 13 42N52'11 76w42'19 5:06:49
Cayuta 49 226 42N16'54 76w41'50 5:06:47
Cayutaville 49 226 42N23'23 76w41'51 5:06:47
Caywood 50 226 42N33'55 76w51'51 5:07:27
Cazenovia 27 14 42N55'48 75w51'11 5:03:25
Cecil Park 60 1 40N58'30 73w49'08 4:55:17
Cedar Bluffs 46 226 43N02'21 73w42'49 4:54:51
Cedar Cliff 36 6 41N35'11 73w57'36 4:55:50
Cedarcrest 26 226 42N48'20 77w42'03 5:10:48
Cedar Flats 44 6 41N14'27 74w01'28 4:56:06
Cedar Hill 1 11 42N32'40 73w46'26 4:55:06
Cedarhurst 30 1 40N37'22 73w43'29 4:54:54
Cedar Knolls 60 6 40N56'53 73w50'27 4:55:22
Cedar Lake 22 13 42N57'29 75w10'47 5:00:43
Cedar Manor 41 1 40N41'26 73w47'27 4:55:10
Cedars 45 20 44N29'28 75w38'13 5:02:33
Cedar Swamp 28 20 43N01'33 77w37'50 5:10:31
Cedarvale 34 13 42N57'57 76w14'59 5:05:00
Cedarville 22 226 42N55'50 75w06'47 5:00:27
Cedarville Station 22 226 42N54'10 75w07'16 5:00:29
Celoron 7 187 42N06'34 79w17'00 5:17:08
Cementon 20 11 42N08'06 73w55'30 4:55:42
Centenary 44 4 41N10'40 73w57'58 4:55:52
Center Berlin 42 11 42N39'39 73w22'09 4:53:29
Center Brunswick 42 220 42N43 73w41 4:54:44
Centerbury Hill 33 211 43N13 75w26 5:01:44
Center Cambridge 58 11 42N59'41 73w27'23 4:53:50
Centereach 52 11 40N51'30 73w06'00 4:52:24
Center Falls 58 226 43N05'57 73w27'32 4:53:50
Centerfield 35 14 42N52'53 77w21'33 5:09:26
Center Lisle 4 226 42N21'30 76w03'43 5:04:15
Center Moriches 52 11 40N48'01 72w47'25 4:51:10
Centerport 6 11 43N02'27 76w35'35 5:06:22
Centerport 52 11 40N53'07 73w22'36 4:53:30
Center Valley 39 140 42N45'28 74w41'10 4:58:45
Center Village 4 17 42N10'03 75w36'49 5:02:27
Centerville 2 226 42N28'47 78w15'00 5:13:00
Centerville 13 226 42N00'54 75w07'56 5:00:32
Centerville 38 226 43N32'52 76w02'41 5:04:11
Centerville 52 11 40N58'10 72w41'32 4:50:46
Centerville 56 215 42N05'03 74w00'49 4:56:03
Center White Creek 58 11 42N58'13 73w22'41 4:53:31
Central 41 1 40N42 73w48 4:55:12
Central Bridge 48 12 42N42'40 74w20'21 4:57:21
Centralia 7 67 42N15'31 79w20'53 5:17:24
Central Islip 52 6 40N47'26 73w12'08 4:52:49
Central Nyack 44 1 41N05'38 73w57'02 4:55:48
Central Square 38 182 43N17'12 76w08'47 5:04:35
Central Valley 36 4 41N19'54 74w07'17 4:56:29
Central White Plains 60 1 41N01 73w47 4:55:08
Centre Island 30 11 40N54'06 73w31'13 4:54:05
Centuck 60 1 40N58 73w51 4:55:24
Ceres 2 22 41N59'58 78w16'09 5:13:05
Chace 61 100 42N39'55 78w03'58 5:12:16
Chadwicks 33 14 43N01'40 75w16'19 5:01:05
Chaffee 15 22 42N34'05 78w28'45 5:13:55
Chamberlain Corners 45 226 44N45 75w08 5:00:32
Chambers 8 14 42N15'44 76w57'25 5:07:50
Champion 23 119 43N57'44 75w41'26 5:02:46
Champion Huddle 23 156 43N59 75w37 5:02:28
Champlain 10 157 44N59'11 73w26'49 4:53:47
Champlain Park 10 86 44N43 73w24 4:53:36
Chapel Hill Estates 60 16 41N17 73w46 4:55:04
Chapin 35 14 42N55'07 77w14'06 5:08:56
Chapinville 39 226 42N44'06 75w10'58 5:00:44
Chappaqua 60 1 41N09'34 73w45'55 4:55:04
Charleston 29 12 42N50'45 74w20'30 4:57:22
Charleston 43 1 40N32'12 74w14'16 4:56:57
Charleston Four Corners 29 7 42N48'10 74w23'58 4:57:36
Charlesworth Corners 29 69 42N57'59 74w41'11 4:58:45
Charlotte 7 67 42N18 79w14 5:16:56
Charlotte 28 226 43N15'18 77w37'02 5:10:28
Charlotte Center 7 67 42N18'16 79w14'17 5:16:57
Charlotteville 48 226 42N32'43 74w39'54 4:58:40

Charlton 46 226 42N56'00 73w58'10 4:55:53
Chase 39 13 42N40'07 74w59'27 4:59:58
Chase Lake 25 15 43N43 75w24 5:01:36
Chase Mills 45 226 44N50'56 75w04'52 5:00:19
Chaseville 39 13 42N32'26 74w51'24 4:59:26
Chasm Falls 17 193 44N45'26 74w13'09 4:56:53
Chateaugay 17 188 44N55'35 74w04'48 4:56:19
Chateaugay 38 226 43N34'26 75w57'45 5:03:51
Chatfield Corner 46 226 43N06'29 73w56'35 4:55:46
Chatham 11 10 42N21'51 73w35'43 4:54:23
Chatham Center 11 11 42N25'05 73w36'52 4:54:27
Chaumont 23 226 44N04'01 76w07'50 5:04:31
Chauncey 60 7 41N00'09 73w51'25 4:55:26
Chautauqua 7 158 42N12'35 79w28'01 5:17:52
Chazy 10 7 44N53'23 73w26'11 4:53:45
Chazy Lake 10 7 44N54 73w48 4:55:12
Chazy Landing 10 7 44N53'14 73w22'43 4:53:31
Chedwel 7 158 42N12'59 79w26'08 5:17:45
Cheektowaga 15 7 42N54 78w45 5:15:00
Chelsea 14 6 41N33'13 73w58'02 4:55:52
Chelsea 43 1 40N36'02 74w11'43 4:56:47
Chemung 8 224 42N00'30 76w37'27 5:06:30
Chenango 4 13 42N12 75w53 5:03:32
Chenango Bridge 4 13 42N10'00 75w51'46 5:03:27
Chenango Forks 4 13 42N14'08 75w50'55 5:03:24
Chenango Lake 9 16 42N35'06 75w26'08 5:01:45
Cheneys Point 7 226 42N06 79w23 5:17:32
Cheningo 12 16 42N39'35 75w59'56 5:04:00
Chepachet 22 226 42N54'39 75w07'17 5:00:29
Cherokee 31 1 40N47 73w58 4:55:52
Cherry Creek 7 107 42N17'40 79w06'00 5:16:24
Cherry Grove 52 11 40N39'32 73w05'22 4:52:21
Cherry Hill 7 20 42N00'39 79w24'42 5:17:39
Cherryplain 42 11 42N37'46 73w21'39 4:53:27
Cherrytown 56 72 41N49'30 74w19'47 4:57:19
Cherry Valley 39 140 42N47'44 74w45'13 4:59:01
Cherry Valley Junction 48 139 42N41 74w29 4:57:56
Cherrywood Shopping Center 30 11 41N04 73w30 4:54:00
Cheshire 35 14 42N49'17 77w19'40 5:09:19
Chester 36 4 41N21'45 74w16'18 4:57:05
Chesterfield 16 226 44N29 73w28 4:53:52
Chester Hill Park 60 1 40N55'24 73w49'22 4:55:17
Chestertown 57 159 43N39'09 73w48'05 4:55:12
Chestnut Hill 34 13 43N07 76w12 5:04:48
Chestnut Ridge 14 11 41N43'51 73w37'48 4:54:31
Chestnut Ridge 32 226 43N09 78w35 5:14:20
Cheviot 11 11 42N07'30 73w54'15 4:55:37
Chichester 56 52 42N06'06 74w18'35 4:57:14
Childs 37 146 43N17'12 78w11'31 5:12:46
Childwold 45 87 44N17'11 74w39'49 4:58:39
Chili 28 15 43N06 77w44 5:10:56
Chili Center 28 15 43N06'26 77w44'45 5:10:59
Chiloway 13 80 41N58'02 75w02'38 5:00:11
Chilson 16 226 43N52'38 73w31'45 4:54:07
Chimney Corners 60 6 41N13'47 73w54'31 4:55:38
China 13 167 42N08'41 75w24'02 5:01:36
Chinatown 31 1 40N42'59 73w59'48 4:55:59
Chipman 45 226 44N46'52 75w11'47 5:00:47
Chipman Corners 6 13 42N37'58 76w22'32 5:05:30
Chipmunk 5 226 42N03'25 78w34'32 5:14:18
Chippewa Bay 45 20 44N26'31 75w45'26 5:03:02
Chittenango 27 226 43N02'42 75w52'01 5:03:28
Chittenango Falls 27 14 42N58'42 75w50'14 5:03:21
Chittenango Springs 27 14 43N01'03 75w51'05 5:03:24
Choconut Center 4 151 42N08'34 75w56'38 5:03:47
Christian Hill 55 13 42N28'43 76w40'21 5:06:41
Christian Hill 57 226 43N44'14 74w04'45 4:56:19
Chuckery Corners 33 11 43N01'56 75w19'46 5:01:19
Church Corners 29 1 42N58'44 74w16'54 4:57:08
Church Street 31 1 40N43 74w00 4:56:00
Churchtown 11 11 42N10'34 73w43'09 4:54:53
Churchville 28 161 43N06'15 77w53'05 5:11:32
Churchville 33 211 43N11'23 75w34'36 5:02:18
Churchville Greene 28 161 43N06 77w53 5:11:32
Churubusco 10 4 44N57'14 73w55'55 4:55:44
Cicero 34 41 43N10'32 76w07'11 5:04:29
Cicero Center 34 14 43N10'44 76w02'28 5:04:10
Cincinnatus 12 226 42N32'32 75w53'46 5:03:35
Circleville 36 11 41N30'51 74w23'02 4:57:32
City Island 3 1 40N50'50 73w47'13 4:55:09
Clairemont Farms 34 13 43N07 76w12 5:04:48
Clare 45 226 44N24'05 75w03'46 5:00:15
Claremont Park 3 1 40N51 73w54 4:55:36
Clarence 15 11 42N58'36 78w35'32 5:14:22
Clarence Center 15 226 43N00'38 78w38'16 5:14:33
Clarendon 37 226 43N11'36 78w03'54 5:12:16
Clark 7 226 42N07'28 79w05'55 5:16:24
Clark Corners 25 156 43N53'01 75w39'40 5:02:39
Clark Corners 38 204 43N26'15 76w25'35 5:05:42
Clark Heights 14 11 41N43'54 73w50'37 4:55:22
Clark Mills 33 11 43N05'32 75w22'48 5:01:31
Clark Point 23 65 43N49'31 76w16'10 5:05:05
Clarksburg 15 153 42N37'11 78w49'54 5:15:20
Clarks Corner 46 226 43N13'17 73w38'31 4:54:34
Clarks Corners 7 226 42N10 79w06 5:16:24
Clarks Mill 58 226 43N07'05 73w34'09 4:54:17
Clarkson 28 226 43N13'59 77w55'40 5:11:43
Clarkstown 44 4 41N06 73w56 4:55:44
Clarksville 1 11 42N34'33 73w57'52 4:55:51
Clarksville 2 226 42N08 78w15 5:13:00
Clarkville 46 7 43N14'36 74w07'24 4:56:30
Claryville 53 226 41N55'06 74w34'22 4:58:17
Clason Point 3 1 40N48'20 73w57'00 4:55:48
Classon 24 1 40N41 73w58 4:55:52
Claverack 11 11 42N13'30 73w44'06 4:54:56
Clay 34 13 43N11'09 76w10'22 5:04:41
Clayburg 10 136 44N35'47 73w50'19 4:55:21
Clayton 23 163 44N14'22 76w05'10 5:04:21
Clayton Center 23 163 44N11'30 76w02'33 5:04:10
Clayville 33 13 42N58'48 75w15'05 5:01:00
Clear Creek 7 20 42N13'15 79w03'38 5:16:15
Clearfield 15 7 42N59 78w45 5:15:00
Clear, Lake 17 176 44N22'03 74w13'59 4:56:56
Cleaver 13 226 42N10'50 75w14'09 5:00:57
Clemons 58 6 43N38'11 73w26'45 4:53:47
Clermont 11 226 42N05'06 73w49'39 4:55:19
Cleveland 38 15 43N14'25 75w53'03 5:03:32
Cleveland Hill 15 7 42N56'41 78w47'04 5:15:08
Cleverdale 57 226 43N28'38 73w38'35 4:54:34
Cliff Haven 10 86 44N39'31 73w26'29 4:53:46
Clifford 38 226 43N22'54 76w17'08 5:05:09
Cliffside 39 13 42N30'50 74w58'58 4:59:56
Clifton 28 226 43N03'08 77w48'54 5:11:16
Clifton 43 1 40N37'12 74w04'39 4:56:19
Clifton 45 25 44N11 74w56 4:59:44
Clifton Gardens 46 11 42N51 73w48 4:55:12
Clifton Heights 15 153 42N44'09 78w55'01 5:15:40
Clifton Knolls 46 11 42N51 73w48 4:55:12
Clifton Park 46 11 42N52 73w44 4:54:56
Clifton Park Center 46 11 42N51'30 73w49'15 4:55:17
Clifton Springs 35 14 42N57'42 77w08'25 5:08:34
Climax 20 11 42N21'57 73w51'05 4:55:24
Clinton 33 11 43N02'54 75w22'44 5:01:31
Clinton Corners 14 226 41N49'48 73w45'46 4:55:03
Clintondale 56 11 41N41'41 74w03'06 4:56:12
Clintondale Station 56 11 41N42'59 74w03'35 4:56:14
Clinton Heights 42 1 42N37'08 73w44'04 4:54:56
Clinton Hollow 14 226 41N50'42 73w48'59 4:55:16
Clinton Mills 10 4 44N57'38 73w52'50 4:55:31
Clinton Park 10 86 44N42 73w26 4:53:44
Clinton Park 42 1 42N37'27 73w43'44 4:54:55
Clintonville 10 226 44N27'56 73w34'59 4:54:20
Clintonville 34 13 42N55'56 76w20'59 5:05:24
Clintonville 39 13 42N36'51 74w57'31 4:59:50
Clint-Wood Center 28 13 43N09 77w33 5:10:12
Clockville 27 226 43N02'30 75w44'42 5:02:59
Clough Corners 4 226 42N20 75w58 5:03:52
Clove 14 226 41N40'15 73w40'31 4:54:42
Clove 48 139 42N40'56 74w34'57 4:58:20
Clover Bank 15 153 42N44'50 78w53'24 5:15:34
Clove Valley 14 226 41N38'07 73w41'20 4:54:45
Clums Corner 42 11 42N45'02 73w34'21 4:54:17
Cluny Point 26 20 42N49'30 77w42'35 5:10:50
Clyde 59 99 43N05'03 76w52'11 5:07:29
Clymer 7 22 42N01'15 79w37'49 5:18:31
Clymer Center 7 22 42N03'12 79w34'41 5:18:19
Clymer Hill 7 22 42N03'39 79w36'55 5:18:28
Cobb 52 11 40N54'04 72w21'20 4:49:25
Cobbtown 23 143 43N43'32 76w02'39 5:04:11
Cobleskill 48 139 42N40'40 74w29'09 4:57:57
Cochecton 53 20 41N42'21 75w03'39 5:00:15
Cochecton Center 53 226 41N39'17 74w58'59 4:59:56
Coeymans 1 1 42N28'26 73w47'34 4:55:10
Coeymans Hollow 1 1 42N28'18 73w53'42 4:55:35
Coffins Mills 45 25 44N10'20 75w05'08 5:00:21
Cohocton 51 14 42N30'08 77w30'27 5:10:02
Cohoes 1 1 42N46'27 73w42'02 4:54:48
Coila 58 11 43N02'09 73w24'05 4:53:36
Cokertown 14 7 42N01'09 73w49'18 4:55:17
Colburns 7 226 42N08'20 79w21'36 5:17:26
Colchester 13 226 42N09'37 75w04'40 5:00:19
Coldbrook 15 1 43N01 78w57 5:15:48
Cold Brook 22 84 43N14'30 75w02'21 5:00:09
Coldbrook 47 6 42N46'43 73w56'39 4:55:47
Cold Brook 56 37 42N00'47 74w16'13 4:57:05
Cold Brook Estates 1 6 42N46 73w56 4:55:44
Colden 15 226 42N38'39 78w41'06 5:14:44
Coldenham 36 11 41N31'32 74w09'12 4:56:37
Colden Hill 36 1 41N31 74w07 4:56:28
Cold Spring 5 20 42N05'49 78w51'54 5:15:28
Cold Spring 6 13 42N56'59 76w34'39 5:06:19
Cold Spring 40 6 41N25'12 73w57'18 4:55:49
Cold Spring Harbor 52 1 40N52'17 73w27'26 4:53:50
Cold Spring Park 16 54 43N59'54 73w28'31 4:53:54
Cold Springs 34 226 43N07'58 76w15'26 5:05:02
Cold Springs 50 226 42N36'20 76w40'37 5:06:42
Cold Springs 51 14 42N22'28 77w16'58 5:09:08
Cold Spring Terrace 52 11 40N51 73w23 4:53:32
Coldwater 28 209 43N08'09 77w44'08 5:10:57
Colegrave 15 22 42N44'10 78w33'18 5:14:13
Colemans Mills 33 222 43N07'46 75w20'47 5:01:23
Coleman Station 14 11 41N54'06 73w31'08 4:54:05
Colesville 4 17 42N10 75w40 5:02:40
Colgate 27 180 42N49 75w33 5:02:12
Collabar 36 11 41N32'03 74w19'02 4:57:16
Collamer 28 13 43N17'50 77w48'48 5:11:15
Collamer 34 41 43N06'17 76w03'38 5:04:15
College 31 1 40N49 73w57 4:55:48
College Park 14 7 42N01'09 73w52'55 4:55:32
College Point 41 1 40N47'15 73w50'47 4:55:23
Colliersville 39 226 42N29'27 74w58'57 4:59:56
Collingwood 34 16 42N52'03 76w05'00 5:04:20
Collingwood Estates 32 226 43N13'44 79w02'54 5:16:12
Collins 15 42 42N29'47 78w55'15 5:15:41
Collins Center 15 42 42N29'37 78w51'06 5:15:24
Collins Landing 23 17 44N18'01 75w58'51 5:03:55
Collinsville 25 77 43N36'37 75w23'04 5:01:32
Colonial Acres 1 11 42N36 73w46 4:55:04
Colonial Acres 60 1 40N58'31 73w45'37 4:55:02
Colonial Heights 14 1 41N42'50 73w51'31 4:55:26
Colonial Heights 60 1 40N57'35 73w50'30 4:55:22
Colonial Park 31 1 40N50 73w56 4:55:44
Colonial Park 33 211 43N13'15 75w26'10 5:01:45
Colonial Springs 52 11 40N45 73w22 4:53:28
Colonial Village 32 199 43N08'06 78w57'58 5:15:52
Colonie 1 1 42N43'04 73w50'02 4:55:20
Colosse 38 14 43N25'13 76w09'33 5:04:38
Colton 45 226 44N33'11 74w56'24 4:59:46
Columbia 22 78 42N56 75w02 5:00:08
Columbia Center 22 78 42N55'57 75w02'15 5:00:09
Columbia University 31 1 40N48 73w58 4:55:52
Columbiaville 11 11 42N19'06 73w45'13 4:55:01
Columbus 9 226 42N41'02 75w22'23 5:01:30
Columbus Circle 31 1 40N48 74w06 4:56:24
Columbus Quarter 9 16 42N42'37 75w19'04 5:01:16
Colvin 34 13 43N01 76w09 5:04:36
Commack 52 11 40N50'34 73w17'36 4:53:10
Como 6 13 42N40'24 76w16'38 5:05:07
Comstock 58 123 43N27'26 73w26'31 4:53:46
Comstock Corners 32 1 43N08'41 78w46'57 5:15:08
Comstock Tract 34 226 43N09 76w20 5:05:20
Concord 15 218 42N32'07 78w43'52 5:14:55
Concord 43 1 40N36'29 74w05'05 4:56:20
Conesus 26 20 42N43'08 77w40'36 5:10:42
Conesus Lake Junction 26 20 42N51'20 77w42'21 5:10:49
Conesville 48 226 42N23'14 74w22'36 4:57:30
Conewango 5 20 42N14'19 79w01'53 5:16:08
Conewango Valley 7 20 42N14'27 79w03'40 5:16:15
Coney Island 24 1 40N34'40 73w59'40 4:55:59
Coney Island 45 207 44N36'22 74w58'19 4:59:53
Conger Corners 33 13 42N55'10 75w24'41 5:01:39
Congers 44 7 41N09'02 73w56'45 4:55:47
Conifer 45 221 44N13'00 74w36'48 4:58:27
Conklin 4 226 42N02'03 75w48'15 5:03:13
Conklin Center 4 226 42N03'22 75w48'26 5:03:14
Conklin Cove 6 13 42N50'32 76w30'19 5:06:01
Conklin Forks 4 151 42N01'25 75w51'25 5:03:26
Conklingville 46 40 43N18'56 73w56'07 4:55:44
Conklin Station 4 226 42N01'21 75w47'51 5:03:11
Connelly 56 11 41N54'36 73w59'30 4:55:58
Connelly Park 7 226 42N08'35 79w23'56 5:17:36
Conquest 6 226 43N07'16 76w38'54 5:06:36
Constable 17 193 44N55'45 74w17'51 4:57:11
Constableville 25 77 43N34'00 75w25'44 5:01:43
Constantia 38 226 43N14'52 76w00'02 5:04:00

Constantia Center 38 15 43N16'50 75w55'20 5:03:41
Continental Village 40 11 41N20'24 73w54'15 4:55:37
Converse 45 226 44N40'49 74w49'30 4:59:18
Cook Corners 7 226 42N28'38 79w15'29 5:17:02
Cook Corners 29 162 42N55'45 74w33'08 4:58:13
Cook Corners 45 226 44N14'31 74w53'07 4:59:32
Cooksburg 1 226 42N25'14 74w12'20 4:56:49
Cooks Falls 13 226 41N56'52 74w58'51 4:59:55
Cooks Mill 17 188 44N57'46 74w07'52 4:56:31
Cookville 19 164 43N00'35 78w19'37 5:13:18
Cooley 53 75 41N52'18 74w42'34 4:58:50
Coolidge Beach 32 226 43N18'21 78w52'03 5:15:28
Cooney Crossing 59 89 43N05'09 77w14'21 5:08:57
Coonrod 33 211 43N14'54 75w31'25 5:02:06
Coons 46 11 42N55'07 73w44'47 4:54:59
Cooper 31 1 40N44 73w59 4:55:56
Coopers Corners 53 197 41N40'17 74w45'05 4:59:00
Coopers Falls 45 226 44N31'04 75w20'19 5:01:21
Coopers Plains 51 13 42N10'56 77w08'31 5:08:34
Cooperstown 39 13 42N42'02 74w55'29 4:59:42
Cooperstown Junction 39 13 42N29'30 74w57'27 4:59:50
Coopersville 17 157 44N56'35 73w24'30 4:53:38
Coopersville 26 226 42N36'13 77w54'42 5:11:39
Copake 11 11 42N06'12 73w33'02 4:54:12
Copake Falls 11 11 42N07'10 73w31'32 4:54:06
Copake Lake 11 11 42N11 73w35 4:54:20
Copenhagen 25 156 43N53'36 75w40'26 5:02:42
Copes Corner 39 226 42N26'21 75w20'53 5:01:24
Copiague 52 11 40N40'53 73w24'01 4:53:36
Coram 52 11 40N52'07 73w00'07 4:52:00
Corbett 13 226 42N02'36 75w01'20 5:00:05
Corbettsville 4 226 42N00'56 75w47'27 5:03:10
Corbin Corner 9 226 42N26'49 75w43'32 5:02:54
Cordova 7 14 42N26'57 79w21'16 5:17:25
Coreys 17 221 44N24'52 74w19'00 4:57:16
Corfu 19 164 42N57'36 78w24'21 5:13:37
Corinth 46 7 43N14'40 73w49'58 4:55:20
Cork 18 43 43N02'41 74w27'40 4:57:51
Corners 55 186 42N28 76w29 5:05:56
Corning 51 13 42N08'34 77w03'18 5:08:13
Corning Manor 51 13 42N07'15 77w00'20 5:08:01
Cornwall 36 165 41N26'41 74w00'58 4:56:04
Cornwall Landing 36 165 41N26'36 74w00'03 4:56:00
Cornwall on the Hudson 36 165 41N27 74w01 4:56:04
Cornwallville 20 226 42N22'05 74w09'31 4:56:38
Corona 41 1 40N44'49 73w51'38 4:55:27
Corrado Corners 22 150 43N01'52 75w04'38 5:00:19
Cortland 12 41 42N36'04 76w10'51 5:04:43
Cortlandt 60 6 41N17 73w54 4:55:36
Cortlandville 12 41 42N36 76w10 5:04:40
Corwin 32 190 43N15'09 78w41'37 5:14:46
Cosmos Heights 12 41 42N35 76w12 5:04:48
Cossayuna 58 213 43N11'01 73w25'38 4:53:43
Coss Corners 51 14 42N16'53 77w21'57 5:09:28
Coteys Corner 45 16 44N46'34 74w40'24 4:58:42
Cottage 5 217 42N25'26 79w02'40 5:16:11
Cottage City 35 14 42N48'40 77w15'35 5:09:02
Cottage Park 7 20 42N14'12 79w29'36 5:17:58
Cottekill 56 11 41N51'05 74w06'09 4:56:25
Cottons 27 226 43N02'30 75w46'56 5:03:08
Cottonwood Cove 26 226 42N45'37 77w43'37 5:10:54
Cottonwood Point 26 226 42N45'02 77w43'36 5:10:54
Country Knolls 46 11 42N55 73w49 4:55:16
Country Life Press 30 11 40N44 73w39 4:54:36
Country Ridge Estates 60 1 41N00 73w40 4:54:40
County Line 32 15 43N20'47 78w27'58 5:13:52
Couse 42 1 42N37'10 73w42'09 4:54:49
Covel Corner 35 226 42N44'58 77w21'49 5:09:27
Cove Neck 30 11 40N52'56 73w30'23 4:54:02
Coventry 9 33 42N18'57 75w38'20 5:02:33
Coventryville 9 149 42N18'48 75w35'55 5:02:24
Covert 50 226 42N34'31 76w41'02 5:06:44
Coveville 46 226 43N03'37 73w35'45 4:54:23
Coveytown Corners 17 141 44N54 74w10 4:56:40
Covington 61 226 42N51'12 78w00'38 5:12:03
Cowan Corner 23 156 44N03'17 75w33'01 5:02:12
Cowdens Corner 7 14 42N24'33 79w16'34 5:17:06
Cowles Settlement 12 226 42N47'17 75w55'34 5:03:42
Cowlesville 61 38 42N50'36 78w28'09 5:13:53
Coxsackie 20 11 42N21'03 73w48'12 4:55:13
Crab Meadow 52 11 40N55'30 73w19'57 4:53:20
Crafts 40 226 41N23'32 73w41'53 4:54:48
Cragsmoor 56 48 41N40'24 74w23'09 4:57:33
Craigie Clair 53 75 41N57'51 74w52'00 4:59:28
Craigs 26 226 42N51'39 77w55'19 5:11:41
Craigsville 36 226 41N21 74w16 4:57:04
Craigville 36 4 41N23'09 74w14'21 4:56:57
Crains Mills 12 16 42N42'34 76w00'21 5:04:01
Cranberry Creek 18 226 43N09'20 74w13'12 4:56:53
Cranberry Lake 45 226 44N13'21 74w50'12 4:59:21
Crandall Corners 58 11 42N57'18 73w34'19 4:54:17
Cranes Corners 22 184 42N59'08 75w07'27 5:00:30
Cranesville 29 1 42N55'02 74w08'07 4:56:32
Cranford 3 1 40N54 73w52 4:55:28
Crary Mills 45 155 44N34'39 75w04'02 5:00:16
Craryville 11 11 42N10'29 73w35'00 4:54:20
Craterclub 16 129 44N17'13 73w21'02 4:53:24
Crawford 56 11 41N39'20 74w19'43 4:57:19
Creek Beach, The 52 11 41N00'34 72w10'54 4:48:44
Creeklocks 56 11 41N52'14 74w02'40 4:56:11
Creekside 15 11 42N41'30 78w46'59 5:15:08
Crescent 46 11 42N49'27 73w44'00 4:54:56
Crescent Beach 28 226 43N17'01 77w39'46 5:10:39
Crescent Beach 43 1 40N38 74w06 4:56:24
Crescent Park 29 226 42N57'38 74w09'43 4:56:39
Crescent Station 1 11 42N47'54 73w44'03 4:54:56
Crestview 5 226 42N05'50 78w29'14 5:13:57
Crest View Heights 54 13 42N04'18 76w07'03 5:04:28
Crestwood 60 1 40N57'36 73w49'29 4:55:18
Crestwood Gardens 60 1 40N58'05 73w49'15 4:55:17
Cribbs Corner 38 226 43N22'38 76w16'12 5:05:05
Crittenden 15 38 42N56'46 78w29'06 5:13:56
Crittenden 28 226 43N06'13 77w38'28 5:10:34
Crocketts 6 226 43N19'38 76w37'40 5:06:31
Crofts Corners 40 6 41N21'53 73w52'03 4:55:28
Croghan 25 226 43N53'45 75w23'34 5:01:34
Crompond 60 6 41N17'42 73w51'57 4:55:28
Cronomer Valley 36 1 41N33'10 74w03'49 4:56:15
Cropseyville 42 11 42N44'56 73w33'28 4:54:14
Crosby 62 14 42N32'55 77w05'49 5:08:23
Crosbyside 57 1 43N25'05 73w41'49 4:54:47
Cross River 60 16 41N15'44 73w36'54 4:54:28
Cross Roads 6 13 42N52'40 76w41'01 5:06:44
Cross Roads Estates 60 16 41N17 73w46 4:55:04
Croton 49 14 42N16 76w51 5:07:24
Crotona Park 3 1 40N50 73w52 4:55:28
Croton Falls 60 133 41N20'50 73w39'41 4:54:39
Croton Heights 60 166 41N14'48 73w47'02 4:55:08
Croton-on-Hudson 60 166 41N12'30 73w53'30 4:55:34
Crotonville 60 166 41N11'15 73w52'14 4:55:29
Crowningshield 16 56 44N19'14 73w30'49 4:54:03
Crown Point 16 138 43N57'01 73w26'15 4:53:45
Crown Point Center 16 138 43N56'30 73w28'10 4:53:53
Crown Village 30 11 40N51 73w27 4:53:48
Crugers 60 6 41N14'00 73w55'23 4:55:42
Crum Creek 18 226 43N02'22 74w42'51 4:58:51
Crum Town 54 154 42N15'19 76w26'42 5:05:47
Crystal Beach 35 14 42N48'49 77w15'50 5:09:03
Crystal Brook 52 11 40N56'52 73w02'33 4:52:10
Crystal Dale 25 226 43N49'17 75w20'00 5:01:20
Crystal Lake 1 226 42N31 74w08 4:56:32
Crystal Lake 5 226 42N26 78w22 5:13:28
Crystal Run 36 1 41N27'34 74w20'28 4:57:22
Crystal Spring 62 13 42N29'16 77w03'08 5:08:13
Cuba 2 20 42N13'03 78w16'32 5:13:06
Cuddebackville 36 21 41N28'02 74w35'39 4:58:23
Cullen 22 78 42N52'56 74w57'45 4:59:51
Culvertown 53 11 41N33'27 74w33'26 4:58:14
Cummings Crossing 12 91 42N46'26 76w07'11 5:04:29
Cummingsville 26 13 42N34'17 77w43'12 5:10:53
Curriers 61 147 42N37'14 78w25'04 5:13:40
Curry 53 74 41N51'30 74w34'54 4:58:20
Currytown 29 7 42N51'29 74w27'52 4:57:51
Curtis 22 214 43N10'23 74w48'41 4:59:15
Curtis 51 226 42N12'26 77w10'12 5:08:41
Curtis Corner 35 47 42N47'22 77w32'35 5:10:10
Cutchogue 52 11 41N00'38 72w29'08 4:49:57
Cutchogue Station 52 11 41N01'17 72w29'54 4:50:00
Cutting 7 226 42N01'27 79w41'46 5:18:47
Cuyler 12 226 42N44'14 75w56'56 5:03:48
Cuylerville 26 13 42N46'37 77w52'16 5:11:29
Cypress Hills 24 1 40N41 73w52 4:55:28
Dadville 25 226 43N48'24 75w28'30 5:01:54
Dahlia 53 75 41N54 74w50 4:59:20
Dairyland 56 48 41N44'49 74w32'16 4:58:09
Daisy 56 11 42N03'21 74w05'17 4:56:21
Dale 61 20 42N49'09 78w10'23 5:12:42
Dalton 26 20 42N32'27 77w57'10 5:11:49
Dalton Crossing 45 226 44N51'13 75w07'21 5:00:29
Damascus 4 226 42N03'21 75w36'38 5:02:27
Dams Corner 33 13 43N07'53 75w34'48 5:02:19
Danby 55 226 42N21'08 76w28'52 5:05:55
Danielstown 57 226 43N15'32 73w47'06 4:55:08
Danley Corners 61 148 42N50'51 78w19'20 5:13:17
Dann Corner 28 226 42N56'49 77w36'48 5:10:27
Dannemora 10 136 44N43'17 73w43'27 4:54:54
Dannemora Crossing 10 20 44N53'43 73w47'28 4:55:10
Dansville 26 13 42N33'39 77w41'47 5:10:47
Danube 22 226 42N59 74w48 4:59:12
Danville 4 167 42N00'32 75w28'45 5:01:55
Darien 19 164 42N54'07 78w21'02 5:13:24
Darien Center 19 164 42N54'04 78w23'20 5:13:33
Darrowsville 57 159 43N36'31 73w48'09 4:55:13
Dashville 56 11 41N49'15 74w02'43 4:56:11
Davenport 13 13 42N28'18 74w50'42 4:59:23
Davenport Center 13 29 42N26'53 74w55'10 4:59:41
Davidson Beach 28 13 43N20'25 77w46'16 5:11:05
Davis Corners 56 37 41N55'04 74w12'38 4:56:51
Davis Crossing 9 226 42N33'45 75w21'28 5:01:26
Davis Park 52 11 40N41'02 73w00'19 4:52:01
Daws 19 142 43N02'40 78w11'33 5:12:46
Day 46 226 43N19 74w00 4:56:00
Day Center 46 226 43N18'32 74w01'01 4:56:04
Days Corners 22 226 42N58'58 75w11'20 5:00:45
Days Rock 22 196 42N58'13 74w57'41 4:59:51
Daysville 38 226 43N31'43 76w10'58 5:04:44
Daysville Corner 38 226 43N32'30 76w11'37 5:04:46
Dayton 5 42 42N25'01 78w58'38 5:15:55
Daytonville 33 13 42N58'38 75w20'36 5:01:22
Dean 7 158 42N19'23 79w26'05 5:17:44
Deansboro 33 11 42N59'42 75w25'44 5:01:43
Deans Corner 40 85 41N22'35 73w38'06 4:54:32
Deans Corners 46 226 43N02'56 73w40'40 4:54:43
Deans Mill 20 1 42N27'00 73w49'53 4:55:20
Debruce 53 75 41N54'49 74w43'39 4:58:55
Decatur 39 226 42N38'39 74w43'32 4:58:54
Deck 22 196 42N57'01 74w52'50 4:59:31
Deckertown 49 14 42N20'37 76w49'56 5:07:20
Deckertown 53 75 41N55'30 74w49'59 4:59:20
Deerfield 33 11 43N07'10 75w13'09 5:00:53
Deerfield 52 11 40N56'09 72w21'54 4:49:28
Deerfield Heights 33 11 43N07'46 75w12'52 5:00:51
Deerhead 16 50 44N21'08 73w32'37 4:54:10
Deerland 21 226 43N56'19 74w27'39 4:57:51
Deer Park 52 11 40N45'42 73w19'47 4:53:19
Deer River 25 156 43N55'47 75w35'22 5:02:21
Deferiet 23 119 44N02'08 75w41'03 5:02:44
Deforest Corners 40 226 41N26'43 73w33'00 4:54:12
Defreestville 42 1 42N39'12 73w41'47 4:54:47
Degrasse 45 226 44N20'59 75w04'34 5:00:18
Degroff 6 12 42N53'01 76w29'58 5:06:00
De Kalb 45 226 44N29'56 75w20'35 5:01:22
DeKalb Junction 45 226 44N30'18 75w16'27 5:01:06
De Lancey 13 226 42N12'20 74w58'16 4:59:53
Delanson 47 98 42N44'43 74w11'19 4:56:45
Delaware 1 1 42N39 73w47 4:55:08
Delaware 53 226 41N46 75w00 5:00:00
Delevan 5 108 42N29'21 78w28'52 5:13:55
Delhi 13 226 42N16'41 74w54'59 4:59:40
Dellwood 15 38 42N55'00 78w34'43 5:14:19
Delmar 1 11 42N37'19 73w49'59 4:55:20
Delphi Falls 34 226 42N52'35 75w54'50 5:03:39
Delray 15 153 42N51 78w46 5:15:04
Dempster Beach 38 204 43N27 76w30 5:06:00
Dempster Corners 18 226 43N05'21 74w34'54 4:58:20
Demster 38 204 43N29'46 76w19'02 5:05:16
Demster Beach 38 204 43N30'51 76w18'33 5:05:14
Denault Corners 42 226 42N36'02 73w31'03 4:54:04
Denison Corner 35 47 42N50'09 77w34'23 5:10:18
Denmark 25 15 43N53'59 75w34'58 5:02:20
Denmark 51 13 42N09'25 77w03'12 5:08:13
Dennies Crossing 18 226 43N04'25 74w18'36 4:57:14
Dennies Hollow 18 226 43N07'39 74w15'08 4:57:01
Denning 56 226 41N57'03 74w29'22 4:57:57
Dennison Corners 7 216 42N29'37 79w08'59 5:16:36
Dennison Corners 22 196 42N57'39 75w00'54 5:00:04
Denniston 36 1 41N27'36 74w06'22 4:56:25
Dennytown 40 6 41N25'35 73w52'07 4:55:28
Denton 36 7 41N24'17 74w24'15 4:57:37
Denton Hills 52 11 40N53 73w22 4:53:28
Denver 13 42 42N12'45 74w34'11 4:58:17
Depauville 23 226 44N08'18 76w03'57 5:04:16
Depew 15 7 42N54'14 78w41'33 5:14:46
De Peyster 45 226 44N33'09 75w26'09 5:01:45
Deposit 4 167 42N03'36 75w25'41 5:01:43
Derby 15 11 42N40'53 78w58'32 5:15:54
Derbys Corners 45 226 44N24'30 75w09'10 5:00:37

Dering Harbor 52 11 41N05'34 72w20'50 4:49:23
Derrick 17 221 44N22'00 74w28'48 4:57:55
De Ruyter 27 226 42N45'30 75w53'05 5:03:32
Desbrough Park 59 33 43N18'09 76w49'53 5:07:20
Deuels Corners 15 11 42N47 78w45 5:15:00
Devereaux 5 226 42N20'01 78w33'55 5:14:16
Devon 52 11 40N59'29 72w06'27 4:48:26
Dewey 28 209 43N11 77w39 5:10:36
Dewey Bridge 58 123 43N25 73w29 4:53:56
DeWitt 34 13 43N02'06 76w03'57 5:04:16
DeWitt Mills 14 219 41N51'20 73w53'00 4:55:32
Dewittville 7 158 42N14'21 79w26'44 5:17:47
Dexter 23 49 44N00'28 76w02'41 5:04:11
Dexterville 38 226 43N19'24 76w30'04 5:06:00
Diamond Hill 22 61 43N03 74w51 4:59:24
Diamond Point 57 226 43N28'45 73w41'15 4:54:45
Diana 25 226 43N36 75w41 5:02:44
Diana Center 25 226 44N04'32 75w26'28 5:01:46
Dibble Corner 9 226 42N25'43 75w42'43 5:02:51
Dibbletown 33 211 43N16'49 75w42'38 5:02:51
Dickersonville 32 226 43N11'26 78w55'50 5:15:43
Dickinson 17 226 44N44'54 74w33'54 4:58:16
Dickinson Center 17 226 44N43'03 74w33'11 4:58:13
Dick-Urban 15 7 42N55 78w42 5:14:48
Diddell 14 6 41N37'24 73w51'09 4:55:25
Dillen 23 226 43N53'17 75w56'57 5:03:48
Dimmick Corners 46 226 43N12 73w39 4:54:36
Dineharts 51 14 42N26'56 77w18'49 5:09:15
Dishaw 45 226 44N50'19 75w02'26 5:00:10
Ditch Plains 52 11 41N02'26 71w55'06 4:47:40
Divine Corners 53 74 41N47'25 74w39'58 4:58:40
Divinity Hill 52 11 40N56'47 72w12'29 4:48:50
Dix 33 211 43N09'56 75w27'45 5:01:51
Dix 49 14 42N20 76w55 5:07:40
Dix Hills 52 11 40N49 73w21 4:53:24
Dobbins Corner 35 41 42N54'22 76w57'48 5:07:51
Dobbs Ferry 60 7 41N00'52 73w52'23 4:55:30
Doctors Crossing 19 145 43N01 78w30 5:14:00
Dodge 7 128 42N00'04 79w05'27 5:16:22
Dogtail Corners 14 11 41N40'17 73w31'44 4:54:07
Dogtown 39 78 42N50'30 75w04'58 5:00:20
Dolgeville 22 168 43N06'03 74w46'24 4:59:06
Dongan Hills 43 1 40N35'18 74w05'48 4:56:23
Doodletown 44 6 41N17'58 74w00'11 4:56:01
Doolins Crossing 23 77 44N05'05 75w40'42 5:02:43
Doonan Corners 13 226 42N20 74w48 4:59:12
Doraville 4 17 42N09'01 75w35'05 5:02:20
Doris Park 38 14 43N14'39 76w01'31 5:04:06
Dorloo 48 13 42N42'46 74w37'24 4:58:30
Dormansville 1 226 42N29'58 73w59'42 4:55:59
Douglas Crossing 23 226 44N10'55 75w49'09 5:03:17
Douglass 16 226 44N30 73w29 4:53:56
Douglaston 41 1 40N46'07 73w44'51 4:54:59
Dover 14 11 41N39 73w34 4:54:16
Dover Furnace 14 11 41N41'03 73w35'16 4:54:21
Dover Plains 14 11 41N44'28 73w34'37 4:54:18
Downsville 13 226 42N04'51 74w59'46 4:59:59
Doxtater Corner 18 226 43N07'00 74w44'01 4:58:56
Doyle 15 7 42N52'46 78w47'06 5:15:08
Drakes Corner 38 226 43N22'36 76w20'34 5:05:22
Dresden 58 6 43N40'21 73w24'40 4:53:39
Dresden 62 12 42N41'02 76w57'22 5:07:49
Dresden Station 58 6 43N33 73w24 4:53:36
Dresserville 6 13 42N42'13 76w19'41 5:05:19
Drews Corner 45 226 44N50'52 75w09'35 5:00:38
Drewville Heights 40 85 41N23'31 73w38'11 4:54:33
Driftwood 7 20 42N07'26 79w19'46 5:17:19
Dryden 55 13 42N29'27 76w17'51 5:05:11
Duane 17 226 44N37 74w15 4:57:00
Duane 47 226 42N45'15 74w08'56 4:56:36
Duane Center 17 226 44N39'34 74w15'52 4:57:03
Duanesburg 47 226 42N45'43 74w08'03 4:56:32
Dublin 50 99 42N59'41 76w55'21 5:07:41
Duboise Corner 55 13 42N29'52 76w33'28 5:06:14
Dudley Settlement 51 14 42N18'15 77w20'25 5:09:22
Duells Corner 15 11 42N44'49 78w44'55 5:15:00
Dugway 38 14 43N27'41 76w04'55 5:04:20
Dumbarton 33 13 43N09'44 75w39'43 5:02:39
Dunbar 4 226 42N06'36 75w43'17 5:02:53
Dundee 62 169 42N31'24 76w58'37 5:07:54
Dunewood 52 11 40N38 73w11 4:52:44
Dunham 33 222 43N06 75w15 5:01:00
Dunham Hollow 42 226 42N35'06 73w29'06 4:53:56
Dunham Manor 33 222 43N07 75w18 5:01:12
Dunkirk 7 134 42N28'46 79w20'03 5:17:20
Dunn Brook 33 226 43N23'14 75w22'55 5:01:32
Dunnsville 1 40 42N44'23 74w00'53 4:56:04
Dunraven 13 226 42N08'03 74w41'51 4:58:47
Dunsbach Ferry 1 1 42N47'31 73w45'24 4:55:02
Dunwoodie 60 1 40N55'42 73w51'51 4:55:27
Dunwoodie Heights 60 1 40N55'31 73w52'06 4:55:28
Durham 20 226 42N23'58 74w10'22 4:56:41
Durhamville 33 13 43N07'14 75w40'17 5:02:41
Durkeetown 58 226 43N14'48 73w31'58 4:54:08
Durland 36 6 41N16'58 74w18'30 4:57:14
Durlandville 36 7 41N21'02 74w23'19 4:57:33
Durso Corner 20 226 42N20'12 74w07'43 4:56:31
Dutcherville 38 15 43N17'20 75w57'27 5:03:50
Dutchess Junction 14 7 41N28'28 73w58'45 4:55:55
Dutch Flats 61 226 42N46'20 78w15'49 5:13:03
Dutch Hollow 36 226 41N14'54 74w16'26 4:57:06
Dutch Hollow 61 226 42N44'14 78w26'42 5:13:47
Dutch Settlement 23 45 44N07'00 75w48'33 5:03:14
Dutch Settlement 38 182 43N19'28 76w04'40 5:04:19
Dutchtown 15 22 42N37'11 78w28'59 5:13:56
Dwaarkill 56 226 41N38'55 74w15'51 4:57:03
Dwelly Corners 48 12 42N46'12 74w20'13 4:57:21
Dyke 51 13 42N13'24 77w01'27 5:08:06
Dykemans 40 226 41N26'03 73w37'08 4:54:29
Dyker Heights 24 1 40N37'17 74w00'36 4:56:02
Dysinger 32 121 43N08'02 78w34'28 5:14:18
Eagle 61 226 42N32'55 78w17'54 5:13:12
Eagle Bay 22 226 43N46'10 74w49'02 4:59:16
Eagle Bridge 42 11 42N57'00 73w23'48 4:53:35
Eagle Center 61 226 42N35 78w15 5:13:00
Eagle Harbor 37 146 43N15'12 78w15'12 5:13:01
Eagle Harbor Station 37 146 43N14'09 78w15'15 5:13:01
Eagle Lake 16 226 43N51 73w25 4:53:40
Eagle Mills 42 220 42N43'45 73w36'15 4:54:25
Eagle Nest 21 226 43N50'59 74w29'09 4:57:57
Eagle Point 26 13 42N48'00 77w43'03 5:10:52
Eagle Valley 36 226 41N09'17 74w13'38 4:56:55
Eagle Village 34 13 43N00'47 75w56'35 5:03:46
Eagleville 27 180 42N52'53 75w38'38 5:02:35
Eagleville 58 213 43N05'04 73w18'48 4:53:15
Earlton 20 11 42N21'20 73w54'04 4:55:36
Earlville 9 13 42N44'23 75w32'44 5:02:11
Earlville 10 188 44N58'13 74w03'01 4:56:12
East Afton 9 226 42N12'25 75w25'26 5:01:42
East Alexander 19 142 42N55'40 78w11'35 5:12:46
East Amboy 38 25 43N22'13 75w54'39 5:03:39
East Amherst 15 11 43N01'06 78w41'49 5:14:47
East Arcade 61 147 42N34'14 78w20'41 5:13:23
East Atlantic Beach 30 11 40N35 73w43 4:54:52
East Aurora 15 170 42N46'04 78w36'49 5:14:27
East Avon 26 20 42N54'33 77w42'24 5:10:50
East Barre 37 146 43N11'13 78w09'02 5:12:36
East Bay 59 226 43N13 76w49 5:07:16
East Bay Park 59 226 43N17'31 76w53'43 5:07:35
East Beekmantown 10 86 44N45'09 73w28'14 4:53:53
East Bend Park 14 1 41N40 73w54 4:55:36
East Bennington 61 226 42N51'31 78w20'15 5:13:21
East Bergen 19 161 43N06'39 77w56'06 5:11:44
East Berkshire 54 226 42N18'23 76w08'38 5:04:35
East Berne 1 40 42N36'59 74w04'30 4:56:18
East Bethany 19 142 42N55'53 78w06'06 5:12:24
East Bloomfield 35 47 42N53'42 77w26'06 5:09:44
East Boston 27 226 43N05'00 75w49'04 5:03:16
East Boylston 38 226 43N41'26 75w55'48 5:03:43
East Branch 13 226 41N59'18 75w08'03 5:00:32
East Brentwood 52 11 40N47'31 73w13'54 4:52:56
East Buskirk 42 11 42N56'40 73w26'04 4:53:44
East Campbell 51 13 42N13'27 77w08'10 5:08:33
East Cayuga Heights 55 186 42N28 76w28 5:05:52
East Chatham 11 10 42N24'38 73w31'30 4:54:06
East Chester 36 4 41N21'16 74w16'39 4:57:07
Eastchester 60 1 40N53'18 73w49'43 4:55:19
East Clarence 15 38 43N00'44 78w35'16 5:14:21
East Cobleskill 48 12 42N40'26 74w23'25 4:57:34
East Cochecton 53 226 41N42'55 75w00'58 5:00:04
East Coldenham 36 1 41N31'10 74w06'33 4:56:26
East Concord 15 218 42N33'07 78w38'26 5:14:34
East Corning 51 13 42N07'32 76w59'12 5:07:57
East Creek 22 61 43N00'26 74w44'38 4:58:59
East Cutchogue 52 11 41N01'39 72w28'15 4:49:53
East DeKalb 45 226 44N28'57 75w18'03 5:01:12
East Delhi 13 226 42N17'56 74w52'45 4:59:31
East Dickinson 17 226 44N46'46 74w29'53 4:58:00
East Durham 20 226 42N22'21 74w05'46 4:56:23
East Eden 15 153 42N40'00 78w49'40 5:15:19
East Elba 19 171 43N03'32 78w08'20 5:12:33
East Elma 15 170 42N48'18 78w35'40 5:14:23
East Elmhurst 41 1 40N45'40 73w51'56 4:55:28
East Elmira 8 13 42N04'17 76w44'07 5:06:56
Eastern Parkway 24 1 40N40'09 73w56'23 4:55:46
East Farmingdale 52 11 40N49 73w27 4:53:48
East Fishkill 14 6 41N33'12 73w47'46 4:55:11
East Flatbush 24 1 40N39'13 73w55'51 4:55:43
East Floyd 33 14 43N16'23 75w16'05 5:01:04
East Frankfort 22 184 43N01'22 75w03'23 5:00:14
East Freetown 12 13 42N33'07 75w59'15 5:03:57
East Gaines 37 146 43N17'25 78w08'08 5:12:33
East Galway 46 226 43N04'18 73w59'20 4:55:57
East Geneva 50 41 42N52'45 76w56'18 5:07:45
East Genoa 6 13 42N38'47 76w30'20 5:06:01
East Glenville 47 226 42N53'40 73w55'42 4:55:43
East Grafton 42 11 42N46'01 73w24'40 4:53:39
East Greenbush 42 1 42N35'27 73w42'08 4:54:49
East Greenville 20 226 42N24'52 73w59'29 4:55:58
East Greenwich 58 1 43N08'44 73w23'53 4:53:36
East Groveland 26 226 42N44'26 77w45'33 5:11:02
East Guilford 9 12 42N20'27 75w24'26 5:01:38
East Half Hollow Hills 52 11 40N48 73w19 4:53:16
East Hamilton 27 180 42N47'57 75w27'57 5:01:52
East Hampton 52 1 40N57'48 71w11'00 4:44:44
East Hartford 58 42 43N20'03 73w23'01 4:53:32
East Hauppauge 52 11 40N50'05 73w09'04 4:52:36
East Hebron 58 213 43N15'42 73w17'13 4:53:09
East Hempstead 30 6 40N42 73w36 4:54:24
East Herkimer 22 183 43N01'49 74w57'52 4:59:51
East Hill 55 186 42N28 76w29 5:05:56
East Hills 30 11 40N47'37 73w37'39 4:54:31
East Hillsdale 11 11 42N10'59 73w30'05 4:54:00
East Homer 12 41 42N39'58 76w06'07 5:04:24
East Hoosick 42 11 42N54'11 73w17'11 4:53:09
East Hounsfield 23 226 43N58'17 75w59'11 5:03:57
East Huntington 52 6 40N52 73w27 4:53:48
East Irvington 60 1 41N02'51 73w50'57 4:55:24
East Islip 52 6 40N43'55 73w11'10 4:52:45
East Ithaca 55 186 42N26'22 76w28'44 5:05:55
East Jefferson 48 226 42N30'14 74w34'49 4:58:19
East Jewett 20 23 42N14'06 74w08'45 4:56:35
East Kilns 10 226 44N28'46 73w47'06 4:55:08
East Kingston 56 11 41N57'14 73w58'06 4:55:52
East Koy 61 226 42N32'27 78w06'17 5:12:25
East Lake Ronkonkoma 52 11 40N49 73w06 4:52:24
East Lancaster 15 7 42N53'45 78w38'18 5:14:33
East Lansing 55 13 42N34'06 76w28'11 5:05:53
East Leon 5 226 42N20'50 78w57'29 5:15:50
East Lindley 51 13 42N02'41 77w05'54 5:08:24
East Line 46 11 42N58'17 73w49'52 4:55:19
East Maine 4 116 42N11'31 75w59'36 5:03:58
East Marion 52 11 41N07'39 72w20'26 4:49:22
East Martinsburg 25 226 43N44'41 75w25'40 5:01:43
East Masonville 13 13 42N15'49 75w18'10 5:01:13
East Massapequa 30 6 40N40 73w26 4:53:44
East McDonough 9 226 42N29'50 75w41'09 5:02:45
East Meadow 30 11 40N42'50 73w33'34 4:54:14
East Meredith 13 29 42N25'17 74w53'14 4:59:33
East Middletown 36 1 41N26'39 74w24'01 4:57:36
Eastmor 42 220 42N41'04 73w37'56 4:54:32
East Moriches 52 11 40N48'18 72w45'41 4:51:03
East Nassau 42 11 42N30'28 73w30'25 4:54:02
East Neck 52 11 40N54 73w23 4:53:32
East Newark 54 226 42N12'12 76w08'55 5:04:36
East New York 24 1 40N40'00 73w52'58 4:55:32
East Nichols 54 36 42N00'24 76w16'59 5:05:08

East Northport 52 7 40N52'36 73w19'30 4:53:18
East Norwich 30 11 40N50'48 73w32'08 4:54:09
East Oakfield 19 26 43N05'53 78w14'51 5:12:59
East Olean 5 101 42N04'48 78w25'13 5:13:41
Easton 58 226 42N59'36 73w33'10 4:54:13
East Otto 5 226 42N23'23 78w45'18 5:15:01
East Palermo 38 182 43N21'04 76w14'00 5:04:56
East Palmyra 59 89 43N05'06 77w09'26 5:08:38
East Park 14 11 41N47'19 73w54'53 4:55:40
East Part 45 105 44N45'56 74w48'24 4:59:14
East Patchogue 52 1 40N46'01 72w59'48 4:51:59
East Pembroke 19 226 42N59'44 78w18'37 5:13:14
East Penfield 28 13 43N07'46 77w24'45 5:09:39
East Pharsalia 9 226 42N33'29 75w43'03 5:02:52
East Pitcairn 45 226 44N13'05 75w13'22 5:00:53
East Pittstown 42 11 42N54'09 73w27'46 4:53:51
East Poestenkill 42 226 42N40'57 73w29'42 4:53:59
Eastport 52 11 40N49'33 72w43'56 4:50:56
East Potter 62 14 42N44'20 77w08'40 5:08:35
East Quogue 52 1 40N50'26 72w34'55 4:50:20
East Randolph 5 20 42N10'22 78w56'53 5:15:48
East Richford 54 226 42N22'17 76w09'16 5:04:37
East Ripley 7 103 42N17'02 79w40'22 5:18:41
East River 12 41 42N38'52 76w06'52 5:04:27
East Rochester 28 13 43N06'31 77w29'16 5:09:57
East Rockaway 30 11 40N38'31 73w40'12 4:54:41
East Rodman 23 45 43N52'12 75w51'13 5:03:25
East Salamanca 5 14 42N09 78w43 5:14:52
East Schodack 42 68 42N33'43 73w38'02 4:54:32
East Schuyler 22 184 43N03'13 75w04'29 5:00:18
East Scott 12 41 42N43'19 76w11'41 5:04:47
East Seneca 15 153 42N50'05 78w42'45 5:14:51
East Setauket 52 11 40N56'29 73w06'23 4:52:26
East Shelby 37 112 43N10'14 78w19'32 5:13:18
East Side 4 151 42N07 75w53 5:03:32
Eastside 52 11 41N00'11 72w08'00 4:48:32
East Sidney 13 104 42N19'48 75w13'57 5:00:56
East Springfield 39 140 42N49'51 74w48'56 4:59:16
East Steamburg 49 13 42N31'46 76w46'18 5:07:05
East Steuben 33 14 43N22'35 75w13'47 5:00:55
East Stone Arabia 29 162 42N57'30 74w31'06 4:58:04
East Syracuse 34 41 43N03'55 76w04'44 5:04:19
East Taghkanic 11 226 42N07'55 73w39'28 4:54:38
East Township 1 40 42N41'59 74w06'05 4:56:24
East Tremont 3 1 40N50'43 73w53'29 4:55:34
East Union 51 14 42N17'52 77w19'30 5:09:18
East Varick 50 12 42N46'12 76w46'11 5:07:05
East Venice 6 13 42N41'27 76w30'03 5:06:00
East Verona 33 211 43N13'05 75w32'57 5:02:12
East Vestal 4 151 42N06 75w59 5:03:56
East Victor 35 19 42N58'28 77w22'52 5:09:31
Eastview 60 6 41N04'53 73w49'47 4:55:19
East Virgil 12 13 42N29'28 76w05'54 5:04:24
East Walden 36 6 41N33'31 74w09'29 4:56:38
East Watertown 23 45 43N57'30 75w51'18 5:03:25
East Waverly 54 224 42N00'38 76w31'06 5:06:04
East Wawarsing 56 48 41N44'58 74w20'56 4:57:24
East Whitehall 58 6 43N32'11 73w19'38 4:53:19
East White Plains 60 1 41N02'20 73w44'53 4:55:00
East Williamson 59 33 43N13'50 77w08'44 5:08:35
East Williston 30 11 40N45'30 73w38'07 4:54:32
East Wilson 32 226 43N14'28 78w45'34 5:15:02
East Windham 20 226 42N20'12 74w09'34 4:56:38
East Windsor 4 226 42N06'40 75w36'32 5:02:26
East Winfield 22 13 42N53'19 75w08'44 5:00:35
Eastwood 34 41 43N03'58 76w06'18 5:04:25
East Woodhull 51 13 42N05'03 77w21'18 5:09:25
East Woods 60 16 41N12'40 73w31'53 4:54:08
East Worcester 39 14 42N37'24 74w40'19 4:58:41
Eaton 27 180 42N50'59 75w36'44 5:02:27
Eaton Corners 27 226 43N08'15 75w53'52 5:03:35
Eaton Corners 47 12 42N48'21 74w14'50 4:56:59
Eatons Neck 52 11 40N54 73w20 4:53:20
Eatonville 22 226 43N04'51 74w55'55 4:59:44
Eavesport 56 11 42N07'02 73w56'10 4:55:45
Eben 45 207 44N37'37 75w03'56 5:00:16
Ebenezer 15 153 42N49'49 78w45'14 5:15:01
Eddy 45 155 44N32'24 75w14'13 5:00:57
Eddy Corners 46 226 43N03'25 73w46'09 4:55:05
Eddyville 5 226 42N19'47 78w45'47 5:15:03
Eddyville 56 11 41N53'39 74w01'35 4:56:06
Eden 15 153 42N39'08 78w53'50 5:15:35
Eden 36 11 41N17'19 74w29'41 4:57:59
Eden Valley 15 153 42N40'44 78w52'20 5:15:29
Edenville 36 6 41N16'33 74w24'41 4:57:39
Edgemere 41 1 40N35'46 73w46'05 4:55:04
Edgemont 60 1 40N59 73w48 4:55:12
Edgewater 6 13 42N46'04 76w28'53 5:05:56
Edgewater 15 1 43N02'47 78w54'36 5:15:38
Edgewater Beach 33 211 43N13'07 75w43'50 5:02:55
Edgewater Park 34 13 42N52'51 76w22'50 5:05:31
Edgewater Park 45 201 44N36'00 75w38'07 5:02:32
Edgewood 20 52 42N08'25 74w12'46 4:56:51
Edgewood 52 11 40N47 73w15 4:53:00
Edgewood Garden 34 41 43N05'13 76w16'08 5:05:05
Edgewood Park 23 17 44N19'47 75w55'08 5:03:41
Edicks 22 196 42N58'03 74w55'48 4:59:43
Edinburg 46 226 43N13'18 74w06'16 4:56:25
Edmeston 39 226 42N41'52 75w14'39 5:00:59
Edson 4 226 42N01'36 75w39'42 5:02:39
Edwards 45 226 44N19'28 75w15'05 5:01:00
Edwards Hill 57 49 43N37'42 74w02'46 4:56:11
Edwards Park 11 11 42N25 73w27 4:53:48
Edwardsville 45 20 44N31'20 75w35'36 5:02:22
Egbertville 43 1 40N34 74w07 4:56:28
Eggertsville 15 7 42N57'48 78w48'15 5:15:13
Egypt 28 13 43N03'51 77w24'28 5:09:38
Eighmyville 14 7 41N56'37 73w51'28 4:55:26
Elayne Meadows 46 11 42N48 73w41 4:54:44
Elba 19 171 43N04'38 78w11'14 5:12:45
Elberta 32 226 43N15'50 78w52'14 5:15:29
Elbow 58 6 43N33 73w24 4:53:36
Elbridge 34 24 43N02'04 76w26'54 5:05:48
Eldred 53 226 41N31'37 74w53'04 4:59:32
Elgin 5 226 42N18'18 78w21'14 5:13:25
Elizabethtown 16 50 44N12'58 73w35'29 4:54:22
Elizabethtown 22 184 42N57'58 75w04'46 5:00:19
Elizaville 11 226 42N03'03 73w47'39 4:55:11
Elka Park 20 23 42N09'33 74w09'28 4:56:38
Elk Brook 13 80 41N58'27 75w03'19 5:00:13
Elk Creek 39 13 42N35'29 74w49'26 4:59:18
Elkdale 5 226 42N12'54 78w45'14 5:15:01
Ellenburg 10 18 44N53'38 73w50'13 4:55:21
Ellenburg Center 10 18 44N51'53 73w53'51 4:55:35
Ellenburg Depot 10 7 44N54'21 73w48'05 4:55:12
Ellenville 56 48 41N43'01 74w23'46 4:57:35
Ellery 7 226 42N10 79w21 5:17:24
Ellery Center 7 226 42N10'58 79w20'50 5:17:23
Ellicott 7 187 42N08 79w13 5:16:52
Ellicott 15 11 42N44'04 78w43'54 5:14:56
Ellicottville 5 172 42N16'30 78w40'23 5:14:42
Ellington 7 226 42N13'00 79w06'29 5:16:26
Ellis 55 226 42N25'31 76w22'54 5:05:32
Ellisburg 23 226 43N43'58 76w08'11 5:04:33
Ellis Hollow 55 186 42N28 76w29 5:05:56
Ellistown 54 224 42N00'31 76w28'40 5:05:55
Ellwood Park 15 1 42N58'32 78w51'12 5:15:25
Elma 15 226 42N51'03 78w38'26 5:14:34
Elma Center 15 226 42N49'47 78w38'11 5:14:33
Elm Beach 50 12 42N42'04 76w44'42 5:06:59
Elmbois 51 181 42N29'03 77w13'49 5:08:55
Elmcrest 34 13 43N07'59 76w14'10 5:04:57
Elmdale 45 178 44N21'37 75w32'37 5:02:10
Elmer Hill 33 211 43N16'47 75w27'00 5:01:48
Elmgrove 28 209 43N10'54 77w43'55 5:10:56
Elm Grove 39 226 42N33'19 75w13'33 5:00:54
Elmhurst 7 187 42N07'05 79w17'38 5:17:11
Elmhurst 41 1 40N44'11 73w52'42 4:55:31
Elmira 8 13 42N05'23 76w48'29 5:07:14
Elmira Heights 8 13 42N07'47 76w49'16 5:07:17
Elmont 30 1 40N42'03 73w42'48 4:54:51
Elm Park 43 1 40N37'53 74w08'57 4:56:36
Elmsford 60 6 41N03'18 73w49'14 4:55:17
Elmsmere 60 7 40N55'42 73w49'16 4:55:17
Elm Tree 7 226 42N09'21 79w28'27 5:17:54
Elm Valley 2 109 42N09'04 77w51'31 5:11:26
Elmwood 6 13 42N49'36 76w31'25 5:06:06
Elnora 46 11 42N53'34 73w49'18 4:55:17
Elpis 33 14 43N17'01 75w49'21 5:03:17
Elsinore 10 14 44N41'37 73w40'02 4:54:40
Elsmere 1 11 42N37'18 73w49'07 4:55:16
Elting Corners 56 11 41N44'28 74w02'07 4:56:08
Eltingville 43 11 40N32'43 74w09'58 4:56:40
Elton 5 226 42N27'03 78w25'45 5:13:43
Elwood 52 11 40N50'43 73w20'08 4:53:21
Elwood Farms 52 11 40N51 73w20 4:53:20
Embarkation 24 1 40N43 73w50 4:55:20
Embogcht 20 226 42N13 73w51 4:55:24
Emerson 6 24 43N06'00 76w36'52 5:06:27
Emerson Hill 43 1 40N36'31 74w05'47 4:56:23
Emeryville 45 178 44N17'42 75w22'04 5:01:28
Eminence 48 13 42N31'31 74w32'09 4:58:09
Emmons 39 14 42N27'48 75w00'44 5:00:03
Emmonsburg 18 226 43N09'11 74w42'36 4:58:50
Empeyville 33 14 43N23'48 75w41'07 5:02:44
Endicott 4 13 42N05'54 76w02'59 5:04:12
Endwell 4 13 42N06'46 76w01'17 5:04:05
Enfield 55 186 42N26'09 76w37'54 5:06:32
Engleville 48 13 42N45'18 74w38'56 4:58:36
Englewood 15 1 42N58 78w51 5:15:24
Ennerdale 35 14 42N52'33 77w10'47 5:08:43
Ensenore 6 13 42N43 76w25 5:05:40
Ephratah 18 226 43N00'03 74w32'34 4:58:10
Eppie Corners 18 43 43N00'19 74w28'16 4:57:53
Erieville 27 226 42N51'06 75w45'21 5:03:01
Erin 8 226 42N11'09 76w40'13 5:06:41
Erwins 51 13 42N06'45 77w08'45 5:08:35
Escarpment 32 199 43N10'07 79w00'25 5:16:02
Esopus 56 11 41N49'40 73w57'56 4:55:52
Esperance 48 12 42N45'40 74w15'25 4:57:02
Esplanade 3 1 40N52 73w51 4:55:24
Essex 16 129 44N18'36 73w21'11 4:53:25
Etna 55 13 42N29'06 76w23'02 5:05:32
Euclid 34 13 43N11'11 76w13'03 5:04:52
Evans 15 11 42N39 79w02 5:16:08
Evans Center 15 11 42N39'29 79w02'06 5:16:08
Evans Corner 50 19 43N01'20 76w46'12 5:07:05
Evans Mills 23 26 44N05'17 75w48'27 5:03:14
Ewells Corner 61 25 42N49'53 78w07'27 5:12:30
Excelsior Springs 26 226 42N45'06 77w42'47 5:10:51
Exeter 39 78 42N48 75w04 5:00:16
Exeter Corner 39 78 42N47'19 75w04'30 5:00:18
Fabius 34 16 42N50'06 75w59'11 5:03:57
Factory Hollow 42 11 42N50'15 73w29'38 4:53:59
Factory Village 46 11 43N01'33 73w52'01 4:55:28
Factoryville 16 138 43N57'06 73w26'31 4:53:46
Fairdale 38 226 43N19'25 76w32'21 5:06:09
Fairfield 22 226 43N08'14 74w54'49 4:59:39
Fairfield 54 154 42N13'57 76w16'44 5:05:07
Fairfield Farms 34 13 43N02 76w01 5:04:04
Fairfield Gardens 1 11 42N42 73w48 4:55:12
Fair Harbor 52 11 40N38'21 73w11'05 4:52:44
Fair Haven 6 226 43N18'59 76w42'09 5:06:49
Fair Haven 12 41 42N46'09 76w16'07 5:05:04
Fairlawn Estates 1 1 42N44 73w45 4:55:00
Fairmount 34 12 43N02'50 76w14'20 5:04:57
Fair Oaks 36 1 41N30'25 74w24'38 4:57:39
Fairport 28 13 43N05'55 77w26'32 5:09:46
Fairview 2 226 42N26'12 78w18'31 5:13:14
Fairview 14 11 41N43'25 73w55'13 4:55:41
Fairview 60 1 41N02'36 73w47'52 4:55:11
Fairview 61 24 42N40'46 78w02'12 5:12:09
Fairville 59 22 43N07'01 77w04'46 5:08:19
Fairweather Corners 46 226 43N01'02 74w03'15 4:56:13
Falconer 7 187 42N07'07 79w11'55 5:16:48
Falcon Manor 32 199 43N06 78w58 5:15:52
Falconwood 15 1 43N01 78w57 5:15:48
Falls 32 199 43N05 79w02 5:16:08
Fallsburg 53 74 41N43'55 74w36'06 4:58:24
Falls Mills 53 226 41N43'51 74w58'57 4:59:56
Fancher 37 146 43N14'41 78w05'29 5:12:22
Fantinekill 56 72 41N48'07 74w18'18 4:57:13
Fargo 19 164 42N55'35 78w26'12 5:13:45
Fargo 23 156 44N02'02 75w34'57 5:02:20
Farleys 6 13 42N49'05 76w42'00 5:06:48
Farleys Point 6 13 42N50 76w42 5:06:48
Farmers Corner 38 96 43N33'03 76w07'38 5:04:31
Farmers Mills 33 11 43N01'25 75w23'52 5:01:35
Farmers Mills 40 226 41N29'44 73w44'23 4:54:58
Farmersville 5 226 42N23'15 78w22'35 5:13:30
Farmersville Station 5 226 42N25'39 78w21'40 5:13:27
Farmingdale 30 11 40N43'57 73w26'45 4:53:47
Farmingdale 36 20 41N24'01 74w14'12 4:56:57
Farmington 35 19 43N01'55 77w19'57 5:09:20
Farmingville 52 11 40N49'52 73w01'48 4:52:07
Farnham 15 22 42N35'40 79w05'29 5:16:22
Farragut 24 1 40N39 73w56 4:55:44
Farrel Corner 22 20 43N10'16 75w04'19 5:00:17
Far Rockaway 41 1 40N36'19 73w45'20 4:55:01
Fawn Ridge 34 226 43N09 76w20 5:05:20
Fay 17 193 44N53'34 74w20'35 4:57:22
Fayette 50 13 42N48'51 76w48'34 5:07:14
Fayette Manor 34 13 43N02 76w01 5:04:04
Fayetteville 34 13 43N01'47 76w00'17 5:04:01
Fayville 46 226 43N08'49 74w07'15 4:56:29
Federal 28 209 43N09 77w37 5:10:28
Federal Reserve 31 1 40N43 73w50 4:55:20
Felters Corners 44 6 41N11'55 74w00'35 4:56:02
Felts Mills 23 119 44N01'20 75w45'49 5:03:03
Fenimore 46 226 43N18'08 73w35'42 4:54:23
Fenner 27 226 42N58'10 75w47'14 5:03:09
Fenner 28 20 43N03'30 77w40'03 5:10:40
Fenton 4 13 42N11 75w50 5:03:20
Fentonville 7 128 42N00'14 79w08'26 5:16:34
Ferenbaugh 51 13 42N11'51 77w00'29 5:08:02
Fergusons Corners 62 41 42N52 76w59 5:07:56
Fergusonville 13 13 42N29'34 74w48'19 4:59:13
Ferndale 53 72 41N46'26 74w44'20 4:58:57
Fernwood 38 226 43N29'43 76w09'03 5:04:36
Fernwood 46 226 43N16'35 73w38'49 4:54:35
Fernwood 53 226 41N52'28 75w04'12 5:00:17

Ferry Village 15
1 42N58'15 78w56'55 5:15:48
Feura Bush 1 11 42N34'40 73w52'45 4:55:31
Fey Mill 33 226 43N26'43 75w32'42 5:02:11
Fickles Corner 9
13 42N15'41 75w49'07 5:03:16
Field Corners 40
135 41N26'52 73w38'42 4:54:35
Field Crossing 39
226 42N40'39 75w01'53 5:00:08
Fields Settlement 23
226 43N56'37 75w58'47 5:03:55
Fieldston 3 1 40N53 73w54 4:55:36
Filer Corners 39
226 42N33 75w15 5:01:00
Fillmore 2 226 42N27'58 78w06'55 5:12:28
Fillmore Corner 34
13 42N59'28 76w01'05 5:04:04
Finchville 36 1 41N25'40 74w34'18 4:58:17
Findley Lake 7
226 42N07'09 79w43'58 5:18:56
Fine 45 226 44N14'52 75w08'17 5:00:33
Fineview 23 163 44N17'15 76w00'45 5:04:03
Finger Lakes Manor 35
14 42N53 77w17 5:09:08
Fink Basin 22 61 43N01'37 74w49'32 4:59:18
Fink Hollow 33 82 43N21'09 75w16'46 5:01:07
Finnegans Corners 36
7 41N21'58 74w21'37 4:57:26
Fintches Corners 6
226 43N16'47 76w38'41 5:06:35
Fire Island Pines 52
11 40N39'55 73w04'07 4:52:16
Fireplace 52 11 41N02'47 72w09'11 4:48:37
Fireplace Lodge Girls Camp 52
11 41N02'58 72w09'09 4:48:37
Firthcliffe 36 11 41N26'21 74w02'44 4:56:11
Firthcliffe Heights 36
1 41N26'54 74w03'28 4:56:14
Fish Creek 25 77 43N31'13 75w32'01 5:02:08
Fish Creek 56 215 42N03'43 74w00'48 4:56:03
Fish Creek Landing 33
211 43N13'15 75w42'01 5:02:48
Fish Creek Station 33
226 43N11'46 75w42'48 5:02:51
Fishers 35 13 43N00'31 77w27'54 5:09:52
Fishers Island 52
11 41N15'25 72w01'28 4:48:06
Fishers Landing 23
163 44N16'35 76w00'30 5:04:02
Fisherville 8 13 42N09'23 76w52'09 5:07:29
Fish House 18 226 43N08'40 74w08'00 4:56:32
Fishkill 14 6 41N32'08 73w53'58 4:55:36
Fishkill Plains 14
6 41N36'25 73w49'51 4:55:19
Fishs Eddy 13 226 41N57'49 75w10'31 5:00:42
Fitch 5 226 42N15'46 78w26'16 5:13:45
Fitch Point 58 1 43N09'00 73w22'49 4:53:31
Fitts Corners 55
13 42N33'49 76w19'25 5:05:18
Five Chimneys Corner 27
60 43N02'00 75w37'10 5:02:29
Five Corners 2
226 42N15 77w47 5:11:08
Five Corners 6 13 42N38'15 76w34'34 5:06:18
Five Corners 9
226 42N38'32 75w19'50 5:01:19
Five Corners 19
26 43N04'41 78w17'15 5:13:09
Five Corners 27
60 43N04'34 75w41'29 5:02:46
Five Corners 33
13 42N53'38 75w22'15 5:01:29
Five Corners 37
146 43N15'46 78w11'35 5:12:46
Fivemile Point 4
20 42N05'28 75w49'24 5:03:18
Five Points 5 226 42N18'10 78w47'45 5:15:11
Five Points 28 27 42N57'41 77w39'52 5:10:39
Five Points 35 41 42N56'56 76w58'43 5:07:55
Five Points 39 13 42N40'43 74w48'47 4:59:15
Flackville 45 201 44N39'55 75w21'28 5:01:26
Flagler Corners 46
11 42N51'17 73w47'42 4:55:11
Flanders 52 11 40N54'12 72w37'05 4:50:28
Flatbrook 11 11 42N22'37 73w25'46 4:53:43
Flatbush 24 1 40N39'07 73w57'34 4:55:50
Flatbush 56 215 42N00'55 73w57'39 4:55:51
Flat Creek 29 162 42N50'34 74w30'07 4:58:00
Flat Creek 48 226 42N25'48 74w24'07 4:57:36
Flatlands 24 1 40N37'16 73w56'07 4:55:44
Fleetwood 60 1 40N55'30 73w50'11 4:55:21
Fleischmanns 13
42 42N09'19 74w31'58 4:58:08
Fleming 6 13 42N51'42 76w34'28 5:06:18
Flemingville 54
205 42N09'53 76w14'57 5:05:00
Flint 35 14 42N51'28 77w06'23 5:08:26
Flint 56 122 41N38'14 74w08'13 4:56:33
Flint Town 33 226 43N23'58 75w26'26 5:01:46
Floodwood 17 221 44N20'01 74w24'24 4:57:38
Floral Park 30 1 40N43'25 73w42'19 4:54:49
Florence 33 226 43N26'18 75w44'59 5:03:00
Florence Hill 33
25 43N25'23 75w47'36 5:03:10
Florida 36 20 41N19'54 74w21'26 4:57:26
Floridaville 6
226 43N14'19 76w29'15 5:05:57
Flowerfield Estates 3
1 40N51 73w53 4:55:32
Flower Hill 30 11 40N48'26 73w40'54 4:54:44
Flowers 4 226 42N02'37 75w41'20 5:02:45
Floyd 33 211 43N13'11 75w20'05 5:01:20
Flushing 41 1 40N45'55 73w49'04 4:55:16
Fluvanna 7 187 42N07'09 79w17'32 5:17:10
Fly Creek 39 13 42N43'06 74w59'01 4:59:56
Flying Point 52
11 40N53'39 72w21'17 4:49:25
Fly Summit 58 4 43N00'45 73w29'05 4:53:56
Folsomdale 61 38 42N49'38 78w26'54 5:13:48
Fonda 29 174 42N57'16 74w22'37 4:57:30
Footes 15 218 42N35'06 78w38'41 5:14:35
Foots Corner 26
226 42N44'47 77w40'40 5:10:43
Ford Corner 28
226 42N58'31 77w31'39 5:10:07
Fordham 3 1 40N51'33 73w53'56 4:55:36
Fordsbush 29 226 42N57'34 74w44'33 4:58:58
Forest 10 20 44N54'07 73w45'23 4:55:02
Forest Avenue Shoppers Town 43
1 40N38 74w08 4:56:32
Forest Beach 34
14 43N13'14 76w05'31 5:04:22
Forestburg 53 226 41N33'00 74w45'06 4:59:00
Forest City 25
226 43N57'07 75w26'33 5:01:46
Forestdale 17 81 44N26'11 73w55'14 4:55:41
Forest Glen 15 1 42N43'54 78w50'55 5:15:24
Forest Glen 56
122 41N42'14 74w07'43 4:56:31
Forest Hills 41 1 40N42'58 73w51'02 4:55:24
Forest Home 55
186 42N27'13 76w28'06 5:05:52
Forest Knolls 60
1 40N56'19 73w46'34 4:55:06
Forest Lawn 28
109 43N14'56 77w30'13 5:10:01
Forest Park 7 225 42N20'02 79w36'18 5:18:25
Forest Park 41 1 40N43 73w50 4:55:20
Forestport 33 226 43N26'31 75w12'27 5:00:50
Forestport Station 33
226 43N27 75w12 5:00:48
Forestville 7 226 42N28'06 79w10'38 5:16:43
Forge Hollow 33
11 42N57'46 75w24'33 5:01:38
Forks 15 7 42N54'14 78w45'16 5:15:01
Forsonville 40 6 41N22'05 73w55'48 4:55:43
Forsyth 7 226 42N17'32 79w39'14 5:18:37
Fort Ann 58 123 43N24'51 73w29'17 4:53:57
FORT CLINTON 44 6 41N19'07 73w59'18 4:55:57
Fort Covington 17
226 44N59'21 74w29'42 4:57:59
Fort Covington Center 17
226 44N56'54 74w27'52 4:57:51
Fort Drum 23 12 44N01 75w48 5:03:12
Fort Edward 58 1 43N16'01 73w35'06 4:54:20
Fort George 31 1 40N52 73w56 4:55:44
Fort Greene 24 1 40N41'37 73w58'03 4:55:52
Fort Hamilton 24
1 40N37'07 74w02'01 4:56:08
Fort Herkimer 22
183 43N01'01 74w57'10 4:59:49
Fort Hill 19 110 43N01'00 77w58'14 5:11:53
Fort Hill 35 13 42N55'01 77w02'37 5:08:10
Fort Hill 52 11 40N52'45 73w24'25 4:53:38
Fort Hill 59 25 43N03'12 76w45'11 5:07:01
Fort Hunter 1 6 42N44'35 73w56'35 4:55:46
Fort Hunter 29 1 42N56'32 74w17'08 4:57:09
Fort Jackson 45
226 44N42'20 74w42'55 4:58:52
Fort Jay 31 1 40N41'28 74w00'59 4:56:04
Fort Johnson 29 1 42N57'30 74w14'00 4:56:56
Fort Miller 58
226 43N09'39 73w34'42 4:54:19
FORT MONTGOMERY 36
6 41N19'26 73w59'14 4:55:57
Fort Niagara Beach 32
226 43N16'04 79w02'16 5:16:09
Fort Ontario 38
204 43N27'57 76w30'31 5:06:02
Fort Plain 29 62 42N55'53 74w37'23 4:58:30
Fort Putnam 36 6 41N23'26 73w57'51 4:55:51
Fort Salonga 52
11 40N54'45 73w18'05 4:53:12
Fortsville 46 226 43N13'48 73w40'56 4:54:44
Fort Ticonderoga 16
6 43N50'29 73w23'17 4:53:33
Fort Tilden 41 1 40N33'44 73w53'29 4:55:34
Fort Wadsworth 43
1 40N36'32 74w03'47 4:56:15
Fort Washington 31
1 40N50 73w56 4:55:44
Fort William Henry 57
1 43N25'14 73w42'35 4:54:50
Foster 54 205 42N07'45 76w08'37 5:04:34
Fosterdale 53 226 41N42'27 74w58'21 4:59:53
Fostertown 36 1 41N33'12 74w02'45 4:56:11
Fosterville 6 13 42N57'29 76w40'24 5:06:42
Foster-Wheeler Junction 26
13 42N34 77w42 5:10:48
Four Mile 5 226 42N01'11 78w27'55 5:13:52
Fourth Lake 57 40 43N21'25 73w49'49 4:55:19
Fowler 45 226 44N16'43 75w23'12 5:01:33
Fowlersville 25
77 43N37'26 75w16'28 5:01:06
Fowlerville 15
226 42N36'08 78w43'01 5:14:52
Fowlerville 26
226 42N53'36 77w50'45 5:11:23
Fowlerville 53
226 41N33'22 74w45'39 4:59:03
Fox 5 226 42N25'05 78w38'32 5:14:34
Fox Hill 46 7 43N11'35 74w02'43 4:56:11
Fox Hills 43 1 40N36'54 74w05'06 4:56:20
Fox Meadow 60 1 41N00'06 73w47'35 4:55:10
Fox Ridge 6 24 43N03'19 76w41'28 5:06:46
Fraleighs 14 7 42N00'12 73w50'04 4:55:20
Francis Corners 46
11 43N00'48 73w46'43 4:55:07
Frankfort 22 150 43N02'20 75w04'15 5:00:17
Frankfort Center 22
184 43N03'04 75w08'41 5:00:35
Franklin 13 104 42N20'26 75w09'56 5:00:40
Franklin Depot 13
13 42N16'57 75w12'35 5:00:50
Franklin D Roosevelt 31
1 40N46 73w58 4:55:52
Franklin Falls 17
81 44N26'12 73w58'15 4:55:53
Franklin Park 34
41 43N04'57 76w04'31 5:04:18
Franklin Springs 33
11 43N02'12 75w23'33 5:01:34
Franklin Square 30
11 40N42'26 73w40'35 4:54:42
Franklinton 48
226 42N31'15 74w18'14 4:57:13
Franklinville 5
108 42N20'13 78w27'30 5:13:50
Franks Corner 12
41 42N35 76w12 5:04:48
Fraser 13 226 42N14'43 74w57'54 4:59:52
Fraser 26 226 42N54'52 77w52'17 5:11:29
Frear Park 42 220 42N44'41 73w40'26 4:54:42
Fredonia 7 14 42N26'24 79w19'55 5:17:20
Freedom 5 226 42N29'05 78w19'53 5:13:20
Freedom Plains 14
11 41N40'21 73w48'00 4:55:12
Freehold 20 226 42N21'33 74w03'01 4:56:12
Freeman 51 13 42N03'20 77w16'22 5:09:05
Freeman Mill 25
226 43N27'39 75w34'44 5:02:19
Freeport 30 175 40N39'27 73w35'01 4:54:20
Freer Corner 39
226 42N28'23 75w15'40 5:01:03
Freetown 52 11 40N58'32 72w10'58 4:48:44
Freetown Corners 12
13 42N31'19 76w02'11 5:04:09
Freeville 55 13 42N30'50 76w20'49 5:05:23
Fremont 51 226 42N23'40 77w37'40 5:10:31
Fremont Center 53
226 41N50'32 75w02'36 5:00:10
Fremont Hills 34
41 43N04 76w04 5:04:16
French Creek 7
226 42N04'04 79w42'14 5:18:49
French Mountain 57
1 43N22'09 73w41'56 4:54:48
Frenchville 33
226 43N19'30 75w21'31 5:01:26
French Woods 13
97 41N55'16 75w11'11 5:00:45
Fresh Kills 43 11 40N33'51 74w11'12 4:56:45
Fresh Meadows 41
1 40N44'05 73w47'38 4:55:11
Fresh Pond 41 1 40N42'25 73w54'14 4:55:37
Fresh Pond Junction 41
1 40N42'14 73w53'31 4:55:34
Fresh Pond Landing 52
11 40N57'54 72w46'21 4:51:05
Frewsburg 7 128 42N03'16 79w09'30 5:16:38
Freysbush 29 62 42N54'33 74w39'48 4:58:39
Friend 62 14 42N39'46 77w11'02 5:08:44
Friendship 2 107 42N12'23 78w08'16 5:12:33
Friends Point 57
226 43N45 73w30 4:54:00
Frink Corner 46
226 43N04'54 73w56'13 4:55:45
Frinks Corner 61
226 42N42'17 78w23'18 5:13:33
Frone Corner 39
226 42N27'30 75w19'14 5:01:17
Frontenac 23 163 44N15'25 76w03'00 5:04:12
Frontier Plaza 28
209 43N08 77w43 5:10:52
Front Street 4
151 42N07 75w56 5:03:44
Frost Hollow 35
226 42N49'36 77w33'53 5:10:16
Frost Valley 56
226 41N59'13 74w30'39 4:58:03
Fruitland 59 226 43N13'27 77w20'16 5:09:21
Fruit Valley 38
204 43N26'07 76w33'51 5:06:15
Fullers 1 6 42N43'33 73w57'39 4:55:51
Fullers 57 226 43N28'39 74w05'42 4:56:23
Fullerville 45
178 44N16'05 75w20'32 5:01:22
Fulmer Valley 2
226 42N05'52 77w49'49 5:11:19
Fulton 38 55 43N19'22 76w25'03 5:05:40
Fultonham 48 226 42N34'06 74w23'45 4:57:35
Fultonville 29
174 42N56'52 74w22'15 4:57:29
Furnace Brook 36
226 41N13 74w17 4:57:08
Furnace Village 59
226 43N14'28 76w49'17 5:07:17
Furnaceville 39
14 42N39'17 74w40'20 4:58:41
Furnaceville 59
226 43N15'08 77w16'27 5:09:06
Furnace Woods 60
11 41N15'53 73w53'11 4:55:33
Furniss 38 204 43N23'43 76w32'01 5:06:08
Fyler Settlement 27
226 43N05'43 75w55'17 5:03:41
Gabriels 17 176 44N25'55 74w10'53 4:56:44
Gabriels Junction 49
14 42N25'17 76w54'14 5:07:37
Gaines 37 146 43N17'06 78w12'56 5:12:52
Gaines Basin 37
146 43N15'31 78w13'24 5:12:54
Gainesville 61 24 42N38'27 78w08'03 5:12:32
Galatia 12 13 42N29'07 76w01'54 5:04:08
Gale 45 87 44N16'03 74w37'53 4:58:32
Galen 59 99 43N04 76w52 5:07:28
Galena 9 200 42N36'47 75w31'52 5:02:07
Galeville 34 13 43N05'24 76w10'24 5:04:42
Galeville 56 11 41N38'11 74w11'29 4:56:46
Galilee 45 201 44N37'01 75w30'30 5:02:02
Gallatin 11 25 42N04 73w43 4:54:52
Gallatinville 11
11 42N02'04 73w40'16 4:54:41
Gallows Hill 60 6 41N19'17 73w54'30 4:55:38
Gallupville 48
226 42N39'45 74w13'59 4:56:56
Galway 46 226 43N01'07 74w01'55 4:56:08
Galway Lake 46
226 43N03 74w12 4:56:48
Gamble Mill 34 13 42N51'25 76w15'09 5:05:01
Ganahgote 56 122 41N41'13 74w10'33 4:56:42
Gang Mills 51 13 42N08'46 77w06'43 5:08:27
Gansevoort 46 226 43N11'46 73w39'08 4:54:37
Garbutt 28 226 43N00'46 77w47'31 5:11:10
Garden City 30
177 40N43'36 73w38'05 4:54:32

Garden City Park 30 11 40N44'27 73w39'47 4:54:39
Garden City South 30 11 40N42'44 73w39'41 4:54:39
Garden Park Estates 1 1 42N40 73w48 4:55:12
Garden Terrace 34 41 43N05'08 76w17'03 5:05:08
Gardenville 15 153 42N51'31 78w45'17 5:15:01
Gardiner 56 122 41N40'47 74w09'03 4:56:36
Gardiners Bay Estates 52 11 41N08 72w20 4:49:20
Gardners Corners 25 226 43N54 75w30 5:02:00
Gardnersville 48 139 42N43'26 74w34'57 4:58:20
Gardnertown 36 1 41N32'06 74w04'14 4:56:17
Gardnerville 36 11 41N20'40 74w29'14 4:57:57
Garfield 42 11 42N32'24 73w23'40 4:53:35
Garland 28 226 43N13'30 77w53'25 5:11:34
Garlinghouse 35 226 42N36'32 77w28'19 5:09:53
Garnerville 44 6 41N12'06 73w59'41 4:55:59
Garnet Lake 57 49 43N32'30 74w00'45 4:56:03
Garoga 18 43 43N02'38 74w31'01 4:58:04
Garrattsville 39 226 42N38'50 75w10'20 5:00:41
Garrison 40 6 41N23'02 73w56'46 4:55:47
Garrison Manor 46 226 42N55'05 73w54'31 4:55:38
Garwoods 2 226 42N27'34 77w49'30 5:11:18
Gaskill 54 205 42N07'48 76w10'55 5:04:44
Gasport 32 121 43N11'57 78w34'35 5:14:18
Gas Spring 2 226 42N24'55 77w50'04 5:11:20
Gates 28 209 43N09 77w41 5:10:44
Gates 46 1 43N05'29 73w38'19 4:54:33
Gates Center 28 209 43N09'12 77w41'28 5:10:46
Gayhead 14 226 41N36 73w47 4:55:08
Gayhead 20 3 42N20'29 73w58'14 4:55:53
Gay Ridge Estates 60 16 41N17 73w46 4:55:04
Gayville 38 14 43N18'21 76w00'50 5:04:03
Geddes 34 13 43N05 76w14 5:04:56
Gedney 60 7 41N01 73w45 4:55:00
Gee Brook 12 226 42N30'33 75w55'07 5:03:40
Geers Corners 45 226 44N10'52 75w20'18 5:01:21
Gees Corner 27 226 43N08'09 75w49'40 5:03:19
Genegantslet 9 226 42N21'01 75w48'39 5:03:15
Genesee 2 226 42N03 78w15 5:13:00
Genesee Falls 61 226 42N34 78w04 5:12:16
Genesee Junction 28 226 43N05'54 77w41'11 5:10:45
Geneseo 26 13 42N47'45 77w49'02 5:11:16
Geneva 35 41 42N52'08 76w58'41 5:07:55
Genoa 6 13 42N40'04 76w32'10 5:06:09
Georgetown 12 226 42N28'09 75w53'36 5:03:34
Georgetown 27 226 42N46'06 75w44'13 5:02:57
Georgetown Square 15 7 42N59 78w45 5:15:00
Georgica 52 11 40N56'43 72w13'13 4:48:53
Georgtown Station 27 180 42N51 75w37 5:02:28
Gerard Park 52 11 41N02'36 72w08'48 4:48:35
German 9 226 42N30 75w50 5:03:20
German Flatts 22 183 42N59 74w59 4:59:56
German Four Corners 9 226 42N29'30 75w51'40 5:03:27
Germantown 2 226 42N09'31 78w16'50 5:13:07
Germantown 11 11 42N08'04 73w53'32 4:55:34
Germantown 36 1 41N22'50 74w42'19 4:58:49
German Village 28 185 43N13'26 77w32'32 5:10:10
Germany Hill 54 205 42N08'56 76w21'10 5:05:25
Germonds 44 4 41N07'13 73w59'37 4:55:58
Gerritsen 24 1 40N35'34 73w55'34 4:55:42
Gerry 7 120 42N11'36 79w14'56 5:17:00
Getman Corners 22 196 42N57'00 75w00'51 5:00:03
Getzville 15 11 43N01'26 78w46'05 5:15:04
Ghent 11 11 42N19'45 73w36'58 4:54:28
Gibson 51 13 42N08'24 77w01'52 5:08:07
Gibson Corners 54 36 42N02'27 76w15'33 5:05:02
Gibson Landing 51 181 42N29'56 77w09'32 5:08:38
Giddingsville 23 143 43N46'42 76w02'09 5:04:09
Gifford 47 226 42N45'03 74w02'56 4:56:12
Gilbert 50 12 42N40'08 76w51'18 5:07:25
Gilbert Corners 40 6 41N23'56 73w52'12 4:55:29
Gilbert Corners 46 226 43N04'05 73w44'12 4:54:57
Gilbert Corners 48 11 42N47'02 74w33'08 4:58:13
Gilbert Mills 38 93 43N18'53 76w18'34 5:05:14
Gilberts Corner 32 145 43N09'18 78w31'14 5:14:05
Gilbertsville 39 226 42N28'17 75w19'34 5:01:18
Gilboa 48 226 42N23'50 74w26'47 4:57:47
Gile 17 226 44N36'46 74w29'55 4:58:00
Gilgo Beach 52 11 40N37'06 73w23'53 4:53:36
Gilmantown 21 11 43N26'17 74w18'59 4:57:16
Girarde 36 11 41N26'36 74w13'41 4:56:55
Gladding Corner 35 47 42N48'06 77w27'05 5:09:48
Glasco 56 215 42N02'37 73w56'52 4:55:47
Glasgow Mills 18 43 43N06'10 74w31'52 4:58:07
Glass Lake 42 226 42N37'48 73w31'53 4:54:08
Gleasons Mill 45 226 44N27'38 74w56'55 4:59:48
Glen 29 174 42N53'39 74w20'42 4:57:23
Glen Aubrey 4 226 42N15'31 76w00'35 5:04:02
Glenburnie 58 226 43N45'48 73w27'24 4:53:50
Glencairn 54 224 42N04'44 76w29'24 5:05:58
Glen Castle 4 151 42N10'44 75w54'25 5:03:38
Glenclyffe 40 6 41N22'05 73w56'56 4:55:48
Glencoe Mills 11 1 42N08'58 73w44'28 4:54:58
Glen Cove 30 1 40N51'44 73w38'03 4:54:32
Glen Cove Landing 30 1 40N51'46 73w39'16 4:54:37
Glendale 25 15 43N42'58 75w25'01 5:01:40
Glendale 41 1 40N42'05 73w53'14 4:55:33
Glendale 60 166 41N11'49 73w50'44 4:55:23
Glen Edith 28 185 43N12'14 77w31'13 5:10:05
Glenerie 56 215 42N02'01 73w58'24 4:55:54
Glenerie Lake Park 56 215 42N00'49 73w59'08 4:55:57
Glenfield 25 15 43N42'37 75w24'09 5:01:37
Glenford 56 11 42N00'09 74w07'36 4:56:30
Glen Grove 51 181 42N26'34 77w11'16 5:08:45
Glenham 14 6 41N31'18 73w55'37 4:55:42
Glen Haven 6 41 42N45'56 76w16'42 5:05:07
Glen Haven 28 185 43N11'35 77w31'54 5:10:08
Glenhaven 33 222 43N07 75w18 5:01:12
Glen Head 30 11 40N50'07 73w37'27 4:54:30
Glen Island 60 1 40N53 73w47 4:55:08
Glen Lake 46 226 41N31 73w42 4:54:48
Glenmark 59 226 43N11'29 76w54'47 5:07:39
Glenmont 1 11 42N36'17 73w46'12 4:55:05
Glenmore 16 226 44N15'15 73w44'35 4:54:58
Glenmore 33 226 43N21'32 75w37'08 5:02:29
Glen Oaks 41 1 40N44'49 73w42'43 4:54:51
Glenora 62 13 42N29'54 76w55'03 5:07:40
Glen Park 23 45 44N00'04 75w58'00 5:03:52
Glenridge 47 4 42N52'01 73w54'36 4:55:38
Glens Falls 57 1 43N18'34 73w38'40 4:54:35
Glen Spey 53 25 41N28'43 74w48'50 4:59:15
Glen, The 57 63 43N35'02 73w51'48 4:55:27
Glenville 26 226 42N46'48 77w36'22 5:10:25
Glenville 47 1 42N55'45 74w03'09 4:56:13
Glenville 60 6 41N03'56 73w50'28 4:55:22
Glenville Center 47 1 42N53'33 73w58'45 4:55:55
Glenwild 46 226 43N08'03 74w03'55 4:56:16
Glen Wild 53 74 41N39'14 74w35'14 4:58:21
Glenwood 15 218 42N37'09 78w39'29 5:14:38
Glenwood 32 199 43N10'06 78w59'49 5:15:59
Glenwood 60 1 40N56'56 73w53'48 4:55:35
Glenwood Landing 30 11 40N49'50 73w38'21 4:54:33
Glenwood Park 36 1 41N30'48 74w03'01 4:56:12
Globe Hotel Corners 6 13 42N47'18 76w22'51 5:05:31
Gloversville 18 46 43N03'10 74w20'39 4:57:23
Godeffroy 36 21 41N26'48 74w36'46 4:58:27
Godfreys Corner 23 17 44N17'38 75w53'17 5:03:33
Golah 28 27 42N58'13 77w42'59 5:10:52
Golden Glow Heights 8 13 42N05'09 76w52'18 5:07:29
Goldens Bridge 60 16 41N17'36 73w40'38 4:54:43
Goldsmith 17 113 44N34'07 73w59'56 4:56:00
Goodrich 54 205 42N06'06 76w17'17 5:05:09
Goodrich Corners 33 211 43N08'55 75w31'42 5:02:07
Goodyear Corners 6 13 42N38'11 76w36'55 5:06:28
Goose Bay 23 17 44N22'00 75w50'48 5:03:23
Goose Bay Estates 52 11 41N04 72w26 4:49:44
Goose Island 58 213 43N15'15 73w25'27 4:53:42
Goosetree 6 13 42N39'17 76w28'30 5:05:54
Gordon Heights 52 11 40N51'31 72w58'16 4:51:53
Gorham 35 14 42N47'56 77w07'55 5:08:32
Gorthey Corners 18 226 43N05'56 74w10'05 4:56:40
Goshen 36 7 41N24'07 74w19'29 4:57:18
Goshen Hills 36 7 41N24 74w20 4:57:20
Gothicville 39 13 42N40'23 74w41'37 4:58:46
Goulds 13 226 41N55'33 75w05'01 5:00:20
Goulds Mill 25 77 43N36'33 75w20'27 5:01:22
Gouverneur 45 178 44N20'12 75w27'48 5:01:51
Governors Island 31 1 40N41 74w01 4:56:04
Gowanda 5 42 42N27'47 78w56'10 5:15:45
Gracie 12 41 42N33'56 76w14'58 5:05:00
Gracie 31 1 40N47 73w58 4:55:52
Grafton 42 11 42N46'08 73w27'05 4:53:48
Graftons Square 38 14 43N26'33 76w09'04 5:04:36
Graham 60 1 41N07'25 73w48'38 4:55:15
Graham Beach 43 1 40N36 74w05 4:56:20
Grahamsville 53 226 41N50'52 74w32'54 4:58:12
Granby Center 38 226 43N19'36 76w27'59 5:05:52
Grandby 38 226 43N18 76w27 5:05:48
Grand Gorge 13 131 42N21'43 74w29'40 4:57:59
Grand Island 15 1 43N01 78w58 5:15:52
Grandview Bay 15 11 42N38 79w03 5:16:12
Grand View Beach 28 226 43N17'52 77w41'00 5:10:44
Grand View Heights 28 226 43N17'43 77w41'37 5:10:46
Grand View-on-Hudson 44 4 41N03'50 73w55'15 4:55:41
Grandview Park 23 163 44N19'10 76w03'20 5:04:13
Grandyle Village 15 1 42N59'47 78w57'19 5:15:49
Grange Landing 35 14 42N45'59 77w19'17 5:09:17
Granger 2 226 42N29 78w01 5:12:04
Grangerville 46 226 43N06'21 73w37'18 4:54:29
Granite 56 72 41N45'36 74w16'10 4:57:05
Granite Springs 60 16 41N18'37 73w45'28 4:55:02
Graniteville 43 1 40N37'29 74w08'56 4:56:36
Grant 22 84 43N19'03 75w03'39 5:00:15
Grant City 43 1 40N34'55 74w06'19 4:56:25
Grant Corner 60 16 41N19'08 73w35'29 4:54:22
Grant Hollow 42 11 42N49'56 73w37'34 4:54:30
Grant Mills 13 226 42N05'03 74w40'51 4:58:43
Grant Park 30 11 40N39 73w42 4:54:48
Grantville 45 226 44N51'34 74w55'17 4:59:41
Granville 58 42 43N24'28 73w15'36 4:53:02
Grapeville 20 11 42N24'44 73w56'01 4:55:44
Graphite 57 226 43N35'04 73w33'48 4:54:15
Grasmere 43 1 40N36'15 74w05'15 4:56:21
Grassy Point 44 6 41N14 73w59 4:55:56
Gravesend 24 1 40N35'51 73w57'56 4:55:52
Gravesville 22 84 43N15'11 75w06'52 5:00:27
Gray 22 84 43N15'53 74w56'51 4:59:47
Graymoor 40 11 41N21'16 73w55'11 4:55:41
Grays Corner 58 6 43N31'49 73w23'09 4:53:33
Grays Corners 46 1 42N49'11 73w45'33 4:55:02
Gray Shores 26 13 42N49'00 77w42'45 5:10:51
Graywood 26 13 42N48'44 77w42'54 5:10:52
Great Bend 23 119 44N02'03 75w43'09 5:02:53
Great Kills 43 1 40N33'15 74w09'07 4:56:36
Great Neck 30 1 40N48'02 73w43'44 4:54:55
Great Neck Estates 30 1 40N47'13 73w44'14 4:54:57
Great Neck Plaza 30 1 40N47'12 73w43'37 4:54:54
Great River 52 11 40N43'16 73w09'29 4:52:38
Great Valley 5 226 42N12'52 78w38'12 5:14:33
Greece 28 209 43N12'35 77w41'36 5:10:46
Greeley Square 31 1 40N45 73w59 4:55:56
Green Acres 15 1 43N00 78w51 5:15:24
Green Acres 30 11 40N39'31 73w43'04 4:54:52
Green Acres Valley 15 1 43N00'26 78w49'54 5:15:20
Greenboro 38 226 43N38'38 75w53'21 5:03:33
Greenburgh 60 7 41N02 73w49 4:55:16
Greenbush 48 139 42N38'47 74w26'39 4:57:47
Green Corners 46 1 43N04'14 74w04'12 4:56:17
Greencrest 7 160 42N26'24 79w25'22 5:17:41
Greendale 11 1 42N12'26 73w50'51 4:55:23
Greene 9 105 42N19'45 75w46'13 5:03:05
Greenfield 46 226 43N06'13 73w51'52 4:55:27
Greenfield Center 46 226 43N07'42 73w50'49 4:55:23
Greenfield Park 56 48 41N43'33 74w29'10 4:57:57
Green Haven 14 226 41N35'14 73w43'06 4:54:52
Greenhaven 60 1 40N57'03 73w42'26 4:54:50
Green Hills 7 160 42N23'32 79w29'37 5:17:58
Greenhurst 7 187 42N07'10 79w18'38 5:17:15
Green Island 1 179 42N44'39 73w41'31 4:54:46
Greenlawn 52 11 40N52'08 73w21'56 4:53:28
Greenpoint 24 1 40N43'25 73w57'05 4:55:48
Greenpoint 52 11 40N43 73w06 4:52:24
Greenport 52 1 41N06'12 72w21'35 4:49:26
Greenport Center 11 1 42N14'27 73w45'46 4:55:03
Greenridge 43 11 40N33'40 74w10'13 4:56:41
Green River 11 11 42N15'43 73w28'22 4:53:53
Greens Crossing 33 13 42N57'29 75w16'38 5:01:07
Green Settlement 23 143 43N51'20 76w02'16 5:04:09
Greens Landing 35 14 42N49'50 77w15'32 5:09:02
Green Street 16 44 44N25'23 73w38'06 4:54:32
Greenvale 30 11 40N48'38 73w37'44 4:54:31
Greenville 20 226 42N24'55 74w01'21 4:56:05
Greenville 36 1 41N21'38 74w37'01 4:58:28
Greenville 51 14 42N25'39 77w30'46 5:10:03
Greenville 56 48 41N52'43 74w24'07 4:57:36
Greenville 60 1 40N59'35 73w49'13 4:55:17
Greenville Center 20 226 42N23'14 74w00'02 4:56:00
Greenway 33 211 43N10'50 75w32'00 5:02:08
Greenway Corners 33 211 43N10'13 75w31'34 5:02:06
Greenwich 58 1 43N05'26 73w29'57 4:54:00
Greenwich Junction 58 213 43N08'59 73w21'12 4:53:25
Greenwich Village 31 1 40N43'42 74w00'12 4:56:01
Greenwood 51 226 42N08'06 77w38'55 5:10:36
Greenwood Lake 36 226 41N13'21 74w17'41 4:57:11
Gregory Landing 6 13 42N48'37 76w18'46 5:05:15
Gregorytown 13 226 42N01'52 75w02'12 5:00:09
Greig 25 119 43N40'53 75w21'18 5:01:25
Greigsville 26 126 42N49'50 77w53'50 5:11:35
Grenell 23 163 44N17'00 76w02'40 5:04:11
Gretna 14 226 41N46'50 73w50'47 4:55:23
Greycourt 36 4 41N21'43 74w15'21 4:57:01
Grey Oaks 60 1 40N57'58 73w52'12 4:55:29
Greystone 60 1 40N58'16 73w53'19 4:55:33
Gridleyville 54 226 42N14'42 76w22'21 5:05:29
Griffin 21 226 43N28'20 74w13'24 4:56:54
Griffins Corners 34 13 42N56'00 76w11'50 5:04:47
Griffins Mills 15 11 42N43'26 78w40'03 5:14:40
Griffiss Air Force Base 33 211 43N13 75w26 5:01:44
Griffiths 7 187 42N07'18 79w19'10 5:17:17
Grindstone 23 163 44N17'00 76w08'35 5:04:34

Griswold 7 15 42N22'02 79W13'48 5:16:55
Griswold 19 164 42N53'26 78W20'43 5:13:23
Grooms Corners 46
4 42N50'06 73W50'39 4:55:23
Grooville 53 75 41N56'33 74W46'04 4:59:04
Grossinger 53 189 41N46 74W44 4:58:56
Groton 55 13 42N35'16 76W22'02 5:05:28
Groton City 55 13 42N36'54 76W17'08 5:05:09
Grotto 55 13 42N33'34 76W24'36 5:05:38
Grout Mill 12 16 42N43'24 76W15'32 5:05:02
Grove 2 226 42N26'11 77W52'06 5:11:28
Groveland 26 13 42N39'53 77W46'12 5:11:05
Groveland Corners 26
13 42N42'06 77W45'07 5:11:00
Grovenor Corners 48
12 42N43'42 74W23'03 4:57:32
Grover 15 7 42N58 78W48 5:15:12
Grover Cleveland Terrace 15
7 42N58'18 78W48'24 5:15:14
Grover Hills 16
54 44N04'39 73W30'43 4:54:03
Grovernor Corners 48
12 42N43 74W20 4:57:20
Grove Springs 51
181 42N28'16 77W09'23 5:08:38
Groveville 14 7 41N30'55 73W56'24 4:55:46
Grymes Hill 43 1 40N37'07 74W05'38 4:56:23
Guideboard 27 16 42N48'33 75W21'07 5:01:24
Guilderland 1 6 42N42'16 73W54'43 4:55:39
Guilderland Center 1
40 42N42'07 73W58'00 4:55:52
Guilderland Gardens 1
1 42N40 73W48 4:55:12
Guilford 9 149 42N24'15 75W29'24 5:01:58
Guilford Center 9
149 42N24'19 75W27'45 5:01:51
Gulf Bridge 38
182 43N17'25 76W03'54 5:04:16
Gulfport 43 1 40N37'47 74W11'46 4:56:47
Gulf Summit 4 226 42N01'08 75W31'51 5:02:07
Gulick 35 226 42N41'30 77W27'23 5:09:50
Gulph 22 226 43N00'37 75W09'35 5:00:38
Gunther Park 60 7 40N56'04 73W51'11 4:55:25
Gurn Spring 46
226 43N10'15 73W43'05 4:54:52
Guyanoga 62 226 42N37'26 77W09'57 5:08:40
Guyler Hill 12
226 42N42'47 75W55'15 5:03:41
Guymard 36 21 41N25'44 74W35'57 4:58:24
Gypsum 35 14 42N58'56 77W07'59 5:08:32
Haberman 41 1 40N43'33 73W55'13 4:55:41
Hadley 46 40 43N19'02 73W50'55 4:55:24
Hadley Bay 7 226 42N08'58 79W24'10 5:17:37
Hagaman 29 226 42N58'28 74W09'05 4:56:36
Hagedorns Mills 46
226 43N04'34 74W06'01 4:56:24
Hagerman 52 11 40N46'14 72W57'52 4:51:51
Hague 57 226 43N44'43 73W29'56 4:54:00
Hague Crossing 45
226 44N43'40 75W14'08 5:00:57
Hailesboro 45 178 44N18'36 75W26'48 5:01:47
Haines Corners 40
7 41N28'25 73W34'57 4:54:20
Haines Falls 20 2 42N11'45 74W05'51 4:56:23
Halcott 20 42 42N13 74W28 4:57:52
Halcott Center 20
42 42N11'18 74W29'30 4:57:58
Halcottsville 13
42 42N12'30 74W36'05 4:58:24
Hale Eddy 13 167 42N00'13 75W23'00 5:01:32
Hale Mills 18 226 43N01'10 74W20'04 4:57:20
Halesite 52 11 40N53'18 73W24'57 4:53:40
Half Acre 6 13 42N55'00 76W37'30 5:06:30
Half Hollow 52 11 40N46'35 73W20'37 4:53:22
Half Hollow Hills 52
11 40N47 73W22 4:53:28
Halfmoon 46 11 42N49'39 73W43'06 4:54:52
Halfmoon Beach 46
1 42N48'11 73W45'16 4:55:01
Halfway 34 24 43N01'31 76W23'32 5:05:34
Halfway House Corners 45
226 44N45 75W08 5:00:32
Halihan Hill 56
11 41N59'28 74W01'42 4:56:07
Hall 35 14 42N47'38 77W04'00 5:08:16
Hallock Landing 52
11 40N57'50 72W56'14 4:51:45
Halls Corner 6 13 42N38'24 76W16'57 5:05:08
Halls Corner 23
77 44N11'59 75W41'57 5:02:48
Halls Corner 46 8 42N59'57 73W48'42 4:55:15
Halls Corner 61
226 42N44'25 78W11'51 5:12:47
Halls Corners 50
226 42N37 77W33 5:10:12
Hallsport 2 109 42N04'31 77W51'09 5:11:25
Hallsville 29 62 42N56'06 74W42'14 4:58:49
Halsey 24 1 40N41 73W55 4:55:40
Halseys Corners 10
86 44N42'28 73W28'10 4:53:53
Halsey Valley 54
226 42N08'29 76W26'22 5:05:45
Halseyville 55 13 42N31'53 76W38'03 5:06:32
Hambletville 13
167 42N05'48 75W23'36 5:01:34
Hamburg 15 153 42N42'57 78W49'47 5:15:19
Hamburg 20 226 42N14'03 73W51'02 4:55:24
Hamburg-on-the-Lake 15
153 42N45 78W51 5:15:24
Hamden 13 226 42N11'28 74W59'42 4:59:59
Hamilton 27 180 42N49'37 75W32'42 5:02:11
Hamilton Beach 41
1 40N39'08 73W49'40 4:55:19
Hamilton Center 27
130 42N47'23 75W29'46 5:01:59
Hamilton Grange 31
1 40N49 73W57 4:55:48
Hamilton Park 43
1 40N38 74W06 4:56:24
Hamlet 7 217 42N22'11 79W08'07 5:16:32
Hamlin 28 226 43N18'11 77W55'17 5:11:41
Hammel 41 1 40N35'16 73W48'38 4:55:15
Hammertown 14 226 41N58'32 73W38'27 4:54:34
Hammond 45 20 44N26'56 75W41'40 5:02:47
Hammonds Corner 38
15 43N28'21 76W23'05 5:05:32
Hammondsport 51
181 42N24'28 77W13'26 5:08:54
Hampshire 51 226 42N09'48 77W31'28 5:10:06
Hampton 58 226 43N31'29 73W15'08 4:53:01
Hampton Bays 52
11 40N52'08 72W31'05 4:50:04
Hampton Beach 52
1 40N48'32 72W35'28 4:50:22
Hamptonburgh 36
11 41N26'06 74W15'38 4:57:03
Hampton Manor 42
1 42N39 73W43 4:54:52
Hampton Park 42 1 42N36'58 73W43'14 4:54:53
Hampton Park 52
11 40N54'33 72W23'41 4:49:35
Hancock 13 97 41N57'14 75W16'51 5:01:07
Hands Creek Landing 52
11 41N01'08 72W12'11 4:48:49
Handsome Eddy 53
20 41N26'34 74W53'28 4:59:34
Hanford Bay 7 216 42N33'26 79W08'37 5:16:34
Hankins 53 20 41N48'51 75W05'14 5:00:21
Hanley Corner 13
42 42N08'04 74W32'38 4:58:11
Hannacroix 20 1 42N25'44 73W48'35 4:55:14
Hannans Corner 28
13 43N04'45 77W26'31 5:09:46
Hannawa Falls 45
207 44N36'44 74W58'17 4:59:53
Hannibal 38 226 43N19'16 76W34'45 5:06:19
Hannibal Center 38
226 43N17'24 76W33'09 5:06:13
Hanover 7 216 42N31 79W08 5:16:32
Hanover 33 11 42N58'01 75W22'41 5:01:31
Hanover Center 7
216 42N31'10 79W08'20 5:16:33
Happy Valley 38
182 43N26'26 75W58'30 5:03:54
Happy Valley 44 4 41N10'09 74W02'52 4:56:11
Harbor 22 184 43N04'55 75W08'53 5:00:36
Harbor Acres 30
11 40N50 73W42 4:54:48
Harbor Green 30
11 40N38'59 73W27'47 4:53:51
Harbor Heights Park 52
11 40N51 73W23 4:53:32
Harbor Hills 30 1 40N47'27 73W44'49 4:54:59
Harbor Isle 30 11 40N36'12 73W39'54 4:54:40
Hardenburg 56 75 42N00'03 74W39'56 4:58:40
Harding Crossing 47
1 42N50'51 73W58'44 4:55:55
Hard Point 6 226 43N05'21 76W39'47 5:06:39
Hardscrabble 13
31 42N19'19 74W34'44 4:58:19
Hardscrabble 52
11 40N58'16 72W13'22 4:48:53
Hardy Corners 2
226 42N21'33 78W18'33 5:13:14
Hardys 61 24 42N37'11 78W10'38 5:12:43
Harford (North Harford Sta) 12
226 42N25'34 76W13'37 5:04:54
Harford Mills 12
226 42N24'41 76W12'06 5:04:48
Harkness 10 86 44N31'25 73W34'12 4:54:17
Harlem 15 7 42N58 78W48 5:15:12
Harlem 31 1 40N48'28 73W56'45 4:55:47
Harlemville 11 1 42N16'13 73W35'41 4:54:23
Harmon-on-Hudson 60
166 41N12 73W53 4:55:32
Harmon Park 47 1 42N53'32 73W55'15 4:55:41
Harmony 7 226 42N03 79W26 5:17:44
Harmony Corners 46
11 42N58'39 73W57'19 4:55:49
Harpersfield 13
226 42N26'18 74W41'16 4:58:45
Harpursville 4 17 42N10'42 75W37'30 5:02:30
Harriet 15 1 42N58 78W51 5:15:24
Harrietstown 17
81 44N23'49 74W09'32 4:56:38
Harrigan 10 188 44N51'09 73W58'01 4:55:52
Harriman 36 4 41N18'30 74W08'42 4:56:35
Harris 53 72 41N42'51 74W43'36 4:58:54
Harrisburg 5 226 42N00'40 78W32'43 5:14:11
Harrisburg 25 226 43N50'32 75W36'11 5:02:25
Harrisburg 57 226 43N24'24 74W04'30 4:56:18
Harris Corners 61
226 42N46'11 78W26'32 5:13:46
Harris Hill 15 7 42N57'53 78W40'40 5:14:43
Harris Hill Manor 8
13 42N05'44 76W54'13 5:07:37
Harrison 60 7 40N58'08 73W42'47 4:54:51
Harrison Grove 32
226 43N16'50 78W57'59 5:15:52
Harrisville 9 15 42N40'48 75W27'48 5:01:51
Harrisville 25
118 44N09'07 75W19'17 5:01:17
Harrower 29 226 42N57'55 74W10'18 4:56:41
Hartfield 7 158 42N16'02 79W28'21 5:17:53
Hartford 58 226 43N21'49 73W23'39 4:53:35
Hartland 32 226 43N14'24 78W34'35 5:14:18
Hart Lot 34 24 43N01 76W28 5:05:52
Hartman 57 226 43N15'49 73W45'01 4:55:00
Hartmans Corners 1
40 42N42'28 73W55'22 4:55:41
Hartsdale 60 7 41N01'08 73W47'55 4:55:12
Harts Hill 33 222 43N07 75W18 5:01:12
Hartson Point 26
226 42N46'21 77W42'47 5:10:51
Hartsville 51 226 42N14'49 77W41'39 5:10:47
Hartwick 39 226 42N39'35 75W02'57 5:00:12
Hartwick Seminary 39
13 42N38'35 74W57'57 4:59:52
Hartwood 53 21 41N32'07 74W41'53 4:58:48
Hartwood Club 53
21 41N30'15 74W43'29 4:58:54
Harvard 13 226 42N01'26 75W06'47 5:00:27
Hasbrouck 53 74 41N47'28 74W36'54 4:58:28
Hasbroucks 21 226 43N52'17 74W38'05 4:58:32
Haselton 16 44 44N24'42 73W46'09 4:55:05
Haselton 33 211 43N13 75W26 5:01:44
Haskell Flats 5
226 42N09'03 78W19'25 5:13:18
Haskinville 51
226 42N25'23 77W33'58 5:10:16
Hastings 38 182 43N22'26 76W09'10 5:04:37
Hastings Center 38
182 43N19'01 76W09'17 5:04:37
Hastings-on-Hudson 60
1 41N00'10 73W52'45 4:55:31
Hatch's Corner 45
226 44N25 75W09 5:00:36
Hatchs Corners 33
211 43N10'41 75W30'28 5:02:02
Hathaway Corners 35
19 42N57'50 77W20'54 5:09:24
Hauppauge 52 11 40N49'32 73W12'11 4:52:49
Haven 53 11 41N32'27 74W31'28 4:58:06
Havens Corner 62
14 42N43'02 77W05'22 5:08:21
Haverling Heights 51
14 42N20'58 77W18'57 5:09:16
Haverstraw 44 6 41N11'51 73W57'54 4:55:52
Haviland 14 11 41N46 73W54 4:55:36
Haviland Hollow 40
7 41N29'04 73W34'16 4:54:17
Hawkeye 10 44 44N31'10 73W51'34 4:55:26
Hawkins Corner 7
226 42N29'33 79W11'34 5:16:46
Hawkins Corner 33
211 43N17'04 75W28'17 5:01:53
Hawkinsville 33
226 43N29'37 75W16'39 5:01:07
Hawley Corners 9
200 42N32'23 75W30'32 5:02:02
Hawleys 13 226 42N10'55 75W00'47 5:00:03
Hawleyton 4 151 42N01'07 75W54'59 5:03:40
Hawthorne 60 6 41N06'26 73W47'47 4:55:11
Hawthorne Hill 47
6 42N47'52 73W52'50 4:55:31
Hawthorne Park 7
225 42N19 79W34 5:18:16
Hawversville 48
226 42N30'52 74W14'35 4:56:58
Haydenville 5 226 42N06'41 78W22'31 5:13:30
Hayground 52 11 40N55'35 72W20'00 4:49:20
Haynersville 42
11 42N47'26 73W34'16 4:54:17
Haynes 9 106 42N28'01 75W32'46 5:02:11
Hayt Corner 55
186 42N28'06 76W32'35 5:06:10
Hayt Corners 50
12 42N41'45 76W47'21 5:07:09
Hazel 53 75 41N55'28 74W52'14 4:59:29
Head Corners 55
186 42N31'29 76W28'23 5:05:54
Head of the Harbor 52
11 40N54'12 73W09'30 4:52:38
Heathcote 60 1 40N59'04 73W46'30 4:55:06
Heatherwood North 52
11 40N56 73W06 4:52:24
Heatherwood South 52
11 40N52 74W49 4:59:16
Heath Grove 34 13 42N53'06 76W17'36 5:05:10
Heath Ridge 60 1 40N58'39 73W46'25 4:55:06
Hebron 58 226 43N17 73W32 4:54:08
Hecla 33 11 43N05'58 75W27'15 5:01:49
Hector 49 226 42N30'02 76W52'22 5:07:29
Hedgesville 51 13 42N08'15 77W24'46 5:09:39
Helena 45 226 44N55'18 74W43'36 4:58:54
Hell Gate 31 1 40N48 73W57 4:55:48
Hemlock 26 226 42N47'39 77W36'24 5:10:26
Hempstead 30 6 40N42'22 73W37'09 4:54:29
Hempstead 44 4 41N08'59 74W02'03 4:56:08
Hempstead Gardens 30
6 40N41'47 73W38'44 4:54:35
Hemstreet Park 42
1 42N54'16 73W40'48 4:54:43
Henderson 23 65 43N50'49 76W10'56 5:04:44
Henderson Harbor 23
65 43N51'51 76W12'08 5:04:49
Hendy Creek 8 13 42N02 76W52 5:07:28
Henrietta 28 20 43N03'33 77W36'45 5:10:27
Hensonville 20 52 42N17'23 74W13'01 4:56:52
Herkimer 22 183 43N01'32 74W59'11 4:59:57
Herkimer Landing 22
226 43N30'34 74W48'54 4:59:16
Hermitage 51 14 42N22'45 77W16'24 5:09:06
Hermitage 61 24 42N38'54 78W11'59 5:12:48
Hermon 45 226 44N28'02 75W13'51 5:00:55
Herrick Grove 23
226 44N03'29 76W11'26 5:04:46
Herricks 30 11 40N45'19 73W40'02 4:54:40
Herrings 23 119 44N01'26 75W39'15 5:02:37
Hertel 15 226 43N27 78W43 5:14:52
Herthum Heights 33
222 43N07 75W18 5:01:12
Hervey Street 20
226 42N20'42 74W07'37 4:56:30
Heslops Corner 39
226 42N28'40 75W18'16 5:01:13
Hessville 29 62 42N52'26 74W41'15 4:58:45
Heuvelton 45 226 44N37'05 75W24'27 5:01:38
Hewittville 45
207 44N42'16 75W00'40 5:00:03
Hewlett 30 1 40N38'35 73W41'46 4:54:47
Hewlett Bay Park 30
1 40N37'59 73W41'45 4:54:47
Hewlett Harbor 30
11 40N38'10 73W40'55 4:54:44
Hewlett Neck 30 1 40N37'24 73W41'55 4:54:48
Hibbards Corner 55
186 42N25'52 76W25'42 5:05:43
Hibernia 14 226 41N48'45 73W45'47 4:55:03
Hickeys Corners 46
226 43N05 73W47 4:55:08
Hickorybush 56 11 41N52'32 74W02'53 4:56:12
Hickory Corners 32
226 43N11'08 78W45'15 5:15:01
Hickory Grove 38
204 43N30'50 76W19'15 5:05:17
Hicks 8 226 42N07'25 76W37'02 5:06:28
Hicksville 30 11 40N46'06 73W31'32 4:54:06
Higgins 2 226 42N13'48 78W05'17 5:12:21

Higgins Bay 21 226 43N24'28 74w32'03 4:58:08
Higginsville 33 13 43N10'37 75w38'50 5:02:35
High Bank 10 136 44N37'36 73w54'55 4:55:40
High Bridge 3 1 40N50'12 73w55'38 4:55:43
High Bridge 34 13 43N00'50 76w00'45 5:04:03
High Falls 20 226 42N09'44 73w58'05 4:55:52
High Falls 25 226 43N55'23 75w22'21 5:01:29
High Falls 56 11 41N49'36 74w07'36 4:56:30
High Flats 45 226 44N35'36 74w53'21 4:59:33
Highland 56 51 41N43'15 73w57'38 4:55:51
Highland Beach 6 12 42N52'39 76w30'56 5:06:04
Highland Falls 36 1 41N22'09 73w58'00 4:55:52
Highland Lake 53 25 41N31'24 74w51'06 4:59:24
Highland Landing 56 51 41N43'04 73w56'55 4:55:48
Highland Mills 36 226 41N20'49 74w07'36 4:56:30
Highland-on-the-Lake 15 11 42N42'29 78w58'42 5:15:55
Highland Park 32 226 43N11'46 78w40'28 5:14:42
Highlands 36 1 41N22 73w59 4:55:56
Highlawn 24 1 40N36 73w58 4:55:52
High Market 25 226 44N05 75w27 5:01:48
High Mills 47 226 42N53'58 73w54'29 4:55:38
Highmount 56 42 42N08'39 74w29'25 4:57:58
High View 53 11 41N33'27 74w27'29 4:57:50
High Woods 56 215 42N02'44 74w01'44 4:56:07
Hiler 15 1 42N58 78w51 5:15:24
Hillburn 44 4 41N07'26 74w10'11 4:56:41
Hill Corners 18 226 43N01'26 74w10'25 4:56:42
Hillcrest 2 226 42N22'45 78w12'20 5:12:49
Hillcrest 4 151 42N08 75w53 5:03:32
Hillcrest 44 4 41N07'40 74w02'29 4:56:10
Hillis 14 11 41N38 73w54 4:55:36
Hillsboro 33 14 43N19'38 75w49'47 5:03:19
Hillsdale 11 11 42N10'44 73w31'35 4:54:06
Hillsdale 58 42 43N22'36 73w19'02 4:53:16
Hillside 33 226 43N21'25 75w23'16 5:01:33
Hillside 41 1 40N42'28 73w47'14 4:55:09
Hillside Heights 30 11 40N45 73w41 4:54:44
Hillside Lake 14 6 41N36 73w53 4:55:32
Hillside Manor 30 11 40N45 73w40 4:54:40
Hillside Park 18 43 43N00 74w22 4:57:28
Hillview 42 1 42N39 73w43 4:54:52
Hilton 28 13 43N17'17 77w47'37 5:11:10
Hiltonville 2 226 42N22'06 77w50'36 5:11:22
Himrod 62 12 42N35'23 76w57'19 5:07:49
Hinckley 33 20 43N18'44 75w07'20 5:00:29
Hinckleyville 28 14 43N12 77w48 5:11:12
Hindsburg 37 146 43N15 78w12 5:12:48
Hinkleyville 28 226 43N12'37 77w51'00 5:11:24
Hinmans Corners 4 151 42N09'38 75w53'51 5:03:35
Hinmansville 38 93 43N14'52 76w21'10 5:05:25
Hinsburg 37 146 43N15'14 78w06'22 5:12:25
Hinsdale 5 20 42N10'04 78w23'15 5:13:33
Hinsdale 34 41 43N06'16 76w08'17 5:04:33
Hitching Corner 22 13 42N53'19 75w09'55 5:00:40
Hoag Corners 42 11 42N33'23 73w30'42 4:54:03
Hobart 13 25 42N22'17 74w40'15 4:58:41
Hoben 2 24 42N00'13 78w05'42 5:12:23
Hobin Corners 33 13 42N53'58 75w18'24 5:01:14
Hoboken 39 226 42N37'37 75w19'22 5:01:17
Hoesville 18 1 43N01'10 74w06'15 4:56:25
Hoffman 32 1 43N04'10 78w49'23 5:15:18
Hoffmans 47 94 42N53'42 74w04'37 4:56:18
Hoffmeister 21 226 43N23'27 74w43'02 4:58:52
Hogansburg 17 226 44N58'26 74w39'49 4:58:39
Hogtown 58 123 43N31'13 73w33'25 4:54:14
Holbrook 52 11 40N48'44 73w04'44 4:52:19
Holbrook Corners 46 226 42N58'26 73w58'37 4:55:54
Holbrook-Holtsville 52 11 40N49 73w04 4:52:16
Holcomb 35 47 42N54'08 77w25'12 5:09:41
Holcombville 57 49 43N41'18 73w59'01 4:55:56
Holiday Manor 35 41 42N52 76w59 5:07:56
Holland 15 22 42N38'28 78w32'31 5:14:10
Holland 41 1 40N35'11 73w49'06 4:55:16
Holland Cove 59 89 43N17'13 77w08'38 5:08:35
Holland Patent 33 14 43N14'30 75w15'26 5:01:02
Holley 37 117 43N13'35 78w01'37 5:12:06
Hollis 41 1 40N42'48 73w46'03 4:55:04
Hollis Court 41 1 40N42 73w44 4:54:56
Holliswood 41 1 40N43 73w50 4:55:20
Hollowville 11 11 42N12'19 73w41'30 4:54:46
Hollywood 45 87 44N14 74w36 4:58:24
Holmes 14 7 41N31'24 73w38'50 4:54:35
Holmesville 9 226 42N30'46 75w24'06 5:01:36
Holton Beach 50 226 42N37'07 76w41'06 5:06:44
Holtsville 52 11 40N48'55 73w02'44 4:52:11
Homecrest 24 1 40N36 73w57 4:55:48
Homer 12 41 42N38'13 76w10'45 5:04:43
Homer Hill 5 226 42N05'44 78w26'56 5:13:48
Homestead Park 60 1 40N54'59 73w46'24 4:55:06
Homewood 34 13 43N02 76w01 5:04:04
Homewood Park 15 7 42N55 78w46 5:15:04

Honeoye 35 47 42N47'24 77w31'02 5:10:04
Honeoye Falls 28 226 42N57'08 77w35'26 5:10:22
Honeoye Park 35 47 42N46'47 77w30'07 5:10:00
Honest Hill 37 226 43N08'43 78w03'58 5:12:16
Honeyville 23 143 43N51'33 75w58'50 5:03:55
Honeywell Corners 18 226 43N02'29 74w08'34 4:56:34
Honk Hill 56 48 41N45'25 74w22'49 4:57:31
Honnedaga 33 14 43N22'52 75w12'04 5:00:48
Honnedaga Lake 33 226 43N27 75w12 5:00:48
Hooker 25 226 43N41'33 75w44'39 5:02:59
Hoopers Valley 54 226 42N01'35 76w23'36 5:05:34
Hoosick 42 11 42N51'45 73w19'43 4:53:19
Hoosick Falls 42 11 42N54'04 73w21'07 4:53:24
Hoosick Junction 42 11 42N55'22 73w21'36 4:53:26
Hope 21 226 43N18'13 74w14'37 4:56:58
Hope Falls 21 7 43N13 74w10 4:56:40
Hope Farm 14 226 41N44 73w40 4:54:40
Hope Valley 21 7 43N13 74w10 4:56:40
Hopewell 35 14 42N54 77w11 5:08:44
Hopewell Center 35 14 42N54'04 77w11'04 5:08:44
Hopewell Junction 14 226 41N35'02 73w48'33 4:55:14
Hopkins Beach 32 226 43N18'05 78w53'18 5:15:33
Hopkinton 45 226 44N41'25 74w42'13 4:58:49
Horace Harding 41 1 40N45 73w44 4:54:56
Horicon 57 226 43N15 73w44 4:54:56
Hornby 51 226 42N14'39 77w02'40 5:08:11
Hornell 51 102 42N19'40 77w39'41 5:10:39
Hornellsville 51 102 42N20 77w40 5:10:40
Horseheads 8 13 42N10'01 76w49'15 5:07:17
Horseshoe 45 87 44N08'05 74w37'56 4:58:32
Horseshoe Hill 60 16 41N11'46 73w34'21 4:54:17
Horton 13 80 41N58'19 75w01'07 5:00:04
Horton Crossing 54 226 42N05'08 76w19'11 5:05:17
Horton Estates 60 16 41N19'26 73w44'44 4:54:59
Hortontown 34 226 43N11'19 76w23'05 5:05:32
Hortontown 40 226 41N29'55 73w47'44 4:55:11
Hortonville 53 226 41N45'51 75w01'50 5:00:07
Hoseaville 13 13 42N28'26 74w48'55 4:59:16
Hoseville 25 15 43N40'53 75w26'42 5:01:47
Houcks Corners 1 11 42N35'44 73w50'06 4:55:20
Houghton 2 226 42N25'24 78w09'27 5:12:38
Hounsfield 23 12 43N57 76w02 5:04:08
Houseville 25 156 44N04 75w35 5:02:20
Housons Corners 48 226 42N36 74w20 4:57:20
Howard 31 1 40N43 74w00 4:56:00
Howard 51 226 42N21'51 77w30'33 5:10:02
Howard Beach 41 1 40N39'28 73w50'12 4:55:21
Howardville 38 25 43N27'46 76w03'11 5:04:13
Howell 36 7 41N22'54 74w20'37 4:57:22
Howells 36 4 41N28'46 74w27'56 4:57:52
Howes 4 226 42N08'09 75w31'28 5:02:06
Howes 61 226 43N35'55 78w14'08 5:12:57
Howes Cave 48 12 42N41'24 74w23'00 4:57:32
Howes Landing 16 6 43N48'55 73w26'11 4:53:45
Howland 6 226 43N04'45 76w40'58 5:06:44
Howland Corners 55 13 42N32'23 76w27'15 5:05:49
Howlett Hill 34 12 43N00'57 76w17'10 5:05:09
Hoxie Corner 14 226 41N42'49 73w42'08 4:54:49
Hub 3 1 40N50 73w54 4:55:36
Hubbard Crossing 23 119 44N03'23 75w39'28 5:02:38
Hubbardsville 27 130 42N49'04 75w27'49 5:01:51
Hubbardtown 54 154 42N12'05 76w19'07 5:05:16
Hubbell Corners 13 31 42N18'02 74w33'18 4:58:13
Huddle 59 226 43N07'21 77w16'20 5:09:05
Hudson 11 1 42N15'10 73w47'29 4:55:10
Hudson Falls 58 1 43N18'02 73w35'11 4:54:21
Hudson Upper 11 1 42N15 73w47 4:55:08
Hughsonville 14 6 41N34'51 73w55'39 4:55:43
Huguenot 36 1 41N25'04 74w37'53 4:58:32
Huguenot 43 1 40N32'14 74w11'42 4:56:47
Huguenot Park 60 1 40N55'22 73w47'41 4:55:11
Hulberton 37 105 43N15'11 78w03'58 5:12:16
Huletts Landing 58 226 43N38'21 73w30'27 4:54:02
Hullsville 54 205 42N09'23 76w10'09 5:04:41
Hulse Landing 52 11 40N58'02 72w48'42 4:51:15
Humaston 33 211 43N15'40 75w35'46 5:02:23
Hume 2 226 42N28'22 78w08'12 5:12:33
Humphrey 5 226 42N12'20 78w32'22 5:14:09
Humphrey Center 5 226 42N14'00 78w31'35 5:14:06
Hungerford Corners 23 65 43N51'02 76w14'02 5:04:56
Hungry Hill 47 6 42N47'21 73w57'10 4:55:49
Hunt 26 20 42N32'49 77w59'40 5:11:59
Hunter 20 52 42N12'49 74w13'09 4:56:53
Hunter Lake 53 53 41N52 74w46 4:59:04
Huntersland 48 226 42N34'15 74w15'36 4:57:02
Hunt Hollow 26 20 42N33'07 77w58'44 5:11:55
Hunt Hollow 35 226 42N39'04 77w28'38 5:09:55
Huntington 52 6 40N52'05 73w25'34 4:53:42

Huntington Bay 52 11 40N53'59 73w24'55 4:53:40
Huntington Beach 52 11 40N53'52 73w23'02 4:53:32
Huntington Station 52 6 40N51'12 73w24'43 4:53:39
Huntingtonville 23 45 43N58'34 75w51'44 5:03:27
Huntly Corners 39 226 42N49'46 75w08'26 5:00:34
Hunts Corner 53 226 41N36'09 75w02'16 5:00:09
Hunts Corners 12 13 42N25'27 76w06'35 5:04:26
Hunts Corners 15 38 43N01'52 78w35'14 5:14:21
Hunts Point 3 1 40N48'45 73w53'04 4:55:32
Hurd Corners 14 7 41N35'22 73w35'02 4:54:20
Hurd Settlement 53 189 41N43'39 74w52'58 4:59:32
Hurlbutville 33 226 43N24'09 75w20'51 5:01:23
Hurley 56 11 41N55'28 74w03'42 4:56:15
Hurleyville 53 74 41N44'08 74w40'29 4:58:42
Huron 59 226 43N14'00 76w52'49 5:07:31
Hurricane 22 84 43N14'49 74w58'43 4:59:55
Hutchinson Crossing 47 1 42N51'11 73w59'52 4:55:59
Hyde Park 14 11 41N47'05 73w56'01 4:55:44
Hyde Park 39 13 42N39'39 74w57'30 4:59:50
Hydesville 59 14 43N04'13 77w06'28 5:08:26
Hydeville 4 20 42N16'58 75w57'06 5:03:48
Hydeville 9 226 42N35'52 75w52'32 5:03:30
Hyndsville 48 139 42N41'08 74w33'43 4:58:15
Idaho 26 226 42N51'42 77w33'21 5:10:13
Idle Hour 52 11 40N44 73w08 4:52:32
Idlewood 15 153 42N43 78w56 5:15:44
Igerna 57 49 43N43'27 73w55'17 4:55:41
Ilion 22 184 43N00'54 75w02'09 5:00:09
Inavale 2 226 42N08'26 78w05'21 5:12:21
Independence 2 226 42N05'17 77w46'54 5:11:08
Index 39 13 42N39'55 74w57'34 4:59:50
Indian Castle 22 61 43N00'29 74w47'23 4:59:10
Indian Cove 6 13 42N46'18 76w28'05 5:05:52
Indian Falls 19 164 43N01'30 78w23'53 5:13:36
Indian Hill 36 4 41N15'36 74w10'27 4:56:42
Indian Kettles 57 226 43N46'24 73w29'20 4:53:57
Indian Lake 21 226 43N46'57 74w16'20 4:57:05
Indian Landing 52 11 40N46'43 72w53'32 4:51:34
Indian Park 36 226 41N12'30 74w18'45 4:57:15
Indian River 25 226 43N58'35 75w22'09 5:01:29
Indian Springs 34 226 43N09 76w20 5:05:20
Indian Village 34 13 42N56'38 76w09'46 5:04:39
Ingalls Crossing 38 93 43N18'17 76w20'56 5:05:24
Ingham Mills 18 61 43N03'27 74w45'51 4:59:03
Ingham Mills Station 22 61 43N02'47 74w47'04 4:59:08
Ingleside 51 226 42N33'39 77w23'38 5:09:35
Ingraham 10 226 44N48'39 73w26'06 4:53:44
Ings 46 226 43N05 73w47 4:55:08
Inlet 21 226 43N45'16 74w47'36 4:59:10
Inman 17 113 44N30 74w07 4:56:28
Interlaken 50 13 42N37'01 76w43'31 5:06:54
Interlaken Beach 50 226 42N37'35 76w41'15 5:06:45
International Junction 15 1 42N58 78w51 5:15:24
Invale 2 226 42N12 78w08 5:12:32
Inverness 26 226 42N53'34 77w52'11 5:11:29
Inwood 30 11 40N37'19 73w44'50 4:54:59
Inwood 31 1 40N51'56 73w55'38 4:55:43
Ionia 34 41 43N05'48 76w22'54 5:05:32
Ionia 35 226 42N55'53 77w29'32 5:09:58
Ira 6 226 43N13'17 76w33'24 5:06:14
Ireland Corners 56 122 41N40'29 74w07'59 4:56:32
Irelandville 49 14 42N24'09 76w54'33 5:07:38
Irish Settlement 22 20 43N09'08 75w03'50 5:00:15
Irish Settlement 45 226 44N28'57 74w52'21 4:59:29
Irishtown 16 49 43N47'56 73w56'27 4:55:46
Irona 17 16 44N54'17 73w42'22 4:54:49
Irondale 14 79 41N58'02 73w31'31 4:54:06
Irondale 22 214 43N09'45 74w46'44 4:59:07
Irondequoit 28 185 43N13 77w35 5:10:20
Irondequoit Manor 28 185 43N13 77w36 5:10:24
Iron Furnace 58 123 43N29'43 73w32'45 4:54:11
Irongate 34 13 43N07 76w12 5:04:48
Ironsides 34 13 42N55'15 76w12'49 5:04:51
Ironton 45 105 44N53'54 74w41'09 4:58:45
Ironville 16 138 43N55'21 73w32'10 4:54:09
Iroquois 15 42 42N31'58 78w59'10 5:15:57
Irvine Mills 5 20 42N03'53 78w38'14 5:14:33
Irving 7 216 42N34'03 79w06'47 5:16:27
Irvington 60 1 41N02'20 73w51'56 4:55:28
Ischua 5 22 42N14'51 78w24'00 5:13:36
Island Cottage Beach 28 226 43N16'38 77w38'50 5:10:35
Island Park 30 11 40N36'15 73w39'21 4:54:37
Isle of San Souci 60 1 40N54'03 73w46'06 4:55:04
Islip 52 6 40N43'47 73w12'39 4:52:51
Islip Manor 52 6 40N44 73w13 4:52:52
Islip Terrace 52 6 40N44'35 73w11'35 4:52:46
Italy 62 226 42N36'42 77w17'32 5:09:10

Italy Hill 62 226 42N35'46 77W14'57 5:09:00
Itaska 4 20 42N17'56 75W54'30 5:03:38
Ithaca 55 186 42N26'26 76W29'49 5:05:59
Ithaca Junction 6
13 42N56 76W33 5:06:12
Ivanhoe 13 13 42N13'56 75W19'34 5:01:18
Ives Corner 42
226 42N41'08 73W31'34 4:54:06
Ives Hollow 22
214 43N08'32 74W49'33 4:59:18
Ives Settlement 9
149 42N23'04 75W27'50 5:01:51
Ivory 7 128 42N04'14 79W05'50 5:16:23
Jackson 58 226 43N04 73W24 4:53:36
Jacksonburg 22
196 43N00'51 74W54'56 4:59:40
Jackson Corners 14
7 42N01'00 73W44'43 4:54:59
Jackson Heights 41
1 40N45'20 73W53'09 4:55:33
Jackson Summit 18
226 43N08'03 74W17'04 4:57:08
Jacksonville 34
93 43N12'54 76W25'18 5:05:41
Jacksonville 55
13 42N30'30 76W36'55 5:06:28
Jacks Reef 34 41 43N05'57 76W25'28 5:05:42
Jamaica 41 1 40N41'29 73W48'22 4:55:13
Jamesport 52 11 40N56'58 72W34'55 4:50:20
Jamestown 7 187 42N05'49 79W14'08 5:16:57
Jamestown West 7
187 42N05 79W17 5:17:08
Jamesville 34 13 42N59'31 76W04'19 5:04:17
Jamison Road 15
170 42N48'18 78W37'17 5:14:29
Janacks Landing Shelter 45
226 44N06'42 74W53'31 4:59:34
Janesville 48 139 42N42'22 74W34'43 4:58:19
Jaquins 7 22 42N01'00 79W36'33 5:18:26
Jasper 51 226 42N07'21 77W30'12 5:10:01
Java 61 226 42N39 78W23 5:13:32
Java Center 61
226 42N39'00 78W23'10 5:13:33
Java Lake 61 147 42N32 78W26 5:13:44
Java Village 61
226 42N40'21 78W26'11 5:13:45
Jay 16 44 44N22'30 73W43'43 4:54:55
Jayville 45 226 44N09'24 75W11'19 5:00:45
Jeddo 37 112 43N15'19 78W27'27 5:13:50
Jefferson 20 226 42N13 73W51 4:55:24
Jefferson 48 226 42N28'52 74W36'39 4:58:27
Jefferson Heights 20
226 42N14'02 73W52'58 4:55:32
Jefferson Mall 28
226 43N05 77W38 5:10:32
Jefferson Park 23
13 43N46'42 76W13'09 5:04:53
Jefferson Plaza 19
142 43N00 78W11 5:12:44
Jefferson Valley 60
16 41N20'17 73W47'28 4:55:10
Jeffersonville 53
226 41N46'51 74W56'03 4:59:44
Jenkinstown 56 11 41N41'49 74W06'07 4:56:24
Jenksville 54 226 42N16'11 76W14'37 5:04:58
Jerden Falls 25
226 44N00'46 75W19'21 5:01:17
Jericho 10 16 44N47'39 73W39'47 4:54:39
Jericho 30 7 40N47'31 73W32'25 4:54:10
Jericho 52 11 40N57'15 72W12'15 4:48:49
Jericon Corners 19
110 43N05'21 77W58'37 5:11:54
Jersalem 10 16 44N48'27 73W44'45 4:54:59
Jersalem Hill 22
226 42N58'39 75W08'47 5:00:35
Jersey Colony 52
11 41N04 72W26 4:49:44
Jerusalem 62 226 42N37 77W08 5:08:32
Jerusalem Corners 15
11 42N40'59 79W00'55 5:16:04
Jewell 33 15 43N13'28 75W48'25 5:03:14
Jewell Corner 46
226 43N11'09 73W37'11 4:54:29
Jewel Manor 34 13 43N07 76W12 5:04:48
Jewett 20 52 42N16'13 74W18'12 4:57:13
Jewett Center 20
52 42N14'11 74W19'04 4:57:16
Jewettville 15 11 42N43'25 78W40'54 5:14:44
Jewettville 23 49 43N57'14 76W05'26 5:04:22
Jobs Corner 51
226 42N23'56 77W33'26 5:10:14
Jockey Hill 56 11 41N59'17 74W03'01 4:56:12
John F Kennedy Intl Airport 41
1 40N40 73W47 4:55:08
Johnsburg 57 11 43N37'06 73W57'42 4:55:51
Johnson 36 11 41N21'58 74W30'25 4:58:02
Johnsonburg 61
226 42N44'15 78W18'35 5:13:14
Johnson City 4
116 42N06'56 75W57'33 5:03:50
Johnson Corners 22
184 43N04'18 75W03'34 5:00:14
Johnson Creek 32
121 43N14'44 78W30'56 5:14:04
Johnsonville 42
11 42N54'52 73W30'51 4:54:03
Johnstown 18 43 43N00'24 74W22'05 4:57:28
Jones Beach 34 13 42N54'17 76W23'40 5:05:35
Jones Beach 37
105 43N22'28 78W08'54 5:12:36
Jones Corners 38
15 43N27'31 76W23'01 5:05:32
Jones Crossing 39
226 42N37'41 75W03'15 5:00:13
Jones Point 34 24 43N06'30 76W27'47 5:05:51
Jones Point 44 11 41N17'10 73W57'23 4:55:50
Jonesville 46 11 42N54'36 73W49'27 4:55:18
Jordan 34 24 43N03'55 76W28'24 5:05:54
Jordanville 22
226 42N54'53 74W57'07 4:59:48
Joscelyn 53 75 41N57'13 74W51'39 4:59:27
Joshua 34 13 42N54'57 76W14'36 5:04:58
Joy 59 108 43N11'32 77W05'36 5:08:22

Juddville 27 14 42N52'52 75W49'59 5:03:20
Junction 19 70 42N55'43 78W01'35 5:12:06
Junction Boulevard 41
1 40N45 73W53 4:55:32
Junius 50 4 42N59 77W11 5:08:44
Kabob 7 67 42N17'00 79W18'56 5:17:16
Kaisertown 36 11 41N30'26 74W17'04 4:57:08
Kallops Corners 56
11 41N51'37 74W04'14 4:56:17
Kalurah 45 226 44N09'36 75W12'38 5:00:51
Kanona 51 14 42N22'20 77W21'58 5:09:28
Karlsfeld 1 1 42N38'56 73W50'32 4:55:22
Karner 1 1 42N43'24 73W51'28 4:55:26
Karrdale 2 226 42N19'16 77W49'16 5:11:17
Karter 23 226 44N01'22 75W30'33 5:02:02
Kasoag 38 25 43N27'41 75W55'26 5:03:42
Kast Bridge 22
183 43N04'12 74W59'26 4:59:58
Katonah 60 1 41N15'32 73W41'09 4:54:45
Katsbaan 56 215 42N06'39 73W58'07 4:55:52
Kattellville 4 13 42N12'00 75W51'34 5:03:26
Kattskill Bay 57
226 43N29 73W38 4:54:32
Kauneonga 53 226 41N41'28 74W50'10 4:59:21
Kauneonga Lake 53
226 41N41 74W50 4:59:20
Kaydeross Park 46
226 43N05 73W47 4:55:08
Kayuta Lake 33
226 43N27 75W12 5:00:48
Keaches Corners 7
226 42N29'30 79W09'46 5:16:39
Kecks Center 18
43 43N00'28 74W27'25 4:57:50
Keefers Corners 1
11 42N35 73W53 4:55:32
Keene 16 226 44N15'22 73W47'33 4:55:10
Keenes 45 178 44N15'46 75W32'31 5:02:10
Keene Valley 16
226 44N11'23 73W47'11 4:55:09
Keeney 12 226 42N47'06 75W57'55 5:03:52
Keepawa 21 226 43N57'27 74W50'23 4:59:22
Keese Mill 17 221 44N25'57 74W17'50 4:57:11
Keeseville 16 20 44N30'18 73W28'50 4:53:55
Keesler Corners 29
62 42N55'03 74W40'48 4:58:43
Kelleys 47 226 42N46'46 74W04'06 4:56:16
Kellogg 45 226 44N43'59 74W43'50 4:58:55
Kelloggsville 6
13 42N47'13 76W21'57 5:05:28
Kelly Corners 13
42 42N10'55 74W36'00 4:58:24
Kellys Corners 34
12 43N00'54 76W15'10 5:05:01
Kelsey 13 97 42N02'43 75W17'55 5:01:12
Kendaia 50 12 42N44'32 76W53'14 5:07:33
Kendall 37 105 43N19'38 78W02'10 5:12:09
Kendall Mills 28
226 43N17'54 77W59'45 5:11:59
Kenilworth 15 1 42N57'41 78W50'18 5:15:21
Kenilworth 30 1 40N49 73W45 4:55:00
Kenka Mills 62 14 42N39'38 77W02'14 5:08:09
Kenmore 15 1 42N57'57 78W52'13 5:15:29
Kennedy 7 20 42N09'26 79W06'08 5:16:25
Kennedy Corner 55
186 42N26'51 76W34'18 5:06:17
Kenoza Lake 53
226 41N44'00 74W57'00 4:59:48
Kensington 15 7 42N56 78W48 5:15:12
Kensington 24 1 40N38'46 73W58'16 4:55:53
Kensington 30 1 40N47'36 73W43'21 4:54:53
Kent (Brice Station) 37
105 43N19'40 78W08'08 5:12:33
Kent 40 226 41N28 73W43 4:54:52
Kent Cliffs 40
226 41N27'18 73W45'16 4:55:01
Kent Corners 40
135 41N28'06 73W39'38 4:54:39
Kent Hills 40 226 41N29'40 73W41'01 4:54:44
Kents Corners 45
226 44N25'58 75W17'51 5:01:11
Kenwells 21 226 43N39'18 74W39'34 4:58:38
Kenwood 1 11 42N37'25 73W46'25 4:55:06
Kenwood 27 60 43N03'29 75W36'45 5:02:27
Kenwood Estates 40
226 41N27 73W40 4:54:40
Kenyonville 37
146 43N18'40 78W16'51 5:13:07
Kerhonkson 56 72 41N46'29 74W17'55 4:57:12
Kerleys Corners 14
7 42N02'34 73W50'54 4:55:24
Kernan 33 222 43N06 75W15 5:01:00
Kerry Siding 13
97 42N01'29 75W15'13 5:01:01
Kerryville 13 97 42N01'40 75W14'20 5:00:57
Ketchums Corners 46
11 43N00'36 73W41'42 4:54:47
Ketchumville 54
226 42N16'16 76W05'56 5:04:24
Keuka 51 226 42N29'31 77W07'20 5:08:29
Keuka Park 62 226 42N36'55 77W05'33 5:08:22
Kew Gardens 41 1 40N42'51 73W49'53 4:55:20
Kiamesha Lake 53
74 41N40'59 74W39'40 4:58:39
Kiantone 7 128 42N01'19 79W11'54 5:16:48
Kidders 50 226 42N38'25 76W41'35 5:06:46
Kildare 17 221 44N19'34 74W31'50 4:58:07
Killawog 4 16 42N24'02 76W01'16 5:04:05
Kill Buck 5 20 42N09'30 78W40'52 5:14:43
Kimball Corners 46
1 43N03'20 74W02'56 4:56:12
Kimball Mill 25
226 44N05'08 75W20'54 5:01:24
Kimball Stand 7
187 42N10'29 79W15'19 5:17:01
Kinderhook 11 11 42N23'43 73W41'54 4:54:48
Kingdom 22 196 42N55'44 74W58'34 4:59:54
King Ferry 6 13 42N39'55 76W37'01 5:06:28
King Ferry Station 6
226 42N39'29 76W39'47 5:06:39
Kings 46 226 43N09'03 73W51'17 4:55:25
Kingsboro 18 226 43N04'02 74W20'30 4:57:22
Kings Bridge 3 1 40N52'43 73W54'20 4:55:37

Kings Bridge Heights 3
1 40N52'20 73W54'04 4:55:36
Kingsbury 58 226 43N21'49 73W31'55 4:54:08
Kings Park 52 11 40N53'10 73W15'28 4:53:02
Kings Point 30 1 40N49'11 73W44'08 4:54:57
Kings School Corner 7
107 42N15'37 79W04'51 5:16:19
Kings Settlement 9
200 42N32 75W31 5:02:04
Kings Station 46
226 43N08'57 73W45'48 4:55:03
Kingston 56 11 41N55'37 73W59'52 4:55:59
Kingstown 52 11 41N00'34 72W09'48 4:48:39
Kingsway 24 1 40N36 73W57 4:55:48
Kipps 36 7 41N25'32 74W17'42 4:57:11
Kirk 9 226 42N36'17 75W38'30 5:02:34
Kirkland 33 11 43N04'40 75W23'01 5:01:32
Kirkville 34 226 43N04'30 75W57'08 5:03:49
Kirkwood 4 20 42N02'23 75W47'51 5:03:11
Kirkwood 51 14 42N32'00 77W27'56 5:09:52
Kirkwood Center 4
20 42N04'54 75W48'24 5:03:14
Kirschnerville 25
226 43N52'59 75W20'14 5:01:21
Kisco Park 60 6 41N11 73W44 4:54:56
Kiskatom 20 226 42N11'58 73W57'41 4:55:51
Kismet 52 11 40N38'03 73W12'14 4:52:49
Kitchawan 60 7 41N13'08 73W47'11 4:55:09
Knapp Creek 5 226 42N00'25 78W30'22 5:14:01
Knapps Corner 14
6 41N37'41 73W55'00 4:55:40
Knappville 18 226 43N13'48 74W39'42 4:58:39
Knickerbocker 31
1 40N43 73W59 4:55:56
Knickerbocker Corner 35
14 42N57'43 77W05'47 5:08:23
Knight Creek 2
109 42N07'45 78W01'04 5:12:04
Knights Eddy 53 1 41N25'30 74W47'09 4:59:09
Knowelhurst 57
226 43N26'38 74W01'14 4:56:05
Knowlesville 37
115 43N14'31 78W18'39 5:13:15
Knowlesville Station 37
115 43N13'41 78W18'26 5:13:14
Knowsville 23 45 43N59 75W56 5:03:44
Knox 1 40 42N40'16 74W06'58 4:56:28
Knoxboro 33 13 42N59'11 75W31'03 5:02:04
Koenig's Point 6
13 42N56 76W33 5:06:12
Kohlertown 53 25 41N46'17 74W56'32 4:59:46
Komar Park 46 11 42N54'41 73W56'44 4:55:47
Kortright 13 226 42N24 74W47 4:59:08
Kortright Center 13
226 42N25'03 74W46'33 4:59:06
Kortright Station 13
226 42N24'22 74W47'46 4:59:11
Kossuth 2 226 42N03'51 78W08'33 5:12:34
Kosterville 25 77 43N36'57 75W20'06 5:01:20
Kraus Landing 38
14 43N11'22 76W01'26 5:04:06
Kringsbush 18 226 43N00'52 74W38'11 4:58:33
Kripplebush 56 11 41N50'25 74W11'40 4:56:47
Krum Corner 55
186 42N29'10 76W34'27 5:06:18
Krumville 56 76 41N53'05 74W14'34 4:56:58
Kuckville 37 146 43N21'38 78W15'57 5:13:04
Kuneytown 50 13 42N50'09 76W46'53 5:07:08
Kyserike 56 11 41N47'51 74W10'24 4:56:42
Kysorville 26 13 42N38'55 77W47'35 5:11:10
Lackawack 56 48 41N46'59 74W25'04 4:57:40
Lackawanna 15 153 42N49'32 78W49'25 5:15:18
Lacona 38 14 43N38'36 76W04'08 5:04:17
Lacy Corners 55
13 42N30'17 76W17'56 5:05:12
Ladentown 44 4 41N11'09 74W04'04 4:56:16
Ladleton 56 226 41N56'27 74W31'07 4:58:04
Lafarges Landing 52
11 41N01'58 72W12'29 4:48:50
La Fargeville 23
226 44N11'41 75W57'59 5:03:52
LaFayette 34 16 42N53'32 76W06'20 5:04:25
Lafayette Corners 55
13 42N35'36 76W17'15 5:05:09
Lafayetteville 14
7 41N57'29 73W44'48 4:54:59
La Grange 14 226 41N40 73W49 4:55:16
Lagrange 36 11 41N26'55 74W17'09 4:57:09
Lagrange 61 226 42N48'06 78W00'50 5:12:03
Lagrangeville 14
226 41N39'03 73W45'48 4:55:03
La Guardia Airport 41
1 40N43 73W50 4:55:20
Laidlaw 5 226 42N23'51 78W24'31 5:13:38
Lairdsville 33 11 43N04'47 75W25'55 5:01:44
Lake 36 226 41N18 74W18 4:57:12
Lake Bluff 59 226 43N16'21 76W56'30 5:07:46
Lake Bonaparte 25
226 44N08'17 75W22'47 5:01:31
Lake Carmel 40
135 41N27'41 73W40'17 4:54:41
Lake Charles 40 7 41N31 73W36 4:54:24
Lake Clear 17 176 44N22 74W14 4:56:56
Lake Colby 17 81 44N21'10 74W08'38 4:56:35
Lake Como 6 41 42N35 76W12 5:04:48
Lake Delaware 13
226 42N14'51 74W49'50 4:59:19
Lake Delta 33 211 43N17'35 75W28'21 5:01:53
Lake Desolation 46
226 43N07'54 73W58'11 4:55:53
Lake Erie Beach 15
11 42N37'27 79W04'02 5:16:16
Lake Gardens 40
17 41N22 73W44 4:54:56
Lake George 57 1 43N25'34 73W42'46 4:54:51
Lake Grove 52 11 40N51'10 73W06'56 4:52:28
Lake Hill 56 11 42N04'02 74W11'15 4:56:45
Lake Huntington 53
226 41N41'03 74W59'35 4:59:58
Lakehurst 60 1 41N04 73W46 4:55:04
Lake Katonah 60 1 41N17'03 73W39'07 4:54:36
Lake Katrine 56
114 41N59'08 73W59'19 4:55:57

Lake Kitchawan 60 16 41N17 73w33 4:54:12
Lakeland 34 13 43N05'25 76w14'27 5:04:58
Lakeland 52 11 40N48'28 73w07'14 4:52:29
Lake Lincolndale 60 16 41N20'30 73w43'20 4:54:53
Lake Lucille 44 4 41N11'10 73w59'42 4:55:59
Lake Luzerne 57 40 43N18'46 73w50'07 4:55:20
Lake Mahopac 40 17 41N22 73w44 4:54:56
Lake Minnewaska 56 11 41N44'07 74w13'00 4:56:52
Lakemont 62 13 42N30'58 76w55'42 5:07:43
Lake Moraine 27 180 42N49 75w33 5:02:12
Lake Osceola 60 16 41N19 73w45 4:55:00
Lake Osiris Colony 36 11 41N34'46 74w10'07 4:56:40
Lake Panamoka 52 11 40N54 72w53 4:51:32
Lake Peekskill 40 6 41N20'05 73w52'53 4:55:32
Lake Placid 16 1 44N16'46 73w58'49 4:55:55
Lake Pleasant 21 226 43N28'15 74w24'47 4:57:39
Lakeport 27 226 43N08'43 75w52'20 5:03:29
Lake Purdy 60 16 41N19'30 73w40'21 4:54:41
Lake Ridge 55 13 42N36'35 76w36'50 5:06:27
Lake Ronkonkoma 52 11 40N50'06 73w07'54 4:52:32
Lake Ronkonkoma Heights 52 11 40N49 73w06 4:52:24
Lake Secor 40 17 41N22 73w44 4:54:56
Lakeside 34 13 43N06'18 76w15'11 5:05:01
Lakeside 36 226 41N21 74w08 4:56:32
Lakeside 37 146 43N22'18 78w15'46 5:13:03
Lakeside 59 226 43N15'20 77w20'19 5:09:21
Lakeside Park 1 11 42N42 73w48 4:55:12
Lakeside Park 7 20 42N14'23 79w29'44 5:17:59
Lakeside Park 37 146 43N19 78w15 5:13:00
Lakeside Park 51 181 42N30'31 77w09'25 5:08:38
Lake Station 36 6 41N17 74w20 4:57:20
Lake Success 30 1 40N46'14 73w43'05 4:54:52
Lake Sunnyside 41 1 40N47 73w47 4:55:08
Lake Sunnyside 57 1 43N22'22 73w38'16 4:54:33
Lake Vanare 57 40 43N22'12 73w47'14 4:55:09
Lakeview 9 226 42N25'55 75w51'57 5:03:28
Lake View 15 153 42N42'40 78w56'11 5:15:45
Lakeview 30 11 40N41'07 73w39'11 4:54:37
Lakeview 38 204 43N30'46 76w25'31 5:05:42
Lake View Terrace 5 226 42N05'57 78w20'53 5:13:24
Lakeville 9 226 42N25'14 75w51'34 5:03:26
Lakeville 26 20 42N50'11 77w42'19 5:10:49
Lakeville 30 11 40N45 73w41 4:54:44
Lakeville 36 226 41N11'50 74w15'39 4:57:03
Lakeville Estates 30 11 40N45 73w41 4:54:44
Lakewood 7 20 42N06'15 79w20'00 5:17:20
Lamberton 7 14 42N24'45 79w23'42 5:17:35
Lambs Corner 1 226 42N26'30 74w04'29 4:56:18
Lambs Corner 61 25 42N49'06 78w04'38 5:12:19
Lambs Corners 1 226 42N25 74w01 4:56:04
Lamont 61 24 42N35'29 78w06'23 5:12:26
Lamont Circle 12 41 42N35 76w12 5:04:48
Lamoreaux Landing 50 226 42N34'31 76w52'35 5:07:30
Lamson 34 93 43N13'03 76w22'13 5:05:29
Lancaster 15 7 42N54'02 78w40'14 5:14:41
Lanesville 20 52 42N07'40 74w15'48 4:57:03
Langdon 4 20 42N04'03 75w47'42 5:03:11
Langdon Corners 45 155 44N36 75w10 5:00:40
Langford 15 153 42N35'15 78w50'32 5:15:22
Langton Corners 19 171 43N05'58 78w11'06 5:12:44
Lansing 38 204 43N26'35 76w27'01 5:05:48
Lansing 55 13 42N29'03 76w28'49 5:05:55
Lansingburgh 42 11 42N47'04 73w40'12 4:54:41
Lansing Station 55 13 42N34'37 76w36'35 5:06:26
Lansingville 55 13 42N35'52 76w33'16 5:06:13
Laona 7 14 42N25'18 79w18'21 5:17:13
Lapala 56 11 41N57 74w00 4:56:00
Lapeer 12 13 42N26'31 76w05'57 5:04:24
Laphams Mills 10 86 44N35'46 73w30'10 4:54:01
Lapla 56 11 41N55'08 74w08'10 4:56:33
Larchmont 60 1 40N55'40 73w45'08 4:55:01
Larchmont Manor 60 1 40N57 73w45 4:55:00
La Salle 32 199 43N04'57 78w58'06 5:15:52
Lassellsville 18 226 43N02'57 74w36'02 4:58:24
Latham 1 1 42N44'49 73w45'34 4:55:02
Latham Corners 9 226 42N27'36 75w23'57 5:01:36
Lattingtown 30 11 40N53'43 73w36'05 4:54:24
Lattintown 56 6 41N38'39 74w00'14 4:56:01
Laughing Waters 52 11 41N02'11 72w25'47 4:49:43
Laurel 52 11 40N58'10 72w33'45 4:50:15
Laurel Hollow 30 11 40N51'24 73w28'12 4:53:53
Laurelton 28 185 43N13 77w36 5:10:24
Laurelton 41 1 40N40'00 73w45'07 4:55:00
Laurens 39 226 42N31'50 75w05'24 5:00:22
Lava 53 226 41N37'00 75w01'10 5:00:05

Laverys Corner 45 16 44N46'09 74w40'18 4:58:41
Lawrence 30 1 40N36'56 73w43'48 4:54:55
Lawrence Beach 30 1 40N37 73w44 4:54:56
Lawrence Farms 60 1 41N10 73w46 4:55:04
Lawrence Park 60 7 40N56'25 73w50'56 4:55:24
Lawrenceville 20 226 42N13'41 73w59'01 4:55:56
Lawrenceville 45 16 44N46'30 74w39'00 4:58:36
Lawrenceville 51 13 41N59'49 77w07'35 5:08:30
Lawrenceville 56 11 41N50'26 74w06'12 4:56:25
Lawtons 15 42 42N32'17 78w55'52 5:15:43
Lawyersville 48 13 42N42'09 74w30'25 4:58:02
Lebanon 27 13 42N46'53 75w38'53 5:02:36
Lebanon 36 226 41N21'36 74w09'31 4:56:38
Lebanon Center 27 13 42N47'06 75w37'12 5:02:29
Lebanon Springs 11 11 42N28'31 73w22'47 4:53:31
Ledgewood Park 20 226 42N12'08 74w00'51 4:56:03
Ledyard 6 13 42N41'43 76w37'19 5:06:29
Lee 33 226 43N16'42 75w34'19 5:02:17
Lee 58 11 42N57'22 73w29'02 4:53:56
Lee Center 33 226 43N18'12 75w31'06 5:02:04
Leeds 20 11 42N15'19 73w54'10 4:55:37
Leedsville 14 11 41N51'19 73w30'51 4:54:03
Leeside 40 226 41N27 73w40 4:54:40
Leesville 48 11 42N47'49 74w38'50 4:58:35
Lefever Falls 56 11 41N51'26 74w03'30 4:56:14
Lefferts 24 1 40N40 73w57 4:55:48
Lefferts Mill 52 11 40N54'00 73w26'43 4:53:47
Lehigh 19 142 42N56'51 78w20'20 5:13:21
Lehigh Valley Junction 50 14 42N56'01 76w47'45 5:07:11
Leibhardt 56 76 41N48 74w13 4:56:52
Leicester 26 13 42N46'19 77w53'49 5:11:35
Leisher Mill 25 226 43N29'07 75w38'19 5:02:33
Lena 39 226 42N37'27 75w05'04 5:00:20
Lenox 27 226 43N03'30 75w42'17 5:02:49
Lenox Basin 27 13 43N05'25 75w42'42 5:02:51
Lenox Furnace 27 226 43N05 75w45 5:03:00
Lenox Hill 31 1 40N46 73w58 4:55:52
Lenox Park 35 41 42N51'28 77w00'53 5:08:04
Lent Hill 51 226 42N31'23 77w25'09 5:09:41
Lentsville 39 140 42N45'01 74w51'35 4:59:26
Leon 5 226 42N17'35 79w01'00 5:16:04
Leonardsville 27 226 42N48'31 75w15'11 5:01:01
Leonta 13 104 42N21'35 75w07'40 5:00:31
Leptondale 36 1 41N34'28 74w05'44 4:56:23
Le Ray 23 226 44N04 75w47 5:03:08
Le Roy 19 70 42N58'42 77w59'04 5:11:56
Le Roy Island 59 226 43N13 76w49 5:07:16
Lester 4 226 42N03'37 75w43'34 5:02:54
Levanna 6 13 42N47'04 76w42'50 5:06:51
Levant 7 187 42N08'00 79w10'55 5:16:44
Levittown 30 11 40N43'33 73w30'53 4:54:04
Lewbeach 53 226 42N00'17 74w47'07 4:59:08
Lewis 16 50 44N16'30 73w33'58 4:54:16
Lewisboro 60 16 41N14'17 73w31'23 4:54:06
Lewis Corners 38 226 43N21'52 76w28'17 5:05:53
Lewiston 32 121 43N10'21 79w02'10 5:16:09
Lewiston Heights 32 199 43N09'57 79w01'42 5:16:07
Lewiston Manor 34 13 43N02 76w06 5:04:24
Lexington 20 226 42N14'25 74w21'57 4:57:28
Leyden 25 77 44N10 75w38 5:02:32
Liberty 53 189 41N48'04 74w44'49 4:58:59
Liberty Gardens 33 211 43N13'20 75w28'30 5:01:54
Libertypole 26 13 42N38'56 77w38'03 5:10:32
Libertyville 56 122 41N43'20 74w08'08 4:56:33
Lick Springs 58 226 43N10'58 73w30'58 4:54:04
Lidell Corners 39 78 42N45'45 75w01'44 5:00:07
Lido Beach 30 11 40N35'20 73w37'33 4:54:30
Liebhardt 56 76 41N51'06 74w16'21 4:57:05
Lighthouse Beach 28 13 43N20'27 77w45'53 5:11:04
Lila 51 226 42N01'16 77w34'20 5:10:17
Lily Dale 7 173 42N21'06 79w19'28 5:17:18
Lima 26 226 42N54'17 77w36'42 5:10:27
Lime Lake 5 22 42N26'04 78w28'48 5:13:55
Limerick 23 49 44N01'45 76w02'36 5:04:10
Limerock 19 70 42N58'43 77w55'09 5:11:41
Limestone 5 20 42N01'38 78w37'47 5:14:31
Limestreet 20 226 42N18'30 73w52'34 4:55:30
Lincklaen 9 226 42N40'32 75w52'38 5:03:31
Lincklaen Center 9 226 42N42'25 75w50'56 5:03:24
Lincoln 27 226 43N02 75w44 5:02:56
Lincoln 59 226 43N11'00 77w20'41 5:09:23
Lincoln 60 1 40N54'31 73w52'40 4:55:31
Lincolndale 60 16 41N19'22 73w43'07 4:54:52
Lincoln Park 15 1 42N58 78w51 5:15:24
Lincoln Park 28 209 43N08'56 77w38'50 5:10:35
Lincoln Park 56 11 41N57'02 73w59'40 4:55:59
Lincolnton 31 1 40N49 73w56 4:55:44
Lincolnville 42 220 42N49'57 73w34'28 4:54:18
Lindbergh Court 1 11 42N42 73w48 4:55:12
Lindbergh Lawns 34 13 43N06'53 76w15'24 5:05:02

Linden 19 142 42N52'37 78w09'49 5:12:39
Linden Acres 14 7 42N00'44 73w52'46 4:55:31
Linden Hill 41 1 40N46 73w49 4:55:16
Lindenhurst 52 9 40N41'12 73w22'26 4:53:30
Linden-Park 43 1 40N35'32 74w05'30 4:56:22
Lindley 51 13 42N01'42 77w08'24 5:08:34
Lindsley Corners 18 226 43N10'22 74w22'09 4:57:29
Linlithgo 11 11 42N10'17 73w50'51 4:55:23
Linlithgo Mills 11 11 42N10'27 73w44'50 4:54:59
Linwood 26 70 42N53'41 77w56'58 5:11:48
Lisbon 45 16 44N43'38 75w19'17 5:01:17
Lisha Kill 1 11 42N45'08 73w52'10 4:55:29
Lisle 4 16 42N21'04 76w00'13 5:04:01
Litchfield 22 226 42N58 75w09 5:00:36
Litchfield 54 224 42N00'33 76w27'35 5:05:50
Lithgow 14 226 41N49'30 73w37'14 4:54:29
Little America 38 226 43N33'42 75w54'02 5:03:36
Little Bow 45 178 44N21'13 75w30'38 5:02:03
Little Britain 36 11 41N28'40 74w07'48 4:56:31
Little Canada 19 142 42N56'45 78w06'42 5:12:27
Little Falls 14 6 41N36 73w53 4:55:32
Little Falls 22 61 43N02'36 74w51'36 4:59:26
Little France 38 182 43N20'52 76w05'49 5:04:23
Little Genesee 2 226 42N01'37 78w12'23 5:12:50
Little Hollow 6 13 42N39'59 76w34'08 5:06:17
Little Neck 41 1 40N45'43 73w44'19 4:54:57
Little Plains 52 11 40N51'02 73w21'58 4:53:28
Little Rapids 21 226 43N55'43 74w52'25 4:59:30
Littlerest 14 226 41N46'15 73w38'40 4:54:35
Little Rock City 5 226 42N12'31 78w42'32 5:14:50
Little Utica 34 93 43N12'58 76w24'07 5:05:36
Little Valley 5 20 42N15'09 78w48'21 5:15:13
Littleville 26 226 42N53'42 77w45'37 5:11:02
Littleville 35 14 42N56'35 77w13'20 5:08:53
Little York 12 16 42N41'45 76w09'53 5:04:40
Little York 36 11 41N17'10 74w26'51 4:57:47
Little York 48 11 42N45'25 74w29'50 4:57:59
Liverpool 34 13 43N06'23 76w13'05 5:04:52
Livingston 11 12 42N08'31 73w46'42 4:55:07
Livingston Manor 53 75 41N54'01 74w49'43 4:59:19
Livingstonville 48 226 42N29'15 74w16'08 4:57:05
Livonia 26 20 42N49'17 77w40'08 5:10:41
Livonia Center 26 20 42N49'17 77w38'20 5:10:33
Lloyd 56 51 41N44'10 74w00'21 4:56:01
Lloyd Harbor 52 11 40N54'12 73w27'37 4:53:50
Lloydsville 39 13 42N49'35 75w14'05 5:00:56
Lochada Lake 53 226 41N29 74w55 4:59:40
Loch Muller 16 49 43N51'58 73w53'24 4:55:34
Loch Sheldrake 53 74 41N46'12 74w39'27 4:58:38
Lock Berlin 59 99 43N04'44 76w56'47 5:07:47
Locke 6 13 42N39'38 76w25'52 5:05:43
Lockpit 59 99 43N02'09 76w48'35 5:07:14
Lockport 32 190 43N10'14 78w41'26 5:14:46
Lockport Junction 32 190 43N09'27 78w45'18 5:15:01
Locksley Park 15 153 42N45'44 78w52'46 5:15:31
Lockwood 54 226 42N05'28 76w33'01 5:06:12
Locust Grove 25 226 43N33'48 75w22'29 5:01:30
Locust Grove 30 7 40N48'36 73w30'09 4:54:01
Locust Manor 41 1 40N41'03 73w46'47 4:55:07
Locust Point 3 1 40N48'57 73w48'09 4:55:13
Locust Valley 30 7 40N52'33 73w35'51 4:54:23
Locustwood 30 11 40N42 73w42 4:54:48
Lodi 50 226 42N36'50 76w49'22 5:07:17
Lodi Center 50 226 42N34'16 76w49'15 5:07:17
Lodi Point 50 226 42N37 77w21 5:09:24
Logan 49 14 42N29'16 76w49'44 5:07:19
Logtown 36 1 41N20'36 74w35'56 4:58:24
Lomala 14 6 41N33'35 73w50'30 4:55:22
Lombard 7 226 42N15'01 79w38'13 5:18:33
Lomond Shore 37 105 43N22'21 78w04'50 5:12:19
Lomontville 56 11 41N53'23 74w07'37 4:56:30
London Terrace 31 1 40N45 74w00 4:56:00
Lonelyville 52 11 40N38'27 73w10'31 4:52:42
Long Beach 30 1 40N35'18 73w39'30 4:54:38
Long Branch 34 13 43N07'05 76w14'37 5:04:58
Long Branch Manor 34 13 43N07 76w12 5:04:48
Long Bridge 34 24 42N58'49 76w26'47 5:05:47
Long Crossing 33 15 43N13'27 75w46'36 5:03:06
Long Eddy 53 20 41N51'03 75w08'02 5:00:32
Long Flat 13 226 42N00'43 75w04'38 5:00:19
Long Island 11 40N50 73w00 4:52:00
Long Island City 41 1 40N44'41 73w56'57 4:55:48
Long Lake 21 34 43N58'22 74w25'17 4:57:41
Long Point Cove 26 226 42N46'29 77w43'29 5:10:54
Long View 7 226 42N07'28 79w23'33 5:17:34
Longwood 3 1 40N49 73w54 4:55:36
Longwood 19 164 42N57'11 78w22'11 5:13:29
Loomis 13 226 42N12'31 75w12'57 5:00:52
Loomis 53 189 41N47'50 74w47'10 4:59:09
Loomis Corner 38 226 43N21'04 76w16'56 5:05:08

Loomises 7 226 42N06'32 79w21'55 5:17:28
Loomis Hill 34 12 43N00'39 76w14'01 5:04:56
Loon Lake 17 113 44N33'06 74w03'26 4:56:14
Loon Lake Junction 17 113 44N30 74w07 4:56:28
Lords Corners 34 13 42N54'37 76w13'18 5:04:53
Lordville 13 97 41N52'09 75w12'56 5:00:52
Lorenz Park 11 1 42N15 73w46 4:55:04
Loring Crossing 12 41 42N37'33 76w08'45 5:04:35
Lorings 12 41 42N35 76w12 5:04:48
Lorraine 23 143 43N45'59 75w57'35 5:03:50
Lost Valley 29 1 42N50'55 74w16'21 4:57:05
Lost Village 45 201 44N37'10 75w29'34 5:01:58
Lotville 18 226 43N07'02 74w41'57 4:58:48
Loudonville 1 1 42N42'17 73w45'19 4:55:01
Louisville 45 226 44N53'51 75w00'58 5:00:04
Lounsberry 54 226 42N03'29 76w20'10 5:05:21
Loveland 15 11 42N44'00 78w41'57 5:14:48
Lowell 33 211 43N08'19 75w30'04 5:02:00
Lower Beechwood 53 226 41N45'29 74w59'01 4:59:56
Lower Chateaugay Lake 17 188 44N56 74w05 4:56:20
Lower Cincinnatus 12 226 42N31'57 75w53'55 5:03:36
Lower Corners 47 1 42N55'43 74w00'49 4:56:03
Lower Genegantslet Corner 9 226 42N18'12 75w48'06 5:03:12
Lower Melville 52 11 40N45'59 73w25'26 4:53:42
Lower Oswegatchie 45 25 44N11'41 75w04'08 5:00:17
Lowerre 60 1 40N54'57 73w53'50 4:55:35
Lower Rotterdam 47 1 42N48 73w58 4:55:52
Lower Rotterdam Junction 47 11 42N51'38 74w01'45 4:56:07
Lower South Bay 34 13 43N12'00 76w03'48 5:04:15
Lower Town Landing 23 163 44N16'12 76w05'29 5:04:22
Low Hampton 58 226 43N35'09 73w17'56 4:53:12
Lowman 8 13 42N01'47 76w43'15 5:06:53
Lowville 25 191 43N47'12 75w29'32 5:01:58
Luce Landing 52 11 40N59'08 72w37'07 4:50:28
Ludingtonville 40 7 41N30'32 73w41'30 4:54:46
Ludlow 60 1 40N55'41 73w54'05 4:55:36
Ludlowville 55 13 42N33'13 76w32'20 5:06:09
Lumberland 53 25 41N29 74w49 4:59:16
Lummisville 59 226 43N14'42 76w54'24 5:07:38
Luna Park 24 1 40N35 73w59 4:55:56
Luther 42 1 42N36'14 73w39'05 4:54:36
Lutheranville 48 226 42N35'05 74w38'29 4:58:34
Luzerne 13 226 41N57'05 75w08'54 5:00:36
Lycoming 38 15 43N29'55 76w23'10 5:05:33
Lyell 28 209 43N10 77w40 5:10:40
Lykers 29 7 42N48'40 74w28'20 4:57:53
Lyme 23 226 44N04 76w12 5:04:48
Lynbrook 30 7 40N39'17 73w40'20 4:54:41
Lynch Tract 33 211 43N13'24 75w26'24 5:01:46
Lyncourt 34 41 43N04 76w09 5:04:36
Lyndon 5 226 42N18 78w21 5:13:24
Lyndon 34 13 43N01'45 76w03'16 5:04:13
Lyndonville 37 15 43N19'36 78w23'21 5:13:33
Lynelle Meadows 34 13 43N07 76w12 5:04:48
Lynwood Estates 1 6 42N46 73w56 4:55:44
Lyon Corner 23 143 43N50'57 76w04'41 5:04:19
Lyon Mountain 10 192 44N43'29 73w54'43 4:55:39
Lyons 59 99 43N03'51 76w59'26 5:07:58
Lyons Corners 2 20 42N16'02 78w15'13 5:13:01
Lyonsdale 25 119 43N37'07 75w18'24 5:01:14
Lyons Falls 25 106 43N37'31 75w22'03 5:01:28
Lyonsville 56 76 41N50'55 74w12'45 4:56:51
Lysander 34 226 43N12'23 76w27'34 5:05:50
Lysander New Community 34 226 43N10'04 76w18'06 5:05:12
Mabbettsville 14 226 41N47'33 73w39'36 4:54:38
MacDonnell Heights 14 1 41N42'34 73w51'46 4:55:27
MacDougall 50 226 42N48'23 76w52'47 5:07:31
Macedon 59 226 43N04'09 77w17'57 5:09:12
Macedon Center 59 226 43N05'39 77w19'15 5:09:17
Machias 5 22 42N25'10 78w29'41 5:13:59
Machias Junction 5 22 42N24'31 78w28'34 5:13:54
Mackey 48 226 42N27'26 74w23'02 4:57:32
Macomb 45 20 44N27 75w34 5:02:16
Madawaska 45 226 44N31'00 74w23'51 4:57:35
Madison 27 180 42N53'56 75w30'45 5:02:03
Madison Center 27 15 42N52'50 75w29'55 5:02:00
Madison Park 52 11 40N51 73w20 4:53:20
Madison Square 31 1 40N45 73w59 4:55:56
Madrid 45 132 44N45'01 75w07'53 5:00:32
Madrid Springs 45 226 44N44'24 75w08'38 5:00:35
Magee 50 19 42N57'40 76w50'47 5:07:23
Magnolia 7 158 42N10'30 79w26'25 5:17:46
Mahopac 40 17 41N22'20 73w44'02 4:54:56
Mahopac Falls 40 17 41N22'19 73w45'44 4:55:03
Mahopac Hills 40 17 41N22 73w44 4:54:56
Mahopac Mines 40 17 41N23'53 73w45'34 4:55:02
Mahopac Point 40 17 41N22 73w44 4:54:56
Mahopac Ridge 40 17 41N22 73w44 4:54:56
Maidstone Park 52 11 41N02'09 72w10'45 4:48:43
Maine 4 226 42N11'33 76w03'41 5:04:15
Main-Mill 15 7 42N59 78w45 5:15:00
Main Settlement 5 226 42N00'48 78w18'52 5:13:15
Malba 41 1 40N47'26 73w49'38 4:55:19
Malcon 50 19 43N00'26 76w51'23 5:07:26
Malden Bridge 11 10 42N28'14 73w35'00 4:54:20
Malden-on-Hudson 56 11 42N05'43 73w56'04 4:55:44
Mallory 38 182 43N19'25 76w07'01 5:04:28
Mallory Corner 39 13 42N25'27 75w17'37 5:01:10
Malone 17 193 44N50'55 74w17'43 4:57:11
Malone Junction 17 193 44N51'28 74w16'27 4:57:06
Malta 46 11 42N58'16 73w47'35 4:55:10
Malta Ridge 46 11 43N00'41 73w47'25 4:55:10
Maltaville 46 11 42N56'44 73w46'56 4:55:08
Maltbie Heights 5 42 42N28 78w56 5:15:44
Malverne 30 194 40N40'44 73w40'28 4:54:42
Malvic Manor 34 13 43N07 76w12 5:04:48
Mamakating 53 11 41N35 74w29 4:57:56
Mamakating Park 53 11 41N36'43 74w32'18 4:58:09
Mamaroneck 60 1 40N56'55 73w43'59 4:54:56
Manchester 35 4 42N58'11 77w13'50 5:08:55
Manchester Bridge 14 1 41N41'04 73w51'59 4:55:28
Manchester Center 35 4 42N58'33 77w10'49 5:08:43
Mandana 34 13 42N51'56 76w24'14 5:05:37
Manhasset 30 6 40N47'52 73w42'00 4:54:48
Manhasset Hills 30 11 40N45 73w41 4:54:44
Manhattan 31 1 40N46 73w59 4:55:56
Manhattan Beach 24 1 40N34'38 73w56'51 4:55:47
Manhattanville 31 1 40N49 73w57 4:55:48
Manhattanville College 60 7 41N02 73w43 4:54:52
Manheim 22 168 43N04 74w48 4:59:12
Manheim Center 22 61 43N02'52 74w47'32 4:59:10
Manitou 40 6 41N19'59 73w57'51 4:55:51
Manitou Beach 28 13 43N19'24 77w42'53 5:10:52
Manlius 34 13 43N00'07 75w58'38 5:03:55
Manning 37 226 43N11'56 78w05'47 5:12:23
Mannings Cove 46 11 43N01'11 73w45'29 4:55:02
Manningville 4 226 42N21'25 76w02'46 5:04:11
Manns Corner 28 27 43N00'10 77w39'59 5:10:40
Mannsville 23 14 43N42'46 76w03'47 5:04:15
Mannville 1 1 42N43 73w44 4:54:56
Manny Corners 29 1 42N56'49 74w08'43 4:56:35
Manorhaven 30 11 40N50'35 73w42'55 4:54:52
Manorkill 48 226 42N23'22 74w19'21 4:57:17
Manorton 11 226 42N05'33 73w47'55 4:55:12
Manorville 52 11 40N52'25 72w48'30 4:51:14
Manorville 56 215 42N08'32 74w02'11 4:56:09
Mansfield 5 226 42N18 78w46 5:15:04
Mapes 2 109 42N02'54 77w55'58 5:11:44
Maple Bay 7 226 42N06 79w23 5:17:32
Maple Beach 26 226 42N44'06 77w43'27 5:10:54
Maplecrest 20 226 42N16'33 74w11'14 4:56:45
Mapledale 33 13 42N54'21 75w15'15 5:01:01
Mapledale 56 42 42N06'39 74w33'48 4:58:15
Maple Flats 33 15 43N16'13 75w51'19 5:03:25
Maple Glen 53 11 41N30'30 74w27'57 4:57:52
Maple Grove 21 7 43N15'22 74w09'15 4:56:37
Maple Grove 34 16 42N53'09 76w11'23 5:04:46
Maple Grove 39 226 42N29'40 75w14'53 5:01:00
Maple Grove 42 226 42N36'53 73w34'10 4:54:17
Maple Hill 38 25 43N27'10 75w51'14 5:03:25
Maple Hill 56 11 41N51'59 74w03'42 4:56:15
Maplehurst 5 226 42N10'48 78w22'55 5:13:32
Maple Point 7 226 42N06'09 79w21'30 5:17:26
Maples 5 226 42N20'02 78w44'07 5:14:56
Maple Shade 46 11 43N01'07 73w43'36 4:54:54
Maple Springs 7 158 42N11'48 79w25'27 5:17:42
Mapleton 6 13 42N50'37 76w36'01 5:06:24
Mapleton 32 1 43N07'23 78w47'58 5:15:12
Mapletown (Blaine) 29 162 42N50'19 74w33'35 4:58:14
Maple Valley 39 226 42N40'46 74w45'52 4:59:03
Maple View 38 14 43N27'26 76w08'44 5:04:35
Maplewood 1 1 42N43 73w44 4:54:56
Maplewood 28 209 43N06'26 77w41'39 5:10:47
Maplewood 53 197 41N40'10 74w44'24 4:58:58
Maplewood 60 1 40N57'48 73w47'21 4:55:09
Marathon 12 13 42N26'30 76w01'57 5:04:08
Marble Hill 3 1 40N53 73w54 4:55:36
Marbletown 56 11 41N53'00 74w06'49 4:56:27
Marbletown 59 14 43N01'14 77w04'00 5:08:16
Marcellus 34 13 42N58'58 76w20'27 5:05:22
Marcellus Falls 34 13 43N00'18 76w20'18 5:05:21
Marcy 24 1 40N42 73w57 4:55:48
Marcy 33 14 43N10'14 75w17'31 5:01:10
Marcy Landing 16 226 44N04'24 73w52'45 4:55:31
Marengo 59 99 43N01'33 76w54'39 5:07:39
Margaretville 13 226 42N08'55 74w38'55 4:58:36
Mariandale 60 1 41N10'28 73w52'03 4:55:28
Mariaville 47 94 42N49'43 74w08'08 4:56:33
Marietta 34 13 42N54'32 76w19'26 5:05:18
Marilla 15 38 42N50'24 78w33'19 5:14:13
Marine Hospital 43 1 40N38 74w06 4:56:24
Mariners Harbor 43 1 40N38'12 74w09'33 4:56:38
Marion 59 89 43N08'36 77w11'22 5:08:45
Mariposa 9 226 42N42'27 75w48'38 5:03:15
Market 14 226 41N52'58 73w44'28 4:54:58
Market 15 153 42N53 78w52 5:15:28
Markhams 5 42 42N23'56 79w00'13 5:16:01
Marlboro 24 1 40N36 73w58 4:55:52
Marlboro 56 6 41N36'20 73w58'19 4:55:53
Marquette 15 1 42N58 78w52 5:15:28
Marshall 2 226 42N19'34 78w12'08 5:12:49
Marshall 33 13 42N57'47 75w19'41 5:01:19
Marshalls 51 14 42N24'42 77w20'43 5:09:23
Marsh Corner 50 12 42N44'20 76w47'31 5:07:10
Marshfield 15 42 42N32'34 78w50'31 5:15:22
Marshville 29 162 42N52'31 74w36'35 4:58:26
Marshville 45 226 44N27'04 75w13'56 5:00:56
Martin 28 27 43N01'33 77w42'20 5:10:49
Martindale 11 11 42N12'25 73w37'56 4:54:32
Martindale Depot 11 11 42N11 73w35 4:54:20
Martinsburg 25 226 43N44'15 75w28'12 5:01:53
Martinsville 32 1 43N02'59 78w50'05 5:15:20
Martinsville 61 24 42N43'17 78w07'59 5:12:32
Martisco 34 13 43N01'02 76w20'06 5:05:20
Martville 6 226 43N16'48 76w37'39 5:06:31
Marvin 7 226 42N01'53 79w44'05 5:18:56
Marycrest 36 226 41N20'11 74w12'34 4:56:50
Maryknoll 60 166 41N11 73w50 4:55:20
Maryland 39 13 42N32'11 74w53'13 4:59:33
Marymount 60 6 41N04 73w51 4:55:24
Marysville 34 24 42N59'02 76w26'58 5:05:48
Masonville 13 226 42N14'31 75w22'40 5:01:31
Maspeth 41 1 40N43'23 73w54'47 4:55:39
Massapequa 30 6 40N40'50 73w28'29 4:53:54
Massapequa Park 30 11 40N40'49 73w27'20 4:53:49
Massawepie 45 221 44N14 74w28 4:57:52
Massena 45 195 44N55'41 74w53'32 4:59:34
Massena Center 45 195 44N57'36 74w49'54 4:59:20
Massena Springs 45 195 44N54'52 74w53'16 4:59:33
Masten Lake 53 11 41N34 74w29 4:57:56
Mastic 52 11 40N48'07 72w50'29 4:51:22
Mastic Beach 52 11 40N46'00 72w51'09 4:51:25
Matinecock 30 11 40N52'34 73w34'37 4:54:18
Matteawan 14 7 41N30 73w58 4:55:52
Matteawan State Hospital 14 7 41N30 73w58 4:55:52
Mattituck 52 11 40N59'28 72w32'05 4:50:08
Mattydale 34 41 43N05'52 76w08'44 5:04:35
Maxwell 26 226 42N58'36 77w46'22 5:11:05
Maybrook 36 11 41N29'02 74w13'05 4:56:52
Maybury Mills 12 41 42N36'03 76w03'58 5:04:16
Mayfair 47 1 42N52'19 73w55'56 4:55:44
Mayfield 18 226 43N06'16 74w15'55 4:57:04
Maynard 33 222 43N08'12 75w15'34 5:01:02
Mays Mills 62 14 42N40'02 76w59'39 5:07:59
Mays Point 50 19 42N59'51 76w45'56 5:07:04
Mayville 7 158 42N15'14 79w30'17 5:18:01
Mayweed Corner 35 47 42N49'52 77w24'53 5:09:40
Maywood 1 11 42N44'38 73w51'48 4:55:27
Maywood 52 11 40N43'21 73w25'30 4:53:42
McClure 4 167 42N02'54 75w29'14 5:01:57
McColloms 17 176 44N30'37 74w18'20 4:57:13
McConnellsville 33 226 43N16'23 75w41'40 5:02:47
McCoon Crossing 22 78 42N53'45 75w03'07 5:00:12
McCormick's Corner 1 6 42N46 73w56 4:55:44
McDonough 9 226 42N29'54 75w46'06 5:03:04
McDuffie Town 50 12 42N45'59 76w47'28 5:07:10
McEwens Corner 45 105 44N45'57 74w41'25 4:58:46
McGraw 12 41 42N35'46 76w05'37 5:04:22
McGraws 51 226 42N04'24 77w43'48 5:10:55
McGrawville 2 226 42N20'57 78w13'40 5:12:55
McIntyre 14 226 41N53'23 73w41'55 4:54:48
McKeever 22 226 43N36'43 75w05'57 5:00:24
McKinley 29 162 42N54'51 74w31'02 4:58:04
McKinneys 55 186 42N28'43 76w30'29 5:06:02
McKinneys Point 55 186 42N28 76w29 5:05:56
McKinstry Hollow 5 226 42N27'38 78w30'36 5:14:02
McKown Park 1 1 42N40 73w48 4:55:12
McKownville 1 1 42N41'02 73w50'53 4:55:24
McKownville Estates 1 1 42N40 73w48 4:55:12
McLaughlin Acres 40 17 41N22'18 73w42'10 4:54:49
McLean 55 13 42N33'07 76w17'29 5:05:10
McMasters Crossing 17 176 44N21'11 74w12'58 4:56:52
McNalls 32 121 43N09'56 78w34'29 5:14:18
McPherson Cove 26 226 42N47'23 77w42'26 5:10:50
McPherson Point 26 226 42N46'48 77w42'50 5:10:51
Meacham 30 11 40N42 73w42 4:54:48
Mead Corner 35 14 42N50'13 77w08'53 5:08:36
Meadowbrook 36 1 41N26'43 74w04'53 4:56:20
Meadowdale 1 40 42N40'14 73w59'03 4:55:56
Meadowmere Park 30 11 40N38'10 73w44'31 4:54:58
Meadow Run 15 153 42N45 78w51 5:15:24

Meadows 28 226 43N13 77W56 5:11:44
Meadow Wood 28 27 42N57'18 77W43'25 5:10:54
Meads Corners 40 226 41N29'01 73W46'08 4:55:05
Meads Creek 51 13 42N16'19 77W06'02 5:08:24
Mechanicstown 36 1 41N26'34 74W23'20 4:57:33
Mechanicville 46 1 42N54'10 73W41'16 4:54:45
Mecklenburg 49 226 42N27'27 76W42'38 5:06:51
Meco 18 226 43N03'21 74W22'58 4:57:32
Mecox 52 11 40N54'40 72W18'17 4:49:13
Medford 52 11 40N49'03 73W00'02 4:52:00
Medina 37 112 43N13'12 78W23'14 5:13:33
Medusa 1 226 42N26'12 74W07'50 4:56:31
Medway 20 11 42N23'50 73W53'19 4:55:33
Melcourt 3 1 40N50 73W54 4:55:36
Mellenville 11 1 42N15'11 73W40'05 4:54:40
Melody Lake 53 197 41N35'41 74W39'56 4:58:40
Melrose 3 1 40N49'28 73W54'39 4:55:39
Melrose 42 11 42N50'31 73W37'23 4:54:30
Melrose Park 6 12 42N54'31 76W32'26 5:06:10
Melville 52 11 40N47'36 73W24'56 4:53:40
Melvin Hill 35 13 42N55'00 77W03'46 5:08:15
Memphis 34 41 43N04'58 76W22'39 5:05:31
Menands 1 11 42N41'31 73W43'30 4:54:54
Mendon 28 226 42N59'52 77W30'17 5:10:01
Mendon Center 28 13 42N59'48 77W33'42 5:10:15
Mendon Farms 28 13 43N00 77W34 5:10:16
Meno 17 226 44N31'45 74W23'43 4:57:35
Menteth Point 35 14 42N53 77W17 5:09:08
Mentz 6 24 43N02 76W38 5:06:32
Menzie Crossing 26 226 42N58'53 77W48'27 5:11:14
Meredith 13 29 42N21'30 74W56'05 4:59:44
Meridale 13 226 42N22'01 74W57'15 4:59:49
Meridian 6 226 43N09'56 76W32'14 5:06:09
Merrick 30 1 40N39'46 73W33'07 4:54:12
Merrick Corner 33 82 43N18'25 75W17'22 5:01:09
Merrickville 13 13 42N16'31 75W10'43 5:00:43
Merriewold 53 197 41N39 74W42 4:58:48
Merriewold Lake 36 226 41N22 74W11 4:56:44
Merriewold Park 53 226 41N34'19 74W43'08 4:58:53
Merrifield 6 13 42N46'58 76W35'07 5:06:20
Merrill 10 136 44N45'53 73W57'31 4:55:50
Merrillsville 27 60 43N01'08 75W40'17 5:02:41
Merrilsville 17 113 44N31'52 74W02'06 4:56:08
Merriweather Campus 30 11 40N48 73W37 4:54:28
Mertensia 35 19 42N57'43 77W21'47 5:09:27
Messenger Bay 27 226 43N09'27 75W48'06 5:03:12
Messengerville 12 13 42N29'20 76W04'30 5:04:18
Methol 13 226 41N55'10 75W00'44 5:00:03
Metropolitan 24 1 40N42 73W57 4:55:48
Mettacahonts 56 76 41N48'46 74W15'17 4:57:01
Mexico 38 14 43N27'34 76W13'45 5:04:55
Michigan Corners 36 1 41N28'01 74W20'53 4:57:24
Michigan Mills 25 226 43N36'13 75W35'52 5:02:23
Middle Bridge 9 144 42N14'43 75W29'18 5:01:57
Middleburg 48 226 42N35'53 74W20'03 4:57:20
Middlebury 61 226 42N50 78W08 5:12:32
Middle Falls 58 226 43N06'02 73W31'31 4:54:06
Middlefield 39 13 42N41'14 74W50'25 4:59:22
Middlefield Center 39 140 42N45'52 74W50'24 4:59:22
Middle Granville 58 42 43N26'00 73W17'02 4:53:08
Middle Grove 46 226 43N05'23 73W55'06 4:55:40
Middle Hope 36 1 41N33'36 74W00'13 4:56:01
Middle Island 52 11 40N53'03 72W56'16 4:51:45
Middleport 27 180 42N47'26 75W33'37 5:02:14
Middleport 32 90 43N12'45 78W28'36 5:13:54
Middlesex 62 226 42N42'17 77W16'19 5:09:05
Middle Sprite 18 226 43N07'14 74W38'21 4:58:33
Middletown 36 1 41N26'45 74W25'24 4:57:42
Middle Village 39 140 42N49'59 74W49'49 4:59:19
Middle Village 41 1 40N42'59 73W52'54 4:55:32
Middleville 22 226 43N08'19 74W58'07 4:59:52
Middleville 52 11 40N53'57 73W17'48 4:53:11
Midhampton 52 11 40N56'59 72W14'28 4:48:58
Midland Beach 43 1 40N34'23 74W05'42 4:56:23
Midtown 31 1 40N45 73W59 4:55:56
Midtown Plaza 28 209 43N09 77W37 5:10:28
Midway 8 14 42N15'05 76W50'16 5:07:21
Midway 55 13 42N33'04 76W29'38 5:05:59
Midway Park 7 158 42N12'05 79W25'28 5:17:42
Midwood 24 1 40N37 73W58 4:55:52
Milan 14 226 41N57'12 73W47'33 4:55:10
Milburn 36 1 41N30'06 74W20'44 4:57:23
Mile of Woods 28 20 43N03'24 77W41'52 5:10:47
Mileses 53 226 41N50'11 75W03'59 5:00:16
Milford 39 15 42N35'26 74W56'44 4:59:47
Milford Center 39 13 42N31'27 74W59'21 4:59:57
Mill Brook 3 1 40N50 73W54 4:55:36
Millbrook 14 39 41N47'06 73W41'40 4:54:47
Millbrook Heights 14 39 41N45'56 73W42'50 4:54:51
Millen Bay 23 226 44N10'09 76W14'39 5:04:59
Miller Corners 29 226 42N49'40 74W14'00 4:56:56
Miller Place 52 11 40N57'35 72W59'48 4:51:59
Millers 37 15 43N19'34 78W27'59 5:13:52
Millers Corner 61 25 42N48'55 78W07'29 5:12:30
Millers Corners 42 1 42N35'07 73W34'12 4:54:17
Millers Crossing 61 20 42N48'38 78W10'10 5:12:41
Millers Mills 22 13 42N55'12 75W04'55 5:00:20
Millers Mills Crossing 22 13 42N54'32 75W05'31 5:00:22
Millersport 15 11 43N05'05 78W41'49 5:14:47
Millerton 14 79 41N57'13 73W30'40 4:54:03
Millertown 42 11 42N54'21 73W30'40 4:54:03
Mill Grove 5 226 42N01'05 78W20'28 5:13:22
Millgrove 15 145 42N56'37 78W33'11 5:14:13
Mill Hook 56 76 41N47'45 74W14'51 4:56:59
Mill Neck 30 11 40N53'13 73W33'20 4:54:13
Mill Point 29 1 42N57 74W11 4:56:44
Millport 8 14 42N15'55 76W50'06 5:07:20
Millsburg 36 11 41N22'22 74W31'33 4:58:06
Mills Corners 18 226 43N03'44 74W07'24 4:56:30
Mills Mills 2 226 42N30'03 78W07'12 5:12:29
Milltown 40 226 41N24'45 73W33'38 4:54:15
Millville 37 112 43N12'27 78W19'30 5:13:18
Millwood 60 7 41N11'32 73W47'52 4:55:11
Milo 62 14 42N37 77W01 5:08:04
Milo Center 62 14 42N38'04 76W59'59 5:08:00
Milo Mills 62 14 42N39'31 77W01'35 5:08:06
Milton 46 226 43N02 73W53 4:55:32
Milton 56 1 41N39'35 73W57'27 4:55:50
Milton 60 1 40N57'43 73W41'19 4:54:45
Milton Center 46 11 43N02'27 73W53'25 4:55:34
Mina 7 226 42N07'48 79W41'18 5:18:45
Minaville 29 1 42N53'09 74W13'01 4:56:52
Minden 29 226 42N56 74W42 4:58:48
Mindenville 29 62 42N59'31 74W43'05 4:58:52
Mineola 30 11 40N44'57 73W38'28 4:54:34
Mineral Springs 48 139 42N40'13 74W27'05 4:57:48
Minerva 16 49 43N47'29 73W59'05 4:55:56
Minetto 38 204 43N23'53 76W28'40 5:05:55
Mineville 16 54 44N05'34 73W31'07 4:54:04
Minisink 36 11 41N20 74W32 4:58:08
Minisink Ford 53 226 41N28'57 74W58'38 4:59:55
Minklers Corners 45 195 44N56 74W54 4:59:36
Minnehaha 22 59 43N39'42 75W04'06 5:00:16
Minoa 34 226 43N04'34 76W00'04 5:04:00
Minsteed 59 226 43N08'57 77W07'14 5:08:29
Mitchellsville 51 14 42N24'29 77W17'24 5:09:10
Model City 32 199 43N11'06 78W59'02 5:15:56
Modena 56 11 41N40'06 74W06'11 4:56:25
Modena Gardens 56 11 41N38'51 74W07'18 4:56:29
Moffitsville 10 136 44N38'19 73W45'23 4:55:02
Mohawk 22 196 43N00'41 75W00'16 5:00:01
Mohawk Gardens 33 211 43N13'35 75W26'24 5:01:46
Mohawk Hill 25 226 43N31'29 75W28'12 5:01:53
Mohawk View 1 1 42N47'01 73W47'20 4:55:09
Mohegan Heights 60 6 40N57'11 73W50'36 4:55:22
Mohegan Lake 60 6 41N19'06 73W51'34 4:55:26
Mohican Lake 53 25 41N31'05 74W49'06 4:59:16
Mohonk Lake 56 11 41N46'07 74W09'22 4:56:37
Moira 17 125 44N49'05 74W33'22 4:58:13
Molyneaux Corners 32 226 43N12'37 78W47'51 5:15:11
Mombaccus 56 72 41N48'54 74W18'43 4:57:15
Mongaup 53 1 41N25'29 74W45'45 4:59:03
Mongaup Valley 53 226 41N40'07 74W47'06 4:59:08
Monroe 36 1 41N19'50 74W11'14 4:56:45
Monsey 44 4 41N06'40 74W04'08 4:56:17
Monsey Heights 44 4 41N07 74W04 4:56:16
Montague 25 226 43N58 75W17 5:01:08
Montario Point 23 14 43N41'30 76W12'05 5:04:48
Montauk 52 11 41N02'09 71W57'18 4:47:49
Montauk Beach 52 11 41N01'33 71W58'03 4:47:52
Montauk Estates 52 11 40N58 72W08 4:48:32
Montauk Station 52 11 41N02'57 71W57'15 4:47:49
Montclair Colony 52 11 41N03'03 72W20'59 4:49:24
Monteola 25 226 43N38'45 75W39'45 5:02:39
Monterey 49 14 42N18'20 77W02'58 5:08:12
Monterey Estates 44 4 41N08 73W56 4:55:44
Montezuma 6 25 43N00'36 76W42'13 5:06:49
Montgomery 36 11 41N31'39 74W14'14 4:56:57
Monticello 53 197 41N39'20 74W41'23 4:58:46
Montoma 56 11 42N01'14 74W07'59 4:56:32
Montour 49 14 42N20 76W49 5:07:16
Montour Falls 49 14 42N20'50 76W50'44 5:07:23
Montrose 60 7 41N15'08 73W55'55 4:55:44
Montville 6 13 42N42'52 76W24'13 5:05:37
Moody 17 221 44N13'40 74W29'07 4:57:56
Mooers 17 198 44N57'48 73W35'16 4:54:21
Mooers Forks 17 198 44N57'29 73W38'28 4:54:34
Moon Beach 6 226 43N23'51 76W38'40 5:06:35
Moons 7 67 42N17'01 79W17'47 5:17:11
Moore Landing 23 17 44N18'01 75W59'28 5:03:58
Moores Mill 14 11 41N42'15 73W44'57 4:55:00
Moorhouse Corner 11 10 42N20'58 73W34'17 4:54:17
Moose River 25 77 44N06 75W40 5:02:40
Moran Corner 28 226 42N57'37 77W37'13 5:10:29
Moravia 6 13 42N42'45 76W25'19 5:05:41
Moreau 46 226 43N14 73W39 4:54:36
Morehouse 21 226 43N27 74W43 4:58:52
Morehouseville 21 226 43N23'27 74W46'27 4:59:06
Moreland 49 14 42N18'28 76W54'26 5:07:38
Morey Park 42 11 42N32'39 73W36'01 4:54:24
Morgan 31 1 40N45 73W59 4:55:56
Morgan Corners 7 226 42N03'13 79W39'35 5:18:38
Morgan Hill 56 11 41N57'20 74W06'39 4:56:27
Morganville 19 70 43N00'08 78W04'28 5:12:18
Moriah 16 54 44N02'46 73W30'20 4:54:01
Moriah Center 16 54 44N03'40 73W30'37 4:54:02
Moriches 52 11 40N48'26 72W49'18 4:51:17
Morley 45 155 44N39'54 75W11'57 5:00:48
Morningside 31 1 40N48 73W57 4:55:48
Morris 39 226 42N32'55 75W14'44 5:00:59
Morrisania 3 1 40N49'45 73W54'25 4:55:38
Morris Heights 3 1 40N50'59 73W55'13 4:55:41
Morrison Heights 36 11 41N30'22 74W12'24 4:56:50
Morrisonville 10 86 44N41'35 73W33'45 4:54:15
Morris Park 3 1 40N51'08 73W51'14 4:55:25
Morris Park 41 1 40N41'25 73W48'59 4:55:16
Morristown 45 20 44N35'11 75W38'55 5:02:36
Morristown Center 45 201 44N35'48 75W35'34 5:02:22
Morrisville 27 29 42N53'55 75W38'26 5:02:34
Morrisville Station 27 226 42N53'29 75W36'16 5:02:25
Morse 38 182 43N22'12 76W08'03 5:04:32
Morse Mill 6 13 42N43'37 76W21'34 5:05:26
Morsston 53 75 41N53'03 74W48'39 4:59:15
Mortimer 28 226 43N05'35 77W38'57 5:10:36
Morton 28 105 43N19'41 77W59'44 5:11:59
Morton Corners 15 218 42N30'40 78W45'55 5:15:04
Morton Corners 55 13 42N35'58 76W20'39 5:05:23
Moscow Hill 27 180 42N47'37 75W24'23 5:01:38
Mosher Corners 55 13 42N35'27 76W24'06 5:05:36
Mosherville 46 226 43N03'42 74W01'09 4:56:05
Moshier Falls 22 226 43N52'12 75W08'23 5:00:34
Mosholu 3 1 40N53 73W52 4:55:28
Mosquito Point 6 226 43N04'46 76W38'51 5:06:35
Mosquito Point 20 226 42N15'37 74W23'57 4:57:36
Mossyglen 51 13 42N08 77W03 5:08:12
Mott Haven 3 1 40N48'32 73W55'24 4:55:42
Motts Corner 35 13 43N01'38 77W24'02 5:09:36
Mottville 34 24 42N58'25 76W26'34 5:05:46
Mountain Dale 53 74 41N41'22 74W31'54 4:58:08
Mountain House 36 226 41N21'30 74W10'30 4:56:42
Mountain Lodge 22 203 43N41'57 74W55'36 4:59:42
Mountain Lodge 36 226 41N23'18 74W08'32 4:56:34
Mountain View 17 30 44N42'10 74W08'20 4:56:33
Mountainville 36 11 41N24'03 74W04'44 4:56:19
Mount Airy 60 166 41N13'04 73W52'46 4:55:31
Mount Arab 45 221 44N10'27 74W36'06 4:58:24
Mount Carmel 3 1 40N52 73W53 4:55:32
Mount Carmel 4 17 42N06'31 75W33'52 5:02:15
Mount Eve 36 7 41N24 74W20 4:57:20
Mount Hope 36 21 41N26'40 74W31'20 4:58:05
Mount Hope 58 123 43N29'50 73W32'51 4:54:11
Mount Hope 60 1 40N59'20 73W52'06 4:55:28
Mount Ivy 44 4 41N11'12 74W02'07 4:56:08
Mount Kisco 60 6 41N12'15 73W43'39 4:54:55
Mount Loretto 43 11 40N31 74W13 4:56:52
Mount Marion 56 215 42N02'19 73W59'13 4:55:57
Mount Marion Park 56 215 42N02'13 73W59'50 4:55:59
Mount Morris 26 13 42N43'32 77W52'28 5:11:30
Mount Pleasant 38 226 43N23'13 76W22'42 5:05:31
Mount Pleasant 46 226 43N09'14 73W58'09 4:55:53
Mount Pleasant 47 1 42N47'51 73W56'53 4:55:48
Mount Pleasant 56 88 42N02'54 74W17'22 4:57:09
Mount Pleasant 60 6 41N05'46 73W47'38 4:55:11
Mount Prosper 53 11 41N35'27 74W32'09 4:58:09
Mount Read 28 185 43N15'10 77W39'34 5:10:38
Mount Riga 14 79 41N59'41 73W30'54 4:54:04
Mount Ross 14 226 42N00'18 73W42'56 4:54:52
Mount Sinai 52 11 40N56'49 73W01'48 4:52:07
Mount Tremper 56 88 42N02'41 74W16'33 4:57:06
Mount Upton 9 226 42N25'35 75W23'01 5:01:32
Mount Vernon 15 153 42N45'14 78W53'27 5:15:34
Mount Vernon 53 11 41N38'54 74W29'49 4:57:59
Mount Vernon 60 1 40N54'45 73W50'15 4:55:21

Mount Vision 39 226 42N34'42 75W03'30 5:00:14
Moyers Corners 34 226 43N10'49 76W15'43 5:05:03
Mud Hill 38 25 43N23'25 75W55'39 5:03:43
Mud Lock 50 14 42N56'47 76W44'11 5:06:57
Mud Mills 59 14 43N04'30 77W04'33 5:08:18
Mud Settlement 38 182 43N17'01 76W06'51 5:04:27
Muitzes Kill 42 68 42N28'36 73W43'53 4:54:56
Mumford 28 226 42N59'34 77W51'38 5:11:27
Mundale 13 226 42N15'17 75W03'00 5:00:12
Mungers Corners 38 226 43N23'49 76W15'25 5:05:02
Munns 27 13 42N58'52 75W34'41 5:02:19
Munnsville 27 13 42N58'37 75W35'14 5:02:21
Munsey Park 30 11 40N47'55 73W40'49 4:54:43
Munsons Corner 50 19 43N01'12 76W48'48 5:07:15
Munsons Corners 12 41 42N34'56 76W12'34 5:04:50
Munsonville 18 226 43N05'20 74W14'24 4:56:58
Murdochs Crossing 37 15 43N19 78W23 5:13:32
Murdock Woods 60 1 40N57'47 73W45'36 4:55:02
Murray 37 105 43N16'26 78W02'46 5:12:11
Murray Hill 60 1 40N59'56 73W47'16 4:55:09
Murray Isle 23 163 44N14 76W05 5:04:20
Murrays Corner 15 145 42N59'55 78W28'40 5:13:55
Muttontown 30 11 40N49'26 73W32'53 4:54:12
Mycenae 34 13 43N02'56 75W55'51 5:03:43
Myers 55 13 42N32'22 76W32'23 5:06:10
Myers Corner 14 6 41N36'22 73W52'24 4:55:30
Myers Grove 36 21 41N26'47 74W36'07 4:58:24
Nanticoke 4 226 42N16'29 76W03'16 5:04:13
Nanuet 44 4 41N05'19 74W00'50 4:56:03
Napanoch 56 48 41N44'38 74W22'19 4:57:29
Napeague 52 1 41N00'34 72W04'07 4:48:16
Naples 35 226 42N36'55 77W24'10 5:09:37
Napoli 5 20 42N11'59 78W53'32 5:15:34
Narrowsburg 53 20 41N36'31 75W03'44 5:00:15
Nashville 7 226 42N27'29 79W04'35 5:16:18
Nashville 32 1 43N04'38 78W51'58 5:15:28
Nassau 42 11 42N30'57 73W36'38 4:54:27
Nassau Farms 52 11 41N01'02 72W27'11 4:49:49
Nassau Point 52 11 41N01 72W29 4:49:56
Nassau Shores 30 11 40N39'43 73W26'26 4:53:46
Natural Bridge 23 226 44N04'08 75W29'39 5:01:59
Natural Dam 45 178 44N20'14 75W30'12 5:02:01
Naumburg 25 191 43N54'04 75W29'40 5:01:59
Nauraushaun 44 4 41N03'25 73W59'34 4:55:58
Navarino 34 13 42N55'39 76W16'27 5:05:06
Nazareth College 28 13 43N09 77W33 5:10:12
Nedrow 34 13 42N58'30 76W08'30 5:04:34
Neelytown 36 11 41N29'01 74W14'39 4:56:59
Nehasane 21 226 44N00'15 74W46'37 4:59:06
Nelliston 29 62 42N56'05 74W36'50 4:58:27
Nelson 27 226 42N55'02 75W46'38 5:03:07
Nelson Corner 45 226 44N22'20 75W41'39 5:02:47
Nelson Corners 40 6 41N24'45 73W54'47 4:55:39
Nelsonville 40 6 41N25'28 73W56'49 4:55:47
Nepera Park 60 1 40N58'33 73W52'03 4:55:28
Neponsit 41 1 40N34'18 73W51'43 4:55:27
Nepperham 60 1 40N57'20 73W52'01 4:55:28
Nesconset 52 11 40N51'07 73W09'16 4:52:37
Netherwood 14 226 41N47'52 73W49'08 4:55:17
Neversink 53 226 41N50'50 74W37'10 4:58:29
Nevis 11 5 42N03'38 73W50'36 4:55:22
New Albion 5 226 42N17'22 78W53'23 5:15:34
Newark 59 14 43N02'48 77W05'44 5:08:23
Newark Valley 54 226 42N13'25 76W11'01 5:04:44
New Baltimore 20 11 42N26'46 73W47'20 4:55:09
New Berlin 9 226 42N37'27 75W19'55 5:01:20
New Berlin Junction 9 149 42N18 75W29 5:01:56
New Boston 12 226 42N40'22 75W55'56 5:03:44
New Boston 25 226 43N48'00 75W44'46 5:02:59
New Bremen 25 226 43N50'16 75W26'26 5:01:46
Newbridge 45 25 44N17'11 74W58'33 4:59:54
New Brighton 43 1 40N38'32 74W05'36 4:56:22
New Britain 11 11 42N27'17 73W29'25 4:53:58
Newburg 61 24 42N41'35 78W07'12 5:12:29
Newburgh 36 1 41N30'12 74W00'39 4:56:03
Newburgh Junction 36 4 41N17'49 74W08'21 4:56:33
New Campbellwood Wye 25 226 43N36'55 75W43'03 5:02:52
New Cassel 30 11 40N45'32 73W34'12 4:54:17
New Castle 60 1 41N11 73W46 4:55:04
New Centerville 38 226 43N34 76W07 5:04:28
New City 44 4 41N08'51 73W59'23 4:55:58
New City Park 44 4 41N08'00 74W00'09 4:56:01
Newcomb 16 226 43N58'10 74W09'54 4:56:40
New Concord 11 10 42N23'43 73W31'37 4:54:06
New Connecticut 54 226 42N16'23 76W08'54 5:04:36
New Dorp 43 1 40N34'26 74W06'59 4:56:28
New Dorp Beach 43 1 40N33'55 74W06'12 4:56:25
New Ebenezer 15 153 42N51'24 78W44'30 5:14:58
New Falconwood 15 1 43N01 78W57 5:15:48
Newfane 32 226 43N17'12 78W42'38 5:14:51
Newfield 55 226 42N21'43 76W35'28 5:06:22
New Forge 11 226 42N06'22 73W40'30 4:54:42
New Hackensack 14 6 41N37'22 73W52'16 4:55:29
New Hamburg 14 6 41N35'18 73W56'44 4:55:47
New Hampton 36 7 41N24'39 74W24'27 4:57:38
New Hartford 33 11 43N04'24 75W17'17 5:01:09
New Haven 38 15 43N28'47 76W18'56 5:05:16
New Hempstead 44 4 41N09 74W02 4:56:08
New Hope 6 13 42N47'53 76W20'51 5:05:23
New Hudson 2 226 42N18 78W15 5:13:00
New Hurley 56 122 41N38'17 74W08'39 4:56:35
New Hyde Park 30 11 40N44'06 73W41'18 4:54:45
Newieden 53 226 41N35'16 74W59'23 4:59:58
New Ireland 4 151 42N10'43 75W57'16 5:03:49
New Kingston 13 226 42N12'49 74W40'57 4:58:44
Newkirk 18 226 43N06'47 74W30'35 4:58:02
Newkirk 24 1 40N39 73W57 4:55:48
New Lebanon 11 11 42N27'50 73W23'49 4:53:35
New Lebanon Center 11 11 42N28'14 73W25'21 4:53:41
New Lisbon 39 226 42N35'16 75W11'04 5:00:44
New London 33 211 43N12'19 75W35'17 5:02:21
New Lots 24 1 40N41 73W52 4:55:28
Newmans Corner 4 13 42N11'25 75W52'53 5:03:32
New Market 32 199 43N06 79W02 5:16:08
New Milford 36 6 41N14'04 74W24'51 4:57:39
New Ohio 4 127 42N13'20 75W42'47 5:02:51
New Oregon 15 153 42N35'18 78W47'31 5:15:10
New Paltz 56 11 41N44'51 74W05'14 4:56:21
Newport 22 20 43N11'09 75W00'53 5:00:04
Newport 28 185 43N12'30 77W32'13 5:10:09
Newport 34 41 43N04'43 76W19'44 5:05:19
Newport 36 11 41N16'33 74W28'11 4:57:53
New Rochelle 60 1 40N54'41 73W46'58 4:55:08
New Russia 16 50 44N09'48 73W36'43 4:54:27
Newrys 20 226 42N26'16 73W59'25 4:55:58
New Salem 1 11 42N37'22 73W58'08 4:55:53
New Salem 56 11 41N53'43 74W00'59 4:56:04
New Scotland 1 11 42N37'43 73W54'50 4:55:39
New Scriba 38 226 43N36'23 75W55'52 5:03:43
New Springville 43 1 40N35'36 74W09'49 4:56:39
New Square 44 4 41N08 74W02 4:56:08
Newstead 15 145 43N01 78W31 5:14:04
New Suffolk 52 11 40N59'29 72W28'35 4:49:54
Newton Falls 45 25 44N12'38 74W59'22 4:59:57
Newton Hook 11 111 42N21'16 73W46'59 4:55:08
Newtonville 1 1 42N43'28 73W45'32 4:55:02
Newtown 15 42 42N32'20 78W57'26 5:15:50
Newtown 46 11 42N52'17 73W43'29 4:54:54
Newtown 52 11 40N52'46 72W30'13 4:50:01
New Utrecht 24 1 40N36'47 73W59'47 4:55:59
New Vernon 36 1 41N30'06 74W29'05 4:57:56
Newville 22 61 42N58'35 74W49'34 4:59:18
New Windsor 36 1 41N28'36 74W01'27 4:56:06
New Woodstock 27 226 42N50'54 75W51'17 5:03:25
New York 31 1 40N42'51 74W00'23 4:56:02
New York Mills 33 222 43N06'19 75W17'30 5:01:10
New York Mills Gardens 33 222 43N07 75W18 5:01:12
Niagara 32 199 43N07 78W59 5:15:56
Niagara Falls 32 199 43N05'40 79W03'25 5:16:14
Niagara Square 15 153 42N53 78W53 5:15:32
Niagara University 32 199 43N08 79W02 5:16:08
Nichols 51 226 42N00'33 77W15'56 5:09:04
Nichols 54 36 42N01'18 76W22'02 5:05:28
Nichols Corners 34 13 42N56'43 76W13'33 5:04:54
Nichols Plaza 23 45 43N59 75W56 5:03:44
Nichols Run 5 226 42N00'12 78W31'15 5:14:05
Nicholsville 38 15 43N16'23 75W57'51 5:03:51
Nicholville 45 226 44N41'50 74W39'35 4:58:38
Niets Crest 7 226 42N07'05 79W23'22 5:17:33
Nile 2 226 42N10'41 78W08'45 5:12:35
Niles 6 13 42N50'15 76W24'50 5:05:39
Nimmonsburg 4 151 42N08 75W53 5:03:32
Nimmonsburg-Chenango Bridge 4 13 42N11 75W53 5:03:32
Ninety Six Corners 33 20 43N20'28 75W05'39 5:00:23
Nineveh 4 17 42N11'39 75W36'10 5:02:25
Nineveh Junction 9 17 42N12'25 75W35'37 5:02:22
Niobe 7 20 42N00'45 79W26'59 5:17:48
Niskayuna 47 1 42N46'47 73W50'46 4:55:23
Nissequoque 52 11 40N54'14 73W11'54 4:52:48
Niverville 11 11 42N26'27 73W39'41 4:54:39
Noble Corner 59 99 43N05'10 76W48'35 5:07:14
Noblesboro 22 84 43N23'45 74W51'44 4:59:27
Noble Shores 38 226 43N32'42 75W52'43 5:03:31
Norfolk 45 226 44N48'03 74W59'29 4:59:58
Normansville 1 11 42N38'03 73W47'53 4:55:12
Norrie Heights 14 219 41N50'21 73W55'32 4:55:42
North 60 1 40N57 73W53 4:55:32
North Afton 9 144 42N16'04 75W32'37 5:02:10
North Alexander 19 25 42N55'46 78W14'31 5:12:58
North Almond 2 226 42N23'26 77W46'12 5:11:05
North Amboy 38 25 43N24'13 75W53'12 5:03:33
North Amityville 52 6 40N41'51 73W25'32 4:53:42
Northampton 18 7 43N13 74W11 4:56:44
Northampton 52 11 40N55 72W38 4:50:32
North Argyle 58 226 43N16'01 73W28'00 4:53:52
North Avon 26 20 42N55'48 77W40'41 5:10:43
North Babylon 52 1 40N42'59 73W19'20 4:53:17
North Bailey 15 7 42N59'26 78W48'17 5:15:13
North Baldwin 30 11 40N39 73W37 4:54:28
North Ballston Spa 46 8 43N01 73W51 4:55:24
North Bangor 17 16 44N50'31 74W24'05 4:57:36
North Barton 54 224 42N07'08 76W29'27 5:05:58
North Bay 33 226 43N13'48 75W44'55 5:03:00
North Bay Shore 52 1 40N44'10 73W15'47 4:53:03
North Beach 41 1 40N45'57 73W52'35 4:55:30
North Belle Isle 34 13 43N05'01 76W15'08 5:05:01
North Bellmore 30 7 40N41'29 73W32'02 4:54:08
North Bellport 52 7 40N46'27 72W56'36 4:51:46
North Bergen 19 110 43N07'25 78W00'49 5:12:03
North Bethlehem 1 1 42N40'12 73W50'47 4:55:23
North Blenheim 48 226 42N28'15 74W26'45 4:57:47
North Bloomfield 35 226 42N56'27 77W34'38 5:10:19
North Bolton 57 226 43N36'06 73W39'17 4:54:37
North Boston 15 11 42N41'08 78W46'37 5:15:06
North Boylston 38 226 43N41'01 76W00'21 5:04:01
North Branch 53 226 41N48'24 74W59'31 4:59:58
North Bridgewater 33 13 42N55'27 75W14'50 5:00:59
North Broadalbin 18 226 43N06'25 74W09'46 4:56:39
North Brookfield 27 13 42N51'01 75W23'28 5:01:34
North Burke 17 141 44N59'12 74W10'29 4:56:42
North Bush 18 43 43N05'05 74W29'34 4:57:58
North Cambridge 58 11 43N01'29 73W27'01 4:53:48
North Cameron 51 20 42N15'13 77W21'54 5:09:28
North Castle 60 1 41N07 73W42 4:54:48
North Cazenovia 27 14 42N59'31 75W52'14 5:03:29
North Chatham 11 10 42N28'19 73W37'56 4:54:32
North Chemung 8 13 42N06'00 76W41'32 5:06:46
North Chili 28 15 43N07'11 77W48'21 5:11:13
North Chittenango 27 226 43N04'52 75W52'23 5:03:30
North Church Corner 38 14 43N30'19 76W13'56 5:04:56
North Clove 14 226 41N42'01 73W40'01 4:54:40
North Clymer 7 22 42N04'30 79W34'22 5:18:17
North Cohocton 51 14 42N33'40 77W27'54 5:09:52
North Colesville 4 127 42N14'28 75W43'19 5:02:53
North Collins 15 42 42N35'43 78W56'29 5:15:46
North Columbia 22 184 42N58'40 75W04'19 5:00:17
North Constantia 38 182 43N20'33 75W59'50 5:03:59
North Corners 45 226 44N44 75W19 5:01:16
North Creek 57 49 43N41'52 73W59'11 4:55:57
North Croghan 23 226 44N02'00 75W30'26 5:02:02
North Croghan Crossing 25 226 44N02'05 75W29'50 5:01:59
North Cuba 2 20 42N14'29 78W16'25 5:13:06
North Dansville 26 13 42N33 77W42 5:10:48
North Darien 19 164 42N58 78W24 5:13:36
North Dock 36 6 41N23'51 73W57'22 4:55:49
Northeast 14 79 41N57 73W32 4:54:08
Northeast Center 14 79 41N55'54 73W32'04 4:54:08
Northeast Henrietta 28 13 43N05 77W31 5:10:04
North East Junction 7 20 42N01'12 79W26'21 5:17:45
North Easton 58 226 43N00'36 73W33'02 4:54:12
North Edmeston 39 226 42N45'24 75W14'15 5:00:57
North Elba 16 1 44N14'36 73W57'17 4:55:49
North End 36 1 41N28 74W24 4:57:36
North Evans 15 11 42N41'49 78W56'30 5:15:46
North Fair Haven 6 226 43N19'58 76W42'00 5:06:48
North Fenton 4 13 42N14'33 75W47'42 5:03:11
Northfield 13 226 42N14'49 75W11'21 5:00:45
North Forest Acres 15 7 43N00'18 78W44'45 5:14:59
North Frankfort 22 184 43N02'32 75W03'34 5:00:14
North Franklin 13 14 42N23'32 75W05'09 5:00:21
North Gage 33 222 43N13'32 75W07'35 5:00:30
North Gainesville 61 24 42N41'04 78W08'01 5:12:32
North Galway 46 1 43N03'08 74W03'31 4:56:14
North Gates 28 209 43N10'35 77W42'06 5:10:48
North Germantown 11 11 42N09'16 73W52'40 4:55:31
North Gouverneur 45 226 44N25'16 75W28'13 5:01:53

North Granville 58 42 43N27'01 73w20'31 4:53:22
North Great River 52 11 40N44'50 73w10'13 4:52:41
North Greece 28 209 43N15'13 77w43'58 5:10:56
North Greenbush 42 1 42N41 73w40 4:54:40
North Greenfield 46 226 43N09'51 73w51'41 4:55:27
North Greenwich 58 1 43N09'31 73w29'10 4:53:57
North Hamlin 28 105 43N20'19 77w54'07 5:11:36
North Hammond 45 20 44N29'00 75w43'47 5:02:55
North Hannibal 38 204 43N21'21 76w32'27 5:06:10
North Harmony 7 226 42N07 79w25 5:17:40
North Harpersfield 13 226 42N28'21 74w41'32 4:58:46
North Hartland 32 150 43N17'20 78w36'18 5:14:25
North Haven 52 11 41N00'46 72w18'48 4:49:15
North Hebron 58 42 43N19'23 73w19'15 4:53:17
North Hempstead 30 1 40N47 73w42 4:54:48
North Highland 40 6 41N26 73w57 4:55:48
North Hills 30 11 40N46'51 73w40'37 4:54:42
North Hillsdale 11 11 42N14'08 73w30'28 4:54:02
North Hoosick 42 11 42N55'41 73w20'36 4:53:22
North Hornell 51 102 42N20'46 77w39'42 5:10:39
North Hudson 16 226 43N57'09 73w43'44 4:54:55
North Huron 59 226 43N15'49 76w53'04 5:07:32
North Ilion 22 184 43N01'19 75w01'44 5:00:07
North Jasper 51 226 42N12 77w24 5:09:36
North Java 61 226 42N41'01 78w20'17 5:13:21
North Jay 16 44 44N23'54 73w40'26 4:54:42
North Kortright 13 13 42N26'10 74w44'23 4:58:58
North Landing 23 13 43N44'08 76w11'05 5:04:44
North Lansing 55 13 42N36'40 76w29'52 5:05:59
North Lawrence 45 105 44N48'18 74w40'31 4:58:42
North Lexington 20 226 42N16'29 74w23'11 4:57:33
North Lindenhurst 52 11 40N42'51 73w22'55 4:53:32
North Litchfield 22 184 43N02 75w04 5:00:16
North Lynbrook 30 7 40N40 73w40 4:54:40
North Macedon 59 226 43N04'56 77w18'17 5:09:13
North Manlius 34 226 43N05'59 75w58'39 5:03:55
North Massapequa 30 6 40N42'03 73w27'45 4:53:51
North Merrick 30 1 40N41'28 73w33'49 4:54:15
North Milton 46 226 43N04'11 73w53'41 4:55:35
North Nassau 42 11 42N34'45 73w32'37 4:54:10
North New Hyde Park 30 11 40N45'17 73w41'16 4:54:45
North Norwich 9 200 42N37'01 75w31'38 5:02:07
North Olean 5 101 42N05'42 78w25'56 5:13:44
North Osceola 25 226 43N34'15 75w42'46 5:02:51
North Patchogue 52 1 40N47'13 73w00'34 4:52:02
North Pelham 60 1 40N55 73w49 4:55:16
North Pembroke 19 142 43N01'16 78w20'10 5:13:21
North Petersburg 42 11 42N49'23 73w19'58 4:53:20
North Pharsalia 9 226 42N36'30 75w42'07 5:02:48
North Pitcher 9 226 42N37'21 75w49'12 5:03:17
North Pole 16 1 44N24'03 73w50'58 4:55:24
Northport 52 7 40N54'03 73w20'37 4:53:22
North Port Byron 6 24 43N03'09 76w37'58 5:06:32
North Reading 49 14 42N27'06 76w58'23 5:07:54
North Ridge 32 226 43N12'45 78w49'34 5:15:18
North Ridgeway 37 112 43N17'27 78w27'56 5:13:52
North River 57 226 43N44'19 74w02'57 4:56:12
North Rockville Centre 30 210 40N40 73w38 4:54:32
North Rose 59 33 43N11'08 76w53'34 5:07:34
North Rush 28 27 43N00'12 77w42'21 5:10:49
North Russell 45 155 44N30'09 75w07'23 5:00:30
North Salem 60 16 41N20'05 73w34'18 4:54:17
North Sanford 4 167 42N09'17 75w27'10 5:01:49
North Schodack 42 1 42N35'04 73w35'55 4:54:24
North Scriba 38 15 43N29'19 76w23'07 5:05:32
North Sea 52 11 40N55'58 72w24'53 4:49:40
North Seaford 30 11 40N47 73w32 4:54:08
North Settlement 20 226 42N20'25 74w17'26 4:57:10
North Sheldon 61 226 42N46'12 78w25'08 5:13:41
North Shore Beach 52 11 40N57 72w56 4:51:44
Northside 51 13 42N08 77w03 5:08:12
North Smithtown 52 6 40N51 73w14 4:52:56
North Spencer 8 226 42N15'21 76w30'28 5:06:02
North Stephentown 42 11 42N35'49 73w22'12 4:53:29
North Sterling 6 226 43N22'11 76w37'25 5:06:30
North Stockholm 45 20 44N46'10 74w56'06 4:59:44
North Syracuse 34 41 43N08'05 76w07'49 5:04:31
North Tarrytown 60 6 41N05'08 73w51'32 4:55:26
North Thurston 51 226 42N16'03 77w16'51 5:09:07
North Tonawanda 32 1 43N02'19 78w51'52 5:15:27
Northtown 15 7 42N58 78w48 5:15:12
Northumberland 46 226 43N07'38 73w35'19 4:54:21
North Urbana 51 181 42N24'46 77w10'02 5:08:40
North Valley Stream 30 7 40N41'06 73w42'08 4:54:49
North Victory 6 226 43N15'22 76w38'35 5:06:34
Northville 18 7 43N13'32 74w10'21 4:56:41
Northville 52 11 40N58'12 72w37'10 4:50:29
North Volney 38 226 43N24'48 76w19'38 5:05:19
North Wantagh 30 6 40N41'36 73w30'29 4:54:02
North Waverly 54 224 42N01'18 76w31'26 5:06:06
North Weedsport 6 24 43N03'32 76w33'34 5:06:14
Northwest Corners 9 226 42N37'46 75w46'26 5:03:06
North Western 33 226 43N20'32 75w21'50 5:01:27
Northwest Landing 52 6 41N00'36 72w14'46 4:48:59
North White Plains 60 1 41N03'18 73w46'02 4:55:04
North Wilmurt 22 82 43N26'59 75w01'01 5:00:04
North Wilna 23 156 44N05'44 75w35'50 5:02:23
North Winfield 22 13 42N55'55 75w11'18 5:00:45
North Wolcott 59 33 43N17'03 76w46'56 5:07:08
Northwood 22 84 43N20'55 75w04'18 5:00:17
North Woodmere 30 1 40N39'00 73w43'28 4:54:54
Northwoods Club 16 226 43N50'43 74w08'46 4:56:35
Norton Hill 20 226 42N24'41 74w04'02 4:56:16
Norton Summit 2 109 42N06'35 78w00'47 5:12:03
Norway 22 226 43N12'30 74w57'09 4:59:49
Norwich 9 200 42N31'52 75w31'26 5:02:06
Norwich Corners 22 14 43N00'52 75w12'45 5:00:51
Norwood 45 105 44N45'05 74w59'41 4:59:59
Noseville 23 45 44N04'31 75w54'57 5:03:40
Nostrand 24 1 40N35 73w57 4:55:48
Nottingham Estates 32 226 43N10'59 78w38'34 5:14:34
Noxon 14 11 41N38'34 73w48'56 4:55:16
Noyack 52 11 40N59'44 72w20'30 4:49:22
Nubia 55 13 42N35'09 76w17'23 5:05:10
Number Four 25 226 43N51'56 75w10'52 5:00:43
Nunda 26 226 42N34'46 77w56'34 5:11:46
Nyack 44 1 41N05'26 73w55'06 4:55:40
Oak Beach 52 11 40N38'21 73w17'20 4:53:09
Oakbrook 44 4 41N06'43 74w00'39 4:56:03
Oakdale 4 116 42N07 75w58 5:03:52
Oakdale 11 1 42N15'04 73w46'50 4:55:07
Oakdale 52 11 40N44'38 73w08'21 4:52:33
Oakes 56 1 41N41'17 73w57'01 4:55:48
Oakfield 19 26 43N03'57 78w16'12 5:13:05
Oak Hill 20 226 42N24'35 74w09'10 4:56:37
Oak Hill 58 11 42N58'15 73w24'16 4:53:37
Oak Hill Landing 11 1 42N11'39 73w51'03 4:55:24
Oakland 26 226 42N34'40 77w58'14 5:11:53
Oakland Gardens 41 1 40N45'14 73w45'59 4:55:04
Oakland Valley 53 21 41N30'25 74w38'58 4:58:36
Oak Orchard 34 13 43N12'21 76w12'46 5:04:51
Oak Orchard 37 112 43N16'27 78w19'58 5:13:20
Oak Point 3 1 40N50 73w54 4:55:36
Oak Point 45 20 44N30'51 75w45'06 5:03:00
Oak Ridge 29 12 42N47'47 74w20'26 4:57:22
Oakridge 34 13 43N07 76w12 5:04:48
Oaks Corners 35 13 42N55'56 77w00'46 5:08:03
Oak Summit 14 226 41N47 73w41 4:54:44
Oaksville 39 13 42N43'29 75w00'19 5:00:01
Oakvale 45 20 44N23'53 75w43'53 5:02:56
Oakville 52 11 40N51'32 72w36'36 4:50:26
Oakwood 6 13 42N53'22 76w38'51 5:06:35
Oakwood 43 1 40N33'50 74w06'59 4:56:28
Oakwood Beach 43 1 40N33'09 74w06'53 4:56:28
Oakwood Heights 43 1 40N38 74w06 4:56:24
Oakwood Heights Station 43 1 40N33'53 74w07'39 4:56:31
Oatka 61 206 42N43'02 78w05'21 5:12:21
Obernburg 53 226 41N50'41 75w00'27 5:00:02
Obi 2 226 42N05'11 78w15'29 5:13:02
Occanum 4 226 42N05'09 75w41'51 5:02:47
Ocean Bay Park 52 11 40N38'55 73w08'26 4:52:34
Ocean Beach 52 11 40N38'48 73w09'27 4:52:38
Oceanside 30 11 40N38'19 73w38'26 4:54:34
Oceola Lake 60 16 41N20'19 73w47'55 4:55:12
Odell 53 226 41N40'46 74w55'04 4:59:40
Odessa 49 14 42N20'12 76w47'20 5:07:09
Ogden 3 1 40N50 73w52 4:55:28
Ogden 28 14 43N10 77w49 5:11:16
Ogden Center 28 14 43N10'20 77w48'17 5:11:13
Ogdensburg 45 201 44N41'39 75w29'12 5:01:57
Ohio 22 226 43N19'20 74w58'44 4:59:55
Ohioville 56 11 41N44'27 74w03'25 4:56:14
Oil Springs Indian Res 5 226 42N14 78w19 5:13:16
Oklahoma 28 226 43N12 77w29 5:09:56
Oklahoma Beach 28 109 43N14'21 77w31'07 5:10:04
Olcott 32 11 43N20'16 78w42'54 5:14:52
Old Bethpage 30 11 40N45'45 73w27'13 4:53:49
Old Brookville 30 11 40N49'55 73w36'19 4:54:25
Old Campbellwood Wye 25 226 43N37'01 75w39'53 5:02:40
Old Central Bridge 48 12 42N42'23 74w19'54 4:57:20
Old Chatham 11 10 42N26'36 73w33'44 4:54:15
Old Chelsa 31 1 40N45 74w00 4:56:00
Old City 22 226 43N09'46 74w59'07 4:59:56
Old Field 52 11 40N57'35 73w07'48 4:52:31
Old Forge 22 203 43N42'36 74w58'29 4:59:54
Old Orchard 26 226 42N49 77w40 5:10:40
Old Orchard Cove 26 226 42N48'03 77w42'15 5:10:49
Old Orchard Point 26 13 42N47'41 77w42'36 5:10:50
Old Place 43 1 40N37'49 74w11'11 4:56:45
Old Town Station 43 1 40N35'45 74w05'15 4:56:21
Old Westbury 30 7 40N47'19 73w36'00 4:54:24
Olean 5 101 42N04'39 78w25'48 5:13:43
Olive 56 37 41N57 74w15 4:57:00
Olivebridge 56 37 41N55'40 74w12'57 4:56:52
Oliverea 56 226 42N03'55 74w27'38 4:57:51
Olmstedville 16 49 43N46'17 73w55'54 4:55:44
Omar 23 17 44N15'42 75w58'26 5:03:54
Omi 11 11 42N19'30 73w40'55 4:54:44
Omro 6 13 42N47'02 76w25'56 5:05:44
Onativia 34 16 42N53'22 76w05'18 5:04:21
Onchiota 17 113 44N29'39 74w07'26 4:56:30
Oneida 27 60 43N05'33 75w39'06 5:02:36
Oneida Castle 33 60 43N04'57 75w38'02 5:02:32
Oneida Corners 57 1 43N22'31 73w37'45 4:54:31
Oneida Lake Beach East 27 226 43N09'59 75w45'53 5:03:04
Oneida Lake Beach West 27 226 43N09'27 75w50'45 5:03:23
Oneida Valley 27 226 43N09'16 75w43'18 5:02:53
Oneonta 39 14 42N27'10 75w03'51 5:00:15
Onesquethaw 1 11 42N35 73w53 4:55:32
Oniad Lake 14 6 41N35 73w53 4:55:32
Oniontown 14 11 41N43'22 73w35'04 4:54:20
Oniontown 27 226 43N07'02 75w49'49 5:03:19
Onleys Station 36 1 41N28 74w24 4:57:36
Onondaga 34 13 42N59 76w12 5:04:48
Onondaga Castle 34 13 42N58'14 76w08'29 5:04:34
Onondaga Hill 34 13 43N00'17 76w11'01 5:04:44
Onondaga Indian Reservation 34 16 42N57 76w09 5:04:36
Onoville 5 226 42N01'37 78w57'56 5:15:52
Ontario 59 33 43N13'15 77w17'00 5:09:08
Ontario Beach 28 226 43N15'36 77w36'41 5:10:27
Ontario Center 59 226 43N13'33 77w18'22 5:09:13
Ontario On the Lake 59 226 43N16'41 77w20'55 5:09:24
Onteo Beach 28 105 43N21'23 77w54'38 5:11:39
Onteora Park 20 23 42N13'12 74w08'09 4:56:33
Oot Park 34 41 43N03'52 76w01'50 5:04:07
Open Meadows 7 226 42N06 79w23 5:17:32
Oppenheim 18 226 43N04'20 74w41'35 4:58:46
Oquaga Lake 4 167 42N04 75w25 5:01:40
Oramel 2 226 42N21'58 78w08'09 5:12:33
Oran 34 226 42N58'41 75w56'00 5:03:44
Orange 49 226 42N20 77w02 5:08:08
Orangeburg 44 4 41N02'47 73w57'00 4:55:48
Orange Lake 36 1 41N32'23 74w05'55 4:56:24
Orangeport 32 121 43N11'54 78w35'46 5:14:23
Orangetown 44 4 41N03 73w57 4:55:48
Orangeville 61 226 42N44 78w15 5:13:00
Orangeville Center 61 226 42N45'01 78w14'55 5:13:00
Orangeville Corners 61 226 42N46 78w19 5:13:16
Orchard Knoll 8 226 42N09'03 76w48'02 5:07:12
Orchard Park 15 11 42N46'03 78w44'39 5:14:59
Orchard Terrace 7 158 42N11'41 79w27'29 5:17:50
Orchard Village 34 12 43N02'34 76w16'53 5:05:08
Oregon 18 226 43N15'32 74w39'18 4:58:37
Oregon 52 11 40N59 72w32 4:50:08
Oregon 57 49 43N33'27 74w07'15 4:56:29

Orient 52 11 41N08'20 72W18'14 4:49:13
Orienta 60 1 40N56'14 73W43'44 4:54:55
Oriental Park 7 226 42N09'20 79W23'06 5:17:32
Orient Point 52 11 41N09'08 72W15'06 4:49:00
Oriskany 33 202 43N09'26 75W19'59 5:01:20
Oriskany Falls 33 202 42N56'21 75W27'41 5:01:51
Orlando 5 226 42N18'16 78W42'59 5:14:52
Orleans 23 22 44N13 75W58 5:03:52
Orleans 35 14 42N55'07 77W06'53 5:08:28
Orleans Four Corners 23 226 44N11'26 75W54'01 5:03:36
Orrs Mill 36 11 41N26'04 74W03'29 4:56:14
Orwell 38 226 43N34'29 75W59'48 5:03:59
Oscawana 60 166 41N13'40 73W54'52 4:55:39
Oscawana Corners 40 6 41N22'42 73W51'23 4:55:26
Oscawana Lake 40 6 41N20 73W52 4:55:28
Osceola 25 118 43N30'00 75W43'21 5:02:53
Osgood Landing 50 14 42N34'20 76W38'44 5:06:35
Ossian 26 13 42N31'16 77W46'47 5:11:07
Ossian Center 26 13 42N34 77W42 5:10:48
Ossining 60 1 41N09'46 73W51'43 4:55:27
Oswegatchie 45 201 44N10'58 75W04'14 5:00:17
Oswego 38 204 43N27'19 76W30'39 5:06:03
Oswego Beach 38 204 43N27'00 76W33'25 5:06:14
Oswego Bitter 34 12 43N03'40 76W21'50 5:05:27
Oswego Center 38 204 43N24'52 76W32'03 5:06:08
Otego 39 104 42N23'50 75W10'26 5:00:42
Otis 28 226 43N15'31 77W52'43 5:11:31
Otisco 34 16 42N51'36 76W13'06 5:04:52
Otisco Valley 34 13 42N49'43 76W13'56 5:04:56
Otisville 36 21 41N28'24 74W32'20 4:58:09
Otsdawa 39 104 42N29'05 75W10'29 5:00:42
Otsego 39 203 42N43 74W58 4:59:52
Otselic 9 226 42N43'21 75W43'13 5:02:53
Otselic Center 9 226 42N42'04 75W44'46 5:02:59
Otter Creek 25 15 43N43'07 75W22'04 5:01:28
Otter Hook 20 66 42N24'15 73W47'58 4:55:12
Otter Kill 36 226 41N22'40 74W17'42 4:57:11
Otter Lake 33 30 43N35'28 75W06'44 5:00:27
Ott Meadows 34 13 43N07 76W12 5:04:48
Otto 5 226 42N21'22 78W49'55 5:15:20
Otto Mills 38 226 43N36'09 75W49'11 5:03:17
Ouaquaga 4 17 42N07'34 75W38'51 5:02:35
Overlook 46 7 43N17'33 73W56'49 4:55:47
Ovid 50 12 42N40'35 76W49'24 5:07:18
Ovid Center 50 226 42N37 77W33 5:10:12
Ovington 24 1 40N38 74W01 4:56:04
Owasco 6 13 42N51'18 76W27'56 5:05:52
Owasco Hill 6 13 42N43'39 76W27'54 5:05:52
Owasco Lake Station 6 13 42N50'26 76W31'36 5:06:06
Owego 54 205 42N06'12 76W15'45 5:05:03
Owens Mills 8 224 42N04'07 76W35'51 5:06:23
Owls Head 17 34 44N44'04 74W10'09 4:56:41
Owls Nest 59 33 43N10'55 77W08'20 5:08:33
Owlsville 48 226 42N27'52 74W25'10 4:57:41
Oxbow 23 226 44N17'14 75W37'24 5:02:30
Oxford 9 106 42N26'31 75W35'53 5:02:24
Oxford 36 226 41N21'03 74W12'59 4:56:52
Oyster Bay 30 7 40N51'56 73W31'57 4:54:08
Oyster Bay Cove 30 7 40N52'15 73W30'41 4:54:03
Ozone Park 41 1 40N40'36 73W50'39 4:55:23
Pacama 56 11 41N55'50 74W10'03 4:56:40
Pachin Mills 14 226 41N59'43 73W39'31 4:54:38
Packwood Corners 50 14 42N53'35 76W55'10 5:07:41
Paddlefords 35 14 42N53 77W17 5:09:08
Paddy Hill 23 45 43N59'59 75W58'58 5:03:56
Padelford 35 14 42N56'25 77W19'05 5:09:16
Page 25 226 43N39'20 75W33'43 5:02:15
Page Brook 9 13 42N15'30 75W45'55 5:03:04
Pages Corner 46 226 43N05'25 73W54'05 4:55:36
Pail Shop Corners 39 13 42N43'26 74W58'51 4:59:55
Paines Corner 61 226 42N50'22 78W00'35 5:12:02
Paines Hollow 22 196 42N57'41 74W54'13 4:59:37
Painted Post 51 13 42N09'43 77W05'40 5:08:23
Palatine 29 11 42N57 74W33 4:58:12
Palatine Bridge 29 162 42N54'39 74W34'28 4:58:18
Palentown 56 72 41N52'44 74W19'19 4:57:17
Palenville 20 226 42N10'28 74W01'14 4:56:05
Palermo 38 226 43N21'54 76W16'58 5:05:08
Palisades 44 4 41N00'40 73W54'50 4:55:39
Palmer 46 7 43N14'43 73W49'04 4:55:16
Palmerville 45 226 44N25'03 75W07'42 5:00:31
Palmyra 59 89 43N03'50 77W14'01 5:08:56
Pamelia 23 45 44N03 75W54 5:03:36
Pamelia Four Corners 23 45 44N05 75W49 5:03:16
Panama 7 226 42N04'30 79W29'00 5:17:56
Panorama Bluff 16 226 44N03'16 73W53'18 4:55:33
Panther Lake 38 15 43N19'34 75W54'03 5:03:36
Pantigo 52 11 40N58'04 72W09'55 4:48:40
Paper Mill Corners 22 214 43N09'08 74W50'45 4:59:23
Paradise 36 21 41N29'48 74W38'42 4:58:35
Paradise Beach 57 1 43N21'02 73W40'49 4:54:43
Paradise Hill 20 11 42N23'01 73W53'23 4:55:34
Paradise Hill 33 13 43N10'06 75W38'26 5:02:34
Paradox 16 226 43N53'29 73W38'46 4:54:35
Parcells Corners 7 226 42N27'28 79W05'49 5:16:23
Paris 33 13 43N00'02 75W18'51 5:01:15
Parish 38 14 43N24'22 76W07'34 5:04:30
Parish Center 38 182 43N24'07 76W04'07 5:04:16
Parishville 45 226 44N37'43 74W48'51 4:59:15
Parishville Center 45 226 44N37'44 74W53'25 4:59:34
Paris Station 33 13 42N57'48 75W18'33 5:01:14
Parkchester 3 1 40N50'20 73W51'39 4:55:27
Parker 9 149 42N24'10 75W27'44 5:01:51
Parkers 25 226 43N43'56 75W40'16 5:02:41
Parkers Corners 1 40 42N44'36 73W59'07 4:55:56
Park Hill 34 41 43N04 76W04 5:04:16
Park Hill 60 1 40N55'25 73W53'26 4:55:34
Parkis Mills 46 226 43N02'23 74W00'48 4:56:03
Park of Edgewater 3 1 40N49'21 73W48'36 4:55:14
Parkside 41 1 40N42'38 73W51'05 4:55:24
Parkside 60 1 40N53'48 73W49'32 4:55:18
Park Slope 24 1 40N40'12 73W59'11 4:55:57
Parkston 53 75 41N54'16 74W46'24 4:59:06
Parksville 53 53 41N51'19 74W45'36 4:59:02
Park Terrace 4 151 42N04'11 75W54'48 5:03:39
Park Village 32 1 43N01'30 78W50'43 5:15:23
Parkville 24 1 40N37'59 73W58'44 4:55:55
Parkway 3 1 40N51 73W52 4:55:28
Parma 28 14 43N16 77W47 5:11:08
Parma Center 28 13 43N15'31 77W47'29 5:11:10
Parma Corners 28 14 43N13'06 77W47'32 5:11:10
Parson Farms 34 12 43N02'12 76W16'50 5:05:07
Parson Mill 25 226 43N26'58 75W34'01 5:02:16
Parsons Beach 41 1 40N46'19 73W45'06 4:55:00
Partello Corners 6 13 42N47'51 76W21'59 5:05:28
Partlow 21 226 43N58'27 74W49'40 4:59:19
Pastime Park 50 41 42N50'22 76W56'32 5:07:46
Pataukunk 56 72 41N47'30 74W18'23 4:57:14
Patchin 15 226 42N39'28 78W44'52 5:14:59
Patchin 31 1 40N45 74W00 4:56:00
Patchinville 51 226 42N31'51 77W35'21 5:10:21
Patchogue 52 1 40N45'56 73W00'56 4:52:04
Patchogue Highlands 52 1 40N46'57 73W01'39 4:52:07
Patent 39 226 42N40'38 75W06'01 5:00:24
Patria 48 13 42N37'02 74W25'43 4:57:43
Patroon 1 1 42N41 73W45 4:55:00
Pattens Mills 58 123 43N22'58 73W36'16 4:54:25
Patterson 40 7 41N30'49 73W36'24 4:54:26
Pattersonville 47 94 42N53'24 74W04'55 4:56:20
Paul Smiths 17 176 44N26'19 74W15'11 4:57:01
Paul Smiths Easy Street 17 176 44N26'23 74W13'48 4:56:55
Pavilion 19 226 42N52'34 78W01'23 5:12:06
Pavilion Center 19 226 42N54'33 78W01'13 5:12:05
Pawling 14 7 41N33'43 73W36'11 4:54:25
Payne Beach 28 13 43N19'53 77W44'12 5:10:57
Paynesville 2 226 42N00'34 77W50'36 5:11:22
Pea Brook 13 226 41N53'40 75W08'54 5:00:36
Peach Lake 40 226 41N26 73W36 4:54:24
Peakville 13 226 41N58'50 75W05'50 5:00:23
Pearl Creek 61 226 42N50'55 78W02'50 5:12:11
Pearl River 44 4 41N03'32 74W01'20 4:56:05
Peas Eddy 13 97 41N56'45 75W13'53 5:00:56
Peasleeville 10 86 44N36'03 73W40'25 4:54:42
Peat Corners 38 182 43N20'18 76W13'49 5:04:55
Pebble Beach 26 226 42N49'56 77W42'29 5:10:50
Peck Hill 34 226 42N59'59 75W55'08 5:03:41
Peck Slip 31 1 40N43 74W00 4:56:00
Pecksport 27 180 42N51'45 75W34'04 5:02:16
Pecksville 14 7 41N31'09 73W41'46 4:54:47
Pecktown 39 226 42N46'23 75W08'47 5:00:35
Peconic 52 11 41N02'52 72W27'49 4:49:51
Peekamoose 56 72 41N55'40 74W22'47 4:57:31
Peekskill 60 1 41N17'24 73W55'15 4:55:41
Pekin 32 226 43N10 78W53 5:15:32
Pekin 38 226 43N32'48 75W57'54 5:03:52
Pelham 60 1 40N54'35 73W48'30 4:55:14
Pelham Manor 60 1 40N53'43 73W48'27 4:55:14
Pelham Parkway 3 1 40N51 73W52 4:55:28
Pellets Island 36 7 41N22'50 74W24'46 4:57:39
Pember Corners 38 204 43N21'25 76W30'39 5:06:03
Pembroke 19 226 42N59'51 78W26'06 5:13:44
Pembroke Center 19 164 42N59'46 78W21'56 5:13:28
Penataquit 52 11 40N43 73W15 4:53:00
Pendleton 32 190 43N05'13 78W43'41 5:14:55
Pendleton Center 32 226 43N06'25 78W46'23 5:15:06
Penelope 4 226 42N24'49 75W53'44 5:03:35
Penfield 28 13 43N07'49 77W28'33 5:09:54
Penfield Center 28 13 43N10'02 77W25'53 5:09:44
Pennellville 38 182 43N16'57 76W16'15 5:05:05
Penn Yan 62 14 42N39'39 77W03'15 5:08:13
Peoria 61 226 42N50'01 77W57'55 5:11:52
Perch River 23 45 44N04'31 76W00'30 5:04:02
Perinton 28 13 43N05 77W27 5:09:48
Perkin 32 226 43N10'06 78W53'07 5:15:32
Perkins Corner 27 14 42N53'47 75W52'51 5:03:31
Perkins Crossing 39 226 42N40'23 75W00'32 5:00:02
Perkinsville 51 226 42N32'23 77W37'43 5:10:31
Perry 61 206 42N42'56 78W00'21 5:12:01
Perry Center 61 206 42N44'56 78W00'22 5:12:01
Perry City 49 13 42N29'31 76W41'42 5:06:47
Perry Mills 10 157 45N00'01 73W30'24 4:54:02
Perrysburg 5 42 42N27'23 79W00'08 5:16:01
Perrys Mills 10 157 44N59 73W26 4:53:44
Perryville 27 226 43N00'25 75W47'59 5:03:12
Persia 5 42 42N23'07 78W56'11 5:15:45
Persons Corners 61 226 42N46'13 78W23'20 5:13:33
Perth 18 226 43N01'03 74W11'40 4:56:47
Peru 10 27 44N34'42 73W31'38 4:54:07
Peru 34 41 43N04'56 76W24'30 5:05:38
Peruton 55 13 42N32'54 76W21'15 5:05:25
Peruville 55 13 42N33'01 76W22'18 5:05:29
Peterboro 27 226 42N58'02 75W41'18 5:02:45
Petersburg 42 11 42N44'58 73W20'26 4:53:22
Petersburg Junction 42 11 42N50'06 73W19'33 4:53:18
Peters Corners 15 38 42N56'29 78W30'46 5:14:03
Peters Corners 18 226 43N09'57 74W24'09 4:57:37
Peter Stuyvesant 31 1 40N44 73W59 4:55:56
Peth 5 226 42N11'40 78W39'34 5:14:38
Petries Corners 25 226 43N48'15 75W21'43 5:01:27
Petrolia 2 226 42N05'22 78W01'07 5:12:04
Petty Corner 6 12 42N55'04 76W30'28 5:06:02
Pharsalia 9 226 42N34'58 75W46'53 5:03:08
Phelps 35 13 42N57'27 77W03'28 5:08:14
Phelps Junction 35 13 42N58'03 77W05'12 5:08:21
Philadelphia 23 77 44N09'16 75W42'33 5:02:50
Philipse Manor 60 6 41N05'44 73W51'54 4:55:28
Philipstown 40 6 41N24 73W55 4:55:40
Phillipsburg 36 1 41N26'16 74W21'35 4:57:26
Phillips Creek 2 226 42N15'29 77W53'38 5:11:35
Phillips Mill 7 226 42N10 79W23 5:17:32
Phillips Mills 7 226 42N09'07 79W22'24 5:17:30
Phillipsport 53 48 41N38'21 74W26'46 4:57:47
Philmont 11 1 42N14'54 73W39'13 4:54:37
Philwold 53 21 41N34'35 74W40'09 4:58:41
Phoenicia 56 88 42N05'05 74W18'57 4:57:16
Phoenix 38 93 43N13'52 76W18'04 5:05:12
Phoenix Mills 39 13 42N40'00 74W56'36 4:59:46
Picketts Corners 10 136 44N39 73W45 4:55:00
Pickettville 45 226 44N36'32 74W49'16 4:59:17
Piercefield 45 87 44N13'55 74W34'12 4:58:17
Pierces Corner 45 178 44N20 75W28 5:01:52
Pierceville 27 180 42N51'00 75W38'14 5:02:33
Piermont 44 7 41N02'31 73W55'07 4:55:40
Pierrepont 45 226 44N32'32 75W00'44 5:00:03
Pierrepont Manor 23 143 43N44'06 76W03'33 5:04:14
Pierstown 39 13 42N46'18 74W54'47 4:59:39
Piffard 26 226 42N49'42 77W51'04 5:11:24
Pike 61 226 42N33'23 78W09'11 5:12:37
Pike Five Corners 61 226 42N35 78W15 5:13:00
Pikes Corner 45 226 44N16'38 75W31'04 5:02:04
Pikeville 2 109 42N03'15 78W02'46 5:12:11
Pilgrim 3 1 40N51 73W51 4:55:24
Pilgrim Corners 36 1 41N27'41 74W26'38 4:57:47
Pilgrimport 59 99 43N05'47 76W58'13 5:07:53
Pillar Point 23 49 43N58'13 76W07'34 5:04:30
Pilot Knob 57 226 43N30'57 73W37'47 4:54:31
Pinckney 25 226 43N51 75W13 5:00:52
Pine 1 1 42N40 73W48 4:55:12
Pine 33 211 43N15'31 75W38'21 5:02:33
Pine Aire 52 11 40N46'14 73W16'28 4:53:06
Pinebrook 60 1 40N57'46 73W46'36 4:55:06
Pinebrook Heights 60 1 40N57'11 73W46'38 4:55:07
Pine Bush 36 20 41N36'29 74W17'58 4:57:12
Pine City 8 13 42N02'12 76W52'11 5:07:29
Pine Corners 62 25 42N44'57 77W15'25 5:09:02
Pine Creek 49 226 42N21'34 77W02'33 5:08:10
Pine Crest 33 211 43N14'20 75W37'23 5:02:30
Pine Grove 25 15 43N45'06 75W22'38 5:01:31
Pine Grove 34 13 42N50'26 76W20'06 5:05:20
Pine Grove 45 16 44N46'27 75W17'08 5:01:09
Pine Grove 47 1 42N45'47 73W59'14 4:55:57
Pine Grove 48 226 42N31'50 74W15'31 4:57:02
Pinegrove Park 1 11 42N42 73W48 4:55:12
Pine Hill 15 7 42N55'12 78W47'37 5:15:10
Pine Hill 33 226 43N18'27 75W39'09 5:02:37
Pine Hill 56 42 42N07'59 74W28'50 4:57:55
Pine Hollow 6 13 42N40'10 76W28'43 5:05:55
Pinehurst 15 153 42N43'56 78W56'07 5:15:44

Pine Island 36 11 41N17'52 74w27'35 4:57:50
Pine Lake 18 226 43N08 74w29 4:57:56
Pine Meadows 38 25 43N31'15 75w54'38 5:03:39
Pine Neck 52 11 40N59'54 72w20'33 4:49:22
Pine Neck-West Tiana 52 11 40N51 72w34 4:50:16
Pine Plains 14 226 41N58'47 73w39'23 4:54:38
Pine Ridge 1 1 42N40 73w48 4:55:12
Pine Ridge Estates 60 1 41N00 73w40 4:54:40
Pinesville 13 226 42N09'19 75w09'50 5:00:39
Pine Tavern 26 13 42N45'13 77w55'44 5:11:43
Pine Valley 8 20 42N13'31 76w50'45 5:07:23
Pineville 13 226 42N10 75w08 5:00:32
Pineville 38 25 43N31'44 76w02'22 5:04:09
Pine Woods 27 180 42N53'13 75w34'46 5:02:19
Pioneer 46 11 43N01 73w51 4:55:24
Piseco 21 226 43N26'54 74w31'08 4:58:05
Pitcairn 45 118 44N10'52 75w16'57 5:01:08
Pitcher 9 226 42N34'51 75w51'55 5:03:28
Pitcher Hill 34 41 43N06'55 76w08'46 5:04:35
Pitcher Springs 9 226 42N35'56 75w49'15 5:03:17
Pitt 31 1 40N43 73w59 4:55:56
Pittsfield 39 226 42N38'19 75w16'54 5:01:08
Pittsford 28 13 43N05'26 77w30'55 5:10:04
Pittstown 42 11 42N50'06 73w29'08 4:53:57
Plaat Clove 20 23 42N08'04 74w05'21 4:56:21
Place Corners 20 226 42N22'01 73w59'31 4:55:58
Plainedge 30 11 40N43'02 73w29'03 4:53:56
Plainfield 39 226 42N50 75w12 5:00:48
Plainfield Center 39 226 42N50'25 75w10'29 5:00:42
Plainview 30 11 40N46'35 73w28'04 4:53:52
Plainville 34 226 43N09'33 76w26'51 5:05:47
Plandome 30 7 40N48'24 73w42'14 4:54:49
Plandome Heights 30 7 40N48'09 73w42'17 4:54:49
Plandome Manor 30 7 40N48'58 73w41'52 4:54:47
Planetarium 31 1 40N47 73w59 4:55:56
Plants Corner 61 226 42N42'16 78w25'06 5:13:40
Plantz Corners 38 226 43N39'58 75w54'42 5:03:39
Plasterville 9 200 42N35'10 75w31'20 5:02:05
Plato 5 226 42N21'05 78w40'17 5:14:41
Platt Cove 20 23 42N10 74w09 4:56:36
Plattekill 56 226 41N37'03 74w04'35 4:56:18
Platten 37 15 43N19'02 78w18'38 5:13:15
Plattsburgh 10 86 44N41'58 73w27'12 4:53:49
Plattsburgh Air Force Base 10 86 44N40 73w27 4:53:48
Plaza 41 1 40N45 73w55 4:55:40
Pleasant Brook 39 226 42N42'59 74w45'50 4:59:03
Pleasantdale 42 11 42N47 73w39 4:54:36
Pleasant Hill 4 4 42N12'25 75w47'12 5:03:09
Pleasant Plains 14 219 41N50'52 73w52'00 4:55:28
Pleasant Plains 43 11 40N31'26 74w12'58 4:56:52
Pleasant Point 38 204 43N27 76w30 5:06:00
Pleasant Point Crossing 38 204 43N29'55 76w20'05 5:05:20
Pleasant Ridge 14 226 41N38'51 73w38'55 4:54:36
Pleasant Ridge Corners 10 86 44N39'15 73w29'48 4:53:59
Pleasantside 60 1 41N16'39 73w53'47 4:55:35
Pleasant Valley 14 226 41N44'40 73w49'18 4:55:17
Pleasant Valley 33 13 42N55'07 75w26'00 5:01:44
Pleasant Valley 51 14 42N23'33 77w15'28 5:09:02
Pleasant Valley 53 226 41N49'34 75w01'33 5:00:06
Pleasant Valley 55 13 42N33'43 76w23'52 5:05:35
Pleasantville 7 158 42N15'39 79w25'43 5:17:43
Pleasantville 60 7 41N07'58 73w47'35 4:55:10
Pleasautdale 42 11 42N47'47 73w40'02 4:54:40
Plessis 23 17 44N16'13 75w51'17 5:03:25
Pletchers Corners 32 199 43N07'13 78w59'51 5:15:59
Plumbrook 45 226 44N50'08 74w54'26 4:59:38
Plutarch 56 11 41N46'41 74w01'39 4:56:07
Plymouth 9 226 42N37'01 75w36'10 5:02:25
Pocantico Hills 60 6 41N05'40 73w50'11 4:55:21
Podunk 55 13 42N31'27 76w39'47 5:06:39
Poestenkill 42 226 42N41'25 73w33'54 4:54:16
Point Au Rouche 10 86 44N42 73w26 4:53:44
Point Breeze 37 105 43N22'12 78w11'26 5:12:46
Point Chautauqua 7 158 42N14 79w27 5:17:48
Point Lookout 30 11 40N35'32 73w34'52 4:54:19
Point o'Woods 52 11 40N39'05 73w07'45 4:52:31
Point Peninsula 23 226 44N00'21 76w13'10 5:04:53
Point Pleasant 7 20 42N14'18 79w29'41 5:17:59
Point Pleasant 28 209 43N12 77w34 5:10:16
Point Rochester 35 226 42N37 77w24 5:09:36
Point Rock 33 226 43N22'50 75w32'51 5:02:11
Point Stockholm 7 187 42N07'12 79w19'04 5:17:16
Point Vivian 23 17 44N18'58 75w57'01 5:03:48
Pokeville 12 41 42N35'24 76w08'02 5:04:32
Poland 22 84 43N13'32 75w03'42 5:00:15
Poland Center 7 226 42N08'07 79w07'27 5:16:30
Polkville 9 200 42N30'56 75w30'31 5:02:02
Polkville 34 41 43N05'36 76w01'54 5:04:08
Pomfret 7 15 42N24 79w21 5:17:24
Pomona 44 4 41N10'01 74w02'37 4:56:10
Pomona Heights 44 4 41N09'58 74w04'09 4:56:17
Pomonok 41 1 40N44 73w47 4:55:08
Pompey 34 14 42N53'56 76w00'59 5:04:04
Pompey Center 34 13 42N55'23 75w57'03 5:03:48
Ponck Hockie 56 11 41N55'29 73w58'24 4:55:54
Pond Eddy 53 25 41N26'25 74w49'25 4:59:18
Pond Settlement 45 226 44N15'37 75w13'21 5:00:53
Ponquogue 52 11 40N51'23 72w30'20 4:50:01
Pontiac 15 42 42N37'26 78w58'10 5:15:53
Poolsburg 11 11 42N26'12 73w46'18 4:55:05
Poolville 27 130 42N46'32 75w30'25 5:02:02
Pope 5 20 42N12'33 79w00'18 5:16:01
Pope Mills 45 226 44N29'05 75w34'52 5:02:19
Popes Ravine 4 151 42N07'06 75w52'11 5:03:29
Poplar Beach 50 12 42N43'34 76w45'41 5:07:03
Poplar Ridge 6 13 42N44'18 76w37'06 5:06:28
Poquott 52 11 40N57'03 73w05'04 4:52:20
Porcaville 17 30 44N41'00 74w11'13 4:56:45
Portage 26 20 42N34 78w00 5:12:00
Portageville 61 20 42N34'11 78w02'25 5:12:10
Port Authority 31 1 40N45 74w00 4:56:00
Port Byron 6 24 43N02'04 76w37'27 5:06:30
Port Chester 60 1 41N00'06 73w39'58 4:54:40
Port Crane 4 151 42N09'51 75w50'02 5:03:20
Port Dickinson 4 151 42N08'00 75w53'48 5:03:35
Port Douglass 16 4 44N29'09 73w25'06 4:53:40
Porter 32 226 43N19 78w59 5:15:56
Porter 58 213 43N17'37 73w16'41 4:53:07
Porter Center 32 226 43N14'58 78w57'28 5:15:50
Porter Corner 62 14 42N32'51 77w02'06 5:08:08
Porter Corners 46 226 43N08'54 73w53'13 4:55:33
Porterville 15 170 42N47'25 78w33'14 5:14:13
Port Ewen 56 11 41N54'19 73w58'36 4:55:54
Port Gibson 35 89 43N02'04 77w09'28 5:08:38
Port Henry 16 54 44N02'54 73w27'37 4:53:50
Port Ivory 43 1 40N38'27 74w10'50 4:56:43
Port Jefferson 52 1 40N56'47 73w04'11 4:52:17
Port Jefferson Station 52 11 40N55'31 73w02'52 4:52:11
Port Jervis 36 1 41N22'30 74w41'35 4:58:46
Port Kent 16 4 44N31'41 73w24'27 4:53:38
Portland 7 160 42N22'47 79w28'04 5:17:52
Portland 55 13 42N31'22 76w31'28 5:06:06
Portlandville 39 15 42N31'49 74w58'03 4:59:52
Port Leyden 25 77 43N34'59 75w20'44 5:01:23
Port Morris 3 1 40N48'05 73w54'36 4:55:38
Port Ontario 38 226 43N34'00 76w11'18 5:04:45
Port Orange 36 21 41N29'12 74w34'32 4:58:18
Port Richmond 43 1 40N37'59 74w08'13 4:56:33
Portville 5 226 42N02'19 78w20'28 5:13:22
Port Washington 30 1 40N49'32 73w41'55 4:54:48
Port Washington North 30 11 40N50'41 73w42'08 4:54:49
Post Creek 8 14 42N14'06 76w57'37 5:07:50
Potsdam 45 207 44N40'11 74w58'54 4:59:56
Potter 62 226 42N42'15 77w12'25 5:08:50
Potter Hill 42 11 42N50'43 73w23'41 4:53:35
Potter Hollow 1 226 42N25'30 74w13'25 4:56:54
Pottersville 57 11 43N43'52 73w49'11 4:55:17
Potterville 56 48 41N49'55 74w22'40 4:57:31
Poughkeepsie 14 1 41N42'01 73w55'17 4:55:41
Poughquag 14 226 41N36'32 73w40'56 4:54:44
Pound Ridge 60 16 41N12'31 73w34'31 4:54:18
Powers Corner 6 13 42N51'34 76w39'53 5:06:40
Powley Place 21 226 43N18'43 74w39'12 4:58:37
Pratt 24 1 40N42 73w58 4:55:52
Pratt Corners 12 16 42N41'15 76w10'09 5:04:41
Prattham 38 14 43N27'22 76w10'49 5:04:43
Pratts 27 180 42N55'17 75w35'26 5:02:22
Prattsburg 51 226 42N31'26 77w17'21 5:09:09
Pratts Hollow 27 180 42N55'22 75w36'11 5:02:25
Prattsville 20 226 42N18'53 74w26'00 4:57:44
Preble 12 91 42N44'07 76w08'55 5:04:36
Pre-emption 35 41 42N52'40 77w01'00 5:08:04
Prendergast Point 7 158 42N11'32 79w26'55 5:17:48
Presho 51 13 42N05'08 77w09'18 5:08:37
Preston 9 226 42N32'02 75w37'25 5:02:30
Preston Center 9 226 42N30'28 75w35'54 5:02:24
Preston Hollow 1 226 42N26'40 74w12'30 4:56:50
Price Home 54 205 42N06'34 76w12'49 5:04:51
Prince 31 1 40N44 74w00 4:56:00
Princes Bay 43 11 40N31'44 74w11'53 4:56:48
Princetown 47 11 42N46'44 74w03'54 4:56:16
Progress 18 226 43N02'35 74w17'51 4:57:11
Prospect 33 82 43N18'15 75w09'09 5:00:37
Prospect Heights 42 1 42N37'02 73w44'24 4:54:58
Prospect Hill 36 21 41N27'31 74w38'20 4:58:33
Prospect Hill 46 11 42N48 73w41 4:54:44
Prospect Park West 24 1 40N40 73w59 4:55:56
Protection 15 22 42N36'31 78w29'40 5:13:59
Providence 46 226 43N06 74w03 4:56:12
Prussian Settlement 33 226 43N27'09 75w30'28 5:02:02
Puckerville 27 226 42N47'12 75w52'33 5:03:30
Pudding Hollow 16 49 43N47'50 74w00'43 4:56:03
Pulaski 38 96 43N34'01 76w07'41 5:04:31
Pulteney 62 226 42N31'30 77w10'03 5:08:40
Pultneyville 59 226 43N16'47 77w11'11 5:08:45
Pulvers 11 1 42N16'49 73w38'55 4:54:36
Pulvers Corners 14 5 41N58'36 73w35'06 4:54:20
Pumpkin Hill 19 17 43N05'49 78w03'59 5:12:16
Pumpkin Hollow 11 11 42N07'41 73w37'11 4:54:29
Pumpkin Hollow 21 226 43N21'03 74w15'44 4:57:03
Pumpkin Hook 58 11 43N01'05 73w17'51 4:53:11
Punkshire Corners 61 147 42N36'03 78w26'50 5:13:47
Purchase 60 7 41N02'27 73w42'54 4:54:52
Purdys 60 16 41N19'33 73w39'20 4:54:37
Purdys Grove 60 1 40N59'33 73w39'59 4:54:40
Purdys Mill 10 16 44N48'30 73w40'16 4:54:41
Purdy Station 60 16 41N20 73w40 4:54:40
Purling 20 226 42N17'03 74w00'21 4:56:01
Putnam 58 29 43N44'48 73w23'51 4:53:35
Putnam Lake 40 226 41N27'43 73w32'48 4:54:11
Putnam Plaza 40 226 41N27 73w40 4:54:40
Putnam Station 58 226 43N44 73w24 4:53:36
Putnam Valley 40 6 41N20'09 73w52'28 4:55:30
Pyrites 45 226 44N30'53 75w11'10 5:00:45
Quackenbush Hill 51 13 42N08 77w03 5:08:12
Quackenkill 42 11 42N46'10 73w31'10 4:54:05
Quail 1 1 42N40 73w47 4:55:08
Quaker Basin 27 226 42N46 75w53 5:03:32
Quaker Hill 14 7 41N34'46 73w32'36 4:54:10
Quaker Ridge 60 1 40N58'15 73w46'50 4:55:07
Quaker Settlement 27 226 42N45'18 75w50'22 5:03:21
Quaker Springs 46 226 43N02'22 73w38'36 4:54:34
Quaker Street 47 98 42N44'05 74w11'12 4:56:45
Quality Hill 27 92 43N04'01 75w46'31 5:03:06
Quarry Heights 60 1 41N04'09 73w45'05 4:55:00
Quarryville 56 215 42N07'11 73w59'15 4:55:57
Queechy 11 11 42N24'17 73w25'18 4:53:41
Queens 41 1 40N43 73w52 4:55:28
Queensbridge 41 1 40N45 73w55 4:55:40
Queensbury 57 123 43N22'38 73w36'49 4:54:27
Queens Village 41 1 40N43'36 73w44'31 4:54:58
Quigley Park 7 226 42N08'11 79w23'46 5:17:35
Quincetree Landing 52 11 41N01'45 72w00'48 4:48:03
Quinneville 4 13 42N14'57 75w46'27 5:03:06
Quioque 52 11 40N49'11 72w37'46 4:50:31
Quogue 52 1 40N49'23 72w36'36 4:50:26
Raceville 58 226 43N27'58 73w16'16 4:53:05
Radio City 31 1 40N46 74w01 4:56:04
Radison 34 226 43N09 76w20 5:05:20
Rainbow Lake 17 176 44N28'01 74w10'24 4:56:42
Rainbow Shores 38 226 43N36'50 76w11'53 5:04:48
Ralmar Park 47 1 42N53'14 73w54'50 4:55:39
Ramapo 44 4 41N08'28 74w10'08 4:56:41
Ramona Beach 38 226 43N32'24 76w13'19 5:04:53
Rampasture 52 11 40N51'07 72w31'44 4:50:07
Randall 29 11 42N54'41 74w26'42 4:57:47
Randall Corner 46 7 43N12'44 73w47'55 4:55:12
Randall Crossing 62 12 42N36'58 76w56'39 5:07:47
Randallsville 27 180 42N47'42 75w34'02 5:02:16
Randelville 36 20 41N20'34 74w20'56 4:57:24
Randolph 5 20 42N09'43 78w58'32 5:15:54
Ransomville 32 226 43N14'19 78w54'36 5:15:38
Rapids 32 190 43N05'54 78w38'28 5:14:34
Raquette Lake 21 226 43N48'47 74w39'28 4:58:38
Raquette River 45 105 44N57'04 74w47'39 4:59:11
Rasbach Corner 18 168 43N06'22 74w44'32 4:58:58
Rathbone 51 20 42N08'02 77w19'17 5:09:17
Ravena 1 1 42N28'06 73w49'00 4:55:16
Ravenwood 1 11 42N42 73w48 4:55:12
Rawson 2 226 42N19'17 78w18'32 5:13:14
Ray 19 142 42N56'00 78w17'51 5:13:11
Ray Brook 16 83 44N18'00 74w05'09 4:56:21
Raymertown 42 220 42N48'50 73w32'06 4:54:08

Raymond 32 190 43N06'25 78W40'03 5:14:40
Raymondville 45 226 44N50'17 74W58'42 4:59:55
Rays Corners 5 20 42N16'11 79W02'45 5:16:11
Rayville 11 11 42N27'51 73W32'20 4:54:09
Readburn 13 226 42N00'40 75W10'28 5:00:42
Reading 49 14 42N25 76W56 5:07:44
Reading Center 49 14 42N25'49 76W55'59 5:07:44
Reber 16 56 44N19'25 73W28'48 4:53:55
Rector 25 226 43N45'20 75W40'38 5:02:43
Rectors 47 1 42N51'44 74W01'01 4:56:04
Redbird 7 67 42N13'49 79W17'58 5:17:12
Red Bunch Corners 18 226 43N04'35 74W15'35 4:57:02
Red Creek 52 11 40N52 72W31 4:50:04
Red Creek 59 33 43N14'50 76W43'26 5:06:54
Red Falls 20 226 42N18'34 74W23'28 4:57:34
Redfield 38 226 43N31'59 75W49'19 5:03:17
Redford 10 226 44N36'30 73W48'17 4:55:13
Red Hook 14 7 41N59'42 73W52'33 4:55:30
Red Hook 24 1 40N40'30 74W00'36 4:56:02
Red Hook Mills 14 7 42N00'36 73W52'18 4:55:29
Red House 5 20 42N06'44 78W48'08 5:15:13
Redman Corners 28 226 43N14'46 77W57'51 5:11:51
Red Mill 38 14 43N25'06 76W08'35 5:04:34
Red Mills 11 11 42N13'15 73W42'44 4:54:51
Red Mills 45 201 44N45'30 75W23'12 5:01:33
Red Mills 55 13 42N31'39 76W19'18 5:05:17
Red Mills 56 226 41N37'41 74W16'22 4:57:05
Redmond Corner 33 137 43N27'52 75W23'25 5:01:34
Red Oaks Mill 14 1 41N39'20 73W52'31 4:55:30
Red Rock 11 10 42N21'25 73W30'39 4:54:03
Red Rock 34 226 43N07'58 76W17'19 5:05:09
Redwood 23 17 44N18'03 75W48'06 5:03:12
Redwood 52 11 40N59'52 72W18'50 4:49:15
Reed Corners 7 14 42N27'04 79W18'25 5:17:14
Reed Corners 35 14 42N50'11 77W12'53 5:08:52
Reeds Corner 26 13 42N35'59 77W40'55 5:10:44
Reedville 23 77 44N06'05 75W39'17 5:02:37
Reeves Park 52 11 40N58'18 72W42'46 4:50:51
Rego Park 41 1 40N43'35 73W51'11 4:55:25
Reidsville 1 11 42N34'00 74W01'28 4:56:06
Relius 6 13 42N55'13 76W39'31 5:06:38
Remington Corners 25 226 44N07'24 75W21'45 5:01:27
Remsen 33 82 43N19'37 75W11'14 5:00:45
Remsenburg 52 11 40N48'27 72W42'33 4:50:50
Renchans 51 14 42N26'25 77W19'31 5:09:18
Reniff 54 226 42N06'59 76W32'47 5:06:11
Rensselaer 42 208 42N38'33 73W44'36 4:54:58
Rensselaer Falls 45 226 44N35'31 75W19'10 5:01:17
Rensselaerville 1 226 42N30'58 74W08'18 4:56:33
Renwick 55 186 42N27'58 76W30'00 5:06:00
Residence Park 60 1 40N54'04 73W47'02 4:55:08
Resort 59 226 43N13'35 76W55'27 5:07:42
Result 20 11 42N21'25 73W56'54 4:55:48
Retsof 26 226 42N50'07 77W52'45 5:11:31
Rexford 46 4 42N51'11 73W53'18 4:55:33
Rexleigh 58 213 43N08'07 73W21'19 4:53:25
Rexville 51 226 42N05'03 77W39'45 5:10:39
Reydon Shores 52 11 41N02'48 72W23'58 4:49:36
Reynales Basin 32 90 43N12'24 78W32'47 5:14:11
Reynolds 42 1 42N53'25 73W39'47 4:54:39
Reynolds Corner 23 45 44N05'25 76W02'34 5:04:10
Reynolds Corners 46 226 43N15'09 73W38'31 4:54:34
Reynoldston 17 226 44N44'35 74W27'00 4:57:48
Reynoldsville 49 14 42N28'01 76W46'14 5:07:05
Rheims 51 181 42N24'03 77W15'15 5:09:01
Rhinebeck 14 64 41N55'36 73W54'47 4:55:39
Rhinecliff 14 11 41N55'10 73W57'06 4:55:48
Rhode Island 9 226 42N40'44 75W48'00 5:03:12
Ricard 38 25 43N29'53 75W55'18 5:03:41
Rice Grove 34 13 42N51'05 76W15'24 5:05:02
Rice Mill 59 226 43N14'02 76W51'30 5:07:26
Rices 23 226 43N55'03 75W58'13 5:03:53
Riceville 5 226 42N26'33 78W36'54 5:14:28
Riceville 18 226 43N05'37 74W16'56 4:57:08
Richardsville 40 226 41N27'49 73W46'32 4:55:06
Richburg 2 25 42N05'18 78W09'13 5:12:37
Richfield 39 78 42N51'26 75W03'16 5:00:13
Richfield Springs 39 78 42N51'12 74W59'09 4:59:57
Richford 54 226 42N21'20 76W12'04 5:04:48
Richland 38 226 43N34'10 76W02'53 5:04:12
Richmond 35 47 42N47 77W31 5:10:04
Richmond 43 1 40N34'26 74W07'51 4:56:31
Richmond Center 35 47 42N48'29 77W31'59 5:10:08
Richmond Hill 41 1 40N41'59 73W49'54 4:55:20
Richmond Valley 43 11 40N31'12 74W13'47 4:56:55
Richmondville 48 13 42N38'03 74W33'52 4:58:15
Richs Corners 37 146 43N13'50 78W08'58 5:12:36
Richville 45 226 44N25'02 75W23'32 5:01:34
Riders 11 11 42N28'22 73W32'37 4:54:10
Riders Mills 11 11 42N28'51 73W33'52 4:54:15
Ridge 26 13 42N40'34 77W54'49 5:11:39
Ridge 52 11 40N53'38 72W53'47 4:51:35
Ridgebury 36 7 41N23'11 74W27'14 4:57:49
Ridgeland 28 20 43N05'27 77W36'38 5:10:27
Ridgelea Heights 32 226 43N12'04 78W40'31 5:14:42
Ridge Mills 33 211 43N14'25 75W26'18 5:01:45
Ridgemont 28 209 43N13 77W41 5:10:44
Ridgeway 37 112 43N16'02 78W23'24 5:13:34
Ridgeway 60 1 41N00'10 73W45'48 4:55:03
Ridgewood 32 190 43N15'01 78W38'51 5:14:35
Ridgewood 33 222 43N06 75W14 5:00:56
Ridgewood 41 1 40N42'00 73W54'22 4:55:37
Rifton 56 11 41N50'15 74W02'16 4:56:09
Riga 28 161 43N04'10 77W53'03 5:11:32
Riggsville 56 72 41N52'19 74W20'21 4:57:21
Rigney Bluff 28 226 43N16'23 77W38'06 5:10:32
Riley Cove 46 11 43N00'48 73W45'54 4:55:04
Ringdahl Court 33 211 43N13 75W26 5:01:44
Rio 36 1 41N23 74W43 4:58:52
Riparius 57 49 43N39'42 73W53'51 4:55:35
Ripley 7 103 42N16'01 79W42'39 5:18:51
Rippleton 27 14 42N54'43 75W52'07 5:03:28
Risingville 51 226 42N13'09 77W18'55 5:09:16
Ritchfield Junction 33 13 42N56'42 75W14'47 5:00:59
River 28 209 43N08 77W38 5:10:32
Riverbank 57 11 43N36'19 73W43'33 4:54:54
Riverdale 3 1 40N54'02 73W54'23 4:55:38
Riverdale 33 211 43N12'37 75W25'58 5:01:44
Rivergate 23 226 44N11'19 75W47'02 5:03:08
Riverhead 52 1 40N55'01 72W39'45 4:50:39
Riverside 4 20 42N00'24 75W45'53 5:03:04
Riverside 46 1 42N55'04 73W40'37 4:54:42
Riverside 51 13 42N09'22 77W04'59 5:08:20
Riverside Estates 52 11 40N55 72W38 4:50:32
Riverside Junction 5 20 42N04'51 78W38'31 5:14:34
Riverside Manors 32 226 43N11'08 79W02'48 5:16:11
Riverside Park 56 11 41N54'55 74W04'37 4:56:18
Riverview 10 136 44N39 73W45 4:55:00
Roanoke 19 70 42N56'37 78W03'08 5:12:13
Roanoke Landing 52 11 40N58'36 72W42'31 4:50:50
Robbins Rest 52 11 40N38'36 73W09'54 4:52:40
Roberts Corner 23 65 43N48'59 76W07'14 5:04:29
Roberts Hill 20 11 42N23'43 73W50'14 4:55:21
Robinson 10 16 44N49'22 73W36'57 4:54:28
Robinson Corners 39 226 42N42'13 75W12'15 5:00:49
Robinwood 21 30 44N02'26 74W45'06 4:59:00
Rochdale 14 1 41N43'06 73W51'11 4:55:25
Rochdale Village 41 1 40N41 73W47 4:55:08
Rochelle Heights 60 1 40N55'32 73W46'55 4:55:08
Rochelle Park 60 1 40N55'04 73W47'10 4:55:09
Rochester 28 209 43N09'17 77W36'57 5:10:28
Rochester Junction 28 226 42N59'02 77W35'36 5:10:22
Rockaway Beach 41 1 40N36 73W49 4:55:16
Rockaway Park 41 1 40N34'48 73W50'12 4:55:21
Rockaway Point 41 1 40N33'38 73W54'56 4:55:40
Rock Beach 28 185 43N14'43 77W34'57 5:10:20
Rock City 5 226 42N00'52 78W28'29 5:13:54
Rock City 11 10 42N24'15 73W34'40 4:54:19
Rock City 14 7 41N58'13 73W49'17 4:55:17
Rock City Falls 46 226 43N04 73W55 4:55:40
Rock Cut 34 13 43N01 76W08 5:04:32
Rockdale 9 226 42N22'41 75W24'29 5:01:38
Rockefeller Center 31 1 40N46 73W59 4:55:56
Rock Falls City 46 226 43N03'43 73W55'03 4:55:40
Rock Glen 61 20 42N41'09 78W07'09 5:12:29
Rock Hill 53 74 41N37'33 74W35'53 4:58:24
Rockhurst 57 226 43N28'26 73W38'09 4:54:33
Rockland 44 4 41N03 73W57 4:55:48
Rockland 53 75 41N56'43 74W54'48 4:59:39
Rockland Lake 44 4 41N08'18 73W56'15 4:55:45
Rock Ledge Beach 37 105 43N22'10 78W13'16 5:12:53
Rock Rift 13 97 42N05'32 75W11'32 5:00:46
Rock Stream 62 22 42N28'16 76W55'40 5:07:43
Rock Tavern 36 11 41N27'58 74W11'30 4:56:46
Rockton 29 1 42N57'12 74W10'21 4:56:41
Rock Valley 13 226 41N53'22 75W05'05 5:00:20
Rockville 2 20 42N18'24 78W09'53 5:12:40
Rockville 36 1 41N29'04 74W24'58 4:57:40
Rockville Centre 30 210 40N39'31 73W38'30 4:54:34
Rockville Lake 2 226 42N21 78W07 5:12:28
Rockwell Mills 9 226 42N26'55 75W23'25 5:01:34
Rockwood 18 43 43N03'29 74W30'16 4:58:01
Rocky Hill 36 6 41N13'46 74W21'13 4:57:25
Rocky Point 10 86 44N43'21 73W24'44 4:53:39
Rocky Point 52 11 40N57'09 72W55'33 4:51:42
Rocky Point Landing 52 11 40N57'55 72W57'19 4:51:49
Rodger Corner 34 13 43N09'43 76W09'30 5:04:38
Rodman 23 226 43N51'04 75W56'28 5:03:46
Roe Park 60 6 41N18'23 73W53'02 4:55:32
Roessleville 1 11 42N41'42 73W48'27 4:55:14
Rogers 10 226 44N27'29 73W36'25 4:54:26
Rogersville 51 226 42N30'53 77W40'16 5:10:41
Rolling Acres 28 14 43N12 77W49 5:11:16
Rolling Hills 28 13 43N05 77W28 5:09:52
Rolling Meadows 56 11 41N55'23 74W03'12 4:56:13
Romanoff 40 226 41N27 73W40 4:54:40
Rombout Ridge 14 1 41N39'45 73W51'59 4:55:28
Rome 16 44 44N26'26 73W41'19 4:54:45
Rome 33 211 43N12'46 75W27'22 5:01:49
Romulus 50 226 42N45'08 76W50'02 5:07:20
Rondaxe 22 203 43N43 74W58 4:59:52
Rondout 56 11 41N55'14 73W59'08 4:55:57
Ronkonkoma 52 11 40N48'55 73W06'46 4:52:27
Ronkonkoma West 52 11 40N49 73W06 4:52:24
Roosa Gap 53 11 41N33 74W26 4:57:44
Roosevelt 30 1 40N40'43 73W35'22 4:54:21
Roosevelt Beach 32 226 43N18'27 78W51'31 5:15:26
Roosevelt Corners 38 182 43N18'16 76W14'27 5:04:58
Roosevelt Field 30 11 40N44 73W39 4:54:36
Rooseveltown 45 226 44N58'22 74W43'53 4:58:56
Root 29 11 42N51 74W28 4:57:52
Root Center 29 7 42N49'23 74W28'34 4:57:54
Rootville 39 226 42N27'25 75W16'17 5:01:05
Rosalyn Heights 30 11 40N47 73W38 4:54:32
Roscoe 53 80 41N55'59 74W54'50 4:59:39
Rose 59 33 43N09'13 76W52'44 5:07:31
Rosebank 43 1 40N36'50 74W04'00 4:56:16
Roseboom 39 140 42N44'30 74W46'37 4:59:06
Rosecrans Park 42 11 42N31'49 73W36'27 4:54:26
Rosedale 41 1 40N39'43 73W44'09 4:54:57
Rosedale 60 1 40N59'36 73W44'36 4:54:58
Rose Grove 52 11 40N57'27 72W23'34 4:49:34
Rose Hill 34 13 42N54'26 76W20'34 5:05:22
Rose Hill 50 41 42N50'58 76W54'36 5:07:38
Roseland 28 226 43N10'53 77W23'12 5:09:33
Roseland Park 35 14 42N52'21 77W15'05 5:09:00
Rosemont Park 42 1 42N39'24 73W42'43 4:54:51
Rosendale 56 11 41N50'38 74W04'57 4:56:20
Roses Point 36 21 41N27'28 74W36'17 4:58:25
Roseton 36 1 41N33'30 73W59'04 4:55:56
Rosiere 23 226 44N07'17 76W14'31 5:04:58
Roslyn 30 11 40N47'59 73W39'05 4:54:36
Roslyn Estates 30 11 40N47'39 73W39'39 4:54:39
Roslyn Harbor 30 11 40N48'59 73W38'15 4:54:33
Roslyn Heights 30 11 40N47'19 73W38'52 4:54:35
Rossburg 2 226 42N29'50 78W04'13 5:12:17
Ross Corners 4 13 42N04'03 76W06'03 5:04:24
Rosses 26 226 42N31'10 77W53'30 5:11:34
Rossie 45 226 44N22'43 75W39'19 5:02:37
Rossman 11 111 42N19'53 73W44'39 4:54:59
Ross Mills 7 187 42N09'36 79W13'21 5:16:53
Ross's Corners 23 143 43N48 76W01 5:04:04
Rosstown 8 13 42N01'27 76W50'29 5:07:22
Rossville 36 226 41N35'31 74W04'10 4:56:17
Rossville 43 11 40N33'20 74W12'50 4:56:51
Rotterdam 47 6 42N49 74W01 4:56:04
Rotterdam Junction 47 11 42N52'28 74W02'49 4:56:11
Rough and Ready 51 226 42N06'27 77W39'09 5:10:37
Round Lake 46 11 42N56'19 73W47'25 4:55:10
Round Top 20 226 42N16'08 74W01'40 4:56:07
Rouses Point 10 157 44N59'38 73W21'55 4:53:28
Rowan Corners 27 14 42N59'04 75W49'01 5:03:16
Roxbury 13 31 42N17'02 74W33'55 4:58:16
Roxbury 41 1 40N33'59 73W53'28 4:55:34
Royalton 32 90 43N12 78W33 5:14:12
Royalton Center 32 121 43N09'49 78W32'19 5:14:09
Ruback Camp 46 1 43N01'30 74W04'00 4:56:16
Ruby 56 13 42N01'05 74W00'55 4:56:04
Ruby Corner 45 20 44N27'08 75W35'48 5:02:23
Rudco 14 1 41N39'00 73W56'30 4:55:46
Rudeston 21 226 43N26'10 74W30'35 4:58:02
Rugby 24 1 40N39 73W56 4:55:44
Rumsey Ridge 32 199 43N09'58 79W01'03 5:16:04
Rural Grove 29 7 42N50'53 74W26'29 4:57:46
Rural Hill 23 13 43N47'39 76W10'25 5:04:42
Rush 28 27 42N59'45 77W38'45 5:10:35
Rushford 2 226 42N23'32 78W15'14 5:13:01
Rushford Lake 2 226 42N23 78W09 5:12:36
Rush Run 8 226 42N14'45 76W45'27 5:07:02
Rushville 62 25 42N45'36 77W13'36 5:08:54
Russell 45 226 44N25'46 75W09'01 5:00:36
Russell Gardens 30 1 40N46'52 73W43'30 4:54:54
Russia 10 136 44N40'25 73W46'57 4:55:08
Russia 22 84 43N15'31 75W04'57 5:00:20
Russ Mills 38 182 43N22'02 76W14'29 5:04:58
Rutland 23 226 43N58 75W47 5:03:08
Rutland Center 23 45 43N57'16 75W48'26 5:03:14
Rutsonville 56 11 41N40'14 74W15'06 4:57:00
Ryder 24 1 40N37 73W56 4:55:44
Rye 60 212 40N58'50 73W41'03 4:54:44
Rye Hills-Rye Brook 60 212 41N00 73W40 4:54:40
Rynex Corners 47 226 42N49'17 74W04'18 4:56:17
Sabael 21 226 43N43'42 74W18'22 4:57:13
Sabattis 21 30 44N04'51 74W42'11 4:58:49
Sabbath Day Point 57 226 43N40'03 73W30'52 4:54:03
Sacandaga 18 7 43N13 74W10 4:56:40

Sacandaga Park 18 7 43N12'58 74w11'23 4:56:46
Sackets Harbor 23 12 43N56'46 76w07'10 5:04:29
Sacketts Harbor 26 13 42N47'47 77w43'16 5:10:53
Sacketts Lake 53 197 41N39 74w42 4:58:48
Saddle Rock 30 1 40N47'39 73w44'56 4:55:00
Saddle Rock Estates 30 1 40N47'37 73w44'32 4:54:58
Sagamore 21 226 43N45'52 74w37'43 4:58:31
Sagaponack 52 11 40N55'31 72w16'43 4:49:07
Sages Cottages 52 11 41N06 72w22 4:49:28
Sages Crossing 9 226 42N35'07 75w20'07 5:01:20
Sagetown 8 13 42N01'36 76w57'27 5:07:50
Sag Harbor 52 6 40N59'52 72w17'35 4:49:10
Sailors Snug Harbor 43 1 40N38 74w06 4:56:24
Saint Albans 41 1 40N41'54 73w45'40 4:55:03
Saint Andrew 36 11 41N34'09 74w08'45 4:56:35
Saint Armand 16 226 44N24 74w02 4:56:08
Saint Bonaventure 5 226 42N05 78w28 5:13:52
Saint Elmo 56 6 41N35'19 74w08'31 4:56:34
Saint George 43 1 40N38'40 74w04'50 4:56:19
Saint Huberts 16 226 44N09'26 73w46'25 4:55:06
Saint James 52 11 40N52'44 73w09'26 4:52:38
Saint James Heights 52 11 40N52 73w10 4:52:40
Saint John Fisher College 28 13 43N07 77w34 5:10:16
Saint Johnsburg 32 1 43N05'19 78w53'24 5:15:34
Saint Johns Place 24 1 40N40 73w57 4:55:48
Saint Johnsville 29 69 42N59'53 74w41'00 4:58:44
Saint Josen 56 76 41N46'53 74w12'31 4:56:50
Saint Josephs 53 226 41N35'24 74w42'38 4:58:51
Saint Lawrence 23 163 44N10'38 76w10'05 5:04:40
Saint Lawrence Park 23 17 44N18'35 75w57'48 5:03:51
Saint Mary's Park 3 1 40N50 73w54 4:55:36
Saint Peters Church 33 211 43N11'29 75w34'25 5:02:18
Saint Regis 17 226 44N59'50 74w39'05 4:58:36
Saint Regis Falls 17 226 44N40'26 74w32'43 4:58:11
Saint Regis Indian Res 17 226 44N59 74w40 4:58:40
Saint Remy 56 11 41N52'57 74w01'18 4:56:05
Saintsville 34 226 43N04'55 75w57'50 5:03:51
Saint Vencent de Paul Camp 15 11 42N39'19 79w03'40 5:16:15
Sala 38 15 43N26'09 76w19'53 5:05:20
Salamanca 5 14 42N09'28 78w42'55 5:14:52
Salem 58 213 43N10'20 73w19'41 4:53:19
Salem Center 60 16 41N19'45 73w35'55 4:54:24
Salem Corner 34 13 42N57'16 75w57'29 5:03:50
Salina 34 13 43N06 76w10 5:04:40
Salisbury 22 214 43N08'03 74w49'28 4:59:18
Salisbury Center 22 214 43N08'33 74w47'13 4:59:09
Salisbury Mills 36 11 41N25'50 74w07'10 4:56:29
Salmon River 10 86 44N42 73w26 4:53:44
Saltaire 52 7 40N38'10 73w11'50 4:52:47
Salt Point 14 226 41N48'24 73w47'37 4:55:10
Salt Springville 29 140 42N51'33 74w44'46 4:58:59
Saltvale 61 206 42N47'02 78w06'36 5:12:26
Sammonsville 18 174 42N59'18 74w26'02 4:57:44
Sampson 50 12 42N43'45 76w54'02 5:07:36
Sampsonville 56 72 41N53'15 74w17'40 4:57:11
Samsondale 44 6 41N12'31 73w58'39 4:55:55
Sanborn 32 1 43N08'12 78w53'06 5:15:32
Sandfordville 45 207 44N43'55 74w53'59 4:59:36
Sand Hill 15 145 43N03'32 78w33'30 5:14:14
Sand Hill 29 62 42N56'39 74w38'01 4:58:32
Sand Hill 39 13 42N22'43 75w15'45 5:01:03
Sand Lake 42 226 42N38'14 73w32'28 4:54:10
Sand Point 26 20 42N50'02 77w42'13 5:10:49
Sand Ridge 38 182 43N15 76w14 5:04:56
Sands Point 30 7 40N51'06 73w43'09 4:54:53
Sandusky 5 226 42N29'45 78w23'05 5:13:32
Sandy Bay 34 13 43N12'19 76w05'01 5:04:20
Sandy Beach 15 1 43N03'23 78w57'36 5:15:50
Sandy Creek 38 226 43N38'39 76w05'11 5:04:21
Sandy Harbour Beach 28 105 43N21'08 77w53'40 5:11:35
Sandy Pond 38 226 43N38'09 76w11'04 5:04:44
Sanford 2 22 42N00'55 78w14'09 5:12:57
Sanford 4 226 42N06'08 75w29'02 5:01:56
Sangerfield 33 13 42N54'50 75w22'46 5:01:31
Sanitaria Springs 4 4 42N09'36 75w45'56 5:03:04
San Remo 52 11 40N52'55 73w13'16 4:52:53
Santa Clara 17 226 44N38'01 74w27'28 4:57:50
Santapoque 52 11 40N43 73w22 4:53:28
Saranac 10 136 44N39'05 73w44'38 4:54:59
Saranac Inn 17 16 44N20'46 74w19'05 4:57:16
Saranac Lake 17 81 44N19'46 74w07'54 4:56:32
Saratoga 46 1 43N04 73w37 4:54:28
Saratoga Lake 46 226 43N03'04 73w43'19 4:54:53
Saratoga Springs 46 1 43N04'59 73w47'06 4:55:08
Sardinia 15 226 42N32'28 78w30'30 5:14:02
Sarles Corners 60 16 41N11'03 73w34'11 4:54:17
Saugerties 56 215 42N04'39 73w57'12 4:55:49
Sauquoit 33 14 43N00'15 75w15'37 5:01:02
Savannah 59 25 43N04'02 76w45'36 5:07:02
Savilton 36 1 41N34'59 74w04'08 4:56:17
Savona 51 20 42N17'19 77w13'07 5:08:52
Sawens 19 164 42N55'40 78w21'16 5:13:25
Sawkill 56 11 41N59'08 74w01'52 4:56:07
Sawyer 2 226 42N04'10 78w05'41 5:12:23
Sawyer 32 1 43N03'53 78w50'42 5:15:23
Sawyer 37 146 43N20'22 78w09'39 5:12:39
Sawyers Corner 6 13 42N58'21 76w35'17 5:06:21
Saxe Corner 23 226 43N45'35 76w06'29 5:04:26
Saxon Park 52 11 40N41 73w13 4:52:52
Saxton 56 226 42N09'28 73w59'41 4:55:59
Sayville 52 7 40N44'09 73w04'57 4:52:20
Scarborough 60 7 41N08'09 73w51'32 4:55:26
Scarsdale 60 1 41N00'18 73w47'06 4:55:08
Scarsdale Downs 60 1 40N59'02 73w46'58 4:55:08
Scarsdale Park 60 1 40N59'00 73w47'37 4:55:10
Schaghticoke 42 11 42N54'00 73w35'09 4:54:21
Schaghticoke Hill 42 11 42N52'43 73w36'22 4:54:25
Schenectady 47 1 42N48'51 73w56'24 4:55:46
Schenevus 39 13 42N32'56 74w49'17 4:59:17
Schepps Corners 34 226 43N06'55 76w00'13 5:04:01
Schermerhorn Landing 45 20 44N24'46 75w47'27 5:03:10
Schodack 42 68 42N32 73w41 4:54:44
Schodack Center 42 68 42N33'16 73w40'37 4:54:42
Schodack Landing 42 68 42N28'46 73w46'12 4:55:05
Schoharie 48 12 42N39'57 74w18'36 4:57:14
Schoharie Junction 48 12 42N43'21 74w19'31 4:57:18
Scholes 2 226 42N21'07 77w55'15 5:11:41
Schonowe 47 1 42N48'36 73w59'40 4:55:59
Schroeppel 38 93 43N16 76w17 5:05:08
Schroon 16 5 43N51 73w46 4:55:04
Schroon Falls 16 226 43N53'57 73w44'57 4:55:00
Schroon Lake 16 5 43N50'19 73w45'41 4:55:03
Schultzville 14 64 41N56 73w54 4:55:36
Schuluski Estates 46 11 42N48 73w41 4:54:44
Schuyler 22 226 43N06 75w06 5:00:24
Schuyler Falls 10 86 44N37'43 73w33'30 4:54:14
Schuyler Lake 39 78 42N46'49 75w01'42 5:00:07
Schuylerville 46 1 43N06'00 73w34'56 4:54:20
Scio 2 109 42N10'17 77w58'44 5:11:55
Sciota 17 198 44N53'45 73w32'59 4:54:12
Sciota 10 226 44N49 73w31 4:54:04
Scipio 6 13 42N48 76w35 5:06:20
Scipio Center 6 13 42N47'01 76w33'34 5:06:14
Scipioville 6 13 42N46'55 76w37'31 5:06:30
Scononda 33 60 43N05'45 75w37'26 5:02:30
Scotchbrush 18 226 43N04'18 74w34'27 4:58:18
Scotchbush 18 226 43N00 74w41 4:58:44
Scotch Bush 29 1 42N51'27 74w11'45 4:56:47
Scotch Church 29 94 42N52'18 74w08'08 4:56:33
Scotch Hill 39 226 42N40'23 75w03'54 5:00:16
Scotchtown 36 1 41N28'53 74w21'38 4:57:27
Scotia 47 7 42N49'35 73w57'53 4:55:52
Scott 12 16 42N43'46 76w14'37 5:04:58
Scottsburg 26 226 42N39'51 77w42'52 5:10:51
Scotts Corner 36 11 41N31'32 74w12'04 4:56:48
Scotts Corners 23 143 43N48 76w01 5:04:04
Scotts Corners 60 16 41N11'21 73w33'04 4:54:12
Scottsville 28 226 43N01'33 77w44'44 5:10:59
Scranton 15 153 42N44'26 78w50'04 5:15:20
Scriba 38 15 43N27'55 76w25'51 5:05:43
Scribner Corners 27 60 43N03'15 75w37'58 5:02:32
Scuttlehole 52 11 40N56'07 72w20'26 4:49:22
Sea Breeze 28 185 43N13'50 77w32'33 5:10:10
Sea Cliff 30 6 40N50'56 73w38'43 4:54:35
Seaford 30 7 40N39'57 73w29'19 4:53:57
Seagate 24 1 40N34'33 74w00'35 4:56:02
Seager 56 42 42N03'42 74w32'42 4:58:11
Seamen's Church Institute 31 1 40N43 74w01 4:56:04
Searingtown 30 11 40N46'29 73w39'22 4:54:37
Searsburg 49 13 42N31'51 76w44'10 5:06:57
Sears Corners 40 226 41N25'43 73w34'40 4:54:19
Searsville 36 11 41N33'49 74w18'27 4:57:14
Seaside 41 1 40N34'59 73w49'43 4:55:19
Seaview 52 11 40N38'49 73w08'58 4:52:36
Second Milo 62 14 42N36'53 77w02'20 5:08:09
Secor Gardens 60 1 40N59'40 73w45'41 4:55:03
Seeley Creek 8 13 42N00'52 76w53'34 5:07:34
Seifert Corners 33 211 43N13'31 75w32'12 5:02:09
Selden 52 11 40N51'59 73w02'10 4:52:09
Selkirk 1 11 42N31'56 73w47'56 4:55:12
Selkirk 38 226 43N34'27 76w12'11 5:04:49
Selkirk Beach 38 226 43N34 76w07 5:04:28
Sellecks Corners 45 226 44N33 74w56 4:59:44
Semans Corner 35 226 42N39'46 77w23'10 5:09:33
Sempronius 6 226 42N43'46 76w18'56 5:05:16
Seneca 35 14 42N50 77w05 5:08:20
Seneca Army Depot 50 12 42N45 76w50 5:07:20
Seneca Castle 35 13 42N53'13 77w05'47 5:08:23
Seneca Falls 50 14 42N54'38 76w47'49 5:07:11
Seneca Heights 5 101 42N04'08 78w25'37 5:13:42
Seneca Hill 38 204 43N24'03 76w28'14 5:05:53
Seneca Knolls 34 13 43N04 76w14 5:04:56
Seneca Mills 62 14 42N39'40 77w00'20 5:08:01
Seneca Point 35 226 42N37 77w24 5:09:36
Sennett 6 24 42N59'41 76w31'59 5:06:08
Sentinel Heights 34 13 42N57'00 76w06'55 5:04:28
Setauket 52 11 40N56'06 73w07'08 4:52:29
Settlers Hill 40 226 41N26 73w36 4:54:24
Seven Hills 40 226 41N27 73w40 4:54:40
Seventh Day Hollow 9 226 42N41'03 75w45'44 5:03:03
Severance 16 226 43N52'33 73w43'51 4:54:55
Severance 28 226 43N03'01 77w43'42 5:10:55
Sevey 45 87 44N17'51 74w43'02 4:58:52
Seward 48 13 42N43'15 74w36'33 4:58:26
Shackport 13 226 42N23'12 74w55'30 4:59:42
Shadigee 37 15 43N22'30 78w23'21 5:13:33
Shady 56 11 42N03'59 74w09'35 4:56:38
Shady Corner Curve 16 1 44N13'02 73w55'53 4:55:44
Shaker Crossing 26 13 42N44'03 77w50'56 5:11:24
Shaker Place 21 226 43N19'27 74w31'29 4:58:06
Shakers 1 11 42N44'22 73w48'42 4:55:15
Shamrock 34 13 42N54'03 76w21'43 5:05:27
Shandaken 56 23 42N07'12 74w23'45 4:57:35
Shandelee 53 75 41N52'44 74w52'18 4:59:29
Sharon 48 11 42N45'40 74w31'59 4:58:08
Sharon Center 48 11 42N46'48 74w35'13 4:58:21
Sharon Springs 48 11 42N47'45 74w37'03 4:58:28
Sharon Station 14 11 41N53'00 73w31'14 4:54:05
Shawangunk 56 226 41N38 74w16 4:57:04
Shaw Corners 46 226 43N04'56 74w01'57 4:56:08
Shawnee 32 1 43N07'41 78w50'17 5:15:21
Sheds 27 226 42N48'40 75w49'50 5:03:19
Sheepshead Bay 24 1 40N35'28 73w56'42 4:55:47
Shekomeko 14 226 41N55'41 73w35'58 4:54:24
Shelby 37 112 43N11 78w23 5:13:32
Shelby Basin 37 112 43N12'57 78w25'51 5:13:43
Shelby Center 37 112 43N11'22 78w23'33 5:13:34
Sheldon 61 226 42N44'14 78w25'08 5:13:41
Sheldon Center 61 226 42N44'16 78w23'19 5:13:33
Sheldon Corners 61 226 42N42 78w27 5:13:48
Sheldon Hall 7 187 42N07'05 79w18'53 5:17:16
Sheldrake 50 226 42N39'54 76w42'07 5:06:48
Sheldrake Springs 50 226 42N39'30 76w45'18 5:07:01
Shelter Island 52 11 41N04'05 72w20'21 4:49:21
Shelter Island Heights 52 11 41N05'02 72w21'23 4:49:26
Shenandoah 14 6 41N31'43 73w47'23 4:55:10
Shenorock 60 16 41N19'54 73w44'19 4:54:57
Shepards Corner 59 99 43N06'18 76w50'23 5:07:22
Shepard Settlement 34 24 42N59'43 76w23'01 5:05:32
Sherburne 9 15 42N40'41 75w29'56 5:02:00
Sherburne Four Corners 9 200 42N38'53 75w32'49 5:02:11
Sheridan 7 226 42N29'18 79w14'15 5:16:57
Sheridan Park 35 41 42N52 76w59 5:07:56
Sherlock Corners 6 13 42N53'48 76w33'59 5:06:16
Sherman 7 22 42N09'33 79w35'44 5:18:23
Sherman Park 60 7 41N07'36 73w46'32 4:55:06
Shermans Bay 7 20 42N05'56 79w20'54 5:17:24
Shermerhorn Landing 45 20 44N27 75w42 5:02:48
Sherrill 33 13 43N04'25 75w35'55 5:02:24
Sherwood 6 13 42N45'39 76w37'18 5:06:29
Sherwood Knolls 34 12 43N02'15 76w15'34 5:05:02
Sherwood Park 42 1 42N36'17 73w43'05 4:54:52
Shin Hollow 36 1 41N24'17 74w36'57 4:58:28
Shinhopple 13 226 42N02'19 75w04'05 5:00:16
Shinnecock Hills 52 11 40N53'27 72w27'51 4:49:51
Shinnecock Indian Res 52 11 40N52 72w25 4:49:40
Shirley 15 42 42N34'36 78w54'50 5:15:39
Shirley 52 11 40N48'05 72w52'05 4:51:28
Shokan 56 11 41N58'24 74w12'45 4:56:51
Sholam 56 48 41N49'15 74w24'39 4:57:39
Shongo 2 226 42N01'05 77w53'50 5:11:35
Shongo 5 20 42N08'19 78w46'42 5:15:07
Shooktown 32 226 43N09'34 78w39'48 5:14:39

Shore Acres 7 226 42N09'01 79w22'49 5:17:31
Shore Acres 28 13 43N20'49 77w51'04 5:11:24
Shore Acres 52 11 41N00'09 72w33'01 4:50:12
Shore Acres 60 1 40N56'49 73w43'28 4:54:54
Shoreham 52 11 40N57'26 72w54'29 4:51:38
Shore Haven 7 225 42N18'50 79w38'31 5:18:34
Shorelands 7 158 42N14'57 79w28'06 5:17:52
Shore Oaks 38 204 43N31'07 76w21'27 5:05:26
Shorewood 49 13 42N25'43 77w06'10 5:08:25
Shorewood 52 11 40N53 73w22 4:53:28
Shortsville 35 4 42N57'21 77w13'16 5:08:53
Short Tract 2 226 42N27'08 78w00'53 5:12:04
Shrub Oak 60 16 41N19'39 73w49'12 4:55:17
Shuetown 25 77 43N37'13 75w19'44 5:01:19
Shultis Corners 56 215 42N03'01 74w04'09 4:56:17
Shumaker Crossing 6 13 42N53'40 76w34'12 5:06:17
Shumla 7 14 42N23'12 79w17'56 5:17:12
Shunpike 14 226 41N49'43 73w42'32 4:54:50
Shurtleff 45 87 44N15'19 74w44'42 4:58:59
Shushan 58 213 43N05'25 73w20'36 4:53:22
Shutter Corners 48 12 42N40'31 74w15'12 4:57:01
Sibleyville 28 226 42N58'01 77w37'07 5:10:28
Sidney 13 12 42N18'53 75w23'31 5:01:34
Sidney Center (Maywood Sta) 13 13 42N17'26 75w15'22 5:01:01
Siegfield Park 52 11 40N50'26 72w56'25 4:51:46
Siena 1 1 42N43 73w46 4:55:04
Sierks 61 148 42N49'18 78w18'11 5:13:13
Sigby Corners 27 15 42N51'50 75w29'34 5:01:58
Sillimans Corners 5 226 42N34 78w29 5:13:56
Siloam 27 226 42N59'05 75w38'30 5:02:34
Silver Bay 57 226 43N41'47 73w30'22 4:54:01
Silver Beach 52 11 41N03'01 72w21'24 4:49:26
Silver Creek 7 216 42N32'39 79w10'01 5:16:40
Silver Lake 36 1 41N28 74w24 4:57:36
Silver Lake 39 226 42N36'05 75w19'58 5:01:20
Silver Lake 61 226 42N42'06 78w01'20 5:12:05
Silver Lake Junction 61 100 42N40'20 78w05'37 5:12:22
Silver Lake Village 36 1 41N28 74w24 4:57:36
Silvernails 11 226 42N00'53 73w41'01 4:54:44
Silver Springs 61 100 42N39'38 78w05'09 5:12:21
Simpsonville 13 13 42N30'14 74w46'59 4:59:08
Sinclair Corner 45 226 44N38'37 74w53'29 4:59:34
Sinclairville 7 67 42N15'50 79w15'32 5:17:02
Sisson 45 207 44N42'20 74w59'14 4:59:57
Sissonville 45 207 44N40 74w59 4:59:56
Skaneateles 34 13 42N56'49 76w25'46 5:05:43
Skaneateles Falls 34 24 42N59'35 76w27'23 5:05:50
Skaneateles Junction 34 24 43N00'40 76w27'28 5:05:50
Skanondaga Heights 34 13 42N52'32 76w24'34 5:05:38
Skerry 17 193 44N46'04 74w22'56 4:57:32
Skinnerville 45 105 44N47'04 74w48'58 4:59:16
Skunks Corner 5 217 42N21'43 79w03'33 5:16:14
Sky Meadow Farms 60 1 41N00 73w40 4:54:40
Sky Ranch 46 226 43N09'00 73w55'05 4:55:40
Skytop 34 13 43N01'13 76w07'25 5:04:30
Slab City 7 22 42N08'01 79w37'05 5:18:28
Slab City 12 91 42N43'07 76w08'07 5:04:32
Slab City 45 207 44N40'11 75w05'33 5:00:22
Slabtown 8 226 42N12 76w48 5:07:12
Slate Hill 36 7 41N23'27 74w28'37 4:57:54
Slaterville Springs 55 226 42N23'44 76w21'03 5:05:24
Slateville 58 42 43N19'50 73w17'23 4:53:10
Sleepy Hollow Manor 60 6 41N06'20 73w51'49 4:55:27
Sleggs Landing 26 13 42N48'23 77w43'02 5:10:52
Sleightsburg 56 11 41N55'00 73w58'37 4:55:54
Slingerlands 1 11 42N37'45 73w51'54 4:55:28
Sliters 42 1 42N36'17 73w36'24 4:54:26
Sloan 15 7 42N53'36 78w47'39 5:15:11
Sloansville 48 12 42N45'25 74w19'51 4:57:19
Sloatsburg 44 4 41N09'16 74w11'36 4:56:46
Slyboro 58 42 43N24'43 73w19'56 4:53:20
Small Corners 33 11 42N58'49 75w25'10 5:01:41
Smallwood 53 226 41N39'55 74w49'11 4:59:17
Smartville 38 14 43N38'29 75w57'46 5:03:51
Smithboro 54 20 42N02'02 76w24'02 5:05:36
Smith Corner 1 226 42N27'55 74w06'05 4:56:24
Smith Corners 22 196 42N56'54 74w51'18 4:59:25
Smithfield 14 11 41N53'08 73w36'02 4:54:24
Smithfield 27 226 42N58 75w40 5:02:40
Smith Landing 20 11 42N07'56 73w54'57 4:55:40
Smith Mills 7 226 42N29'42 79w06'21 5:16:25
Smiths Basin 58 123 43N25 73w29 4:53:56
Smiths Clove 36 226 41N20'46 74w12'04 4:56:48
Smiths Corner 1 226 42N26 74w08 4:56:32
Smiths Corner 61 226 42N37'54 78w15'09 5:13:01
Smiths Corners 18 226 43N03'51 74w22'34 4:57:30
Smiths Mills 7 226 42N28 79w10 5:16:40
Smithtown 52 6 40N51'21 73w12'04 4:52:48
Smithtown Pines 52 6 40N51 73w14 4:52:56
Smith Valley 49 226 42N24'50 76w44'29 5:06:58
Smithville 9 226 42N25 75w46 5:03:04
Smithville 23 12 43N52'34 76w06'01 5:04:24
Smithville Center 9 226 42N24'44 75w43'43 5:02:55
Smithville Flats 9 226 42N23'42 75w48'30 5:03:14
Smyrna 9 226 42N41'14 75w34'16 5:02:17
Snake Hill 46 11 43N00'12 73w44'05 4:54:56
Sneden Landing 44 1 41N00'41 73w54'14 4:55:37
Snowdon 39 226 42N43'57 75w03'49 5:00:15
Snufftown 36 7 41N19'23 74w25'50 4:57:43
Snyder 15 7 42N57'49 78w47'03 5:15:08
Snyder Crossing 34 226 43N04'31 75w59'29 5:03:58
Snyders Corner 42 226 42N40'12 73w37'15 4:54:29
Snyders Corners 5 42 42N21'32 78w54'51 5:15:39
Snyders Lake 42 220 42N43 73w41 4:54:44
Snyderville 11 226 42N05'04 73w45'59 4:55:04
Sodom 40 226 41N24'07 73w35'30 4:54:22
Sodom 57 49 43N38'08 73w59'57 4:56:00
Sodus 59 108 43N14'16 77w03'42 5:08:15
Sodus Center 59 108 43N12'17 77w01'29 5:08:06
Sodus Point 59 22 43N16'18 76w59'22 5:07:57
Soft Maple 25 226 43N55'19 75w14'30 5:00:58
Soldiers Place 15 153 42N55'33 78w52'26 5:15:30
Solon 12 41 42N35'49 76w01'02 5:04:04
Solsville 27 180 42N54'38 75w31'05 5:02:04
Solvay 34 12 43N03'29 76w12'28 5:04:50
Somers 60 16 41N19'41 73w41'10 4:54:45
Somerset 32 226 43N20'51 78w33'22 5:14:13
Somerville 45 178 44N16'59 75w33'25 5:02:14
Sonora 51 226 42N20'02 77w10'01 5:08:40
Sonyea 26 13 42N40'44 77w49'39 5:11:19
Sound Beach 52 11 40N57'22 72w58'06 4:51:52
Soundview 3 1 40N50 73w51 4:55:24
South 60 1 40N55 73w53 4:55:32
South Addison 51 13 42N04'55 77w16'11 5:09:05
South Alabama 19 226 43N04'25 78w20'09 5:13:21
South Albany 1 1 42N33'05 73w50'46 4:55:23
South Albion 38 25 43N31 76w00 5:04:00
South Amenia 14 11 41N47'56 73w32'11 4:54:09
Southampton 52 6 40N53'03 72w23'24 4:49:34
South Amsterdam 29 1 42N56'05 74w11'47 4:56:47
South Apalachin 54 36 42N01'09 76w09'20 5:04:37
South Argyle 58 226 43N11'05 73w29'39 4:53:59
South Attica 61 148 42N47'36 78w15'50 5:13:03
South Avon 26 226 42N51'57 77w46'16 5:11:05
South Barre 37 146 43N09'07 78w09'00 5:12:36
South Bay 27 226 43N09'24 75w44'55 5:03:00
South Bay 58 123 43N31'19 73w30'29 4:54:02
South Bay Village 58 123 43N25 73w29 4:53:56
South Beach 43 1 40N35'25 74w04'02 4:56:16
South Berne 1 226 42N33'30 74w06'02 4:56:24
South Bethlehem 1 11 42N31'54 73w50'52 4:55:23
South Bloomfield 35 47 42N51'40 77w23'23 5:09:34
South Bolivar 2 24 42N00'21 78w06'56 5:12:28
South Bombay 17 125 44N53'24 74w33'17 4:58:13
South Bradford 51 226 42N18'40 77w07'38 5:08:31
South Bristol 35 226 42N43'47 77w23'58 5:09:36
South Brookfield 27 16 42N45'12 75w18'40 5:01:15
South Brooklyn 24 1 40N41'02 73w59'45 4:55:59
South Buffalo 15 153 42N52 78w50 5:15:20
Southburg 61 226 42N40'22 78w20'17 5:13:21
South Butler 59 25 43N07'53 76w45'58 5:07:04
South Byron 19 70 43N02'54 78w03'57 5:12:16
South Cairo 20 3 42N16'37 73w57'26 4:55:50
South Cambridge 58 11 42N57'51 73w28'38 4:53:55
South Cameron 51 13 42N10'26 77w25'50 5:09:43
South Canisteo 51 100 42N11'45 77w33'03 5:10:12
South Carrollton 5 20 42N06'11 78w39'44 5:14:39
South Centerville 36 11 41N23'08 74w31'21 4:58:05
South Chili 28 15 43N03'14 77w46'53 5:11:08
South Clyde 59 99 43N05 76w52 5:07:28
South Colton 45 226 44N30'38 74w53'17 4:59:33
South Columbia 22 78 42N53'21 75w00'27 5:00:02
South Corinth 46 7 43N11'47 73w52'04 4:55:28
South Corning 51 13 42N07'18 77w02'15 5:08:09
South Cortland 12 41 42N33'53 76w13'21 5:04:53
South Cuba 2 20 42N11'59 78w16'25 5:13:06
South Danby 55 226 42N18'23 76w26'36 5:05:46
South Dansville 51 95 42N28'11 77w39'15 5:10:37
South Dayton 5 217 42N21'51 79w03'21 5:16:13
South Dover 14 11 41N39'40 73w33'34 4:54:14
South Durham 20 226 42N19'37 74w05'56 4:56:24
Southeast 40 226 41N24 73w36 4:54:24
South Easton 58 11 42N58'46 73w31'22 4:54:05
Southeast Owasco 6 13 42N45'30 76w27'35 5:05:50
South Edmeston 39 226 42N41'03 75w19'05 5:01:16
South Edwards 45 226 44N16'03 75w12'27 5:00:50
South Fallsburg 53 74 41N42'33 74w37'44 4:58:31
South Farmingdale 30 11 40N43'14 73w26'26 4:53:46
Southfields 36 4 41N14'41 74w10'33 4:56:42
South Floral Park 30 1 40N42'51 73w42'02 4:54:48
South Galway Corner 46 11 43N01'14 73w58'19 4:55:53
Southgate Plaza 15 153 42N51 78w46 5:15:04
South Gilboa 48 226 42N24'54 74w31'54 4:58:08
South Glens Falls 46 1 43N17'57 73w38'08 4:54:33
South Glenwood Landing 30 11 40N49'22 73w38'50 4:54:35
South Granby 38 93 43N15'04 76w24'17 5:05:37
South Granville 58 42 43N22'17 73w17'08 4:53:09
South Greece 28 209 43N11'27 77w43'56 5:10:56
South Greenfield 46 226 43N05'43 73w51'45 4:55:27
South Hamilton 27 13 42N46'04 75w27'19 5:01:49
South Hammond 45 20 44N23'57 75w44'00 5:02:56
South Hannibal 38 226 43N15'45 76w31'28 5:06:06
South Hartford 39 226 42N35 75w04 5:00:16
South Hartford 58 226 43N20'52 73w24'24 4:53:38
South Hartwick 39 226 42N37'00 75w03'31 5:00:14
South Haven 52 11 40N47'57 72w53'44 4:51:35
South Hempstead 30 6 40N40'51 73w36'57 4:54:28
South Highland 40 6 41N22'53 73w54'46 4:55:39
South Hill 55 186 42N25'45 76w29'43 5:05:59
South Holbrook 52 11 40N48 73w04 4:52:16
South Horicon 57 11 43N39'16 73w45'40 4:55:03
South Hornell 51 102 42N18'07 77w39'22 5:10:37
South Hudson Falls 58 1 43N17 73w35 4:54:20
South Huntington 52 6 40N49'25 73w23'57 4:53:36
South Ilion 22 184 42N59'43 75w02'58 5:00:12
South Jamesport 52 11 40N56'11 72w34'40 4:50:19
South Jefferson 48 226 42N27'03 74w34'41 4:58:19
South Jewett 20 52 42N13'24 74w15'23 4:57:02
South Junction 10 86 44N37'59 73w27'16 4:53:49
South Kortright 13 226 42N20'32 74w43'03 4:58:52
South Lake 40 226 41N27 73w40 4:54:40
South Lansing 55 13 42N32'16 76w30'22 5:06:01
South Lebanon 27 13 42N45'33 75w39'30 5:02:38
South Lima 26 226 42N51'19 77w40'32 5:10:42
South Livonia 26 20 42N46'15 77w40'17 5:10:41
South Lockport 32 190 43N09'00 78w41'49 5:14:47
South Manor 52 11 40N51'20 72w49'05 4:51:16
South Millbrook 14 39 41N46'27 73w41'54 4:54:48
South New Berlin 9 226 42N31'46 75w23'08 5:01:33
South New Haven 38 15 43N27'23 76w21'14 5:05:25
South Newstead 15 145 42N57'44 78w30'48 5:14:03
South Nineveh 4 17 42N11 75w38 5:02:32
South Nyack 44 1 41N04'59 73w55'14 4:55:41
Southold 52 6 41N03'53 72w25'36 4:49:42
South Olean 5 101 42N04'26 78w26'28 5:13:46
South Onondaga 34 13 42N55'49 76w12'47 5:04:51
South Otselic 9 226 42N38'48 75w46'54 5:03:08
South Owego 54 205 42N01'28 76w12'52 5:04:51
South Oxford 9 106 42N23'17 75w37'18 5:02:29
South Ozone Park 41 1 40N40'12 73w49'10 4:55:17
South Park 15 153 42N51 78w49 5:15:16
South Plainedge 30 11 40N41 73w28 4:53:52

South Plattsburgh 10 86 44N38'11 73w29'18 4:53:57
South Plymouth 9 226 42N34'53 75w33'53 5:02:16
Southport 8 13 42N03'17 76w49'10 5:07:17
Southport 52 11 40N54'30 72w32'55 4:50:12
South Pulteney 51 181 42N30'03 77w11'18 5:08:45
South Richmond Hill 41 1 40N42 73w50 4:55:20
South Ripley 7 103 42N11'42 79w43'15 5:18:53
South Russell 45 226 44N22'17 75w07'40 5:00:31
South Rutland 23 226 43N54 75w48 5:03:12
South Saint Johnsville 29 62 42N56 74w37 4:58:28
South Salem 60 16 41N16'20 73w33'12 4:54:13
South Schenectady 47 1 42N47'13 73w58'17 4:55:53
South Schodack 42 68 42N30'45 73w42'22 4:54:49
South Schroon 16 5 43N47'42 73w47'33 4:55:10
South Scriba 38 226 43N25'44 76w22'57 5:05:32
South Setauket 52 11 40N54'49 73w06'22 4:52:25
South Shore Plaza 15 153 42N45 78w51 5:15:24
South Side 8 13 42N05 76w48 5:07:12
South Sodus 59 22 43N10'02 76w59'14 5:07:57
South Spafford 34 91 42N46'46 76w13'06 5:04:52
South Stockton 7 67 42N14'40 79w18'56 5:17:16
South Stony Brook 52 1 40N54 73w49 4:55:16
South Thurston 51 226 42N12'09 77w17'43 5:09:11
South Trenton 33 14 43N13'06 75w10'46 5:00:43
South Troupsburg 51 226 42N01'04 77w31'18 5:10:05
South Unadilla 13 13 42N18'48 75w20'20 5:01:21
South Valley 5 226 42N03 79w00 5:16:00
South Valley 39 140 42N42'26 74w42'39 4:58:51
South Valley Stream 30 7 40N39 73w43 4:54:52
South Vandalia 5 22 42N05'00 78w35'26 5:14:22
South Vestal 4 13 42N00'29 76w00'09 5:04:01
Southview 4 151 42N05 75w54 5:03:36
Southville 45 226 44N40'25 74w51'16 4:59:25
South Wales 15 22 42N42'32 78w34'42 5:14:19
South Warsaw 61 24 42N42'36 78w07'50 5:12:31
South Westbury 30 7 40N45 73w34 4:54:16
South Westerlo 1 226 42N26'52 74w01'39 4:56:07
Southwest Hoosick 42 11 42N52'25 73w24'12 4:53:37
Southwest Oswego 38 204 43N24'45 76w34'40 5:06:19
South Wilson 32 226 43N24 78w42 5:14:48
South Windsor 4 226 42N01'39 75w37'22 5:02:29
Southwood 34 13 42N59'46 76w06'33 5:04:26
South Worcester 39 13 42N31'04 74w45'01 4:59:00
Spackenkill 14 1 41N40 73w55 4:55:40
Spafford 34 226 42N48'16 76w15'55 5:05:04
Spafford Landing 34 41 42N47'11 76w16'29 5:05:06
Spafford Valley 34 13 42N49'23 76w14'26 5:04:58
Sparkill 44 4 41N01'52 73w55'39 4:55:43
Sparkle Lake 60 16 41N17 73w46 4:55:04
Sparrow Bush 36 1 41N24'00 74w43'25 4:58:54
Sparta 26 13 42N38 77w42 5:10:48
Sparta 60 166 41N08'41 73w51'50 4:55:27
Spaulding Corner 49 13 42N30'03 76w45'02 5:07:00
Spaulding Furnace 11 226 42N01'40 73w41'43 4:54:47
Spawn Hollow 1 11 42N32'22 73w52'02 4:55:28
Speakers Corner 35 47 42N52'12 77w26'54 5:09:48
Speculator 21 226 43N29'50 74w21'44 4:57:27
Speedsville 55 226 42N18'13 76w15'17 5:05:01
Speigletown 42 11 42N48'16 73w38'05 4:54:32
Spellmans 10 86 44N42 73w26 4:53:44
Spencer 54 226 42N12'35 76w29'37 5:05:58
Spencer Corners 14 79 41N57'48 73w30'10 4:54:01
Spencerport 28 14 43N11'11 77w48'15 5:11:13
Spencer Settlement 33 211 43N10'09 75w28'58 5:01:56
Spencertown 11 10 42N19'24 73w32'47 4:54:11
Speonk 52 11 40N49'10 72w42'21 4:50:49
Sperryville 25 226 43N46'23 75w18'25 5:01:14
Spinnerville 22 184 42N58'03 75w02'26 5:00:10
Split Rock 34 12 43N01'27 76w13'25 5:04:54
Spragues Corner 61 226 42N50'55 78w01'39 5:12:07
Spraguetown 58 1 43N07'58 73w28'43 4:53:55
Spragueville 45 226 44N15'32 75w32'12 5:02:09
Sprakers 29 7 42N53'29 74w30'50 4:58:03
Spring Brook 15 11 42N49'05 78w40'33 5:14:42
Spring Brook Station 15 11 42N50'20 78w40'49 5:14:43
Spring Cove 17 226 44N34'16 74w27'23 4:57:50
Springfield 39 226 42N50'10 74w51'14 4:59:25
Springfield Center 39 226 42N49'44 74w52'37 4:59:30
Springfield Four Corners 39 226 42N50'16 74w52'13 4:59:29
Springfield Gardens 41 1 40N40'41 73w44'49 4:54:59
Spring Glen 56 48 41N39'56 74w25'49 4:57:43
Spring Lake 6 24 43N07'32 76w41'18 5:06:45
Spring Mills 2 226 42N00'28 77w45'50 5:11:03
Springport 6 13 42N51 76w40 5:06:40
Springs 52 11 41N00'58 72w09'35 4:48:38
Springtown 56 11 41N46'56 74w05'14 4:56:21
Springvale 9 200 42N31'10 75w28'26 5:01:54
Spring Valley 44 4 41N06'47 74w02'39 4:56:11
Spring Valley 60 1 41N10'07 73w50'21 4:55:21
Springville 15 218 42N30'30 78w40'03 5:14:40
Springville 52 11 40N52'03 72w31'42 4:50:07
Springwater 26 20 42N38'14 77w35'46 5:10:23
Springwood Village 14 11 41N47 73w55 4:55:40
Sprout Brook 29 162 42N51'03 74w41'08 4:58:45
Sproutville 14 6 41N35 73w51 4:55:24
Spruceton 20 42 42N11'30 74w18'29 4:57:14
Spuyten Duyvil 3 1 40N52'52 73w55'04 4:55:40
Squassux Landing 52 11 40N46'23 72w53'59 4:51:36
Squiretown 52 11 40N53'41 72w31'37 4:50:06
Squirrels Corners 53 226 41N35'58 74w45'00 4:59:00
Staatsburg 14 219 41N50'59 73w55'50 4:55:43
Stacy Basin 33 13 43N11'40 75w37'21 5:02:29
Stadium 3 1 40N50 73w52 4:55:28
Stafford 19 142 42N58'54 78w04'27 5:12:18
Stairs Corners 18 226 43N00'22 74w09'10 4:56:37
Stalbird 45 226 44N24'00 75w12'24 5:00:50
Staleyville 48 7 42N48'42 74w35'58 4:58:24
Stamford 13 32 42N24'26 74w36'53 4:58:28
Stanbro 9 226 42N40'05 75w41'37 5:02:46
Standish 10 192 44N41'21 73w56'58 4:55:48
Stanford 14 226 41N53 73w42 4:54:48
Stanford Heights 1 1 42N45'56 73w53'22 4:55:33
Stanfordville 14 226 41N52'02 73w42'53 4:54:52
Stanley 35 14 42N49'30 77w05'46 5:08:23
Stanley Manor 34 12 43N02'23 76w15'27 5:05:02
Stannards 2 109 42N05'11 77w55'21 5:11:41
Stanwix 33 211 43N11'35 75w26'05 5:01:44
Stanwix Heights 33 211 43N11'03 75w25'44 5:01:43
Stanwood 60 6 41N14'20 73w44'49 4:54:59
Stapleton 43 1 40N37'35 74w04'41 4:56:19
Starbuckville 57 159 43N40'24 73w46'41 4:55:07
Stark 22 226 42N55 74w49 4:59:16
Stark 45 226 44N27'01 74w46'55 4:59:08
Starkey 62 13 42N32'07 76w55'29 5:07:42
Stark School Corner 45 178 44N25'47 75w36'47 5:02:27
Starks Knob 46 226 43N07'18 73w35'17 4:54:21
Starks Landing 33 13 43N10'17 75w38'55 5:02:36
Starkville 22 62 42N55'09 74w46'31 4:59:06
Star Lake 45 25 44N09'35 75w01'55 5:00:08
State Bridge 33 13 43N08'45 75w40'37 5:02:42
State Line 7 226 42N14'40 79w45'32 5:19:02
State Line 14 79 41N57'30 73w29'38 4:53:59
Staten Island 43 1 40N35 74w09 4:56:36
State University 30 11 40N48 73w35 4:54:20
Steamburg 5 20 42N06'29 78w54'16 5:15:37
Steam Valley 5 226 42N05 78w26 5:13:44
Stears Corners 23 143 43N46 75w57 5:03:48
Stebbins Corners 7 22 42N09'46 79w31'35 5:18:06
Stedman 7 158 42N10'10 79w28'37 5:17:54
Steel City 15 153 42N49 78w49 5:15:16
Steele Corners 18 226 43N03'55 74w08'30 4:56:34
Steelton 15 153 42N48 78w49 5:15:16
Steinbeck Corners 40 226 41N27'20 73w36'09 4:54:25
Steinway 41 1 40N46'28 73w54'15 4:55:37
Stella 4 151 42N07 75w56 5:03:44
Stella Niagara 32 121 43N12'07 79w02'33 5:16:10
Stellaville 45 226 44N28'50 75w14'36 5:00:58
Stephens Mills 51 102 42N20 77w40 5:10:40
Stephentown 42 11 42N32'55 73w22'28 4:53:30
Stephentown Center 42 11 42N33'55 73w24'39 4:53:39
Sterling 6 226 43N19'33 76w38'43 5:06:35
Sterling Forest 36 226 41N10'57 74w19'09 4:57:17
Sterlington 44 4 41N08'43 74w11'21 4:56:45
Sterling Valley 6 226 43N20'53 76w37'51 5:06:31
Sterlingville 23 77 44N06'11 75w41'15 5:02:45
Stetsonville 39 226 42N35'59 75w11'50 5:00:47
Steuben 33 82 43N19'12 75w17'00 5:01:08
Steuben Valley 33 14 43N17'37 75w14'42 5:00:59
Stevens Landing 10 226 44N29'14 73w42'45 4:54:51
Stever Mill 18 226 43N03'59 74w09'45 4:56:39
Stewart Corners 6 13 42N44'21 76w31'29 5:06:06
Stewart Corners 22 184 43N02'01 75w11'05 5:00:44
Stewart Corners 38 182 43N16'10 76w14'22 5:04:57
Stewart Landing 18 226 43N08'33 74w35'38 4:58:23
Stewart Manor 30 11 40N43'09 73w41'20 4:54:45
Stickneys 51 14 42N28'09 77w17'58 5:09:12
Stiles 34 226 43N06'50 76w16'37 5:05:06
Stilesville 13 167 42N04'49 75w23'58 5:01:36
Stillham 42 11 42N45'42 73w21'42 4:53:27
Stillman Village 42 11 42N45 73w21 4:53:24
Stillwater 7 187 42N03'32 79w13'08 5:16:53
Stillwater 16 49 43N51'00 74w03'24 4:56:14
Stillwater 38 226 43N33'36 75w55'50 5:03:43
Stillwater 40 29 41N21'27 73w46'29 4:55:06
Stillwater 46 4 42N56'18 73w39'13 4:54:37
Stillwater Hill 60 166 41N10 73w51 4:55:24
Stillwater Junction 46 1 42N55'08 73w41'05 4:54:44
Stirling 52 11 41N06'50 72w22'06 4:49:28
Stissing 14 226 41N54'33 73w40'57 4:54:44
Stittville 33 14 43N13'23 75w17'19 5:01:09
Stockbridge 27 13 42N59'28 75w35'59 5:02:24
Stockholm 45 105 44N45 74w51 4:59:24
Stockholm Center 45 105 44N45'34 74w49'55 4:59:20
Stockport 11 11 42N18'34 73w44'48 4:54:59
Stockport 13 97 41N57 75w17 5:01:08
Stockton 7 173 42N19'03 79w21'22 5:17:25
Stockwell 33 13 42N52'29 75w23'22 5:01:33
Stokes 33 226 43N18 75w31 5:02:04
Stokes Corner 33 211 43N18'13 75w28'25 5:01:54
Stone Arabia 29 62 42N57'13 74w33'32 4:58:14
Stone Church 19 110 43N02'56 77w57'47 5:11:51
Stone Church Corner 50 14 42N57'20 76w52'58 5:07:32
Stonedam 2 226 41N59 77w52 5:11:28
Stone Gate 36 226 41N21 74w11 4:56:44
Stone Mills 23 226 44N06'52 75w58'27 5:03:54
Stone Ridge 29 174 42N55'16 74w25'41 4:57:43
Stone Ridge 56 11 41N51'11 74w08'22 4:56:33
Stony Brook 52 11 40N55'32 73w08'29 4:52:34
Stony Creek 23 65 43N49 76w14 5:04:56
Stony Creek 57 40 43N25'27 73w55'49 4:55:43
Stony Ford 36 7 41N27'34 74w18'19 4:57:13
Stony Hollow 56 11 41N58'19 74w04'49 4:56:19
Stony Point 42 11 42N33'04 73w44'50 4:54:59
Stony Point 44 6 41N13'46 73w59'15 4:55:57
Stoodley Corners 47 1 42N52'08 73w56'01 4:55:44
Stormville 14 17 41N34'13 73w44'45 4:54:59
Stottville 11 11 42N17'10 73w44'21 4:54:57
Stow 7 226 42N09'24 79w24'06 5:17:36
Stowersville 16 56 44N17'12 73w31'18 4:54:05
Straits Corners 54 205 42N08'59 76w22'52 5:05:31
Stratford 18 226 43N10'47 74w41'50 4:58:47
Strathmore 30 11 40N47'31 73w40'40 4:54:43
Stratton 55 226 42N20'49 76w32'29 5:06:10
Streeters Corners 32 226 43N12'08 78w49'33 5:15:18
Street Road 16 226 43N52'49 73w26'59 4:53:48
Stroughs Crossing 23 226 44N11'39 75w51'46 5:03:27
Strykersville 61 226 42N42'18 78w26'55 5:13:48
Sturges Corner 13 13 42N26'56 74w45'24 4:59:02
Stuyvesant 11 66 42N23'25 73w46'55 4:55:08
Stuyvesant 24 1 40N40'46 73w55'54 4:55:44
Stuyvesant Falls 11 11 42N21'19 73w43'53 4:54:56
Sucker Brook 61 206 42N44'48 78w02'04 5:12:08
Suffern 44 7 41N06'53 74w09'00 4:56:36
Suffern Park 44 4 41N06'37 74w07'19 4:56:29
Suffolk Plaza 52 11 40N52 74w49 4:59:16
Sugarbush 17 113 44N32'30 73w58'13 4:55:53
Sugar Loaf 36 226 41N19'15 74w17'09 4:57:09
Sugartown 5 226 42N14'16 78w35'41 5:14:23
Suicide Corners 19 142 42N54'18 78w06'14 5:12:25
Sullivan 27 226 43N03'16 75w50'50 5:03:23
Sullivanville 8 226 42N12'36 76w46'14 5:07:05
Sulphur Springs 23 45 43N55'32 76w01'47 5:04:07
Summerdale 7 225 42N12'50 79w34'14 5:18:17
Summer Hill 6 13 42N38'20 76w19'34 5:05:18
Summerville 28 185 43N15'23 77w36'05 5:10:24
Summit 48 13 42N34'46 74w35'19 4:58:21
Summit Crossing 39 226 42N40'54 75w01'27 5:00:06
Summit Hill 4 151 42N03'32 75w54'59 5:03:40
Summit Park 44 4 41N09'23 74w02'38 4:56:11
Summit Park Mall 32 199 43N06 78w58 5:15:52
Summitville 53 11 41N37'17 74w27'04 4:57:48
Sun 17 141 44N57'10 74w11'04 4:56:44
Sundown 56 226 41N53'16 74w27'38 4:57:51
Sun Haven 60 1 40N55'26 73w46'14 4:55:05
Sunmount 17 221 44N14 74w28 4:57:52

Sunny Brae 60 7 40N55'51 73W49'27 4:55:18
Sunnybrook 40 6 41N23'06 73W51'39 4:55:27
Sunny Shores 26 226 42N45'43 77W42'44 5:10:51
Sunnyside 7 187 42N07'05 79W18'08 5:17:13
Sunnyside 11 11 42N22'40 73W43'51 4:54:55
Sunnyside 41 1 40N44'23 73W56'09 4:55:45
Sunnyside 43 1 40N36'58 74W06'15 4:56:25
Sunrise Terrace 4 151 42N06 75W54 5:03:36
Sunset 24 1 40N38 74W01 4:56:04
Sunset Bay 7 216 42N33'47 79W08'01 5:16:32
Sunset Beach 32 226 43N18'55 78W50'36 5:15:22
Sunset Beach 37 146 43N22'16 78W16'21 5:13:05
Sunset Manor 33 222 43N07 75W18 5:01:12
Sunset View 59 226 43N14'40 76W56'30 5:07:46
Sunside 20 226 42N20'25 74W04'44 4:56:19
SUNY 1 1 42N40 73W48 4:55:12
Surprise 20 226 42N23'33 73W57'01 4:55:48
Suttons Corner 38 93 43N19'27 76W17'17 5:05:09
Svahn Manor 44 4 41N08 73W56 4:55:44
Swain 2 20 42N29 77W51 5:11:24
Swancott Mill 25 77 43N27'44 75W36'12 5:02:25
Swan Lake 53 189 41N45'02 74W46'42 4:59:07
Swartoutville 14 6 41N33'48 73W50'58 4:55:24
Swartwood 8 226 42N13'28 76W36'36 5:06:26
Swastika 10 86 44N30'47 73W45'40 4:55:03
Swazey Acres 46 11 42N48 73W41 4:54:44
Sweden 28 226 43N11 77W56 5:11:44
Sweden Center 28 226 43N10'42 77W56'43 5:11:47
Sweet Meadows 56 1 41N59'58 74W03'00 4:56:12
Sweets 9 226 42N43'24 75W18'18 5:01:13
Sweets Crossing 18 226 43N11'17 74W11'57 4:56:48
Sweets Crossing 34 13 43N01'20 76W21'48 5:05:27
Swenson Drive 14 6 41N36 73W53 4:55:32
Sweyze 52 11 40N55'04 72W43'17 4:50:53
Swift Corner 34 16 42N51'59 76W01'44 5:04:07
Swifts Mills 15 145 43N03'35 78W31'07 5:14:04
Swin 2 226 42N28'40 77W51'13 5:11:25
Swormville 15 11 43N02'18 78W41'51 5:14:47
Sycaway 42 220 42N44'31 73W39'11 4:54:37
Sylva 56 11 41N37'56 74W06'20 4:56:25
Sylvan Beach 33 226 43N11'47 75W43'51 5:02:55
Sylvan Beach 51 181 42N27'53 77W06'31 5:08:26
Sylvan Lake 14 226 41N36'27 73W44'06 4:54:56
Syosset 30 7 40N49'34 73W30'09 4:54:01
Syracuse 34 41 43N02'53 76W08'52 5:04:35
Tabasco 56 72 41N50'51 74W18'04 4:57:12
Taberg 33 226 43N18'13 75W37'02 5:02:28
Tabor Corners 26 226 42N34 77W36 5:10:24
Taborton 42 226 42N38'46 73W29'08 4:53:57
Tacoma 13 226 42N14'07 75W16'49 5:01:07
Taconic Lake 42 11 42N45 73W21 4:53:24
Taghkanic 11 226 42N08'32 73W40'40 4:54:43
Tahawus 16 226 44N03'02 74W03'05 4:56:12
Talcottville 25 226 43N32'00 75W21'56 5:01:28
Talcville 45 226 44N18'35 75W18'23 5:01:14
Tallette 9 16 42N44'24 75W20'01 5:01:20
Tallman 44 4 41N06'40 74W06'01 4:56:24
Tamarack 42 11 42N46'19 73W32'38 4:54:11
Tannersville 20 23 42N11'44 74W08'03 4:56:32
Tappan 44 16 41N01'19 73W56'52 4:55:47
Tarrytown 1 11 42N33'32 73W57'05 4:55:48
Tarrytown 60 6 41N04'34 73W51'33 4:55:26
Tarrytown Heights 60 6 41N04 73W51 4:55:24
Taughannock Falls 55 13 42N31'55 76W36'44 5:06:27
Taunton 34 12 43N01'50 76W12'33 5:04:50
Taylor 12 226 42N34'01 75W53'37 5:03:34
Taylor 26 4 42N56'13 77W52'51 5:11:31
Taylor Center 12 226 42N36'50 75W55'31 5:03:42
Taylor Hollow 15 42 42N31'10 78W55'45 5:15:43
Taylors Corner 45 16 44N46'07 74W37'45 4:58:31
Taylor Settlement 23 143 43N46'58 76W04'30 5:04:18
Taylorshire 15 170 42N44'43 78W39'22 5:14:37
Taylortown 39 203 42N45'50 74W58'55 4:59:56
Taylor Valley 12 13 42N35'35 75W57'10 5:03:49
Teall Beach 50 41 42N48'53 76W56'19 5:07:45
Teboville 17 193 44N48'24 74W14'41 4:56:59
Teed Corners 26 13 42N47'55 77W53'48 5:11:35
Tenantville 46 7 43N17'04 74W06'57 4:56:28
Ten Mile River 53 226 41N36 75W04 5:00:16
Tennanah 53 80 41N56 74W55 4:59:40
Tennanah Lake 53 80 41N53'42 74W58'37 4:59:54
Terminal 43 1 40N38 74W06 4:56:24
Terpening Corners 55 13 42N32'18 76W29'35 5:05:58
Terrace Heights 41 1 40N43'17 73W46'11 4:55:05
Terrace Park 45 201 44N35'53 75W38'07 5:02:32
Terrys Corners 32 121 43N10'27 78W36'02 5:14:24
Terryville 52 11 40N54'32 73W03'56 4:52:16
Texaco Town 19 142 42N54'24 78W03'53 5:12:16
Texas 25 226 43N59'06 75W30'19 5:02:01
Texas 38 14 43N30'46 76W15'05 5:05:00
Texas Valley 12 13 42N29'10 75W58'24 5:03:54
Thayer Corners 17 141 44N55'18 74W08'28 4:56:34
The Bridges 37 105 43N20 78W08 5:12:32
The Cape 56 48 41N44'51 74W26'01 4:57:44
The Elms 38 226 43N39'50 76W10'22 5:04:41
The Forge 17 188 44N56 74W05 4:56:20
The Forks 5 226 42N34 78W29 5:13:56
The Glen 57 63 43N35 73W52 4:55:28
The Landing 52 6 40N51'41 73W11'50 4:52:47
The Narrows 5 226 42N20'11 78W29'14 5:13:57
Thendara 22 59 43N42'00 75W00'08 5:00:01
The Plains 58 11 43N03'10 73W21'32 4:53:26
Theresa 23 226 44N12'55 75W47'51 5:03:11
The Springs 52 11 40N57 72W11 4:48:44
The Terrace 30 11 40N50 73W42 4:54:48
The Vly 56 11 41N51 74W09 4:56:36
Thiells 44 4 41N12'38 74W01'05 4:56:04
Thomas Settlement 23 143 43N48'50 76W04'30 5:04:18
Thomaston 30 1 40N47'10 73W42'51 4:54:51
Thomasville 10 226 44N28'29 73W36'52 4:54:27
Thompson 50 4 43N00'11 76W57'51 5:07:51
Thompson 53 197 41N39 74W40 4:58:40
Thompson Ridge 36 11 41N34'05 74W19'49 4:57:19
Thompsons Corner 33 211 43N17'18 75W46'06 5:03:04
Thompsons Crossing 61 206 42N46'49 78W08'58 5:12:36
Thompsons Lake 1 40 42N38'34 74W02'40 4:56:11
Thompsonville 53 74 41N40'05 74W37'32 4:58:30
Thomson 58 226 43N07'33 73W35'00 4:54:20
Thorn Hill 34 13 42N53'52 76W20'30 5:05:22
Thornton 7 226 42N15'50 79W09'27 5:16:38
Thornton Grove 34 13 42N53'02 76W24'32 5:05:38
Thornton Heights 34 13 42N52'48 76W24'31 5:05:38
Thorntons Corner 59 108 43N10'29 77W00'41 5:08:03
Thornwood 60 7 41N07'24 73W46'46 4:55:07
Thousand Island Park 23 163 44N17'13 76W01'41 5:04:07
Three Mile Bay 23 226 44N04'53 76W11'55 5:04:48
Three Rivers 34 13 43N12'03 76W16'42 5:05:07
Throgs Neck 3 1 40N49'21 73W49'12 4:55:17
Throop 6 24 42N58'33 76W34'16 5:06:17
Throopsville 6 13 42N58'23 76W36'08 5:06:25
Thurman 56 11 41N38 73W57 4:55:48
Thurman 57 226 43N32'00 73W54'59 4:55:40
Thurston 51 226 42N13'22 77W15'52 5:09:03
Thurston Road 28 209 43N08 77W39 5:10:36
Tiana 52 11 40N52'19 72W32'31 4:50:10
Tiana Shores 52 11 40N50 72W35 4:50:20
Ticonderoga 16 6 43N50'55 73W25'26 4:53:42
Tillson 56 11 41N49'44 74W04'08 4:56:17
Tilly Foster 40 85 41N24'59 73W38'59 4:54:36
Times Plaza 24 1 40N41 73W59 4:55:56
Times Square 31 1 40N46 73W59 4:55:56
Timothy Heights 14 11 41N44'21 73W50'19 4:55:21
Tinker Tavern Corner 38 226 43N30'24 76W07'42 5:04:31
Tinkertown 2 226 42N16'04 77W46'05 5:11:04
Tioga 54 226 42N06 76W21 5:05:24
Tioga Center 54 226 42N03'22 76W20'54 5:05:24
Tioga Terrace 54 226 42N04 76W10 5:04:40
Tiona 4 226 42N13 76W11 5:04:44
Tiplady 58 213 43N15'07 73W17'03 4:53:08
Tip Top 22 27 42N13'23 77W47'24 5:11:10
Titusville 14 1 41N40'03 73W52'28 4:55:30
Tivoli 14 5 42N03'30 73W54'35 4:55:38
Toad Harbor 38 14 43N14'29 76W04'31 5:04:18
Toddsville 39 13 42N41'16 74W57'31 4:59:50
Toddville 60 6 41N17'37 73W53'20 4:55:33
Todt Hill 43 1 40N38 74W06 4:56:24
Toggletown 26 226 42N55'07 77W48'47 5:11:15
Toll Corner 39 226 42N28'49 75W16'45 5:01:07
Toll Gate Corner 5 226 42N01'33 78W20'20 5:13:21
Toll Gate Corners 6 13 42N41'44 76W25'14 5:05:41
Tomantown 18 226 43N12'02 74W17'44 4:57:11
Tomhannock 42 11 42N52'08 73W32'39 4:54:11
Tomkins Cove 44 1 41N15'25 73W59'02 4:55:56
Tomlinson Corners 28 13 42N57'53 77W30'10 5:10:01
Tompkins 13 226 42N08 75W16 5:01:04
Tompkins Corners 8 226 42N12'12 76W53'17 5:07:33
Tompkins Corners 40 6 41N23'56 73W48'09 4:55:13
Tompkins Corners 60 1 41N11'28 73W46'59 4:55:08
Tompkins Square 31 1 40N44 73W59 4:55:56
Tompkinsville 43 1 40N38'11 74W05'09 4:56:21
Toms Landing 37 146 43N20'27 78W13'26 5:12:54
Tonawanda 15 1 43N01'13 78W52'50 5:15:31
Tonawanda Indian Reservation 19 226 43N04 78W26 5:13:44
Tonawanda Junction 15 1 42N58 78W51 5:15:24
Tonetta Lake Heights 40 226 41N26 73W36 4:54:24
Topps Henrietta Plaza 28 20 43N05 77W38 5:10:32
Torrey 62 12 42N41 76W59 5:07:56
Tottenville 43 11 40N30'38 74W14'35 4:56:58
Towers Corners 32 226 43N15'29 79W00'34 5:16:02
Towerville 7 67 42N12'31 79W17'44 5:17:11
Towerville Corners 7 187 42N06 79W16 5:17:04
Towlesville 51 14 42N20'01 77W27'22 5:09:49
Towners 40 7 41N28'47 73W36'38 4:54:27
Town Line 15 38 42N53'26 78W34'41 5:14:19
Town Line Station 15 38 42N54'05 78W34'42 5:14:19
Town Pump 28 14 43N09'06 77W51'20 5:11:25
Townsend 49 14 42N20'55 76W57'24 5:07:50
Townsendville 50 226 42N34'22 76W46'57 5:07:08
Toziers Corner 61 226 42N44'15 78W21'45 5:13:27
Tracy Creek 4 13 42N01'10 76W04'49 5:04:19
Trainsmeadow 41 1 40N46 73W53 4:55:32
Transitown 15 7 42N59 78W45 5:15:00
Travers Corners 46 226 43N09'24 73W44'02 4:54:56
Travis 43 1 40N35'35 74W11'18 4:56:45
Treadwell 13 226 42N20'32 75W03'06 5:00:12
Tremont 3 1 40N50'58 73W54'22 4:55:37
Trenton 33 14 43N15 75W12 5:00:48
Trenton Assembly Park 33 14 43N17 75W11 5:00:44
Trenton Falls 33 14 43N16'17 75W09'38 5:00:39
Tressmar 28 209 43N07'36 77W41'25 5:10:46
Triangle 4 226 42N20'23 75W52'50 5:03:31
Triangle Lake 1 226 42N36 74W20 4:57:20
Tribes Hill 29 1 42N57'19 74W17'08 4:57:09
Triborough 31 1 40N48 73W57 4:55:48
Tripoli 12 226 42N44'20 75W57'46 5:03:51
Tripoli 58 123 43N23'27 73W34'48 4:54:19
Tristates 36 1 41N21'38 74W40'56 4:58:44
Trombley Landing 17 226 44N38'12 74W22'34 4:57:30
Troupsburg 51 226 42N02'37 77W32'47 5:10:11
Troutburg 28 105 43N21'52 77W59'25 5:11:58
Trout Creek 13 226 42N12'13 75W16'47 5:01:07
Trout River 17 193 44N59'29 74W18'31 4:57:14
Troy 42 220 42N43'42 73W41'32 4:54:46
Trudeau 16 81 44N20'32 74W07'18 4:56:29
Truesdale Lake 60 16 41N17 73W33 4:54:12
Trumansburg 55 14 42N32'32 76W39'59 5:06:40
Trumbulls Corners 55 226 42N23'01 76W37'58 5:06:32
Truthville 58 42 43N27'01 73W19'31 4:53:18
Truxton 12 16 42N42'43 76W01'44 5:04:07
Tryons Corners 26 226 42N49'02 77W56'31 5:11:46
Tuckahoe 52 11 40N53'56 72W24'41 4:49:39
Tuckahoe 60 6 40N57'01 73W49'40 4:55:19
Tucker Heights 46 11 42N54'36 73W56'15 4:55:45
Tuckers Corner 56 11 41N40'03 74W01'46 4:56:07
Tucker Terrace 45 195 44N56'55 74W58'25 4:59:54
Tudor 31 1 40N45 73W58 4:55:52
Tully 34 91 42N47'53 76W06'35 5:04:26
Tully Center 34 91 42N47'56 76W07'21 5:04:29
Tully Lake Park 34 91 42N47'03 76W08'11 5:04:33
Tully Valley 34 91 42N48 76W06 5:04:24
Tunnel 4 127 42N12'58 75W43'37 5:02:54
Tupper Lake 17 221 44N14 74W28 4:57:52
Turin 25 156 43N37'38 75W24'42 5:01:39
Turnbull Corner 45 226 44N46'29 75W08'47 5:00:35
Turnwood 56 75 42N01'27 74W42'34 4:58:50
Tuscan 39 13 42N35'12 74W46'10 4:59:05
Tuscarora 26 13 42N37'50 77W52'12 5:11:29
Tuscarora 51 226 42N03 77W15 5:09:00
Tuscarora Indian Reservation 32 121 43N10 78W57 5:15:48
Tusten 53 226 41N33'19 75W01'10 5:00:05
Tuthill 56 122 41N41'15 74W09'46 4:56:39
Tuxedo 36 6 41N13 74W11 4:56:44
Tuxedo Park 26 226 42N49'11 77W41'49 5:10:47
Tuxedo Park 36 6 41N11'36 74W11'05 4:56:44
Twelve Corners 28 13 43N07'37 77W33'57 5:10:16
Twilight Park 20 23 42N11'21 74W05'15 4:56:21
Twin Lakes Village 60 16 41N17'57 73W34'13 4:54:17
Twin Orchards 4 13 42N05'50 76W01'36 5:04:06
Two Brooks 17 113 44N34'46 73W58'16 4:55:53
Tylers Corner 38 226 43N30'49 76W09'47 5:04:39
Tylersville 23 226 43N54'03 75W47'59 5:03:12
Tylertown 53 226 41N37'36 74W56'57 4:59:48
Tyner 9 226 42N25'49 75W39'57 5:02:40
Tyre 50 19 42N59'28 76W48'09 5:07:13
Tyrone 49 226 42N24'29 77W03'31 5:08:14
Ulster 56 7 41N59 73W59 4:55:56
Ulster Heights 56 48 41N46'25 74W29'03 4:57:56
Ulster Landing 56 215 41N59'50 73W56'53 4:55:48

Ulster Park 56 11 41N51'21 73W58'39 4:55:55
Ulsterville 56 226 41N36'36 74W20'10 4:57:21
Ulysses 55 13 42N31 76W37 5:06:28
Unadilla 39 13 42N19'31 75W18'46 5:01:15
Unadilla Center 39 13 42N24'15 75W18'33 5:01:14
Unadilla Forks 39 13 42N50'30 75W14'26 5:00:58
Undercliff 16 1 44N20'21 73W58'11 4:55:53
Underwood 16 50 44N05'16 73W40'36 4:54:42
Underwood Club 16 50 44N10 73W37 4:54:28
Underwood Corner 5 20 42N08'55 78W54'14 5:15:37
Uneeda Beach 32 226 43N17'41 78W55'15 5:15:41
Union 4 13 42N07 76W03 5:04:12
Union 27 226 42N52'04 75W53'15 5:03:33
Union Center 4 13 42N09'05 76W04'10 5:04:17
Union Center 56 11 41N51'04 73W59'51 4:55:59
Union Corners 19 70 42N53'42 77W58'47 5:11:55
Union Corners 26 13 42N37'39 77W50'29 5:11:22
Uniondale 30 11 40N42'01 73W35'36 4:54:22
Union Falls 10 44 44N30'26 73W55'01 4:55:40
Union Hill 59 4 43N13'22 77W22'19 5:09:29
Union Mills 18 226 43N05'23 74W08'02 4:56:32
Unionport 3 1 40N49'38 73W51'02 4:55:24
Union Settlement 38 14 43N19'13 76W02'37 5:04:10
Union Springs 6 13 42N50'23 76W41'37 5:06:46
Union Vale 14 226 41N41 73W42 4:54:48
Union Valley 9 226 42N19'27 75W32'32 5:02:10
Union Valley 12 226 42N38'01 75W53'03 5:03:32
Unionville 1 11 42N36'04 73W53'18 4:55:33
Unionville 35 13 42N57'06 77W02'16 5:08:09
Unionville 36 11 41N18'07 74W33'43 4:58:15
Unionville 45 207 44N42'46 74W59'50 4:59:59
Unionville 51 14 42N18'11 77W21'25 5:09:26
Unionville 53 226 41N51'25 74W33'49 4:58:15
United Nations Plaza 31 1 40N45 73W58 4:55:52
United States Public Health 43 1 40N37 74W06 4:56:24
University 34 13 43N02 76W07 5:04:28
University Gardens 30 1 40N46'38 73W43'23 4:54:54
University Heights 3 1 40N51'36 73W54'35 4:55:38
Upper Barbourville 13 167 42N09'36 75W21'21 5:01:25
Upper Beechwood 53 226 41N46'37 74W59'24 4:59:58
Upper Benson 21 7 43N14'57 74W20'12 4:57:21
Upper Brookville 30 11 40N50'19 73W33'56 4:54:16
Upper Fairfield 54 226 42N16'09 76W17'27 5:05:10
Upper Grand View 44 4 41N05 73W56 4:55:44
Upper Hollowville 11 11 42N12'24 73W39'53 4:54:40
Upper Jay 16 226 44N20'11 73W46'34 4:55:06
Upper Lisle 4 226 42N23'46 75W57'27 5:03:50
Upper Mongaup 53 25 41N27'27 74W45'55 4:59:04
Upper Nyack 44 1 41N06'25 73W55'14 4:55:41
Upper Red Hook 14 7 42N01'47 73W50'42 4:55:23
Upper Saint Regis 17 176 44N23'52 74W16'12 4:57:05
Upper Town Landing 23 163 44N15'42 76W06'32 5:04:26
Upper Union 47 6 42N47 73W53 4:55:32
Upperville 9 15 42N42'01 75W36'56 5:02:28
Upson Corners 38 182 43N21'42 76W13'43 5:04:55
Upton 52 11 40N52'10 72W53'14 4:51:33
Upton Lake 14 226 41N50 73W46 4:55:04
Uptonville 28 209 43N12'11 77W38'42 5:10:35
Uptown 56 11 41N57 74W00 4:56:00
Urbana 51 181 42N27'16 77W10'53 5:08:44
Ushers 46 11 42N54'29 73W46'27 4:55:06
Utica 33 222 43N06'03 75W13'59 5:00:56
Utopia 41 1 40N43'38 73W47'13 4:55:09
Vail Mills 18 226 43N03'00 74W13'06 4:56:52
Vails Gate 36 165 41N27'15 74W03'29 4:56:14
Vails Gate Junction 36 165 41N27'36 74W03'43 4:56:15
Vail's Grove 40 226 41N26 73W36 4:54:24
Valatie 11 11 42N24'48 73W40'25 4:54:42
Valatie Colony 11 11 42N26'09 73W40'21 4:54:41
Valcour 10 86 44N36'18 73W26'25 4:53:46
Valentines Beach 34 14 43N11'38 76W02'07 5:04:08
Valhalla 60 7 41N04'29 73W46'32 4:55:06
Valley Brook 29 62 42N56'44 74W39'34 4:58:38
Valley Cottage 44 16 41N07'05 73W57'21 4:55:49
Valley Falls 42 11 42N54'12 73W33'47 4:54:15
Valley Mills 27 13 43N00'43 75W35'24 5:02:22
Valley Pond Estates 60 1 41N18'32 73W43'24 4:54:54
Valley Stream 30 7 40N39'51 73W42'32 4:54:50
Valley View 62 226 42N44'21 77W15'22 5:09:01
Vallonia Springs 4 17 42N10'47 75W32'14 5:02:09
Valois 49 14 42N32'05 76W52'39 5:07:31
Van Allen Park 42 1 42N39'18 73W42'32 4:54:50
Van Brunt 24 1 40N40 73W59 4:55:56
Van Buren 34 226 43N06'49 76W18'09 5:05:13
Van Buren Bay 7 134 42N27'01 79W24'24 5:17:38
Van Buren Point 7 160 42N26'56 79W25'07 5:17:40
Van Burenville 36 1 41N29'55 74W25'41 4:57:43
Van Cortlandtville 60 6 41N18'53 73W54'15 4:55:37
Van Cott 3 1 40N53 73W52 4:55:28
Vandalia 5 22 42N05'46 78W34'48 5:14:19
Van Del 15 11 42N47 78W45 5:15:00
Vanderveer Station 24 1 40N38 73W57 4:55:48
Van Deusenville 29 162 42N50'35 74W41'12 4:58:45
Van Dorn Corner 55 186 42N27'08 76W35'29 5:06:22
Van Etten 8 226 42N11'55 76W33'10 5:06:13
Van Etten Junction 8 226 42N11'19 76W33'33 5:06:14
Van Fleet 51 226 41N59 77W19 5:09:16
Van Hornesville 22 226 42N53'42 74W49'41 4:59:19
Van Keuren 36 20 41N35'25 74W18'36 4:57:14
Van Keurens 14 1 41N38'43 73W56'39 4:55:47
Van Nest 3 1 40N50'54 73W51'51 4:55:27
Van Vleet 51 13 42N02'19 77W17'03 5:09:08
Varick 50 226 42N47 77W19 5:09:16
Varna 55 186 42N27'18 76W26'18 5:05:45
Varysburg 61 226 42N45'48 78W18'36 5:13:14
Vaughns Corners 58 123 43N22'19 73W33'52 4:54:15
Vaughs Corners 58 1 43N18 73W35 4:54:20
Vega 13 42 42N15'19 74W31'49 4:58:07
Venice 6 13 42N43 76W33 5:06:12
Venice Center 6 13 42N44'21 76W33'25 5:06:14
Verbank 14 226 41N43'43 73W42'39 4:54:51
Verbank Village 14 226 41N43'42 73W43'44 4:54:55
Verdoy 1 1 42N45'52 73W48'16 4:55:13
Vermillion 38 226 43N25'01 76W16'41 5:05:07
Vermontville 17 226 44N27'06 74W03'58 4:56:16
Vernal 61 148 42N52 78W17 5:13:08
Vernon 33 13 43N04'46 75W32'23 5:02:10
Vernon Center 33 13 43N03'08 75W30'07 5:02:00
Vernon Park 60 1 40N54'35 73W49'07 4:55:16
Vernon Valley 52 11 40N53'58 73W19'46 4:53:19
Verona 33 13 43N08'17 75W34'16 5:02:17
Verona Beach 33 226 43N11'27 75W43'46 5:02:55
Verona Mills 33 211 43N11'50 75W33'33 5:02:14
Verona Station 33 13 43N08'01 75W35'13 5:02:21
Verplanck 60 7 41N15'10 73W57'37 4:55:50
Versailles 5 42 42N31'08 78W59'46 5:15:59
Vesper 34 91 42N49'03 76W10'54 5:04:44
Vestal 4 13 42N05'06 76W03'15 5:04:13
Vestal Corner 4 13 42N01'58 76W00'55 5:04:04
Vestal Gardens 4 13 42N04 76W01 5:04:04
Veteran 8 226 42N14 76W48 5:07:12
Veteran 56 215 42N04'49 73W59'41 4:55:59
Veterans Administration Faci 19 142 43N00 78W11 5:12:44
Veterans Administration Hosp 15 7 42N56 78W48 5:15:12
Veterans Hospital 34 13 43N02 76W07 5:04:28
Victor 35 19 42N58'57 77W24'33 5:09:38
Victoria 7 226 42N09'51 79W25'39 5:17:43
Victory 6 226 43N11'50 76W39'17 5:06:37
Victory Heights 8 13 42N07 76W49 5:07:16
Victory Mills 46 226 43N05'16 73W35'40 4:54:23
Victory Park 60 1 40N57'09 73W47'40 4:55:11
Vienna 33 226 43N14'22 75W42'10 5:02:49
Viewmonte 11 11 42N05'55 73W52'28 4:55:30
Village 31 1 40N44 74W00 4:56:00
Village of the Branch 52 11 40N51'22 73W11'16 4:52:45
Villenova 7 226 42N23 79W07 5:16:28
Vincent 35 14 42N50'07 77W24'05 5:09:36
Vine Valley 62 226 42N43'25 77W19'30 5:09:18
Vineyard 7 160 42N23'34 79W27'46 5:17:51
Vintonton 48 13 42N30'38 74W28'29 4:57:54
Viola 44 4 41N08'11 74W04'58 4:56:20
Virgil 12 13 42N30'38 76W11'41 5:04:47
Vischer Ferry 46 4 42N47'50 73W49'44 4:55:19
Vista 60 16 41N12'08 73W30'38 4:54:03
Vly, The 56 11 41N53'11 74W12'17 4:56:49
Voak 62 14 42N43'53 77W08'00 5:08:32
Vollentine 5 20 42N06'17 79W00'32 5:16:02
Volney 38 226 43N20'34 76W21'29 5:05:26
Volusia 7 225 42N15'04 79W35'58 5:18:24
Voorheesville 1 11 42N39'14 73W55'45 4:55:43
Vorea 38 14 43N36'03 75W58'21 5:03:53
Vosburg 2 226 42N04'17 78W04'53 5:12:20
Vukote 7 226 42N06'22 79W21'36 5:17:26
Waccabuc 60 16 41N17'26 73W35'45 4:54:23
Waddington 45 226 44N51'52 75W12'16 5:00:49
Wadhams 16 58 44N13'47 73W27'39 4:53:51
Wadhams Park 45 201 44N42 75W29 5:01:56
Wading River 52 11 40N57'01 72W50'35 4:51:22
Wading River Landing 52 11 40N58'00 72W51'15 4:51:25
Wadsworth 26 13 42N49'13 77W53'49 5:11:35
Wadsworth Cove 26 226 42N47'25 77W43'21 5:10:53
Wagon Wheel Landing 16 226 44N02'51 73W50'37 4:55:22
Wagstaff Corner 45 105 44N45'42 74W42'52 4:58:51
Wahmeda 7 158 42N12'59 79W28'42 5:17:55
Wainscott 52 11 40N56'12 72W14'36 4:48:58
Waits 54 205 42N06 76W16 5:05:04
Wakefield 3 1 40N53'52 73W51'10 4:55:25
Walden 15 7 42N54'42 78W47'05 5:15:08
Walden 36 6 41N33'40 74W11'20 4:56:45
Walden Cliffs 15 153 42N43'32 78W57'06 5:15:48
Wales 15 22 42N44 78W31 5:14:04
Wales Center 15 22 42N46'06 78W31'49 5:14:07
Wales Hollow 15 22 42N44'33 78W29'19 5:13:57
Walesville 33 222 43N06'55 75W21'57 5:01:28
Walker 28 13 43N17'53 77W51'39 5:11:27
Walker 38 15 43N29'12 76W26'59 5:05:48
Walkers 61 206 42N43 78W00 5:12:00
Walkers Corners 27 226 43N07'16 75W46'25 5:03:06
Walker Valley 56 6 41N38'01 74W22'42 4:57:31
Walkleys Landing 26 226 42N43'51 77W42'23 5:10:50
Wallace 51 14 42N26'28 77W27'33 5:09:50
Wallington 59 108 43N13'18 77W00'46 5:08:03
Wallins Corners 29 226 42N58'19 74W10'14 4:56:41
Wallkill 56 11 41N36'20 74W11'04 4:56:44
Wallkill Camp 56 122 41N42'58 74W09'45 4:56:39
Walloomsac 42 11 42N55'27 73W19'27 4:53:18
Wall Street 31 1 40N42 74W01 4:56:04
Walmore 32 1 43N07'17 78W55'53 5:15:44
Walton 13 226 42N10'10 75W07'47 5:00:31
Walton Lake 36 226 41N21 74W11 4:56:44
Walton Park 36 226 41N18'35 74W13'46 4:56:55
Walworth 59 226 43N08'21 77W16'21 5:09:05
Wampsville 27 13 43N04'31 75W42'26 5:02:50
Wanakah 15 153 42N44'46 78W54'12 5:15:37
Wanakena 45 226 44N08'02 74W55'17 4:59:41
Wango 7 226 42N25'09 79W05'47 5:16:23
Wantagh 30 6 40N41'01 73W30'38 4:54:03
Wappinger 14 6 41N35 73W54 4:55:36
Wappingers Falls 14 6 41N35'47 73W54'41 4:55:39
Wappingers Lake 14 6 41N37 73W54 4:55:36
Ward 2 226 42N13 77W54 5:11:36
Wardwell 23 143 43N46'03 76W04'07 5:04:16
Wardwell Settlement 23 143 43N48 76W01 5:04:04
Warners 34 41 43N05'07 76W19'46 5:05:19
Warnerville 48 13 42N39'37 74W30'28 4:58:02
Warren 22 226 42N50'50 74W55'17 4:59:41
Warren 23 226 44N08'59 76W12'07 5:04:48
Warrensburg 57 223 43N29'48 73W46'36 4:55:06
Warrens Corners 32 226 43N12'58 78W45'18 5:15:01
Warsaw 61 24 42N44'24 78W07'59 5:12:32
Warwick 36 6 41N15'23 74W21'37 4:57:26
Washington 14 226 41N47 73W41 4:54:44
Washington Bridge 31 1 40N51 73W56 4:55:44
Washington Heights 31 1 40N51'00 73W56'09 4:55:45
Washington Heights 36 1 41N28'12 74W24'58 4:57:40
Washington Hollow 14 226 41N46'55 73W45'30 4:55:02
Washington Lake 36 1 41N31 74W03 4:56:12
Washington Mills 33 11 43N03'00 75W16'24 5:01:06
Washingtonville 36 226 41N25'40 74W09'59 4:56:40
Wassaic 14 11 41N48'14 73W33'33 4:54:14
Waterboro 7 20 42N10'19 79W04'12 5:16:17
Waterburg 55 13 42N30'20 76W40'35 5:06:42
Waterford 46 11 42N47'33 73W40'54 4:54:44
Water Island 52 11 40N40'32 73W01'47 4:52:07
Waterloo 50 14 42N54'17 76W51'47 5:07:27
Waterloo Mills 36 11 41N19'21 74W34'39 4:58:19
Waterman Corner 7 158 42N13'40 79W23'54 5:17:36
Water Mill (Watermill Sta) 52 11 40N54'21 72W21'45 4:49:27
Waterport 37 146 43N19'01 78W15'06 5:13:00
Waterport Station 37 146 43N19'40 78W14'47 5:12:59
Waterside Park 52 11 40N54 73W20 4:53:20
Watertown 23 45 43N58'29 75W54'40 5:03:39
Watertown Center 23 45 43N56'33 75W54'58 5:03:40
Watertown Junction 23 45 43N59 75W56 5:03:44
Watervale 34 13 42N57'00 75W58'57 5:03:56
Water Valley 15 153 42N42'20 78W51'01 5:15:24
Waterville 23 226 43N44'44 75W55'21 5:03:41
Waterville 29 7 42N50'46 74W35'27 4:58:22
Waterville 33 13 42N55'52 75W22'49 5:01:31
Waterville 52 11 41N00'42 72W32'09 4:50:09
Watervliet 1 1 42N43'48 73W42'06 4:54:48
Watervliet Arsenal 1 1 42N43 73W44 4:54:56
Watkins Glen 49 14 42N22'50 76W52'25 5:07:30
Watson 25 156 43N46'33 75W26'11 5:01:45
Watsonville 48 226 42N35'05 74W23'24 4:57:34
Wattlesburg 7 226 42N13'37 79W41'20 5:18:45

Watts Flat 7 20 42N02'14 79w24'44 5:17:39
Watts Flats 7 20 42N06 79w23 5:17:32
Wautoma Beach 28
13 43N20'29 77w48'34 5:11:14
Wave Crest 41 1 40N35'58 73w45'51 4:55:03
Waverly 54 224 42N00'37 76w31'39 5:06:07
Waverly 60 1 40N57'21 73w48'49 4:55:15
Wawarsing 56 48 41N45'32 74w21'28 4:57:26
Wawayanda 36 7 41N24 74w27 4:57:48
Wawbeek 17 221 44N15'16 74w20'13 4:57:21
Wayland 51 35 42N34'04 77w35'24 5:10:22
Wayne 51 226 42N28'15 77w06'21 5:08:25
Wayne Center 59
99 43N09'03 76w57'33 5:07:50
Wayneport 59 13 43N04'22 77w21'41 5:09:27
Wayville 46 11 43N00'03 73w42'30 4:54:50
Weaver Corner 27
226 43N07'22 75w55'41 5:03:43
Webatuck 14 11 41N39'15 73w33'22 4:54:13
Webb 22 226 43N55 74w55 4:59:40
Webbs Crossing 51
102 42N21'59 77w40'57 5:10:44
Webbs Mills 8 13 42N01'25 76w52'54 5:07:32
Weber Corners 39
13 42N42'54 74w39'21 4:58:37
Webster 28 33 43N12'44 77w25'49 5:09:43
Webster Crossing 26
13 42N40'11 77w38'07 5:10:32
Websters Corners 15
11 42N46'54 78w44'46 5:14:59
Wedgewood 49 14 42N20'31 76w53'13 5:07:33
Weed Mines 11 11 42N04'16 73w32'05 4:54:08
Weedsport 6 24 43N02'55 76w33'47 5:06:15
Weekes Corner 6
13 42N39'58 76w35'04 5:06:20
Wegatchie 45 106 44N18'15 75w35'09 5:02:21
Welch Hill 25 156 43N38'10 75w27'39 5:01:51
Welcome 39 226 42N37'25 75w08'42 5:00:35
Wellington Corner 34
13 42N59'13 76w15'38 5:05:03
Wells 21 226 43N23'45 74w17'24 4:57:10
Wells Bridge 39
13 42N22 75w15 5:01:00
Wellsburg 8 13 42N00'58 76w43'38 5:06:55
Wells Corner 33
13 43N00'52 75w29'34 5:01:58
Wellsville 2 109 42N07'19 77w56'54 5:11:48
Wellsville 29 1 42N52'33 74w16'22 4:57:05
Wellwood 38 226 43N24'48 76w15'03 5:05:00
Weltonville 54
226 42N11'47 76w14'49 5:04:59
Wemple 1 11 42N34'27 73w46'34 4:55:06
Wende 15 38 42N56'03 78w32'49 5:14:11
Wendelville 32
226 43N04'16 78w46'15 5:15:05
Wesley 5 42 42N22'23 78w57'28 5:15:50
Wesley Chapel 44
4 41N08 74w06 4:56:24
West Alabama 19
112 43N07'35 78w27'29 5:13:50
West Albany 1 1 42N40'59 73w46'44 4:55:07
West Alden 15 38 42N53'30 78w31'25 5:14:06
West Allen 2 226 42N22'49 78w02'20 5:12:09
West Almond 2 71 42N17'58 77w53'00 5:11:32
West Amboy 38 182 43N23'04 75w59'09 5:03:57
West Amityville 30
6 40N41 73w26 4:53:44
West Athens 20 11 42N17'10 73w50'33 4:55:22
West Babylon 52 1 40N43'05 73w21'17 4:53:25
West Bainbridge 9
149 42N18'50 75w32'38 5:02:11
West Bangor 17 16 44N48'15 74w26'03 4:57:44
West Barre 37 146 43N09'10 78w15'14 5:13:01
West Batavia 19
142 42N58'47 78w17'59 5:13:12
West Bay Shore 52
1 40N42'31 73w16'54 4:53:08
West Beekmantown 10
86 44N46'16 73w33'18 4:54:13
West Bergen 19
110 43N03'58 78w00'18 5:12:01
West Berne 1 226 42N37'44 74w11'04 4:56:44
West Bethany 19
142 42N54'50 78w11'33 5:12:46
West Bloomfield 35
226 42N54'21 77w32'22 5:10:09
West Branch 33
226 43N22'19 75w28'57 5:01:56
West Brighton 28
209 43N07'17 77w37'12 5:10:29
West Brookfield 27
180 42N48'28 75w24'18 5:01:37
Westbrookville 36
21 41N29'55 74w33'32 4:58:14
West Burlington 39
226 42N42'27 75w11'17 5:00:45
Westbury 6 226 43N12'53 76w42'40 5:06:51
Westbury 30 7 40N45'20 73w35'17 4:54:21
Westbury South 30
11 40N45'08 73w33'44 4:54:15
West Bush 18 226 43N04'59 74w22'43 4:57:31
West Butler 59 33 43N10'43 76w48'30 5:07:14
West Cambridge 58
11 42N59'22 73w28'52 4:53:55
West Cameron 51
20 42N13'26 77w25'11 5:09:41
West Camp 56 11 42N07'23 73w56'07 4:55:44
West Canadice Corners 35
226 42N44'13 77w33'09 5:10:13
West Candor 54
154 42N13'13 76w25'05 5:05:40
West Carthage 23
156 43N58'27 75w36'56 5:02:28
West Caton 51 13 42N04'52 77w03'51 5:08:15
West Catskill 20
1 42N13 73w51 4:55:24
West Charlton 46
1 42N57'33 74w01'39 4:56:07
West Chazy 10 7 44N49'14 73w30'27 4:54:02
West Chenango 4
151 42N12'02 75w57'47 5:03:51
Westchester 3 1 40N50'50 73w51'19 4:55:25

Westchester Heights 3
1 40N51 73w51 4:55:24
West Chili 28 15 43N05'46 77w47'22 5:11:09
West Clarksville 2
226 42N07'41 78w14'36 5:12:58
West Colesville 4
151 42N08'36 75w44'57 5:03:00
West Conesville 48
226 42N22'40 74w25'22 4:57:41
West Copake 11 11 42N05'45 73w34'58 4:54:20
West Corners 4 13 42N06'38 76w04'19 5:04:17
West Corners 46
11 43N01'11 73w59'20 4:55:57
West Cornwall 36
11 41N25'51 74w04'08 4:56:17
West Coxsackie 20
11 42N21'38 73w49'02 4:55:16
Westdale 33 25 43N23'16 75w48'56 5:03:16
West Danby 55 226 42N19'08 76w31'33 5:06:06
West Davenport 13
135 42N26'45 74w57'49 4:59:51
West Day 46 7 43N16'02 74w04'12 4:56:17
West Delhi 13 226 42N17'58 75w00'31 5:00:02
West Dryden 55 13 42N31'01 76w24'53 5:05:40
West Durham 20
226 42N23'26 74w14'10 4:56:57
West Eaton 27 226 42N51'16 75w39'23 5:02:38
West Edmeston 39
226 42N45'48 75w16'43 5:01:07
West Ellery 7 158 42N11'43 79w23'54 5:17:36
West Ellicott 7
187 42N06 79w16 5:17:04
West Elmira 8 13 42N04'41 76w50'44 5:07:23
West End 39 14 42N27 75w06 5:00:24
West Endicott 4
13 42N07 76w03 5:04:12
Westerlea 34 12 43N02'52 76w16'31 5:05:06
Westerleigh 43 1 40N37'16 74w07'56 4:56:32
Westerlo 1 226 42N30'54 74w02'45 4:56:11
Western 33 226 43N20 75w23 5:01:32
Western Pine Knolls 1
1 42N40 73w48 4:55:12
Housing 33
226 43N18'20 75w23'00 5:01:32
West Exeter 39
226 42N48'08 75w09'00 5:00:36
Westfall 28 226 43N06'51 77w37'59 5:10:32
West Falls 15 11 42N42'05 78w40'57 5:14:44
West Farms 3 1 40N50'23 73w52'41 4:55:31
Westfield 7 225 42N19'20 79w34'42 5:18:19
Westford 39 13 42N39'00 74w47'53 4:59:12
West Fort Ann 58
123 43N24'35 73w34'27 4:54:18
West Fowler 45
178 44N16'04 75w27'07 5:01:48
West Frankfort 22
184 43N05'16 75w09'57 5:00:40
West Fulton 48
226 42N33'52 74w27'51 4:57:51
West Gaines 37
146 43N16'48 78w17'47 5:13:11
West Galway 18 1 43N00'13 74w06'06 4:56:24
Westgate 28 209 43N08 77w43 5:10:52
West Genesee Terrace 34
12 43N02'52 76w15'39 5:05:03
West Ghent 11 11 42N19'07 73w42'02 4:54:48
West Gilgo Beach 52
11 40N36'46 73w25'12 4:53:41
West Glens Falls 57
6 43N18'00 73w41'04 4:54:44
West Glenville 47
1 42N57 74w11 4:56:44
West Granville 58
42 43N26'52 73w21'47 4:53:27
West Granville Corners 58
6 43N33 73w24 4:53:36
West Greece 28
209 43N13'07 77w45'29 5:11:02
West Greenville 20
226 42N24'42 74w02'22 4:56:09
West Greenwood 51
226 42N09'13 77w42'50 5:10:51
West Groton 55 13 42N36'15 76w26'45 5:05:47
Westhampton 52 6 40N49'28 72w40'00 4:50:40
Westhampton Beach 52
6 40N48'11 72w36'54 4:50:28
West Harpersfield 13
226 42N26'05 74w43'26 4:58:54
West Haverstraw 44
6 41N12'34 73w59'09 4:55:57
West Hebron 58
213 43N13'50 73w22'34 4:53:30
West Hempstead 30
6 40N42'17 73w39'02 4:54:36
West Henrietta 28
20 43N02'24 77w39'43 5:10:39
West Hill 47 1 42N48'56 74w00'46 4:56:03
West Hills 52 11 40N50 73w26 4:53:44
West Hoosick 42
11 42N53'58 73w25'32 4:53:42
West Huntington 52
6 40N51 73w23 4:53:32
West Hurley 56 11 41N59'50 74w06'19 4:56:25
West Islip 52 6 40N42'22 73w18'24 4:53:14
West Jefferson 48
226 42N28'28 74w39'12 4:58:37
West Jewett 20
226 42N15'49 74w19'46 4:57:19
West Junius 35 41 42N57'02 76w58'26 5:07:54
West Kendall 37
105 43N20'09 78w04'34 5:12:18
West Kill 20 42 42N12'30 74w23'13 4:57:33
West Kilns 10 44 44N26'19 73w54'05 4:55:36
West Kortright 13
29 42N24'04 74w51'09 4:59:25
West Laurens 39
226 42N31'47 75w10'19 5:00:41
Westlawn 1 1 42N40 73w48 4:55:12
West Lebanon 11
11 42N29'10 73w28'00 4:53:52
West Lee 33 226 43N18'34 75w33'00 5:02:12
West Leyden 25
226 43N27'34 75w27'51 5:01:51

West Lowville 25
191 43N47'36 75w32'53 5:02:12
West Mahopac 40
17 41N22'15 73w47'26 4:55:10
West Martinsburg 25
226 43N45'34 75w31'04 5:02:04
West Mecox 52 11 40N55 72w21 4:49:24
West Mecox Village 52
11 40N55'02 72w19'43 4:49:19
Westmere 1 6 42N41'28 73w52'09 4:55:29
West Meredith 13
29 42N20'47 75w01'23 5:00:06
West Middleburg 48
226 42N35'44 74w21'13 4:57:25
West Middlebury 61
142 42N51'45 78w09'06 5:12:36
West Milton 46 11 43N02'15 73w55'47 4:55:43
Westminster Park 23
17 44N21'22 75w55'48 5:03:43
West Monroe 38
182 43N16'51 76w04'01 5:04:16
Westmore Estates 1
1 42N40 73w48 4:55:12
Westmoreland 33
11 43N06'58 75w24'15 5:01:37
Westmoreland 52
11 41N03'29 72w22'13 4:49:29
West Mount Vernon 60
1 40N54'44 73w50'54 4:55:24
West Newark 54
226 42N14'35 76w14'12 5:04:57
West New Brighton 43
1 40N38'04 74w06'45 4:56:27
West Newburgh 36
1 41N31 74w03 4:56:12
West Notch 2 226 42N07'32 78w09'20 5:12:37
West Nyack 44 1 41N05'47 73w58'24 4:55:54
Weston 49 13 42N25'15 77w04'30 5:08:18
West Oneonta 39
14 42N28'20 75w07'03 5:00:28
Westons Mills 5
22 42N03'44 78w22'39 5:13:31
Westover 4 116 42N06'57 75w58'33 5:03:54
West Parishville 45
207 44N36'54 74w56'47 4:59:47
West Park 56 11 41N47'40 73w57'36 4:55:50
West Patterson 40
7 41N30'36 73w37'52 4:54:31
West Pawling 14 7 41N35'13 73w39'38 4:54:39
West Perry 61 206 42N43'12 78w01'59 5:12:08
West Perry Center 61
206 42N44'38 78w04'29 5:12:18
West Perrysburg 5
42 42N28'47 79w02'49 5:16:11
West Perth 18 1 43N00'45 74w16'13 4:57:05
West Phoenix 34
93 43N13'32 76w18'18 5:05:13
West Pierrepont 45
155 44N29'33 75w03'36 5:00:14
West Plattsburgh 10
86 44N42'49 73w34'07 4:54:16
West Point 36 6 41N23'29 73w57'23 4:55:50
Westport 16 58 44N11'02 73w26'10 4:53:45
West Portland 7
225 42N21'08 79w31'18 5:18:05
West Potsdam 45
207 44N41'13 75w05'24 5:00:22
West Richmondville 48
13 42N39'07 74w36'50 4:58:27
West Ridge 28 185 43N13 77w39 5:10:36
West Ridgeway 37
112 43N16'04 78w25'11 5:13:41
West Ronkonkoma 52
11 40N49 73w06 4:52:24
West Rush 28 27 42N58'35 77w41'59 5:10:48
West Saint James 52
11 40N51 73w14 4:52:56
West Saint Johnsville 29
62 42N59'58 74w42'03 4:58:48
West Salamanca 5
14 42N09 78w43 5:14:52
West Sand Lake 42
226 42N38'36 73w36'33 4:54:26
West Saugerties 56
215 42N06'45 74w02'55 4:56:12
West Sayville 52
7 40N43'40 73w05'53 4:52:24
West Schuyler 22
222 43N05'54 75w09'06 5:00:36
West Seneca 15
153 42N51 78w48 5:15:12
West Settlement 13
31 42N17'16 74w36'52 4:58:27
West Settlement 20
226 42N19'56 74w22'12 4:57:29
West Shelby 37
112 43N09'33 78w26'14 5:13:45
West Shokan 56 37 41N58'02 74w17'15 4:57:09
West Slaterville 55
226 42N23'38 76w21'48 5:05:27
West Smithtown 52
6 40N51 73w14 4:52:56
West Somerset 32
150 43N19'38 78w36'20 5:14:25
West Sparta 26 13 42N37'37 77w46'24 5:11:06
West Stephentown 42
11 42N34'46 73w28'23 4:53:54
West Stockholm 45
20 44N42'49 74w54'04 4:59:36
West Sweden 28
226 43N08'57 77w59'15 5:11:57
West Taghkanic 11
226 42N07'26 73w43'16 4:54:53
West Tiana 52 11 40N51'35 72w32'39 4:50:11
Westtown 36 11 41N20'12 74w32'25 4:58:10
West Township 1
40 42N41'58 74w09'05 4:56:36
West Turin 25 77 44N07 75w34 5:02:16
West Union 51 226 42N05'42 77w43'33 5:10:54
Westvale 34 13 43N02'51 76w13'15 5:04:53
West Valley 5 226 42N24'10 78w36'37 5:14:26
West Valley Falls 42
11 42N54 73w34 4:54:16

Westview 4 151 42N07 75w56 5:03:44
Westview 26 13 42N33'24 77w49'32 5:11:18
Westview Manor 34 12 43N02'38 76w16'10 5:05:05
Westville 17 193 44N57'45 74w25'02 4:57:40
Westville 39 13 42N37'38 74w52'51 4:59:31
Westville Center 17 193 44N56'41 74w23'47 4:57:35
West Walworth 59 226 43N08'48 77w20'45 5:09:23
West Waterford 46 11 42N48 73w41 4:54:44
West Webster 28 33 43N12'17 77w29'48 5:09:59
West Windsor 4 226 42N05'56 75w45'52 5:03:03
West Winfield 22 13 42N53'07 75w11'37 5:00:46
West Woodstock 27 226 42N50'49 75w52'55 5:03:32
West Yaphank 52 11 40N49 73w00 4:52:00
Wethersfield 61 226 42N39 78w15 5:13:00
Wethersfield Springs 61 226 42N41'09 78w12'22 5:12:49
Wetmore 25 191 43N41'52 75w33'34 5:02:14
Wevertown 57 49 43N38'00 73w56'30 4:55:46
Weyer 15 153 42N43'42 78w54'58 5:15:40
Whaley Lake 14 7 41N31 73w39 4:54:36
Whallonsburg 16 129 44N15'51 73w24'12 4:53:37
Wheatfield 32 1 43N06 78w53 5:15:32
Wheatland 28 226 43N01 77w50 5:11:20
Wheatland Center 28 226 43N00'23 77w49'18 5:11:17
Wheatley 30 11 40N48'20 73w35'30 4:54:22
Wheatville 19 226 43N05'46 78w20'30 5:13:22
Wheeler 51 14 42N25'49 77w19'58 5:09:20
Wheeler Estates 47 11 42N54'11 73w56'20 4:55:45
Wheelers 35 47 42N54 77w25 5:09:40
Wheelertown 22 82 43N23'43 75w03'49 5:00:15
Wheelerville 18 226 43N09'26 74w29'14 4:57:57
Whig Corners 39 13 42N42'35 74w53'41 4:59:35
Whig Hill 38 182 43N17'37 76w04'34 5:04:18
Whipple Corner 55 186 42N28'00 76w34'22 5:06:17
Whippleville 17 193 44N48'35 74w15'44 4:57:03
Whippoorwill 60 1 41N08 73w43 4:54:52
White Birches 60 1 40N58'04 73w46'59 4:55:08
White Church 55 226 42N20'38 76w23'09 5:05:33
White City 28 185 43N15'05 77w35'31 5:10:22
White Corners 27 226 42N54'29 75w36'14 5:02:25
White Creek 58 11 42N58'12 73w17'30 4:53:10
Whiteface 16 1 44N18'40 74w00'11 4:56:01
Whiteface Landing 16 1 44N20'23 73w56'51 4:55:47
White Fathers 17 113 44N30 74w07 4:56:28
Whiteford Hollow 5 226 42N25'10 78w44'03 5:14:56
Whitehall 58 6 43N33'20 73w24'15 4:53:37
Whitehall Corners 60 1 41N16'29 73w42'38 4:54:51
Whitehouse Crossing 14 79 42N01'33 73w31'13 4:54:05
White Lake 33 226 43N31 75w09 5:00:36
White Lake 53 226 41N40'37 74w49'42 4:59:19
Whitelaw 27 226 43N07'56 75w47'28 5:03:10
White Plains 60 1 41N02'02 73w45'48 4:55:03
Whiteport 56 11 41N52'56 74w03'20 4:56:13
Whites 28 15 43N04'35 77w42'34 5:10:50
Whitesboro 33 222 43N07'19 75w17'31 5:01:10
Whiteside Corners 46 226 43N03'53 74w05'30 4:56:22
Whites Store 9 226 42N32 75w23 5:01:32
Whitestone 41 1 40N47'40 73w49'08 4:55:17
White Store 9 226 42N29'09 75w24'14 5:01:37
Whitestown 33 222 43N07 75w19 5:01:16
White Sulphur Springs 53 189 41N47'51 74w49'38 4:59:19
Whitesville 2 226 42N02'16 77w45'46 5:11:03
Whitfield 56 76 41N48'51 74w13'29 4:56:54
Whitman 13 226 42N11'43 75w22'33 5:01:30
Whitney Estates 1 1 42N45'36 73w46'57 4:55:08
Whitney Point 4 36 42N19'44 75w58'05 5:03:52
Whittemore 54 205 42N08'22 76w07'23 5:04:30
Wiccopee 14 226 41N32'20 73w50'48 4:55:23
Wickham Knolls 36 6 41N17 74w20 4:57:20
Wickham Village 36 6 41N17 74w20 4:57:20
Wickman Park 52 11 41N06 72w22 4:49:28
Wicks Corners 6 24 42N57'30 76w27'35 5:05:50
Wilbur 56 11 41N54'35 74w00'18 4:56:01
Wilcox 36 11 41N18'07 74w28'50 4:57:55
Wildwood 45 226 44N33'45 74w54'04 4:59:36
Wildwood 52 11 40N57'52 72w48'45 4:51:15
Wiley Shelter 14 11 41N38'15 73w31'58 4:54:08
Wileytown 39 13 42N42'48 75w02'14 5:00:09
Wileyville 51 226 42N01'39 77w41'49 5:10:47
Willard 50 12 42N40'56 76w52'08 5:07:29
Willet 12 226 42N28'09 75w54'43 5:03:39
Willets 6 13 42N42'39 76w42'17 5:06:49

Williams Bridge 3 1 40N52'38 73w52'00 4:55:28
Williamsburg 24 1 40N42'51 73w57'14 4:55:49
Williams Corner 62 226 42N42'46 77w15'13 5:09:01
Williams Corners 27 29 42N53'34 75w40'24 5:02:42
Williams Grove 34 13 42N50'53 76w15'13 5:05:01
Williams Lake 56 11 41N50 74w05 4:56:20
Williamson 59 33 43N13'26 77w11'11 5:08:45
Williamstown 38 25 43N25'26 75w53'25 5:03:34
Williamsville 15 55 42N57'50 78w44'17 5:14:57
Willing 2 109 42N03 77w54 5:11:36
Williston 15 38 42N49'39 78w31'00 5:14:04
Williston Park 30 11 40N45'23 73w38'43 4:54:35
Willisville 45 207 44N35'36 74w56'19 4:59:45
Willoughby 5 226 42N12'03 78w36'30 5:14:26
Willow 56 11 42N04'35 74w13'42 4:56:55
Willow Beach 35 47 42N44'32 77w30'19 5:10:01
Willow Brook 7 226 42N10'38 79w24'23 5:17:38
Willow Brook 14 226 41N51'42 73w44'40 4:54:59
Willowbrook 43 1 40N36'11 74w08'20 4:56:33
Willow Brook Park 47 1 42N52'55 73w55'15 4:55:41
Willow Creek 55 13 42N31'15 76w34'33 5:06:18
Willowemoc 53 75 41N55'08 74w40'22 4:58:41
Willow Glen 34 24 42N57'48 76w26'11 5:05:45
Willow Glen 46 1 42N55'11 73w43'16 4:54:53
Willow Glen 55 13 42N29'23 76w19'42 5:05:19
Willow Grove 6 24 43N02'18 76w42'58 5:06:52
Willow Grove 44 4 41N13'08 74w02'20 4:56:09
Willow Grove 62 14 42N36'56 77w04'22 5:08:17
Willow Point 4 13 42N06'08 75w59'27 5:03:58
Willow Ridge Estates 15 1 43N00'42 78w48'34 5:15:14
Willsboro 16 56 44N21'26 73w23'33 4:53:34
Willsboro Point 16 56 44N24'31 73w22'43 4:53:31
Willseyville 54 226 42N17'24 76w22'43 5:05:31
Wilmington 16 129 44N23'18 73w48'57 4:55:16
Wilmot Woods 60 1 40N58'48 73w46'51 4:55:07
Wilna 23 156 44N02 75w35 5:02:20
Wilson 32 226 43N18'35 78w49'35 5:15:18
Wilson Corners 6 13 42N44'05 76w23'37 5:05:34
Wilson Creek 54 226 42N17'10 76w08'43 5:04:35
Wilson Park 60 6 41N04 73w51 4:55:24
Wilton 46 226 43N10'48 73w44'41 4:54:59
Winchell 56 37 41N54'57 74w15'21 4:57:01
Winchester 15 153 42N51'53 78w47'13 5:15:09
Wincoma 52 11 40N54'12 73w25'34 4:53:42
Windcrest Park 34 13 43N02'16 76w17'45 5:05:11
Windecker 25 226 43N47'57 75w36'46 5:02:27
Winderest Park 34 12 43N03 76w15 5:05:00
Windham 20 226 42N18'26 74w15'09 4:57:01
Winding Ways 34 13 42N53'20 76w24'39 5:05:39
Windmill Farm 60 1 41N08'51 73w40'53 4:54:44
Windom 15 153 42N47'07 78w47'24 5:15:10
Windsor 4 226 42N04'33 75w38'27 5:02:34
Windsor Beach 28 185 43N15'14 77w35'51 5:10:23
Winebrook Hills 16 226 43N58 74w10 4:56:40
Winfield 22 226 42N54 75w09 5:00:36
Wing 61 226 42N31'57 78w13'10 5:12:53
Wingdale 14 11 41N38'49 73w34'07 4:54:16
Winona 23 143 43N43'08 75w59'11 5:03:57
Winona Lake 36 1 41N31 74w03 4:56:12
Winterton 53 11 41N31'22 74w28'15 4:57:53
Winthrop 45 105 44N47'41 74w47'14 4:59:09
Wirt 2 226 42N08'06 78w09'05 5:12:36
Wiscoy 2 226 42N30'08 78w04'48 5:12:19
Wisner 36 6 41N16'15 74w19'37 4:57:18
Witherbee 16 54 44N05'15 73w32'00 4:54:08
Withey 2 226 42N14'44 77w59'15 5:11:57
Wittenburg 56 11 42N01'30 74w11'46 4:56:47
Wolcott 59 33 43N13'14 76w48'55 5:07:16
Wolcottsburg 15 226 43N03'29 78w38'14 5:14:33
Wolcottsville 32 145 43N06'41 78w31'06 5:14:04
Wolf Hill 1 11 42N36'15 74w00'39 4:56:03
Wolf Lake Landing 22 59 43N36'04 75w01'14 5:00:05
Wolf Pond 17 113 44N38'57 74w04'01 4:56:16
Woodard 34 13 43N08'29 76w11'40 5:04:47
Woodbourne 53 74 41N45'35 74w35'40 4:58:23
Woodbury 30 6 40N49'32 73w28'05 4:53:52
Woodbury 36 4 41N21'52 74w06'23 4:56:26
Woodbury Falls 36 226 41N21 74w08 4:56:32
Woodcliff Park 52 11 40N58'00 72w45'16 4:51:01
Woodgate 33 226 43N31'13 75w09'19 5:00:37
Woodhaven 41 1 40N41'21 73w51'30 4:55:26
Woodhull 33 226 43N26'04 75w12'00 5:00:48
Woodhull 51 226 42N04'49 77w24'32 5:09:38
Woodhull Landing 52 11 40N57'56 72w59'05 4:51:56

Woodinville 14 7 41N34'14 73w37'50 4:54:31
Woodland 34 13 42N52'01 76w21'58 5:05:28
Woodland 56 88 42N03'11 74w19'56 4:57:20
Woodlands 60 1 41N01'25 73w50'06 4:55:20
Woodlawn 3 1 40N53'53 73w52'04 4:55:28
Woodlawn 7 226 42N10'08 79w25'50 5:17:43
Woodlawn 15 153 42N47'52 78w50'49 5:15:23
Woodlawn Beach 15 153 42N48 78w49 5:15:16
Woodmere 30 1 40N37'55 73w42'47 4:54:51
Woodridge 53 72 41N42'38 74w34'29 4:58:18
Woodrow 43 11 40N32'36 74w11'53 4:56:48
Woodruff Heights 47 1 42N52'47 73w55'58 4:55:44
Woods 21 226 43N52'59 74w36'17 4:58:25
Woodsburgh 30 11 40N37'26 73w42'32 4:54:50
Woods Corner 51 13 42N01'53 77w17'42 5:09:11
Woods Corners 22 13 42N51'43 75w11'31 5:00:46
Woods Falls 17 16 44N55'36 73w38'15 4:54:33
Woodside 15 218 42N31'18 78w45'55 5:15:04
Woodside 41 1 40N44'43 73w54'21 4:55:37
Woods Lake 22 73 43N51'08 74w57'06 4:59:48
Woods Mill 23 77 44N07'17 75w34'43 5:02:19
Woods Mills 10 14 44N41'33 73w36'53 4:54:28
Woodstock 20 11 42N19'18 74w00'49 4:56:03
Woodstock 56 11 42N02'27 74w07'07 4:56:28
Woodstream Farms 15 11 43N00'18 78w43'09 5:14:53
Woodsville 26 13 42N34'33 77w43'55 5:10:56
Woodville 23 13 43N45'16 76w09'56 5:04:40
Woodville 35 226 42N40'11 77w21'52 5:09:27
Woodybrook 60 166 41N14'06 73w53'22 4:55:33
Wooglin 7 158 42N15'09 79w27'56 5:17:52
Woolsey 41 1 40N46 73w55 4:55:40
Worcester 39 13 42N35'29 74w45'03 4:59:00
Worley Heights 36 226 41N21 74w11 4:56:44
Worth 23 226 43N47'03 75w52'41 5:03:31
Worth Center 23 226 43N44'33 75w51'17 5:03:25
Worthington 60 1 41N01'51 73w50'10 4:55:21
Wright 48 226 42N40 74w13 4:56:52
Wright 58 29 43N48'01 73w22'52 4:53:31
Wright Park Manor 33 211 43N13 75w26 5:01:44
Wrights Corner 34 93 43N13'04 76w21'32 5:05:26
Wrights Corner 61 25 42N51'31 78w06'15 5:12:25
Wrights Corners 32 190 43N13'21 78w40'38 5:14:43
Wright Settlement 33 211 43N15'03 75w24'55 5:01:40
Wurlitzer Park Village 32 1 43N03'38 78w51'11 5:15:25
Wurtemburg 14 64 41N53'45 73w52'03 4:55:28
Wurtsboro 53 11 41N34'36 74w29'15 4:57:57
Wurtsboro Hills 53 11 41N35'28 74w30'22 4:58:01
Wyandale 15 218 42N33'19 78w45'57 5:15:04
Wyandanch 52 11 40N45'14 73w21'39 4:53:27
Wyantskill 42 220 42N41'48 73w38'41 4:54:35
Wyatts 47 1 42N51'04 74w00'36 4:56:02
Wyckoff 6 13 42N50'31 76w31'40 5:06:07
Wycoff Heights 24 1 40N42 73w55 4:55:40
Wykagyl 60 1 40N56'29 73w47'58 4:55:12
Wykagyl Park 60 1 40N56'30 73w47'09 4:55:09
Wyman Corner 4 4 42N11'59 75w45'58 5:03:04
Wynantskill 42 11 42N42 73w39 4:54:36
Wyomanock 42 11 42N31'02 73w21'39 4:53:27
Wyoming 61 25 42N49'35 78w05'24 5:12:22
Yaddo 46 226 43N04'03 73w45'31 4:55:02
Yagerville 56 48 41N50'43 74w24'48 4:57:39
Yale 50 226 42N48'23 76w55'13 5:07:41
Yaleville 9 149 42N21'36 75w29'56 5:02:00
Yaleville 45 207 44N46'02 74w59'34 4:59:58
Yankee Lake 53 11 41N35'00 74w32'41 4:58:11
Yaphank 52 11 40N50'12 72w55'03 4:51:40
Yates 37 15 43N21 78w23 5:13:32
Yates Center 37 15 43N20'16 78w23'21 5:13:33
Yatesville 62 14 42N40'19 77w08'16 5:08:33
Yellow Mills 59 89 43N03'38 77w15'26 5:09:02
Yonkers 60 1 40N55'52 73w53'57 4:55:36
York 26 226 42N52'16 77w53'08 5:11:33
York 59 226 43N12'00 76w56'37 5:07:46
York Corners 2 109 42N07 77w57 5:11:48
Yorkshire 5 226 42N31'48 78w28'23 5:13:54
Yorktown 60 16 41N17'44 73w48'31 4:55:14
Yorktown Heights 60 16 41N16'15 73w46'41 4:55:07
Yorkville 33 222 43N06'46 75w16'17 5:01:05
Yosts 29 11 42N54'42 74w27'31 4:57:50
Youmans Corner 39 13 42N24'12 75w15'19 5:01:01
Young Hickory 51 226 42N03'10 77w36'32 5:10:26
Youngs 13 13 42N18'00 75w19'07 5:01:16
Youngs 34 13 43N12'23 76w10'01 5:04:40
Youngs Crossing 22 13 42N54'16 75w04'44 5:00:19
Youngstown 32 121 43N14'50 79w03'01 5:16:12
Youngstown Estates 32 226 43N14'12 79w02'51 5:16:11
Youngsville 53 226 41N48'30 74w53'12 4:59:33
Yulan 53 226 41N31'21 74w56'00 4:59:44
Zena 56 11 42N01'00 74w04'36 4:56:18
Zoar 15 42 42N27'24 78w50'22 5:15:21
Zoar 23 143 43N51'31 75w55'22 5:03:41
Zurich 59 226 43N09'02 77w02'37 5:08:10

TIME TABLES

NC # 1

Before 11/18/1883		LMT
11/18/1883	12:00	EST
3/31/1918	02:00	EWT
10/27/1918	02:00	EST
3/30/1919	02:00	EWT
10/26/1919	02:00	EST
2/09/1942	02:00	EWT
9/30/1945	02:00	EST
4/24/1966	02:00	US#1

NC # 2

Before 11/18/1883		LMT
11/18/1883	12:00	EST
3/31/1918	02:00	EWT
10/27/1918	02:00	EST
3/30/1919	02:00	EWT
10/26/1919	02:00	EST
2/09/1942	02:00	EWT
9/30/1945	02:00	EST
4/28/1946	02:00	EDT
9/29/1946	02:00	EST
4/24/1966	02:00	US#1

NC # 3

Before 11/18/1883		LMT
11/18/1883	12:00	EST
3/31/1918	02:00	EWT
10/27/1918	02:00	EST
3/30/1919	02:00	EWT
10/26/1919	02:00	EST
2/09/1942	02:00	EWT
9/30/1945	02:00	EST
5/20/1957	00:00	EDT
9/29/1957	02:00	EST
4/24/1966	02:00	US#1

NC # 4

Before 11/18/1883		LMT
11/18/1883	12:00	EST
3/31/1918	02:00	EWT
10/27/1918	02:00	EST
1/01/1919	02:00	CST
3/30/1919	02:00	CWT
10/26/1919	02:00	CST
2/09/1942	02:00	CWT
9/30/1945	02:00	CST
4/28/1946	02:00	CDT
9/29/1946	02:00	CST
9/28/1947	02:00	EST
4/24/1966	02:00	US#1

COUNTIES

1 Alamance
2 Alexander
3 Alleghany
4 Anson
5 Ashe
6 Avery
7 Beaufort
8 Bertie
9 Bladen
10 Brunswick
11 Buncombe
12 Burke
13 Cabarrus
14 Caldwell
15 Camden
16 Carteret
17 Caswell
18 Catawba
19 Chatham
20 Cherokee
21 Chowan
22 Clay
23 Cleveland
24 Columbus
25 Craven
26 Cumberland
27 Currituck
28 Dare
29 Davidson
30 Davie
31 Duplin
32 Durham
33 Edgecombe
34 Forsyth
35 Franklin
36 Gaston
37 Gates
38 Graham
39 Granville
40 Greene
41 Guilford
42 Halifax
43 Harnett
44 Haywood
45 Henderson
46 Hertford
47 Hoke
48 Hyde
49 Iredell
50 Jackson
51 Johnston
52 Jones
53 Lee
54 Lenoir
55 Lincoln
56 McDowell
57 Macon
58 Madison
59 Martin
60 Mecklenburg
61 Mitchell
62 Montgomery
63 Moore
64 Nash
65 New Hanover
66 Northampton
67 Onslow
68 Orange
69 Pamlico
70 Pasquotank
71 Pender
72 Perquimans
73 Person
74 Pitt
75 Polk
76 Randolph
77 Richmond
78 Robeson
79 Rockingham
80 Rowan
81 Rutherford
82 Sampson
83 Scotland
84 Stanly
85 Stokes
86 Surry
87 Swain
88 Transylvania
89 Tyrrell
90 Union
91 Vance
92 Wake
93 Warren
94 Washington
95 Watauga
96 Wayne
97 Wilkes
98 Wilson
99 Yadkin
100 Yancey

Place		Lat	Long	Time
Aarons Corner 85	1	36N32'17	80w17'46	5:21:11
Abbotts 9	1	34N32	78w43	5:14:52
Abbottsburg 9	1	34N31'01	78w43'31	5:14:54
Aberdeen 63	1	35N07'53	79w25'47	5:17:43
Abingdon 14	2	35N54'40	81w35'46	5:26:23
Abner 62	1	35N29'53	79w54'29	5:19:38
Abshers 97	1	36N22'07	81w06'40	5:24:27
Aces Landing 24	1	34N23'43	78w58'15	5:15:53
Acme 24	1	34N19'32	78w12'18	5:12:49
Acme 36	1	35N15	81w02	5:24:08
Acorn Hill 37	1	36N26'33	76w32'53	5:06:12
Acre 7	1	35N37	76w52	5:07:28
Action 11	1	35N33'41	82w38'21	5:30:33
Acton 11	2	35N35	82w36	5:30:24
Adako 14	1	35N54'15	81w42'15	5:26:49
Adams 95	1	36N13	81w40	5:26:40
Adamsville 96	1	35N22'15	77w57'13	5:11:49
Adcock Crossroads 91	1	36N19'46	78w21'19	5:13:25
Addie 50	2	35N24'21	83w09'36	5:32:38
Addington Mill 57	1	35N06'48	83w23'53	5:33:36
Addor 63	1	35N04'40	79w27'44	5:17:51
Adoniram 39	1	36N33	78w47	5:15:08
Advance 30	1	35N56'28	80w24'34	5:21:38
Advent Crossroads 18	1	35N40'09	81w25'34	5:25:42
Afton 93	1	36N20'19	78w12'59	5:12:52
Aho 95	1	36N09'33	81w37'00	5:26:28
Ahoskie 46	1	36N17'12	76w59'06	5:07:56
Ai 73	1	36N17	78w57	5:15:48
Airboro 96	1	35N21'33	77w59'30	5:11:58
Airlie 42	1	36N20'08	77w53'05	5:11:32
Alamance 1	1	36N02'06	79w29'10	5:17:57
Alarka 87	1	35N21'11	83w26'44	5:33:47
Albemarle 81	1	35N21'00	80w12'01	5:20:48
Albemarle Beach 94	1	35N56'09	76w38'30	5:06:34
Albertson 31	1	35N06'51	77w49'09	5:11:17
Albrittons 54	1	35N11'52	77w39'55	5:10:40
Albrittons Landing 54	1	35N17'48	77w29'42	5:09:59
Alder Branch 15	1	36N15'06	76w01'52	5:04:07
Alert 35	1	36N13'51	78w13'22	5:12:53
Alexander 11	2	35N42	82w37	5:30:28
Alexander Mills 81	1	35N18'38	81w51'32	5:27:26
Alexanders Store 60	1	35N16	80w48	5:23:12
Alexis 36	1	35N23'59	81w07'05	5:24:28
Alfordsville 78	1	34N34'48	79w19'07	5:17:16
Alleghany 29	1	35N32	80w07	5:20:28
Allegheny 58	1	35N59'18	82w40'03	5:30:40
Allen 60	1	35N13'33	80w36'51	5:22:27
Allendale 47	1	34N52	79w17	5:17:08
Allen Grove 42	1	36N18'19	77w38'41	5:10:35
Allen Jay 41	1	35N55'26	79w57'56	5:19:52
Allens Crossroads 90	1	34N54'43	80w24'28	5:21:38
Allens Level 73	1	36N19'31	79w01'16	5:16:05
Allenstand 58	1	35N58'22	82w45'11	5:31:01
Allensville 73	1	36N23'25	78w53'20	5:15:33
Allenton 78	1	34N35'32	78w55'35	5:15:42
All Healing Springs 2	1	35N55	81w10	5:24:40
Alliance 69	1	35N08'41	76w48'09	5:07:13
Alligator 89	1	35N54'52	76w06'46	5:04:27
Alligoods 7	1	35N33'35	76w56'47	5:07:47
Allison 17	1	36N24'32	79w27'52	5:17:51
Allison Ferry 60	1	35N23'19	80w57'28	5:23:50
Allreds 62	1	35N24	79w47	5:19:08
Alma 78	1	34N43'25	79w18'46	5:17:15
Almond 87	2	35N22'11	83w33'55	5:34:16
Alspaugh 34	1	36N08'43	80w15'21	5:21:01
Altamahaw 1	1	36N11'03	79w30'27	5:18:02
Altamont 6	1	35N59'27	81w56'40	5:27:47
Altapass 61	1	35N53'36	82w01'05	5:28:04
Alton 90	1	34N52'51	80w32'31	5:22:10
Amantha 95	1	36N16'43	81w46'48	5:27:07
Amelia 3	1	36N32'33	81w12'12	5:24:49
Amerotron Mill 78	1	34N49	79w11	5:16:44
Amherst 12	1	35N47'56	81w35'47	5:26:23
Amity 49	1	35N44	80w41	5:22:44
Amity Gardens 60	1	35N14	80w47	5:23:08
Amity Hill 49	1	35N41'50	80w46'25	5:23:06
Ammon 9	1	34N48'00	78w34'50	5:14:19
Ammon Ford 9	1	34N47'33	78w35'13	5:14:21
Amostown 85	1	36N31'27	80w03'16	5:20:13
Anderson 17	1	36N16'01	79w20'44	5:17:23
Anderson 28	1	36N04	75w42	5:02:48
Anderson Creek 43	1	35N17'00	78w55'02	5:15:40
Anderson Crossroads 42	1	36N26	77w55	5:11:40
Anderson Landing 10	3	34N02'28	77w56'37	5:11:46
Andersons Crossroads 42	1	36N21'43	77w44'31	5:10:58
Andrews 20	2	35N12'06	83w49'27	5:35:18
Andy Cove 58	1	35N53'41	82w42'47	5:30:51
Angier 43	1	35N30'25	78w44'22	5:14:57
Ansley Heights 95	1	36N08'17	81w42'47	5:26:51
Ansonville 4	1	35N06'16	80w06'34	5:20:26
Antioch 10	1	34N01'22	78w09'07	5:12:36
Antioch 24	1	34N14'22	78w43'07	5:14:52
Antioch 47	1	34N53'08	79w12'31	5:16:50
Antioch 58	1	35N54'27	82w53'16	5:31:33
Antioch 97	1	36N09'12	81w01'17	5:24:05
Apex 92	1	35N43'57	78w51'02	5:15:24
Apple Grove 5	1	36N31'43	81w35'06	5:26:20
Aquadale 84	1	35N13'38	80w13'33	5:20:54
Aquone 57	1	35N12'26	83w37'38	5:34:31
Arabia 47	1	34N57'00	79w07'33	5:16:30
Arapahoe 69	1	35N01'32	76w49'33	5:07:18
Ararat 86	1	36N24'14	80w33'39	5:22:15
Arba 40	1	35N24'04	77w42'09	5:10:49
Arcadia 29	1	35N56'50	80w18'31	5:21:14
Archdale 23	1	35N11'38	81w24'07	5:25:36
Archdale 76	1	35N54'52	79w58'20	5:19:53
Archer 51	1	35N39	78w27	5:13:48
Archers Lodge 51	1	35N41'38	78w22'33	5:13:30
Arcola 93	1	36N17'22	77w58'49	5:11:55
Arden 11	1	35N27'58	82w31'00	5:30:04
Ardmore 34	1	36N05'05	80w16'27	5:21:06
Ardulusa 26	1	34N57'46	78w55'02	5:15:40
Argura 50	1	35N16'03	83w02'28	5:32:10
Arlington 99	1	36N13'38	80w50'01	5:23:20
Armour 24	1	34N20'49	78w15'16	5:13:01
Arnold 29	1	35N53'36	80w16'51	5:21:07
Arrwood Mill 20	1	35N06'38	83w56'27	5:35:46
Artesia 24	1	34N19'20	78w34'31	5:14:18
Arthur 74	1	35N35	77w29	5:09:56
Asbury 19	1	35N36'29	79w12'00	5:16:48
Asbury 62	1	35N30'03	79w46'37	5:19:06
Asbury 85	1	36N31'46	80w25'17	5:21:41
Asbury 92	1	35N47'24	78w44'16	5:14:57
Ash 10	1	34N04'00	78w31'36	5:14:06
Asheboro 76	1	35N42'28	79w48'50	5:19:15
Ashebrook Park 36	1	35N20'32	81w13'35	5:24:54
Asheville 11	2	35N36'03	82w33'15	5:30:13
Ashford 56	1	35N52'17	81w56'53	5:27:48
Ash Hill 86	1	36N23'35	80w34'24	5:22:18
Ashland 5	1	36N26'27	81w39'35	5:26:38
Ashland 17	1	36N19'47	79w31'01	5:18:04
Ashley Heights 47	1	35N05'25	79w22'12	5:17:29
Ashmont 47	1	35N04'13	79w21'19	5:17:25
Ashton 71	1	34N28'31	77w54'05	5:11:36
Ashton Forrest 26	1	35N02	78w57	5:15:48
Ashwood 69	1	35N04'26	76w42'59	5:06:52
Askewville 8	1	36N06'35	76w56'25	5:07:46
Askin 25	1	35N13'13	77w04'01	5:08:16
Aspen 93	1	36N26	77w55	5:11:40
Assembly 44	1	35N32	82w58	5:31:52
Atando 60	1	35N15	80w50	5:23:20
Atando Junction 60	1	35N15'39	80w49'01	5:23:16
Athens 78	1	34N54	79w01	5:16:04
Atkinson 71	1	34N31'42	78w10'17	5:12:41
Atkinson Landing 9	1	34N34'42	78w29'48	5:13:59
Atlantic 16	1	34N53'05	76w20'27	5:05:22
Atlantic Beach 16	1	34N41'56	76w44'26	5:06:58
Atlantic Christian College 98	1	35N44	77w55	5:11:40
Atwell 80	1	35N34	80w41	5:22:44
Atwood 34	1	36N02'59	80w19'36	5:21:18
Auburn 92	1	35N41'35	78w33'20	5:14:13
Audubon 65	3	34N13	77w55	5:11:40
Aulander 8	1	36N13'46	77w06'52	5:08:27
Aumans Crossroads 76	1	35N33'31	79w50'22	5:19:21
Aurelian Springs 42	1	36N21'51	77w48'26	5:11:14
Aurora 7	1	35N18'19	76w47'20	5:07:09
Austin 97	1	36N19'25	80w58'38	5:23:55
Austins Mill 84	1	35N27	80w13	5:20:52
Autryville 82	1	34N59'52	78w38'34	5:14:34
Aventon 64	1	36N09'10	77w57'00	5:11:48
Averasboro 43	1	35N19	78w36	5:14:24
Avery Creek 11	1	35N27'48	82w34'58	5:30:20
Avon 28	1	35N21'07	75w30'39	5:02:03
Avondale 81	1	35N16'10	81w47'27	5:27:10
Axtell 93	1	36N21'45	78w15'24	5:13:02
Aycock Crossing 98	1	35N37'36	78w03'16	5:12:13
Ayden 74	1	35N28'21	77w24'57	5:09:40
Aydlett 27	1	36N19'33	75w54'26	5:03:38
Ayersville 79	1	36N29'13	80w01'31	5:20:06
Azalea 11	1	35N34'48	82w28'17	5:29:53
Azalea 65	3	34N13	77w55	5:11:40
Bacchus 100	1	35N55'40	82w12'20	5:28:49
Bachelor 25	1	34N54'28	76w45'14	5:07:01
Back Creek 76	1	35N45	79w52	5:19:28
Back Landing 89	1	35N55'43	76w19'03	5:05:16
Back Swamp 78	1	34N34	79w07	5:16:28
Badin 84	1	35N24'21	80w07'01	5:20:28
Bagley 51	1	35N34'35	78w10'11	5:12:41
Bahama 32	1	36N09'57	78w52'37	5:15:30
Bailey 61	1	36N03'11	82w19'33	5:29:18
Bailey 64	1	35N46'50	78w07'09	5:12:29
Bailey Camp 14	1	36N06'16	81w38'46	5:26:35
Bailey Town 85	1	36N19'10	80w08'33	5:20:34
Baker Crossroads 23	1	35N23'33	81w27'10	5:25:49
Bakers 90	1	35N01'38	80w36'14	5:22:25
Bakers Crossroads 79	1	36N22'01	79w48'36	5:19:14
Bakers Landing 9	1	34N35'03	78w16'30	5:13:06
Bakersville 61	1	36N00'56	82w09'32	5:28:38
Bakertown 41	1	35N55'48	79w58'03	5:19:52
Bald Creek 100	1	35N54'43	82w25'22	5:29:41
Bald Mountain 95	1	36N18	81w36	5:26:24
Bald Mountain 100	1	35N57'52	82w28'19	5:29:53
Baldwin 5	1	36N20'51	81w31'59	5:26:08
Baldwin 19	1	35N49	79w09	5:16:36
Baldwin 63	1	35N32	79w46	5:19:04
Baldwin Woods 24	1	34N20'33	78w41'22	5:14:45
Balfour 45	1	35N20'47	82w28'20	5:29:53
Balfours 76	1	35N44	79w48	5:19:12

Ball 5 1 36N30 81w30 5:26:00
Ballard 59 1 35N54'13 77w08'57 5:08:36
Ballard Crossroads 37 1 36N24'37 76w47'57 5:07:12
Ballards Crossroads 74 1 35N36 77w35 5:10:20
Ballast Bank 89 1 35N52'01 76w19'25 5:05:18
Ballew Store 100 1 35N55 82w18 5:29:12
Balm 6 1 36N10'11 81w51'09 5:27:25
Balsam 50 2 35N25'36 83w05'07 5:32:20
Balsam Grove 88 1 35N13'46 82w52'26 5:31:30
Baltic 82 1 34N59'37 78w09'36 5:12:38
Baltimore 9 1 34N26'11 78w26'26 5:13:46
Bamboo 95 1 36N11'37 81w36'29 5:26:26
Bandana 61 1 35N58'23 82w10'34 5:28:42
Bandy 18 1 35N38'31 81w05'24 5:24:22
Banks 92 1 35N38'08 78w42'52 5:14:51
Banks Creek 100 1 35N55 82w18 5:29:12
Banks Landing 52 1 35N02'56 77w16'24 5:09:06
Banner 51 1 35N23 78w32 5:14:08
Banner Elk 6 1 36N09'47 81w52'18 5:27:29
Bannertown 34 1 36N15'07 80w15'06 5:21:00
Bannertown 86 1 36N29'08 80w35'25 5:22:22
Banoak 18 1 35N35'10 81w24'33 5:25:38
Barbecue 43 1 35N20'09 79w02'20 5:16:09
Barber 21 1 36N07'21 76w35'34 5:06:22
Barber 80 1 35N43'34 80w38'31 5:22:34
Barber Landing 74 1 35N36'01 77w17'57 5:09:12
Barclaysville 43 1 35N28'07 78w41'40 5:14:47
Barco 27 1 36N23'30 75w58'48 5:03:55
Barfield 46 1 36N23'21 76w54'31 5:07:38
Barham 92 1 35N56'31 78w24'16 5:13:37
Barium Springs 49 1 35N43'08 80w53'54 5:23:36
Barker Heights 45 1 35N18'40 82w26'39 5:29:47
Barkers Creek 50 1 35N24 83w18 5:33:12
Barnard 58 1 35N50'22 82w45'15 5:31:01
Barnardsville 11 1 35N46'39 82w27'18 5:29:49
Barnes Crossroads 21 1 36N15'12 76w37'03 5:06:28
Barnesville 78 1 34N24'31 79w02'49 5:16:11
Barrett 3 1 36N31'38 80w58'06 5:23:52
Barretts Crossing 46 1 36N30 77w00 5:08:00
Barretts Crossroads 46 1 36N28'13 77w03'21 5:08:13
Barriers Mill 13 1 35N21'24 80w25'41 5:21:43
Barringer 49 1 35N41 80w50 5:23:20
Bartlett 15 1 36N17'21 76w05'05 5:04:20
Barton Creek 92 1 35N57 78w39 5:14:36
Bartonsville 46 1 36N28'30 76w57'32 5:07:50
Bass Crossroads 64 1 35N59'03 78w04'44 5:12:19
Bass Landing 21 1 36N10'58 76w43'13 5:06:53
Batarora 10 1 34N14'24 78w08'41 5:12:35
Bat Cave 45 1 35N27'05 82w17'14 5:29:09
Batchelor Crossroads 64 1 35N56'54 78w00'59 5:12:04
Bates Creek 20 1 35N06'47 84w03'11 5:36:13
Bath 7 1 35N28'37 76w48'43 5:07:15
Baton 14 1 35N48'26 81w31'55 5:26:08
Battleboro 33 1 36N02'56 77w44'58 5:11:00
Battleground 6 1 36N14'32 81w55'54 5:27:44
Batts Crossroads 7 1 35N41'25 77w04'49 5:08:19
Baumtown 28 1 35N51'01 75w39'16 5:02:37
Baxter 45 1 35N19'02 82w20'53 5:29:24
Bay 89 1 35N55 76w15 5:05:00
Bayboro 69 1 35N08'34 76w46'14 5:07:05
Bay City 69 1 35N10'45 76w46'15 5:07:05
Bayleaf 92 1 35N56'38 78w38'35 5:14:34
Baynes 17 1 36N16'08 79w18'18 5:17:13
Bay Shore Landing 7 1 35N32'15 76w30'32 5:06:02
Bayshore Park 16 1 34N42 77w06 5:08:24
Bayview 7 1 35N26'12 76w47'32 5:07:10
Beach Land Landing 28 1 35N47'33 75w54'32 5:03:38
Beach Springs 72 1 36N12'33 76w30'54 5:06:04
Beaman Crossroads 82 1 35N07'09 78w24'51 5:13:39
Beams Mill 23 1 35N23'24 81w29'50 5:25:59
Bear Creek 19 1 35N37'00 79w23'06 5:17:32
Bear Creek 38 2 35N16'18 83w43'20 5:34:53
Bear Creek 67 1 34N39'46 77w10'51 5:08:43
Bear Creek Junction 38 1 35N19 83w48 5:35:12
Beard 26 1 35N06'59 78w47'57 5:15:12
Beargrass 59 1 35N45 77w07 5:08:28
Bear Pond 91 1 36N16'37 78w24'22 5:13:37
Bear Poplar 80 1 35N40'33 80w41'37 5:22:46
Bearskin 82 1 35N01 78w30 5:14:00
Bearwallow 45 1 35N27'47 82w18'59 5:29:16
Beasley 94 1 35N54'56 76w32'57 5:06:12
Beaufort 16 1 34N43'05 76w39'51 5:06:39
Beautancus 31 1 35N07'03 78w02'19 5:12:09
Beaverbrook 36 1 35N16'42 81w11'39 5:24:47
Beaver Creek 5 1 36N22'38 81w30'09 5:26:01
Beaver Creek 26 1 35N05'37 78w59'11 5:15:57
Beaverdam 11 2 35N29'50 82w41'13 5:30:45
Beaverdam 26 1 34N54 78w37 5:14:28
Beaverdam 42 1 36N16'14 77w42'26 5:10:50
Beaver Island 85 1 36N23 80w05 5:20:20
Beckford Junction 37 1 36N23'00 76w35'34 5:06:22
Beckwith 7 1 35N31'45 76w46'52 5:07:07
Bectons Old Field Landing 54 1 35N20'07 77w27'16 5:09:49
Beech 11 1 35N42'42 82w28'13 5:29:53
Beech Bottom 6 1 36N04'19 82w00'33 5:28:02
Beech Creek 6 1 36N15'27 81w54'03 5:27:36
Beechertown 57 1 35N16'24 83w40'48 5:34:43
Beech Glen 58 1 35N49'07 82w30'17 5:30:01
Beech Mountain 6 1 36N14 81w56 5:27:44
Bee Log 100 1 35N59'04 82w24'32 5:29:38
Beeson Crossroads 34 1 36N05'10 80w06'05 5:20:24
Belcross 15 1 36N20'52 76w09'18 5:04:37
Belews Creek 34 1 36N14'40 80w04'12 5:20:17
Belfast 96 1 35N25'37 77w58'56 5:11:56
Belgrade 67 1 34N52'48 77w14'07 5:08:56
Belhaven 7 1 35N32'24 76w37'24 5:06:30
Bellair 25 1 35N09'55 77w07'17 5:08:29
Bellarthur 74 1 35N36 77w31 5:10:04
Bellemont 1 1 36N01'32 79w26'36 5:17:46
Bell Fork 67 1 34N45'41 77w24'02 5:09:36
Bell Fork 74 1 35N33'53 77w20'59 5:09:24
Bells 19 1 35N45'05 79w00'31 5:16:02
Bells Crossroads 49 1 35N39'15 80w53'10 5:23:33
Bells Crossroads 71 1 34N25'34 77w57'42 5:11:51
Bells Crossroads 74 1 35N42'32 77w27'48 5:09:51
Bells Fork 74 1 35N36 77w23 5:09:32
Bells Landing 52 1 35N01'48 77w10'47 5:08:43
Bell Swamp 10 1 34N07'59 78w05'47 5:12:23
Belltown 39 1 36N16'09 78w36'41 5:14:27
Bellview 20 1 34N59'28 84w04'02 5:36:16
Belmont 36 1 35N14'34 81w02'15 5:24:09
Belmont 42 1 36N27'53 77w40'48 5:10:43
Belva 58 1 35N56'03 82w44'35 5:30:58
Belvidere 72 1 36N16'07 76w32'10 5:06:09
Belwood 23 1 35N27'50 81w31'19 5:26:05
Benaja 79 1 36N14'59 79w40'39 5:18:43
Benham 97 1 36N17'25 80w55'04 5:23:40
Bennett 19 1 35N33'55 79w32'38 5:18:11
Bensalem 63 1 35N20 79w38 5:18:32
Benson 51 1 35N22'55 78w32'56 5:14:12
Bent Creek 100 1 36N00'45 82w23'10 5:29:33
Benton Crossroads 90 1 34N59 80w33 5:22:12
Benton Heights 90 1 34N59 80w33 5:22:12
Bentons Crossroads 90 1 35N06'14 80w32'12 5:22:09
Bentonsville 51 1 35N20 78w19 5:13:16
Berea 39 1 36N19'14 78w44'31 5:14:58
Berryhill 60 1 35N13 80w57 5:23:48
Berry Mill 57 1 35N13'29 83w21'57 5:33:28
Bertha 27 1 36N16'23 75w54'39 5:03:39
Bertie 8 1 36N03 76w57 5:07:48
Bessemer 41 1 36N05'01 79w44'35 5:18:58
Bessemer City 36 1 35N17'05 81w17'03 5:25:08
Bessie 50 1 35N09'22 83w10'29 5:32:42
Best 96 1 35N20'37 77w50'57 5:11:24
Bests 96 1 35N18 77w47 5:11:08
Beta 50 2 35N23'41 83w11'26 5:32:46
Bethabara 34 1 36N08 80w18 5:21:12
Bethania 34 1 36N10'56 80w20'18 5:21:21
Bethania Station 34 1 36N10'10 80w17'26 5:21:10
Bethany 49 1 35N51 80w52 5:23:28
Bethany 79 1 36N18'26 79w51'32 5:19:26
Bethany Crossroads 26 1 35N03'48 78w41'49 5:14:47
Bethel 2 1 35N44 81w21 5:25:24
Bethel 17 1 36N27'12 79w27'07 5:17:48
Bethel 24 1 34N07'26 78w42'47 5:14:51
Bethel 44 1 35N28'24 82w53'46 5:31:35
Bethel 47 1 34N59 79w13 5:16:52
Bethel 58 1 35N52'59 82w28'38 5:29:55
Bethel 72 1 36N06'50 76w28'55 5:05:56
Bethel 74 1 35N48'25 77w22'45 5:09:31
Bethel 95 1 36N17'36 81w50'58 5:27:24
Bethel Hill 73 1 36N30'16 78w55'02 5:15:40
Bethesda 29 1 35N52'46 80w14'28 5:20:58
Bethesda 32 1 35N56'32 78w50'19 5:15:21
Bethlehem 2 1 35N49'32 81w18'26 5:25:14
Bethlehem 46 1 36N21 76w54 5:07:36
Bettie 16 1 34N47'28 76w35'47 5:06:23
Beulah 48 1 35N25'17 76w29'37 5:05:58
Beulah 51 1 35N36 78w09 5:12:36
Beulah 75 1 35N15 82w38 5:30:32
Beulahtown 51 1 35N35'37 78w10'18 5:12:41
Beulaville 31 1 34N55'25 77w46'27 5:11:06
Beverly Hills 11 1 35N35'08 82w30'17 5:30:01
Biddle Landing 25 1 35N19'03 77w19'34 5:09:18
Big Creek 85 1 36N31 80w23 5:21:32
Big Curve 24 1 34N13'06 78w25'47 5:13:43
Big East Fork 44 1 35N21'51 82w49'13 5:31:17
Biggs Park 78 1 34N36 79w01 5:16:04
Big Junction 38 1 35N18'05 84w01'17 5:36:05
Big Laurel 58 1 35N55'40 82w40'34 5:30:42
Big Laurel 87 1 35N20'21 83w21'07 5:33:24
Big Lick 84 1 35N14'29 80w20'39 5:21:23
Big Pine 58 1 35N47'27 82w48'31 5:31:14
Big Ridge 50 1 35N12'23 83w05'24 5:32:22
Bilboa 32 1 35N57'21 78w51'11 5:15:25
Bills Creek 81 1 35N26'55 82w08'46 5:28:35
Bills Creek Landing 69 1 35N14'37 76w34'47 5:06:19
Biltmore 11 1 35N33'29 82w32'01 5:30:08
Biltmore Forest 11 1 35N32'01 82w31'43 5:30:07
Bina 5 1 36N29'01 81w29'57 5:26:00
Bingham 68 1 35N57 79w12 5:16:48
Bingham Heights 11 1 35N36'38 82w35'09 5:30:21
Bird Cage 24 1 34N20'45 78w50'39 5:15:23
Birdtown 87 1 35N28'07 83w21'08 5:33:25
Biscoe 62 1 35N21'35 79w46'48 5:19:07
Bishop 10 1 34N10'44 78w05'07 5:12:20
Bishops Cross 7 1 35N36'39 76w40'41 5:06:43
Bixby 30 1 35N56'24 80w27'19 5:21:49
Blackberry Inn 11 1 35N42'08 82w25'47 5:29:43
Blackburn 18 1 35N36'57 81w19'52 5:25:19
Black Creek 98 1 35N38'06 77w56'00 5:11:44
Black Ford 47 1 35N05'23 79w08'39 5:16:35
Black Jack 74 1 35N30'06 77w14'53 5:09:00
Black Jack 77 1 35N02 79w50 5:19:20
Blackman 51 1 35N27 78w26 5:13:44
Blackmans Mills 82 1 35N14'52 78w24'29 5:13:38
Blackmon Crossroads 51 1 35N22'06 78w25'43 5:13:43
Black Mountain 11 1 35N37'04 82w19'17 5:29:17
Black Mountain Sanatorium 11 1 35N37 82w19 5:29:16
Blacknel 53 1 35N36'52 79w06'41 5:16:27
Blackrock 8 1 36N03'12 76w44'26 5:06:58
Black Water 86 1 36N23'49 80w37'27 5:22:30
Blackwell 17 1 36N26'33 79w27'50 5:17:51
Blackwood 68 1 35N59'32 79w04'21 5:16:17
Bladenboro 9 1 34N32'19 78w47'16 5:15:09
Bladen Springs 9 1 34N32'14 78w28'31 5:13:54
Blades 25 1 34N53'09 76w46'21 5:07:05
Blaine 62 1 35N29'28 80w03'34 5:20:14
Blanch 17 1 36N30'28 79w17'43 5:17:11
Blands 32 1 35N53'16 78w57'27 5:15:50
Blands Crossroads 54 1 35N10'52 77w42'34 5:10:50
Blanon Landing 24 1 34N22'21 78w14'31 5:12:58
Blantyre 88 1 35N18'00 82w37'34 5:30:30
Blevins Crossroads 3 1 36N32'32 81w00'51 5:24:03
Blevins Store 86 1 36N24 80w43 5:22:52
Blizzards Crossroads 31 1 35N08'11 77w54'07 5:11:36
Bloomingdale 78 1 34N26'26 79w01'14 5:16:05
Bloomington 84 1 35N19'52 80w19'07 5:21:16
Blossomtown 57 1 35N09'01 83w23'37 5:33:34
Blount 94 1 35N54'59 76w36'03 5:06:24
Blounts Creek 7 1 35N20'59 76w57'37 5:07:50
Blowertown 4 1 34N58 80w05 5:20:20
Blowing Rock 95 1 36N08'06 81w40'40 5:26:43
Blue Banks Landing 74 1 35N39'15 77w27'27 5:09:50
Bluefield 9 1 34N29 78w39 5:14:36
Bluefield Crossroads 9 1 34N31'29 78w36'08 5:14:25
Blue Ridge 45 1 35N21'01 82w21'47 5:29:27
Blue Ridge Forest 11 1 35N32'28 82w23'10 5:29:33
Blue Rock 100 1 35N53'26 82w10'47 5:28:43
Blue Springs 47 1 34N57 79w18 5:17:12
Blue Wing Church 50 1 35N29 83w19 5:33:16
Bluff 58 1 35N50'16 82w51'29 5:31:26
Bly 5 1 36N30 81w30 5:26:00
Boardman 24 1 34N26'20 78w56'58 5:15:48
Bobbitt 91 1 36N13'15 78w23'49 5:13:35
Boddies Pond 64 1 35N58 77w58 5:11:52
Boger City 55 1 35N29 81w13 5:24:52
Bogue 16 1 34N41'57 77w02'14 5:08:09
Bohaynee 88 1 35N03'45 83w00'35 5:32:02
Boiling Spring Lakes 10 1 34N01 78w03 5:12:12
Boiling Springs 20 1 35N12'21 84w00'35 5:36:02
Boiling Springs 81 1 35N15'15 81w40'02 5:26:40
Bolivia 10 1 34N04'03 78w08'55 5:12:36
Bolling 42 1 36N27 77w40 5:10:40
Bolton 24 1 34N19'14 78w24'08 5:13:37
Bon Air 34 1 36N07'42 80w14'32 5:20:58
Bonaparte Landing 10 1 33N54 78w27 5:13:48
Bones Ford 26 1 35N07'08 79w04'49 5:16:19
Bonham Heights 16 1 34N42 76w50 5:07:20
Bonlee 19 1 35N38'45 79w24'53 5:17:40
Bonnerton 7 1 35N21'30 76w51'36 5:07:26
Bonnetsville 82 1 34N59'25 78w23'42 5:13:35
Bonnie Doone 26 1 35N05'42 78w57'21 5:15:49
Bonsal 92 1 35N39'37 78w58'26 5:15:54
Boogertown 36 1 35N13'05 81w09'36 5:24:38
Boomer 97 1 36N04'02 81w15'14 5:25:01
Boone 95 1 36N13'00 81w40'29 5:26:42
Boone Field Landing 9 1 34N44'39 78w23'39 5:13:35
Boone Fork 95 1 36N07'20 81w44'19 5:26:57
Boone Landing 10 1 33N54'45 78w20'52 5:13:23
Boones Crossroads 66 1 36N20'19 77w25'08 5:09:41
Boones Hill 86 1 36N28'32 80w34'31 5:22:18
Boone Trail 43 1 35N25'02 78w57'41 5:15:51
Boonford 61 1 35N55'49 82w10'09 5:28:41
Boon Hill 51 1 35N28 78w11 5:12:44
Boon Station 1 1 36N07 79w31 5:18:04
Boonville 99 1 36N13'57 80w42'30 5:22:50
Bostian Heights 80 1 35N33'37 80w31'26 5:22:06
Bostic 81 1 35N21'45 81w50'09 5:27:21
Bostic Yard 81 1 35N22 81w50 5:27:20
Boswell 11 2 35N34'44 82w36'52 5:30:27
Boswellville 98 1 35N40'28 77w58'22 5:11:53
Bottom 86 1 36N28'29 80w46'27 5:23:06
Boulevard 79 1 36N30 79w45 5:19:00
Bowdens 31 1 35N03'25 78w06'57 5:12:28
Bowditch 100 1 35N53'02 82w12'59 5:28:52
Bowlens Creek 100 1 35N52'40 82w17'07 5:29:08
Bowman Bluff 45 1 35N18'13 82w33'43 5:30:15
Bowmore 47 1 34N56'31 79w18'12 5:17:13
Boyd 88 1 35N18 82w39 5:30:36
Boyd Crossroads 74 1 35N31'50 77w11'20 5:08:45
Boyds Fork 7 1 35N32'42 76w50'45 5:07:23
Boyles Chapel 85 1 36N17 80w21 5:21:24
Boylston Creek 88 1 35N18'56 82w39'39 5:30:39
Bracey 78 1 34N32 79w17 5:17:08
Brackett 56 1 35N33 81w57 5:27:48

Bradford Crossroads 49 1 35N47'00 81w00'18 5:24:01
Bradshaw 61 1 36N04 82w17 5:29:08
Braggtown 32 1 36N02'05 78w53'32 5:15:34
Brake 33 1 35N58 77w48 5:11:12
Brandon 5 1 36N32'08 81w30'40 5:26:03
Branon 99 1 36N07'14 80w44'23 5:22:58
Brassfield 32 1 35N55'52 78w51'03 5:15:24
Brasstown 22 1 35N02'22 83w57'25 5:35:50
Braswell 24 1 34N22'07 78w52'04 5:15:28
Braswells Crossroads 42 1 36N05'05 77w22'56 5:09:32
Brendletown 57 1 35N14'25 83w20'26 5:33:22
Brentwood 92 1 35N48 78w38 5:14:32
Brevard 88 1 35N14'00 82w44'04 5:30:56
Brewers Crossroads 66 1 36N30'32 77w36'12 5:10:25
Briarcliff 68 1 35N55'42 79w00'56 5:16:04
Brice 81 1 35N11'29 81w50'59 5:27:24
Brices Crossroads 31 1 34N49'07 78w06'06 5:12:24
Brick Cellar Landing 46 1 36N18'39 76w51'11 5:07:25
Brickhaven 19 1 35N34'29 79w01'45 5:16:07
Brick Landing 10 1 33N54'17 78w23'32 5:13:34
Bricks 33 1 36N06 77w43 5:10:52
Brickton 45 1 35N24'32 82w30'49 5:30:03
Bridgersville 98 1 35N45'22 77w45'06 5:11:00
Bridgeton 25 1 35N07'17 77w01'16 5:08:05
Bridgewater 12 1 35N42'41 81w51'46 5:27:27
Brief 90 1 35N11'24 80w32'01 5:22:08
Briertown 57 1 35N15'44 83w36'45 5:34:27
Brightwater 45 1 35N19'51 82w31'11 5:30:05
Brightwood 41 1 36N07'58 79w45'35 5:19:02
Brindletown 12 1 35N37'30 81w48'03 5:27:12
Brinkleyville 42 1 36N16'34 77w51'14 5:11:25
Britts 78 1 34N32 78w58 5:15:52
Broadbay 34 1 36N03 80w13 5:20:52
Broad Creek 16 1 34N43'14 76w56'12 5:07:45
Broad River 11 1 35N32 82w16 5:29:04
Broadview 41 1 36N07'10 79w47'04 5:19:08
Broadview Estates 88 1 35N14'30 82w43'18 5:30:53
Broadway 24 1 34N18'21 78w51'36 5:15:26
Broadway 53 1 35N27'28 79w03'12 5:16:13
Brocks 67 1 34N55'00 77w31'32 5:10:06
Brogden 51 1 35N25'50 78w14'54 5:13:00
Brogden 96 1 35N17'33 78w02'05 5:12:08
Brook Cove 85 1 36N17'11 80w11'23 5:20:46
Brookford 18 1 35N42'11 81w20'53 5:25:24
Brookhaven 92 1 35N50 78w40 5:14:40
Brooks Crossroads 99 1 36N07'12 80w46'24 5:23:06
Brooksdale 73 1 36N22'27 78w58'51 5:15:55
Brookside 96 1 35N22 77w58 5:11:52
Brookston 91 1 36N21'59 78w20'27 5:13:22
Brookwood 34 1 36N07'35 80w13'47 5:20:55
Brower 76 1 35N34 79w38 5:18:32
Brown Marsh 9 1 34N31 78w38 5:14:32
Brown Mountain Beach 14 1 35N54'28 81w43'36 5:26:54
Browns Crossroads 76 1 35N44'38 79w34'44 5:18:19
Browns Summit 41 1 36N12'45 79w42'50 5:18:51
Brown Town 36 1 35N15'11 81w01'21 5:24:05
Brown Town 71 1 34N20'47 77w44'06 5:10:56
Browntown Crossroads 40 1 35N22'42 77w40'02 5:10:40
Brownwood 5 1 36N16'36 81w33'17 5:26:13
Bruce 41 1 36N12 79w54 5:19:36
Bruce 74 1 35N40'23 77w29'03 5:09:56
Brunswick 24 1 34N17'12 78w42'05 5:14:48
Brush Creek 100 1 35N59 82w13 5:28:52
Brushy Fork 95 1 36N14 81w43 5:26:52
Brushy Mountain 97 1 36N05 81w06 5:24:24
Bryan 86 1 36N22 80w51 5:23:24
Bryan Landing 52 1 35N00'44 77w15'56 5:09:04
Bryantown 66 1 36N16'50 77w21'33 5:09:26
Bryson City 87 2 35N25'51 83w26'51 5:33:47
Bryson Place 87 1 35N31'15 83w25'09 5:33:41
Buck 97 1 36N09'23 81w13'36 5:24:54
Buckeye Ford 45 1 35N15'23 82w23'25 5:29:34
Buckhead 24 1 34N22'28 78w25'06 5:13:40
Buckhorn 68 1 36N05 79w10 5:16:40
Buckhorn Crossroads 98 1 35N40'41 78w06'28 5:12:26
Buckland 37 1 36N28'27 76w45'42 5:07:03
Bucklesberry 54 1 35N13'48 77w43'15 5:10:53
Buckner 58 1 35N51'50 82w29'03 5:29:56
Bucks Corner 16 1 34N43'20 77w04'07 5:08:16
Buck Shoal 99 1 36N07 80w49 5:23:16
Buck Swamp 96 1 35N29 78w03 5:12:12
Buena Vista 8 1 36N07'14 76w57'53 5:07:52
Buena Vista 11 1 35N31'55 82w31'41 5:30:07
Buena Vista 34 1 36N06'41 80w16'57 5:21:08
Buffalo 20 2 35N12'13 83w47'34 5:35:10
Buffalo 49 1 35N42'51 81w02'03 5:24:08
Buffalo City 28 1 35N50'32 75w55'03 5:03:40
Buffalo Cove 14 1 36N05'28 81w31'37 5:26:06
Buford 90 1 34N53 80w33 5:22:12
Bughill 24 1 34N04'43 78w38'39 5:14:35
Buie 78 1 34N44'11 79w08'42 5:16:35
Buies Creek 43 1 35N24'47 78w44'09 5:14:57
Buies Neck 78 1 34N47'51 78w53'42 5:15:35
Buladean 61 1 36N06'30 82w11'42 5:28:47
Bullhead 40 1 35N31 77w47 5:11:08
Bullock 39 1 36N29'28 78w32'43 5:14:11
Bullocks Crossroads 33 1 35N52'46 77w44'27 5:10:58
Bullocksville 91 1 36N27'11 78w20'48 5:13:23
Bunker Hill 77 1 34N57'17 79w46'17 5:19:05
Bunlevel 43 1 35N19 78w47 5:15:08
Bunn 35 1 35N57'39 78w15'14 5:13:01
Bunnlevel 43 1 35N18'34 78w46'50 5:15:07
Bunyan 7 1 35N32'16 76w58'32 5:07:54

Burbage Crossroads 7 1 35N27'01 76w42'12 5:06:49
Burch 86 1 36N16'33 80w46'00 5:23:04
Burden 8 1 36N09'32 77w03'54 5:08:16
Burgaw 71 1 34N33'07 77w55'35 5:11:42
Burger Town 20 1 35N02'57 84w18'16 5:37:13
Burgess 72 1 36N08'05 76w24'27 5:05:38
Burke Chapel 12 1 35N44 81w21 5:25:24
Burkemont 12 1 35N40'54 81w41'59 5:26:48
Burke Park 34 1 36N04'45 80w18'25 5:21:14
Burlington 1 1 36N05'44 79w26'17 5:17:45
Burlington Mills 92 1 35N59 78w30 5:14:00
Burnett Fields 57 1 35N15'40 83w32'29 5:34:10
Burnett Siding 44 1 35N23'45 82w56'19 5:31:45
Burney 9 1 34N43'54 78w43'04 5:14:52
Burningtown 57 1 35N13'52 83w28'16 5:33:53
Burnsville 4 1 35N06'44 80w14'41 5:20:59
Burnsville 100 1 35N55'02 82w18'04 5:29:12
Burnt Chimney Corner 75 1 35N12'25 82w12'15 5:28:49
Burnt Landing 71 1 34N24'39 78w02'08 5:12:09
Burnt Mills 15 1 36N23'39 76w15'55 5:05:04
Burnt Swamp 78 1 34N42 79w07 5:16:28
Burton 32 1 36N02'25 78w49'09 5:15:17
Burton Hills 36 1 35N16'57 81w08'25 5:24:34
Busbee 11 1 35N29'54 82w31'05 5:30:04
Bushy Fork 73 1 36N18'28 79w05'12 5:16:21
Busick 41 1 36N13 79w43 5:18:52
Busick 100 1 35N46'11 82w10'59 5:28:44
Butler Crossroads 24 1 34N05'09 78w38'39 5:14:35
Butlers 8 1 36N03 76w57 5:07:48
Butlers Crossroads 82 1 34N55'23 78w19'52 5:13:19
Butner 39 1 36N07'55 78w45'25 5:15:02
Butters 9 1 34N33'37 78w50'55 5:15:24
Butterwood 42 1 36N21 77w51 5:11:24
Buxton 28 1 35N16'03 75w32'34 5:02:10
Buxton Landing 28 1 35N16'18 75w32'25 5:02:10
Buzzards Crossroads 8 1 36N12 76w46 5:07:04
Bynum 19 1 35N46'26 79w08'33 5:16:34
Byrdville 24 1 34N19'04 78w18'41 5:13:15
Cabarrus 13 1 35N14'13 80w32'31 5:22:10
Cabes Ford 68 1 36N04'46 79w00'27 5:16:02
Cabin 31 1 35N03 77w45 5:11:00
Cable 1 1 36N00 79w28 5:17:52
Cady Landing 37 1 36N27'07 76w56'41 5:07:47
Cahaba 8 1 36N02'25 77w09'24 5:08:38
Caintuck Landing 71 1 34N22'07 78w12'39 5:12:51
Cairo 4 1 34N53'04 79w55'59 5:19:44
Calabash 10 1 33N53'26 78w34'07 5:14:16
Calahaln 30 1 35N55'10 80w39'47 5:22:39
Caldwell 60 1 35N27'13 80w50'35 5:23:22
Caldwell 68 1 36N11'23 79w01'03 5:16:04
Calico 74 1 35N25'06 77w15'18 5:09:01
California 28 1 35N54'15 75w40'51 5:02:43
California 46 1 36N21'28 76w58'43 5:07:55
California 58 1 35N52'00 82w31'11 5:30:05
California 74 1 35N37'59 77w33'25 5:10:14
Call 97 1 36N08'45 81w04'40 5:24:19
Callisons 69 1 35N05'03 76w43'32 5:06:54
Calvander 68 1 35N56'34 79w06'36 5:16:26
Calvert 88 1 35N09'25 82w48'39 5:31:15
Calvin 12 1 35N44'00 81w43'50 5:26:55
Calypso 31 1 35N09'13 78w06'20 5:12:25
Camden 15 1 36N19'42 76w10'20 5:04:41
Camelot 45 1 35N21'29 82w32'07 5:30:08
Cameron 63 1 35N19'36 79w15'20 5:17:01
Campbell 85 1 36N31'40 80w14'15 5:20:57
Campbell Creek 7 1 35N17'37 76w41'28 5:06:46
Campbells Crossroad 47 1 35N05'13 79w13'53 5:16:56
Camp Bryan 25 1 34N50'42 76w59'04 5:07:56
Camp Creek 12 1 35N34'28 81w33'13 5:26:13
Camp Don-Lee 69 1 34N58'27 76w47'17 5:07:09
Camp Glenn 16 1 34N42 76w50 5:07:20
Camp Hardee 7 1 35N28'26 76w59'42 5:07:59
Camp Leach 7 1 35N27'37 76w53'14 5:07:33
Camp Lejeune 67 1 34N40 77w21 5:09:24
Camp Lejeune Central 67 1 34N44 77w24 5:09:36
Camp Lejeune Junction 67 1 34N43 77w22 5:09:28
Camp Occoneechee 81 1 35N24'31 82w12'31 5:28:50
Camp Seagull 69 1 34N58'14 76w47'58 5:07:12
Camp Springs 17 1 36N17'46 79w29'31 5:17:58
Camp Sutton 90 1 34N59 80w33 5:22:12
Cana 30 1 35N58'27 80w34'39 5:22:19
Canada 50 1 35N14 83w01 5:32:04
Canby 62 1 35N13 80w00 5:20:00
Candler 11 2 35N32'11 82w41'35 5:30:46
Candler Heights 11 2 35N32'24 82w42'23 5:30:50
Candor 62 1 35N17'42 79w44'44 5:18:59
Cane 100 1 35N54'18 82w23'11 5:29:33
Cane Brake 88 1 35N03'57 82w53'25 5:31:34
Cane Branch 100 1 35N55 82w18 5:29:12
Cane Creek 20 1 35N05 84w02 5:36:08
Cane Creek 61 1 36N01 82w06 5:28:24
Cane River (P O) 100 1 35N54'52 82w23'29 5:29:34
Canetuck 71 1 34N24 78w10 5:12:40
Caney Fork 50 1 35N19 83w06 5:32:24
Cannon Crossroads 74 1 35N33'06 77w23'02 5:09:32
Cannon Ferry 21 1 36N13 76w37 5:06:28
Canto 11 1 35N42'05 82w45'33 5:31:02
Canton 44 2 35N31'58 82w50'15 5:31:21
Cape Carteret 16 1 34N41'29 77w03'48 5:08:15
Cape Fear 43 1 35N25'30 78w48'54 5:15:16
Cape Fear 65 3 34N13 77w55 5:11:40
Cape Hatteras 48 1 35N30 75w30 5:02:00

Capella 85 1 36N21'42 80w19'00 5:21:16
Cape Lookout 16 1 34N36'19 76w32'12 5:06:09
Capelsie 62 1 35N19'07 79w52'26 5:19:30
Capels Mill 77 1 35N09'21 79w47'47 5:19:11
Capernium 34 1 36N03'15 80w25'01 5:21:40
Caraleigh 92 1 35N45'38 78w38'58 5:14:36
Caraway Landing 69 1 35N19'02 76w34'52 5:06:19
Carbonton 19 1 35N31'13 79w20'57 5:17:24
Carlos 26 1 35N12'34 78w46'19 5:15:05
Carmen 58 1 36N00'17 82w38'28 5:30:34
Carmur 48 1 35N33'08 76w11'25 5:04:46
Caroleen 81 1 35N16'51 81w47'47 5:27:11
Carolina 1 1 36N07'54 79w24'46 5:17:39
Carolina 74 1 35N43 77w17 5:09:08
Carolina Beach 65 3 34N02'06 77w53'38 5:11:35
Carolina Hills 45 1 35N26 82w30 5:30:00
Carolina Pines 92 1 35N44'54 78w39'30 5:14:38
Carpenter 92 1 35N49'14 78w52'19 5:15:29
Carpenter Bottom 6 1 36N04'57 81w59'47 5:27:59
Carr 32 1 35N58 78w45 5:15:00
Carr 68 1 36N12'41 79w13'13 5:16:53
Carrboro 68 1 35N54'36 79w04'32 5:16:18
Carroll 31 1 34N57'07 78w04'35 5:12:18
Carrs 40 1 35N32 77w41 5:10:44
Carson Mill 87 2 35N24'08 83w31'52 5:34:07
Carter 37 1 36N21 76w36 5:06:24
Carter Crossroads 37 1 36N21'26 76w41'05 5:06:44
Cartersville 31 1 34N46'23 77w55'11 5:11:41
Carthage 63 1 35N20'45 79w25'02 5:17:40
Cartoogechaye 57 1 35N07 83w30 5:34:00
Carvers 9 1 34N27'39 78w24'50 5:13:39
Cary 92 1 35N47'29 78w46'53 5:15:08
Casar 23 1 35N30'44 81w37'03 5:26:28
Cash Corner 69 1 35N11'28 76w41'08 5:06:45
Cash Corner No 2 69 1 35N00'05 76w47'31 5:07:10
Cashiers 50 1 35N06'20 83w05'48 5:32:23
Cashoke Landing 8 1 35N56'23 76w44'40 5:06:59
Cason Old Field 4 1 34N50'18 80w05'39 5:20:23
Castalia 64 1 36N04'54 78w03'28 5:12:14
Castle Hayne 65 3 34N21'20 77w54'01 5:11:36
Castoria 40 1 35N32'11 77w40'29 5:10:42
Casville 17 1 36N23'24 79w30'16 5:18:01
Caswell 52 1 35N14'06 77w31'18 5:10:05
Caswell 71 1 34N30 78w09 5:12:36
Caswell Beach 10 1 33N56 78w04 5:12:16
Caswell Landing 54 1 35N17'03 77w29'44 5:09:59
Cataloochee 44 1 35N42 83w04 5:32:16
Catawba 18 1 35N42'26 81w04'33 5:24:18
Catawba Heights 36 1 35N16'28 81w01'41 5:24:07
Catawba Springs 55 1 35N28 81w01 5:24:04
Cates 73 1 36N17'42 78w59'14 5:15:57
Catfish 18 1 35N45'18 81w07'05 5:24:28
Catherine Lake 67 1 34N49'03 77w33'51 5:10:15
Catheys Creek 88 1 35N12 82w47 5:31:08
Cat Square 55 1 35N32'24 81w24'39 5:25:39
Causeway Landing 71 1 34N22'19 78w08'16 5:12:33
Ca-Vel 73 1 36N24 78w59 5:15:56
Cayton 25 1 35N15'49 76w59'24 5:07:58
Cecil 44 1 35N29 82w56 5:31:44
Cedar Bay 10 1 33N56'44 78w32'55 5:14:12
Cedar Creek 26 1 34N57'21 78w45'27 5:15:02
Cedar Falls 76 1 35N45'07 79w43'54 5:18:56
Cedar Fork 31 1 34N52'36 77w42'29 5:10:50
Cedar Fork 92 1 35N51 78w50 5:15:20
Cedar Grove 29 1 35N43'24 80w11'07 5:20:44
Cedar Grove 68 1 36N10'03 79w10'05 5:16:40
Cedar Grove 76 1 35N40'32 79w53'20 5:19:33
Cedar Hill 4 1 35N08'34 80w07'06 5:20:28
Cedar Hill 10 1 34N17'04 78w01'51 5:12:07
Cedar Island 16 1 34N58 76w19 5:05:16
Cedar Lodge 29 1 35N53 80w05 5:20:20
Cedar Mountain 88 1 35N08'36 82w38'35 5:30:34
Cedar Point 16 1 34N41'15 77w04'22 5:08:17
Cedarrock 35 1 36N05 78w09 5:12:36
Cedar Valley 14 1 35N54'10 81w26'05 5:25:44
Ceffo 73 1 36N27'25 79w02'48 5:16:11
Celeste Hinkel 49 1 35N45'25 80w58'32 5:23:54
Celeste Hinkle 49 1 35N51 80w56 5:23:44
Celo 100 1 35N51'18 82w11'53 5:28:48
Center 30 1 35N54'42 80w37'11 5:22:29
Center 99 1 36N08'51 80w42'52 5:22:51
Center Bluff Landing 74 1 35N40'45 77w28'34 5:09:54
Center Grove 41 1 36N10 79w50 5:19:20
Centergrove 73 1 36N17 78w57 5:15:48
Center Hill 21 1 36N12'54 76w36'40 5:06:27
Center Pigeon 44 1 35N30'22 82w51'10 5:31:25
Centerview 13 1 35N29'26 80w37'07 5:22:28
Centerville 35 1 36N11'10 78w06'21 5:12:25
Central 9 1 34N41 78w37 5:14:28
Central 49 1 35N56'13 80w58'00 5:23:52
Central Area 79 1 36N30'25 79w44'42 5:18:59
Central Falls 76 1 35N45'43 79w46'35 5:19:06
Century 92 1 35N47 78w40 5:14:40
Cerro Gordo 24 1 34N19'19 78w55'36 5:15:42
Cessons Mill 46 1 36N15'15 76w50'53 5:07:24
Chadbourn 24 1 34N19'19 78w49'38 5:15:19
Chadwick Acres 67 1 34N31 77w23 5:09:32
Chalybeate 43 1 35N35 78w48 5:15:12

Chalybeate Springs 43
1 35N30'30 78W48'51 5:15:15
Chambersburg 49 1 35N46 80W48 5:23:12
Champion 97 1 36N05 81W22 5:25:28
Chapanoke 72 1 36N15'14 76W22'40 5:05:31
Chapel Hill 58 1 35N56'34 82W42'32 5:30:50
Chapel Hill 68 1 35N54'47 79W03'22 5:16:13
Charity 31 1 34N49'22 77W56'46 5:11:47
Charles 49 1 35N54'50 80W52'20 5:23:29
Charleston 42 1 36N07'12 77W22'33 5:09:30
Charleston 87 1 35N26 83W25 5:33:40
Charlotte 60 1 35N13'37 80W50'36 5:23:22
Charlottetown 60
1 35N13 80W50 5:23:20
Cheek Creek 62 1 35N14 79W52 5:19:28
Cheeks 68 1 36N05 79W12 5:16:48
Cheeks 76 1 35N35'57 79W34'55 5:18:20
Cheeks Cross Roads 68
1 36N06 79W16 5:17:04
Chemway 60 1 35N16'19 80W53'50 5:23:35
Cheoah 38 1 35N20'24 83W44'50 5:34:59
Cherokee 87 1 35N28'27 83W18'54 5:33:16
Cherokee Indian Reservation 87
1 35N29 83W19 5:33:16
Cherry 94 1 35N50'55 76W25'18 5:05:41
Cherry Crossroads 33
1 36N02'54 77W42'09 5:10:49
Cherryfield 88 1 35N10'25 82W48'17 5:31:13
Cherry Grove 17 1 36N18'25 79W27'35 5:17:50
Cherry Grove 24 1 34N14'18 78W57'57 5:15:52
Cherry Landing 74
1 35N35'27 77W16'58 5:09:08
Cherry Lane 3 1 36N26'31 81W01'06 5:24:04
Cherry Point 25 1 34N54 76W54 5:07:36
Cherry Point Landing 25
1 34N56'30 76W52'09 5:07:29
Cherry Ridge Landing 89
1 35N42'12 76W08'30 5:04:34
Cherry Springs 56
1 35N38 82W11 5:28:44
Cherryville 36 1 35N22'43 81W22'45 5:25:31
Chesterfield 12 1 35N48'36 81W39'40 5:26:39
Chestnut Dale 6 1 36N03'59 81W58'48 5:27:55
Chestnut Grove 85
1 36N19'21 80W23'06 5:21:32
Chestnut Hill 5 1 36N30'19 81W21'09 5:25:25
Chestnut Hill 45
1 35N28'29 82W20'34 5:29:22
Chicod 74 1 35N29 77W16 5:09:04
Chimney Rock 81 1 35N26'21 82W14'48 5:28:59
China Grove 80 1 35N34'09 80W34'55 5:22:20
China Grove Cotton Mill 80
1 35N33 80W36 5:22:24
Chinquapin 31 1 34N49'51 77W49'00 5:11:16
Chip 25 1 35N13'45 77W08'12 5:08:33
Chip 62 1 35N15'35 79W53'37 5:19:34
Chocowinity 7 1 35N30'45 77W06'03 5:08:24
Chowan 21 1 36N15'59 76W40'05 5:06:40
Chublake 73 1 36N24 78W59 5:15:56
Church Hill 93 1 36N28'45 78W02'42 5:12:11
Churchill 93 1 36N26 78W05 5:12:20
Churchland 29 1 35N47'10 80W25'04 5:21:40
Church Landing 9
1 34N43'58 78W23'38 5:13:35
Cid 29 1 35N49 80W15 5:21:00
Cisco 21 1 36N11'23 76W38'03 5:06:32
Cityview 34 1 36N06'06 80W12'18 5:20:49
Clairmont 10 1 34N13'57 77W59'19 5:11:57
Claremont 18 1 35N42'52 81W08'47 5:24:35
Clarendon 24 1 34N12'36 78W50'44 5:15:23
Clark 25 1 35N08'45 77W09'37 5:08:38
Clark 44 2 35N26'25 83W04'26 5:32:18
Clarks Crossroads 9
1 34N31'15 78W33'25 5:14:14
Clarks Landing 71
1 34N23'36 77W58'57 5:11:56
Clarksville 30 1 36N00 80W38 5:22:32
Clarkton 9 1 34N29'14 78W39'23 5:14:38
Clarrissa 61 1 36N00'47 82W07'02 5:28:28
Clay 39 1 36N14'33 78W35'17 5:14:21
Clay 41 1 35N58 79W40 5:18:40
Clayroot 74 1 35N22'57 77W15'47 5:09:03
Clayton 51 1 35N39'02 78W27'24 5:13:50
Clearcreek 60 1 35N12 80W45 5:23:00
Clear Run 82 1 34N45'21 78W17'15 5:13:09
Clegg 92 1 35N51'56 78W50'59 5:15:24
Clement 82 1 35N05'44 78W37'44 5:14:31
Clemmons 34 1 36N01'17 80W22'56 5:21:32
Clemmons Station 34
1 35N59'58 80W22'49 5:21:31
Clemmonsville 34
1 36N01 80W23 5:21:32
Clemont 82 1 35N00 78W38 5:14:32
Cleveland 80 1 35N43'59 80W40'38 5:22:43
Cleveland Springs 23
1 35N17 81W32 5:26:08
Clewis Corner 24
1 34N11'11 78W24'09 5:13:37
Clifdale 26 1 35N03'41 79W00'56 5:16:04
Cliffdale 81 1 35N22 81W50 5:27:20
Cliffside 81 1 35N14'17 81W46'12 5:27:05
Clifton 5 1 36N26'48 81W34'16 5:26:17
Cliftonville 98 1 35N49'22 77W56'56 5:11:48
Climax 41 1 35N54'46 79W43'04 5:18:52
Clinchcross 56 1 35N41 82W00 5:28:00
Clinchfield 56 1 35N41'56 81W59'30 5:27:58
Clines 18 1 36N46 81W13 5:24:52
Clingman 97 1 36N10'42 80W55'41 5:23:43
Clinton 82 1 34N59'52 78W19'25 5:13:18
Closs 54 1 35N18'47 77W27'46 5:09:51
Cloverdale 92 1 35N43'41 78W37'11 5:14:29
Clover Garden 1 1 36N11'18 79W27'47 5:17:51
Clyde 44 2 35N32'00 82W54'39 5:31:39
Coakley 33 1 35N55'21 77W25'08 5:09:41
Coalglen 19 1 35N28 79W10 5:16:40
Coal Mine Landing 9
1 34N33'39 78W27'06 5:13:48
Coalville 20 2 35N11'18 83W53'28 5:35:34
Coats 43 1 35N24'28 78W40'20 5:14:41
Coats Crossroads 51
1 35N30'51 78W32'38 5:14:11
Cobbs 98 1 35N48 77W52 5:11:28

Cobbs Crossroad 98
1 35N49'27 77W51'26 5:11:26
Cobb Town 33 1 35N40 77W38 5:10:32
Coburn 11 2 35N32'06 82W45'19 5:31:01
Cockrell Beach 7
1 35N23'57 76W37'38 5:06:31
Coddle Creek 13 1 35N34 80W48 5:23:12
Cofield 46 1 36N21'23 76W54'37 5:07:38
Coggins Mine 62 1 35N29'12 80W01'14 5:20:05
Cognac 77 1 34N57'22 79W36'36 5:18:26
Coinjock 27 1 36N20'34 75W57'10 5:03:49
Cokers Crossroads 96
1 35N24'22 77W50'33 5:11:22
Cokesbury 43 1 35N31'28 78W54'33 5:15:38
Cokesbury 91 1 36N20'55 78W18'16 5:13:13
Cokey 33 1 35N51 77W42 5:10:48
Cold Springs 12 1 35N57'16 81W52'17 5:27:29
Cold Springs 13 1 35N24'54 80W30'48 5:22:03
Cold Water 13 1 35N24'58 80W33'00 5:22:12
Coleman 56 1 35N39'12 82W15'18 5:29:01
Colerain 8 1 36N12'04 76W46'08 5:07:05
Colerain Landing 8
1 36N11'50 76W44'56 5:07:00
Colerian Landing 8
1 36N11'49 76W44'55 5:07:00
Coleridge 76 1 35N38'24 79W36'56 5:18:28
Coleville 85 1 36N32'23 80W13'27 5:20:54
Colewood Acres 93
1 35N48 78W38 5:14:32
Colfax 41 1 36N06'45 80W00'53 5:20:04
Colfax 81 1 35N20 81W46 5:27:04
Colington 28 1 36N00'28 75W42'07 5:02:48
College 32 1 36N00 78W54 5:15:36
College Downs 60
1 35N16 80W48 5:23:12
College Lakes 26
1 35N04 78W53 5:15:32
Collettsville 14
1 35N55'32 81W40'29 5:26:42
Collington 28 1 36N04 75W42 5:02:48
Collinstown 85 1 36N32'43 80W20'14 5:21:21
Collinsville 75 1 35N12'41 82W05'15 5:28:21
Colly 9 1 34N27'36 78W15'17 5:13:01
Colon 53 1 35N31'36 79W09'09 5:16:37
Colonial Heights 26
1 34N56'43 78W56'42 5:15:47
Colonial Heights 92
1 35N41'50 78W40'13 5:14:41
Colony Park 32 1 36N01 78W56 5:15:44
Coltranes Mill 76
1 35N54'21 79W51'24 5:19:26
Columbia 89 1 35N55'03 76W15'09 5:05:01
Columbia Heights 34
1 36N05'25 80W13'40 5:20:55
Columbus 75 1 35N15'11 82W11'50 5:28:47
Combs Fork 52 1 35N03'45 77W31'12 5:10:05
Comet 5 1 36N28'55 81W33'17 5:26:13
Comfort 52 1 35N00'20 77W30'33 5:10:02
Como 46 1 36N30'05 77W00'35 5:08:02
Concord 13 1 35N24'31 80W34'47 5:22:19
Concord 31 1 34N50'15 78W06'59 5:12:28
Concord 73 1 36N26'45 79W04'00 5:16:16
Concord 81 1 35N20'40 81W49'16 5:27:17
Concord 82 1 34N58'58 78W25'01 5:13:40
Concord 100 1 35N52'47 82W19'22 5:29:17
Conetoe 33 1 35N48'56 77W27'22 5:09:49
Congleton 74 1 35N44'59 77W13'46 5:08:55
Coniott Landing 8
1 35N56'45 77W04'19 5:08:17
Connaritsa 8 1 36N11'21 77W04'30 5:08:18
Connellys Springs 12
1 35N44'34 81W30'49 5:26:03
Connestee 88 1 35N14 82W44 5:30:56
Connestee Falls 88
1 35N14 82W44 5:30:56
Connor 98 1 35N44'31 78W08'55 5:12:36
Conoconnara 42 1 36N14 77W29 5:09:56
Conover 18 1 35N42'23 81W13'08 5:24:53
Conrad Hill 29 1 35N48 80W09 5:20:36
Contentnea 40 1 35N30'20 77W43'31 5:10:54
Contentnea Junction 98
1 35N40'41 77W55'58 5:11:44
Contentnea Neck 54
1 35N22 77W29 5:09:56
Conway 66 1 36N26'13 77W13'45 5:08:55
Cooks Crossing 13
1 35N26'54 80W36'54 5:22:28
Cooksville 18 1 35N35'35 81W28'34 5:25:54
Cooktown 61 1 36N03'49 82W09'26 5:28:38
Cooleemee 30 1 35N48'37 80W33'22 5:22:13
Cooleemee Junction 30
1 35N49'31 80W35'02 5:22:20
Cooleys Crossroads 42
1 36N28'57 77W52'53 5:11:32
Cool Run 10 1 33N57'05 78W28'13 5:13:53
Cool Spring 49 1 35N50'41 80W43'58 5:22:56
Cool Springs 53 1 35N28'09 79W12'44 5:16:51
Cool Springs Landing 25
1 35N11'33 77W05'03 5:08:20
Coolvale 10 1 33N57'58 78W02'08 5:12:09
Cooper 82 1 35N09'18 78W37'46 5:14:31
Cooper Gap 75 1 35N22 82W12 5:28:48
Coopers 64 1 35N53 77W58 5:11:52
Copeland 86 1 36N20'18 80W39'01 5:22:36
Copper Ford 45 1 35N21'40 82W19'08 5:29:17
Coral Bay 16 1 34N42 76W50 5:07:20
Corapeake 37 1 36N32'03 76W34'36 5:06:18
Corbett 17 1 36N14'59 79W14'21 5:16:57
Cordova 77 1 34N54'46 79W49'20 5:19:17
Core Creek 16 1 34N49'42 76W41'36 5:06:46
Core Point 7 1 35N25'27 76W51'02 5:07:24
Coreys Crossroads 59
1 35N44'26 77W04'36 5:08:18
Corinth 19 1 35N34'09 78W59'54 5:16:00
Corinth 64 1 36N00'17 78W00'32 5:12:02
Corinth 81 1 35N21'41 81W47'49 5:27:11
Cornatzer 30 1 35N55'25 80W28'48 5:21:55
Cornelius 60 1 35N29'12 80W51'37 5:23:26
Corn Landing 67 1 34N33'25 77W20'23 5:09:22
Cornwall 39 1 36N28'46 78W39'56 5:14:40
Corolla 27 1 36N22'52 75W50'00 5:03:20
Correll Park 80 1 35N39 80W29 5:21:56

Corriher Heights 80
1 35N33'38 80W38'06 5:22:32
Corys 27 1 36N32'19 75W57'49 5:03:51
Costin 71 1 34N34'59 78W06'06 5:12:24
Cottonade 26 1 35N05 78W57 5:15:48
Cotton Grove 29 1 35N44'20 80W15'46 5:21:03
Cotton Patch Landing 7
1 35N24'09 76W58'00 5:07:52
Cottonville 84 1 35N11'54 80W11'24 5:20:46
Coulwood Hills 60
1 35N14 80W55 5:23:40
Council 9 1 34N25'15 78W28'04 5:13:52
Country Park Acres 41
1 36N06 79W49 5:19:16
Countyline 30 1 35N57 80W46 5:23:04
Court House 11 1 35N35 82W30 5:30:00
Court House 15 1 36N21 76W09 5:04:36
Courtney 99 1 36N03'36 80W37'15 5:22:29
Cove 25 1 35N11 77W19 5:09:16
Cove 44 1 35N40'33 82W56'25 5:31:46
Cove City 52 1 35N11'14 77W19'16 5:09:17
Cove Creek 44 1 35N36'23 83W00'41 5:32:03
Cove Creek 95 1 36N18 81W45 5:27:00
Cove Landing 25 1 35N15'15 77W07'26 5:08:30
Covington 17 1 36N27'17 79W21'04 5:17:24
Covington 77 1 35N08'10 79W50'52 5:19:23
Cowans Ford 55 1 35N25'36 80W57'25 5:23:50
Cowarts 50 1 35N17'49 83W06'44 5:32:27
Cowee 57 1 35N15'40 83W24'29 5:33:38
Cowpen Landing 25
1 35N14'18 77W10'03 5:08:40
Cowpen Landing 71
1 34N22'03 77W59'23 5:11:58
Cox Crossing 74 1 35N30'50 77W19'04 5:09:16
Cox Mill 13 1 35N24'30 80W43'42 5:22:55
Coxs Crossroads 7
1 35N22'11 76W57'09 5:07:49
Coxville 74 1 35N24'33 77W19'49 5:09:19
Cozads Mill 57 1 35N09'29 83W23'39 5:33:35
Cozart 39 1 36N06'00 78W46'48 5:15:07
Crab Creek 45 1 35N17 82W34 5:30:16
Crab Orchard 60 1 35N14 80W44 5:22:56
Crab Point 16 1 34N42 76W50 5:07:20
Crab Point Village 16
1 34N45'37 76W43'50 5:06:55
Crabtree 44 1 35N36'06 82W56'29 5:31:46
Craggy 11 2 35N37'53 82W36'06 5:30:24
Cramerton 36 1 35N14'19 81W04'31 5:24:18
Cranberry 6 1 36N08'35 81W58'02 5:27:52
Cranberry Gap 6 1 36N06'58 81W58'58 5:27:56
Craven 80 1 35N37'42 80W19'55 5:21:20
Craven Terrace 25
1 35N06'33 77W03'04 5:08:12
Crawford 27 1 36N26 76W03 5:04:12
Creeches Mill 51
1 35N27'57 78W15'55 5:13:04
Creedmoor 39 1 36N07'20 78W41'11 5:14:45
Creeksville 66 1 36N23'38 77W18'14 5:09:13
Cremo 8 1 36N12 76W46 5:07:04
Crescent 80 1 35N34'31 80W25'13 5:21:41
Creston 5 1 36N25'40 81W37'26 5:26:30
Crestwood 45 1 35N22'03 82W31'13 5:30:05
Creswell 94 1 35N52'13 76W23'33 5:05:34
Cribb Town 24 1 34N12'40 78W47'54 5:15:12
Cricket 97 1 36N10'17 81W11'39 5:24:47
Crims Crossroads 34
1 36N13'12 80W05'17 5:20:21
Crisp 33 1 35N45'02 77W37'32 5:10:30
Croatan 25 1 34N58'06 76W58'08 5:07:53
Croatan 28 1 35N44 75W47 5:03:08
Croatan Shores 28
1 36N01'35 75W39'53 5:02:40
Crockers Nub 51 1 35N41'48 78W10'51 5:12:43
Croft 60 1 35N20'41 80W49'28 5:23:18
Crooked Creek 56
1 35N35 82W10 5:28:40
Crooked Oak 86 1 36N32'02 80W45'32 5:23:02
Cross Landing 89
1 35N52'38 76W20'13 5:05:21
Cross Mill 56 1 35N41 82W00 5:28:00
Crossnore 6 1 36N01'18 81W55'47 5:27:43
Cross Road 86 1 36N30 80W35 5:22:20
Crossway 83 1 34N44'42 79W31'36 5:18:06
Crouse 55 1 35N25'15 81W18'20 5:25:13
Crowder Mountain 36
1 35N15 81W17 5:25:08
Crowders 36 1 35N11'10 81W12'24 5:24:50
Crowells 42 1 36N20 77W35 5:10:20
Crowells Crossroads 42
1 36N13'39 77W33'06 5:10:12
Crumpler 5 1 36N30'14 81W23'40 5:25:35
Crumplers Crossroads 51
1 35N32'25 78W14'10 5:12:57
Crump Town 83 1 34N53'12 79W21'24 5:17:26
Cruso 44 1 35N25'03 82W48'39 5:31:15
Crusoe Island 24
1 34N20 78W42 5:14:48
Crutchfield 86 1 36N16'14 80W43'22 5:22:53
Crutchfield Crossroads 19
1 35N48'30 79W25'58 5:17:44
Culberson 20 1 34N59'30 84W10'04 5:36:40
Culbreth 39 1 36N15'49 78W43'40 5:14:55
Cullasaja 57 1 35N09'54 83W19'26 5:33:18
Cullowhee 50 1 35N18'49 83W10'36 5:32:42
Cumberland 26 1 35N00'17 78W58'03 5:15:52
Cumnock 53 1 35N33'17 79W14'17 5:16:57
Cunning Bluff Landing 71
1 34N25'19 78W07'05 5:12:28
Cunningham 73 1 36N32'17 79W04'43 5:16:19
Currie 71 1 34N27'45 78W06'05 5:12:24
Currituck 27 1 36N26'59 76W00'57 5:04:04
Currituck 48 1 35N31 76W27 5:05:48
Currytown 29 1 35N52'55 80W19'18 5:21:17
Cutshalltown 58 1 35N57'38 82W41'23 5:30:46
Cycle 99 1 36N08'03 80W50'32 5:23:22
Cypress Creek 24
1 34N10'59 78W38'05 5:14:32
Cypress Creek 31
1 34N45'05 77W42'19 5:10:49
Cyrus 67 1 34N45 77W26 5:09:44
Dabney 91 1 36N21'10 78W29'52 5:13:59
Daddysville 35 1 35N54'27 78W13'19 5:12:53
Dale 100 1 36N00 82W14 5:28:56

Dallas 36 1 35N18'59 81w10'35 5:24:42
Dalton 85 1 36N18'32 80w24'05 5:21:36
Dana 45 1 35N19'45 82w22'32 5:29:30
Danbury 85 1 36N24'33 80w12'22 5:20:49
Daniels 55 1 35N30'58 81w18'55 5:25:16
Daniels-Rhyne 55 1 35N27 81w16 5:25:04
Danieltown 81 2 35N17'35 81w54'36 5:27:38
Dan River 17 1 36N29 79w20 5:17:20
Dan River Shores 85 1 36N25'57 80w16'38 5:21:07
Dan Valley 79 1 36N24'30 79w56'30 5:19:46
Darby 97 1 36N07'08 81w30'17 5:26:01
Darden 59 1 35N49'13 76w48'57 5:07:16
Darkridge 6 1 36N09 81w59 5:27:56
Darlington 42 1 36N19'07 77w43'06 5:10:52
Davenport Forks 94 1 35N55'10 76w26'11 5:05:45
Davidson 60 1 35N29'57 80w50'56 5:23:24
Davidson River 88 1 35N15'12 82w41'03 5:30:44
Davidson River Recreational 88 1 35N17'13 82w44'04 5:30:56
Davie Circle 68 1 35N55'07 79w02'16 5:16:09
Davie Crossroads 30 1 35N49'55 80w32'06 5:22:08
Davis 16 1 34N47'50 76w27'38 5:05:51
Davis Landing 9 1 34N32'14 78w16'17 5:13:05
Davis Landing 16 1 34N47'22 76w27'37 5:05:50
Davis Landing 48 1 35N39'41 76w36'06 5:06:24
Davistown 33 1 35N49'43 77w36'49 5:10:27
Davistown 56 1 35N33'42 82w09'08 5:28:37
Dawson 54 1 35N20'42 77w38'12 5:10:33
Dawson Crossroads 42 1 36N09'49 77w31'27 5:10:06
Dawsons Crossroads 54 1 35N16 77w35 5:10:20
Day Book 100 1 35N58'45 82w18'00 5:29:12
Days Crossroads 42 1 36N23'25 77w38'03 5:10:32
Dean 57 1 35N12'51 83w21'35 5:33:26
Deans Mill 57 1 35N14'14 83w28'22 5:33:53
Deans Store 64 1 35N58 77w58 5:11:52
Deaver View 11 2 35N34'52 82w37'26 5:30:30
Debruhls Landing 52 1 35N03'20 77w10'52 5:08:43
Deep Creek 4 1 34N51'10 80w09'32 5:20:38
Deep Gap 95 1 36N14 81w32 5:26:08
Deep River 41 1 36N01'49 79w58'07 5:19:52
Deep Run 54 1 35N08'43 77w42'15 5:10:49
Deerfield 95 1 36N13 81w40 5:26:40
DeGraffenried Park 25 1 35N06'26 77w03'46 5:08:15
Dehart 97 1 36N18'00 81w08'07 5:24:32
De Hart Mill 87 1 35N23'30 83w29'15 5:33:57
Delco 24 1 34N18'56 78w13'30 5:12:54
Delight 23 1 35N28'05 81w38'00 5:26:32
Delight Nixon Crossroads 72 1 36N07'57 76w29'38 5:05:59
Dellaplane 97 1 36N10'59 81w01'45 5:24:07
Dellview 36 1 35N23'19 81w24'36 5:25:38
Dellwood 44 1 35N31'24 83w01'43 5:32:07
Delmar 42 1 36N15'20 77w37'38 5:10:31
Delta 85 1 36N28'28 80w06'05 5:20:24
Delta Landing 82 1 34N38'58 78w15'30 5:13:02
Delway 82 1 34N48'04 78w12'51 5:12:51
Democrat 11 1 35N47'02 82w29'13 5:29:57
Dendron 56 1 35N38'57 82w13'51 5:28:55
Dennis 34 1 36N13'30 80w10'13 5:20:41
Denny 97 1 36N05 81w22 5:25:28
Denton 29 1 35N38'00 80w06'58 5:20:28
Dentons 38 1 35N15'26 83w54'45 5:35:39
Denver 55 1 35N31'52 81w01'48 5:24:07
Deppe 67 1 34N50'54 77w16'58 5:09:08
Derby 77 1 35N08'43 79w38'06 5:18:32
Derita 60 1 35N17'37 80w47'52 5:23:11
Devotion 86 1 36N25'57 80w55'05 5:23:40
Deweese 60 1 35N28 80w50 5:23:20
Dewey Pier 89 1 35N55 76w15 5:05:00
Dexter 39 1 36N23'19 78w30'50 5:14:03
Dickerson 25 1 35N08'14 77w00'47 5:08:03
Dickerson 39 1 36N15'53 78w33'07 5:14:12
Dick Taylor Landing 71 1 34N25'06 78w01'52 5:12:07
Diggs 77 1 34N50'50 79w51'25 5:19:26
Dildys Mill 46 1 36N19'25 76w54'33 5:07:38
Dillard 85 1 36N24'08 80w05'38 5:20:23
Dillingham 11 1 35N45'13 82w24'25 5:29:38
Dillion Ridge 89 1 35N55'51 76w10'55 5:04:44
Dillsboro 50 2 35N22'09 83w15'09 5:33:01
Dillworth 60 1 35N13 80w51 5:23:24
Dimmette 97 1 36N13 80w57 5:23:48
Dinah Landing 7 1 35N28'47 76w55'56 5:07:44
Dismal 82 1 35N06 78w35 5:14:20
Ditch Landing 25 1 35N17'51 77w17'15 5:09:09
Ditch Landing 71 1 34N23'04 78w00'19 5:12:01
Dixie 60 1 35N12'16 80w57'41 5:23:51
Dixie 98 1 35N40'21 77w56'55 5:11:48
Dixie Crossroads 51 1 35N41'27 78w13'09 5:12:53
Dixon 67 1 34N35'09 77w28'49 5:09:55
Dixon Landing 10 1 33N56'45 78w13'24 5:12:54
Dixon Landing 74 1 35N35'46 77w16'02 5:09:04
Dixon Store 73 1 36N29'14 78w51'01 5:15:24
Dobbersville 96 1 35N13'34 78w14'42 5:12:59
Dobson 86 1 36N23'44 80w43'22 5:22:53
Dockery 97 1 36N18'26 81w04'54 5:24:20
Dodgetown 85 1 36N25'57 80w06'07 5:20:24
Dodsons Crossroads 68 1 35N58'20 79w09'49 5:16:39
Doe Creek 10 1 34N00'26 78w18'08 5:13:13
Dogwood Acres 68 1 35N52'50 79w04'42 5:16:19
Dogwood Acres 76 1 35N42 79w49 5:19:16
Dolinger 5 1 36N30 81w30 5:26:00
Dollisons Landing 10 1 34N19'04 78w01'43 5:12:07
Donnaha 34 1 36N13'39 80w25'59 5:21:44
Doolie 49 1 35N36'07 80w53'51 5:23:35
Dora 55 1 35N29'52 81w25'44 5:25:43
Dort 37 1 36N31'46 76w52'12 5:07:29
Dortches 64 1 36N00'40 77w51'28 5:11:26
Dosier 34 1 36N09 80w22 5:21:28
Dothan 24 1 34N02'00 78w44'52 5:14:59
Double Island 100 1 35N57'18 82w12'16 5:28:49
Double Shoals 23 1 35N22'51 81w32'54 5:26:12
Doughton 97 1 36N22'27 80w57'26 5:23:50
Douglas Crossroads 7 1 35N31'43 76w56'59 5:07:48
Dover 23 1 35N17 81w32 5:26:08
Dover 25 1 35N12'58 77w26'14 5:09:45
Dover 63 1 35N26'38 79w43'21 5:18:53
Dover Mill 23 1 35N18'11 81w34'23 5:26:18
Downtown 60 1 35N13 80w51 5:23:24
Downtown 80 1 35N39 80w29 5:21:56
Dozier 34 1 36N11'30 80w24'23 5:21:38
Draco 14 1 35N56'35 81w23'08 5:25:33
Drake 64 1 36N02'17 77w49'04 5:11:16
Drake Park 26 1 35N02 78w57 5:15:48
Draper 79 1 36N31'04 79w41'37 5:18:46
Draughn 33 1 36N04'40 77w33'38 5:10:15
Dresden 5 1 36N27'29 81w32'45 5:26:11
Drew 8 1 36N02'48 77w02'09 5:08:09
Drewry 91 1 36N27'33 78w18'37 5:13:14
Drexel 12 1 35N45'28 81w36'16 5:26:25
Drivers Store 98 1 35N41'47 77w49'07 5:11:16
Druid Hills 45 1 35N19 82w28 5:29:52
Drum Hill 37 1 36N32'30 76w43'32 5:06:54
Drums Crossroads 18 1 35N36'47 81w06'32 5:24:26
Dry Creek 62 1 35N18 79w45 5:19:00
Drysdale Hills 45 1 35N19'27 82w36'03 5:30:24
Dry Wells 64 1 35N47 78w13 5:12:52
Duan 18 1 35N36'54 81w12'46 5:24:51
Duart 9 1 34N47'36 78w49'05 5:15:16
Dublin 9 1 34N39'24 78w43'36 5:14:54
Duck 28 1 36N10'10 75w45'20 5:03:01
Duck Creek 67 1 34N35'44 77w16'57 5:09:08
Ducktown 88 1 35N13'53 82w44'52 5:30:59
Dudley 96 1 35N16'02 78w02'16 5:12:09
Dudley Landing 25 1 35N16'30 77w15'05 5:09:00
Dudley Shoals 14 1 35N51'49 81w22'36 5:25:30
Duff Creek 31 1 34N47'04 78w03'10 5:12:13
Duffies 47 1 34N52'01 79w15'18 5:17:01
Duke 32 1 36N00 78w56 5:15:44
Duke 43 1 35N19 78w40 5:14:40
Dukes 64 1 36N03'35 77w58'42 5:11:55
Dukes Crossroads 7 1 35N28 76w49 5:07:16
Dulah 24 1 34N03'23 78w41'14 5:14:45
Dula Springs 11 1 35N42'42 82w32'24 5:30:10
Dunbars Landing 89 1 35N53'10 76w16'48 5:05:07
Duncan 43 1 35N33'45 78w52'20 5:15:29
Duncans Creek 81 1 35N27 81w43 5:26:52
Dundarrach 47 1 34N55'45 79w09'19 5:16:37
Dunn 43 1 35N18'22 78w36'33 5:14:26
Dunn Crossroads 98 1 35N47'29 77w54'43 5:11:39
Dunns Rock 88 1 35N10'27 82w44'39 5:30:59
Dunns Store 42 1 36N08 77w25 5:09:40
Dupree Crossroads 74 1 35N40 77w38 5:10:32
Dupree Landing 24 1 34N17'33 78w32'58 5:14:12
Dupree Landing 74 1 35N43'41 77w31'10 5:10:05
Durant 72 1 36N08'15 76w17'52 5:05:11
Durants Neck 72 1 36N09 76w19 5:05:16
Durham 32 1 35N59'38 78w53'56 5:15:36
Dutchville 39 1 36N08 78w44 5:14:56
Dysartsville 56 1 35N36'01 81w52'09 5:27:29
Eagle 49 1 36N06 80w46 5:23:04
Eagle Mills 49 1 36N01'25 80w48'01 5:23:12
Eagle Rock 92 1 35N47'28 78w24'31 5:13:38
Eagle Springs 63 1 35N17'29 79w39'11 5:18:37
Eagleton 28 1 36N01'12 75w42'48 5:02:51
Eagletown 66 1 36N16'17 77w13'43 5:08:55
Eakers Corner 23 1 35N25 81w34 5:26:16
Earl 23 1 35N12 81w32 5:26:08
Earleys 46 1 36N15'26 77w01'40 5:08:07
Earpsboro 51 1 35N46'53 78w17'37 5:13:10
Easonburg 64 1 35N54'55 77w52'13 5:11:29
Easons Crossroads 37 1 36N26'55 76w42'01 5:06:48
Easons Store 64 1 35N58 77w48 5:11:12
East Alliance 69 1 35N09 76w49 5:07:16
East Arcadia 9 1 34N22'24 78w20'23 5:13:22
Eastatoe 88 1 35N08 82w47 5:31:08
East Bend 99 1 36N12'59 80w30'46 5:22:03
Eastbrook 10 1 34N16'33 78w02'56 5:12:12
East Carolina University 74 1 35N36 77w23 5:09:32
East Durham 32 1 35N59 78w51 5:15:24
East Fayetteville 26 1 35N02'47 78w51'18 5:15:25
East Flat Rock 45 1 35N16'48 82w25'20 5:29:41
East Fork 88 1 35N07'50 82w46'13 5:31:05
East Franklin 57 1 35N11'26 83w21'50 5:33:27
East Gastonia 36 1 35N16'46 81w09'08 5:24:37
East Goldsboro 16 1 34N45 76w49 5:07:16
East Hamlet 77 1 34N52'54 79w41'08 5:18:45
East Hickory 18 1 35N44 81w21 5:25:24
East Howellsville 78 1 34N41 78w53 5:15:32
East Lake 28 1 35N53'28 75w57'47 5:03:51
East Lake Landing 28 1 35N53'47 75w58'13 5:03:53
East Laport 50 1 35N18'06 83w09'02 5:32:36
East Laurinburg 83 1 34N46'16 79w26'38 5:17:47
East Lumberton 78 1 34N36'37 78w59'33 5:15:58
East Marion 56 1 35N41'03 81w59'31 5:27:58
East Monbo 49 1 35N40'17 80w57'31 5:23:50
Easton View 34 1 36N03'22 80w12'36 5:20:50
Eastover 26 1 35N05'47 78w47'03 5:15:08
East Parkland 92 1 35N44'41 78w37'53 5:14:32
East Rockingham 77 1 34N55'05 79w45'46 5:19:03
East Rocky Mount 33 1 35N58 77w48 5:11:12
East Sanford 53 1 35N30 79w08 5:16:32
East Side Park 77 1 34N57'24 79w45'01 5:19:00
East Side Park 78 1 34N30'15 79w05'36 5:16:22
East Spencer 80 1 35N40'54 80w25'57 5:21:44
East Tabor 24 1 34N09'37 78w50'51 5:15:23
East White Oak 41 1 36N06'04 79w45'45 5:19:03
East Wilmington 65 3 34N13 77w55 5:11:40
East Winston 34 1 36N06'01 80w13'45 5:20:55
Eastwood 63 1 35N14'44 79w26'53 5:17:48
Easy Hill 10 1 34N13'20 78w00'30 5:12:02
Ebbs Chapel 58 1 35N55 82w34 5:30:16
Ebbs Mill 58 1 35N49'16 82w54'26 5:31:38
Ebenezer 20 1 35N09'05 84w03'41 5:36:15
Echo 78 1 34N29'58 79w16'40 5:17:07
Echo Heights 92 1 35N42'04 78w38'53 5:14:36
Echo Park 95 1 36N07'51 81w40'07 5:26:40
Ecusta 88 1 35N16'20 82w42'23 5:30:50
Eden 79 1 36N29'18 79w46'01 5:19:04
Edenburg 47 1 34N54'20 79w18'37 5:17:14
Edenhouse Point 8 1 36N02'33 76w42'27 5:06:50
Edens Landing 71 1 34N25'35 77w34'29 5:10:18
Edenton 21 1 36N03'38 76w36'34 5:06:26
Edgar 76 1 35N51'22 79w54'20 5:19:37
Edgecombe 71 1 34N27'46 77w35'43 5:10:23
Edgemont 14 1 36N00'08 81w46'30 5:27:06
Edgeville 41 1 36N05'35 79w45'44 5:19:03
Edgewood Terrace 63 1 35N13'54 79w34'11 5:18:17
Edmonds 3 1 36N33'38 80w56'37 5:23:46
Edmondson 51 1 35N33'18 78w35'59 5:14:24
Edmundson Crossroads 96 1 35N30'09 77w53'56 5:11:36
Edneyville 45 1 35N25 82w19 5:29:16
Edward 7 1 35N19'27 76w52'32 5:07:30
Edwards 97 1 36N16 80w56 5:23:44
Edwards Crossroads 3 1 36N31'48 81w03'32 5:24:14
Edwards Crossroads 64 1 36N00'55 78w05'40 5:12:23
Edwards Crossroads 66 1 36N24'32 77w18'30 5:09:14
Edwards Fork 42 1 36N07'08 77w23'21 5:09:33
Edwards Junction 25 1 35N06 77w05 5:08:20
Efland 68 1 36N04'52 79w10'10 5:16:41
Egypt 100 1 35N59 82w25 5:29:40
Ela 87 1 35N26'58 83w23'27 5:33:34
Elams 93 1 36N32'28 77w56'35 5:11:46
Elberon 93 1 36N18'47 78w13'10 5:12:53
Elberta 63 1 35N17'05 79w37'58 5:18:32
Elbow Landing 48 1 35N40'20 76w36'17 5:06:25
Eldora 86 1 36N23 80w36 5:22:24
Eldorado 62 1 35N28'01 80w01'46 5:20:07
Eleanors Crossroads 37 1 36N26'12 76w45'30 5:07:02
Elease 26 1 34N51'54 78w47'48 5:15:11
Eleazer 76 1 35N30'53 79w58'08 5:19:53
Elevation 51 1 35N28 78w31 5:14:04
Elf 22 1 35N01'17 83w44'53 5:35:00
Eliah 10 1 34N14'34 78w03'25 5:12:14
Eli Whitney 1 1 35N54'24 79w18'27 5:17:14
Elizabeth 60 1 35N13 80w50 5:23:20
Elizabeth City 70 1 36N18'07 76w13'25 5:04:54
Elizabethtown 9 1 34N37'45 78w36'20 5:14:25
Elkin 86 1 36N14'39 80w50'55 5:23:24
Elkin Valley 86 1 36N16'23 80w51'12 5:23:25
Elk Mountain 11 1 35N38'16 82w35'37 5:30:22
Elk Park 6 1 36N09'26 81w58'42 5:27:55
Elk Shoal 100 1 35N56'32 82w23'27 5:29:34
Elkton 9 1 34N28'00 78w36'20 5:14:25
Elk Valley 6 1 36N10'19 81w54'41 5:27:39
Elkville 97 1 36N04'11 81w24'07 5:25:36
Ellenboro 81 1 35N19'44 81w45'32 5:27:02
Ellendale 2 1 35N55'32 81w16'47 5:25:07
Eller 29 1 36N04 80w14 5:20:56
Ellerbe 77 1 35N04'16 79w45'42 5:19:03
Ellerbe Grove 77 1 34N51'53 79w46'42 5:19:07
Ellijay 57 1 35N11'30 83w16'14 5:33:05
Elliott 82 1 34N59'02 78w12'50 5:12:51
Ellisboro 79 1 36N19'57 79w58'41 5:19:55
Ellis Crossroads 80 1 35N43'28 80w27'57 5:21:52
Ellis Store 8 1 36N03 76w57 5:07:48
Elm City 98 1 35N48'23 77w51'49 5:11:27
Elm Grove 54 1 35N08'43 77w32'12 5:10:09
Elmira Crossroads 74 1 35N25'45 77w12'08 5:08:49
Elm Landing 67 1 34N44'56 77w08'14 5:08:33
Elmore 83 1 34N47'40 79w30'32 5:18:02
Elmores Crossroads 36 1 35N13'22 81w06'04 5:24:24
Elmwood 49 1 35N45'04 80w45'40 5:23:03
Elon College 1 1 36N06'10 79w30'25 5:18:02
Elrod 78 1 34N36'50 79w14'32 5:16:58

Place		Lat	Long	Time
Elroy 96	1	35N20'33	77w54'32	5:11:38
Embro 93	1	36N22'35	78w03'19	5:12:13
Emerald Isle 16	1	34N40'40	76w57'04	5:07:48
Emerald Village 92	1	35N43'08	78w32'53	5:14:12
Emerson 9	1	34N45	78w51	5:15:24
Emerson 24	1	34N10'51	78w51'59	5:15:28
Emery 62	1	35N14'50	79w43'22	5:18:53
Emerywood 41	1	35N58	80w00	5:20:00
Emit 51	1	35N44'23	78w15'25	5:13:02
Emma 11	1	35N35'48	82w35'31	5:30:22
Emmons 29	1	35N41	80w06	5:20:24
Emperor Landing 21	1	36N03'50	76w41'24	5:06:46
Encas 98	1	35N44	77w55	5:11:40
Endy 84	1	35N18	80w17	5:21:08
Enfield 42	1	36N10'51	77w40'01	5:10:40
Engelhard 48	1	35N30'34	75w59'47	5:03:59
Englewood 64	1	35N58	77w48	5:11:12
English 58	1	35N57'01	82w31'37	5:30:06
Enka 11	1	35N32'59	82w39'01	5:30:36
Enka Village 11	1	35N32'27	82w38'41	5:30:35
Ennice 3	1	36N33'12	80w59'46	5:23:59
Eno 68	1	36N02'28	79w00'52	5:16:03
Enochville 80	1	35N31'47	80w40'06	5:22:40
Enola 12	1	35N39'54	81w39'15	5:26:37
Enon 99	1	36N08'23	80w28'09	5:21:53
Enterprise 29	1	35N56'41	80w16'36	5:21:06
Enterprise 93	1	36N27'56	77w56'55	5:11:48
Ephesus 30	1	35N50'31	80w32'46	5:22:11
Ephraim Place 61	1	36N05'16	82w24'13	5:29:37
Epsom 91	1	36N14'43	78w19'44	5:13:19
Erastus 50	1	35N11'26	83w11'16	5:32:45
Erect 76	1	35N32	79w46	5:19:04
Erlanger 29	1	35N50'20	80w15'13	5:21:01
Ernul 25	1	35N15	77w04	5:08:16
Ervintown 67	1	34N54'29	77w33'44	5:10:15
Erwin 43	1	35N19'36	78w40'35	5:14:42
Erwin Heights 29	1	35N54'03	80w04'26	5:20:18
Eskota 100	1	35N47'44	82w18'34	5:29:14
Essex 42	1	36N14'48	77w57'25	5:11:50
Estatoe 61	1	35N54'12	82w07'11	5:28:29
Estelle 17	1	36N30'07	79w14'29	5:16:58
Ether 62	1	35N26'23	79w47'03	5:19:08
Etna (P O) 57	1	35N16'42	83w26'34	5:33:46
Etowah 45	1	35N19'03	82w35'40	5:30:23
Eubanks 68	1	35N58'11	79w04'33	5:16:18
Eufola 49	1	35N43'20	80w59'10	5:23:57
Eure 37	1	36N25'38	76w51'13	5:07:25
Eureka 96	1	35N32'33	77w52'36	5:11:30
Eure Landing 46	1	36N21'22	76w47'42	5:07:11
Evansdale 98	1	35N39'18	77w52'12	5:11:29
Everetts 59	1	35N50'05	77w10'26	5:08:42
Everetts Crossroads 7	1	35N31'22	76w50'33	5:07:22
Everetts Mill 77	1	34N48'51	79w53'32	5:19:34
Evergreen 24	1	34N17'45	78w13'05	5:12:52
Evergreen Estates 26	1	35N02	78w57	5:15:48
Everhardt 80	1	35N33	80w36	5:22:24
Everton 31	1	35N02'16	78w02'46	5:12:11
Ewart 61	1	36N01	82w09	5:28:36
Exum 10	1	34N06'36	78w27'52	5:13:51
Ex-Way 77	1	35N10'19	79w52'19	5:19:29
Ezzelltown 82	1	34N39'55	78w12'09	5:12:49
Fain Ford 20	1	35N15'41	84w02'45	5:36:11
Fair Bluff 24	1	34N18'48	79w02'15	5:16:09
Fairbrook 18	1	35N42'10	81w17'46	5:25:11
Fairfax 87	1	35N27'11	83w50'24	5:35:22
Fairfield 41	1	36N06'00	79w49'08	5:19:17
Fairfield 48	1	35N32'28	76w13'29	5:04:54
Fairfield 90	1	35N03'37	80w23'15	5:21:33
Fairgrove 18	1	35N42'26	81w15'56	5:25:04
Fair Grove 29	1	35N51'07	80w04'40	5:20:19
Fairmont 78	1	34N29'48	79w06'52	5:16:27
Fairntosh 32	1	36N06'22	78w51'03	5:15:24
Fairplains 97	1	36N11'54	81w09'11	5:24:37
Fairport 39	1	36N13'38	78w31'20	5:14:05
Fairview 11	1	35N30'50	82w23'46	5:29:35
Fairview 57	1	35N16'52	83w37'58	5:34:32
Fairview 68	1	36N05'13	79w06'49	5:16:27
Fairview 79	1	36N31'38	79w47'24	5:19:10
Fairview 86	1	36N19'42	80w43'14	5:22:53
Fairview 90	1	35N08'18	80w32'16	5:22:09
Fairview Church 23	1	35N11'42	81w32'03	5:26:08
Fairview Cross Roads 86	1	36N24	80w43	5:22:52
Fairview Park 2	1	35N52'59	81w07'08	5:24:29
Fairway Acres 92	1	35N44'22	78w40'03	5:14:40
Fairway Hills 44	2	35N31'03	82w58'54	5:31:56
Faison 31	1	35N06'58	78w08'11	5:12:33
Faisons 66	1	36N26'40	77w19'30	5:09:18
Faith 80	1	35N35'13	80w27'47	5:21:51
Falcon 26	1	35N11'23	78w38'55	5:14:36
Falkland 74	1	35N41'57	77w30'48	5:10:03
Fallcliff 50	1	35N15'32	83w10'50	5:32:43
Fall Creek 99	1	36N13	80w36	5:22:24
Falling Creek 54	1	35N15'43	77w41'27	5:10:46
Falls 92	1	35N56'23	78w34'47	5:14:19
Fallston 23	1	35N25'44	81w30'06	5:26:00
Fallstown 49	1	35N42	80w56	5:23:44
Farmer 76	1	35N39'12	79w58'38	5:19:55
Farmers Store 5	1	36N30	81w30	5:26:00
Farmington 30	1	36N00'56	80w31'57	5:22:08
Farmville 19	1	35N34'14	79w13'13	5:16:53
Farmville 74	1	35N35'43	77w35'08	5:10:21
Faro 96	1	35N30'41	77w50'39	5:11:23
Farrar 33	1	35N53'43	77w32'35	5:10:10
Farrington 19	1	35N48'06	79w00'51	5:16:03
Faucett 42	1	36N20	77w44	5:10:56
Faucette 1	1	36N11	79w24	5:17:36
Faulkner Crossroads 91	1	36N18'58	78w21'44	5:13:27
Faust 58	1	35N54'40	82w31'49	5:30:07
Fayetteville 26	1	35N03'09	78w52'43	5:15:31
Federal Point 65	3	34N04	77w54	5:11:36
Feezor 29	1	35N41'18	80w16'09	5:21:05
Feltonville 92	1	35N40'59	78w50'02	5:15:20
Fenix 26	1	35N01'59	79w02'06	5:16:08
Fentress 41	1	35N59	79w45	5:19:00
Ferguson 97	1	36N05'08	81w22'07	5:25:28
Fernside 65	3	34N13	77w55	5:11:40
Fero 56	1	35N35'12	81w58'40	5:27:55
Ferrells 64	1	35N53	78w10	5:12:40
Few 32	1	35N56'01	78w53'18	5:15:33
Fiberville 44	2	35N32'24	82w50'54	5:31:24
Fields 54	1	35N17'01	77w43'52	5:10:55
Fieldsboro 40	1	35N36'20	77w40'27	5:10:42
Fields of the Wood 20	1	35N07'24	84w15'27	5:37:02
Fig 5	1	36N27'10	81w36'16	5:26:25
Fillmore 98	1	35N43'07	78w01'54	5:12:08
Finch Mill 98	1	35N45'43	77w59'49	5:11:59
Fines Creek 44	1	35N40'52	82w57'06	5:31:48
Finger 13	1	35N23'05	80w21'29	5:21:26
Finley 14	1	36N04'27	81w35'31	5:26:22
Fipps Crossing 24	1	34N17'39	78w49'37	5:15:18
Fires Creek 22	1	35N04'37	83w51'51	5:35:27
First Landing 94	1	35N55'58	76w23'30	5:05:34
Fisher Creek 50	2	35N24'13	83w11'47	5:32:47
Fisher Park 41	1	36N04'47	79w47'25	5:19:10
Fisher Town 13	1	35N29'41	80w39'50	5:22:39
Fitch 17	1	36N19'25	79w21'43	5:17:27
Fitzgerald 79	1	36N31'59	79w40'24	5:18:42
Five Forks 73	1	36N26'14	79w01'13	5:16:05
Five Forks 78	1	34N28'17	79w12'02	5:16:48
Five Forks 80	1	35N34'33	80w37'05	5:22:28
Five Forks 93	1	36N30'48	78w02'36	5:12:10
Five Points 7	1	35N33'42	76w53'13	5:07:33
Five Points 23	1	35N27'08	81w40'00	5:26:40
Five Points 34	1	36N01'38	80w17'36	5:21:10
Five Points 35	1	35N57'43	78w17'29	5:13:10
Five Points 45	1	35N16'03	82w24'35	5:29:38
Five Points 47	1	35N01'00	79w21'40	5:17:27
Five Points 77	1	34N57'09	79w47'23	5:19:10
Five Points 80	1	35N34'15	80w39'17	5:22:37
Five Points 92	1	35N35'45	78w45'33	5:15:02
Flanner Beach 25	1	34N59'01	76w56'55	5:07:48
Flat Branch 37	1	36N24	76w45	5:07:00
Flat Branch 43	1	35N18'48	78w53'05	5:15:32
Flat Creek 11	1	35N45'10	82w32'48	5:30:11
Flat Gap 12	1	35N43'13	81w34'17	5:26:17
Flat River 73	1	36N18	78w59	5:15:56
Flat Rock 45	1	35N16'16	82w26'30	5:29:46
Flat Rock 85	1	36N23'00	80w23'44	5:21:35
Flat Rock 86	1	36N30'44	80w34'12	5:22:17
Flat Rock 91	1	36N23'28	78w22'05	5:13:28
Flat Rock Forest 45	1	35N16'39	82w26'35	5:29:46
Flats 57	1	35N01	83w19	5:33:16
Flat Shoals 85	1	36N21'54	80w14'38	5:20:59
Flat Springs 1	1	36N15'07	81w56'02	5:27:44
Flat Top 11	1	35N34'06	82w22'54	5:29:32
Flatwood 5	1	36N33'20	81w39'13	5:26:37
Flax Island 37	1	36N26'13	76w56'38	5:07:47
Flay 55	1	35N27'47	81w26'10	5:25:45
Fleetwood 5	1	36N18'22	81w30'49	5:26:03
Fletcher 45	1	35N25'50	82w30'05	5:30:00
Flint Hill 62	1	35N28'41	79w54'54	5:19:40
Flint Hill 76	1	35N48'06	79w55'26	5:19:42
Flint Hill 99	1	36N10'30	80w28'41	5:21:55
Floral College 78	1	34N46'42	79w19'07	5:17:16
Florence 41	1	36N01'31	79w57'33	5:19:50
Florence 69	1	35N08'39	76w37'53	5:06:32
Florence Town 1	1	36N04'39	79w19'00	5:17:16
Flowers 51	1	35N39'13	78w20'43	5:13:23
Flowers Corner 10	1	34N09'45	78w12'29	5:12:50
Flowes Store 13	1	35N17'56	80w33'28	5:22:14
Floytan Crossroads 91	1	36N15'22	78w27'41	5:13:51
Folkstone 67	1	34N32'11	77w30'16	5:10:01
Folly 37	1	36N27	76w37	5:06:28
Folly Fork 37	1	36N29'06	76w34'40	5:06:19
Fontana Dam 38	1	35N26	83w50	5:35:20
Fontana Village 38	1	35N26'08	83w49'09	5:35:17
Fonville 43	1	35N17'24	78w46'12	5:15:05
Footville 99	1	36N03'38	80w42'08	5:22:49
Forbes 61	1	36N00	82w14	5:28:56
Forbush 99	1	36N11'52	80w34'28	5:22:18
Forest 25	1	35N09'41	77w02'51	5:08:11
Forest City 81	1	35N20'02	81w51'55	5:27:28
Forest Grove 95	1	36N18'01	81w48'27	5:27:14
Forest Hill 34	1	36N08'40	80w14'55	5:21:00
Forest Hills 65	3	34N13	77w55	5:11:40
Forest Hills 79	1	36N18'42	79w41'55	5:18:48
Forest Hills 88	1	35N13'06	82w44'10	5:30:57
Forest Hills 92	1	35N42'14	78w37'08	5:14:29
Forestville 92	1	35N57'41	78w31'06	5:14:04
Fork 30	1	35N54	80w34	5:22:16
Fork Mountain 61	1	36N03	82w10	5:28:40
Forks of Ivy 11	1	35N47'30	82w32'21	5:30:09
Fort Barnwell 25	1	35N17'28	77w20'07	5:09:20
Fort Bragg 26	1	35N09	79w00	5:16:00
Fort Caswell 10	1	33N56	78w04	5:12:16
Fort Clark 28	1	35N11'49	75w43'56	5:02:56
Fort Defiance 14	1	36N01'01	81w29'43	5:25:59
Fort Junction 26	1	35N09	78w58	5:15:52
Fort Landing 89	1	35N56'40	76w03'52	5:04:15
Fort Macon 16	1	34N41'48	76w40'49	5:06:43
Fort Macon Village 25	1	34N53	76w54	5:07:36
Fort Raleigh City 28	1	35N56'11	75w42'26	5:02:50
Foscoe 95	1	36N09'42	81w45'57	5:27:04
Foster 50	2	35N23'50	83w10'59	5:32:44
Foster Creek 58	1	35N55'21	82w36'51	5:30:27
Fountain 31	1	34N50'27	77w40'23	5:10:42
Fountain Hill 4	1	35N04'39	80w17'19	5:21:09
Fountain Hill 54	1	35N24'35	77w30'04	5:10:00
Four Oaks 51	1	35N26'41	78w25'38	5:13:43
Fourway 40	1	35N25	77w35	5:10:20
Fowler Crossroads 90	1	35N01'51	80w32'18	5:22:09
Fowler Landing 9	1	34N40'55	78w20'54	5:13:24
Fowlers Crossroads 92	1	35N53'33	78w25'46	5:13:43
Fox Run 32	1	36N08'28	78w57'53	5:15:52
Foys 52	1	35N13	77w26	5:09:44
Foys Landing 67	1	34N37'10	77w25'50	5:09:43
Francisco 85	1	36N30'32	80w21'22	5:21:25
Francis Mill 8	1	36N08'09	77w06'30	5:08:26
Frank 6	1	36N04'14	82w00'10	5:28:01
Franklin 57	1	35N10'56	83w22'54	5:33:32
Franklin 80	1	35N43'16	80w29'57	5:22:00
Franklin Grove 87	1	35N26'08	83w27'47	5:33:51
Franklinton 35	1	36N06'06	78w27'30	5:13:50
Franklinville 76	1	35N44'37	79w41'33	5:18:46
Franktown 67	1	34N54'48	77w30'36	5:10:02
Frazier Crossroads 64	1	35N52'33	78w08'14	5:12:33
Fraziers Crossroads 46	1	36N18'23	77w01'31	5:08:06
Freedom 60	1	35N14	80w53	5:23:32
Freeland 10	1	34N06'25	78w32'15	5:14:09
Freeman 24	1	34N19'01	78w17'04	5:13:08
Freeman Mill 41	1	35N56'17	79w53'26	5:19:34
Fremont 96	1	35N32'43	77w58'30	5:11:54
French Broad 11	1	35N42	82w37	5:30:28
Frenchs Creek 9	1	34N28	78w18	5:13:12
Friendship 20	1	35N04'31	84w11'32	5:36:46
Friendship 31	1	35N03'48	78w02'26	5:12:10
Friendship 41	1	36N05'31	79w57'15	5:19:49
Friendship 92	1	35N41'55	78w54'00	5:15:36
Friendship 99	1	36N14	80w30	5:22:00
Frink Crossing 24	1	34N19'18	78w53'36	5:15:34
Frisco 28	1	35N14'06	75w37'44	5:02:31
Frog Level 74	1	35N34'19	77w26'33	5:09:46
Frog Level 81	1	35N19	81w52	5:27:28
Frog Pond 84	1	35N16'24	80w19'00	5:21:16
Frogsboro 17	1	36N20'43	79w10'56	5:16:44
Frontis 34	1	36N03'58	80w18'31	5:21:14
Fruitland 45	1	35N23'47	82w23'36	5:29:34
Fruitland 77	1	34N55'28	79w39'02	5:18:36
Fruitville 27	1	36N31	75w56	5:03:44
Frying Pan 89	1	35N48'09	76w06'14	5:04:25
Frying Pan Landing 89	1	35N47'58	76w06'17	5:04:25
Fulchers Landing 67	1	34N33'55	77w22'59	5:09:32
Fulchertown 57	1	35N07'20	83w21'30	5:33:26
Fulford 10	1	33N58'03	78w19'49	5:13:19
Fuller Mill 76	1	35N46'40	80w01'22	5:20:05
Fullers 76	1	35N53	80w05	5:20:20
Fulp 85	1	36N18	80w08	5:20:32
Fulton 30	1	35N52	80w27	5:21:48
Funston 10	1	34N06'03	78w01'38	5:12:07
Fuquay-Varina 92	1	35N35'03	78w48'01	5:15:12
Furches 5	1	36N27'12	81w16'52	5:25:07
Furr 84	1	35N15	80w25	5:21:40
Gaddy 78	1	34N27	79w13	5:16:52
Gaddysville 78	1	34N26'55	79w13'25	5:16:54
Gaffey Landing 27	1	36N15'18	75w51'56	5:03:28
Gaineys Place 47	1	34N57'18	79w20'44	5:17:23
Galatia 66	1	36N28'17	77w18'10	5:09:13
Galilee Mission 94	1	35N47'35	76w24'02	5:05:36
Galloway Crossroads 74	1	35N32'46	77w15'43	5:09:03
Gallup Acres 26	1	35N02	78w57	5:15:48
Gamewell 14	1	35N52'09	81w35'47	5:26:23
Gap Civil 3	1	36N31	81w08	5:24:32
Gap Landing 25	1	35N08'32	77w03'58	5:08:16
Garden Creek 56	1	35N42'16	82w02'10	5:28:09
Gardner 98	1	35N44	77w47	5:11:08
Gardner Park 36	1	35N15'15	81w07'52	5:24:31
Gardnerville 74	1	35N23'22	77w17'57	5:09:12
Gardner Webb College 23	1	35N15	81w40	5:26:40
Garland 82	1	34N47'10	78w23'40	5:13:35
Garner 92	1	35N42'40	78w36'52	5:14:27
Garners Store 63	1	35N24'17	79w34'28	5:18:18
Garren Hill 63	1	35N11'14	79w30'08	5:18:01
Garysburg 66	1	36N27'03	77w33'33	5:10:14
Gashes Creek 11	1	35N34'00	82w29'43	5:29:59
Gaskill Landing 16	1	34N43'22	76w33'50	5:06:15
Gaston 66	1	36N30'01	77w38'43	5:10:35
Gastonia 36	1	35N15'43	81w11'15	5:24:45
Gates 37	1	36N30'12	76w46'10	5:07:05
Gatesville 37	1	36N24'12	76w45'12	5:07:01
Gatewood 17	1	36N32'13	79w24'02	5:17:36
Gatlington Landing 37	1	36N30'30	76w54'24	5:07:38
Gause Landing 10	1	33N53'41	78w26'51	5:13:47
Gay 50	1	35N17'29	83w16'24	5:33:06
Gaylord 7	1	35N25'53	76w44'33	5:06:58
Gela 39	1	36N24'52	78w35'25	5:14:22
Genlee 32	1	35N52'15	78w53'30	5:15:34
Genoa 96	1	35N19'34	78w02'26	5:12:10
Gentry Store 73	1	36N27'36	78w55'14	5:15:41
George 66	1	36N19'20	77w13'51	5:08:55
Georges Mill 85	1	36N30'52	80w18'11	5:21:13
Georgetown 11	2	35N37'15	82w39'16	5:30:37
Georgetown 29	1	36N00'54	80w05'59	5:20:24
Georgetown 54	1	35N15'52	77w33'03	5:10:12
Georgeville 13	1	35N18'50	80w27'34	5:21:50
Gerard Landing 7	1	35N25'28	76w57'48	5:07:51
Germanton 85	1	36N15'46	80w13'52	5:20:55
Germantown 48	1	35N25'54	76w27'48	5:05:51

Gerton 45 1 35N28'45 82w20'54 5:29:24
Gethsemane 33 1 36N04'45 77w39'23 5:10:38
Ghio Scholl Station 83
1 34N49'00 79w39'04 5:18:36
Gibbton 69 1 35N05'56 76w43'41 5:06:55
Gibson 83 1 34N45'32 79w36'39 5:18:27
Gibson Landing 9
1 34N32'50 78w26'08 5:13:45
Gibson Mill 83 1 34N50'20 79w28'03 5:17:52
Gibsontown 44 2 35N31'39 82w49'18 5:31:17
Gibsonville 41 1 36N06'20 79w32'33 5:18:10
Giddensville 82 1 35N08'20 78w13'07 5:12:52
Gilead 7 1 35N27'09 76w59'07 5:07:56
Gilford City 41 1 36N04 79w48 5:19:12
Gilkey 81 1 35N26'33 81w58'41 5:27:55
Gill 91 1 36N15'57 78w24'30 5:13:38
Gillburg 91 1 36N16'35 78w22'07 5:13:28
Gilreath 97 1 36N02'59 81w04'43 5:24:19
Glade Creek 3 1 36N31 81w00 5:24:00
Glade Valley 3 1 36N28'18 81w03'06 5:24:12
Glady 11 1 35N30'31 82w43'38 5:30:55
Glady Fork 11 1 35N32 82w41 5:30:44
Glass 13 1 35N28'38 80w37'36 5:22:30
Glen Alpine 12 1 35N43'44 81w46'46 5:27:07
Glen Anna 29 1 35N50'29 80w05'32 5:20:22
Glen Ayre 61 1 36N03'47 82w07'00 5:28:28
Glencoe 1 1 36N08'20 79w25'41 5:17:43
Glendale Springs 5
1 36N20'42 81w22'50 5:25:31
Glendon 63 1 35N28'56 79w25'02 5:17:40
Glenfield 40 1 35N22'59 77w38'35 5:10:34
Glenfield Crossroads 40
1 35N23'35 77w36'59 5:10:28
Glen Forest 32 1 36N01'19 78w48'36 5:15:14
Glenlaurel 56 1 35N50'09 82w06'47 5:28:27
Glen Lennox 68 1 35N54'53 79w01'37 5:16:06
Glenn 68 1 36N01 78w56 5:15:44
Glenola 76 1 35N52'22 79w54'54 5:19:40
Glen Raven 1 1 36N06'47 79w28'36 5:17:54
Glenrock 11 1 35N36 82w33 5:30:12
Glenview 42 1 36N10'03 77w48'43 5:11:15
Glenville 50 1 35N10'24 83w07'46 5:32:31
Glenwood 41 1 36N03'18 79w48'36 5:19:14
Glenwood 56 1 35N36'52 81w58'56 5:27:56
Glenwood 77 1 34N55'55 79w45'31 5:19:02
Glenwood Crossroads 51
1 35N16'03 78w23'44 5:13:35
Glenwood Village 92
1 35N50 78w40 5:14:40
Gliden 21 1 36N19'13 76w36'52 5:06:27
Glisson 31 1 35N06 77w53 5:11:32
Globe 14 1 36N02'46 81w42'30 5:26:50
Gloucester 16 1 34N43'34 76w32'29 5:06:10
Gloucester 88 1 35N13 82w53 5:31:32
Gneiss 57 1 35N08'00 83w16'53 5:33:08
Goat Neck 89 1 35N58'10 76w04'41 5:04:19
Godwin 26 1 35N13'03 78w40'54 5:14:44
Gold 12 1 35N47'35 81w45'44 5:27:03
Golden 81 1 35N22 81w50 5:27:20
Golden Valley 81
1 35N32 81w46 5:27:04
Gold Hill 47 1 34N55'16 79w10'24 5:16:42
Gold Hill 79 1 36N19'05 79w55'51 5:19:43
Gold Hill 80 1 35N31'16 80w20'18 5:21:21
Gold Mine 35 1 36N11 78w05 5:12:20
Gold Mine 57 1 35N03 83w12 5:32:48
Goldpoint 59 1 35N52'13 77w14'30 5:08:58
Gold Rock 64 1 36N04'12 77w48'48 5:11:15
Gold Sand 35 1 36N11'33 78w10'26 5:12:42
Goldsboro 96 1 35N23'05 77w59'35 5:11:58
Goldston 19 1 35N35'35 79w19'43 5:17:19
Gold Valley Crossroads 64
1 35N53'58 78w10'06 5:12:40
Goodluck 45 1 35N26'25 82w26'24 5:29:46
Goodsonville 55 1 35N28 81w15 5:25:00
Goodwin Hills 16
1 35N00'08 76w18'44 5:05:15
Goose Creek 15 1 36N13'41 76w01'42 5:04:07
Goose Creek 90 1 35N07 80w31 5:22:04
Goose Hollow 24 1 34N20'37 78w24'22 5:13:37
Gooseneck 24 1 34N20'43 78w10'12 5:12:41
Goose Nest 59 1 35N59 77w19 5:09:16
Goose Pond 8 1 36N12 76w46 5:07:04
Gordonton 73 1 36N16'51 79w07'38 5:16:31
Gordontown 29 1 35N45'20 80w06'32 5:20:26
Gores Landing 10
1 33N55'27 78w12'42 5:12:51
Gorman 32 1 36N02'11 78w49'25 5:15:18
Goshen 82 1 34N56 78w10 5:12:40
Goshen 97 1 36N09 81w10 5:24:40
Goshen Grove 36 1 35N16'32 81w03'20 5:24:13
Governors Island 87
1 35N26 83w27 5:33:48
Grabtown 8 1 35N57'59 77w02'02 5:08:08
Grace 11 1 35N37'41 82w33'09 5:30:13
Grace Chapel 14 1 35N48 81w26 5:25:44
Grady 71 1 34N27 78w04 5:12:16
Gradys 96 1 35N09'56 77w53'08 5:11:33
Gragg 6 1 36N04'23 81w46'15 5:27:05
Graham 1 1 36N04'08 79w24'03 5:17:36
Graingers 54 1 35N19'11 77w30'37 5:10:02
Grandfather 95 1 36N10 81w52 5:27:28
Grandin 14 1 36N02'38 81w24'58 5:25:40
Grandview 20 1 35N10'03 84w02'43 5:36:11
Grandview Heights 95
1 36N13'08 81w41'02 5:26:44
Grandy 27 1 36N14'31 75w52'46 5:03:31
Granite Falls 14
1 35N47'47 81w25'51 5:25:43
Granite Quarry 80
1 35N36'44 80w26'49 5:21:47
Grant 76 1 35N40 79w45 5:19:00
Grantham 96 1 35N17'49 78w09'50 5:12:39
Granthams 25 1 35N04'12 77w01'17 5:08:05
Grantsboro 69 1 35N08'25 76w50'34 5:07:22
Grape Creek 20 1 35N06'57 84w05'13 5:36:21
Grapevine 58 1 35N48 82w41 5:30:44
Grapevine Landing 89
1 35N43'02 76w03'40 5:04:15
Grapewood 34 1 36N07'11 80w26'19 5:21:45
Graphite 56 1 35N39'38 82w15'07 5:29:00
Grassy Creek 5 1 36N34'25 81w23'20 5:25:33
Grassy Creek 61 1 35N52'56 82w03'25 5:28:14

Grays Chapel 76 1 35N49'07 79w41'56 5:18:48
Grays Creek 26 1 34N57'36 78w50'40 5:15:23
Grayson 5 1 36N32'10 81w41'02 5:26:44
Great Neck 25 1 34N55'48 76w40'30 5:06:42
Great Neck Landing 67
1 34N40'03 77w09'20 5:08:37
Great Swamp 96 1 35N33 78w01 5:12:04
Green Acres 92 1 35N42'32 78w39'00 5:14:36
Greenbank Landing 10
1 34N21'31 78w09'31 5:12:38
Greenbrier Estates 92
1 35N43'03 78w38'45 5:14:35
Green Creek 75 1 35N13'13 82w03'03 5:28:12
Greene 41 1 35N58 79w35 5:18:20
Greene Cove 61 1 36N00'21 82w06'45 5:28:27
Greenevers 31 1 34N50 78w02 5:12:08
Greenhill 44 1 35N35 82w51 5:31:24
Green Hill 81 1 35N24'25 82w02'31 5:28:10
Green Hill 95 1 36N07'24 81w39'29 5:26:38
Greenleaf 96 1 35N24'37 77w59'00 5:11:56
Greenlee 56 1 35N39'53 82w05'51 5:28:23
Green Level 92 1 35N46'55 78w54'15 5:15:37
Green Mountain 100
1 35N59'37 82w15'33 5:29:02
Green Pond 83 1 34N47'04 79w37'58 5:18:32
Green River 45 1 35N13 82w27 5:29:48
Greenriver 75 1 35N22 81w57 5:27:48
Greensboro 41 1 36N04'21 79w47'32 5:19:10
Greens Creek 50 1 35N19'42 83w15'44 5:33:03
Greens Fork 37 1 36N23'39 76w32'45 5:06:11
Green Valley 5 1 36N24'31 81w42'13 5:26:49
Greenville 74 1 35N36'40 77w22'23 5:09:30
Greesons Crossroads 41
1 36N02'05 79w38'20 5:18:33
Gregory 27 1 36N23'02 76w07'24 5:04:30
Gregory Crossroads 67
1 34N54 77w33 5:10:12
Gregory Forks 67
1 34N52'54 77w34'39 5:10:19
Gretna Green 42 1 36N23'23 77w51'13 5:11:25
Greystone 91 1 36N21'38 78w20'58 5:13:24
Griffins Crossroads 4
1 35N01'01 80w13'12 5:20:53
Griffins Crossroads 19
1 35N44'13 79w05'01 5:16:20
Grifton 74 1 35N22'11 77w26'16 5:09:45
Grimesdale 45 1 35N21'50 82w28'32 5:29:54
Grimesland 74 1 35N33'48 77w11'33 5:08:46
Grimshawes 50 1 35N04'33 83w06'38 5:32:27
Grissettown 10 1 33N56'47 78w30'09 5:14:01
Grissom 39 1 36N04'19 78w35'48 5:14:23
Grist 24 1 34N19 78w50 5:15:20
Groometown 41 1 35N59'28 79w52'04 5:19:28
Groomtown 41 1 36N03 79w52 5:19:28
Grove 43 1 35N24 78w40 5:14:40
Grove Hill 93 1 36N20'06 78w00'34 5:12:02
Grovemont 11 1 35N36'35 82w23'14 5:29:33
Grove Park 60 1 35N14'20 80w44'05 5:22:56
Grover 23 1 35N10'28 81w27'00 5:25:48
Groves 36 1 35N16 81w10 5:24:40
Grovestone 11 1 35N36'23 82w21'46 5:29:27
Growers Crossroads 8
1 36N12 76w46 5:07:04
Guide 24 1 34N04'42 78w44'02 5:14:56
Guideway 24 1 34N03'52 78w41'46 5:14:47
Guilford 41 1 36N04'36 79w53'54 5:19:36
Guilford College 41
1 36N05'23 79w53'20 5:19:33
Gulf 19 1 35N33'37 79w16'55 5:17:08
Gulledge 4 1 34N52 80w06 5:20:24
Gulrock 48 1 35N24'51 76w05'24 5:04:22
Gumberry 66 1 36N28'13 77w29'46 5:09:59
Gum Branch 67 1 34N52'11 77w29'47 5:09:59
Gum Corner 27 1 36N25'52 76w05'33 5:04:22
Gum Forks 66 1 36N30'22 77w40'49 5:10:43
Gum Neck 89 1 35N43'48 76w08'37 5:04:34
Gum Neck Landing 89
1 35N41'52 76w06'36 5:04:26
Gum Springs 19 1 35N45'39 79w13'56 5:16:56
Gum Tree 29 1 35N59'46 80w12'01 5:20:48
Guntertown 58 1 35N55'51 82w42'59 5:30:52
Gupton 35 1 36N11'48 78w09'39 5:12:39
Guthrie 34 1 36N07'17 80w09'05 5:20:36
Guyton 9 1 34N32 78w48 5:15:12
Gwaltneys 2 1 35N59 81w12 5:24:48
Hackney 7 1 35N28'11 77w07'10 5:08:29
Haddocks Crossroads 74
1 35N32 77w24 5:09:36
Hadley 19 1 35N49 79w17 5:17:08
Hairtown 43 1 35N16'43 78w59'13 5:15:57
Hale Point Landing 10
1 34N19'50 78w01'53 5:12:08
Half Hell 10 1 34N02'25 78w09'20 5:12:37
Half Moon 67 1 34N49'33 77w27'35 5:09:50
Halifax 42 1 36N19'42 77w35'23 5:10:22
Halifax Crossing 64
1 35N57'29 77w52'20 5:11:29
Hall 37 1 36N26 76w51 5:07:24
Hall Ferry Junction 84
1 35N25'37 80w12'53 5:20:52
Hall Landing 10 1 34N17'59 78w02'06 5:12:08
Halls 46 1 36N17 76w59 5:07:56
Halls 82 1 35N07 78w19 5:13:16
Hallsboro 24 1 34N19'20 78w35'57 5:14:24
Halls Ferry Junction 84
1 35N27 80w13 5:20:52
Halls Ford 87 1 35N21'19 83w30'37 5:34:02
Halls Mills 97 1 36N17'32 81w12'38 5:24:51
Halls Store 82 1 35N06'48 78w32'18 5:14:09
Hallsville 31 1 34N54'26 77w50'21 5:11:21
Hamburg 50 1 35N10 83w08 5:32:32
Hamer 17 1 36N27'23 79w16'30 5:17:06
Hamilton 59 1 35N56'40 77w12'36 5:08:50
Hamilton Crossroads 90
1 35N02'58 80w20'41 5:21:23
Hamilton Lakes 41
1 36N04'59 79w51'13 5:19:25
Hamlet 77 1 34N53'05 79w41'40 5:18:47
Hammond Crossroads 78
1 34N28'30 79w14'08 5:16:57
Hampstead 71 1 34N22'03 77w42'39 5:10:51
Hampton 29 1 35N58 80w22 5:21:28
Hamptonville 99 1 36N05'54 80w45'38 5:23:03

Hamrick 100 1 35N48'35 82w11'57 5:28:48
Hams Crossroads 74
1 35N31'42 77w13'19 5:08:53
Hamtown 41 1 36N06 79w46 5:19:04
Hancock 21 1 36N05'57 76w37'44 5:06:31
Hancock Village 25
1 34N54 76w54 5:07:36
Handy 29 1 35N35'19 80w06'04 5:20:24
Hanes 34 1 36N04'56 80w17'50 5:21:11
Hankins 56 1 35N43'57 82w00'24 5:28:02
Hannersville 29 1 35N49 80w15 5:21:00
Hanrahan 74 1 35N24'25 77w25'39 5:09:43
Happy Acres 88 1 35N07'46 82w42'23 5:30:50
Happy Home 79 1 36N29'46 79w37'43 5:18:31
Happy Valley 14 1 35N59'19 81w33'32 5:26:14
Harbinger 27 1 36N06'07 75w48'52 5:03:15
Hardee Cross Roads 51
1 35N28'24 78w36'29 5:14:26
Hardin 20 1 35N13'34 83w50'40 5:35:23
Hardins 36 1 35N22'45 81w11'26 5:24:46
Hare 3 1 36N28'50 80w58'52 5:23:55
Hares Crossroads 51
1 35N40'13 78w15'07 5:13:00
Hargetts Crossroads 52
1 35N00'10 77w38'13 5:10:33
Hargrove Crossroads 82
1 35N05'39 78w13'44 5:12:55
Harkers Island 16
1 34N41'42 76w33'35 5:06:14
Harlem Heights 4
1 34N58 80w05 5:20:20
Harley 97 1 36N11'34 81w24'53 5:25:40
Harlowe 16 1 34N50'45 76w45'34 5:07:02
Harmony 49 1 35N57'20 80w46'19 5:23:05
Harmony Grove 34
1 36N04'48 80w23'12 5:21:33
Harnett 43 1 35N20'43 78w47'33 5:15:10
Harnett 65 3 34N14 77w51 5:11:24
Harper 51 1 35N18'06 78w19'20 5:13:17
Harpers Crossroads 19
1 35N34'04 79w27'48 5:17:51
Harrell 61 1 36N07 82w12 5:28:48
Harrell Hill 61 1 36N02'24 82w14'13 5:28:57
Harrells 82 1 34N43'39 78w12'05 5:12:48
Harrells Mill 46
1 36N23'08 76w54'18 5:07:37
Harrellsville 46
1 36N18'09 76w47'34 5:07:10
Harrelsonville 24
1 34N20 78w42 5:14:48
Harrelsonville Crossroads 24
1 34N15'16 78w42'34 5:14:50
Harris 63 1 35N18'13 79w32'08 5:18:09
Harris 81 1 35N14'34 81w52'30 5:27:30
Harrisburg 13 1 35N19'25 80w39'22 5:22:37
Harris Crossroads 35
1 35N58'56 78w22'57 5:13:32
Harris Crossroads 91
1 36N24'01 78w25'09 5:13:41
Harris Landing 21
1 36N08'30 76w42'53 5:06:52
Harris Landing 25
1 35N16'55 77w16'35 5:09:06
Harrisons Crossroads 79
1 36N25'13 79w41'24 5:18:46
Harrisville 62 1 35N12'32 79w49'22 5:19:17
Hartland 14 1 35N51'11 81w38'47 5:26:35
Hartman 85 1 36N25'19 80w10'20 5:20:41
Hartsboro 33 1 35N54'55 77w38'48 5:10:35
Hartsease 33 1 35N55'55 77w38'37 5:10:34
Harts Store 85 1 36N29 80w14 5:20:56
Harveytown 54 1 35N16'52 77w34'04 5:10:16
Haslett 37 1 36N31 76w42 5:06:48
Haslin Corners 7
1 35N33'36 76w34'39 5:06:19
Hassell 59 1 35N54'41 77w16'43 5:09:07
Hastings Corner 15
1 36N21'06 76w09'50 5:04:39
Hasty 83 1 34N41'25 79w28'42 5:17:55
Hatcher 82 1 35N05'45 78w12'49 5:12:51
Hatteras 28 1 35N13'09 75w41'26 5:02:46
Havelock 25 1 34N52'44 76w54'06 5:07:36
Havelock Station 25
1 34N52'57 76w55'21 5:07:41
Haw 67 1 34N41'40 77w33'10 5:10:13
Haw Branch 63 1 35N29'50 79w22'16 5:17:29
Haw Branch 67 1 34N56'11 77w37'55 5:10:32
Haw Creek 11 2 35N35'04 82w31'35 5:30:06
Hawfields 1 1 36N03'33 79w18'19 5:17:13
Hawk 61 1 36N01'08 82w05'30 5:28:22
Hawk Branch 100 1 35N57'50 82w22'18 5:29:29
Hawkins Landing 7
1 35N27'07 76w51'10 5:07:25
Hawkside 67 1 34N46'12 77w24'09 5:09:37
Hawra 98 1 35N38'34 78w05'20 5:12:21
Haw River 1 1 36N05'29 79w21'52 5:17:27
Hawtree 93 1 36N30 78w09 5:12:36
Hayes 32 1 35N58'21 78w51'52 5:15:27
Hayesville 22 1 35N02'46 83w49'05 5:35:16
Haymount 26 1 35N03'24 78w54'02 5:15:36
Hayne 82 1 34N58'51 78w35'25 5:14:22
Hays 97 1 36N14'59 81w06'57 5:24:28
Hayti 32 1 36N00 78w54 5:15:36
Haywood 19 1 35N37'12 79w03'51 5:16:15
Hazel Green 11 1 35N35'24 82w35'02 5:30:20
Hazelton 37 1 36N31'05 76w41'58 5:06:48
Hazelwood 44 2 35N28'07 83w00'15 5:32:01
Healing Springs 29
1 35N36'58 80w10'42 5:20:43
Heath Landing 25
1 35N16'07 77w07'50 5:08:31
Heathsville 42 1 36N16'09 77w45'54 5:11:04
Heaton 6 1 36N10'22 81w56'34 5:27:46
Hectors Creek 43
1 35N30 78w51 5:15:24
Hedden Bluff Landing 71
1 34N23'22 78w05'50 5:12:23
Hedrick Grove 29
1 35N46'21 80w10'47 5:20:43
Heflin 51 1 35N42'36 78w12'28 5:12:50
Heilmans Mill 13
1 35N28'58 80w35'02 5:22:20
Helena 73 1 36N17'09 78w57'05 5:15:48

Helens Crossroads 74 1 35N28 77W25 5:09:40
Helton 5 1 36N32'53 81W28'08 5:25:53
Hemby 90 1 35N05 80W41 5:22:44
Hemby Bridge 90 1 35N05 80W41 5:22:44
Hemlock 5 1 36N32 81W40 5:26:40
Henderson 91 1 36N19'46 78W23'58 5:13:36
Hendersonville 45 1 35N19'07 82W27'40 5:29:51
Hendrix 97 1 36N05 81W22 5:25:28
Henrico 66 1 36N32'03 77W49'52 5:11:19
Henrietta 33 1 35N51'28 77W34'59 5:10:20
Henrietta 81 1 35N15'28 81W47'47 5:27:11
Henry 55 1 35N33'30 81W25'33 5:25:42
Henry Landing 82 1 34N36'38 78W18'16 5:13:13
Henry River 12 1 35N41'47 81W25'43 5:25:43
Henrytown 10 1 34N10'23 78W06'28 5:12:26
Hepco 44 1 35N35 82W55 5:31:40
Herrings 82 1 35N08 78W26 5:13:44
Herrings Crossroads 31 1 35N07'17 77W51'58 5:11:28
Herrings Crossroads 82 1 35N10'28 78W23'46 5:13:35
Hertford 72 1 36N11'24 76W27'59 5:05:52
Hertford Village 92 1 35N44'56 78W38'36 5:14:34
Hester 39 1 36N10'12 78W40'22 5:14:41
Hesters Store 73 1 36N16 79W03 5:16:12
Hestertown 78 1 34N35'51 78W59'45 5:15:59
Hewitt 87 2 35N18'32 83W38'52 5:34:35
Hexlena 8 1 36N11'35 77W01'45 5:08:07
Hickmans Crossroads 10 1 33N55'49 78W36'38 5:14:27
Hickmans Cross Roads 24 1 34N27'11 78W49'44 5:15:19
Hickory 18 1 35N43'59 81W20'29 5:25:22
Hickory 64 1 36N07'44 77W48'05 5:11:12
Hickory Crossroads 51 1 35N32'45 78W06'02 5:12:24
Hickory Crossroads 72 1 36N19'13 76W32'42 5:06:11
Hickory Grove 47 1 34N55'25 79W19'29 5:17:18
Hickory Grove 60 1 35N13'43 80W43'15 5:22:53
Hickory Grove 75 1 35N12'36 82W06'15 5:28:25
Hickory Grove Crossroads 9 1 34N44'54 78W25'22 5:13:41
Hickory Knoll 57 1 35N11 83W23 5:33:32
Hickory Mountain 19 1 35N42 79W19 5:17:16
Hickory Point 7 1 35N18 76W47 5:07:08
Hickory Rock 35 1 36N07'27 78W12'37 5:12:50
Hicks Crossroads 60 1 35N25'32 80W55'04 5:23:40
Hicks Crossroads 91 1 36N25'43 78W29'55 5:14:00
Hicks Village 73 1 36N24'18 79W01'20 5:16:05
Hiddenite 2 1 35N54'13 81W05'27 5:24:22
Hidetown 38 1 35N22'17 83W40'49 5:34:43
Higdonville 57 1 35N10'39 83W18'00 5:33:12
Higgins 56 1 35N39 81W57 5:27:48
Higgins 100 1 35N57'34 82W22'49 5:29:31
High Crossroads 64 1 35N48'25 78W02'43 5:12:11
High Falls 63 1 35N29'01 79W31'19 5:18:05
High Hampton 50 1 35N05'59 83W04'56 5:32:20
Highland Park 77 1 34N54'51 79W40'34 5:18:42
Highland Park West 41 1 36N04'08 79W51'26 5:19:26
Highland Pines 77 1 34N54'21 79W44'16 5:18:57
Highlands 57 1 35N03'09 83W11'49 5:32:47
High Point 41 1 35N57'20 80W00'20 5:20:01
High Rock 29 1 35N35'48 80W13'17 5:20:53
High Shoals 36 1 35N24'09 81W12'09 5:24:49
High Shoals 81 1 35N15 81W48 5:27:12
Highsmith 71 1 34N28'30 77W58'56 5:11:56
Highsmiths 82 1 34N55'06 78W29'49 5:13:59
Hightowers 17 1 36N19'37 79W14'37 5:16:58
Hildebran 12 1 35N42'50 81W25'20 5:25:41
Hill 74 1 35N45'43 77W30'52 5:10:03
Hillcrest 47 1 34N59'13 79W11'22 5:16:45
Hill Crest 63 1 35N18'48 79W25'00 5:17:40
Hillcrest 95 1 36N13'16 81W40'05 5:26:40
Hillendale 26 1 35N04 78W53 5:15:32
Hillgirt 45 1 35N21'55 82W29'02 5:29:56
Hilliardston 64 1 36N06'19 77W55'48 5:11:43
Hills 84 1 35N18'47 80W15'40 5:21:03
Hillsborough 68 1 36N04'31 79W06'00 5:16:24
Hills Crossroads 31 1 35N06'50 77W56'31 5:11:46
Hills Crossroads 42 1 36N11'18 77W27'43 5:09:51
Hillsdale 30 1 36N00'18 80W26'23 5:21:46
Hillsdale 41 1 36N12'00 79W50'40 5:19:23
Hilltop 41 1 36N01'50 79W53'05 5:19:32
Hilltop 55 1 35N28 81W15 5:25:00
Hines Crossroads 96 1 35N12'03 77W53'21 5:11:33
Hines Junction 54 1 35N16'08 77W37'11 5:10:29
Hinnes Crossroads 42 1 36N24'12 77W47'59 5:11:12
Hinson 94 1 35N46'03 76W47'50 5:07:11
Hinsons Crossroads 24 1 34N18'21 78W58'45 5:15:55
Hiwassee 22 1 35N02 83W45 5:35:00
Hiwassee Dam 20 1 35N05 84W02 5:36:08
Hiwassee Village 20 1 35N08'56 84W10'17 5:36:41
Hobbs Crossroads 82 1 35N10'19 78W19'22 5:13:17
Hobbsville 37 1 36N20'49 76W36'18 5:06:25
Hobbton 82 1 35N15 78W21 5:13:24
Hobgood 42 1 36N01'47 77W23'53 5:09:36
Hobucken 69 1 35N14'44 76W34'10 5:06:17
Hocutts Crossroads 51 1 35N44'00 78W17'53 5:13:12
Hodges Gap 95 1 36N13 81W40 5:26:40
Hoffman 77 1 35N01'56 79W32'52 5:18:11
Hogback 88 1 35N07 82W55 5:31:40
Hogetown 95 1 36N11'21 81W32'03 5:26:08
Hog Island 63 1 35N11'36 79W17'48 5:17:11
Hoke 94 1 35N44'00 76W48'56 5:07:16
Holden Beach 10 1 33N54'48 78W15'10 5:13:01
Holdens Crossroads 98 1 35N42'24 77W47'00 5:11:08
Holland 92 1 35N34'22 78W46'14 5:15:05
Hollands 74 1 35N43'23 77W28'38 5:09:55
Hollands Crossroads 96 1 35N31'23 78W05'20 5:12:21
Hollemans Crossroads 92 1 35N36'58 78W54'36 5:15:38
Hollifield 56 1 35N41 82W00 5:28:00
Hollis 81 1 35N26'10 81W43'51 5:26:55
Hollister 42 1 36N15'21 77W56'10 5:11:45
Hollow 9 1 34N47 78W50 5:15:20
Holloway 73 1 36N30 78W52 5:15:28
Holly 71 1 34N38 77W43 5:10:52
Holly Grove 29 1 35N49'02 80W11'30 5:20:46
Holly Grove 37 1 36N30'19 76W34'09 5:06:17
Holly Hill 45 1 35N20'39 82W29'48 5:29:59
Holly Ridge 67 1 34N29'43 77W33'19 5:10:13
Holly Springs 16 1 34N47'57 76W54'35 5:07:38
Holly Springs 45 1 35N20'44 82W36'09 5:30:25
Holly Springs 57 1 35N11 83W23 5:33:32
Holly Springs 92 1 35N39'04 78W50'02 5:15:20
Holmesville 78 1 34N21'36 79W08'35 5:16:34
Home Acres 92 1 35N44'23 78W37'57 5:14:32
Homestead 60 1 35N17'00 80W54'48 5:23:39
Hominy 11 2 35N32'45 82W40'35 5:30:42
Honeycutts 82 1 35N03 78W29 5:13:56
Honey Hill 24 1 34N16'31 78W38'00 5:14:32
Honey Island 10 1 34N06 78W32 5:14:08
Honey Pond 10 1 34N01'52 78W29'55 5:14:00
Honey Town 77 1 34N57'00 79W47'02 5:19:08
Honolulu 25 1 35N21'46 77W16'55 5:09:08
Hood Creek Landing 10 1 34N20'18 78W04'39 5:12:19
Hoods 60 1 35N08'14 80W40'59 5:22:44
Hoods Crossroads 60 1 35N07 80W43 5:22:52
Hood Swamp 96 1 35N24'23 77W52'30 5:11:30
Hooker 3 1 36N30'13 81W01'32 5:24:06
Hookerton 40 1 35N25'30 77W35'19 5:10:21
Hooper Hill 10 1 34N19'48 78W04'33 5:12:18
Hoopers Creek 45 1 35N26'20 82W28'01 5:29:52
Hoophole Landing 48 1 35N36'47 76W34'37 5:06:18
Hoop Pole Landing 16 1 34N42'12 76W48'20 5:07:13
Hootentown 7 1 35N32'10 77W01'12 5:08:05
Hootstown 34 1 36N02'56 80W16'01 5:21:04
Hopedale 1 1 36N07'26 79W24'09 5:17:37
Hope Mills 26 1 34N58'13 78W56'44 5:15:47
Hopewell 60 1 35N28'01 80W48'52 5:23:15
Hopewell 81 1 35N22'58 81W44'05 5:26:56
Hopewell 96 1 35N13'34 77W59'17 5:11:57
Hopkins 92 1 35N53'05 78W21'09 5:13:25
Horace 45 1 35N22'18 82W17'48 5:29:11
Horner 39 1 36N19'56 78W34'10 5:14:17
Horneytown 34 1 36N01'10 80W03'37 5:20:14
Horse Creek 5 1 36N31 81W35 5:26:20
Horse Landing 52 1 35N03'59 77W19'30 5:09:18
Horse Neck 78 1 34N49'07 78W54'40 5:15:39
Horsepen Landing 78 1 34N28'50 78W52'23 5:15:30
Horseshoe 15 1 36N27'36 76W23'37 5:05:34
Horse Shoe 45 1 35N20'35 82W33'24 5:30:14
Hosiery Mill 4 1 34N58 80W05 5:20:20
Hothouse 20 1 35N01'15 84W13'57 5:36:56
Hot Springs 58 2 35N53'32 82W49'45 5:31:19
House 74 1 35N39'16 77W21'55 5:09:28
House Creek 92 1 35N51 81W52 5:27:28
Houston 90 1 34N57'26 80W37'42 5:22:31
Houstonville 49 1 36N00'11 80W45'59 5:23:04
Howard Landing 71 1 34N21'17 77W41'19 5:10:45
Howards Creek 55 1 35N29 81W21 5:25:24
Howellsville 78 1 34N41'48 78W55'02 5:15:40
Hubert 67 1 34N42'49 77W14'44 5:08:59
Huckleberry Heights 32 1 36N01 78W56 5:15:44
Huckleberry Spring 32 1 36N02'27 78W57'30 5:15:50
Hudson 14 1 35N50'54 81W29'46 5:25:59
Hufflers Fork 37 1 36N23'46 76W36'26 5:06:26
Huffmantown 67 1 34N57'15 77W33'39 5:10:15
Hughes 6 1 36N03'35 81W57'52 5:27:51
Hugo 54 1 35N23'29 77W31'59 5:10:08
Hulls Crossroads 55 1 35N30'31 81W27'27 5:25:50
Huntdale 61 1 36N01'35 82W19'04 5:29:16
Hunters Bridge 7 1 35N37 76W52 5:07:28
Hunters Mill 37 1 36N24 76W36 5:06:24
Huntersville 60 1 35N24'38 80W50'35 5:23:22
Hunting Creek 97 1 36N10 81W08 5:24:32
Huntley 82 1 35N04'14 78W30'37 5:14:02
Hunts 64 1 35N59'32 78W07'31 5:12:30
Huntsboro 39 1 36N21'33 78W32'17 5:14:09
Huntsville 79 1 36N19 79W59 5:19:56
Huntsville 99 1 36N04'56 80W31'47 5:22:07
Hurdle Mills 73 1 36N16'23 79W02'52 5:16:11
Hurricane 5 1 36N34 81W35 5:26:20
Hurricane 58 1 35N54'51 82W45'28 5:31:02
Husk 5 1 36N35 81W31 5:26:04
Hutson Corner 21 1 36N15'54 76W39'19 5:06:37
Hyatt Creek 44 1 35N27'55 83W01'43 5:32:07
Hydeland 48 1 35N25'35 76W13'12 5:04:53
Hydro 84 1 35N13 80W00 5:20:00
Hymans 25 1 35N09'05 77W10'54 5:08:44
Icard 12 1 35N43'38 81W28'15 5:25:53
Icaria 21 1 36N15'21 76W37'39 5:06:31
Ida 83 1 34N46 79W28 5:17:52
Idalia 7 1 35N16'48 76W47'29 5:07:10
Ida Mill 83 1 34N47'59 79W31'51 5:18:07
Idlewild 5 1 36N17'21 81W26'47 5:25:47
Idlewild 60 1 35N11'19 80W44'39 5:22:59
Ijames Crossroads 30 1 35N56'07 80W38'34 5:22:34
Index 5 1 36N24 81W29 5:25:56
Indian Beach 16 1 34N42 76W50 5:07:20
Indian Cave Park 45 1 35N17'58 82W31'12 5:30:05
Indian Hills 50 1 35N26 83W22 5:33:28
Indian Landing 7 1 35N37'48 76W35'46 5:06:23
Indian Place 50 1 35N14'47 83W05'42 5:32:23
Indian Springs 96 1 35N13'51 77W56'53 5:11:48
Indian Town 15 1 36N20'03 76W04'36 5:04:18
Indian Trail 90 1 35N04'36 80W40'10 5:22:41
Indian Woods 8 1 35N58 77W04 5:08:16
Inez 93 1 36N16'19 78W05'31 5:12:22
Ingalls 6 1 35N58'17 82W00'43 5:28:03
Ingleside 35 1 36N10'34 78W17'47 5:13:11
Ingold 82 1 34N49'36 78W20'51 5:13:23
Ingram 77 1 35N06'01 79W56'17 5:19:45
Ingrams 51 1 35N25 78W25 5:13:40
Institute 54 1 35N21'27 77W42'51 5:10:51
Intelligence 79 1 36N23 79W58 5:19:52
Inverness 47 1 35N10'53 79W14'27 5:16:58
Iotla 57 1 35N14'10 83W23'43 5:33:35
Ipock Landing 25 1 35N15'45 77W07'39 5:08:31
Iredell 10 1 33N55'59 78W35'29 5:14:22
Iron Duff 44 1 35N34'44 82W58'14 5:31:53
Ironhill 24 1 34N08'18 78W47'00 5:15:08
Iron Station 55 1 35N26'29 81W09'23 5:24:38
Ironton 55 1 35N29 81W09 5:24:36
Irving Park 41 1 36N05'43 79W47'58 5:19:12
Irvings Crossroads 54 1 35N04'17 77W38'28 5:10:34
Isenhour 84 1 35N26'59 80W09'24 5:20:38
Isenhour Park 2 1 35N52'06 81W11'16 5:24:45
Island Creek 31 1 34N47 77W56 5:11:44
Island Ford 50 1 35N13'50 83W02'26 5:32:10
Ita 42 1 36N10'28 77W54'39 5:11:39
Ivanhoe 82 1 34N36'38 78W14'32 5:12:58
Ivey Crossroads 78 1 34N25'20 79W05'43 5:16:23
Ivy 58 1 35N48'52 82W30'54 5:30:04
Ivy Hills 44 1 35N31'39 82W59'41 5:31:59
Ivy Ridge 58 2 35N54'42 82W35'19 5:30:21
Jackie Landing 82 1 34N39'09 78W15'17 5:13:01
Jacks Creek 100 1 35N58 82W20 5:29:20
Jackson 66 1 36N23'22 77W25'18 5:09:41
Jackson 90 1 34N52'00 80W41'01 5:22:44
Jackson Creek 76 1 35N41'38 80W00'14 5:20:01
Jackson Hill 29 1 35N34'21 80W09'01 5:20:36
Jackson Line 87 1 35N23'53 83W28'30 5:33:54
Jackson Park 13 1 35N22'33 80W35'59 5:22:24
Jacksons Creek 76 1 35N38 80W07 5:20:28
Jacksons Crossroads 54 1 35N13'24 77W38'46 5:10:35
Jackson Springs 63 1 35N12'34 79W37'34 5:18:30
Jacksons Store 31 1 34N55 77W46 5:11:04
Jacksontown 91 1 36N25'24 78W19'47 5:13:19
Jacksonville 67 1 34N45'14 77W25'50 5:09:43
Jacktown 56 1 35N40'04 81W58'05 5:27:52
Jacobs Fork 18 1 35N36 81W19 5:25:16
Jacocks 72 1 36N08'57 76W15'52 5:05:03
Jakesville 29 1 35N51'13 80W16'48 5:21:07
James City 25 1 35N05'19 77W02'07 5:08:08
Jamestown 41 1 35N59'39 79W56'08 5:19:45
Jamesville 59 1 35N48'40 76W53'49 5:07:35
Janeiro 69 1 34N59'44 76W45'56 5:07:04
Jarman Forks 67 1 34N54 77W33 5:10:12
Jarmantown 67 1 34N58'12 77W37'57 5:10:32
Jarrett Cove 58 1 35N53'54 82W38'37 5:30:34
Jarvisburg 27 1 36N12'10 75W52'01 5:03:28
Jason 40 1 35N22'52 77W46'28 5:11:06
Jasper 25 1 35N12'05 77W12'25 5:08:50
Jefferson 5 1 36N25'13 81W28'25 5:25:54
Jefferson Park 77 1 34N55'04 79W47'07 5:19:08
Jenkins Heights 36 1 35N16'29 81W12'37 5:24:50
Jenkins Meadow 38 1 35N22'55 83W57'11 5:35:49
Jenkins Place 87 1 35N29'06 83W25'27 5:33:42
Jennings 49 1 36N00'43 80W52'50 5:23:31
Jenny Lind 54 1 35N15'25 77W46'42 5:11:07
Jericho 17 1 36N17'13 79W22'00 5:17:28
Jerome 9 1 34N50'33 78W44'03 5:14:56
Jerry 89 1 35N52'55 76W13'38 5:04:55
Jerusalem 30 1 35N48'54 80W30'57 5:22:04
Jessup Mill 85 1 36N31'32 80W22'15 5:21:29
Jessups Landing 9 1 34N32'54 78W26'13 5:13:45
Jeter Mountain Terrace 45 1 35N14'51 82W32'51 5:30:11
Jinnys Branch 10 1 33N54'47 78W23'58 5:13:36
J M Sykes Landing 71 1 34N21'16 78W10'18 5:12:41
Jobs Cabin 97 1 36N15 81W24 5:25:36
Joe (P O) 58 1 35N47'48 82W54'32 5:31:38
Johns 83 1 34N41'59 79W26'35 5:17:46
Johnson Crossroads 51 1 35N31'15 78W36'10 5:14:25
Johnsons Corner 15 1 36N26'04 76W17'56 5:05:12
Johnsons Crossing 19 1 35N36'15 79W24'09 5:17:37

Johnsons Mill 47 1 35N01'14 79W07'47 5:16:31
Johnsons Mills 74 1 35N23'10 77W21'09 5:09:25
Johnsontown 9 1 34N44'31 78W34'18 5:14:17
Johnsontown 29 1 35N52'19 80W06'30 5:20:26
Johnsontown 82 1 34N59'49 78W20'39 5:13:23
Johnsonville 20 1 35N00'41 84W15'47 5:37:03
Johnsonville 43 1 35N16'58 79W06'27 5:16:26
Johns River 14 1 35N56 81W41 5:26:44
Johnstown 9 1 34N38 78W33 5:14:12
Johnstown 55 1 35N26'51 81W21'50 5:25:27
Jollys Old Field Landing 74 1 35N20'53 77W23'30 5:09:34
Jonas Ridge 12 1 35N58'21 81W53'42 5:27:35
Jonathan 44 1 35N33 82W59 5:31:56
Jonathans Creek 44 1 35N37 83W02 5:32:08
Jones 17 1 36N25'45 79W25'49 5:17:43
Jonesboro 53 1 35N27 79W10 5:16:40
Jonesboro Crossing 24 1 34N19'18 78W37'26 5:14:30
Jonesboro Heights 53 1 35N27'24 79W09'08 5:16:37
Jones Corner 52 1 35N03'31 77W12'16 5:08:49
Jones Mill 20 1 35N06'35 83W54'20 5:35:37
Jonestown 34 1 36N03'12 80W20'41 5:21:23
Jonestown 54 1 35N05'02 77W38'34 5:10:34
Jonesville 99 1 36N14'21 80W50'41 5:23:23
Joplor 60 1 35N22'06 80W49'22 5:23:17
Joppa 37 1 36N21'18 76W33'37 5:06:14
Jordan 51 1 35N40'08 78W18'26 5:13:14
Joy 12 1 35N44 81W42 5:26:48
Joyce Mill 85 1 36N32'12 80W24'01 5:21:36
Joyceton 14 1 35N52'02 81W30'29 5:26:02
Joyland 32 1 35N59'28 78W51'17 5:15:25
Joyners Crossing 64 1 35N53'29 77W51'54 5:11:28
Joyners Crossroads 64 1 35N58 77W48 5:11:12
Joynes 97 1 36N22'15 81W04'01 5:24:16
Jubilee 29 1 35N45 80W19 5:21:16
Judkins 93 1 36N23 78W00 5:12:00
Judson 26 1 35N00'07 78W48'33 5:15:14
Jugtown 11 1 35N33'27 82W43'23 5:30:54
Jugtown 63 1 35N30'29 79W39'01 5:18:36
Julian 41 1 35N54'18 79W39'38 5:18:39
Junction 38 1 35N15'54 83W56'16 5:35:45
Juniper 92 1 35N37'54 78W38'30 5:14:34
Junker 60 1 35N15'44 80W45'46 5:23:03
Juno 11 2 35N38'24 82W38'49 5:30:35
Jupiter 11 1 35N45'39 82W35'37 5:30:22
Just 58 1 35N50 82W33 5:30:12
Just Crossroads 1 1 36N11'21 79W16'57 5:17:08
Justice 35 1 36N03'30 78W10'15 5:12:41
Kalmia 61 1 35N55'47 82W01'23 5:28:06
Kannapolis 13 1 35N29'14 80W37'19 5:22:29
Kanuga Pines 45 1 35N16'44 82W29'14 5:29:57
Kappa 30 1 35N54 80W34 5:22:16
Kapps Mill 86 1 36N19 80W52 5:23:28
Katesville 35 1 36N05'20 78W21'58 5:13:28
Kawana 6 1 35N58'50 81W49'24 5:27:18
Keane 32 1 35N58 78W55 5:15:40
Kearney 35 1 36N13'28 78W16'25 5:13:06
Kedron 39 1 36N21'38 78W42'07 5:14:48
Keene 32 1 35N56'57 78W54'16 5:15:37
Keener 82 1 35N06'25 78W19'08 5:13:17
Kelford 8 1 36N10'46 77W13'26 5:08:54
Kellersville 95 1 36N10 81W52 5:27:28
Kellerville 95 1 36N14'43 81W53'52 5:27:35
Kellogs Fork 37 1 36N27'21 76W36'19 5:06:25
Kellum 67 1 34N48'16 77W21'23 5:09:26
Kellumtown 67 1 34N43 77W14 5:08:56
Kelly 9 1 34N27'58 78W19'29 5:13:18
Kellys Crossroads 91 1 36N23'21 78W26'57 5:13:48
Kenansville 31 1 34N57'44 77W57'45 5:11:51
Kendall Chapel 10 1 34N05'23 77W57'47 5:11:51
Kenilworth 11 2 35N34'33 82W32'20 5:30:09
Kenly 51 1 35N35'46 78W07'28 5:12:30
Kennebec 92 1 35N32'24 78W44'51 5:14:59
Kennekeet 28 1 35N42 75W39 5:02:36
Kennel Beach 69 1 35N01'27 76W54'01 5:07:36
Kennells Beach 69 1 35N08 76W51 5:07:24
Kernersville 34 1 36N07'11 80W04'26 5:20:18
Kerr 82 1 34N39'22 78W16'56 5:13:08
Kershaw 69 1 35N02'52 76W44'13 5:06:57
Keys Crossroads 37 1 36N22'08 76W34'51 5:06:19
Kikers 4 1 35N04'32 80W12'41 5:20:51
Kilby 2 1 35N55 81W10 5:24:40
Kilkenny 89 1 35N38'10 76W12'58 5:04:52
Kilkenny Landing 48 1 35N38'31 76W11'41 5:04:47
Kill Devil Hills 28 1 36N01 75W39 5:02:36
Killian Crossroads 18 1 35N33'31 81W03'51 5:24:15
Kimesville 1 1 35N57'08 79W32'23 5:18:10
Kindy Forest 45 1 35N19'18 82W31'01 5:30:04
King 85 1 36N16'50 80W21'34 5:21:26
King Charles 92 1 35N46 78W37 5:14:28
Kingdale 78 1 34N32'40 79W00'53 5:16:04
Kingsboro 33 1 35N58 77W48 5:11:12
Kings Creek 14 1 35N59'32 81W24'07 5:25:36
Kings Crossroads 41 1 36N12'46 79W59'25 5:19:58
Kings Crossroads 74 1 35N40 77W38 5:10:32
Kings Landing 71 1 34N22'27 77W39'09 5:10:37
Kings Mountain 23 1 35N14'42 81W20'29 5:25:22
King Whites Fork 42 1 36N02 77W24 5:09:36
Kinston 54 1 35N15'45 77W34'55 5:10:20
Kinton Fork 39 1 36N18 78W35 5:14:20
Kintons Cross Road 39 1 36N21'13 78W37'52 5:14:31
Kipling 43 1 35N28'47 78W49'17 5:15:17
Kirby 66 1 36N28 77W12 5:08:48
Kirbys Crossing 98 1 35N36'48 78W05'26 5:12:22
Kirkman Crossroad 41 1 35N58'06 79W52'46 5:19:31
Kirkwood 41 1 36N06'16 79W48'34 5:19:14
Kittrell 91 1 36N13'19 78W26'17 5:13:45
Kitty Fork 82 1 35N00 78W20 5:13:20
Kitty Hawk 28 1 36N03'52 75W42'22 5:02:49
Kitty Hawk Beach 28 1 36N05'38 75W42'25 5:02:50
Knightdale 92 1 35N47'15 78W28'51 5:13:55
Knob Creek 23 1 35N30'45 81W32'43 5:26:11
Knob Hill 77 1 34N57'13 79W44'45 5:18:59
Knobs 99 1 36N12 80W49 5:23:16
Knollwood 63 1 35N12'03 79W23'58 5:17:36
Knotts Crossroads 91 1 36N24'23 78W29'34 5:13:58
Knotts Island 27 1 36N31 75W56 5:03:44
Kona 61 1 35N57'00 82W11'31 5:28:46
Koontzville 41 1 36N08'36 79W46'08 5:19:05
Kornbow 26 1 35N05 78W57 5:15:48
Kornegay 31 1 35N03'28 77W49'33 5:11:18
Kross Keys 75 1 35N11 82W11 5:28:44
Kuhns 16 1 34N47'24 77W07'48 5:08:31
Kungsboro 33 1 35N55'04 77W40'16 5:10:41
Kure Beach 65 3 33N59'48 77W54'27 5:11:38
Kyle 57 1 35N13'16 83W36'56 5:34:28
Kyles Crossroads 49 1 35N44'06 80W56'40 5:23:47
Laboratory 55 1 35N26'03 81W15'37 5:25:02
Lackey Hill 87 1 35N26'13 83W26'19 5:33:45
Lackey Store 85 1 36N31'53 80W10'56 5:20:44
Lackey Town 56 1 35N36'42 82W09'54 5:28:40
Ladonia 86 1 36N28'56 80W50'17 5:23:21
Lafayette 26 1 35N02 78W57 5:15:48
Lagoon 9 1 34N38 78W33 5:14:12
La Grange 54 1 35N18'24 77W47'18 5:11:09
Lake Creek 9 1 34N37 78W20 5:13:20
Lakecrest 26 1 35N04 78W53 5:15:32
Lakedale 26 1 35N01'29 78W53'57 5:15:36
Lake Daniel 41 1 36N04'57 79W48'43 5:19:15
Lake Junaluska 44 2 35N31'40 82W57'35 5:31:50
Lake Landing 48 1 35N29 76W02 5:04:08
Lake Lure 81 1 35N25'40 82W12'18 5:28:49
Lake Neighborhood 28 1 35N53'28 75W55'14 5:03:41
Lakeside Village 43 1 35N19'07 78W35'39 5:14:23
Lake Toxaway 88 1 35N07'56 82W56'03 5:31:44
Lakeview 1 1 36N09'18 79W25'25 5:17:42
Lakeview 29 1 35N44'22 80W22'12 5:21:29
Lakeview 63 1 35N14'37 79W18'32 5:17:14
Lakeview Estates 45 1 35N20'00 82W25'39 5:29:43
Lake View Park 18 1 35N44 81W21 5:25:24
Lake Waccamaw 24 1 34N19'08 78W30'01 5:14:00
Lakewood 32 1 35N58 78W55 5:15:40
Lakewood 41 1 36N08'28 79W41'41 5:18:47
Lakewood 45 1 35N17'37 82W29'22 5:29:57
Lake Worth 28 1 35N41'48 75W46'27 5:03:06
Lambert 84 1 35N18'48 80W21'35 5:21:26
Lambs Corner 15 1 36N22'47 76W13'20 5:04:53
Lamm 98 1 35N45'49 78W00'35 5:12:02
Lamm Crossroads 64 1 35N54'34 78W04'00 5:12:16
Lamms Crossroads 98 1 35N40'30 78W02'15 5:12:09
Lancaster 33 1 35N51'29 77W41'36 5:10:46
Lancaster Crossroads 64 1 36N03'45 78W04'59 5:12:20
Landing, Lake 48 1 35N29'24 76W02'13 5:04:09
Landis 80 1 35N32'44 80W36'40 5:22:27
Lane 26 1 35N11'51 78W46'40 5:15:07
Lane Landing 25 1 35N15'23 77W13'40 5:08:55
Lanesboro 4 1 35N00 80W15 5:21:00
Lanes Creek 90 1 34N52 80W23 5:21:32
Lanes Store 81 1 35N29 81W58 5:27:52
Langley Crossroads 64 1 35N54'17 77W54'17 5:11:37
Langley Store 64 1 35N58 77W48 5:11:12
Langston 96 1 35N24'55 77W56'20 5:11:45
Lansdowne 60 1 35N10 80W48 5:23:12
Lansing 5 1 36N29'57 81W30'40 5:26:03
Lanvale 10 1 34N12'13 78W03'26 5:12:14
Lasker 66 1 36N21'00 77W18'21 5:09:13
Lassiter 92 1 35N54'36 78W25'29 5:13:42
Lassiter Crossroads 66 1 36N22'17 77W18'17 5:09:13
Last Chance 48 1 35N27'08 76W04'33 5:04:18
Latham 7 1 35N36'12 77W08'04 5:08:32
Latham Park 41 1 36N05'25 79W48'05 5:19:12
Latham Town 41 1 36N03'03 79W50'41 5:19:23
Lattimore 23 1 35N19'05 81W39'39 5:26:39
Lauada 87 1 35N22'22 83W30'15 5:34:01
Laurel 58 1 35N48 82W41 5:30:44
Laurel Creek 95 1 36N15 81W50 5:27:20
Laurel Hill 11 1 35N32 82W41 5:30:44
Laurel Hill 55 1 35N33'16 81W30'11 5:26:01
Laurel Hill 83 1 34N48'32 79W32'53 5:18:12
Laurel Hills 92 1 35N50 78W40 5:14:40
Laurel Park 45 1 35N18'43 82W30'42 5:30:03
Laurel Park 95 1 36N07'28 81W40'52 5:26:43
Laurel Rock Acres 45 1 35N17'03 82W28'49 5:29:55
Laurel Springs 3 1 36N24'41 81W15'47 5:25:03
Laurinburg 83 1 34N46'26 79W27'47 5:17:51
Laurinburg West 83 1 34N46 79W29 5:17:56
Lawndale 23 1 35N24'50 81W33'48 5:26:15
Lawrence 33 1 36N00'51 77W29'57 5:10:00
Laws 68 1 36N14'23 79W07'08 5:16:29
Lawsons Mill 54 1 35N06'31 77W41'31 5:10:46
Lawsonville 79 1 36N23'34 79W33'50 5:18:15
Lawsonville 85 1 36N29'20 80W13'58 5:20:56
Laxon 95 1 36N14'07 81W32'47 5:26:11
Laytown 14 1 35N54 81W31 5:26:04
Leaksville 79 1 36N30'07 79W46'22 5:19:05
Leaman 63 1 35N26 79W35 5:18:20
Leander 95 1 36N17'11 81W51'32 5:27:26
Leasburg 17 1 36N23'40 79W09'17 5:16:37
Leatherman 57 1 35N17'07 83W22'42 5:33:31
Lebanon 32 1 36N06 78W56 5:15:44
Ledbetter 77 1 34N59'17 79W43'05 5:18:52
Ledger 61 1 35N57'51 82W07'47 5:28:31
Leechville 7 1 35N34'14 76W30'11 5:06:01
Lees 24 1 34N13 78W40 5:14:40
Lees Landing 69 1 35N06'25 76W56'01 5:07:44
Lee's Mill 51 1 35N19'28 78W24'52 5:13:39
Lees Mills 94 1 35N52 76W37 5:06:28
Leesville 92 1 35N54'25 78W43'35 5:14:54
Legerwood 14 1 36N00'51 81W31'12 5:26:05
Leggett 33 1 35N59'27 77W35'00 5:10:20
Leggett Crossroads 78 1 34N26'29 79W05'15 5:16:21
Leggetts Crossroads 7 1 35N40'52 77W09'38 5:08:39
Leicester 11 1 35N39'18 82W41'47 5:30:47
Leland 10 1 34N15'22 78W02'42 5:12:11
Lemley 60 1 35N27 80W54 5:23:36
Lemon Springs 53 1 35N23'22 79W11'41 5:16:47
Lena 26 1 34N54'32 78W47'38 5:15:11
Lennon Crossroads 10 1 33N59'49 78W14'07 5:12:56
Lennons Cross Roads 24 1 34N28'24 78W52'21 5:15:29
Lennoxville 16 1 34N43 76W39 5:06:36
Lenoir 14 1 35N54'50 81W32'21 5:26:09
Lenoir Rhyne 18 1 35N44 81W21 5:25:24
Lenoxville 16 1 34N42'38 76W37'39 5:06:31
Leon 31 1 35N01'44 77W49'13 5:11:17
Lester 54 1 35N16 77W35 5:10:20
Letitia 20 1 35N02'38 84W08'55 5:36:36
Level Cross 76 1 35N53'20 79W48'29 5:19:14
Level Cross 86 1 36N20'40 80W37'44 5:22:31
Levels 89 1 35N55 76W15 5:05:00
Leware 77 1 34N56 79W46 5:19:04
Lewis 39 1 36N22'33 78W35'42 5:14:23
Lewisburg 100 1 35N59'40 82W23'33 5:29:34
Lewis Crossroads 42 1 36N19'56 77W45'10 5:11:01
Lewis Fork 97 1 36N09 81W20 5:25:20
Lewis Landing 71 1 34N24'24 77W36'17 5:10:25
Lewis Point 89 1 35N59'17 76W04'16 5:04:17
Lewiston 8 1 36N07'22 77W10'37 5:08:42
Lewisville 34 1 36N05'49 80W25'10 5:21:41
Lewters Crossroad 66 1 36N30'14 77W15'24 5:09:02
Lexington 29 1 35N49'26 80W15'13 5:21:01
Liberia 93 1 36N21'23 78W05'48 5:12:23
Liberty 20 1 35N07'23 84W17'39 5:37:11
Liberty 76 1 35N51'12 79W34'19 5:18:17
Liberty 80 1 35N34'52 80W20'09 5:21:21
Liberty Hill 62 1 35N13 80W00 5:20:00
Lickskillet 57 1 35N02'51 83W16'53 5:33:08
Lickskillet 93 1 36N15'35 78W09'25 5:12:38
Liddell 54 1 35N10'28 77W48'47 5:11:15
Liledown 2 1 35N53'54 81W13'06 5:24:52
Lilesville 4 1 34N58'03 79W59'05 5:19:56
Lillington 43 1 35N23'57 78W48'58 5:15:16
Lilly 15 1 36N29'07 76W18'11 5:05:13
Lima 25 1 35N11'50 77W08'09 5:08:33
Linberry 76 1 35N51'01 79W42'17 5:18:49
Lincoln Heights 83 1 34N46'55 79W26'49 5:17:47
Lincoln Park 63 1 35N05'11 79W28'20 5:17:53
Lincoln Park 100 1 35N55'34 82W17'50 5:29:11
Lincolnton 55 1 35N28'25 81W15'17 5:25:01
Lindell 40 1 35N32'57 77W48'46 5:11:15
Linden 26 1 35N15'17 78W44'51 5:14:59
Lindley Park 41 1 36N04'08 79W49'57 5:19:20
Lineberry 76 1 35N55 79W43 5:18:52
Linville 6 1 36N03'59 81W52'14 5:27:29
Linville Falls 12 1 35N57'33 81W56'35 5:27:46
Linwood 29 1 35N45'02 80W19'05 5:21:16
Lisbon 9 1 34N31'01 78W31'38 5:14:07
Listening Rock 5 1 36N33'25 81W38'24 5:26:34
Listers Corner 70 1 36N08'29 76W10'18 5:04:41
Litaker 80 1 35N35 80W30 5:22:00
Little Coharie 82 1 34N58 78W31 5:14:04
Little Creek 58 1 35N54'55 82W33'19 5:30:13
Little Easonburg 64 1 35N57'57 77W52'17 5:11:29
Littlefield 74 1 35N26'03 77W25'19 5:09:41
Little Horse Creek 5 1 36N30 81W30 5:26:00
Little Kelly 71 1 34N27'51 77W57'08 5:11:49
Little Kinnakeet 28 1 35N24'23 75W29'31 5:01:58
Little Mountain 56 1 35N43 81W56 5:27:44
Little Pinecreek 58 1 35N48 82W41 5:30:44
Little Port 16 1 34N52'55 76W20'09 5:05:21
Little Prong 10 1 34N06'14 78W30'31 5:14:02
Little Richmond 86 1 36N17'41 80W45'28 5:23:02
Little Richwood 94 1 35N52 76W45 5:07:00
Little River 2 1 35N53'21 81W18'23 5:25:14
Little River 63 1 35N13 79W10 5:16:40
Little River 88 1 35N14'19 82W37'45 5:30:31
Little Rock Creek 61 1 36N05 82W06 5:28:24
Littles Mill 77 1 35N09'09 79W55'05 5:19:40
Littles Quarters 4 1 34N49'21 80W11'58 5:20:48
Little Switzerland 61 1 35N50'57 82W05'26 5:28:22
Littleton 42 1 36N26'04 77W54'44 5:11:39
Livingston Quarters 83 1 34N47'37 79W33'41 5:18:15

Lizard Lick 92 1 35N48'59 78w22'31 5:13:30
Lizzie 40 1 35N30'23 77w37'02 5:10:28
Lizzie Cotton Mills 51 1 35N32 78w17 5:13:08
Lloyd Crossroads 46 1 36N16'46 76w43'32 5:06:54
Loafers Glory 61 1 36N00'47 82w11'15 5:28:45
Lobelia 63 1 35N12'47 79w12'14 5:16:49
Locke 80 1 35N39 80w33 5:22:12
Lock Landing 9 1 34N32'37 78w26'14 5:13:45
Lockwoods Folly 10 1 33N59 78w18 5:13:12
Locust 84 1 35N15'35 80w25'32 5:21:42
Locust Grove 100 1 36N00 82w14 5:28:56
Locust Hill 17 1 36N21'45 79w26'47 5:17:47
Loebs Landing 71 1 34N22'44 78w13'41 5:12:55
Loftins Crossroads 54 1 35N11'59 77w33'42 5:10:15
Logan 81 1 35N25'38 81w53'58 5:27:36
Logan Store 81 1 35N26 81w51 5:27:24
Log Landing 52 1 35N03'14 77w19'21 5:09:17
Log Landing 89 1 35N57'02 76w07'24 5:04:30
Lola 16 1 34N57'28 76w16'47 5:05:07
Lomax 97 1 36N17'36 81w00'04 5:24:00
Lone Hickory 99 1 36N03'28 80w43'02 5:22:52
Long Acre 7 1 35N33 76w56 5:07:44
Long Acres 67 1 34N45 77w26 5:09:44
Long Beach 10 1 33N55 78w07 5:12:28
Long Bluff Landing 71 1 34N25'24 78w08'15 5:12:33
Long Creek 71 1 34N26'31 78w00'36 5:12:02
Long Hill 86 1 36N25 80w33 5:22:12
Longhurst 73 1 36N25'30 78w58'02 5:15:52
Long Island 18 1 35N40'40 80w59'37 5:23:58
Long Pine 4 1 34N49'26 80w13'33 5:20:54
Long Ridge 58 1 35N48'32 82w32'38 5:30:11
Long Shoals 55 1 35N24'53 81w14'26 5:24:58
Longs Store 73 1 36N24'50 79w04'42 5:16:19
Longtown 12 1 35N46'08 81w54'08 5:27:37
Longtown 99 1 36N08'51 80w46'14 5:23:05
Long View 9 1 34N28'30 78w12'09 5:12:49
Longview 18 1 35N43'45 81w23'01 5:25:32
Longwood 10 1 34N00'12 78w32'33 5:14:10
Longwood Park 77 1 34N55 79w41 5:18:44
Loray 49 1 35N49'00 80w58'06 5:23:52
Lost Cove 100 1 36N04'15 82w24'09 5:29:37
Louisburg 35 1 36N05'56 78w18'05 5:13:12
Love Field 50 1 35N21'28 83w12'06 5:32:48
Lovejoy 62 1 35N25'21 79w55'11 5:19:41
Lovelace 97 1 36N06 81w02 5:24:08
Love Valley 49 1 35N59'23 80w59'18 5:23:57
Lovill 95 1 36N14'05 81w44'01 5:26:56
Lowe 78 1 34N38'56 79w06'07 5:16:24
Lowell 36 1 35N16'04 81w06'11 5:24:25
Lowell Mill 51 1 35N33'59 78w09'40 5:12:39
Lower Buck Landing 78 1 34N29'02 78w57'14 5:15:49
Lower Contoe 33 1 35N50 77w28 5:09:52
Lower Fishing Creek 33 1 36N00 77w35 5:10:20
Lower Fork 12 1 35N37 81w34 5:26:16
Lower Hominy 11 1 35N33 82w38 5:30:32
Lower R 33 1 35N47 77w41 5:10:44
Lowes Grove 32 1 35N54'12 78w53'21 5:15:33
Lowesville 55 1 35N25'01 81w00'41 5:24:03
Lowgap 86 1 36N31'32 80w52'03 5:23:28
Low Gap 100 1 35N52'19 82w17'53 5:29:12
Lowland 69 1 35N17'56 76w33'53 5:06:16
Lowrys 4 1 34N52'07 80w10'42 5:20:43
Luart 43 1 35N24'54 78w53'15 5:15:33
Lucama 98 1 35N38'43 78w00'36 5:12:02
Lucia 36 1 35N23'05 81w00'39 5:24:03
Luck 58 1 35N44'09 82w51'59 5:31:28
Lukens 16 1 34N58'14 76w34'28 5:06:18
Lumber Bridge 78 1 34N53'18 79w04'21 5:16:17
Lumber Mill 70 1 36N18'32 76w15'18 5:05:01
Lumberton 78 1 34N37'05 79w00'32 5:16:02
Lumptown 58 1 35N53'33 82w43'32 5:30:54
Lunday 61 1 35N57'15 82w11'43 5:28:47
Luther 11 1 35N32'09 82w44'13 5:30:57
Lyman 31 1 34N51'28 77w44'51 5:10:59
Lynch Beach 69 1 35N09'36 76w41'12 5:06:45
Lynchs Corner 70 1 36N25'22 76w25'17 5:05:41
Lynn 75 1 35N13'42 82w14'05 5:28:56
Lynn Crossroads 32 1 35N55'33 78w45'42 5:15:03
Lyon 39 1 36N07 78w41 5:14:44
Lyon Landing 71 1 34N23'09 78w07'39 5:12:31
Lyons 39 1 36N08'50 78w43'30 5:14:54
Mabel 95 1 36N19'02 81w46'08 5:27:05
Macclesfield 33 1 35N45'07 77w40'13 5:10:41
Macedonia 20 1 35N00 84w10 5:36:40
Macedonia 21 1 36N06'06 76w40'03 5:06:40
Macedonia 92 1 35N44'44 78w44'16 5:14:57
Macedonia 94 1 35N52'31 76w39'55 5:06:40
Machpelah 55 1 35N26'50 81w04'21 5:24:17
Mackeys 94 1 35N56'00 76w36'41 5:06:27
Macks Village 92 1 35N37'39 78w43'10 5:14:53
MacMillan Landing 71 1 34N24'44 77w35'41 5:10:23
Maco 10 1 34N17'13 78w08'47 5:12:35
Macon 93 1 36N26'19 78w05'03 5:12:20
Madison 79 1 36N23'07 79w57'35 5:19:50
Maggie 44 1 35N31'04 83w05'54 5:32:24
Magnolia 12 1 35N43'27 81w41'38 5:26:47
Magnolia 31 1 34N53'47 78w03'16 5:12:13
Magnolia Landing 10 1 34N19'50 78w02'54 5:12:12
Maiden 18 1 35N34'32 81w12'43 5:24:51
Maine 30 1 35N55'52 80w32'45 5:22:11
Makatoka 10 1 34N07'06 78w24'27 5:13:38
Makleyville 48 1 35N27'38 76w32'45 5:06:11
Mallard Cove Landing 52 1 35N03'10 77w18'54 5:09:16
Mallard Creek 60 1 35N18 80w48 5:23:12
Malmo 10 1 34N15'57 78w05'57 5:12:24
Malonee Mill 57 1 35N13'40 83w24'33 5:33:38
Malpass Corner 71 1 34N30'08 78w03'25 5:12:14
Maltby 20 2 35N09'23 83w57'30 5:35:50
Mamers 43 1 35N25'00 78w56'01 5:15:44
Mamie 27 1 36N07'40 75w50'15 5:03:21
Manchester 26 1 35N11'33 78w59'12 5:15:57
Mandale 1 1 35N51'11 79w16'24 5:17:06
Maneys Neck 46 1 36N30 77w01 5:08:04
Mangum 4 1 35N07'22 79w59'15 5:19:57
Mangum 32 1 36N11 78w52 5:15:28
Manly 63 1 35N11'08 79w22'19 5:17:29
Mannings 64 1 35N57 78w05 5:12:20
Manns Harbor 28 1 35N53'08 75w45'47 5:03:03
Mansfield 16 1 34N43'56 76w47'12 5:07:09
Mansfield Park 16 1 34N42 76w50 5:07:20
Manson 93 1 36N25'18 78w17'00 5:13:08
Manteo 28 1 35N54'29 75w40'34 5:02:42
Maple 27 1 36N24'53 76w00'16 5:04:01
Maplecypress 25 1 35N19'33 77w17'58 5:09:12
Maple Grove 14 1 36N00'19 81w43'36 5:26:54
Maple Hill 71 1 34N40'27 77w42'51 5:10:51
Maple Springs 87 1 35N21'25 83w32'01 5:34:08
Maple Springs 97 1 36N10'29 81w22'43 5:25:31
Mapleton 46 1 36N25'36 77w02'06 5:08:08
Mapleville 35 1 36N04'35 78w13'39 5:12:55
Maplewood 77 1 34N55'28 79w45'15 5:19:01
Marble 20 2 35N10'30 83w55'30 5:35:42
Marcus 62 1 35N13 79w38 5:18:32
Maready 31 1 34N48'21 77w47'16 5:11:09
Margaret 35 1 36N01'29 78w13'35 5:12:54
Margaretsville 66 1 36N31'52 77w20'57 5:09:24
Margrace 23 1 35N15 81w20 5:25:20
Maribel 69 1 35N10'00 76w42'25 5:06:50
Marietta 78 1 34N22'07 79w07'21 5:16:29
Marines 67 1 34N34'43 77w21'49 5:09:27
Marion 56 1 35N41'02 82w00'34 5:28:02
Mariposa 55 1 35N24'52 81w03'45 5:24:15
Mark Pine 24 1 34N12'11 78w37'49 5:14:31
Marlboro 74 1 35N34'48 77w35'32 5:10:22
Marler 99 1 36N07'39 80w49'14 5:23:17
Marlwood Acre 60 1 35N12'01 80w42'32 5:22:50
Mar Mac 96 1 35N22 77w58 5:11:52
Marmaduke 93 1 36N20'50 78w04'10 5:12:17
Marsh 86 1 36N18 80w45 5:23:00
Marshall 58 2 35N47'50 82w41'03 5:30:44
Marshallberg 16 1 34N43'40 76w30'58 5:06:04
Mars Hill 58 1 35N49'35 82w32'58 5:30:12
Marsh Landing 52 1 35N02'28 77w17'06 5:09:08
Marshville 90 1 34N59'18 80w22'02 5:21:28
Marston 77 1 34N59'17 79w34'57 5:18:20
Martel Village 11 1 35N37 82w33 5:30:12
Martha 76 1 35N36'39 80w01'08 5:20:05
Martins Creek 20 4 35N01'30 84w01'51 5:36:07
Marvin 90 1 34N59'30 80w48'54 5:23:16
Marys Grove 23 1 35N20'26 81w23'00 5:25:32
Masonboro 65 3 34N10'45 77w50'52 5:11:23
Masons Crossroads 83 1 34N44'04 79w33'42 5:18:15
Mason Store 43 1 35N24 78w49 5:15:16
Masontown 16 1 34N52'10 76w24'57 5:05:40
Massapoag 55 1 35N28 81w15 5:25:00
Mathews Crossroads 64 1 36N05 78w03 5:12:12
Matkins 17 1 36N15'16 79w31'09 5:18:05
Matney 95 1 36N11'30 81w48'40 5:27:15
Matrimony 79 1 36N28 79w55 5:19:40
Matthews 60 1 35N07'00 80w43'26 5:22:54
Matthews Crossroads 64 1 36N03'38 78w02'14 5:12:09
Matthewstown 34 1 36N07 80w10 5:20:40
Maury 40 1 35N28'55 77w35'11 5:10:21
Mavaton 21 1 36N10'26 76w38'33 5:06:34
Maxton 78 1 34N44'06 79w20'57 5:17:24
Mayfield 79 1 36N30'40 79w34'01 5:18:16
Mayhew 49 1 35N33'49 80w54'46 5:23:39
Mayo 79 1 36N27 79w54 5:19:36
Mayodan 79 1 36N24'44 79w58'02 5:19:52
Mayos Crossroads 33 1 35N48 77w23 5:09:32
Mays Crossroads 64 1 36N01'17 78w06'51 5:12:27
Maysville 52 1 34N54'17 77w13'54 5:08:56
Mayview Park 95 1 36N07'49 81w41'11 5:26:45
Mayville Crossing 78 1 34N42'25 78w50'34 5:15:22
Mazeppa 49 1 35N38'30 80w46'51 5:23:07
McAdenville 36 1 35N15'33 81w04'32 5:24:18
Mc Adoo Heights 41 1 36N06'03 79w47'08 5:19:09
McArthur Crossroads 83 1 34N43'05 79w29'18 5:17:57
McClam Crossroads 82 1 35N10'16 78w25'37 5:13:42
McClure Mill 57 1 35N04'55 83w23'22 5:33:33
McConnell 7 1 35N21 76w58 5:07:52
McConnell 63 1 35N27'51 79w30'34 5:18:02
McCray 1 1 36N10'20 79w23'11 5:17:33
McCullen 82 1 35N00 78w20 5:13:20
McCullers 92 1 35N39'39 78w41'46 5:14:47
McDade 68 1 36N11'21 79w10'15 5:16:41
McDaniels 82 1 34N53'00 78w26'50 5:13:47
McDonald 78 1 34N33'14 79w10'33 5:16:42
McDonald Mill 57 1 35N03'52 83w24'10 5:33:37
McDonalds 78 1 34N31 79w09 5:16:36
McFarlan 4 1 34N48'44 79w58'34 5:19:54
McFarland 47 1 35N00'50 79w24'21 5:17:37
McGee Crossroads 51 1 35N31'01 78w34'46 5:14:19
McGee Mill 51 1 35N30'13 78w35'52 5:14:23
McGehees Mill 73 1 36N31'00 79w01'44 5:16:07
McGinnis Crossroads 75 1 35N12'44 82w00'01 5:28:00
McGrady 97 1 36N21 81w14 5:24:56
McGuires 38 1 35N18'08 83w59'45 5:35:59
McKees 9 1 34N29 78w39 5:14:36
McKinney Cove 61 1 36N01'42 82w08'39 5:28:35
McKoy 51 1 35N15'47 78w29'17 5:13:57
McLamb Crossroads 82 1 35N15 78w21 5:13:24
McLauchlin 47 1 35N00 79w07 5:16:28
McLeansville 41 1 36N06'26 79w39'32 5:18:38
McMillan 78 1 34N52'42 78w57'11 5:15:49
McNair Crossing 33 1 35N54'42 77w35'43 5:10:23
McNeills 63 1 35N14 79w20 5:17:20
Meadow 51 1 35N19 78w27 5:13:48
Meadow 85 1 36N18 80w08 5:20:32
Meadow Brook Village 18 1 35N40'28 81w22'58 5:25:32
Meadow Creek 95 1 36N14 81w32 5:26:08
Meadow Landing 78 1 34N29'32 78w57'22 5:15:49
Meadows 85 1 36N22'10 80w10'55 5:20:44
Meadow Summit 79 1 36N30'40 79w43'48 5:18:55
Meadowview 29 1 35N48'19 80w16'57 5:21:08
Meat Camp 95 1 36N17'58 81w40'36 5:26:42
Mebane 1 1 36N05'45 79w16'02 5:17:04
Mechanic 76 1 35N39'11 79w55'45 5:19:43
Medfield 92 1 35N48'23 78w44'44 5:14:59
Medora 33 1 35N55'23 77w44'17 5:10:57
Meege Crossroads 21 1 36N13'32 76w39'22 5:06:37
Melanchton 76 1 35N50'48 79w38'40 5:18:35
Melborne Heights 41 1 35N57'49 79w57'55 5:19:52
Melrose 75 1 35N13'10 82w19'22 5:29:17
Melville 1 1 36N01'18 79w20'01 5:17:20
Melvin Hill 75 1 35N07 82w09 5:28:36
Menola 46 1 36N20'20 77w07'45 5:08:31
Mercer 33 1 35N50'12 77w41'36 5:10:46
Mercer Landing 10 1 33N57'54 78w14'26 5:12:58
Meredith 92 1 35N49 78w43 5:14:52
Meredith College 92 1 35N47 78w40 5:14:40
Merrimon 16 1 34N56'57 76w38'23 5:06:34
Merritt 69 1 35N05'52 76w42'53 5:06:52
Merry Hill 8 1 36N00'42 76w46'22 5:07:05
Merry Oaks 19 1 35N38'30 79w00'28 5:16:02
Mesic 69 1 35N12'01 76w38'39 5:06:35
Metcalf 23 1 35N17 81w32 5:26:08
Method 92 1 35N47'41 78w41'35 5:14:46
Methodist College 26 1 35N04 78w53 5:15:32
Mewborns Crossroads 54 1 35N20'46 77w35'35 5:10:22
Micaville 100 1 35N54'34 82w12'48 5:28:51
Michfield 76 1 35N34'41 79w46'37 5:19:06
Micro 51 1 35N33'49 78w12'17 5:12:49
Middle 21 1 36N11 76w40 5:06:40
Middleburg 91 1 36N23'58 78w19'22 5:13:17
Middle Creek 92 1 35N36 78w44 5:14:56
Middle Creek Mill 57 1 35N04 83w23 5:33:32
Middle Fork 34 1 36N09 80w12 5:20:48
Middle Fork 88 1 35N07'02 82w49'26 5:31:18
Middle River 10 1 34N02'41 78w16'47 5:13:07
Middlesex 64 1 35N47'24 78w12'15 5:12:49
Middleton Heights 83 1 34N46'53 79w27'44 5:17:51
Middletown 48 1 35N28'41 76w00'45 5:04:03
Midland 13 1 35N13'38 80w30'03 5:22:00
Midpine 23 1 35N12'31 81w23'16 5:25:33
Midtown 63 1 35N09'28 79w24'48 5:17:39
Midway 2 1 35N54'26 81w07'08 5:24:29
Midway 7 1 35N30'42 76w54'00 5:07:36
Midway 8 1 36N02'03 76w47'10 5:07:09
Midway 10 1 34N04 78w09 5:12:36
Midway 13 1 35N31 80w38 5:22:32
Midway 29 1 35N57'12 80w13'06 5:20:52
Midway 45 1 35N26'35 82w30'23 5:30:02
Midway 77 1 34N55'50 79w47'22 5:19:09
Midway 79 1 36N16'24 79w47'21 5:19:09
Midway Park 67 1 34N43'33 77w20'30 5:09:22
Milburnie 92 1 35N47'45 78w32'05 5:14:08
Mildred 33 1 35N50'54 77w29'27 5:09:58
Miles 68 1 36N05'10 79w13'36 5:16:54
Miles Crossroad 41 1 35N56'48 79w53'17 5:19:33
Millboro 76 1 35N47'59 79w44'54 5:19:00
Mill Branch 10 1 34N02'25 78w28'24 5:13:54
Mill Bridge 80 1 35N38'48 80w38'15 5:22:33
Millbrook 92 1 35N51'03 78w36'20 5:14:25
Mill Corner 45 1 35N20'07 82w21'16 5:29:25
Mill Creek 5 1 36N19'09 81w33'50 5:26:15
Mill Creek 10 1 34N05'54 78w05'12 5:12:21
Mill Creek 16 1 34N46'33 76w44'51 5:06:59
Mill Crossroads 21 1 36N13'19 76w40'06 5:06:40
Millennium 46 1 36N14'55 77w05'39 5:08:23
Millennium Church 46 1 36N14 77w07 5:08:28
Miller Landing 89 1 35N56'08 76w06'13 5:04:25
Millers 2 1 35N50 81w06 5:24:24
Millers Creek 97 1 36N11'21 81w14'16 5:24:57
Millersville 2 1 35N51'20 81w11'01 5:24:44
Millesville 17 1 36N18'28 79w24'56 5:17:40
Millingport 84 1 35N22'50 80w18'19 5:21:13
Mill Landing 28 1 35N50'21 75w37'04 5:02:28
Mill Neck 46 1 36N30'48 76w59'13 5:07:57
Mill Seat Landing 69 1 35N17'47 76w35'06 5:06:20
Millshoal 57 1 35N14 83w19 5:33:16
Millside 23 1 35N17 81w32 5:26:08
Mill Spring 75 1 35N17'51 82w09'41 5:28:39
Mills Ridge 89 1 35N53'16 76w09'29 5:04:38
Mills River 45 1 35N23'18 82w34'01 5:30:16
Milltown 38 1 35N18'36 83w48'56 5:35:16
Milton 17 1 36N32'20 79w12'32 5:16:50

Milwaukee 66 1 36N24'19 77w13'57 5:08:56
Mimosa Shores 7 1 35N31'10 77w01'04 5:08:04
Mineola 7 1 35N32 77w02 5:08:08
Mineral Springs 4 1 34N56'38 80w14'29 5:20:58
Mineral Springs 90 1 34N56'16 80w40'08 5:22:41
Mingo 82 1 35N11'18 78w34'07 5:14:16
Minneapolis 6 1 36N05'57 81w59'14 5:27:57
Minnesott Beach 69 1 34N58'07 76w48'43 5:07:15
Minpro 61 1 35N55'42 82w05'13 5:28:21
Mint Hill 60 1 35N10'46 80w38'51 5:22:35
Mintons Store 46 1 36N20 77w13 5:08:52
Mintonsville 37 1 36N20'34 76w38'10 5:06:33
Mintz 82 1 34N53'38 78w28'39 5:13:55
Miranda 80 1 35N40 80w44 5:22:56
Misenheimer 84 1 35N29'05 80w17'19 5:21:09
Mission 20 1 35N04'16 83w55'48 5:35:43
Mitchell Landing 24 1 34N21'27 78w12'40 5:12:51
Mitchell Landing 46 1 36N26'12 76w58'06 5:07:52
Mitchells 8 1 36N12 77w02 5:08:08
Mitchell Village 16 1 34N42 76w50 5:07:20
Mitchels Fork 37 1 36N21'00 76w38'11 5:06:33
Mitcheners Crossroads 35 1 36N07'23 78w23'33 5:13:34
Mocksville 30 1 35N53'38 80w33'42 5:22:15
Moffitt Hill 56 1 35N36'20 82w10'34 5:28:42
Mohawk 43 1 35N27 79w03 5:16:12
Mollie 24 1 34N09'04 78w44'27 5:14:58
Momeyer 64 1 35N57'40 78w03'26 5:12:14
Monbo 18 1 35N39'51 80w58'43 5:23:55
Moncure 19 1 35N37'21 79w04'43 5:16:19
Money Island Beach 16 1 34N41'49 76w43'17 5:06:53
Monks Crossroads 82 1 35N15 78w21 5:13:24
Monogram 10 1 33N56'21 78w21'18 5:13:25
Monroe 90 1 34N59'07 80w32'59 5:22:12
Monroeton 79 1 36N17'22 79w44'06 5:18:56
Monroetown 63 1 35N13'07 79w26'43 5:17:47
Monroetown 79 1 36N21 79w41 5:18:44
Montague 71 1 34N26'01 78w03'59 5:12:16
Montclair 26 1 35N02 78w57 5:15:48
Monterey Park 36 1 35N17'49 81w08'35 5:24:34
Montezuma 6 1 36N03'54 81w54'10 5:27:37
Montford Cove 56 1 35N36 82w03 5:28:12
Montford Hills 11 2 35N36'16 82w34'27 5:30:18
Monticello 41 1 36N13'09 79w40'41 5:18:43
Montreat 11 1 35N38'39 82w18'11 5:29:13
Montrose 47 1 35N02'33 79w20'09 5:17:21
Montview 34 1 36N08'24 80w14'12 5:20:57
Moore Landing 71 1 34N24'32 77w35'59 5:10:24
Moores Beach 7 1 35N23'55 76w37'24 5:06:30
Mooresboro 23 1 35N17'55 81w41'57 5:26:48
Moores Chapel 51 1 35N40'55 78w11'25 5:12:46
Moores Corner 69 1 35N02'58 76w41'20 5:06:45
Moores Crossroads 51 1 35N40'40 78w10'11 5:12:41
Moores School House 51 1 35N36 78w07 5:12:28
Moores Springs 85 1 36N25'16 80w17'21 5:21:09
Mooresville 49 1 35N35'05 80w48'37 5:23:14
Mooresville Junction 49 1 35N35 80w49 5:23:16
Mooretown 71 1 34N24'49 77w49'39 5:11:19
Moratock 62 1 35N22 79w54 5:19:36
Moravian Falls 97 1 36N05'48 81w10'57 5:24:44
Mordecai 92 1 35N48 78w38 5:14:32
Morehead 16 1 34N44 76w48 5:07:12
Morehead City 16 1 34N43'22 76w43'35 5:06:54
Morgan Ford 80 1 35N35'09 80w13'29 5:20:54
Morgans Corners 70 1 36N25'02 76w20'58 5:05:24
Morganton 12 1 35N44'43 81w41'06 5:26:44
Morgantown 1 1 36N07'19 79w25'45 5:17:43
Moriah 73 1 36N15'27 78w49'47 5:15:19
Morlan Park 80 1 35N39 80w29 5:21:56
Morning Star 44 1 35N30'46 82w48'54 5:31:16
Morning Star 60 1 35N08 80w42 5:22:48
Morris Field 60 1 35N14 80w53 5:23:32
Morris Landing 67 1 34N28'10 77w30'32 5:10:02
Morrisville 92 1 35N49'24 78w49'33 5:15:18
Mortimer 14 1 35N59'07 81w45'41 5:27:03
Morton 1 1 36N12 79w30 5:18:00
Morton Fork 67 1 34N49'28 77w13'47 5:08:55
Morven 4 1 34N51'50 80w00'05 5:20:00
Moseley Hall 54 1 35N18 77w47 5:11:08
Moss 20 2 35N12'08 83w57'10 5:35:49
Moss 84 1 35N27 80w13 5:20:52
Moss Hill 54 1 35N11'46 77w44'48 5:10:59
Moss Neck 78 1 34N40'02 79w09'11 5:16:37
Mother Vineyard 28 1 35N55'19 75w40'26 5:02:42
Motleta 76 1 35N44'02 79w57'26 5:19:50
Moulton 35 1 36N10'17 78w15'09 5:13:01
Moultonville 82 1 34N59'27 78w15'03 5:13:00
Mountain 50 1 35N12 83w11 5:32:44
Mountain Creek 18 1 35N36 81w01 5:24:04
Mountain Grove 57 1 35N13'11 83w15'29 5:33:02
Mountain Home 45 1 35N22'10 82w29'35 5:29:58
Mountain Island 36 1 35N20'00 80w59'59 5:24:00
Mountain Lake Camp 45 1 35N17'42 82w28'25 5:29:54
Mountain Page 45 1 35N12'35 82w22'06 5:29:28
Mountain Park 86 1 36N22'27 80w51'18 5:23:25
Mountain Valley 45 1 35N12'59 82w29'11 5:29:57
Mountain View 11 1 35N28'20 82w30'15 5:30:01
Mountain View 36 1 35N14'36 81w17'12 5:25:09
Mountain View 68 1 36N04'39 79w04'28 5:16:18
Mountain View 85 1 36N18'32 80w18'15 5:21:13
Mount Airy 86 1 36N29'57 80w36'27 5:22:26
Mount Carmel 62 1 35N13 80w00 5:20:00
Mount Energy 39 1 36N07'31 78w38'30 5:14:34
Mount Gallows 46 1 36N25'04 76w56'53 5:07:48
Mount Gilead 13 1 35N27'00 80w32'46 5:22:11
Mount Gilead 62 1 35N12'53 80w00'09 5:20:01
Mount Gould 8 1 36N07'10 76w45'48 5:07:03
Mount Gould Landing 8 1 36N07'24 76w44'36 5:06:58
Mount Herman 14 1 35N52'53 81w28'58 5:25:56
Mount Hermon 70 1 36N16 76w18 5:05:12
Mount Holly 36 1 35N17'53 81w00'58 5:24:04
Mount Mitchell 13 1 35N29'47 80w33'13 5:22:13
Mount Mitchell 100 1 35N54'44 82w17'29 5:29:10
Mount Mourne 49 1 35N32'35 80w50'51 5:23:23
Mount Olive 9 1 34N35'17 78w35'13 5:14:21
Mount Olive 18 1 35N44 81w21 5:25:24
Mount Olive 24 1 34N25'28 78w47'50 5:15:11
Mount Olive 45 1 35N14'08 82w28'30 5:29:54
Mount Olive 48 1 35N34'33 76w28'14 5:05:53
Mount Olive 85 1 36N19'40 80w20'12 5:21:21
Mount Olive 96 1 35N11'47 78w04'00 5:12:16
Mount Pilgrim 59 1 36N00'35 77w20'11 5:09:21
Mount Pleasant 6 1 36N05 81w56 5:27:44
Mount Pleasant 13 1 35N23'57 80w26'10 5:21:45
Mount Pleasant 20 1 35N00 84w10 5:36:40
Mount Pleasant 48 1 35N24'54 76w05'00 5:04:20
Mount Pleasant 63 1 35N12'19 79w10'16 5:16:41
Mount Pleasant 64 1 35N49'20 78w06'46 5:12:27
Mount Pleasant 77 1 35N04 79w46 5:19:04
Mount Pleasant 92 1 35N33'42 78w40'44 5:14:43
Mount Pleasant 97 1 36N08'56 81w19'15 5:25:17
Mount Pleasant 99 1 36N13'28 80w37'41 5:22:31
Mount Rose 21 1 36N15'22 76w40'15 5:06:41
Mount Sterling 44 1 35N45'43 83w06'14 5:32:25
Mount Tabor 34 1 36N07'08 80w19'11 5:21:17
Mount Tabor 94 1 35N52'12 76w26'32 5:05:46
Mount Tirzah 73 1 36N16'48 78w54'26 5:15:38
Mount Ulla 80 1 35N39'30 80w43'37 5:22:54
Mount Valley 75 1 35N17'09 82w17'39 5:29:11
Mount Vernon 80 1 35N47'15 80w38'49 5:22:35
Mount Vernon 81 1 35N24'38 81w54'31 5:27:38
Mount Vernon Springs 19 1 35N40'04 79w25'32 5:17:42
Mount View 36 1 35N15 81w20 5:25:20
Mount Zion 41 1 36N05'49 79w43'34 5:18:54
Mount Zion 97 1 36N09'12 81w26'46 5:25:47
Moxley 97 1 36N21 81w01 5:24:04
Moyock 27 1 36N31'28 76w10'43 5:04:43
Mud Castle 66 1 36N22'12 77w31'53 5:10:08
Muddy Creek 34 1 36N01'37 80w20'38 5:21:23
Muddy Cross 37 1 36N21'49 76w37'40 5:06:31
Mulberry 14 1 36N02'04 81w38'43 5:26:35
Mulberry 97 1 36N14'22 81w10'51 5:24:43
Mullins Crossroads 42 1 36N06'01 77w28'18 5:09:53
Mundo Vista 76 1 35N45'30 79w54'14 5:19:37
Munks Crossroads 82 1 35N12'24 78w20'13 5:13:21
Murchison 100 1 35N49'47 82w18'58 5:29:16
Murchisontown 53 1 35N21'16 79w08'03 5:16:32
Murdocksville 63 1 35N13'26 79w28'56 5:17:56
Murfreesboro 46 1 36N26'32 77w05'56 5:08:24
Murphey 31 1 34N48'24 77w56'34 5:11:46
Murphy 20 4 35N05'15 84w02'05 5:36:08
Murphy Junction 11 1 35N35'46 82w34'41 5:30:19
Murphytown 9 1 34N40'30 78w21'13 5:13:25
Murrays Hill 18 1 35N40'38 81w05'45 5:24:23
Murraysville 65 3 34N17'44 77w50'52 5:11:23
Murraytown 64 1 35N50'11 78w14'23 5:12:58
Murray Town 71 1 34N36'20 77w53'38 5:11:35
Murrill Landing 52 1 35N02'48 77w17'15 5:09:09
Musgraves Crossroads 96 1 35N30 77w59 5:11:56
Myers 97 1 36N15 81w07 5:24:28
Myers Park 60 1 35N12 80w50 5:23:20
Myrick 42 1 36N26 77w55 5:11:40
Myrtle Grove 65 3 34N08'04 77w52'55 5:11:32
Myrtle Head 10 1 34N08'33 78w29'56 5:14:00
Nags Head 28 1 35N57'26 75w37'28 5:02:30
Nahunta 96 1 35N30'28 78w03'49 5:12:15
Nakina 24 1 34N08'04 78w40'06 5:14:40
Nantahala 87 2 35N17'17 83w40'00 5:34:40
Naples 45 1 35N23'33 82w30'03 5:30:00
Narrow Gap Landing 71 1 34N23'13 78w14'40 5:12:59
Narrow Ridge 63 1 35N07'13 79w33'30 5:18:14
Nashville 64 1 35N58'28 77w57'57 5:11:52
Nathans Creek 5 1 36N26'56 81w23'20 5:25:33
Nations Village 60 1 35N10 80w51 5:23:24
Navassa 10 1 34N15'19 78w00'28 5:12:02
Nebo 56 1 35N42'54 81w55'52 5:27:43
Nebo 99 1 36N13'01 80w39'17 5:22:37
Nebraska 48 1 35N27'27 76w03'49 5:04:15
Needmore 24 1 34N10'25 78w43'04 5:14:52
Needmore 35 1 36N07'20 78w24'51 5:13:39
Needmore 80 1 35N48'34 80w38'06 5:22:32
Needmore 87 1 35N19'36 83w31'23 5:34:06
Neills Creek 43 1 35N26 78w45 5:15:00
Neils Eddy Landing 24 1 34N21'09 78w10'32 5:12:42
Nella 5 1 36N34'09 81w32'51 5:26:11
Nellie 44 1 35N37'35 83w06'45 5:32:27
Nelms 69 1 35N03'05 76w42'19 5:06:49
Nelson 32 1 35N52'56 78w51'01 5:15:24
Nelson Landing 54 1 35N19'09 77w28'51 5:09:55
Neuse 92 1 35N53'50 78w34'10 5:14:17
Neuse Crossroads 92 1 35N53'36 78w33'36 5:14:14
Neuse Forest 25 1 35N06 77w05 5:08:20
Neuse River 92 1 35N51 78w39 5:14:36
Neverson 98 1 35N46 78w04 5:12:16
New Belden 74 1 35N37'06 77w17'42 5:09:11
New Bern 25 1 35N06'30 77w02'40 5:08:11
New Bern Junction 65 3 34N13 77w55 5:11:40
Newbern Landing 27 1 36N09'37 75w51'47 5:03:27
Newberry Landing 94 1 35N58'06 76w27'26 5:05:50
New Bethel 68 1 36N13 78w56 5:15:44
New Bethel 79 1 36N19 79w54 5:19:36
Newbold 26 1 35N04 78w53 5:15:32
New Bridge 11 1 35N37 82w33 5:30:12
New Britton 10 1 34N06 78w32 5:14:08
Newby Landing 72 1 36N07'28 76w18'30 5:05:14
New Candler 11 2 35N32'43 82w40'44 5:30:43
New Castle 97 1 36N11 80w55 5:23:40
Newdale 100 1 35N54'38 82w11'21 5:28:45
Newell 60 1 35N16'46 80w44'09 5:22:57
Newfound 11 1 35N36'15 82w43'55 5:30:56
Newfoundland 89 1 35N56'54 76w07'48 5:04:31
New Haven 3 1 36N31'54 81w09'37 5:24:38
New Hill 92 1 35N40'51 78w56'09 5:15:45
New Holland 48 1 35N26'36 76w10'12 5:04:41
New Home 23 1 35N31 81w37 5:26:28
New Hope 10 1 34N06'31 78w10'01 5:12:40
New Hope 35 1 35N58'07 78w20'09 5:13:21
New Hope 49 1 36N00'53 80w57'24 5:23:50
New Hope 68 1 36N00'36 79w04'27 5:16:18
Newhope 72 1 36N09'21 76w19'03 5:05:16
New Hope 76 1 35N33'17 80w00'56 5:20:04
New Hope 86 1 36N25'11 80w42'43 5:22:51
New Hope 92 1 35N50'22 78w34'51 5:14:19
New Hope 98 1 35N47'43 77w57'03 5:11:48
New Hope Academy 76 1 35N38 80w07 5:20:28
Newhope Proper 72 1 36N11'26 76w22'47 5:05:31
New House 23 1 35N23'34 81w41'31 5:26:46
Newland 6 1 36N05'14 81w55'39 5:27:43
New Lands 89 1 35N50'25 76w16'36 5:05:06
New Leaksville 79 1 36N30 79w45 5:19:00
New Life 24 1 34N07'50 78w50'28 5:15:22
Newlife 97 1 36N15 81w07 5:24:28
New Light 92 1 36N00'46 78w35'51 5:14:23
Newlin 1 1 35N55 79w20 5:17:20
New London 84 1 35N26'35 80w13'10 5:20:53
New Market 76 1 35N49'45 79w51'57 5:19:28
Newport 16 1 34N47'11 76w51'34 5:07:26
New Providence 27 1 36N24'47 76w05'38 5:04:23
New River 95 1 36N14 81w39 5:26:36
New River-Gieger 67 1 34N43 77w27 5:09:48
New Salem 76 1 35N49 79w48 5:19:12
New Salem 90 1 35N07'51 80w22'10 5:21:29
Newsom 29 1 35N32'09 80w11'16 5:20:45
Newton 18 1 35N40'11 81w13'18 5:24:53
Newton Grove 82 1 35N15'25 78w21'09 5:13:25
Newtons Crossroads 82 1 34N41'15 78w09'45 5:12:39
New Town 77 1 34N52'36 79w41'43 5:18:47
New Town 83 1 34N53'48 79w21'53 5:17:28
Niagara 63 1 35N12'26 79w21'21 5:17:25
Nicanor 72 1 36N19'58 76w28'44 5:05:55
Nims 36 1 35N18'34 81w01'50 5:24:07
Nixonton 70 1 36N12'02 76w16'23 5:05:06
Nobles Crossing 24 1 34N17'05 78w50'18 5:15:21
Nobles Crossroads 54 1 35N06'12 77w41'07 5:10:44
Nobles Mill 54 1 35N05'44 77w38'26 5:10:34
Nocho Park 41 1 36N03'57 79w46'17 5:19:05
Norfleet 42 1 36N08'31 77w17'56 5:09:12
Norlina 93 1 36N26'44 78w11'55 5:12:48
Norman 77 1 35N10'13 79w43'23 5:18:54
Normanville 61 1 35N57'47 82w07'04 5:28:28
Norrington Crossroads 43 1 35N21'12 78w54'47 5:15:39
North 34 1 36N08 80w14 5:20:56
North Albemarle 84 1 35N24 80w10 5:20:40
North Asheboro 76 1 35N44'13 79w48'30 5:19:14
North Belmont 36 1 35N16'20 81w02'54 5:24:12
North Brevard 88 1 35N14'44 82w43'05 5:30:52
North Brook 55 1 35N30 81w27 5:25:48
North Burlington 1 1 36N06 79w27 5:17:48
North Catawba 14 1 35N49 81w32 5:26:08
North Charlotte 60 1 35N15 80w50 5:23:20
North Clinton 82 1 35N01 78w18 5:13:12

North Concord 13 1 35N26'03 80W37'15 5:22:29
North Cooleemee 30 1 35N49'09 80W32'59 5:22:12
North Cove 56 1 35N50'09 81W59'21 5:27:57
North Cove Crossing 56 1 35N49'53 82W00'03 5:28:00
North Durham 32 1 36N02 78W53 5:15:32
North Elkin 86 1 36N17'18 80W51'11 5:23:25
North Fork 95 1 36N19'38 81W46'40 5:27:07
Northgate 32 1 36N00 78W54 5:15:36
North Hamlet 77 1 34N54'12 79W41'29 5:18:46
North Harlowe 25 1 34N51'37 76W46'20 5:07:05
North Henderson 91 1 36N20'30 78W23'25 5:13:34
North Hyde Park 41 1 36N07'36 79W48'34 5:19:14
North Kannapolis 80 1 35N31'32 80W36'50 5:22:27
North Lumberton 78 1 34N36 79W01 5:16:04
North River 16 1 34N48'59 76W38'10 5:06:33
North River Corner 16 1 34N46'57 76W37'36 5:06:30
North Rocky Mount 33 1 35N58 77W48 5:11:12
North Roxboro 73 1 36N24 78W59 5:15:56
North Side 39 1 36N05'03 78W44'49 5:14:59
North State Orchards 62 1 35N04 79W46 5:19:04
Northview 53 1 35N31'44 79W11'10 5:16:45
North View 83 1 34N47'29 79W27'29 5:17:50
Northwest 10 1 34N18'46 78W09'41 5:12:39
North Whitakers 64 1 36N07 77W48 5:11:12
North Wilkesboro 97 1 36N09'30 81W08'52 5:24:35
North Winston 34 1 36N07'11 80W14'03 5:20:56
Norton 50 1 35N07'50 83W09'22 5:32:37
Norton 57 1 35N01'00 83W22'52 5:33:31
Norwood 79 1 36N21'09 79W42'47 5:18:51
Norwood 84 1 35N13'10 80W07'09 5:20:29
Norwood Beach 84 1 35N13'58 80W05'57 5:20:24
Norwood Hollow 6 1 36N08'05 81W50'58 5:27:24
Notla 20 1 35N01 84W07 5:36:28
Nutbush 93 1 36N27 78W16 5:13:04
Oakboro 84 1 35N13'32 80W19'45 5:21:19
Oak City 59 1 35N57'49 77W18'30 5:09:14
Oak Crest 34 1 36N08'19 80W16'57 5:21:08
Oakdale 41 1 35N58'54 79W55'43 5:19:43
Oakdale 47 1 34N59 79W13 5:16:52
Oakdale 49 1 35N51 80W56 5:23:44
Oakdale 60 1 35N18'06 80W53'42 5:23:35
Oak Dale Cross Roads 24 1 34N25'11 78W49'07 5:15:16
Oak Forest 11 1 35N29'30 82W31'41 5:30:07
Oak Forest 51 1 35N21'26 78W25'29 5:13:42
Oak Grove 10 1 33N59'38 78W18'18 5:13:13
Oak Grove 20 2 35N12'29 83W53'01 5:35:32
Oakgrove 23 1 35N16'23 81W25'29 5:25:42
Oak Grove 32 1 35N58'53 78W49'15 5:15:17
Oak Grove 41 1 36N02'52 79W47'57 5:19:12
Oak Grove 52 1 35N02'02 77W14'38 5:08:59
Oak Grove 57 1 35N16'48 83W26'49 5:33:47
Oak Grove 86 1 36N30 80W35 5:22:20
Oak Grove 95 1 36N13'29 81W42'33 5:26:50
Oak Grove Inn 51 1 35N34'02 78W11'29 5:12:46
Oak Hill 12 1 35N46'43 81W45'22 5:27:01
Oak Hill 14 1 35N54'11 81W24'55 5:25:40
Oak Hill 39 1 36N26'19 78W43'14 5:14:53
Oak Hill 45 1 35N21'58 82W26'16 5:29:45
Oak Hill 57 1 35N10'17 83W24'28 5:33:38
Oak Hill 83 1 34N57'19 79W23'38 5:17:35
Oak Hill Court 45 1 35N23'10 82W33'47 5:30:15
Oakland 19 1 35N37 79W12 5:16:48
Oakland 64 1 35N59'41 78W02'23 5:12:10
Oakland 78 1 34N50'19 78W57'39 5:15:51
Oakland 88 1 35N06'48 82W58'32 5:31:54
Oak Level 64 1 35N57 77W54 5:11:36
Oakley 11 1 35N33'43 82W30'37 5:30:02
Oakley 74 1 35N45'28 77W17'13 5:09:09
Oak Park 11 1 35N26'52 82W30'30 5:30:02
Oak Park 20 1 35N06'58 84W13'56 5:36:56
Oak Ridge 41 1 36N10'24 79W59'21 5:19:57
Oak Ridge 85 1 36N30'10 80W07'48 5:20:31
Oak Ridge Park 77 1 34N54'49 79W46'24 5:19:06
Oaks 25 1 35N06 77W05 5:08:20
Oaks 68 1 35N57'12 79W15'27 5:17:02
Oakton 78 1 34N29'43 79W02'57 5:16:12
Oakview 41 1 35N59'35 80W01'31 5:20:06
Oakville 93 1 36N29'51 78W06'03 5:12:24
Oakwillow 46 1 36N22'24 76W56'50 5:07:47
Oakwood 41 1 36N02'23 79W51'00 5:19:24
Oakwood Acres 29 1 35N40 80W16 5:21:04
Oakwoods 97 1 36N06'53 81W08'03 5:24:32
Obids 5 1 36N18'30 81W23'14 5:25:33
Occoneechee 68 1 36N05 79W07 5:16:28
Ocean 16 1 34N42'42 76W59'30 5:07:58
Ocean Isle Beach 10 1 33N53 78W26 5:13:44
Oconaluftee Indian Village 87 1 35N29'12 83W19'22 5:33:17
Oconeechee 66 1 36N25 77W31 5:10:04
Ocono Lufty 87 1 35N29 83W19 5:33:16
Ocracoke 48 1 35N06'52 75W58'53 5:03:56
Odell 13 1 35N28 80W44 5:22:56
Odell 93 1 36N21'26 77W56'38 5:11:47
Oden Mill 7 1 35N32'10 76W50'38 5:07:23
Ogburn Crossroads 51 1 35N33'20 78W38'18 5:14:33
Ogburns Crossroads 41 1 36N14'48 79W55'16 5:19:41
Ogburn Station 34 1 36N08'57 80W13'27 5:20:54
Ogden 22 1 35N02 83W57 5:35:48
Ogden 65 3 34N16'20 77W49'08 5:11:17
Ogreeta 20 1 35N09'12 84W08'29 5:36:34
Oine 93 1 36N29'00 78W13'51 5:12:55
Okeewemee 62 1 35N24'27 79W51'15 5:19:25
Okisko 70 1 36N15'33 76W21'18 5:05:25
Ola 44 1 35N40'10 83W05'53 5:32:24
Old 34 1 36N09 80W19 5:21:16
Old Bethlehem 93 1 36N15'12 77W58'49 5:11:55
Old Chapel Crossroads 37 1 36N20'17 76W38'06 5:06:32
Old Cumbee Place 10 1 34N09'31 78W13'11 5:12:53
Old Dock 24 1 34N10'04 78W35'51 5:14:23
Olde Farm 43 1 35N10 78W58 5:15:52
Olde Providence 60 1 35N06'54 80W47'30 5:23:10
Old Ford 7 1 35N38'03 77W03'51 5:08:15
Old Fort 56 1 35N37'44 82W10'51 5:28:43
Old Gilreath 97 1 36N04'27 81W07'03 5:24:28
Old Hundred 83 1 34N49'45 79W35'26 5:18:22
Old Landing 71 1 34N26'54 77W32'39 5:10:11
Old Mill Landing 8 1 35N55'56 77W01'36 5:08:06
Old Murphy 20 1 35N05 84W02 5:36:08
Old Richmond 34 1 36N13 80W24 5:21:36
Olds 27 1 36N10'30 75W51'48 5:03:27
Olds 40 1 35N30 77W37 5:10:28
Old Sneedsboro 4 1 34N49'57 79W56'11 5:19:45
Old Sparta 33 1 35N47'19 77W33'19 5:10:13
Old Town 10 1 34N08'11 77W57'39 5:11:51
Oldtown 34 1 36N09'09 80W17'39 5:21:11
Old Trap 15 1 36N17 76W05 5:04:20
Oleander 65 3 34N13 77W55 5:11:40
Olin 49 1 35N57'09 80W50'24 5:23:22
Olive Branch 90 1 35N06'14 80W19'17 5:21:17
Olive Crossroads 52 1 35N04 77W21 5:09:24
Olive Grove 23 1 35N31 81W37 5:26:28
Olive Hill 57 1 35N12'54 83W27'03 5:33:48
Olive Hill 73 1 36N25'28 79W02'59 5:16:12
Oliver 51 1 35N29'36 78W15'34 5:13:02
Olivers 52 1 35N00'51 77W17'37 5:09:10
Olivers Crossroads 18 1 35N35'20 81W07'25 5:24:30
Olivers Landing 52 1 35N00'48 77W16'26 5:09:06
Olivet 50 1 35N27'16 83W17'48 5:33:11
Olivette 14 2 35N56'46 81W37'01 5:26:28
Olivia 43 1 35N21'34 79W06'36 5:16:26
Olympia 69 1 35N08'20 76W58'16 5:07:53
Olyphic 24 1 33N59'27 78W39'33 5:14:38
O'Neals 51 1 35N42 78W14 5:12:56
Onvil 62 1 35N13 80W00 5:20:00
Ophir 62 1 35N28'40 79W58'45 5:19:55
Ora Mill 23 1 35N18'24 81W35'01 5:26:20
Orange 82 1 35N07'46 78W31'21 5:14:05
Orange Factory 32 1 36N07'38 78W52'33 5:15:30
Orange Grove 68 1 35N58'33 79W11'39 5:16:47
Oregon Hill 79 1 36N26'54 79W38'14 5:18:33
Ore Knob 5 1 36N24'01 81W19'46 5:25:19
Oriental 69 1 35N01'51 76W41'36 5:06:46
Orion 5 1 36N23'51 81W25'16 5:25:41
Orlando 57 1 35N00'12 83W22'46 5:33:31
Ormonds 40 1 35N28 77W33 5:10:12
Ormondsville 40 1 35N28'19 77W32'46 5:10:11
Orrum 78 1 34N27'57 79W00'34 5:16:02
Osborne 77 1 34N48'42 79W48'13 5:19:05
Osborne Knob 56 1 35N50'07 82W06'35 5:28:26
Osbornville 97 1 36N04'32 80W53'52 5:23:35
Osceola 41 1 36N13'40 79W36'57 5:18:28
Osgood 53 1 35N33'14 79W07'43 5:16:31
Osmond 17 1 36N26'49 79W09'31 5:16:38
Ossipee 1 1 36N10'19 79W30'39 5:18:03
Ostwalt 49 1 35N40'57 80W51'41 5:23:27
Oswalt 49 1 35N42 80W53 5:23:32
Oswego 35 1 36N09'00 78W11'51 5:12:47
Oteen 11 1 35N35'14 82W29'29 5:29:58
Othello 5 1 36N21'44 81W26'47 5:25:47
Ottanola 45 1 35N23'30 82W16'43 5:29:07
Otter Creek 33 1 35N43 77W40 5:10:40
Otto 57 1 35N03'36 83W23'16 5:33:33
Otway 16 1 34N46'32 76W33'30 5:06:14
Outlaws Bridge 31 1 35N08'21 77W50'59 5:11:24
Oval 5 1 36N19'49 81W29'18 5:25:57
Overhills 43 1 35N13'15 79W01'55 5:16:08
Overlook 45 1 35N18'28 82W29'02 5:29:56
Overshot 51 1 35N18'23 78W21'48 5:13:27
Owens 26 1 35N02'38 78W56'07 5:15:44
Owltown 11 1 35N36'00 82W43'26 5:30:54
Oxford 39 1 36N18'38 78W35'28 5:14:22
Oxford Park 18 1 35N45'50 81W10'22 5:24:41
Oyster Creek Landing 48 1 35N23'26 76W18'54 5:05:16
Pacolet Valley 75 1 35N12 82W14 5:28:56
Pactolus 74 1 35N37'42 77W13'04 5:08:52
Padgett 67 1 34N40'27 77W35'28 5:10:22
Paint Fork 11 1 35N44'40 82W27'48 5:29:51
Paint Gap 100 1 35N52'45 82W24'28 5:29:38
Paint Rock 58 2 35N55'50 82W53'23 5:31:34
Paint Town 50 1 35N28'09 83W17'34 5:33:10
Palestine 84 1 35N24'15 80W09'52 5:20:39
Palmerville 84 1 35N25'38 80W07'04 5:20:28
Palmyra 42 1 36N04'16 77W20'29 5:09:22
Palo Alto 67 1 34N54 77W14 5:08:56
Palopato 67 1 34N48'17 77W13'11 5:08:53
Pamlico 69 1 35N05'05 76W38'07 5:06:32
Pamlico Beach 7 1 35N23'33 76W36'03 5:06:24
Pantego 7 1 35N35'20 76W39'45 5:06:39
Panther Branch 92 1 35N37 78W39 5:14:36
Panther Creek 44 1 35N38'36 82W58'48 5:31:55
Panther Landing 27 1 36N32'02 76W08'57 5:04:36
Parker 5 1 36N27'28 81W41'22 5:26:45
Parker Landing 74 1 35N42'56 77W29'42 5:09:59
Parkersburg 82 1 34N50'13 78W26'37 5:13:46
Parkers Fork 37 1 36N31'05 76W35'58 5:06:24
Parkers Lower Landing 24 1 34N24'17 78W58'06 5:15:52
Parkers Upper Landing 24 1 34N24'34 78W58'06 5:15:52
Parkhill 12 1 35N42'49 81W47'59 5:27:12
Parkland 92 1 35N44'57 78W38'56 5:14:36
Parks Crossroads 76 1 35N42'13 79W36'18 5:18:25
Park Spring 17 1 36N27'57 79W24'47 5:17:39
Parkstown 96 1 35N22'39 77W49'05 5:11:16
Park Terrace 34 1 36N07'04 80W12'31 5:20:50
Parkton 78 1 34N54'09 79W00'43 5:16:03
Parktown 93 1 36N18'47 78W08'31 5:12:34
Parkville 72 1 36N17'29 76W23'58 5:05:36
Parkway Forest 11 1 35N34'56 82W28'54 5:29:56
Parkwood 13 1 35N25 80W36 5:22:24
Park Wood 32 1 35N54 78W55 5:15:40
Parkwood 63 1 35N25'43 79W29'36 5:17:58
Park Yarn 23 1 35N15 81W20 5:25:20
Parmele 74 1 35N48'59 77W18'52 5:09:15
Parrish Gap 57 1 35N13'31 83W27'12 5:33:49
Parrott Fork 54 1 35N13'17 77W37'01 5:10:28
Parsons Grove Church 62 1 35N16'26 79W51'01 5:19:24
Parsonville 97 1 36N12'58 81W21'45 5:25:27
Paschall 93 1 36N32'30 78W09'29 5:12:38
Pasley 31 1 34N47'07 77W54'03 5:11:36
Pasquotank 70 1 36N16'02 76W20'20 5:05:21
Pates 78 1 34N41'23 79W12'55 5:16:52
Patetown 96 1 35N27'38 77W55'31 5:11:42
Patten 56 1 35N39'03 81W51'37 5:27:26
Patterson 14 1 35N59'57 81W33'51 5:26:15
Patterson Springs 23 1 35N14'07 81W30'53 5:26:04
Pattons Ridge 97 1 36N13'52 81W26'14 5:25:45
Pauls Crossing 84 1 35N25'47 80W18'41 5:21:15
Paw Creek 60 1 35N16'29 80W56'19 5:23:45
Paynes Store 2 1 35N55 81W10 5:24:40
Paynes Tavern 73 1 36N20'30 79W00'40 5:16:03
Peace Haven Estates 34 1 36N07 80W17 5:21:08
Peach 72 1 36N21'16 76W32'13 5:06:09
Peachland 4 1 34N59'37 80W15'53 5:21:04
Peachtree 20 1 35N05'38 83W56'34 5:35:46
Peachtree Landing 71 1 34N21'30 78W03'35 5:12:14
Peacock Crossing 24 1 34N19'36 78W47'59 5:15:12
Peacock Crossroads 96 1 35N29'47 78W02'03 5:12:08
Peacocks Crossroads 51 1 35N19'12 78W27'19 5:13:49
Pea Hill 42 1 36N16'12 77W35'25 5:10:22
Peak Creek 5 1 36N24 81W18 5:25:12
Pearce Crossroads 35 1 35N49 78W19 5:13:16
Pearce Landing 54 1 35N20'13 77W25'01 5:09:40
Pearces 35 1 35N54'59 78W18'26 5:13:14
Pearces Mill 26 1 35N01 78W55 5:15:40
Pea Ridge 75 1 35N19'18 82W05'55 5:28:24
Pea Ridge 94 1 35N57'28 76W28'44 5:05:55
Pea Ridge 99 1 36N08'13 80W51'57 5:23:28
Pecan Grove 42 1 36N08 77W25 5:09:40
Peden 3 1 36N29'54 81W18'31 5:25:14
Pee Dee 4 1 34N56'06 79W53'23 5:19:34
Pee Dee 62 1 35N16'03 80W02'36 5:20:10
Pekin 62 1 35N12'24 79W52'15 5:19:29
Peletier 16 1 34N43'48 77W05'05 5:08:20
Pelham 17 1 36N30'36 79W28'19 5:17:53
Pembroke 78 1 34N40'48 79W11'43 5:16:47
Pender 42 1 36N18'37 77W35'35 5:10:22
Pender Crossroad 98 1 35N48 77W52 5:11:28
Penderlea 71 1 34N39'34 78W03'00 5:12:12
Penders Crossroads 98 1 35N46'07 77W46'19 5:11:05
Pendleton 66 1 36N28'17 77W11'56 5:08:48
Penelo 33 1 35N55'05 77W40'23 5:10:42
Penelope 12 1 35N43'44 81W24'00 5:25:36
Peniel 75 1 35N14'11 82W08'15 5:28:33
Penland 61 1 35N55'48 82W06'44 5:28:27
Penny Hill 74 1 35N45'32 77W30'49 5:10:03
Penrose 88 1 35N16'20 82W38'21 5:30:33
Pensacola 100 1 35N50'52 82W18'04 5:29:14
Peoria 95 1 36N17'26 81W53'37 5:27:34
Peppers 61 1 36N01 82W09 5:28:36
Perch 86 1 36N20 80W26 5:21:44
Perfection 25 1 35N11 77W19 5:09:16
Perkinsville 12 1 35N52'09 81W43'55 5:26:56
Perkinsville 95 1 36N13'08 81W39'34 5:26:38
Perry Landing 52 1 35N00'40 77W16'23 5:09:06
Perrytown 8 1 36N08'16 76W48'16 5:07:13
Persimmon Creek 20 1 35N05 84W02 5:36:08
Peru 67 1 34N33'02 77W22'05 5:09:28
Petche Gap 12 1 35N41'47 81W36'59 5:26:28
Pet Crossroads 92 1 35N49'42 78W30'41 5:14:03
Petersburg 12 1 35N42'23 81W40'16 5:26:41
Petersburg 58 1 35N49'19 82W36'42 5:30:27
Petersburg 67 1 34N55'39 77W32'20 5:10:09
Petersburg Crossing 31 1 34N57'17 77W46'01 5:11:04
Peters Creek 85 1 36N29 80W14 5:20:56
Peters Lake Landing 78 1 34N31'01 78W55'43 5:15:43
Peterson 61 1 36N02'27 82W20'08 5:29:21
Petersville 29 1 35N49'33 80W24'54 5:21:40
Petra Mills 14 1 35N50'26 81W21'43 5:25:27
Pettys Shore 46 1 36N21'51 76W49'40 5:07:19
Pfafftown 34 1 36N09 80W22 5:21:28
Pfaftown 34 1 36N09'09 80W21'45 5:21:27
Pharrs Mill 13 1 35N19'42 80W37'05 5:22:28
Phil 78 1 34N44'53 79W12'51 5:16:51
Philadelphia 77 1 34N57'10 79W43'40 5:18:55

Philadelphus 78 1 34N45'32 79W10'18 5:16:41
Phillips Crossroads 33
1 36N01'10 77W43'15 5:10:53
Phillips Crossroads 52
1 35N05'12 77W26'46 5:09:47
Phillipsville 44
1 35N35 82W52 5:31:28
Phoenix 10 1 34N17'36 78W03'31 5:12:14
Phosphate Junction 7
1 35N31 77W06 5:08:24
Picks 73 1 36N21'10 78W58'49 5:15:55
Piedmont Heights 41
1 36N03'20 79W49'23 5:19:18
Pierces Crossroads 42
1 36N21'32 77W39'39 5:10:39
Pierceville 15 1 36N26'54 76W17'38 5:05:11
Pigeon 44 1 35N33 82W53 5:31:32
Pigeonroost 61 1 36N04'09 82W17'48 5:29:11
Pike Crossroads 96
1 35N29'27 78W03'35 5:12:14
Pike Road 7 1 35N40'58 76W37'40 5:06:31
Pikeville 96 1 35N29'49 77W58'56 5:11:56
Pilands Crossroads 46
1 36N20'44 76W48'42 5:07:15
Pillsboro Landing 74
1 35N41'34 77W29'09 5:09:57
Pilot 29 1 35N52'48 80W07'47 5:20:31
Pilot 35 1 35N53'05 78W15'55 5:13:04
Pilot 86 1 36N23 80W31 5:22:04
Pilot Mountain 86
1 36N23'11 80W28'11 5:21:53
Pinebluff 63 1 35N06'35 79W28'21 5:17:53
Pine Crest 7 1 35N25'10 76W41'23 5:06:46
Pinecroft 41 1 36N01'42 79W50'21 5:19:21
Pine Grove 25 1 34N55'37 76W56'55 5:07:48
Pine Hall 85 1 36N19'28 80W02'59 5:20:12
Pine Harbor 60 1 35N07'03 81W01'49 5:24:07
Pine Hill 63 1 35N02'54 79W24'23 5:17:38
Pine Hill 86 1 36N20'56 80W35'23 5:22:22
Pinehurst 45 1 35N20'42 82W27'41 5:29:51
Pinehurst 63 1 35N11'43 79W28'11 5:17:53
Pine Hurst Park 92
1 35N41'34 78W36'03 5:14:24
Pine Knoll 26 1 34N58'52 78W57'43 5:15:51
Pine Knoll Shores 16
1 34N42 76W50 5:07:20
Pine Level 24 1 34N06'23 78W41'31 5:14:46
Pine Level 51 1 35N30'47 78W14'41 5:12:59
Pinelog 22 1 34N59'50 83W58'06 5:35:52
Pine Log 24 1 34N19'25 78W43'33 5:14:54
Pine Log Village 22
1 34N59'25 83W57'28 5:35:50
Pineola 6 1 36N01'42 81W53'30 5:27:34
Pine Ridge 35 1 35N54'41 78W14'29 5:12:58
Pine Ridge 60 1 35N17'02 80W40'32 5:22:42
Pine Ridge 86 1 36N29'56 80W43'03 5:22:52
Pineridge 94 1 35N52'14 76W41'54 5:06:48
Pine Swamp 5 1 36N18 81W28 5:25:52
Pinetops 33 1 35N47'18 77W38'17 5:10:33
Pinetown 7 1 35N36'37 76W51'42 5:07:27
Pine Tree 98 1 35N44'25 77W47'44 5:11:11
Pine Valley 65 3 34N13 77W55 5:11:40
Pineview 43 1 35N18'22 79W05'23 5:16:22
Pineville 60 1 35N04'59 80W53'33 5:23:34
Piney 14 1 35N52'36 81W40'38 5:26:43
Piney Creek 3 1 36N33'01 81W17'20 5:25:09
Piney Forest Cross Roads 24
1 34N27'25 78W51'49 5:15:27
Piney Green 67 1 34N42'57 77W19'14 5:09:17
Piney Green 82 1 35N01 78W30 5:14:00
Pineygrove 7 1 35N33'53 76W59'13 5:07:57
Piney Grove 10 1 34N02'56 78W10'25 5:12:42
Piney Grove 25 1 34N53 76W54 5:07:36
Piney Grove 33 1 35N55'44 77W28'02 5:09:52
Piney Grove 68 1 36N03'25 79W03'14 5:16:13
Piney Grove 77 1 34N57'18 79W48'38 5:19:15
Piney Grove 82 1 35N09 78W14 5:12:56
Piney Grove Landing 48
1 35N36'01 76W33'25 5:06:14
Piney Island Landing 78
1 34N28'14 78W57'07 5:15:48
Piney Plains 92 1 35N44'44 78W45'17 5:15:01
Piney Ridge 82 1 35N00 78W20 5:13:20
Piney Wood 71 1 34N33'58 78W05'54 5:12:24
Pin Hook 31 1 34N44'51 77W46'18 5:11:05
Pink Hill 54 1 35N03'18 77W44'48 5:10:59
Pinkney 36 1 35N16 81W10 5:24:40
Pinkney 96 1 35N31'31 78W04'00 5:12:16
Pinkston 4 1 35N00'58 80W04'43 5:20:19
Pinnacle 85 1 36N19'45 80W26'00 5:21:44
Pinson 76 1 35N31'32 80W02'01 5:20:08
Pioneer Mills 13
1 35N15'37 80W35'20 5:22:21
Pipkin Place 37 1 36N26'24 76W56'37 5:07:46
Pireway 24 1 34N01'37 78W38'17 5:14:33
Pisgah 76 1 35N32'59 79W52'17 5:19:29
Pisgah Forest 88
1 35N15'15 82W42'01 5:30:48
Pisgah Shadows 88
1 35N16'24 82W37'37 5:30:30
Pitchkettle Landing 25
1 35N16'51 77W15'32 5:09:02
Pitch Landing 46
1 36N17'07 76W50'50 5:07:23
Pittmans Store 64
1 36N06 77W43 5:10:52
Pittsboro 19 1 35N43'12 79W10'39 5:16:43
Plain View 77 1 35N08'41 79W43'10 5:18:53
Plainview 78 1 34N32 79W17 5:17:08
Plain View 82 1 35N14 78W31 5:14:04
Plank Landing 54
1 35N20'16 77W25'51 5:09:43
Plantation Acres 68
1 35N55'24 79W05'39 5:16:23
Plateau 18 1 35N35'36 81W21'32 5:25:26
Plaza 41 1 36N06 79W49 5:19:16
Plaza 60 1 35N14 80W47 5:23:08
Plear 71 1 34N35'45 77W47'45 5:11:11
Pleasant Garden 41
1 35N57'43 79W45'45 5:19:03
Pleasant Gardens 56
1 35N41'20 82W04'42 5:28:19

Pleasant Grove 1
1 36N11'31 79W19'37 5:17:18
Pleasant Grove 11
1 35N41'22 82W31'42 5:30:07
Pleasant Grove 12
1 35N38'01 81W35'02 5:26:20
Pleasant Grove 17
1 36N23'21 79W16'02 5:17:04
Pleasant Grove 31
1 35N05'37 77W50'56 5:11:24
Pleasant Grove 66
1 36N26'21 77W26'41 5:09:47
Pleasant Grove 94
1 35N55'29 76W35'26 5:06:22
Pleasant Hill 1 1 35N52'24 79W28'55 5:17:56
Pleasant Hill 20
1 35N09'25 84W14'49 5:36:59
Pleasant Hill 52
1 35N04'00 77W35'28 5:10:22
Pleasant Hill 66
1 36N31'55 77W32'09 5:10:09
Pleasant Hill 97
1 36N15'26 80W53'01 5:23:32
Pleasant Plains 24
1 34N14'39 78W40'52 5:14:43
Pleasant Plains 46
1 36N17 76W59 5:07:56
Pleasant Ridge 97
1 36N19'10 80W53'16 5:23:33
Pleasant Valley 20
1 35N06'38 84W00'59 5:36:04
Pleasant View 89
1 35N53'21 76W13'59 5:04:56
Pleasantville 63
1 35N19'10 79W27'59 5:17:52
Pleasantville 79
1 36N22'38 79W50'16 5:19:21
Pledger Landing 89
1 35N59'26 76W04'10 5:04:17
Plumtree 6 1 36N01'37 82W00'29 5:28:02
Plyler 84 1 35N22'16 80W16'57 5:21:08
Plymouth 94 1 35N52'00 76W44'56 5:07:00
Pocket 53 1 35N27 79W15 5:17:00
Pocomoke 35 1 36N04'49 78W32'26 5:14:10
Point Caswell 71
1 34N28'05 78W09'36 5:12:38
Point Harbor 27 1 36N04'43 75W47'42 5:03:11
Pole Bridge Crossing 24
1 34N09'31 78W40'56 5:14:44
Polecat Landing 51
1 35N25'32 78W17'10 5:13:09
Pole Creek 11 1 35N33'56 82W42'27 5:30:50
Polkton 4 1 35N00'27 80W12'04 5:20:48
Polkville 23 1 35N25'03 81W38'35 5:26:34
Pollocks 52 1 35N04 77W21 5:09:24
Pollocksville 52
1 35N00'21 77W13'17 5:08:53
Pomona 41 1 36N03'36 79W51'22 5:19:25
Ponderosa 26 1 35N05 78W57 5:15:48
Pond Mountain 5 1 36N32 81W40 5:26:40
Ponzer 48 1 35N35'15 76W29'42 5:05:59
Pookmoke 35 1 36N06 78W27 5:13:48
Pooletown 80 1 35N35'26 80W14'35 5:20:58
Poor Town 46 1 36N16'49 77W01'32 5:08:06
Pope Air Force Base 26
1 35N08 78W59 5:15:56
Pope Crossing 78
1 34N33'58 78W59'53 5:16:00
Popes Landing 78
1 34N33'22 78W58'17 5:15:53
Poplar 61 1 36N04'21 82W20'36 5:29:22
Poplar Branch 27
1 36N16'48 75W53'35 5:03:34
Poplar Branch Landing 27
1 36N14'52 75W52'16 5:03:29
Poplar Grove 75 1 35N23'03 82W07'55 5:28:32
Poplar Grove 82 1 35N06'22 78W13'00 5:12:52
Poplar Grove 95 1 36N11'52 81W42'32 5:26:50
Poplar Point 59 1 35N52 77W10 5:08:40
Poplar Point Landing 59
1 35N55'35 77W07'18 5:08:29
Poplar Springs 85
1 36N16'48 80W19'16 5:21:17
Poplar Tent 13 1 35N24 80W39 5:22:36
Porter 81 1 35N16'09 80W10'09 5:20:41
Porter Junction 7
1 35N31'36 77W05'07 5:08:20
Porterville 9 1 34N27'10 78W33'35 5:14:14
Portsmouth 16 1 35N04'10 76W03'51 5:04:15
Posque Landing 52
1 35N03'20 77W18'05 5:09:12
Possumtrot 100 1 35N54'10 82W25'43 5:29:43
Postell 20 1 35N04'58 84W14'30 5:36:58
Potecasi 66 1 36N21'47 77W14'22 5:08:57
Potters Curve 24
1 34N18'19 78W48'24 5:15:14
Potters Hill 31 1 34N58'07 77W42'38 5:10:51
Pottertown 95 1 36N21'05 81W40'22 5:26:41
Powell Crossroads 37
1 36N20'31 76W39'25 5:06:38
Powells Crossing 24
1 34N20'02 78W51'38 5:15:27
Powells Point 27
1 36N09'26 75W51'33 5:03:26
Powells Store 79
1 36N27 79W39 5:18:36
Powellsville 8 1 36N13'32 76W56'00 5:07:44
Powelltown 88 1 35N07'58 82W48'36 5:31:14
Powers 78 1 34N41'32 78W59'19 5:15:57
Powhatan 51 1 35N36'49 78W25'04 5:13:40
Prathers Creek 3
1 36N30 81W14 5:24:56
Prentiss 57 1 35N07'16 83W22'45 5:33:31
Prescott 7 1 35N11'55 76W48'45 5:07:15
Prestonville 85 1 36N27'27 80W05'54 5:20:24
Prettyman Landing 52
1 35N02'38 77W15'51 5:09:03
Price 79 1 36N32'20 79W54'54 5:19:40
Price Creek 100 1 35N51'58 82W23'02 5:29:32
Pricetown 96 1 35N10'15 77W53'49 5:11:35
Pridgens Landing 71
1 34N23'26 78W14'41 5:12:59

Pridgeons Landing 24
1 34N21'05 78W11'43 5:12:47
Princeton 51 1 35N27'57 78W09'39 5:12:39
Princeville 33 1 35N53'22 77W31'57 5:10:08
Priscilla 36 1 35N16 81W10 5:24:40
Proctor 87 1 35N28'24 83W43'35 5:34:54
Proctorville 78 1 34N28'35 79W02'12 5:16:09
Progress 76 1 35N52'57 79W56'49 5:19:47
Propst Crossroads 18
1 35N37'38 81W22'33 5:25:30
Prospect 10 1 34N02'51 78W19'44 5:13:19
Prospect Hall Landing 9
1 34N48'47 78W49'10 5:15:17
Prospect Hill 17
1 36N14'57 79W11'28 5:16:46
Prosper 24 1 34N15'07 78W15'04 5:13:00
Providence 17 1 36N30'18 79W22'14 5:17:29
Providence 39 1 36N15'15 78W39'43 5:14:39
Providence 56 1 35N38'11 82W03'05 5:28:12
Providence 60 1 35N03'53 80W46'12 5:23:05
Providence Mill 18
1 35N34'55 81W11'45 5:24:47
Proximity 41 1 36N05'33 79W46'39 5:19:07
Pumpkin Center 12
1 35N42'39 81W42'02 5:26:48
Pumpkin Center 55
1 35N31'09 81W08'29 5:24:34
Pumpkin Center 67
1 34N47'29 77W22'22 5:09:29
Pumpkintown 50 1 35N15'14 83W16'56 5:33:08
Pungo 7 1 35N38'12 76W36'44 5:06:27
Puppy Creek Ford 47
1 35N04'07 79W08'03 5:16:32
Purlear 97 1 36N10'55 81W17'04 5:25:08
Purley 17 1 36N28'29 79W21'28 5:17:26
Purnell 92 1 36N00'43 78W33'13 5:14:13
Purvis 78 1 34N35'19 79W15'49 5:17:03
Putnam 63 1 35N26'40 79W28'13 5:17:53
Pyatte 6 1 36N00'46 81W58'09 5:27:53
Quail Ridge 53 1 35N23'36 79W14'07 5:16:56
Quail Roost 32 1 36N11'39 78W54'28 5:15:38
Quaker Gap 85 1 36N21'20 80W17'17 5:21:09
Quaker Meadow 12
1 35N47 81W45 5:27:00
Qualla 50 1 35N26'07 83W19'23 5:33:18
Quarry 97 1 36N10 81W08 5:24:32
Quarter Landing 27
1 36N07'24 75W48'22 5:03:13
Quebec 88 1 35N08'24 82W52'33 5:31:30
Queen 62 1 35N22 79W54 5:19:36
Quewhiffle 47 1 35N02 79W23 5:17:32
Quick 17 1 36N24'19 79W29'48 5:17:59
Quinerly 74 1 35N21'50 77W22'15 5:09:29
Quinland 44 2 35N24'58 83W00'37 5:32:02
Quinns Store 31 1 34N55 77W46 5:11:04
Quitsna 8 1 35N58'11 77W04'03 5:08:16
Quitsna Landing 8
1 35N56'35 77W02'29 5:08:10
Rabontown 10 1 34N10'23 78W10'40 5:12:43
Radford Crossroads 51
1 35N31'12 78W06'52 5:12:27
Radical 97 1 36N21 81W14 5:24:56
Raeford 47 1 34N58'51 79W13'28 5:16:54
Raemon 78 1 34N38'15 79W20'56 5:17:24
Raft Swamp 78 1 34N39 79W06 5:16:24
Rainbow Springs 57
1 35N05'39 83W33'56 5:34:16
Rains Crossroads 51
1 35N30'54 78W08'41 5:12:35
Raleigh 92 1 35N46'19 78W38'20 5:14:33
Rama 60 1 35N10'39 80W46'10 5:23:05
Ramseur 76 1 35N44'00 79W39'10 5:18:37
Ramsey 12 1 35N34'58 81W33'45 5:26:15
Ramseytown 100 1 36N00'02 82W21'27 5:29:26
Randleman 76 1 35N49'04 79W48'12 5:19:13
Randolph 60 1 35N10 80W48 5:23:12
Randolph 74 1 35N36 77W23 5:09:32
Randolph Landing 74
1 35N38'55 77W26'23 5:09:46
Ranger 20 1 35N05 84W02 5:36:08
Rangewood 92 1 35N42'23 78W38'47 5:14:35
Rankin 41 1 36N07'01 79W45'50 5:19:03
Rankin 71 1 34N32 78W10 5:12:40
Ranlo 36 1 35N17'10 81W07'50 5:24:31
Ranlo-Smyre 36 1 35N16 81W10 5:24:40
Ransom 24 1 34N19 78W16 5:13:04
Ransomville 7 1 35N27'08 76W41'08 5:06:45
Rattler Ford 38 1 35N20'52 83W54'15 5:35:37
Ravensford 87 1 35N30'39 83W17'44 5:33:11
Ravenswood 52 1 34N58'44 77W14'04 5:08:56
Rawls 43 1 35N32'13 78W48'56 5:15:16
Raynham 78 1 34N34'27 79W11'43 5:16:47
Raynor 35 1 36N00'30 78W17'05 5:13:08
Raynor Town 96 1 35N23'42 78W08'28 5:12:34
Rays Beach 37 1 36N22'38 76W50'25 5:07:22
Reads Chapel 7 1 35N18'39 76W44'47 5:06:59
Reba 74 1 35N40'26 77W38'22 5:10:33
Rebel Acres 92 1 35N48 78W38 5:14:32
Rebel City 82 1 35N04'57 78W32'56 5:14:12
Reb Kee 71 1 34N36'50 78W11'07 5:12:44
Redallia 74 1 35N29'05 77W22'36 5:09:30
Redbank Landing 72
1 36N12'43 76W17'28 5:05:10
Redbank Landing 74
1 35N36'57 77W20'02 5:09:20
Red Banks 78 1 34N42'10 79W15'04 5:17:00
Red Barn Landing 75
1 35N20'15 82W13'50 5:28:55
Red Brush 86 1 36N28'34 80W41'42 5:22:47
Red Bug 10 1 33N58'51 78W22'28 5:13:30
Redbug 24 1 34N18'30 78W36'44 5:14:27
Redcross 76 1 35N52'56 79W41'46 5:18:47
Red Cross 84 1 35N16'02 80W21'21 5:21:25
Reddies River 97
1 36N11 81W14 5:24:56
Red Hill 9 1 34N28'11 78W25'51 5:13:43
Red Hill 31 1 35N04'44 77W54'34 5:11:38
Red Hill 33 1 36N06 77W43 5:10:52
Red Hill 61 1 36N01'20 82W13'41 5:28:55
Red Hill 82 1 35N08'52 78W23'22 5:13:33
Redhill Landing 25
1 35N14'54 77W12'32 5:08:50
Red House 17 1 36N30 79W09 5:16:36

Redland 30 1 35N59'16 80w28'22 5:21:53
Redmon 58 1 35N47'44 82w43'02 5:30:52
Red Oak 64 1 36N02'18 77w54'24 5:11:38
Red Springs 78 1 34N48'54 79w11'00 5:16:44
Redwood 32 1 36N02'49 78w46'18 5:15:05
Reeds Crossroads 29 1 35N50'41 80w19'58 5:21:20
Reedy Creek 29 1 35N55'11 80w20'02 5:21:20
Reelsboro 69 1 35N08'02 76w54'49 5:07:39
Reems Creek 11 1 35N41 82w33 5:30:12
Reepsville 55 1 35N30'38 81w21'02 5:25:24
Reepville 55 1 35N33 81w24 5:25:36
Reese 95 1 36N19'32 81w49'29 5:27:18
Reeves 24 1 34N03'14 78w36'02 5:14:24
Refuge Mission 62 1 35N23'06 79w57'24 5:19:50
Regal 20 1 35N07'19 84w00'12 5:36:01
Regan 10 1 34N01'01 78w33'57 5:14:16
Register 31 1 34N50 78w02 5:12:08
Rehoboth 66 1 36N20'36 77w22'35 5:09:30
Reid 88 1 35N06'57 82w54'11 5:31:37
Reidsville 79 1 36N21'17 79w39'53 5:18:40
Relief 61 1 36N02'03 82w17'37 5:29:10
Ren 94 1 35N48'29 76w46'35 5:07:06
Rena 99 1 36N11'14 80w48'35 5:23:14
Rennert 78 1 34N48'51 79w04'52 5:16:19
Renston 74 1 35N30'32 77w27'24 5:09:50
Republican 8 1 36N04'56 77w03'37 5:08:14
Research Triangle Park 32 1 36N00 78w55 5:15:40
Rest Haven 7 1 35N25'37 76w43'52 5:06:55
Retreat 44 1 35N27'02 82w54'33 5:31:38
Revere 58 1 35N54'09 82w42'12 5:30:49
Revolution 41 1 36N06'07 79w46'42 5:19:07
Rex 36 1 35N16 81w10 5:24:40
Rex 78 1 34N51'25 79w02'58 5:16:12
Reynolda 34 1 36N07'31 80w17'08 5:21:09
Reynolda Park 34 1 36N07'12 80w17'13 5:21:09
Reynoldson 37 1 36N31'41 76w47'33 5:07:10
Rhamkatte 92 1 35N44'53 78w40'25 5:14:42
Rheasville 42 1 36N24'37 77w42'02 5:10:48
Rhems 25 1 35N04'21 77w10'42 5:08:43
Rhems Landing 25 1 35N03'42 77w08'41 5:08:35
Rhine 5 1 36N25 81w28 5:25:52
Rhodes 8 1 36N10'13 77w07'28 5:08:30
Rhodes-Rhyne 55 1 35N28 81w15 5:25:00
Rhodhiss 14 1 35N46'26 81w25'53 5:25:44
Rhodo 20 1 35N13'03 83w45'08 5:35:01
Rhoney 18 1 35N37'32 81w19'58 5:25:20
Rhyne 60 1 35N17'38 80w58'25 5:23:54
Rhyne Crossroad 71 1 34N33'19 78w00'32 5:12:02
Ricefield 24 1 34N21'57 78w23'46 5:13:35
Rice Mill 58 1 35N54'58 82w40'00 5:30:40
Riceville 11 1 35N37'57 82w28'13 5:29:53
Richards Crossing 71 1 34N20'47 78w00'37 5:12:02
Richardson 9 1 34N33'23 78w50'10 5:15:21
Richfield 84 1 35N28'12 80w15'29 5:21:02
Rich Hill 3 1 35N28'23 80w59'25 5:23:58
Richland 14 1 36N04'47 81w35'54 5:26:24
Richlands 61 1 36N05'11 82w18'52 5:29:15
Richlands 67 1 34N53'57 77w32'49 5:10:11
Richmond Hill 99 1 36N14'42 80w36'39 5:22:27
Richmond Mill 83 1 34N49'14 79w31'42 5:18:07
Richmond Park Extension 77 1 34N57'07 79w45'16 5:19:01
Rich Mountain 50 1 35N19'20 83w02'46 5:32:11
Rich Square 66 1 36N16'26 77w17'05 5:09:08
Rico 24 1 34N26'19 78w37'27 5:14:30
Riddick Crossroads 37 1 36N26'46 76w52'11 5:07:29
Riddicks Landing 46 1 36N31'52 76w55'33 5:07:42
Riddicksville 46 1 36N31'38 76w56'21 5:07:45
Riddle 15 1 36N24 76w06 5:04:24
Ridenhour 84 1 35N25 80w18 5:21:12
Ridge 36 1 35N16 81w10 5:24:40
Ridgecrest 11 1 35N37'14 82w16'58 5:29:08
Ridgefield 41 1 36N06 79w52 5:19:28
Ridge Spring 40 1 35N27'24 77w29'18 5:09:57
Ridgeville 17 1 36N18'01 79w10'51 5:16:43
Ridgeway 93 1 36N26'08 78w14'13 5:12:57
Riegelwood 24 1 34N20'23 78w13'32 5:12:54
Riley 35 1 35N55'53 78w21'12 5:13:25
Riley Hill 92 1 35N51'31 78w25'13 5:13:41
Rimer 13 1 35N28'29 80w29'01 5:21:56
Rimertown 13 1 35N28 80w28 5:21:52
Ringwood 42 1 36N12'40 77w50'51 5:11:23
Rippys 23 1 35N13 81w32 5:26:08
Ritters 63 1 35N28 79w31 5:18:04
River 23 1 35N11 81w43 5:26:52
River Acres 7 1 35N29'50 76w59'34 5:07:58
River Bend 36 1 35N20 81w03 5:24:12
Riverdale 25 1 34N59'45 76w59'13 5:07:57
River Haven 81 1 35N18'55 80w05'09 5:20:21
Rivermont 54 1 35N14'22 77w35'57 5:10:24
River Neck 89 1 35N56'51 76w16'53 5:05:08
River Neck Landing 89 1 35N56'31 76w18'32 5:05:14
Riverside 25 1 36N06 77w05 5:08:20
Riverside 44 1 35N37'05 82w58'05 5:31:52
Riverside 57 1 35N05'27 83w22'42 5:33:31
Riverside 100 1 35N54'43 82w20'48 5:29:23
Roan Landing 10 1 34N21'37 78w06'51 5:12:27
Roanoke Rapids 42 1 36N27'41 77w39'16 5:10:37
Roaring Creek 6 1 36N03'49 82w00'46 5:28:03
Roaring Gap 3 1 36N24'10 80w59'08 5:23:57
Roaring River 97 1 36N12'23 81w00'14 5:24:01
Robbins 63 1 35N26'02 79w35'14 5:18:21
Robbinsville 38 1 35N19'22 83w48'27 5:35:14
Roberdel 77 1 34N58'17 79w44'42 5:18:59
Roberdo 62 1 35N18'48 79w57'00 5:19:48
Roberson Store 59 1 35N49 77w06 5:08:24
Robersonville 59 1 35N49'26 77w15'20 5:09:01
Roberta Mill 13 1 35N21'26 80w38'10 5:22:33
Roberta Mills 13 1 35N25 80w36 5:22:24
Rock Creek 1 1 35N58'28 79w27'57 5:17:52
Rockdale 23 1 35N28'57 81w30'29 5:26:02
Rockfish 47 1 34N59'33 79w03'59 5:16:16
Rockford 86 1 36N16'06 80w38'56 5:22:36
Rock Hill 13 1 35N25 80w36 5:22:24
Rockingham 77 1 34N56'21 79w46'27 5:19:06
Rock Rest 90 1 34N57'16 80w29'01 5:21:56
Rock Ridge 98 1 35N42'07 78w04'03 5:12:16
Rock Spring 74 1 35N36 77w23 5:09:32
Rock Springs 75 1 35N23'44 82w07'51 5:28:31
Rockview 11 1 35N47'07 82w25'47 5:29:43
Rockwell 80 1 35N33'04 80w24'24 5:21:38
Rockwell Park 60 1 35N16 80w48 5:23:12
Rocky Cross 64 1 35N51'47 78w13'20 5:12:53
Rocky Ford 35 1 36N11'59 78w20'37 5:13:22
Rocky Hill 88 1 35N12'57 82w45'16 5:31:01
Rockyhock 21 1 36N10'51 76w41'35 5:06:46
Rocky Knoll 32 1 36N00'58 78w49'26 5:15:18
Rocky Knoll 41 1 36N01'25 79w48'10 5:19:13
Rocky Mount 64 1 35N56'17 77w47'27 5:11:10
Rocky Pass 56 1 35N43 81w56 5:27:44
Rocky Point 71 1 34N26'06 77w53'17 5:11:33
Rocky River 13 1 35N25 80w36 5:22:24
Rocky Springs 2 1 35N57'05 81w06'06 5:24:24
Rocky Springs 62 1 35N13 79w44 5:18:56
Rodanthe 28 1 35N35'36 75w28'06 5:01:52
Rodmans Quarter 7 1 35N32'46 76w46'49 5:07:07
Roduco 37 1 36N27'42 76w48'46 5:07:15
Roe 16 1 34N59'32 76w18'33 5:05:14
Rogers Crossroads 64 1 35N47'09 78w13'02 5:12:52
Rolesville 92 1 35N55'23 78w27'28 5:13:50
Rollins 58 2 35N47'22 82w39'49 5:30:39
Rominger 95 1 36N13'34 81w50'19 5:27:21
Ronda 97 1 36N13'06 80w56'29 5:23:46
Rooks 71 1 34N29'47 78w08'39 5:12:35
Roper 94 1 35N52'40 76w36'56 5:06:28
Roper Springs 42 1 36N25'36 77w52'24 5:11:30
Rose 96 1 35N22 77w58 5:11:52
Rose Bay 48 1 35N27'38 76w23'02 5:05:32
Roseboro 82 1 34N57'10 78w30'32 5:14:02
Roseborough 6 1 36N02'05 81w48'33 5:27:14
Rosebud 85 1 36N18'25 80w10'52 5:20:43
Rosebud 98 1 35N46'00 77w51'28 5:11:26
Rose Hill 31 1 34N49'41 78w01'24 5:12:06
Rose Hill 93 1 36N31'07 78w18'29 5:13:14
Roseland 24 1 34N13'57 78w50'23 5:15:22
Roseland 55 1 35N26'41 81w16'34 5:25:06
Roseland 63 1 35N08'06 79w30'34 5:18:02
Rosemary 42 1 36N27'04 77w40'47 5:10:43
Rosemead 8 1 36N10'48 76w51'59 5:07:28
Rosemont 34 1 36N02'52 80w14'34 5:20:58
Roseneath 42 1 36N04'29 77w28'43 5:09:55
Roseville 73 1 36N21'17 79w02'31 5:16:10
Rosewood 96 1 35N24'48 78w04'16 5:12:17
Rosindale 9 1 34N26'27 78w31'38 5:14:07
Rosin Hill 82 1 35N12'30 78w24'52 5:13:39
Roslin 26 1 34N55'34 78w56'46 5:15:47
Rosman 88 1 35N08'37 82w49'17 5:31:17
Rosser 53 1 35N33'19 79w05'29 5:16:22
Ross Store 85 1 36N20'25 80w13'13 5:20:53
Roten 5 1 36N28'17 81w37'03 5:26:28
Rougemont 32 1 36N13'06 78w55'36 5:15:42
Roughedge 90 1 34N53'57 80w37'26 5:22:30
Roundhill 87 1 35N25'52 83w31'30 5:34:06
Round Peak 86 1 36N30 80w35 5:22:20
Roundtree 74 1 35N28'49 77w28'49 5:09:55
Rover 7 1 35N24'22 77w00'25 5:08:02
Rowan 9 1 34N30'46 78w16'17 5:13:05
Rowan Mill 80 1 35N39 80w30 5:22:00
Rowan Mills 80 1 35N38'53 80w30'20 5:22:01
Rowes Corner 25 1 35N10'20 77w00'19 5:08:01
Rowland 78 1 34N32'11 79w17'30 5:17:10
Roxboro 73 1 36N23'37 78w58'59 5:15:56
Roxobel 8 1 36N12'10 77w14'44 5:08:59
Royal 7 1 35N17'22 76w46'11 5:07:05
Royal 35 1 36N00'54 78w21'30 5:13:26
Royal Mills 92 1 35N59 78w30 5:14:00
Royal Oaks 13 1 35N27'38 80w36'26 5:22:26
Royal Pines 11 1 35N28'30 82w30'58 5:30:04
Rubyatt 62 1 35N12'55 79w43'52 5:18:55
Ruby City 50 1 35N22'38 83w07'06 5:32:28
Rudd 41 1 36N09'57 79w44'35 5:18:58
Ruffin 79 1 36N26'49 79w32'39 5:18:11
Rufus 14 2 35N59'55 81w38'29 5:26:34
Rugby 45 1 35N21'55 82w31'14 5:30:05
Ruggles 42 1 36N16'44 77w35'52 5:10:23
Runion 58 1 35N53'09 82w46'24 5:31:06
Rural Hall 34 1 36N14'25 80w17'37 5:21:10
Rusk 86 1 36N15 80w52 5:23:28
Ruskin 9 1 34N42'35 78w40'29 5:14:42
Russells Creek 10 1 34N08'14 78w07'00 5:12:28
Russellville 4 1 34N59'00 80w08'19 5:20:33
Russ Landing 9 1 34N33'15 78w27'14 5:13:49
Russtown 10 1 33N57'26 78w25'54 5:13:44
Ruth 81 1 35N22'55 81w56'50 5:27:47
Rutherford College 12 1 35N45 81w32 5:26:08
Rutherfordton 81 1 35N22'09 81w57'25 5:27:50
Rutherwood 95 1 36N13'28 81w35'56 5:26:24
Ryes 43 1 35N25'56 79w00'03 5:16:00
Ryland 21 1 36N16'37 76w37'25 5:06:30
Rymers Ferry 38 1 35N26'42 83w52'11 5:35:29
Saconon 45 1 35N20'25 82w21'03 5:29:24
Saddle 3 1 36N33 81w00 5:24:00
Saddletree 78 1 34N43'03 79w01'59 5:16:08
Sadler 79 1 36N24'31 79w37'02 5:18:28
Saint Helena 71 1 34N30'59 77w54'57 5:11:40
Saint John 46 1 36N18'22 77w05'12 5:08:21
Saint Johns 21 1 36N01'50 76w31'37 5:06:06
Saint Johns 46 1 36N18 77w07 5:08:28
Saint Lewis 33 1 35N46'53 77w42'12 5:10:49
Saint Marys 92 1 35N42 78w36 5:14:24
Saint Matthews 92 1 35N48 78w32 5:14:08
Saint Pauls 78 1 34N48'23 78w58'17 5:15:53
Salem 12 1 35N41'55 81w41'50 5:26:47
Salem 34 1 36N05'01 80w14'48 5:20:59
Salem 55 1 35N26'02 81w11'44 5:24:47
Salem 64 1 36N06'52 77w51'42 5:11:27
Salem 70 1 36N11'58 76w07'49 5:04:31
Salem 76 1 35N50'20 79w47'22 5:19:09
Salem 86 1 36N32'17 80w36'05 5:22:24
Salemburg 82 1 35N00'55 78w30'12 5:14:01
Salem Chapel 34 1 36N12 80w12 5:20:48
Sales Ford 20 2 35N07'39 83w59'02 5:35:56
Salisbury 80 1 35N40'15 80w28'28 5:21:54
Salter Path 16 1 34N41'18 76w53'11 5:07:33
Saluda 75 1 35N14'10 82w20'58 5:29:24
Salvo 28 1 35N32'24 75w28'24 5:01:54
Samarcand 63 1 35N17'58 79w41'05 5:18:44
Samaria 64 1 35N51'35 78w10'43 5:12:43
Sandford Landing 67 1 34N30'47 77w23'22 5:09:33
Sand Hill 11 1 35N33'09 82w37'51 5:30:31
Sandhill 69 1 35N06 77w05 5:08:20
Sand Hill Landing 10 1 33N58'01 78w15'07 5:13:00
Sands 95 1 36N15'03 81w38'54 5:26:36
Sandy Bluff Landing 9 1 34N30'46 78w15'11 5:13:01
Sandy Bottom 54 2 35N12'21 77w42'04 5:10:48
Sandy Bottom 58 1 35N51'48 82w46'08 5:31:05
Sandy Bottoms 83 1 34N46'49 79w30'42 5:18:03
Sandycross 37 1 36N22'07 76w33'14 5:06:13
Sandy Cross 64 1 35N53'55 77w56'47 5:11:47
Sandy Cross 79 1 36N21'12 79w44'45 5:18:59
Sandy Grove 29 1 35N47'24 80w12'58 5:20:52
Sandy Grove 47 1 34N56'52 79w05'58 5:16:24
Sandy Hill 10 1 33N58'09 78w13'45 5:12:55
Sandy Landing 7 1 35N29'10 76w41'19 5:06:45
Sandymush 11 1 35N40'21 82w48'41 5:31:15
Sandy Mush 81 1 35N17'21 81w50'41 5:27:23
Sandy Plain 24 1 34N05'28 78w46'30 5:15:06
Sandy Plain 31 1 35N03 77w45 5:11:00
Sandy Plain 92 1 36N03'43 78w41'48 5:14:47
Sandy Plains 23 1 35N16'07 81w22'03 5:25:28
Sandy Plains 75 1 35N14'38 82w05'23 5:28:22
Sandy Ridge 41 1 36N04'33 79w59'44 5:19:59
Sandy Ridge 85 1 36N29'56 80w06'16 5:20:25
Sandy Run 23 1 35N19 81w39 5:26:36
Sanford 53 1 35N28'47 79w10'50 5:16:43
Sans Souci 8 1 35N54'59 76w49'08 5:07:17
Santeetlah 38 1 35N21'22 83w50'18 5:35:21
Sapphire 88 1 35N06'25 83w00'11 5:32:01
Saratoga 98 1 35N39'13 77w46'33 5:11:06
Sarecta 31 1 34N58'44 77w51'28 5:11:26
Sarecta Junction 31 1 34N58 77w58 5:11:52
Sarem 37 1 36N29'00 76w47'31 5:07:10
Sassafras Fork 39 1 36N29 78w34 5:14:16
Sassers Mill 52 1 35N13 77w26 5:09:44
Satterwhite 39 1 36N18 78w35 5:14:20
Saulston 96 1 35N26'24 77w53'53 5:11:36
Saunders 47 1 34N59'25 79w14'24 5:16:58
Saunook 44 2 35N27'06 83w02'41 5:32:11
Sauratown 85 1 36N18 80w08 5:20:32
Savage 37 1 36N29'06 76w35'28 5:06:22
Savages Crossroads 37 1 36N30'07 76w48'40 5:07:15
Savannah 50 1 35N18'33 83w15'35 5:33:02
Saw 80 1 35N33 80w36 5:22:24
Saw Mills 14 1 35N49'29 81w28'29 5:25:54
Saxapahaw 1 1 35N56'50 79w19'20 5:17:17
Saxsony 55 1 35N28 81w15 5:25:00
Sayles Village 11 1 35N34'20 82w30'57 5:30:04
Scalesville 41 1 36N14'10 79w50'41 5:19:23
Scaly Mountain 57 1 35N00'42 83w18'59 5:33:16
Schley 68 1 36N09'09 79w03'42 5:16:15
Scholl 83 1 34N54 79w42 5:18:48
Schoolhouse Landing 7 1 35N24'34 76w35'58 5:06:24
Scotch Grove 83 1 34N46 79w28 5:17:52
Scotch Irish 80 1 35N48 80w38 5:22:32
Scotia 89 1 35N51'34 76w13'03 5:04:52
Scotland Neck 42 1 36N07'46 77w25'14 5:09:41
Scott Creek 50 1 35N25 83w07 5:32:28
Scott Landing 52 1 35N02'57 77w11'11 5:08:45
Scott Park 41 1 36N04'38 79w45'55 5:19:04
Scotts 49 1 35N50'34 81w00'34 5:24:02
Scotts 98 1 35N40'53 78w01'00 5:12:04
Scotts Hill 65 1 34N19'16 77w45'58 5:11:04
Scotts Store 69 1 35N06 77w05 5:08:20
Scottville 3 1 36N28'49 81w18'28 5:25:14
Scranton 48 1 35N29'49 76w27'06 5:05:48
Scuffleton 40 1 35N28 77w25 5:09:40
Scuppernong 94 1 35N54'07 76w27'08 5:05:49
Seaboard 66 1 36N29'24 77w26'30 5:09:46
Sea Breeze 65 3 34N03'47 77w53'30 5:11:34
Seaforth 19 1 35N44'24 79w01'54 5:16:08
Seagate 65 3 34N12'33 77w50'38 5:11:23
Seagrove 76 1 35N32'25 79w46'24 5:19:06
Sealevel 16 1 34N51'44 76w23'17 5:05:33
Sears Landing 71 1 34N25'55 77w33'29 5:10:14
Seaside 10 1 33N53'22 78w29'08 5:13:57
Secession 10 1 33N55'58 78w17'43 5:13:11
Sedalia 41 1 36N04'02 79w37'15 5:18:29
Sedgefield 41 1 36N00'53 79w53'50 5:19:35
Sedgefield 60 1 35N11 80w51 5:23:24
Sedgefield Lakes 41 1 36N03 79w52 5:19:28
Sedgefield Park 41 1 36N03 79w52 5:19:28
Sedges Garden 34 1 36N08 80w14 5:20:56
Sedge-Town 41 1 36N01'50 79w52'06 5:19:28
Seeshore 88 1 35N09'10 82w42'13 5:30:49
Sega Lake 88 1 35N13'08 82w45'47 5:31:03

Place		Lat	Long	Time
Selica 88	1	35N12'00	82w46'42	5:31:07
Selma 51	1	35N32'11	78w17'05	5:13:08
Selma Cotton Mills 51	1	35N32	78w17	5:13:08
Selwin 37	1	36N20'05	76w35'14	5:06:21
Seminole 43	1	35N26'24	79w02'13	5:16:09
Semora 17	1	36N29'54	79w08'57	5:16:36
Senia 6	1	36N05	81w56	5:27:44
Senter 43	1	35N21'20	78w47'38	5:15:11
Sessex 5	1	36N33'42	81w25'09	5:25:41
Setzer Gap 14	1	35N54	81w31	5:26:04
Seven Bridges 78	1	34N44	79w21	5:17:24
Seven Creeks 24	1	34N04'55	78w37'49	5:14:31
Seven Lakes 63	1	35N16'42	79w33'53	5:18:16
Seven Paths 35	1	35N59'51	78w11'02	5:12:44
Seven Springs 96	1	35N13'38	77w50'50	5:11:23
Severn 66	1	36N30'54	77w11'24	5:08:46
Sevier 56	1	35N48'09	82w01'01	5:28:04
Seward 34	1	36N11'11	80w22'10	5:21:29
Sexton 58	1	35N47'51	82w36'52	5:30:27
Seymour Johnson AFB 96	1	35N22	77w58	5:11:52
Shacktown 99	1	36N07'00	80w35'38	5:22:23
Shadberry Landing 94	1	35N57'33	76w28'46	5:05:55
Shady Banks 7	1	35N29'41	76w59'23	5:07:58
Shady Brook 13	1	35N31	80w38	5:22:32
Shady Forest 10	1	33N54	78w27	5:13:48
Shady Grove 30	1	35N57	80w26	5:21:44
Shady Grove 52	1	35N08'24	77w30'26	5:10:02
Shaken 71	1	34N37'04	77w45'34	5:11:02
Shale Brick 29	1	35N53	80w05	5:20:20
Shaleton 90	1	34N59	80w33	5:22:12
Shaleville 58	2	35N54'32	82w51'08	5:31:25
Shallotte 10	1	33N58'23	78w23'10	5:13:33
Shallotte Point 10	1	33N54	78w27	5:13:48
Shallowell 53	1	35N28	79w10	5:16:40
Shallow Ford 57	1	35N17'47	83w29'45	5:33:59
Shanghai 82	1	34N45'54	78w12'28	5:12:50
Shankle 84	1	35N14	80w07	5:20:28
Shankletown 13	1	35N25	80w36	5:22:24
Shannon 78	1	34N50'52	79w08'14	5:16:33
Sharon 15	1	36N29'44	76w18'36	5:05:14
Sharon 49	1	35N46'31	81w04'02	5:24:16
Sharon 60	1	35N09	80w49	5:23:16
Sharonbrook 60	1	35N06'58	80w52'37	5:23:30
Sharpes 2	1	35N54	81w05	5:24:20
Sharpesburg 49	1	35N55	80w58	5:23:52
Sharp Point 74	1	35N40	77w38	5:10:32
Sharpsburg 64	1	35N52'01	77w49'46	5:11:19
Shatley Springs 5	1	36N28'34	81w24'10	5:25:37
Shawboro 27	1	36N24'19	76w05'40	5:04:23
Shaw Heights 26	1	35N05	78w57	5:15:48
Shaw Landing 46	1	36N19'05	76w52'20	5:07:29
Shawneehaw 95	1	36N11	81w49	5:27:16
Shaws 26	1	35N06'51	78w55'51	5:15:43
Shawtown 43	1	35N23'03	78w49'51	5:15:19
Sheffield 30	1	35N57'58	80w40'49	5:22:43
Sheffields 63	1	35N28	79w38	5:18:32
Shelby 23	1	35N17'32	81w32'09	5:26:09
Shell Landing 7	1	35N23'08	76w49'34	5:07:18
Shell Rock Landing 67	1	34N39'12	77w09'52	5:08:39
Shelmerdine 74	1	35N26'52	77w15'44	5:09:03
Shelter Neck 71	1	34N37'12	77w50'34	5:11:22
Shelton 17	1	36N32'08	79w27'30	5:17:50
Shelton Laurel 44	1	35N40'51	83w00'28	5:32:02
Shelton Store 85	1	36N30'40	80w08'34	5:20:34
Sheltontown 86	1	36N29'36	80w33'23	5:22:14
Shepard 32	1	35N58	78w55	5:15:40
Shepherds 49	1	35N38'07	80w49'40	5:23:19
Sherrills Ford 18	1	35N37'13	80w59'12	5:23:57
Sherwood 95	1	36N16'11	81w46'36	5:27:06
Sherwood Forest 11	1	35N35'37	82w25'52	5:29:43
Sherwood Forest 88	1	35N08'39	82w41'15	5:30:45
Sherwood Terrace 88	1	35N08'46	82w40'28	5:30:42
Sherwood Village 41	1	35N56'34	79w59'10	5:19:57
Shields Commissary 42	1	36N08	77w25	5:09:40
Shiloh 11	1	35N33'04	82w31'58	5:30:08
Shiloh 15	1	36N16'23	76w05'08	5:04:21
Shiloh 79	1	36N26'51	79w51'52	5:19:27
Shiloh 81	2	35N17'59	81w56'28	5:27:46
Shiloh Mills 33	1	35N54'28	77w29'35	5:09:58
Shine 40	1	35N26'25	77w47'32	5:11:10
Shines Crossroads 40	1	35N27	77w40	5:10:40
Shingleford Crossing 9	1	34N37'06	78w48'05	5:15:12
Shingle Hollow 81	1	35N28'15	82w04'26	5:28:18
Shinnville 49	1	35N39'31	80w48'12	5:23:13
Shoal 86	1	36N20	80w26	5:21:44
Shoal Creek 20	1	35N06	84w14	5:36:56
Shoal Creek 50	1	35N26	83w22	5:33:28
Shoals 86	1	36N16'26	80w30'41	5:22:03
Shoates 4	1	34N51'55	80w08'27	5:20:34
Shocco 93	1	36N19	78w10	5:12:40
Shoe 97	1	36N16	81w19	5:25:16
Shoeheel Cemetery 51	1	35N37'39	78w12'38	5:12:51
Sholars Crossroads 31	1	34N45'43	77w48'04	5:11:12
Shoofly 39	1	36N13'21	78w43'46	5:14:55
Shookville 57	1	35N08'46	83w13'22	5:32:53
Shooting Creek 22	1	35N01'32	83w40'01	5:34:40
Shopton 60	1	35N10'17	80w57'42	5:23:51
Short Off 57	1	35N03	83w12	5:32:48
Shotwell 92	1	35N44'13	78w26'42	5:13:47
Shoups Ford 12	1	35N35'30	81w33'36	5:26:14
Shuffletown 60	1	35N19'14	80w57'10	5:23:49
Shuford 18	1	35N44	81w21	5:25:24
Shulls Mills 95	1	36N10'25	81w44'38	5:26:59
Shumont 11	1	35N28'15	82w15'32	5:29:02
Shupings Mill 80	1	35N33'05	80w28'54	5:21:56
Sidestown 13	1	35N25	80w36	5:22:24
Sidney 7	1	35N32	76w37	5:06:28
Sidney 24	1	34N11'13	78w47'22	5:15:09
Sidney Crossroads 7	1	35N28'51	76w40'33	5:06:42
Sign Pine 21	1	36N18'32	76w37'28	5:06:30
Sikes Landing 82	1	34N36'30	78w18'24	5:13:14
Siler City 19	1	35N43'24	79w27'45	5:17:51
Silk Hope 19	1	35N46'51	79w22'13	5:17:29
Siloam 86	1	36N17'09	80w33'46	5:22:15
Silver Bluff 44	1	35N28'34	82w52'48	5:31:31
Silver City 47	1	34N59'45	79w13'35	5:16:54
Silver Creek 12	1	35N41	81w48	5:27:12
Silverdale 67	1	34N46'07	77w10'56	5:08:44
Silver Hill 29	1	35N42'37	80w12'24	5:20:50
Silver Hill 69	1	35N10'08	76w50'44	5:07:23
Silver Hill 83	1	34N53'22	79w29'02	5:17:56
Silver Springs 37	1	36N25'03	76w40'20	5:06:41
Silver Springs 63	1	35N05'46	79w28'17	5:17:53
Silverstone 95	1	36N17'17	81w45'07	5:27:00
Silver Valley 29	1	35N43'57	80w06'12	5:20:25
Simmons Bay 24	1	34N08'02	78w37'40	5:14:31
Simmons Corner 52	1	35N05'29	77w13'03	5:08:52
Simmons Landing 89	1	35N53'15	76w19'50	5:05:19
Simpson 74	1	35N35	77w17	5:09:08
Simpsonville 79	1	36N19	79w43	5:18:52
Sims 98	1	35N45'39	78w03'33	5:12:14
Sioux 100	1	36N01'14	82w21'39	5:29:27
Sivey Town 10	1	33N58'02	78w18'24	5:13:14
Six Forks 71	1	34N35'31	77w53'12	5:11:33
Six Forks 92	1	35N54'03	78w39'09	5:14:37
Six Forks Crossroads 92	1	35N51'41	78w28'58	5:13:56
Sixpound 93	1	36N29	78w03	5:12:12
Skibo 26	1	35N03'33	78w58'14	5:15:53
Skinnersville 94	1	35N56'22	76w32'15	5:06:09
Skyco 28	1	35N54	75w40	5:02:40
Skycrest Village 92	1	35N48	78w38	5:14:32
Skyland 11	1	35N29'21	82w31'28	5:30:06
Skyline 63	1	35N15	79w17	5:17:08
Sky Village 45	1	35N19'01	82w30'39	5:30:03
Skyway Terrace 83	1	34N44	79w21	5:17:24
Sladesville 48	1	35N27'49	76w29'23	5:05:58
Slatestone 7	1	35N34'21	76w55'21	5:07:41
Slickrock Ford 57	1	35N11'57	83w31'30	5:34:06
Sligo 27	1	36N27'06	76w04'39	5:04:19
Sloan 31	1	34N46'41	77w49'46	5:11:19
Slocomb 26	1	35N10'38	78w49'26	5:15:18
Slocum 48	1	35N27'21	76w05'22	5:04:21
Slocum Village 25	1	34N53	76w54	5:07:36
Slow Creek 20	1	35N10	83w55	5:35:40
Small 7	1	35N16'48	76w51'13	5:07:25
Small Cross Roads 21	1	36N04	76w36	5:06:24
Smethport 5	1	36N25'35	81w30'07	5:26:00
Smith 31	1	35N00	77w48	5:11:12
Smith Creek 93	1	36N29	78w13	5:12:52
Smith Crossing 24	1	34N19'19	78w38'56	5:14:36
Smithfield 51	1	35N30'30	78w20'23	5:13:22
Smith Grove 30	1	35N57'50	80w30'11	5:22:01
Smiths 78	1	34N39'10	78w52'04	5:15:28
Smiths Bridge 57	1	35N04	83w23	5:33:32
Smiths Corner 15	1	36N18'04	76w03'55	5:04:16
Smiths Crossroads 9	1	34N41'39	78w22'28	5:13:30
Smithtown 7	1	35N31'17	76w39'51	5:06:39
Smithtown 99	1	36N14'09	80w34'40	5:22:19
Smithville 10	1	33N58	78w10	5:12:40
Smithville 60	1	35N29'03	80w52'15	5:23:29
Smithwick 59	1	35N43'35	77w02'12	5:08:09
Smoky Creek 12	1	35N48	81w37	5:26:28
Smyre 36	1	35N16'34	81w07'34	5:24:30
Smyrna 16	1	34N45'33	76w31'40	5:06:07
Snake Bite 8	1	36N05	77w04	5:08:16
Sneads Ferry 67	1	34N33'09	77w23'51	5:09:35
Sneads Grove 83	1	34N46	79w28	5:17:52
Snow Camp 1	1	35N53'36	79w25'49	5:17:43
Snowden 27	1	36N27'24	76w06'32	5:04:26
Snowhill 24	1	34N06'13	78w45'14	5:15:01
Snowhill 40	1	35N27'05	77w40'53	5:10:44
Snow Hill 72	1	36N16'13	76w34'12	5:06:17
Snow Hill 82	1	34N57'38	78w27'18	5:13:49
Snow Hill 85	1	36N29'07	80w11'49	5:20:47
Snow Hill 93	1	36N24'58	78w11'19	5:12:45
Soapstone Mountain 76	1	35N48	79w33	5:18:12
Social Plains 35	1	35N50'53	78w14'52	5:12:59
Soda Hill 95	1	36N16'34	81w38'16	5:26:33
Sodom 58	1	35N48	82w41	5:30:44
Sodyeco 60	1	35N17'49	80w59'54	5:24:00
Solo 95	1	36N16'55	81w37'04	5:26:28
Solola Valley 87	1	35N29'49	83w30'03	5:34:00
Somers 97	1	36N06	80w55	5:23:40
Somers Crossroads 97	1	36N05'00	80w53'48	5:23:35
Somerset 21	1	36N03'37	76w27'43	5:05:51
Somerset Hills 92	1	35N48	78w38	5:14:32
Sophia 76	1	35N49'23	79w51'40	5:19:27
Soul City 93	1	36N24'30	78w16'14	5:13:05
Sound Landing 28	1	36N04'10	75w44'22	5:02:57
Sound Side 28	1	35N57'06	75w37'55	5:02:32
Soundside 89	1	35N57'54	76w14'25	5:04:58
South Albemarle 84	1	35N19	80w11	5:20:44
South Belmont 36	1	35N13'49	81w02'34	5:24:10
South Clinton 82	1	34N57	78w19	5:13:16
South Creek 7	1	35N20'08	76w41'41	5:06:47
Southern Pines 63	1	35N10'26	79w23'33	5:17:34
South Fork 34	1	36N05'23	80w19'07	5:21:16
South Gastonia 36	1	35N13'09	81w12'21	5:24:49
South Goldsboro 96	1	35N21'27	78w00'22	5:12:01
South Greensboro 41	1	36N03	79w49	5:19:16
South Henderson 91	1	36N18'29	78w24'25	5:13:38
South Hominy 11	1	35N29'31	82w44'18	5:30:57
South Lexington 29	1	35N49	80w15	5:21:00
South Lincolnton 55	1	35N27'15	81w14'38	5:24:59
South Lowell 32	1	36N10	78w53	5:15:32
South Lumberton 78	1	34N36	79w01	5:16:04
South Mills 15	1	36N26'44	76w19'40	5:05:19
Southmont 29	1	35N40'04	80w16'02	5:21:04
South Newton 18	1	35N40	81w13	5:24:52
South Point 36	1	35N13	81w06	5:24:24
Southport 10	1	33N55'17	78w01'14	5:12:05
South River 16	1	34N57'31	76w35'50	5:06:23
South River 82	1	34N46	78w21	5:13:24
South Rocky Mount 33	1	35N55'28	77w47'49	5:11:11
South Salisbury 80	1	35N38'37	80w27'46	5:21:51
Southshore Landing 89	1	35N55'10	76w02'59	5:04:12
South Side 34	1	36N04'19	80w14'23	5:20:58
Southside 55	1	35N26'12	81w14'46	5:24:59
South Toe 100	1	35N49	82w11	5:28:44
South Tunis 46	1	36N21'49	76w54'04	5:07:36
South Wadesboro 4	1	34N57'22	80w04'39	5:20:19
South Weldon 42	1	36N24'57	77w36'12	5:10:25
Southwest 54	1	35N12	77w32	5:10:08
South Westfield 86	1	36N27	80w30	5:22:00
South Whitakers 64	1	36N02	77w48	5:11:12
South Whiteville 24	1	34N18'19	78w42'56	5:14:52
South Williams 24	1	34N08	78w49	5:15:16
South Wilmington 65	3	34N13	77w55	5:11:40
South Wilson 98	1	35N44	77w55	5:11:40
Southwood 54	1	35N12'31	77w34'03	5:10:16
Sparkleberry Landing 9	1	34N28'40	78w12'24	5:12:50
Sparta 3	1	36N30'19	81w07'16	5:24:29
Spear 6	1	36N01'20	82w01'26	5:28:06
Speed 33	1	35N58'04	77w26'44	5:09:47
Speedwell 50	1	35N19	83w11	5:32:44
Speights Bridge 40	1	35N33'32	77w44'08	5:10:57
Spellers Ferry Landing 8	1	35N54'53	77w01'31	5:08:06
Spencer 80	1	35N41'32	80w26'06	5:21:44
Spencer Mountain 36	1	35N18'22	81w06'39	5:24:27
Spences Corner 15	1	36N21'03	76w11'46	5:04:47
Spero 76	1	35N42	79w49	5:19:16
Spies 63	1	35N25'18	79w40'08	5:18:41
Spillcorn 58	1	35N57'16	82w39'01	5:30:36
Spilona 51	1	35N29'18	78w28'20	5:13:53
Spindale 81	1	35N21'36	81w55'46	5:27:43
Spiveys Corner 82	1	35N19	78w37	5:14:28
Spokane 76	1	35N32	79w46	5:19:04
Spot 27	1	36N07'05	75w49'10	5:03:17
Spout Springs 43	1	35N16'10	79w03'36	5:16:14
Spray 79	1	36N30'58	79w45'39	5:19:03
Spring Creek 7	1	35N19'27	76w39'23	5:06:38
Spring Creek 58	1	35N47'55	82w51'16	5:31:25
Springdale 36	1	35N17'20	81w08'42	5:24:35
Springfield 41	1	35N55'58	79w59'15	5:19:57
Springfield 83	1	34N46'58	79w31'59	5:18:08
Springfield 97	1	36N15	81w07	5:24:28
Springfield Mills 83	1	34N49	79w32	5:18:08
Spring Garden 25	1	35N12'15	77w09'21	5:08:37
Spring Garden Landing 25	1	35N13'08	77w08'55	5:08:36
Spring Hill 10	1	34N11'39	78w04'10	5:12:17
Spring Hill 42	1	36N12'25	77w26'01	5:09:44
Spring Hill 44	1	35N29'13	82w51'00	5:31:24
Spring Hill 83	1	34N52'58	79w22'58	5:17:32
Spring Hope 25	1	35N11'42	76w58'47	5:07:55
Spring Hope 64	1	35N56'42	78w06'44	5:12:27
Spring Lake 26	1	35N10'04	78w58'23	5:15:54
Spring Valley 41	1	36N03	79w49	5:19:16
Springwood 36	1	35N16'21	81w03'47	5:24:15
Spruce Pine 61	1	35N54'55	82w03'53	5:28:16
Spurgeon 97	1	36N10	81w08	5:24:32
Stacey 79	1	36N25'41	79w34'54	5:18:20
Stackhouse 58	1	35N52'53	82w46'12	5:31:05
Stacy 16	1	34N50'59	76w24'58	5:05:40
Stag Park 71	1	34N31'27	77w50'42	5:11:23
Staley 76	1	35N47'45	79w33'06	5:18:12
Stallings 90	1	35N05'26	80w41'11	5:22:45
Stallings Crossroads 7	1	35N39'33	77w01'47	5:08:07
Stallings Crossroads 35	1	36N05'38	78w09'56	5:12:40
Stamey Branch 6	1	36N05	81w56	5:27:44

Stamey Town 6 1 36N00'17 81w56'48 5:27:47
Stancell 66 1 36N32'37 77w44'25 5:10:58
Stancils Chapel 51 1 35N40'52 78w12'36 5:12:50
Standard 74 1 35N32'54 77w30'07 5:10:00
Stanfield 84 1 35N14'00 80w25'38 5:21:43
Stanhope 64 1 35N51'56 78w04'53 5:12:20
Stanley 36 1 35N21'32 81w05'50 5:24:23
Stanleys Store 30 1 35N54 80w34 5:22:16
Stanleyville 34 1 36N12'08 80w16'52 5:21:07
Stanton 97 1 36N12 81w20 5:25:20
Stantonsburg 98 1 35N36'24 77w49'25 5:11:18
Star 62 1 35N24'07 79w47'04 5:19:08
Starlight 96 1 35N15'59 78w15'31 5:13:02
Starling 67 1 34N42'28 77w13'55 5:08:56
Starmount 60 1 35N10 80w51 5:23:24
Starmount 92 1 35N48 78w38 5:14:32
Starmount Forest 41 1 36N04'46 79w50'40 5:19:23
Startown 18 1 35N38'42 81w16'10 5:25:05
State Road 86 1 36N19'33 80w52'04 5:23:28
Statesville 49 1 35N46'57 80w53'15 5:23:33
State University 92 1 35N48 78w41 5:14:44
Station 74 1 35N41'19 77w21'18 5:09:25
Stave Landing 48 1 35N25'04 76w29'50 5:05:59
Stearns 75 1 35N16'21 82w12'59 5:28:52
Stecoah 38 1 35N22'11 83w41'26 5:34:46
Stedman 26 1 35N00'48 78w41'39 5:14:47
Steeds 62 1 35N28'15 79w46'40 5:19:07
Steel Creek 60 1 35N08 80w57 5:23:48
Steele 80 1 35N41 80w38 5:22:32
Steele Landing 8 1 36N06'34 76w44'12 5:06:57
Steeles 77 1 35N08 79w55 5:19:40
Steen Town 77 1 34N52'16 79w39'12 5:18:37
Steep Pines Fork 16 1 34N43'27 76w38'54 5:06:36
Stella 16 1 34N46'27 77w09'03 5:08:36
Stem 39 1 36N11'59 78w43'21 5:14:53
Stephens Crossroads 79 1 36N28'39 79w36'41 5:18:27
Sterling 60 1 35N06'29 80w53'12 5:23:33
Sterlings 78 1 34N24 79w03 5:16:12
Stevens Mill 96 1 35N20'41 78w07'01 5:12:28
Stewart Crossroads 78 1 34N28'22 79w15'27 5:17:02
Stewarts Mill 41 1 36N02'31 79w39'57 5:18:40
Stewartsville 83 1 34N45 79w27 5:17:48
Stiles 57 1 35N16'49 83w29'06 5:33:56
Still Bluff 71 1 34N25'54 78w08'47 5:12:35
Stilley 7 1 35N20'19 76w55'33 5:07:42
Stilleys Crossroads 98 1 35N43'04 78w11'49 5:12:47
Still Landing 82 1 34N36'09 78w18'11 5:13:13
Stocksville 11 1 35N44'51 82w32'54 5:30:12
Stokes 74 1 35N42'59 77w15'54 5:09:04
Stokesdale 41 1 36N14'13 79w58'47 5:19:55
Stokestown 74 1 35N28 77w25 5:09:40
Stonehaven 60 1 35N10 80w48 5:23:12
Stones Landing 67 1 34N36'27 77w26'37 5:09:46
Stoneville 79 1 36N27'59 79w54'26 5:19:38
Stonewall 69 1 35N08'14 76w44'53 5:07:00
Stonewall Jackson Homes 60 1 35N14 80w53 5:23:32
Stoney Knob 11 1 35N40'48 82w34'22 5:30:17
Stony Creek 17 1 36N15'31 79w25'13 5:17:41
Stony Fork 11 1 35N27'46 82w44'11 5:30:57
Stony Fork 95 1 36N14 81w31 5:26:04
Stony Hill 92 1 35N58'53 78w36'44 5:14:27
Stony Knoll 86 1 36N18'41 80w40'26 5:22:42
Stony Point 2 1 35N51'48 81w02'51 5:24:11
Stony Point 23 1 35N18'18 81w25'58 5:25:44
Storys Crossroads 37 1 36N26'06 76w53'21 5:07:33
Stotts Crossroads 98 1 35N44'26 78w03'47 5:12:15
Stouts 90 1 35N03'19 80w38'23 5:22:34
Stovall 39 1 36N26'53 78w34'14 5:14:17
Stowe 36 1 35N15 81w02 5:24:08
Strabane 54 1 35N11'42 77w46'30 5:11:06
Straits 16 1 34N43'44 76w34'17 5:06:17
Stratford 3 1 36N31'06 81w12'58 5:24:52
Strawberry Hill Landing 10 1 34N20'15 78w03'53 5:12:16
Strawberry Ridge 61 1 35N50'36 82w06'41 5:28:27
Strawhorn Landing 9 1 34N31'10 78w15'53 5:13:04
Strickland Crossroads 51 1 35N22'03 78w22'03 5:13:28
Strickland Crossroads 64 1 35N51'19 78w00'46 5:12:03
Stterwhite 39 1 36N23'11 78w41'12 5:14:45
Stubbs 23 1 35N19'37 81w28'17 5:25:53
Stump Sound 67 1 34N35 77w29 5:09:56
Stumptown 56 1 35N41'24 81w59'05 5:27:56
Stumpy Point 28 1 35N41'54 75w44'27 5:02:58
Sturdivants Crossroads 90 1 34N54'21 80w19'42 5:21:19
Sturgills 5 1 36N33'19 81w29'55 5:26:00
Suburb 10 1 34N00'21 78w08'56 5:12:36
Sugar Fork 57 1 35N08 83w15 5:33:00
Sugar Grove 95 1 36N15'28 81w47'18 5:27:09
Sugar Hill 56 1 35N35'04 82w02'33 5:28:10
Sugar Hill 83 1 34N45'27 79w27'33 5:17:50
Sugar Loaf 2 1 36N00 81w10 5:24:40
Sugar Town 4 1 35N03'20 80w10'57 5:20:44
Suggs Landing 33 1 35N48'59 77w33'07 5:10:12
Suit 20 1 35N05 84w02 5:36:08
Sulphur Springs 11 1 35N34'13 82w37'21 5:30:29
Sulphur Springs 81 2 35N15 81w55 5:27:40
Sulphur Springs 86 1 36N32'23 80w34'29 5:22:18
Summerfield 41 1 36N12'31 79w54'18 5:19:37
Summerhaven 11 1 35N38'17 82w23'30 5:29:34
Summerlin Crossroads 31 1 35N05'03 77w57'28 5:11:50
Summit 41 1 36N06 79w46 5:19:04
Summit 42 1 36N26 77w55 5:11:40
Summit 97 1 36N11 81w17 5:25:08
Summit Hill Landing 74 1 35N35'28 77w16'32 5:09:06
Sumner 41 1 35N59 79w50 5:19:20
Sunburst 44 1 35N24'38 82w55'56 5:31:44
Sunbury 37 1 36N26'27 76w36'43 5:06:27
Sundays Landing 78 1 34N21'12 79w01'32 5:16:06
Sunny Point 10 1 34N39 77w58 5:11:52
Sunny Point 20 1 35N02'01 84w12'31 5:36:50
Sunnyside 12 1 35N41'36 81w39'27 5:26:38
Sunny Side 28 1 35N55'21 75w42'44 5:02:51
Sunnyside 34 1 36N04'09 80w13'15 5:20:53
Sunnyside 36 1 35N19'04 81w18'32 5:25:14
Sunny Side 42 1 36N26 77w55 5:11:40
Sunnyvale 56 1 35N44'22 82w08'44 5:28:35
Sunny View 75 1 35N22'27 82w11'17 5:28:45
Sunrise 96 1 35N22 77w58 5:11:52
Sunrise Beach 18 1 35N45'45 81w05'51 5:24:23
Sunset Beach 10 1 33N52 78w30 5:14:00
Sunset Harbor 10 1 34N04 78w09 5:12:36
Sunset Hills 18 1 35N44 81w21 5:25:24
Sunset Hills 41 1 36N04'26 79w49'23 5:19:18
Sunset Hills 79 1 36N29'50 79w48'42 5:19:15
Sunset Park 44 1 35N35 82w51 5:31:24
Sunshine 81 1 35N26'56 81w48'38 5:27:15
Supply 10 1 34N01'03 78w16'04 5:13:04
Surf City 71 1 34N25'37 77w32'47 5:10:11
Surl 73 1 36N17 78w57 5:15:48
Sussex 5 1 36N34 81w23 5:25:32
Sutherland 5 1 36N23'39 81w41'31 5:26:46
Sutphin 1 1 35N53'21 79w20'49 5:17:23
Suttentown 82 1 35N12'24 78w15'25 5:13:02
Sutton 31 1 34N51'22 77w57'42 5:11:51
Sutton 35 1 35N55'39 78w15'41 5:13:03
Sutton Park 90 1 34N59 80w33 5:22:12
Suttons Corner 9 1 34N38'41 78w35'34 5:14:22
Suttontown 44 1 35N36'20 83w02'46 5:32:11
Suttontown 82 1 35N12'12 78w14'27 5:12:58
Swaimtown 34 1 36N01'47 80w16'32 5:21:06
Swain 94 1 35N53 76w36 5:06:24
Swainsville 23 1 35N17'38 81w39'06 5:26:36
Swan Creek 99 1 36N10'42 80w52'09 5:23:29
Swann 17 1 36N29'29 79w29'00 5:17:56
Swann 43 1 35N22'51 79w06'33 5:16:26
Swannanoa 11 1 35N35'52 82w24'00 5:29:36
Swannanoa Hills 11 1 35N35'34 82w28'18 5:29:53
Swanquarter 48 1 35N24'22 76w19'46 5:05:19
Swansboro 67 1 34N41'15 77w07'10 5:08:29
Swan Station 53 1 35N23 79w07 5:16:28
Swayney 87 1 35N29 83w19 5:33:16
Sweetgum 38 1 35N17'28 83w46'16 5:35:05
Sweetwater 18 1 35N43'50 81w17'59 5:25:12
Sweetwater 22 1 35N04 83w53 5:35:32
Sweetwater 95 1 36N17'33 81w49'12 5:27:17
Swepsonville 1 1 36N01'16 79w21'42 5:17:27
Swift Creek 33 1 36N00 77w43 5:10:52
Swindell 7 1 35N37'24 76w41'25 5:06:46
Swindell Fork 48 1 35N26'31 76w16'47 5:05:07
Swiss 100 1 35N54'51 82w27'00 5:29:48
Sykes Landing 71 1 34N23'32 78w01'22 5:12:05
Sylva 50 2 35N22'25 83w13'34 5:32:54
Tabernacle 76 1 35N46 79w59 5:19:56
Tablerock 12 1 35N50'17 81w48'17 5:27:13
Tabor City 24 1 34N08'55 78w52'37 5:15:30
Talc Mountain 87 2 35N18'49 83w38'28 5:34:34
Talleys Crossing 34 1 36N08'03 80w07'05 5:20:28
Tallulah Gap 38 1 35N19 83w48 5:35:12
Tally Ho 39 1 36N14 78w43 5:14:52
Tamarack 95 1 36N18 81w36 5:26:24
Tants Crossroads 35 1 35N53'54 78w14'02 5:12:56
Tapoco 38 1 35N26'36 83w56'13 5:35:45
Tarawa Terrace 67 1 34N43 77w22 5:09:28
Tarboro 33 1 35N53'48 77w32'10 5:10:09
Tar Corner 15 1 36N28'37 76w17'11 5:05:09
Tarheel 9 1 34N43'59 78w47'25 5:15:10
Tarheel 37 1 36N27'23 76w51'24 5:07:26
Tarheel Landing 9 1 34N44'41 78w47'13 5:15:09
Tar Landing 10 1 34N20'03 78w05'43 5:12:23
Tar Landing 25 1 35N03'59 77w09'55 5:08:40
Tar Landing 59 1 35N48'01 76w56'09 5:07:45
Tar Landing 67 1 34N46'40 77w29'38 5:09:59
Tar Landing 82 1 34N35'44 78w15'06 5:13:00
Tar River 39 1 36N11'59 78w37'47 5:14:31
Tate Street 41 1 36N04 79w54 5:19:36
Tatums 24 1 34N24 78w53 5:15:32
Taylor 98 1 35N47 77w57 5:11:48
Taylor Crossroads 64 1 35N52'56 78w00'16 5:12:01
Taylors Bridge 82 1 34N52'51 78w15'44 5:13:03
Taylors Corner 52 1 35N00'37 77w35'23 5:10:22
Taylors Corners 52 1 35N04 77w21 5:09:24
Taylors Store 8 1 36N01 76w46 5:07:04
Taylors Store 64 1 36N05'23 77w59'15 5:11:57
Taylorsville 2 1 35N55'18 81w10'36 5:24:42
Taylorsville Beach 2 1 35N49'41 81w12'14 5:24:49
Taylortown 63 1 35N12'27 79w29'10 5:17:57
Teachey 31 1 34N46'05 78w00'30 5:12:02
Teaguetown 34 1 36N01'44 80w05'53 5:20:24
Teer 68 1 35N57'37 79w13'50 5:16:55
Tellico 57 1 35N16'32 83w31'40 5:34:07
Tenmile Fork 52 1 35N03'22 77w12'23 5:08:50
Tennelina 58 1 35N55 83w01 5:32:04
Tennessee Acres 41 1 36N06 79w46 5:19:04
Tenney Circle 68 1 35N55'15 79w02'42 5:16:11
Teresita 57 1 35N06'10 83w27'02 5:33:48
Terrace Gardens 45 1 35N20'20 82w28'56 5:29:56
Terra Ceia 7 1 35N36'04 76w45'55 5:07:04
Terra Cotta 41 1 36N03'49 79w52'03 5:19:28
Terrapin Landing 54 1 35N18'07 77w29'16 5:09:57
Terrell 18 1 35N35'21 80w58'42 5:23:55
Terrells 19 1 35N49'13 79w13'51 5:16:55
Terry Fork 58 1 35N49'17 82w26'27 5:29:46
Texaco Beach 15 1 36N17 76w05 5:04:20
Texana 20 1 35N05 84w02 5:36:08
Texans 20 1 35N06'08 84w02'17 5:36:09
Thankful 97 1 36N02'46 81w17'30 5:25:10
The Borough 71 1 34N25'47 78w06'23 5:12:26
Thelma 42 1 36N28'13 77w47'37 5:11:10
Thermal City 81 1 35N31'09 81w58'30 5:27:54
Theta 5 1 36N25 81w28 5:25:52
Thomasboro 10 1 33N56'19 78w33'20 5:14:13
Thomasboro Crossroads 10 1 33N54 78w27 5:13:48
Thomas Crossroads 63 1 35N16'59 79w30'45 5:18:03
Thomas Landing 67 1 34N29'12 77w28'36 5:09:54
Thomas Valley 50 1 35N26 83w22 5:33:28
Thomasville 29 1 35N52'57 80w04'56 5:20:20
Three Forks 87 1 35N38'41 83w15'44 5:33:03
Three Mile 6 1 36N05 81w56 5:27:44
Thurman 25 1 35N02'40 77w00'12 5:08:01
Thurmond 86 1 36N21'59 80w55'43 5:23:43
Tillery 42 1 36N15'06 77w29'09 5:09:57
Timberlake 73 1 36N17 78w57 5:15:48
Timberland 47 1 35N00'15 79w17'24 5:17:10
Timothy 82 1 35N13'31 78w27'37 5:13:50
Tin City 31 1 34N44'25 77w58'43 5:11:55
Tiny Oak Fork 48 1 35N24'24 76w17'18 5:05:09
Tipton Hill 61 1 36N02'04 82w16'04 5:29:04
Toast 86 1 36N30'01 80w37'36 5:22:30
Tobaccoville 34 1 36N14'17 80w22'18 5:21:29
Tobermory 9 1 34N48'33 78w52'38 5:15:31
Todd 5 1 36N18'34 81w35'44 5:26:23
Todds Crossroads 8 1 36N05'10 76w52'38 5:07:31
Toddville 60 1 35N16'26 80w54'48 5:23:39
Toddy 74 1 35N36 77w35 5:10:20
Toecane 61 1 36N00'32 82w11'32 5:28:46
Toe River 6 1 35N59 82w00 5:28:00
Toisnot 98 1 35N49 77w50 5:11:20
Tolar Landing 9 1 34N50'08 78w49'22 5:15:17
Tolarsville 78 1 34N45'40 78w52'21 5:15:29
Toledo 100 1 35N59'13 82w16'11 5:29:05
Toliver 5 1 36N22'06 81w36'01 5:26:24
Toluca 23 1 35N31'45 81w30'40 5:26:03
Tomahawk 82 1 34N42'40 78w19'40 5:13:19
Tom Creek 56 1 35N44'22 82w02'59 5:28:12
Tomotla 20 2 35N08'05 83w59'04 5:35:56
Topia 3 1 36N30'56 81w19'04 5:25:16
Topnot 17 1 36N22'22 79w15'34 5:17:02
Topsail 71 1 34N23'10 77w41'19 5:10:45
Topsail Beach 71 1 34N21'54 77w37'51 5:10:31
Topsy 37 1 36N30'12 76w52'16 5:07:29
Topton 20 2 35N14'49 83w42'12 5:34:49
Town Creek 10 1 34N09'54 78w05'36 5:12:22
Town Creek 98 1 35N48'54 77w48'05 5:11:12
Town Forest 45 1 35N19'14 82w29'17 5:29:57
Townsville 91 1 36N29'40 78w25'26 5:13:42
Townsville Landing 91 1 36N28'45 78w23'38 5:13:35
Tracy 95 1 36N23 81w43 5:26:52
Trading Ford 80 1 35N41'42 80w22'21 5:21:29
Tramway 53 1 35N26'40 79w12'53 5:16:52
Transou 5 1 36N24'14 81w18'02 5:25:12
Trap 8 1 36N12'24 76w52'16 5:07:29
Traphill 97 1 36N20'47 81w01'58 5:24:08
Travis 89 1 35N53'51 76w19'28 5:05:18
Treetop 5 1 36N24 81w29 5:25:56
Trent 54 1 35N10 77w44 5:10:56
Trenton 52 1 35N04'01 77w21'11 5:09:25
Trent Woods 25 1 35N05 77w06 5:08:24
Triangle 55 1 35N29 81w00 5:24:00
Triangle 92 1 35N49 78w50 5:15:20
Trinity 76 1 35N53'40 79w59'28 5:19:58
Trinity 90 1 34N50'59 80w31'52 5:22:07
Triplett 95 1 36N12'11 81w33'32 5:26:14
Trotville 37 1 36N22'08 76w35'53 5:06:24
Trout 5 1 36N23'42 81w36'34 5:26:26
Troutman 49 1 35N42'02 80w53'18 5:23:33
Troxlers Mill 41 1 36N02'25 79w40'59 5:18:44
Troy 62 1 35N21'30 79w53'41 5:19:35
Trust 58 1 35N45'09 82w52'12 5:31:29
Tryon 36 1 35N20'23 81w19'20 5:25:17
Tryon 75 1 35N12'29 82w14'19 5:28:57
Tuckahoe 52 1 35N01 77w36 5:10:24
Tuckasegee 50 1 35N16'13 83w07'22 5:32:29
Tuckaway Park 60 1 35N06'03 80w49'25 5:23:18
Tuckerdale 5 1 36N31'40 81w31'59 5:26:08
Tuckertown 64 1 35N29'12 80w10'26 5:20:42
Tugwell 74 1 35N38'53 77w37'27 5:10:30
Tull Mill 54 1 35N09'11 77w45'58 5:10:56
Tulls 27 1 36N29'28 76w04'27 5:04:18
Tulls Creek 27 1 36N27 76w01 5:04:04
Tulula 38 1 35N16'11 83w45'10 5:35:01
Tumblerville 57 1 35N06'50 83w21'51 5:33:27
Tungsten 91 1 36N30'49 78w28'14 5:13:53
Tunis 46 1 36N23'03 76w53'18 5:07:33
Turkey 82 1 34N59'32 78w11'00 5:12:44
Turkey Ford 86 1 36N23'15 80w39'47 5:22:39
Turlington 43 1 35N21'48 78w39'51 5:14:39
Turnage 33 1 35N41'18 77w39'43 5:10:39
Turnbull 9 1 34N47 78w35 5:14:20
Turnersburg 49 1 35N54'30 80w48'27 5:23:14

Place		Lat	Long	Time
Turners Crossroads 66	1	36N31'59	77w22'38	5:09:31
Turnpike 11	2	35N32'17	82w45'58	5:31:04
Turtle Mountain Indian Res 95	1	36N12	81w33	5:26:12
Tuscarora 25	1	35N09'34	77w12'51	5:08:51
Tuscola Park 44	2	35N31'23	82w57'37	5:31:50
Tusk 16	1	34N44'39	76w31'08	5:06:05
Tuskeegee 38	1	35N24'30	83w43'10	5:34:53
Tusquitee 22	1	35N05'04	83w45'57	5:35:04
Tuxedo 45	1	35N13'31	82w25'47	5:29:43
Twin Lake 10	1	33N54	78w27	5:13:48
Twin Lakes 43	1	35N14'26	78w57'27	5:15:50
Twin Lakes Estates 92	1	35N44'54	78w39'14	5:14:37
Twin Oak 71	1	34N29'44	77w53'51	5:11:35
Twin Oaks 3	1	36N31'39	81w09'48	5:24:39
Tyner 21	1	36N13	76w37	5:06:28
Tyro 29	1	35N48'32	80w22'23	5:21:30
Tyson 84	1	35N14	80w13	5:20:52
Tysonville 92	1	35N49'14	78w42'18	5:14:49
Ulah 76	1	35N38'07	79w49'37	5:19:18
Unahala 87	1	35N21'17	83w24'36	5:33:38
Unaka 20	1	35N11'43	84w08'30	5:36:34
Uncle Jimmys Landing 28	1	35N35'58	75w28'13	5:01:53
Union 46	1	36N20'01	77w01'28	5:08:06
Union 57	1	35N07'04	83w23'46	5:33:35
Union 81	1	35N19'06	81w59'28	5:27:58
Union 88	1	35N05'19	82w58'54	5:31:56
Union 90	1	34N58'53	80w43'25	5:22:54
Union Cross 34	1	36N02'54	80w07'09	5:20:29
Union Grove 7	1	35N39'54	76w36'34	5:06:26
Union Grove 49	1	36N01'28	80w51'59	5:23:28
Union Grove 99	1	36N12'27	80w36'27	5:22:26
Union Hill 45	1	35N21'05	82w20'25	5:29:22
Union Hill 99	1	36N14'25	80w28'54	5:21:56
Union Hope 64	1	35N50'33	78w13'11	5:12:53
Union Mills 81	1	35N29'16	81w57'49	5:27:51
Union Point 16	1	34N47'58	76w51'13	5:07:25
Union Ridge 1	1	36N12'27	79w24'01	5:17:36
Union Ridge 34	1	36N03'06	80w13'31	5:20:54
Unionville 90	1	35N05'14	80w30'33	5:22:02
Unity 80	1	35N47	80w35	5:22:20
University 68	1	36N02'14	79w02'09	5:16:09
University Estates 79	1	36N23'59	79w42'21	5:18:49
U-No 45	1	35N21'32	82w25'17	5:29:41
Upchurch 92	1	35N47'21	78w51'28	5:15:26
Upper 21	1	36N16	76w38	5:06:32
Upper Buck Landing 78	1	34N29'09	78w57'17	5:15:49
Upper Contoe 33	1	35N54	77w24	5:09:36
Upper Creek 12	1	35N52	81w49	5:27:16
Upper Fishing Creek 33	1	36N05	77w38	5:10:32
Upper Fork 12	1	35N39	81w39	5:26:36
Upper Hominy 11	1	35N32	82w43	5:30:52
Upper Little River 43	1	35N24	78w56	5:15:44
Upper Peachtree 20	1	35N05	84w02	5:36:08
Upper Pigeonroost 61	1	36N05'28	82w16'08	5:29:05
Upper Poplar 61	1	36N06'38	82w18'23	5:29:14
Upton 14	1	36N04'12	81w41'44	5:26:47
Upward 45	1	35N17'47	82w23'12	5:29:33
Uree 81	1	35N25'30	82w10'02	5:28:40
Uwharrie 62	1	35N24'54	80w00'14	5:20:01
Vade Mecum 85	1	36N25'07	80w18'25	5:21:14
Valdese 12	1	35N44'26	81w33'48	5:26:15
Vale 6	1	36N05'49	81w56'43	5:27:47
Vale 55	1	35N32'23	81w23'51	5:25:35
Valhalla 21	1	36N08'13	76w39'29	5:06:38
Valhalla 75	1	35N13'29	82w15'53	5:29:04
Valle Crucis 95	1	36N12'33	81w46'43	5:27:07
Valley 6	1	36N05'04	82w02'29	5:28:10
Valley 20	1	35N11	83w51	5:35:24
Valley Hill 45	1	35N17'54	82w29'00	5:29:56
Valley Springs 11	1	35N30'46	82w31'16	5:30:05
Valleytown 20	2	35N11'39	83w48'24	5:35:14
Valley View 34	1	36N09'12	80w19'05	5:21:16
Valmead 14	1	35N56'13	81w32'18	5:26:09
Vanceboro 25	1	35N18'30	77w09'16	5:08:37
Vanceboro Landing 25	1	35N17'50	77w08'44	5:08:35
Vandalia 41	1	36N00'59	79w46'36	5:19:06
Vandemere 69	1	35N11'02	76w39'50	5:06:39
Vander 26	1	35N01'55	78w47'42	5:15:11
Van Eden 71	1	34N37'06	77w57'00	5:11:48
Vannoy 97	1	36N18'48	81w16'24	5:25:06
Vantine 36	1	35N16'53	81w18'03	5:25:12
Varina 92	1	35N35	78w48	5:15:12
Varnum 10	1	34N01	78w16	5:13:04
Varnum Town 10	1	33N56'08	78w14'56	5:13:00
Vashti 2	1	35N59'52	81w06'20	5:24:25
Vass 63	1	35N15'22	79w16'57	5:17:08
Vaughan 93	1	36N25'35	78w00'14	5:12:01
Vein Mountain 56	1	35N33'07	81w57'51	5:27:51
Venable 11	1	35N31'34	82w36'25	5:30:26
Venters 74	1	35N28	77w25	5:09:40
Verona 67	1	34N40'10	77w28'19	5:09:53
Vests 20	1	35N07'25	84w12'20	5:36:49
Vicksboro 93	1	36N18'22	78w16'38	5:13:07
Victory 36	1	35N16	81w10	5:24:40
Victory Village 68	1	35N55	79w01	5:16:04
Vienna 34	1	36N08'15	80w24'08	5:21:37
Viewmont 18	1	35N44'51	81w20'15	5:25:21
Vilas 95	1	36N14'44	81w46'04	5:27:04
Village Landing 25	1	35N17'55	77w17'42	5:09:11
Vina Vista 63	1	35N10'00	79w28'19	5:17:53
Vinegar Hill 24	1	34N10'16	78w49'14	5:15:17
Vinton Woods 36	1	35N18'30	81w09'19	5:24:37
Violet 20	1	35N11'23	84w13'04	5:36:52
Virgilina 39	1	36N33	78w47	5:15:08
Vista 71	1	34N22	77w49	5:11:16
Vixen (P O) 100	1	35N52'25	82w17'54	5:29:12
Volga 58	1	35N44'56	82w40'29	5:30:42
Volunteer 85	1	36N22'04	80w25'12	5:21:41
Vultare 66	1	36N31'01	77w45'55	5:11:04
Waccamaw 10	1	34N04	78w32	5:14:08
Waco 23	1	35N21'41	81w25'44	5:25:43
Wade 26	1	35N09'46	78w44'11	5:14:57
Wade Mills 4	1	34N57'56	80w02'50	5:20:11
Wadesboro 4	1	34N58'05	80w04'37	5:20:18
Wades Point 7	1	35N32	76w37	5:06:28
Wadeville 62	1	35N16'57	79w58'12	5:19:53
Wagoner 5	1	36N24'06	81w23'12	5:25:33
Wagoner 99	1	36N09'25	80w47'40	5:23:11
Wagram 83	1	34N53'16	79w21'59	5:17:28
Wake Crossroads 92	1	35N52'59	78w30'37	5:14:02
Wakefield 92	1	35N49	78w19	5:13:16
Wake Forest 92	1	35N58'47	78w30'36	5:14:02
Wakelon 8	1	36N09'31	76w50'38	5:07:23
Wakulla 78	1	34N47'33	79w15'19	5:17:01
Wakulla 78	1	34N48	79w15	5:17:00
Walkers 71	1	34N32'26	77w51'16	5:11:25
Walkers Crossroads 92	1	35N55'32	78w30'17	5:14:01
Walkersville 90	1	34N56	80w45	5:23:00
Walkertown 11	1	35N39'12	82w20'21	5:29:21
Walkertown 34	1	36N10'31	80w09'12	5:20:37
Walkertown 43	1	35N17'08	78w48'50	5:15:15
Walkertown 80	1	35N33	80w36	5:22:24
Wallace 31	1	34N44'08	77w59'44	5:11:59
Wallace Crossroads 13	1	35N25'06	80w44'44	5:22:59
Wallace Mill 17	1	36N32'03	79w21'08	5:17:25
Walla Watta 7	1	35N35'07	76w52'26	5:07:30
Wallburg 29	1	36N00'36	80w08'22	5:20:33
Walls Landing 77	1	34N58'02	79w51'55	5:19:28
Walnut 58	1	35N50'58	82w44'20	5:30:57
Walnut Cove 85	1	36N17'43	80w08'31	5:20:34
Walnut Creek 33	1	35N53	77w38	5:10:32
Walnut Creek 58	1	35N50'50	82w40'17	5:30:41
Walnut Creek 96	1	35N22	77w58	5:11:52
Walnut Hill 5	1	36N29	81w26	5:25:44
Walser 29	1	35N46'47	80w07'18	5:20:29
Walsh 97	1	36N11	81w17	5:25:08
Walstonburg 40	1	35N36	77w42	5:10:48
Walton Crossroads 37	1	36N21'48	76w38'37	5:06:34
Waltons Store 67	1	34N45	77w26	5:09:44
Wananish 24	1	34N19'19	78w30'02	5:14:00
Wanchese 28	1	35N50'33	75w38'20	5:02:33
Wanets Landing 71	1	34N21'53	78w08'26	5:12:34
Warbler 89	1	35N35	76w14	5:04:56
Ward Corner 24	1	34N07'48	78w41'28	5:14:46
Wards 24	1	34N19	78w50	5:15:20
Wards Corner 71	1	34N32'04	78w04'20	5:12:17
Wards Store 64	1	36N06	77w43	5:10:52
Wardsville 37	1	36N24'24	76w35'07	5:06:20
Warlick 23	1	35N19	81w25	5:25:40
Warne 22	1	34N59'40	83w53'35	5:35:34
Warren Plains 93	1	36N26'33	78w09'38	5:12:39
Warrensville 5	1	36N27'38	81w31'09	5:26:05
Warrenton 93	1	36N23'54	78w09'20	5:12:37
Warren Wilson College 11	1	35N37	82w23	5:29:32
Warrior 14	1	35N54	81w31	5:26:04
Warsaw 31	1	34N59'57	78w05'29	5:12:22
Washburn 23	1	35N19'51	81w37'46	5:26:31
Washburn 81	1	35N23'35	81w49'00	5:27:16
Washington 74	1	35N32'47	77w03'09	5:08:13
Washington Forks 25	1	35N08'32	77w06'16	5:08:25
Washington Heights 74	1	35N32'58	77w02'09	5:08:09
Washington Park 7	1	35N31'57	77w01'58	5:08:08
Wasp 25	1	35N15'22	77w05'12	5:08:21
Watauga 57	1	35N11	83w23	5:33:32
Watauga 95	1	36N11	81w45	5:27:00
Waterlily 27	1	36N22'53	75w55'11	5:03:41
Waterville 44	1	35N46'16	83w06'03	5:32:24
Watery Branch 96	1	35N33'57	77w50'02	5:11:20
Watha 71	1	34N38'25	77w57'40	5:11:51
Watkins 91	1	36N16'52	78w30'20	5:14:01
Watkins Mill 57	1	35N00'21	83w18'32	5:33:14
Watson 90	1	35N04'29	80w25'45	5:21:43
Watson Crossroads 96	1	35N35'08	78w02'53	5:12:12
Watts Crossroads 13	1	35N28'18	80w27'12	5:21:49
Watts Landing 71	1	34N25'17	77w35'28	5:10:22
Waughtown 34	1	36N04'10	80w12'15	5:20:49
Waverly 58	1	35N51'34	82w27'00	5:29:48
Waves 28	1	35N34'00	75w28'08	5:01:53
Waves Landing 28	1	35N34'00	75w28'16	5:01:53
Waxhaw 90	1	34N55'28	80w44'37	5:22:58
Wayah Depot 57	1	35N09'53	83w30'43	5:34:03
Waycross 82	1	34N51'03	78w10'52	5:12:43
Waynesville 44	2	35N29'19	82w59'20	5:31:57
Wayside 47	1	34N59	79w13	5:16:52
Weaver 32	1	36N02'55	78w52'25	5:15:30
Weavers Ford 5	1	36N32'57	81w22'26	5:25:30
Weavers Landing 24	1	34N19'00	78w31'28	5:14:06
Weaverville 11	1	35N41'49	82w33'39	5:30:15
Webb 61	1	36N02'35	82w16'53	5:29:08
Webbs 55	1	35N32	81w02	5:24:08
Webster 50	1	35N20'46	83w13'10	5:32:53
Webster Junction 50	1	35N22	83w14	5:32:56
Webtown 96	1	35N22'07	77w59'16	5:11:57
Weddington 90	1	35N01'20	80w45'40	5:23:03
Weeksville 70	1	36N12'19	76w08'53	5:04:36
Wehutty 20	1	35N05'38	84w17'50	5:37:11
Welch 21	1	36N13	76w37	5:06:28
Welch Creek 24	1	34N25	78w38	5:14:32
Welcome 29	1	35N54'10	80w15'26	5:21:02
Weldon 42	1	36N25'37	77w35'45	5:10:23
Weldons Mill 91	1	36N17'25	78w19'15	5:13:17
Wellons Village 32	1	35N59	78w51	5:15:24
Welmar Heights 26	1	35N02	78w57	5:15:48
Wendell 92	1	35N46'51	78w22'12	5:13:29
Wenona 94	1	35N43'05	76w38'59	5:06:36
Wentworth 79	1	36N24'00	79w46'29	5:19:06
Wesleyan College 64	1	35N58	77w48	5:11:12
Wesley Chapel 90	1	35N00'25	80w40'29	5:22:42
Wesser 87	2	35N19'59	83w35'29	5:34:22
West 31	1	35N00	78w06	5:12:24
Westarea 26	1	35N05	78w57	5:15:48
West Asheville 11	1	35N34'40	82w35'02	5:30:20
West Bend 34	1	36N05'42	80w29'20	5:21:57
Westbrook 9	1	34N28'31	78w25'22	5:13:41
West Brook 13	1	35N31	80w38	5:22:32
Westbrooks 82	1	35N13	78w25	5:13:40
West Burlington 1	1	36N04	79w29	5:17:56
West Canton 44	2	35N32'16	82w51'30	5:31:26
West Concord 13	1	35N23'16	80w35'45	5:22:23
West Cramerton 36	1	35N15'09	81w05'17	5:24:21
West Durham 32	1	36N01	78w56	5:15:44
West End 63	1	35N14'23	79w34'04	5:18:16
Western Hills 84	1	35N16	80w26	5:21:44
Western Prong 24	1	34N27	78w46	5:15:04
Westerwood 41	1	36N04'45	79w48'14	5:19:13
Westfield 86	1	36N28'31	80w26'49	5:21:47
West Gastonia 36	1	35N17'15	81w14'40	5:24:59
West Hamlet 77	1	34N54	79w42	5:18:48
West Haven 11	1	35N28'09	82w34'36	5:30:18
West Hendersonville 45	1	35N19	82w28	5:29:52
West Highlands 34	1	36N05'54	80w16'23	5:21:06
West Hillsborough 68	1	36N04'28	79w07'11	5:16:29
West Howellsville 78	1	34N43	78w56	5:15:44
West Jefferson 5	1	36N24'13	81w29'35	5:25:58
West Jutts Creek 38	1	35N19	83w48	5:35:12
West Landing 54	1	35N19'09	77w28'08	5:09:53
West Lumberton 78	1	34N36	79w01	5:16:04
West Marion 56	1	35N39'28	82w01'32	5:28:06
West Market Street 41	1	36N04	79w50	5:19:20
Westminister 81	1	35N27'01	81w53'21	5:27:33
Westminster 81	1	35N22	81w57	5:27:48
Westmont 76	1	35N42	79w49	5:19:16
Westmore 63	1	35N30'07	79w42'54	5:18:52
West New Bern 25	1	35N06	77w05	5:08:20
West Oaks 34	1	36N04'30	80w18'13	5:21:13
West Onslow Beach 67	1	34N26'52	77w30'28	5:10:02
Westover 92	1	35N47'27	78w42'56	5:14:52
Westover 94	1	35N54'14	76w40'38	5:06:43
West Parkland 92	1	35N44'32	78w38'56	5:14:36
West Philadelphia 63	1	35N22'56	79w39'31	5:18:38
Westport 55	1	35N30'04	80w58'44	5:23:55
West Rockingham 77	1	34N56'35	79w47'14	5:19:09
West Rocky Mount 64	1	35N58	77w48	5:11:12
Westry 64	1	35N57'47	77w53'54	5:11:36
West Salem 34	1	36N04'59	80w15'08	5:21:01
West Salisbury 80	1	35N39	80w29	5:21:56
West Sanford 53	1	35N30	79w12	5:16:48
Westside 80	1	35N33	80w36	5:22:24
Wests Mill (P O) 57	1	35N15'46	83w24'34	5:33:38
West Smithfield 51	1	35N31'37	78w21'20	5:13:25
West Statesville 49	1	35N46	80w56	5:23:44
West Tarboro 33	1	35N54'20	77w32'30	5:10:10
Westview 34	1	36N06'00	80w17'33	5:21:10
West Yanceyville 17	1	36N24'22	79w23'14	5:17:33
Whalebone 28	1	35N54'48	75w36'00	5:02:24
Whaley 6	1	36N14'10	81w55'55	5:27:44
Wharton 7	1	35N32	77w02	5:08:08
Whichard 74	1	35N41'49	77w15'19	5:09:01
Whichard Beach 7	1	35N30'15	77w01'24	5:08:06
Whispering Pines 63	1	35N15'20	79w22'21	5:17:29
Whitakers 64	1	36N06'19	77w42'47	5:10:51
White Bank Landing 52	1	35N03'22	77w20'07	5:09:20
White Cross 68	1	35N55'18	79w11'16	5:16:45
Whitehall Landing 9	1	34N30'59	78w26'09	5:13:45
White Hat Landing 72	1	36N09'05	76w23'00	5:05:32
Whitehead 3	1	36N28'02	81w09'11	5:24:37
White Hill 53	1	35N22'54	79w16'51	5:17:07
Whitehouse 81	1	35N31'37	82w05'31	5:28:22
Whitehurst 74	1	35N45'57	77w19'57	5:09:20
White Lake 9	1	34N38'25	78w29'03	5:13:56
White Level 35	1	36N07'59	78w08'36	5:12:34
White Oak 9	1	34N44'58	78w42'30	5:14:50
Whiteoak 37	1	36N26'46	76w47'14	5:07:09
White Oak 41	1	36N06'23	79w46'24	5:19:06
White Oak 42	1	36N11'07	77w51'26	5:11:26
White Oak 52	1	34N53	77w12	5:08:48
White Oak 64	1	35N55'41	78w02'17	5:12:09
Whiteoak Flats 100	1	36N02'43	82w20'54	5:29:24

White Oak Heights 41 1 36N07'44 79w46'31 5:19:06
White Oak Landing 48 1 35N38'04 76w35'59 5:06:24
White Oaks 88 1 35N15'05 82w42'53 5:30:52
White Plains 48 1 35N27'05 76w01'47 5:04:07
White Plains 86 1 36N26'44 80w38'01 5:22:32
White Pond 78 1 34N26'15 79w11'46 5:16:47
Whitepost 7 1 35N29'29 76w51'05 5:07:24
White Rock 58 1 35N57'09 82w42'06 5:30:48
White Rock 95 1 36N10 81w52 5:27:28
Whites 8 1 36N06 76w47 5:07:08
Whites Chapel Church 76 1 35N49 80w15 5:21:00
Whites Creek 9 1 34N30 78w32 5:14:08
Whites Crossing 24 1 34N13'31 78w43'10 5:14:53
Whites Crossroads 8 1 36N12 76w46 5:07:04
Whites Garage 17 1 36N24 79w20 5:17:20
White Stocking 71 1 34N35'04 77w49'55 5:11:20
White Store 4 1 34N53 80w16 5:21:04
White Sulphur Springs 86 1 36N30 80w35 5:22:20
Whitetown 17 1 36N32'17 79w26'51 5:17:47
Whiteville 24 1 34N20'19 78w42'12 5:14:49
Whitewater 88 1 35N06 83w00 5:32:00
Whitfield Crossroads 54 1 35N14 77w51 5:11:24
Whitford Landing 52 1 35N03'26 77w08'48 5:08:35
Whitley Heights 51 1 35N33'19 78w23'11 5:13:33
Whitley Place 51 1 35N25'35 78w15'49 5:13:03
Whitnel 14 1 35N53'17 81w31'25 5:26:06
Whitney 84 1 35N28'20 80w08'41 5:20:35
Whitsett 41 1 36N04'16 79w33'53 5:18:16
Whitson 61 1 36N05'27 82w18'13 5:29:13
Whittier 87 2 35N26'06 83w21'37 5:33:26
Whitt Town 73 1 36N22'09 79w00'36 5:16:02
Whortonsville 69 1 35N05'44 76w37'44 5:06:31
Whortonville 69 1 35N06 76w43 5:06:52
Whynot 76 1 35N32 79w46 5:19:04
Wiccacanee 66 1 36N27 77w19 5:09:16
Wiggins Crossroads 33 1 35N49'51 77w37'49 5:10:31
Wiggins Crossroads 37 1 36N31'05 76w38'15 5:06:33
Wiggins Mill 98 1 35N41'22 77w56'49 5:11:47
Wilbanks 98 1 35N44'52 77w46'18 5:11:05
Wilbar 97 1 36N14'40 81w17'54 5:25:12
Wilbon 92 1 35N35'51 78w50'14 5:15:21
Wilbourns Store 39 1 36N29'20 78w44'38 5:14:59
Wildacres 56 1 35N49'27 82w06'22 5:28:25
Wildcat Landing 10 1 33N57'02 78w13'51 5:12:55
Wildcat Landing 46 1 36N18'24 76w50'14 5:07:21
Wilders 51 1 35N43 78w21 5:13:24
Wilders Grove 92 1 35N47'55 78w33'53 5:14:16
Wildlife Landing 25 1 35N08'39 77w02'54 5:08:12
Wildwood 16 1 34N44'55 76w49'34 5:07:18
Wilgrove 60 1 35N12'13 80w40'13 5:22:41
Wilkerson Crossroads 98 1 35N42'09 78w06'56 5:12:28
Wilkesboro 97 1 36N08'45 81w09'39 5:24:39
Wilkes Landing 25 1 35N15'05 77w07'37 5:08:30
Wilkinson 7 1 35N36'33 76w41'57 5:06:48
Wilkinson Boulevard 60 1 35N14 80w53 5:23:32
Willard 71 1 34N41'24 77w58'48 5:11:55
Willardville 32 1 36N08'20 78w51'26 5:15:26
Willeyton 37 1 36N30'18 76w43'59 5:06:56
William 19 1 35N49 79w01 5:16:04
Williams 24 1 34N12'15 78w45'47 5:15:03
Williams 96 1 35N11'09 77w58'27 5:11:54
Williamsboro 91 1 36N25'49 78w25'55 5:13:44
Williamsburg 49 1 35N59'01 80w48'50 5:23:15
Williamsburg 79 1 36N16'58 79w35'52 5:18:23
Williams Cross Roads 24 1 34N27'11 78w49'33 5:15:18
Williams Crossroads 92 1 35N39'20 78w39'59 5:14:40
Williams Cross Roads 96 1 35N11 78w04 5:12:16
Williamson Crossroads 24 1 34N21'34 78w55'19 5:15:41
Williamsons 83 1 34N46 79w36 5:18:24
Williamston 59 1 35N51'16 77w03'21 5:08:13
Williams Village 26 1 35N01'48 78w52'10 5:15:29
Willifords Landing 8 1 36N01'18 76w44'56 5:07:00
Willis Landing 16 1 34N41'44 76w47'47 5:07:11
Willis Landing 67 1 34N38'45 77w12'43 5:08:51
Williston 16 1 34N47'21 76w30'20 5:06:01
Willits 50 2 35N22 83w14 5:32:56
Willits-Ochre Hill 50 2 35N24'06 83w07'39 5:32:31
Willow 37 1 36N21 76w36 5:06:24
Willow Branch Landing 8 1 36N04'34 76w43'51 5:06:55
Willow Creek 40 1 35N31'04 77w31'48 5:10:07
Willow Green 40 1 35N28 77w25 5:09:40
Willow Spring 92 1 35N36 78w44 5:14:56
Willow Springs 51 1 35N33'08 78w31'42 5:14:07
Willow Springs 92 1 35N35'44 78w43'54 5:14:56
Wilmar 7 1 35N18 77w09 5:08:36
Wil-Mar Park 13 1 35N25'29 80w36'07 5:22:24
Wilmington 65 3 34N13'32 77w56'42 5:11:47
Wilmington Beach 65 3 34N01'07 77w53'56 5:11:36
Wilmot 50 2 35N24'08 83w18'47 5:33:15
Wilshire Park 11 2 35N35'03 82w36'43 5:30:27
Wilson 11 1 35N35'38 82w25'36 5:29:42
Wilson 98 1 35N43'16 77w54'57 5:11:40
Wilson Creek 14 1 35N58 81w46 5:27:04
Wilson Mills 51 1 35N35'02 78w21'22 5:13:25
Wilsons Creek 6 1 36N02 81w50 5:27:20
Wilsonville 19 1 35N44'11 79w00'02 5:16:00
Wilton 39 1 36N08'31 78w34'37 5:14:18
Wind Blow 77 1 35N10'17 79w40'02 5:18:40
Winders Cross Roads 99 1 36N06 80w46 5:23:04
Windom 100 1 35N55'05 82w15'18 5:29:01
Windsor 8 1 35N59'54 76w56'47 5:07:47
Windsors Crossroads 99 1 36N04'10 80w49'55 5:23:20
Windy Gap 97 1 36N07'06 80w59'23 5:23:58
Winfall 72 1 36N13'08 76w27'51 5:05:51
Wing 61 1 35N56'41 82w08'45 5:28:35
Wingate 90 1 34N59'03 80w26'58 5:21:48
Winnabow 10 1 34N08'57 78w05'38 5:12:23
Winslow 70 1 36N10'46 76w11'56 5:04:48
Winstead Crossroads 64 1 35N50'29 77w55'51 5:11:43
Winsteadville 7 1 35N27'52 76w38'10 5:06:33
Winston-Salem 34 1 36N05'59 80w14'40 5:20:59
Winter Park 65 3 34N12'37 77w53'13 5:11:33
Winterville 74 1 35N31'44 77w24'05 5:09:36
Winton 46 1 36N23'44 76w55'56 5:07:44
Wise 93 1 36N29'11 78w10'16 5:12:41
Wise Forks 52 1 35N13'04 77w30'38 5:10:03
Wisemans View 12 1 35N54'13 81w54'20 5:27:37
Wishart 78 1 34N35 78w55 5:15:40
Witherspoon Crossroad 18 1 35N40'24 81w09'00 5:24:36
Wittenberg 2 1 35N50 81w17 5:25:08
Wittys Crossroads 79 1 36N16'05 79w50'38 5:19:23
Wolf Creek 20 1 35N00'49 84w18'14 5:37:13
Wolf Ford 88 1 35N20'35 82w43'48 5:30:55
Wolf Mountain 50 1 35N12'57 82w59'12 5:31:57
Wolf Pit 77 1 34N53 79w47 5:19:08
Wolfscrape 31 1 35N08 77w59 5:11:56
Wood 35 1 36N11'03 78w03'27 5:12:14
Woodard 8 1 35N54'57 76w51'42 5:07:27
Woodard 98 1 35N44 77w55 5:11:40
Woodburn 10 1 34N15 78w03 5:12:12
Wood Dale 65 3 34N13 77w55 5:11:40
Woodfin 11 1 35N38'00 82w34'56 5:30:20
Woodford 5 1 36N20'42 81w35'27 5:26:22
Woodington 54 1 35N10'26 77w38'09 5:10:33
Woodland 66 1 36N19'53 77w12'47 5:08:51
Woodland Hills 45 1 35N21'42 82w32'13 5:30:09
Wood Landing 69 1 35N04'41 76w54'48 5:07:39
Woodlawn 1 1 36N06'36 79w17'44 5:17:11
Woodlawn 36 1 35N16 81w07 5:24:28
Woodlawn 56 1 35N47'07 82w02'26 5:28:10
Woodleaf 80 1 35N46'08 80w35'28 5:22:22
Woodleigh 27 1 36N31 75w56 5:03:44
Woodley 89 1 35N53'36 76w21'00 5:05:24
Woodrow 25 1 35N06 77w05 5:08:20
Woodrow 44 1 35N28'34 82w53'24 5:31:34
Woods Crossroads 51 1 35N19'33 78w29'45 5:13:59
Woodsdale 73 1 36N29'23 78w57'36 5:15:50
Woodside 71 1 34N25'09 77w38'51 5:10:35
Woodside Hills 11 1 35N33'14 82w40'19 5:30:41
Woodville 8 1 36N06'57 77w11'05 5:08:44
Woodville 20 2 35N11'30 83w52'58 5:35:32
Woodville 72 1 36N14'03 76w19'36 5:05:18
Woodville 86 1 36N30'06 80w28'48 5:21:55
Woodworth 91 1 36N32'17 78w22'45 5:13:31
Wooten Landing 52 1 35N03'24 77w18'36 5:09:14
Wootens Crossroads 24 1 34N26'40 78w44'29 5:14:58
Wootens Crossroads 54 1 35N09'00 77w45'51 5:11:03
Wootentown 7 1 35N32 77w02 5:08:08
Worley 58 1 35N48'20 82w47'28 5:31:10
Worry 12 1 35N49'37 81w44'15 5:26:57
Worthville 76 1 35N48'07 79w46'49 5:19:07
Wrendale 33 1 35N59'10 77w38'45 5:10:35
Wright Place 87 2 35N20'43 83w36'13 5:34:25
Wrightsboro 65 3 34N17'18 77w55'17 5:11:41
Wrightsville 65 3 34N13'14 77w49'03 5:11:16
Wrightsville Beach 65 3 34N12'30 77w47'48 5:11:11
Wyanoke 37 1 36N32'37 76w54'43 5:07:39
Wyatts Cross Roads 24 1 34N25'08 78w49'21 5:15:17
Yadkin 80 1 35N43'16 80w23'57 5:21:36
Yadkin 85 1 36N19 80w22 5:21:28
Yadkin College 29 1 35N53 80w23 5:21:32
Yadkin Junction 65 3 34N13 77w55 5:11:40
Yadkin Junction 80 1 35N40'13 80w27'34 5:21:50
Yadkin Valley 14 1 36N01'20 81w29'25 5:25:58
Yadkinville 99 1 36N08'04 80w39'35 5:22:38
Yamacraw 71 1 34N29'41 78w06'39 5:12:27
Yanceyville 17 1 36N24'14 79w20'11 5:17:21
Yates 5 1 36N17'23 81w27'33 5:25:50
Yates Hill 77 1 34N56'05 79w47'52 5:19:11
Yatesville 7 1 35N37 76w52 5:07:28
Yaupon Beach 10 1 33N54 78w05 5:12:20
Yeatsville 7 1 35N31'42 76w44'26 5:06:58
Yellow Creek 38 1 35N24'50 83w49'55 5:35:20
Yellow Gap 12 1 35N41'10 81w39'05 5:26:36
Yellow Hill Landing 16 1 34N40'40 76w57'28 5:07:50
Yeopim 72 1 36N08'35 76w31'28 5:06:06
York 93 1 36N25 78w17 5:13:08
Youngsville 35 1 36N01'29 78w28'29 5:13:54
Yow Mill 76 1 35N33'08 79w43'22 5:18:53
Zebulon 92 1 35N49'27 78w18'54 5:13:16
Zephyr 86 1 36N22'03 80w48'52 5:23:15
Zion Grove 63 1 35N20'11 79w36'09 5:18:25
Zionville 95 1 36N20'05 81w44'36 5:26:58
Zirconia (Tuxedo Station) 45 1 35N14'30 82w24'59 5:29:40

TIME TABLES

ND # 1

Date	Time	Zone
Before 11/18/1883		LMT
11/18/1883	12:00	CST
3/31/1918	02:00	CWT
10/27/1918	02:00	CST
3/30/1919	02:00	CWT
10/26/1919	02:00	CST
2/09/1942	02:00	CWT
9/30/1945	02:00	CST
4/30/1967	02:00	US#1

ND # 2

Date	Time	Zone
Before 11/18/1883		LMT
11/18/1883	12:00	CST
3/31/1918	02:00	CWT
10/27/1918	02:00	CST
3/30/1919	02:00	CWT
10/26/1919	02:00	CST
2/09/1942	02:00	CWT
9/30/1945	02:00	CST
4/28/1957	02:00	CDT
10/27/1957	02:00	CST
5/31/1958	02:00	CDT
9/02/1958	02:00	CST
5/30/1959	02:00	CDT
9/08/1959	02:00	CST
4/30/1967	02:00	US#1

ND # 3

Date	Time	Zone
Before 11/18/1883		LMT
11/18/1883	12:00	CST
3/31/1918	02:00	CWT
10/27/1918	02:00	CST
3/30/1919	02:00	CWT
10/26/1919	02:00	CST
2/09/1942	02:00	CWT
9/30/1945	02:00	CST
4/28/1957	02:00	CDT
10/27/1957	02:00	CST
4/30/1967	02:00	US#1

ND # 4

Date	Time	Zone
Before 11/18/1883		LMT
11/18/1883	12:00	CST
3/31/1918	02:00	CWT
10/27/1918	02:00	CST
3/30/1919	02:00	CWT
10/26/1919	02:00	CST
2/09/1942	02:00	CWT
9/30/1945	02:00	CST
5/13/1957	00:01	CDT
10/27/1957	02:00	CST
4/30/1967	02:00	US#1

ND # 5

Date	Time	Zone
Before 11/18/1883		LMT
11/18/1883	12:00	CST
3/31/1918	02:00	CWT
10/27/1918	02:00	CST
3/30/1919	02:00	CWT
10/26/1919	02:00	CST
2/09/1942	02:00	CWT
9/30/1945	02:00	CST
4/28/1957	02:00	CDT
5/27/1957	00:01	CST
4/30/1967	02:00	US#1

ND # 6

Date	Time	Zone
Before 11/18/1883		LMT
11/18/1883	12:00	CST
3/31/1918	02:00	CWT
10/27/1918	02:00	CST
3/30/1919	02:00	CWT
10/26/1919	02:00	CST
2/09/1942	02:00	CWT
9/30/1945	02:00	CST
4/28/1957	02:00	CDT
5/25/1957	00:01	CST
4/30/1967	02:00	US#1

ND # 7

Date	Time	Zone
Before 11/18/1883		LMT
11/18/1883	12:00	CST
3/31/1918	02:00	CWT
10/27/1918	02:00	CST
3/30/1919	02:00	CWT
10/26/1919	02:00	CST
2/09/1942	02:00	CWT
9/30/1945	02:00	CST
4/28/1957	02:00	CDT
10/27/1957	02:00	CST
5/31/1958	02:00	CDT
9/02/1958	02:00	CST
5/30/1959	02:00	CDT
9/08/1959	02:00	CST
5/30/1960	02:00	CDT
9/06/1960	02:00	CST
4/30/1967	02:00	US#1

ND # 8

Date	Time	Zone
Before 11/18/1883		LMT
11/18/1883	12:00	CST
3/31/1918	02:00	CWT
10/27/1918	02:00	CST
3/30/1919	02:00	CWT
10/26/1919	02:00	CST
2/09/1942	02:00	CWT
9/30/1945	02:00	CST
4/28/1957	02:00	CDT
10/27/1957	02:00	CST
5/31/1958	02:00	CDT
9/02/1958	02:00	CST
5/30/1959	02:00	CDT
9/08/1959	02:00	CST
5/22/1960	02:00	CDT
9/22/1960	02:00	CST
4/30/1967	02:00	US#1

ND # 9

Date	Time	Zone
Before 11/18/1883		LMT
11/18/1883	12:00	MST
3/31/1918	02:00	MWT
10/27/1918	02:00	MST
3/30/1919	02:00	MWT
10/26/1919	02:00	MST
2/09/1942	02:00	MWT
9/30/1945	02:00	MST
4/30/1967	02:00	US#1

ND # 10

Date	Time	Zone
Before 11/18/1883		LMT
11/18/1883	12:00	MST
3/31/1918	02:00	MWT
10/27/1918	02:00	MST
3/30/1919	02:00	MWT
10/26/1919	02:00	MST
2/09/1942	02:00	MWT
9/30/1945	02:00	MST
5/15/1952	02:00	MDT
9/15/1952	02:00	MST
5/15/1953	02:00	MDT
9/15/1953	02:00	MST
5/15/1954	02:00	MDT
9/15/1954	02:00	MST
5/15/1955	02:00	MDT
9/15/1955	02:00	MST
5/15/1956	02:00	MDT
9/15/1956	02:00	MST
5/15/1957	02:00	MDT
9/15/1957	02:00	MST
5/15/1958	02:00	MDT
9/15/1958	02:00	MST
5/15/1959	02:00	MDT
9/15/1959	02:00	MST
5/15/1960	02:00	CST
4/30/1967	02:00	US#1

COUNTIES

1 Adams
2 Barnes
3 Benson
4 Billings
5 Bottineau
6 Bowman
7 Burke
8 Burleigh
9 Cass
10 Cavalier
11 Dickey
12 Divide
13 Dunn
14 Eddy
15 Emmons
16 Foster
17 Golden Valley
18 Grand Forks
19 Grant
20 Griggs
21 Hettinger
22 Kidder
23 Lamoure
24 Logan
25 McHenry
26 McIntosh
27 McKenzie
28 McLean
29 Mercer
30 Morton
31 Mountrail
32 Nelson
33 Oliver
34 Pembina
35 Pierce
36 Ramsey
37 Ransom
38 Renville
39 Richland
40 Rolette
41 Sargent
42 Sheridan
43 Sioux
44 Slope
45 Stark
46 Steele
47 Stutsman
48 Towner
49 Traill
50 Walsh
51 Ward
52 Wells
53 Williams

Place		Latitude	Longitude	Time
Abercrombie 39	1	46N26'52	96W43'48	6:26:55
Absaraka 9	1	46N58'41	97W23'39	6:29:35
Adams 50	1	48N25'17	98W04'43	6:32:19
Adrian 23	1	46N36'00	98W33'11	6:34:13
Agate 48	1	48N37'22	99W29'34	6:37:58
Akra 34	1	48N46'31	97W43'36	6:30:54
Alamo 53	1	48N34'54	103W28'10	6:53:53
Alexander 27	1	47N50'35	103W38'32	6:54:34
Alfred 23	1	46N36'11	98W59'56	6:36:00
Alice 9	1	46N45'43	97W33'20	6:30:13
Alkabo 12	1	48N51'46	103W53'23	6:55:34
Almont 30	9	46N43'31	101W30'08	6:46:01
Alsen 10	1	48N37'50	98W42'16	6:34:49
Alton 49	1	47N21'20	97W02'43	6:28:11
Ambrose 12	1	48N57'14	103W28'56	6:53:56
Amenia 9	1	47N00'18	97W13'07	6:28:52
Amidon 44	9	46N28'56	103W19'17	6:53:17
Amourdale 48	1	48N52'17	99W22'21	6:37:29
Anamoose 25	1	47N52'57	100W14'27	6:40:58
Aneta 32	1	47N40'46	97W59'16	6:31:57
Anselm 37	1	46N31'43	97W29'43	6:29:59
Antelope 45	9	46N51'21	102W12'08	6:48:49
Antler 5	1	48N58'15	101W16'55	6:45:08
Appam 53	1	48N34'12	103W35'18	6:54:21
Apple Valley 8	1	46N49'18	100W35'51	6:42:23
Ardoch 50	1	48N12'26	97W20'31	6:29:22
Arena 8	1	47N07'38	100W09'43	6:40:39
Argusville 9	1	47N03'08	96W56'03	6:27:44
Arndt 48	1	48N37'48	99W14'06	6:36:56
Arnegard 27	1	47N48'28	103W26'26	6:53:46
Arnold 8	1	46N55'26	100W45'11	6:43:01
Arthur 9	1	47N06'15	97W13'04	6:28:52
Arvilla 18	1	47N55'09	97W29'40	6:29:59
Ashley 26	1	46N01'53	99W22'43	6:37:31
Atcoal 7	1	48N54'05	102W54'41	6:51:39
Auburn 50	1	48N30'25	97W26'22	6:29:45
Aurelia 51	1	48N31	101W53	6:47:32
Avoca 53	1	48N11'06	103W31'25	6:54:06
Avrelia 51	1	48N28'00	101W54'06	6:47:36
Aylmer 35	1	47N56'03	100W11'33	6:40:46
Ayr 9	1	47N02'28	97W29'25	6:29:58
Backoo 34	1	48N50'12	97W42'36	6:30:50
Baden 51	1	48N35'14	102W00'13	6:48:01
Baker 3	1	48N09'38	99W38'50	6:38:35
Baldwin 8	1	47N01'36	100W44'57	6:43:00
Balfour 25	1	47N57'06	100W32'03	6:42:08
Balta 35	1	48N10'00	100W02'12	6:40:09
Banks 27	1	48N02'19	103W11'39	6:52:47
Bantry 25	1	48N29'54	100W36'36	6:42:26
Barks Spur 48	1	48N38	99W06	6:36:24
Barlow 16	1	47N34'11	99W08'15	6:36:33
Barney 39	1	46N16'02	97W00'01	6:28:00
Barrie 39	1	46N34'08	97W07'20	6:28:29
Bartlett 36	1	48N02'41	98W25'55	6:33:44
Barton 35	1	48N30'25	100W10'33	6:40:42
Bathgate 34	1	48N52'38	97W28'33	6:29:54
Battleview 7	1	48N34'44	102W47'31	6:51:10
Bayne 39	1	46N10'03	96W55'39	6:27:43
Beach 17	9	46N55'05	104W00'14	6:56:01
Belcourt 40	1	48N50'21	99W44'40	6:38:59
Belden 31	1	48N09'05	102W21'25	6:49:26
Belfield 45	9	46N53'07	103W11'57	6:52:48
Belmar 5	1	48N39'39	100W19'38	6:41:19
Benedict 28	1	47N49'49	101W04'55	6:44:20
Benson Corner 23	1	46N29'09	98W12'04	6:32:48
Bentley 21	9	46N19'45	102W03'47	6:48:15
Berea 2	1	46N56'03	98W05'41	6:32:23
Bergen 25	1	48N00'06	100W42'51	6:42:51
Berlin 23	1	46N22'43	98W29'22	6:33:57
Berthold 51	1	48N18'47	101W44'12	6:46:57
Berwick 35	1	48N21'40	100W14'46	6:40:59
Beulah 29	9	47N15'48	101W46'39	6:47:07
Big Bend 28	1	47N33	101W13	6:44:52
Binford 20	1	47N33'43	98W20'41	6:33:23
Bisbee 48	1	48N37'33	99W22'39	6:37:31
Bismarck 8	1	46N48'30	100W47'00	6:43:08
Blabon 46	1	47N24'06	97W47'19	6:31:09
Blackmer 39	1	45N58'44	96W36'01	6:26:24
Blaisdell 31	1	48N20'10	102W04'35	6:48:18
Blanchard 49	1	47N20'45	97W13'09	6:28:53
Bloom 47	1	46N54'59	98W36'45	6:34:27
Bluegrass 30	9	46N56'57	101W34'53	6:46:20
Bonetraill 53	1	48N24'59	103W50'17	6:55:21
Bordulac 16	1	47N23'16	98W57'49	6:35:51
Bottineau 5	1	48N49'38	100W26'43	6:41:47
Bounty 12	1	48N54'58	103W10'49	6:52:43
Bowbells 7	1	48N48'11	102W14'44	6:48:59
Bowdon 52	1	47N28'11	99W42'27	6:38:50
Bowesmont 34	1	48N41'24	97W10'40	6:28:43
Bowman 6	9	46N10'59	103W23'40	6:53:35
Braddock 15	1	46N33'52	100W05'26	6:40:22
Brampton 41	1	45N59'41	97W46'33	6:31:06
Brantford 14	1	47N35'52	98W55'21	6:35:41
Breien 30	9	46N22'48	100W56'31	6:43:46
Bremen 52	1	47N44'48	99W23'11	6:37:33
Brinsmade 3	1	48N10'57	99W19'25	6:37:18
Brisbane 19	9	46N20'33	101W29'26	6:45:58
Brittin 8	1	46N42'55	100W24'19	6:41:37
Brocket 36	1	48N12'47	98W21'24	6:33:26
Brooktree Park 9	2	47N00'11	96W53'44	6:27:35
Buchanan 47	1	47N03'45	98W49'43	6:35:19
Bucyrus 1	9	46N03'50	102W47'16	6:51:09
Buffalo 9	1	46N55'11	97W32'57	6:30:12
Buffalo Springs 6	9	46N10'30	103W14'04	6:52:56
Buford 53	1	47N59'55	103W59'27	6:55:58
Burlington 51	1	48N16'31	101W25'42	6:45:43
Burnstad 24	1	46N23'08	99W37'56	6:38:32
Burt 21	9	46N21'55	102W09'17	6:48:37
Butte 28	1	47N50'17	100W39'54	6:42:40
Buttzville 37	1	46N30'29	97W37'46	6:30:31
Buxton 49	1	47N36'07	97W05'49	6:28:23
Caledonia 49	1	47N27'27	96W53'07	6:27:32
Calio 10	1	48N37'52	98W55'57	6:35:44
Calspur 18	2	47N56'00	97W05'16	6:28:21
Calvin 10	1	48N51'09	98W56'06	6:35:44
Cando 48	1	48N29'12	99W12'34	6:36:50
Cannon Ball 43	9	46N23'22	100W35'37	6:42:22
Canton 34	1	48N41	97W40	6:30:40
Carbury 5	1	48N53'27	100W32'39	6:42:11
Carpio 51	1	48N26'33	101W42'51	6:46:51
Carrington 16	1	47N26'59	99W07'33	6:36:30
Carson 19	9	46N25'04	101W33'52	6:46:15
Cartwright 27	9	47N51'35	103W55'33	6:55:42
Cashel 50	1	48N29'05	97W17'54	6:29:12
Casselton 9	1	46N54'02	97W12'39	6:28:51
Cathay 52	1	47N33'12	99W24'31	6:37:38
Cavalier 34	1	48N47'38	97W37'19	6:30:29
Cayuga 41	1	46N04'27	97W23'02	6:29:32
Center 33	9	47N06'59	101W17'57	6:45:12
Central Morton 30	9	46N50	101W30	6:46:00
Central Pierce 35	1	48N09	100W03	6:40:12
Chadwick 43	9	46N09'35	101W02'02	6:44:08
Chaffee 9	1	46N46'28	97W21'08	6:29:25
Chama 17	9	46N54'28	103W54'35	6:55:38
Charbonneau 27	1	47N51'12	103W45'46	6:55:03
Charlson 27	1	48N03'37	102W52'15	6:51:29
Chaseley 52	1	47N27'01	99W49'11	6:39:17
Chola 38	1	48N37'20	101W29'25	6:45:58
Christine 39	1	46N34'25	96W48'05	6:27:12
Churchs Ferry 36	1	48N16'09	99W11'23	6:36:46
Clement 11	1	46N09'16	98W14'38	6:32:59
Clementsville 47	1	47N02'16	98W29'34	6:33:58
Cleveland 47	1	46N53'30	99W07'03	6:36:28
Clifford 49	1	47N20'53	97W24'37	6:29:38
Clifton 35	1	47N53'28	100W02'02	6:40:08
Clyde 10	1	48N46'12	98W53'55	6:35:36
Coburn 37	1	46N37'04	97W22'15	6:29:29
Cogswell 41	1	46N06'25	97W46'54	6:31:08
Cole Ford 25	1	48N31'45	100W27'46	6:41:51
Coleharbor 28	1	47N32'39	101W13'24	6:44:54
Colfax 39	1	46N28'10	96W52'27	6:27:30
Colgan 12	1	48N56'54	103W37'40	6:54:31
Colgate 20	1	47N14'41	97W39'22	6:30:37
Columbus 7	1	48N54'15	102W46'48	6:51:07
Comstock 3	1	48N09'03	99W23'38	6:37:35
Concrete 34	1	48N44'44	97W56'03	6:31:44
Considine 48	1	48N33'43	99W16'58	6:37:08
Conway 50	1	48N14'18	97W40'29	6:30:42
Cooperstown 20	1	47N26'40	98W07'25	6:32:30
Corinth 53	1	48N36'45	103W19'38	6:53:19
Coteau 7	1	48N45'24	102W19'07	6:49:16
Coulee 31	1	48N32'43	102W00'40	6:48:03
Courtenay 47	1	47N13'20	98W33'58	6:34:16
Crary 36	1	48N04'15	98W38'17	6:34:33
Crete 41	1	46N12'01	97W57'45	6:31:51
Crocus 48	1	48N42'32	99W09'40	6:36:39
Croff 27	1	47N44'50	102W56'27	6:51:46
Crosby 12	1	48N54'51	103W17'40	6:53:11
Crystal 34	1	48N35'49	97W40'09	6:30:41
Crystal Springs 22	1	46N52'42	99W28'31	6:37:54
Cuba 2	1	46N49'17	97W51'44	6:31:27
Cummings 49	1	47N30'53	97W04'45	6:28:19
Daglum 45	9	46N42'32	103W01'12	6:52:05
Dahlen 32	1	48N09'29	97W55'45	6:31:43
Daily 2	1	46N43'03	97W58'33	6:31:54
Dakota Boys Ranch 51	1	48N20	101W19	6:45:16
Dana 15	1	46N34'36	100W14'00	6:40:56
Danzig 26	1	46N08'17	99W28'28	6:37:54
Darby 36	1	48N09'13	98W58'02	6:35:52
Davenport 9	1	46N42'51	97W04'11	6:28:17
Dawson 22	1	46N52'07	99W45'04	6:39:00
Dazey 2	1	47N11'26	98W12'05	6:32:48
Deering 25	1	48N23'44	101W03'05	6:44:12
Deisem 23	1	46N26'33	98W47'22	6:35:09
De Lamere 41	1	46N16'02	97W20'05	6:29:20
De Mores 17	9	46N55'19	103W44'31	6:54:58
Denbigh 25	1	48N18'55	100W35'12	6:42:21
Dengate 30	9	46N50'44	101W38'06	6:46:32
Denhoff 42	1	47N28'36	100W15'33	6:41:02
Derrick 36	1	48N28'37	98W33'26	6:34:14
De Sart 44	9	46N22'44	102W57'28	6:51:50
Des Lacs 51	1	48N15'28	101W33'47	6:46:15
Des Lacs Valley 51	1	48N39	102W01	6:48:04
De Villo 39	1	46N03'56	96W38'14	6:26:33

Devils Lake 36 3 48N06'46 98w51'53 6:35:28
Dickey 23 1 46N32'13 98w28'03 6:33:52
Dickinson 45 9 46N52'45 102w47'21 6:51:09
Divide 14 1 47N46'11 99w07'28 6:36:30
Dodge 13 9 47N18'22 102w12'14 6:48:49
Dogden Butte 28
1 47N46 100w50 6:43:20
Donnybrook 51 1 48N30'34 101w53'05 6:47:32
Dore 27 9 47N55'14 104w01'50 6:56:07
Double Ditch Indian Village 8
1 46N56'11 100w54'02 6:43:36
Douglas 51 1 47N51'26 101w30'09 6:46:01
Dover 52 1 47N27'37 99w16'33 6:37:06
Doyon 36 1 48N03'10 98w32'11 6:34:09
Drady 51 1 48N09'07 101w25'31 6:45:42
Drake 25 1 47N55'27 100w22'19 6:41:29
Drayton 34 3 48N34'16 97w10'39 6:28:43
Dresden 10 1 48N49'39 98w28'51 6:33:55
Driscoll 8 1 46N50'39 100w08'28 6:40:34
Duane 11 1 46N04'20 98w32'31 6:34:10
Dundas 14 1 47N38'24 99w01'45 6:36:07
Dunn Center 13 9 47N21'13 102w37'12 6:50:29
Dunning 5 1 48N43'10 101w02'22 6:44:09
Dunseith 40 1 48N48'47 100w03'38 6:40:15
Durbin 9 1 46N48'31 97w08'57 6:28:36
Durupt 47 1 47N05'43 98w28'11 6:33:53
Dwight 39 1 46N18'15 96w44'16 6:26:57
Eagle Nest 30 9 46N51'09 101w55'26 6:47:42
Easby 10 1 48N42'37 98w15'11 6:33:01
East Adams 1 9 46N04 102w12 6:48:48
East Bowman 6 9 46N08 103w15 6:53:00
East Eddy 14 1 47N45 98w43 6:34:52
Eastedge 2 1 46N39'24 97w53'31 6:31:34
East Fairview 27
9 47N51'12 104w02'21 6:56:09
East Foster 16 1 47N28 98w41 6:34:44
East Griggs 20 1 47N27 98w07 6:32:28
East Hettinger 21
9 46N26 102w22 6:49:28
East Kidder 22 1 46N58 99w38 6:38:32
East La Moure 23
1 46N29 98w18 6:33:12
East Logan 24 1 46N27 99w16 6:37:04
East Mercer 29 9 47N23 101w38 6:46:32
East Ramsey 36 1 48N14 98w27 6:33:48
East Sheridan 42
1 47N31 100w12 6:40:48
East Slope 44 9 46N28 103w07 6:52:28
East Stark 45 9 46N48 102w20 6:49:20
Eckelson 2 1 46N56'17 98w19'58 6:33:20
Eckman 5 1 48N39'29 101w03'27 6:44:14
Edgeley 23 1 46N21'33 98w42'55 6:34:52
Edinburg 50 1 48N29'48 97w51'42 6:31:27
Edmore 36 1 48N24'48 98w27'14 6:33:49
Edmunds 47 1 47N14'50 98w58'04 6:35:52
Egeland 48 1 48N37'35 99w05'49 6:36:23
Eland 45 9 46N51'44 102w52'53 6:51:32
Eldridge 47 1 46N54'09 98w51'05 6:35:24
Elgin 19 9 46N24'14 101w50'44 6:47:23
Ellendale 11 1 46N00'10 98w31'36 6:34:06
Elliott 37 1 46N24'08 97w48'52 6:31:15
Elmore 39 8 46N11'45 96w36'18 6:26:25
Embden 9 1 46N48'08 97w25'58 6:29:44
Emerado 18 1 47N55'08 97w21'53 6:29:28
Emerson 13 9 47N11'01 102w38'04 6:50:32
Emmet 51 1 47N38'47 101w39'11 6:46:37
Emrick 52 1 47N35'41 99w30'42 6:38:03
Enderlin 37 1 46N37'23 97w36'04 6:30:24
Englevale 37 1 46N23'34 97w54'47 6:31:39
Enloe 39 1 46N29'59 96w45'26 6:27:02
Epping 53 1 48N16'45 103w21'24 6:53:26
Epworth 31 1 48N06'58 102w13'26 6:48:54
Erie 9 1 47N06'55 97w23'15 6:29:33
Erie Junction 9
1 47N05'36 97w23'03 6:29:32
Esmond 3 1 48N02'09 99w45'42 6:39:03
Essex 36 1 48N07'21 98w44'44 6:34:59
Everest 9 1 46N51'35 97w13'15 6:28:53
Fairdale 50 1 48N29'27 98w13'51 6:32:55
Fairfield 4 9 47N11'22 103w13'18 6:52:53
Fairmount 39 1 46N03'18 96w36'07 6:26:24
Fairview Junction 39
1 46N16'06 96w49'25 6:27:18
Falkirk 28 1 47N21'43 101w05'39 6:44:23
Fallon 30 9 46N30'44 101w05'26 6:44:22
Fargo 9 7 46N52'38 96w47'22 6:27:09
Farmington 39 1 46N16'04 96w45'04 6:27:00
Fayette 13 9 47N15'42 102w56'36 6:51:46
Fessenden 52 1 47N38'57 99w37'44 6:38:31
Fife 9 7 46N53'07 96w57'50 6:27:51
Fillmore 3 1 48N10'49 99w48'01 6:39:12
Fingal 2 1 46N45'38 97w47'24 6:31:10
Finley 46 5 47N30'51 97w50'08 6:31:21
Flasher 30 9 46N27'22 101w13'56 6:44:56
Flaxton 7 1 48N53'55 102w23'31 6:49:34
Fleece 34 1 48N45'37 97w12'23 6:28:50
Flora 3 1 47N57'01 99w25'03 6:37:40
Fonda 40 1 48N40'11 100w01'06 6:40:04
Forbes 11 1 45N56'37 98w46'54 6:35:08
Fordville 50 1 48N13'03 97w47'25 6:31:10
Forest River 50
1 48N12'55 97w28'04 6:29:52
Forest River Colony 18
1 48N10'56 97w42'11 6:30:49
Forfar 5 1 48N34'14 101w17'53 6:45:12
Forman 41 1 46N06'28 97w38'10 6:30:33
Fort Berthold Indian Res 13
1 47N59 102w29 6:49:56
Fort Clark 33 9 47N14'24 101w15'06 6:45:00
Fort Lincoln Estates 8
1 46N49 100w47 6:43:08
Fort Ransom 37 1 46N31'15 97w55'33 6:31:42
Fort Rice 30 1 46N31'34 100w35'02 6:42:20
Fort Totten 3 1 47N58'48 98w59'33 6:35:58
Fort Totten Indian Res 3
1 47N59 99w00 6:36:00
Fortuna 12 1 48N54'36 103w46'44 6:55:07
Fort Yates 43 9 46N05'32 100w37'43 6:42:31
Four Bears 27 1 47N54 102w49 6:51:16
Four Bears Health Center 27
1 47N59 102w29 6:49:56
Foxholm 51 1 48N22'10 101w34'15 6:46:17
Frazier 2 1 47N10 98w27 6:33:48
Freda 19 9 46N20'50 101w10'24 6:44:42
Fredonia 24 1 46N19'34 99w05'37 6:36:22
Fried 47 1 47N02'45 98w39'27 6:34:38
Frontier Village 47
1 46N53'22 99w42'01 6:34:48
Fryburg 4 9 46N52'14 103w18'09 6:53:13
Fullerton 11 1 46N09'55 98w25'36 6:33:42
Funston 25 1 47N59'45 100w15'46 6:41:03
Gackle 24 1 46N37'33 99w08'30 6:36:34
Galchutt 39 1 46N23'15 96w48'33 6:27:14
Galesburg 49 1 47N16'12 97w24'22 6:29:37
Gardar 34 1 48N35'21 97w52'25 6:31:30
Gardena 5 1 48N42'03 100w29'50 6:41:59
Gardner 9 1 47N08'50 96w58'03 6:27:52
Garrison 28 1 47N39'08 101w24'55 6:45:40
Garske 36 1 48N21'28 98w52'37 6:35:30
Gascoyne 6 9 46N07'06 103w04'46 6:52:19
Geneseo 41 1 46N04'26 97w16'42 6:29:07
Genoa 25 1 48N11'37 100w59'38 6:43:59
Gilby 18 1 48N05'07 97w28'13 6:29:53
Gladstone 45 9 46N51'39 102w34'03 6:50:16
Gladys 53 1 48N29'43 103w49'11 6:55:17
Glasston 34 1 48N42'21 97w26'50 6:29:47
Glenburn 38 1 48N30'47 101w13'13 6:44:53
Glenfield 16 1 47N27'12 98w34'01 6:34:16
Glen Ullin 30 9 46N48'54 101w49'46 6:47:19
Glenwood Estates 8
1 46N49 100w47 6:43:08
Glover 11 1 46N14'30 98w08'19 6:32:33
Golden Valley 29
9 47N17'27 102w03'51 6:48:15
Goldwin 47 1 47N08'56 99w12'03 6:36:48
Golva 17 9 46N44'03 103w59'09 6:55:57
Goodrich 42 1 47N28'30 100w07'33 6:40:30
Gorham 4 9 47N08'55 103w18'25 6:53:14
Grace City 16 1 47N33'05 98w48'18 6:35:13
Grafton 50 3 48N24'44 97w24'37 6:29:38
Grand Forks 18 2 47N55'31 97w01'57 6:28:08
Grand Forks Air Force Base 18
1 47N56 97w12 6:28:48
Grand Harbor 36
1 48N10'11 98w59'02 6:35:56
Grandin 9 1 47N14'13 97w00'04 6:28:00
Grand Rapids 23
1 46N26'40 98w22'13 6:33:29
Grano 38 1 48N36'54 101w35'10 6:46:21
Granville 25 1 48N16'04 100w50'32 6:43:22
Grassna 15 1 46N05'16 100w17'43 6:41:11
Grassy Butte 27
9 47N23'33 103w14'51 6:52:59
Great Bend 39 1 46N09'14 96w48'06 6:27:12
Green Acres Estates 8
1 46N49 100w47 6:43:08
Greene 38 1 48N39'23 101w42'03 6:46:48
Greenfield 49 1 47N16'28 97w13'02 6:28:52
Grenora 53 1 48N37'06 103w56'15 6:55:45
Griffin 6 9 46N12'57 103w32'25 6:54:10
Guelph 11 1 46N01'22 98w14'08 6:32:57
Guptill 16 1 47N30'56 99w08'17 6:36:33
Guthrie 25 1 48N00'04 100w22'37 6:41:30
Guyson 24 1 46N17'51 99w12'18 6:36:49
Gwinner 41 1 46N13'33 97w39'44 6:30:39
Hague 15 1 46N01'43 99w59'43 6:39:59
Haley 6 9 45N57'41 103w07'08 6:52:29
Halliday 13 9 47N21'16 102w20'08 6:49:21
Hallson 34 1 48N45'50 97w49'03 6:31:16
Hamar 14 1 47N50'37 98w34'23 6:34:18
Hamberg 52 1 47N45'47 99w30'51 6:38:03
Hamilton 34 1 48N48'31 97w27'09 6:29:49
Hamlet 53 1 48N37'43 103w03'04 6:52:12
Hamlin 41 1 46N09'58 97w17'05 6:29:08
Hampden 36 1 48N32'25 98w39'14 6:34:37
Hample 41 1 46N08'14 97w58'39 6:31:55
Hankinson 39 1 46N04'11 96w54'05 6:27:36
Hanks 53 1 48N36'12 103w48'09 6:55:13
Hanks Corner 34
1 48N45'32 97w56'58 6:31:48
Hannaford 20 1 47N18'48 98w11'10 6:32:45
Hannah 10 1 48N58'18 98w41'29 6:34:46
Hannah Junction 18
1 47N55'31 97w40'00 6:30:40
Hannover 33 9 47N06'41 101w25'34 6:45:42
Hansboro 48 1 48N57'00 99w22'57 6:37:32
Harding 27 9 47N51'12 104w00'53 6:56:04
Harlow 3 1 48N09'49 99w31'07 6:38:04
Harmon 30 9 46N57'06 100w57'08 6:43:49
Hartland 51 1 48N23'58 101w49'12 6:47:17
Harvey 52 1 47N46'11 99w56'06 6:39:44
Harwood 9 2 46N58'46 96w52'49 6:27:31
Hastings 2 1 46N41'02 98w05'39 6:32:23
Hatton 49 1 47N38'23 97w27'11 6:29:49
Havana 41 1 45N57'01 97w37'07 6:30:28
Havelock 21 9 46N28'29 102w44'36 6:50:58
Haynes 1 9 45N58'27 102w28'14 6:49:53
Hazelton 15 1 46N29'05 100w16'45 6:41:07
Hazen 29 9 47N17'40 101w37'20 6:46:29
Heart Butte 19 9 46N29 101w52 6:47:28
Heaton 52 1 47N28'42 99w32'51 6:38:11
Hebron 30 9 46N54'02 102w02'42 6:48:11
Heil 19 9 46N23'15 101w41'58 6:46:48
Heimdal 52 1 47N47'34 99w38'41 6:38:35
Hensel (Canton) 34
1 48N41'18 97w39'58 6:30:40
Hensler 33 9 47N15'37 101w05'04 6:44:20
Herrick 50 1 48N30'50 97w13'41 6:28:55
Herriott 50 1 48N21'16 97w23'20 6:29:33
Hesnault 51 1 48N03'01 101w33'26 6:46:14
Hesper 3 1 47N59'11 99w37'46 6:38:31
Hettinger 1 9 46N00'05 102w38'11 6:50:33
Hickson 9 1 46N40'10 96w48'36 6:27:14
Hillsboro 49 1 47N24'14 97w03'42 6:28:15
Hirschville 13 9 47N04'05 102w33'48 6:50:15
Holmes 18 1 47N42'57 97w17'47 6:29:11
Home On The Range For Boys 17
9 46N55 103w50 6:55:20
Homer 47 1 46N50'52 98w40'16 6:34:41
Honeyford 18 1 48N02'00 97w28'13 6:29:53
Hoople 50 1 48N32'05 97w38'04 6:30:32
Hope 46 1 47N19'20 97w43'19 6:30:53
Horace 9 1 46N45'32 96w54'12 6:27:37
Hovey Mobile Park 10
1 48N29 98w14 6:32:56
Hoving 41 1 46N14'51 97w34'04 6:30:16
Huff 30 10 46N37'26 100w39'05 6:42:36
Hull 15 1 46N01'43 100w07'28 6:40:30
Hunter 9 1 47N11'26 97w13'00 6:28:52
Hurd 5 1 48N38'46 101w13'03 6:44:52
Hurdsfield 52 1 47N26'54 99w55'41 6:39:43
Independence 23
1 46N20'28 98w11'37 6:32:46
Inkster 18 1 48N09'05 97w38'38 6:30:35
Isabel 3 1 48N03'53 99w39'11 6:38:37
Ives 6 9 46N16'15 103w44'20 6:54:57
Jamestown 47 1 46N54'38 98w42'29 6:34:50
Jamestown Junction 47
1 46N51'48 98w40'14 6:34:41
Jessie 20 1 47N32'32 98w14'16 6:32:57
Johnson 47 1 46N58'47 98w30'22 6:34:01
Johnson Ford 19
9 46N34'51 101w45'13 6:47:01
Johnsons Corner 27
1 47N48'15 102w56'28 6:51:46
Johnstown 18 1 48N08'39 97w28'11 6:29:53
Joliette 34 1 48N49'05 97w13'38 6:28:55
Josephine 3 1 47N56'23 99w18'49 6:37:15
Juanita 16 1 47N30'08 98w41'01 6:34:44
Jud 23 1 46N31'34 98w53'43 6:35:35
Judson 30 9 46N49'35 101w16'41 6:45:07
Juno 12 1 48N53'54 103w12'13 6:52:49
Karlsruhe 25 1 48N05'24 100w37'12 6:42:29
Karnak 20 1 47N16'51 98w03'50 6:32:15
Kathryn 2 1 46N40'41 97w58'06 6:31:52
Keene 27 1 47N55'37 102w56'28 6:51:46
Keith 36 1 48N05'36 98w45'08 6:35:01
Kellogg 50 3 48N21'47 97w25'37 6:29:42
Kelso 49 1 47N19'23 97w01'45 6:28:07
Kelvin 40 1 48N56'14 100w03'02 6:40:12
Kempton 18 1 47N49'08 97w36'50 6:30:27
Kenaston 51 1 48N37'07 102w06'44 6:48:27
Kenmare 51 1 48N40'29 102w04'56 6:48:20
Kensal 47 1 47N18'03 98w43'59 6:34:56
Kermit 12 1 48N54'12 103w02'45 6:52:11
Kerry 50 1 48N27'23 97w48'14 6:31:13
Kief 25 1 47N51'27 100w30'40 6:42:03
Killdeer 13 9 47N22'19 102w45'13 6:51:01
Kincaid 7 1 48N53'14 102w47'11 6:51:09
Kindred 9 1 46N38'55 97w01'00 6:28:04
Kintyre 15 1 46N32'59 99w56'57 6:39:48
Kloten 32 1 47N42'58 98w04'30 6:32:18
Kloze 47 1 46N48'02 98w44'22 6:34:57
Knox 3 1 48N20'25 99w41'24 6:38:46
Koldok 2 1 46N55'43 97w43'24 6:30:54
Kongsberg 25 1 47N51'05 100w48'03 6:43:12
Kramer 5 1 48N41'26 100w42'23 6:42:50
Kulm 23 1 46N18'04 98w57'15 6:35:49
Kuroki 5 1 48N55'52 101w08'46 6:44:35
Ladoga 22 1 46N52'34 99w33'45 6:38:15
Lake Jessie 53 1 48N03'38 103w22'35 6:53:30
Lake Metigoshe 5
1 48N50 100w27 6:41:48
Lake Williams 22
1 47N08'05 99w36'51 6:38:27
Lakewood Park 36
1 48N04'18 98w55'45 6:35:43
Lakota 32 1 48N02'34 98w20'09 6:33:21
Lallie 3 1 47N58'42 99w12'56 6:36:52
La Mars 39 1 45N57'53 96w41'24 6:26:46
La Moure 23 1 46N21'26 98w17'39 6:33:11
Landa 5 1 48N53'48 100w54'41 6:43:39
Langdon 10 4 48N45'36 98w22'04 6:33:28
Lankin 50 1 48N18'40 97w55'29 6:31:42
Lansford 5 1 48N37'44 101w22'31 6:45:30
Larimore 18 1 47N54'24 97w37'35 6:30:30
Lark 19 9 46N27'11 101w23'45 6:45:35
Larson 7 1 48N53'23 102w51'29 6:51:26
Lawton 36 1 48N18'10 98w22'08 6:33:29
Leal 2 1 47N06'19 98w19'01 6:33:16
Leeds 3 1 48N17'20 99w26'14 6:37:45
Lefor 45 9 46N40'54 102w33'33 6:50:14
Lehigh 45 9 46N52'04 102w41'39 6:50:47
Lehr 24 1 46N16'47 99w21'07 6:37:24
Leith 19 9 46N21'30 101w38'10 6:46:33
Lemert 16 1 47N30'35 99w15'49 6:37:03
Leonard 9 1 46N39'07 97w14'43 6:28:59
Leroy 34 1 48N55'24 97w45'08 6:31:01
Leverich 35 1 48N26'07 100w05'20 6:40:21
Leyden 34 1 48N52'36 97w48'38 6:31:15
Lidgerwood 39 1 46N04'32 97w09'05 6:28:36
Lignite 7 1 48N52'39 102w33'45 6:50:15
Lincoln Valley 42
1 47N38'18 100w18'14 6:41:13
Linton 15 1 46N16'00 100w13'57 6:40:56
Lisbon 37 1 46N26'30 97w40'51 6:30:43
Litchville 2 1 46N39'13 98w11'38 6:32:47
Lithia 39 1 46N36'58 96w48'47 6:27:15
Little Heart 30
9 46N40'00 100w54'06 6:43:36
Livona 15 1 46N30'08 100w32'48 6:42:11
Logan 51 1 48N08'54 101w09'12 6:44:37
Logan Center 18
1 47N48'10 97w49'05 6:31:16
Loma 10 1 48N37'49 98w31'57 6:34:08
Lonetree 51 1 48N16'57 101w38'36 6:46:34
Loraine 38 1 48N51'56 101w34'03 6:46:16
Lostwood 31 1 48N28'32 102w25'25 6:49:42
Lowell 26 1 45N56'31 99w22'47 6:37:31
Lucca 2 1 46N42'25 97w43'10 6:30:53
Ludden 11 1 46N00'31 98w07'30 6:32:30
Lunds Landing 53
1 48N09'57 103w08'25 6:52:34
Lunds Valley 31
1 48N30'28 102w32'32 6:50:10
Luverne 46 1 47N15'04 97w56'04 6:31:44
Lynchburg 9 1 46N46'28 97w15'45 6:29:03
Lyons 30 9 46N48'40 101w03'10 6:44:13
Maddock 3 1 47N57'45 99w31'47 6:38:07
Magnolia 9 1 46N54'45 97w25'45 6:29:43
Maida 10 1 48N59'55 98w21'52 6:33:27
Makoti 51 1 47N57'40 101w48'15 6:47:13
Mandan 30 10 46N49'36 100w53'21 6:43:33
Mandaree 27 1 47N43'45 102w40'32 6:50:42
Mandt 50 1 48N25'11 97w36'02 6:30:24
Manfred 52 1 47N41'41 99w44'52 6:38:59
Manitou 31 1 48N19'52 102w38'10 6:50:33
Manning 13 9 47N13'48 102w46'11 6:51:05
Mantador 39 1 46N09'55 96w58'37 6:27:54

Place		Latitude	Longitude	Time
Manvel 18	1	48N04'40	97w10'34	6:28:42
Mapes 32	1	48N01'52	98w13'37	6:32:54
Mapleton 9	1	46N53'21	97w03'08	6:28:13
Marion 23	1	46N36'26	98w19'55	6:33:20
Marley 53	1	48N01'30	103w54'16	6:55:37
Marmarth 44	9	46N17'42	103w55'13	6:55:41
Marmon 53	1	48N23'14	103w39'20	6:54:37
Marshall 13	9	47N08'17	102w19'57	6:49:20
Martin 42	1	47N49'36	100w06'53	6:40:28
Mason 9	1	47N04'25	97w19'43	6:29:19
Max 28	1	47N49'16	101w17'54	6:45:12
Maxbass 5	1	48N43'18	101w08'28	6:44:34
Mayville 49	1	47N29'53	97w19'27	6:29:18
Maza 48	1	48N22	99w12	6:36:48
Mazda 44	9	46N17'09	103w51'40	6:55:27
McArthur 34	1	48N52'35	97w13'39	6:28:55
McCanna 18	1	48N00'21	97w42'35	6:30:50
McClusky 42	1	47N29'09	100w26'34	6:41:46
McGregor 53	1	48N35'43	102w55'40	6:51:43
McHenry 16	1	47N34'34	98w35'28	6:34:22
McKenzie 8	1	46N49'27	100w24'47	6:41:39
McLeod 37	1	46N23'37	97w17'57	6:29:12
McVille 32	1	47N45'50	98w10'37	6:32:42
Medberry 23	1	46N22'33	98w37'14	6:34:29
Medicine Hole 13	9	47N26'39	102w53'26	6:51:34
Medina 47	1	46N53'38	99w17'58	6:37:12
Medora (historic Medora) 4	9	46N54'50	103w31'26	6:54:06
Mekinock 18	1	48N00'46	97w21'47	6:29:27
Melville 16	1	47N20'05	99w02'07	6:36:08
Menoken (Burleigh Station) 8	1	46N49'14	100w31'51	6:42:07
Mercer 28	1	47N29'26	100w42'38	6:42:51
Merida 28	1	47N14'34	100w55'44	6:43:43
Merricourt 11	1	46N12'34	98w45'44	6:35:03
Merrifield 18	1	47N50'45	97w06'33	6:28:26
Michigan 32	1	48N01'30	98w07'00	6:32:28
Midway 8	1	46N59'03	100w47'23	6:43:10
Millarton 47	1	46N40'01	98w45'33	6:35:02
Milnor 41	1	46N15'33	97w27'21	6:29:49
Milroy 25	1	48N26'24	100w32'00	6:42:08
Milton 10	1	48N37'35	98w02'32	6:32:10
Minnewaukan 3	1	48N04'17	99w15'07	6:37:00
Minot 51	1	48N13'57	101w17'45	6:45:11
Minot Base 51	1	48N25	101w20	6:45:20
Minto 50	1	48N17'30	97w22'16	6:29:29
Minto West 50	1	48N17	97w31	6:30:04
Moffit 8	1	46N40'38	100w17'27	6:41:10
Mohall 38	1	48N45'48	101w30'46	6:46:03
Monango 11	1	46N10'22	98w35'39	6:34:23
Montpelier 47	1	46N42'01	98w35'23	6:34:22
Mooreton 39	1	46N16'07	96w52'33	6:27:30
Mose 20	1	47N34'43	98w27'16	6:33:49
Moselle 39	1	46N13'55	97w04'59	6:28:20
Mott 21	9	46N22'21	102w19'36	6:49:18
Mountain 34	1	48N41'16	97w51'53	6:31:28
Mount Carmel 10	1	48N56'06	98w23'11	6:33:33
Munich 10	1	48N40'12	98w50'22	6:35:21
Munster 14	1	47N43'13	99w16'17	6:37:05
Murray 49	1	47N25'33	97w16'33	6:29:06
Mylo 40	1	48N38'07	99w37'06	6:38:28
Myra 9	1	46N51'53	97w19'11	6:29:17
Nanson 40	1	48N34'26	99w46'46	6:39:07
Napoleon 24	1	46N30'30	99w46'15	6:39:05
Nash 50	1	48N28'14	97w30'46	6:30:03
Neche 34	1	48N59'10	97w33'16	6:30:13
Nekoma 10	1	48N34'38	98w22'12	6:33:29
Newburg 5	1	48N42'54	100w54'45	6:43:39
New England 21	9	46N32'21	102w52'04	6:51:28
New Hradec 13	9	47N00'00	102w53'02	6:51:32
New Leipzig 19	9	46N22'34	101w56'22	6:47:45
Newman 9	1	46N59'28	97w05'57	6:28:24
New Rockford 14	1	47N40'48	99w08'15	6:36:33
New Salem 30	9	46N50'42	101w24'39	6:45:39
New Town 31	1	47N58'38	102w29'47	6:49:59
Newville 48	1	48N33'31	98w59'13	6:35:57
Niagara 18	1	47N59'47	97w52'12	6:31:29
Nicholson 41	1	46N06'33	97w52'04	6:31:28
Niles 3	1	48N16'52	99w20'56	6:37:24
Nine Mile Corner 51	1	48N48'25	102w05'13	6:48:21
Niobe 51	1	48N41'20	102w12'55	6:48:52
Nolan 9	1	47N08'17	97w33'25	6:30:14
Nome 2	1	46N40'40	97w48'36	6:31:14
Noonan 12	1	48N53'20	103w00'30	6:52:02
Norma 38	1	48N43'44	101w58'22	6:47:53
Norman 9	1	46N39'32	96w56'35	6:27:46
North Almont 30	9	46N50'23	101w30'33	6:46:02
North Billings 4	9	47N10	103w15	6:53:00
North Central Mc Lean 28	1	47N44	101w22	6:45:28
Northeast 12	1	48N54	103w19	6:53:16
Northgate 7	1	48N59'27	102w15'42	6:49:03
North Grand Forks 18	1	47N58'46	97w05'26	6:28:22
North Kidder 22	1	47N10	99w51	6:39:24
North Lemmon 1	9	45N56'46	102w09'26	6:48:38
North Mc Henry 25	1	48N33	100w46	6:43:04
North Nelson 32	1	48N02	98w10	6:32:40
North Pierce 35	1	48N26	99w57	6:39:48
North Ramsey 36	1	48N28	98w37	6:34:28
North Renville 38	1	48N50	101w44	6:46:56
North Sheridan 42	1	47N46	100w20	6:41:20
North Sioux 43	9	46N20	100w41	6:42:44
North Valley City 2	1	46N56'46	97w59'47	6:31:59
Northwood 18	1	47N44'03	97w33'59	6:30:16
Nortonville 23	1	46N33'30	98w44'18	6:34:57
Norway 11	1	46N08'20	98w08'43	6:32:35
Norwich 25	1	48N14'47	100w59'19	6:43:57
Oakdale 13	9	47N28'23	102w51'52	6:51:27

Place		Latitude	Longitude	Time
Oakes 11	1	46N08'19	98w05'24	6:32:22
Oakwood 50	1	48N25'37	97w17'42	6:29:11
Oberon 3	1	47N55'23	99w12'13	6:36:49
Olga 10	1	48N47'54	98w02'15	6:32:09
Olmstead 48	1	48N37'39	99w05'05	6:36:20
Omemee 5	1	48N42'23	100w21'17	6:41:25
Ops 50	1	48N13'40	97w35'48	6:30:23
Oriska 2	1	46N55'50	97w47'19	6:31:09
Orr 18	1	48N05'36	97w40'30	6:30:42
Orrin 35	1	48N05'29	100w09'46	6:40:39
Osnabrock 10	1	48N40'08	98w09'03	6:32:36
Oswald 39	1	46N03'32	96w43'40	6:26:55
Otter Creek 33	9	47N02'57	101w33'17	6:46:13
Overly 5	1	48N40'55	100w08'59	6:40:36
Page 9	1	47N09'35	97w34'15	6:30:17
Palermo 31	1	48N20'23	102w13'43	6:48:55
Parkhurst 47	1	46N58'35	98w45'01	6:35:00
Park River 50	1	48N23'55	97w44'27	6:30:58
Parshall 31	1	47N57'12	102w08'04	6:48:32
Paulson 12	1	48N53'48	103w07'58	6:52:32
Peak 2	1	46N55'56	97w54'46	6:31:39
Pekin 32	1	47N47'27	98w19'40	6:33:19
Pelto 32	1	48N09'31	98w13'39	6:32:55
Pembina 34	4	48N57'59	97w14'36	6:28:58
Penn 36	1	48N13'18	99w05'19	6:36:21
Perella 7	1	48N54'06	102w15'02	6:49:00
Perth 48	1	48N42'59	99w27'27	6:37:50
Peters 24	1	46N23'02	99w42'25	6:38:50
Petersburg 32	1	48N00'40	98w00'04	6:32:00
Petrel 1	9	45N56'54	102w16'36	6:49:06
Pettibone 22	1	47N07'09	99w31'09	6:38:05
Pickardville 42	1	47N28'16	100w34'45	6:42:19
Pick City 29	9	47N30'41	101w27'12	6:45:49
Pickert 46	1	47N26'30	97w48'53	6:31:16
Pierce 8	1	46N47'24	100w41'31	6:42:46
Pierce 44	9	46N21'08	103w04'15	6:52:17
Pillsbury 2	1	47N12'25	97w47'25	6:31:10
Pingree 47	1	47N09'48	98w54'24	6:35:38
Pinkham 9	7	46N55'13	96w54'12	6:27:37
Pisek 50	1	48N18'39	97w42'32	6:30:50
Pitcairn 39	1	46N25'40	96w50'32	6:27:22
Pittsburgh 34	1	48N37'46	97w10'40	6:28:43
Plaza 31	1	48N01'33	101w57'38	6:47:51
Pleasant Lake 3	1	48N21'41	99w48'06	6:39:12
Pleasant Valley 50	1	48N22'10	97w51'51	6:31:27
Poland 50	1	48N11'52	97w13'05	6:28:52
Ponderosa 8	1	46N49	100w47	6:43:08
Porcupine 43	9	46N13'08	101w05'54	6:44:24
Portal 7	1	48N59'45	102w32'57	6:50:12
Portland 49	1	47N29'54	97w22'12	6:29:29
Portland Junction 49	1	47N33'41	97w22'08	6:29:29
Powell 18	1	47N55'11	97w10'39	6:28:43
Power 39	1	46N33'20	97w14'16	6:28:57
Powers Lake 7	1	48N33'46	102w38'51	6:50:35
Prairie Junction 31	1	47N59'29	101w54'08	6:47:37
Prairie View Acres 8	1	46N49	100w47	6:43:08
Preston 49	1	47N18'44	97w13'06	6:28:52
Price 33	9	47N05'09	100w56'28	6:43:46
Prosper 9	2	46N57'47	97w01'10	6:28:05
Raleigh 19	9	46N21'28	101w18'22	6:45:13
Ralston 51	1	48N14'55	101w28'33	6:45:54
Ramsey 36	1	48N09'30	99w05'17	6:36:21
Rangeley 25	1	48N02'34	100w29'26	6:41:58
Raub 28	1	47N44'47	102w02'34	6:48:10
Rawson 27	1	47N49'10	103w32'25	6:54:10
Ray 53	1	48N20'40	103w09'53	6:52:40
Reeder 1	9	46N06'21	102w56'42	6:51:47
Reeves 47	1	46N51'47	98w34'56	6:34:20
Regan 8	1	47N09'29	100w31'40	6:42:07
Regent 21	9	46N25'18	102w33'19	6:50:13
Renville 5	1	48N45'47	101w17'59	6:45:12
Revere 20	1	47N21'20	98w19'42	6:33:19
Reynolds 49	1	47N40'20	97w06'23	6:28:26
Rhame 6	9	46N13'57	103w39'18	6:54:37
Richardton 45	9	46N53'02	102w18'55	6:49:16
Rider 17	9	46N54'51	103w38'13	6:54:33
Riga 25	1	48N17'38	100w42'25	6:42:50
Rising 25	1	48N20'10	100w57'19	6:43:49
Rival 7	1	48N54'06	102w36'41	6:50:27
Riverdale 28	1	47N29'51	101w22'15	6:45:29
Riverdale Junction 28	1	47N29'56	101w10'29	6:44:42
Riverside 9	7	46N53'10	96w54'00	6:27:36
Robinson 22	1	47N08'34	99w46'51	6:39:07
Rock Haven 30	10	46N52'24	100w53'19	6:43:33
Rock Lake 48	1	48N47'25	99w14'45	6:36:59
Rogers 2	1	47N04'22	98w11'57	6:32:48
Rohrville 36	1	48N08'33	98w39'35	6:34:38
Rolette 40	1	48N39'39	99w50'28	6:39:22
Rolla 40	1	48N51'53	99w37'03	6:38:28
Roseglen 28	1	47N45'05	101w50'09	6:47:21
Roseville 49	1	47N26'25	97w23'19	6:29:33
Ross 31	1	48N18'40	102w32'46	6:50:11
Roth 5	1	48N54'28	100w48'08	6:43:13
Rugby 35	1	48N22'08	99w59'45	6:39:59
Ruso 28	1	47N50'18	100w55'59	6:43:44
Russell 5	1	48N40'17	100w54'04	6:43:36
Ruthville 51	1	48N22'18	101w17'54	6:45:12
Rutland 41	1	46N03'11	97w30'31	6:30:02
Ryder 51	1	47N55'03	101w40'39	6:46:43
Saint Anthony 30	9	46N37'01	100w54'46	6:43:39
Saint Benedict 9	1	46N43'28	96w50'28	6:27:22
Saint Gertrude 19	9	46N17'04	101w19'44	6:45:19
Saint Joe 36	1	48N30'49	98w55'37	6:35:42
Saint John 40	1	48N56'40	99w42'38	6:38:51
Saint Michael 3	1	47N59'06	98w52'18	6:35:29
Saint Thomas 34	1	48N37'09	97w26'46	6:29:47
Sanborn 2	1	46N56'32	98w13'26	6:32:54
Sand Hills 37	1	46N26	97w24	6:29:36
Sanger 33	1	47N10'47	100w59'42	6:43:59
San Haven 40	1	48N50'05	100w02'19	6:40:09
Sanish 31	1	47N58'26	102w32'44	6:50:11

Place		Latitude	Longitude	Time
Sarles 10	1	48N56'45	98w59'44	6:35:59
Sawyer 51	1	48N05'23	101w03'12	6:44:13
Schafer 27	1	47N47'58	103w11'10	6:52:45
Schefield 45	9	46N40'29	102w51'15	6:51:25
Schmidt 30	9	46N40'25	100w46'54	6:43:08
Scoria Point 4	9	46N55'52	103w29'06	6:53:56
Scranton 6	9	46N08'53	103w08'33	6:52:34
Selfridge 43	9	46N02'29	100w55'29	6:43:42
Selz 35	1	47N51'26	99w53'29	6:39:34
Sentinel Butte 17	9	46N55'06	103w50'18	6:55:21
Sevenmile Corner 7	1	48N53'40	102w32'44	6:50:11
Sharlow 47	1	46N40'48	98w51'35	6:35:26
Sharon 46	6	47N35'50	97w53'37	6:31:34
Shawnee 18	1	47N57'19	97w45'03	6:31:00
Sheldon 37	1	46N35'09	97w29'27	6:29:58
Shepard 20	1	47N23'23	98w07'54	6:32:32
Sherbrooke 46	1	47N27'39	97w43'09	6:30:53
Sherwood 38	1	48N57'36	101w37'56	6:46:32
Sheyenne 14	1	47N49'41	99w07'11	6:36:29
Shields 19	9	46N14'01	101w07'32	6:44:30
Sibley 2	1	47N13'02	97w57'51	6:31:51
Silva 35	1	48N10'08	99w55'05	6:39:40
Silver Strip 53	1	48N09	103w37	6:54:28
Simcoe 25	1	48N09'23	100w51'59	6:43:28
Sims 30	9	46N46'20	101w29'53	6:46:00
Six Mile Corner 4	9	46N58'50	103w11'25	6:52:46
Skaar 27	9	47N22'24	104w02'23	6:56:10
Skogmo 42	1	47N52	100w30	6:42:00
Solen 43	9	46N23'20	100w47'53	6:43:12
Sonora 39	1	46N04'00	96w44'28	6:26:58
Souris 5	1	48N54'35	100w40'52	6:42:43
Southam 36	1	48N09'30	98w33'06	6:34:12
South Billings 4	9	46N46	103w26	6:53:44
South Dunn 13	9	47N05	102w36	6:50:24
South Grant 19	9	46N12	101w30	6:46:00
South Heart 45	9	46N51'53	102w59'28	6:51:58
South Kidder 22	1	46N47	99w50	6:39:20
South Mc Lean 28	1	47N18	100w55	6:43:40
South Mountrail 31	1	48N01	102w08	6:48:32
South Pierce 35	1	47N57	99w58	6:39:52
South Prairie 51	1	48N03'07	101w17'43	6:45:11
South Renville 38	1	48N32	101w32	6:46:08
South Washington 18	1	47N56	97w12	6:28:48
South Wells 52	1	47N26	99w44	6:38:56
Southwest R 12	1	48N48	103w39	6:54:36
Spiritwood 47	1	46N56'10	98w29'43	6:33:59
Spiritwood Lake 47	1	46N54	98w43	6:34:52
Spotted Horn 27	1	47N42'48	102w42'23	6:50:50
Spring Brook 53	1	48N15'09	103w27'30	6:53:50
Stady 12	1	48N43'14	103w42'20	6:54:49
Stampede 7	1	48N53'14	102w44'14	6:50:57
Standing Rock Indian Res 43	9	46N06	100w38	6:42:32
Stanley 31	1	48N19'02	102w23'24	6:49:34
Stanton 29	9	47N19'16	101w22'52	6:45:31
Starkweather 36	1	48N27'07	98w53'00	6:35:32
State Hospital 47	1	46N54	98w43	6:34:52
State University 9	7	46N53	96w48	6:27:12
Steele 22	1	46N51'17	99w54'56	6:39:40
Sterling 8	1	46N48'50	100w17'28	6:41:10
Stiles 39	1	46N04'31	97w03'08	6:28:13
Still 8	1	47N09'38	100w38'09	6:42:33
Stirum 41	1	46N12'37	97w48'22	6:31:13
Strasburg 15	1	46N08'01	100w09'40	6:40:39
Straubville 41	1	46N02'38	97w53'59	6:31:36
Streeter 47	1	46N39'19	99w21'13	6:37:25
Sully Springs 4	9	46N52'02	103w23'28	6:53:34
Sunny 30	10	46N49'46	100w57'24	6:43:50
Surrey 51	1	48N14'11	101w07'59	6:44:32
Sutton 20	1	47N24'07	98w26'20	6:33:45
Svold 34	1	48N48'28	97w47'47	6:31:11
Sweet Briar 30	9	46N49'28	101w09'16	6:44:37
Sweetwater 36	1	48N12'57	98w52'15	6:35:29
Sydney 47	1	46N43'51	98w46'10	6:35:05
Sykeston 52	1	47N27'54	99w23'57	6:37:36
Taft 49	1	47N27'23	97w04'11	6:28:17
Tagus 31	1	48N20'47	101w56'01	6:47:44
Tappen 22	1	46N52'30	99w38'10	6:38:33
Tasco 5	1	48N41'14	100w15'17	6:41:01
Taylor 45	9	46N54'02	102w25'29	6:49:42
Temple 53	1	48N23'20	103w03'20	6:52:13
Temvik 15	1	46N22'11	100w15'29	6:41:02
Thelan 17	9	46N48'13	103w58'17	6:55:53
Thompson 18	1	47N46'25	97w06'34	6:28:26
Thorne 40	1	48N44'21	99w55'52	6:39:43
Three V Crossing 44	9	46N33'25	103w47'29	6:55:10
Tilden 3	1	48N09'21	99w14'47	6:36:59
Timmer 30	9	46N22'17	101w01'03	6:44:04
Tioga 53	1	48N23'50	102w56'16	6:51:45
Tokio 3	1	47N55'29	98w48'57	6:35:16
Tolley 38	1	48N43'44	101w49'37	6:47:18
Tolna 32	1	47N49'38	98w26'23	6:33:46
Tower City 9	1	46N55'22	97w40'25	6:30:42
Town and Country Shop Ctr 51	1	48N20	101w19	6:45:16
Towner 25	1	48N20'45	100w24'18	6:41:37
Trenton 53	1	48N04'14	103w50'11	6:55:21
Trotters 17	9	47N19'23	103w55'04	6:55:40
Truax 29	9	47N21'30	101w38'47	6:46:35
Truro 5	1	48N41'38	101w26'45	6:45:47
Tunbridge 35	1	48N21'57	100w06'21	6:40:25
Turtle Lake 28	1	47N31'12	100w53'23	6:43:34

Turtle Mountain Indian Res 40	1	48N50	99w45	6:39:00
Turtle Mountains 5	1	48N54	100w20	6:41:20
Tuttle 22	1	47N08'37	99w59'39	6:39:59
Twin Buttes 13	9	47N30'59	102w14'45	6:48:59
Tyler 39	1	46N08'57	96w36'18	6:26:25
Tyler's Western Village 8	1	46N49	100w47	6:43:08
Underwood 28	1	47N27'23	101w08'12	6:44:33
Union 10	1	48N33'28	97w56'55	6:31:48
University 18	1	47N56	97w12	6:28:48
Upham 25	1	48N34'54	100w43'40	6:42:55
Urbana 2	1	46N56'04	98w24'41	6:33:39
Valley City 2	1	46N55'24	98w00'10	6:32:01
Vance 9	1	47N02'02	97w13'03	6:28:52
Vang 10	1	48N54'21	98w07'28	6:32:30
Vashti 47	1	47N11'20	99w04'49	6:36:19
Velva 25	1	48N03'22	100w55'44	6:43:43
Venlo 37	1	46N29'11	97w26'45	6:29:47
Venturia 26	1	45N59'55	99w32'45	6:38:11
Verendrye 25	1	48N07'16	100w44'19	6:42:57
Verona 23	1	46N21'50	98w04'19	6:32:17
Veseleyville 50	1	48N19'31	97w33'25	6:30:14
Voltaire 25	1	48N01'14	100w50'28	6:43:22
Voss 50	1	48N17'47	97w27'18	6:29:49
Wabek 31	1	47N58'19	101w57'22	6:47:49
Wahpeton 39	8	46N15'55	96w36'20	6:26:25
Walcott 39	1	46N32'56	96w56'11	6:27:45
Walden 9	1	47N10'29	97w41'23	6:30:46
Wales 10	1	48N53'45	98w36'08	6:34:25
Walhalla 34	1	48N55'24	97w55'04	6:31:40
Walser Crossing 44	9	46N37'09	103w36'45	6:54:23
Walum 20	1	47N16'11	98w11'39	6:32:47
Warren 9	1	46N43'38	97w00'36	6:28:02
Warsaw 50	1	48N17'46	97w15'16	6:29:01
Warwick 3	1	47N51'18	98w42'35	6:34:50
Washburn 28	1	47N17'21	101w01'43	6:44:07
Wassaic 31	1	48N24'22	102w22'40	6:49:31
Watford City 27	1	47N48'08	103w16'58	6:53:08
Watrous 21	9	46N19'33	102w11'33	6:48:46
Weaver 10	1	48N35'28	98w43'27	6:34:54
Webster 36	1	48N16'56	98w52'33	6:35:30
Wellsburg 52	1	47N49'54	99w45'40	6:39:03
Werner 13	9	47N21'38	102w27'24	6:49:50
West Adams 1	9	46N05	102w46	6:51:04
West Bonetraill 53	1	48N24'07	103w56'54	6:55:48
West Bottineau 5	1	48N46	101w24	6:45:36
West Bowman 6	9	46N05	103w41	6:54:44
Westby 12	1	48N52'13	104w03'05	6:56:12
West Cavalier 10	1	48N46	98w47	6:35:08
West Dickey 11	1	46N07	98w53	6:35:32
West Eddy 14	1	47N43	99w06	6:36:24
West Emmons 15	1	46N17	100w29	6:41:56
West Fargo 9	2	46N52'30	96w54'00	6:27:36
Westfield 15	1	46N01'46	100w12'07	6:40:48
West Foster 16	1	47N27	99w03	6:36:12
West Griggs 20	1	47N28	98w23	6:33:32
West Hettinger 21	9	46N26	102w45	6:51:00
Westhope 5	1	48N54'34	101w01'13	6:44:05
West Logan 24	1	46N28	99w40	6:38:40
West Mc Lean 28	1	47N42	101w55	6:47:40
West Mercer 29	9	47N17	101w57	6:47:48
West Morton 30	9	46N51	101w53	6:47:32
West Oliver 33	9	47N07	101w34	6:46:16
West Sargent 41	1	46N08	97w53	6:31:32
West Slope 44	9	46N27	103w37	6:54:28
West Stark 45	9	46N49	103w06	6:52:24
Wheatland 9	1	46N54'27	97w20'42	6:29:23
Wheelock 53	1	48N17'47	103w15'07	6:53:00
White 5	1	48N41'46	100w37'25	6:42:30
White Earth 31	1	48N22'50	102w46'22	6:51:05
White Shield 28	1	47N39	101w39	6:46:36
Whitman 32	1	48N09'31	98w07'10	6:32:29
Wild Rice 9	1	46N44'47	96w48'33	6:27:14
Wildrose 53	1	48N37'50	103w11'02	6:52:44
Williston 53	1	48N08'00	103w38'00	6:54:32
Willow City 5	1	48N36'16	100w17'38	6:41:11
Wilton 28	1	47N09'31	100w46'59	6:43:08
Wimbledon 2	1	47N10'11	98w27'34	6:33:50
Windsor 47	1	46N53'47	99w02'33	6:36:10
Wing 8	1	47N08'27	100w16'43	6:41:07
Wirch 11	1	46N04'39	98w56'37	6:35:46
Wishek 26	1	46N15'25	99w33'24	6:38:14
Woburn 7	1	48N49'43	102w25'08	6:49:41
Wogansport 8	9	47N02'05	100w52'25	6:43:30
Wolford 35	1	48N29'55	99w42'14	6:38:49
Wolseth 51	1	48N26'47	101w07'25	6:44:30
Woods 9	1	46N40'48	97w11'19	6:28:45
Woodworth 47	1	47N08'33	99w18'10	6:37:13
Wyndmere 39	1	46N16'00	97w07'55	6:28:32
Yellowstone 27	9	47N52	104w00	6:56:00
York 3	1	48N18'46	99w34'23	6:38:18
Youngtown 30	9	46N56'33	101w24'27	6:45:38
Ypsilanti 47	1	46N46'55	98w33'46	6:34:15
Zahl 53	1	48N34'24	103w41'30	6:54:46
Zap 29	9	47N17'11	101w55'20	6:47:41
Zeeland 26	1	45N58'12	99w49'49	6:39:19
Zenith 45	9	46N52'46	103w05'46	6:52:23

TIME TABLES

Zone shifts are uncertain at the zone boundaries for the various changes from Central to Eastern time. During World War II, industrial cities and towns variously ignored the official CWT after February 21, 1943, and used EWT instead, especially during the summer months. We have assumed that the northeast area followed Cleveland, except where newspaper clippings show otherwise. Some of these local differences are not yet documented. During the 1950's, the area observing daylight time gradually spread from the northeast and east westward. But the exact year that particular smaller towns began observing daylight time, and whether the daylight period ended in September or October continues to be uncertain.

OH # 1		
Before 4/01/1893		LMT
4/01/1893	12:00	CST
3/31/1918	02:00	CWT
10/27/1918	02:00	CST
3/30/1919	02:00	CWT
10/26/1919	02:00	CST
9/01/1922	02:00	EST
2/09/1942	02:00	EWT
2/21/1943	02:00	CWT
9/30/1945	02:00	EST
4/30/1967	02:00	US#1

OH # 2		
Before 4/01/1893		LMT
4/01/1893	12:00	CST
3/31/1918	02:00	CWT
10/27/1918	02:00	CST
1/01/1919	02:00	EST
3/30/1919	02:00	EWT
5/17/1919	21:00	CWT
10/26/1919	02:00	CST
3/30/1920	02:00	CDT
10/26/1920	02:00	CST
3/30/1921	02:00	CDT
10/26/1921	02:00	CST
3/30/1922	02:00	CDT
10/26/1922	02:00	CST
3/30/1923	02:00	CDT
10/26/1923	02:00	CST
3/30/1924	02:00	CDT
10/26/1924	02:00	CST
3/30/1925	02:00	CDT
10/26/1925	02:00	CST
3/30/1926	02:00	CDT
9/26/1926	02:00	EST
2/09/1942	02:00	EWT
9/26/1943	02:00	CWT
4/30/1944	02:00	EWT
9/30/1945	02:00	EST
4/25/1948	02:00	EDT
9/26/1948	02:00	EST
4/24/1949	02:00	EDT
9/25/1949	02:00	EST
4/30/1950	02:00	EDT
9/30/1950	02:00	US#5

OH # 3		
Before 4/01/1893		LMT
4/01/1893	12:00	CST
3/31/1918	02:00	CWT
10/27/1918	02:00	CST
3/30/1919	02:00	CWT
10/26/1919	02:00	CST
3/28/1920	02:00	CDT
10/31/1920	02:00	CST
4/02/1921	02:00	CDT
9/25/1921	02:00	CST
4/30/1922	02:00	CDT
9/24/1922	02:00	CST
4/20/1923	02:00	EST
2/09/1942	02:00	EWT
9/26/1943	02:00	CWT
9/30/1945	02:00	EST
4/30/1967	02:00	US#1

OH # 4		
Before 4/01/1893		LMT
4/01/1893	12:00	CST
3/31/1918	02:00	CWT
10/27/1918	02:00	CST
3/30/1919	02:00	CWT
10/26/1919	02:00	CST
8/05/1926	02:00	EST
2/09/1942	02:00	EWT
9/26/1943	02:00	CWT
9/30/1945	02:00	EST
4/30/1967	02:00	US#1

OH # 5		
Before 4/01/1893		LMT
4/01/1893	12:00	CST
3/31/1918	02:00	CWT
10/27/1918	02:00	CST
1/01/1919	02:00	EST
3/30/1919	02:00	EWT
10/26/1919	02:00	EST
2/09/1942	02:00	EWT
2/21/1943	02:00	CWT
9/30/1945	02:00	EST
4/30/1967	02:00	US#1

OH # 6		
Before 4/01/1893		LMT
4/01/1893	12:00	CST
3/31/1918	02:00	CWT
10/27/1918	02:00	CST
1/01/1919	02:00	EST
3/30/1919	02:00	EWT
10/26/1919	02:00	EST
2/09/1942	02:00	EWT
2/21/1943	02:00	CWT
9/30/1945	02:00	EST
4/27/1947	02:00	US#5

OH # 7		
Before 4/01/1893		LMT
4/01/1893	12:00	CST
3/31/1918	02:00	CWT
10/27/1918	02:00	CST
1/01/1919	02:00	EST
3/30/1919	02:00	EWT
10/26/1919	02:00	EST
2/09/1942	02:00	EWT
2/21/1943	02:00	CWT
9/30/1945	02:00	EST
4/25/1948	02:00	EDT
9/26/1948	02:00	EST
4/30/1967	02:00	US#1

OH # 8		
Before 4/01/1893		LMT
4/01/1893	12:00	CST
3/31/1918	02:00	CWT
10/27/1918	02:00	CST
1/01/1919	02:00	EST
3/30/1919	02:00	EWT
10/26/1919	02:00	EST
2/09/1942	02:00	EWT
2/21/1943	02:00	CWT
9/30/1945	02:00	EST
4/25/1948	02:00	EDT
9/26/1948	02:00	EST
4/30/1950	02:00	EDT
9/24/1950	02:00	EST
4/29/1956	02:00	US#5

OH # 9		
Before 4/01/1893		LMT
4/01/1893	12:00	CST
3/31/1918	02:00	CWT
10/27/1918	02:00	CST
1/01/1919	02:00	EST
3/30/1919	02:00	EWT
10/26/1919	02:00	EST
2/09/1942	02:00	EWT
2/21/1943	02:00	CWT
9/30/1945	02:00	EST
4/24/1949	02:00	EDT
9/25/1949	02:00	EST
4/30/1967	02:00	US#1

OH # 10		
Before 4/01/1893		LMT
4/01/1893	12:00	CST
3/31/1918	02:00	CWT
10/27/1918	02:00	CST
1/01/1919	02:00	EST
3/30/1919	02:00	EWT
10/26/1919	02:00	EST
2/09/1942	02:00	EWT
2/21/1943	02:00	CWT
9/30/1945	02:00	EST
4/27/1952	02:00	EDT
9/28/1952	02:00	EST
4/29/1956	02:00	US#5

OH # 11		
Before 4/01/1893		LMT
4/01/1893	12:00	CST
3/31/1918	02:00	CWT
10/27/1918	02:00	CST
1/01/1919	02:00	EST
3/30/1919	02:00	EWT
10/26/1919	02:00	EST
2/09/1942	02:00	EWT
2/21/1943	02:00	CWT
9/30/1945	02:00	EST
4/25/1954	02:00	US#5

OH # 12		
Before 4/01/1893		LMT
4/01/1893	12:00	CST
3/31/1918	02:00	CWT
10/27/1918	02:00	CST
1/01/1919	02:00	EST
3/30/1919	02:00	EWT
10/26/1919	02:00	EST
2/09/1942	02:00	EWT
2/21/1943	02:00	CWT
9/30/1945	02:00	EST
4/24/1955	02:00	EDT
9/25/1955	02:00	EST
4/28/1957	02:00	US#5

OH # 13		
Before 4/01/1893		LMT
4/01/1893	12:00	CST
3/31/1918	02:00	CWT
10/27/1918	02:00	CST
1/01/1919	02:00	EST
3/30/1919	02:00	EWT
10/26/1919	02:00	EST
2/09/1942	02:00	EWT
2/21/1943	02:00	CWT
9/30/1945	02:00	EST
4/24/1955	02:00	US#5

OH # 14		
Before 4/01/1893		LMT
4/01/1893	12:00	CST
3/31/1918	02:00	CWT
10/27/1918	02:00	CST
1/01/1919	02:00	EST
3/30/1919	02:00	EWT
10/26/1919	02:00	EST
2/09/1942	02:00	EWT
2/21/1943	02:00	CWT
9/30/1945	02:00	EST
5/12/1957	02:00	EDT
9/29/1957	02:00	EST
4/28/1963	02:00	EDT
9/29/1963	02:00	EST
4/26/1964	02:00	EDT
9/27/1964	02:00	EST
4/25/1965	02:00	EDT
9/26/1965	02:00	EST
4/24/1966	02:00	US#1

OH # 15		
Before 4/01/1893		LMT
4/01/1893	12:00	CST
3/31/1918	02:00	CWT
10/27/1918	02:00	CST
1/01/1919	02:00	EST
3/30/1919	02:00	EWT
10/26/1919	02:00	EST
2/09/1942	02:00	EWT
2/21/1943	02:00	CWT
9/30/1945	02:00	EST
4/24/1955	02:00	EDT
9/25/1955	02:00	EST
4/29/1956	02:00	EDT
10/28/1956	02:00	EST
4/28/1957	02:00	US#5

OH # 16		
Before 4/01/1893		LMT
4/01/1893	12:00	CST
3/31/1918	02:00	CWT
10/27/1918	02:00	CST
1/01/1919	02:00	EST
3/30/1919	02:00	EWT
10/26/1919	02:00	EST
2/09/1942	02:00	EWT
2/21/1943	02:00	CWT
9/30/1945	02:00	EST
4/28/1957	02:00	US#5

OH # 17		
Before 4/01/1893		LMT
4/01/1893	12:00	CST
3/31/1918	02:00	CWT
10/27/1918	02:00	CST
1/01/1919	02:00	EST
3/30/1919	02:00	EWT
10/26/1919	02:00	EST
2/09/1942	02:00	EWT
2/21/1943	02:00	CWT
9/30/1945	02:00	EST
4/24/1966	02:00	US#2

OH # 18		
Before 4/01/1893		LMT
4/01/1893	12:00	CST
3/31/1918	02:00	CWT
10/27/1918	02:00	CST
1/01/1919	02:00	EST
3/30/1919	02:00	EWT
10/26/1919	02:00	EST
2/09/1942	02:00	EWT
2/21/1943	02:00	CWT
9/30/1945	02:00	EST
6/01/1960	02:00	EDT
9/30/1960	02:00	EST
6/04/1961	02:00	EDT
9/03/1961	02:00	EST
4/29/1962	02:00	EDT
9/30/1962	02:00	EST
6/01/1963	02:00	EDT
8/31/1963	02:00	EST
4/26/1964	02:00	EDT
9/27/1964	02:00	EST
4/25/1965	02:00	US#2

OH # 19		
Before 4/01/1893		LMT
4/01/1893	12:00	CST
3/31/1918	02:00	CWT
10/27/1918	02:00	CST
1/01/1919	02:00	EST
3/30/1919	02:00	EWT
10/26/1919	02:00	EST
2/09/1942	02:00	EWT
2/21/1943	02:00	CWT
9/30/1945	02:00	EST
4/25/1948	02:00	EDT
9/26/1948	02:00	EST
4/28/1957	02:00	US#5

OH # 20		
Before 4/01/1893		LMT
4/01/1893	12:00	CST
3/31/1918	02:00	CWT
10/27/1918	02:00	CST
1/01/1919	02:00	EST
3/30/1919	02:00	EWT
10/26/1919	02:00	EST
2/09/1942	02:00	EWT
2/21/1943	02:00	CWT
9/30/1945	02:00	EST
4/28/1963	02:00	EDT
9/29/1963	02:00	EST
4/26/1964	02:00	EDT
9/27/1964	02:00	EST
4/25/1965	02:00	EDT
9/26/1965	02:00	EST
4/24/1966	02:00	US#1

OH # 21		
Before 4/01/1893		LMT
4/01/1893	12:00	CST
3/31/1918	02:00	CWT
10/27/1918	02:00	CST
1/01/1919	02:00	EST
3/30/1919	02:00	EWT
10/26/1919	02:00	EST
2/09/1942	02:00	EWT
2/21/1943	02:00	CWT
9/30/1945	02:00	EST
4/29/1956	02:00	US#5

OH # 22		
Before 4/01/1893		LMT
4/01/1893	12:00	CST
3/31/1918	02:00	CWT
10/27/1918	02:00	CST
1/01/1919	02:00	EST
3/30/1919	02:00	EWT
10/26/1919	02:00	EST
2/09/1942	02:00	EWT
2/21/1943	02:00	CWT
9/30/1945	02:00	EST
4/24/1955	02:00	US#5

OH # 23		
Before 4/01/1893		LMT
4/01/1893	12:00	CST
3/31/1918	02:00	CWT
10/27/1918	02:00	CST
1/01/1919	02:00	EST
3/30/1919	02:00	EWT
10/26/1919	02:00	EST
2/09/1942	02:00	EWT
2/21/1943	02:00	CWT
9/30/1945	02:00	EST
4/25/1954	02:00	EDT
9/26/1954	02:00	EST
4/24/1955	02:00	EDT
9/25/1955	02:00	EST
4/29/1956	02:00	EDT
9/30/1956	02:00	EST
4/28/1957	02:00	EDT
9/29/1957	02:00	EST
4/27/1958	02:00	EDT
9/28/1958	02:00	EST
4/26/1959	02:00	EDT
9/27/1959	02:00	EST
4/24/1960	02:00	EDT
9/25/1960	02:00	EST
4/30/1961	02:00	EDT
9/24/1961	02:00	EST
4/29/1962	02:00	EDT
9/30/1962	02:00	EST
4/28/1963	02:00	EDT
9/29/1963	02:00	EST
4/26/1964	02:00	EDT
9/27/1964	02:00	EST
4/25/1965	02:00	US#2

OH # 24		
Before 4/01/1893		LMT
4/01/1893	12:00	CST
3/31/1918	02:00	CWT
10/27/1918	02:00	CST
1/01/1919	02:00	EST
3/30/1919	02:00	EWT
10/26/1919	02:00	EST
2/09/1942	02:00	EWT
2/21/1943	02:00	CWT
9/30/1945	02:00	EST
4/24/1955	02:00	EDT
9/25/1955	02:00	EST
4/29/1956	02:00	EDT
9/30/1956	02:00	EST
4/28/1957	02:00	EDT
9/29/1957	02:00	EST
4/27/1958	02:00	EDT
9/28/1958	02:00	EST
4/26/1959	02:00	EDT
9/27/1959	02:00	EST
4/24/1960	02:00	US#2

OH # 25		
Before 4/01/1893		LMT
4/01/1893	12:00	CST
5/01/1914	02:00	EST
3/31/1918	02:00	EWT
10/27/1918	02:00	EST
3/30/1919	02:00	EWT
5/11/1919	02:00	CWT
10/26/1919	02:00	EST
2/09/1942	02:00	EWT
9/26/1943	02:00	CWT
4/30/1944	02:00	EWT
9/24/1944	02:00	CWT
4/29/1945	02:00	EWT
9/30/1945	02:00	EST
4/25/1948	02:00	US#5

OH # 26		
Before 6/15/1890		LMT
6/15/1890	12:00	CST
5/01/1914	02:00	EST
3/31/1918	02:00	EWT
10/27/1918	02:00	EST
3/30/1919	02:00	EWT
5/11/1919	02:00	CWT
10/26/1919	02:00	EST
2/09/1942	02:00	EWT
9/26/1943	02:00	CWT
4/30/1944	02:00	EWT
9/24/1944	02:00	CWT
4/29/1945	02:00	EWT
9/30/1945	02:00	EST
4/25/1948	02:00	US#5

OH # 27		
Before 4/01/1893		LMT
4/01/1893	12:00	CST
3/31/1918	02:00	CWT
10/27/1918	02:00	CST
1/01/1919	02:00	EST
3/30/1919	02:00	CWT
10/26/1919	02:00	CST
3/30/1924	02:00	EST
2/09/1942	02:00	EWT
2/21/1943	02:00	CWT
9/30/1945	02:00	EST
4/30/1967	02:00	US#1

OH # 28		
Before 4/01/1893		LMT
4/01/1893	12:00	CST
3/31/1918	02:00	CWT
10/27/1918	02:00	CST
1/01/1919	02:00	EST
3/30/1919	02:00	CWT
10/26/1919	02:00	CST
3/30/1924	02:00	EST
2/09/1942	02:00	EWT
2/21/1943	02:00	CWT
9/30/1945	02:00	EST
4/27/1947	02:00	EDT
9/28/1947	02:00	EST
4/30/1967	02:00	US#1

OH # 29		
Before 4/01/1893		LMT
4/01/1893	12:00	CST
3/31/1918	02:00	CWT
10/27/1918	02:00	CST
1/01/1919	02:00	EST
3/30/1919	02:00	CWT
10/26/1919	02:00	CST
6/01/1920	02:00	EST
2/09/1942	02:00	EWT
9/26/1943	02:00	CWT
4/01/1944	02:00	EWT
9/03/1944	02:00	CWT
4/01/1945	02:00	EWT
9/30/1945	02:00	EST
4/30/1967	02:00	US#1

OH # 30		
Before 4/01/1893		LMT
4/01/1893	12:00	CST
3/31/1918	02:00	CWT
10/27/1918	02:00	CST
1/01/1919	02:00	EST
3/30/1919	02:00	EWT
6/01/1919	02:00	CWT
10/26/1919	02:00	CST
4/01/1922	02:00	EST
2/09/1942	02:00	EWT
2/21/1943	02:00	CWT
9/30/1945	02:00	EST
4/30/1967	02:00	US#1

OH # 31		
Before 4/01/1893		LMT
4/01/1893	12:00	CST
3/31/1918	02:00	CWT
10/27/1918	02:00	CST
3/30/1919	02:00	CWT

TIME TABLES

10/26/1919 02:00 CST
3/28/1920 02:00 CDT
10/31/1920 02:00 CST
3/26/1921 02:00 CDT
10/02/1921 02:00 CST
11/21/1921 02:00 EST
2/09/1942 02:00 EWT
10/01/1943 00:01 CWT
4/01/1944 00:01 EWT
10/01/1944 00:01 CWT
4/01/1945 00:01 EWT
9/30/1945 02:00 EST
4/25/1948 02:00 EDT
9/26/1948 02:00 EST
4/30/1961 02:00 US#2

OH # 32
Before 4/01/1893 LMT
4/01/1893 12:00 CST
3/31/1918 02:00 CWT
10/27/1918 02:00 CST
3/30/1919 02:00 CWT
10/26/1919 02:00 CST
3/30/1924 02:00 EST
2/09/1942 02:00 EWT
2/21/1943 02:00 CWT
9/30/1945 02:00 EST
4/30/1967 02:00 US#1

OH # 33
Before 4/01/1893 LMT
4/01/1893 12:00 CST
3/31/1918 02:00 CWT
10/27/1918 02:00 CST
3/30/1919 02:00 CWT
10/26/1919 02:00 CST
8/31/1924 00:01 EST
2/09/1942 02:00 EWT
2/21/1943 02:00 CWT
9/30/1945 02:00 EST
4/30/1967 02:00 US#1

OH # 34
Before 4/01/1893 LMT
4/01/1893 12:00 CST
3/31/1918 02:00 CWT
10/27/1918 02:00 CST
3/30/1919 02:00 CWT
10/26/1919 02:00 CST
4/03/1927 02:00 EST
2/09/1942 02:00 EWT
2/21/1943 02:00 CWT
9/30/1945 02:00 EST
4/30/1967 02:00 US#1

OH # 35
Before 4/01/1893 LMT
4/01/1893 12:00 CST
3/31/1918 02:00 CWT
10/27/1918 02:00 CST
3/30/1919 02:00 CWT
10/26/1919 02:00 CST
4/03/1927 02:00 EST
2/09/1942 02:00 EWT
2/21/1943 02:00 CWT
9/30/1945 02:00 EST
4/24/1955 02:00 US#5

OH # 36
Before 4/01/1893 LMT
4/01/1893 12:00 CST
3/31/1918 02:00 CWT
10/27/1918 02:00 CST
3/30/1919 02:00 CWT
10/26/1919 02:00 CST
4/03/1927 02:00 EST
2/09/1942 02:00 EWT
2/21/1943 02:00 CWT
9/30/1945 02:00 EST
4/24/1966 02:00 US#1

OH # 37
Before 4/01/1893 LMT
4/01/1893 12:00 CST
3/31/1918 02:00 CWT
10/27/1918 02:00 CST
3/30/1919 02:00 CWT
10/26/1919 02:00 CST
4/03/1927 02:00 EST
2/09/1942 02:00 EWT
2/21/1943 02:00 CWT
9/30/1945 02:00 EST
4/28/1963 02:00 EDT
9/29/1963 02:00 EST
4/26/1964 02:00 EDT
9/27/1964 02:00 EST
4/25/1965 02:00 EDT
9/26/1965 02:00 EST
4/24/1966 02:00 US#1

OH # 38
Before 4/01/1893 LMT
4/01/1893 12:00 CST
5/01/1914 02:00 EST
3/31/1918 02:00 EWT
10/27/1918 02:00 EST
3/30/1919 02:00 EWT
10/26/1919 02:00 EST
2/09/1942 02:00 EWT
2/21/1943 02:00 CWT
9/30/1945 02:00 EST
4/30/1967 02:00 US#1

OH # 39
Before 1/01/1890 LMT
1/01/1890 12:00 CST
3/31/1918 02:00 CWT
10/27/1918 02:00 CST
3/30/1919 02:00 CWT
10/26/1919 02:00 CST
3/28/1920 02:00 CDT
10/31/1920 02:00 CST
4/03/1921 02:00 CDT
9/25/1921 02:00 CST
4/29/1923 02:00 CDT
9/30/1923 02:00 CST
4/27/1924 02:00 CDT
9/28/1924 02:00 CST
4/26/1925 02:00 CDT
9/27/1925 02:00 CST
4/25/1926 02:00 CDT
9/26/1926 02:00 CST
4/03/1927 02:00 EST
2/09/1942 02:00 EWT
9/26/1943 02:00 CWT
4/02/1944 02:00 EWT
9/03/1944 02:00 CWT
9/30/1945 02:00 EST
4/30/1967 02:00 US#1

OH # 40
Before 4/01/1893 LMT
4/01/1893 12:00 CST
3/31/1918 02:00 CWT
10/27/1918 02:00 CST
3/30/1919 02:00 CWT
5/11/1919 02:00 EWT
10/26/1919 02:00 EST
2/09/1942 02:00 EWT
9/26/1943 02:00 CWT
4/30/1944 02:00 EWT
9/24/1944 02:00 CWT
4/29/1945 02:00 EWT
9/30/1945 02:00 EST
4/25/1948 02:00 EDT
9/26/1948 02:00 EST
4/24/1949 02:00 EDT
9/25/1949 02:00 EST
4/29/1956 02:00 EDT
9/30/1956 02:00 EST
4/28/1957 02:00 EDT
9/29/1957 02:00 EST
4/27/1958 02:00 EDT
10/26/1958 02:00 EST
4/26/1959 02:00 EDT
10/25/1959 02:00 EST
4/24/1960 02:00 EDT
10/30/1960 02:00 EST
4/30/1961 02:00 EDT
10/29/1961 02:00 EST
4/29/1962 02:00 EDT
10/28/1962 02:00 EST
4/28/1963 02:00 EDT
10/27/1963 02:00 EST
5/30/1964 02:00 EDT
9/07/1964 02:00 EST
4/25/1965 02:00 US#2

OH # 41
Before 4/01/1893 LMT
4/01/1893 12:00 CST
3/31/1918 02:00 CWT
10/27/1918 02:00 CST
3/30/1919 02:00 CWT
10/26/1919 02:00 CST
4/05/1925 02:00 EST
2/09/1942 02:00 EWT
9/26/1943 02:00 CWT
4/02/1944 02:00 EWT
9/03/1944 02:00 CWT
9/30/1945 02:00 EST
4/30/1967 02:00 US#1

OH # 42
Before 4/01/1893 LMT
4/01/1893 12:00 CST
3/31/1918 02:00 CWT
10/27/1918 02:00 CST
3/30/1919 02:00 CWT
10/26/1919 02:00 CST
3/28/1920 02:00 CDT
10/31/1920 02:00 CST
4/24/1921 02:00 CDT
9/25/1921 02:00 CST
4/30/1922 02:00 CDT
9/24/1922 02:00 CST
4/29/1923 02:00 CDT
9/30/1923 02:00 CST
4/27/1924 02:00 CDT
9/28/1924 02:00 CST
4/26/1925 02:00 CDT
9/27/1925 02:00 CST
4/25/1926 02:00 CDT
9/26/1926 02:00 EST
2/09/1942 02:00 EWT
9/26/1943 02:00 CWT
4/30/1944 02:00 EWT
9/24/1944 02:00 CWT
4/29/1945 02:00 EWT
9/30/1945 02:00 EST
4/25/1948 02:00 US#5

OH # 43
Before 4/01/1893 LMT
4/01/1893 12:00 CST
3/31/1918 02:00 CWT
10/27/1918 02:00 CST
3/30/1919 02:00 CWT
10/26/1919 02:00 CST
3/28/1920 02:00 CDT
10/31/1920 02:00 CST
4/03/1921 02:00 CDT
9/25/1921 02:00 CST
4/02/1922 02:00 CDT
9/24/1922 02:00 CST
4/01/1923 02:00 CDT
9/30/1923 02:00 CST
4/06/1924 02:00 CDT
9/28/1924 02:00 CST
4/05/1925 02:00 CDT
9/27/1925 02:00 CST
4/04/1926 02:00 CDT
9/26/1926 02:00 EST
2/09/1942 02:00 EWT
9/26/1943 02:00 CWT
4/30/1944 02:00 EWT
9/24/1944 02:00 CWT
4/29/1945 02:00 EWT
9/30/1945 02:00 EST
4/25/1948 02:00 EDT
9/26/1948 02:00 EST
4/30/1950 02:00 EDT
9/30/1950 02:00 US#5

OH # 44
Before 4/01/1893 LMT
4/01/1893 12:00 CST
3/31/1918 02:00 CWT
10/27/1918 02:00 CST
1/01/1919 02:00 EST
3/30/1919 02:00 EWT
5/17/1919 02:00 CWT
10/26/1919 02:00 EST
2/09/1942 02:00 EWT
9/26/1943 02:00 CWT
4/30/1944 02:00 EWT
9/24/1944 02:00 CWT
4/29/1945 02:00 EWT
9/30/1945 02:00 EST
4/30/1967 02:00 US#1

OH # 45
Before 4/01/1893 LMT
4/01/1893 12:00 CST
3/31/1918 02:00 CWT
10/27/1918 02:00 CST
1/01/1919 02:00 EST
3/30/1919 02:00 EWT
5/17/1919 02:00 CWT
10/26/1919 02:00 EST
2/09/1942 02:00 EWT
9/26/1943 02:00 CWT
4/30/1944 02:00 EWT
9/24/1944 02:00 CWT
4/29/1945 02:00 EWT
9/30/1945 02:00 EST
4/28/1946 02:00 US#5

OH # 46
Before 4/01/1893 LMT
4/01/1893 12:00 CST
3/31/1918 02:00 CWT
10/27/1918 02:00 CST
1/01/1919 02:00 EST
3/30/1919 02:00 EWT
5/17/1919 02:00 CWT
10/26/1919 02:00 EST
2/09/1942 02:00 EWT
9/26/1943 02:00 CWT
4/30/1944 02:00 EWT
9/24/1944 02:00 CWT
4/29/1945 02:00 EWT
9/30/1945 02:00 EST
4/25/1948 02:00 US#5

OH # 47
Before 4/01/1893 LMT
4/01/1893 12:00 CST
3/31/1918 02:00 CWT
10/27/1918 02:00 CST
1/01/1919 02:00 EST
3/30/1919 02:00 EWT
5/17/1919 02:00 CWT
10/26/1919 02:00 EST
2/09/1942 02:00 EWT
9/26/1943 02:00 CWT
4/30/1944 02:00 EWT
9/24/1944 02:00 CWT
4/29/1945 02:00 EWT
9/30/1945 02:00 EST
4/25/1948 02:00 EDT
9/26/1948 02:00 EST
4/24/1949 02:00 EDT
9/25/1949 02:00 EST
4/30/1950 02:00 EDT
9/30/1950 02:00 US#5

OH # 48
Before 4/01/1893 LMT
4/01/1893 12:00 CST
3/31/1918 02:00 CWT
10/27/1918 02:00 CST
1/01/1919 02:00 EST
3/30/1919 02:00 EWT
5/17/1919 02:00 CWT
10/26/1919 02:00 EST
2/09/1942 02:00 EWT
9/26/1943 02:00 CWT
4/30/1944 02:00 EWT
9/24/1944 02:00 CWT
4/29/1945 02:00 EWT
9/30/1945 02:00 EST
4/25/1948 02:00 EDT
9/26/1948 02:00 EST
4/24/1949 02:00 EDT
9/25/1949 02:00 EST
4/29/1956 02:00 US#5

OH # 49
Before 4/01/1893 LMT
4/01/1893 12:00 CST
3/31/1918 02:00 CWT
10/27/1918 02:00 CST
1/01/1919 02:00 EST
3/30/1919 02:00 EWT
5/17/1919 02:00 CWT
10/26/1919 02:00 EST
2/09/1942 02:00 EWT
9/26/1943 02:00 CWT
4/30/1944 02:00 EWT
9/24/1944 02:00 CWT
4/29/1945 02:00 EWT
9/30/1945 02:00 EST
4/25/1948 02:00 EDT
9/26/1948 02:00 EST
4/24/1949 02:00 EDT
9/25/1949 02:00 EST
4/29/1951 02:00 EDT
9/30/1951 02:00 EST
4/24/1955 02:00 US#5

OH # 50
Before 4/01/1893 LMT
4/01/1893 12:00 CST
3/31/1918 02:00 CWT
10/27/1918 02:00 CST
1/01/1919 02:00 EST
3/30/1919 02:00 EWT
5/17/1919 02:00 CWT
10/26/1919 02:00 EST
2/09/1942 02:00 EWT
9/26/1943 02:00 CWT
4/30/1944 02:00 EWT
9/24/1944 02:00 CWT
4/29/1945 02:00 EWT
9/30/1945 02:00 EST
4/25/1948 02:00 EDT
9/26/1948 02:00 EST
4/29/1951 02:00 US#5

OH # 51
Before 4/01/1893 LMT
4/01/1893 12:00 CST
3/31/1918 02:00 CWT
10/27/1918 02:00 CST
1/01/1919 02:00 EST
3/30/1919 02:00 EWT
5/17/1919 02:00 CWT
10/26/1919 02:00 EST
2/09/1942 02:00 EWT
9/26/1943 02:00 CWT
4/30/1944 02:00 EWT
9/24/1944 02:00 CWT
4/29/1945 02:00 EWT
9/30/1945 02:00 EST
4/25/1948 02:00 EDT
9/26/1948 02:00 EST
4/24/1949 02:00 EDT
9/25/1949 02:00 EST
4/30/1950 02:00 EDT
9/30/1950 02:00 US#5

OH # 52
Before 4/01/1893 LMT
4/01/1893 12:00 CST
3/31/1918 02:00 CWT
10/27/1918 02:00 CST
1/01/1919 02:00 EST
3/30/1919 02:00 EWT
5/17/1919 02:00 CWT
10/26/1919 02:00 EST
2/09/1942 02:00 EWT
9/26/1943 02:00 CWT
4/30/1944 02:00 EWT
9/24/1944 02:00 CWT
4/29/1945 02:00 EWT
9/30/1945 02:00 EST
4/30/1950 02:00 EDT
9/24/1950 02:00 EST
4/29/1951 02:00 EDT
9/30/1951 02:00 EST
4/27/1952 02:00 EDT
9/28/1952 02:00 EST
4/26/1953 02:00 EDT
9/27/1953 02:00 EST
4/25/1954 02:00 EDT
9/26/1954 02:00 EST
4/24/1955 02:00 EDT
9/25/1955 02:00 EST
4/29/1956 02:00 EDT
9/30/1956 02:00 EST
4/28/1957 02:00 EDT
9/29/1957 02:00 EST
4/27/1958 02:00 EDT
9/28/1958 02:00 EST
4/26/1959 02:00 EDT
9/27/1959 02:00 EST
4/24/1960 02:00 US#2

OH # 53
Before 4/01/1893 LMT
4/01/1893 12:00 CST
3/31/1918 02:00 CWT
10/27/1918 02:00 CST
1/01/1919 02:00 EST
3/30/1919 02:00 EWT
5/17/1919 02:00 CWT
10/26/1919 02:00 EST
2/09/1942 02:00 EWT
9/26/1943 02:00 CWT
4/30/1944 02:00 EWT
9/24/1944 02:00 CWT
4/29/1945 02:00 EWT
9/30/1945 02:00 EST
4/24/1949 02:00 US#5

OH # 54
Before 4/01/1893 LMT
4/01/1893 12:00 CST
3/31/1918 02:00 CWT
10/27/1918 02:00 CST
1/01/1919 02:00 EST
3/30/1919 02:00 EWT
5/17/1919 02:00 CWT
10/26/1919 02:00 EST
2/09/1942 02:00 EWT
9/26/1943 02:00 CWT
4/30/1944 02:00 EWT
9/24/1944 02:00 CWT
4/29/1945 02:00 EWT
9/30/1945 02:00 EST
4/25/1948 02:00 EDT
9/26/1948 02:00 EST
4/24/1949 02:00 EDT
9/25/1949 02:00 EST
4/30/1950 02:00 EDT
9/24/1950 02:00 EST
4/29/1951 02:00 EDT
9/30/1951 02:00 EST
4/27/1952 02:00 EDT
9/28/1952 02:00 EST
4/26/1953 02:00 EDT
9/27/1953 02:00 EST
4/25/1954 02:00 EDT
9/26/1954 02:00 EST
4/24/1955 02:00 EDT
9/25/1955 02:00 EST
4/29/1956 02:00 EDT
10/28/1956 02:00 EST
4/28/1957 02:00 US#5

OH # 55
Before 4/01/1893 LMT
4/01/1893 12:00 CST
3/31/1918 02:00 CWT
10/27/1918 02:00 CST
1/01/1919 02:00 EST
3/30/1919 02:00 EWT
5/17/1919 02:00 CWT
10/26/1919 02:00 EST
2/09/1942 02:00 EWT
9/26/1943 02:00 CWT
4/30/1944 02:00 EWT
9/24/1944 02:00 CWT
4/29/1945 02:00 EWT
9/30/1945 02:00 EST
4/29/1951 02:00 EDT
9/30/1951 02:00 EST
4/24/1955 02:00 US#5

OH # 56
Before 4/01/1893 LMT
4/01/1893 12:00 CST
3/31/1918 02:00 CWT
10/27/1918 02:00 CST
1/01/1919 02:00 EST
3/30/1919 02:00 EWT
5/17/1919 02:00 CWT
10/26/1919 02:00 EST
2/09/1942 02:00 EWT
9/26/1943 02:00 CWT
4/30/1944 02:00 EWT
9/24/1944 02:00 CWT
4/29/1945 02:00 EWT
9/30/1945 02:00 EST
4/29/1951 02:00 EDT
9/30/1951 02:00 EST
4/29/1956 02:00 US#5

OH # 57
Before 4/01/1893 LMT
4/01/1893 12:00 CST
3/31/1918 02:00 CWT
10/27/1918 02:00 CST
1/01/1919 02:00 EST
3/30/1919 02:00 EWT
5/17/1919 02:00 CWT
10/26/1919 02:00 EST
2/09/1942 02:00 EWT
9/26/1943 02:00 CWT
4/30/1944 02:00 EWT
9/24/1944 02:00 CWT
4/29/1945 02:00 EWT
9/30/1945 02:00 EST
4/26/1953 02:00 US#5

OH # 58
Before 4/01/1893 LMT
4/01/1893 12:00 CST
3/31/1918 02:00 CWT
10/27/1918 02:00 CST
1/01/1919 02:00 EST
3/30/1919 02:00 EWT
5/17/1919 02:00 CWT
10/26/1919 02:00 EST
2/09/1942 02:00 EWT
9/26/1943 02:00 CWT
4/30/1944 02:00 EWT
9/24/1944 02:00 CWT
4/29/1945 02:00 EWT
9/30/1945 02:00 EST
4/25/1954 02:00 US#5

OH # 59
Before 4/01/1893 LMT
4/01/1893 12:00 CST
3/31/1918 02:00 CWT
10/27/1918 02:00 CST
1/01/1919 02:00 EST
3/30/1919 02:00 EWT
5/17/1919 02:00 CWT
10/26/1919 02:00 EST
2/09/1942 02:00 EWT
9/26/1943 02:00 CWT
4/30/1944 02:00 EWT
9/24/1944 02:00 CWT
4/29/1945 02:00 EWT
9/30/1945 02:00 EST
4/25/1954 02:00 EDT
9/26/1954 02:00 EST
4/29/1956 02:00 US#5

OH # 60
Before 4/01/1893 LMT
4/01/1893 12:00 CST
3/31/1918 02:00 CWT
10/27/1918 02:00 CST
1/01/1919 02:00 EST
3/30/1919 02:00 EWT
5/17/1919 02:00 CWT

TIME TABLES

Date	Time	Zone
10/26/1919	02:00	EST
2/09/1942	02:00	EWT
9/26/1943	02:00	CWT
4/30/1944	02:00	EWT
9/24/1944	02:00	CWT
4/29/1945	02:00	EWT
9/30/1945	02:00	EST
4/24/1955	02:00	US#5

OH # 61

Date	Time	Zone
Before 4/01/1893		LMT
4/01/1893	12:00	CST
3/31/1918	02:00	CWT
10/27/1918	02:00	CST
1/01/1919	02:00	EST
3/30/1919	02:00	EWT
5/17/1919	02:00	CWT
10/26/1919	02:00	EST
2/09/1942	02:00	EWT
9/26/1943	02:00	CWT
4/30/1944	02:00	EWT
9/24/1944	02:00	CWT
4/29/1945	02:00	EWT
9/30/1945	02:00	EST
4/28/1957	02:00	US#5

OH # 62

Date	Time	Zone
Before 4/01/1893		LMT
4/01/1893	12:00	CST
3/31/1918	02:00	CWT
10/27/1918	02:00	CST
1/01/1919	02:00	EST
3/30/1919	02:00	EWT
5/17/1919	02:00	CWT
10/26/1919	02:00	EST
2/09/1942	02:00	EWT
9/26/1943	02:00	CWT
4/30/1944	02:00	EWT
9/24/1944	02:00	CWT
4/29/1945	02:00	EWT
9/30/1945	02:00	EST
4/27/1958	02:00	US#5

OH # 63

Date	Time	Zone
Before 4/01/1893		LMT
4/01/1893	12:00	CST
3/31/1918	02:00	CWT
10/27/1918	02:00	CST
1/01/1919	02:00	EST
3/30/1919	02:00	EWT
5/17/1919	02:00	CWT
10/26/1919	02:00	EST
2/09/1942	02:00	EWT
9/26/1943	02:00	CWT
4/30/1944	02:00	EWT
9/24/1944	02:00	CWT
4/29/1945	02:00	EWT
9/30/1945	02:00	EST
4/24/1955	02:00	EDT
9/25/1955	02:00	EST
4/29/1956	02:00	EDT
10/28/1956	02:00	US#5

OH # 64

Date	Time	Zone
Before 4/01/1893		LMT
4/01/1893	12:00	CST
3/31/1918	02:00	CWT
10/27/1918	02:00	CST
1/01/1919	02:00	EST
3/30/1919	02:00	EWT
5/17/1919	02:00	CWT
10/26/1919	02:00	EST
2/09/1942	02:00	EWT
9/26/1943	02:00	CWT
4/30/1944	02:00	EWT
9/24/1944	02:00	CWT
4/29/1945	02:00	EWT
9/30/1945	02:00	EST
4/24/1966	02:00	US#2

OH # 65

Date	Time	Zone
Before 4/01/1893		LMT
4/01/1893	12:00	CST
3/31/1918	02:00	CWT
10/27/1918	02:00	CST
1/01/1919	02:00	EST
3/30/1919	02:00	EWT
5/17/1919	02:00	CWT
10/26/1919	02:00	EST
2/09/1942	02:00	EWT
9/26/1943	02:00	CWT
4/30/1944	02:00	EWT
9/24/1944	02:00	CWT
4/29/1945	02:00	EWT
9/30/1945	02:00	EST
4/25/1948	02:00	EDT
9/26/1948	02:00	EST
4/24/1949	02:00	EDT
9/25/1949	02:00	EST
4/26/1953	02:00	EDT
9/27/1953	02:00	EST
4/29/1956	02:00	US#5

OH # 66

Date	Time	Zone
Before 4/01/1893		LMT
4/01/1893	12:00	CST
3/31/1918	02:00	CWT
10/27/1918	02:00	CST
1/01/1919	02:00	EST
3/30/1919	02:00	EWT
5/17/1919	02:00	CWT
10/26/1919	02:00	EST
2/09/1942	02:00	EWT
9/26/1943	02:00	CWT
4/30/1944	02:00	EWT
9/24/1944	02:00	CWT
4/29/1945	02:00	EWT
9/30/1945	02:00	EST
4/24/1949	02:00	EDT
9/25/1949	02:00	EST
4/29/1956	02:00	US#5

OH # 67

Date	Time	Zone
Before 4/01/1893		LMT
4/01/1893	12:00	CST
3/31/1918	02:00	CST
10/27/1918	02:00	CST
1/01/1919	02:00	EST
3/30/1919	02:00	EWT
5/17/1919	02:00	CWT
10/26/1919	02:00	EST
2/09/1942	02:00	EWT
9/26/1943	02:00	CWT
4/30/1944	02:00	EWT
9/24/1944	02:00	CWT
4/29/1945	02:00	EWT
9/30/1945	02:00	EST
4/29/1956	02:00	US#5

OH # 68

Date	Time	Zone
Before 4/01/1893		LMT
4/01/1893	12:00	CST
3/31/1918	02:00	CWT
10/27/1918	02:00	CST
1/01/1919	02:00	EST
3/30/1919	02:00	EWT
5/17/1919	02:00	CWT
10/26/1919	02:00	EST
2/09/1942	02:00	EWT
9/26/1943	02:00	CWT
4/30/1944	02:00	EWT
9/24/1944	02:00	CWT
4/29/1945	02:00	EWT
9/30/1945	02:00	EST
4/29/1956	02:00	EDT
9/30/1956	02:00	EST
4/28/1957	02:00	EDT
9/29/1957	02:00	EST
4/27/1958	02:00	EDT
9/28/1958	02:00	EST
4/26/1959	02:00	EDT
9/27/1959	02:00	EST
4/24/1960	02:00	US#2

OH # 69

Date	Time	Zone
Before 4/01/1893		LMT
4/01/1893	12:00	CST
3/31/1918	02:00	CWT
10/27/1918	02:00	CST
1/01/1919	02:00	EST
3/30/1919	02:00	EWT
5/17/1919	02:00	CWT
10/26/1919	02:00	EST
2/09/1942	02:00	EWT
9/26/1943	02:00	CWT
4/30/1944	02:00	EWT
9/24/1944	02:00	CWT
4/29/1945	02:00	EWT
9/30/1945	02:00	EST
4/28/1957	02:00	EDT
9/29/1957	02:00	EST
4/27/1958	02:00	EDT
9/28/1958	02:00	EST
4/26/1959	02:00	EDT
9/27/1959	02:00	EST
4/24/1960	02:00	EDT
9/25/1960	02:00	EST
4/30/1961	02:00	EDT
9/24/1961	02:00	EST
4/29/1962	02:00	US#2

OH # 70

Date	Time	Zone
Before 4/01/1893		LMT
4/01/1893	12:00	CST
3/31/1918	02:00	CWT
10/27/1918	02:00	CST
1/01/1919	02:00	EST
3/30/1919	02:00	EWT
5/17/1919	02:00	CWT
10/26/1919	02:00	EST
2/09/1942	02:00	EWT
9/26/1943	02:00	CWT
4/30/1944	02:00	EWT
9/24/1944	02:00	CWT
4/29/1945	02:00	EWT
9/30/1945	02:00	EST
4/24/1955	02:00	US#5

OH # 71

Date	Time	Zone
Before 4/01/1893		LMT
4/01/1893	12:00	CST
3/31/1918	02:00	CWT
10/27/1918	02:00	CST
1/01/1919	02:00	EST
3/30/1919	02:00	EWT
5/17/1919	02:00	CWT
10/26/1919	02:00	EST
2/09/1942	02:00	EWT
9/26/1943	02:00	CWT
4/30/1944	02:00	EWT
9/24/1944	02:00	CWT
4/29/1945	02:00	EWT
9/30/1945	02:00	EST
4/25/1948	02:00	EDT
9/26/1948	02:00	EST
4/24/1949	02:00	EDT
9/25/1949	02:00	EST
4/30/1950	02:00	EDT
9/24/1950	02:00	EST
4/29/1951	02:00	EDT
9/30/1951	02:00	EST
4/27/1952	02:00	EDT
9/28/1952	02:00	EST
4/26/1953	02:00	EDT
9/27/1953	02:00	EST
4/25/1954	02:00	EDT
9/26/1954	02:00	EST
4/24/1955	02:00	EDT
9/25/1955	02:00	EST
4/29/1956	02:00	EDT
9/30/1956	02:00	EST
4/28/1957	02:00	EDT
9/29/1957	02:00	EST
4/27/1958	02:00	EDT
9/28/1958	02:00	EST
4/26/1959	02:00	EDT
9/27/1959	02:00	EST
4/24/1960	02:00	US#5

OH # 72

Date	Time	Zone
Before 4/01/1893		LMT
4/01/1893	12:00	CST
3/31/1918	02:00	CWT
10/27/1918	02:00	CST
1/01/1919	02:00	EST
3/30/1919	02:00	EWT
5/17/1919	02:00	CWT
10/26/1919	02:00	EST
2/09/1942	02:00	EWT
9/26/1943	02:00	CWT
4/30/1944	02:00	EWT
9/24/1944	02:00	CWT
4/29/1945	02:00	EWT
9/30/1945	02:00	EST
4/29/1951	02:00	EDT
9/30/1951	02:00	EST
4/27/1952	02:00	EDT
9/28/1952	02:00	EST
4/26/1953	02:00	EDT
9/27/1953	02:00	EST
4/25/1954	02:00	EDT
9/26/1954	02:00	EST
4/24/1955	02:00	EDT
9/25/1955	02:00	EST
4/29/1956	02:00	EDT
9/30/1956	02:00	EST
4/28/1957	02:00	EDT
9/29/1957	02:00	EST
4/27/1958	02:00	EDT
9/28/1958	02:00	EST
4/26/1959	02:00	EDT
9/27/1959	02:00	EST
4/24/1960	02:00	US#2

OH # 73

Date	Time	Zone
Before 4/01/1893		LMT
4/01/1893	12:00	CST
3/31/1918	02:00	CWT
10/27/1918	02:00	CST
1/01/1919	02:00	EST
3/30/1919	02:00	EWT
5/17/1919	02:00	CWT
10/26/1919	02:00	EST
2/09/1942	02:00	EWT
9/26/1943	02:00	CWT
4/30/1944	02:00	EWT
9/24/1944	02:00	CWT
4/29/1945	02:00	EWT
9/30/1945	02:00	EST
4/24/1955	02:00	US#5

OH # 74

Date	Time	Zone
Before 4/01/1893		LMT
4/01/1893	12:00	CST
3/31/1918	02:00	CWT
10/27/1918	02:00	CST
1/01/1919	02:00	EST
3/30/1919	02:00	EWT
5/17/1919	02:00	CWT
10/26/1919	02:00	EST
2/09/1942	02:00	EWT
9/26/1943	02:00	CWT
4/30/1944	02:00	EWT
9/24/1944	02:00	CWT
4/29/1945	02:00	EWT
9/30/1945	02:00	EST
4/28/1946	02:00	EDT
9/29/1946	02:00	EST
4/27/1947	02:00	EDT
9/28/1947	02:00	EST
4/25/1948	02:00	EDT
9/26/1948	02:00	EST
4/24/1949	02:00	EDT
9/25/1949	02:00	EST
4/30/1950	02:00	EDT
9/24/1950	02:00	EST
4/29/1951	02:00	EDT
9/30/1951	02:00	EST
4/27/1952	02:00	EDT
9/28/1952	02:00	EST
4/26/1953	02:00	EDT
9/27/1953	02:00	EST
4/25/1954	02:00	EDT
9/26/1954	02:00	EST
4/24/1955	02:00	EDT
9/25/1955	02:00	EST
4/29/1956	02:00	EDT
9/30/1956	02:00	EST
4/28/1957	02:00	EDT
9/29/1957	02:00	EST
4/27/1958	02:00	EDT
10/26/1958	02:00	EST
4/26/1959	02:00	EDT
10/25/1959	02:00	EST
4/24/1960	02:00	EDT
10/30/1960	02:00	EST
4/30/1961	02:00	EDT
10/01/1961	02:00	EST
4/29/1962	02:00	US#2

OH # 75

Date	Time	Zone
Before 4/01/1893		LMT
4/01/1893	12:00	CST
3/31/1918	02:00	CWT
10/27/1918	02:00	CST
1/01/1919	02:00	EST
3/30/1919	02:00	EWT
5/17/1919	02:00	CWT
10/26/1919	02:00	EST
2/09/1942	02:00	EWT
9/26/1943	02:00	CWT
4/30/1944	02:00	EWT
9/24/1944	02:00	CWT
4/29/1945	02:00	EWT
9/30/1945	02:00	EST
4/28/1946	02:00	EDT
9/29/1946	02:00	EST
4/27/1947	02:00	EDT
9/28/1947	02:00	EST
4/25/1948	02:00	EDT
9/26/1948	02:00	EST
4/24/1949	02:00	EDT
9/25/1949	02:00	EST
4/30/1950	02:00	EDT
9/30/1950	02:00	EST
4/29/1951	02:00	EDT
9/30/1951	02:00	EST
4/27/1952	02:00	EDT
9/28/1952	02:00	EST
4/26/1953	02:00	EDT
9/27/1953	02:00	EST
4/25/1954	02:00	EDT
9/26/1954	02:00	EST
4/24/1955	02:00	EDT
9/25/1955	02:00	EST
4/29/1956	02:00	EDT
9/30/1956	02:00	EST
4/28/1957	02:00	EDT
9/29/1957	02:00	EST
4/27/1958	02:00	EDT
9/07/1958	02:00	EST
4/26/1959	02:00	US#2

OH # 76

Date	Time	Zone
Before 4/01/1893		LMT
4/01/1893	12:00	CST
3/31/1918	02:00	CWT
10/27/1918	02:00	CST
1/01/1919	02:00	EST
3/30/1919	02:00	EWT
5/17/1919	02:00	CWT
10/26/1919	02:00	EST
2/09/1942	02:00	EWT
9/26/1943	02:00	CWT
4/30/1944	02:00	EWT
9/24/1944	02:00	CWT
4/29/1945	02:00	EWT
9/30/1945	02:00	EST
4/27/1958	02:00	EDT
9/28/1958	02:00	EST
4/26/1959	02:00	EDT
9/27/1959	02:00	EST
4/24/1960	02:00	EDT
9/25/1960	02:00	EST
4/30/1961	02:00	EDT
9/24/1961	02:00	EST
4/29/1962	02:00	US#2

OH # 77

Date	Time	Zone
Before 4/01/1893		LMT
4/01/1893	12:00	CST
3/31/1918	02:00	CWT
10/27/1918	02:00	CST
1/01/1919	02:00	EST
3/30/1919	02:00	EWT
5/17/1919	02:00	CWT
10/26/1919	02:00	EST
2/09/1942	02:00	EWT
9/26/1943	02:00	CWT
4/30/1944	02:00	EWT
9/24/1944	02:00	CWT
4/29/1945	02:00	EWT
9/30/1945	02:00	EST
4/28/1946	02:00	EDT
9/29/1946	02:00	EST
4/27/1947	02:00	EDT
9/28/1947	02:00	EST
4/25/1948	02:00	EDT
9/26/1948	02:00	EST
4/24/1949	02:00	EDT
9/25/1949	02:00	EST
4/30/1950	02:00	EDT
9/30/1950	02:00	US#5

OH # 78

Date	Time	Zone
Before 4/01/1893		LMT
4/01/1893	12:00	CST
3/31/1918	02:00	CWT
10/27/1918	02:00	CST
1/01/1919	02:00	EST
3/30/1919	02:00	EWT
5/17/1919	02:00	CWT
10/26/1919	02:00	EST
2/09/1942	02:00	EWT
9/26/1943	02:00	CWT
4/30/1944	02:00	EWT
9/24/1944	02:00	CWT
4/29/1945	02:00	EWT
9/30/1945	02:00	EST
4/25/1954	02:00	EDT
9/26/1954	02:00	EST
4/24/1955	02:00	EDT
9/25/1955	02:00	EST
4/29/1956	02:00	EDT
9/30/1956	02:00	EST
4/28/1957	02:00	EDT
9/29/1957	02:00	EST
4/27/1958	02:00	EDT
9/28/1958	02:00	EST
4/26/1959	02:00	EDT
9/27/1959	02:00	EST
4/24/1960	02:00	EDT
9/25/1960	02:00	EST
4/30/1961	02:00	EDT
9/24/1961	02:00	EST
4/29/1962	02:00	EDT
9/30/1962	02:00	EST
4/28/1963	02:00	EDT
9/29/1963	02:00	EST
4/26/1964	02:00	EDT
9/27/1964	02:00	EST
4/25/1965	02:00	US#2

OH # 79

Date	Time	Zone
Before 4/01/1893		LMT
4/01/1893	12:00	CST
3/31/1918	02:00	CWT
10/27/1918	02:00	CST
1/01/1919	02:00	EST
3/30/1919	02:00	EWT
5/17/1919	02:00	CWT
10/26/1919	02:00	EST
2/09/1942	02:00	EWT
9/26/1943	02:00	CWT
4/30/1944	02:00	EWT
9/24/1944	02:00	CWT
4/29/1945	02:00	EWT
9/30/1945	02:00	EST
4/26/1959	02:00	EDT
9/27/1959	02:00	EST
4/24/1960	02:00	EDT
9/25/1960	02:00	EST
4/30/1961	02:00	EDT
9/24/1961	02:00	EST
4/29/1962	02:00	US#2

OH # 80

Date	Time	Zone
Before 4/01/1893		LMT
4/01/1893	12:00	CST
3/31/1918	02:00	CWT
10/27/1918	02:00	CST
1/01/1919	02:00	EST
3/30/1919	02:00	EWT
5/17/1919	02:00	CWT
10/26/1919	02:00	EST
2/09/1942	02:00	EWT
9/26/1943	02:00	CWT
4/30/1944	02:00	EWT
9/24/1944	02:00	CWT
4/29/1945	02:00	EWT
9/30/1945	02:00	EST
4/24/1955	02:00	US#3

OH # 81

Date	Time	Zone
Before 4/01/1893		LMT
4/01/1893	12:00	CST
3/31/1918	02:00	CWT
10/27/1918	02:00	CST
1/01/1919	02:00	EST
3/30/1919	02:00	EWT
5/17/1919	02:00	CWT
10/26/1919	02:00	EST
2/09/1942	02:00	EWT
9/26/1943	02:00	CWT
4/30/1944	02:00	EWT
9/24/1944	02:00	CWT
4/29/1945	02:00	EWT
9/30/1945	02:00	EST
4/25/1948	02:00	EDT
9/26/1948	02:00	EST
4/24/1949	02:00	EDT
9/25/1949	02:00	EST
4/30/1950	02:00	EDT
9/24/1950	02:00	EST
4/29/1951	02:00	EDT
9/30/1951	02:00	EST
4/27/1952	02:00	EDT
9/28/1952	02:00	EST
4/26/1953	02:00	EDT
9/27/1953	02:00	EST
4/25/1954	02:00	EDT
9/26/1954	02:00	EST
4/24/1955	02:00	EDT
9/25/1955	02:00	EST
4/29/1956	02:00	EDT
10/28/1956	02:00	EST
4/28/1957	02:00	EDT
9/29/1957	02:00	EST
4/27/1958	02:00	EDT
9/28/1958	02:00	EST
4/26/1959	02:00	EDT
9/27/1959	02:00	EST
4/24/1960	02:00	EDT
9/25/1960	02:00	EST
4/30/1961	02:00	EDT
9/24/1961	02:00	EST
4/29/1962	02:00	US#2

OH # 82

Date	Time	Zone
Before 4/01/1893		LMT
4/01/1893	12:00	CST
3/31/1918	02:00	CWT
10/27/1918	02:00	CST
1/01/1919	02:00	EST
3/30/1919	02:00	EWT
5/17/1919	02:00	CWT
10/26/1919	02:00	EST
2/09/1942	02:00	EWT
9/26/1943	02:00	CWT
4/30/1944	02:00	EWT
9/24/1944	02:00	CWT
4/29/1945	02:00	EWT
9/30/1945	02:00	EST
4/27/1958	02:00	EDT
9/28/1958	02:00	EST
4/26/1959	02:00	EDT
9/27/1959	02:00	EST
4/24/1960	02:00	EDT
9/25/1960	02:00	EST
4/30/1961	02:00	EDT
9/24/1961	02:00	EST
4/29/1962	02:00	US#2

OH # 83

Date	Time	Zone
Before 4/01/1893		LMT
4/01/1893	12:00	CST
3/31/1918	02:00	CWT
10/27/1918	02:00	CST
1/01/1919	02:00	EST
3/30/1919	02:00	EWT

TIME TABLES

Date	Time	Zone
5/17/1919	02:00	CWT
10/26/1919	02:00	EST
2/09/1942	02:00	EWT
9/26/1943	02:00	CWT
4/30/1944	02:00	EWT
9/24/1944	02:00	CWT
4/29/1945	02:00	EWT
9/30/1945	02:00	EST
4/29/1951	02:00	EDT
9/30/1951	02:00	EST
4/29/1956	02:00	EDT
9/30/1956	02:00	EST
4/28/1957	02:00	EDT
9/29/1957	02:00	EST
4/27/1958	02:00	EDT
9/28/1958	02:00	EST
4/26/1959	02:00	EDT
9/27/1959	02:00	EST
4/24/1960	02:00	EDT
9/25/1960	02:00	EST
4/30/1961	02:00	EDT
9/24/1961	02:00	EST
4/29/1962	02:00	US#2

OH # 84

Date	Time	Zone
Before	4/01/1893	LMT
4/01/1893	12:00	CST
3/31/1918	02:00	CWT
10/27/1918	02:00	CST
1/01/1919	02:00	EST
3/30/1919	02:00	EWT
5/17/1919	02:00	CWT
10/26/1919	02:00	EST
2/09/1942	02:00	EWT
9/26/1943	02:00	CWT
4/30/1944	02:00	EWT
9/24/1944	02:00	CWT
4/29/1945	02:00	EWT
9/30/1945	02:00	EST
4/28/1946	02:00	EDT
9/29/1946	02:00	EST
4/27/1947	02:00	EDT
9/28/1947	02:00	EST
4/25/1948	02:00	EDT
9/26/1948	02:00	EST
4/24/1949	02:00	EDT
9/25/1949	02:00	EST
4/30/1950	02:00	EDT
9/30/1950	02:00	US#5

OH # 85

Date	Time	Zone
Before	4/01/1893	LMT
4/01/1893	12:00	CST
3/31/1918	02:00	CWT
10/27/1918	02:00	CST
1/01/1919	02:00	EST
3/30/1919	02:00	CWT
10/26/1919	02:00	CST
3/30/1924	02:00	EST
2/09/1942	02:00	EWT
9/26/1943	02:00	CWT
9/30/1945	02:00	EST
4/30/1967	02:00	US#1

OH # 86

Date	Time	Zone
Before	4/01/1893	LMT
4/01/1893	12:00	CST
3/31/1918	02:00	CWT
10/27/1918	02:00	CST
3/30/1919	02:00	CWT
10/26/1919	02:00	CST
3/30/1924	02:00	EST
2/09/1942	02:00	EWT
9/26/1943	02:00	CWT
9/30/1945	02:00	EST
4/30/1967	02:00	US#1

OH # 87

Date	Time	Zone
Before	4/01/1893	LMT
4/01/1893	12:00	CST
3/31/1918	02:00	CWT
10/27/1918	02:00	CST
3/30/1919	02:00	CWT
10/26/1919	02:00	CST
4/03/1927	02:00	EST
2/09/1942	02:00	EWT
9/26/1943	02:00	CWT
9/30/1945	02:00	EST
4/30/1967	02:00	US#1

OH # 88

Date	Time	Zone
Before	2/22/1890	LMT
2/22/1890	12:00	CST
3/31/1918	02:00	CWT
10/27/1918	02:00	CST
3/30/1919	02:00	CWT
10/26/1919	02:00	CST
3/28/1920	02:00	CDT
10/31/1920	02:00	CST
4/02/1921	02:00	CDT
9/25/1921	02:00	CST
4/30/1922	02:00	CDT
9/24/1922	02:00	CST
4/29/1923	02:00	CDT
9/30/1923	02:00	CST
4/27/1924	02:00	CDT
9/28/1924	02:00	CST
4/26/1925	02:00	CDT
9/27/1925	02:00	CST
4/25/1926	02:00	CDT
8/05/1926	02:00	EST
2/09/1942	02:00	EWT
9/26/1943	02:00	CWT
4/30/1944	02:00	EWT
9/24/1944	02:00	CWT
9/30/1945	02:00	EST
4/30/1967	02:00	US#1

OH # 89

Date	Time	Zone
Before	4/01/1893	LMT
4/01/1893	12:00	CST
3/31/1918	02:00	CWT
10/27/1918	02:00	CST
3/30/1919	02:00	CWT
10/26/1919	02:00	CST
8/31/1924	00:01	EST
2/09/1942	02:00	EWT
2/21/1943	02:00	CWT
4/29/1945	02:00	EWT
9/30/1945	02:00	EST
4/30/1967	02:00	US#1

OH # 90

Date	Time	Zone
Before	4/01/1893	LMT
4/01/1893	12:00	CST
3/31/1918	02:00	CWT
10/27/1918	02:00	CST
3/30/1919	02:00	CWT
10/26/1919	02:00	CST
4/25/1926	02:00	EST
2/09/1942	02:00	EWT
10/03/1943	03:00	CWT
4/30/1944	03:00	EWT
9/03/1944	03:00	CWT
4/29/1945	03:00	EWT
9/30/1945	02:00	EST
4/30/1967	02:00	US#1

OH # 91

Date	Time	Zone
Before	4/01/1893	LMT
4/01/1893	12:00	CST
3/31/1918	02:00	CWT
10/27/1918	02:00	CST
3/30/1919	02:00	CWT
10/26/1919	02:00	CST
4/25/1920	02:00	CDT
10/31/1920	02:00	CST
4/24/1921	02:00	CDT
9/25/1921	02:00	CST
4/30/1922	02:00	CDT
9/24/1922	02:00	CST
4/29/1923	02:00	CDT
9/30/1923	02:00	CST
4/27/1924	02:00	CDT
9/28/1924	02:00	CST
4/26/1925	02:00	CDT
9/27/1925	02:00	CST
4/25/1926	02:00	CDT
9/26/1926	02:00	CST
4/03/1927	02:00	EST
2/09/1942	02:00	EWT
2/21/1943	03:00	CWT
4/30/1944	02:00	EWT
9/03/1944	02:00	CWT
4/29/1945	02:00	EWT
5/13/1945	03:00	EST
4/30/1967	02:00	US#1

OH # 92

Date	Time	Zone
Before	4/01/1893	LMT
4/01/1893	12:00	CST
3/31/1918	02:00	CWT
10/27/1918	02:00	CST
3/30/1919	02:00	CWT
10/26/1919	02:00	CST
3/28/1920	02:00	CDT
10/31/1920	02:00	CST
4/03/1921	02:00	CDT
9/25/1921	02:00	CST
3/26/1922	00:00	EST
2/09/1942	02:00	EWT
2/21/1943	02:00	CWT
4/01/1945	02:00	EWT
9/30/1945	02:00	EST
4/30/1967	02:00	US#1

OH # 93

Date	Time	Zone
Before	4/01/1893	LMT
4/01/1893	12:00	CST
3/31/1918	02:00	CWT
10/27/1918	02:00	CST
3/30/1919	02:00	CWT
10/26/1919	02:00	CST
4/01/1922	02:00	EST
2/09/1942	02:00	EWT
9/30/1945	02:00	EST
4/30/1967	02:00	US#1

OH # 94

Date	Time	Zone
Before	4/01/1893	LMT
4/01/1893	12:00	CST
3/31/1918	02:00	CWT
10/27/1918	02:00	CST
3/30/1919	02:00	CWT
10/26/1919	02:00	CST
3/28/1920	02:00	CDT
10/31/1920	02:00	CST
4/03/1921	02:00	CDT
9/25/1921	02:00	CST
4/29/1923	02:00	CDT
9/30/1923	02:00	CST
4/27/1924	02:00	CDT
9/28/1924	02:00	CST
4/26/1925	02:00	CDT
9/27/1925	02:00	CST
4/25/1926	02:00	CDT
9/26/1926	02:00	EST
2/09/1942	02:00	EWT
9/26/1943	02:00	CWT
4/01/1944	02:00	EWT
9/24/1944	02:00	CWT
4/01/1945	02:00	EWT
9/30/1945	02:00	EST
4/30/1967	02:00	US#1

OH # 95

Date	Time	Zone
Before	4/01/1893	LMT
4/01/1893	12:00	CST
3/31/1918	02:00	CWT
10/27/1918	02:00	CST
1/01/1919	02:00	EST
3/30/1919	02:00	CWT
10/26/1919	02:00	CST
6/06/1920	02:00	EST
2/09/1942	02:00	EWT
9/26/1943	02:00	CWT
2/20/1944	02:00	EWT
9/30/1945	02:00	EST
4/27/1952	02:00	EDT
9/28/1952	02:00	EST
4/26/1953	02:00	EDT
9/27/1953	02:00	EST
4/30/1967	02:00	US#1

OH # 96

Date	Time	Zone
Before	4/01/1893	LMT
4/01/1893	12:00	CST
3/31/1918	02:00	CWT
10/27/1918	02:00	CST
1/01/1919	02:00	EST
3/30/1919	02:00	CWT
10/26/1919	02:00	CST
3/28/1920	02:00	CDT
10/31/1920	02:00	CST
4/03/1921	02:00	CDT
9/25/1921	02:00	CST
4/30/1922	02:00	CDT
9/24/1922	02:00	CST
4/29/1923	02:00	CDT
9/30/1923	02:00	CST
3/30/1924	02:00	EST
2/09/1942	02:00	EWT
9/26/1943	02:00	CWT
9/30/1945	02:00	EST
4/30/1967	02:00	US#1

OH # 97

Date	Time	Zone
Before	4/01/1893	LMT
4/01/1893	12:00	CST
3/31/1918	02:00	CWT
10/27/1918	02:00	CST
1/01/1919	02:00	EST
3/30/1919	02:00	CWT
10/26/1919	02:00	CST
3/30/1924	02:00	EST
2/09/1942	02:00	EWT
9/26/1943	02:00	CWT
9/30/1945	02:00	EST
4/30/1967	02:00	US#1

OH # 98

Date	Time	Zone
Before	4/01/1893	LMT
4/01/1893	12:00	CST
3/31/1918	02:00	CWT
10/27/1918	02:00	CST
1/01/1919	02:00	EST
3/30/1919	02:00	CWT
10/26/1919	02:00	CST
3/30/1924	02:00	EST
2/09/1942	02:00	EWT
9/26/1943	02:00	CWT
9/30/1945	02:00	EST
5/14/1964	02:00	EDT
10/25/1964	02:00	EST
4/30/1967	02:00	US#1

OH # 99

Date	Time	Zone
Before	4/01/1893	LMT
4/01/1893	12:00	CST
3/31/1918	02:00	CWT
10/27/1918	02:00	CST
3/30/1919	02:00	CWT
10/26/1919	02:00	CST
8/31/1924	00:01	EST
2/09/1942	02:00	EWT
10/31/1943	02:00	CWT
4/02/1944	02:00	EWT
9/24/1944	02:00	CWT
4/01/1945	02:00	EWT
9/30/1945	02:00	EST
4/30/1967	02:00	US#1

OH # 100

Date	Time	Zone
Before	4/01/1893	LMT
4/01/1893	12:00	CST
3/31/1918	02:00	CWT
10/27/1918	02:00	CST
3/30/1919	02:00	CWT
10/26/1919	02:00	CST
4/03/1927	02:00	EST
2/09/1942	02:00	EWT
9/26/1943	02:00	CWT
4/02/1944	02:00	EWT
9/24/1944	02:00	CWT
9/30/1945	02:00	EST
4/30/1967	02:00	US#1

OH # 101

Date	Time	Zone
Before	4/01/1893	LMT
4/01/1893	12:00	CST
3/31/1918	02:00	CWT
10/27/1918	02:00	CST
3/30/1919	02:00	CWT
10/26/1919	02:00	CST
4/03/1927	02:00	EST
2/09/1942	02:00	EWT
2/21/1943	02:00	CWT
4/02/1944	02:00	EWT
9/24/1944	02:00	CWT
4/01/1945	02:00	EWT
9/30/1945	02:00	EST
4/30/1967	02:00	US#1

OH # 102

Date	Time	Zone
Before	4/01/1893	LMT
4/01/1893	12:00	CST
3/31/1918	02:00	CWT
10/27/1918	02:00	CST
3/30/1919	02:00	CWT
10/26/1919	02:00	CST
3/30/1924	02:00	EST
2/09/1942	02:00	EWT
9/26/1943	02:00	CWT
9/30/1945	02:00	EST
4/30/1967	02:00	US#1

OH # 103

Date	Time	Zone
Before	4/01/1893	LMT
4/01/1893	12:00	CST
3/31/1918	02:00	CWT
10/27/1918	02:00	CST
1/01/1919	02:00	EST
3/30/1919	02:00	EWT
10/26/1919	02:00	EST
2/09/1942	02:00	EWT
9/26/1943	02:00	CWT
9/30/1945	02:00	EST
4/29/1956	02:00	US#5

OH # 104

Date	Time	Zone
Before	4/01/1893	LMT
4/01/1893	12:00	CST
3/31/1918	02:00	CWT
10/27/1918	02:00	CST
1/01/1919	02:00	EST
3/30/1919	02:00	EWT
10/26/1919	02:00	EST
2/09/1942	02:00	EWT
9/26/1943	02:00	CWT
4/01/1944	02:00	EWT
9/24/1944	02:00	CWT
4/01/1945	02:00	EWT
9/30/1945	02:00	EST
4/30/1967	02:00	US#1

OH # 105

Date	Time	Zone
Before	4/01/1893	LMT
4/01/1893	12:00	CST
3/31/1918	02:00	CWT
10/27/1918	02:00	CST
1/01/1919	02:00	EST
3/30/1919	02:00	EWT
10/26/1919	02:00	EST
2/09/1942	02:00	EWT
9/30/1945	02:00	EST
4/25/1948	02:00	EDT
9/26/1948	02:00	EST
4/24/1949	02:00	EDT
9/25/1949	02:00	EST
4/30/1950	02:00	EDT
9/30/1950	02:00	EST
4/29/1951	02:00	EDT
9/30/1951	02:00	EST
4/27/1952	02:00	EDT
9/28/1952	02:00	EST
4/26/1953	02:00	EDT
9/27/1953	02:00	EST
4/25/1954	02:00	EDT
9/26/1954	02:00	EST
4/24/1955	02:00	EDT
9/25/1955	02:00	EST
4/29/1956	02:00	US#2

OH # 106

Date	Time	Zone
Before	4/01/1893	LMT
4/01/1893	12:00	CST
3/31/1918	02:00	CWT
10/27/1918	02:00	CST
1/01/1919	02:00	EST
3/30/1919	02:00	EWT
10/26/1919	02:00	EST
4/27/1941	02:00	EDT
9/28/1941	02:00	EST
2/09/1942	02:00	EWT
9/30/1945	02:00	EST
4/28/1946	02:00	EDT
9/29/1946	02:00	EST
4/27/1947	02:00	EDT
9/28/1947	02:00	EST
4/25/1948	02:00	EDT
9/06/1948	02:00	EST
4/24/1949	02:00	US#3

OH # 107

Date	Time	Zone
Before	4/01/1893	LMT
4/01/1893	12:00	CST
3/31/1918	02:00	CWT
10/27/1918	02:00	CST
3/30/1919	02:00	CWT
10/26/1919	02:00	CST
3/28/1920	02:00	CDT
10/31/1920	02:00	CST
4/03/1921	02:00	CDT
9/25/1921	02:00	CST
4/30/1922	02:00	CDT
9/24/1922	02:00	CST
4/29/1923	02:00	CDT
9/30/1923	02:00	CST
3/30/1924	02:00	EST
2/09/1942	02:00	EWT
2/21/1943	02:00	CWT
4/02/1944	02:00	EWT
9/03/1944	02:00	CWT
4/01/1945	02:00	EWT
9/30/1945	02:00	EST
4/30/1967	02:00	US#1

OH # 108

Date	Time	Zone
Before	4/01/1893	LMT
4/01/1893	12:00	CST
3/31/1918	02:00	CWT
10/27/1918	02:00	CST
3/30/1919	02:00	CWT
10/26/1919	02:00	CST
3/30/1924	02:00	EST
2/09/1942	02:00	EWT
2/21/1943	02:00	CWT
4/02/1944	02:00	EWT
9/03/1944	02:00	CWT
4/01/1945	02:00	EWT
9/30/1945	02:00	EST
4/30/1967	02:00	US#1

OH # 109

Date	Time	Zone
Before	4/01/1893	LMT
4/01/1893	12:00	CST
3/31/1918	02:00	CWT
10/27/1918	02:00	CST
1/01/1919	02:00	EST
3/30/1919	02:00	EWT
6/01/1919	02:00	CWT
10/26/1919	02:00	CST
3/30/1924	02:00	EST
2/09/1942	02:00	EWT
2/21/1943	02:00	CWT
4/02/1944	02:00	EWT
9/03/1944	02:00	CWT
9/30/1945	02:00	EST
4/30/1967	02:00	US#1

OH # 110

Date	Time	Zone
Before	4/01/1893	LMT
4/01/1893	12:00	CST
3/31/1918	02:00	CWT
10/27/1918	02:00	CST
3/30/1919	02:00	CWT
10/26/1919	02:00	CST
4/03/1927	02:00	EST
2/09/1942	02:00	EWT
2/21/1943	02:00	CWT
4/01/1945	02:00	EWT
9/30/1945	02:00	EST
4/30/1967	02:00	US#1

OH # 111

Date	Time	Zone
Before	4/01/1893	LMT
4/01/1893	12:00	CST
3/31/1918	02:00	CWT
10/27/1918	02:00	CST
3/30/1919	02:00	CWT
10/26/1919	02:00	CST
8/31/1924	00:01	EST
2/09/1942	02:00	EWT
2/21/1943	02:00	CWT
4/01/1945	02:00	EWT
9/30/1945	02:00	EST
4/30/1967	02:00	US#1

OH # 112

Date	Time	Zone
Before	4/01/1893	LMT
4/01/1893	12:00	CST
3/31/1918	02:00	CWT
10/27/1918	02:00	CST
1/01/1919	02:00	EST
3/30/1919	02:00	EWT
10/26/1919	02:00	EST
2/09/1942	02:00	EWT
2/21/1943	02:00	CWT
4/01/1945	02:00	EWT
9/30/1945	02:00	EST
4/30/1967	02:00	US#1

OH # 113

Date	Time	Zone
Before	4/01/1893	LMT
4/01/1893	12:00	CST
3/31/1918	02:00	CWT
10/27/1918	02:00	CST
1/01/1919	02:00	EST
3/30/1919	02:00	EWT
10/26/1919	02:00	EST
3/28/1920	02:00	EDT
10/31/1920	02:00	EST
4/24/1921	02:00	EDT
9/25/1921	02:00	EST
4/30/1922	02:00	EDT
9/24/1922	02:00	EST
4/29/1923	02:00	EDT
9/30/1923	02:00	EST
4/27/1924	02:00	EDT
9/28/1924	02:00	EST
4/26/1925	02:00	EDT
9/27/1925	02:00	EST
4/25/1926	02:00	EDT
9/26/1926	02:00	EST
2/09/1942	02:00	EWT
2/21/1943	02:00	CWT
4/01/1945	02:00	EWT
9/30/1945	02:00	EST
4/27/1958	02:00	US#5

OH # 114

Date	Time	Zone
Before	4/01/1893	LMT
4/01/1893	12:00	CST
3/31/1918	02:00	CWT
10/27/1918	02:00	CST
1/01/1919	02:00	EST
3/30/1919	02:00	EWT
10/26/1919	02:00	EST
2/09/1942	02:00	EWT
2/21/1943	02:00	CWT
4/01/1945	02:00	EWT
9/30/1945	02:00	EST
4/25/1954	02:00	US#5

OH # 115

Date	Time	Zone
Before	4/01/1893	LMT
4/01/1893	12:00	CST
3/31/1918	02:00	CWT
10/27/1918	02:00	CST
1/01/1919	02:00	EST
3/30/1919	02:00	EWT
10/26/1919	02:00	EST
2/09/1942	02:00	EWT
2/21/1943	02:00	CWT
4/01/1945	02:00	EWT
9/30/1945	02:00	EST
4/28/1957	02:00	US#5

OH # 116

Date	Time	Zone
Before	4/01/1893	LMT

TIME TABLES

4/01/1893	12:00	CST
3/31/1918	02:00	CWT
10/27/1918	02:00	CST
1/01/1919	02:00	EST
3/30/1919	02:00	EWT
10/26/1919	02:00	EST
2/09/1942	02:00	EWT
2/21/1943	02:00	CWT
4/01/1945	02:00	EWT
9/30/1945	02:00	EST
4/27/1958	02:00	US#5

....

OH # 117

Before 4/01/1893		LMT
4/01/1893	12:00	CST
3/31/1918	02:00	CWT
10/27/1918	02:00	CST
1/01/1919	02:00	EST
3/30/1919	02:00	EWT
6/01/1919	02:00	CWT
10/26/1919	02:00	CST
3/30/1924	02:00	EST
2/09/1942	02:00	EWT
2/21/1943	02:00	CWT
4/01/1945	02:00	EWT
9/30/1945	02:00	EST
4/30/1967	02:00	US#1

....

OH # 118

Before 4/01/1893		LMT
4/01/1893	12:00	CST
3/31/1918	02:00	CWT
10/27/1918	02:00	CST
3/30/1919	02:00	CWT
10/26/1919	02:00	CST
4/03/1927	02:00	EST
2/09/1942	02:00	EWT
2/21/1943	02:00	CWT
4/29/1945	02:00	EWT
9/30/1945	02:00	EST
4/30/1967	02:00	US#1

COUNTIES

1 Adams
2 Allen
3 Ashland
4 Ashtabula
5 Athens
6 Auglaize
7 Belmont
8 Brown
9 Butler
10 Carroll
11 Champaign
12 Clark
13 Clermont
14 Clinton
15 Columbiana
16 Coshocton
17 Crawford
18 Cuyahoga
19 Darke
20 Defiance
21 Delaware
22 Erie
23 Fairfield
24 Fayette
25 Franklin
26 Fulton
27 Gallia
28 Geauga
29 Greene
30 Guernsey
31 Hamilton
32 Hancock
33 Hardin
34 Harrison
35 Henry
36 Highland
37 Hocking
38 Holmes
39 Huron
40 Jackson
41 Jefferson
42 Knox
43 Lake
44 Lawrence
45 Licking
46 Logan
47 Lorain
48 Lucas
49 Madison
50 Mahoning
51 Marion
52 Medina
53 Meigs
54 Mercer
55 Miami
56 Monroe
57 Montgomery
58 Morgan
59 Morrow
60 Muskingum
61 Noble
62 Ottawa
63 Paulding
64 Perry
65 Pickaway
66 Pike
67 Portage
68 Preble
69 Putnam
70 Richland
71 Ross
72 Sandusky
73 Scioto
74 Seneca
75 Shelby
76 Stark
77 Summit
78 Trumbull
79 Tuscarawas
80 Union
81 Van Wert
82 Vinton
83 Warren
84 Washington
85 Wayne
86 Williams
87 Wood
88 Wyandot

Abanaka 81	34	40N45'36	84w41'54	5:38:48
Abbeyville 52	67	41N11'50	81w53'13	5:27:33
Abbottsville 19	34	40N02'15	84w34'42	5:38:19
Aberdeen 8	34	38N39'20	83w45'40	5:35:03
Academia 42	108	40N24'49	82w28'06	5:29:52
Achor 15	78	40N46'27	80w32'31	5:22:10
Acme 52	53	41N01'29	81w47'47	5:27:11
Ada 33	34	40N46'10	83w49'22	5:35:17
Adair 15	67	40N47'37	80w57'22	5:23:49
Adams Mills 60	5	40N09'24	81w56'49	5:27:47
Adamsville 27	27	38N52'31	82w21'20	5:29:25
Adamsville 60	5	40N04'11	81w52'57	5:27:32
Adario 70	5	40N56'04	82w27'01	5:29:48
Addison 27	27	38N53'10	82w08'47	5:28:35
Addyston 31	34	39N08'12	84w42'33	5:38:50
Adelphi 71	34	39N28'00	82w44'50	5:30:59
Adena 41	23	40N13'07	80w52'23	5:23:30
Adrian 74	32	41N00'05	83w19'23	5:33:18
Advance 26	34	41N38'26	84w06'46	5:36:27
Aetnaville 7	23	40N05	80w45	5:23:00
Africa 21	27	40N10'56	82w57'26	5:31:50
Afton 13	34	39N03'41	84w06'01	5:36:24
Ai 26	34	41N37'41	83w56'07	5:35:44
Aid 44	34	38N35'46	82w29'36	5:29:58
Ainger 86	34	41N38'23	84w41'02	5:38:44
Airhill 57	91	39N49'10	84w22'02	5:37:28
Air Line Junction 48	31	41N38'19	83w34'57	5:34:20
Air Material Command 29	34	39N47	84w03	5:36:12
Aitch 56	20	39N47	81w09	5:24:36
Akron 77	2	41N04'53	81w31'09	5:26:05
Alabama Hill 64	27	39N38'04	82w03'06	5:28:12
Albany 5	27	39N13'39	82w12'09	5:28:49
Al Bar Meadows 31	34	39N10'05	84w22'08	5:37:29
Albion 3	44	40N58'27	82w09'50	5:28:39
Alcony 55	34	40N00'41	84w03'29	5:36:14
Alert 9	34	39N19'30	84w46'31	5:39:06
Alexander 5	27	39N15	82w07	5:28:28
Alexanders 18	26	41N22	81w40	5:26:40
Alexandersville 57	91	39N40	84w15	5:37:00
Alexandria 25	27	40N05'20	82w36'45	5:30:27
Alexis 56	20	39N38'11	81w01'53	5:24:08
Alexis Addition 48	31	41N43'11	83w31'37	5:34:06
Alexis Place 48	31	41N42	83w34	5:34:16
Alfred 53	5	39N10'21	81w55'16	5:27:41
Alger 33	34	40N42'22	83w50'38	5:35:23
Alice 27	27	39N01'16	82w22'22	5:29:29
Alikanna 41	106	40N23'15	80w38'10	5:22:33
Alledonia 7	21	39N53'55	80w58'10	5:23:53
Allen Center 80	33	40N14'30	83w28'41	5:33:55
Allensburg 36	34	39N12'16	83w46'38	5:35:07
Allensville 82	34	39N16'21	82w36'25	5:30:26
Allentown 2	90	40N45'17	84w11'41	5:36:47
Allentown 73	34	38N41'46	82w51'30	5:31:26
Alliance 76	51	40N54'55	81w06'22	5:24:25
Alliance Junction 50	67	40N55'15	81w02'33	5:24:10
Alma 71	34	39N11'17	82w58'44	5:31:55
Alpha 29	34	39N43	84w01	5:36:04
Alpine Terrace 13	88	39N05'26	84w17'31	5:37:10
Alpine Village 46	34	40N21	83w41	5:34:44
Alta 70	95	40N43'57	82w34'11	5:30:17
Altamont 41	106	40N20'00	80w37'04	5:22:28
Altamont Hills 41	106	40N19	80w39	5:22:36
Altamont Park 41	106	40N19	80w39	5:22:36
Altitude 56	20	39N45'11	81w01'25	5:24:06
Alton 25	34	39N57'01	83w10'29	5:32:42
Altoona 40	34	39N06'48	82w35'12	5:30:21
Alvada 74	32	41N03'01	83w24'07	5:33:36
Alvordton 86	34	41N39'57	84w26'13	5:37:45
Amanda 23	34	39N38'58	82w44'40	5:30:59
Amberley 31	34	39N12'17	84w25'41	5:37:43
Amberly 25	107	39N56	82w53	5:31:32
Am-Beth Acres 13	88	39N05'08	84w16'51	5:37:07
Amboy 4	72	41N55'38	80w36'55	5:22:28
Amboy 26	34	41N41	83w57	5:35:48
Amelia 13	34	39N01'42	84w13'04	5:36:52
American 2	90	40N46	84w09	5:36:36
Ames 5	5	39N25	82w00	5:28:00
Amesville 5	5	39N24'02	81w57'21	5:27:49
Amherst 47	63	41N23'52	82w13'21	5:28:53
Amherst Heights 76	54	40N49'48	81w30'58	5:26:04
Amith 49	34	40N04'07	83w15'05	5:33:00
Amity 31	34	39N12'20	84w24'15	5:37:37
Amity 42	5	40N28'15	82w22'43	5:29:31
Amity 49	34	40N07	83w16	5:33:04
Amity 57	34	39N47'21	84w22'01	5:37:28
Amlin 25	108	40N04'37	83w10'52	5:32:43
Amlin Heights 29	34	39N44	84w02	5:36:08
Amoy 70	95	40N49'43	82w33'12	5:30:13
Amsden 74	32	41N12'58	83w19'43	5:33:19
Amsterdam 41	67	40N28'25	80w55'23	5:23:42
Amsterdam 45	27	39N57'27	82w22'42	5:29:31
Ancor 31	34	39N08'14	84w19'04	5:37:16
Anderson 31	34	39N05	84w21	5:37:24
Anderson 71	34	39N21'39	83w04'14	5:32:17
Anderson Ferry 31	88	39N04'41	84w37'19	5:38:29
Andersonville 71	34	39N25'40	83w00'35	5:32:02
Andis 44	34	38N33'03	82w31'24	5:30:06
Andover 4	56	41N36'24	80w34'21	5:22:17
Angel 27	27	38N43'15	82w16'10	5:29:05
Angus 74	32	41N11'48	83w17'06	5:33:08
Ankenytown 42	5	40N32'03	82w30'18	5:30:01
Anlo 12	34	39N56'23	83w56'48	5:35:47
Anna 75	34	40N23'40	84w10'22	5:36:41
Annapolis 41	67	40N24'40	80w51'48	5:23:27
Ansonia 19	34	40N12'52	84w38'13	5:38:33
Anthony 5	5	39N14'10	81w58'57	5:27:56
Antioch 49	34	39N45'58	83w16'18	5:33:05
Antioch 56	20	39N39'36	81w04'05	5:24:16
Antiquity 53	20	38N56'49	81w54'23	5:27:38
Antonis 71	34	39N11'02	82w55'39	5:31:43
Antrim 30	5	40N07'13	81w21'31	5:25:26
Antwerp 63	34	41N10'53	84w44'26	5:38:58
Apco 67	67	41N10	81w16	5:25:04
Apex 34	5	40N24'37	80w54'34	5:23:38
Apple 37	34	39N24'10	82w42'26	5:30:50
Apple Creek 85	62	40N45'06	81w50'22	5:27:21
Apple Grove 53	5	38N53'12	81w52'04	5:27:28
Appleton 45	27	40N12'33	82w36'59	5:30:28
Aquilla 28	62	41N34'21	81w09'16	5:24:37
Arabia 44	34	38N39'29	82w28'25	5:29:54
Arbaugh 82	27	39N10'24	82w20'16	5:29:21
Arborcrest Acres 31	34	39N12'48	84w24'52	5:37:39
Arcadia 32	33	41N06'30	83w31'01	5:34:04
Arcanum 19	34	39N59	84w33	5:38:12
Archbold 26	34	41N31'17	84w18'26	5:37:14
Archer 34	21	40N19	81w01	5:24:04
Archers Fork 84	20	39N29'00	81w12'21	5:24:49
Areanum 19	34	39N59'28	84w33'08	5:38:13
Arion 73	34	38N50'46	83w06'14	5:32:25
Arkoe 66	34	39N02'40	83w13'57	5:32:56
Arlington 32	33	40N53'37	83w39'01	5:34:36
Arlington 57	34	39N51'59	84w25'29	5:37:42
Arlington 77	2	41N04'49	81w29'37	5:25:58
Arlington Heights 31	34	39N12'54	84w27'20	5:37:49
Armadale 5	5	39N23'45	81w55'23	5:27:42
Armitage 5	27	39N20'44	82w05'46	5:28:23
Armstrong 85	62	40N54'44	82w00'40	5:28:03
Armstrongs Mills 7	21	39N54'29	80w56'06	5:23:44
Arnheim 8	34	38N56'00	83w49'39	5:35:19
Arnold 80	34	40N08'31	83w15'03	5:33:00
Artanna 42	5	40N19'19	82w18'38	5:29:15
Arthur 63	34	41N11'41	84w21'39	5:37:27
Arwold 55	34	39N58	84w20	5:37:20
Asbury 31	34	39N03'38	84w20'32	5:37:22
Ash 25	27	40N03'19	82w40'09	5:30:41
Ashcraft Ford 60	5	40N09'21	82w08'49	5:28:35
Ashland 3	44	40N52'07	82w19'06	5:29:16
Ashley 21	27	40N24'32	82w57'20	5:31:49
Ashley Corner 73	34	38N46'10	82w47'11	5:31:09
Ash Ridge 8	34	38N54'28	83w45'32	5:35:02
Ashtabula 4	46	41N51'54	80w47'24	5:23:10
Ashton 11	5	39N42'51	81w27'53	5:25:52
Ashville 65	34	39N42'56	82w57'11	5:31:49
Assumption 26	34	41N40'19	83w54'42	5:35:39
Astoria 9	34	39N33'33	84w28'00	5:37:52
Athalia 44	34	38N30'58	82w18'24	5:29:14
Athens 5	97	39N19'45	82w06'05	5:28:24
Atherton 45	5	39N57'38	82w26'10	5:29:45
Atlanta 65	34	39N33'41	83w11'26	5:32:46
Atlas 7	21	39N59	81w11	5:24:44
Atlas 67	67	41N10	81w16	5:25:04
Attica 74	32	41N03'53	82w53'16	5:31:33
Attica Junction 74	32	41N05'13	82w52'38	5:31:31
Atwater 67	67	41N01'26	81w09'49	5:24:39
Atwater Center 67	67	41N01'25	81w08'53	5:24:36
Auburn 9	34	39N23'28	84w42'08	5:38:49
Auburn Center 17	5	40N56'42	82w44'37	5:30:58
Auburn Center 28	67	41N23'14	81w14'47	5:24:59
Auburn Corners 28	67	41N23'14	81w12'59	5:24:52
Augerburg 67	67	41N09'47	81w10'03	5:24:40
Augusta 10	21	40N41'09	81w01'16	5:24:05
Aukerman 85	62	40N57'35	82w01'30	5:28:06
Ault 7	21	40N00	80w46	5:23:04
Aultman 76	67	40N55'42	81w25'03	5:25:40
Aurelius 84	20	39N36	81w26	5:25:44
Aurora 67	46	41N19'11	81w22'48	5:25:31
Austin 71	34	39N26'12	83w13'21	5:32:53
Austinburg 4	72	41N46'19	80w51'17	5:23:25
Austin Square Shopping Ctr 77	67	41N01	81w38	5:26:32
Austintown 50	84	41N06'06	80w45'53	5:23:04
Austin Village 78	45	41N14'33	80w51'34	5:23:26
Autumn Acres 31	34	39N13'26	84w36'19	5:38:25
Ava 61	5	39N50	81w35	5:26:20
Avalon 9	34	39N31'51	84w22'44	5:37:31
Avalon 64	27	39N42	82w26	5:29:44
Avalon Heights 83	34	39N26	84w12	5:36:48
Avis 69	34	41N01'15	84w10'09	5:36:41
Avlon 64	27	39N44'38	82w23'06	5:29:32
Avoca Park 31	34	39N08'20	84w20'28	5:37:22
Avon 47	65	41N27'06	82w02'08	5:28:09
Avondale 7	21	39N58'46	80w44'29	5:22:58
Avondale 31	88	39N08'52	84w29'42	5:37:59
Avondale 46	34	40N29	83w56	5:35:44

Avondale 57 91 39N47'36 84w08'35 5:36:34
Avondale 60 5 39N52'14 82w03'35 5:28:14
Avondale 76 43 40N49'35 81w24'52 5:25:39
Avondale Park 45
27 39N54 82w27 5:29:48
Avon Lake 47 65 41N30'19 82w01'42 5:28:07
Axtel 22 5 41N22'07 82w21'50 5:29:27
Ayersville 20 34 41N14'19 84w17'08 5:37:09
Bachman 57 34 39N51'46 84w27'26 5:37:50
Bacon Flat 1 34 38N57'42 83w21'46 5:33:27
Badgertown 7 21 40N01'47 81w04'56 5:24:20
Bailey 48 34 41N27'43 83w47'16 5:35:09
Bailey Lake 3 44 40N56'45 82w21'35 5:29:26
Baileys Mills 7
21 39N57'21 81w13'44 5:24:55
Bainbridge 28 67 41N23'11 81w20'23 5:25:22
Bainbridge 71 36 39N13'39 83w16'14 5:33:05
Bainbridge Center 28
67 41N26 81w22 5:25:28
Bairdstown 87 34 41N10'22 83w36'29 5:34:26
Baker 19 34 40N03'21 84w42'05 5:38:48
Bakers 47 67 41N09 82w16 5:29:04
Bakersville 16 5 40N21'20 81w38'45 5:26:35
Bald Knobs 53 5 39N01'30 81w50'02 5:27:20
Baldwin 63 34 41N01'08 84w48'07 5:39:12
Ballou 75 34 40N11'59 84w03'37 5:36:14
Ballville 72 32 41N19'40 83w07'56 5:32:32
Baltic 79 16 40N26'24 81w41'57 5:26:48
Baltimore 23 27 39N50'43 82w36'03 5:30:24
Bangorville 70 95 40N33'54 82w33'51 5:30:15
Bangs 42 5 40N21'08 82w33'09 5:30:13
Banker Heights 76
43 40N45'40 81w25'10 5:25:41
Bannock 7 21 40N05'55 80w58'38 5:23:55
Bannon 25 107 39N55'13 82w56'49 5:31:47
Bantam 13 34 38N59'55 84w08'29 5:36:34
Barberton 77 46 41N00'46 81w36'19 5:26:25
Barclay 78 67 41N27'15 80w37'32 5:22:30
Bardwell 8 34 39N02'52 83w55'19 5:35:41
Barlow 84 20 39N23'55 81w39'54 5:26:40
Barnesburg 31 34 39N13'44 84w37'20 5:38:29
Barnesville 7 18 39N59'17 81w10'36 5:24:42
Barnhill 79 16 40N26'53 81w22'09 5:25:29
Barr 79 16 40N30 81w37 5:26:28
Barretts Mills 36
36 39N12'09 83w23'14 5:33:33
Barrick 10 21 40N31'58 81w15'09 5:25:01
Barrick Corners 45
27 40N11'27 82w33'03 5:30:12
Barrs Mills 79 16 40N32'55 81w37'25 5:26:30
Bartles 44 34 38N38 82w40 5:30:40
Bartlett 84 20 39N25'10 81w48'57 5:27:16
Bartley Estates 57
91 39N50 84w13 5:36:52
Bartlow 35 34 41N13 83w56 5:35:44
Barton 7 21 40N06'26 80w50'29 5:23:22
Bartramville 44
37 38N29'33 82w23'05 5:29:32
Barwyn Acres 31
34 39N13'38 84w22'22 5:37:29
Bascom 74 32 41N07'58 83w17'07 5:33:08
Bashan 53 5 39N02'36 81w51'55 5:27:28
Bass Lake 28 67 41N34 81w12 5:24:48
Batavia 13 34 39N04'37 84w10'37 5:36:42
Batemantown 42 27 40N31'33 82w35'46 5:30:23
Bates 87 31 41N35'26 83w34'42 5:34:19
Batesville 61 5 39N54'51 81w16'53 5:25:08
Bath 77 67 41N11'20 81w38'11 5:26:33
Bath Center 77 2 41N10'07 81w38'13 5:26:33
Batson 63 34 41N01'06 84w44'42 5:38:59
Battlesburg 76 67 40N41'53 81w22'13 5:25:29
Baughman 85 62 40N51 81w42 5:26:48
Bay 62 93 41N29 83w00 5:32:00
Bayard 15 67 40N45'02 81w03'54 5:24:16
Bay Bridge 22 5 41N28 82w49 5:31:16
Bays 87 33 41N16'08 83w40'11 5:34:41
Bayshore 72 30 41N25'10 82w56'04 5:31:44
Bayview 4 72 41N32 80w32 5:22:08
Bay View 22 5 41N28'07 82w49'37 5:31:18
Bay Village 18 66 41N29'05 81w55'20 5:27:41
Bazetta 78 45 41N18 80w46 5:23:04
Beach City 76 21 40N39'11 81w34'52 5:26:19
Beachland 18 67 41N35 81w32 5:26:08
Beachwood 18 67 41N27'52 81w30'32 5:26:02
Beacon Hill 9 34 39N16 84w24 5:37:36
Beacon Hill 28 67 41N22'32 81w20'20 5:25:21
Beallsville 56 20 39N50'54 81w02'13 5:24:09
Beals 23 27 39N53'16 82w44'58 5:31:00
Beamsville 19 34 40N11'14 84w35'08 5:38:21
Bear Creek 73 34 38N55'52 83w03'57 5:32:16
Bearfield 64 27 39N41 82w03 5:28:12
Bears Mill 19 34 40N06'39 84w32'27 5:38:10
Beartown 28 67 41N21'30 81w17'25 5:25:10
Beartown 79 16 40N34'29 81w30'51 5:26:03
Beasley Fork 1 34 38N44'59 83w30'59 5:34:04
Beatty 12 39 39N52'54 83w50'25 5:35:22
Beaumont 5 27 39N23'08 82w08'18 5:28:33
Beavan 84 20 39N23 81w14 5:24:56
Beaver 66 34 39N01'50 82w49'28 5:31:18
Beaver Creek 29
34 39N43 84w03 5:36:12
Beaverdam 2 34 40N50 83w59 5:35:56
Beaver Dam Station 2
34 40N49'58 83w58'35 5:35:54
Beaver Mill 36 34 39N10'38 83w24'51 5:33:39
Beaver Park 47 50 41N26'15 82w14'50 5:28:59
Beaver Pond 1 34 38N56'22 83w20'47 5:33:23
Beavertown 57 91 39N41 84w09 5:36:36
Beavertown 84 20 39N28'21 81w06'47 5:24:27
Becker Highlands 41
106 40N22 80w39 5:22:36
Beckett 84 20 39N35'04 81w42'29 5:26:50
Becks Mills 38 5 40N29'16 81w49'10 5:27:17
Bedford 18 70 41N23'35 81w32'12 5:26:09
Bedford Heights 18
70 41N25'01 81w31'39 5:26:07
Beebe 5 5 39N18'46 81w51'29 5:27:26
Beebetown 52 67 41N16'29 81w52'42 5:27:31
Beechcrest 67 67 41N10 81w21 5:25:24
Beechgrove 19 34 39N59'22 84w36'58 5:38:28
Beech-Mar 31 34 39N06'11 84w23'15 5:37:33
Beechview Estates 31
34 39N06'06 84w23'28 5:37:34
Beechwold 25 107 40N03 83w01 5:32:04
Beechwood 41 106 40N22 80w39 5:22:36
Beechwood 68 34 39N35'54 84w30'38 5:38:03
Beechwood 76 67 40N53'29 81w08'03 5:24:32
Belden 47 42 41N14'17 82w01'24 5:28:06
Belfast 13 34 39N10'36 84w08'01 5:36:32
Belfast 36 34 39N03'46 83w31'57 5:34:08
Belfort 76 67 40N48'44 81w14'44 5:24:59
Belknap 34 21 40N13'50 80w52'48 5:23:31
Bellaire 7 6 40N00'58 80w44'33 5:22:58
Bellaire Gardens 51
27 40N37'13 83w07'56 5:32:32
Bellbrook 29 34 39N38'08 84w04'15 5:36:17
Belle Center 46
34 40N30'24 83w44'53 5:35:00
Bellefontaine 46
99 40N21'40 83w45'35 5:35:02
Bellepoint 21 27 40N14'45 83w09'06 5:32:36
Belle Stone School 76
43 40N49'14 81w21'34 5:25:26
Belle Valley 11 5 39N47'26 81w33'23 5:26:14
Belleve 34 21 40N14'32 80w53'43 5:23:35
Belle Vernon 88
32 40N55'35 83w12'07 5:32:48
Belleview Acres 29
34 39N38 84w04 5:36:16
Belleview Heights 68
34 39N51 84w48 5:39:12
Belleview Heights 71
34 39N19'07 83w00'16 5:32:01
Bellevue 39 27 41N16'25 82w50'30 5:31:22
Bellview Heights 7
21 40N01 80w45 5:23:00
Bellville 70 5 40N37'12 82w30'39 5:30:03
Belmont 2 90 40N45 84w06 5:36:24
Belmont 7 13 40N01'45 81w02'21 5:24:09
Belmont 9 34 39N22 84w33 5:38:12
Belmont Park 78
84 41N10'51 80w40'13 5:22:41
Belmont Ridge 7
13 40N09'57 81w10'48 5:24:43
Belmore 69 34 41N09'12 83w56'19 5:35:45
Beloit 50 67 40N55'23 80w59'38 5:23:59
Belpre 84 20 39N16'26 81w34'23 5:26:18
Belvedere 41 106 40N21'28 80w45'55 5:23:04
Bennetts Corners 18
67 41N16'35 81w47'07 5:27:08
Bentley 50 84 41N02 80w33 5:22:12
Bentleyville 18
67 41N24'47 81w24'40 5:25:39
Benton 17 33 40N55'37 83w05'38 5:32:23
Benton 38 5 40N36'09 81w50'49 5:27:23
Benton Ridge 32
34 41N00'17 83w47'39 5:35:11
Bentonville 1 34 38N44'58 83w36'48 5:34:27
Benwood 56 20 39N41'09 81w00'02 5:24:00
Berea 18 46 41N21'58 81w51'16 5:27:25
Bergholz 41 67 40N31'10 80w53'03 5:23:32
Berkey 48 34 41N42'56 83w50'22 5:35:21
Berkley Heights 57
91 39N41 84w09 5:36:36
Berkshire 21 27 40N15'55 82w54'32 5:31:38
Berlin 38 5 40N33'40 81w47'40 5:27:11
Berlin 86 34 41N36'34 84w45'16 5:39:01
Berlin Center 50
67 41N01'28 80w56'52 5:23:47
Berlin Heights 22
9 41N19'31 82w29'36 5:29:58
Berlin Heights Station 22
9 41N21'10 82w29'39 5:29:59
Berlinville 22 9 41N18'09 82w30'53 5:30:04
Bern 5 5 39N25 81w53 5:27:32
Berne 23 27 39N40 82w33 5:30:12
Berne 61 5 39N45 81w31 5:26:04
Bernice 79 16 40N15'52 81w31'10 5:26:05
Berrysville 36 34 39N07'42 83w33'31 5:34:14
Berwick 74 32 41N01'45 83w17'63 5:33:12
Bessemer 5 27 39N27'54 82w11'53 5:28:48
Bethany 9 34 39N23'04 84w22'25 5:37:30
Bethel 13 34 38N57'49 84w04'51 5:36:19
Bethel 49 34 39N43 83w16 5:33:04
Bethel 66 34 39N00'34 83w07'26 5:32:30
Bethesda 7 21 40N00'58 81w04'22 5:24:17
Bethlehem 70 5 40N50'19 82w43'12 5:30:53
Bettsville 74 32 41N14'47 83w14'09 5:32:57
Beulah Beach 22 5 41N23'31 82w26'32 5:29:46
Bevan 84 20 39N24'42 81w13'57 5:24:56
Beverly 84 20 39N32'52 81w38'23 5:26:34
Beverly Gardens 57
34 39N46 84w06 5:36:24
Beverly Hills 13
34 39N11'25 84w16'25 5:37:06
Bevis 31 34 39N15'27 84w36'06 5:38:24
Bexley 25 107 39N58'08 82w56'16 5:31:45
Bidwell 27 27 38N55'07 82w17'57 5:29:12
Big Island 51 33 40N36'44 83w13'01 5:32:52
Biglick 32 33 41N03 83w29 5:33:56
Big Plain 49 34 39N50'19 83w17'21 5:33:09
Big Prairie 38 17 40N40'02 82w05'43 5:28:23
Big Rock 40 34 39N03 82w50 5:31:20
Big Run 5 5 39N21'19 81w52'22 5:27:29
Big Spring 74 32 41N03 83w22 5:33:28
Big Springs 46 33 40N30'02 83w38'08 5:34:33
Billingstown 86
34 41N41'35 84w47'44 5:39:11
Biltmore Gardens 87
31 41N38 83w29 5:33:56
Bingham 56 20 39N50'51 80w57'40 5:23:51
Bingville 6 34 40N36 83w59 5:35:56
Birds Run 30 5 40N10'08 81w38'51 5:26:35
Birmingham 22 5 41N19'48 82w21'39 5:29:27
Birmingham 30 5 40N10'31 81w26'15 5:25:45
Bishopville 58 5 39N30'47 82w02'57 5:28:12
Bismarck 39 32 41N09'54 82w47'14 5:31:09
Blachleyville 85
76 40N45'52 82w04'56 5:28:20
Blackband 79 16 40N25'33 81w32'32 5:26:10
Blackberry Corner 62
93 41N36'13 83w16'51 5:33:07
Blackburn 15 67 40N55 80w51 5:23:24
Black Creek 54 34 40N42 84w44 5:38:56
Blackfork 44 34 38N50'15 82w36'00 5:30:24
Blackfork Junction 40
34 38N51'37 82w36'02 5:30:24
Blackhawk 83 34 39N19'18 84w04'18 5:36:17
Black Horse 67 67 41N09'32 81w16'24 5:25:06
Blackjack 37 27 39N28'04 82w29'03 5:29:58
Blacklick 25 27 39N59'44 82w48'41 5:31:15
Blacklick Estates 25
27 39N54 82w52 5:31:28
Black Run 60 5 40N06'01 82w10'16 5:28:41
Blacktop 30 5 39N58'35 81w28'58 5:25:56
Bladen 27 34 38N39'36 82w11'13 5:28:45
Bladensburg 42 5 40N17'04 82w17'03 5:29:08
Blaine 7 21 40N04'04 80w49'03 5:23:16
Blainesville 7 21 40N07'18 80w53'18 5:23:33
Blairmont 34 21 40N14'20 80w53'24 5:23:34
Blairsville 13 34 38N59'36 84w17'37 5:37:10
Blake 52 60 41N02'49 81w48'55 5:27:16
Blakeslee 86 34 41N31'27 84w43'49 5:38:55
Blanchard 33 33 40N43'55 83w38'37 5:34:34
Blanches Addition 45
27 40N00 82w40 5:30:40
Blanchester 14 34 39N17'35 83w59'20 5:35:57
Blanco 50 73 41N05'08 80w57'35 5:23:50
Blatchford 37 27 39N31'25 82w12'12 5:28:49
Blendon 25 108 40N06 82w55 5:31:40
Blendon Corner 25
108 40N04'49 82w55'44 5:31:43
Blessing 24 34 39N42'09 83w36'13 5:34:25
Blissfield 16 5 40N23'59 81w57'56 5:27:52
Bloom Center 46
34 40N25'02 83w56'44 5:35:47
Bloom Center 87
34 41N12'39 83w35'34 5:34:22
Bloomdale 87 33 41N10'21 83w33'23 5:34:14
Bloomer 55 34 40N11'16 84w24'48 5:37:39
Bloomfield 59 27 40N21'49 82w43'29 5:30:54
Bloomfield 60 5 40N03'01 81w44'33 5:26:58
Bloomfield 84 20 39N33'42 81w12'15 5:24:49
Bloomingburg 24
34 39N36'18 83w23'44 5:33:35
Bloomingdale 41
67 40N20'34 80w49'06 5:23:16
Blooming Grove 59
5 40N42'28 82w43'00 5:30:52
Bloomington 14 34 39N32'13 83w42'23 5:34:50
Bloomingville 22
5 41N21'18 82w43'38 5:30:55
Bloom Junction 73
34 38N48'21 82w41'34 5:30:46
Bloomville 74 32 41N03'07 83w00'54 5:32:04
Blowville 13 34 39N05'51 84w02'42 5:36:11
Blue Ash 31 34 39N13'55 84w22'42 5:37:31
Blue Ball 9 34 39N29'36 84w20'11 5:37:21
Bluebell 30 5 39N53'55 81w35'23 5:26:22
Bluebird Beach 22
67 41N25'07 82w22'44 5:29:31
Blue Creek 1 34 38N46'39 83w19'49 5:33:19
Blue Creek 63 34 41N02 84w38 5:38:32
Blue Jay 31 34 39N13'37 84w44'14 5:38:57
Blue Rock 60 5 39N48'10 81w53'27 5:27:34
Blue Valley Acres 23
27 39N38'23 82w33'30 5:30:14
Bluffton 2 34 40N53'43 83w53'20 5:35:33
Boardman 50 84 41N01'27 80w39'47 5:22:39
Bobo 66 34 39N01'24 82w56'43 5:31:47
Boden 30 5 40N06'54 81w42'09 5:26:49
Bodman 8 34 39N02'40 83w57'58 5:35:52
Bogart 22 5 41N23'45 82w39'04 5:30:36
Bokes Creek 46 33 40N28 83w35 5:34:20
Bolins Mills 82
27 39N13'51 82w17'06 5:29:08
Bolivar 79 16 40N39'00 81w27'08 5:25:49
Bolton 76 67 40N56'23 81w06'55 5:24:28
Bondclay 73 34 38N42'46 82w43'37 5:30:54
Bond Hill 31 88 39N10'29 84w28'02 5:37:52
Boneta 52 53 41N05'58 81w46'31 5:27:06
Bonn 84 20 39N31'53 81w23'08 5:25:33
Bono 48 30 41N38'08 83w16'09 5:33:05
Booktown 72 30 41N23'20 83w06'29 5:32:26
Bookwalter 24 34 39N42'16 83w31'49 5:34:07
Booth 48 30 41N38'17 83w24'43 5:33:39
Booth 79 16 40N13'52 81w32'28 5:26:10
Boston 7 21 39N53'17 81w11'55 5:24:48
Boston 25 5 40N04'33 82w13'38 5:28:55
Boston 36 34 39N12'55 83w30'40 5:34:03
Boston 77 67 41N15'48 81w33'35 5:26:14
Boston Heights 77
67 41N15'53 81w30'48 5:26:03
Boston Mill 77 67 41N14 81w33 5:26:12
Botkins 75 34 40N28'04 84w10'50 5:36:43
Boudes Ferry 8 34 38N52 83w55 5:35:40
Boughtonville 39
5 41N03'09 82w36'41 5:30:27
Boulevard 48 31 41N41'17 83w30'27 5:34:02
Bourneville 71 34 39N16'55 83w09'24 5:32:38
Bowerston 34 21 40N25'31 81w11'17 5:24:45
Bowersville 29 34 39N34'50 83w43'30 5:34:54
Bowling Green 87
33 41N22'29 83w39'05 5:34:36
Bowlusville 11 34 40N01'35 83w47'55 5:35:12
Bowmans Corners 50
67 40N59'17 80w51'28 5:23:26
Boyds Corners 50
67 40N55 81w01 5:24:04
Boydsville 7 21 40N05 80w45 5:23:00
Boys Village 85
76 40N49'56 81w54'07 5:27:36
Braceville 78 67 41N13'42 80w57'17 5:23:49
Bradbury 53 27 39N00'34 82w04'01 5:28:16
Bradford 55 34 40N07'56 84w25'51 5:37:43
Bradley 41 67 40N14'49 80w46'33 5:23:06
Bradner 87 32 41N19'27 83w26'19 5:33:45
Bradrick 44 37 38N26'44 82w24'17 5:29:37
Brady 30 5 40N05'09 81w29'09 5:25:57
Brady 86 34 41N33 84w25 5:37:40
Brady Lake 67 67 41N09'34 81w19'02 5:25:16
Bradyville 1 34 38N41'43 83w40'14 5:34:41
Braffetsville 19
34 39N55'28 84w45'42 5:39:03
Braffettsville 19
34 39N51 84w48 5:39:12
Brailey 26 34 41N33'19 83w55'20 5:35:41
Branch Hill 13 34 39N14'46 84w17'36 5:37:10

Brandon 42 27 40N18'44 82w30'33 5:30:02
Brandt 55 34 39N54'07 84w05'31 5:36:22
Brandywine 17 33 40N51'56 82w56'21 5:31:45
Bratenahl 18 26 41N32'33 81w37'35 5:26:30
Bratton 1 34 39N01 83w26 5:33:44
Brecksville 18 67 41N19'11 81w37'37 5:26:30
Brecon 31 34 39N16'50 84w21'24 5:37:26
Bremen 23 27 39N42'06 82w25'37 5:29:42
Brennersville 68 34 39N48'07 84w34'39 5:38:19
Brentwood 31 34 39N13'42 84w31'47 5:38:07
Brentwood 43 67 41N38'52 81w22'30 5:25:30
Brentwood Estates 41 106 40N22 80w39 5:22:36
Brentwood Lake 47 42 41N18'58 82w04'40 5:28:19
Brewer Heights 71 34 39N20'33 83w01'13 5:32:05
Brewster 76 67 40N42'25 81w35'54 5:26:24
Briarwood Beach 52 73 41N04'36 81w53'47 5:27:35
Brice 25 27 39N55'05 82w49'56 5:31:20
Briceton 63 34 41N05'04 84w37'52 5:38:31
Bridgeport 7 8 40N04'11 80w44'25 5:22:58
Bridgeport 33 33 40N44'45 83w36'07 5:34:24
Bridgeport 80 34 40N09'38 83w23'41 5:33:35
Bridges 36 34 39N20 83w34 5:34:16
Bridgetown 31 34 39N09'11 84w38'14 5:38:33
Bridgeville 60 5 39N58'10 81w52'04 5:27:28
Bridgewater 15 67 40N49'43 80w59'22 5:23:57
Bridgewater 86 34 41N40 84w38 5:38:32
Bridgewater Center 86 34 41N39'29 84w37'51 5:38:31
Brier Hill 50 84 41N07'18 80w40'09 5:22:41
Brigglesville 64 27 39N45'24 82w05'17 5:28:21
Briggs 18 26 41N24 81w43 5:26:52
Briggs 84 20 39N19'32 81w03'39 5:24:15
Briggsdale 25 107 39N55'33 83w03'30 5:32:14
Brighton 12 34 39N55'48 83w33'41 5:34:15
Brighton 47 67 41N10'15 82w18'35 5:29:14
Brighton 87 31 41N38 83w29 5:33:56
Brightwood 79 16 40N26'55 81w23'36 5:25:34
Brilliant 41 67 40N15'53 80w37'35 5:22:30
Brimfield 67 67 41N06'00 81w20'48 5:25:23
Brimfield Station 67 67 41N05'59 81w22'14 5:25:29
Brindle Corner 21 33 40N17'47 83w12'05 5:32:48
Brinkhaven (Gann) 42 5 40N28'10 82w11'39 5:28:47
Brinley 68 34 39N53'40 84w44'23 5:38:58
Brister 56 20 39N47'51 81w16'35 5:25:06
Bristol 58 5 39N41'52 81w43'53 5:26:56
Bristol 64 27 39N40'08 82w13'40 5:28:55
Bristol Village 66 34 39N07'53 82w58'03 5:31:52
Bristolville 78 67 41N23'15 80w52'10 5:23:29
Britney Acres 31 34 39N03'40 84w20'05 5:37:20
Brittain 77 2 41N03'52 81w27'48 5:25:51
Broadacre 41 67 40N21'58 80w47'00 5:23:08
Broadmoor Plaza 57 91 39N48 84w17 5:37:08
Broadview 77 67 41N13'04 81w38'19 5:26:33
Broadview Acres 60 5 39N55 82w01 5:28:04
Broadview Heights 18 67 41N18'50 81w41'07 5:26:44
Broadway 80 33 40N20'28 83w24'44 5:33:39
Broadwell 5 5 39N21'53 81w52'47 5:27:31
Brock 19 34 40N15'59 84w33'31 5:38:14
Brocks Corner 40 34 39N11'26 82w45'38 5:31:03
Brokaw 58 5 39N31'41 81w43'38 5:26:55
Broken Sword 17 32 40N54'24 83w01'01 5:32:04
Bronson 39 5 41N11 82w36 5:30:24
Brookbill 31 88 39N12'41 84w29'50 5:37:59
Brookfield 78 45 41N14'02 80w34'11 5:22:17
Brookgate 18 26 41N25 81w48 5:27:12
Brookhill 31 88 39N12 84w32 5:38:08
Brook Hollow 29 34 39N48 84w01 5:36:04
Brooklyn 18 26 41N26'23 81w44'08 5:26:57
Brooklyn Heights 18 26 41N25'31 81w41'18 5:26:45
Brook Park 18 67 41N23'54 81w48'17 5:27:13
Brooks Corner 40 34 39N12 82w41 5:30:44
Brookside 7 21 40N04'14 80w45'40 5:23:03
Brookside Estates 25 107 40N05 83w01 5:32:04
Brookside Park 78 45 41N15'57 80w50'13 5:23:21
Brookville 57 34 39N50'12 84w24'41 5:37:39
Brookwood 31 88 39N12'05 84w26'28 5:37:46
Broughton 63 34 41N05'23 84w32'07 5:38:08
Brown 55 34 39N56'30 84w04'03 5:36:16
Brown Corner 78 45 41N15'56 80w48'06 5:23:12
Brown Heights 30 5 40N01 81w35 5:26:20
Brownhelm 47 67 41N23'20 82w16'58 5:29:08
Brownhelm Station 47 81 41N24'34 82w17'39 5:29:11
Browns 68 34 39N54'09 84w35'59 5:38:24
Browns Crossroads 33 33 40N36'09 83w31'26 5:34:06
Browns Heights 30 5 40N01'49 81w36'39 5:26:27
Brownstown 8 34 38N58'12 83w50'25 5:35:22
Brownstown 88 33 40N44'16 83w22'12 5:33:29
Brownsville 45 5 39N56'49 82w15'24 5:29:02
Brownsville 56 20 39N35'20 81w05'04 5:24:20
Brownsville 71 34 39N15'38 83w03'02 5:32:12
Browntown 8 34 38N52 83w55 5:35:40
Brunersburg 20 34 41N18'24 84w23'13 5:37:33
Bruno 64 27 39N50'54 82w24'50 5:29:39
Brunswick 52 67 41N14'17 81w50'31 5:27:22
Brunswick Hills 52 67 41N14 81w51 5:27:24
Brush Ridge 51 27 40N41'15 83w09'13 5:32:37
Bryan 86 34 41N28'29 84w33'09 5:38:13
Buchanan 66 34 39N08'59 83w07'25 5:32:30
Buchtel 5 27 39N27'43 82w10'55 5:28:44
Buck 33 34 40N37 83w37 5:34:28
Buckeye 37 34 39N03'16 82w27'33 5:29:50
Buckeye 60 5 39N53'18 81w59'36 5:27:58
Buckeye Addition 42 5 40N24 82w29 5:29:56
Buckeye Lake 45 27 39N56'01 82w28'21 5:29:53
Buckeyeville 30 5 39N57'05 81w36'48 5:26:27
Buckhorn 44 34 38N44'47 82w38'07 5:30:32
Buckhorn Corner 19 34 40N13'23 84w46'31 5:39:06
Buckhorn Furnace 44 34 38N44'11 82w39'08 5:30:37
Buckingham 64 27 39N35'30 82w08'16 5:28:33
Buckland 6 34 40N37'22 84w15'36 5:37:02
Bucks 79 16 40N24 81w39 5:26:36
Bucks Corner 19 34 40N18'33 84w46'31 5:39:06
Buckskin 71 34 39N21 83w18 5:33:12
Bucks Mill 53 5 39N08'30 81w56'48 5:27:47
Bucyrus 17 86 40N48'30 82w58'32 5:31:54
Buena Vista 9 34 39N30 84w23 5:37:32
Buena Vista 24 34 39N25'19 83w29'39 5:33:59
Buena Vista 37 34 39N33'00 82w40'15 5:30:41
Buena Vista 73 34 38N37'48 83w15'41 5:33:03
Buffalo 30 5 39N54'57 81w31'13 5:26:05
Buffalo 40 34 39N05'47 82w38'54 5:30:36
Buford 36 34 39N04'36 83w50'39 5:35:23
Bulah 4 72 41N44 80w47 5:23:08
Bulaville 27 27 38N54'00 82w10'59 5:28:44
Bulkhead 6 34 40N31'14 84w25'17 5:37:41
Bulkhead 46 34 40N25 83w53 5:35:32
Bundysburg 28 67 41N25'12 81w00'30 5:24:02
Bunker Hill 9 34 39N25'02 84w43'23 5:38:54
Bunker Hill 38 5 40N34'22 81w46'59 5:27:08
Bunker Hill 50 67 40N57'33 80w56'09 5:23:45
Burbank 85 62 40N59'19 81w59'42 5:27:59
Burghill 78 67 41N21'34 80w34'07 5:22:16
Burgoon 72 32 41N16'03 83w15'06 5:33:00
Burkettsville 54 34 40N21'07 84w38'32 5:38:34
Burkhardt Center 57 91 39N45'39 84w09'01 5:36:36
Burkhart 56 20 39N47'21 81w15'47 5:25:03
Burlingham 53 27 39N13 82w09 5:28:36
Burlington 26 34 41N34'20 84w18'29 5:37:14
Burlington 44 37 38N24'26 82w32'09 5:30:09
Burlington 45 27 40N14 82w31 5:30:04
Burnetts Corners 85 76 40N46'16 81w58'24 5:27:54
Burnet Woods 31 88 39N09 84w31 5:38:04
Burr Oak 5 27 39N33'03 82w03'50 5:28:15
Burr Oaks 49 34 39N43 83w16 5:33:04
Burr Oaks Heights 49 34 39N42'41 83w16'28 5:33:06
Bursville 54 34 40N37'33 84w43'39 5:38:55
Burton 28 73 41N28'14 81w08'43 5:24:35
Burton City 85 62 40N50'41 81w42'15 5:26:49
Burton Lake 28 67 41N25'43 81w11'13 5:24:45
Burton Station 28 74 41N29'21 81w06'02 5:24:24
Burtonville 14 34 39N24'18 83w48'52 5:35:15
Busenbark 9 34 39N27'56 84w29'08 5:37:57
Bushnell 4 72 41N51'46 80w34'18 5:22:17
Businessburg 7 21 39N55'53 80w51'02 5:23:24
Business Corner 48 34 41N34'25 83w44'16 5:34:57
Busy Corners 72 32 41N25'29 83w18'00 5:33:12
Butler 70 27 40N35'18 82w25'30 5:29:42
Butlers Mill 32 34 41N09'47 83w51'41 5:35:27
Butlerville 83 34 39N18'09 84w05'24 5:36:22
Buzzard Roost 52 73 41N12'56 81w42'33 5:26:50
Byer 40 34 39N10'53 82w37'53 5:30:32
Byesville 30 5 39N58'11 81w32'12 5:26:09
Byhalia 80 33 40N27'13 83w27'20 5:33:49
Byington 66 34 39N05'15 83w17'58 5:33:12
Byrd 8 34 38N50 83w43 5:34:52
Byron 29 34 39N47'10 83w58'51 5:35:55
Cabinet 7 21 40N07'05 81w13'02 5:24:52
Cable 11 34 40N10'13 83w37'42 5:34:31
Cadiz 34 21 40N16'22 80w59'49 5:23:59
Cadiz Junction 34 21 40N21'33 80w55'55 5:23:44
Cadmus 27 34 38N46'01 82w26'13 5:29:45
Caesar Creek 29 34 39N36 83w52 5:35:28
Cain Heights 15 105 40N38 80w35 5:22:20
Cairo 2 34 40N49'55 84w05'10 5:36:21
Cairo 76 43 40N54'16 81w21'38 5:25:27
Calais 56 20 39N51'25 81w16'35 5:25:06
Calamoutier 38 5 40N39'55 81w47'04 5:27:08
Calcutta 15 105 40N40'24 80w34'36 5:22:18
Caldwell 61 5 39N44'52 81w31'00 5:26:04
Caledonia 51 32 40N38'11 82w58'09 5:31:53
California 31 88 39N03'55 84w25'24 5:37:42
Calla 50 67 40N58'21 80w46'15 5:23:05
Camba 40 34 38N57'53 82w36'19 5:30:25
Cambridge 30 116 40N02 81w35 5:26:20
Camden 47 67 41N14'16 82w18'21 5:29:13
Camden 68 34 39N37'44 84w38'55 5:38:36
Cameron 56 20 39N46'01 80w56'42 5:23:47
Camp 66 34 38N58'25 83w06'55 5:32:28
Campbell 50 84 41N04'42 80w35'58 5:22:24
Campbellsport 67 67 41N08'09 81w11'51 5:24:47
Campbellstown 68 34 39N47'16 84w45'37 5:39:02
Camp Bennett 73 34 38N46'23 82w51'38 5:31:27
Camp Calvary 4 72 41N56'39 80w37'31 5:22:30
Camp Creek 66 34 38N59 83w07 5:32:28
Camp Creek 76 67 40N44'04 81w34'25 5:26:18
Camp Dennison 13 34 39N11'53 84w17'20 5:37:09
Camp Ground 23 27 39N43 82w36 5:30:24
Camp Luther 4 72 41N56'28 80w38'48 5:22:35
Camp Oyo 73 34 38N43'33 83w09'09 5:32:37
Camp Park 50 67 41N04'09 80w47'32 5:23:10
Camp Roosevelt 43 67 41N47'29 81w10'03 5:24:40
Camp Washington 31 88 39N08'10 84w32'13 5:38:09
Canaan 85 58 40N56'41 81w56'12 5:27:45
Canaanville 5 27 39N20 82w05 5:28:20
Canal Fulton 76 67 40N53'23 81w35'52 5:26:23
Canal Lewisville 16 5 40N17'57 81w50'11 5:27:21
Canal Winchester 23 27 39N50'34 82w48'17 5:31:13
Candy Town 37 27 39N26 82w14 5:28:56
Canfield 50 67 41N01'30 80w45'40 5:23:03
Cannelville 60 5 39N48'50 81w59'50 5:27:59
Cannon 60 5 39N49'38 82w08'18 5:28:33
Cannons Creek 44 34 38N38'56 82w37'32 5:30:30
Cannons Mills 15 105 40N38 80w35 5:22:20
Canton 76 43 40N47'56 81w22'43 5:25:31
Canton Road 76 54 40N44'50 81w31'02 5:26:04
Canyon Park 50 67 41N04'43 80w59'44 5:23:59
Captina 7 21 39N53'15 80w52'16 5:23:29
Carbondale 5 27 39N22'40 82w16'15 5:29:05
Carbon Hill 37 34 39N30'06 82w14'41 5:28:59
Cardinal Lake 4 72 41N36 80w52 5:23:28
Cardington 59 27 40N30'02 82w53'37 5:31:34
Carey 88 32 40N57'09 83w22'57 5:33:32
Careytown 36 34 39N18'36 83w37'45 5:34:31
Carlisle 11 5 39N44'44 81w21'50 5:25:27
Carlisle 83 34 39N34'55 84w19'13 5:37:17
Carlton 27 27 38N57'49 82w05'55 5:28:24
Carmel 36 34 39N10'01 83w24'30 5:33:38
Caroline 74 32 41N03'08 82w53'37 5:31:34
Carpenter 53 27 39N09'46 82w13'10 5:28:53
Carrington 64 27 39N35'46 82w09'54 5:28:40
Carroll 23 27 39N47'56 82w42'04 5:30:48
Carrollton 10 103 40N34'22 81w05'09 5:24:21
Carrothers 74 32 40N59'53 82w55'20 5:31:41
Carryall 63 34 41N13 84w45 5:39:00
Carsey Toewn 5 27 39N15'01 82w00'30 5:28:02
Carthage 5 5 39N15 81w52 5:27:28
Carthage 31 88 39N11'49 84w28'45 5:37:55
Carthagena 54 34 40N26'12 84w33'36 5:38:14
Carthon 64 27 39N44'56 82w19'55 5:29:20
Carysville 11 34 40N12'43 83w58'51 5:35:55
Cassell 30 5 40N01 81w35 5:26:20
Cassella 54 34 40N24'26 84w33'04 5:38:12
Casstown 55 34 40N03'07 84w07'47 5:36:31
Cassville 34 21 40N13'42 81w06'02 5:24:24
Castalia 22 5 41N24'00 82w48'31 5:31:14
Castine 19 34 39N55'53 84w37'30 5:38:30
Catawba 12 34 39N59'57 83w37'18 5:34:29
Catawba Island 62 93 41N35'07 82w50'13 5:31:21
Catawba Station 11 34 40N01'46 83w39'06 5:34:36
Catbird 1 34 38N44'14 83w33'17 5:34:13
Causeway Manor 4 72 41N37 80w36 5:22:24
Cavallo 16 5 40N24'46 82w10'40 5:28:43
Cavett 81 34 40N56'47 84w34'53 5:38:20
Cawthorn 37 27 39N28'37 82w12'07 5:28:48
Caywood 84 20 39N27'24 81w23'09 5:25:33
Cebee 44 37 38N31'03 82w23'18 5:29:33
Cecil 63 34 41N13'07 84w36'08 5:38:25
Cedar Corners 78 84 41N09'45 80w38'03 5:22:32
Cedar Fork 66 34 39N05'10 83w19'06 5:33:16
Cedar Grove 37 27 39N26'16 82w32'23 5:30:10
Cedar Hill 23 34 39N41'24 82w48'19 5:31:13
Cedarhurst 25 107 39N58 82w52 5:31:28
Cedar Mills 1 34 38N49'23 83w23'34 5:33:34
Cedar Park 78 84 41N09'46 80w38'36 5:22:34
Cedar Point 22 5 41N28'48 82w40'57 5:30:44
Cedar Springs 68 34 39N50'17 84w47'39 5:39:11
Cedar Valley 85 76 40N52'20 82w01'29 5:28:06
Cedarville 29 34 39N44'39 83w48'31 5:35:14
Cedron 13 34 38N48'22 84w03'18 5:36:13
Celeryville 39 5 41N01'47 82w43'55 5:30:56
Celina 54 34 40N32'56 84w34'13 5:38:17
Centenary 27 27 38N47'57 82w16'04 5:29:04
Centennial 48 34 41N43'01 83w44'38 5:34:59
Center 30 5 40N01 81w35 5:26:20
Center 74 32 41N08'32 83w09'28 5:32:38
Center Bend 58 5 39N35'38 81w40'53 5:26:44
Centerburg 42 27 40N18'16 82w41'47 5:30:47
Centerfield 36 34 39N21 83w24 5:33:36
Centerpoint 8 34 38N47'54 83w53'25 5:35:34
Centerpoint 27 34 38N51'05 82w27'00 5:29:48
Center Station 44 34 38N40'42 82w39'46 5:30:39
Centerton 39 5 41N05'00 82w45'12 5:31:01
Center Village 21 27 40N09'55 82w48'28 5:31:14
Centerville 7 21 39N58'33 80w57'56 5:23:52
Centerville 8 34 39N04'51 83w57'09 5:35:49
Centerville 51 33 40N29'41 83w14'36 5:32:58
Centerville 57 34 39N37'42 84w09'34 5:36:38
Centerville 58 5 39N38'23 81w37'26 5:26:30
Centerville 85 79 40N40'06 82w02'28 5:28:10
Central 48 31 41N39 83w32 5:34:08
Central Avenue Park 48 31 41N40'44 83w40'56 5:34:44
Central College 25 108 40N06 82w56 5:31:44
Centreville 27 34 38N55 82w27 5:29:48
Cessna 33 34 40N42 83w43 5:34:52
Ceylon 22 5 41N22'18 82w29'38 5:29:59
Chagrin Falls 28 73 41N25'47 81w23'27 5:25:34
Chagrin Harbor 43 67 41N38 81w25 5:25:40
Chalfants 64 27 39N52'09 82w17'07 5:29:08

Chambersburg 15 67 40N47'15 81W01'55 5:24:08
Chambersburg 27 34 38N41 82W12 5:28:48
Champion 78 45 41N18'00 80W51'00 5:23:24
Chandler 41 67 40N18'28 80W48'16 5:23:13
Chandlersville 60 5 39N53'54 81W49'39 5:27:19
Chapel Hill 64 27 39N37'25 82W03'13 5:28:13
Chapmans 40 34 39N05'21 82W37'06 5:30:28
Chardon 28 73 41N36'51 81W08'57 5:24:36
Charity Rotch 76 54 40N49'27 81W30'29 5:26:02
Charles Mill 3 44 40N44'03 82W21'48 5:29:27
Charlestown 67 67 41N09'47 81W08'53 5:24:36
Charloe 63 34 41N07'53 84W26'02 5:37:44
Charm 38 5 40N30'24 81W47'06 5:27:08
Chase 5 27 39N12'20 82W05'53 5:28:24
Chase 32 89 41N04'23 83W42'32 5:34:50
Chasetown 8 34 39N09'38 83W55'55 5:35:44
Chaseville 61 5 39N53'10 81W27'51 5:25:51
Chaska Beach 22 5 41N24 82W34 5:30:16
Chatfield 17 32 40N57'01 82W56'42 5:31:47
Chatham 45 5 40N09'27 82W27'13 5:29:49
Chatham 52 73 41N05'58 82W01'28 5:28:06
Chattanooga 54 34 40N38'13 84W47'06 5:39:08
Chauncey 5 27 39N23'52 82W07'46 5:28:31
Chautauqua 57 34 39N35'23 84W17'47 5:37:11
Chenoweth 49 34 39N43'52 83W21'27 5:33:26
Cherokee 46 34 40N26'16 83W47'33 5:35:10
Cherry Fork 1 34 38N53'15 83W36'52 5:34:27
Cherry Grove 31 34 39N04'21 84W19'19 5:37:17
Cherry Grove Plaza 31 88 39N06 84W23 5:37:32
Cherry Valley 4 72 41N36'24 80W40'03 5:22:40
Cherry Valley 34 21 40N18'07 80W52'48 5:23:31
Chesapeake 44 37 38N25'40 82W27'26 5:29:50
Cheshire 21 27 40N14'19 82W57'48 5:31:51
Cheshire 27 27 38N56'41 82W06'41 5:28:27
Chesswood Acres 31 34 39N13'25 84W35'38 5:38:23
Chester 53 5 39N05'15 81W55'22 5:27:41
Chester Center 28 67 41N32'03 81W20'17 5:25:21
Chesterfield 26 34 41N40 84W10 5:36:40
Chesterhill 58 5 39N29'18 81W51'58 5:27:28
Chesterland 28 67 41N31'20 81W20'17 5:25:21
Chesterville 59 27 40N28'48 82W41'01 5:30:44
Cheviot 31 88 39N09'25 84W36'48 5:38:27
Chickasaw 54 34 40N26'13 84W29'36 5:37:58
Chickwan 34 21 40N13'57 80W52'58 5:23:32
Chili 16 5 40N22'26 81W45'15 5:27:01
Chillicothe 71 100 39N19'59 82W58'57 5:31:56
Chilo 13 34 38N47'35 84W08'27 5:36:34
Chippewa 85 62 40N57 81W42 5:26:48
Chippewa Lake 52 73 41N03 81W54 5:27:36
Chippewa Lake Park 52 73 41N03'48 81W53'45 5:27:35
Chippewa-on-the-Lake 52 73 41N04'11 81W54'04 5:27:36
Chrisman 49 34 39N49'59 83W22'22 5:33:29
Christiansburg 11 34 40N03'19 84W01'34 5:36:06
Christy 87 33 41N20'34 83W39'56 5:34:40
Christytown 50 67 40N59'59 80W59'10 5:23:57
Chuckery 80 34 40N06'42 83W23'26 5:33:34
Churchill 78 84 41N09'43 80W39'54 5:22:40
Churchtown 84 20 39N28'02 81W32'53 5:26:12
Cincinnati 31 88 39N09'43 84W27'25 5:37:50
Cipper Mills 27 27 38N45'49 82W12'34 5:28:50
Circle Green 41 67 40N29'04 80W52'33 5:23:30
Circle Hill 5 27 39N26 82W14 5:28:56
Circle Hill 55 34 40N04'22 84W24'52 5:37:39
Circleville 65 34 39N36'02 82W56'46 5:31:47
City View Heights 9 34 39N25'22 84W33'05 5:38:12
Claiborne 80 33 40N23'17 83W20'57 5:33:24
Clare 31 34 39N08'22 84W22'37 5:37:30
Claridon 28 67 41N32'19 81W07'45 5:24:31
Claridon 51 27 40N34'59 82W59'49 5:31:59
Clarington 56 20 39N45'56 80W52'17 5:23:29
Clarion 82 27 39N05'27 82W23'00 5:29:32
Clark 16 5 40N26'56 81W54'09 5:27:37
Clark Corners 4 72 41N56 80W36 5:22:24
Clark Corners 52 53 41N03'19 81W43'57 5:26:56
Clarksburg 7 21 40N01 80W51 5:23:24
Clarksburg 71 34 39N30'19 83W09'12 5:32:37
Clarksfield 39 5 41N11'42 82W24'42 5:29:39
Clarkson 15 67 40N44'49 80W36'49 5:22:27
Clarksville 14 34 39N24'05 83W58'53 5:35:56
Clarksville 64 27 39N42'19 82W17'29 5:29:10
Clarktown 73 34 38N51'02 82W54'41 5:31:39
Clay 40 34 38N56'07 82W34'01 5:30:16
Clay Center 62 93 41N33'48 83W21'43 5:33:27
Claylick 25 5 40N03'30 82W17'14 5:29:09
Claysville 30 6 39N56'10 81W40'14 5:26:41
Clayton 1 34 38N44'37 83W40'32 5:34:42
Clayton 55 34 40N09'03 84W22'32 5:37:30
Clayton 57 34 39N51'47 84W21'38 5:37:27
Clearport 23 27 39N37'21 82W40'49 5:30:43
Clearview 5 27 39N17'45 82W07'08 5:28:29
Clearview 47 50 41N26 82W09 5:28:36
Clearview 76 54 40N49'25 81W31'01 5:26:04
Clermontville 13 34 38N55'20 84W15'14 5:37:01
Clertoma 13 34 39N10'18 84W16'58 5:37:08
Cleveland 18 26 41N29'58 81W41'44 5:26:47
Cleveland Heights 18 26 41N31'12 81W33'23 5:26:14
Cleves 31 34 39N09'42 84W44'57 5:39:00
Clifford 73 34 38N55'36 83W01'11 5:32:05
Clifton 12 34 39N47'49 83W49'32 5:35:18
Clifton 31 88 39N09'00 84W31'05 5:38:04
Clifton 84 20 39N32'22 81W33'07 5:26:12
Clifton Farms 9 34 39N30 84W23 5:37:32
Climax 59 27 40N37'50 82W53'17 5:31:33
Cline 56 20 39N36'27 81W09'34 5:24:38
Clinton 25 107 40N02'26 82W57'39 5:31:51
Clinton 77 67 40N56 81W38 5:26:32
Clipper Mills 27 27 38N46 82W11 5:28:44
Clough Heights 13 88 39N05'10 84W18'01 5:37:12
Clover 13 34 38N59'55 84W02'35 5:36:10
Cloverdale 69 34 41N01'15 84W18'16 5:37:13
Cloverdale 87 33 41N20'29 83W34'26 5:34:18
Clover Hill 7 20 39N52'16 80W55'29 5:23:42
Clover Hill 64 27 39N46'36 82W09'49 5:28:39
Clover Hill 78 67 41N29'20 80W52'40 5:23:31
Cluff 31 34 39N07 84W21 5:37:24
Clyde 72 38 41N18'15 82W58'31 5:31:54
Coach Lite Village 48 34 41N36 83W42 5:34:48
Coalburg 78 84 41N11'35 80W35'18 5:22:21
Coalgate 37 27 39N32'13 82W11'06 5:28:44
Coal Grove 44 34 38N30'12 82W38'50 5:30:35
Coal Hill 60 5 39N47'30 81W43'08 5:26:53
Coalport 79 16 40N16'58 81W36'45 5:26:27
Coal Ridge 11 5 39N48'28 81W34'25 5:26:18
Coal Run 84 20 39N34'03 81W34'53 5:26:20
Coalton 40 34 39N06'49 82W36'41 5:30:27
Coats 56 20 39N46'51 81W03'34 5:24:14
Cockrell Run 66 34 38N57'12 82W58'45 5:31:55
Coddingville 52 73 41N08'12 81W42'19 5:26:49
Coitsville 50 84 41N05 80W33 5:22:12
Coitsville Center 50 84 41N05'26 80W34'09 5:22:17
Cokesbury Corners 45 27 40N10'37 82W33'11 5:30:13
Colby 72 30 41N15'48 82W56'47 5:31:47
Cold Springs 12 39 39N55 83W48 5:35:12
Coldwater 54 34 40N28'47 84W37'42 5:38:31
Cole 5 5 39N17'56 81W54'23 5:27:38
Colebrook 4 72 41N32'08 80W45'46 5:23:03
Coleman 15 67 40N47'46 80W48'48 5:23:15
Colerain 7 21 40N07'33 80W48'32 5:23:14
Colerain Heights 31 34 39N14'26 84W35'53 5:38:24
Colerian 71 34 39N27 82W48 5:31:12
Coles Park 73 34 38N47'13 83W00'58 5:32:04
Coletown 19 34 40N08'04 84W42'10 5:38:49
Colfax 23 27 39N44'25 82W30'08 5:30:01
College 42 5 40N22 82W23 5:29:32
College Corner 68 34 39N34'03 84W48'52 5:39:15
College Hill 30 5 40N02'27 81W38'52 5:26:35
College Hill 31 88 39N12'08 84W32'50 5:38:11
College Hill 42 5 40N32'36 82W20'06 5:29:20
College Hills 29 34 39N48 84W01 5:36:04
Collins 39 5 41N15'31 82W29'29 5:29:58
Collinsville 9 34 39N30'55 84W36'34 5:38:26
Collinwood 18 26 41N34 81W34 5:26:16
Colonial Hills 25 107 40N05 83W01 5:32:04
Colton 35 34 41N27'53 83W57'09 5:35:49
Columbia 31 88 39N06'42 84W26'05 5:37:44
Columbia 47 67 41N20 81W57 5:27:48
Columbia 76 54 40N47'01 81W31'22 5:26:05
Columbia 79 16 40N34'30 81W30'26 5:26:02
Columbia 86 34 41N37'59 84W47'19 5:39:09
Columbia Center 45 27 39N59'54 82W41'45 5:30:47
Columbia Center 47 21 41N18'45 81W55'33 5:27:42
Columbia Hills Corners 47 21 41N18'46 81W54'57 5:27:40
Columbiana 15 47 40N53'18 80W41'39 5:22:47
Columbia Station 47 21 41N18'47 81W56'49 5:27:47
Columbus 25 107 39N57'40 82W59'56 5:32:00
Columbus Grove 69 34 40N55'10 84W03'25 5:36:14
Columbus Park 22 5 41N27 82W44 5:30:56
Comet 40 34 39N06'57 82W33'04 5:30:12
Comet 77 67 40N55'21 81W31'33 5:26:06
Commercial Point 65 34 39N46'06 83W03'26 5:32:14
Compton Park 31 34 39N13'52 84W30'26 5:38:02
Compton Woods 31 34 39N13'56 84W29'54 5:38:00
Conant 2 34 40N43'08 84W16'50 5:37:07
Concord 13 34 39N01'19 84W04'49 5:36:19
Concord 19 34 40N05'10 84W34'43 5:38:19
Concord 43 46 41N40'28 81W13'29 5:24:54
Concord 45 27 40N08'35 82W38'17 5:30:33
Condit 21 27 40N15'36 82W47'17 5:31:09
Conesville 16 5 40N11'02 81W53'28 5:27:34
Congo 64 27 39N36'55 82W07'18 5:28:29
Congress 85 62 40N55'33 82W03'11 5:28:13
Congress Lake 76 67 40N58 81W20 5:25:20
Conneaut 4 25 41N56'51 80W33'16 5:22:13
Conneaut Harbor 4 25 41N56 80W36 5:22:24
Connett 5 27 39N24'41 82W15'17 5:29:01
Connor 41 67 40N11'20 80W42'48 5:22:51
Connorville 41 67 40N11'34 80W42'48 5:22:51
Conotton 34 21 40N25'02 81W08'48 5:24:35
Conover 55 34 40N08'07 84W02'47 5:36:11
Constitution 84 20 39N20'53 81W33'17 5:26:13
Continental 69 34 41N06'01 84W15'59 5:37:04
Contreras 9 34 39N31'25 84W48'42 5:39:15
Converse 81 34 40N44'35 84W24'59 5:37:40
Convoy 81 34 40N55'00 84W42'10 5:38:49
Conway Addition 64 27 39N45'05 82W05'18 5:28:21
Cooks 24 34 39N40'59 83W18'26 5:33:14
Cool Ridge Heights 70 95 40N47 82W30 5:30:00
Coolville 5 5 39N13'18 81W47'51 5:27:11
Coon Crossing 36 34 39N09'21 83W23'31 5:33:34
Cooney 86 34 41N39'26 84W44'51 5:38:59
Coonville 37 27 39N23'54 82W20'22 5:29:21
Cooper 74 32 41N10'08 82W58'37 5:31:54
Cooperdale 16 5 40N13'11 82W03'55 5:28:16
Coopersville 66 34 38N57'40 83W02'34 5:32:10
Copley 77 67 41N05'56 81W38'41 5:26:35
Copley Junction 77 67 41N06'17 81W35'57 5:26:24
Cora 27 34 38N49'28 82W22'11 5:29:29
Corinth 78 67 41N23'55 80W37'23 5:22:30
Cork 4 72 41N43'50 80W57'06 5:23:48
Cornelion 78 72 41N29'35 80W31'52 5:22:07
Corner 84 20 39N18'32 81W39'43 5:26:39
Cornersburg 50 84 41N03'46 80W42'41 5:22:51
Cornerville 84 20 39N23'48 81W22'30 5:25:30
Corning 64 27 39N36'09 82W05'18 5:28:21
Corryville 31 88 39N07'35 84W31'30 5:38:06
Corryville 44 37 38N26'08 82W25'18 5:29:41
Cortland 78 71 41N19'49 80W43'32 5:22:54
Cortsville 12 34 39N47'47 83W43'16 5:34:53
Corwin 83 34 39N31'30 84W04'42 5:36:19
Coryville 44 34 38N32'37 82W39'53 5:30:40
Coshocton 16 5 40N16'19 81W51'35 5:27:26
Cosmos 19 34 40N16'02 84W46'46 5:39:07
Cotillion Village 31 88 39N06'25 84W38'25 5:38:34
Cottage Grove 77 2 40N59'19 81W30'44 5:26:03
Cottage Hill 60 5 40N00'58 82W11'18 5:28:45
Coulter 70 44 40N41'33 82W20'39 5:29:23
Country Acres 29 34 39N48 84W01 5:36:04
Country Club Acres 31 34 39N10'52 84W22'46 5:37:31
Country Club Estates 41 106 40N22 80W39 5:22:36
Country Club Highlands 9 34 39N22 84W33 5:38:12
Country Lane Estates 43 67 41N44 81W14 5:24:56
Cove 40 34 39N04 82W39 5:30:36
Covedale 31 88 39N07'16 84W36'23 5:38:26
Coventry 77 2 41N00 81W32 5:26:08
Covington 55 34 40N07'02 84W21'14 5:37:25
Cowlesville 55 34 39N58'53 84W11'12 5:36:45
Cow Run 84 20 39N26'52 81W18'33 5:25:14
Cozaddale 83 34 39N16'17 84W09'43 5:36:39
Crabapple 7 21 40N07'12 80W57'16 5:23:49
Crabtree 73 34 38N53'33 83W06'16 5:32:25
Craig Beach 50 67 41N07'01 80W59'01 5:23:56
Craigton 85 79 40N42'59 82W04'13 5:28:17
Cranberry 17 32 40N57 82W50 5:31:20
Cranberry Prairie 54 34 40N23'33 84W34'50 5:38:19
Crandenbrook 87 31 41N34 83W35 5:34:20
Cranenest 56 20 39N43'37 81W03'45 5:24:15
Cranwood 18 26 41N26 81W34 5:26:16
Craver 13 34 39N08'34 84W10'45 5:36:43
Crawford 34 21 40N18'05 80W59'16 5:23:57
Crawford 88 32 40N55'11 83W20'32 5:33:22
Crawford Corners 52 73 41N00'36 82W03'17 5:28:13
Crayon 11 34 40N12'01 83W53'45 5:35:35
Cream City 41 67 40N33'52 80W43'05 5:22:52
Creola 82 27 39N18'55 82W27'59 5:29:52
Crescent 7 21 40N07'12 80W51'35 5:23:26
Crescent Gardens 76 54 40N48 81W31 5:26:04
Crescentville 31 34 39N18'02 84W26'50 5:37:47
Cresceus Farms 87 31 41N35'05 83W26'25 5:33:46
Crestline 17 28 40N47'15 82W44'12 5:30:57
Creston 85 58 40N59'13 81W53'38 5:27:35
Crestwood Acres 31 34 39N13'57 84W36'18 5:38:25
Crestwood Hills 70 95 40N47 82W30 5:30:00
Cridersville 6 34 40N39'15 84W09'03 5:36:36
Crimson 70 44 40N44'30 82W23'48 5:29:35
Crissey 48 34 41N36'37 83W45'43 5:35:03
Cromers 74 32 41N10'54 83W12'54 5:32:52
Crooked Tree 11 5 39N38'16 81W29'57 5:26:00
Crooksville 64 27 39N46'08 82W05'32 5:28:22
Crosby 31 34 39N17 84W44 5:38:56
Cross Creek 41 106 40N21 80W41 5:22:44
Crossenville 64 27 39N40'50 82W21'23 5:29:26
Crossroads 76 67 40N43'37 81W34'26 5:26:18
Crosstown 8 34 39N05'30 84W00'22 5:36:01
Crosswick 83 34 39N32'38 84W04'44 5:36:19
Croswell 69 34 41N01'15 84W11'52 5:36:47
Croton (P O) 45 27 40N14 82W41 5:30:44
Crown City 27 34 38N35'27 82W16'59 5:29:08
Crownover Mill 65 34 39N37'08 83W13'02 5:32:52
Crown Point 57 91 39N45'03 84W16'02 5:37:04
Crystal Lakes 12 34 39N53'21 84W01'36 5:36:06
Crystal Rock 22 5 41N26'47 82W50'41 5:31:23
Crystal Rock Park 22 5 41N23 82W56 5:31:44
Crystal Springs 76 54 40N50'57 81W32'04 5:26:08
Cuba 14 34 39N21'40 83W51'50 5:35:27
Cuba 69 34 41N03'12 84W11'54 5:36:48
Culbertson Heights 55 34 40N03 84W11 5:36:44
Culler Mill 70 5 40N41'50 82W23'24 5:29:34
Cumberland 30 5 39N51'07 81W39'28 5:26:38
Cumminsville 31 88 39N09'50 84W32'24 5:38:10
Cunningham 24 34 39N34'42 83W33'05 5:34:12

Curtice 48 93 41N37'06 83w22'04 5:33:28
Custar 87 34 41N17'05 83w50'40 5:35:23
Cutler 84 20 39N21'15 81w47'25 5:27:10
Cuyahoga Falls 77 2 41N08'02 81w29'05 5:25:56
Cuyahoga Heights 18 26 41N26'07 81w39'27 5:26:38
Cyclorama Heights 31 88 39N08'26 84w34'50 5:38:19
Cygnet 87 33 41N14'24 83w38'36 5:34:34
Cynthian 75 34 40N18 84w21 5:37:24
Cynthiana 66 34 39N10'25 83w20'55 5:33:24
Dabel 57 91 39N43 84w08 5:36:32
Dadsville 68 34 39N44 84w32 5:38:08
Dague 63 34 41N03'46 84w34'49 5:38:19
Dailyville 66 34 39N09 83w00 5:32:00
Dairy 56 20 39N39'09 80w58'50 5:23:55
Dale 84 5 39N29'20 81w46'00 5:27:04
Dalewood 9 34 39N20 84w25 5:37:40
Daleyville 66 34 39N06'24 83w03'14 5:32:13
Dallas 17 32 40N43 83w03 5:32:12
Dallasburg 83 34 39N16'20 84w11'29 5:36:46
Dalrymple Corners 42 27 40N24'08 82w36'36 5:30:26
Dalton 85 69 40N47'56 81w41'44 5:26:47
Dalzell 84 20 39N33'53 81w18'15 5:25:13
Daman Park 9 34 39N30 84w23 5:37:32
Damascus 35 34 41N23 83w57 5:35:48
Damascus 50 67 40N54'07 80w57'19 5:23:49
Danbury 62 93 41N29'57 82w49'49 5:31:19
Danville 36 34 39N08'41 83w44'17 5:34:57
Danville 42 5 40N26'51 82w15'37 5:29:02
Danville 53 27 39N01'31 82w15'23 5:29:02
Darby Crest 49 34 39N55 83w10 5:32:40
Darbydale 25 34 39N51'13 83w10'59 5:32:44
Darbyville 65 34 39N41'49 83w06'50 5:32:27
Darlington 60 5 39N52'52 82w02'00 5:28:08
Darlington 70 95 40N35'11 82w36'17 5:30:25
Darnell 11 34 40N04'18 83w56'12 5:35:45
Darrowville 77 2 41N12'09 81w26'26 5:25:46
Darrtown 9 34 39N29'44 84w39'41 5:38:39
Dart 84 20 39N29'10 81w16'28 5:25:06
Darwin 53 27 39N08'46 82w01'25 5:28:06
Davisville 40 34 39N05'52 82w36'44 5:30:27
Dawn 19 34 40N13'01 84w34'44 5:38:19
Dawson 75 34 40N15'38 84w19'11 5:37:17
Day Heights 13 34 39N10 84w18 5:37:12
Dayton 57 91 39N45'32 84w11'30 5:36:46
Dayton View 57 91 39N47 84w14 5:36:56
Deacon Creek Corner 78 67 41N23'30 80w50'02 5:23:20
Deadman Crossing 71 34 39N16'21 82w55'41 5:31:43
Deandale 41 106 40N18'33 80w37'00 5:22:28
Deavertown 58 5 39N44'03 82w02'17 5:28:09
Decatur 8 34 38N48'56 83w42'14 5:34:49
Decaturville 84 20 39N20'05 81w45'18 5:27:01
Decker 56 20 39N45'34 81w11'27 5:24:46
DeCliff 51 33 40N36'27 83w20'32 5:33:22
Decrow Corners 45 27 40N11'37 82w35'57 5:30:24
Deep Run 7 21 40N10 80w42 5:22:48
Deerfield 67 67 41N01'28 81w03'01 5:24:12
Deering 44 34 38N30'12 82w35'00 5:30:20
Deer Park 31 34 39N12'19 84w23'41 5:37:35
Deersville 34 21 40N18'27 81w11'12 5:24:45
Defiance 20 110 41N17'04 84w21'21 5:37:25
DeForest 78 75 41N12'10 80w46'47 5:23:07
DeForest Junction 78 75 41N12'19 80w47'27 5:23:10
De Graff 46 34 40N18'43 83w54'57 5:35:40
Dekalb 17 33 40N53'33 82w46'22 5:31:05
Delano 71 34 39N24'25 82w57'20 5:31:49
Delaware 21 117 40N17'55 83w04'05 5:32:16
Delhi 31 88 39N05'42 84w36'19 5:38:25
Delhi Hills 31 88 39N05'34 84w36'46 5:38:27
Delightful 78 67 41N17'10 80w55'31 5:23:42
Delisle 19 34 40N01'10 84w34'27 5:38:18
Dell 84 20 39N24'45 81w21'24 5:25:26
Dellroy 10 21 40N33'16 81w11'59 5:24:48
Delmont 23 27 39N40'58 82w40'51 5:30:43
Delphi 39 5 41N01'52 82w36'28 5:30:26
Delphos 2 34 40N51 84w21 5:37:24
Delta 26 34 41N34'25 84w00'19 5:36:01
Denmark 4 72 41N45 80w42 5:22:48
Denmark 59 27 40N35'12 82w55'05 5:31:40
Denmark Center 4 72 41N45'06 80w40'05 5:22:40
Dennison 79 114 40N23'36 81w20'02 5:25:20
Denson 26 34 41N42'20 84w08'54 5:36:36
Dent 31 34 39N11'09 84w39'05 5:38:36
Denver 71 34 39N11'35 83w03'21 5:32:13
Depew 75 34 40N13'58 84w06'55 5:36:28
Depot 67 67 41N10 81w16 5:25:04
Derby 65 34 39N46'07 83w12'21 5:32:49
Derwent 30 5 39N55'23 81w32'40 5:26:11
Deshler 35 34 41N12'27 83w53'57 5:35:36
Deucher 84 20 39N27'59 81w11'49 5:24:47
Deunquat 88 32 40N55'42 83w07'53 5:32:32
Devil Town 85 76 40N50'43 81w58'25 5:27:54
Devola 84 20 39N28'25 81w28'45 5:25:55
Deweyville 32 34 41N07'54 83w49'12 5:35:17
Dexter 53 27 39N05'14 82w12'47 5:28:51
Dexter City 11 5 39N39'28 81w28'20 5:25:53
Deyarmonville 41 67 40N12'42 80w45'42 5:23:03
Dialton 12 39 40N01'38 83w56'26 5:35:46
Diamond 67 67 41N05'56 81w01'23 5:24:06
Digby 87 33 41N17'40 83w42'33 5:34:50
Dille 7 21 40N00 80w46 5:23:04
Dilles Bottom 7 21 39N55'21 80w46'55 5:23:08
Dillionvale 31 34 39N13'16 84w24'03 5:37:36
Dillon Falls 60 5 39N58'22 82w03'22 5:28:13
Dillonvale 31 34 39N12 84w25 5:37:40
Dillonvale 41 67 40N11'47 80w46'31 5:23:06
Dills 71 36 39N14'36 83w13'01 5:32:52
Dilworth 78 67 41N26 80w37 5:22:28
Dinsmore 75 34 40N26 84w10 5:36:40
Dipple 80 33 40N12'08 83w19'01 5:33:16
Dixie 64 27 39N39'07 82w14'59 5:29:00
Dixie Heights 9 34 39N30 84w23 5:37:32
Dixon 68 34 39N41 84w45 5:39:00
Dixon 81 34 40N57'02 84w48'16 5:39:13
Dixonville 15 105 40N38 80w35 5:22:20
Dlworth 78 67 41N26'50 80w39'58 5:22:40
Doanville 5 27 39N26'06 82w11'29 5:28:46
Dobbston 44 34 38N33'13 82w25'34 5:29:42
Dodds 83 34 39N29'38 84w09'12 5:36:37
Dodgeville 4 72 41N35'08 80w47'49 5:23:11
Dodo 12 34 39N59'00 83w59'34 5:35:58
Dodson 36 34 39N13 83w48 5:35:12
Dodson 57 34 39N51'02 84w26'36 5:37:46
Dodsonville 36 34 39N12'08 83w48'53 5:35:16
Doherty 56 5 39N48'32 81w18'34 5:25:14
Dola 33 33 40N46'59 83w41'34 5:34:46
Dolly Varden 12 34 39N50'33 83w41'33 5:34:46
Doneys 25 107 39N58 82w52 5:31:28
Donnelsville 12 34 39N55'06 83w56'55 5:35:48
Donnersville 7 21 40N07'08 80w58'58 5:23:56
Dorcas 53 5 38N58'20 81w53'23 5:27:34
Dorema 42 5 40N27'01 82w34'29 5:30:18
Dornbusch 31 34 39N14'50 84w36'07 5:38:24
Dorninton 69 34 41N01'14 84w13'02 5:36:52
Dorset 4 72 41N40'49 80w40'03 5:22:40
Douglas 69 34 40N56'32 84w18'03 5:37:12
Dover 79 61 40N31'14 81w28'27 5:25:54
Dowling 87 31 41N28'42 83w35'37 5:34:22
Downard 37 34 39N05'44 82w28'09 5:29:53
Downington 53 27 39N14 82w12 5:28:48
Doylestown 85 67 40N58'12 81w41'48 5:26:47
Drake 60 104 40N01'15 81w59'33 5:27:58
Drakes 64 27 39N35'38 82w07'38 5:28:31
Drakesburg 67 67 41N14'08 81w08'05 5:24:32
Dresden 60 13 40N07'17 82w00'39 5:28:03
Drexel 57 91 39N44'47 84w17'12 5:37:09
Driftwood 4 72 41N01 80w57 5:23:48
Driftwood 43 67 41N51'10 81w00'09 5:24:01
Drinkle 23 34 39N35'28 82w43'42 5:30:55
Dry Ridge 31 34 39N15'33 84w37'09 5:38:29
Dry Run 15 105 40N38 80w35 5:22:20
Dry Run 73 34 38N46'38 83w01'44 5:32:07
Dublin 25 108 40N05'57 83w06'51 5:32:27
Dublin 50 67 41N00'11 80w47'09 5:23:09
Ducat 87 33 41N16'59 83w40'12 5:34:41
Duchouquet 6 34 40N37 84w09 5:36:36
Duck Creek 78 45 41N09'56 80w53'12 5:23:33
Dudley 33 33 40N36 83w29 5:33:56
Dudley 61 5 39N42'02 81w30'32 5:26:02
Duffy 56 20 39N38'38 80w52'20 5:23:29
Duke 73 34 38N59'56 83w14'01 5:32:56
Dull 81 34 40N45'51 84w40'00 5:38:40
Dumontville 23 27 39N46'38 82w36'59 5:30:28
Dunbar 84 20 39N21'34 81w44'31 5:26:58
Dunbridge 87 33 41N27'29 83w36'37 5:34:26
Duncan Falls 60 5 39N52'19 81w54'34 5:27:38
Duncanwood 34 21 40N11'53 80w56'59 5:23:48
Dundas 82 27 39N12'13 82w28'49 5:29:55
Dundee 79 16 40N35'12 81w36'30 5:26:26
Dungannon 15 67 40N44'03 80w52'44 5:23:31
Dungannon 61 5 39N36'54 81w34'21 5:26:17
Dunglen 41 67 40N11'43 80w47'59 5:23:12
Dunham 84 20 39N20'05 81w37'41 5:26:31
Dunkinsville 1 34 38N51'21 83w28'17 5:33:53
Dunkirk 33 33 40N47'21 83w38'36 5:34:34
Dunlap 31 34 39N17'32 84w37'05 5:38:28
Dupont 69 34 41N03'23 84w18'16 5:37:13
Durant 58 5 39N45'01 81w54'39 5:27:39
Durbin 12 39 39N54'42 83w53'28 5:35:34
Durbin 54 34 40N33'36 84w42'30 5:38:50
Durgan 27 27 39N00'29 82w22'01 5:29:28
Dutch Corners 10 21 40N30'40 81w02'16 5:24:09
Dutch Ridge 26 34 41N38'33 83w57'18 5:35:49
Duvall 11 5 39N45'31 81w29'07 5:25:56
Duvall 65 34 39N46'19 82w57'28 5:31:50
Dyesville 53 27 39N07'41 82w13'48 5:28:55
Eagle Beach 62 93 41N31 82w57 5:31:48
Eagle City 12 39 39N58'37 83w50'05 5:35:20
Eagle Mills 82 34 39N19'43 82w41'32 5:30:46
Eagle Point Colony 87 31 41N36'34 83w34'24 5:34:18
Eagleport 58 5 39N44'14 81w54'56 5:27:40
Eagleville 4 72 41N43'00 80w50'10 5:23:21
Eagleville 87 5 41N11'50 83w33'19 5:34:13
Earls Island 75 34 40N22'12 84w21'28 5:37:26
East 10 21 40N41 80w57 5:23:48
East Akron 77 2 41N04'16 81w29'22 5:25:57
East Alliance 50 67 40N54'48 81w04'43 5:24:19
East Ashtabula 4 46 41N53'52 80w47'18 5:23:09
East Bass Lake 28 67 41N35'30 81w10'39 5:24:43
East Batavia Heights 13 34 39N04'41 84w09'14 5:36:37
East Cadiz 34 21 40N18'13 80w56'57 5:23:48
East Cambridge 30 5 40N00'54 81w33'46 5:26:15
East Canton 76 43 40N47'14 81w16'58 5:25:08
East Carlisle 47 42 41N22 82w06 5:28:24
East Carmel 15 67 40N46'37 80w36'51 5:22:27
East Claridon 28 67 41N31'57 81w06'57 5:24:28
East Clayton 5 27 39N27'16 82w16'14 5:29:05
East Cleveland 18 26 41N31'59 81w34'45 5:26:19
East Conneaut 4 25 41N56 80w36 5:22:24
East Danville 36 34 39N06'57 83w43'09 5:34:53
East Defiance 20 34 41N17 84w20 5:37:20
East Delphos 2 34 40N51 84w20 5:37:20
East End 15 105 40N38'14 80w32'05 5:22:08
East End 31 88 39N07 84w25 5:37:40
East Fairfield 15 67 40N49'19 80w38'11 5:22:33
East Farmington 78 67 41N23'27 80w54'48 5:23:39
East Fultonham 60 5 39N51'00 82w07'20 5:28:29
East Gardens 87 31 41N38 83w29 5:33:56
East Goshen 50 67 40N56'42 80w58'14 5:23:53
East Greenville 76 67 40N47'58 81w37'54 5:26:32
Eastlake 43 67 41N39'14 81w27'02 5:25:48
East Lawn 87 31 41N34'35 83w25'38 5:33:43
East Letart 53 5 38N54'22 81w53'01 5:27:32
East Lewistown 50 67 40N56'39 80w41'55 5:22:48
East Liberty 21 27 40N19'36 82w49'03 5:31:16
East Liberty 46 33 40N19'52 83w34'57 5:34:20
East Liberty 77 2 40N58'30 81w29'35 5:25:58
East Liverpool 15 105 40N37'07 80w34'39 5:22:19
East Mansfield 70 95 40N45'29 82w29'22 5:29:57
East Mecca 78 67 41N19 80w43 5:22:52
East Millersport 23 27 39N54'13 82w30'32 5:30:02
East Millfield 5 27 39N25'56 82w05'20 5:28:21
East Monroe 36 34 39N21'31 83w29'56 5:34:00
East Norwalk 39 5 41N16'16 82w34'12 5:30:17
East Norwood 31 88 39N10 84w27 5:37:48
East Norwood 84 20 39N25'01 81w25'43 5:25:43
Easton 30 5 40N02'09 81w25'46 5:25:43
Easton 85 62 40N57'09 81w44'08 5:26:57
East Orwell 4 60 41N32'06 80w50'38 5:23:23
East Palestine 15 46 40N50'02 80w32'26 5:22:10
East Plains 83 34 39N30 84w23 5:37:32
Eastport 79 16 40N25'33 81w21'12 5:25:25
East Richland 7 21 40N04'21 80w57'15 5:23:49
East Ringgold 65 27 39N40'10 82w51'40 5:31:27
East Rochester 15 67 40N44'46 81w02'07 5:24:08
East Side 50 84 41N06'02 80w38'13 5:22:33
East Sparta 76 67 40N40'02 81w21'18 5:25:25
East Springfield 41 67 40N27'02 80w51'38 5:23:27
East Steels Corners 77 2 41N10'51 81w30'31 5:26:02
East Swanton 48 34 41N34'58 83w51'16 5:35:25
East Townsend 39 5 41N14'55 82w29'31 5:29:58
East Trumbull 4 72 41N39'41 80w54'53 5:23:40
East Union 11 5 39N46'04 81w24'03 5:25:36
East Union 85 62 40N47'45 81w49'03 5:27:16
Eastview 57 34 39N46 84w06 5:36:24
Eastwood 8 34 39N02'56 83w59'05 5:35:56
Eaton 47 67 41N18'50 82w01'15 5:28:05
Eaton 68 34 39N44'38 84w38'12 5:38:33
Eaton Estates 47 67 41N18'32 82w00'21 5:28:01
Eber 24 34 39N34'22 83w28'17 5:33:53
Echo 7 21 40N02'09 80w49'44 5:23:19
Echo Lake Glen 52 73 41N13'39 81w43'06 5:26:52
Eckley 10 21 40N37'16 81w01'24 5:24:06
Eckley 26 34 41N33'49 84w14'58 5:37:00
Eckmansville 1 34 38N51'57 83w38'34 5:34:34
Eden 53 5 39N09'24 81w45'33 5:27:02
Eden Park 73 34 38N46'29 82w56'32 5:31:46
Edenton 13 34 39N13'42 84w03'11 5:36:13
Edenville 88 32 40N49'11 83w09'35 5:32:38
Edgefield 24 34 39N36'51 83w38'41 5:34:35
Edgefield 76 43 40N50'20 81w23'13 5:25:33
Edgemont 31 88 39N12'02 84w27'53 5:37:52
Edgerton 86 34 41N26'55 84w44'53 5:39:00
Edgewater 18 26 41N29 81w48 5:27:12
Edgewater Beach 45 5 39N55'31 82w24'39 5:29:39
Edgewater Park 25 107 39N54'29 82w52'58 5:31:32
Edgewood 4 46 41N52'22 80w46'23 5:23:06
Edinburg 67 67 41N05'59 81w08'46 5:24:35
Edison 59 27 40N33'27 82w51'45 5:31:27
Edmunds Switch 73 34 38N48'29 82w45'34 5:31:02
Edon 86 34 41N33'23 84w46'08 5:39:05
Edward 25 107 39N53'00 82w55'51 5:31:43
Edwardsville 83 34 39N20'13 84w01'39 5:36:07
Edwina 56 20 39N42'56 81w09'20 5:24:37
Egypt 6 34 40N23'08 84w25'59 5:37:44
Egypt 7 21 40N05'06 81w07'41 5:24:31
Egypt 73 34 38N50'39 82w48'04 5:31:12
Elfort 73 34 38N50'00 82w39'11 5:30:37
Elleen Gardens 31 88 39N06'01 84w37'04 5:38:28
Ekerts Corners 78 75 41N12'19 80w44'26 5:22:58
Elba 84 20 39N36'29 81w24'48 5:25:39
Elberta Beach 47 67 41N25'42 82w20'25 5:29:22
Eldean 55 34 40N04'40 84w13'21 5:36:53
Eldon 30 5 39N58 81w17 5:25:08
Eldorado 68 34 39N54'07 84w40'30 5:38:42
Elenor 13 34 39N10'37 84w11'49 5:36:47
Elery 35 31 41N17'54 84w04'07 5:36:16
Elgin 81 34 40N44'33 84w28'33 5:37:54
Elida 2 34 40N47'19 84w12'14 5:36:49
Elizabeth 60 5 39N52'31 82w03'43 5:28:15
Elizabethtown 30 5 40N02'09 81w24'24 5:25:38
Elizabethtown 31 34 39N09'31 84w48'17 5:39:13
Elizabethtown 83 34 39N35 84w18 5:37:12
Elk 11 5 39N40'23 81w20'10 5:25:21

Elk Fork 82 27 39N16'57 82W28'06 5:29:52
Elk Lick 13 34 39N01'36 84W07'47 5:36:31
Elkrun 15 67 40N46 80W41 5:22:44
Elkton 15 67 40N45'43 80W41'56 5:22:48
Ellerton 57 34 39N40'39 84W18'34 5:37:14
Ellet 77 2 41N03'05 81W26'08 5:25:45
Elliot 58 5 39N29 81W52 5:27:28
Elliott Crossroads 58
5 39N31'51 81W56'38 5:27:47
Elliottville 5 27 39N18'43 82W07'22 5:28:29
Ellis 60 104 40N02'46 81W58'59 5:27:56
Ellisonville 44
34 38N36'16 82W38'49 5:30:35
Elliston 62 93 41N32'51 83W16'49 5:33:07
Ellsberry 8 34 38N40'45 83W43'16 5:34:53
Ellsworth 50 67 41N01'27 80W51'27 5:23:26
Elm Acres 76 54 40N48 81W31 5:26:04
Elm Center 69 34 41N06'08 84W05'35 5:36:22
Elm Grove 66 34 39N02'47 83W09'50 5:32:39
Elmira 26 34 41N34'45 84W18'30 5:37:14
Elmore 62 93 41N28'34 83W17'45 5:33:11
Elms Acres 76 67 40N47'46 81W35'47 5:26:23
Elmview 2 90 40N41'11 84W09'04 5:36:36
Elmville 36 34 39N03'54 83W27'07 5:33:48
Elmwood 65 34 39N30'02 82W55'41 5:31:43
Elmwood Place 31
88 39N11'14 84W29'17 5:37:57
Elroy 19 34 40N12'23 84W42'34 5:38:50
Elton 76 54 40N43'43 81W36'59 5:26:28
Elyria 47 42 41N22'06 82W06'28 5:28:26
Emerald 1 34 39N00'04 83W39'27 5:34:38
Emerald 63 34 41N12 84W31 5:38:04
Emerson 41 67 40N10'39 80W49'23 5:23:18
Emery Chapel 12
39 39N55 83W48 5:35:12
Emmett 63 34 41N13'49 84W33'14 5:38:13
Empire 41 67 40N30'27 80W37'27 5:22:30
England 3 44 40N50'25 82W14'22 5:28:57
England Station 3
44 40N54 82W22 5:29:28
Englewood 57 34 39N52'39 84W18'08 5:37:13
English Woods 31
88 39N08'23 84W33'25 5:38:14
Eno 27 27 38N58'20 82W14'14 5:28:57
Enoch 61 5 39N39 81W26 5:25:44
Enon 12 34 39N52'41 83W56'13 5:35:45
Enterprise 37 27 39N33'53 82W28'47 5:29:55
Enterprise 68 34 39N41'49 84W30'00 5:38:00
Epworth 70 95 40N50'57 82W27'54 5:29:52
Epworth Heights 13
34 39N14'57 84W16'44 5:37:07
Equity 84 20 39N33'32 81W34'33 5:26:18
Era 65 34 39N44'28 83W14'26 5:32:58
Erastus 54 34 40N30'32 84W42'28 5:38:50
Erhart 52 73 41N11'59 81W58'28 5:27:54
Erie 62 93 41N32 83W01 5:32:04
Erieview 18 26 41N29 81W40 5:26:40
Eris 11 34 40N09'22 83W51'10 5:35:25
Erlin 72 30 41N21'57 83W00'45 5:32:03
Espyville 51 33 40N35'49 83W15'19 5:33:01
Espyville 77 2 41N05 81W33 5:26:12
Esselburn 52 73 41N01'36 82W04'41 5:28:19
Essex 80 33 40N28'57 83W18'57 5:33:16
Esto 42 5 40N20'02 82W13'49 5:28:55
Etna 44 34 38N37'27 82W39'14 5:30:37
Etna 45 27 39N57'26 82W40'55 5:30:44
Euclid 18 70 41N35'35 81W31'37 5:26:06
Euclid Memorial Park Library 18
70 41N35'53 81W31'27 5:26:06
Eureka 27 34 38N40'38 82W11'30 5:28:46
Eureka 50 67 40N54'53 80W40'47 5:22:43
Evansport 20 34 41N25'34 84W23'47 5:37:35
Evanston 31 88 39N08'40 84W28'10 5:37:53
Evanston 55 34 39N56'41 84W11'59 5:36:48
Evansville 78 67 41N09'21 80W45'47 5:23:03
Evendale 31 34 39N15'22 84W25'05 5:37:40
Everett 77 67 41N12'16 81W34'21 5:26:17
Evergreen 27 27 38N53'28 82W16'26 5:29:06
Evergreen 84 20 39N27 81W28 5:25:52
Ewing 37 27 39N28'21 82W26'00 5:29:44
Ewington 27 27 39N00'34 82W21'11 5:29:25
Excello 9 34 39N28'51 84W25'08 5:37:41
Fairborn 29 34 39N49'15 84W01'10 5:36:05
Fairdale 30 5 40N00'53 81W37'15 5:26:29
Fairfax 31 88 39N08'43 84W23'36 5:37:34
Fairfax 36 34 39N02'52 83W35'15 5:34:21
Fairfield 9 34 39N20'45 84W33'38 5:38:15
Fairfield 41 68 40N26'24 80W48'53 5:23:16
Fairfield Beach 23
27 39N54'57 82W28'31 5:29:54
Fairhaven 68 34 39N38'20 84W46'18 5:39:05
Fairhope 76 67 40N49'44 81W17'56 5:25:12
Fairlawn 77 67 41N07'26 81W36'49 5:26:27
Fairmount 31 88 39N07'40 84W33'13 5:38:13
Fair Oaks 13 34 39N05 84W11 5:36:44
Fair Oaks 73 34 38N46'50 82W50'19 5:31:21
Fairplay 9 34 39N20'13 84W35'45 5:38:23
Fairplay 41 67 40N21'46 80W48'58 5:23:16
Fairpoint 7 21 40N07'13 80W55'59 5:23:44
Fairport 43 67 41N45 81W16 5:25:04
Fairport Harbor 43
67 41N45 81W17 5:25:08
Fairview 1 34 38N48'26 83W38'53 5:34:36
Fairview 24 34 39N28'47 83W18'19 5:33:13
Fairview 30 5 39N54'07 81W33'16 5:26:13
Fairview 36 34 39N12'16 83W43'49 5:34:55
Fairview 57 91 39N47'11 84W13'16 5:36:53
Fairview 60 5 39N55'33 82W04'01 5:28:16
Fairview Corners 21
33 40N16'26 83W12'55 5:32:52
Fairview Heights 41
67 40N28 80W36 5:22:24
Fairview Heights 84
20 39N27 81W28 5:25:52
Fairview Lanes 22
5 41N27 82W44 5:30:56
Fairview Park 18
67 41N26'29 81W51'52 5:27:27
Fairway View Estates 2
90 40N44 84W09 5:36:36
Fairwind Acres 31
34 39N14'38 84W21'31 5:37:26
Fallsburg 45 5 40N12'10 82W14'10 5:28:57
Falls Junction 18
67 41N21'24 81W28'00 5:25:52
Fargo 59 27 40N21'29 82W49'53 5:31:20
Far Hills 57 91 39N43 84W10 5:36:40
Farmdale 78 67 41N26'13 80W36'30 5:22:26
Farmer 20 34 41N22'59 84W37'50 5:38:31
Farmers 14 34 39N19'18 83W45'49 5:35:03
Farmerstown 38 5 40N29'14 81W43'33 5:26:54
Farmersville 57
34 39N40'46 84W25'45 5:37:43
Farmington 7 21 40N06'31 80W49'23 5:23:18
Farmington 78 67 41N23'26 80W57'17 5:23:49
Farnham 4 72 41N54'01 80W34'19 5:22:17
Farrington 55 34 40N06'20 84W13'53 5:36:56
Fashion Heights 31
88 39N06'50 84W36'59 5:38:28
Fawcett 1 34 38N52'01 83W24'19 5:33:37
Faxon Hills 31 88 39N07'57 84W26'16 5:37:45
Fay 84 20 39N28'05 81W16'44 5:25:07
Fayette 26 34 41N40'24 84W19'37 5:37:18
Fayetteville 8 34 39N11'12 83W55'56 5:35:44
Fearing 84 20 39N29 81W24 5:25:36
Federal 5 5 39N27'07 81W59'22 5:27:57
Federal Reserve 18
26 41N29 81W40 5:26:40
Federal Reserve 31
88 39N09 84W30 5:38:00
Feed Springs 34
16 40N20'57 81W15'12 5:25:01
Feesburg 8 34 38N52'42 83W59'56 5:36:00
Felicity 13 34 38N50'20 84W05'47 5:36:23
Fernald 31 34 39N16'32 84W41'23 5:38:46
Fernbank 31 34 39N07'32 84W42'09 5:38:49
Fernell Heights 13
34 39N06'42 84W17'20 5:37:09
Fernwood 41 106 40N20'03 80W42'28 5:22:50
Ferristown 8 34 39N14'09 83W55'26 5:35:42
Ferry 29 34 40N36 83W59 5:35:56
Ferry 57 34 39N34'49 84W06'16 5:36:25
Fiat 79 16 40N24'48 81W39'43 5:26:39
Fields 47 42 41N22'06 81W59'52 5:27:59
Fields Terrace 44
37 38N27 82W28 5:29:52
Filburns Island 75
34 40N22'10 84W20'39 5:37:23
Fillmore 84 20 39N18'12 81W44'43 5:26:59
Fincastle 8 34 38N59'30 83W42'53 5:34:52
Findlay 32 89 41N02'39 83W39'00 5:34:36
Findley Gardens 41
67 40N28 80W36 5:22:24
Finney 31 34 39N07'08 84W47'19 5:39:09
Finneytown 31 88 39N12'01 84W31'14 5:38:05
Firebrick 44 34 38N50'21 82W38'44 5:30:35
Firemans Park 64
27 39N55'37 82W26'36 5:29:46
Fireside 74 30 41N13'35 82W54'43 5:31:39
Firestone Park 77
2 41N02'06 81W30'59 5:26:04
Fishback 62 93 41N30 82W52 5:31:28
Fisher 5 27 39N16'45 82W08'42 5:28:35
Fitch 48 31 41N41'47 83W35'27 5:34:22
Fitch 50 84 41N05'26 80W32'42 5:22:11
Fitchville 39 5 41N05'41 82W29'19 5:29:57
Five Corners 42 5 40N19'01 82W35'28 5:30:22
Five Forks 15 67 40N39'46 80W54'36 5:23:38
Five Forks 30 5 40N00'29 81W36'05 5:26:24
Five Forks 44 34 38N36'52 82W33'39 5:30:15
Fivemile 8 34 39N06'20 83W55'53 5:35:44
Five Points 3 95 40N49'19 82W23'36 5:29:34
Five Points 5 27 39N21'08 82W13'35 5:28:54
Five Points 8 34 38N59'18 83W46'12 5:35:05
Five Points 11 34 40N06'03 83W32'38 5:34:11
Five Points 50 67 40N57'31 80W38'33 5:22:34
Five Points 53 5 39N03'19 81W58'17 5:27:53
Five Points 55 34 39N55'11 84W24'56 5:37:40
Five Points 65 34 39N40'28 83W10'49 5:32:43
Five Points 78 67 41N18'41 80W31'09 5:22:05
Five Points 83 34 39N34'07 84W11'35 5:36:46
Five Points 87 31 41N30'27 83W35'39 5:34:23
Flag 11 20 39N41'11 81W18'18 5:25:13
Flatiron 64 27 39N44'43 82W05'52 5:28:23
Flat Iron 83 34 39N31'56 84W14'56 5:37:00
Flat Ridge 30 5 40N07'49 81W40'24 5:26:42
Flat Rock 74 32 41N14'09 82W51'37 5:31:26
Fleatown 45 5 39N59'35 82W24'17 5:29:37
Fleetwood Addition 80
33 40N15 83W22 5:33:28
Fleetwood Park 80
33 40N15'03 83W21'56 5:33:28
Fleming 84 20 39N23'30 81W36'39 5:26:27
Fleming Falls 70
95 40N48'02 82W26'36 5:29:46
Fletcher 55 34 40N08'41 84W06'45 5:36:27
Flicks Corners 67
67 41N05'56 81W00'07 5:24:00
Flint 25 107 40N07'38 83W00'21 5:32:01
Floodwood 5 27 39N26 82W14 5:28:56
Flora 53 5 39N09'53 81W58'42 5:27:55
Florence 7 15 40N07'10 80W42'56 5:22:52
Florence 11 5 39N45'28 81W31'53 5:26:08
Florence 22 9 41N19'24 82W24'50 5:29:39
Florence 49 34 39N50'52 83W32'50 5:34:11
Florida 35 34 41N19'19 84W12'16 5:36:49
Flushing 7 21 40N08'58 81W03'59 5:24:16
Fly 56 20 39N33'53 81W00'31 5:24:02
Folsom 36 34 39N05'42 83W35'34 5:34:22
Footville 4 72 41N39'42 80W58'42 5:23:55
Foraker 33 34 40N40'39 83W44'30 5:34:58
Forest 33 33 40N48'06 83W30'38 5:34:03
Forestdale 44 34 38N30'08 82W36'13 5:30:25
Forest Hill 77 2 41N05'47 81W29'33 5:25:58
Forest Hills 12
39 39N55 83W48 5:35:12
Forest Hills 66
34 39N06'33 83W00'36 5:32:02
Forest Hills Estates 31
88 39N05'10 84W19'19 5:37:17
Forest Park 31 34 39N17'25 84W30'15 5:38:01
Forest Park 57 91 39N47 84W13 5:36:52
Forest Park 62 93 41N32'41 83W22'44 5:33:31
Forest View 41
106 40N22 80W39 5:22:36
Forestville 31 34 39N04'30 84W20'42 5:37:23
Forgy 12 34 39N54'47 83W59'30 5:35:58
Fort Brown 63 34 41N06'43 84W25'13 5:37:41
Fort Fizzle 38 5 40N29'34 82W05'35 5:28:22
Fort Jefferson 19
34 40N01'35 84W39'19 5:38:37
Fort Jennings 69
34 40N54'23 84W17'48 5:37:11
Fort Loramie 75
34 40N21'05 84W22'26 5:37:30
Fort McKinley 57
91 39N47'51 84W15'13 5:37:01
Fort Meigs Place 87
31 41N34 83W35 5:34:20
Fort Miami Addition 48
31 41N35 83W40 5:34:40
Fort Recovery 54
34 40N24'46 84W46'35 5:39:06
Fort Seneca 74 32 41N12'33 83W10'08 5:32:41
Fort Shawnee 2 90 40N41'12 84W08'16 5:36:33
Foster 83 34 39N19'09 84W15'11 5:37:01
Fosterville 50 84 41N04'37 80W40'33 5:22:42
Fosterville 68 34 39N37'33 84W42'12 5:38:49
Fostoria 74 32 41N09'25 83W25'01 5:33:40
Fountain Park 11
34 40N09'54 83W33'15 5:34:13
Fountain Square 31
88 39N06'04 84W30'37 5:38:02
Four Corners 42 5 40N30'27 82W22'52 5:29:31
Fourmans Corners 19
34 40N01'12 84W31'04 5:38:04
Fourmile House Corner 72
32 41N22'22 83W10'36 5:32:42
Fowler 78 67 41N18'40 80W39'21 5:22:37
Fowlers Mill 28
67 41N31'39 81W15'22 5:25:01
Fox 10 21 40N36 80W54 5:23:36
Fox 65 34 39N38'36 83W00'45 5:32:03
Fox Acres 31 34 39N11'44 84W34'12 5:38:17
Fox Chase 25 108 40N06 82W56 5:31:44
Foxhunter Lane 31
34 39N14'09 84W19'00 5:37:16
Foxtown 56 20 39N40'07 81W00'44 5:24:03
Frampton 45 5 40N13'38 82W12'23 5:28:50
Frank 74 32 41N11'23 82W51'29 5:31:26
Frankfort 48 34 41N38'38 83W51'23 5:35:26
Frankfort 71 34 39N24'05 83W10'51 5:32:43
Franklin 83 34 39N33'32 84W18'15 5:37:13
Franklin Furnace 73
34 38N38'42 82W50'56 5:31:24
Franklin Junction 86
34 41N40'19 84W24'52 5:37:39
Franklin Square 15
47 40N51'22 80W47'31 5:23:10
Frazeysburg 60 5 40N07'02 82W07'10 5:28:29
Frazier 60 5 39N52'45 81W58'44 5:27:55
Frederick 55 34 39N55'31 84W16'28 5:37:06
Frederick 73 34 38N48'40 82W46'40 5:31:07
Fredericksburg 85
44 40N40'36 81W52'14 5:27:29
Fredericksdale 11
5 39N48'11 81W25'37 5:25:42
Fredericktown 15
105 40N42'50 80W32'53 5:22:12
Fredericktown 42
5 40N28'52 82W32'27 5:30:10
Fredonia 45 27 40N09'07 82W31'12 5:30:05
Fredricksburg 50
67 41N04'02 80W58'38 5:23:55
Freeburg 76 67 40N50'01 81W08'54 5:24:36
Freedom 67 67 41N14'10 81W08'57 5:24:36
Freedom Station 67
67 41N12'20 81W08'52 5:24:35
Freeland 60 5 39N52'52 81W46'32 5:27:06
Freemans Gardens 48
31 41N38'29 83W36'28 5:34:26
Freeport 34 21 40N12'38 81W15'59 5:25:04
Fremont 72 41 41N21'01 83W07'19 5:32:29
Frenchtown 19 34 40N14'47 84W31'26 5:38:06
Frenchtown 74 32 41N01'44 83W20'37 5:33:22
Fresno 16 5 40N19'57 81W44'30 5:26:58
Friendship 73 34 38N41'52 83W05'38 5:32:23
Friendsville 52
73 41N01'38 81W57'57 5:27:52
Fritchleys Corners 10
21 40N38'03 81W12'50 5:24:51
Frontier Park 31
34 39N13 84W35 5:38:20
Frontier Town 50
84 41N02 80W38 5:22:32
Frost 5 5 39N16'36 81W49'47 5:27:19
Fruitdale 71 34 39N18'06 83W20'23 5:33:22
Fruit Hill 31 34 39N04'32 84W21'52 5:37:27
Fryburg 6 34 40N30'54 84W08'56 5:36:36
Fryburg 38 5 40N36'49 81W49'32 5:27:18
Frys Corners 19
34 40N02'53 84W37'50 5:38:31
Frytown 57 91 39N43'01 84W16'26 5:37:06
Fulda 11 5 39N43'28 81W24'57 5:25:40
Fullertown 28 67 41N29'33 81W17'55 5:25:12
Fulton 59 27 40N27'45 82W49'44 5:31:19
Fultonham 60 5 39N51'20 82W08'30 5:28:34
Funk 85 76 40N45'11 82W06'59 5:28:28
Fursville 25 27 40N00'11 82W42'59 5:30:52
Gabels Corner 72
32 41N19'38 83W11'49 5:32:47
Gage 27 34 38N47'46 82W23'52 5:29:35
Gageville 4 52 41N50'44 80W39'57 5:22:40
Gahanna 25 27 40N01'09 82W52'46 5:31:31
Galatea 87 33 41N10'40 83W38'41 5:34:35
Galaxy Acres 31
34 39N14'27 84W34'52 5:38:19
Galena 21 27 40N12'54 82W52'48 5:31:31
Galetown 72 38 41N15'59 82W59'48 5:31:59
Galion 17 112 40N44'01 82W47'24 5:31:10
Gallia 27 34 38N46 82W23 5:29:32
Gallipolis 27 97 38N48'35 82W12'09 5:28:49
Galloway 25 34 39N54'47 83W09'45 5:32:39
Gallup 35 34 41N11'18 84W01'45 5:36:07
Gambier 42 5 40N22'32 82W23'50 5:29:35
Gambrinus 76 43 40N46'19 81W25'08 5:25:41
Ganges 70 5 40N54'22 82W33'41 5:30:15
Gann 42 5 40N28'10 82W11'39 5:28:47
Gano 9 34 39N18'08 84W24'30 5:37:38

Garden 5 5 39N12'28 81w58'35 5:27:54
Garden 48 34 41N36'15 83w47'47 5:35:11
Garden Acres 12
39 39N57 83w47 5:35:08
Garden Acres 70
95 40N47 82w30 5:30:00
Garden City 73 34 38N42'28 82w51'14 5:31:25
Garden Isle 52 73 41N00'25 82w01'07 5:28:04
Garden Terrace 41
106 40N22 80w39 5:22:36
Gardner 17 5 40N58'55 82w44'38 5:30:59
Garfield 40 34 39N07'25 82w37'12 5:30:29
Garfield 50 67 40N55'06 80w57'19 5:23:49
Garfield Heights 18
26 41N25'01 81w36'22 5:26:25
Garland 55 34 39N56'05 84w22'10 5:37:29
Garrettsville 67
46 41N17'03 81w05'48 5:24:23
Gasper 68 34 39N41 84w38 5:38:32
Gast Corner 51 27 40N27'00 83w13'18 5:32:53
Gasville 84 5 39N31'44 81w19'05 5:25:16
Gates Mills 18 67 41N31'03 81w24'13 5:25:37
Gath 36 34 39N03'48 83w48'15 5:35:13
Gatton Rock 70 27 40N36'07 82w28'27 5:29:54
Gavers 15 67 40N42'25 80w48'21 5:23:13
Gaysport (Blue Rock P O) 60
5 39N48'10 81w53'27 5:27:34
Geauga Lake 67 46 41N20'40 81w22'55 5:25:32
Geeburg 50 67 41N02'56 80w50'19 5:23:21
Gem 11 5 39N39'50 81w25'35 5:25:42
Gem Beach 62 93 41N34'10 82w49'21 5:31:17
Geneva 4 71 41N48'18 80w56'54 5:23:48
Geneva 23 27 39N39'43 82w26'01 5:29:44
Geneva-on-the-Lake 4
71 41N51'34 80w57'15 5:23:49
Genntown 83 34 39N27'37 84w10'15 5:36:41
Genoa 62 93 41N31'05 83w21'33 5:33:26
Genoa 76 54 40N46'58 81w28'00 5:25:52
Genterville 30 5 40N03'53 81w31'48 5:26:07
Genung Corners 43
46 41N47'23 81w02'56 5:24:12
Geography Hall 50
84 41N07'10 80w34'15 5:22:17
Georges Run 41
106 40N18'02 80w37'32 5:22:30
Georgesville 25
107 39N53'27 83w13'19 5:32:53
Georgetown 8 34 38N51'52 83w54'15 5:35:37
Georgetown 24 34 39N26'17 83w30'33 5:34:02
Georgetown 30 5 40N00'12 81w35'25 5:26:22
Georgetown 34 21 40N12'27 80w55'15 5:23:41
Georgetown 68 34 39N54'05 84w32'28 5:38:10
Gepharts 73 34 38N47'12 82w47'40 5:31:11
Gerald 35 34 41N27'25 84w08'39 5:36:35
German 66 34 39N00'10 82w54'20 5:31:37
Germano 34 5 40N24'30 80w56'50 5:23:47
Germantown 57 34 39N37'34 84w22'10 5:37:29
Germantown 84 20 39N35'02 81w19'04 5:25:16
Getaway 44 37 38N29'12 82w28'05 5:29:52
Gettysburg 19 34 40N06'41 84w29'43 5:37:59
Gettysburg 68 34 39N50'26 84w43'14 5:38:53
Geyer 6 34 40N30'30 84w03'50 5:36:15
Ghent 77 2 41N09'30 81w38'13 5:26:33
Gibisonville 37
34 39N29'59 82w34'00 5:30:16
Gibson 30 5 39N58'35 81w24'48 5:25:39
Gibson 54 34 40N23 84w45 5:39:00
Gibsonburg 72 32 41N23'04 83w19'14 5:33:17
Gieringer 31 34 39N11'52 84w44'14 5:38:57
Gilbert 60 104 40N01'17 81w58'36 5:27:54
Gilboa 69 34 41N01'05 83w55'19 5:35:41
Gilead 59 27 40N33 82w50 5:31:20
Gillia 27 34 38N49'49 82w31'04 5:30:04
Gillivan 49 34 39N59'19 83w20'13 5:33:21
Gilmore 79 16 40N17'27 81w26'26 5:25:46
Ginger Hill 50 67 40N58'22 80w34'10 5:22:17
Ginghamsburg 55
34 39N55'47 84w11'58 5:36:48
Girard 78 84 41N09'14 80w42'06 5:22:48
Girton 72 32 41N17'01 83w21'35 5:33:26
Gist Settlement 36
34 39N18'57 83w38'50 5:34:35
Givens 66 34 39N03'11 82w55'28 5:31:42
Glade 40 34 39N00'48 82w46'58 5:31:08
Gladstone 29 34 39N44'37 83w41'06 5:34:44
Glandorf 69 34 41N01'44 84w04'45 5:36:19
Glasgow 15 105 40N39'28 80w41'24 5:22:46
Glasgow 79 16 40N18'31 81w33'03 5:26:12
Glass 84 20 39N32'55 81w07'46 5:24:31
Glass Rock 64 27 39N52'38 82w17'21 5:29:09
Glencoe 7 21 40N00'29 80w53'16 5:23:33
Glencoe 31 34 39N14 84w32 5:38:08
Glendale 31 34 39N16'14 84w27'34 5:37:50
Glendale 44 34 38N34'00 82w45'37 5:31:02
Glendon 24 34 39N30'30 83w33'03 5:34:12
Glen Ebon 5 27 39N24'15 82w11'27 5:28:46
Glen Echo 12 39 40N00'16 83w47'49 5:35:11
Glen Este 13 34 39N05'56 84w15'29 5:37:02
Glenford 64 5 39N53'17 82w19'02 5:29:16
Glengary Heights 25
108 40N06 82w56 5:31:44
Glen Jean 66 34 39N06'46 82w58'39 5:31:55
Glen Karn 19 34 40N00'35 84w47'31 5:39:10
Glenmary 31 34 39N16 84w29 5:37:56
Glenmont 38 5 40N31'12 82w05'51 5:28:23
Glenmoor 15 105 40N39'58 80w37'24 5:22:30
Glenmore 81 34 40N47'05 84w41'54 5:38:48
Glen Nell 40 34 39N08'51 82w37'17 5:30:29
Glenns Run 7 15 40N06 80w44 5:22:56
Glen Ridge Acres 13
34 39N06'10 84w16'03 5:37:04
Glen Robbins 41
67 40N09'40 80w44'36 5:22:58
Glen Roy 40 34 39N06'45 82w34'47 5:30:19
Glen Run 41 67 40N11'42 80w44'45 5:22:59
Glen Summitt 27
27 38N56'49 82w19'27 5:29:18
Glenwillow 18 67 41N21'42 81w28'11 5:25:53
Glenwood 11 5 39N52'02 81w34'27 5:26:18
Glenwood 68 34 39N44 84w32 5:38:08
Gloria Glens Park 52
73 41N03'30 81w53'53 5:27:36
Glouster 5 27 39N30'11 82w05'05 5:28:20
Glynwood 6 34 40N34'58 84w18'58 5:37:16
Gnadenhutten 79
16 40N21'30 81w26'04 5:25:44
Goddard Corners 25
27 40N03'36 82w36'42 5:30:27
Goes 29 34 39N46'00 83w54'58 5:35:40
Golda 7 21 40N07'39 81w10'36 5:24:42
Golden Corners 85
62 40N54'54 81w58'55 5:27:56
Golden Gate 18 67 41N31 81w31 5:26:04
Goldsboro 40 34 39N07'01 82w34'05 5:30:16
Golf Manor 31 88 39N11'14 84w26'47 5:37:47
Golfway Acres 31
34 39N12'27 84w33'58 5:38:16
Gomer 2 34 40N50'42 84w11'14 5:36:45
Good Hope 24 34 39N26'50 83w21'54 5:33:28
Goodland Acres 76
67 40N40'28 81w15'40 5:25:03
Goodwin 56 20 39N40'47 80w54'42 5:23:39
Goodyear Heights 77
2 41N04'41 81w28'04 5:25:52
Gordon 19 34 39N55'50 84w30'31 5:38:02
Gore 37 27 39N34'49 82w17'42 5:29:11
Gorham 26 34 41N40 84w19 5:37:16
Goshen 13 34 39N14'00 84w09'41 5:36:39
Goshen 79 16 40N26'37 81w24'36 5:25:38
Gould 4 72 41N44'56 80w37'21 5:22:29
Gould 41 106 40N19'03 80w39'13 5:22:37
Gould 48 31 41N36'12 83w36'41 5:34:27
Gould Park 25 108 40N04'07 82w53'54 5:31:36
Goulds 41 106 40N19 80w39 5:22:36
Gracey 84 20 39N26'19 81w17'40 5:25:11
Grafton 47 57 41N16'21 82w03'17 5:28:13
Graham 56 20 39N39'24 81w12'08 5:24:49
Graham Corners 16
5 40N11'13 82w05'18 5:28:21
Grand 51 33 40N40 83w21 5:33:24
Grand Prairie 51
32 40N40 83w07 5:32:28
Grand Rapids 87
34 41N24'43 83w51'52 5:35:27
Grand River 43 67 41N44'10 81w16'53 5:25:08
Grandview 84 20 39N30'29 81w04'56 5:24:20
Grandview Heights 11
34 40N11'08 83w58'13 5:35:53
Grandview Heights 25
107 39N58'47 83w02'27 5:32:10
Grandview Homes 2
90 40N43 84w06 5:36:24
Grange Hall 65 34 39N38'00 83w11'07 5:32:44
Granger 52 67 41N09'20 81w43'55 5:26:56
Grant (Grants Station) 33
33 40N42'38 83w34'05 5:34:16
Granville 25 27 40N04'05 82w31'11 5:30:05
Grape Grove 29 34 39N42'59 83w40'54 5:34:44
Grassy Point 33
33 40N33'33 83w35'13 5:34:21
Gratiot 45 5 39N57'04 82w12'58 5:28:52
Gratis 68 34 39N38'52 84w31'38 5:38:07
Grayson 55 34 39N59'42 84w08'40 5:36:35
Graysville 56 20 39N39'56 81w10'26 5:24:42
Graytown 62 93 41N32'34 83w15'40 5:33:03
Greasy Ridge 44
34 38N38'43 82w25'16 5:29:41
Great Bend 53 5 38N57'11 81w48'56 5:27:16
Great Western 7
21 40N04'22 80w59'06 5:23:56
Green Acres 9 34 39N30 84w23 5:37:32
Greenbrier 56 20 39N38'20 81w07'03 5:24:28
Greenbush 8 34 39N04'31 83w55'31 5:35:42
Greenbush 68 34 39N36'05 84w29'55 5:38:00
Green Camp 51 33 40N31'55 83w12'38 5:32:51
Greencastle 23 27 39N46'26 82w45'39 5:31:03
Green Creek 72 30 41N18 83w01 5:32:04
Greendale 37 27 39N32'31 82w16'32 5:29:06
Greene 78 67 41N27'43 80w44'48 5:22:59
Greene Center 78
67 41N27'42 80w45'45 5:23:03
Greenfield 36 34 39N21'07 83w22'58 5:33:32
Greenfield Village 31
88 39N12'13 84w31'29 5:38:06
Greenford 50 67 40N56'38 80w47'30 5:23:10
Green Hills 29 34 39N48 84w01 5:36:04
Greenhills 31 34 39N16'05 84w31'23 5:38:06
Greenland 71 34 39N26'42 83w07'14 5:32:29
Greenmount 57 91 39N41 84w09 5:36:36
Greensburg 77 67 40N55'54 81w27'54 5:25:52
Green Springs 72
30 41N15'22 83w03'06 5:32:12
Greens Run 5 27 39N27'52 82w06'50 5:28:27
Greens Store 40
34 39N04 82w39 5:30:36
Greentown 41 67 40N15'05 80w46'07 5:23:04
Greentown 76 67 40N55'39 81w24'10 5:25:37
Greentree Corners 83
34 39N27'45 84w16'02 5:37:04
Green Valley 42 5 40N24 82w29 5:29:56
Green Valley 44
34 38N33'04 82w42'19 5:30:49
Greenview 57 91 39N49 84w15 5:37:00
Greenville 19 110 40N06'10 84w37'59 5:38:32
Greenwich 39 5 41N01'48 82w30'57 5:30:04
Greenwood 30 5 39N55'29 81w27'43 5:25:51
Greenwood Acres 76
54 40N50'10 81w31'08 5:26:05
Greer 42 5 40N31'20 82w12'01 5:28:48
Greggs 66 34 39N04'17 82w57'27 5:31:50
Greggs Hill 66 34 39N05'40 82w58'23 5:31:54
Gregory 21 27 40N14'25 83w00'47 5:32:03
Grelton 35 34 41N20'30 83w59'59 5:36:00
Gretna 46 33 40N20'48 83w51'31 5:35:26
Griffin 60 5 39N55'23 81w55'35 5:27:42
Griffith 31 34 39N09 84w44 5:38:56
Griffith 56 20 39N43'15 81w06'18 5:24:25
Griggs 4 72 41N44 80w47 5:23:08
Grimms Bridge 15
105 40N40'34 80w32'29 5:22:10
Grodis Corner 62
93 41N36'15 83w15'38 5:33:03
Groesbeck 31 34 39N13'23 84w35'13 5:38:21
Grooms 1 34 39N01'13 83w16'31 5:33:06
Grosvenor 5 27 39N19'58 82w07'52 5:28:31
Groton 22 5 41N21 82w47 5:31:08
Grove City 25 107 39N52'53 83w05'35 5:32:22
Grove City Country Club 25
107 39N51'02 83w04'17 5:32:17
Groveport 25 34 39N51'08 82w53'09 5:31:33
Grover Hill 63 34 41N01'09 84w28'36 5:37:54
Guerne 85 76 40N45'48 81w53'46 5:27:35
Guernsey 30 5 40N10'54 81w35'33 5:26:22
Guilford 15 67 40N47'30 80w51'59 5:23:28
Guilford 52 60 41N01 81w49 5:27:16
Gunnerville 29 34 39N35'01 83w45'46 5:35:03
Gurneyville 14 34 39N30'53 83w52'37 5:35:30
Gustavus 78 67 41N27'43 80w39'57 5:22:40
Gutman 6 34 40N31'10 84w02'38 5:36:11
Guyan 27 34 38N38 82w18 5:29:12
Guysville 5 5 39N17'24 81w55'25 5:27:42
Gypsum 62 93 41N29'36 82w52'33 5:31:30
Hackney 58 5 39N37'57 81w40'38 5:26:43
Hagan Addition 34
23 40N12'53 80w53'05 5:23:32
Hageman 83 34 39N23'24 84w15'54 5:37:04
Hagler 24 34 39N35'17 83w30'50 5:34:03
Hakes Corners 78
75 41N11'48 80w43'44 5:22:55
Hale 33 33 40N32 83w33 5:34:12
Hales Creek 73 34 38N48'40 82w40'32 5:30:42
Haley's Subdivision 79
16 40N33 81w29 5:25:56
Hallett 48 31 41N42'27 83w31'15 5:34:05
Hallock 86 34 41N31'36 84w33'27 5:38:14
Halls Corners 78
84 41N08 80w38 5:22:32
Hallsville 71 34 39N26'38 82w49'38 5:31:19
Hambden 28 67 41N36'15 81w08'45 5:24:35
Hamburg 23 27 39N39'16 82w39'39 5:30:39
Hamburg 68 34 39N53'14 84w40'35 5:38:42
Hamden 82 34 39N09'35 82w31'37 5:30:06
Hamer 36 34 39N10 83w44 5:34:56
Hamer 86 34 41N37'41 84w24'55 5:37:40
Hamersville 8 34 38N55'04 83w59'00 5:35:56
Hametown 77 67 41N01 81w38 5:26:32
Hamilton 9 87 39N23'58 84w33'41 5:38:15
Hamilton 56 20 39N45'54 81w14'29 5:24:58
Hamilton Meadows 25
107 39N51'10 82w58'42 5:31:55
Hamler 35 34 41N13'45 84w02'03 5:36:08
Hamlet 13 34 39N01'08 84w11'59 5:36:48
Hamley Run 5 27 39N23'51 82w10'10 5:28:41
Hammansburg 87 33 41N13'35 83w41'19 5:34:45
Hammond Crossroad 34
21 40N11'03 80w57'22 5:23:49
Hammondsville 41
67 40N33'27 80w42'26 5:22:50
Hancock 32 34 41N09'19 83w51'07 5:35:24
Hanersville 27 27 38N50'08 82w12'55 5:28:52
Hanesville 53 27 39N02'14 82w13'07 5:28:52
Hanford 25 107 39N57'05 82w56'53 5:31:48
Hanging Rock 44
34 38N33'36 82w43'16 5:30:53
Hanley Village 70
95 40N42 82w32 5:30:08
Hannibal 56 20 39N40'02 80w52'20 5:23:29
Hanover 25 5 40N04'47 82w15'40 5:29:03
Hanover 34 23 40N21'58 81w04'09 5:24:17
Hanoverton 15 67 40N45'04 80w56'14 5:23:45
Hanville Corners 39
5 41N07'09 82w36'45 5:30:27
Happy Corners 57
34 39N50'50 84w18'42 5:37:15
Happy Hollow 76
67 40N40 81w21 5:25:24
Happy Hours Addition 73
34 38N46'08 82w52'09 5:31:29
Harbor 4 46 41N53'16 80w48'56 5:23:16
Harbor Hills 45
27 39N58 82w28 5:29:52
Harbor View 48 31 41N41'36 83w26'40 5:33:47
Hard 38 5 40N39'56 81w57'09 5:27:49
Hardin 75 34 40N17'11 84w14'32 5:36:58
Harding 48 34 41N38 83w51 5:35:24
Harding 60 5 39N55 82w01 5:28:04
Hardscrabble 52
67 41N15'37 81w55'40 5:27:43
Hardscrabble 78
45 41N15'33 80w52'06 5:23:28
Hardy 38 5 40N34 81w55 5:27:40
Harewood Acres 31
34 39N11'44 84w23'07 5:37:32
Harlan 83 34 39N19 84w05 5:36:20
Harlan Park 9 34 39N31'40 84w23'15 5:37:33
Harlem 21 27 40N09'06 82w50'22 5:31:21
Harlem Springs 10
21 40N31'15 81w00'12 5:24:01
Harley 23 27 39N51'11 82w41'17 5:30:45
Harmer 84 113 39N24'37 81w27'42 5:25:51
Harmon 76 54 40N42'34 81w33'35 5:26:14
Harmony 12 39 39N55'22 83w41'50 5:34:47
Harper 46 33 40N25'44 83w42'30 5:34:50
Harper 71 34 39N21'53 83w15'42 5:33:03
Harpersfield 4 72 41N45'34 80w56'49 5:23:47
Harpster 88 32 40N44'21 83w15'14 5:33:01
Harriett 30 5 40N01 81w35 5:26:20
Harriett 36 34 39N07'15 83w29'20 5:33:57
Harriettsville 11
5 39N37'53 81w20'16 5:25:21
Harris 62 93 41N29 83w14 5:32:56
Harris 71 36 39N12'56 83w08'28 5:32:34
Harrisburg 25 34 39N48'34 83w10'16 5:32:41
Harrisburg 27 27 38N53'58 82w20'43 5:29:23
Harrisburg 76 67 40N53'36 81w13'39 5:24:55
Harrison 31 34 39N15'43 84w49'12 5:39:17
Harrison Furnace 73
34 38N49'47 82w52'57 5:31:32
Harrison Mills 73
34 38N49'55 82w48'29 5:31:14
Harrisonville 53
27 39N07'35 82w08'02 5:28:32
Harrisville 34 21 40N10'53 80w53'16 5:23:33
Harrod 2 34 40N42'23 83w55'17 5:35:41
Harshasville 1 34 38N54'29 83w32'40 5:34:11
Hartford 78 67 41N18'41 80w34'07 5:22:16
Hartford Croton (P O) 45
27 40N14'21 82w41'14 5:30:45
Hartland 39 5 41N10'31 82w29'27 5:29:58

Hartland Station 39 5 41N12'38 82W29'30 5:29:58
Hartleyville 5 27 39N32'38 82W06'12 5:28:25
Hartsburg 69 34 41N05'33 84W19'28 5:37:18
Hartsgrove 4 72 41N36'18 80W57'13 5:23:49
Hartshorn 56 20 39N42'24 81W13'09 5:24:53
Hartville 76 67 40N57'49 81W19'53 5:25:20
Hartwell 31 34 39N12'48 84W28'07 5:37:52
Harveysburg 83 34 39N30'13 84W00'38 5:36:03
Harwood 36 34 39N07'52 83W50'46 5:35:23
Haselton 50 84 41N05'01 80W37'05 5:22:28
Haskins 87 34 41N27'53 83W42'22 5:34:49
Hasting Hill 73 34 38N46 82W59 5:31:56
Hastings 70 95 40N39'19 82W26'40 5:29:47
Hatch 66 34 39N00'32 83W10'35 5:32:42
Hatton 87 33 41N15'03 83W28'07 5:33:52
Havana 39 5 41N08'14 82W44'50 5:30:59
Haven Park 48 34 41N38'27 83W42'42 5:34:51
Havens 72 32 41N18'21 83W11'34 5:32:46
Havens Corners 25 27 40N01'08 82W48'56 5:31:16
Havensport 23 27 39N48'36 82W40'23 5:30:42
Haven View 55 34 40N00'27 84W03'29 5:36:14
Haverhill 73 34 38N35'05 82W49'56 5:31:20
Haviland 63 34 41N01'08 84W34'51 5:38:19
Hawks 82 27 39N06'41 82W23'14 5:29:33
Hayden 25 108 40N03'32 83W11'49 5:32:47
Haydenville 37 27 39N28'55 82W19'42 5:29:19
Hayes Corners 28 67 41N27'32 81W01'22 5:24:05
Hayes Place 87 31 41N38 83W29 5:33:56
Hayesville 3 44 40N46'23 82W15'45 5:29:03
Hayesville 65 34 39N32'13 82W55'58 5:31:44
Haynes 37 34 39N26'05 82W40'45 5:30:43
Hays Corner 57 91 39N47'48 84W22'01 5:37:28
Hayward 84 20 39N34'21 81W40'22 5:26:41
Hazael 53 5 39N02'56 81W48'18 5:27:13
Hazelwood 31 34 39N15'58 84W21'47 5:37:27
Headleys Corners 25 27 40N00 82W49 5:31:16
Heath 45 5 40N01'22 82W26'41 5:29:47
Heatherdowns 48 31 41N36 83W38 5:34:32
Hebardville 5 27 39N15'12 82W10'05 5:28:40
Hebron 45 27 39N57'42 82W29'29 5:29:58
Hecla 44 34 38N32'57 82W38'20 5:30:33
Hector 69 34 41N06'01 84W13'40 5:36:55
Hedges 63 34 41N05'31 84W30'54 5:38:04
Hegemanns Landing 75 34 40N22'24 84W20'55 5:37:24
Heidelberg Beach 22 5 41N23'16 82W27'16 5:29:49
Helena 30 5 39N55'38 81W36'38 5:26:27
Helena 72 32 41N21 83W18 5:33:12
Helmick 16 5 40N23'30 81W56'28 5:27:46
Hemlock 64 27 39N35'19 82W09'20 5:28:37
Hemlock Grove 53 5 39N07'15 81W59'09 5:27:57
Hempstead 57 91 39N41 84W09 5:36:36
Hendrysburg 7 21 40N03'39 81W10'24 5:24:42
Henley 73 34 38N50'41 83W09'22 5:32:37
Hennings Mill 13 34 39N00'51 84W01'50 5:36:07
Henrietta 47 67 41N20'30 82W18'03 5:29:12
Henry 87 34 41N14 83W43 5:34:52
Hepburn 33 33 40N37'17 83W28'11 5:33:53
Herbert Corners 50 67 41N02'39 80W45'39 5:23:03
Herefork 3 44 41N03'38 82W23'41 5:29:35
Herlan 56 20 39N48'31 81W17'38 5:25:11
Hermanville 85 58 40N54'57 81W54'39 5:27:39
Herrick 41 67 40N12'35 80W49'51 5:23:19
Heslop 84 20 39N30'57 81W17'04 5:25:08
Hessville 72 30 41N24'06 83W14'40 5:32:59
Hestoria 8 34 38N45 83W50 5:35:20
Hewitt 19 34 39N59'21 84W40'59 5:38:44
Hibbetts 10 21 40N38'31 81W06'46 5:24:27
Hickman 45 5 40N08'59 82W18'35 5:29:14
Hickory Corners 50 67 40N58'23 80W51'22 5:23:25
Hickory Grove 62 93 41N29'19 82W55'09 5:31:41
Hickoryville 83 34 39N27'56 83W59'44 5:35:59
Hicks 83 34 39N21'30 84W03'22 5:36:13
Hicksville 20 34 41N17'35 84W45'43 5:39:03
Hideaway Hills 37 27 39N39'17 82W28'38 5:29:55
Hiett 8 34 38N41 83W46 5:35:04
Higby 71 34 39N11'46 82W51'59 5:31:28
Higginsport 8 34 38N47'23 83W58'03 5:35:52
High Hill 60 5 39N49'55 81W45'56 5:27:04
Highland 36 34 39N20'40 83W35'51 5:34:23
Highland Bend 73 34 38N46'20 82W52'13 5:31:29
Highland Heights 18 67 41N33'07 81W28'43 5:25:55
Highland Park 31 88 39N05'26 84W37'07 5:38:28
Highland Park 73 34 38N38'06 82W50'52 5:31:23
Highland Park 76 54 40N48 81W31 5:26:04
Highland Terrace 7 21 40N06'38 80W54'21 5:23:37
Highlandtown 15 21 40N38'03 80W45'25 5:23:02
Highpoint 31 34 39N17'18 84W21'01 5:37:24
Highwater 45 27 40N10'33 82W31'10 5:30:05
Hill Addition 15 105 40N38 80W35 5:22:20
Hill And Hollow 9 34 39N31 84W44 5:38:56
Hill Craft Acres 13 88 39N04'50 84W17'06 5:37:08
Hillcrest 15 105 40N37'42 80W39'27 5:22:38
Hillcrest 76 67 40N53'54 81W07'29 5:24:30
Hillcrest 83 34 39N24'12 84W15'16 5:37:01
Hillcrest 85 76 40N47'44 81W54'21 5:27:37
Hillcrest 86 34 41N35'11 84W32'14 5:38:09
Hill Grove 19 34 40N10'39 84W46'06 5:39:04
Hilliar 42 27 40N19 82W41 5:30:44
Hilliard 25 30 40N02'00 83W09'30 5:32:38
Hillman 8 34 38N52 83W55 5:35:40
Hills 84 20 39N25'59 81W21'44 5:25:27
Hills and Dales 76 43 40N49'47 81W26'42 5:25:47
Hills and Dales Shopping Cen 57 91 39N41 84W09 5:36:36
Hillsboro 36 34 39N12'08 83W36'42 5:34:27
Hillsboro 41 106 40N19 80W39 5:22:36
Hilltop 25 107 39N57 83W05 5:32:20
Hilltop 55 34 39N58 84W10 5:36:40
Hilltop 56 20 39N41'48 81W09'13 5:24:37
Hill Top Acres 31 88 39N13'27 84W29'46 5:37:59
Hinckley 52 73 41N14'18 81W44'43 5:26:59
Hinton 54 34 40N36'41 84W42'31 5:38:50
Hiram 67 46 41N18'45 81W08'38 5:24:35
Hiram Rapids 67 46 41N20'24 81W09'59 5:24:40
Hiramsburg 11 5 39N48'30 81W35'45 5:26:23
Hitchcock 40 34 38N54 82W35 5:30:20
Hoadley 27 34 38N46'52 82W34'18 5:30:17
Hoagland 36 34 39N12'15 83W40'53 5:34:44
Hoagland Corner 78 45 41N16'24 80W46'44 5:23:07
Hoaglin 81 34 40N56'46 84W29'42 5:37:59
Hobson 53 27 38N59'30 82W04'33 5:28:18
Hobson Jucation 53 27 38N59'01 82W04'45 5:28:19
Hocking 5 27 39N22'04 82W15'57 5:29:04
Hockingport 5 5 39N11'17 81W45'07 5:27:00
Hohman 84 20 39N32'28 81W10'40 5:24:43
Holden 6 34 40N36'09 83W52'49 5:35:31
Holgate 35 34 41N14'56 84W07'59 5:36:32
Holiday Acres 31 34 39N12'11 84W22'59 5:37:32
Holiday Valley 12 34 39N48 84W01 5:36:04
Holland 48 34 41N37'18 83W42'42 5:34:51
Hollansburg 19 34 39N59'49 84W47'32 5:39:10
Hollister 5 27 39N30'20 82W06'43 5:28:27
Holloway 7 21 40N09'44 81W07'58 5:24:32
Hollowtown 36 34 39N06'42 83W46'54 5:35:08
Hollywood Estates 31 34 39N12'42 84W32'08 5:38:09
Holman-Stonybrook Shopping C 31 34 39N14 84W20 5:37:20
Holmes 17 32 40N51 83W01 5:32:04
Holmesville 38 5 40N37'46 81W55'28 5:27:42
Holt 41 67 40N30'44 80W45'07 5:23:00
Home Acres 9 34 39N30 84W23 5:37:32
Home Acres 55 34 40N03 84W11 5:36:44
Homedale 25 107 40N03 83W01 5:32:04
Homer 45 27 40N15'10 82W31'04 5:30:04
Homer 52 73 41N02'41 82W07'33 5:28:30
Homerville 52 73 41N01'45 82W07'34 5:28:30
Homeside 7 21 40N03'45 80W54'09 5:23:37
Homeville 22 5 41N27 82W44 5:30:56
Homewood 9 34 39N22 84W33 5:38:12
Homewood 48 34 41N32'34 83W43'57 5:34:56
Homeworth 15 67 40N50'07 81W03'58 5:24:16
Honesty 61 5 39N35'15 81W29'08 5:25:57
Honeytown 85 76 40N47'49 81W52'47 5:27:31
Hooker 23 27 39N44'51 82W39'36 5:30:38
Hooksburg 58 5 39N35'01 81W47'02 5:27:08
Hooks Corner 57 91 39N49'16 84W08'42 5:36:35
Hooper Park 82 27 39N14'26 82W21'06 5:29:24
Hooven 31 34 39N10'41 84W45'33 5:39:02
Hope 82 27 39N19'06 82W20'14 5:29:21
Hopedale 34 21 40N19'31 80W54'05 5:23:36
Hope Furnace 82 27 39N19'55 82W20'26 5:29:22
Hopetown 71 34 39N22'43 82W58'31 5:31:54
Hopewell 41 67 40N13'21 80W42'36 5:22:50
Hopewell 60 5 39N57'20 82W10'15 5:28:41
Hopkinsville 83 34 39N20'20 84W13'11 5:36:53
Horatio 19 34 40N08'58 84W31'30 5:38:06
Horner Hill 53 27 39N06'17 82W05'58 5:28:24
Horns Mill 23 27 39N39'03 82W33'01 5:30:12
Horton 34 21 40N09'43 80W54'28 5:23:38
Horton 46 33 40N27'11 83W33'18 5:34:13
Hoskinsville 11 5 39N46'16 81W35'32 5:26:22
Houcktown 32 33 40N56'07 83W35'39 5:34:23
Houston 75 34 40N15'16 84W20'13 5:37:21
Howard 42 5 40N24'27 82W19'37 5:29:18
Howard Farms Beach 48 30 41N39'14 83W14'44 5:32:59
Howenstein 76 67 40N40 81W21 5:25:24
Howland 78 45 41N14'18 80W44'27 5:22:58
Hoytville 87 34 41N11'24 83W47'05 5:35:08
Hubbard 78 46 41N09'23 80W34'10 5:22:17
Huber Heights 57 34 39N50'38 84W07'29 5:36:30
Huber Ridge 25 108 40N05'19 82W55'00 5:31:40
Hudson 77 47 41N14'24 81W26'27 5:25:46
Hue 82 27 39N23'13 82W30'19 5:30:01
Hughes 9 34 39N23'13 84W24'29 5:37:38
Hulington 13 34 38N59'19 84W09'32 5:36:38
Hull 5 5 39N15'14 81W58'06 5:27:52
Hull Prairie 87 33 41N28'25 83W41'49 5:34:47
Hulls Crossing 87 34 41N32'16 83W41'34 5:34:46
Humboldt 71 36 39N16'38 83W18'50 5:33:15
Hume 2 90 40N39'47 84W12'03 5:36:48
Hunt 42 27 40N19'14 82W28'14 5:29:53
Huntcrest Acres 31 34 39N04'52 84W20'11 5:37:21
Hunter 7 21 39N56'52 81W03'27 5:24:14
Hunterdon 5 27 39N30'37 82W07'18 5:28:29
Huntersville 33 34 40N43'04 83W46'03 5:35:04
Huntington 47 67 41N06'11 82W13'16 5:28:53
Huntington Park 8 34 38N40'16 83W46'11 5:35:05
Hunting Valley 18 67 41N29'21 81W24'07 5:25:36
Huntsburg 43 67 41N32'05 81W03'07 5:24:12
Hunts Corners 39 5 41N13'39 82W45'27 5:31:02
Huntsville 9 34 39N23'29 84W23'01 5:37:32
Huntsville 46 34 40N26'36 83W48'18 5:35:13
Huntsville 65 34 39N32'23 82W46'12 5:31:05
Hurford 34 21 40N14'44 80W53'50 5:23:35
Huron 22 7 41N22'25 82W33'17 5:30:13
Hustead 12 39 39N50'26 83W51'47 5:35:27
Hyatts 21 27 40N13'00 83W05'07 5:32:20
Hyattville 21 27 40N10 83W06 5:32:24
Hyde Park 31 88 39N08'31 84W26'02 5:37:44
Hyde Park 57 91 39N41 84W09 5:36:36
Hyland Park 73 34 38N39 82W52 5:31:28
Iberia 59 27 40N40'13 82W50'37 5:31:22
Idaho 66 34 39N05'17 83W08'31 5:32:34
Ideal 30 5 39N58'48 81W31'58 5:26:08
Idlewild 54 34 40N33'03 84W29'38 5:37:59
Idlewood 31 88 39N08'55 84W28'27 5:37:54
Iler 74 32 41N11'06 83W19'10 5:33:17
Ilesboro 37 27 39N26'05 82W27'12 5:29:49
Immergrun 48 30 41N41'21 83W25'20 5:33:41
Independence 18 26 41N23'40 81W38'27 5:26:34
Independence 20 34 41N17 84W20 5:37:20
Indian Camp 30 5 40N05'40 81W38'45 5:26:35
Indian Hill 31 34 39N10'51 84W20'43 5:37:23
Indian Knolls 13 34 39N10'41 84W16'29 5:37:06
Indian Ridge 31 34 39N14 84W32 5:38:08
Indianview 13 34 39N13'19 84W18'04 5:37:12
Industry 67 67 41N04'38 81W11'40 5:24:47
Infant of Prague Villa 77 2 40N59'37 81W31'14 5:26:05
Ingle Mann 68 34 39N51 84W48 5:39:12
Ingomar 68 34 39N42'43 84W30'00 5:38:00
Ink 74 32 41N07 83W10 5:32:40
Inlet 26 34 41N39'13 84W11'07 5:36:44
Ira 77 67 41N10'53 81W35'04 5:26:20
Iradale 77 2 41N08 81W34 5:26:16
Ireland 5 5 39N15'20 81W46'18 5:27:05
Iron City 46 33 40N22 83W46 5:35:04
Irondale 41 67 40N34'18 80W43'36 5:22:54
Irondale 60 21 40N07 82W02 5:28:08
Ironspot 60 5 39N49'07 82W03'41 5:28:15
Ironton 44 87 38N32'12 82W40'59 5:30:44
Ironton Junction 40 34 39N05'47 82W33'25 5:30:14
Ironville 48 30 41N40'33 83W28'32 5:33:54
Irville 60 5 40N02'57 82W07'38 5:28:31
Irvington 57 91 39N50'26 84W15'37 5:37:02
Irwin 80 34 40N07'21 83W29'22 5:33:57
Island Creek 41 106 40N25 80W40 5:22:40
Island View 46 34 40N30'58 83W53'10 5:35:33
Isle Saint George 62 93 41N43 82W49 5:31:16
Isleta 16 5 40N16'12 81W40'18 5:26:41
Israel 68 34 39N37 84W46 5:39:04
Ithaca 19 34 39N56'14 84W33'12 5:38:13
Ivorydale 31 88 39N10'39 84W29'47 5:37:59
Ivorydale Junction 31 88 39N10'12 84W30'15 5:38:01
Jackson 40 34 39N03'07 82W38'12 5:30:33
Jackson 85 58 40N57'37 81W53'58 5:27:36
Jacksonburgh 9 34 39N32'18 84W30'09 5:38:01
Jackson Center 50 67 41N06 80W52 5:23:28
Jackson Center 75 34 40N26 84W03 5:36:12
Jackson Heights 40 34 39N01'53 82W37'41 5:30:31
Jackson Heights 41 67 40N11 80W41 5:22:44
Jackson Lake 40 34 38N54 82W35 5:30:20
Jackson Special 30 5 39N59'36 81W34'25 5:26:18
Jacksontown 45 5 39N57'34 82W24'47 5:29:39
Jacksonville 1 34 38N54'29 83W26'24 5:33:46
Jacksonville 5 27 39N28'30 82W04'55 5:28:20
Jacksonville 12 39 39N57'31 83W51'53 5:35:28
Jacktown 9 34 39N30 84W23 5:37:32
Jacobsburg 7 21 39N57'54 80W54'16 5:23:37
Jaite 18 26 41N17'18 81W34'26 5:26:18
Jamestown 24 34 39N39'29 83W44'06 5:34:56
Jasper 66 34 39N03 83W03 5:32:12
Jasper Mills 24 34 39N31'07 83W31'14 5:34:05
Jaybird 1 34 38N56'22 83W17'54 5:33:12
Jays 19 34 40N06 84W38 5:38:32
Jaysville 19 34 40N02'53 84W35'57 5:38:24
Jeddo 41 46 40N28 80W36 5:22:24
Jeddoe 67 46 41N16'37 81W08'42 5:24:35
Jefferson 4 72 41N44'19 80W46'12 5:23:05
Jefferson 23 27 39N48'50 82W45'39 5:31:03
Jefferson 85 76 40N48'06 82W01'23 5:28:06
Jefferson Estates 65 34 39N34'00 82W57'09 5:31:49
Jefferson Heights 41 106 40N19 80W39 5:22:36
Jeffersonville 24 34 39N39'13 83W33'50 5:34:15
Jelloway 42 5 40N32'12 82W18'01 5:29:12
Jenera 32 34 40N53'59 83W43'37 5:34:54
Jenkins Addition 60 5 39N55 82W01 5:28:04
Jep 44 34 38N38 82W40 5:30:40
Jericho 9 34 39N32'52 84W40'28 5:38:42
Jericho 56 20 39N37'03 81W06'23 5:24:26
Jerome 80 33 40N09'59 83W10'33 5:32:42
Jeromesville 3 44 40N48'15 82W11'45 5:28:47
Jerry City 87 33 41N15'14 83W36'16 5:34:25
Jersey 25 27 40N03'13 82W43'24 5:30:54
Jerusalem 56 20 39N51'06 81W05'33 5:24:22
Jessup 1 34 39N01'30 83W31'59 5:34:08
Jethro 15 105 40N38 80W35 5:22:20
Jewell 20 34 41N19'33 84W17'08 5:37:09
Jewett 34 11 40N22'04 81W00'20 5:24:01
Jimtown 15 46 40N49'13 80W32'05 5:22:08
Jimtown 82 34 39N21'12 82W43'23 5:30:54
Jobs 37 27 39N30'01 82W10'45 5:28:43
Joetown 58 5 39N39'56 81W55'34 5:27:42

Johnson 11 34 40N08 83W59 5:35:56
Johnson 24 34 39N32'50 83W19'50 5:33:19
Johnson Corners 48 31 41N36'59 83W39'55 5:34:40
Johnsons Corners 77 67 41N01 81W38 5:26:32
Johnston 78 67 41N23'19 80W39'57 5:22:40
Johnston 79 16 40N32'43 81W22'11 5:25:29
Johnstown 45 27 40N09'13 82W41'07 5:30:44
Johnsville 57 34 39N44'43 84W25'25 5:37:42
Jones 21 27 40N16'28 83W00'53 5:32:04
Jonesboro 14 34 39N18'07 83W49'31 5:35:18
Jones City 69 34 40N52'53 84W10'54 5:36:44
Jones Corner 1 34 38N49'11 83W17'33 5:33:10
Jones Farm 31 34 39N14'47 84W20'22 5:37:21
Jonestown 40 34 39N05'42 82W37'57 5:30:32
Jonestown 81 34 40N46'17 84W30'51 5:38:03
Joppa 53 5 39N09'10 81W47'55 5:27:12
Jordanville 15 67 40N46'11 80W45'23 5:23:02
Joy 58 5 39N28'13 81W56'28 5:27:46
Joyce 79 115 40N27'18 81W30'11 5:26:01
Joy, Mount 73 34 38N57'05 83W10'25 5:32:42
Jug Run 41 67 40N12'43 80W44'52 5:22:59
Jugs Corners 59 95 40N40'51 82W38'44 5:30:35
Jumbo 33 5 40N35'42 83W45'29 5:35:02
Jump 33 5 40N36'57 83W47'40 5:35:11
Junction 63 34 41N11'35 84W27'31 5:37:50
Junction City 64 27 39N43'16 82W17'56 5:29:12
Junior Furnace 73 34 38N37'23 82W48'33 5:31:14
Justus 76 67 40N42'16 81W34'45 5:26:19
Kalida 69 34 40N58'58 84W11'58 5:36:48
Kamms Corner 18 26 41N27'01 81W49'05 5:27:16
Kanauga 27 27 38N50'32 82W08'50 5:28:35
Kansas 74 32 41N14'42 83W17'05 5:33:08
Kauke 85 76 40N42'39 81W58'57 5:27:56
Kay Subdivision 83 34 39N35 84W18 5:37:12
Keene 16 5 40N20'42 81W52'06 5:27:28
Keith 61 5 39N39'24 81W33'47 5:26:15
Kelleys Island 22 5 41N35'49 82W42'37 5:30:50
Kelloggsville 4 72 41N51'24 80W37'03 5:22:28
Kemp 2 90 40N43'25 84W13'24 5:36:54
Kendall Heights 76 54 40N49'27 81W30'29 5:26:02
Kendeigh Corner 47 67 41N22'43 82W15'10 5:29:01
Kenilworth 78 67 41N27'44 80W44'15 5:22:57
Kenmore 77 2 41N03 81W34 5:26:16
Kennard 11 34 40N11'35 83W40'47 5:34:43
Kennedy Heights 31 34 39N11'08 84W24'30 5:37:38
Kennonsburg 61 5 39N54'54 81W22'33 5:25:30
Kennvale 73 34 38N38'55 83W08'12 5:32:33
Keno 53 5 39N05'53 81W51'48 5:27:27
Kenricksville 83 34 39N33'04 84W09'56 5:36:40
Kenridge 31 34 39N15'01 84W22'30 5:37:30
Kensington 15 67 40N44'07 80W57'24 5:23:50
Kent 67 46 41N09'13 81W21'29 5:25:26
Kenton 33 111 40N38'49 83W36'35 5:34:26
Kenwood 31 34 39N12'38 84W22'02 5:37:28
Kenwood 34 21 40N13 80W52 5:23:28
Kenwood 48 31 41N40 83W36 5:34:24
Kenwood Hills 31 34 39N10'02 84W22'56 5:37:32
Kenwood Knolls 31 34 39N13'00 84W22'31 5:37:30
Kerr 27 27 38N52'22 82W15'39 5:29:03
Kerr 56 20 39N46'34 81W08'06 5:24:32
Kerr Corner 21 33 40N25'09 83W14'56 5:33:00
Kessler 55 34 39N58 84W20 5:37:20
Kettering 57 91 39N41'22 84W10'08 5:36:41
Kettlersville 75 34 40N26'20 84W15'41 5:37:03
Key 7 21 39N58'30 80W52'13 5:23:29
Keystone 37 34 39N00'36 82W26'55 5:29:48
Keystone 40 34 38N59'17 82W36'33 5:30:26
Kidron 85 69 40N44'27 81W44'42 5:26:59
Kieferville 69 34 41N06'01 84W12'24 5:36:50
Kilbourne 21 27 40N19'48 82W57'27 5:31:50
Kile 49 34 40N07 83W16 5:33:04
Kileville 49 108 40N06'16 83W12'39 5:32:51
Kilgore 10 21 40N27'51 81W00'07 5:24:00
Killbuck 38 5 40N29'42 81W59'05 5:27:56
Kilmer 61 20 39N36'12 81W22'43 5:25:31
Kilvert 5 5 39N20'43 81W52'57 5:27:32
Kimball 22 5 41N18'34 82W42'07 5:30:48
Kimberly 5 27 39N25'38 82W12'55 5:28:52
Kimbolton 30 5 40N09'10 81W34'20 5:26:17
Kincaid Springs 66 34 39N06'08 83W15'52 5:33:03
Kinderhook 65 34 39N34'29 83W04'06 5:32:16
King Corners 78 45 41N15'39 80W44'27 5:22:58
Kingman 14 34 39N30'03 83W56'24 5:35:46
King Mines 30 5 39N59 81W27 5:25:48
Kingsbury 53 5 39N06'41 82W00'21 5:28:01
Kings Corners 59 95 40N39'00 82W37'18 5:30:29
Kingscreek 11 110 40N09'40 83W43'30 5:34:54
Kingsgate 31 34 39N14 84W32 5:38:08
Kings Mills 83 34 39N21'20 84W14'55 5:37:00
Kings Mine 30 5 39N59'24 81W29'05 5:25:56
Kingston 71 34 39N28'26 82W54'39 5:31:39
Kingsville 4 52 41N53'27 80W40'35 5:22:42
Kingsville-on-the-Lake 4 52 41N55'24 80W42'11 5:22:49
Kingsway 72 30 41N25'03 83W08'08 5:32:33
Kinnickinnick 71 34 39N21 83W00 5:32:00
Kinsey 57 34 39N51'14 84W17'34 5:37:10
Kinsman 7 21 40N08'01 80W54'17 5:23:37
Kinsman 78 56 41N26'38 80W35'20 5:22:21
Kiousville 49 34 39N47'50 83W17'41 5:33:11
Kipling 30 5 39N59'46 81W30'03 5:26:00
Kipton 47 67 41N16'05 82W18'08 5:29:13
Kirby 88 33 40N48'47 83W25'07 5:33:40
Kirbyville 8 34 39N07'35 83W58'38 5:35:55
Kirkersville 45 27 39N57'34 82W35'45 5:30:23
Kirkpatrick 51 32 40N41'19 83W00'31 5:32:02
Kirkwood 7 21 40N05 81W11 5:24:44
Kirkwood 75 34 40N12'58 84W11'50 5:36:47
Kirkwood Heights 7 21 40N05 80W45 5:23:00
Kirtland 43 67 41N37'44 81W21'42 5:25:27
Kirtland Hills 43 67 41N37'26 81W18'26 5:25:14
Kitchen 40 34 38N52'11 82W32'34 5:30:10
Kitts Hill 44 34 38N33'41 82W34'39 5:30:19
Kiwanis Lake 28 67 41N26 81W13 5:24:52
Klee 7 21 40N01 80W45 5:23:00
Klines Corner 78 84 41N11'00 80W39'53 5:22:40
Klocks Crossing 14 34 39N15'24 83W50'15 5:35:21
Klondike 21 27 40N16'19 83W08'39 5:32:35
Klondike 78 67 41N19'48 80W46'47 5:23:07
Klondyke 15 105 40N38 80W35 5:22:20
Knockemstiff 71 34 39N16'04 83W07'09 5:32:29
Knollwood 29 34 39N45 84W04 5:36:16
Knollwood Village 65 34 39N37'18 82W53'59 5:31:36
Knox 42 29 40N27'27 82W31'46 5:30:07
Knox 82 27 39N15'58 82W17'09 5:29:09
Knoxdale 63 34 41N11'53 84W40'31 5:38:42
Knoxville 41 67 40N29'32 80W40'51 5:22:43
Kolmont 41 106 40N18'44 80W39'40 5:22:39
Kossuth 6 34 40N39'34 84W20'53 5:37:24
Kreitzer Corner 57 34 39N45'35 84W26'35 5:37:46
Krumroy 77 2 41N00'54 81W28'24 5:25:54
Kunkle 86 34 41N38'12 84W29'43 5:37:59
Kyger 27 27 38N58'53 82W09'18 5:28:37
Kyles 9 34 39N24'58 84W24'28 5:37:38
Kylesburg 45 27 39N58 82W28 5:29:52
Lacarne 62 93 41N30'57 83W02'32 5:32:10
La Croft 15 105 40N38'45 80W35'53 5:22:24
Ladd 66 34 38N59'14 83W10'51 5:32:43
Lafayette 2 34 40N45'37 83W56'55 5:35:48
Lafayette 49 34 39N56'15 83W24'24 5:33:38
Lafayette 52 73 41N08 81W52 5:27:28
LaFeuille Terrace 31 88 39N08'08 84W35'26 5:38:22
Lafferty 7 21 40N06'42 81W01'10 5:24:05
La Grange 44 34 38N31 82W39 5:30:36
Lagrange 47 73 41N14'14 82W07'12 5:28:29
Laings 56 20 39N43'01 81W00'45 5:24:03
Lake Cable 76 43 40N51'36 81W26'55 5:25:48
Lake Fork 3 44 40N44'57 82W08'30 5:28:34
Lakeland 48 30 41N39'36 83W15'28 5:33:02
Lakeland 61 5 39N53'13 81W22'27 5:25:30
Lakeland Beach 38 17 40N39'51 82W06'20 5:28:25
Lakeline 43 67 41N39'34 81W27'16 5:25:49
Lake Lucerne 28 67 41N24'18 81W20'18 5:25:21
Lake Milton 50 73 41N05'58 80W58'14 5:23:53
Lakemont Landing 48 30 41N40'23 83W16'50 5:33:07
Lakemore 77 2 41N01'15 81W26'10 5:25:45
Lake o' Springs 76 43 40N48 81W19 5:25:16
Lakeside 9 34 39N30 84W23 5:37:32
Lakeside 23 27 39N55'19 82W31'04 5:30:04
Lakeside 62 93 41N32'35 82W44'57 5:31:00
Lake Slagle 76 43 40N52'41 81W27'23 5:25:50
Lake Sylvan 12 34 39N55 83W37 5:34:28
Lake View 42 5 40N29'56 82W31'34 5:30:06
Lakeview 46 34 40N29 83W56 5:35:44
Lakeview 61 5 39N55'19 81W26'00 5:25:44
Lakeview 77 2 40N59'53 81W31'25 5:26:06
Lake View Heights 66 34 39N06'26 83W01'50 5:32:07
Lakeville 38 17 40N39'22 82W07'38 5:28:31
Lakewood 18 26 41N28'55 81W47'54 5:27:12
La Mar Heights 5 97 39N18'43 82W06'12 5:28:25
Lamb Corners 25 108 40N06'25 83W11'33 5:32:46
Lamira 7 21 40N01'27 80W59'17 5:23:57
Lancaster 23 96 39N42'49 82W35'58 5:30:24
Landeck 2 34 40N48'04 84W23'17 5:37:33
Landin Park 55 34 40N08'08 84W16'14 5:37:05
Landis 19 34 40N03'15 84W30'11 5:38:01
Lane 43 67 41N45'03 81W10'53 5:24:44
Langsville 53 27 39N02'49 82W10'54 5:28:44
Lanier 68 34 39N42 84W33 5:38:12
Lansing 7 21 40N04'32 80W47'25 5:23:10
Laporte 47 42 41N19'50 82W04'40 5:28:19
Lapperell 66 34 39N07'49 83W16'41 5:33:07
La Rue 51 33 40N35 83W23 5:33:32
Lashley 61 5 39N55'07 81W24'02 5:25:36
Latcha 87 30 41N32'39 83W27'13 5:33:49
Latham 66 34 39N05'56 83W14'48 5:32:59
Lathrop 58 5 39N25'22 81W54'56 5:27:40
Latimer 78 67 41N21'24 80W37'05 5:22:28
Lattasburg 85 62 40N52'43 82W06'31 5:28:26
Lattasville 71 34 39N20'53 83W12'23 5:32:50
Latty 63 34 41N05'19 84W35'07 5:38:20
Laura 55 34 39N59'41 84W24'29 5:37:38
Laurel 13 34 38N57 84W17 5:37:08
Laurel 37 34 39N30 82W34 5:30:16
Laurel Ridge 76 43 40N52 81W20 5:25:20
Laurelville 37 34 39N28'24 82W44'22 5:30:57
Lawco 44 34 38N38'22 82W42'08 5:30:49
Lawndale 76 54 40N47'09 81W32'31 5:26:10
Lawrence Furnace 44 34 38N38'39 82W40'28 5:30:42
Lawrenceville 12 39 39N59'12 83W52'43 5:35:31
Lawshe 1 34 38N56'26 83W28'11 5:33:53
Lawyerdale Estates 31 34 39N06'17 84W21'06 5:37:24
Layhigh 9 34 39N21'42 84W41'46 5:38:47
Layland 16 5 40N26'10 81W58'01 5:27:52
Layman 84 20 39N24'12 81W43'28 5:26:54
Leaper 27 27 38N40'56 82W16'13 5:29:05
Leavittsburg 78 45 41N14'52 80W52'38 5:23:31
Leavittsville 10 21 40N30'49 81W11'47 5:24:47
Lebanon 56 20 39N36'28 81W16'24 5:25:06
Lebanon 83 34 39N26'07 84W12'11 5:36:49
Lecta 44 34 38N40'09 82W22'38 5:29:31
Lee Road 18 26 41N27 81W35 5:26:20
Leesburg 36 34 39N20'42 83W33'11 5:34:13
Lees Creek 14 34 39N25'12 83W38'58 5:34:36
Leesville 10 21 40N27'06 81W12'44 5:24:51
Leesville 17 33 40N47'43 82W47'18 5:31:09
Leetonia 15 47 40N52'38 80W45'20 5:23:01
Lehmkuhl Landing 75 34 40N23'17 84W17'45 5:37:11
Leipsic 69 34 41N05'54 83W59'05 5:35:56
Leipsic Junction 69 34 41N06'23 83W58'41 5:35:55
Leistville 65 34 39N31'47 82W50'20 5:31:21
Leith 84 20 39N27'19 81W09'02 5:24:36
Lelan 83 34 39N26 84W12 5:36:48
Lemert 17 33 40N53'39 83W05'37 5:32:22
Lemon 9 34 39N29'18 84W20'16 5:37:21
Lemoyne 87 32 41N29'45 83W28'27 5:33:54
Lena 55 34 40N08'27 84W01'56 5:36:08
Lenox 4 72 41N40'48 80W45'43 5:23:03
Leo 40 34 39N08'53 82W40'09 5:30:41
Leon 4 72 41N39'13 80W36'58 5:22:28
Leonardsburg 21 27 40N21'27 82W59'23 5:31:58
Lerado 13 34 39N10'29 84W00'30 5:36:02
Lesmil 40 34 39N09'30 82W34'15 5:30:17
Le Sourdsville 9 34 39N26'25 84W25'48 5:37:43
Lester 52 73 41N10'51 81W56'17 5:27:45
Letart 53 5 38N55 81W53 5:27:32
Letart Falls 53 5 38N53'34 81W55'27 5:27:42
Levanna 8 34 38N45'59 83W53'02 5:35:32
Lewis 8 34 38N50 84W00 5:36:00
Lewis Addition 41 106 40N22 80W39 5:22:36
Lewisburg 68 34 39N50'46 84W32'23 5:38:10
Lewis Center 21 27 40N11'54 83W00'37 5:32:02
Lewistown 46 33 40N25'20 83W53'05 5:35:32
Lewisville 56 20 39N45'55 81W13'07 5:24:52
Lexington 70 95 40N40'43 82W34'57 5:30:20
Lexington 76 67 40N57'43 81W06'17 5:24:25
Leyda 10 21 40N40'16 81W08'04 5:24:32
Liars Corner 5 27 39N23'59 82W06'16 5:28:25
Liberty 57 91 39N43 84W15 5:37:00
Liberty Center 35 34 41N26'36 84W00'32 5:36:02
Liberty Plaza 78 84 41N08 80W38 5:22:32
Lick 40 34 39N03 82W37 5:30:28
Licking View 60 5 39N57'14 82W02'00 5:28:08
Lickskillet 71 34 39N15'00 82W48'35 5:31:14
Liebs Island 23 27 39N54 82W33 5:30:12
Liggett Crossing 34 21 40N21'46 80W55'15 5:23:41
Lightsville 19 34 40N17'07 84W42'46 5:38:51
Lilly Chapel 49 34 39N53'20 83W16'54 5:33:08
Lima 2 90 40N44'33 84W06'19 5:36:25
Lima 53 27 39N03'51 82W07'12 5:28:29
Limaville 76 67 40N58'55 81W08'55 5:24:36
Lime City 87 31 41N32'06 83W34'01 5:34:16
Limecrest 12 39 39N55 83W48 5:35:12
Limerick 40 34 39N07'30 82W45'01 5:31:00
Limestone 62 93 41N33'09 83W12'45 5:32:51
Limestone City 12 39 39N54'43 83W52'36 5:35:30
Lincoln 59 27 40N28 82W51 5:31:24
Lincoln Heights 31 34 39N14'20 84W27'20 5:37:49
Lincoln Heights 53 97 39N01'35 82W02'56 5:28:12
Lincoln Heights 70 95 40N46'17 82W29'04 5:29:56
Lincoln Village 25 107 39N57 83W07 5:32:28
Lincolnville 36 34 39N05'55 83W24'07 5:33:36
Lindair Estates 12 39 39N55 83W48 5:35:12
Lindale 13 34 38N59 84W13 5:36:52
Lindentree 10 21 40N36'18 81W18'04 5:25:12
Lindenwald 9 34 39N22'20 84W33'33 5:38:14
Lindsey 72 30 41N25'08 83W13'17 5:32:53
Linndale 18 26 41N26'48 81W46'02 5:27:04
Linnville 44 34 38N33'23 82W28'44 5:29:55
Linnville 45 5 39N57'19 82W20'31 5:29:22
Linton Mills 16 5 40N10'26 81W41'37 5:26:46
Linwood 31 88 39N07'17 84W24'53 5:37:40
Linworth 25 107 40N05 83W01 5:32:04
Lippincott 11 34 40N11'37 83W46'32 5:35:06
Lisbon 12 34 39N51'39 83W38'07 5:34:32
Lisbon 15 67 40N46'19 80W46'06 5:23:04
Lisman 44 34 38N38'10 82W40'50 5:30:43
Litchfield 52 73 41N10'04 82W01'23 5:28:06
Lithopolis 23 34 39N48'10 82W48'23 5:31:14
Little Center 14 34 39N28'56 83W52'11 5:35:29
Little Chicago 65 34 39N43'20 82W57'10 5:31:49
Little Farms 25 107 39N57 83W07 5:32:28
Little Hocking 84 20 39N15'38 81W42'00 5:26:48
Little Mountain 43 67 41N38'06 81W16'26 5:25:06
Little Richmond 57 34 39N46'27 84W26'40 5:37:47
Little Sandusky 88 32 40N44'19 83W12'55 5:32:52
Little Walnut 65 34 39N41'03 82W58'16 5:31:53
Little Washington 70 95 40N41'45 82W28'22 5:29:53
Little York 57 91 39N51'31 84W15'29 5:37:02

Little York 77 67 41N21 81w32 5:26:08
Livingston 25 107 39N56 82w53 5:31:32
Lloyd Corners 45 5 40N00'50 82w24'12 5:29:37
Lloydsville 7 21 40N04'17 80w59'45 5:23:59
Lock 45 27 40N16'17 82w36'39 5:30:27
Lockbourne 25 34 39N48'33 82w58'21 5:31:53
Lockbourne Base 25 34 39N49 82w57 5:31:48
Lockington 75 34 40N12'29 84w14'02 5:36:56
Lockland 31 34 39N14 84w28 5:37:52
Lock Port 86 34 41N32'59 84w23'24 5:37:34
Locks 71 34 39N21 83w00 5:32:00
Lock Two 6 34 40N26 84w22 5:37:28
Lockville 23 27 39N49'07 82w44'01 5:30:56
Lockville Station 23 27 39N50'01 82w44'39 5:30:59
Lockwood 78 67 41N27'41 80w50'50 5:23:23
Lockwood Corners 77 2 41N00'02 81w33'38 5:26:15
Locust Corner 13 34 39N01'29 84w16'32 5:37:06
Locust Fork 84 20 39N26'13 81w31'01 5:26:04
Locust Grove 1 34 38N59'18 83w22'41 5:33:31
Locust Grove 45 5 40N00'10 82w26'16 5:29:45
Locust Grove 50 67 40N56'38 80w45'51 5:23:03
Locust Lake 13 34 39N01'35 84w14'00 5:36:56
Locust Point 62 93 41N31 83w08 5:32:32
Locust Ridge 8 34 38N59'31 84w00'26 5:36:02
Lodi 52 73 41N02'00 82w00'44 5:28:03
Logan 37 27 39N32'24 82w24'26 5:29:38
Logansville 46 34 40N20'44 83w55'50 5:35:43
Logtown 15 67 40N47'03 80w47'37 5:23:10
Lombardsville 73 34 38N49'15 83w07'59 5:32:32
London 49 101 39N53'11 83w26'54 5:33:48
London 70 5 40N54'37 82w37'46 5:30:31
Londonderry 30 5 40N12 81w16 5:25:04
Londonderry 71 34 39N16'00 82w47'26 5:31:10
Long 19 34 40N04'41 84w47'53 5:39:12
Long Beach 62 93 41N36'51 83w06'44 5:32:27
Long Bottom 53 5 39N05'10 81w48'14 5:27:13
Longley 74 32 41N13'21 83w25'16 5:33:41
Long Run 41 67 40N11'42 80w48'57 5:23:16
Longstreth 37 27 39N26 82w14 5:28:56
Longview Heights 5 27 39N18'09 82w05'18 5:28:21
Longvue 84 20 39N27 81w28 5:25:52
Loomis 7 13 40N01'43 81w00'31 5:24:02
Lorain 47 50 41N27'10 82w10'57 5:28:44
Loramie 75 34 40N14 84w22 5:37:28
Lordstown 78 45 41N09'56 80w51'28 5:23:26
Lore City 30 5 39N59'05 81w27'31 5:25:50
Losantville Triangle 31 88 39N07'42 84w30'08 5:38:01
Lostcreek 55 34 40N05 84w04 5:36:16
Lost Creek Addition 2 90 40N43 84w06 5:36:24
Lottridge 5 5 39N13'38 81w53'51 5:27:35
Louden 1 34 39N01'36 83w27'10 5:33:49
Loudon 79 16 40N34'10 81w30'04 5:26:00
Loudonville 3 5 40N38'07 82w14'00 5:28:56
Louisville 1 35 38N59'34 83w27'52 5:33:51
Louisville 76 67 40N50'14 81w15'35 5:25:02
Loveland 31 34 39N16 84w16 5:37:04
Loveland Park 83 34 39N17'59 84w15'48 5:37:03
Lovell 88 33 40N53'26 83w19'54 5:33:20
Lowell 74 32 41N12'25 83w03'19 5:32:13
Lowell 84 20 39N32 81w31 5:26:04
Lowellville 50 84 41N02'07 80w32'12 5:22:09
Lower Newport 84 20 39N21'07 81w20'43 5:25:23
Lower Salem 84 20 39N33'40 81w23'48 5:25:35
Low Gap 16 5 40N14'40 81w37'52 5:26:31
Low Gap 82 27 39N20'30 82w32'44 5:30:11
Loyal Oak 77 67 41N01 81w38 5:26:32
Loys Corners 78 75 41N11'05 80w41'32 5:22:46
Lucas 70 5 40N42 82w25 5:29:40
Lucasburg 30 5 39N57'16 81w34'10 5:26:17
Lucasville 73 34 38N52'46 82w59'49 5:31:59
Lucerne 42 27 40N27'45 82w37'43 5:30:31
Luckey 87 32 41N27'02 83w29'15 5:33:57
Ludington 64 27 39N35'37 82w09'38 5:28:39
Ludlow 84 20 39N35'17 81w39'05 5:26:36
Ludlow Falls 55 34 39N59'53 84w20'20 5:37:21
Lugbill Addition 26 34 41N31 84w18 5:37:12
Luhrig 5 27 39N20'00 82w11'00 5:28:44
Luke Chute 84 5 39N32'17 81w43'11 5:26:53
Lumberton 14 34 39N33'25 83w50'56 5:35:24
Lunda 80 33 40N21'53 83w30'42 5:34:03
Luray 24 34 39N34'37 83w30'53 5:34:04
Luray 45 27 39N57'28 82w31'54 5:30:08
Luttrell 24 34 39N35'05 83w38'59 5:34:36
Lybrand 21 33 40N19'00 83w14'14 5:32:57
Lykens 17 32 40N57'54 83w01'01 5:32:04
Lyme 39 5 41N15 82w48 5:31:12
Lynchburg 15 67 40N44'28 80w59'58 5:24:00
Lynchburg 36 34 39N14'30 83w47'29 5:35:10
Lyndhurst 18 67 41N31'12 81w29'20 5:25:57
Lyndon 71 34 39N21'09 83w18'44 5:33:15
Lynn 33 34 40N38 83w43 5:34:52
Lynn 51 27 40N29'56 83w06'26 5:32:26
Lynns Corners 50 67 41N02'33 80w44'14 5:22:57
Lynnview 31 34 39N14'10 84w33'25 5:38:14
Lynx 1 34 38N46'23 83w24'47 5:33:39
Lyons 26 34 41N41'58 84w04'13 5:36:17
Lyra 73 34 38N44'18 82w44'16 5:30:57
Lytle 83 34 39N33'39 84w08'06 5:36:32
Lytton 26 34 41N39'26 83w57'19 5:35:49
Mabee Corner 40 34 38N54'10 82w43'16 5:30:53
Macedon 54 34 40N28'46 84w45'09 5:39:01
Macedonia 9 34 39N20'55 84w47'45 5:39:11
Macedonia 77 58 41N18'49 81w30'31 5:26:02
Mack 31 34 39N09'29 84w38'59 5:38:36
Macksburg 84 20 39N37'56 81w27'24 5:25:50
Mackstown 21 27 40N08'42 82w52'58 5:31:32
Macochee Castle 46 34 40N15'29 83w43'01 5:34:52
Macon 8 34 38N57'54 83w43'42 5:34:55
Madden Corners 78 45 41N12'38 80w44'26 5:22:58
Maddox 1 34 38N41 83w36 5:34:24
Madeira 31 34 39N11'27 84w21'49 5:37:27
Madison 43 46 41N46'16 81w03'00 5:24:12
Madisonburg 85 76 40N51'28 81w55'33 5:27:42
Madison Hill 85 76 40N47'04 81w56'00 5:27:44
Madison Lake 49 34 39N52'15 83w22'47 5:33:31
Madison Mills 24 34 39N39'13 83w20'23 5:33:22
Madison-on-the-Lake 43 46 41N48 81w04 5:24:16
Madisonville 31 34 39N09'27 84w23'28 5:37:34
Magnetic Springs 80 33 40N21'10 83w15'41 5:33:03
Magnolia 76 21 40N39'04 81w17'57 5:25:12
Mahoning 67 53 41N15'32 81w02'56 5:24:12
Maineville 83 34 39N18'54 84w13'15 5:36:53
Mainsville 64 27 39N42'44 82w14'32 5:28:58
Malaga 56 20 39N51'17 81w08'58 5:24:36
Malinta 35 34 41N19'21 84w02'17 5:36:09
Mallet Creek 52 73 41N10'02 81w55'32 5:27:42
Malta 58 5 39N38'57 81w51'44 5:27:27
Malvern 10 21 40N41'30 81w10'53 5:24:44
Manara 24 34 39N36'09 83w18'47 5:33:15
Manchester 1 34 38N41'17 83w36'34 5:34:26
Manchester 77 2 40N56'13 81w34'10 5:26:17
Mandale 63 34 41N01 84w17 5:37:08
Manhattan 41 106 40N22 80w39 5:22:36
Mannhassett Village 83 34 39N22 84w17 5:37:08
Mansfield 70 95 40N45'30 82w30'56 5:30:04
Mantua 67 46 41N17'02 81w13'27 5:24:54
Mantua Center 67 67 41N18'35 81w14'42 5:24:59
Mantua Corners 67 46 41N18'37 81w13'17 5:24:53
Maple 8 34 38N54'12 84w02'08 5:36:09
Maple Corner 29 34 39N36'30 83w54'24 5:35:38
Maple Grove 28 67 41N24'00 81w06'30 5:24:26
Maple Grove 71 34 39N22'23 83w06'16 5:32:25
Maple Grove 74 32 41N12'53 83w13'33 5:32:54
Maple Heights 18 26 41N24'55 81w33'58 5:26:16
Maple Heights 61 5 39N45 81w31 5:26:04
Maple Lake 41 68 40N26 80w46 5:23:04
Maple Ridge 50 67 40N55'23 81w03'04 5:24:12
Mapleshade 27 27 38N49'17 82w10'36 5:28:42
Mapleton 76 43 40N44'45 81w14'47 5:24:59
Maple Valley 77 2 41N05'02 81w34'13 5:26:17
Maplewood 75 34 40N22'34 84w01'33 5:36:06
Marathon 13 34 39N08'41 84w00'23 5:36:02
Marble Cliff 25 107 39N59'12 83w03'42 5:32:15
Marble Furnace 1 34 38N57 83w24 5:33:36
Marblehead 62 93 41N32 82w44 5:30:56
Marchand 76 43 40N53 81w24 5:25:36
Marcy 18 26 41N26 81w37 5:26:28
Marcy 65 27 39N45'06 82w49'43 5:31:19
Marengo 59 27 40N24'03 82w48'39 5:31:15
Margaretta 22 5 41N25 82w48 5:31:12
Maria Stein 54 34 40N24'28 84w29'36 5:37:58
Mariemont 31 34 39N08'42 84w22'28 5:37:30
Marietta 84 113 39N24'55 81w27'18 5:25:49
Marion 51 98 40N35'19 83w07'43 5:32:31
Mark Center 20 34 41N17'20 84w37'52 5:38:31
Marlain Acres 31 34 39N13'57 84w30'15 5:38:01
Marlan Acres 31 34 39N14 84w32 5:38:08
Marlboro 76 67 40N57'04 81w12'51 5:24:51
Marl City 46 33 40N25'57 83w41'12 5:34:45
Marne 25 5 40N04'16 82w18'34 5:29:14
Marquand Mills 60 5 40N08'45 81w47'51 5:27:11
Marquis 50 67 40N59'17 80w45'51 5:23:03
Marr 56 20 39N37'43 81w13'33 5:24:54
Marseilles 88 33 40N42'05 83w23'34 5:33:34
Marshall 36 34 39N09'07 83w29'06 5:33:56
Marshallville 85 62 40N54'08 81w44'03 5:26:56
Martel 51 27 40N40'08 82w54'37 5:31:38
Martin 62 32 41N33'27 83w20'12 5:33:21
Martinsburg 42 5 40N16'11 82w21'15 5:29:25
Martins Ferry 7 15 40N05'45 80w43'29 5:22:54
Martinsville 14 34 39N19'26 83w48'54 5:35:16
Martinsville 38 5 40N36'52 81w52'05 5:27:28
Mary Ann 45 5 40N09 82w19 5:29:16
Marygrove 48 34 41N35 83w54 5:35:36
Marysville 30 5 39N56'50 81w36'13 5:26:25
Marysville 80 33 40N14'11 83w22'02 5:33:28
Mason 83 34 39N21'36 84w18'36 5:37:14
Mason Heights 83 34 39N22 84w17 5:37:08
Massie 83 34 39N29 84w02 5:36:08
Massieville 71 34 39N15'54 82w58'01 5:31:52
Massillon 76 54 40N47'48 81w31'18 5:26:05
Masury 78 46 41N12'40 80w32'17 5:22:09
Matville 65 34 39N45'50 83w06'01 5:32:24
Maud 9 34 39N21'19 84w23'25 5:37:34
Maumee 48 31 41N33'46 83w39'14 5:34:37
Maustown 9 34 39N24'20 84w27'06 5:37:48
Maximo 76 67 40N52'35 81w10'20 5:24:41
Maxtown 21 27 40N06 82w56 5:31:44
Maxville 64 27 39N37'04 82w20'02 5:29:20
Maybee 70 95 40N46'44 82w37'17 5:30:29
Mayfield 9 34 39N29'41 84w22'22 5:37:29
Mayfield 18 67 41N33'07 81w26'22 5:25:45
Mayfield Heights 18 67 41N31'09 81w27'29 5:25:50
Mayflower Village 76 54 40N48'01 81w33'10 5:26:13
May-Green Shopping Center 18 67 41N31 81w32 5:26:08
May Hill 1 34 39N00'46 83w30'29 5:34:02
Maynard 7 21 40N07'24 80w52'46 5:23:31
Maysville 2 34 40N43'57 83w52'48 5:35:31
Maysville 16 5 40N09'15 81w48'00 5:27:12
Maysville 37 27 39N32'59 82w19'16 5:29:17
Maysville 60 5 39N53'46 82w02'03 5:28:08
Maysville 85 62 40N41'50 81w47'34 5:27:10
McArthur 82 34 39N14'47 82w28'43 5:29:55
McAvan 84 20 39N23'32 81w34'27 5:26:18
McCance 85 62 40N41'52 81w53'03 5:27:32
McCartyville 75 34 40N23'41 84w15'21 5:37:01
McClaimsville 49 34 39N43'43 83w16'18 5:33:05
McClainville 7 21 40N01'24 80w47'35 5:23:10
McClintocksburg 67 58 41N11 80w59 5:23:56
McClure 35 34 41N22'17 83w56'31 5:35:46
McComb 32 34 41N06'27 83w47'34 5:35:10
McConnelsville 58 5 39N38'55 81w51'12 5:27:25
McCoppin Mill 36 34 39N10'57 83w26'19 5:33:45
McCormick 27 27 38N46 82w11 5:28:44
McCracken Corners 15 67 40N55 80w51 5:23:24
McCuneville 64 27 39N37'44 82w14'04 5:28:56
McCutchenville 88 32 40N59'26 83w15'34 5:33:02
McDaniel Crossroad 27 34 38N45'26 82w28'44 5:29:55
McDermott 73 34 38N50'05 83w03'54 5:32:16
McDonald 60 5 39N51'45 81w50'50 5:27:23
McDonald 78 75 41N09'49 80w43'28 5:22:54
McDonaldsville 76 43 40N53'15 81w28'45 5:25:55
McFarlands Corners 28 67 41N24'42 81w20'18 5:25:21
McGaw 73 34 38N38'16 83w13'29 5:32:54
McGill 63 34 41N01'08 84w46'27 5:39:06
McGonigle 9 34 39N26'45 84w40'59 5:38:44
McGuffey 33 34 40N41'34 83w47'08 5:35:09
McGuffey Heights 50 46 41N07'36 80w35'15 5:22:21
McIntyre 41 67 40N18'24 80w46'53 5:23:08
McKay 3 5 40N42'21 82w14'35 5:28:58
McKays Corners 50 84 41N01'27 80w38'04 5:22:32
McKean 45 27 40N10 82w31 5:30:04
McKendree 49 34 39N47'09 83w16'19 5:33:05
McKinley Heights 78 75 41N11'01 80w43'03 5:22:52
McLean 75 34 40N22 84w21 5:37:24
McLeish 5 27 39N32'06 82w06'08 5:28:25
McLuney 64 27 39N44'25 82w06'09 5:28:25
McMorran 46 33 40N23'22 83w50'54 5:35:24
McVitty 33 33 40N45'42 83w32'15 5:34:09
McWhorters Acres 9 34 39N25 84w35 5:38:20
McZena 3 64 40N40 82w07 5:28:28
Mead 7 21 39N58 80w50 5:23:20
Meade 65 34 39N30'17 82w52'37 5:31:30
Meadowbrook 60 5 39N59'52 82w02'07 5:28:08
Meadowbrook Lake 77 2 41N10 81w28 5:25:52
Meadow Lawn 9 34 39N30 84w23 5:37:32
Mecca 78 67 41N23'22 80w44'14 5:22:57
Mechanic 38 5 40N29 81w52 5:27:28
Mechanicsburg 11 34 40N04'19 83w33'23 5:34:14
Mechanicsburg 17 33 40N54 82w46 5:31:04
Mechanicsburg 56 20 39N38'46 81w05'04 5:24:20
Mechanicsburg 85 76 40N49 81w56 5:27:44
Mechanicstown 10 21 40N37'07 80w57'05 5:23:48
Mechanicsville 4 72 41N45'17 80w53'41 5:23:35
Medina 52 73 41N08'18 81w51'50 5:27:27
Medway 12 34 39N53 84w02 5:36:08
Meeker 51 33 40N38'37 83w18'21 5:33:13
Meigs 53 5 39N09'57 81w53'51 5:27:35
Meigs 58 5 39N41'25 81w46'31 5:27:06
Meigsville 58 5 39N38 81w45 5:27:00
Melbern 86 34 41N28'01 84w39'05 5:38:36
Melmore 74 32 41N01'26 83w06'34 5:32:26
Melody Lake 60 5 39N55 82w01 5:28:04
Melrose 63 34 41N05'32 84w25'11 5:37:41
Melvin 14 34 39N28'24 83w43'04 5:34:52
Memphis 14 34 39N24'35 83w36'34 5:34:26
Mendon 54 34 40N40'24 84w31'08 5:38:05
Mentor 43 48 41N39'58 81w20'23 5:25:22
Mentor Headlands 43 48 41N44'23 81w18'43 5:25:15
Mentor-on-the-Lake 43 48 41N42'18 81w21'38 5:25:27
Mentzer 33 33 40N35'48 83w34'54 5:34:20
Mercer 54 34 40N39'18 84w35'08 5:38:21
Mercerville 27 27 38N39'45 82w16'19 5:29:05
Meredith 21 33 40N23'10 83w07'54 5:32:32
Mermill 87 33 41N20 83w39 5:34:36
Merriam 60 5 39N48'12 81w54'00 5:27:36
Merritt 53 5 39N01'42 81w51'04 5:27:24
Mesopotamia 78 67 41N27'30 80w57'19 5:23:49
Metamora 26 34 41N42'42 83w54'35 5:35:38
Metham 16 5 40N22'04 81w59'06 5:27:56
Metzger 71 34 39N23'37 82w57'21 5:31:49
Mexico 88 32 40N59'11 83w11'36 5:32:46
Meyers Lake 76 43 40N48'45 81w25'00 5:25:40
Miami 31 34 39N13 84w42 5:38:48
Miami Grove 31 34 39N14'05 84w18'25 5:37:14
Miami Heights 31 88 39N09'54 84w43'14 5:38:53
Miamisburg 57 34 39N38'34 84w17'12 5:37:09
Miamitown 31 34 39N12'57 84w42'15 5:38:49
Miami University 9 34 39N31 84w44 5:38:56

Miami Villa 57 91 39N50'50 84w10'12 5:36:41
Miamiville 13 34 39N12'45 84w17'58 5:37:12
Mid City 57 91 39N45 84w11 5:36:44
Middle Bass 62 93 41N41 82w50 5:31:20
Middleboro 83 34 39N21'02 84w02'30 5:36:10
Middlebourne 30 5 40N03'04 81w20'12 5:25:21
Middlebranch 76 67 40N53'24 81w19'44 5:25:19
Middleburg 11 5 39N40'28 81w23'23 5:25:34
Middleburg 41 67 40N27'17 80w52'50 5:23:31
Middleburg 46 34 40N17'33 83w34'57 5:34:20
Middleburg Heights 18 67 41N21'41 81w48'47 5:27:15
Middlebury 42 5 40N31 82w35 5:30:20
Middlebury 81 34 40N50'46 84w44'46 5:38:59
Middlefield 28 74 41N27'43 81w04'26 5:24:18
Middle Point 81 34 40N51 84w27 5:37:48
Middleport 53 97 39N00'06 82w02'56 5:28:12
Middleton 15 67 40N50'36 80w39'05 5:22:36
Middleton 37 34 39N04'52 82w29'33 5:29:58
Middleton Corner 29 34 39N34'50 83w51'42 5:35:27
Middletown 9 3 39N30'54 84w23'54 5:37:36
Middletown 11 34 40N11'30 83w37'09 5:34:29
Middletown 17 33 40N46'25 82w47'31 5:31:10
Midland 14 34 39N18'22 83w54'40 5:35:39
Midpark 18 26 41N24 81w46 5:27:04
Midtown 60 5 39N55 82w01 5:28:04
Midvale 79 16 40N26'16 81w22'24 5:25:30
Midway 7 21 40N07'27 80w54'30 5:23:38
Midway 19 34 39N57'20 84w27'53 5:37:52
Midway 49 34 39N44'00 83w28'40 5:33:55
Midway 53 27 39N07'23 82w00'30 5:28:02
Midway 55 34 40N05'33 84w12'53 5:36:52
Midway Mall 47 42 41N22 82w06 5:28:24
Mifflin 3 44 40N46'26 82w21'52 5:29:27
Mifflinville 25 107 40N02'07 82w57'11 5:31:49
Milan 22 38 41N17'51 82w36'20 5:30:25
Miley Crossroads 38 5 40N37'27 82w05'17 5:28:21
Milford 13 34 39N10'31 84w17'40 5:37:11
Milford Center 80 34 40N10'43 83w26'08 5:33:45
Mill 79 16 40N23 81w20 5:25:20
Millbrook 85 76 40N43'38 82w00'30 5:28:02
Millbury 87 30 41N33'58 83w25'29 5:33:42
Millcreek 80 33 40N13 83w14 5:32:56
Milledgeville 24 34 39N35'34 83w35'15 5:34:21
Miller 42 27 40N19 82w30 5:30:00
Miller 44 34 38N32'12 82w18'07 5:29:12
Miller City 69 34 41N06'10 84w07'53 5:36:32
Miller Grove 19 34 40N00'24 84w27'51 5:37:51
Millersburg 38 5 40N33'16 81w55'05 5:27:40
Millers Corners 25 27 40N06'40 82w42'17 5:30:49
Millers Corners 38 5 40N35'56 81w46'52 5:27:07
Millersport 23 27 39N54'00 82w32'03 5:30:08
Millerstown 11 34 40N09'25 83w55'17 5:35:41
Millersville 72 32 41N18'43 83w16'53 5:33:08
Millertown 64 27 39N35'59 82w05'50 5:28:23
Millfield 5 27 39N25'58 82w05'49 5:28:23
Mill Grove 58 5 39N36'04 81w42'47 5:26:51
Millport 15 67 40N42'00 80w53'12 5:23:33
Millport 65 34 39N42'56 82w58'23 5:31:54
Mill Rock 15 67 40N47'53 80w35'30 5:22:22
Mills 27 27 38N50'57 82w14'08 5:28:57
Millsboro 70 95 40N45 82w31 5:30:04
Millsbury 87 30 41N34 83w26 5:33:44
Millville 9 34 39N23'21 84w39'16 5:38:37
Millville 50 67 40N54'21 80w48'24 5:23:14
Millwood 30 5 39N58 81w17 5:25:08
Millwood 42 5 40N27 82w16 5:29:04
Milton Center 87 34 41N19 83w50 5:35:20
Miltonsburg 56 20 39N49 81w10 5:24:40
Miltonville 9 34 39N30'03 84w27'39 5:37:51
Mina 86 34 41N27'14 84w42'40 5:38:51
Mineral 5 27 39N19'26 82w15'53 5:29:04
Mineral City 79 21 40N36'04 81w21'41 5:25:27
Mineral Ridge 78 68 41N08'24 80w46'09 5:23:05
Mineral Springs 1 34 38N53'13 83w19'46 5:33:19
Minersville 53 5 39N01'21 81w59'37 5:27:58
Minerton 82 27 39N04'00 82w24'14 5:29:37
Minerva 76 21 40N43'47 81w06'20 5:24:25
Minerva Junction 10 21 40N42'42 81w09'06 5:24:36
Minerva Park 25 107 40N04'35 82w56'38 5:31:47
Minford 73 34 38N51'32 82w51'44 5:31:27
Mingo 11 34 40N12'29 83w38'18 5:34:33
Mingo Junction 41 106 40N19'18 80w36'36 5:22:26
Minnehan Bend 71 34 39N12'38 83w09'10 5:32:37
Minster 6 34 40N23'35 84w22'34 5:37:30
Misco 64 5 39N43'40 82w04'26 5:28:18
Mishler 67 67 40N59'58 81w21'43 5:25:27
Mississinawa 19 34 40N19 84w45 5:39:00
Mitchaw 48 34 41N42'07 83w45'44 5:35:03
Mitiwanga 22 5 41N23'02 82w27'53 5:29:52
Mizers 79 12 40N16'38 81w34'53 5:26:20
Moats 20 34 41N19'54 84w31'33 5:38:06
Modest 13 34 39N11'35 84w06'26 5:36:26
Modoc 5 27 39N28'06 82w07'48 5:28:31
Moffitt Heights 76 54 40N46'42 81w34'28 5:26:18
Mogadore 77 67 41N02'47 81w23'53 5:25:36
Mohawk 16 5 40N20 82w03 5:28:12
Mohawk Village 16 5 40N19'30 82w04'47 5:28:19
Mohicanville 3 44 40N43'41 82w11'29 5:28:46
Moline 87 31 41N33'31 83w30'41 5:34:03
Momeneetown 48 31 41N39'35 83w24'35 5:33:38
Monclova 48 34 41N33'31 83w43'59 5:34:56
Monclova Gardens 48 34 41N35 83w40 5:34:40
Monday Creek 37 27 39N34'55 82w16'31 5:29:06
Monfort Heights 31 34 39N13 84w35 5:38:20
Monnett 17 32 40N43'03 83w02'24 5:32:10
Mononcue 88 32 40N49'38 83w16'07 5:33:04
Monroe 9 34 39N26'25 84w21'44 5:37:27
Monroe 29 34 39N40'38 83w51'54 5:35:28
Monroe 40 34 38N51'23 82w37'45 5:30:31
Monroe Center 4 72 41N50'40 80w34'18 5:22:17
Monroefield 56 20 39N49'14 81w12'09 5:24:49
Monroe Mills 42 5 40N25 82w20 5:29:20
Monroeville 39 27 41N14'39 82w41'47 5:30:47
Monroeville 41 67 40N35'52 80w50'16 5:23:21
Monterey 13 34 39N08'01 84w04'53 5:36:20
Monterey 54 34 40N27'02 84w47'02 5:39:08
Monterey 69 34 40N57 84w21 5:37:24
Montezuma 54 34 40N29'20 84w32'55 5:38:12
Montgomery 31 34 39N13'41 84w21'15 5:37:25
Montgomery Heights 31 34 39N14'12 84w21'25 5:37:26
Monticello 81 34 40N41'51 84w25'32 5:37:42
Montpelier 86 34 41N35 84w37 5:38:28
Montra 75 34 40N25'55 84w05'42 5:36:23
Montrose 77 2 41N08'08 81w38'15 5:26:33
Montville 43 67 41N36'26 81w03'02 5:24:12
Moons 24 34 39N34 83w31 5:34:04
Moorefield 12 39 39N55 83w48 5:35:12
Moorefield 34 21 40N11'59 81w10'16 5:24:41
Moore Junction 84 20 39N22'45 81w29'55 5:26:00
Moores Fork 13 34 39N11'47 84w01'22 5:36:05
Moores Junction 64 27 39N42'11 82w06'59 5:28:28
Mooresville 71 34 39N19'40 82w51'05 5:31:24
Moraine 57 91 39N42'22 84w13'10 5:36:53
Moreland 85 76 40N42'45 81w56'40 5:27:47
Moreland Corners 25 27 40N01'31 82w42'00 5:30:48
Moreland Hills 18 67 41N26'52 81w25'40 5:25:43
Morgan Center 27 27 38N58'59 82w16'03 5:29:04
Morgan Center 42 5 40N16'50 82w25'03 5:29:40
Morgandale 78 45 41N15'56 80w46'59 5:23:08
Morgan Place 57 34 39N51'49 84w17'07 5:37:08
Morgan Run 16 5 40N16'53 81w47'40 5:27:11
Morgansville 58 5 39N39 81w52 5:27:28
Morgantown 50 84 40N58'24 80w37'57 5:22:32
Morgantown 66 34 39N07'46 83w11'54 5:32:48
Morganville 58 5 39N37'56 81w57'17 5:27:49
Morges 10 21 40N38'07 81w14'45 5:24:59
Morning Sun 68 34 39N38 84w39 5:38:36
Morningview 7 21 40N08'19 80w47'39 5:23:11
Morral 51 32 40N41'16 83w12'45 5:32:51
Morris 42 29 40N26 82w30 5:30:00
Morris Apartments 57 91 39N50 84w13 5:36:52
Morrisons 60 5 39N55 82w01 5:28:04
Morristown 5 27 39N24'52 82w07'14 5:28:29
Morristown 7 21 40N03'47 81w04'28 5:24:18
Morrisville 14 34 39N21'19 83w48'10 5:35:13
Morrow 83 34 39N21'16 84w07'38 5:36:31
Mortimer (North Findlay) 32 33 41N06'34 83w39'01 5:34:36
Moscow 13 34 38N51'25 84w13'45 5:36:55
Moss Run 84 20 39N28'25 81w18'54 5:25:16
Moulton 6 34 40N33'22 84w17'50 5:37:11
Moultrie 15 67 40N47'47 81w04'16 5:24:17
Moundbuilders 45 5 40N07 82w26 5:29:44
Mound Crossing 37 34 39N30'22 82w37'23 5:30:30
Moundsville 61 5 39N45 81w31 5:26:04
Mound View 48 31 41N40 83w24 5:33:36
Mount Adams 31 88 39N06'33 84w29'46 5:37:59
Mount Air 25 107 40N07'57 83w02'11 5:32:09
Mount Airy 31 34 39N11'29 84w34'13 5:38:17
Mount Airy Center 31 88 39N10'00 84w34'53 5:38:20
Mount Auburn 31 88 39N07'05 84w30'13 5:38:01
Mount Blanchard 32 33 40N53'54 83w33'22 5:34:13
Mount Blanco 53 27 39N11'18 82w15'47 5:29:03
Mount Carmel 13 34 39N07 84w21 5:37:24
Mount Carmel 72 30 41N16'16 82w56'13 5:31:45
Mount Carmel Heights 13 34 39N07'06 84w18'04 5:37:12
Mount Carrick 56 20 39N45'08 81w02'49 5:24:11
Mount Cory 32 34 40N56'12 83w49'21 5:35:17
Mount Eaton 85 62 40N41'40 81w42'12 5:26:49
Mount Ephraim 11 5 39N50'50 81w25'05 5:25:40
Mount Everett 84 20 39N27 81w28 5:25:52
Mount Forest Trails 13 34 39N05'57 84w17'58 5:37:12
Mount Gilead 59 27 40N32'57 82w49'39 5:31:19
Mount Healthy 31 34 39N14'01 84w32'45 5:38:11
Mount Healthy Heights 31 34 39N14 84w32 5:38:08
Mount Holly 13 34 39N00'46 84w10'53 5:36:44
Mount Holly 83 34 39N34'18 84w01'57 5:36:08
Mount Hope 38 5 40N37'26 81w47'05 5:27:08
Mount Jefferson 75 34 40N15 84w20 5:37:20
Mount Joy 73 34 38N52 83w11 5:32:44
Mount Liberty 42 27 40N20'48 82w37'49 5:30:31
Mount Lookout 31 88 39N07'44 84w25'49 5:37:43
Mount Olive 13 34 38N53'12 84w05'31 5:36:22
Mount Orab 8 34 39N01'39 83w55'11 5:35:41
Mount Perry 64 27 39N52'43 82w13'12 5:28:53
Mount Pisgah 13 34 38N59'01 84w13'55 5:36:56
Mount Pleasant 41 67 40N10'31 80w47'53 5:23:12
Mount Pleasant 72 30 41N16 82w51 5:31:24
Mount Pleasant 76 43 40N54'28 81w24'20 5:25:37
Mount Pleasant 82 27 39N23'34 82w27'25 5:29:50
Mount Repose 13 34 39N12'02 84w13'28 5:36:54
Mount Saint John 29 34 39N43'07 84w05'59 5:36:24
Mount Saint Joseph 31 88 39N06 84w39 5:38:36
Mount Sinai 66 34 39N08'33 82w47'55 5:31:12
Mount Sterling 49 34 39N43'10 83w15'55 5:33:04
Mount Summit 31 34 39N05'19 84w19'48 5:37:19
Mount Union 76 67 40N54'05 81w06'22 5:24:25
Mount Vernon 42 29 40N23'36 82w29'09 5:29:57
Mount Victory 33 33 40N32'04 83w31'14 5:34:05
Mountview 31 88 39N06'55 84w39'46 5:38:39
Mountville 58 5 39N31'05 81w59'09 5:27:57
Mount Washington 31 88 39N05'15 84w23'11 5:37:33
Mount Zion 11 5 39N52'29 81w31'30 5:26:06
Mowrystown 36 34 39N02'18 83w44'55 5:35:00
Moxahala 64 27 39N39'45 82w08'11 5:28:33
Moxahala Park 60 5 39N55 82w01 5:28:04
Mudsock 25 108 40N00'08 83w10'56 5:32:44
Mudsock 27 34 38N46 82w23 5:29:32
Muhlenberg 65 34 39N42 83w07 5:32:28
Mulberry 13 34 39N11'36 84w14'32 5:36:58
Mulberry Grove 55 34 40N06'09 84w19'47 5:37:19
Mule Town 73 34 38N52'00 82w51'48 5:31:27
Muncie Hollow 72 30 41N23'09 83w05'05 5:32:20
Mungen 87 33 41N16'29 83w39'00 5:34:36
Munks Corners 25 27 39N55'04 82w55'01 5:31:40
Munroe Falls 77 67 41N08'40 81w26'24 5:25:46
Munson 28 67 41N32 81w15 5:25:00
Munson Hill 4 72 41N48'07 80w50'03 5:23:20
Muntanna 69 34 40N58'33 84w18'04 5:37:12
Murdock 83 34 39N17'31 84w12'22 5:36:49
Murlin Heights 57 91 39N51'28 84w11'58 5:36:48
Murray City 37 27 39N30'41 82w09'49 5:28:39
Museville 60 5 39N47'19 81w47'54 5:27:12
Musselman 71 34 39N22'05 83w08'33 5:32:34
Muttonville 68 34 39N39'29 84w41'09 5:38:45
Mutual 11 34 40N04'43 83w38'13 5:34:33
Myers 76 21 40N46'16 81w07'58 5:24:32
Myersville 77 67 40N58'34 81w25'26 5:25:42
Nace Corner 66 34 39N04'02 83w21'45 5:33:27
Naceville 66 34 39N05 83w23 5:33:32
Nankin 3 44 40N55'17 82w16'55 5:29:08
Napier 84 20 39N22'25 81w43'01 5:26:52
Napoleon 35 34 41N23'32 84w07'31 5:36:30
Narva 34 21 40N19'02 80w57'44 5:23:51
Nasby 48 31 41N37'49 83w36'41 5:34:27
Nash Corners 65 34 39N37 82w57 5:31:48
Nashport 60 5 40N04'14 82w10'33 5:28:42
Nashville 19 34 40N05'31 84w44'40 5:38:59
Nashville 38 5 40N35'46 82w06'44 5:28:27
Nashville 55 34 39N57'55 84w16'47 5:37:07
National Road 45 27 39N58 82w28 5:29:52
Navarre 76 54 40N43'28 81w31'20 5:26:05
Naylor 50 67 40N55'06 80w58'23 5:23:54
Neals Corner 8 34 38N57'46 83w58'27 5:35:54
Neapolis 48 34 41N29'34 83w52'24 5:35:30
Nease Settlement 53 5 39N01'18 81w57'20 5:27:49
Neave 19 34 40N02 84w39 5:38:36
Needfull 36 34 39N06'15 83w51'34 5:35:26
Needmore 2 34 40N51 84w20 5:37:20
Needmore 19 34 40N11'45 84w30'10 5:38:01
Neel 8 34 38N46'14 83w42'55 5:34:52
Neelysville 58 5 39N37'37 81w46'40 5:27:07
Neffs 7 10 40N01'38 80w48'55 5:23:16
Negley 15 67 40N47'24 80w32'21 5:22:09
Nellie 16 5 40N20'11 82w04'05 5:28:16
Nelson 67 67 41N18'36 81w03'06 5:24:12
Nelsonville 5 27 39N27'31 82w13'55 5:28:56
Neptune 54 34 40N36'11 84w29'30 5:37:58
Nettle Lake 86 34 41N40'45 84w43'24 5:38:54
Nevada 88 32 40N49'09 83w07'50 5:32:31
Neville 13 34 38N48'36 84w12'44 5:36:51
New Albany 25 27 40N04'52 82w48'32 5:31:14
New Albany 50 67 40N56'32 80w50'10 5:23:21
New Alexander 15 67 40N45 81w02 5:24:08
New Alexandria 41 67 40N17'26 80w40'46 5:22:43
New Antioch 14 34 39N24'26 83w44'46 5:34:59
Newark 45 92 40N03'29 82w24'05 5:29:36
New Athens 34 21 40N11'05 80w59'45 5:23:59
New Baltimore 31 34 39N15'53 84w40'03 5:38:40
New Baltimore 76 67 40N59'04 81w14'59 5:25:00
New Bavaria 35 34 41N12'13 84w10'06 5:36:40
New Bedford 16 5 40N26'41 81w45'55 5:27:04
Newbern 75 34 40N15'05 84w14'28 5:36:58
Newberry 55 34 40N08 84w23 5:37:32
New Bloomington 51 33 40N35'00 83w19'00 5:33:16
New Boston 73 34 38N45'08 82w56'13 5:31:45

New Bremen 6 34 40N26'13 84w22'47 5:37:31
New Buffalo 50 67 40N59'17 80w42'45 5:22:51
Newburgh Heights 18 26 41N27'00 81w39'49 5:26:39
New Burlington 14 34 39N33'43 83w57'56 5:35:52
New Burlington 31 34 39N15'34 84w33'26 5:38:14
Newbury 28 67 41N28 81w15 5:25:00
New California 80 34 40N09'22 83w14'12 5:32:57
New Carlisle 12 34 39N56'10 84w01'32 5:36:06
New Castle 7 21 39N53'27 81w04'33 5:24:18
Newcastle 16 5 40N20'06 82w09'57 5:28:40
New Castle 44 34 38N31 82w39 5:30:36
New Chicago 57 91 39N43'55 84w15'31 5:37:02
New Cleveland 69 34 41N01 84w03 5:36:12
Newcomerstown 79 12 40N16'20 81w36'22 5:26:25
New Concord 60 5 39N59'37 81w44'03 5:26:56
New Cumberland 41 44 40N30 80w36 5:22:24
New Cumberland 79 16 40N37 81w23 5:25:32
New Dover 80 33 40N14'48 83w18'17 5:33:13
Newell 41 67 40N15'37 80w50'11 5:23:21
Newell Run 84 20 39N23'13 81w16'04 5:25:04
New England 5 5 39N20'02 81w56'28 5:27:46
New England 76 54 40N47'46 81w30'06 5:26:00
Newfain 66 34 39N07'11 83w19'03 5:33:16
New Floodwood 5 27 39N24'49 82w11'17 5:28:45
New Franklin 76 67 40N47'54 81w05'32 5:24:22
New Garden 15 67 40N47'43 80w55'35 5:23:42
New Germany 29 34 39N46'29 84w04'48 5:36:19
New Guilford 16 5 40N17'27 82w09'42 5:28:39
New Hagerstown 10 21 40N26'36 81w11'14 5:24:45
New Hampshire 6 34 40N33'22 83w57'10 5:35:49
New Harmony 8 34 39N00'49 84w00'44 5:36:03
New Harrisburg 10 21 40N37'17 81w08'46 5:24:35
New Harrison 19 34 40N06'44 84w31'03 5:38:04
New Haven 31 34 39N16'32 84w44'27 5:38:58
New Haven 39 5 41N01'54 82w40'54 5:30:44
New Holland 65 34 39N33'14 83w15'25 5:33:02
New Hope 8 34 38N57'50 83w54'45 5:35:39
New Hope 68 34 39N47'30 84w42'48 5:38:51
New Jasper 29 34 39N39'15 83w49'10 5:35:17
New Jerusalem 46 33 40N22'26 83w39'27 5:34:38
Newkirk 9 34 39N24'20 84w47'16 5:39:09
New Knoxville 6 34 40N29'37 84w18'53 5:37:16
New Lebanon 57 34 39N44'43 84w23'06 5:37:32
New Lexington 64 109 39N42'50 82w12'31 5:28:50
New Lexington 68 34 39N45'36 84w32'02 5:38:08
New Liberty 15 67 40N51 80w32 5:22:08
New London 39 5 41N05 82w24 5:29:36
New Lyme 4 72 41N36'17 80w46'52 5:23:07
New Lyme Station 4 72 41N35'25 80w50'45 5:23:23
New Madison 19 34 39N58'04 84w42'33 5:38:50
Newman 51 27 40N27 83w11 5:32:44
Newman 76 54 40N49'52 81w33'55 5:26:16
Newmans 51 27 40N29'03 83w11'29 5:32:46
New Mansfield 5 27 39N19'26 82w13'12 5:28:53
New Market 36 34 39N08'07 83w40'08 5:34:41
New Marshfield 5 27 39N19 82w13 5:28:52
New Martinsburg 24 34 39N23'48 83w27'50 5:33:51
New Matamoras 84 20 39N31'28 81w04'02 5:24:16
New Miami 9 34 39N26'05 84w32'13 5:38:09
New Middleton 15 67 40N51'52 80w54'55 5:23:40
New Middletown 50 67 40N57 80w34 5:22:16
New Milford (Rootstown Sta) 67 67 41N06'17 81w12'53 5:24:52
New Moorefield 12 34 39N59'31 83w43'02 5:34:52
New Moscow 16 5 40N16 81w52 5:27:28
New Palestine 13 34 39N00'31 84w18'18 5:37:13
New Paris 68 34 39N51'25 84w47'36 5:39:10
New Petersburg 36 34 39N15'44 83w26'42 5:33:47
New Philadelphia 79 115 40N29'23 81w26'45 5:25:47
New Pittsburg 37 27 39N30'52 82w11'44 5:28:47
New Pittsburg 85 76 40N50'21 82w06'01 5:28:24
New Pittsburgh 39 5 40N59'45 82w43'52 5:30:55
New Plymouth 82 27 39N23'05 82w23'47 5:29:35
New Plymouth Heights 73 34 38N39 82w52 5:31:28
Newport 49 34 39N50'06 83w27'55 5:33:52
Newport 75 34 40N21 84w22 5:37:28
Newport 79 16 40N21'33 81w20'35 5:25:22
Newport 84 20 39N23'27 81w13'37 5:24:54
New Princeton 16 5 40N23'15 82w03'41 5:28:15
New Reading 64 16 39N48'33 82w21'00 5:29:24
New Richland 46 34 40N29'09 83w46'24 5:35:06
New Richmond 13 34 38N56'55 84w16'48 5:37:07
New Riegel 74 32 41N03'05 83w19'07 5:33:16
New Rochester 87 33 41N21'45 83w30'27 5:34:02
New Rome 25 34 39N57'06 83w08'32 5:32:34
New Rumley 34 11 40N24'06 81w01'52 5:24:07
New Salem 23 27 39N50'52 82w28'21 5:29:53
New Salisbury 15 67 40N33 80w43 5:22:52
New Somerset 41 67 40N28 80w36 5:22:24
New Springfield 50 67 40N55'02 80w36'23 5:22:26
New Stark 32 33 40N50 83w39 5:34:36
New Straitsville 64 27 39N34'40 82w14'16 5:28:57
New Strasburg 23 34 39N39'07 82w45'46 5:31:03
Newton Falls 78 58 41N11'18 80w58'42 5:23:55
Newtonsville 13 34 39N10'55 84w05'11 5:36:21
Newtown 31 34 39N07'28 84w21'42 5:37:27
New Town 37 34 39N31'15 82w10'15 5:28:41
Newtown 41 67 40N12 80w46 5:23:04
New Vienna 14 34 39N19'25 83w41'28 5:34:46
Newville 70 5 40N37'49 82w23'08 5:29:33
New Washington 17 32 40N57'44 82w51'16 5:31:25
New Waterford 15 61 40N50'42 80w36'53 5:22:28
New Way 45 27 40N09'15 82w34'25 5:30:18
New Weston 19 34 40N20'14 84w38'36 5:38:34
New Westville 68 34 39N49'21 84w47'33 5:39:10
New Winchester 17 33 40N43'08 82w55'09 5:31:41
Ney 20 34 41N22'52 84w31'22 5:38:05
Nicholsville 13 34 38N57'30 84w10'10 5:36:41
Nile 73 34 38N42 83w09 5:32:36
Niles 78 75 41N10'58 80w45'56 5:23:04
Niles Beach 48 31 41N41'11 83w22'12 5:33:29
Niles Junction 78 67 41N10'16 80w48'12 5:23:13
Nimishillen 76 67 40N51 81w16 5:25:04
Nimisila 77 67 40N56 81w38 5:26:32
Nineveh 19 34 40N02'56 84w32'43 5:38:11
Nipgen 71 36 39N11'28 83w08'58 5:32:36
Noble 18 67 41N36 81w31 5:26:04
Normandy Heights 9 34 39N22 84w33 5:38:12
Norris 55 34 39N58 84w20 5:37:20
Norristown 10 21 40N39'55 80w57'06 5:23:48
North 34 23 40N23 81w06 5:24:24
North Akron 77 2 41N06'28 81w30'38 5:26:03
Northampton 77 2 41N10 81w32 5:26:08
North Auburn 17 33 40N58'03 82w47'32 5:31:10
North Baltimore 87 33 41N10'58 83w40'42 5:34:43
North Bend 31 34 39N09'09 84w44'53 5:39:00
North Benton 50 67 40N59'06 81w00'46 5:24:03
North Benton Station 67 67 40N59'36 81w01'18 5:24:05
North Berne 23 27 39N42'20 82w29'55 5:30:00
North Bloomfield 78 67 41N27'51 80w52'07 5:23:28
North Brewster 76 67 40N43'14 81w35'51 5:26:23
North Bristol 78 67 41N24'32 80w52'09 5:23:29
Northbrook 31 34 39N14'47 84w35'01 5:38:20
North Canton 76 43 40N52'33 81w24'09 5:25:37
North Clippinger 31 34 39N11 84w22 5:37:28
North College Hill 31 88 39N13'06 84w33'03 5:38:12
North Condit 21 27 40N15 82w51 5:31:24
North Creek 69 34 41N08'47 84w13'10 5:36:53
North Dayton 57 91 39N47 84w10 5:36:40
North Eaton 47 42 41N18'48 81w58'53 5:27:56
North Fairfield 39 5 41N06'14 82w36'43 5:30:27
North Feesburg 8 34 38N55 83w59 5:35:56
Northfield 77 67 41N20'42 81w31'43 5:26:07
Northfield Center 77 58 41N18'51 81w32'22 5:26:09
North Findlay 32 33 41N06'34 83w39'01 5:34:36
North Folk Village 71 34 39N21 83w00 5:32:00
North Fork Village 71 34 39N20'09 83w01'45 5:32:07
North Georgetown 15 67 40N51 80w59 5:23:56
North Greenfield 46 33 40N22'39 83w35'22 5:34:21
North Hampton 12 34 39N59 83w56 5:35:44
North Hill 77 2 41N06 81w31 5:26:04
North Hills 37 34 39N32 82w24 5:29:36
North Hills Estates 31 88 39N12'43 84w31'26 5:38:06
North Houston 75 34 40N15 84w20 5:37:20
North Industry 76 43 40N44'20 81w22'01 5:25:28
North Jackson 50 67 41N06'00 80w51'27 5:23:26
North Kenova 44 37 38N26 82w33 5:30:12
North Kingman 14 34 39N30'38 83w56'35 5:35:46
North Kingsville 4 52 41N54'21 80w41'26 5:22:46
Northland 25 107 40N04 82w58 5:31:52
North Lawrence 76 67 40N50'23 81w37'43 5:26:31
North Lewisburg 11 34 40N13'23 83w33'27 5:34:14
North Liberty 42 5 40N32'15 82w24'30 5:29:38
North Lima 50 61 40N56'54 80w39'33 5:22:38
North Madison 43 67 41N48'07 81w02'57 5:24:12
North Monroeville 39 5 41N15 82w42 5:30:48
Northmoor 57 34 39N51 84w18 5:37:12
North Moreland 73 34 38N45'47 82w56'10 5:31:45
North Mount Vernon 42 5 40N24'22 82w28'39 5:29:55
North Olmsted 18 50 41N24'56 81w55'25 5:27:42
North Perry 43 67 41N47 81w09 5:24:36
North Randall 18 67 41N26'05 81w31'33 5:26:06
North Richmond 4 72 41N42'52 80w34'08 5:22:17
Northridge 12 39 39N59'30 83w46'43 5:35:07
Northridge 57 91 39N48'27 84w11'49 5:36:47
North Ridgeville 47 67 41N22'13 82w02'43 5:28:11
North Robinson 17 27 40N47 82w51 5:31:24
North Royalton 18 67 41N18'49 81w43'29 5:26:54
North Sagamore Heights 31 34 39N12'46 84w24'30 5:37:38
North Salem 30 5 40N08'36 81w32'45 5:26:11
North Side 50 84 41N07'05 80w38'49 5:22:35
North Star 19 34 40N19'29 84w34'14 5:38:17
North Summit Shopping Center 77 67 41N19 81w30 5:26:00
North Uniontown 36 34 39N12 83w37 5:34:28
Northup 27 27 38N46'55 82w17'02 5:29:08
Northville 11 34 40N10'55 83w48'44 5:35:15
Northwest 25 107 40N03 83w05 5:32:20
Northwest 86 34 41N40 84w45 5:39:00
Northwood 46 33 40N28'22 83w43'57 5:34:56
Northwood 87 31 41N36'39 83w32'10 5:34:09
North Woodbury 59 95 40N40 82w30 5:30:00
North Zanesville 60 104 39N58'43 82w00'13 5:28:01
Norton 21 27 40N26'02 83w04'26 5:32:18
Norton 77 67 41N02 81w39 5:26:36
Norwalk 39 44 41N14'33 82w36'57 5:30:28
Norwich 60 5 39N59'06 81w47'30 5:27:10
Norwood 31 88 39N09'20 84w27'35 5:37:50
Norwood 84 20 39N25'09 81w26'00 5:25:44
Nottingham 34 21 40N15 81w10 5:24:40
Nova 3 44 41N01'44 82w18'17 5:29:13
Novelty 28 67 41N29'41 81w20'27 5:25:22
Nunda 42 5 40N32'07 82w21'37 5:29:26
Nutwood 78 67 41N18'40 80w38'11 5:22:33
Oak 56 20 39N44'28 80w56'23 5:23:46
Oakdale 5 27 39N31'18 82w05'39 5:28:23
Oakdale 31 34 39N12'40 84w36'21 5:38:25
Oakdale 57 91 39N41 84w09 5:36:36
Oakdale 76 54 40N48 81w31 5:26:04
Oakfield 64 27 39N39'33 82w06'58 5:28:28
Oakfield 78 67 41N24'32 80w51'00 5:23:24
Oakgrove 30 21 40N08'26 81w13'43 5:24:55
Oak Grove 84 20 39N26'55 81w28'00 5:25:52
Oak Harbor 62 93 41N30 83w09 5:32:36
Oak Hill 40 34 38N54 82w35 5:30:20
Oak Hill 42 5 40N24'51 82w14'28 5:28:58
Oak Knoll 51 98 40N33'40 83w08'45 5:32:35
Oakland 9 34 39N30'24 84w24'01 5:37:36
Oakland 14 34 39N28'58 83w54'46 5:35:39
Oakland 23 34 39N35'54 82w45'24 5:31:02
Oakland 40 34 39N05'03 82w42'47 5:30:51
Oakland Park 25 107 40N03 82w58 5:31:52
Oakley 31 88 39N09'13 84w25'30 5:37:42
Oakley Square 31 88 39N09'04 84w26'01 5:37:44
Oak Park 34 21 40N15'06 80w59'56 5:24:00
Oak Ridge 76 54 40N50'23 81w30'17 5:26:01
Oak Run 49 34 39N49 83w21 5:33:24
Oakshade 26 34 41N40'08 84w09'08 5:36:37
Oakthorpe 23 27 39N48'20 82w26'10 5:29:45
Oakview 2 90 40N41'38 84w12'37 5:36:50
Oakwood 18 67 41N23'09 81w29'20 5:25:57
Oakwood 57 91 39N43'31 84w10'27 5:36:42
Oakwood 63 34 41N05'44 84w22'50 5:37:31
Oberlin 47 46 41N17'38 82w13'03 5:28:52
Oberlin Beach 22 5 41N22'58 82w30'28 5:30:02
Obetz 25 107 39N52'44 82w57'03 5:31:48
Oceola 17 33 40N50'41 83w05'38 5:32:23
Oco 7 21 40N06'35 80w59'52 5:23:59
O'Connor Landing 46 33 40N31 83w44 5:34:56
O'Connor Point 46 34 40N29'48 83w51'08 5:35:25
Octa 24 34 39N36'14 83w36'47 5:34:27
Odell 30 5 40N09'03 81w28'37 5:25:54
Ogden 14 34 39N25'51 83w54'41 5:35:39
Ogontz 22 9 41N20'38 82w27'34 5:29:50
Ohio City 81 34 40N46'17 84w36'56 5:38:28
Ohio Furnace 73 34 38N36'10 82w47'05 5:31:08
Ohio Junction 7 15 40N06 80w44 5:22:56
Ohltown 50 67 41N07'42 80w47'07 5:23:08
Okeana 9 34 39N20'52 84w46'03 5:39:04
Oklahoma 68 34 39N47'11 84w38'02 5:38:32
Okolona 35 34 41N21'19 84w13'04 5:36:52
Old Fort 74 32 41N14 83w09 5:32:36
Old Gore 37 27 39N34'39 82w18'18 5:29:13
Old Plymouth Heights 73 34 38N39 82w52 5:31:28
Old Straitsville 64 27 39N35 82w14 5:28:56
Oldtown 29 34 39N43'49 83w56'16 5:35:45
Oldtown Flats 53 5 38N59'48 81w50'33 5:27:22
Old Washington 30 5 40N02'19 81w26'41 5:25:47

Old West End 48 31 41N40 83W33 5:34:12
Olena 39 5 41N09'16 82W32'28 5:30:10
Olive 61 5 39N45 81W31 5:26:04
Olive Branch 13 34 39N05'02 84W13'31 5:36:54
Olive Furnace 44 34 38N45'42 82W37'48 5:30:31
Olive Green 21 27 40N19'09 82W49'49 5:31:19
Olive Green 61 5 39N44'38 81W36'54 5:26:28
Oliver 1 34 38N54 83W30 5:34:00
Olivesburg 70 5 40N53'09 82W25'44 5:29:43
Olivett 7 21 40N01'19 81W08'17 5:24:33
Olmsted Falls 18 50 41N22'30 81W54'30 5:27:38
Olszeski 41 67 40N11'40 80W47'20 5:23:09
Omar 74 32 41N07'27 82W52'17 5:31:29
Omega 66 34 39N09'06 82W54'37 5:31:38
Oneida 9 34 39N28'42 84W23'25 5:37:34
Oneida 10 21 40N41'55 81W08'57 5:24:36
Ontario 70 95 40N45'34 82W35'25 5:30:22
Opperman 30 5 39N53'26 81W36'03 5:26:24
Oran 75 34 40N17'28 84W19'18 5:37:17
Orange 16 5 40N17'17 81W40'59 5:26:44
Orange 18 67 41N26'59 81W28'51 5:25:55
Orange 21 107 40N10'27 83W00'29 5:32:02
Orangeburg 68 34 39N50'19 84W44'49 5:38:59
Orangeville 78 67 41N20'21 80W31'09 5:22:05
Orbiston 37 34 39N29'08 82W10'07 5:28:40
Orchard Beach 22 5 41N24'23 82W24'34 5:29:38
Orchard Island 46 34 40N28'47 83W53'07 5:35:32
Orchard Park Heights 70 95 40N42 82W32 5:30:08
Oregon 48 30 41N38'37 83W29'13 5:33:57
Oregonia 83 34 39N27'03 84W05'46 5:36:23
Oreton 82 27 39N09'50 82W24'46 5:29:39
Oreville 37 27 39N35'05 82W16'08 5:29:05
Orient 65 34 39N48'10 83W09'07 5:32:36
Orland 82 27 39N22'58 82W25'26 5:29:42
Orpheus 40 34 38N57'47 82W27'30 5:29:50
Orrville 85 69 40N50'37 81W45'51 5:27:03
Orwell 4 60 41N32'06 80W52'06 5:23:28
Osborn Corners 77 67 41N12'06 81W40'44 5:26:43
Osceola 83 34 39N20'30 84W03'19 5:36:13
Osgood 19 34 40N20'23 84W29'43 5:37:59
Osnaburg 76 67 40N47 81W16 5:25:04
Ostrander 21 33 40N15'58 83W12'46 5:32:51
Otsego 60 5 40N07'17 81W45'54 5:27:04
Otsego 87 34 41N26'51 83W46'45 5:35:07
Ottawa 69 34 41N01'09 84W02'50 5:36:11
Ottawa Hills 48 31 41N39'51 83W38'36 5:34:34
Otter 80 33 40N16'33 83W25'09 5:33:41
Otterbein 19 34 39N56'45 84W40'18 5:38:41
Otterbein 83 34 39N26'46 84W16'41 5:37:07
Ottokee 26 34 41N36'08 84W08'04 5:36:32
Ottoville 69 34 40N55'56 84W20'20 5:37:21
Otway 73 34 38N51'59 83W11'15 5:32:45
Outville 45 27 39N59'42 82W35'45 5:30:23
Overlook 57 34 39N46 84W06 5:36:24
Overlook Hills 41 106 40N23'01 80W41'32 5:22:46
Overpeck 9 34 39N27'03 84W30'52 5:38:03
Overton 85 76 40N51'53 82W00'37 5:28:02
Owens 51 33 40N31'13 83W09'29 5:32:38
Owens Hill 60 5 39N55 82W01 5:28:04
Owensville 13 34 39N07'21 84W08'09 5:36:33
Owensville 73 34 38N51'04 83W02'25 5:32:10
Oxford 9 34 39N30'25 84W44'43 5:38:59
Ozark 56 20 39N49'36 81W04'55 5:24:20
Padanaram 4 72 41N39'13 80W32'13 5:22:09
Paddison Hills 31 34 39N04'50 84W21'38 5:37:27
Padua 54 34 40N25 84W46 5:39:04
Page Manor 57 34 39N45'57 84W06'35 5:36:26
Paget 21 27 40N19'15 83W00'45 5:32:03
Pagetown 59 27 40N21'26 82W49'06 5:31:16
Pageville 53 27 39N10'00 82W08'12 5:28:33
Paine Crossing 37 27 39N33'13 82W15'30 5:29:02
Painesville 43 46 41N43'28 81W14'45 5:24:59
Painesville-on-the-Lake 43 67 41N46'00 81W13'52 5:24:55
Painters Creek 19 34 40N02'08 84W28'10 5:37:53
Paintersville 29 34 39N35'08 83W49'11 5:35:17
Paint Valley 38 5 40N35'09 82W00'21 5:28:01
Palermo 10 21 40N29'24 81W09'17 5:24:37
Palestine 19 34 40N02'58 84W44'36 5:38:58
Palmyra 42 27 40N32'40 82W32'26 5:30:10
Palmyra 67 67 41N05'56 81W03'06 5:24:12
Palos 5 27 39N31'55 82W04'24 5:28:18
Pancoastburg 24 34 39N37'27 83W15'56 5:33:04
Pandora 69 34 40N56'53 83W57'40 5:35:51
Panhandle 41 67 40N21'31 80W52'08 5:23:29
Panhandle Corners 25 27 40N04'36 82W41'20 5:30:45
Pansy 14 34 39N20'35 83W57'09 5:35:49
Paradise 50 67 40N58'25 80W42'28 5:22:50
Paradise Hill 3 44 40N54 82W22 5:29:28
Paris 67 67 41N09'59 81W03'05 5:24:12
Paris 76 67 40N47'51 81W09'54 5:24:40
Parkdale 31 34 39N17 84W31 5:38:04
Parkertown 22 5 41N20'38 82W47'14 5:31:09
Park Layne 12 34 39N56 84W02 5:36:08
Parkman 28 67 41N22'14 81W03'55 5:24:16
Park Place 31 34 39N14'21 84W28'18 5:37:53
Park Ridge Acres 12 39 39N54'23 83W52'15 5:35:29
Parks Corner 43 67 41N36'40 81W19'42 5:25:19
Parks Mills 25 107 40N02'08 82W55'54 5:31:44
Parkview 18 67 41N25'43 81W52'10 5:27:29
Parkview Heights 31 88 39N12 84W32 5:38:08
Parlett 41 21 40N18'27 80W51'47 5:23:27
Parma 18 26 41N24'17 81W43'23 5:26:54
Parma Heights 18 26 41N23'24 81W45'35 5:27:02
Parral 79 16 40N33'40 81W29'50 5:25:59
Parrott 24 34 39N36'51 83W31'54 5:34:08
Pasadena 57 91 39N41 84W09 5:36:36
Pasco 75 34 40N17'00 84W06'03 5:36:24
Pataskala 45 27 39N59'44 82W40'28 5:30:42
Patmos 50 67 40N58'25 80W54'22 5:23:37
Patriot 27 34 38N46 82W23 5:29:32
Patten Mills 84 5 39N27'26 81W46'54 5:27:08
Patterson 33 33 40N46'50 83W31'33 5:34:06
Pattersonville 10 21 40N44 81W05 5:24:20
Pattin Addition 84 20 39N27 81W28 5:25:52
Pattonville 40 34 39N01'54 82W29'51 5:29:59
Pattytown 55 34 40N01'19 84W24'49 5:37:39
Paulding 63 34 41N08'17 84W34'50 5:38:19
Pavonia 70 95 40N45 82W31 5:30:04
Pawnee 52 73 41N04'03 82W04'37 5:28:18
Paxton 71 36 39N14 83W14 5:32:56
Payne 63 34 41N04'39 84W43'38 5:38:55
Paynes Corner 78 67 41N14'13 80W37'03 5:22:28
Pearl (Chili Station) 16 5 40N22'07 81W43'36 5:26:54
Pearlbrook 18 26 41N27 81W42 5:26:48
Pease 7 21 40N05 80W46 5:23:04
Pebble 66 34 39N08 83W08 5:32:32
Peck 66 34 39N09'22 83W00'59 5:32:04
Pecks Corners 43 67 41N35'02 81W20'57 5:25:24
Pedro 44 34 38N37'49 82W40'03 5:30:40
Peebles 1 34 38N56'56 83W24'21 5:33:37
Pee Pee 66 34 39N08 83W01 5:32:04
Pekin 10 21 40N43'01 81W07'21 5:24:29
Pekin 41 106 40N25'43 80W39'45 5:22:39
Pekin 83 34 39N30'10 84W11'58 5:36:48
Pemberton 75 34 40N17'41 84W01'57 5:36:08
Pemberville 87 32 41N24'39 83W27'40 5:33:51
Penfield 47 67 41N10'07 82W07'17 5:28:29
Penfield Junction 47 50 41N25'31 82W09'36 5:28:38
Peniel 27 34 38N48'14 82W32'02 5:30:08
Peninsula 77 67 41N14'28 81W33'10 5:26:13
Pennsville 58 5 39N34'31 81W51'20 5:27:25
Penn View 4 72 41N37 80W36 5:22:24
Peoli 79 16 40N13'38 81W26'19 5:25:45
Peoria 9 34 39N26'00 84W49'02 5:39:16
Peoria 80 33 40N18'50 83W26'45 5:33:47
Pepper Pike 18 67 41N28'42 81W27'50 5:25:51
Perintown 13 34 39N08 84W14 5:36:56
Perkins 22 5 41N24 82W42 5:30:48
Perkins Corners 50 84 41N06'11 80W42'42 5:22:51
Perry 43 46 41N45'37 81W08'28 5:24:34
Perry Addition 73 34 38N54'37 82W52'19 5:31:29
Perry Center 87 33 41N12'35 83W28'42 5:33:55
Perry Heights 76 54 40N47'43 81W28'25 5:25:54
Perrysburg 87 31 41N33'25 83W37'38 5:34:31
Perrysburg Heights 87 31 41N34 83W35 5:34:20
Perrysville 3 44 40N39'27 82W18'42 5:29:15
Perrysville 10 23 40N27'53 81W05'41 5:24:23
Perryton 45 5 40N08'40 82W12'04 5:28:48
Peru 39 5 41N10'12 82W38'33 5:30:34
Petersburg 10 21 40N34 81W05 5:24:20
Petersburg 40 34 38N59'23 82W44'40 5:30:59
Petersburg 50 67 40N54'45 80W31'50 5:22:07
Petersburgh 10 23 40N30'50 81W06'45 5:24:27
Petrea 40 34 39N04'24 82W36'03 5:30:24
Petroleum 78 45 41N12'04 80W32'13 5:22:09
Pettisville 26 34 41N31'50 84W13'47 5:36:55
Pfeiffer Station 33 5 39N31 81W18 5:25:12
Phalanx 78 46 41N15'39 80W58'44 5:23:55
Pharisburg 80 33 40N20'43 83W18'13 5:33:13
Pherson 65 34 39N39'21 83W07'11 5:32:29
Phillipsburg 57 34 39N54'16 84W24'06 5:37:36
Philo 60 5 39N51'40 81W54'25 5:27:38
Philothea 54 34 40N27'02 84W39'13 5:38:37
Phoneton 55 34 39N53'49 84W08'07 5:36:32
Pickaway 65 34 39N32 82W55 5:31:40
Pickerington 23 27 39N53'03 82W45'13 5:31:01
Pickrelltown 46 34 40N17'59 83W39'37 5:34:38
Piedmont 34 21 40N11 81W12 5:24:48
Pierce 13 34 39N02 84W16 5:37:04
Pierpont 4 72 41N44'57 80W34'07 5:22:16
Pigeon Run 76 54 40N44'56 81W34'23 5:26:18
Pigeye 55 34 39N55'19 84W18'43 5:37:15
Pigtown 10 103 40N43'49 81W03'13 5:24:13
Piketon 66 34 39N04'05 83W00'52 5:32:03
Pikeville 19 34 39N21 83W24 5:33:36
Pine Gap 1 34 38N57'24 83W18'51 5:33:15
Pine Grove 40 34 39N10'17 82W42'00 5:30:48
Pine Grove 44 34 38N36'29 82W42'18 5:30:49
Pinegrove 53 5 39N09'50 81W49'34 5:27:18
Pinehurst 84 20 39N27 81W28 5:25:52
Pine Valley 41 67 40N12'15 80W46'03 5:23:04
Piney Fork 41 67 40N15 80W50 5:23:20
Pinhook 70 5 40N40'56 82W22'42 5:29:31
Pink 73 34 38N45'09 83W15'50 5:33:03
Pinkerman 73 34 38N50'18 82W46'11 5:31:05
Pioneer 86 34 41N40'48 84W33'11 5:38:13
Pipesville 42 5 40N21'02 82W18'41 5:29:15
Piqua 55 34 40N08'41 84W14'33 5:36:58
Pisgah 9 34 39N19'06 84W22'08 5:37:29
Pitchin 12 39 39N50'34 83W45'45 5:35:03
Pitsburg 19 34 39N59 84W29 5:37:56
Pitt 88 32 40N46 83W15 5:33:00
Pittsburgh Junction 34 21 40N21 81W00 5:24:00
Pittsfield 47 67 41N14'13 82W13'09 5:28:53
Placid Meadows 31 88 39N06'04 84W36'35 5:38:26
Plain City 49 34 40N06'27 83W16'03 5:33:04
Plainfield 16 5 40N12'34 81W43'11 5:26:53
Plainview 56 20 39N40'44 81W06'20 5:24:25
Plainville 31 34 39N08'31 84W21'36 5:37:26
Plankton 17 33 40N57 83W11 5:32:44
Planktown 70 5 40N57'27 82W35'09 5:30:21
Plano 24 34 39N29'27 83W17'12 5:33:09
Plantation Acres 31 88 39N12 84W32 5:38:08
Plants 53 5 38N58 81W55 5:27:40
Plantsville 58 5 39N27'08 81W52'33 5:27:30
Plattsburg 12 34 39N53'46 83W36'42 5:34:27
Plattsville 75 34 40N13'56 84W04'39 5:36:19
Playhouse Square 18 26 41N30 81W41 5:26:44
Pleasant 25 34 39N52 83W11 5:32:44
Pleasant Bend 35 34 41N10'49 84W11'24 5:36:46
Pleasant City 30 5 39N54'13 81W32'44 5:26:11
Pleasant Corners 25 107 39N50'38 83W07'37 5:32:30
Pleasant Grove 60 5 39N57'07 81W57'33 5:27:50
Pleasant Grove 71 34 39N13'43 83W07'56 5:32:32
Pleasant Heights 15 105 40N37'56 80W35'21 5:22:21
Pleasant Hill 5 27 39N20 82W05 5:28:20
Pleasant Hill 23 27 39N40'17 82W30'29 5:30:02
Pleasant Hill 41 106 40N25'12 80W39'31 5:22:38
Pleasant Hill 55 34 40N03'06 84W20'40 5:37:23
Pleasant Hills 31 34 39N14'09 84W31'30 5:38:06
Pleasant Home 85 62 40N54'56 82W06'33 5:28:26
Pleasanton 5 27 39N14'26 82W05'36 5:28:22
Pleasant Plain 83 34 39N16'46 84W06'44 5:36:27
Pleasant Ridge 31 34 39N11'00 84W25'29 5:37:42
Pleasant Run 31 34 39N17'59 84W33'49 5:38:15
Pleasant Run Farms 31 34 39N17 84W31 5:38:04
Pleasant Valley 16 5 40N14'44 81W51'15 5:27:25
Pleasant Valley 18 26 41N21'34 81W41'16 5:26:45
Pleasant Valley 66 34 39N03'40 83W05'35 5:32:22
Pleasant Valley 71 34 39N22'21 83W02'25 5:32:10
Pleasant View 24 34 39N39'54 83W38'00 5:34:32
Pleasant View 76 43 40N49'52 81W20'30 5:25:22
Pleasantville 23 27 39N48'35 82W31'20 5:30:05
Plumwood 49 34 40N00'29 83W24'56 5:33:40
Plymouth 4 46 41N49'33 80W44'46 5:22:59
Plymouth 39 27 40N59'44 82W40'02 5:30:40
Plymouth Center 4 46 41N50'13 80W45'15 5:23:01
Poast Town 9 34 39N32'50 84W23'00 5:37:32
Poast Town Heights 9 34 39N35'01 84W23'00 5:37:32
Poetown 8 34 38N55 83W59 5:35:56
Point 25 107 39N56 83W03 5:32:12
Point Isabel 13 34 38N53'40 84W07'54 5:36:32
Point Place 48 31 41N43'08 83W28'46 5:33:55
Point Pleasant 13 34 38N53'40 84W14'02 5:36:56
Point Rock 53 27 39N08'29 82W17'48 5:29:11
Pointview 50 67 40N56'40 80W53'51 5:23:35
Poland 50 84 41N01'27 80W36'54 5:22:28
Poland Center 50 84 41N01'26 80W34'03 5:22:16
Polk 3 44 40N56'40 82W12'56 5:28:52
Polkadotte 44 34 38N35'03 82W22'27 5:29:30
Polo 55 34 40N10'56 84W21'21 5:37:25
Pomeroy 53 97 39N01'39 82W02'02 5:28:08
Pond Run 73 34 38N39'49 83W07'36 5:32:30
Pontiac 39 5 41N11'20 82W43'30 5:30:54
Poplar Grove 66 34 39N02'38 83W18'18 5:33:13
Poplar Ridge 19 34 40N04'31 84W32'44 5:38:11
Portage 87 33 41N19'36 83W39'03 5:34:36
Portage Lakes 77 2 41N00 81W32 5:26:08
Port Clinton 62 93 41N30'43 82W56'16 5:31:45
Porter 27 27 38N55 82W18 5:29:12
Porterfield 84 20 39N18 81W34 5:26:16
Portersville 64 27 39N40'29 82W01'52 5:28:07
Port Homer 41 67 40N28 80W36 5:22:24
Port Jefferson 75 34 40N19'43 84W05'40 5:36:23
Portland 53 5 39N06 81W46 5:27:04
Portsmouth 73 94 38N43'54 82W59'52 5:31:59
Port Union 9 34 39N19'58 84W27'48 5:37:51
Port Washington 79 16 40N20 81W31 5:26:04
Port William 14 34 39N33'07 83W47'11 5:35:09
Possum Woods 12 39 39N55 83W48 5:35:12
Postboy 79 12 40N13'37 81W35'04 5:26:20
Post Town 57 34 39N46'51 84W18'42 5:37:15
Potsdam 55 34 39N57'48 84W25'03 5:37:40
Pottersburg 80 33 40N15'58 83W30'03 5:34:00
Pottery Addition 41 106 40N24'08 80W37'31 5:22:30
Poulton 56 20 39N36'27 81W07'17 5:24:29
Powell 16 5 40N18'21 81W42'07 5:26:48
Powell 21 32 40N09'28 83W04'31 5:32:18

Powellsville 73
34 38N40'00 82w47'01 5:31:08
Powers 26 34 41N41 84w20 5:37:20
Powhatan Point 7
21 39N51'36 80w48'56 5:23:16
Powhattan 11 34 40N02'32 83w41'24 5:34:46
Pratts 32 33 40N55'21 83w30'16 5:34:01
Pratts Fork 5 27 39N11'32 82w01'02 5:28:04
Prattsville 82 27 39N14'19 82w23'29 5:29:34
Pravo 41 67 40N31'09 80w49'58 5:23:20
Prentiss 69 34 41N09'09 84w01'06 5:36:04
Preston Addition 73
34 38N53'17 82w57'39 5:31:51
Price Hill 31 88 39N06'36 84w34'33 5:38:18
Pricetown 36 34 39N08'35 83w48'07 5:35:12
Pricetown 78 67 41N06 81w00 5:24:00
Pride 71 34 39N14'01 82w53'45 5:31:35
Primrose 86 34 41N40'49 84w26'13 5:37:45
Princeton 9 34 39N23'18 84w27'14 5:37:49
Pritchard 67 67 41N08'03 81w00'30 5:24:02
Proctor 67 67 41N10 81w16 5:25:04
Proctorville 44
37 38N26'13 82w22'38 5:29:31
Prospect 51 27 40N27'01 83w11'19 5:32:45
Providence 48 34 41N25'06 83w52'23 5:35:30
Provident 7 21 40N05'41 80w54'33 5:23:38
Provincial Point 31
34 39N07 84w21 5:37:24
Public Square 18
26 41N27 81w44 5:26:56
Pulaski 86 34 41N30'38 84w30'28 5:38:02
Pulaskiville 59
27 40N32'02 82w42'37 5:30:50
Pulse 36 34 39N02 83w56 5:35:44
Pultney 7 21 40N01 80w48 5:23:12
Puntenneyville 1
34 38N40 83w23 5:33:32
Puritan 82 27 39N09'31 82w29'21 5:29:57
Puritas Park 18
26 41N26 81w48 5:27:12
Purity 45 5 40N12'01 82w20'19 5:29:21
Pusheta 6 34 40N31 84w10 5:36:40
Put-in-Bay 62 93 41N39'15 82w49'15 5:31:17
Putnam Place 84
20 39N27 81w28 5:25:52
Pymatuning Park 4
72 41N37 80w36 5:22:24
Pyrmont 57 34 39N48'43 84w27'39 5:37:51
Pyro 40 34 38N55'27 82w31'57 5:30:08
Quaker City 30 5 39N58'12 81w17'58 5:25:12
Quaker Hill 50 67 40N55 81w03 5:24:12
Qualey 84 20 39N21'17 81w45'31 5:27:02
Queen Acres 9 34 39N23'41 84w38'23 5:38:34
Queensboro 10 21 40N31'05 81w13'18 5:24:53
Quincy 46 34 40N17'57 83w58'08 5:35:53
Raab Corners 48
34 41N39'28 83w49'06 5:35:16
Raccoon 27 34 38N55 82w24 5:29:36
Raccoon Island 27
27 38N43'10 82w11'46 5:28:47
Racine 53 5 38N58'16 81w54'52 5:27:39
Radcliff 82 27 39N08'27 82w22'37 5:29:30
Radio Heights 15
105 40N38 80w35 5:22:20
Radnor 21 33 40N23'03 83w09'03 5:32:36
Ragersville 79 16 40N27'09 81w37'35 5:26:30
Raiders Run 31 34 39N12'59 84w22'09 5:37:29
Rainbow 84 20 39N29'40 81w27'56 5:25:52
Rain Rock 45 5 40N11'34 82w17'23 5:29:10
Rainsboro 36 34 39N13'12 83w25'20 5:33:41
Ramsey 41 67 40N11'34 80w50'01 5:23:20
Randall Terrace 71
34 39N19'41 83w00'55 5:32:04
Randle 16 5 40N18'48 81w56'00 5:27:44
Randolph 67 67 41N01'58 81w14'55 5:25:00
Randolph Landing 53
5 39N07'33 81w44'52 5:26:59
Range 49 34 39N43'55 83w25'29 5:33:42
Ransom 68 34 39N44'39 84w34'51 5:38:19
Rappsburg 44 34 38N36'59 82w24'20 5:29:37
Rarden 73 34 38N55'20 83w14'33 5:32:58
Ratchford 40 34 39N07'15 82w30'21 5:30:01
Ratcliffburg 82
34 39N15'46 82w40'53 5:30:44
Rathbone 21 27 40N11'47 83w08'43 5:32:35
Rathbone 84 20 39N26'19 81w27'39 5:25:51
Rathbone Heights 84
20 39N27 81w28 5:25:52
Ravenna 67 46 41N09'27 81w14'32 5:24:58
Rawson 32 34 40N57'32 83w47'03 5:35:08
Ray 82 34 39N12'13 82w41'01 5:30:44
Rayland 41 67 40N10'57 80w41'29 5:22:46
Raymond 80 33 40N20'05 83w27'57 5:33:52
Rays Corners 4 72 41N41'00 80w46'51 5:23:07
Rays Corners 78
45 41N14'14 80w45'57 5:23:04
Reading 15 67 40N50'06 81w01'53 5:24:08
Reading 31 34 39N13'25 84w26'32 5:37:46
Recker Heights 55
34 40N10 84w16 5:37:04
Recovery 54 34 40N26 84w46 5:39:04
Red Bank 31 34 39N08'08 84w23'59 5:37:36
Redbird 43 67 41N48 81w04 5:24:16
Redbush 84 20 39N16'29 81w42'02 5:26:48
Red Coach Farm 57
91 39N41 84w09 5:36:36
Red Diamond 82 27 39N15'14 82w25'46 5:29:43
Redfield 64 27 39N47'18 82w10'07 5:28:40
Red Fox 67 67 41N10 81w21 5:25:24
Redhaw 3 44 40N53'51 82w09'23 5:28:38
Red Lion 83 34 39N29'29 84w14'59 5:37:00
Redoak 8 34 38N48'23 83w47'32 5:35:10
Red River 19 34 40N04'48 84w26'55 5:37:48
Redtown 5 27 39N27'57 82w05'36 5:28:22
Reed 74 32 41N07 82w52 5:31:28
Reeds 8 34 38N46'58 83w54'34 5:35:38
Reedsburg 85 76 40N48'31 82w06'25 5:28:26
Reeds Mill 41 106 40N21'36 80w44'55 5:23:00
Reedsville 53 5 39N07'17 81w44'52 5:26:59
Reedtown 74 32 41N09'07 82w50'50 5:31:23
Reedurban 76 43 40N47'40 81w26'13 5:25:45
Reese 25 107 39N51'58 82w57'10 5:31:49
Reesville 14 34 39N28'56 83w40'37 5:34:42
Reform 45 5 40N08'12 82w15'01 5:29:00
Regina Heights 57
91 39N48'54 84w16'18 5:37:05
Rehm 66 34 39N03'50 82w57'40 5:31:51
Rehoboth 64 27 39N44'37 82w11'39 5:28:47
Reily 9 34 39N26'01 84w45'40 5:39:03
Reinersville 58 5 39N41'12 81w39'40 5:26:39
Relief 84 20 39N35'20 81w41'19 5:26:45
Reminderville 77
67 41N20'45 81w23'43 5:25:35
Remington 31 34 39N13'41 84w19'17 5:37:17
Remsen Corners 52
67 41N11'19 81w44'31 5:26:58
Rendcomb Junction 31
34 39N07'48 84w24'26 5:37:38
Rendville 64 27 39N37'10 82w05'28 5:28:22
Renick 71 34 39N17'54 82w57'14 5:31:49
Renick Junction 71
34 39N18'47 82w56'01 5:31:44
Reno 84 20 39N22'22 81w23'45 5:25:35
Reno Beach 48 30 41N39'48 83w16'10 5:33:05
Renrock 61 5 39N45'29 81w40'22 5:26:41
Rensselaer Park 31
88 39N12 84w29 5:37:56
Republic 74 32 41N07'19 83w00'57 5:32:04
Resaca 49 34 40N02'58 83w23'17 5:33:33
Residence Park 57
91 39N45'18 84w15'44 5:37:03
Revenge 23 27 39N36'12 82w39'07 5:30:36
Rexford 34 21 40N18'59 80w56'51 5:23:47
Reynolds 43 67 41N39'21 81w22'38 5:25:31
Reynoldsburg 25
27 39N57'17 82w48'44 5:31:15
Reynolds Corners 48
31 41N39 83w41 5:34:44
Rhodesdale 41 67 40N11 80w41 5:22:44
Rialto 9 34 39N20 84w25 5:37:40
Rice 69 34 41N09'03 84w17'40 5:37:11
Rice 72 30 41N26 83w06 5:32:24
Riceland 85 62 40N51 81w46 5:27:04
Rices Mills 78 67 41N29'28 80w44'15 5:22:57
Richey 81 34 40N53'39 84w38'53 5:38:36
Richfield 77 67 41N14'23 81w38'18 5:26:33
Richfield Center 48
34 41N41'08 83w49'03 5:35:16
Richfield Heights 77
67 41N12'14 81w37'50 5:26:31
Rich Hill 42 27 40N18 82w41 5:30:44
Rich Hill 60 5 39N52 81w47 5:27:08
Richland 46 33 40N31 83w44 5:34:56
Richland 82 34 39N11'13 82w35'51 5:30:23
Richland Furnace 82
34 39N11'11 82w35'46 5:30:23
Richland Meetinghouse 30
5 39N58'04 81w16'02 5:25:04
Richmond 41 68 40N26'00 80w46'19 5:23:05
Richmond Center 4
72 41N40'49 80w34'07 5:22:16
Richmond Dale 71
34 39N12'07 82w48'50 5:31:15
Richmond Heights 18
67 41N33'10 81w30'37 5:26:02
Richville 76 43 40N45'04 81w28'41 5:25:55
Richwood 80 33 40N25'35 83w17'49 5:33:11
Rickard Acres 9
34 39N33'18 84w21'58 5:37:28
Rickenbacker Air Force Base 25
108 39N49 82w57 5:31:48
Ridgefield 39 5 41N15 82w41 5:30:44
Ridgeland 40 34 39N00'49 82w31'21 5:30:05
Ridgeton 17 33 40N53'59 82w56'42 5:31:47
Ridgeview 47 42 41N22 82w06 5:28:24
Ridgeville 35 34 41N27 84w17 5:37:08
Ridgeville 83 34 39N31'43 84w10'37 5:36:42
Ridgeville Corners 35
34 41N26'16 84w15'27 5:37:02
Ridgeway 33 33 40N30'50 83w34'22 5:34:17
Ridgewood 60 5 39N55 82w01 5:28:04
Ridgewood Heights 57
91 39N44'48 84w16'12 5:37:05
Riggs 4 72 41N48'16 80w32'20 5:22:09
Rigrish 73 34 38N46 82w59 5:31:56
Rigrish Addition 73
34 38N46'41 82w51'16 5:31:25
Rimer 69 34 40N53'04 84w12'41 5:36:51
Rinard Mills 56
20 39N35 81w09 5:24:36
Ringgold 58 5 39N35'25 81w58'47 5:27:55
Rio Grande 27 34 38N52'46 82w22'50 5:29:31
Ripley 8 34 38N44'44 83w50'42 5:35:23
Risingsun 87 32 41N16'10 83w25'30 5:33:42
Rittenours 71 34 39N12'59 82w50'34 5:31:22
Rittman 85 46 40N58'41 81w46'56 5:27:08
River Corners 52
73 41N06'23 82w05'41 5:28:23
Riverdale 66 34 39N00'31 83w03'47 5:32:15
River Edge 18 67 41N25 81w51 5:27:24
Riverlea 25 107 40N04'55 83w01'31 5:32:06
Riverside 31 88 39N04'39 84w36'11 5:38:25
Riverside 57 91 39N47 84w07 5:36:28
Riverside Park 79
16 40N22'46 81w24'11 5:25:37
River Styx 52 73 41N08 81w52 5:27:28
Riverview 7 21 40N03'28 80w44'07 5:22:56
Riverview 60 104 39N58'40 81w59'01 5:27:56
Riverview 84 20 39N22'04 81w32'02 5:26:08
Riverview Heights 31
88 39N03'09 84w24'11 5:37:37
Riviera Park 66
34 39N06'07 83w01'23 5:32:06
Rix Mills 60 5 39N55'27 81w44'47 5:26:59
Roachester 83 34 39N21'24 84w05'49 5:36:23
Roachton 87 31 41N31'20 83w39'45 5:34:39
Roads 40 34 39N04'52 82w32'17 5:30:09
Roanoke 79 16 40N24'35 81w21'09 5:25:25
Roberts 60 5 39N52'37 82w05'22 5:28:21
Robertsburg 21 27 40N25'27 83w09'43 5:32:39
Robertsville 76
67 40N45'47 81w11'23 5:24:46
Robins 30 5 39N57'19 81w30'48 5:26:03
Robtown 65 34 39N43'01 83w03'36 5:32:14
Robyville 41 21 40N12'25 80w52'46 5:23:31
Rochester 11 5 39N49'51 81w31'25 5:26:06
Rochester 47 67 41N07'35 82w18'19 5:29:13
Rochester Place 87
31 41N38 83w29 5:33:56
Rock 79 16 40N18'18 81w21'44 5:25:27
Rockaway 74 32 41N04'59 83w03'15 5:32:13
Rockbridge 37 34 39N34'47 82w31'20 5:30:05
Rock Camp 15 67 40N41'38 80w39'46 5:22:39
Rock Camp 44 34 38N31'47 82w32'55 5:30:12
Rock Creek 4 72 41N39'37 80w51'39 5:23:27
Rock Cut 60 13 40N04'04 81w58'36 5:27:54
Rockdale 9 34 39N25'57 84w27'19 5:37:49
Rockford 54 34 40N41'16 84w38'48 5:38:35
Rockford 79 16 40N28'37 81w18'31 5:25:14
Rock Haven Park 25
5 40N03'23 82w13'46 5:28:55
Rock Hill 7 21 40N08'20 81w06'19 5:24:25
Rockland 84 20 39N16'52 81w36'22 5:26:25
Rock Mill 23 27 39N44'58 82w42'45 5:30:51
Rock Mills 24 34 39N26'35 83w24'33 5:33:38
Rockport 2 34 40N52'20 84w00'02 5:36:00
Rock Springs 53
97 39N03'36 82w00'58 5:28:04
Rockville 1 34 38N37'01 83w16'18 5:33:05
Rockville 76 54 40N41'24 81w30'36 5:26:02
Rock Way 12 39 39N55'39 83w52'43 5:35:31
Rockwood 44 37 38N25'51 82w26'20 5:29:45
Rocky Fork 45 5 40N09'46 82w17'29 5:29:10
Rocky Hill 40 34 38N59'20 82w32'42 5:30:11
Rocky Ridge 62 93 41N32'00 83w12'45 5:32:51
Rocky River 18 26 41N28'32 81w50'22 5:27:21
Rodney 27 27 38N50'57 82w18'15 5:29:13
Rogers 15 67 40N47'29 80w37'35 5:22:30
Rokeby Lock 58 5 39N43'55 81w54'19 5:27:37
Rolandus 53 5 38N57'50 81w49'30 5:27:18
Rollersville 72
32 41N20'27 83w22'42 5:33:31
Rolling Knolls Estate 31
34 39N12'27 84w25'20 5:37:41
Rolling Mill Park 9
34 39N30 84w23 5:37:32
Rome 4 72 41N36'17 80w51'56 5:23:28
Rome 21 27 40N14'47 82w54'42 5:31:39
Rome 44 37 38N26'45 82w21'50 5:29:27
Rome 70 5 40N55'35 82w31'49 5:30:07
Rome Station 4 72 41N36 80w52 5:23:28
Romohr Acres 13
34 39N08'18 84w17'23 5:37:10
Roosevelt 57 91 39N45 84w15 5:37:00
Rootstown 67 67 41N05'56 81w14'34 5:24:58
Roscoe 16 5 40N16 81w52 5:27:28
Rose 10 21 40N36 81w16 5:25:04
Rosedale 20 34 41N17'28 84w41'25 5:38:46
Rosedale 49 34 40N04'41 83w27'18 5:33:49
Rose Farm 64 5 39N44'09 82w04'41 5:28:19
Rose Hill 19 34 40N18'31 84w43'32 5:38:54
Roseland 70 95 40N47'19 82w32'34 5:30:10
Rose Lawn 9 34 39N31'46 84w22'32 5:37:30
Roselawn 31 88 39N11'42 84w27'45 5:37:51
Roselms 63 34 41N01'10 84w25'09 5:37:41
Rosemont 50 67 41N03'48 80w53'12 5:23:33
Rosemoor 24 34 39N37'40 83w40'01 5:34:40
Rosemount 73 34 38N47'10 82w58'45 5:31:55
Roseville 60 5 39N48'26 82w04'17 5:28:17
Rosewood 11 34 40N13'08 83w57'39 5:35:51
Roslyn 57 91 39N41 84w09 5:36:36
Ross 9 34 39N18'44 84w39'02 5:38:36
Rossburg 19 34 40N16'44 84w38'15 5:38:33
Rosseau 58 5 39N34'25 81w56'49 5:27:47
Rossford 87 31 41N36'35 83w33'52 5:34:15
Rossmoyne 31 34 39N12'49 84w23'13 5:37:33
Rossville 9 34 39N25 84w35 5:38:20
Rossville 55 34 40N09'25 84w14'21 5:36:57
Roswell 79 16 40N28'33 81w20'59 5:25:24
Round Bottom 56
20 39N44'06 80w58'10 5:23:53
Roundhead 33 33 40N33'34 83w50'07 5:35:20
Rousculp 2 90 40N42 84w08 5:36:32
Rowenton 4 72 41N40'49 80w43'22 5:22:53
Rowlesville 27 27 39N00'35 82w17'03 5:29:08
Rowsburg 3 44 40N51'31 82w09'21 5:28:37
Roxabell 71 34 39N23'05 83w11'16 5:32:45
Roxanna 29 34 39N34'57 84w00'58 5:36:04
Roxbury 58 5 39N31'22 81w44'54 5:27:00
Royalton 23 27 39N43'39 82w46'00 5:31:04
Royersville 44 34 38N36'38 82w40'38 5:30:43
Rubyville 73 34 38N49'30 82w55'48 5:31:43
Rudolph 87 33 41N17'52 83w40'12 5:34:41
Ruggles 3 44 41N01'46 82w23'33 5:29:34
Ruggles Beach 22
5 41N22'55 82w28'31 5:29:54
Rumley 34 11 40N23 81w01 5:24:04
Rumley 75 34 40N24'49 84w14'36 5:36:58
Runnymede 9 34 39N30 84w23 5:37:32
Rupels 71 34 39N15'07 82w52'14 5:31:29
Rupert 49 34 39N52'57 83w21'12 5:33:25
Rural 13 34 38N46'42 84w05'22 5:36:21
Ruraldale 60 5 39N46'55 81w50'38 5:27:23
Rush 79 16 40N18'38 81w22'05 5:25:28
Rushmore 69 34 40N52'27 84w15'12 5:37:01
Rush Run 41 67 40N13'54 80w40'50 5:22:43
Rushsylvania 46
33 40N27'41 83w40'12 5:34:41
Rushtown 73 34 38N49'58 83w01'12 5:32:05
Rushville 23 27 39N45'52 82w25'54 5:29:44
Rushville 53 5 39N07'26 81w45'37 5:27:02
Russell 28 67 41N28 81w21 5:25:24
Russell 36 34 39N13'10 83w43'43 5:34:55
Russell 59 27 40N30'58 82w50'08 5:31:21
Russell Center 28
67 41N27'45 81w20'27 5:25:22
Russell Heights 15
105 40N35 80w39 5:22:36
Russells 60 5 39N55'23 82w01'56 5:28:08
Russells Point 46
34 40N28'16 83w53'34 5:35:34
Russellville 8 34 38N51'59 83w47'13 5:35:09
Russia 75 34 40N14'04 84w24'34 5:37:38
Rutland 53 27 39N02'43 82w07'50 5:28:31
Ryan 48 31 41N38'43 83w29'41 5:33:59
Rye Beach 22 5 41N24 82w34 5:30:16
Sabina 14 34 39N29'19 83w38'13 5:34:33
Sagamore Hills 77
67 41N19 81w34 5:26:16

Sahara Sands 76 54 40N48 81w31 5:26:04
Saint Albans 45 27 40N05 82w36 5:30:24
Saint Bernard 31 88 39N10'01 84w29'55 5:38:00
Saint Charles 9 34 39N23'29 84w44'33 5:38:58
Saint Clairsville 7 22 40N04'50 80w54'01 5:23:36
Saint Henry 54 34 40N25'03 84w38'23 5:38:34
Saint Joe 7 21 40N01'13 80w48'15 5:23:13
Saint Johns 6 34 40N33'21 84w05'01 5:36:20
Saint Johns (Maria Stein PO) 54 34 40N24'27 84w28'26 5:37:54
Saint Joseph 54 34 40N25'35 84w44'22 5:38:57
Saint Joseph 67 67 41N01'38 81w17'58 5:25:12
Saint Joseph 86 34 41N28 84w45 5:39:00
Saint Louisville 45 5 40N10'22 82w25'08 5:29:41
Saint Martin 8 34 39N12'52 83w53'36 5:35:34
Saint Marys 6 34 40N32'32 84w23'22 5:37:33
Saint Paris 11 34 40N07'42 83w57'35 5:35:50
Saint Pauls 65 34 39N44'50 82w54'46 5:31:39
Saint Peters 54 34 40N27'01 84w44'46 5:38:59
Saint Rosa 54 34 40N24'27 84w31'00 5:38:04
Saint Sebastian 54 34 40N26 84w29 5:37:56
Saint Stephens 74 32 41N01'22 82w57'30 5:31:50
Saint Wendelin 54 34 40N28 84w34 5:38:16
Salem 15 77 40N54'03 80w51'25 5:23:26
Salem 64 27 39N40'57 82w20'08 5:29:21
Salem Center 53 27 39N03'10 82w16'26 5:29:06
Salem Heights 15 77 40N54'03 80w53'28 5:23:34
Salem Heights 31 88 39N04'18 84w22'42 5:37:31
Salesville 30 5 39N58'24 81w20'13 5:25:21
Saline 41 67 40N32 80w42 5:22:48
Salineville 15 67 40N37'21 80w50'17 5:23:21
Salisbury 53 27 39N03 82w03 5:28:12
Salow Corners 78 46 41N12'49 80w32'56 5:22:12
Saltair 13 34 38N55'35 84w08'32 5:36:34
Saltillo 38 5 40N31'15 81w50'52 5:27:23
Saltillo 64 27 39N47'40 82w08'57 5:28:36
Salt Lick 64 27 39N37 82w12 5:28:48
Salt Rock 51 33 40N40 83w15 5:33:00
Salt Run 41 67 40N14'57 80w39'48 5:22:39
Samantha 36 34 39N17'00 83w35'31 5:34:22
Sampleville 68 34 39N44'34 84w34'35 5:38:18
Sand Beach 62 93 41N36'35 83w05'45 5:32:23
Sandburr Corners 48 34 41N36'37 83w44'16 5:34:57
Sand Fork 27 34 38N42'32 82w23'19 5:29:33
Sand Hill 22 5 41N21'41 82w45'20 5:31:01
Sand Hill 73 34 38N41'44 82w51'19 5:31:25
Sandhill 84 20 39N22'44 81w23'16 5:25:33
Sand Ridge 5 27 39N26 82w06 5:28:24
Sand Run 37 34 39N30'54 82w14'15 5:28:57
Sand Run Junction 37 34 39N31'04 82w15'41 5:29:03
Sandusky 22 40 41N26'56 82w42'29 5:30:50
Sandy Corners 25 108 40N04'48 83w09'30 5:32:38
Sandy Hill 21 33 40N17'31 83w08'50 5:32:35
Sandy Springs 1 34 38N36'41 83w17'53 5:33:12
Sandyville 79 16 40N38'25 81w22'21 5:25:29
San Margherita 25 107 39N59'40 83w05'12 5:32:21
Santa Fe 46 34 40N29'29 83w59'39 5:35:59
San Toy 64 27 39N38'20 82w02'07 5:28:08
Sarahsville 11 5 39N48'26 81w28'05 5:25:52
Sardinia 8 34 39N00'28 83w48'31 5:35:14
Sardis 56 20 39N37'22 80w54'46 5:23:39
Sargents 66 34 39N00'12 83w01'23 5:32:06
Saundersville 44 34 38N39'36 82w21'23 5:29:26
Savageville 40 34 39N08'20 82w43'09 5:30:53
Savannah 3 44 40N57'55 82w21'55 5:29:28
Saville Estates 57 34 39N46 84w06 5:36:24
Savona 19 34 39N59'22 84w39'42 5:38:39
Sawyerwood 77 2 41N02'16 81w26'28 5:25:46
Saybrook 4 46 41N49'39 80w52'19 5:23:29
Saybrook-on-the-Lake 4 46 41N52'22 80w53'13 5:23:33
Sayler Park 31 88 39N06'45 84w41'21 5:38:45
Sayre 64 27 39N41'04 82w03'32 5:28:14
Schauers Acres 12 34 39N53 84w02 5:36:08
Schlegels Grove 72 30 41N23'31 83w05'15 5:32:21
Schley 84 20 39N26'34 81w15'19 5:25:01
Schoenbrunn 79 16 40N27'50 81w24'40 5:25:39
Schooley 71 34 39N15'56 82w52'12 5:31:29
Schrader 71 34 39N18'29 82w54'52 5:31:39
Schumm 81 34 40N45'23 84w43'39 5:38:55
Scienceville 50 84 41N06'49 80w37'01 5:22:28
Scio 34 23 40N23'45 81w05'06 5:24:20
Scioto 21 33 40N16'49 83w08'27 5:32:34
Sciotodale 73 34 38N45'17 82w52'08 5:31:29
Scioto Furnace 73 34 38N47'55 82w45'54 5:31:04
Scioto Village 21 27 40N11'35 83w08'34 5:32:34
Sciotoville 73 34 38N45'29 82w53'29 5:31:34
Scipio 9 34 39N23'31 84w49'06 5:39:16
Scipio 74 32 41N05'56 82w57'31 5:31:50
Scotch Ridge 87 33 41N25 83w28 5:33:52
Scotland 28 67 41N31'21 81w21'42 5:25:27
Scott 81 34 40N59'23 84w35'00 5:38:20
Scott Corners 25 27 40N04'28 82w36'20 5:30:25
Scottown 44 34 38N33'01 82w23'20 5:29:33
Scotts Crossing 2 34 40N49'04 84w16'22 5:37:05
Scroggsfield 10 21 40N34'40 80w57'40 5:23:51
Scrub Ridge 1 34 38N52'01 83w23'35 5:33:34
Scudder 54 34 40N34'29 84w44'47 5:38:59
Seal 66 34 39N05 82w58 5:31:52
Seal 88 32 40N52'37 83w09'02 5:32:36
Seaman 1 34 38N56'31 83w34'21 5:34:17
Seamersville 81 34 40N55'56 84w25'01 5:37:40
Sebastian 54 34 40N26'39 84w31'00 5:38:04
Sebring 50 59 40N55'22 81w01'09 5:24:05
Secedar Corners 78 84 41N10 80w36 5:22:24
Sedalia 49 34 39N45 83w29 5:33:56
Sedamsville 31 88 39N05'36 84w34'23 5:38:18
Sedan 73 34 38N56'51 83w07'06 5:32:28
Sego 64 27 39N50'50 82w12'28 5:28:50
Seilcrest Acres 83 34 39N14 84w20 5:37:20
Sellers Point 23 27 39N54 82w33 5:30:12
Selma 12 34 39N47'12 83w42'31 5:34:50
Senecaville 30 5 39N56'03 81w27'45 5:25:51
Senior 83 34 39N23'09 84w05'22 5:36:21
Sentinel 4 72 41N38'05 80w43'18 5:22:53
Seven Hills 18 26 41N23'43 81w40'35 5:26:42
Seven Hills 31 34 39N14 84w32 5:38:08
Seven Mile 9 34 39N28'48 84w33'07 5:38:12
Seventeen 79 16 40N21'22 81w27'21 5:25:49
Seville 52 60 41N00'36 81w51'45 5:27:27
Seward 26 34 41N41'59 84w02'11 5:36:09
Sewellsville 7 21 40N05'53 81w12'48 5:24:51
Shackleton 36 34 39N10'32 83w40'41 5:34:43
Shade 5 27 39N13'33 82w02'19 5:28:09
Shademoore 31 34 39N08'17 84w22'06 5:37:28
Shade River 53 5 39N04'06 81w48'52 5:27:15
Shadeville 25 108 39N49'56 83w00'12 5:32:01
Shady Bend 16 16 40N16'04 81w38'26 5:26:34
Shady Glen 41 67 40N28'48 80w38'24 5:22:34
Shady Glen 71 34 39N21 83w00 5:32:00
Shady Grove 24 34 39N42'12 83w38'32 5:34:34
Shadyside 7 21 39N58'15 80w45'03 5:23:00
Shadyside 15 105 40N38 80w35 5:22:20
Shaker Crossing 57 91 39N41 84w09 5:36:36
Shaker Heights 18 73 41N28'26 81w32'14 5:26:09
Shalersville 67 67 41N14'20 81w13'53 5:24:56
Shandon 9 34 39N19'35 84w42'53 5:38:52
Shane 41 68 40N28'39 80w48'16 5:23:13
Shanesville 79 16 40N30'40 81w39'12 5:26:37
Shannon 60 5 40N05'03 82w05'19 5:28:21
Shannon 72 30 41N24'42 83w04'44 5:32:19
Sharon 25 107 40N05'28 82w57'25 5:31:50
Sharon 40 34 39N03'40 82w40'24 5:30:42
Sharon 61 5 39N44'10 81w33'56 5:26:16
Sharon Center 52 53 41N05'59 81w44'09 5:26:57
Sharon Hills 25 107 40N05 83w01 5:32:04
Sharon Park 2 90 40N44 84w09 5:36:36
Sharon Park 9 34 39N24 84w33 5:38:12
Sharonville 31 34 39N16'05 84w24'48 5:37:39
Sharon West 78 45 41N14 80w31 5:22:04
Sharpeye 19 34 40N06'22 84w44'49 5:38:59
Sharpsburg 54 34 40N22'04 84w42'35 5:38:50
Sharpsburg 58 5 39N26'09 81w54'42 5:27:39
Sharps Crossing 19 34 40N09'04 84w43'57 5:38:56
Shartz Road 83 34 39N35 84w18 5:37:12
Shauck (Johnsville) 59 27 40N37'15 82w39'43 5:30:39
Shawnee 64 27 39N36'17 82w12'42 5:28:51
Shawnee Hills 21 27 40N09'28 83w08'03 5:32:32
Shawnee Hills 29 34 39N39'10 83w47'13 5:35:09
Shawnee Meadows 2 90 40N42 84w08 5:36:32
Shawtown 32 34 41N06'29 83w52'19 5:35:29
Shawtown 59 27 40N29'00 82w57'51 5:31:51
Shawville 47 42 41N22 82w06 5:28:24
Shay 84 20 39N30'37 81w13'02 5:24:52
Sheffield 47 67 41N25'16 82w05'47 5:28:23
Sheffield Center 4 72 41N49'25 80w39'52 5:22:39
Sheffield Lake 47 67 41N29'15 82w06'06 5:28:24
Shelby 70 85 40N52'53 82w39'43 5:30:39
Shell Beach 23 27 39N55'13 82w29'12 5:29:57
Shenandoah 70 5 40N54'42 82w29'58 5:30:00
Shepard 25 107 40N00 82w56 5:31:44
Shepherdstown 7 21 40N09'32 80w56'37 5:23:46
Sheridan 44 37 38N28'08 82w36'02 5:30:24
Sherman 39 5 41N10 82w48 5:31:12
Sherman 77 67 41N01 81w38 5:26:32
Sherman Corners 52 73 41N14'18 81w47'08 5:27:09
Sherritts 44 34 38N41'33 82w31'15 5:30:05
Sherrodsville 10 21 40N29'41 81w14'35 5:24:58
Sherwood 20 34 41N17'14 84w33'13 5:38:13
Sherwood Village 31 34 39N05'04 84w21'53 5:37:28
Shillings Mill 50 67 41N03'30 80w59'10 5:23:57
Shiloh 8 34 38N59'19 83w57'39 5:35:51
Shiloh 13 34 39N38'13 84w06'32 5:36:26
Shiloh 57 91 39N49'07 84w13'43 5:36:55
Shiloh 70 5 40N58'00 82w36'02 5:30:24
Shiltown 50 67 41N03'29 80w55'39 5:23:43
Shinrock 22 9 41N20'46 82w31'17 5:30:05
Shipp 4 72 41N46'56 80w32'09 5:22:09
Shively 54 34 40N35'48 84w38'52 5:38:35
Shively Corners 50 67 41N07'01 80w46'38 5:23:07
Shore 18 67 41N37 81w31 5:26:04
Shoreland 43 67 41N45'52 81w13'39 5:24:55
Short Creek 34 21 40N11 80w55 5:23:40
Short Hills 57 91 39N41 84w09 5:36:36
Short Line Junction 18 67 41N25'20 81w47'49 5:27:11
Shreve 85 79 40N40'53 82w01'19 5:28:05
Shunk 35 34 41N21'49 84w02'20 5:36:09
Shyville 66 34 39N00'27 82w59'09 5:31:57
Siam 74 32 41N05'05 82w52'42 5:31:31
Sidney 75 34 40N17'03 84w09'20 5:36:37
Signal 15 67 40N47'54 80w39'34 5:22:38
Silica 48 34 41N40'53 83w44'32 5:34:58
Silo 67 67 41N18'32 81w16'53 5:25:08
Silver Creek 29 34 39N39 83w44 5:34:56
Silver Creek 33 33 40N34'35 83w40'42 5:34:43
Silver Creek 52 53 41N01 81w44 5:26:56
Silver Lake 77 2 41N09'32 81w27'16 5:25:49
Silver Run 53 27 38N58'35 82w05'28 5:28:22
Silverton 31 34 39N11'34 84w24'02 5:37:36
Simons 4 72 41N32'00 80w32'00 5:22:08
Singing Hills 57 91 39N40 84w15 5:37:00
Sinking Spring 36 34 39N04'22 83w23'13 5:33:33
Sippo 76 67 40N48'59 81w36'05 5:26:24
Sippo Heights 76 54 40N48'19 81w30'09 5:26:01
Sitka 84 20 39N26'52 81w20'19 5:25:21
Siverly 82 34 39N20'56 82w30'00 5:30:00
Six Corners 20 34 41N19'29 84w42'35 5:38:50
Six Mile 57 91 39N44'47 84w18'38 5:37:15
Six Point 56 20 39N43'25 80w59'54 5:24:00
Six Points 87 33 41N16'57 83w33'17 5:34:13
Sixteen Mile Stand 31 34 39N16'22 84w19'39 5:37:19
Skeels Crossroads 54 34 40N34'25 84w47'05 5:39:08
Skit 34 21 40N20'20 80w57'27 5:23:50
Skyline Acres 31 34 39N13'43 84w34'01 5:38:16
Slabtown 2 90 40N47'20 84w03'07 5:36:12
Slate Mills 71 34 39N21'02 83w03'26 5:32:14
Slater 6 34 40N31'40 84w04'24 5:36:18
Slaters 11 5 39N45'56 81w32'22 5:26:09
Slickaway 8 34 38N41'01 83w44'47 5:34:59
Sligo 14 34 39N26'30 83w55'13 5:35:41
Slocum 73 34 38N45'59 82w50'33 5:31:22
Slocum Heights 73 34 38N46'14 82w50'59 5:31:24
Slocums 73 34 38N46 82w59 5:31:56
Slough 23 27 39N47'58 82w45'42 5:31:03
Smith Corners 50 67 40N59'26 80w35'06 5:22:20
Smithfield 41 67 40N16'15 80w46'54 5:23:08
Smith Mill 60 5 39N55'39 81w51'19 5:27:25
Smithville 85 62 40N51'44 81w51'43 5:27:27
Smithville 88 32 40N53'47 83w13'53 5:32:56
Smoketown 76 21 40N40'21 81w32'20 5:26:09
Smoky Corners 1 34 39N01'18 83w21'25 5:33:26
Smyrna 34 21 40N10'18 81w14'38 5:24:59
Snively 85 62 40N45'20 81w40'15 5:26:41
Snodes 50 67 40N57'33 80w59'38 5:23:59
Snowville 53 27 39N10'05 82w05'28 5:28:22
Snyders Mill 12 39 39N56'07 83w51'45 5:35:27
Snyderville 12 39 39N54'04 83w54'49 5:35:39
Soaptown 78 67 41N08'33 80w49'37 5:23:18
Socialville 83 34 39N19'10 84w19'54 5:37:20
Sodom 78 84 41N10'55 80w38'34 5:22:34
Solon 18 46 41N23'23 81w26'29 5:25:46
Somerdale 79 16 40N33'59 81w21'39 5:25:27
Somerford 49 34 39N58 83w30 5:34:00
Somers 68 34 39N37 84w39 5:38:36
Somerset 64 27 39N48'25 82w17'50 5:29:11
Somerton 7 21 39N54'04 81w08'13 5:24:33
Somerville 9 34 39N33'47 84w38'19 5:38:33
Sonora 60 5 39N59'03 81w54'16 5:27:37
South Akron 77 2 41N03'41 81w31'01 5:26:04
South Amherst 47 67 41N21'21 82w15'14 5:29:01
South Arlington 77 2 41N03 81w30 5:26:00
South Bay 42 5 40N29'36 82w31'12 5:30:05
South Beach 36 34 39N10'57 83w28'37 5:33:54
South Bloomfield 65 34 39N43'06 82w59'13 5:31:57
South Bloomingville 37 34 39N25'07 82w35'58 5:30:24
Southbrook 57 91 39N41 84w09 5:36:36
South Charleston 12 34 39N49'31 83w38'04 5:34:32
South Clippinger 31 34 39N10'34 84w21'00 5:37:24
South Condit 21 27 40N14'52 82w47'22 5:31:09
Southdale 57 91 39N41 84w09 5:36:36
South Delta 26 34 41N33'19 84w00'00 5:36:00
South Enon Estates 12 34 39N52 83w56 5:35:44
Southern Hills 57 91 39N41 84w09 5:36:36
Southern Knoll 9 34 39N31 84w44 5:38:56
South Euclid 18 70 41N31'23 81w31'07 5:26:04
South Excello 9 34 39N29 84w25 5:37:40
South Highlands 9 34 39N30'07 84w22'41 5:37:31
South Hill Park 48 34 41N37'46 83w41'56 5:34:48
Southington 78 67 41N18'30 80w57'22 5:23:49
South Kingman 14 34 39N27 83w50 5:35:20
Southland 18 26 41N24 81w46 5:27:04
Southland Shopping Center 51 27 40N35 83w07 5:32:28

South Lebanon 83 34 39N22'15 84w12'48 5:36:51
South Logan 37 33 39N31'44 82w24'30 5:29:38
South Lorain 47 50 41N26'20 82w08'12 5:28:33
South Madison 43 67 41N43'31 81w03'01 5:24:12
South Milford 13 34 39N09'17 84w17'18 5:37:09
South Mount Vernon 42 29 40N22'54 82w29'33 5:29:58
South Newbury 28 67 41N26'21 81w12'29 5:24:50
South New Lyme 4 72 41N34'54 80w46'38 5:23:07
South Olive 11 5 39N40'08 81w29'11 5:25:57
South Park 18 26 41N22 81w40 5:26:40
South Park 88 32 40N48'59 83w17'12 5:33:09
South Perry 37 34 39N29'48 82w40'16 5:30:41
South Plymouth 24 34 39N34'48 83w35'12 5:34:21
South Point 44 37 38N25'04 82w35'11 5:30:21
South Russell 28 67 41N25'53 81w21'56 5:25:28
South Salem 71 34 39N20'10 83w18'24 5:33:14
South Shore Park 48 31 41N41'13 83w24'18 5:33:37
South Side 50 84 41N04'10 80w39'51 5:22:39
South Side 79 16 40N28'37 81w26'59 5:25:48
South Solon 49 34 39N44'16 83w36'48 5:34:27
South Vernon 42 5 40N24 82w29 5:29:56
South Vienna 12 34 39N55'37 83w36'45 5:34:27
South Warsaw 2 90 40N39'30 84w01'57 5:36:08
South Webster 73 34 38N48'48 82w43'37 5:30:54
Southwest 70 95 40N44 82w31 5:30:04
South West Hubbard 78 84 41N10 80w36 5:22:24
South Woodbury 59 27 40N25'11 82w51'25 5:31:26
Southworth 2 34 40N45'50 84w20'24 5:37:22
South Zanesville 60 104 39N53'57 82w00'23 5:28:02
Spanker 57 91 39N51'29 84w14'43 5:36:59
Spargursville 71 34 39N13'31 83w10'02 5:32:40
Sparta 59 27 40N23'41 82w42'02 5:30:48
Speaker's Addition 41 106 40N22 80w39 5:22:36
Specht 10 21 40N38'53 81w00'53 5:24:04
Speidel 7 21 40N00'07 81w06'49 5:24:27
Spellacy 38 5 40N35'38 82w12'46 5:28:51
Spellman Crossing 66 34 39N10'03 83w16'27 5:33:06
Spencer 52 73 41N06'01 82w07'24 5:28:30
Spencer 60 21 40N04 81w54 5:27:36
Spencer Station 30 5 39N57'45 81w16'20 5:25:05
Spencerville 2 34 40N42'32 84w21'13 5:37:25
Spiller 53 5 38N59'37 81w50'24 5:27:22
Spokane 78 67 41N23'25 80w50'59 5:23:24
Spore 17 32 40N51'47 83w02'22 5:32:09
Sprague 56 20 39N40'44 81w13'04 5:24:52
Spratt 60 5 39N52'20 81w43'59 5:26:56
Spreng 3 44 40N46'51 82w09'23 5:28:38
Sprigg 1 34 38N42 83w38 5:34:32
Springboro 83 34 39N33'08 84w14'00 5:36:56
Springbrook 22 5 41N25'54 82w53'12 5:31:33
Springcreek 55 34 40N10 84w11 5:36:44
Springdale 31 34 39N17'13 84w29'07 5:37:56
Springfield 12 39 39N55'27 83w48'32 5:35:14
Spring Grove 15 105 40N37'38 80w37'06 5:22:28
Springhills 11 34 40N15'20 83w52'11 5:35:29
Spring Meadows 31 34 39N13'06 84w31'45 5:38:07
Spring Mill 70 95 40N48'36 82w35'23 5:30:22
Spring Mountain 16 5 40N24'31 82w03'03 5:28:12
Springside 73 34 38N45 82w51 5:31:24
Springvale 13 34 39N13'38 84w11'45 5:36:47
Spring Valley 28 67 41N21'22 81w20'24 5:25:22
Spring Valley 29 34 39N36'32 84w00'28 5:36:02
Spring Valley 47 42 41N22 82w06 5:28:24
Spring Valley 48 34 41N36'20 83w43'51 5:34:55
Springville 74 32 41N00'35 83w23'12 5:33:33
Springville 85 79 40N44'10 82w01'58 5:28:08
Springwood 9 34 39N31 84w44 5:38:56
Sprucevale 15 105 40N42'25 80w34'55 5:22:20
Squires 72 32 41N15'19 83w21'06 5:33:24
Squirrel Town 1 34 38N41'50 83w22'46 5:33:31
Stafford 56 20 39N42'48 81w16'35 5:25:06
Stanberry Park 31 88 39N05'34 84w23'37 5:37:34
Standardsburg 39 5 41N13'03 82w42'19 5:30:49
Standley 35 34 41N16'03 84w13'39 5:36:55
Stanhope 78 56 41N29'54 80w36'15 5:22:25
Stanley 87 31 41N35'31 83w31'07 5:34:04
Stanleyville 84 20 39N28'19 81w24'41 5:25:39
Stanwood 76 54 40N45'30 81w38'02 5:26:32
Starbucktown 14 34 39N28'35 83w47'12 5:35:09
Stark Corners 21 27 40N18'38 82w50'48 5:31:23
Starr 37 27 39N23'49 82w21'40 5:29:27
Starrs Corners 50 67 41N01'28 80w42'42 5:22:51
Station 15 (Philadelphia Rd) 34 16 40N23'19 81w15'35 5:25:02
Staunton 24 34 39N28'31 83w29'00 5:33:56
Staunton 55 34 40N02'24 84w10'51 5:36:43
Steamburg 4 72 41N42'50 80w37'06 5:22:28
Steam Corners 59 95 40N40'52 82w39'52 5:30:39
Steamtown 11 5 39N48'59 81w21'36 5:25:26
Steel Point 19 34 40N01'11 84w32'50 5:38:11
Steel Run 84 20 39N29'37 81w15'47 5:25:03
Steinersville 7 21 39N52'08 80w49'53 5:23:20
Stella 82 27 39N20'55 82w33'07 5:30:12
Stelvideo 19 34 40N09'07 84w33'04 5:38:12
Stemple 10 21 40N37'05 81w05'23 5:24:22
Sterling 85 58 40N58'03 81w50'55 5:27:24
Sterling Heights 83 34 39N35 84w18 5:37:12
Steuben 39 5 41N06'17 82w41'14 5:30:45
Steubenville 41 106 40N22'11 80w38'03 5:22:32
Stewart 5 5 39N18'29 81w53'41 5:27:35
Stewartsville 7 21 40N00'43 80w51'30 5:23:26
Stillwater 79 16 40N19'24 81w18'31 5:25:14
Stillwater Junction 57 91 39N46'50 84w16'10 5:37:05
Stillwell 38 5 40N27'38 82w05'40 5:28:23
Stiversville 53 5 39N06 81w46 5:27:04
Stockdale 66 34 38N57'23 82w51'30 5:31:26
Stockham 73 34 38N44'40 83w01'57 5:32:08
Stockport 58 5 39N32'54 81w47'35 5:27:10
Stockton 9 34 39N19'21 84w30'14 5:38:01
Stock Yards 31 88 39N09 84w33 5:38:12
Stone 60 5 39N47'00 81w54'32 5:27:38
Stone Creek 79 16 40N23'50 81w33'44 5:26:15
Stonelick 13 34 39N07'21 84w11'25 5:36:46
Stoneville 4 72 41N33'23 80w57'46 5:23:51
Stoney Hill 77 67 41N08'09 81w40'05 5:26:40
Stony Prairie 72 32 41N22 83w09 5:32:36
Stony Ridge 50 67 41N05'28 80w48'13 5:23:13
Stony Ridge 87 32 41N30'37 83w30'26 5:34:02
Stonyrill 83 34 39N30 84w23 5:37:32
Storms 71 34 39N14'19 83w10'49 5:32:43
Stoudertown 23 27 39N52'03 82w41'29 5:30:46
Stout 1 34 38N39'50 83w22'45 5:33:31
Stoutsville 23 34 39N36'17 82w49'45 5:31:19
Stovertown 60 5 39N50'29 81w59'13 5:27:57
Stow 77 67 41N09'34 81w26'26 5:25:46
Straitsville 64 27 39N35'41 82w14'45 5:28:59
Strasburg 79 24 40N35'41 81w31'37 5:26:06
Stratford 21 27 40N15'22 83w03'49 5:32:15
Stratford Manor 31 88 39N10'02 84w24'36 5:37:38
Stratton 41 67 40N31'18 80w37'35 5:22:30
Streetsboro 67 67 41N14'21 81w20'46 5:25:23
Stringer 41 67 40N13'58 80w39'45 5:22:39
Stringtown 5 27 39N18'05 81w59'11 5:27:57
Stringtown 8 34 39N07'03 83w59'14 5:35:57
Stringtown 13 34 38N49'20 84w05'54 5:36:24
Stringtown 36 34 39N14'05 83w29'18 5:33:57
Stringtown 57 91 39N49'05 84w18'44 5:37:15
Stringtown 60 5 40N01'44 82w00'51 5:28:03
Stringtown 64 27 39N44'43 82w05'18 5:28:21
Stringtown 65 34 39N30'12 82w46'27 5:31:06
Stringtown 85 79 40N41'00 81w59'32 5:27:58
Strongsville 18 67 41N18'52 81w50'09 5:27:21
Stroup Corners 78 67 41N23 80w59 5:23:56
Stroups 78 67 41N20'21 80w56'08 5:23:45
Struthers 50 84 41N03'09 80w36'29 5:22:26
Stryker 86 34 41N30'13 84w24'51 5:37:39
Stuart Manor 41 106 40N22 80w39 5:22:36
Success 53 5 39N08'06 81w49'57 5:27:20
Suffield 67 67 41N01'23 81w20'51 5:25:23
Suffield Station 67 67 41N01'18 81w22'23 5:25:30
Sugar Bush Knolls 67 67 41N12 81w21 5:25:24
Sugar Creek 5 27 39N22'56 82w04'45 5:28:19
Sugarcreek 79 16 40N30 81w37 5:26:28
Sugar Creek Station 79 16 40N30'11 81w38'28 5:26:34
Sugar Grove 23 27 39N37'35 82w32'55 5:30:12
Sugar Grove 41 67 40N30'28 80w39'26 5:22:38
Sugar Grove 55 34 40N04'46 84w21'09 5:37:25
Sugar Grove 73 34 38N42'43 83w03'40 5:32:15
Sugar Grove Hill 12 39 39N55 83w50 5:35:20
Sugar Ridge 87 33 41N25'44 83w37'21 5:34:29
Sugar Rock 62 93 41N33'56 82w51'21 5:31:25
Sugar Tree Ridge 36 34 39N04'13 83w39'43 5:34:39
Sugar Valley 68 34 39N41'32 84w42'47 5:38:51
Suiter 44 34 38N35'25 82w25'30 5:29:42
Sullivan 3 44 41N01'41 82w13'20 5:28:53
Sulphur Grove 57 34 39N51'39 84w06'17 5:36:25
Sulphur Lick 71 34 39N21'46 83w07'04 5:32:28
Sulphur Springs 17 27 40N52'16 82w52'38 5:31:31
Sulphur Springs 64 27 39N36'02 82w09'59 5:28:40
Summerfield 11 5 39N47'48 81w20'10 5:25:21
Summerford 49 34 39N56'00 83w29'30 5:33:58
Summerside 13 34 39N06'17 84w17'18 5:37:09
Summerside Estates 13 34 39N07'22 84w17'05 5:37:08
Summersville 80 33 40N24'00 83w24'40 5:33:39
Summit 31 88 39N07'36 84w37'19 5:38:29
Summit 56 20 39N46 81w13 5:24:52
Summit 71 34 39N21 83w00 5:32:00
Summit 78 84 41N08'38 80w43'21 5:22:53
Summithill 71 36 39N13'05 83w06'48 5:32:27
Summit Station 45 27 39N59'49 82w45'08 5:31:01
Summitville 15 67 40N40'41 80w53'11 5:23:33
Sumner 53 5 39N08'21 81w55'36 5:27:42
Sunaire 31 88 39N05'46 84w37'42 5:38:31
Sunbury 21 27 40N14'33 82w51'33 5:31:26
Sunbury 57 34 39N36'47 84w21'57 5:37:28
Sundale 13 34 39N13'15 84w16'05 5:37:04
Sundale 60 5 39N58'38 81w47'30 5:27:10
Sunfish 66 34 39N02 83w12 5:32:48
Sunny Acres 41 106 40N22 80w39 5:22:36
Sunnyland 12 39 39N54'14 83w50'58 5:35:24
Sunny Meade 30 5 40N01 81w35 5:26:20
Sunnyside 47 81 41N25'21 82w18'38 5:29:15
Sunrise 44 34 38N29'20 82w32'50 5:30:11
Sunsbury 56 20 39N50 81w02 5:24:08
Sunset Beach 50 67 41N06'49 80w58'19 5:23:53
Sunset Harbor 72 30 41N25'16 82w55'06 5:31:40
Sunset Heights 7 21 40N05'59 80w46'58 5:23:08
Sunset Point 43 67 41N44 81w14 5:24:56
Sunshine 1 34 38N42'56 83w18'56 5:33:16
Sunshine Park 41 106 40N22 80w39 5:22:36
Sun Valley 25 107 39N56 82w53 5:31:32
Superior 73 34 38N40'43 82w42'27 5:30:50
Superior 86 34 41N34 84w38 5:38:32
Surfside 43 67 41N38 81w25 5:25:40
Surrey Hill 78 45 41N13 80w47 5:23:08
Sutton 53 5 39N01 81w55 5:27:40
Swan 82 34 39N21 82w28 5:29:52
Swan Creek 26 34 41N32 83w56 5:35:44
Swan Creek 27 34 38N35'38 82w12'08 5:28:49
Swander 74 32 41N05'43 83w05'36 5:32:22
Swanders 75 34 40N21'38 84w10'23 5:36:42
Swanktown 57 34 39N52'15 84w22'43 5:37:31
Swans 25 5 40N03'45 82w21'00 5:29:24
Swanson 34 67 40N22'47 80w53'19 5:23:33
Swanton 26 34 41N35'19 83w53'28 5:35:34
Swartz Mill 23 27 39N37'56 82w29'39 5:29:59
Swazey 56 20 39N45'50 81w17'16 5:25:09
Swickards Additions 41 106 40N22 80w39 5:22:36
Swift 84 5 39N33'13 81w42'59 5:26:52
Switzer 56 20 39N50'09 80w53'21 5:23:33
Switzerland 56 20 39N49 80w54 5:23:36
Sybene 44 37 38N25'10 82w30'14 5:30:01
Sycamore 31 34 39N17'00 84w19'01 5:37:16
Sycamore 88 32 40N56'59 83w10'15 5:32:41
Sycamore Valley 56 20 39N39'59 81w14'37 5:24:58
Sychar Road 42 5 40N24 82w29 5:29:56
Sylvania 48 34 41N43'08 83w42'47 5:34:51
Symmes 31 34 39N14'49 84w17'47 5:37:11
Symmes Corner 9 34 39N20'16 84w34'11 5:38:17
Syracuse 53 5 38N59'51 81w58'27 5:27:54
Tabor 10 21 40N33'11 81w09'10 5:24:37
Taborville 28 67 41N21'42 81w17'44 5:25:11
Tacoma 7 21 39N59'50 81w08'48 5:24:35
Taft 31 34 39N12 84w25 5:37:40
Talawanda Springs 68 34 39N34'44 84w48'14 5:39:13
Tallmadge 77 2 41N06'05 81w26'31 5:25:46
Tama 54 34 40N37'59 84w37'08 5:38:29
Tampico 19 34 40N02'55 84w47'35 5:39:10
Tappan 34 16 40N21'26 81w12'28 5:24:50
Tarlton 65 34 39N33'21 82w46'34 5:31:06
Tate 13 34 38N58 84w05 5:36:20
Tatmans 64 27 39N36 82w05 5:28:20
Tawawa 75 34 40N14'10 84w01'40 5:36:07
Taylor 80 33 40N21 83w23 5:33:32
Taylor Corners 50 67 41N07'01 80w47'40 5:23:11
Taylor Creek 33 33 40N33 83w41 5:34:44
Taylor Farm Acres 76 54 40N50 81w32 5:26:08
Taylorsburg 57 34 39N49'58 84w17'36 5:37:10
Taylors Creek 31 34 39N12'38 84w40'27 5:38:42
Taylor Station 25 107 39N59'16 82w50'35 5:31:22
Taylorsville 36 34 39N04'38 83w44'03 5:34:56
Taylorsville 57 91 39N51'51 84w09'59 5:36:40
Taylortown 41 67 40N27'39 80w39'29 5:22:38
Taylortown 70 5 40N51'28 82w36'37 5:30:26
Teakwood Acres 31 88 39N12'24 84w32'32 5:38:10
Tedrow 26 34 41N36'12 84w12'22 5:36:49
Teegarden 15 67 40N49'22 80w49'44 5:23:19
Temperanceville 7 21 39N54'28 81w13'47 5:24:55
Tennyson 66 34 39N03'16 83w07'21 5:32:29
Terminal Junction 7 15 40N06 80w44 5:22:56
Terrace Park 31 34 39N09'33 84w18'26 5:37:14
Terre Haute 11 34 40N02'58 83w52'41 5:35:31
Terry Acres 29 34 39N48 84w01 5:36:04
Texas 17 32 40N57 83w06 5:32:24
Texas 35 34 41N25'25 83w57'06 5:35:48
Thacher 65 34 39N33'49 82w53'03 5:31:32
Thackery 11 34 40N03'20 83w55'08 5:35:41
Thatcher 65 34 39N37 82w57 5:31:48
The Avenue 78 45 41N14 80w32 5:22:08
The Bend 20 34 41N17'02 84w30'56 5:38:04
The Eastern 41 67 40N29'49 80w53'46 5:23:35
The Highlands 13 34 39N12'46 84w16'16 5:37:05
Thelma 26 34 41N38'45 84w13'46 5:36:55
Thelma City 50 67 40N55 81w06 5:24:24
The Pines 31 88 39N06'53 84w37'44 5:38:31
The Plains 5 27 39N22'08 82w07'57 5:28:32
The Point 36 36 39N13'53 83w20'53 5:33:24
Thivener 27 27 38N44'10 82w14'43 5:28:59
Thomastown 77 2 41N02'38 81w29'11 5:25:57
Thompson 28 67 41N41'24 81w03'06 5:24:12
Thompson Place 15 105 40N38 80w35 5:22:20
Thorn 64 27 39N54 82w26 5:29:44
Thornport 64 5 39N54'47 82w24'40 5:29:39
Thornville 64 27 39N53'47 82w25'13 5:29:41
Thorny Acres 83 34 39N30 84w23 5:37:32
Thorps 12 39 39N52'48 83w42'26 5:34:50
Three Forks 61 5 39N41'27 81w32'03 5:26:08

Three Locks 71 34 39N15'11 82W54'33 5:31:38
Thrifton 71 34 39N20'36 83W22'01 5:33:28
Thurman 27 27 38N54'00 82W26'45 5:29:47
Thurston 23 27 39N50'25 82W32'46 5:30:11
Tibbetts Corners 78
75 41N10'54 80W43'03 5:22:52
Tick Ridge 84 20 39N21'32 81W42'59 5:26:52
Tiffin 74 1 41N06'52 83W10'41 5:32:43
Tilton Crossroads 45
5 40N10'11 82W14'36 5:28:58
Tiltonsville 41
67 40N10'00 80W42'00 5:22:48
Timberlake 43 67 41N39'57 81W26'36 5:25:46
Tinney 72 32 41N18'46 83W18'41 5:33:15
Tipp City 55 34 39N57'30 84W10'20 5:36:41
Tippecanoe 34 21 40N16'11 81W17'13 5:25:09
Tipton 63 34 41N01'09 84W40'11 5:38:41
Tiro 17 32 40N54'20 82W46'22 5:31:05
Tiverton 16 5 40N25'05 82W08'18 5:28:33
Tobasco 13 88 39N04'06 84W17'52 5:37:11
Tobias 51 32 40N41'18 83W03'59 5:32:16
Toboso 25 5 40N03'23 82W13'06 5:28:52
Tod 17 32 40N51 83W06 5:32:24
Todds 58 5 39N31'29 81W50'49 5:27:23
Toledo 48 31 41N39'50 83W33'19 5:34:13
Toledo Junction 70
95 40N48'46 82W36'58 5:30:28
Tom Corwin 40 34 39N05'56 82W34'42 5:30:19
Tomlison Addition 73
34 38N53'09 82W58'26 5:31:54
Tontogany 87 34 41N25'09 83W44'27 5:34:58
Toots Crossroads 10
103 40N32'20 81W04'06 5:24:16
Top-of-the-Ridge 13
34 39N11'46 84W16'04 5:37:04
Torch 5 5 39N14'22 81W44'57 5:27:00
Toronto 41 80 40N27'51 80W36'04 5:22:24
Totts Corners 50
67 40N59'17 80W47'53 5:23:12
Town and Country Estates 57
91 39N41 84W09 5:36:36
Township School Scotch Ridge 87
33 41N24'09 83W31'24 5:34:06
Townwood 69 34 41N06'34 83W54'02 5:35:36
Tradersville 49
34 39N59'59 83W29'55 5:34:00
Trail 38 5 40N35'25 81W42'23 5:26:50
Trail Run 56 20 39N33 81W04 5:24:16
Tranquility 1 34 38N57'45 83W31'59 5:34:08
Trebeins 29 87 39N42'20 83W59'07 5:35:56
Tremont City 12
34 40N00'40 83W50'10 5:35:21
Trenton 9 34 39N28'51 84W27'28 5:37:50
Triadelphia 58 5 39N41'59 81W57'56 5:27:52
Trimble 5 34 39N29'05 82W04'45 5:28:19
Trinway 60 5 40N08'28 82W00'36 5:28:02
Triumph 78 67 41N29'28 80W44'50 5:22:59
Tri-Village 25
107 40N00 83W03 5:32:12
Trombley 87 33 41N15'14 83W38'43 5:34:35
Tropic 58 5 39N44'15 82W04'17 5:28:17
Trotwood 57 34 39N47'50 84W18'41 5:37:15
Trowbridge 62 93 41N34'48 83W16'52 5:33:07
Troy 55 34 40N02'22 84W12'12 5:36:49
Troyton 21 27 40N23'39 83W04'49 5:32:19
Truetown 5 27 39N26'59 82W06'30 5:28:26
Trumbull 4 72 41N40'41 80W57'15 5:23:49
Truro 25 27 39N56'02 82W53'01 5:31:32
Tucson 71 34 39N21'23 82W49'34 5:31:18
Tulip 1 34 38N44'04 83W24'54 5:33:40
Tunnel 84 20 39N27 81W28 5:25:52
Tunnel Hill 16 5 40N15'17 82W02'57 5:28:12
Tuppers Plains 53
5 39N10'07 81W50'48 5:27:23
Turkey Foot Corner 4
72 41N40'21 80W50'11 5:23:21
Turpin Hills 31
34 39N06'36 84W22'48 5:37:31
Tuscarawas 79 16 40N23'41 81W24'26 5:25:38
Tusculum 31 88 39N07'22 84W25'42 5:37:43
Twenty Mile Stand 83
34 39N18'23 84W16'48 5:37:07
Twightwee 31 34 39N15'07 84W17'12 5:37:09
Twin Lakes 2 90 40N43 84W06 5:36:24
Twin Lakes 67 67 41N10 81W21 5:25:24
Twinsburg 77 67 41N18'45 81W26'25 5:25:46
Twinsburg Heights 77
67 41N20 81W27 5:25:48
Twin Valley 73 34 38N47'25 82W57'09 5:31:49
Tylers Corners 25
27 40N05'44 82W39'47 5:30:39
Tylersville 9 34 39N21'27 84W25'17 5:37:41
Tymochtee 88 32 40N56'57 83W16'13 5:33:05
Tyndall 16 5 40N13'02 81W52'56 5:27:32
Tyrone 16 5 40N15'10 81W58'41 5:27:55
Tyrrell 78 67 41N16'20 80W38'11 5:22:33
Uhrichsville 79
19 40N23'35 81W20'48 5:25:23
Union 57 34 39N53'52 84W18'23 5:37:14
Union City 19 34 40N11'58 84W48'19 5:39:13
Union Corners 19
34 40N04'45 84W29'25 5:37:58
Union Depot 77 2 41N04'38 81W31'02 5:26:04
Union Furnace 37
27 39N27'42 82W21'23 5:29:26
Union Landing Siding 44
34 38N31 82W39 5:30:36
Union Park 9 34 39N18'10 84W24'39 5:37:39
Union Plains 8 34 39N02 83W56 5:35:44
Unionport 41 67 40N21 80W51 5:23:24
Union Ridge 15 78 40N46'28 80W34'33 5:22:18
Union Station 25
27 40N01'17 82W30'46 5:30:03
Uniontown 7 21 40N07'50 80W59'31 5:23:58
Uniontown 76 67 40N58'30 81W24'30 5:25:38
Unionvale 34 21 40N16'20 80W55'38 5:23:43
Unionville 15 47 40N51'19 80W44'15 5:22:57
Unionville 43 72 41N46'49 81W00'11 5:24:01
Unionville 58 5 39N37'43 81W43'27 5:26:54
Unionville 84 20 39N27'08 81W27'29 5:25:50
Unionville Center 80
34 40N08'18 83W20'24 5:33:22
Uniopolis 6 34 40N36'08 84W05'12 5:36:21

Unity 1 34 38N53'30 83W31'24 5:34:06
Unity 15 67 40N51'53 80W33'35 5:22:14
University Heights 18
73 41N29'52 81W32'15 5:26:09
University View 25
107 40N00 83W03 5:32:12
Upland Heights 41
67 40N09'32 80W43'27 5:22:54
Upper 44 34 38N33 82W39 5:30:36
Upper Arlington 9
34 39N30'58 84W22'35 5:37:30
Upper Arlington 25
107 40N00 83W04 5:32:16
Upper Dayton View 57
91 39N47 84W14 5:36:56
Upper Lowell 84
20 39N32'08 81W31'19 5:26:05
Upper Sandusky 88
102 40N49'38 83W16'53 5:33:08
Upton 72 30 41N24'54 83W00'41 5:32:03
Urbana 11 110 40N06'30 83W45'09 5:35:01
Urbancrest 25 107 39N53'51 83W05'13 5:32:21
Urban Hill 76 67 40N50'50 81W37'08 5:26:29
Utica 45 5 40N14'03 82W27'05 5:29:48
Utica 83 34 39N29'51 84W09'37 5:36:38
Utley 5 5 39N23'13 81W54'36 5:27:38
Utopia 13 34 38N46'34 84W03'26 5:36:14
Vadis 7 21 39N55'29 80W49'36 5:23:18
Vails Corners 59
27 40N21'53 82W45'13 5:31:01
Vales Mills 82 27 39N10'40 82W18'53 5:29:16
Valley 15 67 40N51'56 80W56'54 5:23:48
Valley City 52 67 41N14'16 81W55'54 5:27:44
Valley City Station 52
67 41N14'18 81W54'03 5:27:36
Valley Crossing 25
107 39N53'20 82W56'57 5:31:48
Valleydale 31 88 39N12 84W29 5:37:56
Valley Ford 53 27 39N10'00 82W14'41 5:28:59
Valley Glen 41
106 40N18'32 80W41'08 5:22:45
Valley Hi 46 33 40N21 83W41 5:34:44
Valley Juction 31
34 39N10'11 84W46'30 5:39:06
Valley Junction 79
16 40N35'04 81W23'05 5:25:32
Valley View 18 26 41N21'37 81W35'54 5:26:24
Valley View 25
107 39N57'56 83W04'21 5:32:17
Valley View 41 67 40N21'19 80W45'52 5:23:03
Valley View 73 34 38N46'19 83W00'56 5:32:04
Valley View Heights 13
34 39N07'14 84W17'31 5:37:10
Valley View Village 60
5 39N55 82W01 5:28:04
Valleywood 29 34 39N43'22 84W04'30 5:36:18
Vallonia 7 21 39N57'37 80W49'48 5:23:19
Van 46 33 40N30'09 83W36'55 5:34:28
Vanatta 45 5 40N07'33 82W25'46 5:29:43
Van Buren 32 33 41N08'19 83W38'58 5:34:36
Vanburen 45 5 40N07 82W26 5:29:44
Vandalia 57 34 39N53'26 84W11'56 5:36:48
Vanderhoof 5 5 39N12'07 81W51'40 5:27:27
Vandervorts Corners 14
34 39N26'41 83W59'20 5:35:57
Vanlue 32 33 40N58'31 83W28'45 5:33:55
Van Meter 66 34 39N02'32 83W01'37 5:32:06
Van Wert 81 118 40N52'10 84W35'03 5:38:20
Vauces 71 34 39N16'13 82W53'24 5:31:34
Vaughnsville 69
34 40N52'54 84W09'02 5:36:36
Vega 40 34 38N55 82W27 5:29:48
Venedocia 81 34 40N47'11 84W27'25 5:37:50
Venice 22 5 41N26'45 82W46'14 5:31:05
Venice Heights 78
45 41N15'10 80W44'27 5:22:58
Vera Cruz 8 34 39N10'19 83W57'45 5:35:51
Vermilion 22 81 41N25'19 82W21'53 5:29:28
Vermilion-on-the-Lake 47
81 41N25'42 82W19'26 5:29:18
Vermona 13 34 39N06'34 84W17'07 5:37:08
Vernon 44 34 38N42'42 82W38'24 5:30:34
Vernon 70 5 40N54 82W37 5:30:28
Vernon 78 67 41N23'11 80W34'08 5:22:17
Vernon Heights 51
5 40N35 83W07 5:32:28
Vernon Junction 70
5 40N51'01 82W41'15 5:30:45
Verona 68 34 39N54'12 84W29'08 5:37:57
Versailles 19 34 40N13'21 84W29'04 5:37:56
Vesuvius Furnace 44
34 38N36'22 82W37'45 5:30:31
Veterans Administration 57
91 39N46 84W12 5:36:48
Veto 84 20 39N20'30 81W40'21 5:26:41
Vickery 72 30 41N22'55 82W56'06 5:31:44
Vicksville 58 5 39N32'58 82W01'25 5:28:06
Victory Camp 21
27 40N10'52 82W55'54 5:31:44
Vienna 78 82 41N14'16 80W39'52 5:22:39
Vigo 71 34 39N14'52 82W47'35 5:31:10
Viking Village 13
34 39N05'52 84W17'59 5:37:12
Villa 12 39 39N57'55 83W45'31 5:35:02
Villa Nova 6 34 40N32'43 84W25'29 5:37:42
Vincent 47 42 41N25'13 82W06'58 5:28:28
Vincent 84 20 39N22'31 81W40'11 5:26:41
Vine Street 43 67 41N38 81W25 5:25:40
Vinton 27 27 38N58'35 82W20'30 5:29:22
Vinton 82 27 39N14'39 82W26'13 5:29:45
Violet 23 27 39N53 82W46 5:31:04
Virginia 16 5 40N11 81W57 5:27:48
Volunteer Bay 22
5 41N23'55 82W25'13 5:29:41
Vulcan 48 31 41N39'03 83W36'34 5:34:26
Wabash 54 34 40N32'44 84W45'00 5:39:00
Wacker Heights 23
27 39N44'35 82W34'42 5:30:19
Waco 76 43 40N46'43 81W20'50 5:25:23
Wade 84 20 39N26'26 81W10'22 5:24:41
Wadsworth 52 46 41N01'32 81W43'48 5:26:55
Waggoner Place 87
31 41N34 83W35 5:34:20

Wagram 45 27 39N57'24 82W43'50 5:30:55
Wahlsburg 8 34 38N54'49 83W54'10 5:35:37
Wainwright 37 34 39N07'20 82W29'23 5:29:58
Wainwright 79 16 40N25'07 81W25'45 5:25:43
Waite Hill 43 67 41N37'07 81W23'03 5:25:32
Wakefield 19 34 40N08'30 84W36'51 5:38:27
Wakefield 66 34 38N58'13 83W01'12 5:32:05
Wakeman 39 5 41N15'16 82W23'59 5:29:36
Walbridge 87 31 41N35'16 83W29'36 5:33:58
Waldo 51 27 40N27'32 83W04'38 5:32:19
Wales Corners 72
5 41N18'56 82W54'10 5:31:37
Walhonding 16 5 40N21'34 82W08'49 5:28:35
Walhonding 30 5 39N54'16 81W29'51 5:25:59
Wallace Heights 41
67 40N27'29 80W37'48 5:22:31
Wallace Mills 73
34 38N51'30 82W47'50 5:31:11
Walnut 65 27 39N42'34 82W51'07 5:31:24
Walnut Creek 38 5 40N32'29 81W43'19 5:26:53
Walnut Grove 33
33 40N43'05 83W37'26 5:34:30
Walnut Grove 46
33 40N25'38 83W37'24 5:34:30
Walnut Hill 76 54 40N46'53 81W30'03 5:26:00
Walnut Hills 31
88 39N07'37 84W29'03 5:37:56
Walnut Hills 40
34 39N04 82W39 5:30:36
Walnut Hills 76
54 40N48 81W31 5:26:04
Walnutrun 49 34 39N53 83W27 5:33:48
Walser 64 5 39N54'47 82W21'17 5:29:25
Walton 33 5 40N38'21 83W45'56 5:35:04
Walton Hills 18
67 41N21'56 81W33'41 5:26:15
Wamsley 1 34 38N49'45 83W16'37 5:33:06
Wapakoneta 6 118 40N34'04 84W11'37 5:36:46
Ward 37 27 39N31 82W14 5:28:56
Ward Town 8 34 38N45 83W50 5:35:20
Wardwood Acres 31
34 39N14'31 84W35'29 5:38:22
Warner 84 20 39N33'46 81W25'06 5:25:40
Warnock 7 21 40N01'21 80W56'15 5:23:45
Warren 78 45 41N14'15 80W49'07 5:23:16
Warrensburg 21 33 40N18'21 83W10'07 5:32:40
Warrensville 18
67 41N26 81W30 5:26:00
Warrensville Heights 18
67 41N26'06 81W32'11 5:26:09
Warrenton 41 67 40N11'31 80W40'49 5:22:43
Warrentown 30 5 40N04'08 81W29'19 5:25:57
Warsaw 16 5 40N20'07 82W00'25 5:28:02
Warsaw Junction 16
5 40N19'44 82W00'44 5:28:03
Warwick 77 67 40N56 81W38 5:26:32
Warwick 79 16 40N24 81W25 5:25:40
Washington Court House 24
4 39N32'11 83W26'21 5:33:45
Washington Hall 10
103 40N34'24 81W02'41 5:24:11
Washington Mills 29
34 39N38'51 84W02'49 5:36:11
Washingtonville 15
67 40N54'01 80W45'51 5:23:03
Watch Farm Acres 31
88 39N03'52 84W22'46 5:37:31
Watch Hill 31 34 39N03'49 84W22'18 5:37:29
Waterford 42 27 40N32'36 82W37'08 5:30:29
Waterford 84 20 39N32'32 81W38'24 5:26:34
Waterloo 5 27 39N20 82W14 5:28:56
Waterloo 10 103 40N30'55 81W04'15 5:24:17
Waterloo 25 27 39N50'23 82W47'06 5:31:08
Waterloo 44 34 38N42'05 82W28'26 5:29:54
Watertown 84 20 39N27'57 81W38'00 5:26:32
Waterville 48 34 41N30'03 83W43'06 5:34:52
Watheys 10 21 40N39'05 81W01'21 5:24:05
Watkins 80 33 40N12'45 83W14'49 5:32:59
Watson 74 32 41N11'22 83W06'19 5:32:25
Wattsville 10 21 40N34'24 80W55'59 5:23:44
Wauseon 26 34 41N32'57 84W08'30 5:36:34
Waverly 66 34 39N07'36 82W59'08 5:31:57
Waverly Gables 66
34 39N06'57 83W00'24 5:32:02
Way 56 20 39N38'28 81W11'01 5:24:44
Wayland 67 67 41N09'38 81W04'17 5:24:17
Wayne 4 72 41N32'04 80W40'00 5:22:40
Wayne 87 33 41N18'05 83W28'25 5:33:54
Wayne Lakes Park 19
34 40N01'23 84W39'43 5:38:39
Waynesburg 17 33 40N57'37 82W47'33 5:31:10
Waynesburg 76 67 40N40'04 81W15'27 5:25:02
Waynesfield 6 34 40N36'02 83W58'31 5:35:54
Waynesville 83 34 39N31'47 84W05'12 5:36:21
Weathersfield 78
75 41N10 80W45 5:23:00
Weavers 19 34 40N01'35 84W40'42 5:38:43
Weavers Corners 39
5 41N12'06 82W49'29 5:31:18
Weaver Station 19
34 40N06 84W38 5:38:32
Webb 7 21 39N57'17 80W46'43 5:23:07
Webb Summit 37 27 39N35'11 82W21'43 5:29:27
Webertown 36 34 39N14'08 83W50'15 5:35:21
Webster 19 34 40N11'12 84W28'41 5:37:55
Webster 87 33 41N27 83W32 5:34:08
Weems (Smithfield Station) 41
67 40N17'10 80W45'16 5:23:01
Wegee 7 21 39N57'44 80W46'11 5:23:05
Weilersville 85
62 40N50'23 81W51'42 5:27:27
Welcome 38 5 40N32'46 82W01'19 5:28:05
Weller 70 5 40N56 82W27 5:29:48
Wellington 47 55 41N10'08 82W13'05 5:28:52
Wellington Park 31
34 39N14 84W32 5:38:08
Wellman 83 34 39N28'57 84W01'57 5:36:08
Wells 41 67 40N16 80W41 5:22:44
Wellston 40 87 39N07'24 82W31'59 5:30:08
Wellsville 15 105 40N36'10 80W38'57 5:22:36
Welsh 53 27 39N09'02 82W10'23 5:28:42
Welshfield 28 67 41N23'13 81W08'33 5:24:34
Welshtown 53 5 39N01'39 81W59'45 5:27:59

Wendelin 54 34 40N23'57 84w41'24 5:38:46
Wengerlawn 57 34 39N49 84w25 5:37:40
Wernert 48 31 41N42 83w36 5:34:24
Wesley 60 5 39N55'29 82w10'33 5:28:42
Wesley 84 20 39N25 81w48 5:27:12
West 15 67 40N46 81w02 5:24:08
West Akron 77 2 41N04'28 81w32'52 5:26:11
West Alexandria 68 34 39N44'40 84w31'56 5:38:08
West Andover 4 56 41N36'24 80w36'44 5:22:27
Westarado 76 54 40N46'26 81w32'44 5:26:11
West Austintown 50 67 41N05'59 80w47'36 5:23:10
West Bass Lake 28 67 41N36'20 81w10'41 5:24:43
West Bedford 16 5 40N15'33 82w04'36 5:28:18
West Bellaire 7 6 40N01 80w45 5:23:00
West Belpre 84 20 39N18 81w34 5:26:16
West Berlin 21 27 40N15'20 83w00'46 5:32:03
Westboro 14 34 39N16'53 83w54'38 5:35:39
West Brookfield 76 54 40N47'45 81w34'16 5:26:17
West Canaan 85 62 40N56'42 81w59'38 5:27:59
West Carlisle 16 5 40N13'44 82w07'06 5:28:28
West Carlisle 47 42 41N22 82w06 5:28:24
West Carrollton 57 91 39N40'18 84w15'10 5:37:01
West Charleston 55 34 39N55'23 84w08'01 5:36:32
West Chesapeake 44 37 38N27 82w28 5:29:52
West Chester 9 34 39N19'49 84w24'30 5:37:38
West Chester 79 16 40N14'01 81w20'40 5:25:23
West Clarksfield 39 5 41N11'26 82w25'39 5:29:43
West Covington 55 34 40N06'46 84w21'35 5:37:26
West Delta 26 34 41N34'23 84w01'19 5:36:05
West Elkton 68 34 39N35'16 84w33'16 5:38:13
West End 4 46 41N52 80w49 5:23:16
West Enon Estates 12 34 39N52 83w56 5:35:44
Western Hills 31 88 39N07 84w37 5:38:28
Western Reserve Estates 77 67 41N15'51 81w24'39 5:25:39
Western Star 77 67 41N01'32 81w41'17 5:26:45
Westerville 25 27 40N07'34 82w55'45 5:31:43
West Fairport 43 67 41N45 81w17 5:25:08
Westfall 65 34 39N33'29 82w59'57 5:32:00
West Farmington 78 67 41N23'26 80w58'25 5:23:54
Westfield 15 105 40N38 80w35 5:22:20
Westfield 59 27 40N25'56 82w58'55 5:31:56
Westfield Center 52 73 41N01'35 81w56'00 5:27:44
West Florence 68 34 39N44'38 84w45'38 5:39:03
Westhill Heights 50 67 41N01'44 80w50'06 5:23:20
Westhope 35 34 41N17'54 83w56'28 5:35:46
West Independence 32 33 41N04'36 83w26'28 5:33:46
West Jackson 80 33 40N29'03 83w22'43 5:33:31
West Jefferson 49 34 39N56'41 83w16'08 5:33:05
West Jefferson 86 34 41N34'19 84w33'24 5:38:14
West Junction 71 34 39N13'05 82w46'06 5:31:04
West Lafayette 16 5 40N16'31 81w45'04 5:27:00
Westlake 18 67 41N27'19 81w55'05 5:27:40
West Lakeville 4 72 41N56 80w36 5:22:24
West Lancaster 24 34 39N37'22 83w36'35 5:34:26
Westland 58 5 39N33'01 81w53'58 5:27:36
West Lebanon 85 62 40N43'28 81w40'04 5:26:40
West Leipsic 69 34 41N06'26 84w00'09 5:36:01
West Liberty 17 33 40N51'44 82w46'34 5:31:06
West Liberty 46 34 40N15'08 83w45'21 5:35:01
West Liberty 59 27 40N22'40 82w53'27 5:31:34
West Lodi 74 32 41N09'51 82w56'18 5:31:45
West Logan 37 27 39N32'20 82w25'43 5:29:43
West London 49 34 39N53 83w27 5:33:48
West Manchester 68 34 39N54'09 84w37'35 5:38:30
West Mansfield 46 33 40N24'07 83w32'43 5:34:11
West Marietta 84 20 39N27 81w28 5:25:52
West Marysville 80 33 40N24 82w29 5:29:56
West Mecca 78 67 41N23'25 80w46'36 5:23:06
West Middletown 9 3 39N31'25 84w25'05 5:37:40
West Millgrove 87 33 41N14'38 83w29'29 5:33:58
West Milton 55 34 39N57'45 84w19'41 5:37:19
Westminster 2 34 40N41'36 83w58'49 5:35:55
West Newton 2 34 40N39'14 83w53'34 5:35:34
West Oberlin 47 46 41N18 82w13 5:28:52
Weston 87 34 41N20'41 83w47'50 5:35:11
West Park 18 26 41N28 81w47 5:27:08
West Park 32 89 41N01'06 83w40'29 5:34:42
West Park 41 106 40N22 80w39 5:22:36
West Park 76 54 40N46'59 81w31'48 5:26:07
West Point 15 67 40N42'30 80w42'09 5:22:49
West Point 59 27 40N38'21 82w47'06 5:31:08
West Portsmouth 73 34 38N45'30 83w01'45 5:32:07
West Powhatan 7 21 39N52 80w49 5:23:16
West Richfield 77 67 41N14'22 81w39'19 5:26:37
West Rushville 23 27 39N45'50 82w26'51 5:29:47
West Salem 85 62 40N58'17 82w06'36 5:28:26
West Side 50 84 41N06'08 80w41'22 5:22:45
West Sonora 68 34 39N53'20 84w32'28 5:38:10
West Steels Corners 77 2 41N10'51 81w32'12 5:26:09
West Toledo 48 31 41N42 83w34 5:34:16
West Town 51 5 40N35 83w07 5:32:28
West Union 1 34 38N47'40 83w32'43 5:34:11
West Unity 86 34 41N35'10 84w26'06 5:37:44
West View 18 67 41N21'37 81w54'10 5:27:37
Westville 11 34 40N06'34 83w50'17 5:35:21
Westville 50 67 40N54'05 80w59'39 5:23:59
Westville Lake 15 67 40N55 81w01 5:24:04
West Warren 78 45 41N14 80w51 5:23:24
West Wheeling 7 21 40N03'39 80w44'33 5:22:58
West Williamsfield 4 72 41N32'00 80w36'30 5:22:26
Westwood 31 88 39N08'55 84w35'58 5:38:24
Westwood 41 106 40N22 80w39 5:22:36
Westwood 85 76 40N46'53 81w57'36 5:27:50
Westwood Estates 41 106 40N22 80w39 5:22:36
West Woodville 13 34 39N18 83w59 5:35:56
Wetsel 81 34 40N56'48 84w26'10 5:37:45
Weyers 22 5 41N22'25 82w46'03 5:31:04
Weymouth 52 73 41N11'08 81w47'40 5:27:11
Wharton 88 33 40N51'41 83w27'42 5:33:51
Wheat Ridge 1 34 38N53'03 83w30'12 5:34:01
Wheatville 68 34 39N41'17 84w34'34 5:38:18
Wheelersburg 73 34 38N43'49 82w51'20 5:31:25
Wheelers Mill 73 34 38N49'39 82w51'00 5:31:24
Wheeling Creek 7 21 40N04'04 80w46'47 5:23:07
Wherrys Crossroads 10 21 40N37'01 81w06'12 5:24:25
Whetstone 17 32 40N46 82w54 5:31:36
Whigville 11 5 39N49'39 81w22'26 5:25:30
Whipple 84 20 39N31'20 81w24'53 5:25:40
Whipple Heights 76 43 40N48'58 81w26'02 5:25:44
Whisler 65 34 39N29'12 82w49'12 5:31:17
Whistler 65 34 39N29 82w55 5:31:40
White Cottage 60 5 39N52'18 82w05'52 5:28:23
White Eyes 16 5 40N20 81w44 5:26:56
White Fox 39 67 41N11'03 82w21'13 5:29:25
Whitehall 25 107 39N58'00 82w53'08 5:31:33
Whitehouse 48 34 41N31'08 83w48'14 5:35:13
White Oak 8 34 39N00'57 83w52'37 5:35:30
White Oak 24 34 39N41'20 83w20'40 5:33:23
White Oak 31 34 39N12'47 84w35'58 5:38:24
White Oak Meadows 31 34 39N13'38 84w35'59 5:38:24
White Oaks 41 106 40N22 80w39 5:22:36
White Oak Valley 8 34 38N55'12 83w55'37 5:35:42
White Pond 77 67 41N06 81w38 5:26:32
Whites 23 27 39N42'17 82w35'28 5:30:22
Whites Corner 29 34 39N38'15 84w06'36 5:36:26
Whites Landing 72 5 41N25'47 82w54'04 5:31:36
White Sulphur 21 33 40N16'36 83w09'27 5:32:38
Whitetree 31 34 39N12'48 84w25'26 5:37:42
Whiteville 26 34 41N42'42 83w58'35 5:35:54
Whitewater 31 34 39N12 84w46 5:39:04
Whitfield 57 34 39N40'24 84w16'34 5:37:06
Whitney 7 21 40N00'47 80w55'44 5:23:43
Wick 4 49 41N32'03 80w38'51 5:22:35
Wickliffe 43 49 41N36'19 81w27'13 5:25:49
Wickliffe 50 84 41N06'09 80w43'44 5:22:55
Widowville 3 44 40N44'58 82w19'00 5:29:16
Wiggonsville 13 34 38N55'46 84w05'40 5:36:23
Wightmans Grove 72 30 41N25'21 83w03'07 5:32:12
Wilberforce 29 34 39N42'58 83w52'40 5:35:31
Wilbren 64 27 39N43'31 82w10'31 5:28:43
Wildare 78 67 41N20'55 80w48'41 5:23:15
Wildbrook Acres 31 34 39N14'34 84w31'13 5:38:05
Wildwood 9 34 39N30 84w23 5:37:32
Wilgus 44 34 38N37'18 82w27'27 5:29:50
Wilhelm Corner 78 45 41N15'56 80w46'29 5:23:06
Wilkesville 82 27 39N04'28 82w19'34 5:29:18
Wilkins 48 34 41N35'50 83w50'44 5:35:23
Wilkins Corners 45 5 40N07 82w26 5:29:44
Wilkins Run 45 5 40N07'47 82w20'39 5:29:23
Willard 39 5 41N03'11 82w43'35 5:30:54
Willetsville 36 34 39N15'09 83w42'10 5:34:49
Williamsburg 13 34 39N03'15 84w03'11 5:36:13
Williams Center 86 34 41N25'44 84w36'37 5:38:26
Williams Corner 13 34 39N10'21 84w09'39 5:36:39
Williamsdale 9 34 39N26'28 84w31'48 5:38:07
Williamsfield 4 83 41N32'00 80w34'15 5:22:17
Williamsport 15 67 40N43'26 80w38'10 5:22:33
Williamsport 59 27 40N34'46 82w43'48 5:30:55
Williamsport 65 34 39N35'09 83w07'14 5:32:29
Williamstown 32 33 40N50'02 83w39'03 5:34:36
Williston 62 93 41N36'13 83w20'24 5:33:22
Willobee 43 67 41N38 81w25 5:25:40
Willoughby 43 46 41N38'23 81w24'24 5:25:38
Willoughby Hills 43 46 41N35'54 81w25'07 5:25:40
Willow 18 26 41N28 81w39 5:26:36
Willow Brook Heights 76 43 40N52 81w20 5:25:20
Willow Crest 50 67 40N58'24 80w39'03 5:22:36
Willowdell 19 34 40N18'23 84w27'14 5:37:49
Willow Grove 7 6 40N01 80w45 5:23:00
Willow Grove 15 77 40N53'09 80w54'02 5:23:36
Willowick 43 49 41N37'59 81w28'08 5:25:53
Willow Lakes 60 5 39N55 82w01 5:28:04
Willowville 13 34 39N05'44 84w14'54 5:37:00
Willow Wood 44 34 38N33'40 82w28'05 5:29:52
Wills 30 5 40N01 81w23 5:25:32
Wills Creek 16 5 40N10'48 81w51'03 5:27:24
Willshire 81 34 40N44'55 84w47'28 5:39:10
Willshire Heights 83 34 39N35 84w18 5:37:12
Wilmer 22 5 41N23'47 82w41'45 5:30:47
Wilmington 14 34 39N26'43 83w49'43 5:35:19
Wilmot 76 21 40N39'21 81w37'56 5:26:32
Wilson 56 20 39N51'24 81w04'01 5:24:16
Wiltondale 31 34 39N10 83w21 5:33:24
Winameg 26 34 41N37'37 84w03'54 5:36:16
Winchester 1 34 38N56'30 83w39'03 5:34:36
Winchester 40 34 38N59'13 82w32'21 5:30:09
Windchester Hills 20 34 41N17 84w20 5:37:20
Windfall 52 73 41N08'11 81w47'09 5:27:09
Windham 67 53 41N14'06 81w02'58 5:24:12
Windsor 4 72 41N32'06 80w56'04 5:23:44
Windsor 70 95 40N48'30 82w26'08 5:29:45
Windsor 83 34 39N17'05 84w03'00 5:36:12
Windsor Mills 4 72 41N32'06 80w57'45 5:23:51
Winesburg 38 5 40N36'59 81w41'43 5:26:47
Winfield 79 16 40N32'55 81w33'31 5:26:14
Wingett Run 84 20 39N32'12 81w14'36 5:24:58
Wingston 87 33 41N16'11 83w43'40 5:34:55
Winkle 36 34 39N07 83w43 5:34:52
Winklepeck Grove 79 16 40N31'24 81w36'49 5:26:27
Winklers Mill 56 20 39N41'01 80w56'00 5:23:44
Winona 15 67 40N49'41 80w53'47 5:23:35
Winterdale 41 106 40N22 80w39 5:22:36
Winterset 30 5 40N06'14 81w25'00 5:25:40
Wintersville 41 106 40N22'31 80w42'14 5:22:49
Wintondale 31 88 39N12'52 84w30'53 5:38:04
Winton Place 31 88 39N10'27 84w30'57 5:38:04
Winton Terrace 31 88 39N10'56 84w30'43 5:38:03
Wisterman 69 34 41N07'25 84w14'16 5:36:57
Withamsville 13 34 39N03'44 84w17'18 5:37:09
Wittens 56 20 39N35'24 80w58'48 5:23:55
Wolf 79 16 40N19'18 81w34'18 5:26:17
Wolfcale 81 34 40N53'17 84w45'39 5:39:03
Wolf Creek 84 5 39N28'46 81w43'56 5:26:56
Wolfhurst 7 21 40N04'09 80w47'02 5:23:08
Wolfpen 53 27 39N04'31 82w04'40 5:28:19
Wolf Run 41 67 40N28'02 80w53'22 5:23:33
Wonderland 25 107 40N01 82w53 5:31:32
Woodbourne 57 91 39N39 84w12 5:36:48
Woodington 19 34 40N10'42 84w40'40 5:38:43
Woodland 80 33 40N28'44 83w15'27 5:33:02
Woodland Park 13 34 39N11'50 84w04'07 5:36:16
Woodlawn 31 34 39N15'07 84w28'13 5:37:53
Woodlyn 65 34 39N34'12 83w06'51 5:32:27
Woodmere 18 67 41N27'44 81w28'51 5:25:55
Woods 9 34 39N31 84w44 5:38:56
Woodsdale 9 34 39N26'04 84w28'33 5:37:54
Woodsfield 56 14 39N45'45 81w06'56 5:24:28
Woodside 87 33 41N21'08 83w27'59 5:33:52
Woodstock 11 34 40N10'26 83w31'39 5:34:07
Woodview Park 80 33 40N15'44 83w21'26 5:33:26
Woodville 13 34 39N15'18 84w00'40 5:36:03
Woodville 72 32 41N27'05 83w21'57 5:33:28
Woodville Gardens 87 31 41N35'31 83w27'02 5:33:48
Woodworth 50 67 40N59'17 80w39'49 5:22:39
Wooster 85 76 40N48'18 81w56'07 5:27:44
Wooster Heights 70 95 40N46'04 82w27'55 5:29:52
Worstville 63 34 41N04'54 84w40'14 5:38:41
Worthington 25 107 40N05'35 83w01'05 5:32:04
Wortley 60 104 39N57'32 81w58'43 5:27:55
Wren 81 34 40N48'03 84w46'31 5:39:06
Wright-Patterson A F B 29 34 39N47 84w03 5:36:12
Wrightstown 58 5 39N28'34 81w58'25 5:27:54
Wrightsville 1 34 38N42'10 83w30'44 5:34:03
Wrightview 29 34 39N48 84w01 5:36:04
Wrightview Heights 29 34 39N48 84w01 5:36:04
Wrightville 26 107 39N51'39 83w14'52 5:32:59
Wyandot 88 32 40N43'53 83w07'11 5:32:29
Wyoming 31 34 39N13'52 84w27'57 5:37:52
Wyoming Meadows 31 34 39N14'25 84w29'42 5:37:59
Xavier 31 88 39N09 84w29 5:37:56
Xenia 29 87 39N41'05 83w55'47 5:35:43
Yale 62 93 41N36 83w20 5:33:20
Yale 67 67 41N03'45 81w05'55 5:24:24
Yankeeburg 84 20 39N22'49 81w20'36 5:25:22
Yankee Crossing 50 77 40N55'22 80w54'27 5:23:38
Yankee Hills 78 67 41N14'03 80w32'58 5:22:12
Yankee Lake 78 67 41N16'00 80w34'04 5:22:16

Place		Latitude	Longitude	Time
Yankeetown 8	34	38N56'22	84w01'13	5:36:05
Yankeetown 19	34	39N55'47	84w43'20	5:38:53
Yankeetown 24	34	39N39'41	83w16'06	5:33:04
Yarico 44	34	38N39'42	82w24'30	5:29:38
Yates Corners 28	67	41N27'47	81w17'20	5:25:09
Yatesville 24	34	39N40'40	83w26'58	5:33:48
Yellowbud 71	34	39N30'15	83w00'35	5:32:02
Yellow Creek 41	67	40N34'28	80w40'04	5:22:40
Yellow Springs 29	34	39N48'23	83w53'13	5:35:33
Yellowtown 64	27	39N42'05	82w04'06	5:28:16
Yelverton 33	33	40N32'55	83w42'37	5:34:50
Yoder 2	90	40N41'14	84w04'16	5:36:17
Yondota 48	93	41N38'18	83w18'44	5:33:15
York 41	67	40N15'29	80w51'53	5:23:28
York Center 80	33	40N24'28	83w27'12	5:33:49
Yorkshire 19	34	40N19'31	84w29'44	5:37:59
Yorktown 79	16	40N26'48	81w30'56	5:26:04
Yorkville 7	21	40N09'16	80w42'38	5:22:51
Yost 64	5	39N54'31	82w19'58	5:29:20
Youba 5	5	39N14	81w45	5:27:00
Young Hickory 60	5	39N46'46	81w44'58	5:27:00
Youngs 73	34	38N53'55	83w12'22	5:32:49
Youngs Corners 52	73	41N08'10	81w44'07	5:26:56
Youngstown 50	84	41N05'59	80w38'59	5:22:36
Youngsville 1	34	38N55'22	83w34'03	5:34:16
Zahns Corners 66	34	39N03'38	82w57'45	5:31:51
Zaleski 82	27	39N16'56	82w23'42	5:29:35
Zane 46	33	40N17	83w36	5:34:24
Zanesfield 46	33	40N20'18	83w40'38	5:34:43
Zanesville 60	104	39N56'25	82w00'48	5:28:03
Zanesville Terrace 60	5	39N53'58	82w02'02	5:28:08
Zann's Corners 66	34	39N09	83w00	5:32:00
Zeno 60	5	39N47'54	81w44'01	5:26:56
Zenz City 54	34	40N25	84w46	5:39:04
Zimmer 25	107	39N54'24	82w53'54	5:31:36
Zimmerman 29	34	39N43'40	84w03'27	5:36:14
Ziontown 64	16	39N51'13	82w21'44	5:29:27
Zoar 79	16	40N36'51	81w25'21	5:25:41
Zoar 83	34	39N21'03	84w11'30	5:36:46
Zoarville 79	16	40N35'04	81w23'22	5:25:33
Zone 26	34	41N37'22	84w19'41	5:37:19
Zuck 42	5	40N22'41	82w14'11	5:28:57

TIME TABLES

OK # 1

Date	Time	Zone
Before 11/18/1883		LMT
11/18/1883	12:00	CST
3/31/1918	02:00	CWT
10/27/1918	02:00	CST
3/30/1919	02:00	CWT
10/26/1919	02:00	CST
2/09/1942	02:00	CWT
9/30/1945	02:00	CST
4/30/1967	02:00	US#1

OK # 2

Date	Time	Zone
Before 11/18/1883		LMT
11/18/1883	12:00	CST
3/31/1918	02:00	CWT
10/27/1918	02:00	CST
3/30/1919	02:00	CWT
10/26/1919	02:00	CST
2/09/1942	02:00	CWT
9/30/1945	02:00	CST
5/28/1962	02:00	CDT
11/13/1962	02:00	CST
4/30/1967	02:00	US#1

OK # 3

Date	Time	Zone
Before 11/18/1883		LMT
11/18/1883	12:00	CST
3/31/1918	02:00	CWT
10/27/1918	02:00	CST
3/30/1919	02:00	CWT
10/26/1919	02:00	CST
2/09/1942	02:00	CWT
9/30/1945	02:00	CST
6/13/1966	02:00	CDT
10/30/1966	02:00	US#1

OK # 4

Date	Time	Zone
Before 11/18/1883		LMT
11/18/1883	12:00	MST
3/31/1918	02:00	MWT
10/27/1918	02:00	MST
3/30/1919	02:00	MWT
10/26/1919	02:00	MST
3/08/1921	02:00	CST
2/09/1942	02:00	CWT
9/30/1945	02:00	CST
4/30/1967	02:00	US#1

COUNTIES

1 Adair
2 Alfalfa
3 Atoka
4 Beaver
5 Beckham
6 Blaine
7 Bryan
8 Caddo
9 Canadian
10 Carter
11 Cherokee
12 Choctaw
13 Cimarron
14 Cleveland
15 Coal
16 Comanche
17 Cotton
18 Craig
19 Creek
20 Custer
21 Delaware
22 Dewey
23 Ellis
24 Garfield
25 Garvin
26 Grady
27 Grant
28 Greer
29 Harmon
30 Harper
31 Haskell
32 Hughes
33 Jackson
34 Jefferson
35 Johnston
36 Kay
37 Kingfisher
38 Kiowa
39 Latimer
40 Le Flore
41 Lincoln
42 Logan
43 Love
44 McClain
45 McCurtain
46 McIntosh
47 Major
48 Marshall
49 Mayes
50 Murray
51 Muskogee
52 Noble
53 Nowata
54 Okfuskee
55 Oklahoma
56 Okmulgee
57 Osage
58 Ottawa
59 Pawnee
60 Payne
61 Pittsburg
62 Pontotoc
63 Pottawatomie
64 Pushmataha
65 Roger Mills
66 Rogers
67 Seminole
68 Sequoyah
69 Stephens
70 Texas
71 Tillman
72 Tulsa
73 Wagoner
74 Washington
75 Washita
76 Woods
77 Woodward

Place	TT	Lat	Long	Time
Achille 7	1	33N50'00	96w23'13	6:25:33
Acme 26	1	34N47'56	98w01'08	6:32:05
Ada 62	1	34N46'28	96w40'41	6:26:43
Adair 49	1	36N26'12	95w16'16	6:21:05
Adams 70	4	36N45'23	101w04'36	6:44:18
Adamson 61	1	34N55'26	95w32'49	6:22:11
Addielee 1	1	35N57'32	94w38'12	6:18:33
Addington 34	1	34N14'40	97w58'00	6:31:52
Adel 64	1	34N34'45	95w35'39	6:22:23
Admiral 72	1	36N10	95w55	6:23:40
Afton 58	1	36N41'37	94w57'46	6:19:51
Agawam 26	1	34N52'24	97w56'45	6:31:47
Agra 41	1	35N53'49	96w52'31	6:27:30
Ahloso 62	1	34N44'06	96w38'14	6:26:33
Ahpeatone 17	1	34N21	98w18	6:33:12
Akins 68	1	35N30'25	94w41'26	6:18:46
Albany 7	1	33N52'53	96w09'45	6:24:39
Albert 8	1	35N13'58	98w24'40	6:33:39
Albion 64	1	34N39'46	95w05'59	6:20:24
Alcorn 36	1	36N36'47	97w23'34	6:29:34
Alden 8	1	34N58'31	98w35'06	6:34:20
Alderson 61	1	34N54'00	95w41'30	6:22:46
Aledo 22	1	35N49'38	99w07'26	6:36:30
Alex 26	1	34N54'53	97w46'42	6:31:07
Alfalfa 8	1	35N13'08	98w36'25	6:34:26
Alikchi 45	1	34N09'46	95w04'08	6:20:17
Aline 2	1	36N30'35	98w26'55	6:33:48
Allen 62	1	34N52'44	96w24'44	6:25:39
Allison 7	1	33N53'45	96w22'17	6:25:29
Alluwe 53	1	36N36'37	95w29'13	6:21:57
Alma 69	1	34N25'10	97w36'43	6:30:27
Alpers 10	1	34N29'33	97w23'13	6:29:33
Alpha 37	1	35N52'13	98w06'00	6:32:24
Alston 77	1	36N26'10	99w17'24	6:37:10
Alsuma 72	1	36N05'42	95w51'48	6:23:27
Altona 37	1	35N46'59	98w10'15	6:32:41
Altus 33	1	34N38'17	99w20'01	6:37:20
Altus Air Force Base 33	1	34N39	99w19	6:37:16
Alva 76	1	36N48'18	98w39'58	6:34:40
Amabel 60	1	36N00'39	96w50'16	6:27:21
Amber 26	1	35N09'37	97w52'44	6:31:31
Amber Pocasset 26	1	35N08	97w53	6:31:32
America 45	1	33N48'55	94w32'54	6:18:12
Ames 47	1	36N14'45	98w11'06	6:32:44
Amorita 2	1	36N55'28	98w17'29	6:33:10
Anadarko 8	1	35N04'21	98w14'36	6:32:58
Anchor 73	1	35N50'08	95w24'10	6:21:37
Anderson 41	1	35N49'35	96w59'24	6:27:58
Anderson 63	1	35N05'14	96w59'03	6:27:56
Anthon 20	1	35N44'25	99w00'46	6:36:03
Antioch 25	1	34N43'30	97w24'19	6:29:37
Antioch 48	1	34N05	96w46	6:27:04
Antlers 64	1	34N13'52	95w37'12	6:22:29
Apache 8	1	34N53'37	98w21'56	6:33:28
Apache Wye 8	1	35N02'37	98w21'23	6:33:26
Apperson 57	1	36N45'04	96w45'57	6:27:04
Apple 12	1	34N07'39	95w25'02	6:21:40
Aqua Park 68	1	35N37'13	95w04'33	6:20:18
Arapaho 20	1	35N34'40	98w57'51	6:35:51
Arcadia 55	1	35N40'00	97w19'35	6:29:18
Arch 61	1	34N46'28	95w39'39	6:22:39
Ardmore 10	1	34N10'27	97w08'36	6:28:34
Arkoma 40	1	35N21'16	94w26'02	6:17:44
Arlington 41	1	35N34'44	96w40'46	6:26:43
Armstrong 7	1	34N03'05	96w20'42	6:25:23
Arnett 23	1	36N08'06	99w46'28	6:39:06
Arnett 29	1	34N44'50	99w57'53	6:39:52
Arpelar 61	1	34N56'31	95w57'55	6:23:52
Arthur 69	1	34N28	98w00	6:32:00
Artillery Village 16	1	34N38'20	98w24'49	6:33:39
Asher 63	1	34N59'22	96w55'24	6:27:42
Ashland 61	1	34N46'04	96w04'10	6:24:17
Ashley 2	1	36N48'16	98w31'28	6:34:06
Asphaltum 34	1	34N15'36	97w40'29	6:30:42
Atlee 34	1	34N05'36	97w37'56	6:30:32
Atoka 3	1	34N23'09	96w07'41	6:24:31
Atwood 32	1	34N57'22	96w20'18	6:25:21
Autwine 36	1	36N43'19	97w13'47	6:28:55
Avant 57	1	36N29'22	96w03'43	6:24:15
Avard 76	1	36N41'56	98w47'19	6:35:09
Avery 41	1	35N53'03	96w45'07	6:27:00
Avoca 63	1	35N00'50	96w55'49	6:27:43
Aydelotte 63	1	35N26'39	96w54'41	6:27:39
Aylesworth 48	1	34N01'41	96w37'35	6:26:30
Babbs 38	1	34N56'54	99w03'33	6:36:14
Bache 61	1	34N53'39	95w38'54	6:22:36
Bacone 51	1	35N46'01	95w20'24	6:21:22
Bado 47	1	36N13'01	98w44'33	6:34:58
Bailey 26	1	34N42'58	97w47'52	6:31:11
Baker 70	4	36N52'10	101w01'03	6:44:04
Bald Hill 56	1	35N44'25	95w50'13	6:23:21
Baldridge 68	1	35N21'43	94w37'11	6:18:29
Balko 4	4	36N37'48	100w41'04	6:42:44
Ballard 1	1	36N05'40	94w35'21	6:18:21
Banner 9	1	35N30'46	97w50'55	6:31:24
Banty 7	1	34N04'11	96w05'41	6:24:23
Banzet 18	1	36N56'34	95w15'05	6:21:00
Barber 11	1	35N45'26	94w52'03	6:19:28
Barnsdall 57	1	36N33'43	96w09'41	6:24:39
Baron 1	1	35N55'25	94w36'58	6:18:28
Barr 24	1	36N13'57	98w02'00	6:32:08
Bartlesville 74	2	36N44'50	95w58'50	6:23:55
Bashe 40	1	35N18'45	94w26'01	6:17:44
Battiest 45	1	34N23'36	94w55'29	6:19:42
Baum 10	1	34N16'05	96w58'50	6:27:55
Beachton 45	1	34N29'26	94w33'59	6:18:16
Bearden 54	1	35N20'53	96w23'18	6:25:33
Beaver 4	1	36N48'58	100w31'10	6:42:05
Bebee 62	1	34N50'42	96w47'29	6:27:10
Beckwith 21	1	36N11'49	94w42'35	6:18:50
Bedwell 40	1	35N09'35	94w43'00	6:18:52
Bee 35	1	34N07'19	96w34'19	6:26:17
Beggs 56	1	35N44'33	96w04'12	6:24:17
Beland 51	1	35N41'30	95w32'08	6:22:09
Bell 1	1	35N43'05	94w34'33	6:18:18
Bellemont 63	1	35N27'47	96w46'15	6:27:05
Belleville 43	1	33N55'32	97w32'36	6:30:10
Bellvue 19	1	35N54'03	96w23'13	6:25:33
Belmont 63	1	35N29	96w41	6:26:44
Belva 77	1	36N29'56	98w58'29	6:35:54
Belzoni 64	1	34N11'08	95w27'55	6:21:52
Bender 36	1	36N55'59	97w08'14	6:28:33
Bengal 39	1	34N49'58	95w03'42	6:20:15
Benmartin 73	1	35N52	95w31	6:22:04
Bennington 7	1	34N00'16	96w02'15	6:24:09
Bentley 3	1	34N12'53	96w04'43	6:24:19
Berch Hole 11	1	35N49'38	95w06'03	6:20:24
Berlin 65	1	35N27'02	99w37'30	6:38:30
Bernice 21	1	36N36'57	94w55'03	6:19:40
Bessie 75	1	35N23'09	98w59'16	6:35:57
Bethany 55	1	35N31'07	97w37'55	6:30:32
Bethel 16	1	34N35'39	98w09'32	6:32:38
Bethel 45	1	34N21'35	94w50'14	6:19:21
Bethel Acres 63	1	35N19	97w02	6:28:08
Big Cabin 18	1	36N32'16	95w13'16	6:20:53
Big Cedar 40	1	34N38'45	94w38'55	6:18:36
Bigheart 57	1	36N51'06	96w13'32	6:24:54
Big Rocks 64	1	34N13'46	95w34'22	6:22:17
Big Spring 32	1	35N14	96w14	6:24:56
Billings 52	1	36N31'44	97w26'37	6:29:46
Bills Corner 52	1	36N17'24	97w04'02	6:28:16
Binger 8	1	35N18'32	98w20'30	6:33:22
Bishop 23	1	36N07	100w02	6:40:08
Bison 24	1	36N11'47	97w53'23	6:31:34
Bixby 72	1	35N56'31	95w52'59	6:23:32
Black Bear 52	1	36N20'26	97w13'10	6:28:53
Blackburn 59	1	36N22'23	96w35'45	6:26:23
Blackgum 68	1	35N36'35	94w59'22	6:19:57
Blackjack 68	1	35N25'50	94w38'15	6:18:33
Blackland 57	1	36N49'45	96w29'31	6:25:58
Blackwell 36	1	36N48'16	97w16'57	6:29:08
Blair 33	1	34N46'46	99w20'06	6:37:20
Blanch 1	1	35N46'59	94w39'57	6:18:40
Blanchard 44	1	35N08'16	97w39'28	6:30:38
Blanco 61	1	34N45'04	95w46'27	6:23:06
Blanton 24	1	36N25'40	97w55'36	6:31:42
Blocker 61	1	35N03'41	95w34'05	6:22:16
Bloomington 28	1	35N00'06	99w37'50	6:38:31
Blue 7	1	33N59'47	96w13'47	6:24:55
Bluejacket 18	1	36N47'59	95w04'15	6:20:17
Bluff 12	1	34N02	95w42	6:22:48
Boatman 49	1	36N15'30	95w11'03	6:20:44
Boehler 3	1	34N10'15	95w53'00	6:23:32
Boggy Depot 3	1	34N23	96w08	6:24:32
Bois d'Arc 36	1	36N45	97w00	6:28:00
Boise City 13	4	36N43'46	102w30'46	6:50:03
Bokchito 7	1	34N01'02	96w08'33	6:24:34
Bokhoma 45	1	33N49'22	94w34'58	6:18:20
Bokoshe 40	1	35N11'11	94w47'08	6:19:09
Boley 54	1	35N29'36	96w29'00	6:25:56
Bond 46	1	35N28	95w31	6:22:04
Bond 61	1	34N48'51	95w39'15	6:22:37
Boone 8	1	34N53'55	98w27'42	6:33:51
Bordeaux 40	1	35N06'51	94w52'24	6:19:30
Boss 45	1	33N54	94w49	6:19:16
Boswell 12	1	34N01'38	95w52'08	6:23:29
Boudinot 25	1	34N48'48	97w06'29	6:28:26
Boulanger Landing 57	1	36N58'12	96w12'00	6:24:48
Boulangerville 57	1	36N57'23	96w13'05	6:24:52
Boulevard 14	1	35N14	97w25	6:29:40
Bouse Junction 47	1	36N25'18	98w53'19	6:35:33
Bowden 19	1	36N03'46	96w05'13	6:24:21
Bowers 39	1	34N54'44	95w25'08	6:21:41
Bowlegs 67	1	35N08'46	96w40'11	6:26:41
Bowlin Spring 18	1	36N37'08	95w22'39	6:21:31
Bowring 57	1	36N52'41	96w07'11	6:24:29
Box 14	1	34N58'17	97w08'59	6:28:36
Box 68	1	35N34'52	94w58'34	6:19:54
Boyd 4	4	36N42'12	100w49'40	6:43:19
Boynton 51	1	35N38'55	95w39'21	6:22:37
Braden 40	1	35N17'03	94w30'04	6:18:00
Bradley 26	1	34N52'41	97w42'29	6:30:50
Brady 25	1	34N37'22	97w16'56	6:29:08
Braggs 51	1	35N39'48	95w11'52	6:20:47
Braidwood 40	1	34N56'54	94w47'44	6:19:11
Braithwaite 75	1	35N22'25	99w03'29	6:36:14
Braman 36	1	36N55'25	97w20'00	6:29:20
Bray 69	1	34N38'16	97w49'02	6:31:16
Breckinridge 24	1	36N26'13	97w43'53	6:30:56
Brent 68	1	35N28	94w47	6:19:08
Briartown 51	1	35N17'50	95w14'22	6:20:57
Bridgeport 8	1	35N32'47	98w23'03	6:33:32
Briggs 11	1	35N55'37	94w52'28	6:19:30
Brink 76	1	36N50'28	98w36'43	6:34:27
Brinkman 28	1	35N00'36	99w30'59	6:38:04
Bristow 19	1	35N49'50	96w23'27	6:25:34
Bristow Point 61	1	35N07'18	95w36'44	6:22:27
Britton 55	1	35N33'56	97w31'51	6:30:07
Brock 10	1	34N06'57	97w14'21	6:28:57
Broken Arrow 72	1	36N03'09	95w47'26	6:23:10
Broken Bow 45	1	34N01'45	94w44'20	6:18:57
Bromide 35	1	34N25'06	96w29'48	6:25:59
Bromide Junction 35	1	34N24'15	96w25'57	6:25:44
Brooken 31	1	35N20	95w03	6:20:12
Brooksville 63	1	35N11'53	96w58'05	6:27:52
Brown 7	1	34N05'20	96w28'48	6:25:55
Broxton 8	1	34N59'09	98w24'32	6:33:38
Bruno 3	1	34N20'39	96w04'30	6:24:18
Brush Hill 46	1	35N25'12	95w37'41	6:22:31
Brushy 68	1	35N33'25	94w43'31	6:18:54
Bryans Corner (Balko P O) 4	4	36N36'59	100w49'41	6:43:19
Bryant 56	1	35N23'26	96w03'52	6:24:15
Buck Creek Landing 45	1	34N01'35	94w30'41	6:18:03
Bucker 6	1	35N54'51	98w21'26	6:33:26
Buffalo 30	1	36N50'08	99w37'48	6:38:31
Bug Tussle 61	1	35N01'51	95w41'23	6:22:46
Bunch 1	1	35N40'57	94w45'39	6:19:03

Burbank 57 1 36N41'42 96w43'54 6:26:56
Burg 3 1 34N34'50 95w59'45 6:23:59
Burlington 2 1 36N54'00 98w25'21 6:33:41
Burmah 22 1 35N49'37 99w04'28 6:36:18
Burnett 63 1 35N09'21 97w04'50 6:28:19
Burneyville 43 1 33N54'28 97w17'19 6:29:09
Burns Flat 75 1 35N20'56 99w10'12 6:36:41
Burt 71 1 34N27'01 99w04'50 6:36:19
Burton 13 4 36N47'54 102w09'39 6:48:39
Burwell 64 1 34N11'09 95w09'04 6:20:36
Bushyhead 66 1 36N27'41 95w29'38 6:21:59
Butler 20 1 35N38'12 99w11'08 6:36:45
Butner 67 1 35N15'39 96w27'31 6:25:50
Byars 44 1 34N52'27 97w02'59 6:28:12
Byng 62 1 34N51'40 96w39'55 6:26:40
Byron 2 1 36N54'07 98w17'37 6:33:10
Cabaniss 61 1 34N56'30 96w01'28 6:24:06
Cache 16 1 34N37'46 98w37'42 6:34:31
Cache Wye 16 1 34N42'34 98w37'41 6:34:31
Caddo 7 1 34N07'36 96w15'47 6:25:03
Cade 7 1 34N05'55 95w59'23 6:23:58
Cairo 15 1 34N35'26 96w07'54 6:24:32
Caldwell Hill 10
1 34N11'14 97w00'58 6:28:04
Calera 7 1 33N56'04 96w25'42 6:25:43
Calhoun 40 1 35N06'13 94w44'45 6:18:59
Callahan 24 1 36N17'45 97w34'07 6:30:16
Calumet 9 1 35N36'04 98w07'06 6:32:28
Calvin 32 1 34N58'04 96w14'54 6:25:00
Camargo 22 1 36N01'02 99w17'20 6:37:09
Cambria 39 1 34N51 95w34 6:22:16
Cambridge 38 1 35N04'22 99w12'18 6:36:49
Cameron 40 1 35N08'02 94w32'04 6:18:08
Cameron College 16
1 34N37 98w25 6:33:40
Camp Houston 76
1 36N46 99w07 6:36:28
Canadian 61 1 35N10'38 95w39'18 6:22:37
Canadian City 9
1 35N32 97w57 6:31:48
Canadian Fork 61
1 35N14'35 95w31'39 6:22:07
Canadian Shores 61
1 35N10'29 95w44'24 6:22:58
Caney 3 1 34N13'56 96w12'50 6:24:51
Caney Ridge 11 1 35N45'51 94w52'50 6:19:31
Canton 6 1 36N03'13 98w35'17 6:34:21
Canute 75 1 35N25'19 99w16'45 6:37:07
Capitol Hill 55
1 35N26 97w32 6:30:08
Capron 76 1 36N53'48 98w34'38 6:34:19
Carbon 61 1 34N55'34 95w38'20 6:22:33
Carbondale 72 1 36N05'43 96w01'12 6:24:05
Cardin 58 1 36N58'21 94w50'55 6:19:24
Carl 29 1 34N57'29 99w56'24 6:39:46
Carleton 6 1 36N00'52 98w30'54 6:34:04
Carmen 2 1 36N34'44 98w27'43 6:33:51
Carnegie 8 1 35N06'13 98w36'12 6:34:25
Carney 41 1 35N48'30 97w00'45 6:28:03
Carpenter 65 1 35N31'49 99w22'17 6:37:29
Carrier 24 1 36N28'37 98w01'19 6:32:05
Carson 32 1 35N09'57 96w05'18 6:24:21
Carter 5 1 35N13'08 99w30'19 6:38:01
Carter 11 1 35N52 94w58 6:19:52
Carter Nine 57 1 36N44'41 96w39'40 6:26:39
Carter Park 55 1 35N26 97w26 6:29:44
Carters Corner 46
1 35N17'22 95w39'46 6:22:39
Carters Landing 11
1 35N47'50 94w54'13 6:19:37
Cartersville 31
1 35N13'53 94w50'41 6:19:23
Cartoco 60 1 36N05'14 96w42'50 6:26:51
Cartwright 7 1 33N51'10 96w33'42 6:26:15
Carwile 2 1 36N27'48 98w18'03 6:33:12
Casey 59 1 36N16'57 96w40'26 6:26:42
Cashion 37 1 35N47'53 97w40'42 6:30:43
Castaneda 13 4 36N52'52 102w31'15 6:50:05
Castle 54 1 35N28'28 96w22'55 6:25:32
Caston 40 1 34N57'26 94w49'58 6:19:20
Catale 66 1 36N33'39 95w22'18 6:21:29
Catesby 23 1 36N29'35 99w57'45 6:39:51
Cato 37 1 36N08'45 98w01'56 6:32:08
Catoosa 66 1 36N11'20 95w44'44 6:22:59
Cavanal 40 1 34N58'49 94w41'53 6:18:48
Cayuga 21 1 36N38'03 94w40'47 6:18:43
Cedar 39 1 35N01'06 94w59'21 6:19:57
Cedar Crest 49 1 36N06'48 95w13'44 6:20:55
Cedardale 77 1 36N19'08 98w59'46 6:35:59
Cedars 40 1 35N16'27 94w26'33 6:17:46
Cedar Village 50
1 34N26'32 97w08'02 6:28:32
Cement 8 1 34N55'55 98w08'24 6:32:34
Center 62 1 34N47'57 96w48'55 6:27:16
Center Point 39
1 34N56'47 95w18'48 6:21:15
Centerview 63 1 35N26'01 96w39'54 6:26:40
Centerville 38 1 34N43'31 99w06'20 6:36:25
Centerville 61 1 34N52'00 95w31'03 6:22:04
Centrahoma 15 1 34N36'35 96w20'43 6:25:23
Centralia 18 1 36N47'48 95w21'11 6:21:25
Central Washita 75
1 35N17 98w57 6:35:48
Ceres 52 1 36N28'38 97w16'56 6:29:08
Cerrogordo 45 1 33N51 94w39 6:18:36
Cestos 22 1 36N08'39 99w05'36 6:36:22
Chambers 61 1 34N52'11 95w49'28 6:23:18
Chance 1 1 36N03'37 94w39'18 6:18:37
Chandler 41 1 35N42'06 96w52'50 6:27:31
Chase 51 1 35N45 95w22 6:21:28
Chattanooga 16 1 34N25'22 98w39'22 6:34:37
Chatto Crossing 16
1 34N41'08 98w23'14 6:33:33
Checotah 46 1 35N28'12 95w31'22 6:22:05
Cheek 10 1 34N04'42 97w16'56 6:29:08
Chelsea 66 1 36N32'08 95w25'56 6:21:44
Cherokee 2 1 36N45'16 98w21'23 6:33:26
Cherry Tree 1 1 35N44'29 94w38'35 6:18:34
Chester 47 1 36N12'59 98w55'14 6:35:41
Chewey 1 1 36N06'13 94w46'02 6:19:04
Cheyenne 65 1 35N36'50 99w40'16 6:38:41
Cheyenne Valley 47
1 36N22'09 98w39'27 6:34:38

Chickasha 26 1 35N03'09 97w56'10 6:31:45
Chigley 50 1 34N35'36 97w04'41 6:28:19
Childers 53 1 36N46'18 95w32'22 6:22:09
Chilesville 54 1 35N33'07 96w28'35 6:25:54
Chilli 39 1 34N56'31 95w26'11 6:21:45
Chilocco 36 1 36N59'20 97w04'10 6:28:17
Chism 44 1 34N54'46 96w56'12 6:27:45
Chitwood 26 1 34N57 97w56 6:31:44
Chloeta 21 1 36N25'23 94w58'14 6:19:53
Chockie 3 1 34N34'55 95w59'53 6:24:00
Choctaw 55 1 35N29'51 97w16'07 6:29:04
Choska 73 1 36N03 95w42 6:22:48
Chouteau 49 1 36N11'09 95w20'34 6:21:22
Christie 1 1 35N57'29 94w41'24 6:18:46
Cimarron 55 1 35N31 97w29 6:29:56
Cimmaron City 42
1 36N00 97w37 6:30:28
Cisco 45 1 33N54 94w49 6:19:16
Citra 32 1 34N47'47 96w22'34 6:25:30
City View 28 1 34N50'29 99w21'06 6:37:24
Civit 25 1 34N47'21 97w07'31 6:28:30
Claremore 66 1 36N18'45 95w36'57 6:22:28
Clarita 15 1 34N28'58 96w25'59 6:25:44
Clarks Heights 63
1 35N22'35 97w00'02 6:28:00
Clarksville 73 1 35N49'32 95w30'50 6:22:03
Claud 69 1 34N28 98w00 6:32:00
Clayton 64 1 34N35'22 95w21'09 6:21:25
Clear Lake 4 1 36N41'20 100w16'18 6:41:05
Clearview 54 1 35N23'49 96w11'10 6:24:45
Clebit 45 1 34N23'25 95w01'12 6:20:05
Clemscot 10 1 34N20'50 97w27'23 6:29:50
Cleora 21 1 36N34'44 94w58'15 6:19:53
Cleo Springs 47
1 36N24'19 98w26'25 6:33:46
Cleveland 59 1 36N18'36 96w27'50 6:25:51
Clifton 41 1 35N30'57 96w54'42 6:27:39
Clinton 20 1 35N30'56 98w58'01 6:35:52
Clothier 14 1 35N19'11 97w24'52 6:29:39
Cloud Chief 75 1 35N15'09 98w50'34 6:35:22
Cloudy 64 1 34N18'07 95w16'51 6:21:07
Clyde 27 1 36N50'47 97w49'15 6:31:17
Coal Creek 40 1 35N11'20 94w39'38 6:18:39
Coalgate 15 1 34N32'17 96w13'06 6:24:52
Coalton 56 1 35N29'51 95w56'20 6:23:45
Cobalt Junction 10
1 34N09'45 97w30'42 6:30:03
Cobb 7 1 34N05'05 96w24'27 6:25:38
Cocklebur Flat 18
1 36N49'48 95w11'51 6:20:47
Cody 20 1 35N48'19 98w41'25 6:34:46
Cody 59 1 36N19'08 96w42'36 6:26:50
Cogar 8 1 35N20'02 98w07'49 6:32:31
Coil 62 1 34N39'29 96w31'46 6:26:07
Colbert 7 1 33N51'11 96w30'08 6:26:01
Colcord 21 1 36N15'51 94w41'34 6:18:46
Cold Springs 38
1 34N47'45 99w00'17 6:36:01
Cole 44 1 35N06'08 97w34'21 6:30:17
Coleman 35 1 34N16'17 96w25'08 6:25:41
College 60 1 36N07 97w04 6:28:16
Collinsville 72
1 36N21'52 95w50'19 6:23:21
Colony 75 1 35N20'55 98w40'35 6:34:42
Comanche 69 1 34N22'08 97w57'49 6:31:51
Commerce 58 1 36N56'00 94w52'22 6:19:29
Compton 40 1 34N48'16 95w01'16 6:20:05
Concho 9 1 35N36'56 97w59'39 6:31:59
Connerville 35 1 34N26'51 96w38'09 6:26:33
Conrad 13 4 36N36'55 102w22'23 6:49:30
Conser 40 1 34N50'25 94w41'05 6:18:44
Coodys Bluff 53
1 36N41'54 95w33'50 6:22:15
Cook 3 1 34N16'16 96w11'49 6:24:47
Cookietown 17 1 34N16'30 98w27'11 6:33:49
Cookson 11 1 35N42'39 94w55'11 6:19:41
Cooper 57 1 36N48'40 96w45'06 6:27:00
Cooperton 38 1 34N52'03 98w51'59 6:35:28
Copan 74 1 36N53'51 95w55'33 6:23:42
Copeland 21 1 36N39'21 94w49'41 6:19:19
Copic Slab 68 1 35N36'35 94w33'32 6:18:14
Cora 76 1 36N47'52 98w55'00 6:35:40
Corbett 14 1 34N58'24 97w13'45 6:28:55
Cordell 75 1 35N17'26 98w59'17 6:35:57
Corinne 64 1 34N11'09 95w17'28 6:21:10
Corn 75 1 35N22'41 98w46'54 6:35:08
Cornatzar 18 1 36N38'20 95w06'27 6:20:26
Cornish 34 1 34N09'32 97w35'48 6:30:23
Corral Crossing 16
1 34N39'56 98w22'45 6:33:31
Corum 69 1 34N21'44 98w06'14 6:32:25
Cottingham 60 1 35N57'44 96w57'07 6:27:48
Cotton Valley 74
1 36N58'15 95w51'31 6:23:26
Cottonwood 15 1 34N33'21 96w12'13 6:24:49
Cottonwood 68 1 35N22'06 94w32'56 6:18:12
Council Hill 51
1 35N33'20 95w39'04 6:22:36
Counts 61 1 34N40'24 95w34'43 6:22:19
Countyline 69 1 34N26'55 97w33'45 6:30:15
Courtney 43 1 33N56'25 97w30'29 6:30:02
Covington 24 1 36N18'27 97w35'10 6:30:21
Cowden 75 1 35N14'52 98w42'42 6:34:51
Cowden Junction 75
1 35N17'27 98w42'40 6:34:51
Coweta 73 1 35N57'06 95w39'02 6:22:36
Cowlington 40 1 35N18 94w47 6:19:08
Cox City 26 1 34N43'31 97w43'53 6:30:56
Coxs Corner 16 1 34N38'15 98w12'43 6:32:51
Coyle 42 1 35N57'24 97w14'03 6:28:56
Craig 61 1 34N50'25 95w37'38 6:22:31
Cravens 39 1 34N57 95w05 6:20:20
Crawford 65 1 35N49'37 99w47'57 6:39:12
Creata 33 1 34N31'09 99w32'48 6:38:11
Crekola 51 1 35N42'20 95w29'14 6:21:57
Creosote 12 1 34N01 95w31 6:22:04
Crescent 42 1 35N57'09 97w35'40 6:30:23
Crescent Springs 42
1 35N53'47 97w36'08 6:30:25
Criner 44 1 34N58'17 97w33'51 6:30:15
Cromwell 67 1 35N20'24 96w27'25 6:25:50
Cropper 24 1 36N26'28 97w41'23 6:30:46
Cross Roads 32 1 35N00'23 96w14'51 6:24:59

Crossroads 45 1 33N58'57 94w47'27 6:19:10
Crowder 61 1 35N07'26 95w40'11 6:22:41
Crusher 50 1 34N21'02 97w01'45 6:28:07
Crystal 3 1 34N13'36 95w55'48 6:23:43
Cumberland 48 1 34N03'52 96w35'58 6:26:24
Curtis 77 1 36N26'21 99w08'32 6:36:34
Cushing 60 1 35N59'06 96w46'00 6:27:04
Custer City 20 1 35N39'54 98w52'58 6:35:32
Cyril 8 1 34N53'47 98w12'01 6:32:48
Dacoma 76 1 36N39'34 98w33'46 6:34:15
Daisy 3 1 34N32'09 95w44'22 6:22:57
Dale 63 1 35N23'24 97w02'41 6:28:11
Damon 39 1 34N51'18 95w18'27 6:21:14
Dane 47 1 36N13'01 98w37'09 6:34:29
Darrow 6 1 36N05'53 98w23'17 6:33:33
Darwin 3 1 34N14'52 95w46'45 6:23:07
Davenport 41 1 35N42'17 96w45'54 6:27:04
Davidson 71 1 34N14'27 99w04'31 6:36:18
Davis 50 1 34N30'16 97w07'09 6:28:29
Dawes 58 1 36N52'53 94w59'28 6:19:58
Dawson 72 1 36N10'47 95w54'30 6:23:38
Dead Women Crossing 20
1 35N34'04 98w39'02 6:34:36
Deer Creek 27 1 36N48'21 97w31'09 6:30:05
Degnan 39 1 34N56'50 95w21'11 6:21:25
Degroat 66 1 36N20'11 95w36'13 6:22:25
Dela 64 1 34N12'01 95w31'19 6:22:05
Delaware 53 1 36N46'43 95w38'21 6:22:33
Del City 55 1 35N26'31 97w26'26 6:29:46
Delhi 5 1 35N10'29 99w40'34 6:38:42
Dempsey 65 1 35N31'03 99w49'21 6:39:17
Denman 39 1 34N56'12 95w01'32 6:20:06
Dennis 21 1 36N32'21 94w53'02 6:19:32
Denny 50 1 34N34'12 96w50'47 6:27:23
Denoya 57 1 36N42 96w44 6:26:56
Denton 69 1 34N39'59 98w07'27 6:32:30
Dentonville 56 1 35N44'28 96w08'22 6:24:33
Denver 14 1 35N13'57 97w16'55 6:29:08
Depew 19 1 35N48'10 96w30'21 6:26:01
Depot 61 1 34N56 95w46 6:23:04
Devol 17 1 34N11'45 98w35'23 6:34:22
Dewar 56 1 35N27'29 95w56'28 6:23:46
Dewey 74 1 36N47'45 95w56'07 6:23:44
Dibble 44 1 35N02'00 97w37'46 6:30:31
Dickson 10 1 34N11'14 96w59'03 6:27:56
Dighton 56 1 35N28'03 95w53'34 6:23:34
Dillard 10 1 34N11'14 97w24'16 6:29:37
Dill City 75 1 35N16'36 99w08'05 6:36:32
Dilworth 36 1 36N56'29 97w13'40 6:28:55
Disney 49 1 36N28'52 95w00'53 6:20:04
Divide 64 1 34N28'33 95w18'33 6:21:14
Dixie Park 69 1 34N29'14 97w56'57 6:31:48
Dixon 67 1 35N09'34 96w31'17 6:26:05
Dodge 21 1 36N34'25 94w39'21 6:18:37
Doga 57 1 36N34'00 96w47'43 6:27:11
Dog Creek 40 1 35N06'03 94w51'04 6:19:24
Dolberg 62 1 34N37'36 96w55'07 6:27:40
Donaldson 72 1 36N09 95w57 6:23:48
Doolin 70 4 36N47'56 101w59'33 6:47:58
Dotyville 58 1 36N51'32 94w54'31 6:19:38
Dougherty 50 1 34N23'58 97w03'19 6:28:13
Douglas 24 1 36N15'38 97w40'08 6:30:41
Douglas 72 1 36N11'01 95w52'50 6:23:31
Douthat 58 1 36N57'33 94w50'09 6:19:21
Dover 37 1 35N58'53 97w54'39 6:31:39
Dow 61 1 34N52'36 95w36'00 6:22:24
Downtown 55 1 35N29 97w32 6:30:08
Doxey 5 1 35N19'27 99w34'58 6:38:20
Doyle 69 1 34N37 97w30 6:30:00
Drake 50 1 34N23'52 96w57'02 6:27:48
Drakes Corner 60
1 35N59'09 96w52'24 6:27:30
Driftwood 2 1 36N52'45 98w21'33 6:33:26
Dripping Springs 10
1 34N11'13 97w02'17 6:28:09
Drumb 39 1 34N55'47 95w28'51 6:21:55
Drummond 24 1 36N18'01 98w02'08 6:32:09
Drumright 19 1 35N59'18 96w36'03 6:26:24
Dudley 41 1 35N48'41 97w03'58 6:28:16
Duhringe Pass 16
1 34N43'46 98w29'23 6:33:58
Duke 33 1 34N39'41 99w34'11 6:38:17
Dunbar 43 1 33N56'27 97w16'55 6:29:08
Dunbar 64 1 34N27'31 95w33'37 6:22:14
Duncan 69 1 34N30'08 97w57'27 6:31:50
Dundee 10 1 34N13'52 97w32'41 6:30:11
Dunjee Park 55 1 35N30'48 97w18'01 6:29:12
Durant 7 1 33N59'28 96w22'26 6:25:30
Durham 65 1 35N50'31 99w55'28 6:39:42
Durwood 10 1 34N10'36 96w57'52 6:27:51
Dustin 32 1 35N16'14 96w01'50 6:24:07
Dutton 8 1 35N12'14 98w05'39 6:32:23
Eagle City 6 1 35N55'59 98w35'29 6:34:22
Eagletown 45 1 34N02'03 94w34'29 6:18:18
Eakly 8 1 35N18'19 98w33'27 6:34:14
Earl 35 1 34N12'06 96w53'51 6:27:35
Earlsboro 63 1 35N16'03 96w48'11 6:27:13
Eason 63 1 35N00'53 97w07'48 6:28:31
East Bryan 7 1 34N02 96w01 6:24:04
East Canadian 9
1 35N35 97w48 6:31:12
East Cherokee 11
1 35N51 94w51 6:19:24
East Coal 15 1 34N33 96w14 6:24:56
Eastern 55 1 35N29 97w29 6:29:56
Eastern Oklahoma A&M College 39
1 34N55 95w19 6:21:16
Easter Pageant 16
1 34N44'33 98w35'24 6:34:22
East Jackson 33
1 34N43 99w13 6:36:52
East Jesse 62 1 34N34'52 96w30'43 6:26:03
East Jessie 15 1 34N39 96w31 6:26:04
East Johnston 35
1 34N17 96w30 6:26:00
East Junction 20
1 35N31'35 98w57'51 6:35:51
East Logan 42 1 35N52 97w15 6:29:00
East Love 43 1 33N55 97w08 6:28:32
East Major 47 1 36N21 98w14 6:32:56
Eastman 43 1 33N59'18 97w15'52 6:29:03
East Mayes 49 1 36N23 95w05 6:20:20

East McClain 44	1	34N54	97W08	6:28:32
East Murray 50	1	34N30	96W57	6:27:48
East Ninnekah 26	1	34N57	97W56	6:31:44
East Noble 52	1	36N26	97W06	6:28:24
Eastport 45	1	33N47'20	94W28'54	6:17:56
East Roger Mills 65	1	35N43	99W27	6:37:48
Eastside 58	1	36N52'17	94W42'59	6:18:52
East Side 74	2	36N45	95W59	6:23:56
East Tillman 71	1	34N17	98W44	6:34:56
East Tulsa 72	1	36N10'21	95W56'26	6:23:46
Echota 1	1	35N49	94W37	6:18:28
Econtuchka 63	1	35N24'20	96W47'19	6:27:09
Eddy 36	1	36N43'54	97W27'30	6:29:50
Edgewater Acres 66	1	36N26'32	95W37'43	6:22:31
Edgewater Park 16	1	34N49'33	98W22'40	6:33:31
Edith 76	1	36N48'10	99W12'39	6:36:51
Edmond 55	1	35N39'10	97W28'40	6:29:55
Edna 19	1	35N42'14	96W12'37	6:24:50
Elba 66	1	36N24'10	95W40'45	6:22:43
Eldon 11	1	35N55'41	94W50'24	6:19:22
Eldorado 33	1	34N28'19	99W38'52	6:38:35
Elgin 16	1	34N46'49	98W17'31	6:33:10
Eli 11	1	35N59'15	95W11'21	6:20:45
Elk City 5	1	35N24'43	99W24'14	6:37:37
Ellaville 63	1	35N06'05	96W48'33	6:27:14
Ellerville 11	1	36N01'52	94W54'07	6:19:36
Elliott 53	1	36N56'32	95W37'45	6:22:31
Elmer 33	1	34N28'52	99W21'02	6:37:24
Elmore City 25	1	34N37'22	97W23'46	6:29:35
Elmwood 4	4	36N36'59	100W31'20	6:42:05
El Reno 9	1	35N31'56	97W57'17	6:31:49
Emerson Center 17	1	34N21	98W18	6:33:12
Emet 35	1	34N12'09	96W32'31	6:26:10
Empire City 69	1	34N25'13	98W01'36	6:32:06
Emsey 41	1	35N46'03	97W01'27	6:28:06
England 1	1	35N53'04	94W40'04	6:18:40
Enid 24	1	36N23'44	97W52'41	6:31:31
Enos 48	1	34N00	96W43	6:26:52
Enterprise 31	1	35N13'47	95W22'47	6:21:31
Enville 43	1	33N59'01	96W59'10	6:27:57
Eram 56	1	35N37'01	95W45'17	6:23:01
Erick 5	1	35N12'55	99W51'58	6:39:28
Erie 36	1	36N59'56	97W04'31	6:28:18
Erin Springs 25	1	34N48'39	97W36'23	6:30:26
Esau Junction 59	1	36N21'13	96W42'16	6:26:49
Estella 18	1	36N41'05	95W17'13	6:21:09
Ethel 64	1	34N13'46	95W32'38	6:22:11
Etna 24	1	36N22'14	97W44'47	6:30:59
Etta 11	1	35N53	94W54	6:19:36
Eubanks 64	1	34N25'19	95W35'05	6:22:20
Eucha 21	1	36N23'31	94W52'58	6:19:32
Euchee Creek 72	1	36N08	96W03	6:24:12
Eufaula 46	1	35N17'14	95W34'56	6:22:20
Eva 70	4	36N47'54	101W54'23	6:47:38
Eville 43	1	34N00'18	96W59'13	6:27:57
Ewing 20	1	35N31	98W58	6:35:52
Fairfax 57	1	36N34'25	96W42'14	6:26:49
Fairland 58	3	36N45'04	94W50'50	6:19:23
Fairmont 24	1	36N21'20	97W42'19	6:30:49
Fair Oaks 73	1	36N09	95W40	6:22:40
Fairvalley 76	1	36N44'08	99W01'27	6:36:06
Fairview 47	1	36N16'08	98W28'46	6:33:55
Falconhead 43	1	33N54	97W17	6:29:08
Falfa 39	1	34N45	95W03	6:20:12
Fallis 41	1	35N44'54	97W07'13	6:28:29
Fallon 12	1	33N59'52	95W25'00	6:21:40
Falls Creek Assembly 50	1	34N25'35	97W06'39	6:28:27
Fame 46	1	35N21'44	95W38'44	6:22:35
Fanshawe 40	1	34N57'03	94W54'29	6:19:38
Fargo 23	1	36N22'34	99W37'24	6:38:30
Farley 55	1	35N29	97W34	6:30:16
Farmers Hill 45	1	33N55'28	95W01'02	6:20:04
Farris 3	1	34N15'45	95W51'59	6:23:28
Farwell 26	1	34N53'09	98W00'19	6:32:01
Faxon 16	1	34N27'25	98W34'43	6:34:19
Fay 22	1	35N48'48	98W39'27	6:34:38
Featherston 61	1	35N04'43	95W29'23	6:21:58
Felker 45	1	34N02'26	95W03'07	6:20:12
Felt 13	4	36N34'03	102W47'35	6:51:10
Fern 30	1	36N26	99W24	6:37:36
Fewell 64	1	34N31'05	95W03'13	6:20:13
Fillmore 35	1	34N16'27	96W29'45	6:25:59
Finley 64	1	34N19'42	95W29'41	6:21:59
Fisher 72	1	36N07'45	96W08'31	6:24:34
Fite 57	2	36N43'24	96W04'45	6:24:19
Fittstown 62	1	34N36'53	96W38'03	6:26:32
Fitzhugh 62	1	34N39'57	96W46'29	6:27:06
Five Mile 58	1	36N59'00	94W41'34	6:18:46
Fivemile Corner 17	1	34N21'44	98W13'34	6:32:54
Fleetwood 34	1	33N53'48	97W51'03	6:31:24
Fletcher 16	1	34N49'23	98W14'38	6:32:59
Flint 21	1	36N11'14	94W42'28	6:18:50
Flora 3	1	34N31'33	96W01'54	6:24:08
Floris 4	1	36N52'11	100W42'39	6:42:51
Fluor 70	4	36N57'59	101W03'02	6:44:12
Flynn 55	1	35N24'06	97W29'14	6:29:57
Fobb 48	1	33N54'40	96W50'45	6:27:23
Fogel 40	1	34N42'25	94W27'19	6:17:49
Foley 20	1	35N41'02	98W50'57	6:35:24
Folsom 35	1	34N11'36	96W25'13	6:25:41
Foraker 57	1	36N52'20	96W33'55	6:26:16
Foreman 68	1	35N20'05	94W38'12	6:18:33
Forest Hill 40	1	34N55'39	94W37'10	6:18:29
Forest Park 55	1	35N30'15	97W26'45	6:29:47
Forgan 4	1	36N54'25	100W32'20	6:42:09
Forman 68	1	35N24	94W36	6:18:24
Forney 12	1	34N01'47	95W37'10	6:22:29
Forrester 40	1	34N52'20	94W31'35	6:18:06
Fort Cobb 8	1	35N05'52	98W26'07	6:33:44
Fort Coffee 40	1	35N17'21	94W35'03	6:18:20
Fort Gibson 51	1	35N47'51	95W15'01	6:21:00
Fort Reno 9	1	35N32	97W57	6:31:48
Fort Sill 16	1	34N41	98W26	6:33:44
Fort Supply 77	1	36N34'25	99W34'19	6:38:17
Fort Towson 12	1	34N01'07	95W15'58	6:21:04
Fort Washita 7	1	34N06'10	96W32'46	6:26:11
Foss 75	1	35N27'16	99W10'10	6:36:41
Foster 25	1	34N36'59	97W29'20	6:29:57
Four Mile Crossing 16	1	34N41'10	98W26'42	6:33:47
Fowler 41	1	35N30'26	97W03'10	6:28:13
Fox 10	1	34N21'49	97W29'31	6:29:58
Foyil 66	1	36N26'05	95W31'09	6:22:05
Francis 62	1	34N52'25	96W35'43	6:26:23
Frankfort 57	1	36N58'33	96W40'46	6:26:43
Franklin 14	1	35N16'35	97W20'07	6:29:20
Franks 62	1	34N36'23	96W38'33	6:26:34
Frederick 71	1	34N23'31	99W01'05	6:36:04
Freedom 76	1	36N46'08	99W06'45	6:36:27
Frey 19	1	36N01'11	96W36'36	6:26:26
Friendship 33	1	34N41'45	99W13'43	6:36:55
Frink 61	1	34N53'03	95W47'21	6:23:09
Frisco 62	1	34N38'52	96W34'43	6:26:19
Frogville 12	1	33N53'51	95W18'45	6:21:15
Frost 42	1	35N53'03	97W14'48	6:28:59
Fugate 3	1	34N27'26	95W55'18	6:23:41
Gaar Corner 62	1	34N47'48	96W51'42	6:27:27
Gaddy 63	1	35N19'59	97W00'02	6:28:00
Gage 23	1	36N18'56	99W45'26	6:39:02
Gano 60	1	36N00'53	96W45'17	6:27:01
Gans 68	1	35N23'20	94W41'31	6:18:46
Gansel 52	1	36N16'48	97W22'19	6:29:29
Gap 3	1	34N43	95W54	6:23:36
Garber 24	1	36N26'13	97W35'07	6:30:20
Garden City 72	1	36N06'38	96W00'10	6:24:01
Garden Grove 63	1	35N25'10	96W46'15	6:27:05
Garland 31	1	35N19'08	95W03'05	6:20:12
Garnett 72	1	36N11'13	95W49'35	6:23:18
Garvin 45	1	33N57'14	94W56'32	6:19:46
Gas City 69	1	34N26'59	98W05'12	6:32:21
Gate 4	1	36N51'12	100W03'18	6:40:13
Gay 12	1	33N57'13	95W37'23	6:22:30
Geary 9	1	35N37'52	98W19'01	6:33:16
Gene Autry 10	1	34N17'01	97W02'16	6:28:09
Georgetown 51	1	35N48	95W15	6:21:00
Gerlach 77	1	36N26'09	99W27'08	6:37:49
Geronimo 16	1	34N28'52	98W22'58	6:33:32
Gerty 32	1	34N50'12	96W17'22	6:25:09
Gibbon 27	1	36N56'34	97W58'55	6:31:56
Gibson 73	1	35N52'15	95W21'06	6:21:24
Gideon 11	1	36N00'34	95W01'59	6:20:08
Gilbert 27	1	36N47'23	97W56'50	6:31:47
Gilland 57	1	36N31'59	96W09'14	6:24:37
Gilmore 40	1	35N03'10	94W31'22	6:18:05
Glencoe 60	1	36N13'43	96W55'31	6:27:42
Glendale 40	1	34N55'23	94W42'33	6:18:50
Glenn 10	1	34N19	97W08	6:28:32
Glenoak 53	2	36N43'41	95W48'31	6:23:14
Glenpool 72	1	35N57'19	96W00'31	6:24:02
Glover 45	1	34N04'13	94W53'52	6:19:35
Golden 45	1	34N02'04	94W53'46	6:19:35
Goldsby 44	1	35N09	97W29	6:29:56
Goltry 2	1	36N31'57	98W09'05	6:32:36
Good 12	1	34N01	95W31	6:22:04
Goodlake 45	1	33N42'25	94W38'32	6:18:34
Goodland 12	1	33N58'54	95W33'18	6:22:13
Goodnight 42	1	35N57'05	97W08'25	6:28:34
Goodwater 45	1	33N54'36	94W34'23	6:18:18
Goodwell 70	4	36N35'43	101W38'10	6:46:33
Goodwin 23	1	36N11'48	99W56'05	6:39:44
Gore 68	1	35N31'45	95W07'01	6:20:28
Gore Landing 68	1	35N31'23	95W05'44	6:20:23
Goss 3	1	34N33'03	95W41'28	6:22:46
Gotebo 38	1	35N04'13	98W52'19	6:35:29
Gould 29	1	34N40'15	99W46'15	6:39:05
Gowen 39	1	34N52'53	95W28'36	6:21:54
Grace 3	1	34N43	95W54	6:23:36
Gracemont 8	1	35N11'18	98W15'37	6:33:02
Grady 34	1	34N01'13	97W39'55	6:30:40
Graham 10	1	34N20'26	97W26'03	6:29:44
Grainola 57	1	36N56'14	96W39'01	6:26:36
Grainville 36	1	36N50'24	97W13'41	6:28:55
Grandfield 71	1	34N13'42	98W41'03	6:34:44
Grand Lake Towne 49	1	36N30'15	95W01'20	6:20:05
Grandview Heights 51	1	35N42'51	95W21'58	6:21:28
Granite 28	1	34N57'44	99W22'49	6:37:31
Grant 12	1	33N56'35	95W30'48	6:22:03
Gray 4	4	36N33'30	100W49'24	6:43:18
Gray 72	1	36N07'49	96W04'49	6:24:19
Gray Horse 57	1	36N32'59	96W38'51	6:26:35
Grayson 56	1	35N30'11	95W52'21	6:23:29
Greasy 1	1	35N40'02	94W42'02	6:18:48
Green 1	1	35N58'37	94W37'35	6:18:30
Green 49	1	36N23'09	95W17'21	6:21:09
Green Country Estates 11	1	35N52'13	94W59'17	6:19:57
Greenfield 6	1	35N43'43	98W22'33	6:33:31
Green Pastures 55	1	35N31'20	97W20'08	6:29:21
Greenville 43	1	34N00'26	97W07'32	6:28:30
Greenwood 64	1	34N11'32	95W35'15	6:22:21
Greig 55	1	36N47	95W38	6:22:32
Grenade Crossing 16	1	34N40'11	98W22'50	6:33:31
Griggs 13	4	36N36'10	102W07'19	6:48:29
Grimes 65	1	35N27'58	99W45'38	6:39:03
Grove 21	1	36N35'37	94W46'08	6:19:05
Gulf Junction 9	1	35N32	97W57	6:31:48
Gulf Junction 25	1	34N43'44	97W12'11	6:28:49
Gulftown 56	1	35N27'23	95W54'39	6:23:39
Guthrie 42	1	35N52'44	97W25'30	6:29:42
Guymon 70	4	36N40'58	101W28'52	6:45:55
Gypsy 19	1	35N42'42	96W27'33	6:25:50
Haileyville 61	1	34N51'16	95W34'55	6:22:20
Half Bank Crossing 3	1	34N21'11	96W00'19	6:24:01
Hall Addition 72	1	36N08	96W03	6:24:12
Hallett 59	1	36N14'02	96W34'02	6:26:16
Hall Park 14	1	35N14'13	97W24'22	6:29:37
Hamden 12	1	34N08'32	95W33'59	6:22:16
Hamilton 67	1	35N09	96W30	6:26:00
Hammon 65	1	35N37'58	99W22'53	6:37:32
Hammon Junction 65	1	35N39'22	99W22'30	6:37:30
Hanna 46	1	35N12'18	95W53'24	6:23:34
Hanson 68	1	35N26'04	94W41'55	6:18:48
Happyland 62	1	34N47'48	96W32'57	6:26:12
Harden City 62	1	34N36'26	96W35'58	6:26:24
Hardesty 70	4	36N36'59	101W11'25	6:44:46
Hardy 36	1	36N58'15	96W47'53	6:27:12
Harjo 63	1	35N12'48	96W49'39	6:27:19
Harmon 23	1	36N08'41	99W33'36	6:38:14
Harmony Star 66	1	36N18'27	95W28'15	6:21:53
Harrah 55	1	35N29'22	97W09'48	6:28:39
Harris 45	1	33N45'01	94W43'44	6:18:55
Harrisburg 69	1	34N26'05	97W47'22	6:31:09
Harrison 68	1	35N25'12	94W52'02	6:19:28
Hart 62	1	34N42'51	96W55'01	6:27:40
Hartshorne 61	1	34N50'42	95W33'26	6:22:14
Haskell 51	1	35N49'13	95W40'26	6:22:42
Haskew 76	1	36N46	99W07	6:36:28
Hastings 34	1	34N13'36	98W06'35	6:32:26
Hatchetville 8	1	34N56'31	98W26'37	6:33:46
Haw Creek 40	1	34N46'21	94W30'33	6:18:02
Hawley 27	1	36N45'11	98W01'08	6:32:05
Haworth 45	1	33N50'47	94W39'09	6:18:37
Haydenville 54	1	35N35'43	96W15'48	6:25:03
Hayward 24	1	36N16'40	97W30'44	6:30:03
Haywood 61	1	34N53'14	95W56'53	6:23:48
Hazel Dell 63	1	35N26'56	97W00'00	6:28:00
Headrick 33	1	34N37'39	99W08'16	6:36:33
Healdton 10	1	34N13'59	97W29'15	6:29:57
Heavener 40	1	34N53'21	94W36'02	6:18:24
Hectorville 56	1	35N50'31	95W55'30	6:23:42
Helena 2	1	36N32'46	98W16'11	6:33:05
Heman 76	1	36N32'06	98W56'37	6:35:46
Hendrix 7	1	33N46'25	96W24'20	6:25:37
Hennepin 25	1	34N30'32	97W20'48	6:29:23
Hennessey 37	1	36N06'33	97W53'54	6:31:36
Henryetta 56	1	35N26'23	95W58'54	6:23:56
Herd 57	1	36N51'52	96W12'02	6:24:48
Herring 65	1	35N36'36	99W31'03	6:38:04
Hess 33	1	34N27'53	99W16'19	6:37:05
Hester 28	1	34N48'04	99W25'59	6:37:44
Hewitt 10	1	34N10'08	97W24'16	6:29:37
Hext 5	1	35N14'51	99W45'09	6:39:01
Heyburn 19	1	35N54'44	96W17'01	6:25:08
Hiawatha 40	1	34N53'33	94W28'01	6:17:52
Hibsaw 55	1	35N42'13	97W08'26	6:28:34
Hickory 50	1	34N33'24	96W51'36	6:27:26
Hickory Hill 57	1	36N56'45	96W06'36	6:24:26
Hicks Addition 55	1	35N29	97W22	6:29:28
Higgins 39	1	34N48'41	95W26'00	6:21:44
High Hill 12	1	34N08'06	95W17'48	6:21:11
Hightower 33	1	34N37'50	99W15'12	6:37:01
Highway 9 Landing 61	1	35N14'24	95W29'32	6:21:58
Hill 40	1	35N05'40	94W28'09	6:17:53
Hill Chapel 45	1	33N59'10	94W44'53	6:19:00
Hillsdale 24	1	36N33'47	97W59'28	6:31:58
Hill Top 32	1	34N54	96W06	6:24:24
Hinton 8	1	35N28'17	98W21'19	6:33:25
Hird 62	1	34N48'38	96W39'06	6:26:36
Hisle 66	1	36N28'36	95W28'34	6:21:54
Hitchcock 6	1	35N58'08	98W20'53	6:33:24
Hitchita 46	1	35N31'11	95W45'04	6:23:00
Hitchland 70	4	36N29'56	101W19'03	6:45:16
Hobart 38	1	35N01'46	99W05'34	6:36:22
Hochatown 45	1	34N11'38	94W40'32	6:18:42
Hocker 5	1	35N17'24	99W28'25	6:37:54
Hockerville 58	1	36N59'38	94W46'51	6:19:07
Hodgen 40	1	34N50'33	94W37'58	6:18:32
Hoffman 56	1	35N29'21	95W50'33	6:23:22
Hogshooter 74	2	36N41'55	95W51'15	6:23:25
Holdenville 32	1	35N04'49	96W23'56	6:25:36
Holley Creek 45	1	34N01	94W44	6:18:56
Hollis 29	1	34N41'18	99W54'42	6:39:39
Hollister 71	1	34N20'32	98W52'14	6:35:29
Hollow 18	1	36N53'15	95W16'11	6:21:05
Holly Creek 45	1	33N58'41	94W48'59	6:19:16
Hollywood 14	1	35N14	97W25	6:29:40
Homer 62	1	34N46'53	96W37'00	6:26:28
Homestead 6	1	36N08'59	98W23'37	6:33:34
Hominy 57	1	36N24'51	96W23'42	6:25:35
Honobia 64	1	34N32'20	94W56'14	6:19:45
Hontubby 40	1	34N51'01	94W33'57	6:18:16
Hooker 70	4	36N51'36	101W12'47	6:44:51
Hooper 17	1	34N09'33	98W10'25	6:32:42
Hoover 25	1	34N31'16	97W14'49	6:28:59
Hope 69	1	34N34'08	97W50'11	6:31:21
Hopeton 76	1	36N41'17	98W39'56	6:34:40
Hopewell 3	1	34N14'00	96W22'22	6:25:29
Hopkins 13	4	36N47'58	102W04'54	6:48:20
Horntown 32	1	35N05'13	96W14'51	6:24:59
Hotulke 63	1	35N16	96W56	6:27:44
Hough 70	4	36N52'15	101W34'36	6:46:18
Hovey 70	4	36N51'46	101W40'43	6:46:43
Howard 66	1	36N29'43	95W27'31	6:21:50
Howe 40	1	34N57'04	94W38'13	6:18:33
Hoxbar 43	1	34N04'15	97W02'20	6:28:09
Hoyt 31	1	35N16'18	95W18'07	6:21:12
Hucmac 22	1	36N03'27	98W47'45	6:35:11
Hughart 31	1	35N12'09	95W17'46	6:21:11
Hughes 39	1	34N56'57	94W58'18	6:19:53
Hugo 12	1	34N00'38	95W30'34	6:22:02
Hulah 57	1	36N55'43	96W02'06	6:24:08
Hulbert 11	1	35N55'57	95W08'28	6:20:34
Hulen 17	1	34N30'14	98W13'16	6:32:53
Humphreys 33	1	34N33'21	99W14'13	6:36:57
Hunnewell 36	1	36N59'55	97W24'27	6:29:38
Hunter 24	1	36N33'49	97W39'39	6:30:39
Huskey 12	1	33N56'45	95W16'41	6:21:07
Hyde Park 51	1	35N47'22	95W18'14	6:21:13
Hydro 6	1	35N32'58	98W34'40	6:34:19

Place		Latitude	Longitude	Time
Hy 10 Landing 51	1	35N36'55	95W10'36	6:20:42
Iconium 42	1	35N52'09	97W11'15	6:28:45
Idabel 45	1	33N53'44	94W49'34	6:19:18
Imo 24	1	36N21'14	97W58'39	6:31:55
IXL 54	1	35N31'21	96W23'17	6:25:33
Kingston 48	1	33N59'55	96W43'10	6:26:53
Kinta 31	1	35N07'09	95W14'15	6:20:57
Kiowa 61	1	34N43'14	95W53'56	6:23:36
Knowles 4	1	36N52'24	100W11'35	6:40:46
Komalty 38	1	35N02'51	98W59'24	6:35:58
Konawa 67	1	34N57'34	96W45'09	6:27:01
Kosoma 64	1	34N20'54	95W36'46	6:22:27
Krebs 61	1	34N55'40	95W42'56	6:22:52
Kremlin 24	1	36N32'50	97W49'52	6:31:19
Kulli 45	1	33N54	94W49	6:19:16
Kullitukio 45	1	33N51'07	94W43'19	6:18:53
Kusa 56	1	35N26'57	95W55'26	6:23:42
Lacey 37	1	36N06'58	98W05'09	6:32:21
Lafayette 31	1	35N10'26	95W06'12	6:20:25
Lahoma 24	1	36N23'15	98W05'22	6:32:21
Lake 72	1	36N08'24	96W04'54	6:24:20
Lake Aluma 55	1	35N32'13	97W26'27	6:29:46
Lake Creek 28	1	35N01'46	99W24'47	6:37:39
Lake Hiwassee 55	1	35N39'06	97W18'21	6:29:13
Lake Humphreys 69	1	34N39	97W57	6:31:48
Lakeside 7	1	33N57'18	96W33'06	6:26:12
Lakeside Village 16	1	34N47'54	98W23'05	6:33:32
Lake Station 72	1	36N09	96W02	6:24:08
Lake Valley 75	1	35N10'05	98W51'46	6:35:27
Lakeview 42	1	35N47'52	97W25'30	6:29:42
Lakewest 7	1	34N02	95W52	6:23:28
Lamar 32	1	35N05'58	96W07'38	6:24:31
Lamberson 40	1	34N47'41	95W00'48	6:20:03
Lambert 2	1	36N40'59	98W25'22	6:33:41
Lamont 27	1	36N41'26	97W33'22	6:30:13
Lane 3	1	34N17'55	95W59'16	6:23:57
Langley 49	1	36N27'50	95W02'51	6:20:11
Langston 42	1	35N56'42	97W15'18	6:29:01
Lark 48	1	34N00	96W43	6:26:52
Last Chance 54	1	35N32'12	96W15'51	6:25:03
Latham 40	1	35N07'24	94W48'19	6:19:13
Latta 62	1	34N44'49	96W42'20	6:26:49
Laverne 30	1	36N42'35	99W53'35	6:39:34
Laverty 26	1	34N59'26	98W04'30	6:32:18
Lawrence 62	1	34N41'11	96W43'58	6:26:56
Lawrie 42	1	35N57'24	97W25'23	6:29:42
Lawton 16	1	34N36'31	98W23'24	6:33:34
Leach 21	1	36N12'17	94W55'20	6:19:41
Leader 62	1	34N43'44	96W28'37	6:25:54
Lebanon 48	1	33N58'56	96W54'27	6:27:38
Leedey 22	1	35N52'12	99W20'47	6:37:23
Leflore 40	1	34N53'55	94W58'48	6:19:55
Lehigh 15	1	34N28'09	96W12'58	6:24:52
Lela 59	1	36N19'08	96W55'27	6:27:42
Leliaetta 73	1	36N01'02	95W22'04	6:21:28
Lenapah 53	1	36N51'02	95W38'09	6:22:33
Lenna 46	1	35N22'35	95W46'09	6:23:05
Lenora 22	1	36N02'28	99W03'42	6:36:15
Lenox 40	1	34N41'44	94W49'28	6:19:18
Leon 43	1	33N52'45	97W25'44	6:29:43
Leonard 72	1	35N55'13	95W47'57	6:23:12
Lep 57	1	36N47'26	96W43'29	6:26:54
Lequire 31	1	35N06'16	95W06'26	6:20:26
Letitia 16	1	34N34'46	98W12'41	6:32:51
Lewisville 31	1	35N07'12	95W16'36	6:21:06
Lexington 14	1	35N00'53	97W20'07	6:29:20
Libbey 70	4	36N56'14	101W58'28	6:47:54
Liberty 7	1	33N44'10	96W20'33	6:25:22
Liberty 11	1	36N04'29	94W58'50	6:19:55
Liberty 68	1	35N28'39	94W32'32	6:18:10
Liberty 69	1	34N26'57	97W57'52	6:31:51
Lige 38	1	34N39'30	99W01'06	6:36:04
Lillard Park 55	1	35N25'43	97W35'38	6:30:23
Lima 67	1	35N10'26	96W35'58	6:26:24
Limestone 39	1	34N55	95W19	6:21:16
Limestone Gap 3	1	34N36'02	95W58'16	6:23:53
Lincoln 33	1	34N29'38	99W45'36	6:39:02
Lincolnville 58	1	36N56'37	94W45'25	6:19:02
Lindley 47	1	36N12'22	98W13'57	6:32:56
Lindsay 25	1	34N50'05	97W36'08	6:30:25
Linn 48	1	34N07'05	96W37'29	6:26:30
Little 67	1	35N20'53	96W40'18	6:26:41
Little Axe 14	1	35N13'57	97W12'44	6:28:51
Little Chief 57	1	36N39'57	96W38'24	6:26:34
Little City 48	1	34N05'10	96W36'57	6:26:28
Little Ponderosa 4	4	36N57'25	100W52'33	6:43:30
Loco 69	1	34N19'45	97W40'51	6:30:43
Locust Grove 49	1	36N12'00	95W10'03	6:20:40
Lodi 39	1	35N00'33	95W02'31	6:20:10
Logan 4	4	36N34'22	100W13'01	6:40:52
Lona 31	1	35N07	95W14	6:20:56
Lone Grove 10	1	34N10'31	97W15'45	6:29:03
Lone Oak 68	1	35N23'26	94W32'55	6:18:12
Lone Pine 3	1	34N11'20	95W48'51	6:23:15
Lone Wolf 38	1	34N59'22	99W14'57	6:37:00
Long 68	1	35N29'51	94W35'04	6:18:20
Longdale 6	1	36N08'00	98W33'01	6:34:12
Longtown 61	1	35N14'43	95W30'45	6:22:03
Lookeba 8	1	35N21'46	98W22'00	6:33:28
Lookout 76	1	36N57	99W16	6:37:04
Lost City 11	1	35N59'16	95W08'10	6:20:33
Lotsee 72	1	36N08	96W13	6:24:52
Louis 29	1	34N33'55	99W48'04	6:39:12
Loveland 71	1	34N18'19	98W46'17	6:35:05
Lovell 42	1	36N03'25	97W38'06	6:30:32
Loving 40	1	34N52'01	94W28'47	6:17:55
Lowrey 11	1	36N05'53	94W55'19	6:19:41
Loyal 37	1	35N58'16	98W07'14	6:32:29
Lucien 52	1	36N16'29	97W27'16	6:29:49
Ludlow 40	1	34N32'10	94W51'02	6:19:24
Lugert 38	1	34N53'45	99W16'30	6:37:06
Lula 62	1	34N42'02	96W25'55	6:25:44
Lusta 49	1	36N14'33	95W20'13	6:21:21
Luther 55	1	35N39'42	97W11'43	6:28:47
Lutie 39	1	34N55	95W16	6:21:04
Lyman 57	1	36N50'25	96W44'35	6:26:58
Lynn Addition 57	1	36N24	96W13	6:24:52
Lynn Lane 72	1	36N08'52	95W46'46	6:23:07
Lyons 1	1	35N45'04	94W42'39	6:18:51
Mackie 65	1	35N41'10	99W47'39	6:39:11
Macomb 63	1	35N08'48	97W00'31	6:28:02
Macomb-Y 63	1	35N08'47	96W55'35	6:27:42
Madden 53	1	36N42	95W38	6:22:32
Madge 29	1	34N54'01	99W57'29	6:39:50
Madill 48	1	34N05'25	96W46'17	6:27:05
Magruder 47	1	36N12'52	98W13'23	6:32:54
Maguire 14	1	35N07'52	97W17'59	6:29:12
Mallard Bay 73	1	35N51'35	95W16'44	6:21:07
Manard 11	1	35N48	95W15	6:21:00
Manchester 27	1	36N59'38	98W02'14	6:32:09
Mangum 28	1	34N52'19	99W30'14	6:38:01
Manitou 71	1	34N30'27	98W58'59	6:35:56
Mannford 19	1	36N07	96W21	6:25:24
Manning 61	1	34N55	95W33	6:22:12
Mannsville 35	1	34N11'09	96W52'49	6:27:31
Maple 68	1	35N28'17	94W37'35	6:18:30
Maramec 59	1	36N14'31	96W40'48	6:26:43
Marble City 68	1	35N34'49	94W49'15	6:19:17
Marena 60	1	36N04'20	97W12'42	6:28:51
Marietta 43	1	33N56'13	97W06'59	6:28:28
Markham 19	1	36N03'40	96W36'26	6:26:26
Marland 52	1	36N33'39	97W09'03	6:28:36
Marlow 69	1	34N38'53	97W57'28	6:31:50
Marsden 43	1	34N03'20	97W11'43	6:28:47
Marshall 42	1	36N09'14	97W37'31	6:30:30
Martha 33	1	34N43'31	99W23'12	6:37:33
Martin 51	1	35N33'59	95W18'38	6:21:15
Marty 33	1	34N31'46	99W30'27	6:38:02
Masham 59	1	36N26'57	96W51'12	6:27:25
Mason 54	1	35N33'58	96W21'07	6:25:24
Massey Point 61	1	35N03'51	95W38'41	6:22:35
Matoaka 74	2	36N40'43	95W58'41	6:23:55
Matoy 7	1	34N08'06	96W03'35	6:24:14
Maud 67	1	35N07'49	96W46'32	6:27:06
Maxwell 62	1	34N54'12	96W50'38	6:27:23
May 30	1	36N37'01	99W44'49	6:38:59
Mayfield 5	1	35N20'20	99W52'35	6:39:30
Mayhew 12	1	34N03'39	95W53'09	6:23:33
Maysville 25	1	34N49'02	97W24'20	6:29:37
Mazie 49	1	36N06'27	95W21'47	6:21:27
McAlester 61	1	34N56'00	95W46'10	6:23:05
McBride 48	1	33N56'07	96W37'59	6:26:32
McClure 20	1	35N39'05	99W18'19	6:37:13
McCurtain 31	1	35N08'59	94W58'14	6:19:53
McFarlin 66	1	36N12'21	95W31'59	6:22:08
McGee 25	1	34N49'32	96W57'25	6:27:50
McKey 68	1	35N28'57	94W53'05	6:19:32
McKiddyville 14	1	35N05'15	97W12'42	6:28:51
McKnight 29	1	34N45'58	99W54'43	6:39:39
McLain 51	1	35N33'59	95W16'07	6:21:04
McLoud 63	1	35N26'09	97W05'28	6:28:22
McMan 10	1	34N14	97W29	6:29:56
McMillan 48	1	34N05'23	96W56'13	6:27:45
McQueen 29	1	34N40'00	99W42'05	6:38:48
McTees Store 38	1	34N59	99W15	6:37:00
McWillie 2	1	36N32'09	98W21'15	6:33:25
Mead 7	1	33N59'58	96W30'32	6:26:02
Medford 27	1	36N48'25	97W44'00	6:30:56
Medicine Park 16	1	34N43'45	98W30'08	6:34:01
Meeker 41	1	35N30'12	96W54'09	6:27:37
Meers 16	1	34N46'58	98W34'43	6:34:19
Mehan 60	1	36N02'42	96W56'32	6:27:46
Mekko 61	1	35N00'00	95W45'13	6:23:01
Mellette 46	1	35N13'02	95W42'56	6:22:52
Melvin 11	1	34N56	95W54	6:23:36
Memorial 51	1	35N45	95W22	6:21:28
Meno 47	1	36N23'10	98W10'39	6:32:43
Meridian 42	1	35N50'31	97W14'48	6:28:59
Meridian 65	1	35N27'57	99W57'51	6:39:51
Merrick 41	1	35N51'23	97W08'27	6:28:34
Merritt 5	1	35N22'11	99W30'18	6:38:01
Messer 12	1	34N05'14	95W28'09	6:21:53
Metory 11	1	35N50'25	95W02'17	6:20:09
Mexhoma 13	4	36N43'10	102W59'03	6:51:56
Miami 58	1	36N52'28	94W52'38	6:19:31
Micawber 54	1	35N37'28	96W30'43	6:26:03
Middleberg 26	1	35N06'22	97W44'05	6:30:56
Middleton 36	1	36N57'21	97W06'50	6:28:27
Midlothian 41	1	35N38'14	96W55'20	6:27:41
Midway 3	1	34N31	96W13	6:24:52
Midway 41	1	35N29'33	97W05'18	6:28:21
Midway 42	1	36N04'21	97W31'58	6:30:08
Midway 51	1	35N45'17	95W44'54	6:23:00
Midway 54	1	35N36'36	96W33'52	6:26:15
Midway 70	4	36N52'12	101W21'37	6:45:26
Midway Village 55	1	35N27'34	97W26'43	6:29:47
Midwest City 55	1	35N26'58	97W23'47	6:29:35
Milburn 35	1	34N14'27	96W32'56	6:26:12
Milfay 19	1	35N45'18	96W33'56	6:26:16
Mill Creek 35	1	34N24'15	96W49'34	6:27:18
Miller 64	1	34N18'59	95W44'41	6:22:59
Millerton 45	1	33N59'09	95W00'48	6:20:03
Milo 10	1	34N19'57	97W20'21	6:29:21
Milton 40	1	35N09'42	94W51'48	6:19:27
Minco 26	1	35N18'46	97W56'39	6:31:47
Mineral Heights 58	1	36N59	94W50	6:19:20
Mingo 72	1	36N13'14	95W52'07	6:23:28
Mocane 4	1	36N53'37	100W22'20	6:41:29
Moffett 68	1	35N23'25	94W26'48	6:17:47
Mohawk 72	1	36N12'21	95W55'38	6:23:43
Monroe 40	1	34N59'33	94W31'00	6:18:04
Moodys 11	1	36N01'52	94W57'27	6:19:50
Moon 45	1	33N49'27	94W34'17	6:18:17
Moore 14	1	35N20'22	97W29'11	6:29:57
Mooreland 77	1	36N26'21	99W12'16	6:36:49
Moorewood 20	1	35N44'25	99W20'55	6:37:24
Moravia 28	1	35N07'09	99W30'35	6:38:02
Moreville 58	3	36N47'10	94W47'30	6:19:10
Morgans Corner 57	1	36N22'05	96W12'50	6:24:51
Morris 56	1	35N36'27	95W51'36	6:23:26
Morrison 52	1	36N17'50	97W00'28	6:28:02
Morse 54	1	35N32'12	96W16'55	6:25:08
Morvin 63	1	35N12'12	97W00'56	6:28:04
Mound Grove 45	1	34N04'55	95W05'13	6:20:21
Mounds 19	1	35N52'35	96W03'39	6:24:15
Mountain Park 38	1	34N41'50	98W56'57	6:35:48
Mountain View 38	1	35N05'51	98W44'46	6:34:59
Mount Herman 45	1	34N18'21	94W48'51	6:19:15
Mount Scott 16	1	34N46'42	98W31'53	6:34:08
Mount View 16	1	34N47'49	98W10'35	6:32:42
Mount Zion 45	1	33N56'21	95W02'04	6:20:08
Mouser 70	4	36N52'14	101W24'53	6:45:40
Moyers 64	1	34N19'34	95W39'12	6:22:37
Mudsand 12	1	34N02	95W42	6:22:48
Muldrow 68	1	35N24'22	94W35'55	6:18:24
Mulhall 42	1	36N03'53	97W24'24	6:29:38
Muncy (Tracy) 70	4	36N49'12	101W45'44	6:47:03
Murphy 49	1	36N08'49	95W14'40	6:20:59
Murry Spur 40	1	35N15'35	94W32'54	6:18:12
Muse 40	1	34N40'19	94W45'45	6:19:03
Muskogee 51	1	35N44'52	95W22'10	6:21:29
Mustang 9	1	35N23'03	97W43'27	6:30:54
Mutual 77	1	36N13'53	99W10'04	6:36:40
Myers 57	1	36N45'12	96W24'02	6:25:36
Nani-chito 45	1	34N25'20	94W38'48	6:18:35
Nanos 57	1	36N47'47	96W16'09	6:25:05
Narcissa 58	1	36N48'04	94W55'36	6:19:42
Nardin 36	1	36N48'20	97W26'44	6:29:47
Nash 27	1	36N39'58	98W03'00	6:32:12
Nashoba 64	1	34N28'55	95W12'54	6:20:52
Nashville 27	1	36N40	98W03	6:32:12
Natura 56	1	35N44'24	95W56'07	6:23:44
Navina 42	1	35N47'56	97W33'36	6:30:14
Neal 63	1	35N19'59	96W47'22	6:27:09
Nebo 50	1	34N21'41	96W57'09	6:27:49
Needmore 14	1	35N07'52	97W12'43	6:28:51
Neff 40	1	35N03	94W37	6:18:28
Negro Bend 3	1	34N19'33	95W56'07	6:23:44
Neill 25	1	34N49'18	97W30'44	6:30:03
Nelagony 57	1	36N37'35	96W14'31	6:24:58
Nellie 69	1	34N34'46	98W07'27	6:32:30
Nelson 12	1	34N07'38	95W41'06	6:22:44
Neodesha 73	1	36N02'46	95W26'03	6:21:44
Newalla 55	1	35N24'18	97W09'45	6:28:39
New Alluwe 53	1	36N37	95W29	6:21:56
Newby 19	1	35N42'41	96W21'06	6:25:24
Newcastle 44	1	35N14'50	97W35'58	6:30:24
New Cordell 75	1	35N18	98W59	6:35:56
Newkirk 36	1	36N52'56	97W03'11	6:28:13
New Liberty 5	1	35N21'49	99W43'02	6:38:52
New Lima 67	1	35N10'18	96W35'32	6:26:22
New Mannford 19	1	36N07'22	96W21'26	6:25:26
New Oberlin 12	1	33N53'41	95W51'04	6:23:24
Newport 10	1	34N15'10	97W16'28	6:29:06
New Prue 57	1	36N15'11	96W16'14	6:25:05
New Tulsa 58	1	36N55'04	94W42'41	6:18:51
New Tulsa 73	1	36N04	95W40	6:22:40
New Woodville 48	1	33N58	96W39	6:26:36
Nichols Hills 55	1	35N33'03	97W32'55	6:30:12
Nicoma Park 55	1	35N29'28	97W19'22	6:29:17
Nicut 68	1	35N35'02	94W33'33	6:18:14
Nida 35	1	34N08'35	96W29'55	6:26:00
Niles 9	1	35N26'04	98W15'16	6:33:01
Ninnekah 26	1	34N57'00	97W55'32	6:31:42
Noble 14	1	35N08'21	97W23'40	6:29:35
Nobletown 67	1	35N12'11	96W31'46	6:26:07
Noel 76	1	36N46'52	98W43'08	6:34:53
Nolia 64	1	34N28'35	95W09'05	6:20:36
Non 32	1	34N46'40	96W14'26	6:24:58
Norfolk 60	1	35N59	96W46	6:27:04
Norge 26	1	34N59'18	97W59'48	6:31:59
Norman 14	1	35N13'21	97W26'21	6:29:45
Norris 39	1	34N59'56	94W58'13	6:19:53
North Alfalfa 2	1	36N51	98W19	6:33:16
North Atoka 3	1	34N32	95W54	6:23:36
North Beaver 4	1	36N53	100W40	6:42:40
North Canadian 9	1	35N40	97W57	6:31:48
North Central Bryan 7	1	34N04	96W12	6:24:48
North Central Pittsburg 61	1	35N07	95W46	6:23:04
North Central Pontotoc 62	1	34N51	96W37	6:26:28
North Cherokee 11	1	36N04	94W59	6:19:56
North Cleveland 14	1	35N18	97W23	6:29:32
North Craig 18	1	36N55	95W09	6:20:36
North Enid 24	1	36N26'08	97W52'07	6:31:28
North Logan 42	1	36N06	97W30	6:30:00
North Marshall 48	1	34N05	96W48	6:27:12
North McAlester 61	1	34N57'21	95W45'38	6:23:03
North Mc Curtain 45	1	34N24	94W45	6:19:00
North Miami 58	1	36N55'02	94W52'46	6:19:31
North Pole 45	1	34N05'30	94W53'21	6:19:33
North Pushmataha 64	1	34N36	95W16	6:21:04
Northside 72	1	36N11	95W59	6:23:56
North Sobol 64	1	34N11'09	95W14'18	6:20:57
North Village 60	1	35N59'08	96W39'06	6:26:36
Northwest 55	1	35N29	97W32	6:30:08
Notichtown 68	1	35N34'36	95W05'29	6:20:22
Nowata 53	1	36N42'02	95W38'16	6:22:33
Noxie 53	1	36N58'17	95W43'56	6:22:56
Numa 27	1	36N48'12	97W36'21	6:30:25
Nursery 7	1	34N00	96W23	6:25:32

Nuyaka 56 1 35N39'11 96w08'22 6:24:33
Oak Grove 50 1 34N36'53 96w58'00 6:27:52
Oak Grove 60 1 35N59 96w37 6:26:28
Oak Grove 73 1 36N04'30 95w40'20 6:22:41
Oak Hill 45 1 34N02'27 94w50'08 6:19:21
Oakhurst 72 1 36N04'31 96w03'51 6:24:15
Oakland 48 1 34N06'00 96w47'37 6:27:10
Oak Lodge 40 1 35N14'54 94w35'36 6:18:22
Oakman 62 1 34N49'56 96w37'00 6:26:28
Oak Ridge 57 1 36N53'49 96w06'46 6:24:27
Oakridge 72 1 36N04'30 96w02'08 6:24:09
Oaks 21 1 36N09'58 94w51'16 6:19:25
Oakwood 22 1 35N55'54 98w42'17 6:34:49
Oberlin 7 1 33N52'25 95w51'05 6:23:24
Ochelata 74 1 36N36'00 95w58'46 6:23:55
Octavia 40 1 34N31'36 94w42'10 6:18:49
Odetta 38 1 34N39'50 98w50'36 6:35:22
Ogeechee 58 3 36N45'45 94w48'51 6:19:15
Oglesby 74 1 36N37'35 95w51'23 6:23:26
Oil Center 62 1 34N52'07 96w49'26 6:27:18
Oil City 10 1 34N16'28 97w25'05 6:29:40
Oil City 69 1 34N31'23 98w04'22 6:32:17
Oilton 19 1 36N05'04 96w35'00 6:26:20
Okarche 9 1 35N43'33 97w58'34 6:31:54
Okay 73 1 35N51'02 95w19'05 6:21:16
Okeene 6 1 36N06'58 98w19'00 6:33:16
Okemah 54 1 35N25'57 96w18'17 6:25:13
Okesa 57 2 36N42'46 96w08'04 6:24:32
Okfuskee 54 1 35N35'43 96w13'41 6:24:55
Oklahoma City 55
1 35N28'03 97w30'58 6:30:04
Oklahoma College 26
1 35N02 97w57 6:31:48
Oklahoma Hills 69
1 34N28'55 97w55'41 6:31:43
Okmulgee 56 1 35N37'24 95w57'37 6:23:50
Okoee 18 1 36N31'07 95w05'40 6:20:23
Oktaha 51 1 35N34'35 95w28'29 6:21:54
Old Allison 7 1 33N52'53 96w20'13 6:25:21
Old Bennington 7
1 34N02'51 96w01'30 6:24:06
Old Bliss 52 1 36N32'51 97w08'39 6:28:35
Old Farris 3 1 34N14'38 95w52'30 6:23:30
Old Retrop 75 1 35N08'43 99w20'32 6:37:22
Oleta 64 1 34N11'58 95w20'37 6:21:22
Olive 7 1 33N54'28 96w26'52 6:25:47
Olive 19 1 36N01'42 96w28'47 6:25:55
Olney 15 1 34N28'21 96w21'39 6:25:27
Olustee 33 1 34N32'55 99w25'19 6:37:41
Omega 37 1 35N52'13 98w11'51 6:32:47
Onapa 46 1 35N24'21 95w33'11 6:22:13
Oneida 37 1 35N58'15 98w04'01 6:32:16
Oneta 73 1 36N01'08 95w42'28 6:22:50
Ontario 58 1 36N59'15 94w45'46 6:19:03
Oologah 66 1 36N26'49 95w42'29 6:22:50
Oowala 66 1 36N25'24 95w36'52 6:22:27
Opah 57 1 36N45'04 96w17'35 6:25:10
Optima 70 4 36N45'30 101w21'21 6:45:25
Ord 12 1 33N54'36 95w29'57 6:22:00
Orienta 47 1 36N21'36 98w28'25 6:33:54
Oriental 54 1 35N32'11 96w13'43 6:24:55
Orion 47 1 36N13'00 98w46'42 6:35:07
Orlando 42 1 36N08'56 97w22'40 6:29:31
Orr 43 1 34N01'55 97w32'07 6:30:08
Osage 57 1 36N17'34 96w24'56 6:25:40
Osage Hills Estates 72
1 36N08 96w03 6:24:12
Osage Indian Reservation 57
1 36N40 96w20 6:25:20
Osage Junction 57
1 36N32'07 96w43'05 6:26:52
Oscar 34 1 33N59'02 97w45'09 6:31:01
Oseuma 58 3 36N43'47 94w53'26 6:19:34
Oswalt 43 1 34N01'39 97w20'04 6:29:20
Otoe 52 1 36N23'02 97w10'59 6:28:44
Ottawa 58 1 36N51'24 94w47'15 6:19:09
Overbrook 43 1 34N04'02 97w08'27 6:28:34
Owasso 72 1 36N16'10 95w51'16 6:23:25
Owen 74 1 36N59'57 95w55'53 6:23:44
Ozark 33 1 34N38'17 99w12'41 6:36:51
Pacific Junction 9
1 35N32 97w57 6:31:48
Paden 54 1 35N30'28 96w34'02 6:26:16
Page 40 1 34N42'38 94w32'58 6:18:12
Panama 40 1 35N10'02 94w40'20 6:18:41
Panola 39 1 34N55'43 95w12'47 6:20:51
Panoma 70 4 36N50'02 101w15'33 6:45:02
Panther 31 1 35N08'05 94w59'54 6:20:00
Paoli 25 1 34N49'36 97w15'32 6:29:02
Paradise Hill 68
1 35N37'34 95w04'02 6:20:16
Paradise View 49
1 36N08'39 95w18'07 6:21:12
Parallel 22 1 35N53'55 98w49'52 6:35:19
Parker 15 1 34N44'16 96w10'48 6:24:43
Parkersburg 20 1 35N29'33 99w01'24 6:36:06
Park Hill 11 1 35N51'40 94w57'31 6:19:50
Parkland 41 1 35N50'24 96w50'31 6:27:22
Park Wheeler Corner 56
1 35N37'28 96w09'26 6:24:38
Parvin 37 1 36N04'19 98w10'26 6:32:42
Patterson 39 1 34N57'17 95w24'05 6:21:36
Patton 49 1 36N28'36 95w15'20 6:21:01
Pauls Valley 25
1 34N44'24 97w13'19 6:28:53
Pawhuska 57 1 36N40'04 96w20'13 6:25:21
Pawnee 59 1 36N20'16 96w48'13 6:27:13
Paw Paw 68 1 35N19'56 94w30'48 6:18:03
Payne 44 1 34N54'22 97w31'47 6:30:07
Payson 41 1 35N33'01 96w51'18 6:27:25
Payton Crossing 3
1 34N17'30 95w53'29 6:23:34
Peachtree Crossing 16
1 34N41'13 98w22'53 6:33:32
Pearson 63 1 35N04'22 96w55'03 6:27:40
Pearsonia 57 1 36N48'06 96w27'02 6:25:48
Peckham 36 1 36N53'13 97w10'32 6:28:42
Peggs 11 1 36N04'51 95w05'57 6:20:24
Pemeta 19 1 36N01'28 96w36'55 6:26:28
Peno Corner 40 1 35N19'59 94w28'01 6:17:52
Pensacola 49 1 36N27'18 95w07'49 6:20:31
Peoria 58 1 36N54'55 94w40'11 6:18:41
Perkins 60 1 35N58'26 97w02'00 6:28:08
Pernell 25 1 34N33'41 97w30'35 6:30:02
Perry 52 1 36N17'22 97w17'16 6:29:09
Pershing 57 1 36N35'36 96w16'30 6:25:06
Petersburg 34 1 33N57'18 97w34'10 6:30:17
Petes Corner 52
1 36N17'25 97w06'12 6:28:25
Petros 40 1 34N52'10 94w36'31 6:18:26
Pettit 11 1 35N45'53 94w57'55 6:19:52
Pettit Bay 11 1 35N45'09 94w56'35 6:19:46
Pharoah 54 1 35N25'13 96w07'22 6:24:29
Phillips 15 1 34N30'21 96w13'10 6:24:53
Phroso 47 1 36N16'51 98w49'03 6:35:16
Picher 58 1 36N59'13 94w49'50 6:19:19
Pickens 45 1 34N23'47 95w00'42 6:20:03
Pickett 62 1 34N46'55 96w46'28 6:27:06
Pickwick 7 1 33N52'03 96w31'35 6:26:06
Piedmont 9 1 35N38'31 97w44'46 6:30:59
Pierce 46 1 35N26'05 95w42'58 6:22:52
Pike 43 1 33N57'52 97w19'30 6:29:18
Pine Knot Crossing 64
1 34N14'55 95w08'31 6:20:34
Pine Ridge 8 1 35N00'54 98w26'39 6:33:47
Pine Springs 3 1 34N16 95w52 6:23:28
Pine Top 61 1 34N40'38 95w44'30 6:22:58
Piney 1 1 35N53'04 94w32'30 6:18:10
Pink 63 1 35N15'38 97w07'10 6:28:29
Pin Oaks Acres 49
1 36N07'44 95w16'13 6:21:05
Pioneer Park 16
1 34N37 98w25 6:33:40
Piper 47 1 36N10'27 98w16'02 6:33:04
Pirtle 7 1 33N59'20 96w16'03 6:25:04
Pittsburg 61 1 34N42'47 95w50'59 6:23:24
Plainview 28 1 35N04'24 99w43'19 6:38:53
Plainview 45 1 34N06'48 95w07'17 6:20:29
Plainview 76 1 36N50'28 99w14'27 6:36:58
Platter 7 1 33N54'25 96w32'05 6:26:08
Player 19 1 36N05'46 96w36'10 6:26:25
Pleasant Grove 67
1 35N13'29 96w44'14 6:26:57
Pleasant Hill 45
1 33N46'08 94w39'51 6:18:39
Pleasant Valley 60
1 35N59'22 97w18'01 6:29:12
Plunkettville 45
1 34N25 94w29 6:17:56
Plunketville 45
1 34N24'51 94w29'18 6:17:57
Pocasset 26 1 35N11'37 97w57'08 6:31:49
Pocola 40 1 35N13'52 94w28'40 6:17:55
Pollard 45 1 33N51 94w39 6:18:36
Ponca City 36 1 36N42'25 97w05'07 6:28:20
Pond Creek 27 1 36N40'09 97w48'03 6:31:12
Pontotoc 35 1 34N29'19 96w37'32 6:26:30
Poole 55 1 35N36'32 97w13'35 6:28:54
Pooleville 10 1 34N25'10 97w23'58 6:29:36
Port 75 1 35N12'16 99w18'25 6:37:14
Porter 73 1 35N52'15 95w31'20 6:22:05
Porter Hill 16 1 34N46'57 98w23'11 6:33:33
Porum 51 1 35N21'22 95w15'55 6:21:04
Post Oak 43 1 34N04'16 97w25'17 6:29:41
Potapo 3 1 34N28 96w03 6:24:12
Poteau 40 1 35N03'13 94w37'24 6:18:30
Potter 58 1 36N57'24 94w51'52 6:19:27
Powell 48 1 33N57'18 96w51'44 6:27:27
Powers 9 1 35N26'59 97w57'07 6:31:48
Prague 41 1 35N29'12 96w41'05 6:26:44
Prairie Hill 33
1 34N35'38 99w32'38 6:38:11
Prattville 72 1 36N06'16 96w07'06 6:24:28
Prentiss 5 1 35N21'50 99w48'19 6:39:13
Preston 56 1 35N42'41 95w59'29 6:23:58
Price 72 1 36N08'08 96w04'05 6:24:16
Pritchard 7 1 34N05'03 96w08'49 6:24:35
Proctor 1 1 35N57'58 94w46'38 6:19:07
Provence 10 1 34N09'04 97w01'14 6:28:05
Prue 57 1 36N14'17 96w18'59 6:25:16
Pruitt City 10 1 34N25'12 97w30'36 6:30:02
Pryor 49 1 36N19 95w19 6:21:16
Pulaski 19 1 35N48'49 96w26'22 6:25:45
Pumpkin Center 16
1 34N37 98w25 6:33:40
Pumpkin Center 51
1 35N42'46 95w07'37 6:20:30
Pumpkin Center 56
1 35N40'55 95w47'03 6:23:08
Purcell 44 1 35N00'49 97w21'39 6:29:27
Purdy 25 1 34N42'57 97w35'14 6:30:21
Putnam 22 1 35N51'20 98w58'05 6:35:52
Pyramid Corners 18
1 36N50 95w04 6:20:16
Qualls 11 1 35N43'13 95w01'58 6:20:08
Quapaw 58 1 36N57'16 94w47'16 6:19:09
Quay 60 1 36N09'34 96w42'38 6:26:51
Quinlan 77 1 36N27'16 99w02'42 6:36:11
Quinton 61 1 35N07'22 95w22'15 6:21:29
Raiford 46 1 35N16'04 95w47'12 6:23:09
Ralph 20 1 35N30'32 99w00'42 6:36:03
Ralston 59 1 36N30'14 96w43'55 6:26:56
Rambo 59 1 36N16'08 96w53'21 6:27:33
Ramona 74 1 36N31'49 95w55'24 6:23:42
Ranch Acres 72 1 36N08 95w57 6:23:48
Ranchwood Manor 14
1 35N27 97w31 6:30:04
Randlett 17 1 34N10'38 98w27'48 6:33:51
Range 70 4 36N32'38 101w04'58 6:44:20
Rankin 65 1 35N37'28 99w55'27 6:39:42
Ratliff City 10
1 34N26'56 97w30'33 6:30:02
Rattan 64 1 34N12'01 95w24'46 6:21:39
Ravia 35 1 34N14'30 96w45'04 6:27:00
Rayford 50 1 34N26'04 97w05'40 6:28:23
Reagan 35 1 34N20'56 96w43'17 6:26:53
Reams 61 1 35N03'56 95w41'59 6:22:48
Reck 10 1 34N10 97w25 6:29:40
Red Bird 73 1 35N53'08 95w35'19 6:22:21
Redden 3 1 34N30'23 95w50'40 6:23:23
Red Fork 72 1 36N06'21 96w01'29 6:24:06
Red Hill 31 1 35N20'50 94w56'25 6:19:46
Red Horse 55 1 35N28 97w24 6:29:36
Redland 45 1 33N54'36 94w40'25 6:18:42
Redland 68 1 35N18'17 94w37'27 6:18:30
Red Oak 39 1 34N57'03 95w04'48 6:20:19
Red Rock (Redrock P O) 52
1 36N27'33 97w10'43 6:28:43
Reed 28 1 34N54'02 99w41'43 6:38:47
Reeder Ford 68 1 35N34'44 94w31'10 6:18:05
Reeding 37 1 35N47'27 97w46'11 6:31:05
Reeves 51 1 35N45 95w22 6:21:28
Regnier 13 4 36N59'38 102w51'24 6:51:26
Reichert 40 1 34N52'09 94w45'14 6:19:01
Remington 57 1 36N38'40 96w43'15 6:26:53
Remus 63 1 35N20 96w59 6:27:56
Remy 68 1 35N27'23 94w32'02 6:18:08
Renfrow 27 1 36N55'32 97w39'20 6:30:37
Rentiesville 46
1 35N31'17 95w29'41 6:21:59
Retrop 75 1 35N09'35 99w21'34 6:37:26
Rexroat 10 1 34N12'59 97w24'16 6:29:37
Reydon 65 1 35N39'13 99w55'07 6:39:40
Reynolds 3 1 34N39'55 95w55'51 6:23:43
Rhea 22 1 35N50'30 99w14'04 6:36:56
Richards 15 1 34N46 98w23 6:33:32
Richards Spur 16
1 34N46 98w17 6:33:08
Richardsville 46
1 35N28'42 95w40'50 6:22:43
Richland 9 1 35N34'48 97w48'16 6:31:13
Richmond 77 1 36N11'27 99w03'07 6:36:12
Richville 61 1 34N56'16 95w40'27 6:22:42
Ridley 16 1 34N42'13 98w22'40 6:33:31
Ringling 34 1 34N10'42 97w35'32 6:30:22
Ringold 45 1 34N12'54 95w07'30 6:20:30
Ringwood 47 1 36N22'46 98w14'42 6:32:59
Ripley 60 1 36N01'04 96w54'19 6:27:37
Ritts Junction 19
1 35N44'28 96w30'43 6:26:03
Roberta 7 1 33N55'35 96w18'08 6:25:13
Robinson Corner 48
1 34N05'07 96w36'04 6:26:24
Rock Creek 32 1 34N50'24 96w07'37 6:24:30
Rock Island 40 1 35N10'56 94w28'25 6:17:54
Rock Island Junction 9
1 35N32 97w57 6:31:48
Rocky 75 1 35N09'25 99w03'36 6:36:14
Rocky Ford 16 1 34N50'43 98w04'18 6:32:17
Rocky Mountain 1
1 35N48'19 94w46'02 6:19:04
Rocky Point 73 1 36N01'42 95w19'40 6:21:19
Roff 62 1 34N37'39 96w50'26 6:27:22
Rogers 18 1 36N55'01 95w11'51 6:20:47
Roland 68 1 35N25'16 94w30'52 6:18:03
Roll 65 1 35N46'45 99w42'40 6:38:51
Romulus 63 1 35N06'59 96w55'23 6:27:42
Ron 29 1 34N47'32 99w51'34 6:39:26
Roosevelt 38 1 34N50'55 99w01'17 6:36:05
Rose 49 1 36N13'10 95w01'46 6:20:07
Rosedale 44 1 34N55'06 97w11'01 6:28:44
Rosehill 65 1 35N30'31 99w43'01 6:38:52
Rosston 30 1 36N48'48 99w56'01 6:39:44
Rossville 41 1 35N35'38 96w59'55 6:28:00
Row 21 1 36N16'43 94w41'25 6:18:46
Roxana 42 1 36N06'05 97w39'25 6:30:38
Rubottom 43 1 33N56'25 97w27'24 6:29:50
Rufe 45 1 34N07'25 95w08'38 6:20:35
Rush Springs 26
1 34N46'57 97w57'24 6:31:50
Russell 28 1 34N46'05 99w40'01 6:38:40
Russellville 61
1 35N09'06 95w26'06 6:21:44
Russett 35 1 34N11'24 96w48'17 6:27:13
Ruthdale 53 1 36N48'54 95w44'14 6:22:57
Ryan 34 1 34N01'12 97w57'26 6:31:50
Sacred Heart 63
1 35N00'04 96w48'33 6:27:14
Sadie 68 1 35N23'16 94w51'14 6:19:25
Sageeyah 66 1 36N22'16 95w39'10 6:22:37
Saint Louis 63 1 35N04'27 96w51'10 6:27:25
Salem 56 1 35N23'02 95w55'42 6:23:43
Salina 49 1 36N17'34 95w09'11 6:20:37
Sallisaw 68 1 35N27'37 94w47'14 6:19:09
Salt Fork 27 1 36N38'06 97w35'19 6:30:21
Sams Point 61 1 35N11'38 95w41'36 6:22:46
Sand Bluff 12 1 34N07'39 95w47'57 6:23:12
Sand Creek 27 1 36N50'25 98w01'10 6:32:05
Sanders 1 1 35N55'14 94w42'24 6:18:50
Sanders 53 1 36N48'53 95w26'58 6:21:48
Sand Point 7 1 33N57'52 96w33'44 6:26:15
Sand Springs 72
1 36N08'23 96w06'31 6:24:26
Sandy 29 1 34N48'45 99w57'52 6:39:51
Sans Bois 31 1 35N07'50 95w09'21 6:20:37
Santa Fe 69 1 34N25'11 97w41'32 6:30:46
Sapulpa 19 1 35N59'55 96w06'50 6:24:27
Sardis 64 1 34N39'57 95w24'34 6:21:38
Sasakwa 67 1 34N56'55 96w31'30 6:26:06
Satterwhite 25 1 34N33'53 97w24'17 6:29:37
Savanna 61 1 34N49'44 95w50'37 6:23:22
Sawyer 12 1 34N00'49 95w22'17 6:21:29
Sayre 5 1 35N17'28 99w38'23 6:38:34
Schlegel 60 1 36N00'27 96w40'42 6:26:43
Schoeb Switch 2
1 36N46 98w23 6:33:32
Schoolton 67 1 35N23'30 96w27'30 6:25:50
Schulter 56 1 35N30'52 95w57'23 6:23:50
Scipio 61 1 35N03'17 95w57'23 6:23:50
Scott 9 1 35N22'36 98w14'10 6:32:57
Scraper 11 1 36N05'22 94w51'01 6:19:24
Scullin 50 1 34N31'07 96w51'44 6:27:27
Scullyville 40 1 35N15 94w37 6:18:28
Sealy 67 1 34N57'23 96w30'11 6:26:01
Sedan 38 1 34N58'18 98w45'38 6:35:03
Seiling 22 1 36N08'53 98w55'26 6:35:42
Selman 30 1 36N48'07 99w29'26 6:37:58
Seminole 67 1 35N13'28 96w40'13 6:26:41
Sentinel 75 1 35N09'28 99w10'30 6:36:42
Sequoyah 66 1 36N22'24 95w33'38 6:22:15
Sevenmile Corner 7
1 34N06'48 96w08'49 6:24:35
Seven Oaks 68 1 35N28'53 94w43'55 6:18:56
Seward 42 1 35N47'53 97w29'17 6:29:57
Shady Grove 46 1 35N29'35 95w24'57 6:21:40
Shady Grove 68 1 35N23'26 94w30'47 6:18:03
Shady Point 40 1 35N07'48 94w39'30 6:18:38
Shamrock 19 1 35N54'36 96w35'01 6:26:20
Sharon 77 1 36N16'33 99w20'07 6:37:20

Place		Lat.	Long.	Time
Shartel 55	1	35N31	97w32	6:30:08
Shattuck 23	1	36N16'33	99w52'51	6:39:31
Shawnee 63	1	35N19'38	96w55'30	6:27:42
Shay 48	1	33N55'58	96w46'29	6:27:06
Shea 24	1	36N23'03	97w46'50	6:31:07
Sheridan 16	1	34N37	98w25	6:33:40
Sherwood 45	1	34N19'52	94w46'41	6:19:07
Shidler 57	1	36N46'55	96w39'39	6:26:39
Shiloh 42	1	35N48'20	97w09'33	6:28:38
Shinewell 45	1	33N52'52	94w30'47	6:18:03
Shirk 72	1	36N07'19	96w07'38	6:24:31
Shoals 12	1	33N53'52	95w23'51	6:21:35
Shrewder 29	1	34N46'07	99w45'19	6:39:01
Shults 45	1	33N53'44	94w44'21	6:18:57
Sickles 8	1	35N21'46	98w26'51	6:33:47
Sill 16	1	34N41	98w30	6:34:00
Silo 7	1	34N02'29	96w28'26	6:25:54
Silver City 19	1	36N05'25	96w29'39	6:25:59
Simon 43	1	34N04	97w09	6:28:36
Simpson 48	1	34N09'10	96w53'21	6:27:33
Skedee 59	1	36N22'46	96w42'17	6:26:49
Skiatook 57	1	36N22'06	96w00'04	6:24:00
Skullyville (Oak Lodge) 40	1	35N14'54	94w35'36	6:18:22
Slapout 4	1	36N36'57	100w06'30	6:40:26
Slaughterville 14	1	35N05'14	97w20'05	6:29:20
Slick 19	1	35N46'37	96w15'57	6:25:04
Slim 45	1	34N05'03	95w06'15	6:20:25
Smacker 40	1	35N00'48	94w39'52	6:18:39
Smelter Prairie 74	2	36N45	95w59	6:23:56
Smith-Lee 7	1	33N53'13	96w01'28	6:24:06
Smith Village 55	1	35N27'03	97w27'25	6:29:50
Smithville 45	1	34N28	94w39	6:18:36
Sneed Acres 16	1	34N38'11	98w23'23	6:33:34
Snow 64	1	34N23'45	95w24'45	6:21:39
Snyder 38	1	34N39'32	98w57'05	6:35:48
Sobol 64	1	34N09'40	95w14'18	6:20:57
Soldani 57	1	36N45'33	96w47'50	6:27:11
Sooner 26	1	35N13'57	97w51'12	6:31:25
Soonerville 41	1	35N55'39	96w50'14	6:27:21
Soper 12	1	34N01'58	95w41'49	6:22:47
Sorrels 40	1	35N01'45	94w38'48	6:18:35
Southard 6	1	36N03'21	98w28'30	6:33:54
South Beaver 4	1	36N39	100w29	6:41:56
South Bryan 7	1	33N47	96w21	6:25:24
South Canadian 9	1	35N26	97w58	6:31:52
South Central Pontotoc 62	1	34N38	96w39	6:26:36
South Cherokee 11	1	35N48	94w58	6:19:52
South Cleveland 14	1	35N04	97w13	6:28:52
South Coffeyville 53	1	36N59'40	95w37'12	6:22:29
Southeast 72	1	36N06	95w53	6:23:32
South Ellis 23	1	36N05	99w44	6:38:56
South Hughes 32	1	34N53	96w16	6:25:04
South Jefferson 34	1	34N02	97w51	6:31:24
South Kay 36	1	36N41	97w07	6:28:28
South Latimer 39	1	34N45	95w14	6:20:56
South Le Flore 40	1	34N32	94w41	6:18:44
South Marshall 48	1	33N56	96w46	6:27:04
South Roger Mills 65	1	35N28	99w46	6:39:04
Southside 72	1	36N06	95w58	6:23:52
South Village 41	1	35N54'47	96w38'31	6:26:34
South Wagoner 73	1	35N51	95w30	6:22:00
Southwest 55	1	35N26	97w33	6:30:12
South Woods 76	1	36N34	98w42	6:34:48
Spade Mountain 1	1	35N52'39	94w44'46	6:18:59
Sparks 41	1	35N36'29	96w49'15	6:27:17
Spaulding 32	1	35N00'50	96w26'23	6:25:46
Spavinaw 49	1	36N23'28	95w02'47	6:20:11
Speer 12	1	34N06'48	95w33'20	6:22:13
Spelter City 56	1	35N27'30	95w57'47	6:23:51
Spencer 55	1	35N31'22	97w22'37	6:29:30
Spencerville 12	1	34N08'32	95w21'29	6:21:26
Sperry 72	1	36N17'50	95w59'28	6:23:58
Spiro 40	1	35N14'28	94w37'11	6:18:29
Sportsmen Acres 49	1	36N18	95w19	6:21:16
Spring Creek 8	1	35N15'42	98w10'59	6:32:44
Springer 10	1	34N18'52	97w08'33	6:28:34
Spring Hill 14	1	35N00'53	97w15'54	6:29:04
Springhill 73	1	35N48'47	95w34'14	6:22:17
Spring Lake Park 55	1	35N31	97w29	6:29:56
Squaretop 8	1	35N04'31	98w18'05	6:33:12
Sroboda 38	1	34N42'37	98w57'20	6:35:49
Stafford 20	1	35N32'12	99w07'18	6:36:29
Staley 7	1	33N49'36	96w31'47	6:26:07
Stanley 64	1	34N32'24	95w28'10	6:21:53
Stapp 40	1	34N45'18	94w37'25	6:18:30
Star 31	1	35N18'40	94w51'53	6:19:28
Star 61	1	34N40'16	95w32'19	6:22:09
State Capitol 55	1	35N31	97w30	6:30:00
Stealy 44	1	34N55'41	97w24'22	6:29:37
Stecker 8	1	34N57'27	98w18'56	6:33:16
Steedman 62	1	34N48'56	96w28'47	6:25:55
Steel Junction 45	1	34N02'26	94w46'31	6:19:06
Steen 24	1	36N25	97w52	6:31:28
Stella 14	1	35N19'09	97w12'45	6:28:51
Sterling 16	1	34N45'01	98w10'17	6:32:41
Stidham 46	1	35N22'07	95w41'58	6:22:48
Stigler 31	1	35N15'13	95w07'22	6:20:29
Stillwater 60	1	36N06'56	97w03'29	6:28:14
Stilwell 1	1	35N48'52	94w37'42	6:18:31
Stock Yards 55	1	35N27	97w33	6:30:12
Stone Bluff 73	1	35N53'09	95w44'12	6:22:57
Stones Corner 73	1	35N52'16	95w36'23	6:22:26
Stonewall 62	1	34N39'09	96w31'33	6:26:06
Stony Point 1	1	35N50'52	94w41'40	6:18:47
Stony Point 40	1	35N15'10	94w40'06	6:18:40
Story 25	1	34N51'19	97w27'30	6:29:50
Straight 70	4	36N52'36	101w26'54	6:45:48
Strang 49	1	36N24'38	95w07'50	6:20:31
Stratford 25	1	34N47'48	96w57'33	6:27:50
Strawberry Spring 1	1	35N59'23	94w38'58	6:18:36
Stringtown 3	1	34N28'00	96w03'11	6:24:13
Stringtown 17	1	34N21	98w18	6:33:12
Strohm 57	1	36N38'35	96w33'19	6:26:13
Strong City 65	1	35N40'13	99w35'57	6:38:24
Stroud 41	1	35N44'55	96w39'28	6:26:38
Stuart 32	1	34N54'05	96w05'55	6:24:24
Sturgis 13	4	36N53'38	102w04'51	6:48:17
Success 18	1	36N36'46	95w02'05	6:20:08
Sugar Creek 40	1	34N53'23	94w28'43	6:17:55
Sugden 34	1	34N04'55	97w58'41	6:31:55
Sullivan Village 16	1	34N37	98w25	6:33:40
Sulphur 50	1	34N30'28	96w58'05	6:27:52
Summerfield 40	1	34N53'55	94w51'57	6:19:28
Summit 51	1	35N39'57	95w25'21	6:21:41
Sumner 52	1	36N19'08	97w07'16	6:28:29
Sumpter 36	1	36N53'01	97w17'39	6:29:11
Sunkist 12	1	34N08'31	95w53'09	6:23:33
Sunray 69	1	34N24'45	97w57'53	6:31:52
Sunrise 54	1	35N31'14	96w07'22	6:24:29
Sunrise 56	1	35N27'22	95w55'03	6:23:40
Sunset 20	1	35N45'16	98w58'06	6:35:52
Sunset Corner 40	1	35N14'18	94w40'19	6:18:41
Sunsweet 18	1	36N34'57	95w19'26	6:21:18
Swan Lake 8	1	35N14'05	98w30'57	6:34:04
Sweetwater 5	1	35N25'20	99w54'40	6:39:39
Swink 12	1	34N01'04	95w12'07	6:20:48
Sycamore 21	1	36N24'18	94w42'47	6:18:51
Sylvian 67	1	35N20'52	96w33'55	6:26:16
Tabler 26	1	35N02'39	97w49'10	6:31:17
Tabor 19	1	35N48'06	96w15'48	6:25:03
Taft 51	1	35N45'42	95w32'46	6:22:11
Tahlequah 11	1	35N54'55	94w58'11	6:19:53
Tahona 40	1	35N09'41	94w36'11	6:18:25
Tailholt 11	1	35N50'12	94w50'31	6:19:22
Talala 66	1	36N31'47	95w42'04	6:22:48
Talihina 40	1	34N45'05	95w02'52	6:20:11
Tallant 57	1	36N35'51	96w11'25	6:24:46
Taloah 3	1	34N15'32	96w12'08	6:24:49
Taloga 22	1	36N02'19	98w57'48	6:35:51
Tamaha 31	1	35N23'46	94w59'00	6:19:56
Tangier 77	1	36N25'15	99w31'59	6:38:08
Tatums 10	1	34N28'58	97w27'41	6:29:51
Taupa 16	1	34N36'14	98w30'36	6:34:02
Taylor 5	1	35N14'53	99w22'55	6:37:32
Taylor 17	1	34N10'25	98w19'51	6:33:19
Taylor Corner Gin 71	1	34N13'05	98w55'24	6:35:42
Taylor Ferry 73	1	35N56'39	95w16'44	6:21:07
Tecumseh 63	1	35N15'28	96w56'11	6:27:45
Tegarden 76	1	36N47'52	98w58'11	6:35:53
Temple 17	1	34N16'19	98w14'08	6:32:57
Teresita 11	1	36N06'34	94w59'33	6:19:58
Terlton 59	1	36N11'17	96w29'24	6:25:58
Terral 34	1	33N53'48	97w56'10	6:31:45
Texanna 46	1	35N20'50	95w26'12	6:21:45
Texas Junction 9	1	35N32	97w57	6:31:48
Texhoma 70	4	36N30'18	101w46'57	6:47:08
Texola 5	1	35N13'09	99w59'27	6:39:58
Thackerville 43	1	33N47'36	97w08'34	6:28:34
The Village 55	1	35N33'39	97w33'04	6:30:12
Thomas 20	1	35N44'39	98w44'50	6:34:59
Thompson Corner 11	1	35N54'55	95w04'57	6:20:20
Three-Way Corner 8	1	35N17'27	98w24'42	6:33:39
Ti 61	1	34N42'33	95w39'40	6:22:39
Tia Juana 49	1	36N28'44	95w00'11	6:20:01
Tiawah 66	1	36N15'40	95w33'38	6:22:15
Tidal 19	1	35N59	96w37	6:26:28
Tidmore 67	1	35N14	96w41	6:26:44
Tiger 66	1	36N11'19	95w48'16	6:23:13
Tinker Air Force Base 55	1	35N29	97w32	6:30:08
Tip 49	1	36N21'03	95w11'02	6:20:44
Tipton 71	1	34N30'10	99w08'26	6:36:34
Tishomingo 35	1	34N14'10	96w40'42	6:26:43
Titanic 1	1	35N54'03	94w46'19	6:19:05
Todd 18	1	36N40'00	95w03'11	6:20:13
Togo 47	1	36N25'11	98w45'52	6:35:03
Tom 45	1	33N44'09	94w34'22	6:18:17
Tonkawa 36	1	36N40'42	97w18'35	6:29:14
Tonnece 21	1	36N16'43	94w36'42	6:18:27
Toppers 73	1	35N58'14	95w18'34	6:21:14
Topsy 21	1	36N24	95w03	6:20:12
Torpedo 57	2	36N43'37	96w02'34	6:24:10
Touzalin 23	1	36N20'00	99w58'28	6:39:54
Tracy 70	4	36N49'12	101w45'44	6:47:03
Trail 22	1	35N58'07	99w17'47	6:37:11
Treece 58	1	36N59'56	94w50'40	6:19:23
Trestle Ford 40	1	34N59'32	94w28'48	6:17:55
Tribbey 63	1	35N06'55	97w03'11	6:28:13
Trousdale 63	1	35N02'28	97w02'33	6:28:10
Troy 35	1	34N19'38	96w46'53	6:27:08
Tryon 41	1	35N52'11	96w57'49	6:27:51
Tsa La Gi Indian Village 11	1	35N51'59	94w57'30	6:19:50
Tucker 40	1	35N18'13	94w43'48	6:18:55
Tullahassee 73	1	35N50'05	95w26'15	6:21:45
Tulsa 72	1	36N09'14	95w59'33	6:23:58
Tupelo 15	1	34N36'17	96w25'26	6:25:42
Turkey Ford 58	1	36N40'03	94w42'55	6:18:52
Turley 72	1	36N14'31	95w58'32	6:23:54
Turner 43	1	33N56'24	97w18'59	6:29:16
Turpin 4	4	36N52'03	100w52'37	6:43:30
Tushka 3	1	34N19'13	96w10'01	6:24:40
Tuskahoma 64	1	34N37'04	95w16'35	6:21:06
Tuskegee 19	1	35N39'11	96w16'51	6:25:07
Tussy 10	1	34N30'24	97w32'34	6:30:10
Tuttle 26	1	35N17'27	97w48'43	6:31:15
Tuxedo Park 74	2	36N45	95w59	6:23:56
Twin Cities 61	1	34N51	95w36	6:22:24
Twin Hills 56	1	35N37	95w58	6:23:52
Twin Lakes 37	1	35N52'10	97w39'52	6:30:39
Twin Oaks 21	1	36N12'19	94w51'04	6:19:24
Tyler 48	1	34N06'13	96w54'34	6:27:38
Tyner 36	1	36N44'20	97w17'31	6:29:10
Tyrola 62	1	34N54'25	96w41'43	6:26:47
Tyrone 70	4	36N57'15	101w03'54	6:44:16
Ulan 61	1	35N06'58	95w53'10	6:23:33
Ultima Thule 45	1	34N03'33	94w28'43	6:17:55
Uncas 36	1	36N47'44	96w55'46	6:27:43
Unger 12	1	34N01'34	95w46'54	6:23:08
Union 37	1	36N01'44	97w48'03	6:31:12
Union 72	1	36N04'25	95w51'52	6:23:27
Union City 9	1	35N23'30	97w56'28	6:31:46
Union Hill 62	1	34N49'22	96w45'56	6:27:04
Union Valley 62	1	34N41'39	96w34'57	6:26:20
Unity 70	4	36N45'43	101w42'30	6:46:50
Upson 68	1	35N30	94w58	6:19:52
Ury 7	1	34N03'06	96w22'22	6:25:29
Utica 7	1	33N54'05	96w13'16	6:24:53
Valley Brook 55	1	35N24'07	97w28'52	6:29:55
Valley Drive 72	1	36N08	96w03	6:24:12
Valley Park 66	1	36N19	95w37	6:22:28
Valliant 45	1	34N00'08	95w05'37	6:20:22
Vamoosa 67	1	34N59'08	96w40'11	6:26:41
Vance Air Force Base 24	1	36N25	97w52	6:31:28
Vanoss 62	1	34N45'50	96w52'18	6:27:29
Velma 69	1	34N27'36	97w40'25	6:30:42
Vera 74	1	36N26'57	95w52'50	6:23:31
Verden 26	1	35N05'00	98w05'15	6:32:21
Verdigris 66	1	36N14'05	95w41'27	6:22:46
Vernon 46	1	35N12'56	95w55'32	6:23:42
Vian 68	1	35N29'54	94w58'10	6:19:53
Vici 22	1	36N08'59	99w17'52	6:37:11
Victor 40	1	34N57'59	94w47'12	6:19:09
Victory 33	1	34N39'08	99w26'19	6:37:45
Vinco 60	1	35N57'13	97w02'14	6:28:09
Vining 2	1	36N46'03	98w09'50	6:32:39
Vinita 18	1	36N38'19	95w09'14	6:20:37
Vinson 29	1	34N54'02	99w51'34	6:39:26
Virgil 12	1	34N04'11	95w22'56	6:21:32
Vista 63	1	34N58	96w46	6:27:04
Vivian 46	1	35N17'23	95w42'58	6:22:52
Wade 7	1	33N53'20	96w04'33	6:24:18
Wadena 64	1	34N24'09	95w35'48	6:22:23
Wagoner 73	1	35N57'34	95w22'09	6:21:29
Wainwright 51	1	35N36'45	95w33'51	6:22:15
Wakita 27	1	36N53'00	97w55'18	6:31:41
Waldron 2	1	36N59'52	98w10'59	6:32:44
Walls 40	1	35N02'13	94w54'32	6:19:38
Wallville 25	1	34N46'05	97w30'13	6:30:01
Walnut 9	1	35N27	98w14	6:32:56
Walters 17	1	34N21'35	98w18'27	6:33:14
Wandel 37	1	35N53'06	97w44'43	6:30:59
Wanette 63	1	34N57'43	97w01'56	6:28:08
Wann 53	1	36N54'55	95w48'15	6:23:13
Wapanucka 35	1	34N22'26	96w25'27	6:25:42
Ward 40	1	35N14'14	94w43'31	6:18:54
Ward Springs 61	1	34N48'40	96w01'19	6:24:05
Wardville 3	1	34N39'13	96w01'48	6:24:07
Warner 51	1	35N29'39	95w18'19	6:21:13
Warr Acres 55	1	35N31'21	97w37'07	6:30:28
Warren 33	1	34N46'59	99w12'29	6:36:50
Warwick 41	1	35N41'09	97w00'14	6:28:01
Washington 44	1	35N03'32	97w29'03	6:29:56
Washita 8	1	35N06'10	98w20'26	6:33:22
Washita 50	1	34N32'49	97w07'52	6:28:31
Washunga 36	1	36N47'01	96w50'16	6:27:21
Wasseta 7	1	34N04'47	96w18'36	6:25:14
Watchorn 59	1	36N25'12	96w59'47	6:27:59
Waterloo 55	1	35N43'31	97w28'40	6:29:55
Watkins 72	1	35N58'51	96w00'41	6:24:03
Watonga 6	1	35N50'41	98w24'46	6:33:39
Watova 53	1	36N37'02	95w39'20	6:22:37
Watson 45	1	34N26'14	94w33'26	6:18:14
Watts 1	1	36N06'33	94w34'12	6:18:17
Wauhillau 1	1	35N51'25	94w46'23	6:19:06
Waukomis 24	1	36N16'49	97w53'52	6:31:35
Waurika 34	1	34N10'01	97w59'50	6:31:59
Wayne 44	1	34N55'05	97w18'51	6:29:15
Waynoka 76	1	36N34'56	98w52'46	6:35:31
Wealand 58	1	36N53	94w53	6:19:32
Weatherford 20	1	35N31'34	98w42'26	6:34:50
Weathers 61	1	34N39'34	95w35'00	6:22:20
Webb 22	1	35N55'40	99w07'56	6:36:32
Webb City 57	1	36N48'25	96w42'30	6:26:50
Webber Falls 51	1	35N30'39	95w07'47	6:20:31
Webbers Falls 51	1	35N31	95w08	6:20:32
Weeks 7	1	33N52'06	95w50'02	6:23:20
Wekiwa 72	1	36N09'11	96w10'22	6:24:41
Welch 18	1	36N52'25	95w05'44	6:20:23
Weleetka 54	1	35N20'08	96w08'10	6:24:33
Welling 11	1	35N52'40	94w54'03	6:19:36
Wellston 41	1	35N41'39	97w03'47	6:28:15
Welon 33	1	34N39'07	99w20'46	6:37:23
Welty 54	1	35N37'28	96w24'18	6:25:37
Wesley 3	1	34N35'16	95w53'51	6:23:35
West Atoka 3	1	34N17	96w17	6:25:08
West Canadian 9	1	35N38	98w12	6:32:48
West Central Pontotoc 62	1	34N46	96w50	6:27:20
West Central Stephens 69	1	34N31	97w58	6:31:52
West Choctaw 12	1	34N01	95w47	6:23:08
West Cleo 47	1	36N24'20	98w27'54	6:33:52
West Coal 15	1	34N34	96w25	6:25:40

Place		Latitude	Longitude	Time
West Fort Smith 68	1	35N23'49	94w26'23	6:17:46
West Fort Towson 12	1	34N01'22	95w16'25	6:21:06
West Haskell 31	1	35N12	95w19	6:21:16
West Jackson 33	1	34N34	99w33	6:38:12
West Johnston 35	1	34N20	96w34	6:26:16
West Love 43	1	33N57	97w25	6:29:40
West Murray 50	1	34N32	97w07	6:28:28
West Muskogee 51	1	35N44'13	95w24'42	6:21:39
West Point 60	1	36N11'18	96w51'14	6:27:25
Westport 59	1	36N18	96w28	6:25:52
West Siloam Springs 21	1	36N11	94w35	6:18:20
West Texas 70	4	36N47	101w51	6:47:24
West Tulsa 72	1	36N08'06	96w00'08	6:24:01
Westville 1	1	35N59'33	94w34'04	6:18:16
West Woods 76	1	36N50	99w09	6:36:36
Wetumka 32	1	35N14'15	96w14'29	6:24:58
Wewoka 67	1	35N09'31	96w29'35	6:25:58
Wheatland 55	1	35N23'52	97w39'07	6:30:36
Wheeless 13	4	36N43'09	102w53'38	6:51:35
Whippoorwill 57	1	36N54'44	96w07'47	6:24:31
Whitebead 25	1	34N45'39	97w18'01	6:29:12
White Eagle 36	1	36N36'30	97w04'33	6:28:18
Whitefield 31	1	35N15'09	95w14'14	6:20:57
White Oak 11	1	35N43'32	95w01'46	6:20:07
White Oak 18	1	36N37'13	95w15'50	6:21:03
Whitesboro 40	1	34N41'33	94w53'06	6:19:32
Whitmire 1	1	35N56'39	94w39'49	6:18:39
Whittier 72	1	36N09	95w59	6:23:56
Wilburton 39	1	34N55'07	95w18'32	6:21:14
Wildcat Point 11	1	35N45'53	94w55'02	6:19:40
Wildhorse 41	1	35N54'46	96w48'13	6:27:13
Wild Horse 57	1	36N25	96w24	6:25:36
Willard 30	1	36N58'21	99w43'30	6:38:54
Williams 40	1	35N09'53	94w32'54	6:18:12
Willis 48	1	33N53'08	96w49'44	6:27:19
Willow 28	1	35N03'05	99w30'33	6:38:02
Willow View 14	1	35N03'30	97w15'53	6:29:04
Will Rogers 55	1	35N27	97w31	6:30:04
Wilson 3	1	34N20'45	96w21'16	6:25:25
Wilson 10	1	34N09'43	97w25'32	6:29:42
Wilson 56	1	35N30'27	96w02'04	6:24:08
Wilzetta 41	1	35N33'01	96w44'07	6:26:56
Wimer 18	1	37N00	95w37	6:22:28
Winchester 76	1	36N57'26	98w47'49	6:35:11
Winganon 66	1	36N33'14	95w33'39	6:22:15
Winrock Farms 50	1	34N30'56	96w50'22	6:27:21
Wirt 10	1	34N13'51	97w31'53	6:30:08
Wister 40	1	34N58'02	94w43'28	6:18:54
Witcher 55	1	35N35'38	97w25'21	6:29:41
Witteville 40	1	35N05'11	94w39'02	6:18:36
Wolco 57	1	36N32'18	96w04'16	6:24:17
Wolf 67	1	35N05'15	96w39'30	6:26:38
Woodard Corner 54	1	35N31'19	96w09'31	6:24:38
Woodford 10	1	34N20'19	97w17'03	6:29:08
Woodlawn Park 55	1	35N30'41	97w38'59	6:30:36
Woods 55	1	35N26'07	97w15'52	6:29:03
Woodville 48	1	33N58'11	96w39'12	6:26:37
Woodward 77	1	36N26'01	99w23'24	6:37:34
Woolaroc 57	2	36N39'39	96w06'51	6:24:27
Wright City 45	1	34N03'36	95w00'11	6:20:01
Wyandotte 58	1	36N47'36	94w43'30	6:18:54
Wybark 51	1	35N48'41	95w19'53	6:21:20
Wye 63	1	35N09	97w01	6:28:04
Wynnewood 25	1	34N38'36	97w09'51	6:28:39
Wynona 57	1	36N32'46	96w19'37	6:25:18
Yahola 51	1	35N45'45	95w36'24	6:22:26
Yale 60	1	36N06'51	96w41'56	6:26:48
Yanush 39	1	34N42'35	95w18'49	6:21:15
Yarnaby 7	1	33N47'27	96w15'24	6:25:02
Yeager 32	1	35N09'27	96w20'21	6:25:21
Yerby 40	1	35N00'02	94w40'40	6:18:43
Yewed 2	1	36N40'56	98w24'35	6:33:38
Yonkers 73	1	36N03'10	95w15'38	6:21:03
Yost 60	1	36N12'03	97w00'40	6:28:03
Yuba 7	1	33N48'34	96w12'15	6:24:49
Yukon 9	1	35N30'24	97w45'44	6:31:03
Zafra 40	1	34N30'31	94w29'12	6:17:57
Zaneis 10	1	34N10'21	97w29'56	6:30:00
Zeb 11	1	35N49'18	95w03'16	6:20:13
Zena 21	1	36N29'46	94w51'12	6:19:25
Zincville 58	1	36N59'29	94w48'31	6:19:14
Zion 1	1	35N46'57	94w38'05	6:18:32
Zoe 40	1	34N46'04	94w37'41	6:18:31

TIME TABLES

OR # 1
Before 11/18/1883 LMT
11/18/1883 12:00 MST
3/31/1918 02:00 MWT
10/27/1918 02:00 MST
3/30/1919 02:00 MWT
10/26/1919 02:00 MST
2/09/1942 02:00 MWT
9/30/1945 02:00 MST
4/28/1963 02:00 MDT
10/27/1963 02:00 MST
4/26/1964 02:00 MDT
10/25/1964 02:00 MST
4/25/1965 02:00 MDT
10/31/1965 02:00 MST
4/30/1967 02:00 MDT
10/29/1967 02:00 MST
4/28/1968 02:00 MDT
10/27/1968 02:00 MST
4/27/1969 02:00 MDT
10/26/1969 02:00 MST
4/26/1970 02:00 MDT
10/25/1970 02:00 MST
4/25/1971 02:00 MDT
10/31/1971 02:00 MST
4/30/1972 02:00 MDT
10/29/1972 02:00 MST
4/29/1973 02:00 MDT
10/28/1973 02:00 MST
2/03/1974 02:00 MDT
10/27/1974 02:00 MST
2/23/1975 02:00 US#1

OR # 2
Before 11/18/1883 LMT
11/18/1883 12:00 PST
3/31/1918 02:00 PWT
10/27/1918 02:00 PST
3/30/1919 02:00 PWT
10/26/1919 02:00 PST
2/09/1942 02:00 PWT
9/30/1945 02:00 PST
4/30/1950 02:00 PDT
9/24/1950 02:00 PST
4/29/1951 02:00 PDT
9/30/1951 02:00 PST
4/28/1963 02:00 PDT
10/27/1963 02:00 PST
4/26/1964 02:00 PDT
10/25/1964 02:00 PST
4/25/1965 02:00 PDT
10/31/1965 02:00 PST
4/24/1966 02:00 PDT
10/30/1966 02:00 PST
4/30/1967 02:00 US#1

OR # 3
Before 11/18/1883 LMT
11/18/1883 12:00 PST
3/31/1918 02:00 PWT
10/27/1918 02:00 PST
3/30/1919 02:00 PWT
10/26/1919 02:00 PST
2/09/1942 02:00 PWT
9/30/1945 02:00 PST
4/30/1950 02:00 PDT
9/24/1950 02:00 PST
4/29/1951 02:00 PDT
9/30/1951 02:00 PST
4/27/1952 02:00 PDT
9/28/1952 02:00 PST
4/28/1963 02:00 PDT
10/27/1963 02:00 PST
4/26/1964 02:00 PDT
10/25/1964 02:00 PST
4/25/1965 02:00 PDT
10/31/1965 02:00 PST
4/24/1966 02:00 PDT
10/30/1966 02:00 PST
4/30/1967 02:00 US#1

OR # 4
Before 11/18/1883 LMT
11/18/1883 12:00 PST
3/31/1918 02:00 PWT
10/27/1918 02:00 PST
3/30/1919 02:00 PWT
10/26/1919 02:00 PST
2/09/1942 02:00 PWT
9/30/1945 02:00 PST
4/30/1950 02:00 PDT
9/24/1950 02:00 PST
4/29/1951 02:00 PDT
9/30/1951 02:00 PST
5/07/1961 01:00 PDT
9/24/1961 02:00 PST
4/29/1962 02:00 PDT
9/29/1962 02:00 PST
4/28/1963 02:00 PDT
10/27/1963 02:00 PST
4/26/1964 02:00 PDT
10/25/1964 02:00 PST
4/25/1965 02:00 PDT
10/31/1965 02:00 PST
4/24/1966 02:00 PDT
10/30/1966 02:00 PST
4/30/1967 02:00 US#1

OR # 5
Before 11/18/1883 LMT
11/18/1883 12:00 PST
3/31/1918 02:00 PWT
10/27/1918 02:00 PST
3/30/1919 02:00 PWT
10/26/1919 02:00 PST
2/09/1942 02:00 PWT
9/30/1945 02:00 PST
4/30/1950 02:00 PDT
9/24/1950 02:00 PST
4/29/1951 02:00 PDT
9/30/1951 02:00 PST
4/27/1952 02:00 PDT
9/28/1952 02:00 PST
5/07/1961 01:00 PDT
9/24/1961 02:00 PST
4/29/1962 02:00 PDT
9/29/1962 02:00 PST
4/28/1963 02:00 PDT
10/27/1963 02:00 PST
4/26/1964 02:00 PDT
10/25/1964 02:00 PST
4/25/1965 02:00 PDT
10/31/1965 02:00 PST
4/24/1966 02:00 PDT
10/30/1966 02:00 PST
4/30/1967 02:00 US#1

OR # 6
Before 11/18/1883 LMT
11/18/1883 12:00 PST
3/31/1918 02:00 PWT
10/27/1918 02:00 PST
3/30/1919 02:00 PWT
10/26/1919 02:00 PST
2/09/1942 02:00 PWT
9/30/1945 02:00 PST
4/24/1949 02:00 PDT
9/25/1949 02:00 PST
4/30/1950 02:00 PDT
9/24/1950 02:00 PST
4/29/1951 02:00 PDT
9/30/1951 02:00 PST
4/27/1952 02:00 PDT
9/28/1952 02:00 PST
5/07/1961 01:00 PDT
9/24/1961 02:00 PST
4/29/1962 02:00 PDT
9/29/1962 02:00 PST
4/28/1963 02:00 PDT
10/27/1963 02:00 PST
4/26/1964 02:00 PDT
10/25/1964 02:00 PST
4/25/1965 02:00 PDT
10/31/1965 02:00 PST
4/24/1966 02:00 PDT
10/30/1966 02:00 PST
4/30/1967 02:00 US#1

OR # 7
Before 11/18/1883 LMT
11/18/1883 12:00 PST
3/31/1918 02:00 PWT
10/27/1918 02:00 PST
3/30/1919 02:00 PWT
10/26/1919 02:00 PST
2/09/1942 02:00 PWT
9/30/1945 02:00 PST
4/30/1950 02:00 PDT
9/24/1950 02:00 PST
4/29/1951 02:00 PDT
9/30/1951 02:00 PST
4/29/1962 02:00 PDT
9/29/1962 02:00 PST
4/28/1963 02:00 PDT
10/27/1963 02:00 PST
4/26/1964 02:00 PDT
10/25/1964 02:00 PST
4/25/1965 02:00 PDT
10/31/1965 02:00 PST
4/24/1966 02:00 PDT
10/30/1966 02:00 PST
4/30/1967 02:00 US#1

OR # 8
Before 11/18/1883 LMT
11/18/1883 12:00 PST
3/31/1918 02:00 PWT
10/27/1918 02:00 PST
3/30/1919 02:00 PWT
10/26/1919 02:00 PST
2/09/1942 02:00 PWT
9/30/1945 02:00 PST
4/30/1950 02:00 PDT
9/24/1950 02:00 PST
4/29/1951 02:00 PDT
9/30/1951 02:00 PST
4/27/1952 02:00 PDT
9/28/1952 02:00 PST
4/29/1962 02:00 PDT
9/29/1962 02:00 PST
4/28/1963 02:00 PDT
10/27/1963 02:00 PST
4/26/1964 02:00 PDT
10/25/1964 02:00 PST
4/25/1965 02:00 PDT
10/31/1965 02:00 PST
4/24/1966 02:00 PDT
10/30/1966 02:00 PST
4/30/1967 02:00 US#1

OR # 9
Before 11/18/1883 LMT
11/18/1883 12:00 PST
3/31/1918 02:00 PWT
10/27/1918 02:00 PST
3/30/1919 02:00 PWT
10/26/1919 02:00 PST
2/09/1942 02:00 PWT
9/30/1945 02:00 PST
4/30/1950 02:00 PDT
9/24/1950 02:00 PST
4/29/1951 02:00 PDT
9/30/1951 02:00 PST
5/27/1962 02:00 PDT
9/29/1962 02:00 PST
4/28/1963 02:00 PDT
10/27/1963 02:00 PST
4/26/1964 02:00 PDT
10/25/1964 02:00 PST
4/25/1965 02:00 PDT
10/31/1965 02:00 PST
4/24/1966 02:00 PDT
10/30/1966 02:00 PST
4/30/1967 02:00 US#1

OR # 10
Before 11/18/1883 LMT
11/18/1883 12:00 PST
3/31/1918 02:00 PWT
10/27/1918 02:00 PST
3/30/1919 02:00 PWT
10/26/1919 02:00 PST
2/09/1942 02:00 PWT
9/30/1945 02:00 PST
4/24/1949 02:00 PDT
9/25/1949 02:00 PST
4/30/1950 02:00 PDT
9/04/1950 02:00 PST
4/29/1951 02:00 PDT
9/30/1951 02:00 PST
4/27/1952 02:00 PDT
9/28/1952 02:00 PST
5/07/1961 01:00 PDT
9/24/1961 02:00 PST
4/29/1962 02:00 PDT
9/29/1962 02:00 PST
4/28/1963 02:00 PDT
10/27/1963 02:00 PST
4/26/1964 02:00 PDT
10/25/1964 02:00 PST
4/25/1965 02:00 PDT
10/31/1965 02:00 PST
4/24/1966 02:00 PDT
10/30/1966 02:00 PST
4/30/1967 02:00 US#1

OR # 11
Before 11/18/1883 LMT
11/18/1883 12:00 PST
3/31/1918 02:00 PWT
10/27/1918 02:00 PST
3/30/1919 02:00 PWT
10/26/1919 02:00 PST
2/09/1942 02:00 PWT
9/30/1945 02:00 PST
4/30/1950 02:00 PDT
9/24/1950 02:00 PST
4/29/1951 02:00 PDT
9/30/1951 02:00 PST
4/29/1962 02:00 PDT
9/29/1962 02:00 PST
4/28/1963 02:00 PDT
10/27/1963 02:00 PST
4/26/1964 02:00 PDT
10/25/1964 02:00 PST
4/25/1965 02:00 PDT
10/31/1965 02:00 PST
4/24/1966 02:00 PDT
10/30/1966 02:00 PST
4/30/1967 02:00 US#1

OR # 12
Before 11/18/1883 LMT
11/18/1883 12:00 PST
3/31/1918 02:00 PWT
10/27/1918 02:00 PST
3/30/1919 02:00 PWT
10/26/1919 02:00 PST
2/09/1942 02:00 PWT
9/30/1945 02:00 PST
4/25/1948 02:00 PDT
9/26/1948 02:00 PST
4/24/1949 02:00 PDT
9/11/1949 02:00 PST
4/30/1950 02:00 PDT
9/24/1950 02:00 PST
4/29/1951 02:00 PDT
9/30/1951 02:00 PST
4/30/1952 02:00 PDT
9/28/1952 02:00 PST
5/07/1961 01:00 PDT
9/24/1961 02:00 PST
4/29/1962 02:00 PDT
9/29/1962 02:00 PST
4/28/1963 02:00 PDT
10/27/1963 02:00 PST
4/26/1964 02:00 PDT
10/25/1964 02:00 PST
4/25/1965 02:00 PDT
10/31/1965 02:00 PST
4/24/1966 02:00 PDT
10/30/1966 02:00 PST
4/30/1967 02:00 US#1

OR # 13
Before 11/18/1883 LMT
11/18/1883 12:00 PST
3/31/1918 02:00 PWT
10/27/1918 02:00 PST
3/30/1919 02:00 PWT
10/26/1919 02:00 PST
2/09/1942 02:00 PWT
9/30/1945 02:00 PST
4/24/1949 02:00 PDT
9/25/1949 02:00 PST
4/30/1950 02:00 PDT
9/24/1950 02:00 PST
4/29/1951 02:00 PDT
9/30/1951 02:00 PST
4/29/1962 02:00 PDT
9/29/1962 02:00 PST
4/28/1963 02:00 PDT
10/27/1963 02:00 PST
4/26/1964 02:00 PDT
10/25/1964 02:00 PST
4/25/1965 02:00 PDT
10/31/1965 02:00 PST
4/24/1966 02:00 PDT
10/30/1966 02:00 PST
4/30/1967 02:00 US#1

OR # 14
Before 11/18/1883 LMT
11/18/1883 12:00 PST
3/31/1918 02:00 PWT
10/27/1918 02:00 PST
3/30/1919 02:00 PWT
10/26/1919 02:00 PST
2/09/1942 02:00 PWT
9/30/1945 02:00 PST
4/24/1949 02:00 PDT
9/25/1949 02:00 PST
4/30/1950 02:00 PDT
9/24/1950 02:00 PST
4/29/1951 02:00 PDT
9/30/1951 02:00 PST
4/27/1952 02:00 PDT
9/28/1952 02:00 PST
4/29/1962 02:00 PDT
9/29/1962 02:00 PST
4/28/1963 02:00 PDT
10/27/1963 02:00 PST
4/26/1964 02:00 PDT
10/25/1964 02:00 PST
4/25/1965 02:00 PDT
10/31/1965 02:00 PST
4/24/1966 02:00 PDT
10/30/1966 02:00 PST
4/30/1967 02:00 US#1

OR # 15
Before 11/18/1883 LMT
11/18/1883 12:00 PST
3/31/1918 02:00 PWT
10/27/1918 02:00 PST
3/30/1919 02:00 PWT
10/26/1919 02:00 PST
2/09/1942 02:00 PWT
9/30/1945 02:00 PST
4/24/1949 02:00 PDT
9/25/1949 02:00 PST
4/30/1950 02:00 PDT
9/24/1950 02:00 PST
4/29/1951 02:00 PDT
9/30/1951 02:00 PST
4/28/1963 02:00 PDT
10/27/1963 02:00 PST
4/26/1964 02:00 PDT
10/25/1964 02:00 PST
4/25/1965 02:00 PDT
10/31/1965 02:00 PST
4/24/1966 02:00 PDT
10/30/1966 02:00 PST
4/30/1967 02:00 US#1

OR # 16
Before 11/18/1883 LMT
11/18/1883 12:00 PST
3/31/1918 02:00 PWT
10/27/1918 02:00 PST
3/30/1919 02:00 PWT
10/26/1919 02:00 PST
2/09/1942 02:00 PWT
9/30/1945 02:00 PST
4/25/1948 02:00 PDT
9/26/1948 02:00 PST
4/30/1950 02:00 PDT
9/24/1950 02:00 PST
4/29/1951 02:00 PDT
9/30/1951 02:00 PST
4/28/1963 02:00 PDT
10/27/1963 02:00 PST
4/26/1964 02:00 PDT
10/25/1964 02:00 PST
4/25/1965 02:00 PDT
10/31/1965 02:00 PST
4/24/1966 02:00 PDT
10/30/1966 02:00 PST
4/30/1967 02:00 US#1

OR # 17
Before 11/18/1883 LMT
11/18/1883 12:00 PST
3/31/1918 02:00 PWT
10/27/1918 02:00 PST
3/30/1919 02:00 PWT
10/26/1919 02:00 PST
2/09/1942 02:00 PWT
9/30/1945 02:00 PST
4/24/1949 02:00 PDT
9/25/1949 02:00 PST
4/30/1950 02:00 PDT
9/24/1950 02:00 PST
4/29/1951 02:00 PDT
9/30/1951 02:00 PST
5/07/1961 01:00 PDT
9/24/1961 02:00 PST
4/29/1962 02:00 PDT
9/29/1962 02:00 PST
4/28/1963 02:00 PDT
10/27/1963 02:00 PST
4/26/1964 02:00 PDT
10/25/1964 02:00 PST
4/25/1965 02:00 PDT
10/31/1965 02:00 PST
4/24/1966 02:00 PDT
10/30/1966 02:00 PST
4/30/1967 02:00 US#1

COUNTIES

1 Baker
2 Benton
3 Clackamas
4 Clatsop
5 Columbia
6 Coos
7 Crook
8 Curry
9 Deschutes
10 Douglas
11 Gilliam
12 Grant
13 Harney
14 Hood River
15 Jackson
16 Jefferson
17 Josephine
18 Klamath
19 Lake
20 Lane
21 Lincoln
22 Linn
23 Malheur
24 Marion
25 Morrow
26 Multnomah
27 Polk
28 Sherman
29 Tillamook
30 Umatilla
31 Union
32 Wallowa
33 Wasco
34 Washington
35 Wheeler
36 Yamhill

Place		Lat.	Long.	
Abernethy 20	2	43N36'27	122w05'14	8:08:21
Abrams 20	2	43N41'03	122w57'20	8:11:49
Acorn Park 20	8	44N05	123w08	8:12:32
Ada 20	2	43N52'30	124w02'38	8:16:11
Adams 30	2	45N46'03	118w33'41	7:54:15
Adams Point 18	2	42N00'39	121w29'50	8:05:59
Adel 19	2	42N10'39	119w53'51	7:59:35
Adrian 23	1	43N44'27	117w04'15	7:48:17
Advance 3	4	45N19'03	122w42'41	8:10:51
Agate Beach 21	11	44N40'39	124w03'38	8:16:15
Agness 8	2	42N33'24	124w04'04	8:16:16
Aims 3	12	45N27'03	122w12'24	8:08:50
Airlie 27	2	44N45'02	123w19'49	8:13:19
Akin 10	2	43N17'26	123w21'41	8:13:27
Alameda 26	12	45N33'19	122w37'46	8:10:31
Albany 22	13	44N38'12	123w06'17	8:12:25
Albee 30	2	45N12'46	118w54'29	7:55:38
Albina 26	12	45N32'38	122w40'26	8:10:42
Alder 2	2	44N34'57	123w30'28	8:14:02
Alder 32	2	45N23'53	117w17'46	7:49:11
Alder Creek 3	4	45N22'41	122w06'02	8:08:24
Aldervale 29	11	45N46'07	123w50'35	8:15:22
Aldrich Point 4	14	46N11	123w50	8:15:20
Alfalfa 9	8	44N04'39	121w00'57	8:04:04
Algoma 18	3	42N20'50	121w48'52	8:07:15
Alicel 31	2	45N24'16	117w58'44	7:51:55
Alkali Lake 19	2	42N11	120w22	8:01:28
Allegany 6	2	43N25'34	124w01'52	8:16:07
Allston 5	12	45N24	122w39	8:10:36
Alma 20	2	43N53'28	123w28'25	8:13:54
Aloha 34	5	45N29'40	122w51'57	8:11:28

Alpha 20 2 44N09'52 123w41'58 8:14:48
Alpine 2 2 44N19'49 123w21'33 8:13:26
Alpine 25 2 45N36'59 119w31'43 7:58:07
Alpine Junction 2 2 44N20'12 123w17'49 8:13:11
Alsea 2 2 44N22'54 123w35'43 8:14:23
Alston 5 4 46N05'58 123w02'45 8:12:11
Altamont 18 3 42N12'25 121w44'10 8:06:57
Alvadore 20 2 44N07'37 123w15'48 8:13:03
Amelia 23 1 44N23'25 117w37'24 7:50:30
Amity 36 13 45N06'57 123w12'22 8:12:49
Anderson 3 4 45N27'35 122w23'10 8:09:33
Andrews 13 2 42N27'51 118w36'44 7:54:27
Anlauf 10 2 43N42'40 123w13'21 8:12:53
Annex 23 1 44N15 116w58 7:47:52
Antelope 33 2 44N54'39 120w43'18 8:02:53
Antone 35 2 44N28'18 119w48'32 7:59:14
Apex 30 2 45N53'27 118w40'40 7:54:43
Apiary 5 12 46N00'51 123w01'44 8:12:07
Applegate 15 2 42N15'26 123w10'02 8:12:40
Applegate Ford 15 2 42N48'13 122w36'53 8:10:28
Apple Valley 5 4 45N45 122w52 8:11:28
Arago 6 2 43N06'08 124w11'28 8:16:46
Arcadia 23 1 43N55'28 116w59'04 7:47:56
Arch Cape 4 11 45N49'45 123w57'39 8:15:51
Ardenwald 3 12 45N27'20 122w37'43 8:10:31
Ardgour 3 12 45N27'12 122w39'03 8:10:36
Arleta 26 12 45N29'20 122w35'32 8:10:22
Arlington 11 2 45N43'01 120w11'59 8:00:48
Arnaud 26 12 45N28'41 122w32'49 8:10:11
Arock 23 1 42N54'51 117w31'27 7:50:06
Ash 10 2 43N33'09 123w49'14 8:15:17
Ashdale 3 12 45N23'38 122w37'15 8:10:29
Ashland 15 2 42N11'41 122w42'30 8:10:50
Ashwood 16 2 44N44'02 120w45'12 8:03:01
Astoria 4 14 46N11'17 123w49'48 8:15:19
Athena 30 2 45N48'43 118w29'22 7:53:57
Auburn 1 2 44N41'58 117w56'39 7:51:47
Augustine Gilbert Place 13 2 42N52'24 119w21'52 7:57:27
Aumsville 24 2 44N50'28 122w52'11 8:11:29
Aurora 24 2 45N13'52 122w45'17 8:11:01
Austa 20 2 44N00'09 123w38'59 8:14:36
Austin 12 2 44N36'10 118w29'44 7:53:59
Austin Junction 12 2 44N34'27 118w30'02 7:54:00
Avery 2 7 44N32'24 123w16'12 8:13:05
Avon 5 12 45N24 122w39 8:10:36
Awbrey 20 8 44N07'37 123w11'34 8:12:46
Axford 33 2 44N53'00 121w02'56 8:04:12
Azalea 10 2 42N47'44 123w15'33 8:13:02
Bade 30 2 45N54'45 118w25'20 7:53:41
Badger Corner 24 15 44N57'01 122w58'56 8:11:56
Badger Mountain 20 2 44N04 123w23 8:13:32
Bailey Junction 2 2 44N19'57 123w20'13 8:13:21
Bakeoven 33 2 45N05'12 120w50'19 8:03:21
Baker 1 9 44N46'42 117w49'42 7:51:19
Baker Valley 1 2 44N50 117w46 7:51:04
Ballston 27 15 45N04'01 123w19'11 8:13:17
Balm Grove 34 6 45N35'49 123w13'02 8:12:52
Bancroft 6 2 42N56'23 124w00'21 8:16:01
Bandon 6 2 43N07'09 124w24'26 8:17:38
Banks 34 4 45N37'08 123w06'47 8:12:27
Barlow 3 4 45N15'07 122w43'10 8:10:53
Barlow Crossing Forest Camp 33 2 45N13'01 121w36'47 8:06:27
Barnesdale 29 7 45N38'22 123w51'12 8:15:25
Barnett 11 2 45N32'05 120w15'58 8:01:04
Barnhardy 19 2 42N28'30 119w42'45 7:58:51
Barnhart 30 2 45N39'10 118w55'33 7:55:42
Barrett 30 2 45N56'50 118w27'07 7:53:48
Bartlett 32 2 45N59'06 117w27'26 7:49:50
Bartlett Landing 26 12 45N34'40 122w28'46 8:09:55
Barton 3 4 45N23'21 122w24'21 8:09:37
Barton Heights 32 2 45N17'07 116w41'54 7:46:48
Barview 6 2 43N21'16 124w18'43 8:17:15
Barview 29 11 45N34'12 123w56'32 8:15:46
Base Line 26 12 45N31'10 122w27'15 8:09:49
Basque 23 1 42N24'39 117w52'03 7:51:28
Bass 10 2 43N48'48 124w06'56 8:16:28
Bass Haines Place 13 2 42N21'51 118w58'34 7:55:54
Bates 12 2 44N35'35 118w30'27 7:54:02
Batterson 29 11 45N42'05 123w45'26 8:15:02
Battin 3 12 45N27'32 122w34'37 8:10:18
Bay City 29 7 45N31'22 123w53'17 8:15:33
Bayocean 29 11 45N31'40 123w57'04 8:15:48
Bay Park 6 2 43N20'57 124w12'02 8:16:48
Bayshore 21 2 44N26 124w04 8:16:16
Bayside Garden 29 11 45N43 123w54 8:15:36
Bayview 21 2 44N26'33 124w02'02 8:16:08
Beal 18 2 43N34'31 121w30'44 8:06:03
Bear Creek 20 2 44N12'57 123w17'18 8:13:09
Beatty 18 2 42N26'31 121w16'11 8:05:05
Beaver 29 2 45N16'37 123w49'31 8:15:18
Beaver Creek 3 12 45N17'17 122w32'04 8:10:08
Beaver Homes 5 4 46N00'21 122w55'33 8:11:42
Beaver Marsh 18 2 43N08'03 121w48'07 8:07:12
Beaver Springs 5 4 46N02'46 122w56'49 8:11:47
Beaverton 34 12 45N29'14 122w48'09 8:11:13
Beburg 34 12 45N29'05 122w47'44 8:11:11
Beck 20 2 44N02 123w52 8:15:28
Beech Creek 12 2 44N37'10 119w08'52 7:56:35
Beecher 20 2 44N01'53 123w40'31 8:14:42
Belding 29 2 45N42'20 123w30'07 8:14:00
Belfort 29 2 45N44'06 123w36'09 8:14:25
Belknap Springs 20 2 44N11'26 122w02'53 8:08:12
Bell 3 12 45N27'26 122w35'20 8:10:21
Belleview 15 2 42N12 122w42 8:10:48
Bellevue 36 14 45N06'56 123w18'54 8:13:16
Bellfountain 2 2 44N21'50 123w21'15 8:13:25
Bellfountain Junction 2 2 44N21'48 123w17'24 8:13:10
Bellinger Landing 20 8 44N04'13 122w54'27 8:11:38
Bellrose 26 12 45N28'53 122w31'19 8:10:05
Bend 9 8 44N03'30 121w18'51 8:05:15
Bendemeer 34 6 45N34'16 122w53'51 8:11:35
Berlin 22 2 44N31 122w53 8:11:32
Bethany 34 6 45N33'29 122w51'59 8:11:28
Bethel 20 8 44N03'55 123w07'53 8:12:32
Bethel 27 2 45N02'26 123w11'01 8:12:44
Bethel Gospel Park 24 15 45N03'15 122w57'03 8:11:48
Bethel Heights 27 15 45N02'41 123w08'58 8:12:36
Beulah 23 1 43N54'24 118w09'06 7:52:36
Beverly Beach 21 2 44N43'14 124w03'23 8:16:14
Biddle 4 2 46N07'59 123w39'34 8:14:38
Biggs 28 2 45N40'05 120w50'14 8:03:21
Biggs Junction 28 2 45N40'12 120w49'54 8:03:20
Bingham 15 2 42N19 122w58 8:11:52
Bingham Springs 30 2 45N44'32 118w13'51 7:52:55
Birkenfeld 5 4 45N59'27 123w20'11 8:13:21
Bissell 3 4 45N17'39 122w10'41 8:08:43
Blachly 20 3 44N11'42 123w32'02 8:14:08
Black Butte Ranch 9 2 44N17 121w33 8:06:12
Black Place 16 2 44N38'18 120w46'18 8:03:05
Black Rock 27 2 44N52'16 123w29'42 8:13:59
Blaine 29 2 45N16'39 123w42'12 8:14:49
Blaisdell 19 2 42N22'42 120w50'34 8:03:22
Blakeley 30 2 45N44'30 118w36'11 7:54:25
Blalock 11 2 45N42 120w22 8:01:28
Blann Meadow 35 2 44N36'39 119w54'12 7:59:37
Blitzen 13 2 42N36'52 119w04'05 7:56:16
Blodgett 2 2 44N35'50 123w31'06 8:14:04
Blooming 34 6 45N29'15 123w03'00 8:12:12
Bloucher 14 10 45N37'53 121w35'52 8:06:23
Blue Mountain 30 2 45N52'07 118w24'06 7:53:36
Blue River 20 2 44N09'17 122w20'24 8:09:22
Bly 18 2 42N23'52 121w02'26 8:04:10
Boardman 25 2 45N50'24 119w41'58 7:58:48
Boardman Junction 25 2 45N50'03 119w37'19 7:58:29
Bodie 31 2 45N24'39 118w21'51 7:53:27
Bolton 3 12 45N22'19 122w37'26 8:10:30
Bonanza 18 2 42N11'56 121w24'18 8:05:37
Bonifer 30 2 45N40'56 118w21'43 7:53:27
Bonita 23 1 44N15'09 117w49'58 7:51:20
Bonita 34 12 45N25'01 122w45'49 8:11:03
Bonneville 26 4 45N38'10 121w57'03 8:07:48
Bonney Crossing 33 2 45N15'27 121w23'27 8:05:34
Bonnie Lure Park 3 4 45N21 122w21 8:09:24
Bonny Slope 26 12 45N32'45 122w46'55 8:11:08
Booth 10 2 43N50'56 124w05'14 8:16:21
Boring 3 4 45N25'48 122w22'25 8:09:30
Bourbon 28 2 45N16'25 120w42'43 8:02:51
Bourne 1 2 44N49'28 118w11'47 7:52:47
Bowers Junction 34 6 45N35'44 122w54'16 8:11:37
Boyd 33 2 45N29'22 121w04'52 8:04:19
Boyer 29 2 45N04'13 123w43'32 8:14:54
Bradley Corner 34 12 45N27'12 122w46'23 8:11:06
Bradwood 4 2 46N11'49 123w26'16 8:13:45
Brandt 10 2 42N46'17 123w32'54 8:14:12
Braun 5 4 45N47'34 123w13'17 8:12:53
Braymill 18 2 42N36'33 121w48'35 8:07:14
Breitenbush 24 2 44N44 122w09 8:08:36
Breitenbush Hot Springs 24 2 44N46'59 121w58'40 8:07:55
Brenham 10 2 43N45'38 124w06'39 8:16:27
Brewster 22 2 44N34'49 122w52'02 8:11:28
Briarwood 3 12 45N25'49 122w39'34 8:10:38
Brickerville 20 2 44N02 123w52 8:15:28
Bridal Veil 26 4 45N33'33 122w10'27 8:08:42
Bridge 6 2 43N01'27 124w00'21 8:16:01
Bridgeport 1 2 44N29'09 117w44'39 7:50:59
Bridgeport 27 2 44N50'55 123w23'07 8:13:32
Bridgeton 26 12 45N29 122w41 8:10:44
Bridgeview 17 2 42N07'34 123w36'17 8:14:25
Bridlemile 26 12 45N29'36 122w42'33 8:10:50
Briedwell 36 13 45N06'54 123w14'15 8:12:57
Brighton 29 2 45N40'21 123w55'18 8:15:41
Brightwood 3 4 45N22'35 122w00'56 8:08:04
Broadacres 24 10 45N11'17 122w52'05 8:11:28
Broadbent 6 2 43N00'33 124w08'43 8:16:35
Broadmead 27 4 45N04'23 123w16'06 8:13:04
Brockway 10 2 43N06'33 123w27'15 8:13:49
Brogan 23 1 44N14'47 117w30'58 7:50:04
Brookings 8 2 42N03'10 124w16'58 8:17:08
Brooklyn 26 12 45N29'26 122w38'10 8:10:33
Brooks 24 15 45N02'54 122w57'26 8:11:50
Brookwild 3 12 45N27'36 122w36'34 8:10:26
Brothers 9 2 43N48'50 120w36'08 8:02:25
Brownlee 1 2 44N49 116w56 7:47:44
Brownsboro 15 2 42N28'06 122w42'32 8:10:50
Brownsmead 4 2 46N13'04 123w32'22 8:14:09
Browns Mill 17 2 42N12'13 123w19'59 8:13:20
Browns Mountain Crossing 9 2 43N44'38 121w46'55 8:07:08
Brownsville 22 2 44N23'37 122w59'01 8:11:56
Browntown 17 2 42N03'11 123w15'46 8:13:03
Brunks Corner 27 15 44N55'59 123w08'47 8:12:35
Brush College 27 15 44N57 123w05 8:12:20
Bryant 3 12 45N24'15 122w43'17 8:10:53
Buchanan 2 7 44N34 123w16 8:13:04
Buchanan 13 2 43N38'33 118w37'39 7:54:31
Buckboard 23 1 43N34'44 117w38'48 7:50:35
Buck Creek Crossing 19 2 43N04'41 121w13'39 8:04:55
Buck Fork 10 2 43N01 123w18 8:13:12
Buckheaven 34 6 45N22'36 122w59'54 8:12:00
Buckley 28 2 45N22 120w47 8:03:08
Bucks Corners 30 2 45N47'08 119w19'36 7:57:18
Buell 27 15 45N00'59 123w25'02 8:13:40
Buena Vista 27 2 44N46'11 123w08'58 8:12:36
Bullards 6 2 43N09'00 124w23'40 8:17:35
Bull Mountain 34 12 45N25'06 122w49'16 8:11:17
Bullrun 3 4 45N24 122w16 8:09:04
Buncom 15 2 42N10'27 122w59'49 8:11:59
Bunker Hill 6 2 43N21'22 124w12'13 8:16:49
Buoy Depot 4 14 46N11 123w50 8:15:20
Burlingame 26 12 45N28'07 122w41'02 8:10:44
Burlington 26 12 45N38'47 122w50'29 8:11:22
Burns 13 2 43N35'11 119w03'11 7:56:13
Burns Corner 27 2 44N49'48 123w22'30 8:13:30
Burns Junction 23 1 42N46'37 117w51'08 7:51:25
Burnt Woods 21 2 44N36'14 123w37'18 8:14:29
Burpee 21 2 44N36'24 123w54'17 8:15:37
Butte Falls 15 2 42N32'36 122w33'52 8:10:15
Butter Creek Junction 25 2 45N37'09 119w26'11 7:57:45
Butterfield 4 14 46N02'37 123w54'37 8:15:38
Butteville 24 2 45N15'45 122w50'21 8:11:21
Butteville Station 24 2 45N15'35 122w48'11 8:11:13
Buxton 34 4 45N41'20 123w11'23 8:12:46
Bybee Springs 15 2 42N34'29 123w02'36 8:12:10
Byerle 6 2 42N55'24 124w07'15 8:16:29
Byers 10 2 42N55'31 123w30'09 8:14:01
Cabell City 12 2 44N53'43 118w22'02 7:53:28
Cairo 23 1 43N59'46 117w00'29 7:48:02
Cairo Junction 23 1 43N59'20 117w00'16 7:48:01
Calapooia 10 2 43N26 123w17 8:13:08
Calapooia 22 2 44N19'39 122w44'22 8:10:57
Calapooya 22 2 44N24 122w36 8:10:24
California Bar 17 2 42N07'11 123w28'25 8:13:54
Calimus 18 2 42N40'50 121w49'07 8:07:16
Calkins 10 3 43N13'18 123w24'27 8:13:38
Callahan 10 2 43N15'58 123w36'31 8:14:26
Camas Valley 10 2 43N02'04 123w40'22 8:14:41
Cambrai 33 2 45N10'11 121w05'04 8:04:20
Camp Elkanah 31 2 45N14'06 118w26'56 7:53:48
Camp Sherman 16 2 44N28 121w38 8:06:32
Camp Twelve 21 11 44N43 123w55 8:15:40
Campus 2 7 44N34 123w16 8:13:04
Canaan 5 4 45N55'56 122w55'00 8:11:40
Canary 20 2 43N55'41 124w02'03 8:16:08
Canby 3 4 45N15'47 122w41'29 8:10:46
Canemah 3 12 45N20'45 122w37'12 8:10:29
Cannon Beach 4 11 45N53'31 123w57'37 8:15:50
Cannon Beach Junction 4 11 45N56'30 123w55'03 8:15:40
Canyon City 12 2 44N23'23 118w56'57 7:55:48
Canyonville 10 2 42N55'39 123w16'48 8:13:07
Cape Meares 29 2 45N29'24 123w57'27 8:15:50
Capitol Hill 26 12 45N27'56 122w41'47 8:10:47
Carlton 36 2 45N17'40 123w10'31 8:12:42
Carnahan 4 11 46N06'02 123w54'57 8:15:40
Carnation 34 6 45N30'28 123w06'05 8:12:24
Carnes 10 3 43N07'55 123w22'14 8:13:29
Carpenterville 8 2 42N13'13 124w20'18 8:17:21
Carson 1 2 44N56'09 117w10'28 7:48:42
Cartney 22 3 44N10'54 123w10'00 8:12:40
Carus 3 12 45N16'17 122w34'10 8:10:17
Carver 3 12 45N23'41 122w29'46 8:09:59
Cascade Gorge 15 2 42N42'57 122w34'03 8:10:16
Cascade Locks 14 4 45N40'12 121w53'22 8:07:33
Cascade Summit 18 2 43N35 122w02 8:08:08
Cascadia 22 2 44N23'51 122w28'50 8:09:55
Castle 25 2 45N49'44 119w50'06 7:59:20
Cave Junction 17 2 42N09'47 123w38'49 8:14:35
Cayuse 30 2 45N40'37 118w33'20 7:54:13
Cecil 25 2 45N37'05 119w57'28 7:59:50
Cedardale 3 12 45N09'33 122w29'37 8:09:58
Cedar Hills 34 12 45N30'18 122w47'50 8:11:11
Cedarhurst Park 3 4 45N19'52 122w25'30 8:09:42
Cedar Mill 34 12 45N31'30 122w48'35 8:11:14
Cedar Point 6 2 43N10'47 124w12'44 8:16:51
Celilo Village 33 2 45N38'45 120w57'53 8:03:52
Central Point 3 4 45N17'44 122w37'45 8:10:31
Central Point 15 2 42N22'34 122w54'55 8:11:40
Champ 26 12 45N34'28 122w38'16 8:10:33
Champoeg 24 2 45N14'56 122w53'49 8:11:35
Chapman 5 4 45N49'31 122w59'03 8:11:56
Chapman Corner 27 15 44N57'38 123w04'40 8:12:19
Chapman Landing 5 5 45N44'46 122w50'22 8:11:21
Charleston 6 2 43N20'25 124w19'44 8:17:19
Charlestown 30 2 45N53'20 119w17'47 7:57:11
Chatfield 33 2 45N41'55 121w21'13 8:05:25
Chehalem 34 14 45N19'41 122w53'15 8:11:33
Chehalem Mountain 34 4 45N25 123w00 8:12:00
Chelsea 18 3 42N13 121w45 8:07:00
Chemawa 24 2 45N00'06 122w59'29 8:11:58
Chemult 18 2 43N13'00 121w46'54 8:07:08
Cheney 6 2 43N01'25 124w07'42 8:16:31
Chenoweth 33 2 45N37 121w13 8:04:52

Cherry Grove 34
4 45N26'52 123w14'32 8:12:58
Cherry Heights 33
2 45N36'11 121w14'23 8:04:58
Cherryville 3 4 45N22'02 122w09'14 8:08:37
Cheshire 20 2 44N11'23 123w17'04 8:13:08
Chilcoat Junction Shelter 20
2 43N27'08 122w40'44 8:10:43
Chiloquin 18 2 42N34'40 121w51'54 8:07:28
China Town 1 2 44N29'35 117w41'54 7:50:48
Chinchalo 18 2 42N52'00 121w49'10 8:07:17
Chitwood 21 2 44N39'18 123w49'17 8:15:17
Christie 34 4 45N36'20 123w04'30 8:12:18
Christmas Valley 19
2 43N14'11 120w38'09 8:02:33
Chrome 6 2 43N12'53 124w14'42 8:16:59
Cipole 34 4 45N22'29 122w48'38 8:11:15
Clackamas 3 12 45N24'28 122w34'09 8:10:17
Clackamas Heights 3
12 45N22'17 122w34'41 8:10:19
Clarke 25 2 45N50'17 119w35'59 7:58:24
Clarkes 3 4 45N12'56 122w28'12 8:09:53
Clarksville 1 2 44N29'29 117w40'44 7:50:43
Clarnie 26 12 45N32'48 122w32'09 8:10:09
Clarno 33 2 44N54'49 120w28'20 8:01:53
Clatskanie 5 4 46N06'05 123w12'20 8:12:49
Clatskanie Heights 5
4 46N03'22 123w12'57 8:12:52
Clatsop Plains 4
14 46N03 123w55 8:15:40
Clatsop Station 4
8 46N07'44 123w55'36 8:15:42
Clear Creek 5 4 45N48'22 123w16'42 8:13:07
Clear Lake 24 2 45N02'08 123w01'11 8:12:05
Clearwater 10 2 43N15'47 122w25'15 8:09:41
Clem 11 2 45N25'17 120w12'08 8:00:49
Cleo 6 2 43N19'53 124w11'55 8:16:48
Cleveland 10 3 43N17'47 123w28'31 8:13:54
Clifton 4 2 46N12'40 123w27'40 8:13:51
Clifton 14 10 45N42'26 121w33'23 8:06:14
Climax 15 2 42N17'43 122w37'07 8:10:28
Cloverdale 9 2 44N17'29 121w27'06 8:05:48
Cloverdale 20 2 43N55'30 122w57'58 8:11:52
Cloverdale 29 11 45N12'22 123w53'27 8:15:34
Clow Corner 27 2 44N53'52 123w14'02 8:12:56
Coalca 3 4 45N18'31 122w39'41 8:10:39
Coaledo 6 2 43N13'57 124w13'55 8:16:56
Cobb 30 2 45N57'19 118w23'47 7:53:35
Coburg 20 2 44N08'14 123w03'55 8:12:16
Cochran 34 4 45N42'17 123w24'26 8:13:38
Cold Springs 30
2 45N52'43 119w09'52 7:56:39
Cold Springs Junction 30
2 45N54'50 119w08'13 7:56:33
Colestine 15 2 42N03'10 122w38'59 8:10:36
College Crest 20
8 44N04 123w05 8:12:20
College Hill 20
8 44N01'52 123w05'49 8:12:23
Colton 3 4 45N10'20 122w26'12 8:09:45
Columbia City 5
17 45N53'25 122w48'21 8:11:13
Columbia Hall 33
2 45N36 121w11 8:04:44
Comstock 10 2 43N44'22 123w11'07 8:12:44
Concomly 24 2 45N05'48 122w58'32 8:11:54
Concord 3 12 45N24'16 122w38'11 8:10:33
Condon 11 2 45N14'04 120w11'02 8:00:44
Cone Mill 35 2 45N00'45 119w57'10 7:59:49
Conley 31 2 45N22'08 117w59'34 7:51:58
Conners Place 8
2 42N27'43 124w00'18 8:16:01
Conrad Place 18
2 42N36'30 120w54'03 8:03:36
Conroy 2 7 44N33'15 123w20'17 8:13:21
Cook 3 12 45N24'08 122w43'55 8:10:56
Cooper Mountain 34
4 45N28 122w53 8:11:32
Coos Bay 6 2 43N22'05 124w12'57 8:16:52
Cooston 6 2 43N23'42 124w11'03 8:16:44
Copeland Place 23
1 43N25'55 117w44'40 7:50:59
Copper 15 2 42N01'36 123w08'44 8:12:35
Copperfield 1 2 44N58'30 116w51'43 7:47:27
Coquille 6 2 43N10'38 124w11'11 8:16:45
Corbett 26 4 45N31'55 122w17'24 8:09:10
Corbett Station 26
4 45N32'29 122w17'24 8:09:10
Cordes 6 2 43N26'26 124w14'08 8:16:57
Corey Hill 5 4 45N51'43 123w12'17 8:12:49
Cornelius 34 6 45N31'12 123w03'31 8:12:14
Cornelius Pass 26
12 45N35 122w48 8:11:12
Cornell Place 30
2 45N50'59 119w17'18 7:57:09
Cornucopia 1 2 45N00'30 117w11'30 7:48:46
Cornutt 10 2 42N55'31 123w25'54 8:13:44
Coronado Shores 21
11 44N56 124w01 8:16:04
Corvallis 2 7 44N33'53 123w15'39 8:13:03
Corvallis Junction 2
7 44N34'41 123w15'25 8:13:02
Cottage Grove 20
3 43N47'52 123w03'30 8:12:14
Cottrell 3 4 45N27'28 122w18'16 8:09:13
Council Crest 26
12 45N29'20 122w42'05 8:10:48
Country Estate 2
7 44N34 123w16 8:13:04
Courtrock 12 2 44N49 119w25 7:57:40
Cove 31 2 45N17'48 117w48'25 7:51:14
Cove Orchard 36
2 45N22'31 123w09'13 8:12:37
Cow Creek 10 2 42N51'24 123w35'47 8:14:23
Coyote Corner 4
2 45N45'12 123w25'28 8:13:42
Crabtree 22 2 44N38'07 122w53'49 8:11:35
Crale 20 2 43N51'03 122w39'10 8:10:37
Crane 13 2 43N24'55 118w34'38 7:54:19
Crater Lake 18 2 42N54 122w08 8:08:32
Crates 33 2 45N37'41 121w12'49 8:04:51
Crawfordsville 22
2 44N21'26 122w51'24 8:11:26

Crescent 18 2 43N27'45 121w41'40 8:06:47
Crescent Lake 18
2 43N30'34 121w58'06 8:07:52
Crescent Lake Junction 18
2 43N31'42 121w56'35 8:07:46
Creston 23 2 43N30'05 118w00'32 7:52:02
Creston 26 12 45N29 122w36 8:10:24
Creswell 20 2 43N55'05 123w01'24 8:12:06
Criterion 33 2 45N02'33 120w59'48 8:03:59
Crockett 30 2 45N58'25 118w23'47 7:53:35
Crooked River 7
2 44N10 120w30 8:02:00
Crooks 31 2 45N08'52 117w52'05 7:51:28
Cross Hollows 33
2 44N59'40 120w45'05 8:03:00
Crow 20 8 43N59'35 123w20'18 8:13:21
Crowfoot 22 2 44N30'30 122w53'20 8:11:33
Crowley 23 1 43N17'30 117w53'36 7:51:34
Crowley 27 2 44N58'43 123w12'25 8:12:50
Crown Point 6 2 43N19'49 124w18'25 8:17:14
Cruzatte 20 2 43N37'31 122w10'48 8:08:43
Cully 26 12 45N34 122w36 8:10:24
Culp Creek 20 2 43N42'13 122w50'47 8:11:23
Culver 16 2 44N31'33 121w12'43 8:04:51
Currinsville 3 4 45N18'55 122w20'29 8:09:22
Curtin 10 2 43N43'21 123w12'39 8:12:51
Curtis 24 2 45N16'09 122w47'40 8:11:11
Cushman 20 2 43N59'09 124w02'35 8:16:10
Cutler City 21
11 44N55'03 124w00'54 8:16:04
Cutsforth Corner 25
2 45N28'45 119w40'36 7:58:42
Dads Creek 10 2 42N53'25 123w33'34 8:14:14
Dahl Pine 33 2 45N00'52 121w29'57 8:06:00
Dairy 18 2 42N14'07 121w31'12 8:06:05
Dale 12 2 44N59'19 118w56'47 7:55:47
Dallas 27 2 44N55'10 123w18'57 8:13:16
Dalles 33 7 45N35'41 121w10'39 8:04:43
Damascus 3 12 45N25'04 122w27'28 8:09:50
Damascus Heights 3
4 45N26 122w23 8:09:32
Damewoods Place 10
2 43N45'52 123w38'07 8:14:32
Danebo 20 8 44N03'35 123w10'39 8:12:43
Danner 23 1 42N56'40 117w20'21 7:49:21
Dant 33 2 45N02'18 121w06'44 8:04:27
Davidson 33 2 44N58'29 121w04'18 8:04:17
Davies Junction 34
4 45N38'41 123w08'02 8:12:32
Dawson 2 2 44N21'39 123w24'38 8:13:39
Days Creek 10 2 42N58'21 123w10'16 8:12:41
Dayton 36 2 45N13'15 123w04'30 8:12:18
Dayville 12 2 44N28'06 119w32'05 7:58:08
Deadmond Place 19
2 43N07'59 121w09'11 8:04:37
Dead Ox Flat 23
1 44N09 116w57 7:47:48
Deadwood 20 2 44N05'45 123w45'44 8:15:03
Deady 10 2 43N21'16 123w19'29 8:13:18
Dee 14 4 45N35'18 121w37'32 8:06:30
Deerhorn 20 2 44N04'55 122w44'50 8:10:59
Deer Island 5 4 45N55'53 122w50'33 8:11:22
Dehlinger 18 2 42N06'53 121w40'39 8:06:43
Delake 21 11 44N57'45 124w00'54 8:16:04
Delena 5 4 46N05'55 123w04'22 8:12:17
Dellwood 6 2 43N22'09 124w00'46 8:16:03
Dellwood 36 4 45N25'32 123w08'08 8:12:33
Delmar 6 2 43N15'38 124w13'34 8:16:54
Delmoor 4 11 46N10 123w55 8:15:40
DeMoss Springs 28
2 45N30'41 120w40'55 8:02:44
Denmark 8 2 42N53'27 124w27'41 8:17:51
Dennis 23 1 44N05'27 117w19'22 7:49:17
Depoe Bay 21 11 44N48'31 124w03'43 8:16:15
Derry 27 2 44N55'48 123w12'43 8:12:51
Deschutes 9 8 44N09'24 121w15'16 8:05:01
Deschutes Junction 9
8 44N09'37 121w15'28 8:05:02
Detour 34 6 45N30'07 123w06'48 8:12:27
Detroit 24 2 44N44'03 122w08'55 8:08:36
Dever 22 13 44N43'09 123w05'23 8:12:22
Devitt 2 2 44N37'22 123w32'46 8:14:11
Dew Valley 6 2 43N02'24 124w24'47 8:17:39
Dexter 20 2 43N54'58 122w49'18 8:11:17
Diamond 13 2 43N00'44 118w39'54 7:54:40
Diamond Lake 10
2 43N10'44 122w08'16 8:08:33
Diamond Lake Junction 18
2 43N04'51 121w49'27 8:07:18
Dickey Prairie 3
12 45N07'06 122w31'37 8:10:06
Dike 33 2 45N24'32 120w52'00 8:03:28
Dillard 10 2 43N06'11 123w25'36 8:13:42
Dilley 34 6 45N29'27 123w07'20 8:12:29
Dimmick 17 2 42N28'32 123w22'29 8:13:30
Disston 20 2 43N41'54 122w46'08 8:11:05
Dixie 1 2 44N28'07 117w19'58 7:49:20
Dixie 18 2 42N01'50 122w15'41 8:09:03
Dixon 33 2 45N01'46 121w03'53 8:04:16
Dixonville 10 3 43N12'28 123w14'24 8:12:58
Doctor Rankins Place 4
2 45N54'29 123w27'40 8:13:51
Dodge 3 4 45N12'54 122w18'04 8:09:12
Dodson 26 4 45N36'20 122w02'04 8:08:08
Dole 10 2 43N02'20 123w19'51 8:13:19
Dollar 22 2 44N17'28 122w37'52 8:10:31
Dolph 21 2 45N06'21 123w47'19 8:15:09
Dolph Corner 27
2 44N58'07 123w17'55 8:13:12
Donald 24 2 45N13'21 122w50'17 8:11:21
Donna 20 2 44N08'43 122w54'41 8:11:39
Donnybrook 16 2 44N45'16 120w39'00 8:02:36
Dora 6 2 43N09'22 123w57'18 8:15:49
Dorena 20 2 43N43'12 122w51'39 8:11:27
Douglas Gardens 20
3 44N03 123w00 8:12:00
Douglass Ridge 3
4 45N20'34 122w18'02 8:09:12
Dougren 20 2 43N57'48 122w52'58 8:11:32
Dover 3 4 45N19'53 122w13'40 8:08:55
Downing 5 4 46N08'39 123w04'17 8:12:17
Downing 30 2 45N51'30 118w24'49 7:53:39
Downs 24 4 45N02'33 122w47'34 8:11:10

Drain 10 2 43N39'32 123w19'03 8:13:16
Drake Crossing 24
2 44N55'34 122w39'17 8:10:37
Draperville 22
13 44N38'46 123w02'09 8:12:09
Drew 10 2 42N52'55 122w53'54 8:11:36
Drewsey 13 2 43N48'24 118w22'35 7:53:30
Drift Creek 21 2 44N26 124w04 8:16:16
Dry Creek 2 7 44N30'19 123w16'28 8:13:06
Dryden 17 2 42N16'11 123w32'10 8:14:09
Dryland 3 4 45N11'07 122w39'37 8:10:38
Duck Pond 23 2 43N20'59 118w00'15 7:52:01
Dufur 33 2 45N27'12 121w07'46 8:04:31
Duke Landing 36
2 45N08'27 123w01'37 8:12:06
Dukes Valley 14
10 45N42 121w31 8:06:04
Duncan 30 2 45N33'41 118w18'55 7:53:16
Dundee 36 14 45N16'42 123w00'35 8:12:02
Dunes 20 2 43N55 124w06 8:16:24
Dunnean 13 2 43N25'56 118w15'39 7:53:03
Dunthorpe 26 12 45N26'09 122w39'14 8:10:37
Durbin 24 15 44N56'31 122w53'09 8:11:33
Durettes Landing 24
2 45N08'35 123w01'39 8:12:07
Durham 34 12 45N24'08 122w45'06 8:11:00
Durkee 1 2 44N34'56 117w27'49 7:49:51
Duroc 30 2 45N54'18 118w37'09 7:54:29
Eagle Creek 3 4 45N21'27 122w21'28 8:09:26
Eagle Crest Corner 27
15 44N59'05 123w07'53 8:12:32
Eagle Point 15 2 42N28'22 122w48'06 8:11:12
Eagle Valley 1 2 44N51 117w18 7:49:12
Eakin 28 2 45N18'02 120w45'36 8:03:02
East Bend 9 8 44N04 121w16 8:05:04
East Gardiner 10
2 43N43'12 124w04'52 8:16:19
East Gresham 26
12 45N31 122w28 8:09:52
East Lake 9 2 43N40 121w30 8:06:00
East Maupin 33 2 45N10'20 121w04'26 8:04:18
East Milwaukie 3
12 45N26'35 122w37'40 8:10:31
Eastmoreland 26
12 45N28'24 122w37'23 8:10:30
East Parkrose 26
12 45N32 122w31 8:10:04
East Portland 26
12 45N30'56 122w39'33 8:10:38
East Saint Johns 26
12 45N35'29 122w43'09 8:10:53
Eastside 6 2 43N21'49 124w11'30 8:16:46
Eastwood 10 3 43N11 123w22 8:13:28
Echo 30 2 45N44'33 119w11'40 7:56:47
Echo Dell 3 4 45N19'57 122w31'35 8:10:06
Eckman Lake 21 2 44N26 124w04 8:16:16
Eddy Place 23 1 43N27'58 117w28'57 7:49:56
Eddyville 21 2 44N38'05 123w46'31 8:15:06
Edenbower 10 3 43N14'05 123w22'52 8:13:31
Edwards 35 2 45N03'34 120w05'04 8:00:20
Egert Place 18 2 42N21'37 121w33'02 8:06:12
Eightmile 25 2 45N15'20 119w48'54 7:59:16
Eightmile Crossing Campgroun 33
2 45N24'23 121w27'20 8:05:49
Eldorado 23 2 44N25'35 117w44'41 7:50:59
Eldriedge Landing 24
2 45N06'25 123w00'12 8:12:01
Elgarose 10 3 43N15'30 123w29'05 8:13:56
Elgin 31 2 45N33'54 117w54'59 7:51:40
Elk City 21 2 44N37'15 123w52'32 8:15:30
Elk Creek Campground 12
2 44N14'43 118w23'50 7:53:35
Elkhead 10 2 43N32'27 123w11'02 8:12:44
Elkhorn 24 2 44N50'09 122w21'39 8:09:27
Elk Lake 9 8 43N58'54 121w48'17 8:07:13
Elk Rock 26 12 45N26'21 122w39'23 8:10:38
Elkton 10 2 43N38'16 123w34'01 8:14:16
Ella 25 2 45N37'53 119w48'28 7:59:14
Ellendale 27 2 44N55'48 123w21'18 8:13:25
Ellingson Mill 12
2 44N26 118w12 7:52:48
Elliott Prairie 3
4 45N09 122w51 8:11:24
Elmira 20 2 44N03'57 123w21'15 8:13:25
Elmonica 34 12 45N30'46 122w51'13 8:11:25
Elrus 20 2 44N03'09 123w25'13 8:13:41
Elsie 4 2 45N51'57 123w35'37 8:14:22
Elwood 3 4 45N12'30 122w22'08 8:09:29
Emerald Heights 4
14 46N11 123w50 8:15:20
Emerson 33 2 45N32'45 120w58'45 8:03:55
Emigrant Crossing 18
2 43N21'54 121w49'28 8:07:18
Emigrant Springs 28
2 45N37'22 120w33'41 8:02:15
Empire 6 2 43N23'35 124w16'34 8:17:06
Endersby 33 2 45N29'33 121w09'03 8:04:36
Englewood 6 2 43N21'01 124w13'22 8:16:53
Englewood 26 12 45N26'10 122w41'43 8:10:47
Enid 20 8 44N07'08 123w11'02 8:12:44
Enright 29 2 45N43'26 123w34'07 8:14:16
Enterprise 32 2 45N25'35 117w16'40 7:49:07
Eola 27 15 44N57 123w05 8:12:20
Eola Crest 36 13 45N05'56 123w08'22 8:12:33
Eola Village 36
14 45N09'35 123w08'54 8:12:36
Erickson Mill 12
2 44N35'13 119w33'05 7:58:12
Erratic Rock Wayside 36
14 45N08'25 123w17'31 8:13:10
Errol 26 12 45N27'41 122w36'52 8:10:27
Errol Heights 26
12 45N28'07 122w36'30 8:10:26
Erskine 28 2 45N26'18 120w46'39 8:03:07
Estabrook 6 2 43N02'39 124w08'01 8:16:32
Estacada 3 4 45N17'23 122w19'57 8:09:20
Estoos 4 2 46N06'14 123w41'48 8:14:47
Eugene 20 8 44N03'08 123w05'08 8:12:21
Evans 32 2 45N30'06 117w25'18 7:49:41
Evans Valley 15
2 42N32 123w07 8:12:28
Fairbanks 33 2 45N37'27 121w00'03 8:04:00
Fairdale 36 2 45N21'36 123w20'03 8:13:20

Fairfield 24	2	45N08'05	123W00'18	8:12:01
Fair Oaks 3	12	45N25'12	122W38'58	8:10:36
Fairoaks 10	2	43N25'03	123W12'44	8:12:51
Fairview 6	2	43N13'01	124W04'21	8:16:17
Fairview 22	2	44N31	122W53	8:11:32
Fairview 25	2	45N23'08	119W50'32	7:59:22
Fairview 26	12	45N32'19	122W25'58	8:09:44
Fairview 28	2	45N29'50	120W33'47	8:02:15
Fairview 29	2	45N27'28	123W47'16	8:15:09
Falcon Heights 18	2	42N09	121W47	8:07:08
Fall Creek 20	2	43N57'35	122W49'09	8:11:17
Falls City 27	2	44N51'59	123W26'05	8:13:44
Fallsview 3	4	45N13'49	122W31'01	8:10:04
Fanno 34	12	45N27'32	122W47'08	8:11:09
Faraday 3	4	45N16'09	122W18'52	8:09:15
Fargo 24	2	45N14'54	122W48'53	8:11:16
Farley 14	4	45N41'44	121W49'49	8:07:19
Farmington 34	12	45N26'57	122W56'48	8:11:47
Faubion 3	4	45N20'36	121W56'02	8:07:44
Fawn 24	2	44N46'10	122W35'41	8:10:23
Fayetteville 22	2	44N27'40	123W09'46	8:12:39
Federal 26	12	45N29	122W41	8:10:44
Fellers 24	2	45N12'43	122W50'57	8:11:24
Fern Corner 27	2	44N51'13	123W21'24	8:13:26
Ferndale 30	2	45N58'53	118W23'47	7:53:35
Fern Hill 4	14	46N09'53	123W44'09	8:14:57
Fern Hill 5	12	45N24	122W39	8:10:36
Fern Ridge 3	12	45N23'03	122W36'00	8:10:24
Ferns 27	2	44N55	123W19	8:13:16
Fernvale 10	2	42N46'43	123W22'13	8:13:29
Fernwood 3	6	45N07'29	122W28'12	8:09:53
Fields 13	2	42N15'52	118W40'27	7:54:42
Fields 20	2	43N40'53	122W18'10	8:09:13
Finn 20	8	44N03'26	123W12'00	8:12:48
Finn Rock 20	8	44N07'45	122W22'54	8:09:32
Finns Corner 27	2	45N02'37	123W12'22	8:12:49
Fir 26	12	45N33'58	122W35'05	8:10:20
Fir Grove 20	8	44N07'09	123W08'13	8:12:33
Firlock 34	12	45N28'14	122W45'16	8:11:01
Firo 20	2	44N03'59	123W52'45	8:15:31
Fir Villa 27	2	44N55'42	123W16'23	8:13:06
Firwood 3	4	45N22'39	122W13'25	8:08:54
Fischers Mill 3	4	45N20'20	122W26'04	8:09:44
Fisher 21	2	44N17'31	123W50'20	8:15:21
Fishers Corner 3	12	45N17'26	122W33'48	8:10:15
Fishers Mill 3	12	45N23	122W36	8:10:24
Fish Lake Resort 15	2	42N28	122W48	8:11:12
Five Corners 19	2	42N11'11	120W25'59	8:01:44
Flagg 20	2	44N01'31	123W29'54	8:14:00
Flavel 4	11	46N10	123W55	8:15:40
Flora 32	2	45N54'01	117W18'32	7:49:14
Florence 20	2	43N58'58	124W05'55	8:16:24
Flynn 2	2	44N32'28	123W23'08	8:13:33
Foley Springs 20	2	44N09'15	122W05'51	8:08:23
Folkenberg 26	12	45N37'45	122W51'54	8:11:28
Foots Creek 15	2	42N23	123W04	8:12:16
Fords Mill 22	2	44N33'51	122W43'15	8:10:53
Forest Crossing 7	2	44N20'56	121W04'47	8:04:19
Forest Grove 34	6	45N31'12	123W06'34	8:12:26
Forest Grove Junction 34	6	45N32'01	122W53'57	8:11:36
Forest Park 26	12	45N32	122W43	8:10:52
Forfar 21	2	44N38	124W03	8:16:12
Fort Hill 27	15	45N03'39	123W33'15	8:14:13
Fort Klamath 18	2	42N42'17	121W59'41	8:07:59
Fort Klamath Junction 18	2	42N41'42	121W58'18	8:07:53
Fort Rock 19	2	43N21'24	121W03'10	8:04:13
Fort Stevens 4	11	46N12'08	123W57'40	8:15:51
Fortune Branch 10	2	42N46'30	123W18'59	8:13:16
Fort Vannoy 17	2	42N27	123W24	8:13:36
Fort Warner 19	2	42N23'54	120W08'11	8:00:33
Foss 29	11	45N41'47	123W47'47	8:15:11
Fossil 35	2	44N59'54	120W12'54	8:00:52
Foster 22	2	44N24'38	122W40'16	8:10:41
Fourbit Ford 15	2	42N30'02	122W24'15	8:09:37
Four Cabin Corner 21	2	44N57'53	123W45'59	8:15:04
Four Corners 15	2	42N23'21	122W51'28	8:11:26
Four Corners 24	15	44N55'41	122W58'57	8:11:56
Fourmile 6	2	43N00'30	124W24'50	8:17:39
Fox 12	2	44N38'56	119W08'35	7:56:34
Fox Mill 12	2	44N38'20	119W08'37	7:56:35
Fox Valley 24	2	44N45'35	122W33'02	8:10:12
Franklin 20	3	44N09'39	123W18'12	8:13:13
Franz 10	2	43N44'23	124W04'44	8:16:19
Frazier 20	2	43N39'38	122W15'01	8:09:00
Freels 32	2	45N25'59	117W19'10	7:49:17
Freewater 30	2	45N56	118W23	7:53:32
Frenchglen 13	2	42N49'37	118W54'52	7:55:39
Friend 33	2	45N20'49	121W15'58	8:05:04
Frissel Crossing Forest Camp 20	2	43N57'25	122W05'02	8:08:20
Frost Mill 13	2	44N01'51	118W38'12	7:54:33
Fruitdale 17	2	42N22	123W19	8:13:16
Fruitland 24	15	44N56'28	122W55'46	8:11:43
Fruitvale 21	2	44N39'16	123W58'45	8:15:55
Fry 22	13	44N35'18	123W02'14	8:12:09
Fry Place 8	2	42N29'30	124W05'55	8:16:24
Fuego 18	2	42N48'27	121W49'47	8:07:19
Fulton 26	12	45N28'53	122W40'26	8:10:42
Fulton 30	2	45N43'50	118W44'53	7:55:00
Galena 12	2	44N42'38	118W48'55	7:55:16
Gales Creek 34	6	45N35'12	123W12'49	8:12:51
Gales Landing 9	8	43N47'56	121W45'19	8:07:01
Galesville 10	2	42N46'42	123W17'41	8:13:11
Galice 17	2	42N34'11	123W35'46	8:14:23
Galloway 25	2	45N33'29	119W26'41	7:57:47
Gap 20	2	43N44'09	123W03'17	8:12:13
Garden Home 34	12	45N27'58	122W45'08	8:11:01
Gardiner 10	2	43N43'49	124W06'33	8:16:26
Garfield 3	4	45N16'38	122W16'39	8:09:07
Garibaldi 29	11	45N33'36	123W54'35	8:15:38
Garrett Place 19	2	42N17'44	120W32'13	8:02:09
Gasco 26	12	45N34'48	122W45'37	8:11:02
Gaston 34	4	45N26'11	123W08'18	8:12:33
Gates 24	2	44N45'23	122W24'56	8:09:40
Gateway 16	2	44N46'32	121W04'54	8:04:20
Gaylord 6	2	42N57'20	124W06'20	8:16:25
Gazley 10	2	43N01	123W18	8:13:12
Gearhart 4	14	46N01'28	123W54'36	8:15:38
Geer 24	15	44N55'47	122W53'32	8:11:34
Gem 18	2	42N07'39	121W43'07	8:06:52
Geneva 16	2	44N28'25	121W23'26	8:05:34
George 3	4	45N17'42	122W13'43	8:08:55
Gerlinger 27	2	44N55'14	123W12'43	8:12:51
Gervais 24	2	45N06'30	122W53'47	8:11:35
Gibbon 30	2	45N41'59	118W21'50	7:53:27
Gilbert 26	12	45N28'37	122W31'50	8:10:07
Gilbert Station 26	12	45N28'51	122W32'07	8:10:08
Gilchrist 18	2	43N28'38	121W41'03	8:06:44
Gilchrist Junction 18	2	43N21'35	121W48'39	8:07:15
Gillespie Corners 20	8	44N02	123W06	8:12:24
Gilliams 27	2	44N55	123W19	8:13:16
Gladstone 3	12	45N22'51	122W35'37	8:10:22
Gladstone Station 3	12	45N22'42	122W35'31	8:10:22
Gladtidings 3	12	45N29	122W44	8:10:56
Glasgow 6	2	43N26'05	124W12'36	8:16:50
Glenada 20	2	43N57'38	124W06'10	8:16:25
Glen Avon 3	6	45N05'03	122W29'15	8:09:57
Glenbrook 2	2	44N18'50	123W24'19	8:13:37
Glen Brown Place 13	2	42N46'11	118W39'05	7:54:36
Glencoe 34	4	45N36'01	122W59'27	8:11:58
Glencullen 26	12	45N29'14	122W43'09	8:10:53
Glendale 10	2	42N44'11	123W25'20	8:13:41
Glendale Junction 10	2	42N45'18	123W22'16	8:13:29
Glendoveer 26	12	45N32	122W31	8:10:04
Glen Echo 3	12	45N23'12	122W36'15	8:10:25
Gleneden Beach 21	11	44N52'53	124W01'59	8:16:08
Glengary 10	3	43N07'35	123W21'22	8:13:25
Glenmorrie 3	12	45N25	122W42	8:10:48
Glenwood 4	11	46N06'35	123W55'13	8:15:41
Glenwood 20	8	44N02'40	123W02'01	8:12:08
Glenwood 34	4	45N38'58	123W16'11	8:13:05
Glide 10	2	43N18'06	123W06'00	8:12:24
Globe 20	2	44N00'34	123W36'14	8:14:25
Goble 5	4	46N00'58	122W52'27	8:11:30
Goff 28	2	45N43'00	120W40'40	8:02:43
Gold Beach 8	2	42N24'27	124W25'14	8:17:41
Gold Creek 27	15	45N02'58	123W31'59	8:14:08
Golden 17	2	42N40'57	123W19'49	8:13:19
Gold Hill 15	2	42N26	123W03	8:12:12
Goldson 20	3	44N09'48	123W20'29	8:13:22
Golf Junction 3	12	45N27'30	122W39'05	8:10:36
Gooch 24	2	44N45'26	122W31'38	8:10:07
Gooseberry 25	2	45N17'33	119W53'27	7:59:34
Gooseberry Mountain 16	2	44N39'57	120W37'43	8:02:31
Gopher 36	15	45N06	123W24	8:13:36
Goshen 20	3	43N59'44	123W00'37	8:12:02
Government Camp 3	4	45N18'15	121W45'13	8:07:01
Grabenhorst Corner 24	15	44N52'59	123W02'07	8:12:08
Graham 26	12	45N32'00	122W35'51	8:10:23
Grand Ronde 27	2	45N03'37	123W36'29	8:14:26
Grand Ronde Agency 36	2	45N04'48	123W36'38	8:14:27
Grandview 16	2	44N28	121W41	8:06:44
Granite 12	2	44N48'34	118W25'00	7:53:40
Granite Hill 17	2	42N31	123W19	8:13:16
Grant Place 13	2	42N42'14	118W30'34	7:54:02
Grants Pass 17	2	42N26'21	123W19'38	8:13:19
Grass Valley 28	2	45N21'37	120W47'04	8:03:08
Gravelford 6	2	43N06'19	124W04'37	8:16:18
Green 10	2	43N09'38	123W22'00	8:13:28
Green Acres 6	2	43N15'28	124W12'13	8:16:49
Greenacres 10	2	43N41	123W48	8:15:12
Greenberry 2	7	44N27'18	123W16'28	8:13:06
Greenburg 34	12	45N26'20	122W46'23	8:11:06
Green Hills 26	12	45N30'20	122W43'40	8:10:55
Greenhorn 1	2	44N42'29	118W29'25	7:53:58
Greenleaf 20	2	44N06'50	123W39'57	8:14:40
Green Peak 10	2	43N19'59	123W37'44	8:14:31
Green Springs Mountain 15	2	42N07	122W23	8:09:32
Greenville 22	2	44N23'13	122W46'42	8:11:07
Greenville 34	6	45N35'35	123W06'47	8:12:27
Gregory 15	2	42N02'48	122W38'19	8:10:33
Gresham 26	12	45N29'54	122W25'49	8:09:43
Greton 34	12	45N26'17	122W46'47	8:11:07
Griggs 22	2	44N36'23	122W52'13	8:11:29
Grizzly 16	2	44N29'53	120W55'07	8:03:40
Gulliford Crossing 30	2	45N05'36	119W05'40	7:56:23
Gulling 31	2	45N37'13	117W53'07	7:51:32
Gunter 10	2	43N47'54	123W30'32	8:14:02
Gurdane 30	2	45N16'09	119W06'12	7:56:25
Gwendolen 11	2	45N20'53	120W08'25	8:00:34
Hager 18	3	42N11'29	121W41'57	8:06:48
Haig 26	12	45N29'58	122W38'34	8:10:34
Haines 1	2	44N54'42	117W56'16	7:51:45
Haley 3	4	45N26'35	122W22'58	8:09:32
Halfway 1	2	44N52'51	117W06'49	7:48:27
Halls Ferry 24	15	44N54	123W02	8:12:08
Halsey 22	2	44N23'03	123W06'31	8:12:26
Hamilton 12	2	44N44'26	119W18'29	7:57:14
Hamlet 4	2	45N50'47	123W41'58	8:14:48
Hammond 4	11	46N12'01	123W57'01	8:15:48
Hampton 9	2	43N40'22	120W13'58	8:00:56
Hampton 20	2	43N49'13	122W36'00	8:10:24
Hamricks Corner 3	4	45N16	122W41	8:10:44
Happy Hollow 29	11	45N08'33	123W48'09	8:15:13
Happy Valley 3	12	45N26'49	122W31'45	8:10:07
Harbor 8	2	42N03'12	124W15'59	8:17:04
Harborton 26	12	45N36'56	122W48'11	8:11:13
Hardman 25	2	45N10'12	119W40'51	7:58:43
Hardy 33	2	44N59'34	121W03'25	8:04:14
Harlan 21	2	44N32'24	123W41'31	8:14:46
Harmony 3	12	45N26'10	122W34'38	8:10:19
Harmony 28	2	45N26'51	120W36'43	8:02:27
Harmony Point 3	12	45N26'50	122W34'37	8:10:18
Harney 13	2	43N38'36	118W49'18	7:55:17
Harper 23	1	43N51'48	117W36'32	7:50:26
Harper Junction 23	1	43N51'20	117W36'16	7:50:25
Harriman 18	3	42N13	121W45	8:07:00
Harris 2	2	44N34'42	123W27'32	8:13:50
Harrisburg 22	3	44N16'27	123W10'10	8:12:41
Hathaway Mead 29	2	45N27'25	123W49'03	8:15:16
Hauser 6	2	43N29'35	124W13'03	8:16:52
Havana 30	2	45N43'30	118W39'21	7:54:37
Hawthorne 10	2	43N27'23	123W04'47	8:12:19
Hay Creek Ranch 16	2	44N37'06	120W56'18	8:03:45
Hayesville 24	15	44N59'10	122W58'54	8:11:56
Hayward 34	4	45N38'40	123W12'56	8:12:52
Hazeldale 34	12	45N28'00	122W53'31	8:11:34
Hazel Green 24	15	45N00'38	122W55'31	8:11:42
Hazelia 3	12	45N23'19	122W41'28	8:10:46
Hazelwood 26	12	45N32	122W31	8:10:04
Heather 20	2	43N39'37	122W13'34	8:08:54
Hebo 29	11	45N13'50	123W51'44	8:15:27
Heceta Beach 20	2	44N02'01	124W07'48	8:16:31
Heceta Junction 20	2	44N01'04	124W06'00	8:16:24
Helix 30	2	45N50'59	118W39'21	7:54:37
Helvetia 34	6	45N35'45	122W54'58	8:11:40
Hemlock 20	2	43N45'31	122W30'43	8:10:03
Hemlock 26	12	45N33'00	122W29'33	8:09:58
Hemlock 29	2	45N18'57	123W50'08	8:15:21
Hendricks 20	3	44N04'11	122W58'03	8:11:52
Henley 18	2	42N09'08	121W41'52	8:06:47
Heppner 25	2	45N21'12	119W33'24	7:58:14
Heppner Junction 11	2	45N47'34	120W01'35	8:00:06
Herbst Place 29	11	45N11'27	123W50'54	8:15:24
Hereford 1	2	44N29'55	118W02'10	7:52:09
Hereford 3	12	45N22'56	122W35'40	8:10:23
Hermiston 30	2	45N50'26	119W17'18	7:57:09
Hermiston Junction 30	2	45N55'05	119W18'16	7:57:13
Herrmah 34	12	45N22'49	122W47'51	8:11:11
Hidaway Springs 30	2	45N07'52	118W44'12	7:54:57
Highland 3	4	45N14'54	122W24'29	8:09:38
High Rock 3	4	45N09'36	121W53'32	8:07:34
Highway 24	2	45N09	122W51	8:11:24
Hildebrand 18	2	42N17'52	121W28'42	8:05:55
Hilgard 31	2	45N21'08	118W13'37	7:52:54
Hillsboro 34	6	45N31'23	122W59'19	8:11:57
Hillsdale 26	12	45N28'54	122W41'37	8:10:46
Hillside 34	6	45N35'32	123W11'29	8:12:46
Hillsview 3	12	45N27'20	122W24'46	8:09:39
Hines 13	2	43N33'51	119W04'48	7:56:19
Hinkle 30	2	45N47'48	119W18'40	7:57:15
Hito 24	2	45N12'41	122W46'12	8:11:05
Hobsonville 29	7	45N32'57	123W54'03	8:15:36
Holbrook 26	12	45N39'36	122W51'44	8:11:27
Holdman 30	2	45N52'20	118W55'53	7:55:44
Holiday Beach 21	2	44N34'04	124W04'01	8:16:16
Holladay Park 26	12	45N33	122W38	8:10:32
Holland 17	2	42N07'40	123W32'16	8:14:09
Holley 22	2	44N21'16	122W46'56	8:11:08
Hollywood 24	15	44N58	123W00	8:12:00
Hollywood 26	12	45N32'08	122W37'16	8:10:29
Homestead 1	2	45N01'26	116W50'59	7:47:24
Homly 30	2	45N41'08	118W30'48	7:54:03
Hood River 14	10	45N42'20	121W31'13	8:06:05
Hoodview 3	4	45N19'29	122W48'16	8:11:13
Hope 23	1	43N56'44	117W21'52	7:49:27
Hopewell 36	15	45N05'50	123W05'27	8:12:22
Hopmere 24	15	45N03'00	122W59'10	8:11:57
Hopville 27	2	44N48'12	123W07'54	8:12:32
Horton 18	2	42N21'00	121W30'56	8:06:04
Horton 20	3	44N12'36	123W29'32	8:13:58
Hoskins 2	2	44N40'37	123W28'03	8:13:52
Hosley 18	2	42N04'29	121W40'16	8:06:41
Hot Lake 31	2	45N14'41	117W57'24	7:51:50
Hot Springs 18	2	42N06'55	121W17'06	8:05:08
Howell 24	4	45N00	122W53	8:11:32
Hubbard 24	2	45N10'57	122W48'24	8:11:14
Huber 34	12	45N28'31	122W51'01	8:11:24
Hugo 17	2	42N35'05	123W24'05	8:13:36
Hunter Creek 8	2	42N25	124W25	8:17:40
Huntington 1	2	44N21'05	117W15'56	7:49:04
Huntington Junction 23	1	44N20'45	117W36'06	7:50:24
Huron 30	2	45N29'31	118W19'52	7:53:19
Hurricane Grange 32	2	45N20'59	117W16'11	7:49:05
Hutchinson 1	2	44N58'18	117W58'36	7:51:54
Idanha 24	2	44N42'10	122W04'39	8:08:19
Idaville 29	11	45N30'36	123W51'52	8:15:27

Idleyld Park 10 2 43N19'26 123W01'22 8:12:05
Illahe 8 2 42N37'44 124W03'23 8:16:14
Illinois Valley 17 2 42N10 123W39 8:14:36
Imbler 31 2 45N27'35 117W57'40 7:51:51
Imnaha 32 2 45N33'34 116W49'56 7:47:20
Independence 27 2 44N51'05 123W11'08 8:12:45
Indian Crossing 32 2 45N06'41 117W00'51 7:48:03
Indian Ford 9 2 44N21'28 121W36'36 8:06:26
Indian Village 13 2 43N35 119W03 7:56:12
Inglis 5 4 46N07'36 123W09'50 8:12:39
Interlachen 26 12 45N33'07 122W26'44 8:09:47
Ione 25 2 45N30'05 119W49'25 7:59:18
Ironside 23 1 44N19'28 117W56'37 7:51:46
Irrigon 25 2 45N53'45 119W29'25 7:57:58
Irving 20 8 44N06'49 123W09'50 8:12:39
Irvington 26 12 45N32'26 122W39'03 8:10:36
Irvinville 22 2 44N33'43 122W57'26 8:11:50
Isadore 10 2 43N30'11 123W18'59 8:13:16
Island 3 12 45N26 122W37 8:10:28
Island City 31 2 45N20'28 118W02'37 7:52:10
Ivory Pine Mill 18 2 42N29'07 121W05'38 8:04:23
Ivy 4 14 46N11 123W50 8:15:20
Izee 12 2 44N04'02 119W23'06 7:57:32
Jack Shelter 22 2 44N26'54 121W52'15 8:07:29
Jacksonville 15 2 42N18'49 122W57'57 8:11:52
Jacktown 34 12 45N26'59 122W55'07 8:11:40
Jamieson 23 1 44N10'56 117W26'13 7:49:45
Jasper 20 8 43N59'48 122W54'18 8:11:37
Jean 3 12 45N23'54 122W44'19 8:10:57
Jeffers Garden 4 14 46N11 123W50 8:15:20
Jefferson 24 2 44N43'11 123W00'33 8:12:02
Jenne 26 12 45N29'07 122W29'03 8:09:56
Jennings Lodge 3 12 45N23'29 122W36'41 8:10:27
Jerome Prairie 17 2 42N24 123W25 8:13:40
Jewell 4 2 45N56'05 123W30'10 8:14:01
Jewell Junction 4 11 45N51'33 123W33'11 8:14:13
John Day 12 2 44N24'58 118W57'07 7:55:48
Johnson 6 2 43N08'23 124W10'42 8:16:43
Johnson City 3 12 45N26 122W37 8:10:28
Johnson Crossing 5 5 45N43'53 122W52'28 8:11:30
Johnson Landing 5 5 45N43'47 122W51'34 8:11:26
Jonesboro 13 1 43N47'45 117W54'49 7:51:39
Jordan 22 2 44N43'38 122W41'55 8:10:48
Jordan 23 1 42N53 117W29 7:49:56
Jordan 25 2 45N29'44 119W46'25 7:59:06
Jordan Creek 29 2 45N32'55 123W36'02 8:14:24
Jordan Valley 23 1 42N58'27 117W03'12 7:48:13
Joseph 32 2 45N21'16 117W13'43 7:48:55
Judkins 20 8 44N02'34 123W02'55 8:12:12
Judson Landing 27 2 44N49'22 123W07'08 8:12:29
Jumpoff Joe 16 2 44N39'31 120W50'24 8:03:22
Junction City 20 3 44N13'10 123W12'16 8:12:49
Juniper 30 2 45N58'22 119W00'10 7:56:01
Juniper Butte 35 2 44N34'15 119W47'57 7:59:12
Juno 29 2 45N29'23 123W50'39 8:15:23
Juntura 23 1 43N44'41 118W04'43 7:52:19
Kahneeta Hot Springs 33 2 44N51'40 121W12'04 8:04:48
Kamela 31 2 45N26'04 118W23'33 7:53:34
Kansas City 34 6 45N35'46 123W08'45 8:12:35
Kaskela 33 2 44N54'44 121W04'33 8:04:18
Keasey 5 4 45N51'42 123W19'42 8:13:19
Keating 1 9 44N52'27 117W35'22 7:50:21
Keizer 24 15 44N59'25 123W01'30 8:12:06
Kellogg 10 2 43N33'19 123W33'14 8:14:13
Kelly Butte 26 12 45N30 122W33 8:10:12
Kelso 3 4 45N25'07 122W18'25 8:09:14
Kendall 26 12 45N27'52 122W34'40 8:10:19
Keno 18 2 42N07'36 121W55'44 8:07:43
Kent 28 2 45N11'43 120W41'35 8:02:46
Kenton 26 12 45N34'55 122W40'49 8:10:43
Kerby 17 2 42N11'40 123W39'02 8:14:36
Kernville 21 11 44N53'58 124W00'12 8:16:01
Kerry 5 2 46N07'16 123W21'02 8:13:24
Kilts 16 2 44N44 120W45 8:03:00
Kimberly 12 2 44N45'34 119W38'36 7:58:34
Kimmell 32 2 45N41'50 117W46'18 7:51:05
King City 34 12 45N27 122W46 8:11:04
King Cole 18 2 42N07'40 122W14'43 8:08:59
Kings Corner 30 2 45N51'24 118W47'08 7:55:09
Kings Heights 26 12 45N31'46 122W42'24 8:10:50
Kingsley 33 2 45N20'29 121W11'58 8:04:48
Kingston 22 2 44N47'02 122W46'23 8:11:06
Kings Valley 2 2 44N42'25 123W26'00 8:13:44
Kingwood 27 15 44N57 123W05 8:12:20
Kinton 34 12 45N25'24 122W52'36 8:11:30
Kinzua 35 2 44N59'23 120W03'28 8:00:14
Kirk 18 2 42N44'51 121W49'42 8:07:19
Kirkpatrick 26 12 45N28'48 122W32'47 8:10:11
Kishwalks 33 2 44N55'15 121W15'29 8:05:02
Kitson Hot Springs 20 2 43N41'20 122W22'18 8:09:29
Kittleson Place 19 2 42N20'31 120W21'13 8:01:25
Kiwanda Beach 29 2 45N21 123W11 8:12:44
K Junction 27 2 44N54'28 123W35'32 8:14:22
Klamath Agency 18 2 42N37'06 121W55'58 8:07:44
Klamath Falls 18 3 42N13'30 121W46'50 8:07:07
Klamath Junction 15 2 42N08'30 122W36'51 8:10:27
Kloan 33 2 45N32'57 120W54'02 8:03:36
Klondike 28 2 45N34'58 120W36'45 8:02:27
Knappa 4 2 46N11'07 123W35'05 8:14:20
Knappa Junction 4 2 46N10'11 123W34'58 8:14:20
Kneeland Place 32 2 45N36'22 116W31'27 7:46:06
Knight 3 12 45N26'47 122W38'48 8:10:35
Kokel Corner 3 12 45N02'43 122W31'52 8:10:07
Kopplein 2 2 44N43'00 123W29'51 8:13:59
Krewson 10 2 43N40'48 123W18'01 8:13:12
Kroll 10 2 43N47'33 124W07'29 8:16:30
Labish Village 24 15 45N01'10 122W58'16 8:11:53
Lacomb 22 2 44N35'07 122W44'32 8:10:58
Ladd 3 12 45N25'00 122W40'08 8:10:41
Ladd Hill 3 4 45N16'28 122W51'18 8:11:25
Ladds Circle 26 12 45N30'31 122W38'53 8:10:36
Lafayette 36 2 45N14'40 123W06'49 8:12:27
La Grande 31 2 45N19'29 118W05'12 7:52:21
Lakebrook 24 2 45N01'42 123W02'57 8:12:12
Lakecreek 15 2 42N25'21 122W37'30 8:10:30
Lake Grove 3 12 45N25 122W42 8:10:48
Lake of the Woods 18 2 42N22'44 122W12'40 8:08:51
Lake Oswego 3 12 45N25'15 122W40'10 8:10:41
Lake Shore 18 2 42N13 121W53 8:07:32
Lakeside 6 2 43N34'33 124W10'26 8:16:42
Lakeview 19 3 42N11'20 120W20'41 8:01:23
Lakewood 3 12 45N25 122W42 8:10:48
Lakin Place 7 2 44N26'06 120W35'06 8:02:20
Lamm Crossing 18 2 42N53'36 121W41'30 8:06:46
Lancaster 20 3 44N15'11 123W11'40 8:12:47
Lancaster 23 1 44N06'53 117W21'48 7:49:27
Langdon 10 2 42N46'34 123W34'17 8:14:17
Langell 18 2 42N14 121W07 8:04:28
Langell Valley 18 2 42N00'35 121W13'40 8:04:55
Langlois 8 2 42N55'25 124W26'59 8:17:48
Langrell 1 2 44N54'21 117W08'42 7:48:35
La Pine 9 2 43N40'14 121W30'09 8:06:01
Larson Place 15 2 42N48'39 122W37'26 8:10:30
Larwood 22 2 44N42 122W51 8:11:24
Latham 20 2 43N46'32 123W03'40 8:12:15
Latourell 26 4 45N32'27 122W13'12 8:08:53
Latourell Falls 26 4 45N38 121W57 8:07:48
Laurel 34 6 45N25'07 122W59'26 8:11:58
Laurel Grove 6 2 43N01'33 124W24'49 8:17:39
Laurelhurst 26 12 45N31'35 122W37'18 8:10:29
Laurelwood 34 4 45N25'23 123W04'47 8:12:19
Laurelwood Academy 34 4 45N26 123W08 8:12:32
Lava 9 8 43N55'19 121W24'51 8:05:39
Lawen 13 2 43N26'35 118W48'00 7:55:12
Leaburg 20 8 44N06'27 122W40'33 8:10:42
Lebanon 22 2 44N32'12 122W54'21 8:11:37
Lee 6 2 43N08 124W11 8:16:44
Lee's Camp 29 12 45N27 122W30 8:10:00
Lee Thomas Crossing 19 2 42N36'17 120W50'57 8:03:24
Lehman Hot Springs 30 2 45N09'11 118W39'39 7:54:39
Leland 17 2 42N38'19 123W26'23 8:13:46
Lena 25 2 45N24'00 119W16'51 7:57:07
Leneve 6 2 43N12'23 124W16'21 8:17:05
Lents 26 12 45N28'48 122W33'58 8:10:16
Lents Junction 26 12 45N28'36 122W33'13 8:10:13
Lenz 14 4 45N37'47 121W31'23 8:06:06
Lenz 18 2 42N56'17 121W49'07 8:07:16
Leona 10 2 43N41'43 123W17'17 8:13:09
Lewis 33 2 45N41'27 117W05'37 7:48:22
Lewis And Clark 4 2 46N07 123W51 8:15:24
Lewisburg 2 2 44N37'45 123W14'25 8:12:58
Lewisville 27 2 44N47'18 123W20'39 8:13:23
Lexington 25 2 45N26'43 119W41'00 7:58:44
Libby 6 2 43N20'16 124W13'58 8:16:56
Liberal 3 12 45N11'35 122W35'04 8:10:20
Liberty 22 2 44N24 122W36 8:10:24
Liberty 24 15 44N53'18 123W03'33 8:12:14
Lilleas 4 2 46N06'18 123W41'49 8:14:47
Lime 1 2 44N24'24 117W18'37 7:49:14
Lincoln 15 2 42N06'32 122W24'07 8:09:36
Lincoln 27 15 45N01'12 123W04'58 8:12:20
Lincoln Beach 21 11 44N51'02 124W02'44 8:16:11
Lincoln City 21 11 44N57'30 124W01'00 8:16:04
Lindbergh 5 4 46N04'30 122W54'18 8:11:37
Link 27 2 44N45'32 123W23'21 8:13:33
Linnemann 26 12 45N29'19 122W28'08 8:09:53
Linnton 26 12 45N35'56 122W47'09 8:11:09
Linslaw 20 2 44N00'02 123W40'58 8:14:44
Little Albany 21 2 44N25 123W54 8:15:36
Little Alps 1 2 44N57'57 118W10'55 7:52:44
Little Valley 23 1 43N53'47 117W30'38 7:50:03
Lockhart Crossing 12 2 44N10'10 118W13'41 7:52:55
Lockit 33 2 45N29'55 120W50'10 8:03:21
Locoda 5 4 46N09'45 123W08'46 8:12:35
Locust Grove 28 2 45N35'56 120W47'16 8:03:09
Logan 3 12 45N20'37 122W25'18 8:09:41
Logsden 21 2 44N44'36 123W47'35 8:15:10
London 20 2 43N48 123W04 8:12:16
London Springs 20 2 43N38'05 123W05'24 8:12:22
Lone Elder 3 4 45N13'50 122W40'47 8:10:43
Lone Pine 18 2 42N33'20 121W37'07 8:06:28
Lonerock 11 2 45N05'21 119W52'55 7:59:32
Lone Rock Place 18 2 42N18'36 121W34'53 8:06:20
Lone Star 22 2 44N34'39 122W19'19 8:09:17
Lone Tree 31 2 45N17'10 118W01'19 7:52:05
Long Creek 12 2 44N42'51 119W06'11 7:56:25
Long Pass 22 2 44N30'20 122W52'18 8:11:29
Long Tom 20 2 44N02'59 123W23'18 8:13:33
Long Tom Station 20 3 44N11'20 123W27'10 8:13:49
Lookingglass 10 2 43N10'43 123W29'06 8:13:56
Looking Glass 31 2 45N42'35 117W50'18 7:51:21
Lorane 20 2 43N50'16 123W14'16 8:12:57
Lorella 18 2 42N08'14 121W16'17 8:05:05
Lostine 32 2 45N29'15 117W25'53 7:49:44
Lost River 18 2 42N02'45 121W37'46 8:06:31
Love Station 17 2 42N20'40 123W34'01 8:14:16
Lowell 20 2 43N55'07 122W46'57 8:11:08
Lower Bridge 9 2 44N21 121W11 8:04:44
Luce Place 10 2 43N53'24 123W39'19 8:14:37
Lukarilla 4 2 45N49'39 123W36'02 8:14:24
Lunnville 36 2 45N21'02 123W10'25 8:12:42
Luse 23 1 43N59'46 117W04'25 7:48:18
Luther 3 12 45N27'39 122W35'06 8:10:20
Lyons 24 2 44N46'29 122W36'50 8:10:27
Mabel 20 2 44N12'53 122W49'33 8:11:18
Mack Landing 21 11 44N51'34 123W56'46 8:15:47
Macksburg 3 4 45N12'50 122W39'36 8:10:38
Macleay 24 15 44N54'29 122W53'10 8:11:33
Madras 16 11 44N38'01 121W07'42 8:04:31
Madras Station 16 11 44N39'00 121W07'58 8:04:32
Mahan 34 6 45N31'54 122W59'31 8:11:58
Malheur City 23 2 44N24'47 117W43'26 7:50:54
Malheur Junction 23 1 43N59'45 116W58'13 7:47:53
Malin 18 2 42N00'46 121W24'27 8:05:38
Malone 18 2 42N01'11 121W33'30 8:06:14
Manhattan Beach 29 11 45N37'50 123W56'25 8:15:46
Manning 34 6 45N39'54 123W09'45 8:12:39
Manzanita 29 2 45N43'07 123W56'02 8:15:44
Maple Grove 27 2 44N46'42 123W20'39 8:13:23
Mapleton 20 2 44N01'53 123W51'25 8:15:26
Maplewood 26 12 45N28'12 122W43'44 8:10:55
Marcola 20 2 44N10'21 122W51'34 8:11:26
Marial 8 2 42N42'45 123W53'16 8:15:33
Marion 24 2 44N44'57 122W56'28 8:11:46
Marion Forks 22 2 44N36'56 121W56'49 8:07:47
Market 6 2 43N20 124W14 8:16:56
Marlene Village 34 12 45N31'01 122W49'04 8:11:16
Marmot 3 4 45N23'48 122W06'52 8:08:27
Marquam 3 4 45N04'24 122W41'09 8:10:45
Marquam Hill 26 12 45N29'57 122W41'18 8:10:45
Marshall Place 10 2 42N59'19 122W57'07 8:11:48
Marshland 5 4 46N06'41 123W17'04 8:13:08
Martin Manor 34 12 45N30 122W47 8:11:08
Marval 2 2 44N37'23 123W33'42 8:14:15
Marylhurst 3 12 45N24 122W39 8:10:36
Mason Additions 7 2 44N18 120W51 8:03:24
Massinger Corner 3 4 45N15'07 122W29'48 8:09:59
Maupin 33 2 45N10'31 121W04'49 8:04:19
Maxville 32 2 45N44'46 117W33'21 7:50:13
Mayger 5 4 46N09'49 123W06'25 8:12:26
May Park 31 2 45N20 118W04 7:52:16
Mayville 11 2 45N04'57 120W11'28 8:00:46
Maywood 20 2 44N03'16 123W17'53 8:13:12
Maywood Park 26 12 45N33 122W34 8:10:16
Mazama 18 2 43N00'26 121W48'38 8:07:15
McBee 30 2 45N38'58 118W52'30 7:55:30
McCormac 6 2 43N20'25 124W11'48 8:16:47
McCormmach 30 2 45N44'53 118W44'30 7:54:59
McCoy 27 2 45N02'32 123W12'55 8:12:52
McCredie Springs 20 2 43N42'36 122W17'16 8:09:09
McDermitt 23 1 41N59'52 117W43'02 7:50:52
McDonald 28 2 45N35'20 120W24'32 8:01:38
McEwen 1 2 44N42'03 118W06'13 7:52:25
McKay 30 2 45N29'59 118W36'53 7:54:28
McKee 24 2 45N09 122W51 8:11:24
McKee Bridge 15 2 42N19 122W58 8:11:52
McKenzie 20 2 44N08 122W27 8:09:48
McKenzie Bridge 20 2 44N10'31 122W09'46 8:08:39
McKinley 6 2 43N11'20 124W01'30 8:16:06
McLean Place 13 2 42N24'41 118W37'22 7:54:29
McLeod 15 2 42N39'45 122W41'12 8:10:45
McMinnville 36 14 45N12'37 123W11'51 8:12:47
McNary 30 2 45N55'10 119W17'17 7:57:09
McNulty 5 17 45N50'26 122W50'26 8:11:22
Meacham 30 2 45N30'24 118W25'13 7:53:41
Meacham Corner 34 6 45N41'39 123W03'52 8:12:15
Meadowbrook 3 12 45N29 122W44 8:10:56
Meadow View 20 3 44N13 123W12 8:12:48
Mecca 16 2 44N46'17 121W12'26 8:04:50
Meda 29 11 45N08'48 123W54'53 8:15:40
Medford 15 3 42N19'36 122W52'28 8:11:30
Medical Springs 31 2 45N01'02 117W37'39 7:50:31
Mehama 24 2 44N47'25 122W37'05 8:10:28
Melco Landing 21 11 44N51'21 123W57'58 8:15:52
Melrose 10 2 43N14'52 123W27'28 8:13:50
Melrose Acres 7 2 44N18 120W51 8:03:24

Melville 4 14 46N03'37 123w50'32 8:15:22
Menefee 3 12 45N25'39 122w38'38 8:10:35
Merle 34 6 45N32'36 122w53'56 8:11:36
Merlin 17 2 42N31'03 123w25'07 8:13:40
Merrill 18 2 42N01'31 121w35'58 8:06:24
Messner 25 2 45N50'58 119w40'44 7:58:43
Metolius 16 2 44N35'12 121w10'38 8:04:43
Metzger 34 12 45N26'48 122w45'28 8:11:02
Middle Grove 24 15 44N58'12 122w57'51 8:11:51
Middle Siuslaw 20 2 44N09 123w46 8:15:04
Middleton 34 14 45N20'38 122w51'48 8:11:27
Midland 18 2 42N07'51 121w49'09 8:07:17
Midway 15 2 42N23'23 122w53'14 8:11:33
Midway 30 2 45N46'33 118w39'06 7:54:36
Midway 34 6 45N24'41 122w57'33 8:11:50
Midway 36 2 45N05'10 123w39'38 8:14:39
Mikkalo 11 2 45N28'16 120w14'01 8:00:56
Miles Crossing 4 14 46N09'09 123w50'18 8:15:21
Military Crossing 18 2 42N57'02 121w40'09 8:06:41
Mill City 22 2 44N45'15 122w28'37 8:09:54
Miller 22 2 44N21'37 123w09'53 8:12:40
Miller 26 12 45N37'09 122w48'32 8:11:14
Miller 28 2 45N38'23 120w53'29 8:03:34
Miller Place 13 2 42N49'31 119w12'16 7:56:49
Millersburg 22 13 44N40'52 123w03'37 8:12:14
Millican 9 8 43N52'45 120w55'08 8:03:41
Millington 6 2 43N19'57 124w11'47 8:16:47
Millwood 10 2 43N23'07 123w32'42 8:14:11
Milo 10 2 42N55'51 123w02'55 8:12:12
Milton-Freewater 30 2 45N55'58 118w23'12 7:53:33
Milwaukie 3 12 45N26'47 122w38'17 8:10:33
Milwaukie Heights 3 12 45N25'49 122w38'00 8:10:32
Minam 32 2 45N37'19 117w43'20 7:50:53
Mineral 1 2 44N32'08 117w09'08 7:48:37
Minerva 20 2 44N04'15 123w57'33 8:15:50
Minnow 20 2 43N53'59 122w44'23 8:10:58
Minski Place 21 2 44N58'48 123w51'27 8:15:26
Minthorn 30 2 45N40'14 118w36'10 7:54:25
Minto 24 15 44N55'20 123w03'17 8:12:13
Mission 30 16 45N40'14 118w40'57 7:54:44
Mist 5 4 45N59'47 123w15'19 8:13:01
Mistletoe 15 2 42N08'09 122w37'48 8:10:31
Mitchell 22 2 44N18'20 122w41'20 8:10:45
Mitchell 27 2 44N46'53 123w17'05 8:13:08
Mitchell 35 2 44N34'00 120w09'08 8:00:37
Mitchell Corner 24 15 44N56'23 122w59'22 8:11:57
Modeville 27 2 44N47'28 123w07'55 8:12:32
Modoc Point 18 2 42N26'42 121w52'02 8:07:28
Mohawk 20 3 44N03 123w00 8:12:00
Mohawk Junction 20 3 44N02'28 122w59'08 8:11:57
Mohawk Post 20 2 44N08'39 122w54'52 8:11:39
Mohler 29 11 45N42'27 123w51'42 8:15:27
Molalla 3 5 45N08'51 122w34'33 8:10:18
Monett 20 2 43N46'17 123w04'39 8:12:19
Monitor 24 2 45N06'06 122w44'49 8:10:59
Monkland 28 2 45N29'09 120w37'32 8:02:30
Monmouth 27 2 44N50'55 123w13'58 8:12:56
Monroe 2 2 44N18'51 123w17'44 8:13:11
Montavilla 26 12 45N31'09 122w34'40 8:10:19
Montgomery Ranch 9 8 44N04 121w18 8:05:12
Monument 12 2 44N49'10 119w25'12 7:57:41
Moody 21 2 44N35'55 123w56'48 8:15:47
Moody 33 2 45N37'35 120w54'40 8:03:39
Moores Crossing 12 2 44N26'13 119w18'46 7:57:15
Morgan 25 2 45N33'10 119w55'10 7:59:41
Morgan Landing 21 11 44N50'00 123w58'08 8:15:53
Morgan Landing 26 12 45N40'38 122w46'36 8:11:06
Moro 28 2 45N29'03 120w43'48 8:02:55
Mosier 33 2 45N41'01 121w23'46 8:05:35
Motanic 31 2 45N23'03 118w20'10 7:53:21
Mountain Air Park 3 4 45N21'33 121w59'22 8:07:57
Mountaindale 34 6 45N37'30 123w02'16 8:12:09
Mount Angel 24 4 45N04'05 122w47'56 8:11:12
Mount Hood 3 4 45N22 122w05 8:08:20
Mount Hood 14 4 45N32'17 121w34'02 8:06:16
Mount Vernon 12 2 44N25'04 119w06'45 7:56:27
Mount View 15 2 42N06'44 122w22'59 8:09:32
Mowich 18 2 43N22'18 121w49'40 8:07:19
Mowrey Landing 21 11 44N48'51 123w58'14 8:15:53
Moyina 18 2 42N14'00 121w32'55 8:06:12
Mulino 3 4 45N13'18 122w34'51 8:10:19
Mulloy 34 4 45N20'02 122w47'21 8:11:09
Multnomah 26 12 45N28'11 122w42'22 8:10:49
Multnomah Falls 26 4 45N34'38 122w06'56 8:08:28
Mundorf 3 4 45N16 122w41 8:10:44
Munkers 22 2 44N42 122w51 8:11:24
Munley 25 2 45N48'40 119w28'24 7:57:54
Munra 30 16 45N40'16 118w43'47 7:54:55
Munson 22 2 44N25'57 123w09'49 8:12:39
Murphy 17 2 42N20'52 123w19'56 8:13:20
Murphys Camp 10 2 43N41 123w48 8:15:12
Myrick 30 2 45N48'16 118w42'48 7:54:51
Myrtle Creek 10 2 43N01'13 123w17'31 8:13:10
Myrtle Point 6 2 43N03'54 124w08'16 8:16:33
Naef 3 12 45N24'10 122w37'42 8:10:31
Namorf 23 1 43N46'43 117w43'53 7:50:56
Napton 23 1 43N40'32 117w03'31 7:48:14
Narrows 13 2 43N35 119w03 7:56:12
Narrows 22 2 44N26'21 122w47'06 8:11:08
Nashville 21 2 44N39'13 123w36'26 8:14:26
Nasoma 34 12 45N22'18 122w47'11 8:11:09
Natal 5 4 45N58'34 123w11'39 8:12:47
Natron 20 8 44N01'07 122w55'19 8:11:41
Navy Heights 4 14 46N11'24 123w46'41 8:15:07
Neahkahnie 29 11 45N43 123w54 8:15:36
Neahkahnie Beach 29 11 45N43'46 123w56'22 8:15:45
Neawanna Station 4 14 46N00'38 123w54'18 8:15:37
Necanicum Junction 4 11 45N54'10 123w45'30 8:15:02
Nedonna 29 11 45N34 123w55 8:15:40
Nedonna Beach 29 11 45N38'39 123w56'20 8:15:45
Needy 3 4 45N10'22 122w42'05 8:10:48
Nehalem 29 2 45N43'13 123w53'34 8:15:34
Nehalem Junction 29 11 45N41'59 123w52'30 8:15:30
Nekoma 20 2 44N02'47 123w45'19 8:15:01
Nelscott 21 11 44N56'37 124w01'13 8:16:05
Nelson 1 2 44N32'23 117w25'04 7:49:40
Nelson Place 35 2 44N29'31 119w44'58 7:59:00
Neotsu 21 11 45N00'05 123w58'48 8:15:55
Nesika Beach 8 2 42N30'23 124w24'44 8:17:39
Neskowin 29 11 45N06'25 123w58'59 8:15:56
Nesmith 34 12 45N27'37 122w45'32 8:11:02
Netarts 29 11 45N26'06 123w56'41 8:15:47
Newberg 36 14 45N18'01 122w58'19 8:11:53
New Bridge 1 2 44N48'02 117w11'20 7:48:45
New Era 3 4 45N18'03 122w39'28 8:10:38
Newhope 17 2 42N21'28 123w22'01 8:13:28
New Idaho 19 2 42N11 120w22 8:01:28
New Idanha 22 2 44N41'52 122w04'22 8:08:17
New Pine Creek 19 2 41N59'39 120w17'46 8:01:11
Newport 21 7 44N38'13 124w03'08 8:16:13
Newport Heights 21 2 44N38'40 124w01'24 8:16:06
New Princeton 13 2 43N16'59 118w34'54 7:54:20
Newton 34 6 45N30'19 122w57'23 8:11:50
Newton Creek 10 3 43N11 123w22 8:13:28
Niagara 24 2 44N45'29 122w20'06 8:09:20
Nimrod 20 8 44N06'50 122w25'21 8:09:41
Ninety-one 3 4 45N10'22 122w43'18 8:10:53
Nixon 22 2 44N23 123w05 8:12:20
Nolin 30 2 45N41'00 119w05'58 7:56:24
Nonpareil 10 2 43N24'28 123w10'01 8:12:40
Noon 2 2 44N32'44 123w23'49 8:13:35
North Albany 2 13 44N39'11 123w06'02 8:12:24
North Bayside 6 2 43N30 124w10 8:16:40
North Beach 20 2 43N53'37 124w06'32 8:16:26
North Bend 6 2 43N24'24 124w13'23 8:16:54
North Fork 30 2 45N31'25 118w17'04 7:53:08
North Fork Crossing Forest C 3 4 45N12'35 122w09'10 8:08:37
North Howell 24 2 45N01'53 122w52'20 8:11:29
North Junction (Davidson) 33 2 44N58'29 121w04'18 8:04:17
North Plains 34 4 45N35'50 122w59'32 8:11:58
North Portland 26 12 45N36'38 122w42'08 8:10:49
North Powder 31 2 45N01'43 117w55'08 7:51:41
North Santiam 24 2 44N46'04 122w52'39 8:11:31
North Side 24 2 45N00 122w47 8:11:08
North Siuslaw 20 2 44N06 123w59 8:15:56
North Sweet Home 22 2 44N28 122w42 8:10:48
North Umpqua 10 2 43N17 123w01 8:12:04
Nortons 21 2 44N39'50 123w42'03 8:14:48
Norway 6 2 43N06'04 124w09'20 8:16:37
Norwood 34 12 45N21'34 122w45'10 8:11:01
Noti 20 2 44N03'33 123w26'51 8:13:47
Nye 30 2 45N37'38 118w58'44 7:55:55
Nyssa 23 1 43N52'37 116w59'38 7:47:59
Oakbrook 33 2 45N19'22 120w58'34 8:03:54
Oakdale 27 2 44N55 123w19 8:13:16
Oak Grove 3 12 45N25'01 122w38'20 8:10:33
Oak Grove 14 10 45N39'46 121w35'15 8:06:21
Oak Grove 27 2 44N58'22 123w10'16 8:12:41
Oakland 10 2 43N25'20 123w17'50 8:13:11
Oaklawn 3 4 45N07'10 122w43'42 8:10:55
Oak Park 24 15 44N57'52 122w58'57 8:11:56
Oakridge 20 3 43N44'48 122w27'38 8:09:51
Oaks 10 2 43N11'15 123w21'39 8:13:27
Oak Springs 33 2 45N13'15 121w04'52 8:04:19
Oakville 22 2 44N30'45 123w11'07 8:12:44
O'Brien 17 2 42N04'03 123w42'07 8:14:48
Oceanlake 21 11 44N58'32 124w00'41 8:16:03
Oceanside 29 11 45N27'40 123w58'00 8:15:52
Ochoco 7 2 44N22 120w46 8:03:04
Odell 14 4 45N37'38 121w32'31 8:06:10
Odell Lake 18 2 43N32'57 121w57'49 8:07:51
Oklahoma Hill 4 2 46N08'36 123w24'17 8:13:37
Olalla 10 2 43N04'02 123w33'12 8:14:13
Old Colton 3 4 45N10'20 122w24'49 8:09:39
Old Johnson Mill 10 2 42N47'45 122w52'21 8:11:29
Old Kelly Mill 35 2 44N29'40 120w18'39 8:01:15
Old Town 10 2 43N25 123w18 8:13:12
Olene 18 2 42N10'19 121w37'47 8:06:31
Olex 11 2 45N29'50 120w10'04 8:00:40
Olney 4 2 46N06'01 123w45'23 8:15:02
Olson 27 2 44N46'43 123w36'10 8:14:25
Ona 21 2 44N30'15 124w01'16 8:16:05
O'Neil 7 2 44N19'51 121w05'12 8:04:21
O'Neil Corners 3 4 45N16'15 122w39'38 8:10:39
Oneonta 26 4 45N35'16 122w05'02 8:08:20
Ontario 23 1 44N01'36 116w57'43 7:47:51
Ontario Heights 23 1 44N04'14 117w01'21 7:48:05
Opal City 16 2 44N26'41 121w12'45 8:04:51
Opal Springs 16 2 44N29'27 121w17'46 8:05:11
Ophir 8 2 42N33'48 124w22'54 8:17:32
Orchard View 36 14 45N14'26 123w16'12 8:13:05
Ordnance 30 2 45N48'15 119w24'56 7:57:40
Oregon Caves 17 2 42N10 123w39 8:14:36
Oregon City 3 12 45N21'27 122w36'20 8:10:25
Oregon Trunk Junction 33 2 45N38'42 120w59'04 8:03:56
Orenco 34 6 45N31'40 122w54'39 8:11:39
Oretech 18 3 42N13 121w45 8:07:00
Oretown 29 11 45N09'14 123w57'15 8:15:49
Orient 26 4 45N28'03 122w21'05 8:09:24
Orleans 22 13 44N34'13 123w11'22 8:12:45
Orrs Corner 27 2 44N54'37 123w14'02 8:12:56
Ortley 33 2 45N39'22 121w17'13 8:05:09
Orville 24 2 44N51'14 123w08'47 8:12:35
Oswego 3 12 45N25'15 122w40'10 8:10:41
Otis 21 2 45N01'28 123w56'43 8:15:47
Otis Junction 21 2 45N01'10 123w56'50 8:15:47
Otter Rock 21 11 44N44'50 124w03'37 8:16:14
Outlook 3 12 45N23'11 122w31'15 8:10:05
Overland 6 2 43N14'44 124w13'22 8:16:53
Overstreet 23 1 43N46'30 117w03'10 7:48:13
Owyhee 23 1 43N47'42 117w03'15 7:48:13
Owyhee Corners 23 1 43N53 117w00 7:48:00
Oxbow 1 2 45N02 116w51 7:47:24
Oxman 1 2 44N37'55 117w31'15 7:50:05
Oysterville 21 2 44N34'41 124w00'03 8:16:00
Pacific City 29 11 45N12'09 123w57'42 8:15:51
Pacific Grange Hall 4 11 46N05'52 123w54'54 8:15:40
Page 22 13 44N36'54 123w06'27 8:12:26
Page Place 23 1 43N26'42 117w33'23 7:50:14
Paisley 19 2 42N41'38 120w32'42 8:02:11
Palestine 2 13 44N41'05 123w09'32 8:12:38
Palmer Junction 31 2 45N42'28 117w50'30 7:51:22
Paradise 32 2 45N56'18 117w13'15 7:48:53
Paradise Park 3 4 45N18'58 122w23'01 8:09:32
Parkdale 14 4 45N31'12 121w35'44 8:06:23
Parker 27 2 44N46'21 123w12'13 8:12:49
Parker Place 18 2 42N19'03 121w32'35 8:06:10
Parkersburg 6 2 43N08'35 124w20'28 8:17:22
Parkers Mill 25 2 45N05'16 119w34'26 7:58:18
Park Place 3 12 45N22'34 122w34'53 8:10:20
Parkrose 26 12 45N33'35 122w33'33 8:10:14
Parliament 32 2 45N34'22 116w35'57 7:46:24
Paterson Junction 25 2 45N53'46 119w33'26 7:58:14
Patton 34 4 45N26'50 123w08'28 8:12:34
Paulina 7 2 44N08'02 119w57'42 7:59:51
Paxton 16 2 44N42'40 121w05'47 8:04:23
Peck 10 2 42N53'45 123w32'14 8:14:09
Pedee 27 2 44N45'13 123w24'46 8:13:39
Peel 10 2 43N15'32 123w01'55 8:12:08
Pelican City 18 3 42N15'12 121w47'46 8:07:11
Pendair 30 16 45N40'23 118w50'13 7:55:21
Pendair Heights 30 16 45N41'15 118w50'34 7:55:22
Pendleton 30 16 45N40'20 118w47'15 7:55:09
Pendleton Junction 30 16 45N40 118w48 7:55:12
Peninsula Junction 26 12 45N35'35 122w42'37 8:10:50
Penn 20 2 44N01'47 123w31'43 8:14:07
Peoria 22 2 44N26'56 123w12'22 8:12:49
Perry 31 2 45N20'55 118w09'56 7:52:40
Perrydale 27 4 45N02'34 123w15'16 8:13:01
Persist 15 2 42N46'00 122w36'22 8:10:25
Petersburg 33 7 45N36'40 121w04'37 8:04:18
Philomath 2 2 44N32'25 123w21'59 8:13:28
Phoenix 15 2 42N16'32 122w49'01 8:11:16
Piedmont 26 12 45N33'55 122w40'01 8:10:40
Pike 36 2 45N22'35 123w15'37 8:13:02
Pikes Crossing 18 2 42N41'53 120w55'55 8:03:44
Pilot Rock 30 2 45N29'00 118w49'44 7:55:19
Pinckney 27 15 44N56'54 123w02'56 8:12:12
Pine 1 2 44N51'41 117w05'17 7:48:21
Pine City 25 2 45N34'53 119w24'57 7:57:40
Pine Grove 14 10 45N42 121w31 8:06:04
Pine Grove 18 3 42N10'55 121w40'12 8:06:41
Pine Grove 33 2 45N06'32 121w21'45 8:05:27
Pinehurst 15 2 42N07'04 122w21'54 8:09:28
Pine Ridge 18 2 42N35'39 121w51'38 8:07:27
Pioneer 21 2 44N38'53 123w52'08 8:15:29
Pioneer 26 12 45N31 122w41 8:10:44
Pirtle 22 13 44N35'58 123w08'11 8:12:33
Pistol River 8 2 42N16'38 124w23'37 8:17:34
Pittsburg 5 4 45N54'03 123w09'04 8:12:36
Placer 17 2 42N37'56 123w18'51 8:13:15
Plainview 9 8 44N14'01 121w27'45 8:05:51
Plainview 22 2 44N29'00 123w00'43 8:12:03
Pleasant Center 32 2 45N18'53 117w07'20 7:48:29
Pleasantdale 36 2 45N11'04 123w03'30 8:12:14
Pleasant Hill 20 2 43N57'58 122w55'50 8:11:43
Pleasant Home 26 12 45N27'51 122w20'07 8:09:20
Pleasant Valley 1 9 44N40'28 117w37'46 7:50:31
Pleasant Valley 17 2 42N33'26 123w23'05 8:13:32
Pleasant Valley 26 12 45N28 122w27 8:09:48
Pleasant Valley 29 2 45N21'56 123w48'10 8:15:13
Plum Trees 8 2 42N48'51 124w21'20 8:17:25

Plush 19 2 42N24'42 119w54'10 7:59:37
Pocahontas 1 2 44N48'52 117w58'16 7:51:53
Poe Place 13 2 42N15'40 118w36'07 7:54:24
Poe Valley 18 2 42N14 121w31 8:06:04
Poindexter Place 19 2 42N42'33 119w28'21 7:57:53
Point Terrace 20 2 44N00'41 123w54'36 8:15:38
Poison Creek 13 2 43N43'06 119w01'43 7:56:07
Polk Station 27 2 44N55 123w19 8:13:16
Pollard 17 2 42N40'44 123w27'17 8:13:49
Pondosa 31 2 45N00'29 117w38'30 7:50:34
Pony Village 6 2 43N24 124w14 8:16:56
Pope Corner 4 11 45N52'25 123w33'34 8:14:14
Porterville 12 2 44N47'45 118w23'39 7:53:35
Portland 26 12 45N31'25 122w40'30 8:10:42
Portland Heights 26 12 45N30'21 122w42'07 8:10:48
Portland Intl Airport 26 12 45N34 122w34 8:10:16
Portland Zoo Railway 26 12 45N30 122w42 8:10:48
Port Orford 8 2 42N44'45 124w29'46 8:17:59
Post 7 2 44N10 120w29 8:01:56
Potter 22 2 44N25'27 123w09'50 8:12:39
Powell Butte 7 2 44N15 121w01 8:04:04
Powell Butte 26 12 45N29 122w31 8:10:04
Powellhurst 26 12 45N30'15 122w32'11 8:10:09
Powell Valley 26 12 45N29'12 122w23'32 8:09:34
Power City 30 2 45N54'43 119w18'10 7:57:13
Powers 6 2 42N53'01 124w04'19 8:16:17
Powwatka 32 2 45N53'00 117w28'40 7:49:55
Prahl 3 4 45N17'15 122w46'40 8:11:07
Prairie City 12 2 44N27'48 118w42'32 7:54:50
Pratum 24 15 44N57'33 122w52'39 8:11:31
Prescott 5 4 46N02'57 122w53'10 8:11:33
Princeton 13 2 43N15 118w35 7:54:20
Prineville 7 8 44N18 120w51 8:03:24
Prineville Junction 9 2 44N18'45 121w09'47 8:04:39
Pringle 24 15 44N55'13 123w01'36 8:12:06
Progress 34 12 45N27'26 122w46'51 8:11:07
Promise 32 2 45N50'30 117w32'35 7:50:10
Prospect 15 2 42N45'04 122w29'16 8:09:57
Prosper 6 2 43N08'51 124w22'21 8:17:29
Provolt 15 2 42N17'15 123w13'45 8:12:55
Prunedale 30 2 45N56'59 118w25'57 7:53:44
Pryor 20 2 43N44'01 122w23'49 8:09:35
Pulp 3 12 45N19'55 122w39'08 8:10:37
Quartz 1 9 44N43'11 117w46'27 7:51:06
Quartz Mountain 19 2 42N19'21 120w48'52 8:03:15
Quatama 34 12 45N31'24 122w53'17 8:11:33
Quinaby 24 15 45N02'07 122w59'56 8:12:00
Quincy 5 4 46N08'38 123w09'32 8:12:38
Quines Creek 10 2 42N46'45 123w16'14 8:13:05
Quinton 11 2 45N42'16 120w31'38 8:02:07
Rafton 26 12 45N38'32 122w49'28 8:11:18
Rainbow 20 2 44N10'01 122w14'08 8:08:57
Rainier 5 4 46N05'21 122w56'05 8:11:44
Rainrock 20 2 44N04'26 123w51'05 8:15:24
Rajneesh 33 2 44N55 120w43 8:02:52
Rajneeshpuram 33 2 44N50 120w29 8:01:56
Raleigh Hills 34 12 45N29'01 122w45'14 8:11:01
Ramapo 26 12 45N28'50 122w31'49 8:10:07
Ramsey Hall 33 2 45N27 121w08 8:04:32
Rand 17 2 42N35'47 123w35'06 8:14:20
Randolph 6 2 43N10'05 124w21'19 8:17:25
Redbell 10 2 43N20'21 123w19'45 8:13:19
Redess 13 2 43N28'15 118w53'45 7:55:35
Redland 3 2 45N20'37 122w29'30 8:09:58
Redmond 9 8 44N16'22 121w10'22 8:04:41
Reed 20 2 44N10'23 123w50'01 8:15:20
Reeds Mill 25 2 45N05'45 119w36'21 7:58:25
Reedsport 10 2 43N42'09 124w05'44 8:16:23
Reedville 34 12 45N29'52 122w54'04 8:11:36
Remote 6 2 43N00'22 123w53'29 8:15:34
Rennie Landing 20 2 44N07'29 122w28'06 8:09:52
Reservation 30 2 45N40 118w34 7:54:16
Reston 10 2 43N07'49 123w37'08 8:14:29
Reuben 5 4 46N00'32 122w52'34 8:11:30
Reuben 10 2 42N44'10 123w29'28 8:13:58
Rex 36 14 45N18'59 122w54'27 8:11:38
Rhinehart 31 2 45N29'55 117w55'59 7:51:44
Rhododendron 3 4 45N19'47 121w54'36 8:07:38
Rice 33 2 45N30'20 121w02'35 8:04:10
Rice Hill 10 2 43N31'35 123w18'13 8:13:13
Richardson 20 2 44N00'21 123w41'56 8:14:48
Richland 1 2 44N46'09 117w10'03 7:48:40
Richmond 35 2 44N43'52 119w59'28 7:59:58
Rickreall 27 2 44N55'51 123w13'38 8:12:55
Riddle 10 2 42N57'04 123w21'47 8:13:27
Rieckens Corner 13 2 42N44'58 119w04'08 7:56:17
Rieth 30 2 45N39'40 118w52'13 7:55:29
Riley 13 2 43N32'30 119w30'10 7:58:01
Riley Huff Place 13 2 42N32'37 118w42'20 7:54:49
Ring 30 2 45N59'45 118w46'41 7:55:07
Ringtail Pine 10 2 43N15'33 122w29'11 8:09:57
Ritner 27 2 44N43'41 123w26'35 8:13:46
Ritter 12 2 44N53'33 119w08'33 7:56:34
River Crest 3 12 45N23 122w36 8:10:24
Riverdale 26 12 45N27'03 122w39'36 8:10:38
River Grove 3 12 45N23'29 122w43'56 8:10:56
River Junction 26 12 45N37'57 122w49'26 8:11:18
River Road 20 8 44N05 123w08 8:12:32
Riversdale 10 2 43N15'56 123w25'13 8:13:41
Riverside 22 13 44N36'25 123w09'23 8:12:38
Riverside 23 2 43N32'30 118w09'29 7:52:38
Riverton 6 2 43N09'27 124w16'24 8:17:06
Riverview 5 4 45N52 123w11 8:12:44
Riverview 20 3 44N13 123w12 8:12:48
Riverwood 26 12 45N26'39 122w39'45 8:10:39
Roads End 21 11 45N00'23 124w00'21 8:16:01
Roberts 7 2 44N04'53 120w41'01 8:02:44
Roberts 22 2 44N29'40 122w28'46 8:09:55
Roberts 24 15 44N54'08 123w05'57 8:12:24
Roberts Butte 32 2 45N38'29 117w12'35 7:48:50
Robertson 3 12 45N26'04 122w38'19 8:10:33
Robideau Landing 9 2 43N46'10 121w49'56 8:07:20
Robinette 1 2 44N45'10 117w01'46 7:48:07
Robinson 34 12 45N26'58 122w47'06 8:11:08
Robinsonville 12 2 44N42'50 118w29'01 7:53:56
Robinwood 3 12 45N23'34 122w38'45 8:10:35
Rockaway 29 7 45N36'49 123w56'31 8:15:46
Rock Creek 1 2 44N54'51 118w02'05 7:52:08
Rock Creek 11 2 45N34'22 120w17'46 8:01:11
Rockford 14 10 45N40'45 121w33'12 8:06:13
Rock Hill 22 2 44N28'59 122w56'53 8:11:48
Rock Point 15 2 42N25'56 123w05'52 8:12:23
Rockville 23 1 43N17'31 117w06'11 7:48:25
Rockwood 26 12 45N31'09 122w28'33 8:09:54
Rocky Ford 18 2 42N53'41 121w27'46 8:05:51
Rocky Ford 23 1 43N26'09 117w06'30 7:48:26
Rocky Point 18 3 42N28'51 122w04'59 8:08:20
Rogers 1 2 44N37'16 117w50'08 7:51:21
Rogers 6 2 43N27'20 124w13'53 8:16:56
Rogue Elk 15 2 43N50 123w14 8:12:56
Rogue River 15 2 42N26'10 123w10'15 8:12:41
Rome 23 1 42N50'21 117w37'38 7:50:31
Rondowa 32 2 45N43'30 117w46'59 7:51:08
Rooster Rock 26 4 45N32'28 122w15'07 8:09:00
Roseburg 10 3 43N13'00 123w20'26 8:13:22
Rosebush 28 2 45N18'05 120w43'05 8:02:52
Rose City Park 26 12 45N32 122w36 8:10:24
Rosedale 24 15 44N51'17 123w03'37 8:12:14
Rose Lodge 21 11 45N00'38 123w52'45 8:15:31
Rosemont 3 12 45N22'10 122w38'43 8:10:35
Rosewood 3 12 45N23'53 122w43'55 8:10:56
Ross 30 2 45N27'42 118w25'07 7:53:40
Rothe 3 12 45N23'50 122w37'13 8:10:29
Round Prairie 10 3 43N05'18 123w22'06 8:13:28
Rowena 33 2 45N40'21 121w16'02 8:05:04
Rowland 22 2 44N17'41 123w04'35 8:12:18
Roy 34 4 45N35'41 123w04'52 8:12:19
Royal 20 2 43N49'30 123w07'47 8:12:31
Ruby 26 12 45N30'55 122w27'13 8:09:49
Ruch 15 2 42N14'12 123w02'28 8:12:10
Ruckel Junction 30 2 45N37'43 118w07'55 7:52:32
Ruckles 10 2 43N02'30 123w19'46 8:13:19
Rufus 28 2 45N41'42 120w44'05 8:02:56
Ruggs 25 2 45N15'49 119w41'08 7:58:45
Rural Dell 3 4 45N08'57 122w39'00 8:10:36
Russellville 26 12 45N31'09 122w33'24 8:10:14
Rutledge 28 2 45N20'17 120w38'46 8:02:35
Rye Valley 1 2 44N21 117w16 7:49:04
Safley 10 2 43N42'05 123w15'35 8:13:02
Sage Hen Crossing 19 2 42N11'37 120w04'01 8:00:16
Saginaw 20 3 43N49'58 123w02'39 8:12:11
Sago 31 2 45N04'36 117w50'54 7:51:24
Sailor 20 2 44N03'04 123w25'51 8:13:43
Saint Benedict 24 4 45N03 122w46 8:11:04
Saint Helens 5 17 45N51'51 122w48'19 8:11:13
Saint Johns 26 12 45N35'25 122w45'12 8:11:01
Saint Johns Junction 26 12 45N34'12 122w42'33 8:10:50
Saint Joseph 36 14 45N14'18 123w08'37 8:12:34
Saint Louis 24 2 45N07'22 122w56'28 8:11:46
Saint Paul 24 2 45N12'41 122w58'32 8:11:54
Salado 21 2 44N33'13 123w47'08 8:15:09
Salem 24 15 44N56'35 123w02'02 8:12:08
Salisbury 1 2 44N39'12 117w52'20 7:51:29
Salmon 3 4 45N22'04 122w01'24 8:08:06
Salmonberry 29 2 45N44'58 123w38'54 8:14:36
Salmon Harbor 10 2 43N42 124w06 8:16:24
Salt Creek 27 2 44N59'45 123w21'06 8:13:24
Sams Valley 15 2 42N29'30 122w58'27 8:11:54
Sandhill Crossing 18 2 42N35'43 120w53'11 8:03:33
Sand Hollow 25 2 45N35'11 119w32'30 7:58:10
Sandlake 29 11 45N18'12 123w55'20 8:15:41
Sandy 3 5 45N23'51 122w15'37 8:09:02
San Marine 21 2 44N21'14 124w05'34 8:16:22
Santa Clara 20 2 44N06'13 123w07'48 8:12:31
Santiam Junction 22 2 44N26'12 121w56'22 8:07:45
Santiam Terrace 22 2 44N26'35 122w48'36 8:11:14
Sargent Place 23 1 44N24'18 117w40'49 7:50:43
Saunders Lake 6 2 43N24 124w14 8:16:56
Scappoose 5 5 45N45'16 122w52'35 8:11:30
Schefflin 34 6 45N34'14 123w02'46 8:12:11
Schmore Place 18 2 42N17'08 121w34'21 8:06:17
Scholls 34 6 45N24'30 122w55'16 8:11:41
Scio 22 2 44N42'18 122w50'53 8:11:24
Scofield 34 4 45N43'08 123w12'47 8:12:51
Scottsburg 10 2 43N39'15 123w48'56 8:15:16
Scotts Mills 24 2 45N02'35 122w40'02 8:10:40
Seal Rock 21 2 44N29'57 124w04'58 8:16:20
Searose Beach 20 2 44N13'57 124w06'26 8:16:26
Seaside 4 14 45N59'36 123w55'17 8:15:41
Seekseequa Junction 16 2 44N40'31 121w17'25 8:05:10
Seghers 34 4 45N27'38 123w08'03 8:12:32
Sellwood 26 12 45N27'53 122w39'05 8:10:36
Selma 17 2 42N16'45 123w36'53 8:14:28
Seneca 12 2 44N08'05 118w58'14 7:55:53
Sentinel Hill 26 12 45N29'23 122w41'41 8:10:47
Service Creek 35 2 44N47'52 120w00'26 8:00:02
Seven Oaks 15 2 42N23'33 122w56'13 8:11:45
Sevier 32 2 45N35'29 117w34'40 7:50:19
Sewell 34 6 45N31'33 122w57'11 8:11:49
Shadowood 3 12 45N22'44 122w41'36 8:10:46
Shady 10 2 43N10'30 123w21'33 8:13:26
Shady Cove 15 2 42N37 122w49 8:11:16
Shady Dell 3 12 45N08'36 122w32'16 8:10:09
Shady Grove 15 2 42N36'39 122w48'41 8:11:15
Shady Pine 18 3 42N18'30 121w48'09 8:07:13
Shaff 24 2 44N48'35 122w51'52 8:11:27
Shale City 15 2 42N16'25 122w35'13 8:10:21
Shanahan Place 19 2 43N05'18 121w18'05 8:05:12
Shangri-La Mill 10 2 42N47'06 122w52'02 8:11:28
Shaniko 33 2 45N00'14 120w45'04 8:03:00
Shaniko Junction 33 2 44N55'17 120w56'42 8:03:47
Shannon 20 2 44N01'50 123w35'52 8:14:23
Sharps Corner 30 2 45N55'05 119w19'18 7:57:17
Shaw 24 2 44N51 122w52 8:11:28
Sheaville 23 1 43N07'38 117w02'59 7:48:12
Shedd 22 2 44N27'42 123w06'33 8:12:26
Shelburn 22 2 44N44'10 122w52'10 8:11:29
Sherar 33 2 45N15'13 121w02'27 8:04:10
Sheridan 36 15 45N05'58 123w23'37 8:13:34
Sherwood 34 4 45N21'24 122w50'20 8:11:21
Shiloh Basin 5 17 45N52 122w48 8:11:12
Shipley 36 15 45N05'58 123w25'28 8:13:42
Shorewood 6 2 43N27'15 124w13'01 8:16:52
Shrock 2 7 44N28'28 123w16'44 8:13:07
Shutler 11 2 45N38'00 120w10'03 8:00:40
Shutter Landing 6 2 43N32'48 124w09'25 8:16:38
Siboco 20 2 43N58'06 124w03'21 8:16:13
Sidney 24 2 44N47'00 123w06'30 8:12:26
Siletz 21 2 44N43'19 123w55'08 8:15:41
Siltcoos 20 2 43N53'21 124w03'45 8:16:15
Silver Falls City 24 2 44N52'19 122w38'58 8:10:36
Silver Lake 19 2 43N07'41 121w02'42 8:04:11
Silverton 24 4 45N00'19 122w46'55 8:11:08
Silverton Hills 24 2 44N59 122w43 8:10:52
Silvies 12 2 44N01'59 118w56'03 7:55:44
Silvies Landing 12 2 44N00'54 118w56'36 7:55:46
Simnasho 33 2 44N58'23 121w20'56 8:05:24
Simon Landing 24 2 45N03'24 123w03'13 8:12:13
Simpson 27 2 44N46'48 123w18'05 8:13:12
Simpson Place 35 2 44N29'11 120w15'08 8:01:01
Sinamox 33 2 45N22'04 120w54'03 8:03:36
Siskiyou 15 2 42N04'30 122w36'21 8:10:25
Sisters 9 2 44N17'28 121w32'53 8:06:12
Sitkum 6 2 43N08'54 123w51'36 8:15:26
Siuslaw 20 2 44N03'32 123w48'56 8:15:16
Six Corners 34 4 45N22'04 122w50'45 8:11:23
Sixes 8 2 42N49'13 124w28'55 8:17:56
Skelley 10 2 43N35'56 123w21'34 8:13:26
Skipanon 4 11 46N10 123w55 8:15:40
Skull Spring 23 1 43N29'55 117w47'25 7:51:10
Skyland 3 12 45N25 122w42 8:10:48
Skyline 26 12 45N39 122w51 8:11:24
Smeltz 30 2 45N54'10 118w40'20 7:54:41
Smithfield 27 2 44N59'01 123w15'47 8:13:03
Smith Lake 26 12 45N36 122w41 8:10:44
Smiths Ford 10 2 43N17'46 122w55'00 8:11:40
Smock 33 2 45N15 121w10 8:04:40
Snooseville Corner 34 6 45N43'24 123w04'12 8:12:17
Sodaville 22 2 44N29'05 122w52'14 8:11:29
Sonny 14 10 45N42'11 121w37'20 8:06:29
Southbeach 21 2 44N36'46 124w02'51 8:16:11
South Corvallis 2 7 44N32 123w18 8:13:12
South Grants Pass 17 2 42N25 123w20 8:13:20
South Junction 33 2 44N51'15 121w04'31 8:04:18
South Lake Oswego 3 12 45N24'29 122w40'20 8:10:41
South Lebanon 22 2 44N32 122w54 8:11:36
South Medford 15 2 42N20 122w57 8:11:48
South Oswego 3 12 45N25 122w42 8:10:48
Southport 6 2 43N17'54 124w13'09 8:16:53
South Scappoose 5 4 45N44'35 122w52'42 8:11:31
South Side 20 8 44N02 123w06 8:12:24
South Siuslaw 20 2 43N56 124w03 8:16:12
South Sweet Home 22 2 44N22 122w32 8:10:08
South Umpqua 10 2 42N51 123w08 8:12:32
Sparks 30 16 45N35'28 118w48'47 7:55:15
Sparta 1 2 44N52'16 117w19'23 7:49:18
Speaker 17 2 42N43'00 123w17'34 8:13:10
Speece 11 2 45N23'51 120w08'56 8:00:36
Spicer 22 2 44N35'13 122w56'51 8:11:47
Spitzenberg 5 4 45N49'33 122w56'42 8:11:47
Spofford 30 2 45N58'27 118w20'26 7:53:22
Spongs Landing 24 15 45N01'14 123w04'17 8:12:17
Spoos Mill 35 2 44N31'06 119w58'30 7:59:54
Sprague River 18 2 42N27'20 121w30'11 8:06:01
Spray 35 2 44N50'04 119w47'36 7:59:10

Springbrook 36 14 45N19'04 122w56'40 8:11:47
Springdale 26 12 45N31'09 122w19'43 8:09:19
Springfield 20 3 44N02'47 123w01'15 8:12:05
Springfield Junction 20 8 44N02'15 123w02'15 8:12:09
Springwater 3 4 45N15'03 122w20'18 8:09:21
Stafford 3 4 45N21'27 122w43'17 8:10:53
Staleys Junction 34 4 45N40'58 123w11'42 8:12:47
Stanfield 30 2 45N46'50 119w12'58 7:56:52
Stanfield Junction 30 2 45N45'46 119w12'09 7:56:49
Stanley 3 12 45N27'29 122w36'11 8:10:25
Stanton 30 2 45N55'20 118w41'27 7:54:46
Starkey 31 2 45N13'18 118w25'29 7:53:42
Starkey Corner 34 4 45N34'23 123w00'11 8:12:01
Starvation Heights 15 2 42N29'08 123w10'01 8:12:40
Stauffer 19 2 43N29'04 120w06'54 8:00:28
Stayton 24 2 44N48'03 122w47'36 8:11:10
Steamboat 10 2 43N20'44 122w44'04 8:10:56
Steamboat 15 2 42N04'33 123w12'14 8:12:49
Stearns 9 2 43N46'25 121w27'30 8:05:50
Steeds Crossing 33 2 45N15'48 121w24'40 8:05:39
Steinman 15 2 42N05'40 122w35'24 8:10:22
Stephens 10 2 43N23'01 123w23'28 8:13:34
Stewart Lennox Addition 18 3 42N13 121w45 8:07:00
Stewarts 35 2 45N00'16 120w04'35 8:00:18
Stewarts Crossing 12 2 44N27'58 119w28'14 7:57:53
Still 1 2 44N32'57 117w08'46 7:48:35
Stimson Mill 34 4 45N28'07 123w11'14 8:12:45
Strassel 34 4 45N42'36 123w14'37 8:12:58
Stratton Place 19 2 43N10'37 121w09'32 8:04:38
Strawberry 25 2 45N33'34 119w39'48 7:58:39
Stukel 18 2 42N06'51 121w42'25 8:06:50
Sturgill 1 2 44N41'13 117w05'04 7:48:20
Sublimity 24 2 44N49'47 122w47'36 8:11:10
Sulphur Springs 10 2 43N47'00 123w54'00 8:15:36
Summer Lake 19 2 42N58'23 120w46'35 8:03:06
Summerville 31 2 45N29'19 118w00'07 7:52:00
Summit 2 2 44N38'17 123w34'39 8:14:19
Summit 14 4 45N38'04 121w33'19 8:06:13
Sumner 6 2 43N16'55 124w08'59 8:16:36
Sumpter 1 2 44N44'45 118w12'04 7:52:48
Sundstrom Place 12 2 44N20'51 119w36'29 7:58:26
Sunnycrest 36 2 45N18'07 123w01'00 8:12:04
Sunnyside 3 12 45N25'37 122w31'35 8:10:06
Sunnyside 24 15 44N50'42 123w01'32 8:12:06
Sunnyside 30 2 45N57'45 118w24'04 7:53:36
Sunny Valley 17 2 42N38'21 123w22'28 8:13:30
Sunriver 9 8 44N04 121w18 8:05:12
Sunset 1 2 44N53'43 117w02'34 7:48:10
Sunset 3 12 45N21'36 122w37'44 8:10:31
Sunset Beach 4 11 46N10 123w55 8:15:40
Sunset Landing 21 11 44N53'05 123w56'11 8:15:45
Suplee 7 2 44N04'10 119w40'32 7:58:42
Surf Pines 4 11 46N10 123w55 8:15:40
Surprise Valley 10 2 43N01 123w18 8:13:12
Susanville 12 2 44N42'48 118w46'58 7:55:08
Sutherlin 10 2 43N23'25 123w18'41 8:13:15
Suver 27 2 44N44'35 123w12'22 8:12:49
Svensen 4 2 46N10'15 123w39'29 8:14:38
Svensen Junction 4 2 46N09'56 123w39'31 8:14:38
Swain 20 3 44N12'21 123w12'02 8:12:48
Swedetown 5 4 46N02'29 123w06'24 8:12:26
Sweet Home 22 2 44N23'52 122w44'06 8:10:56
Swisshome 20 2 44N03'29 123w47'53 8:15:12
Sycamore 26 12 45N28'40 122w30'24 8:10:02
Sylvan 26 12 45N30'33 122w44'04 8:10:56
Sylvester Place 13 2 43N40'26 119w07'04 7:56:28
Table Rock 15 2 42N27'05 122w54'42 8:11:39
Taft 21 11 44N56'02 124w01'16 8:16:05
Takilma 17 2 42N03'06 123w37'06 8:14:28
Talbot 24 2 44N45'40 123w05'42 8:12:23
Talent 15 2 42N14'45 122w47'15 8:11:09
Tallman 22 2 44N33'55 122w58'02 8:11:52
Tangent 22 2 44N32'29 123w06'25 8:12:26
Tarter 27 2 44N45'47 123w20'08 8:13:21
Taylor Place (Site) 19 2 42N30'43 120w39'56 8:02:40
Taylorville 4 2 46N08'29 123w23'53 8:13:36
Teeters Landing (Site) 18 2 42N05'04 121w53'01 8:07:32
Telegraph Hill 6 2 43N22'23 124w12'56 8:16:52
Telocaset 31 2 45N06'04 117w49'31 7:51:18
Templeton 6 2 43N32'45 124w05'55 8:16:24
Tenmile 10 2 43N05'47 123w33'47 8:14:15
Tennessee 22 2 44N35 122w55 8:11:40
Terrebonne 9 2 44N21'11 121w10'36 8:04:42
Texum 18 2 42N10'34 121w46'52 8:07:07
Tharp 10 2 43N39'04 124w05'39 8:16:23
Thatcher 34 6 45N33'54 123w08'25 8:12:34
The Dalles 33 7 45N35'41 121w10'39 8:04:43
Thielson 27 2 44N55'16 123w12'00 8:12:48
Thirtymile 11 2 45N10'10 120w09'27 8:00:38
Thornberry 28 2 45N37'56 120w45'44 8:03:03
Thorn Creek Butte 12 2 44N16'59 119w21'09 7:57:25
Thorn Hollow 30 2 45N41'02 118w27'32 7:53:50
Three Forks 12 2 44N17'00 119w37'40 7:58:31
Three Lynx 3 4 45N07'35 122w04'13 8:08:17
Three Pines 17 2 42N33'57 123w23'51 8:13:35
Three Rocks 21 11 45N02'41 123w59'53 8:16:00
Thurston 20 8 44N03'12 122w54'55 8:11:40
Tide 20 2 44N04'00 123w50'20 8:15:21
Tide Creek 5 4 45N56 122w51 8:11:24
Tidewater 21 2 44N24'41 123w53'57 8:15:36
Tiernan 20 2 44N00'58 123w56'20 8:15:45
Tierra Del Mar 29 11 45N15'08 123w57'48 8:15:51
Tigard 34 12 45N25'53 122w46'13 8:11:05
Tillamook 29 2 45N27'23 123w50'34 8:15:22
Tiller 10 2 42N55'43 122w57'00 8:11:48
Timber 34 4 45N43'12 123w17'36 8:13:10
Timber Grove 3 4 45N12'03 122w26'42 8:09:47
Timbuktu 34 4 45N31'57 123w23'27 8:13:34
Tioga 6 2 43N15'28 123w48'56 8:15:16
Tobias 34 5 45N29'44 122w52'48 8:11:31
Toketee Falls 10 2 43N16'33 122w26'59 8:09:48
Toledo 21 2 44N37'18 123w56'14 8:15:45
Tollgate 30 2 45N49 118w25 7:53:40
Tolo 15 2 42N25'28 122w58'13 8:11:53
Tolovana Park 4 11 45N52'20 123w57'31 8:15:50
Tompkins Landing 36 2 45N06'32 123w00'33 8:12:02
Tongue Point Naval Base 4 14 46N11'49 123w46'14 8:15:05
Tongue Point Village 4 14 46N11'49 123w46'14 8:15:05
Tonquin 34 4 45N21'01 122w47'34 8:11:10
Top 12 2 44N49 119w25 7:57:40
Tophill 34 4 45N45'08 123w11'42 8:12:47
Tracy 3 4 45N18'10 122w17'24 8:09:10
Trail 15 2 42N38'55 122w48'34 8:11:14
Trece 34 12 45N25'42 122w45'46 8:11:03
Treharne 5 4 45N50'31 123w13'07 8:12:52
Trenholm 5 4 45N53'44 122w57'51 8:11:51
Trent 20 2 43N56'35 122w51'34 8:11:26
Triangle Lake 20 2 44N08 123w35 8:14:20
Tri City 10 2 42N58'51 123w19'19 8:13:17
Trojan 5 4 46N02'00 122w53'03 8:11:32
Trout Creek 13 2 43N55'38 118w56'20 7:55:45
Troutdale 26 12 45N32'22 122w23'10 8:09:33
Troy 32 2 45N56'49 117w27'02 7:49:48
Tryon 26 12 45N27 122w42 8:10:48
Tualatin 34 12 45N23'03 122w45'46 8:11:03
Tucke Place 13 2 42N51'46 119w13'35 7:56:54
Tulsa 22 2 44N23'26 123w09'53 8:12:40
Tumalo 9 2 44N09'00 121w19'47 8:05:19
Turner 24 2 44N50'36 122w57'06 8:11:48
Tuskan 33 2 45N13'23 121w04'52 8:04:19
Twelvemile Corner 26 12 45N31'09 122w25'59 8:09:44
Twickenham 35 2 44N44'38 120w10'15 8:00:41
Twin Rocks 29 11 45N35'52 123w56'41 8:15:47
Twomile 6 2 43N03'29 124w24'48 8:17:39
Tyee 10 2 43N26'22 123w34'27 8:14:18
Tygh Valley 33 2 45N14'51 121w10'19 8:04:41
Ukiah 30 2 45N08'03 118w55'53 7:55:44
Umapine 30 2 45N58'36 118w29'43 7:53:59
Umatilla 30 2 45N55'03 119w20'29 7:57:22
Umatilla Indian Reservation 30 2 45N40 118w33 7:54:12
Umli 18 2 43N26'55 121w56'57 8:07:48
Umpqua 10 2 43N21'56 123w28'02 8:13:52
Union 31 2 45N12'31 117w51'51 7:51:27
Union Creek 10 2 42N52'11 123w34'28 8:14:18
Union Creek 15 2 42N54'26 122w26'40 8:09:47
Union Gap 10 2 43N24'24 123w18'46 8:13:15
Union Junction 31 2 45N12'24 117w54'32 7:51:38
Union Mills 3 4 45N11'59 122w33'27 8:10:14
Union Point 22 2 44N20'55 122w59'04 8:11:56
Unionvale 36 2 45N08'36 123w03'34 8:12:14
United Junction 26 12 45N37'49 122w49'17 8:11:17
Unity 1 2 44N26'15 118w11'30 7:52:46
Unity 20 2 43N58 122w49 8:11:16
University of Oregon 20 8 44N04 123w05 8:12:20
University Park 26 12 45N34'35 122w43'39 8:10:55
Upper Crossing 13 2 42N31'25 118w47'08 7:55:09
Upper Farm 21 2 44N45 123w47 8:15:08
Upper Highland 3 4 45N14'09 122w25'44 8:09:43
Upper Siuslaw 20 2 43N55 123w22 8:13:28
Upper Soda 22 2 44N24'23 122w16'54 8:09:08
Upper Walla Walla 30 2 45N56 118w17 7:53:08
Vadis 34 6 45N36'06 123w02'01 8:12:08
Valby 25 2 45N19'00 119w50'25 7:59:22
Vale 23 1 43N58'56 117w14'14 7:48:57
Valle Vista 34 6 45N35'57 122w53'24 8:11:34
Valley Falls 19 2 42N29'03 120w16'51 8:01:07
Valley Junction 27 15 45N03'44 123w34'15 8:14:17
Valsetz 27 2 44N50'18 123w39'14 8:14:37
Van 13 2 43N59'24 118w41'14 7:54:45
Vandervert Ranch 9 8 44N04 121w18 8:05:12
Van Horn 14 10 45N39'25 121w30'25 8:06:02
Vanport 26 12 45N35 122w41 8:10:44
Vansycle 30 2 45N56'53 118w43'19 7:54:53
Vaughn 20 2 44N01'26 123w26'09 8:13:45
Veatch 20 2 43N45'22 123w06'07 8:12:24
Venator 13 2 43N20'53 118w18'15 7:53:13
Veneta 20 2 44N02'56 123w20'59 8:13:24
Verboort 34 6 45N32'59 123w05'08 8:12:21
Verdure 22 2 44N31'57 123w09'35 8:12:38
Vermont Hills 26 12 45N28'39 122w43'36 8:10:54
Vernonia 5 4 45N51'32 123w11'30 8:12:46
Vida 20 2 44N08'46 122w34'07 8:10:16
Villa Ridge 26 12 45N26'35 122w44'28 8:10:58
Vincent 31 2 45N41'13 117w46'35 7:51:06
Vinemaple 4 11 45N53'19 123w32'35 8:14:10
Vinson 30 2 45N28'03 119w05'36 7:56:22
Viola 3 4 45N17'54 122w24'33 8:09:38
Vista 24 15 44N54 123w02 8:12:08
Voltage 13 2 43N15'41 118w48'22 7:55:13
Voorhies 15 2 42N17'37 122w50'25 8:11:22
Votaw 34 14 45N19'54 122w53'08 8:11:33
Waconda 24 2 45N04'32 122w58'33 8:11:54
Waconda Beach 21 2 44N23'16 124w05'18 8:16:21
Wagontire 13 2 43N14'59 119w52'29 7:59:30
Wakefield 29 2 45N44'26 123w42'14 8:14:49
Wakonda Beach 21 2 44N26 124w04 8:16:16
Walden 20 2 43N48 123w04 8:12:16
Waldport 21 2 44N25'37 124w04'03 8:16:16
Waldron 35 2 44N43'28 120w01'39 8:00:07
Walker 20 2 43N51'15 123w02'19 8:12:09
Walkers Corner 27 2 44N58'46 123w13'03 8:12:52
Wallace 3 4 45N16'34 122w47'17 8:11:09
Wallace Bridge 27 15 45N04 123w29 8:13:56
Wallinch 27 2 44N45'34 123w22'20 8:13:29
Wallowa 32 2 45N34'13 117w31'38 7:50:07
Walterville 20 2 44N04'08 122w48'10 8:11:13
Walton 20 2 44N01'51 123w35'03 8:14:20
Wamic 33 2 45N13'42 121w16'05 8:05:04
Wankers Corner 3 12 45N22'31 122w42'03 8:10:48
Wapato 36 2 45N24'23 123w07'22 8:12:29
Wapinitia 33 2 45N06'52 121w15'19 8:05:01
Warm Springs 16 2 44N45'49 121w15'54 8:05:04
Warm Springs Indian Res 16 2 44N46 121w16 8:05:04
Warner 6 2 42N59'15 124w09'25 8:16:38
Warner Valley 19 2 42N29 119w47 7:59:08
Warren 5 4 45N49'09 122w50'52 8:11:23
Warrendale 26 4 45N36'46 122w00'52 8:08:03
Warrenton 4 8 46N09'55 123w55'21 8:15:41
Wasco 28 2 45N35'31 120w41'49 8:02:47
Waterbury Mill 12 2 44N39'30 119w07'41 7:56:31
Waterloo 22 2 44N29'39 122w49'27 8:11:18
Waterman 30 2 45N53'18 118w32'27 7:54:10
Waterman 35 2 44N37'10 119w53'21 7:59:33
Waterview 5 17 45N54'33 122w49'13 8:11:17
Watseco 29 11 45N35'11 123w56'48 8:15:47
Watson 26 12 45N28'15 122w33'59 8:10:16
Watts 18 2 42N27'21 121w01'24 8:04:06
Watts 34 6 45N32'30 123w10'02 8:12:40
Wauna 4 2 46N09'26 123w24'18 8:13:37
Waverly Heights 3 12 45N27'00 122w38'50 8:10:35
Wayland 30 2 45N54'20 118w34'34 7:54:18
Weatherby 1 2 44N29'55 117w22'13 7:49:29
Weaver 10 2 43N00'28 123w18'34 8:13:14
Weaver Place 13 2 42N38'45 118w50'08 7:55:21
Webfoot 28 2 45N35'06 120w31'07 8:02:04
Wecoma Beach (Post Office) 21 11 44N59'20 124w00'23 8:16:02
Wedderburn 8 2 42N25'47 124w24'50 8:17:39
Welches 3 4 45N19'42 121w57'35 8:07:50
Weldwood 22 2 44N31'15 122w54'06 8:11:36
Wellsdale 2 13 44N42'05 123w11'37 8:12:46
Wells Landing 27 2 44N47'09 123w07'57 8:12:32
Wemme 3 4 45N20'56 121w57'53 8:07:52
Wenaha Forks 32 2 45N57'03 117w47'35 7:51:10
Wendling 20 2 44N11'26 122w47'50 8:11:11
Wendson 20 2 43N59'51 124w01'19 8:16:05
West 4 11 46N04'36 123w54'45 8:15:39
Westfall 23 1 43N59'31 117w42'29 7:50:50
Westfir 20 2 43N45'27 122w29'43 8:09:59
West Haven 34 12 45N31'04 122w46'06 8:11:04
Westimber 34 4 45N42'30 123w18'35 8:13:14
Westlake 20 2 43N53'00 124w06'50 8:16:27
Westland 30 2 45N48'08 119w22'17 7:57:29
West Linn 3 12 45N21'57 122w36'40 8:10:27
West Main 15 2 42N22 122w56 8:11:44
Westmoreland 26 12 45N28'35 122w38'45 8:10:35
West Oak 20 2 43N43 122w28 8:09:52
Weston 30 2 45N48'50 118w25'25 7:53:42
Weston Landing 36 2 45N12'07 123w02'46 8:12:11
Westport 4 2 46N07'58 123w22'25 8:13:30
West Portland 26 12 45N27'18 122w43'53 8:10:56
West Portland Park 26 12 45N26'49 122w43'28 8:10:54
West Powellhurst 26 12 45N29 122w33 8:10:12
West Rainier 5 12 45N24 122w39 8:10:36
West Saint Helens 5 17 45N51'28 122w49'34 8:11:18
West Salem 27 15 44N56'21 123w03'35 8:12:14
West Scio 22 2 44N42'40 122w52'54 8:11:32
West Side 19 2 42N06'48 120w29'33 8:01:58
West Side 20 8 44N05 123w08 8:12:32
West Slope 34 12 45N29'56 122w45'48 8:11:03
West Stayton 24 2 44N47'12 122w51'56 8:11:28
West Sweet Home 22 2 44N26 122w44 8:10:56
West Union 34 6 45N34'00 122w53'34 8:11:34
West Vale 23 1 43N58 117w22 7:49:28
Westwood 3 12 45N26 122w37 8:10:28
West Woodburn 24 2 45N09'18 122w53'41 8:11:35
Wetmore 35 2 44N59'14 119w53'30 7:59:34
Wetzels Corner 3 12 45N25'05 122w26'02 8:09:44
Weyerhaeuser Townsite 18 3 42N13 121w45 8:07:00
Wheatland 36 15 45N05'34 123w02'56 8:12:12
Wheeler 29 7 45N41'21 123w52'46 8:15:31
Wheeler Heights 29 11 45N41'06 123w53'22 8:15:33
Whiskey Dick 33 2 44N56'00 121w04'55 8:04:20
Whiskey Hill 3 4 45N10'35 122w44'48 8:10:59
Whitaker 22 2 44N33'31 122w52'19 8:11:29

White City 15 2 42N26'15 122w51'28 8:11:26
Whitehouse Place 19 2 42N33'08 120w34'30 8:02:18
Whitely Landing County Park 20 8 44N07'00 123w06'24 8:12:26
Whites Landing 36 2 45N07'33 123w00'39 8:12:03
Whiteson 36 14 45N09'06 123w11'44 8:12:47
Whitewater 3 4 45N07'47 122w04'36 8:08:18
Whitford 34 12 45N28'20 122w46'20 8:11:05
Whitney 1 2 44N39'34 118w17'23 7:53:10
Whitwood Court 26 12 45N35'08 122w46'15 8:11:05
Wichita 3 12 45N27'08 122w35'51 8:10:23
Wichita Station 3 12 45N27'26 122w36'05 8:10:24
Wicopee 20 2 43N40'21 122w15'41 8:09:03
Wigrich 27 2 44N48'22 123w08'56 8:12:36
Wigrich Landing 27 2 44N49'30 123w08'35 8:12:34
Wilark 5 4 45N45 122w52 8:11:28
Wilbur 10 2 43N19'16 123w20'22 8:13:21
Wilcox 28 2 45N07'43 120w40'00 8:02:40
Wilderville 17 2 42N22'57 123w27'57 8:13:52
Wildwood 3 4 45N21'16 121w58'48 8:07:55
Wildwood Campground 35 2 44N29'03 120w20'13 8:01:21
Wilhoit 3 12 45N03'10 122w34'00 8:10:16
Wilkesboro 34 4 45N36'32 123w05'41 8:12:23
Willamette 3 12 45N20'40 122w39'57 8:10:40
Willamette City 20 2 43N44'47 122w29'01 8:09:56
Willamette Heights 26 12 45N32'07 122w42'59 8:10:52
Willamina 36 15 45N04'44 123w29'05 8:13:56
Willbridge 26 12 45N33'43 122w44'34 8:10:58
Williams 17 2 42N13'08 123w16'22 8:13:05
Willowcreek 23 1 43N59 117w15 7:49:00
Willowdale 16 2 44N48'20 120w56'31 8:03:46
Willows 11 2 45N47'07 120w02'54 8:00:12
Willsburg Junction 3 12 45N27'31 122w38'05 8:10:32
Wilson 26 12 45N28'48 122w30'47 8:10:03
Wilson Beach 29 2 45N27 123w50 8:15:20
Wilson Corner 3 12 45N25'57 122w26'03 8:09:44
Wilsonia 3 12 45N25'28 122w39'33 8:10:38
Wilsonville 3 4 45N18'00 122w46'21 8:11:05
Wimer 15 2 42N32'20 123w08'52 8:12:35
Winant 21 2 44N35'01 124w00'04 8:16:00
Winberry 20 2 43N57'13 122w42'41 8:10:51
Winch 36 14 45N04'45 123w15'53 8:13:04
Winchester 10 2 43N16'49 123w21'09 8:13:25
Winchester Bay 10 2 43N40'38 124w10'25 8:16:42
Windmaster Corner 14 10 45N42 121w31 8:06:04
Wind Rock 12 2 44N53'11 118w35'50 7:54:23
Winema Beach 29 11 45N12 123w53 8:15:32
Wing 1 2 44N50'08 117w52'57 7:51:32
Wingville 1 2 44N50'23 117w55'14 7:51:41
Winlock 35 2 44N54'44 119w53'21 7:59:33
Winona 17 2 42N33'38 123w17'45 8:13:11
Winona 27 15 44N55'46 123w04'44 8:12:19
Winston 10 2 43N07'21 123w24'41 8:13:39
Winterville 6 2 43N07'29 124w22'03 8:17:28
Wistful Vista 16 2 44N38 121w08 8:04:32
Witch Hazel 34 6 45N30'02 122w55'48 8:11:43
Wocus 18 2 42N16'22 121w48'28 8:07:14
Wolf Creek 17 2 42N41'44 123w23'39 8:13:35
Wonder 17 2 42N21'52 123w32'04 8:14:08
Woodburn 24 2 45N08'38 122w51'15 8:11:25
Woodraffe 22 2 44N17'46 122w38'59 8:10:36
Woods 29 11 45N12'51 123w57'13 8:15:49
Woods Landing 36 2 45N11'43 123w01'07 8:12:04
Woodson 5 4 46N06'53 123w19'23 8:13:18
Woodstock 26 12 45N28'45 122w36'26 8:10:26
Wood Village 26 12 45N32'04 122w25'03 8:09:40
Worden 18 2 42N02'44 121w51'55 8:07:28
Wren 2 2 44N35'16 123w25'38 8:13:43
Wrentham 33 2 45N32'13 120w59'26 8:03:58
Wyeth 14 4 45N41'27 121w46'07 8:07:04
Yachats 21 2 44N18'41 124w06'13 8:16:25
Yamhill 36 2 45N20'30 123w11'10 8:12:45
Yampo 36 13 45N05'51 123w09'37 8:12:38
Yamsay 18 2 43N04'02 121w48'20 8:07:13
Yankton 5 17 45N52'01 122w53'08 8:11:33
Yaquina 21 2 44N36'08 124w00'27 8:16:02
Yoakum 30 2 45N40'22 119w02'36 7:56:10
Yoder 3 4 45N08'18 122w40'50 8:10:43
Yoncalla 10 2 43N35'55 123w16'56 8:13:08
Yonna 18 2 42N16'05 121w27'59 8:05:52
Young 24 2 44N49'29 122w51'51 8:11:27
Zena 27 15 45N00'32 123w07'42 8:12:31
Zigzag 3 4 45N20'39 121w56'31 8:07:46
Zumwalt 32 2 45N37'51 116w58'09 7:47:53

TIME TABLES

The law requiring that birth times be recorded in EST was in effect until April 12, 1971. But this law was infrequently observed. Daylight time was widely observed during the 1950's. However this is not fully documented for smaller towns.

PA # 1

Before 4/13/1887		LMT
4/13/1887	12:00	EST
3/31/1918	02:00	EWT
10/27/1918	02:00	EST
3/30/1919	02:00	EWT
10/26/1919	02:00	EST
2/09/1942	02:00	EWT
9/30/1945	02:00	US#2

PA # 2

Before 4/13/1887		LMT
4/13/1887	12:00	EST
3/31/1918	02:00	EWT
10/27/1918	02:00	EST
3/30/1919	02:00	EWT
10/26/1919	02:00	EST
4/24/1938	02:00	US#2

PA # 3

Before 4/13/1887		LMT
4/13/1887	12:00	EST
3/31/1918	02:00	EWT
10/27/1918	02:00	EST
3/30/1919	02:00	EWT
10/26/1919	02:00	EST
4/27/1941	02:00	US#2

PA # 4

Before 4/13/1887		LMT
4/13/1887	12:00	EST
3/31/1918	02:00	EWT
10/27/1918	02:00	EST
3/30/1919	02:00	EWT
10/26/1919	02:00	EST
2/09/1942	02:00	EWT
9/30/1945	02:00	EST
4/27/1947	02:00	US#2

PA # 5

Before 4/13/1887		LMT
4/13/1887	12:00	EST
3/31/1918	02:00	EWT
10/27/1918	02:00	EST
3/30/1919	02:00	EWT
10/26/1919	02:00	EST
2/09/1942	02:00	EWT
9/30/1945	02:00	EST
4/24/1949	02:00	US#2

PA # 6

Before 4/13/1887		LMT
4/13/1887	12:00	EST
3/31/1918	02:00	EWT
10/27/1918	02:00	EST
3/30/1919	02:00	EWT
10/26/1919	02:00	EST
2/09/1942	02:00	EWT
9/30/1945	02:00	EST
4/29/1956	02:00	US#2

PA # 7

Before 4/13/1887		LMT
4/13/1887	12:00	EST
3/31/1918	02:00	EWT
10/27/1918	02:00	EST
3/30/1919	02:00	EWT
10/26/1919	02:00	EST
2/09/1942	02:00	EWT
9/30/1945	02:00	EST
4/26/1953	02:00	US#2

PA # 8

Before 4/13/1887		LMT
4/13/1887	12:00	EST
3/31/1918	02:00	EWT
10/27/1918	02:00	EST
3/30/1919	02:00	EWT
10/26/1919	02:00	EST
4/26/1931	02:00	US#2

PA # 9

Before 4/13/1887		LMT
4/13/1887	12:00	EST
3/31/1918	02:00	EWT
10/27/1918	02:00	EST
3/30/1919	02:00	EWT
10/26/1919	02:00	EST
4/24/1921	02:00	US#2

PA # 10

Before 4/13/1887		LMT
4/13/1887	12:00	EST
3/31/1918	02:00	EWT
10/27/1918	02:00	EST
3/30/1919	02:00	EWT
10/26/1919	02:00	EST
4/26/1925	02:00	US#2

PA # 11

Before 4/13/1887		LMT
4/13/1887	12:00	EST
3/31/1918	02:00	EWT
10/27/1918	02:00	EST
3/30/1919	02:00	EWT
10/26/1919	02:00	EST
4/24/1921	02:00	EDT
9/25/1921	02:00	EST
4/30/1922	02:00	EDT
9/24/1922	02:00	EST
4/29/1923	02:00	EDT
9/30/1923	02:00	EST
4/27/1924	02:00	EDT
9/28/1924	02:00	EST
4/26/1925	02:00	EDT
9/27/1925	02:00	EST
4/25/1926	02:00	EDT
9/26/1926	02:00	EST
4/24/1927	02:00	EDT
9/25/1927	02:00	EST
4/29/1928	02:00	EDT
9/30/1928	02:00	EST
4/28/1929	02:00	EDT
9/29/1929	02:00	EST
4/27/1930	02:00	EDT
9/28/1930	02:00	EST
4/26/1931	02:00	EDT
9/27/1931	02:00	EST
4/24/1932	02:00	EDT
9/25/1932	02:00	EST
4/30/1933	02:00	EDT
9/24/1933	02:00	EST
4/29/1934	02:00	EDT
9/30/1934	02:00	EST
4/28/1935	02:00	EDT
9/29/1935	02:00	EST
4/26/1936	02:00	EDT
9/27/1936	02:00	EST
4/25/1937	02:00	EDT
9/26/1937	02:00	EST
4/24/1938	02:00	EDT
9/25/1938	02:00	EST
4/30/1939	02:00	EDT
9/24/1939	02:00	EST
4/28/1940	02:00	EDT
9/29/1940	02:00	EST
4/27/1941	02:00	EDT
9/28/1941	02:00	EST
2/09/1942	02:00	EWT
9/30/1945	02:00	EST
4/28/1946	02:00	EDT
9/29/1946	02:00	EST
4/27/1947	02:00	EDT
9/28/1947	02:00	EST
4/25/1948	02:00	EDT
9/26/1948	02:00	EST
4/24/1949	02:00	EDT
9/25/1949	02:00	EST
4/30/1950	02:00	EDT
9/24/1950	02:00	EST
4/29/1951	02:00	EDT
9/30/1951	02:00	EST
4/27/1952	02:00	EDT
9/28/1952	02:00	EST
4/26/1953	02:00	EDT
9/27/1953	02:00	EST
4/25/1954	02:00	EDT
9/26/1954	02:00	EST
4/24/1955	02:00	EDT
9/25/1955	02:00	EST
4/29/1956	02:00	EDT
9/30/1956	02:00	EST
4/28/1957	02:00	EDT
9/29/1957	02:00	EST
4/27/1958	02:00	EDT
9/28/1958	02:00	EST
4/26/1959	02:00	EDT
9/27/1959	02:00	EST
4/24/1960	02:00	EDT
9/25/1960	02:00	EST
4/30/1961	02:00	EDT
9/24/1961	02:00	EST
4/29/1962	02:00	US#2

PA # 12

Before 4/13/1887		LMT
4/13/1887	12:00	EST
3/31/1918	02:00	EWT
10/27/1918	02:00	EST
3/30/1919	02:00	EWT
10/26/1919	02:00	EST
4/28/1929	02:00	US#2

PA # 13

Before 4/13/1887		LMT
4/13/1887	12:00	EST
3/31/1918	02:00	EWT
10/27/1918	02:00	EST
3/30/1919	02:00	EWT
10/26/1919	02:00	EST
4/27/1930	02:00	US#2

PA # 14

Before 4/13/1887		LMT
4/13/1887	12:00	EST
3/31/1918	02:00	EWT
10/27/1918	02:00	EST
3/30/1919	02:00	EWT
10/26/1919	02:00	EST
4/30/1933	02:00	US#2

PA # 15

Before 4/13/1887		LMT
4/13/1887	12:00	EST
3/31/1918	02:00	EWT
10/27/1918	02:00	EST
3/30/1919	02:00	EWT
10/26/1919	02:00	EST
4/28/1935	02:00	US#2

PA # 16

Before 4/13/1887		LMT
4/13/1887	12:00	EST
3/31/1918	02:00	EWT
10/27/1918	02:00	EST
3/30/1919	02:00	EWT
10/26/1919	02:00	EST
4/24/1932	02:00	EDT
9/25/1932	02:00	EST
4/24/1938	02:00	US#2

PA # 17

Before 4/13/1887		LMT
4/13/1887	12:00	PA#8
9/30/1945	02:00	EST
4/24/1949	02:00	US#2

PA # 18

Before 4/13/1887		LMT
4/13/1887	12:00	EST
3/31/1918	02:00	EWT
10/27/1918	02:00	EST
3/30/1919	02:00	EWT
10/26/1919	02:00	EST
4/29/1934	02:00	EDT
9/30/1934	02:00	EST
4/28/1935	02:00	EDT
9/29/1935	02:00	EST
4/26/1936	02:00	EDT
9/27/1936	02:00	EST
2/09/1942	02:00	EWT
9/30/1945	02:00	EST
4/28/1946	02:00	US#2

PA # 19

Before 4/13/1887		LMT
4/13/1887	12:00	PA#8
4/29/1956	02:00	EDT
9/30/1956	02:00	EST
4/28/1957	02:00	US#2

PA # 20

Before 4/13/1887		LMT
4/13/1887	12:00	EST
3/31/1918	02:00	EWT
10/27/1918	02:00	EST
3/30/1919	02:00	EWT
10/26/1919	02:00	EST
4/28/1935	02:00	EDT
9/29/1935	02:00	EST
2/09/1942	02:00	EWT
9/30/1945	02:00	EST
4/28/1946	02:00	US#2

PA # 21

Before 4/13/1887		LMT
4/13/1887	12:00	EST
3/31/1918	02:00	EWT
10/27/1918	02:00	EST
3/30/1919	02:00	EWT
10/26/1919	02:00	EST
5/05/1935	02:00	EDT
9/29/1935	02:00	PA#1
4/30/1967	02:00	US#1

PA # 22

Before 4/13/1887		LMT
4/13/1887	12:00	EST
3/31/1918	02:00	EWT
10/27/1918	02:00	EST
3/30/1919	02:00	EWT
10/26/1919	02:00	EST
4/30/1939	02:00	EDT
9/24/1939	02:00	EST
2/09/1942	02:00	EWT
9/30/1945	02:00	EST
4/29/1951	02:00	US#2

PA # 23

Before 4/13/1887		LMT
4/13/1887	12:00	EST
3/31/1918	02:00	EWT
10/27/1918	02:00	EST
3/30/1919	02:00	EWT
10/26/1919	02:00	EST
4/29/1934	02:00	US#2

PA # 24

Before 4/13/1887		LMT
4/13/1887	12:00	PA#2
9/25/1938	02:00	EST
4/27/1941	02:00	US#2

PA # 25

Before 4/13/1887		LMT
4/13/1887	12:00	EST
3/31/1918	02:00	EWT
10/27/1918	02:00	EST
3/30/1919	02:00	EWT
10/26/1919	02:00	EST
4/30/1939	02:00	US#2

PA # 26

Before 4/13/1887		LMT
4/13/1887	12:00	EST
3/31/1918	02:00	EWT
10/27/1918	02:00	EST
3/30/1919	02:00	EWT
10/26/1919	02:00	EST
4/30/1933	02:00	EDT
9/24/1933	02:00	PA#2
4/30/1967	02:00	US#1

PA # 27

Before 4/13/1887		LMT
4/13/1887	12:00	EST
3/31/1918	02:00	EWT
10/27/1918	02:00	EST
3/30/1919	02:00	EWT
10/26/1919	02:00	EST
4/28/1940	02:00	US#2

PA # 28

Before 4/13/1887		LMT
4/13/1887	12:00	EST
3/31/1918	02:00	EWT
10/27/1918	02:00	EST
3/30/1919	02:00	EWT
10/26/1919	02:00	EST
4/26/1936	02:00	US#2

PA # 29

Before 4/13/1887		LMT
4/13/1887	12:00	EST
3/31/1918	02:00	EWT
10/27/1918	02:00	EST
3/30/1919	02:00	EWT
10/26/1919	02:00	EST
4/28/1940	02:00	EDT
9/29/1940	02:00	EST
4/27/1941	02:00	EDT
9/28/1941	02:00	EST
2/09/1942	02:00	EWT
9/30/1945	02:00	EST
4/26/1953	02:00	US#2

PA # 30

Before 4/13/1887		LMT
4/13/1887	12:00	EST
3/31/1918	02:00	EWT
10/27/1918	02:00	EST
3/30/1919	02:00	EWT
10/26/1919	02:00	EST
4/24/1932	02:00	EDT
9/25/1932	02:00	EST
4/26/1936	02:00	US#2

PA # 31

Before 4/13/1887		LMT
4/13/1887	12:00	EST
3/31/1918	02:00	EWT
10/27/1918	02:00	EST
3/30/1919	02:00	EWT
10/26/1919	02:00	EST
4/24/1932	02:00	EDT
9/25/1932	02:00	EST
4/30/1933	02:00	EDT
9/24/1933	02:00	EST
4/29/1934	02:00	EDT
9/30/1934	02:00	EST
4/24/1938	02:00	US#2

PA # 32

Before 4/13/1887		LMT
4/13/1887	12:00	PA#8
9/27/1931	02:00	EST
4/30/1932	02:00	US#2

PA # 33

Before 4/13/1887		LMT
4/13/1887	12:00	EST
3/31/1918	02:00	EWT
10/27/1918	02:00	EST
3/30/1919	02:00	EWT
10/26/1919	02:00	EST
4/27/1941	02:00	EDT
9/28/1941	02:00	EST
2/09/1942	02:00	EWT
9/30/1945	02:00	EST
4/28/1946	02:00	EDT
9/29/1946	02:00	EST
4/27/1947	02:00	EDT
9/28/1947	02:00	EST
4/25/1948	02:00	EDT
9/26/1948	02:00	EST
4/24/1949	02:00	EDT
9/25/1949	02:00	EST
4/30/1950	02:00	EDT
9/24/1950	02:00	EST
4/29/1951	02:00	EDT
9/30/1951	02:00	EST
4/27/1952	02:00	EDT
9/28/1952	02:00	EST
4/26/1953	02:00	EDT
9/27/1953	02:00	EST
4/25/1954	02:00	EDT
9/26/1954	02:00	EST
4/24/1955	02:00	EDT
10/30/1955	02:00	EST
4/29/1956	02:00	EDT
9/30/1956	02:00	EST
4/28/1957	02:00	EDT
9/29/1957	02:00	EST
4/27/1958	02:00	EDT
9/28/1958	02:00	EST
4/26/1959	02:00	EDT
9/27/1959	02:00	EST
4/24/1960	02:00	EDT
9/25/1960	02:00	EST
4/30/1961	02:00	US#2

PA # 34

Before 4/13/1887		LMT
4/13/1887	12:00	PA#3
2/09/1942	02:00	EWT
9/30/1945	02:00	EST
4/27/1947	02:00	EDT
9/28/1947	02:00	EST
4/25/1948	02:00	EDT
9/26/1948	02:00	EST
4/24/1949	02:00	EDT
9/25/1949	02:00	EST
4/30/1950	02:00	EDT
9/24/1950	02:00	EST
4/29/1951	02:00	EDT
9/30/1951	02:00	EST
4/27/1952	02:00	EDT
9/28/1952	02:00	EST
4/29/1956	02:00	US#2

PA # 35

Before 4/13/1887		LMT
4/13/1887	12:00	EST
3/31/1918	02:00	EWT
10/27/1918	02:00	EST
3/30/1919	02:00	EWT
10/26/1919	02:00	EST
4/27/1941	02:00	EDT
9/28/1941	02:00	EST
2/09/1942	02:00	EWT
9/30/1945	02:00	EST
4/26/1953	02:00	US#2

PA # 36

Before 4/13/1887		LMT
4/13/1887	12:00	EST
3/31/1918	02:00	EWT
10/27/1918	02:00	EST
3/30/1919	02:00	EWT
10/26/1919	02:00	EST
4/27/1941	02:00	EDT
9/28/1941	02:00	EST
2/09/1942	02:00	EWT
9/30/1945	02:00	EST
4/27/1947	02:00	EDT
9/28/1947	02:00	EST
4/25/1948	02:00	EDT
9/26/1948	02:00	EST
4/24/1949	02:00	EDT
9/25/1949	02:00	EST
4/30/1950	02:00	EDT
9/24/1950	02:00	EST
4/29/1951	02:00	EDT
9/30/1951	02:00	EST
4/27/1952	02:00	EDT
9/28/1952	02:00	EST
4/26/1953	02:00	EDT
9/27/1953	02:00	EST
4/25/1954	02:00	EDT
9/26/1954	02:00	EST
4/24/1955	02:00	EDT
9/25/1955	02:00	EST
4/29/1956	02:00	EDT
9/30/1956	02:00	EST
4/28/1957	02:00	US#2

PA # 37

Before 4/13/1887		LMT
4/13/1887	12:00	EST
3/31/1918	02:00	EWT
10/27/1918	02:00	EST
3/30/1919	02:00	EWT
10/26/1919	02:00	EST
4/27/1941	02:00	EDT
9/28/1941	02:00	EST
2/09/1942	02:00	EWT
9/30/1945	02:00	EST
4/29/1956	02:00	US#2

PA # 38

Before 4/13/1887		LMT
4/13/1887	12:00	EST
3/31/1918	02:00	EWT
10/27/1918	02:00	EST
3/30/1919	02:00	EWT
10/26/1919	02:00	EST
4/27/1941	02:00	EDT
9/28/1941	02:00	EST
2/09/1942	02:00	EWT
9/30/1945	02:00	EST
4/30/1950	02:00	US#2

PA # 39

Before 4/13/1887		LMT
4/13/1887	12:00	PA#8
9/27/1931	02:00	EST
4/28/1940	02:00	EDT
9/29/1940	02:00	EST
4/27/1941	02:00	EDT
9/28/1941	02:00	EST
2/09/1942	02:00	EWT
9/30/1945	02:00	EST
4/28/1946	02:00	EDT
9/29/1946	02:00	EST
4/27/1947	02:00	EDT
9/28/1947	02:00	EST
4/25/1948	02:00	EDT
9/26/1948	02:00	EST
4/24/1949	02:00	EDT
9/25/1949	02:00	EST
4/30/1950	02:00	EDT
9/24/1950	02:00	EST
4/29/1951	02:00	EDT
9/30/1951	02:00	EST
4/27/1952	02:00	EDT
9/28/1952	02:00	EST
4/26/1953	02:00	EDT
9/27/1953	02:00	EST
4/25/1954	02:00	EDT
9/26/1954	02:00	EST
4/24/1955	02:00	EDT
9/25/1955	02:00	EST
4/29/1956	02:00	EDT
10/28/1956	02:00	EST
4/28/1957	02:00	EDT

TIME TABLES

10/27/1957 02:00 EST
4/27/1958 02:00 EDT
9/28/1958 02:00 EST
4/26/1959 02:00 US#2
....
PA # 40
Before 4/13/1887 LMT
4/13/1887 12:00 PA#1
9/28/1947 02:00 EST
4/26/1953 02:00 US#2
....
PA # 41
Before 4/13/1887 LMT
4/13/1887 12:00 PA#1
9/29/1946 02:00 EST
4/24/1949 02:00 US#2
....
PA # 42
Before 4/13/1887 LMT
4/13/1887 12:00 PA#1
4/24/1955 02:00 EDT
9/25/1955 02:00 EST
4/29/1956 02:00 EDT
9/30/1956 02:00 EST
4/28/1957 02:00 EDT
9/29/1957 02:00 EST
4/27/1958 02:00 US#2
....
PA # 43
Before 4/13/1887 LMT
4/13/1887 12:00 PA#1
9/29/1946 02:00 EST
4/26/1953 02:00 US#2
....
PA # 44
Before 4/13/1887 LMT
4/13/1887 12:00 PA#1
4/24/1955 02:00 EDT
9/25/1955 02:00 EST
4/29/1956 02:00 US#2
....
PA # 45
Before 4/13/1887 LMT
4/13/1887 12:00 EST
3/31/1918 02:00 EWT
10/27/1918 02:00 EST
3/30/1919 02:00 EWT
10/26/1919 02:00 EST
4/28/1935 02:00 EDT
9/29/1935 02:00 EST
4/26/1936 02:00 EDT
9/27/1936 02:00 EST
2/09/1942 02:00 EWT
9/30/1945 02:00 EST
4/28/1946 02:00 EDT
9/29/1946 02:00 EST
4/27/1947 02:00 EDT
9/28/1947 02:00 EST
4/25/1948 02:00 EDT
9/26/1948 02:00 EST
4/24/1949 02:00 EDT
9/25/1949 02:00 EST
4/30/1950 02:00 EDT
9/24/1950 02:00 EST
4/29/1951 02:00 EDT
9/30/1951 02:00 EST
4/27/1952 02:00 EDT
9/28/1952 02:00 EST
4/26/1953 02:00 EDT
9/27/1953 02:00 EST
4/25/1954 02:00 EDT
9/26/1954 02:00 EST
4/24/1955 02:00 EDT
9/25/1955 02:00 EST
4/29/1956 02:00 US#2
....
PA # 46
Before 4/13/1887 LMT
4/13/1887 12:00 PA#8
4/29/1934 02:00 EDT
10/27/1934 02:00 US#2
....
PA # 47
Before 4/13/1887 LMT
4/13/1887 12:00 PA#8
4/26/1936 02:00 EDT
10/25/1936 02:00 US#2
....
PA # 48
Before 4/13/1887 LMT
4/13/1887 12:00 PA#4
9/28/1952 02:00 EST
4/29/1956 02:00 US#2
....
PA # 49
Before 4/13/1887 LMT
4/13/1887 12:00 EST
3/31/1918 02:00 EWT
10/27/1918 02:00 EST
3/30/1919 02:00 EWT
10/26/1919 02:00 EST
4/26/1936 02:00 EDT
9/27/1936 02:00 EST
4/28/1940 02:00 US#2
....
PA # 50
Before 4/13/1887 LMT
4/13/1887 12:00 EST
3/31/1918 02:00 EWT
10/27/1918 02:00 EST
3/30/1919 02:00 EWT
10/26/1919 02:00 EST
2/09/1942 02:00 EWT
9/30/1945 02:00 EST
4/27/1947 02:00 EDT
9/28/1947 02:00 EST
4/25/1948 02:00 EDT
9/26/1948 02:00 EST
4/24/1949 02:00 EDT
9/25/1949 02:00 EST
4/30/1950 02:00 EDT
9/24/1950 02:00 EST
4/29/1951 02:00 EDT
9/30/1951 02:00 EST
4/27/1952 02:00 EDT
9/28/1952 02:00 EST
4/26/1953 02:00 EDT
9/27/1953 02:00 EST
4/25/1954 02:00 EDT
9/26/1954 02:00 EST
4/24/1955 02:00 EDT
9/25/1955 02:00 EST
4/29/1956 02:00 EDT
9/30/1956 02:00 EST
4/28/1957 02:00 EDT
9/29/1957 02:00 EST
4/27/1958 02:00 EDT
9/28/1958 02:00 EST
4/26/1959 02:00 EDT
9/27/1959 02:00 EST
4/24/1960 02:00 EDT
9/25/1960 02:00 EST
4/30/1961 02:00 US#2
....
PA # 51
Before 4/13/1887 LMT
4/13/1887 12:00 EST
3/31/1918 02:00 EWT
10/27/1918 02:00 EST
3/30/1919 02:00 EWT
10/26/1919 02:00 EST
2/09/1942 02:00 EWT
9/30/1945 02:00 EST
4/25/1948 02:00 US#2
....
PA # 52
Before 4/13/1887 LMT
4/13/1887 12:00 EST
3/31/1918 02:00 EWT
10/27/1918 02:00 EST
3/30/1919 02:00 EWT
10/26/1919 02:00 EST
2/09/1942 02:00 EWT
9/30/1945 02:00 EST
4/25/1948 02:00 EDT
9/26/1948 02:00 EST
4/26/1953 02:00 US#2
....
PA # 53
Before 4/13/1887 LMT
4/13/1887 12:00 EST
3/31/1918 02:00 EWT
10/27/1918 02:00 EST
3/30/1919 02:00 EWT
10/26/1919 02:00 EST
2/09/1942 02:00 EWT
9/30/1945 02:00 EST
4/25/1948 02:00 EDT
9/26/1948 02:00 EST
4/24/1949 02:00 EDT
9/25/1949 02:00 EST
4/30/1950 02:00 EDT
9/24/1950 02:00 EST
4/29/1951 02:00 EDT
9/30/1951 02:00 EST
4/27/1952 02:00 EDT
9/28/1952 02:00 EST
4/26/1953 02:00 EDT
9/27/1953 02:00 EST
4/25/1954 02:00 EDT
9/26/1954 02:00 EST
4/24/1955 02:00 EDT
10/30/1955 02:00 EST
4/29/1956 02:00 EDT
10/28/1956 02:00 EST
4/28/1957 02:00 EDT
10/27/1957 02:00 EST
4/27/1958 02:00 EDT
9/28/1958 02:00 EST
4/26/1959 02:00 EDT
9/27/1959 02:00 EST
4/24/1960 02:00 EDT
9/25/1960 02:00 EST
4/30/1961 02:00 US#2
....
PA # 54
Before 4/13/1887 LMT
4/13/1887 12:00 EST
3/31/1918 02:00 EWT
10/27/1918 02:00 EST
3/30/1919 02:00 EWT
10/26/1919 02:00 EST
2/09/1942 02:00 EWT
9/30/1945 02:00 EST
4/27/1947 02:00 EDT
9/28/1947 02:00 EST
4/25/1948 02:00 EDT
9/26/1948 02:00 EST
4/24/1949 02:00 EDT
9/25/1949 02:00 EST
4/30/1950 02:00 EDT
9/24/1950 02:00 EST
4/29/1951 02:00 EDT
9/30/1951 02:00 EST
4/27/1952 02:00 EDT
9/28/1952 02:00 EST
4/26/1953 02:00 EDT
9/27/1953 02:00 EST
4/25/1954 02:00 EDT
9/26/1954 02:00 EST
4/24/1955 02:00 EDT
10/02/1955 02:00 EST
4/29/1956 02:00 EDT
9/30/1956 02:00 EST
4/28/1957 02:00 EDT
9/29/1957 02:00 EST
4/27/1958 02:00 EDT
9/28/1958 02:00 EST
4/26/1959 02:00 EDT
9/27/1959 02:00 EST
4/24/1960 02:00 EDT
9/25/1960 02:00 EST
4/30/1961 02:00 EDT
9/24/1961 02:00 EST
4/29/1962 02:00 US#2
....
PA # 55
Before 4/13/1887 LMT
4/13/1887 12:00 EST
3/31/1918 02:00 EWT
10/27/1918 02:00 EST
3/30/1919 02:00 EWT
10/26/1919 02:00 EST
2/09/1942 02:00 EWT
9/30/1945 02:00 EST
4/25/1948 02:00 EDT
9/26/1948 02:00 EST
4/24/1949 02:00 EDT
9/25/1949 02:00 EST
4/30/1950 02:00 EDT
9/24/1950 02:00 EST
4/29/1951 02:00 EDT
9/30/1951 02:00 EST
4/27/1952 02:00 EDT
9/28/1952 02:00 EST
4/26/1953 02:00 EDT
9/27/1953 02:00 EST
4/25/1954 02:00 EDT
9/26/1954 02:00 EST
4/24/1955 02:00 EDT
9/25/1955 02:00 EST
4/29/1956 02:00 EDT
9/30/1956 02:00 EST
4/28/1957 02:00 EDT
9/29/1957 02:00 EST
4/27/1958 02:00 EDT
9/28/1958 02:00 EST
4/26/1959 02:00 EDT
9/27/1959 02:00 EST
4/24/1960 02:00 EDT
9/25/1960 02:00 EST
4/30/1961 02:00 US#2
....
PA # 56
Before 4/13/1887 LMT
4/13/1887 12:00 EST
3/31/1918 02:00 EWT
10/27/1918 02:00 EST
3/30/1919 02:00 EWT
10/26/1919 02:00 EST
2/09/1942 02:00 EWT
9/30/1945 02:00 EST
4/30/1950 02:00 US#2
....
PA # 57
Before 4/13/1887 LMT
4/13/1887 12:00 EST
3/31/1918 02:00 EWT
10/27/1918 02:00 EST
3/30/1919 02:00 EWT
10/26/1919 02:00 EST
2/09/1942 02:00 EWT
9/30/1945 02:00 EST
4/25/1948 02:00 EDT
9/26/1948 02:00 EST
4/26/1953 02:00 EDT
9/27/1953 02:00 EST
4/25/1954 02:00 EDT
9/26/1954 02:00 EST
4/24/1955 02:00 EDT
10/09/1955 02:00 EST
4/29/1956 02:00 EDT
9/30/1956 02:00 EST
4/28/1957 02:00 EDT
9/29/1957 02:00 EST
4/27/1958 02:00 EDT
9/28/1958 02:00 EST
4/26/1959 02:00 EDT
9/27/1959 02:00 EST
4/24/1960 02:00 US#2
....
PA # 58
Before 4/13/1887 LMT
4/13/1887 12:00 PA#3
9/01/1941 02:00 PA#1
4/30/1967 02:00 US#1
....
PA # 59
Before 4/13/1887 LMT
4/13/1887 12:00 EST
3/31/1918 02:00 EWT
10/27/1918 02:00 EST
3/30/1919 02:00 EWT
10/26/1919 02:00 EST
2/09/1942 02:00 EWT
9/30/1945 02:00 EST
4/29/1951 02:00 US#2
....
PA # 60
Before 4/13/1887 LMT
4/13/1887 12:00 EST
3/31/1918 02:00 EWT
10/27/1918 02:00 EST
3/30/1919 02:00 EWT
10/26/1919 02:00 EST
2/09/1942 02:00 EWT
9/30/1945 02:00 EST
4/29/1951 02:00 EDT
9/30/1951 02:00 EST
4/29/1956 02:00 US#2
....
PA # 61
Before 4/13/1887 LMT
4/13/1887 12:00 EST
3/31/1918 02:00 EWT
10/27/1918 02:00 EST
3/30/1919 02:00 EWT
10/26/1919 02:00 EST
4/27/1941 02:00 EDT
9/26/1941 02:00 PA#1
4/30/1967 02:00 US#1
....
PA # 62
Before 4/13/1887 LMT
4/13/1887 12:00 EST
3/31/1918 02:00 EWT
10/27/1918 02:00 EST
3/30/1919 02:00 EWT
10/26/1919 02:00 EST
2/09/1942 02:00 EWT
9/30/1945 02:00 EST
4/26/1953 02:00 EDT
9/27/1953 02:00 EST
4/25/1954 02:00 EDT
9/26/1954 02:00 EST
4/24/1955 02:00 EDT
10/02/1955 00:00 EST
4/29/1956 02:00 EDT
9/30/1956 02:00 EST
4/28/1957 02:00 EDT
9/29/1957 02:00 EST
4/27/1958 02:00 EDT
9/28/1958 02:00 EST
4/26/1959 02:00 EDT
9/27/1959 02:00 EST
4/24/1960 02:00 US#2
....
PA # 63
Before 4/13/1887 LMT
4/13/1887 12:00 PA#7
4/24/1955 02:00 EDT
9/25/1955 02:00 EST
4/29/1956 02:00 EDT
9/30/1956 02:00 EST
4/28/1957 02:00 EDT
9/29/1957 02:00 EST
4/27/1958 02:00 EDT
9/28/1958 02:00 EST
4/26/1959 02:00 EDT
9/27/1959 02:00 EST
4/24/1960 02:00 US#2
....
PA # 64
Before 4/13/1887 LMT
4/13/1887 12:00 EST
3/31/1918 02:00 EWT
10/27/1918 02:00 EST
3/30/1919 02:00 EWT
10/26/1919 02:00 EST
2/09/1942 02:00 EWT
9/30/1945 02:00 EST
4/25/1954 02:00 US#2
....
PA # 65
Before 4/13/1887 LMT
4/13/1887 12:00 EST
3/31/1918 02:00 EWT
10/27/1918 02:00 EST
3/30/1919 02:00 EWT
10/26/1919 02:00 EST
2/09/1942 02:00 EWT
9/30/1945 02:00 EST
4/24/1955 02:00 US#2
....
PA # 66
Before 4/13/1887 LMT
4/13/1887 12:00 EST
3/31/1918 02:00 EWT
10/27/1918 02:00 EST
3/30/1919 02:00 EWT
10/26/1919 02:00 EST
2/09/1942 02:00 EWT
9/30/1945 02:00 EST
4/29/1956 02:00 EDT
9/30/1956 02:00 EST
4/28/1957 02:00 US#2
....
PA # 67
Before 4/13/1887 LMT
4/13/1887 12:00 EST
3/31/1918 02:00 EWT
10/27/1918 02:00 EST
3/30/1919 02:00 EWT
10/26/1919 02:00 EST
4/26/1931 02:00 EDT
9/27/1931 02:00 EST
4/24/1932 02:00 EDT
9/25/1932 02:00 EST
4/30/1933 02:00 EDT
9/24/1933 02:00 EST
4/29/1934 02:00 EDT
9/30/1934 02:00 EST
4/28/1935 02:00 EDT
9/29/1935 02:00 EST
4/26/1936 02:00 EDT
9/27/1936 02:00 EST
4/25/1937 02:00 EDT
9/26/1937 02:00 EST
4/24/1938 02:00 EDT
9/25/1938 02:00 EST
4/30/1939 02:00 EDT
9/24/1939 02:00 EST
4/28/1940 02:00 EDT
9/29/1940 02:00 EST
4/27/1941 02:00 EDT
9/28/1941 02:00 EST
2/09/1942 02:00 EWT
9/30/1945 02:00 EST
4/28/1946 02:00 EDT
9/29/1946 02:00 EST
4/27/1947 02:00 EDT
9/28/1947 02:00 EST
4/25/1948 02:00 EDT
9/26/1948 02:00 EST
4/24/1949 02:00 EDT
9/25/1949 02:00 EST
4/30/1950 02:00 EDT
9/24/1950 02:00 EST
4/29/1951 02:00 EDT
9/30/1951 02:00 EST
4/27/1952 02:00 EDT
9/28/1952 02:00 EST
4/26/1953 02:00 EDT
9/27/1953 02:00 EST
4/25/1954 02:00 EDT
9/26/1954 02:00 EST
4/24/1955 02:00 EDT
10/30/1955 02:00 EST
4/29/1956 02:00 EDT
10/28/1956 02:00 EST
4/28/1957 02:00 EDT
9/29/1957 02:00 EST
4/27/1958 02:00 EDT
9/28/1958 02:00 EST
4/26/1959 02:00 US#2
....
PA # 68
Before 4/13/1887 LMT
4/13/1887 12:00 PA#3
4/27/1958 02:00 EDT
9/28/1958 02:00 EST
4/26/1959 02:00 EDT
9/27/1959 02:00 EST
4/24/1960 02:00 EDT
9/25/1960 02:00 EST
4/30/1961 02:00 US#2
....
PA # 69
Before 4/13/1887 LMT
4/13/1887 12:00 EST
3/31/1918 02:00 EWT
10/27/1918 02:00 EST
3/30/1919 02:00 EWT
10/26/1919 02:00 EST
2/09/1942 02:00 EWT
9/30/1945 02:00 EST
4/28/1946 02:00 EDT
9/29/1946 02:00 EST
4/27/1947 02:00 EDT
9/28/1947 02:00 EST
4/29/1951 02:00 US#2
....
PA # 70
Before 4/13/1887 LMT
4/13/1887 12:00 EST
3/31/1918 02:00 EWT
10/27/1918 02:00 EST
3/30/1919 02:00 EWT
10/26/1919 02:00 EST
2/09/1942 02:00 EWT
9/30/1945 02:00 EST
4/28/1946 02:00 EDT
9/29/1946 02:00 EST
4/27/1947 02:00 EDT
9/28/1947 02:00 EST
4/25/1948 02:00 EDT
9/26/1948 02:00 EST
4/24/1949 02:00 EDT
9/25/1949 02:00 EST
4/30/1950 02:00 EDT
9/24/1950 02:00 EST
4/29/1951 02:00 EDT
9/30/1951 02:00 EST
4/27/1952 02:00 EDT
9/28/1952 02:00 EST
4/26/1953 02:00 EDT
9/27/1953 02:00 EST
4/25/1954 02:00 EDT
9/26/1954 02:00 EST
4/29/1956 02:00 EDT
9/30/1956 02:00 EST
4/28/1957 02:00 EDT
9/29/1957 02:00 EST
4/27/1958 02:00 US#2
....
PA # 71
Before 4/13/1887 LMT
4/13/1887 12:00 PA#3
9/28/1952 02:00 EST
4/29/1956 02:00 US#2
....
PA # 72
Before 4/13/1887 LMT
4/13/1887 12:00 EST
3/31/1918 02:00 EWT
10/27/1918 02:00 EST
3/30/1919 02:00 EWT
10/26/1919 02:00 EST
4/30/1933 02:00 EDT
9/24/1933 02:00 EST
4/27/1941 02:00 EDT
9/28/1941 02:00 EST
2/09/1942 02:00 EWT
9/30/1945 02:00 EST
4/28/1946 02:00 EDT
9/29/1946 02:00 EST
4/27/1947 02:00 EDT
9/28/1947 02:00 EST
4/25/1948 02:00 EDT
9/26/1948 02:00 EST
4/24/1949 02:00 EDT
9/25/1949 02:00 EST
4/30/1950 02:00 EDT
9/24/1950 02:00 EST
4/29/1956 02:00 US#2
....
PA # 73
Before 4/13/1887 LMT
4/13/1887 12:00 PA#1
4/24/1955 02:00 EDT
9/25/1955 02:00 EST
4/29/1956 02:00 EDT
9/30/1956 02:00 EST
4/28/1957 02:00 EDT
9/29/1957 02:00 EST
4/27/1958 02:00 EDT
9/28/1958 02:00 EST
4/26/1959 02:00 EDT
9/27/1959 02:00 EST
4/24/1960 02:00 US#2

TIME TABLES

PA # 74
Before 4/13/1887 LMT
4/13/1887 12:00 EST
3/31/1918 02:00 EWT
10/27/1918 02:00 EST
3/30/1919 02:00 EWT
10/26/1919 02:00 EST
4/24/1921 02:00 EDT
9/25/1921 02:00 EST
4/30/1922 02:00 EDT
9/24/1922 02:00 EST
4/29/1923 02:00 EDT
9/30/1923 02:00 EST
4/27/1924 02:00 EDT
9/28/1924 02:00 EST
4/26/1925 02:00 EDT
9/27/1925 02:00 EST
4/25/1926 02:00 EDT
9/26/1926 02:00 EST
4/24/1927 02:00 EDT
9/25/1927 02:00 EST
4/29/1928 02:00 EDT
9/30/1928 02:00 EST
4/28/1929 02:00 EDT
9/29/1929 02:00 EST
4/27/1930 02:00 EDT
9/28/1930 02:00 EST
4/26/1931 02:00 EDT
9/27/1931 02:00 EST
4/24/1932 02:00 EDT
9/25/1932 02:00 EST
4/30/1933 02:00 EDT
9/24/1933 02:00 EST
4/29/1934 02:00 EDT
9/30/1934 02:00 EST
4/28/1935 02:00 EDT
9/29/1935 02:00 EST
4/26/1936 02:00 EDT
9/27/1936 02:00 EST
4/25/1937 02:00 EDT
9/26/1937 02:00 EST
4/24/1938 02:00 EDT
9/25/1938 02:00 EST
4/30/1939 02:00 EDT
9/24/1939 02:00 EST
4/28/1940 02:00 EDT
9/29/1940 02:00 EST
4/27/1941 02:00 EDT
9/28/1941 02:00 EST
2/09/1942 02:00 EWT
9/30/1945 02:00 EST
4/28/1946 02:00 EDT
9/29/1946 02:00 EST
4/27/1947 02:00 EDT
9/28/1947 02:00 EST
4/25/1948 02:00 EDT
9/26/1948 02:00 EST
4/24/1949 02:00 EDT
9/25/1949 02:00 EST
4/30/1950 02:00 EDT
9/24/1950 02:00 EST
4/29/1951 02:00 EDT
9/30/1951 02:00 EST
4/27/1952 02:00 EDT
9/28/1952 02:00 EST
4/26/1953 02:00 EDT
9/27/1953 02:00 EST
4/25/1954 02:00 EDT
9/26/1954 02:00 EST
4/24/1955 02:00 EDT
10/30/1955 02:00 EST
4/29/1956 02:00 EDT
9/30/1956 02:00 EST
4/28/1957 02:00 EDT
9/29/1957 02:00 EST
4/27/1958 02:00 EDT
9/28/1958 02:00 EST
4/26/1959 02:00 EDT
9/27/1959 02:00 EST
4/24/1960 02:00 US#2

PA # 75
Before 4/13/1887 LMT
4/13/1887 12:00 PA#3
4/28/1946 02:00 EDT
9/29/1946 02:00 EST
4/27/1947 02:00 EDT
9/28/1947 02:00 EST
4/25/1948 02:00 EDT
9/26/1948 02:00 EST
4/24/1949 02:00 EDT
9/25/1949 02:00 EST
4/30/1950 02:00 EDT
9/24/1950 02:00 EST
4/29/1951 02:00 EDT
9/30/1951 02:00 EST
4/27/1952 02:00 EDT
9/28/1952 02:00 EST
4/26/1953 02:00 EDT
9/27/1953 02:00 EST
4/25/1954 02:00 EDT
9/26/1954 02:00 EST
4/24/1955 02:00 EDT
9/25/1955 02:00 EST
4/29/1956 02:00 EDT
9/30/1956 02:00 EST
4/28/1957 02:00 US#2

PA # 76
Before 4/13/1887 LMT
4/13/1887 12:00 EST
3/31/1918 02:00 EWT
10/27/1918 02:00 EST
3/30/1919 02:00 EWT
10/26/1919 02:00 EST
2/09/1942 02:00 EWT
9/30/1945 02:00 EST
4/28/1946 02:00 EDT
9/29/1946 02:00 EST
4/27/1947 02:00 EDT
9/28/1947 02:00 EST
4/25/1948 02:00 EDT
9/26/1948 02:00 EST
4/24/1949 02:00 EDT
9/25/1949 02:00 EST
4/30/1950 02:00 EDT
9/24/1950 02:00 EST
4/29/1951 02:00 EDT
9/30/1951 02:00 EST
4/27/1952 02:00 EDT
9/28/1952 02:00 EST
4/26/1953 02:00 EDT
9/27/1953 02:00 EST
4/25/1954 02:00 EDT
9/26/1954 02:00 EST
4/24/1955 02:00 EDT
9/25/1955 02:00 EST
4/29/1956 02:00 EDT
10/28/1956 02:00 EST
4/28/1957 02:00 EDT
9/29/1957 02:00 EST
4/27/1958 02:00 EDT
9/28/1958 02:00 EST
4/26/1959 02:00 US#2

PA # 77
Before 4/13/1887 LMT
4/13/1887 12:00 EST
3/31/1918 02:00 EWT
10/27/1918 02:00 EST
3/30/1919 02:00 EWT
10/26/1919 02:00 EST
4/27/1930 02:00 EDT
9/28/1930 02:00 EST
4/26/1931 02:00 EDT
9/27/1931 02:00 EST
4/24/1932 02:00 EDT
9/25/1932 02:00 EST
4/30/1933 02:00 EDT
9/24/1933 02:00 EST
4/29/1934 02:00 EDT
9/30/1934 02:00 EST
4/28/1935 02:00 EDT
9/29/1935 02:00 EST
4/26/1936 02:00 EDT
9/27/1936 02:00 EST
4/25/1937 02:00 EDT
9/26/1937 02:00 EST
4/24/1938 02:00 EDT
9/25/1938 02:00 EST
4/30/1939 02:00 EDT
9/24/1939 02:00 EST
4/28/1940 02:00 EDT
9/29/1940 02:00 EST
4/27/1941 02:00 EDT
9/28/1941 02:00 EST
2/09/1942 02:00 EWT
9/30/1945 02:00 EST
4/28/1946 02:00 EDT
9/29/1946 02:00 EST
4/29/1956 02:00 EDT
9/30/1956 02:00 EST
4/28/1957 02:00 US#2

PA # 78
Before 4/13/1887 LMT
4/13/1887 12:00 EST
3/31/1918 02:00 EWT
10/27/1918 02:00 EST
3/30/1919 02:00 EWT
10/26/1919 02:00 EST
4/27/1924 02:00 US#2

PA # 79
Before 4/13/1887 LMT
4/13/1887 12:00 EST
3/31/1918 02:00 EWT
10/27/1918 02:00 EST
3/30/1919 02:00 EWT
10/26/1919 02:00 EST
2/09/1942 02:00 EWT
9/30/1945 02:00 EST
4/27/1947 02:00 EDT
9/28/1947 02:00 EST
4/25/1948 02:00 EDT
9/26/1948 02:00 EST
4/24/1949 02:00 EDT
9/25/1949 02:00 EST
4/30/1950 02:00 EDT
9/24/1950 02:00 EST
4/29/1951 02:00 EDT
9/30/1951 02:00 EST
4/27/1952 02:00 EDT
9/28/1952 02:00 EST
4/26/1953 02:00 EDT
9/27/1953 02:00 EST
4/25/1954 02:00 EDT
9/26/1954 02:00 EST
4/24/1955 02:00 EDT
9/25/1955 02:00 EST
4/29/1956 02:00 EDT
9/30/1956 02:00 EST
4/28/1957 02:00 EDT
9/29/1957 02:00 EST
4/27/1958 02:00 EDT
9/28/1958 02:00 EST
4/26/1959 02:00 US#2

PA # 80
Before 4/13/1887 LMT
4/13/1887 12:00 EST
3/31/1918 02:00 EWT
10/27/1918 02:00 EST
3/30/1919 02:00 EWT
10/26/1919 02:00 EST
4/24/1932 02:00 US#2

PA # 81
Before 4/13/1887 LMT
4/13/1887 12:00 PA#1
4/24/1955 02:00 EDT
9/25/1955 02:00 EST
4/29/1956 02:00 EDT
9/30/1956 02:00 EST
4/28/1957 02:00 EDT
9/29/1957 02:00 EST
4/27/1958 02:00 EDT
9/28/1958 02:00 EST
4/26/1959 02:00 EDT
9/27/1959 02:00 EST
4/24/1960 02:00 EDT
9/25/1960 02:00 EST
4/30/1961 02:00 US#2

PA # 82
Before 4/13/1887 LMT
4/13/1887 12:00 EST
3/31/1918 02:00 EWT
10/27/1918 02:00 EST
3/30/1919 02:00 EWT
10/26/1919 02:00 EST
2/09/1942 02:00 EWT
9/30/1945 02:00 EST
4/28/1946 02:00 EDT
9/29/1946 02:00 EST
4/27/1947 02:00 EDT
9/28/1947 02:00 EST
4/25/1948 02:00 EDT
9/26/1948 02:00 EST
4/24/1949 02:00 EDT
9/25/1949 02:00 EST
4/30/1950 02:00 EDT
9/24/1950 02:00 EST
4/29/1951 02:00 EDT
9/30/1951 02:00 EST
4/27/1952 02:00 EDT
9/28/1952 02:00 EST
4/26/1953 02:00 EDT
9/27/1953 02:00 EST
4/25/1954 02:00 EDT
9/26/1954 02:00 EST
4/24/1955 02:00 EDT
9/25/1955 02:00 EST
4/29/1956 02:00 EDT
9/30/1956 02:00 EST
4/28/1957 02:00 EDT
9/29/1957 02:00 EST
4/27/1958 02:00 EDT
9/28/1958 02:00 EST
4/26/1959 02:00 US#2

PA # 83
Before 4/13/1887 LMT
4/13/1887 12:00 EST
3/31/1918 02:00 EWT
10/27/1918 02:00 EST
3/30/1919 02:00 EWT
10/26/1919 02:00 EST
4/30/1939 02:00 EDT
9/24/1939 02:00 EST
2/09/1942 02:00 EWT
9/30/1945 02:00 EST
4/28/1946 02:00 EDT
9/29/1946 02:00 EST
4/27/1947 02:00 EDT
9/28/1947 02:00 EST
4/25/1948 02:00 EDT
9/26/1948 02:00 EST
4/24/1949 02:00 EDT
9/25/1949 02:00 EST
4/30/1950 02:00 EDT
9/24/1950 02:00 EST
4/29/1951 02:00 EDT
9/30/1951 02:00 EST
4/27/1952 02:00 EDT
9/28/1952 02:00 EST
4/26/1953 02:00 EDT
9/27/1953 02:00 EST
4/25/1954 02:00 EDT
9/26/1954 02:00 EST
4/24/1955 02:00 EDT
9/25/1955 02:00 EST
4/29/1956 02:00 EDT
9/30/1956 02:00 EST
4/28/1957 02:00 EDT
9/29/1957 02:00 EST
4/27/1958 02:00 EDT
9/28/1958 02:00 EST
4/26/1959 02:00 EDT
9/27/1959 02:00 EST
4/24/1960 02:00 EDT
9/25/1960 02:00 EST
4/30/1961 02:00 US#2

PA # 84
Before 4/13/1887 LMT
4/13/1887 12:00 EST
3/31/1918 02:00 EWT
10/27/1918 02:00 EST
3/30/1919 02:00 EWT
10/26/1919 02:00 EST
4/29/1934 02:00 EDT
9/30/1934 02:00 EST
4/28/1935 02:00 EDT
9/29/1935 02:00 EST
4/26/1936 02:00 EDT
9/27/1936 02:00 EST
4/25/1937 02:00 EDT
9/26/1937 02:00 EST
4/24/1938 02:00 EDT
9/25/1938 02:00 EST
4/30/1939 02:00 EDT
9/24/1939 02:00 EST
4/28/1940 02:00 EDT
9/29/1940 02:00 EST
4/27/1941 02:00 EDT
9/28/1941 02:00 EST
2/09/1942 02:00 EWT
9/30/1945 02:00 EST
4/28/1946 02:00 EDT
9/29/1946 02:00 EST
4/27/1947 02:00 EDT
9/28/1947 02:00 EST
4/25/1948 02:00 EDT
9/26/1948 02:00 EST
4/24/1949 02:00 EDT
9/25/1949 02:00 EST
4/30/1950 02:00 EDT
9/24/1950 02:00 EST
4/29/1951 02:00 EDT
9/30/1951 02:00 EST
4/27/1952 02:00 EDT
9/28/1952 02:00 EST
4/26/1953 02:00 EDT
9/27/1953 02:00 EST
4/25/1954 02:00 EDT
9/26/1954 02:00 EST
4/24/1955 02:00 EDT
9/25/1955 02:00 EST
4/29/1956 02:00 US#2

PA # 85
Before 4/13/1887 LMT
4/13/1887 12:00 EST
3/31/1918 02:00 EWT
10/27/1918 02:00 EST
3/30/1919 02:00 EWT
10/26/1919 02:00 EST
4/24/1938 02:00 EDT
9/25/1938 02:00 EST
4/30/1939 02:00 EDT
9/24/1939 02:00 EST
4/28/1940 02:00 EDT
9/29/1940 02:00 EST
4/27/1941 02:00 EDT
9/28/1941 02:00 EST
2/09/1942 02:00 EWT
9/30/1945 02:00 EST
4/28/1946 02:00 EDT
9/29/1946 02:00 EST
4/27/1947 02:00 EDT
9/28/1947 02:00 EST
4/25/1948 02:00 EDT
9/26/1948 02:00 EST
4/24/1949 02:00 EDT
9/25/1949 02:00 EST
4/30/1950 02:00 EDT
9/24/1950 02:00 EST
4/29/1951 02:00 EDT
9/30/1951 02:00 EST
4/27/1952 02:00 EDT
9/28/1952 02:00 EST
4/26/1953 02:00 EDT
9/27/1953 02:00 EST
4/25/1954 02:00 EDT
9/26/1954 02:00 EST
4/24/1955 02:00 EDT
9/25/1955 02:00 EST
4/29/1956 02:00 EDT
9/30/1956 02:00 EST
4/28/1957 02:00 EDT
9/29/1957 02:00 EST
4/27/1958 02:00 EDT
9/28/1958 02:00 EST
4/26/1959 02:00 EDT
9/27/1959 02:00 EST
4/24/1960 02:00 US#2

PA # 86
Before 4/13/1887 LMT
4/13/1887 12:00 EST
3/31/1918 02:00 EWT
10/27/1918 02:00 EST
3/30/1919 02:00 EWT
10/26/1919 02:00 EST
4/24/1938 02:00 EDT
9/25/1938 02:00 EST
4/30/1939 02:00 EDT
9/24/1939 02:00 EST
4/28/1940 02:00 EDT
9/29/1940 02:00 EST
4/27/1941 02:00 EDT
9/28/1941 02:00 EST
2/09/1942 02:00 EWT
9/30/1945 02:00 EST
4/29/1956 02:00 US#2

PA # 87
Before 4/13/1887 LMT
4/13/1887 12:00 PA#3
9/29/1946 02:00 EST
4/29/1956 02:00 US#2

PA # 88
Before 4/13/1887 LMT
4/13/1887 12:00 EST
3/31/1918 02:00 EWT
10/27/1918 02:00 EST
3/30/1919 02:00 EWT
10/26/1919 02:00 EST
2/09/1942 02:00 EWT
9/30/1945 02:00 EST
4/27/1947 02:00 EDT
9/28/1947 02:00 EST
4/25/1948 02:00 EDT
9/26/1948 02:00 EST
4/24/1949 02:00 EDT
9/25/1949 02:00 EST
4/30/1950 02:00 EDT
9/24/1950 02:00 EST
4/29/1951 02:00 EDT
9/30/1951 02:00 EST
4/27/1952 02:00 EDT
9/28/1952 02:00 EST
4/26/1953 02:00 EDT
9/27/1953 02:00 EST
4/25/1954 02:00 EDT
9/26/1954 02:00 EST
4/24/1955 02:00 EDT
9/25/1955 02:00 EST
4/29/1956 02:00 US#2

PA # 89
Before 4/13/1887 LMT
4/13/1887 12:00 PA#5
4/24/1955 02:00 EDT
9/25/1955 02:00 EST
4/29/1956 02:00 EDT
9/30/1956 02:00 EST
4/28/1957 02:00 EDT
9/29/1957 02:00 EST
4/27/1958 02:00 US#2

PA # 90
Before 4/13/1887 LMT
4/13/1887 12:00 EST
3/31/1918 02:00 EWT
10/27/1918 02:00 EST
3/30/1919 02:00 EWT
10/26/1919 02:00 EST
4/29/1928 02:00 US#2

PA # 91
Before 4/13/1887 LMT
4/13/1887 12:00 EST
3/31/1918 02:00 EWT
10/27/1918 02:00 EST
3/30/1919 02:00 EWT
10/26/1919 02:00 EST
4/28/1940 02:00 EDT
9/02/1940 02:00 EST
4/27/1941 02:00 EDT
9/28/1941 02:00 EST
2/09/1942 02:00 EWT
9/30/1945 02:00 EST
4/28/1946 02:00 EDT
9/29/1946 02:00 EST
4/27/1947 02:00 EDT
9/28/1947 02:00 EST
4/25/1948 02:00 EDT
9/26/1948 02:00 EST
4/24/1949 02:00 EDT
9/25/1949 02:00 EST
4/30/1950 02:00 EDT
9/24/1950 02:00 EST
4/29/1951 02:00 EDT
9/30/1951 02:00 EST
4/27/1952 02:00 EDT
9/28/1952 02:00 EST
4/26/1953 02:00 EDT
9/27/1953 02:00 EST
4/25/1954 02:00 EDT
9/26/1954 02:00 EST
4/24/1955 02:00 EDT
9/25/1955 02:00 EST
4/29/1956 02:00 EDT
10/28/1956 02:00 EST
4/28/1957 02:00 EDT
9/29/1957 02:00 EST
4/27/1958 02:00 EDT
9/28/1958 02:00 EST
4/26/1959 02:00 EDT
9/27/1959 02:00 EST
4/24/1960 02:00 US#2

PA # 92
Before 4/13/1887 LMT
4/13/1887 12:00 EST
3/31/1918 02:00 EWT
10/27/1918 02:00 EST
3/30/1919 02:00 EWT
10/26/1919 02:00 EST
2/09/1942 02:00 EWT
9/30/1945 02:00 EST
4/25/1948 02:00 EDT
9/26/1948 02:00 EST
4/26/1953 02:00 EDT
9/27/1953 02:00 EST
4/25/1954 02:00 EDT
9/26/1954 02:00 EST
4/24/1955 02:00 EDT
9/25/1955 02:00 EST
4/29/1956 02:00 EDT
9/30/1956 02:00 EST
4/28/1957 02:00 EDT
9/29/1957 02:00 EST
4/27/1958 02:00 EDT
9/28/1958 02:00 EST
4/26/1959 02:00 EDT
9/27/1959 02:00 EST
4/24/1960 02:00 US#2

PA # 93
Before 4/13/1887 LMT
4/13/1887 12:00 EST
3/31/1918 02:00 EWT
10/27/1918 02:00 EST
3/30/1919 02:00 EWT
10/26/1919 02:00 EST
2/09/1942 02:00 EWT
9/30/1945 02:00 EST
4/27/1947 02:00 EDT
9/28/1947 02:00 EST
4/29/1956 02:00 US#2

PA # 94
Before 4/13/1887 LMT
4/13/1887 12:00 EST
3/31/1918 02:00 EWT
10/27/1918 02:00 EST
3/30/1919 02:00 EWT
10/26/1919 02:00 EST
2/09/1942 02:00 EWT
9/30/1945 02:00 EST
4/24/1955 02:00 EDT
9/25/1955 02:00 EST
4/29/1956 02:00 EDT
9/30/1956 02:00 EST
4/28/1957 02:00 EDT

TIME TABLES

9/29/1957	02:00	EST
4/27/1958	02:00	EDT
9/28/1958	02:00	EST
4/26/1959	02:00	EDT
9/27/1959	02:00	EST
4/24/1960	02:00	US#2

PA # 95

Before 4/13/1887		LMT
4/13/1887	12:00	EST
3/31/1918	02:00	EWT
10/27/1918	02:00	EST
3/30/1919	02:00	EWT
10/26/1919	02:00	EST
4/24/1921	02:00	EDT
9/25/1921	02:00	EST
4/30/1922	02:00	EDT
9/24/1922	02:00	EST
4/29/1923	02:00	EDT
9/30/1923	02:00	EST
4/27/1924	02:00	EDT
9/28/1924	02:00	EST
4/26/1925	02:00	EDT
9/27/1925	02:00	EST
4/25/1926	02:00	EDT
9/26/1926	02:00	EST
4/24/1927	02:00	EDT
9/25/1927	02:00	EST
4/29/1928	02:00	EDT
9/30/1928	02:00	EST
4/28/1929	02:00	EDT
9/29/1929	02:00	EST
4/27/1930	02:00	EDT
9/28/1930	02:00	EST
4/26/1931	02:00	EDT
9/27/1931	02:00	EST
4/24/1932	02:00	EDT
9/25/1932	02:00	EST
4/30/1933	02:00	EDT
9/24/1933	02:00	EST
4/29/1934	02:00	EDT
9/30/1934	02:00	EST
4/28/1935	02:00	EDT
9/29/1935	02:00	EST
4/26/1936	02:00	EDT
9/27/1936	02:00	EST
4/25/1937	02:00	EDT
9/26/1937	02:00	EST
4/24/1938	02:00	EDT
9/25/1938	02:00	EST
4/30/1939	02:00	EDT
9/24/1939	02:00	EST
4/28/1940	02:00	EDT
9/29/1940	02:00	EST
4/27/1941	02:00	EDT
9/28/1941	02:00	EST
2/09/1942	02:00	EWT
9/30/1945	02:00	EST
4/28/1946	02:00	EDT
9/29/1946	02:00	EST
4/27/1947	02:00	EDT
9/28/1947	02:00	EST
4/25/1948	02:00	EDT
9/26/1948	02:00	EST
4/24/1949	02:00	EDT
9/25/1949	02:00	EST
4/30/1950	02:00	EDT
9/24/1950	02:00	EST
4/29/1951	02:00	EDT
9/30/1951	02:00	EST
4/27/1952	02:00	EDT
9/28/1952	02:00	EST
4/26/1953	02:00	EDT
9/27/1953	02:00	EST
4/25/1954	02:00	EDT
9/26/1954	02:00	EST
4/24/1955	02:00	EDT
10/30/1955	02:00	EST
4/29/1956	02:00	EDT
10/28/1956	02:00	EST
4/28/1957	02:00	EDT
9/29/1957	02:00	EST
4/27/1958	02:00	EDT
9/28/1958	02:00	EST
4/26/1959	02:00	US#2

PA # 96

Before 4/13/1887		LMT
4/13/1887	12:00	EST
3/31/1918	02:00	EWT
10/27/1918	02:00	EST
3/30/1919	02:00	EWT
10/26/1919	02:00	EST
4/24/1921	02:00	EDT
9/25/1921	02:00	EST
4/30/1922	02:00	EDT
9/24/1922	02:00	EST
4/29/1923	02:00	EDT
9/30/1923	02:00	EST
4/27/1924	02:00	EDT
9/28/1924	02:00	EST
4/26/1925	02:00	EDT
9/27/1925	02:00	EST
4/25/1926	02:00	EDT
9/26/1926	02:00	EST
4/24/1927	02:00	EDT
9/25/1927	02:00	EST
4/29/1928	02:00	EDT
9/30/1928	02:00	EST
4/28/1929	02:00	EDT
9/29/1929	02:00	EST
4/27/1930	02:00	EDT
9/28/1930	02:00	EST
4/26/1931	02:00	EDT
9/27/1931	02:00	EST
4/24/1932	02:00	EDT
9/25/1932	02:00	EST
4/30/1933	02:00	EDT
9/24/1933	02:00	EST
4/29/1934	02:00	EDT
9/30/1934	02:00	EST
4/28/1935	02:00	EDT
9/29/1935	02:00	EST
4/26/1936	02:00	EDT
9/27/1936	02:00	EST
4/25/1937	02:00	EDT
9/26/1937	02:00	EST
4/24/1938	02:00	EDT
9/25/1938	02:00	EST
4/30/1939	02:00	EDT
9/24/1939	02:00	EST
4/28/1940	02:00	EDT
9/29/1940	02:00	EST
4/27/1941	02:00	EDT
9/28/1941	02:00	EST
2/09/1942	02:00	EWT
9/30/1945	02:00	EST
4/26/1953	02:00	US#2

PA # 97

Before 4/13/1887		LMT
4/13/1887	12:00	EST
3/31/1918	02:00	EWT
10/27/1918	02:00	EST
3/30/1919	02:00	EWT
10/26/1919	02:00	EST
4/30/1932	02:00	US#2

PA # 98

Before 4/13/1887		LMT
4/13/1887	12:00	EST
3/31/1918	02:00	EWT
10/27/1918	02:00	EST
3/30/1919	02:00	EWT
10/26/1919	02:00	EST
2/09/1942	02:00	EWT
9/30/1945	02:00	EST
4/25/1954	02:00	US#3

PA # 99

Before 4/13/1887		LMT
4/13/1887	12:00	PA#3
9/21/1948	02:00	EST
4/24/1949	02:00	US#2

PA # 100

Before 4/13/1887		LMT
4/13/1887	12:00	EST
3/31/1918	02:00	EWT
10/27/1918	02:00	EST
3/30/1919	02:00	EWT
10/26/1919	02:00	EST
2/09/1942	02:00	EWT
9/30/1945	02:00	EST
4/28/1946	02:00	EDT
9/29/1946	02:00	EST
4/27/1947	02:00	EDT
9/28/1947	02:00	EST
4/25/1948	02:00	EDT
9/26/1948	02:00	EST
4/24/1949	02:00	EDT
9/25/1949	02:00	EST
4/30/1950	02:00	EDT
9/24/1950	02:00	EST
4/29/1951	02:00	EDT
9/30/1951	02:00	EST
4/27/1952	02:00	EDT
9/28/1952	02:00	EST
4/26/1953	02:00	EDT
9/27/1953	02:00	EST
4/25/1954	02:00	EDT
9/26/1954	02:00	EST
4/24/1955	02:00	EDT
9/25/1955	02:00	EST
4/29/1956	02:00	EDT
10/28/1956	02:00	EST
4/28/1957	02:00	EDT
9/29/1957	02:00	EST
4/27/1958	02:00	US#2

PA # 101

Before 4/13/1887		LMT
4/13/1887	12:00	PA#8
4/24/1955	02:00	EDT
9/25/1955	02:00	EST
4/29/1956	02:00	EDT
10/28/1956	02:00	EST
4/28/1957	02:00	EDT
10/27/1957	02:00	EST
4/27/1958	02:00	EDT
9/28/1958	02:00	EST
4/26/1959	02:00	US#2

PA # 102

Before 4/13/1887		LMT
4/13/1887	12:00	EST
3/31/1918	02:00	EWT
10/27/1918	02:00	EST
3/30/1919	02:00	EWT
10/26/1919	02:00	EST
4/28/1940	02:00	EDT
9/29/1940	02:00	EST
4/27/1941	02:00	EDT
9/01/1941	02:00	EST
2/09/1942	02:00	EWT
9/30/1945	02:00	EST
4/28/1946	02:00	US#2

PA # 103

Before 4/13/1887		LMT
4/13/1887	12:00	EST
3/31/1918	02:00	EWT
10/27/1918	02:00	EST
3/30/1919	02:00	EWT
10/26/1919	02:00	EST
2/09/1942	02:00	EWT
9/30/1945	02:00	EST
6/01/1946	02:00	EDT
8/31/1946	02:00	EST
4/25/1948	02:00	EDT
9/26/1948	02:00	EST
4/26/1953	02:00	US#2

PA # 104

Before 4/13/1887		LMT
4/13/1887	12:00	PA#3
9/15/1947	02:00	EST
4/25/1948	02:00	US#2

PA # 105

Before 4/13/1887		LMT
4/13/1887	12:00	EST
3/31/1918	02:00	EWT
10/27/1918	02:00	EST
3/30/1919	02:00	EWT
10/26/1919	02:00	EST
2/09/1942	02:00	EWT
9/30/1945	02:00	EST
4/25/1948	02:00	EDT
9/26/1948	02:00	EST
4/24/1949	02:00	EDT
9/04/1949	02:00	EST
4/30/1950	02:00	US#2

PA # 106

Before 4/13/1887		LMT
4/13/1887	12:00	EST
3/31/1918	02:00	EWT
10/27/1918	02:00	EST
3/30/1919	02:00	EWT
10/26/1919	02:00	EST
2/09/1942	02:00	EWT
9/30/1945	02:00	EST
4/27/1947	02:00	EDT
9/28/1947	02:00	EST
4/29/1948	02:00	EDT
9/01/1948	02:00	EST
4/24/1949	02:00	US#2

PA # 107

Before 7/01/1887		LMT
7/01/1887	12:00	EST
3/31/1918	02:00	EWT
10/27/1918	02:00	EST
3/30/1919	02:00	EWT
10/26/1919	02:00	EST
4/17/1921	02:00	EDT
10/23/1921	02:00	EST
4/16/1922	02:00	EDT
10/22/1922	02:00	EST
4/15/1923	02:00	EDT
10/28/1923	02:00	EST
4/20/1924	02:00	EDT
10/26/1924	02:00	EST
4/19/1925	02:00	EDT
10/25/1925	02:00	EST
4/18/1926	02:00	EDT
10/24/1926	02:00	EST
4/17/1927	02:00	EDT
10/23/1927	02:00	EST
4/15/1928	02:00	EDT
10/28/1928	02:00	EST
4/21/1929	02:00	EDT
10/27/1929	02:00	EST
4/20/1930	02:00	EDT
10/26/1930	02:00	EST
4/19/1931	02:00	EDT
10/25/1931	02:00	EST
4/17/1932	02:00	EDT
10/23/1932	02:00	EST
4/16/1933	02:00	EDT
10/22/1933	02:00	EST
4/15/1934	02:00	EDT
10/28/1934	02:00	EST
4/21/1935	02:00	EDT
10/27/1935	02:00	EST
4/19/1936	02:00	EDT
10/25/1936	02:00	EST
4/18/1937	02:00	EDT
10/24/1937	02:00	EST
4/17/1938	02:00	EDT
10/23/1938	02:00	EST
4/16/1939	02:00	EDT
10/22/1939	02:00	EST
5/13/1940	02:00	EDT
9/02/1940	02:00	EST
4/27/1941	02:00	EDT
9/28/1941	02:00	EST
2/09/1942	02:00	EWT
9/30/1945	02:00	EST
4/28/1946	02:00	EDT
9/29/1946	02:00	EST
4/27/1947	02:00	EDT
9/28/1947	02:00	EST
4/25/1948	02:00	EDT
9/26/1948	02:00	EST
4/24/1949	02:00	EDT
9/25/1949	02:00	EST
4/30/1950	02:00	EDT
9/24/1950	02:00	EST
4/29/1951	02:00	EDT
9/30/1951	02:00	EST
4/27/1952	02:00	EDT
9/28/1952	02:00	EST
4/26/1953	02:00	EDT
9/27/1953	02:00	EST
4/25/1954	02:00	EDT
9/26/1954	02:00	EST
4/24/1955	02:00	EDT
9/25/1955	02:00	EST
4/29/1956	02:00	EDT
9/30/1956	02:00	EST
4/28/1957	02:00	EDT
9/29/1957	02:00	EST
4/27/1958	02:00	EDT
9/28/1958	02:00	EST
4/26/1959	02:00	EDT
9/27/1959	02:00	EST
4/24/1960	02:00	US#2

PA # 108

Before 4/13/1887		LMT
4/13/1887	12:00	PA#2
9/24/1939	02:00	EST
5/01/1941	02:00	EDT
10/01/1941	02:00	EST
2/09/1942	02:00	EWT
9/30/1945	02:00	EST
4/29/1951	02:00	US#2

PA # 109

Before 4/13/1887		LMT
4/13/1887	12:00	PA#3
9/26/1948	02:00	EST
4/30/1949	02:00	US#2

PA # 110

Before 4/13/1887		LMT
4/13/1887	12:00	PA#4
4/30/1950	02:00	EDT
9/30/1950	02:00	EST
4/29/1951	02:00	EDT
9/30/1951	02:00	EST
4/27/1952	02:00	EDT
9/28/1952	02:00	EST
4/29/1956	02:00	US#2

PA # 111

Before 4/13/1887		LMT
4/13/1887	12:00	PA#1
9/26/1948	02:00	EST
4/27/1949	02:00	US#2

PA # 112

Before 4/13/1887		LMT
4/13/1887	12:00	EST
3/31/1918	02:00	EWT
10/27/1918	02:00	EST
3/30/1919	02:00	EWT
10/26/1919	02:00	EST
4/30/1933	02:00	EDT
9/24/1933	02:00	EST
4/25/1937	02:00	EDT
9/26/1937	02:00	EST
2/09/1942	02:00	EWT
9/30/1945	02:00	EST
4/28/1946	02:00	EDT
9/29/1946	02:00	EST
4/27/1947	02:00	EDT
9/28/1947	02:00	EST
4/25/1948	02:00	EDT
9/26/1948	02:00	EST
4/24/1949	02:00	EDT
9/25/1949	02:00	EST
4/30/1950	02:00	EDT
9/30/1950	02:00	EST
4/29/1951	02:00	EDT
9/30/1951	02:00	EST
4/27/1952	02:00	EDT
9/28/1952	02:00	EST
4/26/1953	02:00	EDT
9/27/1953	02:00	EST
4/25/1954	02:00	EDT
9/26/1954	02:00	EST
4/24/1955	02:00	EDT
10/30/1955	02:00	EST
4/29/1956	02:00	EDT
9/30/1956	02:00	EST
4/28/1957	02:00	EDT
9/29/1957	02:00	EST
4/27/1958	02:00	EDT
9/28/1958	02:00	EST
4/26/1959	02:00	US#2

PA # 113

Before 4/13/1887		LMT
4/13/1887	12:00	EST
3/31/1918	02:00	EWT
10/27/1918	02:00	EST
3/30/1919	02:00	EWT
10/26/1919	02:00	EST
2/09/1942	02:00	EWT
9/30/1945	02:00	EST
4/28/1946	02:00	EDT
10/31/1946	02:00	US#2

PA # 114

Before 1/01/1887		LMT
1/01/1887	12:00	EST
3/31/1918	02:00	EWT
10/27/1918	02:00	EST
3/30/1919	02:00	EWT
10/26/1919	02:00	EST
3/28/1920	02:00	EDT
10/31/1920	02:00	EST
4/24/1921	02:00	US#2

PA # 115

Before 4/13/1887		LMT
4/13/1887	12:00	EST
3/31/1918	02:00	EWT
10/27/1918	02:00	EST
3/30/1919	02:00	EWT
10/26/1919	02:00	EST
2/09/1942	02:00	EWT
9/30/1945	02:00	EST
4/25/1948	02:00	EDT
9/26/1948	02:00	EST
4/24/1949	02:00	EDT
9/25/1949	02:00	EST
4/30/1950	02:00	EDT
9/30/1950	02:00	US#2

PA # 116

Before 4/13/1887		LMT
4/13/1887	12:00	EST
3/31/1918	02:00	EWT
10/27/1918	02:00	EST
3/30/1919	02:00	EWT
10/26/1919	02:00	EST
2/09/1942	02:00	EWT
9/30/1945	02:00	EST
4/25/1948	02:00	EDT
9/26/1948	02:00	EST
4/30/1949	02:00	EDT
9/25/1949	02:00	US#2

PA # 117

Before 4/13/1887		LMT
4/13/1887	12:00	PA#3
4/30/1950	02:00	EDT
9/30/1950	02:00	EST
4/29/1951	02:00	EDT
9/30/1951	02:00	EST
4/27/1952	02:00	EDT
9/28/1952	02:00	EST
4/26/1953	02:00	EDT
9/27/1953	02:00	EST
4/25/1954	02:00	EDT
9/26/1954	02:00	EST
4/24/1955	02:00	EDT
10/30/1955	02:00	EST
4/29/1956	02:00	EDT
9/30/1956	02:00	EST
4/28/1957	02:00	US#2

PA # 118

Before 4/13/1887		LMT
4/13/1887	12:00	PA#8
9/29/1940	02:00	EST
5/01/1941	02:00	EDT
10/01/1941	02:00	US#2

PA # 119

Before 4/13/1887		LMT
4/13/1887	12:00	EST
3/31/1918	02:00	EWT
10/27/1918	02:00	EST
3/30/1919	02:00	EWT
10/26/1919	02:00	EST
4/30/1933	02:00	EDT
9/24/1933	02:00	EST
4/29/1934	02:00	EDT
9/30/1934	02:00	EST
4/28/1935	02:00	EDT
9/29/1935	02:00	EST
4/26/1936	02:00	EDT
9/27/1936	02:00	EST
4/25/1937	02:00	EDT
9/26/1937	02:00	EST
4/24/1938	02:00	EDT
9/25/1938	02:00	EST
4/30/1939	02:00	EDT
9/24/1939	02:00	EST
4/28/1940	02:00	EDT
9/29/1940	02:00	EST
4/27/1941	02:00	EDT
9/28/1941	02:00	EST
2/09/1942	02:00	EWT
9/30/1945	02:00	EST
4/28/1946	02:00	EDT
9/29/1946	02:00	EST
4/27/1947	02:00	EDT
9/28/1947	02:00	EST
4/25/1948	02:00	EDT
9/26/1948	02:00	EST
4/24/1949	02:00	EDT
9/25/1949	02:00	EST
4/30/1950	02:00	EDT
9/30/1950	02:00	EST
4/29/1951	02:00	US#2

PA # 120

Before 4/13/1887		LMT
4/13/1887	12:00	EST
3/31/1918	02:00	EWT
10/27/1918	02:00	EST
3/30/1919	02:00	EWT
10/26/1919	02:00	EST
6/14/1937	02:00	EDT
9/02/1937	02:00	EST
6/03/1939	02:00	EDT
9/04/1939	02:00	EST
4/28/1940	02:00	EDT
9/29/1940	02:00	EST
4/27/1941	02:00	EDT
9/28/1941	02:00	EST
2/09/1942	02:00	EWT
9/30/1945	02:00	EST
4/28/1946	02:00	EDT
9/29/1946	02:00	EST
4/27/1947	02:00	EDT
9/28/1947	02:00	EST
4/25/1948	02:00	EDT
9/26/1948	02:00	EST
4/24/1949	02:00	EDT
9/25/1949	02:00	EST
4/30/1950	02:00	EDT
9/24/1950	02:00	EST
4/29/1951	02:00	EDT
9/23/1951	02:00	EST
4/27/1952	02:00	EDT
9/28/1952	02:00	EST
4/26/1953	02:00	EDT
9/27/1953	02:00	EST
4/25/1954	02:00	EDT
9/26/1954	02:00	EST
4/24/1955	02:00	EDT
9/25/1955	02:00	EST
4/29/1956	02:00	EDT
9/30/1956	02:00	EST
4/28/1957	02:00	US#2

PA # 121

Before 4/13/1887		LMT
4/13/1887	12:00	EST
3/31/1918	02:00	EWT
10/27/1918	02:00	EST
3/30/1919	02:00	EWT
10/26/1919	02:00	EST

TIME TABLES

3/28/1920 02:00 EDT
10/30/1920 02:00 EST
4/24/1921 02:00 EDT
9/25/1921 02:00 EST
4/30/1922 02:00 EDT
9/24/1922 02:00 EST
4/29/1923 02:00 EDT
9/30/1923 02:00 EST
4/27/1924 02:00 EDT
9/28/1924 02:00 EST
4/26/1925 02:00 EDT
9/27/1925 02:00 EST
4/25/1926 02:00 EDT
9/26/1926 02:00 EST
4/24/1927 02:00 EDT
9/25/1927 02:00 EST
4/29/1928 02:00 EDT
9/30/1928 02:00 EST
4/28/1929 02:00 EDT
9/29/1929 02:00 EST
4/27/1930 02:00 EDT
9/28/1930 02:00 EST
4/26/1931 02:00 EDT
9/27/1931 02:00 EST
4/24/1932 02:00 EDT
9/25/1932 02:00 EST
4/29/1933 00:01 EDT
9/31/1933 00:01 EST
4/28/1934 00:01 EDT
9/29/1934 00:01 EST
5/04/1935 00:01 EDT
9/28/1935 00:01 EST
5/02/1936 00:01 EDT
10/03/1936 00:01 EST
5/01/1937 00:01 EDT
10/02/1937 00:01 EST
4/30/1938 00:01 EDT
10/01/1938 00:01 EST
4/29/1939 00:01 EDT
9/30/1939 00:01 EST
5/04/1940 00:01 EDT
9/28/1940 00:01 EST
5/03/1941 00:01 EDT
10/04/1941 00:01 EST
2/09/1942 02:00 EWT
9/30/1945 02:00 EST
4/28/1946 02:00 EDT
9/29/1946 02:00 EST
4/27/1947 02:00 EDT
9/28/1947 02:00 EST
4/25/1948 02:00 EDT
9/26/1948 02:00 EST
4/24/1949 02:00 EDT
9/25/1949 02:00 EST
4/30/1950 02:00 EDT
9/24/1950 02:00 EST
4/29/1951 02:00 EDT
9/30/1951 02:00 EST
4/27/1952 02:00 EDT
9/28/1952 02:00 EST
4/26/1953 02:00 EDT
9/27/1953 02:00 EST
4/25/1954 02:00 EDT
9/26/1954 02:00 EST
4/24/1955 02:00 EDT
10/30/1955 02:00 EST
4/29/1956 02:00 EDT
9/30/1956 02:00 EST
4/28/1957 02:00 EDT
9/29/1957 02:00 EST
4/27/1958 02:00 EDT
9/28/1958 02:00 EST
4/26/1959 02:00 US#2
....
PA # 122
Before 4/13/1887 LMT
4/13/1887 12:00 PA#6
9/27/1964 02:00 EST
4/25/1965 02:00 US#2
....
PA # 123
Before 4/13/1887 LMT
4/13/1887 12:00 EST
3/31/1918 02:00 EWT
10/27/1918 02:00 EST
3/30/1919 02:00 EWT
10/26/1919 02:00 EST
2/09/1942 02:00 EWT
9/30/1945 02:00 EST
4/30/1950 02:00 EDT
9/30/1950 02:00 EST
4/29/1951 02:00 US#2

COUNTIES

1 Adams
2 Allegheny
3 Armstrong
4 Beaver
5 Bedford
6 Berks
7 Blair
8 Bradford
9 Bucks
10 Butler
11 Cambria
12 Cameron
13 Carbon
14 Centre
15 Chester
16 Clarion
17 Clearfield
18 Clinton
19 Columbia
20 Crawford
21 Cumberland
22 Dauphin
23 Delaware
24 Elk
25 Erie
26 Fayette
27 Forest
28 Franklin
29 Fulton
30 Greene
31 Huntingdon
32 Indiana
33 Jefferson
34 Juniata
35 Lackawanna
36 Lancaster
37 Lawrence
38 Lebanon
39 Lehigh
40 Luzerne
41 Lycoming
42 McKean
43 Mercer
44 Mifflin
45 Monroe
46 Montgomery
47 Montour
48 Northampton
49 Northumberland
50 Perry
51 Philadelphia
52 Pike
53 Potter
54 Schuylkill
55 Snyder
56 Somerset
57 Sullivan
58 Susquehanna
59 Tioga
60 Union
61 Venango
62 Warren
63 Washington
64 Wayne
65 Westmoreland
66 Wyoming
67 York

Aaronsburg 14 52 40N53'59 77w27'13 5:09:49
Abbott 53 6 41N34'56 77w47'05 5:11:08
Abbottstown 1 1 39N53'11 76w59'06 5:07:56
Aberdeen 35 4 41N21'31 75w29'39 5:01:59
Aberdeen 36 2 40N10'36 76w37'25 5:06:30
Abington 46 2 40N07'14 75w07'06 5:00:28
Abrahams 46 90 40N06'46 75w22'39 5:01:31
Abrahamsville 64 6 41N45'51 75w07'26 5:00:30
Academia 34 7 40N29'47 77w28'34 5:09:54
Academy Corners 59 6 41N57 77w26 5:09:44
Acahela 45 94 41N06 75w36 5:02:24
Accomac 67 1 40N02'42 76w33'50 5:06:15
Acheson 63 6 40N11'42 80w27'05 5:21:48
Acker 50 1 40N29'50 77w03'37 5:08:14
Ackermanville 48 17 40N50'21 75w13'11 5:00:53
Ackworth 15 13 40N00'28 75w40'07 5:02:40
Acme 65 6 40N07'36 79w25'44 5:17:43
Acmetonia 2 14 40N32'27 79w48'58 5:19:16
Acosta 56 6 40N06'37 79w04'09 5:16:17
Adah 26 51 39N53'47 79w55'20 5:19:41
Adams 3 6 40N56'28 79w38'33 5:18:34
Adamsburg 65 3 40N18'42 79w39'23 5:18:38
Adams Corner 10 6 41N02 80w03 5:20:12
Adams Crossing 11 6 40N32'33 78w52'49 5:15:31
Adamsdale 54 27 40N38'10 76w07'42 5:04:31
Adams Hill 65 25 40N20 79w43 5:18:52
Adamstown 36 27 40N14'28 76w03'24 5:04:14
Adamsville 20 63 41N30'40 80w22'12 5:21:29
Adamsville 67 1 39N52'58 76w37'17 5:06:29
Addingham 23 9 39N57 75w18 5:01:12
Addison 56 53 39N44'50 79w20'22 5:17:21
Adelaide 26 104 40N02'36 79w37'27 5:18:30
Admire 67 39 39N57'43 76w52'15 5:07:29
Adrian 3 15 40N53'05 79w32'17 5:18:09
Adrian Furnace 17 56 41N07'55 78w47'02 5:15:08
Adrian Mines 33 51 40N59'05 78w57'38 5:15:51
Advance 32 72 40N42'31 79w15'44 5:17:03
Africa 28 51 39N50 77w55 5:11:40
Ahrensville 61 9 41N27'16 79w38'45 5:18:35
Aiden Lair 46 1 40N09 75w12 5:00:48
Aiken 42 6 41N52'41 78w34'41 5:14:19
Ailston 67 1 39N44'39 76w18'57 5:05:16
Airville 67 1 39N49'56 76w24'24 5:05:38
Airydale 31 85 40N29'04 77w52'04 5:11:28
Aitch 31 3 40N22'27 78w09'34 5:12:38
Ajax 61 109 41N21'16 79w47'27 5:19:10
Akeley 62 6 41N57'53 79w07'52 5:16:31
Akersville 29 6 39N58'42 78w11'53 5:12:48
Akron 36 28 40N09'24 76w12'09 5:04:49
Aladdin 3 2 40N41'30 79w39'25 5:18:38
Alaska 33 34 41N10'39 79w05'46 5:16:23
Alaska 49 27 40N47'01 76w26'16 5:05:45
Alba 8 7 41N42'18 76w49'43 5:07:19
Albany 26 56 40N02'16 79w52'18 5:19:29
Albany 39 56 40N37'00 75w52'01 5:03:28
Albert 40 6 41N07'13 75w55'53 5:03:44
Alberts Corners 40 20 41N14 75w52 5:03:28
Albidale 46 1 40N09 75w03 5:00:12
Albion 25 7 41N53'26 80w22'00 5:21:28
Albion 33 51 40N57'32 78w56'50 5:15:47
Albrightsville 13 94 41N00'52 75w36'05 5:02:24
Alburtis 39 13 40N30'39 75w36'12 5:02:25
Alcoa Center 65 14 40N32'18 79w38'43 5:18:35
Aldan 23 9 39N55'17 75w17'18 5:01:09
Alden 40 21 41N10'55 76w00'46 5:04:03
Aldenville 64 6 41N38'48 75w21'51 5:01:27
Alderson 40 6 41N22 76w02 5:04:08
Aldham 15 8 40N05'26 75w32'30 5:02:10
Aldovin 66 59 41N37'02 75w56'19 5:03:45
Aleppo 30 7 39N49'26 80w26'47 5:21:47
Alexander Springs 44 6 40N37'42 77w40'28 5:10:42
Alexandria 31 7 40N33'23 78w05'53 5:12:24
Alfarata 31 7 40N33'59 78w07'07 5:12:28
Alfarata 44 1 40N39'45 77w27'26 5:09:50
Alford 58 59 41N48'24 75w46'30 5:03:06
Alica 26 51 40N00'29 79w55'43 5:19:43
Alice 65 6 40N09'51 79w27'36 5:17:50
Alicia 26 51 40N02 79w55 5:19:40
Alinda 50 6 40N20'47 77w17'05 5:09:08
Aline 55 6 40N40'50 76w59'15 5:07:57
Aliquippa 4 13 40N38'12 80w14'25 5:20:58
Allandale 21 12 40N14 76w57 5:07:48
Allegany 53 6 41N52 77w54 5:11:36
Allegheny 2 114 40N28 80w01 5:20:04
Allegheny Acres 2 114 40N36'55 79w52'13 5:19:29
Allegheny Furnace 7 33 40N29'23 78w24'27 5:13:38
Allegheny Springs 62 3 41N49'36 79w18'15 5:17:13
Alleghenyville 6 101 40N14'03 75w59'20 5:03:57
Allemans 17 54 40N43'36 78w24'15 5:13:37
Allen 21 1 40N10 77w05 5:08:20
Allen 48 13 40N43 75w29 5:01:56
Allen Crest 39 13 40N39 75w30 5:02:00
Allendale 11 63 40N19'07 78w43'32 5:14:54
Allendale 21 12 40N13'26 76w53'26 5:07:34
Allendale Farms 23 9 39N58 75w22 5:01:28
Allen Junction 39 13 40N37'55 75w23'28 5:01:34
Allenport 31 85 40N22'25 77w52'13 5:11:29
Allenport 63 115 40N05'53 79w50'57 5:19:24
Allens 41 82 41N14'31 76w58'47 5:07:55
Allens Crossroads 65 1 40N08'10 79w50'35 5:19:22
Allens Mills 33 6 41N11'58 78w54'28 5:15:38
Allensville 44 7 40N32'09 77w49'02 5:11:16
Allentown 39 13 40N37 75w29 5:01:56
Allenvale 56 6 40N04'48 79w08'32 5:16:34
Allenwood 60 73 41N06'27 76w53'55 5:07:36
Alliance Furnace 65 104 40N06'50 79w43'08 5:18:53
Allis Hollow 8 60 41N50'36 76w18'22 5:05:13
Allison 26 51 39N59'20 79w51'54 5:19:28
Allison Heights 26 51 39N59'10 79w52'44 5:19:31
Allison Park 2 114 40N33 79w58 5:19:52
Allport 11 92 40N39'40 78w45'29 5:15:02
Allport 17 4 40N58'01 78w12'06 5:12:48
Almaden 17 63 40N45'46 78w24'00 5:13:36
Almedia 19 4 41N00'52 76w22'53 5:05:32
Almont 9 8 40N21'51 75w20'05 5:01:20
Alpha 48 17 40N51'07 75w17'07 5:01:08
Alpine 67 12 40N04'43 76w52'23 5:07:30
Alpsville 2 8 40N18'20 79w47'45 5:19:11
Alsace 6 101 40N23 75w52 5:03:28
Alsace Manor 6 101 40N23'59 75w51'39 5:03:27
Alta Manor 7 33 40N31'54 78w24'17 5:13:37
Altamont 54 27 40N47'10 76w13'31 5:04:54
Altenwald 28 100 39N50'42 77w36'14 5:10:25
Althom 62 6 41N45'12 79w18'11 5:17:13
Althouse 56 79 39N53'17 79w01'52 5:16:07
Altman 37 112 40N58'32 80w16'44 5:21:07
Alton 15 13 39N57 75w36 5:02:24
Alton Park 39 13 40N33'42 75w29'54 5:02:00
Altoona 7 33 40N31'07 78w23'42 5:13:35
Altor 15 13 39N58'13 75w40'12 5:02:41
Alum Bank 5 6 40N10'50 78w36'50 5:14:27
Alum Rock 16 1 41N10'02 79w37'17 5:18:29
Aluta 48 8 40N46'15 75w19'02 5:01:16
Alvan 5 6 40N08'46 78w08'58 5:12:36
Alverda 32 6 40N37'49 78w51'26 5:15:26
Alverton 65 111 40N08'24 79w35'15 5:18:21
Amaranth 29 6 39N47'51 78w16'42 5:13:07
Amasa 35 1 41N32 75w32 5:02:08
Ambau 67 95 39N51'05 76w53'36 5:07:34
Amberson 28 1 40N10'13 77w40'39 5:10:43
Ambler 46 8 40N09'16 75w13'19 5:00:53
Ambler Farms 23 9 39N53 75w18 5:01:12
Ambler Highlands 46 9 40N07 75w14 5:00:56
Ambridge 4 13 40N35'21 80w13'31 5:20:54
Ambridge Heights 2 13 40N35'30 80w12'43 5:20:51
Ambrose 32 6 40N46'21 79w06'31 5:16:26
Amend 26 80 39N52'22 79w47'22 5:19:09
Amesville 17 4 40N49'51 78w24'02 5:13:36
Amity 9 13 40N30'33 75w17'11 5:01:09
Amity 63 6 40N02'22 80w12'19 5:20:49
Amity Hall 50 51 40N24 77w02 5:08:08
Amityville 6 8 40N18'00 75w44'12 5:02:57
Amsbry 11 55 40N32'11 78w33'23 5:14:14
Amsterdam 43 6 41N08'02 80w08'02 5:20:32
Amwell 63 3 40N05 80w12 5:20:48
Analomink 45 23 41N03'04 75w13'15 5:00:53
Anchor 36 2 40N08'14 76w34'54 5:06:20
Ancient Oaks 39 13 40N32'50 75w35'23 5:02:22
Andalusia 9 9 40N04'10 74w58'18 4:59:53
Anderson 17 6 41N03'30 78w39'39 5:14:39
Anderson 44 73 40N32'23 77w38'45 5:10:35
Andersonburg 50 6 40N21'00 77w28'07 5:09:52
Anderson Creek 17 7 41N08'45 78w32'49 5:14:11
Andersons Corner 20 3 41N47'40 80w01'26 5:20:06
Andersontown 67 1 40N04'45 76w49'43 5:07:19
Andover 29 66 39N56'47 78w05'03 5:12:20
Andreas 54 1 40N45'06 75w47'34 5:03:10
Andrews Bridge 36 23 39N58 76w00 5:04:00
Andrews Plan 4 13 40N37 80w16 5:21:04
Andrews Settlement 53 6 41N54'00 77w54'16 5:11:37
Angelica 6 101 40N15'41 75w57'14 5:03:49
Angels 64 6 41N16'41 75w22'04 5:01:28
Anise 46 8 40N19'35 75w32'08 5:02:08
Anita 33 51 41N00'05 78w57'48 5:15:51
Ankeny 56 6 40N08'16 79w06'37 5:16:26
Annaline Village 23 90 39N50 75w25 5:01:40
Annandale 10 6 41N05'28 79w53'35 5:19:34
Annin 42 7 41N53 78w19 5:13:16
Annin Creek 42 7 41N54'05 78w15'38 5:13:03
Annisville 10 6 41N04'57 79w47'50 5:19:11
Annville 38 8 40N19'46 76w30'56 5:06:04
Anselma 15 8 40N04'53 75w38'32 5:02:34
Ansonia 59 6 41N44'47 77w25'43 5:09:43
Ansonville 17 54 40N50'51 78w33'57 5:14:16
Antes Fort 41 7 41N11'30 77w13'27 5:08:54
Anthracite 38 8 40N16'27 76w23'54 5:05:36
Antis 7 50 40N36 78w20 5:13:20
Antrim 59 6 41N38'02 77w17'14 5:09:09
Apolacon 58 6 41N57 76w06 5:04:24
Apollo 3 4 40N34'53 79w34'00 5:18:16
Appenzell 45 23 40N59'34 75w21'20 5:01:25
Applebachsville 9 13 40N28'57 75w16'24 5:01:06
Appletree Hill 9 9 40N09'37 74w50'38 4:59:23
Applewold 3 15 40N48'31 79w31'19 5:18:05
Apps 48 8 40N45'58 75w34'55 5:02:20
Aqua 28 42 39N54'43 77w37'02 5:10:28
Aquashicola 13 8 40N48'40 75w35'26 5:02:22
Aqueduct 50 51 40N24 77w02 5:08:08
Aquetong 9 8 40N21'05 75w00'13 5:00:01
Ararat 58 59 41N49'46 75w31'30 5:02:06
Arbor 67 1 39N52 76w37 5:06:28
Arbuckle 25 58 41N58'58 79w51'51 5:19:27
Arcadia 32 6 40N46'52 78w51'10 5:15:25

Arcadia 36 1 39N47 76w11 5:04:44
Archbald 35 1 41N29'41 75w32'14 5:02:09
Arch Rock 34 7 40N36'27 77w25'07 5:09:40
Arch Spring 7 11 40N36'21 78w12'11 5:12:49
Arcola 46 8 40N09'09 75w27'25 5:01:50
Ardara 65 25 40N21'28 79w44'07 5:18:56
Arden 63 3 40N12'18 80w15'33 5:21:02
Ardenheim 31 81 40N27'51 77w59'00 5:11:56
Arden Mines 63 3 40N13'07 80w15'53 5:21:04
Ardmore 46 9 40N00'24 75w17'09 5:01:09
Ardmore Manor 23 9 40N01 75w17 5:01:08
Ardmore Park 23 9 39N59'38 75w17'52 5:01:11
Ardsley 46 9 40N07'16 75w09'20 5:00:37
Arendtsville 1 1 39N55'23 77w17'56 5:09:12
Arensburg 26 6 39N57'10 79w57'00 5:19:48
Argentine 10 6 41N05'39 79w49'10 5:19:17
Argus 9 8 40N21'59 75w23'00 5:01:32
Aristes 19 27 40N49'06 76w20'19 5:05:21
Arlingham 46 9 40N06'55 75w12'13 5:00:49
Arlingham Hills 46 9 40N06 75w15 5:01:00
Arlington 23 9 39N58 75w18 5:01:12
Arlington 64 6 41N24'43 75w19'34 5:01:18
Arlington Heights 45 23 40N59'24 75w13'00 5:00:52
Arlington Knolls 39 13 40N39'24 75w29'50 5:01:59
Arlington Park 2 114 40N23 79w49 5:19:16
Armagh 32 7 40N27'13 79w01'56 5:16:08
Armbrust 65 111 40N13'25 79w33'05 5:18:12
Armenia 8 7 41N45 76w52 5:07:28
Armstrong 10 6 41N05'39 80w03'07 5:20:12
Arndts 48 80 40N47'58 75w28'38 5:01:55
Arnold 65 14 40N34'48 79w46'01 5:19:04
Arnold City 26 1 40N06'59 79w49'31 5:19:18
Arnot 59 6 41N39'45 77w07'24 5:08:30
Arnots Addition 54 27 40N43'05 76w12'01 5:04:48
Arona 65 3 40N16'09 79w39'42 5:18:39
Aronimink 23 9 39N57'02 75w19'08 5:01:17
Aronimink Estates 23 9 39N57 75w18 5:01:12
Aronimink Heights 23 9 39N57 75w18 5:01:12
Aronimink Park 23 9 39N57 75w18 5:01:12
Aronwald 23 90 40N00'53 75w24'52 5:01:39
Arrowhead Lake 45 1 41N09'06 75w34'25 5:02:18
Arroyo 24 59 41N23'27 78w52'50 5:15:31
Arsenal 2 114 40N28 79w57 5:19:48
Artemas 5 6 39N44'49 78w26'21 5:13:45
Arthurs 16 37 41N16'15 79w23'27 5:17:34
Arundel Village 46 1 40N11 75w10 5:00:40
Asaph 59 6 41N46'15 77w24'19 5:09:37
Asbury 19 4 41N07'35 76w20'12 5:05:21
Asbury 25 107 42N04'19 80w10'56 5:20:44
Ashbury 19 4 41N05 76w25 5:05:40
Ashcom 5 6 40N00'13 78w25'10 5:13:41
Asherton 49 6 40N47'17 76w49'27 5:07:18
Ashfield 13 80 40N47'04 75w42'50 5:02:51
Ashland 17 4 40N52'17 78w20'00 5:13:20
Ashland 54 27 40N46'54 76w20'46 5:05:23
Ashley 40 20 41N12'37 75w53'49 5:03:35
Ashmead Village 46 9 40N03'42 75w05'58 5:00:24
Ashtola 56 123 40N11'49 78w46'48 5:15:07
Ashtree 30 6 39N46'22 80w21'41 5:21:27
Ashville 11 63 40N33'36 78w32'56 5:14:12
Askam 40 20 41N11'55 75w57'17 5:03:49
Aspers 1 1 39N58'46 77w13'23 5:08:54
Aspinwall 2 114 40N29'29 79w54'18 5:19:37
Aston 23 90 39N52 75w26 5:01:44
Aston Manor 23 90 39N51 75w22 5:01:28
Aston Mills 23 90 39N52'27 75w26'55 5:01:48
Astral 61 109 41N20'38 79w46'20 5:19:05
Asylum 8 60 41N42'47 76w20'02 5:05:20
Atco 64 6 41N37'16 75w05'10 5:00:21
Atglen 15 8 39N56'57 75w58'26 5:03:54
Athens 8 1 41N57'26 76w31'06 5:06:04
Athol 6 8 40N18 75w44 5:02:56
Atkinson Mills 44 7 40N27'19 77w49'06 5:11:16
Atlantic 17 59 40N50'41 78w23'43 5:13:35
Atlantic 20 59 41N30'17 80w20'21 5:21:21
Atlantic 26 51 39N46'41 79w54'57 5:19:40
Atlantic 65 3 40N21'27 79w19'11 5:17:17
Atlas 49 27 40N47'59 76w25'41 5:05:43
Atlasburg 63 6 40N20'28 80w22'59 5:21:32
Atwells Crossing 10 6 41N06'18 79w55'14 5:19:41
Atwood 3 6 40N45'17 79w16'00 5:17:04
Auburn 54 3 40N35'54 76w05'37 5:04:22
Auburn Center 58 6 41N41'23 76w02'13 5:04:09
Auburn Four Corners 58 60 41N43'12 75w58'50 5:03:55
Aucheys 54 1 40N34'30 76w10'00 5:04:40
Audenried 13 42 40N54'38 75w59'31 5:03:58
Audubon 46 90 40N07'40 75w25'56 5:01:44
Aughwick 31 85 40N20'12 77w51'38 5:11:27
Augustaville 49 82 40N48'26 76w44'30 5:06:58
Aultman 32 6 40N33'50 79w15'40 5:17:03
Austin 53 6 41N37'52 78w05'30 5:12:22
Austinburg 59 6 41N59'35 77w29'42 5:09:59
Austin Heights 35 18 41N22'58 75w44'36 5:02:58
Austinville 8 7 41N50'20 76w52'27 5:07:30
Autumn Leaves 64 6 41N55'44 75w20'05 5:01:20
Avalon 2 114 40N30'03 80w04'04 5:20:16
Avella 63 6 40N16'30 80w27'39 5:21:51
Avery 66 59 41N38'19 75w55'53 5:03:44
Avis 18 7 41N11'05 77w18'51 5:09:15
Avoca 40 1 41N20'23 75w44'12 5:02:57
Avon 38 8 40N20'44 76w23'25 5:05:34
Avondale 15 8 39N49'24 75w47'01 5:03:08
Avondale 40 20 41N13'22 75w58'56 5:03:56
Avondale Hill 40 20 41N13'38 75w59'01 5:03:56
Avondale Knolls 23 90 39N54 75w22 5:01:28
Avon Heights 38 8 40N21'09 76w22'31 5:05:30
Avonia 25 68 42N02'44 80w16'12 5:21:05
Avonmore 65 116 40N31'44 79w27'42 5:17:51
Avoy 64 6 41N26'41 75w20'24 5:01:22
Axemann 14 70 40N53'24 77w45'38 5:11:03
Ayers Crossroads 8 6 41N51'41 76w40'02 5:06:40
Ayers Hill 53 66 41N43'43 77w57'57 5:11:52
Ayr 29 66 39N54 78w01 5:12:04
Azelta 59 6 41N50'22 77w29'07 5:09:56
Bachmanville 22 31 40N14'33 76w35'42 5:06:23
Backup Corners 62 6 41N55'02 79w09'01 5:16:36
Backus 42 6 41N48'08 78w33'51 5:14:15
Bacon Mill 67 1 39N49'03 76w32'11 5:06:09
Bacton 15 47 40N03 75w35 5:02:20
Baden 4 13 40N38'06 80w13'42 5:20:55
Baederwood 46 9 40N06'24 75w08'33 5:00:34
Bagdad 25 35 41N57'07 80w01'28 5:20:06
Bagdad 65 4 40N39'11 79w38'40 5:18:35
Baggaley 65 3 40N16'06 79w22'22 5:17:29
Baidland 63 1 40N11'41 79w58'16 5:19:53
Bailey 50 1 40N29 77w08 5:08:32
Baileys Corner 8 7 41N43 76w47 5:07:08
Baileyville 14 6 40N42'29 77w59'08 5:11:57
Bainbridge 36 2 40N05'27 76w40'04 5:06:40
Bair 67 67 39N54'19 76w49'41 5:07:19
Bairdford 2 6 40N37'52 79w52'54 5:19:32
Bairdstown 32 35 40N25'57 79w16'45 5:17:07
Baker 15 8 39N50'08 75w48'25 5:03:14
Bakers Crossroad 11 63 40N37'27 78w41'43 5:14:47
Bakers Summit 5 3 40N15'45 78w25'18 5:13:41
Baker Station 15 1 39N49 75w50 5:03:20
Baker Station 63 3 40N04'31 80w13'35 5:20:54
Bakerstown 2 6 40N39'03 79w56'12 5:19:45
Bakerstown Station 2 56 40N39'19 79w58'22 5:19:53
Bakersville 56 6 40N02'32 79w13'00 5:16:52
Bakerton 11 63 40N36'10 78w44'42 5:14:59
Bala 46 9 39N59'57 75w14'00 5:00:56
Bala-Cynwyd 46 9 40N00'27 75w14'04 5:00:56
Bald Eagle 7 11 40N43'19 78w11'08 5:12:45
Bald Eagle 18 7 41N07 77w31 5:10:04
Bald Eagle 67 1 39N46'13 76w25'42 5:05:43
Bald Hill 17 6 41N04'47 78w17'36 5:13:10
Bald Hill 30 6 39N44'38 80w01'00 5:20:04
Bald Hill Church 30 6 39N44'00 80w00'55 5:20:04
Baldwin 2 114 40N23'08 79w57'40 5:19:51
Baldwin 23 90 39N51'44 75w20'11 5:01:21
Baldwin Furnace 65 7 40N21'05 79w03'02 5:16:12
Balliet 13 80 40N46'43 75w42'41 5:02:51
Balliettsville 39 13 40N40'42 75w34'27 5:02:18
Balls Mills 41 7 41N19'05 77w01'38 5:08:07
Balltown 27 3 41N36'05 79w10'21 5:16:41
Bally 6 3 40N24'08 75w35'15 5:02:21
Balsam 59 6 41N42'11 77w20'56 5:09:24
Balsinger 26 80 39N53'46 79w47'57 5:19:12
Bamford 36 97 40N05'06 76w23'21 5:05:33
Banard Town 4 8 40N46 80w20 5:21:20
Bandanna (Pleasant Hill) 67 1 39N44'19 76w56'15 5:07:45
Banetown 63 3 40N04'42 80w13'42 5:20:55
Baney Settlement 17 6 41N04'06 78w25'26 5:13:42
Banfield 3 4 40N38'11 79w36'21 5:18:25
Bangor 48 17 40N51'56 75w12'25 5:00:50
Banian Junction 17 6 40N48'50 78w26'12 5:13:45
Banksville 2 114 40N24'30 80w02'02 5:20:08
Banner Ridge 17 122 40N51 78w43 5:14:52
Bannerville 55 1 40N43'56 77w20'53 5:09:24
Banning 26 104 40N07'10 79w45'06 5:19:00
Baoba 52 6 41N28'53 75w05'30 5:00:22
Barbours 41 82 41N23'35 76w47'59 5:07:12
Barclay 8 60 41N39'21 76w37'36 5:06:30
Bard 5 6 39N57 78w39 5:14:36
Bardwell 66 59 41N33'40 75w51'45 5:03:27
Baresville 67 1 39N48 76w59 5:07:56
Bareville 36 28 40N05'32 76w09'22 5:04:37
Barkeyville 61 6 41N11'31 79w58'33 5:19:54
Barking 2 14 40N31'58 79w46'56 5:19:08
Barlow 1 1 39N45'19 77w13'49 5:08:55
Barlow Heights 46 8 40N12'42 75w32'42 5:02:11
Barlow Knoll 1 1 39N50'43 77w13'35 5:08:54
Barmouth 46 9 40N01 75w15 5:01:00
Barnards 32 59 40N49'31 79w13'48 5:16:55
Barners Hill 65 25 40N20'53 79w44'19 5:18:57
Barnes 11 63 40N36'44 78w45'25 5:15:02
Barnes 33 34 41N07'17 79w04'59 5:16:20
Barnes 62 3 41N40'41 79w01'41 5:16:07
Barnesboro 11 92 40N39'45 78w46'49 5:15:07
Barnes Gap 29 6 39N44'37 78w21'21 5:13:25
Barneston 15 27 40N06'16 75w48'37 5:03:14
Barnesville 54 27 40N48'52 76w01'52 5:04:07
Barnett 27 6 41N22 79w10 5:16:40
Barnettstown 31 6 40N12'40 78w10'38 5:12:43
Barneytown 31 85 40N24 77w56 5:11:44
Barnitz 21 16 40N07'17 77w13'36 5:08:54
Barnsley 15 3 39N45'56 75w59'21 5:03:57
Barr 11 92 40N37 78w49 5:15:16
Barree 31 6 40N35'07 78w06'03 5:12:24
Barren Hill 46 90 40N05'14 75w15'48 5:01:03
Barret Plan 4 13 40N37 80w16 5:21:04
Barrett 17 1 41N00'38 78w23'21 5:13:33
Barrett 45 84 41N12 75w16 5:01:04
Barronvale 56 4 39N57'06 79w16'18 5:17:05
Barrs Corners 61 6 41N16'43 79w43'11 5:18:53
Barr Slope 32 6 40N42'47 79w00'58 5:16:04
Barrville 44 73 40N39'47 77w40'37 5:10:42
Barry 54 27 40N43 76w25 5:05:40
Barry Heights 46 90 40N08 75w21 5:01:24
Bart 36 23 39N56 76w04 5:04:16
Barto 6 2 40N23'28 75w36'38 5:02:27
Barton 32 6 40N47'33 79w03'15 5:16:13
Bartonsville 45 1 41N00'18 75w16'48 5:01:07
Bartville 36 23 39N53'28 76w04'07 5:04:16
Basket 6 101 40N23'24 75w49'35 5:03:18
Bassards Corners 46 80 40N48 75w32 5:02:08
Bastress 41 64 41N10'33 77w08'15 5:08:33
Bath 48 13 40N43'32 75w23'40 5:01:35
Bath Addition 9 9 40N06'27 74w51'56 4:59:28
Bath Junction 48 13 40N43'19 75w22'53 5:01:32
Bath Manor 9 9 40N08 74w51 4:59:24
Battle Hollow 33 6 41N00'21 78w59'49 5:15:59
Bauerstown 2 114 40N29'45 79w58'36 5:19:54
Baumgardner 36 8 39N57'38 76w16'52 5:05:07
Baumstown 6 8 40N16'49 75w48'19 5:03:13
Bausman 36 8 40N01'27 76w19'52 5:05:19
Bavington 63 6 40N25'33 80w21'53 5:21:28
Baxter 33 6 41N08'04 79w09'00 5:16:36
Bayard Park 48 12 40N38'05 75w20'47 5:01:23
Beachdale 56 79 39N54'13 79w00'45 5:16:03
Beach Haven 40 1 41N04'06 76w10'34 5:04:42
Beach Lake 64 6 41N36'06 75w09'01 5:00:36
Beachly 56 53 39N46'26 79w18'29 5:17:14
Beacon Lodge 31 85 40N22'27 77w48'47 5:11:15
Beadling 2 114 40N21'37 80w04'21 5:20:17
Beale 34 6 40N30 77w31 5:10:04
Beallsville 63 51 40N03'55 80w01'26 5:20:06
Beans Cove 5 6 39N47'37 78w34'35 5:14:18
Bear Creek 40 1 41N10'43 75w45'24 5:03:02
Bear Creek Junction 40 60 41N05'43 75w46'55 5:03:08
Bear Gap 49 1 40N49'56 76w30'22 5:06:01
Bear Lake 62 6 41N59'36 79w30'11 5:18:01
Bear Lick 28 51 39N53'37 77w56'35 5:11:46
Bear Rocks 26 6 40N07'22 79w27'43 5:17:51
Bear Run Junction 54 3 40N48'08 76w11'29 5:04:46
Bears Crossroads 21 16 40N11'54 77w20'24 5:09:22
Bear Swamp 18 7 41N08'28 77w39'02 5:10:36
Beartown 28 100 39N44'42 77w30'04 5:10:00
Beartown 36 27 40N06'41 75w58'40 5:03:55
Bear Valley 49 27 40N46'21 76w34'40 5:06:19
Beatty 65 3 40N18'06 79w25'07 5:17:40
Beatty Hills 23 9 39N58 75w22 5:01:28
Beaufort Farms 22 12 40N17 76w53 5:07:32
Beaumont 66 6 41N24'36 75w59'48 5:03:59
Beaver 4 19 40N41'43 80w18'18 5:21:13
Beaver Acres 2 114 40N28 80w05 5:20:20
Beaver Brook 40 42 40N55'05 75w59'23 5:03:58
Beaver Center 20 6 41N48'08 80w28'03 5:21:52
Beaverdale 11 63 40N19'17 78w41'48 5:14:47
Beaverdale 49 27 40N48 76w25 5:05:40
Beaverdam 14 64 40N50'29 77w32'52 5:10:11
Beaver Dam 25 3 41N55'38 79w45'02 5:19:00
Beaver Falls 4 8 40N45'07 80w19'10 5:21:17
Beaver Lake 41 6 41N17'37 76w35'29 5:06:22
Beaver Meadows 13 42 40N55'41 75w54'54 5:03:40
Beavers Mill 6 8 40N21'25 75w48'36 5:03:14
Beaver Springs 55 6 40N44'46 77w12'35 5:08:50
Beavertown 7 51 40N22'20 78w14'14 5:12:57
Beavertown 31 6 40N16'26 78w04'39 5:12:19
Beavertown 55 6 40N45'13 77w10'11 5:08:41
Beavertown 67 1 40N06'28 77w03'11 5:08:13
Beaver Valley 11 54 40N43 78w31 5:14:04
Beaver Valley 19 4 40N55'20 76w16'58 5:05:08
Beccaria 17 54 40N46'12 78w26'54 5:13:48
Bechtelsville 6 2 40N22'24 75w37'46 5:02:31
Beckersville 6 101 40N13'52 75w54'28 5:03:38
Becks 54 49 40N41 76w12 5:04:48
Beckville 54 27 40N38'30 76w11'51 5:04:47
Bedford 5 70 40N01'07 78w30'15 5:14:01
Bedford Springs 5 70 39N59'50 78w30'36 5:14:02
Bedminster 9 1 40N25'33 75w10'46 5:00:43
Beechcliff 2 114 40N26'47 80w11'36 5:20:46
Beech Creek 18 7 41N04'33 77w35'20 5:10:21
Beechersville 1 1 39N55'02 77w17'23 5:09:10
Beech Flats 8 103 41N37'59 76w48'56 5:07:16
Beech Glen 57 6 41N19'45 76w35'17 5:06:21
Beech Grove 24 6 41N20'08 78w41'36 5:14:46
Beech Grove 41 6 41N26'40 77w11'30 5:08:46
Beech Grove 64 59 41N36'06 75w18'05 5:01:12
Beechmont 2 114 40N23'34 80w09'36 5:20:38
Beechton 33 5 41N14'05 78w51'03 5:15:24
Beechtree 33 5 41N12'36 78w49'15 5:15:17
Beechview 2 114 40N24'38 80w01'30 5:20:06
Beechwood 12 106 41N29'06 78w23'28 5:13:34
Beechwood Park 23 90 39N52 75w23 5:01:32
Beechwoods 33 56 41N11'19 78w51'01 5:15:24
Beegleton 5 6 39N54'53 78w30'56 5:14:04
Beeman 59 59 41N57'18 77w07'02 5:08:28
Beersville 48 13 40N44'47 75w28'16 5:01:53
Beesons 26 80 39N52 79w42 5:18:48
Beham 63 6 40N01'18 80w30'40 5:22:03
Bela 16 1 41N03'00 79w34'40 5:18:19
Belair Park 36 8 40N04 76w19 5:05:16
Belardy 9 9 40N06'02 74w52'42 4:59:31
Belden 5 70 40N04'33 78w30'21 5:14:01
Belfast 29 60 39N53 78w09 5:12:36
Belfast 48 8 40N46'50 75w16'42 5:01:07
Belfast Junction 48 12 40N46'04 75w16'22 5:01:05

Belford 17 6 41N07'41 78W05'00 5:12:20
Belian Village 35
18 41N20'40 75W42'23 5:02:50
Belknap 3 59 40N53'57 79W18'11 5:17:13
Bell Acres 2 13 40N35 80W10 5:20:40
Bellaire 36 2 40N11'29 76W34'31 5:06:18
Bellasylva 66 6 41N27'25 76W14'21 5:04:57
Bella Vista 41 82 41N14'52 76W52'49 5:07:31
Belle Bridge 2 8 40N18'02 79W51'57 5:19:28
Bellefield 2 114 40N26'50 79W56'33 5:19:46
Bellefonte 14 70 40N54'48 77W46'43 5:11:07
Bellegrove 38 8 40N22'01 76W32'57 5:06:12
Bellemont 36 9 39N59'41 76W06'06 5:04:24
Belle Valley 25
107 42N06'15 80W01'18 5:20:05
Belle Vernon 26 1 40N07'30 79W52'00 5:19:28
Belleview Heights 25
107 42N05'24 80W00'06 5:20:00
Belleville 44 6 40N36'18 77W43'33 5:10:54
Bellevue 2 114 40N29'38 80W03'07 5:20:12
Bellevue 67 1 39N45'38 76W23'56 5:05:36
Bell Mountain 35
18 41N26 75W40 5:02:40
Bell Point 65 4 40N32'42 79W33'02 5:18:12
Bellrun 42 7 42N00 78W16 5:13:04
Bells 65 110 40N15'17 79W15'44 5:17:03
Bells Camp 42 102 41N58'48 78W33'14 5:14:13
Bells Landing 17
122 40N55'01 78W38'59 5:14:36
Bells Mills 33 51 40N57'10 78W55'23 5:15:42
Bellton 4 121 40N49'48 80W18'25 5:21:14
Belltown 24 6 41N21'24 79W02'30 5:16:10
Belltown 44 1 40N42'46 77W25'01 5:09:40
Bellwood 7 50 40N36'12 78W19'30 5:13:18
Belmar 2 114 40N28'00 79W53'46 5:19:35
Belmar 61 6 41N19'59 79W46'30 5:19:06
Belmar Park 37
112 41N00'23 80W22'37 5:21:30
Belmont 11 74 40N17'14 78W53'23 5:15:34
Belmont Corner 64
59 41N44'26 75W27'24 5:01:50
Belmont Hills 46
9 40N02'03 75W15'29 5:01:02
Belmont Homes 11
74 40N17 78W53 5:15:32
Belmont Terrace 46
90 40N06'18 75W22'01 5:01:28
Belsano 11 63 40N31'10 78W52'17 5:15:29
Belsano Crossing 11
63 40N30'57 78W51'40 5:15:27
Belsena 17 6 40N50'56 78W26'36 5:13:46
Belsena Mills 17
6 40N50 78W26 5:13:44
Belton 4 121 40N52 80W16 5:21:04
Beltzhoover 2 114 40N25'11 80W00'08 5:20:01
Beltzville 13 8 40N50'24 75W38'09 5:02:33
Ben Avon 2 114 40N30'29 80W05'00 5:20:20
Ben Avon 32 72 40N35'41 79W09'42 5:16:39
Ben Avon Heights 2
114 40N30'49 80W04'24 5:20:18
Bencetown 32 6 40N43'28 78W59'54 5:16:00
Benders Junction 48
13 40N48'52 75W23'43 5:01:35
Bendersville 1 1 39N58'57 77W14'59 5:09:00
Bendertown 19 4 41N08'55 76W19'02 5:05:16
Benedicks 67 1 40N00 76W58 5:07:52
Benedicts 67 1 40N01'36 76W55'42 5:07:43
Benezette 24 6 41N19'00 78W23'12 5:13:33
Benfer 55 6 40N46'22 77W12'32 5:08:50
Benharts 6 101 40N22'40 75W54'41 5:03:39
Benjamin 2 7 40N38'01 79W50'24 5:19:22
Benjamin 9 8 40N25 75W23 5:01:32
Benner 14 9 40N52 77W48 5:11:12
Bennetts Corner 9
8 40N17'23 75W06'03 5:00:24
Benroy 67 67 39N56'43 76W40'22 5:06:41
Bensalem 9 9 40N06 74W57 4:59:48
Bens Creek 11 55 40N23'54 78W37'41 5:14:31
Bens Creek 56 74 40N16'57 78W56'12 5:15:45
Benson 56 74 40N12'30 78W55'41 5:15:43
Bentley Creek 8 7 41N56'47 76W42'49 5:06:51
Bentleyville 63
51 40N07'00 80W00'31 5:20:02
Benton 19 56 41N11'42 76W23'02 5:05:32
Benton 36 1 39N46'35 76W15'05 5:05:00
Benvenue 22 1 40N24'14 77W00'35 5:08:02
Benzinger 24 36 41N26 78W33 5:14:12
Berge Run 53 6 41N29'18 78W03'07 5:12:12
Bergey 46 8 40N18'08 75W25'23 5:01:42
Berkeley Hills 2
114 40N31'54 80W00'14 5:20:01
Berkley 6 101 40N25'45 75W56'05 5:03:44
Berkleys Mill 56
79 39N50'43 79W00'00 5:16:00
Berkshire Heights 6
101 40N19 75W59 5:03:56
Berlin 56 6 39N55'14 78W57'29 5:15:50
Berlin Junction 1
1 39N51'21 77W02'09 5:08:09
Berlinsville 48 8 40N46'07 75W34'27 5:02:18
Bermudian 67 1 40N01'10 77W02'09 5:08:09
Bern 6 101 40N24 75W59 5:03:56
Berne 6 80 40N31'26 76W00'07 5:04:00
Bernharts 6 101 40N23 75W56 5:03:44
Bernice 57 60 41N28'13 76W22'55 5:05:32
Bernville 6 3 40N26 76W07 5:04:28
Berrysburg 22 4 40N36'07 76W48'44 5:07:15
Berrytown 8 7 41N53'24 76W46'02 5:07:04
Bertha 63 7 40N22'39 80W25'57 5:21:44
Berwick 19 1 41N03'16 76W14'01 5:04:56
Berwick Heights 19
1 41N04'55 76W14'55 5:05:00
Berwinsdale 17 54 40N49'09 78W35'51 5:14:23
Berwyn 15 90 40N02'41 75W26'21 5:01:45
Besco 63 6 39N59'06 80W01'26 5:20:06
Bessemer 2 114 40N23'40 79W51'16 5:19:25
Bessemer (Walford Station) 37
1 40N58'29 80W29'38 5:21:59
Bessemer 65 111 40N07'41 79W33'19 5:18:13
Bessemer Junction 2
114 40N23'33 79W50'21 5:19:21
Bessemer Terrace 2
114 40N24 79W50 5:19:20
Best 2 114 40N22 79W54 5:19:36
Best Station 39 8 40N45 75W37 5:02:28
Bethany 64 59 41N36'47 75W17'05 5:01:08
Bethayres 46 9 40N06'50 75W04'17 5:00:17
Bethel 2 114 40N20'39 80W02'35 5:20:10
Bethel 6 1 40N28'28 76W17'30 5:05:10
Bethel 11 54 40N29 78W43 5:14:52
Bethel 43 117 41N11'33 80W23'19 5:21:33
Bethel 57 6 41N33'13 76W36'28 5:06:26
Bethel 64 59 41N33'50 75W11'24 5:00:46
Bethelboro 26 104 39N56'06 79W40'14 5:18:41
Bethel Hill 46 8 40N11'02 75W19'07 5:01:16
Bethel, Mount 48
8 40N54'17 75W06'43 5:00:27
Bethel Park 2 114 40N20 80W01 5:20:04
Bethesda 36 1 39N50'45 76W18'15 5:05:13
Bethlehem 17 122 40N51'42 78W43'50 5:14:55
Bethlehem 48 13 40N37'33 75W22'15 5:01:29
Bethlehem View 48
12 40N38'27 75W21'14 5:01:25
Bethton 9 8 40N19 75W19 5:01:16
Betula 42 93 41N40'15 78W23'38 5:13:35
Betz 17 6 40N50'43 78W26'10 5:13:45
Betzwood 46 90 40N06'38 75W25'12 5:01:41
Beuchler 54 9 40N32'57 76W26'20 5:05:45
Beula 11 54 40N28'36 78W46'20 5:15:05
Beulah 2 114 40N27 79W50 5:19:20
Beulah 17 6 40N48'31 78W24'37 5:13:38
Beulah Land 41 6 41N28'42 77W26'33 5:09:46
Beverly 36 2 40N10'58 76W36'43 5:06:27
Beverly Estates 36
8 40N04'27 76W18'08 5:05:13
Beverly Heights 38
8 40N24'21 76W28'30 5:05:54
Beverly Hills 7
33 40N31'52 78W24'52 5:13:39
Beverly Hills 23
9 39N57'34 75W16'45 5:01:07
Beyer 32 6 40N47'11 79W12'05 5:16:48
Biddle 65 25 40N20 79W41 5:18:44
Bidwell 26 53 39N51'22 79W25'29 5:17:42
Bidwell Hill 64 4 41N22'50 75W22'35 5:01:30
Biesecker Gap 28
100 39N47'15 77W32'03 5:10:08
Big Beaver 4 121 40N49 80W22 5:21:28
Big Bend 43 66 41N17'04 80W19'11 5:21:17
Big Bend 62 120 41N50'27 79W00'16 5:16:01
Big Cove Tannery 29
66 39N50'56 78W02'59 5:12:12
Big Creek 13 8 40N50'44 75W38'54 5:02:36
Biggerstown 41 6 41N15'09 76W31'53 5:06:08
Bigler 17 6 40N59'05 78W18'24 5:13:14
Biglerville 1 56 39N55'49 77W14'54 5:09:00
Big Mine Run 54
27 40N47'15 76W19'04 5:05:16
Big Mine Run Junction 54
27 40N47 76W21 5:05:24
Bigmount 67 1 40N00 76W58 5:07:52
Big Mountain 49
27 40N46'14 76W32'02 5:06:08
Big Mountain 67
39 39N57'27 76W56'06 5:07:44
Big Pond 8 7 41N52'58 76W42'18 5:06:49
Big Run 14 7 41N04'53 77W40'05 5:10:40
Big Run 22 1 40N34'14 76W44'39 5:06:59
Big Run 33 51 40N58'01 78W52'43 5:15:31
Big Shanty 42 6 41N50'15 78W39'18 5:14:37
Big Spring 14 70 40N54'33 77W46'53 5:11:08
Big Spring 21 82 40N07'47 77W24'20 5:09:37
Big Spring 28 70 39N46'43 77W43'11 5:10:53
Bilger Rocks 17 6 40N59'38 78W35'33 5:14:22
Billing 16 6 41N16'57 79W30'41 5:18:03
Billmeyer 36 1 40N04'20 76W39'05 5:06:36
Bingen 48 13 40N33'26 75W21'12 5:01:25
Bingham 42 6 41N49'01 78W36'44 5:14:27
Bingham 53 6 41N57 77W47 5:11:08
Bingham Center 53
6 41N57'14 77W46'36 5:11:06
Binnstown 63 114 40N00'55 79W58'04 5:19:52
Bino 28 1 39N48 77W44 5:10:56
Birch 18 7 41N11'44 77W58'35 5:11:54
Birchardville 58
60 41N50'51 76W00'47 5:04:03
Birchrunville 15
8 40N07'46 75W38'17 5:02:33
Birchtown 58 1 41N39'09 75W31'06 5:02:04
Birch Valley 9 9 40N10'01 74W49'41 4:59:19
Birchwood Lakes 52
3 41N15'16 74W55'08 4:59:41
Birdell 15 9 40N04'22 75W51'40 5:03:27
Bird in Hand 36
96 40N02'19 76W10'57 5:04:44
Birdsboro 6 8 40N15'52 75W48'16 5:03:13
Birdville 2 14 40N38'16 79W43'16 5:18:53
Birdville 31 85 40N24'07 77W56'32 5:11:46
Birmingham 15 13 39N54'18 75W35'41 5:02:23
Birmingham 31 11 40N38'52 78W11'44 5:12:47
Bishop 63 114 40N19'14 80W11'14 5:20:45
Bishtown 17 6 41N01'28 78W21'39 5:13:27
Bitner 26 105 39N58'57 79W42'46 5:18:51
Bittersville 67 1 39N55'29 76W32'52 5:06:11
Bittinger 1 1 39N50'16 77W00'53 5:08:04
Bittners Mill 56
51 39N50'59 78W49'04 5:15:16
Bitumen 18 7 41N17'59 77W52'44 5:11:31
Bixby Corner 8 6 41N56'31 76W21'42 5:05:27
Bixler 50 6 40N22'13 77W24'10 5:09:37
Black 8 41 41N49'10 76W26'20 5:05:45
Black 56 4 39N55 79W08 5:16:32
Black Ash 20 6 41N35'28 79W54'02 5:19:36
Black Baron 36 1 39N44'07 76W11'31 5:04:46
Black Bear 6 101 40N20 75W53 5:03:32
Blackburn 65 25 40N23'22 79W44'51 5:18:59
Black Creek 40 1 40N59 76W11 5:04:44
Black Creek Junction 13
60 40N55'54 75W49'22 5:03:17
Black Diamond 63
1 40N11'33 79W54'09 5:19:37
Blackfield 56 4 39N54'24 79W05'18 5:16:21
Blackgap 28 1 39N55 77W34 5:10:16
Blackhawk 4 8 40N42'47 80W27'23 5:21:50
Black Horse 15 32 39N59'08 75W57'19 5:03:49
Black Horse 23 90 39N55'02 75W25'22 5:01:41
Black Horse 46 90 40N06'29 75W18'41 5:01:15
Black Horse Tavern 1
1 39N49'08 77W17'01 5:09:08
Black Lick 32 98 40N28'45 79W12'00 5:16:48
Blacklog 34 6 40N25'26 77W40'52 5:10:43
Blackman 40 20 41N15 75W53 5:03:32
Black Ridge 2 114 40N27'17 79W51'10 5:19:25
Blackrock 67 1 39N43'18 76W51'41 5:07:27
Blacks 61 1 41N12'29 79W45'29 5:19:02
Blacks Corner 20
77 41N41'14 80W11'22 5:20:45
Blackstone 65 4 40N39'43 79W39'08 5:18:37
Blacksville 30 6 39N43'16 80W12'45 5:20:51
Blacktown 43 66 41N10'00 80W10'25 5:20:42
Black Walnut 66 6 41N39 76W10 5:04:40
Blackwell 59 6 41N33'23 77W22'46 5:09:31
Blackwood 54 9 40N38'30 76W19'39 5:05:19
Blain 50 6 40N20'18 77W30'46 5:10:03
Blain City 17 54 40N45'23 78W32'00 5:14:08
Blaine 63 6 40N11 80W24 5:21:36
Blaine Hill 2 8 40N16'25 79W52'31 5:19:30
Blainsburg 63 56 40N01'56 79W52'52 5:19:31
Blainsport 36 1 40N16'50 76W08'24 5:04:34
Blair 7 33 40N24 78W25 5:13:40
Blairfour 7 6 40N13'57 78W10'07 5:12:40
Blairs Corners 16
6 41N10'59 79W33'51 5:18:15
Blairs Mills 31 6 40N17'01 77W43'07 5:10:52
Blairsville 32 35 40N25'52 79W15'40 5:17:03
Blairtown 30 1 39N53'20 80W11'12 5:20:45
Blakely 35 18 41N28'51 75W35'42 5:02:23
Blakes 59 6 41N41 77W04 5:08:16
Blakeslee 45 94 41N05'33 75W35'35 5:02:22
Blanchard 2 7 40N39'26 79W49'43 5:19:19
Blanchard 14 7 41N03'51 77W35'53 5:10:24
Blanco 3 6 40N46'36 79W21'16 5:17:25
Blandburg 11 63 40N41'13 78W24'40 5:13:39
Blandon 6 101 40N26'28 75W53'14 5:03:33
Blanket Hill 3 15 40N45'54 79W25'21 5:17:41
Blawnox 2 114 40N29'36 79W51'39 5:19:27
Bleakley Hill 61
109 41N24'17 79W49'35 5:19:18
Bliem Corners 40
1 41N08'21 75W58'44 5:03:55
Bloom 17 7 41N01 78W38 5:14:32
Bloomfield 2 114 40N27'39 79W57'04 5:19:48
Bloomingdale 13
80 40N49'29 75W51'02 5:03:24
Bloomingdale 36 8 40N04'47 76W18'11 5:05:13
Bloomingdale 40 1 41N14'18 76W11'56 5:04:48
Blooming Glen 9 1 40N22'10 75W14'55 5:01:00
Blooming Grove 52
6 41N22'14 75W09'18 5:00:37
Blooming Grove 67
1 39N47'41 76W56'40 5:07:47
Bloomington 17 7 40N56'20 78W31'03 5:14:04
Bloomington 35 4 41N19'50 75W28'37 5:01:54
Blooming Valley 20
6 41N40'52 80W02'28 5:20:10
Bloomsburg 6 80 40N25'46 76W00'49 5:04:03
Bloomsburg 19 4 41N00'13 76W27'19 5:05:49
Bloomsdale Gardens 9
9 40N09 74W51 4:59:24
Bloserville 21 1 40N10 77W24 5:09:36
Bloss 59 6 41N40 77W07 5:08:28
Blossburg 59 59 41N40'46 77W03'51 5:08:15
Blosser Hill 26 7 39N44'45 79W53'50 5:19:35
Blosserville 21 1 40N14'24 77W21'45 5:09:27
Blossom Hill 36 8 40N05'24 76W19'15 5:05:17
Blossom Valley 36
8 40N04 76W19 5:05:16
Blough 56 6 40N10'18 78W54'30 5:15:38
Blowtown 33 34 41N17'45 78W56'06 5:15:44
Blue Ball (West Decatur P O) 17
4 40N55'39 78W16'49 5:13:07
Blue Ball 36 27 40N07'07 76W02'51 5:04:11
Blue Bell 46 8 40N09'08 75W16'00 5:01:04
Blue Bell Farms 46
8 40N10 75W17 5:01:08
Blue Bell Gardens 46
8 40N10 75W17 5:01:08
Blue Goose 11 92 40N35'08 78W49'08 5:15:17
Blue Goose Mine 16
1 41N03 79W39 5:18:36
Blue Hill 55 82 40N48 76W52 5:07:28
Blue Jay 27 3 41N33'03 79W07'42 5:16:31
Blue Knob 7 51 40N21'16 78W33'14 5:14:13
Blue Marsh 6 101 40N22'02 76W02'12 5:04:09
Blue Mountain Camps 45
23 41N00 75W11 5:00:44
Blue Mountain Pines 45
17 40N54'08 75W14'34 5:00:58
Blue Ridge 9 9 40N07'52 74W52'00 4:59:28
Blue Ridge Summit 28
1 39N43'27 77W28'18 5:09:53
Bluestone 41 6 41N22'50 77W26'25 5:09:46
Bluff 30 6 39N48'18 80W18'20 5:21:13
Blystone Mill 20
3 41N48 80W03 5:20:12
Blythe 54 27 40N44 76W07 5:04:28
Blytheburn 40 20 41N07'32 75W57'14 5:03:49
Blythedale 2 8 40N14'57 79W48'04 5:19:12
Blythewood 9 8 40N21 75W13 5:00:52
Boalsburg 14 9 40N46'32 77W47'34 5:11:10
Boardman 17 122 40N52'40 78W27'49 5:13:51
Bobbys Corners 43
117 41N12'05 80W27'22 5:21:49
Bobtown 30 7 39N45'40 79W58'54 5:19:56
Bocktown 4 13 40N32'36 80W18'01 5:21:12
Bodines 41 7 41N27'01 76W58'22 5:07:53
Boeckel Landing 67
1 39N48'06 76W18'42 5:05:15
Boggstown 28 1 40N04 77W50 5:11:20
Boggsville 3 2 40N45'32 79W40'16 5:18:41
Bogus Corners 25
107 42N03'36 79W55'53 5:19:44
Bohemia 52 6 41N29'49 75W04'04 5:00:16
Bohrmans Mill 54
27 40N38 76W10 5:04:40
Boiling Springs 21
2 40N08'59 77W07'43 5:08:31
Bolivar 65 7 40N23'49 79W09'07 5:16:36

Bolivar Run 42 102 41N57 78W39 5:14:36
Boltz 32 7 40N25'15 79W00'11 5:16:01
Bon Air 11 74 40N20'16 78W52'09 5:15:29
Bon Air 23 9 39N58'01 75W19'07 5:01:16
Bonair 46 1 40N11'11 75W05'53 5:00:24
Bon Aire 10 3 40N53 79W53 5:19:32
Bondsville 15 46 40N01'18 75W45'39 5:03:03
Bon Meade 2 13 40N32'46 80W14'25 5:20:58
Bonnair 67 3 39N45'09 76W45'21 5:07:01
Bonneauville 1 1 39N48'43 77W08'15 5:08:33
Bonnie Brook 10 3 40N51'59 79W49'46 5:19:19
Bonny Brook 21 16 40N10'41 77W11'09 5:08:45
Bonnymeade 63 6 40N21'44 80W21'30 5:21:26
Bonus 10 6 41N07'03 79W43'00 5:18:52
Booher Corners 43 6 41N20'52 80W01'03 5:20:04
Booker 17 6 40N51'09 78W26'16 5:13:45
Boone 56 6 40N00'33 78W50'55 5:15:24
Booneville 18 7 41N01'12 77W21'28 5:09:26
Boon Terrace 63 2 40N14'50 80W11'54 5:20:48
Booth Corner 23 90 39N50'21 75W29'40 5:01:59
Boothwyn 23 90 39N49'48 75W26'31 5:01:46
Boothwyn Highlands 23 90 39N50 75W25 5:01:40
Boot Jack 24 36 41N22'53 78W41'12 5:14:45
Boquet 65 3 40N22'53 79W36'09 5:18:25
Bordell 42 6 41N52'31 78W32'13 5:14:09
Bordnersville 38 1 40N26'39 76W31'51 5:06:07
Borie 53 66 41N41'09 77W57'09 5:11:49
Borland Manor 63 2 40N15'34 80W09'34 5:20:38
Borough 4 19 40N41 80W20 5:21:20
Bortondale 23 90 39N54'06 75W24'23 5:01:38
Bossards Corner 48 8 40N46'28 75W31'46 5:02:07
Bossardsville 45 23 40N55'40 75W16'18 5:01:05
Boston 2 9 40N18'43 79W49'24 5:19:18
Boston Run 54 3 40N48'11 76W11'22 5:04:45
Boswell 56 6 40N09'41 79W01'45 5:16:07
Botts 67 67 39N57 76W42 5:06:48
Boulevard 51 9 40N02 75W04 5:00:16
Boulevard Manor 40 20 41N14'48 75W49'52 5:03:19
Bourne 8 60 41N51 76W30 5:06:00
Bourne Mills 8 60 41N48'09 76W37'50 5:06:31
Bovard 10 6 41N04'25 79W58'19 5:19:53
Bovard 65 99 40N19'11 79W30'13 5:18:01
Bowdertown 32 63 40N45'39 78W50'53 5:15:24
Bower 17 122 40N53'41 78W40'32 5:14:42
Bower Hill 2 114 40N22'24 80W05'38 5:20:23
Bowers 6 8 40N29'14 75W44'33 5:02:58
Bowersville 33 51 40N55'22 78W51'52 5:15:27
Bowest 26 104 39N59'15 79W35'27 5:18:22
Bowie 43 6 41N15'29 80W06'23 5:20:26
Bowling Green 23 90 39N55'09 75W22'51 5:01:31
Bowman Addition 67 1 39N48 76W59 5:07:56
Bowman Creek 66 6 41N25'47 76W01'11 5:04:05
Bowmans 54 3 40N49'26 76W08'23 5:04:34
Bowmansdale 21 12 40N09'58 76W58'42 5:07:55
Bowmans Store 67 1 39N46 76W50 5:07:20
Bowmanstown 13 8 40N47'59 75W39'44 5:02:39
Bowmansville 36 27 40N11'48 76W01'04 5:04:04
Bowood 26 51 39N48'58 79W50'59 5:19:24
Boyce 2 114 40N19'04 80W06'37 5:20:26
Boyd 49 6 40N56'08 76W35'54 5:06:24
Boyds Mills 64 6 41N38'26 75W08'26 5:00:34
Boydstown 10 6 40N56'16 79W50'47 5:19:23
Boydtown 49 27 40N47'17 76W31'48 5:06:07
Boyer 2 114 40N18'54 80W01'49 5:20:07
Boyers 10 6 41N06'30 79W53'57 5:19:36
Boyers Junction 6 8 40N26'26 75W46'14 5:03:05
Boyertown 6 2 40N20'01 75W38'16 5:02:33
Boynton 56 79 39N46'00 79W04'01 5:16:16
Brackenridge 2 14 40N36'29 79W44'29 5:18:58
Brackney 58 6 41N59'23 75W55'38 5:03:43
Braddock 2 114 40N24'12 79W52'07 5:19:28
Braddock 63 3 40N08'43 80W13'48 5:20:55
Braddock Hills 2 114 40N25'02 79W51'55 5:19:28
Braddock, Mount 26 80 39N56'34 79W38'41 5:18:35
Braden Plan 30 6 39N58'10 80W02'49 5:20:11
Bradenville 65 3 40N19'17 79W20'25 5:17:22
Bradford 42 102 41N57'21 78W38'39 5:14:35
Bradford Hills 15 13 40N00'11 75W38'54 5:02:36
Bradford Woods 2 6 40N38'15 80W04'55 5:20:20
Bradley Junction 11 54 40N33'06 78W40'02 5:14:40
Bradleytown 61 6 41N33'21 79W51'42 5:19:27
Bradys Bend 3 1 40N59'47 79W37'47 5:18:31
Braeburn 65 14 40N36'43 79W42'42 5:18:51
Brainerd Center 45 23 40N56'57 75W17'50 5:01:11
Braintrim 66 59 41N38 76W08 5:04:32
Brallier 5 6 40N04'09 78W19'56 5:13:20
Braman 64 6 41N49 75W05 5:00:20
Branch 54 27 40N41 76W17 5:05:08
Branch Dale 54 27 40N40'09 76W19'23 5:05:18
Branchton 10 6 41N04'21 79W59'09 5:19:57
Branchville 25 107 41N57'36 80W08'28 5:20:34
Brandamore 15 9 40N03'13 75W49'13 5:03:17
Brandon 61 6 41N18'58 79W51'03 5:19:24
Brandonville 54 56 40N51'39 76W09'59 5:04:40
Brandt 58 59 41N57'34 75W32'43 5:02:11
Brandtsville 21 12 40N08'35 77W03'44 5:08:15
Brandy Camp 24 6 41N19'15 78W41'16 5:14:45
Brandywine Homes 15 9 39N59 75W50 5:03:20
Brandywine Manor 15 9 40N03'41 75W48'36 5:03:14
Brandywine Summit 23 4 39N52'20 75W32'53 5:02:12
Brandywine Village 46 90 40N05'50 75W22'21 5:01:29
Brant Hill 30 1 39N48'42 80W12'25 5:20:50
Bratton 44 7 40N29 77W42 5:10:48
Brave 30 6 39N43'29 80W15'37 5:21:02
Braznell 26 51 40N01'29 79W51'14 5:19:25
Breadysville 9 1 40N12 75W05 5:00:20
Breakneck 26 104 40N02'27 79W32'27 5:18:10
Bredinsburg 61 109 41N23'41 79W46'22 5:19:05
Bredinville 10 3 40N50'48 79W54'39 5:19:39
Breedtown 61 74 41N35'59 79W42'29 5:18:50
Breezewood 2 114 40N33 80W01 5:20:04
Breezewood 5 6 39N59'57 78W14'20 5:12:57
Breezy Corner 6 8 40N24'40 75W50'48 5:03:23
Breezy Point 29 66 39N59'05 78W02'47 5:12:11
Breinigsville 39 9 40N32'12 75W37'54 5:02:32
Brenizer 65 35 40N24'10 79W16'06 5:17:04
Brent 37 6 41N06'49 80W10'02 5:20:40
Brentwood 2 114 40N22'14 79W58'30 5:19:54
Breslau 40 20 41N14'00 75W56'06 5:03:44
Bressler 22 12 40N13'46 76W49'13 5:07:17
Breton Hills 9 1 40N12 75W05 5:00:20
Bretonville 17 6 40N51'07 78W33'58 5:14:16
Briarbrook 40 20 41N14 75W52 5:03:28
Briarcliff 23 9 39N54 75W18 5:01:12
Briar Creek 19 1 41N02'45 76W16'57 5:05:08
Briarwood 9 1 42N08 75W53 5:03:32
Brick Church 3 15 40N41'10 79W27'20 5:17:49
Bricker Crossroads 10 2 40N44'27 79W43'29 5:18:54
Brickerville 36 8 40N13'33 76W18'10 5:05:13
Brick Tavern 9 13 40N27'23 75W23'06 5:01:32
Bridesburg 51 9 40N00'01 75W04'12 5:00:17
Bridgeburg 3 15 40N52'09 79W29'03 5:17:56
Bridge Point 9 8 40N16'59 75W07'50 5:00:31
Bridgeport 1 1 39N55'56 77W18'43 5:09:15
Bridgeport 13 60 41N03'06 75W46'09 5:03:05
Bridgeport 17 7 40N58'31 78W33'05 5:14:12
Bridgeport 36 8 40N02'21 76W15'54 5:05:04
Bridgeport 46 90 40N06'18 75W20'44 5:01:23
Bridgeport 50 6 40N19'47 77W17'13 5:09:09
Bridgeport 65 111 40N07'45 79W31'58 5:18:08
Bridgeton 9 7 40N33 75W06 5:00:24
Bridgeton 67 1 39N47'27 76W25'15 5:05:41
Bridgetown 9 97 40N11'18 74W55'52 4:59:43
Bridge Valley 9 8 40N16'46 75W05'05 5:00:20
Bridgeville 2 114 40N21'22 80W06'37 5:20:26
Bridgewater 4 19 40N42'19 80W18'05 5:21:12
Bridgewater 9 9 40N05'52 74W55'11 4:59:41
Bridgewater 23 90 39N51'52 75W23'54 5:01:36
Bridgewater Farms 23 90 39N52 75W23 5:01:32
Brier Hill 26 51 39N58'49 79W49'42 5:19:19
Briggsville 40 1 41N02'27 76W08'16 5:04:33
Brighton 4 8 40N42 80W22 5:21:28
Brighton 23 9 39N58 75W18 5:01:12
Brightside 9 9 40N08 74W51 4:59:24
Brightwood 2 114 40N20'26 80W01'58 5:20:08
Brillhart 67 67 39N54'33 76W45'18 5:07:01
Brinker 10 3 40N49'46 79W49'48 5:19:19
Brinkerton 16 6 41N04'38 79W21'35 5:17:26
Brinkerton 65 99 40N13'22 79W31'35 5:18:06
Brintons 15 13 39N57 75W36 5:02:24
Brintons Corners 4 121 40N51'10 80W10'56 5:20:44
Briquette 2 10 40N22 79W51 5:19:24
Brisbin 17 4 40N50'17 78W21'17 5:13:25
Briscoe Springs 43 6 41N10 80W05 5:20:20
Bristol 9 9 40N06'02 74W51'08 4:59:25
Bristol Terrace Number One 9 9 40N06'52 74W51'11 4:59:25
Bristol Terrace Number Two 9 9 40N07'10 74W51'20 4:59:25
Bristoria 30 6 39N52'25 80W24'32 5:21:38
Brittains Corner 15 8 40N06'00 75W28'43 5:01:55
Brittany Farms 9 2 40N20 75W18 5:01:12
Britton Run 20 56 41N47'41 79W44'33 5:18:58
Broad Acres 43 6 41N10'37 80W05'02 5:20:20
Broad Axe 46 1 40N08'20 75W14'40 5:00:59
Broad Ford 26 104 40N02'50 79W36'31 5:18:26
Broadlawn Highlands 2 114 40N19'34 80W04'21 5:20:17
Broad Street 40 42 40N58 76W00 5:04:00
Broad Top City 31 6 40N12'08 78W08'28 5:12:34
Broadview 2 14 40N37 79W44 5:18:56
Broadway 40 1 41N14'50 76W12'54 5:04:52
Broadway Manor 9 9 40N08 74W51 4:59:24
Brock 30 6 39N44'33 80W10'23 5:20:42
Brockie 67 67 39N57 76W42 5:06:48
Brockport 24 5 41N15'35 78W43'37 5:14:54
Brockton 54 1 40N44'54 76W04'08 5:04:17
Brockway 33 5 41N14'57 78W47'59 5:15:12
Brodbecks 67 1 39N46'14 76W49'41 5:07:19
Brodhead 48 13 40N40'50 75W20'29 5:01:22
Brodheadsville 45 1 40N55'28 75W23'39 5:01:35
Brogue 67 1 39N52'18 76W29'00 5:05:56
Brogueville 67 1 39N50'35 76W31'55 5:06:08
Brokenstraw 62 3 41N51 79W19 5:17:16
Brommerstown 54 1 40N35'51 76W09'21 5:04:37
Brookdale 11 74 40N23 78W50 5:15:20
Brookdale 58 50 41N58'38 75W48'42 5:03:15
Brookes Mills 7 33 40N28 78W25 5:13:40
Brookfield 15 13 39N51'11 75W35'49 5:02:23
Brookfield 59 6 41N59'40 77W35'37 5:10:22
Brookhaven 23 90 39N52'09 75W22'58 5:01:32
Brookhaven Gardens 23 90 39N52 75W23 5:01:32
Brookland 53 6 41N49'44 77W47'52 5:11:11
Brookline 2 114 40N23'31 80W01'05 5:20:04
Brookline 23 9 39N58'56 75W18'19 5:01:13
Brooklyn 58 59 41N45'04 75W48'26 5:03:14
Brooklyn 59 59 41N54'33 77W08'30 5:08:34
Brook Park 60 70 40N58 76W54 5:07:36
Brookside 2 114 40N19'55 80W03'20 5:20:13
Brookside 21 82 40N04'56 77W24'49 5:09:39
Brookside 25 107 42N08'19 79W59'23 5:19:58
Brookside 41 7 41N23'28 77W15'14 5:09:01
Brookside 54 9 40N36 76W23 5:05:32
Brookside 66 59 41N34'30 75W56'09 5:03:45
Brookside Farms 2 114 40N20 80W05 5:20:20
Brooks Mill 7 3 40N22'25 78W25'23 5:13:42
Brookston 27 3 41N37'03 78W58'43 5:15:55
Brookthorpe Hills 23 9 39N59'00 75W20'47 5:01:23
Brookvale 26 104 40N01 79W35 5:18:20
Brookville 33 34 41N09'40 79W05'00 5:16:20
Brookwater Park 46 8 40N12 75W28 5:01:52
Broomall 23 1 39N58'53 75W21'25 5:01:26
Brothersvalley 56 6 39N55 78W59 5:15:56
Brotherton 56 6 39N58'17 78W57'29 5:15:50
Broughton 2 114 40N19'33 79W59'12 5:19:57
Broughton Hollow 59 6 41N40'08 77W18'43 5:09:15
Browfield 26 80 39N51'25 79W42'44 5:18:51
Brownbacks 15 118 40N10'29 75W37'07 5:02:28
Browndale 64 59 41N39 75W28 5:01:52
Brownfield 26 80 39N51 79W43 5:18:52
Brown Hill 20 3 41N47'27 79W55'57 5:19:44
Brownlee 59 6 41N40'04 77W15'26 5:09:02
Brown Mills 28 42 39N49'47 77W42'07 5:10:48
Brown Row 26 105 39N58'11 79W36'38 5:18:27
Browns 40 1 41N20'41 75W43'43 5:02:55
Brownsburg 9 8 40N19'05 74W55'14 4:59:41
Browns Crossroads 3 6 40N55'38 79W37'39 5:18:31
Brownsdale 10 6 40N46'26 79W58'00 5:19:52
Browns Mill 6 8 40N18'09 75W46'55 5:03:08
Brownstone 22 12 40N16 76W43 5:06:52
Brownstown 3 4 40N32'54 79W30'48 5:18:03
Brownstown 11 74 40N20'04 78W56'18 5:15:45
Brownstown 26 1 40N06'17 79W50'01 5:19:20
Brownstown 36 28 40N07'25 76W12'51 5:04:51
Brownsville 6 80 40N22'01 76W04'35 5:04:18
Brownsville 26 1 40N01'25 79W53'03 5:19:32
Brownsville 28 1 39N54'03 77W31'17 5:10:05
Brownton 67 7 39N52'11 76W33'44 5:06:15
Browntown 8 6 41N39'03 76W14'26 5:04:58
Browntown 40 1 41N18'35 75W47'16 5:03:09
Browntown 63 6 40N16'44 80W27'54 5:21:52
Browntown 65 25 40N20'02 79W43'59 5:18:56
Bruce 67 1 39N47'42 76W26'43 5:05:47
Bruceton 2 114 40N19'05 79W58'48 5:19:55
Bruin 10 6 41N03'17 79W43'37 5:18:54
Brumbaugh 5 6 40N10'46 78W28'15 5:13:53
Brumbaugh Crossing 31 3 40N23'29 78W08'07 5:12:32
Brunnerville 36 8 40N11'05 76W17'06 5:05:08
Brush Creek 29 6 39N56 78W14 5:12:56
Brushmeadway 7 33 40N25 78W24 5:13:36
Brush Run 1 1 39N51'43 77W05'53 5:08:24
Brushton 2 114 40N27'24 79W53'39 5:19:35
Brushtown 1 1 39N47'52 77W02'47 5:08:11
Brushtown 21 1 40N05'26 77W19'02 5:09:16
Brush Valley 32 6 40N32'10 79W04'00 5:16:16
Brushville 8 6 41N48'36 76W11'17 5:04:45
Brushville 58 59 41N54'57 75W37'42 5:02:31
Bryan 3 59 40N49'58 79W17'26 5:17:10
Bryan 26 104 40N03 79W39 5:18:36
Bryan 30 6 39N52'31 80W28'44 5:21:55
Bryan Hill 32 72 40N38 79W09 5:16:36
Bryan Hill Manor 32 72 40N38'34 79W07'51 5:16:31
Bryan Mill 41 6 41N15'45 76W42'52 5:06:51
Bryansville 67 7 39N44'53 76W21'12 5:05:25
Bryant 2 114 40N34 80W00 5:20:00
Bryn Athyn 46 1 40N07'53 75W04'04 5:00:16
Bryn Gweled 9 1 40N11 75W03 5:00:12
Bryn Mawr 2 114 40N18'14 80W05'13 5:20:21
Bryn Mawr 46 9 40N01'11 75W18'18 5:01:13
Brysonia 1 1 39N57'05 77W18'29 5:09:14
Buchanan Summit 28 51 39N55'08 77W56'43 5:11:47
Bucher 17 6 40N50 78W26 5:13:44
Buchers Mills 62 3 41N45'40 79W10'12 5:16:41
Buck 36 27 39N52'21 76W13'45 5:04:55
Buck 40 6 41N10 75W41 5:02:44
Buckeye 65 111 40N07'19 79W33'02 5:18:12
Buck Hill Falls 45 84 41N11'16 75W15'58 5:01:04
Buckhorn 11 63 40N32'51 78W28'54 5:13:56
Buckhorn 19 4 41N01'09 76W30'03 5:06:00
Buckingham 9 8 40N19'25 75W03'37 5:00:14
Buckingham Valley 9 8 40N18'35 75W03'00 5:00:12
Buckman Village 23 90 39N51 75W22 5:01:28
Buckmanville 9 8 40N18'54 74W58'29 4:59:54
Buck Mountain 13 60 40N58'48 75W48'48 5:03:15
Buck Mountain 54 27 40N49'16 76W05'57 5:04:24
Buck Run 15 9 39N55'26 75W50'57 5:03:24
Buck Run 32 6 40N41'05 78W59'30 5:15:58
Buck Run 54 27 40N42'27 76W19'38 5:05:19
Buckstown 56 6 40N04'16 78W51'43 5:15:27
Bucksville 9 1 40N30'23 75W11'17 5:00:45
Bucktoe 9 97 40N11'38 74W54'23 4:59:38
Bucktown 15 8 40N10'29 75W39'45 5:02:39
Buck Valley 29 6 39N45'59 78W17'00 5:13:08
Budaville 63 6 40N09'43 80W27'59 5:21:52
Buells Corners 20 56 41N50 79W41 5:18:44
Buena Vista 2 8 40N16'38 79W47'58 5:19:12
Buena Vista 7 11 40N40 78W13 5:12:52
Buena Vista 10 6 40N58'40 79W46'22 5:19:05
Buena Vista 26 104 40N01'11 79W42'40 5:18:51

Buena Vista 28 100 39N45 77W34 5:10:16
Buena Vista 36 23 40N01'15 75W58'47 5:03:55
Buena Vista Springs 28 100 39N43'55 77W30'12 5:10:01
Buffalo 63 6 40N13'35 80W21'38 5:21:27
Buffalo Creek 3 7 40N49'08 79W39'40 5:18:39
Buffalo Crossroads 60 70 40N57'48 76W58'09 5:07:53
Buffalo Mills 3 7 40N50'24 79W38'37 5:18:34
Buffalo Mills 5 7 39N56'00 78W38'46 5:14:35
Buffalo Run 14 63 40N49'42 77W57'45 5:11:51
Buffalo Springs 38 8 40N17'31 76W20'06 5:05:20
Buffalo Valley 3 6 40N50 79W38 5:18:32
Buffington 26 51 39N55'44 79W50'29 5:19:22
Buffington 32 6 40N31 78W57 5:15:48
Buhl 43 117 41N15 80W30 5:22:00
Buhls Station 10 6 40N47'55 80W01'33 5:20:06
Bulger 63 64 40N22'42 80W19'41 5:21:19
Bullion 61 6 41N14'47 79W53'52 5:19:35
Bullis Mills 42 40 41N59'05 78W21'04 5:13:24
Bullskin 26 111 40N05 79W32 5:18:08
Bull Tavern 15 8 40N07'02 75W29'15 5:01:57
Bully Hill 61 109 41N22'08 79W49'35 5:19:18
Bumpville 8 41 41N54'15 76W23'10 5:05:33
Bunches 67 12 40N10'53 76W52'44 5:07:31
Bungalow Park 39 13 40N34'55 75W31'35 5:02:06
Bunker Hill 34 6 40N26'15 77W32'12 5:10:09
Bunker Hill 38 8 40N23'38 76W29'05 5:05:56
Bunkertown 34 1 40N39'03 77W14'30 5:08:58
Bunola 2 8 40N14'14 79W57'03 5:19:48
Burd Coleman Village 38 8 40N16'00 76W25'06 5:05:40
Burdette 30 6 39N58'05 80W26'48 5:21:47
Burds Crossing 65 3 40N19'43 79W18'42 5:17:15
Burgettstown 63 4 40N22'55 80W23'35 5:21:34
Burholme 51 9 40N03'40 75W05'01 5:00:20
Burkhelder 56 79 39N52'51 79W02'00 5:16:08
Burlington 8 60 41N46'47 76W36'28 5:06:26
Burnham 44 73 40N38'19 77W34'08 5:10:17
Burning Bush 5 7 39N56'17 78W34'50 5:14:19
Burning Well 42 75 41N40 78W49 5:15:16
Burnside 17 6 40N48'46 78W47'09 5:15:09
Burnside 23 9 39N55 75W19 5:01:16
Burnside 49 27 40N45'59 76W33'28 5:06:14
Burnstown 37 121 40N52 80W16 5:21:04
Burnt Cabins 29 6 40N04'41 77W53'45 5:11:35
Burnt Mills 15 8 39N50'06 75W39'01 5:02:36
Burnt Mills 36 1 39N56'29 76W18'24 5:05:14
Burnwood 58 6 41N47'10 75W30'26 5:02:02
Burrell 65 35 40N25'01 79W15'59 5:17:04
Burrows 53 6 41N41'37 77W45'00 5:11:00
Burson Plan 30 6 39N58'03 80W03'00 5:20:12
Bursonville 9 12 40N32'16 75W14'26 5:00:58
Burtville 42 6 41N47'20 78W12'19 5:12:49
Bush Addition 14 70 40N54'17 77W47'21 5:11:09
Bushkill 52 3 41N05'36 75W00'08 5:00:01
Bushkill Center 48 8 40N47'37 75W19'30 5:01:18
Bush Patch 35 18 41N22'25 75W44'49 5:02:59
Bustleton 51 9 40N04'57 75W01'55 5:00:08
Bute 26 80 39N57'14 79W41'57 5:18:48
Butler 10 3 40N51'40 79W53'44 5:19:35
Butler Junction 10 2 40N40'24 79W41'38 5:18:47
Buttermilk Falls 65 110 40N15'49 79W17'28 5:17:10
Butternut Grove 41 82 41N21'14 76W53'52 5:07:35
Buttonwood 40 20 41N13'19 75W56'34 5:03:46
Buttonwood 41 7 41N29'59 77W08'06 5:08:32
Buttonwood Glen 9 8 40N21 75W13 5:00:52
Buttonwood Manor 9 8 40N21 75W13 5:00:52
Butts 14 7 41N01'38 77W54'41 5:11:39
Butztown 48 13 40N39'11 75W19'42 5:01:19
Buyerstown 36 23 40N00'41 76W02'46 5:04:11
Buzz 30 6 39N47'14 80W19'14 5:21:17
Byers 15 80 40N04'41 75W40'52 5:02:43
Byersdale 4 13 40N37'25 80W13'29 5:20:54
Byrnedale 24 7 41N17'31 78W30'16 5:14:01
Byrnesville 19 27 40N47'47 76W20'22 5:05:21
Byromtown 27 6 41N31'27 79W03'02 5:16:12
Bywood 23 9 39N57'29 75W16'02 5:01:04
Bywood Heights 23 9 39N58 75W18 5:01:12
Cabel 49 27 40N48'53 76W35'10 5:06:21
Cable Hollow 62 6 41N57'49 79W04'58 5:16:20
Cabot 10 6 40N45'53 79W46'00 5:19:04
Cacoosing 6 101 40N20'59 76W00'30 5:04:02
Cadis 8 6 41N58'44 76W14'34 5:04:58
Cadogan 3 15 40N45'14 79W34'53 5:18:20
Caernarvon 6 27 40N10 75W53 5:03:32
Cains 36 23 40N01'37 75W57'16 5:03:49
Cairnbrook 56 63 40N07'08 78W49'06 5:15:16
Caldwell 18 76 41N08 77W28 5:09:52
Caledonia 24 7 41N17'14 78W27'37 5:13:50
Caledonia Park 28 1 39N54'15 77W28'44 5:09:55
Calico Corner 9 9 40N07'43 74W58'09 4:59:53
California 9 13 40N28'32 75W20'51 5:01:23
California 47 73 41N04'00 76W43'36 5:06:54
California 63 1 40N03'56 79W53'31 5:19:34
California Furnace 65 110 40N11'30 79W12'30 5:16:50
Calkins 64 6 41N39'19 75W09'21 5:00:37
Callapoose 64 4 41N22'17 75W24'20 5:01:37
Callensburg 16 6 41N07'33 79W33'31 5:18:14
Callery 10 6 40N44'26 80W02'12 5:20:09
Callimont 56 79 39N49 79W02 5:16:08
Caln 15 46 39N59'27 75W46'50 5:03:07
Caln Meeting House 15 46 40N00'26 75W45'53 5:03:04
Calumet 65 6 40N12'39 79W29'08 5:17:57
Calvert 41 7 41N24'01 76W58'00 5:07:52
Calvert Hills 7 33 40N31'07 78W24'41 5:13:39
Calvin 31 6 40N20'12 78W01'39 5:12:07
Camargo 36 27 39N54'58 76W10'31 5:04:42
Cambra 40 6 41N11'53 76W18'22 5:05:13
Cambria City 11 74 40N20'24 78W55'50 5:15:43
Cambridge 15 27 40N04'53 75W56'16 5:03:45
Cambridge Springs 20 3 41N48'13 80W03'24 5:20:14
Camden Hill 2 114 40N22 79W54 5:19:36
Cameron 12 106 41N27'15 78W10'33 5:12:42
Cameron 49 6 40N56'03 76W42'28 5:06:50
Cameron 60 70 40N58'27 76W58'37 5:07:54
Cammal 41 6 41N24 77W28 5:09:52
Camp Akiba 45 17 40N56 75W19 5:01:16
Campbells Mill 32 98 40N28'08 79W13'46 5:16:55
Campbelltown 38 31 40N16'39 76W35'08 5:06:21
Campbelltown 42 75 41N42'43 78W39'11 5:14:37
Campbellville 57 6 41N32'53 76W33'15 5:06:13
Camp Curtin 22 12 40N17 76W53 5:07:32
Camp Grove 49 51 40N43 76W51 5:07:24
Camp Hill 2 114 40N25 80W05 5:20:20
Camp Hill 21 12 40N14'23 76W55'13 5:07:41
Camp Jo-Ann 65 14 40N31 79W41 5:18:44
Camp Mystic 25 3 41N48 80W03 5:20:12
Camp Perry 43 6 41N24 80W11 5:20:44
Campton 2 14 40N37 79W44 5:18:56
Camptown 8 6 41N43'52 76W14'06 5:04:56
Canaan 64 6 41N34 75W24 5:01:36
Canaan Grove 38 25 40N17'23 76W15'38 5:05:03
Canadensis 45 84 41N11'34 75W15'09 5:01:01
Canadohta Lake 20 58 41N54 79W51 5:19:24
Canal 61 6 41N29 79W57 5:19:48
Canal Center 61 59 41N28'19 79W56'03 5:19:44
Canan 7 33 40N27'43 78W25'48 5:13:43
Canan Station 7 33 40N31 78W25 5:13:40
Candlebrook 46 90 40N05 75W22 5:01:28
C and M Junction 17 56 41N05'02 78W45'29 5:15:02
Candor 63 51 40N23'31 80W18'33 5:21:14
Cannelton 4 8 40N47'56 80W28'33 5:21:54
Canoe 32 51 40N53 78W57 5:15:48
Canoe Camp 59 59 41N50 77W01 5:08:04
Canoe Creek 7 33 40N28'42 78W16'18 5:13:05
Canoe Furnace 16 6 41N11'20 79W31'05 5:18:04
Canoe Ridge 32 51 40N51'49 78W56'10 5:15:45
Canonsburg 63 2 40N15'45 80W11'15 5:20:45
Canton 8 103 41N39'23 76W51'13 5:07:25
Canyon Vista 57 6 41N27'58 76W33'54 5:06:16
Caprivi 21 16 40N14'38 77W13'55 5:08:56
Carbon 8 60 41N38'59 76W39'43 5:06:39
Carbon 13 8 40N48 75W36 5:02:24
Carbon 31 6 40N13 78W10 5:12:40
Carbon 43 117 41N09'52 80W22'40 5:21:31
Carbon 65 99 40N17'25 79W33'38 5:18:15
Carbon Center 10 3 40N52'23 79W47'37 5:19:10
Carbondale 35 1 41N34'25 75W30'08 5:02:01
Cardale 26 51 39N57'24 79W51'59 5:19:28
Cardiff 11 63 40N29'42 78W50'03 5:15:20
Cardington 23 9 39N58 75W18 5:01:12
Carley Brook 64 59 41N37'40 75W14'08 5:00:57
Carlim 7 3 40N29'13 78W10'12 5:12:41
Carlisle 21 16 40N12'05 77W11'21 5:08:45
Carlisle Barracks 21 2 40N13 77W10 5:08:40
Carlisle Junction 21 2 40N07'27 77W10'37 5:08:42
Carlisle Springs 21 16 40N16'15 77W09'53 5:08:40
Carlson 24 75 41N35'02 78W50'22 5:15:21
Carlton 43 59 41N28'34 80W01'12 5:20:05
Carman 24 59 41N21'57 78W49'29 5:15:18
Carmichaels 30 51 39N53'48 79W58'29 5:19:54
Carmona 43 6 41N07'20 80W06'11 5:20:25
Carnegie 2 114 40N24'31 80W05'01 5:20:20
Carney 65 3 40N18'23 79W26'50 5:17:47
Carnot 2 13 40N31'01 80W13'18 5:20:53
Carnwath 17 6 40N51'48 78W30'45 5:14:03
Carpenter Corner 43 6 41N20 80W06 5:20:24
Carpenter Hollow 66 44 41N32'53 75W49'01 5:03:16
Carpenter Town 35 44 41N33'43 75W42'33 5:02:50
Carpentertown 65 111 40N11'07 79W31'00 5:18:04
Carrick 2 114 40N23'47 79W59'26 5:19:58
Carrick Valley 28 1 40N03'35 77W51'56 5:11:28
Carrier 33 59 41N08 79W11 5:16:44
Carroll 18 7 41N02'55 77W12'36 5:08:50
Carroll Park 19 4 41N00 76W25 5:05:40
Carroll Park 23 9 39N59 75W16 5:01:04
Carrolltown 11 63 40N36'10 78W42'32 5:14:50
Carrolltown Road 11 63 40N35'51 78W43'41 5:14:55
Carroll Valley 1 1 39N47 77W22 5:09:28
Carson 2 114 40N25 79W59 5:19:56
Carsontown 41 6 41N24'28 77W19'59 5:09:20
Carsonville 22 24 40N29'03 76W46'02 5:07:04
Carter 10 6 41N07'11 80W01'55 5:20:08
Carter Camp 53 6 41N44 77W39 5:10:36
Cartin 22 4 40N35'06 76W50'58 5:07:24
Cartwright 24 5 41N16'28 78W43'52 5:14:55
Cartwrights Crossing 42 75 41N40'06 78W44'58 5:15:00
Carver Court 15 9 39N59 75W50 5:03:20
Carversville 9 8 40N23'11 75W03'47 5:00:15
Carverton 40 20 41N20'14 75W51'55 5:03:28
Casanova 14 4 40N57'17 78W10'04 5:12:40
Cascade 41 7 41N27 76W54 5:07:36
Casey Highlands 9 1 40N10'46 75W03'54 5:00:16
Casey Tract 9 1 40N13 75W01 5:00:04
Casey Village 9 1 40N11'42 75W02'51 5:00:11
Cashtown 1 1 39N53'04 77W21'35 5:09:26
Cashtown 28 42 39N52'04 77W44'12 5:10:57
Cassandra 11 55 40N24'31 78W38'27 5:14:34
Casselman 56 4 39N53'08 79W12'42 5:16:51
Cassville 31 6 40N17'35 78W01'38 5:12:07
Castanea 18 76 41N07'29 77W25'48 5:09:43
Caste Village 2 114 40N22 79W58 5:19:52
Castile 30 6 39N59'19 80W07'35 5:20:30
Castle Fin 67 1 39N46'06 76W19'43 5:05:19
Castle Garden 12 7 41N19'53 78W08'26 5:12:34
Castle Rock 23 90 39N58'27 75W26'26 5:01:46
Castle Rocks 18 7 41N05'52 77W14'31 5:08:58
Castle Shannon 2 114 40N21'53 80W01'21 5:20:05
Castle Valley 9 2 40N17'14 75W09'34 5:00:38
Castlewood 37 112 40N55'30 80W16'28 5:21:06
Castor 51 9 40N02 75W04 5:00:16
Cataract 17 6 41N10 78W04 5:12:16
Catasauqua 39 13 40N39'17 75W28'30 5:01:54
Catawissa 19 4 40N57'07 76W27'36 5:05:50
Catfish 16 7 41N00'23 79W35'13 5:18:21
Catharine 7 3 40N31 78W12 5:12:48
Cats Run Junction 26 51 39N50'06 79W55'13 5:19:41
Cavettsville 65 25 40N22'32 79W45'41 5:19:03
Ceasetown 40 1 41N15'28 76W00'48 5:04:03
Cecil 63 114 40N19'46 80W10'16 5:20:41
Cedarbrook 46 9 40N04'59 75W09'37 5:00:38
Cedarbrook Hills 46 9 40N05 75W09 5:00:36
Cedar Brook-Melrose Park 46 9 40N05 75W07 5:00:28
Cedar Cliff 21 12 40N13'42 76W54'11 5:07:37
Cedar Cliff Manor 21 12 40N14 76W57 5:07:48
Cedar Grove 46 8 40N17'23 75W38'06 5:02:32
Cedar Heights 46 8 40N05'03 75W17'23 5:01:10
Cedar Hill 44 6 40N39'14 77W37'49 5:10:31
Cedar Hollow 15 8 40N04'21 75W31'23 5:02:06
Cedarhurst 2 114 40N23 80W04 5:20:16
Cedar Knoll 15 9 40N01'54 75W49'39 5:03:19
Cedar Lane 36 27 40N07 76W02 5:04:08
Cedar Ledge 8 103 41N38'22 76W52'15 5:07:29
Cedar Pines 41 6 41N30'34 77W27'23 5:09:50
Cedar Ridge 1 1 39N50'46 77W06'41 5:08:27
Cedar Run 41 6 41N31 77W27 5:09:48
Cedars 46 8 40N12'45 75W22'08 5:01:29
Cedar Springs 18 76 41N04'53 77W28'48 5:09:55
Cedarville 15 8 40N13'37 75W40'19 5:02:41
Celia 4 121 40N48'54 80W13'44 5:20:55
Cementon 39 13 40N41'21 75W30'29 5:02:02
Centennial 1 1 39N48'55 77W03'33 5:08:14
Centennial 14 63 40N46'39 78W02'35 5:12:10
Centennial Hills 9 1 40N12 75W05 5:00:20
Center 2 14 40N28'39 79W45'33 5:19:02
Center 34 7 40N35 77W24 5:09:36
Center Bridge 9 8 40N24'01 74W58'48 4:59:55
Center Hill 3 15 40N47'51 79W34'44 5:18:19
Center Mills 1 1 39N57'20 77W12'41 5:08:51
Center Moreland 66 59 41N25'12 75W55'50 5:03:43
Centerport 6 80 40N29'10 76W00'28 5:04:02
Center Road 20 7 41N42'43 80W25'02 5:21:40
Center Square 36 28 40N06'18 76W12'00 5:04:48
Center Square 46 8 40N10 75W17 5:01:08
Center Square 50 6 40N17'45 77W33'01 5:10:12
Center Square Greens 46 90 40N08 75W21 5:01:24
Centertown 43 6 41N13'43 80W02'41 5:20:11
Center Union 31 81 40N32'18 77W57'40 5:11:51
Center Valley 3 15 40N42'26 79W34'12 5:18:17
Center Valley 39 13 40N31'45 75W23'37 5:01:34
Centerville 5 70 39N49'46 78W39'00 5:14:36
Centerville 20 7 41N44'10 79W45'48 5:19:03
Centerville 32 7 40N23'22 79W04'25 5:16:18
Centerville 36 8 40N03'37 76W23'28 5:05:34
Centerville 50 1 40N33'25 77W03'01 5:08:12
Centerville 63 51 40N02'43 79W58'33 5:19:54
Centerville 65 111 40N09'33 79W41'38 5:18:47
Centerville 67 3 39N48'03 76W44'17 5:06:57
Central 19 6 41N17'48 76W22'24 5:05:30
Central 65 111 40N10'39 79W35'07 5:18:20
Central City 14 70 40N57'00 77W47'49 5:11:11
Central City 56 63 40N06'38 78W48'08 5:15:13
Central Highlands 2 8 40N17 79W50 5:19:20
Centralia 19 27 40N48'15 76W20'27 5:05:22
Central Manor 36 26 39N59'57 76W25'35 5:05:42
Central Oak Heights 60 70 41N00'41 76W52'14 5:07:29
Central Park 2 8 40N17 79W50 5:19:20
Central Wharf 2 114 40N24 79W54 5:19:36
Centre 34 7 40N32'39 77W18'38 5:09:15
Centre 50 6 40N21'22 77W24'27 5:09:38
Centre Hall 14 64 40N50'51 77W41'11 5:10:45
Centre Hill 14 64 40N49'07 77W38'49 5:10:35
Century 26 51 40N00'37 79W53'10 5:19:33
Cereal 65 25 40N18'52 79W43'26 5:18:54
Ceres 42 7 41N58 78W16 5:13:04
Cessna 5 70 40N05'40 78W31'33 5:14:06

Cetronia 39 13 40N35'12 75w31'48 5:02:07
Ceylon 30 51 39N51'43 79w58'51 5:19:55
Chadds Ford 23 13 39N52'18 75w35'30 5:02:22
Chadds Ford Junction 15 13 39N52'08 75w35'47 5:02:23
Chadville 26 80 39N51'59 79w45'07 5:19:00
Chaffee 24 6 41N34'49 78w56'03 5:15:44
Chain 54 1 40N44'15 75w56'44 5:03:47
Chain Bridge 9 1 40N12 75w05 5:00:20
Chaintown 65 111 40N05'49 79w39'20 5:18:37
Chalfant 2 114 40N24'31 79w50'21 5:19:21
Chalfont 9 2 40N17'18 75w12'34 5:00:50
Chalkhill 26 6 39N50'39 79w37'01 5:18:28
Challenge 24 5 41N17'19 78w41'21 5:14:45
Chalybeat 5 70 40N01'41 78w29'06 5:13:56
Chambersburg 28 42 39N56'15 77w39'41 5:10:39
Chambers Hill 22 12 40N16 76w49 5:07:16
Chambers Mill 63 3 40N05'58 80w14'37 5:20:58
Chambersville 32 72 40N42'19 79w09'29 5:16:38
Chamouni 26 115 40N03'31 79w52'24 5:19:30
Champion 63 51 40N25'21 80w17'28 5:21:10
Champion 65 6 40N04'30 79w21'30 5:17:26
Chanceford 67 1 39N53 76w29 5:05:56
Chandler Plan 3 15 40N46 79w32 5:18:08
Chandlers Valley 62 3 41N56'03 79w18'14 5:17:13
Chaneysville 5 6 39N49'25 78w29'22 5:13:57
Chapel 6 2 40N26'10 75w32'45 5:02:11
Chapel Downs 2 14 40N33 79w49 5:19:16
Chapel Hill 46 1 40N09 75w03 5:00:12
Chapman 39 13 40N35'21 75w36'15 5:02:25
Chapman 48 13 40N45'38 75w24'18 5:01:37
Chapman 55 51 40N41'14 76w53'13 5:07:33
Chapman Lake 35 1 41N32 75w32 5:02:08
Chapmanville 61 6 41N35'35 79w50'18 5:19:21
Charleroi 63 1 40N08'16 79w53'54 5:19:36
Charleston 43 117 41N14'13 80w21'38 5:21:27
Charleston 59 6 41N46'06 77w14'41 5:08:59
Charlestown 3 6 40N57'38 79w15'23 5:17:02
Charlestown 15 8 40N05'55 75w33'12 5:02:13
Charlestown 28 51 39N51'36 77w56'05 5:11:44
Charlesville 5 70 39N56'55 78w30'16 5:14:01
Charlies Grove 11 6 40N31'52 78w53'37 5:15:34
Charlottsville 7 11 40N38'41 78w16'38 5:13:07
Charlton 18 76 41N10'42 77w21'03 5:09:24
Charlton 22 12 40N19 76w48 5:07:12
Charmian 28 1 39N44'34 77w27'54 5:09:52
Charming Forge 6 56 40N23'22 76w10'21 5:04:41
Charnita 1 1 39N47 77w22 5:09:28
Charteroak 31 81 40N40'40 77w54'35 5:11:38
Charter Oaks 25 107 42N05'18 80w08'16 5:20:33
Charterwood 2 114 40N33 80w01 5:20:04
Chartiers 30 6 39N57'29 80w03'04 5:20:12
Chartiers Terrace 2 114 40N25 80w05 5:20:20
Chase 40 20 41N17'05 75w57'48 5:03:51
Chatham 15 8 39N51'12 75w49'19 5:03:17
Chatham Park 23 9 40N00 75w18 5:01:12
Chatham Run 18 76 41N10'17 77w21'56 5:09:28
Chatham Village 23 9 40N00 75w18 5:01:12
Chatwood 15 13 39N57'59 75w35'23 5:02:22
Chauncey 40 20 41N15 75w57 5:03:48
Checkerville 8 7 41N54'36 76w45'38 5:07:03
Chelsea 23 90 39N52'01 75w28'06 5:01:52
Cheltenham 46 9 40N03'39 75w05'40 5:00:23
Chelten Hills 46 9 40N04'43 75w08'50 5:00:35
Chemung 41 7 41N35'26 76w50'21 5:07:21
Cherokee Ranch 6 101 40N24 75w55 5:03:40
Cherry City 2 114 40N29'41 79w57'47 5:19:51
Cherry Corner 17 122 40N53'09 78w38'29 5:14:34
Cherrydale 46 90 40N05 75w16 5:01:04
Cherry Flats 59 59 41N43'54 77w10'30 5:08:42
Cherry Grove 31 6 40N17'52 78w03'51 5:12:15
Cherry Grove 62 6 41N41'46 79w08'41 5:16:35
Cherry Hill 25 7 41N54 80w22 5:21:28
Cherryhill 32 6 40N39 79w00 5:16:00
Cherry Hill 48 8 40N45'29 75w18'35 5:01:14
Cherry Lane 3 4 40N34'09 79w33'36 5:18:14
Cherry Mills 57 60 41N30'13 76w27'33 5:05:50
Cherry Ridge 64 59 41N31'54 75w16'44 5:01:07
Cherry Run 14 7 41N03'19 77w58'44 5:11:55
Cherry Run 60 6 40N50'58 77w21'17 5:09:25
Cherry Run 62 3 41N38'03 78w59'48 5:15:59
Cherrytown 8 6 41N40'52 76w16'46 5:05:07
Cherrytown 31 3 40N17'38 78w14'31 5:12:58
Cherry Tree 32 63 40N43'35 78w48'25 5:15:14
Cherrytree 61 9 41N31'58 79w43'07 5:18:52
Cherry Valley 10 6 41N09'25 79w47'57 5:19:12
Cherry Valley 63 6 40N21'02 80w20'55 5:21:24
Cherryville 48 8 40N45'14 75w32'20 5:02:09
Cherryville 54 27 40N34 76w24 5:05:36
Chesney Downs 23 9 39N56 75w20 5:01:20
Chester 23 90 39N50'58 75w21'22 5:01:25
Chesterfield 17 54 40N47'38 78w28'12 5:13:53
Chester Heights 23 4 39N53'24 75w28'33 5:01:54
Chester Hill 17 113 40N53'23 78w13'43 5:12:55
Chester Plaza 23 90 39N51'44 75w24'42 5:01:39
Chester Springs 15 8 40N05'42 75w37'02 5:02:28
Chester Valley Knoll 15 8 40N02 75w31 5:02:04
Chesterville 15 8 39N46'40 75w48'40 5:03:15
Chestnut Crossroads 21 82 40N03'01 77w27'11 5:09:49
Chestnut Grove 17 7 41N01'30 78w39'37 5:14:38
Chestnut Grove 32 72 40N38'28 79w07'55 5:16:32
Chestnut Grove 41 6 41N11'07 76w35'04 5:06:20
Chestnut Hill 25 107 42N04'52 80w05'28 5:20:22
Chestnut Hill 36 26 40N02'53 76w26'23 5:05:46
Chestnut Hill 48 12 40N42'45 75w12'53 5:00:52
Chestnut Hill 51 9 40N04'37 75w12'28 5:00:50
Chestnut Hill 67 1 40N03'49 77w05'09 5:08:21
Chestnut Level 36 27 39N49'22 76w12'58 5:04:52
Chestnut Ridge 26 51 39N58'49 79w48'24 5:19:14
Chestnut Ridge 36 8 40N03'20 76w22'23 5:05:30
Chestnut View 36 8 40N02'28 76w22'13 5:05:29
Chest Springs 11 63 40N34'48 78w36'26 5:14:26
Cheswick 2 119 40N32'30 79w47'58 5:19:12
Chevy Chase Heights 32 72 40N38'12 79w08'40 5:16:35
Chewton 37 121 40N53'20 80w19'34 5:21:18
Cheyney 23 4 39N55'42 75w31'23 5:02:06
Chickaree 11 63 40N26'45 78w52'55 5:15:32
Chickasaw 3 64 40N55 79w28 5:17:52
Chickies 36 26 40N03'25 76w31'30 5:06:06
Chickory 11 74 40N21 78w54 5:15:36
Chicora 10 6 40N56'53 79w44'35 5:18:58
Childs 35 1 41N33'21 75w31'14 5:02:05
Chillisquaque 49 70 40N56'33 76w51'19 5:07:25
China Hall 9 9 40N06 74w56 4:59:44
Chinchilla 35 45 41N28'30 75w40'39 5:02:43
Chippewa 4 8 40N46 80w23 5:21:32
Chippewa 41 83 41N14'16 76w46'38 5:07:07
Choconut 58 6 41N58'43 76w00'00 5:04:00
Christiana 36 23 39N57'17 75w59'50 5:03:59
Christian Corner 13 80 40N49'51 75w32'59 5:02:12
Christian Springs 48 8 40N44'03 75w20'28 5:01:22
Christleys Mills 10 6 41N04'46 80w04'26 5:20:18
Christmans 13 80 40N58'05 75w38'40 5:02:35
Christmansville 13 1 40N58'35 75w40'31 5:02:42
Christy Manor 3 15 40N44'18 79w31'44 5:18:07
Chrome 15 3 39N44'00 75w58'58 5:03:56
Chrystal 53 6 41N57'35 78w01'49 5:12:07
Chulasky 49 6 40N57'14 76w39'54 5:06:40
Church Hill 15 27 40N06'38 75w51'00 5:03:24
Church Hill 26 51 39N52'47 79w52'53 5:19:32
Church Hill 27 6 41N34'00 79w22'57 5:17:32
Church Hill 28 51 39N50'17 77w51'44 5:11:27
Church Hill 44 73 40N40'55 77w35'56 5:10:24
Church Hill Manor 44 73 40N40 77w36 5:10:24
Churchill 2 114 40N26'18 79w50'36 5:19:22
Churchill Valley 2 114 40N27'32 79w50'02 5:19:20
Churchtown 21 1 40N09'54 77w05'04 5:08:20
Churchtown 36 27 40N07'59 75w57'54 5:03:52
Churchville 5 7 40N09'53 78w30'45 5:14:03
Churchville 9 56 40N11'10 75w01'09 5:00:05
Churchville 16 6 41N06'12 79w25'12 5:17:41
Churchville 48 8 40N45'07 75w15'02 5:01:00
Cinnamon Hills 46 90 40N05 75w22 5:01:28
Circle Ville 14 9 40N47'21 77w54'23 5:11:38
Circleville 65 25 40N19'41 79w44'15 5:18:57
Cisna Run 50 6 40N21'09 77w25'53 5:09:44
Cito 29 66 39N52'33 77w59'36 5:11:58
Claghorn 32 98 40N29'16 79w04'31 5:16:18
Clairton 2 8 40N17'32 79w52'55 5:19:32
Clairton Junction 2 114 40N22 79w54 5:19:36
Clamtown 54 27 40N48 75w58 5:03:52
Clappertown 7 3 40N24'11 78w16'32 5:13:06
Clapp Farm 61 9 41N25 79w42 5:18:48
Clapp Lease 61 6 41N23'57 79w31'45 5:18:07
Clappville 20 7 41N41'47 79w47'41 5:19:11
Clara 53 6 41N53'34 78w06'10 5:12:25
Clarence 14 7 41N02'53 77w56'26 5:11:46
Clarendon 62 3 41N46'48 79w05'36 5:16:22
Clarendon Heights 62 3 41N47'29 79w06'20 5:16:25
Claridge 65 3 40N21'56 79w37'21 5:18:29
Clarington 27 6 41N19'57 79w07'24 5:16:30
Clarion 16 37 41N12'53 79w23'08 5:17:33
Clarion Junction 16 37 41N14'13 79w25'02 5:17:40
Clark 43 6 41N17'10 80w25'40 5:21:43
Clark Manor 4 13 40N37 80w16 5:21:04
Clarksburg 32 6 40N32'01 79w22'56 5:17:32
Clarks Green 35 45 41N29'34 75w42'00 5:02:48
Clarks Mills 43 6 41N23'35 80w11'02 5:20:44
Clarks Summit 35 45 41N29'19 75w42'32 5:02:50
Clarkstown 41 83 41N11'55 76w43'33 5:06:54
Clarksville 30 6 39N58'22 80w02'39 5:20:11
Clarksville Hill 63 6 39N58'56 80w02'21 5:20:09
Claussville 39 13 40N36'51 75w39'15 5:02:37
Clay 36 30 40N13'06 76w15'21 5:05:01
Clayford 26 80 39N53'41 79w46'31 5:19:06
Clay Hill 28 42 39N49'11 77w40'30 5:10:42
Claylick 28 51 39N46'00 77w53'38 5:11:35
Claypoole Heights 32 72 40N37'17 79w11'35 5:16:46
Claysburg 7 3 40N17'48 78w27'00 5:13:48
Claysville 63 6 40N07'04 80w24'38 5:21:39
Clayton 6 2 40N25'05 75w34'26 5:02:18
Claytonia 10 6 41N00'35 79w58'02 5:19:52
Clearbrook 23 9 39N56 75w16 5:01:04
Clearbrook Village 46 1 40N11 75w06 5:00:24
Clearfield 17 1 41N01'38 78w26'22 5:13:45
Clearfield 48 8 40N48'03 75w20'50 5:01:23
Clearfield Junction 17 1 41N00'04 78w23'48 5:13:35
Clear Ridge 5 6 39N58'10 78w22'03 5:13:28
Clear Ridge 29 6 40N05'21 77w59'43 5:11:59
Clear Run 17 56 41N08'15 78w45'18 5:15:01
Clear Spring 38 8 40N19'59 76w32'54 5:06:12
Clear Spring 67 1 40N03'31 77w03'47 5:08:15
Clearview 36 8 40N03'45 76w18'06 5:05:12
Clearview Estates 4 13 40N37 80w16 5:21:04
Clearville 5 6 39N55'00 78w23'03 5:13:32
Clemo 64 6 41N30'14 75w19'28 5:01:18
Cleona 38 8 40N20'14 76w28'33 5:05:54
Clermont 42 59 41N41'22 78w29'19 5:13:57
Cleveland 19 27 40N52 76w27 5:05:48
Cleversburg 21 82 40N02'15 77w27'59 5:09:52
Cleversburg Junction 21 82 40N03'01 77w27'54 5:09:52
Cliff Mine 2 114 40N27 80w12 5:20:48
Clifford 58 59 41N38'56 75w35'57 5:02:24
Clifton 2 114 40N19'52 80w04'06 5:20:16
Clifton 22 80 40N13'44 76w43'28 5:06:54
Clifton 35 4 41N13'22 75w32'49 5:02:11
Clifton Heights 23 9 39N55'45 75w17'48 5:01:11
Climax 3 6 40N59'03 79w22'35 5:17:30
Climax 32 29 40N23'07 79w07'28 5:16:30
Clinton 2 6 40N29'22 80w17'41 5:21:11
Clinton 3 2 40N42'23 79w35'12 5:18:21
Clinton 10 2 40N43'27 79w47'09 5:19:09
Clinton 26 6 40N02'57 79w27'48 5:17:51
Clintondale 18 76 41N01'02 77w31'16 5:10:05
Clintonville 61 6 41N11'57 79w52'23 5:19:30
Cloe 33 51 40N56'13 78w55'58 5:15:44
Clonmell 15 1 39N52'56 75w49'35 5:03:18
Clover 33 34 41N09 79w10 5:16:40
Clover Creek 7 51 40N18'23 78w16'46 5:13:07
Cloverdale Park 46 8 40N16 75w15 5:01:00
Clover Hill 63 51 40N05'09 79w58'45 5:19:55
Cloverly Acres 22 1 40N33'10 76w56'09 5:07:45
Clover Park 6 101 40N19 75w57 5:03:48
Clover Run 17 122 40N56'02 78w46'49 5:15:07
Clune 32 6 40N34 79w18 5:17:12
Cly 67 80 40N07'26 76w44'12 5:06:57
Clyde 32 29 40N26'59 79w04'13 5:16:17
Clyde 48 13 40N42'29 75w23'43 5:01:35
Clymer 32 52 40N40'05 79w00'43 5:16:03
Clymer 59 6 41N51'24 77w35'55 5:10:24
Coal 49 27 40N48 76w33 5:06:12
Coal Brook 26 104 40N01 79w35 5:18:20
Coal Cabin Beach 67 1 39N44 76w19 5:05:16
Coal Castle 54 49 40N43'22 76w14'44 5:04:59
Coal Center 63 1 40N04'06 79w54'07 5:19:36
Coal City 61 6 41N18'39 79w48'48 5:19:15
Coaldale 5 6 40N10'02 78w12'56 5:12:52
Coaldale 14 4 40N56'10 78w09'38 5:12:39
Coaldale 22 1 40N34 76w42 5:06:48
Coaldale 54 80 40N49'22 75w54'26 5:03:38
Coal Glen 33 5 41N12'42 78w51'18 5:15:25
Coal Hill 61 9 41N23'27 79w35'02 5:18:20
Coal Hollow 10 2 40N43'46 79w46'40 5:19:07
Coal Hollow 24 36 41N20'42 78w36'38 5:14:27
Coal Junction 56 6 40N08'10 79w03'44 5:16:15
Coalmont 31 6 40N12'40 78w12'01 5:12:48
Coalport 13 80 40N52 75w44 5:02:56
Coalport 17 54 40N44'52 78w32'05 5:14:08
Coal Run 17 4 40N51 78w16 5:13:04
Coal Run 32 6 40N33'26 79w17'42 5:17:11
Coal Run 49 27 40N47'38 76w31'22 5:06:05
Coal Run 56 79 39N46'36 79w04'56 5:16:20
Coaltown 10 6 41N02'40 79w58'22 5:19:53
Coaltown 37 112 41N02'21 80w20'50 5:21:23
Coal Valley 2 6 40N19'05 79w54'10 5:19:37
Coatesville 15 9 39N58'59 75w49'27 5:03:18
Cobalt Ridge 9 9 40N09'23 74w52'10 4:59:29
Cobblesville 21 1 40N05'07 77w19'57 5:09:20
Cobbs Corners 62 56 41N50 79w41 5:18:44
Cobham 62 6 41N43'26 79w20'03 5:17:20
Coburn 7 33 40N29'43 78w25'48 5:13:43
Coburn 14 52 40N51'47 77w27'53 5:09:52
Cocalico 36 28 40N17'19 76w12'13 5:04:49
Cocalico House 36 28 40N16'54 76w12'14 5:04:49
Cochran Acres 4 13 40N37 80w16 5:21:04
Cochrans Mill 2 8 40N17'30 79w57'41 5:19:51
Cochrans Mills 3 15 40N40'12 79w27'30 5:17:50
Cochranton 20 59 41N31'12 80w02'55 5:20:12
Cochranville 15 8 39N53'30 75w55'19 5:03:41
Cocolamus 34 6 40N38'52 77w12'46 5:08:51
Codding 8 60 41N49'13 76w36'31 5:06:26
Coder 33 34 41N08'41 79w06'49 5:16:27
Codorus 67 3 39N47 76w47 5:07:08
Codorus Furnace 67 1 40N03'03 76w39'29 5:06:38
Coffeetown 38 31 40N19'33 76w35'26 5:06:22
Coffeetown 39 13 40N38'55 75w34'41 5:02:19
Coffeetown 48 12 40N37'08 75w12'29 5:00:50
Coffeys Crossing 63 3 40N09'31 80w20'06 5:21:20
Coffman 26 6 40N03'06 79w22'56 5:17:32
Cogan House 41 6 41N25 77w10 5:08:40
Cogan Station 41 7 41N19 77w05 5:08:20
Coggins Corner 64 6 41N37'01 75w22'22 5:01:29

Coheva 38 8 40N20'45 76W27'01 5:05:48
Coilton 48 12 40N42'34 75W14'42 5:00:59
Cokeburg 63 51 40N06'04 80W04'03 5:20:16
Cokeburg Junction 63 51 40N06'31 80W01'54 5:20:08
Coldbrook 26 104 40N02'27 79W34'35 5:18:18
Cold Point 46 90 40N06'41 75W16'19 5:01:05
Cold Run 6 8 40N11'48 75W49'59 5:03:20
Cold Spring 8 6 41N35'22 76W44'00 5:06:56
Cold Spring 15 8 40N15 75W39 5:02:36
Cold Spring 28 1 39N55 77W34 5:10:16
Cold Spring 31 81 40N31'28 77W59'54 5:12:00
Cold Spring 38 27 40N31 76W34 5:06:16
Cold Spring 64 59 41N43'44 75W17'53 5:01:12
Cold Spring 67 3 39N49'47 76W49'58 5:07:20
Colebrook 18 7 41N13 77W32 5:10:08
Colebrook 38 7 40N14'17 76W30'41 5:06:03
Colebrookdale 6 2 40N18'27 75W39'09 5:02:37
Colegrove 42 93 41N43'43 78W23'10 5:13:33
Cole Hill 36 23 40N00'47 75W58'05 5:03:52
Coleman 56 6 40N03'10 78W57'49 5:15:51
Colemanville 36 1 39N54'02 76W20'35 5:05:22
Colerain 31 6 40N37'34 78W06'54 5:12:28
Colerain Forge 31 6 40N37 78W08 5:12:32
Coles 54 3 40N49 76W08 5:04:32
Colesburg 53 66 41N50'09 77W56'24 5:11:46
Coles Creek 19 6 41N14'29 76W21'54 5:05:28
Coles Mill 19 6 41N11'21 76W28'48 5:05:55
Colesville 39 13 40N34'19 75W23'34 5:01:34
Coleville 14 70 40N54'34 77W47'50 5:11:11
Coleville 42 93 41N53'42 78W30'58 5:14:04
Colfax 31 81 40N21'54 78W00'40 5:12:03
College 14 9 40N48 77W49 5:11:16
College 46 12 40N41 75W14 5:00:56
College Heights 6 101 40N22'27 75W53'54 5:03:36
College Hill 4 8 40N46'40 80W19'27 5:21:18
College Misericordia 40 20 41N20 75W56 5:03:44
College Park 46 9 40N06 75W15 5:01:00
College Park 60 70 40N56'54 76W53'06 5:07:32
Collegeville 46 8 40N11'08 75W27'07 5:01:48
Colley 57 6 41N32'04 76W17'12 5:05:09
Collier 2 114 40N23 80W07 5:20:28
Collier 26 80 39N51'01 79W46'44 5:19:07
Collingdale 23 9 39N54'42 75W16'39 5:01:07
Collins 36 27 39N52'48 76W07'59 5:04:32
Collinsburg 65 61 40N13'27 79W46'07 5:19:04
Collinsville 67 1 39N51'24 76W27'04 5:05:48
Collomsville 41 82 41N08'51 77W08'36 5:08:34
Colmar 46 8 40N16'02 75W15'14 5:01:01
Colon 33 34 41N05'45 79W04'36 5:16:18
Colona 4 13 40N40 80W17 5:21:08
Colonial Crest 22 12 40N16 76W49 5:07:16
Colonial Hills 6 101 40N16'54 76W00'57 5:04:04
Colonial Hills 44 73 40N33'56 77W36'44 5:10:27
Colonial Manor 36 8 40N02 76W20 5:05:20
Colonial Park 22 12 40N18'02 76W48'36 5:07:14
Colonial Park 23 9 39N56 75W20 5:01:20
Colonial Park 36 28 40N05 76W11 5:04:44
Colonial Park 49 6 41N00'15 76W50'22 5:07:21
Colonial Village 46 90 40N04'22 75W23'38 5:01:35
Colonial Village 61 9 41N26'38 79W41'06 5:18:44
Columbia 36 26 40N02'01 76W30'17 5:06:01
Columbia Cross Roads 8 7 41N50'09 76W48'08 5:07:13
Columbia Hill 19 4 41N02'29 76W33'56 5:06:16
Columbus 62 3 41N56'27 79W34'55 5:18:20
Colver 11 54 40N32'36 78W47'17 5:15:09
Colwyn 23 9 39N54'44 75W15'15 5:01:01
Colyer 14 64 40N47'03 77W40'34 5:10:42
Colza 62 3 41N54'55 79W36'20 5:18:25
Comly 47 6 41N07'10 76W43'45 5:06:55
Commerce 51 9 39N58 75W09 5:00:36
Commodore 32 6 40N42'47 78W56'37 5:15:46
Compass 15 23 40N01'21 75W56'34 5:03:46
Comps Crossroads 56 51 39N48'00 78W47'33 5:15:10
Compton 2 14 40N37'29 79W44'26 5:18:58
Compton 56 79 39N45'42 79W07'21 5:16:29
Conashaugh 52 3 41N16'16 74W50'58 4:59:24
Concord 25 7 41N53'33 79W44'06 5:18:56
Concord 28 1 40N15'06 77W42'02 5:10:48
Concordville 23 4 39N53'06 75W31'14 5:02:05
Concrete Bridge Crossing 11 63 40N32'14 78W52'03 5:15:28
Condit Crossing 63 3 40N03'56 80W13'49 5:20:55
Condron 11 63 40N36'25 78W30'31 5:14:02
Conemaugh 11 74 40N21 78W54 5:15:36
Conestoga 15 56 40N08'32 75W50'07 5:03:20
Conestoga 36 8 39N56'26 76W20'48 5:05:23
Conestoga Farms 23 1 39N52 75W35 5:02:20
Conestoga Gardens 36 8 40N01'56 76W16'39 5:05:07
Conestoga Woods 36 8 40N02'16 76W16'31 5:05:06
Coneville 53 29 41N54'14 78W03'54 5:12:16
Conewago 36 2 40N09'29 76W39'38 5:06:39
Conewago Heights 67 1 40N05'08 76W43'01 5:06:52
Conewango 62 120 41N53 79W11 5:16:44
Confluence 56 53 39N48'46 79W21'25 5:17:26
Conger 63 3 40N01'38 80W14'54 5:21:00
Congo 46 2 40N21'03 75W35'03 5:02:20
Congress Hill 17 6 41N05'57 78W16'48 5:13:07
Congruity 65 6 40N23'54 79W30'14 5:18:01
Conifer 33 6 41N04'59 79W08'20 5:16:33
Conklin Hill 64 6 41N44'14 75W05'00 5:00:20
Connaughton 46 90 40N04'47 75W18'51 5:01:15
Conneaut Center 20 7 41N42'44 80W27'01 5:21:48
Conneaut Lake 20 6 41N36'12 80W18'20 5:21:13
Conneaut Lake Park 20 6 41N38'08 80W18'54 5:21:16
Conneautville 20 6 41N45'28 80W22'05 5:21:28
Conneautville Station 20 6 41N45'38 80W24'09 5:21:37
Connellsville 26 104 40N01'04 79W35'23 5:18:22
Conners Mill 36 27 39N53'40 76W06'53 5:04:28
Connersville 49 27 40N47'32 76W25'32 5:05:42
Connerton 54 27 40N47'58 76W16'26 5:05:06
Connoquenessing 10 6 40N49'04 80W00'52 5:20:03
Conoy 36 2 40N07 76W40 5:06:40
Conpitt Junction 65 29 40N22'33 79W06'10 5:16:25
Conrad 53 6 41N36'36 77W53'27 5:11:34
Conshohocken 46 90 40N04'45 75W18'07 5:01:12
Conshohocken Station 46 90 40N03'37 75W20'22 5:01:21
Constitution 67 1 39N43'16 76W24'54 5:05:40
Content 33 6 41N06'36 79W08'41 5:16:35
Continental 51 9 39N57 75W09 5:00:36
Continental Number 2 26 80 39N52'43 79W45'58 5:19:04
Conway 4 13 40N39'35 80W14'22 5:20:57
Conyngham 40 42 40N59'31 76W03'25 5:04:14
Cook 65 6 40N11 79W19 5:17:16
Cooke 21 1 40N02 77W19 5:09:16
Cookport 32 6 40N41'58 78W54'44 5:15:39
Cooks 31 6 40N12'41 78W05'15 5:12:21
Cooksburg 16 6 41N20'00 79W12'35 5:16:50
Cooks Mills 5 51 39N44'55 78W44'33 5:14:58
Cooks Run 18 7 41N18 77W51 5:11:24
Cooks Summit 3 15 40N42'24 79W32'23 5:18:10
Cook Tomb 27 6 41N19'43 79W11'48 5:16:47
Coolbaugh 45 84 41N12 75W25 5:01:40
Coolbaughs 45 1 41N06 75W00 5:00:00
Coolidge Hollow 59 6 41N41'24 77W17'34 5:09:10
Coolspring 26 80 39N54'13 79W40'48 5:18:43
Coolspring 33 6 41N02'35 79W05'02 5:16:20
Cool Spring 43 66 41N17'35 80W14'26 5:20:58
Cool Valley 63 2 40N17'23 80W09'24 5:20:38
Coon Corners 20 77 41N40 80W07 5:20:28
Coon Hunter 55 6 40N46'33 77W03'19 5:08:13
Coon Island 63 6 40N06'42 80W27'42 5:21:51
Coons Corners 20 77 41N42'58 80W12'35 5:20:50
Coontown 42 75 41N40'08 78W43'19 5:14:53
Cooper Corners 66 59 41N35'16 75W55'25 5:03:42
Coopersburg 39 13 40N30'41 75W23'27 5:01:34
Coopersdale 11 74 40N21'20 78W56'15 5:15:45
Cooper Settlement 17 6 41N01'53 78W06'29 5:12:26
Cooperstown 10 6 40N42'49 79W55'48 5:19:43
Cooperstown 61 6 41N29'55 79W52'14 5:19:29
Cooperstown 65 3 40N18'21 79W21'56 5:17:28
Coopersville 36 23 39N56'15 76W02'08 5:04:09
Copella 48 13 40N48'00 75W22'08 5:01:29
Copes Bridge 15 13 39N57 75W36 5:02:24
Copesville 15 13 39N57'32 75W39'23 5:02:38
Coplay 39 13 40N40'12 75W29'45 5:01:59
Coral 32 71 40N29'57 79W10'27 5:16:42
Coraopolis 2 114 40N31'06 80W10'01 5:20:40
Coraopolis Heights 2 114 40N30 80W10 5:20:40
Corbett 53 6 41N40'58 77W46'34 5:11:06
Corbettown 33 51 40N58'01 79W10'56 5:16:44
Cordelia 36 26 40N03'05 76W28'29 5:05:54
Corduroy 24 75 41N30'35 78W56'05 5:15:44
Corinne 15 13 39N54'19 75W40'20 5:02:41
Cork Lane 40 1 41N18'35 75W47'15 5:03:09
Corliss 2 114 40N27'14 80W03'55 5:20:16
Corner Ketch 15 46 40N02'13 75W45'00 5:03:00
Corner Store 15 8 40N07'03 75W30'19 5:02:01
Corning 39 13 40N27'05 75W31'51 5:02:07
Cornish 26 7 39N45'27 79W49'33 5:19:18
Cornog 15 80 40N04'36 75W45'18 5:03:01
Cornplanter 61 9 41N28 79W40 5:18:40
Cornpropst 31 81 40N30 78W01 5:12:04
Cornwall 38 8 40N16'25 76W24'23 5:05:38
Cornwall Center 38 8 40N16'38 76W24'48 5:05:39
Cornwall Furnace 38 8 40N16'14 76W24'22 5:05:37
Cornwall Junction 38 8 40N20'33 76W26'25 5:05:46
Cornwells Heights 9 9 40N04'36 74W56'57 4:59:48
Corpers Homes 46 90 40N05 75W16 5:01:04
Corrine 15 13 39N57 75W36 5:02:24
Corry 25 3 41N55'13 79W38'26 5:18:34
Corsica 33 6 41N10'52 79W12'09 5:16:49
Corsons 46 90 40N06'30 75W16'30 5:01:06
Cortez 33 51 41N01'01 78W58'58 5:15:56
Cortez 35 6 41N27'55 75W27'27 5:01:50
Corwins Corners 42 102 41N55'56 78W34'53 5:14:20
Corydon 42 6 41N56 78W51 5:15:24
Coryland 8 7 41N54'02 76W51'31 5:07:26
Coryville 42 93 41N52'57 78W23'55 5:13:36
Coseytown 28 1 39N43'46 77W47'10 5:11:09
Cosmus 3 7 40N56'46 79W32'34 5:18:10
Cossart 15 13 39N50'51 75W35'53 5:02:24
Costello 53 6 41N35'36 78W03'35 5:12:14
Cosytown 28 1 39N48 77W44 5:10:56
Cottage 31 81 40N37'15 77W59'05 5:11:56
Cottage Grove 37 112 41N05'39 80W19'04 5:21:16
Cottage Hill 16 6 41N00'37 79W20'51 5:17:23
Cottageville 9 8 40N22'36 75W04'45 5:00:19
Cottles Corner 5 6 40N08'12 78W20'30 5:13:22
Cotton Town 7 3 40N16'46 78W28'52 5:13:55
Couchtown 50 6 40N19'28 77W27'45 5:09:51
Coudersport 53 66 41N46'29 78W01'15 5:12:05
Coudley 17 4 41N04'19 78W14'21 5:12:57
Coulter 2 8 40N17'47 79W48'06 5:19:12
Coulter 33 51 41N00'38 79W04'32 5:16:18
Coulters 2 8 40N18 79W48 5:19:12
Council Crest 40 42 40N58 76W00 5:04:00
Country Acres 46 90 40N05 75W16 5:01:04
Country Club Estates 23 9 39N55 75W19 5:01:16
Country Club Estates 36 8 40N04 76W19 5:05:16
Country Club Heights 36 8 40N03'59 76W16'29 5:05:06
Country Gardens 36 28 40N05 76W11 5:04:44
Country Hills 65 25 40N20 79W43 5:18:52
County Line 46 1 40N09'54 75W03'38 5:00:15
Coupon 11 33 40N32'12 78W30'55 5:14:04
Courtdale 40 20 41N16'48 75W54'45 5:03:39
Courtney 63 1 40N13'07 79W58'08 5:19:53
Courtneys Mills 43 70 41N06'47 80W04'28 5:20:18
Covalt 29 6 39N49'21 78W08'43 5:12:35
Cove 50 51 40N21'17 76W58'41 5:07:55
Covedale 7 3 40N28'57 78W10'23 5:12:42
Cove Gap 28 51 39N51'57 77W56'34 5:11:46
Coventryville 15 8 40N10'24 75W41'23 5:02:46
Coverdale 2 114 40N19'31 80W02'15 5:20:09
Coverdale 7 3 40N28 78W12 5:12:48
Coverdale 37 8 40N52'44 80W21'51 5:21:27
Cover Hill 11 74 40N19'32 78W53'21 5:15:33
Covert 8 7 41N44'56 76W51'12 5:07:25
Coverts 37 112 40N59'40 80W24'59 5:21:40
Coveville 45 84 41N12'44 75W16'06 5:01:04
Coveytown 57 60 41N32'48 76W27'15 5:05:49
Covington 59 59 41N44'41 77W04'39 5:08:19
Covode 32 51 40N52'51 79W00'57 5:16:04
Cowan 60 6 40N57'27 77W00'50 5:08:03
Cowanesque 59 6 41N55'59 77W29'51 5:09:59
Cowansburg 65 4 40N15'16 79W45'14 5:19:01
Cowanshannock 3 6 40N48 79W18 5:17:12
Cowans Village 28 51 40N00'06 77W54'51 5:11:39
Cowansville 3 6 40N53'16 79W35'19 5:18:21
Cowden 63 2 40N19'04 80W11'50 5:20:47
Coxeville 13 42 40N56 75W55 5:03:40
Coxton 40 1 41N21 75W46 5:03:04
Coy 32 71 40N31'45 79W08'29 5:16:34
Coy Junction 32 71 40N32'11 79W09'10 5:16:37
Coyle 21 2 40N08'46 77W10'43 5:08:43
Coyleville 10 6 40N51'12 79W43'43 5:18:55
Coyne Lock 67 1 39N46'02 76W16'27 5:05:06
Crabapple 30 6 39N55'11 80W28'32 5:21:54
Crabtree 65 3 40N21'44 79W28'15 5:17:53
Crabtree Hollow 9 9 40N09'14 74W50'03 4:59:20
Cracker Jack 63 1 40N10'03 79W57'53 5:19:52
Crackersport 39 13 40N36'06 75W33'45 5:02:15
Crafton 2 114 40N26'06 80W03'59 5:20:16
Craig 35 44 41N33'19 75W39'52 5:02:39
Craighead 21 16 40N08'49 77W10'14 5:08:41
Craigs 54 3 40N49'56 76W08'39 5:04:35
Craigs Meadow 45 23 41N02'12 75W08'16 5:00:33
Craigsville 3 6 40N51'08 79W38'59 5:18:36
Craley 67 2 39N56'51 76W30'39 5:06:03
Cramer 32 7 40N25'11 78W59'34 5:15:58
Cranberry 40 42 40N58 76W00 5:04:00
Cranberry 61 1 41N20'59 79W42'37 5:18:50
Cranberry Ridge 40 42 40N58 76W00 5:04:00
Cranesville 25 7 41N54'18 80W20'38 5:21:23
Crates 16 6 41N06'38 79W16'12 5:17:05
Crawford 18 7 41N06 77W16 5:09:04
Crawford Corners 61 6 41N10'22 79W46'03 5:19:04
Crawfordtown 33 51 40N59'24 78W58'10 5:15:53
Creamery 46 8 40N13'12 75W25'00 5:01:40
Creamton 64 6 41N40'26 75W22'43 5:01:31
Creekside 32 72 40N40'44 79W11'16 5:16:45
Creighton 2 14 40N35'14 79W46'43 5:19:07
Crenshaw 33 5 41N14'55 78W45'44 5:15:03
Crescent 2 13 40N33 80W14 5:20:56
Crescentdale 37 121 40N53 80W20 5:21:20
Crescent Heights 63 51 40N03'19 79W56'15 5:19:45
Crescent Hills 2 114 40N28'15 79W49'30 5:19:18
Crescent Lake 45 84 41N04'29 75W22'59 5:01:32
Crescentville 51 9 40N02'40 75W06'05 5:00:24
Cresco 45 84 41N09'14 75W16'51 5:01:07
Creslo 11 63 40N19'59 78W45'34 5:15:02
Cresmont 54 27 40N47 76W14 5:04:56
Cress 28 100 39N44'08 77W33'53 5:10:16
Cresson 11 55 40N27'35 78W35'31 5:14:22
Cressona 54 27 40N37'36 76W11'35 5:04:46
Crestmont 18 76 41N10'34 77W22'19 5:09:29
Crestmont 46 2 40N08'08 75W07'42 5:00:31
Crestmont Village 4 13 40N37 80W16 5:21:04
Crestview 46 1 40N11 75W06 5:00:24
Crestview 63 1 40N10'53 79W51'49 5:19:27
Creswell 36 8 39N57'43 76W26'05 5:05:44
Crete 32 6 40N35'49 79W14'34 5:16:58

Criders Corners 10 6 40N41'09 80w06'03 5:20:24
Croft 17 6 41N04'46 78w20'04 5:13:20
Crolls Mills 10 6 41N01'14 80w02'39 5:20:11
Cromby 15 8 40N08'52 75w31'42 5:02:07
Cromwell 31 6 40N14 77w55 5:11:40
Crooked Creek 31 81 40N30 78w01 5:12:04
Crooked Creek 59 6 41N51'21 77w14'15 5:08:57
Crookham 63 114 40N12'33 79w59'04 5:19:56
Crosby 42 93 41N44'42 78w23'26 5:13:34
Cross Creek 63 6 40N19'44 80w24'34 5:21:38
Cross Fork 53 6 41N29'00 77w48'53 5:11:16
Crossgrove 55 1 40N44'15 77w19'13 5:09:17
Crossingville 20 6 41N49'47 80w14'21 5:20:57
Cross Keys 1 1 39N52'15 77w01'40 5:08:07
Cross Keys 7 33 40N26'45 78w25'58 5:13:44
Cross Keys 9 8 40N19'39 75w07'43 5:00:31
Cross Keys 34 6 40N21'28 77w42'14 5:10:49
Crosskill Mills 6 25 40N26'52 76w21'11 5:05:25
Crossland 26 104 40N02'14 79w36'21 5:18:25
Cross Mill 67 1 39N47'56 76w32'28 5:06:10
Crossroads 48 13 40N46'20 75w25'14 5:01:41
Cross Roads 67 1 39N49'10 76w34'37 5:06:18
Cross Village 13 42 40N56'07 75w55'36 5:03:42
Crosswicks 46 9 40N05'48 75w05'30 5:00:22
Crown 16 6 41N23'23 79w16'16 5:17:05
Crows Mills 30 6 39N55'40 80w30'21 5:22:01
Croydon 9 9 40N05'14 74w54'14 4:59:37
Croydon Acres 9 9 40N05'54 74w54'08 4:59:37
Croydon Heights 9 9 40N05'46 74w53'43 4:59:35
Croyland 24 59 41N21'27 78w49'02 5:15:16
Croyle 11 63 40N22 78w45 5:15:00
Crozar Terrace 23 90 39N51 75w22 5:01:28
Crozer Park Gardens 23 90 39N51 75w22 5:01:28
Crozierville 23 90 39N53'06 75w26'40 5:01:47
Crucible 30 6 39N56'54 79w57'54 5:19:52
Crumb 56 123 40N08'54 78w43'37 5:14:54
Crum Creek Manor 23 90 39N52'52 75w22'39 5:01:31
Crum Lynne 23 9 39N52'20 75w19'42 5:01:19
Crystal 26 51 39N44'51 79w49'29 5:19:18
Crystal 53 6 41N55 78w01 5:12:04
Crystal Lake 58 59 41N39 75w28 5:01:52
Crystal Spring 29 6 39N56'59 78w13'44 5:12:55
Crystal Springs 27 6 41N32'10 79w19'48 5:17:19
Cuba Mills 34 7 40N35'26 77w24'25 5:09:38
Cuddy 2 114 40N21 80w09 5:20:36
Cuddy Hill 2 114 40N20'57 80w09'39 5:20:39
Culbertson 28 6 40N15'11 77w45'14 5:11:01
Culmerville 2 6 40N39'15 79w50'21 5:19:21
Culp 7 33 40N34'49 78w15'37 5:13:02
Culpepper Woods 46 90 40N05 75w16 5:01:04
Cumberland Park 21 12 40N14 76w57 5:07:48
Cumberland Valley 5 51 39N49 78w39 5:14:36
Cumberland Village 30 51 39N53'57 79w58'07 5:19:52
Cumbola 54 27 40N42'42 76w08'17 5:04:33
Cumiskey 8 6 41N34'08 76w19'27 5:05:18
Cummings 41 6 41N20 77w20 5:09:20
Cummingstown 21 16 40N12 77w11 5:08:44
Cummingswood Park 65 6 40N08 79w26 5:17:44
Cumminsville 21 1 40N07'15 77w18'58 5:09:16
Cumru 6 101 40N18 75w57 5:03:48
Cuneo 24 36 41N21 78w37 5:14:28
Cunningham 10 2 40N40'39 79w49'23 5:19:18
Cupola 15 27 40N05'57 75w50'44 5:03:23
Curfew 26 104 40N02'29 79w45'31 5:19:02
Curley Hill 9 8 40N21 75w13 5:00:52
Curllsville 16 6 41N05'55 79w26'49 5:17:47
Curren Terrace 46 90 40N08 75w21 5:01:24
Curry 2 114 40N19'55 79w59'09 5:19:57
Curry Hill 40 20 41N14'17 75w57'49 5:03:51
Curry Run 17 122 40N54'45 78w39'58 5:14:40
Currys Mills 10 6 41N05'17 80w03'51 5:20:15
Curryville 7 51 40N16'33 78w20'19 5:13:21
Curtin 14 6 40N58'20 77w44'39 5:10:59
Curtis Hills 46 9 40N05 75w09 5:00:36
Curtis Park 14 113 40N54 78w13 5:12:52
Curtis Park 23 9 39N54 75w17 5:01:08
Curtisville 2 6 40N38'32 79w51'04 5:19:24
Curwensville 17 1 40N58'32 78w31'31 5:14:06
Cush Creek 32 63 40N46'18 78w51'20 5:15:25
Cush Cushion Crossing 32 6 40N43'16 78w51'48 5:15:27
Cussewago 20 6 41N48 80w13 5:20:52
Custards 20 59 41N31'49 80w09'34 5:20:38
Custer City 42 102 41N54'21 78w39'07 5:14:36
Custis Woods 46 9 40N07 75w10 5:00:40
C V Junction 59 59 41N58'56 77w07'25 5:08:30
Cyclone 42 6 41N49'56 78w35'10 5:14:21
Cymbria 11 92 40N39'27 78w44'54 5:15:00
Cymbria Mine 11 92 40N40 78w47 5:15:08
Cynwyd Estates 46 9 40N01 75w15 5:01:00
Cynwyd Hills 46 9 40N01 75w15 5:01:00
Cypher 5 6 40N05'33 78w18'41 5:13:15
Cyrus 61 1 41N14'23 79w48'34 5:19:14
Daggett 59 6 41N56'55 76w55'35 5:07:42
Dagus 24 36 41N21'42 78w36'58 5:14:28
Daguscahonda 24 36 41N25'10 78w39'21 5:14:37

Dagus Mines 24 36 41N21'14 78w36'21 5:14:25
Dahoga 24 7 41N35'57 78w43'27 5:14:54
Daisytown 11 74 40N19'09 78w54'04 5:15:36
Daisytown 63 51 40N03'16 79w55'56 5:19:44
Dale 6 2 40N24'58 75w36'58 5:02:28
Dale 11 74 40N18'46 78w54'16 5:15:37
Dale 17 6 41N00'41 78w17'35 5:13:10
Dale Summit 14 9 40N50'09 77w47'38 5:11:11
Daleville 15 23 39N51'51 75w53'07 5:03:32
Daleville 35 4 41N18'18 75w30'51 5:02:03
Dalevue 14 9 40N47'45 77w49'46 5:11:19
Daley 56 63 40N05'09 78w44'18 5:14:57
Dallas 40 1 41N20'10 75w57'49 5:03:51
Dallas City 42 102 41N56'27 78w33'21 5:14:13
Dallastown 67 7 39N53'58 76w38'26 5:06:34
Dalmatia 49 51 40N39'15 76w54'10 5:07:37
Dalton 35 44 41N32'03 75w44'11 5:02:57
Damascus 64 6 41N42'11 75w04'07 5:00:16
Danboro 9 8 40N21'16 75w07'59 5:00:32
Danielsville 48 80 40N47'40 75w31'39 5:02:07
Dannersville 48 13 40N44'37 75w26'07 5:01:44
Danville 47 70 40N57'48 76w36'47 5:06:27
Darby 23 9 39N55'06 75w15'34 5:01:02
Darbytown 64 6 41N36'39 75w04'11 5:00:17
Dark Water 54 27 40N44'07 76w12'00 5:04:48
Darling 23 4 39N54'12 75w28'12 5:01:53
Darlington 4 64 40N48'34 80w25'22 5:21:41
Darlington 23 90 39N55 75w22 5:01:28
Darlington 65 110 40N15'27 79w17'19 5:17:09
Darlington Corners 15 13 39N55'11 75w34'37 5:02:18
Darragh 65 3 40N15'59 79w40'44 5:18:43
Dartmouth Hills 46 90 40N05 75w22 5:01:28
Dauberville 6 80 40N27'49 75w58'56 5:03:56
Daugherty 4 8 40N45 80w17 5:21:08
Dauphin 22 12 40N22'02 76w55'53 5:07:44
Daves Gap 29 60 39N54'37 78w11'30 5:12:46
Davidsburg 67 1 39N59'01 76w53'41 5:07:35
Davidson 26 104 39N43'22 79w52'49 5:19:31
Davidson 57 6 41N20 76w28 5:05:52
Davidson Heights 4 13 40N35 80w16 5:21:04
Davidsville 56 74 40N13'37 78w56'12 5:15:45
Davis 32 72 40N44'28 79w09'32 5:16:38
Davis Grove 46 1 40N11 75w10 5:00:40
Davistown 26 6 40N02'29 79w24'13 5:17:37
Davistown 30 6 39N46'07 80w01'27 5:20:06
Davisville 9 1 40N10'59 75w03'33 5:00:14
Dawson 26 104 40N02'49 79w39'17 5:18:37
Dawson Manor 46 1 40N11 75w06 5:00:24
Dawson Ridge 4 19 40N42 80w19 5:21:16
Dawson Run 27 35 41N32'12 79w26'24 5:17:46
Day 16 37 41N11'12 79w15'54 5:17:04
Daylesford 15 90 40N02'20 75w27'38 5:01:51
Dayton 3 59 40N52'49 79w14'32 5:16:58
Dayton 22 1 40N34'36 76w38'56 5:06:36
Deal 56 79 39N49 79w02 5:16:08
Dean 11 33 40N37'19 78w30'03 5:14:00
Deanville 3 6 40N57'00 79w23'55 5:17:36
Deardorffs Mill 1 1 40N01'31 77w04'52 5:08:19
Dearth 26 80 39N56'29 79w47'41 5:19:11
Deckard 20 59 41N31'28 79w58'33 5:19:54
Deckers Point 32 6 40N45'40 78w58'48 5:15:55
Deckertown 58 89 41N39'36 75w49'40 5:03:19
Dee 3 64 40N56'06 79w26'37 5:17:46
Deegan (Goff Station) 10 6 41N07'31 79w52'45 5:19:31
Deemers Crossroads 33 6 41N07'07 78w55'41 5:15:43
Deemston 63 51 40N02 80w02 5:20:08
Deep Run 9 8 40N24'28 75w10'26 5:00:42
Deep Valley 30 6 39N45'17 80w28'11 5:21:53
Deer Creek 43 6 41N27 80w08 5:20:32
Deercroft 46 90 40N05 75w16 5:01:04
Deer Lake 26 6 39N51'00 79w35'22 5:18:21
Deer Lake 54 80 40N37'30 76w03'39 5:04:15
Deer Lick 30 6 39N58'53 80w16'45 5:21:07
Deer Park 9 8 40N21'03 74w59'32 4:59:58
Deffenbaugh 26 51 39N51'09 79w52'26 5:19:30
Defiance 5 51 40N09'40 78w13'48 5:12:55
Degolia 42 102 41N54'53 78w39'05 5:14:36
Deibler 49 6 40N52'44 76w37'41 5:06:31
Delabole 48 17 40N51'07 75w14'34 5:00:58
Delamater Corners 20 6 41N41'56 80w00'08 5:20:01
De Lancey 33 51 40N59 78w58 5:15:52
Delano 54 60 40N50'20 76w04'17 5:04:17
Delaware Grove 43 66 41N18'13 80w17'43 5:21:11
Delaware Run 49 73 41N08'12 76w51'05 5:07:24
Delaware Water Gap 45 23 41N00 75w09 5:00:36
Delhill Corners 25 91 42N09'18 79w51'48 5:19:27
Dellville 50 51 40N21'50 77w06'58 5:08:28
Delmar 59 6 41N43 77w20 5:09:20
Delmont 65 6 40N24'47 79w34'14 5:18:17
Delphene 30 6 39N49'48 80w22'49 5:21:31
Delphi 46 8 40N16'10 75w28'15 5:01:53
Delps 48 80 40N48'07 75w27'01 5:01:48
Delroy 67 2 39N58'17 76w34'26 5:06:18
Delta 67 1 39N43'37 76w19'37 5:05:18
Delta Manor 48 13 40N39'27 75w24'27 5:01:38
Demmler 2 114 40N23 79w49 5:19:16
Dempseytown 61 109 41N30'47 79w46'42 5:19:07
Demunds Corners 40 20 41N22'50 75w56'39 5:03:47
Denbeau Heights 63 51 40N01'27 79w54'59 5:19:40
Denbo 63 51 40N00'44 79w55'55 5:19:44
Denholm 34 7 40N36'03 77w26'01 5:09:44
Denison 65 3 40N17'26 79w27'51 5:17:51
Dennis Mills 19 1 41N03'37 76w19'07 5:05:16
Dennison 40 60 41N06 75w50 5:03:20

Dennys Corners 20 77 41N40'25 80w13'29 5:20:54
Dennys Mill 10 2 40N46'50 79w43'54 5:18:56
Denton 32 6 40N49'37 79w10'57 5:16:44
Denton Hill 53 66 41N45'37 77w52'51 5:11:31
Dents Run 24 7 41N21'29 78w16'03 5:13:04
Denver 36 28 40N13'59 76w08'15 5:04:33
Deodate 22 2 40N12'48 76w37'18 5:06:29
Deringer 40 60 40N56 76w10 5:04:40
Derrick City 42 102 41N58'14 78w34'18 5:14:17
Derringer 40 60 40N56'59 76w08'40 5:04:35
Derringer Corners 37 6 40N55'33 80w27'54 5:21:52
Derrs 19 6 41N11'18 76w27'42 5:05:51
Derry 19 4 41N04'33 76w36'59 5:06:28
Derry 65 3 40N20'02 79w18'00 5:17:12
Derry Church 22 31 40N17 76w39 5:06:36
Derstines 9 2 40N20'39 75w18'32 5:01:14
Derwood Park 23 9 39N53 75w21 5:01:24
Derwyn 46 9 40N01 75w15 5:01:00
De Sale 10 1 41N08'26 79w49'30 5:19:18
Deshon Manor 10 3 40N53 79w53 5:19:32
Desire 33 6 41N01'31 78w53'26 5:15:34
Detters Mill 67 1 40N00'51 76w55'39 5:07:43
De Turksville 54 9 40N34'36 76w19'50 5:05:19
Devault 15 8 40N04'28 75w32'08 5:02:09
Devon 15 90 40N02'57 75w25'46 5:01:43
Dewart 49 73 41N06'33 76w52'37 5:07:30
Dewey Corner 41 83 41N19'41 76w49'21 5:07:17
Dewey Heights 39 13 40N41'01 75w30'47 5:02:03
Dexter 59 74 41N43'11 77w22'59 5:09:32
De Young 24 6 41N34 78w54 5:15:36
Diamond 16 7 41N01'16 79w28'59 5:17:56
Diamond 61 74 41N36'26 79w47'55 5:19:12
Diamondtown 49 27 40N48'04 76w25'04 5:05:40
Diamondville 32 6 40N39'54 78w58'03 5:15:52
Dias 32 7 40N28'52 79w02'41 5:16:11
Dice 60 6 40N53'16 77w02'18 5:08:09
Dick 65 4 40N15'29 79w44'08 5:18:57
Dickerson Run 26 104 40N02'44 79w40'00 5:18:40
Dickey 28 51 39N52'05 77w53'45 5:11:35
Dickeys Mountain 29 6 39N46'47 78w04'40 5:12:19
Dickinson 21 1 40N06'48 77w20'07 5:09:20
Dicksonburg 20 6 41N42'19 80w21'08 5:21:25
Dickson City 35 18 41N28'17 75w36'29 5:02:26
Diebertsville 39 8 40N41'05 75w38'48 5:02:35
Dieffenbach 47 6 41N04'28 76w41'06 5:06:44
Diehl 5 70 39N55'44 78w29'17 5:13:57
Diehltown 17 54 40N47'10 78w33'55 5:14:16
Dieners Hall 54 49 40N41 76w12 5:04:48
Dietrich 22 4 40N31'42 76w49'35 5:07:18
Dilliner 30 7 39N45'06 79w55'31 5:19:42
Dillinger 39 13 40N33 75w31 5:02:04
Dillingerville 39 13 40N28'40 75w29'07 5:01:56
Dillontown 64 6 41N52'07 75w16'00 5:01:04
Dillsburg 67 1 40N06'39 77w02'07 5:08:08
Dillsburg Junction 21 12 40N12'58 77w01'57 5:08:08
Dilltown 32 6 40N27'59 79w00'10 5:16:01
Dilworthtown 15 13 39N53'57 75w34'03 5:02:16
Dime 3 4 40N39'22 79w31'59 5:18:08
Dimeling 17 1 41N02 78w27 5:13:48
Dimmsville 34 1 40N36'21 77w08'11 5:08:33
Dimock 58 60 41N44'47 75w53'55 5:03:36
Dingman 51 1 41N21 74w55 4:59:40
Dingmans Ferry 52 3 41N13'12 74w52'18 4:59:29
Dinsmore 63 7 40N22'50 80w25'50 5:21:43
Dipple Manor 40 42 40N59'01 76w01'19 5:04:05
Distant 3 6 40N58'10 79w21'25 5:17:26
District 6 9 40N26 75w40 5:02:40
Divide 19 6 41N15'24 76w26'03 5:05:44
Dividing Ridge 56 6 39N56 78w57 5:15:48
Dixon 66 59 41N33'28 75w53'53 5:03:36
Dixon Corner 33 34 41N16'34 78w58'14 5:15:53
Dixonville 32 6 40N42'59 79w00'26 5:16:02
Doane 59 6 41N34'22 77w20'07 5:09:20
Dock Hollow 3 2 40N41'55 79w40'10 5:18:41
Dock Junction 25 107 42N06'21 80w07'08 5:20:29
Doe Run 15 9 39N54'58 75w49'05 5:03:16
Dog Town 3 15 40N46'49 79w31'34 5:18:06
Dogtown 19 4 40N57'38 76w17'27 5:05:10
Dogtown 29 6 39N43'49 78w10'02 5:12:40
Dogtown 38 1 40N16'00 76w17'07 5:05:08
Dogtown 40 1 41N08'21 76w08'48 5:04:35
Dogtown 55 82 40N48 76w52 5:07:28
Dogtown 59 7 41N34'45 76w55'28 5:07:42
Dogwood Acres 9 1 40N11 75w03 5:00:12
Dogwood Hollow 9 9 40N08'33 74w50'25 4:59:22
Dolf 67 1 39N46'59 76w32'45 5:06:11
Dolington 9 8 40N15'54 74w53'45 4:59:35
Dombach Manor 36 8 40N04 76w19 5:05:16
Donaghmore 38 8 40N20 76w26 5:05:44
Donaldson 54 9 40N38'09 76w24'44 5:05:39
Donaldson 62 3 41N39'32 79w00'48 5:16:03
Donaldsons Crossroads 63 2 40N16'23 80w07'37 5:20:30
Donation 31 81 40N34'00 77w56'17 5:11:45
Donegal 65 6 40N06'45 79w22'58 5:17:32
Donegal Heights 36 2 40N06'00 76w31'01 5:06:04
Donegal Springs 36 2 40N06'00 76w34'00 5:06:16
Donerville 36 8 40N02'14 76w24'31 5:05:38
Donley 63 6 40N09'01 80w25'41 5:21:43

Donnally Mills 50
1 40N31'01 77w14'14 5:08:57
Donnelly 65 111 40N08'39 79w35'57 5:18:24
Donnellytown 21
16 40N17'08 77w05'53 5:08:24
Donner Crossroads 43
59 41N25'40 80w22'50 5:21:31
Donohoe 65 3 40N18'51 79w28'29 5:17:54
Donora 63 1 40N10'24 79w51'28 5:19:26
Donsfort 63 6 40N11'25 80w30'01 5:22:00
Dooleyville 49 27 40N47'25 76w25'50 5:05:43
Dora 30 51 39N48 79w55 5:19:40
Dora 33 51 40N58'00 79w09'38 5:16:39
Doris 11 74 40N20 78w56 5:15:44
Dorlan 15 13 40N02'51 75w43'01 5:02:52
Dormont 2 114 40N23'45 80w02'00 5:20:08
Dorneyville 39 13 40N34'30 75w31'12 5:02:05
Dornsife 49 51 40N44'44 76w47'22 5:07:09
Dorothy 65 3 40N18'10 79w23'37 5:17:34
Dorrance 40 6 41N06'17 76w00'31 5:04:02
Dorset 54 1 40N42'08 75w52'35 5:03:30
Dorseyville 2 114 40N34'37 79w53'20 5:19:33
Dott 29 6 39N48'51 78w11'21 5:12:45
Dotter 61 1 41N12'42 79w43'23 5:18:54
Dotters Corners 45
9 40N56'41 75w31'14 5:02:05
Doty Roundtop 32
6 40N49'04 78w56'53 5:15:48
Dotyville 62 74 41N40'12 79w36'01 5:18:24
Doubling Gap 21 1 40N10 77w24 5:09:36
Dougherty 11 33 40N37'03 78w27'39 5:13:51
Doughertys Mills 10
6 41N02'16 80w01'48 5:20:07
Douglass 2 1 40N14'38 79w48'45 5:19:15
Douglass 6 28 40N18 75w40 5:02:40
Douglassville 6 8 40N15'28 75w43'36 5:02:54
Doutyville 49 27 40N48 76w33 5:06:12
Dover 67 1 40N00'06 76w51'02 5:07:24
Dowler Junction 17
6 40N49'42 78w47'29 5:15:10
Dowlin 15 13 40N02'19 75w42'25 5:02:50
Down East 15 8 40N02 75w31 5:02:04
Downey 56 6 39N58'04 78w52'49 5:15:31
Downieville 10 6 40N40'49 80w00'05 5:20:00
Downing Hills 15
46 40N00 75w42 5:02:48
Downingtown 15 80 40N00'23 75w42'13 5:02:49
Doylesburg 28 1 40N12'48 77w42'01 5:10:48
Doyles Mills 34 7 40N29'04 77w30'54 5:10:04
Doylestown 9 8 40N18'36 75w07'49 5:00:31
Doylestown 28 1 40N11'51 77w43'18 5:10:53
Draco 67 1 39N45'04 76w32'09 5:06:09
Drake 43 6 41N07'01 80w11'17 5:20:45
Drakes Creek 13
60 40N58'18 75w42'42 5:02:51
Drakes Mills 20 3 41N49'47 80w04'56 5:20:20
Draketown 18 76 41N06'47 77w28'10 5:09:53
Draketown 25 107 41N54'40 80w04'33 5:20:18
Draketown 56 53 39N51'10 79w22'03 5:17:28
Drane 17 4 40N52'44 78w16'48 5:13:07
Draper 59 6 41N39'24 77w22'07 5:09:28
Drauckers 17 56 41N03 78w43 5:14:52
Dravosburg 2 114 40N21'02 79w53'11 5:19:33
Dreher 64 6 41N18 75w21 5:01:24
Drehersville 54 1 40N38'33 76w01'04 5:04:04
Dreibelbis 6 1 40N33'17 75w52'47 5:03:31
Drennen 2 14 40N31'25 79w42'05 5:18:48
Dresher 46 9 40N08'27 75w10'02 5:00:40
Drexelbrook 23 9 39N57 75w18 5:01:12
Drexel Gardens 23
9 39N57 75w18 5:01:12
Drexel Heights 48
13 40N41 75w22 5:01:28
Drexel Hill 23 9 39N56'49 75w17'33 5:01:10
Drexel Hills 21
12 40N13'33 76w52'55 5:07:32
Drexel Manor 23 9 39N57 75w18 5:01:12
Drexel Park 23 9 39N57 75w18 5:01:12
Drexel Plaza 23 9 39N56 75w16 5:01:04
Drifting 17 6 41N01'27 78w06'31 5:12:26
Drifton 40 42 41N00'00 75w54'21 5:03:37
Driftwood 12 64 41N20'23 78w08'04 5:12:32
Drinker 35 4 41N23'42 75w27'54 5:01:52
Driscoll 11 54 40N31'46 78w39'45 5:14:39
Drocton 18 73 41N20 77w45 5:11:00
Dromgold 50 6 40N20'46 77w11'31 5:08:46
Druid Hills 40 20 41N19'46 75w57'50 5:03:51
Drummond 24 5 41N18'24 78w43'42 5:14:55
Drumore 36 1 39N47'30 76w15'55 5:05:04
Drumore Center 36
27 39N50'15 76w12'58 5:04:52
Drums 40 42 41N01'05 75w59'43 5:03:59
Drury Run 18 73 41N19'47 77w46'44 5:11:07
Dry Hill 26 104 40N03'39 79w36'50 5:18:27
Dry Run 28 1 40N10'03 77w45'15 5:11:01
Dry Tavern 13 80 40N48'25 75w43'17 5:02:53
Dry Tavern 30 6 39N56'21 80w00'45 5:20:03
Dry Top 14 70 40N57'24 77w47'48 5:11:11
Drytown 36 1 39N51'39 76w17'34 5:05:10
Dry Valley Crossroads 60
70 40N53'30 76w54'53 5:07:40
Dryville 6 9 40N27'51 75w45'00 5:03:00
Dublin 9 8 40N22'18 75w12'07 5:00:48
Dublin Mills 29 6 40N07'14 78w01'36 5:12:06
Du Bois 17 56 41N07'09 78w45'37 5:15:02
Duboistown 41 82 41N13'21 77w02'14 5:08:09
Duckrun 37 112 40N54'33 80w16'14 5:21:05
Dudley 31 6 40N12'19 78w10'54 5:12:44
Duff City 4 13 40N36'05 80w07'45 5:20:31
Duffield 28 42 39N53'01 77w34'34 5:10:18
Dugan Hill 26 51 39N52'03 79w51'28 5:19:26
Duhring 27 6 41N28 79w07 5:16:28
Duke Center 42 6 41N57'08 78w28'49 5:13:55
Dumas 56 53 39N47'08 79w19'10 5:17:17
Dunbar 26 105 39N58'40 79w36'53 5:18:28
Duncan 59 6 41N39'07 77w15'29 5:09:02
Duncannon 50 51 40N23'53 77w01'24 5:08:06
Duncansville 7 33 40N25'24 78w26'03 5:13:44
Duncott 54 49 40N42'43 76w14'38 5:04:59
Dundaff 58 1 41N39'14 75w33'07 5:02:12
Dundore 55 51 40N43'43 76w51'22 5:07:25
Dungarvin 31 6 40N42'32 78w04'56 5:12:20
Dunkard 30 7 39N44'28 79w58'30 5:19:54

Dunkelbergers 49
27 40N46'00 76w44'00 5:06:56
Dunkle 63 6 40N12'47 80w25'08 5:21:41
Dunlap 9 9 40N11'19 74w52'10 4:59:29
Dunlap Creek Junction 26
51 40N02 79w55 5:19:40
Dunlap Creek Village 26
1 39N58'08 79w52'10 5:19:29
Dunlevy 63 115 40N06'36 79w51'06 5:19:24
Dunlo 11 63 40N17'39 78w43'15 5:14:53
Dunminning 23 90 40N00 75w23 5:01:32
Dunmore 35 18 41N25'11 75w37'58 5:02:32
Dunn 63 3 40N10 80w16 5:21:04
Dunning 8 7 41N56'00 76w47'56 5:07:12
Dunningsville 63
2 40N11'08 80w04'53 5:20:20
Dunningtown 65 6 40N25'16 79w34'57 5:18:20
Dunns Eddy 62 3 41N51 79w14 5:16:56
Dunnstable 18 76 41N11 77w24 5:09:36
Dunnstown 18 76 41N08'45 77w25'18 5:09:41
Dunring 27 6 41N30'36 78w59'52 5:15:59
Dupont 40 1 41N19'30 75w44'45 5:02:59
Duquesne 2 10 40N22'53 79w51'36 5:19:26
Duquesne Heights 2
114 40N26'07 80w01'13 5:20:05
Duquesne Wharf 2
10 40N22 79w51 5:19:24
Durbin 30 6 39N55'05 80w29'06 5:21:56
Durell 8 60 41N43'31 76w22'05 5:05:28
Durham 9 1 40N34'32 75w13'25 5:00:54
Durham Furnace 9
12 40N34'46 75w11'51 5:00:47
Durlach 36 30 40N13'53 76w13'48 5:04:55
Durrell 8 41 41N46 76w27 5:05:48
Durward 53 6 41N49'35 78w08'16 5:12:33
Duryea 40 1 41N20'38 75w44'20 5:02:57
Duryea Junction 40
1 41N21 75w46 5:03:04
Dushore 57 60 41N31'27 76w24'04 5:05:36
Dutch Corner 5 70 40N05'23 78w25'41 5:13:43
Dutch Hill 16 1 41N03'54 79w38'17 5:18:33
Dutch Hill 26 51 40N00'23 79w58'14 5:19:53
Dutch Hill 43 112 41N14'16 80w23'49 5:21:35
Dutch Settlement 11
63 40N23 78w40 5:14:40
Dutchtown 28 51 39N53'49 77w55'23 5:11:42
Dutton Mill 15 13 39N58'52 75w30'46 5:02:03
Dyberry 64 59 41N38'11 75w15'34 5:01:02
Dyerstown 9 8 40N20'27 75w07'31 5:00:30
Dykeman Spring 21
82 40N02'31 77w30'56 5:10:04
Dysart 11 63 40N35'48 78w31'02 5:14:04
Dysertown 11 55 40N26'39 78w35'38 5:14:23
Eagle 15 80 40N04'40 75w41'17 5:02:45
Eagle Farms 23 9 40N00 75w18 5:01:12
Eagle Foundry 31
6 40N12 78w08 5:12:32
Eagle Heights 23
9 40N00 75w18 5:01:12
Eaglehurst 25 107 42N05'44 80w09'49 5:20:39
Eagle Point 6 8 40N32'42 75w45'42 5:03:03
Eagle Rock 61 9 41N27'09 79w34'32 5:18:18
Eagles Mere 57 6 41N24'39 76w34'56 5:06:20
Eagles Mere Park 57
6 41N25 76w35 5:06:20
Eagleton Fields 18
7 41N12'07 77w38'07 5:10:32
Eagleville 14 7 41N03'23 77w35'35 5:10:22
Eagleville 46 90 40N09'34 75w24'31 5:01:38
Eakin Corner 61 6 41N10'24 79w48'49 5:19:15
Earlington 46 1 40N19'15 75w22'22 5:01:29
Earlston 5 6 40N00'22 78w22'13 5:13:29
Earlville 6 8 40N19'00 75w44'14 5:02:57
Earlyville 24 36 41N21'41 78w37'20 5:14:29
Earnestville 14 4 40N50'57 78w17'00 5:13:08
East Allen 48 13 40N42 75w25 5:01:40
East Allentown 39
13 40N36'23 75w26'52 5:01:47
East Altoona 7 33 40N32'50 78w21'54 5:13:28
East Ararat 58 6 41N47'32 75w29'10 5:01:57
East Athens 8 1 41N57'36 76w30'21 5:06:01
East Bangor 48 17 40N52'46 75w11'03 5:00:44
East Beech 18 7 41N04'37 77w33'01 5:10:12
East Benton 35 44 41N34'36 75w39'35 5:02:38
East Berlin 1 1 39N56'15 76w58'44 5:07:55
East Berlin 64 6 41N35'29 75w05'47 5:00:23
East Berwick 40 1 41N03'43 76w13'22 5:04:53
East Bethlehem 63
6 40N00 80w00 5:20:00
East Bloomsburg 19
4 40N59'26 76w26'07 5:05:44
East Bradford 15
13 39N58 75w39 5:02:36
East Bradford 42
102 41N57 78w39 5:14:36
East Brady 16 1 40N59'09 79w36'48 5:18:27
East Branch 33 51 41N01'59 79w03'04 5:16:12
East Branch 62 56 41N47'55 79w33'56 5:18:16
East Brandywine 15
46 40N02 75w45 5:03:00
Eastbrook 37 112 41N02'29 80w16'42 5:21:07
East Brunswick 54
1 40N41 76w00 5:04:00
East Buffalo 60
70 40N56 76w55 5:07:40
East Buffalo 63 3 40N11 80w16 5:21:04
East Butler 10 3 40N52'40 79w50'48 5:19:23
East Caln 15 13 40N01 75w41 5:02:44
East Cameron 49
27 40N47 76w26 5:05:44
East Canton 8 103 41N39'41 76w47'43 5:07:11
East Carnegie 2
114 40N24'56 80w04'32 5:20:18
East Carroll 11
63 40N35 78w41 5:14:44
East Charleston 59
59 41N50 77w01 5:08:04
East Chillisquaque 49
6 41N00 76w48 5:07:12
East Cocalico 36
28 40N14 76w06 5:04:24
East Conemaugh 11
74 40N20'55 78w53'02 5:15:32

East Connellsville 26
104 40N01 79w35 5:18:20
East Coventry 15
8 40N12 75w37 5:02:28
East Deer 2 14 40N35 79w47 5:19:08
East Donegal 36 2 40N06 76w34 5:06:16
East Drumore 36
27 39N52 76w10 5:04:40
East Du Bois 17
56 41N07 78w46 5:15:04
East Earl 36 27 40N06'36 76w01'59 5:04:08
East End 7 33 40N31'13 78w22'39 5:13:31
East End 14 70 40N54'49 77w45'13 5:11:01
East End 17 1 41N02 78w27 5:13:48
East Fairfield 20
59 41N33 80w05 5:20:20
East Falls 51 9 40N00'52 75w11'31 5:00:46
East Faxon 41 82 41N15 76w58 5:07:52
East Fayetteville 28
1 39N54'02 77w33'19 5:10:13
East Ferney 18 7 41N11'46 77w33'17 5:10:13
East Finley 63 6 40N01'25 80w23'16 5:21:33
East Franklin 3
15 40N51 79w34 5:18:16
East Fredericktown 26
51 39N59 79w55 5:19:40
East Fredricktown 26
6 40N00'10 79w59'37 5:19:58
East Freedom 7 3 40N21'27 78w25'48 5:13:43
East Germantown 51
9 40N03 75w10 5:00:40
East Goshen 15 13 40N00 75w33 5:02:12
East Greenville 46
2 40N24'23 75w30'08 5:02:01
East Hanover 38 8 40N23'51 76w35'32 5:06:22
East Hempfield 36
8 40N04 76w23 5:05:32
East Herrick 8 6 41N48'20 76w13'02 5:04:52
East Hickory 27 6 41N35'02 79w24'07 5:17:36
East Hill 41 6 41N20'44 77w19'01 5:09:16
East Hills 48 13 40N39'30 75w20'37 5:01:22
East Honesdale 64
22 41N33'46 75w14'51 5:00:59
East Hopewell 67
1 39N48 76w32 5:06:08
East Huntingdon 65
111 40N08 79w36 5:18:24
East Jermyn 35 1 41N31'32 75w32'43 5:02:11
East Kane 42 75 41N39'17 78w47'31 5:15:10
East Keating 18 7 41N19 77w58 5:11:52
East Kittanning 3
15 40N48'56 79w30'59 5:18:04
East Lackawannock 43
66 41N12 80w17 5:21:08
East Lampeter 36
8 40N02 76w14 5:04:56
Eastland 36 3 39N45'16 76w06'56 5:04:28
Eastland Hills 28
100 39N44'55 77w33'44 5:10:15
Eastland Hills 36
8 40N02'07 76w15'17 5:05:01
East Lansdowne 23
9 39N56'44 75w15'42 5:01:03
East Lawn 48 8 40N45'01 75w17'41 5:01:11
Eastlawn Gardens 46
8 40N45 75w18 5:01:12
East Lawrenceville 59
59 41N58'56 77w04'35 5:08:18
East Lemon 66 59 41N35'10 75w51'58 5:03:28
East Lenox 58 59 41N42'02 75w38'38 5:02:35
East Lewisburg 49
70 40N58'08 76w52'19 5:07:29
East Liberty 2
114 40N27'38 79w55'23 5:19:42
East Lynn 58 60 41N39'32 75w54'00 5:03:36
East Mahanoy Junction 54
27 40N48'41 76w02'36 5:04:10
East Mahoning 32
6 40N49 79w03 5:16:12
East Manchester 67
67 40N03 76w42 5:06:48
East Marianna 63
6 40N01'18 80w05'37 5:20:22
East Marlborough 15
8 39N53 75w43 5:02:52
East McKeesport 2
114 40N22'59 79w48'24 5:19:14
East Mead 20 77 41N38 80w04 5:20:16
East Millsboro 26
6 39N58'52 79w59'37 5:19:58
East Mines 54 27 40N42'37 76w11'29 5:04:46
East Monongahela 2
1 40N12'08 79w55'01 5:19:40
Eastmont 2 114 40N26'10 79w48'43 5:19:15
Eastmont 11 74 40N18 78w55 5:15:40
Eastmont 67 1 40N01'43 76w49'41 5:07:19
East Moravia 37
112 40N55'40 80w22'07 5:21:28
East Muncy 41 83 41N12 76w47 5:07:08
East Nantmeal 15
1 40N08 75w43 5:02:52
East New Castle 37
112 40N58'27 80w19'03 5:21:16
East Newport 50 1 40N29 77w08 5:08:32
East Norriton 46
8 40N10 75w21 5:01:24
East Norwegian 54
27 40N43 76w10 5:04:40
East Nottingham 15
3 39N45 75w58 5:03:52
East Oakmont 2 10 40N31'23 79w48'42 5:19:15
Easton 16 7 41N07'38 79w32'28 5:18:10
Easton 48 12 40N41'18 75w13'16 5:00:53
Easton Anglers 45
84 41N10'43 75w09'42 5:00:39
East Oreland 46 9 40N07 75w11 5:00:44
East Penn 13 80 40N46 75w44 5:02:56
East Pennsboro 21
12 40N17 76w56 5:07:44
East Petersburg 36
8 40N06'00 76w21'16 5:05:25
East Pikeland 15
8 40N08 75w34 5:02:16

East Pittsburgh 2
114 40N23'44 79W50'20 5:19:21
East Point 59 7 41N35'13 77W02'24 5:08:10
East Prospect 67
2 39N58'19 76W31'13 5:06:05
East Providence 5
6 40N01 78W16 5:13:04
East Riverside 26
51 39N55'54 79W55'39 5:19:43
East Rochester 4
13 40N42'00 80W16'06 5:21:04
East Rockhill 9 8 40N27 75W21 5:01:24
East Run 32 6 40N45'07 78W55'23 5:15:42
East Rush 58 60 41N45'37 75W59'52 5:03:59
East Saint Clair 5
6 40N08 78W34 5:14:16
East Salem 34 7 40N36'32 77W14'18 5:08:57
East Sandy 61 109 41N19'52 79W46'08 5:19:05
East Saxton 5 51 40N13'14 78W14'10 5:12:57
East Shamburg 61
6 41N34'09 79W36'38 5:18:27
East Sharon 53 29 41N58'40 78W08'53 5:12:36
East Sharpsburg 7
3 40N19'57 78W22'10 5:13:29
East Side 13 60 41N03'41 75W46'11 5:03:05
East Smethport 42
93 41N48'31 78W25'11 5:13:41
East Smithfield 8
6 41N51'52 76W37'33 5:06:30
East Springfield 25
68 41N57'54 80W24'27 5:21:38
East Sterling 64
6 41N19'36 75W20'14 5:01:21
East Stroudsburg 45
23 40N59'58 75W10'54 5:00:44
East Swiftwater 45
84 41N06'20 75W18'26 5:01:14
East Taylor 11 74 40N22 78W53 5:15:32
East Texas 39 13 40N32'51 75W33'42 5:02:15
East Titusville 20
74 41N37'19 79W38'33 5:18:34
East Towanda 8 41 41N45'54 76W26'00 5:05:44
Easttown 15 90 40N02 75W26 5:01:44
Easttown Woods 15
90 40N03 75W26 5:01:44
East Troy 8 7 41N46'12 76W44'15 5:06:57
East Union 54 60 40N53 76W08 5:04:32
East Uniontown 26
80 39N54 79W42 5:18:48
Eastvale 4 8 40N46'00 80W18'54 5:21:16
East Vandergrift 65
4 40N35'53 79W33'41 5:18:15
East View 30 1 39N53'37 80W13'48 5:20:55
Eastville 18 7 41N02'08 77W13'34 5:08:54
East Vincent 15
118 40N11 75W35 5:02:20
Eastvue 2 114 40N27'57 79W48'08 5:19:13
East Washington 63
3 40N10'25 80W14'16 5:20:57
East Waterford 34
6 40N22'13 77W36'18 5:10:25
East Wayne 20 6 41N34'20 79W54'29 5:19:38
East Weissport 13
8 40N50'14 75W41'08 5:02:45
East Wheatfield 32
7 40N27 79W01 5:16:04
East Whiteland 15
47 40N03 75W33 5:02:12
Eastwick 51 9 39N53'25 75W14'34 5:00:58
East William Penn (Shaft PO) 54
27 40N48'44 76W13'16 5:04:53
Eastwood 2 114 40N27'41 79W51'43 5:19:27
Eastwood 65 99 40N31'07 79W31'07 5:18:04
East Yoe 67 1 39N54'58 76W37'47 5:06:31
East York 67 67 39N58'25 76W41'12 5:06:45
Eatonville 66 59 41N30'52 75W57'41 5:03:51
Eau Claire 10 1 41N08'10 79W47'54 5:19:12
Ebenezer 22 80 40N14'06 76W46'34 5:07:06
Ebenezer 38 8 40N21'28 76W27'28 5:05:50
Ebensburg 11 54 40N29'06 78W43'30 5:14:54
Ebensburg Junction 11
55 40N29'56 78W39'42 5:14:39
Eberhardt 2 114 40N34 80W00 5:20:00
Eberleys Mill 21
12 40N13'32 76W54'21 5:07:37
Ebervale 40 42 40N59'10 75W56'30 5:03:46
Echo 3 59 40N51'00 79W19'39 5:17:19
Echo 11 74 40N22'37 78W51'28 5:15:26
Echo Lake 45 23 41N00 75W11 5:00:44
Echo Reach 9 9 40N03'54 74W56'50 4:59:47
Echo Valley 23 90 39N59'30 75W25'57 5:01:44
Echo Valley 54 9 40N36'00 76W23'32 5:05:34
Eckenrode Mill 11
57 40N35'54 78W39'10 5:14:37
Eckert 39 13 40N37 75W31 5:02:04
Eckley 40 60 40N59'36 75W51'46 5:03:27
Eckville 6 56 40N37'58 75W57'11 5:03:49
Economy 4 13 40N37 80W11 5:20:44
Eddington 9 9 40N05'04 74W56'43 4:59:47
Eddington Gardens 9
9 40N05'57 74W57'20 4:59:49
Eddystone 23 90 39N51'36 75W20'41 5:01:23
Eddyville 3 6 40N56'34 79W16'40 5:17:07
Ededburg 6 80 40N33'59 75W57'39 5:03:51
Edella 35 44 41N30'49 75W39'38 5:02:39
Edelman 48 8 40N47'25 75W15'55 5:01:04
Eden 17 6 41N06'35 78W20'33 5:13:22
Eden 36 27 40N04'13 76W16'12 5:05:05
Edenborn 26 51 39N53'03 79W52'55 5:19:32
Edenburg 6 80 40N33 75W59 5:03:56
Eden Croft 46 1 40N09 75W03 5:00:12
Edendale 14 4 40N50'15 78W16'02 5:13:04
Eden Heights 36 8 40N04'19 76W16'15 5:05:05
Eden Park 2 10 40N19'54 79W50'42 5:19:23
Edenton 15 3 39N51'24 75W55'58 5:03:44
Edenville 28 42 39N57'27 77W48'15 5:11:13
Edgeboro 9 8 40N14'08 74W55'50 4:59:43
Edgebrook 2 114 40N23'32 80W00'48 5:20:03
Edgecliff 65 14 40N35'59 79W43'26 5:18:54
Edgegrove 1 1 39N49'06 77W02'00 5:08:08
Edge Hill 46 9 40N06'12 75W09'49 5:00:39
Edgely 9 9 40N07'43 74W50'05 4:59:20
Edgemere 52 6 41N15'23 74W59'02 4:59:56
Edgemont 22 12 40N17'07 76W50'59 5:07:24
Edgemont 23 4 39N58'29 75W27'03 5:01:48
Edgemont 48 8 40N46'41 75W33'05 5:02:12
Edgemont Farms 15
90 40N00 75W23 5:01:32
Edges Mill 15 46 40N00 75W42 5:02:48
Edgewater 2 14 40N31 79W50 5:19:20
Edgewater Park 9
9 40N12 74W49 4:59:16
Edgewater Terrace 65
3 40N17'10 79W21'05 5:17:24
Edgewood 2 114 40N25'55 79W52'54 5:19:32
Edgewood 32 72 40N34'51 79W13'20 5:16:53
Edgewood 40 42 41N02'51 75W57'25 5:03:50
Edgewood 49 27 40N47'18 76W34'22 5:06:17
Edgewood 56 64 40N01 79W05 5:16:20
Edgewood Acres 2
114 40N26 79W53 5:19:32
Edgewood Grove 56
6 40N01 79W05 5:16:20
Edgewood Park 9 9 40N12 74W49 4:59:16
Edgewood Park 23
9 39N58 75W22 5:01:28
Edgeworth 2 13 40N33'04 80W11'35 5:20:46
Edie 56 6 40N05'12 79W07'38 5:16:31
Edinboro 25 3 41N52'27 80W07'55 5:20:32
Edinburg 37 112 41N00'52 80W26'13 5:21:45
Edison 9 8 40N16'49 75W07'47 5:00:31
Edisonville 36 96 39N59 76W11 5:04:44
Edmon 3 4 40N31'35 79W29'36 5:17:58
Edna 65 3 40N19 79W39 5:18:36
Edna Number One 65
3 40N18'03 79W39'06 5:18:36
Edna Number Two 65
25 40N17'34 79W41'20 5:18:45
Edwards Crossing 11
63 40N32'04 78W50'36 5:15:22
Edwardsville 40
20 41N16'10 75W55'00 5:03:40
Effort 45 1 40N56'21 75W26'07 5:01:44
Egypt 17 1 41N03'38 78W19'54 5:13:20
Egypt 33 5 41N14'46 78W56'15 5:15:45
Egypt 39 13 40N40'48 75W31'49 5:02:07
Egypt Corners 61
1 41N21'17 79W43'46 5:18:55
Egypt Mills 52 6 41N07'32 74W57'22 4:59:49
Ehrenfeld 11 63 40N22'17 78W46'40 5:15:07
Eichelbergertown 5
6 40N08'35 78W17'47 5:13:11
Eidenau 10 6 40N47'30 80W05'46 5:20:23
Eighty Four 63 2 40N10'54 80W08'00 5:20:32
Ekastown 10 2 40N42'40 79W46'36 5:19:06
Elam 23 4 39N51'18 75W32'29 5:02:10
Elbell 33 51 40N54'40 78W54'35 5:15:38
Elberta 7 33 40N30'51 78W19'20 5:13:17
Elbinsville 5 6 39N45'17 78W28'33 5:13:54
Elbon 24 5 41N18'14 78W41'11 5:14:45
Elbridge 59 6 41N55'15 77W16'28 5:09:06
Elbrook 28 100 39N49'04 77W36'25 5:10:26
Elco 63 115 40N04'39 79W52'10 5:19:29
Elder 11 63 40N41 78W41 5:14:44
Elderberry Pond 9
9 40N09'35 74W49'29 4:59:18
Elders Ridge 32
116 40N29 79W27 5:17:48
Eldersville 63 6 40N21'07 80W28'43 5:21:55
Elderton 3 6 40N41'42 79W20'30 5:17:22
El-Do Lake 45 8 40N57'35 75W32'04 5:02:08
Eldora 36 1 39N47'28 76W11'04 5:04:44
Eldora 63 1 40N10'15 79W53'38 5:19:35
Eldorado 7 33 40N28'20 78W25'28 5:13:42
Eldorado 10 6 41N05'29 79W44'50 5:18:59
Eldred 42 40 41N57'28 78W23'08 5:13:33
Eldred Center 62
3 41N44'43 79W33'23 5:18:14
Eldredsville 57 6 41N32'40 76W37'57 5:06:32
Elephant 9 8 40N25'29 75W14'31 5:00:58
Eleven Mile 53 6 41N58'56 77W59'11 5:11:57
Elfinwild 2 114 40N32'59 79W57'31 5:19:50
Elgin 25 7 41N54'11 79W44'38 5:18:59
Elgin Park 23 90 40N00 75W23 5:01:32
Elim 11 74 40N19 78W56 5:15:44
Elimsport 41 6 41N07'40 77W01'15 5:08:05
Elizabeth 2 8 40N16'09 79W53'24 5:19:34
Elizabethtown 36
2 40N09'10 76W36'11 5:06:25
Elizabethville 22
4 40N32'56 76W48'44 5:07:15
Elk City 16 6 41N14'39 79W30'07 5:18:00
Elk Creek 25 7 41N54 80W18 5:21:12
Elkdale 15 1 41N01 75W20 5:01:20
Elkdale 58 59 41N40'54 75W33'13 5:02:13
Elk Grove 57 6 41N18'22 76W24'26 5:05:38
Elkhorn 2 8 40N13'19 79W57'50 5:19:51
Elkin 32 6 40N48'14 79W06'30 5:16:26
Elkins Park 46 9 40N04'37 75W07'38 5:00:31
Elk Lake 58 60 41N45'06 75W57'02 5:03:48
Elkland 59 6 41N59'10 77W18'40 5:09:15
Elk Lick 56 79 39N46 79W07 5:16:28
Elk Park 26 6 39N45'43 79W27'09 5:17:49
Elk Run Junction 33
51 40N56 78W58 5:15:52
Elkview 15 7 39N48'30 75W53'44 5:03:35
Ellendale Forge 22
12 40N23'58 76W51'10 5:07:25
Ellen Gowan 54 27 40N49'02 76W10'36 5:04:42
Ellenton 41 103 41N32'22 76W48'16 5:07:13
Ellerslie 9 9 40N06'27 74W55'00 4:59:40
Elliger Park 46 9 40N07 75W14 5:00:56
Elliott 2 114 40N27'00 80W03'33 5:20:14
Elliottsburg 50 6 40N23'20 77W17'21 5:09:09
Elliotts Mills 37
6 41N02'06 80W08'37 5:20:34
Elliottson 21 16 40N12'00 77W16'22 5:09:05
Elliottsville 26
6 39N46'10 79W37'36 5:18:30
Ellisburg 53 6 41N55'52 77W53'37 5:11:34
Ellport 37 121 40N51'50 80W15'33 5:21:02
Ellrod 2 10 40N21 79W51 5:19:24
Ellsworth 63 51 40N06'43 80W01'03 5:20:04
Ellwell 8 6 41N34'30 76W15'50 5:05:03
Ellwood City 37
121 40N52 80W17 5:21:08
Elm 36 1 40N12'14 76W20'57 5:05:24
Elmdale 35 4 41N24'42 75W27'39 5:01:51
Elmer 53 6 41N55'10 77W37'25 5:10:30
Elm Grove 26 105 39N59'20 79W41'52 5:18:47
Elmhurst 35 4 41N22'40 75W32'42 5:02:11
Elmo 16 6 41N16'25 79W32'16 5:18:09
Elmora 11 63 40N36 78W45 5:15:00
Elmwood 51 9 39N55'04 75W13'42 5:00:55
Elmwood 67 67 39N58'10 76W41'55 5:06:48
Elmwood Terrace 9
9 40N10'04 74W52'36 4:59:30
Elora 10 6 40N59'38 79W59'23 5:19:58
Elrama 63 8 40N15'07 79W55'31 5:19:42
Elrico 65 6 40N28 79W31 5:18:04
Elroy 46 8 40N16'55 75W20'12 5:01:21
Elstie 11 63 40N31'12 78W31'55 5:14:08
Elstonville 36 8 40N12'28 76W25'12 5:05:41
Elton 11 123 40N16'47 78W48'09 5:15:13
Elverson 15 56 40N09'24 75W49'59 5:03:20
Elwood Park 63 3 40N09'50 80W16'57 5:21:08
Elwyn 23 90 39N54'28 75W24'38 5:01:39
Elwyn Terrace 36
8 40N09'22 76W23'13 5:05:33
Elysburg 49 1 40N51'52 76W33'10 5:06:13
Emanuelsville 48
13 40N45'37 75W27'38 5:01:51
Emblem 2 10 40N19'04 79W47'08 5:19:09
Embreeville 15 8 39N55'48 75W44'05 5:02:56
Emeigh 11 92 40N41'41 78W47'14 5:15:09
Emerald 30 6 39N59 80W03 5:20:12
Emerald 39 8 40N44'42 75W38'06 5:02:32
Emerickville 33
34 41N07'57 78W59'18 5:15:57
Emigh Run 32 63 40N44 78W49 5:15:16
Emigsville 67 67 40N01'18 76W43'42 5:06:55
Emilie 9 9 40N09'14 74W51'20 4:59:25
Emlenton 61 1 41N10'38 79W42'29 5:18:50
Emmaus 39 13 40N32'22 75W29'50 5:01:59
Emmaus Junction 39
13 40N32'56 75W29'18 5:01:57
Emmaville 29 6 39N54'37 78W14'59 5:13:00
Emmons 57 6 41N18'26 76W26'20 5:05:45
Emporium 12 106 41N30'44 78W14'07 5:12:56
Emsworth 2 114 40N30'36 80W05'41 5:20:23
End 29 6 40N06'02 78W06'57 5:12:28
Endeavor 27 6 41N35'22 79W23'07 5:17:32
Enders 22 24 40N29'30 76W51'00 5:07:24
Energy 37 112 40N55'46 80W15'54 5:21:04
Enfield 46 9 40N05'46 75W11'49 5:00:47
Engleside 36 8 40N01'23 76W18'17 5:05:13
Engles Lake 45 84 41N06 75W20 5:01:20
Engles Mill 56 79 39N45'10 79W03'41 5:16:15
Englesville 6 2 40N19'04 75W38'34 5:02:34
Englewood 54 27 40N47'02 76W14'32 5:04:58
English Center 41
6 41N26'14 77W16'48 5:09:07
Enhaut 22 12 40N13'54 76W49'38 5:07:19
Enid 29 6 40N05 78W10 5:12:40
Enlow 2 51 40N27'15 80W14'00 5:20:56
Ennisville 31 81 40N38'10 77W50'48 5:11:23
Enoch 56 6 40N04'40 79W05'59 5:16:24
Enola 21 12 40N17'24 76W56'03 5:07:44
Enon 63 64 39N58'30 80W25'15 5:21:41
Enon Valley (Enon Station) 37
6 40N51'17 80W27'26 5:21:50
Enterline 22 24 40N27'48 76W50'34 5:07:22
Enterprise 32 6 40N49'42 78W57'50 5:15:51
Enterprise 43 6 41N09'51 80W02'21 5:20:09
Enterprise 49 27 40N46 76W30 5:06:00
Enterprise 62 74 41N37'44 79W34'19 5:18:17
Entlerville 21 1 40N15'45 77W20'46 5:09:23
Entriken 31 6 40N20'02 78W11'57 5:12:48
Ephrata 36 30 40N10'47 76W10'45 5:04:43
Equinunk 64 6 41N51'21 75W13'27 5:00:54
Erbs Mill 36 1 39N51'46 76W20'17 5:05:21
Ercildoun 15 9 39N56'47 75W50'22 5:03:21
Erdenheim 46 9 40N05'31 75W12'51 5:00:51
Erdman 22 1 40N38'44 76W41'24 5:06:46
Erhard 17 6 40N50'42 78W30'11 5:14:01
Erie 25 107 42N07'45 80W05'07 5:20:20
Erie Heights 25
107 42N05'06 80W06'33 5:20:26
Erie Junction 33
5 41N14'35 78W46'26 5:15:06
Erlen 46 9 40N03 75W08 5:00:32
Erly 50 6 40N24'32 77W20'21 5:09:21
Ernest 32 72 40N40'41 79W09'43 5:16:39
Ernest 46 90 40N06'14 75W19'05 5:01:16
Erney 67 1 40N06'10 76W49'59 5:07:20
Erwinna 54 1 40N30'02 75W04'23 5:00:18
Eshbach 6 2 40N23'06 75W37'13 5:02:29
Eshcol 50 1 40N27'22 77W18'20 5:09:13
Esplen 2 114 40N27'27 80W03'03 5:20:12
Espy 19 4 41N00'22 76W24'37 5:05:38
Espyville 20 7 41N36'23 80W29'40 5:21:59
Essen 2 114 40N21'43 80W04'57 5:20:20
Essington 23 9 39N51'43 75W17'51 5:01:11
Estella 57 6 41N30'38 76W37'22 5:06:29
Esterly 6 101 40N20 75W53 5:03:32
Esther 4 19 40N40 80W24 5:21:36
Estherton 22 12 40N17 76W53 5:07:32
Etna 2 114 40N30'15 79W56'57 5:19:48
Etna Furnace 7 3 40N31'24 78W10'47 5:12:43
Etters 67 1 40N09 76W45 5:07:00
Euclid 10 3 40N59'36 79W55'45 5:19:43
Eulalia 53 66 41N45 78W00 5:12:00
Eureka 11 123 40N15 78W50 5:15:20
Eureka 46 8 40N14'40 75W11'33 5:00:46
Eureka 65 6 40N08'48 79W44'12 5:18:57
Eustontown 38 8 40N20 76W26 5:05:44
Evans 26 80 39N54 79W44 5:18:56
Evansburg 46 8 40N10'51 75W25'46 5:01:43
Evans City 10 108 40N46'09 80W03'47 5:20:15
Evans Falls 66 59 41N27'57 76W01'06 5:04:04
Evans Manor 26 80 39N55'11 79W40'57 5:18:44
Evanstown 65 3 40N15'53 79W41'22 5:18:45
Evansville 6 80 40N28'33 75W53'42 5:03:35
Evansville 19 1 41N04'23 76W17'43 5:05:11
Evendale 34 6 40N40'23 77W10'28 5:08:42
Everett 5 70 40N00'41 78W22'25 5:13:30
Evergreen 2 114 40N30'22 79W59'27 5:19:58
Evergreen 8 60 41N37'12 76W24'52 5:05:39

Evergreen Park 39 13 40N38'29 75w29'06 5:01:56
Everhartville 50 1 40N29 77w08 5:08:32
Everson 26 111 40N05'28 79w35'16 5:18:21
Ewalt 2 114 40N28 80w01 5:20:04
Ewen 40 1 41N18'36 75w48'39 5:03:15
Ewings Mill 32 6 40N34'31 78w59'33 5:15:58
Ewingsville 2 114 40N23'58 80w06'46 5:20:27
Excelsior 49 27 40N46'23 76w29'48 5:05:59
Excelsior Corner 62 6 41N41'47 79w28'58 5:17:56
Exchange 47 6 41N06'47 76w41'03 5:06:44
Exeter 40 1 41N19'14 75w49'10 5:03:17
Exmoor 54 9 40N32'00 76w24'44 5:05:39
Experiment 2 114 40N18'33 79w58'33 5:19:54
Export 65 6 40N25'05 79w37'33 5:18:30
Exton 15 13 40N01'44 75w37'16 5:02:29
Eyer 31 11 40N41'21 78w10'35 5:12:42
Eyers Grove 19 6 41N05'19 76w31'03 5:06:04
Eynon 35 18 41N29'44 75w34'29 5:02:18
Factory Hill 26 105 39N57'58 79w36'14 5:18:25
Factoryville 48 17 40N49'29 75w12'36 5:00:50
Factoryville 66 44 41N33'47 75w46'59 5:03:08
Fades 40 20 41N19'14 76w07'16 5:04:29
Fagleysville 46 2 40N16'35 75w33'55 5:02:16
Fagundus 62 6 41N37'57 79w26'00 5:17:44
Fair Acres 67 12 40N14 76w51 5:07:24
Fairbank 26 51 39N56'36 79w50'59 5:19:24
Fairbanks 65 116 40N29'03 79w29'08 5:17:57
Fairbrook 14 6 40N43'38 77w56'16 5:11:45
Fairchance 26 51 39N49'29 79w45'17 5:19:01
Fairdale 30 51 39N53'13 79w58'06 5:19:52
Fairdale 58 60 41N48'37 75w57'42 5:03:51
Fairfield 1 1 39N47'14 77w22'08 5:09:29
Fairfield 25 107 42N10'07 80w00'07 5:20:00
Fairfield 63 6 40N00'48 80w04'17 5:20:17
Fairfield Heights 32 98 40N28'06 79w10'46 5:16:43
Fairfiled (Greene P O) 36 1 39N47'05 76w13'29 5:04:54
Fair Grounds 30 6 39N56 80w03 5:20:12
Fairhaven Heights 2 114 40N23 79w49 5:19:16
Fair Hill 9 8 40N19'11 75w16'51 5:01:07
Fairhope 26 1 40N06'49 79w50'24 5:19:22
Fairhope 56 51 39N50'24 78w47'32 5:15:10
Fairland 36 8 40N08'54 76w21'17 5:05:25
Fairlawn 41 7 41N17'34 77w03'44 5:08:15
Fairless Hills 9 97 40N10'46 74w51'20 4:59:25
Fairless Junction 9 97 40N10'35 74w53'51 4:59:35
Fairmont 26 6 39N56'29 79w26'29 5:17:46
Fairmount 36 27 39N48'52 76w07'43 5:04:31
Fairmount 40 6 41N17 76w16 5:05:04
Fairmount 51 9 39N59 75w10 5:00:40
Fairmount 64 6 41N55'01 75w25'07 5:01:40
Fairmount 65 25 40N19'20 79w42'48 5:18:51
Fairmount City 16 6 41N00'29 79w18'48 5:17:15
Fairmount Springs 40 6 41N14'52 76w18'27 5:05:14
Fairoaks 2 13 40N34'46 80w13'01 5:20:52
Fairoaks 46 1 40N11 75w10 5:00:40
Fairplain 25 68 42N02'17 80w18'13 5:21:13
Fairplay 1 1 39N44'32 77w17'10 5:09:09
Fairview 4 8 40N41'32 80w28'13 5:21:53
Fairview 7 33 40N31'24 78w24'35 5:13:38
Fairview 10 6 41N00'52 79w44'35 5:18:58
Fairview 17 4 41N02'04 78w13'56 5:12:56
Fairview 23 90 39N52'18 75w20'42 5:01:23
Fairview 24 36 41N21'50 78w33'21 5:14:13
Fairview 25 68 42N01'53 80w15'20 5:21:01
Fairview 28 100 39N47'59 77w33'19 5:10:13
Fairview 31 6 40N12'42 78w02'16 5:12:09
Fairview 33 51 40N56'30 78w57'04 5:15:48
Fairview 43 66 41N19'33 80w13'49 5:20:55
Fairview 44 73 40N33'11 77w35'32 5:10:22
Fairview 49 27 40N47'02 76w34'13 5:06:17
Fairview Drive 67 1 39N48 76w59 5:07:56
Fairview Heights 2 114 40N31'07 79w51'27 5:19:26
Fairview Heights 6 80 40N25'51 76w00'28 5:04:02
Fairview Heights 40 20 41N09'26 75w53'20 5:03:33
Fairview Heights 42 102 41N58'25 78w35'46 5:14:23
Fairview Hills 40 20 41N14 75w52 5:03:28
Fairview Knolls 46 12 40N41 75w14 5:00:56
Fairview Park 15 13 39N57 75w36 5:02:24
Fairview Park 36 8 40N01'47 76w21'39 5:05:27
Fairview Park 40 20 41N14 75w52 5:03:28
Fairview Park 67 12 40N11'11 76w50'54 5:07:24
Fairview Village 46 90 40N09'28 75w23'15 5:01:33
Fairville 15 8 39N50'39 75w37'52 5:02:31
Fairville 60 70 40N58 76w54 5:07:36
Falconcrest 15 13 39N57 75w36 5:02:24
Fall Brook 59 6 41N40'38 76w59'10 5:07:57
Fallentimber 11 54 40N41'12 78w29'58 5:14:00
Fallen Timbers 26 7 39N44 79w52 5:19:28
Falling Spring 28 42 39N54'16 77w35'59 5:10:24
Falling Spring 50 6 40N21'07 77w12'42 5:08:51
Fallowfield 63 51 40N09 79w57 5:19:48
Falls 66 6 41N27'38 75w50'57 5:03:24
Falls Creek 33 59 41N08'42 78w48'17 5:15:13
Fallsdale 64 6 41N40'42 75w09'17 5:00:37
Fallsington 9 9 40N11'14 74w49'09 4:59:17
Fallston 4 19 40N43'32 80w18'57 5:21:16
Falmouth 36 2 40N07'46 76w42'51 5:06:51
Fannett 28 1 40N12 77w43 5:10:52
Fannettsburg 28 1 40N03'54 77w49'47 5:11:19
Faraday Park 23 9 39N54 75w20 5:01:20
Farmbrook 9 9 40N08'34 74w50'09 4:59:21
Farmdale 36 2 40N04'07 76w28'07 5:05:52
Farmers 67 39 39N55'03 76w54'41 5:07:39
Farmers Mills 14 64 40N51'56 77w36'28 5:10:26
Farmers Valley 8 52 41N47'17 76w49'49 5:07:19
Farmers Valley 42 93 41N51'39 78w26'56 5:13:48
Farmersville 36 30 40N07'39 76w09'55 5:04:40
Farmersville 48 12 40N39'59 75w18'21 5:01:13
Farmington 6 9 40N31'43 75w40'12 5:02:41
Farmington 26 6 39N48'26 79w33'57 5:18:16
Farmington 39 13 40N35'25 75w25'56 5:01:44
Farmington Hill 59 59 41N55'21 77w14'29 5:08:58
Farm School 9 8 40N17'58 75w09'34 5:00:38
Farquhar Estates 67 67 39N57 76w42 5:06:48
Farragut 41 82 41N17'35 76w54'25 5:07:38
Farrandsville 18 7 41N10'30 77w30'46 5:10:03
Farrell 43 117 41N12'44 80w29'49 5:21:59
Farview 6 101 40N19 75w57 5:03:48
Farwell 18 73 41N19'58 77w42'53 5:10:52
Fassett 8 7 41N59'10 76w46'25 5:07:06
Faunce 17 122 40N54'44 78w26'09 5:13:45
Fauncetown 20 6 41N37'09 79w51'26 5:19:26
Fawn Grove 67 1 39N43'40 76w27'08 5:05:49
Faxon 41 82 41N14'54 76w58'39 5:07:55
Fayette 26 51 39N49'20 79w55'09 5:19:41
Fayette 34 1 40N39 77w16 5:09:04
Fayette 37 6 41N06'14 80w18'36 5:21:14
Fayette City 26 1 40N06'01 79w50'27 5:19:22
Fayetteville 2 51 40N26'20 80w12'50 5:20:51
Fayetteville 28 1 39N54'40 77w33'01 5:10:12
Fayfield 67 67 39N58'02 76w40'59 5:06:44
Fay Terrace 43 59 41N24 80w23 5:21:32
Fearnot 54 27 40N38'38 76w38'12 5:06:33
Feasterville 9 1 40N08'38 75w00'20 5:00:01
Federal 2 114 40N22'43 80w08'53 5:20:36
Federal Reserve 2 114 40N27 79w58 5:19:52
Federal Reserve 51 9 39N57 75w09 5:00:36
Federal Square 22 12 40N16 76w53 5:07:32
Fell 35 1 41N36 75w29 5:01:56
Fellsburg 65 1 40N10'59 79w49'28 5:19:18
Fells Corners 35 4 41N18'11 75w32'00 5:02:08
Fellwick 46 9 40N07 75w14 5:00:56
Felton 67 7 39N51'17 76w33'53 5:06:16
Feltonville 23 90 39N50'45 75w23'45 5:01:35
Feltonville 51 9 40N01'18 75w07'34 5:00:30
Fenelton 10 6 40N52'13 79w43'35 5:18:54
Fenmore 67 1 39N50'15 76w31'37 5:06:06
Ferguson 2 114 40N34 80w00 5:20:00
Ferguson 26 105 39N57'33 79w37'23 5:18:30
Fergusonville 9 9 40N06'59 74w54'02 4:59:36
Fermanagh 34 7 40N36 77w23 5:09:32
Fern 16 6 41N17'57 79w32'34 5:18:10
Fern Brook 40 20 41N19'48 75w56'30 5:03:46
Ferndale 9 1 40N32'01 75w10'45 5:00:43
Ferndale 11 74 40N17'20 78w54'54 5:15:40
Ferndale 49 27 40N46'52 76w34'25 5:06:18
Ferndale 54 1 40N52'55 76w14'40 5:04:59
Ferney 18 7 41N13'27 77w33'48 5:10:15
Fernglen 36 1 39N48'37 76w15'59 5:05:04
Fern Glen 40 60 40N56'48 76w09'33 5:04:38
Fern Hill 15 13 39N58'46 75w35'28 5:02:22
Fernridge 45 84 41N04'18 75w33'59 5:02:16
Fern Rock 51 9 40N02'38 75w08'23 5:00:34
Fern Village 46 1 40N11 75w06 5:00:24
Fernville 19 4 41N00'14 76w27'51 5:05:51
Fernway 10 6 40N48 80w08 5:20:32
Fernwood 17 63 40N46'25 78w23'55 5:13:36
Fernwood 23 9 39N56 75w16 5:01:04
Ferrellton 56 6 40N08'51 79w02'27 5:16:10
Ferrelton 56 6 40N07 78w57 5:15:48
Ferris 10 6 41N06'04 79w51'38 5:19:27
Ferris Corners 20 3 41N47'39 79w57'45 5:19:51
Fertigs 61 6 41N21'02 79w35'00 5:18:20
Fertility 36 8 40N01'37 76w14'36 5:04:58
Fetterville 36 27 40N06'35 76w00'25 5:04:02
Fetzertown 14 70 40N59'20 77w49'40 5:11:19
Feys Grove 40 6 41N05'23 76w00'18 5:04:01
Fiddlergreen 62 3 41N44'46 79w32'31 5:18:10
Fiddlers Green 11 63 40N22'17 78w39'35 5:14:38
Fiddletown 45 9 40N52'01 75w26'36 5:01:46
Fidelity 51 9 39N57 75w09 5:00:36
Fiedler 14 6 40N54'17 77w23'28 5:09:34
Fieldmore Springs 20 74 41N38 79w40 5:18:40
Fieldsons Crossroads 30 51 39N47'24 79w56'26 5:19:46
Fifficktown 11 74 40N22 78w51 5:15:24
Fiketown 26 6 39N44'28 79w29'19 5:17:57
Filbert 26 51 39N56'35 79w51'15 5:19:25
Filer Corners 43 6 41N18'14 80w07'35 5:20:30
Filetown 48 8 40N46'23 75w18'03 5:01:12
Fillmore 14 70 40N51'32 77w52'36 5:11:30
Finch Hill 35 1 41N34 75w32 5:02:08
Findlay 2 6 40N29 80w18 5:21:12
Findley 43 66 41N13 80w11 5:20:44
Finland 9 2 40N23'03 75w25'11 5:01:41
Finley Mills 33 51 40N56 78w58 5:15:52
Finleyville 5 51 40N10 78w13 5:12:52
Finleyville 63 114 40N15'08 80w00'11 5:20:01
Finlyville 5 51 40N09'10 78w11'11 5:12:45
Finney 63 3 40N09'25 80w19'04 5:21:16
Finton 11 54 40N42'55 78w31'06 5:14:04
First Fork 12 6 41N27'12 78w02'58 5:12:12
Fiscal 67 3 39N43'39 76w47'38 5:07:11
Fisher 16 6 41N15'59 79w14'34 5:16:58
Fisher 63 1 40N10'12 79w54'29 5:19:38
Fisher Corners 23 90 39N52'21 75w26'43 5:01:47
Fisherdale 19 1 40N51'15 76w26'40 5:05:47
Fisher Heights 10 3 40N55'31 79w57'15 5:19:49
Fisher Heights 63 1 40N11 79w54 5:19:36
Fishermans Paradise 14 9 40N52'50 77w47'35 5:11:10
Fishers Corner 23 90 39N51 75w22 5:01:28
Fishers Ferry 49 82 40N46'09 76w50'42 5:07:23
Fishertown 5 6 40N07'18 78w35'09 5:14:21
Fishertown 11 74 40N21'05 78w46'26 5:15:06
Fisherville 15 46 40N00'54 75w45'13 5:03:01
Fisherville 22 24 40N30'04 76w53'03 5:07:32
Fishingcreek 19 6 41N08 76w21 5:05:24
Fiske 11 54 40N40'34 78w30'20 5:14:01
Fisk Mill 58 60 41N53'25 75w53'37 5:03:34
Fitz Henry 65 6 40N10'04 79w45'22 5:19:01
Fitzwatertown 46 9 40N07'28 75w09'36 5:00:38
Five Corners 20 7 41N42'12 79w44'50 5:18:59
Five Forks 5 6 39N51'39 78w24'32 5:13:38
Five Forks 26 6 39N43'16 79w32'50 5:18:11
Five Forks 28 100 39N48'05 77w36'32 5:10:26
Five Locks 6 80 40N31'34 75w59'11 5:03:57
Five Points 1 1 39N56'54 77w06'07 5:08:24
Five Points 4 6 40N40'59 80w28'50 5:21:55
Five Points 6 9 40N31'16 75w42'22 5:02:49
Five Points 9 9 40N11'31 74w49'09 4:59:17
Five Points 10 6 41N02'51 79w54'30 5:19:38
Five Points 15 8 39N49'57 75w42'28 5:02:50
Five Points 16 6 41N07'18 79w25'59 5:17:44
Five Points 17 122 40N47'37 78w40'20 5:14:41
Five Points 19 6 41N14'38 76w19'47 5:05:19
Five Points 24 7 41N16'27 78w35'58 5:14:24
Five Points 25 3 41N58'17 79w42'04 5:18:48
Five Points 32 72 40N43'41 79w13'07 5:16:52
Five Points 40 6 40N59'01 76w09'08 5:04:37
Five Points 43 6 41N24'19 80w01'11 5:20:05
Five Points 46 9 40N06'24 75w11'20 5:00:45
Five Points 48 17 40N53'18 75w09'14 5:00:37
Five Points 49 6 41N07'23 76w46'21 5:07:05
Five Points 53 6 41N30'31 77w58'09 5:11:53
Five Points 61 6 41N17'54 79w52'42 5:19:31
Five Points 65 99 40N24'11 79w31'23 5:18:06
Fivepointville 36 28 40N10'58 76w03'05 5:04:12
Flaggs Manor 15 1 39N51'28 75w54'35 5:03:38
Flat Rock 14 63 40N49'30 78w06'24 5:12:26
Flat Rock 26 6 39N46'11 79w28'37 5:17:54
Flatwoods 26 104 40N01'42 79w43'34 5:18:54
Fleetville 35 44 41N35'53 75w42'54 5:02:52
Fleetwing Estates 9 9 40N09 74w51 4:59:24
Fleetwood 6 8 40N27'14 75w49'06 5:03:16
Fleming 14 7 40N54 77w53 5:11:32
Fleming Summit 32 6 40N43'26 78w54'16 5:15:37
Flemington 18 76 41N07'35 77w28'19 5:09:53
Flickerville 29 6 39N51'23 78w14'19 5:12:57
Flicksville 48 15 40N50'39 75w12'07 5:00:48
Flinton 11 54 40N43 78w31 5:14:04
Flintville 38 8 40N18'31 76w19'47 5:05:19
Flora 32 51 40N53'32 78w52'19 5:15:29
Floradale 1 1 39N57'31 77w14'55 5:09:00
Floreffe 2 8 40N15'27 79w55'12 5:19:41
Florence 63 6 40N25'56 80w26'02 5:21:44
Florida Park 23 90 39N58'41 75w25'47 5:01:43
Florin 36 2 40N07 76w31 5:06:04
Florys Mill 36 8 40N04'53 76w21'03 5:05:24
Flourtown 46 9 40N06'12 75w12'46 5:00:51
Flourtown Gardens 46 9 40N06 75w15 5:01:00
Flowing Spring 7 33 40N28'20 78w16'06 5:13:04
Flushing 9 9 40N07'06 74w54'25 4:59:38
F M Corners 43 117 41N13'11 80w28'16 5:21:53
Fogelsville 39 13 40N34'59 75w37'59 5:02:32
Folcroft 23 9 39N53'27 75w17'03 5:01:08
Foley 56 51 39N49'46 78w49'06 5:15:16
Foley Corner 57 60 41N28'36 76w25'12 5:05:41
Foleys Siding 2 114 40N22 80w00 5:20:00
Folsom 23 9 39N53'23 75w19'32 5:01:18
Folstown 40 20 41N09'39 76w00'37 5:04:02
Fombell 4 121 40N48'34 80w12'07 5:20:48
Font 15 46 40N00 75w42 5:02:48
Fontaine 15 27 40N07'16 75w51'41 5:03:27
Fontana 38 8 40N17'03 76w29'58 5:06:00
Footedale 26 51 39N54'33 79w49'31 5:19:18
Foot of Ten 7 33 40N24'57 78w27'20 5:13:49
Forbes Road 65 99 40N21'14 79w31'19 5:18:05
Force 24 7 41N15'28 78w30'05 5:14:00
Ford City 3 15 40N46'20 79w31'48 5:18:07
Ford Cliff 3 15 40N45 79w32 5:18:08
Fordham 33 51 40N54'54 79w02'00 5:16:08
Fordview 3 15 40N46'13 79w31'23 5:18:06
Fordville 67 39 39N57'05 76w54'46 5:07:39
Fordyce 30 1 39N50'51 80w04'52 5:20:19
Foreman 5 70 40N04'40 78w23'30 5:13:34
Forest Castle 40 1 41N20 75w49 5:03:16
Forest City 58 59 41N39'05 75w28'01 5:01:52
Forest City Station 64 59 41N39'00 75w27'28 5:01:50
Forest Grove 2 114 40N28'45 80w07'50 5:20:31
Forest Grove 9 8 40N17'32 75w03'34 5:00:14
Forest Hill 60 64 40N58'28 77w02'59 5:08:12

Forest Hills 2 114 40N25'11 79w51'01 5:19:24
Forest Hills 36 28 40N05 76w11 5:04:44
Forest Hills Manor 46 1 40N09 75w03 5:00:12
Forest Inn 13 8 40N50 75w42 5:02:48
Forest Knolls 46 8 40N04 76w26 5:05:44
Forest Lake 58 6 41N53'03 75w57'35 5:03:50
Forest Lake Park 52 6 41N28 75w03 5:00:12
Forest Park 9 2 40N20 75w18 5:01:12
Forest Park 40 20 41N11'32 75w47'07 5:03:08
Forest Park 52 1 41N08'21 75w01'07 5:00:04
Forestville 10 6 41N06'21 80w00'22 5:20:01
Forestville 15 1 39N49'01 75w54'40 5:03:39
Forestville 54 49 40N41'32 76w18'06 5:05:12
Forestville 57 6 41N29'13 76w36'09 5:06:25
Forge 7 11 40N40 78w13 5:12:52
Forks 19 4 41N05 76w25 5:05:40
Forks Church 3 4 40N40'28 79w35'39 5:18:23
Forkston 66 6 41N31'42 76w07'34 5:04:30
Forksville 57 6 41N29 76w36 5:06:24
Fort Couch 21 12 40N14'46 76w54'17 5:07:37
Fortenia 64 22 41N34'39 75w17'38 5:01:11
Fort Fetter 7 33 40N25'42 78w24'33 5:13:38
Fort Hill 56 53 39N49'49 79w16'22 5:17:05
Fort Hunter 22 12 40N20'46 76w54'45 5:07:39
Fort Littleton 29 6 40N03'46 77w57'50 5:11:51
Fort Loudon 28 51 39N54'53 77w54'18 5:11:37
Fort Miffin 51 9 39N52'31 75w12'48 5:00:51
Fortney 67 12 40N05'56 76w54'26 5:07:38
Fort Pittsburgh 2 114 40N26'28 80w00'36 5:20:02
Fort Robertson 50 6 40N21'38 77w23'04 5:09:32
Fortuna 46 8 40N15'32 75w15'54 5:01:04
Fort Washington 46 9 40N08'30 75w12'34 5:00:50
Forty Fort 40 20 41N16'44 75w52'43 5:03:31
Forward 56 63 40N07'53 78w51'54 5:15:28
Forwardstown 56 6 40N13'07 79w01'48 5:16:07
Fossilville 5 6 39N52'01 78w41'41 5:14:47
Foster 32 116 40N31'57 79w26'25 5:17:46
Foster 61 6 41N19'30 79w48'20 5:19:13
Foster Brook 42 102 41N58'30 78w37'03 5:14:28
Foster Corner 61 109 41N24'50 79w51'12 5:19:25
Fosters Corner 61 9 41N28'28 79w44'05 5:18:56
Fosters Mills 3 6 40N54'18 79w38'03 5:18:32
Fostoria 7 11 40N37'06 78w19'15 5:13:17
Foundryville 19 1 41N04'42 76w14'09 5:04:57
Fountain 14 7 41N02'22 77w55'24 5:11:42
Fountain 54 27 40N39'19 76w26'49 5:05:47
Fountain Dale 1 1 39N44'25 77w26'01 5:09:44
Fountain Hill 39 13 40N36'05 75w23'44 5:01:35
Fountain House 20 59 41N44 80w07 5:20:28
Fountain House Corners 20 77 41N41'59 80w06'50 5:20:27
Fountain Springs 54 27 40N47 76w21 5:05:24
Fountainville 9 8 40N20'28 75w09'03 5:00:36
Fountian Springs 54 27 40N46'16 76w19'30 5:05:18
Four Corners 24 75 41N31'46 78w56'01 5:15:44
Four Points 24 36 41N17'11 78w37'05 5:14:28
Foustown 67 67 39N59'42 76w46'19 5:07:05
Foustwell 56 6 40N13'05 78w53'59 5:15:36
Fowler Heights 32 72 40N38'22 79w08'22 5:16:33
Fowlersville 19 1 41N03'37 76w19'44 5:05:19
Foxburg 16 1 41N08'35 79w40'48 5:18:43
Foxburg 33 51 40N57'44 78w52'45 5:15:31
Fox Chapel 2 114 40N31 79w53 5:19:32
Fox Chase 36 8 40N04 76w19 5:05:16
Fox Chase 51 9 40N04'52 75w04'50 5:00:19
Fox Chase Manor 46 9 40N05 75w07 5:00:28
Foxcroft 23 9 39N59'43 75w21'20 5:01:25
Foxdale 65 111 40N13 79w36 5:18:24
Fox Hill 28 100 39N48'44 77w33'17 5:10:13
Fox Hill 40 20 41N15'46 75w49'02 5:03:16
Fox Hill 53 6 41N51'08 77w46'15 5:11:05
Fox Ridge 2 114 40N33'39 80w01'54 5:20:08
Foxtown 65 111 40N13'31 79w35'10 5:18:21
Foxtown Hill 45 23 40N58'38 75w10'45 5:00:43
Foxwood Park 23 9 39N58 75w22 5:01:28
Frackville 54 27 40N47'02 76w13'50 5:04:55
Frackville Junction 54 27 40N47'12 76w13'53 5:04:56
Frailey 54 9 40N38 76w25 5:05:40
Francis 25 68 41N57'34 80w15'54 5:21:04
Francis Mine 63 6 40N23 80w24 5:21:36
Franconia 46 8 40N18'28 75w21'29 5:01:26
Frank 2 8 40N16 79w48 5:19:12
Frankford 51 9 40N01'41 75w05'07 5:00:20
Frankfort Springs 4 6 40N28'44 80w26'34 5:21:46
Franklin 11 74 40N20'32 78w53'06 5:15:32
Franklin 15 1 39N44'34 75w50'56 5:03:24
Franklin 61 109 41N23'52 79w49'54 5:19:20
Franklin Center 23 90 39N55 75w22 5:01:28
Franklin Center 25 68 41N56'08 80w13'30 5:20:54
Franklin Corners 25 7 41N53 80w08 5:20:32
Franklindale 8 60 41N42'10 76w33'17 5:06:13
Franklin Farms 63 3 40N09'18 80w16'14 5:21:05
Franklin Forks 58 60 41N55'05 75w50'52 5:03:23
Franklin Furnace 28 42 39N57'33 77w49'19 5:11:17
Franklin Furnace 47 6 40N59'19 76w39'05 5:06:36
Franklin Hill 58 50 41N58 75w45 5:03:00
Franklin Junction 40 20 41N13'22 75w54'13 5:03:37
Franklin Park 2 114 40N35 80w06 5:20:24
Franklin Pike Corners 20 77 41N36'48 80w08'55 5:20:36
Franklintown 67 1 40N04'36 77w01'43 5:08:07
Franklinville 31 6 40N38'47 78w05'26 5:12:22
Franklinville 46 8 40N10'46 75w16'41 5:01:07
Frankstown 7 33 40N26'38 78w21'18 5:13:25
Frazer 15 47 40N01'56 75w33'23 5:02:14
Frazier Mill 10 6 40N45'11 79w51'17 5:19:25
Frederick 46 8 40N18 75w32 5:02:08
Fredericksburg 3 6 41N01'05 79w41'17 5:18:45
Fredericksburg 7 51 40N19'00 78w31'08 5:14:05
Fredericksburg 20 77 41N38'45 80w10'37 5:20:42
Fredericksburg 38 1 40N26'37 76w25'43 5:05:43
Fredericksville 6 9 40N27'11 75w41'22 5:02:45
Fredericktown 63 6 40N00'09 79w59'54 5:20:00
Fredericktown Hill 63 6 40N00'05 80w00'04 5:20:00
Fredonia 43 66 41N19'18 80w15'32 5:21:02
Fredrick 46 8 40N18'10 75w31'47 5:02:07
Freeburg 55 4 40N45'47 76w56'23 5:07:46
Freedom 4 13 40N41'15 80w15'15 5:21:01
Freehold 62 6 41N57 79w26 5:17:44
Freeland 40 42 41N01'00 75w53'51 5:03:35
Freeman 42 59 41N41'26 78w39'09 5:14:37
Freemansburg 48 12 40N37'35 75w20'46 5:01:23
Freemansburg Heights 48 13 40N39 75w21 5:01:24
Freemanville 6 101 40N16'48 75w56'19 5:03:45
Freemont 15 3 39N44'42 76w04'00 5:04:16
Freeport 3 2 40N40'26 79w41'06 5:18:44
Freeport 25 91 42N14'23 79w49'59 5:19:20
Freeport 30 6 39N46 80w25 5:21:40
Freeport Junction 3 2 40N41 79w41 5:18:44
Freeport Mills 38 8 40N24'06 76w24'50 5:05:39
Frenchs Corners 3 15 40N53'56 79w30'06 5:18:00
French Settlement 41 82 41N12'39 77w00'47 5:08:03
Frenchtown 20 6 41N36'43 80w01'19 5:20:05
Frenchtown 41 6 41N12'51 76w38'46 5:06:35
Frenchville 17 6 41N06'17 78w13'13 5:12:53
Freys Grove 22 80 40N12'56 76w43'26 5:06:54
Freysville 67 1 39N55'41 76w36'23 5:06:26
Freytown 35 6 41N17'50 75w26'44 5:01:47
Fricks 9 8 40N17 75w16 5:01:04
Fricks Lock 15 8 40N13'20 75w35'45 5:02:23
Friedens 39 8 40N44'04 75w36'59 5:02:28
Friedens 56 6 40N03'00 78w59'55 5:16:00
Friedensburg 54 27 40N36'09 76w14'28 5:04:58
Friedensville 39 13 40N33'33 75w23'42 5:01:35
Friendship Heights 26 51 39N46'58 79w55'02 5:19:40
Friendship Village 15 9 39N59 75w50 5:03:20
Friendsville 58 6 41N55'01 76w02'45 5:04:11
Friesville 7 3 40N17'40 78w27'45 5:13:51
Frills Corners 16 6 41N23'44 79w22'06 5:17:28
Frinks 53 66 41N48'54 77w59'03 5:11:56
Frisbie 54 1 40N39'51 76w03'59 5:04:16
Frisco 4 121 40N50'52 80w16'05 5:21:04
Fritztown 6 101 40N17'43 76w04'08 5:04:17
Frizzleburg 37 51 41N04'35 80w27'18 5:21:49
Frogtown 3 1 40N57'04 79w39'26 5:18:38
Frogtown 16 6 41N06'39 79w18'59 5:17:16
Frogtown 31 6 40N42'53 78w06'36 5:12:26
Frogtown 63 6 40N12'31 80w30'20 5:22:01
Frogtown 67 12 40N10'53 76w51'30 5:07:26
Froman 63 114 40N14'03 79w59'19 5:19:57
Frostburg 33 51 40N57'52 79w02'01 5:16:08
Frugality 11 54 40N39'11 78w29'20 5:13:57
Fruittown 14 64 40N46'39 77w39'55 5:10:40
Fruitville 36 8 40N04 76w19 5:05:16
Fruitville 46 8 40N15'23 75w32'28 5:02:10
Frush Valley 6 101 40N23'49 75w54'36 5:03:38
Frutcheys 45 23 41N00 75w11 5:00:44
Fryburg 16 6 41N21'13 79w26'18 5:17:45
Frye 63 1 40N11'02 79w56'08 5:19:45
Frystown 6 25 40N26'59 76w20'04 5:05:20
Frysville 36 30 40N10'11 76w06'08 5:04:25
Fuhrmans Mill 67 1 39N45'29 76w55'27 5:07:42
Fuller 26 6 40N05'50 79w44'44 5:18:59
Fuller 33 34 41N05'53 78w59'05 5:15:56
Fullerton 39 13 40N37'54 75w28'25 5:01:54
Fullerton 42 6 41N59'11 78w31'04 5:14:04
Fulmor 46 17 40N09'56 75w06'18 5:00:25
Fulmor Heights 46 1 40N11 75w06 5:00:24
Fulton 36 1 39N47 76w11 5:04:44
Fulton Run 32 72 40N39'51 79w12'10 5:16:49
Furlong 9 8 40N17'46 75w04'57 5:00:20
Furnace Hill 26 105 39N58'23 79w36'20 5:18:25
Furnace Hill 43 117 41N10'14 80w27'57 5:21:52
Furnace Run 3 15 40N51'10 79w33'00 5:18:12
Furniss 36 1 39N47'38 76w13'20 5:04:53
Gabby Heights 63 3 40N09'11 80w15'38 5:21:03
Gabelsville 6 2 40N20'13 75w39'21 5:02:37
Gaffney 42 75 41N45'23 78w36'22 5:14:25
Gahagen 56 63 40N03'44 78w48'08 5:15:13
Gaibleton 32 6 40N43'29 79w06'06 5:16:24
Gaines 59 6 41N45'07 77w33'28 5:10:14
Gaines Junction 59 6 41N44'50 77w34'26 5:10:18
Gale 63 3 40N01'57 80w21'26 5:21:26
Galena Hill 61 109 41N23'40 79w50'36 5:19:22
Galeton 53 6 41N43'59 77w38'32 5:10:34
Galilee 64 6 41N44'06 75w08'24 5:00:34
Gallagher 18 7 41N16 77w27 5:09:48
Gallagherville 15 46 39N59'56 75w43'38 5:02:55
Gallatin 2 1 40N11'51 79w53'21 5:19:33
Gallatin 26 51 39N49'26 79w55'05 5:19:40
Gallitzin 11 55 40N28'56 78w33'07 5:14:12
Galloway 61 109 41N25'29 79w49'03 5:19:16
Gallows Harbor 17 4 41N03'21 78w15'47 5:13:03
Gallows Hill 9 12 40N31'50 75w13'20 5:00:53
Gamble 41 7 41N23 76w56 5:07:44
Gambles 63 2 40N12'38 80w07'52 5:20:31
Ganister 7 3 40N28'29 78w13'34 5:12:54
Gans 26 51 39N44'34 79w49'28 5:19:18
Gap 36 23 39N59'14 76w01'15 5:04:05
Gapsville 5 6 39N57'12 78w14'31 5:12:58
Garards Fort 30 6 39N48'57 80w01'36 5:20:06
Gardeau 42 75 41N37'16 78w13'28 5:12:54
Garden City 2 114 40N26'51 79w46'47 5:19:07
Garden City 23 90 39N52'35 75w22'15 5:01:29
Gardendale 23 90 39N50'32 75w26'48 5:01:47
Garden Hills 36 8 40N01'49 76w21'22 5:05:25
Garden View 41 82 41N15'15 77w02'47 5:08:11
Garden View 44 7 40N42'37 77w35'24 5:10:22
Gardenville 9 8 40N22'21 75w06'29 5:00:26
Gardner 14 11 40N44'37 78w13'47 5:12:55
Gardner 37 112 41N00 80w21 5:21:24
Gardner Hill 24 7 41N16'51 78w33'23 5:14:14
Gardners 1 1 40N00'20 77w12'26 5:08:50
Garfield 6 1 40N25'50 76w02'24 5:04:10
Gargol 1 1 40N00'57 77w10'23 5:08:42
Garland 62 7 41N48'58 79w26'39 5:17:47
Garman 11 92 40N40 78w47 5:15:08
Garmantown 11 92 40N40'47 78w48'30 5:15:14
Garrett 56 79 39N51'47 79w03'30 5:16:14
Garrettford 23 9 39N57 75w18 5:01:12
Garrett Hill 23 90 40N01'37 75w20'16 5:01:21
Garretts Run 3 15 40N47'36 79w30'47 5:18:03
Garrison 30 6 39N43'46 80w25'22 5:21:41
Garvers Ferry 65 2 40N39'56 79w41'25 5:18:46
Garvey Melton 2 114 40N20'55 80w02'25 5:20:10
Gascola 2 114 40N27'08 79w47'46 5:19:11
Gaskill 33 6 40N57 78w51 5:15:24
Gastonville 63 114 40N15'26 79w59'46 5:19:59
Gastow 3 6 40N42'33 79w18'57 5:17:16
Gastown 3 6 40N40 79w18 5:17:12
Gatchellville 67 1 39N46'08 76w28'02 5:05:52
Gates 26 51 39N53'23 79w54'41 5:19:39
Gatesburg 14 6 40N44'41 78w00'19 5:12:01
Gateway Center 2 114 40N27 79w59 5:19:56
Gauff Hill 39 13 40N35'29 75w24'56 5:01:40
Gayly 2 114 40N26'39 80w08'49 5:20:35
Gaysport 7 33 40N25'39 78w23'52 5:13:35
Gazzam 17 54 40N52'01 78w34'28 5:14:18
Gearhartville 17 113 40N53'21 78w15'06 5:13:00
Gebhart 56 4 39N56'39 79w10'39 5:16:43
Geeseytown 7 33 40N26'55 78w20'45 5:13:23
Geiger 56 6 40N02'03 79w02'26 5:16:10
Geigertown 6 8 40N12'09 75w50'12 5:03:21
Geistown 11 74 40N17'27 78w52'09 5:15:29
Gelatt 58 6 41N48'24 75w35'00 5:02:20
General Warren Village 15 8 40N02'30 75w31'25 5:02:06
General Wayne 46 9 40N01 75w15 5:01:00
Genesee 53 6 41N59'21 77w51'58 5:11:28
Geneva 20 59 41N33'45 80w13'31 5:20:54
Geneva Hill 4 8 40N46 80w20 5:21:20
Georges 26 51 39N50 79w46 5:19:04
Georges Station 65 99 40N19'04 79w29'17 5:17:57
Georgetown 1 56 39N43'23 77w05'47 5:08:23
Georgetown 3 4 40N38'18 79w36'13 5:18:25
Georgetown 4 6 40N38'29 80w29'53 5:22:00
Georgetown (Bart P O) 36 23 39N56'15 76w05'01 5:04:20
Georgetown 40 20 41N13'38 75w52'09 5:03:29
Georgetown 48 8 40N43'30 75w20'17 5:01:21
Georgeville 32 6 40N50'02 79w05'39 5:16:23
German 26 51 39N53 79w52 5:19:28
German Corners 39 8 40N42 75w42 5:02:48
Germania 53 6 41N38'51 77w39'38 5:10:39
Germans 13 8 40N45'52 75w44'27 5:02:58
German Settlement 14 7 41N03'53 78w00'18 5:12:01
Germansville 39 8 40N42'05 75w42'26 5:02:50
Germantown 1 56 39N46'09 77w08'54 5:08:36
Germantown 11 63 40N21'24 78w39'59 5:14:40
Germantown 19 27 40N47'13 76w21'49 5:05:27
Germantown 28 1 39N55'14 77w32'45 5:10:11
Germantown 51 9 40N02'36 75w10'50 5:00:43
Germantown 52 6 41N25'09 75w04'21 5:00:17
Germany 1 56 39N44' 77w06 5:08:24
Germany 32 7 40N25'13 79w07'01 5:16:28
Geryville 9 2 40N24'55 75w28'32 5:01:54
Getty Heights 32 72 40N36'45 79w10'37 5:16:42
Gettysburg 1 1 39N49'51 77w13'53 5:08:56
Gettysburg Junction 21 16 40N12 77w11 5:08:44
Ghennes Heights 63 1 40N09'14 79w56'23 5:19:46
Ghent 8 60 41N51'47 76w26'23 5:05:46

Gibbon Glade 26 6 39N44'23 79W35'41 5:18:23
Gibbs Hill 42 3 41N44'33 78W54'46 5:15:39
Gibraltar 6 8 40N17'03 75W52'20 5:03:29
Gibson 58 6 41N48'12 75W38'40 5:02:35
Gibson 63 51 40N08'03 79W59'40 5:19:59
Gibsonia 2 114 40N37'48 79W58'11 5:19:53
Gibsonton 65 1 40N08'01 79W52'56 5:19:32
Gideon 56 6 40N04'35 79W02'43 5:16:11
Gifford 42 6 41N51'29 78W35'48 5:14:23
Gilbert 45 1 40N54'57 75W26'23 5:01:46
Gilberton 54 27 40N47'58 76W12'46 5:04:51
Gilbertsville 46
2 40N19'12 75W36'38 5:02:27
Gilfoyle 27 6 41N26'21 79W10'55 5:16:44
Gilkeson 63 2 40N13'15 80W06'22 5:20:25
Gillespie 26 1 40N05'00 79W49'44 5:19:19
Gillett 8 7 41N57'04 76W47'41 5:07:11
Gill Hall 2 8 40N17'57 79W57'44 5:19:51
Gillingham 17 6 41N07'03 78W18'42 5:13:15
Gillintown 14 7 41N01'58 77W59'24 5:11:58
Gilmore 26 80 39N49'48 79W48'11 5:19:13
Gilmore 30 6 39N45 80W20 5:21:20
Gilmore 42 102 41N58'15 78W33'58 5:14:16
Gilmore 63 51 40N22 80W14 5:20:56
Gilmore Acres 2
114 40N28 79W50 5:19:20
Gilpin 3 4 40N40 79W36 5:18:24
Gilpin 32 6 40N42'30 79W06'01 5:16:24
Ginger Hill 63 1 40N11'41 79W59'54 5:20:00
Ginter 17 63 40N46'21 78W22'56 5:13:32
Ginther 54 27 40N51'37 76W00'11 5:04:01
Gipsy 32 6 40N48'26 78W52'36 5:15:30
Girard 25 68 42N00'01 80W19'06 5:21:16
Girard Junction 25
68 42N00'47 80W22'18 5:21:29
Girard Manor 54 3 40N52'02 76W06'05 5:04:24
Girardville 54 27 40N47'29 76W17'02 5:05:08
Girdland 64 59 41N40'55 75W12'11 5:00:49
Girty 3 6 40N38'50 79W24'40 5:17:39
Gitts Run 67 1 39N48 76W59 5:07:56
Gladden 2 114 40N20'21 80W10'44 5:20:43
Gladden Heights 63
51 40N21'43 80W14'46 5:20:59
Glade 56 6 39N59'45 78W51'59 5:15:28
Glade 62 3 41N49'39 79W07'15 5:16:29
Glade City 56 79 39N49'07 78W59'42 5:15:59
Glade Mills 10 6 40N43'28 79W55'28 5:19:42
Glades 26 6 39N43'51 79W31'21 5:18:05
Glades 67 67 40N00'36 76W40'50 5:06:43
Gladhill (Greenstone P O) 1
1 39N45'06 77W27'00 5:09:48
Gladstone 23 9 39N56 75W16 5:01:04
Gladwyne 46 9 40N02'26 75W16'46 5:01:07
Glasgow 4 6 40N38'44 80W30'22 5:22:01
Glasgow 11 54 40N42'27 78W26'46 5:13:47
Glasgow 46 8 40N15'49 75W39'40 5:02:39
Glass City 14 113 40N52'17 78W12'55 5:12:52
Glassmere 2 14 40N34'35 79W46'50 5:19:07
Glassport 2 8 40N19'29 79W53'33 5:19:34
Glassworks 30 51 39N48'07 79W54'52 5:19:39
Glatfelters 67 3 39N52'28 76W45'03 5:07:00
Gleason 59 103 41N38'01 76W55'56 5:07:44
Gleasonton 18 7 41N21'15 77W42'12 5:10:49
Glen Acres 15 13 39N57 75W36 5:02:24
Glen Ashton Farms 9
9 40N06'12 74W54'59 4:59:40
Glenburn 35 44 41N31'25 75W43'27 5:02:54
Glen Campbell 32
6 40N49'15 78W49'38 5:15:19
Glen Carbon 54 49 40N42'54 76W18'41 5:05:15
Glencoe 56 6 39N49'16 78W50'45 5:15:23
Glendale 2 114 40N23'47 80W05'45 5:20:23
Glendale 9 8 40N19'56 75W00'21 5:00:01
Glendale 40 1 41N20'20 75W42'21 5:02:49
Glendale Gardens 23
9 39N54 75W18 5:01:12
Glendon 48 12 40N39'58 75W14'11 5:00:57
Glendon 54 3 40N49 76W08 5:04:32
Glendower 54 49 40N42'45 76W19'26 5:05:18
Glen Eden 10 6 40N43'39 80W06'42 5:20:27
Glen Eyre 52 6 41N27'56 75W04'38 5:00:19
Glenfield 2 114 40N31 80W08 5:20:32
Glen Forney 28
100 39N46'17 77W30'08 5:10:01
Glenhall 15 13 39N55'49 75W42'50 5:02:51
Glen Hazel 24 7 41N32'17 78W36'45 5:14:27
Glen Hope 17 54 40N47'48 78W30'00 5:14:00
Glenhurst 46 1 40N09 75W04 5:00:16
Glen Iron 60 6 40N52'02 77W12'05 5:08:48
Glen Junction 40
60 40N57'22 76W10'48 5:04:43
Glenlake 9 97 40N10'36 74W53'35 4:59:34
Glenloch 15 97 40N01'48 75W35'06 5:02:20
Glen Lyon 40 1 41N10'30 76W04'30 5:04:18
Glenmar Gardens 25
107 42N03'51 80W02'32 5:20:10
Glen Mawr 41 81 41N18'49 76W39'13 5:06:37
Glen Mills 23 4 39N55'09 75W29'31 5:01:58
Glenmoore 15 1 40N05'20 75W46'20 5:03:05
Glen Moore 36 8 40N03'43 76W18'43 5:05:15
Glennville 15 3 39N52'42 75W57'10 5:03:49
Glenolden 23 9 39N54'00 75W17'22 5:01:09
Glen Richey 17 1 40N56'56 78W28'41 5:13:55
Glen Riddle 23 90 39N53'38 75W26'03 5:01:44
Glen Rock 67 3 39N47'35 76W43'50 5:06:55
Glenrose 15 9 39N56'36 75W51'38 5:03:27
Glen Roy 15 3 39N46'00 76W02'59 5:04:12
Glenruadh 25 107 42N05'50 80W10'23 5:20:42
Glen Savage 56 1 39N54'35 78W46'58 5:15:08
Glenshaw 2 114 40N31'58 79W58'04 5:19:52
Glenside 46 9 40N06'08 75W09'09 5:00:37
Glenside Gardens 46
9 40N07 75W10 5:00:40
Glenside Heights 46
9 40N07 75W10 5:00:40
Glen Summit 40 20 41N08'46 75W51'38 5:03:27
Glen Union 18 7 41N15'13 77W36'37 5:10:26
Glenview 2 114 40N31 79W58 5:19:52
Glenville 67 3 39N45'25 76W48'56 5:07:16
Glenwall Village 4
13 40N37 80W16 5:21:04
Glenwillard 2 13 40N33'35 80W13'28 5:20:54
Glenwood 2 114 40N24'19 79W56'39 5:19:47
Glenwood 22 12 40N17'27 76W50'47 5:07:23
Glenwood 25 107 42N05'26 80W04'33 5:20:18
Glenwood 58 89 41N39'06 75W43'13 5:02:53
Glenworth 54 49 40N41 76W12 5:04:48
Glessner 56 6 40N11'33 79W02'28 5:16:10
Globe Mills 55 6 40N48'22 76W59'31 5:07:58
Glosser View 41
82 41N13'55 77W07'11 5:08:29
Glyde 63 51 40N07'32 80W08'13 5:20:33
Glyndon 20 56 41N50 79W41 5:18:44
Gnatstown 67 1 39N52'03 76W55'45 5:07:43
Gobbler Knob 17 7 41N11'05 78W34'21 5:14:17
Godard 25 107 42N02'21 80W00'38 5:20:03
Godfrey 3 4 40N41'28 79W37'33 5:18:30
Goehring 4 121 40N48'54 80W12'48 5:20:51
Goff 10 6 41N06 79W54 5:19:36
Goheenville 3 64 40N54'24 79W22'20 5:17:29
Gold 53 6 41N52'19 77W50'15 5:11:21
Golden Hill 66 6 41N39 76W10 5:04:40
Goldenridge 9 9 40N08'45 74W51'14 4:59:25
Golden Rod Farms 17
1 41N01'02 78W24'05 5:13:36
Goldenville 1 56 39N53'33 77W14'32 5:08:58
Gold Mine 38 27 40N31'34 76W32'15 5:06:09
Goldsboro (Etters P O) 67
1 40N09'09 76W45'02 5:07:00
Golf Villa 23 9 40N00 75W18 5:01:12
Golinza 27 6 41N26'23 79W19'44 5:17:19
Good 28 100 39N45 77W34 5:10:16
Good Hope 21 12 40N16'09 76W59'07 5:07:56
Good Hope Mill 21
12 40N15'59 76W58'47 5:07:55
Good Intent 63 6 40N02'13 80W26'44 5:21:47
Goodmans Corners 61
6 41N22 79W29 5:17:56
Goods Corner 11
74 40N22'19 78W52'46 5:15:31
Good Spring 54 9 40N37'29 76W29'07 5:05:56
Goodtown 56 6 39N53'36 78W58'43 5:15:55
Goodville 34 6 40N35'33 77W12'02 5:08:48
Goodville 36 27 40N07'32 76W00'13 5:04:01
Goodyear 21 1 40N02'47 77W12'18 5:08:49
Goosetown 15 9 39N58'14 75W46'47 5:03:07
Goram 67 1 39N52'26 76W24'29 5:05:38
Gordon 54 27 40N45'06 76W20'11 5:05:21
Gordonville 36 9 40N01'12 76W08'02 5:04:32
Gorman Summit 32
6 40N47'39 78W53'13 5:15:33
Gorton 14 7 40N59'39 78W02'27 5:12:10
Gosford 3 15 40N50'59 79W30'37 5:18:02
Goshen 17 6 41N05'01 78W24'26 5:13:38
Goshen 36 1 39N47'16 76W09'57 5:04:40
Goshenville 15 13 39N59'42 75W32'41 5:02:11
Gosser Hill 65 4 40N37'22 79W36'34 5:18:26
Goss Run Junction 17
4 40N49'55 78W19'57 5:13:20
Gouglersville 6
101 40N16'25 76W01'10 5:04:05
Gouldsboro 64 4 41N14'41 75W27'20 5:01:49
Gouldtown 62 6 41N59'42 79W05'18 5:16:21
Gowen 40 60 40N56'51 76W10'45 5:04:43
Gowen City 49 1 40N45'20 76W32'02 5:06:08
Gracedale 40 20 41N10'16 75W52'02 5:03:28
Gracedale County Home 48
8 40N44'22 75W20'14 5:01:21
Grace Park 23 9 39N54 75W20 5:01:20
Graceton 32 71 40N30'21 79W09'59 5:16:40
Graceville 5 6 40N03'05 78W14'38 5:12:59
Gracey 29 66 40N04'54 78W03'40 5:12:15
Gradwohl Terrace 48
13 40N39 75W21 5:01:24
Gradyville 23 4 39N56'35 75W28'11 5:01:53
Grafton 32 98 40N28'24 79W12'33 5:16:50
Graham 17 6 40N54'49 78W14'51 5:12:59
Graham Crossing 26
105 39N59'18 79W39'37 5:18:38
Grampian 17 7 40N57'57 78W36'48 5:14:27
Grampian Hills 41
82 41N15'34 77W00'12 5:08:01
Grand Central 48
17 40N50'39 75W15'52 5:01:03
Grand Valley 62 6 41N43'16 79W32'16 5:18:09
Grandview 3 15 40N49'11 79W30'43 5:18:03
Grand View 5 6 40N02'15 78W45'30 5:15:02
Grandview 24 36 41N25'17 78W32'54 5:14:12
Grandview 32 72 40N36'50 79W08'43 5:16:35
Grandview 61 9 41N28'01 79W39'52 5:18:39
Grandview 63 1 40N10'05 79W52'11 5:19:29
Grandview Heights 36
8 40N03'23 76W17'20 5:05:09
Grand View Heights 46
90 40N08'06 75W19'41 5:01:19
Grandview Park 24
36 41N26 78W34 5:14:16
Grand View Park 46
8 40N12 75W28 5:01:52
Grandview Terrace 67
67 39N57 76W42 5:06:48
Grange 33 61 40N56 78W58 5:15:52
Grange Corners 20
6 40N47 79W14 5:16:56
Grange Hall Center 20
6 40N47 79W14 5:16:56
Grangeville 67 1 39N48 76W59 5:07:56
Granite 1 1 39N49 77W11 5:08:44
Grant 32 6 40N47 78W57 5:15:48
Grant City 37 6 40N59'17 80W10'17 5:20:41
Grantham 21 12 40N09'23 76W59'48 5:07:59
Grant Station 24
6 41N19 78W23 5:13:32
Grantville 22 1 40N22'40 76W38'48 5:06:35
Granville 44 73 40N33'13 77W37'33 5:10:30
Granville 63 51 40N04'04 79W54'31 5:19:38
Granville Center 8
7 41N43'04 76W42'26 5:06:50
Granville Summit 8
7 41N43'04 76W46'46 5:07:07
Grapeville 65 99 40N19'31 79W36'21 5:18:25
Grassflat 17 6 41N00'09 78W06'53 5:12:28
Grassmere Park 19
6 41N16'30 76W22'41 5:05:31
Grassy Island 35
18 41N28'16 75W34'57 5:02:20
Graterford 46 8 40N13'32 75W27'18 5:01:49
Gratton 32 98 40N28 79W12 5:16:48
Gratz 22 1 40N36'42 76W43'08 5:06:53
Gratztown 65 61 40N13'46 79W47'13 5:19:09
Gravel Lick 16 6 41N19'00 79W14'31 5:16:58
Gravel Lick 53 6 41N30'39 77W48'05 5:11:12
Gravel Pit 5 6 39N52'43 78W41'21 5:14:45
Gravel Place 45
23 41N01'06 75W11'45 5:00:47
Gravers 51 9 40N04'38 75W12'08 5:00:49
Gravity 64 59 41N28'19 75W22'49 5:01:31
Gray 7 11 40N39'24 78W15'15 5:13:01
Gray 30 6 39N56 80W23 5:21:32
Gray 41 7 41N25'19 77W01'32 5:08:06
Gray 56 6 40N08'09 79W05'35 5:16:22
Graybill 67 67 39N55'25 76W48'04 5:07:12
Graydon 67 1 39N51'15 76W39'19 5:06:37
Grays 65 98 40N23'45 79W14'24 5:16:58
Grays Landing 26
51 39N49'56 79W55'08 5:19:41
Graysville 30 6 39N55'55 80W23'06 5:21:32
Graysville 31 6 40N41'29 78W01'41 5:12:07
Grazier 56 6 40N11 78W59 5:15:56
Grazierville 7 11 40N39'13 78W15'54 5:13:04
Greason 21 16 40N11'34 77W17'26 5:09:10
Great Belt 10 3 40N48'31 79W48'12 5:19:13
Great Bend 58 50 41N58'18 75W44'37 5:02:58
Greater Point Marion 26
7 39N45'00 79W53'58 5:19:36
Greble 38 25 40N25'50 76W21'17 5:05:25
Greece City 10 6 40N57'38 79W49'51 5:19:19
Greeley 52 6 41N25'16 74W59'44 4:59:59
Green Acres 67 67 39N59 76W46 5:07:04
Greenawald 39 56 40N36'12 75W52'21 5:03:29
Greenawalds 39 13 40N37'38 75W31'02 5:02:04
Greenback 49 27 40N46'52 76W31'21 5:06:05
Greenbank 36 27 40N07 76W05 5:04:20
Green Briar 33 34 41N19'17 78W55'41 5:15:43
Greenbrier 14 64 40N51 77W34 5:10:16
Greenbrier 23 90 40N00 75W23 5:01:32
Greenbrier 49 6 40N42'47 76W40'59 5:06:44
Greenbrook 9 9 40N08'49 74W50'06 4:59:20
Greenburr 18 7 41N00'21 77W21'17 5:09:25
Greenbury 54 49 40N41 76W12 5:04:48
Greencastle 28 70 39N47'25 77W43'41 5:10:55
Greencrest Park 43
59 41N20'45 80W24'19 5:21:37
Greendale 3 15 40N48'19 79W23'14 5:17:33
Greendale 42 75 41N39'51 78W46'53 5:15:08
Greene 36 1 39N47 76W14 5:04:56
Greene Junction 26
104 40N01 79W35 5:18:20
Greenes Landing 8
1 41N55'51 76W31'31 5:06:06
Greenfield 2 13 40N25'17 79W56'37 5:19:46
Greenfield 11 63 40N30'45 78W32'17 5:14:09
Greenfield 43 66 41N11'56 80W21'47 5:21:27
Greenfield Manor 6
101 40N21 75W56 5:03:44
Green Fields 22 1 40N35 76W37 5:06:28
Green Grove 14 64 40N52'44 77W33'07 5:10:12
Green Grove 35 18 41N31'28 75W36'30 5:02:26
Green Hill 15 13 39N59'45 75W35'58 5:02:24
Green Hill 29 66 39N59'38 78W05'08 5:12:21
Green Hill 67 67 39N57 76W42 5:06:48
Green Hills 23 9 39N54 75W17 5:01:08
Greenland 36 8 40N01'49 76W14'04 5:04:56
Green Lane 46 8 40N20'12 75W28'10 5:01:53
Green Lane Farms 21
12 40N13'19 76W53'54 5:07:36
Green Lawn 15 1 39N53'16 75W50'31 5:03:22
Greenlawn Park 9
9 40N08 74W51 4:59:24
Greenmount 1 1 39N45'51 77W16'26 5:09:06
Green Oaks 61 9 41N25'51 79W35'49 5:18:23
Greenock 2 3 40N18'44 79W48'25 5:19:14
Green Park 50 6 40N23 77W19 5:09:16
Green Point 38 1 40N28'51 76W33'07 5:06:12
Green Ridge 23 90 39N52 75W23 5:01:32
Green Ridge 35 18 41N25'33 75W38'44 5:02:35
Green Ridge 40 42 40N57'32 76W00'30 5:04:02
Green Ridge 67 67 39N59 76W46 5:07:04
Greenridge Farms 46
1 40N09 75W03 5:00:12
Greensboro 30 51 39N47'28 79W54'47 5:19:39
Greensburg 65 99 40N18'05 79W32'21 5:18:09
Greens Landing 8
1 41N58 76W31 5:06:04
Green Spring 21 1 40N08'57 77W27'51 5:09:51
Green Springs 1 1 39N50'56 77W00'13 5:08:01
Greenstone 1 1 39N54 77W01 5:08:04
Greentown 52 6 41N19'18 75W18'21 5:01:13
Green Tree 2 114 40N24'42 80W02'45 5:20:11
Green Tree 15 8 40N02'16 75W29'42 5:01:59
Green Valley 2
114 40N23 79W49 5:19:16
Green Valley 33
34 41N03'41 79W02'29 5:16:10
Green Valley Acres 23
9 39N58 75W18 5:01:12
Greenview Park 23
9 40N00 75W18 5:01:12
Green Village 28
42 39N59'35 77W36'31 5:10:26
Greenville 17 6 41N00'38 78W36'16 5:14:25
Greenville 43 69 41N24'16 80W23'29 5:21:34
Greenwald 65 3 40N21'37 79W27'16 5:17:49
Greenwich 6 8 40N34 75W49 5:03:16
Greenwich 11 92 40N41'08 78W49'08 5:15:17
Greenwood 7 33 40N32'09 78W21'28 5:13:26
Greenwood 19 6 41N08'04 76W28'53 5:05:56
Greenwood 26 104 40N01 79W35 5:18:20
Greenwood 28 1 39N54'21 77W31'11 5:10:05
Greenwood 35 18 41N22'20 75W42'07 5:02:48
Greenwood Heights 26
104 40N00'22 79W36'07 5:18:24
Greenwood Hills 22
12 40N13'05 76W46'19 5:07:05
Greenwood Village 10
3 40N52'50 79W57'24 5:19:50
Gregg 2 114 40N24'23 80W09'53 5:20:40
Gregory 40 20 41N15'49 75W56'42 5:03:47

Greisemersville 6 2 40N21'16 75w45'24 5:03:02
Grenoble 9 1 40N12 75w05 5:00:20
Gresham 20 74 41N37'25 79w43'12 5:18:53
Greshville 6 2 40N19'06 75w39'49 5:02:39
Gretna 63 3 40N14'45 80w18'12 5:21:13
Grieder 21 16 40N12'49 77w18'51 5:09:15
Grier City 54 27 40N49'43 76w03'22 5:04:13
Griers Corner 9 8 40N21'44 75w11'05 5:00:44
Griesemersville 6 2 40N20 75w38 5:02:32
Griffin 26 80 39N50'24 79w53'30 5:19:34
Griffiths 42 75 41N41'42 78w43'06 5:14:52
Griffithtown 11 63 40N30'06 78w50'46 5:15:23
Grill 6 101 40N17'55 75w56'27 5:03:46
Grimesville 41 82 41N14'54 77w04'03 5:08:16
Grimms Crossroads 67 1 39N54'36 76w32'58 5:06:12
Grimville 39 8 40N34'40 75w47'06 5:03:08
Grindstone 26 51 40N00'58 79w49'51 5:19:19
Gringo 4 13 40N33'50 80w16'18 5:21:05
Grisemore 32 6 40N38'50 78w52'43 5:15:31
Groffdale 36 27 40N05'29 76w07'47 5:04:31
Grovania 19 6 40N58'26 76w31'31 5:06:06
Grove 12 6 41N22 78w03 5:12:12
Grove 15 13 40N00'17 75w38'06 5:02:32
Grove Chapel 32 72 40N38 79w09 5:16:36
Grove City 43 70 41N09'28 80w05'20 5:20:21
Grove Mill 67 1 39N45'52 76w31'09 5:06:05
Grover 8 7 41N36'52 76w52'03 5:07:28
Groveton 2 114 40N30'14 80w08'26 5:20:34
Grugan 18 7 41N15 77w36 5:10:24
Grundys Corner 9 9 40N06'26 74w54'07 4:59:36
Gruversville 9 8 40N30'03 75w19'21 5:01:17
Gruvertown 48 17 40N49'22 75w09'04 5:00:36
Guenot Settlement 17 6 41N04'50 78w08'37 5:12:34
Guernsey 1 1 39N56'50 77w13'58 5:08:56
Guffey 42 59 41N45'33 78w41'37 5:14:46
Guffey 65 25 40N17'20 79w45'57 5:19:04
Guilford 28 42 39N51'55 77w36'46 5:10:27
Guilford Springs 28 42 39N53'50 77w40'33 5:10:42
Guitonville 27 6 41N28'33 79w15'31 5:17:02
Guldens 1 1 39N51'30 77w08'21 5:08:33
Gulich 17 63 40N46 78w24 5:13:36
Gulph Mills 46 90 40N04'11 75w20'25 5:01:22
Gump 30 1 39N48'20 80w11'44 5:20:47
Gum Run 40 1 40N57'07 76w07'49 5:04:31
Gum Stump 14 70 40N58'49 77w50'59 5:11:24
Gum Tree 15 9 39N59 75w50 5:03:20
Gurnee 59 6 41N48'11 77w31'18 5:10:05
Gurney Hill 61 109 41N23'10 79w50'16 5:19:21
Guth 39 13 40N37 75w31 5:02:04
Guthriesville 15 46 40N01'59 75w45'50 5:03:03
Guthsville 39 13 40N37'09 75w35'12 5:02:21
Guyasuta 2 114 40N30 79w56 5:19:44
Guys Mills 20 6 41N37'48 79w58'40 5:19:55
Gwynedd 46 8 40N12'06 75w15'20 5:01:01
Gwynedd Heights 46 8 40N12'18 75w15'45 5:01:03
Gwynedd Square 46 8 40N13'18 75w18'11 5:01:13
Gwynedd Valley 46 8 40N11'03 75w15'24 5:01:02
Haafsville 39 9 40N34'44 75w39'41 5:02:39
Haags Mill 64 6 41N17'21 75w19'52 5:01:19
Haas 54 1 40N42'02 76w29'41 5:05:59
Hackelbernie 13 80 40N52 75w44 5:02:56
Hackett 63 114 40N14'52 80w01'19 5:20:05
Hacklebernie 13 80 40N51'27 75w46'18 5:03:05
Hackney 63 6 40N01'54 80w13'05 5:20:52
Haddenville 26 80 39N55'46 79w46'17 5:19:05
Haddock 54 42 40N52'53 76w00'22 5:04:01
Hadley 43 6 41N24'50 80w14'00 5:20:56
Haffey 2 114 40N29 79w50 5:19:20
Hagero 56 123 40N10'53 78w48'51 5:15:15
Hagersville 9 8 40N24'25 75w15'02 5:01:00
Hahnstown 36 30 40N10'16 76w07'26 5:04:30
Hahntown 65 25 40N19'06 79w43'07 5:18:52
Haines 14 6 40N54 77w22 5:09:28
Haines Acres 67 67 39N59 76w46 5:07:04
Hale 17 4 40N47'19 78w20'41 5:13:23
Haleeka 41 7 41N19 77w05 5:08:20
Half Falls 50 24 40N29'19 76w57'07 5:07:48
Halfmoon 14 63 40N46 78w02 5:12:08
Halford Hills 46 90 40N08 75w21 5:01:24
Halfville 36 8 40N11'18 76w19'32 5:05:18
Halfway 38 8 40N20 76w26 5:05:44
Half Way House 46 8 40N17'06 75w38'28 5:02:34
Halifax 22 24 40N28'05 76w55'56 5:07:44
Hall 2 114 40N26 79w47 5:19:08
Hallam (Hellam P O) 67 1 40N00'17 76w36'16 5:06:25
Hallman 15 8 40N06'44 75w35'32 5:02:22
Hallowell 46 1 40N11'51 75w07'55 5:00:32
Halls 41 83 41N12 76w47 5:07:08
Hallstead 58 50 41N57'40 75w44'37 5:02:58
Hallston 10 6 41N01'13 79w59'07 5:19:56
Hallton 24 6 41N24'07 78w55'57 5:15:44
Hallwood 40 1 41N13'27 76w07'25 5:04:30
Halsey 42 75 41N40'22 78w40'53 5:14:44
Hamburg 6 80 40N33'20 75w58'56 5:03:56
Hametown 67 3 39N47'54 76w40'46 5:06:43
Hamill 32 6 40N49 78w59 5:15:56
Hamilton 33 7 40N55'27 79w04'52 5:16:19
Hamilton 49 82 40N51'26 76w46'15 5:07:05
Hamiltonban 1 1 39N48 77w24 5:09:36
Hamilton Park 36 8 40N02 76w20 5:05:20
Hamilton Square 45 23 40N55'28 75w17'42 5:01:11
Hamlin 38 1 40N26'53 76w22'34 5:05:30
Hamlin 64 6 41N24'13 75w23'56 5:01:36
Hamlin Station 42 93 41N42'39 78w23'41 5:13:35
Hammersley Fork 18 7 41N25'57 77w55'15 5:11:41
Hammett 25 107 42N04'00 79w58'08 5:19:53
Hammond 59 59 41N52'58 77w11'42 5:08:47
Hammondville 26 111 40N07'14 79w32'02 5:18:08
Hamorton 15 8 39N52'06 75w39'21 5:02:37
Hampden 6 101 40N21 75w55 5:03:40
Hampden 21 12 40N15 76w58 5:07:52
Hampshire Heights 65 99 40N18 79w34 5:18:16
Hampton 1 1 39N55'46 77w03'31 5:08:14
Hampton 2 114 40N35 79w57 5:19:48
Hampton Station 61 9 41N23'13 79w33'48 5:18:15
Hancock 6 9 40N30'17 75w40'58 5:02:44
Haneyville 18 76 41N19'32 77w28'31 5:09:54
Hanlin 63 6 40N23 80w24 5:21:36
Hannah 14 6 40N46'02 78w05'52 5:12:23
Hannahstown 10 6 40N46'12 79w47'26 5:19:10
Hannastown 65 3 40N21'13 79w29'49 5:17:59
Hannasville 61 59 41N28'40 79w56'53 5:19:48
Hann Hill 43 117 41N12'38 80w26'50 5:21:47
Hannoverdale 22 31 40N19'16 76w42'15 5:06:49
Hanover 40 21 41N11'08 75w58'57 5:03:56
Hanover 48 13 40N39'42 75w24'46 5:01:39
Hanover 67 1 39N48'02 76w59'00 5:07:56
Hanover Acres 39 13 40N36'46 75w26'50 5:01:47
Hanoverdale 22 1 41N09 79w41 5:18:44
Hanover Green 40 20 41N13'05 75w57'06 5:03:48
Hanover Heights 15 8 40N15 75w39 5:02:36
Hanover Junction 67 3 39N50'32 76w46'33 5:07:06
Hanoverville 48 13 40N40'58 75w22'31 5:01:30
Hansotte Plan 3 15 40N46 79w32 5:18:08
Happy Valley 40 1 41N19'39 75w50'06 5:03:20
Harbor 37 112 41N02'07 80w24'34 5:21:38
Harborcreek 25 107 42N09'59 79w57'11 5:19:49
Harbor Woods 15 47 40N03 75w33 5:02:12
Harding 40 6 41N21'45 75w48'38 5:03:15
Hardy 2 114 40N36'32 79w58'05 5:19:52
Hardy Hill 26 105 39N57'51 79w36'07 5:18:24
Harford 58 59 41N46'56 75w42'07 5:02:48
Harford Heights 65 25 40N20 79w43 5:18:52
Harkness 8 7 41N51'19 76w42'26 5:06:50
Harlan 16 59 41N07'56 79w12'49 5:16:51
Harlansburg 37 112 41N01'27 80w11'20 5:20:45
Harleigh 40 42 40N58'50 75w58'18 5:03:53
Harlem 6 2 40N27'29 75w35'16 5:02:21
Harleysville 46 8 40N16'46 75w23'15 5:01:33
Harmar 2 14 40N33 79w50 5:19:20
Harmar Heights 2 14 40N33'23 79w49'09 5:19:17
Harmarville 2 114 40N31'52 79w50'55 5:19:24
Harmonsburg 20 6 41N39'39 80w19'05 5:21:16
Harmontown 53 6 41N55'19 77w51'16 5:11:25
Harmonville 46 90 40N05'43 75w17'11 5:01:09
Harmony 10 6 40N48'05 80w07'39 5:20:31
Harmony 17 7 40N46'52 78w43'44 5:14:55
Harmony 33 51 40N58'06 78w58'14 5:15:53
Harmony Grove 67 1 40N00'37 76w54'29 5:07:38
Harmony Hill 15 46 40N00 75w42 5:02:48
Harmony Junction 10 6 40N47'46 80w06'12 5:20:25
Harmonyville 15 8 40N11'21 75w43'24 5:02:54
Harnedsville 56 53 39N47'51 79w19'41 5:17:19
Harpers 48 8 40N46'45 75w33'25 5:02:14
Harper Tavern 38 8 40N24'14 76w34'41 5:06:19
Harper Village 2 13 40N37 80w16 5:21:04
Harriman 9 9 40N08 74w51 4:59:24
Harris 14 6 40N48 77w45 5:11:00
Harris Acres 14 9 40N46'42 77w48'57 5:11:16
Harrisburg 22 12 40N16'25 76w53'05 5:07:32
Harrison 2 14 40N37 79w44 5:18:56
Harrison City 65 3 40N21'15 79w38'55 5:18:36
Harrison Valley 53 6 41N56'31 77w38'59 5:10:36
Harrisonville 29 66 39N59'15 78w03'35 5:12:14
Harristown 36 9 40N00'24 76w05'03 5:04:20
Harrisville 10 6 41N08'12 80w00'34 5:20:02
Harrity 13 8 40N50'24 75w40'05 5:02:40
Harrow 9 1 40N29'28 75w10'29 5:00:42
Harshaville 4 6 40N32'30 80w24'39 5:21:39
Hartfield 59 6 41N34'33 77w09'55 5:08:40
Hartleton 60 6 40N54'02 77w09'23 5:08:38
Hartley 5 70 40N01'17 78w27'10 5:13:49
Hartley 60 6 40N53 77w13 5:08:52
Hartranft 46 90 40N08 75w21 5:01:24
Hartsfield 59 6 41N33 77w06 5:08:24
Hartstown 20 63 41N33'09 80w22'46 5:21:31
Hartsville 9 1 40N13'42 75w05'43 5:00:23
Harvey Junction 40 20 41N16 75w54 5:03:36
Harveys Lake 40 6 41N23'00 76w01'30 5:04:06
Harveys Run 33 59 41N10'21 78w47'16 5:15:09
Harveyville 40 1 41N12'50 76w14'47 5:04:59
Harwick 2 119 40N33'24 79w48'19 5:19:13
Harwood (Harwood Mines P O) 40 42 40N56'38 76w01'11 5:04:05
Harwood Park 23 9 39N58 75w18 5:01:12
Haslets Corner 61 109 41N29'45 79w49'29 5:19:18
Hasson Heights 61 9 41N25 79w42 5:18:48
Hastings 11 92 40N39'54 78w42'45 5:14:51
Hastings 27 3 41N36'25 79w06'00 5:16:24
Hatboro 46 17 40N10'27 75w06'26 5:00:26
Hatchtown 20 56 41N46'44 79w39'02 5:18:36
Hatfield 26 80 39N52'40 79w44'22 5:18:57
Hatfield 46 8 40N16'47 75w17'59 5:01:12
Hatton 21 16 40N08'18 77w09'29 5:08:38
Haucks 54 27 40N49'52 76w02'13 5:04:09
Hauto 13 1 40N50'39 75w53'29 5:03:34
Haverford 46 9 40N00'47 75w17'41 5:01:11
Haverford Park Apartments 23 9 40N01 75w17 5:01:08
Havertown 23 9 39N58'51 75w18'32 5:01:14
Hawkey 65 111 40N07'19 79w35'34 5:18:22
Hawkeye 65 111 40N08 79w35 5:18:20
Hawk Run 17 113 40N55'26 78w12'23 5:12:50
Hawksville 36 27 39N54'37 76w09'53 5:04:40
Hawley 64 6 41N28'33 75w10'57 5:00:44
Hawstone 34 73 40N35'42 77w29'56 5:10:00
Hawthorn 16 6 41N01 79w17 5:17:08
Hawthorne 16 6 41N01'12 79w16'29 5:17:06
Haycock 9 8 40N30 75w18 5:01:12
Haycock Run 9 8 40N25 75w23 5:01:32
Haydentown 26 51 39N47'20 79w46'15 5:19:05
Hayesville 15 3 39N49'13 75w57'54 5:03:52
Hayfield 20 77 41N43 80w13 5:20:52
Haymaker 42 40 41N59'53 78w24'42 5:13:39
Haynie 16 37 41N15 79w28 5:17:52
Hays 2 114 40N23'22 79w56'03 5:19:44
Hays 26 80 39N52'35 79w47'03 5:19:08
Hays Corner 40 6 41N21'10 75w59'34 5:03:58
Hays Grove 21 1 40N05'37 77w22'17 5:09:29
Hays Mill 56 79 39N51'03 78w58'24 5:15:54
Haysville 2 114 40N31'35 80w09'33 5:20:38
Haysville 10 6 40N59'55 79w45'17 5:19:01
Hayti 15 9 39N58'58 75w50'30 5:03:22
Hazard 13 8 40N47'42 75w38'21 5:02:33
Hazel Hurst 42 6 41N42'21 78w34'58 5:14:20
Hazel Kirk 63 1 40N10'29 79w57'35 5:19:50
Hazelton Mills 42 6 41N53'55 78w43'09 5:14:53
Hazelwood 2 13 40N24'48 79w56'22 5:19:45
Hazen 4 121 40N49'00 80w14'43 5:20:59
Hazen 33 6 41N12'24 78w58'14 5:15:53
Hazle 40 42 40N58 76w00 5:04:00
Hazlebrook 40 42 40N58'36 75w53'11 5:03:33
Hazleton 40 42 40N57'30 75w58'30 5:03:54
Hazleton Junction 54 27 40N51'51 76w00'50 5:04:03
Hazle Village 40 42 40N58 76w00 5:04:00
Hazzard 63 1 40N11 79w54 5:19:36
Headlee Heights 30 6 39N48'54 79w58'21 5:19:53
Heart Lake 58 60 41N51'08 75w47'40 5:03:11
Hearts Content 62 6 41N40'54 79w14'51 5:16:59
Heath 33 6 41N20 79w01 5:16:04
Heath 43 6 41N05'52 80w04'24 5:20:18
Heatherwold 23 90 39N54 75w22 5:01:28
Heath Station 33 6 41N24 78w56 5:15:44
Heathville 33 6 41N05'23 79w10'51 5:16:43
Heaton 46 17 40N09'24 75w06'24 5:00:26
Hebe 49 51 40N39'41 76w44'06 5:06:56
Heberling 21 1 40N11'32 77w29'24 5:09:58
Hebron 38 8 40N20'20 76w23'59 5:05:36
Hebron 53 6 41N50'31 78w04'01 5:12:16
Hebron Center 53 8 41N52'43 78w01'06 5:12:04
Heckscherville 54 49 40N43'08 76w16'45 5:05:07
Heckton 22 12 40N21'08 76w54'58 5:07:40
Hecktown 48 13 40N41'35 75w20'07 5:01:20
Hecla 54 1 40N42'08 76w00'08 5:04:01
Hector 53 6 41N51'45 77w37'08 5:10:29
Heebnerville 46 8 40N12'24 75w19'04 5:01:16
Hegarty Crossroads 17 54 40N46'57 78w28'05 5:13:52
Hegins 54 27 40N39'05 76w29'53 5:06:00
Heidelberg 2 114 40N23'32 80w05'28 5:20:22
Heidlersburg 1 1 39N56'57 77w08'47 5:08:35
Heilman 3 15 40N45'36 79w28'23 5:17:54
Heilmandale 38 8 40N22'09 76w28'40 5:05:55
Heilwood 32 6 40N37'15 78w54'55 5:15:40
Heise Run 59 6 41N46'10 77w21'14 5:09:25
Heistersburg 26 6 39N57'46 79w55'54 5:19:44
Helen 26 80 39N58'16 79w46'52 5:19:07
Helen Furnace 16 37 41N17'32 79w18'43 5:17:15
Helen Mills 24 5 41N16'37 78w42'17 5:14:49
Helfenstein 49 27 40N44'57 76w27'13 5:05:49
Helfrick Spring Apartments 39 13 40N39 75w30 5:02:00
Helixville 5 6 40N04'27 78w42'17 5:14:49
Hellam 67 1 40N00'17 76w36'16 5:06:25
Hellen Mills 24 6 40N45 76w04 5:04:16
Hellertown 48 13 40N34'46 75w20'28 5:01:22
Hellings Corner 9 97 40N09'14 74w53'49 4:59:35
Helvetia 17 56 41N02'52 78w46'27 5:15:06
Hemlock 19 4 41N01 76w31 5:06:04
Hemlock 62 120 41N50'57 79w03'28 5:16:14
Hemlock Farms 52 6 41N19'36 75w02'13 5:00:09
Hemlock Grove 52 6 41N18'39 75w18'15 5:01:13
Hemlock Grove 57 6 41N21 76w35 5:06:20
Hempfield 36 26 40N03'17 76w26'21 5:05:45
Henderson 16 37 41N10'28 79w16'37 5:17:06
Henderson 17 59 40N51'38 78w23'00 5:13:32
Henderson 43 6 41N20 80w06 5:20:24
Henderson Park 46 90 40N05'35 75w21'46 5:01:27
Henderson Station 61 6 41N17'44 79w59'37 5:19:58
Hendersonville 10 6 40N41'25 80w04'28 5:20:18
Hendersonville 43 6 41N18'05 80w02'08 5:20:09

Hendersonville 63 114 40N17'57 80W09'09 5:20:37
Hendleton 6 101 40N19 75W57 5:03:48
Hendricks 46 8 40N18'18 75W27'48 5:01:51
Henlein 43 69 41N22'49 80W21'28 5:21:26
Henningsville 6 13 40N28'00 75W40'17 5:02:41
Henrietta 7 51 40N15'53 78W17'51 5:13:11
Henry Clay 26 6 39N46 79W27 5:17:48
Henrys Bend 61 9 41N27'46 79W36'03 5:18:24
Henrys Mills 62 6 41N38'14 79W02'37 5:16:10
Henryville 45 84 41N05'37 75W14'30 5:00:58
Hensel 36 27 39N49'18 76W12'04 5:04:48
Hensingerville 39 13 40N29'45 75W35'26 5:02:22
Hepburn 41 7 41N20 77W03 5:08:12
Hepburn Heights 41 7 41N18'41 77W04'27 5:08:18
Hepburnia 17 7 40N56'47 78W36'56 5:14:28
Hepburnville 41 7 41N18'17 77W04'02 5:08:16
Hephzibah 15 9 39N57'02 75W48'30 5:03:14
Hepler 54 1 40N41'30 76W34'40 5:06:19
Herbert 26 51 39N56'37 79W49'51 5:19:19
Hercules 46 8 40N45 75W16 5:01:04
Hereford 6 1 40N26'57 75W33'09 5:02:13
Heritage Hills 2 8 40N17 79W50 5:19:20
Herman 10 3 40N49'48 79W48'41 5:19:15
Herminie 65 25 40N15'48 79W43'04 5:18:52
Herminie Number Two 65 3 40N16'43 79W41'34 5:18:46
Hermitage 43 117 41N14'00 80W26'56 5:21:48
Hermit Spring 62 6 41N40'41 79W11'03 5:16:44
Herndon 49 51 40N42'34 76W50'34 5:07:22
Hero 30 2 39N43'27 80W20'54 5:21:24
Herrick Center 58 59 41N44'31 75W29'23 5:01:58
Herrick Corner 58 59 41N44'26 75W28'52 5:01:55
Herrickville 8 6 41N48'23 76W15'24 5:05:02
Herrville 36 8 39N56'47 76W15'26 5:05:02
Hershey 22 31 40N17'09 76W39'02 5:06:36
Hershey Heights 1 1 39N48 76W59 5:07:56
Hershey Mill 15 13 40N00'46 75W33'23 5:02:14
Heshbon 32 98 40N28'19 79W05'41 5:16:23
Heshbon Park 41 82 41N14 77W01 5:08:04
Hessdale 36 96 39N56'37 76W12'38 5:04:51
Hessl 40 1 41N03'56 76W11'14 5:04:45
Hesston 31 3 40N25'15 78W06'37 5:12:26
Hetlerville 19 1 41N00'52 76W15'41 5:05:03
Hettesheimer Corners 66 6 41N25'48 76W03'43 5:04:15
Heverly 17 54 40N44'30 78W30'09 5:14:01
Hewitt 5 6 39N45'17 78W30'56 5:14:04
Hiawatha 64 6 41N55 75W28 5:01:52
Hibbs 26 51 39N55'54 79W52'58 5:19:32
Hickernell 20 6 41N47'37 80W17'52 5:21:11
Hickman 2 114 40N22'59 80W09'21 5:20:37
Hickory 63 51 40N17'56 80W18'32 5:21:14
Hickory Corner 10 3 40N55'57 80W00'09 5:20:01
Hickory Corners 43 117 41N14'00 80W27'20 5:21:49
Hickory Corners 49 6 40N39'21 76W51'52 5:07:27
Hickory Grove 58 59 41N58'06 75W40'18 5:02:41
Hickory Heights 37 112 41N00 80W21 5:21:24
Hickory Hill 5 51 40N11'42 78W13'14 5:12:53
Hickory Hill 15 3 39N44'54 75W55'16 5:03:41
Hickory Hills 9 9 40N12 74W49 4:59:16
Hickorytown 21 16 40N11'48 77W07'40 5:08:31
Hickorytown 46 90 40N06'48 75W17'05 5:01:08
Hickox 53 6 41N58'34 77W51'23 5:11:26
Hicks Ferry 40 1 41N04 76W15 5:05:00
Hicks Hill 3 116 40N32 79W28 5:17:52
Hicks Run 12 7 41N21'47 78W14'18 5:12:57
Hicksville 3 116 40N32'14 79W27'08 5:17:49
Hickton 63 6 40N22'16 80W21'49 5:21:27
Hidden Valley 46 90 40N05 75W22 5:01:28
Hiestand 15 118 40N10'07 75W36'19 5:02:25
Higbee 30 6 39N50'27 80W24'22 5:21:37
Higgins Corner 10 6 41N06'18 79W50'31 5:19:22
Higgins Corners 10 6 41N05 79W50 5:19:20
Highcliff 2 114 40N31'36 80W03'02 5:20:12
Highfield 10 3 40N51 79W54 5:19:36
Highhouse 26 80 39N51'58 79W48'36 5:19:14
High Lake 64 6 41N48'50 75W18'22 5:01:13
Highland 2 114 40N28'20 79W55'11 5:19:41
Highland 4 8 40N49 80W25 5:21:40
Highland 6 80 40N18'40 76W05'38 5:04:23
Highland 8 60 41N44'14 76W31'46 5:06:07
Highland 40 20 41N20 75W54 5:03:36
Highland 65 99 40N21'41 79W31'33 5:18:06
Highland Acres 36 8 40N02 76W17 5:05:08
Highland Corners 24 75 41N33'37 78W51'04 5:15:24
Highland Farms 9 1 40N13 75W01 5:00:04
Highland Fling 11 6 40N35'32 78W26'51 5:13:47
Highland Meadows 2 8 40N17 79W50 5:19:20
Highland Park 9 8 40N20'48 75W18'04 5:01:12
Highland Park 11 74 40N17 78W53 5:15:32
Highland Park 21 12 40N13'54 76W54'06 5:07:36
Highland Park 23 9 39N57'55 75W16'19 5:01:05
Highland Park 25 107 42N05'24 80W07'43 5:20:31
Highland Park 44 73 40N37'15 77W34'06 5:10:16
Highland Park 48 12 40N39'31 75W15'49 5:01:03
Highlands 40 42 41N00'48 75W52'59 5:03:32
Highland View 9 1 40N13 75W01 5:00:04
High Meadows 23 90 39N55 75W22 5:01:28
Highmount 67 1 40N01'52 76W34'34 5:06:18
High Park 46 1 40N11 75W06 5:00:24
Highrock 67 1 39N48'55 76W28'45 5:05:55
Highspire 22 12 40N12'39 76W47'29 5:07:10
Highton 9 8 40N19'20 74W59'20 4:59:57
Highville 67 8 39N56'48 76W25'01 5:05:40
Hilborn 41 6 41N29'08 77W29'48 5:09:59
Hildebrand 67 3 39N44'38 76W45'11 5:07:01
Hileman Heights 7 33 40N29'32 78W23'38 5:13:35
Hill Church 6 2 40N20 75W38 5:02:32
Hill Church 63 2 40N14'41 80W10'28 5:20:42
Hill City 61 1 41N21'13 79W38'43 5:18:35
Hillcrest 2 114 40N20'55 80W02'00 5:20:08
Hill Crest 26 104 40N01 79W35 5:18:20
Hillcrest 43 117 41N14 80W29 5:21:56
Hill Crest 46 9 40N05'40 75W10'52 5:00:43
Hillcrest 67 67 39N56'16 76W42'15 5:06:49
Hillcroft 67 67 39N56'46 76W42'16 5:06:49
Hilldale 2 8 40N14'57 79W52'40 5:19:31
Hilldale 10 6 41N00'24 79W47'57 5:19:12
Hilldale 40 20 41N17'21 75W50'12 5:03:21
Hillegass 46 2 40N22'18 75W31'14 5:02:05
Hiller 26 1 40N00'37 79W54'04 5:19:36
Hilliards 10 6 41N05'09 79W50'01 5:19:20
Hillman 32 51 40N54'17 78W51'01 5:15:24
Hills (Lawrence P O) 63 114 40N18'22 80W07'15 5:20:29
Hillsboro 56 123 40N10'55 78W51'16 5:15:25
Hillsdale 32 6 40N45'06 78W53'07 5:15:32
Hillsdale 58 89 41N41'03 75W48'09 5:03:13
Hillsgrove 57 6 41N26'38 76W42'27 5:06:50
Hillside 39 13 40N36'34 75W35'44 5:02:23
Hillside 40 20 41N17'50 75W55'31 5:03:42
Hillside 54 49 40N41 76W12 5:04:48
Hillside 65 3 40N22'05 79W15'39 5:17:03
Hillside Junction 35 18 41N20'54 75W43'05 5:02:52
Hillside Village 9 8 40N21 75W13 5:00:52
Hills Terrace 54 3 40N48'58 76W09'00 5:04:36
Hillsview 65 110 40N16'43 79W10'23 5:16:42
Hillsville 37 1 41N00'28 80W29'49 5:21:59
Hilltop 9 13 40N29'33 75W22'45 5:01:31
Hill Top Acres 3 15 40N46 79W32 5:18:08
Hilltop Acres 36 8 40N01'59 76W16'06 5:05:04
Hilltown 1 1 39N53'38 77W21'33 5:09:26
Hilltown 9 8 40N22 75W18 5:01:12
Hillville 3 6 41N01'50 79W36'01 5:18:24
Hilton 67 1 40N00 76W58 5:07:52
Hinkletown 9 1 40N24'16 75W07'25 5:00:30
Hinkletown 36 30 40N08'53 76W07'19 5:04:29
Hinkson Corner 23 90 39N54 75W22 5:01:28
Hinterleiter 6 8 40N30'50 75W43'58 5:02:56
Hiyasota 56 6 40N11 78W59 5:15:56
Hoadleys 64 59 41N30'33 75W17'09 5:01:09
Hoagland 43 66 41N12'16 80W16'56 5:21:08
Hoagland Vista 57 6 41N29'08 76W43'37 5:06:54
Hoban Heights 66 59 41N28'19 75W53'43 5:03:35
Hobart 67 1 39N44'34 76W54'17 5:07:37
Hobbie 40 1 41N04'36 76W04'36 5:04:18
Hoblet 8 6 41N51'02 76W39'23 5:06:38
Hoblitzell 5 51 39N50 78W43 5:14:52
Hockersville 21 1 40N06'32 77W21'07 5:09:24
Hockersville 22 31 40N15'48 76W39'09 5:06:37
Hoernerstown 22 12 40N17'14 76W43'29 5:06:54
Hoffer 55 51 40N40'34 76W56'08 5:07:45
Hoffman 39 8 40N45 75W37 5:02:28
Hoffmansville 46 8 40N19'40 75W33'28 5:02:14
Hogestown 21 12 40N14'45 77W01'59 5:08:08
Hogsett 26 80 39N54'42 79W42'45 5:18:51
Hoguetown 11 55 40N28'00 78W36'04 5:14:24
Hohls Crossing 6 8 40N16'20 75W50'17 5:03:21
Hokendauqua 39 13 40N39'43 75W29'29 5:01:58
Hokes 67 3 39N44'17 76W50'25 5:07:22
Holbrook 30 6 39N51'19 80W18'35 5:21:14
Holden 16 59 41N10'02 79W13'21 5:16:53
Holicong 9 8 40N20'08 75W02'52 5:00:11
Holiday Park 2 14 40N29 79W44 5:18:56
Holland 9 8 40N10'22 74W59'35 4:59:58
Holland Heights 36 8 40N04'28 76W15'19 5:05:01
Hollars Hill 40 42 40N56'56 76W00'28 5:04:02
Hollenback 8 6 41N36'14 76W14'50 5:04:59
Hollenback 40 6 41N04 76W05 5:04:20
Hollentown 11 54 40N41'23 78W27'54 5:13:52
Hollers Hill 40 42 40N58 76W00 5:04:00
Holley Heights 67 67 39N58 76W47 5:07:08
Hollidaysburg 7 33 40N25'38 78W23'21 5:13:33
Hollinger 36 8 40N02 76W20 5:05:20
Hollisters 35 4 41N19'07 75W30'02 5:02:00
Hollisterville 64 4 41N23'28 75W26'20 5:01:45
Hollo 48 8 40N43'22 75W17'45 5:01:11
Hollsopple 56 66 40N12'45 78W55'45 5:15:43
Holly Hill 9 9 40N09'45 74W50'21 4:59:21
Hollywood 17 7 41N14'31 78W32'28 5:14:10
Hollywood 40 42 40N59'41 75W59'45 5:03:59
Hollywood 46 9 40N05'23 75W05'38 5:00:23
Hollywood 67 67 39N57 76W42 5:06:48
Hollywood Heights 67 67 39N56'57 76W41'20 5:06:45
Holme Circle 51 9 40N03'22 75W01'43 5:00:07
Holmes 23 9 39N54'15 75W18'32 5:01:14
Holmesburg 51 9 40N02'29 75W01'42 5:00:07
Holt 4 64 40N37'22 80W22'11 5:21:29
Holters Croosing 14 63 41N01 77W39 5:10:36
Holtwood 36 7 39N49'55 76W19'40 5:05:19
Holtz 67 1 39N56'32 76W36'13 5:06:25
Homans Corner 5 51 40N12'59 78W16'30 5:13:06
Home 32 6 40N44'22 79W06'20 5:16:25
Homeacre 10 3 40N51'33 79W56'23 5:19:46
Home Acres 67 67 39N57 76W42 5:06:48
Homecamp 17 6 41N05 78W39 5:14:36
Homeland 36 8 40N03'50 76W17'13 5:05:09
Home Park 39 13 40N40'56 75W30'59 5:02:04
Homer 53 66 41N43 78W01 5:12:04
Homer City 32 71 40N32'36 79W09'45 5:16:39
Homer Gap 7 33 40N33'50 78W24'16 5:13:37
Homestead 2 114 40N24'21 79W54'44 5:19:39
Homestead Park 2 114 40N24 79W54 5:19:36
Homesville 54 27 40N47 76W21 5:05:24
Hometown 54 27 40N49'25 75W58'50 5:03:55
Homets Ferry 8 60 41N41'56 76W19'23 5:05:18
Homeville 2 114 40N23'06 79W52'43 5:19:31
Homeville 15 3 39N51'39 75W59'13 5:03:57
Homewood 2 114 40N27'05 79W54'29 5:19:38
Homewood 4 121 40N48'50 80W19'46 5:21:19
Homewood 67 1 40N06'35 77W02'40 5:08:11
Honeoye 53 29 41N59'27 78W08'00 5:12:32
Honesdale 64 22 41N34'36 75W15'33 5:01:02
Honey Brook 15 27 40N05'39 75W54'42 5:03:39
Honey Creek 44 7 40N41'23 77W33'33 5:10:14
Honey Grove 34 6 40N24'08 77W33'09 5:10:13
Honey Hole 40 42 41N02'28 75W57'16 5:03:49
Honey Pot 40 21 41N12 76W00 5:04:00
Honeytown 19 4 41N09'57 76W19'03 5:05:16
Hood 9 8 40N21'39 74W57'48 4:59:51
Hoodville 61 1 41N11 79W43 5:18:52
Hooker 10 6 40N59'49 79W49'54 5:19:20
Hooks 3 64 40N55'38 79W29'17 5:17:57
Hookstown 4 6 40N35'57 80W28'23 5:21:54
Hoosicks Mill 3 6 40N48'08 79W14'11 5:16:57
Hoover 26 51 39N52'38 79W51'10 5:19:25
Hoover 62 3 41N39'57 79W01'25 5:16:06
Hooverhurst 32 6 40N48'17 78W51'19 5:15:25
Hoovers 62 3 41N42 79W02 5:16:08
Hooversville 56 6 40N08'49 78W54'44 5:15:39
Hooverville 65 7 40N24'46 79W01'38 5:16:07
Hop Bottom 58 89 41N42'21 75W46'00 5:03:04
Hopeland 36 28 40N14'01 76W15'45 5:05:03
Hope Mills 43 66 41N11'25 80W13'39 5:20:55
Hope, Mount 26 105 39N57'40 79W43'22 5:18:53
Hopeville 48 13 40N38'44 75W17'10 5:01:09
Hopewell 5 6 40N08'08 78W16'05 5:13:04
Hopewell 15 3 39N46'45 76W01'00 5:04:04
Hopewell 65 6 40N04'16 79W20'40 5:17:23
Hopewell Center 67 1 39N47'51 76W30'28 5:06:02
Hoppenville 46 2 40N22'42 75W27'38 5:01:51
Hoppers Mill 54 1 40N46'57 75W51'50 5:03:27
Hoppestown 41 6 41N26'10 76W46'28 5:07:06
Hopwood 26 80 39N52'38 79W42'08 5:18:49
Horatio 33 51 40N55'45 79W00'57 5:16:04
Hormtown 33 6 41N08'47 78W55'10 5:15:41
Hornbrook 8 41 41N49'18 76W28'47 5:05:55
Hornby 25 91 42N06'58 79W51'47 5:19:27
Horners Mill 26 6 40N06'33 79W18'54 5:17:16
Hornerstown 11 74 40N18'51 78W54'45 5:15:39
Hornig 36 8 40N04'50 76W14'40 5:04:59
Horning 2 114 40N20'15 79W59'30 5:19:58
Horningford 44 73 40N30'36 77W41'17 5:10:45
Horn Siding 62 7 41N50'51 79W28'51 5:17:55
Horrell 7 33 40N27'11 78W17'22 5:13:09
Horseshoe Heights 36 8 40N02 76W17 5:05:08
Horsham 46 1 40N10'42 75W07'44 5:00:31
Horton City 24 5 41N17'54 78W43'58 5:14:56
Hortons Corners 8 6 41N40 76W16 5:05:04
Hosensack 39 13 40N27'13 75W29'50 5:01:59
Hosensock 54 27 40N49'08 76W04'37 5:04:18
Hospital 46 90 40N08 75W21 5:01:24
Host 6 1 40N24'56 76W12'25 5:04:50
Hostetter 65 3 40N15'58 79W23'55 5:17:36
Hottelville 27 6 41N21'11 79W09'22 5:16:37
House Landing Strip 59 6 41N33'26 77W06'55 5:08:28
Houserville 14 9 40N49'26 77W49'45 5:11:19
Houseville 10 6 40N43'34 79W50'35 5:19:22
Houston 63 2 40N14'47 80W12'42 5:20:51
Houston City 40 1 41N20'14 75W44'00 5:02:56
Housum 28 42 39N52'13 77W43'57 5:10:56
Houtzdale 17 4 40N49'30 78W21'05 5:13:24
Hovey 3 1 41N08 79W41 5:18:44
Howard 2 114 40N24 79W54 5:19:36
Howard 12 106 41N31 78W14 5:12:56
Howard 14 63 41N00'51 77W39'30 5:10:38
Howard 42 102 41N53'11 78W39'08 5:14:37
Howard Siding 12 106 41N28'35 78W19'25 5:13:18
Howe 33 34 41N12'54 79W06'09 5:16:25
Howell 21 12 40N13'21 76W58'03 5:07:52
Howell Park 2 8 40N17 79W50 5:19:20
Howellville 15 90 40N03'34 75W28'12 5:01:53
Howersville 48 8 40N46'13 75W30'42 5:02:03
Howerton 48 13 40N41 75W22 5:01:28
Howertown 48 13 40N41'48 75W27'58 5:01:52
Hoytdale 4 121 40N50'57 80W19'46 5:21:19
Hoytville 59 6 41N35'16 77W17'57 5:09:12
Hublersburg 14 63 40N57'39 77W36'37 5:10:26
Hubley 54 27 40N38 76W37 5:06:28
Huckenberry 17 6 40N57'57 78W07'32 5:12:30
Hudson 17 113 40N53'03 78W14'35 5:12:58
Hudson 40 20 41N16'29 75W50'11 5:03:21
Hudsondale 13 60 40N55'00 75W51'20 5:03:25
Huefner 16 6 41N18'50 79W23'17 5:17:33
Huey 16 7 41N04'51 79W30'30 5:18:02
Huff 32 29 40N23 79W04 5:16:16
Huffs Church 6 13 40N31 75W36 5:02:24
Huffs Corner 8 6 41N53'16 76W36'25 5:06:26
Hughes Park 46 90 40N05'09 75W20'53 5:01:24

Hughestown 40 1 41N19'37 75W46'25 5:03:06
Hughesville 41 81 41N14'28 76W43'27 5:06:54
Hughs 40 1 41N14'26 76W03'55 5:04:16
Hulltown 26 104 40N02'34 79W38'52 5:18:35
Hulmenville 9 97 40N08'35 74W54'41 4:59:39
Hulmeville 9 97 40N09 74W55 4:59:40
Hulmeville Park 9
97 40N10 74W55 4:59:40
Hulton 2 14 40N31 79W50 5:19:20
Humbert 56 53 39N51'22 79W18'56 5:17:16
Humbolt 40 42 40N56'14 76W02'35 5:04:10
Hummels Store 6
101 40N18 75W59 5:03:56
Hummelstown 22 12 40N15'55 76W42'31 5:06:50
Hummels Wharf 55
82 40N49'54 76W50'10 5:07:21
Humphreys 65 99 40N18 79W34 5:18:16
Humphreys Corner 61
6 41N14'48 79W48'36 5:19:14
Humphreyville 15
9 39N57'34 75W52'40 5:03:31
Humpreys 65 3 40N14'49 79W28'41 5:17:55
Hundred Spring 31
11 40N40 78W13 5:12:52
Hungerford 67 27 39N45'23 76W40'41 5:06:43
Hungry Hollow 3 4 40N38'29 79W34'03 5:18:16
Hunker 65 111 40N12'15 79W37'15 5:18:29
Hunlock 40 1 41N12'34 76W04'56 5:04:20
Hunlock Creek 40
1 41N12'21 76W03'59 5:04:16
Hunlock Gardens 40
1 41N12'43 76W02'52 5:04:11
Hunsecker 36 8 40N05'08 76W14'40 5:04:59
Hunter 27 35 41N28'27 79W29'52 5:17:59
Hunter 49 27 40N45'27 76W45'34 5:07:02
Hunter Hill 46 90 40N07 75W16 5:01:04
Hunters Run 21 56 40N04'19 77W11'44 5:08:47
Hunterstown 1 1 39N52'56 77W09'38 5:08:39
Huntersville 41
83 41N18'48 76W45'45 5:07:03
Huntingdon 31 81 40N29'05 78W00'38 5:12:03
Huntingdon Furnace 31
11 40N39'25 78W06'51 5:12:27
Huntingdon Heights 65
25 40N20 79W43 5:18:52
Huntingdon Manor 36
28 40N05 76W11 5:04:44
Huntingdon Meadows 46
1 40N09 75W03 5:00:12
Huntingdon Valley 46
1 40N07'21 75W03'50 5:00:15
Hunting Park 51 9 40N01 75W09 5:00:36
Huntington Mills 40
1 41N11'26 76W14'02 5:04:56
Huntley 12 7 41N22'02 78W09'10 5:12:37
Huntley 17 7 41N13'13 78W23'33 5:13:34
Huntsdale 21 16 40N06'08 77W18'28 5:09:14
Huntsville 40 20 41N18'23 75W58'29 5:03:54
Huron 26 51 39N52'25 79W55'10 5:19:41
Husband 56 6 40N02'30 79W06'07 5:16:24
Huskin 56 63 40N07 78W49 5:15:16
Huston 56 53 39N49'46 79W22'32 5:17:30
Huston Run 63 114 40N14'03 79W59'20 5:19:57
Hustons Mill 21
12 40N15'19 77W02'16 5:08:09
Hustontown 29 6 40N02'56 78W01'38 5:12:07
Hutchins 42 59 41N39'44 78W37'39 5:14:31
Hutchinson 26 80 39N51'45 79W42'11 5:18:49
Hutchinson 65 61 40N13'34 79W43'55 5:18:56
Hyde 17 1 41N00'09 78W27'49 5:13:51
Hyde Park 6 101 40N22'38 75W55'32 5:03:42
Hyde Park 35 18 41N24'56 75W41'13 5:02:45
Hyde Park 65 4 40N37'57 79W35'24 5:18:22
Hydes 24 5 41N16 78W44 5:14:56
Hydetown 20 7 41N39'09 79W43'38 5:18:55
Hyde Villa 6 101 40N23 75W56 5:03:44
Hyndman 5 51 39N49'23 78W43'06 5:14:52
Hynemansville 39
1 40N35'36 75W42'45 5:02:51
Hyner 18 7 41N19'54 77W38'40 5:10:35
Hyner View 18 7 41N19'35 77W37'27 5:10:30
Hyson Hill 67 1 39N47'43 76W34'08 5:06:17
Icedale 15 27 40N04'01 75W49'43 5:03:19
Icedale Mobile Homes 15
27 40N06 75W55 5:03:40
Ickesburg 50 7 40N27'21 77W21'07 5:09:24
Idaho 3 6 40N39'13 79W20'50 5:17:23
Idamar 32 7 40N43'44 79W00'11 5:16:01
Idaville 1 1 40N00'53 77W12'11 5:08:49
Ideal 32 6 40N37'59 79W04'06 5:16:16
Idetown 40 6 41N20'49 76W01'32 5:04:06
Idlewood 2 114 40N25'42 80W04'30 5:20:18
Idlewood 9 97 40N09'52 74W56'53 4:59:48
Imler 5 7 40N12'24 78W31'23 5:14:06
Imlertown 5 70 40N05'32 78W28'11 5:13:53
Immaculata 15 8 40N01 75W35 5:02:20
Imperial 2 51 40N26'58 80W14'41 5:20:59
Independence 4 13 40N34'20 80W18'34 5:21:14
Independence 55
51 40N40'51 76W53'43 5:07:35
Independence 63 6 40N15'14 80W30'28 5:22:02
Independence, Mount 26
80 39N55'52 79W38'39 5:18:35
India 65 29 40N22'35 79W07'11 5:16:29
Indiana 32 72 40N37'17 79W09'10 5:16:37
Indian Creek 9 9 40N08'41 74W51'58 4:59:28
Indian Creek 26 6 39N58'08 79W30'42 5:18:03
Indian Crossing 42
40 41N58'25 78W24'18 5:13:37
Indian Head 25 35 41N53'58 79W59'43 5:19:59
Indian Head 26 6 40N01'29 79W23'43 5:17:35
Indian Hills 13 8 40N51'12 75W41'20 5:02:45
Indian King 15 13 39N57 75W36 5:02:24
Indian Lake 56 63 40N02'48 78W51'09 5:15:25
Indianland 48 8 40N45'40 75W33'14 5:02:13
Indian Mountain Lake 13
1 41N00'11 75W30'31 5:02:02
Indianola 2 14 40N34'10 79W51'50 5:19:27
Indian Orchard 64
59 41N32'50 75W12'50 5:00:51
Indian Pines 2
114 40N26 80W04 5:20:16
Indian Point 52 2 41N17'08 74W50'05 4:59:20
Indian Run 43 6 41N09'04 80W15'52 5:21:03
Indian Springs Estates 32
72 40N36'15 79W10'54 5:16:44
Indiantown 38 8 40N24'35 76W34'50 5:06:19
Indiantown 56 6 40N00'23 79W13'05 5:16:52
Indian Town Gap 22
12 40N20 76W50 5:07:20
Indian Village 1
1 39N48 76W59 5:07:56
Industry (Frank P O) 2
8 40N15'52 79W47'33 5:19:10
Industry 4 19 40N38'40 80W24'59 5:21:40
Inez 53 66 41N43'12 78W01'19 5:12:05
Ingleby 14 6 40N50'50 77W25'40 5:09:43
Inglenook 22 24 40N24'47 76W58'53 5:07:56
Ingleside 11 74 40N15'33 78W53'28 5:15:34
Inglesmith 5 6 39N45'05 78W22'55 5:13:32
Ingomar 2 114 40N34'51 80W03'40 5:20:15
Ingram 2 114 40N26'46 80W04'04 5:20:16
Inkerman 40 1 41N17'56 75W48'47 5:03:15
Intercourse 36 23 40N02'15 76W06'19 5:04:25
Inwood 38 1 40N28'32 76W31'16 5:06:05
Iola 19 6 41N08'11 76W31'55 5:06:08
Iona 38 8 40N20 76W26 5:05:44
Irish Meeting House 9
8 40N23'40 75W12'20 5:00:49
Irishtown 1 1 39N50'17 77W02'58 5:08:12
Irishtown 17 7 40N58'34 78W39'58 5:14:40
Irishtown 26 105 39N56'49 79W36'09 5:18:25
Irishtown 36 1 40N01'43 76W09'33 5:04:38
Irishtown 42 6 41N48'59 78W40'17 5:14:41
Irishtown 43 66 41N12'48 80W07'30 5:20:30
Irona 38 8 40N19'16 76W22'17 5:05:29
Iron Bridge 65
111 40N06'59 79W33'05 5:18:12
Iron City 27 6 41N33'29 79W01'36 5:16:06
Iron Ridge 67 1 39N50'26 76W54'43 5:07:39
Ironsides 15 8 40N08'02 75W32'29 5:02:10
Iron Springs 1 1 39N46'32 77W23'49 5:09:35
Ironstone 6 2 40N18'04 75W40'25 5:02:42
Ironton 39 13 40N40'12 75W34'05 5:02:16
Ironville 7 11 40N39'27 78W13'00 5:12:52
Ironville 36 26 40N03'23 76W27'47 5:05:51
Irvin 2 114 40N22 79W54 5:19:36
Irvine 62 3 41N50'21 79W16'07 5:17:04
Irving 54 9 40N31'58 76W26'21 5:05:45
Irvona 17 54 40N46'28 78W33'13 5:14:13
Irwin 65 25 40N19'28 79W42'05 5:18:48
Isabella 15 1 40N07'15 75W50'18 5:03:21
Isabella 26 51 39N56'38 79W56'11 5:19:45
Iselin 32 6 40N33'34 79W23'12 5:17:33
Iselin Heights 17
56 41N07'38 78W47'07 5:15:08
Island Park 49 82 40N52 76W47 5:07:08
Island Plain 58
59 41N57'17 75W42'19 5:02:49
Ithan 23 90 40N01'48 75W22'00 5:01:28
Itley 25 7 41N53 80W08 5:20:32
Iva 36 9 39N57'47 76W08'09 5:04:33
Ivarea 25 7 41N54'13 80W15'58 5:21:04
Ivyland 9 1 40N12'28 75W04'23 5:00:18
Ivy Mills 23 4 39N54 75W28 5:01:52
Ivy Rock 46 90 40N05'38 75W18'59 5:01:16
Ivywood 10 2 40N42'39 79W51'07 5:19:24
Jacks Mountain 1
1 39N45'16 77W24'09 5:09:37
Jackson 19 6 41N11'42 76W27'18 5:05:49
Jackson 25 107 42N01'43 80W00'36 5:20:02
Jackson 58 6 41N50'17 75W35'28 5:02:22
Jackson Center 43
6 41N16'22 80W08'21 5:20:33
Jackson Center 59
6 41N56'23 76W58'56 5:07:56
Jackson Corner 31
81 40N35'47 77W51'44 5:11:27
Jackson Crossing 62
120 41N50'36 79W13'01 5:16:52
Jackson Hall 28
42 39N56 77W40 5:10:40
Jackson Knolls 37
112 41N00 80W21 5:21:24
Jackson Knolls Gardens 37
112 40N57'16 80W25'41 5:21:43
Jackson Mills 5 6 39N58'19 78W16'17 5:13:05
Jackson Summit 59
6 41N56'36 77W01'01 5:08:04
Jacksonville 9 1 40N13'46 75W03'17 5:00:13
Jacksonville 14
63 40N59'32 77W37'56 5:10:32
Jacksonville 32 6 40N32'27 79W16'55 5:17:08
Jacksonville 36
23 39N59'05 76W02'36 5:04:10
Jacksonville 39
56 40N40'15 75W49'44 5:03:19
Jacksonville 48
13 40N42'19 75W24'32 5:01:38
Jacksonwald 6 101 40N19'28 75W51'00 5:03:24
Jacksville 10 6 41N01'01 80W06'47 5:20:27
Jacktown 65 25 40N19'48 79W43'40 5:18:55
Jacktown Acres 65
25 40N20 79W43 5:18:52
Jacobs Creek 65 6 40N07'59 79W44'31 5:18:58
Jacobs Mills 67 1 39N49'57 76W55'42 5:07:43
Jacobus 67 3 39N52'59 76W42'39 5:06:51
Jaffa Mosque 7 33 40N30'25 78W24'36 5:13:38
Jalappa 6 80 40N31'43 76W02'16 5:04:09
James City 24 75 41N37'12 78W50'21 5:15:21
James Creek 31 3 40N23 78W10 5:12:40
James Manor 9 8 40N21 75W13 5:00:52
Jamestown 11 63 40N24'16 78W39'20 5:14:37
Jamestown 13 8 40N50'39 75W42'41 5:02:51
Jamestown 43 63 41N29'05 80W26'16 5:21:45
Jamesville 48 13 40N44'06 75W25'12 5:01:41
Jamison 9 8 40N15'17 75W05'23 5:00:22
Jamison 26 80 39N54 79W44 5:18:56
Jamison 27 35 41N30'47 79W27'12 5:17:49
Jamison City 19 6 41N18'23 76W21'40 5:05:27
Jamisonville 10 3 40N56'38 79W55'29 5:19:42
Janesville (Smithmill P O) 17
63 40N45'36 78W25'18 5:13:41
Japan 40 20 40N59'33 75W54'38 5:03:39
Jarrettown 46 1 40N09'18 75W10'32 5:00:42
Jay 24 7 41N18 78W30 5:14:00
J & B Junction 42
59 41N44 78W39 5:14:36
Jeanesville 40 42 40N58 76W00 5:04:00
Jeannette 65 3 40N19'41 79W36'56 5:18:28
Jeanville 40 42 40N55'39 75W58'15 5:03:53
Jeddo 40 6 40N59'44 75W53'48 5:03:35
Jednota 22 80 40N12'16 76W45'32 5:07:02
Jefferis 26 80 39N54'25 79W48'27 5:19:14
Jefferis Crossing 26
80 39N54 79W44 5:18:56
Jefferson 16 6 41N12'11 79W33'19 5:18:13
Jefferson 30 6 39N55'48 80W03'33 5:20:14
Jefferson 54 1 40N35'04 76W07'48 5:04:31
Jefferson 63 6 40N17'09 80W29'56 5:22:00
Jefferson (Codorus PO) 67
3 39N49'02 76W50'31 5:07:22
Jefferson Center 10
3 40N46'32 79W50'06 5:19:20
Jefferson Junction 58
59 41N57'28 75W33'28 5:02:14
Jeffersonville 46
90 40N07'44 75W22'21 5:01:29
Jenkins 40 20 41N18 75W48 5:03:12
Jenkins Corner 36
1 39N43'53 76W09'12 5:04:37
Jenkintown 46 9 40N05'45 75W07'32 5:00:30
Jenkintown Manor 46
9 40N05 75W07 5:00:28
Jenks 27 6 41N28 79W07 5:16:28
Jenks 66 59 41N28'36 75W58'35 5:03:54
Jenners 56 6 40N08'35 79W02'35 5:16:10
Jenners Crossroads 56
6 40N09'05 79W02'59 5:16:12
Jennerstown 56 6 40N09'35 79W04'00 5:16:16
Jennersville 15 1 39N49'23 75W52'12 5:03:29
Jenningsville 66
59 41N34'59 76W08'39 5:04:35
Jericho 12 116 41N19'19 78W04'37 5:12:18
Jericho 64 6 41N19'09 75W23'27 5:01:34
Jericho Mills 34
7 40N36'47 77W20'15 5:09:21
Jericho Valley 9
8 40N22 74W56 4:59:44
Jermyn 35 1 41N31'51 75W32'45 5:02:11
Jerome 56 74 40N12'32 78W59'02 5:15:56
Jersey Mills 41 6 41N21'26 77W24'25 5:09:38
Jersey Shore 41
73 41N12 77W15 5:09:00
Jerseytown 19 4 41N05'19 76W34'43 5:06:19
Jessup 35 1 41N28'07 75W33'45 5:02:15
Jewell 2 114 40N18'41 80W03'56 5:20:16
Jewtown 32 6 40N37'53 78W54'22 5:15:37
Jim Thorpe 13 80 40N52'33 75W43'58 5:02:56
Jimtown 56 6 40N01'39 79W13'41 5:16:55
J M Junction 32 6 40N36'15 79W17'45 5:17:11
Joanna 6 56 40N10'25 75W51'44 5:03:27
Joanna Furnace 6
27 40N11'22 75W53'19 5:03:33
Joanna Heights 6
1 40N11'07 75W51'18 5:03:25
Jobs Corners 59 6 41N55'54 76W56'10 5:07:45
Joffre 63 6 40N22'45 80W21'38 5:21:27
Johnsburg 56 6 39N52'10 78W50'37 5:15:22
Johnsonburg 24 36 41N29'26 78W40'31 5:14:42
Johnsonburg 32 6 40N53'10 78W52'41 5:15:31
Johnson Greene 40
20 41N13'55 75W58'06 5:03:52
Johnsons Corner 23
1 39N50'57 75W32'18 5:02:09
Johnsons Mill 29
6 39N44'57 78W08'52 5:12:35
Johnston 28 1 39N45'30 77W45'19 5:11:01
Johnstown 11 74 40N19'36 78W55'20 5:15:41
Johnstown 38 1 40N16'42 76W19'00 5:05:16
Johnstown 60 6 40N56'24 77W03'11 5:08:13
Johnsville 9 1 40N11'27 75W04'08 5:00:17
John Wanamaker 51
9 39N57 75W09 5:00:36
Jo Jo 42 75 41N38'09 78W51'05 5:15:24
Joliett 54 9 40N36'43 76W27'14 5:05:49
Joller 31 6 40N12'14 78W04'01 5:12:16
Jollytown 30 2 39N43'42 80W19'19 5:21:17
Jonas 45 9 40N58'03 75W30'44 5:02:03
Jones 24 7 41N34 78W40 5:14:40
Jones Mills 65 6 40N05'19 79W20'27 5:17:22
Jones Terrace 46
12 40N41 75W14 5:00:56
Jonestown 19 4 41N07'45 76W18'16 5:05:13
Jonestown 38 1 40N24'49 76W28'43 5:05:55
Jonestown 54 49 40N41'58 76W16'18 5:05:05
Jonestown 63 1 40N07'46 79W58'26 5:19:54
Jonesville 13 9 40N51'07 75W32'29 5:02:10
Jordan 39 8 40N42 75W42 5:02:48
Jordan Park Apartments 39
13 40N39 75W30 5:02:00
Jordan Valley 39
8 40N42'46 75W42'50 5:02:51
Josephine 32 98 40N28'38 79W10'54 5:16:44
Josephtown 4 19 40N40'12 80W19'53 5:21:20
Joyce 37 112 40N58'19 80W18'58 5:21:16
Joy, Mount 17 1 41N03'10 78W26'10 5:13:45
Joy, Mount 65 111 40N08'42 79W30'08 5:18:01
Jubilee 35 4 41N20'49 75W27'22 5:01:49
Jugtown 28 100 39N50'30 77W36'19 5:10:25
Jugtown 54 1 40N32'14 75W04'33 5:00:18
Julian 14 7 40N51'51 77W56'23 5:11:46
Jumonville 26 80 39N53'06 79W38'55 5:18:36
Juneau 32 51 40N53'18 78W57'46 5:15:51
Junedale 13 42 40N55'24 75W56'31 5:03:46
June Meadows 46 1 40N09 75W03 5:00:12
Juniata 7 33 40N32'18 78W22'54 5:13:32
Juniata 26 105 39N59'48 79W41'26 5:18:46
Juniata 50 1 40N29 77W12 5:08:48
Juniata 51 9 40N00'30 75W06'33 5:00:26
Juniata Crossing 5
6 39N59'40 78W16'08 5:13:05
Juniata Furnace 50
1 40N27'19 77W10'07 5:08:40
Juniata Gap 7 33 40N32'56 78W25'46 5:13:43
Juniata Terrace 44
73 40N35 77W35 5:10:20
Juniper Circle 39
13 40N38'24 75W29'33 5:01:58

Just A Farm 46 1 40N09 75w03 5:00:12
Justus 35 45 41N30'08 75w38'25 5:02:34
Kahletown 33 6 41N16'21 79w09'27 5:16:38
Kaiserville 66 59 41N36'42 75w58'57 5:03:56
Kammerer 63 2 40N11'01 80w02'53 5:20:12
Kane 42 75 41N39'46 78w48'41 5:15:15
Kanesholm 42 75 41N40'29 78w43'38 5:14:55
Kaneville 61 9 41N30'15 79w42'10 5:18:49
Kantner 56 6 40N06'06 78w56'14 5:15:45
Kanty 25 107 42N07'16 80w00'08 5:20:01
Kantz 55 82 40N46'37 76w54'04 5:07:36
Kantz Corners 20
59 41N31'05 80w03'34 5:20:14
Kaolin 15 8 39N47'55 75w43'39 5:02:55
Kapp 49 82 40N54'24 76w49'58 5:07:20
Kapp Heights 49
82 40N53'59 76w48'30 5:07:14
Karen 63 51 40N02 79w55 5:19:40
Karns 2 14 40N37'50 79w42'14 5:18:49
Karns City 10 1 40N59'38 79w43'32 5:18:54
Karthaus 14 6 41N07'15 78w06'51 5:12:27
Kaseville 47 6 40N59'53 76w35'40 5:06:23
Kashner 43 6 41N22'51 80w18'17 5:21:13
Kasiesville 28 51 39N44'55 77w53'29 5:11:34
Kaska 54 27 40N44'24 76w06'27 5:04:26
Kasson 42 93 41N44'55 78w31'35 5:14:06
Kasson Brook 66 6 41N28'18 76w08'53 5:04:36
Katellen 48 13 40N49'29 75w22'04 5:01:28
Kato 14 7 41N05'05 77w51'59 5:11:28
Kauffman 28 42 39N50'02 77w42'23 5:10:50
Kaufmann 26 6 39N54'06 79w27'58 5:17:52
Kaufmann's 2 114 40N22 80w03 5:20:12
Kaufmann's-McKnight Road 2
114 40N33 80w01 5:20:04
Kaylor 3 7 40N58'52 79w40'05 5:18:40
Kaylor 11 55 40N29'46 78w39'47 5:14:39
Kaywin 39 13 40N38'09 75w24'07 5:01:36
Keal Run 32 51 40N52'37 78w49'57 5:15:20
Kearney 5 51 40N08'25 78w13'23 5:12:54
Kearsarge 25 107 42N03'57 80w05'35 5:20:22
Keating 18 7 41N15'32 77w54'16 5:11:37
Keating Junction 18
7 41N18 77w51 5:11:24
Keating Summit 53
75 41N40'51 78w10'53 5:12:44
Keborts Corners 20
6 41N35'22 80w11'41 5:20:47
Kecksburg 65 111 40N11'05 79w27'39 5:17:51
Kedron Park 23 9 39N54 75w20 5:01:20
Keech 53 6 41N59 77w52 5:11:28
Keefers 49 6 40N52'31 76w43'18 5:06:53
Keelersburg 66 59 41N27'18 75w53'48 5:03:35
Keelersville 9 8 40N24'58 75w15'10 5:01:01
Keenan 10 6 41N06'15 79w52'24 5:19:30
Keeney 67 27 39N45'34 76w39'43 5:06:39
Keeneyville 59 6 41N51'38 77w18'18 5:09:13
Keeny Row 26 51 39N57'14 79w53'13 5:19:33
Keepville 25 7 41N52'06 80w23'42 5:21:35
Keewaydin 17 6 41N06'16 78w09'20 5:12:37
Keffer 65 110 40N15 79w14 5:16:56
Keffers 54 9 40N36'45 76w27'53 5:05:52
Kegg 5 6 39N58'55 78w43'14 5:14:53
Kehler 54 8 40N41'39 76w31'39 5:06:07
Kehley Run Junction 54
27 40N49 76w12 5:04:48
Keifertown 65 111 40N06'12 79w34'45 5:18:19
Keisters 10 6 41N02'09 80w00'43 5:20:03
Keisterville 26
80 39N57'41 79w46'58 5:19:08
Kelayres 54 60 40N54'03 76w00'14 5:04:01
Kellersburg 3 6 40N58'10 79w25'28 5:17:42
Kellers Church 9
8 40N25 75w23 5:01:32
Kellersville 45
23 40N56'36 75w17'41 5:01:11
Kellerville 34 6 40N39'35 77w09'39 5:08:39
Kellettville 27 6 41N32'17 79w16'05 5:17:04
Kellogg 8 60 41N40'41 76w27'36 5:05:50
Kelly 3 15 40N46 79w32 5:18:08
Kelly 60 70 41N00 76w55 5:07:40
Kellyburg 41 7 41N26'18 76w52'41 5:07:31
Kelly Crossroads 60
70 41N00'59 76w56'09 5:07:45
Kelly Point 60 70 40N59'31 76w56'09 5:07:45
Kellytown 17 122 40N53'23 78w27'37 5:13:50
Kellytown 59 59 41N49'51 77w05'30 5:08:22
Kellyville 23 9 39N57 75w18 5:01:12
Kelton 15 1 39N48'31 75w52'42 5:03:31
Kemblesville 15 1 39N44'56 75w49'28 5:03:18
Kemmererville 45
23 40N56'00 75w14'38 5:00:59
Kempton 6 56 40N37'34 75w51'10 5:03:25
Kempville 6 8 40N29'41 75w48'54 5:03:16
Kendall 4 6 40N32'03 80w29'17 5:21:57
Kendall Creek 42
102 41N57 78w39 5:14:36
Kendigtown 9 8 40N20'51 75w08'28 5:00:34
Kendrick 17 4 40N49'06 78w22'52 5:13:31
Kenhorst 6 101 40N18'38 75w56'23 5:03:46
Kenilworth 15 8 40N13'53 75w38'04 5:02:32
Kenmar 41 82 41N15'12 76w57'35 5:07:50
Kenmawr 2 114 40N28'56 80w06'52 5:20:27
Kennard 43 59 41N27'54 80w20'12 5:21:21
Kennedy 2 114 40N29 80w06 5:20:24
Kennedy 59 6 41N40'48 77w25'43 5:09:43
Kennedy Mill 37 6 40N59'34 80w11'04 5:20:44
Kennells Mill 56
51 39N46'17 78w47'56 5:15:12
Kennerdell 61 6 41N15'59 79w50'27 5:19:22
Kenneth 26 1 40N03'55 79w51'09 5:19:25
Kennett Square 15
8 39N50'48 75w42'43 5:02:51
Kenny 2 114 40N22 79w54 5:19:36
Kenny Row 26 51 39N56 79w50 5:19:20
Kennywood 2 114 40N23'16 79w51'54 5:19:28
Kenrock 31 6 40N13'59 78w10'15 5:12:41
Kensington 51 9 39N59'09 75w07'56 5:00:32
Kent 32 6 40N33 79w17 5:17:08
Kenwick Village 36
8 40N05'33 76w18'43 5:05:15
Kenwood 32 6 40N38'48 78w56'44 5:15:47
Keown 2 114 40N35'09 80w02'43 5:20:11
Keown Station 2
114 40N32'40 80w01'47 5:20:07
Kepner 54 1 40N41'49 75w55'13 5:03:41
Kepple Hill 3 4 40N36'41 79w34'07 5:18:16
Kepples 10 2 40N43'00 79w42'00 5:18:48
Kepples Corners 10
1 40N57'54 79w42'26 5:18:50
Kernsville 39 13 40N37'58 75w35'56 5:02:24
Kernville 11 74 40N19'10 78w55'09 5:15:41
Kerr 3 2 40N44'05 79w38'43 5:18:35
Kerr 17 114 41N02'01 78w25'24 5:13:42
Kerrmoor 17 7 40N53'33 78w34'56 5:14:20
Kerrs Corners 25
91 42N12'19 79w46'18 5:19:05
Kerrs Corners 43
6 41N10'18 80w03'09 5:20:13
Kerrsville 21 16 40N11'08 77w19'14 5:09:17
Kerrtown 20 77 41N37'45 80w09'41 5:20:39
Kersey 24 36 41N21'44 78w35'47 5:14:23
Kesslerville 48 8 40N47'13 75w14'36 5:00:58
Ketcham 40 20 41N21'36 75w54'50 5:03:39
Ketner 24 7 41N32'21 78w37'50 5:14:31
Keys 67 1 39N52'53 76w32'11 5:06:09
Keyser Valley 35
18 41N25'32 75w41'47 5:02:47
Keystone 24 5 41N16 78w44 5:14:56
Keystone 40 20 41N16'39 75w47'46 5:03:11
Keystone 50 12 40N19'34 77w03'19 5:08:13
Keystone 56 79 39N48'23 78w59'09 5:15:57
Keystone 65 25 40N16'03 79w42'29 5:18:50
Khedive 30 51 39N53'02 80w02'11 5:20:09
Kibbeville 53 6 41N58'38 78w04'00 5:12:16
Kidder 13 94 41N04 75w40 5:02:40
Kidders Corner 25
7 41N54'39 80w24'05 5:21:36
Kilbuck 2 114 40N31 80w06 5:20:24
Kilgore 61 6 41N15'44 80w00'00 5:20:00
Killinger 22 1 40N33'44 76w55'23 5:07:42
Kimberton 15 8 40N07'50 75w34'21 5:02:17
Kimble Corners 25
58 41N55'02 79w51'59 5:19:28
Kimbles 52 6 41N28'06 75w07'19 5:00:29
Kimmel 31 6 40N12'34 78w03'22 5:12:13
Kimmel 32 72 40N42'50 79w08'26 5:16:34
Kimmel 56 4 39N58'10 79w12'35 5:16:50
Kimmell 5 7 40N15 78w30 5:14:00
Kimmelton 56 6 40N04'02 78w57'13 5:15:49
Kim Plan 65 25 40N20 79w43 5:18:52
Kinderhook 36 26 40N03'08 76w29'57 5:06:00
Kindts Corner 6
80 40N27'42 75w55'57 5:03:44
King 5 7 40N14'38 78w27'52 5:13:51
King of Prussia 46
90 40N05'21 75w23'47 5:01:35
Kingsdale 1 56 39N43'28 77w07'09 5:08:29
Kingsley 27 59 41N32 79w16 5:17:04
Kingsley 58 59 41N45'35 75w45'09 5:03:01
Kings Manor 46 90 40N05'54 75w20'43 5:01:23
Kingston 40 20 41N15'42 75w53'50 5:03:35
Kingston 65 3 40N17'31 79w20'29 5:17:22
Kingsville 16 6 41N07'54 79w15'51 5:17:03
Kingswood Estates 45
9 40N51'50 75w28'18 5:01:53
Kingswood Park 9
9 40N08 74w51 4:59:24
Kingview 26 111 40N05'55 79w34'35 5:18:18
Kingwood 56 4 39N54'05 79w16'08 5:17:05
Kinkora Heights 50
51 40N22'23 77w01'29 5:08:06
Kinlock 65 14 40N32'59 79w44'12 5:18:57
Kinney 53 6 41N59'24 77w56'41 5:11:47
Kinport 11 63 40N44 78w49 5:15:16
Kinter Crossing 32
6 40N36'23 78w51'47 5:15:27
Kintersburg 32 6 40N42'55 79w04'45 5:16:19
Kintnersville 9 1 40N33'25 75w10'48 5:00:43
Kinzers (Kinzer Station) 36
23 39N59'54 76w03'43 5:04:15
Kinzua Beach 62
120 41N51'11 78w57'18 5:15:49
Kinzua Heights 62
6 41N52'07 78w56'08 5:15:45
Kipps Run 49 6 40N56'45 76w39'34 5:06:38
Kirby 30 1 39N48'10 80w07'02 5:20:28
Kirbyville 6 8 40N28'27 75w51'32 5:03:26
Kirchberg 48 13 40N35'23 75w18'55 5:01:16
Kirkland 15 13 40N00'36 75w36'03 5:02:24
Kirklyn 23 9 39N58'09 75w17'28 5:01:10
Kirks Mills 36 3 39N45'19 76w06'23 5:04:26
Kirkwood 36 3 39N51'22 76w04'38 5:04:19
Kirwan Heights 2
114 40N22'07 80w06'07 5:20:24
Kishacoquillas 44
6 40N38'15 77w39'46 5:10:39
Kiskimere 3 4 40N37'11 79w35'02 5:18:20
Kiskiminetas 3 4 40N35 79w29 5:17:56
Kiskiminetas Junction 65
2 40N40'38 79w40'00 5:18:40
Kis-Lyn 40 42 41N00'20 75w59'14 5:03:57
Kissel Hill 36 8 40N08'21 76w17'52 5:05:11
Kissimmee 55 6 40N47'43 77w05'08 5:08:21
Kissingers Mill 16
7 41N01'42 79w33'53 5:18:16
Kistler 44 85 40N22'48 77w52'07 5:11:28
Kistler 50 6 40N23'22 77w26'03 5:09:44
Kitches Corners 43
59 41N24 80w23 5:21:32
Kittanning 3 15 40N48'59 79w31'20 5:18:05
Kittanning Heights 3
15 40N50 79w33 5:18:12
Kittatinny 13 8 40N47'23 75w39'46 5:02:39
Klahr 7 3 40N17'57 78w30'47 5:14:03
Klapperthall Junction 6
101 40N18'55 75w54'31 5:03:38
Klecknersville 48
13 40N46'32 75w25'24 5:01:42
Kleinfeltersville 38
25 40N18'03 76w14'58 5:05:00
Kleinville 46 2 40N23'35 75w28'10 5:01:53
Kline 16 6 41N17'54 79w35'06 5:18:20
Kline 54 60 40N54 76w00 5:04:00
Klines Corner 6 9 40N31'26 75w41'12 5:02:45
Klines Grove 49
82 40N54'19 76w41'22 5:06:45
Klines Mill 56 6 40N10'34 79w05'46 5:16:23
Klinesville 36 26 40N02'52 76w30'34 5:06:02
Klinesville 39 8 40N34'37 75w51'12 5:03:25
Klingerstown 54 1 40N39'37 76w41'23 5:06:46
Klondike 42 6 41N51'37 78w48'02 5:15:12
Klondyke 44 73 40N36'08 77w34'50 5:10:19
Knapp 59 6 41N45 77w18 5:09:12
Knauers 6 101 40N14'48 75w59'52 5:03:59
Knauertown 15 1 40N10'17 75w43'38 5:02:55
Kneass 49 51 40N43'41 76w48'34 5:07:14
Knechts 48 8 40N48'39 75w20'08 5:01:21
Knepper 28 100 39N49'57 77w34'15 5:10:17
Knightsbridge 2
114 40N26 80w04 5:20:16
Knightsville 31
85 40N14'31 78w00'43 5:12:03
Knob 4 19 40N41'51 80w11'17 5:20:45
Knobsville 29 66 40N00'27 77w57'47 5:11:51
Knobville 44 7 40N43'10 77w31'38 5:10:07
Knoebels Grove 49
27 40N52'42 76w30'22 5:06:01
Knousetown 34 1 40N39'24 77w04'42 5:08:19
Knowlton 53 6 41N46'17 78w07'39 5:12:31
Knowltonwood 23
90 39N54 75w23 5:01:32
Knox 4 121 40N52 80w16 5:21:04
Knox 16 35 41N14'04 79w32'15 5:18:09
Knox Dale 33 34 41N05'10 79w01'36 5:16:06
Knoxlyn 1 1 39N49'51 77w19'02 5:09:16
Knoxville 2 114 40N25'11 79w59'42 5:19:59
Knoxville 26 51 40N00'57 79w52'36 5:19:30
Knoxville 59 6 41N57'26 77w26'21 5:09:45
Kohinoor Junction 54
27 40N49 76w12 5:04:48
Kohlmeyer Corner 10
6 41N08'37 79w50'46 5:19:23
K O Junction 43
59 41N28'27 80w21'53 5:21:28
Koonsville 40 1 41N10'09 76w09'40 5:04:39
Koontzville 5 70 39N56'16 78w28'09 5:13:53
Koppel 4 121 40N50'03 80w19'21 5:21:17
Korn Krest 40 20 41N13'05 75w56'39 5:03:47
Kossuth 16 6 41N17'05 79w34'27 5:18:18
Kraft Mill 67 1 39N49'13 76w52'38 5:07:31
Kralltown 67 1 40N01'11 76w58'59 5:07:56
Krassdale 39 2 40N25'53 75w29'06 5:01:56
Kratz 46 8 40N18'57 75w28'18 5:01:53
Kratzerville 55
82 40N51'36 76w53'46 5:07:35
Krause 34 6 40N23'05 77w43'32 5:10:54
Kraussdale 39 2 40N25 75w31 5:02:04
Krayn 11 123 40N16'09 78w43'37 5:14:54
Kreamer 55 6 40N48'11 76w57'51 5:07:51
Krebs 17 1 40N59'06 78w24'26 5:13:38
Krebs 54 1 40N50'59 76w12'01 5:04:48
Kregar 26 6 40N07'17 79w18'22 5:17:13
Kreidersville 48
13 40N43'09 75w29'42 5:01:59
Kremis 43 59 41N20'50 80w18'42 5:21:15
Kresgeville 45 1 40N53'49 75w30'12 5:02:01
Kreutz Creek 67 1 40N00'14 76w37'07 5:06:28
Kricks Mill 6 1 40N24'47 76w10'11 5:04:41
Kricktown 6 101 40N18 76w00 5:04:00
Krings 56 74 40N16'28 78w54'16 5:15:37
Krocksville 39 13 40N34'23 75w34'09 5:02:17
Krumrine 14 9 40N48 77w52 5:11:28
Krumsville 39 1 40N34'43 75w47'51 5:03:11
Kuhl 25 107 42N05'31 79w57'51 5:19:51
Kuhnsville 39 13 40N35'32 75w35'21 5:02:21
Kuhntown 30 6 39N46'22 80w16'17 5:21:05
Kulp 19 4 40N53'53 76w21'03 5:05:24
Kulpmont 49 27 40N47'36 76w28'22 5:05:53
Kulps 49 27 40N47'34 76w36'33 5:06:26
Kulps Corner 9 8 40N22'55 75w13'12 5:00:53
Kulpsville 46 8 40N14'34 75w20'13 5:01:21
Kulptown 6 8 40N14'40 75w47'46 5:03:11
Kunkle 40 20 41N22'42 75w58'58 5:03:56
Kunkletown 45 9 40N50'52 75w26'55 5:01:48
Kushequa 42 75 41N44'54 78w37'19 5:14:29
Kutztown 6 8 40N31'02 75w46'40 5:03:07
Kutztown 38 25 40N23'55 76w19'20 5:05:17
Kylers Corners 24
36 41N19'15 78w38'21 5:14:33
Kylertown 17 6 40N59'36 78w10'03 5:12:40
Kyleville 67 1 39N49'07 76w23'15 5:05:33
Kyttle 40 6 41N18'40 76w11'18 5:04:45
La Anna 52 84 41N14'53 75w19'59 5:01:20
La Belle 26 51 40N00'28 79w58'45 5:19:55
Laboratory 63 3 40N09'18 80w12'49 5:20:51
La Bott 67 39 39N55'15 76w53'47 5:07:35
Lacey Park 9 1 40N11'10 75w05'20 5:00:21
Laceyville 66 59 41N38'45 76w09'42 5:04:39
Lack 34 6 40N22 77w41 5:10:44
Lackawannock 43 6 41N12 80w21 5:21:24
Lackawaxen 52 59 41N28'55 74w59'11 4:59:57
Laddsburg 8 60 41N34'29 76w25'03 5:05:40
Ladona 53 66 41N46 78w01 5:12:04
Lafayette 42 6 41N47'37 78w40'48 5:14:43
Lafayette Hill 46
90 40N06 75w16 5:01:04
Lafayette Park 46
90 40N05 75w16 5:01:04
Lafayetteville 5
6 40N12'06 78w27'14 5:13:49
Lafferty Hill 2
114 40N23 79w59 5:19:56
Laflin 40 1 41N17'20 75w48'21 5:03:13
La Gonda 63 3 40N11 80w16 5:21:04
Lahaska 9 8 40N20'47 75w01'55 5:00:08
Laidig 29 66 40N01'42 78w05'00 5:12:20
Laings Garden 9 9 40N08 74w51 4:59:24
Laird 3 6 40N50 79w38 5:18:32
Laird Crossing 3
6 40N52'13 79w37'59 5:18:32
Lairdsville 41 6 41N13'45 76w36'48 5:06:27
La Jose 17 122 40N50 78w41 5:14:44
Lake Ariel 64 59 41N27'14 75w22'59 5:01:32
Lake Carey 66 59 41N35'45 75w56'03 5:03:44
Lake City 24 59 41N21'53 78w53'09 5:15:33
Lake City 25 68 42N00'51 80w20'44 5:21:23
Lake Como 64 6 41N50'59 75w20'14 5:01:21

Lake Denise 65 3 40N14'10 79W42'00 5:18:48
Lake Harmony 13 94 41N03'38 75W35'29 5:02:22
Lake Lynn 26 7 39N44 79W52 5:19:28
Lakemont 7 33 40N28'22 78W23'19 5:13:33
Lakemont Terrace 7 33 40N31 78W25 5:13:40
Lake Naomi Estates 45 84 41N06'54 75W27'34 5:01:50
Lake Pleasant 25 58 41N54 79W51 5:19:24
Lake Run 26 51 39N43'41 79W51'39 5:19:27
Lake Sheridan 35 89 41N38 75W47 5:03:08
Lakeside 9 9 40N09'05 74W49'00 4:59:16
Lakeside 58 50 41N51'26 75W39'30 5:02:38
Laketon 40 6 41N21'56 76W03'29 5:04:14
Laketon Heights 2 114 40N27'50 79W51'19 5:19:25
Lakeview 58 59 41N51'50 75W37'05 5:02:28
Lakeview Heights 22 12 40N16 76W49 5:07:16
Lakeville 64 7 41N26'17 75W16'37 5:01:06
Lake Winola 66 6 41N30 75W50 5:03:20
Lakewood 25 107 42N05'31 80W10'26 5:20:42
Lakewood 64 6 41N51'07 75W22'54 5:01:32
Lamar 18 76 41N00'58 77W31'53 5:10:08
Lamartine 16 37 41N13'21 79W38'03 5:18:32
Lambert 26 51 39N54'48 79W52'20 5:19:29
Lamberton 26 51 39N54'49 79W52'45 5:19:31
Lambertsville 56 6 40N04'27 78W54'48 5:15:39
Lambs Creek 59 59 41N50'39 77W05'56 5:08:24
Lamokin Village 23 90 39N51 75W22 5:01:28
Lamonaville 27 6 41N28'12 79W01'36 5:16:06
Lamont 24 75 41N36'44 78W48'26 5:15:14
Lamonts Corners 43 117 41N15'25 80W27'05 5:21:48
Lamott 46 9 40N04'04 75W08'27 5:00:34
Lampeter 36 8 39N59'24 76W14'24 5:04:58
Lanark 39 13 40N33'06 75W25'59 5:01:44
Lancaster 36 8 40N02'16 76W18'21 5:05:13
Lancaster Junction 36 8 40N07'53 76W24'09 5:05:37
Lancasterville 46 9 40N07'05 75W14'54 5:01:00
Landenberg 15 8 39N46'38 75W46'18 5:03:05
Lander 62 6 41N58'01 79W14'18 5:16:57
Landingville 54 27 40N37'34 76W07'26 5:04:30
Landisburg 50 6 40N20'33 77W18'27 5:09:14
Landis Farms 36 8 40N04 76W19 5:05:16
Landis Store 6 2 40N25'35 75W39'40 5:02:39
Landis Valley 36 8 40N05'37 76W16'51 5:05:07
Landisville 9 8 40N20'57 75W06'49 5:00:27
Landisville 36 97 40N05'43 76W24'37 5:05:38
Landon Station 26 1 40N04'43 79W49'29 5:19:18
Landreth Manor 9 9 40N08 74W51 4:59:24
Landrus 59 6 41N38'32 77W12'23 5:08:50
Landstreet 56 6 40N11'29 78W54'38 5:15:39
Lane 3 2 40N41 79W41 5:18:44
Lanesboro 58 59 41N57'25 75W35'07 5:02:20
Lanes Mills 33 5 41N13'12 78W46'34 5:15:06
Laneville 3 2 40N40'46 79W41'27 5:18:46
Langdon 25 107 42N04'37 80W01'41 5:20:07
Langdon 40 1 41N19'10 75W43'32 5:02:54
Langdon 41 7 41N31 76W57 5:07:48
Langdondale 5 6 40N07'49 78W15'15 5:13:01
Langeloth 63 6 40N21'54 80W24'51 5:21:39
Langford Hills 23 9 39N58 75W22 5:01:28
Langhorne 9 97 40N10'28 74W55'23 4:59:42
Langhorne Gables 9 97 40N10 74W55 4:59:40
Langhorne Gardens 9 97 40N10'49 74W53'15 4:59:33
Langhorne Manor 9 97 40N10'01 74W55'05 4:59:40
Langhorne Terrace 9 97 40N10'18 74W56'59 4:59:48
Langville 33 6 41N02'08 79W10'36 5:16:42
Lansdale 46 8 40N14'29 75W17'03 5:01:08
Lansdowne 23 9 39N56'17 75W16'20 5:01:05
Lansdowne Park Gardens 23 9 39N55 75W16 5:01:04
Lanse 17 6 40N58'30 78W07'47 5:12:31
Lansford 13 80 40N49'54 75W52'58 5:03:32
Lantz 49 82 40N50'13 76W46'12 5:07:05
Lantz Corners 42 59 41N42'30 78W41'37 5:14:46
Lapark 36 9 40N01 76W08 5:04:32
Lapidea Hills 23 90 39N54 75W22 5:01:28
La Plume 35 44 41N33'24 75W45'15 5:03:01
Laporte 57 6 41N25'26 76W29'40 5:05:59
Laquin 8 60 41N37'56 76W39'04 5:06:36
Larabee 42 40 41N54'16 78W22'45 5:13:31
Larchmont 23 90 39N59'15 75W22'59 5:01:32
Larchmont Square 23 90 39N58'37 75W23'23 5:01:34
Lardintown 10 2 40N42'18 79W48'46 5:19:15
Large 2 8 40N18 79W54 5:19:36
Larimer 65 25 40N20'43 79W43'36 5:18:54
Larke 7 3 40N25'39 78W12'22 5:12:49
Larkin Knoll 23 90 39N50 75W25 5:01:40
Larkins Corner 23 90 39N50 75W25 5:01:40
Larksville 40 20 41N14'42 75W55'52 5:03:43
Larrys Creek 41 6 41N13'10 77W12'50 5:08:51
Larryville 41 6 41N14'23 77W13'03 5:08:52
Larue 67 3 39N49'13 76W45'38 5:07:03
Lashley 29 6 39N45'34 78W16'52 5:13:07
Lathrop 58 89 41N41 75W49 5:03:16
Latimore 1 1 40N02'44 77W07'17 5:08:29
La Trappe 9 97 40N07'49 74W58'46 4:59:55
Latrobe 65 3 40N19'16 79W22'47 5:17:31
Lattimer 40 42 40N59'38 75W57'42 5:03:51
Lattimer Mines 40 42 41N00 75W57 5:03:48
Laubach 19 6 41N15'38 76W22'45 5:05:31
Lauffer 65 111 40N09'00 79W35'15 5:18:21
Laughlin Corner 4 6 40N39 80W30 5:22:00
Laughlintown 65 110 40N12'43 79W11'53 5:16:48
Laurel 15 8 39N56'17 75W46'26 5:03:06
Laurel 21 1 40N00 77W12 5:08:48
Laurel 67 1 39N49'31 76W30'36 5:06:02
Laurel Bend 9 9 40N08 74W51 4:59:24
Laureldale 6 101 40N23'17 75W55'06 5:03:40
Laurel Falls 56 79 39N49'01 79W07'09 5:16:29
Laurel Gardens 2 114 40N31'39 80W01'31 5:20:06
Laurel Gardens 40 42 40N58 76W00 5:04:00
Laurel Grove 28 1 40N09'09 77W42'39 5:10:51
Laurel Hill 26 105 39N58'16 79W42'55 5:18:52
Laurel Hill 36 27 40N04'23 76W05'04 5:04:20
Laurel Hill 63 51 40N22'03 80W13'51 5:20:55
Laurel Junction 54 27 40N50'26 76W03'29 5:04:14
Laurella 64 22 41N35'37 75W12'34 5:00:50
Laurel Lake 58 6 41N57'25 75W55'07 5:03:40
Laurel Mountain Village 56 6 40N10'08 79W08'23 5:16:34
Laurel Park 60 6 40N52'14 77W10'43 5:08:43
Laurel Run 40 20 41N13'20 75W51'48 5:03:27
Laurel Summit 56 6 40N06'57 79W10'32 5:16:42
Laurelton 60 6 40N52'59 77W11'56 5:08:48
Laurelville 36 27 40N07 76W05 5:04:20
Laurelville 65 111 40N08'35 79W29'05 5:17:56
Laurys Station 39 8 40N43'23 76W31'50 5:06:07
Lausanne 13 60 40N58 75W49 5:03:16
Lavansville 56 6 40N00'57 79W09'13 5:16:37
Lavelle 54 27 40N45'48 76W22'59 5:05:32
Laverock 46 9 40N05'42 75W10'53 5:00:44
Lavery 25 7 41N52'48 80W13'33 5:20:54
Lawn 38 2 40N13'12 76W32'22 5:06:09
Lawndale 51 9 40N03'01 75W05'31 5:00:22
Lawnherst 46 12 40N41 75W14 5:00:56
Lawnton 22 12 40N15'30 76W48'15 5:07:13
Lawrence 63 114 40N18 80W07 5:20:28
Lawrence Corners 59 59 41N51'40 77W00'31 5:08:02
Lawrence Junction 37 112 40N58'04 80W22'41 5:21:31
Lawrence Park 23 9 39N58'05 75W20'30 5:01:22
Lawrence Park 25 107 42N09 80W01 5:20:04
Lawrenceville 2 114 40N28'03 79W57'39 5:19:51
Lawrenceville 35 1 41N21'21 75W44'53 5:03:00
Lawrenceville 59 59 41N59'51 77W07'35 5:08:30
Lawsonham 16 7 40N59'46 79W29'06 5:17:56
Lawson Heights 65 3 40N17'30 79W23'22 5:17:33
Lawsville Center 58 60 41N56'20 75W50'34 5:03:22
Lawton 58 6 41N47'09 76W04'16 5:04:17
Layfield 46 2 40N19'04 75W34'11 5:02:17
Layton 26 6 40N05'25 79W43'25 5:18:54
Leacock 36 27 40N05'08 76W12'31 5:04:50
Leaders Heights 67 67 39N54'23 76W43'09 5:06:53
Leaf Park 36 8 40N02 76W20 5:05:20
Leak Run 2 114 40N26'38 79W47'48 5:19:11
Leaman Place 36 9 40N00'26 76W07'00 5:04:28
Leamersville 7 33 40N22'06 78W25'38 5:13:43
Learn Settlement 32 6 40N41'16 78W56'55 5:15:48
Leasureville 10 2 40N44'49 79W42'14 5:18:49
Leather Corner Post 39 13 40N37'15 75W38'19 5:02:33
Leatherwood 16 6 41N01'48 79W23'29 5:17:34
Lebanon 38 8 40N20'27 76W24'42 5:05:39
Lebanon Church 2 114 40N22 79W54 5:19:36
Lebo 50 6 40N21 77W18 5:09:12
Le Boeuf 25 35 41N53 79W57 5:19:48
Le Boeuf Gardens 25 35 41N55'47 79W58'56 5:19:56
Lebo Vista 41 6 41N23'21 77W28'07 5:09:52
Leck Kill 49 1 40N43'00 76W37'49 5:06:31
Leckrone 26 51 39N51'41 79W52'13 5:19:29
Lecontes Mills 17 6 41N04'59 78W17'01 5:13:08
Lederach 46 8 40N15'42 75W24'23 5:01:38
Ledgedale 52 6 41N22'14 75W19'45 5:01:19
Ledy 28 7 39N51'28 77W32'35 5:10:10
Lee 40 1 41N09'13 76W05'06 5:04:20
Leechburg 2 4 40N30'16 79W45'49 5:19:03
Leechburg 3 4 40N37'37 79W36'21 5:18:25
Leechs Corners 43 59 41N25'53 80W20'04 5:21:20
Leedon Estates 23 9 39N53 75W20 5:01:20
Leedon Gardens 23 9 39N53 75W20 5:01:20
Lee Mine 40 21 41N12 76W00 5:04:00
Lee Park 40 20 41N13'52 75W54'54 5:03:40
Leeper 16 6 41N22'13 79W18'16 5:17:13
Leesburg 43 6 41N08'04 80W13'13 5:20:53
Leesburg Station 43 6 41N08'35 80W14'29 5:20:58
Lees Crossroads 21 82 40N04'11 77W26'32 5:09:46
Lees Mill 15 3 39N44'17 76W04'48 5:04:19
Leesport 6 80 40N26'49 75W58'00 5:03:52
Leet 2 13 40N35 80W12 5:20:48
Leetonia 59 6 41N35'59 77W29'44 5:09:59
Leetsdale 2 13 40N33'47 80W12'31 5:20:50
Lehigh 35 6 41N16'28 75W27'15 5:01:49
Lehigh Furnace 39 8 40N44'33 75W40'49 5:02:43
Lehigh Gap 39 8 40N46'36 75W36'31 5:02:26
Lehighton 13 80 40N50'01 75W42'51 5:02:51
Lehigh University 48 13 40N36 75W23 5:01:32
Lehigh Valley 39 13 40N38 75W23 5:01:32
Lehman 40 6 41N19'01 76W01'22 5:04:05
Lehman 67 95 39N51'52 76W51'31 5:07:26
Leibeyville 54 1 40N43'43 75W52'17 5:03:29
Leibharts Corner 67 2 39N59'28 76W29'54 5:06:00
Leidighs 21 12 40N08'40 77W05'29 5:08:22
Leidy 18 7 41N24'19 77W55'20 5:11:41
Leidytown 9 90 40N19'05 75W14'40 5:00:59
Leinbachs 6 101 40N23'33 75W59'41 5:03:59
Leiperville 23 90 39N52'01 75W20'27 5:01:22
Leiphart Mill 67 1 39N59'13 76W36'11 5:06:25
Leisenring 26 104 39N59'54 79W38'35 5:18:34
Leith 26 80 39N53'04 79W43'35 5:18:54
Leithsville 48 13 40N33'13 75W20'11 5:01:21
Lemasters 28 51 39N51'40 77W51'35 5:11:26
Lemon 66 59 41N36'58 75W56'34 5:03:46
Lemont 14 9 40N48'38 77W49'07 5:11:16
Lemont Furnace 26 80 39N54'50 79W40'10 5:18:41
Lemoyne 21 12 40N14'28 76W53'40 5:07:35
Lenape 15 13 39N54'46 75W37'55 5:02:32
Lenape Heights 3 15 40N46 79W31 5:18:04
Lenape Park 3 15 40N46 79W32 5:18:08
Lenhartsville 6 1 40N34'22 75W53'18 5:03:33
Lenker Manor 22 12 40N16 76W49 5:07:16
Lenkerville 22 1 40N32'02 76W57'34 5:07:50
Lenni 23 4 39N53'38 75W26'53 5:01:48
Lenni Heights 23 90 39N54 75W26 5:01:44
Lennox Park 23 90 39N52 75W23 5:01:32
Lenover 15 32 39N57'19 75W56'49 5:03:47
Lenox 58 89 41N42'42 75W40'24 5:02:42
Lenoxville 58 6 41N39'44 75W38'15 5:02:33
Leola 36 28 40N05'16 76W11'07 5:04:44
Leolyn 41 7 41N35'12 76W53'13 5:07:33
Leona 8 52 41N49'18 76W44'44 5:06:59
Leonard 17 1 41N02 78W27 5:13:48
Leonardsville 13 94 41N04'31 75W41'33 5:02:46
Leopard 15 90 40N01'14 75W27'09 5:01:49
Leopard Lakes 15 90 40N03 75W26 5:01:44
LeRaysville 8 6 41N50'19 76W10'50 5:04:43
Lerchs 48 13 40N41'59 75W25'03 5:01:40
Lernerville 10 2 40N44'17 79W45'45 5:19:03
Leroy 8 7 41N40'33 76W42'27 5:06:50
Leslie Run 13 60 40N59'46 75W43'40 5:02:55
Lester 23 9 39N52'15 75W16'59 5:01:08
Letort 36 26 39N58'34 76W24'24 5:05:38
Letterkenny 28 1 40N04 77W41 5:10:44
Letterkenny Army Depot 28 42 39N56 77W40 5:10:40
Level Corner 41 64 41N12'07 77W11'18 5:08:45
Level Green 65 25 40N23'36 79W43'14 5:18:53
Levittown 9 9 40N09'18 74W49'45 4:59:19
Lewisberry 67 12 40N08'06 76W51'36 5:07:26
Lewisburg 60 70 40N57'52 76W53'05 5:07:32
Lewis Corner 53 6 41N54'03 77W55'44 5:11:43
Lewis Corners 58 59 41N53'45 75W39'48 5:02:39
Lewis Crossing 26 51 39N52'03 79W52'10 5:19:29
Lewis Mills 15 27 40N05'57 75W49'44 5:03:19
Lewis Run 42 6 41N52'15 78W39'42 5:14:39
Lewistown 44 73 40N35'57 77W34'18 5:10:17
Lewistown 54 27 40N43'57 76W01'42 5:04:07
Lewistown Junction 44 73 40N35'25 77W34'40 5:10:19
Lewisville 15 1 39N43'21 75W52'31 5:03:30
Lewisville 32 6 40N30'38 79W19'17 5:17:17
Lewisville 53 6 41N54 77W46 5:11:04
Lexington 36 8 40N11'18 76W18'00 5:05:12
Liberty 2 10 40N19'31 79W51'23 5:19:26
Liberty 26 104 40N02'33 79W39'39 5:18:39
Liberty 42 6 41N42'33 78W12'59 5:12:52
Liberty 59 6 41N33'30 77W06'18 5:08:25
Liberty Corners 8 41 41N46 76W27 5:05:48
Liberty Square 36 1 39N48 76W15 5:05:00
Library 2 114 40N17'23 80W00'36 5:20:02
Library Junction 63 114 40N17'15 80W03'16 5:20:13
Lickdale 38 1 40N27'00 76W30'44 5:06:03
Licking 16 6 41N08 79W33 5:18:12
Licking Creek 29 66 39N59 78W05 5:12:20
Lickingville 16 6 41N22'40 79W22'07 5:17:28
Liewellyn Corners 40 20 41N13'59 75W48'05 5:03:12
Lightner 67 67 39N58 76W47 5:07:08
Light Street 19 4 41N02'10 76W25'26 5:05:42
Ligonier 65 110 40N14'35 79W14'16 5:16:57
Lilly 11 55 40N25'33 78W37'13 5:14:29
Lillyville 4 121 40N50'39 80W14'12 5:20:57
Lima 23 4 39N55'02 75W26'27 5:01:46
Lime Bluff 41 83 41N13'46 76W45'39 5:07:03
Limehill 8 6 41N43'29 76W17'08 5:05:09
Limekiln 6 8 40N21 75W48 5:03:12
Limeport 39 13 40N30'32 75W26'51 5:01:47
Limerick 46 8 40N13'51 75W31'21 5:02:05
Limerick Center 46 8 40N14'11 75W32'12 5:02:09
Lime Ridge 19 4 41N01'40 76W20'23 5:05:22
Limerock 36 8 40N09'32 76W20'27 5:05:22
Limestone 16 37 41N07'43 79W19'38 5:17:19
Limestoneville 47 70 41N02'21 76W44'53 5:07:00
Lime Valley 36 8 39N57'47 76W13'49 5:04:55
Limeville 36 23 40N00'07 75W58'50 5:03:55
Lincoln 2 8 40N17 79W50 5:19:20

Lincoln 36 30 40N11'47 76w12'05 5:04:48
Lincoln Acres 65 25 40N20 79w43 5:18:52
Lincoln Colliery 54 9 40N36 76w23 5:05:32
Lincoln Falls 57 6 41N31'01 76w39'46 5:06:39
Lincoln Heights 6 8 40N16 75w48 5:03:12
Lincoln Heights 65 3 40N18'26 79w37'02 5:18:28
Lincoln Hill 63 3 40N09'13 80w17'34 5:21:10
Lincoln Park 2 114 40N28 79w50 5:19:20
Lincoln Park 6 101 40N18'53 75w59'09 5:03:57
Lincoln Park 23 9 39N54 75w17 5:01:08
Lincoln Terrace 48 12 40N41'30 75w15'24 5:01:02
Lincoln University 15 3 39N48'01 75w55'22 5:03:41
Lincolnville 20 7 41N47'37 79w50'18 5:19:21
Lincolnway 67 67 39N58 76w47 5:07:08
Linconia 9 97 40N07'32 74w58'58 4:59:56
Lindaville 58 89 41N43'40 75w48'53 5:03:16
Lindbergh 40 20 41N06'38 75w56'39 5:03:47
Lindberg Heights 46 8 40N13'42 75w31'54 5:02:08
Lindberg Terrace 46 118 40N11 75w33 5:02:12
Linden 41 64 41N13'51 77w08'23 5:08:34
Linden 63 2 40N13'41 80w08'28 5:20:34
Linden Grove 2 114 40N22'02 80w00'55 5:20:04
Linden Hall 14 64 40N47'49 77w45'40 5:11:03
Linds Crossing 7 33 40N26'31 78w19'19 5:13:17
Lindsey 33 51 40N56 78w58 5:15:52
Line Lexington 9 8 40N17'21 75w15'41 5:01:03
Line Mountain 49 6 40N42'45 76w33'27 5:06:14
Linesville 20 7 41N39'22 80w25'27 5:21:42
Linfield 46 8 40N12'36 75w34'13 5:02:17
Linglestown 22 12 40N20'02 76w47'22 5:07:09
Linhart 2 114 40N25'21 79w48'53 5:19:16
Linn 26 51 40N01'34 79w51'26 5:19:26
Linntown 60 70 40N57'32 76w53'58 5:07:36
Linville Circle 36 8 40N01'50 76w15'55 5:05:04
Linwood 23 90 39N49'35 75w25'33 5:01:42
Linwood Terrace 23 90 39N50 75w25 5:01:40
Lionville 15 13 40N03'13 75w39'37 5:02:38
Lippincott 30 1 39N56'20 80w07'09 5:20:29
Lisbon 61 1 41N11'50 79w47'40 5:19:11
Lisburn 21 12 40N10'04 76w54'38 5:07:39
Listie 56 6 40N01'41 79w00'49 5:16:03
Listonburg 56 53 39N45'17 79w18'52 5:17:15
Litchfield 8 6 41N58'03 76w25'50 5:05:43
Lithia Spring 49 82 40N55'15 76w45'49 5:07:03
Lithia Springs 49 82 40N54 76w48 5:07:12
Lithia Valley 66 44 41N34 75w47 5:03:08
Lititz 36 8 40N09'26 76w18'26 5:05:14
Little Beaver 37 6 40N53 80w28 5:21:52
Little Britain 36 1 39N46'44 76w07'01 5:04:28
Little Chapel 64 6 41N25'08 75w22'10 5:01:29
Little Chicago 30 51 39N51'36 79w57'39 5:19:51
Little Cooley 20 7 41N44'26 79w53'39 5:19:35
Little Corners 20 77 41N40 80w07 5:20:28
Little Gap 13 9 40N49'58 75w31'22 5:02:05
Little Germany 50 6 40N23'02 77w15'55 5:09:04
Little Hickory 27 6 41N32'27 79w23'52 5:17:35
Little Hope 25 91 42N05'56 79w49'09 5:19:17
Little Italy 9 1 40N16'05 75w01'27 5:00:06
Little Jack Corners 5 6 40N09'28 78w21'23 5:13:26
Little Kansas 44 7 40N29'16 77w48'40 5:11:15
Little Mahanoy 49 6 40N46 76w46 5:07:04
Little Marsh 59 6 41N52'36 77w24'06 5:09:36
Little Meadows 58 6 41N59'26 76w07'52 5:04:31
Little Roundtop 34 7 40N39'08 77w21'27 5:09:26
Littles Corners 20 77 41N42'47 80w13'56 5:20:56
Littlestown 1 56 39N44'40 77w05'18 5:08:21
Little Summit 26 105 39N59'23 79w40'17 5:18:41
Little Summit 45 84 41N05'57 75w24'47 5:01:39
Little Summit 63 51 40N07'02 80w06'41 5:20:27
Littletown 32 6 40N31'13 79w01'34 5:16:06
Little Washington 15 46 40N02'53 75w47'07 5:03:08
Little Washington 21 1 40N10 77w24 5:09:36
Live Easy 30 51 39N51'47 79w56'14 5:19:45
Liverpool 50 1 40N34'29 76w59'22 5:07:57
Livonia 14 6 40N58'50 77w17'31 5:09:10
Lizard Creek Junction 13 8 40N47'34 75w39'38 5:02:39
Llandrilla 46 9 40N01 75w15 5:01:00
Llanerch 23 9 39N58'17 75w17'58 5:01:12
Llanerch Manor 23 9 40N00 75w18 5:01:12
Llanfair 11 63 40N17'08 78w43'24 5:14:54
Llangelan Hills 23 90 40N00 75w23 5:01:32

Llewellyn 54 27 40N40'22 76w16'46 5:05:07
Lloydell 11 63 40N18'51 78w41'31 5:14:46
Lloydsville 65 3 40N18'38 79w24'04 5:17:36
Lloydville 11 63 40N40'12 78w24'24 5:13:38
Llyswen 7 33 40N28'42 78w24'12 5:13:37
Loag 15 27 40N07'44 75w48'48 5:03:15
Lobachsville 6 101 40N24'34 75w44'07 5:02:56
Lochiel 60 70 40N56'54 76w57'17 5:07:49
Lochland 39 8 40N41'51 75w44'07 5:02:56
Loch Lomond Junction 14 113 40N54'58 78w11'51 5:12:47
Lochvale 32 6 40N51'54 78w50'57 5:15:24
Locke Mills 44 7 40N42'38 77w31'25 5:10:06
Lock Haven 18 76 41N08'13 77w26'50 5:09:47
Lock No 4 63 1 40N08 79w54 5:19:36
Lockport 18 76 41N08'27 77w26'28 5:09:46
Lockport 44 73 40N32'35 77w39'33 5:10:38
Lockport 48 8 40N44'12 75w34'27 5:02:18
Lockport 65 7 40N23'30 79w07'20 5:16:29
Locksley 23 4 39N55'47 75w30'26 5:02:02
Lockview 63 1 40N09'26 79w54'36 5:19:38
Lockville 66 20 41N25'01 75w52'41 5:03:31
Lockwood 12 106 41N31'44 78w16'28 5:13:06
Locust 19 27 40N53 76w23 5:05:32
Locust 32 6 40N51'23 78w58'22 5:15:53
Locustdale 19 27 40N46'38 76w22'35 5:05:30
Locust Gap 49 27 40N46'18 76w26'30 5:05:46
Locust Grove 14 64 40N49'09 77w34'53 5:10:20
Locust Grove 15 13 39N57 75w36 5:02:24
Locust Grove 36 67 40N04'48 76w39'34 5:06:38
Locust Grove 55 6 40N40'28 76w56'51 5:07:47
Locust Hill 26 7 39N45'16 79w52'10 5:19:29
Locust Lakes Village 45 1 41N08'43 75w32'40 5:02:11
Locust Point 21 12 40N11'50 77w03'51 5:08:15
Locust Ridge 2 114 40N30 79w59 5:19:56
Locust Run 34 6 40N33'17 77w16'23 5:09:06
Locust Spring 67 1 39N56'00 76w34'30 5:06:18
Locust Summit 49 27 40N46'19 76w24'15 5:05:37
Locust Valley 39 13 40N29'44 75w24'28 5:01:38
Locust Valley 54 6 41N48'16 76w03'43 5:04:15
Lodi 54 1 40N33'05 75w05'04 5:00:20
Lofty 54 42 40N52'06 76w01'48 5:04:07
Logan 7 33 40N30 78w24 5:13:36
Logan 32 6 40N49'00 78w52'04 5:15:28
Logan 51 9 40N01'42 75w09'07 5:00:36
Logan Mills 18 7 41N00'24 77w22'59 5:09:32
Logans Ferry 2 14 40N34 79w45 5:19:00
Logans Ferry Heights 2 14 40N32'43 79w45'17 5:19:01
Logansport 3 15 40N46 79w32 5:18:08
Loganton 18 7 41N02'03 77w18'25 5:09:14
Loganville 67 3 39N51'20 76w42'28 5:06:50
Log Pile 63 3 40N09'47 80w17'34 5:21:10
Logue 53 6 41N33'32 77w57'01 5:11:48
Loleta 24 6 41N23'56 79w04'47 5:16:19
London 43 6 41N08'37 80w08'56 5:20:36
London Britain 15 1 39N45 75w47 5:03:08
London Grove 15 8 39N50 75w49 5:03:16
Lonely Acres 11 63 40N33'03 78w41'35 5:14:46
Lone Pine 63 3 40N04'27 80w10'21 5:20:41
Long Acre Park 23 9 39N56 75w16 5:01:04
Long Branch 63 115 40N06'13 79w52'10 5:19:29
Longbridge 65 110 40N16'09 79w17'45 5:17:11
Long Brook 57 6 41N22'15 76w29'08 5:05:57
Longfellow 44 73 40N30'16 77w40'26 5:10:42
Longlevel 67 26 40N01 76w32 5:06:08
Longmead Farms 51 9 40N05'11 74w58'20 4:59:53
Long Pond 45 84 41N03'12 75w27'48 5:01:51
Long Run 11 92 40N39'41 78w49'18 5:15:17
Long Run 13 8 40N51'20 75w42'01 5:02:48
Longs Crossroad 11 63 40N40'04 78w34'36 5:14:18
Longsdale 6 13 40N29'14 75w40'16 5:02:41
Longsdorf 21 1 40N06'07 77w20'24 5:09:22
Longstown 67 67 39N59 76w46 5:07:04
Longswamp 6 9 40N29'53 75w39'19 5:02:37
Long Valley 8 60 41N38'59 76w34'06 5:06:16
Longview 2 114 40N20'52 80w00'54 5:20:04
Longwood 15 8 39N52'03 75w40'15 5:02:41
Lookabough Corners 3 4 40N39'51 79w36'15 5:18:25
Lookout 64 6 41N47 75w11 5:00:44
Loomis Park 40 20 41N12'14 75w58'13 5:03:53
Loop 7 33 40N25'19 78w21'43 5:13:27
Loop 32 6 40N53'59 79w09'57 5:16:40
Loop Station 7 33 40N25 78w24 5:13:36
Lopez 57 6 41N27'28 76w20'02 5:05:20
Lorain 11 74 40N17'56 78w53'33 5:15:34
Lorane 6 101 40N17'18 75w51'18 5:03:25
Lorberry 54 9 40N36'06 76w26'43 5:05:47
Lorberry Junction 54 27 40N35'19 76w24'47 5:05:39
Lords Valley 52 6 41N22'03 75w03'46 5:00:15
Lorenton 59 6 41N32'40 77w17'09 5:09:09
Loretto 11 55 40N30'11 78w37'50 5:14:31
Loretto Road 11 55 40N30'32 78w39'19 5:14:37
Loschs 34 1 40N38'40 77w08'45 5:08:35
Losh Run 50 51 40N27'18 77w01'55 5:08:08
Lost Creek 54 27 40N48'23 76w14'50 5:04:59
Lottsville 62 6 41N57'06 79w26'01 5:17:44
Loucks Mills 53 6 41N50'42 77w42'05 5:10:48
Louden Hill 58 60 41N46'18 75w53'55 5:03:36
Loux Corner 9 8 40N20'49 75w13'26 5:00:54
Louxs Corner 9 13 40N27'48 75w18'40 5:01:15
Lovedale 2 8 40N16'39 79w52'05 5:19:28
Lovejoy 32 6 40N42'26 78w57'30 5:15:50

Lovell 25 3 41N54'22 79w42'09 5:18:49
Lovelton 66 59 41N32'21 76w11'19 5:04:45
Lovely 5 6 40N12'34 78w36'19 5:14:25
Lover 63 1 40N06'45 79w57'02 5:19:48
Lovi 4 6 40N40'48 80w09'17 5:20:37
Lowber 26 1 40N04'09 79w50'10 5:19:21
Lowber 65 61 40N14'45 79w46'16 5:19:05
Lowell 55 1 40N43'48 77w17'46 5:09:11
Lower 13 8 40N49 75w34 5:02:16
Lower Allen 21 12 40N13 76w56 5:07:44
Lower Alsace 6 101 40N20 75w53 5:03:32
Lower Askam 40 20 41N11'39 75w58'16 5:03:53
Lower Augusta 49 82 40N48 76w48 5:07:12
Lower Brownville 54 27 40N49'03 76w13'03 5:04:52
Lower Burrell 65 14 40N33'11 79w45'27 5:19:02
Lower Chanceford 67 1 39N49 76w23 5:05:32
Lower Chichester 23 90 39N50 75w25 5:01:40
Lower Dutchtown 11 55 40N25'02 78w37'46 5:14:31
Lower Frankford 21 1 40N14 77w18 5:09:12
Lower Frederick 46 8 40N17 75w29 5:01:56
Lower Gwynedd 46 8 40N11 75w14 5:00:56
Lower Heidelberg 6 101 40N21 76w03 5:04:12
Lower Hopewell 15 3 39N47'03 76w01'20 5:04:05
Lower Longswamp 6 9 40N29'27 75w38'42 5:02:35
Lower Macungie 39 13 40N33 75w34 5:02:16
Lower Mahanoy 49 51 40N40 76w53 5:07:32
Lower Makefield 9 9 40N14 74w50 4:59:20
Lower Merion 46 90 40N02 75w18 5:01:12
Lower Mifflin 21 1 40N14 77w26 5:09:44
Lower Milford 39 13 40N28 75w28 5:01:52
Lower Moreland 46 1 40N08 75w03 5:00:12
Lower Mount Bethel 46 15 40N48 75w10 5:00:40
Lower Nazareth 48 8 40N43 75w20 5:01:20
Lower Orchard 9 9 40N09 74w51 4:59:24
Lower Oxford 15 3 39N48 75w59 5:03:56
Lower Paxton 22 12 40N19 76w48 5:07:12
Lower Peanut 26 6 39N58'28 79w45'46 5:19:03
Lower Pottsgrove 46 8 40N16 75w36 5:02:24
Lower Providence 46 90 40N08 75w26 5:01:44
Lower Sagon 49 6 40N53 76w41 5:06:44
Lower Salford 46 8 40N16 75w24 5:01:36
Lower Saucon 48 13 40N36'22 75w16'58 5:01:08
Lower Southampton 9 1 40N09 74w59 4:59:56
Lower Swatara 22 80 40N13 76w46 5:07:04
Lower Tannersville 45 84 41N01'54 75w18'01 5:01:12
Lower Turkeyfoot 56 53 39N52 79w21 5:17:24
Lower Tyrone 26 104 40N04 79w39 5:18:36
Lower Whyel 65 4 40N13'25 79w40'56 5:18:44
Lower Windsor 67 2 39N58 76w32 5:06:08
Lower Yoder 11 74 40N20 78w57 5:15:48
Lowhill 39 1 40N39 75w39 5:02:36
Lowhill 63 114 40N00'36 79w57'04 5:19:48
Lowville 25 7 42N01'29 79w49'18 5:19:17
Loyalhanna 65 116 40N19'21 79w21'45 5:17:27
Loyalhanna Woodlands Number 65 3 40N27'04 79w26'29 5:17:46
Loyalsockville 41 82 41N19'15 76w54'35 5:07:38
Loyalton 22 1 40N34'08 76w45'43 5:07:03
Loyalville 40 20 41N20'10 76w05'58 5:04:24
Loysburg 5 6 40N09'39 78w22'31 5:13:30
Loysburg Gap 5 6 40N09'35 78w21'58 5:13:28
Loysville 50 6 40N21'56 77w20'23 5:09:23
Lucerne Mines 32 71 40N33'32 79w09'05 5:16:36
Lucesco 65 4 40N38 79w37 5:18:28
Luces Corners 20 6 41N36'58 79w50'00 5:19:20
Lucinda 16 6 41N18'30 79w22'12 5:17:29
Luciusboro 32 71 40N30'38 79w07'21 5:16:29
Lucket 11 55 40N27'49 78w37'12 5:14:29
Lucknow 22 12 40N19'39 76w53'10 5:07:33
Lucky 67 1 39N54'13 76w26'45 5:05:47
Lucon 46 2 40N14'06 75w24'58 5:01:40
Lucullus 41 6 41N22'08 77w32'25 5:10:10
Lucy Crossing 46 12 40N41 75w14 5:00:56
Lucy Furnace 44 85 40N23'36 77w53'10 5:11:33
Ludlow 42 3 41N43'42 78w56'37 5:15:46
Ludwigs Corner 15 80 40N06'56 75w41'38 5:02:47
Luke Fidler 49 27 40N48 76w33 5:06:12
Lumber 12 7 41N27 78w11 5:12:44
Lumber City 17 7 40N55'27 78w34'31 5:14:18
Lumber City 44 73 40N39'37 77w36'04 5:10:24
Lumberville 9 1 40N24'24 75w02'18 5:00:09
Lundys Lane 25 7 41N53'33 80w20'21 5:21:21
Lungerville 41 6 41N16'39 76w30'44 5:06:03
Lurgan 28 56 40N05'38 77w37'53 5:10:32

Lushbaugh 12 6 41N25'23 78w01'54 5:12:08
Luthersburg 17 56 41N03'12 78w43'10 5:14:53
Luthers Mills 8 41 41N46'56 76w34'00 5:06:16
Lutztown 21 16 40N12 77w11 5:08:44
Lutzville 5 6 40N00'29 78w26'09 5:13:45
Luxor 65 3 40N20'03 79w28'42 5:17:55
Luzerne 26 51 39N59'57 79w57'47 5:19:51
Luzerne 40 20 41N17'08 75w54'05 5:03:36
Lycippus 65 3 40N13'44 79w25'45 5:17:43
Lycoming 41 7 41N18 77w06 5:08:24
Lykens 22 1 40N34'00 76w42'03 5:06:48
Lyleville 17 54 40N44'21 78w32'25 5:14:10
Lymanville 58 60 41N38'55 75w57'12 5:03:49
Lymehurst 41 82 41N14'49 76w57'09 5:07:49
Lynces Junction 20 6 41N37'27 80w19'50 5:21:19
Lynch 27 6 41N36'08 79w03'02 5:16:12
Lynchville 24 36 41N26'14 78w33'49 5:14:15
Lyndell 15 80 40N03'34 75w44'42 5:02:59
Lyndon 36 8 40N00'22 76w17'48 5:05:11
Lyndora 10 3 40N51'08 79w55'38 5:19:43
Lynn 39 1 40N40 75w47 5:03:08
Lynn 58 60 41N39'52 75w56'17 5:03:45
Lynnewood Gardens 46 9 40N05 75w07 5:00:28
Lynnport 39 1 40N40'31 75w48'19 5:03:13
Lynnville 39 1 40N38'49 75w45'07 5:03:00
Lynnwood 26 1 40N07'27 79w50'37 5:19:22
Lynnwood 40 20 41N14'05 75w55'55 5:03:44
Lynnwood Park 23 9 40N00 75w18 5:01:12
Lynoak 6 101 40N19 75w57 5:03:48
Lynwood 6 101 40N19 75w57 5:03:48
Lyona 20 6 41N41'36 79w58'06 5:19:52
Lyons 6 8 40N28'55 75w45'29 5:03:02
Lyons Run Mine 65 25 40N22 79w44 5:18:56
Lyon Station 6 8 40N29 75w45 5:03:00
Lyonstown 14 70 40N56'15 77w44'34 5:10:58
Lyon Valley 39 1 40N37'44 75w40'14 5:02:41
Mabel 54 27 40N42'36 76w25'29 5:05:42
Mable 54 27 40N47 76w21 5:05:24
Mable Hill 30 7 39N46'29 79w56'19 5:19:45
Mac 8 60 41N48'27 76w35'00 5:06:20
Macada 48 13 40N39'24 75w21'21 5:01:25
MacArthur 4 13 40N37 80w16 5:21:04
Macdonaldton 56 6 39N54'58 78w55'14 5:15:41
Macedonia 8 41 41N45'37 76w23'15 5:05:33
Macedonia 34 7 40N36'41 77w26'36 5:09:46
Mackeyville 18 76 41N03'16 77w27'42 5:09:51
Macungie 39 13 40N30'57 75w33'20 5:02:13
Maddensville 31 6 40N07'36 77w57'30 5:11:50
Madera 17 6 40N49'42 78w26'07 5:13:44
Madge 24 75 41N40 78w49 5:15:16
Madison 65 3 40N14'50 79w40'39 5:18:43
Madisonburg 14 64 40N55'34 77w31'03 5:10:04
Madisonville 35 4 41N21'31 75w28'32 5:01:54
Madley 5 6 39N53'53 78w40'24 5:14:42
Magee 62 6 41N42'06 79w21'23 5:17:26
Magill Heights 2 114 40N37'15 79w51'38 5:19:27
Magnolia Gardens 9 9 40N08 74w51 4:59:24
Magnolia Hill 9 9 40N09'50 74w50'05 4:59:20
Mahaffey 17 6 40N52'22 78w43'28 5:14:54
Mahanoy City 54 3 40N48'45 76w08'31 5:04:34
Mahanoy Plane 54 3 40N47'40 76w14'32 5:04:58
Mahantango 55 6 40N38'56 76w56'34 5:07:46
Mahoning 3 64 40N55'57 79w27'34 5:17:50
Mahoning 26 105 39N58'24 79w37'29 5:18:30
Mahoningtown 37 112 40N58'28 80w22'21 5:21:29
Maiden Creek 6 80 40N26'53 75w53'55 5:03:36
Main 19 4 40N59 76w23 5:05:32
Mainesburg 59 59 41N47'02 76w59'55 5:08:00
Mainland 46 8 40N15'21 75w21'38 5:01:27
Mainsville 28 82 40N00'54 77w30'54 5:10:04
Mainville 19 4 40N58'33 76w22'29 5:05:30
Maitland 44 73 40N37'50 77w30'11 5:10:01
Maizeville 54 27 40N47'53 76w13'21 5:04:53
Majeriks Corners 25 35 41N56 79w59 5:19:56
Makefield Village 9 9 40N12 74w49 4:59:16
Malden Place 63 51 40N02'15 79w55'51 5:19:43
Malta 49 6 40N37'04 76w54'34 5:07:38
Maltby 40 20 41N16 75w54 5:03:36
Malvern 15 8 40N02'10 75w30'51 5:02:03
Mammoth 65 111 40N12'03 79w27'48 5:17:51
Mamont 65 6 40N28'55 79w35'26 5:18:22
Manada Gap 22 12 40N23'50 76w42'37 5:06:50
Manadahill 22 1 40N21'08 76w42'54 5:06:52
Manatawny 6 101 40N23'01 75w43'59 5:02:56
Manayunk 51 9 40N01'28 75w12'52 5:00:51
Mance 56 79 39N49'54 78w56'13 5:15:45
Manchester 2 114 40N27'18 80w01'12 5:20:05
Manchester 67 35 40N03'47 76w43'07 5:06:52
Manchester Beach 25 107 42N04'38 80w14'14 5:20:57
Mandata 49 51 40N41'00 76w49'37 5:07:18
Manhattan 59 6 41N44'49 77w32'18 5:10:09
Manheim 36 2 40N09'48 76w23'43 5:05:35
Manifold 63 2 40N11'42 80w13'08 5:20:53
Manito 65 3 40N16'21 79w23'55 5:17:36
Manitto Haven 65 3 40N25'26 79w25'56 5:17:44
Mann 5 6 39N46 78w24 5:13:36
Mannitto Haven 65 3 40N24 79w25 5:17:40
Manns Choice 5 6 40N00'09 78w35'29 5:14:22
Mannsville 50 1 40N25'33 77w16'02 5:09:04
Manoa 23 9 39N58'35 75w19'06 5:01:16
Manoa Heights 23 9 40N00 75w18 5:01:12
Manor 32 6 40N37'57 78w59'02 5:15:56
Manor 65 25 40N20'02 79w40'13 5:18:41
Manor Heights 3 15 40N45'05 79w31'48 5:18:07
Manor Hill 31 81 40N37'07 77w55'16 5:11:41
Manor Park Terrace 3 15 40N46 79w32 5:18:08
Manor Ridge 36 8 40N02'17 76w21'59 5:05:28
Manorville 3 15 40N47'14 79w31'12 5:18:05
Manown 2 1 40N11'52 79w54'16 5:19:37
Mansfield 59 59 41N48'26 77w04'40 5:08:19
Mansville 65 6 40N10'39 79w19'32 5:17:18
Mantz 54 1 40N43'56 75w49'48 5:03:19
Mantzville 54 1 40N46'04 75w52'13 5:03:29
Maple Beach 9 9 40N05'10 74w52'09 4:59:29
Maple Crest 15 47 40N03 75w33 5:02:12
Mapledale 61 109 41N23'03 79w51'40 5:19:27
Maple Glen 46 1 40N10'45 75w10'51 5:00:43
Maple Glen 63 51 40N00'56 79w58'37 5:19:54
Maple Grove 6 13 40N29'28 75w36'56 5:02:28
Maple Grove 15 3 39N46'08 75w56'20 5:03:45
Maple Grove 16 7 41N01'48 79w30'42 5:18:03
Maple Grove 19 56 41N10'39 76w23'06 5:05:32
Maple Grove 26 6 40N03'43 79w22'12 5:17:29
Maple Grove 64 6 41N56'43 75w25'13 5:01:41
Maple Grove Park 6 101 40N18 75w59 5:03:56
Maple Hill 41 82 41N10'29 76w57'08 5:07:49
Maple Hill 54 27 40N48'50 76w10'40 5:04:43
Maple Hill 59 6 41N41'24 77w09'58 5:08:40
Maple Lake 35 4 41N19'34 75w34'25 5:02:18
Maple Manor 40 42 40N58 76w00 5:04:00
Maple Point 9 97 40N12'02 74w54'03 4:59:36
Maple Ridge 56 6 40N12'39 78w54'49 5:15:39
Maple Shade 9 9 40N06'00 74w53'44 4:59:35
Maple Shade 61 1 41N19'58 79w40'33 5:18:42
Maple Summit 57 6 41N33'34 76w46'35 5:07:06
Mapleton 31 85 40N23'37 77w56'29 5:11:46
Mapleton Depot 31 85 40N24 77w56 5:11:44
Mapletown 30 51 39N48'16 79w56'38 5:19:47
Maplewood 9 8 40N21 75w13 5:00:52
Maplewood 64 6 41N25'54 75w26'13 5:01:45
Maplewood Heights 40 20 41N20'20 75w56'21 5:03:45
Maplewood Park 23 9 39N56 75w18 5:01:12
Maplewood Terrace 65 99 40N16'58 79w31'52 5:18:07
Marble 16 6 41N20'20 79w26'18 5:17:45
Marble City 5 6 40N08'48 78w18'21 5:13:13
Marble Hall 46 90 40N05'29 75w15'06 5:01:00
Marburg 67 95 39N47'05 76w53'10 5:07:33
Marchand 32 6 40N51'27 79w01'23 5:16:06
Marcus Hook 23 90 39N49'09 75w25'08 5:01:41
Marcy 66 59 41N34'24 75w55'03 5:03:40
Marengo 14 6 40N43'52 78w01'53 5:12:08
Margaret 3 15 40N46'49 79w22'17 5:17:29
Margaretta Furnace 67 1 39N57'55 76w32'13 5:06:09
Margo Gardens 9 9 40N07'13 74w52'09 4:59:29
Marguerite 65 3 40N15'49 79w27'49 5:17:51
Maria 5 51 40N13'04 78w24'26 5:13:38
Maria Furnace 1 1 39N46'30 77w24'19 5:09:37
Marianna 63 7 40N01'29 80w06'01 5:20:24
Mariasville 61 1 41N12'32 79w39'39 5:18:39
Marienville 27 6 41N28'08 79w07'24 5:16:30
Marietta 36 26 40N03'25 76w33'09 5:06:13
Marion 28 42 39N51'26 77w41'44 5:10:47
Marion Center 32 6 40N46'12 79w03'01 5:16:12
Marion Heights 49 27 40N48'15 76w27'55 5:05:52
Marion Hill 4 8 40N43'49 80w17'46 5:21:11
Mark Acres 65 25 40N20 79w43 5:18:52
Markelsville 50 1 40N27'56 77w13'56 5:08:56
Markes 28 51 39N52'28 77w52'19 5:11:29
Market Square 51 9 40N04 75w12 5:00:48
Markham 23 4 39N53'27 75w30'22 5:02:01
Markle 65 4 40N34'21 79w38'38 5:18:35
Marklesburg 31 3 40N22'59 78w10'24 5:12:42
Markleton 56 4 39N51'38 79w13'38 5:16:55
Markleysburg 26 6 39N43'59 79w27'11 5:17:49
Markton 33 51 41N00'38 79w03'52 5:16:15
Markvue Manor 65 25 40N20 79w43 5:18:52
Marlboro 15 8 39N53'44 75w42'16 5:02:49
Marlborough 46 2 40N22 75w27 5:01:48
MarLin 54 27 40N40'42 76w14'44 5:04:59
Marple 23 9 39N58'39 75w22'44 5:01:31
Marple Gardens 23 9 39N58 75w22 5:01:28
Marple Heights 23 9 39N58 75w22 5:01:28
Marple Summit Estates 23 9 39N58 75w22 5:01:28
Marple Woods 23 9 39N58 75w22 5:01:28
Marron 17 7 40N51'42 78w37'10 5:14:29
Mars 10 3 40N41'45 80w00'43 5:20:03
Marsh 15 1 40N09 75w50 5:03:20
Marsh 28 100 39N45 77w34 5:10:16
Marshall 2 6 40N39 80w06 5:20:24
Marshall Heights 32 98 40N27'51 79w11'36 5:16:46
Marshall Hollow 40 1 41N13'19 76w16'25 5:05:06
Marshalls Creek 45 85 41N02'35 75w07'40 5:00:31
Marshall Terrace 23 90 39N50 75w25 5:01:40
Marshallton 15 13 39N56'59 75w40'50 5:02:43
Marshallton 49 27 40N47'12 76w32'23 5:06:10
Marshbrook 35 44 41N38'14 75w40'40 5:02:43
Marshburg 42 6 41N51'16 78w45'17 5:15:01
Marsh Creek 59 6 41N46'34 77w23'55 5:09:36
Marsh Hill 41 7 41N28'37 76w58'28 5:07:54
Marshlands 59 6 41N42'48 77w34'44 5:10:19
Marsh Run 67 12 40N12'00 76w48'50 5:07:15
Marshview 8 41 40N40'31 76w23'06 5:05:32
Marshwood 35 1 41N26'10 75w34'03 5:02:16
Marsteller 11 92 40N39'02 78w48'30 5:15:14
Marstown 54 9 40N32'23 76w22'42 5:05:31
Martha Furnace 14 7 40N50'05 78w00'27 5:12:02
Martic 36 1 39N53 76w18 5:05:12
Martic Forge 36 1 39N54'19 76w19'40 5:05:19
Marticville 36 1 39N55'35 76w18'26 5:05:14
Martin 26 51 39N48'23 79w54'36 5:19:38
Martin 67 95 39N53'17 76w50'27 5:07:22
Martindale 11 63 40N21'36 78w37'57 5:14:32
Martindale 36 27 40N09'11 76w05'20 5:04:21
Martinsburg 7 51 40N18'40 78w19'28 5:13:18
Martinsburg Junction 7 51 40N18'32 78w20'22 5:13:21
Martins Corner 15 9 40N02'32 75w51'37 5:03:26
Martins Creek 48 15 40N47'00 75w11'12 5:00:45
Martins Creek Junction 48 17 40N49'39 75w12'02 5:00:48
Martins Crossroads 34 73 40N33'33 77w29'55 5:10:00
Martins Ferry 30 51 39N48 79w55 5:19:40
Martinsville 67 1 39N56'25 76w31'30 5:06:06
Martintown 32 6 40N38'32 78w51'07 5:15:24
Martzville 19 1 41N04'07 76w16'02 5:05:04
Marvel Gardens 23 9 39N53 75w21 5:01:24
Marvindale 42 93 41N43'46 78w32'29 5:14:10
Marwood 10 6 40N46'44 79w46'24 5:19:06
Maryd 54 27 40N45'36 76w03'23 5:04:14
Marysville 5 51 40N11'28 78w15'38 5:13:03
Marysville 14 63 40N47'58 77w57'19 5:11:49
Marysville 22 12 40N20'33 76w55'49 5:07:43
Marywood College 35 18 41N25 75w39 5:02:36
Mascot 17 59 40N51'02 78w24'05 5:13:36
Mascot 36 1 40N03'42 76w09'17 5:04:37
Mason 61 109 41N28'25 79w50'50 5:19:23
Mason and Dixon 28 1 39N43'17 77w45'16 5:11:01
Mason-Dixon 28 1 39N43'17 77w45'16 5:11:01
Masontown 26 51 39N50'48 79w54'00 5:19:36
Masseyburg 31 81 40N39'34 77w55'39 5:11:43
Masten 41 7 41N30'26 76w49'15 5:07:17
Mastersonville 36 8 40N11'48 76w29'15 5:05:57
Masthope 52 6 41N32'09 75w01'43 5:00:07
Matamoras 22 24 40N26'24 76w56'01 5:07:44
Matamoras 52 3 41N22'07 74w42'02 4:58:48
Mateer 3 15 40N38'31 79w28'24 5:17:54
Mather 30 6 39N56'05 80w04'26 5:20:18
Mattawana 44 7 40N29'46 77w43'47 5:10:55
Matternville 14 63 40N49'50 77w57'58 5:11:52
Matterstown 22 4 40N34'21 76w50'52 5:07:23
Matthews Run 62 3 41N54'16 79w20'41 5:17:23
Mattie 5 6 39N55'10 78w17'54 5:13:12
Mausdale 47 6 40N59'11 76w38'07 5:06:32
Maxatawny 6 9 40N32'33 75w41'21 5:02:45
Maxwell 26 51 40N00'38 79w58'13 5:19:53
Mayberry 47 6 40N55 76w33 5:06:12
Mayburg 27 3 41N42 79w02 5:16:08
Mayes 17 54 40N49'32 78w37'11 5:14:29
Mayfair 49 82 40N51'01 76w37'50 5:06:31
Mayfair 51 9 40N02'01 75w02'04 5:00:08
Mayfield 35 1 41N32'17 75w32'11 5:02:09
Mayfield 65 111 40N08'10 79w35'53 5:18:24
Mayfield East 67 67 39N58 76w44 5:06:56
Mayport 16 6 41N02'01 79w15'06 5:17:00
Maysville 3 6 40N33'47 79w27'03 5:17:48
Maysville 43 59 41N24'16 80w27'10 5:21:49
Maysville 49 27 40N47 76w33 5:06:12
Maytown 36 2 40N04'31 76w34'57 5:06:20
Maytown 67 12 40N05'59 76w52'22 5:07:29
Mayville 37 112 41N05'14 80w18'45 5:21:15
Maze 34 6 40N36'44 77w11'45 5:08:47
Mazeppa 60 70 40N59'01 76w59'19 5:07:57
McAdams 63 51 40N23'10 80w16'05 5:21:04
McAdoo 54 60 40N54'36 75w59'30 5:03:58
McAdoo Heights 54 60 40N53'30 75w59'43 5:03:59
McAlevys Fort 31 81 40N38'23 77w49'54 5:11:20
McAlisters Crossroads 2 13 40N30'56 80w16'06 5:21:04
McAlisterville 34 1 40N38'10 77w16'30 5:09:06
McBride 10 3 40N47'51 79w55'29 5:19:42
McCalmont 10 6 40N49'10 79w56'41 5:19:47
McCalmont 33 51 41N02 78w58 5:15:52
McCance 65 110 40N15 79w14 5:16:56
McCandless 2 114 40N34 80w02 5:20:08
McCarroll Corner 57 6 41N27'58 76w15'22 5:05:01
McCarthey 17 54 40N49'42 78w30'36 5:14:02
McCartney 17 7 40N50 78w26 5:13:44
McCartys Corner 52 2 41N17'30 74w51'48 4:59:27
McCaslin 37 112 41N00'47 80w15'25 5:21:02
McCauley 16 6 41N22'04 79w26'17 5:17:45
McCauley 17 4 40N50 78w21 5:13:24
McChesneytown 65 3 40N19 79w23 5:17:32
McClarran 65 3 40N19'30 79w28'06 5:17:52
McCleary 4 64 40N36'32 80w24'02 5:21:36
McClellan 22 24 40N28 76w56 5:07:44
McClellandtown 26 51 39N53'13 79w52'01 5:19:28
McClellan Heights 67 67 39N57 76w42 5:06:48
McClintock 61 9 41N27'22 79w41'19 5:18:45
McClure 26 111 40N06'14 79w33'15 5:18:13
McClure 55 1 40N42'25 77w18'53 5:09:16
McConnellsburg 29 66 39N55'57 77w59'57 5:12:00
McConnells Mill 37 112 40N57'10 80w10'13 5:20:41
McConnells Mills 63 2 40N15'09 80w14'57 5:21:00
McConnellstown 31 81 40N27'09 78w04'55 5:12:20
McCormick 32 6 40N50'09 79w06'33 5:16:26
McCoys Corners 43 70 41N07'37 80w05'48 5:20:23
McCoysville 34 7 40N27'11 77w34'05 5:10:16
McCracken 30 7 39N51'13 80w28'34 5:21:54
McCrays 27 6 41N29'26 79w05'42 5:16:23

McCrea 21 1 40N14'39 77W26'37 5:09:46
McCrea Furnace 3
6 40N55'34 79W17'28 5:17:10
McCullochs Mills 34
6 40N25'25 77W35'11 5:10:21
McCullough 65 25 40N21'52 79W38'20 5:18:33
McDermott 67 1 39N44'56 76W25'06 5:05:40
McDonald 63 51 40N22'15 80W14'06 5:20:56
McDowell Corners 43
6 41N10 80W05 5:20:20
McElhattan 18 64 41N09'35 77W21'42 5:09:27
McEwensville 49
73 41N04'22 76W49'05 5:07:16
McFann 10 6 40N43'37 79W56'32 5:19:46
McGarey 33 34 41N04'55 79W07'00 5:16:28
McGees Mills 17 6 40N52'54 78W45'46 5:15:03
McGillstown 38 1 40N23'19 76W31'31 5:06:06
McGovern 63 2 40N13'44 80W13'00 5:20:52
McGrann 3 15 40N46'53 79W31'18 5:18:05
McGregor 3 59 40N53 79W15 5:17:00
McHaddon 3 15 40N47'19 79W35'37 5:18:22
McHenry 41 6 41N24 77W28 5:09:52
McIlhaney 45 1 40N55'19 75W21'35 5:01:26
McIntyre 32 6 40N34'11 79W17'45 5:17:11
McIntyre 41 7 41N31 76W57 5:07:48
McKeages Crossing 32
63 40N43'24 78W48'56 5:15:16
McKean 25 107 42N00 80W09 5:20:36
McKean 42 6 41N49'06 78W33'28 5:14:14
McKeansburg 54 1 40N40'42 76W01'26 5:04:06
McKee 7 3 40N21'35 78W25'03 5:13:40
McKee 50 1 40N25'39 77W13'17 5:08:53
McKees Half Falls 55
51 40N39'41 76W55'06 5:07:40
McKeesport 2 10 40N20'52 79W51'52 5:19:27
McKees Rocks 2
114 40N27'56 80W03'57 5:20:16
McKimm 4 121 40N50'05 80W15'29 5:21:02
McKinley 24 75 41N36'12 78W51'19 5:15:25
McKinley 46 9 40N05'05 75W07'02 5:00:28
McKinley Hill 26
7 39N43'50 79W54'04 5:19:36
McKinney 28 1 40N09'07 77W36'50 5:10:27
McKnight 2 114 40N33 80W02 5:20:08
McKnightstown 1 1 39N52'14 77W19'33 5:09:18
McKnightstown Station 1
1 39N51'25 77W19'29 5:09:18
McKnight Village 2
114 40N33 80W01 5:20:04
McLallen Corners 25
3 41N52'47 80W02'58 5:20:12
McLane 25 107 41N56'10 80W07'36 5:20:30
McLaughlin Corners 20
7 41N43'34 79W42'32 5:18:50
McMichaels 45 1 40N59'42 75W23'55 5:01:36
McMinns Summit 33
5 41N12'10 78W46'32 5:15:06
McMurray 63 114 40N16'40 80W05'03 5:20:20
McNees 3 15 40N47'51 79W26'43 5:17:47
McNett 41 7 41N34 76W51 5:07:24
McPherron 17 122 40N46'21 78W36'57 5:14:28
McPhersons Corner 61
9 41N23'58 79W35'07 5:18:20
McQueston Corners 43
6 41N25 80W14 5:20:56
McSherrystown 1 6 39N48'26 77W00'42 5:08:03
McSparren 36 7 39N45'54 76W12'30 5:04:50
McVeytown 44 7 40N29'57 77W44'30 5:10:58
McVille 3 2 40N43'33 79W36'11 5:18:25
McWilliams 3 6 40N57'57 79W15'08 5:17:01
Mead 62 3 41N47 79W05 5:16:20
Meade Heights 22
80 40N12'24 76W45'16 5:07:01
Meadetown 67 1 39N48'59 76W31'13 5:06:05
Meadia Heights 36
8 40N02 76W17 5:05:08
Meadowbrook 26 80 39N52'22 79W42'57 5:18:52
Meadowbrook 46 9 40N06'45 75W04'43 5:00:19
Meadowbrook Manor 15
47 40N03 75W33 5:02:12
Meadowdale 56 6 40N07'33 79W06'48 5:16:27
Meadow Gap 31 6 40N09'36 77W55'52 5:11:43
Meadow Lands 63 2 40N13'09 80W13'15 5:20:53
Meadowood 10 3 40N51 79W56 5:19:44
Meadowview 49 1 40N50'49 76W35'32 5:06:22
Meadowview Estates 36
28 40N05 76W11 5:04:44
Meadow Wood 4 13 40N37 80W16 5:21:04
Meadville 20 77 41N38'29 80W09'06 5:20:36
Meadville Junction 20
6 41N38'20 80W20'43 5:21:23
Mechanic Grove 36
27 39N50'55 76W09'32 5:04:38
Mechanicsburg 4 6 40N33'42 80W24'11 5:21:37
Mechanicsburg 21
12 40N12'51 77W00'32 5:08:02
Mechanics Grove 36
27 39N54 76W10 5:04:40
Mechanicsville 9
8 40N20'38 75W04'30 5:00:18
Mechanicsville 16
37 41N10'06 79W20'03 5:17:20
Mechanicsville 36
8 40N07'03 76W22'47 5:05:31
Mechanicsville 39
13 40N39'00 75W32'17 5:02:09
Mechanicsville 47
6 40N57'59 76W35'13 5:06:21
Mechanicsville 51
9 40N06'34 74W57'56 4:59:52
Mechanicsville 54
49 40N41'22 76W11'10 5:04:45
Mechesneytown 65
116 40N18'53 79W21'32 5:17:26
Meckesville 13 94 40N59'59 75W33'08 5:02:13
Mecks Corner 50 1 40N23'10 77W08'35 5:08:34
Meckville 6 1 40N28'17 76W22'53 5:05:32
Media 23 90 39N55'00 75W23'17 5:01:33
Medix Run 24 7 41N17'24 78W23'51 5:13:35
Meeker 40 20 41N18'49 76W03'58 5:04:16
Megargee 15 9 39N59 75W50 5:03:20
Meharg 10 3 40N47'10 79W53'56 5:19:36
Mehoopany 66 59 41N33'48 76W03'39 5:04:15
Meiser 55 6 40N47 77W03 5:08:12
Meisertown 45 84 41N04'50 75W16'08 5:01:05
Meiserville 55 6 40N40'09 76W58'21 5:07:53
Melcroft 26 6 40N03'07 79W23'22 5:17:33
Mellingertown 65
111 40N08'43 79W31'06 5:18:04
Mellotts Mill 29
6 40N01'02 78W02'19 5:12:09
Melrose 6 101 40N20 75W53 5:03:32
Melrose 26 51 39N59'31 79W57'23 5:19:50
Melrose 58 59 41N55'47 75W30'15 5:02:01
Melrose Park 46 9 40N03'42 75W07'56 5:00:32
Mench 5 6 39N58'24 78W19'29 5:13:18
Mendenhall 15 8 39N51'14 75W38'30 5:02:34
Mendon 65 111 40N10'46 79W41'02 5:18:44
Menges Mill 1 56 39N43'17 77W06'12 5:08:25
Menges Mills 67
95 39N51'39 76W53'43 5:07:35
Menno 44 7 40N34'42 77W46'13 5:11:05
Mentcle 32 6 40N38'14 78W52'57 5:15:32
Mercer 43 66 41N13'37 80W14'24 5:20:58
Mercersburg 28 51 39N49'40 77W54'13 5:11:37
Mercersburg Junction 28
51 39N51'26 77W53'26 5:11:34
Mercur 8 41 41N48'09 76W19'41 5:05:19
Meredith 3 6 40N47'48 79W17'36 5:17:10
Meredith 33 51 41N05'21 78W57'02 5:15:48
Meridian 10 3 40N50'54 79W57'44 5:19:51
Merion 46 9 40N00 75W15 5:01:00
Merion Golf Manor 23
9 40N01 75W17 5:01:08
Merion Park 46 90 40N02 75W18 5:01:12
Merion Square 46
90 40N02 75W18 5:01:12
Merion Station 46
90 40N02 75W18 5:01:12
Merion View 46 90 40N05 75W22 5:01:28
Meriwether Farms 15
13 39N57 75W36 5:02:24
Merlin 15 8 40N06'11 75W34'47 5:02:19
Merrian 49 27 40N46'42 76W24'34 5:05:38
Merrill 4 19 40N39'59 80W21'19 5:21:25
Merrittstown 26
51 39N58'22 79W52'40 5:19:31
Merryall 8 6 41N41'55 76W13'51 5:04:55
Mertztown 6 9 40N30'21 75W39'57 5:02:40
Mertz Town 13 80 40N49'12 75W45'28 5:03:02
Merwin 65 4 40N32 79W39 5:18:36
Merwinsburg 45 1 40N57'58 75W28'04 5:01:52
Merwood 23 9 40N00 75W18 5:01:12
Meshoppen 66 59 41N36'51 76W02'49 5:04:11
Messmore 26 51 39N52'42 79W50'42 5:19:23
Metal 28 1 40N00'50 77W52'45 5:11:31
Metamora Station 39
13 40N38'15 75W31'54 5:02:08
Metcalf 65 14 40N37'23 79W41'27 5:18:46
Metzler 56 6 39N55'14 79W16'45 5:17:07
Mexico 34 7 40N32'15 77W21'13 5:09:25
Mexico 47 70 41N01'16 76W44'55 5:07:00
Meyersdale 56 79 39N48'49 79W01'30 5:16:06
Meyersville 39 13 40N38'47 75W32'55 5:02:12
Mickley Gardens 39
13 40N39 75W30 5:02:00
Mickleys 39 13 40N38'50 75W29'45 5:01:59
Mickleys Gardens 39
13 40N38'59 75W30'20 5:02:01
Middleboro 25 107 41N59'49 80W08'36 5:20:34
Middleburg 40 60 41N04'12 75W46'26 5:03:06
Middleburg 55 6 40N47'31 77W02'45 5:08:11
Middlebury 59 6 41N52 77W16 5:09:04
Middlebury Center 59
6 41N50'37 77W16'29 5:09:06
Middle Churches 65
111 40N09 79W33 5:18:12
Middle City 51 9 39N57 75W10 5:00:40
Middle Creek 55 1 40N45'40 77W15'30 5:09:02
Middle Lancaster 10
6 40N51'16 80W07'25 5:20:30
Middle Paxton 22
12 40N23 76W55 5:07:40
Middleport 54 1 40N43'46 76W05'09 5:04:21
Middlesex 21 16 40N14'04 77W08'11 5:08:33
Middle Smithfield 45
1 41N06 75W06 5:00:24
Middle Spring 21
82 40N05'00 77W32'30 5:10:10
Middleswarth 55 6 40N47 77W03 5:08:12
Middle Taylor 11
74 40N22 78W55 5:15:40
Middleton 17 122 40N53'08 78W44'46 5:14:59
Middletown 8 7 41N55'38 76W41'57 5:06:48
Middletown 22 80 40N11'59 76W43'53 5:06:56
Middletown 31 51 40N13'19 78W12'46 5:12:51
Middletown 42 6 41N53'00 78W33'05 5:14:12
Middletown 48 13 40N38'38 75W19'58 5:01:20
Middletown 65 111 40N15'42 79W37'15 5:18:29
Middletown Center 58
6 41N52'34 76W05'25 5:04:22
Middletown Heights 23
90 39N55 75W22 5:01:28
Midland 4 2 40N37'57 80W26'48 5:21:47
Midland 63 2 40N15'32 80W13'06 5:20:52
Midmont 24 59 41N36'39 78W36'27 5:14:26
Midvale 28 100 39N43'21 77W32'35 5:10:10
Midvale 40 20 41N16'01 75W51'49 5:03:27
Midvalley 19 27 40N49 76W23 5:05:32
Midway 1 1 39N48'30 77W00'11 5:08:01
Midway 9 9 40N07'54 74W53'18 4:59:33
Midway 38 8 40N18'28 76W24'40 5:05:39
Midway 63 51 40N22'09 80W17'35 5:21:10
Midway 65 99 40N15'54 79W33'41 5:18:15
Midway Manor 39
13 40N37'54 75W25'36 5:01:42
Miedel Hill 65
111 40N06'43 79W36'23 5:18:26
Miffin Cross Roads 19
4 40N58'15 76W18'56 5:05:16
Mifflin 34 7 40N34'10 77W24'11 5:09:37
Mifflinburg 60 4 40N55'03 77W02'53 5:08:12
Mifflin Junction 2
114 40N20'52 79W57'05 5:19:48
Mifflintown 34 7 40N34'11 77W23'50 5:09:35
Mifflinville (Creasy Sta) 19
1 41N01'56 76W18'30 5:05:14
Milan 8 60 41N54'27 76W31'25 5:06:06
Milanville 64 6 41N40'17 75W03'56 5:00:16
Milbell 65 61 40N13'08 79W42'35 5:18:50
Mildred 57 6 41N28'41 76W22'43 5:05:31
Mile Run 49 82 40N48'12 76W46'23 5:07:06
Miles 14 6 40N57 77W24 5:09:36
Milesburg 14 70 40N56'30 77W47'07 5:11:08
Milesville 2 1 40N11 79W54 5:19:36
Milford 52 2 41N19'20 74W48'10 4:59:13
Milford 56 6 39N57'11 79W06'16 5:16:25
Milford Manor 9 9 40N12 74W49 4:59:16
Milford Mills 15
80 40N03'54 75W43'43 5:02:55
Milford Park 39
13 40N28'40 75W31'40 5:02:07
Milford Square 9
2 40N26'13 75W23'57 5:01:36
Milfred Terrace 63
6 39N59'27 80W00'10 5:20:01
Militia Hill 46 9 40N07 75W14 5:00:56
Millardsville 38
25 40N22'53 76W16'09 5:05:05
Millbach 38 1 40N19'57 76W14'18 5:04:57
Millbach Springs 38
1 40N18'40 76W14'36 5:04:58
Millbank 23 9 39N58 75W18 5:01:12
Millbank 65 110 40N15'46 79W16'06 5:17:04
Millbourne 23 9 39N57'48 75W15'02 5:01:00
Millbrook 14 9 40N48 77W52 5:11:28
Millbrook 43 6 41N14'55 80W03'40 5:20:15
Millburn 43 6 41N10'07 80W13'50 5:20:55
Mill City 66 44 41N29'45 75W50'11 5:03:21
Mill Creek 31 85 40N26'08 77W55'54 5:11:44
Mill Creek 54 49 40N41'52 76W11'02 5:04:44
Mill Creek 59 59 41N52'53 77W07'35 5:08:30
Mill Creek Corner 6
8 40N33'32 75W44'55 5:03:00
Mill Creek Falls 9
9 40N08'02 74W52'29 4:59:30
Millcreek Township 25
107 42N08 80W09 5:20:36
Milledgeville 43
59 41N28'13 80W03'45 5:20:15
Miller Heights 48
13 40N39 75W21 5:01:24
Miller Manor 48
13 40N42'01 75W26'22 5:01:45
Miller Run 56 6 40N09 78W55 5:15:40
Millers 20 3 41N48 80W03 5:20:12
Millers 48 15 40N49'35 75W15'54 5:01:04
Millers 54 1 40N43'54 75W49'03 5:03:16
Millersburg 22 1 40N32'22 76W57'40 5:07:51
Millers Corner 54
60 40N55'24 76W09'09 5:04:37
Millers Crossroads 49
82 40N50'55 76W41'13 5:06:45
Millersdale 65 3 40N16'30 79W37'51 5:18:31
Miller Shaft 11
63 40N22'45 78W39'47 5:14:39
Millers Station 20
3 41N48'38 79W59'41 5:19:59
Millerstown 2 14 40N39'00 79W47'57 5:19:12
Millerstown 7 51 40N16'44 78W17'55 5:13:12
Millerstown 16 6 41N18'22 79W27'10 5:17:49
Millerstown 50 1 40N32'58 77W09'18 5:08:37
Millersville 36 8 39N59'52 76W21'16 5:05:25
Millerton 59 6 41N59'00 76W56'20 5:07:45
Millertown 19 4 41N03'48 76W28'09 5:05:53
Millertown 26 6 40N01'28 79W22'54 5:17:32
Mill Grove 19 4 40N52'58 76W21'09 5:05:25
Mill Grove 65 61 40N12'45 79W44'24 5:18:58
Mill Hall 18 76 41N06'26 77W29'05 5:09:56
Millheim 14 52 40N53'27 77W28'37 5:09:54
Milligantown 65 6 40N33'30 79W40'34 5:18:42
Mill Lane 15 8 40N03'00 75W32'59 5:02:12
Millmont 60 7 40N53'09 77W08'23 5:08:34
Mill Park 46 8 40N15 75W39 5:02:36
Millport 36 28 40N08'11 76W15'13 5:05:01
Millport 53 6 41N55'30 78W07'11 5:12:29
Millrift 52 6 41N24'33 74W44'37 4:58:58
Mill Run 7 3 40N30'29 78W26'09 5:13:45
Mill Run 17 7 41N13'49 78W33'04 5:14:12
Mill Run 26 6 39N57'04 79W27'17 5:17:49
Mill Run Junction 26
6 39N57'50 79W27'12 5:17:49
Mills 53 6 41N56'46 77W41'12 5:10:45
Millsboro 26 7 39N59'12 79W59'38 5:19:59
Millstone 24 6 41N21'15 79W04'20 5:16:17
Milltown 2 10 40N30'34 79W47'42 5:19:11
Milltown 8 1 41N59'34 76W30'32 5:06:02
Milltown 15 13 39N57'57 75W32'45 5:02:11
Milltown 50 6 40N21'24 77W17'12 5:09:09
Milltown 62 3 41N42'25 79W02'53 5:16:12
Millvale 2 114 40N28'48 79W58'43 5:19:55
Millview 57 6 41N30'22 76W35'30 5:06:22
Mill Village 25
59 41N52'35 79W58'18 5:19:53
Millville 19 7 41N07'13 76W31'49 5:06:07
Millway 36 8 40N09'40 76W14'10 5:04:57
Millwood 65 3 40N21'09 79W16'43 5:17:07
Milmont Park 23 9 39N53 75W20 5:01:20
Milnesville 40 42 40N59'25 75W58'59 5:03:56
Milnor 28 1 39N45'17 77W44'43 5:10:59
Milroy 44 7 40N42'50 77W35'27 5:10:22
Milton 3 59 40N54'35 79W13'01 5:16:52
Milton 49 70 41N00'43 76W50'53 5:07:24
Milton Grove 36 2 40N09'44 76W31'55 5:06:08
Milwaukee 35 45 41N25'21 75W46'41 5:03:07
Mina 53 66 41N44'38 78W05'12 5:12:21
Mineral 61 6 41N19 79W58 5:19:52
Mineral Point 11
74 40N22'46 78W50'08 5:15:21
Mineral Spring 56
79 39N54'11 78W59'58 5:16:00
Mineral Springs 17
1 40N59'53 78W21'50 5:13:27
Miners Mills 40
20 41N16'01 75W49'56 5:03:20
Miners Village 38
8 40N16'01 76W23'56 5:05:36
Minersville 11 74 40N20'32 78W55'33 5:15:42

Minersville 54 27 40n41'26 76w15'45 5:05:03
Minerville 8 60 41n37'01 76w37'54 5:06:32
Minesite 39 13 40n35 75w28 5:01:52
Mingo 46 8 40n10'07 75w31'25 5:02:06
Mingoville 14 63 40n55'56 77w38'54 5:10:36
Minisink Hills 45 23 41n00 75w08 5:00:32
Minister 27 3 41n37'08 79w08'55 5:16:36
Minnequa 8 103 41n40'26 76w50'03 5:07:20
Minnis Corner 43 59 41n29'04 80w20'20 5:21:21
Minooka 35 18 41n22'45 75w41'34 5:02:46
Miola 16 37 41n14'58 79w20'52 5:17:23
Miquon 46 90 40n03'36 75w15'57 5:01:04
Miquon Hills 46 90 40n05 75w17 5:01:08
Misertown 45 84 41n06 75w15 5:01:00
Mishler Corners 25 7 41n56'06 80w12'18 5:20:49
Mission Hill 36 8 40n04 76w19 5:05:16
Mitchell Creek 59 59 41n56'06 77w06'23 5:08:26
Mitchell Park 46 1 40n11 75w06 5:00:24
Mix Run 12 7 41n20'22 78w11'34 5:12:46
Mixtown 59 6 41n50'50 77w35'16 5:10:21
Mocanaqua 40 1 41n08'28 76w08'21 5:04:33
Mocking Bird Hill 65 25 40n20 79w43 5:18:52
Model Village 23 90 39n50 75w25 5:01:40
Modena 15 9 39n58'00 75w48'00 5:03:12
Moffitt Sterling 30 7 39n45'28 79w56'11 5:19:45
Moffitty 30 7 39n45 79w56 5:19:44
Mogees 46 90 40n08 75w21 5:01:24
Mogees Station 46 90 40n06'28 75w19'12 5:01:17
Mohns Hill 6 101 40n16'33 76w02'47 5:04:11
Mohnton 6 101 40n17'09 75w59'05 5:03:56
Mohrsville 6 80 40n28'26 75w58'38 5:03:55
Molino 54 1 40n36'33 76w01'32 5:04:06
Mollenauer 2 114 40n21'12 80w01'31 5:20:06
Molltown 6 8 40n28'38 75w52'51 5:03:31
Monaca 4 13 40n41'14 80w16'18 5:21:05
Monaghan 67 12 40n08 76w58 5:07:52
Monarch 26 105 39n58'45 79w39'26 5:18:38
Monessen 65 1 40n08'54 79w53'17 5:19:33
Mongul 28 82 40n04'42 77w35'32 5:10:22
Moninger 63 2 40n14'30 80w12'46 5:20:51
Moniteau 10 6 41n03'47 79w53'59 5:19:36
Monocacy 6 8 40n15'30 75w46'54 5:03:08
Monocacy Station 6 8 40n16 75w46 5:03:04
Monongahela 63 1 40n12'11 79w55'35 5:19:42
Monongahela Junction 2 10 40n22 79w51 5:19:24
Monroe 9 1 40n34'22 75w11'33 5:00:46
Monroe 10 2 40n42'26 79w42'51 5:18:51
Monroe 16 6 41n11'39 79w35'27 5:18:22
Monroe Furnace 31 81 40n41'49 77w53'35 5:11:34
Monroe Heights 2 114 40n25'01 79w45'09 5:19:01
Monroeton 8 60 41n42'45 76w28'30 5:05:54
Monroeville 2 114 40n26 79w45 5:19:00
Monroeville Mall 2 114 40n26 79w47 5:19:08
Mont Alto 28 7 39n50'39 77w33'31 5:10:14
Montandon 49 70 40n57'55 76w51'04 5:07:24
Mont Clare 46 8 40n08'20 75w30'10 5:02:01
Montdale 35 18 41n32'02 75w36'36 5:02:26
Montebello 50 51 40n25'41 77w04'26 5:08:18
Montello 6 101 40n18'44 76w02'14 5:04:09
Monterey 6 8 40n32'18 75w43'31 5:02:54
Monterey 28 1 39n44'17 77w28'18 5:09:53
Monterey 36 28 40n04'13 76w10'17 5:04:41
Montgomery 41 82 41n10'13 76w52'38 5:07:31
Montgomery Ferry 50 1 40n29'56 76w58'23 5:07:54
Montgomery Square 46 8 40n15 75w15 5:01:00
Montgomeryville 46 8 40n14'50 75w14'39 5:00:59
Montmorenci 24 36 41n29'54 78w44'26 5:14:58
Montour 2 114 40n27 79w58 5:19:52
Montour 19 4 40n59 76w30 5:06:00
Montour Junction 2 114 40n30 80w10 5:20:40
Montoursville 41 82 41n15'15 76w55'15 5:07:41
Montrose 6 101 40n18'23 75w59'17 5:03:57
Montrose 58 60 41n50'02 75w52'39 5:03:31
Montrose Hill 2 114 40n30'13 79w51'21 5:19:25
Montsera 21 16 40n06'32 77w17'03 5:09:08
Monument 14 7 41n06'40 77w42'17 5:10:49
Monvue 26 51 39n51 79w54 5:19:36
Moon 2 13 40n30'32 80w14'22 5:20:57
Moon Crest 2 114 40n30 80w10 5:20:40
Moon Run 2 114 40n27'11 80w06'35 5:20:26
Moonstown 38 1 40n16'53 76w18'26 5:05:14
Moore 48 9 40n47 75w25 5:01:40
Mooredale 21 16 40n07'39 77w17'34 5:09:10
Mooresburg 47 56 40n58'58 76w42'18 5:06:49
Moores Corners 10 6 41n02'25 80w06'39 5:20:27
Moorestown 48 13 40n46'43 75w22'12 5:01:29
Moorhead 25 91 42n11'09 79w54'13 5:19:37
Moorheadville 25 91 42n11'31 79w54'37 5:19:38
Moors Mill 21 16 40n06'55 77w16'54 5:09:08
Moosehead 40 60 41n07'11 75w47'37 5:03:10
Moosic 35 18 41n21'12 75w44'19 5:02:57
Morado 4 8 40n47'17 80w19'59 5:21:20
Morann 17 4 40n47'11 78w22'02 5:13:28
Moravia 37 121 40n55'16 80w22'35 5:21:30
Moravian 48 13 40n38 75w23 5:01:32
Mordansville 19 4 41n04'01 76w29'56 5:06:00
Morea (Morea Colliery P O) 54 3 40n47'22 76w10'18 5:04:41
Morea Colliery 54 3 40n48 76w10 5:04:40
Moreland 41 6 41n11'21 76w39'09 5:06:37
Moreland Farms 46 1 40n11 75w06 5:00:24
Moreland Manor 46 1 40n11 75w06 5:00:24
Morewood 46 1 40n11 75w06 5:00:24
Morewood 65 111 40n08'53 79w33'48 5:18:15
Morford 30 7 39n47'49 80w28'42 5:21:55
Morgan 2 114 40n21'15 80w08'24 5:20:34
Morgan 26 104 39n55'33 79w39'32 5:18:38
Morgan Hill 2 114 40n21'08 80w09'10 5:20:37
Morgans Hill 46 12 40n41 75w14 5:00:56
Morgans Land 17 54 40n49'58 78w32'24 5:14:10
Morgantown 6 3 40n09'18 75w53'25 5:03:34
Morganza 63 2 40n16'25 80w09'28 5:20:38
Morningside 2 114 40n28'57 79w55'47 5:19:43
Morrell 26 105 39n59 79w37 5:18:28
Morris 59 6 41n35'42 77w17'33 5:09:10
Morris Crossroads 26 7 39n45'12 79w51'27 5:19:26
Morrisdale 17 7 40n56'56 78w13'32 5:12:54
Morris Run 59 6 41n40'38 77w01'06 5:08:04
Morrisville 9 9 40n12'41 74w47'18 4:59:09
Morrisville 30 1 39n53'41 80w09'43 5:20:39
Morrows Corner 3 15 40n54'28 79w32'27 5:18:10
Morstein 15 8 40n01'00 75w35'14 5:02:21
Morton 23 9 39n54'35 75w19'26 5:01:18
Mortonville 15 9 39n56'47 75w46'41 5:03:07
Morwood 46 8 40n18'55 75w23'32 5:01:34
Morysville 6 2 40n19'28 75w39'05 5:02:36
Moscow 35 4 41n20'12 75w31'08 5:02:05
Moselem 6 80 40n30'02 75w53'04 5:03:32
Moselem Springs 6 8 40n29'08 75w50'20 5:03:21
Mosgrove 3 7 40n52'08 79w28'32 5:17:54
Moshannon 11 55 40n24'42 78w37'34 5:14:30
Moshannon 14 7 41n01'56 78w00'19 5:12:01
Mosherville 8 7 41n58'37 76w54'25 5:07:38
Mosiertown 20 59 41n46'21 80w12'23 5:20:50
Mosserville 39 1 40n41'39 75w45'47 5:03:03
Moss Plan 4 19 40n42 80w17 5:21:08
Mossville 40 6 41n16'19 76w16'46 5:05:07
Mostoller 56 6 40n04'19 78w56'30 5:15:46
Mottarns Mill 32 6 40n50'07 79w03'28 5:16:14
Moudy Hill 11 63 40n22'53 78w41'23 5:14:46
Moulstown 67 1 39n51'07 76w55'59 5:07:44
Mount Aetna 6 25 40n25'09 76w17'44 5:05:11
Mountaindale 11 54 40n41'36 78w25'30 5:13:42
Mountain Green 28 1 40n07'00 77w48'44 5:11:15
Mountain Grove 40 4 40n58'53 76w12'40 5:04:51
Mountainhome 45 84 41n10'25 75w16'17 5:01:05
Mountain Lake 8 41 41n45'44 76w35'01 5:06:20
Mountain Top 36 27 40n06'24 75w57'11 5:03:49
Mountain Top 40 20 41n10'10 75w52'40 5:03:31
Mountainville 39 13 40n34'29 75w27'09 5:01:49
Mount Air 37 6 40n54'06 80w26'30 5:21:46
Mount Airy 16 7 41n05'39 79w31'20 5:18:05
Mount Airy 36 28 40n03'58 76w01'04 5:04:04
Mount Airy 51 9 40n03'50 75w11'13 5:00:45
Mount Airy Terrace 40 20 41n18'58 75w56'31 5:03:46
Mount Allen 21 12 40n10'45 76w58'27 5:07:54
Mount Alton 42 6 41n47'39 78w37'41 5:14:31
Mount Ararat 38 8 40n22'59 76w28'50 5:05:55
Mount Bethel 48 8 40n54 75w07 5:00:28
Mount Braddock 26 104 39n57 79w39 5:18:36
Mount Carbon 54 49 40n40'29 76w11'19 5:04:45
Mount Carmel 30 6 39n46'18 80w30'42 5:22:03
Mount Carmel 49 27 40n47'49 76w24'44 5:05:39
Mount Carmel Junction 49 27 40n47'00 76w26'08 5:05:45
Mount Chestnut 10 3 40n53'16 79w58'51 5:19:55
Mount Chestnut Springs 10 3 40n53'11 79w59'30 5:19:58
Mount Cobb 35 6 41n24'48 75w29'37 5:01:58
Mount Dallas 5 6 40n00'43 78w23'43 5:13:35
Mount Eagle 14 63 40n58'55 77w42'21 5:10:49
Mount Etna 7 3 40n31'13 78w10'22 5:12:41
Mount Gretna 38 8 40n14'51 76w28'11 5:05:53
Mount Gretna Heights 38 8 40n14'53 76w27'53 5:05:52
Mount Herman 63 3 40n02'56 80w14'02 5:20:56
Mount Holly Springs 21 2 40n07'06 77w11'25 5:08:46
Mount Hope 1 56 39n48'12 77w25'40 5:09:43
Mount Hope 17 1 40n59'24 78w24'35 5:13:38
Mount Hope 20 6 41n35'38 79w57'28 5:19:50
Mount Hope 36 8 40n13'19 76w25'19 5:05:41
Mount Independence 26 80 39n55 79w40 5:18:40
Mount Jackson 37 112 40n57'44 80w26'08 5:21:45
Mount Jewett 42 38 41n43'32 78w38'19 5:14:33
Mount Joy 17 1 41n02 78w27 5:13:48
Mount Joy 36 2 40n06'35 76w30'13 5:06:01
Mount Joy 65 111 40n09 79w33 5:18:12
Mount Laffee 54 49 40n43'01 76w13'44 5:04:55
Mount Laurel 40 42 40n56'04 75w59'38 5:03:59
Mount Lebanon 2 114 40n21'19 80w02'59 5:20:12
Mount Misery 1 1 39n50'23 77w02'38 5:08:11
Mount Morris 30 6 39n43'59 80w04'05 5:20:16
Mount Nebo 2 114 40n33'10 80w06'19 5:20:25
Mount Nebo 36 1 39n53'01 76w19'31 5:05:18
Mount Nebo 65 111 40n07'20 79w36'26 5:18:26
Mount Oliver 2 114 40n24'51 79w59'17 5:19:57
Mount Patrick 50 1 40n31'38 76w59'19 5:07:57
Mount Penn 6 101 40n19'41 75w53'28 5:03:34
Mount Pleasant 1 1 39n44'01 77w04'33 5:08:18
Mount Pleasant 6 1 40n24'17 76w03'55 5:04:16
Mount Pleasant 9 90 40n19'49 75w14'17 5:00:57
Mount Pleasant 34 7 40n33'19 77w22'52 5:09:31
Mount Pleasant 36 23 39n55'53 76w06'12 5:04:25
Mount Pleasant 38 8 40n16'57 76w31'47 5:06:07
Mount Pleasant 44 7 40n43'35 77w36'33 5:10:26
Mount Pleasant 48 17 40n48'23 75w09'20 5:00:37
Mount Pleasant 49 82 40n53'34 76w44'36 5:06:58
Mount Pleasant 50 6 40n19'08 77w32'43 5:10:11
Mount Pleasant 54 49 40n42'38 76w20'13 5:05:21
Mount Pleasant 59 6 41n33'29 77w17'07 5:09:08
Mount Pleasant 65 111 40n08'56 79w32'29 5:18:10
Mount Pleasant 67 1 40n08'13 76w57'48 5:07:51
Mount Pleasant Mills 55 6 40n43'23 77w00'58 5:08:04
Mount Pocono 45 84 41n07'19 75w21'54 5:01:28
Mount Rock 21 82 40n09'38 77w19'03 5:09:16
Mount Rock 28 82 40n01'18 77w33'54 5:10:16
Mount Rock 44 73 40n36'48 77w34'19 5:10:17
Mount Royal 67 1 40n02'21 76w53'17 5:07:33
Mount Sterling 26 51 39n50'46 79w56'07 5:19:44
Mount Tabor 1 1 40n00'48 77w14'23 5:08:58
Mount Tabor 3 6 40n59'15 79w13'04 5:16:52
Mount Top 67 1 40n03'31 76w59'22 5:07:57
Mount Troy 2 114 40n28 80w01 5:20:04
Mount Union 28 1 39n55 77w34 5:10:16
Mount Union 31 85 40n23'04 77w52'57 5:11:32
Mount Vernon 2 8 40n17'30 79w48'40 5:19:15
Mount Vernon 15 3 39n48'34 76w01'34 5:04:06
Mount Vernon 65 14 40n33'24 79w45'11 5:19:01
Mountville 36 8 40n02'21 76w25'52 5:05:43
Mount Washington 2 114 40n25'51 80w00'38 5:20:03
Mount Wilson 38 8 40n15'22 76w30'36 5:06:02
Mount Wolf 67 7 40n03'47 76w42'15 5:06:49
Mount Zion 21 16 40n07'45 77w10'28 5:08:42
Mount Zion 38 8 40n24'00 76w22'55 5:05:32
Mount Zion 40 1 41n20 75w49 5:03:16
Mount Zion 45 23 41n00'59 75w13'35 5:00:54
Mount Zion 67 67 40n00'08 76w41'00 5:06:44
Moween 65 116 40n28'54 79w25'56 5:17:44
Mowersville 28 82 40n06'43 77w34'56 5:10:20
Mowry 17 6 41n03'36 78w08'27 5:12:34
Mowry 54 27 40n45'44 76w24'16 5:05:37
Moxham 11 74 40n17'39 78w54'28 5:15:38
Moyer 26 104 40n02'58 79w33'57 5:18:16
Moyers 54 27 40n33'07 76w15'01 5:05:00
Moyers Grove 40 1 41n03'38 76w03'53 5:04:16
Moylan 23 90 39n55 75w23 5:01:32
Moylan-Rose Valley Station 23 90 39n54'20 75w23'18 5:01:33
Mozart 9 8 40n16'33 75w03'15 5:00:13
Muddy Creek 10 3 40n58'20 79w58'17 5:19:53
Muddy Creek Forks 67 1 39n48'29 76w28'32 5:05:54
Mud Run 13 1 40n59'23 75w42'46 5:02:51
Muff 3 59 40n53'04 79w20'18 5:17:21
Muhlenberg 6 101 40n22'59 75w56'21 5:03:45
Muhlenberg 40 1 41n12 76w04 5:04:16
Muhlenberg Park 6 101 40n23 75w56 5:03:44
Muhlenburg 40 1 41n13'44 76w09'34 5:04:38
Muir 54 27 40n35'32 76w31'08 5:06:05
Mullertown 67 1 39n48 76w59 5:07:56
Mumbauersville 9 2 40n25'06 75w27'36 5:01:50
Mummasburg 1 1 39n53'08 77w17'23 5:09:10
Muncy 41 83 41n12'20 76w47'09 5:07:09
Muncy Creek 41 83 41n12 76w45 5:07:00
Muncy Valley 57 6 41n20'33 76w35'08 5:06:21
Munderf 33 34 41n17'04 78w56'59 5:15:48
Mundys Corner 11 74 40n26'41 78w50'29 5:15:22
Munhall 2 114 40n23'32 79w54'01 5:19:36
Munhall Terrace 2 114 40n22 79w54 5:19:36
Munntown 63 2 40n13'56 80w05'23 5:20:22
Munson 17 7 40n57'17 78w10'24 5:12:42
Munster 11 55 40n28'06 78w39'16 5:14:37
Murdock 56 6 39n57'29 79w05'57 5:16:24
Murdocksville 2 6 40n29 80w18 5:21:12
Murphy Siding 26 104 40n01 79w35 5:18:20
Murray 38 1 40n29'59 76w31'41 5:06:07
Murray 57 6 41n28'19 76w20'39 5:05:23
Murrell 36 30 40n10'07 76w10'03 5:04:40
Murrinsville 10 6 41n08'36 79w53'03 5:19:32
Murry Hill 63 2 40n16'32 80w09'27 5:20:38
Murrysville 65 114 40n25'42 79w41'52 5:18:47
Muse 63 2 40n17'34 80w12'02 5:20:48
Muse Junction 63 2 40n18'47 80w11'44 5:20:47
Musellmans Crossing 14 7 41n05'28 77w55'09 5:11:41
Musselman Grove 7 3 40n17'25 78w30'19 5:14:01
Musser 14 6 40n43'34 77w59'05 5:11:56
Mustard 2 8 40n14'06 79w49'08 5:19:17

Mutual 65 99 40N14'12 79W29'52 5:17:59
Muzette 27 6 41N28'22 79W14'02 5:16:56
Myersbrook 65 6 40N04'20 79W17'28 5:17:10
Myersburg 8 41 41N47'49 76W22'46 5:05:31
Myerstown 21 1 40N02'37 77W11'23 5:08:46
Myerstown 38 25 40N22'28 76W18'11 5:05:13
Mylo Park 11 54 40N29 78W43 5:14:52
Myobeach 66 59 41N36'07 76W04'55 5:04:20
Myoma 10 6 40N44 80W02 5:20:08
Myonia 10 6 40N43'48 80W01'33 5:20:06
Myrtle 42 7 41N58'54 78W14'31 5:12:58
Mystic 25 3 41N48 80W03 5:20:12
Mystic Park 20 7 41N40'26 79W45'53 5:19:04
Naces Corner 9 2 40N20'05 75W12'25 5:00:50
Nacetown 38 8 40N23'19 76W21'09 5:05:25
Naceville 9 8 40N21'05 75W22'22 5:01:29
Nadine 2 114 40N28'35 79W52'09 5:19:29
Naginey 44 7 40N42'15 77W33'07 5:10:12
Nagles Crossroad 11
63 40N38'13 78W35'34 5:14:22
Nan Lynn Gardens 9
1 40N12 75W05 5:00:20
Nansen 24 75 41N34'56 78W51'47 5:15:27
Nanticoke 40 21 41N12'19 76W00'19 5:04:01
Nantilly 21 12 40N10'11 76W58'06 5:07:52
Nantmeal Village 15
80 40N08'29 75W42'17 5:02:49
Nanty Glo 11 63 40N28'20 78W50'01 5:15:20
Naomi 26 1 40N06'25 79W50'30 5:19:22
Napier 5 6 40N02'13 78W33'31 5:14:14
Napierville 36 30 40N11 76W11 5:04:44
Narberth 46 9 40N00'30 75W15'39 5:01:03
Narbrook Park 23
9 40N00 75W16 5:01:04
Narrows Creek 17
56 41N08'05 78W42'02 5:14:48
Narrowsville 9 7 40N34'12 75W07'45 5:00:31
Narvon 36 27 40N06'10 75W58'41 5:03:55
Nashua 37 51 41N04'43 80W23'57 5:21:36
Nashville 32 6 40N47'48 78W55'38 5:15:43
Nashville 67 95 39N53'57 76W51'10 5:07:25
Nassau Village 23
9 39N53 75W20 5:01:20
Natalie 49 27 40N49'02 76W27'48 5:05:51
National Hill 2
114 40N20'44 80W09'26 5:20:38
Natrona 2 14 40N36'52 79W43'11 5:18:53
Natrona Heights 2
14 40N37'24 79W43'48 5:18:55
Naumanstown 36 8 40N09'45 76W25'56 5:05:44
Nauvoo 59 6 41N33'52 77W12'34 5:08:50
Nauvoo 67 12 40N09'26 76W53'06 5:07:32
Naval Hospital 51
9 39N55 75W11 5:00:44
Navarro 48 13 40N41 75W22 5:01:28
Nay Aug 35 18 41N23'57 75W35'13 5:02:21
Nazareth 48 8 40N44'25 75W18'36 5:01:14
Nealeys 10 6 40N57'15 80W04'56 5:20:20
Nealmont 7 11 40N39'58 78W13'10 5:12:53
Neason Hill 20 77 41N37'42 80W08'42 5:20:35
Neath 8 6 41N52'24 76W08'08 5:04:33
Nebo 26 6 40N03'34 79W21'53 5:17:28
Nebo 30 6 39N56'44 80W26'50 5:21:47
Nebraska 27 6 41N28'09 79W23'01 5:17:32
Nebraska 35 1 41N31'27 75W32'15 5:02:09
Nectarine 61 6 41N11'45 79W55'54 5:19:44
Ned 30 6 39N43'33 80W28'57 5:21:56
Needful 17 6 41N00 78W21 5:13:24
Needmore 29 6 39N50'45 78W08'42 5:12:35
Neelyton 31 6 40N09'39 77W49'22 5:11:17
Neff 31 7 40N32'37 78W05'03 5:12:20
Neffs 39 8 40N41'40 75W36'36 5:02:26
Neffs Mills 31 81 40N38'09 77W57'51 5:11:51
Neffsville 36 8 40N06'00 76W18'20 5:05:13
Neiffer 46 8 40N15'46 75W31'14 5:02:05
Neil Corner 30 51 39N53'59 79W59'04 5:19:56
Neiltown 27 6 41N36'20 79W30'21 5:18:01
Neiman 67 3 39N49'08 76W47'39 5:07:11
Nekoda 50 1 40N35'09 77W06'00 5:08:24
Nellie 26 104 40N01'30 79W40'41 5:18:43
Nelson 59 59 41N58'42 77W14'11 5:08:57
Nemacolin 30 51 39N52'42 79W55'30 5:19:42
Neola 45 23 40N57'32 75W20'26 5:01:22
Nesbit Corners 43
6 41N16'35 80W07'31 5:20:30
Nescopeck 40 1 41N03'07 76W13'16 5:04:53
Nescopeck Pass 40
20 41N04'34 75W57'33 5:03:50
Neshaminy 9 8 40N13'46 75W08'21 5:00:33
Neshaminy Falls 9
97 40N09'12 74W57'35 4:59:50
Neshaminy Hills 9
97 40N09'34 74W57'33 4:59:50
Neshaminy Valley 9
9 40N06 74W56 4:59:44
Neshaminy Woods 9
97 40N09'53 74W57'25 4:59:50
Neshannock 43 112 41N12'57 80W23'46 5:21:35
Neshannock Falls 37
6 41N04'58 80W17'52 5:21:11
Nesquehoning 13 1 40N51'52 75W48'41 5:03:15
Nesquehoning Junction 13
80 40N52'22 75W45'20 5:03:01
Nether Providence 23
90 39N54 75W22 5:01:28
Nettle Hill 30 6 39N47'48 80W22'59 5:21:32
Neversink 6 8 40N18'27 75W53'16 5:03:33
Neville 2 114 40N31 80W08 5:20:32
Neville Island 2
114 40N31 80W08 5:20:32
New Albany 8 60 41N36'00 76W26'32 5:05:46
New Alexandria 65
3 40N23'55 79W25'20 5:17:41
New Athens 16 7 41N00'49 79W32'13 5:18:09
New Baltimore 56
6 39N59'09 78W46'23 5:15:06
New Baltimore 67
1 39N48 76W59 5:07:56
New Beaver 37 121 40N53 80W22 5:21:28
New Bedford 37 6 41N05'50 80W30'18 5:22:01
New Berlin 60 6 40N52'44 76W59'14 5:07:57
New Berlinville 6
2 40N20'43 75W38'00 5:02:32
Newberry 41 82 41N14'23 77W03'11 5:08:13
Newberry 67 12 40N08 76W48 5:07:12
Newberrytown 67 1 40N07'50 76W47'33 5:07:10
New Bethlehem 16
87 41N00'06 79W19'54 5:17:20
New Bloomfield 50
1 40N25'11 77W11'12 5:08:45
Newboro 26 51 39N56'02 79W50'42 5:19:23
New Boston 54 3 40N47'49 76W09'09 5:04:37
Newbridge 28 1 40N08'48 77W43'36 5:10:54
New Bridgeville 67
1 39N54'45 76W29'20 5:05:57
New Brighton 4 19 40N43'49 80W18'37 5:21:14
New Britain 9 56 40N17'56 75W10'53 5:00:44
New Buena Vista 5
6 40N00'32 78W41'55 5:14:48
New Buffalo 50 3 40N27'15 76W58'12 5:07:53
Newburg 7 33 40N31'18 78W25'31 5:13:42
Newburg (LaJose P O) 17
122 40N50'07 78W40'38 5:14:43
Newburg 21 82 40N08'14 77W33'18 5:10:13
Newburg 31 6 40N17'00 78W07'58 5:12:32
Newburg 48 8 40N42'11 75W19'48 5:01:19
Newburg Homes 48
12 40N42'11 75W16'30 5:01:06
New Castle 37 112 41N00'13 80W20'50 5:21:23
New Castle 54 27 40N43'48 76W12'43 5:04:51
New Castle Junction 37
112 40N57'55 80W22'10 5:21:29
New Centerville 15
90 40N04'13 75W25'47 5:01:43
New Centerville 56
4 39N56'33 79W11'29 5:16:46
Newchester 1 1 39N54'12 77W05'45 5:08:23
New Columbia 60
70 41N02'27 76W52'02 5:07:28
New Columbus 13 1 40N52'06 75W48'56 5:03:16
New Columbus 40 6 41N10'24 76W17'38 5:05:11
Newcomer 26 80 39N52'45 79W47'33 5:19:10
New Cumberland 21
12 40N13'56 76W53'06 5:07:32
New Cumberland Army Depot 67
12 40N16 76W53 5:07:32
New Danville 36 8 39N59'11 76W18'55 5:05:16
New Derry 65 3 40N21'02 79W19'00 5:17:16
New Eagle 63 1 40N12'28 79W56'50 5:19:47
Newell 26 115 40N04'32 79W53'54 5:19:36
Newelltown 59 7 41N35'00 76W54'44 5:07:39
New England 2 8 40N20'05 79W55'38 5:19:43
New Enterprise 5
6 40N10'13 78W24'26 5:13:38
New Era 8 60 41N37'37 76W21'01 5:05:24
Newfield 2 114 40N30'04 79W47'46 5:19:11
Newfield 53 6 41N52'48 77W48'51 5:11:15
Newfield Junction 53
6 41N52'06 77W49'21 5:11:17
New Florence 65 7 40N22'49 79W04'32 5:16:18
Newfoundland 64 6 41N18'26 75W19'13 5:01:17
New Franklin 28
42 39N52'51 77W38'10 5:10:33
New Freedom 67 27 39N44'16 76W42'06 5:06:48
New Freeport 30 6 39N45'35 80W25'33 5:21:42
New Galena 9 2 40N19'49 75W11'17 5:00:45
New Galilee 4 8 40N50'08 80W23'59 5:21:36
New Garden 15 8 39N48'51 75W45'09 5:03:01
New Geneva 26 51 39N47'18 79W54'34 5:19:38
New Germantown 50
6 40N18'32 77W34'12 5:10:17
New Germany 11 63 40N24'44 78W45'19 5:15:01
New Grenada 29 6 40N08'04 78W05'16 5:12:21
New Hamburg 43 66 41N19'31 80W20'31 5:21:22
New Hanover 46 2 40N17'52 75W34'54 5:02:20
New Hanover Square 46
8 40N18'38 75W32'20 5:02:09
Newhard 39 8 40N43'29 75W37'01 5:02:28
New Holland 36 27 40N06'06 76W05'08 5:04:21
New Hope 9 8 40N21'51 74W57'06 4:59:48
New Ireland 25 58 41N52'47 79W55'40 5:19:43
New Jerusalem 6 8 40N26'53 75W44'51 5:02:59
New Kensington 65
14 40N34'11 79W45'54 5:19:04
New Kingstown 21
56 40N13'59 77W04'48 5:08:19
Newkirk 54 27 40N47'26 75W59'36 5:03:58
New Lancaster 21
82 40N04'31 77W25'03 5:09:40
New Lebanon 43 6 41N24'53 80W04'30 5:20:18
New Lexington 56
4 39N56'14 79W14'13 5:16:57
Newlin 15 8 39N55 75W44 5:02:56
Newlin 19 4 40N53'06 76W23'04 5:05:32
Newlinville 15 9 39N58'23 75W49'44 5:03:19
New London 15 3 39N46'57 75W52'33 5:03:30
New London 17 54 40N47'19 78W26'00 5:13:44
New London 62 6 41N41 79W24 5:17:36
Newlonsburg 65
114 40N25'28 79W39'53 5:18:40
New Mahoning 13 8 40N47'51 75W48'38 5:03:15
Newmanstown 38 1 40N20'58 76W12'49 5:04:51
Newmansville 16 6 41N25'43 79W22'07 5:17:28
New Market 67 12 40N14 76W51 5:07:24
New Milford 58 50 41N52'21 75W43'39 5:02:55
New Millport 17 6 40N53'37 78W32'20 5:14:09
New Milltown 36
23 40N01'15 76W03'33 5:04:14
New Mines 54 27 40N40'31 76W19'40 5:05:19
New Oxford 1 88 39N51'49 77W03'22 5:08:13
New Paris 5 6 40N06'23 78W38'42 5:14:35
New Park 67 1 39N44'05 76W30'21 5:06:01
New Philadelphia 54
27 40N43'10 76W06'58 5:04:28
Newport 37 121 40N54'00 80W21'17 5:21:25
Newport 50 1 40N28'40 77W07'51 5:08:31
Newport Center 40
21 41N11'21 76W01'33 5:04:06
Newportville 9 9 40N07'25 74W54'01 4:59:36
Newportville Terrace 9
9 40N07'19 74W54'25 4:59:38
New Providence 36
27 39N55'31 76W11'54 5:04:48
New Richmond 20 6 41N43'17 79W57'05 5:19:48
New Ringgold 54 1 40N41'09 75W59'58 5:04:00
Newry 7 33 40N23'37 78W26'09 5:13:45
New Salem 3 6 40N59'17 79W14'40 5:16:59
New Salem 26 51 39N55'27 79W50'09 5:19:21
New Schaefferstown 6
1 40N26 76W07 5:04:28
New Sewickley 4 6 40N43 80W13 5:20:52
New Shaefferstown 6
3 40N27'12 76W10'04 5:04:40
New Sheffield 4
13 40N35'56 80W16'49 5:21:07
Newside 39 8 40N41'26 75W38'41 5:02:35
New Smithville 39
8 40N34'47 75W43'43 5:02:55
New Stanton 65
111 40N13'09 79W36'35 5:18:26
New Texas 2 14 40N29'48 79W45'11 5:19:01
New Texas 36 1 39N44'57 76W09'51 5:04:39
Newton 40 44 41N13'21 75W53'44 5:03:35
Newtonburg 17 122 40N55'07 78W45'39 5:15:03
Newton Center 35
45 41N26'51 75W47'03 5:03:08
Newton Hamilton 44
85 40N23'30 77W50'14 5:11:21
Newton Junction 54
3 40N48'11 76W08'10 5:04:33
Newton Lake 35 1 41N34 75W32 5:02:08
Newtown 2 114 40N24'59 79W48'53 5:19:16
Newtown 9 8 40N13'45 74W56'14 4:59:45
Newtown 11 74 40N20'47 78W51'33 5:15:26
New Town 14 4 40N50'57 78W15'42 5:13:03
Newtown 30 7 39N45'25 79W58'12 5:19:53
Newtown 36 26 40N04'27 76W29'35 5:05:58
Newtown 39 9 40N33'02 75W39'40 5:02:39
Newtown 40 20 41N13 75W54 5:03:36
Newtown 54 9 40N39'02 76W20'54 5:05:24
Newtown Heights 23
90 39N58'58 75W24'46 5:01:39
Newtown Square 23
8 39N59'12 75W24'05 5:01:36
New Tripoli 39 1 40N40'51 75W45'08 5:03:01
New Vernon 43 6 41N24'57 80W07'19 5:20:29
Newville 9 2 40N18'20 75W13'13 5:00:53
Newville 21 1 40N10'23 77W23'56 5:09:36
Newville 36 4 40N08'49 76W37'47 5:06:31
New Virginia 43
117 41N13'10 80W24'23 5:21:38
New Washington 17
122 40N49'24 78W42'20 5:14:49
New Wilmington 37
6 41N07'20 80W19'59 5:21:20
Niagara 64 59 41N44 75W26 5:01:44
Niantic 46 2 40N22'44 75W34'19 5:02:17
Nicetown 51 9 40N00'47 75W09'26 5:00:38
Nichola 3 6 40N52'22 79W41'07 5:18:44
Nicholson 66 89 41N37'34 75W46'51 5:03:07
Nickel Mines 36 9 40N01 76W08 5:04:32
Nickleville 61 1 41N16'30 79W38'52 5:18:35
Nicklin 61 109 41N23'54 79W53'08 5:19:33
Nicktown 11 92 40N36'48 78W48'13 5:15:13
Nicodemus 28 100 39N47'18 77W36'07 5:10:24
Nilan 26 51 39N43'58 79W53'03 5:19:32
Niles 61 109 41N23'52 79W54'54 5:19:40
Niles Valley 59 6 41N49'30 77W17'16 5:09:09
Ninepoints 36 23 39N54'48 76W02'44 5:04:11
Nine Row 11 54 40N32'39 78W47'52 5:15:11
Nineveh 16 27 41N15'53 79W36'07 5:18:24
Nineveh 30 6 39N57'41 80W18'29 5:21:14
Nippenose 41 6 41N11 77W13 5:08:52
Nisbet 41 64 41N13'05 77W06'49 5:08:27
Nittany 14 63 40N59'51 77W33'23 5:10:14
Niver Junction 56
6 39N54'06 78W57'44 5:15:51
Niverton 56 6 39N43'51 79W07'55 5:16:32
Nixon 10 3 40N53 79W53 5:19:32
Nixon 58 6 41N56'19 76W08'10 5:04:33
Noble 46 9 40N06'20 75W07'31 5:00:30
Noblestown 2 51 40N23'28 80W11'56 5:20:48
Nockamixon 9 1 40N31 75W11 5:00:44
Noel 11 55 40N28'59 78W39'45 5:14:39
Nolo 32 6 40N34'20 78W57'35 5:15:50
Nook 34 7 40N30'25 77W31'40 5:10:07
Nordmont 57 6 41N22'45 76W28'27 5:05:54
Normal 13 8 40N50 75W42 5:02:48
Normal Square 13
8 40N47'20 75W48'04 5:03:12
Normalville 26 6 39N59'55 79W26'54 5:17:48
Norman 33 34 41N06'26 79W05'34 5:16:22
Normandy 51 56 40N06'12 74W59'46 4:59:59
Norristown 46 90 40N07'17 75W20'25 5:01:22
Norrisville 20 6 41N42'57 80W16'13 5:21:05
Norritonville 46
8 40N09'52 75W20'10 5:01:21
North 8 41 41N48 76W28 5:05:52
North Abington 35
44 41N33 75W42 5:02:48
Northampton 48 13 40N41'10 75W29'50 5:01:59
Northampton Hills 9
1 40N11 75W03 5:00:12
North Annville 38
1 40N21 76W32 5:06:08
North Apollo 3 4 40N35'46 79W33'21 5:18:13
North Ardmore 46
9 40N00 75W17 5:01:08
North Aronimink 23
9 39N58 75W18 5:01:12
North Bangor 48
17 40N54'17 75W11'40 5:00:47
North Barnesboro 11
92 40N40'12 78W47'27 5:15:10
North Beaver 37
112 40N57 80W26 5:21:44
North Belle Vernon 65
1 40N07'45 79W52'06 5:19:28
North Bend 18 7 41N21'00 77W42'09 5:10:49
North Bessemer 2
114 40N29'36 79W47'51 5:19:11
North Bethlehem 63
51 40N06 80W06 5:20:24
North Bingham 53
6 41N59'14 77W45'43 5:11:03
North Braddock 2
114 40N23'56 79W50'28 5:19:22
North Branch 66 6 41N33 76W11 5:04:44
Northbrook 15 8 39N55'13 75W41'21 5:02:45

Northbrook Hills 36 8 40N04 76w19 5:05:16
North Buffalo 3 15 40N45'46 79w35'02 5:18:20
North Butler 10 3 40N53 79w53 5:19:32
North Catasauqua 48 13 40N39'35 75w28'38 5:01:55
North Centre 19 6 41N04'32 76w22'48 5:05:31
North Charleroi 63 1 40N09'04 79w54'28 5:19:38
North Codorus 67 95 39N52 76w49 5:07:16
North Connellsville 26 104 40N02 79w35 5:18:20
North Coplay 39 13 40N40'49 75w30'11 5:02:01
North Cornwall 38 8 40N17'10 76w25'01 5:05:40
North Coventry 15 8 40N13 75w41 5:02:44
North East 25 91 42N12'56 79w50'04 5:19:20
North Edinburg 37 112 41N01'13 80w26'22 5:21:45
North End 40 20 41N16 75w51 5:03:24
North Essington 23 9 39N52 75w17 5:01:08
North Fayette 2 51 40N25 80w14 5:20:56
North Fogelsville 39 9 40N35'41 75w37'51 5:02:31
North Fork 53 6 41N58'50 77w37'27 5:10:30
North Franklin 63 3 40N09 80w16 5:21:04
North Fredericktown 63 6 40N00'35 80w00'01 5:20:00
North Freedom 33 6 41N01'19 79w12'36 5:16:50
North Ghent 8 60 41N53'31 76w26'32 5:05:46
North Hamilton 9 8 40N21 75w13 5:00:52
North Heidelberg 6 1 40N23'45 76w08'04 5:04:32
North Hills 46 9 40N07 75w10 5:00:40
North Hills 49 70 41N01'30 76w50'33 5:07:22
North Hopewell 67 1 39N49 76w36 5:06:24
North Huntingdon 65 25 40N20 79w44 5:18:56
North Irwin 65 25 40N20'15 79w42'49 5:18:51
North Jackson 58 59 41N53'14 75w34'56 5:02:20
North Larchmont 23 90 40N00 75w23 5:01:32
North Lebanon 38 8 40N22 76w25 5:05:40
North Liberty 43 6 41N05'34 80w05'40 5:20:23
North Londonderry 38 1 40N20 76w35 5:06:20
North Mahoning 32 6 40N53 79w03 5:16:12
North Manheim 54 27 40N39 76w09 5:04:36
North Manor 26 104 40N01'33 79w35'41 5:18:23
North McKees Rocks 2 114 40N28 80w05 5:20:20
North Mehoopany 66 59 41N34'33 76w03'45 5:04:15
North Middleton 21 16 40N14 77w12 5:08:48
North Mills 43 66 41N18'09 80w10'56 5:20:44
Northmoreland 66 6 41N26 75w56 5:03:44
North Mountain 41 6 41N17'32 76w33'10 5:06:13
North Newton 21 1 40N09 77w27 5:09:48
North Oakland 10 6 40N55'19 79w47'37 5:19:10
North Orwell 8 60 41N54'45 76w18'54 5:05:16
North Park 9 9 40N10'00 74w49'00 4:59:16
North Philadelphia 51 9 40N00 75w10 5:00:40
North Philipsburg 14 113 40N54'27 78w12'29 5:12:50
North Pine Grove 16 6 41N23'43 79w13'20 5:16:53
North Point 5 51 40N10 78w13 5:12:52
North Point 32 6 40N54'13 79w07'54 5:16:32
North Radcliffe 9 9 40N08 74w51 4:59:24
North Rochester 4 19 40N42'22 80w16'17 5:21:05
North Rome 8 41 41N52'21 76w24'05 5:05:36
North Sandy 61 6 41N23'18 80w00'00 5:20:00
North Scottdale 65 111 40N06'34 79w33'59 5:18:16
North Scranton 35 18 41N26 75w40 5:02:40
North Sewickley 4 121 40N50'35 80w16'12 5:21:05
North Shenango 20 7 41N36 80w28 5:21:52
North Side 2 114 40N27'26 80w00'26 5:20:02
North Springfield 25 51 41N59'40 80w25'31 5:21:42
North Strabane 63 2 40N14 80w09 5:20:36
North Sulger 33 6 41N10'24 78w57'17 5:15:49
North Towanda 8 41 41N47'16 76w27'15 5:05:49
Northumberland 49 82 40N53'30 76w47'52 5:07:11
North Vandergrift 3 4 40N36'26 79w33'35 5:18:14
North Versailles 2 9 40N23 79w49 5:19:16
Northvue 10 3 40N55'14 79w55'56 5:19:44
North Wales 46 8 40N12'39 75w16'43 5:01:07
North Warren 62 120 41N52'27 79w09'09 5:16:37
North Washington 10 6 41N02'52 79w48'49 5:19:15
North Washington 65 4 40N31'58 79w35'53 5:18:24
North Water Gap 45 23 41N00'16 75w08'12 5:00:33
North Waynesburg 30 100 39N45 77w34 5:10:16
North Weissport 13 8 40N50'09 75w41'55 5:02:48
North Whitehall 39 8 40N40 75w35 5:02:20
Northwood 7 11 40N41'07 78w13'48 5:12:55
North Woodbury 7 51 40N17 78w19 5:13:16
Northwood Heights 48 12 40N42'08 75w16'00 5:01:04
North York 67 67 39N58'41 76w44'00 5:06:56
Norvelt 65 111 40N12'29 79w29'52 5:17:59
Norwegian 54 49 40N41 76w14 5:04:56
Norwich 42 6 41N39'34 78w22'25 5:13:30
Norwin Heights 65 25 40N20 79w43 5:18:52
Norwood 2 114 40N28 80w05 5:20:20
Norwood 23 9 39N53'30 75w18'00 5:01:12
Norwood Acres 23 9 39N53 75w18 5:01:12
Norwood Park 23 9 39N53 75w18 5:01:12
Nossville 31 6 40N14'01 77w45'57 5:11:04
Notre Dame Hills 39 13 40N38'22 75w25'22 5:01:41
Nottingham 9 1 40N08 74w58 4:59:52
Nottingham 15 3 39N45'19 76w00'54 5:04:04
Nova 28 1 39N43'54 77w49'11 5:11:17
Nowrytown 32 116 40N31'52 79w25'49 5:17:43
Noxen 40 6 41N25'17 76w03'32 5:04:14
Noyes 18 7 41N17 77w50 5:11:20
Nuangola 40 1 41N09'18 75w58'43 5:03:55
Nuangola Station 40 20 41N08'57 75w56'44 5:03:47
Number Fifty Six 51 9 39N57 75w09 5:00:36
Number Five Mine 43 66 41N08'30 80w10'41 5:20:43
Number Thirty-Seven 11 123 40N15'04 78w51'36 5:15:26
Numidia 19 27 40N52'50 76w24'09 5:05:37
NuMine 3 6 40N47'46 79w17'00 5:17:08
Nuremberg 54 60 40N56'22 76w10'19 5:04:41
Nyesville 28 42 40N01'46 77w37'23 5:10:30
Oakbottom 36 27 39N54 76w10 5:04:40
Oakbourne 15 4 39N56'25 75w34'42 5:02:19
Oakdale 2 114 40N23'53 80w11'09 5:20:45
Oakdale 40 20 40N59'31 75w55'14 5:03:41
Oakdale Manor 9 9 40N12 74w49 4:59:16
Oakeola 23 9 39N54 75w18 5:01:12
Oakford 9 1 40N08'54 74w57'51 4:59:51
Oakford Park 65 3 40N20 79w37 5:18:28
Oak Forest 30 1 39N50'31 80w14'21 5:20:57
Oak Grove 1 56 39N43'54 77w06'50 5:08:27
Oak Grove 17 4 40N57'18 78w12'32 5:12:50
Oak Grove 45 85 41N02'52 75w06'54 5:00:28
Oak Grove 47 56 41N00'28 76w43'10 5:06:53
Oak Grove 54 9 40N36 76w23 5:05:32
Oak Grove 63 3 40N11'36 80w16'15 5:21:05
Oak Grove 65 110 40N15'34 79w12'06 5:16:48
Oak Hall 14 9 40N47'38 77w48'10 5:11:13
Oak Hill 2 114 40N25'33 79w48'47 5:19:15
Oak Hill 17 6 41N09'10 78w07'20 5:12:29
Oak Hill 35 18 41N21'57 75w43'00 5:02:52
Oak Hill 36 3 39N46'55 76w05'24 5:04:22
Oak Hill 61 109 41N24'46 79w50'24 5:19:22
Oakhurst 11 74 40N21'29 78w56'41 5:15:47
Oakland 2 114 40N26'31 79w57'46 5:19:51
Oakland 11 74 40N18'23 78w53'16 5:15:33
Oakland 37 112 40N59'23 80w22'11 5:21:29
Oakland 43 66 41N14'11 80w13'08 5:20:53
Oakland 58 59 41N57'00 75w36'19 5:02:25
Oakland Beach 20 6 41N36 80w19 5:21:16
Oakland Mills 34 1 40N36'52 77w19'02 5:09:16
Oak Lane 46 9 40N03'23 75w07'18 5:00:29
Oaklane Manor 46 9 40N05 75w08 5:00:32
Oakleigh 22 12 40N15'29 76w49'15 5:07:17
Oakley 58 59 41N44'12 75w45'17 5:03:01
Oaklyn 49 82 40N51'30 76w45'16 5:07:01
Oakmont 2 14 40N31'18 79w50'33 5:19:22
Oakmont 11 74 40N17 78w53 5:15:32
Oakmont 23 9 39N59'13 75w18'30 5:01:14
Oakmont Park 23 9 40N00 75w18 5:01:12
Oak Park 46 8 40N14'42 75w18'12 5:01:13
Oak Park 49 82 40N54'50 76w45'38 5:07:03
Oak Park Trailer Camp 46 8 40N17 75w18 5:01:12
Oak Ridge 3 6 41N00'27 79w17'46 5:17:11
Oak Ridge 17 6 40N50'58 78w29'48 5:13:59
Oakryn 36 1 39N46'36 76w08'30 5:04:34
Oaks 46 8 40N07'54 75w27'36 5:01:50
Oak Shade 36 27 39N48'16 76w06'46 5:04:27
Oak Tree 32 6 40N48'38 79w03'01 5:16:12
Oaktree Hollow 9 9 40N08'52 74w50'27 4:59:22
Oakview 23 9 39N57 75w18 5:01:12
Oakview Park 23 9 39N57 75w18 5:01:12
Oakville 21 23 40N07'34 77w27'20 5:09:49
Oakville 65 3 40N19 79w23 5:17:32
Oakwood 37 112 41N00 80w22 5:21:28
Oakwood Park 40 20 41N15 75w53 5:03:32
Oalmer Park 46 12 40N41 75w14 5:00:56
Obelisk 46 8 40N17'17 75w30'42 5:02:03
Oberlin 22 12 40N14'29 76w48'54 5:07:16
Oberlin Gardens 22 12 40N14'37 76w49'22 5:07:17
Observatory 2 114 40N29 80w01 5:20:04
Ochre Mill 40 60 41N07'42 75w46'51 5:03:07
Odell 63 51 40N06'46 80w06'31 5:20:26
Odenthal 11 63 40N23 78w40 5:14:40
Odenwelder 46 12 40N41 75w14 5:00:56
Odin 53 66 41N41'52 78w05'12 5:12:21
O'Donnell 33 6 41N05'46 78w56'18 5:15:45
Ogden 23 90 39N49'47 75w27'24 5:01:50
Ogdensburg 59 7 41N36'55 76w58'15 5:07:53
Ogdonia 57 6 41N24'41 76w42'21 5:06:49
Ogle 10 6 40N42'15 80w06'16 5:20:25
Ogle 56 6 40N13 78w43 5:14:52
Ogletown 56 123 40N12'09 78w42'12 5:14:49
Ogontz 46 9 40N04 75w07 5:00:28
Ogontz Campus 46 2 40N07 75w07 5:00:28
O'Hara 2 114 40N30 79w54 5:19:36
Ohio 2 114 40N33 80w06 5:20:24
Ohiopyle 26 4 39N52'18 79w29'33 5:17:58
Ohioview 4 19 40N39'14 80w23'17 5:21:33
Ohioville 4 6 40N40'45 80w29'42 5:21:59
Ohl 33 6 41N05'00 79w09'40 5:16:39
Oil City 11 55 40N24'08 78w38'25 5:14:34
Oil City 61 9 41N26'02 79w42'24 5:18:50
Oil Creek 61 9 41N25 79w42 5:18:48
Oklahoma 17 56 41N06'50 78w44'01 5:14:56
Oklahoma 65 4 40N34'53 79w34'27 5:18:18
Okome 41 6 41N26'14 77w24'48 5:09:39
Olanta 17 122 40N55'00 78w30'24 5:14:02
Old Boston 40 1 41N17'36 75w46'07 5:03:04
Old Clarendon 62 3 41N46'26 79w06'07 5:16:24
Old Concord 63 3 40N00'31 80w20'13 5:21:21
Old Crabtree 65 3 40N21'00 79w26'19 5:17:45
Olde Hickory 36 8 40N04 76w19 5:05:16
Old Enon 37 6 40N51 80w27 5:21:48
Old Forge 28 100 39N47'40 77w29'04 5:09:56
Old Forge 35 18 41N22'16 75w44'07 5:02:56
Old Fort 14 64 40N50'07 77w40'19 5:10:41
Old Frame 26 51 39N48'27 79w51'45 5:19:27
Old Furnace (Shirley Mine) 4 6 40N47'43 80w10'13 5:20:41
Old Junction 56 6 40N01 79w05 5:16:20
Old Line 36 8 40N06 76w22 5:05:28
Old Lycoming 41 82 41N16 77w05 5:08:20
Old Meadow 65 111 40N06 79w35 5:18:20
Old Mountain House 29 6 40N01'08 78w11'21 5:12:45
Old Orchard 46 12 40N41 75w14 5:00:56
Old Port 34 7 40N31'30 77w23'30 5:09:34
Old Shade Furnace 56 63 40N09'06 78w49'39 5:15:19
Old Side 14 7 41N03'41 77w56'27 5:11:46
Old Stanton 65 111 40N13'38 79w36'22 5:18:25
Old Zionsville 39 13 40N29'11 75w31'14 5:02:05
Old Zollarsville 63 6 40N00'40 80w04'33 5:20:18
Oleona 53 6 41N33'22 77w42'07 5:10:48
Oleopolis 61 9 41N27'20 79w37'03 5:18:28
Oley 6 1 40N22 75w46 5:03:04
Oley Furnace 6 101 40N24'30 75w47'20 5:03:09
Oley Line 6 8 40N20'38 75w48'17 5:03:13
Oliphant Furnace 26 80 39N50'32 79w43'34 5:18:54
Oliveburg 33 51 40N59'27 79w01'36 5:16:06
Oliver 26 80 39N55'03 79w43'03 5:18:52
Oliver Manor 61 9 41N26'06 79w40'44 5:18:43
Oliver Mills 40 20 41N13'01 75w50'32 5:03:22
Olivet 3 116 40N35'12 79w24'42 5:17:39
Olmsted 53 66 41N45'02 78w03'57 5:12:16
Olmsville 59 6 41N39'24 77w24'09 5:09:37
Olney 51 9 40N02'28 75w07'27 5:00:30
Olyphant 35 18 41N28'06 75w36'12 5:02:25
Onberg 32 6 40N40'01 79w03'19 5:16:13
Oneida 10 3 40N54'19 79w53'04 5:19:32
Oneida 31 81 40N33 77w58 5:11:52
Oneida 54 60 40N54'27 76w07'33 5:04:30
Oneida Junction 40 42 40N58 76w00 5:04:00
Oniontown 43 59 41N20'48 80w20'26 5:21:22
Onnalinda 11 63 40N18'34 78w40'46 5:14:43
Ono 38 1 40N24'10 76w32'06 5:06:08
Onspaugh Corners 20 77 41N38'50 80w12'32 5:20:50
Ontario 63 51 40N06'12 80w04'29 5:20:18
Ontelaunee 6 80 40N25'01 75w56'41 5:03:47
Opp 41 83 41N12 76w47 5:07:08
Oppenheimer 5 70 40N07'25 78w28'17 5:13:53
Oppermans Corner 15 8 40N04'42 75w38'04 5:02:32
Option 2 114 40N20'47 79w58'25 5:19:54
Orange 19 6 41N06 76w25 5:05:40
Orange 40 20 41N23'19 75w53'38 5:03:35
Orangeville 19 4 41N04'41 76w24'53 5:05:40
Orbisonia 31 6 40N14'34 77w53'36 5:11:34
Orchard Beach 25 91 42N14'29 79w49'44 5:19:19
Orchard Crest 21 12 40N12'51 76w59'11 5:07:57
Orchard Crossing 7 11 40N40 78w13 5:12:52
Orchard Hill 65 111 40N08'49 79w31'43 5:18:07
Orchard Hills 3 4 40N35'10 79w31'54 5:18:08
Orchard Hills 23 90 39N55 75w22 5:01:28
Orchard Park 36 8 40N04 76w19 5:05:16
Orefield 39 13 40N38'05 75w35'05 5:02:20
Oregon 36 28 40N00'00 76w14'43 5:04:59
Oregon 64 59 41N39 75w13 5:00:52
Oregon Hill 41 6 41N31'27 77w18'26 5:09:14
Ore Hill 7 3 40N17'37 78w24'04 5:13:36
Oreland 46 9 40N07'06 75w10'41 5:00:43
Oreland Gardens 46 9 40N07 75w11 5:00:44
Oreminea 7 3 40N24'17 78w15'20 5:13:01
Ore Valley 67 67 39N55'53 76w39'27 5:06:38
Oreville 6 9 40N31'07 75w41'25 5:02:46
Orient 26 51 39N57'04 79w51'15 5:19:25
Oriental 34 1 40N38'00 77w00'23 5:08:02
Oriole 41 6 41N08'28 77w12'37 5:08:50
Ormrod 39 13 40N40'16 75w33'19 5:02:13
Ormsby 42 6 41N48'32 78w32'31 5:14:10
Orners Corner 7 33 40N33'30 78w23'27 5:13:34
Orrstown 28 1 40N03'31 77w36'37 5:10:26
Orrtanna 1 4 39N50'42 77w21'40 5:09:27

Orrville 2 119 40N33 79W47 5:19:08
Orson 64 6 41N48'49 75W26'54 5:01:48
Orville 2 14 40N32'59 79W47'03 5:19:08
Orville 46 8 40N15'59 75W17'33 5:01:10
Orviston 18 7 41N06'23 77W45'09 5:11:01
Orwell 8 6 41N53'02 76W16'39 5:05:07
Orwig 67 27 39N45'39 76W37'42 5:06:31
Orwigsburg 54 1 40N39'17 76W06'04 5:04:24
Orwin 54 27 40N35'02 76W31'59 5:06:08
Osborn 43 6 41N27'43 80W17'21 5:21:09
Osborne 2 13 40N31'54 80W10'09 5:20:41
Oscar 3 59 40N50'25 79W22'17 5:17:29
Osceola 59 6 41N58'55 77W20'34 5:09:22
Osceola Mills 17
4 40N51'00 78W16'15 5:13:05
Osgood 43 59 41N26'41 80W22'04 5:21:28
Oshanter 17 1 40N56'07 78W27'42 5:13:51
Ostend 17 122 40N52'09 78W43'09 5:14:53
Osterburg 5 7 40N10'10 78W31'14 5:14:05
Osterhout 66 59 41N30'35 75W53'56 5:03:36
Oswayo 53 6 41N55'16 78W01'07 5:12:04
Ottawa 47 6 41N04'54 76W42'14 5:06:49
Otterbein 28 82 40N07'13 77W36'05 5:10:24
Otter Creek 43 59 41N24 80W18 5:21:12
Otto 42 6 41N57 78W29 5:13:56
Otto 49 4 40N43'08 76W47'53 5:07:12
Ottown 5 6 40N01 78W22 5:13:28
Ottsville 9 1 40N28'23 75W09'41 5:00:39
Ott Town 5 6 39N58'41 78W26'48 5:13:47
Outcrop 26 51 39N45'57 79W49'31 5:19:18
Outlet 40 20 41N20'21 76W03'38 5:04:15
Outwood 54 9 40N32'39 76W28'35 5:05:54
Oval 41 64 41N09'04 77W10'10 5:08:41
Overbrook 2 114 40N23'06 79W59'37 5:19:58
Overbrook 51 9 39N59'21 75W14'37 5:00:58
Overbrook Hills 46
9 39N59 75W16 5:01:04
Overfield 66 6 41N31 75W50 5:03:20
Overholt Acres 65
25 40N20 79W43 5:18:52
Overleigh 46 9 40N01 75W15 5:01:00
Overlook 36 8 40N04 76W19 5:05:16
Overlook 49 27 40N49'12 76W34'31 5:06:18
Overlook Heights 14
9 40N48'26 77W53'04 5:11:32
Overlook Springs 39
13 40N32'10 75W28'36 5:01:54
Overshot 8 41 41N45'43 76W31'27 5:06:06
Overton 8 60 41N34'12 76W30'12 5:06:01
Overview 21 12 40N19'08 76W55'24 5:07:42
Owassee 59 6 41N42'48 77W27'25 5:09:50
Owens Corners 25
91 42N06'58 79W55'12 5:19:41
Owensdale 26 104 40N04'35 79W36'14 5:18:25
Owl Hollow 8 6 41N58'56 76W20'20 5:05:21
Owls Nest 24 75 41N28'17 78W53'16 5:15:33
Owltown 61 9 41N30'26 79W39'06 5:18:36
Oxford 15 3 39N47'07 75W58'45 5:03:55
Oxford Valley 9 9 40N10'52 74W52'00 4:59:28
Oyster Point 36 8 40N03'31 76W24'14 5:05:37
Packer 13 80 40N54 75W53 5:03:32
Packerton 13 8 40N51'18 75W43'10 5:02:53
Packerton Junction 13
8 40N51'48 75W43'17 5:02:53
Paddytown 56 53 39N50'55 79W16'31 5:17:06
Pageville 25 7 41N51'36 80W16'00 5:21:04
Paine 24 36 41N21'44 78W34'34 5:14:18
Paint 56 123 40N14'37 78W50'57 5:15:24
Painter Run 59 59 41N51'36 77W03'29 5:08:14
Painters Crossroads 23
4 39N52'51 75W32'50 5:02:11
Paintersville 44
6 40N38'58 77W27'09 5:09:49
Paintersville 65
111 40N13 79W36 5:18:24
Paintertown 65 25 40N20 79W43 5:18:52
Paint Mills 16 37 41N15'05 79W24'51 5:17:39
Paisley 30 51 39N51'45 79W57'18 5:19:49
Palestine 17 4 41N01'23 78W13'18 5:12:53
Paletown 9 8 40N25'35 75W18'58 5:01:16
Pallas 55 51 40N42'44 76W57'13 5:07:49
Palm 46 2 40N25'41 75W32'00 5:02:08
Palmdale 22 31 40N17'52 76W37'08 5:06:29
Palmer 20 6 41N45'39 80W25'46 5:21:43
Palmer 26 51 39N54'42 79W55'12 5:19:41
Palmer 46 8 40N42 75W16 5:01:04
Palmer Heights 48
12 40N41'14 75W15'46 5:01:03
Palmerton 13 8 40N48'05 75W36'38 5:02:27
Palmertown 32 98 40N28'17 79W10'54 5:16:44
Palmyra 38 31 40N18'32 76W35'37 5:06:22
Palo Alto 5 51 39N45'49 78W45'01 5:15:00
Palo Alto 54 49 40N41'14 76W10'21 5:04:41
Palomino Farms 9
8 40N14'22 75W07'47 5:00:31
Pancake 14 7 41N03'08 77W55'05 5:11:40
Pancoast 33 6 41N07'43 78W49'23 5:15:18
P and W Patch 63
6 40N15'50 80W28'39 5:21:55
Panic 33 6 41N02'10 78W56'51 5:15:47
Panorama Village 14
9 40N47'03 77W48'37 5:11:14
Pansy 33 6 41N02'30 79W09'06 5:16:36
Pansy Hill 38 8 40N20'56 76W27'56 5:05:52
Panther 18 7 41N06'23 77W49'50 5:11:19
Panther 52 6 41N16'48 75W17'59 5:01:12
Paoli 15 8 40N02'31 75W28'36 5:01:54
Paper Mill 19 4 41N01'47 76W26'28 5:05:46
Paper Mills 46 1 40N08'24 75W04'28 5:00:18
Paradise 36 9 40N00'35 76W07'44 5:04:31
Paradise 54 9 40N34'08 76W22'53 5:05:32
Paradise Crossing 45
84 41N07'40 75W20'26 5:01:22
Paradise Falls 45
84 41N09 75W17 5:01:08
Paradise Furnace 31
3 40N18'44 78W07'32 5:12:30
Paradise Valley 45
84 41N07'19 75W16'52 5:01:07
Pardee 17 113 40N56'17 78W12'15 5:12:49
Pardee 60 7 40N51'38 77W16'20 5:09:05
Pardeesville 40
42 41N00'06 75W58'00 5:03:52
Pardoe 43 66 41N13'05 80W08'42 5:20:35
Pardus 33 6 41N08'45 78W53'14 5:15:33
Paris 63 6 40N24'13 80W30'46 5:22:03
Park 65 4 40N37 79W34 5:18:16
Parkchester 15 13 39N57 75W36 5:02:24
Park Crest 54 27 40N49'00 76W02'51 5:04:11
Parker 3 6 41N05'45 79W40'58 5:18:44
Parker City 3 6 41N05 79W41 5:18:44
Parker Ford 15 8 40N11'58 75W35'03 5:02:20
Parkers Glen 52 6 41N26'10 74W53'11 4:59:33
Parkersville 15
13 39N53'20 75W38'47 5:02:35
Parkesburg 15 32 39N57'31 75W55'11 5:03:41
Park Forest Village 14
9 40N48'24 77W55'02 5:11:40
Park Gate 37 121 40N51'15 80W18'27 5:21:14
Park Heights 67 1 39N48 76W59 5:07:56
Parkhill 11 74 40N21'38 78W52'17 5:15:29
Park Hills 14 9 40N47'51 77W53'58 5:11:36
Park Hills 67 1 39N48 76W59 5:07:56
Parkland 9 97 40N09'32 74W55'56 4:59:44
Parkland Heights 9
97 40N09'25 74W56'32 4:59:46
Park Manor 6 101 40N19 75W57 5:03:48
Park Meadows 65
25 40N20 79W43 5:18:52
Park Place 54 3 40N50'18 76W05'54 5:04:24
Parks 3 4 40N39 79W32 5:18:08
Parks Crossroad 58
60 41N49'02 76W01'03 5:04:04
Parkside 23 90 39N51'51 75W22'44 5:01:31
Parkside 45 84 41N06'04 75W15'03 5:01:00
Parkside Courts 39
13 40N36'17 75W32'00 5:02:08
Parkside Manor 23
90 39N52 75W23 5:01:32
Parkstown 11 74 40N19'35 78W52'46 5:15:31
Parkstown 37 112 41N00'59 80W24'24 5:21:38
Parktown Estates 9
9 40N12 74W49 4:59:16
Parkvale 58 89 41N43'04 75W52'21 5:03:29
Park View 2 114 40N30'06 79W55'53 5:19:44
Parkview Gardens 39
13 40N39 75W30 5:02:00
Park View Heights 14
70 40N55'04 77W45'30 5:11:02
Parkville 67 1 39N46'52 76W57'49 5:07:51
Parkway Center 2
114 40N26 80W03 5:20:12
Park Way Manor 39
13 40N35'18 75W32'59 5:02:12
Parkwood 32 6 40N37'08 79W18'05 5:17:12
Park Wynne Estates 23
9 39N58 75W22 5:01:28
Parnassus 65 14 40N33'25 79W45'44 5:19:03
Parrish 27 6 41N29'29 78W59'49 5:15:59
Parrs Mill 19 4 40N54'25 76W28'21 5:05:53
Parryville 13 8 40N49'05 75W40'23 5:02:42
Parsons 40 20 41N15'36 75W50'32 5:03:22
Parsonsville 17 4 40N50'48 78W19'57 5:13:20
Parsonville 10 6 41N03'34 79W48'35 5:19:14
Parsonville 17 4 40N50 78W21 5:13:24
Parvin 18 76 41N03'33 77W30'57 5:10:04
Paschall 51 9 39N56 75W14 5:00:56
Passer 9 8 40N31'02 75W19'56 5:01:20
Passmore 6 2 40N22 75W38 5:02:32
Patagonia 43 117 41N14'52 80W30'44 5:22:03
Patchel Run 61
109 41N25 79W50 5:19:20
Patchinville 17
63 40N44 78W49 5:15:16
Patchville 17 6 40N46'50 78W46'37 5:15:06
Patience 5 70 39N52'24 78W36'39 5:14:27
Patricksburg 49
51 40N46'23 76W48'01 5:07:12
Patterson 4 8 40N45 80W20 5:21:20
Patterson Grove 40
1 41N13'54 76W14'25 5:04:58
Patterson Heights 4
8 40N44'22 80W19'46 5:21:19
Patterson Hill 2
8 40N16'49 79W52'15 5:19:29
Pattersons Mill 63
6 40N17'32 80W26'55 5:21:48
Patterson Township 4
8 40N46 80W20 5:21:20
Pattersonville 54
1 40N50'22 76W13'39 5:04:55
Patton 11 57 40N37'23 78W39'09 5:14:37
Pattonville 3 15 40N46'30 79W31'16 5:18:05
Paulton 65 4 40N34'14 79W34'30 5:18:18
Paupack 52 6 41N23'46 75W11'48 5:00:47
Pavia 5 7 40N15'26 78W35'05 5:14:20
Paxinos 49 1 40N51'02 76W34'51 5:06:19
Paxinosa 48 12 40N42'42 75W12'04 5:00:48
Paxtang 22 12 40N15'32 76W49'56 5:07:20
Paxtang Manor 22
12 40N16 76W49 5:07:16
Paxton 22 1 40N35'46 76W56'15 5:07:45
Paxtonia 22 12 40N19'02 76W47'41 5:07:11
Paxtonville 55 6 40N46'13 77W05'03 5:08:20
Peacedale 15 3 39N44'42 75W54'25 5:03:38
Peaceful Valley 10
6 41N03'10 79W49'48 5:19:19
Peach Bottom 36 7 39N45'03 76W13'34 5:04:54
Peach Bottom Village 36
1 39N47 76W11 5:04:44
Peach Glen 1 1 40N01'23 77W13'49 5:08:55
Peale 17 6 40N59'52 78W04'54 5:12:20
Pealertown 19 4 41N07'05 76W21'47 5:05:27
Peanut 37 112 41N00'31 80W28'14 5:21:53
Peanut 65 3 40N20'09 79W18'56 5:17:16
Pearl 61 6 41N16'31 79W55'20 5:19:41
Pebble Acres 9 8 40N21 75W13 5:00:52
Pebble Hill 9 8 40N21 75W13 5:00:52
Pecan 61 6 41N20'08 79W53'07 5:19:32
Pechin 26 105 39N57'47 79W36'56 5:18:28
Pecks Pond 52 6 41N16'59 75W05'33 5:00:22
Peckville 35 1 41N28'35 75W34'25 5:02:18
Pemberton 31 11 40N37'19 78W10'07 5:12:40
Pen Argyl 48 17 40N52'07 75W15'19 5:01:01
Penarth 46 9 40N01 75W15 5:01:00
Penbrook 22 12 40N16'31 76W50'54 5:07:24
Penbryn 59 7 41N35'48 76W52'35 5:07:30
Pencoyd 46 9 40N02 75W15 5:01:00
Pendle Hill 23 90 39N54'33 75W22'09 5:01:29
Penfield 17 7 41N12'30 78W34'33 5:14:18
Penfield 23 9 39N58'50 75W17'21 5:01:09
Penfield Downs 46
9 39N59 75W16 5:01:04
Penllyn 46 8 40N10'12 75W14'44 5:00:59
Pen Mar 28 100 39N43'13 77W30'25 5:10:02
Penn 65 3 40N19'44 79W38'29 5:18:34
Penn Allen 48 8 40N43'56 75W21'56 5:01:28
Pennbrook 46 8 40N15 75W17 5:01:08
Penn Center 51 9 39N57 75W10 5:00:40
Penncraft 26 6 39N57'36 79W54'48 5:19:39
Penndel 9 97 40N09'07 74W55'01 4:59:40
Pennersville 28
100 39N43'36 77W28'45 5:09:55
Pennfield 9 9 40N08 74W51 4:59:24
Penn Five 14 4 40N49'37 78W16'08 5:13:05
Penn Forest 13 1 40N58 75W39 5:02:36
Penn Glyn 65 25 40N19'27 79W41'22 5:18:45
Penn Hall 14 64 40N51'39 77W33'28 5:10:14
Penn Haven Junction 13
60 40N56'42 75W44'50 5:02:59
Penn Heights 67 1 39N48 76W59 5:07:56
Penn Hill 36 1 39N46'50 76W10'45 5:04:43
Penn Hill Apartments 23
9 39N52 75W20 5:01:20
Penn Hill Homes 23
9 39N52 75W20 5:01:20
Penn Hills 2 114 40N28 79W52 5:19:28
Pennhurst 15 8 40N11'28 75W34'30 5:02:18
Pennington 31 11 40N41'42 78W09'37 5:12:38
Pennline 20 7 41N42'44 80W30'42 5:22:03
Penn Pines 23 9 39N56 75W18 5:01:12
Penn Pitt 30 51 39N47'21 79W55'30 5:19:42
Penn Ridge 2 114 40N27'49 79W48'46 5:19:15
Penn Rose 2 114 40N29 79W50 5:19:20
Penn Rose Park 36
8 40N04'30 76W18'59 5:05:16
Penn Run 32 6 40N37'07 79W00'41 5:16:03
Pennsburg 46 2 40N23'27 75W29'33 5:01:58
Pennsbury 15 1 39N52 75W37 5:02:28
Pennsbury Heights 9
9 40N12 74W49 4:59:16
Pennsbury Village 2
114 40N26 80W04 5:20:16
Penns Creek 55 6 40N51'35 77W03'20 5:08:13
Pennsdale 41 81 41N14'35 76W47'49 5:07:11
Pennside 6 101 40N20'14 75W52'44 5:03:31
Pennside 25 7 41N51'02 80W24'05 5:21:36
Penns Park 9 8 40N15'57 74W59'54 5:00:00
Penn Square 46 90 40N08'34 75W18'53 5:01:16
Pennsville 26 104 40N04'18 79W33'47 5:18:15
Pennsville 48 13 40N44'55 75W30'17 5:02:01
Penns Woods 65 25 40N20 79W43 5:18:52
Pennsylvania Furnace 31
6 40N42'21 78W00'14 5:12:01
Penn Valley 9 9 40N10'47 74W47'47 4:59:11
Penn Valley 46 9 40N00 75W16 5:01:04
Penn Valley Terrace 9
97 40N10 74W55 4:59:40
Penn View 14 6 40N50'47 77W27'10 5:09:49
Penn Village 46 8 40N15 75W39 5:02:36
Pennville 67 1 39N47'22 76W59'54 5:08:00
Penn Wood 5 70 40N01'44 78W25'57 5:13:44
Pennwyn 6 101 40N17'39 75W58'38 5:03:55
Penn Wynne 46 9 39N59'10 75W16'33 5:01:06
Pennypack Woods 51
9 40N03'15 75W00'59 5:00:04
Penobscot 40 20 41N09'59 75W51'52 5:03:27
Penoke 27 6 41N30'22 79W04'16 5:16:17
Penowa 63 6 40N17'13 80W30'12 5:22:01
Penryn 36 1 40N12'18 76W22'07 5:05:28
Pensyls Mill 19 4 40N54'11 76W29'22 5:05:57
Pentland 67 1 39N47'27 76W51'15 5:07:25
Pequea 36 8 39N53'17 76W22'03 5:05:28
Percy 26 80 39N55'57 79W39'06 5:18:36
Perdix 50 51 40N21'20 76W57'30 5:07:50
Perkasie 9 8 40N22'19 75W17'35 5:01:10
Perkiomen Heights 46
2 40N22'34 75W30'58 5:02:04
Perkiomen Junction 15
8 40N06'59 75W28'32 5:01:54
Perkiomen Village 46
8 40N12 75W28 5:01:52
Perkiomenville 46
8 40N19'27 75W28'42 5:01:55
Perrine Corners 43
6 41N17'19 80W04'18 5:20:17
Perrymont 2 114 40N33 80W01 5:20:04
Perryopolis 26 6 40N05'13 79W45'03 5:19:00
Perrys Corners 43
6 41N11'52 80W04'44 5:20:19
Perry Square 25
107 42N08 80W05 5:20:20
Perrysville 2 114 40N32'05 80W01'59 5:20:08
Perryville 16 6 41N05'53 79W40'01 5:18:40
Perryville 41 7 41N19'16 77W05'59 5:08:24
Perryville 65 116 40N30'46 79W31'24 5:18:06
Peru 14 70 40N51'17 77W46'01 5:11:04
Perulack 34 6 40N20'34 77W38'26 5:10:34
Peru Mills 34 6 40N22'29 77W41'14 5:10:45
Petersburg 31 81 40N34'21 78W02'50 5:12:11
Petersburg 43 6 41N26'21 80W15'18 5:21:01
Petersburg 67 1 39N54'03 76W34'42 5:06:19
Peters Corner 9 8 40N22'32 75W02'31 5:00:10
Peters Creek 2 8 40N18 79W54 5:19:36
Peters Store 39 8 40N45 75W37 5:02:28
Petersville 10 6 40N49'26 80W00'41 5:20:03
Petersville 48 13 40N45'09 75W28'40 5:01:55
Petroleum Center 61
9 41N30'58 79W40'57 5:18:44
Petrolia 10 6 41N01'00 79W43'04 5:18:52
Pettis 20 77 41N40 80W07 5:20:28
Pew 16 6 41N02 79W15 5:17:00
Pheasant Hill 36
8 40N04 76W19 5:05:16
Philadelphia 51 9 39N57'08 75W09'51 5:00:39
Philipsburg 14
113 40N53'47 78W13'15 5:12:53
Philipsburg 63 1 40N03'42 79W52'53 5:19:32
Philipston 16 1 40N58'27 79W35'26 5:18:22

Phillips 26 80 39N56'21 79W43'45 5:18:55
Phillips 59 6 41N56'21 77W29'01 5:09:56
Phillipston 16 7 41N02 79W30 5:18:00
Phillipsville 15 9 40N00'04 75W53'51 5:03:35
Phillipsville 25 7 42N02'12 79W53'06 5:19:32
Philmont 46 1 40N09 75W03 5:00:12
Philmont Manor 46 1 40N09 75W03 5:00:12
Philmont Park 46 1 40N09 75W03 5:00:12
Phoenix Park 54 49 40N40'57 76W17'25 5:05:10
Phoenixville 15 8 40N07'49 75W30'55 5:02:04
Piatt 41 64 41N13 77W13 5:08:52
Piatt 57 6 41N33'03 76W43'01 5:06:52
Pickering 15 8 40N06'33 75W31'41 5:02:07
Picture Rocks 41 6 41N16'47 76W42'48 5:06:51
Pierce 2 8 40N18 79W54 5:19:36
Pierce 3 6 41N02 79W15 5:17:00
Pierceville 67 3 39N45'15 76W46'48 5:07:07
Pigeon 27 6 41N31'50 79W03'05 5:16:12
Pigs Ear 24 6 41N33'48 78W56'14 5:15:45
Pikeland 15 8 40N06'01 75W36'43 5:02:27
Pikes Creek 40 20 41N18'23 76W05'47 5:04:23
Pikes Peak 32 6 40N35'54 79W00'40 5:16:03
Piketown 22 12 40N22'43 76W45'22 5:07:01
Pikeville 6 101 40N23'54 75W43'26 5:02:54
Pilgerts 6 13 40N28'28 75W39'14 5:02:37
Pilgrim Gardens 23 9 39N57'23 75W19'29 5:01:18
Pilgrimham 16 6 41N14'01 79W36'11 5:18:25
Pillow 22 4 40N38'27 76W48'10 5:07:13
Pilltown 56 6 40N10'17 79W00'48 5:16:03
Pindleton 11 63 40N30'23 78W48'36 5:15:14
Pine 18 7 41N09'59 77W18'50 5:09:15
Pine 59 6 41N36'37 77W24'24 5:09:38
Pine Avenue 25 107 42N06 80W03 5:20:12
Pine Bank 30 6 39N45'25 80W18'35 5:21:14
Pine City 16 37 41N18'18 79W30'28 5:18:02
Pinecreek 33 34 41N09'33 79W03'32 5:16:14
Pinecrest 9 97 40N10 74W55 4:59:40
Pinecroft 7 33 40N34'07 78W21'01 5:13:24
Pinedale 54 1 40N38 76W05 5:04:20
Pine Flats 32 6 40N39'33 78W55'13 5:15:41
Pine Flats 52 6 41N14'26 75W06'08 5:00:25
Pine Forge 6 8 40N16'58 75W41'28 5:02:46
Pine Furnace 3 15 40N51'13 79W25'46 5:17:43
Pine Glen 14 6 41N05'20 78W03'25 5:12:14
Pine Glen 44 7 40N30'06 77W40'50 5:10:43
Pine Grove 11 55 40N29'07 78W37'15 5:14:29
Pine Grove 17 1 40N58'44 78W27'12 5:13:49
Pine Grove 36 3 39N47'40 76W02'50 5:04:11
Pine Grove 50 6 40N22'56 77W26'40 5:09:47
Pine Grove 54 27 40N32'54 76W23'06 5:05:32
Pine Grove 58 89 41N39'28 75W48'03 5:03:12
Pine Grove Furnace 21 1 40N02'00 77W17'56 5:09:12
Pine Grove Mills 14 9 40N44'01 77W53'09 5:11:33
Pine Hall 14 9 40N46'34 77W53'07 5:11:32
Pine Hill 3 15 40N48'59 79W31'57 5:18:08
Pine Hill 54 49 40N41'57 76W17'09 5:05:09
Pine Hill 56 6 39N53'14 78W59'24 5:15:58
Pinehurst 4 13 40N36'14 80W11'05 5:20:44
Pine Junction 54 60 40N50'20 76W04'03 5:04:16
Pine Mill 64 6 41N47'09 75W14'35 5:00:58
Pine Ridge 23 90 39N55'10 75W22'21 5:01:29
Pine Run 9 8 40N19'51 75W08'44 5:00:35
Pine Run 41 64 41N14'16 77W10'40 5:08:43
Pine Summit 19 6 41N10'40 76W33'53 5:06:16
Pine Swamp 15 1 40N11'01 75W47'09 5:03:09
Pineton 32 6 40N36'04 78W54'07 5:15:36
Pinetown 67 12 40N07'12 76W54'04 5:07:36
Pinetree 65 111 40N06'46 79W36'04 5:18:24
Pine Valley 62 3 41N58'03 79W31'08 5:18:05
Pine View 40 20 41N08'08 75W56'54 5:03:48
Pineville 9 8 40N17'46 75W00'22 5:00:01
Pineville 62 6 41N37'55 79W30'20 5:18:01
Pine Waters 6 101 40N25'14 75W42'27 5:02:50
Pinewood 9 9 40N09'24 74W49'16 4:59:17
Piney 16 6 41N08 79W28 5:17:52
Piney Fork 2 114 40N17'23 79W59'47 5:19:59
Pink 64 6 41N28'43 75W20'07 5:01:20
Pinkerton 56 4 39N50'50 79W14'23 5:16:58
Pinney Corners 20 6 41N43'01 80W01'17 5:20:05
Pinola 28 82 40N02'15 77W35'31 5:10:22
Piolett 16 6 41N03'24 79W24'10 5:17:37
Pioneer 61 9 41N31'52 79W39'55 5:18:40
Piper 17 6 41N11'05 78W08'44 5:12:35
Pipersville 9 1 40N25'31 75W08'23 5:00:34
Pitcairn 2 114 40N24'11 79W46'42 5:19:07
Pithole City 61 9 41N31'15 79W35'14 5:18:21
Pitman 54 1 40N42'54 76W31'16 5:06:05
Pitt Gas 30 6 39N58'48 80W01'41 5:20:07
Pittock 2 114 40N29'13 80W05'05 5:20:20
Pitts 59 6 41N44'39 77W16'13 5:09:05
Pittsburgh 2 114 40N26'26 79W59'46 5:19:59
Pittsburgh Valley 36 8 39N57 76W21 5:05:24
Pittsfield 62 7 41N50'08 79W22'54 5:17:32
Pittston 40 1 41N19'33 75W47'23 5:03:10
Pittston Junction 40 1 41N20'30 75W47'10 5:03:09
Pittsville 61 6 41N15'22 79W44'27 5:18:58
Plainfield 21 2 40N12'11 77W17'25 5:09:10
Plainfield 46 15 40N49 75W15 5:01:00
Plainfield 67 1 40N10'11 76W45'53 5:07:04
Plain Grove 37 6 41N03'15 80W08'35 5:20:34
Plains 40 20 41N16'31 75W51'02 5:03:24
Plainsville 40 20 41N17'25 75W51'00 5:03:24
Plainview 1 1 39N55'34 77W09'52 5:08:39
Plainville 38 31 40N15'57 76W34'32 5:06:18
Plane Bank 11 55 40N24'33 78W37'48 5:14:31
Planebrook 15 8 40N02'22 75W34'27 5:02:18
Plank 59 6 41N34'16 77W14'47 5:08:59
Platea 25 7 41N57'01 80W19'42 5:21:19
Plateau Heights 20 77 41N40 80W07 5:20:28
Plattsville 11 92 40N41'32 78W44'46 5:14:59
Plaza 10 3 40N53 79W53 5:19:32
Plaza Heights 67 1 39N48 76W59 5:07:56
Pleasant 62 3 41N48 79W11 5:16:44
Pleasant Corners 39 8 40N41'00 75W41'27 5:02:46
Pleasant Gap 14 70 40N52'05 77W44'49 5:10:59
Pleasant Grove 36 1 39N43'51 76W11'39 5:04:47
Pleasant Grove 60 6 40N55'57 77W07'58 5:08:32
Pleasant Grove 63 6 40N04'35 80W21'25 5:21:26
Pleasant Grove 65 110 40N11'06 79W17'10 5:17:09
Pleasant Grove 67 80 40N07'11 76W44'39 5:06:59
Pleasant Hall 28 1 40N03'11 77W39'15 5:10:37
Pleasant Hill 11 74 40N21'43 78W55'25 5:15:42
Pleasant Hill 17 6 41N00'26 78W07'50 5:12:31
Pleasant Hill 23 90 39N55 75W22 5:01:28
Pleasant Hill 25 107 42N04'26 80W00'08 5:20:01
Pleasant Hill 26 104 40N00'54 79W30'30 5:18:02
Pleasant Hill 32 72 40N38'32 79W08'09 5:16:33
Pleasant Hill 37 121 40N53'20 80W11'40 5:20:47
Pleasant Hill 38 8 40N20'10 76W26'31 5:05:46
Pleasant Hill 67 1 39N48 76W59 5:07:56
Pleasant Hills 2 114 40N20'08 79W57'39 5:19:51
Pleasant Hills 22 12 40N33'58 76W55'08 5:07:41
Pleasant Mount 64 59 41N44'23 75W26'05 5:01:44
Pleasant Ridge 29 66 39N55'41 78W06'28 5:12:26
Pleasant Run 46 8 40N20'54 75W32'31 5:02:10
Pleasant Union 56 79 39N45'49 78W52'13 5:15:29
Pleasant Unity 65 3 40N14'22 79W27'04 5:17:48
Pleasant Valley 6 80 40N24'08 76W03'31 5:04:14
Pleasant Valley 7 33 40N30'09 78W23'25 5:13:34
Pleasant Valley 9 13 40N31'16 75W17'35 5:01:10
Pleasant Valley 26 104 40N03'07 79W31'43 5:18:07
Pleasant Valley 54 9 40N33'46 76W22'16 5:05:29
Pleasant Valley 65 3 40N22'44 79W40'26 5:18:42
Pleasant View 3 4 40N36'38 79W34'27 5:18:18
Pleasantview 4 8 40N46 80W20 5:21:20
Pleasant View 14 70 40N55'34 77W46'43 5:11:07
Pleasant View 22 12 40N15'48 76W43'55 5:06:56
Pleasant View 34 7 40N27'24 77W29'31 5:09:58
Pleasant View 67 1 39N54'10 76W35'26 5:06:22
Pleasant View Heights 63 51 40N05'26 80W04'55 5:20:20
Pleasant View Summit 40 60 41N12'44 75W39'50 5:02:39
Pleasant Village 7 33 40N31 78W25 5:13:40
Pleasantville 2 14 40N37'19 79W44'13 5:18:57
Pleasantville 5 6 40N11 78W37 5:14:28
Pleasantville 61 6 41N35'32 79W34'47 5:18:19
Pleasureville 67 67 39N59'49 76W42'25 5:06:50
Pleasureville Heights 67 67 39N59 76W46 5:07:04
Plowville 6 101 40N12'51 75W54'34 5:03:38
Plum 2 14 40N29 79W47 5:19:08
Plum 61 74 41N38 79W40 5:18:40
Plumbridge 9 9 40N09 74W51 4:59:24
Plumbsock 63 3 40N01'30 80W15'15 5:21:01
Plum Corner 61 6 41N31'55 79W51'54 5:19:28
Plum Creek 2 14 40N29 79W44 5:18:56
Plumer 61 9 41N29'57 79W38'31 5:18:34
Plummer 26 51 39N52'14 79W51'56 5:19:28
Plum Run 29 6 39N45'56 78W07'05 5:12:28
Plumsock 15 90 39N58'21 75W27'47 5:01:51
Plumsteadville 9 8 40N23'14 75W08'49 5:00:35
Plumville 32 6 40N47'35 79W10'51 5:16:43
Plunketts Creek 41 6 41N24 76W47 5:07:08
Plymouth 40 20 41N14'25 75W56'42 5:03:47
Plymouth Center 46 90 40N07 75W16 5:01:04
Plymouth Junction 40 20 41N14'41 75W55'37 5:03:42
Plymouth Meeting 46 90 40N06'08 75W16'29 5:01:06
Plymouth Valley 46 90 40N08 75W21 5:01:24
Plymptonville 17 1 41N02'09 78W26'23 5:13:46
Pocahontas 56 79 39N44'28 78W57'31 5:15:50
Pocono 45 84 41N04 75W18 5:01:12
Pocono Lake 45 3 41N06'19 75W28'35 5:01:54
Pocono Lake Preserve 45 84 41N06 75W28 5:01:52
Pocono Manor 45 84 41N06'00 75W21'33 5:01:26
Pocono Mountain Lake Estates 13 94 41N04'53 75W41'48 5:02:47
Pocono Park 45 23 41N00 75W13 5:00:52
Pocono Pines 45 84 41N06'24 75W27'17 5:01:49
Pocono Playhouse 45 84 41N10'27 75W16'29 5:01:06
Pocono Summit 45 84 41N64'40 75W23'12 5:01:33
Pocono Summit Estates 45 84 41N07'20 75W22'49 5:01:31
Pocopson 15 13 39N54'01 75W37'34 5:02:30
Pogue 31 6 40N12'38 77W55'42 5:11:43
Point 5 6 40N04'39 78W36'02 5:14:24
Point 49 82 40N56 76W47 5:07:08
Point Breeze 2 114 40N27'16 79W55'19 5:19:41
Point Breeze 26 6 39N47'43 79W40'26 5:18:42
Point Breeze 49 27 40N45'18 76W33'18 5:06:13
Point Breeze 51 9 39N55 75W11 5:00:44
Point Hill 61 109 41N24'06 79W49'17 5:19:17
Point Lookout 63 3 40N06'59 80W15'43 5:21:03
Point Marion 26 7 39N44'20 79W53'56 5:19:36
Point Phillip 48 13 40N47'47 75W24'57 5:01:40
Point Pleasant 9 1 40N25'21 75W04'00 5:00:16
Point View 7 3 40N29'22 78W14'31 5:12:58
Point View 29 6 39N48'37 78W15'51 5:13:03
Poke Run 65 6 40N29'25 79W35'49 5:18:23
Pokeytown 56 6 40N07 78W57 5:15:48
Poland 30 7 39N45 79W56 5:19:44
Poland Mines 30 7 39N45'56 79W56'44 5:19:47
Polen 30 6 39N52'02 80W30'15 5:22:01
Polk 61 6 41N22'01 79W55'46 5:19:43
Polk Junction 61 6 41N22 79W56 5:19:44
Polktown 28 100 39N45'35 77W37'51 5:10:31
Polk Valley 48 13 40N34'12 75W18'16 5:01:13
Polkville 19 6 41N14'04 76W26'00 5:05:44
Pomeroy 15 32 39N57'51 75W53'13 5:03:33
Pomeroy Heights 15 32 39N58'13 75W53'10 5:03:33
Pond Bank 28 42 39N52'22 77W32'30 5:10:10
Pond Creek 40 60 41N02'40 75W50'43 5:03:23
Pond Eddy 52 6 41N25'52 74W49'24 4:59:18
Pond Hill 40 1 41N07'34 76W06'12 5:04:25
Pont 25 7 41N51'05 80W18'21 5:21:13
Pools Corner 9 8 40N18'49 75W06'21 5:00:25
Poorman Side 14 7 41N03'49 77W55'24 5:11:42
Poplar Bridge 45 85 41N04'22 75W06'53 5:00:28
Poplar Grove 26 104 40N02'06 79W34'48 5:18:19
Poplar Grove 36 8 40N13'55 76W18'57 5:05:16
Poplars 67 67 39N59'19 76W48'20 5:07:13
Porkey 27 3 41N36'43 79W09'57 5:16:40
Portage 11 63 40N23'19 78W40'21 5:14:41
Portage Creek 42 6 41N49 78W17 5:13:08
Port Allegany 42 3 41N48'39 78W16'48 5:13:07
Port Ann 55 6 40N49'27 77W08'54 5:08:36
Port Barnett 33 34 41N09'23 79W03'04 5:16:12
Port Blanchard 40 1 41N18'11 75W49'44 5:03:19
Port Bowkley 40 20 41N16'25 75W51'36 5:03:26
Port Carbon 54 27 40N41'47 76W10'09 5:04:41
Port Clinton 54 80 40N34'56 76W01'29 5:04:06
Porter 33 51 40N56'02 79W10'08 5:16:41
Porters Corners 20 6 41N30'18 80W15'28 5:21:02
Porters Mill 15 8 40N11'23 75W38'49 5:02:35
Porters Sideling 67 1 39N49'31 76W53'42 5:07:35
Portersville 10 6 40N55'22 80W08'33 5:20:34
Port Griffith 40 1 41N19 75W47 5:03:08
Port Indian 46 90 40N08 75W21 5:01:24
Port Jenkins 40 60 41N04'57 75W46'17 5:03:05
Port Kennedy 46 90 40N05 75W22 5:01:28
Portland 48 8 40N55'23 75W05'49 5:00:23
Portland Mills 24 59 41N22'41 78W50'04 5:15:20
Port Matilda 14 63 40N47'58 78W03'16 5:12:13
Port Perry 2 114 40N23'27 79W50'59 5:19:24
Port Providence 46 8 40N07'41 75W29'35 5:01:58
Port Richmond 51 9 39N58'36 75W06'02 5:00:24
Port Royal 34 7 40N32'00 77W23'09 5:09:33
Port Royal 65 6 40N10'07 79W46'04 5:19:04
Port Trevorton 55 51 40N42'26 76W51'59 5:07:28
Port Vue 2 10 40N20'09 79W52'12 5:19:29
Possum Hollow 37 121 40N51'20 80W20'14 5:21:21
Potetown 7 3 40N20 78W24 5:13:36
Potosi 67 3 39N49'14 76W40'24 5:06:42
Potter Brook 59 6 41N54'48 77W36'13 5:10:25
Pottersdale 17 6 41N09'57 78W03'46 5:12:15
Potters Mills 14 64 40N47'45 77W37'32 5:10:30
Potterville 8 60 41N52'50 76W14'08 5:04:57
Potts Grove 49 6 40N59'37 76W47'22 5:07:09
Pottstown 46 8 40N14'43 75W39'00 5:02:36
Pottstown Landing 15 8 40N14'11 75W39'55 5:02:40
Pottsville 54 49 40N41'08 76W11'45 5:04:47
P&OV Junction 2 114 40N28 80W05 5:20:20
Powder Valley 39 13 40N27'58 75W31'29 5:02:06

Powell 8 60 41N42'17 76w30'26 5:06:02
Powells Valley 22 24 40N26'00 76w56'00 5:07:44
Powelton 14 4 40N49 78w14 5:12:56
Powys 41 7 41N20'52 77w05'34 5:08:22
Poyntelle 64 6 41N49'14 75w25'13 5:01:41
Prattville 8 6 41N50'48 76w07'55 5:04:32
Preisser Crossing 11 54 40N33'06 78w48'54 5:15:16
Prentisvale 42 40 41N56'00 78w26'21 5:13:45
Prescott 38 8 40N21'05 76w21'17 5:05:25
Prescottville 33 6 41N05'10 78w51'38 5:15:27
President 61 6 41N27'28 79w33'30 5:18:14
Presidential Heights 2 114 40N33 80w01 5:20:04
Presque Isle 25 107 42N08 80w09 5:20:36
Presston 2 114 40N28 80w05 5:20:20
Presto 2 114 40N22'25 80w07'05 5:20:28
Preston 40 20 41N12'25 75w54'21 5:03:37
Preston 42 75 41N41'34 78w51'05 5:15:24
Preston 64 6 41N51 75w25 5:01:40
Preston Corner 64 6 41N49'14 75w22'12 5:01:29
Preston Hill 54 27 40N47 76w17 5:05:08
Preston Park 64 6 41N52'52 75w21'23 5:01:26
Pretoria 56 6 40N11 78w59 5:15:56
Price 45 84 41N08 75w13 5:00:52
Priceburg 35 18 41N27 75w37 5:02:28
Pricedale 65 1 40N07'53 79w50'40 5:19:23
Pricetown 6 8 40N25'36 75w49'20 5:03:17
Priceville 64 6 41N48'38 75w11'37 5:00:46
Prichard 40 1 41N15'18 76w08'05 5:04:32
Primos 23 9 39N55'13 75w18'25 5:01:14
Primrose 54 49 40N41'39 76w16'55 5:05:08
Primrose 63 51 40N21'20 80w16'05 5:21:04
Princeton 37 112 40N57'50 80w13'54 5:20:56
Pringle 40 20 41N16'41 75w53'51 5:03:35
Pritchard 59 59 41N59'11 77w09'28 5:08:38
Pritchards Corner 43 117 41N16'46 80w29'01 5:21:56
Prittstown 26 111 40N05'54 79w33'16 5:18:13
Proctor 41 82 41N25'12 76w48'28 5:07:14
Progress 22 12 40N17'06 76w49'54 5:07:20
Promised Land 52 6 41N18'34 75w12'38 5:00:51
Prompton 64 7 41N34'58 75w19'32 5:01:18
Prospect 10 6 40N54'16 80w02'48 5:20:11
Prospect 11 74 40N20'04 78w54'45 5:15:39
Prospect Gardens 36 8 40N02 76w17 5:05:08
Prospect Heights 48 13 40N39 75w21 5:01:24
Prospect Hill 35 18 41N28 75w36 5:02:24
Prospective 46 1 40N12'42 75w11'10 5:00:45
Prospect Park 12 106 41N31'01 78w12'57 5:12:52
Prospect Park 23 9 39N53'16 75w18'31 5:01:14
Prospect Park 48 12 40N39'55 75w16'31 5:01:06
Prospectville 46 1 40N13 75w11 5:00:44
Prosperity 63 3 40N02'49 80w17'42 5:21:11
Prouty Place Camp 53 6 41N39'27 77w54'46 5:11:39
Providence 35 18 41N26'02 75w39'42 5:02:39
Providence 36 78 39N55 76w14 5:04:56
Providence Downe 23 90 39N55 75w22 5:01:28
Providence Square 46 8 40N12 75w28 5:01:52
Providence Village 23 90 39N54 75w22 5:01:28
Provins Works 26 51 39N51 79w54 5:19:36
Pughtown 15 8 40N10'00 75w39'57 5:02:40
Pulaski 37 51 41N06'48 80w25'57 5:21:44
Pulasri 4 8 40N44 80w18 5:21:12
Punxsutawney 33 51 40N56'37 78w58'16 5:15:53
Purcell 5 6 39N47'18 78w22'03 5:13:28
Purchase Line 32 6 40N44'11 78w55'45 5:15:43
Puritan 11 63 40N21'56 78w38'38 5:14:35
Puritan 26 51 39N52'42 79w51'40 5:19:27
Puseyville 36 3 39N50'58 76w06'44 5:04:27
Putnam 59 59 41N45 77w05 5:08:20
Putnamville 62 6 41N55'44 79w11'43 5:16:47
Putneyville 3 6 40N56'48 79w19'04 5:17:16
Puttstown 31 51 40N13'29 78w14'05 5:12:56
Puzzletown 7 33 40N22'37 78w29'24 5:13:58
P & W Patch 63 6 40N17 80w28 5:21:52
Pyles Mills 37 121 40N52'28 80w10'39 5:20:43
Pymatuning 43 59 41N20 80w25 5:21:40
Pyrra 3 15 40N43'15 79w25'33 5:17:42
Quakake 54 60 40N51'06 76w02'11 5:04:09
Quaker City 6 56 40N39'34 75w52'45 5:03:31
Quaker Hills 36 8 40N00'55 76w20'17 5:05:21
Quaker Lake 58 6 41N59 75w56 5:03:44
Quakertown 9 8 40N26'30 75w20'31 5:01:22
Quaker Valley 1 1 39N56 77w15 5:09:00
Quarry Glen 8 41 41N48'21 76w27'50 5:05:51
Quarryville 36 27 39N53'49 76w09'50 5:04:39
Quecreek 56 6 40N05'23 79w04'46 5:16:19
Queen 5 7 40N15'33 78w30'28 5:14:02
Queen 27 6 41N37'32 79w21'49 5:17:27
Queen City 19 4 40N54'54 76w26'10 5:05:45
Queen Junction 10 3 40N58'09 79w55'45 5:19:43
Queens Grant 9 9 40N12 74w49 4:59:16
Queens Run 18 76 41N10'54 77w28'37 5:09:54
Queenstown 3 6 41N00'23 79w37'56 5:18:32
Quemahoning 56 6 40N08 78w58 5:15:52
Quentin 38 8 40N16'46 76w26'19 5:05:45
Quicks Bend 8 6 41N38 76w15 5:05:00
Quicktown 35 4 41N21'59 75w27'14 5:01:49
Quiet Dell 30 6 39N48'05 80w30'44 5:22:03
Quiggleville 41 7 41N19'42 77w06'40 5:08:27
Quincy 28 100 39N48'12 77w34'29 5:10:18
Quincy Hollow 9 9 40N09'13 74w51'45 4:59:27
Quinlan Corners 35 4 41N19'37 75w33'50 5:02:15
Quinlantown 8 6 41N35'45 76w37'54 5:06:32
Quinns Corner 52 2 41N18'59 74w50'47 4:59:23
Quinsonia 28 100 39N50'11 77w36'09 5:10:25
Quitman 49 1 40N54'23 76w33'54 5:06:16
Raberts Corner 39 1 40N41'29 75w46'45 5:03:07
Raccoon 4 64 40N36 80w22 5:21:28
Rachelwood 65 29 40N17'32 79w05'49 5:16:23
Racine 4 8 40N46 80w20 5:21:20
Radebaugh 65 99 40N18'46 79w34'44 5:18:19
Rader 16 37 41N10'07 79w15'22 5:17:01
Radnor 23 90 40N02'46 75w21'37 5:01:26
Radnor Station 23 90 40N02'23 75w22'08 5:01:29
Rager Summit 44 1 40N41'25 77w21'10 5:09:25
Rahn 54 80 40N48 75w56 5:03:44
Rahns 46 8 40N12'33 75w27'12 5:01:49
Railroad 67 27 39N45'38 76w41'55 5:06:48
Raineytown 26 104 40N02'25 79w38'39 5:18:35
Rainsburg 5 6 39N53'39 78w30'59 5:14:04
Ralph 26 51 39N55'42 79w53'26 5:19:34
Ralpho 49 1 40N51 76w33 5:06:12
Ralphton 56 6 40N06'49 79w01'14 5:16:05
Ralston 41 7 41N30'23 76w57'16 5:07:49
Ramey 17 6 40N47'53 78w23'51 5:13:35
Ramsay Terrace 65 111 40N09'23 79w32'25 5:18:10
Ramsaytown 33 34 41N04'50 79w04'01 5:16:16
Ramsey 41 6 41N17'04 77w19'29 5:09:18
Ranavilla 21 12 40N14 76w57 5:07:48
Rand 2 114 40N23 79w59 5:19:56
Rand 60 6 40N55'53 77w05'48 5:08:23
Randolph 20 6 41N38 79w57 5:19:48
Randolph 56 6 40N09'02 79w00'09 5:16:01
Ranges Corners 25 3 41N55'06 79w44'37 5:18:58
Rankin 2 114 40N24'45 79w52'46 5:19:31
Ranshaw 49 27 40N47'09 76w31'06 5:06:04
Ransom 35 1 41N23'39 75w49'20 5:03:17
Rapho 36 1 40N10 76w27 5:05:48
Raricks 54 1 40N54'03 76w14'03 5:04:56
Rasler Run 26 6 40N00'27 79w28'40 5:17:55
Rasleytown 48 17 40N48'53 75w15'59 5:01:04
Rasselas 24 59 41N36'26 78w37'10 5:14:29
Rathbun 24 106 41N29'06 78w26'19 5:13:45
Rathmel 33 6 41N05'40 78w50'24 5:15:22
Rattigan 10 6 40N54'03 79w42'27 5:18:50
Raubenstine 67 1 39N44'03 76w59'47 5:07:59
Raubs Mills 55 1 40N43'28 77w16'02 5:09:04
Raubsville 48 12 40N38'08 75w11'36 5:00:46
Rauchtown 18 7 41N07'22 77w14'11 5:08:57
Rausch Creek 54 9 40N36'43 76w25'36 5:05:42
Rauschs 54 1 40N39'52 75w59'34 5:03:58
Raven Creek 19 6 41N12 76w23 5:05:32
Raven Run 54 27 40N48'58 76w15'14 5:05:01
Ravine 54 27 40N34'28 76w24'15 5:05:37
Rawlinsville 36 1 39N52'56 76w16'09 5:05:05
Rayburn 3 15 40N50 79w29 5:17:56
Raymilton 61 6 41N20'08 79w58'34 5:19:54
Raymond 53 6 41N51'35 77w51'44 5:11:27
Rayne 32 6 40N44'17 79w01'49 5:16:07
Raytown 32 6 40N50 78w50 5:15:20
Rea 63 6 40N16'38 80w23'51 5:21:35
Reade 11 63 40N41 78w26 5:13:44
Reading 6 101 40N20'08 75w55'38 5:03:43
Reading Gardens 6 101 40N20 75w53 5:03:32
Reading Mines 56 6 40N07 78w57 5:15:48
Reading Number Three 56 6 40N05'16 78w57'40 5:15:51
Reagantown 65 111 40N08'22 79w38'56 5:18:36
Reamstown 36 28 40N12'41 76w07'25 5:04:30
Reamstown Heights 36 28 40N13 76w07 5:04:28
Rebel Hill 46 90 40N05 75w17 5:01:08
Rebersburg 14 6 40N56'40 77w26'43 5:09:47
Rebuck 49 6 40N43'20 76w44'09 5:06:57
Rector 65 110 40N11'48 79w14'20 5:16:57
Red Bank 60 64 40N57'03 77w03'14 5:08:13
Red Barn 32 71 40N31'28 79w09'33 5:16:38
Redbird 11 63 40N22'38 78w39'44 5:14:39
Red Bridge 28 42 39N57'45 77w38'24 5:10:34
Red Bridge 42 75 41N40 78w49 5:15:16
Red Cedar Hill 9 9 40N09'15 74w50'54 4:59:24
Redclyffe 16 6 41N23'41 79w09'09 5:16:37
Red Cross 49 4 40N42'40 76w47'11 5:07:09
Redds Mill 63 1 40N08'46 79w58'41 5:19:55
Red Hill 7 33 40N31 78w25 5:13:40
Red Hill 40 6 41N15'27 76w16'09 5:05:05
Red Hill 46 2 40N22'22 75w28'53 5:01:56
Red Hot 2 7 40N39'47 79w50'10 5:19:21
Redington 48 13 40N38'17 75w17'19 5:01:09
Red Lion 6 13 40N28'50 75w36'59 5:02:28
Red Lion 15 8 39N52'41 75w40'55 5:02:44
Red Lion 67 7 39N54'03 76w36'22 5:06:25
Red Mill 11 63 40N30'52 78w54'07 5:15:36
Red Mill 14 64 40N48'02 77w38'42 5:10:35
Red Mill 33 56 41N09'18 78w49'20 5:15:17
Redmond 10 6 41N05'00 80w02'07 5:20:08
Red Oak 35 6 41N26'25 75w29'12 5:01:57
Red Rock 40 6 41N17'23 76w18'06 5:05:12
Red Rock 42 102 41N57'57 78w33'11 5:14:13
Red Rose Gate 9 9 40N09 74w51 4:59:24
Red Run 36 28 40N11'03 76w04'57 5:04:20
Red Schoolhouse Corner 64 59 41N41'26 75w21'08 5:01:25
Redstone 26 51 40N04'29 79w48'14 5:19:13
Redstone Junction 26 80 39N55 79w43 5:18:52
Reduction 65 6 40N11'01 79w46'16 5:19:05
Reeceville 15 9 40N01'40 75w47'45 5:03:11
Reed 22 3 40N25 76w58 5:07:52
Reed 49 1 40N52'11 76w35'40 5:06:23
Reeder 9 8 40N21'12 74w58'52 4:59:55
Reeders 45 1 41N01'08 75w20'11 5:01:21
Reeds Corners 25 107 41N58'46 80w06'34 5:20:26
Reeds Furnace 43 6 41N20'03 80w00'18 5:20:01
Reeds Gap 34 6 40N26'04 77w36'41 5:10:27
Reeds Road 15 46 40N00 75w42 5:02:48
Reedsville 44 73 40N39'50 77w35'46 5:10:23
Reels Corners 56 63 40N03'29 78w49'41 5:15:19
Reese 7 33 40N26'04 78w18'09 5:13:13
Reesedale 3 15 40N55'50 79w28'08 5:17:53
Reesers Summit 67 12 40N12'04 76w51'57 5:07:28
Rees Mill 30 1 39N54'43 80w13'24 5:20:54
Reevesdale 54 27 40N46'54 76w00'44 5:04:03
Refton 36 8 39N56'50 76w13'59 5:04:56
Regan Junction 11 63 40N32'35 78w51'08 5:15:25
Regency Park 2 14 40N29 79w44 5:18:56
Register 40 6 41N11'48 76w16'18 5:05:05
Rehrersburg 6 1 40N27'27 76w14'41 5:04:59
Reidsburg 16 37 41N09'02 79w24'12 5:17:37
Reiffton 6 101 40N19'11 75w52'26 5:03:30
Reightown 7 50 40N36'08 78w20'01 5:13:20
Reilly 40 60 41N05'31 75w52'54 5:03:32
Reilly 54 9 40N40 76w20 5:05:20
Reillys 11 57 40N37'49 78w40'11 5:14:41
Reimold 67 1 39N45'29 76w37'09 5:06:29
Reinerton 54 27 40N35'32 76w31'58 5:06:08
Reinholds 36 56 40N15'56 76w07'01 5:04:28
Reinoeldville 38 8 40N20 76w26 5:05:44
Reissing 63 114 40N20'34 80w11'57 5:20:48
Reistville 38 25 40N19'38 76w18'11 5:05:13
Reitz 33 6 41N13'18 78w54'00 5:15:36
Reitz 56 63 40N08'15 78w48'40 5:15:15
Relay 67 1 39N55'29 76w38'56 5:06:36
Reliance 46 8 40N18'51 75w20'22 5:01:21
Rembrant 32 6 40N41'43 79w00'33 5:16:02
Remoeldville 38 8 40N21'28 76w25'21 5:05:41
Rene Mont 54 1 40N40'41 75w58'01 5:03:52
Renfrew 10 6 40N48'24 79w57'54 5:19:52
Rennerdale 2 114 40N23'54 80w08'30 5:20:34
Reno 61 109 41N24'35 79w45'09 5:19:01
Renovo 18 73 41N19'35 77w45'04 5:11:00
Renton 2 14 40N30'06 79w43'36 5:18:54
Renton Junction 2 14 40N29 79w44 5:18:56
Republic 26 51 39N57'45 79w52'37 5:19:30
Republican 63 1 40N04 79w54 5:19:36
Reserve 2 114 40N29 79w59 5:19:56
Reservoir 7 33 40N24'24 78w22'50 5:13:31
Reservoir Heights 22 1 40N32'15 76w55'58 5:07:44
Reservoir Hill 26 104 39N59'55 79w34'52 5:18:19
Resler 49 6 40N46'54 76w45'30 5:07:02
Ressaca 45 1 41N06'41 75w05'42 5:00:23
Retort 14 4 40N49 78w14 5:12:56
Retta 58 6 41N43'45 76w03'30 5:04:14
Revere 9 1 40N30'55 75w09'41 5:00:39
Revloc 11 54 40N29'32 78w45'52 5:15:03
Rew 42 6 41N54'05 78w32'22 5:14:09
Reward 50 1 40N33'19 77w04'43 5:08:19
Rexford 59 6 41N45'04 77w30'14 5:10:01
Rexis 32 6 40N29'11 78w55'21 5:15:41
Rexmont 38 8 40N16'38 76w22'58 5:05:32
Rextown 39 8 40N45'00 75w38'16 5:02:33
Reyburn 40 1 41N09 76w10 5:04:40
Reynolds 54 27 40N44'27 75w58'28 5:03:54
Reynoldsdale 5 6 40N08'51 78w33'28 5:14:14
Reynolds Heights 43 59 41N20'42 80w23'40 5:21:35
Reynolds Mill 67 67 39N53'42 76w44'34 5:06:58
Reynoldstown 53 6 41N54'13 77w53'10 5:11:33
Reynoldsville 33 48 41N05'49 78w53'20 5:15:33
Rhawnhurst 51 9 40N03'42 75w03'22 5:00:13
Rheems 36 2 40N07'48 76w34'15 5:06:17
Rhoads 14 7 41N00'35 77w52'36 5:11:30
Rhone 40 21 41N12 76w00 5:04:00
Ribold 10 6 40N47'55 79w59'44 5:19:59
Ribot 31 81 40N35'10 78w01'38 5:12:07
Rice 40 1 41N09 75w57 5:03:48
Rices Landing 30 6 39N56'43 79w59'45 5:19:59
Riceville 20 7 41N46'39 79w48'11 5:19:13
Richards Grove 41 6 41N15'13 76w29'31 5:05:58
Richardsville 33 6 41N14'24 79w00'45 5:16:03
Richboro 9 1 40N12'54 75w00'40 5:00:03
Richboro Manor 9 1 40N13 75w01 5:00:04
Richeyville 63 51 40N03'12 80w00'08 5:20:01
Richfield 34 6 40N41'19 77w06'47 5:08:27
Richfol 63 2 40N16 80w11 5:20:44
Rich Hill 9 13 40N24'22 75w20'12 5:01:21
Rich Hill 63 2 40N13'00 80w13'55 5:20:56
Richland 2 56 40N38 79w57 5:19:48
Richland 11 33 40N35'48 78w29'09 5:13:57
Richland 23 9 39N57'47 75w18'58 5:01:16
Richland 38 25 40N21'33 76w15'31 5:05:02
Richland Center 9 8 40N25'53 75w17'52 5:01:11
Richlandtown 9 13 40N28'12 75w19'15 5:01:17
Richmond 48 17 40N50'44 75w08'34 5:00:34
Richmond 51 9 39N59'36 75w06'02 5:00:24
Richmondale 35 59 41N38'14 75w28'55 5:01:56
Richmond Furnace 28 51 39N57'47 77w54'03 5:11:36
Richvale 31 6 40N16'50 77w46'31 5:11:06
Rickenbach 6 80 40N25'34 75w57'41 5:03:51
Ricketts 40 6 41N23'28 76w16'41 5:05:07
Rico 32 6 40N33'00 79w01'13 5:16:05
Riddle Crossroads 61 6 41N12'01 79w50'40 5:19:23
Riddlesburg 5 51 40N09'43 78w15'17 5:13:01
Riddlewood 23 90 39N54'20 75w25'58 5:01:44
Riderville 42 6 41N52 78w40 5:14:40
Ridgebury 8 7 41N58'24 76w43'19 5:06:53
Ridgemont 14 63 40N49'41 77w56'56 5:11:48

Ridge Park 6 101 40N19 75W57 5:03:48
Ridge Valley 9 8 40N22'39 75W22'39 5:01:31
Ridgeview 22 12 40N19 76W48 5:07:12
Ridge View 65 111 40N08'27 79W32'48 5:18:11
Ridgeview Park 65 3 40N20 79W18 5:17:12
Ridgeville 47 6 40N58'07 76W33'55 5:06:16
Ridgewood 6 8 40N18'03 75W53'54 5:03:36
Ridgewood 40 20 41N16'38 75W48'47 5:03:15
Ridgewood Farm 15 13 39N57 75W36 5:02:24
Ridgewood Park 23 9 40N00 75W18 5:01:12
Ridgway 24 36 41N25'13 78W43'44 5:14:55
Ridley 23 9 39N53 75W20 5:01:20
Ridley Farms 23 9 39N54 75W20 5:01:20
Ridley Gardens 23 9 39N55 75W19 5:01:16
Ridley Park 23 9 39N52'52 75W19'27 5:01:18
Ridley Parkview 23 9 39N53 75W20 5:01:20
Riegelsville 9 12 40N35'39 75W11'41 5:00:47
Rienze 8 60 41N39'07 76W20'11 5:05:21
Rife 22 1 40N32'54 76W52'51 5:07:31
Riggles Gap 7 33 40N34'48 78W23'03 5:13:32
Riggs 8 60 41N50'17 76W34'35 5:06:18
Riggs 30 6 39N51'37 80W27'11 5:21:49
Riker 33 51 40N56'45 78W56'26 5:15:46
Rileyville 64 59 41N42'56 75W13'47 5:00:55
Rillton 65 25 40N17'21 79W43'53 5:18:56
Rimer 3 7 40N56'10 79W31'32 5:18:06
Rimersburg 16 43 41N02'29 79W30'12 5:18:01
Rimerton 3 64 40N55 79W28 5:17:52
Rinely 67 1 39N48'06 76W35'51 5:06:23
Ringdale 57 60 41N27'08 76W26'45 5:05:47
Ringertown 65 6 40N25'06 79W35'08 5:18:21
Ringgold 33 6 40N59'41 79W10'05 5:16:40
Ringing Hill 46 8 40N15 75W39 5:02:36
Ringing Rock Park 46 8 40N15 75W39 5:02:36
Ringlands 63 3 40N01'35 80W13'51 5:20:55
Ringtown 6 9 40N30'48 75W41'55 5:02:48
Ringtown 54 56 40N51'31 76W13'48 5:04:55
Rippletown 40 6 41N07'23 75W56'15 5:03:45
Risher Mine Siding 2 114 40N22 79W54 5:19:36
Rising Sun 39 8 40N42'08 75W35'48 5:02:23
Rismiller 48 17 40N50'23 75W18'57 5:01:16
Rita 40 60 41N07'20 75W52'54 5:03:32
Ritchie 18 7 41N17'55 77W36'34 5:10:26
Riterville 42 59 41N46'10 78W39'44 5:14:39
Rittenhouse 40 1 41N15'19 76W14'06 5:04:56
Rittenhouse Gap 6 13 40N33 75W34 5:02:16
Ritters Crossroads 41 6 41N12'18 76W35'09 5:06:21
Ritterville 39 13 40N37'16 75W25'38 5:01:43
Ritzie Village 22 12 40N23'40 76W46'56 5:07:08
River Hill 2 1 40N12'16 79W54'40 5:19:39
Riverside 11 74 40N17'00 78W55'21 5:15:41
Riverside 35 18 41N29'09 75W33'24 5:02:14
Riverside 49 6 40N57'19 76W37'45 5:06:31
Riverside Junction 35 18 41N28 75W37 5:02:28
Riverton 48 17 40N49'40 75W05'11 5:00:21
River Valley 2 14 40N32'46 79W49'18 5:19:17
River View 3 6 40N36'18 79W34'46 5:18:19
Riverview 4 8 40N46 80W20 5:21:20
Riverview 16 6 40N59'23 79W34'26 5:18:18
Riverview 17 1 41N00'14 78W27'22 5:13:49
Riverview 18 7 41N10'07 77W30'36 5:10:02
River View 63 1 40N12'43 79W57'37 5:19:50
Riverview Acres 39 8 40N45 75W37 5:02:28
River View Park 6 101 40N23'33 75W57'33 5:03:50
Rixford 42 6 41N55'34 78W29'40 5:13:59
Roadside 28 100 39N45'48 77W31'55 5:10:08
Roaring Branch 41 7 41N33'56 76W57'11 5:07:49
Roaring Brook 35 4 41N23 75W33 5:02:12
Roaring Brook 40 1 41N15'23 76W07'13 5:04:29
Roaring Creek 47 1 40N55'56 76W31'25 5:06:06
Roaring Spring 7 3 40N20'09 78W23'28 5:13:34
Robb 65 29 40N23'32 79W02'17 5:16:09
Robbins 65 10 40N17'46 79W46'59 5:19:08
Robert Bruce West 46 1 40N11 75W06 5:00:24
Roberts 56 6 39N58'44 79W05'23 5:16:22
Robertsdale 31 6 40N11'03 78W06'56 5:12:28
Robertsville 33 51 40N56 78W58 5:15:52
Robeson 6 8 40N15 75W52 5:03:28
Robeson Crossing 6 101 40N16'34 75W50'52 5:03:23
Robeson Extension 7 3 40N28'01 78W12'00 5:12:48
Robesonia 6 56 40N21'06 76W08'05 5:04:32
Robindale 32 29 40N24'03 79W02'13 5:16:09
Robin Hood Lakes 45 8 40N58'04 75W31'59 5:02:08
Robinson 32 7 40N24'15 79W08'23 5:16:34
Robinson 37 1 41N01'41 80W29'42 5:21:59
Robinson 63 51 40N27'01 80W20'13 5:21:21
Robinsonville 5 6 39N48'56 78W20'21 5:13:21
Rocherty 38 8 40N18'08 76W26'58 5:05:48
Rochester 4 19 40N42'08 80W17'12 5:21:09
Rochester Mills 32 6 40N49'07 78W59'09 5:15:57
Rock 54 9 40N36 76W23 5:05:32
Rockdale 9 9 40N06'30 74W52'54 4:59:32
Rockdale 10 3 40N46'40 79W52'59 5:19:32
Rockdale 20 3 41N48 79W58 5:19:52
Rockdale 23 90 39N53'16 75W26'22 5:01:45
Rockdale 28 1 39N51'35 77W48'48 5:11:15
Rockdale 33 56 41N10'36 78W50'31 5:15:22
Rockdale 35 1 41N17'32 75W36'43 5:02:27
Rockdale 39 8 40N43'00 75W33'44 5:02:15
Rockdale Acres 20 3 41N46'01 79W55'26 5:19:42
Rockefeller 49 82 40N50 76W44 5:06:56
Rockey 67 1 39N53'56 76W31'05 5:06:04
Rock Falls Park 10 6 41N02'15 80W01'58 5:20:08
Rock Glen 40 1 40N57'55 76W11'05 5:04:44
Rockhill 9 8 40N24 75W24 5:01:36
Rockhill 31 56 40N14'30 77W54'00 5:11:36
Rockhill 36 8 39N57'45 76W21'46 5:05:27
Rockhill Furnace 31 6 40N15 77W54 5:11:36
Rockhill Station 9 8 40N24'21 75W18'26 5:01:14
Rockingham 56 63 40N07 78W49 5:15:16
Rock Lake 64 59 41N44 75W26 5:01:44
Rockland 61 7 41N13'56 79W45'07 5:19:00
Rockledge 46 9 40N04'52 75W05'24 5:00:22
Rockmere 61 9 41N25'53 79W39'34 5:18:38
Rock Point 37 121 40N51'34 80W18'48 5:21:15
Rockport 13 60 40N57'54 75W45'49 5:03:03
Rockrimmin Ridge 36 28 40N05 76W11 5:04:44
Rock Run 15 9 39N59 75W50 5:03:20
Rocksprings 14 6 40N42'32 77W58'04 5:11:52
Rocks Works 26 80 39N50'14 79W53'46 5:19:35
Rockton 17 6 41N04'32 78W39'12 5:14:37
Rocktown 65 111 40N10'26 79W35'36 5:18:22
Rockville 3 15 40N43'59 79W26'31 5:17:46
Rockville 5 7 39N55'51 78W40'17 5:14:41
Rockville 11 74 40N21'29 78W46'56 5:15:08
Rockville 14 6 40N56'24 77W27'35 5:09:50
Rockville 15 27 40N04'40 75W51'20 5:03:25
Rockville 16 6 41N02'26 79W23'04 5:17:32
Rockville 22 12 40N20'10 76W54'18 5:07:37
Rockville 34 7 40N34'34 77W24'35 5:09:38
Rockville 37 6 41N00'10 80W10'25 5:20:42
Rockville 44 6 40N36'40 77W46'04 5:11:04
Rockville 48 80 40N47'04 75W29'53 5:02:00
Rockville 67 3 39N46'43 76W46'31 5:07:06
Rockwood 38 8 40N22'49 76W27'05 5:05:48
Rockwood 56 4 39N54'56 79W09'09 5:16:37
Rockwood Station 56 4 39N54'39 79W09'38 5:16:39
Rock Works 26 51 39N51 79W54 5:19:36
Rocky Forest 66 6 41N38'04 76W11'52 5:04:47
Rocky Glen 35 18 41N22 75W43 5:02:52
Rocky Grove 61 109 41N24'18 79W49'56 5:19:20
Rocky Hill 15 13 39N58'35 75W32'10 5:02:09
Rocky Ridge 9 8 40N23'43 75W19'29 5:01:18
Rocky Valley 9 13 40N30'06 75W22'03 5:01:28
Rodi 2 114 40N27'58 79W49'34 5:19:18
Rodman 7 3 40N20 78W24 5:13:36
Rodney 65 6 40N09'09 79W25'00 5:17:40
Roeders 54 1 40N34'00 76W11'44 5:04:47
Roedersville 54 9 40N35'10 76W19'30 5:05:18
Roelofs 9 8 40N13'01 74W51'43 4:59:27
Roemersville 52 6 41N17'05 75W14'59 5:01:00
Rogers Mill 26 6 39N59'32 79W24'40 5:17:39
Rogers Stop 63 1 40N07'38 79W55'22 5:19:41
Rogerstown 26 104 40N00'05 79W37'36 5:18:30
Rogersville 30 1 39N52'52 80W16'23 5:21:06
Rogertown 62 3 41N49'22 79W06'16 5:16:25
Rohrerstown 36 8 40N03'10 76W21'37 5:05:26
Rohrsburg 19 4 41N08'00 76W25'21 5:05:41
Roler 67 1 40N00 76W58 5:07:52
Rolfe 24 36 41N30 78W41 5:14:44
Rolling Glen 15 47 40N03 75W33 5:02:12
Rolling Hills 6 101 40N19 75W57 5:03:48
Rolling Hills 39 13 40N39 75W30 5:02:00
Rolling Park 23 90 39N51 75W22 5:01:28
Rolling Stone 17 4 41N03'21 78W09'14 5:12:37
Romansville 15 9 39N57'07 75W44'28 5:02:58
Rome 8 60 41N51'30 76W20'28 5:05:22
Romney 26 6 40N02'44 79W24'10 5:17:37
Romola 14 63 41N03'25 77W41'22 5:10:45
Ronco 26 51 39N52'11 79W55'14 5:19:41
Ronks 36 1 40N01'34 76W10'08 5:04:41
Rook 2 114 40N24'51 80W04'09 5:20:17
Roots 7 50 40N36'48 78W21'41 5:13:27
Roots Crossing 7 11 40N40 78W13 5:12:52
Rootville 20 7 41N46'29 79W52'16 5:19:29
Rosas 52 6 41N26'29 74W48'34 4:59:14
Roscoe 63 115 40N04'46 79W51'57 5:19:28
Rose 33 34 41N08 79W06 5:16:24
Roseann 44 7 40N41'38 77W35'29 5:10:22
Roseboro 32 51 40N51'45 78W58'19 5:15:53
Rosebud 17 54 40N45'15 78W32'30 5:14:10
Roseburg 50 1 40N25'50 77W20'28 5:09:22
Rosecrans 18 7 41N03'21 77W18'42 5:09:15
Rose Crest 2 114 40N26 79W47 5:19:08
Rosedale 2 114 40N29'11 79W50'15 5:19:21
Rosedale 9 13 40N28'08 75W23'26 5:01:34
Rosedale 15 1 39N50'52 75W39'52 5:02:39
Rosedale 26 80 39N54 79W44 5:18:56
Rosedale Heights 2 114 40N29 79W50 5:19:20
Rosegarden 67 12 40N08'52 77W00'41 5:08:03
Rose Gardens 61 9 41N24'36 79W40'20 5:18:41
Roseglen 46 9 40N02'50 75W15'23 5:01:02
Rose Glen 50 1 40N24'13 77W05'05 5:08:20
Rosehill 51 9 40N01 75W09 5:00:36
Roselawn 7 33 40N31 78W25 5:13:40
Rosemont 46 90 40N01'32 75W19'27 5:01:18
Rosemont Terrace 39 13 40N37'48 75W24'55 5:01:40
Rosengrant 66 59 41N30'23 75W59'09 5:03:57
Rose Point 37 112 40N58'12 80W11'12 5:20:45
Roses 27 6 41N27'16 79W09'24 5:16:38
Roseto 48 17 40N52'50 75W12'54 5:00:52
Rose Tree 23 90 39N56'03 75W23'26 5:01:34
Rosetree Woods 23 9 39N58 75W22 5:01:28
Rose Valley 23 90 39N53'46 75W23'07 5:01:32
Rose Valley 46 1 40N09'55 75W12'26 5:00:50
Rose Valley Acres 23 90 39N55 75W22 5:01:28
Roseville 33 34 41N10'40 79W08'47 5:16:35
Roseville 36 8 40N04'43 76W17'42 5:05:11
Roseville 59 59 41N51'56 76W57'28 5:07:50
Roseville 67 1 40N03'50 76W55'05 5:07:40
Rosewood Gardens 9 1 40N12 75W05 5:00:20
Rosewood Park 9 1 40N12'21 75W06'50 5:00:27
Roslyn 46 2 40N07'54 75W08'17 5:00:33
Ross Common 45 17 40N51'54 75W18'23 5:01:14
Rossford 3 15 40N45'05 79W32'18 5:18:09
Rossiter 32 51 40N53'40 78W55'53 5:15:44
Rossland 45 1 40N52'16 75W23'50 5:01:35
Rosslyn Farms 2 114 40N25'32 80W05'39 5:20:23
Rossmere 36 8 40N03'22 76W17'50 5:05:11
Rossmoyne 21 12 40N11'50 76W56'39 5:07:47
Rossmoyne 32 6 40N49'29 79W07'40 5:16:31
Rossmoyne Manor 21 12 40N12'39 76W57'04 5:07:48
Ross Siding 41 6 41N24 77W28 5:09:52
Rosston 3 15 40N45'03 79W33'06 5:18:12
Rossville 67 1 40N03 76W56 5:07:44
Rostraver 65 1 40N10 79W49 5:19:16
Rote 18 76 41N04'44 77W25'14 5:09:41
Rothsville 36 28 40N09'04 76W15'05 5:05:00
Rough and Ready 54 1 40N40'46 76W37'41 5:06:31
Roulette 53 6 41N46'48 78W09'15 5:12:37
Round Head 6 9 40N30'31 76W18'36 5:05:14
Round Knob 5 51 40N08'59 78W11'34 5:12:46
Round Top 1 1 39N47'45 77W13'53 5:08:56
Roundtop 34 1 40N39'49 77W19'21 5:09:17
Roundtop 59 6 41N42'25 77W15'09 5:09:01
Roundtown 67 67 40N01'04 76W45'21 5:07:01
Rouseville 61 9 41N28'08 79W41'28 5:18:46
Rouzerville 28 100 39N44'12 77W32'07 5:10:08
Rowena 56 6 40N07'08 78W55'26 5:15:42
Rowenna 36 64 40N03'55 76W36'42 5:06:27
Rowes Run 26 51 40N00'34 79W49'02 5:19:16
Rowland 52 59 41N28'16 75W02'33 5:00:10
Rowland Park 46 9 40N05 75W08 5:00:32
Roxborough 51 9 40N02'17 75W13'22 5:00:53
Roxbury 11 74 40N18'04 78W55'28 5:15:42
Roxbury 21 12 40N12'02 77W03'02 5:08:12
Roxbury 28 1 40N06'37 77W39'44 5:10:39
Roxbury 55 6 39N56'51 78W54'19 5:15:37
Royal 26 51 39N59 79W49 5:19:16
Royal 58 89 41N40'01 75W37'04 5:02:28
Royalton 22 80 40N11'14 76W43'49 5:06:55
Royer 7 3 40N25'19 78W16'25 5:13:06
Royersford 46 118 40N11'03 75W32'18 5:02:09
Roystone 62 3 41N43'20 78W58'15 5:15:53
Roytown 56 6 40N06'02 79W08'02 5:16:32
Rozel Park 9 1 40N11 75W03 5:00:12
Ruble 26 51 39N48 79W49 5:19:16
Ruble Mill 26 51 39N46'54 79W47'43 5:19:11
Ruchsville 39 13 40N39'10 75W32'44 5:02:11
Rudes Corner 64 59 41N45'05 75W21'01 5:01:24
Rudytown 67 12 40N14 76W51 5:07:24
Ruff Creek 30 1 39N57'32 80W10'29 5:20:42
Ruffs Dale 65 111 40N10'30 79W36'30 5:18:26
Ruggles 66 6 41N23'18 76W03'22 5:04:13
Rule Corners 40 1 41N09'10 75W57'51 5:03:51
Rumbels 40 42 41N01'51 75W59'06 5:03:56
Rumilla 46 8 40N19 75W19 5:01:16
Rummel 56 123 40N13'04 78W48'30 5:15:14
Rummerfield 8 6 41N44'38 76W18'25 5:05:14
Rundell 20 6 41N45'31 80W17'04 5:21:08
Runville 14 70 40N57'52 77W50'25 5:11:22
Rupert 19 4 40N58'45 76W28'28 5:05:54
Ruppletown 54 7 40N33'39 75W06'59 5:00:28
Ruppsville 39 13 40N34'49 75W36'03 5:02:24
Rural Ridge 2 14 40N35'08 79W49'44 5:19:19
Rural Valley 3 6 40N47'57 79W18'53 5:17:16
Rural Valley 63 6 40N11'13 80W20'56 5:21:24
Ruscombmanor 6 8 40N26 75W49 5:03:16
Rush 58 60 41N47'00 76W02'48 5:04:11
Rushboro 58 60 41N43'57 76W02'08 5:04:09
Rush Crossroads 30 6 39N48'22 80W15'26 5:21:02
Rushland 9 56 40N15'27 75W01'52 5:00:07
Rushtown 49 6 40N55'04 76W37'48 5:06:31
Rushville 58 59 41N46'57 76W07'21 5:04:29
Russell 62 6 41N56'29 79W08'07 5:16:32
Russell City 24 6 41N34'17 78W54'32 5:15:38
Russell Hill 66 59 41N32 75W57 5:03:48
Russellton 2 14 40N36'41 79W50'14 5:19:21
Russellville 15 3 39N50'32 75W56'30 5:03:46
Russellville 31 3 40N18'19 78W14'02 5:12:56
Rutan 30 6 39N53'42 80W20'24 5:21:22
Rutherford 22 12 40N16 76W49 5:07:16
Rutherford Heights 22 12 40N16'02 76W46'24 5:07:06
Ruthford 11 63 40N20 78W45 5:15:00
Ruthfred Acres 2 114 40N19'05 80W03'22 5:20:13
Rutland 59 59 41N52 76W59 5:07:56
Rutledge 23 9 39N54'06 75W19'44 5:01:19
Rutledgedale 64 6 41N42'37 75W10'45 5:00:43
Ryan 54 60 40N48 76W04 5:04:16
Ryans Corner 9 8 40N15'46 74W58'11 4:59:53
Rydal 46 9 40N06'23 75W06'32 5:00:26
Ryde 44 7 40N26'08 77W45'33 5:11:02
Rye 50 12 40N20 77W02 5:08:08
Rye 67 1 39N52'41 76W39'48 5:06:39
Ryeland 6 1 40N21'07 76W10'45 5:04:43
Ryers 51 9 40N03'49 75W05'15 5:00:21
Ryerson Station 30 6 39N53'33 80W28'30 5:21:54
Rynd Farm 61 9 41N28'57 79W41'42 5:18:47
Ryot 5 6 40N08'45 78W38'13 5:14:33
Sabinsville 59 6 41N52'04 77W31'32 5:10:06
Sabula 17 56 41N09'23 78W40'08 5:14:41
Sackett 24 75 41N31'53 78W54'14 5:15:37
Sackville 23 90 39N53'16 75W22'59 5:01:32
Saco 8 60 41N48'39 76W32'07 5:06:08
Saco 35 4 41N24'49 75W28'17 5:01:53
Sacramento 54 27 40N38'04 76W35'21 5:06:21

Sadlers Corner 61 9 41N23'50 79w37'29 5:18:30
Sadsbury Meeting House 36 8 39N58'15 75w59'28 5:03:58
Sadsburyville 15 32 39N58'54 75w53'30 5:03:34
Saegers 41 83 41N11'21 76w49'46 5:07:19
Saegersville 39 8 40N42'02 75w41'24 5:02:46
Saegertown 20 59 41N43'08 80w08'52 5:20:35
Safe Harbor 36 8 39N55'48 76w22'47 5:05:31
Sagamore 3 6 40N46'48 79w13'41 5:16:55
Sagamore 26 6 40N01'57 79w23'53 5:17:36
Sagamore Estates 52 6 41N22'07 74w54'14 4:59:37
Saginaw 67 1 40N03'54 76w40'23 5:06:42
Sagon 49 27 40N48'15 76w29'43 5:05:59
Saint Albans 23 90 39N59'19 75w23'25 5:01:34
Saint Augustine 11 63 40N36'47 78w34'43 5:14:19
Saint Benedict 11 92 40N37'39 78w43'47 5:14:55
Saint Boniface 11 57 40N40'00 78w40'52 5:14:43
Saint Charles 16 6 40N59'43 79w23'28 5:17:34
Saint Clair 2 114 40N24'59 79w58'18 5:19:53
Saint Clair 54 27 40N43'14 76w11'29 5:04:46
Saint Clair 65 99 40N16'07 79w32'55 5:18:12
Saint Clair Acres 2 114 40N20 80w05 5:20:20
Saint Clairsville 5 7 40N09'24 78w30'37 5:14:02
Saint Davids 23 90 40N02'27 75w22'44 5:01:31
Saint George 61 6 41N14'57 79w47'28 5:19:10
Saint Joe 10 6 40N54'16 79w46'26 5:19:06
Saint Johns 40 42 41N01'41 76w00'23 5:04:02
Saint Joseph 58 6 41N55'40 75w59'34 5:03:58
Saint Lawrence 6 101 40N19'37 75w52'20 5:03:29
Saint Lawrence 11 57 40N41'55 78w37'32 5:14:30
Saint Leonard 9 8 40N12'05 74w57'33 4:59:50
Saint Martins 51 9 40N04'04 75w11'50 5:00:47
Saint Marys 24 36 41N25'40 78w33'40 5:14:15
Saint Marys Seminary 46 90 40N02'30 75w20'28 5:01:22
Saint Michael 11 63 40N20'13 78w46'16 5:15:05
Saint Nicholas 54 3 40N48'16 76w10'41 5:04:43
Saint Paul 56 79 39N46'32 79w06'23 5:16:26
Saint Pauls Church 51 9 40N04'29 75w12'11 5:00:49
Saint Peters 15 56 40N10'48 75w43'52 5:02:55
Saint Petersburg 16 1 41N09'42 79w39'11 5:18:37
Saint Thomas 28 1 39N55'03 77w47'53 5:11:12
Saint Vincent 65 3 40N19 79w23 5:17:32
Saint Vincent College 65 3 40N19 79w23 5:17:32
Saint Vincent Shaft 65 3 40N17'02 79w24'00 5:17:36
Salco 56 6 39N56 78w57 5:15:48
Salem 17 56 41N04'19 78w44'31 5:14:58
Salem 28 42 39N59'06 77w39'16 5:10:37
Salem 43 59 41N26'04 80w19'55 5:21:20
Salem 55 82 40N48'44 76w54'05 5:07:36
Salem Harbor 9 9 40N06 74w56 4:59:44
Salemville 5 6 40N08'54 78w25'59 5:13:44
Salford 46 8 40N17'45 75w27'17 5:01:49
Salford Heights 46 8 40N17 75w23 5:01:32
Salfordville 46 8 40N18 75w26 5:01:44
Salida 2 114 40N20'43 80w00'37 5:20:02
Salina 65 116 40N31'18 79w29'54 5:18:00
Salisbury 56 79 39N45'10 79w04'52 5:16:19
Salisbury Heights 36 23 40N02'02 76w00'41 5:04:03
Salisbury Junction 56 79 39N49'32 79w01'58 5:16:08
Salix 11 63 40N18'00 78w45'56 5:15:04
Salladasburg 41 6 41N16'38 77w13'34 5:08:54
Sally Ann 6 9 40N28'20 75w43'37 5:02:54
Salona 18 76 41N05'03 77w27'48 5:09:51
Saltillo 31 6 40N12'38 78w00'25 5:12:02
Saltlick 26 6 40N03 79w24 5:17:36
Saltsburg 32 116 40N29'11 79w27'06 5:17:48
Salunga 36 97 40N06'03 76w25'30 5:05:42
Saluvia 29 66 40N00'19 78w06'13 5:12:25
Sample 2 114 40N34'46 79w58'06 5:19:52
Sample Heights 2 114 40N30 79w59 5:19:56
Sample Run 32 6 40N39'38 79w01'24 5:16:06
Sampson 25 107 42N00'33 79w59'52 5:19:59
Sampson 63 1 40N10'26 79w52'59 5:19:32
Sanatoga 46 8 40N14'42 75w35'44 5:02:23
Sanatoga Park 46 8 40N15 75w39 5:02:36
Sanbourn 17 4 40N54'04 78w23'51 5:13:35
Sand Beach 22 31 40N18'31 76w40'07 5:06:40
Sandertown 11 55 40N28'12 78w35'33 5:14:22
Sand Hill 38 8 40N21'34 76w25'55 5:05:44
Sandhill 45 17 40N56'41 75w18'27 5:01:14
Sand Hill 65 111 40N10'06 79w33'02 5:18:12
Sand Patch 56 79 39N47'53 78w58'23 5:15:54
Sandrock 30 6 39N44'42 80w24'00 5:21:36
Sand Springs 40 20 41N03'44 75w57'51 5:03:51
Sandts Eddy 46 12 40N41 75w14 5:00:56
Sandy 17 56 41N06'28 78w46'17 5:15:05
Sandy Bank 23 90 39N55 75w22 5:01:28
Sandy Creek 2 114 40N28'31 79w50'55 5:19:24
Sandy Hill 46 90 40N08 75w21 5:01:24
Sandy Hollow 16 7 41N00'29 79w33'03 5:18:12
Sandy Hook 28 42 39N59'42 77w46'41 5:11:07
Sandy Lake 43 6 41N20'55 80w04'57 5:20:20
Sandy Lick 10 2 40N42'45 79w43'46 5:18:55
Sandy Plains 63 6 39N59'52 80w01'46 5:20:07
Sandy Point 10 6 41N09'53 79w45'48 5:19:03
Sandy Ridge 14 4 40N48'53 78w14'09 5:12:57
Sandy Run 30 51 39N48 79w55 5:19:40
Sandy Run 40 20 41N01'10 75w51'26 5:03:26
Sandy Valley 33 6 41N07'38 78w52'08 5:15:29
Sandyville 52 6 41N08'35 75w02'09 5:00:09
Sanford 62 3 41N46'10 79w32'10 5:18:09
Sankertown 11 55 40N28 78w35 5:14:20
Santiago (Tyre P O) 2 51 40N26'03 80w16'15 5:21:05
Sarah Furnace 16 7 41N00'29 79w35'52 5:18:23
Sardis 65 14 40N29'30 79w41'31 5:18:46
Sartwell 42 40 41N52'47 78w21'00 5:13:24
Sarver 10 2 40N43'53 79w44'46 5:18:59
Sarverville 10 2 40N43'10 79w45'21 5:19:01
Sassamansville 46 2 40N20'31 75w34'21 5:02:17
Satterfield 57 60 41N29'25 76w24'32 5:05:38
Satterfield Junction 57 60 41N31 76w24 5:05:36
Saulsburg 31 81 40N37'14 77w53'42 5:11:35
Savage 56 6 39N46'24 79w12'18 5:16:49
Savan 32 6 40N49'18 78w59'51 5:15:59
Saverys Mill 15 13 39N52'59 75w38'37 5:02:34
Saville 50 6 40N26'18 77w23'46 5:09:35
Sawtown 61 9 41N22'09 79w34'30 5:18:18
Sawyer City 42 102 41N56'39 78w35'28 5:14:22
Saxonburg 10 6 40N45'14 79w48'37 5:19:14
Saxton 5 51 40N12'55 78w14'41 5:12:59
Saybrook 62 3 41N43'23 79w03'08 5:16:13
Saylorsburg 45 17 40N53'44 75w19'26 5:01:18
Saylorsville 13 94 41N02'26 75w41'38 5:02:47
Sayre 8 1 41N58'44 76w30'57 5:06:04
Scab Hill 65 25 40N19'21 79w43'01 5:18:52
Scalp Level 11 123 40N14'59 78w50'57 5:15:24
Scammells Corner 9 9 40N14'11 74w51'10 4:59:25
Scandia 62 6 41N54'46 79w02'08 5:16:09
Scarlan Hill 11 55 40N24'14 78w37'56 5:14:32
Scarlets Mill 6 8 40N14 75w51 5:03:24
Scattertown 24 7 41N14'54 78w31'29 5:14:06
Scenery Hill 63 51 40N05 80w04 5:20:16
Scenic Hills 23 9 39N56 75w20 5:01:20
Schades Corner 15 8 40N13'47 75w40'02 5:02:40
Schaefferstown 38 25 40N17'54 76w17'41 5:05:11
Scheidy 39 13 40N41'35 75w33'42 5:02:15
Schellsburg 5 6 40N02'56 78w38'40 5:14:35
Schenley 3 2 40N41'04 79w39'43 5:18:39
Schenley Heights 2 114 40N27'05 79w57'33 5:19:50
Scherersville 39 13 40N37'43 75w30'36 5:02:02
Schnecksville 39 8 40N40'04 75w36'27 5:02:26
Schoeneck 36 28 40N14'29 76w10'28 5:04:42
Schoeneck 48 8 40N45'19 75w18'31 5:01:14
Schoenersville 48 13 40N39'48 75w25'30 5:01:42
Schoentown 54 27 40N42 76w10 5:04:40
Schofer 6 8 40N32'19 75w42'55 5:02:52
Schoffner Corner 33 34 41N18'35 78w55'41 5:15:43
Schofield Corners 43 6 41N25'11 80w09'22 5:20:37
Schollard 43 6 41N08'22 80w12'52 5:20:51
School Lane 36 8 40N02 76w20 5:05:20
School Lane Hills 36 8 40N02 76w18 5:05:12
Schracktown 18 7 41N01'38 77w19'56 5:09:20
Schubert 6 1 40N29'51 76w13'16 5:04:53
Schultzville 6 2 40N23'05 75w36'12 5:02:25
Schultzville 35 45 41N28'56 75w45'57 5:03:04
Schuster Heights 10 2 40N41'24 79w42'24 5:18:50
Schuyler 47 6 41N05'38 76w44'07 5:06:56
Schuylkill 51 9 39N56 75w11 5:00:44
Schuylkill Haven 54 27 40N37'50 76w10'17 5:04:41
Schuylkill Hills 46 90 40N08 75w21 5:01:24
Schweibinzville 56 6 39N54'02 79w18'39 5:17:15
Schwenksville 46 8 40N15'22 75w27'51 5:01:51
Sciota 45 17 40N55'46 75w18'59 5:01:16
Sconnelltown 15 13 39N56'10 75w37'32 5:02:30
Scotch Hill 16 6 41N19'36 79w15'56 5:17:04
Scotch Hollow 17 4 40N52'11 78w18'09 5:13:13
Scotia 2 8 40N18 79w54 5:19:36
Scotia 14 63 40N47'59 77w56'47 5:11:47
Scotland 28 42 39N58'07 77w35'15 5:10:21
Scotrun 45 84 41N03'57 75w19'13 5:01:17
Scott 35 1 41N34'10 75w37'57 5:02:32
Scott Center 64 6 41N56'20 75w23'43 5:01:35
Scottdale 65 111 40N06'01 79w35'14 5:18:21
Scott Haven 65 1 40N15'20 79w47'22 5:19:09
Scotts Crossing 62 3 41N56'08 79w35'43 5:18:23
Scottsville 4 13 40N34'58 80w15'32 5:21:02
Scottsville 66 59 41N35'46 76w05'48 5:04:23
Scott Township 2 114 40N25 80w05 5:20:20
Scranton 35 18 41N24'32 75w39'46 5:02:39
Scrubgrass 61 1 41N12 79w47 5:19:08
Scullton 56 4 39N56'52 79w18'47 5:17:15
Scyoc 50 6 40N22 77w36 5:10:24
Seagers 41 83 41N12 76w47 5:07:08
Seal 15 13 39N54'11 75w35'28 5:02:22
Seamentown 32 6 40N42'35 78w55'46 5:15:43
Seanor 56 74 40N12'43 78w53'55 5:15:36
Searights 26 80 39N56'41 79w48'50 5:19:15
Sebring 59 6 41N35'42 77w06'37 5:08:26
Secane 23 9 39N54'50 75w18'09 5:01:13
Secane Highlands 23 9 39N56 75w18 5:01:12
Sechrist Mill 67 7 39N51'46 76w35'27 5:06:22
Sedwicks Mill 10 6 41N09'53 79w47'06 5:19:08
Seeger Place 31 6 40N41'48 77w46'05 5:11:04
Seek 54 80 40N49 75w55 5:03:40
Seelyville 64 22 41N34'39 75w16'53 5:01:08
Seemsville 48 13 40N43'20 75w27'31 5:01:50
Seger 65 3 40N21'54 79w17'08 5:17:09
Seiberlingville 39 9 40N36'32 75w44'07 5:02:56
Seidersville 48 13 40N35'16 75w23'06 5:01:32
Seiple 39 13 40N38'34 75w31'10 5:02:05
Seipstown 39 9 40N35'25 75w40'48 5:02:43
Seisholtzville 6 13 40N28'11 75w36'16 5:02:25
Seitzland 67 3 39N47'07 76w43'24 5:06:54
Seitzville 67 3 39N49'48 76w45'44 5:07:03
Seldersville 11 63 40N30'14 78w51'48 5:15:27
Selea 31 6 40N09'21 77w59'31 5:11:58
Selinsgrove 55 82 40N47'56 76w51'45 5:07:27
Selinsgrove Junction 49 82 40N48'06 76w50'22 5:07:21
Selkirk 62 74 41N41'14 79w34'50 5:18:19
Sellersville 9 8 40N21'14 75w18'19 5:01:13
Seltzer 54 27 40N41'43 76w14'03 5:04:56
Seminole 3 6 40N57'17 79w20'35 5:17:22
Seneca 61 9 41N22'43 79w42'15 5:18:49
Seneca Valley 65 25 40N20 79w43 5:18:52
Sereno 19 6 41N09'15 76w31'18 5:06:05
Sergeant 42 7 41N38'02 78w45'08 5:15:01
Seven Pines 34 7 40N28'11 77w27'45 5:09:51
Seven Points 49 2 40N49'24 76w42'45 5:06:51
Seven Springs 56 6 40N01'23 79w17'51 5:17:11
Seven Stars 1 1 39N51'31 77w17'51 5:09:11
Seven Stars 15 118 40N09'48 75w35'41 5:02:23
Seven Stars 31 6 40N39'30 78w04'55 5:12:20
Seven Stars 34 1 40N36'48 77w06'19 5:08:25
Seven Stars 46 90 40N06'01 75w18'04 5:01:12
Seven Valleys 67 3 39N51'20 76w46'08 5:07:05
Seward 65 7 40N24'51 79w01'13 5:16:05
Sewickley 2 13 40N32'11 80w11'05 5:20:44
Sewickley Heights 2 13 40N34 80w09 5:20:36
Sewickley Hills 2 114 40N34'54 80w08'13 5:20:33
Seybertown 3 1 40N59 79w37 5:18:28
Seyfert 6 8 40N17'18 75w53'02 5:03:32
Seyoc 50 6 40N17'55 77w38'59 5:10:36
Shade 56 63 40N07 78w50 5:15:20
Shade Gap 31 6 40N10'51 77w51'58 5:11:28
Shadeland 20 6 41N48'56 80w22'35 5:21:30
Shades Glen 40 60 41N10'36 75w41'04 5:02:44
Shade Valley 31 6 40N17 77w43 5:10:52
Shadle 55 111 40N42'18 76w59'31 5:07:58
Shado-Wood Village 32 72 40N36'33 79w12'06 5:16:48
Shadow Shuttle 2 114 40N27'09 79w49'12 5:19:17
Shady Grove 28 100 39N46'40 77w40'08 5:10:41
Shady Plain 3 4 40N36'43 79w26'18 5:17:45
Shadyside 2 114 40N27'05 79w56'28 5:19:46
Shaffer 17 56 41N07'27 78w44'04 5:14:56
Shaffers Corner 26 80 39N51 79w43 5:18:52
Shaffers Corners 35 45 41N25'25 75w47'25 5:03:10
Shaffersville 31 81 40N34'11 78w08'38 5:12:35
Shaft 54 27 40N49 76w12 5:04:48
Shaft 56 6 39N54'14 78w56'08 5:15:45
Shafton 65 25 40N19'51 79w41'36 5:18:46
Shaler 2 114 40N32 79w58 5:19:52
Shalercrest 2 114 40N31 79w57 5:19:48
Shamburg 16 6 41N09'20 79w27'55 5:17:52
Shamburg 61 74 41N33'36 79w37'43 5:18:31
Shamokin 49 27 40N47'20 76w33'33 5:06:14
Shamokin Dam 55 82 40N50'55 76w49'12 5:07:17
Shamrock 26 80 39N55'04 79w48'24 5:19:14
Shamrock 30 6 39N43'18 80w16'11 5:21:05
Shamrock 49 1 40N51'39 76w35'06 5:06:20
Shamrock 56 6 39N56'14 79w06'53 5:16:28
Shamrock Station 6 9 40N30'09 75w38'56 5:02:36
Shaner 65 25 40N16'52 79w46'31 5:19:06
Shaners Crossroads 65 4 40N38 79w37 5:18:28
Shanesville 6 2 40N21'51 75w41'52 5:02:47
Shanks Mill 1 1 39N43'33 77w21'50 5:09:27
Shanksville 56 6 40N01'04 78w54'27 5:15:38
Shanktown 32 6 40N42 78w58 5:15:52
Shankweilers 39 13 40N39'01 75w35'55 5:02:24
Shannondale 16 6 41N04'52 79w13'57 5:16:56
Shannon Heights 2 114 40N29'21 79w49'50 5:19:19
Shanor Heights 10 3 40N54'02 79w54'34 5:19:38
Sharon 43 117 41N13'59 80w29'37 5:21:58
Sharon Center 53 29 41N56'25 78w08'45 5:12:35
Sharon Hill 23 9 39N54'23 75w16'19 5:01:05
Sharon Park 23 9 39N54 75w17 5:01:08
Sharpe 29 6 39N48'59 78w07'07 5:12:28
Sharpe Hill 2 114 40N30'12 79w56'15 5:19:45
Sharpsburg 2 114 40N29'40 79w55'36 5:19:42
Sharpsburg 31 85 40N31'13 77w50'05 5:11:20
Sharps Hill 2 114 40N30 79w56 5:19:44
Sharpsville 43 117 41N15'33 80w28'20 5:21:53
Sharrertown 63 51 40N03'17 79w57'35 5:19:50

Shartlesville 6 1 40N30'46 76w06'17 5:04:25
Shavertown 40 20 41N20 75w56 5:03:44
Shawanese 40 6 41N21'05 76w02'04 5:04:08
Shaw Mine 63 51 40N22 80w14 5:20:56
Shaw Mines 56 79 39N47'51 79w03'10 5:16:13
Shawmont 51 9 40N03'10 75w14'11 5:00:57
Shawmut 24 5 41N17'14 78w44'01 5:14:56
Shawnee 44 73 40N35'01 77w31'23 5:10:06
Shawnee on Delaware 45 23 41N00'44 75w06'40 5:00:27
Shaws 20 77 41N40 80w07 5:20:28
Shaws Corners 20 59 41N33'40 80w06'32 5:20:26
Shaws Landing 20 59 41N33'05 80w06'53 5:20:28
Shawtown 65 25 40N20'05 79w42'19 5:18:49
Shawville 17 1 41N04'09 78w21'30 5:13:26
Shawwood Park 10 6 40N57'50 80w07'40 5:20:31
Shay 3 6 40N44'11 79w27'18 5:17:49
Shaytown 53 29 41N54'22 78w10'22 5:12:41
Shazen 11 92 40N42'05 78w45'29 5:15:02
Sheakleyville 43 6 41N26'34 80w12'29 5:20:50
Shearersburg 65 4 40N36'54 79w39'16 5:18:37
Sheatown 40 21 41N11'36 76w00'54 5:04:04
Sheeder 15 118 40N09'06 75w37'13 5:02:29
Sheerlund Forest 6 101 40N19 75w57 5:03:48
Sheffield 62 3 41N42'14 79w02'09 5:16:09
Sheffield Junction 27 3 41N35'00 78w59'30 5:15:58
Shehawken 64 6 41N53'22 75w23'36 5:01:34
Shelander Hollow 62 3 41N42'23 79w01'06 5:16:04
Shellsville 22 3 40N22'00 76w40'15 5:06:41
Shelltown 7 3 40N27'23 78w12'24 5:12:50
Shelly 9 13 40N28'51 75w22'21 5:01:29
Shellytown 7 3 40N24'32 78w12'34 5:12:50
Shelocta 32 6 40N39'21 79w18'08 5:17:13
Shelvey 24 36 41N22'11 78w39'01 5:14:36
Shenandoah 54 27 40N49'13 76w12'04 5:04:48
Shenandoah Heights 54 1 40N49'39 76w12'26 5:04:50
Shenandoah Junction 54 27 40N49 76w12 5:04:48
Shenango 43 59 41N22'47 80w23'57 5:21:36
Shenkel 15 8 40N15 75w39 5:02:36
Shenks Ferry 67 1 39N53'58 76w23'11 5:05:33
Shepherdstown 21 12 40N10'39 76w59'30 5:07:58
Sheppton 54 60 40N53'51 76w07'05 5:04:28
Sheraden 2 114 40N27'34 80w04'39 5:20:19
Sherersville 39 13 40N37 75w31 5:02:04
Sheridan 38 1 40N21'19 76w13'23 5:04:54
Sheridan 54 27 40N35'14 76w34'07 5:06:16
Sherman 64 6 41N59'15 75w25'36 5:01:42
Shermans Dale 50 6 40N19'27 77w10'24 5:08:42
Shermansville 20 6 41N37'33 80w22'27 5:21:30
Sherrett 3 6 40N56'05 79w34'17 5:18:17
Sherwin 10 3 41N00'16 79w56'44 5:19:47
Sheshequin 8 60 41N51'19 76w29'28 5:05:58
Shetters Grove 67 67 39N58 76w44 5:06:56
Shettleston 14 7 41N04'46 77w53'35 5:11:34
Shickshinny 40 1 41N09'11 76w09'02 5:04:36
Shields 2 13 40N33 80w10 5:20:40
Shieldsburg 65 3 40N23'33 79w26'17 5:17:45
Shillington 6 101 40N18'28 75w57'57 5:03:52
Shiloh 17 6 41N02'30 78w17'30 5:13:10
Shiloh 67 67 39N58'41 76w47'51 5:07:11
Shimersville 48 13 40N37'03 75w19'51 5:01:19
Shimerville 39 13 40N29'42 75w31'36 5:02:06
Shimpstown 28 51 39N47'25 77w54'00 5:11:36
Shindle 44 1 40N40'10 77w24'49 5:09:39
Shinerville 57 6 41N29'15 76w22'56 5:05:32
Shingiss 63 2 40N14'24 80w12'35 5:20:50
Shinglebury 59 6 41N53'33 77w17'49 5:09:11
Shinglehouse 53 29 41N57'49 78w11'28 5:12:46
Shingletown 14 9 40N45'48 77w49'33 5:11:18
Shintown 18 73 41N18'26 77w48'06 5:11:12
Shipmans Eddy 62 120 41N49'47 79w05'14 5:16:21
Shippensburg 21 82 40N03'02 77w31'14 5:10:05
Shippenville 16 37 41N15'01 79w27'35 5:17:50
Shippingport 4 6 40N37'55 80w24'51 5:21:39
Shiremanstown 21 12 40N13'24 76w57'14 5:07:49
Shire Oaks 63 8 40N14'37 79w56'48 5:19:47
Shirks Corner 46 8 40N16'49 75w26'08 5:01:45
Shirksville 38 1 40N25'43 76w25'21 5:05:41
Shirley 31 85 40N21 77w52 5:11:28
Shirleysburg 31 85 40N17'52 77w52'28 5:11:30
Shoaf 26 51 39N50'27 79w48'31 5:19:14
Shober 56 79 39N53'29 79w01'22 5:16:05
Shocks Mills 36 26 40N04 76w33 5:06:12
Shoemaker 11 63 40N23'39 78w38'46 5:14:35
Shoemakers 45 23 41N04'41 75w01'41 5:00:07
Shoemakers 54 3 40N49'52 76w07'49 5:04:31
Shoemakersville 6 80 40N30'03 75w58'13 5:03:53
Shoenberger 31 11 40N38'00 78w11'10 5:12:45
Shoenersville 39 13 40N35 75w28 5:01:52
Shohola 52 6 41N28'30 74w54'56 4:59:40
Shohola Falls 52 6 41N23'27 74w57'59 4:59:52
Shope Gardens 22 80 40N12 76w43 5:06:52
Shorbes Hill 67 1 39N48 76w59 5:07:56
Short Run 53 6 41N35'23 77w46'55 5:11:08
Shortsville 59 6 41N51'58 77w21'39 5:09:27
Shortys Place 29 6 40N01'11 78w09'43 5:12:39
Shraders 44 7 40N41'52 77w33'14 5:10:13
Shreiners 36 8 40N04'35 76w20'52 5:05:23
Shreiners 55 82 40N51'56 76w50'39 5:07:23
Shrewsbury 67 27 39N46'07 76w40'48 5:06:43
Shumans 19 4 40N57'12 76w18'09 5:05:13
Shunk 57 6 41N32'46 76w44'35 5:06:58
Sibleyville 25 35 41N59'01 80w02'49 5:20:11
Sickler Hill 40 20 41N13'39 75w58'37 5:03:54
Sickles Corner 7 33 40N33'14 78w16'59 5:13:08
Siddonsburg 67 1 40N08'45 76w57'59 5:07:52
Sidley 25 47 40N03'56 75w33'46 5:02:15
Sidman (Lovett Station) 11 63 40N19'50 78w44'42 5:14:59
Sidney 32 51 40N52'38 78w48'34 5:15:14
Siegfried 48 13 40N41 75w22 5:01:28
Sigel 33 6 41N17 79w07 5:16:28
Siglerville 44 7 40N44'22 77w31'58 5:10:08
Sigmund 39 13 40N28'24 75w33'33 5:02:14
Sigsbee 30 51 39N49'40 79w57'23 5:19:50
Siko 64 59 41N40'26 75w15'13 5:01:01
Siles 9 97 40N09'20 74w58'16 4:59:53
Silkworth 40 1 41N16'20 76w05'12 5:04:21
Silvara 8 6 41N41'55 76w08'05 5:04:32
Silver Creek 54 27 40N43'58 76w08'01 5:04:32
Silverdale 9 8 40N20'51 75w16'17 5:01:05
Silver Ford Heights 44 85 40N22'38 77w50'55 5:11:24
Silver Lake 9 8 40N14 74w56 4:59:44
Silver Lake 58 6 41N58 75w56 5:03:44
Silver Lake 67 12 40N08 76w52 5:07:28
Silver Mills 5 6 39N45'23 78w21'51 5:13:27
Silver Spring 36 8 40N03'51 76w26'15 5:05:45
Silver Spring 52 2 41N17'58 74w50'57 4:59:24
Silverton 54 27 40N39'31 76w16'15 5:05:05
Silverville 10 2 40N42'16 79w43'23 5:18:54
Simmonstown 36 23 39N58'32 75w59'39 5:03:59
Simpson 35 1 41N35'30 75w29'08 5:01:57
Simpson Store 63 6 39N58'42 80w23'54 5:21:36
Singersville 22 12 40N22'38 76w54'43 5:07:39
Sinking Spring 6 101 40N19'38 76w00'41 5:04:03
Sinking Valley 7 33 40N31 78w25 5:13:40
Sinnemahoning 12 116 41N19'09 78w05'48 5:12:23
Sinsheim 67 95 39N48'17 76w51'59 5:07:28
Siousca 15 9 40N00'15 75w49'16 5:03:17
Sipes Mill 29 6 39N54'38 78w09'10 5:12:37
Sipesville 56 6 40N05'57 79w05'29 5:16:22
Sister 48 8 40N53'54 75w09'13 5:00:37
Sistersville 3 15 40N47'10 79w36'45 5:18:27
Sitka 26 105 39N59'29 79w36'42 5:18:27
Siverly 61 9 41N25'14 79w41'37 5:18:46
Six Mile Run 5 51 40N10 78w13 5:12:52
Six Points 10 6 41N08'26 79w45'18 5:19:01
Sizerville 12 106 41N35'19 78w11'49 5:12:47
Skelp 7 33 40N37'11 78w16'06 5:13:04
Skeltontown 20 3 41N48'44 80w06'43 5:20:27
Skidmore 37 112 41N00 80w21 5:21:24
Skinners Eddy 66 6 41N38'29 76w08'49 5:04:35
Skippack 46 8 40N13'22 75w23'57 5:01:36
Skyline Heights 67 67 39N59 76w46 5:07:04
Skyline View 22 1 40N20'21 76w43'33 5:06:54
Skytop 45 84 41N13'40 75w14'19 5:00:57
Slab 67 7 39N47'46 76w20'12 5:05:21
Slabtown 3 64 40N52'39 79w23'40 5:17:35
Slabtown 17 63 40N44 78w49 5:15:16
Slabtown 19 27 40N54'18 76w24'33 5:05:38
Slabtown 28 26 39N49'39 77w33'26 5:10:14
Slackwater 36 8 39N58'56 76w21'23 5:05:26
Slatedale 39 8 40N44'40 75w39'25 5:02:38
Slatefield 48 80 40N47'45 75w29'52 5:01:59
Slateford 48 8 40N56'46 75w06'52 5:00:27
Slate Hill 67 1 39N44'21 76w17'23 5:05:10
Slate Lick 3 2 40N46'01 79w38'35 5:18:34
Slate Ridge 1 1 39N44'02 77w05'29 5:08:22
Slate Run 41 6 41N28'22 77w30'07 5:10:00
Slate Valley 48 80 40N45'23 75w34'39 5:02:19
Slateville 39 56 40N39'50 75w52'03 5:03:28
Slatington 39 8 40N44'54 75w36'44 5:02:27
Slickport 11 92 40N40'23 78w42'36 5:14:50
Slickville 65 6 40N27'35 79w31'24 5:18:06
Sligo 2 2 40N38'36 79w41'31 5:18:46
Sligo 16 6 41N06'33 79w29'25 5:17:58
Slippery Rock 10 6 41N03'50 80w03'24 5:20:14
Slippery Rock Park 10 6 41N01'27 80w00'56 5:20:04
Slocum 40 1 41N07'55 76w02'46 5:04:11
Slocum Corners 40 1 41N08'43 76w01'18 5:04:05
Slonaker 15 118 40N10'38 75w37'58 5:02:32
Slovan 63 6 40N21'33 80w23'24 5:21:34
Smallwood 63 51 40N04'06 79w55'07 5:19:40
Smeltzer 3 6 40N48'25 79w15'33 5:17:02
Smethport 42 93 41N48'40 78w26'42 5:13:47
Smicksburg 32 6 40N52'11 79w10'16 5:16:41
Smiley 26 80 39N50'19 79w48'11 5:19:13
Smiley 58 6 41N46'50 75w35'16 5:02:21
Smith 32 98 40N26'54 79w14'10 5:16:57
Smith 63 6 40N22 80w23 5:21:32
Smith Bridge 30 6 39N55 80w26 5:21:44
Smith Corner 7 33 40N21'27 78w29'21 5:13:57
Smith Corners 61 6 41N10'51 79w52'04 5:19:28
Smithdale 2 1 40N13'40 79w47'30 5:19:10
Smithfield 26 51 39N48'11 79w48'29 5:19:14
Smithfield 31 81 40N30 78w01 5:12:04
Smithfield 45 85 41N02 75w08 5:00:32
Smithfield Center 31 81 40N29 78w02 5:12:08
Smith Gap 45 9 40N50'04 75w26'05 5:01:44
Smith Gardens 67 1 40N04 76w43 5:06:52
Smithland 16 6 41N01'13 79w24'21 5:17:37
Smithmill 17 63 40N46 78w25 5:13:40
Smithport 32 6 40N50'09 78w52'36 5:15:30
Smiths 67 95 39N53 76w52 5:07:28
Smiths Corner 9 1 40N25'27 75w06'20 5:00:25
Smiths Corners 61 6 41N17'57 79w46'20 5:19:05
Smiths Ferry 4 6 40N38'51 80w30'08 5:22:01
Smiths Station 67 1 39N48'54 76w55'32 5:07:42
Smith Summit 33 5 41N13'36 78w49'38 5:15:19
Smithton 65 6 40N09'14 79w44'29 5:18:58
Smithtown 9 1 40N26 75w09 5:00:36
Smithtown 33 56 41N08'40 78w51'11 5:15:25
Smithville 36 27 39N55'35 76w15'09 5:05:01
Smock 26 6 39N59'53 79w47'00 5:19:08
Smokeless 32 29 40N23 79w04 5:16:16
Smoke Run 17 6 40N47'41 78w25'40 5:13:43
Smoketown 9 13 40N23'54 75w19'42 5:01:19
Smoketown 28 42 39N56'56 77w34'33 5:10:18
Smoketown 36 8 40N02'21 76w11'59 5:04:48
Smoketown 48 8 40N42'37 75w20'51 5:01:23
Smullton 14 52 40N56'10 77w26'24 5:09:46
Smyerstown 32 51 40N53 78w56 5:15:44
Smyrna 36 23 39N56'47 76w02'38 5:04:11
Snake Spring Valley 5 70 40N02 78w25 5:13:40
Snedekerville 8 7 41N53'41 76w48'03 5:07:12
Snively Corners 16 6 41N14'49 79w37'14 5:18:29
Snowball Gate 9 9 40N09 74w51 4:59:24
Snowden 2 114 40N16'42 79w57'55 5:19:52
Snowdenville 15 118 40N11'27 75w36'04 5:02:24
Snow Shoe 14 7 41N01'51 77w56'59 5:11:48
Snows Mill 58 60 41N47'54 75w59'07 5:03:56
Snyder Corner 67 1 39N55'11 76w31'42 5:06:07
Snyders 54 1 40N43'16 75w51'43 5:03:27
Snydersburg 16 6 41N19'58 79w21'21 5:17:25
Snydersville 45 23 40N57'30 75w17'31 5:01:10
Snydertown 14 63 40N59'03 77w35'10 5:10:21
Snydertown 31 81 40N23'02 78w03'41 5:12:15
Snydertown 49 6 40N52'09 76w40'20 5:06:41
Snydertown 65 3 40N10'14 79w35'12 5:18:21
Snyderville 3 59 40N53 79w15 5:17:00
Sober 14 64 40N51 77w34 5:10:16
Social Island 28 42 39N53'05 77w42'42 5:10:51
Soho 2 114 40N26'15 79w58'58 5:19:56
Soldier 33 6 41N03'45 78w50'39 5:15:23
Solebury 9 8 40N22'50 75w00'31 5:00:02
Solomons Gap 40 20 41N10'45 75w53'00 5:03:32
Somerfield 56 53 39N45'14 79w23'30 5:17:34
Somerset 56 6 40N00'30 79w04'42 5:16:19
Somers Lane 59 59 41N58'03 77w06'39 5:08:27
Somerton 51 56 40N07'24 75w00'55 5:00:04
Somerville 3 1 40N57'38 79w39'15 5:18:37
Sonestown 57 6 41N21'13 76w33'16 5:06:13
Sonman 11 63 40N23'42 78w39'34 5:14:38
Sopertown 8 7 41N52'32 76w54'17 5:07:37
Soradoville 44 1 40N40'47 77w24'46 5:09:39
Soudersburg 36 96 40N00'54 76w09'19 5:04:37
Souderton 46 8 40N18'42 75w19'32 5:01:18
Soukesburg 11 74 40N21'11 78w46'56 5:15:08
South Abington 35 45 41N29 75w42 5:02:48
South Altoona 7 33 40N29'20 78w24'34 5:13:38
Southampton 9 1 40N10'27 75w02'39 5:00:11
South Annville 38 8 40N18 76w31 5:06:04
South Ardmore 23 9 40N00 75w18 5:01:12
South Auburn 58 59 41N39'54 76w04'50 5:04:19
South Beaver 4 6 40N46 80w27 5:21:48
South Bend 3 6 40N37'40 79w22'11 5:17:29
South Bethlehem 3 6 40N59'58 79w20'28 5:17:22
South Bradford 42 102 41N55'45 78w39'11 5:14:37
South Branch 8 60 41N38'54 76w26'42 5:05:47
South Buffalo 3 2 40N44 79w38 5:18:32
South Burgettstown 63 6 40N23 80w24 5:21:36
South Canaan 64 6 41N30'19 75w24'45 5:01:39
South Carnegie 2 114 40N25 80w05 5:20:20
South Centre 19 6 41N02 76w21 5:05:24
South Clarksville 30 6 39N59 80w03 5:20:12
South Clearfield 17 1 41N02 78w27 5:13:48
South Coatesville 15 9 39N58'27 75w49'13 5:03:17
South Connellsville 26 104 39N59'48 79w35'10 5:18:21
South Coventry 15 8 40N11 75w40 5:02:40
South Creek 8 7 41N57 76w47 5:07:08
Southdale 40 1 41N09'05 76w16'09 5:05:05
South Duquesne 2 10 40N22 79w51 5:19:24
South Easton 48 12 40N40'47 75w12'45 5:00:51
South Eaton 66 59 41N29'32 75w54'33 5:03:38
Southerwood 65 6 40N08 79w26 5:17:44
South Fayette 2 114 40N21 80w09 5:20:36
South Fork 11 62 40N22'02 78w47'30 5:15:10
South Franklin 63 3 40N07 80w18 5:21:12
South Gibson 58 6 41N44'03 75w37'50 5:02:31
South Greensburg 65 99 40N16'42 79w32'42 5:18:11
South Hanover 22 31 40N17 76w43 5:06:52

South Heidelberg 6
80 40N19 76w06 5:04:24
South Heights 4
13 40N34'25 80w14'09 5:20:57
South Hermitage 36
27 40N03'35 75w58'52 5:03:55
South Hill 8 60 41N50'09 76w15'50 5:05:03
South Hills 2 114 40N23'31 80w02'16 5:20:09
South Huntingdon 65
4 40N11 79w43 5:18:52
South Lakemont 7
33 40N27'57 78w23'34 5:13:34
South Lebanon 38
8 40N20 76w23 5:05:32
South Londonderry 38
2 40N14 76w33 5:06:12
South Mahoning 32
6 40N53 79w09 5:16:36
South Manheim 54
27 40N36 76w09 5:04:36
South Meadville 20
77 41N40 80w07 5:20:28
South Media 23 90 39N54'32 75w23'01 5:01:32
South Middleton 21
2 40N09 77w10 5:08:40
Southmont 11 74 40N18'38 78w56'20 5:15:45
South Montrose 58
60 41N47'50 75w53'30 5:03:34
South Mountain 28
1 39N50'47 77w29'17 5:09:57
South New Castle 37
112 40N58'40 80w20'43 5:21:23
South Newton 21 1 40N05 77w24 5:09:36
South Oil City 61
9 41N25 79w42 5:18:48
South Park 2 114 40N18 80w00 5:20:00
South Perkasie 9
8 40N25 75w23 5:01:32
South Philipsburg 14
113 40N53'09 78w13'16 5:12:53
South Pottstown 15
8 40N14'22 75w39'05 5:02:36
South Pymatuning 43
117 41N18 80w29 5:21:56
South Renovo 18
73 41N19'23 77w44'55 5:11:00
South Shenango 20
63 41N32 80w27 5:21:48
South Side 35 18 41N24 75w40 5:02:40
Southside 67 1 39N46'52 76w23'42 5:05:35
South Sterling 52
65 41N15'51 75w20'54 5:01:24
South Strabane 63
3 40N08'18 80w09'49 5:20:39
South Tamaqua 54
27 40N45'28 75w56'41 5:03:47
South Temple 6
101 40N23'53 75w55'19 5:03:41
South Terrace 48
13 40N36'28 75w20'59 5:01:24
South Towanda 8
41 41N45'03 76w26'37 5:05:46
South Union 26 80 39N53 79w44 5:18:56
South Union 59 7 41N34'05 76w59'57 5:08:00
South Uniontown 26
80 39N53'33 79w44'50 5:18:59
South Versailles 2
9 40N18 79w48 5:19:12
Southview 63 51 40N19'40 80w15'33 5:21:02
Southwark 51 9 39N56 75w09 5:00:36
South Warren 8 6 41N53'30 76w11'39 5:04:47
South Waverly 8 1 41N59'51 76w32'15 5:06:09
Southwest 65 111 40N11'56 79w31'16 5:18:05
Southwest Greensburg 65
99 40N17'28 79w32'50 5:18:11
South Whitehall 39
13 40N36 75w32 5:02:08
South Williamsport 41
82 41N13'55 76w59'58 5:08:00
South Woodbury 5
6 40N10 78w25 5:13:40
Southwood Hills 67
67 39N57 76w42 5:06:48
Sowash 65 3 40N19'37 79w28'21 5:17:53
Spaces Corners 3
15 40N50'23 79w27'57 5:17:52
Spaces Corners 16
6 41N04'00 79w19'17 5:17:17
Spangler 11 92 40N38'34 78w46'23 5:15:06
Spangsville 6 2 40N21'23 75w44'34 5:02:58
Sparta 20 56 41N48 79w42 5:18:48
Sparta 63 3 40N01'43 80w19'08 5:21:17
Spartansburg 20
56 41N49'26 79w41'02 5:18:44
Spears Grove 34 6 40N16'20 77w42'23 5:10:50
Spechty Kopf 22 1 40N31'22 76w40'13 5:06:41
Speeceville 22 51 40N22'28 76w59'40 5:07:59
Speedwell 36 8 40N12'31 76w19'20 5:05:17
Speers 63 1 40N07'28 79w52'48 5:19:31
Spencers Corners 35
1 41N36'17 75w34'00 5:02:16
Spencertown 59 7 41N37'06 76w53'57 5:07:36
Spike Island 14 4 40N50'38 78w16'07 5:13:04
Spike Island 35
18 41N21'06 75w43'09 5:02:53
Spilt Rock 13 94 41N03'42 75w36'47 5:02:27
Spindletown 33 51 40N59'19 78w56'02 5:15:44
Spindley City 11
55 40N32'16 78w34'22 5:14:17
Spinnerstown 9 8 40N26'20 75w26'15 5:01:45
Split Rock 13 94 41N04 75w36 5:02:24
Sporting Hill 21
12 40N14'10 76w58'20 5:07:53
Sporting Hill 36
8 40N08'38 76w25'13 5:05:41
Sportsburg 33 51 40N55'17 79w00'32 5:16:02
Spraggs 30 6 39N46'50 80w12'59 5:20:52
Sprankle Mills 33
6 41N00'07 79w06'50 5:16:27
Spring Bank 14 52 40N55'24 77w29'00 5:09:56
Springboro 20 6 41N48'02 80w22'09 5:21:29
Spring Brook 35 1 41N18'08 75w36'37 5:02:26
Spring Church 3 4 40N36'22 79w29'21 5:17:57

Spring City 15
118 40N10'36 75w32'53 5:02:12
Spring Creek 39
13 40N32'03 75w36'09 5:02:25
Spring Creek 62 7 41N52'33 79w31'32 5:18:06
Springdale 2 119 40N32'27 79w47'03 5:19:08
Springdale 67 1 39N57'02 76w42'54 5:06:52
Springdell 15 9 39N54'24 75w50'07 5:03:20
Springettsbury 67
67 39N59 76w41 5:06:44
Springfield 8 7 41N50'57 76w44'46 5:06:59
Springfield 21 1 40N10 77w24 5:09:36
Springfield 23 9 39N55'50 75w19'14 5:01:17
Springfield Falls 43
6 41N08'38 80w13'18 5:20:53
Springfield Junction 7
3 40N28'28 78w13'43 5:12:55
Springfield Park 23
9 39N56 75w20 5:01:20
Spring Garden 9 8 40N14 74w56 4:59:44
Spring Garden 36
23 40N00 76w06 5:04:24
Spring Garden 54
27 40N38 76w10 5:04:40
Spring Garden 60
73 41N06'50 76w55'43 5:07:43
Spring Garden 65
111 40N09 79w33 5:18:12
Spring Garden 67
67 39N57 76w43 5:06:52
Spring Glen 54 27 40N37'34 76w37'16 5:06:29
Spring Grove 67
95 39N52'28 76w51'58 5:07:28
Springhaven 38 1 40N16'30 76w17'44 5:05:11
Springhaven Estates 23
90 39N54 75w22 5:01:28
Spring Hill 2 114 40N27'44 79w59'41 5:19:59
Spring Hill 8 6 41N42'10 76w11'07 5:04:44
Spring Hill 11 63 40N22'35 78w40'13 5:14:41
Spring Hill 23 9 39N56 75w18 5:01:12
Springhill 26 51 39N43'53 79w48'11 5:19:13
Springhope 5 6 40N06'11 78w35'59 5:14:24
Spring House 46 8 40N11'07 75w13'41 5:00:55
Springlawn 15 1 39N44'09 75w52'03 5:03:28
Spring Meadow 5 6 40N09'22 78w34'57 5:14:20
Spring Mill 46 90 40N04'32 75w16'50 5:01:07
Spring Mills 14
64 40N51'12 77w34'04 5:10:16
Springmont 6 101 40N19'35 76w00'00 5:04:00
Spring Mount 31 6 40N42'51 78w08'31 5:12:34
Spring Mount 46 8 40N16'32 75w27'25 5:01:50
Spring Plains 67
67 39N58'57 76w38'49 5:06:35
Spring Run 28 1 40N08'31 77w46'26 5:11:06
Springs 56 6 39N44'01 79w08'58 5:16:36
Springton 15 1 40N04'33 75w46'13 5:03:05
Springtown 9 13 40N33'23 75w17'23 5:01:10
Springtown 28 1 40N04'50 77w49'12 5:11:17
Springtown 40 20 41N04'24 75w59'27 5:03:58
Springtown 49 73 41N06'46 76w51'07 5:07:24
Springvale 67 1 39N53'41 76w35'01 5:06:20
Spring Valley 6
101 40N24 75w55 5:03:40
Spring Valley 9 8 40N19'01 75w04'54 5:00:20
Spring Valley 17
4 40N58'46 78w21'27 5:13:26
Spring Valley 48
13 40N33'09 75w21'33 5:01:26
Spring Valley Estates 28
42 39N56 77w40 5:10:40
Springville 21 2 40N09 77w09 5:08:36
Springville 36 23 40N02'53 76w01'13 5:04:05
Springville 58 60 41N41'51 75w55'05 5:03:40
Springville 61 6 41N22 79w56 5:19:44
Sproul 7 3 40N16'21 78w27'39 5:13:51
Spruce 18 6 41N08'52 78w00'09 5:12:01
Spruce 32 6 40N40'47 78w51'30 5:15:26
Spruce Creek 31 7 40N36'34 78w08'09 5:12:33
Spruce Grove 36 3 39N48'24 76w04'02 5:04:16
Spruce Hill 34 6 40N28'38 77w27'04 5:09:48
Spruces 15 9 39N57'49 75w49'10 5:03:17
Sprucetown 26 7 39N45'10 79w54'39 5:19:39
Spry 67 67 39N55'06 76w41'07 5:06:44
Squab Hollow 24
36 41N21'05 78w40'03 5:14:40
Square Corner 1 1 39N48'34 77w06'23 5:08:26
Squirrel Hill 2
114 40N26'17 79w55'10 5:19:41
Squirrel Hill 16
6 41N02'19 79w24'43 5:17:39
Stacktown 36 2 40N05'20 76w38'26 5:06:34
Stafore Estates 48
13 40N39'43 75w24'17 5:01:37
Stahlstown 65 6 40N09'00 79w19'59 5:17:20
Stairville 40 1 41N07'52 76w00'44 5:04:03
Stalker 64 6 41N49'34 75w07'15 5:00:29
Stambaugh 26 80 39N55 79w40 5:18:40
Standard 65 111 40N09'34 79w32'11 5:18:09
Standard Shaft 65
111 40N09'53 79w32'00 5:18:08
Standing Stone 8
60 41N44'22 76w21'42 5:05:27
Stanfordville 58
60 41N57'25 75w49'47 5:03:19
Stanhope 54 9 40N32'05 76w21'08 5:05:25
Stanley 17 56 41N03'25 78w47'29 5:15:10
Stanleys Corner 61
9 41N23'42 79w38'15 5:18:33
Stanton 33 34 41N05'18 79w06'44 5:16:27
Stanton Corner 64
6 41N37'32 75w06'55 5:00:28
Stanton Heights 2
114 40N28'41 79w56'21 5:19:45
Stanton Heights 65
111 40N12'45 79w36'01 5:18:24
Stanwood 9 9 40N06'26 74w57'10 4:59:49
Stanwood Gardens 9
9 40N06 74w56 4:59:44
Starbrick 62 120 41N50'25 79w12'20 5:16:49
Starford 32 6 40N42'06 78w57'33 5:15:50
Star Junction 63
6 40N03'45 79w45'50 5:19:03
Starks 35 18 41N20'55 75w44'09 5:02:57

Starkville 66 89 41N36'21 75w50'05 5:03:20
Starlight 64 6 41N54'18 75w19'53 5:01:20
Starners 21 1 40N01'37 77w13'15 5:08:53
Starners Station 21
1 40N00 77w12 5:08:48
Starr 27 6 41N31'43 79w21'38 5:17:27
Starr 62 6 41N44'09 79w31'22 5:18:05
Starrucca 64 59 41N53'59 75w28'16 5:01:53
Starview 67 1 40N02'54 76w41'19 5:06:45
Star Village 48
13 40N35'34 75w23'14 5:01:33
State College 14
9 40N47'36 77w51'37 5:11:26
State Hill 6 101 40N21'47 76w01'42 5:04:07
State Hill 15 23 40N00'22 75w56'17 5:03:45
State Line 5 51 39N43'30 78w46'04 5:15:04
Stateline 25 7 42N16 79w43 5:18:52
State Line 28 1 39N43'29 77w43'29 5:10:54
Steamburg 20 7 41N44'16 80w28'14 5:21:53
Steam Valley 41 7 41N27'30 77w07'52 5:08:31
Steel City 48 13 40N37'40 75w19'41 5:01:19
Steelstown 38 8 40N21'16 76w34'35 5:06:18
Steelton 22 12 40N14'07 76w50'30 5:07:22
Steelville 15 23 39N54'17 75w50'38 5:03:59
Steene 64 1 41N35'24 75w21'03 5:01:24
Steffins Hill 4 8 40N46 80w20 5:21:20
Steins 54 27 40N39'59 76w18'24 5:05:14
Steinsburg 9 13 40N27'58 75w25'17 5:01:41
Steinsville 39 56 40N39'27 75w51'20 5:03:25
Stemlersville 13
8 40N50'50 75w36'30 5:02:26
Sterling 17 4 40N49'49 78w20'32 5:13:22
Sterling 64 6 41N20'28 75w23'25 5:01:34
Sterling Run 12 7 41N24'53 78w11'57 5:12:48
Sterlingworth 39
13 40N35'06 75w32'24 5:02:10
Sterrettania 25
107 42N00'16 80w12'12 5:20:49
Stetlersville 39
13 40N37'26 75w33'31 5:02:14
Steuben 20 7 41N41 79w49 5:19:16
Steuben 41 6 41N23'39 77w09'32 5:08:38
Steuben 48 13 40N41'30 75w22'01 5:01:28
Stevens 8 56 41N46 76w10 5:04:40
Stevens 36 28 40N12'58 76w09'20 5:04:37
Stevenson 8 60 41N37'23 76w26'06 5:05:44
Stevens Point 58
59 41N57'36 75w31'25 5:02:06
Stevenstown 67 1 40N06'05 76w59'16 5:07:57
Stevensville 8 6 41N45'38 76w10'36 5:04:42
Stewardson 53 6 41N33 77w44 5:10:56
Stewart 26 6 39N53 79w29 5:17:56
Stewarton 26 6 39N55'24 79w28'39 5:17:55
Stewart Run 27 6 41N32'56 79w29'50 5:17:59
Stewartstown 67 1 39N45'13 76w35'30 5:06:22
Stewartsville 65
25 40N20'24 79w45'17 5:19:01
Stewartville 20 7 41N36'03 80w25'39 5:21:43
Stickney 42 102 41N57'43 78w48'20 5:15:13
Sticks 67 3 39N44'49 76w48'16 5:07:13
Stiefler Corner 5
7 40N16'14 78w31'42 5:14:07
Stier 46 17 40N53 75w12 5:00:48
Stifflertown 17
63 40N44'01 78w48'08 5:15:13
Stiles 39 13 40N39'55 75w30'31 5:02:02
Stiles Crossing 32
6 40N35'29 78w52'20 5:15:29
Still Creek 54 27 40N51'21 76w00'01 5:04:00
Stilleys Siding 2
8 40N18 79w54 5:19:36
Stillwater 19 6 41N08'56 76w21'58 5:05:28
Stillwater Lake Estates 45
84 41N07'05 75w24'18 5:01:37
Stiltz 67 3 39N43'16 76w45'55 5:07:04
Stines Corner 6 1 40N37'22 75w45'51 5:03:03
Stobo 4 13 40N39'47 80w15'47 5:21:03
Stockdale 63 115 40N05'00 79w50'54 5:19:24
Stockertown 48 8 40N45'14 75w15'45 5:01:03
Stockport 64 6 41N53'40 75w16'39 5:01:07
Stockton 40 42 40N58 76w00 5:04:00
Stoddartsville 40
94 41N07'47 75w37'43 5:02:31
Stokesdale 59 6 41N46'39 77w18'35 5:09:14
Stoneboro 43 66 41N20'21 80w06'19 5:20:25
Stone Church 46 8 40N54 75w07 5:00:28
Stonedale 2 114 40N32'57 80w07'19 5:20:29
Stone Glen 22 12 40N23'05 76w53'15 5:07:33
Stoneham 62 3 41N47'57 79w05'59 5:16:24
Stone Hill 36 8 39N57'15 76w21'12 5:05:25
Stone House 16 37 41N11'25 79w21'43 5:17:27
Stone House Corner 8
6 41N48'53 76w08'14 5:04:33
Stonehurst 23 1 39N57'22 75w15'28 5:01:02
Stonehurst Hills 23
9 39N58 75w18 5:01:12
Stonemont 54 1 40N33'23 76w13'39 5:04:55
Stoner 67 1 40N00'14 76w34'37 5:06:18
Stone Row 5 6 40N09 78w16 5:13:04
Stonerstown 5 51 40N13'00 78w15'28 5:13:02
Stonersville 6 8 40N18'59 75w48'16 5:03:13
Stonerville 26 4 39N51'36 79w30'42 5:18:03
Stonetown 6 8 40N18'12 75w49'40 5:03:19
Stonevilla 65 99 40N17'40 79w31'04 5:18:04
Stoneybreak 29 6 39N45 78w11 5:12:44
Stonington 49 82 40N51'07 76w40'17 5:06:41
Stonybreak 29 6 39N46'00 78w14'49 5:12:59
Stonybrook 9 9 40N09'01 74w49'47 4:59:19
Stonybrook 67 67 39N59'13 76w38'40 5:06:35
Stonybrook Heights 67
67 39N59 76w46 5:07:04
Stonycreek 11 74 40N18'14 78w53'28 5:15:34
Stony Creek 54 3 40N34'53 76w03'44 5:04:15
Stony Creek Mills 6
101 40N20'44 75w52'13 5:03:29
Stony Fork 59 6 41N40'23 77w21'45 5:09:27
Stony Point 9 1 40N31 75w11 5:00:44
Stony Point 20 6 41N34'27 80w19'37 5:21:18
Stony Point 28 1 40N07'41 77w48'17 5:11:13
Stony Point 30 6 39N55'37 80w04'57 5:20:20
Stony Point 50 6 40N22'13 77w28'43 5:09:55
Stony Run 34 1 40N39'06 77w09'12 5:08:37
Stony Run 39 1 40N37'07 75w49'06 5:03:16

Stoopville 9 8 40N15'56 74W56'58 4:59:48
Stormstown 14 63 40N47'36 78W01'01 5:12:04
Stormville 45 23 40N57'06 75W14'38 5:00:59
Stottsville 15 32 39N57'34 75W53'19 5:03:33
Stouchsburg 6 1 40N22'48 76W13'57 5:04:56
Stoufferstown 28 42 39N55'40 77W37'51 5:10:31
Stoughstown 21 82 40N06'49 77W24'37 5:09:38
Stouts 48 13 40N36'22 75W14'41 5:00:59
Stover 31 11 40N40'38 78W12'07 5:12:48
Stoverdale 22 12 40N16 76W43 5:06:52
Stovers Mill 16 1 41N07'57 79W35'43 5:18:23
Stoverstown 67 95 39N53'03 76W49'03 5:07:16
Stowe 46 8 40N15'09 75W40'40 5:02:43
Stowell 66 6 41N34'27 76W12'07 5:04:48
Stowe Township 2 114 40N28 80W05 5:20:20
Stoystown 56 6 40N06'12 78W56'59 5:15:48
Straban 1 1 39N52 77W10 5:08:40
Strabane 63 2 40N15'03 80W11'53 5:20:48
Strafford 15 90 40N03'03 75W24'17 5:01:37
Straight Creek 24 59 41N35'51 78W28'05 5:13:52
Strangford 32 98 40N25'48 79W13'16 5:16:53
Strasburg 36 96 39N58'59 76W11'04 5:04:44
Strattanville 16 37 41N12'08 79W19'40 5:17:19
Strausstown 6 1 40N29'32 76W11'00 5:04:44
Strawberry Ridge 47 6 41N04'27 76W39'07 5:06:36
Strawbridge 41 6 41N18'50 76W37'25 5:06:30
Strawntown 9 13 40N28'18 75W16'20 5:01:05
Straw Pump 65 25 40N20 79W43 5:18:52
Street Road 9 1 40N09'29 75W00'56 5:00:04
Streights 24 7 41N34'14 78W37'21 5:14:29
Stremmels 1 1 39N49 77W11 5:08:44
Strickersville 15 1 39N44'02 75W47'36 5:03:10
Strickhousers 67 3 39N50'19 76W48'32 5:07:14
Strickler 67 26 40N00'40 76W33'05 5:06:12
Stricklerstown 38 1 40N19'30 76W13'34 5:04:54
Strinestown 67 1 40N05'28 76W45'42 5:07:03
Stringtown 3 15 40N45'51 79W31'25 5:18:06
Stringtown 5 51 39N45'02 78W45'08 5:15:01
Stringtown 30 51 39N54'37 79W56'22 5:19:45
Strobleton 16 6 41N22'04 79W24'31 5:17:38
Strodes Mills 44 73 40N33'03 77W40'24 5:10:42
Stronach 17 7 40N57'56 78W35'21 5:14:21
Strong 49 27 40N47'55 76W26'18 5:05:45
Strongstown 32 6 40N33'10 78W55'19 5:15:41
Stroud 45 23 41N01 75W13 5:00:52
Stroudsburg 45 23 40N59'12 75W11'42 5:00:47
Struble 14 9 40N46'58 77W52'35 5:11:30
Strum 26 51 39N48 79W49 5:19:16
Studa 63 6 40N18'13 80W26'49 5:21:47
Stull 66 6 41N25'02 76W05'31 5:04:22
Stump Creek 33 6 41N00'45 78W50'15 5:15:21
Stumptown 17 4 40N51'42 78W15'48 5:13:03
Stumptown 36 28 40N03'43 76W10'02 5:04:40
Sturgeon 2 51 40N23'05 80W12'40 5:20:51
Sturgis 35 18 41N29'40 75W35'07 5:02:20
Suburban Village 15 13 39N57 75W36 5:02:24
Sudan 63 1 40N09'50 79W58'04 5:19:52
Suedburg 54 9 40N31'37 76W28'12 5:05:53
Sugarcreek 61 109 41N25'17 79W52'53 5:19:32
Sugar Grove 62 6 41N58'57 79W20'20 5:17:21
Sugar Hill 33 5 41N14'35 78W52'41 5:15:31
Sugar Hill 63 3 40N09'08 80W18'37 5:21:14
Sugar Loaf 40 6 40N59 76W05 5:04:20
Sugar Notch 40 20 41N11'49 75W55'43 5:03:43
Sugar Run 8 6 41N38'32 76W14'31 5:04:58
Sugartown 15 8 40N00'00 75W30'30 5:02:02
Sulger 33 34 41N09'58 78W59'03 5:15:56
Sullivan 26 80 39N52 79W42 5:18:48
Sullivan 59 59 41N48 76W57 5:07:48
Sulphur Springs 5 6 39N57'50 78W36'29 5:14:26
Sulphur Springs 50 51 40N24 77W02 5:08:08
Sumerson 24 6 41N19'35 78W19'57 5:13:20
Summerdale 21 12 40N18'32 76W55'40 5:07:43
Summerhill 11 63 40N22'41 78W45'39 5:15:03
Summer Hill 19 1 41N05'32 76W15'17 5:05:01
Summerhill 36 3 39N46'26 76W04'27 5:04:18
Summerville 33 6 41N06'58 79W11'13 5:16:45
Summerville 58 50 41N58 75W45 5:03:00
Summit 11 55 40N27'28 78W34'20 5:14:17
Summit 42 102 41N56'34 78W31'55 5:14:08
Summit Grove Camp 67 27 39N44 76W42 5:06:48
Summit Hill 13 80 40N49'29 75W52'17 5:03:29
Summit Lawn 39 13 40N33'33 75W26'02 5:01:44
Summit Mills 56 79 39N48'32 79W04'33 5:16:18
Summit Station 54 1 40N33'50 76W12'17 5:04:49
Sumneytown 46 8 40N19'44 75W27'05 5:01:48
Sunbeam 28 42 39N56 77W40 5:10:40
Sunbrook 7 33 40N26'00 78W26'00 5:13:44
Sunbury 49 82 40N51'45 76W47'41 5:07:11
Suncliff 32 6 40N33'28 79W00'31 5:16:02
Sundale 9 1 40N28'50 75W06'37 5:00:26
Sunderlinville 53 6 41N49'40 77W38'20 5:10:33
Sunflower 4 6 40N43'53 80W14'23 5:20:58
Sunnybrook 46 9 40N06'48 75W11'52 5:00:47
Sunnybrook Estates 23 9 39N53 75W18 5:01:12
Sunnyburn 67 1 39N48'20 76W22'16 5:05:29
Sunny Rest Lodge 13 8 40N49'20 75W39'00 5:02:36
Sunny Side 2 1 40N11'53 79W53'00 5:19:32
Sunnyside 3 15 40N48'49 79W27'56 5:17:52
Sunny Side 5 6 40N08'31 78W17'09 5:13:09
Sunnyside 36 8 40N01'34 76W16'43 5:05:07
Sunnyside 37 112 40N58'11 80W24'29 5:21:38
Sunnyside 49 27 40N48'59 76W34'44 5:06:19
Sunnyside 53 29 41N57'05 78W11'11 5:12:45
Sunol 43 6 41N28'27 80W08'44 5:20:35
Sunset 38 8 40N21'53 76W25'04 5:05:40
Sunset Hills 4 13 40N37 80W16 5:21:04
Sunset Manor 67 67 39N58 76W44 5:06:56
Sunset Pines 18 76 41N08'49 77W28'17 5:09:53
Sunset Valley 37 112 41N04'03 80W18'34 5:21:14
Sunset Valley 65 25 40N18'19 79W44'22 5:18:57
Sunshine 26 51 39N48'59 79W55'00 5:19:40
Sunshine 40 1 41N09 76W10 5:04:40
Sun Valley 45 1 40N58'55 75W27'59 5:01:52
Sun Village 23 90 39N51 75W22 5:01:28
Sunville 61 6 41N33'07 79W50'06 5:19:20
Superior 26 51 39N59'31 79W53'35 5:19:34
Superior 65 3 40N21'19 79W20'18 5:17:21
Suplee 15 27 40N05'58 75W52'46 5:03:31
Surrey Hills 23 90 40N00 75W23 5:01:32
Surveyor 17 1 41N04'26 78W19'31 5:13:18
Suscon 40 1 41N18'08 75W43'22 5:02:53
Susquehanna 58 59 41N56'36 75W36'00 5:02:24
Susquehanna Bridge 17 1 41N02 78W27 5:13:48
Susquehanna Depot 58 59 41N57 75W36 5:02:24
Sutersville 65 1 40N14'10 79W47'58 5:19:12
Sutton 16 59 41N08'54 79W12'56 5:16:52
Sutton Mill 61 1 41N11'25 79W46'55 5:19:08
Swales 34 1 40N39'16 77W13'41 5:08:55
Swamproot 43 6 41N08'33 80W03'10 5:20:13
Swan Acres 2 114 40N33 80W01 5:20:04
Swanville 25 107 42N03'54 80W11'41 5:20:47
Swart 30 1 39N56 80W15 5:21:00
Swarthmore 23 9 39N54'07 75W21'01 5:01:24
Swarthmorwood 23 9 39N54 75W20 5:01:20
Swarts 30 1 39N57'20 80W15'11 5:21:01
Swartzville 36 1 40N13'59 76W04'43 5:04:19
Swatara 22 31 40N16'36 76W40'00 5:06:40
Swatara Crest 22 80 40N14'46 76W47'07 5:07:08
Swatara Station 22 31 40N17 76W39 5:06:36
Swede Hill 65 99 40N16'40 79W34'17 5:18:17
Swedeland 46 90 40N05'16 75W19'53 5:01:20
Sweden 53 66 41N48'07 77W52'16 5:11:29
Sweden Valley 53 66 41N45'23 77W57'02 5:11:48
Swedesburg 46 90 40N06'15 75W19'45 5:01:19
Swedetown 11 92 40N40'29 78W41'57 5:14:48
Swedetown 65 111 40N06 79W35 5:18:20
Sweeney Plan 65 1 40N08 79W52 5:19:28
Sweeneys Crossroads 65 1 40N10'37 79W48'21 5:19:13
Sweet Valley 40 6 41N16'56 76W08'42 5:04:35
Sweetwater 28 1 40N01'40 77W53'05 5:11:32
Swengel 60 6 40N53'32 77W07'37 5:08:30
Swiftwater 45 84 41N05'43 75W19'31 5:01:18
Swineford 55 6 40N47 77W03 5:08:12
Swissdale 18 76 41N10'41 77W26'01 5:09:44
Swissmont 24 106 41N28'36 78W29'16 5:13:57
Swissvale 2 114 40N25'25 79W52'59 5:19:32
Switzer 39 1 40N38'52 75W42'53 5:02:52
Swoyerville 40 20 41N17'30 75W52'30 5:03:30
Syberton 11 55 40N30'30 78W34'59 5:14:20
Sybertsville 40 6 41N00'05 76W04'36 5:04:18
Sycamore 30 1 39N55'36 80W14'42 5:20:59
Sycamore Mills 23 90 39N56'45 75W25'17 5:01:41
Sygan 2 114 40N21'14 80W08'13 5:20:33
Sygan Hill 2 114 40N21'22 80W08'06 5:20:32
Sykesville 33 56 41N03'01 78W49'21 5:15:17
Sylmar 15 3 39N43'23 76W01'41 5:04:07
Sylvan 28 51 39N45'12 78W01'19 5:12:05
Sylvan Dell 6 101 40N20 75W53 5:03:32
Sylvan Dell 41 82 41N13'50 76W56'28 5:07:46
Sylvan Grove 17 4 41N01'46 78W09'17 5:12:37
Sylvan Hills 7 33 40N25 78W24 5:13:36
Sylvania 8 7 41N48'18 76W51'26 5:07:26
Sylvan Lane 56 79 39N44'37 79W06'44 5:16:27
Sylvester 59 6 41N57'49 77W33'33 5:10:14
Sylvis 17 92 40N44'11 78W43'23 5:14:54
Syner 38 8 40N20'57 76W35'17 5:06:21
Table Rock 1 1 39N54'48 77W13'18 5:08:53
Tabor 51 9 40N02'19 75W08'33 5:00:34
Tacony 51 9 40N01'52 75W02'41 5:00:11
Tadmor 48 8 40N43'47 75W21'29 5:01:26
Tafton 52 6 41N24'16 75W11'00 5:00:44
Taintor 42 6 41N48'22 78W39'59 5:14:40
Tait 33 34 41N05'28 79W02'58 5:16:12
Takitezy 61 109 41N24'48 79W55'11 5:19:41
Talcose 15 13 39N59'13 75W39'58 5:02:40
Talley Cavey 2 114 40N35'24 79W56'52 5:19:47
Tallmanville 64 6 41N52'21 75W24'08 5:01:37
Tallyho 42 59 41N46'01 78W43'07 5:14:52
Talmage 36 28 40N00'00 76W12'49 5:04:51
Talmer 19 6 41N14'10 76W28'50 5:05:55
Tamanend 54 27 40N50'37 76W02'23 5:04:10
Tamaqua 54 27 40N47'50 75W58'11 5:03:53
Tamarack 18 7 41N25'28 77W50'55 5:11:24
Tambine 24 36 41N31'47 78W40'45 5:14:43
Tamiment 52 6 41N08'32 75W01'39 5:00:07
Tanguy 23 4 39N57'01 75W30'39 5:02:03
Tank 40 6 40N58 76W05 5:04:20
Tanners Falls 64 59 41N39'39 75W17'19 5:01:09
Tannersville 45 84 41N02'24 75W18'22 5:01:13
Tannertown 60 6 40N58'15 77W02'17 5:08:09
Tannery 40 60 41N02'17 75W45'46 5:03:03
Tanoma 32 6 40N42'01 79W02'45 5:16:11
Tarentum 2 14 40N36'05 79W45'36 5:19:02
Tarrs 65 111 40N10'12 79W35'54 5:18:24
Tarrtown 3 15 40N51'08 79W31'09 5:18:05
Tatamy 48 15 40N44'27 75W15'27 5:01:02
Tatesville 5 6 40N03'35 78W21'27 5:13:26
Taxville 67 1 39N57'30 76W48'54 5:07:16
Taylor 35 18 41N23'41 75W42'25 5:02:50
Taylor Highlands 31 81 40N30'23 78W01'02 5:12:04
Tayloria 36 3 39N47'42 76W04'11 5:04:17
Taylorstown 63 6 40N09'35 80W22'42 5:21:31
Taylorstown Station 63 6 40N09'00 80W22'17 5:21:29
Taylorsville 9 8 40N17'19 74W52'44 4:59:31
Taylorsville 32 6 40N42'40 78W58'36 5:15:54
Taylorville 54 27 40N44'29 76W23'27 5:05:34
Teagarden Homes 30 6 39N58'34 80W02'58 5:20:12
Tearing Run 32 71 40N31'40 79W09'14 5:16:37
Teedyskung Lake 52 6 41N28 75W03 5:00:12
Teepleville 20 3 41N45'09 79W56'18 5:19:45
Telescope 53 6 41N46'53 77W44'22 5:10:57
Telford 46 2 40N19'19 75W19'42 5:01:19
Tell 31 6 40N15 77W46 5:11:04
Temple 6 101 40N24'31 75W55'19 5:03:41
Templeton 3 64 40N55'02 79W27'40 5:17:51
Ten Mile 63 6 40N01'14 80W09'24 5:20:38
Tenmile Bottom 61 9 41N23 79W42 5:18:48
Tenth Avenue 39 13 40N38 75W23 5:01:32
Terminal 23 9 39N58 75W18 5:01:12
Terrace 2 114 40N23'27 79W53'23 5:19:34
Terre Hill 36 27 40N09'26 76W03'03 5:04:12
Terry 8 60 41N39 76W20 5:05:20
Terrytown 8 6 41N40'10 76W16'49 5:05:07
Texas 41 6 41N32'06 77W15'11 5:09:01
Texas 64 22 41N33 75W15 5:01:00
Texas Corner 5 6 40N07'55 78W24'05 5:13:36
Tharptown 49 27 40N48 76W33 5:06:12
The Pines 1 1 39N53'38 77W06'56 5:08:28
Thielman Crossroads 10 3 40N41'45 80W02'59 5:20:12
Thomas 63 2 40N14'15 80W05'39 5:20:23
Thomas Crossroads 65 110 40N14'25 79W11'51 5:16:47
Thomasdale 56 6 40N13'14 79W00'44 5:16:03
Thomas Mill 56 74 40N13'33 78W59'15 5:15:57
Thomas Mills 11 57 40N39'42 78W39'48 5:14:39
Thomas Mills 56 6 40N11 78W59 5:15:56
Thomasville 67 39 39N55'43 76W51'03 5:07:24
Thompson 58 6 41N51'49 75W30'53 5:02:04
Thompson No 1 26 51 39N56'36 79W52'59 5:19:32
Thompsons Mills 20 74 41N40'23 79W40'50 5:18:43
Thompsontown 17 122 40N49'03 78W37'56 5:14:32
Thompsontown 34 7 40N33'52 77W14'15 5:08:57
Thompsontown Station 34 7 40N33'07 77W14'12 5:08:57
Thompsonville 63 2 40N17'27 80W06'30 5:20:26
Thornburg 2 114 40N26'04 80W04'57 5:20:20
Thornbury 15 4 39N55 75W34 5:02:16
Thorndale 15 46 39N59'34 75W44'44 5:02:59
Thorndale 57 60 41N25'28 76W25'16 5:05:41
Thorndale Heights 15 46 40N00 75W42 5:02:48
Thornhurst 35 6 41N10'42 75W34'51 5:02:19
Thornridge 9 9 40N10'25 74W49'26 4:59:18
Thornton 23 4 39N54'26 75W31'55 5:02:08
Thornton Junction 25 68 41N59'29 80W22'32 5:21:30
Thornwood 65 111 40N06'47 79W35'08 5:18:21
Threemile 24 75 41N31'59 78W53'03 5:15:32
Three Springs 31 6 40N11'42 77W59'00 5:11:56
Three Springs Run 59 6 41N33'57 77W15'23 5:09:02
Three Tuns 46 1 40N10'42 75W11'36 5:00:46
Throop 35 18 41N27'05 75W36'44 5:02:27
Thumptown 59 74 41N42'10 77W23'29 5:09:34
Tiadaghton 59 6 41N38'50 77W26'45 5:09:47
Tidal 3 64 40N57'28 79W29'47 5:17:59
Tide 32 71 40N33'17 79W07'50 5:16:31
Tidedale 32 71 40N33 79W10 5:16:40
Tidioute 62 6 41N41 79W24 5:17:36
Tiffany 58 60 41N50'13 75W49'16 5:03:17
Tilden 6 80 40N33 76W01 5:04:04
Tilden 67 67 39N57'24 76W39'30 5:06:38
Tillotson 20 58 41N50'02 79W49'05 5:19:16
Timberly Heights 10 3 40N54'44 79W55'33 5:19:42
Timberwyck 23 90 39N55 75W22 5:01:28
Timblin 33 6 40N57'59 79W11'54 5:16:48
Timbuck 42 6 41N48'11 78W41'53 5:14:48
Time 30 6 39N57 80W19 5:21:16
Tingley 58 50 41N54'11 75W44'06 5:02:56
Tinicum 9 1 40N26'54 75W06'29 5:00:26
Tioga 59 59 41N54'31 77W08'00 5:08:32
Tioga Junction 59 59 41N57'28 77W06'27 5:08:26
Tiona 62 3 41N44'49 79W04'03 5:16:16
Tionesta 27 35 41N29'43 79W27'22 5:17:49
Tippecanoe 26 6 40N00'46 79W47'41 5:19:11
Tippery 61 1 41N22'39 79W38'15 5:18:33
Tipton 7 50 40N38'09 78W17'46 5:13:11
Tire Hill 56 74 40N16'07 78W54'58 5:15:40
Tirzah 58 6 41N45'00 75W33'40 5:02:15
Titlows Corner 15 8 40N13'40 75W39'18 5:02:37
Titusville 20 74 41N37'37 79W40'26 5:18:42
Tivoli 41 81 41N17'53 76W41'30 5:06:46
Toboyne 50 6 40N17 77W36 5:10:24
Toby 16 7 41N04'54 79W32'52 5:18:11
Toby 24 36 41N19'39 78W37'56 5:14:32
Tobyhanna 45 84 41N10'38 75W25'02 5:01:40
Tobyhanna Army Depot 45 84 41N11 75W25 5:01:40
Todd 31 6 40N15'36 78W04'36 5:12:18
Todmorron 23 90 39N54 75W22 5:01:28
Toftrees 14 9 40N48 77W52 5:11:28
Toland 21 1 40N04'11 77W12'44 5:08:51
Tolna 67 27 39N45'43 76W39'07 5:06:36
Tomb 41 6 41N14 77W15 5:09:00
Tombs Run 41 6 41N15'09 77W19'33 5:09:18
Tomhicken (Sugarloaf P O) 40 6 40N58'10 76W05'45 5:04:23
Tompkins 59 59 41N58'36 77W11'28 5:08:46

Tompkinsville 35
1 41N35'23 75w36'52 5:02:27
Tomstown 28 100 39N47'34 77w33'43 5:10:15
Tooley Corners 35
4 41N20'23 75w34'50 5:02:19
Toonerville 61 74 41N34'11 79w41'28 5:18:46
Top 3 15 40N42'36 79w26'45 5:17:47
Topton 6 9 40N30'12 75w42'06 5:02:48
Torbert 41 7 41N13'14 77w19'04 5:09:16
Torpedo 62 3 41N46'45 79w27'57 5:17:52
Torrance 65 98 40N25'02 79w13'23 5:16:54
Torresdale 51 9 40N03'17 75w00'17 5:00:01
Torrey 64 59 41N37'58 75w11'33 5:00:46
Toughkenamon 15 8 39N49'53 75w45'28 5:03:02
Towamencin 46 8 40N15 75w19 5:01:16
Towamensing 13 80 40N52 75w35 5:02:20
Towanda 8 41 41N46'03 76w26'35 5:05:46
Tower City 54 27 40N35'21 76w33'10 5:06:13
Tower Hill Number One 26
51 39N57'02 79w52'38 5:19:31
Tower Hill Number Two 26
51 39N58'02 79w53'47 5:19:35
Towerville 15 9 39N57'20 75w50'57 5:03:24
Towner 8 41 41N53'02 76w22'51 5:05:31
Town Hill 40 1 41N10'45 76w15'20 5:05:01
Town Line 40 1 41N09 76w10 5:04:40
Townville 20 6 41N40'40 79w52'48 5:19:31
Trachsville 13 9 40N52'51 75w31'47 5:02:07
Tracy 25 7 41N52'32 80w28'18 5:21:53
Trade City 32 6 40N52'43 79w04'29 5:16:18
Tradesville 9 2 40N16'15 75w09'48 5:00:39
Trafford 65 114 40N23'08 79w45'33 5:19:02
Trailwood 40 20 41N15 75w53 5:03:32
Trainer 23 90 39N49'39 75w24'53 5:01:40
Transfer 43 6 41N19'44 80w25'59 5:21:44
Trappe 46 8 40N11'56 75w28'36 5:01:54
Trauger 65 3 40N13'58 79w27'46 5:17:51
Traymore 9 1 40N13'49 75w03'58 5:00:16
Tredyffrin 15 90 40N04 75w26 5:01:44
Treehaven 2 114 40N20 80w02 5:20:08
Trees Mills 65 6 40N25'51 79w32'45 5:18:11
Treichlers 48 8 40N44'03 75w32'39 5:02:11
Tremont 54 9 40N37'42 76w23'15 5:05:33
Trent 56 6 39N59'05 79w14'38 5:16:59
Trenton 54 3 40N50'17 76w05'27 5:04:22
Tresckow 13 42 40N54'48 75w58'01 5:03:52
Tresslarville 64
6 41N27'17 75w23'58 5:01:36
Treveskyn (Cuddy P O) 2
114 40N20'55 80w09'18 5:20:37
Trevorton 49 56 40N46'52 76w40'24 5:06:42
Trevose 9 1 40N08'21 74w58'53 4:59:56
Trevose Heights 9
1 40N09'04 74w59'15 4:59:57
Trewigtown 46 8 40N16'38 75w15'38 5:01:03
Trexler 6 56 40N38'08 75w51'13 5:03:25
Trexlertown 39 13 40N32'53 75w36'22 5:02:25
Tri Mills 19 6 41N15'42 76w20'45 5:05:23
Trimmer Manor 67
67 39N58 76w44 5:06:56
Trindle Springs 21
12 40N12'23 77w01'25 5:08:06
Tripoli 11 54 40N32'41 78w46'38 5:15:07
Triumph 30 6 39N46'39 80w20'39 5:21:23
Triumph 62 7 41N45 79w24 5:17:36
Trooper 46 90 40N08'59 75w24'08 5:01:37
Trotter 26 104 40N00'31 79w37'19 5:18:29
Trotwood 2 114 40N20 80w05 5:20:20
Trout Corners 43
117 41N14'00 80w28'16 5:21:53
Troutman 10 6 40N59'17 79w47'39 5:19:11
Trout Run 41 7 41N23'10 77w03'26 5:08:14
Trouts Crossing 65
111 40N09 79w33 5:18:12
Troutville 17 56 41N01'32 78w47'08 5:15:09
Trowbridge 59 6 41N57'30 76w58'47 5:07:55
Troxelville 55 6 40N48'11 77w12'20 5:08:49
Troy 8 52 41N47'09 76w47'18 5:07:09
Troy 17 113 40N54'54 78w13'00 5:12:52
Troy Center 20 7 41N38'33 79w49'34 5:19:18
Troy Hill 2 114 40N28'08 79w58'44 5:19:55
Troy Hill 3 15 40N49 79w32 5:18:08
Truce 36 27 39N53'24 76w14'17 5:04:57
Trucksville 40 20 41N18'14 75w55'57 5:03:44
Trucksville Gardens 40
20 41N18'44 75w55'14 5:03:41
Truemans 27 3 41N37'07 79w08'02 5:16:32
Truesdale Terrace 40
20 41N10'40 75w57'31 5:03:50
Truittsburg 16 6 41N03'44 79w17'03 5:17:08
Truman 12 106 41N28'37 78w22'08 5:13:29
Trumbauersville 9
13 40N24'38 75w22'43 5:01:31
Trunkeyville 27 6 41N36'47 79w24'08 5:17:37
Truxall 65 4 40N32'55 79w32'27 5:18:10
Tryonville 20 7 41N42'06 79w47'06 5:19:08
Trythall 15 56 40N10'48 75w45'09 5:03:01
Tuckerton 6 101 40N24'17 75w56'14 5:03:45
Tullytown 9 9 40N08'21 74w48'54 4:59:16
Tulpehocken 6 25 40N26 76w16 5:05:04
Tuna 42 102 41N59'46 78w37'03 5:14:28
Tunkhannock 66 59 41N32'19 75w56'49 5:03:47
Tunnelhill 11 55 40N28'41 78w32'28 5:14:10
Tunnelton 32 116 40N27'37 79w23'20 5:17:33
Turbett 34 7 40N31 77w22 5:09:28
Turbotville 49 6 41N06'07 76w46'17 5:07:05
Turkey City 16 1 41N11'07 79w36'49 5:18:27
Turkeyfoot 28 42 39N53'20 77w43'23 5:10:54
Turkeyfoot 63 51 40N03'07 80w01'30 5:20:06
Turkey Run 54 27 40N48'29 76w12'13 5:04:49
Turkeytown 65 61 40N11'42 79w43'49 5:18:55
Turner 20 63 41N30'28 80w28'55 5:21:56
Turner 43 66 41N14'26 80w11'12 5:20:45
Turnersville 20
63 41N30'36 80w28'37 5:21:54
Turnersville 35 4 41N18'51 75w28'33 5:01:54
Turnip Hole 16 1 41N09'09 79w35'22 5:18:21
Turnpike 67 27 39N46 76w41 5:06:44
Turn Villa 45 23 41N04'09 75w02'37 5:00:10
Turtle Creek 2
114 40N24'21 79w49'31 5:19:18
Turtlepoint 42 7 41N52'18 78w20'24 5:13:22
Turtleville 60 70 40N55'30 76w51'52 5:07:27

Tuscarora 34 7 40N31'16 77w19'53 5:09:20
Tuscarora 54 27 40N46'12 76w02'16 5:04:09
Tuscarora Summit 28
51 39N54'57 77w57'25 5:11:50
Tusculum 21 82 40N02'17 77w30'57 5:10:04
Tusseyville 14 64 40N47'50 77w40'44 5:10:43
Tweedale 15 3 39N47'41 76w01'45 5:04:07
Twenty Row 11 54 40N32'17 78w47'36 5:15:10
Twickinham Village 46
9 40N07 75w10 5:00:40
Twilight 63 1 40N06'46 79w53'20 5:19:33
Twin Bridge Farm 15
13 39N57 75w36 5:02:24
Twin Bridges 63 1 40N07'54 79w55'35 5:19:42
Twin Brooks 67 67 39N58 76w44 5:06:56
Twin Grove Park 38
1 40N30'43 76w30'53 5:06:04
Twin Hollows 14 6 41N10'22 77w58'04 5:11:52
Twin Lakes 52 6 41N23'22 74w53'51 4:59:35
Twin Oaks 9 9 40N09 74w51 4:59:24
Twin Oaks 23 90 39N50'20 75w25'21 5:01:41
Twin Oaks 61 1 41N20'13 79w41'02 5:18:44
Twin Oaks Farms 23
90 39N52 75w23 5:01:32
Twin Rocks 11 63 40N29'48 78w51'58 5:15:28
Two Lick 32 71 40N34'03 79w09'51 5:16:39
Twomile 42 6 41N49'57 78w17'46 5:13:11
Two Taverns 1 1 39N46'42 77w09'57 5:08:40
Tyler 17 7 41N14'25 78w31'27 5:14:06
Tyler 58 60 41N43'07 75w54'44 5:03:39
Tylerdale 63 3 40N10'51 80w15'04 5:21:00
Tyler Hill 64 6 41N41'42 75w06'30 5:00:26
Tylersburg 16 6 41N23'05 79w19'21 5:17:17
Tylersport 46 1 40N20'58 75w22'53 5:01:32
Tylersville 18 7 40N59'26 77w25'31 5:09:42
Tyre 2 51 40N26 80w17 5:21:08
Tyrone 7 11 40N40'14 78w14'20 5:12:57
Tyrone Forge 7 11 40N39'38 78w13'05 5:12:52
Tyrrell 8 6 41N55'31 76w17'03 5:05:08
Uhdey 8 41 41N43'27 76w24'14 5:05:37
Uhlers Crossing 48
8 40N45'02 75w13'59 5:00:56
Uhlerstown 54 1 40N31'31 75w04'25 5:00:18
Uledi 26 80 39N53'46 79w47'26 5:19:10
Ulster 8 60 41N50'45 76w30'08 5:06:01
Ulysses 53 6 41N54'14 77w45'44 5:11:03
Unamis 56 53 39N44'34 79w17'08 5:17:09
Undercliff 2 114 40N30'43 79w56'49 5:19:47
Unicorn 36 27 39N50'12 76w09'08 5:04:37
Union 36 3 39N50'27 76w03'39 5:04:15
Union Center 59
103 41N37'08 76w56'50 5:07:47
Union City 25 58 41N53'58 79w50'44 5:19:23
Union Corner 49 1 40N54'00 76w34'40 5:06:19
Union Dale 58 59 41N43'00 75w29'33 5:01:58
Union Deposit 22
31 40N17'25 76w40'56 5:06:44
Union Furnace 31
11 40N36'46 78w09'48 5:12:39
Union Grove 36 27 40N09'02 76w01'26 5:04:06
Union Hill 13 8 40N49'41 75w41'38 5:02:47
Union Hill 58 6 41N47'02 75w37'25 5:02:30
Union Mills 44 6 40N36'21 77w41'59 5:10:48
Union, Mount 28 1 39N54'19 77w30'12 5:10:01
Union Square 36 8 40N10'57 76w27'51 5:05:51
Uniontown 26 80 39N54 79w44 5:18:56
Uniontown 32 63 40N42'17 78w49'51 5:15:19
Uniontown 49 27 40N48'15 76w34'23 5:06:18
Uniontown 61 109 41N23'12 79w50'56 5:19:24
Uniontown 67 1 40N07 77w02 5:08:08
Uniontown North 26
80 39N54 79w44 5:18:56
Union Trust 2 114 40N27 79w59 5:19:56
Union Valley 37
112 40N56'12 80w20'32 5:21:22
Unionville 4 19 40N44'43 80w12'28 5:20:50
Unionville 6 8 40N14'43 75w42'43 5:02:51
Unionville 10 3 40N56'29 79w57'44 5:19:51
Unionville 13 1 40N57'50 75w41'18 5:02:45
Unionville 14 70 40N54'26 77w52'33 5:11:30
Unionville 15 8 39N53'43 75w44'05 5:02:56
Unionville 46 8 40N17'54 75w17'00 5:01:08
Union Water Works 38
8 40N21'57 76w31'28 5:06:06
United 65 111 40N13'06 79w29'17 5:17:57
Unity 2 3 40N29'32 79w46'47 5:19:07
Unity House 52 6 41N08 75w02 5:00:08
Unity Junction 2
14 40N29'53 79w47'10 5:19:09
Unityville 41 6 41N13'59 76w30'58 5:06:04
Universal 2 114 40N28'23 79w47'49 5:19:11
University Heights 48
13 40N35'46 75w23'24 5:01:34
University Park 14
9 40N48'07 77w51'24 5:11:26
Uno 67 1 40N06'12 76w59'01 5:07:56
Upland 15 8 39N53'11 75w46'29 5:03:06
Upland 23 90 39N51'09 75w22'59 5:01:32
Upland Park 23 9 40N00 75w18 5:01:12
Upland Terrace 46
9 40N01 75w15 5:01:00
Upper Allen 21 12 40N11 76w59 5:07:56
Upper Augusta 49
82 40N53 76w45 5:07:00
Upper Bern 6 1 40N31 76w06 5:04:24
Upper Black Eddy 54
9 40N33'55 75w06'00 5:00:24
Upper Brownville 54
27 40N49'09 76w13'10 5:04:53
Upper Burrell 65
6 40N33 79w40 5:18:40
Upper Chichester 23
90 39N50 75w26 5:01:44
Upper Darby 23 9 39N55'42 75w16'27 5:01:06
Upper Dublin 46 1 40N09 75w11 5:00:44
Upper Dutchtown 11
55 40N25'12 78w38'20 5:14:33
Upper Emilie 9 9 40N09'38 74w50'57 4:59:24
Upper Exeter 40 1 41N24'25 75w50'17 5:03:21
Upper Fairfield 41
6 41N18 76w52 5:07:28
Upper Frankford 21
1 40N14 77w22 5:09:28

Upper Frederick 46
8 40N19 75w31 5:02:04
Upper Glasgow 46
8 40N16'09 75w39'52 5:02:39
Upper Gwynedd 46
8 40N13 75w17 5:01:08
Upper Hanover 46
2 40N25 75w31 5:02:04
Upper Hillville 16
6 41N02'14 79w36'41 5:18:27
Upper Lawn 38 31 40N34'27 76w21'15 5:05:25
Upper Leacock 36
8 40N05 76w12 5:04:48
Upper Lehigh 40
20 41N01'56 75w54'26 5:03:38
Upper Macungie 39
13 40N34 75w37 5:02:28
Upper Mahanoy 49
1 40N43 76w38 5:06:32
Upper Mahantango 54
1 40N40 76w37 5:06:28
Upper Makefield 9
8 40N18 74w54 4:59:36
Upper Merion 46
90 40N05 75w22 5:01:28
Upper Middletown 26
6 39N57'58 79w45'17 5:19:01
Upper Mifflin 21
1 40N12 77w30 5:10:00
Upper Milford 39
13 40N30 75w31 5:02:04
Upper Mill 21 2 40N06'11 77w10'46 5:08:43
Upper Moreland 46
2 40N10 75w06 5:00:24
Upper Mount Bethel 46
8 40N54 75w08 5:00:32
Upper Nazareth 48
8 40N44 75w21 5:01:24
Upper Octoraro 15
32 39N58'25 75w55'17 5:03:41
Upper Orchard 9 9 40N09 74w51 4:59:24
Upper Oxford 15 3 39N51 75w57 5:03:48
Upper Paxton 22 1 40N34 76w55 5:07:40
Upper Peanut 26 6 39N58'44 79w46'45 5:19:07
Upper Pittston 40
1 41N20'17 75w47'12 5:03:09
Upper Pottsgrove 46
8 40N17 75w38 5:02:32
Upper Reese 7 33 40N26'20 78w19'12 5:13:17
Upper Sagon 49 6 40N53 76w41 5:06:44
Upper Saint Clair 2
114 40N20 80w05 5:20:20
Upper Salford 46
8 40N18 75w27 5:01:48
Upper Saucon 39
13 40N32 75w25 5:01:40
Upper Southampton 9
1 40N11 75w02 5:00:08
Upper Strasburg 28
1 40N03'37 77w42'33 5:10:50
Upper Tulpehocken 6
1 40N30 76w10 5:04:40
Upper Turkeyfoot 56
6 39N54 79w17 5:17:08
Upper Two Lick 32
71 40N35'26 79w08'20 5:16:33
Upper Tyrone 26
111 40N05 79w35 5:18:20
Upper Uwchlan 15
80 40N05 75w43 5:02:52
Upper Whyel 65 3 40N13'53 79w40'53 5:18:44
Upper Yoder 11 74 40N18 78w57 5:15:48
Upsonville 58 60 41N54'53 75w48'12 5:03:13
Upton 28 1 39N48'19 77w48'25 5:11:14
Uptown 2 114 40N27 79w59 5:19:56
Urban 49 51 40N40'52 76w46'19 5:07:05
Urey 32 6 40N50'37 78w49'34 5:15:18
Uriah 21 1 40N02'32 77w10'36 5:08:42
Ursina 56 53 39N49'03 79w19'41 5:17:19
U S Naval Base 51
9 39N53 75w10 5:00:40
Uswick 64 6 41N27'02 75w14'52 5:00:59
Utahville 17 54 40N44'36 78w28'13 5:13:53
Utica 61 59 41N26'08 79w57'27 5:19:50
Uwchland 15 80 40N05 75w41 5:02:44
Vail 7 11 40N40 78w13 5:12:52
Valcourt 43 6 41N06'58 80w07'06 5:20:28
Valemont Heights 2
10 40N30'14 79w48'53 5:19:16
Valencia 10 6 40N40'29 79w59'23 5:19:58
Valier 33 51 40N54'57 79w02'42 5:16:11
Vallamont Hills 41
82 41N15'21 77w01'25 5:08:06
Valley Camp 65 14 40N35'07 79w46'00 5:19:04
Valley Corners 25
58 41N59'14 79w53'38 5:19:35
Valley Falls 46 1 40N06'42 75w03'18 5:00:13
Valley Forge 15 8 40N05'49 75w28'12 5:01:53
Valley Forge 67
67 39N59'04 76w42'28 5:06:50
Valley Forge Estates 15
90 40N02 75w22 5:01:28
Valley Forge Homes 46
90 40N05 75w22 5:01:28
Valley Forge Manor 46
8 40N08 75w31 5:02:04
Valley Furnace 54
27 40N43 76w07 5:04:28
Valley Glenn 38 1 40N20'42 76w36'58 5:06:28
Valley Green 23 9 39N57 75w18 5:01:12
Valley Junction 67
95 39N48'41 76w52'23 5:07:30
Valley View 11 74 40N20 78w56 5:15:44
Valley View 14 70 40N53'55 77w49'52 5:11:19
Valley View 23 9 39N58'52 75w23'04 5:01:32
Valley View 36 8 40N08'51 76w23'03 5:05:32
Valley View 54 27 40N38'45 76w32'22 5:06:09
Valley View Acres 23
90 40N00 75w23 5:01:32
Valley View Farms 23
9 39N56 75w20 5:01:20
Valley View Heights 3
15 40N46 79w32 5:18:08

Van 61 1 41N19'04 79W39'18 5:18:37
Van Buren 3 6 40N59'00 79W34'27 5:18:18
Van Buren 63 3 40N04'38 80W17'27 5:21:10
Vance 63 3 40N09'55 80W11'39 5:20:47
Vances Mill 26 80 39N57'08 79W43'49 5:18:55
Vanceville 63 2 40N08'26 80W04'46 5:20:19
Vanderbilt 26 104 40N01'59 79W39'42 5:18:39
Vandergrift 65 4 40N36'10 79W33'54 5:18:16
Vandergrift Heights 65 4 40N37 79W34 5:18:16
Vandling 35 59 41N37'59 75W28'15 5:01:53
Vandyke 34 7 40N31'55 77W17'37 5:09:10
Van Emman 63 2 40N16'40 80W08'39 5:20:35
Vankirk 63 3 40N07'15 80W14'35 5:20:58
Van Meter 65 6 40N08'20 79W44'45 5:18:59
Van Ormer 11 54 40N40'24 78W29'34 5:13:58
Vanport 4 19 40N41'04 80W19'45 5:21:19
Van Reeds Mill 6 101 40N21'56 75W59'40 5:03:59
Van Voorhis 63 51 40N09'22 79W58'28 5:19:54
Van Voorhis Hill 63 51 40N04'26 80W02'34 5:20:10
Van Wert 34 7 40N34'59 77W17'51 5:09:11
Varden 64 6 41N29'01 75W23'46 5:01:35
Vaux Town 9 8 40N21 75W13 5:00:52
Vawter 8 6 41N55'34 76W24'24 5:05:38
Venango 20 3 41N46'21 80W06'48 5:20:27
Venango 61 109 41N22'27 79W48'03 5:19:12
Venetia 63 114 40N14'48 80W02'33 5:20:10
Venice 63 2 40N19'16 80W13'08 5:20:53
Venturetown 62 120 41N51'48 79W09'18 5:16:37
Venus 61 6 41N22'00 79W28'42 5:17:55
Vera Cruz 36 1 40N15'20 76W05'19 5:04:21
Vera Cruz 39 13 40N30'20 75W29'49 5:01:59
Verdilla 55 82 40N44'36 76W54'03 5:07:36
Vermilion Hill 9 97 40N10'50 74W49'44 4:59:19
Vernfield 46 8 40N17'50 75W24'33 5:01:38
Vernon 20 77 41N38 80W13 5:20:52
Vernon 66 59 41N26'48 75W57'27 5:03:50
Vernondale 25 107 42N04'06 80W12'06 5:20:48
Vernon Park 51 9 40N02 75W10 5:00:40
Verona 2 14 40N30'23 79W50'36 5:19:22
Versailles 2 9 40N18'56 79W49'53 5:19:20
Vestaburg 63 51 40N00'58 79W59'24 5:19:58
Vesta Heights 63 6 40N00'48 79W59'45 5:19:59
Vesta No 6 63 51 40N02 79W58 5:19:52
Vesta Number Six 63 51 40N00'09 79W56'16 5:19:45
Vetera 11 54 40N34'21 78W46'53 5:15:08
Veterans Hospital 2 114 40N27 79W58 5:19:52
Veterans Hospital 40 20 41N15 75W53 5:03:32
Viall Hill 8 60 41N41'09 76W19'01 5:05:16
Vicksburg 7 33 40N22'03 78W24'53 5:13:40
Vicksburg 60 70 40N56'19 76W59'18 5:07:57
Victor 17 113 40N52'49 78W15'29 5:13:02
Victoria 26 4 39N51'07 79W27'29 5:17:50
Victoria Furnace 22 12 40N24'59 76W52'34 5:07:30
Victory 61 7 41N19 79W54 5:19:36
Victory Heights 61 109 41N21'47 79W45'44 5:19:03
Victory Hills 63 1 40N11'29 79W53'34 5:19:34
Vienna 63 6 40N06 80W31 5:22:04
Viennese Woods 2 114 40N30 79W59 5:19:56
Village 2 114 40N20 80W05 5:20:20
Village Green 23 90 39N52'10 75W25'40 5:01:43
Villa Green 67 67 39N57'13 76W41'59 5:06:48
Villa Maria 37 6 41N04'25 80W30'27 5:22:02
Villa Maria Infirmary 6 1 40N18'25 76W05'46 5:04:23
Villanova 23 90 40N02'14 75W20'58 5:01:24
Vincent 15 118 40N11 75W33 5:02:12
Vinco 11 74 40N24'18 78W51'21 5:15:25
Vinemont 6 1 40N16'55 76W04'53 5:04:20
Vineyard 44 7 40N25'29 77W47'02 5:11:08
Vintage 36 9 40N00'03 76W04'48 5:04:19
Vintondale 11 63 40N28'53 78W55'08 5:15:41
Violet Hill 67 1 39N56'30 76W42'41 5:06:51
Violet Wood 9 9 40N08'17 74W51'00 4:59:24
Vira 44 73 40N39'05 77W32'00 5:10:08
Virginia Mills 1 1 39N48'10 77W22'35 5:09:30
Virginville 6 8 40N31'26 75W52'24 5:03:30
Vista 65 8 40N16'42 79W47'44 5:19:11
Vogansville 36 28 40N07'26 76W07'49 5:04:31
Vogleyville 10 3 40N50'57 79W51'41 5:19:27
Volant 37 6 41N06'49 80W15'33 5:21:02
Vosburg 66 59 41N33'40 76W00'17 5:04:01
Vowinckel 16 6 41N24'41 79W13'44 5:16:55
Vroman Hill 8 7 41N44'29 76W39'43 5:06:39
Vrooman 20 74 41N43'33 79W38'59 5:18:36
Vulcan 54 27 40N48'38 76W06'33 5:04:26
Wabank 36 8 39N59'54 76W19'49 5:05:19
Wabash 2 114 40N26 80W03 5:20:12
Waddle 14 63 40N50'02 77W56'06 5:11:44
Wadesville 54 49 40N42'59 76W12'45 5:04:51
Wadsworth 10 3 40N51'47 79W48'58 5:19:16
Wadsworth 51 9 40N04 75W10 5:00:40
Wagner 44 1 40N40'53 77W23'19 5:09:33
Wagners 45 1 41N07'10 75W31'34 5:02:06
Wagnersville 48 13 40N39'04 75W18'39 5:01:15
Wago Junction 67 7 40N05'14 76W41'43 5:06:47
Wagontown 15 9 40N00'38 75W50'35 5:03:22
Wahlville 10 6 40N48'19 80W03'17 5:20:13
Wahneta 50 1 40N27'15 77W11'21 5:08:45
Wahnetah 13 80 40N52 75W44 5:02:56
Wakefield (Peach Botton P O) 36 1 39N46'25 76W10'46 5:04:43
Wakena 65 116 40N29'23 79W28'53 5:17:56
Walbert 39 13 40N36'40 75W34'07 5:02:16
Walcksville 13 8 40N52'09 75W39'22 5:02:37
Waldheim Park 39 13 40N34'14 75W27'13 5:01:49
Walkchalk 3 15 40N50'07 79W34'37 5:18:18
Walker Lake 52 6 41N25'08 74W55'08 4:59:41
Walkers Mill 2 114 40N23'45 80W07'50 5:20:31
Walkertown 42 6 41N57'32 78W30'14 5:14:01
Walkertown 63 51 40N03'16 79W56'44 5:19:47
Walkton 13 80 40N49'07 75W32'54 5:02:12
Wall 2 114 40N23'37 79W47'11 5:19:09
Wallace 15 80 40N05'18 75W44'41 5:02:59
Wallace City 4 13 40N40'37 80W11'24 5:20:46
Wallace Corners 61 6 41N21'09 79W59'17 5:19:57
Wallace Junction 25 68 42N00'48 80W19'11 5:21:17
Wallaceton 17 7 40N57'35 78W17'21 5:13:09
Wallaceville 61 74 41N33'45 79W48'10 5:19:13
Waller 19 6 41N13'57 76W25'25 5:05:42
Walley Mill 10 6 41N02'37 79W46'38 5:19:07
Wallingford 23 90 39N53'27 75W21'48 5:01:27
Wallingford Hills 23 90 39N54 75W22 5:01:28
Wallis Run 41 7 41N25'04 76W51'34 5:07:26
Wall Rose 4 13 40N38'03 80W09'39 5:20:39
Walls Corners 35 44 41N32'20 75W47'20 5:03:09
Wallsville 35 44 41N34'32 75W42'43 5:02:51
Walltown 17 7 40N57'53 78W38'35 5:14:34
Walmo 37 112 41N02'11 80W21'22 5:21:25
Walnut 4 8 40N49 80W25 5:21:40
Walnut 34 7 40N31'29 77W29'23 5:09:58
Walnut Bend 61 9 41N25 79W42 5:18:48
Walnut Bottom 21 1 40N05'22 77W24'15 5:09:37
Walnut Gardens 39 13 40N39 75W30 5:02:00
Walnut Grove 11 74 40N18'37 78W53'47 5:15:35
Walnut Grove 50 1 40N27'26 77W15'36 5:09:02
Walnut Hill 26 80 40N05'37 79W34'08 5:18:17
Walnut Hill 30 7 39N44'26 79W54'34 5:19:38
Walnut Hill 46 9 40N05'49 75W04'42 5:00:19
Walnutport 48 8 40N45'15 75W35'57 5:02:24
Walnuttown 6 8 40N26'58 75W50'35 5:03:22
Walsall 11 74 40N15'56 78W53'34 5:15:34
Walsh 17 56 41N09'54 78W38'01 5:14:32
Walston 33 51 40N57'54 78W59'42 5:15:59
Walston Junction 33 51 40N56 78W58 5:15:52
Walter Chapel 2 14 40N35'22 79W49'36 5:19:18
Walters 48 12 40N42'12 75W15'09 5:01:01
Waltersburg 26 80 39N58'49 79W45'51 5:19:03
Walther 2 114 40N19'43 80W03'17 5:20:13
Walton 17 6 41N04'18 78W17'59 5:13:12
Walton 53 6 41N47'23 77W45'52 5:11:03
Waltonville 22 12 40N14'25 76W40'58 5:06:44
Waltrous 59 6 41N44'37 77W34'35 5:10:18
Waltz 65 111 40N10 79W37 5:18:28
Waltz Mill 65 4 40N12'31 79W40'04 5:18:40
Waltzvale 17 6 40N47'23 78W29'19 5:13:37
Wampum 37 121 40N53'17 80W20'18 5:21:21
Wanamakers 39 56 40N39'39 75W50'46 5:03:23
Wanamie 40 21 41N10'24 76W02'09 5:04:09
Wandin Junction 32 6 40N40'36 78W57'42 5:15:51
Wanneta 25 7 41N54 80W22 5:21:28
Wapwallopen 40 1 41N04'28 76W07'52 5:04:31
Ward 23 4 39N52'49 75W30'43 5:02:03
Ward 59 7 41N41 76W56 5:07:44
Wardville 50 1 40N35'00 77W08'38 5:08:35
Warfordsburg 29 6 39N45'06 78W11'16 5:12:45
Warminster 9 1 40N12'24 75W06'00 5:00:24
Warminster Heights 9 1 40N11'13 75W04'55 5:00:20
Warminster Village 9 1 40N12'05 75W06'13 5:00:25
Warner 63 1 40N08'19 79W56'08 5:19:45
Warnertown 45 84 40N09'44 75W27'22 5:01:49
Warren 62 120 41N50'38 79W08'43 5:16:35
Warren Center 8 6 41N56'16 76W10'52 5:04:43
Warrendale 2 6 40N39'12 80W04'47 5:20:19
Warrenham 8 6 41N58'18 76W09'11 5:04:37
Warrens Mill 56 79 39N46'46 78W57'26 5:15:50
Warrensville 41 82 41N19'35 76W56'45 5:07:47
Warrington 9 8 40N14'57 75W08'04 5:00:32
Warrior Ridge 31 81 40N32'33 78W01'56 5:12:08
Warrior Run 40 20 41N11'29 75W57'03 5:03:48
Warrior Run 49 6 41N05'50 76W48'21 5:07:13
Warriors Mark 31 6 40N42'12 78W07'48 5:12:31
Warsaw 33 6 41N12'54 78W57'13 5:15:49
Warsaw 35 18 41N26'23 75W36'59 5:02:28
Warwick 15 1 40N09'54 75W47'03 5:03:08
Washington 21 1 40N12'08 77W28'42 5:09:55
Washington 63 3 40N10'26 80W14'47 5:20:59
Washington Boro 36 26 39N59'33 76W28'03 5:05:52
Washington Crossing 9 1 40N17'36 74W52'15 4:59:29
Washington Heights 21 12 40N14'49 76W53'47 5:07:35
Washington Hill 46 8 40N15'09 75W37'50 5:02:31
Washington Junction 2 114 40N21'10 80W01'40 5:20:07
Washington, Mount 26 6 39N48'52 79W34'49 5:18:19
Washington Square 46 90 40N08'55 75W18'28 5:01:14
Washingtonville 47 6 41N03'06 76W40'30 5:06:42
Wassergass 48 13 40N35'09 75W17'30 5:01:10
Waterfall 29 6 40N07'39 78W03'47 5:12:15
Waterford 25 35 41N56'34 79W59'05 5:19:56
Waterford 65 110 40N15'16 79W10'04 5:16:40
Waterloo 34 6 40N17'18 77W41'41 5:10:47
Waterloo Mills 15 90 40N01'23 75W25'16 5:01:41
Waterman 32 71 40N31'51 79W07'37 5:16:30
Waterside 5 51 40N14 78W22 5:13:28
Waterson 16 37 41N10'38 79W17'24 5:17:10
Water Street 31 81 40N34'17 78W08'18 5:12:33
Waterton 40 1 41N09 76W10 5:04:40
Waterville 41 6 41N18'35 77W21'42 5:09:27
Watkins 11 63 40N37'34 78W45'41 5:15:03
Watrous 59 6 41N45 77W34 5:10:16
Watson Crossing 62 3 41N47 79W06 5:16:24
Watson Farm 27 6 41N28 79W07 5:16:28
Watson Run 20 6 41N35'23 80W13'02 5:20:52
Watsontown 49 73 41N05'04 76W51'51 5:07:27
Watters 10 6 40N45'29 80W01'56 5:20:08
Wattersonville 3 6 40N58'52 79W33'15 5:18:13
Watts 50 3 40N28 76W59 5:07:56
Wattsburg 25 7 42N00'13 79W48'40 5:19:15
Waverly 35 45 41N31'35 75W42'21 5:02:49
Waverly Heights 23 9 39N57 75W18 5:01:12
Waverly Manor 23 9 39N57 75W18 5:01:12
Wawa 23 4 39N54'06 75W27'36 5:01:50
Wawaset 15 13 39N57 75W36 5:02:24
Wayland 20 77 41N37'43 80W04'10 5:20:17
Waymart 64 1 41N34'49 75W24'31 5:01:38
Wayne 23 90 40N02'38 75W23'17 5:01:33
Waynecastle 28 1 39N46'22 77W39'01 5:10:36
Wayne Heights 28 100 39N44'37 77W33'15 5:10:13
Wayne Junction 51 9 40N01'21 75W09'35 5:00:38
Waynesboro 28 100 39N45'21 77W34'41 5:10:19
Waynesburg 30 1 39N53'47 80W10'46 5:20:43
Waynesville 22 24 40N27'08 76W52'46 5:07:31
Weather 13 60 40N56'30 75W49'43 5:03:19
Weatherly 13 60 40N57 75W50 5:03:20
Weaverland 36 27 40N08'12 76W03'31 5:04:14
Weaver Mill 65 110 40N12 79W15 5:17:00
Weavers Old Stand 65 111 40N13'15 79W33'06 5:18:12
Weaversville 48 13 40N41'19 75W27'15 5:01:49
Weavertown 6 8 40N18'21 75W45'09 5:03:01
Weavertown 36 96 40N02'19 76W09'29 5:04:38
Weavertown 38 8 40N21'23 76W23'35 5:05:34
Weavertown 63 2 40N15'34 80W10'29 5:20:42
Weber City 12 106 41N30'14 78W15'39 5:13:03
Weber Hills 25 107 42N04'12 80W03'45 5:20:15
Webster 54 27 40N43'55 75W59'07 5:03:56
Webster 65 114 40N11'06 79W50'56 5:19:24
Websters Mill 29 66 39N51'36 78W02'07 5:12:08
Wech Corners 40 20 41N08'46 75W54'22 5:03:37
Weeds Corners 25 107 42N01'48 79W56'00 5:19:44
Weedville 24 7 41N16'36 78W29'31 5:13:58
Wegley 65 25 40N20 79W43 5:18:52
Wehnwood 7 33 40N32'13 78W24'10 5:13:37
Wehrum 32 6 40N28'15 78W57'00 5:15:48
Weidasville 39 8 40N38'18 75W38'45 5:02:35
Weiders Crossing 48 8 40N47'03 75W36'20 5:02:25
Weidmanville 36 30 40N12'18 76W12'55 5:04:52
Weigelstown 67 1 39N59'01 76W49'22 5:07:17
Weigh Scale 49 27 40N48 76W33 5:06:12
Weigletown 37 112 40N58'42 80W16'04 5:21:04
Weikert 60 7 40N51'30 77W17'44 5:09:11
Weilersville 39 13 40N31'41 75W36'38 5:02:27
Weimer 32 6 40N41'24 79W01'07 5:16:04
Weinel Crossroads 65 4 40N36'52 79W37'24 5:18:30
Weir Lake 45 9 40N54'49 75W25'11 5:01:41
Weisel 9 8 40N25'38 75W15'24 5:01:02
Weisenberg 39 9 40N36 75W42 5:02:48
Weishample 54 27 40N41'37 76W26'47 5:05:47
Weis Library 25 107 42N02'54 80W10'12 5:20:41
Weissport 13 8 40N49'44 75W41'57 5:02:48
Weldbank 62 3 41N45'37 79W04'48 5:16:19
Weldon 46 9 40N06'36 75W08'42 5:00:35
Wellersburg 56 6 39N43'58 78W51'02 5:15:24
Welliversville 19 4 41N05'52 76W28'34 5:05:54
Wells 32 6 40N49'42 79W08'42 5:16:35
Wellsboro 59 6 41N44'55 77W18'03 5:09:12
Wellsboro Junction 59 6 41N47'14 77W18'16 5:09:13
Wells Creek 56 6 40N02'16 78W59'42 5:15:59
Wells Hollow 8 60 41N51'35 76W14'43 5:04:59
Wells Tannery 29 6 40N05'28 78W10'00 5:12:40
Wellsville 67 1 40N03'05 76W56'13 5:07:45
Welsh Hill 58 59 41N43 75W29 5:01:56
Welsh Run 28 1 39N45'53 77W51'09 5:11:25
Welty 65 111 40N09 79W33 5:18:12
Weltys 28 100 39N45 77W34 5:10:16
Weltytown 65 3 40N12'30 79W26'46 5:17:47
Wendel 65 25 40N17'44 79W41'12 5:18:45
Wenksville 1 1 39N59'24 77W18'39 5:09:15
Wennersville 39 13 40N36'39 75W32'53 5:02:12
Wentlings Corners 16 6 41N11'32 79W32'45 5:18:11
Werkheiser 48 8 40N47'09 75W15'59 5:01:04
Werleys Corner 39 1 40N37'59 75W43'26 5:02:54
Wernersville 6 80 40N19'48 76W04'51 5:04:19
Wertz 7 3 40N27'20 78W14'51 5:12:59
Wertzville 21 12 40N17'01 77W02'39 5:08:11
Wescosville 39 13 40N34'00 75W33'12 5:02:13
Wesley 61 6 41N13'41 79W57'41 5:19:51
Wesley Chapel 11 74 40N23'19 78W51'45 5:15:27
Wesleyville 25 107 42N08'25 80W00'55 5:20:04
West 31 6 40N38 77W59 5:11:56

West Abington 35
44 41N32 75w46 5:03:04
West Acres 60 70 40N58 76w54 5:07:36
West Alexander 63
6 40N06'18 80w30'29 5:22:02
West Aliquippa 4
13 40N37 80w16 5:21:04
West Ambler 46 1 40N09 75w12 5:00:48
West Amity 63 6 40N02'22 80w13'20 5:20:53
West Annville 38
8 40N20 76w31 5:06:04
West Apollo 65 4 40N35 79w34 5:18:16
West Athens 8 1 41N56'55 76w31'21 5:06:05
West Auburn 58 6 41N43'13 76w06'24 5:04:26
Westaway 46 90 40N05 75w16 5:01:04
West Bangor 48 17 40N52'45 75w14'21 5:00:57
West Bangor 67 1 39N43'48 76w18'48 5:05:15
West Beaver 55 1 40N45 77w19 5:09:16
West Beech 14 7 41N03'32 77w34'42 5:10:19
West Bellevue 2
114 40N30 80w04 5:20:16
West Bend 26 6 39N58'23 79w58'24 5:19:54
West Berwick 19 1 41N04 76w15 5:05:00
West Bethany 65
111 40N09'45 79w35'58 5:18:24
West Bethlehem 63
6 40N02 80w05 5:20:20
West Bingham 53 6 41N56'40 77w49'00 5:11:16
West Bolivar 65 7 40N23'38 79w09'24 5:16:38
West Bowmans 13 8 40N47'48 75w40'27 5:02:42
West Bradford 15
46 39N58 75w43 5:02:52
West Branch 11 92 40N39'41 78w47'10 5:15:09
West Branch 53 6 41N41 77w42 5:10:48
West Brandywine 15
9 40N03 75w49 5:03:16
West Bridgewater 4
19 40N42 80w19 5:21:16
West Bristol 9 9 40N06'05 74w53'08 4:59:33
Westbrook Park 23
9 39N56'07 75w18'31 5:01:14
West Brownsville 63
1 40N01'27 79w53'27 5:19:34
West Brunswick 54
1 40N38 76w04 5:04:16
West Buffalo 60 6 40N57 77w03 5:08:12
West Burlington 8
7 41N45'49 76w40'30 5:06:42
West Caln 15 9 40N01 75w53 5:03:32
West Cameron 49 1 40N45'19 76w38'23 5:06:34
West Carroll 11
63 40N36 78w44 5:14:56
West Catasauqua 39
13 40N38'44 75w28'29 5:01:54
West Chester 15
13 39N57'38 75w36'21 5:02:25
West Chillisquaque 49
70 40N58 76w51 5:07:24
West Clifford 58
59 41N41'05 75w37'07 5:02:28
West Cocalico 36
28 40N16 76w09 5:04:36
Westcolang 52 59 41N30'46 75w00'20 5:00:01
Westcolang Park 64
6 41N30'52 75w02'20 5:00:09
West Conshohocken 46
90 40N04'11 75w19'00 5:01:16
West Cornwall 38
8 40N16 76w27 5:05:48
West Creek 12 106 41N29'41 78w16'42 5:13:07
West Cressona 54
27 40N38 76w12 5:04:48
West Damascus 64
6 41N42'00 75w10'18 5:00:41
West Decatur 17 4 40N56 78w17 5:13:08
West Deer 2 6 40N38 79w52 5:19:28
West Derry 65 3 40N19'23 79w18'46 5:17:15
West Donegal 36 2 40N08 76w37 5:06:28
West Earl 36 28 40N08 76w11 5:04:44
West Easton 48 12 40N40'43 75w14'14 5:00:57
West Eldred 42 40 41N57'24 78w24'14 5:13:37
West Elizabeth 2
8 40N16'15 79w53'58 5:19:36
West Ellwood Junction 4
121 40N50 80w20 5:21:20
West End 2 114 40N26'25 80w02'08 5:20:09
West End 5 6 39N57'07 78w44'56 5:15:00
West End 22 12 40N16 76w53 5:07:32
West Enola 21 12 40N16 76w55 5:07:40
West Etna 2 114 40N31 79w57 5:19:48
West Export 65 6 40N25'19 79w38'10 5:18:33
West Fairfield 65
29 40N20'58 79w07'35 5:16:30
West Fairview 21
12 40N16'30 76w54'57 5:07:40
Westfall 51 2 41N23 74w45 4:59:00
West Falls 66 6 41N27'38 75w51'24 5:03:26
West Fayetteville 28
1 39N55'00 77w34'28 5:10:18
Westfield 59 6 41N55'09 77w32'21 5:10:09
Westfield Terrace 67
12 40N14 76w51 5:07:24
West Finley 63 6 39N59'35 80w27'48 5:21:51
Westford 20 63 41N33'27 80w28'44 5:21:55
West Ford City 3
15 40N45'36 79w33'48 5:18:15
West Franklin 3 6 40N51 79w39 5:18:36
West Franklin 8
60 41N41'48 76w37'38 5:06:31
West Freedom 16 6 41N06'26 79w37'28 5:18:30
West Gate Hills 23
9 39N58'23 75w19'37 5:01:18
Westgate Hills 48
13 40N38'42 75w24'19 5:01:37
West Goshen 15 13 39N59 75w36 5:02:24
West Goshen Hills 15
13 39N57 75w36 5:02:24
West Goshen Park 15
13 39N57 75w36 5:02:24
West Greene 25 7 42N00'51 79w56'27 5:19:46
West Grove 15 1 39N49'19 75w49'40 5:03:19
West Hamburg 6 80 40N32'51 76w00'09 5:04:01
West Hanover 22
12 40N22 76w45 5:07:00
West Hazleton 40
42 40N57'31 75w59'47 5:03:59
West Hemlock 47 6 41N02 76w35 5:06:20
West Hempfield 36
26 40N04 76w27 5:05:48
West Hickory 27 6 41N34'07 79w24'30 5:17:38
West Hill 21 16 40N12'11 77w18'49 5:09:15
West Hills Estates 41
82 41N14'47 77w03'16 5:08:13
West Hills Shopping Center 2
114 40N30 80w10 5:20:40
West Hoffman 2
114 40N34 80w00 5:20:00
West Homestead 2
114 40N23'38 79w54'44 5:19:39
Westinghouse Village 23
9 39N52'08 75w17'47 5:01:11
West Jeannette 65
3 40N20 79w37 5:18:28
West Jonestown 38
1 40N24'45 76w29'51 5:05:59
West Keating 18 7 41N13 78w02 5:12:08
West Kittanning 3
15 40N48'37 79w31'47 5:18:07
West Lampeter 36
8 40N00 76w16 5:05:04
West Lancaster 36
8 40N02'12 76w21'21 5:05:25
Westland 63 2 40N16'38 80w16'24 5:21:06
West Lawn 6 101 40N19'47 75w59'41 5:03:59
West Lawn 60 70 40N57'07 76w54'06 5:07:36
West Lebanon 32 6 40N36'09 79w21'14 5:17:25
West Lebanon 38 8 40N20'38 76w26'49 5:05:47
West Leechburg 65
4 40N38'02 79w37'15 5:18:29
West Leisenring 26
80 39N57'33 79w41'51 5:18:47
West Lenox 58 59 41N43'15 75w41'58 5:02:48
West Leroy 8 103 41N39'54 76w44'24 5:06:58
West Liberty 2
114 40N24'08 80w00'53 5:20:04
West Liberty 10 6 41N00'25 80w03'10 5:20:13
West Liberty 17
56 41N04'44 78w47'14 5:15:09
West Library 2
114 40N17'41 80w01'34 5:20:06
Westline 42 6 41N46'31 78w46'21 5:15:05
West Mahanoy 54
27 40N48 76w15 5:05:00
West Mahoning 32
6 40N53 79w09 5:16:36
West Manayunk 46
9 40N01'36 75w14'20 5:00:57
West Manchester 67
39 39N57 76w52 5:07:28
West Manheim 67 1 39N43'21 76w55'05 5:07:40
West Marietta 36
26 40N04 76w33 5:06:12
West Marlborough 15
8 39N54 75w48 5:03:12
West Mayfield 4
121 40N46'48 80w20'19 5:21:21
West Mead 20 77 41N38 80w08 5:20:32
West Meyersdale 56
79 39N48'52 79w02'06 5:16:08
West Middlesex 43
117 41N10'27 80w27'13 5:21:49
West Middletown 63
6 40N14'34 80w25'39 5:21:43
West Mifflin 2
114 40N22 79w54 5:19:36
West Millcreek 25
107 42N04'28 80w09'54 5:20:40
West Milton 60 70 41N01'12 76w52'19 5:07:29
Westminster 25
107 42N04'51 80w08'28 5:20:34
Westminster 40 20 41N16'42 75w46'33 5:03:06
Westminster Manor 2
114 40N20 80w05 5:20:20
West Monocacy 6 8 40N15 75w44 5:02:56
Westmont 7 33 40N30'07 78w25'01 5:13:40
Westmont 11 74 40N18'56 78w57'07 5:15:48
Westmont 38 8 40N20'53 76w28'12 5:05:53
West Monterey 16
1 41N02'55 79w39'42 5:18:39
Westmoreland City 65
3 40N19'52 79w40'38 5:18:43
West Moshannon 17
4 40N49'37 78w21'51 5:13:27
West Myerstown 38
25 40N23 76w18 5:05:12
West Nanticoke 40
21 41N13'18 76w00'56 5:04:04
West Nantmeal 15
1 40N07 75w49 5:03:16
West New Castle 37
112 41N00'14 80w21'53 5:21:28
West New Kensington 2
14 40N33'49 79w46'28 5:19:06
West Newton 65 61 40N12'35 79w46'02 5:19:04
West Nicholson 66
89 41N38'16 75w51'54 5:03:28
West Norriton 46
90 40N08 75w22 5:01:28
West Nottingham 15
3 39N45 76w03 5:04:12
Weston 8 60 41N40'58 76w30'35 5:06:02
Weston 40 1 40N56'29 76w08'33 5:04:34
Weston Place 54
27 40N49'26 76w13'04 5:04:52
Westover 17 7 40N45'01 78w40'16 5:14:41
West Overton 65
111 40N07'03 79w33'52 5:18:15
Westover Woods 46
90 40N08 75w21 5:01:24
West Park 2 114 40N28'27 80w04'40 5:20:19
West Park 51 9 39N59 75w14 5:00:56
West Pen Argyl 48
17 40N51'26 75w16'15 5:01:05
West Penn 54 1 40N44'27 75w57'41 5:03:51
West Pennsboro 21
1 40N11 77w20 5:09:20
West Perry 55 6 40N42 77w06 5:08:24
West Pike 53 6 41N46'34 77w42'51 5:10:51
West Pikeland 15
8 40N05 75w37 5:02:28
West Pike Run 63
51 40N04 79w57 5:19:48
West Pittsburg 37
112 40N55'58 80w21'49 5:21:27
West Pittston 40
1 41N19'39 75w47'36 5:03:10
West Pittston Junction 40
112 40N56 80w22 5:21:28
West Plaza 25 107 42N08 80w09 5:20:36
West Point 11 74 40N22'59 78w50'37 5:15:22
West Point 46 8 40N12'24 75w17'59 5:01:12
West Point Marion 30
7 39N44'23 79w54'16 5:19:37
Westport 18 7 41N18'06 77w50'26 5:11:22
West Pottsgrove 46
28 40N17 75w40 5:02:40
West Providence 5
6 40N01 78w21 5:13:24
West Reading 6
101 40N20'01 75w56'52 5:03:47
West Renovo 18 73 41N19'20 77w45'59 5:11:04
West Ridge 25 107 42N04 80w09 5:20:36
West Ridge 36 8 40N01'13 76w21'26 5:05:26
West Rockhill 9 2 40N25 75w27 5:01:48
West Sadsbury 15
8 39N58 75w57 5:03:48
West Saint Clair 5
6 40N11 78w38 5:14:32
West Salem 43 63 41N24 80w26 5:21:44
West Salisbury 56
79 39N45'15 79w05'43 5:16:23
West Saxonburg 10
6 40N44'48 79w50'48 5:19:23
West Scranton 35
18 41N25 75w41 5:02:44
West Sheffield 62
3 41N42 79w02 5:16:08
West Shenango 20
63 41N31 80w30 5:22:00
West Side 40 21 41N12 76w00 5:04:00
West Side 65 61 40N13 79w46 5:19:04
West Spring Creek 62
3 41N50'44 79w34'11 5:18:17
West Springfield 25
7 41N56'45 80w28'28 5:21:54
West Sunbury 10 6 41N00'26 79w53'47 5:19:35
West Tarentum 2
14 40N35'47 79w46'14 5:19:05
West Taylor 11 74 40N22 78w57 5:15:48
West Telford 46 2 40N20 75w20 5:01:20
West Torresdale 51
9 40N04'24 74w59'19 4:59:57
Westtown 15 4 39N55'51 75w33'08 5:02:13
Westtown Acres 15
13 39N57 75w36 5:02:24
West Union 30 1 40N00'09 80w16'15 5:21:05
West Valley 3 15 40N50'10 79w25'24 5:17:42
West Vandergrift 65
4 40N36'02 79w35'02 5:18:20
West Vernon 20 6 41N35'49 80w15'55 5:21:04
West View 2 114 40N31'20 80w02'04 5:20:08
Westview Heights 37
112 40N59'48 80w22'36 5:21:30
Westville 33 5 41N12'50 78w50'13 5:15:21
West Vincent 15 8 40N08 75w39 5:02:36
West Warren 8 6 41N56'09 76w15'06 5:05:00
West Wayne 23 90 40N02'19 75w24'08 5:01:37
West Waynesburg 30
1 39N54'01 80w12'13 5:20:49
West Wheatfield 32
7 40N26 79w07 5:16:28
West Whiteland 15
13 40N01 75w37 5:02:28
West William Penn 54
27 40N48'27 76w14'15 5:04:57
West Willow 36 8 39N58'22 76w17'18 5:05:09
West Wilmerding 2
114 40N23'55 79w49'16 5:19:17
West Winfield 10
6 40N47'39 79w41'50 5:18:47
Westwood 2 114 40N25'45 80w02'24 5:20:10
Westwood 11 74 40N19 78w56 5:15:44
Westwood 15 9 39N58'18 75w51'13 5:03:25
Westwood Heights 39
13 40N36'11 75w32'29 5:02:10
Westwood Hills 2
10 40N20 79w52 5:19:28
Westwood Park 23
9 40N00 75w18 5:01:12
West Wyoming 40
20 41N19'11 75w50'47 5:03:23
West Wyomissing 6
101 40N19'28 75w59'28 5:03:58
West York 67 67 39N57'09 76w45'06 5:07:00
West Zollarsville 63
6 40N01'31 80w05'21 5:20:21
Wetherill Junction 54
27 40N45'24 76w12'13 5:04:49
Wetherills Corner 46
90 40N07'27 75w26'10 5:01:45
Wetmore 42 75 41N41'42 78w52'33 5:15:30
Wetona 8 7 41N49'46 76w41'56 5:06:48
Wexford 2 114 40N37'35 80w03'22 5:20:13
Weyant 5 7 40N12'48 78w33'23 5:14:14
Wharton 53 6 41N31'54 78w01'12 5:12:05
Wharton Furnace 26
6 39N49'30 79w38'11 5:18:33
Wheatfield 50 1 40N24 77w05 5:08:20
Wheatland 36 8 40N02'22 76w21'05 5:05:24
Wheatland 43 117 41N12'03 80w29'53 5:22:00
Wheatland Hills 36
8 40N02 76w18 5:05:12
Wheat Sheaf 9 9 40N09'45 74w47'57 4:59:12
Wheeler 26 104 40N00'14 79w36'13 5:18:25
Wheelerville 57 6 41N34'28 76w47'07 5:07:08
Wheelock 25 3 41N58'47 79w40'12 5:18:41
Whetham 18 7 41N16'08 77w35'28 5:10:22

Whig Hill 27 59 41N33'39 79w17'47 5:17:11
Whipkeys-Dam 56 4 39N52 79w14 5:16:56
Whiskerville 10 6 41N04'32 79w51'10 5:19:25
Whitaker 2 114 40N23'54 79w53'24 5:19:34
White 26 6 40N04'12 79w26'14 5:17:45
White 32 116 40N28'53 79w25'24 5:17:42
White Bear 6 8 40N16 75w48 5:03:12
White Deer 60 70 41N04'52 76w52'30 5:07:30
Whitehall 1 56 39N47'27 77w06'35 5:08:26
Whitehall 2 114 40N21'40 79w59'28 5:19:58
Whitehall 39 13 40N39 75w30 5:02:00
White Hall 47 6 41N06'59 76w37'55 5:06:32
Whitehall Park 46 90 40N08 75w21 5:01:24
White Haven 40 60 41N03'38 75w46'28 5:03:06
White Hill 21 12 40N13'49 76w55'15 5:07:41
White Horse 9 8 40N22'28 75w18'45 5:01:15
Whitehorse 15 90 39N59'23 75w28'08 5:01:53
White Horse 36 23 40N02'05 75w59'39 5:03:59
White House 26 51 39N45'10 79w47'41 5:19:11
Whiteland Crest 15 47 40N01'14 75w37'20 5:02:29
Whiteland Farms 15 8 40N02 75w31 5:02:04
Whiteley 30 1 39N49 80w08 5:20:32
Whitemarsh 46 9 40N07'19 75w13'01 5:00:52
Whitemarsh Downs 46 9 40N07 75w11 5:00:44
Whitemarsh Estates 46 90 40N05 75w16 5:01:04
Whitemarsh Greens 46 90 40N05 75w16 5:01:04
Whitemarsh Hills 46 90 40N05 75w16 5:01:04
Whitemarsh Valley Farms 46 90 40N05 75w16 5:01:04
White Marsh Village 23 9 39N56 75w20 5:01:20
White Mill Crossing 11 63 40N31'39 78w53'23 5:15:34
White Mills 64 59 41N31'34 75w12'14 5:00:49
White Oak 2 8 40N20'15 79w48'34 5:19:14
White Oak 36 8 40N12'18 76w23'33 5:05:34
White Pine 41 7 41N24'46 77w13'20 5:08:53
White Rock 36 3 39N49'17 76w05'24 5:04:22
White Rocks 28 1 39N52'11 77w31'19 5:10:05
Whitesburg 3 15 40N44'35 79w23'52 5:17:35
Whites Crossing 35 1 41N34 75w32 5:02:08
Whites Ferry 66 59 41N32 75w57 5:03:48
Whites Hill 65 111 40N14'23 79w34'02 5:18:16
Whiteside 17 4 40N48'00 78w21'13 5:13:25
White Spring 22 12 40N23'59 76w50'45 5:07:23
White Springs 60 6 40N52'59 77w05'17 5:08:21
Whitestown 10 6 40N52'36 80w02'32 5:20:10
Whites Valley 64 59 41N42'07 75w22'13 5:01:29
White Township 4 8 40N46 80w20 5:21:20
White Valley 6 6 40N24'57 79w35'55 5:18:24
Whitewood 9 9 40N08'22 74w51'44 4:59:27
Whitfield 6 101 40N19 76w00 5:04:00
Whitford 15 47 40N00'52 75w38'17 5:02:33
Whitney 65 3 40N15'12 79w24'38 5:17:39
Whitneyville 59 59 41N46'23 77w12'03 5:08:48
Whitpain 46 8 40N10 75w17 5:01:08
Whitsett 26 6 40N06'15 79w45'03 5:19:00
Wick 10 6 41N05'51 79w59'43 5:19:59
Wick City 3 15 40N49'38 79w31'33 5:18:06
Wickerham Manor 63 1 40N10'13 79w55'04 5:19:40
Wickerton 15 1 39N47'42 75w49'30 5:03:18
Wickham Village 4 13 40N37 80w16 5:21:04
Wickhaven 26 6 40N07'23 79w46'23 5:19:06
Wiconisco 22 1 40N34'24 76w41'30 5:06:46
Widener College 23 90 39N51 75w22 5:01:28
Widnoon 3 64 40N57'40 79w28'03 5:17:52
Wiegletown 37 112 41N00 80w21 5:21:24
Wiester 65 6 40N29 79w37 5:18:28
Wiggans 54 3 40N49 76w08 5:04:32
Wigwam 42 6 41N59'52 78w27'46 5:13:51
Wila 50 1 40N29'02 77w10'26 5:08:42
Wilawana 8 1 41N59'15 76w37'03 5:06:28
Wilber 56 6 40N07'26 78w54'27 5:15:38
Wilbur 39 13 40N33'39 75w28'26 5:01:54
Wilbur 56 6 40N07 78w57 5:15:48
Wilburton 19 27 40N49'05 76w22'01 5:05:28
Wilco Hill 65 114 40N23 80w04 5:20:16
Wilcox 24 64 41N34'32 78w41'19 5:14:45
Wildcat 16 7 41N01'31 79w28'48 5:17:55
Wilden Acres 46 12 40N41 75w14 5:00:56
Wildwood 2 114 40N35'39 79w58'13 5:19:53
Wildwood 60 6 40N52'11 77w03'03 5:08:12
Wildwood Springs 11 55 40N30'12 78w36'07 5:14:24
Wiley 67 1 39N43'20 76w32'37 5:06:10
Wiley Heights 30 51 39N54 79w58 5:19:52
Wilgus 32 6 40N47'02 78w53'09 5:15:33
Wilkes-Barre 40 20 41N14'45 75w52'54 5:03:32
Wilkins 2 114 40N25 79w50 5:19:20
Wilkinsburg 2 114 40N26'30 79w52'56 5:19:32
Wilko Hill 65 114 40N11'49 79w51'23 5:19:26
Willet 32 72 40N43'45 79w12'31 5:16:50
William Penn Annex 51 9 40N00 75w09 5:00:36
William Penn Manor 48 13 40N39'39 75w20'06 5:01:20
Williams 33 51 40N56 78w58 5:15:52
Williams 56 51 39N49'50 78w46'15 5:15:05
Williamsburg 7 3 40N27'43 78w12'00 5:12:48
Williamsburg 16 37 41N10'46 79w23'44 5:17:35
Williams Corner 15 8 40N06'30 75w30'44 5:02:03
Williams Corner 58 60 41N51'32 75w49'54 5:03:20
Williams Grove 21 12 40N09'06 77w02'06 5:08:08
Williamson 28 1 39N51'11 77w47'52 5:11:11
Williamsport 41 82 41N14'28 77w00'05 5:08:00
Williamstown 22 1 40N34'48 76w37'05 5:06:28
Williamstown 63 6 39N58'45 80w02'28 5:20:10
Williams Valley Junction 54 27 40N35'49 76w33'47 5:06:15
Williamsville 42 59 41N37'46 78w34'31 5:14:18
Williard 59 6 41N41'26 77w15'48 5:09:03
Willistown 15 8 39N57'40 75w29'47 5:01:59
Willock 2 114 40N21'05 79w57'43 5:19:51
Willopenn 9 1 40N11 75w03 5:00:12
Willowburn 23 90 40N02'13 75w22'00 5:01:28
Willowdale 15 8 39N52'27 75w43'05 5:02:52
Willow Grove 37 112 40N57'12 80w22'59 5:21:32
Willow Grove 46 2 40N08'38 75w06'58 5:00:28
Willow Grove Naval Air Sta 46 2 40N09 75w07 5:00:28
Willow Hill 28 1 40N06'29 77w47'19 5:11:09
Willow Lake 54 27 40N38'47 76w10'30 5:04:42
Will O Wood 9 9 40N09'34 74w49'49 4:59:19
Willow Springs 19 4 41N02'18 76w19'01 5:05:16
Willow Springs 65 25 40N20 79w43 5:18:52
Willow Street 36 8 39N58'45 76w16'36 5:05:06
Willow Tree 30 6 39N48'34 79w59'21 5:19:57
Willow View Heights 36 8 40N02 76w17 5:05:08
Wills Creek 5 51 39N50'05 78w43'02 5:14:52
Wilmer 15 8 40N07'22 75w32'15 5:02:09
Wilmer 24 6 41N21'42 78w20'59 5:13:24
Wilmerding 2 114 40N23'27 79w48'37 5:19:14
Wilmington 37 6 41N06 80w20 5:21:20
Wilmore 11 63 40N23'19 78w43'08 5:14:53
Wilmore Heights 11 63 40N22'40 78w42'58 5:14:52
Wilmot 8 6 41N35'41 76w18'35 5:05:14
Wilpen 65 110 40N16'52 79w11'44 5:16:47
Wilshire Hills 67 8 39N58'36 76w38'11 5:06:33
Wilson 2 8 40N18'36 79w53'30 5:19:34
Wilson 48 12 40N41'02 75w14'32 5:00:58
Wilson Creek 56 4 39N55'03 79w06'13 5:16:25
Wilson Mills 61 6 41N32'59 79w54'40 5:19:39
Wilsons Corner 15 8 40N08'44 75w36'25 5:02:26
Wilsonville 52 6 41N27'07 75w10'46 5:00:43
Wimmers 35 59 41N24'15 75w28'53 5:01:56
Winburne 17 7 40N57'58 78w08'43 5:12:35
Windber 56 123 40N14'23 78w50'07 5:15:20
Winder Village 9 9 40N06'22 74w52'27 4:59:30
Windfall 8 7 41N42'20 76w46'27 5:07:06
Wind Gap 48 17 40N50'53 75w17'31 5:01:10
Windham 8 6 41N58'18 76w17'30 5:05:10
Windham Center 8 6 41N57'52 76w19'36 5:05:18
Windham Summit 8 6 41N57'40 76w21'52 5:05:27
Winding Heights 21 12 40N11'32 76w58'21 5:07:53
Winding Hill 21 12 40N11'15 76w59'10 5:07:57
Winding Hill Heights 21 12 40N12 77w00 5:08:00
Windom 36 26 40N00'28 76w24'01 5:05:36
Wind Ridge 30 6 39N54'46 80w26'04 5:21:44
Windsor 67 1 39N54'58 76w35'05 5:06:20
Windsor Castle 6 80 40N32'21 75w56'01 5:03:44
Windsor Farms 22 12 40N17 76w53 5:07:32
Windsor Park 21 12 40N12'54 76w58'36 5:07:54
Windward Heights 10 3 40N54'15 79w54'26 5:19:38
Windy City 24 75 41N37'08 78w52'34 5:15:30
Windy Gap 30 7 39N47'46 80w27'14 5:21:49
Winfield 10 2 40N46 79w44 5:18:56
Winfield 60 70 40N54'33 76w51'20 5:07:25
Winfield Junction 10 2 40N42'30 79w42'11 5:18:49
Wingate 14 70 40N56'05 77w48'51 5:11:15
Wingerton 28 1 39N44'00 77w40'12 5:10:41
Winona Homes 23 9 39N53 75w18 5:01:12
Winslow 33 6 40N55'28 78w53'03 5:15:32
Winstead 26 7 39N45'32 79w55'42 5:19:43
Winterburn 17 7 41N10'48 78w36'08 5:14:25
Winterdale 64 6 41N57'25 75w21'01 5:01:24
Winterset 11 55 40N30'08 78w41'19 5:14:45
Winterstown 67 1 39N50'07 76w37'06 5:06:28
Wintersville 6 25 40N25'29 76w15'55 5:05:04
Wireton 2 13 40N33'51 80w13'45 5:20:55
Wiscasset 45 84 41N06'09 75w20'08 5:01:21
Wishaw 33 6 41N02'34 78w54'31 5:15:38
Wismer 9 1 40N24'56 75w06'54 5:00:28
Wismer PO 9 1 40N24'30 75w06'10 5:00:25
Wissahickon Village 46 90 40N05 75w16 5:01:04
Wissingers 57 6 41N28'55 76w41'39 5:06:47
Wissingertown 11 74 40N20'31 78w50'52 5:15:23
Wissinoming 51 9 40N01'20 75w03'49 5:00:15
Witinski Villa 40 20 41N10'48 75w56'53 5:03:48
Witmer 36 8 40N02'53 76w12'42 5:04:51
Wittenberg 56 79 39N46'56 78w55'21 5:15:41
Wittmer 2 114 40N31'18 79w56'55 5:19:48
Woddale 26 111 40N05'28 79w31'30 5:18:06
Wolf 41 81 41N16 76w44 5:06:56
Wolf Creek 43 6 41N13 80w04 5:20:16
Wolfdale 63 3 40N11'34 80w17'17 5:21:09
Wolf Run 42 6 41N52'17 78w32'46 5:14:11
Wolfsburg 5 70 40N02'47 78w31'48 5:14:07
Wolfs Corners 16 6 41N24'57 79w23'15 5:17:33
Wolfs Crossroads 49 2 40N49'49 76w44'22 5:06:57
Wolfs Store 14 7 40N57'36 77w23'06 5:09:32
Wolftown 2 114 40N24 79w52 5:19:28
Wolverton 49 6 40N55'14 76w42'49 5:06:51
Womelsdorf 6 56 40N21'42 76w11'04 5:04:44
Wood 5 6 40N10'06 78w08'12 5:12:33
Wood 9 9 40N08'26 74w50'50 4:59:23
Woodbine 10 6 40N54'10 79w48'51 5:19:15
Woodbine 67 1 39N47'05 76w24'22 5:05:37
Woodbourne 9 97 40N11'32 74w53'21 4:59:33
Woodbridgetown 26 51 39N46'28 79w48'07 5:19:12
Woodburn 58 60 41N45'26 75w54'21 5:03:37
Woodbury 5 51 40N13'35 78w22'01 5:13:28
Woodchoppertown 6 2 40N20'55 75w43'03 5:02:52
Woodcock 20 3 41N45'17 80w05'09 5:20:21
Woodcock Grange 20 3 41N43'01 80w06'16 5:20:25
Woodcrest 15 13 39N58'44 75w34'28 5:02:18
Wooddale 26 111 40N09 79w33 5:18:12
Wooddale 45 23 41N04'53 75w10'41 5:00:43
Woodglen 26 6 40N02'11 79w47'59 5:19:12
Woodhill 9 8 40N17'30 74w56'23 4:59:46
Wood Hill 61 7 41N12'46 79w44'48 5:18:59
Woodhouse 58 60 41N44'00 75w54'50 5:03:39
Woodland 17 7 40N59'54 78w20'30 5:13:22
Woodland 44 73 40N41'40 77w37'31 5:10:30
Woodland Heights 61 9 41N24'35 79w42'43 5:18:51
Woodland Park 41 82 41N14 77w01 5:08:04
Woodland View 67 67 39N59'53 76w44'05 5:06:56
Woodlawn 4 13 40N37'04 80w14'47 5:20:59
Woodlawn 36 8 40N02'24 76w19'48 5:05:19
Woodlawn 39 13 40N36'48 75w31'23 5:02:06
Woodlawn 65 3 40N20 79w37 5:18:28
Woodlyn 23 9 39N52'20 75w20'15 5:01:21
Woodlyn Manor 23 9 39N53 75w21 5:01:24
Woodlyn Park 23 9 39N53 75w21 5:01:24
Woodmere Park 23 9 40N00 75w18 5:01:12
Woodmont 46 1 40N09'27 75w04'22 5:00:17
Woodrow 63 6 40N17 80w22 5:21:28
Woodruff 30 6 39N50'39 80w19'04 5:21:16
Woodside 9 8 40N13'18 74w52'33 4:59:30
Woodside 26 51 39N50'00 79w50'55 5:19:24
Woodside 40 20 41N00'42 75w53'49 5:03:35
Woodside 67 1 40N07'19 76w46'55 5:07:08
Woodstock 28 1 39N56'19 77w35'02 5:10:20
Woodstown 56 6 40N11 78w59 5:15:56
Woodvale 11 74 40N20'07 78w54'14 5:15:37
Woodvale Heights 11 74 40N19 78w54 5:15:36
Woodview 23 90 40N00 75w23 5:01:32
Woodville 2 114 40N22'55 80w05'27 5:20:22
Woodville 15 8 39N52'13 75w47'55 5:03:12
Woodward 14 6 40N53'55 77w21'23 5:09:26
Woodwards Corner 15 9 39N58'29 75w43'29 5:02:54
Woodycrest 14 9 40N48'48 77w53'54 5:11:36
Woolrich 18 7 41N11'41 77w22'36 5:09:30
Wopsononock 7 6 40N34'05 78w27'06 5:13:48
Worcester 46 8 40N12'04 75w20'49 5:01:23
Worden Place 40 6 41N21'48 76w01'45 5:04:07
Worleytown 28 1 39N44'40 77w46'37 5:11:06
Worman 6 8 40N18'55 75w41'41 5:02:47
Wormleysburg 21 12 40N15'46 76w54'51 5:07:39
Worthington 3 6 40N50'15 79w37'56 5:18:32
Worthville 33 6 41N01'28 79w08'18 5:16:33
Woxall 46 8 40N18'38 75w26'57 5:01:48
Wright 40 6 41N07 75w55 5:03:40
Wrighter Corner 64 6 41N50'20 75w28'22 5:01:53
Wrights 42 6 41N44'41 78w14'38 5:12:59
Wrights Corners 42 93 41N52'56 78w29'36 5:13:58
Wrightsdale 36 1 39N45'02 76w08'06 5:04:32
Wrightstown 9 1 40N16'00 74w59'01 4:59:56
Wrights View 57 6 41N22'40 76w30'58 5:06:04
Wrightsville 62 3 41N54'52 79w25'32 5:17:42
Wrightsville 67 26 40N01'32 76w31'49 5:06:07
Wurtemburg 37 121 40N51'23 80w15'03 5:21:00
Wyalusing 8 60 41N40'05 76w15'44 5:05:03
Wyano 65 4 40N11'50 79w41'51 5:18:47
Wyattville 61 109 41N27'01 79w53'49 5:19:35
Wycombe 9 1 40N16'56 75w01'09 5:00:05
Wydnor 48 13 40N34'54 75w23'17 5:01:33
Wyebrooke 15 27 40N06 75w55 5:03:40
Wylandville 63 2 40N11'38 80w08'02 5:20:32
Wylie 2 8 40N16'42 79w52'45 5:19:31
Wyncote 46 9 40N05'40 75w08'57 5:00:36
Wyncote Hills 46 9 40N05 75w09 5:00:36
Wyncroft 23 90 39N55 75w22 5:01:28
Wyndham Hills 67 67 39N56'23 76w44'02 5:06:56
Wyndmoor 46 9 40N04'52 75w11'23 5:00:46
Wyndmoor Valley 46 9 40N07 75w11 5:00:44
Wynglade Park 23 9 40N00 75w18 5:01:12
Wynn 26 80 39N54 79w44 5:18:56
Wynnefield 51 9 39N59'23 75w14'17 5:00:57
Wynnewood 46 9 40N00'10 75w16'16 5:01:05
Wyoanna 66 1 41N25'50 75w50'02 5:03:20
Wyola 23 90 40N00'29 75w25'08 5:01:41
Wyoming 40 20 41N18'42 75w50'16 5:03:21
Wyoming Camp Ground 40 20 41N20 75w56 5:03:44
Wyomissing 6 101 40N19'46 75w57'56 5:03:52
Wyomissing Hills 6 101 40N20'15 75w58'48 5:03:55
Wyside 12 116 41N18'53 78w04'51 5:12:19
Wysox 8 41 41N46'28 76w23'59 5:05:36

Yardley 9	9	40N14'44	74W50'47	4:59:23
Yardley Farms 9	9	40N12	74W49	4:59:16
Yarnell 14	70	40N59'52	77W48'40	5:11:15
Yatesboro 3	6	40N48'00	79W20'04	5:17:20
Yatesville 40	1	41N18'12	75W47'13	5:03:09
Yatesville 54	27	40N49'30	76W10'18	5:04:41
Yeadon 23	9	39N56'20	75W15'21	5:01:01
Yeagertown 44	73	40N38'35	77W34'51	5:10:19
Yeakle Mill 28	51	39N44'02	78W02'05	5:12:08
Yellow Creek 5	6	40N07'49	78W19'54	5:13:20
Yellow Hammer 27	3	41N36'00	79W18'35	5:17:14
Yellow House 6	8	40N19'23	75W45'18	5:03:01
Yellowood 9	9	40N07'43	74W51'52	4:59:27
Yellow Spring 7	3	40N31'02	78W12'25	5:12:50
Yerkes 46	8	40N10'11	75W27'50	5:01:51
Yocumtown 67	9	40N09'30	76W48'15	5:07:13
Yoe 67	7	39N54'32	76W38'14	5:06:33
York 67	67	39N57'45	76W43'41	5:06:55
Yorkana 67	2	39N58'35	76W35'04	5:06:20
York Furnace 67	8	39N52'20	76W22'54	5:05:32
York Gardens 46	1	40N11	75W06	5:00:24
York Haven 67	80	40N06'39	76W42'58	5:06:52
Yorklyn 67	67	39N59	76W46	5:07:04
York Run 26	80	39N49'57	79W46'47	5:19:07
York Run Junction 26	80	39N49'01	79W48'11	5:19:13
Yorkshire 67	67	39N57'24	76W39'30	5:06:38
York Springs 1	1	40N00'32	77W06'57	5:08:28
Yostville 35	4	41N17'48	75W33'18	5:02:13
Youngdale 18	7	41N08'59	77W21'56	5:09:28
Youngsburg 15	9	39N57'00	75W49'11	5:03:17
Youngstown 26	80	39N55'51	79W39'29	5:18:38
Youngstown 40	42	41N00'22	75W54'25	5:03:38
Youngstown 65	3	40N16'47	79W21'57	5:17:28
Youngsville 48	80	40N46'52	75W28'38	5:01:55
Youngsville 62	3	41N51'08	79W19'08	5:17:17
Youngwood 65	111	40N14'25	79W34'37	5:18:18
Yount 5	70	40N03'43	78W28'22	5:13:53
Yukon 65	4	40N12'45	79W40'59	5:18:44
Zaner 19	6	41N07'49	76W21'31	5:05:26
Zebley Corner 23	90	39N50'05	75W29'56	5:02:00
Zediker 63	3	40N10'19	80W10'30	5:20:42
Zeigler 67	1	39N45'20	76W36'29	5:06:26
Zelienople 10	86	40N47'40	80W08'13	5:20:33
Zenith 40	1	41N01'50	76W11'21	5:04:45
Zenners 54	27	40N45'11	75W57'27	5:03:50
Zeno 10	6	40N46'41	80W01'06	5:20:04
Zerbe 54	9	40N39'25	76W20'48	5:05:23
Zerby 14	52	40N50'46	77W31'17	5:10:05
Zieglerville 46	8	40N17	75W29	5:01:56
Zimmerman 56	6	40N02'54	79W06'33	5:16:26
Zinns Mill 38	8	40N17'33	76W25'44	5:05:43
Zion 14	70	40N54'51	77W41'06	5:10:44
Zion 40	1	41N20	75W49	5:03:16
Zion Grove 54	1	40N54'09	76W12'32	5:04:50
Zion Heights 8	60	41N50'47	76W14'54	5:05:00
Zionhill 9	13	40N29'03	75W23'39	5:01:35
Zion Hill 16	6	41N08'22	79W30'20	5:18:01
Zions View 67	67	40N03'10	76W46'07	5:07:04
Zionsville 39	13	40N28'47	75W30'20	5:02:01
Zollarsville 63	6	40N02	80W06	5:20:24
Zooks Corner 36	8	40N04'46	76W15'08	5:05:01
Zooks Dam 34	7	40N35	77W24	5:09:36
Zora 1	1	39N43'51	77W22'08	5:09:29
Zucksville 48	12	40N43'07	75W14'41	5:00:59
Zullinger 28	100	39N46'12	77W37'48	5:10:31

TIME TABLES

Before	3/28/1899	LMT
3/28/1899	12:00	AST
5/03/1942	00:00	AWT
9/30/1945	02:00	AST

COUNTIES

1 Adjuntas	21 Cidra	41 Lajas	61 Rio Grande
2 Aguada	22 Coamo	42 Lares	62 Sabana Grande
3 Aguadilla	23 Comerio	43 Las Marias	63 Salinas
4 Aguas Buenas	24 Corozal	44 Las Piedras	64 San German
5 Aibonito	25 Culebra	45 Loiza	65 San Juan
6 Anasco	26 Dorado	46 Luquillo	66 San Lorenzo
7 Arecibo	27 Fajardo	47 Manati	67 San Sebastian
8 Arroyo	28 Florida	48 Maricao	68 Santa Isabel
9 Barceloneta	29 Guanica	49 Maunabo	69 Toa Alta
10 Barranquitas	30 Guayama	50 Mayaguez	70 Toa Baja
11 Bayamon	31 Guayanilla	51 Moca	71 Trujillo Alto
12 Cabo Rojo	32 Guaynabo	52 Morovis	72 Utuado
13 Caguas	33 Gurabo	53 Naguabo	73 Vega Alta
14 Camuy	34 Hatillo	54 Naranjito	74 Vega Baja
15 Canovanas	35 Hormigueros	55 Orocovis	75 Vieques
16 Carolina	36 Humacao	56 Patillas	76 Villalba
17 Catano	37 Isabela	57 Penuelas	77 Yabucoa
18 Cayey	38 Jayuya	58 Ponce	78 Yauco
19 Ceiba	39 Juana Dias	59 Quebradillas	
20 Ciales	40 Juncos	60 Rincon	

Place	Latitude	Longitude	Time
Aceitunas 51	18N26'43	67W03'55	4:28:16
Acevedo 43	18N15'50	66W59'02	4:27:56
Adjuntas 1	18N09'53	66W43'21	4:26:53
Aguacate 3	18N30'15	67W06'22	4:28:25
Aguada 2	18N22'53	67W11'19	4:28:45
Aguadilla 3	18N25'46	67W09'16	4:28:37
Aguas Buenas 4	18N15'32	66W06'12	4:24:25
Aguas Claras 19	18N15'17	65W39'14	4:22:37
Aguas Saladas Blancas 39	18N01'59	66W29'48	4:25:59
Aguilita 39	18N01'31	66W32'06	4:26:08
Aibonito 5	18N08'31	66W15'59	4:25:04
Alcantavilla 14	18N28'45	66W51'13	4:27:25
Aldea Cintron 27	18N17'58	65W38'42	4:22:35
Alegria 11	18N22'36	66W11'52	4:24:47
Algarrobo 30	17N58'57	66W05'05	4:24:20
Alianza 14	18N27'13	66W51'14	4:27:25
Allende 7	18N24'14	66W36'13	4:26:25
Almacigo Bajo 78	18N03'24	66W52'00	4:27:28
Altagracia 47	18N26'24	66W28'40	4:25:55
Altamesa 65	18N22'57	66W05'39	4:24:23
Altamira 65	18N23'59	66W06'16	4:24:25
Altavista 58	18N00'51	66W35'12	4:26:21
Amelia 32	18N26'13	66W07'02	4:24:28
Amuelas 39	18N02'03	66W30'21	4:26:01
Anasco 6	18N17'05	67W08'24	4:28:34
Angeles 72	18N17'13	66W47'59	4:27:12
Anton Ruiz 36	18N11'14	65W48'32	4:23:14
Aquilino 6	18N15'20	67W07'09	4:28:29
Arecibo 7	18N28'28	66W42'58	4:26:52
Arenal 63	17N58'41	66W18'57	4:25:16
Arenales 3	18N28'49	67W07'06	4:28:28
Arenas 29	18N01'30	66W54'31	4:27:38
Arenas 45	18N27'01	65W53'52	4:23:35
Arroyo 8	17N58'04	66W03'42	4:24:15
Arturo Lluberas 78	18N02'53	66W51'49	4:27:27
Arus 39	18N00'08	66W31'43	4:26:07
Asomante 5	18N07'55	66W16'43	4:25:07
Asomante 7	18N22'53	66W35'48	4:26:23
Bahomamey 67	18N20	66W59	4:27:56
Bairoa 13	18N15'40	66W02'27	4:24:10
Bajadero 7	18N25'43	66W41'01	4:26:44
Bajandas 36	18N09'35	65W46'55	4:23:08
Balboa 50	18N12'17	67W08'02	4:28:32
Baldorioty de Castro 58	18N00'45	66W37'40	4:26:31
Baldrich 65	18N24'48	66W03'46	4:24:15
Ballaja 7	18N25'40	66W37'38	4:26:31
Ballaja 12	18N04'51	67W08'18	4:28:33
Balneario de Cana Gorda 29	17N57'17	66W52'59	4:27:32
Banos de Coamo 22	18N02'23	66W22'28	4:25:30
Barceloneta 9	18N27'09	66W32'20	4:26:09
Barinas 78	18N00'56	66W50'37	4:27:22
Barranca 7	18N27'56	66W45'14	4:27:01
Barrancas 10	18N13'32	66W18'50	4:25:15
Barrancas 30	17N57'00	66W07'48	4:24:31
Barranquitas 10	18N11'19	66W18'24	4:25:14
Barriada Jaime L Drew 58	18N02'05	66W37'09	4:26:29
Barriada Monte Santo 75	18N07'59	65W27'06	4:21:48
Barrio Indios 31	17N59'42	66W48'47	4:27:15
Barrio Nuevo 11	18N16'47	66W11'37	4:24:46
Bartolo 61	18N21'48	65W50'20	4:23:21
Bayamon 11	18N24'02	66W09'31	4:24:38
Bayamoncito 23	18N14'19	66W10'14	4:24:41
Bayamon Gardens 11	18N22'47	66W10'49	4:24:43
Bayaney 34	18N22'16	66W47'37	4:27:10
Bay View 17	18N26'56	66W08'07	4:24:32
Beatriz 18	18N09'35	66W05'47	4:24:23
Belgie 58	18N00'31	66W36'35	4:26:26
Beltran 27	18N20'34	65W38'01	4:22:32
Belvedere 12	18N05'36	67W11'09	4:28:45
Benitez 45	18N16'29	65W52'56	4:23:32
Berio 24	18N16'21	66W20'40	4:25:23
Besosa 30	17N58'30	66W12'10	4:24:49
Betances 12	18N01'50	67W08'07	4:28:32
Beverly Hills 32	18N20'06	66W05'44	4:24:23
Biafara 7	18N24'38	66W39'44	4:26:39
Bizarreta 39	17N59'51	66W27'27	4:25:50
Blasina 61	18N22'38	65W49'04	4:23:16
Boca Chica 39	17N59'11	66W31'44	4:26:07
Boqueron 12	18N01'44	67W10'10	4:28:41
Boqueron 39	18N03'57	66W30'16	4:26:01
Boqueron 46	18N21'11	65W41'16	4:22:45
Boquillas 47	18N27'52	66W29'19	4:25:57
Borinquen 58	18N01'36	66W36'48	4:26:27
Borras 46	18N21'23	65W41'34	4:22:46
Botijas 55	18N14'36	66W22'03	4:25:28
Branderi 30	17N58'09	66W05'21	4:24:21
Brenas 73	18N28'09	66W20'29	4:25:22
Bucana 58	18N00'26	66W35'30	4:26:22
Bucarabones 69	18N23'53	66W13'08	4:24:53
Bucare 65	18N21'59	66W05'15	4:24:21
Buenaventura 16	18N22'36	65W56'25	4:23:46
Buena Vista 7	18N25'50	66W41'12	4:26:45
Buena Vista 18	18N07'16	66W10'45	4:24:43
Buena Vista 36	18N07'03	65W47'55	4:23:12
Buena Vista 50	18N11'55	67W08'21	4:28:33
Buena Vista 58	18N00'29	66W35'53	4:26:24
Buen Consejo 65	18N23'48	66W02'44	4:24:11
Buenos Aires 65	18N26'26	66W03'47	4:24:15
Buyones 58	17N59'37	66W33'04	4:26:12
Cabo Rojo 12	18N05'19	67W08'46	4:28:35
Cacao 22	18N07'01	66W20'42	4:25:23
Caguas 13	18N14'10	66W02'56	4:24:12
Caguax 13	18N14'21	66W01'53	4:24:08
Calzada 58	18N00'37	66W34'02	4:26:16
Camaceyes 3	18N28'05	67W08'44	4:28:35
Camarones 20	18N20'28	66W30'30	4:26:02
Cambalache 78	18N01'34	66W49'48	4:27:19
Cambute 16	18N21'49	65W55'17	4:23:41
Campamento 33	18N15'19	65W58'47	4:23:55
Campamento Borinquen 29	17N58'26	66W52'09	4:27:29
Campamento Buena Vista 64	18N09'08	66W59'39	4:27:59
Campamento Crozier 7	18N19'27	66W41'09	4:26:45
Campamento de Ninos 61	18N20'35	65W45'20	4:23:01
Campamento Eliza Colberg 61	18N20'28	65W49'43	4:23:19
Campamento Guajataca 67	18N22'20	66W55'06	4:27:40
Campamento Guavate 18	18N06'58	66W03'53	4:24:16
Campamento Pinones 45	18N26'38	65W57'28	4:23:50
Campamento Punta Lima 53	18N11'02	65W42'03	4:22:48
Campamento Radley 7	18N20'08	66W43'03	4:26:52
Campamento Real 56	18N04'37	66W03'20	4:24:13
Campamento Santana 62	18N08'27	66W58'07	4:27:52
Campamento Susua 78	18N04'20	66W54'26	4:27:38
Campamento Zarzal 61	18N20'53	65W47'11	4:23:09
Campanilla 70	18N25'24	66W14'14	4:24:57
Campo Alegre 47	18N26'17	66W27'50	4:25:51
Campo Rico 45	18N20'30	65W53'45	4:23:35
Campo Tortuguero 74	18N27'33	66W25'15	4:25:41
Camuy 14	18N29'09	66W50'43	4:27:23
Cana 11	18N21'11	66W11'19	4:24:45
Canaboncito 13	18N12'49	66W05'23	4:24:22
Canas 29	18N00'16	66W53'25	4:27:34
Candelaria 70	18N24'22	66W12'33	4:24:50
Canovanas 45	18N22'52	65W54'06	4:23:36
Canta Gallo 32	18N21'20	66W07'17	4:24:29
Cantagallo 40	18N14'40	65W56'07	4:23:44
Cantera 65	18N25'36	66W02'36	4:24:10
Cantero 26	18N27'30	66W14'26	4:24:58
Canto de Sapo 16	18N20'59	65W58'04	4:23:52
Caonillas 5	18N09'17	66W15'21	4:25:01
Capa 51	18N22'44	67W03'28	4:28:14
Caparra Hills 32	18N24'22	66W06'10	4:24:25
Caparra Terrace 65	18N24'05	66W05'11	4:24:21
Capitanejo 39	17N59'36	66W29'42	4:25:59
Carmelita 61	18N23'03	65W45'39	4:23:03
Carmen 30	18N02'01	66W10'11	4:24:41
Carola 61	18N22'42	65W47'38	4:23:11
Carolina 16	18N22'58	65W57'28	4:23:50
Carraizo Alto 71	18N20'40	66W32'49	4:26:11
Carrizales 34	18N29'02	66W47'25	4:27:10
Carro 10	18N11'30	66W20'18	4:25:21
Casa Blanca 20	18N14'16	66W31'20	4:26:05
Casa Blanca 46	18N20'59	65W42'34	4:22:50
Caserio Dr Gandara 58	18N00'50	66W36'06	4:26:24
Caserio Dr Pila 58	18N01'18	66W36'15	4:26:25
Casilla del Gobernador 18	18N04'17	66W08'35	4:24:34
Castaner 42	18N10'57	66W49'57	4:27:20
Catano 65	18N26'36	66W07'07	4:24:28
Cayey 18	18N06'50	66W09'59	4:24:40
Cayuco 72	18N17'35	66W44'23	4:26:58
Cayures 68	18N00'10	66W22'28	4:25:30
Ceiba 19	18N15'58	65W38'56	4:22:36
Ceiba 73	18N26'54	66W21'04	4:25:24
Celada 33	18N16'25	65W57'59	4:23:52
Central Aguirre 63	17N57	66W13	4:24:52
Central Cambalache 7	18N27'31	66W41'51	4:26:47
Central Guamani 30	17N57'52	66W10'48	4:24:43
Central Los Canos 7	18N25'47	66W43'02	4:26:52
Centro Calvache 60	18N18'56	67W13'38	4:28:55
Centro Palmar 3	18N24'02	67W07'51	4:28:31
Centro Puntas 60	18N21'55	67W15'50	4:29:03
Cercadillo 7	18N27'23	66W38'59	4:26:36
Cerrillos 12	18N08'13	67W08'55	4:28:36
Cerrillos 58	18N04'09	66W34'13	4:26:17
Cerro Corazon 8	18N00'54	66W05'02	4:24:20
Cerro Gordo 20	18N18'15	66W29'04	4:25:56
Cerro Gordo 73	18N28'58	66W20'41	4:25:23
Cerro Tumbado 30	18N01'27	66W05'43	4:24:23
Cespedes 76	18N08'25	66W28'05	4:25:52
Charco Hondo 7	18N24'58	66W42'44	4:26:51
Chardon 68	17N58'32	66W25'49	4:25:43
Chun Chin 30	17N58'06	66W11'50	4:24:47
Ciales 20	18N20'17	66W28'09	4:25:53
Cidra 21	18N10'40	66W09'42	4:24:39
Cimarrona 30	17N59'53	66W11'26	4:24:46
Cintrona Segunda 58	17N59'54	66W33'28	4:26:14
Clausells 58	18N00'46	66W38'00	4:26:32
Coabey 38	18N12'34	66W33'40	4:26:15
Coamo 22	18N04'55	66W21'30	4:25:26
Coco 63	18N00'33	66W15'35	4:25:02
Colinas de la Parguera 41	17N58'45	67W03'31	4:28:14
College Park 65	18N23'07	66W05'18	4:24:21
Collores 38	18N12'01	66W37'21	4:26:29
Colonia Lujan 75	18N07'24	65W26'35	4:21:46
Colonia Providencia 56	17N59'22	66W00'14	4:24:01
Colonia Puerto Real 75	18N06'45	65W28'55	4:21:56
Coloso 2	18N23'02	67W09'38	4:28:39
Columbia 49	18N00'23	65W54'25	4:23:38
Combate 74	18N25'54	66W25'53	4:25:44
Comerio 23	18N13'12	66W13'35	4:24:54
Cometa 36	18N08'41	65W49'45	4:23:19
Comunas 77	18N05'21	65W50'39	4:23:23
Concordia 8	17N58'54	66W02'14	4:24:09
Condado 65	18N27'23	66W04'16	4:24:17
Conde Avila 12	18N07'05	67W10'15	4:28:41
Condelaria 50	18N11'52	67W09'15	4:28:37
Constancia 58	18N00'24	66W35'59	4:26:24
Consumo 50	18N12'39	67W01'57	4:28:08
Convento 27	18N21'12	65W39'41	4:22:39
Coqui 63	17N58'34	66W13'39	4:24:55
Corazon 30	17N59'41	66W05'07	4:24:20
Corcega 60	18N19'11	67W14'34	4:28:58
Corcovado 34	18N27'38	66W46'36	4:27:06
Cordova Davila 47	18N25'52	66W28'59	4:25:56
Cornelia 12	18N09'13	67W10'13	4:28:41
Corozal 1	18N04'56	66W42'22	4:26:49
Corozal 24	18N20'35	66W19'02	4:25:16
Corozo 12	17N59'02	67W11'05	4:28:44
Corrales 3	18N26'53	67W06'50	4:28:27
Corral Viejo 58	18N04'55	66W39'12	4:26:37
Coto 64	18N05'55	67W03'03	4:28:12
Coto Laurel 58	18N03'06	66W33'06	4:26:12
Coto Norte 47	18N27'00	66W27'08	4:25:49
Coto Sur 47	18N25'15	66W27'51	4:25:51
Country Club 16	18N24'42	65W59'31	4:23:58
Cristina 39	18N03'02	66W30'01	4:26:00
Cruce Davila 9	18N25'58	66W33'57	4:26:16
Cruce Magueyes 9	18N25'12	66W34'18	4:26:17
Cuarto de Tierra 58	18N00'37	66W32'18	4:26:09
Cuatro Calles 12	18N01'42	67W08'22	4:28:33
Cuatro Calles 34	18N25'51	66W47'44	4:27:11

Cuatro Calles 39 18N02'42 66w27'32 4:25:50
Cuatro Caminos 12 18N02'53 67w08'53 4:28:36
Cuba 51 18N23'38 67w06'19 4:28:25
Cucharillas 17 18N26'15 66w09'15 4:24:37
Cuebas 57 18N02'52 66w42'40 4:26:51
Cuesta de las Piedras 50 18N11'06 67w08'36 4:28:34
Culebra 25 18N18'19 65w18'40 4:21:15
Daguao 53 18N13'42 65w41'01 4:22:44
De Diego 65 18N22'46 66w04'13 4:24:17
Delicias 12 18N06'18 67w09'22 4:28:37
Descalabrado 68 18N00'30 66w26'06 4:25:44
Desembarcadero Mosquito 75 18N08'04 65w30'43 4:22:03
Destino 75 18N07'49 65w26'12 4:21:45
Desvio Dolores 61 18N23'07 65w51'23 4:23:26
Desvio Valdes 7 18N29'01 66w39'47 4:26:39
Dewey 25 18N18 65w18 4:21:12
Divisoria 55 18N09'50 66w30'39 4:26:03
Domingo Ruiz 7 18N26'51 66w40'56 4:26:44
Dominguito 7 18N25'23 66w44'54 4:27:00
Dorado 26 18N27'39 66w16'05 4:25:04
Dos Bocas 72 18N20'24 66w40'16 4:26:41
Dos Pinos 65 18N24'24 66w02'19 4:24:09
Duque 53 18N14'29 65w45'03 4:23:00
El Alto 47 18N28'15 66w29'27 4:25:58
El Banco 53 18N14'10 65w42'20 4:22:49
El Bronce 58 18N02'08 66w34'44 4:26:19
El Brujo 12 18N03'06 67w06'52 4:28:27
El Cachete 9 18N25'51 66w31'42 4:26:07
El Campamento 20 18N22 66w28 4:25:52
El Cantito 47 18N27'00 66w30'38 4:26:03
El Cerro 12 18N03'28 67w10'59 4:28:44
El Chino 30 18N03'04 66w05'49 4:24:23
El Cinco 13 18N12'36 66w00'23 4:24:02
El Cinco 35 18N08'23 67w07'17 4:28:29
El Comandante 16 18N24'12 65w59'32 4:23:58
El Combate 12 17N58'49 67w12'45 4:28:51
El Condado 13 18N14'19 66w02'19 4:24:09
El Coto 7 18N27'46 66w44'13 4:26:57
El Coto 26 18N25'55 66w17'14 4:25:09
El Dique 7 18N25'16 66w42'50 4:26:51
Eleanor Roosevelt 65 18N25'06 66w03'52 4:24:15
Electra 36 18N08'41 65w50'32 4:23:22
El Espino 6 18N16'50 67w06'59 4:28:28
El Espino 7 18N24'35 66w37'35 4:26:30
El Faro 31 18N00'12 66w47'20 4:27:09
El Guano 72 18N16'00 66w42'26 4:26:50
Elizabeth 12 18N04'51 67w11'02 4:28:44
El Laberinto 32 18N18'57 66w06'09 4:24:25
El Madrigal 58 18N02'21 66w38'13 4:26:33
El Mango 40 18N14'10 65w52'48 4:23:31
El Minao 65 18N21'32 66w05'10 4:24:21
El Naranjito 13 18N10'31 66w01'53 4:24:08
El Ocho 11 18N20'41 66w11'46 4:24:47
El Pajuil 34 18N25'49 66w47'18 4:27:09
El Polvorin 26 18N25'55 66w17'02 4:25:08
El Porton 11 18N20'28 66w12'01 4:24:48
El Pueblito 47 18N25'50 66w26'54 4:25:48
El Pueblo del Nino 61 18N22'58 65w51'15 4:23:25
El Pulguero 47 18N27'43 66w28'16 4:25:53
El Recreo 64 18N04'40 67w01'54 4:28:08
El Retiro 64 18N04'43 67w02'04 4:28:08
El Rosario 78 18N01'43 66w51'26 4:27:26
El Saco 34 18N24'48 66w47'50 4:27:11
El Salto 67 18N17'47 66w54'38 4:27:39
El Tumbao 29 18N00'25 66w54'01 4:27:36
El Valle 41 18N02'35 67w03'21 4:28:13
El Verde 13 18N13'36 66w03'11 4:24:13
El Verde 61 18N20'27 65w49'34 4:23:18
El Vigia 58 18N01'20 66w37'16 4:26:29
Ensenada 29 17N58'15 66w56'02 4:27:44
Escuela Dr Liborio Cordova 20 18N20'25 66w26'07 4:25:44
Escuela La Prieta 23 18N15'04 66w11'44 4:24:47
Escuela Negroni 12 18N02'22 67w07'41 4:28:31
Espanta Sueno 27 18N19'23 65w39'33 4:22:38
Esperanza 13 18N12'32 66w04'05 4:24:16
Esperanza 53 18N13'13 65w42'38 4:22:51
Esperanza 58 17N59'49 66w34'28 4:26:18
Esperanza 63 17N57'53 66w15'26 4:25:02
Esperanza 75 18N05'57 65w28'16 4:21:53
Espinosa 73 18N25'02 66w19'09 4:25:17
Estacion Botija 53 18N12'32 65w42'28 4:22:50
Estacion Naguabo 53 18N12'22 65w43'48 4:22:55
Estacion Santa Isabel 68 17N59'14 66w24'00 4:25:36
Estebania 35 18N09'22 67w09'18 4:28:37
Extension Country Club 16 18N25'00 65w59'52 4:23:59
Extension Mariani 58 18N00'21 66w37'28 4:26:30
Factor 7 18N26'40 66w38'07 4:26:32
Fagot 58 18N00'56 66w36'05 4:26:24
Fairview 71 18N22'08 65w55'12 4:23:41
Fajardo 27 18N19'37 65w39'08 4:22:37
Faria 11 18N22'21 66w11'52 4:24:47
Faro La Fortaleza 65 18N27'59 66w07'25 4:24:30
Feliciano 3 18N27'56 67w07'33 4:28:30
Fermina 36 18N10'42 65w51'16 4:23:25
Finca Juanita 41 18N00'15 67w03'14 4:28:13
Finca La Corza 50 18N12'20 67w04'10 4:28:17
Finca Marini 50 18N13'02 67w04'59 4:28:20
Finca Pinones 45 18N26'57 65w57'30 4:23:50
Finca San Miguel 6 18N15'21 67w05'17 4:28:21
Flamboyant Gardens 11 18N23'31 66w09'39 4:24:39
Flamingo Garden 11 18N22'35 66w09'59 4:24:40
Floral Park 65 18N25'12 66w03'12 4:24:13
Florida 9 18N21'55 66w34'03 4:26:16
Florida 53 18N14'19 65w46'57 4:23:08
Forest Hills 11 18N23'18 66w09'50 4:24:39
Fort Bundy 53 18N12'59 65w41'36 4:22:46
Fortuna 27 18N18'20 65w38'47 4:22:35
Fortuna 58 17N59'46 66w32'33 4:26:10
Fortuna 63 17N58'57 66w15'26 4:25:02
Fraternidad 29 18N00'42 66w54'27 4:27:38
Fuerte San Cristobal 65 18N28'10 66w06'41 4:24:27
Fuerte San Geronimo 65 18N27'55 66w05'08 4:24:21
Fuig 29 17N59'23 66w54'59 4:27:40
Galateo Bajo 3 18N27'27 67w00'13 4:28:01
Galicias 39 17N59'45 66w30'54 4:26:04
Gandara 21 18N10'39 66w08'47 4:24:35
Garcia 12 18N08'45 67w09'22 4:28:37
Garden Hills 32 18N24'03 66w06'52 4:24:27
Garita 12 18N05'52 67w10'31 4:28:42
Garona 49 18N00'46 65w55'35 4:23:42
Garrochales 7 18N27'35 66w36'41 4:26:27
Guanabana 12 18N00'47 67w07'03 4:28:28
Guanajibo 35 18N08'43 67w08'17 4:28:33
Guanajibo Castillo 50 18N10'00 67w09'19 4:28:37
Guanica 29 17N58'25 66w54'30 4:27:38
Guaniquilla 12 18N03'58 67w10'48 4:28:43
Guaraguao 58 18N07'38 66w40'14 4:26:41
Guayabal 39 18N05'00 66w30'06 4:26:00
Guayabo Dulce 1 18N11'29 66w48'43 4:27:15
Guayama 30 17N59'10 66w06'51 4:24:27
Guayanilla 31 18N01'16 66w47'32 4:27:10
Guaydia 31 18N01'33 66w47'22 4:27:09
Guaynabo 32 18N21'34 66w06'41 4:24:27
Guaypao 57 18N00'57 66w43'56 4:26:56
Gurabo 33 18N15'23 65w58'24 4:23:54
Hacienda Aldea 20 18N17'22 66w32'38 4:26:11
Hacienda Alicia 6 18N15'12 67w06'07 4:28:24
Hacienda Alomar 68 17N57'36 66w23'33 4:25:34
Hacienda Altura 68 18N00'06 66w24'55 4:25:40
Hacienda Amelia 39 18N00'43 66w28'16 4:25:53
Hacienda Americo 78 18N08'31 66w48'56 4:27:16
Hacienda Anadon 39 18N05'30 66w32'22 4:26:09
Hacienda Ana Maria 58 18N03'20 66w33'57 4:26:16
Hacienda Arbela 78 18N09'31 66w49'28 4:27:18
Hacienda Arbona 39 18N05'22 66w32'20 4:26:09
Hacienda Arcadia 75 18N07'36 65w31'17 4:22:05
Hacienda Artau 72 18N14'53 66w44'19 4:26:57
Hacienda Asuncion 78 18N09'56 66w49'55 4:27:20
Hacienda Balare 48 18N11'27 66w58'45 4:27:55
Hacienda Ballester 42 18N13'10 66w53'00 4:27:32
Hacienda Barrancas 58 18N02'16 66w35'30 4:26:22
Hacienda Batiz 58 18N06'25 66w39'45 4:26:39
Hacienda Beatriz Soledad 41 18N01'38 67w02'06 4:28:08
Hacienda Belgodere 31 18N06'18 66w46'14 4:27:05
Hacienda Bermudez 43 18N15'00 67w04'14 4:28:17
Hacienda Bianchi 1 18N10'19 66w47'21 4:27:09
Hacienda Buena Vista 42 18N11'45 66w50'46 4:27:23
Hacienda Buena Vista 68 18N01'33 66w22'22 4:25:29
Hacienda Burenes 58 18N06'15 66w38'34 4:26:34
Hacienda Butler 72 18N17'11 66w35'33 4:26:22
Hacienda Candelaria 78 18N08'40 66w54'53 4:27:40
Hacienda Cano Verde 58 18N01'00 66w35'06 4:26:20
Hacienda Carbonell 72 18N16'29 66w37'48 4:26:31
Hacienda Carmelita 58 18N08'42 66w36'43 4:26:27
Hacienda Carmen 63 17N58'36 66w17'32 4:25:10
Hacienda Casey 43 18N15'08 67w04'35 4:28:18
Hacienda Catalina 31 18N05'48 66w47'38 4:27:11
Hacienda Chesari 31 18N07'03 66w46'34 4:27:06
Hacienda Cintrona Primera 39 18N01'04 66w31'10 4:26:05
Hacienda Cipriano 50 18N14'27 67w03'48 4:28:15
Hacienda Clavell 63 18N02'14 66w13'01 4:24:52
Hacienda Colom 20 18N16'41 66w31'13 4:26:05
Hacienda Concepcion 78 18N08'05 66w49'26 4:27:18
Hacienda Constancia 43 18N12'50 66w56'31 4:27:46
Hacienda Constanza 50 18N12'37 67w05'28 4:28:22
Hacienda Corcega 64 18N07'53 67w01'12 4:28:05
Hacienda Corega 22 18N08'11 66w19'16 4:25:17
Hacienda Cortada 58 18N08'25 66w35'09 4:26:21
Hacienda Coto 64 18N06'11 67w04'10 4:28:17
Hacienda Cristina 39 18N02'47 66w30'15 4:26:01
Hacienda Delicias 48 18N12'13 66w59'28 4:27:58
Hacienda Desengano 41 18N01'23 67w06'35 4:28:26
Hacienda El Banco 38 18N10'27 66w39'07 4:26:36
Hacienda El Fenix 1 18N12'19 66w48'48 4:27:15
Hacienda El Progreso 72 18N10'57 66w39'54 4:26:40
Hacienda El Semil 76 18N07'52 66w31'14 4:26:05
Hacienda El Tesoro 58 18N07'18 66w36'04 4:26:24
Hacienda Esmeralda 68 18N01'09 66w22'25 4:25:30
Hacienda Esperanza 1 18N10'35 66w47'52 4:27:11
Hacienda Esperanza 43 18N14'22 67w02'43 4:28:11
Hacienda Espino 43 18N15'05 66w55'18 4:27:41
Hacienda Eugenia 6 18N17'59 67w11'17 4:28:45
Hacienda Fajardo 50 18N12'11 67w01'47 4:28:07
Hacienda Fe 58 18N01'31 66w32'37 4:26:10
Hacienda Felicia 30 17N58'29 66w04'54 4:24:20
Hacienda Felicita 56 18N00'32 66w01'32 4:24:06
Hacienda Fernandez Rosal 78 18N06'44 66w50'00 4:27:20
Hacienda Figueroa 55 18N11'32 66w30'47 4:26:03
Hacienda Flor de Alba 20 18N17'13 66w30'55 4:26:04
Hacienda Florida 68 17N57'52 66w23'57 4:25:36
Hacienda Florida 78 18N01'53 66w50'48 4:27:23
Hacienda Fortuna 48 18N09'41 66w51'51 4:27:27
Hacienda Garau 20 18N16'16 66w32'55 4:26:12
Hacienda Gloria 31 18N06'52 66w46'03 4:27:04
Hacienda Grande 53 18N13'16 65w42'06 4:22:48
Hacienda Gripinas 38 18N11'52 66w34'37 4:26:18
Hacienda Guayo 39 18N06'50 66w32'02 4:26:08
Hacienda Hucar 63 18N00'50 66w14'24 4:24:58
Hacienda Iberia 42 18N11'31 66w51'31 4:27:26
Hacienda Indiera 48 18N09'55 66w52'17 4:27:29
Hacienda Jauca 38 18N11'13 66w38'26 4:26:34
Hacienda Josefa 43 18N12'14 66w56'55 4:27:48
Hacienda Josefa 58 18N02'54 66w39'50 4:26:39
Hacienda Juanita 43 18N14'25 67w00'49 4:28:03
Hacienda Julia 30 18N00'53 66w12'02 4:24:48
Hacienda Julia 35 18N07'26 67w05'34 4:28:22
Hacienda Jurutungo 58 18N08'29 66w34'35 4:26:18
Hacienda La Abras 7 18N20'15 66w36'30 4:26:26
Hacienda La Balear 1 18N12'01 66w49'49 4:27:19
Hacienda La Catalana 72 18N16'25 66w36'04 4:26:24
Hacienda La Concordia 58 18N05'11 66w33'50 4:26:15
Hacienda La Delfina 48 18N09'18 66w55'23 4:27:42
Hacienda La Esperanza 72 18N11'34 66w40'46 4:26:43
Hacienda La Gloria 58 18N08'13 66w37'46 4:26:31
Hacienda La Isolina 72 18N17'47 66w35'27 4:26:22
Hacienda La Juanita 78 18N08'31 66w50'45 4:27:23
Hacienda La Luisa 78 18N08'59 66w54'18 4:27:37
Hacienda Lamberti 43 18N15'48 67w03'54 4:28:16
Hacienda La Milagrosa 43 18N13'14 67w00'10 4:28:01
Hacienda La Mocha 58 18N07'48 66w38'00 4:26:32
Hacienda La Ratina 12 18N06'14 67w07'45 4:28:31
Hacienda La Rosita 78 18N08'10 66w54'33 4:27:38
Hacienda Las Magas 39 18N06'22 66w32'20 4:26:09
Hacienda Las Pinas 78 18N08'14 66w51'55 4:27:28
Hacienda La Vega 48 18N10'17 66w55'06 4:27:40
Hacienda Lealtad 42 18N14'07 66w53'04 4:27:32
Hacienda Leonor 78 18N08'03 66w50'00 4:27:20
Hacienda Limon 38 18N16'51 66w35'39 4:26:23
Hacienda Limon 76 18N09'35 66w26'44 4:25:47
Hacienda Llanada 48 18N10'52 66w53'44 4:27:35
Hacienda Los Planes 38 18N11'32 66w35'19 4:26:21
Hacienda Loyola 57 18N05'41 66w45'33 4:27:02
Hacienda Luciana 39 18N03'41 66w30'44 4:26:03
Hacienda Luisa 41 18N01'33 67w03'52 4:28:15
Hacienda Manuela 48 18N11'30 66w55'22 4:27:41
Hacienda Maraguez 58 18N05'21 66w35'40 4:26:23
Hacienda Margarita 63 17N58'25 66w18'19 4:25:13
Hacienda Maria 52 18N18'49 66w26'42 4:25:47
Hacienda Maria Antonia 48 18N10'21 66w51'03 4:27:24
Hacienda Marques 72 18N17'25 66w34'32 4:26:18
Hacienda Mata 6 18N15'55 67w04'43 4:28:19

Hacienda Matilde 58 17N59'47 66w38'14 4:26:33
Hacienda Mejias 78 18N07'24 66w48'37 4:27:14
Hacienda Mercado 39 18N03'38 66w30'19 4:26:01
Hacienda Merle 43 18N13'22 67w01'35 4:28:06
Hacienda Miramar 39 18N07'59 66w32'22 4:26:09
Hacienda Miranda 39 18N01'25 66w27'21 4:25:49
Hacienda Mogote 78 18N06'53 66w48'37 4:27:14
Hacienda Molina 58 18N05'48 66w38'05 4:26:32
Hacienda Monserrate 42 18N11'33 66w52'51 4:27:31
Hacienda Monserrate 58 18N04'31 66w34'36 4:26:18
Hacienda Morales 6 18N16'28 67w05'45 4:28:23
Hacienda Noez 1 18N09'22 66w45'56 4:27:04
Hacienda Oliva 57 18N03'56 66w44'56 4:27:00
Hacienda Olivieri 31 18N07'48 66w46'35 4:27:06
Hacienda Pales 68 17N58'29 66w21'30 4:25:26
Hacienda Paraiso 58 18N06'13 66w34'22 4:26:17
Hacienda Penonales 20 18N17'52 66w30'49 4:26:03
Hacienda Piedra Gorda 72 18N18'56 66w35'26 4:26:22
Hacienda Pietri 1 18N10'27 66w46'18 4:27:05
Hacienda Pintado 78 18N07'28 66w48'55 4:27:16
Hacienda Plato Indio 43 18N13'33 67w02'02 4:28:08
Hacienda Polmares 48 18N10'44 67w01'08 4:28:05
Hacienda Poncena 39 18N03'13 66w32'37 4:26:10
Hacienda Porvenir 42 18N15'32 66w52'47 4:27:31
Hacienda Potala 39 18N00'10 66w30'38 4:26:03
Hacienda Ralate 20 18N12'46 66w30'53 4:26:04
Hacienda Recurso 50 18N11'42 67w03'55 4:28:16
Hacienda Resolucion 41 18N01'33 67w04'57 4:28:20
Hacienda Restaurada 58 18N00'13 66w35'21 4:26:21
Hacienda Resurreccion 78 18N08'23 66w51'02 4:27:24
Hacienda Retiro 50 18N11'51 67w01'17 4:28:05
Hacienda Reynes 20 18N16'46 66w32'57 4:26:12
Hacienda Ripoli 1 18N12'27 66w48'07 4:27:12
Hacienda Rivera 1 18N13'11 66w48'42 4:27:15
Hacienda Roig 78 18N06'21 66w50'22 4:27:21
Hacienda Rolon 50 18N11'44 67w02'19 4:28:09
Hacienda Rosali 58 18N07'31 66w34'41 4:26:19
Hacienda Rosario 1 18N08'40 66w46'44 4:27:07
Hacienda Salome 50 18N14'41 67w05'01 4:28:20
Hacienda San Alberto 1 18N12'42 66w49'09 4:27:17
Hacienda San Antonio 48 18N11'23 66w59'57 4:28:00
Hacienda San Carlos 39 18N08'17 66w33'32 4:26:14
Hacienda San Clemente 39 18N08'34 66w32'45 4:26:11
Hacienda San Isidoro 56 17N58'47 65w58'22 4:23:53
Hacienda San Jose 1 18N13'16 66w46'52 4:27:07
Hacienda San Jose 7 18N21'48 66w35'32 4:26:22
Hacienda San Lorenzo 78 18N09'21 66w51'03 4:27:24
Hacienda San Narciso 58 18N08'14 66w36'44 4:26:27
Hacienda San Pedro 67 18N16'30 66w56'02 4:27:44
Hacienda Santa Anita 78 18N07'41 66w48'06 4:27:12
Hacienda Santa Barbara 20 18N15'21 66w33'47 4:26:15
Hacienda Santa Clara 78 18N08'52 66w49'55 4:27:20
Hacienda Santa Elena 1 18N13'18 66w43'26 4:26:54
Hacienda Santa Elena 20 18N18'21 66w31'58 4:26:08
Hacienda Santa Maria 48 18N08'31 66w51'46 4:27:27
Hacienda Santa Rita 48 18N10'24 66w58'55 4:27:56
Hacienda Santa Rita 58 18N07'45 66w35'29 4:26:22
Hacienda Santa Rosa 1 18N09'29 66w47'28 4:27:10
Hacienda Santa Rosa 38 18N11'08 66w37'15 4:26:29
Hacienda Santiago 48 18N11'29 66w54'49 4:27:39
Hacienda Tabonuco 20 18N10'11 66w31'11 4:26:05
Hacienda Teresa 48 18N12'02 66w58'05 4:27:52
Hacienda Teresa 58 18N01'16 66w33'10 4:26:13
Hacienda Teresa 63 17N57'53 66w16'28 4:25:06
Hacienda Tetuan 72 18N16'36 66w36'36 4:26:26
Hacienda Tres Hermanas 72 18N14'04 66w44'17 4:26:57
Hacienda Ursula 39 18N00'22 66w29'15 4:25:57
Hacienda Usera 58 18N05'49 66w36'51 4:26:27
Hacienda Vaquinas 1 18N09'23 66w46'57 4:27:08
Hacienda Vega Grande 38 18N16'35 66w34'53 4:26:20
Hacienda Veremos 50 18N13'46 67w03'08 4:28:13
Hacienda Vertedero 39 18N06'31 66w33'05 4:26:12
Hacienda Vicario 78 18N07'35 66w49'55 4:27:20
Hacienda Vilella 42 18N13'26 66w51'37 4:27:26
Hacienda Vista Alegre 58 18N04'06 66w32'54 4:26:12
Hacienda Yani 58 18N07'25 66w34'36 4:26:18
Hatillo 34 18N29'18 66w49'33 4:27:18
Hato Abajo 7 18N26'58 66w44'52 4:26:59
Hato Arriba 67 18N21'28 67w02'04 4:28:08
Hato Candal 61 18N22'35 65w47'15 4:23:09
Hato Rey 65 18N25 66w03 4:24:12
Hato Tejas 11 18N24'27 66w11'23 4:24:46
Hato Viejo 20 18N21'56 66w28'36 4:25:54
Hector A Pinero 65 18N25'32 66w03'15 4:24:13
Helechal 10 18N09'42 66w18'39 4:25:15
Highland Park 65 18N23'30 66w01'10 4:24:05
Higuey 3 18N25'30 67w09'16 4:28:37
Higuillals 7 18N26'50 66w43'35 4:26:54
Higuillar 26 18N26'27 66w17'33 4:25:10
Honduras 45 18N26'02 65w52'12 4:23:29
Hormigueros 35 18N08'30 67w07'40 4:28:31
Hoya Grande 35 18N09'26 67w07'38 4:28:31
Hoyo Mulas 16 18N23'57 65w57'09 4:23:49
Hucares 53 18N11'22 65w42'35 4:22:50
Humacao 36 18N09'06 65w49'40 4:23:19
Hyde Park 65 18N24'34 66w03'42 4:24:15
Iglesia 3 18N25'53 67w09'15 4:28:37
Iglesia Arenale Altos 3 18N27'22 67w00'59 4:28:04
Iglesia Ceiba Alta 3 18N27'21 67w05'19 4:28:21
Iglesia del Nino Jesus 52 18N21'47 66w24'43 4:25:39
Iglesia Virgen de la Provide 23 18N15'01 66w11'40 4:24:47
Imbery 9 18N26'20 66w33'10 4:26:13
Indiera Alta 48 18N09'13 66w53'06 4:27:32
Ingenio 70 18N26'39 66w13'35 4:24:54
Isabela 37 18N30'10 67w01'29 4:28:06
Isabel Josefa 12 18N06'23 67w07'37 4:28:30
Isabel Segunda (Vieques) 75 18N09'04 65w26'35 4:21:46
Isidra 27 18N20'28 65w38'32 4:22:34
Isleta 51 18N22'32 67w06'32 4:28:26
Islote 7 18N29'21 66w35'50 4:26:23
Jacaguas 39 18N03'23 66w31'43 4:26:07
Jacana 22 18N04'55 66w17'48 4:25:11
Jagual 66 18N09'49 65w59'45 4:23:59
Jaguas 57 18N04'42 66w43'34 4:26:54
Jaguas 63 17N58'15 66w15'54 4:25:04
Jagueyes 70 18N06'44 66w30'32 4:26:02
Jajome 18 18N03'55 66w09'38 4:24:39
Jardines de Arecibo 7 18N28'21 66w45'05 4:27:00
Jardines de Caparra 11 18N23'45 66w07'50 4:24:31
Jardines del Caribe 58 18N00'52 66w38'57 4:26:36
Jardines de Monte Hatillo 65 18N23'24 66w00'39 4:24:03
Jardines de Ponce 58 18N02'39 66w35'42 4:26:23
Jarealito 7 18N28'52 66w41'28 4:26:46
Jauca 68 17N58'16 66w21'58 4:25:28
Jayuya 38 18N13'14 66w35'31 4:26:22
Jayuya Abajo 38 18N13'12 66w36'57 4:26:28
Jobos 3 18N29'56 67w04'19 4:28:17
Jobos 30 17N57'26 66w09'57 4:24:40
Josefa 6 18N16'40 67w07'17 4:28:29
Josefa 27 18N18'51 65w39'00 4:22:36
Josefa 30 17N57'07 66w09'22 4:24:37
Jose Mercado 13 18N13'10 66w01'27 4:24:06
Joya de los Santos 7 18N28'04 66w44'13 4:26:57
Joyuda 12 18N07'01 67w10'58 4:28:44
Juana Diaz 39 18N03'16 66w30'25 4:26:02
Juana Matos 17 18N26'19 66w07'49 4:24:31
Juncos 40 18N13'46 65w55'17 4:23:41
Junio 36 18N11'16 65w47'11 4:23:09
Korea 61 18N22'41 65w46'54 4:23:08
La Aldea 7 18N26'09 66w36'26 4:26:26
La Aldea 11 18N22'44 66w10'31 4:24:42
La Alhambra 58 18N01'03 66w36'17 4:26:25
La Alianza 7 18N23'58 66w36'10 4:26:25
La Arena 11 18N25'09 66w11'11 4:24:45
La Barra 13 18N16'56 66w02'41 4:24:11
La Bayamonesa 13 18N18'17 66w03'50 4:24:15
La Boca 9 18N29'00 66w32'19 4:26:09
La Capital 31 18N02'34 66w48'57 4:27:16
La Casa de Piedra 59 18N25'40 66w55'27 4:27:42
La Ceramica 16 18N25'16 65w59'01 4:23:56
La Changa 13 18N17'59 66w03'44 4:24:15
La Cuesta 34 18N25'14 66w49'00 4:27:16
La Cumbre 65 18N21'43 66w04'34 4:24:18
La Dolores 61 18N22'39 65w51'22 4:23:25
La Esperanza 7 18N23'02 66w44'50 4:26:59
La Esperanza 32 18N22'03 66w06'42 4:24:27
La Estancita 72 18N15'13 66w45'45 4:27:03
La Fe 53 18N12'50 65w45'44 4:23:03
La Glorieta 47 18N27'33 66w28'59 4:25:56
La Gonzalez 67 18N20'01 66w59'52 4:27:59
La Granja 74 18N25'30 66w24'17 4:25:37
La Guaba 5 18N05'22 66w16'16 4:25:05
La Guinea 7 18N25'25 66w43'31 4:26:54
La Guitarra 23 18N12'19 66w15'20 4:25:01
Lajas 41 18N03'07 67w03'35 4:28:14
Lajas Arriba 41 18N02'22 67w00'41 4:28:03
La Joya 29 18N00'10 66w52'26 4:27:30
La Jurado 13 18N11'24 66w05'27 4:24:22
La Luna 29 17N58'51 66w53'25 4:27:34
La Marina 45 18N20'42 65w53'45 4:23:35
Lamboglia 56 17N58'48 65w58'22 4:23:53
La Mina 2 18N21'26 67w10'09 4:28:41
La Monserrate 70 18N26'58 66w14'21 4:24:57
La Muda 32 18N19'52 66w05'57 4:24:24
La Parada 67 18N18'25 67w01'26 4:28:06
La Pica 14 18N28'01 66w51'55 4:27:28
La Pica 38 18N09'39 66w39'00 4:26:36
La Pica 62 18N03'52 66w57'18 4:27:49
La Placita 18 18N07'31 66w10'52 4:24:43
La Plata 5 18N09'23 66w14'00 4:24:56
La Playa 72 18N17'08 66w39'51 4:26:39
La Plaza 13 18N08'27 66w02'34 4:24:10
La Plena 63 18N02'55 66w12'18 4:24:49
La Pradera 13 18N10'38 66w03'38 4:24:15
La Puente 6 18N16'44 67w11'19 4:28:45
La Quinta 78 18N01'42 66w51'46 4:27:27
La Rambla 58 18N01'43 66w36'02 4:26:24
La Rampla 13 18N13'12 66w05'06 4:24:20
Lares 42 18N17'48 66w52'39 4:27:31
La Romana 7 18N24'22 66w36'01 4:26:24
Las Americas 65 18N24'11 66w04'28 4:24:18
Las Arenas 12 18N01'35 67w08'59 4:28:36
Las Arenas 69 18N23'32 66w12'52 4:24:51
Las Cantaras 7 18N22'38 66w40'18 4:26:41
Las Carolinas 13 18N15'22 66w03'55 4:24:16
Las Carreras 45 18N25'54 65w50'21 4:23:21
Las Casas 65 18N25'55 66w02'29 4:24:10
Las Claras 7 18N26'51 66w41'38 4:26:47
Las Coles 61 18N23'09 65w46'19 4:23:05
Las Corozas 2 18N22'01 67w10'39 4:28:43
Las Croabas 27 18N22'00 65w37'35 4:22:30
Las Cruces 16 18N23'45 65w59'04 4:23:56
Las Cruces 21 18N10'13 66w05'52 4:24:23
Las Cunetas 7 18N26'49 66w45'18 4:27:01
Las Delicias 58 18N02'10 66w38'45 4:26:35
Las Flores 22 18N02'56 66w21'50 4:25:27
Las Guaras 62 18N03'42 66w58'46 4:27:55
Las Guasimas 8 17N58'50 66w04'21 4:24:17
Las Llanadas 7 18N23'53 66w41'43 4:26:47
Las Lomas 39 18N03'50 66w30'37 4:26:02
Las Lomas 65 18N23'37 66w05'44 4:24:23
Las Mareas 30 17N56'24 66w08'42 4:24:35
Las Marias 6 18N17'43 67w08'48 4:28:35
Las Marias 22 18N03'27 66w23'17 4:25:33
Las Mercedes 7 18N27'29 66w43'15 4:26:53
Las Mercedes 44 18N10'38 65w52'03 4:23:28
Las Mercedes 45 18N25'20 65w53'31 4:23:34
Las Monjitas 58 18N02'22 66w35'10 4:26:21
Las Ochenta 63 17N59'12 66w19'06 4:25:16
La Soledad 50 18N14'37 67w08'13 4:28:33
Las Ollas 68 18N02'06 66w25'29 4:25:42
Las Palmas 8 17N59'11 66w01'52 4:24:07
Las Palmas 12 17N59'13 67w08'04 4:28:32
Las Palmas 17 18N25'33 66w08'40 4:24:35
Las Piedras 44 18N11'06 65w52'00 4:23:28
Las Pinas 40 18N15'13 65w55'05 4:23:40
Las Torres 44 18N13'16 65w50'01 4:23:20
Las Tres T 61 18N21'43 65w48'21 4:23:13
La Suiza 36 18N08'45 65w48'21 4:23:13
Las Vegas 17 18N26'00 66w08'44 4:24:35
Las Vegas 60 18N11'14 67w01'52 4:28:07
Las Viudas 39 18N03'14 66w31'40 4:26:07
La Torre 45 18N27'28 65w58'52 4:23:55
La Tosca 6 18N17'59 67w12'33 4:28:50
La Trocha 74 18N26'35 66w22'55 4:25:32
Laura 77 18N04'24 65w53'21 4:23:33
Lavadero 35 18N07'55 67w06'01 4:28:24
La Vega 10 18N11'25 66w19'01 4:25:16
La Vega 37 18N24'16 67w00'10 4:28:01
La Vega 61 18N21'01 65w46'09 4:23:05
La Zanja 63 18N02'01 66w18'48 4:25:15
Lechuga 34 18N27'12 66w48'13 4:27:13
Leprocomio 71 18N21'42 66w01'44 4:24:07
Levittown 70 18N27'07 66w10'55 4:24:44
Limas 78 18N00'14 66w49'59 4:27:20
Limon 50 18N11'21 67w04'16 4:28:17
Limones 53 18N15'10 65w42'26 4:22:50
Limones 77 18N05'08 65w54'10 4:23:37
Llanos 41 18N01'53 67w06'35 4:28:26
Llanos Tuna 12 18N04'14 67w07'56 4:28:32
Loiza 65 18N27'03 66w03'11 4:24:13
Loiza Aldea 45 18N26'00 65w52'52 4:23:31
Loiza Valley 45 18N22'37 65w54'51 4:23:39
Lomas Verdes 11 18N22'36 66w08'59 4:24:36
Los Angeles 16 18N25'52 66w00'28 4:24:02
Los Caobos 32 18N24'25 66w05'55 4:24:24
Los Colericos 7 18N28'27 66w43'41 4:26:55
Los Indios 31 18N00'17 66w48'18 4:27:13
Los Llanos 22 18N03'26 66w24'22 4:25:37
Los Maestros 65 18N24'28 66w02'06 4:24:08
Los Magos 69 18N26'07 66w11'22 4:24:45
Los Molinos 47 18N28'18 66w29'11 4:25:57
Los Muertos 7 18N22'20 66w39'56 4:26:40
Los Naranjos 74 18N28'27 66w23'42 4:25:35
Los Pampanos 58 18N00'01 66w38'01 4:26:32
Los Penas 65 18N23'55 66w01'22 4:24:05
Los Perros 36 18N09'52 65w46'57 4:23:08
Los Puertos 22 18N02'37 66w23'43 4:25:35
Los Puertos 26 18N26'10 66w18'37 4:25:14
Los Rabanos 42 18N11 66w50 4:27:20
Lucchetti 78 18N02'08 66w50'42 4:27:23
Luis Cintron 27 18N18'17 65w38'35 4:22:34
Luis Llorens Torres 65 18N27'00 66w02'31 4:24:10
Luquillo 46 18N22'28 65w43'01 4:22:52
Luyando 2 18N21'59 67w09'28 4:28:38
Mabi 27 18N18'45 65w41'06 4:22:44
Macana 31 18N03'28 66w46'26 4:27:06
Machuchal 62 18N02'47 66w56'39 4:27:47
Macun 70 18N24'23 66w12'53 4:24:52
Magas Abajo 31 18N01'20 66w47'01 4:27:08
Magas Arriba 31 18N01'10 66w46'10 4:27:05
Magdalena 63 17N58'26 66w16'50 4:25:07
Magnolia Gardens 11 18N22'42 66w10'06 4:24:40
Maguayo 41 18N00'44 67w05'02 4:28:20
Magueyes 29 18N01'18 66w53'18 4:27:33
Magueyes 58 18N02'44 66w38'59 4:26:36
Maizales 53 18N14'05 65w45'38 4:23:03
Malecon 50 18N13'19 67w09'40 4:28:39
Maleza 3 18N28'45 67w07'43 4:28:31

Malpica 61	18N21'21	65w52'07	4:23:28
Mameyal 26	18N28'30	66w16'29	4:25:06
Mameyes (Palmer P O) 61	18N22'20	65w46'14	4:23:05
Manati 47	18N25'46	66w29'33	4:25:58
Mani 50	18N14'34	67w10'12	4:28:41
Mantilla 3	18N27'00	67w00'51	4:28:03
Manzanillo 39	17N58'38	66w32'14	4:26:09
Maracayo 14	18N29'05	66w51'10	4:27:25
Maraguez 58	18N05'28	66w34'45	4:26:19
Margarita 12	18N05'26	67w06'34	4:28:26
Margarita 39	18N07'00	66w32'21	4:26:09
Margarita 46	18N21'19	65w41'57	4:22:48
Maria Jimenez 33	18N16'00	65w56'31	4:23:46
Mariana 16	18N20'08	65w57'13	4:23:49
Mariana 53	18N14'18	65w42'44	4:22:51
Mariani 58	18N00'32	66w37'06	4:26:28
Maricao 48	18N10'58	66w58'49	4:27:55
Marruecos 65	18N26'31	66w04'15	4:24:17
Martin Pena 65	18N25'45	66w03'11	4:24:13
Martorell 77	18N04'41	65w53'55	4:23:36
Marueno 58	18N05'03	66w40'04	4:26:40
Mata y Orsini 6	18N16'07	67w04'48	4:28:19
Matias 2	18N22'18	67w13'29	4:28:54
Matilde 42	18N16'12	66w50'37	4:27:22
Matojillo 14	18N25'57	66w50'52	4:27:23
Maunabo 49	18N00'33	65w53'59	4:23:36
Mayaguez 50	18N12'11	67w08'24	4:28:34
Mayaguez Terrace 50	18N13'03	67w08'53	4:28:36
Mayo 36	18N07'56	65w48'22	4:23:13
Medianía Alta 45	18N25'35	65w50'38	4:23:23
Media Quijada 31	17N59'06	66w50'16	4:27:21
Medina 24	18N18'01	66w17'56	4:25:12
Melillas 44	18N12'31	65w50'38	4:23:23
Membrillo 14	18N28'57	66w52'15	4:27:29
Milagros 42	18N15'25	66w51'19	4:27:25
Minillas 64	18N04'45	66w58'59	4:27:56
Mini Mini 45	18N25'27	65w50'42	4:23:23
Miraflores 7	18N25'32	66w39'07	4:26:36
Miraflores 36	18N07'37	65w47'51	4:23:11
Miramar 50	18N12'52	67w09'21	4:28:37
Miramar 65	18N27'15	66w05'03	4:24:20
Miranda 74	18N23'19	66w23'03	4:25:32
Moca 51	18N23'48	67w06'49	4:28:27
Monserrate 16	18N24'25	65w56'57	4:23:48
Monserrate 46	18N22'53	65w43'52	4:22:55
Monserrate 74	18N26'19	66w21'36	4:25:26
Montana 3	18N29'24	67w05'58	4:28:24
Montana 7	18N21'48	66w36'25	4:26:26
Montebello 47	18N22'12	66w31'25	4:26:06
Monte Carlo 74	18N26'56	66w23'31	4:25:34
Monteflores 65	18N26'23	66w03'21	4:24:13
Monte Grande 7	18N27'53	66w41'42	4:26:47
Monte Grande 12	18N05'22	67w06'28	4:28:26
Monterrey 73	18N25'24	66w18'50	4:25:15
Mora 3	18N28'12	67w01'58	4:28:08
Morales Diaz 12	18N02'23	67w07'38	4:28:31
Morals 13	18N14'01	66w03'33	4:24:14
Morovis 52	18N19'40	66w24'25	4:25:38
Moscou 75	18N09'02	65w25'59	4:21:44
Muelle de Ponce 58	17N58'10	66w37'15	4:26:29
Munoz Grillo 13	18N10'39	66w05'27	4:24:22
Munoz Rivera 32	18N22'34	66w06'25	4:24:26
Munoz Torruellas 43	18N15'24	66w59'09	4:27:57
Naguabo 53	18N12'49	65w44'07	4:22:56
Naranjales 43	18N12'42	66w59'57	4:28:00
Naranjito 54	18N18'10	66w14'43	4:24:59
Negrito 20	18N19'39	66w32'02	4:26:08
Nemesio Canales 65	18N25'22	66w04'47	4:24:19
Nogueras 21	18N08'49	66w09'58	4:24:40
Notre Dame 13	18N14'00	66w02'42	4:24:11
Nuevo 3	18N25'40	67w09'16	4:28:37
Obrero 7	18N28'29	66w44'33	4:26:58
Obrero 65	18N26'10	66w03'10	4:24:13
Ocean Park 65	18N27'15	66w03'17	4:24:13
Oceanview 7	18N28'20	66w44'11	4:26:57
Ojo De Agua 74	18N27'03	66w23'59	4:25:36
Olimpo 30	18N00'14	66w06'31	4:24:26
Olivares 41	18N00'15	67w04'16	4:28:17
Ollas Hondas 39	18N02'56	66w31'46	4:26:07
Oriente 7	18N26'36	66w42'53	4:26:52
Orocovis 55	18N13'44	66w23'29	4:25:34
Ortiga 76	18N10'04	66w26'52	4:25:47
Ortiz 24	18N19'43	66w19'13	4:25:17
Padilla 24	18N19'26	66w20'42	4:25:23
Pajaro Puertorriqueno 11	18N21'55	66w11'21	4:24:45
Pajaros 69	18N22'14	66w13'02	4:24:52
Palmarejo 24	18N19'12	66w17'51	4:25:11
Palmarejo 41	18N02'32	67w04'38	4:28:19
Palmarejo 45	18N23'53	65w53'27	4:23:34
Palmarejo 58	18N02'39	66w33'13	4:26:13
Palma Sola 76	18N05'49	66w27'36	4:25:50
Palmer 61	18N22'20	65w46'14	4:23:05
Palo Alto 47	18N25'25	66w26'54	4:25:48
Palo Blanco 7	18N25'45	66w38'57	4:26:36
Paloma 34	18N26'19	66w48'18	4:27:13
Palomar 14	18N27'16	66w52'31	4:27:30
Palomas 23	18N14'04	66w15'24	4:25:02
Palomas 78	18N00'56	66w52'25	4:27:30
Palo Seco 70	18N27'47	66w08'42	4:24:35
Parabueyon 12	18N05'41	67w09'45	4:28:39
Parada de Senal Fulminante 41	18N03'43	67w02'27	4:28:10
Parada de Senal Irizarry 41	18N02'01	67w01'31	4:28:06
Paraiso 27	18N17'02	65w42'04	4:22:48
Parcelas Falu 65	18N24'18	66w00'59	4:24:04
Parcelas Penuelas 68	18N00'03	66w20'30	4:25:22
Parguera 41	17N58'36	67w02'55	4:28:12
Park Gardens 65	18N23'27	66w01'57	4:24:08
Parkhurst 44	18N10'44	65w52'32	4:23:30
Parkside 32	18N24'34	66w06'12	4:24:25
Parkville 32	18N22'12	66w05'51	4:24:23
Parque 65	18N27'17	66w03'38	4:24:15
Paso Seco 68	18N00'17	66w23'25	4:25:34
Pastillito 39	18N00'39	66w29'11	4:25:57
Pastillo 39	17N59'38	66w29'07	4:25:56
Pastillo 58	18N02'21	66w39'45	4:26:39
Pastillo Cana 58	18N02'29	66w39'53	4:26:40
Pasto Viejo 36	18N10'21	65w47'26	4:23:10
Patagonia 36	18N08'48	65w50'03	4:23:20
Patillas 56	18N00'30	66w00'58	4:24:04
Paulina 46	18N21'20	65w40'54	4:22:44
Pellejas 1	18N12'19	66w42'06	4:26:48
Pena Cortada 50	18N13'27	67w09'35	4:28:38
Pena Pobre 53	18N13'03	65w49'21	4:23:17
Penuelas 57	18N03'30	66w43'19	4:26:53
Penuelas 68	18N00'40	66w21'05	4:25:24
Perchas 67	18N18'38	66w58'52	4:27:55
Perez Morris 65	18N25'02	66w03'14	4:24:13
Pica 30	17N57'54	66w07'27	4:24:30
Pico 64	18N07'51	67w02'39	4:28:11
Piedra Aguzada 39	18N02'24	66w29'36	4:25:58
Piedras Blancas 31	18N01'08	66w47'56	4:27:12
Pina 69	18N22'06	66w13'30	4:24:54
Pinas 23	18N11'11	66w13'41	4:24:55
Pinones 45	18N27'08	65w57'28	4:23:50
Pitahaya 8	17N59'46	66w03'05	4:24:12
Pitahaya 36	18N11'02	65w49'33	4:23:18
Pitahaya 46	18N20'39	65w43'01	4:22:52
Plan Bonito 12	18N08'40	67w09'50	4:28:39
Plantaje 69	18N26'42	66w10'25	4:24:42
Playa Cortada 68	17N58'43	66w26'30	4:25:46
Playa de Fajardo 27	18N20'05	65w37'58	4:22:32
Playa de Guanica 29	17N58'01	66w54'31	4:27:38
Playa de Guayanes 77	18N03'49	65w49'20	4:23:17
Playa de Guayanilla 31	18N00'29	66w46'20	4:27:05
Playa de Humacao 36	18N10'09	65w44'37	4:22:58
Playa de Naguabo 53	18N11'32	65w43'01	4:22:52
Playa de Ponce 58	17N59'02	66w37'16	4:26:29
Playa de Salinas 68	17N57'52	66w18'03	4:25:12
Playa de Santa Isabel 68	17N57'26	66w24'35	4:25:38
Playa Grande 50	18N15'27	67w10'45	4:28:43
Playa Pajaro 50	18N03'01	67w52'00	4:31:28
Playa Sardinera 27	18N20'51	65w38'11	4:22:33
Playita 77	18N02'48	65w54'28	4:23:38
Playita Cortada 68	17N59'13	66w26'22	4:25:45
Playita Machete 30	17N57'05	66w06'51	4:24:27
Poblado Cerro Gordo 73	18N28'58	66w20'41	4:25:23
Poblado Medianía Alta 45	18N25'35	65w50'38	4:23:23
Poblados Abalos 50	18N11	67w09	4:28:36
Poblado Santana 7	18N26'54	66w40'14	4:26:41
Poblado Sitios 31	18N01'30	66w47'36	4:27:10
Poblados Jacaguas 39	18N03'23	66w31'43	4:26:07
Pole Ojea 12	17N58'37	67w11'08	4:28:45
Ponce 58	18N00'47	66w36'52	4:26:27
Ponce de Leon 32	18N22'23	66w06'03	4:24:24
Ponce De Leon 58	18N00'29	66w37'27	4:26:30
Providencia 56	17N59'22	66w00'14	4:24:01
Proyecto Barracon 75	18N08'16	65w27'29	4:21:50
Pueblito de Ponce 37	18N26'09	66w58'04	4:27:52
Pueblo Norte 12	18N05'29	67w08'49	4:28:35
Pueblo Nuevo 12	18N05'26	67w09'02	4:28:36
Pueblo Nuevo 14	18N27'45	66w51'17	4:27:25
Pueblo Nuevo 48	18N10'59	66w58'34	4:27:54
Pueblo Seco 71	18N22'13	66w01'31	4:24:06
Pueblo Sur 12	18N05'12	67w08'45	4:28:35
Puente Blanco 17	18N25'45	66w08'07	4:24:32
Puerto de Jobos 30	17N57'15	66w11'02	4:24:44
Puerto Maunabo 49	17N59'39	65w53'17	4:23:33
Puerto Nuevo 65	18N24'49	66w04'56	4:24:20
Puerto Nuevo Norte 65	18N25'04	66w05'23	4:24:22
Puerto Real 12	18N04'39	67w11'21	4:28:45
Pugnado Afuera 74	18N25'52	66w24'52	4:25:39
Punta Brava 11	18N24'26	66w10'13	4:24:41
Punta Brava 14	18N26'22	66w52'45	4:27:31
Punta Brava 58	18N00'28	66w32'02	4:26:08
Punta Las Marias 65	18N27'13	66w02'25	4:24:10
Punta Santiago 36	18N10'06	65w44'55	4:23:00
Punto Cubano 26	18N24'26	66w18'30	4:25:14
Quebrada 14	18N21'31	66w49'57	4:27:20
Quebrada Grande 10	18N11'12	66w16'36	4:25:06
Quebrada Seca 19	18N14'19	65w39'55	4:22:40
Quebradillas 59	18N28'33	66w56'20	4:27:45
Quemados 66	18N11'04	65w59'14	4:23:57
Quinta Esperanza 58	17N58'13	66w34'05	4:26:16
Rabo del Buey 63	18N02'13	66w14'27	4:24:58
Radioville 7	18N28'40	66w45'06	4:27:00
Rafael Arroyo 9	18N21'59	66w32'49	4:26:11
Rafael Capo 34	18N24'33	66w46'57	4:27:08
Ramon Colon 67	18N18'49	65w58'37	4:23:54
Ramon Nevares 65	18N24'02	66w04'02	4:24:16
Ramon Pabon 52	18N20'08	66w22'10	4:25:29
Real Abajo 58	18N04'46	66w33'58	4:26:16
Real Anon 58	18N07'17	66w34'23	4:26:18
Real Arriba 58	18N05'52	66w33'49	4:26:15
Recio 56	17N58'25	65w57'31	4:23:50
Regadera 73	18N26'30	66w19'57	4:25:20
Reparto Sevilla 65	18N24'15	66w01'13	4:24:05
Reparto Universitario 65	18N23'46	66w02'30	4:24:10
Reunion 30	17N57'27	66w08'35	4:24:34
Rexmanor 30	17N59'07	66w06'14	4:24:25
Rinco 58	18N03'00	66w32'39	4:26:11
Rincon 60	18N20'32	67w15'01	4:29:00
Rio 44	18N13'48	65w51'33	4:23:26
Rio Abajo 36	18N09'10	65w48'12	4:23:13
Rio Abajo 74	18N25'32	66w23'12	4:25:33
Rio Blanco 53	18N13'13	65w47'20	4:23:09
Rio Canas 39	18N03'04	66w25'36	4:25:42
Rio Canas Abajo 39	18N02'25	66w28'05	4:25:52
Rio Grande 61	18N22'56	65w49'54	4:23:20
Rio Hondo 23	18N12'53	66w15'00	4:25:00
Rio Jueyes 22	18N01'23	66w20'00	4:25:20
Rio Lajas 26	18N23'48	66w16'05	4:25:04
Rio Piedras 65	18N23'58	66w03'01	4:24:12
Rivera y Lomas 54	18N19'46	66w16'13	4:25:05
Riverview 11	18N25'01	66w10'24	4:24:42
Robles 5	18N08'08	66w14'56	4:25:00
Rodriguez Hevia 21	18N11'40	66w10'14	4:24:41
Rolling Hills 16	18N22'55	65w59'03	4:23:56
Roosevelt 66	18N11'51	65w57'55	4:23:52
Rosa Maria 16	18N23'13	65w57'10	4:23:49
Rosario 64	18N09'52	67w04'46	4:28:19
Royal Gardens 11	18N22'41	66w10'47	4:24:43
Royal Town 11	18N22'04	66w10'20	4:24:41
Rucio 57	18N05'38	66w41'32	4:26:46
Sabalos 50	18N10'43	67w08'59	4:28:36
Sabana 11	18N19'55	66w11'16	4:24:45
Sabana 46	18N19'36	65w43'41	4:22:55
Sabana 74	18N27'46	66w21'32	4:25:26
Sabana Abajo 16	18N24'42	65w58'59	4:23:56
Sabana Alta 12	18N07'01	67w09'05	4:28:36
Sabana Eneas 64	18N05'17	67w04'53	4:28:20
Sabana Gardens 16	18N24'59	65w58'22	4:23:53
Sabana Grande 62	18N04'47	66w57'39	4:27:51
Sabana Hoyos 7	18N26'09	66w36'51	4:26:27
Sabana Hoyos 22	18N02'20	66w19'53	4:25:20
Sabana Llana 63	18N01'35	66w15'06	4:25:00
Sabana Llana Abajo 39	18N01'17	66w31'42	4:26:07
Sabana Llana Arriba 39	18N02'00	66w30'48	4:26:03
Sabana Seca 47	18N25'04	66w28'31	4:25:54
Sabana Seca 70	18N25'44	66w11'06	4:24:44
Sabanetas 58	18N00'52	66w35'06	4:26:20
Sagrado Corazon 65	18N22'37	66w03'10	4:24:13
Saint Just 71	18N22'12	66w00'44	4:24:03
Saldana 27	18N17'35	65w42'19	4:22:49
Salinas 29	17N56'12	66w57'15	4:27:49
Salinas 63	17N58'46	66w17'54	4:25:12
Samuel Davila 61	18N21'06	65w49'15	4:23:17
San Agustin 64	18N07'45	67w04'27	4:28:18
San Agustin 65	18N23'48	66w02'19	4:24:09
Sana Muerto 55	18N14'35	66w24'28	4:25:38
San Anton 58	18N00'20	66w36'22	4:26:25
San Antonio 3	18N29'39	67w05'56	4:28:24
San Antonio 26	18N27'03	66w18'11	4:25:13
San Antonio 58	18N00'27	66w37'59	4:26:32
San Cristobal 53	18N13'07	65w43'42	4:22:55
San Diego 22	18N06'00	66w20'15	4:25:21
Sandin 74	18N29'14	66w24'42	4:25:39
San Eladio 53	18N12'56	65w47'08	4:23:09
San Felipe 63	17N58'20	66w12'56	4:24:52
San Fernando 65	18N22'24	66w03'48	4:24:15
San Francisco 7	18N27'02	66w42'51	4:26:51
San Francisco 65	18N22'53	66w04'55	4:24:20
San Gerardo 65	18N22'35	66w03'27	4:24:14
San German 64	18N05'01	67w02'43	4:28:11
San Isidro 45	18N23'45	65w53'06	4:23:32
San Isidro 62	18N04'42	66w57'17	4:27:49
San Jose 47	18N26'24	66w29'18	4:25:57
San Jose 50	18N10'40	67w10'23	4:28:42
San Jose 65	18N25'12	66w02'00	4:24:08
San Jose 70	18N24'01	66w15'22	4:25:01
San Juan 65	18N28'06	66w06'22	4:24:25
San Lorenzo 51	18N22'14	67w06'32	4:28:26
San Lorenzo 66	18N11'29	65w57'41	4:23:51
San Luis 7	18N27'12	66w36'28	4:26:26
San Luis 53	18N12'15	65w42'42	4:22:51
San Martin 65	18N23'43	66w00'18	4:24:01
San Miquel 46	18N22'11	65w42'07	4:22:48
San Pedro 7	18N24'36	66w41'58	4:26:48
San Pedro 27	18N18'44	65w39'43	4:22:39
San Ramon 64	18N04'33	67w01'03	4:28:04
San Sebastian 11	18N22'21	66w11'17	4:24:45
San Sebastian 67	18N20'19	66w59'26	4:27:58
Santa Ana 65	18N24'12	66w03'43	4:24:15
Santa Barbara 3	18N26'00	67w09'18	4:28:37
Santa Barbara 7	18N28'10	66w42'17	4:26:49
Santa Barbara 38	18N13'11	66w36'22	4:26:25
Santa Barbara 45	18N23'47	65w55'12	4:23:41
Santa Clara 21	18N10'17	66w08'57	4:24:36
Santa Clara 58	18N01'24	66w36'09	4:26:25
Santa Clara 66	18N11'55	65w58'17	4:23:53
Santa Cruz 58	17N59'01	66w35'45	4:26:23
Santa Elena 30	17N58'22	66w05'58	4:24:24
Santa Elena 31	18N01'42	66w47'29	4:27:10
Santa Isabel 68	17N58'05	66w24'19	4:25:37
Santa Juanita 11	18N21'53	66w09'42	4:24:39
Santa Maria 19	18N16'32	65w38'27	4:22:34
Santa Maria 58	18N00'22	66w37'06	4:26:28
Santa Maria 62	18N04'33	66w57'28	4:27:50
Santa Maria 65	18N22'41	66w05'14	4:24:21
Santa Maria 75	18N09'15	65w25'57	4:21:44
Santa Marta 64	18N04'53	67w01'46	4:28:07
Santa Monica 11	18N23'33	66w10'28	4:24:42
Santana 7	18N26'54	66w40'14	4:26:41
Santa Rita 27	18N19'15	65w38'34	4:22:34
Santa Rita 65	18N24'16	66w03'24	4:24:14
Santa Rosa 11	18N23'18	66w08'32	4:24:34
Santa Rosa Tres 32	18N22'11	66w08'02	4:24:32
Santa Teresa 36	18N08'33	65w48'28	4:23:14
Santa Teresita 65	18N27'04	66w02'44	4:24:11
Santiago 3	18N29'34	67w04'00	4:28:16
Santiago 68	17N59'53	66w21'08	4:25:25
Santiago Iglesias 65	18N23'06	66w05'59	4:24:24
Santiago y Lima 53	18N12'24	65w42'22	4:22:49
Santo Domingo 57	18N03'55	66w45'10	4:27:01
Santurce 50	18N11'50	67w08'26	4:28:34
San Turce 65	18N27	66w05	4:24:20
San Vicente 46	18N21'21	65w44'27	4:22:58
Seboruco 57	18N01'12	66w43'18	4:26:53

Place	Latitude	Longitude	Time
Segui 20	18N18'40	66w34'03	4:26:16
Segundo Castillo 50	18N09'59	67w09'00	4:28:36
Selgas 9	18N21'47	66w34'00	4:26:16
Semil 76	18N07'28	66w31'01	4:26:04
Serrano 39	17N59'40	66w30'01	4:26:00
Shanghai 53	18N12'35	65w44'42	4:22:59
Sierra Bayamon 11	18N24'13	66w10'13	4:24:41
Sierra Brava 65	18N21'07	66w05'38	4:24:23
Sierra Linda 11	18N23'00	66w10'54	4:24:44
Soroco 27	18N22'16	65w37'34	4:22:30
Sosa 12	18N01'24	67w09'28	4:28:38
Suarez 45	18N25'56	65w51'14	4:23:25
Suchville 32	18N23'50	66w07'16	4:24:29
Sumidero 4	18N13'14	66w07'45	4:24:31
Summit Hills 65	18N24'06	66w06'12	4:24:25
Suromar 53	18N11'23	65w43'38	4:22:55
Susua 62	18N02'07	66w54'42	4:27:39
Tablonal 2	18N23'53	67w10'02	4:28:40
Tablones 53	18N14'35	65w44'44	4:22:59
Tabonuco 42	18N17'07	66w53'18	4:27:33
Tallaboa 57	17N59'49	66w43'00	4:26:52
Tallaboa Alta 57	18N03'11	66w42'02	4:26:48
Tallaboa Poniente 57	18N02'02	66w44'04	4:26:56
Tamarindo 3	18N26'15	67w09'20	4:28:37
Tiburones 9	18N26'01	66w34'52	4:26:19
Tiburones 58	17N59'09	66w32'29	4:26:10
Tintillo 11	18N24'25	66w07'46	4:24:31
Tio 11	18N22'20	66w10'32	4:24:42
Toa Alta 69	18N23'25	66w14'55	4:25:00
Toa Baja 70	18N26'45	66w15'36	4:25:02
Toita 18	18N07'57	66w11'25	4:24:46
Toma de Agua 45	18N21'18	65w54'03	4:23:36
Tomas de Castro 13	18N11'23	66w01'36	4:24:06
Torrecillas 20	18N20'27	66w26'06	4:25:44
Torres 5	18N08'47	66w16'34	4:25:06
Torrimar 32	18N23'23	66w07'04	4:24:28
Tosquero 2	18N23'24	67w12'14	4:28:49
Tras Talleres 65	18N26'52	66w04'47	4:24:19
Tres Hermanos 6	18N17'11	67w11'25	4:28:46
Trujillo Alto 71	18N21'24	66w00'28	4:24:02
Trujillo Bajo 16	18N22'12	65w57'21	4:23:49
Truman 65	18N25'10	66w02'24	4:24:10
Tuque 58	17N59'20	66w39'26	4:26:38
Turabo 13	18N13'09	66w03'47	4:24:15
Union 58	17N59'42	66w32'45	4:26:11
United States Navel Reservoi 65	18N24'39	66w05'40	4:24:23
University Gardens 65	18N24'28	66w03'56	4:24:16
Utuado 72	18N16'03	66w42'03	4:26:48
Uvero Desembarcadero 50	18N02'53	67w54'17	4:31:37
Valencia 11	18N24'06	66w11'30	4:24:46
Valencia 40	18N13'41	65w55'08	4:23:41
Valle Arriba Heights 16	18N24'40	65w58'27	4:23:54
Van Scoy 11	18N21'03	66w11'47	4:24:47
Vapor 27	18N18'21	65w40'22	4:22:41
Varela 7	18N22'41	66w37'52	4:26:31
Vavas 58	18N00'04	66w34'42	4:26:19
Vayas 58	18N03'15	66w35'04	4:26:20
Vazquez 63	18N04'04	66w14'20	4:24:57
Vega Alta 73	18N24'51	66w19'54	4:25:20
Vega Baja 74	18N26'47	66w23'17	4:25:33
Vegas 18	18N07'50	66w06'36	4:24:26
Velazquez 68	17N58'31	66w25'02	4:25:40
Ventura 58	18N01'00	66w32'37	4:26:10
Vertedero 5	18N04'56	66w14'44	4:24:59
Victoria 3	18N24'24	67w09'17	4:28:37
Vieques 45	18N25'37	65w50'00	4:23:20
Vieques 75	18N09'04	65w26'35	4:21:46
Villa Andalucia 65	18N23'03	66w01'39	4:24:07
Villa Blanca 13	18N14'44	66w03'04	4:24:12
Villa Borinquen 13	18N10'37	66w02'43	4:24:11
Villa Borinquen 65	18N24'53	66w05'23	4:24:22
Villa Caparra 32	18N24'35	66w06'41	4:24:27
Villa Capri 65	18N23'38	66w01'53	4:24:08
Villa Carolina 16	18N23'59	65w57'45	4:23:51
Villa Clementina 32	18N22'11	66w05'40	4:24:23
Villa Contessa 11	18N22'52	66w10'09	4:24:41
Villa de Rey 13	18N13'00	66w03'42	4:24:15
Villa Espana 11	18N24'03	66w08'21	4:24:33
Villa Esperanza 58	18N01'18	66w36'07	4:26:24
Villa Flores 58	18N00'37	66w35'27	4:26:22
Villa Fontana 16	18N24'23	65w58'26	4:23:54
Villa Graciela 40	18N14'23	65w55'25	4:23:42
Villa Grillasca 58	18N00'08	66w37'26	4:26:30
Villalba 76	18N07'45	66w29'33	4:25:58
Villa Mar 16	18N26'41	66w01'44	4:24:07
Villa Milagros 78	18N01'37	66w51'42	4:27:27
Villa Nevares 65	18N23'38	66w04'11	4:24:17
Villa Palmeras 65	18N26'32	66w03'02	4:24:12
Villa Perez 1	18N11'34	66w46'46	4:27:07
Villa Prades 65	18N24'32	66w01'31	4:24:06
Villa Rica 11	18N23'53	66w10'16	4:24:41
Villodas 30	17N58'37	66w10'46	4:24:43
Vinet 3	18N24'07	67w08'01	4:28:32
Vista Alegre 11	18N23'48	66w09'45	4:24:39
Vista Alegre 49	18N00'49	65w53'53	4:23:36
Vistamar 16	18N25'46	65w58'45	4:23:55
Vista Verde 50	18N11'13	67w09'14	4:28:37
Volcan 11	18N24'40	66w11'07	4:24:44
Yabucoa 77	18N03'09	65w52'47	4:23:31
Yauco 78	18N02'13	66w51'01	4:27:24
Yeguada 14	18N28'52	66w52'58	4:27:32
Yuquiyu 46	18N20'53	65w43'44	4:22:55
Zanja Blanca 22	18N06'08	66w24'30	4:25:38
Zanja Negra 22	18N05'48	66w23'57	4:25:36

TIME TABLES

RI # 1

Before 11/18/1883		LMT
11/18/1883	12:00	EST
3/31/1918	02:00	EWT
10/27/1918	02:00	EST
3/30/1919	02:00	EWT
10/26/1919	02:00	EST
4/29/1923	02:00	EDT
9/30/1923	02:00	EST
4/27/1924	02:00	EDT
9/28/1924	02:00	EST
4/26/1925	02:00	EDT
9/27/1925	02:00	EST
4/25/1926	02:00	EDT
9/26/1926	02:00	EST
4/24/1927	02:00	EDT
9/25/1927	02:00	EST
4/29/1928	02:00	EDT
9/30/1928	02:00	EST
4/28/1929	02:00	EDT
9/29/1929	02:00	EST
4/27/1930	02:00	EDT
9/28/1930	02:00	EST
4/26/1931	02:00	EDT
9/27/1931	02:00	EST
4/24/1932	02:00	EDT
9/25/1932	02:00	EST
4/30/1933	02:00	EDT
9/24/1933	02:00	EST
4/29/1934	02:00	EDT
9/30/1934	02:00	EST
4/28/1935	02:00	EDT
9/29/1935	02:00	EST
4/26/1936	02:00	EDT
9/27/1936	02:00	EST
4/25/1937	02:00	EDT
9/26/1937	02:00	EST
4/24/1938	02:00	EDT
10/01/1938	02:00	EST
4/30/1939	02:00	EDT
9/24/1939	02:00	EST
4/28/1940	02:00	EDT
9/29/1940	02:00	EST
4/27/1941	02:00	EDT
9/28/1941	02:00	EST
2/09/1942	02:00	US#2

RI # 2

Before 11/18/1883		LMT
11/18/1883	12:00	EST
3/31/1918	02:00	EWT
10/27/1918	02:00	EST
3/30/1919	02:00	EWT
10/26/1919	02:00	EST
4/27/1924	02:00	EDT
9/28/1924	02:00	EST
4/26/1925	02:00	EDT
9/27/1925	02:00	EST
4/25/1926	02:00	EDT
9/26/1926	02:00	EST
4/24/1927	02:00	EDT
9/25/1927	02:00	EST
4/29/1928	02:00	EDT
9/30/1928	02:00	EST
4/28/1929	02:00	EDT
9/29/1929	02:00	EST
4/27/1930	02:00	EDT
9/28/1930	02:00	EST
4/26/1931	02:00	EDT
9/27/1931	02:00	EST
4/24/1932	02:00	EDT
9/25/1932	02:00	EST
4/30/1933	02:00	EDT
9/24/1933	02:00	EST
4/29/1934	02:00	EDT
9/30/1934	02:00	EST
4/28/1935	02:00	EDT
9/29/1935	02:00	EST
4/26/1936	02:00	EDT
9/27/1936	02:00	EST
4/25/1937	02:00	EDT
9/26/1937	02:00	EST
4/24/1938	02:00	EDT
10/01/1938	02:00	EST
4/30/1939	02:00	EDT
9/24/1939	02:00	EST
4/28/1940	02:00	EDT
9/29/1940	02:00	EST
4/27/1941	02:00	EDT
9/28/1941	02:00	EST
2/09/1942	02:00	US#2

COUNTIES

1 Bristol
2 Kent
3 Newport
4 Providence
5 Washington

Place	TT	Lat	Long	Time
Abbott Run 4	1	41n57'19	71w23'22	4:45:33
Abbott Run Valley 4	1	41n55	71w24	4:45:36
Adamsville 3	1	41n33'16	71w07'54	4:44:32
Albion 4	1	41n57'04	71w27'18	4:45:49
Allendale 4	1	41n51'00	71w28'16	4:45:53
Allenton 5	1	41n32'38	71w28'06	4:45:52
Alton 5	1	41n26'15	71w43'04	4:46:52
Annawomscutt 1	1	41n44'25	71w20'40	4:45:23
Anthony 2	1	41n41'42	71w32'59	4:46:12
Apple Blossom 4	1	41n47	71w26	4:45:44
Apponaug 2	1	41n42'01	71w27'37	4:45:50
Arcadia 5	1	41n30	71w43	4:46:52
Arctic 2	1	41n42'11	71w31'44	4:46:07
Arkwright 4	1	41n43'43	71w32'56	4:46:12
Arlington 4	1	41n47	71w26	4:45:44
Armington Corner 4	1	41n47'53	71w21'50	4:45:27
Arnold Mills 4	1	41n58'42	71w23'33	4:45:34
Arnold's Neck 2	1	41n42	71w26	4:45:44
Ashaway 5	1	41n25'24	71w47'10	4:47:09
Ashton 5	1	41n56'20	71w25'52	4:45:43
Atlantic Beach 5	1	41n22	71w50	4:47:20
Auburn 4	1	41n46'26	71w25'42	4:45:43
Austin 5	1	41n35	71w32	4:46:08
Avondale 5	1	41n20'04	71w50'09	4:47:21
Barberville 5	1	41n32'21	71w41'57	4:46:48
Barrington 1	1	41n44'26	71w18'33	4:45:14
Bartons Corner 2	1	41n39'46	71w29'54	4:46:00
Bayridge 2	1	41n40	71w28	4:45:52
Bayside 2	1	41n42'04	71w22'36	4:45:30
Bay Spring 1	1	41n44'53	71w20'50	4:45:23
Bay View 4	1	41n49	71w22	4:45:28
Beach Terrace 1	1	41n43'01	71w17'03	4:45:08
Bellefonte 4	1	41n47	71w26	4:45:44
Belleville 5	1	41n33'14	71w28'09	4:45:53
Berkeley 4	1	41n55'47	71w25'24	4:45:42
Bethel 5	1	41n25'43	71w47'28	4:47:10
Beverage Hill 4	1	41n53	71w23	4:45:32
Birch Swamp Corner 1	1	41n45'07	71w15'42	4:45:03
Bishop Heights 4	1	41n49'35	71w33'29	4:46:14
Black Plain 5	1	41n35'04	71w39'10	4:46:37
Bliss Corners 3	1	41n37'35	71w08'43	4:44:35
Block Island 5	1	41n10	71w34	4:46:16
Bonnet Shores 5	1	41n28'57	71w25'19	4:45:41
Boon Lake 5	1	41n35	71w32	4:46:08
Bowdish Lake 4	1	41n55	71w40	4:46:40
Boyden Heights 4	1	41n49	71w22	4:45:28
Bradford 5	1	41n23'56	71w44'51	4:46:59
Branch Village 4	1	41n59'55	71w32'57	4:46:12
Brenton Village 3	1	41n28'28	71w20'21	4:45:21
Bridgeport 3	1	41n38	71w12	4:44:48
Bridgeton 4	1	41n57'56	71w42'20	4:46:49
Bridgetown 5	1	41n29'14	71w26'44	4:45:47
Briggs Beach 3	1	41n30	71w10	4:44:40
Bristol 1	1	41n40'30	71w16'16	4:45:05
Bristol Colony 3	1	41n36	71w20	4:45:20
Bristol Ferry 3	1	41n37'57	71w15'15	4:45:01
Bristol Highlands 1	1	41n41'46	71w17'16	4:45:09
Bristol Narrows 1	1	41n41	71w16	4:45:04
Broadway 3	1	41n30	71w19	4:45:16
Brookfield 4	1	41n47	71w26	4:45:44
Brown 4	1	41n49	71w26	4:45:44
Brudickville 5	1	41n25'04	71w43'49	4:46:55
Brush Neck Cove 2	1	41n42	71w26	4:45:44
Bullocks Point 4	1	41n49	71w22	4:45:28
Burdickville 5	1	41n24	71w45	4:47:00
Burrillville 4	1	41n57	71w40	4:46:40
Buttonwoods 2	1	41n41'07	71w25'09	4:45:41
Canonchet 5	1	41n44'24	71w44'56	4:47:00
Carolina 5	1	41n27'25	71w39'50	4:46:39
Carpenters Beach 5	1	41n26	71w30	4:46:00
Carpenters Corner 4	1	41n49'18	71w21'24	4:45:26
Cedar Grove 5	1	41n35	71w32	4:46:08
Cedar Point 3	1	41n29	71w22	4:45:28
Cedar Tree Point 2	1	41n42	71w26	4:45:44
Centerdale 4	1	41n51'23	71w28'45	4:45:55
Centerville 2	1	41n41'47	71w31'23	4:46:06
Centerville 5	1	41n31'20	71w44'49	4:46:59
Central Falls 4	1	41n53'26	71w23'34	4:45:34
Charlestown 5	1	41n22'59	71w38'32	4:46:34
Charlestown Beach 5	1	41n22'05	71w37'42	4:46:31
Chepachet 4	1	41n54'54	71w40'19	4:46:41
Chepiwanoxet 2	1	41n40'22	71w26'55	4:45:48
Cherry Valley 4	1	41n52'15	71w40'30	4:46:42
Cherry Valley Beach 4	1	41n55	71w40	4:46:40
Chopmist 4	1	41n49'31	71w40'15	4:46:41
Clarks Village 3	1	41n27'45	71w23'28	4:45:34
Clarkville 4	1	41n55'20	71w47'30	4:47:10
Clayville 4	1	41n46'40	71w40'34	4:46:42
Clyde 2	1	41n43'09	71w31'24	4:46:06
Coasters Harbor 3	1	41n30	71w19	4:45:16
Coddington Point 3	1	41n30	71w19	4:45:16
Coggeshall 1	1	41n41'59	71w14'22	4:44:57
Cold Spring Beach 5	1	41n33'60	71w26'38	4:45:47
Cold Springs Beach 5	1	41n38	71w27	4:45:48
Coles 2	1	41n43'45	71w23'38	4:45:35
Columbia Heights 5	1	41n26'32	71w38'19	4:46:33
Colvintown 2	1	41n43'05	71w34'20	4:46:17
Common Fence Point 3	1	41n36	71w15	4:45:00
Commons 3	1	41n30	71w10	4:44:40
Comstock Gardens 4	1	41n46'39	71w31'24	4:46:06
Conanicut Park 3	1	41n33'42	71w21'53	4:45:28
Conimicut 2	1	41n43'27	71w23'00	4:45:32
Cooks Corner 3	1	41n36'16	71w31'19	4:46:05
Corey's Lane 3	1	41n36	71w15	4:45:00
Coventry 2	1	41n42	71w34	4:46:16
Cowesett 2	1	41n40'52	71w27'42	4:45:51
Cranston 4	1	41n46'47	71w26'16	4:45:45
Crescent Park 4	1	41n49	71w22	4:45:28
Crompton 2	1	41n41'05	71w30'51	4:46:03
Cross Mills 5	1	41n23	71w45	4:47:00
Cumberland 4	1	41n57	71w25	4:45:40
Cumberland Hill 4	1	41n58'36	71w27'33	4:45:50
Curtis Corner 5	1	41n27'14	71w31'44	4:46:07
Darlington 4	1	41n53'06	71w21'49	4:45:27
Davisville 5	1	41n36'48	71w28'33	4:45:54
Diamond Hill 4	1	41n59'16	71w24'45	4:45:39
Dryden Heights 2	1	41n44	71w24	4:45:36
Dunn Corners 5	1	41n21'05	71w46'09	4:47:05
Dunn Landing 5	1	41n10'53	71w36'25	4:46:26
Durfee Hill 4	1	41n55	71w40	4:46:40
Dyerville 4	1	41n49'33	71w27'31	4:45:50
Eagleville 3	1	41n39'28	71w09'10	4:44:37
East Greenwich 2	1	41n39'37	71w27'23	4:45:50
East Matunuck 5	1	41n26	71w30	4:46:00
East Natick 2	1	41n43'07	71w28'57	4:45:56
East Providence 4	1	41n48'49	71w22'14	4:45:29
East Providence Center 4	1	41n50'04	71w20'54	4:45:24
East Providence Wharf 4	1	41n49	71w22	4:45:28
East Side 4	1	41n50	71w24	4:45:36
East Warren 1	1	41n44	71w16	4:45:04
Echo Lake 4	1	41n55	71w40	4:46:40
Eden Park 4	1	41n47	71w26	4:45:44
Edgewood 4	1	41n46'53	71w23'53	4:45:36
Ellis Flats 5	1	41n27'21	71w41'55	4:46:48
Elmwood 4	1	41n47'52	71w25'36	4:45:42
Enos 4	1	41n47	71w26	4:45:44
Escoheag 3	1	41n30'13	71w46'55	4:47:04
Esmond 4	1	41n52'20	71w29'42	4:45:59
Exeter 5	1	41n34'39	71w32'17	4:46:09
Fairbanks Corner 2	1	41n42'28	71w45'26	4:47:02
Fairlawn 4	1	41n52'34	71w24'48	4:45:39
Fairmount 4	1	42n00	71w30	4:46:00
Finast 4	1	41n49	71w22	4:45:28
Fisherville 5	1	41n33'53	71w33'46	4:46:15
Fiskeville 4	1	41n44'03	71w32'55	4:46:12
Fogland Point 3	1	41n38	71w12	4:44:48
Folly Landing 2	1	41n40'52	71w26'57	4:45:48
Forestdale 4	1	41n56'45	71w42'01	4:46:48
Fort Adams 3	1	41n30	71w19	4:45:16
Fort Ninigret 5	1	41n22'50	71w38'59	4:46:36
Foster 4	2	41n51'13	71w45'31	4:47:02
Fountain Spring 4	1	41n51'42	71w31'54	4:46:08
Frenchtown 2	1	41n37'38	71w29'35	4:45:58
Friar 4	1	41n49	71w26	4:45:44
Fruit Hill 4	1	41n50	71w28	4:45:52
Frys Corner 2	1	41n38'44	71w29'45	4:45:59
Galilee 5	1	41n22'36	71w30'49	4:46:03
Garden City 4	1	41n45'44	71w27'08	4:45:49
Gaspee Point 2	1	41n44	71w24	4:45:36
Gazzaville 4	1	41n56'23	71w38'50	4:46:35
Geneva 4	1	41n50	71w28	4:45:52
Georgiaville 4	1	41n53'13	71w30'32	4:46:02
Glendale 4	1	41n58'34	71w37'59	4:46:32
Globe 4	1	41n59'25	71w31'27	4:46:06
Glocester 4	1	41n53	71w40	4:46:40
Goat Island 3	1	41n30	71w19	4:45:16
Gortons Corner 2	1	41n40'54	71w40'05	4:46:40
Gould 5	1	41n27'30	71w31'15	4:46:05
Graniteville 4	1	41n51'41	71w29'35	4:45:58
Grants Mills 4	1	42n00'25	71w24'59	4:45:40
Greene 2	1	41n41'28	71w44'47	4:46:59
Green Hill 5	1	41n22'04	71w35'43	4:46:23
Greenville 4	1	41n52'16	71w33'09	4:46:13
Greenwood 2	1	41n42'30	71w26'41	4:45:47
Greystone 4	1	41n51'59	71w29'27	4:45:58
Hamilton 5	1	41n32'54	71w26'30	4:45:46
Hamiltons Corner 3	1	41n36'30	71w30'39	4:46:03
Hamlet 4	1	42n00'03	71w30'19	4:46:01
Hampden Meadows 1	1	41n44	71w19	4:45:16
Harmony 4	1	41n53'16	71w35'50	4:46:23
Harris 2	1	41n43'28	71w31'59	4:46:08
Harrisville 4	1	41n57'56	71w40'30	4:46:42
Haversham 5	1	41n20'50	71w44'14	4:46:57
Highland Beach 2	1	41n41'47	71w22'01	4:45:28
Hillsdale 5	1	41n31'17	71w38'27	4:46:34
Hillsgrove 2	1	41n43'34	71w26'23	4:45:46
Hog Island 3	1	41n41	71w16	4:45:04
Homestead 3	1	41n37'23	71w18'28	4:45:14
Hope 4	1	41n44'00	71w33'47	4:46:15
Hope Valley 5	1	41n30'27	71w43'00	4:46:52
Hopkins Hollow 2	1	41n40'11	71w45'12	4:47:01
Hopkinton 5	1	41n27'40	71w46'41	4:47:07
Howard 4	1	41n47	71w28	4:45:52
Hoxsie 2	1	41n43'59	71w24'41	4:45:39
Hughesdale 4	1	41n48'29	71w29'39	4:45:59
Indian Lake Shores 5	1	41n28'29	71w27'41	4:45:51
Isaacs Corner 5	1	41n09'51	71w33'50	4:46:15
Island Park 3	1	41n37'24	71w13'40	4:44:55
Jackson 4	1	41n44'19	71w33'00	4:46:12
Jamestown 3	1	41n29'49	71w22'04	4:45:28
Jamestown Shores 3	1	41n31'47	71w23'23	4:45:34
Jerusalem 5	1	41n22'36	71w31'05	4:46:04
Johnston 4	1	41n50	71w30	4:46:00
Kent Corner 4	1	41n46'19	71w21'06	4:45:24
Kent Heights 4	1	41n49	71w22	4:45:28
Kenyon 5	1	41n26'49	71w37'34	4:46:30
Kettle Corner 2	1	41n42'27	71w23'56	4:45:36
Kiefeer Park 5	1	41n35'22	71w26'05	4:45:44
Kingston 5	1	41n28'49	71w31'23	4:46:06
Kingston Station 5	1	41n29'02	71w34'37	4:46:18
Kitts Corner 2	1	41n38'35	71w37'28	4:46:30
Knightsville 4	1	41n46'53	71w27'46	4:45:51
Lafayette 5	1	41n34'14	71w28'40	4:45:55
Lake Bel Air 4	1	42n00	71w30	4:46:00
Lake Mishnock 2	1	41n41	71w34	4:46:16
Lakewood 2	1	41n44'52	71w24'03	4:45:36
Langworthy Corner 5	1	41n20'31	71w46'09	4:47:05
Laurel Hill 4	1	41n57	71w42	4:46:48
Laurel Park 1	1	41n43'07	71w15'49	4:45:03
Lawtons 3	1	41n33'24	71w18'10	4:45:13
Leonard Corner 4	1	41n48'39	71w21'35	4:45:26
Liberty 5	1	41n32'24	71w34'26	4:46:18
Lime Rock 4	1	41n55'43	71w27'03	4:45:48
Lincoln 4	1	41n55	71w26	4:45:44
Lincoln Park 2	1	41n44'15	71w26'04	4:45:44
Lippitt 2	1	41n43'17	71w31'31	4:46:06
Lippitt Estate 4	1	41n57'22	71w25'14	4:45:41
Little Compton 3	1	41n30'36	71w10'18	4:44:41
Longmeadow 2	1	41n42'00	71w22'27	4:45:30
Lonsdale 4	1	41n54'26	71w24'15	4:45:37
Luther Corner 4	1	41n48'30	71w20'23	4:45:22

Lymansville 4 1 41N50'29 71w28'23 4:45:54
Manton 4 1 41N50'11 71w28'08 4:45:53
Manville 4 1 41N58'11 71w28'27 4:45:54
Maple Root Village 2
1 41N41 71w34 4:46:16
Mapleville 4 1 41N56'53 71w38'57 4:46:36
Marieville 4 1 41N52'06 71w26'04 4:45:44
Matunuck 5 1 41N22'42 71w32'47 4:46:11
McGowan Corners 5
1 41N22'44 71w45'44 4:47:03
Melville 3 1 41N35'13 71w17'02 4:45:08
Meshanticut 4 1 41N45'60 71w28'19 4:45:53
Middletown 3 1 41N32'44 71w17'31 4:45:10
Millville 5 1 41N34'27 71w40'57 4:46:44
Misquamicut 5 1 41N19'20 71w48'37 4:47:14
Mohegan 4 1 41N59'09 71w37'23 4:46:30
Mohegan Bluffs 5
1 41N10 71w34 4:46:16
Mooresfield 5 1 41N29'26 71w29'18 4:45:57
Moosehorn Corner 2
1 41N39'12 71w32'35 4:46:10
Moosup Valley 4 1 41N44'13 71w45'40 4:47:03
Moscow 5 1 41N31'22 71w44'31 4:46:58
Mount Saint Joseph College 5
1 41N26 71w30 4:46:00
Mount Vernon 4 1 41N51 71w46 4:47:04
Mount View 5 1 41N38'08 71w24'40 4:45:39
Nannaquaket 3 1 41N38 71w12 4:44:48
Narragansett 5 1 41N26 71w27 4:45:48
Narragansett Beach 5
1 41N26'14 71w27'06 4:45:48
Narragansett Heights 3
1 41N38 71w12 4:44:48
Narragansett Pier 5
1 41N25'56 71w27'25 4:45:50
Nasonville 4 1 41N58'54 71w37'02 4:46:28
Natick 2 1 41N43'12 71w29'32 4:45:58
Nausauket 2 1 41N41'25 71w26'19 4:45:45
Naval Training Station 3
1 41N30 71w19 4:45:16
Nayatt 1 1 41N43'37 71w20'11 4:45:21
New Harbor 5 1 41N10 71w34 4:46:16
Newport 3 1 41N29'24 71w18'48 4:45:15
New Shoreham 5 1 41N10'18 71w33'30 4:46:14
Nichols Corner 2
1 41N38'52 71w28'30 4:45:54
Nooseneck 2 1 41N37'50 71w37'52 4:46:31
North 4 1 41N50 71w26 4:45:44
North Foster 4 1 41N49'53 71w45'04 4:47:00
North Kingstown 5
1 41N36 71w27 4:45:48
North Providence 4
1 41N51 71w28 4:45:52
North Quidnessett 5
1 41N38'19 71w25'10 4:45:41
North Scituate 4
1 41N49'54 71w35'16 4:46:21
North Smithfield 4
1 41N59 71w33 4:46:12
North Tiverton 3
1 41N39'53 71w11'31 4:44:46
Norwood 2 1 41N45'07 71w25'43 4:45:43
Oakland 4 1 41N57'26 71w38'54 4:46:36
Oakland Beach 2 1 41N41'33 71w23'58 4:45:36
Oaklawn 4 1 41N45'07 71w28'40 4:45:55
Oak Valley 4 1 41N57'56 71w36'01 4:46:24
Old Harbor 5 1 41N10 71w34 4:46:16
Old Harbor Landing 5
1 41N09'58 71w32'57 4:46:12
Olney Arnold Estates 4
1 41N47 71w26 4:45:44
Olneyville 4 1 41N48'53 71w26'49 4:45:47
Palace Garden 2 1 41N44'32 71w24'05 4:45:36
Pascoag 4 1 41N57'20 71w42'10 4:46:49
Pawtucket 4 1 41N52'43 71w22'59 4:45:32
Pawtuxet 2 1 41N45'46 71w23'26 4:45:34
Peace Dale 5 1 41N27'04 71w29'47 4:45:59
Peck Corner 1 1 41N45'28 71w20'27 4:45:22
Perryville 5 1 41N23'59 71w33'42 4:46:15
Pettaquamscutt Lake Shores 5
1 41N29'35 71w26'47 4:45:47
Phenix 2 1 41N43'11 71w31'59 4:46:08
Phillipsdale 4 1 41N50'49 71w21'59 4:45:28
Pine Hill 5 1 41N34'40 71w37'40 4:46:31
Places Corner 3 1 41N37'29 71w30'45 4:46:03
Pleasant View 4 1 41N53 71w23 4:45:32
Plum Beach 5 1 41N31'24 71w24'58 4:45:40
Plum Point 5 1 41N30 71w25 4:45:40

Poccasett Heights 3
1 41N38 71w15 4:45:00
Point Judith 5 1 41N21'55 71w29'14 4:45:57
Pontiac 4 1 41N43'52 71w28'45 4:45:55
Popasquash Point 1
1 41N41 71w16 4:45:04
Poplar Point 5 1 41N38 71w27 4:45:48
Portsmouth 3 1 41N36'08 71w15'03 4:45:00
Portsmouth Park 3
1 41N37'06 71w14'29 4:44:58
Potowomut 2 1 41N39'50 71w25'21 4:45:41
Potter Hill 5 1 41N24'49 71w47'58 4:47:12
Pottersville 3 1 41N31'30 71w07'60 4:44:32
Potterville 4 1 41N43'07 71w40'12 4:46:41
Primrose 4 1 41N57'15 71w33'25 4:46:14
Print Works 4 1 41N47 71w26 4:45:44
Providence 4 1 41N49'26 71w24'48 4:45:39
Prudence Island 3
1 41N36 71w20 4:45:20
Prudence Park 3 1 41N36'15 71w19'49 4:45:19
Quaker Hill 3 1 41N36 71w15 4:45:00
Quidnessett 5 1 41N37'38 71w27'14 4:45:49
Quidnick 2 1 41N41'47 71w32'15 4:46:09
Quinnville 4 1 41N55'57 71w26'02 4:45:44
Quonochontaug 5 1 41N20'08 71w42'32 4:46:50
Quonochontaug Beach 5
1 41N19'54 71w43'20 4:46:53
Rice City 2 1 41N42'42 71w45'12 4:47:01
Rice Plat 4 1 41N50 71w35 4:46:20
Richmond 5 1 41N29 71w39 4:46:36
River Point 2 1 41N43'01 71w31'04 4:46:04
Riverside 4 1 41N46'02 71w21'55 4:45:28
River View 2 1 41N42'40 71w22'14 4:45:29
Rockville 3 1 41N31'11 71w45'42 4:47:03
Rocky Brook 5 1 41N27'13 71w30'14 4:46:01
Rodman Crossing 5
1 41N26'20 71w29'14 4:45:57
Round Top 4 1 41N59'59 71w42'03 4:46:48
Rumford 4 1 41N50'43 71w21'09 4:45:25
Rumstick Point 1
1 41N44 71w19 4:45:16
Sachuest 3 1 41N28'49 71w14'31 4:44:58
Sakonnet 3 1 41N27'45 71w11'42 4:44:47
Sandy Point 2 1 41N40 71w28 4:45:52
Sandy Point 5 1 41N10 71w34 4:46:16
Saunderstown 5 1 41N30'28 71w25'30 4:45:42
Saundersville 4 1 41N48'56 71w34'29 4:46:18
Saylesville 4 1 41N53'55 71w24'49 4:45:39
Saylesville Highlands 4
1 41N53'27 71w25'17 4:45:41
Scarborough Hills 5
1 41N23'19 71w28'40 4:45:55
Scituate 4 2 41N49 71w37 4:46:28
Seaweed Beach 5 1 41N22'15 71w29'25 4:45:58
Shady Harbor 5 1 41N20'55 71w43'17 4:46:53
Shannock 5 1 41N26'54 71w38'14 4:46:33
Shawomet 2 1 41N43'01 71w22'34 4:45:30
Shelter Harbor 5
1 41N20'24 71w42'02 4:46:48
Shippee Corner 2
1 41N38'35 71w31'20 4:46:05
Shores Acres 5 1 41N34'57 71w26'12 4:45:45
Simmons Corner 4
1 41N48'54 71w44'04 4:46:56
Simmonsville 4 1 41N48'04 71w30'07 4:46:00
Slatersville 4 1 42N00'01 71w34'49 4:46:19
Slocum 5 1 41N31'50 71w30'60 4:46:04
Smithfield 4 1 41N55'19 71w32'60 4:46:12
Snug Harbor 5 1 41N23'20 71w31'14 4:46:05
Social 4 1 42N00'14 71w30'32 4:46:02
Sockannosset 4 1 41N47 71w26 4:45:44
South Ferry 5 1 41N29'32 71w25'18 4:45:41
South Foster 4 1 41N49'22 71w42'15 4:46:49
South Hopkinton 5
1 41N24'43 71w45'33 4:47:02
South Kingstown 5
1 41N27 71w32 4:46:08
South Portsmouth 3
1 41N32'41 71w15'42 4:45:03
South Warren 1 1 41N44 71w16 4:45:04
Spencer Corner 2
1 41N39'26 71w31'38 4:46:07
Sprague Park 5 1 41N23 71w28 4:45:52
Spragueville 4 1 41N53'26 71w32'30 4:46:10
Spring Green 2 1 41N44'24 71w24'44 4:45:39
Spring Grove 4 1 41N54'47 71w39'11 4:46:37
Spring Lake 2 1 41N40'47 71w34'39 4:46:19

Spring Lake Beach 4
1 41N58 71w38 4:46:32
Squantum 4 1 41N49 71w22 4:45:28
Stillmanville 5 1 41N23'29 71w49'24 4:47:18
Stillwater 4 1 41N54'28 71w31'23 4:46:06
Summit 2 1 41N41 71w44 4:46:56
Tarbox Corner 2 1 41N38'30 71w32'49 4:46:11
Tarkiln 4 1 41N57'18 71w36'24 4:46:26
The Anchorage 3 1 41N31 71w18 4:45:12
The Hummocks 3 1 41N36 71w15 4:45:00
Thornton 4 1 41N47'39 71w28'44 4:45:55
Tiverton 3 1 41N37'33 71w12'50 4:44:51
Tiverton Four Corners 3
1 41N38 71w12 4:44:48
Tonomy Hill 3 1 41N30 71w19 4:45:16
Touisset 1 1 41N42'56 71w14'06 4:44:56
Touisset Highlands 1
1 41N42'39 71w14'26 4:44:58
Tripps Corner 5 1 41N32'33 71w36'05 4:46:24
Tuckertown 5 1 41N25'49 71w32'35 4:46:10
Tuckertown Four Corners 5
1 41N25'42 71w33'35 4:46:14
Tug Hollow 5 1 41N33'35 71w38'44 4:46:35
Tunipus 3 1 41N30 71w10 4:44:40
Union Village 4 1 41N59'28 71w32'23 4:46:10
Usquepaug 5 1 41N30'11 71w36'34 4:46:26
Valley Falls 4 1 41N54'24 71w23'28 4:45:34
Vaughn Hollow 2 1 41N43'10 71w45'23 4:47:02
Wakefield 5 1 41N26'14 71w30'07 4:46:00
Waldron Corners 4
1 41N52'26 71w36'12 4:46:25
Walnut Hill 4 1 42N00 71w30 4:46:00
Warren 1 1 41N43'49 71w16'59 4:45:08
Warren Point 3 1 41N30 71w10 4:44:40
Warwick 2 1 41N41'31 71w22'45 4:45:31
Warwick Neck 2 1 41N43 71w23 4:45:32
Washington 2 1 41N41'18 71w34'02 4:46:16
Washington Park 4
1 41N47 71w26 4:45:44
Watch Hill 5 1 41N22 71w50 4:47:20
Watchmocket Square 4
1 41N49 71w22 4:45:28
Waterford 4 1 42N00'44 71w32'19 4:46:09
Waterman Four Corners 4
1 41N50 71w35 4:46:20
Weekapaug 5 1 41N19'51 71w45'20 4:47:01
Weekapaug Beach 5
1 41N19'49 71w41'45 4:46:47
Wescott 4 1 41N53'11 71w41'25 4:46:46
West Barrington 1
1 41N44'37 71w20'31 4:45:22
Westcott 2 1 41N42'53 71w29'46 4:45:59
Westcott Beach 4
1 41N55 71w40 4:46:40
Westerly 5 1 41N22'39 71w49'40 4:47:19
West Gloucester 4
1 41N55'00 71w47'34 4:47:10
West Greenville 4
1 41N52'39 71w34'19 4:46:17
West Greenwich 2
1 41N37 71w37 4:46:28
West Greenwich Center 2
1 41N41 71w44 4:46:56
West Kingston 5 1 41N28'59 71w33'07 4:46:12
West Warwick 2 1 41N42'22 71w31'25 4:46:06
Weybosset Hill 4
1 41N49 71w25 4:45:40
Whipple 4 1 41N57'50 71w39'29 4:46:38
Whitehall 3 1 41N30'51 71w16'39 4:45:07
White Rock 5 1 41N24'01 71w50'21 4:47:21
Wickford 5 1 41N34'26 71w27'43 4:45:51
Wightmans Corner 3
1 41N37'12 71w32'11 4:46:09
Wildes Corner 2 1 41N42'21 71w25'06 4:45:40
Wild Goose Point 5
1 41N38 71w27 4:45:48
Wood Estates 2 1 41N41 71w34 4:46:16
Woodlawn 4 1 41N52'00 71w23'59 4:45:36
Wood River Junction 5
1 41N26'10 71w41'42 4:46:47
Woods Corner 3 1 41N37'25 71w32'40 4:46:11
Woodville 4 1 41N51'44 71w26'47 4:45:47
Woodville 5 1 41N27'34 71w43'09 4:46:53
Woonsocket 4 1 42N00'10 71w30'55 4:46:04
Wyoming 5 1 41N30'55 71w42'07 4:46:48
Yorktown Manor 5
1 41N38 71w27 4:45:48

TIME TABLES

Date	Time	Zone
Before 11/18/1883		LMT
11/18/1883	12:00	EST
3/31/1918	02:00	EWT
10/27/1918	02:00	EST
3/30/1919	02:00	EWT
10/26/1919	02:00	EST
2/09/1942	02:00	EWT
9/30/1945	02:00	EST
4/30/1967	02:00	US#1

COUNTIES

1 Abbeville
2 Aiken
3 Allendale
4 Anderson
5 Bamberg
6 Barnwell
7 Beaufort
8 Berkeley
9 Calhoun
10 Charleston
11 Cherokee
12 Chester
13 Chesterfield
14 Clarendon
15 Colleton
16 Darlington
17 Dillon
18 Dorchester
19 Edgefield
20 Fairfield
21 Florence
22 Georgetown
23 Greenville
24 Greenwood
25 Hampton
26 Horry
27 Jasper
28 Kershaw
29 Lancaster
30 Laurens
31 Lee
32 Lexington
33 McCormick
34 Marion
35 Marlboro
36 Newberry
37 Oconee
38 Orangeburg
39 Pickens
40 Richland
41 Saluda
42 Spartanburg
43 Sumter
44 Union
45 Williamsburg
46 York

Place	Lat	Long	Time
Abbeville 1	34N10'41	82W22'45	5:29:31
Abingdon 11	34N59'32	81W29'59	5:26:00
Abney Crossroads 28	34N30'31	80W30'51	5:22:03
Adamsburg 44	34N47'28	81W32'35	5:26:10
Adams Crossing 37	34N39'08	82W51'59	5:31:28
Adams Landing 14	33N31'39	80W26'18	5:21:45
Adams Run 10	32N43'14	80W20'54	5:21:24
Adamsville Crossroads 35	34N41'17	79W35'45	5:18:23
Adger 20	34N26'11	81W07'33	5:24:30
Adrian 26	33N56'48	79W01'04	5:16:04
Aiken 2	33N33'37	81W43'11	5:26:53
Albemarle 10	32N48	80W00	5:20:00
Alcolu 14	33N45'03	80W12'52	5:20:51
Alcot 31	34N15'02	80W10'49	5:20:43
Alexander Crossroads 16	34N11'49	79W55'50	5:19:43
Algary 24	34N23	82W21	5:29:24
Alice Mill 39	34N50	82W37	5:30:28
Allen 26	33N55'16	79W02'27	5:16:10
Allendale 3	33N00'28	81W18'31	5:25:14
Allentown 22	33N37'33	79W21'02	5:17:24
Alliance 20	34N21	81W08	5:24:32
Allsbrook 26	34N01'12	78W56'48	5:15:47
Almeda 25	32N49'47	81W02'58	5:24:12
Alston 20	34N14'36	81W19'01	5:25:16
Alta Vista 40	34N02	80W59	5:23:56
Alvin 8	33N20'56	79W48'59	5:19:16
American Spinning 23	34N52	82W23	5:29:32
Ampere 24	34N12	82W09	5:28:36
Anderson 4	34N30'12	82W39'01	5:30:36
Andrews 45	33N27'04	79W33'40	5:18:15
Angelus 13	34N35'48	80W19'12	5:21:17
Angle Siding 7	32N27	80W44	5:22:56
Anne 22	33N28'22	79W15'14	5:17:01
Annieville 22	33N32'41	79W19'48	5:17:19
Ansel 23	34N56	82W13	5:28:52
Antioch 28	34N14'23	80W28'08	5:21:53
Antioch 29	34N42'09	80W40'37	5:22:42
Antioch 45	33N28'47	79W35'48	5:18:23
Antreville 1	34N18'14	82W32'33	5:30:10
Anvil Rock 29	34N34'23	80W43'01	5:22:52
Appalachie 42	34N57'40	82W12'44	5:28:51
Appleton 3	33N02'36	81W21'47	5:25:27
Appleton Mills 4	34N31	82W39	5:30:36
Aragon Mills 12	34N43	81W13	5:24:52
Ararat 8	32N58'42	80W00'13	5:20:01
Arborville 1	34N17'32	82W20'51	5:29:23
Arcadia 42	34N57'29	81W59'27	5:27:58
Arcadia Heights 42	34N57'22	82W00'00	5:28:00
Arcadia Lakes 40	34N03'13	80W57'41	5:23:51
Ard Crossroads 45	33N47'01	79W26'12	5:17:45
Ardincaple 40	34N02	81W04	5:24:16
Ariail 39	34N50'32	82W38'41	5:30:35
Ariel Cross Roads 34	34N04'34	79W18'11	5:17:13
Arkwright 42	34N55'26	81W55'59	5:27:44
Arlington 42	34N56	82W13	5:28:52
Armenia 12	34N46'06	81W17'35	5:25:10
Arthurtown 40	33N57'41	81W00'01	5:24:00
Asbury 11	35N04	81W38	5:26:32
Ashepoo 15	32N44'24	80W33'02	5:22:12
Ashepoo Crossing 15	32N45'27	80W37'09	5:22:29
Ashepoo Siding 15	32N38'12	80W30'03	5:22:00
Ashland 31	34N20'23	80W11'54	5:20:48
Ashleigh 6	33N18'03	81W19'04	5:25:16
Ashley Heights 10	32N55'57	80W03'16	5:20:13
Ashley Junction 10	32N52'08	79W59'45	5:19:59
Ashton 15	33N00'57	80W58'15	5:23:53
Ashwood 31	34N06'32	80W19'00	5:21:16
Atkins 31	34N02'16	80W06'56	5:20:28
Atlantic Beach 26	33N48'09	78W43'00	5:14:52
Attaway 41	34N00	81W46	5:27:04
Auburn 16	34N22'31	79W58'34	5:19:54
Averill 3	33N04'27	81W30'49	5:26:03
Avondale 10	32N47'17	79W59'24	5:19:58
Awendaw 10	33N02'15	79W36'48	5:18:27
Aynor 26	33N59'59	79W11'59	5:16:48
Babbtown 23	34N41	82W11	5:28:44
Bachman Chapel 36	34N15'07	81W30'28	5:26:02
Back Swamp 21	34N16'25	79W43'34	5:18:54
Badham 18	33N11'44	80W36'41	5:22:27
Baggette Crossroads 14	33N37'36	80W08'15	5:20:33
Baileys Landing 7	32N20'45	80W53'15	5:23:33
Baker Crossroads 26	33N59'37	79W03'24	5:16:14
Baker Crossroads 45	33N48'31	79W51'29	5:19:26
Baker Hill 27	32N22'23	81W07'17	5:24:29
Baldock 3	33N04'45	81W25'25	5:25:42
Bald Rock 44	34N43	81W37	5:26:28
Baldwin Mills 12	34N43	81W13	5:24:52
Ballentine 40	34N07'27	81W14'15	5:24:57
Ballentine Landing 40	34N06'44	81W14'42	5:24:59
Balltown 2	33N35'29	81W43'29	5:26:54
Bamberg 5	33N17'49	81W02'06	5:24:08
Baptist Hill 10	32N43'59	80W16'08	5:21:05
Barfield Mill 28	34N29'02	80W31'48	5:22:07
Barkersville 25	32N42'20	80W56'13	5:23:45
Barksdale 30	34N34'10	82W05'15	5:28:21
Barnes 4	34N18	82W40	5:30:40
Barnes Station 4	34N15'33	82W40'51	5:30:43
Barnhill 22	33N42'08	79W22'33	5:17:30
Barnwell 6	33N14'41	81W21'32	5:25:26
Barr 32	33N59	81W14	5:24:56
Barr Crossing 32	33N56'22	81W17'35	5:25:10
Barrell Landing 7	32N17'42	80W55'51	5:23:43
Barrelville 10	32N41'10	80W21'04	5:21:24
Barrineau Crossroads 14	33N52'19	79W54'33	5:19:38
Bartell Crossroads 45	33N45'33	79W34'43	5:18:19
Barton 3	32N55'20	81W17'12	5:25:09
Bascomville 12	34N41'56	80W58'36	5:23:54
Bashan 27	32N33'05	80W56'47	5:23:47
Bass Crossroads 17	34N21'31	79W24'54	5:17:40
Batesburg 32	33N54'28	81W32'51	5:26:11
Batesville 23	34N51'02	82W13'51	5:28:55
Bath 2	33N30'16	81W52'09	5:27:29
Baton Rouge 12	34N41'49	81W20'39	5:25:23
Battle Creek 37	34N44'53	83W17'25	5:33:10
Baxter Forks 26	33N58'26	79W01'04	5:16:04
Bayboro 26	34N00'34	79W01'21	5:16:05
Bay Springs 13	34N37'52	80W09'56	5:20:40
Bay View 40	34N02	80W59	5:23:56
Bazen Crossroads 21	33N54'43	79W31'58	5:18:08
Beard 14	33N51'41	80W02'26	5:20:10
Bears Bluff 10	32N38'41	80W15'14	5:21:01
Bear Swamp 10	32N50	80W05	5:20:20
Beaufort 7	32N25'53	80W40'12	5:22:41
Beaufort 29	34N42	80W47	5:23:08
Beaufort County Landing 7	32N19'24	80W36'20	5:22:25
Beaufort Station 7	32N28	80W42	5:22:48
Beckhamville 12	34N35'25	80W55'12	5:23:41
Beck Landing 15	32N48'16	80W25'08	5:21:41
Beech Island 2	33N25'38	81W53'28	5:27:34
Belcher Crossroads 33	34N02'43	82W25'31	5:29:42
Bel-Clear Heights 2	33N31	81W56	5:27:44
Beldoc 3	33N04	81W29	5:25:56
Belin 22	33N31'04	79W08'38	5:16:35
Belle Isle Gardens 22	33N18'12	79W17'58	5:17:12
Belle Mead 23	34N51	82W23	5:29:32
Bellinger 27	32N17	81W04	5:24:16
Bells 15	33N00	80W49	5:23:16
Bells Crossroads 15	32N58'44	80W51'06	5:23:24
Bells Crossroads 23	34N46'52	82W12'52	5:28:51
Bell Town 29	34N37'55	80W50'49	5:23:23
Belmont 23	34N51	82W24	5:29:36
Belmont 40	34N03'57	81W00'50	5:24:03
Belsep Crossroads 14	33N36'43	80W23'37	5:21:34
Belton 4	34N31'22	82W29'40	5:29:59
Belvedere 2	33N31'51	81W56'42	5:27:47
Belvedere 40	34N02	80W59	5:23:56
Belvedere Estates 8	32N55	80W00	5:20:00
Ben Avon 42	34N56'11	81W52'46	5:27:31
Bendale 40	34N03	81W02	5:24:08
Bennett 10	32N51'43	80W01'33	5:20:06
Bennetts Point 15	32N33'39	80W27'17	5:21:49
Bennettsville 35	34N37'02	79W41'06	5:18:44
Berea 23	34N53'07	82W27'22	5:29:49
Berkeley Hills 8	32N55'04	80W00'19	5:20:01
Berlin 2	33N40'25	81W18'14	5:25:13
Berry Hill 10	32N46'32	80W10'22	5:20:41
Berrys Crossroads 17	34N19'08	79W29'29	5:17:58
Berrys Landing 27	32N25'19	81W12'13	5:24:49
Bethany 46	35N07'01	81W18'23	5:25:14
Bethear 2	33N39	81W22	5:25:28
Beth Eden 36	34N21'11	81W37'22	5:26:29
Bethel 22	33N26'28	79W29'30	5:17:58
Bethera 8	33N12'05	79W47'18	5:19:09
Bethesda 13	34N38'28	80W02'52	5:20:11
Bethune 28	34N24'53	80W20'56	5:21:24
Beufordtown 8	33N17'02	79W44'37	5:18:58
Beverly 39	34N48'22	82W40'06	5:30:40
Biddle 20	34N22	81W05	5:24:20
Bigcreek 41	34N11	81W52	5:27:28
Bingham 17	34N26'06	79W32'36	5:18:10
Birdstown Crossroads 16	34N27'46	79W59'37	5:19:58
Birdtown 29	34N37'48	80W26'01	5:21:44
Bishopville 31	34N13'05	80W14'55	5:21:00
Blacks 41	33N54'59	81W40'37	5:26:42
Blacksburg 11	35N07'16	81W30'58	5:26:04
Blackstock 12	34N33'30	81W09'09	5:24:37
Blackville 6	33N21'28	81W16'15	5:25:05
Blair 20	34N25'17	81W23'47	5:25:35
Blair Mills 4	34N31	82W30	5:30:00
Blairville 46	34N57	81W20	5:25:20
Blake 15	32N41'30	80W46'10	5:23:05
Blakedale 24	34N13'29	82W11'39	5:28:47
Blakely 45	33N29'40	79W45'25	5:19:02
Blakley Crossroads 29	34N35'02	80W50'49	5:23:23
Bleases Crossroads 41	34N03'31	81W48'47	5:27:15
Blenheim 35	34N30'38	79W39'11	5:18:37
Bloomingvale 45	33N27	79W35	5:18:20
Bloomville 14	33N38'05	80W09'42	5:20:39
Blossom 21	34N00	79W34	5:18:16
Blountville 25	32N41'47	80W51'06	5:23:24
Blue Brick 34	34N13'24	79W31'05	5:18:04
Blue Heaven 1	34N24'53	82W16'05	5:29:04
Bluehouse Corners 15	32N46'12	80W41'58	5:22:48
Blue Ridge 23	35N02'32	82W18'19	5:29:13
Blue Town 35	34N37	79W41	5:18:44
Bluff Estates 40	33N59	80W57	5:23:48
Bluffton 7	32N14'13	80W51'38	5:23:27
Blythewood 40	34N12'51	80W58'27	5:23:54
Bobcat Landing 5	33N20'13	81W01'12	5:24:05
Boiling Springs 6	33N08'06	81W25'53	5:25:44
Boiling Springs 42	35N02'47	81W58'55	5:27:56
Bolen Town 38	33N28'30	81W01'03	5:24:04
Bolon Hall Landing 27	32N25'10	80W51'06	5:23:24
Bon Air Terrace 43	33N56'29	80W22'46	5:21:31
Bonds Crossroads 30	34N26'39	81W46'22	5:27:05
Boney 40	34N14'44	80W57'50	5:23:51
Bonham 44	34N46'36	81W38'48	5:26:35
Bonneau 8	33N18'19	79W57'29	5:19:50
Bonneau Beach 8	33N19'11	80W00'02	5:20:00
Bonniview Estates 2	33N30'54	81W42'46	5:26:51
Bookgreen 22	33N33	79W02	5:16:08
Bookman 40	34N09'46	81W09'12	5:24:37
Boones Creek 37	34N55'12	82W57'04	5:31:48
Booth 26	33N57'01	79W03'36	5:16:14
Bordeaux 33	33N55'35	82W25'15	5:29:41
Borden 43	34N04'03	80W28'42	5:21:55
Bostick 21	33N55'55	79W29'15	5:17:57
Bostick Landing 21	33N56'01	79W28'35	5:17:54
Bouknight 19	33N47'17	81W50'13	5:27:21
Bounty Land 37	34N42'26	82W59'28	5:31:58
Bowling Green 46	35N08'59	81W12'45	5:24:51
Bowman 38	33N20'55	80W40'59	5:22:44
Bowyer 38	33N18'22	80W25'14	5:21:41
Boyd 27	32N26'43	80W53'47	5:23:35
Boyden Arbor 40	34N01'26	80W56'45	5:23:47
Boyd Hill 46	34N56'22	81W02'40	5:24:11
Boykin 28	34N07'00	80W34'54	5:22:20
Boykin 35	34N43'57	79W38'40	5:18:35
Bradley 24	34N02'57	82W14'41	5:28:59
Bradleyville 2	33N30'44	81W56'21	5:27:45
Bram Landing 7	32N11'54	80W43'09	5:22:53
Branchville 38	33N15'04	80W48'57	5:23:16
Brand 30	34N31	82W00	5:28:00
Brandon 23	34N51	82W26	5:29:44
Brannon 42	35N03	82W05	5:28:20
Branwood 23	34N52	82W25	5:29:40
Brasstown 37	34N44'41	83W14'16	5:32:57
Brazen Crossroads 21	34N00	79W34	5:18:16
Breeden 35	34N39'11	79W39'34	5:18:38

Name	Lat	Long	Code
Breeze Hill 2	33N31	81w51	5:27:24
Breezewood 24	34N04'17	82w08'48	5:28:35
Brent 43	34N01'10	80w22'13	5:21:29
Brentwood 10	32N51'23	80w00'41	5:20:03
Brewerton 30	34N24	82w15	5:29:00
Brewton 7	32N39'03	80w48'22	5:23:13
Briarcliffe Acres 26	33N39	78w56	5:15:44
Briars 7	32N34'52	80w41'58	5:22:48
Brickhouse Crossroads 36	34N27'13	81w42'14	5:26:49
Brighton 25	32N36'45	81w16'26	5:25:06
Brighton Beach 7	32N12'55	80w50'55	5:23:24
Brightsville 35	34N46	79w36	5:18:24
Bristow 35	34N25'09	79w37'07	5:18:28
Britton 43	33N51'01	80w17'25	5:21:10
Britton Neck 34	33N54'46	79w20'26	5:17:22
Britts 33	33N55	82w18	5:29:12
Broadway 14	33N44	80w28	5:21:52
Broadway Lake 4	34N31	82w39	5:30:36
Brock 37	34N39'02	83w04'55	5:32:20
Brockington 45	33N43'52	79w48'13	5:19:13
Brocks Mill 13	34N45'26	79w59'43	5:19:59
Brogden 43	33N48'43	80w15'45	5:21:03
Bronson Crossroads 17	34N26'59	79w19'25	5:17:18
Brook Forest 23	34N49	82w24	5:29:36
Brook Green Park 21	34N12	79w45	5:19:00
Brooklyn 29	34N42	80w47	5:23:08
Brooksville 26	33N54'22	78w39'32	5:14:38
Brown Bay 26	33N54'25	79w05'22	5:16:21
Brownlee Crossroads 1	34N14'44	82w31'36	5:30:06
Browns Crossroads 36	34N22'06	81w31'43	5:26:07
Browns Hill 2	33N21'27	81w51'25	5:27:26
Browns Landing 3	33N02'57	81w32'42	5:26:11
Brownsville 18	33N01'43	80w11'54	5:20:48
Brownsville 35	34N23'32	79w35'33	5:18:22
Brownway 26	33N47'51	79w09'59	5:16:40
Broxton 15	33N01	80w57	5:23:48
Bruner 40	33N55'15	80w50'30	5:23:22
Brunson 25	32N55'31	81w11'15	5:24:45
Brunson Crossroads 19	33N49'55	82w03'13	5:28:13
Brunson Crossroads 45	33N44'36	79w28'29	5:17:54
Brunsons Store 43	33N52'38	80w13'58	5:20:56
Brushy Creek 4	34N45	82w31	5:30:04
Bryan Landing 7	32N10'34	80w49'30	5:23:18
Bryans Crossroads 45	33N43'52	79w49'18	5:19:17
Buck Hall 10	33N03'11	79w33'36	5:18:14
Buckingham Landing 7	32N13'48	80w47'58	5:23:12
Bucklick 20	34N27'04	80w54'13	5:23:37
Bucksport 26	33N39'53	79w06'10	5:16:25
Buck Stand 1	34N16'26	82w22'36	5:29:30
Bucksville 26	33N43'07	79w03'47	5:16:15
Buffalo 33	33N56'58	82w22'22	5:29:29
Buffalo 44	34N43'32	81w41'01	5:26:44
Buford 29	34N44'40	80w37'01	5:22:28
Bullock Creek 46	34N51'15	81w24'43	5:25:39
Bunker Hill 17	34N27'02	79w25'11	5:17:41
Bunker Hill 26	33N50'01	79w13'10	5:16:53
Burch Crossroads 21	34N08'43	79w43'43	5:18:55
Burgan 26	33N51'00	79w11'41	5:16:47
Burgess 26	33N36'23	79w03'21	5:16:13
Burkett Landing 21	33N54'24	79w38'37	5:18:34
Burnettown 2	33N30'55	81w50'57	5:27:24
Burns Mill 37	34N45'57	83w01'41	5:32:07
Burnt Church Crossroads 15	32N48'29	80w29'30	5:21:58
Burr Hill 15	32N55'53	80w30'48	5:22:03
Burton 7	32N26'08	80w43'27	5:22:54
Bush River 36	34N19'18	81w45'39	5:27:03
Butler Crossroads 21	33N56'37	79w33'49	5:18:15
Bynum 45	33N40	79w50	5:19:20
Byrd 18	33N10'08	80w31'02	5:22:04
Byrds Crossroads 21	33N57'21	79w52'06	5:19:28
Cades 45	33N47'11	79w46'58	5:19:08
Caesars Head 23	35N06'20	82w37'25	5:30:30
Caines 22	33N18'18	79w12'48	5:16:51
Cainhoy 8	32N55'45	79w49'53	5:19:20
Caldwell 15	33N02'30	80w54'14	5:23:37
Caldwell Crossroad 12	34N34'25	80w58'20	5:23:53
Calhoun 39	34N41'33	82w49'54	5:31:20
Calhoun Falls 1	34N05'32	82w35'45	5:30:23
Calhoun Mill 33	34N01'58	82w28'16	5:29:53
Callison 24	34N00'52	82w07'33	5:28:30
Calvert 42	34N56'39	82w00'22	5:28:01
Cambridge 24	34N04'39	81w57'31	5:27:50
Camden 28	34N14'47	80w36'26	5:22:26
Cameron 9	33N33'27	80w42'53	5:22:52
Campbell 4	34N30'39	82w33'29	5:30:14
Campbell Crossroads 13	34N38'31	80w10'16	5:20:41
Camp Branch 21	33N54'30	79w49'05	5:19:16
Camp Branch 25	32N48'37	81w01'24	5:24:06
Camp Cox 29	35N02'01	80w53'24	5:23:34
Camp Creek 29	34N45'39	80w41'45	5:22:47
Camp Croft 42	34N54'38	81w51'11	5:27:25
Campfield 22	33N22	79w17	5:17:08
Camp Gravatt 2	33N44'17	81w35'07	5:26:20
Camp Ground 40	34N11	81w04	5:24:16
Camp Long 2	33N40'41	81w37'11	5:26:29
Camp Oak 37	34N51'29	83w02'03	5:32:08
Campobello 42	35N06'56	82w09'01	5:28:36
Camp Rawl 2	33N39'17	81w28'52	5:25:55
Camp Saint Christopher 10	32N33'56	80w10'55	5:20:44
Campton 42	35N01'43	82w03'51	5:28:15
Canaan 18	32N57'56	80w17'40	5:21:11
Canaan 38	33N19'43	80w56'28	5:23:46
Canaan 42	34N53'35	81w55'56	5:27:44
Canady Crossroads 15	33N03'21	80w37'13	5:22:29
Canady Landing 10	32N48'55	80w24'18	5:21:37
Canadys 15	33N03'21	80w37'13	5:22:29
Cane Savannah 43	33N54'06	80w27'02	5:21:48
Cannons Camp Ground 42	35N00'34	81w51'40	5:27:27
Canon Hill 26	33N47'10	79w11'35	5:16:46
Cantey 28	34N20'40	80w40'43	5:22:43
Capehart 7	32N28	80w48	5:23:12
Capitol 40	34N01	81w00	5:24:00
Capitol View 40	33N59	80w57	5:23:48
Capwells Crossroads 10	32N46'45	80w16'07	5:21:04
Carem 44	34N41'54	81w34'05	5:26:16
Carlisle 42	35N03'25	81w56'16	5:27:45
Carlisle 44	34N35'34	81w27'46	5:25:51
Carmel 29	34N36	80w40	5:22:40
Carmichael Crossroads 17	34N27'49	79w17'16	5:17:09
Carnes Crossroad 8	33N03'48	80w05'36	5:20:22
Carolina Mills 17	34N25	79w22	5:17:28
Caromi Village 8	33N00	80w06	5:20:24
Carris 45	33N30'44	79w49'46	5:19:19
Carter Landing 17	34N08'45	79w32'38	5:18:11
Carters Crossroads 16	34N08'24	80w06'50	5:20:27
Carters Crossroads 22	33N39'19	79w19'01	5:17:16
Cartersville 21	34N05'10	80w01'44	5:20:07
Cartwheel Landing 26	34N06'00	79w14'26	5:16:58
Carver Heights 40	34N02	80w59	5:23:56
Carvers Bay 22	33N44	79w29	5:17:56
Cash 13	34N37'06	79w52'39	5:19:31
Cashion Crossroads 11	35N05'23	81w30'29	5:26:02
Cashville 42	34N48'26	82w07'48	5:28:31
Caskey 29	34N44'41	80w50'14	5:23:21
Cassatt 28	34N21'52	80w26'10	5:21:45
Catarrh 13	34N33'56	80w22'03	5:21:28
Catawba 46	34N51'10	80w54'41	5:23:39
Catchall 43	34N00'34	80w29'26	5:21:58
Cateechee 39	34N46'14	82w46'26	5:31:06
Catfish Landing 34	33N58'01	79w28'55	5:17:56
Causey 26	34N15'48	79w05'54	5:16:24
Cauthens Crossroads 29	34N37'12	80w46'11	5:23:05
Cayce 32	33N57'56	81w04'27	5:24:18
Cedar Creek 40	34N11'04	81w07'55	5:24:32
Cedar Creek 45	33N21'31	79w39'21	5:18:37
Cedar Creek Landing 8	33N03'10	79w52'55	5:19:32
Cedar Grove 26	33N50'10	79w07'28	5:16:30
Cedar Rock 39	34N52'26	82w38'25	5:30:34
Cedar Springs 1	34N04'51	82w18'07	5:29:12
Cedar Springs 10	32N39	80w08	5:20:32
Cedar Swamp 45	33N39'24	79w40'03	5:18:40
Cedar Terrace 40	33N59	80w57	5:23:48
Celriver 46	34N56	81w01	5:24:04
Cementon 38	33N20	80w25	5:21:40
Centenary 34	34N01'51	79w21'21	5:17:25
Center Crossroads 22	33N41'36	79w19'02	5:17:16
Centerville 10	32N44'02	79w58'08	5:19:53
Centerville 17	34N24'41	79w29'33	5:17:58
Centerville 18	32N59'44	80w10'14	5:20:41
Central 39	34N43'27	82w46'53	5:31:08
Central Crossroads 14	33N53'16	79w54'47	5:19:39
Central Pacolet 42	34N54'48	81w44'55	5:27:00
Central-Shiloh 1	34N15'36	82w20'38	5:29:23
Challedon 32	34N03'53	81w09'28	5:24:38
Chandler 10	32N54'16	79w44'09	5:18:57
Chandlers 45	33N40'48	79w29'20	5:17:57
Chapin 32	34N09'57	81w21'00	5:25:24
Chapmans Crossroads 41	34N07'10	81w47'56	5:27:12
Chappells 36	34N10'47	81w52'01	5:27:28
Charity 8	33N00'21	79w51'00	5:19:24
Charleston 10	32N46'35	79w55'52	5:19:43
Charleston Base 10	32N54	80w04	5:20:16
Charleston Crossroads 1	34N04'52	82w29'02	5:29:56
Charleston Heights 10	32N51'25	79w58'15	5:19:53
Charleston Yard 10	32N51	79w55	5:19:40
Chauga Heights 37	34N40'30	83w08'31	5:32:34
Chavistown 35	34N41'41	79w46'05	5:19:04
Cheddar 4	34N34'41	82w29'47	5:29:59
Cheohee 37	34N54'08	83w02'52	5:32:11
Cheraw 13	34N41'51	79w53'01	5:19:32
Cherokee 42	34N56	81w56	5:27:44
Cherokee Falls 11	35N03'53	81w32'33	5:26:10
Cherokee Forest 23	34N53'50	82w19'49	5:29:19
Cherokee Springs 42	35N02'59	81w53'28	5:27:34
Cherry Grove Beach 26	33N50	78w39	5:14:36
Cherry Hill 8	33N13'43	79w56'36	5:19:46
Cherry Hill 45	33N25'05	79w36'08	5:18:25
Cherry Point Landing 7	32N19'34	80w55'02	5:23:40
Cherry Road 46	34N56	81w01	5:24:04
Cherrys Crossing 37	34N39'18	82w50'07	5:31:20
Chesnee 42	35N08'54	81w51'40	5:27:27
Chester 12	34N42'17	81w12'52	5:24:51
Chesterfield 13	34N44'09	80w05'18	5:20:21
Chestnut Crossroads 26	33N55'26	78w45'47	5:15:03
Chestnut Hills 23	34N49	82w24	5:29:36
Chestnut Springs 23	35N10'27	82w24'12	5:29:37
Chickasaw Point 37	34N31	82w59	5:31:56
Chick Springs 23	34N55'37	82w16'51	5:29:07
Chicora 8	33N16'01	80w06'35	5:20:26
Chicora Place 10	32N52	79w59	5:19:56
Childsbury 8	33N05'49	79w56'03	5:19:44
Chinners 26	33N58'50	79w08'44	5:16:35
Chinquapin Falls 32	33N49'31	81w31'21	5:26:05
Chisolm 7	32N32'15	80w36'10	5:22:25
Choppee 22	33N34'16	79w22'59	5:17:32
Citadel 10	32N48	79w57	5:19:48
City View 23	34N51'41	82w25'54	5:29:44
Clambank 22	33N20'06	79w11'41	5:16:47
Claremont 43	33N58'25	80w33'35	5:22:14
Clarks Crossroads 45	33N47'45	79w49'04	5:19:16
Clarks Hill 33	33N40'15	82w10'23	5:28:42
Clatworthy Crossroads 1	34N03'32	82w22'27	5:29:30
Claussen 21	34N07'51	79w37'52	5:18:31
Clayton 20	34N29'16	81w25'09	5:25:41
Clearmont 37	34N40'09	83w03'38	5:32:15
Clear Pond 5	33N11'17	81w01'45	5:24:07
Clearspring 23	34N43	82w18	5:29:12
Clearwater 2	33N29'48	81w53'32	5:27:34
Cleland Crossroads 25	32N56'20	81w07'05	5:24:28
Clemson 39	34N41'00	82w50'15	5:31:21
Clemson University 39	34N41	82w48	5:31:12
Cleora 19	33N50'29	82w03'00	5:28:12
Clevedale 42	34N55'48	82w02'26	5:28:10
Cleveland 23	35N04'20	82w31'39	5:30:07
Clifton 42	34N58'46	81w49'05	5:27:16
Clifton Station 42	34N59'49	81w49'10	5:27:17
Climax 32	34N03'58	81w27'31	5:25:50
Clinton 30	34N28'21	81w52'51	5:27:31
Clio 35	34N34'46	79w32'48	5:18:11
Clover 46	35N06'40	81w13'36	5:24:54
Clubhouse Crossroads 18	32N53'52	80w19'22	5:21:17
Clubhouse Crossroads 32	33N57'36	81w24'08	5:25:37
Clyburn 28	34N25'07	80w35'58	5:22:24
Clyde 16	34N23'07	80w11'05	5:20:44
Coachmans Corners 18	32N58'04	80w18'07	5:21:12
Coats Crossroad 28	34N30'30	80w38'12	5:22:33
Cochrantown 26	33N51	79w03	5:16:12
Cohen Hill 10	32N51'23	80w02'35	5:20:10
Cohens Bluff Landing 3	32N50'29	81w25'36	5:25:42
Cokesbury 24	34N17'21	82w12'29	5:28:50
Cold Point 30	34N25'10	82w02'46	5:28:11
Colemans Crossroads 41	34N06'19	81w46'28	5:27:06
Coles Crossing 21	34N09'59	79w45'50	5:19:03
College Acres 2	33N29'45	81w41'43	5:26:47
Colleton 15	33N02'23	80w52'57	5:23:32
Colliers 19	33N42'31	82w04'40	5:28:19
Collins 12	34N48	81w01	5:24:04
Collins Creek 10	33N09'26	79w24'39	5:17:39
Colonel Creek Landing 20	34N22'08	80w47'50	5:23:11
Columbia 40	34N00'02	81w02'00	5:24:08
Comingtee 8	33N04'46	79w55'02	5:19:40
Conch Creek 22	33N39'56	79w12'07	5:16:48
Concord 4	34N33'16	82w38'47	5:30:35
Concord 46	35N03'00	81w03'53	5:24:16
Concord Crossroads 3	32N59'31	81w25'20	5:25:41
Coneross 37	34N40	83w06	5:32:24
Conestee 23	34N46'05	82w21'00	5:29:24
Congaree 40	33N54'16	80w47'43	5:23:11
Converse 42	34N59'31	81w50'06	5:27:20
Converse Heights 42	34N57'00	81w54'46	5:27:39
Conway 26	33N50'09	79w02'53	5:16:12
Cook 45	33N38'32	79w29'04	5:17:56
Cook Corner 45	33N25'11	79w37'38	5:18:31
Cooke Crossroads 18	32N56'53	80w12'21	5:20:49
Cook Landing 27	32N11'42	81w00'02	5:24:00
Cooks Crossroads 30	34N43'27	82w09'56	5:28:40
Cool Branch 20	34N32'57	81w22'47	5:25:31
Cooley Springs 42	35N08'28	81w56'55	5:27:48
Cool Spring 26	33N58'30	79w08'14	5:16:33
Cooper (P O) 45	33N44'04	79w36'13	5:18:25
Cooper River Landing 7	32N08'01	80w52'09	5:23:29
Coosaw 7	32N32'42	80w46'25	5:23:06
Coosawhatchie 27	32N35'19	80w55'39	5:23:43
Cope 38	33N22'40	81w00'26	5:24:02
Copp Landing 7	32N18'22	80w50'40	5:23:23
Cordesville 8	33N07'55	79w53'01	5:19:32
Cordova 38	33N26'07	80w55'16	5:23:41
Corinth 37	34N42'44	82w53'46	5:31:35
Cornwell 12	34N36'26	81w10'46	5:24:43
Coronaco 24	34N15'35	82w05'40	5:28:23
Cote Bas Landing 8	33N00'53	79w55'27	5:19:42
Cottageville 15	32N56'12	80w28'52	5:21:55
Cotton Valley 17	34N28'42	79w17'05	5:17:08
Couchton 2	33N33'41	81w37'20	5:26:29
Couchtown 2	33N34	81w44	5:26:56
Country Club Estates 46	34N56	81w01	5:24:04
Courtenay 37	34N42'47	82w55'11	5:31:41
Coward 21	33N58'23	79w44'50	5:18:59
Cowden 2	33N17'12	81w47'47	5:27:11
Cow Head Landing 22	33N34'31	79w24'33	5:17:38
Cowpens 42	35N01'00	81w48'15	5:27:13
Cox 36	34N17	81w37	5:26:28
Crane Forest 40	34N03	81w02	5:24:08
Crayton Manor Apartments 4	34N31	82w39	5:30:36
Craytonville 4	34N26'10	82w28'59	5:29:56
Crescent 42	34N46'15	82w06'41	5:28:27
Crescent Beach 26	33N48'27	78w42'04	5:14:48
Creston 9	33N35'50	80w38'52	5:22:35
Crestview 16	34N12	79w45	5:19:00
Cribb Crossroads 22	33N38'40	79w17'06	5:17:08

Crocketts Crossroad 29 34N41'31 80w47'16 5:23:09
Crocketville 25 32N54'59 81w04'39 5:24:19
Croft 2 33N37'20 81w42'04 5:26:48
Cromer Crossroads 36 34N25'22 81w39'20 5:26:37
Crooks Crossroads 45 33N46'42 79w24'38 5:17:39
Crosland Park 2 33N34'54 81w42'04 5:26:48
Cross 8 33N19'38 80w08'55 5:20:36
Cross Anchor 42 34N38'34 81w51'29 5:27:26
Cross Hill 30 34N18'17 81w58'59 5:27:56
Cross Keys 44 34N37'55 81w46'37 5:27:06
Cross Plains 23 35N05'54 82w25'16 5:29:41
Cross Roads 37 34N35'51 82w58'35 5:31:54
Crosswell 39 34N50'58 82w29'39 5:29:59
Crouch 41 34N00 81w46 5:27:04
Crowburg 13 34N47'06 80w26'46 5:21:47
Cumberland 22 33N21'45 79w26'06 5:17:44
Cummings 25 32N47'13 80w59'26 5:23:58
Cunningham 42 34N59'47 82w03'32 5:28:14
Cusac Crossroads 21 34N01'02 79w50'47 5:19:23
Cypress Crossroads 31 34N13'00 80w08'06 5:20:32
Cypress Fork 14 33N45 80w13 5:20:52
Cypress Fork Crossroads 14 33N44'49 80w04'29 5:20:18
Dacusville 39 34N56'07 82w33'32 5:30:14
Daisy 26 33N59'43 78w52'03 5:15:28
Dale 7 32N33'23 80w41'24 5:22:46
Dalewood 24 34N18 82w40 5:30:40
Dalzell 43 34N01'00 80w25'49 5:21:43
Danwood 21 34N05 79w46 5:19:04
Darlington 16 34N17'59 79w52'35 5:19:30
Darraugh 1 34N13'19 82w19'49 5:29:19
Daufuskie Island 7 32N06'15 80w53'08 5:23:33
Davidson 25 32N43'29 80w54'03 5:23:36
Davis Crossroads 14 33N34'07 80w19'59 5:21:20
Davis Hill 15 32N55'04 80w32'34 5:22:10
Davis Landing 34 34N01'38 79w18'28 5:17:14
Davis Station 14 33N36'09 80w15'53 5:21:04
Davistown 21 34N01'22 79w31'53 5:18:08
Dawkins 20 34N21'20 81w22'06 5:25:28
Deadfall Crossroads 36 34N12'21 81w42'11 5:26:49
Deans 4 34N24'07 82w41'16 5:30:45
Deas Mill 46 34N52'21 81w04'19 5:24:17
Deerfield 27 32N22'56 81w05'48 5:24:23
Deer Park 10 32N58'16 80w04'00 5:20:16
DeKalb 28 34N22'38 80w35'46 5:22:23
Delemar Crossroads 18 32N50'46 80w17'04 5:21:08
Dellwood 23 34N52'41 82w21'41 5:29:27
Delmar 41 34N01'12 81w31'21 5:26:05
DeLoach 25 32N39'35 81w10'45 5:24:43
Delphia 46 34N56'27 81w13'48 5:24:55
Delta 44 34N32'23 81w33'41 5:26:15
Denmark 5 33N19'21 81w08'33 5:24:34
Denny 41 34N03'55 81w42'52 5:26:51
Denny Corner 22 33N18'12 79w14'05 5:16:56
Denny Terrace 40 34N03'55 81w03'49 5:24:15
Dentsville 40 34N03'50 80w57'30 5:23:50
Denver 4 34N34'31 82w44'12 5:30:57
Deweys Hill 10 32N53'34 79w58'40 5:19:55
Dillard Crossroads 42 34N49'14 82w05'53 5:28:24
Dillon 17 34N24'59 79w22'17 5:17:29
Dinber 12 34N47'37 81w12'25 5:24:50
Dinkins 43 33N57'08 80w23'13 5:21:33
Dinkins Mill 43 34N02'26 80w32'05 5:22:08
Dixiana 32 33N55'09 81w03'34 5:24:14
Dixie 29 34N42 80w47 5:23:08
Dixie Crossing 43 33N55'41 80w33'21 5:22:13
Dixon Crossroads 37 34N36'33 83w08'50 5:32:35
Dodd Hill 42 35N00'57 82w01'17 5:28:05
Doddville 42 35N03 82w05 5:28:20
Dog Bluff 26 33N57'09 79w13'29 5:16:54
Dog Bluff Landing 26 33N57'58 79w20'11 5:17:21
Donalds 1 34N22'37 82w20'51 5:29:23
Doneraile 16 34N19 79w53 5:19:32
Dongola 26 33N45'26 79w11'14 5:16:45
Dorange 18 33N13'21 80w42'25 5:22:50
Dorchester 10 32N50'58 79w59'18 5:19:57
Dorchester 18 33N08'23 80w23'40 5:21:35
Dorchester Estates 18 33N01 80w11 5:20:44
Dorchester-Waylyn 10 32N52 79w59 5:19:56
Dosheno 4 34N28'40 82w27'07 5:29:48
Douglas 29 34N39'53 80w48'35 5:23:14
Douglass 20 34N27'31 81w14'56 5:25:00
Dovesville 16 34N24'08 79w53'43 5:19:35
Downs Siding 24 34N14'41 82w13'14 5:28:53
Doyle 26 33N57'43 79w09'07 5:16:36
Drake 35 34N28'21 79w40'02 5:18:40
Drawd 15 32N50'52 80w37'30 5:22:30
Drayton 10 32N50'45 80w03'25 5:20:14
Drayton 42 34N58'04 81w54'24 5:27:38
Draytonville 11 35N02'58 81w35'38 5:26:23
Drexel Lake Hills 40 34N02 80w58 5:23:52
Drigger Crossroad 15 32N55'44 80w34'49 5:22:19
Driggerstown 8 33N01'49 80w05'29 5:20:22
Dry Branch 2 33N26'00 81w43'06 5:26:52
DuBose 43 34N03'12 80w20'46 5:21:23
Dubose Crossroads 16 34N15'24 79w58'57 5:19:56
DuBose Crossroads 31 34N04'43 80w19'02 5:21:16
DuBose Park 28 34N14'52 80w35'00 5:22:20
Dudley 13 34N46'51 80w29'52 5:21:59
Duew 1 34N20 82w23 5:29:32
Due West 1 34N20'00 82w23'17 5:29:33
Duford 26 34N11'28 79w03'51 5:16:15
Dukes 25 32N53'51 81w14'17 5:24:57
Dunbar 22 33N31'47 79w21'18 5:17:25
Dunbar 35 34N32'01 79w33'41 5:18:15
Dunbar Landing 22 33N32'08 79w21'01 5:17:24
Duncan 42 34N56'16 82w08'43 5:28:35
Duncan Township 23 34N33'47 82w16'04 5:29:04
Dunean 23 34N49'29 82w25'10 5:29:41
Dunes 26 33N39 78w56 5:15:44
Dunkins Mill 43 34N06 80w32 5:22:08
Dunlape Crossroads 31 34N03'54 80w08'07 5:20:32
Dupont 10 32N48 80w00 5:20:00
Dupont Station 10 32N47'17 80w01'16 5:20:05
Durant 14 33N49'47 80w09'16 5:20:37
Dusty Bend 28 34N15 80w36 5:22:24
Dutch Fork 40 34N04 81w08 5:24:32
Dutchman 42 34N50 81w52 5:27:28
Dwight Crossroads 29 34N44'39 80w37'34 5:22:30
Dyson 24 34N09'42 81w55'57 5:27:44
Eadytown 8 33N24'44 80w08'50 5:20:35
Earle 45 33N27'53 79w38'11 5:18:33
Earle Homes 4 34N31 82w39 5:30:36
Earles 45 33N27 79w35 5:18:20
Earles Grove 37 34N34'00 82w59'31 5:31:58
Earlwood Park 16 34N19'44 79w53'30 5:19:34
Early Branch 25 32N44'44 80w55'41 5:23:43
Earlys Crossroads 16 34N18'01 79w58'27 5:19:54
Easley 39 34N49'47 82w36'06 5:30:24
Eastatoe 39 34N59 82w48 5:31:12
East Gaffney 11 35N04'48 81w37'59 5:26:32
East Gantt 23 34N46'05 82w23'05 5:29:32
East Greer 42 34N56 82w13 5:28:52
East Hartsville 16 34N23 80w05 5:20:20
East Hopewell 11 35N04 81w26 5:25:44
Eastmont 40 33N59 80w57 5:23:48
Eastover 40 33N52'36 80w41'35 5:22:46
East Spartanburg 42 34N55'57 81w53'30 5:27:34
East View 23 34N38'23 82w26'14 5:29:45
Eau Claire 40 34N02'04 81w02'43 5:24:11
Ebenezer 21 34N10'33 79w51'06 5:19:24
Ebenezer 37 34N46'48 83w00'02 5:32:00
Ebenezer 46 34N57'25 81w02'48 5:24:11
Eden 30 34N37 82w07 5:28:28
Edgefield 19 33N47'22 81w55'47 5:27:43
Edgemoor 12 34N48'20 81w00'42 5:24:03
Edgewater Park 10 32N46'18 80w00'06 5:20:00
Edgewood 40 34N02 80w59 5:23:56
Edisto Beach 10 32N28'45 80w20'06 5:21:20
Edisto Club 5 33N24'10 81w09'23 5:24:38
Edisto Island 10 32N33'36 80w16'48 5:21:07
Edmund 32 33N51'41 81w12'01 5:24:48
Edwards 45 33N33'51 79w57'18 5:19:49
Effingham 21 34N03'28 79w45'12 5:19:01
Ehrhardt 5 33N05'48 81w00'52 5:24:03
Eison Crossroads 36 34N28'07 81w38'11 5:26:33
Ekom 30 34N25'53 82w08'27 5:28:34
Elgin 28 34N10'15 80w47'40 5:23:11
Elgin 29 34N40'22 80w43'09 5:22:53
Elim 21 34N02'51 79w47'53 5:19:12
Elko 6 33N22'49 81w22'47 5:25:31
Ellerbees Mill 43 34N04'04 80w31'55 5:22:08
Elliott 31 34N06'25 80w09'50 5:20:39
Elloree 38 33N31'51 80w34'20 5:22:17
Ellwood 8 33N06'39 79w56'11 5:19:45
Elmwood Park 2 33N30'15 81w42'12 5:26:49
Elsie 32 33N55'55 81w20'03 5:25:20
Embree 5 33N15'28 80w53'32 5:23:34
Emory 41 33N59'14 81w42'13 5:26:49
Engleside 42 35N08'41 82w10'06 5:28:40
English Crossroads 31 34N06'56 80w13'21 5:20:53
Enola 42 35N00'55 81w52'04 5:27:28
Enoree 42 34N39'23 81w57'55 5:27:52
Enos 9 33N47'50 81w02'47 5:24:11
Enterprise Landing 26 33N40'08 79w03'39 5:16:15
Epworth 24 34N05'19 82w02'32 5:28:10
Equinox Mill 4 34N31 82w39 5:30:36
Erwin 29 34N41'30 80w48'55 5:23:16
Estill 25 32N45'17 81w14'32 5:24:58
Ethon Crossroads 32 33N55'52 81w18'47 5:25:15
Eulala 41 34N00 81w46 5:27:04
Eulonia 34 33N59'11 79w23'01 5:17:32
Eureka 2 33N41'38 81w46'02 5:27:04
Eutaw Springs 38 33N24'24 80w18'04 5:21:12
Eutawville 38 33N23'40 80w20'51 5:21:23
Evans 12 34N40'11 81w11'27 5:24:46
Evans Mill 13 34N43'36 80w21'01 5:21:24
Evergreen 21 34N04'06 79w40'45 5:18:43
Evergreen Hills 4 34N31'10 82w41'11 5:30:45
Fairfax 3 32N57'32 81w14'12 5:24:57
Fairfield 7 32N13 80w45 5:23:00
Fairfield Terrace 40 34N03 81w02 5:24:08
Fairforest 42 34N57'23 82w00'37 5:28:02
Fairforest Finishing Plant 42 34N58 82w01 5:28:04
Fairmont 42 34N53'57 82w03'29 5:28:14
Fairmont Mills 42 34N55'43 82w03'36 5:28:14
Fair Play 37 34N30'40 82w59'08 5:31:57
Fairs Crossroads 1 34N16'52 82w25'55 5:29:44
Fairview 7 32N34'59 80w47'24 5:23:10
Fairview 23 34N56'48 82w16'11 5:29:05
Fairview 36 34N08'12 81w28'07 5:25:52
Fairview 37 34N44'45 82w58'07 5:31:52
Fairview Crossroads 32 33N45'31 81w21'59 5:25:28
Fairview Heights 42 34N57'55 81w55'15 5:27:41
Farewell Corner 8 33N13'22 79w44'51 5:18:59
Farrell Crossroads 5 33N12'51 80w52'21 5:23:29
Farrells Mill 6 33N20'19 81w21'06 5:25:24
Farrels Crossroads 5 33N15 80w49 5:23:16
Farrow Terrace 40 34N03 81w02 5:24:08
Feasterville 20 34N30'08 81w21'38 5:25:27
Fechtig 25 32N46'08 80w57'51 5:23:51
Federal 23 34N51 82w23 5:29:32
Felder 38 33N25'57 80w51'05 5:23:24
Felderville 38 33N27'48 80w32'38 5:22:11
Fendall 21 34N08'20 79w41'17 5:18:45
Fennell Hill Landing 3 32N55'40 81w29'23 5:25:58
Fenwick 15 32N39'05 80w27'06 5:21:48
Fenwick Crossroads 10 32N43'14 80w04'57 5:20:20
Fenwick Hills 10 32N39 80w08 5:20:32
Ferguson Landing 38 33N25'50 80w16'52 5:21:07
Ferndale 10 32N54 80w00 5:20:00
Fersners 38 33N32'20 80w45'59 5:23:04
Filbert 46 35N02'55 81w15'16 5:25:01
Fingerville 42 35N08'02 82w00'24 5:28:02
Finklea 26 34N05'53 78w58'43 5:15:55
Finland 5 33N21'57 81w05'36 5:24:22
Fisher Hill 13 34N40'34 79w55'53 5:19:44
Five Forks 4 34N37'58 82w40'14 5:30:41
Five Forks 17 34N28'45 79w19'17 5:17:17
Five Forks 23 34N48'17 82w13'47 5:28:55
Five Forks 35 34N33'07 79w35'52 5:18:23
Five Points 37 34N43'28 83w07'30 5:32:30
Five Points 40 34N00 81w00 5:24:00
Five Points 46 35N05'30 81w05'54 5:24:24
Flat Rock 4 34N25'26 82w39'07 5:30:36
Flat Rock 28 34N28'13 80w38'03 5:22:32
Flat Shoals 37 34N51'28 83w00'55 5:32:04
Fleet 21 33N57'32 79w31'36 5:18:06
Fleming Crossroad 29 34N40'39 80w45'43 5:23:03
Fletcher 35 34N42'51 79w35'44 5:18:23
Flinns Crossroads 16 34N19'25 80w02'30 5:20:10
Flint Hill 20 34N24'27 80w57'04 5:23:48
Florence 21 34N11'43 79w45'46 5:19:03
Florence West 21 34N11 79w48 5:19:12
Floyd 16 34N22'15 79w54'14 5:19:37
Floydale 17 34N19'25 79w20'11 5:17:21
Floyd Dale 17 34N19 79w20 5:17:20
Floyds 26 34N10 79w03 5:16:12
Floyds Crossroads 26 34N12'52 79w06'28 5:16:26
Folly Beach 10 32N39'18 79w56'26 5:19:46
Folly Field 7 32N12'07 80w41'26 5:22:46
Forbes Corner 22 33N28'52 79w25'39 5:17:43
Forest 18 33N08 80w24 5:21:36
Forest 33 35N01 82w44 5:30:56
Forest Acres 40 34N01'09 80w59'24 5:23:58
Forest Beach 7 32N13 80w45 5:23:00
Forest Lake 40 34N01 80w57 5:23:48
Foreston 14 33N37'54 80w03'43 5:20:15
Forest View 23 34N53'20 82w21'57 5:29:28
Fork 4 34N31 82w53 5:31:32
Fork 17 34N17'17 79w16'32 5:17:06
Fork Hill Crossroads 29 34N39'51 80w37'14 5:22:29
Fork Shoals 23 34N37'21 82w18'25 5:29:14
Forney 26 33N50'07 79w10'27 5:16:42
Forrest Hills 17 34N20'40 79w26'34 5:17:46
Fort Bull 10 32N50'30 80w03'23 5:20:14
Fort Corner 10 33N04'44 79w37'33 5:18:30
Fort Fremont 7 32N18'30 80w38'17 5:22:33
Fort Jackson 40 34N01 81w00 5:24:00
Fort Lawn 12 34N42'07 80w53'42 5:23:35
Fort Mill 46 35N00'26 80w56'43 5:23:47
Fort Motte 9 33N44'20 80w41'34 5:22:46
Fort Moultrie 10 32N45'32 79w51'29 5:19:26
Fortner 39 35N04 82w31 5:30:04
Foster Corner 22 33N19'14 79w25'30 5:17:42
Foster Mill 42 34N51'21 81w49'40 5:27:19
Fosters Crossroads 29 34N47'11 80w50'29 5:23:22
Fountain Inn 23 34N41'20 82w11'45 5:28:47
Four Holes 38 33N16'42 80w26'00 5:21:44
Four Mile 10 32N48 79w52 5:19:28
Fowler 45 33N42'09 79w41'49 5:18:47
Foxtown 2 33N42'47 81w34'11 5:26:17
Foxville 43 33N53'09 80w33'22 5:22:13
Fraserville 22 33N26'34 79w07'53 5:16:32
Fredonia 32 33N55'38 81w27'44 5:25:51
Freedman 10 32N32'11 80w17'42 5:21:11
Freemont 26 33N56'34 78w44'45 5:14:59
Frieds Bay 26 34N01'51 78w46'17 5:15:05
Friendfield 21 33N58'54 79w40'23 5:18:42
Friendfield 22 33N20'09 79w14'16 5:16:57
Friendship 4 34N29'54 82w22'52 5:29:31
Friendship 24 34N02'31 81w57'35 5:27:50
Friendship 34 34N01'00 79w26'08 5:17:45
Friendship 37 34N37'42 82w55'01 5:31:40
Friendship 46 34N55'14 80w54'53 5:23:40
Fripp Island 7 32N24 80w35 5:22:20
Fripp Landing 7 32N21'33 80w51'00 5:23:24
Frogmore 7 32N23'48 80w34'35 5:22:18
Frost 40 34N04'34 81w05'09 5:24:21
Fruit Hill 41 34N00 81w46 5:27:04
Fulton 35 34N46'41 79w47'31 5:19:10
Fulton Crossroads 43 33N43'40 80w30'38 5:22:03
Furman 25 32N40'53 81w11'18 5:24:45
Gable 14 33N49'30 80w06'34 5:20:26
Gaddys Crossroads 17 34N23'58 79w15'28 5:17:02
Gadsden 40 33N50'44 80w45'58 5:23:04
Gaffney 11 35N04'18 81w39'00 5:26:36
Gaillard Crossroads 43 34N02'57 80w26'05 5:21:44
Gaines Crossroads 24 34N03'50 82w05'12 5:28:21
Galavon 17 34N29'50 79w27'08 5:17:49
Galaxy 40 33N59 80w57 5:23:48
Galivants Ferry 26 34N03'22 79w14'48 5:16:59
Gandy 16 34N26'29 79w51'25 5:19:26
Gantt 23 34N48'00 82w25'28 5:29:42
Gap Creek 23 35N09'03 82w29'30 5:29:58
Gapway 34 34N09'27 79w14'49 5:16:59
Garden City Beach 26 33N34'25 79w00'10 5:16:01
Gardens Corner 7 32N36'02 80w45'41 5:23:03
Gardner Crossroads 21 34N02'34 79w39'29 5:18:38

Place	Latitude	Longitude	Time
Garnett 25	32N36'22	81w14'44	5:24:59
Gary 36	34N21'08	81w43'54	5:26:56
Gaston 32	33N49'01	81w06'04	5:24:24
Gaston Mill 28	34N27'04	80w34'47	5:22:19
Gayle Mill 12	34N43	81w13	5:24:52
Gaylords Crossroads 23	34N44'30	82w11'29	5:28:46
Genoa 35	34N27'22	79w39'44	5:18:39
Georgetown 22	33N22'36	79w17'41	5:17:11
Georgieville 22	33N29'35	79w05'21	5:16:21
Germantown 10	33N11'43	79w26'51	5:17:47
Gettysville 18	32N54'06	80w21'51	5:21:27
Gibbs Crossroads 21	34N01'35	79w36'02	5:18:24
Gibson 10	32N41'56	80w15'32	5:21:02
Gifford 25	32N51'34	81w14'21	5:24:57
Gilbert 32	33N55'27	81w23'38	5:25:35
Gilbert Crossroads 26	33N43'30	79w10'05	5:16:40
Gillespie 13	34N34	80w03	5:20:12
Gilliard 22	33N30'51	79w12'37	5:16:50
Gillisonville 27	32N35'56	80w59'37	5:23:58
Gilmania 27	32N36'42	80w54'39	5:23:39
Givhans 18	33N00'41	80w20'16	5:21:21
Glasgow Landing 27	32N08'07	80w59'28	5:23:58
Glass Hill 26	33N51	79w03	5:16:12
Glassy 23	35N07'23	82w18'48	5:29:15
Glendale 42	34N56'41	81w50'16	5:27:21
Glenn Springs 42	34N48'44	81w50'24	5:27:22
Glenwood 39	34N49'54	82w34'53	5:30:20
Gloverville 2	33N31'33	81w49'49	5:27:19
Gloverville 15	32N54'00	80w29'37	5:21:58
Gluck 4	34N27'07	82w40'01	5:30:40
Glymphville 36	34N23'43	81w25'17	5:25:41
Godsey 24	34N10'06	81w58'03	5:27:52
Golden Grove 23	34N44'02	82w26'38	5:29:47
Golightly 42	34N51'26	81w53'08	5:27:33
Gooch Crossroad 29	34N41'35	80w48'14	5:23:13
Gooches 29	34N42	80w47	5:23:08
Good Hope 22	33N39'23	79w18'18	5:17:13
Good Hope 41	34N02'07	81w53'27	5:27:34
Goodhope Landing 15	32N57'56	80w25'07	5:21:40
Good Hope Landing 27	32N11'16	80w59'27	5:23:58
Goodwins Crossroads 30	34N32'15	81w55'09	5:27:41
Goose Creek 8	32N58'51	80w01'58	5:20:08
Gordonville 45	33N41'12	79w26'44	5:17:47
Goretown 26	34N01'36	78w49'17	5:15:17
Goshen 10	32N43'58	80w11'36	5:20:46
Goshen Hill 44	34N31'16	81w33'48	5:26:15
Goucher 11	34N58'53	81w41'50	5:26:47
Gourdin 45	33N29'00	79w53'46	5:19:35
Govan 5	33N13'20	81w10'35	5:24:42
Gowensville 23	35N11	82w11	5:28:44
Grace 29	34N42'28	80w50'36	5:23:22
Grahams Crossroads 26	34N01'10	78w48'32	5:15:14
Grahamville 26	33N49'17	78w54'40	5:15:39
Grahamville 27	32N28'26	80w57'49	5:23:51
Gramling 42	35N04'36	82w07'58	5:28:32
Graniteville 2	33N33'49	81w48'29	5:27:14
Granthams Crossroads 16	34N25'49	80w07'25	5:20:30
Grassy Pond 11	35N08'13	81w40'21	5:26:41
Gravel Hill 38	33N28'50	80w58'23	5:23:54
Graves 22	33N23'36	79w22'09	5:17:29
Gray Court 30	34N36'29	82w06'49	5:28:27
Grays 27	32N40'25	81w01'14	5:24:05
Grays Hill 7	32N29'36	80w44'33	5:22:58
Grays Landing 2	33N16'20	81w50'03	5:27:20
Great Branch 38	33N30'23	80w57'23	5:23:50
Great Falls 12	34N34'30	80w54'08	5:23:37
Greeleyville 45	33N34'51	79w59'21	5:19:57
Green Bay 8	33N00'53	79w45'20	5:19:01
Green Bay 22	33N26'39	79w31'10	5:18:05
Greenbrier 20	34N22	81w05	5:24:20
Green Hill 13	34N28'33	80w08'57	5:20:36
Green Pond 15	32N43'54	80w36'52	5:22:27
Green Pond 42	34N48'00	82w04'50	5:28:19
Green Sea 26	34N07'34	78w58'33	5:15:54
Greenview 40	34N03	81w02	5:24:08
Greenville 23	34N51'09	82w23'39	5:29:35
Greenwood 24	34N11'43	82w09'43	5:28:39
Greenwood Shores 24	34N10'56	81w55'56	5:27:44
Greenwood Village 24	34N11'34	82w10'23	5:28:42
Greer 23	34N56'19	82w13'38	5:28:55
Greer Mill 23	34N56	82w13	5:28:52
Gregg Camp 21	34N11'49	79w38'23	5:18:34
Greggs Landing 18	32N55'42	80w09'15	5:20:37
Grenadier 32	34N02'23	81w08'03	5:24:32
Grendel Mills 24	34N12	82w09	5:28:36
Grendel Village 24	34N12'08	82w09'18	5:28:37
Gresham 34	33N55'48	79w24'41	5:17:39
Grissett 26	33N50'55	79w01'19	5:16:05
Groover Landing 27	32N29'07	81w13'07	5:24:52
Grove Hall 8	33N02'43	80w04'40	5:20:19
Grover 18	33N06'18	80w35'42	5:22:23
Guess 13	34N46	80w14	5:20:56
Guiton Crossing 26	33N51'23	79w08'51	5:16:35
Gurley 26	34N00'09	78w59'15	5:15:57
Guthriesville 46	34N53'53	81w12'29	5:24:50
Hadden Crossroads 42	34N56'06	82w00'12	5:28:01
Hadden Heights 42	34N56'09	82w01'02	5:28:04
Haddock 38	33N28'55	80w53'49	5:23:35
Hagan 8	33N03'26	79w54'33	5:19:38
Hagan Landing 8	33N03'39	79w54'58	5:19:40
Hagood 43	34N03'25	80w34'19	5:22:17
Hagoods Mill 6	33N12'48	81w18'53	5:25:16
Hale 39	34N49'37	82w32'21	5:30:09
Halleytown 14	33N39'30	80w16'01	5:21:04
Halls Mill 25	32N54'35	81w09'57	5:24:40
Halsellville 12	34N43	81w13	5:24:52
Hamburg 2	33N28'47	81w57'29	5:27:50
Hamer 17	34N28'40	79w19'52	5:17:19
Hammetts Crossroads 31	34N08'57	80w18'35	5:21:14
Hammond 4	34N33'16	82w36'02	5:30:24
Hammond 26	33N54'18	78w51'13	5:15:25
Hammond 28	34N08'22	80w35'04	5:22:20
Hammond Crossroads 9	33N42'52	80w52'20	5:23:29
Hampton 25	32N52'15	81w06'35	5:24:26
Hampton Heights 23	34N53'59	82w20'49	5:29:23
Hampton Park Terrace 10	32N48	79w57	5:19:48
Hanahan 8	32N55'06	80w01'20	5:20:05
Hancock 29	34N54'29	80w48'39	5:23:15
Hand 26	33N51'21	78w48'27	5:15:14
Hand B Junction 15	33N03'24	80w55'59	5:23:44
Hankinson 2	33N19'50	81w49'58	5:27:20
Hannah 21	33N52'59	79w34'50	5:18:19
Hardeeville 27	32N17'13	81w04'51	5:24:19
Hardy 19	33N31	81w56	5:27:44
Harleyville 18	33N12'52	80w26'53	5:21:48
Harmony 19	33N48'01	81w50'27	5:27:22
Harmony 46	34N50'24	80w57'21	5:23:49
Harper Crossroads 45	33N28'02	79w33'58	5:18:16
Harris 24	34N13'12	82w12'11	5:28:49
Harris Springs 30	34N19'54	82w01'36	5:28:06
Harristown 8	33N21'22	79w53'10	5:19:33
Harts Bluff 18	32N55'36	80w23'52	5:21:35
Hartsville 16	34N22'26	80w04'25	5:20:18
Harveytown 42	34N57'20	82w08'40	5:28:35
Harvin 14	33N46'01	80w13'43	5:20:55
Haskell Heights 40	34N03	81w02	5:24:08
Hattieville 6	33N06'44	81w36'41	5:26:27
Hayes Crossroads 3	33N04'12	81w16'31	5:25:06
Hayne Station 42	34N57'47	81w57'40	5:27:51
Hazel Farm 7	32N24'30	80w39'39	5:22:39
Hazelwood Acres 40	33N59	80w57	5:23:48
Healing Springs 6	33N23'38	81w16'25	5:25:06
Heath Springs 29	34N35'35	80w40'32	5:22:42
Heathwood Park 2	33N31'28	81w53'18	5:27:33
Hebron 45	33N47	79w47	5:19:08
Hebron Crossroads 45	33N48'59	79w53'14	5:19:33
Heineman 45	33N33'09	79w56'01	5:19:44
Helena 36	34N16'58	81w38'28	5:26:34
Hemingway 45	33N45'13	79w26'52	5:17:47
Hemlock 12	34N43	81w13	5:24:52
Hendersonville 15	32N47'26	80w43'32	5:22:54
Hendricks 39	34N55'44	82w35'30	5:30:22
Hendricks Corner 26	33N49'17	79w10'59	5:16:44
Henry 45	33N41'07	79w29'52	5:17:59
Heriots Crossroads 43	34N13	80w15	5:21:00
Hermitage Mill 28	34N14'32	80w35'21	5:22:21
Hester 1	34N04'13	82w35'14	5:30:21
Hibernia 41	33N53'09	81w35'08	5:26:21
Hicklin Crossing 12	34N47'27	81w02'54	5:24:12
Hickory Bluff 7	32N13'20	80w45'25	5:23:02
Hickory Grove 26	33N51	79w03	5:16:12
Hickory Grove 41	34N05'18	81w44'04	5:26:56
Hickory Grove 46	34N58'59	81w25'00	5:25:40
Hickory Hill 10	32N45'17	80w06'02	5:20:24
Hickory Hill 15	32N39'57	80w37'51	5:22:31
Hickory Tavern 30	34N31'16	82w11'20	5:28:45
Hicks Store 37	34N37'59	83w00'52	5:32:03
Higgins 41	34N07'38	81w44'53	5:27:00
High Hill Crossroads 17	34N20'38	79w13'03	5:16:52
Highland 23	35N05'15	82w19'16	5:29:17
Highland Park 8	32N55'03	80w01'07	5:20:04
Highland Park 38	33N25'32	80w52'52	5:23:31
High Point 4	34N29'37	82w27'30	5:29:50
High Point 13	34N45'05	80w26'13	5:21:45
Highway Four Forty One 43	33N55	80w21	5:21:24
Hilda 6	33N16'24	81w14'50	5:24:59
Hillcrest 42	34N58'00	81w53'41	5:27:35
Hillcrest 43	34N02'06	80w27'53	5:21:52
Hillcrest Acres 4	34N31	82w30	5:30:00
Hillcrest Heights 4	34N37	82w29	5:29:56
Hillside 16	34N15'24	79w47'10	5:19:09
Hilton 40	34N08'13	81w18'23	5:25:14
Hilton Head 7	32N13	80w45	5:23:00
Hilton Head Island 7	32N12'58	80w45'10	5:23:01
Hobbs Crossroads 43	34N00'35	79w57'11	5:19:49
Hobbyville 42	34N41'48	81w55'54	5:27:44
Hobcaw Point 10	32N49'12	79w53'39	5:19:35
Hodges 24	34N17'15	82w14'40	5:28:59
Hoffmeyer Crossing 21	34N12'25	79w50'18	5:19:21
Hogeye Crossroads 45	33N49'00	79w49'24	5:19:18
Hollands Store 4	34N23	82w42	5:30:48
Holland Store 4	34N23'30	82w48'29	5:31:14
Hollman Crossroads 21	34N05'45	79w53'36	5:19:34
Hollow Creek 2	33N24'26	81w47'19	5:27:09
Hollow Creek 32	34N00'19	81w24'38	5:25:39
Holly Hill 38	33N19'21	80w24'50	5:21:39
Holly Ridge 15	33N02'49	80w26'23	5:21:46
Holly Springs 37	34N42'28	83w11'43	5:32:47
Holly Springs 42	35N00'15	82w10'35	5:28:42
Hollywood 10	32N44'03	80w14'31	5:20:58
Hollywood 41	34N00	81w46	5:27:04
Hollywood Hills 40	34N03	81w02	5:24:08
Holmesville 17	34N21	79w10	5:16:40
Holtson Crossroads 41	33N54	81w33	5:26:12
Homeland Park 4	34N28'14	82w40'15	5:30:41
Homewood 26	33N53'02	79w02'55	5:16:12
Honea Path 4	34N26'47	82w23'30	5:29:34
Honey Hill 8	33N11'25	79w34'33	5:18:18
Hoodtown 46	34N54'01	81w24'08	5:25:37
Hopewell 45	33N40'26	79w24'58	5:17:40
Hopewell 46	34N55'36	81w26'29	5:25:46
Hopkins 40	33N54'15	80w52'38	5:23:31
Horatio 43	34N01'16	80w33'58	5:22:16
Horeb 20	34N22	81w05	5:24:20
Hornsboro 13	34N47'52	80w17'20	5:21:09
Horrel Hill 40	33N57'06	80w50'34	5:23:22
Horry 26	33N56'13	79w08'04	5:16:32
Horsegall 25	32N51	81w05	5:24:20
Horse Landing 7	32N14'18	80w46'56	5:23:08
Howard 26	34N06'44	78w52'34	5:15:30
Howards Crossroads 16	34N17'30	79w46'29	5:19:06
Howe 21	34N08'02	79w45'30	5:19:02
Howells 26	33N58'35	78w59'54	5:16:00
Hoyt Heights 43	33N55	80w21	5:21:24
Hudsons Mill 15	32N55'26	80w48'19	5:23:13
Huets Crossroads 19	33N46'22	81w53'14	5:27:33
Huger 8	33N05'47	79w48'13	5:19:13
Huggins Crossroads 22	33N41'39	79w20'42	5:17:23
Hughes 5	33N08'11	81w00'59	5:24:04
Hughes Landing 26	33N53'22	79w15'44	5:17:03
Hulls Island 26	34N01'35	78w47'21	5:15:09
Humbert Woods 10	32N44'36	80w07'01	5:20:28
Hunley Park 10	32N52	80w03	5:20:12
Hunts Crossroads 16	34N25'55	80w02'51	5:20:11
Hunts Mill 13	34N39'39	80w01'16	5:20:05
Hyman 21	33N59'44	79w35'47	5:18:23
Independents 40	33N56'40	80w54'14	5:23:37
India Hook 46	35N00'26	81w01'19	5:24:05
Indian 45	33N45	79w35	5:18:20
Indiantown 45	33N43'30	79w33'35	5:18:14
Industrial 46	34N56	81w01	5:24:04
Ingleside 42	35N11	82w11	5:28:44
Ingram Beach 26	33N48'47	78w41'12	5:14:45
Inman 42	35N02'49	82w05'25	5:28:22
Inman Mills 42	35N02'29	82w06'16	5:28:25
Irmo 32	34N05'09	81w11'00	5:24:44
Iron Crossroads 15	32N52'22	80w29'20	5:21:57
Irvines Landing 24	34N14'10	82w00'38	5:28:03
Irwin 29	34N42	80w49	5:23:16
Iseman Crossroads 16	34N16'07	79w57'11	5:19:49
Island of Palms 10	32N47'24	79w47'04	5:19:08
Islandton 15	32N54'32	80w56'08	5:23:45
Island View Landing 46	35N01'31	81w02'36	5:24:10
Isle of Palms 10	32N47	79w48	5:19:12
Italy 22	33N26'54	79w32'28	5:18:10
Iva 4	34N18'23	82w39'50	5:30:39
Jackson 2	33N19'31	81w47'17	5:27:09
Jackson 22	33N29'57	79w11'57	5:16:48
Jacksonboro 15	32N46'12	80w27'17	5:21:49
Jacksonham 29	34N56	00w45	5:23:00
Jackson Mill 42	34N56'56	82w04'59	5:28:20
Jacksonville 2	33N30'10	81w50'35	5:27:22
Jalapa 36	34N20'40	81w41'08	5:26:45
Jaluco 26	33N46'40	78w58'36	5:15:54
James Crossroads 14	33N37'53	80w12'59	5:20:52
James Island 10	32N44	79w57	5:19:48
Jamestown 8	33N17'09	79w41'34	5:18:46
Jamestown 21	34N13'42	79w36'16	5:18:25
Jamestown 26	33N49'44	79w04'21	5:16:17
Jamison 38	33N34'55	80w49'05	5:23:16
Jason 37	34N39'52	83w04'44	5:32:19
Jasper 27	32N20'34	80w56'58	5:23:48
Jedburg 18	33N03'20	80w14'19	5:20:57
Jefferson 13	34N39'00	80w23'21	5:21:33
Jenkinsville 20	34N16'02	81w17'19	5:25:09
Jennings 20	34N14'25	81w09'20	5:24:37
Jennys 3	32N57	81w14	5:24:56
Jericho 10	32N45'32	80w19'00	5:21:16
Jernigan Crossroads 16	34N12'18	79w56'51	5:19:47
Jernigans Crossroads 26	34N06'48	78w54'08	5:15:37
Joanna 30	34N24'53	81w48'41	5:27:15
Jocassee 37	34N58'15	82w56'15	5:31:45
Johns 44	34N50	81w41	5:26:44
Johns Island 10	32N47'32	80w06'30	5:20:26
Johns Mill 37	34N37'33	83w06'28	5:32:26
Johnson City 42	34N57'55	81w59'21	5:27:57
Johnson Corner 22	33N28'00	79w21'53	5:17:28
Johnson Crossroads 2	33N23'28	81w41'05	5:26:44
Johnson Crossroads 19	33N46'18	82w03'08	5:28:13
Johnson Crossroads 21	34N02'05	79w49'21	5:19:17
Johnsons Landing 3	32N59'48	81w29'27	5:25:58
Johnsonville 21	33N49'04	79w26'58	5:17:48
Johnston 19	33N49'55	81w48'04	5:27:12
Johnstown 2	33N29'34	81w52'35	5:27:30
Jones Crossroads 2	33N45'54	81w32'40	5:26:11
Jones Crossroads 21	34N04'16	79w51'57	5:19:28
Jones Crossroads 26	33N58'29	79w10'50	5:16:43
Jones Crossroads 29	34N39'03	80w45'59	5:23:04
Jones Crossroads 41	33N58'05	81w39'13	5:26:37
Jonestown 26	33N56'47	79w14'28	5:16:58
Jonesville 15	32N44'10	80w48'58	5:23:16
Jonesville 44	34N50'09	81w40'52	5:26:43
Jordan 14	33N36'21	80w12'33	5:20:50
Jordan 23	35N02'35	82w15'09	5:29:01
Jordania 37	34N41	82w56	5:31:44
Jordan Mill 28	34N24'25	80w30'28	5:22:02
Jordanville 26	33N53'57	79w14'14	5:16:57
Joshua 10	32N51'14	80w00'52	5:20:03
Judson 23	34N51	82w26	5:29:44

Juniper Bay 26 33N52'16 79w10'11 5:16:41
Kathwood 2 33N20'39 81w50'40 5:27:23
Kathwood 32 33N59 81w05 5:24:20
Keitts Crossroads 36 34N20'37 81w30'38 5:26:03
Kellehan Crossroads 45 33N35'26 79w40'46 5:18:43
Kelly 44 34N48'44 81w35'50 5:26:23
Kellytown 16 34N21'11 80w08'23 5:20:34
Kellytown 28 34N14'52 80w44'03 5:22:56
Kelsey Cove Landing 15 32N57'23 80w24'23 5:21:38
Kelton 44 34N50'00 81w34'47 5:26:19
Kemper 17 34N19'41 79w11'59 5:16:48
Kennedy Crossroads 21 34N04'45 79w35'09 5:18:21
Kennedy Mill 44 34N51'13 81w46'05 5:27:04
Kensington 8 33N07'49 79w50'25 5:19:22
Kensington 22 33N22 79w17 5:17:08
Kent 22 33N25'44 79w28'57 5:17:56
Keowee 1 34N23'13 82w25'32 5:29:42
Keowee 37 34N41'43 82w52'43 5:31:31
Kershaw 29 34N33'06 80w35'02 5:22:20
Ketchuptown 26 34N06'07 79w09'20 5:16:37
Key 35 34N31 79w39 5:18:36
Keys Field 26 33N44'36 79w04'05 5:16:16
Kibler 36 34N13'54 81w26'58 5:25:48
Kiffs Crossroads 31 34N10'43 80w08'37 5:20:34
Kilgore 42 34N41'34 81w59'44 5:27:59
Killgo 28 34N15 80w36 5:22:24
Killian 40 34N08'17 80w56'47 5:23:47
Kimberly 13 34N39'45 79w57'32 5:19:50
Kinards 36 34N22'49 81w46'39 5:27:07
King Circle 29 34N42 80w47 5:23:08
King Creek Landing 3 32N55'15 81w28'58 5:25:56
Kingsburg 21 33N52'49 79w27'08 5:17:49
Kings Creek 11 35N04'26 81w26'13 5:25:45
Kingstree 45 33N40'03 79w49'51 5:19:19
Kingville 40 33N48'20 80w41'52 5:22:47
Kirkland 28 34N17'46 80w36'41 5:22:27
Kirkley Mill 28 34N29'52 80w30'45 5:22:03
Kirksey 24 34N01'52 82w02'30 5:28:10
Kirkwood 28 34N15 80w36 5:22:24
Kitchings Mill 2 33N34'42 81w28'39 5:25:55
Kittredge 8 33N04'10 79w58'35 5:19:54
Kline 6 33N07'33 81w20'34 5:25:22
Klondike 26 33N41'27 79w07'05 5:16:28
Kneece 32 33N52'18 81w30'41 5:26:03
Knightsville 18 33N00'41 80w14'17 5:20:57
Knotty Branch 26 33N55'15 79w09'30 5:16:38
Knox 12 34N43'18 81w04'52 5:24:19
Konig 26 33N42'42 78w55'19 5:15:41
Koonce 34 34N08'12 79w17'32 5:17:10
Kress 27 32N38'36 80w53'04 5:23:32
Ladson 10 32N59'08 80w06'36 5:20:26
La France 4 34N36'43 82w45'55 5:31:04
Lake City 21 33N52'15 79w45'20 5:19:01
Lake Forest 23 34N52'15 82w20'30 5:29:22
Lake Lanier 23 35N11 82w11 5:28:44
Lakemont 23 35N03'53 82w37'47 5:30:31
Lake Murray Shores 41 34N04'29 81w29'04 5:25:56
Lake Shores 24 34N16'33 82w03'42 5:28:15
Lakeside 23 34N46'37 82w25'47 5:29:43
Lake Swamp 16 34N13 80w00 5:20:00
Lake Taro 23 34N46'02 82w17'03 5:29:08
Lake View 17 34N20'44 79w09'57 5:16:40
Lakewood 26 33N37'37 78w57'48 5:15:51
Lakewood 46 35N01'15 81w02'42 5:24:11
Lamar 16 34N10'07 80w03'46 5:20:15
Lambert 22 33N19'33 79w34'21 5:18:17
Lambrick 38 33N18'22 80w44'05 5:22:56
Lambs 10 32N53'11 80w04'05 5:20:16
Lancaster 29 34N43'13 80w46'16 5:23:05
Lando 12 34N46'34 81w00'37 5:24:02
Landrum 42 35N10'30 82w11'22 5:28:45
Lands End 7 32N24 80w35 5:22:20
Landsford 12 34N46'28 80w55'17 5:23:41
Lane 45 33N31'17 79w52'44 5:19:31
Lanes Creek 22 33N29'58 79w21'48 5:17:27
Lanford 30 34N38'00 81w58'30 5:27:54
Langfords Crossroads 40 34N12'29 80w54'28 5:23:38
Langley 2 33N31'04 81w50'39 5:27:23
Lathem 39 34N50 82w37 5:30:28
Latimer 1 34N07'55 82w35'34 5:30:22
Latta 17 34N20'13 79w25'53 5:17:44
Laughlin 34 34N11'45 79w28'33 5:17:54
Laurel Bay 7 32N27 80w47 5:23:08
Laurel Hill 10 32N43'18 80w17'12 5:21:09
Laurel Hill Plantation 10 33N03'14 79w32'55 5:18:12
Laurens 30 34N29'56 82w00'52 5:28:03
Lawson 42 34N58'39 81w54'41 5:27:39
Lawton 7 32N08'36 80w47'19 5:23:09
Lawtonville Crossroads 25 32N45'16 81w16'15 5:25:05
Leawood 23 34N53'30 82w24'12 5:29:37
Lebanon 4 34N37'05 82w41'29 5:30:46
Lebanon 20 34N24'41 81w12'18 5:24:49
Lee Crossroads 21 33N52'17 79w39'59 5:18:40
Leeds 12 34N37'46 81w23'47 5:25:35
Lees 5 33N20'54 81w12'43 5:24:51
Leesburg 40 34N00'59 80w42'20 5:22:49
Lees Crossroads 13 34N43'35 80w11'18 5:20:45
Lees Crossroads 16 34N18'00 80w05'09 5:20:21
Leesville 32 33N54'59 81w30'49 5:26:03
Legareville 10 32N39'17 80w03'11 5:20:13
Lena 25 32N45'12 81w12'55 5:24:52
Leo 21 33N50'00 79w36'55 5:18:28
Leslie 46 34N53'26 80w57'24 5:23:50
Lester 35 34N40'45 79w39'04 5:18:36
Level Land 1 34N19'39 82w28'33 5:29:54
Levy 27 32N12'10 81w01'45 5:24:07
Lewis 12 34N43 81w13 5:24:52
Lewis Crossroads 16 34N19'44 79w58'08 5:19:53
Lewis Turnout 12 34N46'43 81w08'01 5:24:32
Lexington 32 33N58'53 81w14'11 5:24:57
Liberty 39 34N47'16 82w41'33 5:30:46
Liberty Hill 10 32N54 80w00 5:20:00
Liberty Hill 28 34N28'41 80w48'07 5:23:12
Liberty Hill 33 33N55'07 82w10'26 5:28:42
Lickville 23 34N37'04 82w20'05 5:29:20
Lighthouse Landing 7 32N10'55 80w44'21 5:22:57
Lima 23 35N05'21 82w26'51 5:29:47
Limehouse 27 32N12'45 81w04'15 5:24:17
Limehouse Station 10 32N46'17 80w04'49 5:20:19
Limerick 8 33N08'09 79w48'55 5:19:16
Limestone 19 33N54'12 82w02'02 5:28:08
Limp 41 33N59'17 81w51'09 5:27:25
Lincoln Shire 40 34N03 81w02 5:24:08
Lincolnville 10 33N00'24 80w09'20 5:20:37
Lingles Crossroads 29 34N45'23 80w37'46 5:22:31
Lions Beach 8 33N12 80w01 5:20:04
Litchfield Beach 22 33N26 79w07 5:16:28
Little Africa 42 35N10'02 82w01'37 5:28:06
Little Camden 40 34N00 81w03 5:24:12
Little Edisto 10 32N35'59 80w20'41 5:21:23
Little Hell Landing 3 33N03'40 81w33'49 5:26:15
Little Mountain 36 34N11'46 81w24'45 5:25:39
Little River 26 33N52'23 78w36'52 5:14:27
Little Rock 17 34N28'35 79w24'12 5:17:37
Little Texas 23 34N58'04 82w23'57 5:29:36
Littleton 40 34N10'44 81w10'33 5:24:42
Little Town 26 33N57'33 78w44'15 5:14:57
Little Vista Heights 42 34N56'24 81w54'48 5:27:39
Live Oak 26 34N03'20 78w56'20 5:15:45
Livingston 38 33N33'12 81w07'08 5:24:29
Lobeco 7 32N33'09 80w44'37 5:22:58
Lockhart 44 34N47'11 81w27'44 5:25:51
Lockhart Junction 44 34N49'08 81w39'08 5:26:37
Lockhart Olk Field 28 34N25'24 80w32'05 5:22:08
Locust Hill 23 35N01'04 82w23'02 5:29:32
Locust Tree Landing 26 33N57'28 79w19'57 5:17:20
Lodge 15 33N04'04 80w57'14 5:23:49
Lodge Hall 22 33N19'58 79w28'29 5:17:54
Log Jam Landing 14 33N31'13 80w18'09 5:21:13
Lone Oak 42 34N59'32 81w58'48 5:27:55
Lone Star 9 33N37'31 80w35'23 5:22:22
Long Bay Estates 26 33N39 78w56 5:15:44
Long Bottom Ford 37 34N53'58 83w11'09 5:32:45
Long Branch 6 33N19'19 81w23'17 5:25:33
Long Branch 30 34N30'49 81w53'44 5:27:35
Longcreek 37 34N46'24 83w15'33 5:33:02
Long Creek Landing 15 32N56'07 80w24'11 5:21:37
Long Point 26 34N01'28 78w52'50 5:15:31
Long Ridge 8 33N12 80w01 5:20:04
Longs 26 33N56'18 78w44'00 5:14:56
Longshore 36 34N16'27 81w44'47 5:26:59
Longtown 20 34N20'51 80w50'15 5:23:21
Longwood 7 32N19'21 80w36'36 5:22:26
Longwood Landing 26 33N36'21 79w05'08 5:16:21
Lopers Crossroads 3 32N56'00 81w16'03 5:25:04
Loris 26 34N03'22 78w53'26 5:15:34
Lota 24 34N15'09 82w02'43 5:28:11
Lotts Crossroads 18 33N02'27 80w14'58 5:21:00
Lower Topsaw Landing 22 33N36'29 79w09'06 5:16:36
Lowndes Landing 15 32N52'06 80w24'14 5:21:37
Lowndesville 1 34N12'45 82w38'59 5:30:36
Lowrys 12 34N48'14 81w14'22 5:24:57
Lucknow 31 34N17'33 80w20'16 5:21:21
Lugoff 28 34N13'38 80w41'22 5:22:45
Lundy Crossroads 26 33N53'03 79w10'43 5:16:43
Lunn 16 34N20'29 79w58'14 5:19:53
Luray 25 32N48'49 81w14'24 5:24:58
Lydia 16 34N17'20 80w06'45 5:20:27
Lydia Mills 30 34N27'31 81w54'07 5:27:36
Lykes 40 33N56'19 80w54'11 5:23:37
Lykesland 40 33N54 80w53 5:23:32
Lyman 42 34N56'53 82w07'39 5:28:31
Lynchburg 31 34N03'36 80w04'18 5:20:17
Lynches Mill 21 34N01'33 79w48'46 5:19:15
Lyndhurst 6 33N15 81w22 5:25:28
Lynwood 2 33N30'27 81w51'38 5:27:27
MacArthurs Junction 1 34N25'19 82w16'54 5:29:08
Macbeth 8 33N16'05 79w58'24 5:19:54
Macedon 32 33N49'02 81w12'50 5:24:51
Macedonia 11 35N04'14 81w45'38 5:27:03
Macedonia 36 34N06'20 81w26'32 5:25:46
Maddens 30 34N27'34 82w03'13 5:28:13
Madison 2 33N33'23 81w48'39 5:27:15
Madison 37 34N37'56 83w12'29 5:32:50
Mallory 17 34N23'18 79w30'48 5:18:03
Malta 43 33N52'37 80w35'03 5:22:20
Mangums 13 34N46 80w23 5:21:32
Manning 14 33N41'42 80w12'40 5:20:51
Manning Crossroads 17 34N28'24 79w27'38 5:17:51
Manville 31 34N09'14 80w18'13 5:21:13
Maple 23 34N55'46 82w14'13 5:28:57
Maple Crossroads 26 33N54'48 79w00'52 5:16:03
Marietta 23 35N01'15 82w30'06 5:30:00
Marine Corps Air Station 7 32N27 80w44 5:22:56
Marion 34 34N10'41 79w24'03 5:17:36
Marlboro 35 34N32'12 79w43'58 5:18:56
Mars Bluff 21 34N12'19 79w39'20 5:18:37
Martin 3 33N04'08 81w28'36 5:25:54
Martin Corner 45 33N24'34 79w42'26 5:18:50
Martin Crossroads 30 34N37'45 82w01'50 5:28:07
Martins Crossroads 45 33N41'59 79w57'27 5:19:50
Martins Landing 10 32N50'36 80w23'40 5:21:35
Martins Landing 25 32N39'02 81w23'35 5:25:34
Martins Point Landing 10 32N53'45 79w50'20 5:19:21
Mary 26 33N52'24 79w06'19 5:16:25
Mary Louise 42 35N05'27 81w50'46 5:27:23
Marysville 22 33N25'39 79w09'05 5:16:36
Maryville 10 32N47'32 79w59'43 5:19:59
Maryville 22 33N20'33 79w17'49 5:17:11
Maryville 42 34N54'59 81w45'25 5:27:02
Mas Old Field Landing 15 33N03'15 80w26'59 5:21:48
Masons Cross Road 4 34N33'26 82w46'31 5:31:06
Mathews Heights 24 34N08'40 82w08'03 5:28:32
Mathews Village 24 34N09'56 82w08'57 5:28:36
Mathis Corner 21 34N05'40 79w41'50 5:18:47
Mauldin 23 34N46'43 82w18'37 5:29:14
Mauldins Mill 25 32N52 81w07 5:24:28
May 17 34N21 79w10 5:16:40
Maybinton 36 34N27'08 81w28'33 5:25:54
Mayesville 43 33N59'15 80w12'30 5:20:50
Mayfair 23 34N53 82w21 5:29:24
May Hilltop 17 34N19'02 79w13'12 5:16:53
Mayo 42 35N05'02 81w51'36 5:27:26
Mayo Mills 42 35N05 81w52 5:27:28
Mayson Crossroads 19 33N56'11 82w07'19 5:28:29
Maysville 13 34N48'39 80w10'01 5:20:40
McBee 13 34N28'08 80w15'22 5:21:01
McBeth 8 33N18 79w58 5:19:52
McCaskill 28 34N07'24 80w42'14 5:22:49
McClellanville 10 33N05'17 79w27'41 5:17:51
McColl 35 34N40'07 79w32'44 5:18:11
McConnells 46 34N52'07 81w13'40 5:24:55
McCormick 33 33N54'48 82w17'37 5:29:10
McCormick Crossroads 17 34N29'43 79w28'46 5:17:55
McCutchens Crossroads 31 34N08'45 80w14'06 5:20:56
McKelvey Crossroads 23 34N36'28 82w22'09 5:29:29
McKennon 13 34N32'48 80w07'41 5:20:31
McKenzie Crossroads 21 33N54'47 79w54'31 5:19:38
McKeown 12 34N37'03 81w10'57 5:24:44
McLaughlin Crossroads 16 34N13'23 80w03'30 5:20:14
McPhersonville 25 32N41'30 80w55'10 5:23:41
McQueen Crossroads 26 34N04'26 79w08'38 5:16:35
Meadow Brook 16 34N15'39 79w46'37 5:19:06
Meadows 44 34N43 81w37 5:26:28
Mean Crossroads 44 34N48'29 81w43'56 5:26:56
Mechanicsville 16 34N20'41 79w45'27 5:19:02
Mechanicsville 31 34N13 80w15 5:21:00
Meeks 21 34N12'07 79w42'43 5:18:51
Meggett 10 32N43'04 80w14'21 5:20:57
Melrose 2 33N25 81w41 5:26:44
Melrose 10 32N47'32 80w02'49 5:20:11
Mepkin 8 33N06'53 79w57'09 5:19:49
Merchant 41 34N00 81w46 5:27:04
Meriwether 33 33N39'10 82w09'35 5:28:38
Mexico 46 34N56'16 81w00'18 5:24:01
Middendorf 13 34N31'18 80w09'47 5:20:39
Midland Park 10 32N55'14 80w02'27 5:20:10
Midland Valley 2 33N33'05 81w49'16 5:27:17
Midway 5 33N17'00 80w58'42 5:23:55
Midway 9 33N30'52 80w38'06 5:22:32
Midway 29 34N36'56 80w31'17 5:22:05
Midway Crossroads 22 33N42'05 79w19'43 5:17:19
Midway Crossroads 29 34N37'14 80w30'06 5:22:00
Midway Crossroads 45 33N46'01 79w32'54 5:18:12
Midway Village 26 33N39 78w56 5:15:44
Miley 25 32N56'52 81w01'55 5:24:08
Milford 43 33N44'49 80w32'00 5:22:08
Milford Springs 24 34N12 82w09 5:28:36
Mill Branch 21 34N03'53 79w33'05 5:18:12
Miller Crossing 46 34N58'46 81w05'02 5:24:20
Miller Crossroads 22 33N42'31 79w18'54 5:17:16
Miller Hill 10 32N43'07 80w01'18 5:20:05
Millers Crossroads 19 33N44'39 82w06'04 5:28:24
Millers Ford 15 32N54'49 80w42'54 5:22:52
Millers Mill 1 34N13'01 82w18'23 5:29:14
Millett 3 33N04'52 81w32'09 5:26:09
Millford 43 33N44 80w28 5:21:52
Mill Stone Landing 27 32N17'10 81w07'10 5:24:29
Mill Village 35 34N37 79w41 5:18:44
Millwood 45 33N35'57 79w44'40 5:18:59
Millwood Gardens 43 33N54'46 80w22'45 5:21:31
Milton 30 34N21'08 81w53'24 5:27:34
Mineral Springs Park 16 34N19'37 79w53'01 5:19:32
Minton Mill 28 34N30'21 80w24'34 5:21:38
Minturn 17 34N31'01 79w28'21 5:17:53
Mitchellville 27 32N27'42 80w59'32 5:23:58
Mitford 20 34N31'38 80w57'20 5:23:49
Mixville 2 33N32'31 81w48'59 5:27:16
Modoc 33 33N44'00 82w12'21 5:28:49
Monaghan 23 34N51'56 82w25'45 5:29:43
Monarch Mills 44 34N43'06 81w35'48 5:26:23
Moncks Corner 8 33N11'45 80w00'48 5:20:03
Monetta 2 33N51'00 81w36'35 5:26:26
Monroe Crossroads 35 34N32'42 79w39'19 5:18:37

Place	Latitude	Longitude	Time
Montague 23	34N54'58	82W26'29	5:29:46
Mont Clare 16	34N23'48	79W49'17	5:19:17
Montgomery 40	34N08'01	81W08'04	5:24:32
Monticello 20	34N21'09	81W17'55	5:25:12
Montmorenci 2	33N31'40	81W38'12	5:26:33
Montrose 13	34N38'08	79W52'23	5:19:30
Moody Cove 37	34N55'56	83W04'15	5:32:17
Moonville 23	34N43'01	82W23'16	5:29:33
Moore 42	34N50'00	81W59'32	5:27:58
Moore Crossroads 45	33N51'02	79W50'24	5:19:22
Moorefield 8	33N17'19	80W10'08	5:20:41
Moores Corner 10	33N06'00	79W28'09	5:17:53
Moores Crossroads 3	32N58'44	81W19'33	5:25:18
Moores Crossroads 45	33N47	79W47	5:19:08
Moores Landing 10	32N56'23	79W39'27	5:18:38
Moreland 8	33N00'33	79W53'43	5:19:35
Moreland Landing 8	33N00'34	79W54'00	5:19:36
Morgan 11	35N07	81W47	5:27:08
Morgan 27	32N18'13	81W04'57	5:24:20
Morgana 19	33N36'25	82W03'16	5:28:13
Morningside 23	34N53'04	82W20'30	5:29:22
Morrell 21	34N08	79W57	5:19:48
Morris Acres 10	32N39	80W08	5:20:32
Morrisville 45	33N36'25	79W32'20	5:18:09
Moselle 15	32N57'57	81W00'46	5:24:03
Moss 19	33N47	81W56	5:27:44
Motbridge 43	34N04	80W05	5:20:20
Mountain Brook 40	33N59	80W57	5:23:48
Mountain Lake Colony 23	35N04'21	82W37'23	5:30:30
Mountain Rest 37	34N51	83W07	5:32:28
Mountain View 42	35N05'14	81W55'46	5:27:43
Mount Beulah 2	33N26'36	81W32'11	5:26:09
Mount Carmel 33	34N00'26	82W30'26	5:30:02
Mount Croghan 13	34N46'11	80W13'41	5:20:55
Mount Gallagher 30	34N23'43	82W11'18	5:28:45
Mount Holly 8	33N02'03	80W02'05	5:20:08
Mount Olive 26	34N14	79W09	5:16:36
Mount Olive 30	34N22'48	82W09'13	5:28:37
Mount Pisgah 28	34N33'29	80W26'43	5:21:47
Mount Pleasant 10	32N47'38	79W51'46	5:19:27
Mount Rena 22	33N31'05	79W07'47	5:16:31
Mount Tabor 22	33N37'04	79W11'42	5:16:47
Mount View 23	35N01'52	82W21'23	5:29:26
Mountville 30	34N21'46	81W58'04	5:27:52
Mount Willing 41	34N00	81W46	5:27:04
Mount Zion 21	33N57'04	79W33'13	5:18:13
Mount Zion 28	34N16	80W32	5:22:08
Mouzon 45	33N44'04	79W55'37	5:19:42
Moyd 22	33N20'28	79W22'10	5:17:29
Mudlick 36	34N16'10	81W52'11	5:27:29
Mulberry Landing 22	33N35'03	79W06'09	5:16:25
Muldrow Mill 16	34N11'59	79W53'05	5:19:32
Mullins 34	34N12'20	79W15'17	5:17:01
Munster 40	34N03'12	81W03'58	5:24:16
Murad 27	32N29'45	80W52'13	5:23:29
Murray 32	33N57'12	81W25'01	5:25:40
Murray Landing 10	32N50'02	79W59'15	5:19:57
Murraysville 8	33N10'52	80W06'06	5:20:24
Murrells Inlet 22	33N33'03	79W02'30	5:16:10
Myers 10	32N49'00	79W57'02	5:19:48
Myrtle Beach 26	33N41'20	78W53'13	5:15:33
Myrtle Island 7	32N12'42	80W51'54	5:23:28
Myrtle Ridge 26	33N41'18	78W54'52	5:15:39
Naval Base 10	32N51	79W55	5:19:40
Naval Hospital 7	32N27	80W44	5:22:56
Ned Swamp 26	33N52'18	79W07'53	5:16:32
Neeses 38	33N31'54	81W07'24	5:24:30
Neighbors Crossroads 30	34N27'29	81W48'24	5:27:14
Nesmith 45	33N39'32	79W30'49	5:18:03
Nevadum 27	32N27'31	80W53'22	5:23:33
Nevadun 27	32N29	80W59	5:23:56
Nevitt Forest 4	34N31	82W39	5:30:36
Newberry 36	34N16'28	81W37'08	5:26:29
New Cut 29	34N46'43	80W40'24	5:22:42
New Cut Landing 10	32N42'21	80W10'41	5:20:43
New Easley Highway 23	34N51	82W26	5:29:44
New Ellenton 2	33N25'17	81W41'09	5:26:45
New Holland 2	33N41'39	81W29'27	5:25:58
New Holland Crossroads 2	33N42'03	81W28'50	5:25:55
New Hope 21	34N01'03	79W45'04	5:19:00
New Hope 22	33N21'02	79W28'16	5:17:53
Newland 8	33N12'15	79W36'59	5:18:28
New Landing 27	32N30'46	81W13'50	5:24:55
New Light 4	34N35'21	82W48'11	5:31:13
New Market 16	34N24'05	80W08'33	5:20:34
New Market 24	34N09'46	82W08'05	5:28:32
Newport 46	34N59'23	81W06'04	5:24:24
New Prospect 42	35N07'56	82W02'39	5:28:11
Newry 37	34N43'30	82W54'36	5:31:38
Newtonville 35	34N42'30	79W38'18	5:18:33
New Town 17	34N25	79W22	5:17:28
New Zion 14	33N50'39	80W01'46	5:20:07
Neyles 15	32N49'30	80W33'31	5:22:14
Nichols 34	34N14'01	79W08'56	5:16:36
Nicholson Village 2	33N33'16	81W39'16	5:26:37
Nicholtown 23	34N50'25	82W22'17	5:29:29
Nimmons 39	34N59	82W48	5:31:12
Nine Times 39	34N54'54	82W50'39	5:31:23
Ninety Six 24	34N10'30	82W01'27	5:28:06
Nixons Crossroads 26	33N51'27	78W39'38	5:14:39
Nixonville 26	33N50'04	78W53'08	5:15:33
Nixville 25	32N44'34	81W09'08	5:24:37
Noisette Creek 10	32N52	79W56	5:19:44
Norman Landing 18	32N59'04	80W24'31	5:21:38
Norris 39	34N45'36	82W45'14	5:31:01
North 38	33N36'56	81W06'08	5:24:25
North Anderson 4	34N31	82W39	5:30:36
North Augusta 2	33N30'06	81W57'55	5:27:52
Northbridge 10	32N48	80W00	5:20:00
North Charleston 10	32N51'16	79W58'30	5:19:54
North Conway 26	33N51'10	79W03'03	5:16:12
North Forest Beach 7	32N13	80W45	5:23:00
Northgate 21	34N12	79W45	5:19:00
Northgate 23	34N52'47	82W23'02	5:29:32
North Hartsville 16	34N23'37	80W04'11	5:20:17
North Litchfield Beach 22	33N26	79W07	5:16:28
North Mullins 34	34N13'01	79W15'27	5:17:02
North Myrtle Beach 26	33N49	78W40	5:14:40
North Pacolet 42	35N09'56	82W05'06	5:28:20
North Santee 22	33N13'48	79W22'37	5:17:30
North Summerville 18	33N01	80W11	5:20:44
North Winyah Heights 22	33N22	79W17	5:17:08
Norway 38	33N27'06	81W07'32	5:24:30
Norwood Crossroad 43	33N58'04	79W56'30	5:19:46
Oak Corner 8	33N10'08	79W42'30	5:18:50
Oak Dale 14	33N51	80W02	5:20:08
Oakey Bay 26	33N50'37	79W08'00	5:16:32
Oak Grove 2	33N44'56	81W31'28	5:26:06
Oak Grove 9	33N46'41	80W58'01	5:23:52
Oakgrove 10	32N37'36	80W12'47	5:20:51
Oak Grove 17	34N21'05	79W32'34	5:18:10
Oak Grove 21	34N08'27	79W34'11	5:18:17
Oak Grove 22	33N23'09	79W27'39	5:17:51
Oak Hill 2	33N25	81W41	5:26:44
Oakhurst 29	34N33	80W35	5:22:20
Oakland 7	32N27	80W44	5:22:56
Oakland 10	32N47'07	80W02'07	5:20:08
Oakland Crossroads 17	34N32'20	79W21'59	5:17:28
Oakland Mill 36	34N17	81W37	5:26:28
Oakley 8	33N07'26	80W01'09	5:20:05
Oak Ridge 29	34N36	80W40	5:22:40
Oak Ridge 45	33N25'15	79W38'40	5:18:35
Oakvale 23	34N42	82W27	5:29:48
Oakway 37	34N36'04	83W01'33	5:32:06
Oakwood 2	33N30'59	81W35'11	5:26:21
Oatland 22	33N29'42	79W20'51	5:17:23
Oats 16	34N15'12	80W04'40	5:20:19
Ocean Drive 26	33N49'06	78W40'25	5:14:42
Ocean Drive Beach 26	33N49	78W40	5:14:40
Ocean Forest 26	33N43'47	78W50'18	5:15:21
Oceanview 10	32N43'04	79W56'02	5:19:44
Oceda 22	33N21'05	79W38'14	5:18:33
Ogden 46	34N51'45	81W05'41	5:24:23
Okatie 27	32N21'07	80W58'42	5:23:55
Olanta 21	33N56'07	79W55'58	5:19:44
Olar 5	33N10'49	81W11'08	5:24:45
Old Cordesville 8	33N10'39	79W55'01	5:19:40
Old House 27	32N27'34	80W53'48	5:23:35
Old Joe 8	33N03'20	79W48'29	5:19:14
Old Madison 37	34N36'45	83W11'47	5:32:47
Old Morrisville 45	33N35'54	79W30'27	5:18:02
Old Pickens 37	34N47'10	82W53'20	5:31:33
Old Point Station 46	34N57'35	81W02'56	5:24:12
Old Town 10	32N48'16	79W59'05	5:19:56
Olga 39	35N02	82W30	5:30:00
Olin 22	33N25'30	79W27'55	5:17:52
Oliver Crossroads 17	34N23'04	79W15'50	5:17:03
Olympia 40	33N58'35	81W01'48	5:24:07
O'Neal 23	35N00'26	82W16'52	5:29:07
Opossum Point Landing 7	32N10'37	80W46'23	5:23:06
Ora 30	34N34'54	81W59'45	5:27:59
Orangeburg 38	33N29'30	80W51'21	5:23:25
Orrs 12	34N43'01	81W07'25	5:24:30
Orrville 4	34N31	82W39	5:30:36
Orum 21	34N00	79W34	5:18:16
Osborn 10	32N45'20	80W20'47	5:21:23
Osceola 29	34N51	80W51	5:23:24
Oswego 43	34N00'26	80W17'16	5:21:09
Otranto 10	32N57'54	80W02'40	5:20:11
Outland 45	33N43'36	79W22'22	5:17:29
Overbrook 23	34N51'35	82W22'41	5:29:31
Owdoms 41	33N59'04	81W52'47	5:27:31
Owens 22	33N41'36	79W23'07	5:17:32
Owens Crossroad 6	33N09'24	81W24'04	5:25:36
Owings 30	34N37'51	82W08'01	5:28:32
Oyster Point 10	32N43'19	79W55'43	5:19:43
Pacolet 42	34N53'56	81W45'43	5:27:03
Pacolet Mills 42	34N55'21	81W44'34	5:26:58
Pacolet Park 42	34N55'14	81W44'32	5:26:58
Padgett Landing 15	32N50'43	80W23'59	5:21:36
Padgetts 15	33N04'18	80W53'11	5:23:33
Pageland 13	34N46'23	80W23'31	5:21:34
Paint Hill 28	34N14'12	80W33'39	5:22:15
Palmer Subdivision 4	34N31	82W39	5:30:36
Palmerville 8	33N15'14	79W38'52	5:18:35
Palmetto 16	34N15'07	79W49'39	5:19:19
Palmetto Bluff 7	32N12'28	80W53'04	5:23:32
Palmetto Fort 10	32N48	79W52	5:19:28
Palmetto Plaza 43	33N55	80W21	5:21:24
Pamplico 21	33N59'45	79W34'13	5:18:17
Panola 14	33N39'22	80W24'42	5:21:39
Panola 24	34N12	82W09	5:28:36
Panola Village 24	34N10'11	82W08'57	5:28:36
Paramount Park 23	34N49	82W24	5:29:36
Paris 23	34N53'38	82W21'45	5:29:27
Parker Crossroads 21	34N10'34	79W36'58	5:18:28
Parkers Ferry 10	32N45'36	80W23'47	5:21:35
Parkers Ferry Landing 15	32N51'33	80W24'14	5:21:37
Parkersville 22	33N27'14	79W07'24	5:16:30
Parkhill 19	33N45'43	81W53'45	5:27:35
Park Hills 42	34N56'06	81W57'00	5:27:48
Park Place 23	34N52'10	82W24'32	5:29:38
Parks Mill 33	33N51'11	82W13'35	5:28:54
Parksville 33	33N47'10	82W13'11	5:28:53
Parler 38	33N29'36	80W30'38	5:22:03
Parlersville 38	33N30'42	80W30'24	5:22:02
Parr 20	34N15'57	81W19'58	5:25:20
Parris Island 7	32N20	80W41	5:22:44
Parrot Point 10	32N43'43	79W54'41	5:19:39
Patrick 13	34N34'28	80W02'46	5:20:11
Patterson Mill 6	33N10'42	81W28'45	5:25:55
Pauline 42	34N49'59	81W52'21	5:27:29
Pawleys Island 22	33N25'59	79W07'18	5:16:29
Paxville 14	33N44'19	80W21'27	5:21:26
Peachtree Landing 26	33N41'40	79W02'55	5:16:12
Peach Valley 42	34N58	81W57	5:27:48
Peak 36	34N14'26	81W19'25	5:25:18
Pecan Terrace 23	34N49	82W24	5:29:36
Pecan Way Terrace 38	33N30	80W52	5:23:28
Peedee 34	34N12'21	79W32'21	5:18:09
Pee Dee Crossroads 26	33N50'18	79W13'22	5:16:53
Pelham 42	34N51'25	82W13'27	5:28:54
Pelion 32	33N45'47	81W14'42	5:24:59
Pelzer 4	34N38'32	82W27'22	5:29:49
Pendleton 39	34N39'06	82W47'02	5:31:08
Peniel Crossroads 21	34N05'19	79W51'23	5:19:26
Percival Crossroads 37	34N40	83W06	5:32:24
Perkins Crossroads 21	34N06'17	79W49'11	5:19:17
Perrot 21	34N02'03	79W35'57	5:18:24
Perry 2	33N37'36	81W18'42	5:25:15
Peters Ferry Landing 26	33N56'13	79W19'04	5:17:16
Petersfield 22	33N40'46	79W13'50	5:16:55
Philip 10	32N53'15	79W48'51	5:19:15
Philson Crossroads 30	34N32'49	81W48'40	5:27:15
Phinney 37	34N43'40	83W00'09	5:32:01
Phoenix 24	34N04'38	82W06'40	5:28:27
Pickens 39	34N53'00	82W42'27	5:30:50
Pickens Mill 39	34N53	82W42	5:30:48
Pickensville 39	34N48'43	82W36'06	5:30:24
Picket Post 37	34N49'43	83W02'57	5:32:12
Piedmont 4	34N42'08	82W27'53	5:29:52
Piedmont Park 23	34N54'31	82W21'53	5:29:28
Piercetown 4	34N39'24	82W35'34	5:30:22
Pierpont 10	32N49'46	80W02'33	5:20:10
Pimlico 8	33N12	80W01	5:20:04
Pinckney Colony 7	32N19'02	80W53'53	5:23:36
Pinckney Crossroad 43	33N59'36	80W29'41	5:21:59
Pinckney Landing 7	32N20'32	80W50'22	5:23:21
Pinckneyville 44	34N50'34	81W28'07	5:25:52
Pinecrest 10	32N48'06	80W01'02	5:20:04
Pine Grove 8	33N02'36	79W59'19	5:19:57
Pine Hill Landing 15	32N50'07	80W23'59	5:21:36
Pine House Crossroads 19	33N44'07	81W51'21	5:27:25
Pinehurst 18	33N01	80W11	5:20:44
Pinehurst 24	34N12	82W09	5:28:36
Pinehurst-Sheppard Park 18	33N01	80W11	5:20:44
Pine Island 26	33N44'11	78W55'34	5:15:42
Pineland 10	33N02'36	79W35'15	5:18:21
Pineland 27	32N36'00	81W09'35	5:24:38
Pine Landing 10	32N36'10	80W23'15	5:21:33
Pine Ridge 16	34N23'42	80W09'47	5:20:39
Pineridge 32	33N54'37	81W06'17	5:24:25
Pineville 8	33N25'41	80W01'46	5:20:07
Pinewood 40	33N53'09	80W51'26	5:23:26
Pinewood 43	33N44'25	80W27'49	5:21:51
Piney Grove 42	35N01	81W48	5:27:12
Pinopolis 8	33N14	80W02	5:20:08
Pisgah 43	34N08'34	80W29'09	5:21:57
Pitch Landing 8	33N14'48	79W34'41	5:18:19
Pitch Landing 26	33N50'02	79W15'08	5:17:01
Pitmon Crossroad 29	34N34'56	80W46'56	5:23:08
Pittman Corner 17	34N21'44	79W17'38	5:17:11
Pittsburg 24	33N59'12	82W00'12	5:28:01
Plains 13	34N39	80W23	5:21:32
Plantersville 22	33N33'19	79W12'56	5:16:52
Platt Spring 26	33N37'32	78W57'56	5:15:52
Playcards 26	34N03'16	79W00'22	5:16:01
Pleasant Grove 22	33N29'18	79W29'16	5:17:57
Pleasant Hill 22	33N40'52	79W22'06	5:17:28
Pleasant Hill 29	34N37'11	80W41'06	5:22:44
Pleasant Hill Landing 8	33N14'42	79W31'16	5:18:05
Pleasant Lane 19	33N54'57	81W59'26	5:27:58
Pleasant Plain 29	34N36'58	80W34'05	5:22:16
Pleasant Valley 23	34N49	82W24	5:29:36
Pleasant Valley 29	35N00'06	80W51'21	5:23:25
Plum Branch 33	33N50'55	82W15'36	5:29:02
Plumfield Landing 16	34N30'04	79W49'30	5:19:18
Pocalla Springs 43	33N52'18	80W21'16	5:21:25
Pocataligo 27	32N38'13	80W51'49	5:23:27
Poe 23	34N52	82W23	5:29:32
Polecat Landing 26	34N05'04	79W14'57	5:17:00
Polk Village 7	32N27	80W44	5:22:56
Polly Landing 14	33N30'33	80W25'38	5:21:43
Polson Crossroads 16	34N17'44	80W01'21	5:20:05
Pomaria 36	34N16'06	81W25'12	5:25:41
Ponpon 10	32N45'42	80W26'06	5:21:44
Pontiac 40	34N07'42	80W51'18	5:23:25
Poovey Estate 29	34N42	80W47	5:23:08
Pope Crossroads 22	33N42'06	79W18'14	5:17:13
Poplar Forks 26	33N55'59	79W02'03	5:16:08
Poplar Hill 26	33N59'33	79W05'57	5:16:24
Poplar Hill 45	33N43'36	79W26'58	5:17:48
Poplar Springs 30	34N26'34	82W12'48	5:28:51
Poplar Springs 42	34N51'57	82W03'10	5:28:13

Poppenheim Crossing 8 32N58'06 80w00'07 5:20:00
Porcher Bluff 10 32N51'30 79w45'51 5:19:03
Port Hill 22 33N42'58 79w17'33 5:17:10
Port Hill Landing 22 33N43'03 79w17'15 5:17:09
Port Royal 7 32N22'44 80w41'34 5:22:46
Port Royal Plantation 7 32N13 80w45 5:23:00
Possum Corner 27 32N41'03 80w58'34 5:23:54
Post Foot Landing 22 33N30'35 79w18'04 5:17:12
Poston 21 33N52'25 79w25'35 5:17:42
Poston Crossroads 21 33N54'16 79w32'53 5:18:12
Poverty Hill 19 33N33'47 82w00'42 5:28:03
Powdersville 4 34N47'30 82w29'35 5:29:58
Pregnall 18 33N09'22 80w27'53 5:21:52
Price Crossroads 21 34N10'04 79w41'17 5:18:45
Price Landing 8 33N16'28 79w34'53 5:18:20
Prices Landing 15 32N58'38 80w25'05 5:21:40
Priceville 32 33N59'55 81w24'34 5:25:38
Primus 29 34N40'52 80w38'21 5:22:33
Princeton 23 34N30'03 82w17'22 5:29:09
Princeville 26 34N04'50 78w56'16 5:15:45
Pringle Bend 15 32N50'52 80w35'17 5:22:21
Pringletown 8 33N08'37 80w18'22 5:21:13
Pritchard 7 32N14'38 81w00'07 5:24:00
Pritchardville 7 32N14'16 80w57'52 5:23:51
Privateer 43 33N49'59 80w24'52 5:21:39
Privetts 26 33N58'08 79w00'10 5:16:01
Promised Land 24 34N07'42 82w14'23 5:28:58
Prospect Crossroads 21 33N49'52 79w33'18 5:18:13
Prosperity 36 34N12'33 81w32'00 5:26:08
Providence 32 34N00'59 81w15'37 5:25:02
Pumpkintown 39 35N00'10 82w39'11 5:30:37
Puncheon Creek 22 33N26'35 79w30'39 5:18:03
Purrysburg 27 32N17'50 81w07'10 5:24:29
Purrysburg Landing 27 32N18'14 81w07'20 5:24:29
Quarantine 22 33N13'46 79w12'16 5:16:49
Quick Crossroads 35 34N43'01 79w44'24 5:18:58
Quinby 21 34N14 79w44 5:18:56
Quinby Estates 21 34N12 79w45 5:19:00
Quinby Forest 21 34N12 79w45 5:19:00
Quinns Crossroad 43 33N59'21 80w20'43 5:21:23
Rabon Crossroads 26 33N58'34 79w05'52 5:16:23
Rabon Crossroads 28 34N18'05 80w44'31 5:22:58
Rainbow Falls 2 33N34'56 81w52'08 5:27:29
Rains 34 34N05'51 79w18'57 5:17:16
Ramsey Grove 22 33N28'41 79w17'25 5:17:10
Rantowles 10 32N46'58 80w08'56 5:20:36
Ravenel 10 32N45'47 80w15'01 5:21:00
Ravenwood 40 34N02'02 80w58'03 5:23:52
Rayflin 32 33N45'14 81w25'31 5:25:42
Red Bank 32 33N55'55 81w14'19 5:24:57
Red Bank Landing 8 32N57'06 79w55'55 5:19:44
Red Bluff 35 34N36'40 79w30'21 5:18:01
Red Bluff Crossroads 26 34N03 78w53 5:15:32
Red Bluff Landing 3 32N52'19 81w27'04 5:25:48
Red Hill 22 33N34'24 79w25'43 5:17:43
Red Hill 26 33N49'14 79w01'09 5:16:05
Red Hill 31 34N10'08 80w24'41 5:21:39
Red Oak Corner 15 32N57'50 80w26'48 5:21:47
Red River 46 34N57'39 80w57'56 5:23:52
Red Star 32 34N01'35 81w28'00 5:25:52
Red Top 10 32N48'09 80w07'22 5:20:29
Reevesville 18 33N12'20 80w38'53 5:22:36
Register Crossroads 16 34N16'18 80w05'01 5:20:20
Rehobeth 26 33N57'54 79w14'23 5:16:58
Reidville 42 34N51'46 82w06'52 5:28:27
Rembert 43 34N05'44 80w32'01 5:22:08
Renfrew 23 34N58'47 82w27'38 5:29:51
Renno 30 34N28'22 81w46'09 5:27:05
Retreat 37 34N37'40 83w03'25 5:32:14
Return 37 34N38'23 82w59'44 5:31:59
Reynold 6 33N22'00 81w19'50 5:25:19
Rhems 22 33N35'34 79w26'29 5:17:46
Rheuark Landing 26 33N43'50 79w02'33 5:16:10
Rhodes Crossroads 15 32N57'31 80w42'36 5:22:50
Rhodes Crossroads 31 34N00'20 80w10'26 5:20:42
Ribault Park 7 32N27 80w44 5:22:56
Rice Crossroads 22 33N39'44 79w14'42 5:16:59
Rice Hope 8 33N05'25 79w55'59 5:19:44
Ricetown 27 32N31'01 80w58'01 5:23:52
Richardson Landing 8 33N18'30 79w58'36 5:19:54
Richburg 12 34N42'57 81w01'11 5:24:05
Rich Hill Crossroads 29 34N39'22 80w39'10 5:22:37
Richland 37 34N40'40 83w01'32 5:32:06
Richland 41 33N57'10 81w41'38 5:26:47
Richland Springs 41 34N00 81w46 5:27:04
Richmond 8 33N04'31 79w52'44 5:19:31
Richmond Hills 23 34N52 82w23 5:29:32
Richtex 20 34N11'00 81w10'55 5:24:44
Ridgecrest 2 33N36'45 81w43'10 5:26:53
Ridge Cut 25 32N45 80w56 5:23:44
Ridgeland 27 32N28'50 80w58'50 5:23:55
Ridge Road Crossroads 32 34N00'10 81w28'20 5:25:53
Ridge Spring 41 33N50'43 81w39'43 5:26:39
Ridgeville 18 33N05'44 80w18'56 5:21:16
Ridgeway 20 34N18'27 80w57'38 5:23:51
Ridgewood 10 33N00 80w06 5:20:24
Ridgewood 40 34N03 81w02 5:24:08
Riley 9 33N37'21 80w47'59 5:23:12
Rimini 14 33N40'09 80w30'02 5:22:00
Rion 20 34N18'25 81w07'31 5:24:30
Ritter 15 32N47 80w38 5:22:32
Rivelon 38 33N28'22 80w53'55 5:23:36
River 41 34N07 81w44 5:26:56
Riverdale 7 32N22'30 80w50'23 5:23:22
Riverdale 17 34N25 79w22 5:17:28
River Falls 23 35N07'26 82w32'31 5:30:10
Riverland 10 32N42'28 79w57'50 5:19:51
Riverland Terrace 10 32N45'43 79w59'25 5:19:58
Rivers Annex 10 32N48 79w57 5:19:48
Riverside 23 34N52'15 82w25'46 5:29:43
Riverside 29 34N46'16 80w50'28 5:23:22
Riverside Park 40 33N51 80w56 5:23:44
Riverview 46 35N00'09 80w58'48 5:23:55
Robat 44 34N47'50 81w30'12 5:26:01
Robbins Neck 16 34N27'56 79w48'08 5:19:13
Robertville 27 32N35'11 81w11'55 5:24:48
Robinson 16 34N28 80w15 5:21:00
Robinson Crossroad 28 34N31'14 80w38'43 5:22:35
Rock Bluff 45 33N40 79w50 5:19:20
Rock Hill 20 34N15'06 81w15'19 5:25:01
Rock Hill 46 34N55'29 81w01'31 5:24:06
Rockland 10 32N36'45 80w12'10 5:20:49
Rockton 20 34N20'50 81w05'15 5:24:21
Rockville 10 32N36'02 80w11'42 5:20:47
Rocky Bluff Crossroads 43 33N58'46 80w17'53 5:21:12
Rocky Bottom 39 35N02'45 82w48'09 5:31:13
Rocky Fork 37 34N51'41 83w04'10 5:32:17
Rocky River 1 34N18 82w40 5:30:40
Roddey 46 34N52'15 80w56'13 5:23:45
Rodgers 14 33N33'16 80w15'32 5:21:02
Rodman 12 34N46'07 81w05'18 5:24:21
Roebuck 42 34N52'46 81w57'59 5:27:52
Rogers Crossroads 16 34N15'57 79w53'17 5:19:33
Rogers Crossroads 22 33N41'55 79w20'58 5:17:24
Rome 45 33N38'52 79w26'19 5:17:45
Ropers Crossroads 19 33N40'54 81w59'06 5:27:56
Rosa Lees Crossroads 16 34N21'33 80w00'22 5:20:01
Rose Hill 7 32N39'06 80w47'57 5:23:12
Rose Hill 22 33N35'58 79w24'16 5:17:37
Roseida 7 32N27 80w44 5:22:56
Rosemont 10 32N50 79w58 5:19:52
Rosemont 22 33N23'36 79w17'02 5:17:08
Rosinville 18 33N11 80w35 5:22:20
Rossville 12 34N36'12 80w59'34 5:23:58
Rotalata 19 33N43'34 81w50'36 5:27:22
Round O 15 32N56'13 80w32'28 5:22:10
Rouse 25 32N53'07 81w16'32 5:25:06
Rowell 12 34N47'38 80w55'15 5:23:41
Rowesville 38 33N22'11 80w50'14 5:23:21
Ruby 13 34N44'42 80w10'59 5:20:44
Ruffin 15 33N00'16 80w48'57 5:23:16
Runnymede 10 32N52'56 80w05'47 5:20:23
Rushville 24 34N00'48 82w09'59 5:28:40
Russell 37 34N54 83w09 5:32:36
Russell Lake Landing 18 33N03'44 80w27'25 5:21:50
Russellville 8 33N23'49 79w58'19 5:19:53
Saint Andrews 10 32N46'54 79w59'07 5:19:56
Saint Andrews 32 33N51 80w56 5:23:44
Saint Charles 31 34N03'59 80w13'06 5:20:52
Saint George 18 33N11'09 80w34'33 5:22:18
Saint Helena 7 32N24 80w36 5:22:24
Saint Matthews 9 33N39'53 80w46'41 5:23:07
Saint Paul 14 33N34'41 80w23'42 5:21:35
Saint Paul Forks 26 33N53'21 79w02'11 5:16:09
Saint Pauls 10 32N45 80w17 5:21:08
Saint Pauls 22 33N34'33 79w11'09 5:16:45
Saint Phillips 36 34N18'05 81w30'38 5:26:03
Saint Stephen 8 33N24'15 79w55'19 5:19:41
Salak 24 34N09'29 82w12'26 5:28:50
Salem 21 33N53'16 79w30'45 5:18:03
Salem 37 34N53'23 82w58'36 5:31:54
Salem Crossroads 20 34N25'17 81w17'53 5:25:12
Salem Crossroads 26 33N57'16 79w07'40 5:16:31
Salkehatchie 15 32N42'22 80w48'48 5:23:15
Salley 2 33N33'56 81w18'13 5:25:13
Sallie Hill 21 34N09'07 79w54'30 5:19:38
Salters 45 33N35'45 79w51'12 5:19:25
Saluca 24 34N12 82w09 5:28:36
Saluda 41 34N00'05 81w46'20 5:27:05
Saluda Gardens 32 33N59 81w05 5:24:20
Saluda Terrace 32 33N59 81w05 5:24:20
Salvesburg Landing 27 32N28'30 80w51'00 5:23:24
Samaria 32 33N54 81w33 5:26:12
Sampit 22 33N21'50 79w27'32 5:17:50
Sampson Landing 34 33N47'53 79w15'24 5:17:02
Sanders Corner 43 34N00'10 80w32'27 5:22:10
Sandridge 8 33N15'18 80w18'58 5:21:16
Sand Ridge 26 33N48'59 79w05'31 5:16:22
Sandwood 40 34N02 80w58 5:23:52
Sandy 10 32N48'54 80w05'01 5:20:20
Sandy Flat 23 34N59'38 82w20'42 5:29:23
Sandy Ford 37 34N51'38 83w14'48 5:32:59
Sandy River 12 34N39'23 81w19'37 5:25:18
Sandy Run 9 33N47'59 80w57'51 5:23:51
Sandy Run 38 33N19'22 80w42'57 5:22:52
Sandy Springs 4 34N35'43 82w45'00 5:31:00
Sansbury Crossroads 21 34N03'38 79w55'24 5:19:42
Sans Souci 23 34N52'40 82w25'27 5:29:42
Sans Souci Heights 23 34N52 82w23 5:29:32
Santee 38 33N28'30 80w29'12 5:21:57
Santee Circle 8 33N14'37 79w57'52 5:19:51
Santuc 44 34N38'04 81w31'22 5:26:05
Sapps Crossroads 29 34N48'32 80w37'53 5:22:32
Saratt 11 34N53'45 81w32'25 5:26:10
Sardinia 14 33N50'03 80w04'59 5:20:20
Sardis 21 34N02'25 79w56'39 5:19:47
Sarvis Crossroads 26 34N02'28 78w58'02 5:15:52
Sato 5 33N19 81w09 5:24:36
Savannah Bluff 26 33N51 79w03 5:16:12
Saxon 42 34N57'40 81w58'03 5:27:52
Saylors Crossing 4 34N23'56 82w30'22 5:30:01
Scanlonville 10 32N48'42 79w53'52 5:19:35
Schofield 5 33N07'57 81w12'00 5:24:48
Schultz Hill 2 33N29'01 81w56'52 5:27:47
Scotia 25 32N40'51 81w14'37 5:24:58
Scott 7 32N20'47 80w37'24 5:22:30
Scott 35 34N32'04 79w41'32 5:18:46
Scottsville 31 33N57'24 80w10'01 5:20:40
Scranton 21 33N55'03 79w44'39 5:18:59
Seaboard Junction 13 34N42 79w53 5:19:32
Seabrook 7 32N31'40 80w46'00 5:23:04
Seabrook 15 32N31'34 80w24'27 5:21:38
Seabrook Landing 7 32N15'33 80w44'27 5:22:58
Sea Pines 7 32N13 80w45 5:23:00
Seaside 10 32N42'41 79w56'30 5:19:46
Secessionville 10 32N42'20 79w56'22 5:19:45
Sedalia 44 34N36'14 81w43'29 5:26:54
Segars 16 34N23'02 80w07'55 5:20:32
Seiglers Crossroads 2 33N38'41 81w39'26 5:26:38
Seigling 3 33N02'39 81w18'55 5:25:16
Seivern 2 33N39 81w22 5:25:28
Sellers 34 34N17'01 79w28'23 5:17:54
Selma 17 34N25 79w22 5:17:28
Seloc 14 33N52'52 80w00'31 5:20:02
Selvern 2 33N42'54 81w24'36 5:25:38
Seneca 37 34N41'08 82w57'12 5:31:49
Sevenmile 10 32N51'56 79w59'53 5:20:00
Seven Prongs 26 33N39'56 79w04'45 5:16:19
Shady Rest 35 34N37 79w41 5:18:44
Shamokin 28 34N19'32 80w36'12 5:22:25
Shannon Hill 31 34N15'05 80w12'15 5:20:49
Shannontown 43 33N54 80w20 5:21:20
Sharon 46 34N57'03 81w20'28 5:25:22
Sharon Park 23 34N54'07 82w27'02 5:29:48
Sharp 40 34N10'27 80w57'03 5:23:48
Sharpes Hill 32 33N48'56 81w09'16 5:24:37
Shaw 43 33N58 80w29 5:21:56
Shaw Air Force Base 43 33N58 80w29 5:21:56
Shaw Heights 43 33N59'04 80w28'58 5:21:56
Sheldon 7 32N36'05 80w47'36 5:23:10
Shell 26 33N54'08 78w54'49 5:15:39
Shell Point 7 32N27 80w44 5:22:56
Shelton 20 34N29'50 81w25'13 5:25:41
Shepard 28 34N19'26 80w32'29 5:22:10
Sheppard Crossroads 24 33N57'42 82w02'50 5:28:11
Sheppard Park 18 33N01 80w11 5:20:44
Sherwood Archer 42 33N34 81w44 5:26:56
Sherwood Forest 23 34N49'56 82w21'14 5:29:25
Shiloh 13 34N40'26 80w05'57 5:20:24
Shiloh 29 34N46'29 80w47'26 5:23:10
Shiloh 37 34N40'03 82w53'36 5:31:34
Shiloh 43 33N56'24 80w02'28 5:20:10
Shipyard Plantations 7 32N13 80w45 5:23:00
Shirley 25 32N39'36 81w18'59 5:25:16
Shoals Junction 24 34N21'22 82w18'11 5:29:13
Shoreswood 42 34N57 81w58 5:27:52
Shulerville 8 33N11'14 79w37'56 5:18:32
Sidney 15 32N59'58 80w34'07 5:22:16
Sigsbee 42 34N59'12 82w00'32 5:28:02
Silver 14 33N40'40 80w21'27 5:21:26
Silverstreet 36 34N13'04 81w42'56 5:26:52
Simmonsville 8 33N14'54 79w38'26 5:18:34
Simmonsville 22 33N25'10 79w10'42 5:16:43
Simpson 20 34N18'30 81w02'44 5:24:11
Simpson Crossing 8 33N14'58 79w58'31 5:19:54
Simpsonville 23 34N44'13 82w15'16 5:29:01
Sims 40 33N57'17 80w57'26 5:23:50
Sinclair Crossroads 17 34N31'38 79w27'54 5:17:52
Singletary Forks 45 33N21'25 79w41'30 5:18:46
Singleton 9 33N41'31 80w43'47 5:22:55
Singleton Crossroads 26 33N50'08 79w11'44 5:16:47
Sixmile 10 32N51'04 79w58'44 5:19:55
Six Mile 39 34N48'26 82w49'15 5:31:17
Six Points 2 33N18'29 81w44'39 5:26:59
Sixty Six 38 33N18'20 80w49'35 5:23:18
Skyland 23 35N02'34 82w16'00 5:29:04
Skyview Terrace 40 33N51 80w56 5:23:44
Slandsville 18 32N58'49 80w14'30 5:20:58
Slansville 18 33N01 80w11 5:20:44
Slater 23 35N01'54 82w29'43 5:29:59
Slighs 36 34N11'54 81w27'02 5:25:48
Smallwood 20 34N16'57 80w57'02 5:23:48
Smith 8 33N03'28 79w46'12 5:19:05
Smith 46 34N56 81w01 5:24:04
Smithboro 34 34N16'13 79w18'13 5:17:13
Smith Ford 11 34N59'48 81w29'08 5:25:57
Smith Mills 22 33N44 79w29 5:17:56
Smiths Turnout 12 34N49'16 81w06'56 5:24:28
Smoaks 15 33N05'22 80w48'51 5:23:15
Smyrna 36 34N16'24 81w42'29 5:26:50
Smyrna 46 35N02'33 81w24'23 5:25:38
Snelling 6 33N14'23 81w27'22 5:25:49
Sniders Crossroads 15 32N53'20 80w51'12 5:23:25
Snoddy 42 34N56'11 82w04'26 5:28:18
Snowden 10 32N50'29 79w50'48 5:19:23
Snow Junction 45 33N40'08 79w28'18 5:17:53
Snow Town 45 33N35'03 79w30'55 5:18:04
Socastee 26 33N41'00 78w59'55 5:16:00
Society Hill 16 34N30'45 79w51'04 5:19:24
Sol Legare Island 10 32N47 79w56 5:19:44

Solomons Crossroads 3 32N47'40 81W19'21 5:25:17
South Bennettsville 35 34N37 79W41 5:18:44
South Congaree 32 33N54'39 81W08'09 5:24:33
Southern 42 35N00 81W58 5:27:52
Southern Shops 42 35N00 81W59 5:27:56
South Forest Estates 23 34N49 82W24 5:29:36
South Greenwood 24 34N09'52 82W08'13 5:28:33
South Hartsville 16 34N23 80W05 5:20:20
South Hills 44 34N41'15 81W36'26 5:26:26
South Lynchburg 31 34N03'08 80W03'40 5:20:15
South Mullins 34 34N12 79W15 5:17:00
South Santee 10 33N10'24 79W25'04 5:17:40
Southside 11 34N57 81W41 5:26:44
Southside 21 34N12 79W45 5:19:00
South Union 37 34N33'04 83W03'07 5:32:12
South Windermere 10 32N46'33 79W58'49 5:19:55
Spanish Wells 7 32N11'30 80W46'43 5:23:07
Spartanburg 42 34N56'58 81W55'56 5:27:44
Speaks Mill 25 32N46'22 81W08'37 5:24:34
Speigner 41 33N54'15 81W43'57 5:26:56
Spiderweb 2 33N24'36 81W49'53 5:27:20
Spring Branch 34 34N14'31 79W23'35 5:17:34
Springdale 2 33N36'25 81W51'14 5:27:25
Springdale 29 34N42 80W47 5:23:08
Springdale 32 33N57'33 81W06'33 5:24:26
Springdell 29 34N49'25 80W52'54 5:23:32
Springfield 38 33N29'48 81W16'46 5:25:07
Spring Gully 22 33N23'14 79W24'35 5:17:38
Spring Hill 26 33N56'25 79W05'44 5:16:23
Spring Hill 31 34N09'05 80W26'19 5:21:45
Spring Hill 40 34N10'32 81W17'15 5:25:09
Springmaid Beach 26 33N39 78W56 5:15:44
Spring Mills 29 34N33 80W35 5:22:20
Springs Park 29 34N36'22 80W52'56 5:23:32
Springwood 40 34N02 80W59 5:23:56
Squires 17 34N18'05 79W14'43 5:16:59
Stafford 25 32N40'12 81W09'54 5:24:40
Staley Crossroads 9 33N40'09 80W57'40 5:23:51
Stallsville 18 32N59'47 80W10'56 5:20:44
Stalvey 26 33N41'06 78W58'09 5:15:53
Star Bluff Crossroads 26 33N51'22 78W45'28 5:15:02
Stark Terrace 40 34N03 81W02 5:24:08
Starr 4 34N22'37 82W41'45 5:30:47
Startex 42 34N55'42 82W05'57 5:28:24
Stateburg 43 33N57'27 80W32'06 5:22:08
State College 38 33N30 80W52 5:23:28
State Park 40 34N05'26 80W57'59 5:23:52
Stave Landing 34 34N10'37 79W11'28 5:16:46
Steamboat Landing 10 32N36'07 80W17'35 5:21:10
Steedman 32 33N55 81W28 5:25:52
Steel Creek Landing 3 33N05'42 81W36'43 5:26:27
Steele Crossing 40 34N54'23 81W03'34 5:24:14
Stephens Crossroads 26 33N53'04 78W41'16 5:14:45
Stewart Crossroads 29 34N48'06 80W35'53 5:22:24
Stiefeltown 2 33N33'08 81W47'45 5:27:11
Stilton 38 33N32'11 80W50'19 5:23:21
Stockman 36 34N13 81W32 5:26:08
Stokes 15 32N57'33 80W43'33 5:22:54
Stokes 25 32N38'30 81W10'14 5:24:41
Stokes 43 33N46'25 80W21'17 5:21:25
Stokes Bluff Landing 25 32N33'26 81W16'58 5:25:08
Stokes Bridge 31 34N13 80W15 5:21:00
Stomp Springs 30 34N28'11 81W44'04 5:26:56
Stoneboro 28 34N32'24 80W44'14 5:22:57
Stone Lake 23 34N52'26 82W22'50 5:29:31
Stone Park 10 32N46'48 80W01'00 5:20:04
Stone Station 42 34N50'46 81W55'32 5:27:42
Stoney Hill 36 34N10'02 81W34'30 5:26:18
Stono 10 32N43'48 79W58'57 5:19:56
Stono Station 10 32N45'39 80W06'22 5:20:25
Stony Landing 8 33N11'35 79W58'10 5:19:53
Stony Point 24 34N16'34 82W07'38 5:28:31
Stover 20 34N33'03 81W01'09 5:24:05
Strangeville 38 33N30 80W52 5:23:28
Stratford Forest 23 34N56'11 82W27'18 5:29:49
Strawberry 8 33N05'29 80W01'51 5:20:07
Strawberry 22 33N19'48 79W15'16 5:17:01
Strawberry Landing 8 33N05'31 79W56'40 5:19:47
Strother 20 34N23'37 81W23'42 5:25:35
Stuart Point 7 32N32 80W46 5:23:04
Stuckey 45 33N44 79W31 5:18:04
Suggs Crossroads 16 34N14'42 80W02'14 5:20:09
Sullivan Crossroads 19 33N55'16 82W06'56 5:28:28
Sullivans Island 10 32N45'47 79W50'13 5:19:21
Summer Hill 2 33N30'21 81W57'17 5:27:49
Summerland 32 33N54 81W33 5:26:12
Summerton 14 33N36'29 80W21'05 5:21:24
Summerville 18 33N01'06 80W10'33 5:20:42
Summit 32 33N55'29 81W25'20 5:25:41
Summit View 23 34N51 82W24 5:29:36
Sumter 43 33N55'13 80W20'30 5:21:22
Sumter Junction 43 33N50'07 80W33'58 5:22:16
Sunny Brook 2 33N40'36 81W48'47 5:27:15
Sunny Side 22 33N33'58 79W01'41 5:16:07
Sunnyside 42 34N56 82W13 5:28:52
Sunset 39 34N58'39 82W47'57 5:31:12
Surfside Beach 26 33N36'21 78W58'24 5:15:54
Suttons 45 33N23'38 79W44'38 5:18:59
Swansea 32 33N44'17 81W05'53 5:24:24
Sweden 5 33N22'44 81W08'07 5:24:32
Sweetwater 2 33N35'08 81W56'27 5:27:46
Switzer 42 34N48'18 82W01'42 5:28:07
Switzerland 27 32N25'39 81W00'32 5:24:02
Sycamore 3 33N02'08 81W13'20 5:24:53
Sylvia Lane 10 32N47'21 80W02'53 5:20:12
Syracuse 16 34N13'52 79W58'03 5:19:52
Taft 45 33N30'03 79W46'57 5:19:08
Talatha 2 33N23'42 81W42'17 5:26:49
Tamassee 37 34N52'49 83W01'11 5:32:05
Tanglewood 23 34N51 82W26 5:29:44
Tarboro 27 32N31'54 81W09'16 5:24:37
Tatum 35 34N38'38 79W35'12 5:18:21
Taxahaw 29 34N41'23 80W31'01 5:22:04
Taylors 23 34N55'13 82W17'47 5:29:11
Taylors Crossroads 36 34N15'58 81W29'53 5:26:00
Tega Cay 46 35N01'27 81W01'41 5:24:07
Temperance Hill 34 34N17'19 79W22'48 5:17:31
Ten Mile 10 32N53'14 79W44'39 5:18:59
Terrell Crossroad 45 33N50'42 79W52'41 5:19:31
Terry Creek 23 35N07'49 82W26'59 5:29:48
Testo 32 33N47'37 81W12'47 5:24:51
Thayer 15 32N52'28 80W37'44 5:22:31
The Dunes 26 33N39 78W56 5:15:44
The Farms 8 32N55 80W00 5:20:00
The Groves 10 32N48'09 79W53'04 5:19:32
Thicketty 11 35N00'59 81W43'30 5:26:54
Thomas Corner 8 33N09'38 79W42'54 5:18:52
Thompson Corner 10 33N07'37 79W35'05 5:18:20
Thor 32 33N42'38 81W15'32 5:25:02
Thorn Hill 28 34N28 80W41 5:22:44
Three Trees 10 32N43'48 79W55'55 5:19:44
Thursa 31 34N15'16 80W17'15 5:21:09
Tibwin 10 33N04'35 79W30'38 5:18:03
Tigerville 23 35N04'06 82W22'07 5:29:28
Tillman 27 32N27'48 81W06'27 5:24:26
Timmonsville 21 34N08'05 79W56'24 5:19:46
Tina 9 33N36'07 80W36'42 5:22:27
Tirzah 46 34N59'46 81W08'37 5:24:34
Tisdale 45 33N29'15 79W39'23 5:18:38
Tobys Bluff 15 32N54'39 80W59'21 5:23:57
Toddville 26 33N45'31 79W04'35 5:16:18
Tokeena Crossroads 37 34N41 82W56 5:31:44
Tomotley 7 32N37'54 80W48'55 5:23:16
Tompkins 26 33N55'38 79W14'34 5:16:58
Toney Creek 4 34N33'15 82W25'21 5:29:41
Totness 9 33N44'33 80W48'01 5:23:12
Townville 4 34N33'49 82W53'55 5:31:36
Toxaway 4 34N29'46 82W37'47 5:30:31
Traber 39 34N46'22 82W42'26 5:30:50
Tradesville 29 34N46'07 80W32'50 5:22:11
Tranquil Acres 18 33N01 80W11 5:20:44
Travelers Rest 23 34N58'03 82W26'37 5:29:46
Trenton 19 33N44'38 81W50'27 5:27:22
Triangle 4 34N31 82W30 5:30:00
Trinity 36 34N14'56 81W44'09 5:26:57
Trio 45 33N29'09 79W43'04 5:18:52
Troy 24 33N59'15 82W17'53 5:29:12
Tuckertown 44 34N31'34 81W29'10 5:25:57
Tugtown 38 33N18'52 80W20'06 5:21:20
Turbeville 14 33N53'26 80W01'07 5:20:04
Turkey 45 33N35 79W36 5:18:24
Turkey Pond 8 33N14'22 79W38'16 5:18:33
Turnbridge Landing 27 32N07'47 81W00'49 5:24:03
Twelvemile 26 33N49'23 79W12'43 5:16:51
Twin Lake Hill 40 33N59 80W57 5:23:48
Tyger 42 34N56'11 82W10'45 5:28:43
Tyler Crossroads 22 33N40'25 79W17'14 5:17:09
Tylersville 30 34N34'52 81W55'16 5:27:41
Ulmer 3 33N05'50 81W12'30 5:24:50
Una 16 34N16'12 80W08'05 5:20:32
Una 42 34N58'08 81W58'14 5:27:53
Union 29 34N42'56 80W37'17 5:22:29
Union 36 34N16'06 81W31'56 5:26:08
Union 44 34N42'55 81W37'26 5:26:30
Union Bleachery 23 34N52 82W23 5:29:32
Union Crossroads 14 33N48'05 79W59'12 5:19:57
Union Crossroads 45 33N38'17 79W25'29 5:17:42
Unity 29 34N47'51 80W41'57 5:22:48
University 40 34N01 81W00 5:24:00
Upper Topsaw Landing 22 33N37'29 79W09'41 5:16:39
Utica 37 34N40'41 82W55'54 5:31:44
Valencia Heights 40 34N00 81W00 5:24:00
Valentine 25 32N49'24 81W15'28 5:25:02
Valley Falls 42 35N00'57 81W58'30 5:27:54
Vance 38 33N26'01 80W25'23 5:21:42
Van Wyck 29 34N51'30 80W50'46 5:23:23
Varnville 25 32N51'01 81W04'46 5:24:19
Vaucluse 2 33N36'45 81W48'36 5:27:14
Vaughans Crossroads 16 34N12'31 80W06'09 5:20:25
Vaughanville 36 34N14'36 81W54'47 5:27:39
Venters 21 33N47'04 79W26'57 5:17:48
Verdery 24 34N06'33 82W14'58 5:29:00
Victor Mills 42 34N55'39 82W12'59 5:28:52
Waccamaw 22 33N29 79W07 5:16:28
Wachesaw Landing 22 33N33'38 79W05'06 5:16:20
Waddell Gardens 7 32N27 80W44 5:22:56
Wade Heights 24 34N10'50 82W08'28 5:28:34
Wadmalaw Island 10 32N40'15 80W14'05 5:20:56
Wadsworth 42 34N56'49 81W59'46 5:27:59
Wagener 2 33N39'08 81W21'41 5:25:27
Walhalla 37 34N45'53 83W03'51 5:32:15
Walker 6 33N24'46 81W18'05 5:25:12
Wallace 35 34N43'12 79W50'30 5:19:22
Walnut Grove 42 34N47'39 81W54'51 5:27:39
Walterboro 15 32N54'18 80W40'01 5:22:40
Wambaw Corner 10 33N11'43 79W27'48 5:17:51
Wampee 8 33N14'35 80W01'54 5:20:08
Wampee 26 33N51'37 78W44'04 5:14:56
Wando 8 32N56'00 79W49'55 5:19:20
Wando Woods 10 32N51'06 80W02'12 5:20:09
Wappoola 8 33N05'52 79W59'25 5:19:58
Ward 41 33N51'28 81W43'48 5:26:55
Ware Place 23 34N37'40 82W23'28 5:29:34
Ware Shoals 24 34N23'54 82W14'49 5:28:59
Warren Crossroads 10 32N49'13 80W16'24 5:21:06
Warren Crossroads 28 34N20'00 80W47'14 5:23:09
Warrenville 2 33N33'03 81W48'15 5:27:13
Warsaw 45 33N30'30 79W33'02 5:18:12
Washington 8 33N16'09 79W40'09 5:18:41
Washington Heights 42 34N56'18 81W56'29 5:27:46
Wateree 40 33N48'25 80W38'15 5:22:33
Waterloo 30 34N21'05 82W03'34 5:28:14
Watkins Store 2 33N25 81W41 5:26:44
Watsonia 41 33N51 81W37 5:26:28
Watts 1 34N08'18 82W29'24 5:29:58
Watts Mills 30 34N31 82W00 5:28:00
Wattsville 30 34N31'23 81W59'42 5:27:59
Waverly Mills 22 33N28'23 79W06'54 5:16:36
Waylyn 10 32N51'22 79W59'43 5:19:59
Weddell 40 34N05'13 80W56'00 5:23:44
Wedgefield 43 33N53'33 80W31'06 5:22:04
Weeks 15 33N02'48 80W37'36 5:22:30
Weeks Landing 9 33N41'24 80W36'00 5:22:24
Welcome 4 34N34'52 82W43'16 5:30:53
Welcome 23 34N49'35 82W26'21 5:29:45
Wellford 42 34N57'03 82W06'22 5:28:25
Wells 38 33N22'17 80W28'51 5:21:55
Wells Crossroads 31 34N04'04 80W09'46 5:20:39
Wertz Crossroads 9 33N38'24 80W47'20 5:23:09
Wesleyan 39 34N43 82W47 5:31:08
West Anderson 4 34N30'07 82W41'18 5:30:45
West Andrews 45 33N27'10 79W34'50 5:18:19
Westcliff 23 35N02 82W30 5:30:00
West Columbia 32 33N59'36 81W04'27 5:24:18
West Florence 21 34N12 79W45 5:19:00
West Gantt 23 34N47'08 82W24'45 5:29:39
West Greenville 23 34N50'35 82W25'47 5:29:43
West Hartsville 16 34N21'56 80W06'33 5:20:26
West Marion 34 34N11'21 79W25'24 5:17:42
Westminster 37 34N39'53 83W05'48 5:32:23
Weston 40 33N52'22 80W49'01 5:23:16
Westover Acres 32 33N59 81W05 5:24:20
West Pelzer 4 34N38'41 82W28'13 5:29:53
West Springs 44 34N46'15 81W46'55 5:27:08
West Store Crossroads 19 33N45'21 82W03'08 5:28:13
West Union 37 34N45'35 83W02'35 5:32:10
West View 42 34N55'30 81W59'36 5:27:58
Westville 23 34N51'02 82W26'44 5:29:47
Westville 28 34N27'24 80W35'57 5:22:24
Wexford 13 34N46'41 80W09'42 5:20:39
Whaley 6 33N26'27 81W17'55 5:25:12
Wheeland 36 34N09'25 81W26'21 5:25:45
Whetsell 38 33N20'01 80W35'25 5:22:22
Whetstone 37 34N50'28 83W11'28 5:32:46
Whipper-Barnoy 10 32N51'44 79W59'14 5:19:57
White Bluff 29 34N33 80W35 5:22:20
White Bluff Corssroads 29 34N39'36 80W33'36 5:22:14
Whitehall 15 32N43'18 80W41'26 5:22:46
Whitehall 24 34N04'55 82W12'40 5:28:51
Whitehall 32 34N03'22 81W08'50 5:24:35
Whitehall Terrace 10 32N48 79W52 5:19:28
White Horse 23 34N48'53 82W26'24 5:29:46
White Horse Heights 23 34N51'39 82W27'33 5:29:50
White Oak 20 34N28'27 81W07'00 5:24:28
White Oak 26 33N52'13 79W04'00 5:16:16
White Plains 4 34N40'23 82W31'58 5:30:08
White Plains 11 34N59'37 81W44'14 5:26:57
White Plains Crossroad 30 34N19'30 81W55'13 5:27:41
White Point Landing 10 32N38'13 80W16'38 5:21:07
White Pond 2 33N25'35 81W28'27 5:25:54
White Pond 26 34N05'36 78W55'35 5:15:42
White Rock 40 34N08'42 81W16'33 5:25:06
Whites Crossroads 16 34N09'36 80W01'09 5:20:05
Whites Pond Crossroad 43 33N58'57 80W19'44 5:21:19
White Stone 42 34N54'10 81W49'02 5:27:16
Whitesville 8 33N08'50 80W03'42 5:20:15
Whitetown 33 33N51'29 82W12'34 5:28:50
Whitmire 36 34N30'10 81W36'42 5:26:27
Whitney 42 34N59'03 81W55'36 5:27:42
Whitney Heights 42 34N58'40 81W55'30 5:27:42
Wiggins 15 32N36'16 80W32'38 5:22:11
Wilder 8 33N18 79W58 5:19:52
Wiles Crossroads 9 33N42'35 80W40'01 5:22:40
Wilkes Crossroads 16 34N12'21 80W02'21 5:20:09
Wilkins 7 32N29'05 80W36'03 5:22:24
Wilkinsville 11 34N58'18 81W31'59 5:26:08
Wilksburg 12 34N44'42 81W23'10 5:25:33
Williams 15 33N02'04 80W50'34 5:23:22
Williamsburg 45 33N28 79W39 5:18:36
Williams Estate 29 34N42 80W47 5:23:08
Williams Hill 22 33N43'26 79W18'55 5:17:16
Williamston 4 34N37'06 82W28'41 5:29:55
Willington 33 33N58'19 82W28'01 5:29:52
Williston 6 33N24'09 81W25'13 5:25:41
Willow Creek Siding 21 34N05'28 79W38'51 5:18:35
Willow Springs Park 2 33N31'17 81W54'50 5:27:39
Willtown Bluff 10 32N40'45 80W24'48 5:21:39
Wilson 14 33N39'47 80W07'07 5:20:28
Wilson Crossroads 16 34N13'22 79W53'48 5:19:35
Wilson Landing 26 33N50'01 79W00'11 5:16:01

Place	Latitude	Longitude	Time
Wilsons Cross Roads 16	34N18	79w53	5:19:32
Wilsons Landing 8	33N26'54	80w09'43	5:20:39
Windhams Crossroads 16	34N12'02	80w02'02	5:20:08
Windom Corner 8	33N08'02	79w42'45	5:18:51
Windsor 2	33N28'54	81w30'50	5:26:03
Windsor Estates 40	34N02	80w59	5:23:56
Windsor Lake Park 40	34N02	80w58	5:23:52
Windsor Park 13	34N42	79w53	5:19:32
Windy Hill 21	34N12	79w45	5:19:00
Windy Hill Beach 26	33N49	78w40	5:14:40
Wineberg Crossroads 16	34N16'57	79w58'37	5:19:54
Winnsboro 20	34N22'50	81w05'12	5:24:21
Winnsboro Mills 20	34N21'42	81w05'08	5:24:21
Winona 21	34N12'26	79w36'12	5:18:25
Winterseat 33	33N58'46	82w12'07	5:28:48
Winthrop College 46	34N56	81w01	5:24:04
Wisacky 31	34N08'53	80w11'37	5:20:46
Witherbee 8	33N09'42	79w49'48	5:19:19
Wolfton 38	33N35'18	80w58'55	5:23:56
Woodburn Hills 42	34N57	81w51	5:27:24
Woodbury 34	33N45'46	79w14'49	5:16:59
Woodfield 40	34N02	80w58	5:23:52
Woodfields 23	34N47'23	82w23'11	5:29:33
Woodford 38	33N40'02	81w06'34	5:24:26
Woodland 8	33N02'16	79w54'24	5:19:38
Woodland Hills 32	34N02'05	81w07'38	5:24:31
Woodland Landing 8	33N02'44	79w54'57	5:19:40
Woodlawn 33	33N37'33	82w07'56	5:28:32
Woodrow 31	34N05'41	80w22'41	5:21:31
Woodruff 42	34N44'22	82w02'14	5:28:09
Woods Chapel 42	34N56	82w11	5:28:44
Woods Crossroads 3	32N59'06	81w20'52	5:25:23
Woodside 23	34N51'14	82w25'59	5:29:44
Woodstock 10	32N57'47	80w05'20	5:20:21
Woodville 10	32N55'52	79w43'45	5:18:55
Woodville 23	34N39'00	82w23'20	5:29:33
Woodward 20	34N31'38	81w10'18	5:24:41
Workman 45	33N44'03	79w58'04	5:19:52
Worthams Ferry 26	33N55'25	78w40'15	5:14:41
Yarborough Crossroads 16	34N14'39	80w01'17	5:20:05
Yauhannah 22	33N37'55	79w11'19	5:16:45
Yeamans Hall 8	32N55	80w00	5:20:00
Yellow House Landing 8	32N54'30	79w55'30	5:19:42
Yemassee 25	32N41'24	80w51'03	5:23:24
Yenome 6	33N11'00	81w20'49	5:25:23
Yonges Island 10	32N41'36	80w13'51	5:20:55
Yorba Village 7	32N36	80w48	5:23:12
York 46	34N59'39	81w14'32	5:24:58
Youngs 30	34N40'14	82w04'51	5:28:19
Zemp 31	34N16'14	80w19'37	5:21:18
Zion 34	34N15'35	79w19'05	5:17:16
Zion Hill 42	34N59'00	81w51'56	5:27:28

TIME TABLES

SD # 1		
Before 11/18/1883		LMT
11/18/1883	12:00	CST
3/31/1918	02:00	CWT
10/27/1918	02:00	CST
3/30/1919	02:00	CWT
10/26/1919	02:00	CST
2/09/1942	02:00	CWT
9/30/1945	02:00	CST
4/30/1967	02:00	US#1

SD # 2		
Before 11/18/1883		LMT
11/18/1883	12:00	CST
3/31/1918	02:00	CWT
10/27/1918	02:00	CST
3/30/1919	02:00	CWT
10/26/1919	02:00	CST
2/09/1942	02:00	CWT
9/30/1945	02:00	CST
5/13/1957	02:00	CDT
9/29/1957	02:00	CST
4/30/1967	02:00	US#1

SD # 3		
Before 11/18/1883		LMT
11/18/1883	12:00	MST
3/31/1918	02:00	MWT
10/27/1918	02:00	MST
3/30/1919	02:00	MWT
10/26/1919	02:00	MST
2/09/1942	02:00	MWT
9/30/1945	02:00	MST
4/30/1967	02:00	US#1

SD # 4		
Before 11/18/1883		LMT
11/18/1883	12:00	MST
3/31/1918	02:00	MWT
10/27/1918	02:00	MST
3/30/1919	02:00	MWT
10/26/1919	02:00	MST
2/09/1942	02:00	MWT
9/30/1945	02:00	MST
4/24/1966	02:00	US#1

COUNTIES

1 Aurora
2 Beadle
3 Bennett
4 Bon Homme
5 Brookings
6 Brown
7 Brule
8 Buffalo
9 Butte
10 Campbell
11 Charles Mix
12 Clark
13 Clay
14 Codington
15 Corson
16 Custer
17 Davison
18 Day
19 Deuel
20 Dewey
21 Douglas
22 Edmunds
23 Fall River
24 Faulk
25 Grant
26 Gregory
27 Haakon
28 Hamlin
29 Hand
30 Hanson
31 Harding
32 Hughes
33 Hutchinson
34 Hyde
35 Jackson
36 Jerauld
37 Jones
38 Kingsbury
39 Lake
40 Lawrence
41 Lincoln
42 Lyman
43 McCook
44 McPherson
45 Marshall
46 Meade
47 Mellette
48 Miner
49 Minnehaha
50 Moody
51 Pennington
52 Perkins
53 Potter
54 Roberts
55 Sanborn
56 Shannon
57 Spink
58 Stanley
59 Sully
60 Todd
61 Tripp
62 Turner
63 Union
64 Walworth
65 Washabaugh
66 Yankton
67 Ziebach

Place	TT	Lat	Long	Time
Aberdeen 6	1	45N27'53	98w29'10	6:33:57
Academy 11	1	43N27'23	99w04'46	6:36:19
Ada 52	3	45N21	102w24	6:49:36
Adrian 22	1	45N33	99w11	6:36:44
Agar 59	1	44N50'18	100w04'27	6:40:18
Agency 54	1	45N31	97w02	6:28:08
Ahnberg 5	1	44N18'15	97w03'24	6:28:14
Ajax 51	3	43N53'51	103w10'53	6:52:44
Akaska 64	1	45N19'57	100w07'13	6:40:29
Alban 25	1	45N12	96w32	6:26:08
Albee 25	1	45N03'08	96w33'11	6:26:13
Albion 4	1	42N57	97w56	6:31:44
Alcester 63	1	43N01'17	96w37'50	6:26:31
Alden 29	1	44N41	99w06	6:36:24
Alexandria 30	1	43N39'13	97w46'57	6:31:08
Allen 3	3	43N16'51	101w55'26	6:47:42
Alliance 50	1	43N54	96w29	6:25:56
Allison 6	1	45N49	98w40	6:34:40
Allison Crossing 67	3	45N11'56	101w55'01	6:47:40
Alpena 36	1	44N10'53	98w21'55	6:33:28
Alpha 29	1	44N35	98w59	6:35:56
Alsen 63	1	42N57'40	96w48'19	6:27:13
Alsville 28	1	44N35'12	97w07'40	6:28:31
Altamont 19	1	44N50'23	96w41'21	6:26:45
Alto 32	1	44N19'48	100w07'37	6:40:30
Alto 54	1	45N26	97w10	6:28:40
Alton 5	1	44N19	96w35	6:26:20
Altoona 2	1	44N35	98w24	6:33:36
America 7	1	43N33	99w11	6:36:44
Ames 29	1	44N16'09	99w05'04	6:36:20
Amherst 45	1	45N44'17	97w55'15	6:31:41
Anderson 52	3	45N41	102w16	6:49:04
Andover 18	1	45N24'37	97w54'08	6:31:37
Anina 36	1	43N59	98w38	6:34:32
Annin 42	1	43N59	100w04	6:40:16
Antelope 60	4	43N18'11	100w37'44	6:42:31
Antelope Valley 19	1	44N56	96w29	6:25:56
Appleby 14	1	44N49'01	97w03'01	6:28:12
Applegate 42	1	44N08	100w05	6:40:20
Appomattox 53	1	45N08	100w07	6:40:28
Arcade 24	1	44N56	99w01	6:36:04
Ardmore 23	3	43N01'10	103w39'21	6:54:37
Arena 53	1	45N12	99w52	6:39:28
Argentine 23	3	43N26	103w59	6:55:56
Argo 5	1	44N30	96w42	6:26:48
Argonne 48	1	44N04'24	97w38'18	6:30:33
Argyle 16	3	43N32'06	103w38'51	6:54:35
Arlington 38	1	44N21'52	97w07'58	6:28:32
Arlington Beach 5	1	44N32'02	97w05'51	6:28:23
Armour 21	1	43N19'07	98w20'47	6:33:23
Arpan 9	3	44N47'18	103w38'55	6:54:36
Artas 10	1	45N53'17	99w48'22	6:39:13
Artesian 55	1	44N00'33	97w55'14	6:31:41
Artichoke 53	1	44N56	100w06	6:40:24
Ashton 57	1	44N59'42	98w29'51	6:33:59
Astoria 19	1	44N33'30	96w32'49	6:26:11
Athboy 15	3	45N34'27	101w55'20	6:47:41
Athol 57	1	45N00'32	98w35'46	6:34:23
Aurora 5	1	44N17'03	96w41'07	6:26:44
Aurora Center 1	1	43N31'37	98w35'22	6:34:21
Avance 46	3	44N55'06	102w14'50	6:48:59
Avon 4	1	43N00'18	98w03'34	6:32:14
Avon Springs 53	1	44N56	99w45	6:39:00
Badger 38	1	44N29'07	97w12'16	6:28:49
Badnation 47	4	43N39'06	100w22'10	6:41:29
Badus 39	1	44N09	97w11	6:28:44
Bailey 42	1	43N48	99w41	6:38:44
Baltic 49	1	43N45'41	96w44'24	6:26:58
Bancroft 38	1	44N29'17	97w44'59	6:31:00
Bangor 5	1	44N20	97w03	6:28:12
Barnard 6	1	45N43'57	98w29'46	6:33:59
Batesland 3	3	43N07'46	102w06'06	6:48:24
Bath 6	1	45N28'06	98w19'24	6:33:18
Bath Corner 6	1	45N27'33	98w19'45	6:33:19
Bear Butte 46	3	44N28'28	103w18'25	6:53:14
Bear Creek 20	3	45N03'44	101w26'44	6:45:47
Beardsley 33	1	43N17'54	97w58'55	6:31:56
Beaver 48	1	43N53	97w47	6:31:08
Beaver Creek 61	1	43N03	100w10	6:40:40
Beaver Crossing 40	3	44N22'58	104w00'12	6:56:01
Beck 52	3	45N10	102w39	6:50:36
Becker 54	1	45N33	96w50	6:27:20
Beebe 22	1	45N26'53	99w11'42	6:36:47
Belford 1	1	43N53	98w22	6:33:28
Belle 22	1	45N33	98w54	6:35:36
Belle Fourche 9	3	44N40'17	103w51'06	6:55:24
Belle Plaine 57	1	44N51	98w09	6:32:36
Belle Prairie 2	1	44N14	97w55	6:31:40
Belleview 48	1	44N09	97w26	6:29:44
Belvidere 35	3	43N49'55	101w16'16	6:45:05
Bemis 19	1	44N50'06	96w50'53	6:27:24
Benchmark 40	3	44N13'31	103w34'40	6:54:19
Benclare 49	1	43N30'20	96w28'43	6:25:55
Bend 46	3	44N13'40	103w00'35	6:52:02
Benedict 55	1	44N04	97w54	6:31:36
Beotia 57	1	45N11	98w12	6:32:48
Beresford 63	1	43N04'50	96w46'24	6:27:06
Berne 16	3	43N49'03	103w38'18	6:54:33
Bethel 13	1	42N57	97w06	6:28:24
Bethlehem 46	3	44N17	103w31	6:54:04
Betts 17	1	43N42'23	98w08'45	6:32:35
Big Bend 51	3	44N03'56	103w24'51	6:53:39
Big Buffalo 35	3	43N52	102w01	6:48:04
Big Sioux 63	1	42N32	96w30	6:26:00
Big Springs 63	1	42N56'17	96w36'26	6:26:26
Big Stone City 25	1	45N17'30	96w27'45	6:25:51
Bijou Hills 7	1	43N31'05	99w08'58	6:36:36
Billsburg 27	3	44N24'02	101w40'47	6:46:43
Bison 52	3	45N31'13	102w27'39	6:49:51
Bixby 52	3	45N08'54	102w33'41	6:50:15
Black 61	1	43N23	99w57	6:39:48
Black Dog 42	1	43N42	99w34	6:38:16
Blackhawk 46	3	44N09'04	103w18'27	6:53:14
Black Horse 15	3	45N42'57	101w22'49	6:45:31
Blackpipe 3	3	43N20'38	101w16'27	6:45:06
Blacktail 40	3	44N22'12	103w45'35	6:55:02
Blendon 17	1	43N48	98w16	6:33:04
Blinsmon 50	1	43N54	96w35	6:26:20
Blom 19	1	44N35	96w42	6:26:48
Bloomfield 57	1	44N37'57	98w05'55	6:32:24
Bloomingdale 13	1	42N55'28	96w57'23	6:27:50
Blooming Valley 25	1	45N15	97w10	6:28:40
Blue Bell 16	3	43N43'00	103w28'55	6:53:56
Blumengard Colony 24	1	45N10	99w07	6:36:28
Blunt 32	1	44N30'44	99w59'30	6:39:58
Boneita Springs 46	3	44N26'42	102w33'43	6:50:15
Bonesteel 26	1	43N04'35	98w56'39	6:35:47
Bon Homme 4	1	42N53	97w46	6:31:04
Bon Homme Colony 4	1	42N52	97w32	6:30:08
Bonilla 2	1	44N34'58	98w29'56	6:34:00
Booge 49	1	43N38'45	96w27'35	6:25:50
Bossko 54	1	45N46	97w10	6:28:40
Bovee 11	1	43N19'24	98w46'07	6:35:04
Bovine 37	1	44N08	100w52	6:43:28
Bowdle 22	1	45N27'11	99w39'13	6:38:37
Box Elder 51	3	44N06'45	103w04'04	6:52:16
Bradley 12	1	45N05'26	97w38'36	6:30:34
Brainard 6	1	45N44	98w24	6:33:36
Bramhall 34	1	44N30	99w22	6:37:28
Brandon 49	1	43N35'41	96w34'18	6:26:17
Brandon Terrace 49	1	43N35	96w34	6:26:16
Brandt 19	1	44N39'49	96w37'26	6:26:30
Brantford 28	1	44N46	97w23	6:29:32
Brentford 57	1	45N09'37	98w19'21	6:33:17
Bretton 32	1	44N31	99w51	6:39:24
Bridger 67	3	44N32'45	101w54'39	6:47:39
Bridgewater 43	1	43N33'06	97w30'26	6:30:02
Bristol 18	1	45N20'41	97w44'53	6:31:00
Britton 45	1	45N47'30	97w45'02	6:31:00
Broadland 2	1	44N29'33	98w20'56	6:33:24
Brookfield 43	1	43N49	97w20	6:29:20
Brookings 5	1	44N18'41	96w47'53	6:27:12
Brooklyn 41	1	43N07	96w52	6:27:28
Brothersfield 62	1	43N28	97w06	6:28:24
Brownsville 40	3	44N16'31	103w41'38	6:54:47
Bruce 5	1	44N26'17	96w53'23	6:27:34
Brunson 61	1	43N28	99w48	6:39:12
Bryan 11	1	43N08	98w17	6:33:08
Bryant 28	1	44N35'26	97w28'01	6:29:52
Buffalo 31	3	45N35'03	103w32'44	6:54:11
Buffalo Gap 16	3	43N29'30	103w18'45	6:53:15
Buffalo Trading Post 49	1	43N47	96w56	6:27:44
Bull Creek 61	1	43N28	99w35	6:38:20
Bullhead 15	3	45N45'56	101w04'49	6:44:19
Bunker 58	3	44N14'19	101w06'05	6:44:24
Burbank 13	1	42N44'43	96w49'44	6:27:19
Burdette 29	1	44N42'18	98w48'00	6:35:12
Burdick 52	3	45N47	102w23	6:49:32
Burdock 23	3	43N27'11	103w59'34	6:55:58
Burk 49	1	43N48	96w50	6:27:20
Burke 26	1	43N10'57	99w17'30	6:37:10
Burkmere 24	1	45N02'55	99w18'41	6:37:15
Burr Oak 2	1	44N14	98w38	6:34:32
Bushnell 5	1	44N19'43	96w38'32	6:26:34
Butler 18	1	45N15'32	97w42'43	6:30:51
Cactus Flats 35	3	43N50'08	101w53'38	6:47:35
Cadillac 15	3	45N52	101w01	6:44:04
Cambria 6	1	45N33	98w17	6:33:08
Campbell 29	1	44N41	99w16	6:37:04
Camp Crook 31	3	45N33'01	103w58'27	6:55:54
Canadaville 51	3	43N55'23	103w31'25	6:54:06
Canistota 43	1	43N35'52	97w17'25	6:29:10
Canning 32	1	44N23'47	100w01'54	6:40:08
Canova 48	1	43N52'52	97w30'15	6:30:01
Canton 41	1	43N18'03	96w35'33	6:26:22
Canyon City 51	3	44N05'06	103w36'19	6:54:25
Capa 37	3	44N06'32	100w58'40	6:43:55
Capital 33	1	43N13	97w42	6:30:48
Capitola 57	1	44N45	98w02	6:32:08
Caputa 51	3	43N59'38	102w58'54	6:51:56
Carl 44	1	45N48	98w48	6:35:12
Carlisle 6	1	45N39	98w40	6:34:40
Carlock 26	1	43N04'55	99w26'04	6:37:44
Carlton 29	1	44N46	98w53	6:35:32
Carlyle 2	1	44N15	98w24	6:33:36
Carpenter 12	1	44N38'15	97w54'59	6:31:40
Carr 53	1	45N07	99w46	6:39:04
Carroll 11	1	43N28	98w46	6:35:04
Carter 61	3	43N23'14	100w12'08	6:40:49
Carthage 48	1	44N10'16	97w42'58	6:30:52
Cascade Springs 23	3	43N20'00	103w33'00	6:54:12
Cash 52	3	45N36	102w39	6:50:36
Castalia 11	1	43N23	99w00	6:36:00
Castle Rock 9	3	44N57'52	103w25'26	6:53:42
Castlewood 28	1	44N43'22	97w01'47	6:28:07
Cattron 53	1	44N57	100w15	6:41:00
Cavour 2	1	44N22'12	98w02'15	6:32:09
Cedar 29	1	44N21	99w14	6:36:56
Cedar Butte 47	3	43N34'37	101w01'05	6:44:04
Cedar Canyon 46	3	45N01'25	102w41'24	6:50:46
Cedar Grove Colony 7	1	43N31'49	98w48'27	6:35:14
Cedar Lake 3	3	43N04	101w18	6:45:12
Center 1	1	43N33	98w37	6:34:28
Center 43	1	43N44	97w23	6:29:32
Center Point 62	1	43N10	97w14	6:28:56
Centerville 62	1	43N07'10	96w57'40	6:27:51
Central City 40	3	44N21'57	103w46'19	6:55:05
Central Point 18	1	45N17	97w18	6:29:12
Chamberlain 7	1	43N48'39	99w19'49	6:37:19
Chance 52	3	45N24'36	102w16'51	6:49:07
Chancellor 62	1	43N22'20	96w59'12	6:27:57
Chase 67	3	44N56'28	101w37'41	6:46:31
Chaudoin 52	3	45N15	102w24	6:49:36
Chautauqua 39	1	43N58'49	97w03'35	6:28:14
Chelsea 24	1	45N10'07	98w44'21	6:34:57

Cherry Creek 67
3 44N36'20 101w29'58 6:46:00
Chery 36 1 44N09 98w38 6:34:32
Chester 39 1 43N53'42 96w55'34 6:27:42
Cheyenne 51 3 44N23 102w11 6:48:44
Cheyenne Crossing 40
3 44N17'46 103w52'08 6:55:29
Cheyenne River Indian Res 20
3 45N00 101w13 6:44:52
Childstown 62 1 43N18 97w20 6:29:20
Choteau Creek 11
1 43N09 98w10 6:32:40
Civil Bend 63 1 42N37 96w39 6:26:36
Claire City 54 1 45N51'26 97w06'12 6:28:25
Clare 50 1 44N04 96w42 6:26:48
Claremont 6 1 45N40'19 98w00'55 6:32:04
Clark 12 1 44N52'40 97w43'58 6:30:56
Clark Colony 57
1 44N47'22 97w58'48 6:31:55
Clarno 39 1 43N54 97w18 6:29:12
Clayton 33 1 43N26'37 97w39'27 6:30:38
Clearfield 61 1 43N10'06 100w01'40 6:40:07
Clear Lake 19 1 44N44'45 96w40'50 6:26:43
Clearwater 48 1 43N59 97w26 6:29:44
Clinton 48 1 43N59 97w47 6:31:08
Cloverleaf Colony 48
1 44N10'57 97w32'12 6:30:09
Cloyd Valley 22
1 45N22 99w31 6:38:04
Clyde 2 1 44N20 98w17 6:33:08
Coal Springs 52
3 45N26'30 102w06'26 6:48:26
Cody 47 4 43N38 100w32 6:42:08
Colfax Corner 13
1 43N00'40 97w01'19 6:28:05
Collins 12 1 44N35 97w40 6:30:40
Colman 50 1 43N58'57 96w48'51 6:27:15
Colome 61 1 43N15'38 99w42'53 6:38:52
Colton 49 1 43N47'10 96w55'38 6:27:43
Columbia 6 1 45N36'47 98w18'44 6:33:15
Commerce 49 1 43N31 96w42 6:26:48
Como 29 1 44N15 99w13 6:36:52
Conata 51 3 43N43'43 102w11'18 6:48:45
Concord 39 1 44N04 97w18 6:29:12
Conde 57 1 45N09'26 98w05'50 6:32:23
Condon 61 1 43N33 99w42 6:38:48
Cooper 1 1 43N48 98w37 6:34:28
Corn Creek 47 3 43N31 101w10 6:44:40
Cornwall 57 1 44N40 98w17 6:33:08
Corona 54 1 45N20'02 96w45'46 6:27:03
Corsica 21 1 43N25'31 98w24'25 6:33:38
Corson 49 1 43N36'59 96w34'17 6:26:17
Cortlandt 22 1 45N27 98w46 6:35:04
Cottonwood 35 3 43N58'01 101w54'20 6:47:37
Cottonwood Lake 22
1 45N28 99w31 6:38:04
Cottonwood Valley 47
4 43N36 100w54 6:43:36
Council House 42
1 44N04'40 99w35'19 6:38:21
Crandall 18 1 45N09'19 97w57'19 6:31:49
Crandon 57 1 44N46'29 98w27'28 6:33:50
Craven 22 1 45N26'32 98w55'29 6:35:42
Craven Corner 22
1 45N26'52 98w55'32 6:35:42
Crazy Horse 16 3 43N46 103w36 6:54:24
Creighton 51 3 44N15'18 102w12'27 6:48:50
Cresbard 24 1 45N10'12 98w56'53 6:35:48
Creston 51 3 43N54'38 102w41'54 6:50:48
Crocker 12 1 45N06'19 97w47'04 6:31:08
Crook City 40 3 44N26'29 103w37'59 6:54:32
Crooked Creek 51
3 43N57 102w23 6:49:32
Crooks 49 1 43N39'53 96w48'38 6:27:15
Cross Plains 33
1 43N27 97w57 6:31:48
Crow 36 1 44N04 98w52 6:35:28
Crow Creek Indian Res 8
1 44N03 99w26 6:37:44
Crow Lake 36 1 43N57'27 98w44'19 6:34:57
Crystal Lake 1 1 43N38 98w38 6:34:32
Cunningham 53 1 45N02 99w52 6:39:28
Curlew 61 1 43N33 100w11 6:40:44
Custer 16 3 43N46'00 103w35'54 6:54:24
Cuthbert 55 1 43N58'04 98w13'25 6:32:54
Dahlberg 54 1 45N51'21 97w11'06 6:28:44
Dale 36 1 44N09 98w31 6:34:04
Dalesburg 13 1 42N58'37 96w54'14 6:27:37
Dallas 26 1 43N14'10 99w31'00 6:38:04
Dalzell 46 3 44N20'37 102w23'46 6:49:35
Daneville 62 1 43N08 97w06 6:28:24
Danforth 29 1 44N15'15 98w52'59 6:35:32
Dante 11 1 43N02'19 98w11'02 6:32:44
Date 52 3 45N22'02 102w40'45 6:50:43
Davis 62 1 43N15'27 96w59'43 6:27:59
Day 12 1 44N51 97w40 6:30:40
Deadwood 40 3 44N22'36 103w43'45 6:54:55
Dearborn 2 1 44N20 98w24 6:33:36
Deerfield 51 3 44N01'02 103w50'01 6:55:20
De Grey 32 1 44N17'09 99w55'03 6:39:40
Delaney 15 3 45N36 101w55 6:47:40
Delapre 41 1 43N28 96w49 6:27:16
Delaware 41 1 43N13 96w52 6:27:28
Dell Rapids 49 1 43N49'34 96w42'21 6:26:49
Delmont 21 1 43N16'03 98w09'43 6:32:39
Dempster 28 1 44N37'55 96w57'05 6:27:48
Denby 56 3 43N03'39 102w20'14 6:49:21
Dennis 23 3 43N15'41 103w51'59 6:55:28
Denver 38 1 44N23 97w12 6:28:48
De Smet 38 1 44N23'15 97w33'00 6:30:12
Devoe 24 1 45N05'30 98w52'42 6:35:31
Dewey 16 3 43N31'51 104w02'26 6:56:10
De Witt 52 3 45N47 102w07 6:48:28
Dexter 14 1 45N06 97w17 6:29:08
Dezera 11 1 43N09'55 98w30'05 6:34:00
Diamond 54 1 45N44'14 96w41'28 6:26:46
Diana 55 1 43N59 97w54 6:31:36
Dickens 26 1 43N07 99w29 6:37:56
Dimock 33 1 43N28'27 97w59'07 6:31:56
Dixon 26 1 43N23'00 99w28'22 6:37:53
Dog Ear 61 1 43N13 99w57 6:39:48
Doland 57 1 44N53'45 98w06'01 6:32:24
Dolton 62 1 43N29'27 97w23'07 6:29:32
Dorman 42 1 43N59 99w50 6:39:20
Douglas 34 1 44N41 99w29 6:37:56
Draper 37 1 43N55'34 100w32'24 6:42:10
Dryden 23 3 43N10 103w18 6:53:12
Dry Wood Lake 54
1 45N36 97w07 6:28:28
Dudley 23 3 43N18'41 103w49'04 6:55:16
Duell 52 3 45N21 102w39 6:50:36
Dumarce 45 1 45N47 97w24 6:29:36
Dumont 40 3 44N14'19 103w47'54 6:55:12
Dunkel 37 1 43N52 100w31 6:42:04
Dupree 67 3 45N02'51 101w36'02 6:46:24
Duxbury 57 1 45N14'28 98w29'41 6:33:59
Eagle 7 1 43N34'19 99w05'26 6:36:22
Eagle Butte 20 3 45N00'09 101w13'59 6:44:56
Eakin 59 1 44N36'56 100w01'58 6:40:08
Earling 42 1 43N53 99w57 6:39:48
East Choteau 21
1 43N14 98w10 6:32:40
Easter 54 1 45N37 96w55 6:27:40
East Hanson 6 1 45N22 98w02 6:32:08
East Rondell 6 1 45N17 98w17 6:33:08
East Sioux Falls 49
1 43N31'37 96w36'30 6:26:26
Eden 45 1 45N37'00 97w25'10 6:29:41
Edens 26 1 43N18 99w28 6:37:52
Edgemont 23 3 43N18'04 103w49'30 6:55:18
Edgerton 30 1 43N43 97w40 6:30:40
Edison 49 1 43N43 96w35 6:26:20
Edna 42 1 43N44 99w55 6:39:40
Egan 50 1 43N59'57 96w38'55 6:26:36
Egeland 18 1 45N11 97w18 6:29:12
Elbon 27 3 44N16'51 101w41'17 6:46:45
Elida 53 1 44N57 99w53 6:39:32
Elk Point 63 1 42N41'00 96w41'00 6:26:44
Elkton 5 1 44N14'10 96w28'51 6:25:55
Elliott 55 1 43N54 98w16 6:33:04
Ellis 49 1 43N33'45 96w49'49 6:27:19
Ellis Corner 49
1 43N36'06 96w49'50 6:27:19
Elliston 61 1 43N13 99w35 6:38:20
Ellisville 24 1 44N57 99w30 6:38:00
Ellston 26 1 43N02 99w08 6:36:32
Ellsworth 46 3 44N10 103w06 6:52:24
Ellsworth Air Force Base 46
3 44N10 103w06 6:52:24
Elmira 14 1 44N56 97w04 6:28:16
Elmore 40 3 44N18'56 103w53'13 6:55:33
Elm Springs 46 3 44N18'48 102w31'38 6:50:07
Elm Springs Colony 33
1 43N33 97w59 6:31:56
Elrod 12 1 44N53'11 97w34'24 6:30:18
Elroy 24 1 45N07 99w30 6:38:00
Elvira 8 1 44N03 98w59 6:35:56
Emanuel 4 1 43N07 97w56 6:31:44
Emerson 24 1 45N12 99w01 6:36:04
Emery 30 1 43N36'06 97w37'20 6:30:29
Emmet 63 1 42N58'58 96w44'45 6:26:59
Empire 9 3 44N37 103w24 6:53:36
Englewood 40 3 44N17'49 103w47'03 6:55:08
Englewood 52 3 45N16 102w07 6:48:28
Enning 46 3 44N34'32 102w33'46 6:50:15
Epiphany 30 1 43N50'57 97w39'41 6:30:39
Erskine 23 3 43N25'59 103w33'52 6:54:15
Erwin 38 1 44N29'15 97w26'41 6:29:47
Esmond 38 1 44N15'44 97w46'16 6:31:05
Estelline 28 1 44N34'29 96w54'07 6:27:36
Ethan 17 1 43N32'52 97w59'16 6:31:57
Eureka 44 1 45N46'10 99w37'09 6:38:29
Exline 57 1 44N51 98w39 6:34:36
Fair 33 1 43N13 97w56 6:31:44
Fairburn 16 3 43N41'10 103w12'40 6:52:51
Fairfax 26 1 43N01'39 98w53'17 6:35:33
Fairfield 2 1 44N30 98w16 6:33:04
Fairland 42 1 43N53 99w28 6:37:52
Fairpoint 46 3 44N44'54 102w47'46 6:51:11
Fairview 41 1 43N13'18 96w29'23 6:25:58
Faith 46 3 45N01'23 102w02'08 6:48:09
Farmer 30 1 43N43'26 97w41'17 6:30:45
Farmingdale 51 3 43N57'33 102w53'00 6:51:32
Farwell 55 1 43N51'02 97w54'40 6:31:39
Faulkton 24 1 45N02'06 99w07'25 6:36:30
Fayette 53 1 45N12 100w07 6:40:28
Fedora 48 1 44N00'32 97w47'26 6:31:10
Ferney 6 1 45N19'50 98w05'51 6:32:23
Firesteel 20 3 45N25'29 101w17'05 6:45:08
Five Points 51 3 43N58'17 103w33'00 6:54:12
Flandreau 50 1 44N02'58 96w35'42 6:26:23
Flandreau Indian Reservation 50
1 44N03 96w35 6:26:20
Flat Butte 51 3 43N52 102w05 6:48:20
Flat Creek 52 3 45N52 102w16 6:49:04
Fleetwood 49 1 43N35 96w34 6:26:16
Flint Rock 52 3 45N05 102w03 6:48:12
Florence 14 1 45N03'17 97w19'46 6:29:19
Floyd 55 1 44N09 98w02 6:32:08
Foley 14 1 44N50'22 97w08'50 6:28:35
Folsom 16 3 43N49'31 102w52'10 6:51:29
Forbes 11 1 43N27 98w53 6:35:32
Fordham 12 1 44N46 97w55 6:31:40
Forestburg 55 1 44N01'20 98w06'28 6:32:26
Forest City 53 1 45N02 100w15 6:41:00
Fort 45 1 45N38 97w32 6:30:08
Fort Pierre 58 4 44N21'13 100w22'24 6:41:30
Fort Randall 26
1 43N01'28 98w37'26 6:34:30
Fort Thompson 8
1 44N04'07 99w26'15 6:37:45
Fountain 22 1 45N27 98w54 6:35:36
Fourmile 16 3 43N43'58 103w40'30 6:54:42
Foxton 12 1 44N45 97w33 6:30:12
Frankfort 57 1 44N52'36 98w18'18 6:33:13
Franklin 39 1 43N53'30 97w04'07 6:28:16
Franklyn 6 1 45N43 98w40 6:34:40
Frederick 6 1 45N49'57 98w30'21 6:34:01
Fredlund 52 3 45N41 102w39 6:50:36
Freedom 24 1 45N12 99w09 6:36:36
Freeman 33 1 43N21'09 97w26'13 6:29:45
Fremont 50 1 44N09 96w50 6:27:20
Froehlich Addition 49
1 43N31 96w42 6:26:48
Fruitdale 9 3 44N40'06 103w41'48 6:54:47
Fuller 14 1 45N01 97w16 6:29:04
Fulton 30 1 43N43'29 97w49'24 6:31:18
Galena 40 3 44N20'01 103w38'26 6:54:34
Gales 1 1 43N38 98w44 6:34:56
Gallup 57 1 45N04'14 98w29'42 6:33:59
Gannvalley 8 1 44N02'00 98w59'15 6:35:57
Garden City 12 1 44N57'30 97w34'52 6:30:19
Garden Prairie 6
1 45N17 98w10 6:32:40
Garland 6 1 45N39 98w24 6:33:36
Garretson 49 1 43N43'03 96w30'09 6:26:01
Gary 19 1 44N47'33 96w27'20 6:25:49
Gayville 66 1 42N53'17 97w10'19 6:28:41
Geddes 11 1 43N15'13 98w41'42 6:34:47
Gem 6 1 45N22 98w20 6:33:20
Geneseo 54 1 45N22 96w41 6:26:44
Georgia 25 1 45N01 96w42 6:26:48
German 33 1 43N18 97w56 6:31:44
Gettysburg 53 1 45N00'42 99w57'19 6:39:49
Gilbert 29 1 44N35 98w46 6:35:04
Glad Valley 67 3 45N23'57 101w46'38 6:47:07
Glen 22 1 45N28 99w24 6:37:36
Glencross 20 3 45N26'54 100w55'15 6:43:41
Glendale 29 1 44N18 99w05 6:36:20
Glendale Colony 57
1 44N47'58 98w17'14 6:33:09
Glendo 52 3 45N42 102w53 6:51:32
Glenham 64 1 45N31'58 100w16'16 6:41:05
Glover 22 1 45N23 99w24 6:37:36
Goodwill 54 1 45N34'01 97w04'11 6:28:17
Goodwin 19 1 44N52'45 96w50'54 6:27:24
Goose Lake 11 1 43N13 98w34 6:34:16
Gorman 53 1 44N55'37 100w04'28 6:40:18
Gossage Memorial 51
3 44N04'15 103w15'01 6:53:00
Graceland 14 1 44N56 97w26 6:29:44
Graceville Colony 39
1 44N00 97w22 6:29:28
Grafton 48 1 44N09 97w33 6:30:12
Grand 29 1 44N29 98w45 6:35:00
Grandfield 27 3 44N26 101w13 6:44:52
Grand Meadow 49
1 43N43 96w58 6:27:52
Grand River 52 3 45N53 102w38 6:50:32
Grand Valley 15
3 45N41 101w55 6:47:40
Grange 19 1 44N35 96w49 6:27:16
Grant Center 25
1 45N12 96w42 6:26:48
Gray Goose 32 1 44N30'17 100w21'01 6:41:24
Great Bend 58 1 44N56 98w25 6:33:40
Greenfield 6 1 45N49 98w17 6:33:08
Greenfield 13 1 42N52'50 96w50'43 6:27:23
Green Grass 20 3 45N10'16 101w14'44 6:44:59
Greenland 43 1 43N37 97w11 6:28:44
Greenleaf 29 1 44N35 99w07 6:36:28
Green Valley 48
1 44N04 97w40 6:30:40
Greenway 44 1 45N54'35 99w42'38 6:38:51
Greenwood 11 1 42N55'23 98w23'17 6:33:33
Greenwood 40 3 44N13'13 103w33'40 6:54:15
Greenwood 61 1 43N38 100w02 6:40:08
Greenwood Colony 21
1 43N12'48 98w09'03 6:32:36
Gregory 26 1 43N13'56 99w25'48 6:37:43
Grenville 18 1 45N28'01 97w23'36 6:29:34
Gretna 22 1 45N27'02 99w30'52 6:38:03
Grindstone 27 3 44N08'21 101w58'01 6:47:52
Grosse 7 1 43N55'38 99w17'10 6:37:09
Groton 6 1 45N26'51 98w05'54 6:32:24
Grouse Creek 42
1 43N59 99w57 6:39:48
Groveland 57 1 44N56 98w40 6:34:40
Grovena 50 1 43N59 96w35 6:26:20
Grover 14 1 44N48'50 97w16'06 6:29:04
Gustave 31 3 45N16'52 103w58'29 6:55:54
Hague 12 1 44N40 97w47 6:31:08
Hall 52 3 45N20 102w32 6:50:08
Hamill 61 1 43N35'41 99w40'52 6:38:43
Hamlin 28 1 44N46 96w57 6:27:48
Hammer 54 1 45N51'19 97w01'15 6:28:05
Hancock 4 1 42N52 98w03 6:32:12
Hanna 40 3 44N15'42 103w50'43 6:55:23
Hanson 30 1 43N43 97w54 6:31:36
Harding 31 3 45N23'54 103w49'56 6:55:20
Harmon 54 1 45N47 96w43 6:26:52
Harney 51 3 43N53'33 103w23'15 6:53:33
Harrington 3 3 43N10'16 101w15'15 6:45:01
Harrisburg 41 1 43N25'53 96w41'49 6:26:47
Harrison 21 1 43N25'47 98w31'37 6:34:06
Harrold 32 1 44N31'28 99w44'20 6:38:57
Hart 54 1 45N47 96w55 6:27:40
Hartford 49 1 43N37'23 96w56'32 6:27:46
Hartford Beach 54
1 45N24'20 96w40'51 6:26:43
Hartley 27 3 44N24'04 101w48'36 6:47:14
Havana 19 1 44N46 96w49 6:27:16
Haydraw 46 3 44N26'42 102w43'17 6:50:53
Hayes 58 3 44N22'13 101w01'16 6:44:05
Hayti 28 1 44N39'26 97w12'17 6:28:49
Hayward 51 3 43N52'18 103w20'02 6:53:20
Hayward Addition 49
1 43N31 96w42 6:26:48
Hazel 28 1 44N45'35 97w22'45 6:29:31
Hecla 6 1 45N52'59 98w09'06 6:32:36
Henden 48 1 44N04 97w26 6:29:44
Henry 14 1 44N52'38 97w27'58 6:29:52
Heppner 23 3 43N14'49 103w32'58 6:54:12
Hereford 46 3 44N23'14 102w53'42 6:51:35
Herman 39 1 43N59 97w11 6:28:44
Hermosa 16 3 43N50'23 103w11'26 6:52:46
Herreid 10 1 45N50'05 100w04'08 6:40:17
Herrick 26 1 43N06'54 99w11'15 6:36:45
Hetland 38 1 44N22'41 97w14'05 6:28:56
Hiawatha Beach 54
1 45N28'12 96w44'39 6:26:59
Hickman 45 1 45N38 97w48 6:31:12
Hidden Timber 60
4 43N13'46 100w25'16 6:41:41
Hidewood 19 1 44N40 96w50 6:27:20
Highmore 34 1 44N31'17 99w26'28 6:37:46
Hiland 29 1 44N19 98w53 6:35:32
Hilland 27 3 44N16'58 101w51'22 6:47:25
Hill City 51 3 43N55'57 103w34'29 6:54:18

Hillhead 45 1 45N50'06 97w23'30 6:29:34
Hillsdale 24 1 44N56 98w54 6:35:36
Hillside 21 1 43N28'08 98w12'43 6:32:51
Hillside 22 1 45N17 99w24 6:37:36
Hill Side 63 1 42N56'21 96w47'06 6:27:08
Hillside Colony 57
1 44N44'20 98w02'44 6:32:11
Hillsview 44 1 45N39'53 99w33'29 6:38:14
Hilmoe 42 1 43N48 100w10 6:40:40
Hisega 51 3 44N03'12 103w24'05 6:53:36
Hisle 65 3 43N24'21 101w45'05 6:47:00
Hitchcock 2 1 44N37'47 98w24'33 6:33:38
Hoffman 44 1 45N50 99w03 6:36:12
Holabird 34 1 44N31'23 99w35'52 6:38:23
Holden 29 1 44N40 98w53 6:35:32
Holland 21 1 43N28 98w32 6:34:08
Holmquist 18 1 45N20'22 97w39'10 6:30:37
Holsclaw 61 1 43N08 100w10 6:40:40
Home 62 1 43N28 96w59 6:27:56
Homer 18 1 45N32 97w48 6:31:12
Hooker 62 1 43N12'00 97w01'28 6:28:06
Hoover 9 3 45N06'45 103w16'00 6:53:04
Hope 42 1 43N59 100w18 6:41:12
Hopper 1 1 43N43 98w22 6:33:28
Horse Creek 52 3 45N53 102w53 6:51:32
Hosmer 22 1 45N34'44 99w28'28 6:37:54
Hot Springs 23 3 43N25'54 103w28'26 6:53:54
Houghton 6 1 45N45'47 98w12'36 6:32:50
Hoven 53 1 45N14'37 99w46'36 6:39:06
Howard 48 1 44N00'39 97w31'35 6:30:06
Howell 29 1 44N46 99w00 6:36:00
Howes 46 3 44N37'10 102w03'05 6:48:12
Hub City 13 1 42N57'13 96w54'15 6:27:37
Hudgins 52 3 45N41 102w07 6:48:28
Hudson 41 1 43N07'49 96w27'14 6:25:49
Huffton 6 1 45N36'59 98w05'34 6:32:22
Huggins 61 1 43N02 100w05 6:40:20
Hulbert 29 1 44N25 98w45 6:35:00
Humboldt 49 1 43N38'43 97w04'25 6:28:18
Huntimer 49 1 43N50'03 96w55'47 6:27:43
Huntley 22 1 45N28 99w09 6:36:36
Hurley 62 1 43N16'59 97w05'20 6:28:21
Huron 2 1 44N21'48 98w12'50 6:32:51
Huron Colony 2 1 44N33'52 98w12'23 6:32:50
Huron Colony 12
1 44N46'07 97w54'32 6:31:38
Ideal 61 1 43N32'33 99w54'08 6:39:37
Igloo 23 3 43N12'09 103w51'23 6:55:26
Illinois 34 1 44N46 99w29 6:37:56
Imlay 51 3 43N43'10 102w23'49 6:49:35
Imogene 52 3 45N08'26 102w42'45 6:50:51
Indian Creek 35
3 43N57 101w23 6:45:32
Interior 35 3 43N43'37 101w59'01 6:47:56
Iona 42 1 43N32'35 99w25'28 6:37:42
Ipswich 22 1 45N26'40 99w01'44 6:36:07
Irene 66 1 43N04'59 97w09'37 6:28:38
Iron Lightning 67
3 45N03 101w36 6:46:24
Iroquois 38 1 44N22'01 97w51'02 6:31:24
Irwin 61 1 43N18 99w36 6:38:24
Isabel 20 3 45N23'39 101w25'45 6:45:43
James 6 1 45N27'58 98w12'44 6:32:51
James Valley Junction 2
1 44N22'50 98w17'43 6:33:11
Jamesville 66 1 43N06'10 97w29'00 6:29:56
Jasper 30 1 43N43 97w47 6:31:08
Java 64 1 45N30'12 99w53'10 6:39:33
Jefferson 63 1 42N36'09 96w33'32 6:26:14
Jewett 35 3 43N57 101w34 6:46:16
Johnson Siding 51
3 44N05'05 103w26'15 6:53:45
Johnsonville 19
1 44N32'40 96w47'07 6:27:08
Jolly 9 3 44N37'17 103w49'29 6:55:18
Jolly Dump 9 3 44N35'37 103w52'03 6:55:28
Jones 26 1 43N07 99w21 6:37:24
Jordan 61 1 43N23 100w04 6:40:16
Jordan Junction 61
1 43N23'06 100w01'44 6:40:07
Joubert 21 1 43N25'39 98w39'59 6:34:40
Junction City 63
1 42N47'12 96w47'09 6:27:09
Junction Ranger Station 16
3 43N50'46 103w41'39 6:54:47
Junius 39 1 44N00'23 97w14'38 6:28:59
Kadoka 35 3 43N50'02 101w30'34 6:46:02
Kadoka Junction 35
3 43N50'09 101w31'19 6:46:05
Kampeska 14 1 44N52'48 97w16'06 6:29:04
Karinen 31 3 45N54'02 103w40'28 6:54:42
Kassel 33 1 43N18 97w34 6:30:16
Kaylor 33 1 43N11'17 97w50'18 6:31:21
Keldron 15 3 45N55'55 101w48'33 6:47:14
Kellogg 2 1 44N14 98w31 6:34:04
Kenel 15 3 45N51'30 100w27'34 6:41:50
Kennebec 42 1 43N54'13 99w51'41 6:39:27
Kennedy 11 1 43N13 98w18 6:33:12
Kent 22 1 45N17 98w54 6:35:36
Keyapaha 61 1 43N06'34 100w08'15 6:40:33
Keystone 51 3 43N53'44 103w25'04 6:53:40
Kidder 45 1 45N52'59 97w42'47 6:30:51
Kilborn 25 1 45N17 96w48 6:27:12
Kimball 7 1 43N44'48 98w57'29 6:35:50
King 61 1 43N33 99w48 6:39:12
Kingsburg 4 1 42N54'52 97w55'51 6:31:43
Kirley 27 3 44N31'25 101w18'41 6:45:15
Kolls 37 1 44N02 100w38 6:42:32
Kones Corner 28
1 44N43'53 97w06'26 6:28:26
Kosciusko 18 1 45N30 97w17 6:29:08
Kranzburg 14 1 44N53'33 96w55'07 6:27:40
Kulm 33 1 43N18 98w03 6:32:12
Kyle 56 3 43N25'30 102w10'34 6:48:42
La Belle 45 1 45N53 97w25 6:29:40
LaBolt 25 1 45N03'03 96w40'35 6:26:42
Lacy 58 3 44N29'44 100w42'03 6:42:48
LaDelle 57 1 44N40'31 98w07'07 6:32:28
Ladner 31 3 45N49'38 103w43'39 6:54:55
Lafayette 42 1 43N59 99w35 6:38:20
Lafoon 24 1 45N02 99w01 6:36:04
Lake Andes 11 1 43N09'23 98w32'28 6:34:10
Lake Byron 2 1 44N35 98w10 6:32:40
Lake Campbell 50
1 44N19 96w47 6:27:08
Lake City 45 1 45N43'31 97w24'51 6:29:39
Lake Creek 51 3 44N02 102w04 6:48:16
Lake Flat 51 3 44N02 102w18 6:49:12
Lake George 11 1 43N28 99w00 6:36:00
Lake Hendricks 5
1 44N29 96w29 6:25:56
Lake Hill 51 3 44N02 102w11 6:48:44
Lake Norden 28 1 44N34'50 97w12'32 6:28:50
Lake Preston 38
1 44N21'49 97w22'37 6:29:30
Lakeside 46 3 44N11 102w35 6:50:20
Lake Sinai 5 1 44N15 97w04 6:28:16
Laketon 5 1 44N30 97w04 6:28:16
Lake View 39 1 43N59 97w04 6:28:16
Lakeview 60 4 43N06'13 100w44'52 6:42:59
Lamro 61 1 43N23 99w50 6:39:20
Landing Creek 26
1 43N17 98w37 6:34:28
Lane 36 1 44N04'11 98w25'29 6:33:42
Langford 45 1 45N36'09 97w49'48 6:31:19
Lansing 6 1 45N48 98w09 6:32:36
Lantry 20 3 45N00'52 101w25'52 6:45:43
La Plant 20 3 45N08'41 100w39'04 6:42:36
La Prairie 57 1 45N13 98w22 6:33:28
La Roche 11 1 43N28 99w07 6:36:28
La Valley 41 1 43N23 96w45 6:27:00
Lead 40 3 44N21'08 103w45'53 6:55:04
Lebanon 53 1 45N04'11 99w46'10 6:39:05
Lee 54 1 45N27 96w54 6:27:36
Lees Corner 8 1 44N04'39 99w19'30 6:37:18
Lemmon 52 3 45N56'27 102w09'32 6:48:38
Lennox 41 1 43N21'15 96w53'30 6:27:34
Leola 44 1 45N43'22 98w56'26 6:35:46
Le Roy 39 1 44N04 97w04 6:28:16
Lesterville 66 1 43N02'22 97w35'43 6:30:23
Le Sueur 38 1 44N30 97w46 6:31:04
Letcher 55 1 43N53'50 98w08'18 6:32:33
Lien 54 1 45N53 96w55 6:27:40
Lily 18 1 45N10'53 97w40'59 6:30:44
Limestone 23 3 43N10 103w11 6:52:44
Linden Beach 54
1 45N24'17 96w38'54 6:26:36
Linn 29 1 44N51 98w53 6:35:32
Lisbon 17 1 43N38 98w09 6:32:36
Little Buffalo 35
3 43N52 101w51 6:47:24
Littleburg 60 4 43N02'42 100w27'06 6:41:48
Little Eagle 15
3 45N40'33 100w48'14 6:43:13
Little Oak 15 3 45N31 101w10 6:44:40
Lockwood 54 1 45N22 96w34 6:26:16
Lodgepole 52 3 45N48'17 102w39'37 6:50:38
Lodi 13 1 42N58'57 96w59'01 6:27:56
Lodi 57 1 44N51 98w24 6:33:36
Lone Rock 50 1 43N53 96w29 6:25:56
Lone Tree 50 1 43N58'44 96w43'44 6:26:55
Long Hollow 54 1 45N41 97w10 6:28:40
Long Lake 44 1 45N51'24 99w12'17 6:36:49
Long Lake Colony 44
1 45N36'24 98w49'09 6:35:17
Longvalley 65 3 43N20 101w30 6:46:00
Loomer 23 3 43N02 103w08 6:52:32
Loomis 17 1 43N47'38 98w06'15 6:32:25
Lowe 19 1 44N56 96w35 6:26:20
Lower Brule 42 1 44N04'44 99w34'52 6:38:19
Lower Brule Indian Res 42
1 44N05 99w35 6:38:20
Lowry 64 1 45N18'58 99w58'56 6:39:56
Loyalton 22 1 45N17'11 99w16'45 6:37:07
Lucas 26 1 43N17'23 99w12'58 6:36:52
Lucerne 27 3 44N14'21 101w31'33 6:46:06
Ludlow 31 3 45N50'04 103w22'34 6:53:30
Lund 42 1 43N59 100w11 6:40:44
Lura 25 1 45N11 97w07 6:28:28
Lyman 42 1 43N52'52 99w44'21 6:38:57
Lyon 7 1 43N53 98w59 6:35:56
Lyons 49 1 43N43'23 96w52'03 6:27:28
Lyonville 7 1 43N52'40 98w58'13 6:35:53
Macs Corner 34 1 44N15'07 99w26'28 6:37:46
Madison 39 1 44N00'22 97w06'49 6:28:27
Madra 44 1 45N55'48 99w42'58 6:38:52
Madsen Beach 54
1 45N27'37 96w44'22 6:26:57
Mahto 15 3 45N45'31 100w40'33 6:42:42
Maitland 40 3 44N23'51 103w48'04 6:55:12
Maltby 52 3 45N26 102w45 6:51:00
Manchester 38 1 44N22'09 97w43'13 6:30:53
Manderson 56 3 43N14'07 102w28'13 6:49:53
Mansfield 57 1 45N14'35 98w33'45 6:34:15
Maple Leaf 15 3 45N55'29 100w53'25 6:43:34
Mapleton 49 1 43N38 96w42 6:26:48
Marcus 46 3 44N39'29 102w16'22 6:49:05
Marcy Colony 33
1 43N24 97w59 6:31:56
Marietta 23 3 43N23'31 103w55'08 6:55:41
Marindahl 66 1 43N02 97w13 6:28:52
Marion 62 1 43N25'23 97w15'37 6:29:02
Marksville 20 1 45N04'10 100w22'37 6:41:30
Marlar 36 1 44N09 98w52 6:35:28
Marlow 45 1 45N55'15 97w23'07 6:29:32
Marshfield 52 3 45N36 102w27 6:49:48
Martin 3 3 43N10'21 101w43'56 6:46:56
Marty 11 1 42N59'33 98w25'29 6:33:42
Marvin 25 1 45N15'41 96w54'44 6:27:39
Mathews 38 1 44N15 97w34 6:30:16
Mattison 27 3 44N18 101w20 6:45:20
Maurice 40 3 44N23'52 103w53'50 6:55:35
Maurine 46 3 45N01'23 102w35'35 6:50:22
Mawl Springs 51
3 44N05'14 102w48'00 6:51:12
Maxwell Colony 33
1 43N10'56 97w38'03 6:30:32
Maydell 12 1 45N01 97w33 6:30:12
Mayfield 66 1 43N04'57 97w19'06 6:29:16
Mazeppa 25 1 45N12 96w58 6:27:52
McClure 42 1 44N09 100w11 6:40:44
McCook Lake 63 1 42N36 96w34 6:26:16
McGee 51 3 44N02'17 103w23'01 6:53:32
McIntosh 15 3 45N55'17 101w20'57 6:45:24
McKinley 45 1 45N47 97w17 6:29:08
McLaughlin 15 3 45N48'52 100w48'36 6:43:14
McNeely 61 1 43N12 99w50 6:39:20
Meadow 52 3 45N31'45 102w12'57 6:48:52
Meckling 13 1 42N50'33 97w04'09 6:28:17
Medary 5 1 44N12'35 96w47'11 6:27:09
Media 36 1 44N04 98w38 6:34:32
Mellette 57 1 45N09'16 98w29'50 6:33:59
Melrose 25 1 45N17 96w40 6:26:40
Menno 33 1 43N14'23 97w34'39 6:30:19
Mercier 6 1 45N28 98w40 6:34:40
Merritt 51 3 44N08'27 103w34'05 6:54:16
Merton 12 1 44N46 97w39 6:30:36
Metzgerville 17
1 43N32'31 98w15'44 6:33:03
Middleton 62 1 43N18 96w59 6:27:56
Midland 27 3 44N04'18 101w09'18 6:44:37
Midway 49 1 43N42'12 96w42'40 6:26:51
Midway 63 1 42N51'59 96w47'10 6:27:09
Midway 66 1 43N07'33 97w23'56 6:29:36
Milbank 25 1 45N13'09 96w38'07 6:26:32
Milesville 27 3 44N27'29 101w40'44 6:46:43
Milford 2 1 44N35 98w02 6:32:08
Millard 24 1 45N08'58 99w11'40 6:36:47
Millboro 61 1 43N04'23 99w58'07 6:39:52
Miller 29 1 44N31'06 98w59'17 6:35:57
Miller Dale Colony 29
1 44N24'00 99w06'45 6:36:27
Milltown 33 1 43N25'25 97w48'05 6:31:12
Mina 22 1 45N26'00 98w45'30 6:35:02
Miner 48 1 44N04 97w47 6:31:08
Minnekahta 23 3 43N25'50 103w41'16 6:54:45
Minnesota 54 1 45N53 97w02 6:28:08
Miranda 24 1 44N58'19 98w57'50 6:35:51
Miscol 15 3 45N40'37 101w09'43 6:44:39
Mission 60 4 43N18'21 100w39'28 6:42:38
Mission Hill 66
1 42N55'24 97w16'43 6:29:07
Mission Ridge 58
4 44N40'27 100w46'11 6:43:05
Mitchell 17 1 43N42'34 98w01'46 6:32:07
Mobridge 64 1 45N32'14 100w25'39 6:41:43
Modena 22 1 45N33 99w39 6:38:36
Moe 41 1 43N09'22 96w36'31 6:26:26
Moenville 27 3 44N28'30 101w15'23 6:45:02
Molan 33 1 43N13 97w27 6:29:48
Mondamin 29 1 44N16 99w05 6:36:20
Monroe 62 1 43N29'11 97w12'53 6:28:52
Montpelier 22 1 45N23 99w16 6:37:04
Montrose 43 1 43N41'55 97w11'00 6:28:44
Moreau 20 1 45N21'21 100w23'51 6:41:35
Moreau 52 3 45N13 102w17 6:49:08
Morgan 37 3 43N57 101w00 6:44:00
Moritz 19 1 44N50'02 96w33'39 6:26:15
Morningside 2 1 44N21'57 98w11'17 6:32:45
Morningside 42 1 43N34 99w35 6:38:20
Morristown 15 3 45N56'19 101w43'22 6:46:53
Morton 18 1 45N17 97w26 6:29:44
Mosher 47 4 43N28'06 100w17'52 6:41:11
Mound City 10 1 45N43'31 100w04'05 6:40:16
Mount Pleasant 12
1 44N56 97w40 6:30:40
Mount Vernon 17
1 43N42'30 98w15'36 6:33:02
Mud Butte 46 3 45N00'17 102w52'38 6:51:31
Mullen 37 3 43N46 100w45 6:43:00
Murdo 37 1 43N53'18 100w42'45 6:42:51
Murphy 51 3 44N02'40 103w07'36 6:52:30
Mussman 37 1 43N57 100w25 6:41:40
Myersville 51 3 44N06'12 103w44'19 6:54:57
Myron 24 1 45N07 99w01 6:36:04
Mystic 51 3 44N04'37 103w38'28 6:54:34
Nahant 40 3 44N10'36 103w45'18 6:55:01
Nahon 6 1 45N23'08 98w24'22 6:33:37
Nance 2 1 44N35 98w41 6:34:44
Naomi 41 1 43N19'50 96w55'27 6:27:42
Napa Junction 66
1 42N56'28 97w27'12 6:29:49
Naples 12 1 44N46'18 97w30'41 6:30:03
Navan 15 3 45N52 101w23 6:45:32
Nemo 40 3 44N11'39 103w30'16 6:54:01
Newark 45 1 45N55'46 97w47'28 6:31:10
New Effington 54
1 45N51'23 96w55'12 6:27:41
Newell 9 3 44N42'53 103w25'13 6:53:41
New Elm Springs Colony 33
1 43N29'20 97w49'43 6:31:19
New Holland 21 1 43N25'38 98w36'32 6:34:26
New Hope 6 1 45N17 98w40 6:34:40
Newport 45 1 45N38 97w55 6:31:40
New Underwood (Underwood Sta 51
3 44N05'36 102w50'09 6:51:21
New Witten 61 1 43N26 100w05 6:40:20
Nihart 16 3 43N39'23 103w35'26 6:54:22
Nisland 9 3 44N40'23 103w33'11 6:54:13
Nora 63 1 42N56'21 96w42'24 6:26:50
Norbeck 24 1 45N11'03 99w12'44 6:36:51
Nordland 45 1 45N50 97w31 6:30:04
Norris 47 3 43N28'24 101w11'45 6:44:47
North Bryant 22
1 45N33 99w16 6:37:04
North Detroit 6
1 45N48 98w02 6:32:08
North Eagle Butte 20
3 45N00 101w13 6:44:52
North Riverside 53
1 45N12 100w13 6:40:52
North Shore 14 1 44N56'55 97w12'23 6:28:50
North Sioux City 63
1 42N31'38 96w28'58 6:25:56
Northville 57 1 45N09'20 98w34'44 6:34:19
Norton Acres 49
1 43N31 96w42 6:26:48
Norway Center 41
1 43N07'38 96w37'41 6:26:31
Novak 40 3 44N12'59 103w33'05 6:54:12
Nowlin 27 3 44N02'59 101w18'08 6:45:13
Nunda 39 1 44N09'44 97w01'07 6:28:04
Nutley 18 1 45N33 97w26 6:29:44
Oacoma 42 1 43N47'46 99w23'43 6:37:35
Oak Gulch 18 1 45N11 97w56 6:31:44
Oak Hollow 33 1 43N13 98w02 6:32:08
Oak Lake 5 1 44N30 96w35 6:26:20
Oakwood 5 1 44N25 96w56 6:27:44
Odessa 22 1 45N23 99w39 6:38:36

Oelrichs 23 3 43N10'44 103w13'49 6:52:55
Oglala 56 3 43N11'19 102w44'21 6:50:57
Ohio 29 1 44N19 98w59 6:35:56
Okaton 37 3 43N53'10 100w53'29 6:43:34
Okobojo 59 1 44N38'57 100w23'43 6:41:35
Okreek 60 4 43N21'44 100w23'09 6:41:33
Ola 7 1 43N36'03 99w12'37 6:36:50
Oldham 38 1 44N13'39 97w18'27 6:29:14
Olean 57 1 45N08 98w02 6:32:08
Olivet 33 1 43N14'27 97w40'30 6:30:42
Olsonville 60 4 43N07'40 100w36'31 6:42:26
Onaka 24 1 45N11'34 99w27'57 6:37:52
Oneida 55 1 44N04 98w02 6:32:08
O'Neil 24 1 45N07 99w23 6:37:32
Oneota 6 1 45N43 98w32 6:34:08
One Road 54 1 45N33 97w08 6:28:32
Onida 59 1 44N42'29 100w03'34 6:40:14
Ontario 29 1 44N46 99w14 6:36:56
Opal 46 3 44N53'33 102w29'17 6:49:57
Opdahl 28 1 44N40 97w19 6:29:16
Oral 23 3 43N24'18 103w16'07 6:53:04
Ordway 6 1 45N34'43 98w24'42 6:33:39
Oreville 51 3 43N52'03 103w37'21 6:54:29
Orient 24 1 44N54'01 99w05'20 6:36:21
Orland 39 1 43N53'30 97w11'20 6:28:45
Ortley 54 1 45N19'56 97w11'43 6:28:47
Orton 58 4 44N42'37 100w50'30 6:43:22
Osceola 38 1 44N28'03 97w50'18 6:31:21
Oslo 5 1 44N15 96w56 6:27:44
Ottumwa 27 3 44N14'01 101w20'48 6:45:23
Owanka 51 3 44N01'20 102w35'13 6:50:21
Owattonna 53 1 44N57 100w00 6:40:00
Oxford 28 1 44N45 97w13 6:28:52
Pahapesto 61 1 43N38 100w10 6:40:40
Palatine 1 1 43N48 98w23 6:33:32
Palisade 49 1 43N43 96w28 6:25:52
Palmyra 6 1 45N54 98w40 6:34:40
Parade 20 3 45N01'26 101w06'15 6:44:25
Park 29 1 44N51 98w59 6:35:56
Parker 62 1 43N23'51 97w08'10 6:28:33
Parkston 33 1 43N23'56 97w59'00 6:31:56
Parmelee 60 3 43N19'23 101w01'34 6:44:06
Parnell 5 1 44N14 96w35 6:26:20
Patricia 3 3 43N17'14 101w30'42 6:46:03
Patten 1 1 43N54 98w44 6:34:56
Pearl Creek 2 1 44N14 98w02 6:32:08
Pearl Creek Colony 2
1 44N19'43 97w54'48 6:31:39
Pearsons Corner 66
1 43N10'10 97w19'05 6:29:16
Pedro 51 3 44N25'12 102w07'07 6:48:28
Peever 54 1 45N32'35 96w57'16 6:27:49
Pelican 14 1 44N51 97w11 6:28:44
Pembrook 22 1 45N33 98w49 6:35:16
Peninsula Park 39
1 43N56'45 97w00'32 6:28:02
Perkins 4 1 42N51'56 98w00'36 6:32:02
Philip 27 3 44N02'22 101w39'53 6:46:40
Philip Junction 35
3 43N57'57 101w39'39 6:46:39
Phipps 14 1 45N01 97w26 6:29:44
Pickerel 18 1 45N28 97w23 6:29:32
Pickstown 11 1 43N04'02 98w31'54 6:34:08
Piedmont 46 3 44N13'54 103w23'19 6:53:33
Pierpont 18 1 45N29'44 97w49'51 6:31:19
Pierre 32 1 44N22'06 100w21'02 6:41:24
Pine Creek 47 4 43N31 100w52 6:43:28
Pine Ridge 56 3 43N01'32 102w33'21 6:50:13
Pine Ridge Indian Res 56
3 43N01 102w33 6:50:12
Plain Center 11
1 43N08 98w24 6:33:36
Plainfield 7 1 43N43 98w51 6:35:24
Plainview 46 3 43N01 102w33 6:50:12
Plainview 48 3 44N36'08 102w09'40 6:48:39
Plainview Colony 22
1 45N34'54 99w00'22 6:36:01
Plana 6 1 45N31'09 98w18'32 6:33:14
Plankinton 1 1 43N42'56 98w29'05 6:33:56
Plano 30 1 43N48 97w54 6:31:36
Plateau 52 3 45N31 102w53 6:51:32
Plato 29 1 44N51 98w46 6:35:04
Platte 11 1 43N23'13 98w50'39 6:35:23
Platte Colony 11
1 43N28'11 99w07'32 6:36:30
Pleasant Grove 7
1 43N32 98w58 6:35:52
Pleasant Lake 1
1 43N38 98w30 6:34:00
Pleasant Ridge 15
3 45N31 101w24 6:45:36
Pluma 40 3 44N21'31 103w44'16 6:54:57
Plummer 7 1 43N53 98w51 6:35:24
Pollock 10 1 45N54'05 100w17'17 6:41:09
Polo 29 1 44N46'46 99w06'33 6:36:26
Porcupine 56 3 43N14'23 102w19'50 6:49:19
Portage 6 1 45N54 98w04 6:32:16
Portland 19 1 44N56 96w42 6:26:48
Potato Creek 65
3 43N32'04 101w59'23 6:47:58
Powell 22 1 45N17'19 99w01'50 6:36:07
Powell 27 3 44N02'39 101w29'25 6:45:58
Prairie 63 1 43N02 96w45 6:27:00
Prairie City 52
3 45N31'47 102w48'14 6:51:13
Prairie View 16
3 45N52 101w31 6:46:04
Prairie Village 39
1 44N00'22 97w10'02 6:28:40
Presho 42 1 43N54'35 100w03'30 6:40:14
Preston 5 1 44N30 96w57 6:27:48
Preston 40 3 44N21'28 103w53'14 6:55:33
Pringle 16 3 43N36'31 103w35'36 6:54:22
Progressive 61 1 43N27 100w10 6:40:40
Promise 20 3 45N19'58 100w36'12 6:42:25
Prospect 47 3 43N41 101w05 6:44:20
Prosper 17 1 43N38 98w01 6:32:04
Provo 23 3 43N11'28 103w49'28 6:55:18
Pukwana 7 1 43N46'41 99w10'52 6:36:43
Pulaski 24 1 45N07 99w08 6:36:32
Pumpkin Center 49
1 43N32'36 97w05'18 6:28:21
Pure Water 47 4 43N27 100w37 6:42:28

Putney 6 1 45N33'37 98w10'30 6:32:42
Quinn 51 3 43N59'17 102w07'33 6:48:30
Raber 32 1 44N18 99w51 6:39:24
Racine 18 1 45N22 97w25 6:29:40
Rainbow 52 3 45N31 102w24 6:49:36
Rainy Creek 51 3 44N18 102w11 6:48:44
Ralph 31 3 45N46'36 103w03'56 6:52:16
Rames 61 1 43N02 99w49 6:39:16
Ramona 39 1 44N07'10 97w12'58 6:28:52
Ramsey 43 1 43N48 97w11 6:28:44
Randolph 6 1 45N14'34 98w12'34 6:32:50
Rapid City 51 3 44N04'50 103w13'50 6:52:55
Raritan 18 1 45N27 97w33 6:30:12
Rauville 14 1 44N58'47 97w06'20 6:28:25
Ravenna 55 1 43N54 97w54 6:31:36
Ravinia 11 1 43N08'12 98w25'35 6:33:42
Raymond 12 1 44N54'45 97w56'19 6:31:45
Red Elm 67 3 45N03'19 101w47'01 6:47:08
Redfern 51 3 44N00'09 103w38'40 6:54:35
Redfield 57 1 44N52'33 98w31'06 6:34:04
Red Fish 47 4 43N48 101w00 6:44:00
Redig 31 3 45N16'16 103w32'52 6:54:11
Red Iron Lake 45
1 45N41 97w17 6:29:08
Red Lake 7 1 43N43 99w11 6:36:44
Redowl 46 3 44N41'52 102w33'10 6:50:13
Red Rock 49 1 43N38 96w28 6:25:52
Red Scaffold 67
3 44N46'01 101w50'36 6:47:22
Red Shirt 56 3 43N40'03 102w53'54 6:51:36
Redstone 48 1 44N09 97w47 6:31:08
Ree 11 1 42N56 98w17 6:33:08
Ree Heights 29 1 44N31'07 99w11'59 6:36:48
Reliance 42 1 43N52'44 99w36'10 6:38:25
Renel Heights 51
3 44N10 103w06 6:52:24
Renner 49 1 43N38'44 96w43'41 6:26:55
Renner Corner 49
1 43N38'43 96w42'40 6:26:51
Reno 51 3 43N54'53 103w37'01 6:54:28
Reva 31 3 45N32'43 103w05'02 6:52:20
Revillo 25 1 45N01'00 96w34'15 6:26:17
Rex 42 1 43N53 99w42 6:38:48
Rhoades 26 1 43N13 99w20 6:37:20
Rhoda 11 1 43N18 98w45 6:35:00
Richfield 57 1 44N50 98w02 6:32:08
Richland 63 1 42N45'34 96w39'09 6:26:37
Richmond 6 1 45N31'22 98w37'07 6:34:28
Rich Valley 37 1 44N02 100w25 6:41:40
Ridgeland 15 3 45N31 100w36 6:42:24
Ridgeview 20 3 45N05'06 100w48'00 6:43:12
Ring Thunder 47
4 43N26 100w52 6:43:28
Riverside 30 1 43N43'22 97w56'53 6:31:48
Riverside Colony 2
1 44N29'11 98w08'20 6:32:33
Riverview 50 1 44N09 96w43 6:26:52
Robins 23 3 43N16 103w11 6:52:44
Rochford 51 3 44N07'28 103w43'09 6:54:53
Rock Creek 48 1 43N53 97w40 6:30:40
Rockdale 29 1 44N25 99w06 6:36:24
Rockerville 51 3 43N57'29 103w21'29 6:53:26
Rockford 52 3 45N42 102w23 6:49:32
Rockham 24 1 44N54'14 98w49'28 6:35:18
Rockport 30 1 43N39 97w47 6:31:08
Rockport Colony 30
1 43N34'55 97w50'19 6:31:21
Rocky Ford 23 3 43N17'11 103w35'52 6:54:23
Rocky Ford 47 3 43N46 101w08 6:44:32
Rockyford 56 3 43N29'50 102w30'06 6:50:00
Rolling Green 15
3 45N47 101w54 6:47:36
Roscoe 22 1 45N26'55 99w20'18 6:37:21
Rose 42 1 43N48 99w55 6:39:40
Rosebud 60 4 43N13'58 100w51'11 6:43:25
Rosebud Indian Reservation 60
3 43N14 100w51 6:43:24
Rosedale Colony 30
1 43N43 98w02 6:32:08
Rosefield 62 1 43N23 97w20 6:29:20
Rose Hill 29 1 44N19 98w45 6:35:00
Roseland 61 1 43N38 99w40 6:38:40
Rosette 22 1 45N33 99w03 6:36:12
Rosholt 54 2 45N52'00 96w43'52 6:26:55
Roslyn 18 1 45N29'43 97w29'26 6:29:58
Roswell 48 1 44N00'26 97w41'44 6:30:47
Roubaix 40 3 44N16'33 103w39'57 6:54:40
Rouse 11 1 42N56 98w10 6:32:40
Rousseau 32 1 44N18'59 100w04'16 6:40:17
Rowe 42 1 44N09 100w19 6:41:16
Rowena 49 1 43N31'13 96w33'20 6:26:13
Roy 53 1 45N01 99w46 6:39:04
Rudebusch Corner 54
1 45N25'42 97w09'15 6:28:37
Rudolph 6 1 45N20'53 98w32'09 6:34:09
Rumford 23 3 43N07'36 103w41'51 6:54:47
Rumpus Ridge 43
1 43N34'50 97w11'18 6:28:45
Running Bird 47
4 43N36 101w00 6:44:00
Running Water 4
1 42N48 98w01 6:32:04
Rusk 18 1 45N17 97w33 6:30:12
Ruskin Park 55 1 44N00'20 98w05'46 6:32:23
Rutland 39 1 44N05'22 96w58'01 6:27:52
Saint Charles 26
1 43N05'13 99w05'42 6:36:23
Saint Francis 60
4 43N08'40 100w54'17 6:43:37
Saint Lawrence 29
1 44N31'04 98w56'15 6:35:45
Saint Onge 40 3 44N32'48 103w43'14 6:54:53
Salem 43 1 43N43'27 97w23'19 6:29:33
Sanator 16 3 43N41'48 103w36'19 6:54:25
Sand Creek 2 1 44N20 98w38 6:34:32
Sangamon 22 1 45N33 99w24 6:37:36
Sanner 53 1 45N01 100w07 6:40:28
Sansarc 58 3 44N30'24 101w02'04 6:44:08
Saratoga 24 1 45N07 99w16 6:37:04
Savo 6 1 45N54 98w25 6:33:40
Savoy 40 3 44N21'09 103w55'51 6:55:43
Scandinavia 19 1 44N35 96w32 6:26:08
Scenic 51 3 43N46'47 102w33'16 6:50:13

Schaeferville 51
3 44N07'17 103w17'42 6:53:11
Schmidt Landing 54
1 45N22'47 96w33'38 6:26:15
Schriever 26 1 43N07 98w58 6:35:52
Scotch Cap 52 3 45N31 102w39 6:50:36
Scotland 4 1 43N08'59 97w43'02 6:30:52
Scovil 37 1 43N57 100w53 6:43:32
Seim 52 3 45N46 102w15 6:49:00
Selby 64 1 45N30'23 100w01'54 6:40:08
Seneca 24 1 45N03'42 99w30'42 6:38:03
Sevenmile Corner 35
3 43N50'09 101w39'36 6:46:38
Shadehill 52 3 45N45'56 102w10'44 6:48:43
Shady Beach 54 1 45N24'13 96w37'54 6:26:32
Sharon 33 1 43N18 97w49 6:31:16
Sharps Corner 56
3 43N23'23 102w23'53 6:49:36
Sheffield 2 1 44N24'47 98w04'25 6:32:18
Shelby 6 1 45N42 98w11 6:32:44
Shelby 8 1 43N56'53 99w11'13 6:36:45
Sheridan 14 1 44N51 97w04 6:28:16
Sherman 49 1 43N45'33 96w28'33 6:25:54
Shindler 41 1 43N28'30 96w38'54 6:26:36
Shyne 51 3 44N06 102w26 6:49:44
Sidney 52 3 45N42 102w46 6:51:04
Signal 11 1 43N17 98w52 6:35:28
Silver City 51 3 44N05'04 103w33'48 6:54:15
Silver Creek 55
1 44N04 98w09 6:32:36
Silverlake 33 1 43N28 97w28 6:29:52
Sinai 5 1 44N14'40 97w02'26 6:28:10
Sioux 42 1 43N46 100w17 6:41:08
Sioux Falls 49 1 43N33'00 96w42'00 6:26:48
Sioux Falls Junction 50
1 43N58'45 96w41'21 6:26:45
Sioux Valley 63
1 42N52 96w37 6:26:28
Sisseton 54 1 45N39'53 97w02'58 6:28:12
Sisseton Indian Reservation 54
1 45N40 97w03 6:28:12
Sitka 64 1 45N31'01 100w11'09 6:40:45
Skyway 51 3 44N10 103w06 6:52:24
Slim Butte 56 3 43N04'34 102w49'13 6:51:17
Smith 7 1 43N43 99w05 6:36:20
Smiths Park 39 1 43N56'06 96w59'48 6:27:59
Smithwick 23 3 43N18'05 103w13'04 6:52:52
Snake Creek 15 3 45N35'05 100w35'08 6:42:21
So Dak Park 54 1 45N25 96w52 6:27:28
Soldier Creek 60
4 43N19'25 100w53'16 6:43:33
Sommerville 52 3 45N46'29 102w10'29 6:48:42
Sorum 52 3 45N26'59 102w55'44 6:51:43
South Creek 37 3 44N03 100w59 6:43:56
South Dakota Park 54
1 45N25'03 96w42'02 6:26:48
South Detroit 6
1 45N43 98w02 6:32:08
South Forest City 53
1 44N57 100w21 6:41:24
South Riverside 53
1 45N07 100w15 6:41:00
South Shore 14 1 45N06'21 96w55'42 6:27:43
Spain 45 1 45N42'11 97w47'08 6:31:09
Spearfish 40 3 44N29'27 103w51'32 6:55:26
Spencer 43 1 43N43'39 97w35'34 6:30:22
Spink 63 1 42N51'07 96w44'48 6:26:59
Spink Colony 57
1 44N44'48 98w17'30 6:33:10
Spirit Lake 38 1 44N30 97w35 6:30:20
Spirit Mound 13
1 42N52 96w57 6:27:48
Split Rock 49 1 43N32 96w35 6:26:20
Spokane 16 3 43N50'29 103w22'46 6:53:31
Spottswood 57 1 44N39'08 98w30'19 6:34:01
Spring Creek 50
1 44N09 96w35 6:26:20
Spring Creek 60
4 43N07'03 101w01'20 6:44:05
Spring Creek Colony 44
1 45N54'33 98w52'42 6:35:31
Springfield 4 1 42N51'15 97w53'49 6:31:35
Spring Grove 54
1 45N27'47 97w02'59 6:28:12
Spring Hill 29 1 44N25 99w14 6:36:56
Spring Valley 62
1 43N17 97w05 6:28:20
Spring Valley Colony 36
1 44N02'26 98w53'12 6:35:33
Stamford 35 3 43N53'42 101w05'19 6:44:21
Standing Rock Indian Res 15
3 45N46 101w05 6:44:20
Stanley Corner 43
1 43N32'36 97w23'15 6:29:33
Star 13 1 43N03 97w05 6:28:20
Star Prairie 61
1 43N13 100w05 6:40:20
Starr 33 1 43N28 98w03 6:32:12
Stena 45 1 45N48 97w54 6:31:36
Stephan 34 1 44N14'53 99w27'10 6:37:49
Sterling 5 1 44N25 96w49 6:27:16
Stewart 61 1 43N07 99w43 6:38:52
Stickney 1 1 43N35'21 98w26'13 6:33:45
Stockholm 25 1 45N05'59 96w48'06 6:27:12
Stone Bridge 28
1 44N36'08 97w03'34 6:28:14
Stoneville 46 3 44N44'01 102w39'15 6:50:37
Stony Butte 42 1 44N04 100w10 6:41:12
Storla 1 1 43N51'49 98w21'04 6:33:24
Strandburg 25 1 45N02'39 96w45'37 6:27:02
Stratford 6 1 45N18'59 98w18'16 6:33:13
Stratosphere Bowl 51
3 43N58'36 103w20'43 6:53:23
Strool 52 3 45N30'02 102w48'16 6:51:13
Sturgis 46 3 44N24'35 103w30'31 6:54:02
Sully 61 1 43N23 99w36 6:38:24
Sulphur 46 3 44N52'36 102w54'47 6:51:39
Summit 54 1 45N18'16 97w02'10 6:28:09
Sumner 57 1 45N01 98w10 6:32:40
Sunnyside 51 3 44N13 102w18 6:49:12
Sunnyview 5 1 44N20'41 96w47'06 6:27:08
Sun Prairie 43 1 43N48 97w27 6:29:48

Surprise Valley 47 3 43N29 101w01 6:44:04
Susquehanna 33 1 43N23 98w04 6:32:16
Sverdrup 49 1 43N43 96w42 6:26:48
Swan Lake 62 1 43N13 97w06 6:28:24
Sweet 33 1 43N13 97w35 6:30:20
Swett 3 3 43N10'19 101w57'04 6:47:48
Sylvia 42 1 43N44 100w02 6:40:08
Table Mountain 31 3 45N53 103w37 6:54:28
Tabor 4 1 42N56'55 97w39'31 6:30:38
Tacoma Park 6 1 45N32'35 98w14'48 6:32:59
Tamworth 24 1 45N01 99w09 6:36:36
Taopi 49 1 43N48 96w58 6:27:52
Tea 41 1 43N26'47 96w50'08 6:27:21
Terraville 40 3 44N21'44 103w45'51 6:55:03
Terry 40 3 44N20'01 103w48'59 6:55:16
Teton 58 1 44N17'13 100w30'27 6:42:02
Tetonka 57 1 45N07 98w18 6:33:12
Thatcher 20 3 45N01'19 100w55'38 6:43:43
Theresa 2 1 44N25 98w17 6:33:08
Thomas 28 1 44N45'39 97w12'33 6:28:50
Thorp 12 1 45N01 97w41 6:30:44
Three Rivers 57 1 44N57 98w31 6:34:04
Thunder Butte 67 3 45N13 101w40 6:46:40
Thunder Hawk 15 3 45N56'18 101w58'28 6:47:54
Tigerville 51 3 43N58'36 103w38'22 6:54:33
Tilford 46 3 44N18'01 103w25'46 6:53:43
Timber Lake 20 3 45N26 101w05 6:44:20
Tinton 40 3 44N22'50 104w02'53 6:56:12
Tobin 17 1 43N33 98w09 6:32:36
Tolstoy 53 1 45N12'29 99w36'50 6:38:27
Tomahawk 40 3 44N12'43 103w31'41 6:54:07
Toronto 19 1 44N34'23 96w38'32 6:26:34
Torrey Lake 7 1 43N33 98w50 6:35:20
Tracy 42 1 44N04 100w11 6:40:44
Trail 52 3 45N55 102w16 6:49:04
Trail City 20 3 45N28'21 100w43'30 6:42:54
Trent 50 1 43N54'23 96w39'13 6:26:37
Trenton 5 1 44N15 96w42 6:26:48
Tripp 33 1 43N13'32 97w57'56 6:31:52
Trojan 40 3 44N20'32 103w50'15 6:55:21
Troy 25 1 45N02'15 96w51'54 6:27:28
Truro 1 1 43N32 98w30 6:34:00
Tschetter Colony 33 1 43N22 97w41 6:30:44
Tulare 57 1 44N44'17 98w30'34 6:34:02
Tunerville 19 1 44N53'25 96w40'51 6:26:43
Turkey Ridge 62 1 43N14'37 97w16'45 6:29:07
Turkey Valley 66 1 43N07 97w13 6:28:52
Turner 62 1 43N13 96w59 6:27:56
Turton 57 1 45N02'59 98w05'43 6:32:23
Tuthill 3 3 43N09'21 101w29'36 6:45:58
Twin 31 3 45N53 103w00 6:52:00
Twin Brooks 25 1 45N12'21 96w46'45 6:27:07
Twin Butte 15 3 45N31 101w56 6:47:44
Twin Lake 55 1 43N59 98w16 6:33:04
Tyndall 4 1 42N59'36 97w51'45 6:31:27
Union Center 46 3 44N33'39 102w40'08 6:50:41
Unityville 43 1 43N48'05 97w27'08 6:29:49
University 5 1 44N19 96w47 6:27:08
Upper Red Owl 46 3 44N44 102w39 6:50:36
Usta 52 3 45N13'13 102w09'45 6:48:39
Utica 66 1 42N58'52 97w29'46 6:29:59
Vail 52 3 45N36 102w46 6:51:04
Vale 9 3 44N37'13 103w24'06 6:53:36
Valley Springs 49 1 43N34'57 96w28'03 6:25:52
Valleyview 66 1 42N58'02 97w16'43 6:29:07
Van Metre 37 3 44N09'34 100w47'36 6:43:10
Van Order 34 1 44N25 99w21 6:37:24
Vayland 29 1 44N29'37 98w47'55 6:35:12
Veblen 45 1 45N51'47 97w17'14 6:29:09
Vedin Corner 66 1 43N04'57 97w23'55 6:29:36
Verdon 6 1 45N14'38 98w05'50 6:32:23
Vermillion 13 1 42N46'46 96w55'44 6:27:43
Vermont 22 1 45N17 99w16 6:37:04
Vessey 31 3 45N53 103w08 6:52:32
Vestal Springs 16 3 43N49'43 103w41'09 6:54:45
Vetal 3 3 43N12'52 101w22'35 6:45:30
Viborg 62 1 43N10'13 97w04'52 6:28:19
Vickers 52 3 45N26 102w31 6:50:04
Victor 54 1 45N52'08 96w49'57 6:27:20
Victoria 40 3 44N23'42 103w54'26 6:55:38
Vienna 12 1 44N42'11 97w30'04 6:30:00
Viewfield 46 3 44N12'43 102w49'45 6:51:19
Viking 52 3 45N53 102w45 6:51:00
Vilas 48 1 44N00'38 97w35'49 6:30:23
Villa Ranchaero 51 3 44N08 103w04 6:52:16
Villa Trailer Court 51 3 44N10 103w06 6:52:24
Viola 36 1 43N59 98w30 6:34:00
Virgil 2 1 44N17'27 98w25'26 6:33:42
Virginia 20 3 45N14'33 100w34'03 6:42:16
Virginia 63 1 43N00 96w32 6:26:08
Vivian 42 1 43N55'37 100w17'30 6:41:10
Volga 5 1 44N19'25 96w55'34 6:27:42
Volin 66 1 42N57'26 97w10'48 6:28:43
Volunteer 46 3 44N30'43 103w07'57 6:52:32
Vrooman 52 3 45N05 102w46 6:51:04
Wachter 44 1 45N54 98w47 6:35:08
Wacker 44 1 45N54 99w02 6:36:08
Wagner 11 1 43N04'47 98w17'34 6:33:10
Wahehe 11 1 42N58 98w24 6:33:36
Wakonda 13 1 43N00'30 97w06'23 6:28:26
Wakpala 15 3 45N39'26 100w32'05 6:42:08
Waldro 7 1 43N48 98w58 6:35:52
Walker 15 3 45N54'37 101w05'24 6:44:22
Wall 51 3 43N59'33 102w14'28 6:48:58
Wallace 14 1 45N05'10 97w28'32 6:29:54
Wall Lake 49 1 43N33 96w57 6:27:48
Walnut Grove 21 1 43N28 98w25 6:33:40
Walshtown 66 1 43N02 97w20 6:29:20
Wanblee 66 3 43N34'10 101w39'36 6:46:38
Warbonnet 51 3 43N59'57 103w07'58 6:52:32
War Creek 37 1 44N08 100w30 6:42:00
Ward 50 1 44N09'17 96w27'36 6:25:50
Warner 6 1 45N19'33 98w29'42 6:33:59
Wasta 51 3 44N04'07 102w26'43 6:49:47
Watauga 15 3 45N55'22 101w32'33 6:46:10
Watertown 14 1 44N53'58 97w06'53 6:28:28
Waubay 18 1 45N19'55 97w18'17 6:29:13
Waverly 14 1 44N59'55 96w58'17 6:27:53
Weaver 61 1 43N18 99w57 6:39:48
Weber 44 1 45N53 99w54 6:35:36
Webster 18 1 45N19'56 97w31'11 6:30:05
Webster Grove 49 1 43N31 96w42 6:26:48
Wecota 24 1 45N10'21 99w07'02 6:36:28
Wellington 49 1 43N33 97w05 6:28:20
Wendte 58 3 44N14'40 100w39'53 6:42:40
Wentworth 39 1 43N59'50 96w57'50 6:27:51
Wesley 24 1 45N07 98w46 6:35:04
Wessington 2 1 44N27'15 98w41'48 6:34:47
Wessington Springs 36 1 44N04'45 98w34'09 6:34:17
West Britton 45 1 45N47'32 97w50'15 6:31:21
Westerville 13 1 42N46 96w55 6:27:40
West Fork 27 3 44N26'45 101w32'53 6:46:12
West Hanson 6 1 45N22 98w10 6:32:40
Weston 45 1 45N43 97w55 6:31:40
Westover 37 1 43N44'52 100w39'57 6:42:40
West Point 7 1 43N54 99w14 6:36:56
Westport 6 1 45N38'56 98w29'48 6:33:59
Westreville 13 1 42N55'27 97w01'23 6:28:06
West Rondell 6 1 45N17 98w24 6:33:36
Weta 35 3 43N46'28 101w42'59 6:46:52
Wetonka 44 1 45N37'31 98w46'03 6:35:04
Wewela 61 1 43N00'38 99w46'50 6:39:07
Wheatland 18 1 45N11 97w26 6:29:44
Wheaton 29 1 44N47 98w45 6:35:00
Whetstone 26 1 43N13 98w59 6:35:56
White 5 1 44N26'05 96w38'58 6:26:36
White Butte 52 3 45N56'26 102w21'43 6:49:27
White Hill 52 3 45N36 102w53 6:51:32
Whitehorse 20 3 45N16'14 100w53'10 6:43:33
White Lake 1 1 43N43'49 98w42'48 6:34:51
White Owl 48 3 44N35'32 102w25'49 6:49:43
White River 47 4 43N34'05 100w44'42 6:42:59
White Rock 54 1 45N55'00 96w34'17 6:26:17
Whiteside 2 1 44N30 98w40 6:34:40
White Swan 11 1 43N05 98w31 6:34:04
Whitewood 40 3 44N27'40 103w38'17 6:54:33
Whitney 52 3 45N34 102w03 6:48:12
Whitten 61 1 43N26'14 100w05'01 6:40:20
Wicksville 51 3 44N05'46 102w35'17 6:50:21
Wilbur 7 1 43N37 98w50 6:35:20
William Hamilton 34 1 44N35 99w22 6:37:28
Williams Creek 37 1 43N49 100w24 6:41:36
Willow 44 1 45N44 98w48 6:35:12
Willow Creek 61 1 43N07 99w57 6:39:48
Willow Lake 12 1 44N37'39 97w38'12 6:30:33
Wilmot 54 1 45N24'31 96w51'27 6:27:26
Winfred 39 1 43N59'50 97w21'43 6:29:27
Winner 61 1 43N22'36 99w51'31 6:39:26
Winship 6 1 45N55'22 98w31'06 6:34:04
Winsor 5 1 44N25 97w04 6:28:16
Wismer 45 1 45N47 97w27 6:29:48
Witten 61 1 43N26 100w05 6:40:20
Wittenberg 33 1 43N19 97w42 6:30:48
Wolf Creek 33 1 43N20'51 97w37'24 6:30:30
Wolf Creek Colony 33 1 43N15 97w41 6:30:44
Wolsey 2 1 44N24'28 98w28'28 6:33:54
Wood 47 4 43N29'49 100w28'37 6:41:54
Woodland 12 1 45N02 97w48 6:31:12
Woodville 40 3 44N17'28 103w45'17 6:55:01
Woonsocket 55 1 44N03'13 98w16'31 6:33:06
Worthen 30 1 43N33 97w55 6:31:40
Worthing 41 1 43N19'45 96w45'45 6:27:03
Wortman 61 1 43N08 100w04 6:40:16
Wounded Knee 56 3 43N08'26 102w21'55 6:49:28
Wright 61 1 43N13 100w10 6:40:40
Wyandotte 52 3 45N16 102w50 6:51:20
Yale 2 1 44N26'02 97w59'23 6:31:58
Yankton 66 1 42N52'16 97w23'49 6:29:35
Yankton Indian Reservation 11 1 43N08 98w26 6:33:44
Yellowhorse Ford 20 3 45N16'49 100w47'48 6:43:11
Zell 24 1 44N53'49 98w43'41 6:34:55
Zeona 52 3 45N11'36 102w54'43 6:51:39
Zickrick 37 1 43N47 100w31 6:42:04

TIME TABLES

TN # 1
Before 11/18/1883 LMT
11/18/1883 12:00 EST
3/31/1918 02:00 EWT
10/27/1918 02:00 EST
3/30/1919 02:00 EWT
10/26/1919 02:00 EST
2/09/1942 02:00 EWT
9/30/1945 02:00 EST
4/30/1967 02:00 US#1

TN # 2
Before 11/18/1883 LMT
11/18/1883 12:00 EST
3/31/1918 02:00 EWT
10/27/1918 02:00 EST
3/30/1919 02:00 EWT
10/26/1919 02:00 EST
2/09/1942 02:00 EWT
9/30/1945 02:00 EST
4/28/1946 02:00 EDT
7/01/1946 00:01 EST
4/30/1967 02:00 US#1

TN # 3
Before 11/18/1883 LMT
11/18/1883 12:00 CST
3/31/1918 02:00 CWT
10/27/1918 02:00 CST
3/30/1919 02:00 CWT
10/26/1919 02:00 CST
2/09/1942 02:00 CWT
9/30/1945 02:00 CST
4/30/1967 02:00 US#1

TN # 4
Before 11/18/1883 LMT
11/18/1883 12:00 CST
3/31/1918 02:00 CWT
10/27/1918 02:00 CST
3/30/1919 02:00 CWT
10/26/1919 02:00 CST
7/06/1941 00:01 CDT
9/28/1941 02:00 CST
2/09/1942 02:00 CWT
9/30/1945 02:00 CST
5/09/1946 00:01 CDT
9/29/1946 02:00 CST
5/11/1947 00:01 CDT
9/28/1947 00:01 CST
4/25/1948 00:01 CDT
9/26/1948 00:01 CST
4/29/1956 00:01 CDT
10/28/1956 00:01 CST
4/30/1967 02:00 US#1

TN # 5
Before 11/18/1883 LMT
11/18/1883 12:00 CST
3/31/1918 02:00 CWT
10/27/1918 02:00 CST
3/30/1919 02:00 CWT
10/26/1919 02:00 CST
2/09/1942 02:00 CWT
9/30/1945 02:00 CST
5/02/1948 00:01 CDT
8/22/1948 00:01 CST
4/30/1967 02:00 US#1

TN # 6
Before 11/18/1883 LMT
11/18/1883 12:00 CST
3/31/1918 02:00 CWT
10/27/1918 02:00 CST
3/30/1919 02:00 CWT
10/26/1919 02:00 CST
7/14/1941 00:01 CDT
9/28/1941 02:00 CST
2/09/1942 02:00 CWT
9/30/1945 02:00 CST
4/25/1948 00:01 CDT
8/22/1948 02:00 CST
4/30/1967 02:00 US#1

TN # 7
Before 11/18/1883 LMT
11/18/1883 12:00 CST
3/31/1918 02:00 CWT
10/27/1918 02:00 CST
3/30/1919 02:00 CWT
10/26/1919 02:00 CST
7/28/1941 00:01 CDT
9/08/1941 00:01 CST
2/09/1942 02:00 CWT
9/30/1945 02:00 CST
4/30/1967 02:00 US#1

TN # 8
Before 11/18/1883 LMT
11/18/1883 12:00 CST
3/31/1918 02:00 CWT
10/27/1918 02:00 CST
3/30/1919 02:00 CWT
10/26/1919 02:00 CST
7/21/1941 00:01 CDT
9/28/1941 00:01 CST
2/09/1942 02:00 CWT
9/30/1945 02:00 CST
4/30/1967 02:00 US#1

TN # 9
Before 11/18/1883 LMT
11/18/1883 12:00 CST
3/31/1918 02:00 CWT
10/27/1918 02:00 CST
3/30/1919 02:00 CWT
10/26/1919 02:00 CST
7/21/1941 00:01 CDT
9/28/1941 02:00 CST
2/09/1942 02:00 CWT
9/30/1945 02:00 CST
4/30/1967 02:00 US#1

TN # 10
Before 11/18/1883 LMT
11/18/1883 12:00 CST
3/31/1918 02:00 CWT
10/27/1918 02:00 CST
3/30/1919 02:00 CWT
10/26/1919 02:00 CST
7/21/1941 00:01 CDT
9/28/1941 02:00 CST
2/09/1942 02:00 CWT
9/30/1945 02:00 CST
5/02/1948 00:01 CDT
9/26/1948 00:01 CST
4/30/1967 02:00 US#1

TN # 11
Before 11/18/1883 LMT
11/18/1883 12:00 CST
3/31/1918 02:00 CWT
10/27/1918 02:00 CST
3/30/1919 02:00 CWT
10/26/1919 02:00 CST
2/09/1942 02:00 CWT
9/30/1945 02:00 CST
4/25/1948 00:01 CDT
9/26/1948 00:01 CST
4/30/1967 02:00 US#1

TN # 12
Before 11/18/1883 LMT
11/18/1883 12:00 CST
3/31/1918 02:00 CWT
10/27/1918 02:00 CST
3/30/1919 02:00 CWT
10/26/1919 02:00 CST
7/24/1941 00:01 CDT
9/28/1941 02:00 CST
2/09/1942 02:00 CWT
9/30/1945 02:00 CST
4/30/1967 02:00 US#1

TN # 13
Before 11/18/1883 LMT
11/18/1883 12:00 CST
3/31/1918 02:00 CWT
10/27/1918 02:00 CST
3/30/1919 02:00 CWT
10/26/1919 02:00 CST
7/24/1941 00:01 CDT
9/28/1941 02:00 CST
2/09/1942 02:00 CWT
9/30/1945 02:00 CST
5/18/1947 00:01 CDT
9/28/1947 00:01 CST
5/02/1948 00:01 CDT
9/26/1948 00:01 CST
4/30/1967 02:00 US#1

TN # 14
Before 11/18/1883 LMT
11/18/1883 12:00 CST
3/31/1918 02:00 CWT
10/27/1918 02:00 CST
3/30/1919 02:00 CWT
10/26/1919 02:00 CST
8/06/1941 00:01 CDT
9/15/1941 00:01 CST
2/09/1942 02:00 CWT
9/30/1945 02:00 CST
4/30/1967 02:00 US#1

TN # 15
Before 11/18/1883 LMT
11/18/1883 12:00 CST
3/31/1918 02:00 CWT
10/27/1918 02:00 CST
3/30/1919 02:00 CWT
10/26/1919 02:00 CST
7/21/1941 00:01 CDT
9/28/1941 02:00 CST
2/09/1942 02:00 CWT
9/30/1945 02:00 CST
5/01/1948 00:01 CDT
9/20/1948 00:01 CST
4/30/1967 02:00 US#1

TN # 16
Before 11/18/1883 LMT
11/18/1883 12:00 CST
3/31/1918 02:00 CWT
10/27/1918 02:00 CST
3/30/1919 02:00 CWT
10/26/1919 02:00 CST
8/10/1941 00:01 CDT
9/07/1941 00:01 CST
2/09/1942 02:00 CWT
9/30/1945 02:00 CST
4/30/1967 02:00 US#1

TN # 17
Before 11/18/1883 LMT
11/18/1883 12:00 CST
3/31/1918 02:00 CWT
10/27/1918 02:00 CST
3/30/1919 02:00 CWT
10/26/1919 02:00 CST
8/06/1941 00:01 CDT
9/07/1941 00:01 CST
2/09/1942 02:00 CWT
9/30/1945 02:00 CST
4/30/1967 02:00 US#1

TN # 18
Before 11/18/1883 LMT
11/18/1883 12:00 CST
3/31/1918 02:00 CWT
10/27/1918 02:00 CST
3/30/1919 02:00 CWT
10/26/1919 02:00 CST
7/28/1941 00:01 CDT
9/28/1941 02:00 CST
2/09/1942 02:00 CWT
9/30/1945 02:00 CST
4/30/1967 02:00 US#1

TN # 19
Before 11/18/1883 LMT
11/18/1883 12:00 CST
3/31/1918 02:00 CWT
10/27/1918 02:00 CST
3/30/1919 02:00 CWT
10/26/1919 02:00 CST
7/28/1941 00:01 CDT
9/28/1941 02:00 CST
2/09/1942 02:00 CWT
9/30/1945 02:00 CST
5/25/1947 00:01 CDT
9/28/1947 00:01 CST
4/30/1967 02:00 US#1

TN # 20
Before 11/18/1883 LMT
11/18/1883 12:00 CST
3/31/1918 02:00 CWT
10/27/1918 02:00 CST
3/30/1919 02:00 CWT
10/26/1919 02:00 CST
7/28/1941 00:01 CDT
9/28/1941 00:01 CST
2/09/1942 02:00 CWT
9/30/1945 02:00 CST
4/30/1967 02:00 US#1

TN # 21
Before 11/18/1883 LMT
11/18/1883 12:00 CST
3/31/1918 02:00 CWT
10/27/1918 02:00 CST
3/30/1919 02:00 CWT
10/26/1919 02:00 CST
8/07/1941 00:01 CDT
9/28/1941 02:00 CST
2/09/1942 02:00 CWT
9/30/1945 02:00 CST
4/30/1967 02:00 US#1

TN # 22
Before 11/18/1883 LMT
11/18/1883 12:00 CST
3/31/1918 02:00 CWT
10/27/1918 02:00 CST
3/30/1919 02:00 CWT
10/26/1919 02:00 CST
7/14/1941 00:01 CDT
9/28/1941 00:01 CST
2/09/1942 02:00 CWT
9/30/1945 02:00 CST
4/30/1967 02:00 US#1

TN # 23
Before 11/18/1883 LMT
11/18/1883 12:00 CST
3/31/1918 02:00 CWT
10/27/1918 02:00 CST
3/30/1919 02:00 CWT
10/26/1919 02:00 CST
8/10/1941 12:00 CDT
9/13/1941 12:00 CST
2/09/1942 02:00 CWT
9/30/1945 02:00 CST
4/30/1967 02:00 US#1

TN # 24
Before 11/18/1883 LMT
11/18/1883 12:00 CST
3/31/1918 02:00 CWT
10/27/1918 02:00 CST
3/30/1919 02:00 CWT
10/26/1919 02:00 CST
8/06/1941 18:00 CDT
9/06/1941 00:01 CST
2/09/1942 02:00 CWT
9/30/1945 02:00 CST
4/30/1967 02:00 US#1

TN # 25
Before 11/18/1883 LMT
11/18/1883 12:00 CST
3/31/1918 02:00 CWT
10/27/1918 02:00 CST
3/30/1919 02:00 CWT
10/26/1919 02:00 CST
8/09/1941 00:01 CDT
9/15/1941 00:01 CST
2/09/1942 02:00 CWT
9/30/1945 02:00 CST
4/30/1967 02:00 US#1

TN # 26
Before 11/18/1883 LMT
11/18/1883 12:00 CST
3/31/1918 02:00 CWI
10/27/1918 02:00 CST
3/30/1919 02:00 CWT
10/26/1919 02:00 CST
7/29/1941 00:01 CDT
9/08/1941 00:01 CST
2/09/1942 02:00 CWT
9/30/1945 02:00 CST
4/30/1967 02:00 US#1

TN # 27
Before 11/18/1883 LMT
11/18/1883 12:00 CST
3/31/1918 02:00 CWT
10/27/1918 02:00 CST
3/30/1919 02:00 CWT
10/26/1919 02:00 CST
2/09/1942 02:00 CWT
9/30/1945 02:00 CST
4/25/1948 00:01 CDT
9/26/1948 00:01 CST
4/30/1967 02:00 US#1

TN # 28
Before 11/18/1883 LMT
11/18/1883 12:00 CST
3/31/1918 02:00 CWT
10/27/1918 02:00 CST
3/30/1919 02:00 CWT
10/26/1919 02:00 CST
7/14/1941 00:01 CDT
9/08/1941 00:01 CST
2/09/1942 02:00 CWT
9/30/1945 02:00 CST
4/30/1967 02:00 US#1

TN # 29
Before 11/18/1883 LMT
11/18/1883 12:00 CST
3/31/1918 02:00 CWT
10/27/1918 02:00 CST
3/30/1919 02:00 CWT
10/26/1919 02:00 CST
7/27/1941 00:01 CDT
9/28/1941 02:00 CST
2/09/1942 02:00 CWT
9/30/1945 02:00 CST
4/30/1967 02:00 US#1

TN # 30
Before 11/18/1883 LMT
11/18/1883 12:00 CST
3/31/1918 02:00 CWT
10/27/1918 02:00 CST
3/30/1919 02:00 CWT
10/26/1919 02:00 CST
7/14/1941 00:01 CDT
9/28/1941 02:00 CST
2/09/1942 02:00 CWT
9/30/1945 02:00 CST
4/26/1948 00:01 CDT
9/26/1948 00:01 CST
4/30/1967 02:00 US#1

TN # 31
Before 11/18/1883 LMT
11/18/1883 12:00 CST
3/31/1918 02:00 CWT
10/27/1918 02:00 CST
3/30/1919 02:00 CWT
10/26/1919 02:00 CST
7/13/1941 00:01 CDT
9/28/1941 02:00 CST
2/09/1942 02:00 CWT
9/30/1945 02:00 CST
4/30/1967 02:00 US#1

TN # 32
Before 11/18/1883 LMT
11/18/1883 12:00 CST
3/31/1918 02:00 CWT
10/27/1918 02:00 CST
3/30/1919 02:00 CWT
10/26/1919 02:00 CST
7/07/1941 00:01 CDT
9/28/1941 02:00 CST
2/09/1942 02:00 CWT
9/30/1945 02:00 CST
4/30/1967 02:00 US#1

TN # 33
Before 11/18/1883 LMT
11/18/1883 12:00 CST
3/31/1918 02:00 CWT
10/27/1918 02:00 CST
3/30/1919 02:00 CWT
10/26/1919 02:00 CST
7/21/1941 00:01 CDT
9/28/1941 02:00 CST
2/09/1942 02:00 CWT
9/30/1945 02:00 CST
5/25/1947 00:01 CDT
9/28/1947 00:01 CST
4/30/1967 02:00 US#1

TN # 34
Before 11/18/1883 LMT
11/18/1883 12:00 CST
3/31/1918 02:00 CWT
10/27/1918 02:00 CST
3/30/1919 02:00 CWT
10/26/1919 02:00 CST
7/06/1941 00:01 CDT
9/28/1941 02:00 CST
2/09/1942 02:00 CWT
9/30/1945 02:00 CST
4/25/1948 00:01 CDT
9/26/1948 00:01 CST
4/30/1967 02:00 US#1

TN # 35
Before 11/18/1883 LMT
11/18/1883 12:00 CST
3/31/1918 02:00 CWT
10/27/1918 02:00 CST
3/30/1919 02:00 CWT
10/26/1919 02:00 CST
7/08/1941 00:01 CDT
9/28/1941 02:00 CST
2/09/1942 02:00 CWT
9/30/1945 02:00 CST
5/02/1948 00:01 CDT
9/26/1948 00:01 CST
4/30/1967 02:00 US#1

TN # 36
Before 11/18/1883 LMT
11/18/1883 12:00 CST
3/31/1918 02:00 CWT
10/27/1918 02:00 CST
3/30/1919 02:00 CWT
10/26/1919 02:00 CST
7/16/1941 00:01 CDT
9/28/1941 02:00 CST
2/09/1942 02:00 CWT
9/30/1945 02:00 CST
4/30/1967 02:00 US#1

TN # 37
Before 11/18/1883 LMT
11/18/1883 12:00 CST
3/31/1918 02:00 CWT
10/27/1918 02:00 CST
3/30/1919 02:00 CWT
10/26/1919 02:00 CST
7/06/1941 00:01 CDT
9/28/1941 02:00 CST
2/09/1942 02:00 CWT
9/30/1945 02:00 CST
5/03/1948 00:01 CDT
9/26/1948 00:01 CST
4/30/1967 02:00 US#1

TN # 38
Before 11/18/1883 LMT
11/18/1883 12:00 CST
3/31/1918 02:00 CWT
10/27/1918 02:00 CST
3/30/1919 02:00 CWT
10/26/1919 02:00 CST
7/08/1941 00:01 CDT
9/28/1941 02:00 CST
2/09/1942 02:00 CWT
9/30/1945 02:00 CST
4/25/1948 00:01 CDT
9/26/1948 00:01 CST
4/30/1967 02:00 US#1

TN # 39
Before 11/18/1883 LMT
11/18/1883 12:00 CST
3/31/1918 02:00 CWT
10/27/1918 02:00 CST
3/30/1919 02:00 CWT
10/26/1919 02:00 CST
5/12/1940 02:00 CDT
9/08/1940 02:00 CST
8/06/1941 00:01 CDT
9/28/1941 02:00 CST
2/09/1942 02:00 CWT
9/30/1945 02:00 CST
4/30/1967 02:00 US#1

TN # 40
Before 11/18/1883 LMT
11/18/1883 12:00 CST
3/31/1918 02:00 CWT
10/27/1918 02:00 CST
3/30/1919 02:00 CWT
10/26/1919 02:00 CST
8/06/1941 00:01 CDT
9/28/1941 02:00 CST
2/09/1942 02:00 CWT
9/30/1945 02:00 CST
4/30/1967 02:00 US#1

TN # 41
Before 11/18/1883 LMT
11/18/1883 12:00 CST
3/31/1918 02:00 CWT
10/27/1918 02:00 CST
3/30/1919 02:00 CWT
10/26/1919 02:00 CST
2/09/1942 02:00 CWT
9/30/1945 02:00 CST
5/02/1948 00:01 CDT
9/26/1948 00:01 CST
4/30/1967 02:00 US#1

TN # 42
Before 11/18/1883 LMT
11/18/1883 12:00 CST
3/31/1918 02:00 CWT
10/27/1918 02:00 CST
3/30/1919 02:00 CWT
10/26/1919 02:00 CST
7/06/1941 00:01 CDT
9/28/1941 02:00 CST
2/09/1942 02:00 CWT
9/30/1945 02:00 CST
5/26/1947 00:01 CDT
9/27/1947 23:59 CST
5/23/1948 23:59 CDT
9/26/1948 00:01 CST
4/30/1967 02:00 US#1

TN # 43
Before 11/18/1883 LMT
11/18/1883 12:00 CST
3/31/1918 02:00 CWT
10/27/1918 02:00 CST
3/30/1919 02:00 CWT
10/26/1919 02:00 CST
7/06/1941 00:01 CDT
9/28/1941 02:00 CST
2/09/1942 02:00 CWT
9/30/1945 02:00 CST
4/25/1948 00:01 CDT
9/26/1948 00:01 CST
4/30/1967 02:00 US#1

TN # 44
Before 11/18/1883 LMT
11/18/1883 12:00 CST
3/31/1918 02:00 CWT
10/27/1918 02:00 CST

TIME TABLES

3/30/1919 02:00 CWT
10/26/1919 02:00 CST
8/10/1941 12:00 CDT
9/08/1941 00:01 CST
2/09/1942 02:00 CWT
9/30/1945 02:00 CST
4/30/1967 02:00 US#1
....
TN # 45
Before 11/18/1883 LMT
11/18/1883 12:00 CST
3/31/1918 02:00 CWT
10/27/1918 02:00 CST
3/30/1919 02:00 CWT
10/26/1919 02:00 CST
8/09/1941 00:01 CDT
9/26/1941 02:00 CST
2/09/1942 02:00 CWT
9/30/1945 02:00 CST
4/30/1967 02:00 US#1
....
TN # 46
Before 11/18/1883 LMT
11/18/1883 12:00 CST
3/31/1918 02:00 CWT
10/27/1918 02:00 CST
3/30/1919 02:00 CWT
10/26/1919 02:00 CST
7/13/1941 00:01 CDT
9/29/1941 00:01 CST
2/09/1942 02:00 CWT
9/30/1945 02:00 CST
4/30/1967 02:00 US#1
....
TN # 47
Before 11/18/1883 LMT
11/18/1883 12:00 CST
3/31/1918 02:00 CWT
10/27/1918 02:00 CST
3/30/1919 02:00 CWT
10/26/1919 02:00 CST
8/07/1941 00:01 CDT
8/28/1941 00:01 CST
2/09/1942 02:00 CWT
9/30/1945 02:00 CST
4/30/1967 02:00 US#1
....
TN # 48
Before 11/18/1883 LMT
11/18/1883 12:00 CST
3/31/1918 02:00 CWT
10/27/1918 02:00 CST
3/30/1919 02:00 CWT
10/26/1919 02:00 CST
7/10/1941 00:01 CDT
9/28/1941 02:00 CST
2/09/1942 02:00 CWT
9/30/1945 02:00 CST
5/13/1946 00:01 CDT
9/29/1946 00:01 CST
6/13/1947 00:01 CDT
9/26/1947 00:01 CST
4/25/1948 00:01 CDT
9/26/1948 00:01 CST
4/30/1967 02:00 US#1
....
TN # 49
Before 11/18/1883 LMT
11/18/1883 12:00 CST
3/31/1918 02:00 CWT
10/27/1918 02:00 CST
3/30/1919 02:00 CWT
10/26/1919 02:00 CST
7/06/1941 00:01 CDT
9/28/1941 02:00 CST
2/09/1942 02:00 CWT
9/30/1945 02:00 CST
4/30/1967 02:00 US#1
....
TN # 50
Before 11/18/1883 LMT
11/18/1883 12:00 CST
3/31/1918 02:00 CWT
10/27/1918 02:00 CST
3/30/1919 02:00 CWT
10/26/1919 02:00 CST
7/06/1941 00:01 CDT
9/28/1941 02:00 CST
2/09/1942 02:00 CWT
9/30/1945 02:00 CST
4/30/1967 02:00 US#1
....
TN # 51
Before 11/18/1883 LMT
11/18/1883 12:00 CST
3/31/1918 02:00 CWT
10/27/1918 02:00 CST
3/30/1919 02:00 CWT
10/26/1919 02:00 CST
2/09/1942 02:00 CWT
9/30/1945 02:00 CST
9/28/1947 02:00 EST
4/30/1967 02:00 US#1
....
TN # 52
Before 11/18/1883 LMT
11/18/1883 12:00 CST
3/31/1918 02:00 CWT
10/27/1918 02:00 CST
3/30/1919 02:00 CWT
10/26/1919 02:00 CST
7/23/1941 00:01 CDT
9/28/1941 02:00 CST
2/09/1942 02:00 CWT
9/30/1945 02:00 CST
9/28/1947 02:00 EST
4/30/1967 02:00 US#1
....
TN # 53
Before 11/18/1883 LMT
11/18/1883 12:00 CST
3/31/1918 02:00 CWT
10/27/1918 02:00 CST
3/30/1919 02:00 CWT
10/26/1919 02:00 CST
7/21/1941 00:01 CDT
9/28/1941 00:01 CST
2/09/1942 02:00 CWT
9/30/1945 02:00 CST
9/28/1947 02:00 EST
4/30/1967 02:00 US#1
....
TN # 54
Before 11/18/1883 LMT
11/18/1883 12:00 CST
3/31/1918 02:00 CWT
10/27/1918 02:00 CST
3/30/1919 02:00 CWT
10/26/1919 02:00 CST
7/21/1941 00:01 CDT
9/28/1941 02:00 CST
2/09/1942 02:00 CWT
9/30/1945 02:00 CST
9/28/1947 02:00 EST
4/30/1967 02:00 US#1
....
TN # 55
Before 11/18/1883 LMT
11/18/1883 12:00 CST
3/31/1918 02:00 CWT
10/27/1918 02:00 CST
3/30/1919 02:00 CWT
10/26/1919 02:00 CST
7/22/1941 00:01 CDT
9/28/1941 02:00 CST
2/09/1942 02:00 CWT
9/30/1945 02:00 CST
9/28/1947 02:00 EST
4/30/1967 02:00 US#1
....
TN # 56
Before 11/18/1883 LMT
11/18/1883 12:00 CST
3/31/1918 02:00 CWT
10/27/1918 02:00 CST
3/30/1919 02:00 CWT
10/26/1919 02:00 CST
2/09/1942 02:00 CWT
9/30/1945 02:00 CST
4/03/1960 02:00 EST
4/30/1967 02:00 US#1
....
TN # 57
Before 11/18/1883 LMT
11/18/1883 12:00 CST
3/31/1918 02:00 CWT
10/27/1918 02:00 CST
3/30/1919 02:00 CWT
10/26/1919 02:00 CST
7/21/1941 00:01 CDT
9/28/1941 02:00 CST
2/09/1942 02:00 CWT
9/30/1945 02:00 CST
4/03/1960 02:00 EST
4/30/1967 02:00 US#1
....
TN # 58
Before 11/18/1883 LMT
11/18/1883 12:00 CST
3/31/1918 02:00 CWT
10/27/1918 02:00 CST
3/30/1919 02:00 CWT
10/26/1919 02:00 CST
7/28/1941 00:01 CDT
9/28/1941 02:00 CST
2/09/1942 02:00 CWT
9/30/1945 02:00 CST
4/03/1960 02:00 EST
4/30/1967 02:00 US#1
....
TN # 59
Before 11/18/1883 LMT
11/18/1883 12:00 CST
3/31/1918 02:00 CWT
10/27/1918 02:00 CST
3/30/1919 02:00 CWT
10/26/1919 02:00 CST
7/21/1941 00:01 CDT
9/28/1941 02:00 CST
2/09/1942 02:00 CWT
9/30/1945 02:00 CST
4/27/1946 02:00 EST
4/30/1967 02:00 US#1
....
TN # 60
Before 11/18/1883 LMT
11/18/1883 12:00 CST
3/31/1918 02:00 CWT
10/27/1918 02:00 CST
3/30/1919 02:00 CWT
10/26/1919 02:00 CST
7/26/1941 00:01 CDT
9/28/1941 02:00 CST
2/09/1942 02:00 CWT
9/30/1945 02:00 CST
4/27/1946 02:00 EST
4/30/1967 02:00 US#1
....
TN # 61
Before 11/18/1883 LMT
11/18/1883 12:00 CST
3/31/1918 02:00 CWT
10/27/1918 02:00 CST
3/30/1919 02:00 CWT
10/26/1919 02:00 CST
7/21/1941 00:01 CDT
9/28/1941 00:01 CST
2/09/1942 02:00 CWT
9/30/1945 02:00 CST
4/27/1947 02:00 CDT
9/28/1947 02:00 CST
4/25/1948 00:01 CDT
9/26/1948 00:01 CST
8/14/1949 02:00 EST
4/30/1967 02:00 US#1
....
TN # 62
Before 11/18/1883 LMT
11/18/1883 12:00 CST
3/31/1918 02:00 CWT
10/27/1918 02:00 CST
3/30/1919 02:00 CWT
10/26/1919 02:00 CST
7/23/1941 00:01 CDT
9/28/1941 02:00 CST
2/09/1942 02:00 CWT
9/30/1945 02:00 CST
9/29/1947 02:00 EST
4/30/1967 02:00 US#1
....
TN # 63
Before 11/18/1883 LMT
11/18/1883 12:00 CST
3/31/1918 02:00 CWT
10/27/1918 02:00 CST
3/30/1919 02:00 CWT
10/26/1919 02:00 CST
2/09/1942 02:00 CWT
9/30/1945 02:00 CST
4/28/1946 00:01 EST
4/30/1967 02:00 US#1
....
TN # 64
Before 11/18/1883 LMT
11/18/1883 12:00 CST
3/31/1918 02:00 CWT
10/27/1918 02:00 CST
3/30/1919 02:00 CWT
10/26/1919 02:00 CST
7/20/1941 23:00 CDT
9/28/1941 02:00 CST
2/09/1942 02:00 CWT
9/30/1945 02:00 CST
4/28/1946 00:01 EST
4/30/1967 02:00 US#1
....
TN # 65
Before 11/18/1883 LMT
11/18/1883 12:00 CST
3/31/1918 02:00 CWT
10/27/1918 02:00 CST
3/30/1919 02:00 CWT
10/26/1919 02:00 CST
7/21/1941 00:01 CDT
9/28/1941 00:01 CST
2/09/1942 02:00 CWT
9/30/1945 02:00 CST
4/28/1946 00:01 EST
4/30/1967 02:00 US#1
....
TN # 66
Before 11/18/1883 LMT
11/18/1883 12:00 CST
3/31/1918 02:00 CWT
10/27/1918 02:00 CST
3/30/1919 02:00 CWT
10/26/1919 02:00 CST
7/23/1941 00:01 CDT
9/28/1941 00:01 CST
2/09/1942 02:00 CWT
9/30/1945 02:00 CST
4/28/1946 00:01 EST
4/30/1967 02:00 US#1
....
TN # 67
Before 11/18/1883 LMT
11/18/1883 12:00 CST
3/31/1918 02:00 CWT
10/27/1918 02:00 CST
3/30/1919 02:00 CWT
10/26/1919 02:00 CST
7/21/1941 00:01 CDT
9/28/1941 02:00 CST
2/09/1942 02:00 CWT
9/30/1945 02:00 CST
4/28/1946 00:01 EST
4/30/1967 02:00 US#1
....
TN # 68
Before 11/18/1883 LMT
11/18/1883 12:00 CST
3/31/1918 02:00 CWT
10/27/1918 02:00 CST
3/30/1919 02:00 CWT
10/26/1919 02:00 CST
7/22/1941 00:01 CDT
9/28/1941 02:00 CST
2/09/1942 02:00 CWT
9/30/1945 02:00 CST
4/28/1946 00:01 EST
4/30/1967 02:00 US#1
....
TN # 69
Before 11/18/1883 LMT
11/18/1883 12:00 CST
3/31/1918 02:00 CWT
10/27/1918 02:00 CST
3/30/1919 02:00 CWT
10/26/1919 02:00 CST
7/20/1941 23:00 CDT
9/28/1941 02:00 CST
2/09/1942 02:00 CWT
9/30/1945 02:00 CST
4/28/1946 00:01 EST
4/30/1967 02:00 US#1
....
TN # 70
Before 11/18/1883 LMT
11/18/1883 12:00 CST
3/31/1918 02:00 CWT
10/27/1918 02:00 CST
3/30/1919 02:00 CWT
10/26/1919 02:00 CST
7/21/1941 00:01 CDT
9/28/1941 02:00 CST
2/09/1942 02:00 CWT
9/30/1945 02:00 CST
5/05/1946 00:01 EST
4/30/1967 02:00 US#1
....
TN # 71
Before 11/18/1883 LMT
11/18/1883 12:00 CST
3/31/1918 02:00 CWT
10/27/1918 02:00 CST
3/30/1919 02:00 CWT
10/26/1919 02:00 CST
7/21/1941 00:01 CDT
9/28/1941 02:00 CST
2/09/1942 02:00 CWT
9/30/1945 02:00 CST
4/27/1947 02:00 EST
4/30/1967 02:00 US#1
....
TN # 72
Before 11/18/1883 LMT
11/18/1883 12:00 CST
3/31/1918 02:00 CWT
10/27/1918 02:00 CST
3/30/1919 02:00 CWT
10/26/1919 02:00 CST
7/21/1941 00:01 CDT
9/28/1941 02:00 CST
2/09/1942 02:00 CWT
9/30/1945 02:00 CST
4/28/1947 00:01 EST
4/30/1967 02:00 US#1
....
TN # 73
Before 11/18/1883 LMT
11/18/1883 12:00 CST
3/31/1918 02:00 CWT
10/27/1918 02:00 CST
3/30/1919 02:00 CWT
10/26/1919 02:00 CST
7/28/1941 00:01 CDT
9/28/1941 02:00 CST
2/09/1942 02:00 CWT
9/30/1945 02:00 CST
4/28/1947 00:01 EST
4/30/1967 02:00 US#1
....
TN # 74
Before 11/18/1883 LMT
11/18/1883 12:00 CST
3/31/1918 02:00 CWT
10/27/1918 02:00 CST
3/30/1919 02:00 CWT
10/26/1919 02:00 CST
7/21/1941 00:01 CDT
9/28/1941 02:00 CST
2/09/1942 02:00 CWT
9/30/1945 02:00 CST
8/21/1949 02:00 EST
4/30/1967 02:00 US#1
....
TN # 75
Before 11/18/1883 LMT
11/18/1883 12:00 CST
3/31/1918 02:00 CWT
10/27/1918 02:00 CST
1/01/1919 02:00 EST
3/30/1919 02:00 EWT
10/26/1919 02:00 EST
2/09/1942 02:00 EWT
9/30/1945 02:00 EST
4/30/1967 02:00 US#1

COUNTIES

1 Anderson
2 Bedford
3 Benton
4 Bledsoe
5 Blount
6 Bradley
7 Campbell
8 Cannon
9 Carroll
10 Carter
11 Cheatham
12 Chester
13 Claiborne
14 Clay
15 Cocke
16 Coffee
17 Crockett
18 Cumberland
19 Davidson
20 Decatur
21 Dekalb
22 Dickson
23 Dyer
24 Fayette
25 Fentress
26 Franklin
27 Gibson
28 Giles
29 Grainger
30 Greene
31 Grundy
32 Hamblen
33 Hamilton
34 Hancock
35 Hardeman
36 Hardin
37 Hawkins
38 Haywood
39 Henderson
40 Henry
41 Hickman
42 Houston
43 Humphreys
44 Jackson
45 Jefferson
46 Johnson
47 Knox
48 Lake
49 Lauderdale
50 Lawrence
51 Lewis
52 Lincoln
53 Loudon
54 McMinn
55 McNairy
56 Macon
57 Madison
58 Marion
59 Marshall
60 Maury
61 Meigs
62 Monroe
63 Montgomery
64 Moore
65 Morgan
66 Obion
67 Overton
68 Perry
69 Pickett
70 Polk
71 Putnam
72 Rhea
73 Roane
74 Robertson
75 Rutherford
76 Scott
77 Sequatchie
78 Sevier
79 Shelby
80 Smith
81 Stewart
82 Sullivan
83 Sumner
84 Tipton
85 Trousdale
86 Unicoi
87 Union
88 Van Buren
89 Warren
90 Washington
91 Wayne
92 Weakley
93 White
94 Williamson
95 Wilson

Abiff 22 3 35N58'34 87W19'03 5:49:16
Acklen 19 4 36N08 86W48 5:47:12
Acme Mill 54 71 35N33'00 84W34'06 5:38:16
Acorn 62 67 35N28'03 84W13'32 5:36:54
Acton 55 3 35N00'29 88W27'34 5:53:50
Adair 57 3 35N42'51 88W57'39 5:55:51
Adams 74 3 36N34'56 87W03'56 5:48:16
Adams Crossroads 22
3 36N10'53 87W31'15 5:50:05
Adams Mill 90 63 36N08'25 82W35'53 5:30:24
Adamsville 55 3 35N14'09 88W23'26 5:53:34
Addison 54 54 35N22'42 84W31'17 5:38:05
Adkins Mill 65 56 36N10'54 84W51'43 5:39:27
Adolphus 53 68 35N44'28 84W25'32 5:37:42
Aethra 51 3 35N33'40 87W19'27 5:49:18
Aetna 41 3 35N39'18 87W30'17 5:50:01
Aetna 58 8 35N00'43 85W29'41 5:41:59
Afton 30 65 36N11'38 82W44'20 5:30:57
Airport 19 4 36N08 86W42 5:46:48
Airport Estates 19
4 36N06 86W45 5:47:00
Air View 31 3 35N26 85W43 5:42:52
Akard Addition 82
2 36N33'29 82W16'43 5:29:07
Akeman Crossroad 61
54 35N37'36 84W45'05 5:39:00
Akin Landing 20 3 35N26'30 88W02'31 5:52:10
Akins Corner 84 3 35N29'12 89W46'09 5:59:05
Alamo 17 14 35N47'05 89W07'02 5:56:28
Alanthus Hill 34
51 36N33'55 83W23'30 5:33:34
Albany 30 65 36N14'31 82W54'40 5:31:39
Alberton 39 25 35N41'59 88W18'59 5:53:16
Albright 83 42 36N23 86W26 5:45:44
Alcoa 5 64 35N47'22 83W58'26 5:35:54
Aldenwood Park 47
67 35N53'39 84W01'39 5:36:07
Alder Branch 78
60 35N55'18 83W33'18 5:34:13
Alder Springs 7
66 36N22'09 84W00'23 5:36:02
Alder Springs 87
52 36N14'17 83W51'53 5:35:28
Alexander Ford 41
3 35N50'07 87W42'50 5:50:51
Alexander Mill 30
65 36N08'15 82W45'34 5:31:02
Alexander Springs 50
29 35N22'38 87W16'09 5:49:05
Alexandria 21 3 36N04'39 86W02'00 5:44:08
Alfred Reagan Place 78
59 35N42'09 83W28'15 5:33:53
Algood 71 34 36N11'45 85W26'55 5:41:48
Allardt 25 3 36N22'51 84W53'04 5:39:32
Allen Grove 15 65 35N50'28 83W13'03 5:32:52
Allens 38 24 35N38'28 89W11'26 5:56:46
Allens Chapel 21
3 35N57 85W49 5:43:16
Allensville 78 60 35N49 83W33 5:34:12
Alley Ford 65 56 36N04'53 84W40'16 5:38:41
Allingham 73 62 36N01'39 84W20'26 5:37:22
Allisona 94 3 35N45'17 86W41'31 5:46:46
Allons 67 3 36N26'31 85W20'41 5:41:23
Alloway 18 15 35N48'00 84W52'32 5:39:30
Allred 67 3 36N19'50 85W11'23 5:40:46
Almaville 75 3 35N51'55 86W34'52 5:46:19
Almira 84 3 35N29 89W43 5:58:52
Alnwick 5 64 35N44'53 84W02'16 5:36:09
Alpha 32 67 36N10'37 83W22'58 5:33:32
Alpha Heights 32
67 36N11'05 83W23'17 5:33:33
Alpine 67 3 36N23'41 85W13'01 5:40:52
Altamont 31 3 35N25'46 85W43'23 5:42:54
Alta Vista 54 71 35N27'50 84W36'58 5:38:28
Alto 26 18 35N16'14 85W57'11 5:43:49
Alton Hill 56 3 36N32 86W02 5:44:08
Alton Park 33 61 35N00'11 85W19'00 5:41:16
Alumwell 37 70 36N28'52 83W00'07 5:32:00
Amanda 93 3 35N56 85W28 5:41:52
Amherst 47 67 35N57'31 84W01'54 5:36:08
Amis 37 70 36N25'06 82W57'09 5:31:49
Amis Chapel 37 70 36N28 82W51 5:31:24
Amity Heights 82
2 36N35 82W11 5:28:44
Amqui 19 4 36N16'34 86W42'33 5:46:50
Anchor Mill 2 6 35N32'17 86W32'00 5:46:08
Anderson 16 13 35N22'39 86W10'47 5:44:43
Anderson 26 18 34N59'38 85W54'11 5:43:37
Anderson 67 3 36N10'22 85W14'05 5:40:56
Anderson 82 1 36N32'25 82W19'17 5:29:17
Anderson Heights 82
1 36N32 82W19 5:29:16
Andersonville 1
62 36N12 84W02 5:36:08
Anes 59 3 35N33'31 86W45'03 5:47:00
Angeltown 83 50 36N32'50 86W20'59 5:45:24
Anglea 83 50 36N29 86W19 5:45:16
Anglers Cove 73
67 35N49'13 84W31'55 5:38:08
Annadale 6 53 35N09'57 84W53'06 5:39:32
Annadel 65 56 36N10'36 84W39'57 5:38:40
Anthony Hill 28 3 35N08'09 87W06'26 5:48:26
Anthras 7 51 36N32'45 83W59'25 5:35:58
Antioch 2 3 35N47'23 88W58'27 5:55:54
Antioch 19 4 36N03'36 86W40'20 5:46:41
Antioch 21 3 35N51'26 85W43'01 5:42:52
Antioch 38 3 35N26'41 89W20'49 5:57:23
Antioch 39 25 35N41'04 88W26'33 5:53:46
Antioch 44 27 36N16'31 85W39'30 5:42:38
Antioch 53 68 35N48 84W16 5:37:04
Antioch 63 32 36N26'40 87W24'07 5:49:36
Antioch 84 3 35N35'09 89W32'33 5:58:10
Antioch Harbor Resort 40
3 36N21'39 88W07'41 5:52:31
Antioch Landing 40
3 36N23'34 88W05'55 5:52:24
Apalachia 70 73 35N10'05 84W19'22 5:37:17
Apison 33 61 35N01'26 85W01'26 5:40:06
Apollo Shores 72
70 35N44'46 84W44'57 5:39:00
Appleton 50 29 35N01'25 87W14'00 5:48:56
Applewood 33 61 35N08'53 85W20'11 5:41:21
Arcadia 82 2 36N35'07 82W27'29 5:29:50
Archer 59 30 35N27 86W48 5:47:12
Archville 70 72 35N07'58 84W31'32 5:38:06
Arcott 14 11 36N31'12 85W33'18 5:42:13
Arden 62 71 35N25'18 84W24'34 5:37:38
Ardmore 28 3 34N59'31 86W50'48 5:47:23
Arkland 60 3 35N40'33 87W12'02 5:48:48
Arline 5 64 35N47'38 84W05'41 5:36:23
Arlington 42 3 36N19 87W42 5:50:48
Arlington 47 67 36N00'18 83W56'01 5:35:44
Arlington 79 40 35N17'46 89W39'41 5:58:39
Armathwaite 25 3 36N22'27 84W46'56 5:39:08
Arminda 47 67 36N03'03 83W47'47 5:35:11
Armona 5 64 35N47'14 84W00'51 5:36:03
Armour 60 31 35N37 87W02 5:48:08
Armour Village 60
3 35N37'58 87W09'29 5:48:38
Arms Mill 87 52 36N15 83W48 5:35:12
Arno 94 3 35N48'11 86W44'30 5:46:58
Arnold Engineering Developme 16
13 35N21 86W12 5:44:48
Arnolds Chapel 71
3 36N09 85W38 5:42:32
Arp 49 28 35N46'24 89W36'09 5:58:25
Arrington 94 3 35N52'05 86W42'33 5:46:50
Arrow 60 9 35N30'44 87W11'35 5:48:46
Arrowhead 47 67 35N53'08 83W56'15 5:35:45
Arthur 13 51 36N32'53 83W40'15 5:34:41
Asbury 16 12 35N27'49 85W58'38 5:43:55
Asbury 38 3 35N26'58 89W19'56 5:57:20
Asbury 47 67 35N57'09 83W49'33 5:35:18
Asbury 69 3 36N34'53 85W04'00 5:40:16
Asbury 81 3 36N23'43 87W52'41 5:51:31
Asbury 90 75 36N19'15 82W23'40 5:29:35
Ashburn 74 35 36N37'16 86W49'43 5:47:19
Ashburn Ford 18
15 36N09'06 84W59'54 5:40:00
Ashbury 81 3 36N19 87W50 5:51:20
Ashland 91 3 35N26'10 87W40'03 5:50:40
Ashland City 11
10 36N16'27 87W03'51 5:48:15
Ashland Ford 91 3 35N26'29 87W40'14 5:50:41
Ashland Hills 63
32 36N30'23 87W17'48 5:49:11
Ashley Oaks 47 67 35N54'31 84W06'10 5:36:25
Ashport 49 3 35N45'36 89W47'08 5:59:09
Ashport Landing 49
3 35N45'37 89W47'22 5:59:09
Ashwood 60 31 35N34'46 87W08'38 5:48:35
Asia 26 19 35N14'38 86W05'25 5:44:22
Aspen Hill 28 22 35N06'02 87W00'14 5:48:01
Athendale 60 31 35N40'28 87W04'41 5:48:19
Athens 54 71 35N26'34 84W35'35 5:38:22
Atoka 84 3 35N26'28 89W46'41 5:59:07
Atwood 9 3 35N58'23 88W40'41 5:54:43
Auburntown 8 3 35N56'51 86W05'50 5:44:23
Austin 36 23 35N12'06 88W14'21 5:52:57
Austins Mill 37
70 36N22'24 83W00'24 5:32:02
Austin Springs 90
75 36N22'59 82W20'58 5:29:24
Austin Springs 92
3 36N29'30 88W38'04 5:54:32
Austral 70 72 35N14'02 84W32'43 5:38:11
Avoca 82 1 36N31'54 82W14'47 5:28:59
Avondale 19 4 36N12'14 86W46'38 5:47:07
Avondale 27 8 35N50 88W55 5:55:40
Avondale 29 55 36N18'09 83W27'46 5:33:51
Avondale 33 61 35N03'16 85W15'35 5:41:02
Avondale 83 43 36N19'55 86W32'58 5:46:12
Avondale Springs 29
55 36N18'38 83W27'45 5:33:51
Ayers 23 16 36N04'45 89W38'31 5:58:34
Aymett Town 28 22 35N10'34 86W57'35 5:47:50
Babbs Mill 30 65 36N15'49 82W46'38 5:31:07
Bacchus 13 51 36N30'33 83W36'14 5:34:25
Bachelder 51 3 35N32'34 87W19'16 5:49:17
Backwoods 10 1 36N10'34 82W09'01 5:28:36
Bacon Gap 73 67 35N52 84W31 5:38:04
Bagdad 44 3 36N23 85W52 5:43:48
Baggettsville 74
3 36N28'36 86W43'49 5:46:55
Bailey 79 40 35N03'03 89W43'43 5:58:55
Baileyton 30 65 36N20'03 82W50'13 5:31:21
Bailey Town 15 65 35N57'26 83W16'51 5:33:07
Bain 3 3 36N10'01 88W08'53 5:52:36
Bairds Mills 95
34 36N06'08 86W19'54 5:45:20
Baker Bluff 82 2 36N28'00 82W27'59 5:29:52
Baker Crossroads 18
15 35N59'46 85W06'38 5:40:27
Bakers 19 4 36N22'20 86W45'36 5:47:02
Bakers Crossroads 93
3 36N00'48 85W33'08 5:42:13
Bakersworks 22 3 36N04'38 87W15'48 5:49:03
Bakerton 14 3 36N30'46 85W48'17 5:43:13
Bakertown 19 4 36N06 86W45 5:47:00
Bakertown 64 33 35N15'31 86W19'49 5:45:19
Bakerville 43 3 35N56'37 87W52'27 5:51:30
Bakewell 33 61 35N20'36 85W07'59 5:40:32
Bald Crossing 90
63 36N15'45 82W31'05 5:30:04
Bald Point 29 55 36N24'40 83W21'39 5:33:27
Baldwin Ford 34
51 36N35'46 83W18'21 5:33:13
Bales Ford 34 51 36N34'55 83W20'00 5:33:20
Ball Camp 47 67 35N57'10 84W07'19 5:36:29
Ball Play 70 72 35N04 84W44 5:38:56
Balltown 54 54 35N20 84W32 5:38:08
Balmoral 33 61 35N06'26 85W20'48 5:41:23
Baltimore 15 65 35N59'03 83W03'34 5:32:14
Bangham 71 34 36N11 85W28 5:41:52
Banner 78 59 35N43 83W31 5:34:04
Banner Hill 86 1 36N07'50 82W25'29 5:29:42
Banner Springs 25
3 36N14'52 84W55'52 5:39:43
Baptist 19 4 36N09 86W47 5:47:08
Baptist Ridge 14
3 36N29'02 85W31'27 5:42:06
Barefoot 56 3 36N38'09 86W11'32 5:44:46
Barfield 75 37 35N47'06 86W25'36 5:45:42
Bargerton 39 25 35N43'55 88W29'08 5:53:57
Barkertown 31 3 35N23'30 85W33'11 5:42:13
Barley Ford 34 51 36N35'40 83W18'51 5:33:15
Barnard 73 67 35N46 84W34 5:38:16
Barnardsville 73
67 35N52 84W31 5:38:04
Barnes 69 3 36N33'23 85W14'50 5:40:59
Barnes 90 75 36N21'11 82W18'38 5:29:15
Barnes Ford 18 15 35N58'44 84W51'04 5:39:24
Barnesville 50 29 35N26'07 87W23'08 5:49:33
Barr 49 3 35N52'56 89W43'52 5:58:55
Barren Plain 74 3 36N36'05 86W55'10 5:47:41
Barretville 79 40 35N22'25 89W45'48 5:59:03
Barrons Corner 27
21 36N04'12 88W56'07 5:55:44
Barthelia 85 45 36N20'42 86W15'22 5:45:01
Bartlebaugh 33 61 35N06'59 85W10'01 5:40:40
Bartlett 79 40 35N12'16 89W52'26 5:59:30
Barton Mill 54 71 35N31'09 84W36'34 5:38:26
Barton Springs 32
67 36N14'11 83W14'07 5:32:56
Bass Bay 3 3 36N16'56 87W58'33 5:51:54
Bates 41 3 35N54'36 87W22'28 5:49:30
Bates Hill 89 46 35N43'50 85W55'53 5:43:44
Bath Springs 20 3 35N26'23 88W05'16 5:52:21
Batley 1 62 36N01'45 84W17'18 5:37:09
Baucom 16 12 35N32'06 86W13'20 5:44:53
Baugh 28 3 35N04'23 86W51'02 5:47:24
Baugh Spring 6 53 35N10'38 84W59'13 5:39:57
Baxter 71 3 36N09'13 85W38'37 5:42:34
Bazel Town 73 67 35N57'43 84W32'01 5:38:08
Beacon 20 3 35N37'42 88W10'59 5:52:44
Beans Creek 26 18 35N03'42 86W14'48 5:44:59
Bean Station 29
55 36N20'37 83W17'03 5:33:08
Bear Creek 76 58 36N33 84W27 5:37:48
Bearden 47 67 35N55'58 84W00'10 5:36:01
Beard Ford 50 29 35N27'08 87W26'09 5:49:45
Beardstown 68 3 35N42'44 87W47'57 5:51:12
Bear Spring 81 3 36N28'31 87W45'17 5:51:01
Bear Stand 10 1 36N16'43 82W05'18 5:28:21
Beartown 82 2 36N34'12 82W35'44 5:30:23
Bearwallow 11 10 36N17'54 86W59'43 5:47:59
Bear Wallow 59 3 35N41'21 86W45'39 5:47:03
Beasley 59 3 35N40'48 86W39'07 5:46:36
Beasley Crossroads 94
3 35N52'04 87W08'50 5:48:35
Beaver 84 3 35N30'09 89W48'39 5:59:15
Beaverdam Springs 41
3 35N40'55 87W36'16 5:50:25
Beaver Hill 67 3 36N14'05 85W17'36 5:41:10
Beaver Ridge 47
67 35N58 83W58 5:35:52
Beckwith 95 49 36N12'24 86W27'32 5:45:50
Bedford 2 3 35N27'49 86W34'25 5:46:18
Beech Bluff 57 3 35N35'47 88W37'53 5:54:32
Beech Bottom 56 3 36N27'55 86W00'29 5:44:02
Beech Creek 37 70 36N27 82W47 5:31:08
Beech Fork 7 66 36N14'04 84W18'18 5:37:13
Beech Grove 1 62 36N14'04 84W11'24 5:36:46
Beech Grove 11 10 36N19'36 87W11'28 5:48:46
Beechgrove 16 12 35N37'37 86W14'25 5:44:58
Beech Grove 23 3 36N07'46 88W49'04 5:55:16
Beech Grove 29 55 36N22'01 83W28'11 5:33:53
Beech Grove 37 70 36N17'31 83W00'33 5:32:02
Beech Grove 47 67 36N08'43 83W54'52 5:35:39
Beech Grove 60 3 35N37'11 86W58'21 5:47:53
Beech Grove 85 45 36N25'09 86W05'36 5:44:22
Beech Hill 26 3 35N13'20 86W17'38 5:45:11
Beech Hill 28 22 35N13'47 86W53'21 5:47:33
Beech Hill 56 3 36N28'16 86W06'23 5:44:26
Beechnut City 82
1 36N34'02 82W20'00 5:29:20
Beech Springs 78
60 35N57'48 83W37'02 5:34:28
Beechwood 2 5 35N39'05 86W20'17 5:45:21
Beechwood 47 64 35N52'10 83W58'14 5:35:53
Beeler Mill 29 55 36N19'27 83W37'18 5:34:29
Beersheba Springs 31
3 35N28'00 85W39'15 5:42:37
Bel Air 60 31 35N37'37 87W02'43 5:48:11
Bel-Aire 16 13 35N21'39 86W14'14 5:44:57
Bel Aire 75 37 35N51 86W23 5:45:32
Bel-Aire Heights 26
18 35N11'55 86W06'17 5:44:25
Bel-Air Estates 63
32 36N34'10 87W24'00 5:49:36
Belfast 59 3 35N25'15 86W42'09 5:46:49
Belk 21 3 35N50'33 85W41'58 5:42:48
Bella Mara Estates 73
70 35N45'45 84W42'19 5:38:49
Bella Vista Acres 33
61 35N01'27 85W09'40 5:40:39
Bell Bridge 47 67 36N01'02 84W03'01 5:36:12
Bell Buckle 2 5 35N35'30 86W21'15 5:45:25
Bell Campground 47
67 36N01'48 84W03'38 5:36:15
Belle-Aire 47 67 35N52'12 84W09'56 5:36:40
Belle Aire 93 3 35N56 85W28 5:41:52
Belle Brook Estate 82
2 36N35 82W11 5:28:44
Belle Eagle 38 24 35N41'07 89W13'47 5:56:55
Bellefounte 6 53 35N14'44 84W47'43 5:39:11
Belle Meade 5 64 35N44'26 83W58'02 5:35:52
Belle Meade 19 4 36N05'45 86W51'25 5:47:26
Belle Meade 36 23 35N13'07 88W13'35 5:52:54
Belleview 52 9 35N02'43 86W35'49 5:46:23
Belleview Estates 54
54 35N16'47 84W32'53 5:38:12
Belleville 52 9 35N16'22 86W33'14 5:46:13
Bellevue 19 4 36N03'53 86W56'22 5:47:45
Bellevue Estates 54
54 35N20 84W32 5:38:08
Bells 17 3 35N42'40 89W05'15 5:56:21
Bellsburg 22 3 36N16'33 87W11'20 5:48:45
Bells Mill 31 3 35N17'27 85W52'46 5:43:31
Bell Town 11 9 36N06'46 87W09'29 5:48:38
Belltown 62 67 35N25'45 84W15'02 5:37:00
Belltown 70 73 35N00'17 84W21'23 5:37:26
Belltown Hill 70
73 35N01'30 84W19'56 5:37:20
Belltown Mill 62
67 35N25'30 84W15'17 5:37:01
Bellview 4 15 35N44'46 85W10'40 5:40:43
Bellview 52 9 35N09 86W35 5:46:20
Bellwood 95 34 36N15'12 86W08'50 5:44:35

Belmont 1 62 36N14'44 84w01'51 5:36:07
Belmont 16 12 35N25'17 86w06'46 5:44:27
Belmont 24 3 35N23'20 89w29'09 5:57:57
Belmont 45 67 36N00'37 83w19'03 5:33:16
Belmont West 47
67 35N56'09 84w06'21 5:36:25
Belvidere 26 18 35N07'45 86w11'12 5:44:45
Belvins 37 70 36N27'41 82w56'10 5:31:45
Bemis 57 14 35N34'34 88w49'17 5:55:17
Bending Chestnut 94
48 35N57 86w53 5:47:32
Benhill 94 3 35N52'17 86w43'35 5:46:54
Benjestown 79 39 35N15'06 90w03'19 6:00:13
Ben Stockton 25 3 36N26 84w56 5:39:44
Benton 70 72 35N10'27 84w39'13 5:38:37
Benton Cut 3 3 36N14'54 88w02'01 5:52:08
Benton Springs 70
72 35N08'48 84w37'17 5:38:29
Benton Station 70
72 35N11'15 84w41'00 5:38:44
Berclair 79 40 35N06 89w54 5:59:36
Berea 28 22 35N15'30 86w58'06 5:47:52
Berea 89 11 35N48'32 85w42'16 5:42:49
Bergmantown 31 3 35N21'19 85w46'33 5:43:06
Berkshire Wood 47
67 35N56'47 84w05'11 5:36:21
Berlin 59 30 35N31'47 86w49'28 5:47:18
Berry 22 3 36N10'32 87w23'13 5:49:33
Berry Hill 19 4 36N07'01 86w45'59 5:47:04
Berry's Chapel 94
48 35N59 86w52 5:47:28
Bertha 34 51 36N34 83w03 5:32:12
Bessie 48 3 36N29'17 89w29'58 5:58:00
Bethany 30 65 36N05'13 82w43'24 5:30:54
Bethany 89 46 35N42'23 85w51'15 5:43:25
Bethel 1 62 36N10'16 84w04'36 5:36:18
Bethel 9 3 36N02'08 88w26'55 5:53:48
Bethel 11 10 36N22'17 87w10'42 5:48:43
Bethel 21 3 35N51'30 85w51'03 5:43:24
Bethel 28 3 35N00'06 87w03'12 5:48:13
Bethel 38 24 35N44'37 89w16'45 5:57:07
Bethel 60 3 35N48'05 87w07'06 5:48:28
Bethel 68 3 35N35'18 87w50'37 5:51:22
Bethel Springs 55
3 35N14'01 88w36'23 5:54:26
Bethesda 30 65 36N14 82w41 5:30:44
Bethesda 93 3 35N49'20 85w20'33 5:41:22
Bethesda 94 3 35N45'40 86w47'35 5:47:10
Bethlehem 11 4 36N18'07 87w04'58 5:48:20
Bethlehem 36 3 35N15'18 88w21'01 5:53:24
Bethlehem 40 3 36N27'35 88w15'49 5:53:03
Bethlehem 62 67 35N31 84w22 5:37:28
Bethlehem 94 48 36N00'03 86w53'06 5:47:32
Bethpage 83 50 36N28'54 86w18'43 5:45:15
Betsy Willis 16
12 35N25 85w58 5:43:52
Beulah 30 65 36N08'43 83w08'46 5:32:35
Beverly 47 67 36N01'54 83w54'04 5:35:36
Beverly Hills 47
67 36N03 83w53 5:35:32
Bible Hill 20 3 35N42'11 88w08'38 5:52:35
Bidwell 52 9 35N16'31 86w37'42 5:46:31
Big Barren Creek 13
51 36N25 83w41 5:34:44
Big Boy Junction 23
16 36N02'10 89w29'59 5:58:00
Bigbyville 60 31 35N31'14 87w04'48 5:48:19
Big Cherokee 90
75 36N14'10 82w27'49 5:29:51
Big Creek 34 51 36N29'29 83w21'16 5:33:25
Big Creek 37 70 36N28'25 82w56'36 5:31:46
Big Creek 62 67 35N27'51 84w17'57 5:37:12
Big Ivy 36 23 35N07'03 88w03'02 5:52:12
Big Lick 18 15 35N48'26 85w01'17 5:40:05
Big Mountain 65
51 36N02 84w20 5:37:20
Big Piney 53 68 35N41'15 84w20'00 5:37:20
Big Ridge Park 87
52 36N15 83w48 5:35:12
Big Rock 81 3 36N34'50 87w45'36 5:51:02
Big Rock Ford 91
3 35N28'10 87w49'44 5:51:19
Big Sandy 3 3 36N14'05 88w05'07 5:52:20
Big Sandy 90 63 36N18'31 82w35'14 5:30:21
Big Spring 5 64 35N46 84w08 5:36:32
Big Spring 10 1 36N19'01 82w14'34 5:28:58
Big Spring 61 54 35N23'44 84w54'00 5:39:36
Big Springs 5 64 35N43'42 84w06'05 5:36:24
Big Springs 34 51 36N35'20 82w55'26 5:31:42
Big Springs 57 3 35N29 88w43 5:54:52
Big Springs 67 22 36N26'06 85w15'58 5:41:04
Big Springs 75 36 35N42'39 86w16'22 5:45:05
Big War Creek 34
51 36N27 83w14 5:32:56
Bilbrey 71 3 36N10'25 85w19'57 5:41:20
Biltmore 10 1 36N22'20 82w13'33 5:28:54
Binfield 5 64 35N42'18 84w04'28 5:36:18
Bingham 94 48 35N55'48 86w58'06 5:47:52
Binghamton 79 39 35N09 89w59 5:59:56
Birchwood 33 61 35N21'45 84w59'32 5:39:58
Bird Crossroads 78
60 35N49 83w33 5:34:12
Bird Mill 50 29 35N05'59 87w17'58 5:49:12
Birds Bower 38 3 35N27'42 89w25'09 5:57:41
Birdsong Dock 3 3 35N58'09 88w02'48 5:52:11
Birdsong Heights 3
3 35N58'45 88w02'57 5:52:12
Birnam Wood 33 61 35N08'19 85w20'15 5:41:21
Bishop 23 16 36N00'17 89w19'41 5:57:19
Bitter End 10 1 36N12'42 82w02'25 5:28:10
Bivens 28 3 35N23'13 86w57'08 5:47:49
Black Center 3 3 36N04'15 88w05'14 5:52:21
Black Creek 76 58 36N22'51 84w36'21 5:38:25
Black Fox 6 53 35N06'45 84w55'39 5:39:43
Black Fox 29 55 36N17 83w36 5:34:24
Black Jack 16 12 35N26'08 86w06'18 5:44:25
Black Jack 74 3 36N38'00 86w33'50 5:46:15
Blackman 75 37 35N52'31 86w29'54 5:46:00
Black Oak 47 67 36N01'07 83w58'21 5:35:53
Black Oak 76 58 36N29'24 84w36'24 5:38:26
Black Oak 93 3 35N59'43 85w30'57 5:42:04
Blackwell 29 55 36N17 83w31 5:34:04

Blackwell Crossing 59
3 35N23'47 86w40'52 5:46:43
Blaine 29 55 36N09'15 83w42'15 5:34:49
Blair 73 67 35N59'33 84w25'15 5:37:41
Blair Gap 82 2 36N27'01 82w40'47 5:30:43
Blakeville 52 9 35N15'34 86w40'31 5:46:42
Blanche 52 9 35N02'35 86w45'16 5:47:01
Blaney Forest 33
61 35N00'15 85w15'30 5:41:02
Blanton Chapel 16
12 35N28 86w05 5:44:20
Bledsoe 52 9 35N20'08 86w34'41 5:46:19
Bledsoe 83 50 36N30'56 86w15'56 5:45:04
Blevins 10 1 36N13'58 82w09'21 5:28:37
Block 7 66 36N20'31 84w15'17 5:37:01
Block City 37 70 36N32'32 82w40'39 5:30:43
Blockhouse 5 64 35N42'11 83w56'12 5:35:45
Blondy 51 3 35N33'37 87w31'58 5:50:08
Bloomingdale 82 1 36N35'04 82w29'22 5:29:57
Blooming Grove 28
22 35N12'29 86w58'19 5:47:53
Bloomington 69 3 36N34'49 85w11'34 5:40:46
Bloomington Heights 82
2 36N33'44 82w32'34 5:30:10
Bloomington Springs 71
3 36N11'47 85w37'13 5:42:29
Blossom 37 70 36N27'40 82w45'04 5:31:00
Blount Beach 5 64 35N47'00 83w53'45 5:35:35
Blount Hills 5 64 35N46 83w58 5:35:52
Blountville 82 1 36N31'59 82w19'37 5:29:18
Blowing Springs 1
62 36N08'06 84w09'04 5:36:36
Blue Bank 48 3 36N21'06 89w25'30 5:57:42
Blue Creek 28 22 35N20'05 86w55'10 5:47:41
Bluefields 19 4 36N09 86w41 5:46:44
Blue Gem 65 51 35N59'47 84w27'10 5:37:49
Blue Goose 39 25 35N42'12 88w34'36 5:54:18
Blue Grass 47 67 35N51'53 84w03'35 5:36:14
Blue Hill 89 46 35N48'37 85w54'47 5:43:39
Blue Mill 15 65 35N51'22 82w59'43 5:31:59
Blue Ridge 82 2 36N33'15 82w13'07 5:28:52
Blue Sky 68 3 35N45'55 87w52'47 5:51:31
Blue Spring 10 1 36N21'28 82w06'58 5:28:28
Blue Spring 33 61 35N13'12 85w04'22 5:40:17
Blue Springs 6 53 35N05'03 84w54'32 5:39:38
Blue Springs 21 3 35N52'45 85w50'40 5:43:23
Blue Springs 73
54 35N44'31 84w40'02 5:38:40
Blue Springs Resort 73
54 35N44'11 84w40'03 5:38:40
Bluewing 8 3 35N47'09 85w59'30 5:43:58
Bluff City 82 1 36N28'27 82w15'40 5:29:03
Bluff Creek 80 3 36N13'01 85w57'23 5:43:50
Bluff Springs 89
3 35N49'07 85w45'43 5:43:03
Bluffton 15 65 35N48'38 83w10'33 5:32:42
Bluhmtown 21 3 35N54'14 85w52'47 5:43:31
Blunts Landing 68
3 35N36'31 88w01'46 5:52:07
Board Valley 93 3 36N02'25 85w22'31 5:41:30
Boatland 25 3 36N26 84w56 5:39:44
Bobs Landing 20 3 35N26'53 88w02'41 5:52:11
Bobtown 16 18 35N11'06 85w54'57 5:43:40
Bodenham 28 22 35N14'01 87w09'21 5:48:37
Boggess Crossroad 61
54 35N36'06 84w40'17 5:38:41
Bogota 23 16 36N09'50 89w26'18 5:57:45
Bohannon Addition 54
71 35N25'54 84w36'10 5:38:25
Bohannons Landing 20
3 35N43'45 88w02'04 5:52:08
Bold Spring 43 3 35N58'01 87w40'45 5:50:43
Boles 14 3 36N37'06 85w39'56 5:42:40
Bolivar 35 3 35N15'22 88w59'16 5:55:57
Bolton 79 40 35N19'16 89w45'38 5:59:03
Boma 71 3 36N07'37 85w40'57 5:42:44
Bon Air 83 50 36N35'41 86w21'29 5:45:26
Bon Air 93 3 35N56'28 85w21'45 5:41:27
Bon Aqua 41 3 35N57'12 87w19'37 5:49:18
Bon Aqua Junction 41
3 35N55'40 87w18'39 5:49:15
Bond 41 3 35N43'27 87w24'02 5:49:36
Bon De Croft 93 3 35N54 85w22 5:41:28
Bone Cave 88 3 35N46'30 85w35'06 5:42:20
Bonham 72 74 35N43'14 84w53'47 5:39:35
Bonicord 23 16 35N57'16 89w19'18 5:57:17
Bonnertown 50 29 35N00'22 87w17'53 5:49:12
Bonneville Estates 47
67 35N59'44 84w05'04 5:36:20
Bonny Kate 47 67 35N56 83w54 5:35:36
Bonsack 67 3 36N12'27 85w10'25 5:40:42
Bonta Vista Estates 47
67 36N05'28 83w56'12 5:35:45
Bonwood 57 3 35N39 88w53 5:55:32
Boom 69 3 36N30'57 85w10'11 5:40:41
Boomer 15 65 35N49'40 82w57'39 5:31:51
Boone 90 75 36N22'41 82w26'15 5:29:45
Boones Creek 90
75 36N23'32 82w24'42 5:29:39
Booneville 52 9 35N16'27 86w27'52 5:45:51
Boonshill 52 9 35N12'45 86w44'31 5:46:58
Boothspoint 23 16 36N06'45 89w36'10 5:58:25
Bordeaux 19 4 36N11'38 86w49'53 5:47:20
Borden Village 82
2 36N32'09 82w32'29 5:30:10
Boston 94 3 35N50'34 87w01'57 5:48:08
Bottle Hollow 2 6 35N24'25 86w21'44 5:45:27
Bowen 29 55 36N17 83w31 5:34:04
Bowman 18 15 35N57 85w02 5:40:08
Bowmantown 90 63 36N17'53 82w34'33 5:30:18
Box Elder 36 3 35N15'13 88w18'34 5:53:14
Boxwood Hills 47
67 35N54'02 84w08'05 5:36:32
Boyce 33 61 35N04'37 85w15'26 5:41:02
Boyd 47 67 35N50'45 84w10'37 5:36:42
Boyds Creek 78 60 35N55'24 83w39'33 5:34:38
Boydsville 92 3 36N30'07 88w31'23 5:54:06
Boynton Valley 16
12 35N33'27 86w08'40 5:44:35
Brace 50 29 35N22'21 87w18'17 5:49:13
Brackentown 83 50 36N35'56 86w23'12 5:45:33
Bradburn Hill 30
65 36N11'30 82w48'25 5:31:14

Bradbury 73 67 35N52'13 84w23'24 5:37:34
Braden 24 3 35N22'46 89w34'05 5:58:16
Bradford 27 21 36N04'35 88w48'36 5:55:14
Bradleytown 23 16 36N03 89w29 5:57:56
Bradshaw 28 3 35N11'37 86w52'15 5:47:29
Bradyville 8 3 35N44'23 86w09'56 5:44:40
Braemar 10 1 36N16'55 82w09'18 5:28:37
Brainerd 33 61 35N01'12 85w14'25 5:40:58
Brainerd Hills 33
74 35N01'01 85w11'55 5:40:48
Brakebill 62 67 35N31 84w22 5:37:28
Branchville 2 3 35N22'58 86w36'48 5:46:27
Branchville 26 18 35N03'46 86w17'38 5:45:11
Bransford 83 50 36N30'15 86w16'12 5:45:05
Bratcher 89 46 35N42 85w46 5:43:04
Bratchers Crossroads 89
3 35N46'10 85w54'42 5:43:39
Brattontown 56 3 36N31'59 86w03'25 5:44:14
Braxton 8 3 35N49 86w04 5:44:16
Bray 34 51 36N25'24 83w19'40 5:33:19
Brayton 4 15 35N28'56 85w11'00 5:40:44
Braytown 1 62 36N09'29 84w22'40 5:37:30
Brazil 27 8 35N55'03 89w03'45 5:56:15
Breedenton 61 54 35N32'38 84w48'03 5:39:12
Brentlawn 74 35 36N30 86w53 5:47:32
Brentwood 47 67 35N57'22 84w05'43 5:36:23
Brentwood 94 3 36N01'59 86w46'58 5:47:08
Brentwood Mall 94
3 36N02 86w47 5:47:08
Brentwood Station 94
3 36N01'18 86w47'33 5:47:10
Brevards Landing 3
3 35N49'51 87w58'15 5:51:53
Brewer Addition 54
71 35N26'07 84w35'54 5:38:24
Brewstertown 65
51 36N21 84w35 5:38:20
Briar Thicket 15
65 36N06'35 83w07'43 5:32:31
Briarwood 16 13 35N22'35 86w12'47 5:44:51
Briarwood 63 32 36N30'56 87w23'04 5:49:32
Briceville 1 62 36N10'42 84w11'07 5:36:44
Brick Church 28
22 35N12 87w02 5:48:08
Brick Mill 5 64 35N39'25 84w06'12 5:36:25
Bride 84 44 35N36'01 89w43'22 5:58:53
Bridgeport 15 65 35N57'11 83w07'02 5:32:28
Bridwell Heights 82
1 36N32'54 82w27'21 5:29:49
Brier Hill 50 29 35N21'49 87w21'59 5:49:28
Bright Hope 30 65 36N05'43 82w58'17 5:31:53
Brighton 52 9 35N04'48 86w26'21 5:45:45
Brighton 84 3 35N29'02 89w43'30 5:58:54
Brims Corner 17
14 35N48'02 89w10'20 5:56:41
Bristol 82 2 36N35'42 82w11'20 5:28:45
Britton Ford 2 3 35N35'24 86w37'22 5:46:29
Britton Ford 40 3 36N15 88w09 5:52:36
Brittontown 30 65 36N16'22 82w47'12 5:31:09
Britts Landing 68
3 35N47'17 87w58'27 5:51:54
Brittsville 61 54 35N21'12 84w54'28 5:39:38
Broad Acres 47 67 36N01'54 84w02'52 5:36:11
Broadmoor 23 16 36N12'20 89w27'40 5:57:51
Broadview 17 3 35N50'23 89w15'35 5:57:02
Broadview 26 18 35N11'09 86w11'58 5:44:48
Broadview 60 31 35N29'35 87w05'53 5:48:24
Broadway 39 25 35N39 88w23 5:53:32
Brockdell 4 15 35N31'41 85w19'26 5:41:18
Brodies Landing 20
3 35N42'59 88w02'14 5:52:09
Bromley Ford 50
29 35N06'03 87w32'22 5:50:09
Brookfield Acres 47
67 36N05'19 83w51'42 5:35:27
Brooklin 19 4 36N03'01 86w36'53 5:46:28
Brooks Ferry 44
27 36N21 85w39 5:42:36
Brooks Ford 34 70 36N32'15 83w07'37 5:32:30
Brookside 7 66 36N15'10 84w20'54 5:37:24
Brookside Mill 15
65 36N00'56 83w05'51 5:32:23
Brotherton 71 34 36N11'20 85w22'45 5:41:31
Browder 53 68 35N48 84w16 5:37:04
Browder 58 8 35N04 85w39 5:42:36
Brown Crossroads 50
29 35N03'51 87w23'29 5:49:34
Brown Ellis 73 67 35N52'18 84w32'48 5:38:11
Brownington 26 18 35N14'41 86w16'00 5:45:04
Browningtown 26
18 35N21 86w12 5:44:48
Brown Mill 26 18 35N05'22 86w16'12 5:45:05
Browns 15 65 35N47'05 83w06'50 5:32:27
Browns 56 3 36N29'22 85w58'18 5:43:53
Browns Mill 75 3 35N54'08 86w16'51 5:45:07
Brownsport Landing 20
3 35N33'02 87w59'55 5:52:00
Browns Shop 59 3 35N19'16 86w42'11 5:46:49
Brownsville 38 24 35N35'38 89w15'44 5:57:03
Brownsville 42 3 36N21'36 87w43'21 5:50:53
Browntown 18 9 35N57'33 85w12'18 5:40:49
Broylesville 90
63 36N12'50 82w36'10 5:30:25
Bruceton 9 3 36N02'17 88w14'40 5:52:59
Bruceville 23 16 36N02 89w23 5:57:32
Brundige 92 3 36N25'46 88w39'24 5:54:38
Bruner Crossing 26
18 35N14'53 86w07'01 5:44:28
Bruner Grove 15
65 36N04'30 83w06'58 5:32:28
Brunswick 79 40 35N16'02 89w46'07 5:59:04
Brush Creek 77 3 35N24'41 85w23'05 5:41:32
Brush Creek 80 3 36N07'02 86w01'40 5:44:07
Brush Creek 94 3 36N00'26 87w04'53 5:48:20
Bruton Branch 36
3 35N04'33 88w10'53 5:52:44
Bryan Hill 72 74 35N29'50 85w00'09 5:40:01
Bryan Mill 16 12 35N33'59 85w56'16 5:43:45
Bryant Station 60
3 35N30'42 86w53'22 5:47:33
Bryson 28 3 35N05'55 86w51'42 5:47:27
Bryson Mountain 13
51 36N33'57 83w48'45 5:35:15

Brysonville 8 3 35N53'00 86W06'14 5:44:25
Buchanan 40 3 36N26 88W12 5:52:48
Buchanan Crossing 52
9 35N09'42 86W31'00 5:46:04
Buchanan Landing 40
3 36N24'56 88W06'42 5:52:27
Buckeye 7 66 36N24'26 84W17'37 5:37:10
Bucklick 65 56 36N10'02 84W51'32 5:39:26
Buck Lodge 83 50 36N35 86W31 5:46:04
Buckner 21 3 36N00'17 85W45'05 5:43:00
Bucks Mill 52 9 34N59'28 86W31'21 5:46:05
Bucksnort 41 3 35N53'08 87W41'04 5:50:44
Bucktown 36 23 35N16'12 88W11'42 5:52:47
Bucktown 53 68 35N46'52 84W16'53 5:37:08
Buena Vista 9 3 35N58'35 88W17'22 5:53:09
Buffalo 1 62 36N08'13 84W23'15 5:37:33
Buffalo 41 3 35N41'15 87W29'17 5:49:57
Buffalo 43 3 35N53'08 87W48'24 5:51:14
Buffalo 82 1 36N29'32 82W18'21 5:29:13
Buffalo Springs 29
55 36N13'04 83W33'47 5:34:15
Buffalo Valley 51
3 35N27'13 87W36'48 5:50:27
Buffalo Valley 71
3 36N08'29 85W47'12 5:43:09
Buffat Heights 47
67 36N00'52 83W52'45 5:35:31
Bufords 28 3 35N19'55 87W01'32 5:48:06
Bugscuffle 2 5 35N29'58 86W18'55 5:45:16
Bugtussle 56 3 36N37'25 85W52'35 5:43:30
Buladeen 10 1 36N27'35 82W01'07 5:28:04
Bullards Gap 44
27 36N21 85W39 5:42:36
Bull Creek 76 58 36N25 84W29 5:37:56
Bullet Creek 62
70 35N16'44 84W25'34 5:37:42
Bullpen Landing 79
40 35N18'04 90W06'48 6:00:27
Bull Run 19 4 36N16 87W04 5:48:16
Bulls Gap 37 70 36N15'25 83W05'10 5:32:21
Bumpus Cove 86 75 36N09'15 82W29'15 5:29:57
Bumpus Mills 81 3 36N36'17 87W50'15 5:51:21
Bunch Ford 91 3 35N27'05 87W49'59 5:51:20
Buncombe 82 1 36N30'42 82W19'02 5:29:16
Bungalow Town 5
64 35N45'40 83W59'33 5:35:58
Bunker Hill 28 22 35N08'22 86W52'35 5:47:30
Bunker Hill 75 3 35N42'36 86W35'58 5:46:24
Bunker Hill 82 1 36N25'11 82W14'57 5:29:00
Buntontown 46 1 36N17'30 81W58'24 5:27:54
Buntyn 79 39 35N07 89W57 5:59:48
Burbank 10 1 36N08'55 82W06'07 5:28:24
Burchfield Heights 47
67 35N59'18 84W10'57 5:36:44
Burem 37 70 36N24'54 82W55'13 5:31:41
Burgen 8 3 35N43'43 86W07'21 5:44:29
Burger 54 71 35N23'56 84W26'39 5:37:47
Burke 18 9 35N46'28 85W01'01 5:40:04
Burlington 47 67 35N59'26 83W52'45 5:35:31
Burlington Heights 6
53 35N12'15 84W51'40 5:39:27
Burlison 84 3 35N33'25 89W46'44 5:59:07
Burns 22 3 36N03'12 87W18'45 5:49:15
Burnt Church 36
23 35N14 88W14 5:52:56
Burristown 44 3 36N23'12 85W32'31 5:42:10
Burrus Landing 48
3 36N22'00 89W30'17 5:58:01
Burrville 65 56 36N17'38 84W45'06 5:39:00
Burt 8 3 35N46'09 86W07'46 5:44:31
Burton 37 70 36N24 83W00 5:32:00
Burton Mill 53 68 35N40'15 84W16'10 5:37:05
Burtons Landing 20
3 35N40'03 88W01'12 5:52:05
Burwood 94 3 35N48'45 86W59'00 5:47:56
Busby 50 29 35N06'24 87W24'35 5:49:38
Bushtown 33 61 35N02'58 85W16'03 5:41:04
Bussell Ford 13
51 36N32'56 83W34'56 5:34:20
Busselltown 53 68 35N46'31 84W14'04 5:36:56
Busseltown 20 3 35N40'21 88W02'08 5:52:09
Busy Corner 16 12 35N31'42 86W09'30 5:44:38
Butler 46 1 36N21'12 82W01'57 5:28:08
Butlers Landing 14
11 36N29'23 85W33'42 5:42:15
Bybee 15 65 36N02'53 83W10'46 5:32:43
Bybee 89 46 35N42 85W46 5:43:04
Byington 47 67 35N58'05 84W07'06 5:36:28
Byrdstown 69 3 36N34'28 85W07'44 5:40:31
Cabin Row 63 3 36N22 87W18 5:49:12
Cabo 12 3 35N25'50 88W28'27 5:53:54
Cactus Cove 5 64 35N50'33 84W05'50 5:36:23
Cades 27 8 35N58'33 88W47'00 5:55:08
Cades Cove 5 64 35N40 83W45 5:35:00
Caffey 55 3 35N03'29 88W29'41 5:53:59
Cagle 77 3 35N28'30 85W27'40 5:41:51
Caigletown 43 3 35N54'21 87W51'01 5:51:24
Cain Mill 32 67 36N15'55 83W11'55 5:32:48
Cainsville 95 49 35N59'07 86W14'56 5:45:00
Cairo 17 14 35N49'24 89W09'58 5:56:40
Cairo 83 42 36N21'39 86W21'49 5:45:27
Cairo Bend 95 34 36N14'20 86W24'01 5:45:36
Calderwood 5 64 35N30'33 83W59'39 5:35:59
Caldwell 2 6 35N30'13 86W22'56 5:45:32
Calfkiller 71 3 36N09 85W16 5:41:04
Calhoun 16 12 35N28 86W05 5:44:20
Calhoun 54 54 35N17'47 84W44'53 5:39:00
Calico 61 54 35N31'31 84W50'04 5:39:20
Calistia 74 3 36N30'46 88W39'57 5:46:40
Callie 94 48 35N49'56 86W51'01 5:47:24
Calls 16 12 35N20'46 86W00'19 5:44:01
Cal Place 26 19 35N02'20 86W03'44 5:44:15
Camargo 52 9 35N04'56 86W38'09 5:46:33
Cambria 54 54 35N16'54 84W32'11 5:38:09
Cambridge 89 3 35N47'35 85W41'45 5:42:47
Camden 3 7 36N03'32 88W05'52 5:52:23
Camelot 37 70 36N26'54 83W03'20 5:32:13
Camelot 47 67 35N59'48 84W06'33 5:36:26
Campaign 89 3 35N46'15 85W37'43 5:42:31
Camp Austin 65 51 35N59 84W33 5:38:12
Campbell Army Airfield 63
3 36N38 87W28 5:49:52
Campbell Junction 18
15 36N02'37 85W10'09 5:40:41
Campbells 60 3 35N29 86W59 5:47:56
Campbells Station 60
3 35N26'48 86W59'20 5:47:57
Campbellsville 28
3 35N20'14 87W07'50 5:48:31
Camp Creek 30 65 36N05'14 82W45'50 5:31:03
Camp Ground 25 3 36N11'20 85W03'08 5:40:13
Camp Ground 66 3 36N23'38 88W47'19 5:55:09
Camp Jordan 33 61 35N00'15 85W11'16 5:40:45
Camp Marymount 94
3 35N59 87W07 5:48:28
Camp Monterey Lake 71
3 36N09 85W16 5:41:04
Camp Ocoee 70 72 35N04'45 84W38'52 5:38:35
Camp Placid 82 1 36N31'15 82W20'25 5:29:22
Camp Tom Howard 82
1 36N32'20 81W59'36 5:27:58
Camp Wildwood 90
75 36N20'17 82W21'15 5:29:25
Canaan 60 31 35N35'08 87W10'59 5:48:44
Canaan 63 3 36N24'15 87W29'28 5:49:58
Canaan Grove 84
44 35N26'37 89W35'23 5:58:22
Canadaville 24 3 35N09'08 89W35'37 5:58:22
Canby Hills 47 67 35N57'00 84W03'40 5:36:15
Candlewyck 82 2 36N35 82W11 5:28:44
Cane Ridge 19 4 36N05 86W39 5:46:36
Caney Branch 30
65 36N02'48 82W59'00 5:31:56
Caney Creek 70 72 35N05'42 84W32'53 5:38:12
Caney Hollow 36 3 35N00'16 88W13'02 5:52:52
Caney Spring 59
30 35N27 86W48 5:47:12
Capital Hill 76
58 36N25 84W29 5:37:56
Capitol Hill 26
18 35N17'28 86W03'55 5:44:16
Capleville 79 40 35N01'14 89W53'52 5:59:35
Car Branch 13 51 36N26 83W36 5:34:24
Cardiff 73 70 35N53'26 84W37'52 5:38:31
Carlisle 81 3 36N25'29 87W45'25 5:51:02
Carlock 44 27 36N25'25 85W32'49 5:42:11
Carlock 54 54 35N17'29 84W33'09 5:38:13
Carlton 5 64 35N49'28 84W01'34 5:36:06
Carnegie 90 75 36N19'41 82W20'29 5:29:22
Carpenter Addition 47
67 36N02'43 83W48'37 5:35:14
Carpenter Campground 5
64 35N40'20 84W00'17 5:36:01
Carriage Hill 33
61 35N06'42 85W20'53 5:41:24
Carroll 57 3 35N43'06 88W49'12 5:55:17
Carroll Reece 90
75 36N19 82W21 5:29:24
Carson Spring 15
65 35N55'38 83W15'51 5:33:03
Carter 10 1 36N24'46 82W04'50 5:28:19
Carter 47 67 36N01'15 83W42'51 5:34:51
Carter Crossroads 2
3 35N40'10 86W31'30 5:46:06
Carters Creek 60
31 35N43'02 86W59'41 5:47:59
Carter Shields Place 5
64 35N35'22 83W47'55 5:35:12
Cartersville 60 3 35N43'16 87W14'44 5:48:59
Cartertown 78 59 35N44'14 83W29'06 5:33:56
Carthage 80 41 36N15'08 85W57'06 5:43:48
Carthage Junction 80
3 36N10'04 85W54'48 5:43:39
Cartwright 77 3 35N16'42 85W27'30 5:41:50
Cartwright 80 3 36N23'33 85W52'12 5:43:29
Caryville 7 66 36N17'56 84W13'24 5:36:54
Cash Point 52 9 35N01'05 86W48'19 5:47:13
Cassville 93 3 35N57'19 85W36'06 5:42:24
Castalian Springs 83
50 36N23'37 86W18'29 5:45:14
Castle Heights 15
65 35N57'13 83W09'33 5:32:38
Catalpa 59 3 35N19'10 86W42'43 5:46:51
Cataska 62 70 35N13'58 84W19'36 5:37:18
Cat Corner 66 3 36N12'49 89W24'51 5:57:39
Cates 48 3 36N26'37 89W28'39 5:57:55
Catlettsburg 78
60 35N54'16 83W34'52 5:34:19
Cato 85 3 36N23'50 86W02'03 5:44:08
Caton 78 60 35N48'01 83W27'03 5:33:48
Catons Grove 15
65 35N47'32 83W12'26 5:32:50
Catoosa 65 56 36N03'15 84W40'21 5:38:41
Cave 93 3 35N51 85W31 5:42:04
Cave Creek 73 67 35N48'50 84W23'15 5:37:33
Cave Mill 5 64 35N47'57 83W53'17 5:35:33
Cave Spring 13 51 36N30'17 83W33'24 5:34:14
Cave Spring 63 3 36N29'10 87W35'58 5:50:24
Cavvia 9 3 35N53 88W09 5:52:36
Cawood 13 51 36N27 83W55 5:35:40
Caywood Ford 82 2 36N30'49 82W07'48 5:28:31
Cedar Bluff 47 67 35N55'35 84W05'40 5:36:23
Cedar Bluff 78 60 35N51'16 83W26'06 5:33:44
Cedarbluff 85 3 36N12 86W18 5:45:12
Cedar Chapel 35 3 35N24'08 89W10'02 5:56:40
Cedar Creek 30 65 36N01'26 82W54'09 5:31:37
Cedar Creek Landing 68
3 35N32'56 87W59'26 5:51:58
Cedar Crest North 47
67 36N04'04 83W59'00 5:35:56
Cedarfork 13 51 36N27 83W34 5:34:16
Cedar Fork 73 68 35N41'03 04W31'57 5:38:08
Cedar Grove 2 3 35N38'39 86W37'34 5:46:30
Cedar Grove 9 3 35N49'01 88W35'44 5:54:23
Cedar Grove 10 1 36N18'30 82W18'49 5:29:15
Cedar Grove 39 3 35N28'55 88W16'04 5:53:04
Cedar Grove 43 3 35N56'46 87W48'39 5:51:15
Cedar Grove 69 3 36N33'26 85W03'22 5:40:13
Cedar Grove 73 67 35N50'42 84W27'46 5:37:51
Cedar Grove 82 1 36N28'48 82W11'19 5:28:45
Cedar Grove 83 42 36N20'41 86W26'35 5:45:46
Cedar Hill 74 3 36N33'05 86W59'57 5:48:00
Cedar Lane 30 65 36N21'25 82W39'44 5:30:39
Cedar Point Landing 84
3 35N27'55 89W59'26 5:59:58
Cedars 95 49 36N06 86W25 5:45:40
Cedar Springs 47
67 35N54'41 84W05'11 5:36:21
Cedar Springs 54
71 35N25'09 84W37'01 5:38:28
Cedar Valley 82 2 36N35 82W11 5:28:44
Celina 14 11 36N33'00 85W30'19 5:42:01
Center 17 3 35N47 89W00 5:56:00
Center 40 3 36N23 88W29 5:53:56
Center 50 29 35N21'14 87W27'06 5:49:48
Center 62 70 35N22 84W18 5:37:12
Center Ford 18 9 35N56'56 84W51'32 5:39:26
Center Grove 26
18 35N17'59 86W13'37 5:44:54
Center Grove 44
27 36N15'50 85W36'31 5:42:26
Center Hill 8 3 35N47'37 85W57'44 5:43:51
Center Hill 39 3 35N32'38 88W23'39 5:53:35
Center Point 12 3 35N23 88W26 5:53:44
Center Point 50
29 35N06'19 87W20'04 5:49:20
Center Point 77 3 35N18 85W22 5:41:28
Center Point 81 3 36N29 87W50 5:51:20
Center Point 93 3 35N53'10 85W36'55 5:42:28
Center Point Lula 12
3 35N27'58 88W22'22 5:53:29
Center Star 36 23 35N09'52 88W04'12 5:52:17
Center Star 41 3 35N41'54 87W19'43 5:49:19
Centersville 30
65 36N16'38 82W40'23 5:30:42
Centersville 53
68 35N42'52 84W12'27 5:36:50
Centertown 89 3 35N43'30 85W55'14 5:43:41
Centerview 15 65 36N04 83W09 5:32:36
Centerview 36 23 35N17'07 88W10'25 5:52:42
Centerville 30 65 36N13 82W38 5:30:32
Centerville 41 3 35N46'44 87W28'01 5:49:52
Centerville 95 34 36N17'22 86W12'24 5:44:50
Central 10 1 36N19'34 82W17'23 5:29:10
Central 27 8 35N58 88W57 5:55:48
Central 49 28 35N48'13 89W32'14 5:58:09
Central Heights 82
1 36N32 82W19 5:29:16
Central Point 29
55 36N17 83W31 5:34:04
Central State Hospital 19
4 36N08 86W42 5:46:48
Centreville 95 34 36N12 86W18 5:45:12
Cerro Gordo 36 23 35N18'13 88W10'50 5:52:43
Chalet Village 78
59 35N42'27 83W32'42 5:34:11
Chalklevel 3 3 35N59'12 88W03'54 5:52:16
Chalk Level 37 70 36N21'28 82W59'42 5:31:59
Chalybeate 88 3 35N33'31 85W30'40 5:42:03
Chambers 55 3 35N04'50 88W23'09 5:53:33
Champ 52 9 35N09'19 86W23'07 5:45:32
Chanceytown 70 73 35N03'11 84W23'02 5:37:32
Chandler 5 64 35N50'17 83W59'03 5:35:56
Chantay Acres 60
31 35N38'26 87W01'19 5:48:05
Chanute 69 3 36N36'21 85W03'35 5:40:14
Chapel Hill 39 25 35N35'55 88W29'12 5:53:57
Chapel Hill 59 3 35N37'35 86W41'36 5:46:46
Chapel Hill 60 9 35N38'01 87W15'06 5:49:00
Chapman Grove 73
67 35N49'18 84W34'50 5:38:19
Chapmans 28 22 35N10'35 87W01'10 5:48:05
Chapmansboro 11 9 36N18'44 87W08'29 5:48:34
Charity 64 3 35N09 86W35 5:46:20
Charleston 6 53 35N17'14 84W45'30 5:39:02
Charleston 84 3 35N29'45 89W30'32 5:58:02
Charleys Branch 1
62 36N11'35 84W20'00 5:37:20
Charlotte 22 3 36N10'38 87W20'23 5:49:22
Charlotte Park 19
4 36N08'59 86W53'06 5:47:32
Chaseville 3 3 35N52'38 88W06'47 5:52:27
Chaska 7 66 36N31'44 84W04'39 5:36:19
Chattanooga 33 61 35N02'44 85W18'35 5:41:14
Cheap Hill 11 9 36N19'57 87W09'22 5:48:37
Cheeks Crossroads 32
67 36N15'01 83W12'45 5:32:51
Chennault Ford 52
9 35N08'55 86W30'42 5:46:03
Cherokee 29 55 36N12'26 83W29'52 5:33:59
Cherokee 90 75 36N16'27 82W23'04 5:29:32
Cherokee Heights 5
64 35N46 83W58 5:35:52
Cherokee Hills 73
67 35N51'29 84W30'17 5:38:01
Cherokee Hills 78
60 35N51'45 83W30'50 5:34:03
Cherokee Park 5
64 35N46 83W58 5:35:52
Cherokee Ridge 47
67 36N00'16 84W01'01 5:36:04
Cherokee Woods 33
61 35N04'23 85W12'34 5:40:50
Cherry 49 3 35N40'36 89W42'30 5:58:50
Cherrybrook 47 67 36N00'46 84W00'42 5:36:03
Cherry Corner 59
3 35N19'56 86W49'42 5:47:19
Cherry Crossroads 14
3 36N35'35 85W43'57 5:42:56
Cherry Hill 21 3 36N04'27 85W43'40 5:42:55
Cherry Valley 95
9 36N05'54 86W09'50 5:44:39
Cherrywood 9 3 36N05'34 88W30'52 5:54:03
Chesney 87 52 36N13'48 83W42'45 5:34:51
Chesterfield 39
25 35N38'04 88W16'01 5:53:04
Chestnutbloom 32
67 36N13 83W17 5:33:08
Chestnut Bluff 17
3 35N51'45 89W19'59 5:57:20
Chestnut Grove 34
70 36N31'20 83W06'44 5:32:27
Chestnut Grove 68
3 35N37'48 87W48'34 5:51:14
Chestnut Grove 74
3 36N24'48 86W54'27 5:47:38
Chestnut Grove 81
3 36N29 87W50 5:51:20

Chestnut Grove 87 52 36N15 83w48 5:35:12
Chestnut Hill 3 3 36N05'34 88w00'20 5:52:01
Chestnut Hill 45 67 35N55'48 83w20'25 5:33:22
Chestnut Hill 83 50 36N33'15 86w24'00 5:45:36
Chestnut Mound 80 3 36N12'10 85w49'35 5:43:18
Chestnut Ridge 64 9 35N20'05 86w32'18 5:46:09
Chestnut Valley 62 70 35N25'51 84w10'26 5:36:42
Chestoa 86 1 36N06'20 82w26'43 5:29:47
Chestua 62 67 35N31 84w22 5:37:28
Chestuee 6 53 35N07'50 84w46'51 5:39:07
Chestuee 62 67 35N27'59 84w25'02 5:37:40
Chewalla 55 3 35N00'48 88w38'47 5:54:35
Chic 23 16 35N56'47 89w38'48 5:58:35
Chickamauga 33 61 35N02 85w11 5:40:44
Chickasaw Heights 40 26 36N18'38 88w18'20 5:53:13
Childers Hill 36 3 35N04'42 88w19'30 5:53:18
Childress 82 1 36N25'40 82w15'49 5:29:03
Chilhowee 5 64 35N33'26 84w00'38 5:36:03
Chilhowee Hills 47 67 36N00'27 83w51'01 5:35:24
Chilhowee View 5 64 35N42'52 83w55'18 5:35:41
China Grove 27 21 36N08 88w55 5:55:40
Chinquapin Grove 82 1 36N26'35 82w12'48 5:28:51
Chinubee 50 29 35N07'23 87w31'07 5:50:04
Chipman 83 50 36N26'55 86w16'45 5:45:07
Chittum 13 51 36N27 83w34 5:34:16
Choptack 37 70 36N24'15 83w05'51 5:32:23
Chota 5 64 35N37'01 84w02'13 5:36:09
Choto Estates 47 64 35N49'18 84w08'50 5:36:35
Choto Hills 5 64 35N48'53 84w08'08 5:36:33
Christiana 75 36 35N42'36 86w23'58 5:45:36
Christian Bend 37 70 36N28'30 82w47'41 5:31:11
Christianburg 62 71 35N32'13 84w26'35 5:37:46
Christie Hill 5 64 35N46 83w58 5:35:52
Christmasville 9 3 36N05'36 88w38'51 5:54:35
Christmasville 38 24 35N40'58 89w17'42 5:57:11
Chuckey 30 65 36N12'57 82w41'18 5:30:45
Church Hill 37 70 36N31'20 82w42'49 5:30:51
Churchton 23 16 36N07'09 89w10'39 5:56:43
Churchwell Landing 36 3 35N04'56 88w17'32 5:53:10
Cinder Ford 81 3 36N20'26 87w53'26 5:51:34
Citico Beach 62 67 35N32'12 84w06'27 5:36:26
Clack Branch 50 29 35N05'43 87w28'27 5:49:54
Clacks Gap 73 67 35N56 84w33 5:38:12
Clairfield 13 51 36N33'00 83w57'01 5:35:48
Clareville 27 21 36N12 89w01 5:56:04
Clark Addition 5 64 35N46 83w58 5:35:52
Clarketown 10 1 36N10'19 82w12'44 5:28:51
Clarkrange 25 3 36N11'00 85w01'03 5:40:04
Clarksburg 9 3 35N52'18 88w23'35 5:53:34
Clarksville 63 32 36N31'47 87w21'34 5:49:26
Clarksville Base 63 3 36N38 87w28 5:49:52
Clarktown 93 3 35N55'59 85w18'36 5:41:14
Claxton 1 62 36N02'30 84w06'36 5:36:26
Claxton 54 71 35N18'14 84w38'40 5:38:35
Claybrook 57 3 35N42'30 88w38'03 5:54:32
Clay Hill 59 3 35N34'10 86w40'27 5:46:42
Claylick 22 3 36N09'31 87w13'01 5:48:52
Claysville 18 15 35N58'09 85w08'58 5:40:36
Clayton 66 3 36N27'33 89w14'19 5:56:57
Clearbranch 86 1 36N03'15 82w30'59 5:30:04
Clearmont 89 3 35N43'31 85w58'58 5:43:56
Clear Springs 30 65 36N13 82w38 5:30:32
Clear Springs 47 67 36N08'49 83w52'50 5:35:31
Clear Springs 54 54 35N27'44 84w45'54 5:39:04
Clearwater 54 71 35N30'19 84w39'03 5:38:36
Clementsville 14 3 36N36'42 85w43'33 5:42:54
Cleveland 6 53 35N09'34 84w52'36 5:39:30
Clevenger 15 65 35N58 83w11 5:32:44
Click Mill 15 65 35N53'49 83w05'05 5:32:20
Cliffside 82 2 36N30'54 82w31'16 5:30:05
Cliff Springs 67 3 36N10'50 85w09'03 5:40:36
Clifton 91 3 35N23'13 87w59'43 5:51:59
Clifton Hills 33 61 35N00'33 85w17'47 5:41:11
Clifton Junction 91 3 35N18'31 87w56'56 5:51:48
Clifty 93 9 35N54'01 85w13'12 5:40:53
Climer 6 53 35N10'33 84w45'29 5:39:02
Clinchmore 7 66 36N13'10 84w16'56 5:37:08
Clinch View 1 62 36N05'10 84w08'18 5:36:33
Clinton 1 62 36N06'12 84w07'55 5:36:32
Clopton 84 3 35N27'38 89w40'17 5:58:41
Cloud Creek 37 70 36N24'13 83w08'16 5:32:33
Cloud Ford 82 2 36N35'22 82w36'20 5:30:25
Clouds 13 51 36N27'33 83w38'57 5:34:36
Clouse Hill 31 3 35N16 85w44 5:42:56
Clovercroft 94 48 35N55'25 86w46'00 5:47:04
Cloverdale 66 3 36N14'02 89w19'49 5:57:19
Cloverdale 79 40 35N20 89w53 5:59:32
Clover Hill 5 64 35N42'16 84w02'59 5:36:12
Cloverhill 19 4 36N09'23 86w39'30 5:46:38
Cloverport 35 3 35N23'51 89w01'03 5:56:04
Club Springs 80 3 36N09'28 85w51'30 5:43:26
Clydeton Landing 43 3 36N10'30 87w55'10 5:51:41
Coal Chute 10 1 36N20 82w13 5:28:52
Coalfield 65 51 36N01'44 84w25'15 5:37:41
Coal Hill 65 51 35N59'45 84w27'36 5:37:50
Coal Hill 76 58 36N18'28 84w36'47 5:38:27
Coaling 22 3 36N18'02 87w15'48 5:49:03
Coalmont 31 3 35N20'15 85w42'15 5:42:49
Cobbs 17 3 35N43 89w05 5:56:20
Coble 41 3 35N46'59 87w37'57 5:50:32
Cochran 59 30 35N25'23 86w48'06 5:47:12
Coffee Landing 36 3 35N16'14 88w17'35 5:53:10
Coffee Ridge 86 1 36N01'26 82w30'32 5:30:02
Coile 54 71 35N25'41 84w39'06 5:38:36
Coker Creek 62 70 35N15'56 84w17'09 5:37:09
Cold Spring 4 15 35N39'37 85w08'45 5:40:35
Cold Spring 46 1 36N30'24 81w49'22 5:27:17
Cold Spring 82 1 36N34'27 82w04'04 5:28:16
Cold Springs 5 64 35N44 83w49 5:35:16
Cold Springs 37 70 36N31'10 82w50'56 5:31:24
Coldwater 52 9 35N05'04 86w44'01 5:46:56
Coleman Heights 59 30 35N26'38 86w46'59 5:47:08
Colesburg 22 3 36N03'45 87w20'44 5:49:23
Coles Store 71 3 36N09 85w38 5:42:32
Coletown 70 73 35N00'14 84w22'12 5:37:29
College 4 15 35N22 85w23 5:41:32
College 5 64 35N46 83w58 5:35:52
Collegedale 33 61 35N03'11 85w03'01 5:40:12
College Grove 94 3 35N47'18 86w40'28 5:46:42
College Hill 72 74 35N29'11 85w01'19 5:40:05
College Park 10 1 36N17'50 82w18'36 5:29:14
College Park Estates 5 64 35N43'09 83w56'34 5:35:46
Collier Landing 63 3 36N27'26 87w32'16 5:50:09
Colliers Corner 45 67 36N06'20 83w24'00 5:33:36
Collierville 79 40 35N02'31 89w39'52 5:58:39
Collins 31 3 35N22'50 85w34'28 5:42:18
Collins 37 70 36N24 83w00 5:32:00
Collins Mill 13 51 36N25'02 83w45'48 5:35:03
Collins Mill 54 54 35N34'53 84w40'21 5:38:41
Collinwood 91 3 35N10'27 87w44'16 5:50:57
Colonial Heights 82 2 36N29'06 82w30'12 5:30:01
Colonial Village 47 67 35N55'10 83w52'58 5:35:32
Columbia 60 31 35N36'54 87w02'07 5:48:08
Columbia Gardens 60 31 35N36'58 87w04'37 5:48:18
Columbia Hill 67 3 36N11'55 85w12'31 5:40:50
Columbus Hill 44 27 36N23'11 85w37'20 5:42:29
Combs 13 51 36N30'04 83w41'22 5:34:45
Comfort 58 8 35N07'39 85w44'32 5:42:58
Commerce 95 9 36N08'24 86w06'12 5:44:25
Como 40 3 36N17'35 88w30'44 5:54:03
Compton 76 37 35N54'17 86w19'44 5:45:19
Conasauga 1 62 35N59 84w18 5:37:12
Conasauga 54 54 35N19'47 84w28'36 5:37:54
Conasauga 70 72 35N00'16 84w43'46 5:38:55
Conasauga Heights 1 62 36N01'54 84w11'57 5:36:48
Conasauga Mill 62 70 35N18'37 84w21'25 5:37:26
Concord 9 3 35N55'45 88w21'57 5:53:28
Concord 27 8 35N58'43 88w49'59 5:55:20
Concord 43 3 36N13'48 87w46'07 5:51:04
Concord 47 67 35N52'07 84w08'31 5:36:34
Concord 72 74 35N35'51 84w54'36 5:39:38
Concord 75 3 35N44'29 86w33'18 5:46:13
Condon 87 67 36N10'52 83w47'38 5:35:11
Condra 58 3 35N15'52 85w28'00 5:41:52
Conkintown 82 2 36N27'58 82w39'49 5:30:39
Conklin 90 75 36N11'24 82w32'26 5:30:10
Conner Heights 78 60 35N46'16 83w32'34 5:34:10
Conway 28 3 35N05'28 86w57'13 5:47:49
Conyersville 40 3 36N26'59 88w17'39 5:53:11
Cooke Landing 72 74 35N35'14 84w48'24 5:39:14
Cookeville 71 34 36N09'46 85w30'06 5:42:00
Cook Mill 45 67 35N59'36 83w33'50 5:34:15
Cook Mill 73 68 35N41'37 84w32'07 5:38:08
Cooktown 25 3 36N20'23 85w07'27 5:40:30
Cool Springs 27 21 36N09'46 89w08'19 5:56:33
Cooper Ford 51 29 35N28'11 87w26'27 5:49:46
Cooper Mill 4 15 35N37'51 85w09'10 5:40:37
Coopers 9 3 36N02 88w15 5:53:00
Coopertown 74 3 36N26'15 86w58'02 5:47:52
Copperhill 70 73 34N59'20 84w22'15 5:37:29
Copper Ridge 47 67 36N07'56 83w54'49 5:35:39
Coptown 26 18 35N00'03 86w10'25 5:44:42
Coran 37 70 36N21'34 83w00'42 5:32:03
Corbandale 63 3 36N26'55 87w30'47 5:50:03
Corbin Hill 65 51 36N02 84w20 5:37:20
Cordell 76 58 36N20'13 84w26'58 5:37:48
Corder Crossroads 52 9 35N05'08 86w28'24 5:45:54
Cordova 79 40 35N09'20 89w46'34 5:59:06
Corinth 47 67 36N03'54 83w53'05 5:35:32
Corinth 83 50 36N34'40 86w25'32 5:45:42
Cornersville 59 3 35N21'41 86w50'23 5:47:22
Coro Lake 79 39 35N04 90w04 6:00:16
Corona 84 3 35N26'43 90w04'57 6:00:20
Corryton 47 67 36N09'13 83w46'57 5:35:08
Cortner 2 3 35N28'06 86w16'35 5:45:06
Cortners Mill 2 3 35N28'30 86w16'21 5:45:05
Cosby 15 65 35N49'02 83w14'49 5:32:59
Coster Yards 47 67 35N59'12 83w56'37 5:35:46
Cottage Grove 40 3 36N22'45 88w28'45 5:53:55
Cottage Home 95 49 35N59'27 86w02'00 5:44:08
Cotton Lake 84 44 35N33'43 89w30'19 5:58:01
Cotton Patch Crossroads 42 3 36N21'09 87w57'00 5:51:48
Cottonport 61 54 35N31 84w47 5:39:08
Cottontown 83 50 36N27'05 86w32'17 5:46:09
Cottonwood Grove 48 3 36N13'43 89w31'30 5:58:06
Cotula 7 66 36N28'42 84w03'15 5:36:13
Couchville 19 4 36N12 86w37 5:46:28
Coulter Shoals 53 64 35N47'59 84w10'59 5:36:44
Coulterville 33 61 35N24'36 85w06'18 5:40:25
Counce 36 3 35N02'32 88w16'24 5:53:06
Country Club Estates 82 2 36N35 82w11 5:28:44
County Corner 9 3 35N49'03 88w10'51 5:52:43
County Line 29 55 36N20 83w22 5:33:28
Countyline 64 33 35N19'23 86w22'08 5:45:29
Courtland 74 3 36N28'12 86w50'39 5:47:23
Courtland Place 30 65 35N56'38 82w49'03 5:31:16
Cove Creek 7 66 36N18 84w13 5:36:52
Cove Creek 10 1 36N12 82w05 5:28:20
Cove Creek Cascades 78 60 35N45'46 83w37'14 5:34:29
Cove Lake Estates 7 66 36N18'02 84w12'37 5:36:50
Covington 84 44 35N33'51 89w38'47 5:58:35
Cowan 26 18 35N09'52 86w00'38 5:44:03
Cowan Springs 5 64 35N45'01 83w48'33 5:35:14
Cowanstown 46 1 36N20 82w00 5:28:00
Cowards 47 67 35N58 83w58 5:35:52
Cowden 59 30 35N30'53 86w46'18 5:47:05
Cowenville 80 3 36N09 85w57 5:43:48
Cow Ford 68 3 35N34'08 87w49'12 5:51:17
Coxburg 3 3 35N53'57 88w02'10 5:52:09
Coxville 17 3 35N49'59 89w01'32 5:56:06
Cozette 20 3 35N45'30 88w04'07 5:52:16
Crab Orchard 18 9 35N54'33 84w52'41 5:39:31
Crabtree 10 1 36N12'14 82w06'15 5:28:25
Crackers Neck 46 1 36N23'39 81w49'06 5:27:16
Craft Spring 30 65 36N16'24 82w48'37 5:31:14
Craggie Hope 11 9 36N05'33 87w09'00 5:48:36
Craigfield 94 3 35N54'49 87w11'13 5:48:45
Crandull 46 1 36N32'49 81w53'46 5:27:35
Cranmore Cove 72 74 35N30'05 85w03'03 5:40:12
Craveltown 80 3 36N23 85w57 5:43:48
Cravens Landing 36 23 35N18'20 88w12'17 5:52:49
Cravenstown 67 3 36N18'18 85w07'40 5:40:31
Crawford 67 3 36N16'09 85w09'39 5:40:39
Creek Side 60 31 35N35'40 87w01'38 5:48:07
Creekwood 2 6 35N28'00 86w28'41 5:45:55
Crenshaw 47 67 35N53'18 83w56'16 5:35:45
Crescent 75 37 35N45'02 86w26'34 5:45:46
Crescent View 28 22 35N09'10 87w01'23 5:48:06
Creson 52 9 35N10'07 86w33'05 5:46:12
Creston 18 15 36N00'31 85w04'31 5:40:18
Crestwood 73 67 35N50'17 84w30'02 5:38:00
Crestwood Hills 47 67 35N55'43 84w04'32 5:36:18
Crewstown 50 29 35N10'48 87w26'28 5:49:46
Crieve Hall 19 4 36N06 86w45 5:47:00
Crippen Gap 47 67 36N02 83w56 5:35:44
Crisp Spring 8 3 35N39'55 85w52'41 5:43:31
Crockett 66 3 36N17'53 89w02'34 5:56:10
Crockett Mills 17 3 35N52'03 89w10'09 5:56:41
Cromwell Crossroads 91 3 35N08'12 87w49'42 5:51:19
Cronanville 48 3 36N26'04 89w28'38 5:57:55
Cross 82 1 36N33'38 82w17'24 5:29:10
Cross Anchor 30 65 36N13 82w48 5:31:12
Cross Bridges 60 9 35N32 87w12 5:48:48
Cross Keys 94 3 35N48 86w40 5:46:40
Crossland 40 3 36N30'03 88w22'49 5:53:31
Cross Lanes 56 3 36N31'20 86w08'58 5:44:36
Cross Plains 74 3 36N32'55 86w41'46 5:46:47
Crossroads 3 3 36N00'02 88w08'51 5:52:35
Crossroads 17 3 35N44'36 89w07'59 5:56:32
Cross Roads 21 3 35N57'25 85w52'02 5:43:28
Cross Roads 23 3 35N53'12 89w19'54 5:57:20
Crossroads 36 23 35N17'59 88w07'25 5:52:30
Crossroads 41 3 35N43'09 87w31'02 5:50:04
Cross Roads 50 29 35N19'01 87w20'55 5:49:24
Cross Roads 56 3 36N36'48 86w09'11 5:44:37
Crossroads 79 40 35N07'40 89w39'26 5:58:38
Crossroads 91 3 35N03'46 87w43'40 5:50:55
Crosstown 84 3 35N26'44 89w47'33 5:59:10
Crossville 18 15 35N56'56 85w01'37 5:40:06
Crouch Crossroad 90 75 36N22'40 82w24'29 5:29:38
Crow 22 3 36N03 87w19 5:49:16
Crowley Store 92 3 36N08'12 88w41'34 5:54:46
Crowtexas 36 23 35N16'28 88w06'43 5:52:27
Crucifer 39 3 35N38'46 88w33'00 5:54:12
Crump 36 3 35N13'18 88w19'05 5:53:16
Crump Landing 36 3 35N12'57 88w18'33 5:53:14
Crunk 74 3 36N25'26 86w53'37 5:47:34
Crystal 66 3 36N27'46 89w10'32 5:56:42
Crystal Springs 52 9 35N04'27 86w27'39 5:45:51
Cuba 37 70 36N22'39 83w07'52 5:32:31
Cuba 79 40 35N21'05 89w59'14 5:59:57
Cuba Landing 43 3 35N52'45 87w55'58 5:51:44
Cub Creek 44 27 36N24'01 85w42'57 5:42:52
Culleoka 60 3 35N28'46 86w58'59 5:47:56
Culpepper 8 3 35N49'06 86w08'34 5:44:34
Culvahouse 61 54 35N41'47 84w41'59 5:38:48
Cumberland City 81 3 36N23'36 87w38'11 5:50:33
Cumberland Estates 47 67 35N59'02 84w00'46 5:36:03

Cumberland Furnace 22 3 36N16'07 87w21'35 5:49:26
Cumberland Gap 13 51 36N35'58 83w40'07 5:34:40
Cumberland Heights 19 4 36N11'47 86w46'49 5:47:07
Cumberland Heights 31 3 35N24'20 85w41'48 5:42:47
Cumberland Heights 63 3 36N29'27 87w23'58 5:49:36
Cumberland Homesteads 18 15 35N54'30 84w56'43 5:39:47
Cumberland Plateau 4 15 35N39 85w15 5:41:00
Cumberland Spring 72 74 35N31'29 85w02'13 5:40:09
Cumberland Springs 64 3 35N20'29 86w17'43 5:45:11
Cumberland Springs 72 74 35N01 85w11 5:40:44
Cumberland View 7 66 36N20 84w11 5:36:44
Cumberland View Estates 1 62 36N13'55 84w08'33 5:36:34
Cummings Crossroads 83 50 36N28'42 86w34'34 5:46:18
Cummingsville 88 3 35N48'30 85w27'44 5:41:51
Cunningham 63 3 36N23'36 87w23'14 5:49:33
Curlee 8 3 35N46'39 86w09'34 5:44:38
Currie 27 21 36N02'35 89w02'34 5:56:10
Curtistown 88 3 35N34'24 85w35'00 5:42:20
Curve 49 28 35N48'17 89w27'24 5:57:50
Cusick 53 67 35N51'04 84w13'18 5:36:53
Cusick 78 60 35N50'52 83w42'34 5:34:50
Cypress 17 14 35N45'40 89w04'05 5:56:16
Cypress 55 3 35N01'41 88w42'29 5:54:50
Cypress Creek 40 3 36N26 88w12 5:52:48
Cypress Inn 91 3 35N00'43 87w49'00 5:51:16
Cyruston 52 9 35N09 86w35 5:46:20
Daisy 33 61 35N14'52 85w11'11 5:40:45
Dale Acres 33 61 35N07'25 85w14'45 5:40:59
Dale Hollow 14 11 36N33 85w30 5:42:00
Dalewood 19 4 36N12'20 86w42'57 5:46:52
Dallas Crest 33 61 35N05'31 85w17'35 5:41:10
Dallas Gardens 33 61 35N12'35 85w09'44 5:40:39
Dallas Heights 33 61 35N05'10 85w17'46 5:41:11
Dallas Hills 33 61 35N12'29 85w08'54 5:40:36
Damascus 46 1 36N26'21 81w54'44 5:27:39
Damon 36 3 35N00'41 88w19'45 5:53:19
Dancyville 24 3 35N24'28 89w17'38 5:57:11
Dandridge 45 67 36N00'55 83w24'54 5:33:40
Daniels Landing 68 3 35N49'10 87w58'05 5:51:52
Daniels Point Landing 49 3 35N46'28 89w47'51 5:59:11
Dante 47 67 36N01'36 83w59'35 5:35:58
Darden 39 3 35N38'17 88w13'01 5:52:52
Darkey Springs 93 3 35N53'48 85w35'22 5:42:21
Daus 77 3 35N18'52 85w26'03 5:41:44
Davidson 25 3 36N16'39 85w06'18 5:40:25
Davidson 69 3 36N34'05 85w01'21 5:40:05
Davis 53 68 35N43'59 84w15'12 5:37:01
Davis Chapel 9 3 36N00 88w25 5:53:40
Davis Ford 5 64 35N46'40 83w51'14 5:35:25
Davis Ford 51 3 35N27'39 87w32'59 5:50:12
Davis Springs 86 1 36N10'37 82w16'33 5:29:06
Davy Crockett 30 65 36N13 82w48 5:31:12
Daylight 89 46 35N44'45 85w51'27 5:43:26
Days Crossroads 56 3 36N30'37 85w59'15 5:43:57
Daysville 18 9 35N53'41 84w46'12 5:39:05
Dayton 72 74 35N29'38 85w00'45 5:40:03
Daytona Hills 33 61 35N06 85w17 5:41:08
Dayton Spur 18 15 35N57'36 84w59'32 5:39:58
Dean 76 58 36N20'41 84w21'14 5:37:25
Deanburg 12 3 35N24'44 88w48'21 5:55:13
Deane Hill 47 67 35N55'45 84w01'10 5:36:05
Deans 41 3 35N44'15 87w28'26 5:49:54
DeArmond 73 67 35N58'05 84w29'00 5:37:56
Deason 75 5 35N36'12 86w26'12 5:45:45
Decatur 61 54 35N30'53 84w47'25 5:39:10
Decatur Hills 61 54 35N31'53 84w48'01 5:39:12
Decaturville 20 3 35N35'03 88w07'10 5:52:29
Decherd 26 18 35N12'35 86w04'46 5:44:19
Deep Springs 1 62 36N05 84w03 5:36:12
Deep Springs 45 67 35N59'25 83w31'00 5:34:04
Deerfield 50 29 35N18'10 87w28'30 5:49:54
Deerfield Acres 82 2 36N32'36 82w09'46 5:28:39
Deer Lodge 65 56 36N12'05 84w45'33 5:39:02
Deermont 65 68 36N01'34 84w35'20 5:38:21
Defeated 80 41 36N19'35 85w54'30 5:43:38
Delano 70 72 35N15'54 84w33'12 5:38:13
De Lap 7 66 36N20'54 84w09'23 5:36:38
Delina 59 3 35N16'04 86w44'10 5:46:57
Dellrose 52 9 35N06'47 86w48'05 5:47:12
Dellwood 5 64 35N46'17 83w54'52 5:35:39
Del Rio 15 65 35N55'11 83w01'33 5:32:06
Demory 7 66 36N20'11 84w03'58 5:36:16
Denmark 42 3 36N20'18 87w43'45 5:50:55
Denmark 57 3 35N31'58 89w00'14 5:56:01
Dennis Cove 10 1 36N17 82w10 5:28:40
Denny Seminary 71 3 36N05 85w44 5:42:56
Densons Landing 68 3 35N45'55 87w59'05 5:51:56
Denton 15 65 35N50'59 83w11'14 5:32:45
Denton Crossroads 14 3 36N35'01 85w39'18 5:42:37
Dentville 54 54 35N16'54 84w36'25 5:38:26
Denver 8 3 35N50 86w10 5:44:40
Denver 43 3 36N02'49 87w55'15 5:51:41
DePriest Bend 68 3 35N44'17 87w48'39 5:51:15
De Rossett 93 3 35N57'02 85w18'32 5:41:14
DeRusk 30 65 36N06'55 82w52'10 5:31:29
Desha 83 42 36N25'45 86w21'51 5:45:27
Detroit 84 3 35N35'20 89w48'49 5:59:15
Devonia 1 62 36N09 84w23 5:37:32
Diana 28 3 35N17'02 86w51'20 5:47:25
Dibrell 89 3 35N48'43 85w47'31 5:43:10
Dickel 16 13 35N21 86w12 5:44:48
Dickey Landing 20 3 35N23'35 88w09'50 5:52:39
Dickson 22 3 36N04'37 87w23'16 5:49:33
Dickson Town 28 3 35N02'47 86w52'44 5:47:31
Difficult 80 3 36N22'09 85w53'32 5:43:34
Dill 4 15 35N36 85w11 5:40:44
Dilley 13 51 36N33 83w59 5:35:56
Dillton 75 37 35N48'02 86w19'23 5:45:18
Disco 5 64 35N47'09 84w09'30 5:36:38
Dismal 21 3 36N00 85w58 5:43:52
Disney 7 66 36N14'55 84w10'17 5:36:41
Ditty 71 3 36N05'38 85w34'50 5:42:19
Dixie 66 3 36N25'43 89w12'21 5:56:49
Dixie Lee 58 8 35N02'36 85w41'10 5:42:45
Dixie Lee Junction 53 67 35N51'38 84w13'33 5:36:54
Dixie Mills 20 3 35N36'53 88w10'58 5:52:44
Dixon Springs 80 3 36N21'32 86w03'09 5:44:13
Dixonville 84 3 35N25'23 89w56'45 5:59:47
Doaks Crossroads 95 34 36N06'32 86w14'37 5:44:58
Dockery 6 53 35N07'02 84w53'24 5:39:34
Doddsville 11 10 36N20'32 87w13'45 5:48:55
Dodson 73 70 35N52'35 84w37'00 5:38:28
Dodson 93 3 35N48'45 85w22'23 5:41:30
Dodson Branch 44 27 36N18'45 85w31'56 5:42:08
Dodson Estates 19 4 36N12 86w37 5:46:28
Doeville 46 1 36N23'22 81w58'12 5:27:53
Dog Hill 17 3 35N50'27 89w16'59 5:57:08
Dogtown 10 1 36N19'57 82w08'42 5:28:35
Dogtown 31 3 35N20'58 85w41'13 5:42:45
Dogwood 18 67 35N49'50 84w48'41 5:39:15
Dogwood 73 67 35N47'15 84w25'21 5:37:41
Dogwood Flat 41 3 35N50'34 87w20'50 5:49:23
Dogwood Shores 73 67 35N45'33 84w26'22 5:37:45
Dollar 9 3 35N54'36 88w15'36 5:53:02
Dolomite 42 3 36N21'40 87w39'28 5:50:38
Donegan Crossing 22 3 36N05'59 87w27'54 5:49:52
Donelson 19 4 36N09'45 86w40'12 5:46:41
Donnels Chapel 75 3 35N50 86w10 5:44:40
Donoho 80 41 36N18'46 85w52'05 5:43:28
Doran Addition 82 2 36N35'13 82w33'00 5:30:12
Dortch Landing 81 3 36N23'46 88w00'33 5:52:02
Dorton 18 15 35N57'10 84w57'22 5:39:49
Dossett 1 62 36N03'45 84w13'29 5:36:54
Doss Ford 74 3 36N35'11 86w44'12 5:46:57
Dotson 29 55 36N20'08 83w29'50 5:33:59
Dotson Branch 44 3 36N11 85w28 5:41:52
Dotson's Camp Ground 29 55 36N17 83w36 5:34:24
Dotsontown 30 65 36N14'18 82w39'56 5:30:40
Dotsonville 63 3 36N28'57 87w29'11 5:49:57
Double Bridges 49 3 35N54'18 89w27'13 5:57:49
Double Springs 54 71 35N19'16 84w38'05 5:38:32
Double Springs 71 3 36N10'16 85w35'51 5:42:23
Double Springs 75 37 35N50'08 86w19'56 5:45:20
Double Springs 82 2 36N26'05 82w33'54 5:30:16
Double Top 25 3 36N29'10 85w03'24 5:40:14
Douglas 52 9 35N08'54 86w29'27 5:45:58
Douglas 94 48 35N52'17 86w50'44 5:47:23
Douglas Estates 45 67 35N59'56 83w21'40 5:33:27
Dover 81 3 36N29'16 87w50'18 5:51:21
Dover Landing 81 3 36N26'59 88w02'48 5:52:11
Dowelltown 21 3 36N00'54 85w56'37 5:43:46
Dowler Heights 33 61 35N10'53 85w20'26 5:41:22
Doyle 93 3 35N51'11 85w30'45 5:42:03
Doyle Springs 78 60 35N46'03 83w43'25 5:34:54
Drake Forest 33 61 35N01'56 85w08'29 5:40:34
Drapers Crossroads 56 3 36N30'43 85w54'32 5:43:38
Dresden 92 47 36N17'29 88w42'29 5:54:50
Driftwood 82 2 36N35 82w11 5:28:44
Drop 93 3 35N56 85w28 5:41:52
Drummonds 84 3 35N27'48 89w54'36 5:59:38
Dry Creek 90 75 36N12'24 82w26'07 5:29:44
Dry Hill 46 1 36N19'35 81w57'04 5:27:48
Dry Hill 49 3 35N50'17 89w28'50 5:57:55
Dry Hill 73 70 35N54'36 84w39'17 5:38:37
Duck Creek 34 51 36N29'28 83w13'24 5:32:54
Duck River 41 3 35N44 87w17 5:49:08
Ducktown 70 73 35N02'09 84w22'58 5:37:32
Ducktown 90 63 36N20'09 82w37'45 5:30:31
Dudney Hill 44 27 36N19'56 85w37'44 5:42:31
Due West 19 4 36N16 86w43 5:46:52
Duff 7 66 36N26'48 84w04'03 5:36:16
Dukedom 92 3 36N30'08 88w42'54 5:54:52
Dulaney 30 65 36N08'01 82w54'54 5:31:40
Dull 22 3 36N12'20 87w17'07 5:49:08
Dumplin 45 67 36N00'19 83w33'30 5:34:14
Dumplin Mill 45 67 35N59'50 83w33'49 5:34:15
Dunbar 20 3 35N27'32 88w08'40 5:52:35
Duncan 5 64 35N47'55 83w57'53 5:35:52
Duncan Hills 33 61 35N05'22 85w19'14 5:41:17
Duncantown 26 18 35N19'31 86w02'26 5:44:10
Duncanville 59 30 35N27'06 86w50'29 5:47:22
Dunlap 77 3 35N22'17 85w23'26 5:41:34
Dunn 50 29 35N11'39 87w20'24 5:49:22
Dunn Creek 78 60 35N48 83w23 5:33:32
Duo 13 51 36N28'59 83w37'54 5:34:32
Duplex 94 48 35N44'49 86w50'14 5:47:21
Duplex Mission 94 48 35N44'51 86w51'35 5:47:26
DuPont 78 60 35N49'34 83w42'08 5:34:49
DuPont Springs 78 60 35N48'30 83w40'47 5:34:43
Durhamville 49 28 35N40'05 89w29'35 5:57:58
Dutch 29 55 36N17 83w36 5:34:24
Dutch Valley 1 62 36N06'52 84w12'31 5:36:50
Dycus 44 3 36N24 85w48 5:43:12
Dyer 27 21 36N04'00 88w59'38 5:55:59
Dyersburg 23 16 36N02'04 89w23'08 5:57:33
Dykes 87 52 36N21'55 83w49'58 5:35:20
Dykes Crossroads 18 15 35N59'46 85w04'44 5:40:19
Dykes Mill 37 2 36N26'17 82w42'11 5:30:49
Dyllis 73 67 35N57'49 84w25'09 5:37:41
Dyson Grove 46 1 36N20 82w00 5:28:00
Eads 79 40 35N12'16 89w38'57 5:58:36
Eagan 13 51 36N33'07 83w58'37 5:35:54
Eagle Creek 3 3 35N54'48 87w59'14 5:51:57
Eagle Furnace 73 70 35N46'16 84w44'11 5:38:57
Eagle Point 73 70 35N45'49 84w45'13 5:39:01
Eagle Point Cabin Area 73 70 35N45'41 84w44'20 5:38:57
Eagleton Village 5 64 35N47'42 83w55'55 5:35:44
Eagleville 75 36 35N44'30 86w38'59 5:46:36
Earleyville 89 46 35N45'27 85w51'28 5:43:26
East 19 4 36N11 86w45 5:47:00
East Acres 79 40 35N20 89w53 5:59:32
East Brainerd 33 61 34N59'45 85w09'01 5:40:36
Eastbrook 26 18 35N14'05 86w09'32 5:44:38
East Chattanooga 33 61 35N03'55 85w14'57 5:41:00
East Chester 12 3 35N28 88w32 5:54:08
East Cleveland 6 53 35N09'39 84w51'28 5:39:26
East Cyruston 52 9 35N09'25 86w42'55 5:46:52
Eastdale 33 61 35N02'32 85w14'20 5:40:57
East Due West 19 4 36N16 86w43 5:46:52
East Erin 42 3 36N17 87w36 5:50:24
East Etowah 54 54 35N19'23 84w31'05 5:38:04
East Fork 78 60 35N50'42 83w25'03 5:33:40
Eastgate Center 33 61 35N02 85w14 5:40:56
East Hill 58 8 35N03'53 85w34'31 5:42:18
East Jamestown 25 3 36N27'53 84w52'24 5:39:30
East Junction 79 39 35N04'32 90w03'06 6:00:12
East Kingsport 82 2 36N33 82w31 5:30:04
East Lake 33 61 35N00'19 85w16'45 5:41:07
Eastland 93 3 35N53'53 85w14'13 5:40:57
East Memphis 79 39 35N07 89w57 5:59:48
East Miller's Cove 5 64 35N44 83w49 5:35:16
East Perryville Landing 20 3 35N37'04 88w02'00 5:52:08
Eastport 15 65 35N57'33 83w10'25 5:32:42
East Ridge 33 61 35N00'51 85w15'07 5:41:00
Eastside 8 3 35N49 86w04 5:44:16
East Side 10 1 36N20'18 82w11'56 5:28:48
East Side 22 3 36N03 87w19 5:49:16
East Siding 1 62 36N05 84w08 5:36:32
East Springbrook 5 64 35N47'51 83w58'29 5:35:54
East Sweetwater 62 67 35N36'26 84w24'50 5:37:39
East Union 57 3 35N36'18 88w46'01 5:55:04
East View 6 54 35N07'17 84w52'42 5:39:31
Eastview 30 65 36N09'59 82w48'23 5:31:14
Eastview 55 3 35N04'32 88w32'42 5:54:11
East View 61 54 35N20'22 84w55'59 5:39:44
Eastwood 47 67 36N01'40 83w47'05 5:35:08
Eastwood 75 3 36N00'23 86w34'00 5:46:16
Eaton 27 8 35N58'08 89w07'55 5:56:32
Eaton Crossroad 53 68 35N50'11 84w17'39 5:37:11
Eaton Forest 53 68 35N50'05 84w19'06 5:37:16
Ebenezer 47 67 35N53'46 84w04'14 5:36:17
Ebenezer 58 8 35N04'21 85w34'48 5:42:19
Ebenezer 59 30 35N16'38 86w46'59 5:47:08
Echo Valley 47 67 35N54'18 84w03'48 5:36:15
Eden Corner 74 3 36N31'03 86w44'46 5:46:59
Eden of the Lake 72 74 35N43'45 84w43'38 5:38:55
Edenwold 19 4 36N17'24 86w41'37 5:46:46
Edgefield 82 2 36N35 82w11 5:28:44
Edgemont 15 65 35N57'53 83w15'20 5:33:01
Edgemont 82 2 36N34'43 82w11'02 5:28:44
Edgemoor 1 62 36N00'53 84w09'27 5:36:38
Edgewater 72 74 35N29'19 84w59'58 5:40:00
Edgewood 22 3 36N10'54 87w31'51 5:50:07
Edgewood 23 16 36N05'03 89w13'39 5:56:55
Edgewood Acres 5 64 35N48'30 83w56'11 5:35:45
Edgewood Heights 1 62 36N02'24 84w08'15 5:36:33
Edgewood Hills 72 74 35N42'16 84w52'32 5:39:30
Edith 49 28 35N50'54 89w31'59 5:58:08
Edna 45 67 36N09 83w25 5:33:40
Edward Grove 38 3 35N42'19 89w25'39 5:57:43
Edwards Point 33 61 35N08'54 85w22'13 5:41:29
Edwina 15 65 35N54'41 83w10'21 5:32:41
Egam 52 9 35N11'14 86w38'50 5:46:35

Egan 95 34 36N13'19 86w20'45 5:45:23
Egypt 79 40 35N14'34 89w55'31 5:59:42
Egypt 84 3 35N29'28 89w47'02 5:59:08
Eidson 37 70 36N30'40 83w01'43 5:32:07
Elba 24 3 35N06'39 89w34'28 5:58:18
Elbethel 2 6 35N31'06 86w30'24 5:46:02
Elbridge 66 3 36N15'37 89w19'19 5:57:17
Elgin 76 58 36N19'56 84w36'23 5:38:26
Elijah Oliver Place 5 64 35N35'50 83w51'03 5:35:24
Elizabeth 17 3 35N57'52 89w10'39 5:56:43
Elizabethton 10 1 36N20'55 82w12'39 5:28:51
Elkhead 31 3 35N19 85w53 5:43:32
Elkhorn 40 26 36N20'02 88w09'33 5:52:38
Elkins 26 18 35N15'36 86w07'57 5:44:32
Elkins 41 3 35N49'21 87w28'49 5:49:55
Elkins Landing 20 3 35N33'44 88w00'20 5:52:01
Elk Mills 10 1 36N16'21 81w59'24 5:27:58
Elk Mill Village 52 9 35N09'44 86w34'00 5:46:16
Elkmont 78 59 35N39'13 83w34'50 5:34:19
Elkmont Springs 28 3 35N00'18 86w52'01 5:47:28
Elkton 28 3 35N03'08 86w53'19 5:47:33
Elk Valley 7 66 36N29'01 84w14'45 5:36:59
Ellejoy 5 60 35N48'34 83w45'19 5:35:01
Ellendale 79 40 35N13'50 89w49'33 5:59:18
Ellis Mill 62 70 35N23'23 84w22'26 5:37:30
Ellis Mills 42 3 36N18'24 87w33'27 5:50:14
Elmore 17 3 35N47'41 89w19'41 5:57:19
Elmore 18 15 36N07'06 85w04'46 5:40:19
Elmore Park 79 40 35N11'58 89w51'24 5:59:26
Elm Springs 29 55 36N17 83w36 5:34:24
Elmwood 80 3 36N13'33 85w53'05 5:43:32
Elora 52 9 35N00'48 86w21'21 5:45:25
Elverton 73 67 35N58'43 84w26'35 5:37:46
Elysian Grove 43 3 36N01'35 87w51'32 5:51:26
Elza 1 62 36N03'09 84w12'11 5:36:49
Embreeville 90 75 36N10'52 82w27'31 5:29:50
Emerts Cove 78 60 35N49 83w33 5:34:12
Emery Mill 4 15 35N39'08 85w11'00 5:40:44
Emmett 82 2 36N31'52 82w06'51 5:28:27
Emory Gap 73 67 35N55'00 84w34'30 5:38:18
Emory Heights 1 62 36N01'23 84w13'20 5:36:53
Emory Heights 73 67 35N55'51 84w31'38 5:38:07
Emory Valley 1 62 36N01'37 84w12'44 5:36:51
Englewood 54 71 35N25'28 84w29'15 5:37:57
Englewood 66 3 36N25 89w03 5:56:12
English Creek 15 65 35N54'05 83w13'28 5:32:54
English Mountain Resort 78 60 35N49 83w33 5:34:12
Enigma 80 3 36N08 85w47 5:43:08
Eno 22 3 36N03'35 87w27'12 5:49:49
Enon 56 3 36N35'41 85w54'40 5:43:39
Ensor 71 3 36N10'04 85w39'28 5:42:38
Enterprise 37 70 36N20'46 82w55'43 5:31:43
Enterprise 60 9 35N28'18 87w10'46 5:48:43
Enville 12 3 35N23'05 88w25'39 5:53:43
Ephesus 9 3 36N07'40 88w17'19 5:53:09
Ephraim Bales Place 78 59 35N41'47 83w28'11 5:33:53
Epperson 62 70 35N15'31 84w20'00 5:37:20
Epworth 94 48 35N52'25 86w47'30 5:47:10
Erasmus 18 15 35N53'13 85w11'06 5:40:44
Erie 53 68 35N38'51 84w34'29 5:38:18
Erin 42 3 36N19'06 87w41'41 5:50:47
Ernestville 86 1 36N04'17 82w30'10 5:30:01
Erwin 86 1 36N08'42 82w25'01 5:29:40
Essary Springs 35 3 35N00'43 88w47'53 5:55:12
Estes Kefauver 90 75 36N19 82w21 5:29:24
Estes Pond 48 3 36N25'59 89w26'56 5:57:48
Estill Springs 26 18 35N16'14 86w07'41 5:44:31
Ethridge 50 29 35N19'25 87w18'13 5:49:13
Etowah 54 54 35N19'24 84w31'30 5:38:06
Etter 69 3 36N33'41 85w05'53 5:40:24
Euchee 61 54 35N40'33 84w43'01 5:38:52
Eulia 56 3 36N31'28 86w10'22 5:44:41
Eureka 6 53 35N16'18 84w51'34 5:39:26
Eureka 46 1 36N33'22 81w46'11 5:27:05
Eureka 73 70 35N50'28 84w40'14 5:38:41
Eurekaton 38 3 35N25'58 89w13'09 5:56:53
Eva 3 3 36N03'52 88w00'15 5:52:01
Evanston 34 51 36N30'27 83w17'14 5:33:09
Evansville 23 16 36N02'03 89w25'18 5:57:41
Eve Mills 62 67 35N38'38 84w18'45 5:37:15
Evensville 72 74 35N33'52 84w57'17 5:39:49
Evergreen 10 1 36N10'40 82w01'16 5:28:05
Evins Mill 21 3 35N57 85w49 5:43:16
Ewingville 94 48 35N55'18 86w51'28 5:47:26
Excell 63 32 36N29'10 87w15'36 5:49:02
Factory 91 3 35N19 87w46 5:51:04
Fagin 62 67 35N33'17 84w19'07 5:37:16
Fair Acres 82 2 36N32'46 82w31'59 5:30:08
Fairfax Heights 33 61 35N06'34 85w15'51 5:41:03
Fairfield 2 5 35N34'00 86w17'07 5:45:08
Fairfield 32 67 36N13 83w17 5:33:08
Fairfield 41 3 35N50'05 87w25'58 5:49:44
Fairfield 83 50 36N37'11 86w20'44 5:45:23
Fairfield Glade 18 15 36N00'01 84w53'11 5:39:33
Fair Garden 78 60 35N49 83w33 5:34:12
Fairgrounds 2 6 35N29 86w27 5:45:48
Fairlane 62 67 35N37'37 84w27'17 5:37:49
Fairlane Estates 2 6 35N30'14 86w28'44 5:45:55
Fairmount 33 61 35N10'53 85w19'25 5:41:18
Fairmount 82 2 36N35'06 82w10'16 5:28:41
Fair Oaks 47 67 35N58'16 84w02'08 5:36:09
Fairview 5 64 35N42'55 84w00'34 5:36:02
Fairview 6 53 35N13'18 84w49'30 5:39:18
Fairview 10 1 36N11'51 82w13'08 5:28:53
Fairview 14 3 36N32'55 85w18'42 5:41:15
Fairview 16 12 35N26'08 86w13'14 5:44:53
Fairview 25 3 36N29'59 85w00'22 5:40:01
Fairview 29 55 36N23'03 83w21'33 5:33:26
Fairview 30 65 36N13'19 82w45'41 5:31:03
Fairview 33 61 35N08'04 85w11'12 5:40:45
Fairview 50 29 35N02'32 87w27'19 5:49:49
Fairview 54 71 35N27'17 84w33'38 5:38:15
Fairview 56 3 36N30'40 86w10'41 5:44:43
Fairview 57 3 35N45'49 88w50'28 5:55:22
Fairview 59 30 35N26'19 86w47'57 5:47:12
Fairview 73 67 35N47'46 84w34'10 5:38:17
Fairview 76 58 36N25 84w29 5:37:56
Fair View 81 3 36N29'45 87w53'50 5:51:35
Fairview 82 1 36N29'25 82w21'03 5:29:24
Fairview 89 46 35N38'26 85w43'08 5:42:53
Fairview 90 75 36N18'48 82w31'58 5:30:08
Fairview 91 3 35N02'39 87w40'33 5:50:42
Fairview 94 3 35N58'55 87w07'17 5:48:29
Fairview Heights 45 67 35N58'22 83w31'31 5:34:06
Fairview Heights 60 31 35N37'17 87w02'26 5:48:10
Faix 69 3 36N30'51 85w07'32 5:40:30
Falcon 55 3 35N08'41 88w36'05 5:54:24
Fall Branch 90 63 36N25'05 82w37'26 5:30:30
Fall Creek 2 3 35N33'48 86w32'31 5:46:10
Falling Water 33 61 35N12'11 85w15'13 5:41:01
Fall River 50 29 35N08'04 87w13'06 5:48:52
Falls Mill 26 18 35N05'55 86w15'41 5:45:03
Fanchers Mills 93 3 35N59'57 85w36'58 5:42:28
Fancy 92 47 36N21'59 88w39'16 5:54:37
Farmer Mill 10 1 36N14'09 81w57'52 5:27:51
Farmers Exchange 41 3 35N33 87w34 5:50:16
Farmers Union Landing 36 3 35N21'47 88w12'17 5:52:49
Farmers Valley 68 3 35N29 87w50 5:51:20
Farmington 59 30 35N30'04 86w42'39 5:46:51
Farner 70 73 35N09'15 84w18'55 5:37:16
Farragut 47 67 35N53'04 84w09'13 5:36:37
Farrar Hill 16 12 35N34'41 86w09'44 5:44:39
Farris Chapel 26 19 35N11 86w07 5:44:28
Farrport 5 64 35N49'14 83w58'44 5:35:55
Faulkner Springs 89 46 35N43'02 85w45'42 5:43:03
Faxon 3 3 36N15'19 88w00'07 5:52:00
Fayette Corners 24 3 35N21'58 89w12'34 5:56:50
Fayetteville 52 9 35N09'07 86w34'14 5:46:17
Federal Reserve 19 4 36N09 86w47 5:47:08
Felker 6 53 35N01'49 84w48'00 5:39:12
Fennel Store 29 55 36N09 83w42 5:34:48
Fernvale 94 48 35N57'16 87w04'45 5:48:19
Fernwood 32 67 36N09'34 83w18'21 5:33:13
Field Crest 60 31 35N36'17 87w05'06 5:48:20
Fielden Store 45 67 36N06 83w33 5:34:12
Fikes Mill 60 3 35N41'46 87w13'12 5:48:53
Fincastle 7 66 36N24'35 84w02'52 5:36:11
Findlay 93 3 35N57'28 85w28'47 5:41:55
Finger 55 3 35N21'30 88w35'56 5:54:24
Finley 23 16 36N02'09 89w28'47 5:57:55
Finney Patch 15 65 35N51'50 83w08'11 5:32:33
Fishers Landing 20 3 35N34'23 88w00'44 5:52:03
Fisherville 79 40 35N09'33 89w39'49 5:58:39
Fishery 86 1 36N08 82w25 5:29:40
Fish Springs 10 1 36N19'02 82w03'31 5:28:14
Fisk University 19 4 36N09 86w47 5:47:08
Fitzhughs Landing 81 3 36N29'56 87w51'38 5:51:27
Five Forks 20 3 35N41'16 88w10'23 5:52:42
Five Forks 36 3 35N23'16 88w14'39 5:52:59
Five Points 28 22 35N10'57 86w56'03 5:47:44
Five Points 50 29 35N02'45 87w18'40 5:49:15
Five Points 57 3 35N31'06 88w39'59 5:54:40
Five Points 72 74 35N26'41 85w01'03 5:40:04
Flag Branch 30 65 36N13 82w48 5:31:12
Flag Pond 86 1 36N00'55 82w33'26 5:30:14
Flat Branch 31 3 35N18'24 85w42'29 5:42:50
Flat Creek 2 6 35N23'28 86w24'30 5:45:38
Flat Gap 45 67 36N03'44 83w28'40 5:33:55
Flat Hollow 7 66 36N27 83w55 5:35:40
Flat Rock 80 3 36N13'32 86w06'10 5:44:25
Flat Rock Ford 65 51 35N58'09 84w40'15 5:38:41
Flat Top 33 61 35N21'27 85w13'29 5:40:54
Flatwood 84 3 35N33 89w48 5:59:12
Flatwood 89 46 35N47'02 85w53'49 5:43:35
Flatwoods 50 3 35N18'02 87w21'02 5:49:24
Flat Woods 68 3 35N28'37 87w49'39 5:51:19
Flewellyn 74 35 36N28'53 86w58'28 5:47:54
Flint Springs 6 53 35N02'04 84w54'22 5:39:37
Flintville 52 9 35N03'45 86w25'11 5:45:41
Flippin 49 28 35N47'14 89w29'34 5:57:58
Floraton 75 3 35N47'32 86w15'25 5:45:02
Florence 75 37 35N55'07 86w28'06 5:45:52
Flourville 90 75 36N18 82w28 5:29:52
Flowers 3 3 36N04 88w06 5:52:24
Flowertown 16 12 35N23'38 86w14'32 5:44:58
Fly 60 3 35N47'22 87w09'31 5:48:38
Flynns Lick 44 27 36N19'35 85w42'49 5:42:51
Fochee 53 68 35N44 84w21 5:37:24
Foot of Island Forty Landing 79 39 35N15'14 90w06'05 6:00:24
Forbus 25 3 36N33'10 84w59'30 5:39:58
Ford 53 68 35N49'54 84w14'36 5:36:58
Ford Crossing 90 75 36N16'21 82w30'16 5:30:01
Fordtown 7 66 36N21'56 84w07'07 5:36:28
Fordtown 82 2 36N27'10 82w30'13 5:30:01
Forest Chapel 83 50 36N34 86w15 5:45:00
Forest Grove 19 4 36N21'28 86w52'58 5:47:32
Forest Grove 61 54 35N31 84w47 5:39:08
Forest Heights 53 68 35N49'39 84w14'09 5:36:57
Forest Highlands 33 61 35N07'13 85w16'08 5:41:05
Forest Hill 5 64 35N42'10 83w57'59 5:35:52
Forest Hill 43 3 36N06'12 87w47'27 5:51:10
Forest Hill 79 40 35N03'47 89w45'33 5:59:02
Forest Hills 2 6 35N28'52 86w25'18 5:45:41
Forest Hills 19 4 36N04'06 86w50'39 5:47:23
Forest Hills 47 67 35N56'33 83w59'12 5:35:57
Forest Hills 59 30 35N26'53 86w48'29 5:47:14
Forest Hills 82 2 36N35 82w11 5:28:44
Forest Home 94 48 35N58'33 86w55'37 5:47:42
Forest Mill 16 12 35N30'57 86w02'13 5:44:09
Forest Park 33 61 35N10'51 85w17'17 5:41:09
Forge Ridge 13 51 36N34'22 83w34'49 5:34:19
Forked Deer 38 3 35N46'27 89w23'06 5:57:32
Fork Mountain 1 62 36N07'36 84w25'12 5:37:41
Fork of Pike 21 3 36N00 85w58 5:43:52
Fork Ridge 13 51 36N34'49 83w47'56 5:35:12
Forks of River 47 67 35N57'35 83w50'16 5:35:21
Forks of The River 80 3 36N13 85w51 5:43:24
Forrest Hills 60 31 35N37'25 87w03'13 5:48:13
Forrest Park 16 13 35N21'18 86w11'32 5:44:46
Fort Campbell 63 3 36N36 87w33 5:50:12
Fort Cheatham 33 61 35N00'44 85w16'32 5:41:06
Fort Harry 78 67 35N38'19 83w28'28 5:33:54
Fort Henry 81 3 36N30'26 88w00'57 5:52:04
Fort Loudon 62 68 35N35'45 84w12'23 5:36:50
Fort Loudon Estates 53 68 35N46'53 84w13'55 5:36:56
Fort Nashborough 19 4 36N09'47 86w46'31 5:47:06
Fort Pillow 49 3 35N39'48 89w44'20 5:58:57
Fort Robinson 82 2 36N33'18 82w35'25 5:30:22
Forty Five 24 3 35N03'26 89w18'32 5:57:14
Forty Forks 55 3 35N17'37 88w34'56 5:54:20
Foster Crossroads 76 58 36N34'59 84w33'20 5:38:13
Fosterville 75 3 35N39'18 86w24'11 5:45:37
Foundry Hill 40 3 36N24'35 88w21'18 5:53:25
Fountain City 47 67 36N01'55 83w56'15 5:35:45
Fountaincrest 47 67 36N04'27 83w56'30 5:35:46
Fountain Head 83 50 36N33'03 86w29'42 5:45:59
Fountain Heights 60 3 35N32'41 86w57'59 5:47:52
Four Points 27 21 36N06'36 88w51'28 5:55:26
Four Points 45 60 36N01'10 83w36'38 5:34:27
Four Points 48 16 35N58'34 89w23'27 5:57:34
Fourville 90 75 36N23'31 82w20'51 5:29:35
Four Way 2 6 35N29 86w27 5:45:48
Foust 33 61 35N00'58 85w17'20 5:41:09
Fowler Grove 15 65 36N02'55 83w08'03 5:32:32
Fowlers 3 3 36N04 88w06 5:52:24
Fowlkes 48 16 35N58'14 89w23'10 5:57:33
Fox Bluff 11 10 36N18'58 87w11'25 5:48:46
Foxbranch 34 51 36N34 83w03 5:32:12
Fox Fire 47 67 35N52'35 84w03'51 5:36:15
Fox Hills 5 64 35N52'20 83w59'23 5:35:57
Frankewing 28 3 35N11'33 86w51'04 5:47:24
Frankfort 65 56 36N06'09 84w48'13 5:39:13
Franklin 94 48 35N55'30 86w52'08 5:47:29
Fraterville 1 62 36N11'48 84w10'20 5:36:41
Frayser 79 39 35N13'03 90w00'12 6:00:01
Fredonia 16 12 35N32'24 86w06'24 5:44:26
Fredonia 38 3 35N24'12 89w26'02 5:57:44
Fredonia 63 32 36N26'23 87w13'07 5:48:52
Fredonia 77 3 35N23'57 85w25'56 5:41:44
Free Hills 14 11 36N33'59 85w29'27 5:41:58
Freeland 40 3 36N29'57 88w11'39 5:52:47
Freemont 31 3 35N21'41 85w44'06 5:42:56
Freeway 47 67 36N05'00 83w56'31 5:35:46
Freewill 44 27 36N17'51 85w35'09 5:42:21
Fremont 66 3 36N26'17 89w11'51 5:56:47
French Broad 15 65 35N55 83w01 5:32:04
Frettin 35 3 35N04 88w53 5:55:32
Friendship 4 15 35N36'34 85w04'05 5:40:16
Friendship 17 3 35N54'32 89w14'43 5:56:59
Friendship 28 22 35N13'58 86w54'56 5:47:40
Friendship 37 70 36N26'45 83w10'19 5:32:41
Friendship 82 1 36N32'45 82w00'59 5:28:04
Friends Station 45 67 36N05'41 83w34'45 5:34:19
Friendsville 5 64 35N45'37 84w08'09 5:36:33
Frierson Town 60 9 35N31'34 87w10'48 5:48:43
Frisco 37 70 36N32 82w41 5:30:44
Frog Jump 27 8 35N54'56 89w00'30 5:56:02
Frog Pond 22 3 36N07'34 87w13'47 5:48:55
Frog Pond 56 3 36N32'47 85w58'12 5:43:53
Front Street 79 39 35N08 90w03 6:00:12
Frost 1 62 36N05'38 84w17'05 5:37:08
Frost Bottom 1 62 36N05'20 84w16'53 5:37:08
Frost Ford 34 51 36N31'51 83w09'02 5:32:36
Fruitland 27 21 35N53'36 88w55'55 5:55:44
Fruitvale 17 3 35N44'48 89w00'50 5:56:07
Fruit Valley 2 3 35N45 86w32 5:46:08
Fry 32 67 36N13 83w17 5:33:08
Fugate Ford 13 51 36N32'52 83w24'43 5:33:39
Fuller 46 1 36N31'23 81w48'29 5:27:14
Fulton 49 3 35N36'43 89w52'57 5:59:32
Furnace 41 3 35N53'36 87w38'26 5:50:34
Furnace 46 1 36N29 81w48 5:27:12
Furnace Landing 91 3 35N23'13 88w01'11 5:52:05
Gabtown 90 63 36N23'24 82w36'58 5:30:28
Gadsden 2 3 35N46'33 88w59'24 5:55:58

Gail 12 3 35N26 88W39 5:54:36
Gainesboro 44 27 36N21'20 85W39'32 5:42:38
Gainesville 84 3 35N24'48 89W36'33 5:58:26
Gainsville 84 44 35N25 89W32 5:58:08
Gaitherville 50
29 35N14'44 87W21'55 5:49:28
Galaxy Heights 33
61 35N07'34 85W15'30 5:41:02
Galbraith Springs 37
70 36N22'09 83W10'45 5:32:43
Galen 56 3 36N34'36 85W57'43 5:43:51
Galewood 47 67 35N53'53 84W01'48 5:36:07
Gallatin 83 42 36N23'18 86W26'48 5:45:47
Gallaway 24 3 35N19'33 89W36'58 5:58:28
Galloway Landing 45
67 36N00'33 83W24'28 5:33:38
Galloway Mill 82
1 36N29'56 82W17'56 5:29:12
Gandy 50 29 35N13'12 87W24'14 5:49:37
Gann 27 20 36N00'31 88W44'13 5:54:57
Gant 60 3 35N39'22 87W09'54 5:48:40
Gap Creek 10 1 36N17'08 82W13'57 5:28:56
Gap of the Ridge 56
3 36N31'36 86W06'40 5:44:27
Gap Spring 6 53 35N00'20 84W47'06 5:39:08
Garber 90 75 36N13'08 82W27'41 5:29:51
Gardner 92 3 36N21'30 88W53'53 5:55:36
Garland 47 64 35N51'29 84W06'30 5:36:26
Garland 84 3 35N35'18 89W45'09 5:59:01
Garner Ford 26 3 35N11'27 86W17'48 5:45:11
Garrard Ford 36 3 35N18'13 88W03'34 5:52:14
Garrard Landing 20
3 35N23'36 88W06'16 5:52:25
Garrett 20 3 35N36'07 88W10'34 5:52:42
Garrettsburg 9 3 35N57'23 88W16'35 5:53:06
Garretts Mill 67
22 36N25'35 85W17'54 5:41:12
Gassaway 8 3 35N56'23 85W59'44 5:43:59
Gates 49 3 35N50'18 89W24'22 5:57:37
Gates Ford 4 15 35N27'51 85W18'45 5:41:15
Gath 89 46 35N46'48 85W47'27 5:43:10
Gatlinburg 78 59 35N42'51 83W30'37 5:34:02
Gattistown 52 9 35N12'29 86W23'45 5:45:35
Gause 74 3 36N26'12 87W03'03 5:48:12
Gaylan Heights 33
61 35N04'22 85W13'48 5:40:55
Genesis 18 15 36N06'33 84W55'02 5:39:40
Geneva 91 3 35N07'17 87W37'20 5:50:29
Gennett Camp 7 66 36N14'03 84W17'29 5:37:10
Gentry 71 3 36N10'53 85W44'46 5:42:59
Georgetown 6 61 35N17'11 84W56'46 5:39:47
Georgetown 27 8 36N00'46 88W57'18 5:55:49
Georgetown 54 54 35N24'07 84W41'19 5:38:45
George W Lee 79
39 35N08 90W03 6:00:12
Georgia Crossing 26
18 35N11'18 86W02'45 5:44:11
Germantown 11 10 36N13'42 87W07'45 5:48:31
Germantown 19 4 36N16'46 86W52'25 5:47:30
Germantown 79 40 35N05'12 89W48'36 5:59:14
Gernt 25 56 36N26'43 84W42'53 5:38:52
Gerren Heights 4
15 35N34'57 85W08'07 5:40:32
Gibbs 47 67 36N07 83W51 5:35:24
Gibbs 66 3 36N24'40 89W00'14 5:56:01
Gibbs Crossroads 56
3 36N26'57 85W52'50 5:43:31
Gibson 27 21 35N52'31 88W50'48 5:55:23
Gibsontown 82 2 36N33'04 82W32'43 5:30:11
Gibson Wells 27 8 35N52'50 89W02'22 5:56:09
Gift 84 44 35N33'08 89W33'52 5:58:15
Gilchrist 55 3 35N12'20 88W25'34 5:53:42
Giles Town 79 40 35N19'28 90W02'35 6:00:10
Gillises Mills 36
23 35N08'08 88W02'07 5:52:08
Gilmore 57 3 35N41'16 88W48'25 5:55:14
Gilreath Mill 25
3 36N33'16 85W01'57 5:40:08
Gilt Edge 84 3 35N33'04 89W49'28 5:59:18
Gin House Lake 84
3 35N27 89W49 5:59:16
Gin Landing 20 3 35N26'59 88W02'40 5:52:11
Gismonda 3 3 35N57'33 88W07'05 5:52:28
Gladdice 44 27 36N20'47 85W48'20 5:43:13
Glade 78 59 35N44'24 83W27'44 5:33:51
Glades 65 56 36N14'33 84W47'24 5:39:10
Glades 78 59 35N43 83W31 5:34:04
Gladeville 95 49 36N06'45 86W24'59 5:45:40
Gladstone 90 75 36N11'04 82W34'24 5:30:18
Glass 66 3 36N15'53 89W15'13 5:57:01
Gleason 92 3 36N12'49 88W36'45 5:54:27
Glen 16 12 35N21'35 85W55'01 5:43:40
Glen Alice 73 70 35N48'21 84W44'26 5:38:58
Glen Alpine 82 2 36N29'12 82W35'38 5:30:23
Glencliff 19 4 36N07'21 86W43'06 5:46:52
Glendale 19 4 36N07 86W52 5:47:28
Glendale 33 61 35N06'25 85W19'53 5:41:20
Glendale 50 29 35N06'37 87W23'14 5:49:33
Glendale 53 68 35N43'52 84W12'26 5:36:50
Glendale 60 31 35N32'26 86W59'19 5:47:57
Glendale 90 63 36N19'38 82W36'24 5:30:26
Glendale Estates 28
22 35N11'56 87W00'43 5:48:03
Glenkirk Landing 91
3 35N24'34 87W58'04 5:51:52
Glenmary 76 58 36N18'39 84W37'29 5:38:30
Glenmore Estates 5
64 35N50'10 83W57'20 5:35:49
Glenobey 25 3 36N23'07 85W00'33 5:40:02
Glenview 16 12 35N28'37 86W04'49 5:44:19
Glenview 19 4 36N07'41 86W42'01 5:46:48
Glenwilde 22 3 36N16 87W22 5:49:28
Glenwood 33 61 35N02'13 85W16'02 5:41:04
Glenwood 43 3 36N01'48 87W49'13 5:51:17
Glenwood 47 67 36N02'17 84W00'10 5:36:01
Glenwylde 22 3 36N17'44 87W20'38 5:49:23
Glimp 49 3 35N41'58 89W38'40 5:58:35
Globe 59 30 35N26'06 86W52'21 5:47:29
Glover Crossroad 74
3 36N26'57 86W56'48 5:47:47
Glover Hill 58 8 35N03'47 85W39'06 5:42:36
Gnat Grove 59 30 35N17'57 86W48'47 5:47:15
Gnat Hill 16 12 35N37'27 86W08'25 5:44:34
Goat City 27 21 35N49'39 88W45'36 5:55:02
Gobey 65 51 36N08'56 84W35'59 5:38:24
Godwin 60 31 35N39'06 87W02'58 5:48:12
Goffton 71 34 36N06'14 85W26'26 5:41:46
Goin 13 51 36N25'24 83W43'20 5:34:53
Golddust 49 28 35N43'31 89W51'31 5:59:26
Goldpoint 33 61 35N06 85W15 5:41:00
Goodbars 89 3 35N44'27 85W36'05 5:42:24
Goodfield 61 54 35N27'59 84W49'33 5:39:18
Good Hope 7 66 36N35 84W08 5:36:32
Good Hope 23 16 36N03'33 89W17'10 5:57:09
Good Hope 55 3 35N15'21 88W29'19 5:53:57
Goodlettsville 19
4 36N19'23 86W42'48 5:46:51
Good Luck 27 21 36N07'13 88W54'25 5:55:38
Goodrich 41 3 35N50'41 87W28'43 5:49:55
Goodspring 28 3 35N08'36 87W06'05 5:48:24
Goodsprings 54 54 35N19'58 84W33'36 5:38:14
Goose Horn 56 3 36N26'33 85W49'34 5:43:18
Gooseneck 1 62 36N13'18 84W01'38 5:36:07
Gooseneck 5 64 35N45'10 84W06'26 5:36:26
Gordon 28 22 35N12'15 87W03'02 5:48:12
Gordonsburg 51 3 35N34'11 87W25'26 5:49:42
Gordonsville 80 3 36N10'21 85W55'47 5:43:43
Gorman 43 3 36N06'16 87W42'28 5:50:50
Goshen 37 70 36N27'55 82W44'23 5:30:58
Gossburg 16 12 35N39'43 86W12'58 5:44:52
Graball 27 20 35N52'21 88W44'41 5:54:59
Graball 59 30 35N18'33 86W48'31 5:47:14
Graball 83 50 36N28'57 86W26'17 5:45:45
Grady 54 54 35N20'46 84W30'59 5:38:04
Graham 41 3 35N52'27 87W27'45 5:49:51
Graham Mill 90 75 36N10'38 82W32'40 5:30:11
Grand Junction 35
3 35N02'56 89W11'13 5:56:45
Grandmother Ford 43
3 35N51'10 87W43'25 5:50:54
Grandview 30 65 36N15'47 82W43'15 5:30:53
Grandview 36 23 35N22'54 88W07'04 5:52:28
Grandview 47 67 35N54'33 83W51'31 5:35:26
Grandview 72 74 35N44'37 84W50'24 5:39:22
Grandview Terrace 82
2 36N35 82W11 5:28:44
Granite 1 62 36N07'48 84W09'51 5:36:39
Grant 33 61 35N17'33 85W14'09 5:40:57
Grant 80 3 36N11'20 86W04'20 5:44:17
Grantsboro 7 66 36N18'53 84W04'05 5:36:16
Granville 44 3 36N16'16 85W47'43 5:43:11
Grasshopper 33 61 35N22 85W00 5:40:00
Grassland 94 48 35N57 86W53 5:47:32
Grassy Cove 18 15 35N50'26 84W55'05 5:39:40
Grassy Creek 70
73 35N00'09 84W26'22 5:37:45
Grassy Fork 15 65 35N49'02 83W05'29 5:32:22
Gratio 66 3 36N15'31 89W25'31 5:57:42
Gravel Hill 55 3 35N05'12 88W31'28 5:54:06
Gravel Hill 90 63 36N13 82W38 5:30:32
Gravelly Hill 45
67 36N06'05 83W28'58 5:33:56
Gravelly Hills 5
64 35N49'44 84W07'57 5:36:32
Gravelotte 11 10 36N16 87W04 5:48:16
Graveltown 80 3 36N21'04 85W57'49 5:43:51
Graveston 47 67 36N09'34 83W49'32 5:35:18
Gray 90 75 36N25'11 82W28'36 5:29:54
Gray Acres 82 2 36N35 82W11 5:28:44
Graymere Manor 60
31 35N35'35 87W04'44 5:48:19
Graysburg 30 65 36N18'52 82W40'50 5:30:43
Grays Camp 66 3 36N27'27 89W21'34 5:57:26
Grays Crossing 2
6 35N29'54 86W24'03 5:45:36
Grays Crossing 42
3 36N19'50 87W45'07 5:51:00
Graysville 72 74 35N26'49 85W05'04 5:40:20
Graytown 41 3 35N47'27 87W23'59 5:49:36
Green Acres 28 22 35N11'09 87W03'12 5:48:13
Green Acres 47 67 35N58 83W58 5:35:52
Green Acres 73 67 35N50'38 84W30'41 5:38:03
Green Acres 82 2 36N31'32 82W31'54 5:30:08
Greenback 53 68 35N39'40 84W10'20 5:36:41
Greenbrier 11 10 36N16'35 87W07'05 5:48:28
Green Brier 69 3 36N36'46 85W07'53 5:40:32
Greenbrier 74 3 36N25'39 86W48'17 5:47:13
Greenbrier 78 60 35N41'00 83W38'19 5:34:33
Greenbrier 94 3 35N50'42 87W08'30 5:48:34
Greeneville 30 65 36N09'47 82W49'52 5:31:19
Green Field 28 3 35N08'31 87W03'30 5:48:14
Greenfield 92 3 36N09'12 88W48'02 5:55:12
Greenfield Bend 60
3 35N40'58 87W16'23 5:49:06
Greenfields 82 2 36N32'04 82W32'10 5:30:09
Green Grove 56 3 36N27'53 86W10'23 5:44:42
Greenhaw 26 18 35N13'23 86W00'36 5:44:02
Greenhill 45 67 36N01'34 83W28'58 5:33:56
Green Hill 89 46 35N49'54 85W47'44 5:43:11
Green Hill 95 49 36N13'22 86W32'58 5:46:12
Green Hills 19 4 36N06'13 86W49'00 5:47:16
Green Hills 60 31 35N37 87W02 5:48:08
Green Hills Village 19
4 36N06 86W50 5:47:20
Greenland 37 70 36N30'09 82W47'12 5:31:09
Greenlawn 95 49 36N14'36 86W33'43 5:46:15
Green Meadow 5 64 35N46'41 84W00'09 5:36:01
Green Meadow 6 53 35N07'22 84W53'37 5:39:34
Green Pine 10 1 36N16'11 82W16'39 5:29:07
Green Pond 67 3 36N12'38 85W10'37 5:40:42
Greens Crossroad 89
46 35N47'20 85W42'56 5:42:52
Greens Mill 33 61 35N10'35 85W13'35 5:40:54
Greens View 16 18 35N13'03 85W55'07 5:43:40
Greentown 58 3 35N17'27 85W39'32 5:42:38
Greenvale 95 9 35N59'59 86W11'52 5:44:47
Green Valley 47
67 35N55'25 84W03'56 5:36:16
Green Valley 56 3 36N36'35 86W02'25 5:44:10
Green Village 37
70 36N32'10 82W40'37 5:30:42
Greenway 47 67 36N01'14 83W55'22 5:35:41
Greenwood 44 3 36N22'35 85W32'38 5:42:11
Greenwood 56 3 36N30'30 85W51'43 5:43:27
Greenwood 75 3 35N42'28 86W38'45 5:46:35
Greenwood 90 75 36N15'38 82W25'33 5:29:42
Greenwood 95 34 36N08'47 86W14'05 5:44:56
Greenwood Forest 47
67 36N03'19 83W56'15 5:35:45
Greenwood Heights 47
67 35N58'28 84W01'24 5:36:06
Greer Ford 4 15 35N32'46 85W14'01 5:40:56
Greivertown 18 67 35N50'07 84W47'34 5:39:10
Greystone 30 65 36N06'01 82W42'28 5:30:50
Greystone Estates 82
2 36N35 82W11 5:28:44
Greystone Heights 78
59 35N43'02 83W30'57 5:34:04
Griffen 24 3 35N16'34 89W30'01 5:58:00
Griffin Corner 79
40 35N19'33 89W59'08 5:59:57
Griffintown 11 10 36N10'57 87W08'15 5:48:33
Griffith 4 15 35N03 88W35 5:54:20
Griffith Creek 58
8 35N17'02 85W33'00 5:42:12
Grigsby 37 70 36N19'26 82W59'46 5:31:59
Grimsley 25 3 36N16'01 84W59'04 5:39:56
Grinders 41 3 35N48 87W27 5:49:48
Grizzard 27 21 36N01'42 88W59'08 5:55:57
Gronanville 48 3 36N23 89W29 5:57:56
Gross Crossroad 82
1 36N27'21 82W20'58 5:29:24
Gruetli 31 3 35N22'15 85W39'36 5:42:38
Gudger 62 67 35N28'28 84W25'27 5:37:42
Guild 58 8 35N03 85W32 5:42:08
Gulf Park 47 67 35N55'59 84W06'35 5:36:26
Gulfwood 47 67 35N55'49 84W05'11 5:36:21
Gum 75 37 35N44'41 86W19'33 5:45:18
Gum Creek 26 18 35N17'33 86W00'25 5:44:02
Gumdale 20 3 35N31'06 87W59'35 5:51:58
Gum Flat 17 3 35N42'54 88W59'02 5:55:56
Gum Spring 15 65 35N59'28 83W13'16 5:32:53
Gum Spring 93 3 35N52'46 85W34'18 5:42:17
Gum Springs 50 29 35N11'30 87W17'31 5:49:10
Gum Springs 52 9 35N05'19 86W24'32 5:45:38
Gum Springs 56 3 36N26'40 85W56'43 5:43:47
Gunnings 82 1 36N31'55 82W23'08 5:29:33
Guntown 37 70 36N23'40 82W59'20 5:31:57
Guys 55 3 35N02'05 88W33'31 5:54:14
Habersham 7 66 36N29'51 84W04'25 5:36:18
Hackberry 63 3 36N26'05 87W26'04 5:49:44
Hagys Corner 79
40 35N24'14 89W46'00 5:59:04
Haigler Ridge 40
3 36N16'08 88W07'49 5:52:31
Hale 90 75 36N19'08 82W28'01 5:29:52
Hale Mill 18 9 35N50'27 85W08'14 5:40:33
Hales Camp 75 38 35N59'46 86W29'33 5:45:58
Hales Crossroads 32
67 36N08'39 83W15'16 5:33:01
Hales Point 49 3 35N54'36 89W37'37 5:58:30
Halesville 21 3 36N00 85W58 5:43:52
Haletown 58 8 35N02 85W32 5:42:08
Haley 2 5 35N29'18 86W18'39 5:45:15
Half Acre 8 3 35N52'05 85W55'20 5:43:41
Half Moon Shores 73
54 35N43'44 84W40'10 5:38:41
Halfway 18 56 36N05'57 84W50'54 5:39:24
Hallbrook 47 67 36N04'56 83W55'10 5:35:41
Hall Ford 18 56 36N09'05 84W54'11 5:39:37
Halls 49 3 35N52'32 89W23'46 5:57:35
Halls Creek 43 3 36N11'24 87W49'19 5:51:17
Halls Crossroads 47
67 36N04'49 83W56'33 5:35:46
Halls Hill 75 37 35N52'11 86W14'06 5:44:56
Halls Mill 2 3 35N33'12 86W34'55 5:46:20
Hall Town 83 50 36N30'13 86W33'49 5:46:15
Haltown 85 45 36N25'38 86W08'06 5:44:32
Hamble 22 3 36N18'25 87W17'00 5:49:08
Hambright 70 72 35N12'45 84W30'44 5:38:03
Hamburg 36 3 35N05'41 88W18'15 5:53:13
Hamburg 58 8 35N00'24 85W42'09 5:42:49
Hamillville 33 61 35N07'28 85W13'58 5:40:56
Hamilton Mill 52
9 35N06'31 86W46'44 5:47:07
Hamlin Town 13 51 36N33'57 83W56'04 5:35:44
Hampshire 60 3 35N35'48 87W17'35 5:49:10
Hampton 10 1 36N17'03 82W10'22 5:28:41
Hampton Mill 30
65 36N06'46 82W41'02 5:30:44
Hampton Station 63
32 36N36'49 87W13'32 5:48:54
Handleyton 74 3 36N35'58 86W37'46 5:46:31
Haney 20 3 35N29'46 88W08'24 5:52:34
Hanging Limb 67 3 36N14'13 85W09'43 5:40:39
Happy Hill 28 3 35N22'15 86W59'48 5:47:59
Happy Top 18 9 35N45 84W50 5:39:20
Happy Valley 5 64 35N36'32 83W57'27 5:35:50
Happy Valley 10 1 36N18 82W18 5:29:12
Happy Valley Landing 84
3 35N25'34 90W08'05 6:00:32
Harbin 73 70 35N52'13 84W38'15 5:38:33
Harbison 47 67 36N10 83W49 5:35:16
Harbison Crossroads 47
67 36N07'15 83W51'10 5:35:25
Harbor Heights 33
61 35N05'48 85W11'55 5:40:48
Harbuck 70 73 35N05'32 84W22'19 5:37:29
Hardin Barn Landing 68
3 35N26'08 88W02'06 5:52:08
Hardin Estates 53
68 35N48'30 84W14'24 5:36:58
Hardin Ford 36 23 35N18'18 88W04'40 5:52:19
Hardin Ford 50 29 35N05'24 87W31'48 5:50:07
Hardin Landing 68
3 35N26'41 88W02'26 5:52:10
Hardin Valley 47
67 35N56 84W11 5:36:44
Hardison Mill 60
31 35N36'37 86W49'23 5:47:18
Hardscrabble 8 3 35N53'37 86W06'07 5:44:24
Hardy 67 3 36N19'06 85W26'26 5:41:46
Hardy Acres 60 31 35N38'44 87W01'13 5:48:05
Hargiss 67 3 36N13'18 85W09'59 5:40:40
Harmon 46 1 36N31'43 81W54'31 5:27:38
Harmony 26 18 35N10 86W12 5:44:48
Harmony 44 27 36N24'19 85W36'06 5:42:24
Harmony 88 3 35N47 85W35 5:42:20
Harmony 90 75 36N23'41 82W33'59 5:30:16

Harmony Grove 15
65 35N53'22 82w59'52 5:31:59
Harmony Hills 82
2 36N34'50 82w30'14 5:30:01
Harms 52 9 35N09'17 86w39'03 5:46:36
Harpeth 94 48 35N47'56 86w50'39 5:47:23
Harpeth Valley 22
3 36N10'51 87w10'03 5:48:40
Harpeth Valley Park 19
4 36N10 86w46 5:47:04
Harr 82 2 36N35'15 81w59'33 5:27:58
Harrill Hills 47
67 36N02'35 83w55'09 5:35:41
Harriman 73 67 35N56'02 84w33'09 5:38:13
Harriman Junction 73
67 35N56'28 84w33'59 5:38:16
Harris 66 3 36N26'48 88w56'59 5:55:48
Harrisburg 78 60 35N51'49 83w29'02 5:33:56
Harris Ford 77 3 35N23'32 85w21'53 5:41:28
Harris Hills 33
61 34N59'31 85w10'50 5:40:43
Harris Mill 86 1 36N00'31 82w32'23 5:30:10
Harrison 33 61 35N06'49 85w08'17 5:40:33
Harrison Bluff 33
61 35N08'52 85w09'29 5:40:38
Harrison Hills 53
68 35N48'34 84w17'22 5:37:09
Harrison Point 33
61 35N07'24 85w08'26 5:40:34
Harrogate 13 51 36N34'56 83w39'25 5:34:38
Harrtown 82 1 36N33'38 82w23'10 5:29:33
Hartford 15 65 35N49'00 83w08'36 5:32:34
Hartmantown 90 75 36N21'57 82w34'09 5:30:17
Hartsville 85 45 36N23'27 86w10'02 5:44:40
Hartsville Junction 83
50 36N26'58 86w19'36 5:45:18
Harwell 28 22 35N07'05 87w00'21 5:48:01
Hassell Landing 20
3 35N23'28 88w01'12 5:52:05
Hatchertown 78 60 35N43'54 83w37'56 5:34:32
Hatchie 57 3 35N26'15 89w04'39 5:56:19
Hatfield Ford 18
15 35N58'05 84w50'46 5:39:23
Hathaway 48 3 36N13'34 89w39'35 5:58:38
Havana 36 23 35N22'01 88w05'56 5:52:24
Havley Springs 32
67 36N13'44 83w18'39 5:33:15
Havron Chapel 58
8 35N04 85w39 5:42:36
Hawkinsville 23 3 35N54'30 89w17'02 5:57:08
Haws Crossroads 90
63 36N22'57 82w37'00 5:30:28
Hawthorne 2 6 35N22'16 86w29'55 5:46:00
Haydenburg 44 3 36N25'14 85w44'36 5:42:58
Hayes Fork 81 3 36N29 87w50 5:51:20
Hayesville 30 65 36N01'13 82w48'30 5:31:14
Hayesville 56 3 36N38'01 86w05'40 5:44:23
Haynes 48 3 36N18'28 89w28'33 5:57:54
Haynesfield 82 2 36N34'05 82w11'40 5:28:47
Hays 24 3 35N04 89w24 5:57:36
Haysboro 19 4 36N13'56 86w42'50 5:46:51
Hays Crossing 24
3 35N03'38 89w28'00 5:57:52
Haysville 56 3 36N37'00 86w05'00 5:44:20
Hazel 40 3 36N30'08 88w19'31 5:53:18
Head of Barren 13
51 36N26 83w36 5:34:24
Heard 69 3 36N23 85w19 5:41:16
Heath 46 1 36N27'16 81w45'18 5:27:01
Heather Heights 47
67 35N59'32 84w05'14 5:36:21
Heatoncreek 10 1 36N12 82w05 5:28:20
Hebbertsburg 18
15 36N01'02 84w47'41 5:39:11
Hebron 35 3 35N09'54 88w53'35 5:55:34
Hegler Ford 65 56 36N07'17 84w48'50 5:39:15
Heiskell 47 67 36N04'54 84w03'14 5:36:13
Helena 25 3 36N26 84w56 5:39:44
Helenwood 76 58 36N25'47 84w32'39 5:38:11
Heloise 23 16 36N03'02 89w40'32 5:58:42
Helton 21 3 36N03'57 85w56'43 5:43:47
Heltonville 29 55 36N17'31 83w23'59 5:33:36
Hematite 63 3 36N27'22 87w26'55 5:49:48
Hembree 76 58 36N13'46 84w25'14 5:37:41
Hemlock Park 82 2 36N30'10 82w30'16 5:30:01
Henard Mill 37 70 36N28'58 82w59'16 5:31:57
Henardtown 37 70 36N23'03 83w00'46 5:32:03
Henderson 12 3 35N26'21 88w38'29 5:54:34
Henderson Springs 78
60 35N48'19 83w35'33 5:34:22
Hendersonville 83
43 36N18'17 86w37'12 5:46:29
Hendon 4 15 35N25'11 85w14'30 5:40:58
Hendron 47 67 35N56 83w54 5:35:36
Henley 26 18 35N12'35 86w05'42 5:44:23
Henning 49 3 35N40'22 89w34'24 5:58:18
Henrietta 11 10 36N24'19 87w12'13 5:48:49
Henry 40 3 36N12'14 88w25'11 5:53:41
Henry Crossing 29
55 36N16'06 83w33'01 5:34:12
Henry Crossroads 78
60 35N57'28 83w35'38 5:34:23
Henry Ford 18 15 36N04'41 84w52'48 5:39:31
Henrys Crossroads 78
60 36N00 83w38 5:34:32
Henry Street 32
67 36N13 83w17 5:33:08
Henryville 50 29 35N23'31 87w23'39 5:49:35
Hensley Chapel 93
3 35N56 85w28 5:41:52
Herbert Domain 4
15 35N45'33 85w14'39 5:40:59
Heritage Hills 5
64 35N43'19 83w58'02 5:35:52
Hermitage 19 4 36N11'46 86w37'21 5:46:29
Hermitage Hills 19
4 36N12'05 86w37'59 5:46:32
Hermitage Springs 14
3 36N34'51 85w46'53 5:43:08
Hermon 30 65 36N12 82w44 5:30:56
Hiawassee 89 3 35N36'54 85w53'40 5:43:35
Hickerson 16 13 35N21 86w12 5:44:48
Hickey 7 66 36N21'16 84w15'52 5:37:03
Hickey 71 3 36N05'54 85w42'20 5:42:49
Hickman 80 3 36N08'38 85w56'26 5:43:46
Hickory 45 60 36N02'33 83w39'21 5:34:37
Hickory Bend 19 4 36N09 86w41 5:46:44
Hickory Corners 12
3 35N20'36 88w42'09 5:54:49
Hickory Flat 9 3 35N49'22 88w35'28 5:54:22
Hickory Flats 39
3 35N27'44 88w21'36 5:53:26
Hickory Flats 55
3 35N14'11 88w25'43 5:53:43
Hickory Forks 20
3 35N40'55 88w09'59 5:52:40
Hickory Grove 4
15 35N28'14 85w12'03 5:40:48
Hickory Grove 27
8 35N59'07 89w00'46 5:56:03
Hickory Grove 83
50 36N23'11 86w17'34 5:45:10
Hickory Grove 89
46 35N42 85w46 5:43:04
Hickory Heights 50
29 35N13'41 87w18'41 5:49:15
Hickory Heights 59
30 35N26'41 86w46'03 5:47:04
Hickory Hill 64 3 35N15'22 86w20'48 5:45:23
Hickory Hill Estates 16
13 35N24'09 86w13'09 5:44:53
Hickory Hills 33
61 35N02'47 85w10'25 5:40:42
Hickory Hills 47
67 35N54'40 84w01'33 5:36:06
Hickory Point 38
3 35N26'42 89w17'47 5:57:11
Hickory Point 63
32 36N26'02 87w14'53 5:49:00
Hickory Star Landing 87
52 36N15 83w48 5:35:12
Hickory Tree 82 1 36N29'28 82w09'07 5:28:36
Hickory Valley 33
61 35N02'26 85w10'10 5:40:41
Hickory Valley 35
3 35N09'13 89w07'40 5:56:31
Hickory Valley 87
52 36N15 83w48 5:35:12
Hickory Withe 24
3 35N14'38 89w35'19 5:58:21
Hicks Chapel 58 8 35N12 85w31 5:42:04
Hicks Crossing 78
60 35N54'00 83w43'45 5:34:55
Hicksville 57 3 35N38'14 88w49'21 5:55:17
Hico 9 3 36N05'28 88w29'22 5:53:57
Hidden Hills 47
67 35N58'31 84w02'15 5:36:09
Hidden Valley 47
67 35N56'16 84w05'02 5:36:20
High Bluff 47 67 35N53'30 83w50'36 5:35:22
Highcliff 7 66 36N34'56 84w04'34 5:36:18
Highland 25 3 36N16'07 85w05'56 5:40:24
Highland 44 27 36N21'45 85w46'26 5:43:06
Highland 66 3 36N24'42 89w01'01 5:56:04
Highland 67 22 36N17'38 85w15'48 5:41:03
Highland 83 50 36N37'28 86w22'23 5:45:30
Highland 91 3 35N13'55 87w44'15 5:50:57
Highland Academy 83
50 36N35 86w31 5:46:04
Highland Acres 5
64 35N44'14 83w59'30 5:35:58
Highland Forest 73
70 35N51'12 84w41'21 5:38:45
Highland Heights 19
4 36N13 86w46 5:47:04
Highland Heights 28
22 35N10'43 87w03'09 5:48:13
Highland Heights 60
31 35N35'40 87w02'29 5:48:10
Highland Heights 79
40 35N10 89w54 5:59:36
Highland Park 7
66 36N21'37 84w08'09 5:36:33
Highland Park 33
61 35N01'43 85w16'20 5:41:05
Highland Park 47
67 36N03'02 83w55'32 5:35:42
Highland Park 53
68 35N48'38 84w15'20 5:37:01
Highland Park 60
31 35N36'19 87w02'26 5:48:10
Highland Park 82
2 36N32'12 82w31'18 5:30:05
Highland Springs 29
55 36N13'46 83w38'34 5:34:34
Highlandview 47
67 35N56 83w54 5:35:36
High Point 7 66 36N18'18 84w13'49 5:36:55
High Point 15 65 36N06'22 83w09'49 5:32:39
High Point 65 56 36N09'01 84w49'34 5:39:18
High Point 76 58 36N28'31 84w32'31 5:38:10
Highway One Hundred 19
4 36N07 86w52 5:47:28
Hilham 67 3 36N24'51 85w26'30 5:41:46
Hill 60 3 35N32'53 86w56'55 5:47:48
Hillard 9 3 35N57'06 88w24'27 5:53:38
Hillcrest 16 12 35N27'07 86w06'42 5:44:27
Hillcrest 32 67 36N12'50 83w16'31 5:33:06
Hillcrest 59 30 35N26'29 86w48'10 5:47:13
Hillcrest 82 1 36N27'28 82w16'37 5:29:06
Hilldale 63 32 36N32 87w22 5:49:28
Hilliard 9 3 36N00 88w25 5:53:40
Hillsboro 16 12 35N24'45 85w58'13 5:43:53
Hillsdale 56 3 36N26'46 86w03'31 5:44:14
Hillsview 54 54 35N23'19 84w48'05 5:39:12
Hilltop 2 6 35N22'29 86w21'34 5:45:26
Hilltop 40 26 36N20'27 88w20'38 5:53:23
Hilltop 63 1 36N28'07 87w23'26 5:49:34
Hilltop 75 38 35N58'20 86w32'01 5:46:08
Hill Top 90 75 36N19 82w21 5:29:24
Hillvale 1 62 36N10'31 84w05'45 5:36:23
Hillville 38 3 35N27'19 89w10'10 5:56:41
Hillwood 19 4 36N07 86w52 5:47:28
Himesville 2 6 35N25'52 86w26'04 5:45:44
Hindscreek 1 62 36N05 84w08 5:36:32
Hinds Creek Valley 87
52 36N15 83w48 5:35:12
Hinkle 36 3 35N24'28 88w18'01 5:53:12
Hinkledale 9 3 36N05'36 88w35'56 5:54:24
Hinson Springs 39
25 35N37'40 88w25'28 5:53:42
Hinton Crossing 11
10 36N22'00 87w14'51 5:48:59
Hitchcox 4 15 35N36 85w11 5:40:44
Hite Ford 43 3 35N55'43 87w48'19 5:51:13
Hiwassee 70 72 35N10'59 84w27'58 5:37:52
Hiwassee College 62
67 35N33'28 84w21'45 5:37:27
Hix Mill Ford 2 6 35N24'24 86w25'35 5:45:42
Hixon 31 3 35N26'47 85w48'34 5:43:14
Hixson 33 61 35N08'26 85w13'58 5:40:56
Hobbs Hill 31 3 35N16'32 85w43'39 5:42:55
Hodges 45 67 36N04'37 83w38'29 5:34:34
Hodgetown 33 61 35N21'57 85w07'35 5:40:30
Hodson 17 3 35N55'44 89w10'56 5:56:44
Hoggtown 80 41 36N15 85w57 5:43:48
Hohenwald 51 3 35N32'52 87w33'07 5:50:12
Holiday City 79
40 35N03 89w54 5:59:36
Holiday Hills 36
3 35N01'04 88w12'50 5:52:51
Holiday Hills 73
67 35N46'59 84w36'49 5:38:27
Holiday Shores 73
67 35N53'47 84w28'58 5:37:56
Holladay 3 3 35N52'14 88w08'45 5:52:35
Holladay 71 34 36N11 85w28 5:41:52
Holland Ford 65
56 36N07'22 84w50'06 5:39:20
Holland Mill 30
65 36N18'27 82w46'56 5:31:08
Holloway 95 34 36N08'24 86w19'15 5:45:17
Hollow Rock 9 3 36N02'17 88w16'25 5:53:06
Hollow Springs 8
3 35N40'23 86w07'12 5:44:29
Holly Creek 91 29 35N05'11 87w36'09 5:50:25
Holly Grove 38 3 35N39'23 89w07'44 5:56:31
Holly Grove 59 30 35N27'36 86w44'43 5:46:59
Holly Grove 84 3 35N31'47 89w44'21 5:58:57
Holly Heights 33
61 35N17'11 85w08'45 5:40:35
Holly Leaf 27 3 36N02'54 88w41'48 5:54:47
Holly Springs 62
70 35N16'29 84w22'48 5:37:31
Holly Springs 67
22 36N25'08 85w23'59 5:41:36
Hollywood 33 61 35N08 85w19 5:41:16
Hollywood 60 3 35N28'42 87w02'53 5:48:12
Hollywood 79 39 35N11 89w57 5:59:48
Holston 82 75 36N29'09 82w23'57 5:29:36
Holston Heights 82
2 36N32'33 82w33'52 5:30:15
Holston Hills 47
67 35N59'56 83w50'22 5:35:21
Holston Hills 82
2 36N30'16 82w30'48 5:30:03
Holston Institute 82
1 36N32 82w19 5:29:16
Holston Valley 82
1 36N33'56 82w04'11 5:28:17
Holtland 59 3 35N41'32 86w41'41 5:46:47
Holton 7 66 36N33'54 84w02'14 5:36:09
Holts Corner 59 3 35N41'33 86w41'36 5:46:46
Holtsville 36 3 35N18'44 88w14'51 5:52:59
Holttown 15 65 36N04'40 83w12'20 5:32:49
Holy Hill 46 1 36N28'47 81w49'21 5:27:17
Homaway Village 16
13 35N23'15 86w13'36 5:44:54
Homestead 18 15 35N57 85w02 5:40:08
Homeway Village 16
13 35N21 86w12 5:44:48
Honeycutt 37 70 36N25'44 82w52'40 5:31:31
Hood Lake 50 29 35N12'47 87w20'02 5:49:20
Hoodoo 16 12 35N38'18 86w10'34 5:44:42
Hookers Bend 36 3 35N19'14 88w12'55 5:52:52
Hoop 13 51 36N27 83w34 5:34:16
Hoovers Gap 75 36 35N43 86w24 5:45:36
Hopewell 6 53 35N14'05 84w53'17 5:39:33
Hopewell 9 3 35N54'02 88w38'00 5:54:32
Hopewell 13 51 36N33'54 83w27'19 5:33:49
Hopewell 19 4 36N13'29 86w37'33 5:46:30
Hopewell 27 21 36N04'52 89w04'42 5:56:19
Hopewell 84 3 35N29 89w43 5:58:52
Hopewell Mill 62
67 35N31'15 84w15'34 5:37:02
Hopewell Springs 62
67 35N31'46 84w16'10 5:37:05
Hopkins Crossing 43
3 36N05'04 87w46'25 5:51:06
Hopson 10 1 36N13'31 82w08'16 5:28:33
Hornbeak 66 3 36N19'52 89w17'47 5:57:11
Horner 68 3 35N31'47 87w53'58 5:51:36
Hornertown 41 3 35N39'31 87w35'15 5:50:21
Hornet 78 60 35N45'18 83w43'29 5:34:54
Hornsby 35 3 35N13'39 88w49'46 5:55:19
Horse Creek 30 65 36N09'46 82w39'48 5:30:39
Horseshoe 10 1 36N20'09 82w07'07 5:28:28
Horsleys 56 3 36N28'10 86w07'05 5:44:28
Hortense 22 3 36N08'56 87w25'52 5:49:43
Horton Ford 34 51 36N34'23 82w56'22 5:31:45
Housley 10 1 36N26'44 82w02'41 5:28:11
Housley Addition 54
71 35N25'44 84w36'28 5:38:26
Houston 91 3 35N14'29 87w55'04 5:51:40
Howard 62 67 35N35 84w15 5:37:00
Howard 68 3 35N37'37 88w00'58 5:52:04
Howard Ford 25 3 36N20'30 84w50'57 5:39:24
Howard Hill 82 2 36N33'22 82w35'02 5:30:20
Howard Mill 65 56 36N06'09 84w43'00 5:38:52
Howard Quarter 13
51 36N28'26 83w24'40 5:33:39
Howards Landing 79
40 35N16'53 90w06'40 6:00:27
Howards Landing 84
3 35N30'35 90w00'36 6:00:02
Howard Springs 18
15 35N57'26 85w04'57 5:40:20
Howardville 33 61 35N00'20 84w59'52 5:39:59

Howell 52 9 35N13'48 86W36'40 5:46:27
Howell Hill 52 9 35N03'43 86W31'04 5:46:04
Howley 9 3 35N53'04 88W32'21 5:54:09
Hubbard 5 64 35N45'28 83W53'00 5:35:32
Hubertville 74 35 36N33'20 86W48'01 5:47:12
Huckleberry 33 61 35N15'37 85W12'40 5:40:51
Huddle Mill 82 1 36N30'58 82W27'29 5:29:50
Hudson 50 29 35N19'52 87W24'03 5:49:36
Huffman 65 56 36N16'45 84W39'12 5:38:37
Hugarth 25 3 36N26 84W56 5:39:44
Hughell Crossing 18 15 36N00'23 85W07'14 5:40:29
Hughes Loop 27 20 35N57'20 88W46'24 5:55:06
Hughett 76 58 36N19'16 84W30'34 5:38:02
Hughey 52 9 35N12'29 86W41'34 5:46:46
Hulan Hollow 86 1 36N08'35 82W24'23 5:29:38
Hull Mill 30 65 36N12'57 82W56'00 5:31:44
Humboldt 27 8 35N49'11 88W54'57 5:55:40
Hunnicutt Mill 45 67 36N03'04 83W27'44 5:33:51
Hunter 7 66 36N21'44 84W08'26 5:36:34
Hunter 10 1 36N22'18 82W09'32 5:28:38
Hunters Point 95 34 36N17'50 86W15'48 5:45:03
Huntersville 57 3 35N36'55 88W58'56 5:55:56
Huntingdon 9 3 36N00'02 88W25'41 5:53:43
Hunting Hills West 47 67 35N57'34 84W03'34 5:36:14
Huntland 26 18 35N03'04 86W16'11 5:45:05
Huntsville 53 68 35N46'37 84W16'57 5:37:08
Huntsville 76 58 36N24'35 84W29'26 5:37:58
Hurdlow 64 3 35N10'26 86W20'15 5:45:21
Hurley 36 3 35N08'17 88W21'57 5:53:28
Huron 39 3 35N35'17 88W31'56 5:54:08
Hurricane 44 27 36N24'46 85W38'17 5:42:33
Hurricane 95 34 36N03'14 86W18'41 5:45:15
Hurricane Hill 49 28 35N45 89W32 5:58:08
Hurricane Mills 43 3 35N58'16 87W46'55 5:51:08
Hurst Mill 13 51 36N25'53 83W31'22 5:34:05
Hustburg 43 3 35N58'58 87W57'35 5:51:50
Hutchings 93 3 35N56 85W28 5:41:52
Hutsell 54 71 35N27'37 84W36'22 5:38:25
Hygeia Springs 74 3 36N24'47 86W47'28 5:47:10
Hyndsver 92 3 36N22'13 88W46'03 5:55:04
Iconium 8 3 35N46'34 86W01'18 5:44:05
Idaho 50 29 35N05'37 87W17'34 5:49:10
Idaville 84 3 35N25'53 89W42'39 5:58:51
Ideal Valley 72 74 35N41'46 84W52'46 5:39:31
Idlewild 27 8 36N01'47 88W48'29 5:55:14
Idlewild 54 71 35N28'52 84W42'14 5:38:49
Idlewild 60 31 35N37'23 87W03'26 5:48:14
Idlewood Acres 47 67 36N01'44 84W00'28 5:36:02
Idol 29 55 36N22'00 83W24'06 5:33:36
Ilford 7 66 36N29'45 84W03'48 5:36:15
Imperial Estates 47 67 35N59'22 84W05'47 5:36:23
Independence 34 51 36N31 83W02 5:32:08
Independence 67 3 36N26 85W15 5:41:00
India 40 26 36N19'57 88W15'29 5:53:02
Indian Bluff 1 62 36N11 84W11 5:36:44
Indian Cave 29 55 36N09 83W42 5:34:48
Indian Hills 33 61 35N02'50 85W13'36 5:40:54
Indian Mound 21 3 35N56 85W28 5:41:52
Indian Mound 81 3 36N30'03 87W41'37 5:50:46
Indian Ridge 29 55 36N09 83W42 5:34:48
Indian Springs 82 1 36N32 82W26 5:29:44
Ingleside Hill 54 71 35N27'05 84W34'43 5:38:19
Inglewood 19 4 36N12'51 86W43'49 5:46:55
Inman 58 8 35N06'37 85W31'34 5:42:06
Inskip 47 67 36N00'47 83W57'31 5:35:50
Irish Cut 15 65 35N57'34 83W09'41 5:32:39
Iron Bridge Landing 40 3 36N22'06 88W05'11 5:52:21
Iron City 50 29 35N01'26 87W34'53 5:50:20
Iron Hill 22 3 35N59'21 87W19'22 5:49:17
Ironsburg 62 70 35N14'15 84W20'48 5:37:23
Irving College 89 3 35N35'02 85W42'48 5:42:51
Irwin 87 52 36N19'48 83W49'47 5:35:19
Irwinton Shores 73 54 35N45'16 84W39'45 5:38:39
Isabella 70 73 35N01'40 84W21'19 5:37:25
Isbell 60 31 35N32'02 87W08'52 5:48:35
Isham 76 58 36N35'51 84W26'20 5:37:45
Island Home 47 67 35N57'21 83W53'05 5:35:32
Island Number Forty Landing 79 40 35N17'14 90W06'45 6:00:27
Isoline 18 15 35N57 85W02 5:40:08
Isom 60 3 35N37'58 87W18'16 5:49:13
Ivy 62 70 35N16'10 84W25'26 5:37:42
Ivy Bluff 8 3 35N39'39 86W01'53 5:44:08
Ivydell 7 66 36N23'40 84W07'55 5:36:32
Ivy Point 19 4 36N20'55 86W47'33 5:47:10
Ivyton 67 3 36N24'13 85W09'07 5:40:36
Jacksboro 7 66 36N19'48 84W11'02 5:36:44
Jacks Creek 12 3 35N28'07 88W31'15 5:54:05
Jackson 57 14 35N36'52 88W48'50 5:55:15
Jackson Heights 60 31 35N38'25 87W00'33 5:48:02
Jackson Heights 75 37 35N51 86W23 5:45:32
Jackson Range Station 39 3 35N32'22 88W30'46 5:54:03
Jackson Square 1 62 36N01'29 84W14'25 5:36:58
Jackson Suburban 57 14 35N36 88W49 5:55:16
Jacksonville 66 3 36N18'00 89W19'10 5:57:17
Jakestown 75 37 35N51 86W23 5:45:32
Jalapa 62 70 35N20'39 84W21'43 5:37:27
Jamestown 25 3 36N25'39 84W55'55 5:39:44
Jamestown 84 3 35N33'04 89W51'44 5:59:27
Jarrell 9 3 36N03'55 88W34'23 5:54:18
Jasper 58 8 35N04'27 85W37'34 5:42:30
Jaybird 15 65 35N57'57 83W12'04 5:32:48
Jaybird 32 67 36N15'26 83W14'21 5:32:57
Jeannette 20 3 35N44'27 88W05'58 5:52:24
Jearoldstown 30 65 36N21'47 82W42'09 5:30:49
Jefferson 21 3 35N53'40 85W42'40 5:42:51
Jefferson City 45 67 36N07'20 83W29'33 5:33:58
Jefferson Estates 45 67 36N09 83W25 5:33:40
Jefferson Springs 75 38 36N00'05 86W27'30 5:45:50
Jellico 7 66 36N35'16 84W07'37 5:36:30
Jena 53 68 35N39'17 84W09'21 5:36:37
Jenkins Hill 78 60 35N49 83W33 5:34:12
Jenkins Mill 15 65 35N47'13 83W14'32 5:32:58
Jenkins Village 14 3 36N31'08 85W48'26 5:43:14
Jenkinsville 23 16 36N03'07 89W24'57 5:57:40
Jennings Bluff Landing 68 3 35N35'37 88W01'08 5:52:05
Jere Baxter 19 4 36N13 86W44 5:46:56
Jeremiah 71 34 36N13'33 85W24'15 5:41:37
Jernigan Town 74 3 36N31'20 86W41'05 5:46:44
Jersey 33 61 35N04'11 85W11'34 5:40:46
Jerusalem 52 9 35N14'36 86W47'04 5:47:08
Jessie 89 46 35N45'13 85W44'32 5:42:58
Jeter Landing 68 3 35N25'32 88W00'57 5:52:04
Jewell 92 47 36N20'10 88W36'23 5:54:26
Jewett 18 15 35N46'18 84W56'10 5:39:45
Jimtown 15 65 35N58'16 83W10'07 5:32:40
Joelton 19 4 36N18'47 86W51'55 5:47:28
John Sevier 47 67 36N02'24 83W48'56 5:35:16
Johnson City 90 75 36N18'48 82W21'13 5:29:25
Johnson Ford 36 23 35N22'22 88W04'47 5:52:19
Johnsons Chapel 21 3 35N56 85W28 5:41:52
Johnsons Crossroads 83 50 36N29'39 86W35'35 5:46:22
Johnsons Grove 17 3 35N46'02 89W11'44 5:56:47
Johnsons Mill 41 3 35N46'36 87W13'51 5:48:55
Johnsons Store 37 70 36N32 82W41 5:30:44
Johnsonville 43 3 36N03'36 87W57'10 5:51:49
Johnstown 16 13 35N21 86W12 5:44:48
Johntown 85 45 36N21'52 86W04'25 5:44:18
Jones 38 3 35N40'20 89W08'29 5:56:34
Jonesboro 90 75 36N17'39 82W28'25 5:29:54
Jones Chapel 69 3 36N34 85W08 5:40:32
Jones Cove 78 60 35N49'46 83W19'35 5:33:18
Jones Ford 25 3 36N09'41 84W56'38 5:39:47
Jones Mill 40 3 36N26'47 88W27'38 5:53:51
Jonestown 28 3 35N23'41 87W12'46 5:48:51
Jones Valley 41 3 35N45'35 87W15'13 5:49:01
Jonesville 25 3 36N11'00 84W56'14 5:39:45
Jonesville 73 63 35N58'59 84W23'29 5:37:34
Joppa 29 55 36N14'15 83W36'55 5:34:28
Joppa 93 3 35N49'23 85W38'10 5:42:33
Jordonia 19 4 36N12'33 86W51'55 5:47:28
Jug Town 75 37 35N51 86W23 5:45:32
Jumbo 9 3 35N51'59 88W29'26 5:53:58
Junction 15 65 35N48'11 83W00'50 5:32:03
Juno 39 25 35N41'53 88W31'14 5:54:05
Kalida 73 62 36N00'10 84W21'26 5:37:26
Kansas 83 42 36N27'10 86W22'50 5:45:31
Kansas City 90 75 36N11'35 82W28'10 5:29:53
Karns 47 67 35N58'55 84W06'50 5:36:27
Kaywood 16 13 35N21'00 86W13'48 5:44:55
Kedron 28 3 35N03'02 87W02'43 5:48:11
Kedron 60 3 35N42'08 86W53'54 5:47:36
Keebler Crossroads 90 75 36N21'52 82W28'45 5:29:55
Keefe 48 3 36N20'08 89W26'31 5:57:46
Keeling 34 3 35N26'16 89W28'24 5:57:54
Keenburg 10 1 36N23'13 82W13'38 5:28:55
Keese 26 18 35N12'21 86W05'54 5:44:24
Keister 45 67 36N08'11 83W27'50 5:33:51
Kellertown 2 5 35N32'02 86W17'19 5:45:09
Kelley Town 73 63 36N02'15 84W21'40 5:37:27
Kellys Landing 68 3 35N31'54 87W58'38 5:51:55
Kelso 52 9 35N07'33 86W28'07 5:45:52
Keltonburg 21 3 35N52'34 85W44'50 5:42:59
Kemmer Hill 72 74 35N40'40 84W52'08 5:39:29
Kempville 80 41 36N20'48 85W51'48 5:43:27
Kendricks Creek 82 2 36N31 82W32 5:30:08
Kenneytown 30 65 36N16'23 82W51'32 5:31:26
Kenton 66 3 36N12'08 89W00'44 5:56:03
Kenwood 63 32 36N34'41 87W23'26 5:49:34
Kepler 37 70 36N24'07 82W53'07 5:31:32
Kerrville 79 40 35N22'53 89W51'32 5:59:26
Ketchen 76 66 36N34'14 84W19'02 5:37:16
Ketner Mill 58 8 35N08'17 85W31'02 5:42:04
Kettle Mills 60 3 35N40'34 87W17'23 5:49:10
Key 93 3 35N56 85W28 5:41:52
Key Corner 49 3 35N55'53 89W29'26 5:57:58
Keyes Point 49 28 35N43'17 89W54'37 5:59:38
Key Ford 25 3 36N20'16 84W48'18 5:39:13
Keys Chapel 2 6 35N29 86W27 5:45:48
Keys Mill 90 75 36N20'54 82W31'04 5:30:04
Key Station 46 1 36N23 81W43 5:26:52
Keystone 90 75 36N19'23 82W19'56 5:29:20
Khotan 1 62 36N04'36 84W20'00 5:37:20
Kidwell 13 51 36N34'51 83W54'26 5:35:38
Killians Chapel 31 3 35N26 85W43 5:42:52
Kilsyth 7 66 36N25'43 84W04'59 5:36:20
Kimball 58 8 35N02'52 85W40'19 5:42:41
Kimberlin Heights 47 67 35N55'50 83W45'05 5:35:00
Kimbro 19 4 36N01'45 86W36'48 5:46:27
Kimbrough Crossroad 45 67 36N06'45 83W20'35 5:33:22
Kimery 92 3 36N10'49 88W51'53 5:55:28
Kimmins 51 3 35N37'13 87W32'16 5:50:09
Kincaid 62 67 35N34'18 84W16'58 5:37:08
Kincheloe Mill 90 63 36N25'02 82W33'30 5:30:14
Kinderhook 60 3 35N47'42 87W11'21 5:48:45
King 7 66 36N33 83W57 5:35:48
King Arthur Court 47 67 35N59'57 84W06'53 5:36:28
Kingfield 94 48 35N55'36 87W02'21 5:48:09
Kingsley Station 47 67 35N55'06 83W55'47 5:35:43
Kings Point 33 61 35N05'25 85W14'02 5:40:56
Kingsport 82 2 36N32'54 82W33'43 5:30:15
King Springs 90 75 36N19 82W21 5:29:24
Kings Ridge 33 61 35N09'32 85W14'34 5:40:58
Kingston 73 67 35N52'51 84W30'31 5:38:02
Kingston Heights 73 67 35N53'19 84W32'08 5:38:09
Kingston Hills 47 67 35N54'52 84W02'27 5:36:10
Kingston Springs 11 9 36N06'07 87W06'54 5:48:28
Kingston Woods 47 67 35N54'25 84W02'37 5:36:10
Kinneys 74 35 36N31'42 86W56'44 5:47:47
Kinzel Springs 5 64 35N41'13 83W47'47 5:35:11
Kirby 56 3 36N28'44 86W54'30 5:43:38
Kirk 24 3 35N06'07 89W37'31 5:58:30
Kirkland 52 9 35N03'44 86W37'45 5:46:31
Kirkland 94 3 35N48'26 86W39'46 5:46:39
Kirkstall 1 62 36N02'24 84W11'27 5:36:46
Kirkwood 63 32 36N35'36 87W12'55 5:48:52
Kiser 5 68 35N44'28 84W10'00 5:36:40
Kissling Crossing 26 19 35N10'03 86W07'54 5:44:32
Kitchens 51 3 35N28'51 87W34'11 5:50:17
Kite 37 70 36N24 83W00 5:32:00
Kittrell 75 3 35N49'25 86W14'41 5:44:59
Kittrell Landing 68 3 35N29'16 87W58'43 5:51:55
Kleburne 60 31 35N44'21 86W58'22 5:47:53
Kline 26 19 35N11 86W07 5:44:28
Klondike 37 70 36N26'20 83W07'54 5:32:32
Knapp 1 62 36N13 84W09 5:36:36
Knob Creek 49 28 35N52'51 89W31'52 5:58:07
Knob Creek 50 29 35N10'57 87W28'44 5:49:55
Knob Creek 78 60 35N50'11 83W44'17 5:34:57
Knob Creek Mill 90 75 36N20'56 82W24'16 5:29:37
Knollwood 33 61 35N06'58 85W17'09 5:41:09
Knox Park 54 71 35N27'01 84W34'38 5:38:19
Knoxville 47 67 35N57'38 83W55'15 5:35:41
Kodak 78 60 35N58'28 83W37'37 5:34:30
Koko 38 3 35N28'44 89W16'18 5:57:05
Kyles Ford 34 51 36N34'15 83W02'36 5:32:10
Laager 31 3 35N22'21 85W35'56 5:42:24
Lacher Ford 91 3 35N24'28 87W46'19 5:51:05
Laconia 24 3 35N16'56 89W15'07 5:57:00
Lacy 35 3 35N06'40 88W51'28 5:55:26
Laddie Village 73 67 35N52'46 84W30'16 5:38:01
Ladds 58 8 35N00'38 85W32'49 5:42:11
Ladins Landing 36 23 35N23'12 88W08'57 5:52:36
Lafayette 56 3 36N31'16 86W01'35 5:44:06
La Follette 7 66 36N22'58 84W07'12 5:36:29
LaGrange 24 3 35N02'43 89W14'37 5:56:58
Laguardo 95 34 36N17'47 86W26'37 5:45:46
Lake City 1 62 36N13'04 84W09'17 5:36:37
Lake Crest 82 2 36N28'54 82W29'26 5:29:58
Lake Drive 48 3 36N21'47 89W26'01 5:57:44
Lake Forest 47 67 35N55'36 83W52'04 5:35:28
Lakeharbor 73 67 35N48'31 84W36'10 5:38:25
Lake Harbor Estates 33 61 35N07'51 85W08'52 5:40:35
Lake Hills 16 13 35N24'45 86W11'59 5:44:48
Lake Hills 33 61 35N04'52 85W11'34 5:40:46
Lakemont 5 64 35N51'14 83W57'39 5:35:51
Lakemont Cabin Area 37 70 36N21'05 83W10'43 5:32:43
Lakemont Heights 73 70 35N50'57 84W41'47 5:38:47
Lakemoor 47 67 35N56 83W54 5:35:36
Lakemoore 32 67 36N15'10 83W16'58 5:33:08
Lakemore Hills 47 67 35N55'38 83W58'50 5:35:55
Lake Placid 12 3 35N26 88W39 5:54:36
Lakeshore Estates 33 61 35N07'23 85W09'21 5:40:37
Lake Side 33 61 35N06 85W15 5:41:00
Lakeside 62 67 35N36'39 84W16'56 5:37:08
Lakeside 72 74 35N42'37 84W45'07 5:39:00
Lakeside Park 33 61 35N11'25 85W10'02 5:40:40
Lakesite 33 61 35N12'31 85W07'37 5:40:30
Lake Tansi 18 15 35N57 85W02 5:40:08
Lake Tullahoma Estates 16 13 35N23'45 86W12'13 5:44:49
Lakeview 5 64 35N49'24 84W03'45 5:36:15
Lakeview 26 19 35N01'54 86W01'50 5:44:07
Lakeview 32 67 36N11'29 83W18'42 5:33:15
Lakeview 73 67 35N51'18 84W32'48 5:38:11
Lakeview 74 35 36N33'17 86W48'34 5:47:14
Lakeview Estates 5 64 35N51'47 83W57'44 5:35:51
Lake View Heights 73 67 35N56 84W33 5:38:12
Lakeview Manor 40 3 36N15 88W09 5:52:36
Lake View Park 45 67 36N01'28 83W23'53 5:33:36
Lake Vista 33 61 35N04'42 85W10'37 5:40:42
Lakewood 9 3 35N59'58 88W29'15 5:53:57
Lakewood 19 4 36N14'35 86W38'08 5:46:33
Lakewood 33 61 35N22'51 85W02'24 5:40:10
Lakewood 47 67 35N52'17 84W06'25 5:36:26
Lakewood Village 72 74 35N40'34 84W47'53 5:39:12

Lamar 79 39 35N06 89w59 5:59:56
Lambert 24 3 35N18'46 89w29'04 5:57:56
Lamont 74 35 36N37'27 86w45'26 5:47:02
Lamontville 6 54 35N21'17 84w49'01 5:39:16
Lancaster 80 3 36N07'39 85w51'15 5:43:25
Lancaster Hill 80 3 36N07'38 85w52'56 5:43:32
Lancelot Acres 28 22 35N11'01 87w03'13 5:48:13
Lanceville 15 65 35N56'13 82w54'25 5:31:38
Lancing 65 56 36N07'14 84w39'14 5:38:37
Landmark 47 67 35N56'47 84w03'26 5:36:14
Lane 23 16 36N11'39 89w21'44 5:57:27
Laneview 27 8 36N01'25 88w53'55 5:55:36
Lanier 5 64 35N38 84w03 5:36:12
Lankford Town 31 3 35N14'58 85w44'14 5:42:57
Lansdell Park 33 61 34N59'28 85w12'52 5:40:51
Lantana 18 9 35N52'36 85w06'04 5:40:24
Lanton 60 31 35N37 87w02 5:48:08
Lapata 23 16 36N04'58 89w10'56 5:56:44
Largo 20 3 35N33'00 88w05'47 5:52:23
Lascassas 75 3 35N55'49 86w17'28 5:45:10
Lassiter Corner 66 3 36N21'36 89w22'01 5:57:28
Latham 92 47 36N25'24 88w42'51 5:54:51
Laurel 1 62 36N05'07 84w11'01 5:36:44
Laurel 78 60 35N46'37 83w24'21 5:33:37
Laurel Bloomery 46 1 36N33'58 81w45'35 5:27:02
Laurel Bluff 73 67 35N47'52 84w31'22 5:38:05
Laurel Brook 72 74 35N29'40 85w06'44 5:40:27
Laurelburg 88 3 35N43'18 85w34'50 5:42:19
Laurel Cove 88 3 35N45 85w27 5:41:48
Laurel Fork 10 1 36N12'21 82w00'10 5:28:01
Laurel Grove 1 62 36N07'02 84w14'08 5:36:57
Laurel Hill 12 3 35N18'53 88w42'37 5:54:50
Laurel Hill 21 3 36N06'10 85w48'47 5:43:15
Laurel Hill 50 29 35N24'11 87w30'35 5:50:02
La Vergne 75 3 36N00'56 86w34'55 5:46:20
Lavinia 9 3 35N50'57 88w39'39 5:54:39
Law 39 25 35N45'47 88w36'19 5:54:25
Law Chapel 5 64 35N46 83w58 5:35:52
Lawnville 73 67 35N52'36 84w27'25 5:37:50
Lawrence 57 3 35N38'55 88w47'26 5:55:10
Lawrenceburg 50 29 35N14'32 87w20'05 5:49:20
Lawson Crossroad 5 64 35N39'15 83w47'51 5:35:11
Lawson Mill 34 51 36N28'17 83w18'34 5:33:14
Lawson Mill 89 3 35N37'42 85w49'15 5:43:17
Lawton 55 3 35N10 88w35 5:54:20
Lazy Acres 47 67 36N00'27 84w03'26 5:36:14
Leach 9 3 35N55'58 88w29'14 5:53:57
Leadvale 15 67 36N04'18 83w14'08 5:32:57
Leama 75 37 35N51 86w23 5:45:32
Leaman 34 51 36N32 83w13 5:32:52
Leanna 75 37 35N56'19 86w25'52 5:45:43
Leapwood 55 3 35N18'21 88w27'22 5:53:49
Lea Springs 29 55 36N10'40 83w41'00 5:34:44
Leatherwood 91 3 35N23'39 87w50'52 5:51:23
Leatherwood Ford 76 58 36N28'38 84w40'10 5:38:41
Lebanon 6 53 35N03'05 84w57'31 5:39:50
Lebanon 36 3 35N22'12 88w17'38 5:53:11
Lebanon 95 34 36N12'29 86w17'28 5:45:10
Lebanon, Mount 84 44 35N36'25 89w42'26 5:58:50
Ledbetter 27 20 35N56'04 88w43'45 5:54:55
Ledbetter Landing 3 3 35N50'04 87w58'11 5:51:53
Ledfords Mill 64 12 35N24'11 86w16'34 5:45:06
Lee 4 15 35N36 85w11 5:40:44
Leemans Corner 95 34 36N07'55 86w14'57 5:45:00
Leesburg 90 75 36N17'32 82w32'40 5:30:11
Lees Corner 60 3 35N41'49 86w49'57 5:47:20
Lees Station 4 15 35N33'15 85w15'10 5:41:01
Lee Valley 37 70 36N27'47 83w08'37 5:32:34
Leeville 95 34 36N11'27 86w25'03 5:45:40
Leftwich 60 31 35N34'23 86w52'00 5:47:28
Legate 81 3 36N33'16 87w41'55 5:50:48
Lego Landing 39 3 35N29'18 87w59'06 5:51:56
Leighs Chapel 84 44 35N34 89w42 5:58:48
Leighton 57 3 35N33'25 89w03'23 5:56:14
Leinart 1 62 36N05 84w08 5:36:32
Leinarts 1 62 36N06'28 84w11'24 5:36:46
Leipers Fork 94 3 35N53'44 86w59'52 5:47:59
Lenoir City 53 69 35N47'50 84w15'22 5:37:01
Lenow 79 40 35N11'11 89w43'50 5:58:55
Lenox 23 16 36N05'21 89w29'54 5:58:00
Leoma 50 29 35N09'41 87w20'53 5:49:24
Leonard 82 2 36N35 82w11 5:28:44
Leonardtown 82 1 36N35'31 82w16'30 5:29:06
Leoni 8 3 35N46'28 85w58'59 5:43:56
Lesters 28 22 35N04'10 87w00'18 5:48:01
Lewisburg 59 30 35N26'57 86w47'20 5:47:09
Lewis Chapel 77 3 35N22 85w23 5:41:32
Lewis Lane 37 70 36N33'21 82w37'35 5:30:30
Lewis Park 51 3 35N33 87w34 5:50:16
Lewis Store 16 12 35N38 86w14 5:44:56
Lexie 26 18 35N08'53 86w18'05 5:45:12
Lexie Crossroads 26 18 35N08'27 86w17'09 5:45:09
Lexington 39 25 35N39'03 88w23'36 5:53:34
Liberty 3 3 36N06'01 88w06'30 5:52:26
Liberty 20 3 35N26'46 88w12'53 5:52:52
Liberty 21 3 36N00'24 85w58'04 5:43:52
Liberty 26 19 35N08'01 86w06'21 5:44:25
Liberty 28 3 35N03'34 86w58'05 5:47:52
Liberty 44 3 36N16'32 85w45'25 5:43:02
Liberty 46 1 36N29 81w48 5:27:12
Liberty 52 9 35N06'43 86w32'31 5:46:10
Liberty 55 3 35N01'11 88w25'14 5:53:41
Liberty 65 51 36N06 84w36 5:38:24
Liberty 77 3 35N16'26 85w27'54 5:41:52
Liberty 83 50 36N33'56 86w19'13 5:45:17
Liberty 90 63 36N08'31 82w37'21 5:30:29
Liberty 92 3 36N12'48 88w42'30 5:54:50
Liberty Grove 50 29 35N02'29 87w22'59 5:49:32
Liberty Hill 15 65 36N04'39 83w10'27 5:32:42
Liberty Hill 24 3 35N18'08 89w16'51 5:57:07
Liberty Hill 28 3 35N19'50 87w11'26 5:48:46
Liberty Hill 29 55 36N19'03 83w36'52 5:34:27
Liberty Hill 30 65 36N18'23 82w41'25 5:30:46
Liberty Hill 54 71 35N22'56 84w26'15 5:37:45
Liberty Hill 64 3 35N09'32 86w20'46 5:45:23
Liberty Hill 72 74 35N35'55 85w02'07 5:40:08
Liberty Hill 94 3 35N58'53 87w11'00 5:48:44
Liberty Hill 95 49 36N02'36 86w03'47 5:44:15
Lick Creek 3 3 36N19'16 88w01'19 5:52:05
Lick Creek 20 3 35N39 88w07 5:52:28
Lick Creek Landing 3 3 36N19'42 88w00'47 5:52:03
Lick Creek Landing 68 3 35N41'09 88w01'04 5:52:04
Licklog 15 65 35N51'54 83w09'50 5:32:39
Lick Skillet 20 3 35N29'26 88w12'21 5:52:49
Lickskillet 87 52 36N17'15 83w48'02 5:35:12
Lickton 19 4 36N18'05 86w48'36 5:47:14
Life 39 25 35N36'52 88w28'43 5:53:55
Lightfoot 49 28 35N44'52 89w38'33 5:58:34
Lillamay 11 10 36N13'55 87w02'58 5:48:12
Lillard Mill 59 30 35N35'12 86w47'05 5:47:08
Lillydale 86 1 36N07'40 82w24'19 5:29:37
Lily Grove 13 51 36N26'33 83w42'49 5:34:51
Limbs 92 3 36N14 88w50 5:55:20
Limestone 90 63 36N13'41 82w37'50 5:30:31
Limestone Cove 86 1 36N10'51 82w15'43 5:29:03
Linary 18 15 35N51'51 84w59'26 5:39:58
Lincoln 52 9 35N00'54 86w30'27 5:46:02
Lincoln Park 47 67 35N59'51 83w55'51 5:35:43
Lincoln Park 59 30 35N27'47 86w48'34 5:47:14
Lincoya Hills 19 4 36N10'47 86w40'36 5:46:42
Linden 68 3 35N37'02 87w50'22 5:51:21
Lindenwood 66 3 36N28 89w03 5:56:12
Lindsay Mill 7 66 36N15'36 84w08'45 5:36:35
Liners 63 3 36N22'56 87w34'16 5:50:17
Line Spring 78 60 35N41'48 83w39'08 5:34:37
Link 75 36 35N43'00 86w30'23 5:46:02
Linsdale 70 54 35N15'05 84w37'41 5:38:31
Linton 19 4 36N01'38 87w00'37 5:48:02
Linwood 95 34 36N09'28 86w11'07 5:44:44
Lipe 3 3 36N02'27 88w10'46 5:52:43
Lisbon 35 3 35N06'22 88w54'55 5:55:40
Little Barren 87 52 36N21'56 83w45'21 5:35:01
Little Bigby 60 3 35N35 87w05 5:48:20
Little Cherokee 90 75 36N14'07 82w26'24 5:29:46
Little Cove 78 60 35N45'31 83w36'21 5:34:25
Little Crab 25 3 36N27'25 85w03'23 5:40:14
Little Creek 13 51 36N33'09 83w34'22 5:34:17
Little Creek 19 4 36N16'44 86w47'08 5:47:09
Little Crooked Creek Landing 3 3 36N13'36 87w57'33 5:51:50
Little Doe 46 1 36N27'09 81w52'49 5:27:31
Little Earren 13 51 36N26 83w36 5:34:24
Little Emory 73 67 35N57'27 84w29'00 5:37:56
Little Hope 75 37 35N51 86w23 5:45:32
Little Hope 91 3 35N19 87w46 5:51:04
Littlelot 41 3 35N47'20 87w19'23 5:49:18
Little Milligan 10 1 36N18'53 82w01'06 5:28:04
Little River 5 64 35N51'02 83w56'31 5:35:46
Little Rock Mills 41 3 35N50'53 87w17'53 5:49:12
Little Spring Landing 20 3 35N28'23 88w01'48 5:52:07
Little Texas 94 48 35N48'02 86w46'59 5:47:08
Little White Oak 7 66 36N31'27 84w03'13 5:36:13
Litton 4 15 35N44'18 85w02'10 5:40:09
Litz Manor 82 2 36N31'24 82w31'00 5:30:04
Lively 59 31 35N40'03 86w47'41 5:47:11
Liverworth 63 3 36N24'01 87w19'35 5:49:18
Livesay Mill 34 51 36N33'29 83w02'19 5:32:09
Livingston 67 22 36N23'00 85w19'23 5:41:18
Loafers Corner 75 3 35N59'05 86w32'48 5:46:11
Lobelville 68 3 35N46'19 87w47'02 5:51:08
Locke 79 40 35N19'56 90w01'36 6:00:06
Lockertsville 11 10 36N20'45 87w07'15 5:48:29
Lockes Mill 52 9 35N12'59 86w26'40 5:45:47
Lockmiller Addition 54 71 35N25'49 84w36'03 5:38:24
Locust Grove 23 16 36N10'27 89w15'25 5:57:02
Locust Mountain 90 63 36N20'25 82w34'35 5:30:18
Locust Springs 30 65 36N18'19 82w47'54 5:31:12
Lodge 58 8 35N01 85w43 5:42:52
Lodi 50 29 35N13'21 87w33'09 5:50:13
Lofton 75 3 35N55'43 86w16'21 5:45:05
Logans Lake 55 3 35N22 88w36 5:54:24
Lois 64 3 35N13'57 86w21'56 5:45:28
Lomax Crossroads 51 3 35N33'24 87w34'44 5:50:19
London 15 65 35N52'11 83w00'08 5:32:01
Lone Mountain 13 51 36N23'26 83w35'06 5:34:20
Lone Mountain 76 58 36N15'38 84w29'23 5:37:58
Lone Oak 63 3 36N23 87w20 5:49:20
Lone Oak 77 3 35N12'02 85w21'51 5:41:27
Lone Star 82 2 36N28'21 82w37'22 5:30:29
Lonewood 88 3 35N46'30 85w17'37 5:41:10
Long Branch 33 61 35N10'19 85w14'11 5:40:57
Long Branch 50 29 35N09'22 87w25'29 5:49:42
Long Creek 15 65 35N59'13 83w01'16 5:32:05
Long Creek 56 3 36N33'26 86w05'35 5:44:22
Long Ford 70 72 35N14'13 84w29'05 5:37:56
Long Ford 78 60 35N49'09 83w27'48 5:33:51
Long Hollow 7 66 36N22'32 84w05'58 5:36:24
Long Island 82 2 36N31'10 82w33'09 5:30:13
Long Rock 9 3 36N00 88w25 5:53:40
Longs Bend 37 70 36N26'47 82w49'37 5:31:18
Longs Mills 54 71 35N27 84w36 5:38:24
Longtown 24 3 35N20'29 89w30'51 5:58:03
Longview 2 6 35N38'28 86w31'46 5:46:07
Lonoke 27 21 36N12 89w01 5:56:04
Lonsdale 47 67 35N59'08 83w57'26 5:35:50
Lookout Mountain 33 61 34N59'39 85w20'58 5:41:24
Lookout Valley 33 61 35N01 85w20 5:41:20
Loonewood 88 3 35N45 85w27 5:41:48
Loretto 50 29 35N04'40 87w26'23 5:49:46
Lorraine 72 74 35N43'19 84w49'40 5:39:19
Lost Creek 93 3 35N52'38 85w21'45 5:41:27
Lost Mountain 30 65 36N13 82w48 5:31:12
Lott Landing 36 23 35N23'57 88w05'36 5:52:22
Loudon 53 68 35N43'58 84w20'02 5:37:20
Loudon City Park 53 68 35N43'28 84w22'39 5:37:31
Louise 63 3 36N16 87w22 5:49:28
Louisville 5 64 35N49'18 84w02'53 5:36:12
Lousie 63 3 36N22'15 87w23'57 5:49:36
Lovejoy 67 3 36N11'24 85w10'05 5:40:40
Lovelace 30 65 36N24'27 82w39'25 5:30:38
Love Lady 69 3 36N35'21 85w09'34 5:40:38
Loveland 47 67 36N01'05 83w52'09 5:35:29
Lovell 47 67 35N53'44 84w08'14 5:36:33
Lovell Heights 47 67 35N53'49 84w07'45 5:36:31
Love Station 86 1 36N07'14 82w26'05 5:29:44
Lovetown 60 9 35N38'37 87w15'04 5:49:00
Lower Forked Deer Landing 49 3 35N46'50 89w45'20 5:59:01
Lower Holly Creek 91 29 35N03'31 87w36'03 5:50:24
Lower Mill 33 61 35N10'04 85w13'19 5:40:53
Lower Mockeson 50 29 35N04'05 87w16'31 5:49:06
Lower Rutherford Creek 60 3 35N39 86w57 5:47:48
Lowland 32 67 36N09 83w12 5:32:48
Lowryville 36 23 35N06'15 88w05'56 5:52:24
Luckett 49 28 35N43'41 89w40'28 5:58:42
Lucky 89 46 35N47'51 85w50'34 5:43:22
Lucy 79 40 35N18'00 89w55'38 5:59:43
Lulaville 29 66 36N15'28 83w34'32 5:34:18
Luminary 4 15 35N41'44 85w00'03 5:40:00
Luna 59 30 35N22'09 86w43'50 5:46:55
Lunns Store 59 3 35N38 86w42 5:46:48
Lupton City 33 61 35N06'20 85w15'51 5:41:03
Luray 39 3 35N35'29 88w34'33 5:54:18
Lusk 4 15 35N22 85w23 5:41:32
Luskville 54 54 35N16'30 84w39'40 5:38:39
Luther 34 51 36N27'39 83w14'25 5:32:58
Luttrell 53 68 35N39'14 84w31'45 5:38:07
Luttrell 87 52 36N11'58 83w44'31 5:34:58
Lutts 91 3 35N09'04 87w56'17 5:51:45
Lyles 41 3 35N55'11 87w20'42 5:49:23
Lynchburg 64 33 35N16'59 86w22'27 5:45:30
Lynn 27 21 36N06'20 88w51'36 5:55:26
Lynn Garden 82 2 36N34'37 82w34'04 5:30:16
Lynnville 28 3 35N22'36 87w00'22 5:48:01
Lyons View 47 67 35N55'39 83w59'29 5:35:58
Macedonia 9 3 36N07'40 88w26'15 5:53:45
Macedonia 54 71 35N22'00 84w27'15 5:37:49
Macedonia 66 3 36N13'16 88w58'59 5:55:56
Macedonia 93 3 36N02'08 85w31'53 5:42:08
Mace's Hill 80 3 36N19 86w01 5:44:04
Macon 24 3 35N09'11 89w29'23 5:57:58
Maddox 36 23 35N09'39 88w13'08 5:52:53
Madge 79 3 35N22'52 89w40'00 5:58:40
Madie 48 3 36N16'54 89w27'41 5:57:51
Madison 19 4 36N15'22 86w42'50 5:46:51
Madison College 19 4 36N16 86w43 5:46:52
Madison Hall 57 3 35N33'48 88w52'11 5:55:29
Madisonville 62 67 35N31'11 84w21'49 5:37:27
Maggart 80 3 36N13 85w53 5:43:32
Maggies Mill 70 72 35N14'03 84w28'17 5:37:53
Magnolia 42 3 36N15'18 87w52'17 5:51:29
Mahan Village 65 51 36N10'05 84w29'21 5:37:57
Mahoney Mill 5 64 35N47'06 84w06'07 5:36:24
Major 95 34 36N04'49 86w20'23 5:45:22
Malesus 57 3 35N32'34 88w49'36 5:55:18
Mallory 79 39 35N04 90w04 6:00:16
Mallorys 94 48 35N57 86w53 5:47:32
Malone 28 3 35N03'46 87w12'14 5:48:49
Maloney Heights 47 67 35N56 83w54 5:35:36
Maloneyville 47 67 36N05'11 83w50'07 5:35:20
Manchester 16 12 35N28'54 86w05'19 5:44:21
Manchester Park 33 61 35N06'51 85w16'37 5:41:06
Manila 54 71 35N27'45 84w28'43 5:37:55
Mankinville 75 37 35N47'29 86w21'24 5:45:26
Manlyville 40 3 36N13'25 88w10'17 5:52:41
Manring 13 51 36N33'30 83w48'50 5:35:15
Mansfield 40 3 36N10'38 88w17'10 5:53:09
Mansford 26 19 35N11 86w07 5:44:28
Manskers Island 19 4 36N16 86w43 5:46:52
Manson 25 3 36N26 84w56 5:39:44

Maple Grove 14 3 36N27 85W21 5:41:24
Maple Grove 56 3 36N33'18 86W02'54 5:44:12
Maple Grove 57 3 35N35'03 88W42'58 5:54:52
Maple Grove 61 54 35N42'43 84W41'20 5:38:45
Maple Hill 82 2 36N33'49 82W16'13 5:29:05
Maplehurst 82 1 36N28 82W15 5:29:00
Maples 1 62 36N09'17 84W07'25 5:36:30
Maple Spring 15 65 35N54'06 83W17'20 5:33:09
Maple Spring 41 3 35N39'27 87W22'27 5:49:30
Maplewood 19 4 36N13'47 86W43'50 5:46:55
Marble City 47 67 35N57'09 83W57'53 5:35:52
Marbledale 47 67 35N57'28 83W49'07 5:35:16
Marble Hall 37 70 36N24 83W00 5:32:00
Marble Hill 5 64 35N43'06 84W08'26 5:36:34
Marble Hill 64 3 35N12'12 86W19'24 5:45:18
Marble Plains 26 19 35N11 86W07 5:44:28
Marbleton 86 1 36N14'27 82W19'36 5:29:18
Marbuts 28 3 35N01'38 87W10'04 5:48:40
Marguerite 32 67 36N15'21 83W15'29 5:33:02
Marimont 33 74 35N01'20 85W11'05 5:40:44
Marion 13 51 36N32'25 83W55'38 5:35:43
Marion 63 3 36N19'43 87W26'02 5:49:44
Markham 48 3 36N23 89W29 5:57:56
Marlow 1 62 36N03'48 84W14'36 5:36:58
Marlyn Hills 82 2 36N33'05 82W12'56 5:28:52
Marmor 5 64 35N47'17 84W07'02 5:36:28
Marrowbone 11 10 36N14'35 87W00'25 5:48:02
Marshall 37 70 36N34'22 82W39'40 5:30:39
Marshall Heights 59 30 35N26'46 86W48'05 5:47:12
Marshall Hill 54 71 35N31'41 84W35'30 5:38:22
Mars Hill 50 29 35N15'54 87W17'23 5:49:10
Martel 53 68 35N49'18 84W13'11 5:36:53
Martel Estates 53 68 35N48'43 84W14'04 5:36:56
Martha 95 34 36N13'47 86W25'37 5:45:42
Martha Washington 25 3 36N11 85W01 5:40:04
Martin 92 3 36N20'36 88W51'01 5:55:24
Martin Creek 71 3 36N09 85W38 5:42:32
Martin Landing 20 3 35N25'11 88W04'36 5:52:18
Martins Mills 91 3 35N12'07 87W57'07 5:51:48
Martin Springs 58 8 35N10'00 85W47'23 5:43:10
Marvin 30 65 36N14'53 82W59'56 5:32:00
Marvins Bluff Landing 68 3 35N34'57 88W00'43 5:52:03
Mary Chapel 29 55 36N20 83W22 5:33:28
Marys Grove 52 9 35N00 86W40 5:46:40
Maryville 5 64 35N45'23 83W58'14 5:35:53
Mascot 47 67 35N38'10 83W22'40 5:33:31
Mashburn 54 67 35N26'10 84W31'48 5:38:07
Mason 84 44 35N24'42 89W31'58 5:58:08
Mason Grove 2 3 35N45'52 88W57'29 5:55:50
Mason Hall 66 21 36N12'24 89W05'37 5:56:22
Mason Springs 13 51 36N29'21 83W32'21 5:34:09
Massengill Mill 29 55 36N12'20 83W33'22 5:34:13
Masseyville 12 3 35N17'37 88W42'23 5:54:50
Match 60 31 35N37 87W02 5:48:08
Matlock Ford 41 3 35N53'21 87W28'53 5:49:56
Maupin Row 90 75 36N19 82W21 5:29:24
Maury City 17 3 35N48'53 89W13'32 5:56:54
Maury Junction 17 3 35N52'29 89W12'13 5:56:49
Maxey 23 16 36N07'59 89W18'59 5:57:16
Maxwell 26 18 35N05'33 86W13'22 5:44:53
May Acres 45 67 36N09 83W25 5:33:40
Mayday 90 75 36N12'36 82W29'50 5:29:59
Mayland 18 9 36N02'48 85W12'00 5:40:48
Maymead 46 1 36N24'57 81W50'14 5:27:21
Maynardville 87 52 36N15'02 83W47'51 5:35:11
Mays Landing 36 3 35N23'53 88W02'08 5:52:09
Mayview Heights 47 67 36N02'46 84W00'35 5:36:02
McAllister Hill 70 73 35N01'41 84W20'46 5:37:23
McAllisters Crossroads 63 3 36N21'09 87W21'00 5:49:24
McAnna 66 3 36N20 89W10 5:56:40
McBurg 52 9 35N11'05 86W48'48 5:47:15
McCains 60 31 35N31'05 87W03'20 5:48:13
McClamerys Stand 91 3 35N10 87W44 5:50:56
McCloud 37 70 36N22'00 82W58'12 5:31:53
McClures Bend 80 41 36N15 85W57 5:43:48
McCoinsville 44 27 36N18'57 85W38'11 5:42:33
McConnell 66 3 36N25'22 88W51'06 5:55:24
McCookville 78 60 35N45'49 83W31'18 5:34:05
McCormack Crossing 60 3 35N45'11 86W57'02 5:47:48
McCullough 23 16 36N02 89W23 5:57:32
McCutchen Heights 66 3 36N22'14 89W03'53 5:56:16
McDaniel 94 3 35N50'02 86W41'45 5:46:47
McDonald 6 53 35N06'48 84W58'58 5:39:56
McDonald Hill 37 70 36N23'30 82W58'46 5:31:55
McElroy 88 3 35N47'32 85W33'49 5:42:15
McEwen 43 3 36N06'28 87W37'59 5:50:32
McFarland 70 73 35N10'20 84W23'42 5:37:35
McGeetown 70 73 35N02'06 84W19'29 5:37:18
McGhee 62 68 35N36'41 84W12'32 5:36:50
McGinnis Ford 18 9 35N55'59 84W54'24 5:39:38
McGlamerys Stand 91 3 35N08'48 87W44'42 5:50:59
McHarg 70 73 35N00'17 84W24'02 5:37:36
McIllwain 3 3 35N51'46 88W04'47 5:52:19
McKenzie 9 3 36N07'57 88W31'07 5:54:04
McKinley 90 75 36N18'33 82W24'38 5:29:39
McKinnon 42 3 36N18'58 87W54'25 5:51:38
McKnight 60 3 35N47'31 87W08'19 5:48:33
McLemoresville 9 3 35N59'14 88W34'28 5:54:18
McLin's Corner 17 3 35N54 89W15 5:57:00
McMahan 78 60 35N54'57 83W40'22 5:34:41
McMillan 47 67 36N02'37 83W47'29 5:35:10
McMinnville 89 46 35N41 85W46 5:43:04
McMinnville Plaza 89 46 35N42 85W46 5:43:04
McMullens 5 68 35N42'59 84W10'22 5:36:41
McNairy 55 3 35N18'43 88W37'38 5:54:31
McPheeter Bend 37 70 36N29'24 82W43'19 5:30:53
McPherson Landing 72 54 35N33'16 84W50'47 5:39:23
Meacham 23 16 36N07'57 89W20'54 5:57:24
Meades Quarry 47 67 35N57'08 83W51'56 5:35:28
Meadorville 56 3 36N28'28 86W02'10 5:44:09
Meadow 53 68 35N41'51 84W09'52 5:36:39
Meadow Branch 29 55 36N20 83W22 5:33:28
Meadow Brook 5 64 35N46'55 83W56'55 5:35:48
Meadow Mead 40 26 36N18'25 88W17'29 5:53:10
Meadow View 33 61 35N17 84W57 5:39:48
Meadowview 50 29 35N15'25 87W20'48 5:49:23
Meadowview Gardens 73 67 35N56 84W33 5:38:12
Meagsville 44 27 36N21 85W39 5:42:36
Mecca 54 71 35N21'15 84W25'16 5:37:41
Mechanicsville 8 3 35N57 85W49 5:43:16
Medford 1 62 36N10'52 84W08'38 5:36:35
Medina 27 21 35N48'10 88W46'29 5:55:06
Medon 57 3 35N27'26 88W52'07 5:55:28
Meigs Cabin Area 61 54 35N41'14 84W42'37 5:38:50
Melbourne 1 62 36N10'46 83W59'35 5:35:58
Melrose 5 64 35N44'45 83W50'07 5:35:20
Melrose 19 4 36N07 86W47 5:47:08
Melrose Park 16 12 35N29'43 86W06'03 5:44:24
Melville 33 61 35N14'00 85W11'33 5:40:46
Melville Hill 33 61 35N16 85W11 5:40:44
Melvine 4 15 35N43'58 85W03'29 5:40:14
Melwood 12 3 35N14 88W36 5:54:24
Memorial 14 3 36N32 85W51 5:43:24
Memphis 79 39 35N08'58 90W02'56 6:00:12
Memphis State University 79 39 35N07 89W57 5:59:48
Mengelwood 23 16 36N02'43 89W32'37 5:58:10
Mentor 5 64 35N49'18 84W00'43 5:36:03
Mercer 57 3 35N28'45 89W02'32 5:56:10
Meredith Cave 7 66 36N23 84W07 5:36:28
Meridian 18 15 35N53'24 84W55'54 5:39:44
Merry Oaks 19 4 36N09'51 86W41'06 5:46:44
Metal Ford 51 3 35N27'51 87W31'18 5:50:05
Meux Corner 38 3 35N26'23 89W24'21 5:57:37
Michie 55 3 35N03'22 88W26'07 5:53:44
Middlebrook Acres 47 67 35N56'28 84W03'38 5:36:15
Middlebrook Heights 47 67 35N57'22 83W59'30 5:35:58
Middleburg 35 3 35N11'52 89W05'15 5:56:21
Middleburg 39 3 35N35'29 88W15'24 5:53:02
Middle City 23 16 36N02'10 89W26'06 5:57:44
Middle Creek 78 60 35N49'17 83W32'21 5:34:09
Middle Fork 39 3 35N32'09 88W29'12 5:53:57
Middle Landing 48 3 36N21'12 89W25'02 5:57:40
Middle Settlement 5 64 35N47'50 84W03'19 5:36:13
Middleton 35 3 35N03'52 88W53'27 5:55:34
Middle Valley 33 61 35N11'45 85W11'05 5:40:44
Middle Valley Estates 33 61 35N10'02 85W12'10 5:40:49
Midfields 82 2 36N34'12 82W34'48 5:30:19
Midland 75 3 35N40'12 86W28'50 5:45:55
Midtown 73 67 35N52'46 84W33'51 5:38:15
Midtown Heights 73 67 35N52'35 84W33'24 5:38:14
Midvale 33 61 35N05'19 85W18'41 5:41:15
Midway 2 5 35N25'45 86W19'22 5:45:17
Midway 14 3 36N33'13 85W36'33 5:42:26
Midway 15 65 35N52'11 83W01'50 5:32:07
Midway 16 18 35N12'33 85W52'58 5:43:32
Midway 17 3 35N42'52 88W59'55 5:56:00
Midway 21 3 35N57'16 85W45'18 5:43:01
Midway 23 16 36N00'21 89W41'21 5:58:45
Midway 30 65 36N10'36 82W59'49 5:31:59
Midway 37 70 36N33'45 82W52'24 5:31:30
Midway 40 3 36N29'16 88W29'53 5:54:00
Midway 46 1 36N24'49 81W46'05 5:27:04
Midway 47 67 36N04 83W41 5:34:44
Midway 66 3 36N23'11 88W57'48 5:55:51
Midway 69 3 36N30'00 85W10'41 5:40:43
Midway 73 67 35N46'34 84W33'06 5:38:12
Midway 90 75 36N18'00 82W25'26 5:29:42
Mifflin 12 3 35N33'10 88W34'48 5:54:19
Milan 27 20 35N55'11 88W45'32 5:55:02
Milburnton 30 65 36N18'41 82W38'43 5:30:35
Miles Crossroads 14 3 36N32'33 85W44'19 5:42:57
Mile Straight 33 61 35N12'57 85W13'40 5:40:55
Milky Way 28 22 35N12 87W02 5:48:08
Mill Brook 90 63 36N15'58 82W37'38 5:30:31
Mill Creek 1 62 36N14'42 84W00'48 5:36:03
Mill Creek 40 3 36N26'57 88W24'09 5:53:37
Mill Creek 41 3 35N55 87W21 5:49:24
Mill Creek 46 1 36N22'22 81W51'35 5:27:26
Mill Creek 65 56 36N15'48 84W35'18 5:38:21
Mill Creek 71 34 36N11 85W28 5:41:52
Milldale 74 35 36N35'24 86W45'49 5:47:03
Milledgeville 55 3 35N22'22 88W22'03 5:53:28
Miller 24 3 35N20'57 89W16'57 5:57:08
Miller 90 75 36N18'35 82W26'02 5:29:44
Miller Cove 5 64 35N42'35 83W49'03 5:35:16
Miller Flats 37 70 36N26'15 82W52'21 5:31:29
Miller's Cove 5 64 35N44 83W49 5:35:16
Millersville 83 50 36N22'16 86W42'36 5:46:50
Millertown 47 67 36N02'27 83W50'37 5:35:22
Millican 78 60 35N49 83W33 5:34:12
Millican Grove 78 60 35N54'18 83W30'30 5:34:02
Milligan College 10 1 36N18 82W18 5:29:12
Millington 79 40 35N20'29 89W53'50 5:59:35
Mill Point 82 1 36N34'39 82W21'37 5:29:26
Mill Seat 60 3 35N50'21 87W12'16 5:48:49
Millsfield 23 16 36N08'29 89W22'57 5:57:32
Mill Spring 45 67 36N09'23 83W31'32 5:34:06
Millstone 18 9 35N55'12 84W47'40 5:39:11
Milltown 43 3 35N59'53 87W35'40 5:50:23
Milltown 44 3 36N23'37 85W47'58 5:43:12
Milltown 59 30 35N35'02 86W47'12 5:47:09
Millview 94 48 35N52'44 86W47'27 5:47:10
Millville 52 9 35N07'36 86W48'47 5:47:15
Milo 4 15 35N41 84W52 5:39:28
Milton 75 3 35N55'47 86W10'54 5:44:44
Mimms 19 4 36N06 86W45 5:47:00
Mimosa 52 9 35N13'13 86W31'09 5:46:05
Mimosa Estates 5 64 35N50'52 83W58'06 5:35:52
Mimosa Heights 5 64 35N50'18 83W58'01 5:35:52
Mineral Park 6 53 35N06'02 85W00'23 5:40:02
Mineral Springs 58 8 35N05'25 85W32'04 5:42:08
Mineral Springs 67 3 36N09'42 85W13'31 5:40:54
Minersville 1 62 36N09'39 84W12'26 5:36:50
Minnick 66 3 36N16'05 89W21'57 5:57:28
Minnow Ford 28 3 35N03'50 87W04'31 5:48:18
Minor Hill 28 3 35N03'19 87W09'27 5:48:38
Mint 5 64 35N38'30 84W02'19 5:36:09
Minton Mill 13 51 36N31'23 83W41'11 5:34:45
Miser Station 5 64 35N46'42 84W05'26 5:36:22
Mission Oaks 33 61 34N59'18 85W15'25 5:41:02
Miston 23 16 36N09'53 89W29'25 5:57:58
Mitchell 74 3 36N37'37 86W34'05 5:46:16
Mitchell Ford 29 55 36N09'41 83W39'51 5:34:39
Mitchell Springs 90 75 36N22'48 82W35'10 5:30:21
Mitchellville 83 50 36N37'55 86W32'27 5:46:10
Mixie 9 3 36N08'02 88W19'54 5:53:20
Mobra 93 3 35N52'54 85W15'36 5:41:02
Moccasin 91 3 35N24'12 87W44'26 5:50:58
Mockingbird Hill 47 67 35N54'01 83W58'57 5:35:56
Model 81 3 36N39 87W59 5:51:56
Moffatt 66 3 36N19'36 89W05'28 5:56:22
Mohawk 30 65 36N12'03 83W03'10 5:32:13
Mohawk Crossroad 30 65 36N13'17 83W01'45 5:32:07
Molasses Point Landing 84 3 35N25'32 90W06'56 6:00:28
Mole 37 70 36N28'51 82W45'17 5:31:01
Molino 52 9 35N06'26 86W40'29 5:46:42
Mona 75 37 35N59'14 86W25'17 5:45:41
Monoville 80 3 36N18'25 85W58'25 5:43:54
Monroe 67 3 36N26'13 85W14'33 5:40:58
Montague 19 4 36N14'53 86W43'11 5:46:53
Montague 72 74 35N27'24 85W05'52 5:40:23
Monteagle 58 3 35N14'24 85W50'23 5:43:22
Monterey 71 3 36N08'51 85W16'06 5:41:04
Montezuma 12 3 35N23'37 88W41'36 5:54:46
Montgomery 20 3 35N27'55 88W09'23 5:52:38
Montgomery 76 58 36N19'33 84W22'15 5:37:29
Montvale 5 64 35N46 83W58 5:35:52
Moodyville 69 3 36N32'17 85W04'31 5:40:18
Mooney 91 3 35N24'39 87W53'38 5:51:35
Mooneyham 88 3 35N44'44 85W20'15 5:41:21
Moons 40 3 36N15 88W09 5:52:36
Moore 64 33 35N17 86W21 5:45:24
Moore Crossing 58 8 34N59'53 85W38'23 5:42:34
Moore Ford 2 6 35N28'28 86W24'03 5:45:36
Mooreland Heights 47 67 35N54'59 83W53'22 5:35:33
Mooresburg 37 70 36N20'47 83W13'42 5:32:55
Mooresburg Springs 37 70 36N22'19 83W13'50 5:32:55
Moores Camp (Devonia P O) 1 62 36N08'58 84W23'09 5:37:33
Moores Chapel 27 20 35N55 88W46 5:55:04
Mooresville 59 30 35N26'24 86W54'51 5:47:39
Mooring 48 3 36N18'50 89W30'57 5:58:04
Moorman 24 3 35N18'40 89W23'15 5:57:33
Moralfa 5 64 35N47'32 84W06'16 5:36:25
Morgan Springs 72 74 35N33'41 85W06'07 5:40:24
Morganton 53 68 35N38'36 84W13'38 5:36:55
Morgantown 72 74 35N30'12 85W01'45 5:40:07
Morganville 58 8 35N12 85W31 5:42:04
Morley 7 66 36N33'04 84W02'54 5:36:12
Morny 19 4 36N17'17 86W53'38 5:47:35
Morrell Mill 28 3 35N04'39 86W52'21 5:47:29
Morris Chapel 3 3 36N04 88W06 5:52:24
Morris Chapel 36 3 35N19'26 88W21'08 5:53:25
Morrison 89 3 35N36'10 85W55'11 5:43:41
Morrison City 82 2 36N35'29 82W34'25 5:30:18
Morrison Creek 44 27 36N19'50 85W35'40 5:42:23
Morristown 32 67 36N12'50 83W17'42 5:33:11
Morton Hill 38 3 35N28'17 89W17'19 5:57:09
Moscow 24 3 35N03'43 89W24'14 5:57:37
Mosheim 30 65 36N11'22 82W57'31 5:31:50
Moshina Heights 47 67 35N59'07 83W48'06 5:35:12
Moss 14 3 36N35'21 85W37'01 5:42:28

Mossy Grove 65 51 35N56 84w33 5:38:12
Mossy Spring 87 52 36N21'17 83w55'14 5:35:41
Motch 13 51 36N34'57 83w47'03 5:35:08
Mountain City 46 1 36N28'28 81w48'18 5:27:13
Mountain Dale 86 1 36N08 82w25 5:29:40
Mountain Home 90 75 36N18'38 82w22'24 5:29:30
Mountain View 16 12 35N28 86w05 5:44:20
Mountain View 72 74 35N29'11 85w01'56 5:40:08
Mountain View 76 58 36N22'55 84w35'09 5:38:21
Mountain View Acres 26 19 35N11'43 86w05'48 5:44:23
Mount Airy 69 3 36N32'48 85w05'02 5:40:20
Mount Airy 77 3 35N26'25 85w20'54 5:41:24
Mount Ararat 8 3 35N54'07 85w56'40 5:43:47
Mount Carmel 20 3 35N30'03 88w00'02 5:52:00
Mount Carmel 30 65 36N15'05 82w57'12 5:31:49
Mount Carmel 37 70 36N32'43 82w39'40 5:30:39
Mount Carmel 84 44 35N29'52 89w38'56 5:58:36
Mount Carmel 90 75 36N09'02 82w35'24 5:30:22
Mount Crest 4 15 35N40'11 85w14'24 5:40:58
Mount Denson 74 35 36N32'35 86w53'20 5:47:33
Mount Gilead 39 3 35N45'57 88w32'23 5:54:10
Mount Harmony 6 54 35N18'44 84w51'35 5:39:26
Mount Harmony 54 71 35N31'13 84w30'18 5:38:01
Mount Herman 64 6 35N21'30 86w29'03 5:45:56
Mount Herman 92 3 36N09 88w48 5:55:12
Mount Hope 91 3 35N21'33 87w44'52 5:50:59
Mount Horeb 45 67 36N05'28 83w26'25 5:33:46
Mount Joy 60 9 35N31'29 87w15'41 5:49:03
Mount Juliet 95 49 36N12'00 86w31'07 5:46:04
Mount Lebanon 20 3 35N34'31 88w03'01 5:52:12
Mount Lebanon 50 29 35N14'47 87w27'58 5:49:52
Mount Leo 89 46 35N40'16 85w45'19 5:43:01
Mount Moriah 3 3 35N57'44 88w02'42 5:52:11
Mount Nebo 50 29 35N03'27 87w32'14 5:50:09
Mount Olive 31 3 35N42 85w46 5:43:04
Mount Olive 47 67 35N54'29 83w56'21 5:35:45
Mount Olive 58 8 35N12'06 85w32'49 5:42:11
Mount Olive 75 37 35N53'15 86w26'27 5:45:46
Mount Orange 27 8 35N57'24 89w00'12 5:56:01
Mount Pelia 92 3 36N19'03 88w56'58 5:55:48
Mount Pisgah 93 3 35N49 85w36 5:42:24
Mount Pleasant 30 65 36N10'10 82w54'25 5:31:38
Mount Pleasant 40 3 36N29'11 88w14'55 5:53:00
Mount Pleasant 60 9 35N32'03 87w12'25 5:48:50
Mount Pleasant 71 34 36N11 85w28 5:41:52
Mount Pleasant 76 58 36N21 84w35 5:38:20
Mount Tabor 5 64 35N45'56 84w01'19 5:36:05
Mount Tabor 20 3 35N37'23 88w06'59 5:52:28
Mount Tucker Addition 82 1 36N32'41 82w17'46 5:29:11
Mount Union 44 27 36N16'13 85w31'31 5:42:06
Mount Union 69 3 36N32'11 85w06'23 5:40:26
Mount Vernon 5 64 35N48'28 84w07'15 5:36:29
Mount Vernon 18 9 35N52 84w41 5:38:44
Mount Vernon 62 67 35N24'42 84w21'52 5:37:27
Mount Vernon 75 3 35N44'04 86w36'49 5:46:27
Mount Vernon 83 50 36N32'07 86w20'32 5:45:22
Mount View 19 4 36N03'16 86w37'08 5:46:29
Mount View 31 3 35N17'34 85w51'55 5:43:28
Mount View 76 58 36N21 84w35 5:38:20
Mount Vinson 55 3 35N11'26 88w23'40 5:53:35
Mount Zion 11 9 36N20'09 86w58'36 5:47:54
Mount Zion 50 29 35N08'55 87w28'45 5:49:55
Mount Zion 55 3 35N21'31 88w24'09 5:53:37
Mount Zion 62 67 35N31'30 84w11'37 5:36:46
Mount Zion 63 3 36N19'46 87w22'29 5:49:30
Mount Zion 89 46 35N34'16 85w49'14 5:43:17
Mourberry 93 3 35N56 85w28 5:41:52
Mousetail Landing 68 3 35N40'33 88w00'53 5:52:04
Mowbray 33 61 35N16'36 85w13'20 5:40:53
Mowls Mill 37 70 36N23'49 82w51'40 5:31:27
Mud Creek 16 12 35N35'44 86w00'48 5:44:03
Muddy Pond 67 3 36N12'30 85w06'46 5:40:27
Mudsink 94 48 35N54'37 86w48'47 5:47:15
Mudtavern 19 4 36N09'04 86w41'30 5:46:46
Mudville 79 40 35N22'39 89w44'18 5:58:57
Mulberry 52 9 35N12'38 86w27'37 5:45:50
Mulberry Gap 34 51 36N32 83w13 5:32:52
Mulberry Hill 81 3 36N29 87w50 5:51:20
Mule Hollow 47 67 35N58'48 83w51'02 5:35:24
Mullican 78 60 35N54 83w29 5:33:56
Mulloy 83 50 36N32'59 86w37'24 5:46:30
Munford 84 3 35N26'57 89w48'54 5:59:16
Murfreesboro 75 37 35N50'44 86w23'25 5:45:34
Murphy Hills 47 67 36N03'52 83w55'12 5:35:41
Murphy Mill 13 51 36N29'04 83w32'53 5:34:12
Murray Hills 33 61 35N05'35 85w12'12 5:40:49
Murray Store 54 71 35N37'01 84w37'27 5:38:30
Murrelltown 37 70 36N28'53 83w07'40 5:32:31
Myers 26 19 35N12'49 86w08'00 5:44:32
Nameless 44 3 36N15'18 85w42'37 5:42:50
Nance 17 14 35N50'05 89w07'15 5:56:29
Nance Landing 36 3 35N24'11 88w02'36 5:52:10
Nankipoo 49 3 35N52'25 89w29'17 5:57:57
Napier 51 3 35N33 87w34 5:50:16
Narrow Valley 29 55 36N17 83w31 5:34:04
Nars Ford 62 67 35N25'15 84w15'32 5:37:02
Nash 71 3 36N03'35 85w39'21 5:42:37
Nash Landing 36 3 35N04'18 88w17'27 5:53:10
Nashville 19 4 36N09'57 86w47'04 5:47:08
Natco 60 31 35N38'32 87w03'15 5:48:13
Natural Bridge 15 65 36N00 83w06 5:32:24
Nauvoo 23 16 36N05'37 89w24'51 5:57:39
Naval Air Station Memphis 79 40 35N20 89w53 5:59:32
Naval Hospital 79 40 35N20 89w53 5:59:32
Neapolis 60 31 35N42'38 86w58'32 5:47:54
Neboville 27 21 36N03'24 89w07'49 5:56:31
Needmore 32 67 36N18'14 83w09'53 5:32:40
Needmore 55 3 35N04'33 88w27'28 5:53:50
Needmore 59 30 35N27'13 86w46'20 5:47:05
Needmore 60 9 35N32'43 87w14'01 5:48:56
Needmore 63 3 36N27'58 87w34'43 5:50:19
Neely 57 3 35N32'34 88w57'10 5:55:49
Neely Crossroads 14 3 36N30'12 85w27'04 5:41:48
Neil 26 18 35N02'06 86w18'55 5:45:16
Nelsontown 82 2 36N33'22 82w32'57 5:30:12
Nemo 65 56 36N04'01 84w39'09 5:38:37
Neptune 11 10 36N20'59 87w12'17 5:48:49
Neubert 47 67 35N54'03 83w49'15 5:35:17
Neva 46 1 36N23'35 81w51'50 5:27:27
Newark 93 3 36N11 85w28 5:41:52
Newbern 23 16 36N06'46 89w15'42 5:57:03
New Bethel 24 3 35N05'40 89w32'04 5:58:08
New Bethel 54 54 35N18'39 84w34'01 5:38:16
New Bethel 82 1 36N25'34 82w21'11 5:29:25
New Boston 40 26 36N20'10 88w26'35 5:53:46
New Canton 37 70 36N31'17 82w45'30 5:31:02
Newcastle 35 3 35N13'13 89w10'31 5:56:42
Newcomb 7 66 36N33'13 84w09'58 5:36:40
New Corinth 29 55 36N12'06 83w36'55 5:34:28
New Deal 83 50 36N31'02 86w33'49 5:46:15
New Dellrose 52 9 35N06'34 86w48'33 5:47:14
New Due West 19 4 36N16 86w43 5:46:52
Newell Station 78 60 35N53 83w43 5:34:52
New Enterprise 27 21 35N54'20 88w50'59 5:55:24
New Era 18 15 35N47'22 85w05'16 5:40:21
New Era 78 60 35N50'28 83w36'07 5:34:24
New Era Landing 68 3 35N30'09 87w58'34 5:51:54
New Harmony 4 15 35N32'44 85w07'58 5:40:32
New Harmony 36 23 35N18'45 88w09'29 5:52:38
New Harmony 56 3 36N29'21 86w05'34 5:44:22
New Haven 76 58 36N29'43 84w35'07 5:38:20
New Herman 2 6 35N20'06 86w26'36 5:45:46
New Hope 11 10 36N19'51 87w16'10 5:49:05
New Hope 34 51 36N28'20 83w10'47 5:32:43
New Hope 36 3 35N11'40 88w20'15 5:53:21
New Hope 37 70 36N23'37 82w51'19 5:31:25
New Hope 40 3 36N11'30 88w15'14 5:53:01
New Hope 42 3 36N15'31 87w50'22 5:51:21
New Hope 43 3 36N02'20 87w38'20 5:50:33
New Hope 44 3 36N23'06 85w30'34 5:42:02
New Hope 52 9 35N02'17 86w29'27 5:45:58
New Hope 55 3 35N03'01 88w29'43 5:53:59
New Hope 58 8 35N01 85w43 5:42:52
New Hope 94 3 36N01'04 87w09'35 5:48:38
New Hope Landing 3 3 36N19'25 88w05'06 5:52:20
New Johnsonville 43 3 36N01'16 87w58'01 5:51:52
New Lawton 55 3 35N12'16 88w28'13 5:53:53
New Loyston 87 52 36N13'37 83w55'22 5:35:41
Newmansville 30 65 36N16'44 82w45'34 5:31:02
New Markam 48 3 36N23 89w29 5:57:56
New Market 45 67 36N06'14 83w33'10 5:34:13
New Markham 48 3 36N27'21 89w24'02 5:57:36
New Middleton 80 3 36N10'29 86w00'21 5:44:01
New Midway 73 67 35N50'26 84w25'07 5:37:40
Newport 15 65 35N58'01 83w11'16 5:32:45
New Prospect 50 29 35N13'28 87w15'04 5:49:00
New Providence 53 68 35N46'40 84w20'59 5:37:24
New Providence 63 3 36N32'55 87w22'45 5:49:31
New River 76 58 36N22'57 84w32'55 5:38:12
New Safford 39 3 35N43'44 88w12'15 5:52:49
New Salem 33 61 35N14'25 85w09'11 5:40:37
New Salem 44 27 36N18'50 85w40'11 5:42:41
Newsom 19 4 36N04'48 86w59'50 5:47:59
New Tazewell 13 51 36N26'33 83w35'59 5:34:24
Newton 18 15 35N47'41 85w12'45 5:40:51
Newton 70 73 34N59'38 84w22'16 5:37:29
Newtown 2 3 35N41'24 86w31'24 5:46:06
New Town 36 23 35N14'16 88w14'20 5:52:57
New Town 59 3 35N22'22 86w50'23 5:47:22
New Town 60 3 35N45'13 86w55'02 5:47:40
Newtown 70 73 34N59 84w22 5:37:28
Newtown 76 58 36N24'13 84w26'59 5:37:48
New Union 16 12 35N31'57 86w04'51 5:44:19
New Victory 90 75 36N18 82w28 5:29:52
New Zion 9 3 36N01'50 88w31'43 5:54:07
New Zion 56 3 36N34'11 86w10'24 5:44:42
Nickletown 58 8 35N05'27 85w35'40 5:42:23
Nicks Creek 7 66 36N25 84w29 5:37:56
Ninemile 4 15 35N41'59 85w05'44 5:40:23
Niota 54 71 35N30'48 84w32'43 5:38:11
Nix Landing 3 3 35N51'17 87w57'06 5:51:48
Nixon 36 3 35N06'53 88w15'24 5:53:02
Noah 16 12 35N34'30 86w11'31 5:44:46
Nobles 40 26 36N21'19 88w13'11 5:52:53
Nolensville 94 3 35N57'08 86w40'10 5:46:41
Nonaburg 54 71 35N24'44 84w27'41 5:37:51
Norene 95 49 36N03'24 86w14'33 5:44:58
Norma 76 58 36N20'13 84w23'08 5:37:33
Normandy 2 3 35N27'07 86w15'36 5:45:02
Norris 1 62 36N11'44 84w04'05 5:36:16
Norris Ford 65 56 36N08'14 84w52'21 5:39:29
Norris Park 1 62 36N13'30 84w04'41 5:36:19
North 19 4 36N10 86w48 5:47:12
North 79 39 35N10 90w01 6:00:04
Northbrook 47 67 36N02'55 83w58'54 5:35:56
North Cannon 8 3 35N52 86w03 5:44:12
North Carolina Landing 36 3 35N03'43 88w15'53 5:53:04
North Chattanooga 33 61 35N03'45 85w18'32 5:41:14
North Cleveland 6 53 35N10'31 84w52'05 5:39:28
Northcott 82 2 36N34'22 82w32'03 5:30:08
Northcutts Cove 31 3 35N42 85w46 5:43:04
Northeast 19 4 36N13 86w46 5:47:04
Northern Hills 33 61 35N08'42 85w14'34 5:40:58
North Etowah 54 54 35N20'31 84w31'45 5:38:07
North Fork Holston 82 2 36N34 82w36 5:30:24
North Glen Estates 33 61 35N08'11 85w15'20 5:41:01
North Hills 47 67 36N00'19 83w54'30 5:35:38
North Huntingdon 9 3 36N03 88w23 5:53:32
North Johnson City 90 75 36N20'40 82w22'37 5:29:30
North Knoxville 47 67 36N00'07 83w54'45 5:35:39
North Liberty 54 71 35N29'55 84w36'40 5:38:27
North of The River 44 3 36N24 85w44 5:42:56
Northpoint 62 67 35N37'20 84w28'41 5:37:55
Northport 15 65 35N58'30 83w10'47 5:32:43
North Riverside 51 3 35N33 87w34 5:50:16
Northshore Estates 33 61 35N06'58 85w12'44 5:40:51
Northshore Woods 47 67 35N53'46 84w01'35 5:36:06
North Side 57 3 35N39 88w53 5:55:32
North Side 80 3 36N21 85w57 5:43:48
North Springs 44 3 36N28'01 85w45'19 5:43:01
Northwoods 33 61 35N09'10 85w15'04 5:41:00
Norwood 1 62 36N01'49 84w19'25 5:37:18
Norwood 47 67 36N00'15 83w58'54 5:35:56
Notchy Creek 62 67 35N27'55 84w22'18 5:37:29
Nough 15 65 35N52'55 83w00'38 5:32:03
Nubia 83 50 36N38'07 86w21'46 5:45:27
Nucarbon 50 29 35N10 87w21 5:49:24
Number One 83 42 36N23 86w26 5:45:44
Nunnelly 41 3 35N51'34 87w28'09 5:49:53
Nutbush 38 3 35N41'53 89w24'29 5:57:38
Oak City 78 60 35N53'55 83w42'10 5:34:49
Oakdale 37 70 36N28 82w51 5:31:24
Oakdale 56 3 36N33'52 86w07'21 5:44:29
Oakdale 65 56 35N59'08 84w33'12 5:38:13
Oak Dale 67 3 36N25'09 85w12'21 5:40:49
Oakdale 74 3 36N28'29 86w42'44 5:46:51
Oakdale 93 3 35N56 85w28 5:41:52
Oakfield 57 3 35N42'48 88w47'38 5:55:11
Oak Grove 7 66 36N15'03 84w08'42 5:36:35
Oak Grove 10 1 36N17'53 82w15'29 5:29:02
Oak Grove 12 3 35N24'10 88w34'54 5:54:20
Oak Grove 13 51 36N33'13 83w29'51 5:33:59
Oak Grove 14 3 36N35'49 85w42'12 5:42:49
Oak Grove 22 3 36N00'27 87w28'56 5:49:56
Oak Grove 26 18 35N15'26 86w00'00 5:44:00
Oak Grove 28 3 35N05'44 87w06'59 5:48:28
Oak Grove 33 61 35N01'14 85w16'54 5:41:08
Oak Grove 36 23 35N16'28 88w13'47 5:52:55
Oak Grove 40 3 36N23'16 88w10'05 5:52:40
Oak Grove 45 67 36N02'19 83w21'04 5:33:24
Oak Grove 47 67 36N02'32 83w52'42 5:35:31
Oak Grove 51 3 35N27'17 87w32'20 5:50:09
Oak Grove 53 68 35N48'08 84w18'55 5:37:16
Oak Grove 58 8 35N07'36 85w30'58 5:42:04
Oak Grove 62 67 35N34'39 84w18'43 5:37:15
Oak Grove 67 3 36N22'33 85w15'42 5:41:03
Oak Grove 70 72 35N10'52 84w37'11 5:38:29
Oak Grove 83 50 36N34'14 86w22'48 5:45:31
Oak Grove 84 44 35N34 89w42 5:58:48
Oak Grove 87 52 36N21'12 83w49'08 5:35:17
Oak Grove 89 3 35N41'59 85w57'45 5:43:51
Oak Grove 90 75 36N24'42 82w25'29 5:29:42
Oak Grove Heights 47 67 35N58'02 84w06'43 5:36:27
Oak Hill 15 65 36N00'09 82w59'12 5:31:57
Oak Hill 18 15 35N59'22 85w00'36 5:40:02
Oak Hill 19 4 36N05'16 86w46'59 5:47:08
Oak Hill 40 3 36N26'17 88w05'19 5:52:21
Oak Hill 50 29 35N09'49 87w16'27 5:49:06
Oak Hill 59 3 35N27'19 86w42'45 5:46:51
Oak Hill 67 3 36N16'11 85w20'15 5:41:21
Oak Hill 69 3 36N36'08 85w13'15 5:40:53
Oak Hill 73 67 35N44'36 84w37'10 5:38:29
Oak Hill 82 2 36N34'16 82w11'58 5:28:48
Oak Hill North 33 61 35N08'48 85w15'41 5:41:03
Oak Hills Estates 73 62 35N59'08 84w20'00 5:37:20
Oakhurst 5 64 35N46 83w58 5:35:52
Oakknob 56 3 36N32 86w02 5:44:08
Oakland 24 3 35N13'44 89w30'54 5:58:04
Oakland 40 26 36N16'40 88w13'46 5:52:55
Oakland 45 67 36N03'03 83w28'18 5:33:53
Oakland 47 67 36N01'54 83w54'39 5:35:39
Oakland 74 3 36N30'02 86w49'50 5:47:19
Oakland 89 46 35N42 85w46 5:43:04
Oakland 90 63 36N16'17 82w37'15 5:30:29
Oakland 95 34 36N16'15 86w20'33 5:45:22
Oakleigh Estates 82 2 36N35 82w11 5:28:44
Oakley 67 3 36N30'28 85w18'38 5:41:15

Oak Park 26 13 35N20'45 86W13'05 5:44:52
Oakplain 11 10 36N16 87W04 5:48:16
Oak Plains 63 32 36N25'45 87W10'09 5:48:41
Oak Ridge 1 62 36N00'37 84W16'11 5:37:05
Oakridge 63 3 36N23'39 87W27'30 5:49:50
Oak View 5 64 35N44 83W49 5:35:16
Oakview 38 24 35N38'50 89W19'00 5:57:16
Oakview 82 1 36N33'26 82W20'25 5:29:22
Oakville 79 40 35N03'54 89W56'27 5:59:46
Oakwood 6 53 35N13'17 84W48'41 5:39:15
Oakwood 63 3 36N32'09 87W34'46 5:50:19
Obed Junction 65
56 36N04'46 84W45'50 5:39:03
Obey City 67 3 36N10'25 85W10'05 5:40:40
Obion 66 3 36N15'32 89W11'30 5:56:46
Ocana 83 43 36N18 86W37 5:46:28
Ocoee 70 72 35N07'20 84W43'08 5:38:53
O'Connors 93 3 35N56 85W28 5:41:52
Odd Fellows Hall 28
22 35N18'15 86W57'29 5:47:50
Odens Bend 83 42 36N23 86W26 5:45:44
Offset 82 2 36N36'23 81W55'11 5:27:41
Offutt 1 62 36N10'08 84W07'49 5:36:31
Ogden 72 74 35N30'31 85W06'05 5:40:24
Oglesby 19 4 36N06 86W45 5:47:00
Okalona 67 22 36N19'35 85W20'24 5:41:22
Okolona 10 1 36N16'16 82W19'08 5:29:17
Okolona 37 70 36N34'55 82W46'22 5:31:05
Okra 69 3 36N36'57 85W07'19 5:40:29
Old Antioch 44 27 36N24'34 85W32'07 5:42:08
Old Cumberland 4
15 35N32'55 85W22'21 5:41:29
Olde Mill 33 61 35N10'03 85W13'36 5:40:54
Old Englewood 54
71 35N24'31 84W29'12 5:37:57
Old Ferry Landing 35
3 35N23'29 89W04'34 5:56:18
Old Fields Place 43
3 36N05'25 87W50'13 5:51:21
Oldfort 70 72 35N03'55 84W43'57 5:38:56
Old Fremont 66 3 36N26'10 89W10'22 5:56:41
Old Glory 5 64 35N46'35 84W01'32 5:36:06
Oldham 78 60 35N46'34 83W28'56 5:33:56
Old Hickory 19 4 36N15'35 86W38'52 5:46:35
Old Hometown 79
39 35N02 90W03 6:00:12
Old Lawton 55 3 35N12'46 88W28'10 5:53:53
Old Middleton 80
3 36N10'34 85W59'37 5:43:58
Old Patty 70 54 35N14'44 84W36'54 5:38:28
Old Salem 26 18 35N05'02 86W15'02 5:45:00
Old Springville 40
3 36N17'17 88W08'43 5:52:35
Old Sweetwater 62
68 35N38'52 84W25'35 5:37:42
Oldtown 15 65 35N58'48 83W09'57 5:32:40
Old Washington 72
74 35N32'04 84W54'26 5:39:38
Old Well Crossing 89
3 35N37'21 85W53'04 5:43:32
Old Winesap 18 15 35N47'25 85W09'55 5:40:40
Old Zion 93 3 35N58'21 85W33'50 5:42:15
Olive Branch 49
28 35N45 89W32 5:58:08
Olivehill 36 3 35N16'26 88W01'56 5:52:08
Oliver Springs 73
63 36N02'40 84W20'40 5:37:23
Olivet 28 3 35N17'39 87W01'38 5:48:07
Olivet 36 23 35N12'51 88W12'01 5:52:48
Oneida 76 58 36N29'53 84W30'46 5:38:03
Only 41 3 35N51'42 87W41'30 5:50:46
Ooltewah 33 61 35N04'30 85W03'44 5:40:15
Opossum 49 28 35N42'35 89W33'52 5:58:15
Opossum Creek Pines 33
61 35N18'21 85W05'53 5:40:24
Oral 73 67 35N50'00 84W21'23 5:37:26
Orchard Knob 58
61 35N02'23 85W16'41 5:41:07
Orchard View 73
63 35N59'42 84W22'38 5:37:31
Orebank 82 2 36N33'20 82W28'05 5:29:52
Ore Springs 92 47 36N17'41 88W34'41 5:54:19
Orgains Crossroads 63
32 36N26'20 87W22'09 5:49:29
Orlinda 74 3 36N36'03 86W43'00 5:46:52
Orme 58 8 35N00'43 85W48'17 5:43:13
Orrs 59 3 35N25'26 86W43'23 5:46:54
Orysa 49 28 35N37'20 89W29'52 5:57:59
Osage 40 26 36N21'21 88W24'42 5:53:39
Osborne Ford 59
30 35N29'46 86W45'43 5:47:03
Oslin 59 30 35N31'42 86W45'51 5:47:03
Ostella 59 30 35N19'22 86W47'31 5:47:10
Oswego 7 66 36N35 84W08 5:36:32
Otes 37 70 36N18'32 83W01'23 5:32:06
Otter Creek Junction 18
15 35N56'08 84W55'55 5:39:44
Ottinger 15 65 36N03'23 83W02'43 5:32:11
Ottway 30 65 36N16'02 82W52'01 5:31:28
Overall 75 37 35N48'28 86W28'23 5:45:54
Overlook 5 64 35N46 83W58 5:35:52
Overstreets 14 11 36N33 85W30 5:42:00
Overton 79 40 35N14'49 89W59'44 5:59:59
Ovilla 50 29 35N18'48 87W33'40 5:50:15
Ovoca 16 13 35N24'34 86W12'16 5:44:49
Owens Landing 20
3 35N24'54 88W03'23 5:52:14
Owl City 38 3 35N43'37 89W11'31 5:56:46
Owl City 48 3 36N20'04 89W25'46 5:57:43
Owlhollow 26 19 35N11 86W07 5:44:28
Owl Hoot 48 3 36N11'28 89W32'02 5:58:08
Oxmore Hills 47
67 35N59'39 84W06'17 5:36:25
Ozone 18 9 35N52'55 84W48'33 5:39:14
Ozone 67 3 36N30'30 85W17'00 5:41:08
Pactolus 82 2 36N29'56 82W31'18 5:30:05
Padgett Mill 15
65 35N50'44 83W13'35 5:32:54
Pailo 4 15 35N28'14 85W19'12 5:41:17
Paine Spring 72
74 35N34'28 85W00'32 5:40:02
Painter Spring 82
1 36N35'38 82W03'10 5:28:13
Painter Spring 90
1 36N07'28 82W35'50 5:30:23
Paint Rock 73 68 35N44'39 84W30'53 5:38:04
Palestine 12 3 35N17'15 88W46'38 5:55:07
Palestine 39 25 35N35'27 88W26'31 5:53:46
Palestine 40 3 36N15'32 88W24'07 5:53:36
Palestine 74 35 36N30 86W53 5:47:32
Pall Mall 25 3 36N33'02 84W58'04 5:39:52
Palmer 31 3 35N21'04 85W34'04 5:42:16
Palmersville 92 3 36N24'12 88W35'14 5:54:21
Palmetto 59 3 35N29'31 86W39'52 5:46:39
Palmyra 63 3 36N26 87W29 5:49:56
Pandora 46 1 36N25'18 81W56'30 5:27:46
Pan Gap 33 61 35N03'06 85W22'04 5:41:28
Papaw 34 55 36N25'16 83W21'45 5:33:27
Paperville 82 2 36N34'28 82W08'30 5:28:34
Paragon Mills 19
4 36N06 86W45 5:47:00
Parham 83 50 36N27 86W32 5:46:08
Paris 40 26 36N18'07 88W19'36 5:53:18
Paris Landing 40
3 36N26'29 88W04'42 5:52:19
Parkburg 57 3 35N27'56 88W48'16 5:55:13
Park City 47 67 35N59'12 83W53'37 5:35:34
Parker 23 16 35N59'52 89W16'59 5:57:08
Parker 69 3 36N35'21 85W06'00 5:40:24
Parker Crossroads 39
3 35N47'37 88W23'27 5:53:34
Parker Ford 18 15 36N01'01 85W01'20 5:40:05
Parkey 34 51 36N32 83W13 5:32:52
Park Grove 50 29 35N18'42 87W22'23 5:49:30
Park Lane 63 32 36N33'37 87W23'39 5:49:35
Park Settlement 78
60 35N43'15 83W41'37 5:34:46
Park Shore 33 61 35N06 85W15 5:41:00
Parkshore Estates 33
61 35N10'31 85W09'56 5:40:40
Park Station 60 3 35N31'36 86W55'00 5:47:40
Parksville 70 72 35N05'57 84W39'03 5:38:36
Parkview 73 70 35N50'16 84W41'44 5:38:47
Parkway Village 79
40 35N03'51 89W54'22 5:59:37
Parragon 71 34 36N11'39 85W24'41 5:41:39
Parrottsville 15
65 36N00'33 83W05'33 5:32:22
Parry 94 48 35N52'37 86W52'53 5:47:32
Parsons 20 3 35N38'59 88W07'36 5:52:30
Paschall 94 48 35N57 86W53 5:47:32
Pasquo 19 4 36N02'04 86W58'26 5:47:54
Pate Hill 30 65 36N05'50 83W02'26 5:32:10
Patriot Landing 68
3 35N28'13 88W01'32 5:52:06
Patterson 75 3 35N49'23 86W36'34 5:46:26
Patterson Crossroads 13
51 36N33'57 83W38'50 5:34:35
Patterson Landing 36
3 35N24'58 88W03'52 5:52:15
Patterson Mill 70
73 34N59'26 84W26'23 5:37:46
Pattersonville 24
3 35N08'19 89W18'12 5:57:13
Patty 70 72 35N16 84W33 5:38:12
Paulette 87 52 36N11'29 83W53'24 5:35:34
Pawpaw Plains 73
67 35N52'11 84W20'15 5:37:21
Payne Cove 31 3 35N19 85W53 5:43:32
Paynes Store 85 3 36N23'19 86W15'45 5:45:03
Peabody 7 66 36N27'01 84W04'33 5:36:18
Peach 28 3 35N02'46 87W13'27 5:48:54
Peak 1 62 36N03'49 84W07'17 5:36:29
Peakland 61 54 35N37'41 84W45'47 5:39:03
Peanut 15 65 36N00 83W06 5:32:24
Pea Ridge 21 3 36N00 85W58 5:43:52
Pea Ridge 50 29 35N12'57 87W27'58 5:49:52
Pearl City 52 9 35N08'12 86W41'48 5:46:47
Peavine 18 15 36N01'32 84W53'47 5:39:35
Pebble Hill 55 3 35N05'57 88W25'30 5:53:42
Peckerwood Point 84
3 35N27'06 89W52'55 5:59:32
Pedigo 47 67 36N06'04 83W59'36 5:35:58
Peeled Chestnut 93
3 35N57'47 85W39'21 5:42:37
Peewee 7 66 36N15'41 84W16'34 5:37:06
Pegram 11 9 36N06'02 87W03'04 5:48:12
Pelham 31 3 35N18'36 85W52'51 5:43:31
Pence 23 16 36N10 89W29 5:57:56
Pennine 72 74 35N38'12 84W53'47 5:39:35
Pennington Bend 19
4 36N09 86W41 5:46:44
Pennington Chapel 87
52 36N17 83W36 5:34:24
Peoples Landing 68
3 35N48'46 87W58'07 5:51:52
Peppertown 50 29 35N00'21 87W23'25 5:49:34
Perkins Bluff Landing 36
3 35N12'39 88W18'45 5:53:15
Perkins Hill 60
31 35N37 87W02 5:48:08
Perogue Ford 41 3 35N49'19 87W41'06 5:50:44
Perrin Hollow 29
55 36N09 83W42 5:34:48
Perry 57 3 35N39 88W53 5:55:32
Perryville 20 3 35N37'14 88W02'30 5:52:10
Persia 37 70 36N20'23 83W00'11 5:32:01
Peter Cable Place 5
64 35N35'17 83W49'17 5:35:17
Petersburg 37 70 36N24'41 82W58'27 5:31:54
Petersburg 52 9 35N19'11 86W38'15 5:46:33
Peters Landing 68
3 35N28'50 87W59'24 5:51:58
Peters Mill 47 67 35N58'02 83W42'08 5:34:49
Petros 65 51 36N05'45 84W26'33 5:37:46
Pettyjohn Mill 82
1 36N31'49 82W26'52 5:29:47
Petway 11 10 36N12'54 87W09'09 5:48:37
Peytona 83 43 36N22'06 86W30'53 5:46:04
Peytonsville 94
48 35N49'06 86W46'46 5:47:07
Phiferes 88 3 35N39'55 85W26'45 5:41:47
Philadelphia 44 3 36N12 85W37 5:42:28
Philadelphia 53
68 35N40'46 84W24'14 5:37:37
Philadelphia 60 3 35N33'20 86W55'11 5:47:41
Philadelphia 90
63 36N10'11 82W38'12 5:30:33
Philippi 21 3 35N59'18 85W46'16 5:43:05
Phillippy 48 3 36N28'58 89W22'34 5:57:30
Phillips 36 23 35N14'27 88W13'07 5:52:52
Phillips Ford 67
3 36N12'58 85W07'33 5:40:30
Phipps Bend 37 70 36N27'58 82W48'40 5:31:15
Pickwatina Place 54
71 35N26'04 84W37'52 5:38:31
Pickwick 36 3 35N03 88W18 5:53:12
Pickwick Dam 36 3 35N03 88W14 5:52:56
Piedmont 31 3 35N16'03 85W51'22 5:43:25
Piedmont 45 67 36N01'33 83W31'40 5:34:07
Pierce 10 1 36N21'04 82W02'36 5:28:10
Pierce Station 66
3 36N28'15 88W54'54 5:55:40
Pigeon Forge 78
60 35N47'18 83W33'16 5:34:13
Pigeon River Estates 78
60 35N49 83W33 5:34:12
Pigeon Roost 43 3 36N06'11 87W48'29 5:51:14
Pikeville 4 15 35N36'20 85W11'20 5:40:45
Pillowville 92 3 36N09'09 88W39'41 5:54:39
Pilot Knob 30 65 36N16'05 82W59'45 5:31:59
Pilot Knob 83 42 36N23 86W26 5:45:44
Pilot Mountain 65
56 36N11'58 84W39'38 5:38:39
Pine Creek 88 3 35N37'37 85W26'12 5:41:45
Pine Crest 7 66 36N16'34 84W07'44 5:36:31
Pine Crest 10 1 36N17'57 82W19'05 5:29:16
Pine Grove 30 65 36N22'00 82W44'11 5:30:57
Pine Grove 53 68 35N44 84W21 5:37:24
Pine Grove 78 60 35N48'57 83W34'41 5:34:19
Pine Grove 88 3 35N45 85W27 5:41:48
Pine Haven 25 3 36N27'12 84W56'15 5:39:45
Pinehaven 79 40 35N20 89W53 5:59:32
Pine Hill 6 53 35N04'06 84W58'41 5:39:55
Pine Hill 14 3 36N34'06 85W38'47 5:42:35
Pine Hill 40 3 36N28'15 88W08'34 5:52:34
Pine Hill 58 8 35N12 85W31 5:42:04
Pine Hill 76 58 36N30'23 84W28'16 5:37:53
Pineland 61 54 35N31 84W47 5:39:08
Pine Orchard 65
51 35N58'05 84W39'14 5:38:37
Pine Point 40 3 36N15 88W09 5:52:36
Piner Ford 60 3 35N50'14 87W12'29 5:48:50
Pine Ridge 45 67 36N06 83W17 5:33:08
Pine Ridge 70 73 35N08'13 84W18'42 5:37:15
Pine Springs 47
67 35N52'34 84W04'39 5:36:19
Pine Top 35 3 35N18'11 88W48'03 5:55:12
Pine Top 53 68 35N48 84W16 5:37:04
Pinetree Estates 33
61 35N11'48 85W11'33 5:40:46
Pine View 68 3 35N43'50 87W56'04 5:51:44
Pineview Heights 16
13 35N22'00 86W13'51 5:44:55
Pineville 32 67 36N13'34 83W15'09 5:33:01
Pinewood 41 3 35N54'41 87W28'11 5:49:53
Piney 65 68 36N00'54 84W33'30 5:38:14
Piney 88 3 35N45 85W27 5:41:48
Piney Flats 82 1 36N25'10 82W18'15 5:29:13
Piney Grove 10 1 36N13'02 82W14'16 5:28:57
Piney Grove 35 3 35N18'03 88W49'31 5:55:18
Piney Grove 36 23 35N17'23 88W04'32 5:52:18
Piney Grove 54 54 35N21'44 84W36'02 5:38:24
Piney Shores Estates 72
74 35N40'47 84W49'05 5:39:16
Piney Woods 33 61 34N59'16 85W18'59 5:41:16
Pinhook 71 3 36N08'00 85W18'48 5:41:15
Pinhook 87 52 36N16'47 83W49'03 5:35:16
Pinkney 50 29 35N09'25 87W32'37 5:50:10
Pinnacle 11 9 36N21'00 86W56'23 5:47:46
Pinnacle 78 60 35N44'53 83W24'51 5:33:39
Pinson 57 3 35N29'24 88W43'14 5:54:53
Pioneer 7 66 36N25'03 84W18'51 5:37:15
Pioneer Village 73
70 35N46'26 84W43'16 5:38:53
Piperton 24 3 35N02'42 89W37'18 5:58:29
Pisgah 21 3 35N57 85W49 5:43:16
Pisgah 28 22 35N10'49 86W54'43 5:47:39
Pisgah 79 40 35N09'31 89W42'35 5:58:50
Pisgah 92 47 36N22'46 88W43'03 5:54:52
Pittman Center 78
59 35N45'33 83W23'46 5:33:35
Pittsburg Landing 36
3 35N09'08 88W19'22 5:53:17
Plainfield 5 64 35N46'11 83W57'32 5:35:50
Plain Grove 69 3 36N31'10 85W13'45 5:40:55
Plainview 75 36 35N41'59 86W20'42 5:45:23
Plainview 87 52 36N12 83W45 5:35:00
Plainview Heights 16
13 35N21'03 86W11'37 5:44:46
Plant 43 3 36N00'59 87W54'45 5:51:39
Plantation Hills 47
67 36N00'09 83W53'52 5:35:35
Plateau 18 15 36N04'58 85W06'41 5:40:27
Plateau of The Barrens 8
3 35N43 86W02 5:44:08
Pleasant Garden 86
1 36N08'02 82W18'39 5:29:15
Pleasant Grove 2
6 35N25'03 86W32'15 5:46:09
Pleasant Grove 15
65 35N53'35 83W10'23 5:32:42
Pleasant Grove 20
3 35N25'44 88W09'43 5:52:39
Pleasant Grove 45
60 36N02'07 83W38'09 5:34:33
Pleasant Grove 52
9 35N03'33 86W36'16 5:46:25
Pleasant Grove 58
8 35N04 85W39 5:42:36
Pleasant Grove 60
3 35N29'12 86W59'08 5:47:57
Pleasant Grove 76
58 36N33 84W27 5:37:48
Pleasant Grove 83
50 36N36'00 86W13'31 5:44:54
Pleasant Hill 3 3 35N57'46 88W12'10 5:52:49
Pleasant Hill 12
3 35N24'25 88W26'48 5:53:47

Pleasant Hill 14 3 36N27 85w21 5:41:24
Pleasant Hill 18 9 35N58'35 85w11'38 5:40:47
Pleasant Hill 20 3 35N28'58 88w09'04 5:52:36
Pleasant Hill 30 65 36N08'08 82w38'48 5:30:35
Pleasant Hill 37 70 36N17'08 83w03'53 5:32:16
Pleasant Hill 39 25 35N40'01 88w19'56 5:53:20
Pleasant Hill 40 3 36N10'49 88w11'38 5:52:47
Pleasant Hill 49 3 35N40'13 89w39'26 5:58:38
Pleasant Hill 56 3 36N34'06 86w04'19 5:44:17
Pleasant Hill 61 73 35N39'48 84w42'30 5:38:50
Pleasant Hill 64 33 35N17'41 86w19'19 5:45:17
Pleasant Hill 70 72 34N59 84w22 5:37:28
Pleasant Hill 75 3 35N46'17 86w35'50 5:46:23
Pleasant Hill 78 60 35N49 83w33 5:34:12
Pleasant Hills 47 67 35N59'44 84w00'07 5:36:00
Pleasant Hills 60 3 35N35'25 87w06'08 5:48:25
Pleasant Point 13 51 36N26 83w36 5:34:24
Pleasant Point 50 29 35N08'10 87w22'57 5:49:32
Pleasant Ridge 8 3 35N52'47 86w02'09 5:44:09
Pleasant Ridge 26 18 35N03 86w16 5:45:04
Pleasant Ridge 47 67 35N59'29 84w00'49 5:36:03
Pleasant Shade 80 3 36N22'41 85w56'59 5:43:48
Pleasant Vale 30 65 36N15'19 82w41'50 5:30:47
Pleasant Valley 50 29 35N18'10 87w13'18 5:48:53
Pleasant Valley 56 3 36N27'37 86w07'10 5:44:29
Pleasant Valley 90 75 36N20'53 82w30'58 5:30:04
Pleasant View 8 3 35N44'29 85w59'42 5:43:59
Pleasant View 11 9 36N23'39 87w02'12 5:48:09
Pleasant View 53 68 35N49'35 84w17'23 5:37:10
Pleasant View Landing 79 40 35N19'45 90w05'36 6:00:22
Pleasantville 41 3 35N40'01 87w41'54 5:50:48
Plunkets Creek 80 3 36N11 85w56 5:43:44
Pocahontas 16 12 35N38'14 86w02'43 5:44:11
Pocahontas 35 3 35N03'09 88w48'13 5:55:13
Poga 10 1 36N14'44 81w57'30 5:27:50
Point Pleasant 15 65 36N06'50 83w12'37 5:32:50
Point Pleasant 20 3 35N23'21 88w11'21 5:52:45
Point Pleasant Landing 20 3 35N23'09 88w11'19 5:52:45
Polecat 43 3 35N57'24 87w52'50 5:51:31
Polk 66 3 36N18'29 89w07'04 5:56:28
Pollard 42 3 36N16'34 87w40'41 5:50:43
Pollards Mill 36 23 35N02'52 88w05'52 5:52:23
Pomona 18 15 35N57'15 85w06'57 5:40:28
Pomona 22 3 36N02'01 87w20'52 5:49:23
Pond 22 3 36N06'17 87w25'44 5:49:43
Ponderosa 73 67 35N52'40 84w32'07 5:38:08
Ponderosa Hills 47 67 36N02'43 84w02'01 5:36:08
Ponders 73 67 35N45'43 84w33'21 5:38:13
Pond Grove 73 70 35N52'01 84w40'03 5:38:40
Pond Hill 54 71 35N33'06 84w36'54 5:38:28
Pondville 83 50 36N35'08 86w21'05 5:45:24
Poor 35 3 35N02'11 88w53'37 5:55:34
Pope 57 3 35N35 88w52 5:55:28
Pope 68 3 35N37'07 87w59'22 5:51:57
Poplar 1 62 36N02'48 84w18'37 5:37:14
Poplar Corner 38 3 35N39'35 89w05'57 5:56:24
Poplar Creek 60 3 35N40'34 87w12'33 5:48:50
Poplar Grove 1 62 36N05 84w08 5:36:32
Poplar Grove 13 51 36N33'22 83w31'56 5:34:08
Poplar Grove 43 3 35N58'34 87w35'20 5:50:21
Poplar Grove 49 16 35N55'47 89w25'17 5:57:41
Poplar Grove 71 34 36N11 85w28 5:41:52
Poplar Grove 82 2 36N27'51 82w35'10 5:30:21
Poplar Hill 28 3 35N01'51 86w57'35 5:47:50
Poplar Hill 54 71 35N27 84w36 5:38:24
Poplar Ridge 23 16 36N12'26 89w14'43 5:56:59
Poplar Springs 9 25 35N53'48 88w25'02 5:53:40
Poplar Springs 39 25 35N43'06 88w33'22 5:54:13
Poplar Springs 53 68 35N44'44 84w17'32 5:37:10
Poplar Springs 67 3 36N20'05 85w29'04 5:41:56
Poplar Springs 73 67 35N52'27 84w24'55 5:37:40
Poplar Top 60 3 35N36'49 87w08'35 5:48:34
Poplins Crossroads 2 3 35N34'48 86w35'03 5:46:20
Porter 22 3 35N59'03 87w16'39 5:49:07
Porter Court 40 26 36N19'21 88w19'28 5:53:18
Porterfield 8 3 35N52'47 86w09'42 5:44:39
Porter Ford 36 3 35N19'13 88w01'47 5:52:07
Porter Gap 49 3 35N54'55 89w29'50 5:57:59
Porters 60 31 35N31'26 87w09'23 5:48:38
Portland 83 50 36N34'54 86w30'59 5:46:04
Port Royal 63 3 36N33'13 87w08'31 5:48:34
Port Serena 33 61 35N11'02 85w10'16 5:40:41
Postelle 70 73 35N02'39 84w24'15 5:37:37
Post Oak 3 3 36N04'21 88w08'13 5:52:33
Post Oak 71 34 36N11 85w28 5:41:52
Postoak 73 70 35N52'24 84w37'51 5:38:31
Poteet 67 3 36N24 85w14 5:40:56
Potter Ford 18 15 36N04'21 84w54'10 5:39:37
Pottsville 60 31 35N38'16 86w49'31 5:47:18
Powder Springs 29 55 36N15'13 83w40'11 5:34:41
Powell 47 67 36N01'54 84w01'41 5:36:07
Powell Heights 47 67 36N02'21 84w01'49 5:36:07
Powell Landing 48 3 36N12'34 89w39'42 5:58:39
Powells Crossroads 58 8 35N11'22 85w29'09 5:41:57
Powell Station 47 67 36N03 84w02 5:36:08
Powers 24 3 35N14'15 89w24'49 5:57:39
Prairie Creek 33 61 35N11'43 85w08'14 5:40:33
Prairie Peninsula 33 61 35N11'35 85w08'51 5:40:35
Prairie Plains 16 12 35N20'37 85w57'58 5:43:52
Presbytery Camp 82 2 36N33'36 82w06'25 5:28:26
Presley Ridge 20 3 35N26'20 88w14'45 5:52:59
Pressmens Home 37 70 36N27 83w04 5:32:16
Prestige 49 28 35N45 89w32 5:58:08
Preston Woods 82 2 36N32'27 82w29'24 5:29:58
Price 49 3 35N40 89w45 5:59:00
Price 93 3 35N56 85w28 5:41:52
Primm Springs 41 3 35N49'15 87w15'00 5:49:00
Princeton 90 75 36N21'27 82w22'00 5:29:28
Probst 70 72 35N10'52 84w29'05 5:37:56
Proctor City 48 3 36N25'14 89w26'47 5:57:47
Promise 22 3 36N12'35 87w19'53 5:49:20
Prospect 5 64 35N48'41 83w48'09 5:35:13
Prospect 6 53 35N10'37 84w55'06 5:39:40
Prospect 28 3 35N01'47 87w00'11 5:48:01
Prospect 52 9 35N04'50 86w33'47 5:46:15
Prospect 53 68 35N43'41 84w25'27 5:37:42
Prospect 54 71 35N22'03 84w25'11 5:37:41
Prosperity 56 3 36N29'14 85w52'27 5:43:30
Prosperity 95 49 35N58'49 86w03'32 5:44:14
Protemus 66 3 36N20 89w10 5:56:40
Providence 5 64 35N50'58 83w47'11 5:35:09
Providence 19 4 36N04'22 86w43'28 5:46:54
Providence 31 3 35N16'43 85w53'51 5:43:35
Providence 51 3 35N26'42 87w34'59 5:50:20
Providence 57 3 35N39'00 89w03'51 5:56:15
Providence 83 50 36N35'23 86w18'46 5:45:15
Pruden 13 51 36N35 83w54 5:35:36
Pryor Ridge 58 8 35N16 85w44 5:42:56
Puckett 75 3 35N45 86w32 5:46:08
Pulaski 28 22 35N11'59 87w01'51 5:48:07
Pumpkin Center 5 64 35N34'16 84w05'40 5:36:23
Pumpkintown 56 3 36N35'14 85w54'39 5:43:39
Puncheon Camp 29 55 36N18'53 83w32'21 5:34:09
Punkton 15 65 35N55 83w01 5:32:04
Purdy 55 3 35N13'36 88w31'50 5:54:07
Pursley 43 3 36N04'19 87w52'49 5:51:31
Puryear 40 3 36N26'39 88w20'04 5:53:20
Pyburn 36 3 35N05'28 88w15'15 5:53:01
Pyburn Place 58 8 35N11'06 85w43'26 5:42:54
Quebeck 93 3 35N49'00 85w34'01 5:42:16
Quercus 50 29 35N26'25 87w25'47 5:49:43
Quincy 17 14 35N50'02 89w04'52 5:56:19
Quito 84 3 35N24'47 89w56'04 5:59:44
Raccoon Valley 87 52 36N13'46 83w50'31 5:35:22
Rader 30 65 36N10'15 82w55'55 5:31:44
Radmoor 33 61 35N00'48 85w10'29 5:40:42
Rafter 62 70 35N23'33 84w10'42 5:36:43
Ragsdale 16 12 35N30'06 86w00'57 5:44:04
Raines 79 39 35N02 90w03 6:00:12
Raleigh 79 40 35N12'21 89w54'49 5:59:39
Rally Hill 60 31 35N40'07 86w49'52 5:47:19
Ralston 92 3 36N19'36 88w48'00 5:55:12
Ramah 50 29 35N04'38 87w19'47 5:49:19
Ramer 55 3 35N04'10 88w37'20 5:54:29
Ramsey 47 67 35N58'38 83w50'40 5:35:23
Ramsey 79 40 35N17'54 90w02'30 6:00:10
Randolph 84 3 35N30'59 89w53'19 5:59:33
Range 10 1 36N22 82w17 5:29:08
Ranger 57 3 35N39 88w53 5:55:32
Range Turkeytown 10 1 36N22'08 82w15'56 5:29:04
Rankin 15 65 36N03'08 83w12'55 5:32:52
Rankin Cove 58 8 35N02'18 85w34'47 5:42:19
Ransom Stand 91 23 35N01'52 87w57'42 5:51:51
Rascal Town 50 29 35N00'26 87w26'32 5:49:46
Rather 24 3 35N03'46 89w18'11 5:57:13
Raulstontown 58 8 35N01'13 85w42'22 5:42:49
Raus 2 3 35N23'44 86w19'45 5:45:19
Raven Branch 15 65 35N51'05 83w06'03 5:32:24
Ravenscroft 93 3 35N58'38 85w17'43 5:41:11
Rayon City 19 4 36N16'12 86w39'54 5:46:40
Rayon Terrace 10 1 36N20 82w13 5:28:52
Rays 67 3 36N13'11 85w19'37 5:41:18
Rays Chapel 2 3 35N38 86w42 5:46:48
Raysville 64 3 35N19'49 86w18'59 5:45:16
Readyville 8 3 35N49'41 86w10'29 5:44:42
Reagan 39 3 35N31'18 88w20'33 5:53:22
Reagan 54 71 35N33'05 84w30'51 5:38:03
Rebel Acres 28 22 35N11'58 87w00'56 5:48:04
Red Ash 7 66 36N18'48 84w14'12 5:36:57
Red Bank 5 64 35N38'36 83w46'06 5:35:04
Red Bank 33 61 35N06'44 85w17'39 5:41:11
Red Bankwhite Oak 33 61 35N07 85w17 5:41:08
Red Boiling Springs 56 3 36N32'00 85w51'00 5:43:24
Red Hill 6 53 35N04'30 84w52'52 5:39:31
Red Hill 13 51 36N30'30 83w43'46 5:34:55
Red Hill 16 12 35N28 86w05 5:44:20
Red Hill 25 3 36N32'46 85w02'03 5:40:08
Red Hill 50 29 35N18'21 87w24'56 5:49:40
Red Hill 58 8 35N13'29 85w30'33 5:42:02
Red House 29 55 36N09 83w42 5:34:48
Red Oak 52 3 35N14'38 86w48'32 5:47:14
Red Row 60 9 35N31'34 87w11'37 5:48:46
Redstone 82 2 36N35 82w11 5:28:44
Red Sulphur Springs 36 3 35N00'25 88w14'15 5:52:57
Red Walnut 20 3 35N28'09 88w10'37 5:52:42
Redwine 15 65 36N05'39 83w11'35 5:32:46
Reeders Crossing 22 3 36N03'55 87w16'36 5:49:06
Reed Spring 53 68 35N40 84w24 5:37:36
Reeds Store 75 3 35N48 86w40 5:46:40
Reedtown 15 65 35N58 83w11 5:32:44
Reel Cove 58 8 35N12 85w31 5:42:04
Reesetown 70 73 35N03'42 84w21'11 5:37:25
Reeves 90 75 36N18'49 82w25'28 5:29:42
Rehoboth 23 16 36N01'56 89w15'20 5:57:01
Reidtown 15 65 35N58'50 83w16'47 5:33:07
Reliance 13 51 36N34'26 83w48'24 5:35:14
Reliance 70 72 35N11'13 84w29'57 5:38:00
Remy 7 66 36N29'09 84w03'08 5:36:13
Rennbore 47 67 35N55'46 84w07'16 5:36:29
Reubensville 74 50 36N35'29 86w35'33 5:46:22
Reverie 84 3 35N32 90w00 6:00:00
Revilo 50 29 35N08'22 87w16'07 5:49:04
Rheatown 30 65 36N13'52 82w41'45 5:30:47
Rhyan Springs 67 3 36N27'48 85w14'16 5:40:57
Rialto 84 44 35N37'26 89w36'26 5:58:26
Rice Bend 86 1 36N01 82w33 5:30:12
Riceville 54 54 35N23'05 84w41'35 5:38:46
Rich 28 3 35N23'14 87w07'25 5:48:30
Rich Acres 90 75 36N19 82w21 5:29:24
Richard City 58 8 34N59'39 85w43'30 5:42:54
Richardson 84 3 35N26 89w47 5:59:08
Richardson Cove 78 60 35N48'57 83w26'01 5:33:44
Richardsons 84 3 35N30'41 89w56'24 5:59:46
Richardsons Landing 84 3 35N30'56 89w56'10 5:59:45
Rich Creek 59 3 35N34'02 86w42'01 5:46:48
Richland 19 4 36N09'14 86w51'28 5:47:26
Richland 29 55 36N08'15 83w39'56 5:34:40
Richmond 2 3 35N23'08 86w35'31 5:46:22
Richs Crossing 26 18 35N02'28 86w18'09 5:45:13
Richville 14 3 36N33'44 85w36'21 5:42:25
Richwood 23 16 36N02 89w23 5:57:32
Richwoods 23 16 36N00'23 89w30'22 5:58:01
Rickman 67 3 36N15'45 85w22'32 5:41:30
Riddles Store 54 71 35N36'33 84w32'32 5:38:10
Riddle Store 54 71 35N36 84w28 5:37:52
Riddleton 80 3 36N19'17 86w01'05 5:44:04
Ridenour 87 52 36N13'35 83w57'10 5:35:49
Ridge 13 51 36N27 83w34 5:34:16
Ridgedale 18 9 35N56 85w28 5:41:52
Ridgedale 33 61 35N01'19 85w16'11 5:41:05
Ridgedale 47 67 35N59'03 84w01'43 5:36:07
Ridgedale 82 2 36N35 82w11 5:28:44
Ridgefields 82 2 36N32'43 82w36'08 5:30:25
Ridge Lake North 33 61 35N08'36 85w11'34 5:40:46
Ridgely 48 3 36N15'48 89w29'16 5:57:57
Ridgeside (Shepherd Hills) 33 61 35N01'57 85w15'09 5:41:01
Ridgetop 51 3 35N36 87w18 5:49:12
Ridgetop 74 3 36N23'42 86w46'46 5:47:07
Ridgeview 32 67 36N12'05 83w20'18 5:33:21
Ridgeview Heights 47 67 36N06'08 83w50'25 5:35:22
Ridgeville 64 33 35N16'24 86w18'00 5:45:12
Ridgewood 7 62 36N15'19 84w10'55 5:36:44
Ridgewood Acres 33 61 35N03'10 85w14'41 5:40:59
Ridley 60 31 35N33'06 87w11'28 5:48:46
Riggs Crossroads 94 3 35N42'48 86w41'52 5:46:47
Right 36 3 35N19 88w21 5:53:24
Riley 13 51 36N32'28 83w25'55 5:33:44
Rinda 92 3 36N09 88w48 5:55:12
Ringgold 63 32 36N35'38 87w25'05 5:49:40
Rinnie 18 15 36N08'55 85w02'04 5:40:08
Riovista 10 1 36N20'05 82w15'42 5:29:03
Ripley 49 28 35N44'43 89w31'47 5:58:07
Ritchie 13 51 36N27 83w34 5:34:16
Ritta 47 67 36N03'26 83w52'01 5:35:28
Riva Lake Camp 26 19 35N11 86w07 5:44:28
Riverdale 47 67 35N57'51 83w45'49 5:35:03
River Heights 36 3 35N13'12 88w18'47 5:53:15
River Heights 60 31 35N38'08 87w02'14 5:48:09
River Hill 86 1 36N06'27 82w27'06 5:29:48
River Hill 93 3 35N49'22 85w26'03 5:41:44
River Hills 33 61 35N05'28 85w16'07 5:41:08
Rivermont 33 61 35N06'05 85w16'21 5:41:05
River Oaks 33 61 35N07'03 85w08'21 5:40:33
Riversburg 28 22 35N16'11 87w02'38 5:48:11
Riverside 16 12 35N28 86w05 5:44:20
Riverside 19 4 36N13 86w50 5:47:20
Riverside 51 3 35N26'57 87w35'51 5:50:23
Riverside 60 31 35N37'25 87w01'36 5:48:06
Riverside 79 39 35N07 89w59 5:59:56
Riverside 82 1 36N29'11 82w11'50 5:28:47
Riverside Park 33 61 35N04'08 85w16'03 5:41:04

Riverton 25 3 36N27'01 85W05'14 5:40:21
River View 13 51 36N32'30 83W37'58 5:34:32
Riverview 29 55 36N17'12 83W22'05 5:33:28
Riverview 33 61 35N04'08 85W17'04 5:41:08
Riverview 82 2 36N32'13 82W33'19 5:30:13
Riverview 86 1 36N07'21 82W26'40 5:29:47
Riverview 88 3 35N41'25 85W34'41 5:42:19
Rives 66 3 36N21'20 89W02'53 5:56:12
Roan Hill 90 75 36N18'18 82W20'45 5:29:23
Roan Mountain 10
1 36N11'46 82W04'14 5:28:17
Roaring Springs 30
65 36N17'47 82W46'39 5:31:07
Roark Cove 16 18 35N14'49 85W55'49 5:43:43
Robbins 69 3 36N34 85W08 5:40:32
Robbins 76 58 36N21'12 84W35'22 5:38:21
Roberts 57 3 35N40'34 88W59'43 5:55:59
Roberts 71 3 36N06'50 85W41'24 5:42:46
Roberts Ford 7 66 36N14'17 84W19'59 5:37:20
Robertson 12 3 35N15'56 88W43'07 5:54:52
Robertson Fork 59
3 35N23 87W00 5:48:00
Robinson Crossroads 47
67 35N56'57 84W09'32 5:36:38
Robinson Landing 72
54 35N31'35 84W52'59 5:39:32
Robinson Mill 53
68 35N43'22 84W19'21 5:37:17
Robison 9 3 35N59'42 88W13'55 5:52:56
Roby 12 3 35N27'55 88W24'03 5:53:36
Rock Bridge 83 50 36N30'50 86W23'00 5:45:32
Rock City 80 41 36N15'47 86W03'11 5:44:13
Rock City 82 2 36N34'03 82W26'09 5:29:45
Rock Creek 59 3 35N31 86W44 5:46:56
Rock Creek 69 3 36N26 84W56 5:39:44
Rock Creek 86 1 36N09'32 82W24'13 5:29:37
Rockdale 60 9 35N28'16 87W15'23 5:49:02
Rockdale 75 38 36N03'47 86W27'53 5:45:52
Rockford 5 64 35N49'39 83W56'27 5:35:46
Rock Haven 29 55 36N20'29 83W23'14 5:33:33
Rock Hill 34 51 36N34 83W03 5:32:12
Rock Hill 39 25 35N37'26 88W19'19 5:53:17
Rock Hill 82 1 36N24'35 82W16'21 5:29:05
Rock House 85 3 36N22'08 86W06'05 5:44:24
Rock Island 89 3 35N47'32 85W36'48 5:42:27
Rockland 83 43 36N18'04 86W38'31 5:46:34
Rockledge 16 18 35N08'52 85W58'03 5:43:52
Rockport 3 3 35N56'31 88W01'03 5:52:04
Rockport Landing 3
3 35N56'35 88W00'48 5:52:03
Rock Springs 22 3 36N18'45 87W16'15 5:49:05
Rock Springs 23
16 36N01'56 89W16'46 5:57:07
Rock Springs 39 3 35N47'52 88W26'45 5:53:47
Rock Springs 75
38 35N59 86W31 5:46:04
Rock Springs 82 2 36N27'55 82W33'15 5:30:13
Rockvale 75 3 35N45'26 86W31'53 5:46:08
Rockville 62 67 35N36'01 84W22'06 5:37:28
Rockwood 73 70 35N51'56 84W41'06 5:38:44
Rockwood Hill 30
65 36N07'42 82W51'38 5:31:27
Rocky Branch 5 64 35N44'27 83W50'28 5:35:22
Rocky Ford 7 66 36N21'31 84W12'10 5:36:49
Rocky Fork 75 38 35N59 86W31 5:46:04
Rocky Fork 86 1 36N02'06 82W33'08 5:30:13
Rocky Grove 78 60 35N49 83W15 5:33:00
Rocky Hill 47 67 35N54'10 84W01'17 5:36:05
Rocky Mound 56 3 36N36'27 86W09'57 5:44:40
Rocky Point 71 34 36N11 85W28 5:41:52
Rocky Ridge 67 3 36N26'36 85W11'34 5:40:46
Rocky Spring 62
67 35N29'20 84W20'16 5:37:21
Rocky Springs 82
75 36N26'49 82W22'10 5:29:29
Roddy 72 74 35N46'18 84W46'26 5:39:06
Rodemer 41 3 35N53'44 87W25'11 5:49:41
Roe 32 67 36N10'57 83W18'13 5:33:13
Roe Junction 32
67 36N10'26 83W18'26 5:33:14
RoEllen 23 16 36N01'25 89W16'53 5:57:08
Rogana 83 50 36N26'42 86W20'01 5:45:20
Rogers 18 9 35N59'41 84W45'51 5:39:03
Rogers Creek 54
71 35N30'10 84W41'30 5:38:46
Rogers Springs 35
3 35N03'00 88W58'32 5:55:54
Rogersville 37 70 36N24'26 83W00'20 5:32:01
Rolling Acres 45
67 36N09 83W25 5:33:40
Rolling Brook 6
53 35N11'05 84W48'46 5:39:15
Rolling Fields 60
31 35N36'29 87W03'33 5:48:14
Rolling Hills 32
67 36N11'37 83W17'12 5:33:09
Rolling Hills 59
30 35N26'28 86W48'55 5:47:16
Rollingwood 33 61 35N03'07 85W13'25 5:40:54
Rome 80 3 36N15'43 86W04'18 5:44:17
Romeo 30 65 36N17'28 82W56'09 5:31:45
Roneys Store 66 3 36N23'21 89W17'39 5:57:11
Rose Creek 55 3 35N12'19 88W41'49 5:54:47
Rosedale 1 62 36N10'19 84W20'56 5:37:24
Rose Hill 57 3 35N39 88W53 5:55:32
Rose Hill 87 52 36N18'24 83W45'37 5:35:02
Rosemark 79 40 35N21'45 89W46'20 5:59:05
Rose Valley 81 3 36N30 87W42 5:50:48
Roseville 2 5 35N27'28 86W18'06 5:45:12
Roslin 25 3 36N13'23 84W55'33 5:39:42
Ross Camp Ground 37
70 36N32 82W41 5:30:44
Rosser 9 3 36N01'51 88W21'13 5:53:25
Rossview 63 32 36N33'38 87W14'06 5:48:56
Rossville 24 3 35N02'54 89W32'33 5:58:10
Rossville Junction 24
3 35N02'30 89W32'37 5:58:10
Rotherwood Heights 37
2 36N33'25 82W37'12 5:30:29
Rotherwood Hills 37
2 36N32'39 82W37'13 5:30:29
Rough Point 44 27 36N21'37 85W44'11 5:42:57
Round Pond 63 32 36N27'24 87W22'40 5:49:31
Round Top 95 49 36N00'17 86W02'41 5:44:11
Routon 40 3 36N13'46 88W22'20 5:53:29
Rover 2 3 35N40'23 86W35'48 5:46:23
Rowland 89 3 35N44'45 85W40'58 5:42:44
Roy 57 3 35N30'47 88W47'13 5:55:09
Royal 2 6 35N29 86W27 5:45:48
Royal Blue 7 66 36N22'56 84W15'38 5:37:03
Royal Oaks 16 12 35N27'06 86W05'23 5:44:22
Royal Oaks 60 31 35N38'12 87W02'46 5:48:11
Royer Estates 75
37 35N51 86W23 5:45:32
Rozells Mill 52 9 35N01'09 86W31'31 5:46:06
Ruby Falls 33 61 35N01'08 85W20'22 5:41:21
Rucker 75 37 35N45'09 86W23'16 5:45:33
Rudderville 94 48 35N50'26 86W44'28 5:46:58
Rudolph 38 24 35N42'13 89W15'02 5:57:00
Rugby 65 56 36N21'37 84W42'03 5:38:48
Ruppertown 51 3 35N25'26 87W35'39 5:50:23
Rural Hill 19 4 36N04'02 86W37'52 5:46:31
Rural Vale 62 70 35N18'42 84W21'35 5:37:26
Rushy Springs 45
67 36N07'26 83W21'41 5:33:27
Ruskin 22 3 36N09'39 87W31'09 5:50:05
Russel Fork 7 66 36N27 84W04 5:36:16
Russell Crossroad 30
65 36N05'59 82W55'39 5:31:43
Russell Crossroads 39
3 35N36'47 88W34'06 5:54:16
Russell Fork 7 66 36N27'32 84W03'07 5:36:12
Russell Hill 56 3 36N25'54 85W53'50 5:43:35
Russell Mill 13
51 36N26'49 83W51'52 5:35:27
Russellville 32
67 36N15'31 83W11'43 5:32:47
Rutherford 27 21 36N07'39 88W59'09 5:55:57
Ruthledge Ford 16
18 35N18'22 85W56'36 5:43:46
Ruthledge Hill 16
3 35N18'31 85W56'28 5:43:46
Ruthton 82 2 36N32'51 82W07'37 5:28:30
Ruthville 92 3 36N26'19 88W47'49 5:55:11
Rutledge 29 55 36N16'51 83W30'54 5:34:04
Rutledge Falls 16
12 35N25'13 86W08'10 5:44:33
Rutledge Hills 16
12 35N25 85W58 5:43:52
Ryall Springs 33
61 35N00'17 85W06'55 5:40:28
Sadie 10 1 36N25'57 82W03'19 5:28:13
Sadler 71 3 36N13'25 85W44'10 5:42:57
Sadlersville 74 3 36N36'36 87W07'05 5:48:28
Safely 89 46 35N42 85W46 5:43:04
Safford 39 3 35N38 88W13 5:52:52
Safley 89 46 35N36'57 85W42'32 5:42:50
Sagetown 70 72 35N11 84W39 5:38:36
Sailors Rest 63 3 36N23 87W38 5:50:32
Saint Andrews 16
18 35N12'40 85W53'33 5:43:34
Saint Bethlehem 63
3 36N34'19 87W18'00 5:49:12
Saint Clair 37 70 36N19'50 83W05'14 5:32:21
Saint Clair 72 74 35N44'01 84W48'30 5:39:14
Saint Elmo 33 61 34N59'48 85W19'48 5:41:19
Saint James 30 65 36N01'42 82W57'11 5:31:49
Saint John 14 3 36N35'40 85W18'26 5:41:14
Saint Joseph 50
29 35N02'10 87W30'24 5:50:02
Saint Marys 50 29 35N02'06 87W25'08 5:49:41
Saint Paul 84 3 35N26 89W47 5:59:08
Sainville 16 12 35N30'35 85W54'46 5:43:39
Sal City 26 19 35N03'21 86W02'57 5:44:12
Sale Creek 33 61 35N22'56 85W06'32 5:40:26
Salem 15 65 36N01'19 83W02'27 5:32:10
Salem 51 3 35N36'54 87W27'30 5:49:50
Salem 63 32 36N27'35 87W19'49 5:49:19
Salem 75 3 35N48'33 86W28'08 5:45:55
Salem 84 3 35N26'10 89W44'11 5:58:57
Salem 92 3 36N14 88W50 5:55:20
Saltillo 36 3 35N22'40 88W12'34 5:52:50
Salt Lick 41 3 35N55'34 87W32'59 5:50:12
Samburg 66 3 36N22'51 89W21'17 5:57:25
Sampson 4 15 35N40'33 85W16'20 5:41:05
Sanders 31 3 35N16 85W44 5:42:56
Sanders Crossing 31
3 35N16'54 85W44'53 5:43:00
Sandhill 75 3 36N01'19 86W32'32 5:46:10
Sandhill 92 3 36N13'45 88W39'32 5:54:38
Sandlick 13 51 36N23'47 83W40'55 5:34:44
Sand Ridge 39 25 35N40'45 88W28'47 5:53:55
Sand Springs 71 3 36N07'48 85W20'26 5:41:22
Sand Switch 16 18 35N13'18 85W52'42 5:43:31
Sandy 25 3 36N17'31 85W04'27 5:40:18
Sandy 46 1 36N23'48 81W47'24 5:27:10
Sandy Hook 60 9 35N29'00 87W14'15 5:48:57
Sandy Lane 62 70 35N22 84W18 5:37:12
Sandy Point 3 3 36N02'46 88W10'05 5:52:40
Sandy Ridge 45 67 35N57'22 83W22'35 5:33:30
Sandy Springs 74
3 36N26'52 87W00'39 5:48:03
Sanford 54 54 35N20'30 84W43'13 5:38:53
Sanford Hill 12 3 35N26'05 88W39'11 5:54:37
Sango 63 32 36N30'23 87W13'15 5:48:53
Santa Fe 60 3 35N44'06 87W07'41 5:48:31
Saratoga Springs 4
15 35N42'56 85W14'43 5:40:59
Sardis 15 65 35N58 83W11 5:32:44
Sardis 39 3 35N26'32 88W17'37 5:53:10
Saulpaws Landing 20
3 35N45'37 87W59'40 5:51:59
Saulsbury 35 3 35N02'49 89W05'16 5:56:21
Saundersville 83
43 36N19'33 86W33'52 5:46:15
Savannah 36 23 35N13'29 88W14'57 5:53:00
Sawdust 60 3 35N40'05 87W11'24 5:48:46
Sawyers Mill 3 3 36N02'11 88W11'31 5:52:46
Scaife 79 39 34N59'50 90W01'58 6:00:08
Scandlyn 73 63 36N00'36 84W23'05 5:37:32
Scarboro 1 67 35N58'59 84W13'21 5:36:53
Scattersville 83
50 36N35'27 86W34'04 5:46:16
Scenic Heights 26
19 35N11'52 86W05'55 5:44:24
Scenic Point Estates 47
64 35N47'50 84W08'10 5:36:33
Scoot Mill 30 65 36N09'02 83W07'56 5:32:32
Scott 61 54 35N39'17 84W45'04 5:39:00
Scott Hill 9 3 35N54'21 88W28'50 5:53:55
Scottsboro 19 4 36N12'38 86W55'40 5:47:43
Scotts Hill 20 3 35N30'54 88W14'43 5:52:59
Scotts Mill 60 9 35N29'59 87W08'54 5:48:36
Screamer 60 9 35N26'38 87W09'35 5:48:38
Scribner 60 3 35N30'06 86W56'46 5:47:47
Seaton Spring 78
60 35N48'41 83W29'45 5:33:59
Sebowisha 80 3 36N08'17 85W52'08 5:43:29
Seeber Flats 1 62 36N10'07 84W12'57 5:36:52
Self Landing 20 3 35N25'19 88W01'18 5:52:05
Selmer 55 3 35N10'12 88W35'32 5:54:22
Sengtown 83 50 36N36'48 86W26'15 5:45:45
Sentertown 47 67 36N03'02 83W49'48 5:35:19
Sentinel Heights 72
74 35N30'09 84W59'56 5:40:00
Sequatchie 58 8 35N06'56 85W35'37 5:42:22
Sequatchie Valley 4
15 35N36 85W12 5:40:48
Sequoia Grove 6
53 35N12'45 84W50'52 5:39:23
Sequoyah Estates 62
67 35N30'32 84W22'50 5:37:31
Sequoyah Heights 5
64 35N46'12 84W10'04 5:36:40
Sequoyah Hills 33
61 35N11'53 85W09'15 5:40:37
Sequoyah Hills 47
67 35N56'10 83W58'29 5:35:54
Sequoyah Landing Cabin Area 1
62 36N15'32 84W03'14 5:36:13
Serles 35 3 35N10'09 88W50'37 5:55:22
Servilla 70 72 35N14'07 84W27'42 5:37:51
Seth 60 9 35N32'52 87W17'23 5:49:10
Seven Cedars 54
54 35N20'42 84W32'00 5:38:08
Seven Islands 47
67 35N56 83W54 5:35:36
Sevenoaks 47 67 35N54'26 84W05'42 5:36:23
Sevier Home 47 67 35N53'45 83W52'22 5:35:29
Sevierville 78 60 35N52'05 83W33'43 5:34:15
Sewanee 16 18 35N12'11 85W55'16 5:43:41
Sewee 61 54 35N35'32 84W40'45 5:38:43
Sewee Landing 61
54 35N33'53 84W47'53 5:39:12
Sexton 28 3 35N02'39 87W12'05 5:48:48
Seymour 78 60 35N53'26 83W43'29 5:34:54
Seymour Heights 78
60 35N52'38 83W45'43 5:35:03
Shackle Island 83
43 36N22'14 86W37'00 5:46:28
Shacklett 11 9 36N07'29 87W05'53 5:48:24
Shaddon Mill 5 68 35N36'20 84W10'15 5:36:41
Shadowlawn 79 40 35N17 89W40 5:58:40
Shadrick Hill 31
3 35N16'04 85W42'10 5:42:49
Shadtown 86 1 36N13'46 82W19'09 5:29:17
Shady Acres 16 12 35N27'43 86W04'15 5:44:17
Shady Grove 16 12 35N37'09 85W59'07 5:43:56
Shady Grove 33 61 35N15'15 85W07'11 5:40:29
Shady Grove 36 3 35N23'47 88W14'56 5:53:00
Shady Grove 44 3 36N15'03 85W40'48 5:42:43
Shady Grove 45 67 35N58'42 83W29'03 5:33:56
Shady Grove 47 67 35N52 84W08 5:36:32
Shady Grove 52 9 35N06'15 86W20'07 5:45:20
Shady Grove 63 32 36N27'50 87W11'05 5:48:44
Shady Grove 65 56 36N06'13 84W40'29 5:38:42
Shady Grove 78 60 35N47'02 83W27'42 5:33:51
Shady Grove 85 3 36N22'06 86W08'15 5:44:33
Shady Grove 93 3 35N54'29 85W34'37 5:42:18
Shady Grove Duck River 41
3 35N43'25 87W16'43 5:49:07
Shady Hill 39 25 35N34'00 88W19'13 5:53:17
Shady Rest 33 61 35N00'07 85W08'20 5:40:33
Shady Rest 89 46 35N42'59 85W43'29 5:42:54
Shady Valley 46 1 36N31'09 81W55'41 5:27:43
Shallowford 86 1 36N08 82W25 5:29:40
Shandy 35 3 35N17'37 88W57'33 5:55:50
Shannondale 47 67 36N03'04 83W54'41 5:35:39
Shannon Hills 33
61 35N10'51 85W12'53 5:40:52
Shannon Landing 20
3 35N24'15 88W02'20 5:52:09
Sharon 92 3 36N14'00 88W49'28 5:55:18
Sharondale 16 13 35N21'34 86W14'40 5:44:59
Sharon Park 60 31 35N35'53 87W02'48 5:48:11
Sharp Place 25 3 36N30'32 84W49'40 5:39:19
Sharps Chapel 87
52 36N21 83W50 5:35:20
Sharpsville 75 37 35N52'29 86W16'58 5:45:08
Shaver Town 80 3 36N10'20 86W02'20 5:44:09
Shaw 38 24 35N43'18 89W20'08 5:57:21
Shawanee 13 51 36N34'50 83W38'20 5:34:33
Shawnette 91 3 35N11'02 87W40'16 5:50:41
Shea 7 66 36N14'17 84W19'48 5:37:19
Shearin Ford 2 3 35N34'31 86W38'00 5:46:32
Shelby Center 79
40 35N12 89W54 5:59:36
Shelby Farms 79
40 35N09'13 89W51'07 5:59:24
Shelby Forest 79
40 35N19 89W54 5:59:36
Shelbyville 2 6 35N29'00 86W27'37 5:45:50
Shelbyville Mills (Royal Sta 2
6 35N28'19 86W29'18 5:45:57
Shell Creek 10 1 36N11'21 82W02'34 5:28:10
Shellsford 89 46 35N40'22 85W42'42 5:42:51
Shenandoah Heights 10
1 36N19 82W21 5:29:24
Shepherd 33 61 35N02'20 85W11'31 5:40:46
Shepherd Forest 33
61 35N07'52 85W19'43 5:41:19
Shepp (Shepards Station) 38
3 35N30'04 89W20'47 5:57:23
Sherril Heights 62
67 35N30'13 84W23'00 5:37:32
Sherrilltown 95 9 36N02'56 86W12'10 5:44:49
Sherwood 26 18 35N04'34 85W55'24 5:43:42

Sherwood Estates 1 62 36N02'04 84w08'30 5:36:34
Sherwood Forest 6 53 35N06'43 84w51'13 5:39:25
Sheybogan 8 3 35N45'11 86w03'13 5:44:13
Shiloh 2 5 35N31'49 86w15'04 5:45:00
Shiloh 9 3 35N49'58 88w12'27 5:52:50
Shiloh 36 3 35N06'55 88w21'42 5:53:27
Shiloh 37 70 36N28'55 83w05'58 5:32:24
Shiloh 44 3 36N11 85w28 5:41:52
Shiloh 63 3 36N21'53 87w30'05 5:50:00
Shiloh 75 37 35N51'40 86w19'50 5:45:19
Shingles Landing 81 3 36N29'48 87w45'14 5:51:01
Shingletown 46 1 36N33'01 81w47'17 5:27:09
Shining Rock 21 3 35N57 85w49 5:43:16
Shipetown 47 67 36N04'28 83w45'47 5:35:03
Shipley 71 34 36N11 85w28 5:41:52
Shipps Bend 41 3 35N48 87w27 5:49:48
Shirley 25 3 36N20'43 84w46'43 5:39:07
Shirley Crossing 29 55 36N15'38 83w34'01 5:34:16
Shirleyton 58 8 35N14'12 85w29'43 5:41:59
Shofner 66 3 36N24'10 88w58'52 5:55:55
Shooks 47 67 35N54'49 83w49'43 5:35:19
Shooks Gap 5 64 35N53'03 83w47'32 5:35:10
Shop Springs 95 34 36N07'40 86w12'44 5:44:51
Shore Acres 33 61 35N18'44 85w04'38 5:40:19
Short Creek 75 3 35N40'22 86w21'39 5:45:27
Short Tail Springs 33 61 35N07 85w08 5:40:32
Shouns 46 1 36N26'43 81w47'59 5:27:12
Shubert 51 3 35N32'00 87w34'12 5:50:17
Siam 10 1 36N20'52 82w09'01 5:28:36
Sibley 36 3 35N18'53 88w16'19 5:53:05
Sides Place 58 3 35N12'54 85w43'41 5:42:55
Sideview 83 42 36N23 86w26 5:45:44
Sidonia 92 3 36N14'38 88w54'21 5:55:37
Siglo 60 31 35N35'14 87w07'46 5:48:31
Signal Hills 33 61 35N05'56 85w19'59 5:41:20
Signal Mountain 33 61 35N07'21 85w20'38 5:41:23
Silcott Ford 76 58 36N24'15 84w35'33 5:38:22
Silerton 35 3 35N20'25 88w48'22 5:55:13
Silica 7 66 36N19'25 84w14'36 5:36:58
Siloam 56 3 36N32'46 86w12'46 5:44:51
Silvacola 82 1 36N34'22 82w22'56 5:29:32
Silver City 32 67 36N13'15 83w09'53 5:32:40
Silver Creek 59 3 35N30'07 86w52'29 5:47:30
Silverdale 33 61 35N03'32 85w08'13 5:40:33
Silver Grove 82 1 36N29'46 82w12'27 5:28:50
Silver Hill 75 37 36N00'05 86w22'02 5:45:28
Silver Lake 46 1 36N32'18 81w46'33 5:27:06
Silver Point 71 3 36N05'26 85w43'47 5:42:55
Silver Ridge 53 68 35N48 84w16 5:37:04
Silver Springs 95 49 36N11'41 86w27'12 5:45:49
Silverton 42 3 36N12'21 87w39'30 5:50:38
Simonton 84 3 35N29 89w43 5:58:52
Sims Ford 36 3 35N19'45 88w02'37 5:52:10
Sims Ridge 50 29 35N12'48 87w32'50 5:50:11
Sims Spring 2 6 35N30'39 86w36'57 5:46:28
Singleton 2 6 35N25'44 86w22'20 5:45:29
Singleton 5 64 35N51'30 83w58'30 5:35:54
Singtown 83 50 36N35 86w31 5:46:04
Sitka 27 20 35N51'48 88w45'27 5:55:02
Sixmile 5 64 35N39'35 83w57'43 5:35:51
Skaggston 47 67 36N05'15 83w45'36 5:35:02
Skinem 52 9 35N05'26 86w35'19 5:46:21
Skinner Crossroad 30 65 36N10'45 83w04'48 5:32:19
Skullbone 27 21 36N05'02 88w45'40 5:55:03
Skyline Park 33 61 35N08'55 85w19'32 5:41:18
Slatestone 1 62 36N11'09 84w11'47 5:36:47
Slatesville 95 9 36N06 86w08 5:44:32
Slayden 22 3 36N17'41 87w28'13 5:49:53
Slick Rock 76 58 36N18'14 84w30'16 5:38:01
Slickrock Ford 91 3 35N26'18 87w43'56 5:50:56
Slide 37 70 36N21 82w59 5:31:56
Sloanville 79 40 35N21'12 89w57'11 5:59:49
Smarden 94 3 35N50'00 87w05'01 5:48:20
Smartt 89 3 35N38'25 85w50'12 5:43:21
Smith Chapel 44 3 36N11 85w28 5:41:52
Smithfield 62 70 35N16'51 84w15'02 5:37:00
Smithland 52 9 35N07'18 86w23'08 5:45:33
Smiths Chapel 56 3 36N32 85w51 5:43:24
Smiths Fork 36 3 35N17 88w02 5:52:08
Smith Shoals 82 2 36N27'32 82w27'44 5:29:51
Smith Springs 19 4 36N09 86w41 5:46:44
Smithtown 4 15 35N28'16 85w12'59 5:40:52
Smithtown 58 8 35N04'52 85w44'06 5:42:56
Smithville 21 3 35N57'38 85w48'51 5:43:15
Smithwood 47 67 36N01'40 83w55'20 5:35:41
Smoky Junction 76 58 36N17'14 84w21'47 5:37:27
Smoky Landing Dock 5 64 35N46'29 84w08'17 5:36:33
Smoky View Estates 5 64 35N45'49 84w02'21 5:36:09
Smyrna 9 3 35N57'23 88w19'54 5:53:20
Smyrna 59 3 35N34'40 86w41'53 5:46:48
Smyrna 69 3 36N33'39 85w09'59 5:40:40
Smyrna 75 38 35N58'58 86w31'07 5:46:04
Smyrna 89 46 35N37'58 85w42'50 5:42:51
Sneedville 34 51 36N31'47 83w13'03 5:32:52
Snell 75 37 35N51 86w23 5:45:32
Snodgrass 13 51 36N26'43 83w37'33 5:34:30
Snow Hill 33 61 35N10'46 85w02'40 5:40:11
Snows Hill 21 3 35N59'03 85w52'36 5:43:30
Soddy 33 61 35N17'19 85w10'00 5:40:40
Soddy-Daisy 33 61 35N14'10 85w11'55 5:40:48
Soddy Lake Heights 33 61 35N16'41 85w08'09 5:40:33
Solo 84 44 35N35'02 89w35'59 5:58:24
Solway 47 67 35N58'48 84w10'53 5:36:44
Somerville 24 17 35N14'37 89w21'00 5:57:24
South 19 4 36N09 86w45 5:47:00
Southall 94 48 35N53'33 86w55'35 5:47:42
South Berlin 59 30 35N30'02 86w50'12 5:47:21
South Bradley 6 53 35N03 84w56 5:39:44
South Cannon 8 3 35N46 86w04 5:44:16
South Carthage 80 41 36N14'31 85w57'07 5:43:48
South Cleveland 6 53 35N08'28 84w52'20 5:39:29
South Clinton 1 62 36N04'19 84w08'00 5:36:32
South Columbia 60 31 35N37 87w02 5:48:08
South Covington 84 44 35N34 89w42 5:58:48
South Daisy 33 61 35N16 85w11 5:40:44
South Dyersburg 23 16 36N01'10 89w23'28 5:57:34
Southern Hills 60 31 35N35'24 87w02'03 5:48:08
South Etowah 54 54 35N20 84w32 5:38:08
South Fork 48 16 35N56'09 89w23'21 5:57:33
South Fulton 66 3 36N30'03 88w52'31 5:55:30
Southgate 79 39 35N04 90w04 6:00:16
South Hall 5 64 35N46'37 83w58'58 5:35:56
South Harriman 73 67 35N55'14 84w33'51 5:38:15
South Huntingdon 9 3 35N55 88w29 5:53:56
South Knoxville 47 67 35N56'35 83w53'56 5:35:36
Southland Mall 79 39 35N02 90w03 6:00:12
South Liberty 54 54 35N21'48 84w37'37 5:38:30
South Pittsburg 58 8 35N00'44 85w42'16 5:42:49
Southport 60 3 35N28'14 87w05'56 5:48:24
Southside 36 3 35N02'44 88w21'06 5:53:24
Southside 60 31 35N37 87w02 5:48:08
Southside 63 3 36N22'17 87w17'44 5:49:11
South Side 80 3 36N11 86w00 5:44:00
South Tunnel 83 50 36N28'49 86w27'58 5:45:52
Sowell Ford 60 31 35N35'33 86w53'05 5:47:32
Spanish Trails 47 67 35N56'55 84w05'30 5:36:22
Sparkman 88 3 35N48'22 85w30'47 5:42:03
Sparta 93 3 35N55'33 85w27'51 5:41:51
Spear Springs 37 70 36N24 83w00 5:32:00
Speck 76 58 36N26'55 84w41'04 5:38:44
Speedwell 13 51 36N27'31 83w52'19 5:35:29
Speiden 28 3 35N12'35 86w50'36 5:47:22
Spencer 88 3 35N44'50 85w28'00 5:41:52
Spencer Hill 60 9 35N26'55 87w09'50 5:48:39
Spencers Mill 22 3 36N03 87w19 5:49:16
Spivey 56 3 36N35'43 85w49'38 5:43:19
Spot 41 3 35N53'10 87w35'29 5:50:22
Spout Springs 66 3 36N25'38 89w18'35 5:57:14
Springbrook 5 64 35N47 83w59 5:35:56
Spring City 72 74 35N41'31 84w51'39 5:39:27
Spring Creek 40 3 36N12'19 88w12'45 5:52:51
Spring Creek 50 29 35N12'47 87w26'50 5:49:47
Spring Creek 54 54 35N25'04 84w43'31 5:38:54
Spring Creek 57 3 35N46'00 88w40'38 5:54:43
Spring Creek 68 3 35N39'15 87w59'24 5:51:58
Spring Creek 89 3 35N33'51 85w37'09 5:42:29
Springdale 13 51 36N25'27 83w31'28 5:34:06
Springdale 82 2 36N30'52 82w33'32 5:30:14
Springers Station 50 29 35N08'20 87w23'13 5:49:33
Springfield 74 35 36N30'33 86w53'06 5:47:32
Spring Hill 38 3 35N27'03 89w16'37 5:57:06
Spring Hill 39 3 35N40'54 88w34'09 5:54:17
Spring Hill 42 3 36N20'18 87w36'17 5:50:25
Spring Hill 60 3 35N45'04 86w55'48 5:47:43
Spring Hill 93 3 36N00'18 85w23'19 5:41:33
Spring Place 47 67 36N01'26 83w51'16 5:35:25
Springvale 32 67 36N11'51 83w12'22 5:32:49
Spring Valley 33 61 35N07'20 85w18'45 5:41:15
Springville 40 3 36N14'57 88w09'11 5:52:37
Spruce Pine 37 70 36N23'13 83w12'49 5:32:51
Spurgeon 90 75 36N26'22 82w27'21 5:29:49
Squirrel Flat 25 3 36N29'26 84w58'10 5:39:53
Stacy 37 70 36N25'49 82w47'43 5:31:11
Staffords Store 92 3 36N05'46 88w41'39 5:54:47
Staffordtown 70 73 34N59'53 84w23'19 5:37:33
Stahlman 19 4 36N10 86w47 5:47:08
Stainville 1 62 36N12'26 84w18'51 5:37:15
Stakely Mill 62 67 35N26'37 84w21'12 5:37:25
Stanfield 7 66 36N28 84w17 5:37:08
Stanfill 7 66 36N27'35 84w17'15 5:37:09
Stanley Junction 76 58 36N27'14 84w29'40 5:37:59
Stanton 38 3 35N27'44 89w24'07 5:57:36
Stantonville 55 3 35N12 88w27 5:53:48
Starkeytown 78 60 35N43'58 83w34'36 5:34:18
Star Point 69 3 36N34'18 85w09'43 5:40:39
Statesville 95 9 36N01'10 86w07'30 5:44:30
State University 90 75 36N19 82w21 5:29:24
Static 69 3 36N37'18 85w05'10 5:40:21
Station Camp 83 50 36N27 86w32 5:46:08
Statonville 55 3 35N09'30 88w25'33 5:53:42
Staunton Mill 30 65 36N07'24 82w50'39 5:31:23
Stayton 22 3 36N16'37 87w19'37 5:49:18
Stegall 39 25 35N33'25 88w26'39 5:53:47
Stella 28 3 35N02'20 87w05'05 5:48:20
Stephen Holston 82 2 36N35 82w11 5:28:44
Stephens 65 51 36N03'36 84w26'45 5:37:47
Stephenson 16 12 35N23'52 85w55'35 5:43:42
Sterling Park 33 61 35N10'35 85w12'48 5:40:51
Stewart 42 3 36N19'14 87w50'29 5:51:22
Stewart Hill 90 75 36N18'28 82w30'29 5:30:02
Stiles Ford 64 9 35N08'22 86w22'09 5:45:29
Stinger 23 16 35N57'27 89w34'45 5:58:19
Stinking Creek 7 66 36N23 84w07 5:36:28
Stiversville 60 3 35N26'32 87w02'32 5:48:10
Stock Creek 47 67 35N56 83w54 5:35:36
Stockton 25 3 36N24'19 84w49'22 5:39:17
Stockton Valley 53 68 35N44 84w21 5:37:24
Stokes 23 16 35N57'34 89w13'13 5:56:53
Stokes Crossing 2 5 35N32 86w20 5:45:20
Stokes Mill 1 62 36N10'49 83w58'39 5:35:55
Stone 44 27 36N23'39 85w39'39 5:42:39
Stonebrook 47 67 35N57'03 84w03'25 5:36:14
Stone River 19 4 36N12 86w37 5:46:28
Stone River Estates 19 4 36N12 86w37 5:46:28
Stones River Homes 75 38 36N00'23 86w29'42 5:45:59
Stonewall 80 3 36N11'25 85w53'56 5:43:36
Stoney Fork 76 58 36N18 84w13 5:36:52
Stony Creek 10 1 36N24 82w05 5:28:20
Stony Gap 34 51 36N32 83w13 5:32:52
Stony Point 22 3 36N15'49 87w31'08 5:50:05
Stony Point 37 70 36N29'24 82w49'20 5:31:17
Stowers 65 56 36N13'53 84w49'01 5:39:16
Strahl 37 70 36N21'14 82w57'23 5:31:50
Strauss Mill 16 12 35N33'35 86w07'28 5:44:30
Strawberry Plains 45 67 36N03'47 83w41'10 5:34:45
Striggersville 37 70 36N26'32 82w59'26 5:31:58
Stringtown 8 49 35N56'56 86w01'39 5:44:07
Stringtown 27 21 36N10'00 89w01'42 5:56:07
Stringtown 36 3 35N21'50 88w10'34 5:52:42
Stringtown 39 25 35N37'02 88w22'57 5:53:32
Stringtown 63 3 36N28'40 87w33'33 5:50:14
Stringtown 93 3 35N53'34 85w18'07 5:41:12
Stroudsville 74 3 36N28'57 87w06'25 5:48:26
Stuart Heights 33 61 35N05'55 85w17'05 5:41:08
Sturdivant Crossing 57 3 35N27'09 89w03'57 5:56:16
Suburban Hills 47 67 35N54'53 84w04'05 5:36:16
Suburban Hills 54 54 35N24'38 84w40'39 5:38:43
Sugar Creek 44 27 36N26'07 85w37'29 5:42:30
Sugar Creek 46 1 36N35'53 81w43'41 5:26:55
Sugar Forks 45 67 36N01'27 83w24'14 5:33:37
Sugar Grove 6 53 35N04'23 84w48'53 5:39:16
Sugar Grove 73 67 35N54'50 84w27'55 5:37:52
Sugar Grove 83 50 36N37'37 86w16'03 5:45:04
Sugar Hill 68 3 35N33'06 87w49'14 5:51:17
Sugarlimb 53 68 35N46'15 84w18'38 5:37:15
Sugar Tree 20 3 35N49'45 88w02'10 5:52:09
Sugartree Ford 28 22 35N05'54 86w59'14 5:47:57
Suggs Creek 95 49 36N07'07 86w29'43 5:45:59
Sullivan Gardens 82 2 36N28'40 82w35'36 5:30:22
Sulphur 67 22 36N18'24 85w22'41 5:41:31
Sulphura 83 50 36N32'20 86w24'46 5:45:39
Sulphur Creek 41 3 35N40 87w42 5:50:48
Sulphur Spring 32 67 36N10'03 83w17'33 5:33:10
Sulphur Springs 1 62 36N05 84w08 5:36:32
Sulphur Springs 11 10 36N14'58 87w03'15 5:48:13
Sulphur Springs 52 9 35N13'05 86w40'16 5:46:41
Sulphur Springs 58 8 35N12 85w31 5:42:04
Sulphur Springs 69 3 36N33'48 85w04'01 5:40:16
Sulphur Springs 90 63 36N20'53 82w32'33 5:30:10
Sulphur Well Landing 40 3 36N21'37 88w07'08 5:52:29
Sumac 28 22 35N14'46 86w56'27 5:47:46
Summer City 4 15 35N34'27 85w06'58 5:40:28
Summerfield 31 3 35N15'13 85w47'57 5:43:12
Summer Shade 67 3 36N27 85w21 5:41:24
Summersville 82 2 36N27'53 82w31'51 5:30:07
Summertown 33 61 35N10'06 85w18'09 5:41:13
Summertown 50 29 35N26'05 87w18'46 5:49:15
Summit 33 61 35N04'11 85w06'03 5:40:24
Summit 37 70 36N15 83w05 5:32:20
Summit 63 32 36N32 87w22 5:49:28
Summit Knobs 33 61 35N04 85w10 5:40:40
Summitville 16 12 35N33'34 85w59'33 5:43:58
Sunbright 65 56 36N14'36 84w40'12 5:38:41
Sunkist Beach 48 3 36N21'09 89w27'09 5:57:49
Sunny Brook 82 2 36N32'43 82w13'44 5:28:55
Sunnyhill 38 3 35N32'05 89w14'57 5:57:00
Sunny Hills 82 2 36N35 82w11 5:28:44
Sunnyside 30 65 36N07'32 82w48'41 5:31:15
Sunnyside 34 51 36N32 83w13 5:32:52
Sunny Side 40 26 36N18'25 88w13'50 5:52:55
Sunnyside 53 68 35N39'08 84w23'23 5:37:34
Sunnyside 60 31 35N35'20 87w04'51 5:48:19
Sunnyside 66 3 36N22'58 88w58'34 5:55:54
Sunnyside 82 1 36N32'29 82w27'20 5:29:49
Sunrise 41 3 35N40'59 87w26'23 5:49:46
Sunrise 47 67 36N04'23 83w47'29 5:35:10
Sunrise 56 3 36N34'12 85w53'52 5:43:35

Sunset 69 3 36N31'54 85w09'37 5:40:38
Sunset Hill 32 67 36N11'57 83w20'44 5:33:23
Sunset Hills 82 2 36N30'40 82w30'53 5:30:04
Surgoinsville 37 70 36N28'15 82w51'07 5:31:24
Surprise 61 71 35N38'46 84w38'02 5:38:32
Susong 32 67 36N10'19 83w11'33 5:32:46
Sutherland 46 1 36N36'15 81w48'37 5:27:14
Swallow Bluff Landing 20 3 35N23'12 88w08'35 5:52:34
Swan Bluff 41 3 35N42'51 87w25'43 5:49:43
Swann Chapel 45 67 36N01 83w25 5:33:40
Swannsylvania 45 67 36N01 83w25 5:33:40
Sweetgum 88 3 35N47'36 85w24'33 5:41:38
Sweet Lips 12 3 35N24'30 88w31'20 5:54:05
Sweeton Hill 31 3 35N20'04 85w43'03 5:42:52
Sweetwater 62 67 35N36'05 84w27'40 5:37:51
Swift 36 23 35N20'38 88w08'28 5:52:34
Sycamore 11 10 36N19'19 87w03'11 5:48:13
Sycamore 13 51 36N27 83w29 5:33:56
Sycamore 71 34 36N11 85w28 5:41:52
Sycamore 94 3 35N49'01 86w59'51 5:47:59
Sycamore Hall 13 51 36N27 83w34 5:34:16
Sycamore Landing 43 3 35N56'14 87w54'53 5:51:40
Sycamore Swamp 52 9 35N04'38 86w23'35 5:45:34
Sycamore Valley 56 3 36N31'02 85w55'41 5:43:43
Sykes 80 3 36N07'24 85w58'40 5:43:55
Sylco 70 72 35N02'02 84w35'55 5:38:24
Sylvia 22 3 36N10'18 87w25'32 5:49:42
Tabernacle 84 24 35N31'21 89w34'37 5:58:18
Tabor 18 15 35N57 85w02 5:40:08
Tackett Creek 7 66 36N32'20 84w00'29 5:36:02
Taft 52 9 35N01'14 86w43'05 5:46:52
Talbott 45 67 36N09'09 83w24'55 5:33:40
Tallassee 5 64 35N32'48 84w03'36 5:36:14
Talley 59 3 35N21'23 86w41'00 5:46:44
Tampico 29 55 36N11'47 83w33'43 5:34:15
Tanglewood 80 41 36N16'31 85w59'16 5:43:57
Tan Rara Oesta 47 67 35N52'58 84w06'50 5:36:27
Tantallon 26 18 35N06'06 85w56'06 5:43:44
Tara Estates 16 13 35N23'06 86w11'57 5:44:48
Tariffville 62 67 35N29'12 84w10'43 5:36:43
Tarkiln Ford 93 9 35N52'38 85w13'23 5:40:54
Tarlton 31 3 35N29'35 85w39'11 5:42:37
Tarpley 28 22 35N08'32 86w59'36 5:47:58
Tarsus 63 3 36N25'25 87w32'21 5:50:09
Tasso 6 53 35N12'42 84w48'15 5:39:13
Tate 9 3 35N57'26 88w27'47 5:53:51
Tate Springs 29 55 36N20'24 83w20'45 5:33:23
Tatesville 31 3 35N22'00 85w33'40 5:42:15
Tatumville 23 16 36N02'33 89w11'39 5:56:47
Taylor Crossroads 2 3 35N38'48 86w34'12 5:46:17
Taylor Crossroads 22 3 36N12'07 87w26'20 5:49:45
Taylor Hill 72 74 35N28'52 85w01'37 5:40:06
Taylor Mill 90 63 36N18'51 82w34'13 5:30:17
Taylors 24 3 35N14 89w21 5:57:24
Taylors 93 3 36N00'49 85w21'44 5:41:27
Taylors Crossing 39 3 35N31'29 88w15'08 5:53:01
Taylors Crossroads 67 3 36N30'38 85w15'09 5:41:01
Taylorsville 60 3 35N38'09 87w16'27 5:49:06
Taylorsville 95 34 36N16'32 86w11'59 5:44:48
Taylortown 26 18 35N08'48 86w13'23 5:44:54
Taylortown 43 3 35N55'57 87w43'46 5:50:55
Taylortown 52 9 35N11'57 86w45'16 5:47:01
Tazewell 13 51 36N27'15 83w34'10 5:34:17
Teachers College 19 4 36N09 86w47 5:47:08
Teague 35 3 35N24'39 88w54'55 5:55:40
Tekoa 47 67 35N59'16 84w02'31 5:36:10
Telford 90 63 36N14'56 82w32'43 5:30:11
Tellico Hills 54 71 35N27'51 84w35'13 5:38:21
Tellico Plains 62 70 35N21'46 84w17'39 5:37:11
Temperance Hall 21 3 36N05'02 85w54'03 5:43:36
Temple Acres 47 67 36N06'01 83w55'31 5:35:42
Temple Ford 2 6 35N29'52 86w31'37 5:46:06
Templeton 23 16 36N09'24 89w13'44 5:56:55
Templow 85 3 36N26'09 86w14'13 5:44:57
Ten Mile 61 54 35N40'00 84w39'53 5:38:40
Tennemo 23 16 36N09'39 89w34'08 5:58:17
Tennemo Landing 23 16 36N09'34 89w35'11 5:58:21
Tennessee City 22 3 36N05'35 87w30'53 5:50:04
Tennessee Hills 82 2 36N32'10 82w14'24 5:28:58
Tennessee Ridge 42 3 36N18'43 87w46'24 5:51:06
Terrace View 73 70 35N45'03 84w43'32 5:38:54
Terrell 92 3 36N23'06 88w56'38 5:55:47
Terry 9 3 35N54'10 88w34'43 5:54:19
Terry Creek 7 66 36N28 84w17 5:37:08
Terry Estates 28 22 35N10'46 87w02'54 5:48:12
Tharpe 81 3 36N34'25 87w56'04 5:51:44
The Crossroads 58 8 35N03'08 85w50'30 5:43:22
Theodore 51 3 35N33'18 87w32'25 5:50:10
Theta 60 3 35N46'43 87w03'01 5:48:12
The Wye 1 62 36N12'53 84w09'58 5:36:40
The Y 90 75 36N18'00 82w22'56 5:29:32
Thick 59 3 35N39'32 86w44'03 5:46:56
Third Creek 47 67 35N58'13 84w00'12 5:36:01
Thomas 71 3 36N05'01 85w38'43 5:42:35
Thomas Addition 82 2 36N34'30 82w33'02 5:30:12
Thomas Bridge 82 1 36N28 82w15 5:29:00
Thomas Springs 18 15 35N50'45 85w12'50 5:40:51
Thomasville 11 10 36N24'50 87w08'01 5:48:32
Thompson Crossroads 36 3 35N15'43 88w02'57 5:52:12
Thompson Mill 34 51 36N34'58 83w22'07 5:33:28
Thompsons Crossroads 22 3 36N09'00 87w31'54 5:50:08
Thompsons Station 94 3 35N48'07 86w54'41 5:47:39
Thompsons Store 14 11 36N36'24 85w25'22 5:41:41
Thorn Grove 47 67 36N00'16 83w41'36 5:34:46
Thorn Hill 29 55 36N21'30 83w25'03 5:33:40
Thornton 47 67 35N52'56 84w08'53 5:36:36
Thornton Heights 47 67 35N52 84w08 5:36:32
Three Churches 91 3 35N10 87w44 5:50:56
Three Forks 26 19 35N03'08 86w06'22 5:44:25
Three Forks 76 58 36N27'00 84w34'12 5:38:17
Three Oaks 50 29 35N21'56 87w16'20 5:49:05
Three Oaks 52 9 35N02'12 86w32'28 5:46:10
Three Point 49 3 35N41'33 89w41'59 5:58:48
Three Points 47 67 36N03'48 83w46'16 5:35:05
Three Springs 32 67 36N15 83w12 5:32:48
Three Way 27 8 35N50 88w55 5:55:40
Throckmorton 81 3 36N25'42 87w38'12 5:50:33
Thula 30 65 36N09'49 83w05'23 5:32:22
Thurman 20 3 35N25'31 88w11'55 5:52:48
Thurman Addition 78 60 35N49 83w33 5:34:12
Tibbs 38 24 35N41'55 89w20'49 5:57:23
Tidwell 22 3 36N00'43 87w20'06 5:49:20
Tiftonia 33 61 35N01'13 85w21'58 5:41:28
Tiger Tail 23 16 35N56'10 89w34'47 5:58:19
Tigertown 32 67 36N11'44 83w16'46 5:33:07
Tiger Valley 10 1 36N13'42 82w11'12 5:28:45
Tigrett 23 16 35N57'05 89w14'24 5:56:58
Tilghman 27 21 36N09'03 89w05'15 5:56:21
Timbercrest 47 67 35N57'09 84w00'44 5:36:03
Timberlake 39 25 35N42'36 88w22'54 5:53:32
Timberlake 47 67 35N54'43 83w57'56 5:35:52
Timberlinks 33 61 35N07'48 85w20'49 5:41:23
Timber Ridge 30 65 36N07'10 82w56'22 5:31:45
Timesville 33 61 35N09'18 85w19'52 5:41:19
Timothy 67 3 36N29'21 85w24'25 5:41:38
Tinch 25 3 36N26 84w56 5:39:44
Tin Cup 3 3 36N02'44 88w06'02 5:52:24
Tinsleys Bottom 44 3 36N33 85w30 5:42:00
Tioga 1 62 36N07'40 84w24'18 5:37:37
Tiprell 13 51 36N34'57 83w40'44 5:34:43
Tipton 47 67 35N56 83w54 5:35:36
Tipton 84 3 35N24'49 89w49'11 5:59:17
Tipton Oliver Place 5 64 35N35'18 83w48'46 5:35:15
Tiptonville 48 3 36N22'42 89w28'19 5:57:53
Tiptop 4 15 35N38'36 85w13'04 5:40:52
Titus 7 66 36N23'30 84w16'45 5:37:07
Tobaccoport 81 3 36N38'32 87w53'24 5:51:34
Todd Town 18 9 35N53'13 85w13'22 5:40:53
Tolley Town 10 1 36N11'26 82w13'05 5:28:52
Tom Murray 57 3 35N39 88w53 5:55:32
Tomotla Ford 62 68 35N34'34 84w10'41 5:36:43
Tom Town 15 65 35N50'43 83w01'00 5:32:04
Toomy 76 58 36N28'01 84w35'40 5:38:23
Toone 35 3 35N21'08 88w57'09 5:55:49
Top of the World Estates 5 64 35N33 84w06 5:36:24
Topside 47 67 35N52'33 83w57'35 5:35:50
Topsy 91 3 35N25'32 87w42'11 5:50:49
Toqua 62 67 35N35 84w15 5:37:00
Torbet 31 3 35N21'24 85w37'42 5:42:31
Tottys 41 3 35N44 87w17 5:49:08
Tottys Bend 41 3 35N47'04 87w22'08 5:49:29
Toulon 38 3 35N44'18 89w24'56 5:57:40
Towee 70 72 35N11 84w30 5:38:00
Town Acres 30 65 36N09'32 82w48'31 5:31:14
Town Creek 13 51 36N27 83w55 5:35:40
Towne Hills 33 61 35N08'51 85w14'18 5:40:57
Townsend 5 64 35N40'31 83w45'21 5:35:01
Tracy City 31 3 35N15'37 85w44'10 5:42:57
Trade 46 1 36N20'57 81w44'45 5:26:59
Trails West 47 67 35N54'53 84w03'08 5:36:13
Tranquillity 54 54 35N33'27 84w40'39 5:38:43
Travisville 69 3 36N35'04 84w59'38 5:39:59
Treadway 34 51 36N25'07 83w13'28 5:32:54
Treeville 47 67 36N02 84w02 5:36:08
Tremont 5 64 35N37'15 83w40'39 5:34:43
Trenton 27 8 35N58'50 88w56'29 5:55:46
Trent Valley 34 51 36N29'51 83w11'32 5:32:46
Trentville 47 67 36N01'40 83w43'13 5:34:53
Trevecca-College 19 4 36N09 86w45 5:47:00
Trevilion 7 66 36N33 84w03 5:36:12
Trezevant 9 3 36N00'41 88w37'22 5:54:29
Trigg 28 3 35N18'42 86w51'07 5:47:24
Trigonia 53 68 35N36'47 84w11'17 5:36:45
Trimble 23 16 36N12'11 89w11'27 5:56:46
Trinity 43 3 36N09'49 87w49'51 5:51:19
Trinity 94 48 35N54'37 86w45'14 5:47:01
Triune 94 3 35N52 86w43 5:46:52
Trotters Landing 43 3 35N59'27 88w00'06 5:52:00
Trousdale 8 3 35N40'10 85w56'20 5:43:45
Trousdale 83 42 36N23'51 86w24'08 5:45:37
Troy 66 3 36N20'19 89w09'50 5:56:39
Trundle Crossroad 78 60 35N53'11 83w44'07 5:34:56
Tuckahoe 47 67 36N04 83w41 5:34:44
Tucker Ford 2 3 35N34'09 86w37'35 5:46:30
Tuckers Corner 27 8 36N00'18 88w50'44 5:55:23
Tuckers Crossroads 95 34 36N11'56 86w10'26 5:44:42
Tullahoma 16 13 35N21'43 86w12'34 5:44:50
Tulu 55 3 35N03'46 88w23'38 5:53:35
Tumbling 92 3 36N14'28 88w32'33 5:54:10
Tupper Town 65 51 36N03'09 84w20'43 5:37:23
Turkeyfoot 33 61 35N06'27 85w10'20 5:40:41
Turkey Track 50 29 35N23'23 87w34'26 5:50:18
Turley 7 66 36N18 84w13 5:36:52
Turnbull 22 3 36N03 87w19 5:49:16
Turner Ford 18 3 36N08'51 84w55'28 5:39:42
Turner Landing 20 3 35N27'44 88w02'30 5:52:10
Turners Station 83 50 36N36'37 86w16'06 5:45:04
Turnersville 74 3 36N29'16 87w02'24 5:48:10
Turnpike 38 24 35N36 89w16 5:57:04
Turtletown 70 73 35N07'37 84w21'13 5:37:25
Tusculum 19 4 36N03'32 86w43'00 5:46:52
Tusculum 30 65 36N10'30 82w45'32 5:31:02
Tusculum College 30 65 36N10 82w46 5:31:04
Twin Oak 71 3 36N09 85w38 5:42:32
Twin Oaks 82 2 36N35'38 81w58'12 5:27:53
Twinton 67 3 36N17'03 85w07'40 5:40:31
Two Chestnut 83 50 36N26'49 86w37'01 5:46:28
Twomey 41 3 35N45'58 87w27'51 5:49:51
Tylersville 23 16 36N00'15 89w32'29 5:58:10
Tyner 33 61 35N03'46 85w09'26 5:40:38
Tyner Hills 33 61 35N03'27 85w09'00 5:40:36
Tyson 27 21 36N08'34 89w04'13 5:56:17
Uceba 5 64 35N53 83w43 5:34:52
Una 19 4 36N05'50 86w39'17 5:46:37
Unaka Springs 86 1 36N05'51 82w26'30 5:29:46
Underhill 21 3 36N02 85w54 5:43:36
Underwood 56 3 36N36'39 85w59'13 5:43:57
Unicoi 86 1 36N11'43 82w20'59 5:29:24
Union 38 24 35N35'05 89w07'10 5:56:29
Union 65 51 36N04'15 84w29'09 5:37:57
Union 73 67 35N54'08 84w25'20 5:37:41
Union 89 46 35N42'46 85w42'04 5:42:48
Union Camp 56 3 36N32 86w02 5:44:08
Union Central 27 8 35N57'52 88w47'11 5:55:09
Union City 66 3 36N25'27 89w03'25 5:56:14
Union Cross 39 3 35N45'35 88w27'17 5:53:49
Union Grove 5 64 35N45'09 84w05'35 5:36:22
Union Grove 54 71 35N35'50 84w34'18 5:38:17
Union Grove 60 3 35N35'56 86w57'19 5:47:49
Union Grove 78 67 35N56'38 83w32'28 5:34:10
Union Heights 32 67 36N10'58 83w14'55 5:33:00
Union Hill 14 3 36N33'05 85w41'46 5:42:47
Union Hill 19 4 36N20'03 86w46'45 5:47:07
Union Hill 39 3 35N31 88w20 5:53:20
Union Hill 50 29 35N05'21 87w19'58 5:49:20
Union Hill 84 3 35N26 89w47 5:59:08
Union McMinn 54 71 35N31 84w32 5:38:08
Union Ridge 2 5 35N30'37 86w15'53 5:45:04
Union Temple 30 65 36N17'53 82w44'08 5:30:57
Union Valley 78 60 35N55'14 83w42'38 5:34:51
Unionville 2 3 35N37'18 86w35'33 5:46:22
Unionville 48 16 35N57'06 89w26'10 5:57:45
Unitia 53 68 35N45'05 84w10'25 5:36:42
Unity 20 3 35N24'41 88w09'23 5:52:38
Unity 67 3 36N28'43 85w19'31 5:41:18
University of Tennessee 47 67 35N57 83w56 5:35:44
University of The South 26 18 35N12 85w55 5:43:40
University View 16 18 35N11'35 85w56'14 5:43:45
Upchurch 30 65 36N14'32 82w46'26 5:31:06
Upper Big Bigby 60 9 35N30 87w12 5:48:48
Upper Holly Creek 91 29 35N06'36 87w36'27 5:50:26
Upper Mockeson 50 29 35N04'12 87w18'08 5:49:13
Upper Shady 46 1 36N30'15 81w56'20 5:27:45
Upper Shell Creek 10 1 36N10'03 82w01'54 5:28:08
Upper Sinking 41 3 35N40'01 87w38'48 5:50:35
Upper Windrock 1 62 36N05'31 84w20'27 5:37:22
Uptonville 57 3 35N27'17 88w58'44 5:55:55
Uptown 47 67 35N59 83w56 5:35:44
Uptown Nashville 19 4 36N10 86w47 5:47:08
Utah 20 3 35N35'25 88w03'30 5:52:14
Vaden 43 3 36N06 87w38 5:50:32
Valdeau 33 61 35N05'01 85w19'06 5:41:16
Vale 9 3 36N06'24 88w15'32 5:53:02
Valleybrook 33 61 35N09'20 85w12'48 5:40:51
Valley Creek 13 51 36N34'19 83w54'43 5:35:39
Valley Forge 10 1 36N18'23 82w11'36 5:28:46
Valley Hills 82 2 36N35 82w11 5:28:44
Valleyhome 32 67 36N13 83w17 5:33:08
Valley View 1 62 36N06 84w08 5:36:32
Valleyview 33 61 35N01'22 85w07'03 5:40:28
Valley View 46 1 36N29 81w48 5:27:12
Valleyview 75 3 35N58'21 86w19'24 5:45:18
Valley View Heights 1 62 36N01'41 84w09'28 5:36:38
Van Benber Springs 13 51 36N27 83w55 5:35:40
Van Blarcom 19 4 36N09 86w51 5:47:24
Van Buren 35 3 35N07'53 89w04'31 5:56:18
Vance 82 2 36N31'20 82w12'47 5:28:51
Vancel Mill 13 51 36N31'24 83w37'59 5:34:32
Vandever 18 9 35N49'51 85w05'31 5:40:22
Van Dyke 40 26 36N13'17 88w18'04 5:53:12
Van Hill 37 70 36N23'19 82w48'48 5:31:15

Vanleer 22 3 36N14'06 87w26'38 5:49:47
Vannatta 2 6 35N36'57 86w28'55 5:45:56
Vanntown 52 9 35N00'32 86w27'22 5:45:49
Vardy 34 51 36N32 83w13 5:32:52
Vasper 7 66 36N16'16 84w11'42 5:36:47
Vaughn's Gap 19 4 36N07 86w52 5:47:28
Vaughns Grove 27 8 36N00'07 88w51'22 5:55:25
Venable Spring 59 31 35N36'27 86w46'56 5:47:08
Verdun 76 58 36N29'41 84w32'27 5:38:10
Vernon 41 3 35N52'10 87w29'47 5:49:59
Vernon Heights 82 2 36N29'44 82w34'00 5:30:16
Verona 59 30 35N31'50 86w46'11 5:47:05
Versailles 75 3 35N43'46 86w32'29 5:46:10
Vervilla 89 3 35N35'44 85w52'17 5:43:29
Vesta 95 34 36N03'54 86w24'48 5:45:39
Vestal 47 67 35N55'37 83w55'20 5:35:41
Viar 23 16 36N01'04 89w19'41 5:57:19
Victoria 58 8 35N09'13 85w33'15 5:42:13
Victory 7 66 36N23'27 84w00'32 5:36:02
Vildo 35 3 35N24'20 89w06'13 5:56:25
Village Green 47 67 35N53'03 84w10'03 5:36:40
Vine 95 34 36N01'52 86w21'28 5:45:26
Vinegar Hill 82 2 36N33'04 82w06'11 5:28:25
Vine Ridge 67 3 36N15'38 85w07'08 5:40:29
Vineyard Landing 72 74 35N35'32 84w47'35 5:39:10
Vinta Mill 28 3 35N04'11 86w56'21 5:47:45
Viola 89 3 35N32'18 85w51'33 5:43:26
Virtue 47 67 35N51'23 84w10'43 5:36:43
Vise 20 3 35N35 88w07 5:52:28
Vise Landing 20 3 35N30'28 87w58'39 5:51:55
Volunteer Heights 18 15 35N55'59 85w02'21 5:40:09
Vonore 62 67 35N35'24 84w14'31 5:36:58
Voorhies 51 3 35N26'57 87w33'40 5:50:15
Vose 5 64 35N47'31 83w57'51 5:35:51
Vulcan 58 8 35N00'24 85w31'48 5:42:07
Waco 28 3 35N22'33 87w01'55 5:48:08
Waconda Point 33 61 35N08'04 85w07'59 5:40:32
Wade 75 38 35N57'39 86w29'44 5:45:59
Walden 33 61 35N09'53 85w18'05 5:41:12
Walden Creek 78 60 35N47'14 83w37'36 5:34:30
Waldensia 18 9 35N54'48 84w47'31 5:39:10
Waldens Ridge 72 74 35N01 85w11 5:40:44
Wales 28 22 35N14'56 87w04'58 5:48:20
Walker 79 39 35N04 90w04 6:00:16
Walker Ford 4 15 35N28'53 85w16'51 5:41:07
Walker Ford 30 65 36N03'52 82w52'58 5:31:32
Walkers Landing 3 3 35N49'02 87w58'31 5:51:54
Walkertown 30 65 36N15'35 82w45'24 5:31:02
Walkertown 36 23 35N11'07 88w14'36 5:52:58
Wallace Acres 59 30 35N27'39 86w46'46 5:47:07
Walland 5 64 35N43'41 83w48'48 5:35:15
Walling 93 3 35N48'29 85w35'58 5:42:24
Walnut Grove 2 3 35N40'54 86w32'34 5:46:10
Walnut Grove 7 62 36N17'49 83w59'34 5:35:58
Walnut Grove 26 18 35N06'31 86w14'20 5:44:57
Walnut Grove 27 21 36N12 89w01 5:56:04
Walnut Grove 36 23 35N02'24 88w03'04 5:52:12
Walnut Grove 46 1 36N26'16 81w45'15 5:27:01
Walnut Grove 61 54 35N32'08 84w44'24 5:38:58
Walnut Grove 78 60 35N52'58 83w28'11 5:33:53
Walnut Grove 82 1 36N26'12 82w14'33 5:28:58
Walnut Grove 83 50 36N29'03 86w36'47 5:46:27
Walnut Grove 84 3 35N35'31 89w46'50 5:59:07
Walnut Grove 85 3 36N23'23 86w14'30 5:44:58
Walnut Hill 17 3 35N42'55 89w02'51 5:56:11
Walnut Hill 73 67 35N57'02 84w32'02 5:38:08
Walnut Hill 82 2 36N34'11 82w15'25 5:29:02
Walnut Log 66 3 36N28'04 89w18'56 5:57:16
Walnut Shade 56 3 36N34'28 85w49'48 5:43:19
Walter Crossroad 30 65 36N07'00 82w58'00 5:31:52
Walterhill 75 3 35N57'00 86w22'40 5:45:31
Walts Landing 79 40 35N23'33 90w02'39 6:00:11
Wa-Ni Village 29 55 36N13'22 83w27'16 5:33:49
Ware Branch 33 61 35N15'34 85w05'17 5:40:21
Warren 24 3 35N14'18 89w26'34 5:57:46
Warrenburg 30 65 36N07'38 83w05'40 5:32:23
Warrens Bluff 39 25 35N36'55 88w19'08 5:53:17
Warrensburg 30 65 36N11 82w59 5:31:56
Wartburg 65 51 36N06'17 84w35'50 5:38:23
Wartrace 2 5 35N31'38 86w20'01 5:45:20
Warwicktown 87 52 36N13'52 83w52'47 5:35:31
Washburn 29 55 36N17'24 83w35'28 5:34:22
Washington 72 74 35N01 85w11 5:40:44
Washington College 90 63 36N13 82w38 5:30:32
Washington Heights 33 61 35N05'15 85w10'15 5:40:41
Washington Heights 47 67 36N00'49 84w04'25 5:36:18
Washplace Ford 68 3 35N33'35 87w49'19 5:51:17
Wasp 15 65 35N51'16 82w55'56 5:31:44
Watauga 10 1 36N22'14 82w17'49 5:29:11
Watauga Flats 90 1 36N22'43 82w18'42 5:29:15
Watauga Point 10 1 36N19'37 82w16'01 5:29:04
Water Fork Mill 30 65 36N06'52 82w44'35 5:30:58
Waterloo 67 3 36N18'06 85w27'59 5:41:52
Watertown 5 64 35N44'17 83w47'17 5:35:09
Watertown 95 9 36N06'01 86w07'55 5:44:32
Water Valley 60 3 35N44'28 87w11'22 5:48:45
Waterville 6 53 35N06'27 84w51'50 5:39:27
Watkins 21 3 35N55'26 85w51'18 5:43:25
Watson 18 15 35N59'35 84w49'08 5:39:17
Watson 41 3 35N42'03 87w29'13 5:49:57
Watt Heights 54 54 35N17'34 84w44'27 5:38:58
Watts Bar Dam (Post Office) 72 74 35N37'16 84w47'16 5:39:09
Watts Bar Estates 72 74 35N44'13 84w43'11 5:38:53
Waucheesi 62 70 35N21'26 84w10'33 5:36:42
Waverly 43 3 36N05'02 87w47'41 5:51:11
Waycross 37 70 36N35'35 82w38'55 5:30:36
Wayland Springs 50 29 35N03'42 87w34'29 5:50:18
Waynesboro 91 3 35N19'10 87w45'44 5:51:03
Wayside 89 46 35N42 85w46 5:43:04
Weakley 28 22 35N15'52 87w11'19 5:48:45
Weakly 28 3 35N15 87w20 5:49:20
Wear Valley 78 60 35N42'50 83w39'12 5:34:37
Weaver 82 1 36N31'37 82w11'06 5:28:44
Webber City 50 29 35N20'48 87w16'56 5:49:08
Webbs Chapel 21 3 35N57 85w49 5:43:16
Webbs Jungle 2 5 35N37'33 86w17'34 5:45:10
Webbs Landing 68 3 35N35'47 88w01'20 5:52:05
Webbtown 56 3 36N30'01 85w58'07 5:43:52
Webster 73 70 35N52'08 84w38'00 5:38:32
Wedgewood Hills 47 67 35N54'13 84w04'52 5:36:19
Welch Camp 7 66 36N14'20 84w18'35 5:37:14
Welch Crossroad 87 52 36N21'21 83w50'41 5:35:23
Welchland 88 3 35N38'52 85w31'00 5:42:04
Well Spring 7 66 36N27 83w55 5:35:40
Wellsville 5 64 35N36'25 84w05'14 5:36:21
Wellwood 38 3 35N36'57 89w06'28 5:56:26
Wesleyanna 54 71 35N21'46 84w33'34 5:38:14
West 19 4 36N09 86w51 5:47:24
West 27 20 35N50'26 88w45'15 5:55:01
Westavia Woods 47 67 35N56'45 84w02'14 5:36:09
Westborough 47 67 35N56'37 84w03'21 5:36:13
Westbourne 7 66 36N29'37 84w01'46 5:36:07
West Bradley 6 53 35N13 84w56 5:39:44
West Britts Landing 20 3 35N47'13 87w58'44 5:51:55
West Chester 12 3 35N24 88w41 5:54:44
West Cyruston 52 9 35N08'09 86w45'03 5:47:00
Westel 18 57 35N51'47 84w45'19 5:39:01
West Emory 47 67 35N52'48 84w05'26 5:36:22
West End 4 15 35N37'07 85w12'11 5:40:49
West End 15 65 35N58'11 83w12'22 5:32:49
West End Heights 95 34 36N12'55 86w19'09 5:45:17
West Erin 42 3 36N18 87w45 5:51:00
West Forest 47 67 35N56'50 84w03'06 5:36:12
West Fork 67 3 36N24 85w14 5:40:56
West Greene 30 65 36N13 82w48 5:31:12
West Harpeth 94 48 35N50'33 86w54'00 5:47:36
West Haven 47 67 35N58'26 83w58'47 5:35:55
West Haven 60 31 35N36'21 87w04'32 5:48:18
West Hills 47 67 35N56'14 84w01'28 5:36:06
West Hills 73 67 35N55'30 84w33'56 5:38:16
West Hima 36 23 35N11'19 88w14'33 5:52:58
West Junction 79 39 35N03'58 90w05'48 6:00:23
West Knoxville 47 67 35N58'13 83w57'19 5:35:49
Westlyn 47 67 35N54'53 84w01'42 5:36:07
West Maryville 5 64 35N45'23 83w58'45 5:35:55
West Meade 16 12 35N28'16 86w04'17 5:44:17
West Meade 19 4 36N07'04 86w53'14 5:47:33
West Meade 60 31 35N36'05 87w03'36 5:48:14
West Mill 18 15 35N56'02 85w11'03 5:40:44
West Miller Cove 5 64 35N44 83w49 5:35:16
Westmoreland 83 50 36N33'43 86w14'53 5:45:00
Westmoreland Heights 47 67 35N55'19 84w00'18 5:36:01
West Mousetail Landing 20 3 35N40'33 88w01'07 5:52:04
West Myers 15 65 35N56'11 83w04'55 5:32:20
West Nashville 19 4 36N09 86w51 5:47:24
West Oneida 76 58 36N30'13 84w31'51 5:38:07
Westover 57 3 35N36'39 88w52'36 5:55:30
Westpoint 50 29 35N07'59 87w32'01 5:50:08
Westport 9 3 35N53'47 88w19'02 5:53:16
West Ridge 37 70 36N33'03 82w38'48 5:30:35
West Riverside 89 46 35N40'11 85w47'07 5:43:08
West Robbins 76 51 36N21'29 84w36'42 5:38:27
West Sandy Landing 40 3 36N19'23 88w07'20 5:52:29
West Shiloh 55 3 35N08'55 88w23'00 5:53:32
Westside 28 29 35N11'18 87w12'48 5:48:51
Westside Heights 26 13 35N20'59 86w13'32 5:44:54
West Springbrook 5 64 35N47'51 83w59'00 5:35:56
West Union 79 40 35N22'13 89w58'00 5:59:52
West Union 92 47 36N17'31 88w39'02 5:54:36
West View 33 61 35N00'02 85w06'01 5:40:24
West View 47 67 35N57'40 83w57'54 5:35:52
West View Park 82 2 36N33'45 82w34'38 5:30:19
Westwood 16 13 35N28'13 86w05'45 5:44:23
Westwood 60 31 35N35'47 87w05'32 5:48:22
Westwood 79 39 35N04 90w04 6:00:16
Westwood Estates 1 62 36N07'00 84w08'17 5:36:33
Westwood Gardens 57 3 35N37'48 88w49'47 5:55:19
Westwood Hills 5 64 35N43'24 83w59'17 5:35:57
Westwood Homes 16 12 35N29'15 86w03'45 5:44:15
Wetmore 70 72 35N15'21 84w33'05 5:38:12
Wheel 2 6 35N29'19 86w37'47 5:46:31
Wheelerton 28 3 35N05'22 86w50'12 5:47:21
Whispering Hills 47 67 36N03'24 83w59'42 5:35:59
Whitaker 2 6 35N27'07 86w37'35 5:46:30
White 79 40 35N06 89w54 5:59:36
White Acres 59 30 35N27'09 86w49'07 5:47:16
White Bluff 22 3 36N06'27 87w13'15 5:48:53
White Bridge 19 4 36N07 86w52 5:47:28
White City 31 3 35N14'50 85w42'10 5:42:49
White Fern 39 3 35N38'23 88w35'43 5:54:23
White Ford 2 6 35N32'56 86w38'21 5:46:33
White Ford 65 56 36N07'46 84w48'10 5:39:13
Whitehaven 79 39 35N01'38 90w01'45 6:00:07
Whitehead 59 30 35N28'48 86w47'20 5:47:09
Whitehead Hill 10 1 36N13'40 82w09'27 5:28:38
White Hill 83 3 36N24'35 86w41'26 5:46:46
White Hill 88 3 35N39'18 85w34'19 5:42:17
White Hollow 87 52 36N20'48 83w53'43 5:35:35
White Horn 37 70 36N17'04 83w03'22 5:32:13
Whitehouse 41 3 35N54'50 87w36'23 5:50:26
White House 83 3 36N28'13 86w39'05 5:46:36
Whiteleyville 44 3 36N26'43 85w40'19 5:42:41
White Oak 7 66 36N32'05 84w02'05 5:36:08
White Oak 33 61 35N05'30 85w18'32 5:41:14
White Oak 56 3 35N35'57 85w59'11 5:43:57
White Oak 65 51 35N59 84w33 5:38:12
Whiteoak 94 3 35N50'18 87w09'13 5:48:37
White Oak Flat 22 3 36N12'42 87w15'40 5:49:03
White Oaks 16 12 35N27'40 86w03'43 5:44:15
White Pine 45 67 36N06'27 83w17'13 5:33:09
White Pine Ford 18 15 36N04'30 85w01'39 5:40:07
White Rock 10 1 36N13'14 82w08'00 5:28:32
Whitesand 30 65 36N02'57 82w49'16 5:31:17
Whitesburg 32 67 36N16'18 83w08'24 5:32:34
White Schoolhouse Corners 65 51 36N02 84w20 5:37:20
Whites Creek 19 4 36N15'57 86w49'51 5:47:19
White's Creek 72 74 35N41 84w52 5:39:28
Whiteside 58 8 34N59'14 85w29'52 5:41:59
White Station 79 40 35N06'07 89w51'35 5:59:26
Whiteville 35 3 35N19'35 89w08'58 5:56:36
Whitfield 41 3 35N46'59 87w37'08 5:50:29
Whitleyville 44 3 36N27 85w40 5:42:40
Whitlock 40 26 36N22'15 88w21'25 5:53:26
Whitthorne 9 3 35N54'52 88w38'45 5:54:35
Whittle Springs 47 67 36N01'03 83w54'57 5:35:40
Whitwell 58 8 35N12'05 85w31'09 5:42:05
Widow Town 78 60 35N49 83w33 5:34:12
Wilbur 10 1 36N20'20 82w07'06 5:28:28
Wilcox 17 3 35N56'08 89w09'15 5:56:37
Wilder 25 3 36N15'58 86w05'20 5:40:22
Wilder Chapel 26 18 35N13 86w05 5:44:20
Wildersville 39 3 35N46'53 88w21'37 5:53:26
Wildwood 5 64 35N48'13 83w52'17 5:35:29
Wildwood Lake 6 53 35N09 84w52 5:39:28
Wildwood Mill 8 3 35N44'04 86w00'18 5:44:01
Wilhoite Mills 59 3 35N35'36 86w41'51 5:46:47
Wilkerson 13 51 36N33 83w57 5:35:48
Wilkinson Corner 38 3 35N27'08 89w19'06 5:57:16
Wilkinstown 20 3 35N37'43 88w09'14 5:52:37
Wilkinsville 84 3 35N24'11 89w53'48 5:59:35
Willard 85 45 36N26'50 86w11'00 5:44:44
Willardtown 45 67 36N01'29 83w34'45 5:34:19
Willette 56 3 36N26'28 85w51'02 5:43:24
Williams 49 28 35N45 89w32 5:58:08
Williams 56 3 36N33'11 86w01'15 5:44:05
Williamsburg 54 54 35N21'14 84w31'46 5:38:07
Williams Crossroads 21 3 36N02'16 85w42'16 5:42:49
Williams Mill 13 51 36N24'14 83w34'52 5:34:19
Williamsport 60 3 35N41'12 87w13'10 5:48:53
Williams Springs 29 55 36N20'14 83w34'44 5:34:19
Willis 34 51 36N35'09 83w01'01 5:32:04
Willis 38 3 35N28'43 89w16'38 5:57:07
Willis Springs 70 72 35N00'34 84w41'13 5:38:45
Williston 24 3 35N09'27 89w22'06 5:57:28
Willow Grove 2 5 35N25'39 86w17'40 5:45:11
Willow Grove 14 3 36N35'13 85w20'32 5:41:22
Wills 46 1 36N32'01 81w47'37 5:27:10
Wilson Hill 59 30 35N24'56 86w51'54 5:47:28
Wilson Station 62 67 35N25 84w29 5:37:56
Wilsonville 15 65 35N58'23 83w14'20 5:32:57
Wilton Springs 15 65 35N52'44 83w11'12 5:32:45
Winchester 26 19 35N11'09 86w06'44 5:44:27
Winchester Springs 26 19 35N14'46 86w10'39 5:44:43
Windle 67 22 36N20'10 85w22'43 5:41:31
Windletown 67 3 36N15'51 85w08'48 5:40:35
Windrock 1 62 36N05'06 84w19'52 5:37:19
Windrow 75 3 35N47'55 86w33'18 5:46:13
Windsor Park 47 67 35N58'44 84w00'01 5:36:00
Windy City 57 3 35N44'30 88w54'24 5:55:38
Windy Hill 82 2 36N35 82w11 5:28:44
Winesap 4 15 35N46'05 85w09'56 5:40:40
Winfield 76 58 36N33'21 84w27'06 5:37:48
Wingo 9 3 36N03'08 88w35'05 5:54:20
Winklers Crossroads 56 3 36N36'21 85w50'31 5:43:22
Winn Crossing 59 3 35N38'43 86w41'58 5:46:48

Winner 10 1 36N23'49 82w06'33 5:28:26
Winn Springs 36 3 35N00'39 88w12'35 5:52:50
Winona 76 58 36N22'36 84w27'01 5:37:48
Winslow 65 67 35N59'29 84w27'24 5:37:50
Winton Town 16 12 35N28'23 85w54'59 5:43:40
Wirmingham 67 3 36N29'05 85w11'19 5:40:45
Withamtown 83 50 36N32'48 86w18'14 5:45:13
Witt 32 67 36N09'00 83w16'59 5:33:08
Wixtown 56 3 36N32'29 86w08'19 5:44:33
Wolf Creek 15 65 35N55'24 82w56'42 5:31:47
Wolf Creek 21 3 36N05 85w44 5:42:56
Wolf Creek 50 29 35N00'56 87w32'34 5:50:10
Wolf Creek 72 74 35N38'43 84w51'20 5:39:25
Wolf River 25 3 36N33 84w58 5:39:52
Wolverine 66 3 36N18'27 89w09'52 5:56:39
Womack 89 46 35N45'06 85w49'29 5:43:18
Wood 62 67 35N34'36 84w29'04 5:37:56
Woodbine 19 4 36N07'13 86w44'36 5:46:58
Woodbury 8 3 35N49'39 86w04'18 5:44:17
Woodby Hill 86 1 36N12'04 82w14'26 5:28:58
Woodcliff 71 3 36N09 85w16 5:41:04
Wooddale 47 67 36N00'54 83w45'35 5:35:02
Wooded Acres 47 67 35N58'36 84w01'45 5:36:07
Woodfield Park 47 67 35N54'20 83w49'53 5:35:20
Woodland 38 3 35N33'52 89w05'56 5:56:24
Woodland Acres 40 26 36N20'08 88w15'18 5:53:01
Woodland Acres 47 67 35N54'00 84w02'06 5:36:08
Woodland Heights 33 61 35N04'22 85w19'32 5:41:18
Woodland Heights 36 23 35N14'26 88w14'39 5:52:59
Woodland Heights 41 3 35N45'22 87w28'40 5:49:55
Woodland Mills 66 3 36N29'18 89w06'54 5:56:28
Woodlawn 18 15 35N57 85w02 5:40:08
Woodlawn 30 65 36N18'09 82w52'47 5:31:31
Woodlawn 53 68 35N48 84w16 5:37:04
Woodlawn 63 3 36N32'39 87w30'38 5:50:03
Woodlawn 90 75 36N16'23 82w27'33 5:29:50
Woodlawn 91 3 35N10'09 87w43'40 5:50:55
Woodmore 33 74 35N02'13 85w13'28 5:40:54
Woodrow 28 9 35N10'00 86w50'00 5:47:20
Woodrow 82 1 36N31'00 82w27'52 5:29:51
Woods Ferry 83 42 36N23 86w26 5:45:44
Woodstock 79 40 35N16'23 89w58'56 5:59:56
Woods Valley 22 3 36N18'06 87w24'31 5:49:38
Woodville 12 3 35N15'35 88w45'19 5:55:01
Woodville 38 3 35N46'00 89w26'12 5:57:45
Woody 18 15 35N57 85w02 5:40:08
Wooldridge 7 66 36N34'36 84w11'02 5:36:44
Woolworth 43 3 36N13'07 87w43'11 5:50:53
Wrencoe 19 4 36N06 86w45 5:47:00
Wright 48 3 36N26'14 89w25'07 5:57:40
Wright 84 3 35N29 89w43 5:58:52
Wrigley 41 3 35N54'03 87w20'51 5:49:23
Wyatt Landing 20 23 35N23'08 88w07'41 5:52:31
Wyatts Chapel 81 3 36N29 87w50 5:51:20
Wyatt Village 29 55 36N19'20 83w16'56 5:33:08
Wyly 3 3 36N04 88w06 5:52:24
Wynn 7 66 36N28'13 84w03'06 5:36:12
Wynnburg 48 3 36N19'43 89w28'24 5:57:54
Wyricktown 47 67 36N03'20 83w43'59 5:34:56
Yager 89 46 35N43'53 85w48'52 5:43:15
Yankeetown 93 3 35N59'18 85w25'23 5:41:42
Yarbro Landing 20 3 35N28'47 88w00'07 5:52:00
Yateston 93 3 35N53'14 85w35'36 5:42:22
Yeary Mill 34 51 36N34'47 83w26'39 5:33:47
Yell 59 30 35N22'09 86w47'13 5:47:09
Yellow Creek 42 3 36N16'43 87w34'07 5:50:16
Yellow Springs 20 3 35N48'39 88w07'23 5:52:30
Yett Addition 78 60 35N49 83w33 5:34:12
Yettland Park 78 60 35N52'35 83w34'43 5:34:19
Yoakum Crossroad 13 51 36N29'55 83w46'32 5:35:06
Yokley 28 3 35N24'57 87w06'31 5:48:26
York Landing 63 3 36N27'33 87w31'44 5:50:07
Yorkville 27 21 36N05'58 89w07'08 5:56:29
Young Bend 21 3 35N55'15 85w43'38 5:42:55
Youngs Crossing 57 3 35N44'22 88w50'51 5:55:23
Youngville 74 35 36N35'07 86w49'33 5:47:18
Yount Town 34 51 36N26'34 83w14'16 5:32:57
Y Section 90 75 36N19 82w21 5:29:24
Yukon 52 9 35N04'29 86w39'57 5:46:40
Yuma 9 3 35N50'51 88w20'12 5:53:21
Yum Yum 24 3 35N20'43 89w21'50 5:57:27
Zacharytown 47 67 36N08'21 83w43'40 5:34:55
Zack 3 3 36N04 88w06 5:52:24
Zenith 25 56 36N25'39 84w44'13 5:38:57
Zion 60 31 35N35'54 87w08'37 5:48:34
Zion Grove 78 60 35N49 83w33 5:34:12
Zion Hill 37 70 36N28'37 82w52'37 5:31:30
Zion Hill 54 71 35N23'53 84w31'16 5:38:05

TIME TABLES

TX # 1

Before 11/18/1883		LMT
11/18/1883	12:00	CST
3/31/1918	02:00	CWT
10/27/1918	02:00	CST
3/30/1919	02:00	CWT
10/26/1919	02:00	CST
2/09/1942	02:00	CWT
9/30/1945	02:00	CST
4/30/1967	02:00	US#1

TX # 2

Before 11/18/1883		LMT
11/18/1883	12:00	MST
3/31/1918	02:00	MWT
10/27/1918	02:00	MST
3/30/1919	02:00	MWT
10/26/1919	02:00	MST
2/09/1942	02:00	MWT
9/30/1945	02:00	MST
4/30/1967	02:00	US#1

TX # 3

Before 11/18/1883		LMT
11/18/1883	12:00	CST
3/31/1918	02:00	CWT
10/27/1918	02:00	CST
11/27/1918	02:00	MST
3/30/1919	02:00	MWT
10/26/1919	02:00	MST
3/07/1921	02:00	CST
2/09/1942	02:00	CWT
9/30/1945	02:00	CST
4/30/1967	02:00	US#1

COUNTIES

1 Anderson
2 Andrews
3 Angelina
4 Aransas
5 Archer
6 Armstrong
7 Atascosa
8 Austin
9 Bailey
10 Bandera
11 Bastrop
12 Baylor
13 Bee
14 Bell
15 Bexar
16 Blanco
17 Borden
18 Bosque
19 Bowie
20 Brazoria
21 Brazos
22 Brewster
23 Briscoe
24 Brooks
25 Brown
26 Burleson
27 Burnet
28 Caldwell
29 Calhoun
30 Callahan
31 Cameron
32 Camp
33 Carson
34 Cass
35 Castro
36 Chambers
37 Cherokee
38 Childress
39 Clay
40 Cochran
41 Coke
42 Coleman
43 Collin
44 Collingsworth
45 Colorado
46 Comal
47 Comanche
48 Concho
49 Cooke
50 Coryell
51 Cottle
52 Crane
53 Crockett
54 Crosby
55 Culberson
56 Dallam
57 Dallas
58 Dawson
59 Deaf Smith
60 Delta
61 Denton
62 De Witt
63 Dickens
64 Dimmit
65 Donley
66 Duval
67 Eastland
68 Ector
69 Edwards
70 Ellis
71 El Paso
72 Erath
73 Falls
74 Fannin
75 Fayette
76 Fisher
77 Floyd
78 Foard
79 Fort Bend
80 Franklin
81 Freestone
82 Frio
83 Gaines
84 Galveston
85 Garza
86 Gillespie
87 Glasscock
88 Goliad
89 Gonzales
90 Gray
91 Grayson
92 Gregg
93 Grimes
94 Guadalupe
95 Hale
96 Hall
97 Hamilton
98 Hansford
99 Hardeman
100 Hardin
101 Harris
102 Harrison
103 Hartley
104 Haskell
105 Hays
106 Hemphill
107 Henderson
108 Hidalgo
109 Hill
110 Hockley
111 Hood
112 Hopkins
113 Houston
114 Howard
115 Hudspeth
116 Hunt
117 Hutchinson
118 Irion
119 Jack
120 Jackson
121 Jasper
122 Jeff Davis
123 Jefferson
124 Jim Hogg
125 Jim Wells
126 Johnson
127 Jones
128 Karnes
129 Kaufman
130 Kendall
131 Kenedy
132 Kent
133 Kerr
134 Kimble
135 King
136 Kinney
137 Kleberg
138 Knox
139 Lamar
140 Lamb
141 Lampasas
142 La Salle
143 Lavaca
144 Lee
145 Leon
146 Liberty
147 Limestone
148 Lipscomb
149 Live Oak
150 Llano
151 Loving
152 Lubbock
153 Lynn
154 McCulloh
155 McLennan
156 McMullen
157 Madison
158 Marion
159 Martin
160 Mason
161 Matagorda
162 Maverick
163 Medina
164 Menard
165 Midland
166 Milam
167 Mills
168 Mitchell
169 Montague
170 Montgomery
171 Moore
172 Morris
173 Motley
174 Nacogdoches
175 Navarro
176 Newton
177 Nolan
178 Nueces
179 Ochiltree
180 Oldham
181 Orange
182 Palo Pinto
183 Panola
184 Parker
185 Parmer
186 Pecos
187 Polk
188 Potter
189 Presidio
190 Rains
191 Randall
192 Reagan
193 Real
194 Red River
195 Reeves
196 Refugio
197 Roberts
198 Robertson
199 Rockwall
200 Runnels
201 Rusk
202 Sabine
203 San Augustine
204 San Jacinto
205 San Patricio
206 San Saba
207 Schleicher
208 Scurry
209 Shackelford
210 Shelby
211 Sherman
212 Smith
213 Somervell
214 Starr
215 Stephens
216 Sterling
217 Stonewall
218 Sutton
219 Swisher
220 Tarrant
221 Taylor
222 Terrell
223 Terry
224 Throckmorton
225 Titus
226 Tom Green
227 Travis
228 Trinity
229 Tyler
230 Upshur
231 Upton
232 Uvalde
233 Val Verde
234 Van Zandt
235 Victoria
236 Walker
237 Waller
238 Ward
239 Washington
240 Webb
241 Wharton
242 Wheeler
243 Wichita
244 Wilbarger
245 Willacy
246 Williamson
247 Wilson
248 Winkler
249 Wise
250 Wood
251 Yoakum
252 Young
253 Zapata
254 Zavala

Abbott 109	1	31N53'05	97W04'23	6:28:18
Abell City 186	1	31N15'00	102W39'30	6:50:38
Abercrombie 20	1	29N01'55	95W45'11	6:23:01
Abercrombie 227	1	30N20'19	97W43'31	6:30:54
Aberdeen 44	3	35N02'16	100W08'56	6:40:36
Aberfoyle 116	1	33N18'18	96W01'30	6:24:06
Abernathy 152	1	33N49'56	101W50'33	6:47:22
Abilene 221	1	32N26'55	99W43'58	6:38:56
Abilene Christian College 221	1	32N28	99W44	6:38:56
Abington 38	1	34N32'40	100W12'25	6:40:50
Ables Springs 129	1	32N45	96W29	6:25:56
Abner 129	1	32N37'40	96W11'29	6:24:46
Abram 108	1	26N11'58	98W24'39	6:33:39
Acacia Lake 31	1	25N55	97W29	6:29:56
Academy 14	1	30N58'51	97W20'29	6:29:22
Acala 115	2	31N20'02	105W54'50	7:03:39
Acampo 209	1	32N42'46	99W26'36	6:37:46
Ace 187	1	30N32'10	94W49'27	6:19:18
Ackerly 58	1	32N31'35	101W42'56	6:46:52
Acme 99	1	34N19'00	99W49'25	6:39:18
Acton 111	1	32N26'48	97W41'24	6:30:46
Acuff 152	1	33N35'42	101W37'11	6:46:29
Acworth 194	1	33N46'27	94W56'58	6:19:48
Adair 223	1	32N57'46	102W15'15	6:49:01
Adams 139	1	33N42'17	95W29'16	6:21:57
Adams 207	1	30N56'04	100W15'52	6:41:03
Adams Gardens 31	1	26N11	97W39	6:30:36
Adamsville 141	1	31N18'04	98W10'07	6:32:40
Addicks 101	1	29N46'56	95W38'32	6:22:34
Addielou 194	1	33N48'53	95W12'59	6:20:52
Addison 57	1	32N57'42	96W49'44	6:27:19
Addran 112	1	33N17'39	95W36'10	6:22:25
Adel 143	1	29N20'58	97W10'22	6:28:41
Adell 184	1	32N53'04	97W55'19	6:31:41
Ad Hall 166	1	30N51	96W59	6:27:56
Adina 144	1	30N25'17	97W10'20	6:28:41
Adkins 15	1	29N23'34	98W14'13	6:32:57
Admiral 30	1	32N17'47	99W17'51	6:37:11
Adobe Crossing 186	1	31N03'10	102W18'25	6:49:14
Adrian 180	3	35N16'29	102W39'53	6:50:40
Adsul 176	1	30N38'34	93W50'34	6:15:22
Advance 184	1	32N56'28	97W55'37	6:31:42
Ady 188	3	35N29'08	102W07'55	6:48:32
Aero Vista 71	2	31N49'27	106W23'17	7:05:33
Afton 63	1	33N45'46	100W48'59	6:43:16
Agnes 184	1	32N58'45	97W47'18	6:31:09
Agua Dulce 178	1	27N46'53	97W54'30	6:31:38
Agua Nueva 124	1	26N54'05	98W36'00	6:34:24
Aguilares 240	1	27N26'54	99W05'13	6:36:21
Aiken 77	1	34N08'32	101W31'31	6:46:06
Aiken 210	1	31N41'23	94W19'55	6:17:20
Aikin Grove 194	1	33N33'20	95W02'54	6:20:12
Air 160	1	30N45	99W14	6:36:56
Airlawn 57	1	32N50	96W50	6:27:20
Airport City 15	1	29N31'58	98W18'04	6:33:12
Air Terminal 165	1	32N00	102W05	6:48:20
Airville 14	1	31N04'37	97W09'48	6:28:39
Alabama Creek 228	1	31N03	95W08	6:20:32
Alamo 108	1	26N11'00	98W07'22	6:32:29
Alamo Alto 71	2	31N27	106W05	7:04:20
Alamo Heights 15	1	29N29'05	98W27'56	6:33:52
Alamo Village 136	1	29N25'40	100W23'41	6:41:35
Alanreed 90	3	35N12'45	100W44'02	6:42:56
Alazan 174	1	31N40	94W38	6:18:32
Alba 250	1	32N47'34	95W38'03	6:22:32
Albany 209	1	32N43'24	99W17'49	6:37:11
Albert 86	1	30N11'37	98W36'05	6:34:24
Albert Thomas 101	1	29N47	95W23	6:21:32
Albion 194	1	33N51'32	95W01'50	6:20:07
Alco 3	1	31N21'07	94W34'13	6:18:17
Alcoa 166	1	30N33'51	97W03'59	6:28:16
Alderbranch 1	1	31N41'19	95W27'28	6:21:50
Aldine 101	1	29N55'56	95W22'48	6:21:31
Aldine Estates 101	1	29N55	95W20	6:21:20
Aldine Gardens 101	1	29N55	95W20	6:21:20
Aldine Meadows 101	1	29N55	95W20	6:21:20
Aledo 184	1	32N41'45	97W36'07	6:30:24
Alejandrenas 253	1	26N46'37	99W08'24	6:36:34
Aleman 97	1	31N37'56	98W02'31	6:32:10
Alexander 72	1	32N03'32	98W12'21	6:32:49
Alexanders Store 210	1	31N46	93W52	6:15:28
Aley 107	1	32N26	96W05	6:24:20
Alfalfa 71	2	31N45'19	106W22'52	7:05:31
Alfred 125	1	27N52'49	97W59'04	6:31:56
Algerita 206	1	31N13'40	98W51'10	6:35:25
Algoa 84	1	29N24'08	95W10'09	6:20:41
Alice 125	1	27N45'07	98W04'10	6:32:17
Alice Rural 125	1	27N41	98W05	6:32:20
Alief 101	1	29N42'39	95W35'46	6:22:23
Allamoore 115	2	31N04'41	105W00'11	7:00:01
Allen 43	1	33N06'11	96W40'13	6:26:41
Allendale 101	1	29N41'38	95W14'46	6:20:59
Allendale 243	1	33N51'27	98W35'36	6:34:22

Allenfarm 21 1 30N23'57 96w14'37 6:24:58
Allenhurst 116 1 29N00'33 95w50'40 6:23:23
Allen Point 74 1 33N38'41 95w54'27 6:23:38
Allens Chapel 74 1 33N34 96w00 6:24:00
Allens Point 74 1 33N35 95w54 6:23:36
Alleyton 45 1 29N42'23 96w29'10 6:25:57
Allison 111 1 32N32'25 97w57'44 6:31:51
Allison 242 3 35N36'21 100w06'01 6:40:24
Allison 249 1 33N15'59 97w25'35 6:29:42
Allmon 77 1 33N52'53 101w30'46 6:46:03
Allred 251 1 32N59'10 102w53'15 6:51:33
Alma 70 1 32N17'07 96w32'45 6:26:11
Almeda 101 1 29N36'14 95w25'01 6:21:40
Almeda Plaza 101 1 29N38'03 95w25'06 6:21:40
Almira 34 1 33N06'00 94w26'43 6:17:47
Almont 19 1 33N30 94w37 6:18:28
Aloe 235 1 28N45'59 97w04'33 6:28:18
Alpine 22 1 30N21'30 103w39'38 6:54:39
Alsa (Unino) 234 1 32N49'06 96w02'01 6:24:08
Alsdorf 70 1 32N24'18 96w32'08 6:26:09
Altair 45 1 29N34'16 96w27'14 6:25:49
Alta Loma 84 1 29N22'12 95w04'51 6:20:19
Alto 37 1 31N39'01 95w04'21 6:20:17
Alto Bonito 214 1 26N18'26 98w38'24 6:34:34
Alto Colorado 24 1 27N09'23 98w07'36 6:32:30
Altoga 43 1 33N14'59 96w29'21 6:25:57
Alton 108 1 26N17'13 98w18'47 6:33:15
Alto Springs 73 1 31N17'09 96w40'13 6:26:41
Altuda 22 3 30N18'07 103w27'27 6:53:50
Alum 247 1 29N17'42 97w57'52 6:31:51
Alum Creek 11 1 30N04'03 97w13'02 6:28:52
Alvarado 126 1 32N24'23 97w12'41 6:28:51
Alvery Junction 226 1 31N28'53 100w25'01 6:41:40
Alvin 20 1 29N25'25 95w14'38 6:20:59
Alvord 249 1 33N21'30 97w41'40 6:30:47
Amanda 136 1 29N22'18 100w39'27 6:42:38
Amarillo 188 3 35N13'19 101w49'51 6:47:19
Ambia 139 1 33N35'34 95w39'32 6:22:38
Ambrose 91 1 33N41'26 96w23'06 6:25:32
Amelia 123 1 30N04'11 94w11'27 6:16:46
Ames 50 1 31N31'15 97w46'45 6:31:07
Ames 146 1 30N03'13 94w44'36 6:18:58
Amherst 139 1 33N43'40 95w28'45 6:21:55
Amherst 140 1 34N00'37 102w24'54 6:49:40
Amistad 233 1 29N21 100w50 6:43:20
Amistad Acres 233 1 29N30'54 101w10'01 6:44:40
Amistad Village 233 1 29N27'40 101w01'43 6:44:07
Amity 47 1 32N03'33 98w53'00 6:35:32
Ammans Crossing 130 1 29N53'41 98w40'15 6:34:41
Ammansville 75 1 29N47'20 96w51'30 6:27:26
Amphion 7 1 28N59'54 98w38'07 6:34:32
Amy 60 1 33N22 95w41 6:22:44
Anacacho 136 1 29N11'27 100w18'01 6:41:12
Anadarko 201 1 31N55'41 94w52'34 6:19:30
Anahuac 101 1 29N46'22 94w40'57 6:18:44
Anarene 5 1 33N29'06 98w39'57 6:34:40
Anchor 20 1 29N09 95w27 6:21:48
Anchorage 7 1 29N04'02 98w42'20 6:34:49
Ander 88 1 28N51'27 97w20'31 6:29:22
Anderson 93 1 30N29'13 95w59'12 6:23:57
Anderson Ways 84 1 29N15'38 94w54'22 6:19:37
Andice 246 1 30N46'55 97w51'07 6:31:24
Andrews 2 1 32N19'07 102w32'43 6:50:11
Angel City 88 1 28N42'59 97w32'27 6:30:10
Angeles 195 1 31N54'05 103w57'43 6:55:51
Angelo State University 226 1 31N28 100w27 6:41:48
Angler 250 1 32N35'38 95w15'12 6:21:01
Angleton 20 1 29N10'09 95w25'54 6:21:44
Angleton South 20 1 29N09 95w27 6:21:48
Angus 175 1 32N00'22 96w25'58 6:25:44
Anhalt 46 1 29N47'38 98w28'31 6:33:54
Anna 43 1 33N20'56 96w32'54 6:26:12
Annarose 149 1 28N20 98w07 6:32:28
Annaville 178 1 27N50'18 97w34'58 6:30:20
Anneta 184 1 32N42'53 97w40'33 6:30:42
Anneville 249 1 33N07'01 97w34'18 6:30:17
Annona 194 1 33N34'50 94w54'55 6:19:40
Ansley Place 22 3 30N14'36 103w08'17 6:52:33
Anson 127 1 32N45'23 99w53'45 6:39:35
Anson Jones 101 1 29N47 95w22 6:21:28
Antelope 119 1 33N26'30 98w22'10 6:33:29
Antelope Crossing 50 1 31N14'48 97w52'18 6:31:29
Anthony 71 2 31N59'57 106w36'18 7:06:25
Anthony 74 1 33N40'36 96w22'23 6:25:30
Antioch 25 1 31N46'28 98w46'38 6:35:07
Antioch 34 1 33N11'07 94w15'20 6:17:01
Antioch 60 1 33N22'40 95w48'01 6:23:12
Antioch 107 1 32N13'56 95w33'50 6:22:15
Antioch 126 1 32N18'46 97w11'52 6:28:47
Antioch 157 1 31N04'02 95w42'40 6:22:51
Antioch 210 1 31N51'15 94w04'37 6:16:18
Antioch 212 1 32N12'07 95w15'31 6:21:02
Anton 110 1 33N48'40 102w09'48 6:48:39
Apolonia 93 1 30N29'35 95w54'35 6:23:38
Appelt Hill 143 1 29N31'05 96w54'31 6:27:38
Appleby 174 1 31N42'58 94w36'17 6:18:25
Apple Springs 228 1 31N13'24 94w57'58 6:19:52
Aquilla 109 1 31N51'05 97w13'04 6:28:52
Arah 208 1 32N45'29 101w08'05 6:44:32
Aransas Pass 205 1 27N54'33 97w08'59 6:28:36
Arbala 112 1 32N59'15 95w39'11 6:22:37
Arbor 113 1 31N17'39 95w17'40 6:21:11
Arbor 183 1 32N15'12 94w30'50 6:18:03
Arcade 68 1 31N48'10 102w26'44 6:49:47
Arcadia 84 1 29N22'59 95w07'12 6:20:29
Arcadia 210 1 31N45'47 94w20'25 6:17:22
Arcadia Park 57 1 32N44'58 96w54'37 6:27:38
Archer City 5 1 33N35'44 98w37'31 6:34:30
Arcola 79 1 29N29'45 95w27'56 6:21:52
Arcola Junction 79 1 29N30'10 95w27'44 6:21:51
Arden 118 1 31N26'37 100w46'00 6:43:04
Ardis Heights 116 1 33N08'21 96w04'22 6:24:17
Argenta 149 1 28N10'11 97w50'49 6:31:23
Argo 225 1 33N15'18 94w53'41 6:19:35
Argyle 61 1 33N07'16 97w10'59 6:28:44
Ariola 100 1 30N22 94w19 6:17:16
Arispe 115 2 31N09'04 105w16'28 7:01:06
Arizona 236 1 30N47'22 95w28'04 6:21:52
Arkansas City 214 1 26N39'40 98w26'02 6:33:44
Arlam 201 1 31N52'34 94w32'02 6:18:08
Arlie 38 1 34N43'04 100w05'26 6:40:22
Arlington 220 1 32N44'08 97w06'28 6:28:26
Arlington Downs 220 1 32N43 97w06 6:28:24
Arlington Heights 178 1 27N50'05 97w33'59 6:30:16
Arlington Heights 220 1 32N44 97w23 6:29:32
Armstrong 75 1 29N43'25 97w12'34 6:28:50
Armstrong 131 1 26N55'27 97w47'28 6:31:10
Armstrong Landing 34 1 33N13'38 94w16'43 6:17:07
Arneckeville 62 1 28N59'32 97w16'19 6:29:05
Arnett 50 1 31N26'42 97w53'28 6:31:34
Arnett 110 1 33N29'33 102w17'29 6:49:10
Arney 35 3 34N41'14 102w06'09 6:48:25
Arno 195 1 31N39'47 103w38'08 6:54:33
Arnold 43 1 33N16'11 96w19'51 6:25:19
Arp 212 1 32N13'31 95w03'27 6:20:14
Arroyo 31 1 26N11 97w39 6:30:36
Art 160 1 30N44 99w07 6:36:28
Artesia Wells 142 1 28N16'47 99w17'03 6:37:08
Arthur City 139 1 33N52'13 95w30'22 6:22:01
Arvana 58 1 32N48'35 101w54'52 6:47:39
Asa 155 1 31N24'51 97w03'14 6:28:13
Ash 107 1 32N12 95w51 6:23:24
Ash 113 1 31N11'42 95w41'31 6:22:46
Ashby 161 1 28N42 96w13 6:24:52
A Sherton 64 1 28N26'30 99w45'36 6:39:02
Ashland 230 1 32N41'26 94w42'15 6:18:49
Ashmore 83 1 32N54'55 102w16'41 6:49:07
Ashtola 65 3 35N00'23 101w02'35 6:44:10
Ashwood 116 1 29N06'14 95w52'16 6:23:29
Ashworth 129 1 32N35 96w17 6:25:08
Asia 187 1 31N00 94w50 6:19:20
Askew 112 1 33N04 95w28 6:21:52
Aspermont 217 1 33N08'00 100w13'37 6:40:54
Astin 198 1 30N42'24 96w33'47 6:26:15
Astrodome 101 1 29N42 95w25 6:21:40
Atascosa 15 1 29N16'00 98w43'54 6:34:56
Atascosito Crossing (Histcl) 45 1 29N39'43 96w27'01 6:25:48
Atco 155 1 31N28'47 97w14'42 6:28:59
Ater 50 1 31N31'23 97w51'39 6:31:27
Athens 107 1 32N12'17 95w51'19 6:23:25
Atlanta 34 1 33N06'49 94w09'51 6:16:39
Atlas 139 1 33N34'07 95w37'00 6:22:28
Atlee 142 1 28N02 99w21 6:37:24
Atoy 37 1 31N46'26 95w00'47 6:20:03
Atreco 123 1 29N58'46 93w52'57 6:15:32
Attoyac 174 1 31N33'31 94w21'28 6:17:26
Atwell 30 1 32N15'40 99w08'02 6:36:32
Aubrey 61 1 33N18'15 96w59'09 6:27:57
Auburn 70 1 32N17'50 97w04'37 6:28:18
Audelia 57 1 32N54'33 96w43'01 6:26:52
Augusta 113 1 31N31'53 95w19'50 6:21:19
Augustus 85 1 33N07'50 101w17'57 6:45:12
Aurora 249 1 33N03'38 97w30'11 6:30:01
Austin 227 1 30N16'01 97w44'34 6:30:58
Austonio 113 1 31N11'08 95w38'18 6:22:33
Austwell 29 1 28N23'24 96w50'31 6:27:22
Authon 184 1 32N52'06 97w56'37 6:31:46
Avalon 70 1 32N12'19 96w47'23 6:27:10
Avant Prairie 81 1 31N36'34 96w10'50 6:24:43
Avenger Village 177 1 32N27'34 100w27'19 6:41:49
Avery 194 1 33N33'07 94w46'51 6:19:07
Avinger 34 1 32N53'59 94w33'22 6:18:13
Avoca 127 1 32N51'56 99w42'56 6:38:52
Avonak 101 1 30N05'40 95w30'24 6:22:02
Avondale 31 1 26N13'27 97w42'55 6:30:52
Avondale 220 1 32N58'04 97w25'13 6:29:41
Axtell 155 1 31N39'29 96w58'16 6:27:53
Azle 220 1 32N53'42 97w32'44 6:30:11
Back 90 3 35N21'53 100w36'34 6:42:26
Bacliff 101 1 29N30'24 94w59'32 6:19:58
Bacon 243 1 33N59'36 98w32'42 6:34:11
Bader 163 1 29N22'17 98w57'16 6:35:49
Badger 68 1 31N43'44 102w36'50 6:50:27
Bagby 74 1 33N29'04 95w55'09 6:23:41
Bagwell 194 1 33N39'43 95w09'38 6:20:39
Bahia Mar 31 1 26N05 97w08 6:28:32
Bailey 74 1 33N26'56 96w09'56 6:24:40
Baileyboro 9 1 34N01'36 102w49'09 6:51:17
Bailey Prairie 20 1 29N09'06 95w30'31 6:22:02
Baileyville 166 1 31N03'09 96w49'42 6:27:19
Bainer 110 1 33N51'40 102w14'22 6:48:57
Bainville 128 1 28N44'43 97w55'57 6:31:44
Baird 30 1 32N23'38 99w23'38 6:37:35
Baker 51 1 34N12'05 100w06'39 6:40:27
Baker 184 1 32N34'46 97w43'37 6:30:54
Bakers Crossing 233 1 29N57'43 101w08'51 6:44:35
Bakersfield 186 1 30N53'28 102w17'51 6:49:11
Balch Springs 57 1 32N43'43 96w37'21 6:26:29
Balcones Heights 15 1 29N29'16 98w33'05 6:34:12
Bald Hill 3 1 31N14'22 94w38'41 6:18:35
Bald Prairie 198 1 31N13'24 96w25'57 6:25:44
Baldridge 186 1 31N01'40 102w37'12 6:50:29
Baldwin 102 1 32N42'21 94w14'03 6:16:56
Ballard Crossing 97 1 31N32'23 98w05'18 6:32:21
Ballinger 200 1 31N44'17 99w56'49 6:39:47
Balm 49 1 33N44'48 96w58'35 6:27:54
Balmorhea 195 1 30N59'03 103w44'39 6:54:59
Balsora 249 1 33N06'58 97w51'06 6:31:24
Bammel 101 1 30N00'24 95w27'48 6:21:51
Banana Junction 155 1 31N34 97w10 6:28:40
Bancroft 181 1 30N06'40 93w47'56 6:15:12
Bandera 10 1 29N43'35 99w04'24 6:36:18
Bandera Falls 10 1 29N40'37 98w57'47 6:35:51
Bangs 25 1 31N43'01 99w07'56 6:36:32
Bankersmith 130 1 30N07'32 98w49'16 6:35:17
Bannas Junction 155 1 31N36'11 97w11'40 6:28:47
Banquete 178 1 27N48'21 97w47'45 6:31:11
Barado 236 1 30N37'26 95w28'46 6:21:55
Barbarosa 94 1 29N42'04 98w00'10 6:32:01
Barclay 73 1 31N04'35 97w06'33 6:28:26
Bardwell 70 1 32N16'08 96w41'45 6:26:47
Barker 101 1 29N47'03 95w41'05 6:22:44
Barkman 19 1 33N31'31 94w14'39 6:16:59
Barksdale 69 1 29N43'30 100w02'01 6:40:08
Barnes 187 1 30N53'35 94w41'48 6:18:47
Barnhart 118 1 31N07'40 101w10'13 6:44:41
Barnum 187 1 30N56'41 94w40'21 6:18:41
Barrett 101 1 29N52'47 95w03'46 6:20:15
Barry 175 1 32N05'57 96w38'09 6:26:33
Barstow 238 1 31N27'40 103w23'36 6:53:34
Bartholomew Crossing 224 1 33N03'08 99w19'35 6:37:18
Bartlett 246 1 30N47'41 97w25'31 6:29:42
Bartley Woods 74 1 33N29'20 96w01'37 6:24:06
Barton 198 1 30N55'11 96w42'41 6:26:51
Bartons Chapel 119 1 33N13 98w10 6:32:40
Bartonville 61 1 33N04'23 97w07'53 6:28:32
Barwise 77 1 33N59'50 101w31'34 6:46:06
Bascom 212 1 32N19'22 95w13'02 6:20:52
Basin Junction 22 1 29N20'03 103w15'22 6:53:01
Basin Springs 91 1 33N43'36 96w50'12 6:27:21
Bassett 19 1 33N19'00 94w33'39 6:18:15
Bastrop 11 1 30N06'37 97w18'54 6:29:16
Bastrop Bayou 20 1 29N09 95w27 6:21:48
Bastrop Beach 20 1 29N06'42 95w22'20 6:21:29
Bateman 11 1 29N57'04 97w28'30 6:29:54
Batesville 254 1 28N57'03 99w37'03 6:38:28
Bath 236 1 30N35'40 95w37'25 6:22:30
Batson 100 1 30N14'57 94w36'25 6:18:26
Battle 155 1 31N33'09 96w53'21 6:27:33
Bautista 171 3 35N43'12 102w01'28 6:48:06
Baxter 107 1 32N10'06 95w44'56 6:23:00
Bay City 161 1 28N58'57 95w58'09 6:23:53
Bay Harbor 84 1 29N07'38 95w04'06 6:20:16
Bay Oaks 101 1 29N39 95w01 6:20:04
Bayou 202 1 31N21 93w51 6:15:24
Bayou Chantilly 84 1 29N27 95w03 6:20:12
Bay Plaza 101 1 29N46 95w00 6:20:00
Bayside 196 1 28N05'37 97w12'52 6:28:51
Bayside Terrace 101 1 29N37'37 95w00'49 6:20:03
Baytown 101 1 29N44'07 94w58'38 6:19:55
Bayview 31 1 26N07'42 97w23'53 6:29:36
Bayview 84 1 29N30'53 95w00'15 6:20:01
Baywood 101 1 29N34 95w01 6:20:04
Bazette 175 1 32N11'00 96w16'19 6:25:05
Beach 170 1 30N19'11 95w25'16 6:21:41
Beach City 36 1 29N39'44 94w53'24 6:19:34
Beacon 73 1 31N10'57 96w48'41 6:27:15
Beacon Hill 15 1 29N28 98w32 6:34:08
Beadle 161 1 28N54 96w03 6:24:12
Bear Creek 34 1 32N55'47 94w27'01 6:17:48
Bear Creek 204 1 30N26'57 95w13'15 6:20:53
Beard 8 1 29N40'38 96w15'03 6:25:00
Bear Grass 145 1 31N22 96w09 6:24:36
Beasley 79 1 29N29'50 95w55'04 6:23:40
Beasley Crossing 154 1 31N27'22 99w06'30 6:36:26
Beattie 47 1 32N02'17 98w41'32 6:34:46
Beatty Place 22 3 30N22'09 103w20'07 6:53:20
Beaukiss 246 1 30N26'34 97w14'39 6:28:59
Beaumont 123 1 30N05'09 94w06'06 6:16:24
Beaumont Place 101 1 29N50'13 95w11'58 6:20:48
Beauxart Gardens 123 1 29N57'38 94w02'05 6:16:08
Beaverdam 19 1 33N38'11 94w40'16 6:18:41
Bebe 89 1 29N24'54 97w38'13 6:30:33
Beck 140 1 33N57'23 102w32'11 6:50:09
Becker 129 1 32N29'34 96w12'24 6:24:50
Beckmann 15 1 29N36'33 98w36'07 6:34:24
Beckville 183 1 32N14'34 94w27'19 6:17:49
Becton 152 1 33N47'01 101w38'50 6:46:35
Bedford 220 1 32N50'38 97w08'34 6:28:34
Bedias 93 1 30N46'32 95w56'57 6:23:48
Bee Cave 227 1 30N18'30 97w56'41 6:31:47
Beech Grove 121 1 30N51'21 94w07'16 6:16:29
Bee House 50 1 31N24 98w05 6:32:20
Beeville 13 1 28N24'02 97w44'53 6:31:00
Behring Store 94 1 29N35 97w58 6:31:52
Bel Air 102 1 32N31'06 94w22'24 6:17:30

Belcherville 169 1 33N48'09 97w49'55 6:31:20
Belco 14 1 31N08'09 97w20'21 6:29:21
Belding 186 1 30N47'28 103w01'29 6:52:06
Belen 71 2 31N41'09 106w18'43 7:05:15
Belfalls 14 1 31N10'23 97w12'12 6:28:49
Belgrade 176 1 30N41'08 93w39'48 6:14:39
Belk 139 1 33N50'42 95w42'53 6:22:52
Bellaire 101 1 29N42'20 95w27'31 6:21:50
Bellaire Junction 101 1 29N43'37 95w26'51 6:21:47
Bellaire West 101 1 29N41'47 95w34'30 6:22:18
Bell Branch 70 1 32N14'36 96w55'31 6:27:42
Bellco 242 3 35N22'50 100w30'32 6:42:02
Belle Plain 30 1 32N18'39 99w21'38 6:37:27
Belle Plain 171 3 35N52 101w58 6:47:52
Bellevue 39 1 33N38'11 98w00'49 6:32:03
Bellmead 155 1 31N35'38 97w06'31 6:28:26
Bell Place Windmill 122 1 30N37'11 104w29'23 6:57:58
Bells 91 1 33N36'37 96w24'38 6:25:39
Bellview 190 1 32N46'57 95w41'51 6:22:47
Bellville 8 1 29N57'00 96w15'25 6:25:02
Belmena 166 1 30N54'31 96w54'30 6:27:38
Belmont 89 1 29N31'23 97w41'01 6:30:44
Belott 113 1 31N25'50 95w18'21 6:21:13
Belt Junction 220 1 32N42'00 97w21'12 6:29:25
Belton 14 1 31N03'21 97w27'51 6:29:51
Ben 250 1 32N40'48 95w32'28 6:22:10
Ben Arnold 166 1 30N57'49 96w59'16 6:27:57
Benavides 66 1 27N35'55 98w24'28 6:33:38
Ben Bolt 125 1 27N38'50 98w04'52 6:32:19
Benbrook 220 1 32N40'23 97w27'37 6:29:50
Benchley 198 1 30N44'54 96w27'30 6:25:50
Bend 206 1 31N06 98w31 6:34:04
Bendetsen 146 1 30N19'24 95w05'58 6:20:24
Ben Franklin 60 1 33N28'36 95w46'07 6:23:04
Benge Corner 165 1 31N42'50 102w00'34 6:48:02
Ben Hur 147 1 31N30'37 96w43'39 6:26:55
Benjamin 138 1 33N35'02 99w47'31 6:39:10
Bennett 184 1 32N43'08 98w02'51 6:32:11
Bennett Place 22 1 30N13'27 103w04'07 6:52:16
Benoit 200 1 31N46'58 99w49'43 6:39:19
Benonine 242 3 35N13'37 100w00'51 6:40:03
Bentonville 125 1 27N46'32 97w57'28 6:31:50
Ben Wheeler 234 1 32N26'45 95w42'13 6:22:49
Berclair 88 1 28N31'50 97w35'27 6:30:22
Berea 113 1 31N20'03 95w18'40 6:21:15
Berea 158 1 32N48'22 94w24'07 6:17:36
Berger 14 1 31N09'49 97w19'10 6:29:17
Bergheim 130 1 29N49'38 98w34'30 6:34:18
Bergs Mill 15 1 29N20'07 98w27'10 6:33:49
Bergstrom Air Force Base 227 1 30N13 97w40 6:30:40
Bering 187 1 30N53'00 94w51'50 6:19:27
Berlin 239 1 30N10'16 96w26'44 6:25:47
Bernardo 45 1 29N45'38 96w23'31 6:25:34
Bernecker 76 1 32N33'39 100w33'43 6:42:15
Bernstein 98 3 36N23'39 101w21'24 6:45:26
Berryville 107 1 32N05'18 95w28'18 6:21:53
Bertram 246 1 30N44'37 98w03'19 6:32:13
Bess 66 1 28N20 98w07 6:32:28
Bessie Heights 181 1 30N02'42 93w55'10 6:15:41
Bessmay 121 1 30N27'45 93w57'11 6:15:49
Best 192 1 31N13'28 101w37'15 6:46:29
Bethany 183 1 32N22 94w03 6:16:12
Bethard 57 1 32N54'13 96w41'28 6:26:46
Bethel 1 1 31N55'12 95w55'12 6:23:41
Bethel 57 1 32N57'36 96w58'35 6:27:54
Bethel 70 1 32N24 96w50 6:27:20
Bethel 112 1 33N04'43 95w24'32 6:21:38
Bethel 184 1 32N41'46 97w49'21 6:31:17
Bethel 200 1 31N39'05 99w54'30 6:39:38
Bethel 230 1 32N41'33 94w45'49 6:19:03
Bethlehem 34 1 33N08'56 94w30'44 6:18:03
Bethlehem 109 1 31N57 97w19 6:29:16
Bethlehem 230 1 32N39'28 94w47'38 6:19:11
Betner 139 1 33N40 95w31 6:22:04
Bettie 230 1 32N48'30 94w57'40 6:19:51
Bettis 74 1 33N44'46 96w08'36 6:24:34
Beulah 3 1 31N11'07 94w40'06 6:18:40
Beulah 147 1 31N27'27 96w33'06 6:26:12
Beverly 155 1 31N32 97w09 6:28:36
Beverly Hills 43 1 33N04'09 96w29'22 6:25:57
Beverly Hills 155 1 31N31'17 97w09'13 6:28:37
Beversville 246 1 30N28 97w24 6:29:36
Bevil Oaks 123 1 30N09 94w16 6:17:04
Bexar 15 1 29N13'31 98w41'15 6:34:45
Beyer Crossing 164 1 30N54'05 99w54'54 6:39:40
Beyersville 246 1 30N30'35 97w19'46 6:29:19
Biardstown 139 1 33N32'19 95w30'19 6:22:01
Big Bend National Park 22 1 29N16 103w17 6:53:08
Bigby Corner 87 1 31N42'25 101w39'04 6:46:36
Bigfoot 82 1 29N02'48 98w51'59 6:35:28
Biggers 43 1 33N09'17 96w32'49 6:26:11
Biggs 71 2 31N50 106w23 7:05:32
Biggs Field 71 2 31N50 106w23 7:05:32
Big Hill 147 1 31N28'03 96w40'24 6:26:42
Big Lake 192 1 31N11'29 101w27'36 6:45:50
Big Rock 107 1 32N21'33 95w56'27 6:23:46
Big Sandy 230 1 32N35'01 95w06'31 6:20:26
Big Spring 114 1 32N15'01 101w28'42 6:45:55
Big Springs 201 1 32N04'02 94w58'02 6:19:52
Big Square 35 3 34N23'05 102w28'09 6:49:53
Big Wells 64 1 28N34'23 99w34'06 6:38:16
Billington 147 1 31N40 96w58 6:27:52
Biloxi 176 1 30N44 93w39 6:14:36
Birch 26 1 30N22'54 96w40'37 6:26:42
Birdville 220 1 32N48 97w15 6:29:00
Birome 109 1 31N48'47 96w57'45 6:27:51
Birthright 112 1 33N16'20 95w33'53 6:22:16
Biry 163 1 29N13'14 99w01'04 6:36:04
Bisbee 220 1 32N36'32 97w11'02 6:28:44
Bishop 178 1 27N35'09 97w47'56 6:31:12
Bi-Stone 147 1 31N41'10 96w25'21 6:25:41
Bivins 34 1 33N01'10 94w11'56 6:16:48
Bixby 31 1 26N09'05 97w51'12 6:31:25
Black 185 3 34N40'57 102w36'32 6:50:26
Black Ankle 203 1 31N31'25 94w00'16 6:16:01
Black Bass 253 1 26N52'39 99w15'17 6:37:01
Blackberry 93 1 30N23'52 95w51'24 6:23:26
Black Flat 5 1 33N41'48 98w50'22 6:35:21
Blackfoot 1 1 31N56'46 95w50'06 6:23:20
Black Hill 7 1 28N59'40 98w19'28 6:33:18
Blackjack 37 1 32N03'03 95w06'15 6:20:25
Black Jack 198 1 30N53'18 96w31'41 6:26:07
Blackjack 202 1 31N09'46 93w55'56 6:15:44
Blackland 155 1 31N28'44 96w53'10 6:27:33
Blackland 199 1 32N53'58 96w20'58 6:25:24
Black Oak 112 1 32N58'20 95w25'50 6:21:43
Blackwell 177 1 32N05'12 100w19'02 6:41:16
Blackwell Crossing 25 1 31N51'17 99w11'44 6:36:47
Blair 221 1 32N25'17 100w03'35 6:40:14
Blakeney 194 1 33N51'55 95w05'04 6:20:20
Blanchard 187 1 30N44'12 95w03'19 6:20:13
Blanco 16 1 30N05'52 98w25'16 6:33:41
Blanconia 13 1 28N23'54 97w24'43 6:29:39
Bland 14 1 31N12'46 97w30'51 6:30:03
Bland 181 1 30N05'29 93w45'26 6:15:02
Bland Lake 203 1 31N35'24 94w06'41 6:16:27
Blanket 47 1 31N49'26 98w47'12 6:35:09
Blanket Springs 167 1 31N35'10 98w46'45 6:35:07
Blanks 28 1 29N53 97w40 6:30:40
Blanton 109 1 32N06'24 97w18'58 6:29:16
Blanton 200 1 31N49'17 99w52'14 6:39:29
Bleakwood 176 1 30N41'32 93w49'20 6:15:17
Bledsoe 40 1 33N37'09 103w01'15 6:52:05
Bleiblerville 8 1 30N00'28 96w26'50 6:25:47
Blessing 161 1 28N52'16 96w13'04 6:24:52
Blevins 73 1 31N13'23 97w12'30 6:28:50
Blewett 232 1 29N11'05 100w01'49 6:40:07
Blix 3 1 31N15'46 94w52'01 6:19:28
Blocker 102 1 32N34 94w25 6:17:40
Blodgett 225 1 33N04'06 95w06'31 6:20:26
Bloomburg 34 1 33N08'16 94w03'26 6:16:14
Bloomdale 43 1 33N14'50 96w40'45 6:26:43
Bloomfield 49 1 33N26'40 97w00'55 6:28:04
Blooming Grove 175 1 32N05'31 96w42'56 6:26:52
Bloomington 235 1 28N38'51 96w53'32 6:27:34
Blossom 139 1 33N39'41 95w23'08 6:21:33
Blowout 16 1 30N26'49 98w34'38 6:34:19
Blox 121 1 30N58'26 93w58'30 6:15:54
Blue 144 1 30N23'30 97w08'50 6:28:35
Bluegrove 39 1 33N40'26 98w13'47 6:32:55
Blue Haven Estates 116 1 32N43 96w00 6:24:00
Blue Mound 220 1 32N51'23 97w20'19 6:29:21
Blue Ridge 43 1 33N17'52 96w24'05 6:25:36
Blue Ridge 73 1 31N16'34 96w44'28 6:26:58
Blue Springs 203 1 31N16'35 94w04'26 6:16:18
Bluetown 31 1 26N04'26 97w49'22 6:31:17
Bluett 249 1 33N09'27 97w26'17 6:29:45
Blue Water Key 107 1 32N18 95w29 6:21:56
Bluff Dale 72 1 32N21'03 98w01'16 6:32:05
Bluff Springs 184 1 32N46 97w28 6:29:52
Bluff Springs 227 1 30N09'27 97w46'07 6:31:04
Bluffton 150 1 30N49'14 98w29'28 6:33:58
Bluff View 25 1 31N43'12 99w00'29 6:36:02
Blum 109 1 32N08'33 97w23'49 6:29:35
Blumenthal 86 1 30N13'18 98w44'29 6:34:58
Bluntzer 178 1 27N53'49 97w46'58 6:31:08
Bob Harris 101 1 29N42 95w12 6:20:48
Bobville 170 1 30N20'52 95w46'57 6:23:08
Bobwyn 57 1 32N39'13 96w35'57 6:26:24
Boca Chica 31 1 25N55 97w29 6:29:56
Boden 188 3 35N23'57 102w03'48 6:48:15
Boedecker Junction 45 1 29N28'44 96w21'33 6:25:26
Boerne 130 1 29N47'40 98w43'54 6:34:56
Bogata 194 1 33N28'14 95w12'49 6:20:51
Bogus Springs 34 1 33N01 94w12 6:16:48
Bois d'Arc 1 1 31N46 95w38 6:22:32
Boise 180 3 35N12'52 102w51'33 6:51:26
Boldtville 15 1 29N21'48 98w21'38 6:33:27
Boles Home 116 1 32N56'50 96w06'08 6:24:25
Bolin 56 3 36N08'22 102w38'05 6:50:32
Boling 241 1 29N15'51 95w56'37 6:23:46
Bolivar 61 1 33N21'30 97w14'42 6:28:59
Bolivar Peninsula 84 1 29N25 94w38 6:18:32
Bomarton 12 1 33N30'27 99w25'33 6:37:42
Bona 91 1 33N42'41 96w28'29 6:25:54
Bon Ami 121 1 30N42'48 93w52'57 6:15:32
Bonanza 112 1 32N58'51 95w43'13 6:22:53
Bonanza 170 1 30N23 95w42 6:22:48
Bonham 74 1 33N34'38 96w10'41 6:24:43
Bonita 169 1 33N45'32 97w35'39 6:30:23
Bonita Junction 174 1 31N38'58 94w39'48 6:18:39
Bonner 108 1 26N12 98w15 6:33:00
Bonnerville 81 1 31N50'26 96w10'09 6:24:41
Bonney 20 1 29N18'59 95w26'52 6:21:47
Bonnie View 196 1 28N10'03 97w17'59 6:29:12
Bono 126 1 32N19'25 97w30'15 6:30:01
Bonus 241 1 29N27'05 96w16'50 6:25:07
Bon Wier 176 1 30N44'23 93w38'35 6:14:34
Booker 148 3 36N27'12 100w32'13 6:42:09
Boone 95 1 34N14'41 101w48'42 6:47:15
Boonsville 249 1 33N04'06 97w51'47 6:31:27
Boonville 21 1 30N40'14 96w19'28 6:25:18
Booth 79 1 29N31'47 95w38'59 6:22:36
Boothe 77 1 33N58'30 101w12'06 6:44:48
Bootleg 59 3 34N49'44 102w48'49 6:51:15
Boquillas Crossing 22 1 29N11'19 102w56'42 6:51:47
Boracho 55 1 31N04'38 104w23'17 6:57:33
Borden 45 1 29N41'28 96w42'06 6:26:48
Borderland 71 2 31N53'00 106w35'43 7:06:23
Bordersville 101 1 30N00'04 95w17'37 6:21:10
Borger 117 3 35N40'04 101w23'49 6:45:35
Bor-ley Heights 123 1 30N09'50 94w11'15 6:16:45
Borrachio 189 1 29N43'52 104w32'36 6:58:10
Bosque 18 1 31N51'17 97w36'13 6:30:25
Bosqueville 155 1 31N36'32 97w11'42 6:28:47
Boss 220 1 32N33'20 97w30'28 6:30:02
Bostick 212 1 32N23'14 95w16'19 6:21:05
Boston 19 1 33N26'29 94w25'10 6:17:41
Botines 240 1 27N45'22 99w26'15 6:37:45
Bouchard 57 1 32N54'25 96w45'33 6:27:02
Bounce 165 1 31N57'09 102w09'33 6:48:38
Bovina 185 3 34N30'49 102w52'57 6:51:32
Bowers City 90 3 35N25'08 100w55'00 6:43:40
Bowie 169 1 33N33'32 97w50'54 6:31:24
Bowser 206 1 31N24'20 98w57'43 6:35:51
Box Canyon Estates 233 1 29N31'42 101w10'03 6:44:40
Box Church 147 1 31N32 96w32 6:26:08
Boxelder 194 1 33N28'47 94w52'54 6:19:32
Box Quarter 198 1 30N59 96w41 6:26:44
Boxwood 230 1 32N47'01 94w45'17 6:19:01
Boyce 70 1 32N22'41 96w44'15 6:26:57
Boyd 74 1 33N39'07 96w10'46 6:24:43
Boyd 249 1 33N04'43 97w33'54 6:30:16
Boyd Lodge 208 1 32N35 101w00 6:44:00
Boydston 90 3 35N10'58 101w00'29 6:44:02
Boynton 3 1 31N14'08 94w25'46 6:17:43
Boys Ranch 180 3 35N32 102w15 6:49:00
Boz 70 1 32N18'29 96w55'44 6:27:43
Bozar 167 1 31N28 98w34 6:34:16
Brachfield 201 1 32N02'45 94w38'54 6:18:36
Bracken 46 1 29N36'35 98w19'15 6:33:17
Brackettville 136 1 29N18'37 100w25'03 6:41:40
Brad 182 1 32N45'06 98w30'27 6:34:02
Bradford 1 1 31N59'19 95w45'59 6:23:04
Bradshaw 221 1 32N05'54 99w53'51 6:39:35
Brady 154 1 31N08'06 99w20'05 6:37:20
Brady 210 1 31N39'54 94w12'13 6:16:49
Bragg 100 1 30N25'08 94w33'51 6:18:15
Branch 43 1 33N08 96w37 6:26:28
Branchville 166 1 30N53'03 96w45'49 6:27:03
Brand 208 1 32N47'32 100w57'37 6:43:50
Brandon 109 1 32N02'44 96w57'37 6:27:50
Branom 112 1 33N11'53 95w48'55 6:23:16
Bransford 220 1 32N53'59 97w10'05 6:28:40
Branton 67 1 32N06 98w58 6:35:52
Brashear 112 1 33N07'07 95w44'00 6:22:56
Brazoria 20 1 29N02'39 95w34'08 6:22:17
Brazos 182 1 32N39'41 98w07'18 6:32:29
Brazos Point 18 1 32N11'13 97w37'08 6:30:29
Brazosport 20 1 29N00 95w21 6:21:24
Breckenridge 215 1 32N45'20 98w54'07 6:35:36
Bremond 198 1 31N09'54 96w40'36 6:26:42
Brenham 239 1 30N10'00 96w23'51 6:25:35
Brentwood Manor 235 1 28N48 96w59 6:27:56
Breslau 143 1 29N31'22 96w59'47 6:27:59
Briar 249 1 32N59'42 97w32'33 6:30:10
Briargrove 101 1 29N44'45 95w29'22 6:21:57
Briaroaks 126 1 32N33 97w20 6:29:20
Briary 166 1 31N02'40 96w53'30 6:27:34
Brice 96 1 34N42'20 100w53'45 6:43:35
Brickel 211 3 36N17'15 102w08'53 6:48:36
Bridge City 181 1 30N01'14 93w50'44 6:15:23
Bridgeport 249 1 33N12'36 97w45'16 6:31:01
Briggs 27 1 30N53'22 97w55'29 6:31:42
Bright Star 190 1 32N49'58 95w40'27 6:22:42
Brinker 112 1 33N07'38 95w29'32 6:21:58
Briscoe 242 3 35N35'01 100w17'22 6:41:09
Bristol 70 1 32N27'41 96w34'11 6:26:17
Britton 70 1 32N32'54 97w04'03 6:28:16
Britton Davis 71 2 31N51'37 106w25'19 7:05:41
Broaddus 203 1 31N18'24 94w16'08 6:17:05
Broadview 152 1 33N38'12 101w55'39 6:47:43
Broadway 54 1 33N42'13 101w04'20 6:44:17
Broadway 139 1 33N31'13 95w34'24 6:22:18
Broadway Junction 139 1 33N31'21 95w35'22 6:22:21
Brock 184 1 32N40'34 97w56'26 6:31:46
Brock Junction 184 1 32N42'10 97w57'23 6:31:50
Brogado 195 1 30N59 103w44 6:54:56
Bronco 251 1 33N15'25 103w03'31 6:52:14
Bronson 202 1 31N20'38 94w00'48 6:16:03
Bronte 41 1 31N53'14 100w17'29 6:41:10
Brooke Army Medical Center 15 1 29N27 98w27 6:33:48
Brookeland 202 1 31N09'09 93w59'36 6:15:58
Brookesmith 25 1 31N33'01 99w07'06 6:36:28
Brookhaven 14 1 31N10'49 97w37'33 6:30:30
Brookhaven 101 1 29N40'29 95w21'46 6:21:27
Brook Hollow 57 1 32N49 96w51 6:27:24
Brooks Air Force Base 15 1 29N21 98w26 6:33:44
Brooks Crossing 141 1 31N06'58 98w03'18 6:32:13
Brookshire 237 1 29N47'09 95w57'03 6:23:48
Brookside 20 1 29N36 95w19 6:21:16

Brookside Village 101 1 29N35 95w20 6:21:20
Brookston 139 1 33N37'23 95w41'57 6:22:48
Broome 216 1 31N45'34 100w50'13 6:43:21
Brotherton 74 1 33N34'34 96w06'33 6:24:26
Brown 159 1 32N25'33 101w44'12 6:46:57
Browndell 121 1 31N06'32 93w57'46 6:15:51
Brownfeld Corner 150 2 31N59'01 105w07'43 7:00:31
Brownfield 223 1 33N10'52 102w16'26 6:49:06
Brown Hill 89 1 29N46'08 97w18'53 6:29:16
Browning 212 1 32N23'01 95w05'02 6:20:20
Brownlee 177 1 32N24'57 100w38'05 6:42:32
Brownsboro 28 1 29N47'01 97w36'32 6:30:26
Brownsboro 107 1 32N18'08 95w36'48 6:22:27
Brownsville 31 1 25N54'05 97w29'50 6:29:59
Brownwood 25 1 31N42'33 98w59'27 6:35:58
Brownwood 181 1 30N06'51 93w44'06 6:14:56
Broyles 1 1 31N46 95w38 6:22:32
Bruceville 155 1 31N19'09 97w14'11 6:28:57
Brumley 230 1 32N52'46 95w00'53 6:20:04
Brundage 64 1 28N34 99w40 6:38:40
Bruner 181 1 30N05'19 93w45'14 6:15:01
Bruni 240 1 27N25'33 98w50'26 6:35:22
Brunswick 113 1 31N34'54 95w03'42 6:20:15
Brushie Prairie 220 1 31N59'39 96w45'18 6:27:01
Brushy 37 1 32N05'34 95w08'47 6:20:35
Brushy 111 1 32N23'11 97w49'36 6:31:18
Brushy Creek 1 1 31N57'27 95w36'53 6:22:28
Bryan 21 1 30N40'27 96w22'11 6:25:29
Bryan 249 1 33N05'55 97w25'05 6:29:40
Bryans Mill 34 1 33N14'06 94w29'52 6:17:59
Bryarly 194 1 33N44'47 94w53'26 6:19:34
Bryden 171 3 36N01'24 101w57'17 6:47:49
Bryson 119 1 33N09'40 98w23'07 6:33:32
B U 155 1 31N31 97w08 6:28:32
Buchanan Dam 115 1 30N44'23 98w25'51 6:33:43
Buck 187 1 30N43 94w56 6:19:44
Buckeye 161 1 28N53'43 96w02'52 6:24:11
Buck Hollow 134 1 30N29'24 100w01'13 6:40:05
Buckholts 166 1 30N52'22 97w07'29 6:28:30
Buckhorn 8 1 30N02'18 96w11'59 6:24:48
Buckhorn 176 1 30N45'59 93w40'53 6:14:44
Buckingham 57 1 32N56'11 96w43'29 6:26:54
Buckner 43 1 33N13'03 96w39'48 6:26:39
Buckner 184 1 32N35'23 97w54'08 6:31:37
Buda 105 1 30N05'06 97w50'24 6:31:22
Buena Vista 15 1 29N16'16 98w27'40 6:33:51
Buena Vista 31 1 26N14'41 97w20'55 6:29:24
Buena Vista 71 2 31N48'30 106w32'22 7:06:09
Buena Vista 186 1 31N12'40 102w38'25 6:50:34
Buenos 85 1 33N17'57 101w29'14 6:45:57
Buenos Aires 22 1 29N05'06 103w28'07 6:53:52
Buffalo 42 1 31N47'26 99w12'27 6:36:50
Buffalo 107 1 32N16'20 96w16'47 6:25:07
Buffalo 145 1 31N27'49 96w03'28 6:24:14
Buffalo 167 1 31N28'53 98w53'51 6:35:35
Buffalo Gap 221 1 32N16'45 99w49'47 6:39:19
Buffalo Gap 227 1 30N22'50 97w57'06 6:31:48
Buffalo Springs 39 1 33N33'23 98w08'22 6:32:33
Buffalo Springs 56 3 36N29'12 102w45'32 6:51:02
Buford 71 2 31N38'56 106w16'39 7:05:07
Buford 168 1 32N27'41 100w51'23 6:43:26
Bug Tussle 74 1 33N29'01 95w56'36 6:23:46
Bula 9 1 33N54'41 102w38'15 6:50:33
Bulah 37 1 31N41'07 95w13'00 6:20:52
Bulcher 49 1 33N48'01 97w25'46 6:29:43
Bullard 212 1 32N08'23 95w19'12 6:21:17
Bullock 67 1 32N30'56 98w41'11 6:34:45
Bulverde 46 1 29N44'37 98w27'10 6:33:49
Buna 121 1 30N25'58 93w57'44 6:15:51
Bunavista 117 3 35N39'13 101w26'49 6:45:47
Buncomb 183 1 32N09 94w20 6:17:20
Bundy Crossing 157 1 30N55'27 96w12'15 6:24:49
Bunger 252 1 33N00'49 98w35'37 6:34:22
Bunker Hill 56 3 36N07'35 102w52'26 6:51:30
Bunker Hill 101 1 29N47 95w32 6:22:08
Bunker Hill 121 1 30N23'49 93w56'33 6:15:46
Bunker Hill 139 1 33N49'50 95w46'15 6:23:05
Bunker Hill Village 101 1 29N46'02 95w31'47 6:22:07
Bunyan 72 1 32N10'08 98w21'53 6:33:28
Burbank Gardens 57 1 32N44 96w59 6:27:56
Burchard Place 195 1 31N30'15 103w51'22 6:55:25
Burford 158 1 32N47'09 94w22'59 6:17:32
Burgess 14 1 30N56 97w14 6:28:56
Burkburnett 243 1 34N05'52 98w34'13 6:34:17
Burke 3 1 31N13'54 94w46'06 6:19:04
Burkett 42 1 31N59'45 99w13'31 6:36:54
Burkeville 176 1 30N59'59 93w40'04 6:14:40
Burleigh 8 1 29N55'10 96w09'00 6:24:36
Burleson 126 1 32N32'31 97w19'14 6:29:17
Burlington 166 1 31N00'54 96w59'47 6:27:59
Burnell 128 1 28N40'50 97w49'57 6:31:20
Burnet 27 1 30N45'29 98w13'41 6:32:55
Burnett 74 1 33N33'20 96w01'44 6:24:07
Burns 19 1 33N31'05 94w17'20 6:17:09
Burns City 49 1 33N30'45 97w02'14 6:28:09
Burr 241 1 29N18'28 96w00'26 6:24:02
Burrantown 113 1 31N29'33 95w12'17 6:20:49
Burris 152 1 33N31'29 101w46'45 6:47:07
Burrow 116 1 32N59 96w20 6:25:20
Burton 126 1 32N17'36 97w26'39 6:29:47
Burton 239 1 30N10'55 96w35'43 6:26:23
Busby 76 1 32N37'22 100w25'14 6:41:41
Bushland 188 3 35N11'31 102w03'51 6:48:15
Bustamante 253 1 27N00'02 99w06'42 6:36:27
Busterville 110 1 33N25 102w09 6:48:36
Butler 11 1 30N19'14 97w17'47 6:29:11
Butler 81 1 31N39'49 95w55'24 6:23:42
Buzzard Peak Crossing 224 1 33N02'06 99w21'32 6:37:26
Byers 39 1 34N04'05 98w11'25 6:32:46
Bynum 109 1 31N58'18 97w00'10 6:28:01
Byrd 70 1 32N12'38 96w39'58 6:26:40
Byrds 25 1 31N54'48 99w02'30 6:36:10
Byrdtown 139 1 33N36'44 95w21'53 6:21:28
Byrne 226 1 31N19'05 100w28'36 6:41:54
Cactus 171 3 36N03'10 101w54'44 6:47:39
Cactus 240 1 27N54'24 99w23'37 6:37:34
Caddo 215 1 32N43'05 98w40'05 6:34:40
Caddo 247 1 29N17'33 97w54'10 6:31:37
Caddo Mills 116 1 33N03'56 96w13'39 6:24:55
Cadiz 13 1 28N25'37 97w56'21 6:31:45
Caesar 13 1 28N39'19 97w53'53 6:31:36
Cain City 86 1 30N11'49 98w48'45 6:35:15
Calallen 178 1 27N52'02 97w37'22 6:30:29
Calaveras 247 1 29N13'19 98w15'35 6:33:02
Calder Highlands 123 1 30N05'48 94w08'39 6:16:35
Calder Terrace 123 1 30N05'20 94w09'27 6:16:38
Caldwell 26 1 30N31'52 96w41'34 6:26:46
Caldwell 152 1 33N45'57 101w57'26 6:47:50
Caldwell Crossing 155 1 31N37'26 97w20'04 6:29:20
Caldwood 123 1 30N04'37 94w09'26 6:16:38
Caldwood Acres 123 1 30N03'41 94w09'13 6:16:37
Caledonia 201 1 31N55'26 94w31'36 6:18:06
Calf Creek 154 1 30N58'43 99w28'07 6:37:52
Calgary 203 1 31N37'02 94w07'09 6:16:29
Calgary Woods 101 1 29N51'48 95w18'52 6:21:15
Calina 147 1 31N45'23 96w41'59 6:26:48
Call 176 1 30N35 93w48 6:15:12
Callaghan 240 1 27N52'35 99w24'01 6:37:36
Callan 164 1 31N03'30 99w41'29 6:38:46
Calliham 156 1 28N28'49 98w21'00 6:33:24
Callisburg 49 1 33N41'52 97w00'31 6:28:02
Call Junction 121 1 30N35'32 93w54'56 6:15:40
Calvary 250 1 32N45'28 95w31'37 6:22:06
Calvary Church 50 1 31N25'58 97w46'58 6:31:08
Calvert 198 1 30N58'40 96w40'25 6:26:42
Calvert Junction 198 1 30N56'31 96w44'14 6:26:57
Calvin 11 1 30N07 97w19 6:29:16
Camden 187 1 30N55'01 94w44'03 6:18:56
Cameron 166 1 30N51'11 96w58'36 6:27:54
Camey 61 1 33N05'00 96w51'21 6:27:25
Camilla 204 1 30N35'58 95w03'28 6:20:14
Camp Alzafar 130 1 29N48 98w45 6:35:00
Campbell 116 1 33N08'53 95w57'04 6:23:48
Campbellton 7 1 28N44'50 98w18'08 6:33:13
Camp Bullis 15 1 29N23 98w36 6:34:24
Camp Dallas 61 1 33N08'23 96w59'19 6:27:57
Camp Hulen 161 1 28N42'23 96w14'35 6:24:58
Campo Alto 108 1 26N12'17 98w07'34 6:32:30
Camp Providence 187 1 30N43 94w56 6:19:44
Camp Ruby 187 1 30N43 94w56 6:19:44
Camps 92 1 32N27 94w44 6:18:56
Camp San Saba 154 1 31N00 99w16 6:37:04
Camp Scenic 133 1 30N04 99w14 6:36:56
Camp Springs 208 1 32N38 100w46 6:43:04
Camp Stanley 15 1 29N26 98w30 6:34:00
Camp Stewart 133 1 30N04 99w20 6:37:20
Campti 210 1 31N49'34 94w02'24 6:16:10
Camp Verde 133 1 29N54 99w06 6:36:24
Camp Willow 94 1 29N39'56 98w04'06 6:32:16
Camp Wood 193 1 29N40'09 100w00'43 6:40:03
Cana 234 1 32N34'28 96w00'52 6:24:03
Canaan 91 1 33N33'16 96w24'05 6:25:36
Canada Verde 247 1 29N08 98w09 6:32:36
Canadian 106 3 35N54'46 100w22'54 6:41:32
Canadian River Breaks 188 3 35N17 101w52 6:47:28
Canary 157 1 30N59'36 96w10'41 6:24:43
Candelaria 189 1 30N08'18 104w40'57 6:58:44
Cane Junction 241 1 29N10'28 95w59'55 6:24:00
Caney 112 1 33N08 95w36 6:22:24
Caney 161 1 28N57'48 95w51'16 6:23:25
Caney 194 1 33N40'15 94w52'54 6:19:32
Caney City 107 1 32N13'31 96w01'58 6:24:08
Cannon 91 1 33N26'19 96w29'01 6:25:56
Canton 234 1 32N33'23 95w51'47 6:23:27
Cantu 108 1 26N18'56 98w18'30 6:33:14
Canutillo 71 2 31N54'41 106w35'59 7:06:24
Canyon 152 1 33N35'34 101w43'52 6:46:55
Canyon 191 3 34N58'49 101w55'06 6:47:40
Canyon City 46 1 29N52'25 98w11'15 6:32:45
Canyon Creek 43 1 32N57 96w44 6:26:56
Canyon Creek Square 43 1 32N57 96w44 6:26:56
Canyon Lake 46 1 29N42 98w08 6:32:32
Canyon Lake Forest 46 1 29N51'42 98w15'46 6:33:03
Canyon Springs 46 1 29N52'21 98w17'14 6:33:09
Canyon Valley 54 1 33N24'04 101w20'05 6:45:20
Capitol 227 1 30N17 97w44 6:30:56
Capitola 76 1 32N37'20 100w29'32 6:41:58
Caplen 84 1 29N29'58 94w31'23 6:18:06
Capps Corner 169 1 33N48'08 97w30'27 6:30:02
Cap Rock 54 1 33N29 101w24 6:45:36
Caps 221 1 32N22'23 99w50'48 6:39:23
Caradan 167 1 31N33'13 98w28'37 6:33:54
Carancahua 120 1 28N41'47 96w23'22 6:25:33
Carbon 67 1 32N16'14 98w49'42 6:35:19
Carbondale 19 1 33N18'54 94w26'28 6:17:46
Cardiff 237 1 29N47'09 95w54'21 6:23:37
Cardinal 107 1 32N12 95w51 6:23:24
Carey 38 1 34N28'16 100w19'31 6:41:18
Carey Estates 101 1 29N34 95w01 6:20:04
Cargray 33 3 35N31'00 101w10'30 6:44:42
Carlisle 152 1 33N34'40 101w58'36 6:47:54
Carlisle 228 1 30N52'25 95w12'24 6:20:50
Carlos 93 1 30N35'40 96w04'40 6:24:19
Carlsbad 41 1 31N36'19 100w38'35 6:42:34
Carlson 227 1 30N25'39 97w27'06 6:29:48
Carlton 97 1 31N55'05 98w10'18 6:32:41
Carmine 75 1 30N08'57 96w41'09 6:26:45
Carmona 187 1 30N59'24 94w57'23 6:19:50
Carnes 99 1 34N23'58 99w44'16 6:38:57
Caro 174 1 31N45'18 94w42'20 6:18:49
Carolina 236 1 30N47'37 95w23'48 6:21:35
Carpenter 247 1 29N22'41 98w11'04 6:32:44
Carpenters Bluff 91 1 33N45'16 96w24'46 6:25:39
Carr 235 1 28N44'08 96w45'17 6:27:01
Carretas Crossing 31 1 26N01'10 97w17'30 6:29:10
Carricitos 31 1 26N02'42 97w42'34 6:30:50
Carrizo Springs 64 1 28N31'18 99w51'37 6:39:26
Carroll 212 1 32N28'38 95w31'12 6:22:05
Carrollton 57 1 32N57'13 96w53'24 6:27:34
Carson 74 1 33N42'07 96w00'20 6:24:01
Carswell Air Force Base 220 1 32N45 97w26 6:29:44
Carta Valley 69 1 29N47'36 100w40'28 6:42:42
Carter 61 1 33N11'25 97w06'05 6:28:24
Carter 184 1 32N54'24 97w44'28 6:30:58
Carterville 34 1 33N04'09 94w28'19 6:17:53
Carterville 102 1 32N36'04 94w35'09 6:18:21
Carthage 183 1 32N09'26 94w20'14 6:17:21
Cartwright 129 1 32N39'33 96w16'17 6:25:05
Cartwright 250 1 32N52'19 95w22'16 6:21:29
Casa Blanca 125 1 28N00'02 97w54'13 6:31:37
Casa de Peidras 222 1 29N51'12 101w54'58 6:47:40
Casa de Piedra 22 1 29N06'05 103w03'15 6:52:13
Casa Piedra 189 1 29N44'18 104w03'13 6:56:13
Casey 71 2 31N35 106w14 7:04:56
Cash 116 1 32N59'40 96w06'28 6:24:26
Cason 172 1 33N02'19 94w48'53 6:19:16
Cass 34 1 33N11'42 94w03'47 6:16:15
Castell 150 1 30N42'03 98w57'22 6:35:49
Castle Hill Estates 220 1 32N52'02 97w30'56 6:30:04
Castle Hills 15 1 29N31'23 98w30'58 6:34:04
Castolon 22 1 29N07'59 103w30'50 6:54:03
Castor 167 1 31N22'08 98w30'36 6:34:02
Castroville 163 1 29N21'20 98w52'42 6:35:31
Catarina 64 1 28N20'43 99w36'47 6:38:27
Cat Spring 8 1 29N50'43 96w19'32 6:25:18
Causey Place 22 1 30N13'20 103w06'23 6:52:26
Cave Springs 102 1 32N34 94w25 6:17:40
Caves Spring 34 1 32N58'00 94w23'57 6:17:36
Caviness 139 1 33N45'28 95w36'47 6:22:27
Cavitt 50 1 31N22'32 97w31'06 6:30:04
Cawthon 21 1 30N25'06 96w14'34 6:24:58
Cayote 18 1 31N46'07 97w27'26 6:29:50
Cayuga 1 1 31N57'25 95w58'28 6:23:54
Cedar Creek 11 1 30N05'13 97w30'02 6:30:00
Cedar Creek 237 1 30N11'40 96w03'36 6:24:14
Cedar Grove 3 1 31N23'05 94w43'58 6:18:56
Cedar Hill 57 1 32N35'18 96w57'21 6:27:49
Cedar Hill 77 1 34N08'36 101w12'14 6:44:49
Cedar Lake 161 1 28N54'03 95w38'12 6:22:33
Cedar Mills 91 1 33N49'43 96w49'10 6:27:17
Cedar Park 246 1 30N30'18 97w49'12 6:31:17
Cedar Point 36 1 29N46 95w00 6:20:00
Cedar Point 174 1 31N42'17 94w29'11 6:17:57
Cedar Springs 73 1 31N10'40 96w55'09 6:27:41
Cedar Springs 230 1 32N52'08 94w44'04 6:18:56
Cedarvale 129 1 32N34'11 96w05'29 6:24:22
Cedar Valley 227 1 30N13'20 97w57'20 6:31:49
Cedarview 57 1 32N34'47 96w57'59 6:27:52
Cee Vee 51 1 34N13 100w27 6:41:48
Cego 73 1 31N14'42 97w09'44 6:28:39
Cele 227 1 30N26'28 97w31'20 6:30:05
Celeste 116 1 33N17'39 96w11'40 6:24:47
Celina 43 1 33N19'28 96w47'03 6:27:08
Center 147 1 31N32 96w32 6:26:08
Center 210 1 31N47'43 94w10'44 6:16:43
Center City 167 1 31N28'13 98w24'31 6:33:38
Center Grove 225 1 33N07'43 94w50'17 6:19:21
Center Line 26 1 30N21 96w32 6:26:08
Center Mill 111 1 32N33'14 97w45'51 6:31:03
Center Plains 219 1 34N22'22 101w53'07 6:47:32
Center Point 32 1 33N00 94w58 6:19:52
Center Point 70 1 32N11 96w53 6:27:32
Center Point 114 1 32N14 101w28 6:45:52

Place	Code	Latitude	Longitude	Time
Center Point 116	1	33N08	96W07	6:24:28
Center Point 133	1	29N56'38	99W02'10	6:36:09
Center Point 183	1	32N19	94W31	6:18:04
Center Point 220	1	32N56'07	97W32'34	6:30:10
Centerview 145	1	31N16	95W59	6:23:56
Centerville 57	1	32N52'39	96W37'12	6:26:29
Centerville 145	1	31N15'28	95W58'41	6:23:55
Centerville 228	1	31N10'49	95W02'34	6:20:10
Centex 105	1	29N54'07	97W54'52	6:31:39
Central 3	1	31N25'38	94W48'30	6:19:14
Central 220	1	32N45	97W20	6:29:20
Central Gardens 123	1	29N59'43	94W00'50	6:16:03
Central Heights 123	1	29N57	93W59	6:15:56
Central Heights 174	1	31N42'18	94W40'36	6:18:42
Centralia 228	1	31N15'28	95W02'23	6:20:10
Central Park 101	1	29N45	95W19	6:21:16
Cereal 77	1	34N12'09	101W31'17	6:46:05
Cestohowa 128	1	29N00'35	97W56'04	6:31:44
Chaffee Village 14	1	31N07'46	97W45'41	6:31:03
Chaffin Crossing 42	1	31N27'21	99W23'55	6:37:36
Chaffin Place 189	1	29N58'51	104W27'26	6:57:50
Chalk 51	1	33N52'42	100W13'23	6:40:54
Chalk Bluff 155	1	31N34	97W10	6:28:40
Chalk Hill 201	1	32N21'10	94W39'03	6:18:36
Chalk Mountain 72	1	32N09'15	97W54'38	6:31:39
Chalmers 116	1	29N04'15	95W57'41	6:23:51
Chalybeate 250	1	32N58	95W17	6:21:08
Chamberlin 56	3	36N08'55	102W23'02	6:49:32
Chambersville 43	1	33N18'22	96W38'08	6:26:33
Chambliss 43	1	33N17'41	96W29'42	6:25:59
Champion 177	1	32N21'31	100W37'12	6:42:29
Chance 26	1	30N21	96W32	6:26:08
Chancellor 186	1	30N41'33	103W10'25	6:52:42
Chandler 107	1	32N18'28	95W28'47	6:21:55
Chaney 67	1	32N21'54	98W37'13	6:34:29
Channelview 101	1	29N46'33	95W06'52	6:20:27
Channelwood 101	1	29N46	95W09	6:20:36
Channey Crossing 21	1	30N43'13	96W10'03	6:24:40
Channing 103	3	35N41'01	102W19'47	6:49:19
Chapel Hill 212	1	32N18'40	95W11'30	6:20:46
Chapin 111	1	32N32'16	97W40'31	6:30:42
Chapman 201	1	32N08'59	94W37'59	6:18:32
Chapman Ranch 178	1	27N35	97W27	6:29:48
Chappel 206	1	31N03'20	98W34'14	6:34:17
Chappell Hill 239	1	30N08'33	96W15'24	6:25:02
Charco 88	1	28N44'25	97W36'55	6:30:28
Charleston 57	1	32N46	96W37	6:26:28
Charleston 60	1	33N23'11	95W32'01	6:22:08
Charlie 39	1	34N05'46	98W18'55	6:33:16
Charlotte 7	1	28N51'42	98W42'22	6:34:49
Chase 13	1	28N22	97W40	6:30:40
Chase Field 13	1	28N23	97W42	6:30:48
Chat 109	1	32N01	97W07	6:28:28
Chatfield 175	1	32N14'29	96W24'26	6:25:38
Chatt 109	1	31N56'37	97W05'22	6:28:21
Cheapside 89	1	29N16'41	97W24'10	6:29:37
Cheek 123	1	29N59'00	94W12'09	6:16:49
Chenango 20	1	29N15'14	95W27'31	6:21:50
Cheneyboro 175	1	31N57'27	96W20'54	6:25:24
Cherokee 206	1	30N58'56	98W42'26	6:34:50
Cherokee 229	1	30N51'40	94W29'23	6:17:58
Cherokee Landing 37	1	32N03'44	95W25'41	6:21:43
Cherry Mountain 86	1	30N22'57	98W55'23	6:35:42
Cherry Spring 86	1	30N28'59	99W00'32	6:36:02
Chester 238	1	30N55'34	94W35'47	6:18:23
Chesterville 45	1	29N36'35	96W12'26	6:24:50
Cheyenne 248	1	31N59	103W08	6:52:32
Chico 249	1	33N17'45	97W47'55	6:31:12
Chicota 139	1	33N52'08	95W34'15	6:22:17
Chief 129	1	32N35	96W17	6:25:08
Chihuahua 108	1	26N13'29	98W24'48	6:33:39
Childress 38	1	34N25'35	100W12'13	6:40:49
Chillicothe 99	1	34N15'23	99W30'59	6:38:04
Chilton 73	1	31N16'48	97W03'50	6:28:15
China 123	1	30N02'52	94W20'08	6:17:21
China Creek 206	1	31N15'32	98W47'22	6:35:09
China Grove 15	1	29N23'19	98W20'55	6:33:24
China Grove 20	1	29N18'45	95W27'23	6:21:50
China Grove 208	1	32N31'48	100W49'01	6:43:16
China Springs 155	1	31N39'08	97W18'27	6:29:14
Chinati 189	1	29N33	104W23	6:57:32
Chinquapin 161	1	28N45'27	95W46'25	6:23:06
Chinquapin 203	1	31N24'10	94W05'57	6:16:24
Chinquapin Landing 161	1	28N44'57	95W45'58	6:23:04
Chipley 235	1	28N47'11	97W02'08	6:28:09
Chireno 174	1	31N29'57	94W21'06	6:17:24
Chisholm 199	1	32N50'17	96W22'17	6:25:29
Chispa 122	1	30N44'40	104W41'49	6:58:47
Chita 228	1	30N56'11	95W12'29	6:20:50
Choate 128	1	28N45'52	97W44'34	6:30:58
Chocolate Bayou 20	1	29N24	95W14	6:20:56
Chocolate Springs 20	1	29N18'16	95W15'43	6:21:03
Choice 210	1	31N41'58	94W08'43	6:16:35
Chriesman 26	1	30N35'57	96W46'14	6:27:05
Christine 7	1	28N47'20	98W29'49	6:33:59
Christoval 226	1	31N11'36	100W29'54	6:42:00
Chub 165	1	32N01'26	102W01'08	6:48:05
Chuckville 67	1	32N05'57	98W53'59	6:35:36
Chumley 203	1	31N30'37	94W00'02	6:16:00
Chunky 188	3	35N23'58	101W50'25	6:47:22
Church Hill 201	1	32N09	94W48	6:19:12
Churchill Bridge 20	1	29N02	95W34	6:22:16
Cibolo 94	1	29N33'41	98W13'36	6:32:54
Cielo Vista 71	2	31N47'16	106W22'48	7:05:31
Cima 229	1	30N56'24	94W24'06	6:17:36
Cipres 108	1	26N41'19	98W19'11	6:33:17
Circle 37	1	31N48'04	95W00'31	6:20:02
Circle 140	1	34N11	102W14	6:48:56
Circle Back 9	1	34N04	102W32	6:50:08
Circleville 246	1	30N38'14	97W26'07	6:29:44
Cisco 67	1	32N23'17	98W58'44	6:35:55
Cistern 75	1	29N48'56	97W13'06	6:28:52
Citrus City 108	1	26N19'34	98W23'06	6:33:32
City, Arroyo 31	1	26N19'58	97W26'21	6:29:45
City-by-the-Sea 4	1	27N57'05	97W06'17	6:28:25
Clairemont 132	1	33N09'59	100W45'08	6:43:01
Clairette 72	1	32N02'21	98W07'07	6:32:28
Clara 243	1	33N57	98W40	6:34:40
Clardy 139	1	33N31'33	95W25'55	6:21:44
Clarendon 65	3	34N56'16	100W53'16	6:43:33
Clareville 13	1	28N19'20	97W52'15	6:31:29
Clark 146	1	30N23'31	94W45'58	6:19:04
Clarks 29	1	28N37	96W38	6:26:32
Clarkson 166	1	30N59'42	96W55'29	6:27:42
Clarksville 194	1	33N36'38	95W03'09	6:20:13
Clarksville City 92	1	32N31'46	94W54'10	6:19:37
Clarktown 202	1	31N10'19	93W45'49	6:15:03
Clarkwood 178	1	27N47'03	97W32'22	6:30:09
Claude 6	3	35N06'42	101W21'46	6:45:27
Clauene 110	1	33N27'42	102W22'32	6:49:30
Clawson 3	1	31N24'02	94W47'33	6:19:10
Clay 26	1	30N23'21	96W20'36	6:25:22
Clays Corner 185	3	34N23'09	102W42'58	6:50:52
Clayton 123	1	29N57	93W59	6:15:56
Clayton 183	1	32N05'53	94W28'29	6:17:54
Claytonville 76	1	32N36'54	100W31'32	6:42:06
Claytonville 219	1	34N22'31	101W34'28	6:46:18
Clear Creek 106	3	35N56'22	100W19'32	6:41:18
Clear Lake 43	1	33N04'41	96W29'42	6:25:59
Clear Lake City 101	1	29N33	95W07	6:20:28
Clear Lake Shores 84	1	29N32'50	95W01'55	6:20:08
Clear Springs 94	1	29N40'33	98W03'34	6:32:14
Clear Springs 174	1	31N28'02	94W23'13	6:17:33
Clearview 11	1	30N02'33	97W20'07	6:29:20
Clearwater 80	1	33N00'00	95W12'04	6:20:48
Clearwater Cove 205	1	28N05'24	97W52'03	6:31:28
Cleburne 126	1	32N20'51	97W23'11	6:29:33
Clegg 149	1	28N07'21	98W15'54	6:33:04
Clemons 237	1	29N50'33	96W02'27	6:24:10
Clemville 161	1	28N59'45	96W08'27	6:24:34
Cleo 134	1	30N36'13	99W52'29	6:39:30
Cleta 191	3	34N55'31	101W55'34	6:47:42
Cleveland 42	1	31N40'36	99W15'12	6:37:01
Cleveland 146	1	30N20'28	95W05'07	6:20:20
Clever Creek 210	1	31N12	100W30	6:42:00
Click 150	1	30N33'47	98W34'25	6:34:18
Cliffside 188	3	35N15'54	101W55'56	6:47:44
Clifton 18	1	31N46'56	97W34'35	6:30:18
Clifton 234	1	32N43	96W00	6:24:00
Clifton Beach 36	1	29N30'40	94W58'37	6:19:54
Climax 43	1	33N12'17	96W26'58	6:25:48
Climax 174	1	31N29'19	94W41'35	6:18:46
Cline 232	1	29N14'35	100W04'57	6:40:20
Clint 71	2	31N35'32	106W13'25	7:04:54
Clinton 62	1	29N06	97W17	6:29:08
Clinton 116	1	33N06'12	96W14'08	6:24:57
Clinton Park 101	1	29N44'25	95W15'26	6:21:02
Clodine 79	1	29N42'26	95W41'16	6:22:45
Cloptins Crossing 105	1	29N58'49	98W06'55	6:32:28
Close City 85	1	33N12'39	101W29'12	6:45:57
Cloudy 57	1	32N44	96W59	6:27:56
Cloverleaf 101	1	29N46'41	95W10'18	6:20:41
Clower 234	1	32N32'34	95W41'40	6:22:47
Club Lake Estates 212	1	32N20	95W18	6:21:12
Clute 20	1	29N01'28	95W23'55	6:21:36
Clutter Point 74	1	33N30'29	96W05'36	6:24:22
Clyde 30	1	32N24'21	99W29'36	6:37:58
Coady 101	1	29N47'03	95W00'58	6:20:04
Coahoma 114	1	32N17'47	101W18'21	6:45:13
Coal Mine 163	1	29N13'35	98W48'43	6:35:15
Coalville 182	1	32N34'32	98W19'55	6:33:20
Cobb 129	1	32N42'51	96W06'00	6:24:24
Coble 110	1	33N35'42	102W30'09	6:50:01
Coburn 148	3	36N03'59	100W09'11	6:40:37
Cochran 8	1	30N01'43	96W07'45	6:24:31
Cockrell Hill 57	1	32N44'10	96W53'12	6:27:33
Codman 197	3	35N38'24	100W45'11	6:43:01
Coesfield 49	1	33N49'06	97W01'54	6:28:08
Coffee City 107	1	32N06'57	95W29'57	6:22:00
Coffeeville 230	1	32N49'45	94W45'27	6:19:02
Cofferville 140	1	34N00'39	102W19'31	6:49:18
Coit 147	1	31N22'59	96W40'16	6:26:41
Coke 250	1	32N55'30	95W26'06	6:21:44
Colaboz 31	1	26N08	97W38	6:30:32
Coldhill 212	1	32N20	95W18	6:21:12
Coldspring 204	1	30N35'32	95W07'45	6:20:31
Cold Springs 50	1	31N14'30	97W36'59	6:30:28
Coldwater 56	3	36N27'19	102W37'45	6:50:31
Cole 57	1	32N42'02	96W55'14	6:27:41
Coleman 42	1	31N49'38	99W25'34	6:37:42
Coletoville 235	1	28N45'33	97W08'45	6:28:35
Coleyville 51	1	34N14'02	100W22'44	6:41:31
Colfax 234	1	32N30'37	95W43'57	6:22:56
Colita 187	1	30N53'01	95W00'34	6:20:02
Collado 55	1	30N56'53	104W53'11	6:59:33
College Hill 19	1	33N24'56	94W36'46	6:18:27
Collegeport 161	1	28N43'30	96W10'29	6:24:42
College Station 21	1	30N37'40	96W20'03	6:25:20
Colleyville 220	1	32N52'51	97W09'17	6:28:37
Collier 195	1	31N10'03	103W34'59	6:54:20
Collin 43	1	33N11'55	96W48'58	6:27:16
Collins 121	1	31N00'04	93W58'28	6:15:54
Collinsville 91	1	33N33'41	96W54'39	6:27:39
Colmesneil 229	1	30N54'28	94W25'19	6:17:41
Cologne 88	1	28N42'19	97W10'53	6:28:44
Colonial 155	1	31N33	97W10	6:28:40
Colony 75	1	29N46'08	97W10'43	6:28:43
Colorado 11	1	29N59'08	97W08'02	6:28:32
Colorado City 168	1	32N23'17	100W51'51	6:43:27
Colquitt 129	1	32N47'43	96W21'26	6:25:26
Coltexo 90	3	35N26	100W48	6:43:12
Colton 227	1	30N08'58	97W41'49	6:30:47
Columbia Heights 15	1	29N22'11	98W31'35	6:34:06
Columbus 45	1	29N42'23	96W32'22	6:26:09
Comal 46	1	29N38'43	98W13'24	6:32:54
Comanche 47	1	31N53'50	98W36'12	6:34:25
Comanche Crossing 89	1	29N34'24	97W16'15	6:29:05
Combes 31	1	26N14'54	97W44'01	6:30:56
Combine 129	1	32N35'18	96W30'30	6:26:02
Cometa 254	1	28N39'52	100W01'08	6:40:05
Comfort 130	1	29N58'03	98W54'17	6:35:37
Commerce 116	1	33N14'49	95W53'59	6:23:36
Como 112	1	33N03'38	95W28'19	6:21:53
Comptons 22	1	29N05'19	103W04'52	6:52:19
Comstock 233	1	29N41'03	101W10'23	6:44:42
Comyn 47	1	32N04'22	98W28'12	6:33:53
Concan 232	1	29N29'42	99W42'44	6:38:51
Concepcion 66	1	27N23'46	98W21'27	6:33:26
Concho 48	1	31N32'12	99W48'40	6:39:15
Concord 3	1	31N07'24	94W15'09	6:17:01
Concord 37	1	32N04'12	95W02'46	6:20:11
Concord 81	1	31N31'29	96W03'24	6:24:14
Concord 116	1	33N06'52	96W09'21	6:24:37
Concord 145	1	31N15'24	96W08'39	6:24:35
Concord 201	1	31N54'59	94W35'18	6:18:21
Concord 230	1	32N49'31	94W54'38	6:19:39
Concordia 178	1	27N36'08	97W42'24	6:30:50
Concrete 62	1	29N14'17	97W17'34	6:29:10
Cone 54	1	33N47'50	101W23'14	6:45:33
Conlen 56	3	36N14'07	102W14'13	6:48:57
Connell 181	1	30N06'05	93W59'40	6:15:59
Connor 157	1	30N57'53	95W48'45	6:23:15
Conoley 166	1	30N33'29	97W10'14	6:28:41
Conquista Crossing 128	1	28N56'33	98W03'25	6:32:14
Conroe 170	1	30N18'42	95W27'21	6:21:49
Content 200	1	31N59	99W38	6:38:32
Converse 15	1	29N31'04	98W18'57	6:33:16
Conway 33	3	35N12'28	101W22'51	6:45:31
Coody Crossing 224	1	33N06'02	99W28'16	6:37:53
Cook 49	1	33N36'43	97W07'39	6:28:31
Cooks Point 26	1	30N37	96W37	6:26:28
Cooks Store 1	1	31N50	95W50	6:23:20
Cookville 225	1	33N11'08	94W51'15	6:19:25
Cool 184	1	32N48'00	98W00'03	6:32:00
Coolidge 147	1	31N45'14	96W38'59	6:26:36
Cooper 60	1	33N22'24	95W41'17	6:22:45
Cooper Creek 61	1	33N14'25	97W04'52	6:28:19
Copano Village 4	1	28N05'16	97W03'29	6:28:14
Copeland 212	1	32N14'23	95W16'18	6:21:05
Copeville 43	1	33N04'46	96W24'55	6:25:40
Coppell 57	1	32N57'16	97W00'53	6:28:04
Copperas Cove 50	1	31N07'26	97W54'10	6:31:37
Copper Canyon 61	1	33N07	97W11	6:28:44
Corbet 175	1	32N00'23	96W32'12	6:26:09
Corbyn 46	1	29N38'55	98W14'05	6:32:56
Cordele 120	1	29N08'05	96W37'47	6:26:31
Corinth 61	1	33N09'14	97W03'52	6:28:15
Corinth 127	1	32N51'15	99W52'08	6:39:29
Corinth 145	1	31N22'22	96W00'10	6:24:01
Corinth 169	1	33N50'41	97W31'18	6:30:05
Corinth 234	1	32N41	95W43	6:22:52
Corlena 56	3	36N19'13	102W56'20	6:51:45
Corley 19	1	33N19'34	94W23'39	6:17:35
Corner School 73	1	31N28'47	96W50'36	6:27:22
Cornersville 112	1	32N58	95W17	6:21:08
Corner Windmill 22	1	29N39'05	103W04'46	6:52:19
Corner Windmill 55	1	31N03'52	104W52'12	6:59:29

Corner Windmill 122 1 30N51'37 103w44'56 6:55:00
Corner Windmill 135 1 33N37'08 100w30'42 6:42:03
Corner Windmill 165 1 31N50'01 102w09'14 6:48:37
Corner Windmill 180 3 35N33'22 102w50'07 6:51:20
Corner Windmill 233 1 30N09'35 100w55'09 6:43:41
Cornett 34 1 33N07'46 94w34'28 6:18:18
Corn Hill 246 1 30N48'24 97w36'53 6:30:28
Cornudas 115 2 31N46'47 105w28'14 7:01:53
Coronado 71 2 31N44 106w21 7:05:24
Coronado Hills 71 2 31N49'41 106w31'37 7:06:06
Corpus Christi 178 1 27N48'01 97w23'46 6:29:35
Corpus Christi West 178 1 27N51 97w45 6:31:00
Corral City 61 1 33N07 97w11 6:28:44
Corrigan 187 1 30N59'48 94w49'37 6:19:18
Corry 140 1 34N01'36 102w06'03 6:48:24
Corsicana 175 1 32N05'43 96w28'07 6:25:52
Corsicana Junction 175 1 32N06 96w31 6:26:04
Coryell 50 1 31N32'46 97w37'05 6:30:28
Cost 89 1 29N26'14 97w31'43 6:30:07
Cotton 74 1 33N35 96w11 6:24:44
Cotton 93 1 30N49'53 95w53'40 6:23:35
Cotton Center 74 1 33N30'35 96w07'18 6:24:29
Cotton Center 95 1 33N59'35 101w59'33 6:47:58
Cottondale 249 1 33N03'57 97w42'16 6:30:49
Cotton Flat 165 1 31N55'44 102w03'34 6:48:14
Cotton Gin 81 1 31N40'51 96w21'37 6:25:26
Cotton Mill 91 1 33N45 96w34 6:26:16
Cotton Patch 62 1 28N59'02 97w36'58 6:30:28
Cottonwood 21 1 30N49'43 96w20'02 6:25:20
Cottonwood 72 1 32N05'21 98w17'22 6:33:09
Cottonwood 146 1 29N55'01 94w30'58 6:18:04
Cottonwood 155 1 31N49'38 97w02'29 6:28:10
Cottonwood 157 1 30N54'47 96w00'10 6:24:01
Cottonwood 230 1 32N12'21 99w12'15 6:36:49
Cotulla 142 1 28N26'12 99w14'05 6:36:56
Coughlin 181 1 30N11'12 93w51'28 6:15:26
Coughran 7 1 28N56'39 98w24'48 6:33:39
Country Campus 236 1 30N43 95w33 6:22:12
Country Club Estates 68 1 31N52 102w22 6:49:28
Country Club Terrace 235 1 28N48 96w59 6:27:56
County Line 32 1 33N00 94w58 6:19:52
County Line 95 1 33N41 102w00 6:48:00
County Line 174 1 31N43'18 94w56'14 6:19:45
Coupland 246 1 30N27'35 97w23'18 6:29:33
Courchesne 71 2 31N47'38 106w31'54 7:06:08
Courtney 93 1 30N16'01 96w03'35 6:24:14
Courtney 159 1 32N08'48 101w54'20 6:47:37
Cove 36 1 29N46 95w00 6:20:00
Cove 181 1 30N04'12 93w44'24 6:14:58
Cove City 181 1 30N04 93w45 6:15:00
Cove Springs 37 1 32N00'35 95w20'46 6:21:23
Covington 109 1 32N10'42 97w15'28 6:29:02
Cowden Place 248 1 31N43'33 102w48'12 6:51:13
Cowley 43 1 33N00'35 96w46'25 6:27:06
Cox 230 1 32N44 94w57 6:19:48
Coxville 227 1 30N24'05 97w40'44 6:30:43
Coyanosa 186 1 31N14'34 103w03'51 6:52:15
Coy City 128 1 28N49'28 98w02'24 6:32:10
Coymack 73 1 31N10'48 96w50'32 6:27:22
Coyote Corner 2 1 32N06'25 102w43'26 6:50:54
Coyote Place 115 2 31N44'46 105w51'19 7:03:25
Cozart 221 1 32N23'07 99w57'46 6:39:51
Cozy Corner 75 1 29N51'34 96w50'50 6:27:23
Crabapple 86 1 30N26'34 98w50'14 6:35:21
Crabb 79 1 29N32'17 95w42'35 6:22:50
Crabbs Prairie 236 1 30N45'14 95w38'56 6:22:36
Craft 37 1 31N55'05 95w14'07 6:20:56
Crafton 249 1 33N22'09 97w54'20 6:31:37
Craig 201 1 32N09 94w48 6:19:12
Crandall 129 1 32N37'40 96w27'20 6:25:49
Crane 52 1 31N23'50 102w20'59 6:49:24
Cranell 196 1 28N10'04 97w23'33 6:29:34
Cranes Mill 46 1 29N55'14 98w17'24 6:33:10
Cranfills Gap 18 1 31N46'25 97w49'32 6:31:18
Crawford 155 1 31N32'03 97w26'34 6:29:46
Creagleville 234 1 32N41 95w43 6:22:52
Creath 113 1 31N26'52 95w13'23 6:20:54
Crecy 228 1 31N12'04 95w03'18 6:20:13
Creechville 70 1 32N20'33 96w31'44 6:26:07
Creedmoor 227 1 30N05'23 97w44'01 6:30:56
Crescent 241 1 29N19 96w06 6:24:24
Crescent Center 205 1 27N52'46 97w19'19 6:29:17
Crescent Heights 107 1 32N12 95w51 6:23:24
Cresson 111 1 32N31'57 97w37'03 6:30:28
Cresthaven 15 1 29N31 98w31 6:34:04
Crestwood 68 1 31N52 102w22 6:49:28
Crews 200 1 31N58 99w58 6:39:52
Crimcrest 201 1 32N09'00 94w49'02 6:19:16
Crisp 70 1 32N23'52 96w34'51 6:26:19
Crockett 113 1 31N19'05 95w27'23 6:21:50
Crockett Heights 53 1 30N42'11 101w06'52 6:44:27
Cronin 1 1 31N40'34 95w36'59 6:22:28
Crosby 101 1 29N54'42 95w03'43 6:20:15
Crosbyton 54 1 33N39'36 101w14'15 6:44:57
Cross 93 1 30N48'36 96w06'10 6:24:25
Cross 156 1 28N55 98w33 6:34:12
Cross Cut 25 1 32N02'01 99w07'56 6:36:32
Cross Plains 230 1 32N07'34 99w09'54 6:36:40
Cross Road 194 1 33N41'58 95w16'23 6:21:06
Crossroads 32 1 32N55'55 94w57'39 6:19:51
Cross Roads 47 1 31N57 98w44 6:34:56
Crossroads 60 1 33N26'44 95w42'18 6:22:49
Cross Roads 61 1 33N18 96w59 6:27:56
Cross Roads 76 1 32N47'55 100w30'29 6:42:02
Crossroads 102 1 32N26'54 94w14'15 6:16:57
Cross Roads 107 1 32N02'56 95w58'02 6:23:52
Cross Roads 145 1 31N05'00 95w55'26 6:23:42
Crossroads 166 1 30N57'51 96w47'28 6:27:10
Crossroads 192 1 31N33'54 101w36'25 6:46:26
Cross Roads 201 1 32N19'52 94w47'32 6:19:10
Crossroads Community Centery 34 1 33N04'22 94w34'54 6:18:20
Crossroads School (Abandoned 200 1 31N39'21 100w06'32 6:40:26
Crossroad Store 18 1 31N44'02 97w39'54 6:30:40
Croton 63 1 33N40'33 100w44'51 6:42:59
Crow 108 1 26N14'46 98w31'09 6:34:05
Crow 250 1 32N36'56 95w18'34 6:21:14
Crowell 78 1 33N59'02 99w43'28 6:38:54
Crowley 220 1 32N34'44 97w21'44 6:29:27
Crown 7 1 28N56'28 98w44'23 6:34:58
Crowther 156 1 28N35'18 98w23'30 6:33:34
Crume Gin 77 1 34N16'21 101w31'11 6:46:05
Crusher 115 2 31N04'01 104w57'43 6:59:51
Cruz Calle 66 1 27N23'12 98w16'13 6:33:05
Cryer Creek 175 1 32N07'45 96w39'24 6:26:38
Crystal Beach 84 1 29N27'25 94w38'22 6:18:33
Crystal City 254 1 28N40'38 99w49'40 6:39:19
Crystal Falls 215 1 32N53'44 98w54'00 6:35:36
Crystal Lake 1 1 31N46 95w38 6:22:32
Cuadrilla 71 2 31N31'59 106w12'00 7:04:48
Cuatro Caminos 195 1 30N51'21 103w35'36 6:54:22
Cuba 126 1 32N18'50 97w16'08 6:29:05
Cude Crossing Windmill 82 1 28N52'44 99w12'18 6:36:49
Cuero 62 1 29N05'37 97w17'20 6:29:09
Cuevitas 108 1 26N15'45 98w34'40 6:34:19
Cuevitas 124 1 26N49'32 98w51'40 6:35:27
Culleoka 43 1 33N07'52 96w29'30 6:25:58
Cumby 112 1 33N08'14 95w50'21 6:23:21
Cummins Crossing 166 1 30N48'08 97w09'53 6:28:40
Cundiff 119 1 33N19'00 97w59'53 6:32:00
Cuney 37 1 32N01'55 95w25'02 6:21:40
Cunningham 139 1 33N25'35 95w21'26 6:21:26
Currie 175 1 31N51'49 96w26'36 6:25:46
Curry Crossing 14 1 31N12'10 97w38'14 6:30:33
Curtis 121 1 30N55'16 94w03'52 6:16:15
Curvitas 108 1 26N14 98w34 6:34:16
Cushing 174 1 31N48'52 94w50'25 6:19:22
Cusseta 34 1 33N09'44 94w27'26 6:17:50
Custer City 49 1 33N40'58 97w02'59 6:28:12
Cut 113 1 31N13 95w29 6:21:56
Cut and Shoot 170 1 30N19 95w28 6:21:52
Cutbert 168 1 32N28'53 101w01'54 6:44:08
Cuthand 194 1 33N28'03 95w03'19 6:20:13
Cuthbert 168 1 32N24 100w52 6:43:28
Cuyler 33 3 35N23'21 101w16'21 6:45:05
Cyclone 14 1 31N01'39 97w09'02 6:28:36
Cypress 80 1 33N02'38 95w16'08 6:21:05
Cypress 101 1 29N58'08 95w41'49 6:22:47
Cypress Bend 101 1 29N51 95w30 6:22:00
Cypress Creek 133 1 30N01'02 98w58'36 6:35:54
Cypress Creek Estates 101 1 29N58 95w42 6:22:48
Cypress Mill 16 1 30N22'51 98w15'01 6:33:00
Dabney 232 1 29N09'44 100w05'57 6:40:24
Dacosta 235 1 28N43'12 96w52'22 6:27:29
Dacus 170 1 30N26'49 95w47'33 6:23:10
Dads Corner 5 1 33N44'46 98w41'16 6:34:45
Daffan 227 1 30N21 97w33 6:30:12
Daingerfield 172 1 33N01'54 94w43'18 6:18:53
Daisetta 146 1 30N06'47 94w38'34 6:18:34
Dalby Springs 19 1 33N22'08 94w40'46 6:18:43
Dale 28 1 29N55'38 97w33'51 6:30:15
Dale Crest 234 1 32N41 95w43 6:22:52
Dalhart 56 3 36N03'34 102w30'46 6:50:03
Dallam 21 1 30N25'12 96w12'58 6:24:52
Dallardsville 187 1 30N37'42 94w37'54 6:18:32
Dallas 57 1 32N47'00 96w48'00 6:27:12
Dal-nor 57 1 32N57 96w53 6:27:32
Dalrock 57 1 32N54'38 96w31'51 6:26:07
Dalton 34 1 33N12'17 94w35'48 6:18:23
Dalton 61 1 33N17'57 97w12'16 6:28:49
Dalworth 57 1 32N44 96w59 6:27:56
Dalworthington Gardens 220 1 32N42'10 97w09'18 6:28:37
Dalys 113 1 31N29 95w29 6:21:56
Dalzell 25 1 31N37'45 99w02'13 6:36:09
Damon 20 1 29N17'25 95w44'04 6:22:56
Danbury 20 1 29N13'41 95w20'41 6:21:23
Danciger 20 1 29N10'17 95w49'07 6:23:16
Danevang 241 1 29N03'26 96w12'26 6:24:50
Daniel 113 1 31N19 95w27 6:21:48
Daniels 183 1 32N03'57 94w22'30 6:17:30
Daniels 239 1 30N11'55 96w12'20 6:24:49
Danner 74 1 33N40'31 96w06'48 6:24:27
Danville 92 1 32N24'03 94w49'36 6:19:18
Daphine 80 1 33N16'00 95w07'46 6:20:31
Darco 102 1 32N24'32 94w26'08 6:17:45
Darden 19 1 33N18'00 94w34'51 6:18:19
Darilek 247 1 29N03'10 98w13'54 6:32:56
Darling 162 1 28N59'34 100w23'57 6:41:36
Darrouzett 148 3 36N26'46 100w19'28 6:41:18
Datura 147 1 31N43'27 96w36'46 6:26:27
Daugherty 190 1 32N52 95w46 6:23:04
Dauphin 107 1 32N11'13 95w54'59 6:23:40
Davenport 194 1 33N55'30 95w08'11 6:20:33
Davidson 26 1 30N28'19 96w37'51 6:26:31
Davilla 166 1 30N47'08 97w16'29 6:29:06
Davis 7 1 28N47'58 98w45'25 6:35:02
Davis Prairie 147 1 31N25'13 96w31'31 6:26:06
Davisville 3 1 31N24'10 94w42'37 6:18:50
Davisville 145 1 31N16 95w59 6:23:56
Dawn 59 3 34N54'37 102w11'58 6:48:48
Dawson 175 1 31N53'38 96w42'52 6:26:51
Dayton 146 1 30N02'47 94w53'06 6:19:32
Deadwood 183 1 32N08'23 94w08'30 6:16:34
Deal 33 3 35N35'43 101w34'18 6:46:17
Dean 39 1 33N57'01 98w20'45 6:33:23
Dean 110 1 33N41 102w00 6:48:00
Deanville 26 1 30N25'55 96w45'21 6:27:01
Deanwright 1 1 31N44'11 95w32'33 6:22:10
De Berry 183 1 32N18'14 94w09'59 6:16:40
Decatur 249 1 33N14'03 97w35'09 6:30:21
Decker 177 1 32N05 100w19 6:41:16
Decker 227 1 30N18'23 97w37'03 6:30:28
Decker Prairie 170 1 30N07'51 95w39'08 6:22:37
Deco 101 1 29N58'02 95w32'19 6:22:09
Deep Water Point Estates 43 1 33N03'24 96w27'07 6:25:48
Deep Well Crossing 112 1 33N18'24 95w41'42 6:22:47
Deer Creek 39 1 33N38'11 98w17'14 6:33:09
Deer Park 101 1 29N42'18 95w07'25 6:20:30
De Kalb 19 1 33N30'31 94w36'58 6:18:28
Delaware Junction 25 1 31N47'11 98w52'07 6:35:28
Delba 74 1 33N22'30 96w19'51 6:25:19
Delbert L Atkinson 101 1 29N39 95w11 6:20:44
DeLeon 47 1 32N06'39 98w32'08 6:34:09
Delhi 28 1 29N49'38 97w23'43 6:29:35
Delia 147 1 31N42'24 96w46'03 6:27:04
Dell City 150 2 31N56'19 105w12'03 7:00:48
Del Mar 31 1 26N00'41 97w09'07 6:28:36
Del Mar 240 1 27N34'10 99w29'08 6:37:57
Del Mar Hills 240 1 27N31 99w30 6:38:00
Delmer 37 1 31N49'35 95w13'09 6:20:53
Delmita 214 1 26N40'47 98w24'44 6:33:39
Del Monte 123 1 29N57 93w59 6:15:56
Del Norte Acres 71 2 31N52'02 106w26'05 7:05:44
Del Norte Heights 71 2 31N45'27 106w21'53 7:05:28
Delray 183 1 32N09'12 94w27'35 6:17:50
Del Rio 233 1 29N21'45 100w53'47 6:43:35
Delrose 230 1 32N47'08 94w57'21 6:19:49
Del Valle 227 1 30N12'38 97w39'16 6:30:37
Delwin 51 1 33N52'35 100w23'55 6:41:36
Demarco 27 1 30N41'36 98w15'14 6:33:01
Democrat 47 1 31N54 98w36 6:34:24
Democrat Crossing 21 1 30N48'38 96w10'29 6:24:42
Denhawken 247 1 29N10'30 97w55'08 6:31:41
Denison 91 1 33N45'20 96w32'11 6:26:09
Denman Crossroads 234 1 32N23'55 95w53'25 6:23:34
Denning 203 1 31N30'52 94w14'42 6:16:59
Dennis 184 1 32N37'07 97w55'35 6:31:42
Denny 73 1 31N18 96w38 6:26:32
Denson Spring 1 1 31N29 95w29 6:21:56
Denton 30 1 32N15'31 99w32'21 6:38:09
Denton 61 1 33N12'53 97w07'58 6:28:32
Denver City 251 1 32N57'52 102w49'43 6:51:19
Denver Harbor 101 1 29N47 95w19 6:21:16
Denworth 90 3 35N23'38 100w36'27 6:42:26
Deport 139 1 33N31'34 95w18'56 6:21:16
Derby 82 1 28N46'16 99w07'42 6:36:31
Derden 109 1 32N11'01 97w19'42 6:29:19
Dermott 208 1 32N51'16 101w00'55 6:44:04
Dernal 235 1 28N41'43 96w56'39 6:27:47
Desdemona 67 1 32N16'13 98w33'00 6:34:12
Desert 43 1 33N23'18 96w24'06 6:25:36
De Soto 57 1 32N35'23 96w51'24 6:27:26
Dessau 227 1 30N24'12 97w38'17 6:30:33
Detmold 166 1 30N39'00 97w12'50 6:28:51
Detroit 194 1 33N39'41 95w15'59 6:21:04
Devers 146 1 30N01'38 94w35'29 6:18:22
Devils Shores 233 1 29N37'15 100w56'12 6:43:45
Devine 163 1 29N08'23 98w54'18 6:35:37
Dew 81 1 31N35'42 96w08'23 6:24:34
Dewalt 79 1 29N33'23 95w33'23 6:22:14
Dewees 247 1 29N01'13 98w10'19 6:32:41
Dewey 169 1 33N32 97w33 6:30:12
Deweyville 176 1 30N17'51 93w44'36 6:14:58
Dewville 89 1 29N22'40 97w48'39 6:31:15
Dexter 49 1 33N49'07 96w57'48 6:27:51
Dextra 174 1 31N48'34 94w55'50 6:19:43
D'Hanis 163 1 29N19'49 99w16'46 6:37:07
Dial 74 3 33N29'47 95w52'04 6:23:28
Dial 117 3 35N47'51 101w23'30 6:45:34
Dialville 37 1 31N51'26 95w13'49 6:20:55
Diana 230 1 32N42'35 94w45'07 6:19:00
Diboll 3 1 31N11'13 94w46'51 6:19:07
Dicey 184 1 32N48'26 97w41'56 6:30:48
Dickens 63 1 33N37'18 100w50'10 6:43:21
Dickinson 84 1 29N27'38 95w03'04 6:20:12
Dickson Cove 116 1 32N54 96w05 6:24:20
Dickworsham 39 1 33N45'05 98w06'55 6:32:28
Dido 220 1 32N47 97w21 6:29:24
Dies 100 1 30N23'19 94w23'45 6:17:35
Dike 112 1 33N14'19 95w28'55 6:21:56
Dilley 82 1 28N40'02 99w10'13 6:36:41
Dilworth 89 1 29N30'28 97w17'06 6:29:08
Dilworth 194 1 33N42'09 94w58'48 6:19:55

Place	Code	Latitude	Longitude	Time
Dime Box 144	1	30N21'23	96w49'20	6:27:17
Dimmitt 35	3	34N33'03	102w18'41	6:49:15
Dimple 194	1	33N42'51	95w04'17	6:20:17
Dinero 149	1	28N13'34	97w57'41	6:31:51
Ding Dong 14	1	31N07	97w46	6:31:04
Dingerville 157	1	31N04'25	95w50'47	6:23:23
Dinkins 21	1	30N25'17	96w10'36	6:24:42
Dinsmore 241	1	29N19'01	96w03'01	6:24:12
Direct 139	1	33N49'15	95w50'11	6:23:21
Dirgin 201	1	32N15'25	94w35'19	6:18:21
Dittlinger 46	1	29N40'51	98w10'44	6:32:43
Divide 41	1	31N54	100w29	6:41:56
Divot 82	1	28N45'45	99w15'31	6:37:02
Dix 159	1	32N06'04	101w51'54	6:47:28
Dixie 91	1	33N43'00	96w54'16	6:27:37
Dixon 116	1	33N04'09	96w01'36	6:24:06
Doans 244	1	34N20'37	99w15'19	6:37:01
Dobbin 170	1	30N21'55	95w46'33	6:23:06
Dobrowolski 7	1	28N53'33	98w38'33	6:34:34
Doc Brown 181	1	30N05'04	93w45'58	6:15:04
Dodd 35	1	34N20'06	102w28'43	6:49:55
Dodd City 74	1	33N34'31	96w04'29	6:24:18
Dodge 236	1	30N44'43	95w23'52	6:21:35
Dodson 44	3	34N46'00	100w01'25	6:40:06
Dog Ridge 14	1	31N03'14	97w30'23	6:30:02
Dogwood 229	1	30N47	94w25	6:17:40
Dogwood Acres 101	1	30N05'20	95w10'21	6:20:41
Dolan 3	1	31N05'17	94w25'54	6:17:44
Dolen 146	1	30N25'30	94w53'51	6:19:35
Domino 34	1	33N15'54	94w06'54	6:16:28
Donahoe 14	1	30N48'57	97w19'58	6:29:20
Donelton 116	1	32N57	95w56	6:23:44
Donie 81	1	31N28'37	96w13'20	6:24:53
Donna 108	1	26N10'12	98w03'06	6:32:12
Don-Tol 241	1	29N13'22	95w54'59	6:23:40
Doole 154	1	31N23'44	99w35'55	6:38:24
Dorchester 91	1	33N31'49	96w41'21	6:26:45
Dorman 241	1	29N22'55	96w13'07	6:24:52
Doss 34	1	33N00	94w22	6:17:28
Doss 86	1	30N26'40	99w07'49	6:36:31
Dot 73	1	31N15	97w30	6:30:00
Dothan 67	1	32N23	98w59	6:35:56
Dotson 74	1	33N44'21	96w02'08	6:24:09
Dotson 183	1	32N00'17	94w31'47	6:18:07
Doty 181	1	30N09'36	93w56'45	6:15:47
Double Bayou 36	1	29N41'33	94w37'44	6:18:31
Double Ford 167	1	31N17'22	98w35'51	6:34:23
Double Mountain 217	1	33N08'09	100w24'33	6:41:38
Double Oak 61	1	33N07	97w11	6:28:44
Doucette 229	1	30N49'05	94w25'43	6:17:43
Doud 152	1	33N33'16	101w56'10	6:47:45
Dougherty 77	1	33N57	101w05	6:44:20
Dougherty 190	1	32N57'20	95w46'08	6:23:05
Doughtery 173	1	33N56'30	101w05'10	6:44:21
Douglas 212	1	32N21'03	95w04'05	6:20:16
Douglass 174	1	31N40'04	94w52'50	6:19:31
Douglassville 34	1	33N11'31	94w21'12	6:17:25
Doule 147	1	31N32	96w32	6:26:08
Douro 68	1	31N45'42	102w31'31	6:50:06
Dowling 123	1	30N00'59	94w02'14	6:16:09
Downing 47	1	32N01'26	98w33'01	6:34:12
Downs 155	1	31N27'14	97w04'11	6:28:17
Downsville 155	1	31N27'20	97w04'00	6:28:16
Doyle 147	1	31N34'24	96w30'18	6:26:01
Dozier 44	3	35N04'52	100w20'37	6:41:22
Draco 249	1	33N06'17	97w44'39	6:30:59
Drane 175	1	32N02'41	96w35'14	6:26:21
Drasco 200	1	32N04'35	99w59'14	6:39:57
Draw 153	1	33N10	101w48	6:47:12
Dreka 210	1	31N40'29	93w57'22	6:15:49
Dresden 175	1	32N01'50	96w40'49	6:26:43
Drews Landing 187	1	30N32'37	94w51'39	6:19:27
Dreyer 89	1	29N22'01	97w16'22	6:29:05
Dreyfoos 106	3	35N59'17	100w02'24	6:40:10
Driftwood 105	1	30N07'22	98w01'50	6:32:07
Dripping Springs 105	1	30N11'24	98w05'11	6:32:21
Driscoll 178	1	27N40'27	97w44'54	6:31:00
Drop 61	1	33N07'51	97w21'20	6:29:25
Dryden 222	1	30N02'40	102w06'51	6:48:27
Dryden Crossing (Cable) 222	1	29N48'39	102w08'52	6:48:35
Dry Valley 169	1	33N33'16	97w41'26	6:30:46
Dubina 75	1	29N43'43	96w49'58	6:27:20
Dublin 72	1	32N05'06	98w20'30	6:33:22
Dudley 30	1	32N15'29	99w36'17	6:38:25
Duff 210	1	31N38'21	94w07'44	6:16:31
Duffau 72	1	32N04'56	98w01'18	6:32:05
Dug Ford 224	1	33N00'50	99w23'07	6:37:32
Duke 79	1	29N30'16	95w29'09	6:21:57
Duke Crossing 167	1	31N33'13	98w47'56	6:35:12
Dulin 25	1	31N31'54	99w05'55	6:36:24
Dull 142	1	28N26'41	98w55'51	6:35:43
Dumas 171	3	35N51'56	101w58'22	6:47:53
Dumas Junction 188	3	35N12'46	101w48'07	6:47:12
Dumont 135	1	33N48'35	100w30'57	6:42:04
Dunagan 3	1	31N20'47	94w36'54	6:18:28
Dunbar 190	1	32N52	95w46	6:23:04
Duncans Woods 181	1	30N06	93w46	6:15:04
Duncanville 57	1	32N39'06	96w54'29	6:27:38
Dundee 5	1	33N44'25	98w54'07	6:35:36
Dunlap 51	1	34N08'26	100w17'46	6:41:11
Dunlap 227	1	30N14'55	97w33'34	6:30:14
Dunlay 163	1	29N20'54	98w59'25	6:35:58
Dunn 208	1	32N34'01	100w53'06	6:43:32
Dunnam 101	1	30N04'31	95w09'59	6:20:40
Dunnan 170	1	29N47	95w23	6:21:32
Dunns Fort 198	1	30N51'53	96w25'43	6:25:43
Duplex 74	1	33N46'40	96w08'20	6:24:33
Dupre 235	1	28N50'37	97w00'38	6:28:03
Durango 73	1	31N12'17	97w07'49	6:28:31
Durant 3	1	31N25'01	94w50'01	6:19:20
Durenville 167	1	31N29'38	98w34'33	6:34:18
Durham 116	1	33N21'02	95w58'43	6:23:55
Duster 47	1	32N06'17	98w40'35	6:34:42
Dye 169	1	33N37'14	97w36'44	6:30:27
Dye Mound 169	1	33N42	97w31	6:30:04
Dyersdale 101	1	29N53'29	95w15'27	6:21:02
Dyess Air Force Base 221	1	32N25	99w48	6:39:12
Eagle Acres 220	1	32N59'09	97w31'07	6:30:04
Eagle Flat 115	2	31N06'35	105w07'56	7:00:32
Eagle Ford 57	1	32N47'05	96w54'02	6:27:36
Eagle Lake 45	1	29N35'22	96w20'00	6:25:20
Eagle Mountain 220	1	32N49	97w24	6:29:36
Eagle Mountain Acres 220	1	32N39	97w14	6:28:56
Eagle Pass 162	1	28N42'32	100w29'57	6:42:00
Earle 15	1	29N15'47	98w29'26	6:33:58
Earls 184	1	32N44'08	97w44'34	6:30:58
Early 25	1	31N44'31	98w56'43	6:35:47
Earlywine 239	1	30N12'59	96w18'26	6:25:14
Earth 140	1	34N13'59	102w24'27	6:49:38
East Afton 63	1	33N44'53	100w44'33	6:42:58
East Austin 227	1	30N16	97w42	6:30:48
East Bernard 41	1	29N31'51	96w04'15	6:24:17
East Bexar 15	1	29N27	98w19	6:33:16
East Caney 112	1	33N07'54	95w27'24	6:21:50
East Central 71	2	31N39	106w15	7:05:00
East Columbia 20	1	29N08'28	95w36'56	6:22:28
East Crockett 53	1	30N46	101w12	6:44:48
East Delta 60	1	33N23'36	95w30'46	6:22:03
East Direct 139	1	33N46	95w39	6:22:36
East Ector 68	1	31N54	102w24	6:49:36
Easter 35	3	34N38'44	102w23'47	6:49:35
Easterly 198	1	31N06'19	96w23'02	6:25:32
Eastex Oaks Village 101	1	29N56	95w17	6:21:08
Eastgate 146	1	30N03	94w53	6:19:32
East Grand 57	1	32N47	96w45	6:27:00
East Grayson 91	1	33N40	96w26	6:25:44
East Hamilton 210	1	31N35'45	93w50'30	6:15:22
East Haven 101	1	29N38'23	95w15'08	6:21:01
East Houston 101	1	29N49'46	95w16'11	6:21:05
Eastland 67	1	32N24'05	98w49'02	6:35:16
East Liberty 210	1	31N40'04	94w01'58	6:16:08
East Mayfield 202	1	31N21	93w51	6:15:24
East Mountain 230	1	32N35'37	94w51'19	6:19:25
East Oak Cliff 57	1	32N44	96w49	6:27:16
Easton 201	1	32N23'14	94w34'58	6:18:20
East Point 250	1	32N49'52	95w17'51	6:21:11
East River 101	1	30N18	95w07	6:20:28
East Side 58	1	32N44	101w58	6:47:52
East Side 183	1	32N18	94w10	6:16:40
East Stamford 127	1	33N00	99w42	6:38:48
East Sweden 154	1	31N10'02	99w15'21	6:37:01
East Tawakoni 190	1	32N53'03	95w55'44	6:23:43
East Tempe 187	1	30N43	94w56	6:19:44
East Terrell 222	1	30N14	102w00	6:48:00
East Tom Green 226	1	31N27	100w15	6:41:00
Eastvale 61	1	33N03	97w03	6:28:12
East View 92	1	32N22	94w52	6:19:28
East Waco 155	1	31N33'25	97w05'48	6:28:23
Eastwood 101	1	29N43	95w19	6:21:16
Eaton 198	1	30N58'22	96w20'22	6:25:21
Ebenezer 32	1	32N58'19	94w52'51	6:19:31
Ebenezer 121	1	31N02'16	94w09'39	6:16:39
Ebony 167	1	31N30'09	98w53'51	6:35:35
Echo 42	1	31N55'41	99w19'03	6:37:16
Echo 181	1	30N09'09	93w43'56	6:14:56
Echols 147	1	31N41'09	96w38'14	6:26:33
Eckert 86	1	30N24'51	98w44'11	6:34:57
Ecleto 128	1	29N02'46	97w45'04	6:31:00
Eclipse 121	1	30N45'09	93w58'40	6:15:55
Ector 74	1	33N34'38	96w16'23	6:25:06
Edcouch 108	1	26N17'37	97w57'37	6:31:50
Eddy 155	1	31N17'40	97w15'07	6:29:00
Eden 48	1	31N12'58	99w50'43	6:39:23
Ederville 220	1	32N45'26	97w12'38	6:28:51
Edgar 62	1	29N12'18	97w14'02	6:28:56
Edge 21	1	30N53	96w18	6:25:12
Edgecliff 220	1	32N40	97w21	6:29:24
Edgecliff Village 220	1	32N39'27	97w20'33	6:29:22
Edgewater Beach 227	1	30N24'11	97w59'55	6:32:00
Edgewood 234	1	32N41'53	95w53'06	6:23:32
Edgeworth 14	1	30N57'05	97w08'25	6:28:34
Edgeworth Place 101	1	29N53'06	95w18'30	6:21:14
Edhube 74	1	33N31'35	96w13'03	6:24:52
Edinburg 108	1	26N18'05	98w09'47	6:32:39
Edith 41	1	31N54'12	100w36'37	6:42:26
Edmonson 95	1	34N16'57	101w53'59	6:47:36
Edna 120	1	28N58'42	96w38'45	6:26:35
Edna Hill 72	1	31N57'23	98w19'48	6:33:19
Edom 234	1	32N22'20	95w36'31	6:22:26
Edroy 205	1	27N58'24	97w40'33	6:30:42
Edwards 39	1	33N49'34	98w01'50	6:32:07
Edwards Place 22	3	30N24'09	103w25'01	6:53:40
Egan 126	1	32N27'10	97w17'58	6:29:12
Egypt 170	1	30N13'15	95w33'41	6:22:15
Egypt 241	1	29N24'17	96w14'12	6:24:57
Eichelberger Crossing 155	1	31N37'00	97w18'28	6:29:14
Eight Mile 102	1	32N34	94w25	6:17:40
El Bernardo 20	1	29N02'24	95w39'09	6:22:37
Elbert 224	1	33N15'58	98w59'37	6:35:58
Elberta 212	1	32N17'33	95w14'47	6:20:59
Elbow 114	1	32N09'37	101w30'42	6:46:03
El Calaboz 31	1	26N01'51	97w38'52	6:30:35
El Campo 241	1	29N11'47	96w16'10	6:25:05
El Carro 125	1	27N54'36	98w09'41	6:32:39
El Centro 214	1	26N41	98w25	6:33:40
Elderville 92	1	32N22'20	94w43'42	6:18:55
Eldon 36	1	29N48'54	94w55'03	6:19:40
Eldorado 207	1	30N51'36	100w36'02	6:42:24
Eldorado Center 175	1	31N51'04	96w37'40	6:26:31
Eldridge 45	1	29N28'04	96w21'18	6:25:25
Electra 243	1	34N01'45	98w55'07	6:35:40
Electric City 117	3	35N42'37	101w24'45	6:45:39
Elevation 166	1	30N39'12	96w49'07	6:27:16
El Gato 108	1	26N09'13	98w05'57	6:32:24
Elgin 11	1	30N20'58	97w22'12	6:29:29
Eli 96	1	34N41'37	100w37'42	6:42:31
Eliasville 252	1	32N57'35	98w45'54	6:35:04
El Indio 162	1	28N30'42	100w18'39	6:41:15
Elizabeth 123	1	30N04'35	94w11'19	6:16:45
Elizabethtown 61	1	33N01'18	97w16'35	6:29:06
El Jardin 31	1	25N55	97w29	6:29:56
El Jardin Del Mar 101	1	29N35'54	94w59'16	6:19:57
Elk 155	1	31N36'59	96w56'08	6:27:45
Elkhart 1	1	31N37'30	95w34'45	6:22:19
Ella 125	1	27N28'24	98w06'20	6:32:25
El Lago 101	1	29N34	95w01	6:20:04
Ellen 95	1	34N01'17	101w37'34	6:46:30
Ellinger 75	1	29N50'21	96w42'18	6:26:49
Elliot 198	1	30N57'13	96w34'06	6:26:16
Elliott 244	1	34N09'00	99w03'19	6:36:13
Ellsworth 91	1	33N42'16	96w34'51	6:26:19
Ellwood 152	1	33N34	101w54	6:47:36
El Martillo 137	1	27N20'26	97w26'53	6:29:48
Elmaton 161	1	28N53'10	96w08'23	6:24:34
Elmdale 221	1	32N25'50	99w38'22	6:38:33
Elmendorf 15	1	29N15'21	98w19'57	6:33:20
Elm Flat 175	1	32N05'01	96w18'00	6:25:12
Elm Grove 28	1	29N53'26	97w29'14	6:29:57
Elm Grove 37	1	31N52'18	95w06'04	6:20:24
Elm Grove 75	1	29N45'16	97w13'54	6:28:56
Elm Grove 206	1	31N25'39	99w03'20	6:36:13
Elm Grove 241	1	29N26'31	96w19'32	6:25:18
Elm Grove 246	1	30N41'06	97w19'11	6:29:17
Elmina 236	1	30N33'34	95w28'31	6:21:54
Elm Mott 155	1	31N40'18	97w05'55	6:28:24
Elmo 129	1	32N43'19	96w09'53	6:24:40
Elmont 91	1	33N25'22	96w38'15	6:26:33
Elmtown 1	1	31N53'45	95w37'42	6:22:31
Elmwood 1	1	31N55'10	95w37'51	6:22:31
Eloise 73	1	31N07'22	96w48'30	6:27:14
El Oso 128	1	28N44'05	98w00'07	6:32:00
El Paso 71	2	31N45'31	106w29'11	7:05:57
El Refugio 214	1	26N20'24	98w45'20	6:35:01
Elroy 227	1	30N07'14	97w30'06	6:30:02
Elsa 108	1	26N17'35	97w59'34	6:31:58
El Sauz 214	1	26N34'25	98w52'17	6:35:29
Elstone 163	1	29N21	99w08	6:36:32
El Tesoro 111	1	32N23'33	97w38'54	6:30:36
Elton 63	1	33N42'16	100w50'28	6:43:22
El Toro 120	1	28N56'52	96w42'18	6:26:49
Elva 70	1	32N31'36	96w47'40	6:27:11
Elwood 74	1	33N48'42	96w04'25	6:24:18
Elwood 157	1	31N03'31	95w49'31	6:23:18
Elwood 234	1	32N44'18	95w56'58	6:23:48
Ely 74	1	33N31'22	96w18'45	6:25:15
Elysian Fields 102	1	32N22'06	94w10'58	6:16:44
Emberson 139	1	33N45'39	95w39'08	6:22:37
Emblem 112	1	33N14'50	95w45'57	6:23:04
Emerson 222	1	30N08'55	102w32'09	6:50:09
Emerson Place 101	1	29N52'46	95w19'01	6:21:16
Emhouse 175	1	32N09'45	96w34'37	6:26:18
Emilee 229	1	30N47	94w25	6:17:40
Eminence 101	1	29N50'01	94w41'28	6:18:46
Emmaus 37	1	32N00'54	95w02'55	6:20:12
Emmett 220	1	31N59'15	96w47'33	6:27:10
Emory 190	1	32N52'28	95w45'55	6:23:04
Enchanted Oaks 107	1	32N22	95w59	6:23:56
Encinal 142	1	28N02'27	99w21'15	6:37:25
Encino 24	1	26N56'09	98w08'06	6:32:32
Energy 47	1	31N46	98w22	6:33:28
Engelman 108	1	26N18	98w00	6:32:00
Engle 75	1	29N40'51	97w00'33	6:28:02
Engleman Gardens 108	1	26N19'52	98w01'08	6:32:05
English 20	1	29N22'26	95w31'39	6:22:07
English 74	1	33N32'59	96w08'08	6:24:33
English 194	1	33N37'39	94w51'33	6:19:26
English Crossing 10	1	29N40'53	98w58'32	6:35:54
Enloe 60	1	33N25'58	95w39'26	6:22:38
Ennis 70	1	32N19'45	96w37'30	6:26:30
Enoch 230	1	32N43'12	94w59'54	6:20:00
Enochs 9	1	33N52'23	102w45'34	6:51:02
Enon 230	1	32N46'14	95w01'46	6:20:07
Enos 237	1	29N47	95w57	6:23:48
Enright 21	1	30N30'21	96w17'47	6:25:11
Ensign 70	1	32N15'55	96w36'55	6:26:28
Enterprise 37	1	31N58	95w16	6:21:04
Enterprise 74	1	33N31'18	96w20'59	6:25:24
Enterprise 234	1	32N43	96w00	6:24:00
Eola 48	1	31N23'55	100w05'20	6:40:21
Eolian 215	1	32N40'00	99w00'57	6:36:04
Era 49	1	33N29'43	97w17'16	6:29:09
Erath 155	1	31N37'59	97w15'48	6:29:03
Erin 121	1	30N46'46	93w59'48	6:15:59
Erna 164	1	30N45'02	99w29'08	6:37:57
Erwin 93	1	30N29'09	96w03'35	6:24:14
Esbon 150	1	30N52	98w49	6:35:16
Escobares 214	1	26N24'37	98w57'44	6:35:51
Escobas 253	1	27N03'44	99w01'24	6:36:06
Eskota 76	1	32N31'29	100w14'48	6:40:59

Esperanza 115 2 31N09'34 105w42'36 7:02:50
Esperson 146 1 29N57'19 94w55'02 6:19:40
Esseville 149 1 28N41'06 98w12'19 6:32:49
Estacado 54 1 33N45'08 101w33'41 6:46:15
Estelle 57 1 32N51'58 97w00'46 6:28:03
Estelline 96 1 34N32'48 100w26'16 6:41:45
Estes 4 1 27N57'49 97w06'00 6:28:24
Estes 102 1 32N26'18 94w40'00 6:18:40
Estes Addition 249
1 33N00 97w29 6:29:56
Ethel 91 1 33N32'37 96w50'38 6:27:23
Etholen 115 2 31N11'32 105w25'26 7:01:42
Etoile 174 1 31N23'12 94w26'09 6:17:45
Etter 171 3 36N01'45 101w59'01 6:47:56
Eubank Acres 227
1 30N23'06 97w40'57 6:30:44
Eula 30 1 32N20'32 99w33'41 6:38:15
Eulalie 201 1 31N54 94w24 6:17:36
Euless 220 1 32N50'13 97w04'54 6:28:20
Eulogy 18 1 32N04 97w30 6:30:00
Eunice 145 1 31N19'09 95w49'05 6:23:16
Eunice 219 3 34N28'14 101w46'04 6:47:04
Eureka 80 1 33N20'57 95w18'21 6:21:13
Eureka 175 1 32N00'45 96w17'44 6:25:11
Eureka 209 1 32N34'56 99w03'22 6:36:13
Eustace 107 1 32N18'25 96w00'23 6:24:02
Evadale 121 1 30N21'17 94w04'21 6:16:17
Evans 34 1 32N56'28 94w15'09 6:17:01
Evant 50 1 31N28'34 98w09'06 6:32:36
Evelyn 107 1 32N18'25 95w31'57 6:22:08
Everett 180 3 35N13'32 102w19'43 6:49:19
Evergreen 108 1 26N20'18 98w03'23 6:32:14
Evergreen 204 1 30N33'39 95w14'18 6:20:57
Everitt 204 1 30N18 95w07 6:20:28
Everman 220 1 32N37'51 97w17'20 6:29:09
Ewelder 205 1 28N06'57 97w26'50 6:29:47
Ewell 230 1 32N51'45 94w55'00 6:19:40
Ewing 3 1 31N22'21 94w29'25 6:17:58
Exchange Park 57
1 32N50 96w50 6:27:20
Exell 171 3 35N37'50 101w58'27 6:47:54
Exum 103 3 36N01'37 102w11'38 6:48:47
Eylau 19 1 33N22'45 94w06'58 6:16:28
Ezzell 143 1 29N16'56 96w54'02 6:27:36
Fabens 71 2 31N30'08 106w09'29 7:04:38
Fada 250 1 32N36'37 95w17'41 6:21:11
Fairbanks 101 1 29N51'09 95w31'27 6:22:06
Fairchilds 79 1 29N25'52 95w46'48 6:23:07
Fairdale 202 1 31N13'49 93w39'42 6:14:39
Fairfield 81 1 31N43'28 96w09'54 6:24:40
Fairland 27 1 30N38'38 98w17'04 6:33:08
Fairlie 116 1 33N18'48 95w57'29 6:23:50
Fairmont 77 1 34N15'11 101w03'34 6:44:14
Fairmount 202 1 31N11'48 93w43'59 6:14:56
Fair Oaks 147 1 31N29'12 96w18'26 6:25:14
Fair Park 57 1 32N47 96w46 6:27:04
Fair Play 183 1 32N08'49 94w31'52 6:18:07
Fairview 6 3 35N06'13 101w32'29 6:46:10
Fairview 9 1 34N06'08 102w37'01 6:50:28
Fairview 18 1 31N39 97w28 6:29:52
Fairview 21 1 30N39'07 96w26'06 6:25:44
Fairview 34 1 32N56'47 94w22'41 6:17:31
Fairview 43 1 33N09'28 96w37'53 6:26:32
Fairview 83 1 32N41'48 102w32'10 6:50:09
Fairview 97 1 31N29'14 98w13'11 6:32:53
Fairview 101 1 29N45 95w24 6:21:36
Fairview 111 1 32N30'53 97w48'05 6:31:12
Fairview 114 1 32N21'21 101w31'07 6:46:04
Fairview 201 1 31N52 94w59 6:19:56
Fairview 206 1 31N16'57 98w45'29 6:35:02
Fairview 247 1 29N06'44 98w19'22 6:33:17
Fairview 249 1 33N01'09 97w32'44 6:30:11
Fairy 97 1 31N50'45 97w58'56 6:31:56
Faker 32 1 33N00 94w58 6:19:52
Falcon 253 1 26N38'16 99w05'43 6:36:23
Falcon Heights 214
1 26N33'31 99w07'22 6:36:29
Falcon Lake 253
1 26N52'17 99w15'19 6:37:01
Falcon Mesa 253
1 26N52'21 99w17'21 6:37:09
Falcon Shores 253
1 26N53'44 99w15'11 6:37:01
Falcon Village 214
1 26N33'40 99w08'03 6:36:32
Falfurrias 24 1 27N13'36 98w08'38 6:32:35
Fall Creek 111 1 32N23'52 97w39'04 6:30:36
Fallon 147 1 31N34'51 96w24'22 6:25:37
Falls City 128 1 28N58'57 98w01'02 6:32:04
Famuliner 40 1 33N40'49 102w51'56 6:51:28
Fannett 123 1 29N55'33 94w15'02 6:17:00
Fannin 88 1 28N41'43 97w14'08 6:28:57
Fargo 244 1 34N17'41 99w16'38 6:37:07
Farmer 54 1 33N47'00 101w27'24 6:45:50
Farmer 252 1 33N20'47 98w33'17 6:34:13
Farmers Branch 57
1 32N55'35 96w53'45 6:27:35
Farmers Valley 244
1 34N09 99w18 6:37:12
Farmersville 43
1 33N09'48 96w21'35 6:25:26
Farmington 91 1 33N28'08 96w38'42 6:26:35
Farnsworth 179 3 36N19'16 100w57'57 6:43:52
Farrar 147 1 31N27'24 96w16'50 6:25:07
Farrsville 176 1 30N59'00 93w48'26 6:15:14
Farwell 185 3 30N15'00 103w15'00 6:53:00
Fashing 7 1 28N47'32 98w08'22 6:32:33
Fate 199 1 32N56'29 96w22'52 6:25:31
Faubion Crossing 141
1 31N23'26 98w11'23 6:32:46
Faught 139 1 33N44'14 95w25'14 6:21:41
Faulkner 139 1 33N51'32 95w20'24 6:21:22
Fawil 176 1 30N43'34 93w42'27 6:14:50
Fayburg 43 1 33N16'09 96w23'15 6:25:33
Fayetteville 75
1 29N54'20 96w40'21 6:26:41
Fays Corner 108
1 26N05'38 98w11'58 6:32:48
Faysville 108 1 26N25 98w08 6:32:32
Fedor 144 1 30N18'57 97w03'09 6:28:13
Felicia 146 1 30N01'26 94w30'28 6:18:02
Fellowship 210 1 31N56'16 94w01'54 6:16:08
Fentress 28 1 29N45'21 97w46'34 6:31:06

Fergus 116 1 33N08 96w07 6:24:28
Ferguson 121 1 31N02'09 94w08'21 6:16:33
Ferguson Crossing 93
1 30N36'27 96w10'53 6:24:44
Ferris 70 1 32N32'02 96w39'55 6:26:40
Fetzer 237 1 30N14'28 95w49'03 6:23:16
Field Creek 150
1 30N54'05 98w56'41 6:35:47
Fieldton 140 1 34N02'21 102w13'22 6:48:53
Fife 154 1 31N23'25 99w23'03 6:37:32
Figridge 101 1 29N45'46 94w22'36 6:17:30
Files Valley 109
1 32N13'21 97w04'36 6:28:18
Fincastle 107 1 32N07'45 95w34'03 6:22:16
Fink 91 1 33N48'13 96w40'37 6:26:42
Finlay 115 2 31N15'31 105w37'46 7:02:31
Finley 74 1 33N44'46 96w11'09 6:24:45
Finney 95 1 34N16'39 101w42'57 6:46:52
Finney 135 1 33N46'53 100w22'46 6:41:31
First Crossing 46
1 29N45'54 98w08'29 6:32:34
First Crossing 232
1 29N29'42 99w42'38 6:38:51
Fischer 46 1 29N58'36 98w15'56 6:33:04
Fish Branch 204
1 30N30 95w00 6:20:00
Fisher 76 1 32N47'37 100w23'22 6:41:33
Fisk 42 1 31N40'15 99w29'20 6:37:57
Fisk Crossing 25
1 31N35'38 98w49'18 6:35:17
Fitze 174 1 31N47'08 94w32'03 6:18:08
Fitzhugh 105 1 30N14'42 98w01'37 6:32:06
Fivemile 58 1 32N37'52 101w53'21 6:47:33
Fivemile Crossing 164
1 30N54'46 99w42'30 6:38:50
Five Points 70 1 32N16'41 96w54'04 6:27:36
Five Points 178
1 27N51'20 97w37'46 6:30:31
Flagg 35 3 34N25'34 102w24'34 6:49:38
Flag Springs 74
1 33N30'59 96w00'41 6:24:03
Flamingo Bay 101
1 29N34 95w01 6:20:04
Flanagan 201 1 32N19 94w31 6:18:04
Flat 50 1 31N18'31 97w37'47 6:30:31
Flat Fork 210 1 31N52'51 94w12'39 6:16:51
Flatonia 75 1 29N41'15 97w06'30 6:28:26
Flat Prairie 74
1 33N27'45 95w58'41 6:23:55
Flat Rock 231 1 31N13'33 101w50'56 6:47:24
Flatrock Crossing (Ford) 163
1 29N34'21 99w24'07 6:37:36
Flatrock Ford 105
1 30N04'13 97w53'26 6:31:34
Flats 190 1 32N50'18 95w52'57 6:23:32
Flat Top 217 1 33N01'28 100w05'51 6:40:23
Flatwood 234 1 32N27 95w42 6:22:48
Fleming 47 1 31N48'47 98w28'20 6:33:53
Fletcher 100 1 30N15'56 94w11'20 6:16:45
Flint 212 1 32N12'14 95w20'54 6:21:24
Flint Creek 252
1 33N06 98w35 6:34:20
Flo 145 1 31N25'05 95w54'46 6:23:39
Flomot 173 1 34N13'37 100w59'19 6:43:57
Flora 112 1 33N15'16 95w25'59 6:21:44
Florence 246 1 30N50'28 97w47'36 6:31:10
Florence Hill 57
1 32N40'23 97w00'54 6:28:04
Floresville 247
1 29N08'00 98w09'21 6:32:37
Florey 2 1 32N27'10 102w35'22 6:50:21
Flour Bluff 178
1 27N40'25 97w16'43 6:29:07
Flour Bluff Junction 178
1 27N47'06 97w29'33 6:29:58
Flowella 24 1 27N12'58 98w03'51 6:32:15
Flower Grove 159
1 32N29'57 101w53'07 6:47:32
Flower Hill 11 1 29N57'54 97w07'53 6:28:32
Flower Mound 61
1 33N00'52 97w05'48 6:28:23
Floy 75 1 29N46'58 97w05'56 6:28:24
Floyd 116 1 33N08'55 96w14'41 6:24:59
Floydada 77 1 33N59'04 101w20'14 6:45:21
Flugrath 22 1 30N06'10 98w31'10 6:34:05
Fluvanna 208 1 32N53'08 101w08'54 6:44:36
Flynn 145 1 31N09'03 96w07'27 6:24:30
Foard City 78 1 33N52'51 99w47'58 6:39:12
Fodice 113 1 31N10'22 95w18'06 6:21:12
Follett 148 3 36N26'02 100w08'28 6:40:34
Folley 173 1 34N17'33 100w56'15 6:43:45
Folsom 188 3 35N14'09 101w42'19 6:46:49
Folsom 210 1 31N51'07 94w15'38 6:17:03
Foncine 43 1 33N08 96w37 6:26:28
Fondren 101 1 29N32 95w07 6:20:28
Foot 43 1 33N08 96w37 6:26:28
Forbes 121 1 30N30'33 93w55'38 6:15:43
Ford Oaks 227 1 30N10'22 97w49'55 6:31:20
Fords Corner 203
1 31N28'54 94w00'21 6:16:01
Fords Prairie 75
1 29N53'45 97w09'36 6:28:38
Fordtran 235 1 29N04'01 97w00'30 6:28:02
Forest 37 1 31N31 95w01 6:20:04
Forestburg 169 1 33N31'59 97w33'23 6:30:14
Forest Chapel 139
1 33N51'54 95w37'01 6:22:28
Forest Cove 101
1 29N56 95w17 6:21:08
Forest Glade 147
1 31N37'50 96w31'18 6:26:05
Forest Grove 43
1 33N07'12 96w36'32 6:26:26
Forest Grove 107
1 32N18 95w29 6:21:56
Forest Heights 181
1 30N14'17 93w45'31 6:15:02
Forest Hill 139
1 33N35 95w54 6:23:36
Forest Hill 220
1 32N40'19 97w16'08 6:29:05
Forest Hill 250
1 32N50'11 95w25'04 6:21:40

Forest Hills 212
1 32N20 95w18 6:21:12
Forney 129 1 32N44'53 96w28'18 6:25:53
Forreston 70 1 32N15'22 96w51'54 6:27:28
Forsan 114 1 32N06'35 101w21'57 6:45:28
Fort Belknap Park 252
1 33N12 98w44 6:34:56
Fort Bliss 71 2 31N48 106w25 7:05:40
Fort Chadbourne 41
1 32N00'02 100w17'21 6:41:09
Fort Clark Springs 136
1 29N18'21 100w25'18 6:41:41
Fort Crockett 84
1 29N16'18 94w48'56 6:19:16
Fort Davis 122 1 30N35'17 103w53'39 6:55:35
Fort Gates 50 1 31N23'25 97w41'03 6:30:44
Fort Griffin 209
1 32N55'55 99w13'47 6:36:55
Fort Hancock 115
2 31N17'54 105w50'41 7:03:23
Fort Hood 14 1 31N08 97w45 6:31:00
Fort Inge 232 1 29N10'39 99w45'51 6:39:03
Fort Lancaster 53
1 30N40'00 101w41'44 6:46:47
Fort McIntosh 240
1 27N30'27 99w31'17 6:38:05
Fort McKavett 164
1 30N49'37 100w06'23 6:40:26
Fort Parker 147
1 31N33'49 96w32'49 6:26:11
Fort Quitman 115
2 31N03'45 105w35'00 7:02:20
Fort Ringgold 214
1 26N23 98w49 6:35:16
Fort Sam Houston 15
1 29N27 98w27 6:33:48
Fort Spunky 111
1 32N19'31 97w38'41 6:30:35
Fort Stockton 186
1 30N53'38 102w52'44 6:51:31
Fort Travis 84 1 29N21'48 94w45'27 6:19:02
Fort Wolters 182
1 32N50 98w04 6:32:16
Fort Worth 220 1 32N43'31 97w19'14 6:29:17
Foster 79 1 29N39'01 95w49'55 6:23:20
Foster 223 1 33N03'54 102w17'27 6:49:10
Foster Place 101
1 29N41'39 95w21'06 6:21:24
Foster Store 26
1 30N32 96w42 6:26:48
Fosterville 1 1 32N00'38 95w36'52 6:22:27
Fostoria 170 1 30N19'34 95w09'58 6:20:40
Fouke 250 1 32N37'40 95w16'26 6:21:06
Fountain 21 1 30N40'20 96w29'01 6:25:56
Four Corners 20
1 29N02 95w34 6:22:16
Four Corners 31
1 25N55'13 97w27'58 6:29:52
Four Corners 170
1 30N19 95w28 6:21:52
Four Corner Windmill 53
1 30N37'37 101w33'48 6:46:15
Four Corner Windmill 192
1 31N17'31 101w35'58 6:46:24
Fourmile Crossing 22
1 30N12'20 103w10'49 6:52:43
Fourmile Crossing 164
1 30N54'50 99w51'09 6:39:25
Four Points 227
1 30N24'13 97w51'12 6:31:25
Fourth Crossing 46
1 29N50'33 98w10'03 6:32:40
Four Way 171 3 35N41 102w20 6:49:20
Fowlerton 142 1 28N27'55 98w48'38 6:35:15
Fowlkes 243 1 33N59'36 98w50'03 6:35:20
Fox 184 1 32N46'19 97w54'15 6:31:37
Frame 39 1 33N48'53 98w13'17 6:32:53
Frame Switch 246
1 30N34 97w25 6:29:40
Francis 181 1 30N05'22 93w46'35 6:15:06
Francitas 120 1 28N51'34 96w20'18 6:25:21
Frankel City 2 1 32N23'03 102w46'54 6:51:08
Frankell 215 1 32N37'27 98w43'05 6:34:52
Franklin 198 1 31N01'33 96w29'06 6:25:56
Franklin Center 208
1 32N43'47 101w01'52 6:44:07
Frankston 1 1 32N03'09 95w30'22 6:22:01
Frankston Lake 1
1 32N03 95w30 6:22:00
Fratt 15 1 29N31'02 98w23'48 6:33:35
Fred 229 1 30N34'35 94w10'34 6:16:42
Fredericksburg 86
1 30N16'30 98w52'18 6:35:29
Fredonia 92 1 32N24'13 94w47'45 6:19:11
Fredonia 160 1 30N55'55 99w06'47 6:36:27
Fredonia Hill 174
1 31N35'32 94w39'52 6:18:39
Freedom 155 1 31N33 97w08 6:28:32
Freeland 126 1 32N11'49 97w33'58 6:30:16
Freemound 49 1 33N33'38 97w28'34 6:29:54
Freeneytown 201
1 31N57'05 94w52'05 6:19:28
Freeport 20 1 28N57'14 95w21'34 6:21:26
Freer 66 1 27N52'57 98w37'03 6:34:28
Freestone 81 1 31N32'32 96w14'52 6:24:59
Freeway Oaks 170
1 29N47 95w23 6:21:32
Freiheit 46 1 29N43'01 98w04'07 6:32:16
Freisburg 45 1 29N52'15 96w32'47 6:26:11
Frenstat 26 1 30N23'50 96w39'11 6:26:37
Fresenius 100 1 30N22'32 94w14'14 6:16:57
Fresno 79 1 29N32'19 95w26'50 6:21:47
Freyburg 75 1 29N45'27 96w57'59 6:27:52
Friars 201 1 32N13'54 94w54'15 6:19:37
Friday 228 1 31N06'29 95w15'43 6:21:03
Friendly Corner 15
1 29N29'50 98w11'42 6:32:47
Friendship 58 1 32N37'58 102w01'53 6:48:08
Friendship 60 1 33N18'47 95w44'44 6:22:59
Friendship 121 1 30N46'54 93w52'26 6:15:30
Friendship 140 1 33N59'15 102w34'24 6:50:18
Friendship 145 1 31N17'40 96w06'32 6:24:26
Friendship 212 1 32N29'24 95w01'20 6:20:05

Friendship 228 1 31N13'36 95w11'19 6:20:45
Friendship 230 1 32N46'50 94w53'42 6:19:35
Friendship 246 1 30N42'50 97w19'48 6:29:19
Friendswood 84 1 29N31'45 95w12'03 6:20:48
Friona 185 3 34N38'30 102w43'25 6:50:54
Frio Town 82 1 29N01'09 99w18'09 6:37:13
Frisco 43 1 33N09'02 96w49'24 6:27:18
Fritch 117 3 35N38'23 101w36'10 6:46:25
Frog 129 1 32N43'06 96w08'24 6:24:34
Frog Hop 139 1 33N30'37 95w32'15 6:22:09
Frognot 43 1 33N18'13 96w21'34 6:25:26
Front 183 1 32N18 94w10 6:16:40
Fronton 214 1 26N24'24 99w05'01 6:36:20
Frosa 147 1 31N37'38 96w41'50 6:26:47
Frost 175 1 32N04'48 96w48'23 6:27:14
Fruitdale 57 1 32N42'25 96w46'08 6:27:05
Fruitland 169 1 33N30'06 97w47'43 6:31:11
Fruitvale 234 1 32N40'59 95w48'11 6:23:13
Frydek 8 1 29N45'11 96w05'17 6:24:21
Fulbright 194 1 33N32'54 95w15'03 6:21:00
Fulda 12 1 33N41'14 99w01'22 6:36:05
Fuller 242 3 35N14'29 100w04'53 6:40:20
Fuller Springs 3
1 30N15 95w32 6:22:08
Fullerville 208
1 32N55'31 101w03'54 6:44:16
Fulshear 79 1 29N41'23 95w53'58 6:23:36
Fulton 4 1 28N03'40 97w02'27 6:28:10
Fulton Beach 4 1 28N04 97w02 6:28:08
Funston 127 1 32N45'05 99w47'59 6:39:12
Fuqua 146 1 30N26'49 94w44'10 6:18:57
Furguson 95 1 34N07'43 101w44'54 6:47:00
Furney Richardson 81
1 31N38 96w17 6:25:08
Fussel 201 1 31N58 94w49 6:19:16
Gadston 139 1 33N28'51 95w35'14 6:22:21
Gageby 242 3 35N37'11 100w20'23 6:41:22
Gage Corner Windmill 135
1 33N40'17 100w29'58 6:42:00
Gail 17 1 32N46'13 101w26'42 6:45:47
Gainesmore 161 1 28N55'03 95w41'27 6:22:46
Gainesville 49 1 33N37'33 97w07'59 6:28:32
Gainesville 102
1 32N36'59 94w19'09 6:17:17
Gainesville 150
1 30N40'39 98w31'16 6:34:05
Galena Park 101
1 29N44 95w14 6:20:56
Galilee 212 1 32N15'58 95w25'42 6:21:43
Galilee 236 1 30N41'48 95w38'22 6:22:33
Gallatin 37 1 31N53'27 95w08'43 6:20:35
Gallaway 183 1 31N58 93w57 6:15:48
Galle 94 1 29N44'17 97w54'50 6:31:39
Galloway 34 1 33N02'08 94w11'16 6:16:45
Galloway 123 1 29N58'20 94w12'49 6:16:51
Galveston 84 1 29N18 94w48 6:19:12
Galveston Island 84
1 29N14 94w56 6:19:44
Gamblin 250 1 32N53'29 95w34'58 6:22:20
Ganado 120 1 29N02'25 96w30'48 6:26:03
Gandy 27 1 30N43'07 98w13'53 6:32:56
Gannon 76 1 32N33'24 100w28'59 6:41:56
Gano 246 1 30N37 97w12 6:28:48
Garceno 214 1 26N24'22 98w56'21 6:35:45
Garciasville 214
1 26N19'08 98w41'37 6:34:46
Garden Acres 220
1 32N35'40 97w18'08 6:29:13
Garden City 87 1 31N51'50 101w28'51 6:45:55
Garden City 101
1 29N51 95w27 6:21:48
Gardendale 68 1 32N01'13 102w22'47 6:49:31
Gardendale 142 1 28N31'00 99w12'57 6:36:52
Gardendale 178 1 27N42'17 97w22'51 6:29:31
Garden Ridge 46
1 29N30 98w25 6:33:40
Garden Valley 38
1 34N23 100w04 6:40:16
Garden Valley 212
1 32N31 95w25 6:21:40
Garden Villas 235
1 28N48 96w59 6:27:56
Garfield 62 1 29N02'32 97w39'06 6:30:36
Garfield 227 1 30N11'14 97w33'27 6:30:14
Garland 19 1 33N30'59 94w40'09 6:18:41
Garland 57 1 32N54'45 96w38'19 6:26:33
Garner 184 1 32N49'59 97w59'06 6:31:56
Garrett 70 1 32N21'48 96w39'16 6:26:37
Garretts Bluff 139
1 33N52'17 95w43'14 6:22:53
Garrison 174 1 31N49'27 94w29'27 6:17:58
Garth 101 1 29N46 95w00 6:20:00
Gartman View 47
1 31N56'29 98w34'16 6:34:17
Garvin 249 1 33N05 97w34 6:30:16
Garwood 45 1 29N26'58 96w23'48 6:25:35
Gary 170 1 30N19'38 95w43'26 6:22:54
Gary 183 1 32N01'43 94w22'15 6:17:29
Garza Crossing 15
1 29N16'59 98w36'49 6:34:27
Gasco 57 1 32N39 96w56 6:27:44
Gasoline 23 1 34N22 101w03 6:44:12
Gastonia 129 1 32N36'42 96w24'08 6:25:37
Gatesville 50 1 31N26'06 97w44'37 6:30:58
Gatewood 101 1 29N55 95w20 6:21:20
Gause 166 1 30N47'06 96w43'16 6:26:53
Gay Hill 75 1 29N53'11 96w45'37 6:27:02
Gay Hill 239 1 30N16'18 96w29'38 6:25:59
Gaylord 148 3 36N26'30 100w26'25 6:41:46
Gem 106 3 35N47'07 100w07'23 6:40:30
Geneva 202 1 31N28'37 93w55'02 6:15:40
Genoa 101 1 29N37'23 95w11'49 6:20:47
Gentry 188 3 35N17'46 101w59'31 6:47:58
Gentry Crossing 224
1 33N03'21 99w20'26 6:37:22
Gentrys Mill 97
1 31N47'31 98w13'31 6:32:54
George 157 1 30N58'18 96w06'32 6:24:26
Georges Creek 213
1 32N17'38 97w38'15 6:30:33
Georgetown 246 1 30N37'57 97w40'37 6:30:42
George West 149
1 28N19'56 98w07'02 6:32:28

Georgia 139 1 33N45'14 95w49'52 6:23:19
Gerald 155 1 31N33 97w09 6:28:36
Germania 165 1 32N03'53 101w56'23 6:47:46
Geronimo 94 1 29N39'46 97w58'00 6:31:52
Gethsemane 158 1 32N48'09 94w06'33 6:16:26
Gholson 155 1 31N42'03 97w12'58 6:28:52
Gibtown 119 1 33N01'55 97w56'53 6:31:48
Giddings 144 1 30N10'57 96w56'10 6:27:45
Gifford 57 1 32N53'52 96w45'56 6:27:04
Gilbert 3 1 30N15 95w32 6:22:08
Gilbert Landing 101
1 29N47'59 95w03'21 6:20:13
Gilbreth 250 1 32N53'46 95w33'34 6:22:14
Gilburg 123 1 30N08'37 94w10'13 6:16:41
Gilchrist 101 1 29N30'44 94w29'20 6:17:57
Giles 65 3 34N49'08 100w35'08 6:42:21
Gill 102 1 32N23'34 94w20'27 6:17:22
Gillett 128 1 29N07'41 97w47'05 6:31:08
Gilliland 138 1 33N43'53 99w40'59 6:38:44
Gillis 172 1 33N01'34 94w45'50 6:19:03
Gilmer 181 1 30N06 93w46 6:15:04
Gilmer 230 1 32N43'43 94w56'32 6:19:46
Gilpin 63 1 33N24'54 100w42'58 6:42:52
Gilson Groves 64
1 28N16'09 99w45'19 6:39:01
Ginger 190 1 32N50'59 95w43'10 6:22:53
Ginsite 51 1 33N56'52 100w21'39 6:41:27
Girard 132 1 33N21'44 100w39'45 6:42:39
Girvin 186 1 31N03'46 102w23'17 6:49:33
Gist 121 1 30N16'27 93w54'20 6:15:37
Givens 139 1 33N41'36 95w30'18 6:22:01
Gladewater 92 1 32N32'11 94w56'33 6:19:46
Gladewater 225 1 33N14'40 94w56'44 6:19:47
Gladewater Park 92
1 32N30'41 94w58'37 6:19:54
Glad Tidings 100
1 30N22 94w19 6:17:16
Gladwater 225 1 33N09 94w58 6:19:52
Gladys 123 1 30N00'06 94w04'18 6:16:17
Gladys 169 1 33N37'03 97w30'59 6:30:04
Glass 213 1 32N03 97w45 6:31:00
Glaze City 89 1 29N24'25 97w17'18 6:29:09
Glazier 106 3 36N00'41 100w15'48 6:41:03
Glecker 143 1 29N41 96w54 6:27:36
Glen Cove 42 1 31N51'57 99w38'14 6:38:33
Glen Cove 84 1 29N32'54 95w02'54 6:20:12
Glencrest 220 1 32N42 97w16 6:29:04
Glendale 228 1 31N00'56 95w18'03 6:21:12
Glenfawn 201 1 31N54'49 94w51'24 6:19:26
Glen Flora 241 1 29N20'50 96w11'35 6:24:46
Glen Hill 199 1 32N53'41 96w28'27 6:25:54
Glenn 63 1 33N46'51 100w50'48 6:43:23
Glenn Heights 57
1 32N37 96w51 6:27:24
Glenrio 180 3 35N10'43 103w02'31 6:52:10
Glen Rose 213 1 32N14'04 97w45'18 6:31:01
Glenwood 230 1 32N38'27 94w50'38 6:19:23
Glidden 45 1 29N42'02 96w35'10 6:26:21
Globe 139 1 33N44'41 95w42'19 6:22:49
Glory 139 1 33N32'00 95w32'21 6:22:09
Gluck 188 3 35N21'57 101w48'44 6:47:15
Gober 14 1 31N05'54 97w22'07 6:29:28
Gober 74 1 33N20'00 96w05'18 6:24:21
Godley 126 1 32N26'56 97w31'35 6:30:06
Goforth 105 1 30N01'18 97w47'35 6:31:10
Gold 86 1 30N17 98w52 6:35:28
Golden 250 1 32N43'46 95w33'46 6:22:15
Golden Acres 101
1 29N40'14 95w09'10 6:20:37
Goldfinch 82 1 28N51'31 98w52'23 6:35:30
Goldsboro 42 1 32N03'36 99w40'51 6:38:43
Goldsmith 68 1 31N58'50 102w36'53 6:50:28
Goldthwaite 167
1 31N26'59 98w34'14 6:34:17
Golfcrest 101 1 29N41'28 95w17'55 6:21:12
Goliad 88 1 28N40'05 97w23'17 6:29:33
Golinda 73 1 31N22'39 97w04'57 6:28:20
Golly 62 1 28N56'36 97w15'41 6:29:03
Gomez 223 1 33N10'54 102w22'39 6:49:31
Gonzales 89 1 29N30'05 97w27'08 6:29:49
Goober Hill 210
1 31N39'05 93w55'51 6:15:43
Goodfellow Air Force Base 226
1 31N28 100w27 6:41:48
Good Hope 143 1 29N27'07 96w53'58 6:27:36
Good Hope 210 1 31N48 94w11 6:16:44
Goodland 40 1 33N52'22 102w58'32 6:51:54
Goodland 198 1 30N52'55 96w40'04 6:26:40
Goodlett 99 3 34N20'06 99w52'47 6:39:31
Goodlow Park 175
1 32N06'55 96w13'05 6:24:52
Goodnight 6 3 35N02'04 101w11'09 6:44:45
Goodnight 175 1 32N07'18 96w09'34 6:24:38
Goodrich 187 1 30N36'19 94w56'47 6:19:47
Good Springs 201
1 32N03'22 94w54'38 6:19:39
Goodville 73 1 31N12 97w02 6:28:08
Goodwill 26 1 30N38'29 96w37'37 6:26:30
Goodwill 239 1 30N14'31 96w11'05 6:24:44
Goodwin 203 1 31N25'33 94w16'13 6:17:05
Gordon 153 1 33N12 101w23 6:45:32
Gordon 182 1 32N32'54 98w22'08 6:33:29
Gordon Junction 182
1 32N32'04 98w19'04 6:33:16
Gordonville 91 1 33N47'44 96w51'10 6:27:25
Goree 138 1 33N28'02 99w31'27 6:38:06
Gore Landing 100
1 30N24'38 94w07'10 6:16:29
Gorman 67 1 32N12'49 98w40'13 6:34:41
Goshen 184 1 32N57'39 97w44'47 6:30:59
Goshen 236 1 30N43 95w33 6:22:12
Gospel Hill 236
1 30N49'44 95w21'18 6:21:25
Gossett 129 1 32N26 96w05 6:24:20
Gough 60 1 33N20'38 95w48'01 6:23:12
Gould 37 1 32N03'20 95w09'02 6:20:36
Gouldbusk 42 1 31N33'17 99w28'35 6:37:54
Gover 91 1 33N44'09 96w25'26 6:25:42
Gozar 195 1 31N12'48 103w55'41 6:55:43
Graball 239 1 30N15'54 96w08'03 6:24:32
Graceton 230 1 32N42'52 94w47'20 6:19:09
Grady 146 1 30N20'28 95w06'05 6:20:24
Grady 159 1 32N18'24 101w55'48 6:47:43

Graford 182 1 32N56'15 98w14'48 6:32:59
Graham 85 1 33N09'02 101w28'09 6:45:53
Graham 252 1 33N06'25 98w35'21 6:34:21
Graham Chapel 85
1 33N12 101w23 6:45:32
Granbury 111 1 32N26'31 97w47'38 6:31:11
Grand Bluff 183
1 32N16'18 94w20'35 6:17:22
Grandfalls 238 1 31N20'21 102w51'05 6:51:24
Grand Lake 170 1 30N19 95w28 6:21:52
Grand Prairie 57
1 32N44'45 96w59'51 6:27:59
Grand Saline 234
1 32N40'24 95w42'33 6:22:50
Grandview 19 1 33N26 94w04 6:16:16
Grandview 58 1 32N54'36 101w59'50 6:47:59
Grandview 126 1 32N16'13 97w10'44 6:28:43
Grange Hall 102
1 32N34 94w25 6:17:40
Granger 246 1 30N43'03 97w26'33 6:29:46
Grangerland 170
1 30N15'09 95w19'45 6:21:19
Granite Shoals 27
1 30N35 98w24 6:33:36
Granite Shoals Lake Shores 150
1 30N40 98w26 6:33:44
Granjeno 108 1 26N08'04 98w18'16 6:33:13
Granville 3 1 31N16'52 94w50'18 6:19:22
Grapeland 113 1 31N29'30 95w28'42 6:21:55
Grapetown 86 1 30N08'50 98w49'05 6:35:16
Grapevine 220 1 32N56'03 97w04'40 6:28:19
Grassland 153 1 33N12 101w23 6:45:32
Grass Pond Colony 247
1 29N15'04 98w07'45 6:32:31
Gratis 181 1 30N08'56 93w49'47 6:15:19
Gravel Slough 57
1 32N32 96w40 6:26:40
Gray 158 1 32N47'15 94w04'24 6:16:18
Grayback 244 1 33N59'26 99w10'26 6:36:42
Grayburg 100 1 30N07'15 94w24'40 6:17:39
Gray Crossing 247
1 29N10'12 97w59'41 6:31:59
Gray Mule 77 1 34N17'20 101w05'38 6:44:23
Grays Chapel 1 1 31N46 95w38 6:22:32
Grays Prairie 129
1 32N28'19 96w20'57 6:25:24
Graytown 247 1 29N12'28 98w19'14 6:33:17
Great Southwest 220
1 32N45 97w06 6:28:24
Green 128 1 28N44'19 97w52'20 6:31:29
Green Acres 212
1 32N20 95w18 6:21:12
Greenfield Acres 68
1 31N52 102w22 6:49:28
Green Hill 225 1 33N14'53 94w59'45 6:19:59
Green Lake 29 1 28N31'45 96w47'36 6:27:10
Greenock 18 1 31N45'58 97w20'43 6:29:23
Greens Bayou 101
1 29N45'56 95w12'22 6:20:49
Greens Bluff 1 1 31N52'12 95w58'09 6:23:53
Greens Crossing 246
1 30N50'08 97w54'05 6:31:36
Greenshores 227
1 30N20'23 97w49'01 6:31:16
Green Valley 61
1 33N18'48 97w03'50 6:28:15
Greenview 112 1 33N01'20 95w43'00 6:22:52
Greenview Hills 57
1 32N51 96w58 6:27:52
Greenville 116 1 33N08 96w07 6:24:28
Greenvine 239 1 30N06'53 96w33'29 6:26:14
Greenwood 112 1 33N06'09 95w19'22 6:21:17
Greenwood 165 1 32N01'39 101w53'43 6:47:35
Greenwood 184 1 32N45'08 97w51'37 6:31:26
Greenwood 194 1 33N48'42 94w59'00 6:19:56
Greenwood 249 1 33N22'51 97w28'27 6:29:54
Greenwood Village 101
1 29N52'56 95w20'06 6:21:20
Gregg 227 1 30N21 97w33 6:30:12
Greggton 92 1 32N29'53 94w47'35 6:19:10
Gregory 205 1 27N55'19 97w17'23 6:29:10
Gresham 212 1 32N13'45 95w20'57 6:21:24
Grey Forest 15 1 29N36'55 98w40'50 6:34:43
Gribble 57 1 32N54'01 96w54'37 6:27:38
Grice 230 1 32N48'22 95w07'08 6:20:29
Griffin 37 1 32N02'17 95w04'31 6:20:18
Griffing 123 1 29N55 93w56 6:15:44
Griffing Park 123
1 29N55'03 93w55'27 6:15:42
Griffith 40 1 33N45'29 103w01'09 6:52:05
Griffith 70 1 32N22'09 97w04'41 6:28:19
Grigsby 210 1 31N39'18 94w23'29 6:17:34
Grimes 177 1 32N27'32 100w10'42 6:40:43
Grindstone 81 1 31N44 96w10 6:24:40
Grisham 35 1 34N20'02 102w01'01 6:48:04
Grisham Pumping Station 55
1 31N27'04 104w11'52 6:56:47
Grit 160 1 30N47 99w19 6:37:16
Grit 190 1 32N47 95w38 6:22:32
Groceville 170 1 30N20'27 95w20'02 6:21:20
Groesbeck 147 1 31N31'27 96w32'01 6:26:08
Groom 90 3 35N12'13 101w06'23 6:44:26
Grossville 160 1 30N41'02 99w12'04 6:36:48
Grosvenor 25 1 31N52'56 99w08'59 6:36:36
Groves 123 1 29N56'53 93w55'01 6:15:40
Groveton 228 1 31N03'17 95w07'32 6:20:30
Grow 135 1 33N48'35 100w17'54 6:41:12
Grubbe 112 1 32N57'48 95w35'57 6:22:24
Grub Hill 109 1 32N05'10 97w16'44 6:29:07
Gruenau 62 1 29N04'14 97w34'02 6:30:16
Gruene 46 1 29N44'17 98w06'13 6:32:25
Gruhlkey 180 3 35N15'55 102w44'37 6:50:58
Grulla 214 1 26N16 98w39 6:34:36
Gruver 98 3 36N15'54 101w24'21 6:45:37
Guadalupe 235 1 28N45'06 96w55'21 6:27:41
Guadalupe Heights 133
1 29N59'46 99w05'59 6:36:24
Guajillo 66 1 27N45 98w05 6:32:20
Guda 73 1 31N21'31 97w01'57 6:28:08
Gude 81 1 31N45'22 96w28'07 6:25:52
Guerra 124 1 26N52'58 98w53'36 6:35:34
Guffey 123 1 30N01'07 94w04'55 6:16:20
Guilbeau 15 1 29N24 98w30 6:34:00

Guild 186 1 30N57'21 102w52'30 6:51:30
Gulf 161 1 28N43'16 95w53'30 6:23:34
Gulf Camp 238 1 31N35 102w53 6:51:32
Gulf Hill 161 1 28N45'25 95w55'47 6:23:43
Gulf Park 20 1 28N57'39 95w24'49 6:21:39
Gum Springs 34 1 33N08'58 94w21'38 6:17:27
Gum Springs 102
1 32N27'35 94w40'35 6:18:42
Gum Springs 201
1 32N04'54 94w55'37 6:19:42
Gun Barrel City 107
1 32N20'04 96w09'04 6:24:36
Gunsight 215 1 32N32'29 98w52'15 6:35:29
Gunter 43 1 33N26'52 96w44'50 6:26:59
Gunter 250 1 32N52'07 95w37'46 6:22:31
Gus 26 1 30N27'19 96w51'27 6:27:26
Gustine 47 1 31N50'42 98w24'09 6:33:37
Guthrie 135 1 33N37'14 100w19'21 6:41:17
Guy 79 1 29N20'38 95w46'58 6:23:08
Guys Store 145 1 31N16 95w59 6:23:56
Gwinns Crossing (Historical) 45
1 29N32'23 96w28'15 6:25:53
Haby Crossing 232
1 29N19'42 99w56'49 6:39:47
Hacienda Heights 71
2 31N44'34 106w21'11 7:05:25
Hackberry 15 1 29N24 98w28 6:33:52
Hackberry 51 1 33N55'56 100w08'50 6:40:35
Hackberry 69 1 29N55'38 100w00'44 6:40:03
Hackberry 85 1 33N17'13 101w33'21 6:46:13
Hackberry 143 1 29N34'41 96w52'46 6:27:31
Hackberry Crossing 233
1 30N13'07 101w39'25 6:46:38
Haeckerville 94
1 29N33'42 98w13'01 6:32:52
Hagansport 80 1 33N20'29 95w14'57 6:21:00
Hagerville 113 1 31N20'40 95w04'52 6:20:19
Hahn 241 1 29N16'52 96w23'48 6:25:35
Haid 241 1 29N13 96w02 6:24:08
Hail 74 1 33N30'03 96w03'26 6:24:14
Hainesville 250
1 32N43'03 95w21'51 6:21:27
Halbert 210 1 31N46 93w52 6:15:28
Hale Center 95 1 34N03'51 101w50'36 6:47:22
Halesboro 194 1 33N27'43 95w18'11 6:21:13
Halfway 95 1 34N11'17 101w57'07 6:47:48
Hall 158 1 32N49'08 94w19'43 6:17:19
Hall 206 1 31N17'06 99w03'05 6:36:12
Hallettsville 143
1 29N26'37 96w56'27 6:27:46
Hallmark Crossing 141
1 31N05'08 98w03'04 6:32:12
Halls Bluff 113
1 31N21'16 95w39'26 6:22:38
Hallsburg 155 1 31N32'19 96w57'21 6:27:49
Halls Store 183
1 32N22 94w03 6:16:12
Hallsville 102 1 32N30'15 94w34'26 6:18:18
Halsell 39 1 33N43'10 98w20'40 6:33:23
Halsted 75 1 29N54'26 96w46'53 6:27:08
Haltom City 220
1 32N47'58 97w16'08 6:29:05
Hamby 221 1 32N31'07 99w37'51 6:38:31
Hamilton 97 1 31N42'13 98w07'25 6:32:30
Hamlin 76 1 32N53'05 100w07'34 6:40:30
Hammetts Crossing 227
1 30N20'24 98w08'16 6:32:33
Hammond 198 1 31N05'42 96w42'49 6:26:51
Hamon 89 1 29N23'44 97w22'00 6:29:28
Hampton 229 1 30N56 94w36 6:18:24
Hamrick 42 1 31N51'30 99w28'47 6:37:55
Hamshire 123 1 29N51'41 94w18'44 6:17:15
Hancock 58 1 32N49'08 101w51'46 6:47:27
Handley 220 1 32N43'57 97w13'04 6:28:52
Handy 166 1 30N39 97w00 6:28:00
Hanger 91 1 33N42'40 96w45'27 6:27:02
Hankamer 101 1 29N51'29 94w37'36 6:18:30
Hannibal 72 1 32N22'25 98w20'07 6:33:20
Hanover 166 1 30N48'13 96w49'17 6:27:17
Hansford 98 3 36N12'05 101w18'06 6:45:12
Hanson 210 1 31N58 94w03 6:16:12
Happy 219 3 34N44'37 101w51'15 6:47:25
Happy Hill 126 1 32N28'07 97w14'11 6:28:57
Happy Hollow 232
1 29N37'18 99w45'12 6:39:01
Happy Union 95 1 34N01'15 101w41'46 6:46:47
Happy Valley 174
1 31N50'10 94w46'57 6:19:08
Happy Valley 221
1 32N07'57 100w06'32 6:40:26
Harbin 72 1 32N07'00 98w16'23 6:33:06
Harbor Grove 61
1 33N06'45 97w03'01 6:28:12
Hardin 146 1 30N09'08 94w44'20 6:18:57
Hardin-Simmons 221
1 32N28 99w44 6:38:56
Hardy 169 1 33N34'35 97w31'13 6:30:05
Hardy Heights 101
1 29N53'00 95w22'02 6:21:28
Hare 246 1 30N40'15 97w16'22 6:29:05
Hargill 108 1 26N26'32 98w00'49 6:32:03
Harker Heights 14
1 31N05 97w39 6:30:36
Harkeyville 206
1 31N12'38 98w47'07 6:35:08
Harlandale 15 1 29N21 98w29 6:33:56
Harlem 79 1 29N36'56 95w42'45 6:22:51
Harleton 102 1 32N40'35 94w34'28 6:18:18
Harlingen 31 1 26N11'25 97w41'45 6:30:47
Harmaston 101 1 29N58'39 95w09'32 6:20:38
Harmon 139 1 33N31'14 95w49'19 6:23:17
Harmony 1 1 31N45'29 95w47'37 6:23:10
Harmony 26 1 30N26'55 96w39'24 6:26:38
Harmony 107 1 32N18'52 96w15'58 6:25:04
Harmony 112 1 33N00'16 95w20'43 6:21:23
Harmony 128 1 29N03'05 97w49'06 6:31:16
Harmony 132 1 33N02'26 100w33'44 6:42:15
Harmony 184 1 32N41'42 97w47'46 6:31:11
Harmony 201 1 32N16 94w59 6:19:56
Harmony 203 1 31N36'59 94w11'04 6:16:44
Harmony 236 1 30N43'58 95w28'36 6:21:54
Harmony Hill 201
1 32N19 94w31 6:18:04

Harper 86 1 30N17'59 99w14'38 6:36:59
Harpers Crossing 112
1 33N18'39 95w38'50 6:22:35
Harpersville 215
1 32N36'00 98w56'02 6:35:44
Harrells 176 1 30N39'55 93w49'50 6:15:19
Harriet 226 1 31N32'49 100w19'06 6:41:16
Harrisburg 101 1 29N43'05 95w16'46 6:21:07
Harrisburg 121 1 31N00'42 93w53'23 6:15:34
Harrisdale 68 1 31N52 102w22 6:49:28
Harrison 155 1 31N31'21 96w59'55 6:28:00
Harrold 244 1 34N04'50 99w01'55 6:36:08
Hart 35 1 34N23'06 102w06'55 6:48:28
Hartburg 176 1 30N15'27 93w45'52 6:15:03
Hart Camp 140 1 33N55 102w20 6:49:20
Hartex 5 1 33N49'14 98w40'37 6:34:42
Hartland 24 1 26N49'28 98w08'50 6:32:35
Hartley 103 3 35N53'08 102w23'47 6:49:35
Hartman 19 1 33N22'42 94w10'06 6:16:40
Harts Bluff 194
1 33N23'50 94w57'21 6:19:49
Hart Spur 220 1 32N50 97w10 6:28:40
Hartzo 158 1 32N46 94w21 6:17:24
Harvard 32 1 33N03'35 94w58'05 6:19:52
Harvest Heights 101
1 29N51 95w27 6:21:48
Harvey 21 1 30N39'17 96w16'30 6:25:06
Harwood 89 1 29N39'56 97w30'18 6:30:01
Hasima 20 1 29N01'41 95w46'27 6:23:06
Haskell 104 1 33N09'27 99w44'00 6:38:56
Haslam 210 1 31N58'02 94w01'37 6:16:06
Haslet 220 1 32N58'29 97w20'51 6:29:23
Hasse 47 1 31N56'11 98w29'18 6:33:57
Hastings 20 1 29N30'31 95w15'05 6:21:00
Hatchel 200 1 31N51'00 99w56'56 6:39:48
Hatchetville 112
1 33N15'34 95w31'46 6:22:07
Hathaway 100 1 30N07'39 94w28'54 6:17:56
Havana 108 1 26N14'41 98w30'33 6:34:02
Hawdon 79 1 29N28'43 95w28'20 6:21:53
Hawkins 250 1 32N35'18 95w12'14 6:20:49
Hawkinsville 161
1 28N53'15 95w40'10 6:22:41
Hawley 127 1 32N36'43 99w48'50 6:39:15
Hawthorne 210 1 31N36'17 94w01'47 6:16:07
Hawthorne 236 1 30N32'04 95w23'42 6:21:35
Hawthorne Place 101
1 29N51'25 95w21'52 6:21:27
Hay City 105 1 30N02'50 97w59'17 6:31:57
Hayden 234 1 32N43 96w00 6:24:00
Hayford Crossing 224
1 33N03'35 99w21'24 6:37:26
Haymond 22 1 30N08'37 103w01'08 6:52:05
Haynesville (Punkin Center) 243
1 34N05'29 98w54'56 6:35:40
Hays Crossing 42
1 31N28'12 99w26'00 6:37:44
Hays Spring 113
1 31N28'14 95w31'54 6:22:08
Hayward Junction 174
1 31N35'20 94w38'56 6:18:36
Hazeldell 47 1 31N52'53 98w19'54 6:33:20
Headsville 198 1 31N15'40 96w29'44 6:25:59
Heafer 15 1 29N20'36 98w35'02 6:34:20
Heaker 101 1 29N38'33 95w28'09 6:21:53
Heakers 101 1 29N38'00 95w29'56 6:22:00
Heald 242 3 35N14 100w36 6:42:24
Hearne 198 1 30N52'42 96w35'34 6:26:22
Heath 199 1 32N50'11 96w28'29 6:25:54
Heaton 90 3 35N32'53 100w48'30 6:43:14
Hebbronville 124
1 27N18'23 98w40'41 6:34:43
Hebert 123 1 29N59'07 94w03'42 6:16:15
Hebron 61 1 33N01'35 96w51'48 6:27:27
Heckville 152 1 33N45'17 101w39'53 6:46:40
Hedley 65 3 34N52'01 100w39'36 6:42:38
Hedwigs Hill 160
1 30N39'56 99w06'42 6:36:27
Hedwig Village 101
1 29N46'38 95w31'01 6:22:04
Hefner 138 1 33N31'59 99w31'59 6:38:08
Hegar 237 1 30N06'57 95w49'39 6:23:19
Heidelberg 108 1 26N11'48 97w52'48 6:31:31
Heidenheimer 14
1 31N01'05 97w18'09 6:29:13
Heights 84 1 29N23'19 94w55'49 6:19:43
Helbig 123 1 30N07'47 94w08'32 6:16:34
Heldnfelt 205 1 28N07'59 97w51'30 6:31:26
Helena 128 1 28N57'13 97w49'23 6:31:18
Helmic 228 1 31N10'50 94w59'11 6:19:57
Helms 45 1 29N39'01 96w30'10 6:26:01
Helotes 15 1 29N34'40 98w41'22 6:34:45
Helotes Park Estates 15
1 29N37 98w41 6:34:44
Helotes Ranch Acres 15
1 29N37 98w41 6:34:44
Hemming 49 1 33N25'53 97w05'08 6:28:21
Hemphill 202 1 31N20'26 93w50'48 6:15:23
Hempstead 237 1 30N05'50 96w04'41 6:24:19
Henderson 201 1 32N09'11 94w47'57 6:19:12
Hendrix 116 1 33N01'18 96w14'05 6:24:56
Henkhaus 143 1 29N30'37 97w09'08 6:28:37
Henly 105 1 30N11'40 98w12'38 6:32:51
Hennessey 101 1 29N47'05 95w32'38 6:22:11
Henning 174 1 31N50 94w30 6:18:00
Henrietta 39 1 33N49'02 98w11'42 6:32:47
Henrys Chapel 37
1 32N08 95w07 6:20:28
Herbert 79 1 29N35'21 95w35'37 6:22:22
Hereford 59 3 34N48'54 102w23'50 6:49:35
Heritage Hills 227
1 30N22 97w41 6:30:44
Herman 249 1 33N10'02 97w31'56 6:30:08
Hermits Cove 190
1 32N53'58 95w53'07 6:23:32
Hermleigh 208 1 32N38'06 100w45'32 6:43:02
Hermosa 195 1 31N22'35 103w38'28 6:54:34
Herndon 177 1 32N28'55 100w12'48 6:40:51
Herring 1 1 31N45'32 95w24'03 6:21:36
Herring 226 1 31N28 100w27 6:41:48
Herty 3 1 31N21'22 94w40'59 6:18:44
Hester 175 1 32N06 96w31 6:26:04
Hewitt 155 1 31N27'44 97w11'44 6:28:47

Hext 164 1 30N52'08 99w31'42 6:38:07
Heyser 29 1 28N35'08 96w50'09 6:27:21
Hickey 201 1 32N05'39 94w52'20 6:19:29
Hickmuntown 227
1 30N23 97w45 6:31:00
Hickory Creek 61
1 33N07'20 97w02'34 6:28:10
Hickory Creek 116
1 33N21'55 96w09'24 6:24:38
Hickory Grove 61
1 33N07 97w02 6:28:08
Hickory Hill 32
1 32N56'11 95w00'44 6:20:03
Hickory Ridge 202
1 31N12'45 93w38'31 6:14:34
Hicks 144 1 30N32'25 96w59'19 6:27:57
Hicksbaugh 229 1 30N33'42 94w21'00 6:17:24
Hicks Crossing 206
1 31N10'01 98w30'19 6:34:01
Hickston 89 1 29N36'10 97w16'29 6:29:06
Hico 97 1 31N58'58 98w02'00 6:32:08
Hidalgo 108 1 26N06'00 98w15'46 6:33:03
Hidden Acres 205
1 28N06'54 97w51'26 6:31:26
Hidden Echo 101
1 30N03'13 95w07'09 6:20:29
Hidden Hill 61 1 33N06'44 97w03'42 6:28:15
Hidden Valley 101
1 29N51 95w27 6:21:48
Hideaway Hill 149
1 28N11'12 97w53'36 6:31:34
Higginbotham 83
1 32N54'04 102w59'30 6:51:58
Higgins 123 1 30N03'28 94w05'07 6:16:20
Higgins 148 3 36N07'11 100w01'26 6:40:06
High 139 1 33N36'44 95w44'49 6:22:59
Highbank 73 1 31N10'11 96w50'00 6:27:20
High Hill 75 1 29N43'04 96w55'37 6:27:42
High Island 101
1 29N34'00 94w23'36 6:17:34
Highland 57 1 32N52'36 96w54'54 6:27:40
Highland 72 1 32N09'17 98w26'44 6:33:47
Highland 126 1 32N10'19 97w32'58 6:30:12
Highland 155 1 31N32'04 97w21'05 6:29:24
Highland Acres 91
1 33N46 96w40 6:26:40
Highland Acres 101
1 29N51 95w27 6:21:48
Highland Acres 116
1 32N57 95w56 6:23:44
Highland Addition 101
1 29N51 95w27 6:21:48
Highland Addition 184
1 32N58 97w41 6:30:44
Highland Bayou 84
1 29N21 95w01 6:20:04
Highland Estates 235
1 28N48 96w59 6:27:56
Highland Heights 101
1 29N51'48 95w25'40 6:21:43
Highland Hills 15
1 29N22 98w27 6:33:48
Highland Park 57
1 32N50 96w48 6:27:12
Highlands 101 1 29N49'07 95w03'21 6:20:13
Highland Village 61
1 33N05'30 97w02'47 6:28:11
Highland Village 101
1 29N45 95w29 6:21:56
Highland Waters 10
1 29N45'05 99w08'08 6:36:33
Hightower 146 1 30N23'29 94w58'19 6:19:53
High Valley 206
1 31N04'57 98w32'09 6:34:09
Hiland Shores 91
1 33N46 96w40 6:26:40
Hilburn 35 1 34N21'56 102w05'24 6:48:22
Hilda 160 1 30N35'12 99w06'51 6:36:27
Hilda Siding 94
1 29N35'17 98w04'13 6:32:17
Hilger 74 1 33N37'19 96w05'48 6:24:23
Hill 11 1 30N07 97w19 6:29:16
Hillard 33 3 35N36'21 101w24'42 6:45:39
Hill City 111 1 32N18'28 97w50'54 6:31:24
Hill Country Village 15
1 29N34'56 98w29'26 6:33:58
Hillcrest 20 1 29N23 95w13 6:20:52
Hill Crest 21 1 30N40 96w22 6:25:28
Hillcrest 45 1 29N44'55 96w36'03 6:26:24
Hillebrandt 123
1 29N55'59 94w06'47 6:16:27
Hillister 229 1 30N40'03 94w22'52 6:17:31
Hillje 241 1 29N08'55 96w20'35 6:25:22
Hills 144 1 30N13 97w07 6:28:28
Hillsboro 109 1 32N00'39 97w07'47 6:28:31
Hillshire 101 1 29N47'26 95w29'20 6:21:57
Hillside Gardens 101
1 29N55 95w20 6:21:20
Hilltop 86 1 30N23'51 98w58'06 6:35:52
Hilltop Lakes 145
1 31N04'45 96w12'13 6:24:49
Hilshire Village 101
1 29N47 95w29 6:21:56
Hilton 91 1 33N34'14 96w37'14 6:26:29
Hinckley 139 1 33N40 95w31 6:22:04
Hindes 7 1 28N43'00 98w47'24 6:35:10
Hindman 58 1 32N53'10 101w52'40 6:47:31
Hines 244 1 34N09 99w18 6:37:12
Hinkles Ferry 20
1 29N02 95w34 6:22:16
Hiram 129 1 32N38'36 96w06'29 6:24:26
Hitchcock 84 1 29N20'53 95w00'57 6:20:04
Hitchland 98 3 36N29'56 101w19'05 6:45:16
Hitson 76 1 32N53'40 100w12'41 6:40:51
Hix 26 1 30N41'52 96w39'43 6:26:39
Hoard 250 1 32N38'29 95w23'14 6:21:33
Hoban 195 1 31N11'39 103w34'32 6:54:18
Hobbs 14 1 31N03'07 97w26'21 6:29:45
Hobbs 76 1 32N46'53 100w35'29 6:42:22
Hobby 79 1 29N35'08 95w29'30 6:21:58
Hobson 128 1 28N57'26 97w59'06 6:31:56
Hochheim 62 1 29N18'44 97w17'29 6:29:10
Hockley 101 1 30N01'36 95w50'39 6:23:23

Hockley Mine 101
1 30N02 95w51 6:23:24
Hodges 127 1 32N35'21 99w52'07 6:39:28
Hodgson 19 1 33N28'19 94w41'09 6:18:45
Hoefer 45 1 29N36'07 96w14'33 6:24:58
Hoen 155 1 31N46'53 96w59'07 6:27:56
Hogansville 190
1 32N52'30 95w40'09 6:22:41
Hogeye 116 1 33N17'49 96w09'47 6:24:39
Hogg 26 1 30N26'07 96w47'54 6:27:12
Hogg 198 1 31N08'37 96w41'15 6:26:45
Hogpen Crossing 146
1 30N03'25 94w30'41 6:18:03
Holcombs Store 37
1 31N48 95w09 6:20:36
Holden 147 1 31N39'11 96w26'50 6:25:47
Holder 25 1 31N54'46 98w58'43 6:35:55
Holiday 61 1 33N03 97w03 6:28:12
Holiday Beach 4
1 28N10'07 97w00'36 6:28:02
Holiday Estates 116
1 32N43 96w00 6:24:00
Holiday Hills 190
1 32N57 95w56 6:23:44
Holland 14 1 30N52'41 97w24'05 6:29:36
Holland Quarters 183
1 32N10'08 94w25'33 6:17:42
Hollicott Crossing 180
3 35N31'58 102w22'45 6:49:31
Holliday 5 1 33N48'58 98w41'41 6:34:47
Hollis 157 1 31N01 95w55 6:23:40
Holly 113 1 31N07'47 95w20'13 6:21:21
Holly Grove 187
1 30N31'06 94w42'27 6:18:50
Holly Springs 32
1 32N55'32 94w48'57 6:19:16
Holly Springs 121
1 30N53'49 93w53'02 6:15:32
Holly Springs 174
1 31N45'15 94w34'50 6:18:19
Holly Springs 234
1 32N26'04 95w46'34 6:23:06
Hollywood 123 1 29N57 93w59 6:15:56
Hollywood Park 15
1 29N36'01 98w29'13 6:33:57
Holman 75 1 29N47'46 96w47'46 6:27:11
Holt 117 3 36N01'20 101w13'47 6:44:55
Holt 206 1 31N22'21 99w01'50 6:36:07
Homer 3 1 31N17'20 94w38'17 6:18:33
Homer Junction 154
1 31N09'53 99w30'35 6:38:02
Hondo 163 1 29N20'50 99w08'28 6:36:34
Honea 170 1 30N19'06 95w35'58 6:22:24
Honey Creek 46 1 29N48'18 98w30'03 6:34:00
Honey Grove 74 1 33N35'00 95w54'35 6:23:38
Honey Island 100
1 30N23'43 94w26'26 6:17:46
Hood 49 1 33N32'34 97w20'56 6:29:24
Hooks 19 1 33N27'58 94w17'18 6:17:09
Hoot 19 1 33N19'45 94w02'54 6:16:12
Hoot and Holler Crossing 244
1 33N57'17 99w14'22 6:36:57
Hoover 90 3 35N35'38 100w51'01 6:43:24
Hoover 139 1 33N35'07 95w20'21 6:21:21
Hoovers Valley 27
1 30N46 98w14 6:32:56
Hope 143 1 29N12'59 96w59'51 6:27:59
Hopewell 80 1 33N07'06 95w09'20 6:20:37
Hopewell 113 1 31N15'30 95w21'42 6:21:27
Hopewell 145 1 31N20'39 95w49'16 6:23:17
Horizon City 71
2 31N41'33 106w12'25 7:04:50
Horn Hill 147 1 31N34'08 96w38'00 6:26:32
Hornsby 227 1 30N14'50 97w34'59 6:30:20
Hornsby Bend 227
1 30N16 97w42 6:30:48
Horsehead Crossing 186
1 31N14'07 102w29'00 6:49:56
Hortense 187 1 30N50'45 94w42'15 6:18:49
Horton 60 1 33N15'44 95w49'14 6:23:17
Horton 121 1 31N04'13 93w57'46 6:15:51
Horton 183 1 32N18 94w10 6:16:40
Hoskins 20 1 29N00'34 95w23'03 6:21:32
Hostyn 75 1 29N50'44 96w55'10 6:27:41
Hot Springs 22 1 29N10'55 102w59'30 6:51:58
Hot Wells 101 1 29N57'24 95w40'54 6:22:44
Houmont Park 101
1 29N50'32 95w12'22 6:20:49
House Crossing 50
1 31N11'08 97w48'31 6:31:14
Houston 101 1 29N45'47 95w21'47 6:21:27
Houston Heights 101
1 29N47'52 95w23'52 6:21:35
Hovey 186 3 30N36'39 103w22'01 6:53:28
Howard 70 1 32N17'26 96w46'15 6:27:05
Howards 176 1 30N44'55 93w47'02 6:15:08
Howardwick 65 3 35N02'14 100w54'23 6:43:38
Howe 91 1 33N30'31 96w36'43 6:26:27
Howellville 101
1 29N43 95w35 6:22:20
Howland 139 1 33N31'59 95w38'19 6:22:33
Howth 237 1 30N10'07 96w03'54 6:24:16
Hoxie 246 1 30N39'15 97w20'45 6:29:23
Hoyt 250 1 32N47 95w38 6:22:32
Hoyte 166 1 30N47'05 96w54'55 6:27:40
Hub 185 3 34N38 102w43 6:50:52
Hubbard 19 1 33N27'59 94w38'18 6:18:33
Hubbard 109 1 31N50'54 96w47'49 6:27:11
Huber 210 1 31N49'34 94w19'14 6:17:17
Hubert 205 1 27N58'40 97w42'19 6:30:49
Huckabay 72 1 32N20'41 98w17'53 6:33:12
Hudd 208 1 32N55'35 100w40'46 6:42:43
Hudson 3 1 31N19 94w50 6:19:20
Hudson 101 1 29N54'08 95w30'08 6:22:01
Hudson Chapel 37
1 31N43'53 95w09'10 6:20:37
Hudsonville 74 1 33N42'39 96w02'23 6:24:10
Huff Creek 121 1 30N56'13 93w53'15 6:15:33
Huffins 34 1 32N59'57 94w08'08 6:16:33
Huffman 101 1 30N01'37 95w05'08 6:20:21
Hufsmith 101 1 30N07'19 95w35'47 6:22:23
Huggins 39 1 33N50'10 98w04'12 6:32:17
Hughes 235 1 28N45'05 96w58'16 6:27:53
Hughes Springs 34
1 32N59'54 94w37'50 6:18:31
Hulen Park 84 1 29N23 94w57 6:19:48
Hull 146 1 30N08'46 94w38'32 6:18:34
Hulldale 207 1 31N01'17 100w32'35 6:42:10
Hulver 96 1 34N31'38 100w30'55 6:42:04
Humble 101 1 29N59'55 95w15'43 6:21:03
Humble 112 1 33N01'00 95w22'02 6:21:28
Humble Camp 101
1 29N35'54 95w11'08 6:20:45
Humble Government Wells Camp 66
1 27N53 98w37 6:34:28
Humble Heights 101
1 29N56 95w17 6:21:08
Hume 37 1 31N56'40 95w19'57 6:21:20
Hungerford 241 1 29N23'56 96w04'36 6:24:18
Hunt 116 1 33N08 96w07 6:24:28
Hunt 133 1 30N04 99w20 6:37:20
Hunt Crossing 246
1 30N41'25 97w48'45 6:31:15
Hunter 46 1 29N48'25 98w01'24 6:32:06
Hunters Creek Village 101
1 29N46'13 95w29'43 6:21:59
Huntington 3 1 31N16'39 94w34'35 6:18:18
Huntoon 179 3 36N27'21 100w37'50 6:42:31
Huntsville 236 1 30N43'24 95w33'02 6:22:12
Hurlwood 152 1 33N34'36 102w02'15 6:48:09
Hurnville 39 1 33N57'31 98w10'09 6:32:41
Huron 109 1 32N02'23 97w21'35 6:29:26
Hurst 220 1 32N49'24 97w10'13 6:28:41
Hurstown 210 1 31N41'49 94w01'44 6:16:07
Hurst Springs 50
1 31N47 97w35 6:30:20
Hutchins 57 1 32N38'57 96w42'46 6:26:51
Hutto 246 1 30N32'33 97w32'47 6:30:11
Huxley 210 1 31N45'44 93w52'37 6:15:30
Hyatt 229 1 30N34'31 94w24'08 6:17:37
Hye 22 1 30N14'32 98w34'11 6:34:17
Hylton 177 1 32N07'41 100w12'09 6:40:49
Hyman 168 1 32N08'17 101w08'05 6:44:32
Hynds City 169 1 33N54'42 97w43'17 6:30:53
Iago 241 1 29N16'40 95w57'49 6:23:51
Iatan 168 1 32N22 101w01 6:44:04
Ida 91 1 33N34'30 96w29'23 6:25:58
Idalou 152 1 33N39'59 101w40'57 6:46:44
Idlewild 57 1 32N44 96w59 6:27:56
Idyle Hour Acres 227
1 30N25'34 97w40'29 6:30:42
Iglehart 227 1 30N15'31 97w42'24 6:30:50
Ike 70 1 32N24'13 96w46'12 6:27:05
Ike 149 1 28N23'28 98w09'15 6:32:37
Illinois Bend 169
1 33N52'54 97w29'13 6:29:57
Impact 221 1 32N30 99w45 6:39:00
Imperial 186 1 31N16'22 102w41'32 6:50:46
Inadale 208 1 32N32'27 100w40'58 6:42:44
Inari 196 1 28N30'50 97w03'14 6:28:13
Independence 239
1 30N19'09 96w20'47 6:25:23
India 70 1 32N31'30 96w36'57 6:26:28
Indian Creek 25
1 31N31'23 98w58'47 6:35:55
Indian Gap 97 1 31N39'46 98w24'47 6:33:39
Indian Hills 176
1 31N01'58 93w45'33 6:15:02
Indian Hot Springs 115
2 30N49'34 105w19'01 7:01:16
Indianola 29 1 28N30'42 96w29'14 6:25:57
Indian Rock 230
1 32N44 94w57 6:19:48
Indio 189 1 29N43'03 104w32'14 6:58:09
Industrial 57 1 32N47 96w49 6:27:16
Industry 8 1 29N58'20 96w30'07 6:26:00
Inez 235 1 28N54'13 96w47'16 6:27:09
Ingleside 205 1 27N52'39 97w12'41 6:28:51
Ingleside-on-the-Bay 205
1 27N49'45 97w13'23 6:28:54
Ingram 133 1 30N04'38 99w14'24 6:36:58
Inks Lake Village 150
1 30N45 98w25 6:33:40
Inwood 57 1 32N55'50 96w49'17 6:27:17
Iola 93 1 30N46'18 96w04'29 6:24:18
Iona 184 1 32N40'52 97w33'14 6:30:13
Iowa Colony 20 1 29N28'56 95w24'55 6:21:40
Iowa Park 243 1 33N57'05 98w40'06 6:34:40
Ira 208 1 32N34'55 101w00'06 6:44:00
Iraan 186 1 30N54'50 101w53'51 6:47:35
Irby 104 1 33N10'47 99w31'20 6:38:05
Iredell 18 1 31N59'06 97w52'18 6:31:29
Ireland 50 1 31N34'00 97w57'54 6:31:52
Irene 109 1 31N59'31 96w52'16 6:27:29
Ironton 37 1 31N55'08 95w22'24 6:21:30
Irving 57 1 32N48'50 96w56'55 6:27:48
Irvington 101 1 29N50 95w23 6:21:32
Irwin 56 3 36N11'30 102w18'41 6:49:15
Iser 115 2 31N22'15 105w55'20 7:03:41
Isla 71 2 31N29'14 106w12'21 7:04:49
Isla 202 1 31N26 93w51 6:15:24
Island 84 1 29N18 94w50 6:19:20
Island 157 1 31N02 95w45 6:23:00
Islitas 240 1 27N40'01 99w39'10 6:38:37
Italy 70 1 32N11'02 96w53'04 6:27:32
Itasca 109 1 32N09'34 97w08'59 6:28:36
Iuka 7 1 29N02'44 98w44'17 6:34:57
Ivan 215 1 32N52'28 98w43'59 6:34:56
Ivanhoe 74 1 33N42'47 96w08'37 6:24:34
Iverson 109 1 32N07 96w57 6:27:48
Izoro 141 1 31N17'39 98w04'31 6:32:18
Jacinto City 101
1 29N46'02 95w14'01 6:20:56
Jacksboro 119 1 33N13'06 98w09'30 6:32:38
Jackson 158 1 32N44'10 94w34'52 6:18:19
Jackson 210 1 31N56'02 94w03'35 6:16:14
Jackson 234 1 32N28'53 95w55'46 6:23:43
Jackson Crossing 50
1 31N14'54 97w50'15 6:31:21
Jacksonville 37
1 31N57'49 95w16'13 6:21:05
Jacobia 116 1 33N13'12 96w03'15 6:24:13
Jacobs 201 1 32N16 94w59 6:19:56
Jagoe 61 1 33N10'25 97w08'56 6:28:36
Jamaica Beach 84
1 29N18 94w50 6:19:20
James 113 1 31N22 95w11 6:20:44
James 210 1 31N51'33 94w06'56 6:16:28
James 230 1 32N41'36 94w44'34 6:18:58
James Moody 235
1 28N48 96w59 6:27:56
Jamestown 176 1 30N55'22 93w49'34 6:15:18
Jamestown 212 1 32N35'09 95w35'03 6:22:20
J and E Junction 121
1 30N40'08 93w53'22 6:15:33
J and L Ranchland 101
1 29N56 95w17 6:21:08
Jappa 27 1 30N45 98w03 6:32:12
Jardin 116 1 33N19'46 95w55'05 6:23:40
Jarrell 246 1 30N49'29 97w36'15 6:30:25
Jarvis 1 1 31N45'18 95w26'41 6:21:47
Jarvis College 250
1 32N35 95w12 6:20:48
Jasper 121 1 30N55'12 93w59'47 6:15:59
Jasper Heights 102
1 32N32'44 94w19'26 6:17:18
Java 37 1 31N47'03 95w19'12 6:21:17
Jayell 30 1 32N23'10 99w19'24 6:37:18
Jay Ray 45 1 29N40'01 96w25'47 6:25:43
Jayton 132 1 33N14'53 100w34'24 6:42:18
Jean 252 1 33N17'46 98w36'58 6:34:28
Jeanetta 101 1 29N43'14 95w31'33 6:22:06
Jeans 229 1 31N01 94w23 6:17:32
Jeddo 11 1 29N48'31 97w18'52 6:29:15
Jefferson 158 1 32N45'26 94w20'42 6:17:23
Jenkins 157 1 30N58'30 95w51'32 6:23:26
Jenkins 172 1 32N58'34 94w43'06 6:18:52
Jennings 139 1 33N34'47 95w27'58 6:21:52
Jensen Drive 101
1 29N48 95w20 6:21:20
Jentsch Acres 46
1 29N41'35 98w09'27 6:32:38
Jericho 65 3 35N10'23 100w54'28 6:43:38
Jericho 210 1 31N42'21 94w14'16 6:16:57
Jermyn 119 1 33N15'51 98w23'17 6:33:33
Jersey Village 101
1 29N53'15 95w33'46 6:22:15
Jester 175 1 31N57 96w37 6:26:28
Jewell 155 1 31N30'10 97w11'45 6:28:47
Jewett 145 1 31N21'41 96w08'38 6:24:35
J Frank Dobie 15
1 29N24 98w25 6:33:40
Jiba 129 1 32N30'55 96w16'33 6:25:06
Jim Ned 221 1 32N10 99w50 6:39:20
Jinks Branch 246
1 30N38'04 97w53'28 6:31:34
Joaquin 210 1 31N57'56 94w03'13 6:16:13
Joe 91 1 33N47'58 96w31'49 6:26:07
Joel 59 3 34N51'38 102w18'04 6:49:12
Joe Pool 57 1 32N43 96w51 6:27:24
John Allen 101 1 29N47 95w24 6:21:36
Johnfarris 77 1 34N13'12 101w12'39 6:44:51
John Foster 101
1 29N42 95w12 6:20:48
Johnson 170 1 30N12'01 95w27'43 6:21:51
Johnson 223 1 33N13'36 102w27'47 6:49:51
Johnson City 16
1 30N16'36 98w24'42 6:33:39
Johnson Space Center 101
1 29N34 95w05 6:20:20
Johnsons Station 220
1 32N41'31 97w07'40 6:28:31
Johnstone 233 1 29N22'52 100w45'31 6:43:02
Johnstown 170 1 30N19 95w28 6:21:52
Johnstown 234 1 32N43 96w00 6:24:00
Johnsue 237 1 29N47'09 95w52'35 6:23:30
Johnsville 72 1 32N08'45 98w01'33 6:32:06
Johntown 194 1 33N25'22 95w10'10 6:20:41
Joiner 75 1 29N53'19 96w47'25 6:27:10
Joinerville 201
1 32N10'40 94w54'02 6:19:36
Joliet 28 1 29N46'09 97w40'44 6:30:43
Jolly 39 1 33N51'50 98w20'57 6:33:24
Jollyville 227 1 30N26'33 97w46'29 6:31:06
Jonah 246 1 30N38'16 97w32'26 6:30:10
Jones 234 1 32N36'30 95w40'27 6:22:42
Jonesboro 50 1 31N36'52 97w52'35 6:31:30
Jones Creek 20 1 28N58'06 95w27'18 6:21:49
Jones Creek 241
1 29N17'12 96w18'45 6:25:15
Jones Prairie 166
1 30N57'46 96w50'05 6:27:20
Jonestown 227 1 30N29'43 97w55'23 6:31:42
Jonesville 102 1 32N29'52 94w06'39 6:16:27
Joplin 119 1 33N05'37 97w59'40 6:31:59
Joppa 27 1 30N49'31 98w01'53 6:32:08
Jordan 11 1 29N56'26 97w21'16 6:29:25
Jordans Store 210
1 31N46 93w52 6:15:28
Josephine 43 1 33N03'40 96w18'25 6:25:14
Joshua 126 1 32N27'41 97w23'16 6:29:33
Josselet 104 1 33N14'05 99w42'14 6:38:49
Josserand 228 1 31N02'06 95w05'22 6:20:21
Jot 'Em Down 60
1 33N25 95w56 6:23:44
Jourdanton 7 1 28N55'04 98w32'46 6:34:11
Joy 39 1 33N34'34 98w12'56 6:32:52
Joy 212 1 32N34 94w55 6:19:40
Jozye 157 1 31N01 95w55 6:23:40
Jubilee Springs 14
1 31N10'36 97w29'56 6:30:00
Jud 104 1 33N16'56 99w57'29 6:39:50
Judkins 68 1 31N43'03 102w37'56 6:50:32
Judson 92 1 32N34'57 94w45'12 6:19:01
Juilliard 188 3 35N19'07 101w48'33 6:47:14
Julian 131 1 26N47'42 97w57'18 6:31:49
Juliff 79 1 29N27'00 95w28'31 6:21:54
Jumbo 35 3 34N42'14 102w16'54 6:49:08
Junction 134 1 30N29'21 99w46'18 6:39:05
Junction Windmill 133
1 30N16'10 99w42'00 6:38:48
Juno 233 1 30N09'06 101w06'54 6:44:28
Jupiter Pharmacy 57
1 32N57 96w44 6:26:56
Justiceburg 85 1 33N02'34 101w12'09 6:44:49
Justin 61 1 33N05'05 97w17'45 6:29:11
Kadane Corner 243
1 33N51'28 98w50'18 6:35:21
Kaffir 219 3 34N38'00 101w49'13 6:47:17

Place		Latitude	Longitude	Time
Kalgary 54	1	33N24'32	101w08'53	6:44:36
Kamay 243	1	33N51'28	98w48'28	6:35:14
Kamey 29	1	28N38'09	96w44'35	6:26:58
Kanawha 194	1	33N51'41	95w15'10	6:21:01
Kane 108	1	26N12'32	98w16'00	6:33:04
Karen 170	1	30N15'22	95w42'05	6:22:48
Karnack 102	1	32N40'04	94w10'13	6:16:41
Karnes City 128	1	28N53'05	97w54'02	6:31:36
Karon 149	1	28N28'43	98w00'07	6:32:00
Katemcy 160	1	30N54'45	99w15'13	6:37:01
Katy 101	1	29N47'08	95w49'27	6:23:18
Kaufman 129	1	32N35'20	96w18'31	6:25:14
Kayare 31	1	26N11	97w39	6:30:36
Kay Bee Heights 50	1	31N07'06	97w49'52	6:31:19
Kearny 64	1	28N20'30	99w32'09	6:38:09
Keechi 145	1	31N31'00	95w57'11	6:23:49
Keefer 170	1	30N10'47	95w11'54	6:20:48
Keeler 126	1	32N32'16	97w22'03	6:29:28
Keelersville 246	1	30N44'09	97w31'05	6:30:04
Keenan 170	1	30N19'15	95w38'43	6:22:35
Keene 126	1	32N23'48	97w19'25	6:29:18
Keeter 249	1	33N02'04	97w36'46	6:30:27
Keith 93	1	30N38'42	96w06'04	6:24:24
Keithton 121	1	30N51'58	93w55'24	6:15:42
Kelland Heights 15	1	29N24'13	98w38'50	6:34:35
Keller 220	1	32N56'04	97w15'05	6:29:00
Keller Corner 31	1	25N55	97w29	6:29:56
Kellerville 242	3	35N22'18	100w30'09	6:42:01
Kellogg 116	1	33N12'33	96w09'03	6:24:36
Kelly 43	1	33N21'45	96w37'07	6:26:28
Kelly Air Force Base 15	1	29N23	98w35	6:34:20
Kellyville 158	1	32N46'45	94w24'33	6:17:38
Kelsay 124	1	26N57	98w08	6:32:32
Kelsay 214	1	26N20'29	98w44'23	6:34:58
Kelsey 230	1	32N43'54	95w02'58	6:20:12
Kelton 242	3	35N24'03	100w06'45	6:40:27
Keltys 3	1	31N21'41	94w45'03	6:19:00
Kemah 84	1	29N32'33	95w01'13	6:20:05
Kemp 129	1	32N26'33	96w13'47	6:24:55
Kempner 141	1	31N04'51	98w00'08	6:32:01
Kendalia 130	1	29N58'08	98w31'19	6:34:05
Kendleton 79	1	29N27'02	95w59'40	6:23:59
Kenedy 128	1	28N49'08	97w50'54	6:31:24
Kenefick 146	1	30N06'32	94w51'29	6:19:26
Kennard 113	1	31N21'34	95w10'59	6:20:44
Kennedale 220	1	32N38'48	97w13'32	6:28:54
Kennedy Shores 31	1	25N55	97w29	6:29:56
Kennemer Crossing 139	1	33N27'15	95w31'53	6:22:08
Kenney 8	1	30N02'51	96w19'36	6:25:18
Kensing 60	1	33N24'21	95w25'53	6:21:44
Kent 55	1	31N04'09	104w13'00	6:56:52
Kentucky Town 91	1	33N31'18	96w26'19	6:25:45
Kentwood Manor 15	1	29N35'56	98w27'42	6:33:51
Kenwood 57	1	32N42'43	96w54'13	6:27:37
Kenwood Place 101	1	29N55	95w20	6:21:20
Keokuk 102	1	32N30'39	94w30'06	6:18:00
Kerens 175	1	32N07'59	96w13'39	6:24:55
Kermit 248	1	31N51'27	103w05'32	6:52:22
Kerrick 56	3	36N29'44	102w14'32	6:48:58
Kerrville 133	1	30N02'50	99w08'24	6:36:34
Kevin 146	1	30N18	95w07	6:20:28
Key 58	1	32N44	101w48	6:47:12
Keys Crossing 25	1	31N28'44	99w01'31	6:36:06
Kickapoo 1	1	32N03	95w30	6:22:00
Kildare 34	1	32N56'35	94w14'53	6:17:00
Kildare Junction 34	1	32N54'30	94w11'18	6:16:45
Kilgore 88	1	28N46'10	97w17'47	6:29:11
Kilgore 92	1	32N23'10	94w52'32	6:19:30
Killeen 14	1	31N07'01	97w43'39	6:30:55
Kilowatt 181	1	30N06	93w46	6:15:04
Kimball 18	1	32N04	97w30	6:30:00
Kimball 98	3	36N19'41	101w16'24	6:45:06
Kimbro 227	1	30N21	97w33	6:30:12
Kinard Estates 181	1	30N10'27	93w47'25	6:15:10
Kincheonville 227	1	30N12'12	97w50'05	6:31:20
King 50	1	31N22'46	97w54'52	6:31:39
King 103	3	35N54'16	102w43'07	6:50:52
King 194	1	33N35	94w55	6:19:40
King City 146	1	30N18	95w07	6:20:28
Kingola 244	1	34N08	99w09	6:36:36
Kingsbury 94	1	29N38'52	97w49'40	6:31:19
Kingsland 115	1	30N39'29	98w26'25	6:33:46
Kingsley 57	1	32N54	96w37	6:26:28
Kingsmill 90	3	35N29'18	101w03'33	6:44:14
Kingsmill Camp 90	3	35N29'55	101w02'32	6:44:10
Kingston 116	1	33N15'10	96w10'35	6:24:42
Kings Village 227	1	30N26'08	97w41'21	6:30:45
Kingsville 137	1	27N30'56	97w51'21	6:31:25
Kingsville Station 137	1	27N30	97w49	6:31:16
Kingswood 57	1	32N34'17	96w58'28	6:27:54
Kinkler 143	1	29N32'02	96w53'56	6:27:36
Kinsloe 92	1	32N26'01	94w49'27	6:19:18
Kinwood 101	1	29N54'42	95w18'08	6:21:13
Kiomatia 194	1	33N53'21	95w13'22	6:20:53
Kirby 15	1	29N27'47	98w23'07	6:33:32
Kirbyville 121	1	30N39'37	93w53'33	6:15:34
Kirk 147	1	31N35'13	96w43'40	6:26:55
Kirkland 38	1	34N22'45	100w03'40	6:40:15
Kirkpatrick Addition 212	1	32N20	95w18	6:21:12
Kirtley 75	1	29N58'01	97w05'51	6:28:23
Kirvin 81	1	31N45'59	96w19'48	6:25:19
Kitalou 152	1	33N39'17	101w43'36	6:46:54
Kitchenville 227	1	30N14	97w47	6:31:08
Kittrell 236	1	30N57	95w23	6:21:32
Kleberg 57	1	32N40'17	96w36'56	6:26:28
Klein 101	1	30N02'51	95w31'56	6:22:08
Klondike 58	1	32N33'32	101w57'24	6:47:50
Klondike 60	1	33N19'47	95w45'28	6:23:02
Klump 239	1	30N07'13	96w29'26	6:25:58
Knapp 208	1	32N39'05	101w07'05	6:44:28
Knickerbocker 226	1	31N15'59	100w37'22	6:42:29
Knight Crossing 154	1	31N25'55	99w20'26	6:37:22
Knights Bluff Landing 34	1	33N14'20	94w15'19	6:17:01
Knippa 232	1	29N17'42	99w38'13	6:38:33
Knob Hill 72	1	32N15'32	98w08'34	6:32:34
Knoblaw 180	3	35N32'59	102w53'41	6:51:35
Knolle 125	1	27N58'26	97w49'27	6:31:18
Knott 114	1	32N24'09	101w38'27	6:46:34
Knox City 138	1	33N25'05	99w49'07	6:39:16
Knoxville 134	1	30N18	99w15	6:37:00
Koerth 143	1	29N18'32	96w59'47	6:27:59
Kohrville 101	1	30N00'43	95w35'07	6:22:20
Kokernot 89	1	29N26'34	97w15'59	6:29:04
Kokomo 67	1	32N16'58	98w42'17	6:34:49
Komensky 143	1	29N34'19	97w02'45	6:28:11
Koockville 160	1	30N45'25	99w14'59	6:37:00
Koppe 21	1	30N34'20	96w19'34	6:25:18
Kopperl 18	1	32N04'11	97w30'13	6:30:01
Kosciusko 247	1	29N06'19	97w57'01	6:31:48
Kosmos 4	1	27N56'29	97w06'57	6:28:28
Kosse 147	1	31N18'27	96w37'54	6:26:32
Kossuth 1	1	31N44'32	95w29'55	6:22:00
Kountze 100	1	30N22'17	94w18'44	6:17:15
Kovar 11	1	29N54'06	97w12'49	6:28:51
Krebsville 8	1	29N59'25	96w35'04	6:26:20
Krem 57	1	32N54	96w37	6:26:28
Kress 219	1	34N21'59	101w44'53	6:47:00
Kreutzberg 130	1	29N51'48	98w40'30	6:34:42
Kriebaum Place 22	1	30N12'32	103w05'13	6:52:21
Krugerville 61	1	33N18	96w59	6:27:56
Krum 61	1	33N15'41	97w14'16	6:28:57
Kubala Store 62	1	29N04'09	97w29'27	6:29:58
Kurten 21	1	30N47'13	96w15'50	6:25:03
Kyle 105	1	29N59'20	97w52'37	6:31:30
Kyote 7	1	29N01'35	98w47'23	6:35:10
La Aura Crossing 31	1	26N01'32	97w19'22	6:29:17
La Bahia 239	1	30N08'39	96w38'12	6:26:33
Laban 45	1	29N41'05	96w28'09	6:25:53
Labatt 247	1	29N08	98w09	6:32:36
La Belle 123	1	29N52'46	94w09'39	6:16:39
La Blanca 108	1	26N17'33	98w02'15	6:32:09
La Casa 215	1	32N36'03	98w41'21	6:34:45
La Casita 214	1	26N19'24	98w42'54	6:34:52
Laceola 157	1	30N58'18	95w59'12	6:23:57
La Cerda 174	1	31N26'16	94w23'50	6:17:35
Lackland 15	1	29N23	98w37	6:34:28
Lackland Air Force Base 15	1	29N23	98w36	6:34:24
Lackland City 15	1	29N23'20	98w38'45	6:34:35
Lackland Heights 15	1	29N24'18	98w39'17	6:34:37
Lackland Terrace 15	1	29N24'41	98w38'33	6:34:34
La Coste 163	1	29N18'38	98w48'35	6:35:14
La Cour 146	1	30N04	94w48	6:19:12
Lacy 228	1	31N03	95w08	6:20:32
Lacy-Lakeview 155	1	31N37'45	97w06'09	6:28:25
Lacyville 174	1	31N30'18	94w36'25	6:18:26
Ladonia 74	1	33N25'29	95w56'46	6:23:47
LaFayette 230	1	32N53'54	94w51'21	6:19:25
La Feria 31	1	26N09'31	97w49'25	6:31:18
Lafitte 45	1	29N39'43	96w15'45	6:25:03
La Fruta 205	1	28N02'26	97w51'33	6:31:26
Lagarto 149	1	28N07'09	97w57'19	6:31:49
La Gloria 125	1	27N16'52	98w07'59	6:32:32
La Gloria 214	1	26N43'11	98w31'16	6:34:05
Lago Vista 227	1	30N27'36	97w59'17	6:31:57
La Grange 75	1	29N54'19	96w52'35	6:27:30
La Grulla (Grulla PO) 214	1	26N16'09	98w38'49	6:34:35
La Guna 71	2	31N47'21	106w31'20	7:06:05
Laguna 232	1	29N25'08	100w00'19	6:40:01
Laguna Heights 31	1	26N04'47	97w15'13	6:29:01
Laguna Park 18	1	31N51'33	97w22'46	6:29:31
Laguna Seca 108	1	26N29'43	98w11'39	6:32:47
Laguna Vista 31	1	26N06'02	97w17'24	6:29:10
Lahey 223	1	33N07'22	102w20'02	6:49:20
La India 24	1	27N10'18	98w07'39	6:32:31
Laird Hill 201	1	32N21'11	94w54'19	6:19:37
La Isla 71	2	31N30	106w12	7:04:48
Lajitas 22	1	29N15'41	103w46'34	6:55:06
La Joya 108	1	26N14'48	98w28'52	6:33:55
La Junta 184	1	32N55'11	97w35'58	6:30:24
La Junta 189	1	29N35'37	104w24'38	6:57:39
Lake 249	1	33N13	97w46	6:31:04
Lake Alaska 20	1	29N09	95w27	6:21:48
Lake Barbara 20	1	29N01'30	95w23'21	6:21:33
Lake Brownwood 25	1	31N50'08	99w00'27	6:36:02
Lake Cherokee 92	1	32N09	94w48	6:19:12
Lake Corsicana 175	1	32N06	96w31	6:26:04
Lake Creek 60	1	33N26'50	95w35'16	6:22:21
Lake Creek 155	1	31N30'33	96w57'01	6:27:48
Lake Crest Estates 220	1	32N51'41	97w24'48	6:29:39
Lake Cypress 101	1	29N58	95w42	6:22:48
Lake Dallas 61	1	33N07'09	97w01'31	6:28:06
Lake Estates 170	1	30N23	95w42	6:22:48
Lake Forest 220	1	32N57'03	97w31'07	6:30:04
Lakefront Lodge 253	1	26N52'58	99w16'22	6:37:05
Lake Halbert 175	1	32N06	96w31	6:26:04
Lake Hills 10	1	29N35'03	98w56'55	6:35:48
Lake Jackson 20	1	29N02'01	95w26'03	6:21:44
Lake Jackson Farms 20	1	29N03'27	95w28'17	6:21:53
Lake Kiowa 49	1	33N38	97w08	6:28:32
Lakeland 170	1	30N19	95w28	6:21:52
Lakeland Heights 57	1	32N43'22	96w58'54	6:27:56
Lakeland Hills 227	1	30N16	97w48	6:31:12
Lakeland Park 227	1	30N23	97w45	6:31:00
Lake Medina Highlands 10	1	29N34'04	98w57'25	6:35:50
Lakenon 109	1	32N03'07	97w01'27	6:28:06
Lake Placid 94	1	29N35	97w58	6:31:52
Lakeport 92	1	32N24	94w42	6:18:48
Lake Shore 25	1	31N49'47	99w05'26	6:36:22
Lake Shore Estates 220	1	32N37'51	97w29'04	6:29:56
Lakeshore Gardens 205	1	28N07'45	97w52'10	6:31:29
Lakeside 45	1	29N33'53	96w19'43	6:25:19
Lakeside 71	2	31N44'49	106w23'52	7:05:35
Lakeside 84	1	29N33'08	95w03'32	6:20:14
Lakeside 220	1	32N49	97w28	6:29:52
Lakeside City 5	1	33N52	98w33	6:34:12
Lakeside Hieghts 150	1	30N40	98w26	6:33:44
Lakeside Village 18	1	32N01'15	97w29'37	6:29:58
Lake Tanglewood 191	3	35N11	101w51	6:47:24
Lake Thomas 208	1	32N35	101w00	6:44:00
Laketon 90	3	35N32'37	100w37'57	6:42:32
Lake Victor 27	1	30N54'32	98w11'35	6:32:46
Lakeview 14	1	31N03	97w28	6:29:52
Lakeview 57	1	32N42'37	96w59'06	6:27:56
Lakeview 77	1	33N52'36	101w15'25	6:45:02
Lakeview 96	1	34N40'29	100w41'56	6:42:48
Lakeview 123	1	29N54'48	93w53'54	6:15:36
Lakeview 153	1	33N19'35	102w03'00	6:48:12
Lakeview 155	1	31N36	97w06	6:28:24
Lakeview 181	1	30N13'12	94w06'30	6:16:26
Lake View 201	1	32N09'49	94w48'16	6:19:13
Lakeview 219	3	34N31'46	101w55'11	6:47:41
Lake View 233	1	29N27'18	100w56'39	6:43:47
Lakeview Assembly 1	1	31N39'30	95w41'09	6:22:45
Lakeview Estates 234	1	32N43	96w00	6:24:00
Lakeway 227	1	30N22'04	97w59'29	6:31:58
Lakewood 57	1	32N49	96w45	6:27:00
Lakewood 101	1	29N46	95w00	6:20:00
Lakewood 181	1	30N07'42	93w58'40	6:15:55
Lakewood Harbor 18	1	31N54'13	97w25'10	6:29:41
Lakewood Heights 101	1	30N01'19	95w06'51	6:20:27
Lakewood Heights 205	1	28N06'09	97w51'47	6:31:27
Lake Worth 220	1	32N48'17	97w26'41	6:29:47
Lake Worth Village 220	1	32N48	97w27	6:29:48
La Leona 31	1	26N16'03	97w27'31	6:29:50
Laman 172	1	32N59'06	94w39'16	6:18:37
Lamar 4	1	28N08'21	97w00'19	6:28:01
Lamar 210	1	31N46'47	94w15'20	6:17:01
Lamar Park 178	1	27N44	97w24	6:29:36
La Marque 84	1	29N23	94w58	6:19:52
Lamar Tech 123	1	30N03	94w06	6:16:24
Lamar Terrace 101	1	29N43'53	95w28'05	6:21:52
Lamasco 74	1	33N41'42	96w03'59	6:24:16
Lamesa 58	1	32N44'15	101w57'02	6:47:48
Lamkin 47	1	31N49'23	98w15'50	6:33:03
Lamont 187	1	30N39'26	94w57'06	6:19:48
Lampasas 141	1	31N03'49	98w10'53	6:32:44
Lanark 34	1	33N10'55	94w08'57	6:16:36
Lancaster 57	1	32N35'31	96w45'21	6:27:01
Landa Park Highlands 46	1	29N43'10	98w08'23	6:32:34
Landergin 180	3	35N16'10	102w33'27	6:50:14
Landrum 31	1	26N02'37	97w41'54	6:30:48
Lane 116	1	33N18'07	96w15'44	6:25:03
Lane City 241	1	29N12'57	96w01'34	6:24:06
Lanely 81	1	31N36'02	96w03'59	6:24:14
Laneport 246	1	30N41'26	97w16'43	6:29:07
Lane Prairie 126	1	32N21	97w23	6:29:32
Laneville 201	1	31N58'27	94w48'49	6:19:15
Langtry 233	1	29N49	101w34	6:46:16
Lanham 97	1	31N45'09	97w57'08	6:31:49
Lanier 34	1	32N56'07	94w22'25	6:17:30
Lanius 221	1	32N31'07	99w44'39	6:38:59
Lannius 74	1	33N36'29	96w03'21	6:24:13
Lansing 102	1	32N30'28	94w37'34	6:18:30
Lantana 31	1	26N11'34	97w34'43	6:30:19
La Paloma 31	1	26N02'44	97w40'02	6:30:40
La Para 149	1	28N22'00	97w57'14	6:31:49
La Parita 7	1	28N50'49	98w35'35	6:34:22
La Parra Landing 131	1	27N15'18	97w38'25	6:30:34
La Penusca 31	1	26N04'39	97w29'39	6:29:59
Lapham 15	1	29N33	98w31	6:34:04
La Porte 101	1	29N39'56	95w01'09	6:20:05
La Pryor 254	1	28N56'27	99w50'58	6:39:24
La Puerta 214	1	26N20'39	98w44'41	6:34:59
Laredo 240	1	27N30'22	99w30'26	6:38:02
La Reforma 214	1	26N41'07	98w22'27	6:33:30
Lariat 185	3	34N19'49	102w54'27	6:51:38
Larissa 37	1	32N03'21	95w19'29	6:21:18
Lark 33	3	35N12'27	101w14'23	6:44:58
Larue 107	1	32N07'00	95w40'28	6:22:42

La Salle 120 1 28N47'29 96w40'08 6:26:41
LaSalle 147 1 31N31'59 96w25'07 6:25:40
Lasara 245 1 26N27'52 97w54'39 6:31:39
Lasca 115 2 31N14'04 105w28'28 7:01:54
Las Flores 82 1 28N41'49 98w56'28 6:35:46
Las Gallinas 7 1 29N06'44 98w29'18 6:33:57
Las Lulas 189 1 30N01'33 104w41'43 6:58:47
Las Milpas 108 1 26N07'05 98w11'57 6:32:48
Las Palmas 253 1 26N57'08 99w16'29 6:37:06
Las Rusias 31 1 26N03'13 97w45'26 6:31:02
Lassater 158 1 32N50'02 94w30'09 6:18:01
Las Tiendas 240 1 27N54'09 99w38'21 6:38:33
Las Vegas 64 1 28N32'52 99w29'22 6:37:57
Las Yescas 31 1 26N13'21 97w30'20 6:30:01
Latch 230 1 32N41'48 95w04'08 6:20:17
Latex 183 1 32N21 94w06 6:16:24
Latexo 113 1 31N23'42 95w28'26 6:21:54
La Tijera 108 1 26N10 98w03 6:32:12
Latium 239 1 30N04'49 96w33'37 6:26:14
La Tuna 71 2 31N58'51 106w35'24 7:06:22
Lauback 94 1 29N37'41 97w56'24 6:31:46
Laughlin 233 1 29N21 100w46 6:43:04
Laughlin Air Force Base 233 1 29N21 100w50 6:43:20
Laureles 31 1 26N06'32 97w29'38 6:29:59
Laurel Heights 15 1 29N27 98w30 6:34:00
Laurel Hill 204 1 30N36'10 95w12'47 6:20:51
Lautz 211 3 36N11'14 102w01'53 6:48:08
Lavender 147 1 31N32'04 96w39'20 6:26:37
La Vernia 247 1 29N21'22 98w06'55 6:32:28
La Villa 108 1 26N17'54 97w55'42 6:31:43
Lavon 43 1 33N01'39 96w26'02 6:25:44
Lavon Beach Estates 43 1 33N06'50 96w26'59 6:25:48
Lavon Lake Lodges 43 1 33N02'16 96w30'08 6:26:01
Lavon Shores Estates 43 1 33N06'22 96w28'43 6:25:55
Law 21 1 30N40 96w22 6:25:28
La Ward 120 1 28N50'37 96w27'50 6:25:51
Lawn 221 1 32N08'05 99w44'58 6:39:00
Lawrence 129 1 32N44'32 96w20'33 6:25:22
Lawrence Springs 234 1 32N38'33 95w47'14 6:23:09
Lawson 57 1 32N42'08 96w33'53 6:26:16
Lawson Crossing 181 1 30N07'51 94w05'17 6:16:21
Lawsonville 201 1 31N56'07 94w36'02 6:18:24
Lazare 99 1 34N16'59 99w59'50 6:39:59
Lazbuddie 185 3 34N23'35 102w36'39 6:50:27
Leaday 42 1 31N34'04 99w40'22 6:38:41
League City 84 1 29N30'26 95w05'41 6:20:23
Leagueville 107 1 32N13'51 95w39'18 6:22:37
Leakey 193 1 29N43'43 99w45'40 6:39:03
Leal 7 1 28N54'50 98w21'36 6:33:26
Leander 246 1 30N34'43 97w51'10 6:31:25
Leary 19 1 33N27'36 94w12'27 6:16:50
Lebanon 43 1 33N06'47 96w48'19 6:27:13
Lebanon 109 1 31N48'37 97w16'13 6:29:05
Lebanon 126 1 32N22'07 97w26'48 6:29:47
Ledbetter 75 1 30N09'02 96w47'28 6:27:10
Ledbetter Hills 57 1 32N41'32 96w55'33 6:27:42
Lee 33 3 35N18'00 101w29'48 6:45:59
Leedale 14 1 30N59'11 97w11'52 6:28:47
Lees 87 1 32N04'34 101w29'11 6:45:57
Leesburg 32 1 32N59'15 95w05'01 6:20:20
Lee Spring 212 1 32N12'45 95w22'18 6:21:29
Leesville 89 1 29N24'24 97w44'41 6:30:59
Lefman 241 1 29N15'45 96w03'17 6:24:13
Lefors 90 3 35N26'11 100w48'19 6:43:13
Leggett 187 1 30N49'04 94w52'13 6:19:29
Legion 133 1 30N01'22 99w06'58 6:36:28
Lehman 49 1 33N37'18 102w47'53 6:51:12
Leigh 102 1 32N36'16 94w07'53 6:16:32
Lela 242 3 35N13'39 100w20'33 6:41:22
Lelavale 100 1 30N24'12 94w29'02 6:17:56
Lelia Lake 65 3 34N54'04 100w46'13 6:43:05
Leming 7 1 29N04'22 98w29'02 6:33:56
Lemley 184 1 32N49'03 97w52'46 6:31:31
Lemonville 181 1 30N12'51 93w50'44 6:15:23
Lena 75 1 29N53'06 97w02'06 6:28:08
Lenorah 159 1 32N18'16 101w52'33 6:47:30
Lenox 22 3 30N14'11 103w22'42 6:53:31
Lenz 128 1 28N47'25 97w58'36 6:31:54
Leo 49 1 33N27'10 97w23'40 6:29:35
Leo 144 1 30N21'57 96w59'05 6:27:56
Leona 145 1 31N09'16 95w58'08 6:23:53
Leonard 74 1 33N22'46 96w14'50 6:24:59
Leonidas 170 1 30N18'56 95w32'01 6:22:08
Leon Junction 50 1 31N20'27 97w35'38 6:30:23
Leon Springs 15 1 29N39'53 98w37'44 6:34:31
Leon Valley 15 1 29N29'42 98w37'06 6:34:28
Leroy 155 1 31N43'53 97w01'03 6:28:04
Lesley 96 1 34N40'37 100w48'56 6:43:16
Le Tourneau 92 1 32N27 94w44 6:18:56
Levelland 110 1 33N35'14 102w22'39 6:49:31
Leveretts Chapel 201 1 32N16 94w59 6:19:56
Le Verte 121 1 30N31'46 93w55'39 6:15:43
Levi 155 1 31N22'37 97w07'19 6:28:29
Levinson 55 1 31N05'56 104w07'03 6:56:28
Levita 50 1 31N30'53 97w53'16 6:31:33
Lewisville 61 1 33N02'46 96w59'38 6:27:59
Lewisville 237 1 30N04'07 96w06'50 6:24:27
Lewisville Valley 61 1 33N03 97w03 6:28:12
Lexington 144 1 30N25'08 97w00'41 6:28:03
Libby 174 1 31N40 94w38 6:18:32
Liberty 34 1 32N53'04 94w26'53 6:17:48
Liberty 42 1 31N43'41 99w13'51 6:36:55
Liberty 112 1 33N01'14 95w39'46 6:22:39
Liberty 146 1 30N03'28 94w47'43 6:19:11
Liberty 152 1 33N41'38 101w46'00 6:47:04
Liberty 166 1 30N46'37 96w51'07 6:27:24
Liberty 174 1 31N44'09 94w54'03 6:19:36
Liberty 176 1 30N55'23 93w43'21 6:14:53
Liberty 194 1 33N36'47 95w13'53 6:20:56
Liberty 201 1 32N13'00 94w36'33 6:18:26
Liberty City 92 1 32N26'43 94w56'54 6:19:48
Liberty Grove 57 1 32N57'28 96w31'40 6:26:07
Liberty Grove 60 1 33N19'52 95w41'49 6:22:47
Liberty Hill 109 1 31N57 97w19 6:29:16
Liberty Hill 166 1 30N40'25 97w08'35 6:28:34
Liberty Hill 204 1 30N30'53 95w08'36 6:20:34
Liberty Hill 225 1 33N13'34 94w54'00 6:19:36
Liberty Hill 246 1 30N39'53 97w55'20 6:31:41
Lider 95 1 34N10'33 101w37'25 6:46:30
Liggett 57 1 32N51 96w58 6:27:52
Lightner 48 1 31N07'34 99w37'01 6:38:28
Lilac 166 1 30N37 97w12 6:28:48
Lilbert 174 1 31N44 94w54 6:19:36
Lillard 100 1 30N21'18 94w07'05 6:16:28
Lillian 126 1 32N30'23 97w11'14 6:28:45
Lilly 44 3 34N51 100w10 6:40:40
Lily Island 187 1 30N54'14 94w42'34 6:18:50
Lime City 50 1 31N23'40 97w31'37 6:30:06
Limestone 147 1 31N38'31 96w23'46 6:25:35
Lincoln 144 1 30N17'14 96w57'47 6:27:51
Lincoln Park 61 1 33N18 96w59 6:27:56
Lindale 212 1 32N30'56 95w24'33 6:21:38
Linda Vista 253 1 26N52'55 99w16'46 6:37:07
Lindberg 220 1 32N40'56 97w12'51 6:28:51
Linden 34 1 33N00'44 94w21'55 6:17:28
Lindenau 62 1 29N07'03 97w22'14 6:29:29
Lindsay 49 1 33N38'09 97w13'21 6:28:53
Lingleville 72 1 32N14'40 98w22'38 6:33:31
Link Five 101 1 29N42'15 95w05'41 6:20:23
Linkwood Estates 220 1 32N44 97w31 6:30:04
Linn 108 1 26N33'35 98w07'18 6:32:29
Linn Flat 174 1 31N47'23 94w43'54 6:18:56
Linwood 37 1 31N39'51 94w59'25 6:19:58
Lipan 111 1 32N31'06 98w02'44 6:32:11
Lipscomb 148 3 36N14'00 100w16'14 6:41:05
Lissie 241 1 29N33'21 96w13'30 6:24:54
Littig 227 1 30N19'10 97w26'57 6:29:48
Little Cypress 181 1 30N09'52 93w45'21 6:15:01
Little Elm 61 1 33N09'45 96w56'14 6:27:45
Little Elm 147 1 31N26'20 96w42'25 6:26:50
Littlefield 140 1 33N55'02 102w19'28 6:49:18
Little Hope 250 1 32N46'46 95w15'24 6:21:02
Little Mexico 186 1 30N54 102w53 6:51:32
Little New York 89 1 29N33'03 97w18'23 6:29:14
Little Ridge 43 1 33N03'46 96w27'16 6:25:49
Little River 14 1 30N59'19 97w21'57 6:29:28
Lively 12 1 33N35'43 99w10'46 6:36:43
Lively 129 1 32N24'35 96w19'23 6:25:18
Live Oak 15 1 29N33'54 98w20'10 6:33:21
Live Oak 48 1 31N08'20 99w55'45 6:39:43
Liveoak 182 1 32N31 98w03 6:32:12
Live Oak Resorts 109 1 32N00'37 97w21'44 6:29:27
Liverpool 20 1 29N17'41 95w16'43 6:21:07
Livingston 187 1 30N42'39 94w55'58 6:19:44
Llano 150 1 30N45'33 98w40'29 6:34:42
Lobo 55 1 30N48'50 104w45'09 6:59:01
Lochridge 20 1 29N21'10 95w31'51 6:22:07
Locker 195 1 31N22'46 103w31'32 6:54:06
Locker 206 1 31N22'38 98w53'48 6:35:35
Lockett 244 1 34N04'52 99w22'39 6:37:31
Lockettville 110 1 33N23'30 102w19'02 6:49:16
Lockhart 28 1 29N53'05 97w40'11 6:30:41
Lockney 77 1 34N07'28 101w26'28 6:45:46
Loco 38 1 34N43'03 100w09'08 6:40:37
Locust 91 1 33N47'50 96w46'20 6:27:05
Locust Grove 148 3 36N06'51 100w21'59 6:41:28
Lodi 158 1 32N52'34 94w16'46 6:17:07
Lodwick 158 1 32N46 94w21 6:17:24
Loeb 100 1 30N11'40 94w11'34 6:16:46
Loebau 144 1 30N17'15 96w54'18 6:27:37
Logan 183 1 32N04'42 94w03'13 6:16:13
Lohn 154 1 31N19'25 99w24'35 6:37:38
Loire 247 1 29N06'35 98w23'43 6:33:35
Lois 49 1 33N27'22 97w13'12 6:28:53
Lois 101 1 29N49'58 95w30'13 6:22:01
Lolaville 43 1 33N05'50 96w48'18 6:27:13
Lolita 120 1 28N50'21 96w32'32 6:26:10
Loma 236 1 30N40'49 95w48'33 6:23:14
Loma Alta 156 1 28N07'14 98w30'53 6:34:04
Loma Alta 233 1 29N55'04 100w46'27 6:43:06
Loma Pelona 189 1 29N32'07 104w18'13 6:57:13
Loma Terrace 71 2 31N43'53 106w19'53 7:05:20
Loma Vista 247 1 29N01'16 98w14'46 6:32:59
Loma Vista 254 1 28N57 99w37 6:38:28
Lomax 101 1 29N40'49 95w03'55 6:20:16
Lomax 114 1 32N06'59 101w38'23 6:46:34
Lometa 141 1 31N13'01 98w23'35 6:33:34
Lomo Alta 156 1 28N28 98w33 6:34:12
London 134 1 30N40'36 99w34'34 6:38:18
Lone Camp 182 1 32N40'45 98w16'06 6:33:04
Lone Cedar 70 1 32N08'55 96w45'04 6:27:00
Lone Elm 70 1 32N24 96w50 6:27:20
Lone Grove 150 1 30N48'45 98w34'31 6:34:18
Lone Mountain 230 1 32N44 94w57 6:19:48
Lone Oak 15 1 29N22'00 98w14'40 6:32:59
Lone Oak 37 1 31N44'22 95w11'54 6:20:48
Lone Oak 45 1 29N54'05 96w34'54 6:26:20
Lone Oak 116 1 32N59'48 95w56'24 6:23:46
Lone Oak 139 1 33N29'10 95w19'32 6:21:18
Lone Oak 175 1 32N07'07 96w45'34 6:27:02
Lone Pine 1 1 31N46 95w38 6:22:32
Lone Pine 230 1 32N50'40 94w54'24 6:19:38
Lone Star 14 1 31N06'10 97w41'55 6:30:48
Lone Star 37 1 31N57'12 95w02'16 6:20:09
Lone Star 77 1 34N16'27 101w24'57 6:45:40
Lone Star 172 1 32N56'38 94w42'25 6:18:50
Lone Star 194 1 33N33'44 95w09'21 6:20:37
Lone Star 225 1 33N14'02 94w49'46 6:19:19
Lone Willow 126 1 32N16'07 97w28'28 6:29:54
Long Branch 67 1 32N16 98w50 6:35:20
Long Branch 73 1 31N15'31 96w41'41 6:26:47
Long Branch 183 1 32N04'22 94w34'04 6:18:16
Long Crossing 232 1 29N28'56 99w32'59 6:38:12
Longfellow 186 1 30N09'42 102w38'17 6:50:33
Long Hollow 145 1 31N17'36 96w15'55 6:25:04
Longhorn 15 1 29N31'51 98w24'07 6:33:36
Long Lake 1 1 31N38'58 95w46'51 6:23:07
Long Mott 29 1 28N28'56 96w45'37 6:27:02
Long Point 79 1 29N23'26 95w43'58 6:22:56
Long Point 102 1 32N42 94w07 6:16:28
Longpoint 239 1 30N14'11 96w31'40 6:26:07
Longview 92 1 32N30'02 94w44'25 6:18:58
Longview Heights 102 1 32N30'21 94w40'46 6:18:43
Longworth 76 1 32N39'01 100w20'43 6:41:23
Looneyville 174 1 31N45'47 94w50'39 6:19:23
Loop 83 1 32N54'55 102w24'56 6:49:40
Lopeno 253 1 26N42'40 99w06'35 6:36:26
Lopezville 108 1 26N14'16 98w09'34 6:32:38
Lora 197 3 35N44'27 100w33'26 6:42:14
Loraine 168 1 32N24'40 100w42'43 6:42:51
Lorena 155 1 31N23'11 97w12'55 6:28:52
Lorenzo 54 1 33N40'14 101w32'05 6:46:08
Los Angeles 108 1 26N34'40 98w08'22 6:32:33
Los Angeles 142 1 28N27'56 99w00'00 6:36:00
Los Barreras 214 1 26N23'11 98w55'13 6:35:41
Los Coyotes 245 1 26N25 97w48 6:31:12
Los Cuates 31 1 26N04'50 97w29'47 6:29:59
Los Ebanos 108 1 26N14'35 98w33'41 6:34:15
Los Fresnos 31 1 26N04'17 97w28'34 6:29:54
Los Garzas 214 1 26N21'49 98w53'36 6:35:34
Los Indios 31 1 26N02'56 97w44'41 6:30:59
Los Jardines 15 1 29N25 98w34 6:34:16
Los Lomas 149 1 28N08'15 97w53'16 6:31:33
Los Ojuelos 240 1 27N24'10 98w59'46 6:35:59
Losoya 15 1 29N14'00 98w27'22 6:33:49
Los Saenz 214 1 26N24 99w00 6:36:00
Lost Creek Place 136 1 29N36'32 100w10'45 6:40:43
Los Velas 214 1 26N20'16 98w46'51 6:35:07
Lott 73 1 31N12'12 97w02'11 6:28:09
Lotta 102 1 32N34'41 94w06'14 6:16:25
Louetta 101 1 30N00'23 95w33'39 6:22:15
Louise 241 1 29N06'40 96w24'11 6:25:37
Louis Granger Place 22 1 30N08'55 103w10'52 6:52:43
Love 34 1 32N58'14 94w36'31 6:18:26
Love Chapel 34 1 33N00 94w38 6:18:32
Lovelace 109 1 32N05'20 97w07'42 6:28:31
Lovelady 113 1 31N07'36 95w26'43 6:21:47
Lovell Lake 123 1 29N56'32 94w07'32 6:16:30
Loving 252 1 33N15'51 98w30'37 6:34:02
Lowake 48 1 31N33'58 100w04'32 6:40:18
Lowe 168 1 32N11'45 100w50'18 6:43:21
Lowry Crossing 43 1 33N08 96w37 6:26:28
Loyal Valley 160 1 30N34'32 99w00'27 6:36:02
Loyola Beach 137 1 27N20'00 97w41'40 6:30:47
Loy Place (Abandoned) 22 1 29N47'35 103w39'59 6:54:40
Lozano 31 1 26N11'20 97w32'27 6:30:10
Lozier 222 1 29N56'06 101w49'12 6:47:17
Lubbock 152 1 33N34'40 101w51'17 6:47:25
Lucas 43 1 33N05'03 96w34'35 6:26:18
Lucas 123 1 29N59'53 94w04'08 6:16:17
Luckenbach 86 1 30N10'44 98w45'27 6:35:02
Lucky Ridge 249 1 33N02'10 97w40'05 6:30:40
Lueders 127 1 32N48'05 99w37'07 6:38:28
Luella 91 1 33N34'10 96w33'03 6:26:12
Lufkin 3 1 31N20'17 94w43'44 6:18:55
Lufkin Junction 212 1 32N20 95w18 6:21:12
Luke Wilson 5 1 33N43'04 98w33'00 6:34:12
Luling 28 1 29N40'49 97w38'50 6:30:35
Lull 108 1 26N20'31 98w09'51 6:32:39
Lull 233 1 29N45'10 101w17'34 6:45:10
Lumberton 100 1 30N15'11 94w11'23 6:16:46
Lumkins 70 1 32N14'37 96w51'51 6:27:27
Lums Chapel 140 1 33N50 102w20 6:49:20
Luna 81 1 31N33'08 96w13'02 6:24:52
Lunas 22 1 29N12'55 103w32'04 6:54:08
Lund 227 1 30N24'23 97w23'46 6:29:35
Lusk 224 1 32N58'15 99w01'54 6:36:08
Luther 114 1 32N26'37 101w27'23 6:45:50
Lutie 44 3 35N01'23 100w13'20 6:40:53
Luxello 15 1 29N36'05 98w18'50 6:33:15
Lyday Crossing 74 1 33N27'48 95w52'39 6:23:31
Lydia 194 1 33N26'46 94w45'16 6:19:01
Lyford 245 1 26N24'43 97w47'22 6:31:09
Lynchburg 101 1 29N47'13 95w03'19 6:20:13

Lynchburg Landing 101
1 29N45'56 95w04'40 6:20:19
Lyncrest 101 1 29N52 95w20 6:21:20
Lyndon B Johnson Space Ctr 101
1 29N34 95w05 6:20:20
Lynn Grove 93 1 30N17'06 96w01'51 6:24:07
Lyons 26 1 30N23'10 96w33'47 6:26:15
Lyra 182 1 32N33'19 98w28'07 6:33:52
Lytle 7 1 29N13'59 98w47'46 6:35:11
Lytle 220 1 32N38'28 97w19'57 6:29:20
Lytton Springs 28
1 30N00'16 97w36'44 6:30:27
Mabank 129 1 32N21'59 96w06'02 6:24:24
Mabelle 12 1 33N40'12 99w08'20 6:36:33
Mabry 194 1 33N36'48 95w07'05 6:20:28
Mac Bain 173 1 33N53'37 100w58'28 6:43:54
Macdona 15 1 29N19'32 98w41'27 6:34:46
Macedonia 8 1 29N50'39 96w09'16 6:24:37
Macedonia 19 1 33N26 94w04 6:16:16
Macedonia 32 1 33N02'51 94w58'24 6:19:54
Macedonia 146 1 30N15'45 94w53'23 6:19:34
Macedonia 158 1 32N43'45 94w31'38 6:18:07
Macey 21 1 30N56'56 96w15'49 6:25:03
Machovec 171 3 35N56'38 101w59'11 6:47:57
Mackay 241 1 29N16'11 96w08'58 6:24:36
Macomb 91 1 33N35'53 96w51'21 6:27:25
Macon 80 1 33N05'19 95w07'39 6:20:31
Macune 203 1 31N24'57 94w09'36 6:16:38
Macy 21 1 30N54 96w24 6:25:36
Madero 108 1 26N10'13 98w19'52 6:33:19
Madisonville 157
1 30N56'59 95w54'41 6:23:39
Madras 194 1 33N39'30 94w58'55 6:19:56
Magasco 202 1 31N16'50 93w58'30 6:15:54
Magers Crossing 232
1 29N34'35 99w43'29 6:38:54
Magic City 242 3 35N21'27 100w22'41 6:41:31
Magnet 241 1 29N09'02 95w59'12 6:23:57
Magnolia 170 1 30N12'33 95w45'02 6:23:00
Magnolia 204 1 30N28'59 95w11'36 6:20:46
Magnolia Beach 29
1 28N33'36 96w32'33 6:26:10
Magnolia Gardens 101
1 29N53'11 95w06'45 6:20:27
Magnolia Hills 229
1 30N46'41 94w28'36 6:17:54
Magnolia Park 101
1 29N43'56 95w17'31 6:21:10
Magnolia Springs 121
1 30N44'07 94w01'35 6:16:06
Magoun 148 3 36N22'35 100w01'59 6:40:08
Magpetco 123 1 29N58 93w59 6:15:56
Magwalt 248 1 31N55'25 103w06'51 6:52:27
Maha 227 1 30N05'25 97w40'34 6:30:42
Mahl 174 1 31N44'01 94w40'34 6:18:42
Mahomet 27 1 30N49'18 97w55'54 6:31:44
Mahoney 112 1 33N11'33 95w29'37 6:21:58
Main Place 57 1 32N47 96w47 6:27:08
Majors 80 1 33N06'10 95w13'10 6:20:53
Malakoff 107 1 32N10'10 96w00'44 6:24:03
Mallard 169 1 33N40 97w43 6:30:52
Malone 109 1 31N55'04 96w53'40 6:27:35
Malta 19 1 33N29'17 94w31'19 6:18:05
Malvado 222 1 29N58'04 101w52'04 6:47:28
Malvern 113 1 31N20'07 95w42'12 6:22:49
Mambrino 111 1 32N22'27 97w44'41 6:30:59
Manchaca 227 1 30N08'26 97w49'58 6:31:20
Manchester 101 1 29N43'05 95w15'42 6:21:03
Manchester 194 1 33N50'33 95w09'44 6:20:39
Manda 227 1 30N24'09 97w28'05 6:29:52
Mangum 67 1 32N19'12 98w51'33 6:35:26
Manheim 144 1 30N13'50 97w01'51 6:28:07
Mankin 107 1 32N09 96w05 6:24:20
Mankins 5 1 33N46'57 98w47'48 6:35:11
Mankins Mill 215
1 32N39'10 99w03'29 6:36:14
Mann 195 1 31N24'12 103w31'12 6:54:05
Mann Crossing 15
1 29N18'21 98w39'42 6:34:39
Manning 3 1 31N08'19 94w32'10 6:18:09
Manor 227 1 30N20'26 97w33'24 6:30:14
Mansfield 220 1 32N33'47 97w08'29 6:28:34
Manson 120 1 28N59'33 96w36'56 6:26:28
Mantu 101 1 29N47'51 95w05'24 6:20:22
Manvel 20 1 29N27'45 95w21'28 6:21:26
Maple 40 1 33N50'55 102w53'53 6:51:36
Maple Crest Acres 181
1 30N08'06 93w58'52 6:15:55
Maple Springs 225
1 33N21'20 95w00'19 6:20:01
Mapleton 113 1 31N08'24 95w40'07 6:22:40
Marak 166 1 30N54'06 97w04'06 6:28:16
Marathon 22 1 30N12'18 103w14'39 6:52:59
Marble Falls 27
1 30N34'41 98w16'21 6:33:05
March Trailer Court 116
1 32N43 96w00 6:24:00
Marco 154 1 31N08'24 99w34'48 6:38:19
Marfa 189 1 30N18'28 104w01'07 6:56:04
Margaret 78 1 34N02'58 99w39'03 6:38:36
Margie 145 1 31N13'45 96w07'51 6:24:31
Marie 200 1 31N53 100w18 6:41:12
Marietta 34 1 33N10'24 94w32'32 6:18:10
Marilee 43 1 33N24'13 96w45'40 6:27:03
Marilla 44 3 34N58'47 100w23'50 6:41:35
Marion 94 1 29N34'16 98w08'24 6:32:34
Marion West 158
1 32N48 94w30 6:18:00
Marjorie 166 1 30N37'52 97w05'02 6:28:20
Markham 161 1 28N57'36 96w03'54 6:24:16
Markley 252 1 33N21'30 98w26'52 6:33:47
Markout 129 1 32N42'24 96w29'32 6:25:58
Marlin 73 1 31N18'22 96w53'52 6:27:35
Marly 75 1 29N52'17 97w01'59 6:28:08
Marquez 145 1 31N14'21 96w15'12 6:25:01
Marsh 188 3 35N32'23 101w55'18 6:47:41
Marshall 102 1 32N32'41 94w22'02 6:17:28
Marshall Ford 227
1 30N23'30 97w53'18 6:31:33
Marshall Springs 225
1 33N13'19 95w04'50 6:20:19
Marshy Springs 81
1 31N31'25 96w06'04 6:24:24
Marston 187 1 30N45'29 94w54'31 6:19:38
Mart 155 1 31N32'32 96w50'00 6:27:20
Martha 146 1 30N05'12 94w55'05 6:19:40
Martin 3 1 31N02'47 94w24'01 6:17:36
Martindale 28 1 29N50'43 97w50'26 6:31:22
Martinez 15 1 29N25'07 98w20'08 6:33:21
Martins Mills 234
1 32N24'58 95w47'24 6:23:10
Martin Springs 112
1 33N05'12 95w33'53 6:22:16
Martinsville 174
1 31N38'33 94w24'50 6:17:39
Marvin 139 1 33N36'28 95w28'56 6:21:56
Marvin 198 1 30N54'52 96w42'10 6:26:49
Maryetta 119 1 33N17'54 98w04'29 6:32:18
Mary Hardin-Baylor 14
1 31N03 97w28 6:29:52
Maryneal 177 1 32N14'07 100w27'00 6:41:48
Marystown 126 1 32N27'35 97w19'11 6:29:17
Marysville 49 1 33N46'14 97w20'02 6:29:20
Mason 160 1 30N44'55 99w13'49 6:36:55
Mason 202 1 31N14'44 93w46'07 6:15:04
Mason Crossing 50
1 31N12'19 97w42'55 6:30:52
Massa 203 1 31N16'17 94w07'42 6:16:31
Massey Lake 1 1 31N48'43 95w52'05 6:23:28
Masterson 33 3 35N24'40 101w37'09 6:46:29
Masterson 171 3 35N38'09 101w57'35 6:47:50
Matador 173 1 34N00'43 100w49'18 6:43:17
Matagorda 161 1 28N41'26 95w58'02 6:23:52
Mathis 205 1 28N05'39 97w49'40 6:31:19
Matilda 120 1 28N57'33 96w40'45 6:26:43
Matinburg 230 1 32N54'08 95w02'40 6:20:11
Matthews 45 1 29N29'57 96w19'21 6:25:17
Matthews Place 22
3 30N13'58 103w01'27 6:52:06
Mattox 176 1 30N59'59 93w46'24 6:15:06
Mattson 104 1 33N15'07 99w35'51 6:38:23
Maud 19 1 33N19'58 94w20'33 6:17:22
Maudlowe 196 1 28N25'35 96w53'26 6:27:34
Mauriceville 181
1 30N12'12 93w51'58 6:15:28
Maurin 89 1 29N30 97w27 6:29:48
Maverick 200 1 31N50'00 100w11'41 6:40:47
Maxdale 14 1 30N59'23 97w50'07 6:31:20
Maxey 139 1 33N42'12 95w45'04 6:23:00
Maxey Town 203 1 31N26'36 94w07'21 6:16:29
Maxwell 28 1 29N52'51 97w47'35 6:31:10
Maxwell Crossing 184
1 32N37'15 97w56'13 6:31:45
May 25 1 31N58'46 98w55'11 6:35:41
Maydelle 37 1 31N48'02 95w18'08 6:21:13
Mayer 188 3 35N15'43 101w44'16 6:46:57
Mayfair 101 1 29N41'15 95w19'10 6:21:17
Mayfield 95 1 34N06'28 101w59'21 6:47:57
Mayfield 109 1 32N05'47 97w11'38 6:28:47
Mayflower 176 1 31N05'24 93w43'25 6:14:54
Mayflower 201 1 32N19'51 94w36'16 6:18:25
Mayhill 61 1 33N11 97w04 6:28:16
Maynard 204 1 30N31'19 95w19'40 6:21:19
Mayo 128 1 28N54'18 97w55'20 6:31:41
Maypearl 70 1 32N18'47 97w00'41 6:28:03
Mays Crossing 128
1 28N56'46 98w03'49 6:32:15
Maysfield 166 1 30N53'49 96w51'03 6:27:24
McAdoo 63 1 33N44'02 101w00'21 6:44:01
McAllen 108 1 26N12'11 98w13'47 6:32:55
McBeth 20 1 29N09 95w27 6:21:48
McBride 33 3 35N31'05 101w29'37 6:45:58
McCamey 231 1 31N08'09 102w13'26 6:48:54
McCaulley 76 1 32N46'55 100w12'13 6:40:49
McClanahan 73 1 31N21'25 96w49'42 6:27:19
McClelland 210 1 31N39'48 94w04'40 6:16:19
McColl 108 1 26N12 98w15 6:33:00
McCook 108 1 26N29'00 98w23'26 6:33:34
McCoy 7 1 28N51'37 98w20'51 6:33:23
McCoy 77 1 33N52'05 101w26'14 6:45:45
McCoy 129 1 32N50 96w06 6:24:24
McCoy 183 1 32N02 94w22 6:17:28
McCoy 194 1 33N34'36 95w07'32 6:20:30
McCroskey 116 1 29N05'57 95w57'34 6:23:50
McDade 11 1 30N17'01 97w14'15 6:28:57
McDonald 169 1 33N32'26 97w49'26 6:31:18
McElroy 202 1 31N11'58 93w59'42 6:15:59
McFadden 123 1 30N00'55 94w01'51 6:16:07
McFaddin 235 1 28N33'13 97w00'49 6:28:03
McFarland Place 22
1 30N11'15 103w02'14 6:52:09
McGalin 121 1 30N27 93w57 6:15:48
McGregor 155 1 31N26'38 97w24'32 6:29:38
McHattie 79 1 29N32'29 95w50'46 6:23:23
McKee 171 3 36N01 101w49 6:47:16
McKeichan Crossing 224
1 33N00'54 99w14'59 6:37:00
McKibben 98 3 36N07'33 101w20'19 6:45:21
McKinney 43 1 33N11'51 96w36'54 6:26:28
McKinney Springs 22
1 29N23'16 103w04'33 6:52:18
McKnight 65 3 34N54'26 100w33'25 6:42:14
McKnight 201 1 32N00'15 94w54'20 6:19:37
McLean 90 3 35N13'57 100w35'58 6:42:24
McLendon 199 1 32N50'46 96w23'23 6:25:34
McLendon-Chisholm 199
1 32N53 96w30 6:26:00
McLeod 34 1 32N56'40 94w04'48 6:16:19
McMahan 28 1 29N51'09 97w31'09 6:30:05
McMillin 206 1 31N12 98w44 6:34:56
McMurray 221 1 32N25 99w46 6:39:04
McNair 101 1 29N48'14 96w01'17 6:20:05
McNair Village 14
1 31N08'02 97w45'32 6:31:02
McNary 115 2 31N14'53 105w47'45 7:03:11
McNeil 28 1 29N42'29 97w35'03 6:30:20
McNeil 227 1 30N27'10 97w43'13 6:30:53
McNorton 178 1 27N48'42 97w32'20 6:30:09
McQueeney 94 1 29N35'31 98w01'59 6:32:08
McRoy 129 1 32N49'25 96w06'26 6:24:26
Meaders 57 1 32N53'17 96w48'44 6:27:15
Meador Grove 14
1 31N17'07 97w27'24 6:29:50
Meadow 223 1 33N20'13 102w12'22 6:48:49
Mecca 157 1 30N59'02 96w04'00 6:24:16
Medical Center 57
1 32N49 96w49 6:27:16
Medicine Mound 99
1 34N11'16 99w35'39 6:38:23
Medill 139 1 33N47'35 95w24'30 6:21:38
Medina 10 1 29N47'47 99w14'46 6:36:59
Medina Base 15 1 29N23 98w36 6:34:24
Meeker 123 1 30N04'58 94w15'29 6:17:02
Meeks 14 1 30N59'31 97w07'01 6:28:28
Megargel 5 1 33N27'03 98w55'27 6:35:42
Meldrum 210 1 31N55'17 94w20'05 6:17:20
Melendy 101 1 29N52'49 95w34'15 6:22:17
Melissa 43 1 33N17'09 96w34'21 6:26:17
Melo 88 1 28N37'27 97w25'12 6:29:41
Melody Hills 220
1 32N49'49 97w18'33 6:29:14
Melon 82 1 28N50'28 99w06'49 6:36:27
Melrose 88 1 28N48'12 97w31'23 6:30:06
Melrose 92 1 32N22 94w52 6:19:28
Melrose 174 1 31N33'41 94w28'35 6:17:54
Melrose Park 101
1 29N52'12 95w22'17 6:21:29
Melton 116 1 33N08 96w07 6:24:28
Melvin 154 1 31N11'42 99w34'46 6:38:19
Memorial Park 101
1 29N47 95w32 6:22:08
Memphis 96 1 34N43'29 100w32'01 6:42:08
Menard 164 1 30N55'03 99w47'10 6:39:09
Mendiates 66 1 27N58'55 98w14'58 6:33:00
Mendota 106 3 35N48'05 100w29'52 6:41:59
Mendoza 28 1 30N00'17 97w41'09 6:30:45
Menlow 109 1 31N52'10 97w09'37 6:28:38
Mentone 151 1 31N42'18 103w35'56 6:54:24
Mentz 45 1 29N45'00 96w26'12 6:25:45
Mercedes 108 1 26N08'58 97w54'48 6:31:39
Mercer's Gap 47
1 31N54 98w36 6:34:24
Merchandise Mart 57
1 32N47 96w48 6:27:12
Mercury 154 1 31N24'44 99w09'26 6:36:38
Mereta 226 1 31N27'25 100w08'26 6:40:34
Meridian 18 1 31N55'23 97w39'23 6:30:38
Merit 116 1 33N13'00 96w17'14 6:25:09
Merito 108 1 26N15'23 98w13'14 6:32:53
Merkel 221 1 32N28'14 100w00'45 6:40:03
Merle 26 1 30N26'57 96w27'44 6:25:51
Merrelltown 227
1 30N27'16 97w41'41 6:30:47
Merrick 159 1 32N23'04 101w50'23 6:47:22
Mertens 109 1 32N03'30 96w53'47 6:27:35
Mertzon 118 1 31N15'42 100w49'01 6:43:16
Mesa 71 2 31N32 106w10 7:04:40
Mesilla Park 90
3 35N33'57 100w57'07 6:43:48
Mesquite 17 1 32N52'13 101w37'47 6:46:31
Mesquite 57 1 32N46'00 96w35'56 6:26:24
Metcalf Gap 182
1 32N33 98w30 6:34:00
Metz 68 1 31N42'12 102w39'24 6:50:38
Mewshaw 37 1 31N46'49 95w21'33 6:21:26
Mexia 147 1 31N40'47 96w28'55 6:25:56
Mexico 116 1 32N54 96w05 6:24:20
Meyerland 101 1 29N41'05 95w28'02 6:21:52
Meyers Village 68
1 31N52 102w22 6:49:28
Meyersville 62 1 28N55'41 97w18'44 6:29:15
Miami 197 3 35N41'29 100w38'16 6:42:33
Mickey 77 1 34N07 101w27 6:45:48
Mico 163 1 29N32'38 98w55'22 6:35:41
Middleburg 99 1 34N15'24 99w48'35 6:39:14
Middle Crossing 50
1 31N12'53 97w47'38 6:31:11
Middleton 145 1 31N10'30 95w51'50 6:23:27
Middle Water 103
3 35N51 102w47 6:51:08
Middlewell 171 3 35N45'53 102w07'27 6:48:30
Mideity 139 1 33N50'32 95w30'51 6:22:03
Midfield 161 1 28N56'15 96w12'28 6:24:50
Midkiff 231 1 31N37'58 101w50'22 6:47:21
Midland 165 1 31N59'50 102w04'39 6:48:19
Midline 170 1 30N15'28 95w08'42 6:20:35
Midlothian 70 1 32N28'56 96w59'39 6:27:59
Midway 14 1 31N05'15 97w25'39 6:29:43
Midway 20 1 28N57'14 95w20'12 6:21:21
Midway 34 1 33N05'21 94w34'55 6:18:20
Midway 53 1 30N54'37 101w09'38 6:44:39
Midway 58 1 32N41'10 101w47'10 6:47:09
Midway 74 1 33N34'13 96w13'17 6:24:53
Midway 97 1 31N42'05 98w12'19 6:32:49
Midway 107 1 32N11'10 95w56'46 6:23:47
Midway 109 1 32N05'31 97w00'05 6:28:00
Midway 114 1 32N16'28 101w22'12 6:45:29
Midway 116 1 33N18'12 96w09'05 6:24:36
Midway 125 1 28N01'13 98w05'42 6:32:23
Midway 143 1 29N21'52 97w10'23 6:28:42
Midway 145 1 31N22'02 95w57'19 6:23:49
Midway 147 1 31N32'33 96w43'44 6:26:55
Midway 152 1 33N32'22 101w34'59 6:46:20
Midway 157 1 31N01'33 95w45'01 6:23:00
Midway 170 1 30N18 95w07 6:20:28
Midway 194 1 33N42'26 95w13'30 6:20:54
Midway 205 1 27N57'13 97w21'01 6:29:24
Midway 208 1 32N43'58 100w40'57 6:42:44
Midway 212 1 32N28'16 95w06'10 6:20:25
Midway 225 1 33N16'02 94w56'43 6:19:47
Midway 230 1 32N51'27 94w57'06 6:19:48
Midway Crossing 244
1 33N57'46 99w12'39 6:36:51
Midyett 183 1 32N18 94w10 6:16:40
Miguel 82 1 28N55'24 90w49'13 6:35:17
Mikeska 149 1 28N17'08 98w02'57 6:32:12
Milam 202 1 31N25'56 93w50'44 6:15:23
Milano 166 1 30N42'37 96w51'47 6:27:27
Milburn 154 1 31N26'15 99w06'34 6:36:26
Mildred 175 1 32N02'06 96w22'36 6:25:30
Mile High 115 2 31N16'16 105w24'43 7:01:39
Miles 200 1 31N35'50 100w10'55 6:40:44
Milford 70 1 32N07'28 96w56'42 6:27:47
Military Crossing 154
1 31N26'50 99w16'53 6:37:08
Mill Creek 239 1 30N09'19 96w29'35 6:25:58
Miller Grove 32
1 33N00 94w58 6:19:52

Miller Grove 112
1 33N01'27 95w48'09 6:23:13
Millers 22 1 29N52'27 102w42'56 6:50:52
Millersview 48 1 31N24'31 99w45'19 6:39:01
Millett 142 1 28N34'54 99w11'56 6:36:48
Millheim 8 1 29N52'18 96w14'53 6:25:00
Millican 21 1 30N28'06 96w12'08 6:24:49
Milligan 43 1 33N11'09 96w32'49 6:26:11
Mill Pond 174 1 31N40 94w38 6:18:32
Mills 91 1 33N43'46 96w32'44 6:26:11
Millsap 184 1 32N44'53 98w00'32 6:32:02
Millsville 205 1 27N54'45 97w11'07 6:28:44
Mill Town 228 1 30N57'31 95w22'25 6:21:30
Millwood 43 1 32N59'45 96w25'05 6:25:40
Milo Center 59 3 34N58'59 102w24'06 6:49:36
Milton 139 1 33N30'53 95w22'27 6:21:30
Milvid 146 1 30N27'30 94w47'47 6:19:11
Mims 20 1 29N05'13 95w17'13 6:21:09
Minchin 61 1 33N10'45 97w09'12 6:28:37
Minden 201 1 32N00'48 94w42'26 6:18:50
Mineola 250 1 32N39'47 95w29'17 6:21:57
Minera 240 1 27N43'19 99w45'28 6:39:02
Mineral 13 1 28N32'54 97w54'14 6:31:37
Mineral Heights 116
1 33N06'36 96w06'57 6:24:28
Mineral Wells 182
1 32N48'30 98w06'45 6:32:27
Minerva 166 1 30N45'29 96w59'16 6:27:57
Mingo 61 1 33N14'48 97w03'38 6:28:15
Mings Chapel 230
1 32N44 94w57 6:19:48
Mingus 182 1 32N32'16 98w25'19 6:33:41
Minnetex 101 1 29N36'59 95w21'18 6:21:25
Minter 139 1 33N28'14 95w23'32 6:21:34
Minters Chapel 220
1 32N57 97w07 6:28:28
Mirando City 240
1 27N26'22 99w00'03 6:36:00
Mission 108 1 26N12'56 98w19'30 6:33:18
Mission Hills 71
2 31N47'20 106w29'44 7:05:59
Mission Valley 46
1 29N42 98w08 6:32:32
Mission Valley 235
1 28N53'56 97w11'38 6:28:47
Missouri City 79
1 29N37'06 95w32'15 6:22:09
Mitchell 67 1 32N20'43 99w03'39 6:36:15
Mitchell Crossing 154
1 31N24'56 99w19'51 6:37:19
Mitchell Place 22
3 30N14'31 103w09'28 6:52:38
Mittie 37 1 31N58'18 95w13'44 6:20:55
Mixon 37 1 32N05'19 95w12'36 6:20:50
M K Crossing 224
1 33N00'05 99w23'33 6:37:34
Mobeetie 242 3 35N30'47 100w26'29 6:41:46
Mofeta 222 1 30N03'15 102w13'32 6:48:54
Moffatt 14 1 31N11'59 97w28'05 6:29:52
Moffett 3 1 30N15 95w32 6:22:08
Moffitt 3 1 31N23'53 94w38'35 6:18:34
Moline 141 1 31N23'01 98w18'37 6:33:14
Monadale 246 1 30N33 97w33 6:30:12
Monahans 238 1 31N35'39 102w53'32 6:51:34
Monaville 237 1 29N57'02 96w02'19 6:24:09
Monkstown 74 1 33N47'27 95w55'41 6:23:43
Monroe 201 1 32N20'07 94w44'15 6:18:57
Monroe City 101
1 29N47'05 94w35'06 6:18:20
Mont 143 1 29N27 96w56 6:27:44
Montague 169 1 33N39'53 97w43'13 6:30:53
Montague Village 50
1 31N07 97w50 6:31:20
Montalba 1 1 31N52'35 95w43'57 6:22:56
Mont Belvieu 36
1 29N50'51 94w53'26 6:19:34
Monte Alto 108 1 26N22'22 97w58'17 6:31:53
Monte Christo 108
1 26N22'56 98w17'48 6:33:11
Monte Grande 31
1 26N16'06 97w31'08 6:30:05
Montell 232 1 29N32'16 100w00'40 6:40:03
Monteola 13 1 28N41'51 97w54'56 6:31:40
Monterey 3 1 31N13'48 94w23'43 6:17:35
Monterey 158 1 32N50'07 94w02'53 6:16:12
Montfort 175 1 32N13'20 96w20'57 6:25:24
Montgomery 170 1 30N23'17 95w41'46 6:22:47
Montgomery Gardens 212
1 32N20 95w18 6:21:12
Monthalia 89 1 29N28'07 97w36'30 6:30:26
Monticello 225 1 33N05'45 95w05'08 6:20:21
Montopolis 227 1 30N14'35 97w41'25 6:30:46
Montoya 71 2 31N51'02 106w34'49 7:06:19
Moody 155 1 31N18'29 97w21'40 6:29:27
Moonshine Hill 101
1 30N00'10 95w14'10 6:20:57
Moore 21 1 30N46'13 96w19'51 6:25:19
Moore 82 1 29N03'18 99w00'36 6:36:02
Mooredale 79 1 29N18'38 95w49'41 6:23:19
Moore Grove 236
1 30N34'26 95w32'29 6:22:10
Moore Hill 187 1 30N41'25 95w01'55 6:20:08
Moore's Chapel 74
1 33N35 96w11 6:24:44
Moores Crossing 227
1 30N10'07 97w39'49 6:30:39
Moore Station 107
1 32N07 95w41 6:22:44
Mooresville 73 1 31N18'09 97w08'34 6:28:34
Mooring 21 1 30N41'22 96w33'19 6:26:13
Morales 120 1 29N07'38 96w45'44 6:27:03
Moran 209 1 32N32'51 99w09'56 6:36:40
Moravia 143 1 29N35'22 96w59'05 6:27:56
Morey 123 1 29N52'52 94w16'57 6:17:08
Morgan 18 1 32N01'07 97w36'29 6:30:26
Morgan Bluff 181
1 30N12'32 93w43'15 6:14:53
Morgan Mill 72 1 32N23'17 98w10'01 6:32:40
Morgans Point 101
1 29N40'45 94w59'23 6:19:58
Morgan's Point Resort 14
1 31N03 97w28 6:29:52
Morita 114 1 32N11'04 101w38'00 6:46:32

Morrill 113 1 31N35'37 95w03'52 6:20:15
Morris Grove 112
1 33N02'13 95w18'51 6:21:15
Morrison Falls 94
1 29N33'51 98w01'12 6:32:05
Morris Ranch 86
1 30N17 98w52 6:35:28
Morse 98 3 36N03'45 101w28'30 6:45:54
Morse Junction 117
3 36N01'56 101w28'25 6:45:54
Morton 40 1 33N43'30 102w45'32 6:51:02
Morton 102 1 32N40'11 94w39'28 6:18:38
Morton Valley 67
1 32N28 98w49 6:35:16
Moscow 187 1 30N54'47 94w49'30 6:19:18
Moselle 220 1 32N37'45 97w21'13 6:29:25
Moser 222 1 30N29'33 101w55'55 6:47:44
Mosheim 18 1 31N37'34 97w35'59 6:30:24
Moss Bluff 146 1 29N56'14 94w45'47 6:19:03
Moss Hill 146 1 30N14'50 94w44'29 6:18:58
Mossy Grove 236
1 30N51'07 95w45'04 6:23:00
Mostyn 170 1 30N13'41 95w41'24 6:22:46
Moulton 143 1 29N34'29 97w08'33 6:28:34
Mound 50 1 31N21'06 97w38'14 6:30:33
Mound City 113 1 31N34'36 95w24'20 6:21:37
Mountain 50 1 31N25 97w43 6:30:52
Mountain City 105
1 30N02'13 97w53'12 6:31:33
Mountain Creek 57
1 32N44 96w59 6:27:56
Mountain Home 133
1 30N10 99w22 6:37:28
Mountain Peak 70
1 32N24'45 97w01'02 6:28:04
Mountain Springs 49
1 33N28'49 97w02'37 6:28:10
Mountain View 71
2 31N51'59 106w24'52 7:05:39
Mountain View 109
1 32N06'44 97w04'33 6:28:18
Mount Bethel 116
1 33N02'54 96w06'33 6:24:26
Mount Blanco 54
1 33N48'56 101w11'34 6:44:46
Mount Calm 109 1 31N45'22 96w52'44 6:27:31
Mount Calvary 183
1 32N09 94w20 6:17:20
Mount Carmel 243
1 34N02 98w55 6:35:40
Mount Enterprise 201
1 31N55'04 94w40'51 6:18:43
Mount Enterprise 250
1 32N40 95w29 6:21:56
Mount Evergreen 123
1 30N09'06 94w10'29 6:16:42
Mount Gainor 105
1 30N08'37 98w08'05 6:32:32
Mount Herman 210
1 31N41'53 94w18'05 6:17:12
Mount Houston 101
1 29N53'27 95w18'20 6:21:13
Mount Joy 60 1 33N28'30 95w37'14 6:22:29
Mount Joy Crossing 60
1 33N29'01 95w36'59 6:22:28
Mount Lucas 149
1 28N11'12 97w56'46 6:31:47
Mount Mitchell 172
1 33N07'19 94w48'15 6:19:13
Mount Morian 236
1 30N43'34 95w29'29 6:21:58
Mount Olive 120
1 29N04'00 96w41'39 6:26:47
Mount Olive 143
1 29N23'33 97w05'59 6:28:24
Mount Pleasant 221
1 32N23'49 99w58'17 6:39:53
Mount Pleasant 225
1 33N09'24 94w58'05 6:19:52
Mount Selman 37
1 32N04'05 95w17'02 6:21:08
Mount Sharp 105
1 30N10 98w05 6:32:20
Mount Sylvan 212
1 32N27'26 95w28'07 6:21:52
Mount Union 121
1 30N41'56 94w01'20 6:16:05
Mount Vernon 80
1 33N11'19 95w13'16 6:20:53
Mount Wesley 133
1 30N04'28 99w09'33 6:36:38
Mount Zion 170 1 30N29'38 95w25'55 6:21:44
Mount Zion 237 1 29N47 95w57 6:23:48
Moursund 235 1 28N53'10 97w03'27 6:28:14
Mozelle 42 1 31N35'56 99w29'33 6:37:58
Mozo 246 1 30N41'29 97w31'29 6:30:06
Muddig 116 1 33N25 95w56 6:23:44
Mudville 21 1 30N40'49 96w33'03 6:26:12
Muehlsville 94 1 29N32'59 98w02'35 6:32:10
Muellersville 239
1 30N05'42 96w25'28 6:25:42
Muenster 49 1 33N39'06 97w22'34 6:29:30
Mull 125 1 27N45'37 98w13'00 6:32:52
Mulberry 74 1 33N43'16 96w16'51 6:25:07
Mulberry Springs 102
1 32N35'58 94w36'22 6:18:25
Muldoon 75 1 29N48'56 97w04'15 6:28:17
Muleshoe 9 1 34N13'35 102w43'24 6:50:54
Mulkey 35 3 34N27'56 102w12'49 6:48:51
Mullin 167 1 31N33'24 98w39'55 6:34:40
Mullins Crossing 226
1 31N32'10 100w13'05 6:40:52
Mullins Prairie 75
1 29N54 96w52 6:27:28
Mumford 198 1 30N44'03 96w33'53 6:26:16
Muncy 77 1 34N03'59 101w23'28 6:45:34
Munday 138 1 33N26'57 99w37'21 6:38:29
Munger 147 1 31N47'45 96w42'22 6:26:49
Mungerville 58 1 32N46'24 102w05'27 6:48:22
Munson 199 1 32N53'48 96w17'53 6:25:12
Murchison 107 1 32N16'42 95w44'58 6:23:00
Murdo 180 3 35N36'34 102w21'02 6:49:24
Murphy 43 1 33N00'54 96w36'46 6:26:27

Murray 252 1 33N03'23 98w53'41 6:35:35
Murryhill 152 1 33N33 101w53 6:47:32
Musgrove 250 1 32N57'19 95w13'39 6:20:55
Mustang 61 1 33N19'14 96w54'10 6:27:37
Mustang 73 1 31N15'04 96w38'30 6:26:34
Mustang 147 1 31N45 96w39 6:26:36
Mustang Beach 178
1 27N48'12 97w05'26 6:28:22
Mykawa 101 1 29N37'14 95w18'16 6:21:13
Myra 49 1 33N37'26 97w18'51 6:29:15
Myrtle 101 1 29N39'00 95w24'16 6:21:37
Myrtle Springs 234
1 32N36'35 95w55'48 6:23:43
Naaman 57 1 32N57'13 96w37'37 6:26:30
Naclina 174 1 31N22'25 94w27'09 6:17:49
Nacogdoches 174
1 31N36'12 94w39'19 6:18:37
Nada 45 1 29N24'17 96w23'10 6:25:33
Nadeau 84 1 29N23'03 94w56'40 6:19:47
Nancy 3 1 31N06'20 94w25'50 6:17:43
Napier 204 1 30N29'01 95w00'21 6:20:01
Naples 172 1 33N12'11 94w40'48 6:18:43
Narcisso 51 1 34N00'01 100w28'23 6:41:54
Naruna 27 1 30N59'19 98w19'02 6:33:16
Nash 19 1 33N26'32 94w07'50 6:16:31
Nash 70 1 32N15'56 96w48'45 6:27:15
Nassau Bay 101 1 29N47 95w23 6:21:32
Nat 174 1 31N42'48 94w49'35 6:19:18
Natalia 163 1 29N11'22 98w51'44 6:35:27
Natural Bridge Caverns 15
1 29N30 98w25 6:33:40
Navarro 175 1 31N59'54 96w22'41 6:25:31
Navarro Mills 175
1 31N57'28 96w40'55 6:26:44
Navasota 93 1 30N23'16 96w05'15 6:24:21
Navidad 120 1 29N03'55 96w46'08 6:27:05
Navo 61 1 33N13'14 96w55'47 6:27:43
Nazareth 35 3 34N32'39 102w06'08 6:48:25
Neale 155 1 31N31'22 97w01'26 6:28:06
Neals Valley 70
1 32N20 96w38 6:26:32
Necessity 215 1 32N38'54 98w46'29 6:35:06
Nechanitz 75 1 30N02'44 96w49'36 6:27:18
Neches 1 1 31N52'00 95w29'44 6:21:59
Neches Indian Village 37
1 31N39 95w04 6:20:16
Neches Junction 123
1 29N55 93w56 6:15:44
Nederland 123 1 29N58'27 93w59'32 6:15:58
Needmore 9 1 34N01'59 102w44'13 6:50:57
Needmore 60 1 33N19'25 95w50'22 6:23:21
Needmore 203 1 31N07'56 94w03'12 6:16:13
Needmore 223 1 33N19'36 102w19'34 6:49:18
Needville 79 1 29N23'57 95w50'15 6:23:21
Negley 194 1 33N45'36 95w05'06 6:20:20
Negro Crossing 226
1 31N21'13 100w32'11 6:42:09
Neinda 127 1 32N47'48 100w05'33 6:40:22
Nell 149 1 28N42'39 98w04'17 6:32:17
Nelleva 21 1 30N27'16 96w11'10 6:24:45
Nelson 70 1 32N18'49 96w51'24 6:27:26
Nelson City 130
1 29N52'38 98w47'42 6:35:11
Nelsonville 8 1 29N58'35 96w24'11 6:25:37
Nelta 112 1 33N18'08 95w28'35 6:21:54
Nemo 213 1 32N15'35 97w39'06 6:30:36
Nena 70 1 32N19'37 96w51'20 6:27:25
Neri 111 1 32N21'49 97w46'29 6:31:06
Nesbit 198 1 31N05'53 96w35'48 6:26:23
Nesbitt 102 1 32N35'37 94w27'14 6:17:49
Nesbitt 198 1 31N10 96w41 6:26:44
Neuville 210 1 31N40'41 94w08'32 6:16:34
Nevada 43 1 33N02'32 96w22'25 6:25:30
Newark 249 1 33N00'04 97w29'03 6:29:56
Newark Beach 249
1 32N59'40 97w30'33 6:30:02
New Baden 198 1 31N03'03 96w25'44 6:25:43
New Berlin 94 1 29N27'50 98w06'03 6:32:24
New Birthright 112
1 33N16'20 95w35'03 6:22:20
New Blox 121 1 30N58'55 93w59'11 6:15:57
New Boston 19 1 33N27'35 94w24'55 6:17:40
New Braunfels 46
1 29N42'10 98w07'27 6:32:30
New Bremen 8 1 29N55'26 96w24'16 6:25:37
Newburg 47 1 31N54 98w36 6:34:24
Newby 145 1 31N21'36 96w10'41 6:24:43
New Caney 170 1 30N09'18 95w12'40 6:20:51
Newcastle 252 1 33N11'38 98w44'18 6:34:57
New Clarkson 166
1 31N00'21 96w54'19 6:27:37
New Colony 14 1 30N57'43 97w09'46 6:28:39
New Colony 34 1 33N02'52 94w17'56 6:17:12
New Corn Hill 246
1 30N46'10 97w35'14 6:30:21
New Davy 62 1 29N03'20 97w36'45 6:30:27
New Deal 152 1 33N44'14 101w50'10 6:47:21
New Fountain 163
1 29N23'11 99w03'35 6:36:14
Newgulf 241 1 29N15'18 95w53'59 6:23:36
Newgulf Junction 241
1 29N14'02 95w55'10 6:23:41
New Harmony 210
1 31N46 93w52 6:15:28
New Harmony 212
1 32N24'51 95w27'57 6:21:52
New Harp 169 1 33N27'09 97w34'21 6:30:17
New Hebron 102 1 32N21 94w06 6:16:24
New Home 153 1 33N19'35 101w54'42 6:47:39
New Hope 19 1 33N26'32 94w42'12 6:18:49
New Hope 37 1 31N55'24 95w18'30 6:21:14
New Hope 43 1 33N12'36 96w33'54 6:26:16
New Hope 57 1 32N48'50 96w35'44 6:26:23
New Hope 61 1 33N14'04 96w59'18 6:27:57
New Hope 80 1 33N01'05 95w10'08 6:20:41
New Hope 107 1 32N15'02 95w35'46 6:22:23
New Hope 127 1 32N52'06 99w47'57 6:39:12
New Hope 147 1 31N24'40 96w16'52 6:25:07
New Hope 201 1 32N20'37 94w46'15 6:19:05
New Hope 204 1 30N18 95w07 6:20:28
New Hope 212 1 32N10'16 95w18'52 6:21:15
New Hope 250 1 32N39'23 95w25'05 6:21:40
New Katy 227 1 30N20'49 97w31'29 6:30:06

New Liberty 34 1 33N10'18 94w15'25 6:17:02
Newlin 96 1 34N35'23 100w26'38 6:41:47
New London 201 1 32N14'19 94w56'25 6:19:46
New Lynn 153 1 33N12'41 101w39'54 6:46:40
Newman 71 2 31N52 106w26 7:05:44
New Mesquite 43 1 33N07'00 96w26'00 6:25:44
New Mine 32 1 33N00 94w58 6:19:52
New Mobeetie 242 3 35N31'55 100w26'28 6:41:46
New Moore 153 1 33N01'19 102w01'56 6:48:08
New Mountain 230 1 32N49'43 94w48'37 6:19:14
Newport 39 1 33N28'04 98w00'58 6:32:04
Newport 101 1 29N54 95w04 6:20:16
New Prospect 201 1 32N12'05 94w44'04 6:18:56
New Salem 182 1 32N37'01 98w05'54 6:32:24
New Salem 201 1 31N56'29 94w57'34 6:19:50
Newsome 32 1 32N58'38 95w08'19 6:20:33
New Summerfield 37 1 31N58'50 95w05'37 6:20:22
New Sweden 227 1 30N24'30 97w30'46 6:30:03
Newt 74 1 33N50'19 95w53'55 6:23:36
New Taiton 241 1 29N18'33 96w20'29 6:25:22
Newton 176 1 30N50'54 93w45'26 6:15:02
Newtonville 89 1 29N39'07 97w11'41 6:28:47
New Ulm 8 1 29N53'31 96w29'24 6:25:58
New Waverly 236 1 30N32'15 95w28'59 6:21:56
New Wehdem 8 1 30N10 96w24 6:25:36
New Willard 187 1 30N47'48 94w53'34 6:19:34
New York 107 1 32N10'04 95w40'08 6:22:41
Neylandville 116 1 33N11'58 96w00'11 6:24:01
Niblock 154 1 31N08'28 99w23'30 6:37:34
Nicholas 198 1 30N46'56 96w35'40 6:26:23
Nickel 89 1 29N33'19 97w13'07 6:28:52
Nickelberry 34 1 33N10 94w33 6:18:12
Nickel Creek 55 1 32N25 104w14 6:56:56
Nickleberry 34 1 33N08'48 94w31'12 6:18:05
Niederwald 28 1 30N00'33 97w43'40 6:30:55
Nigton 228 1 31N13 94w58 6:19:52
Nile 166 1 30N37 97w12 6:28:48
Nimitz 15 1 29N33 98w31 6:34:04
Nimrod 67 1 32N16'20 99w03'08 6:36:13
Nineteen Mile Crossing 232 1 29N23'52 100w00'06 6:40:00
Nineveh 145 1 31N23'00 95w48'21 6:23:13
Nix 141 1 31N04 98w11 6:32:44
Nixon 89 1 29N16'02 97w45'51 6:31:03
Noack 246 1 30N33'27 97w18'15 6:29:13
Nobility 74 1 33N22'33 96w21'58 6:25:28
Noble 139 1 33N33'07 95w47'38 6:23:11
Nockenut 247 1 29N20'46 97w54'41 6:31:39
Nocona 169 1 33N47'12 97w43'32 6:30:54
Noelke 118 1 31N08'55 100w55'45 6:43:43
Nogalus 228 1 31N15'19 95w05'17 6:20:21
Nolan 177 1 32N16'25 100w14'32 6:40:58
Nolanville 14 1 31N04'43 97w36'19 6:30:25
Nolte 94 1 29N34'28 98w01'51 6:32:07
Nome 123 1 30N02'08 94w25'27 6:17:42
Nona 100 1 30N20'00 94w17'30 6:17:10
Noodle 127 1 32N36'08 100w03'06 6:40:12
Noonan 163 1 29N16'08 98w54'06 6:35:36
Noonday 102 1 32N33'14 94w35'17 6:18:21
Noonday 212 1 32N14'08 95w24'21 6:21:37
Nopal 62 1 29N07'53 97w34'39 6:30:19
Nopal 189 1 30N17'17 103w55'34 6:55:42
Nordheim 62 1 28N55'15 97w36'34 6:30:26
Norias 131 1 26N47'23 97w46'33 6:31:06
Noria Willie 24 1 27N05'07 98w07'37 6:32:30
Normandy 162 1 28N54'36 100w35'51 6:42:23
Normangee 145 1 31N01'46 96w06'52 6:24:27
Normanna 13 1 28N31'46 97w46'55 6:31:08
Normans Crossing 246 1 30N29'28 97w29'23 6:29:58
Norrick 242 3 35N12'46 100w08'10 6:40:33
Norse 18 1 31N47 97w35 6:30:20
North Abilene 127 1 32N32'41 99w46'09 6:39:05
North Amarillo 188 3 35N14 101w48 6:47:12
North Austin 227 1 30N18 97w43 6:30:52
Northaven 57 1 32N53 96w51 6:27:24
North Beach 178 1 27N49'15 97w23'24 6:29:34
North Broadway 15 1 29N33 98w29 6:33:56
North Cedar 228 1 31N13 94w58 6:19:52
North Cleveland 146 1 30N21 95w06 6:20:24
North College 152 1 33N34 101w52 6:47:28
North Cowden 68 1 32N00'16 102w30'45 6:50:03
Northcrest 155 1 31N38 97w06 6:28:24
Northcrest Estates 235 1 28N48 96w59 6:27:56
North Elm 166 1 30N55'56 97w02'53 6:28:12
Northfield 173 1 34N17'14 100w35'54 6:42:24
Northgate 235 1 28N48 96w59 6:27:56
North Georgetown 246 1 30N38'50 97w40'37 6:30:42
North Groesbeck 99 1 34N25'05 99w50'29 6:39:22
North Houston 101 1 29N55'31 95w30'54 6:22:04
North Houston Heights 101 1 29N52 95w20 6:21:20
North Jefferson 158 1 32N46 94w21 6:17:24
North Jim Hogg 124 1 27N14 98w45 6:35:00
Northlake 61 1 33N08 97w16 6:29:04
Northline Terrace 101 1 29N50 95w23 6:21:32
North Loop 15 1 29N31'40 98w27'33 6:33:50
North Oaks 227 1 30N22 97w41 6:30:44
North Pitchfork Corner Windm 63 1 33N33'56 100w37'49 6:42:31
North Port Arthur 123 1 29N55 93w56 6:15:44
North Prairie 73 1 31N20'30 97w05'00 6:28:20
North Randall 191 3 35N06 101w52 6:47:28
North Richland Hills 220 1 32N50'03 97w13'43 6:28:55
North River 38 1 34N40 100w12 6:40:48
Northrup 144 1 30N06'01 96w58'12 6:27:53
North Rusk 37 1 31N48 95w09 6:20:36
North Salem 145 1 31N18'51 96w04'25 6:24:18
North San Pedro 178 1 27N48 97w41 6:30:44
North Shadydale 101 1 29N50'41 95w18'39 6:21:15
North Shepherd 101 1 29N47 95w23 6:21:32
North Sherman 91 1 33N38 96w36 6:26:24
North Sherman Junction 91 1 33N39'43 96w35'25 6:26:22
North Shore 101 1 30N01'35 95w13'23 6:20:54
North Shore Acres 227 1 30N24'54 97w57'45 6:31:51
Northside 244 1 34N18'17 99w17'51 6:37:11
North Texarkana 19 1 33N26 94w04 6:16:16
North Uvalde 232 1 29N13 99w47 6:39:08
North Vidor 181 1 30N09 94w01 6:16:04
Northwest 220 1 32N53 97w29 6:29:56
Northwest 227 1 30N20 97w44 6:30:56
North Zulch 157 1 30N55'03 96w06'29 6:24:26
Norton 200 1 31N52'15 100w07'33 6:40:30
Norwood 203 1 31N24'18 94w12'43 6:16:51
Notla 179 3 36N24 100w48 6:43:12
Notrees 68 1 31N55'02 102w45'19 6:51:01
Nottawa 241 1 29N32'20 96w08'55 6:24:36
Novice 42 1 31N59'22 99w37'24 6:38:30
Novice 139 1 33N47'17 95w23'05 6:21:32
Novohrad 143 1 29N36'20 97w02'55 6:28:12
Noxville 134 1 30N23'23 99w28'01 6:37:52
Nueces 178 1 27N48'50 97w27'42 6:29:51
Nugent 127 1 32N41'38 99w40'02 6:38:40
Nunnelee 74 1 33N36'59 96w13'17 6:24:53
Nursery 235 1 28N55'24 97w05'54 6:28:24
Nuway 71 2 31N56'14 106w35'50 7:06:23
Nye 240 1 27N33'34 99w30'24 6:38:02
Oakalla 27 1 30N59'10 97w55'30 6:31:42
Oak Cliff 57 1 32N44'21 96w48'39 6:27:15
Oak Dale 72 1 32N13 98w13 6:32:52
Oakdale 80 1 33N16'24 95w18'11 6:21:13
Oakdale 112 1 33N16'55 95w31'01 6:22:04
Oak Flat 3 1 31N16'27 94w30'52 6:18:03
Oak Flat 174 1 31N48'08 94w47'43 6:19:11
Oak Flats 201 1 31N56'50 94w46'00 6:19:04
Oak Forest 89 1 29N29'55 97w35'04 6:30:20
Oak Grove 19 1 33N32'10 94w41'16 6:18:45
Oak Grove 34 1 33N03'45 94w12'18 6:16:49
Oak Grove 70 1 32N15'33 96w35'00 6:26:20
Oak Grove 112 1 33N18'20 95w33'18 6:22:13
Oak Grove 204 1 30N26'25 95w12'54 6:20:52
Oak Grove 220 1 32N34'46 97w17'32 6:29:10
Oak Grove 250 1 32N49'17 95w20'41 6:21:23
Oak Hill 121 1 30N47'56 94w06'46 6:16:27
Oak Hill 126 1 32N20'05 97w22'11 6:29:29
Oak Hill 201 1 32N16'26 94w41'41 6:18:47
Oak Hill 227 1 30N14'07 97w51'35 6:31:26
Oakhurst 204 1 30N44'13 95w18'57 6:21:16
Oak Island 16 1 29N13'39 98w33'34 6:34:14
Oak Island 36 1 29N39'40 94w41'22 6:18:45
Oak Knoll 220 1 32N48 97w15 6:29:00
Oak Lake 155 1 31N36 97w06 6:28:24
Oakland 20 1 28N59'30 95w26'37 6:21:46
Oakland 37 1 31N48'51 95w13'09 6:20:53
Oakland 45 1 29N36'05 96w49'47 6:27:19
Oakland 74 1 33N40'15 96w09'18 6:24:37
Oakland 119 1 33N25'08 98w17'24 6:33:10
Oakland 181 1 30N06 93w46 6:15:04
Oakland 201 1 32N09 94w48 6:19:12
Oakland 234 1 32N34'16 95w45'19 6:23:01
Oakland Estates 15 1 29N32'15 98w35'59 6:34:24
Oak Park 133 1 30N03 99w09 6:36:36
Oak Ridge 19 1 33N30 94w37 6:18:28
Oak Ridge 129 1 32N45 96w29 6:25:56
Oak Ridge 174 1 31N40 94w38 6:18:32
Oak Ridge 184 1 32N45 97w43 6:30:52
Oaks 13 1 28N36'31 98w01'53 6:32:08
Oaks 220 1 32N47 97w24 6:29:36
Oak Village 235 1 28N43'08 97w09'00 6:28:36
Oakville 149 1 28N26'56 98w06'06 6:32:24
Oakwood 145 1 31N35'05 95w50'56 6:23:24
Oates Prairie 101 1 29N47'48 95w14'32 6:20:58
Oatmeal 246 1 30N41'48 98w05'39 6:32:23
Oberly Crossing 130 1 29N55'11 98w35'15 6:34:21
Obregon 42 1 31N43'19 99w13'56 6:36:56
O'Brien 104 1 33N22'48 99w50'36 6:39:22
Ocaw 155 1 31N37'23 97w04'40 6:28:19
Ocee 155 1 31N33'21 97w21'19 6:29:25
Ochoa 189 1 29N40'01 104w30'01 6:58:00
Ocker 14 1 31N04'14 97w08'36 6:28:34
Odds 147 1 31N24'32 96w42'56 6:26:52
Odell 244 3 34N20'45 99w25'07 6:37:40
Odem 205 1 27N57'01 97w34'55 6:30:20
Odessa 68 1 31N50'44 102w22'02 6:49:28
Odlaw 136 1 29N14'06 100w10'05 6:40:40
Odom 234 1 32N22'41 96w01'52 6:24:07
O'Donnell 153 1 32N57'49 101w49'56 6:47:20
O'Donnell Place 88 1 28N26'45 97w19'56 6:29:20
Oenaville 14 1 31N07'39 97w13'41 6:28:55
O'Farrell 34 1 33N07'28 94w19'14 6:17:17
Ogburn 250 1 32N50'24 95w13'20 6:20:53
Ogden 12 1 33N30'29 99w12'51 6:36:51
Ogden 46 1 29N38'03 98w15'30 6:33:02
Ogden 78 1 34N05'27 100w07'23 6:40:30
Ogg 191 3 34N50'07 101w53'23 6:47:34
Oglesby 50 1 31N25'06 97w30'25 6:30:02
Ohio 97 1 31N32'21 98w05'09 6:32:21
Oil City 117 3 35N44'49 101w30'47 6:46:03
Oilla 181 1 30N05'51 93w53'27 6:15:34
Oilton 240 1 27N27'56 98w58'26 6:35:54
Ojo de Angua 137 1 27N27'52 97w25'18 6:29:41
Ojuelas 240 1 27N26 99w00 6:36:00
Oklahoma 170 1 30N09'19 95w35'37 6:22:22
Oklahoma Flat 110 1 33N47'10 102w24'02 6:49:36
Oklahoma Lane 185 3 34N23 103w02 6:52:08
Oklaunion 244 1 34N07'46 99w08'33 6:36:34
Okra 67 1 32N16 98w50 6:35:20
Ola 129 1 32N34'31 96w10'31 6:24:42
Olcott 101 1 29N35'41 95w10'14 6:20:41
Old Beekley Place 22 3 30N13'39 103w13'27 6:52:54
Old Boston 19 1 33N24'14 94w24'58 6:17:40
Old Brazoria 20 1 29N03'19 95w33'54 6:22:16
Old Burk Place 118 1 31N23'49 101w02'54 6:44:12
Old Caseyville Crossing 252 1 33N00'46 98w36'49 6:34:27
Old Christian Place 55 1 31N32'26 104w16'49 6:57:07
Old Corbett Place 22 1 30N01'30 103w02'37 6:52:10
Old Davy 62 1 29N05'00 97w37'37 6:30:30
Old Diana 230 1 32N44'26 94w44'35 6:18:58
Old Dime Box 144 1 30N22'37 96w51'46 6:27:27
Old Edith Lochausen Place 22 1 30N06'54 103w05'20 6:52:21
Old Elwood 157 1 31N04'18 95w48'10 6:23:13
Olden 67 1 32N25'08 98w45'02 6:35:00
Oldenburg 75 1 29N58'35 96w45'53 6:27:04
Old Farm Crossing (Ford) 180 3 35N31'17 102w35'58 6:50:24
Old Flatonia 75 1 29N39'46 97w05'26 6:28:22
Old Freitag Place 118 1 31N27'21 101w05'40 6:44:23
Old Glory 217 1 33N07'47 100w03'20 6:40:13
Oldham 57 1 32N52'21 96w52'51 6:27:31
Old House Place 195 1 31N13'10 103w58'37 6:55:54
Old Houston Place 87 1 32N01'16 101w42'10 6:46:49
Old Junction School 86 1 30N14'36 98w36'22 6:34:25
Old Larissa 37 1 32N08 95w19 6:21:16
Old Laurel 176 1 30N27 93w57 6:15:48
Old London 201 1 32N13'36 94w56'40 6:19:47
Old Mobeetie 242 3 35N31 100w26 6:41:44
Old Moulton 143 1 29N35'16 97w10'35 6:28:42
Old Ocean 20 1 29N04'47 95w44'58 6:23:00
Old Oscar Nance Place 22 3 30N29'00 103w11'31 6:52:46
Old Parker Place 22 3 30N29'18 103w12'40 6:52:51
Old Patterson Place 115 2 31N02'18 105w20'32 7:01:22
Old Place Windmill 122 1 30N54'26 103w50'10 6:55:21
Old Place Windmills 2 1 32N10'27 102w32'00 6:50:08
Old Reed Place 22 1 30N04'55 103w07'35 6:52:30
Old River 26 1 30N30 96w27 6:25:48
Old River Terrace 101 1 29N46 95w09 6:20:36
Old Round Rock (vacated) 246 1 30N30'52 97w40'53 6:30:44
Old Saint Marys 196 1 28N06'06 97w12'31 6:28:50
Old Salem 19 1 33N27'05 94w31'37 6:18:06
Old Salem 176 1 30N37 93w53 6:15:32
Old Santa Elena 214 1 26N43'20 98w28'34 6:33:54
Old Union 19 1 33N20'23 94w27'56 6:17:52
Old Union 147 1 31N24'31 96w24'58 6:25:40
Old Union 220 1 32N55'33 97w07'37 6:28:30
Old Union 225 1 33N11'15 94w54'49 6:19:39
Old Waverly 204 1 30N31'44 95w21'09 6:21:25
Oletha 147 1 31N21'30 96w24'46 6:25:39
Olfen 200 1 31N36'34 99w57'37 6:39:50
Olin 97 1 31N52'38 98w06'24 6:32:26
Olivia 29 1 28N38'18 96w27'19 6:25:49
Ollie 187 1 30N47'25 94w46'48 6:19:07
Olmito 31 1 26N01'17 97w32'02 6:30:08
Olmos 13 1 28N14'29 97w49'05 6:31:16
Olmos 94 1 29N26'26 98w02'01 6:32:08
Olmos 214 1 26N21'33 98w46'57 6:35:08
Olmos Park 15 1 29N28'43 98w29'14 6:33:57
Olney 252 1 33N22'14 98w45'09 6:35:01
Olton 140 1 34N11'00 102w08'03 6:48:32
Omaha 172 1 33N10'50 94w44'38 6:18:59
Omen 212 1 32N13'02 95w06'14 6:20:25
Onalaska 187 1 30N48'20 95w06'58 6:20:28
Onion Creek 70 1 32N13'27 96w37'17 6:26:29
Opdyke 110 1 33N35'35 102w16'30 6:49:06
Opelika 107 1 32N17'49 95w40'27 6:22:42
Oplin 230 1 32N08'19 99w33'30 6:38:14
O'Quinn 75 1 29N49'18 96w58'22 6:27:53
Ora 3 1 31N16'38 94w25'39 6:17:43
Oran 182 1 32N57'45 98w09'34 6:32:38
Orange 181 1 30N05'34 93w44'11 6:14:57
Orangedale 13 1 28N26'21 97w49'33 6:31:18
Orangefield 181 1 30N04'29 93w51'20 6:15:25

Orange Grove 125
1 27N57'23 97w56'12 6:31:45
Orangeville 74 1 33N28'42 96w20'22 6:25:21
Orchard 79 1 29N36'14 95w58'10 6:23:53
Ore City 230 1 32N48'00 94w43'14 6:18:53
Orelia 82 1 28N41'10 98w50'53 6:35:24
Orient 177 1 32N30'37 100w24'18 6:41:37
Orient 226 1 31N39 100w20 6:41:20
Orla 151 1 31N49'30 103w54'30 6:55:38
Orme 220 1 32N43 97w06 6:28:24
Orozimbo 20 1 29N15'12 95w34'37 6:22:18
Orrs 158 1 32N50'33 94w31'28 6:18:06
Ort 55 1 31N17'48 104w21'21 6:57:25
Orton Hill (reduced usage) 174
1 31N35'48 94w38'16 6:18:33
Orvil 240 1 27N38'21 99w29'09 6:37:57
Osage 50 1 31N31'28 97w33'52 6:30:15
Oscar 14 1 31N03'02 97w15'43 6:29:03
Osceola 109 1 32N07'50 97w13'37 6:28:54
Osman 233 1 29N53'27 101w39'08 6:46:37
Otey 20 1 29N17'08 95w32'43 6:22:11
Otis Chalk 114 1 32N07 101w22 6:45:28
Ottine 89 1 29N35'52 97w35'02 6:30:20
Otto 73 1 31N26'56 96w48'31 6:27:14
Ovalo 221 1 32N10'22 99w48'27 6:39:14
Overcup Landing 34
1 33N14'16 94w21'58 6:17:28
Overland 112 1 33N09'19 95w44'50 6:22:59
Overton 201 1 32N16'28 94w58'42 6:19:55
Ovilla 70 1 32N31'35 96w53'10 6:27:33
Owens 25 1 31N50'52 98w55'32 6:35:42
Owens 54 1 33N33'30 101w21'09 6:45:25
Owensville 198 1 31N04'22 96w31'09 6:26:05
Owentown 212 1 32N26'08 95w11'44 6:20:47
Owl Creek 14 1 31N13'38 97w30'41 6:30:03
Owlett Green 234
1 32N30'07 95w39'49 6:22:39
Oxford 150 1 30N36'14 98w42'14 6:34:49
Oyster Creek 20
1 29N00'10 95w19'54 6:21:20
Ozona 53 1 30N42'36 101w12'01 6:44:48
Pacio 60 1 33N25'54 95w32'24 6:22:10
Packery 239 1 30N10 96w24 6:25:36
Padgett 252 1 33N18'03 98w54'36 6:35:38
Paducah 51 1 34N00'44 100w18'06 6:41:12
Pafford Crossing 232
1 29N40'38 101w00'13 6:44:01
Pagoda 228 1 30N57 95w23 6:21:32
Paige 11 1 30N12'36 97w06'53 6:28:28
Paint Creek 104
1 33N03'46 99w40'21 6:38:41
Paint Crossing 224
1 33N03'02 99w22'14 6:37:29
Paint Rock 48 1 31N30'30 99w55'11 6:39:41
Paisano Annex 71
2 31N46 106w26 7:05:44
Pakan 242 3 35N17'05 100w25'52 6:41:43
Palacios 161 1 28N42'28 96w13'02 6:24:52
Palafox 240 1 27N47'59 99w52'18 6:39:29
Palava 76 1 32N34'40 100w20'09 6:41:21
Palestine 1 1 31N45'43 95w37'50 6:22:31
Palestine 112 1 33N05'04 95w48'23 6:23:14
Palestine 187 1 30N56 94w36 6:18:24
Palito Blanco 125
1 27N05'29 98w11'20 6:32:45
Palmer 70 1 32N25'52 96w40'03 6:26:40
Palmetal 31 1 26N11'44 97w39'47 6:30:39
Palmetto 79 1 29N32'08 95w27'58 6:21:52
Palmetto 204 1 30N44 95w19 6:21:16
Palm Grove 31 1 25N51'09 97w25'03 6:29:40
Palm Harbor 4 1 27N58'13 97w05'37 6:28:22
Palmhurst 108 1 26N15'29 98w19'04 6:33:16
Palmview 108 1 26N17 98w10 6:32:40
Palm Village 31
1 25N55 97w29 6:29:56
Palo Alto 178 1 27N39'41 97w47'50 6:31:11
Palo Alto Heights 15
1 29N19'49 98w33'23 6:34:14
Paloduro 6 3 34N49'01 101w11'16 6:44:45
Paloma 162 1 28N53'03 100w25'28 6:41:42
Palo Pinto 182 1 32N46'02 98w17'54 6:33:12
Paluxy 111 1 32N16'14 97w54'26 6:31:38
Pamela Heights 101
1 29N37'37 95w26'57 6:21:48
Pampa 90 3 35N32'10 100w57'34 6:43:50
Pancake 50 1 31N37'03 97w47'58 6:31:12
Pandale 233 1 30N11'03 101w33'02 6:46:12
Pandora 247 1 29N15'00 97w50'15 6:31:21
Panhandle 33 3 35N20'44 101w22'48 6:45:31
Panhandle 34 1 33N13'16 94w20'45 6:17:23
Panna Maria 128
1 28N57'29 97w53'50 6:31:35
Panola 183 1 32N21'28 94w05'28 6:16:22
Panorama Estates 116
1 32N43 96w00 6:24:00
Panorama Village 170
1 30N19 95w28 6:21:52
Pantego 220 1 32N42'51 97w09'22 6:28:37
Pantera 22 1 28N59'14 103w12'13 6:52:49
Pantex 33 3 35N20 101w35 6:46:20
Panther Junction 22
1 29N19'42 103w12'17 6:52:49
Papalote 13 1 28N10'20 97w36'06 6:30:24
Papalote Colorado 189
1 29N29'32 104w00'52 6:56:03
Papalote del Norte 24
1 27N03'27 98w04'11 6:32:17
Papalote Escondido 189
1 29N28'33 103w59'55 6:56:00
Papalote Llano 189
1 29N25'59 103w56'46 6:55:47
Papalote Seco 189
1 29N27'31 103w54'19 6:55:37
Paradise 249 1 33N09'00 97w41'13 6:30:45
Paris 139 1 33N39'39 95w33'19 6:22:13
Park 75 1 29N54 96w52 6:27:28
Park Cities 57 1 32N50 96w47 6:27:08
Parker 26 1 30N36'17 96w31'17 6:26:05
Parker 43 1 33N03'19 96w37'18 6:26:29
Parker 126 1 32N14'38 97w16'51 6:29:07
Park Glen 101 1 29N44 95w35 6:22:20
Park Hill Estate 15
1 29N27 98w30 6:34:00
Park Place 101 1 29N41'32 95w16'38 6:21:07
Parks Corner Windmill 82
1 28N45'34 99w18'51 6:37:15
Park Springs 249
1 33N24'19 97w49'07 6:31:16
Parkview Estates 94
1 29N35 97w58 6:31:52
Parkwood 121 1 30N27 93w57 6:15:48
Parkwood Estates 101
1 29N55'20 95w18'32 6:21:14
Parmerton 185 3 34N34'47 102w48'07 6:51:12
Parnell 96 1 34N31'23 100w36'12 6:42:25
Parsley Crossing 97
1 31N34'03 98w06'43 6:32:27
Partwood Crossing 180
3 35N31'10 102w40'41 6:50:43
Parvin 61 1 33N15'12 96w52'12 6:27:29
Pasadena 101 1 29N41'27 95w12'32 6:20:50
Pasche 48 1 31N12'59 99w41'11 6:38:45
Pastura 127 1 32N57'37 100w01'09 6:40:05
Patilo 72 1 32N30'09 98w10'06 6:32:40
Patman 34 1 32N54 94w33 6:18:12
Patrich 201 1 31N55 94w41 6:18:44
Patricia 58 1 32N33'16 102w01'12 6:48:05
Patrick 57 1 32N34'26 96w37'52 6:26:31
Patrick 155 1 31N41'03 97w14'52 6:28:59
Patroon 210 1 31N37'22 93w58'51 6:15:55
Pattison 237 1 29N49'30 95w59'41 6:23:59
Patton 155 1 31N39 97w28 6:29:52
Patton 170 1 30N12 95w10 6:20:40
Pattonville 139
1 33N34'45 95w23'31 6:21:34
Pauline 99 1 34N18 99w44 6:38:56
Pauline 107 1 32N20'16 96w03'13 6:24:13
Paul Junction 154
1 31N09'24 99w16'21 6:37:05
Pauls Store 210
1 31N46 93w52 6:15:28
Pawelekville 128
1 29N03'08 97w56'00 6:31:44
Pawnee 13 1 28N39'09 98w00'09 6:32:01
Paxton 210 1 31N57'28 94w09'54 6:16:40
Payne 158 1 32N51'05 94w17'20 6:17:09
Paynes 79 1 29N36'01 95w36'49 6:22:27
Paynes Corner 83
1 32N43'32 102w47'40 6:51:11
Payne Springs 107
1 32N16'41 96w04'00 6:24:16
Payton 16 1 30N06'49 98w18'18 6:33:13
Peaceful Valley 212
1 32N20 95w18 6:21:12
Peace Valley Harbor 149
1 28N07'47 97w53'49 6:31:35
Peach Creek 21 1 30N32'18 96w11'40 6:24:47
Peach Creek 241
1 29N19 96w06 6:24:24
Peach Tree Village 238
1 30N56'41 94w36'47 6:18:27
Peacock 217 1 33N10'56 100w23'56 6:41:36
Peadenville 182
1 32N55'13 98w04'28 6:32:18
Pearl 50 1 31N24'36 98w02'05 6:32:08
Pearland 20 1 29N33'48 95w17'09 6:21:09
Pearl City 62 1 29N10'51 97w14'37 6:28:58
Pear Ridge 123 1 29N55'12 93w56'16 6:15:45
Pearsall 82 1 28N53'31 99w05'41 6:36:23
Pearson 163 1 29N16'16 98w52'09 6:35:29
Pearsons Chapel 113
1 31N08 95w27 6:21:48
Pear Valley 154
1 31N18'36 99w29'37 6:37:58
Peary Place 178
1 27N40'44 97w19'28 6:29:18
Peaster 184 1 32N52'19 97w51'59 6:31:28
Peavy 3 1 31N17'42 94w48'38 6:19:15
Pebble Beach 43
1 33N05 96w25 6:25:40
Pebble Beach Sunset Acres 43
1 33N05'01 96w27'02 6:25:48
Pecan Crossing 168
1 32N10'00 100w50'03 6:43:20
Pecan Gap 60 1 33N26'13 95w50'47 6:23:23
Pecangrove 50 1 31N25 97w31 6:30:04
Pecan Heights 32
1 33N00'07 94w56'31 6:19:46
Pecan Park 101 1 29N42'28 95w17'23 6:21:10
Pecan Springs 206
1 31N00'51 99w03'46 6:36:15
Pecan Wells 97 1 31N34'35 98w22'16 6:33:29
Pecos 195 1 31N25'22 103w29'34 6:53:58
Peden 220 1 32N57'09 97w32'01 6:30:08
Pedigo 229 1 30N47 94w25 6:17:40
Peel Junction 170
1 30N22'48 95w42'36 6:22:50
Peeltown 129 1 32N24'18 96w22'51 6:25:31
Peerless 112 1 33N15'42 95w42'00 6:22:48
Peggy 7 1 28N44'22 98w10'42 6:32:43
Pelham 220 1 31N57'34 96w48'18 6:27:13
Pendell 18 1 31N42'49 97w32'28 6:30:10
Pendelton 202 1 31N21 93w51 6:15:24
Pendleton 14 1 31N11'42 97w20'54 6:29:24
Penelope 109 1 31N51'36 96w55'35 6:27:42
Peniel 116 1 33N09'46 96w07'36 6:24:30
Penitas 108 1 26N13'49 98w26'40 6:33:47
Penland 91 1 33N40'37 96w27'14 6:25:49
Pennington 228 1 31N11'28 95w14'07 6:20:56
Penwell 68 1 31N44'23 102w35'28 6:50:22
Peoria 109 1 31N58'41 97w13'18 6:28:53
Pep 110 1 33N49 102w33 6:50:12
Percilla 113 1 31N32'49 95w23'56 6:21:36
Perezville 108 1 26N13'27 98w24'01 6:33:36
Perico 56 3 36N16'35 102w51'50 6:51:27
Pernitas Point 149
1 28N03'35 97w54'16 6:31:37
Perrin 119 1 33N02'02 98w04'08 6:32:17
Perrin Air Force Base 119
1 33N43 96w40 6:26:40
Perry 73 1 31N25'04 96w54'54 6:27:40
Perry Landing 20
1 28N58'47 95w29'21 6:21:57
Perryton 179 3 36N24'00 100w48'08 6:43:13
Perryville 250 1 32N51'56 95w09'27 6:20:38
Pershing 227 1 30N15'33 97w43'07 6:30:52
Personville 147
1 31N30'45 96w20'11 6:25:21
Pert 1 1 31N55'20 95w32'49 6:22:11
Pescadito 240 1 27N30'37 99w15'26 6:37:02
Peters 8 1 29N51'35 96w11'11 6:24:45
Petersburg 95 1 33N52'10 101w35'49 6:46:23
Peterson 123 1 29N57 93w59 6:15:56
Peterson Landing 20
1 29N14'35 95w13'45 6:20:55
Peters Prairie 194
1 33N32'35 95w00'17 6:20:01
Petersville 62 1 29N18'45 97w12'59 6:28:52
Petrolia 39 1 34N00'47 98w13'55 6:32:56
Petronila 178 1 27N40'18 97w38'08 6:30:33
Petteway 198 1 31N11'04 96w32'16 6:26:09
Pettibone 166 1 30N50'59 97w04'50 6:28:19
Pettigrew 74 1 33N38'44 96w01'09 6:24:05
Pettit 47 1 31N51 98w24 6:33:36
Pettit 110 1 33N41'49 102w31'27 6:50:06
Pettits 22 1 28N59'54 103w17'01 6:53:08
Pettus 13 1 28N37'04 97w48'07 6:31:12
Petty 139 1 33N36'09 95w48'35 6:23:14
Petty 153 1 33N16'59 101w58'49 6:47:55
Pettys Chapel 175
1 32N06 96w31 6:26:04
Pettytown 28 1 29N54'26 97w27'33 6:29:50
Peveto 181 1 30N08'08 93w49'11 6:15:17
Pezuna del Caballo 55
1 31N34'02 104w41'50 6:58:47
Pflugerville 227
1 30N26'21 97w37'11 6:30:29
Phalba 234 1 32N25'25 95w58'39 6:23:55
Pharr 108 1 26N11'40 98w11'00 6:32:44
Pheasant 161 1 28N48'05 96w13'04 6:24:52
Phelan 11 1 30N09'31 97w19'33 6:29:18
Phelps 236 1 30N41'46 95w26'39 6:21:47
Phillips 117 3 35N41'28 101w21'48 6:45:27
Phillips 230 1 32N34'44 94w57'43 6:19:51
Phillipsburg 239
1 30N05'41 96w22'00 6:25:28
Phillips Camp 98
3 36N29'51 101w27'49 6:45:51
Philrich 117 3 35N39 101w26 6:45:44
Philview Camp 117
3 35N39 101w26 6:45:44
Phoenix 15 1 29N22'54 98w32'29 6:34:10
Pickens 107 1 32N15'14 95w55'21 6:23:41
Pickett 175 1 32N00'45 96w28'36 6:25:54
Pickton 112 1 33N01'41 95w23'34 6:21:34
Pickwick 182 1 32N56 98w15 6:33:00
Pidcoke 50 1 31N16'44 97w53'17 6:31:33
Piedmont 93 1 30N31'14 96w05'40 6:24:23
Pierce 241 1 29N14'20 96w11'59 6:24:48
Pierce Junction 101
1 29N40'13 95w23'46 6:21:35
Pierces Chapel 37
1 31N58 95w16 6:21:04
Pike 43 1 33N19'20 96w18'10 6:25:13
Pila Blanca 66 1 27N48'22 98w28'21 6:33:53
Pilgrim 89 1 29N17'35 97w31'18 6:30:05
Pilgrims Rest 190
1 32N52 95w46 6:23:04
Pilot Grove 91 1 33N20'16 96w25'28 6:25:42
Pilot Knob 227 1 30N09'50 97w41'34 6:30:46
Pilot Point 61 1 33N23'47 96w57'37 6:27:50
Pine 32 1 32N54'47 94w58'09 6:19:53
Pine Branch 194
1 33N28'53 95w06'47 6:20:27
Pine Crest 123 1 30N07'12 94w07'18 6:16:29
Pine Forest 112
1 33N06'45 95w23'04 6:21:32
Pine Forest 181
1 30N10'52 94w02'03 6:16:08
Pine Grove 37 1 31N52'53 95w19'48 6:21:19
Pine Grove 101 1 29N56 95w17 6:21:08
Pine Grove 176 1 30N46'15 93w48'35 6:15:14
Pine Grove 181 1 30N06'31 93w45'28 6:15:02
Pine Hill 37 1 31N59'31 95w00'47 6:20:03
Pine Hill 112 1 33N03'39 95w19'12 6:21:17
Pinehill 201 1 32N06'16 94w36'18 6:18:25
Pine Hill 236 1 30N40'46 95w33'47 6:22:15
Pinehurst 170 1 30N10'15 95w40'56 6:22:44
Pinehurst 181 1 30N05'38 93w44'45 6:14:59
Pine Island 123
1 30N03'22 94w16'38 6:17:07
Pine Lake 170 1 30N23 95w42 6:22:48
Pineland 202 1 31N14'52 93w58'27 6:15:54
Pine Mills 250 1 32N44'29 95w17'21 6:21:09
Pine Prairie 236
1 30N47'10 95w33'35 6:22:14
Pine Ridge 100 1 30N12'10 94w21'01 6:17:24
Pine Springs 19
1 33N37'16 94w44'37 6:18:58
Pine Springs 55
1 31N53'33 104w48'54 6:59:16
Pine Springs 212
1 32N23'53 95w16'00 6:21:04
Pine Trail Estates 212
1 32N11'27 95w27'12 6:21:49
Pine Valley 3 1 31N12 94w47 6:19:08
Pine Valley 236
1 30N39'37 95w27'08 6:21:49
Pineview 250 1 32N54'28 95w09'36 6:20:38
Pinewood 92 1 32N27 94w44 6:18:56
Pinewood Estates 100
1 30N06 94w09 6:16:36
Piney Grove 170
1 30N13 95w45 6:23:00
Piney Grove 230
1 32N54'06 95w06'19 6:20:25
Piney Point 101
1 29N47 95w32 6:22:08
Piney Point Village 101
1 29N45'35 95w31'01 6:22:04
Pin Hook 139 1 33N48'34 95w19'09 6:21:17
Pinkerton 104 1 33N11'55 99w50'29 6:39:22
Pinnacle 230 1 32N34 95w00 6:20:00
Pin Oak 11 1 30N05'07 97w05'06 6:28:20
Pinto 136 1 29N16'52 100w35'17 6:42:21
Pioneer 67 1 32N06'41 99w05'14 6:36:21
Pioneer Town 105
1 29N59'09 98w06'28 6:32:26
Pipe Creek 10 1 29N43'24 98w56'08 6:35:45

Pirtle 201 1 32N18'17 94W51'19 6:19:25
Pisek 45 1 29N55'00 96W34'58 6:26:20
Pisgah 174 1 31N42'20 94W31'22 6:18:05
Pitner Junction 201
1 32N17'22 94W52'06 6:19:28
Pitts 170 1 29N56 95W17 6:21:08
Pittsburg 32 1 32N59'43 94W57'56 6:19:52
Pittsville 170 1 30N03'49 95W14'34 6:20:58
Placedo 235 1 28N41'28 96W49'40 6:27:19
Placid 154 1 31N19'31 99W11'03 6:36:44
Plains 17 1 32N54'44 101W38'39 6:46:35
Plains 251 1 33N11'19 102W49'39 6:51:19
Plains Assembly 77
1 33N53'12 101W20'20 6:45:21
Plains Junction 96
1 34N33'29 100W26'10 6:41:45
Plainview 61 1 33N17'30 97W18'55 6:29:16
Plainview 95 1 34N11'05 101W42'23 6:46:50
Plainview 104 1 33N01'13 99W49'25 6:39:18
Plainview 113 1 31N13'23 95W15'41 6:21:03
Plainview 127 1 32N51'55 99W57'12 6:39:49
Plainview 174 1 31N32'00 94W34'28 6:18:18
Plainview 202 1 31N15 93W58 6:15:52
Plainview 241 1 29N06'47 96W19'27 6:25:18
Planeport 71 2 31N49'34 106W26'03 7:05:44
Plano 43 1 33N01'11 96W41'55 6:26:48
Plantation 20 1 29N02 95W26 6:21:44
Plantersville 93
1 30N19'58 95W51'42 6:23:27
Plaska 96 1 34N36'21 100W38'47 6:42:35
Plata 189 1 29N52'34 104W01'02 6:56:04
Plateau 55 1 31N04 104W34 6:58:16
Platt 3 1 31N24'53 94W36'29 6:18:26
Pleak 79 1 29N29'20 95W48'27 6:23:14
Pleasant Glade 220
1 32N53 97W06 6:28:24
Pleasant Grove 73
1 31N07'49 96W54'12 6:27:37
Pleasant Grove 74
1 33N25'54 95W54'27 6:23:38
Pleasant Grove 147
1 31N25'42 96W38'08 6:26:33
Pleasant Grove 167
1 31N22'23 98W25'39 6:33:43
Pleasant Grove 201
1 32N01'16 94W57'19 6:19:49
Pleasant Grove 230
1 32N34 95W00 6:20:00
Pleasant Grove 250
1 32N55'33 95W23'53 6:21:36
Pleasant Hill 16
1 30N17 98W25 6:33:40
Pleasant Hill 34
1 33N03'11 94W23'49 6:17:35
Pleasant Hill 67
1 32N16'15 98W57'27 6:35:50
Pleasant Hill 79
1 29N39'17 95W53'28 6:23:34
Pleasant Hill 166
1 30N31'47 97W04'12 6:28:17
Pleasant Hill 187
1 31N00'31 94W47'51 6:19:11
Pleasant Hill 227
1 30N11'27 97W46'38 6:31:07
Pleasant Hill 239
1 30N10 96W24 6:25:36
Pleasant Hill 251
1 33N01'20 102W39'48 6:50:39
Pleasanton 7 1 28N58'01 98W28'42 6:33:55
Pleasant Point 126
1 32N29'09 97W11'50 6:28:47
Pleasant Ridge 107
1 32N03 95W30 6:22:00
Pleasant Ridge 145
1 31N11'58 95W55'25 6:23:42
Pleasant Ridge 183
1 32N06'16 94W20'05 6:17:20
Pleasant Run 57
1 32N36'02 96W52'44 6:27:31
Pleasant Springs 145
1 31N18'53 95W54'05 6:23:36
Pleasant Valley 57
1 32N57'10 96W34'11 6:26:17
Pleasant Valley 85
1 33N16'17 101W30'14 6:46:01
Pleasant Valley 116
1 33N07'25 96W16'22 6:25:05
Pleasant Valley 140
3 34N17'55 102W33'36 6:50:14
Pleasant Valley 182
1 32N49 98W04 6:32:16
Pleasant Valley 188
3 35N15'29 101W49'50 6:47:19
Pleasant Valley 243
1 33N56'20 98W35'21 6:34:21
Pleasant Valley Crossing 105
1 30N00'01 98W11'58 6:32:48
Pledger 76 1 32N45'32 100W17'16 6:41:09
Pledger 161 1 29N10'56 95W54'30 6:23:38
Plemons 117 3 35N48'03 101W18'31 6:45:14
Plover 220 1 32N35'29 97W29'07 6:29:56
Pluck 187 1 31N00'40 94W44'36 6:18:58
Plum 75 1 29N56'05 96W58'02 6:27:52
Plum Creek 81 1 31N35'53 95W59'07 6:23:56
Plum Grove 70 1 32N11'44 96W59'21 6:27:57
Plum Grove 146 1 30N12'52 95W05'41 6:20:23
Plummer Crossing 247
1 29N07'34 97W58'09 6:31:53
Podo 116 1 29N06'44 95W54'03 6:23:36
Poe 174 1 31N27'28 94W36'18 6:18:25
Poe Prairie 184
1 32N45 98W01 6:32:04
Poesville 18 1 32N01 97W36 6:30:24
Poetry 129 1 32N45 96W29 6:25:56
Point 190 1 32N55'53 95W52'16 6:23:29
Pointblank 204 1 30N44'44 95W12'45 6:20:51
Point Comfort 29
1 28N40'46 96W33'36 6:26:14
Point Enterprise 147
1 31N39'32 96W25'31 6:25:42
Point Loma 205 1 28N06'40 97W51'47 6:31:27
Polar 132 1 32N51 101W01 6:44:04
Pollok 3 1 31N26'47 94W52'19 6:19:29
Polytechnic 220
1 32N43 97W16 6:29:04
Pomeroy 33 3 35N26'33 101W30'20 6:46:01
Pomona 37 1 32N00'42 95W16'47 6:21:07
Ponder 61 1 33N10'58 97W17'13 6:29:09
Pond Springs 227
1 30N27'01 97W47'06 6:31:08
Pone 201 1 32N02'18 94W53'05 6:19:32
Ponta 37 1 31N58 95W16 6:21:04
Pontotoc 160 1 30N54'33 98W58'47 6:35:55
Pony 200 1 31N45 99W57 6:39:48
Poole 190 1 32N56'59 95W40'01 6:22:40
Poolville 184 1 32N58'30 97W51'28 6:31:26
Poorboy Landing 34
1 33N13'30 94W18'07 6:17:12
Pope City 102 1 32N41'04 94W18'24 6:17:14
Pops Landing Campground 158
1 32N47'43 94W38'23 6:18:34
Porfirio 245 1 26N24'07 97W36'26 6:30:26
Port Acres 123 1 29N54'06 94W01'55 6:16:08
Portairs 178 1 27N45 97W25 6:29:40
Port Alto 29 1 28N39'35 96W24'47 6:25:39
Port Aransas 178
1 27N50'01 97W03'39 6:28:15
Port Arthur 123
1 29N53'55 93W55'43 6:15:43
Port Bolivar 84
1 29N22'50 94W45'51 6:19:03
Port Brownsville 31
1 25N55 97W25 6:29:40
Porter 170 1 30N06'08 95W13'46 6:20:55
Porter Springs 113
1 31N16'14 95W36'32 6:22:26
Port Harlingen 31
1 26N11'56 97W36'04 6:30:24
Port Ingleside 205
1 27N49'24 97W11'42 6:28:47
Port Isabel 31 1 26N04'23 97W12'30 6:28:50
Portland 205 1 27N52'37 97W19'25 6:29:18
Port Lavaca 29 1 28N36'53 96W37'33 6:26:30
Port Mansfield 245
1 26N33'16 97W25'29 6:29:42
Port Neches 123
1 29N59'28 93W57'30 6:15:50
Port O'Connor 29
1 28N26'53 96W24'20 6:25:37
Port Sullivan 198
1 30N51'57 96W41'43 6:26:47
Portway Acres 31
1 25N55 97W29 6:29:56
Porvenir 189 1 30N34 104W29 6:57:56
Posey 112 1 33N16'00 95W39'33 6:22:38
Posey 152 1 33N28'57 101W42'35 6:46:50
Post 85 1 33N11'27 101W22'40 6:45:31
Post Oak 60 1 33N23'53 95W36'10 6:22:25
Post Oak 74 1 33N42'52 96W05'01 6:24:20
Postoak 81 1 31N38 96W17 6:25:08
Post Oak 113 1 31N08 95W27 6:21:48
Postoak 119 1 33N27'25 98W08'34 6:32:34
Post Oak 139 1 33N42'57 95W19'24 6:21:18
Post Oak Bend 129
1 32N38'18 96W18'17 6:25:13
Postoak Point 8
1 29N53 96W29 6:25:56
Poteet 7 1 29N02'25 98W34'04 6:34:16
Poth 247 1 29N04'10 98W04'54 6:32:20
Potosi 221 1 32N19'45 99W39'22 6:38:37
Potters Point 158
1 32N46 94W21 6:17:24
Pottsboro 91 1 33N45'33 96W40'09 6:26:41
Pottsville 97 1 31N40'23 98W19'31 6:33:18
Powderly 139 1 33N48'40 95W31'27 6:22:06
Powell 175 1 32N07'03 96W19'25 6:25:18
Powell 203 1 31N07'26 94W05'19 6:16:21
Powell Crossing 184
1 32N37'04 97W54'18 6:31:37
Powell Point 79
1 29N28'45 96W01'21 6:24:05
Poynor 107 1 32N04'27 95W35'53 6:22:24
Prade Ranch 193
1 30N10 99W22 6:37:28
Praesel 166 1 30N37'51 97W00'35 6:28:02
Praha 75 1 29N40'05 97W04'01 6:28:16
Prairie Dell 14
1 30N53'02 97W34'48 6:30:19
Prairie Grove 3
1 31N10'09 94W43'09 6:18:53
Prairie Grove 147
1 31N34'15 96W25'22 6:25:41
Prairie Hill 147
1 31N39'18 96W47'19 6:27:09
Prairie Hill 239
1 30N14'55 96W22'37 6:25:30
Prairie Lea 28 1 29N43'56 97W45'12 6:31:01
Prairie Mountain 150
1 30N33'38 98W52'45 6:35:31
Prairie Point 49
1 33N29'43 97W28'27 6:29:54
Prairie Point 74
1 33N31'18 96W04'50 6:24:19
Prairie Springs 126
1 32N33 97W20 6:29:20
Prairie Valley 75
1 29N56'52 96W59'46 6:27:59
Prairie Valley 109
1 31N52'37 97W19'41 6:29:19
Prairie Valley 169
1 33N47 97W44 6:30:56
Prairie View 237
1 30N05'35 95W59'15 6:23:57
Prairieville 129
1 32N28'47 96W06'10 6:24:25
Prattville 60 1 33N25'26 95W35'21 6:22:21
Preble 184 1 32N46'51 97W57'40 6:31:51
Preiss Heights 46
1 29N44'25 98W07'08 6:32:29
Premont 125 1 27N21'37 98W07'24 6:32:30
Presidio 189 1 29N33'38 104W22'18 6:57:29
Preston 57 1 32N52 96W48 6:27:12
Preston 91 1 33N52'56 96W37'58 6:26:32
Preston Road Highlands 43
1 33N00 96W49 6:27:16
Preston Shores 91
1 33N46 96W40 6:26:40
Price 60 1 33N23'49 95W43'47 6:22:55
Price 123 1 29N57 93W59 6:15:56
Price 201 1 32N08'02 94W56'34 6:19:46
Prices 37 1 31N53'57 95W25'38 6:21:43
Priddy 167 1 31N40'31 98W30'31 6:34:02
Pride 58 1 32N56'14 102W04'38 6:48:19
Primera 31 1 26N13'32 97W45'28 6:31:02
Primrose 220 1 32N36'41 97W25'59 6:29:44
Primrose 234 1 32N27 95W42 6:22:48
Princeton 43 1 33N10'48 96W29'52 6:25:59
Pringle 117 3 35N56'57 101W27'21 6:45:49
Pritchett 230 1 32N39'42 95W01'06 6:20:04
Proctor 47 1 31N59'14 98W25'46 6:33:43
Proffitt 252 1 33N11'31 98W52'22 6:35:29
Proffitt Crossing 252
1 33N13'53 98W53'02 6:35:32
Progreso 63 1 26N05'31 97W57'25 6:31:50
Progress 9 1 34N16'58 102W48'34 6:51:14
Progress 182 1 32N49 98W04 6:32:16
Promenade 57 1 32N57 96W44 6:26:56
Prospect 39 1 33N28'58 98W11'28 6:32:46
Prospect 158 1 32N50'29 94W21'58 6:17:28
Prosper 43 1 33N14'10 96W48'03 6:27:12
Providence 3 1 31N19'27 94W47'46 6:19:11
Providence 77 1 34N15'25 101W31'14 6:46:05
Providence 187 1 30N39'55 94W53'37 6:19:34
Providence 234 1 32N41 95W43 6:22:52
Provident City 45
1 29N16'57 96W37'55 6:26:32
Pruett 34 1 32N46 94W21 6:17:24
Pruitt 34 1 32N53'30 94W21'28 6:17:26
Pruitt 234 1 32N34'03 95W38'28 6:22:34
Pruitt Lake 34 1 32N57'06 94W30'09 6:18:01
Pueblo Nuevo 189
1 30N07'18 104W39'37 6:58:38
Pueblo Vitoria 195
1 30N57'59 103W46'34 6:55:06
Puente 188 3 35N26'44 101W53'07 6:47:32
Puerto Rico 108
1 26N38'57 98W20'43 6:33:23
Pullman 188 3 35N11'46 101W42'22 6:46:49
Pumphrey 200 1 32N02'19 100W02'17 6:40:09
Pumpkin 204 1 30N32 95W29 6:21:56
Pumpkin Center 58
1 32N51'01 102W02'59 6:48:12
Pumpkin Center 67
1 32N19'12 98W49'43 6:35:19
Pumpville 233 1 29N56'36 101W44'14 6:46:57
Punkin Center 99
3 34N17'18 99W52'50 6:39:31
Punkin Center 184
1 32N45'23 97W43'47 6:30:55
Purdon 175 1 31N56'56 96W36'59 6:26:28
Purley 80 1 33N05'28 95W15'43 6:21:03
Purmela 50 1 31N29'01 97W57'43 6:31:51
Pursley 175 1 31N55'04 96W32'37 6:26:10
Purves 72 1 32N00'12 98W16'12 6:33:05
Putnam 30 1 32N22'15 99W11'32 6:36:46
Pyote 238 1 31N32'05 103W07'33 6:52:30
Pyron 208 1 32N27 100W33 6:42:12
Quail 44 3 34N54'35 100W23'53 6:41:36
Quanah 99 1 34N17'52 99W44'24 6:38:58
Quarry 239 1 30N18 96W30 6:26:00
Quebec 189 1 30N30'38 104W23'57 6:57:36
Queen City 34 1 33N08'55 94W09'00 6:16:36
Quemado 162 1 28N56'52 100W37'25 6:42:30
Quicksand 176 1 30N51 93W45 6:15:00
Quihi 163 1 29N23'29 99W01'47 6:36:07
Quincy 102 1 32N31'24 94W25'13 6:17:41
Quinf 166 1 30N52'37 96W58'39 6:27:55
Quinlan 116 1 32N54'37 96W08'07 6:24:32
Quinn 121 1 30N22'57 94W02'04 6:16:08
Quintana 20 1 28N55'59 95W18'29 6:21:14
Quintana 196 1 28N20'48 97W08'42 6:28:35
Quintana Beach 20
1 28N55'23 95W18'59 6:21:16
Quitaque 23 1 34N21'58 101W03'24 6:44:14
Quitman 250 1 32N47'45 95W27'03 6:21:48
Rabb 178 1 27N48'01 97W45'00 6:31:00
Rabbs 143 1 29N27 96W56 6:27:44
Rabbs Prairie 75
1 29N57'48 96W53'25 6:27:34
Raccoon Bend 8 1 30N00'42 96W07'58 6:24:32
Racetrack 60 1 33N22 95W41 6:22:44
Rachal 24 1 26N53'23 98W08'06 6:32:32
Radio Junction 141
1 31N04'36 98W10'06 6:32:40
Radium 127 1 32N49'45 99W59'42 6:39:59
Ragtown 139 1 33N50'21 95W44'51 6:22:59
Ragtown 210 1 31N40'12 93W53'22 6:15:33
Rainbow 213 1 32N15'55 97W42'50 6:30:51
Raisin 235 1 28N44'31 97W07'10 6:28:29
Raleigh 175 1 32N00'32 96W41'55 6:26:48
Ralls 54 1 33N40'27 101W23'14 6:45:33
Ramah 210 1 31N57 94W15 6:17:00
Rambo 34 1 32N55'04 94W05'28 6:16:22
Ramireno 253 1 27N00'24 99W23'04 6:37:32
Ramirez 66 1 27N20'43 98W24'34 6:33:38
Ramona 108 1 26N10 97W59 6:31:56
Ramsdell 242 3 35N11'30 100W26'26 6:41:46
Ramsey 45 1 29N39'13 96W24'04 6:25:36
Ranchito 31 1 26N01'31 97W37'48 6:30:31
Rancho Allegre Addition 125
1 27N45 98W05 6:32:20
Rancho Viejo 124
1 27N19 98W41 6:34:44
Rand 129 1 32N32'20 96W10'34 6:24:42
Randado 124 1 27N04'49 98W52'41 6:35:31
Randolph 74 1 33N29'02 96W15'08 6:25:01
Randolph Air Force Base 15
1 29N32 98W19 6:33:16
Ranger 67 1 32N28'11 98W40'43 6:34:43
Rangerville 31 1 26N05'22 97W44'54 6:31:00
Rankin 70 1 32N12'20 96W42'23 6:26:50
Rankin 231 1 31N13'21 101W56'15 6:47:45
Ratama 82 1 28N40 99W10 6:36:40
Ratcliff 113 1 31N23'29 95W08'22 6:20:33
Ratcliff 203 1 31N32 94W07 6:16:28
Ratcliff 214 1 26N16'55 98W37'35 6:34:30
Ratibor 14 1 31N05'14 97W12'44 6:28:51
Ratler 167 1 31N22'52 98W46'08 6:35:05

Rattan 60 1 33N24'55 95W46'54 6:23:08
Rattlesnake Crossing 100 1 30N14'47 94W32'50 6:18:11
Ravenna 74 1 33N40'22 96W14'29 6:24:58
Rawlins 57 1 32N50'17 96W44'11 6:26:57
Rayburn 146 1 30N24'48 94W55'27 6:19:42
Rayford 170 1 30N07'38 95W25'40 6:21:43
Rayland 78 1 34N03'52 99W28'53 6:37:56
Raymond 39 1 33N52'41 98W23'46 6:33:35
Raymondville 245 1 26N29 97W47 6:31:08
Rayner Junction 45 1 29N33'12 96W19'43 6:25:19
Ray Point 149 1 28N30'50 98W05'17 6:32:21
Raywood 146 1 30N02'30 94W40'19 6:18:41
Razor 139 1 33N52'55 95W38'27 6:22:34
Reagan 73 1 31N13'05 96W46'56 6:27:08
Reagan Wells 232 1 29N32'19 99W50'12 6:39:21
Reagor Springs 70 1 32N19'43 96W45'38 6:27:03
Realitos 66 1 27N26'40 98W31'41 6:34:07
Reavilon 116 1 33N09'25 96W05'48 6:24:23
Redbank 19 1 33N31'33 94W15'31 6:17:02
Red Bird 57 1 32N39 96W56 6:27:44
Red Bird Addition 57 1 32N40'07 96W55'06 6:27:40
Red Bluff 101 1 29N36'38 94W59'27 6:19:58
Red Bluff 195 1 31N53'41 103W55'01 6:55:40
Red Bluff Crossing 141 1 31N12'44 98W33'58 6:34:16
Red Bluff Crossing 217 1 32N59'23 100W21'34 6:41:26
Red Branch 91 1 33N48'45 96W53'52 6:27:35
Red Branch 228 1 31N04'05 95W24'21 6:21:37
Red Cut Heights 19 1 33N26 94W04 6:16:16
Redfield 174 1 31N40'46 94W39'53 6:18:40
Red Fish Cove 84 1 29N05'58 95W06'29 6:20:26
Redford 189 1 29N26'59 104W11'20 6:56:45
Red Gate 108 1 26N29'47 98W08'01 6:32:32
Red Hill 34 1 33N07'23 94W22'16 6:17:29
Red Hill 109 1 32N05'47 97W20'12 6:29:21
Red Hill 147 1 31N29'14 96W30'46 6:26:03
Red Lake 81 1 31N40'14 95W57'19 6:23:49
Redland 3 1 31N24'15 94W43'16 6:18:53
Redland 145 1 31N14'40 96W01'53 6:24:08
Redland 234 1 32N22'36 95W29'54 6:22:00
Redlawn 37 1 31N41'09 95W05'46 6:20:23
Red Level 201 1 32N20'24 94W58'04 6:19:52
Redlick 19 1 33N27'53 94W10'15 6:16:41
Redmond Terrace 21 1 30N37 96W20 6:25:20
Red Mud 63 1 33N25'36 100W59'56 6:44:00
Red Oak 70 1 32N31'03 96W48'15 6:27:13
Red Oak 129 1 32N35 96W17 6:25:08
Red Ranger 14 1 31N00'23 97W10'48 6:28:43
Red Rock 11 1 29N57'34 97W26'45 6:29:47
Red Springs 12 1 33N36'46 99W24'42 6:37:39
Red Springs 19 1 33N24'21 94W11'35 6:16:46
Red Springs 212 1 32N31'55 95W16'14 6:21:05
Red Top 252 1 33N10'32 98W34'06 6:34:16
Redtown 3 1 31N24'56 94W56'20 6:19:45
Redwater 19 1 33N21'29 94W15'15 6:17:01
Redwood 94 1 29N48'36 97W54'40 6:31:39
Reeds Settlement 194 1 33N42'13 94W55'35 6:19:42
Reedville 28 1 29N52'46 97W50'46 6:31:23
Reese 37 1 32N01'23 95W23'31 6:21:34
Reese 152 1 33N36 102W02 6:48:08
Reese 181 1 30N12'04 93W45'05 6:15:00
Reese Air Force Base 152 1 33N35 101W51 6:47:24
Reese Village 152 1 33N35'41 102W01'18 6:48:05
Refuge 113 1 31N30'04 95W24'03 6:21:36
Refugio 196 1 28N18'18 97W16'30 6:29:06
Regency 167 1 31N25'13 98W51'02 6:35:24
Rehburg 239 1 30N15'16 96W33'44 6:26:15
Rehm 103 3 35N57'59 102W38'39 6:50:35
Rehobeth 183 1 32N09 94W20 6:17:20
Reilly Springs 112 1 33N00'21 95W32'42 6:22:11
Reinhardt 57 1 32N50'06 96W41'20 6:26:45
Rek Hill 75 1 29N55'56 96W38'24 6:26:34
Reklaw 201 1 31N51'45 94W59'15 6:19:57
Relampago 63 1 26N05'05 97W55'06 6:31:40
Reliance 21 1 30N44'35 96W14'20 6:24:57
Remolino 214 1 26N23'12 98W54'26 6:35:38
Rendon 220 1 32N34'34 97W14'28 6:28:58
Renner 43 1 32N59'25 96W46'26 6:27:06
Reno 139 1 33N39'47 95W27'44 6:21:51
Reno 184 1 32N56'39 97W34'37 6:30:18
Retreat 109 1 32N08'04 97W28'26 6:29:54
Retreat 175 1 32N02'02 96W28'27 6:25:54
Retta 220 1 32N33'08 97W14'07 6:28:56
Rexville 8 1 29N43'34 96W12'47 6:24:51
Reyes 66 1 27N50'20 98W25'38 6:33:43
Reynard 113 1 31N24'37 95W39'16 6:22:37
Reynolds 76 1 32N50'34 100W14'05 6:40:56
Reynolds Crossing 224 1 33N02'08 99W19'22 6:37:17
Rhea 185 3 34N40'16 102W56'55 6:51:48
Rhea Mills 43 1 33N15'44 96W43'58 6:26:56
Rhineland 138 1 33N31'47 99W39'17 6:38:37
Rhode Island 81 1 31N48'55 96W13'52 6:24:55
Rhome 249 1 33N03'12 97W28'18 6:29:53
Rhonesboro 230 1 32N45'16 95W08'26 6:20:34
Ricardo 137 1 27N25'16 97W51'03 6:31:24
Rice 175 1 32N14'37 96W29'54 6:26:00
Rice 212 1 32N20 95W18 6:21:12
Rices Crossing 246 1 30N28'46 97W27'29 6:29:50
Rices Crossing School 246 1 30N29'40 97W27'18 6:29:49
Richards 93 1 30N32'15 95W50'21 6:23:21
Richardson 57 1 32N56'53 96W43'46 6:26:55
Richardson Heights Village 57 1 32N57 96W44 6:26:56
Richland 175 1 31N55'36 96W25'45 6:25:43

Richland 190 1 32N56 95W52 6:23:28
Richland Hills 220 1 32N48'57 97W13'40 6:28:55
Richland Park 220 1 32N49 97W12 6:28:48
Richland Springs 206 1 31N16'10 98W56'41 6:35:47
Richmond 79 1 29N34'55 95W45'38 6:23:03
Richwood 20 1 29N03'21 95W24'35 6:21:38
Richwood Village 20 1 29N02 95W24 6:21:36
Rickels 249 1 33N11'00 97W49'43 6:31:19
Riderville 183 1 32N11'35 94W22'53 6:17:32
Ridge 167 1 31N34 98W40 6:34:40
Ridge 198 1 31N09 96W19 6:25:16
Ridgecrest 21 1 30N40 96W22 6:25:28
Ridgecrest 181 1 30N09'57 93W44'53 6:15:00
Ridgeheights 165 1 31N57'12 102W03'44 6:48:15
Ridgeway 112 1 33N10'49 95W46'09 6:23:05
Ridings 74 1 33N41'58 96W11'03 6:24:44
Ridout 247 1 29N04'56 98W08'28 6:32:34
Riesel 155 1 31N28'29 96W55'23 6:27:42
Riggs Ford 50 1 31N13'04 97W39'16 6:30:37
Rincon 214 1 26N30'51 98W35'33 6:34:22
Ringgold 169 1 33N49'13 97W56'36 6:31:46
Rio Farms 108 1 26N18 97W58 6:31:52
Rio Frio 193 1 29N38'09 99W44'11 6:38:57
Rio Grande City 214 1 26N22'46 98W49'12 6:35:17
Rio Hondo 31 1 26N14'06 97W34'54 6:30:20
Riomedina 163 1 29N26'22 98W53'02 6:35:32
Rio Pecos 52 1 31N05 102W21 6:49:24
Rio Rico 63 1 26N03'21 97W53'23 6:31:34
Rios 66 1 27N27'05 98W15'53 6:33:04
Rio Vista 126 1 32N14'00 97W22'27 6:29:30
Rising Star 67 1 32N05'45 98W57'48 6:35:51
Rita 26 1 30N41'12 96W36'31 6:26:26
Ritchie 155 1 31N28'45 97W13'35 6:28:54
Riverbottom 204 1 30N45 95W13 6:20:52
Riverby 74 1 33N50'39 95W55'46 6:23:43
River Creek Acres 149 1 28N17'54 98W02'49 6:32:11
Riverdale 88 1 28N40'22 97W32'36 6:30:10
River Hill 183 1 32N09 94W20 6:17:20
River Hills 227 1 30N20'20 97W50'57 6:31:24
River Oaks 57 1 32N37'33 96W54'45 6:27:39
River Oaks 101 1 30N11 95W42 6:22:48
River Oaks 220 1 32N46'37 97W23'39 6:29:35
Riverside 220 1 32N47 97W18 6:29:12
Riverside 236 1 30N51'10 95W24'12 6:21:37
Riverside Crest 101 1 30N00'59 95W14'13 6:20:57
Riverside Terrace 101 1 29N42'30 95W21'24 6:21:26
River Spur 254 1 28N39'38 99W48'10 6:39:13
River Terrace 101 1 30N05'59 95W08'45 6:20:35
Riverton 195 1 31N45'12 103W46'16 6:55:05
Riviera 137 1 27N17'54 97W48'53 6:31:16
Riviera Beach 137 1 27N18 97W49 6:31:16
Roach 34 1 33N04'10 94W16'18 6:17:05
Roane 175 1 32N10'26 96W22'48 6:25:31
Roanoke 61 1 33N00'14 97W13'32 6:28:54
Roans Prairie 93 1 30N35'03 95W56'37 6:23:46
Roaring Springs 173 1 33N53'58 100W51'24 6:43:26
Robards 15 1 29N32'11 98W32'18 6:34:09
Robberson 214 1 26N39'04 98W35'16 6:34:21
Robbins 145 1 31N15'19 96W07'21 6:24:29
Robert Lee 41 1 31N53'32 100W29'04 6:41:56
Robertson 54 1 33N33'51 101W30'48 6:46:03
Robertson 121 1 30N17'35 93W54'34 6:15:38
Robinson 155 1 31N28'03 97W06'52 6:28:27
Robinson Arms Landing 195 1 31N57'50 103W57'42 6:55:51
Robstown 178 1 27N47'24 97W40'07 6:30:40
Roby 76 1 32N44'41 100W22'38 6:41:31
Roch 47 1 32N01'26 98W27'17 6:33:49
Rochelle 154 1 31N13'28 99W12'39 6:36:51
Rochester 104 1 33N18'57 99W51'20 6:39:25
Rock Creek 23 1 34N27'48 101W26'04 6:45:44
Rock Creek 155 1 31N40'01 97W14'29 6:28:58
Rock Crossing 244 1 33N58'52 99W08'56 6:36:36
Rockdale 112 1 33N06'47 95W38'14 6:22:33
Rockdale 166 1 30N39'19 97W00'04 6:28:00
Rockett 70 1 32N28'11 96W45'49 6:27:03
Rockford 139 1 33N29'16 95W27'02 6:21:48
Rock Hill 37 1 31N58'22 95W01'22 6:20:05
Rockhill 43 1 33N12'14 96W48'08 6:27:13
Rock Hill 250 1 32N48 95W27 6:21:48
Rockhouse 8 1 29N53 96W29 6:25:56
Rock Island 45 1 29N31'51 96W34'30 6:26:18
Rock Island 146 1 30N04'07 94W42'03 6:18:48
Rock Island 158 1 32N51'48 94W39'49 6:18:39
Rock Island 187 1 31N00 94W50 6:19:20
Rock Island 237 1 30N10'21 96W07'30 6:24:30
Rockland 229 1 31N00'54 94W22'53 6:17:32
Rockledge 65 3 35N10'31 100W49'08 6:43:17
Rockne 11 1 29N59'44 97W25'51 6:29:43
Rockport 4 1 28N01'13 97W03'15 6:28:13
Rock Springs 18 1 31N41'09 97W24'59 6:29:40
Rocksprings 69 1 30N00'56 100W12'18 6:40:49
Rock Springs 80 1 32N58'29 95W15'19 6:21:01
Rock Springs 158 1 32N47'28 94W32'06 6:18:08
Rockwall 199 1 32N55'52 96W27'34 6:25:50
Rockwell 139 1 33N35'28 95W32'58 6:22:12
Rockwood 42 1 31N30'03 99W22'23 6:37:30
Rocky Branch 172 1 33N06'41 94W41'52 6:18:47
Rocky Creek 22 1 30N15'12 98W31'36 6:34:06

Rocky Hill 73 1 31N20'51 96W56'54 6:27:48
Rocky Hill 86 1 30N13'28 98W47'36 6:35:10
Rocky Mound 32 1 33N01'08 95W01'19 6:20:05
Roddy 234 1 32N25'02 96W02'08 6:24:09
Rodet 168 1 32N23'21 100W48'22 6:43:13
Rodney 175 1 31N49'18 96W36'41 6:26:27
Roganville 121 1 30N48'00 93W54'12 6:15:37
Rogers 14 1 30N55'53 97W13'35 6:28:54
Rogers 74 1 33N32'30 96W14'50 6:24:59
Rogers 221 1 32N10'27 99W41'06 6:38:44
Rogers Hill 155 1 31N43'52 97W11'55 6:28:48
Rogerslacy 108 1 26N16'37 97W52'38 6:31:31
Roland 43 1 33N16'42 96W38'57 6:26:36
Rolla 44 3 34N48'19 100W18'37 6:41:14
Rolling Hills 116 1 32N57 95W56 6:23:44
Rolling Oaks 234 1 32N43 96W00 6:24:00
Rollingwood 227 1 30N16'36 97W47'27 6:31:10
Rollover 101 1 29N30'21 94W30'24 6:18:02
Roma 214 1 26N24 99W05 6:36:20
Roma-Los Saenz 214 1 26N24'17 99W00'56 6:36:04
Romayor 146 1 30N27'04 94W50'35 6:19:22
Romero 103 3 35N43'39 102W55'51 6:51:43
Romney 67 1 32N14'29 98W57'27 6:35:50
Rooneys Place 22 1 29N05'44 103W04'06 6:52:16
Roosevelt 134 1 30N29'27 100W03'17 6:40:13
Roosevelt 152 1 33N34'53 101W40'26 6:46:42
Ropesville 110 1 33N24'48 102W09'14 6:48:37
Rosalie 194 1 33N28'35 95W10'41 6:20:43
Rosanky 11 1 29N55'45 97W17'36 6:29:10
Roscoe 177 1 32N26'45 100W32'18 6:42:09
Rosebud 73 1 31N04'22 96W58'42 6:27:55
Rose City 181 1 30N06'09 94W03'06 6:16:12
Rosedale 73 1 31N13 96W47 6:27:08
Rosedale 123 1 30N08'05 94W09'52 6:16:39
Rosedale Acres 123 1 30N09'01 94W11'11 6:16:45
Rose Hill 57 1 32N51'11 96W35'09 6:26:21
Rose Hill 101 1 30N04'14 95W42'12 6:22:49
Rose Hill 204 1 30N34'52 95W05'37 6:20:22
Rose Hill Acres 100 1 30N12 94W12 6:16:48
Rosenberg 79 1 29N33'25 95W48'30 6:23:14
Rosenfeld 22 1 30N06'12 102W45'06 6:51:00
Rosenthal 155 1 31N25'02 97W05'57 6:28:24
Rosevine 202 1 31N25'13 93W58'30 6:15:54
Rosewood 230 1 32N45'01 95W04'51 6:20:19
Rosharon 20 1 29N21'07 95W27'36 6:21:50
Rosita 66 1 27N47'10 98W25'49 6:33:43
Rosita 214 1 26N23'58 98W55'39 6:35:43
Ross 20 1 29N03'03 95W25'16 6:21:41
Ross 155 1 31N43'06 97W07'08 6:28:29
Ross City 114 1 32N14 101W28 6:45:52
Rosser 129 1 32N27'45 96W27'11 6:25:49
Rosslyn 101 1 29N50'07 95W28'45 6:21:55
Rosston 49 1 33N29'00 97W26'31 6:29:46
Rossville 7 1 29N05'28 98W40'49 6:34:43
Roswell 18 1 31N47 97W35 6:30:20
Rotan 76 1 32N51'07 100W27'55 6:41:52
Rotherwood 101 1 30N04'59 95W29'47 6:21:59
Rough Creek Crossing 206 1 31N07'48 98W32'41 6:34:11
Round Mott 241 1 29N13'44 96W27'33 6:25:50
Round Mountain 16 1 30N25'53 98W20'40 6:33:23
Round Prairie 175 1 32N02'07 96W10'41 6:24:43
Round Prairie 198 1 31N17'45 96W21'51 6:25:27
Round Rock 246 1 30N30'29 97W40'43 6:30:43
Round Timber 12 1 33N26'09 99W04'13 6:36:17
Round Top 75 1 30N03'54 96W41'45 6:26:47
Roundup 110 1 33N46 102W06 6:48:24
Rowden 230 1 32N12'14 99W20'37 6:37:22
Rowena 200 1 31N38'49 100W02'45 6:40:11
Rowland 169 1 33N56'46 97W41'15 6:30:45
Rowlett 57 1 32N54'10 96W33'49 6:26:15
Roxton 139 1 33N32'46 95W43'32 6:22:54
Roy 35 3 34N27'59 102W12'48 6:48:51
Royal Lane 57 1 32N54 96W48 6:27:12
Royalty 238 1 31N22'20 102W52'00 6:51:28
Royder 21 1 30N31'39 96W18'17 6:25:13
Roy Miller 178 1 27N47 97W26 6:29:44
Roy Royall 101 1 29N52 95W20 6:21:20
Royse City 199 1 32N58'30 96W19'56 6:25:20
Royston 76 1 32N48'42 100W17'53 6:41:12
Roznov 75 1 29N59'03 96W42'29 6:26:50
Rubboard Crossing 232 1 29N41'54 101W00'24 6:44:02
Rucker 47 1 32N09'54 98W36'09 6:34:25
Rudolph 131 1 26N41'07 97W46'07 6:31:04
Rugby 194 1 33N29'44 95W16'01 6:21:04
Rugeley 161 1 28N57'37 95W49'22 6:23:17
Ruhff 176 1 30N16'26 93W43'57 6:14:56
Ruidosa 189 1 29N58'58 104W40'44 6:58:43
Rule 104 1 33N11'04 99W53'36 6:39:34
Rumley 141 1 31N10'22 98W04'04 6:32:16
Runge 128 1 28N52'59 97W42'46 6:30:51
Rural Shade 175 1 32N03'00 96W08'21 6:24:33
Rushing 175 1 31N48 96W28 6:25:52
Rush Prairie 175 1 32N05 96W48 6:27:12
Rusk 37 1 31N47'45 95W09'00 6:20:36
Russell 145 1 31N22'38 95W51'00 6:23:24
Russell Crossing 246 1 30N40'20 97W45'01 6:31:00
Russellville 173 1 33N55'13 100W41'21 6:42:45
Russeltown 31 1 26N04'57 97W34'54 6:30:20
Rutersville 75 1 29N56'51 96W47'49 6:27:11
Rutland 3 1 31N11'15 94W47'38 6:19:11
Rye 146 1 30N27'09 94W46'07 6:19:04
Rye 198 1 30N43'45 96W29'24 6:25:58
Rylie 57 1 32N41'26 96W38'14 6:26:33
Rymers 161 1 28N51'22 95W56'29 6:23:46
Sabanno 67 1 32N11'07 99W05'25 6:36:22

Sabathany 184 1 32N54'17 97W36'44 6:30:27
Sabinal 232 1 29N19'02 99W27'58 6:37:52
Sabine 123 1 29N43'11 93W52'17 6:15:29
Sabine Pass 123
1 29N44'00 93W53'39 6:15:35
Sabinetown 202 1 31N24'10 93W42'30 6:14:50
Sachse 57 1 32N58'34 96W35'42 6:26:23
Sacul 174 1 31N49'29 94W55'07 6:19:40
Sadler 91 1 33N40'57 96W50'53 6:27:24
Sagerton 104 1 33N04'37 99W57'19 6:39:49
Saginaw 220 1 32N51'36 97W21'49 6:29:27
Saint Clair City 212
1 32N08 95W07 6:20:28
Saint Elmo 81 1 31N56'16 96W10'54 6:24:44
Saint Francis 33
3 35N15'42 101W37'21 6:46:29
Saint Francis Village 220
1 32N35 97W22 6:29:28
Saint Hedwig 15
1 29N24'51 98W11'59 6:32:48
Saint James 89 1 29N34'01 97W36'16 6:30:25
Saint Jo 169 1 33N41'41 97W31'20 6:30:05
Saint John 143 1 29N37'52 96W57'11 6:27:49
Saint Johns Colony 28
1 29N58'15 97W33'29 6:30:14
Saint Lawrence 87
1 31N42'09 101W32'15 6:46:09
Saint Louis 212
1 32N20 95W18 6:21:12
Saint Paul 43 1 33N01 96W32 6:26:08
Saint Paul 73 1 31N18 96W53 6:27:32
Saint Paul 145 1 31N30'06 95W45'32 6:23:02
Saint Paul 205 1 28N05'57 97W33'20 6:30:13
Saint Paul 237 1 30N06'31 96W07'43 6:24:31
Salado 14 1 30N56'49 97W32'18 6:30:09
Salado Junction 15
1 29N27'01 98W25'03 6:33:40
Salem 11 1 29N50'34 97W19'39 6:29:19
Salem 37 1 31N45'36 95W08'18 6:20:33
Salem 166 1 30N48'56 97W01'25 6:28:06
Salem 176 1 30N32'32 93W46'04 6:15:04
Salem 212 1 32N10'28 95W01'20 6:20:05
Salem 235 1 28N59'19 96W54'39 6:27:39
Salem 250 1 32N49'31 95W37'07 6:22:28
Salesville 182 1 32N54'44 98W05'16 6:32:21
Saline 164 1 30N43'20 99W33'11 6:38:13
Salineno 214 1 26N30'58 99W06'43 6:36:27
Salmon 1 1 31N34'22 95W29'53 6:22:00
Salona 169 1 33N32'50 97W44'51 6:30:59
Salter 198 1 31N02'04 96W44'42 6:26:59
Salt Flat 115 2 31N45 105W05 7:00:20
Salt Gap 154 1 31N18'13 99W35'56 6:38:24
Saltillo 112 1 33N11'04 95W19'34 6:21:18
Saltlick Mill 122
1 30N44'29 103W37'40 6:54:31
Salty 166 1 30N35'36 97W07'57 6:28:32
Sam Fordyce 108
1 26N14'56 98W31'43 6:34:07
Sam Houston 101
1 29N47 95W23 6:21:32
Sam Houston College 236
1 30N43 95W33 6:22:12
Samnorwood 44 3 35N03'08 100W16'49 6:41:07
Sample 89 1 29N13'07 97W31'23 6:30:06
Sam Rayburn 121
1 30N55 94W00 6:16:00
San Angelo 226 1 31N27'49 100W26'12 6:41:45
San Angelo Junction 42
1 31N46'34 99W22'03 6:37:28
San Antonio 15 1 29N25'26 98W29'36 6:33:58
San Antonio Viejo 124
1 26N57'19 98W49'57 6:35:20
San Augustine 203
1 31N31'47 94W06'21 6:16:25
San Benito 31 1 26N07'56 97W37'51 6:30:31
San Carlos 108 1 26N17'43 98W04'18 6:32:17
San Carlos 214 1 26N40'45 98W51'12 6:35:25
Sanco 41 1 32N00'30 100W31'25 6:42:06
Sand 58 1 32N42'15 102W10'19 6:48:41
Sanderson 222 1 30N08'32 102W23'37 6:49:34
Sand Flat 126 1 32N19'22 97W17'17 6:29:09
Sand Flat 234 1 32N37'38 95W39'01 6:22:36
Sand Flats 145 1 31N32'53 95W48'40 6:23:15
Sandhill 77 1 33N59'36 101W28'45 6:45:55
Sand Hill 81 1 31N43'20 95W55'50 6:23:43
Sandhill 112 1 33N19'48 95W32'34 6:22:10
Sand Hill 230 1 32N44 94W57 6:19:48
Sandia 125 1 28N01'20 97W52'45 6:31:31
San Diego 66 1 27N45'49 98W14'19 6:32:57
Sandjack 176 1 30N38'22 93W42'27 6:14:50
Sand Lake 70 1 32N25'46 96W29'33 6:25:58
Sandoval 246 1 30N38'24 97W17'25 6:29:10
Sandow 166 1 30N33'52 97W04'21 6:28:17
Sand Ridge 113 1 31N06'26 95W41'05 6:22:44
Sand Ridge 241 1 29N25'05 96W15'07 6:25:00
Sand Springs 114
1 32N16'57 101W21'02 6:45:24
Sandune 146 1 30N07'27 94W46'27 6:19:06
Sandusky 91 1 33N45'58 96W53'31 6:27:34
Sandy 16 1 30N21'38 98W28'09 6:33:53
Sandy Acres 165
1 31N57'07 102W04'35 6:48:18
Sandy Corner 241
1 29N11 96W17 6:25:08
Sandy Creek 166
1 30N43 96W52 6:27:28
Sandy Fork 89 1 29N41'05 97W25'01 6:29:40
Sandy Harbor 150
1 30N35 98W20 6:33:20
Sandy Hill 239 1 30N16'40 96W19'32 6:25:18
Sandy Point 20 1 29N23'07 95W28'51 6:21:55
San Elizario 71
2 31N35'06 106W16'20 7:05:05
San Felipe 8 1 29N47'34 96W06'02 6:24:24
Sanford 117 3 35N42'07 101W32'03 6:46:08
San Francisco 22
1 29N53'36 102W24'13 6:49:37
San Gabriel 166
1 30N41'39 97W11'45 6:28:47
Sanger 61 1 33N21'47 97W10'25 6:28:42
San Geromino 15
1 29N37'22 98W47'37 6:35:10

San Ignacio de Loyola 214
1 26N18'55 98W41'37 6:34:46
San Isidro 214 1 26N42'59 98W27'13 6:33:49
San Jacinto 188
3 35N12 101W53 6:47:32
San Jacinto 236
1 30N37'19 95W43'15 6:22:53
San Jose 15 1 29N20'47 98W31'46 6:34:07
San Jose 66 1 27N35'00 98W18'20 6:33:13
San Jose 71 2 31N43'16 106W21'45 7:05:27
San Juan 108 1 26N11'20 98W09'18 6:32:37
San Juan 178 1 27N46'01 97W32'19 6:30:09
San Juan Community 108
1 26N17 98W10 6:32:40
San Leanna 8 1 30N17 97W44 6:30:56
San Leon 84 1 29N28'59 94W55'19 6:19:41
San Manuel 108 1 26N33'51 98W07'15 6:32:29
San Marcos 105 1 29N52'59 97W56'28 6:31:46
San Martine 195
1 31N09'28 104W04'11 6:56:17
San Pablo 240 1 27N37'10 98W48'32 6:35:14
San Patricio 205
1 27N57'15 97W46'18 6:31:05
San Pedro 31 1 25N58'53 97W35'46 6:30:23
San Pedro 178 1 27N47'18 97W40'41 6:30:43
San Perlita 245
1 26N30'03 97W38'22 6:30:33
San Ramon 240 1 27N55'58 99W23'14 6:37:33
San Roman 214 1 26N45'10 98W50'29 6:35:22
San Saba 206 1 31N11'44 98W43'04 6:34:52
Sansom Park Village 220
1 32N48'21 97W24'10 6:29:37
Santa Anna 42 1 31N44'31 99W19'17 6:37:17
Santa Anna 214 1 26N40'04 98W33'51 6:34:15
Santa Catarina 214
1 26N39'18 98W34'38 6:34:19
Santa Clara 94 1 29N30'42 98W07'16 6:32:29
Santa Cruz 66 1 27N24'11 98W16'05 6:33:04
Santa Cruz 214 1 26N21'15 98W46'05 6:35:04
Santa Elena 214
1 26N45'35 98W29'10 6:33:57
Santa Elena Crossing 22
1 29N07'17 103W31'25 6:54:06
Santa Margarita 214
1 26N29'32 99W05'33 6:36:22
Santa Maria 31 1 26N04'42 97W50'57 6:31:24
Santa Monica 245
1 26N21'43 97W35'08 6:30:21
Santa Rita 192 1 31N13'24 101W39'24 6:46:38
Santa Rosa 31 1 26N15'23 97W49'29 6:31:18
Santo 182 1 32N36'11 98W12'54 6:32:52
Santo Tomas 240
1 27N44'38 99W45'04 6:39:00
San Vicente Crossing 22
1 29N07'48 103W00'52 6:52:03
San Ygnacio 253
1 27N02'32 99W26'23 6:37:46
Sapoak 72 1 32N27'17 98W14'51 6:32:59
Saragosa 195 1 31N01'26 103W39'40 6:54:39
Saratoga 100 1 30N17'02 94W31'45 6:18:07
Sarber 158 1 32N49'01 94W27'44 6:17:51
Sarco 88 1 28N40 97W23 6:29:32
Sardis 34 1 33N00'18 94W32'27 6:18:10
Sardis 70 1 32N25'43 96W54'21 6:27:37
Sardis 76 1 32N45'20 100W29'44 6:41:59
Sardis 210 1 31N48'06 94W05'38 6:16:23
Sargent 57 1 32N44'13 96W46'46 6:27:07
Sargent 161 1 28N50'06 95W39'52 6:22:39
Sarita 131 1 27N13'17 97W47'20 6:31:09
Sash 74 1 33N44'50 95W54'40 6:23:39
Saspamco 247 1 29N14'03 98W17'44 6:33:11
Satin 73 1 31N20'47 97W01'53 6:28:08
Satsuma 101 1 29N54'11 95W36'11 6:22:25
Sattler 46 1 29N50'52 98W10'31 6:32:42
Saturn 89 1 29N42 97W18 6:29:12
Sauer 166 1 30N51 96W59 6:27:56
Sauney Stand 239
1 30N05'36 96W13'21 6:24:53
Savage 54 1 33N35'34 101W25'57 6:45:44
Savoy 74 1 33N35'57 96W21'59 6:25:28
Saxet 210 1 31N57'57 94W17'55 6:17:12
Sayard 226 1 31N28 100W27 6:41:48
Sayers 11 1 30N07 97W19 6:29:16
Sayers 15 1 29N22'26 98W17'19 6:33:09
Sayersville 11 1 30N13'54 97W19'37 6:29:18
Scallorn 167 1 31N19'46 98W28'26 6:33:54
Scatter Branch 116
1 33N14'23 95W58'06 6:23:52
Scenic Woods 101
1 29N51'38 95W18'02 6:21:12
Scharbauer City 68
1 32N01'25 102W25'48 6:49:43
Schattel 82 1 28N57'11 98W51'28 6:35:26
Schertz 94 1 29N33'07 98W16'10 6:33:05
Schoenau 8 1 29N53 96W29 6:25:56
Schoolerville 97
1 31N36'59 98W10'58 6:32:44
School Land 89 1 29N16 97W46 6:31:04
Schroeder 88 1 28N48'55 97W13'27 6:28:54
Schulenburg 75 1 29N40'54 96W54'10 6:27:37
Schumansville 94
1 29N38'42 98W04'35 6:32:18
Schwab City 187
1 30N35'33 94W49'52 6:19:19
Schwertner 246 1 30N48'55 97W30'50 6:30:03
Scissors 108 1 26N08'22 98W03'13 6:32:13
Scobee 27 1 30N38'44 98W18'57 6:33:16
Scofield 26 1 30N21'13 96W26'23 6:25:46
Scotland 5 1 33N39'36 98W28'13 6:33:53
Scott 234 1 32N35'40 96W01'19 6:24:05
Scott Crossing 104
1 33N04'39 99W32'36 6:38:10
Scotts Corner 76
1 32N48'32 100W35'58 6:42:24
Scotts Crossing 115
1 30N56'18 104W54'24 6:59:38
Scotts Crossing 150
1 30N43'41 98W48'48 6:35:15
Scottsville 102
1 32N32'25 94W14'17 6:16:57
Scranton 67 1 32N18'18 99W06'24 6:36:26
Scrapping Valley 176
1 31N09'13 93W51'30 6:15:26

Scroggins 80 1 32N58'25 95W11'04 6:20:44
Scurlock 88 1 28N40'50 97W18'45 6:29:15
Scurry 129 1 32N31'07 96W22'50 6:25:31
Sea Breeze 36 1 29N43'08 94W22'28 6:17:30
Seabrook 101 1 29N33'50 95W01'31 6:20:06
Sea Crest Park 36
1 29N46 95W00 6:20:00
Seadrift 29 1 28N24'54 96W42'48 6:26:51
Seagoville 57 1 32N38'22 96W32'17 6:26:09
Seagraves 83 1 32N56'39 102W33'52 6:50:15
Sea Isle 84 1 29N08'34 95W02'36 6:20:10
Seale 147 1 31N18'47 96W22'21 6:25:29
Sealy 8 1 29N46'50 96W09'25 6:24:38
Seaman 146 1 30N21'57 95W02'09 6:20:09
Seaton 14 1 31N03'27 97W12'57 6:28:52
Seawillow 28 1 29N49'23 97W36'19 6:30:25
Sebastian 245 1 26N20'33 97W47'24 6:31:10
Sebastopol 228 1 30N54'34 95W14'58 6:21:00
Seclusion 143 1 29N18'02 96W41'44 6:26:47
Seco Mines 162 1 28N45'10 100W29'43 6:41:59
Second Corinth 237
1 30N08'35 96W07'02 6:24:28
Second Crossing 46
1 29N46'43 98W09'36 6:32:38
Second Crossing 232
1 29N30'54 99W41'49 6:38:47
Security 170 1 30N19'40 95W14'21 6:20:57
Sedalia 43 1 33N25 96W34 6:26:16
Sedwick 209 1 32N36'11 99W12'15 6:36:49
Seeligson 125 1 27N24'32 98W06'56 6:32:28
Sefcikville 14 1 31N06 97W21 6:29:24
Seger 198 1 30N55'16 96W37'23 6:26:30
Seglar 15 1 29N16 98W44 6:34:56
Segno 187 1 30N34'37 94W41'10 6:18:45
Segovia 134 1 30N25'09 99W40'12 6:38:41
Seguin 94 1 29N34'07 97W57'52 6:31:51
Sejita 66 1 27N18'12 98W26'22 6:33:45
Selden 72 1 32N08'38 98W06'23 6:32:26
Selfs 74 1 33N41'32 95W54'51 6:23:39
Selma 15 1 29N35'03 98W18'20 6:33:13
Selma 169 1 33N29'15 97W53'18 6:31:33
Selman 154 1 31N15'13 99W06'03 6:36:24
Selman City 201
1 32N11 94W58 6:19:52
Seminary Hill 220
1 32N41 97W20 6:29:20
Seminole 83 1 32N43'08 102W38'40 6:50:35
Senate 119 1 33N10'27 98W17'38 6:33:11
Senior 15 1 29N17 98W39 6:34:36
Senterfitt 141 1 31N11'52 98W26'13 6:33:45
Serbin 144 1 30N07'39 96W59'55 6:28:00
Serna 15 1 29N30 98W25 6:33:40
Seth 100 1 30N17'55 94W11'01 6:16:44
Seth Ward 95 1 34N12'42 101W41'23 6:46:46
Settegast 101 1 29N50'29 95W17'03 6:21:08
Settles Addition 114
1 32N14 101W28 6:45:52
Seven Heart Crossing 195
1 31N09'48 104W01'25 6:56:06
Seven Knobs 213
1 32N09'07 97W44'56 6:31:00
Seven L Crossing 99
3 34N11'20 99W52'28 6:39:30
Sevenmile Corner 231
1 31N19'17 101W56'33 6:47:46
Seven Oaks 187 1 30N51'07 94W52'01 6:19:28
Seven Pines 92 1 32N35'29 94W49'08 6:19:17
Seven Points 107
1 32N19'13 96W12'46 6:24:51
Seven Sisters 66
1 28N01 98W31 6:34:04
Seventeen Mile Crossing 226
1 31N32'49 100W09'50 6:40:39
Seward Junction 246
1 30N39'13 97W52'31 6:31:30
Sexton 202 1 31N33'46 93W54'39 6:15:39
Sexton City 201
1 32N16 94W59 6:19:56
Seymore 112 1 32N59'27 95W35'43 6:22:23
Seymour 12 1 33N35'39 99W15'36 6:37:02
Seymour West 12
1 33N36 99W22 6:37:28
Shadow Glen 101
1 29N46 95W09 6:20:36
Shadowland 194 1 33N31'07 95W16'56 6:21:08
Shady Grove 3 1 31N10'51 94W45'04 6:19:00
Shady Grove 27 1 30N49'05 98W04'46 6:32:19
Shady Grove 37 1 31N50'45 95W01'26 6:20:06
Shady Grove 49 1 33N34'01 96W58'21 6:27:53
Shady Grove 57 1 32N48'11 97W01'12 6:28:05
Shady Grove 74 1 33N32'14 96W03'15 6:24:13
Shady Grove 113
1 31N14'02 95W19'25 6:21:18
Shady Grove 133
1 29N58'49 99W04'40 6:36:19
Shady Grove 175
1 31N57 96W37 6:26:28
Shady Grove 190
1 32N54'11 95W44'52 6:22:59
Shady Grove 212
1 32N26'30 95W16'55 6:21:08
Shady Grove 230
1 32N40'53 95W07'57 6:20:32
Shady Oaks 220 1 32N50 97W10 6:28:40
Shady Shores 61
1 33N09'54 97W01'45 6:28:07
Shady Trees 101
1 29N56 95W17 6:21:08
Shafter 189 1 29N49'12 104W18'10 6:57:13
Shallowater 152
1 33N41'20 101W59'52 6:47:59
Shamrock 57 1 32N35'57 96W53'14 6:27:33
Shamrock 242 3 35N12'51 100W14'55 6:41:00
Shamrock Shores 25
1 31N49'13 99W05'56 6:36:24
Shankleville 176
1 30N58'12 93W42'24 6:14:50
Shannon 39 1 33N28'26 98W15'31 6:33:02
Sharon 212 1 32N20 95W18 6:21:12
Sharp 166 1 30N45'04 97W09'21 6:28:37
Sharpstown 101 1 29N42 95W31 6:22:04
Sharyland 108 1 26N12'39 98W17'16 6:33:09
Shaufler 177 1 32N24'08 100W26'14 6:41:45

Shavano Park 15
1 29N35'05 98w33'08 6:34:13
Shaw 222 1 30N01'43 102w00'20 6:48:01
Shaw Bend 206 1 31N12 98w44 6:34:56
Shawnee 3 1 31N12'49 94w29'56 6:18:00
Shawnee Prairie 3
1 31N10'46 94w32'37 6:18:10
Shawnee Shores Estates 116
1 32N54 96w05 6:24:20
Shaws Bend 45 1 29N44'11 96w38'22 6:26:33
Shawville 41 1 31N51'00 100w17'59 6:41:12
Sheeks 146 1 29N58'52 94w58'30 6:19:54
Sheerin 171 3 35N58'15 101w52'55 6:47:32
Sheerin Junction 171
3 36N01'27 101w52'56 6:47:32
Sheffield 34 1 32N56'12 94w15'13 6:17:01
Sheffield 186 1 30N41'25 101w49'20 6:47:17
Shelby 8 1 30N01'17 96w35'53 6:26:24
Shelbyville 210
1 31N45'41 94w04'42 6:16:19
Sheldon 101 1 29N52'04 95w07'41 6:20:31
Shell Ridge 4 1 27N59'49 97w03'36 6:28:14
Shenandoah 170 1 30N19 95w28 6:21:52
Shep 221 1 32N03 100w07 6:40:28
Shepherd 204 1 30N29'52 94w59'47 6:19:59
Sheppard Air Force Base 243
1 33N59 98w31 6:34:04
Shepphard 176 1 30N27 93w57 6:15:48
Shepton 43 1 33N01'38 96w47'40 6:27:11
Sheridan 45 1 29N29'36 96w40'15 6:26:41
Sherlock 148 3 36N26'44 100w13'25 6:40:54
Sherman 91 1 33N38'08 96w36'31 6:26:26
Sherman Junction 91
1 33N39'18 96w33'04 6:26:12
Sherry 194 1 33N32'36 95w06'10 6:20:25
Sherwood 118 1 31N16'52 100w47'42 6:43:11
Sherwood Place 101
1 29N52'24 95w19'16 6:21:17
Sherwood Shores 27
1 30N35 98w20 6:33:20
Shields 42 1 31N35'35 99w25'26 6:37:42
Shiloh 11 1 30N07 97w19 6:29:16
Shiloh 57 1 32N57'04 96w39'52 6:26:39
Shiloh 72 1 32N00'40 98w20'19 6:33:21
Shiloh 92 1 32N34'18 94w51'43 6:19:27
Shiloh 146 1 29N56'55 94w42'31 6:18:50
Shiloh 147 1 31N37'53 96w27'44 6:25:51
Shiner 143 1 29N25'44 97w10'13 6:28:41
Shirley 112 1 33N03'07 95w40'42 6:22:43
Shiro 93 1 30N36'47 95w53'17 6:23:33
Shive 97 1 31N36'44 98w14'04 6:32:56
Shoemaker Place 22
1 30N13'09 103w08'32 6:52:34
Shoreacres 101 1 29N37'12 95w00'35 6:20:02
Short 210 1 31N43'04 94w11'01 6:16:44
Shortall 141 1 31N04'31 98w04'53 6:32:20
Shorts Corner 15
1 29N32'53 98w24'39 6:33:39
Shotgun Crossing 190
1 32N55'15 95w42'24 6:22:50
Shumla 233 1 29N46'52 101w23'50 6:45:35
Sidney 47 1 31N56'57 98w44'13 6:34:57
Sid Place 22 1 29N50'01 103w39'09 6:54:37
Sierra Blanca 115
2 31N10'28 105w21'24 7:01:26
Sierra Chino 22
1 29N02'24 103w24'48 6:53:39
Siesta Shores 253
1 26N51'28 99w15'12 6:37:01
Silas 201 1 31N49'26 94w23'52 6:17:35
Siloam 19 1 33N21'48 94w34'23 6:18:18
Siloam 47 1 31N50'27 98w20'18 6:33:21
Siloam 246 1 30N25'33 97w17'02 6:29:08
Silsbee 100 1 30N20'56 94w10'40 6:16:43
Silver 41 1 32N04'15 100w40'56 6:42:44
Silver City 74 1 33N29'17 95w59'57 6:24:00
Silver City 166
1 30N54'35 96w57'00 6:27:48
Silver City 175
1 31N58'28 96w38'25 6:26:34
Silver City 194
1 33N51'10 95w03'34 6:20:14
Silver Lake 234
1 32N40'11 95w35'44 6:22:23
Silverton 23 1 34N28'27 101w18'15 6:45:13
Silver Valley 42
1 31N57'23 99w32'45 6:38:11
Simmons 149 1 28N24'21 98w16'49 6:33:07
Simmons Bottom 146
1 30N09'25 94w53'07 6:19:32
Simmonsville 14
1 32N44 94w57 6:19:48
Simmonsville 176
1 30N57'37 93w37'56 6:14:32
Simms 19 1 33N21'01 94w30'26 6:18:02
Simms 59 3 35N02'00 102w39'26 6:50:38
Simonton 79 1 29N40'45 95w58'37 6:23:54
Simpsonville 161
1 28N42 96w13 6:24:52
Sims 21 1 30N39'58 96w33'05 6:26:12
Simsboro 81 1 31N40'27 96w18'57 6:25:16
Sinclair City 212
1 32N11'54 95w04'47 6:20:19
Singleton 93 1 30N39'07 95w57'30 6:23:50
Sinton 205 1 28N02'11 97w30'32 6:30:02
Sipe Springs 47
1 32N05'26 98w47'02 6:35:08
Sisterdale 130 1 29N58'22 98w43'14 6:34:53
Sivells Bend 49
1 33N50'59 97w13'25 6:28:54
Sixmile Crossing 226
1 31N28'08 100w20'29 6:41:22
Six Point 95 1 34N05'37 101w48'01 6:47:12
Six Points 178 1 27N46 97w24 6:29:36
Sixteen Corner Windmill 2
1 32N22'26 102w15'04 6:49:00
Sixteen Mile Crossing 226
1 31N32'31 100w10'41 6:40:43
Skeeterville 206
1 31N21'14 98w57'45 6:35:51
Skellytown 33 3 35N34'31 101w11'02 6:44:44
Skidmore 13 1 28N15'14 97w41'07 6:30:44
Skinner Town 187
1 31N02'05 94w48'12 6:19:13
Skyscraper Shadows 101
1 29N37'11 95w16'31 6:21:06
Slab Crossing 97
1 31N31'33 98w04'51 6:32:19
Slabtown 139 1 33N28'18 95w32'06 6:22:08
Slater 50 1 31N20'36 97w58'10 6:31:53
Slate Shoals 139
1 33N51'11 95w24'32 6:21:38
Slaton 152 1 33N26'14 101w38'35 6:46:34
Slay 175 1 32N05 96w48 6:27:12
Slayden 89 1 29N34'31 97w32'01 6:30:08
Slide 152 1 33N24'50 101w55'46 6:47:43
Slidell 249 1 33N21'35 97w23'29 6:29:34
Sligo 251 1 33N02'44 102w41'52 6:50:47
Slocum 1 1 31N37'52 95w27'43 6:21:51
Slutter 45 1 29N42 96w33 6:26:12
Smada 79 1 29N34'52 95w34'48 6:22:19
Small 234 1 32N42 95w53 6:23:32
Smeltertown 71 2 31N47'00 106w31'34 7:06:06
Smetana 21 1 30N39'07 96w27'25 6:25:50
Smiley 89 1 29N16'03 97w38'08 6:30:33
Smith 14 1 31N03'19 97w21'04 6:29:24
Smithdale 38 1 34N35'45 100w11'53 6:40:48
Smithfield 220 1 32N52'15 97w12'54 6:28:52
Smith Grove 113
1 31N08'20 95w23'07 6:21:32
Smith Hill 19 1 33N32'24 94w17'41 6:17:11
Smithland 158 1 32N48'50 94w10'05 6:16:40
Smith Oaks 91 1 33N38'54 96w29'31 6:25:58
Smith Place 186
1 30N45'19 103w12'28 6:52:50
Smith Point 36 1 29N32'12 94w45'37 6:19:02
Smiths Bend 18 1 31N49'48 97w18'15 6:29:13
Smithson Valley 46
1 29N48'46 98w20'13 6:33:21
Smith Springs 72
1 32N13 98w13 6:32:52
Smithville 11 1 30N00'30 97w09'33 6:28:38
Smithville 89 1 29N31'26 97w36'28 6:30:26
Smithwick 27 1 30N33'38 98w08'41 6:32:35
Smitty 107 1 32N12 95w51 6:23:24
Smoot 227 1 30N16'27 97w39'05 6:30:36
Smyer 110 1 33N35'03 102w09'46 6:48:39
Smyrna 34 1 33N04'41 94w05'03 6:16:20
Smyrna 102 1 32N43'34 94w37'49 6:18:31
Smyrna 169 1 33N28'36 97w44'00 6:30:56
Smyth Crossing 232
1 29N07'13 99w53'13 6:39:33
Snap 183 1 32N09 94w20 6:17:20
Sneedville 51 1 33N52'48 100w16'44 6:41:07
Snipe 20 1 29N07'24 95w28'55 6:21:56
S N Junction 226
1 31N25'17 100w27'45 6:41:51
Snook 26 1 30N29'19 96w27'51 6:25:51
Snow 145 1 31N03 96w07 6:24:28
Snow Hill 43 1 33N10 96w22 6:25:28
Snow Hill 187 1 30N59'37 94w48'32 6:19:14
Snow Hill 204 1 30N42'23 95w13'14 6:20:53
Snyder 95 1 34N06'29 101w43'50 6:46:55
Snyder 208 1 32N43'04 100w55'02 6:43:40
Socorro 71 2 31N39'16 106w18'10 7:05:13
Soda 187 1 30N43 94w56 6:19:44
Soda Springs 28
1 29N43'07 97w35'56 6:30:24
Soda Springs 184
1 32N45 98w01 6:32:04
Sodville 205 1 27N58'10 97w28'23 6:29:54
Solino 108 1 26N29'17 98w07'57 6:32:32
Solis 22 1 29N03'40 103w05'57 6:52:24
Solis Landing 22
1 29N02'39 103w06'18 6:52:25
Solms 46 1 29N39'56 98w10'14 6:32:41
Somerset 15 1 29N13'34 98w39'27 6:34:38
Somerville 26 1 30N20'45 96w31'41 6:26:07
Sommers Mill 14
1 30N58'11 97w25'53 6:29:44
Soncy 188 3 35N11'20 101w56'31 6:47:46
Sonoma 70 1 32N20'25 96w36'35 6:26:26
Sonora 218 1 30N34'00 100w38'35 6:42:34
Sorghumville 113
1 31N03'24 95w30'30 6:22:02
Sorrelle 241 1 29N20'20 96w09'34 6:24:38
Sorters 170 1 29N47 95w23 6:21:32
Soules Chapel 230
1 32N44 94w57 6:19:48
Sour Lake 100 1 30N08'24 94w24'39 6:17:39
South 21 1 30N37 96w20 6:25:20
South Amarillo 188
3 35N10 101w53 6:47:32
South Austin 227
1 30N14 97w47 6:31:08
South Bend 252 1 33N00'16 98w40'05 6:34:40
South Bexar 15 1 29N16 98w29 6:33:56
South Bosque 155
1 31N28'54 97w17'16 6:29:09
South Brazos 20
1 30N31 96w16 6:25:04
South Brice 96 1 34N41'00 100w53'43 6:43:35
South Dallas 57
1 32N45 96w46 6:27:04
Southeast 220 1 32N37 97w12 6:28:48
South Elm 166 1 30N56'50 97w07'48 6:28:31
South End 123 1 30N03 94w06 6:16:24
South Fort Worth 220
1 32N44 97w20 6:29:20
South Gale 91 1 33N45 96w34 6:26:16
South Groveton 228
1 31N03 95w08 6:20:32
South Hanlon 215
1 32N43'39 98w52'39 6:35:31
South Haven 114
1 32N11'03 101w28'53 6:45:56
South Houston 101
1 29N39'46 95w14'07 6:20:56
South Jim Hogg 124
1 26N56 98w49 6:35:16
South Jonestown Hills 227
1 30N28'10 97w56'16 6:31:45
Southlake 220 1 32N56'28 97w08'02 6:28:32
Southland 85 1 33N21'43 101w32'59 6:46:12
Southland 241 1 29N11 96w17 6:25:08
Southland Acres 220
1 32N40'31 97w06'58 6:28:28
South Laredo 240
1 27N31 99w30 6:38:00
South Lawn 101 1 29N41'38 95w22'24 6:21:30
South Liberty 146
1 30N01'44 94w47'31 6:19:10
Southmayd (Southmayde Sta) 91
1 33N37'49 96w46'08 6:27:05
Southmore 101 1 29N44 95w22 6:21:28
South Mountain 50
1 31N25'39 97w40'38 6:30:43
South Oak Cliff 57
1 32N43 96w48 6:27:12
South Padre Island 31
1 26N06'12 97w09'52 6:28:39
South Park 101 1 29N40 95w20 6:21:20
South Plains 77
1 34N13'28 101w18'33 6:45:14
South Post Oak 101
1 29N39 95w29 6:21:56
South Purmela 50
1 31N28'11 97w58'19 6:31:53
South Rockwall 199
1 32N52 96w23 6:25:32
South Salem 145
1 31N16'04 96w04'17 6:24:17
South San Antonio 15
1 29N22 98w33 6:34:12
South Sand Hills 9
1 33N57 102w49 6:51:16
South San Pedro 178
1 27N47 97w41 6:30:44
South Shore 102
1 32N40'12 94w04'58 6:16:20
Southside Place 101
1 29N42'21 95w26'12 6:21:45
South Sulphur 116
1 33N15'54 96w00'35 6:24:02
South Temple 14
1 31N06 97w21 6:29:24
South Texarkana 19
1 33N24'08 94w02'34 6:16:10
South Texas Medical Center 15
1 29N30 98w35 6:34:20
Southton 15 1 29N17'46 98w25'06 6:33:40
Southwest 220 1 32N38 97w27 6:29:48
Sowells Bluff 74
1 33N45'02 96w11'41 6:24:47
Sowers 57 1 32N49'42 96w59'35 6:27:58
Spade 140 1 33N55'34 102w09'11 6:48:37
Spade 168 1 32N15'01 100w58'08 6:43:53
Spanish Camp 241
1 29N19 96w06 6:24:24
Spanish Fort 169
1 33N56'44 97w37'00 6:30:28
Spanish Village 4
1 28N16'33 96w52'50 6:27:31
Sparenberg 58 1 32N35'02 101w50'23 6:47:22
Sparks 14 1 30N55'42 97w21'34 6:29:26
Sparks Crossing 141
1 31N04'15 98w08'06 6:32:32
Speaks 143 1 29N15'19 96w42'00 6:26:48
Spear 21 1 30N36'05 96w20'12 6:25:21
Spearman 98 3 36N11'54 101w11'31 6:44:46
Speegleville 155
1 31N33'21 97w15'08 6:29:01
Spicewood 27 1 30N28'31 98w09'22 6:32:37
Spillers Store 145
1 31N09 95w58 6:23:52
Spivey Crossing 109
1 31N47'18 97w19'27 6:29:18
Splawn 166 1 30N55'12 96w59'08 6:27:57
Splendora 170 1 30N13'58 95w09'39 6:20:39
Spofford 136 1 29N10'30 100w24'48 6:41:39
Spooner 181 1 30N06 93w46 6:15:04
Spraberry 165 1 31N55'23 101w49'31 6:47:18
Spring 101 1 30N04'47 95w25'01 6:21:40
Spring Branch 46
1 29N53'23 98w25'30 6:33:42
Spring Creek 86
1 30N17 98w52 6:35:28
Spring Creek 206
1 31N21'11 98w49'18 6:35:17
Spring Creek 224
1 33N22'12 98w57'40 6:35:51
Spring Creek Acres 235
1 28N48 96w59 6:27:56
Springdale 34 1 33N13'59 94w07'59 6:16:32
Springdale 97 1 31N36'46 98w18'53 6:33:16
Springfield 1 1 31N59'12 95w48'18 6:23:13
Springfield 125
1 27N45 98w05 6:32:20
Springfield 147
1 31N39'34 96w28'57 6:25:56
Spring Hill 19 1 33N36'16 94w40'18 6:18:41
Spring Hill 32 1 33N00'30 94w54'00 6:19:36
Spring Hill 61 1 33N17'56 96w56'09 6:27:45
Spring Hill 74 1 33N36'32 96w00'36 6:24:02
Spring Hill 92 1 32N33'46 94w48'07 6:19:12
Spring Hill 94 1 29N35 97w58 6:31:52
Spring Hill 175
1 31N56'10 96w42'36 6:26:50
Spring Hill 204
1 30N34'51 95w12'44 6:20:51
Spring Hills 170
1 30N07'11 95w25'28 6:21:42
Springlake 140 1 34N13'54 102w18'20 6:49:13
Spring Seat 145
1 31N12'25 96w02'13 6:24:09
Springtown 97 1 31N48'07 98w11'22 6:32:45
Springtown 184 1 32N57'57 97w41'00 6:30:44
Spring Valley 101
1 29N47'22 95w30'12 6:22:01
Spring Valley 155
1 31N23'59 97w17'23 6:29:10
Sprinkle 227 1 30N18 97w43 6:30:52
Spur 63 1 33N28'35 100w51'19 6:43:25
Spurger 229 1 30N41'33 94w10'39 6:16:43
Spurlin 97 1 31N50'37 98w08'19 6:32:33
Squaw Mountain 119
1 33N21'40 98w19'14 6:33:17
Stacy 154 1 31N28'37 99w35'51 6:38:23

Staff 67 1 32N21'33 98W42'22 6:34:49
Stafford 79 1 29N36'57 95W33'27 6:22:14
Stag Creek 47 1 32N00'43 98W45'24 6:35:02
Stagecoach 170 1 30N13 95W45 6:23:00
Stairtown 28 1 29N43'05 97W43'39 6:30:55
Staley (Embryfield) 204 1 30N50'01 95W17'31 6:21:10
Stallwitz Lake 171 3 35N48'36 102W00'54 6:48:04
Stamford 127 1 32N56'43 99W48'09 6:39:13
Stampede 14 1 31N16'55 97W24'13 6:29:37
Stamps 230 1 32N45'27 94W47'16 6:19:09
Standart 136 1 29N20'32 100W37'04 6:42:28
Stanfield 39 1 33N58'09 97W59'58 6:32:00
Stanton 159 1 32N07'45 101W47'17 6:47:09
Staples 94 1 29N46'52 97W50'09 6:31:21
Star 167 1 31N28'06 98W18'57 6:33:16
Star Harbor 107 1 32N10 96W01 6:24:04
Stark 181 1 30N07'53 93W52'03 6:15:28
Starrville 212 1 32N28'11 95W06'57 6:20:28
Startzville 46 1 29N50'40 98W16'25 6:33:06
State Line 83 1 32N43'36 103W03'52 6:52:15
Steele Hill 63 1 33N26'46 100W47'16 6:43:09
Steeltown 123 1 29N57 93W55 6:15:40
Steen 62 1 29N19'18 97W18'45 6:29:15
Steep Hollow 21 1 30N41'42 96W17'26 6:25:10
Stegall 9 1 34N00'12 102W57'21 6:51:49
Stekoll Camp 117 3 35N46'42 101W22'42 6:45:31
Stellar 75 1 29N53'25 97W08'25 6:28:34
Stephen Creek 204 1 30N41'32 95W11'02 6:20:44
Stephens Crossing 184 1 32N37'07 97W57'51 6:31:51
Stephenville 72 1 32N13'14 98W12'07 6:32:48
Sterley 77 1 34N12'40 101W23'50 6:45:35
Sterling City 216 1 31N50'10 100W59'04 6:43:56
Sterrett 70 1 32N28'26 96W49'52 6:27:19
Sterrett Hill 183 1 32N17'22 94W23'32 6:17:34
Stevens 211 3 36N25'08 101W55'29 6:47:42
Stewards Mill 81 1 31N49'24 96W12'05 6:24:48
Stewart 201 1 32N17'51 94W38'52 6:18:35
Stewart Heights 101 1 29N46 95W00 6:20:00
Stieren 89 1 29N40 97W30 6:30:00
Stiles 192 1 31N24'24 101W33'57 6:46:16
Stillwell Crossing 22 1 29N23'55 102W49'06 6:51:16
Stilson 146 1 30N01'07 94W55'07 6:19:40
Stinnett 117 3 35N49'37 101W26'33 6:45:46
Stith 127 1 32N32'47 99W56'38 6:39:47
Stockard 107 1 32N16'46 95W57'30 6:23:50
Stockdale 247 1 29N14'12 97W57'35 6:31:50
Stockholm 108 1 26N25 97W48 6:31:12
Stockman 210 1 31N46'45 94W24'23 6:17:38
Stock Yards 220 1 32N47 97W21 6:29:24
Stolz 150 1 30N46'37 98W33'24 6:34:14
Stoneburg 169 1 33N40'16 97W54'18 6:31:37
Stone City 21 1 30N37'48 96W32'30 6:26:10
Stoneham 93 1 30N20'30 95W54'44 6:23:39
Stonewall 86 1 30N14'09 98W39'51 6:34:39
Stony 61 1 33N13'27 97W21'08 6:29:25
Stormville 250 1 32N48 95W27 6:21:48
Stout 250 1 32N52'19 95W17'47 6:21:11
Stowell 101 1 29N47'23 94W22'59 6:17:32
Stowers Corner Windmill 133 1 30N01'40 99W30'09 6:38:01
Strain 100 1 30N07'59 94W32'55 6:18:12
Stranger 73 1 31N19'36 96W43'27 6:26:54
Stratford 211 3 36N20'10 102W04'18 6:48:17
Stratton 62 1 29N09'05 97W09'00 6:28:36
Stratton Ridge 20 1 28N58 95W25 6:21:40
Strawn 182 1 32N33'07 98W29'52 6:33:59
Streeter 160 1 30N45'53 99W22'34 6:37:30
Streetman 81 1 31N52'38 96W19'29 6:25:18
Strickland 202 1 31N15 93W58 6:15:52
Strickland Crossing 202 1 31N19'36 93W56'18 6:15:45
Stricklin Springs 102 1 32N25'54 94W09'09 6:16:37
String Prairie 11 1 29N53'08 97W20'48 6:29:23
Stringtown 14 1 31N01'25 97W14'27 6:28:58
Stringtown 176 1 30N54'28 93W37'30 6:14:30
Stringtown 201 1 32N07'04 94W54'10 6:19:37
Stringtown 202 1 31N11'30 93W55'32 6:15:42
Strip Crossing 180 3 35N30'58 102W39'19 6:50:37
Structure 246 1 30N21 97W22 6:29:28
Stryker Creek Junction 37 1 31N53'21 95W01'46 6:20:07
Stuart Place 22 1 29N56'22 102W36'37 6:50:26
Stuart Place 31 1 26N10'40 97W45'27 6:31:02
Stubblefield 113 1 31N18'51 95W06'35 6:20:26
Stubbs 129 1 32N24'31 96W17'15 6:25:09
Study Butte 22 1 29N19 103W37 6:54:28
Stumptown 202 1 31N09'21 93W68'01 6:15:52
Sturdivant 182 1 32N45'55 98W03'59 6:32:16
Sturgeon 49 1 33N45'26 96W58'31 6:27:54
Sturgis Mill 202 1 31N21 93W51 6:15:24
Styx 129 1 32N21'47 96W19'40 6:25:19
Sublett 220 1 32N38'41 97W07'59 6:28:32
Sublime 143 1 29N28'43 96W47'50 6:27:11
Sudan 140 1 34N04'04 102W31'26 6:50:06
Sudduth 27 1 30N39'29 98W15'09 6:33:01
Suffolk 230 1 32N44 94W57 6:19:48
Sugar Land 79 1 29N37'10 95W38'05 6:22:32
Sugar Valley 116 1 29N03'45 95W50'22 6:23:21
Suggs 118 1 31N07'20 101W04'37 6:44:18
Sullivan 94 1 29N39 97W50 6:31:20
Sullivan City 108 1 26N16'38 98W33'48 6:34:15
Sulphur 19 1 33N18'46 94W03'20 6:16:13
Sulphur 228 1 31N03'32 94W58'38 6:19:55
Sulphur Bluff 112 1 33N19'57 95W23'53 6:21:36
Sulphur Springs 3 1 31N09 94W26 6:17:44
Sulphur Springs 112 1 33N08'18 95W36'03 6:22:24
Sulphur Springs 201 1 31N53'47 94W45'54 6:19:04
Sul Ross 22 1 30N20 103W39 6:54:36
Summerfield 185 3 34N44'17 102W30'24 6:50:02
Summerfield 230 1 32N43'12 95W01'33 6:20:06
Summerville 89 1 29N27'18 97W28'13 6:29:53
Sumner 139 1 33N44'25 95W40'22 6:22:41
Sun 91 1 33N45 96W34 6:26:16
Sundown 110 1 33N27'22 102W29'20 6:49:57
Sunniland 149 1 28N35'15 98W13'07 6:32:52
Sunnylane 27 1 30N55'47 98W08'10 6:32:33
Sunnyside 35 1 34N20'52 102W18'11 6:49:13
Sunny Side 101 1 29N39'50 95W22'04 6:21:28
Sunnyside 123 1 30N04'13 94W08'49 6:16:35
Sunny Side 237 1 29N53'18 96W04'08 6:24:17
Sunnyside 247 1 29N08'23 98W03'08 6:32:13
Sunny Side PO 237 1 29N54'33 96W03'57 6:24:16
Sunnyslope 19 1 33N26 94W04 6:16:16
Sunnyvale 57 1 32N47'47 96W33'38 6:26:15
Sun Oil Camp 214 1 26N41 98W25 6:33:40
Sunray 171 3 36N01'00 101W49'27 6:47:18
Sunrise 73 1 31N17 96W53 6:27:32
Sunrise 203 1 31N30'41 94W04'31 6:16:18
Sunrise Acres 71 2 31N51'38 106W26'41 7:05:47
Sunrise Beach Village 150 1 30N45 98W41 6:34:44
Sunset 138 1 33N26'51 99W42'46 6:38:51
Sunset 152 1 33N34 101W57 6:47:48
Sunset 169 1 33N27'07 97W45'59 6:31:04
Sunset Heights 68 1 31N52 102W22 6:49:28
Sunset Valley 227 1 30N13'32 97W48'12 6:31:13
Sunshine 97 1 31N51'48 98W08'40 6:32:35
Suntide 178 1 27N49 97W31 6:30:04
Sunview 158 1 32N48 94W43 6:18:52
Surf Oaks 101 1 29N35'20 94W59'46 6:19:59
Surfside 20 1 28N56'35 95W17'51 6:21:11
Surfside Beach 20 1 28N56'39 95W17'19 6:21:09
Sutherland Springs 247 1 29N16'23 98W03'23 6:32:14
Sutton 198 1 30N49'16 96W31'47 6:26:07
Suttons Mill 174 1 31N29'17 94W22'51 6:17:31
Swamp City 92 1 32N34 94W55 6:19:40
Swan 212 1 32N26'05 95W22'01 6:21:28
Swan Lagoon 101 1 29N47 95W23 6:21:32
Swanson Hill 1 1 31N46 95W38 6:22:32
Swansons Landing 102 1 32N40'29 94W03'21 6:16:13
Swartout 187 1 30N38'18 95W00'17 6:20:01
Swearingen 51 1 34N08'55 100W08'51 6:40:35
Sweeny 20 1 29N02'19 95W41'54 6:22:48
Sweeny Switch 149 1 28N06 97W50 6:31:20
Sweet Home 143 1 29N20'42 97W04'17 6:28:17
Sweetwater 47 1 31N54 98W36 6:34:24
Sweetwater 177 1 32N28'15 100W24'20 6:41:37
Swenson 217 1 33N12'25 100W18'42 6:41:15
Swift 174 1 31N37'12 94W28'59 6:17:56
Swiss Alp 75 1 29N46'56 96W54'33 6:27:38
Sycamore 176 1 31N00 93W40 6:14:40
Sycamore 249 1 33N19'25 97W29'23 6:29:58
Sylvan 139 1 33N38'39 95W26'02 6:21:44
Sylvan Beach 101 1 29N40 95W02 6:20:08
Sylvester 76 1 32N43'15 100W15'14 6:41:01
Tabor 21 1 30N47'44 96W22'15 6:25:29
Tacoma 183 1 32N09 94W20 6:17:20
Tacubaya 24 1 26N55'11 98W16'27 6:33:06
Tadmor 113 1 31N25'54 95W10'32 6:20:42
Taft 205 1 27N58'43 97W23'54 6:29:36
Taft Southwest 205 1 27N59 97W24 6:29:36
Tahoka 153 1 33N10'00 101W47'36 6:47:10
Taiton 241 1 29N11 96W17 6:25:08
Talbert Crossing 99 1 34N20'58 99W46'49 6:39:07
Talco 225 1 33N21'45 95W06'16 6:20:25
Talley 22 1 28N58'59 103W11'01 6:52:44
Talpa 42 1 31N46'35 99W42'33 6:38:50
Talty 129 1 32N40'59 96W23'07 6:25:32
Tam Anne 35 3 34N31'51 102W31'08 6:50:05
Tamberg 75 1 29N54'33 96W43'09 6:26:53
Tamega 27 1 30N45 98W03 6:32:12
Tamina 170 1 30N10'42 95W26'29 6:21:46
Tanglewood 144 1 30N29'51 96W59'10 6:27:57
Tankersley 226 1 31N20'58 100W38'35 6:42:34
Tanner Settlement 146 1 30N12'33 94W42'13 6:18:49
Tarkington Prairie 146 1 30N18 95W07 6:20:28
Tarleton 72 1 32N13 98W13 6:32:52
Tarpley 10 1 29N39'25 99W16'34 6:37:06
Tarrant 220 1 32N49'00 97W04'37 6:28:18
Tarver 109 1 31N57 97W19 6:29:16
Tarzan 159 1 32N18'19 101W58'29 6:47:54
Tascosa 180 3 35N30'40 102W15'03 6:49:00
Tate Springs 220 1 32N40'52 97W11'35 6:28:46
Tatsie 198 1 30N47'36 96W36'07 6:26:24
Tatsie Crossing 198 1 30N48'03 96W36'23 6:26:26
Tatum 201 1 32N18'57 94W30'59 6:18:04
Tavener 79 1 29N32'24 95W59'21 6:23:57
Taylor 246 1 30N34'14 97W24'33 6:29:38
Taylor Lake Village 101 1 29N35 95W03 6:20:12
Taylorsville 28 1 29N53'45 97W29'52 6:29:59
Taylor Town 139 1 33N27'23 95W27'00 6:21:48
Taylorville 74 1 33N25 96W03 6:24:12
Tazewell 112 1 33N03'24 95W37'11 6:22:29
T C U 220 1 32N44 97W20 6:29:20
Teague 81 1 31N37'37 96W17'01 6:25:08
Teaselville 212 1 32N08'52 95W24'16 6:21:37
Tech 152 1 33N34 101W52 6:47:28
Tecifie 177 1 32N30'31 100W19'24 6:41:18
Tecula 37 1 32N01'11 95W12'33 6:20:50
Tehuacana 147 1 31N44'28 96W32'48 6:26:11
Telegraph 134 1 30N19'38 99W54'21 6:39:37
Telephone 74 1 33N46'52 96W01'04 6:24:04
Telferner 235 1 28N50'55 96W53'25 6:27:34
Telico 70 1 32N22'19 96W30'44 6:26:03
Tell 38 1 34N22'33 100W23'40 6:41:35
Temco 121 1 30N21'35 94W04'00 6:16:16
Temple 14 1 31N05'53 97W20'33 6:29:22
Tenaha 210 1 31N56'37 94W14'38 6:16:59
Teneryville 92 1 32N32'14 94W48'28 6:19:14
Tenmile 58 1 32N35'52 101W54'54 6:47:40
Tenmile Crossing 25 1 31N38'32 98W52'38 6:35:31
Tenmile Crossing 164 1 30N53'01 99W37'47 6:38:31
Tenneryville 92 1 32N27 94W44 6:18:56
Tennessee Colony 1 1 31N50'07 95W50'19 6:23:21
Tennyson 41 1 31N44'30 100W17'09 6:41:09
Terlingua 22 1 29N19'17 103W36'56 6:54:28
Terlingua Abaja 22 1 29N11'36 103W36'25 6:54:26
Terrell 129 1 32N44'09 96W16'30 6:25:06
Terrell Hills 15 1 29N28'29 98W27'02 6:33:48
Terrell Wells 15 1 29N20'22 98W30'56 6:34:04
Terry 181 1 30N05'58 93W55'57 6:15:44
Terrys Chapel 73 1 31N04 96W58 6:27:52
Terryville 62 1 29N11'23 97W04'15 6:28:17
Tesco 177 1 32N29'40 100W14'34 6:40:58
Tesnus 22 1 30N07'05 102W53'51 6:51:35
Texarkana 19 1 33N25'30 94W02'51 6:16:11
Texas City 84 1 29N23'01 94W54'09 6:19:37
Texas City Junction 84 1 29N20'58 94W56'21 6:19:45
Texas City Terminal Junction 84 1 29N19'49 94W57'56 6:19:52
Texhoma 211 3 36N29'53 101W46'57 6:47:08
Texla 181 1 30N13'12 93W52'51 6:15:31
Texline 56 3 36N22'40 103W01'25 6:52:06
Texon 192 1 31N13'29 101W41'21 6:46:45
Texroy 117 3 35N38'04 101W17'45 6:45:11
Thalia 78 1 33N59'05 99W32'15 6:38:09
Thayer 108 1 26N09 97W55 6:31:40
The Crossroads 166 1 30N44'50 97W07'55 6:28:32
Thedford 212 1 32N29'04 95W23'47 6:21:35
The Grove 50 1 31N16'23 97W31'30 6:30:06
The Heights 20 1 29N24 95W14 6:20:56
The Knobbs 144 1 30N17 97W15 6:29:00
Thelma 15 1 29N12'50 98W30'05 6:34:00
Thelma 147 1 31N34'59 96W36'39 6:26:27
The Meadows 79 1 29N38 95W33 6:22:12
Theon 246 1 30N45'46 97W35'49 6:30:23
Thermo 112 1 33N06'08 95W30'57 6:22:04
Thicket 100 1 30N23'44 94W37'48 6:18:31
Third Crossing 46 1 29N48'11 98W09'48 6:32:39
Third Crossing 232 1 29N32'10 99W42'47 6:38:51
Thomas 230 1 32N51'39 95W04'02 6:20:16
Thomas Crossing 3 1 31N22'19 94W31'42 6:18:07
Thomaston 62 1 28N59'50 97W09'17 6:28:37
Thompson 101 1 29N51 95W30 6:22:00
Thompson Grove 56 3 36N24'52 102W48'14 6:51:13
Thompsons 79 1 29N29'51 95W35'05 6:22:20
Thompsonville 89 1 29N42'09 97W22'54 6:29:32
Thompsonville 124 1 27N12'19 98W56'24 6:35:46
Thornberry 39 1 34N03'29 98W23'20 6:33:33
Thorndale 166 1 30N36'49 97W12'19 6:28:49
Thorne 91 1 33N38'00 96W47'11 6:27:09
Thorn Hill 46 1 29N44'35 98W05'56 6:32:24
Thornton 147 1 31N24'39 96W34'19 6:26:17
Thorntonville 238 1 31N34'58 102W55'13 6:51:41
Thorp Spring 111 1 32N28'26 97W49'35 6:31:18
Thrall 246 1 30N35'25 97W17'48 6:29:11
Three Corner Windmill 238 1 31N38'07 103W03'35 6:52:14
Three Leagues 159 1 32N29'44 101W58'18 6:47:53
Three Oaks 247 1 28N58'35 98W10'01 6:32:40
Three Points 227 1 30N27'05 97W39'43 6:30:39
Three Rivers 149 1 28N27'36 98W10'56 6:32:44
Three States 34 1 33N01'09 94W02'33 6:16:10
Thrift 243 1 34N07'34 98W37'18 6:34:29
Thrifty 25 1 31N48'39 99W07'54 6:36:32
Throckmorton 224 1 33N10'43 99W10'38 6:36:43
Thurber 72 1 32N30'26 98W25'01 6:33:40
Tidehaven 161 1 28N54 96W09 6:24:36
Tidwell 116 1 33N12'34 96W06'04 6:24:24
Tidwell Prairie 198 1 31N05'23 96W39'26 6:26:38
Tiffin 67 1 32N29'47 98W39'46 6:34:39
Tigertown 139 1 33N42'49 95W48'15 6:23:13
Tigerville 187 1 30N42'09 95W04'25 6:20:18

Tigua 71 2 31N44'30 106w21'49 7:05:27
Tilden 156 1 28N27'42 98w32'56 6:34:12
Tilmon 28 1 29N47'51 97w33'11 6:30:13
Timber Cove 101 1 29N34 95w01 6:20:04
Timberlake 101 1 29N58 95w42 6:22:48
Timberlane Acres 170 1 30N05'16 95w14'19 6:20:57
Timesville 145 1 31N31'33 95w47'02 6:23:08
Timothy 175 1 32N14 96w25 6:25:40
Timpson 210 1 31N54'13 94w23'42 6:17:35
Tinaja 22 1 29N44'19 102w52'50 6:51:31
Tin Top 111 1 32N35'51 97w48'46 6:31:15
Tin Top 161 1 28N47'03 96w07'26 6:24:30
Tioga 91 1 33N28'00 96w55'05 6:27:40
Tira 112 1 33N19'35 95w34'28 6:22:18
Tivoli 196 1 28N27'18 96w53'16 6:27:33
Tivydale 86 1 30N15'02 99w05'57 6:36:24
Tobe Hahn 123 1 30N06 94w09 6:16:36
Toco 139 1 33N38 95w42 6:22:48
Tod 101 1 29N34 95w01 6:20:04
Todd 93 1 30N16'04 95w50'22 6:23:21
Todd City 1 1 31N55'08 95w28'39 6:21:55
Todville 101 1 29N33'59 95w00'48 6:20:03
Togo 11 1 29N57'01 97w13'08 6:28:53
Tokio 223 1 33N10'53 102w16'29 6:49:06
Toland 177 1 32N26'58 100w08'59 6:40:36
Tolar 111 1 32N23'20 97w55'13 6:31:41
Tolbert 244 1 34N13'09 99w23'46 6:37:35
Toledo 176 1 31N10'27 93w33'40 6:14:15
Tolosa 129 1 32N22'14 96w14'25 6:24:58
Toluca 63 1 26N04'14 97w56'38 6:31:47
Tomball 101 1 30N05'49 95w36'57 6:22:28
Tom Bean 91 1 33N31'12 96w29'01 6:25:56
Tomlinson Hill 73 1 31N15'56 96w59'16 6:27:57
Tool 107 1 32N26 96w05 6:24:20
Topsey 50 1 31N13'08 97w59'05 6:31:56
Torian 125 1 27N42'52 98w04'35 6:32:18
Tornillo 71 2 31N26'43 106w05'16 7:04:21
Toto 184 1 32N58 97w52 6:31:28
Tours 155 1 31N45'35 97w02'15 6:28:09
Tow 150 1 30N53'00 98w28'20 6:33:53
Town Bluff 229 1 30N47 94w25 6:17:40
Town Hall 57 1 32N46 96w37 6:26:28
Toyah 195 1 31N18'53 103w47'34 6:55:10
Toyahvale 195 1 30N56'39 103w47'20 6:55:09
Tracy 166 1 30N44'30 97w05'49 6:28:23
Trading Post 227 1 30N18'17 97w56'08 6:31:45
Trammells 79 1 29N32'04 95w32'14 6:22:09
Travis 73 1 31N08'07 97w00'09 6:28:01
Travis Peak 227 1 30N35 98w20 6:33:20
Trawick 174 1 31N46'15 94w44'35 6:18:58
Treichel 101 1 30N04'53 95w39'05 6:22:36
Trent 177 1 32N29'22 100w07'34 6:40:30
Trenton 74 1 33N25'50 96w20'18 6:25:21
Tres Papalotes 22 1 29N27'24 103w46'32 6:55:06
Trevat 228 1 31N07'11 94w56'46 6:19:47
Triangle 73 1 31N16'53 96w59'23 6:27:58
Tribune 91 1 33N35'54 96w35'25 6:26:22
Tri Cities 107 1 32N12 95w51 6:23:24
Trickham 42 1 31N35'15 99w13'49 6:36:55
Trinidad 107 1 32N00'30 96w05'27 6:24:22
Trinity 228 1 30N56'42 95w22'31 6:21:30
Trinity Mills 57 1 32N58'53 96w55'38 6:27:43
Trinity Park 43 1 33N05'16 96w32'30 6:26:10
Trio 232 1 29N24'08 99w33'29 6:38:14
Tripp 57 1 32N47'41 96w33'37 6:26:14
Tropical Acres 235 1 28N48 96w59 6:27:56
Troup 212 1 32N08'40 95w07'13 6:20:29
Trout Creek 176 1 30N37'02 93w48'33 6:15:14
Troy 14 1 31N12'24 97w18'09 6:29:13
Truby 127 1 32N38'43 99w55'30 6:39:42
Truce 119 1 33N24'47 98w01'50 6:32:07
True 252 1 33N16'47 98w43'42 6:34:55
Trumbull 70 1 32N29'25 96w39'55 6:26:40
Truscott 138 1 33N45'15 99w48'39 6:39:15
Tubbs Corner 52 1 31N22'57 102w37'00 6:50:28
Tucker 1 1 31N40'24 95w44'52 6:22:59
Tuckers Corner 19 1 33N25'38 94w42'32 6:18:50
Tuff 10 1 29N46'08 99w24'12 6:37:37
Tulane 181 1 30N05'44 93w50'19 6:15:21
Tuleta 13 1 28N34'14 97w47'49 6:31:11
Tulia 219 3 34N32'09 101w45'29 6:47:02
Tulip 74 1 33N48'29 96w07'52 6:24:31
Tulsita 13 1 28N38'34 97w48'57 6:31:16
Tundra 234 1 32N27'50 95w52'49 6:23:31
Tunis 26 1 30N32'41 96w31'37 6:26:06
Tupelo 175 1 32N15 96w30 6:26:00
Turcotte 131 1 27N00'25 97w47'42 6:31:11
Turkey 96 1 34N23'33 100w53'50 6:43:35
Turkey Creek 34 1 32N57'18 94w34'19 6:18:17
Turkey Hollow 246 1 30N28'56 97w44'33 6:30:58
Turlington 81 1 31N41'41 96w03'15 6:24:13
Turnbaugh Corner 68 1 31N58'47 102w40'56 6:50:44
Turnersville 50 1 31N37'02 97w44'19 6:30:57
Turnersville 227 1 30N05'33 97w46'51 6:31:07
Turnertown (Selman City P O) 201 1 32N11'23 94w56'58 6:19:48
Turney 37 1 31N54'32 95w11'42 6:20:47
Turtle Bayou 36 1 29N46 94w42 6:18:48
Tuscola 221 1 32N12'34 99w47'47 6:39:11
Tuxedo 127 1 32N55'58 99w57'05 6:39:48
Twentymile Crossing 164 1 30N54'44 99w29'32 6:37:58
Twichell 179 3 36N26'15 100w43'43 6:42:55
Twin City 91 1 33N42'12 96w34'12 6:26:17
Twin Grove 148 3 36N19'43 100w26'16 6:41:45
Twin Mill 103 3 35N57'21 102w48'30 6:51:14
Twin Mountains 252 1 33N06'34 98w34'57 6:34:20
Twin Sisters 16 1 30N00'09 98w24'18 6:33:37
Twitchell 179 3 36N24 100w48 6:43:12
Twitty 242 3 35N18'50 100w14'09 6:40:57
Two F Crossing 217 1 33N18'18 100w01'08 6:40:05
T W U 61 1 33N13 97w08 6:28:32
Tye 206 1 32N27'27 99w52'16 6:39:29
Tyler 212 1 32N21'04 95w18'03 6:21:12
Tylers Bluff 49 1 33N42 97w31 6:30:04
Tynan 13 1 28N10'09 97w45'26 6:31:02
Type 11 1 30N21 97w22 6:29:28
Tyson 109 1 31N47'55 97w14'21 6:28:57
Uhland 28 1 29N57'27 97w47'09 6:31:09
Umbarger 188 3 34N57'16 102w06'18 6:48:25
Uncertain 102 1 32N42'43 94w07'16 6:16:29
Underwood 95 1 33N59'09 101w50'35 6:47:22
Union 21 1 30N51'47 96w18'36 6:25:14
Union 58 1 32N40'25 102w03'49 6:48:15
Union 80 1 33N08'04 95w16'25 6:21:06
Union 152 1 33N24'50 101w46'21 6:47:05
Union 208 1 32N43'44 100w59'50 6:43:59
Union 223 1 33N02'11 102w13'17 6:48:53
Union 247 1 29N19'12 97w50'40 6:31:23
Union Bower 57 1 32N51 96w58 6:27:52
Union Center 67 1 32N10'14 98w57'37 6:35:50
Union Grove 14 1 31N00'01 97w36'06 6:30:24
Union Grove 138 1 33N25'24 99w52'06 6:39:28
Union Grove 230 1 32N34'16 94w55'13 6:19:41
Union High 175 1 31N54 96w43 6:26:52
Union Hill 14 1 31N10'23 97w32'45 6:30:11
Union Hill 18 1 32N04 97w30 6:30:00
Union Hill 61 1 33N24'06 97w07'55 6:28:32
Union Hill 74 1 33N27'51 96w16'50 6:25:07
Union Hill 230 1 32N48'51 94w58'49 6:19:55
Union Hill 239 1 30N12'10 96w36'48 6:26:27
Union Springs 174 1 31N40 94w38 6:18:32
Union Valley 116 1 32N55'38 96w15'03 6:25:00
Union Valley 129 1 32N41'50 96w18'01 6:25:12
Union Valley 247 1 29N16 97w46 6:31:04
Unity 139 1 33N45'55 95w45'15 6:23:01
Unity 247 1 29N11'50 98w03'13 6:32:13
Universal City 15 1 29N32'52 98w17'27 6:33:10
University 227 1 30N17 97w44 6:30:56
University Hill 61 1 33N11 97w04 6:28:16
University of Dallas 57 1 32N51 96w58 6:27:52
University of Texas at El Pa 71 2 31N47 106w30 7:06:00
University Park 15 1 29N28 98w35 6:34:20
University Park 57 1 32N51 96w48 6:27:12
University Park 243 1 33N52 98w33 6:34:12
Upper Meyersville 62 1 28N55'09 97w20'46 6:29:23
Upshaw 174 1 31N40 94w53 6:19:32
Upton 11 1 30N00'40 97w15'50 6:29:03
Urbana 204 1 30N33'37 94w57'24 6:19:50
Urebeno 253 1 26N56'44 99w18'52 6:37:15
Utley 11 1 30N10'54 97w25'14 6:29:41
Utopia 232 1 29N36'54 99w31'36 6:38:06
Uvalde 232 1 29N12'34 99w47'09 6:39:09
Vahlsing 205 1 28N07'25 97w47'59 6:31:12
Vair 228 1 31N16'51 94w54'48 6:19:39
Valdasta 43 1 33N17'38 96w28'15 6:25:53
Valdina Farms 163 1 29N29'39 99w22'49 6:37:31
Valentine 122 1 30N35'14 104w29'46 6:57:59
Valera 42 1 31N45'10 99w32'49 6:38:11
Valleycreek 74 1 33N25 96w03 6:24:12
Valley Farms 175 1 32N18'28 96w24'19 6:25:37
Valley Grove 201 1 31N52'44 94w48'30 6:19:14
Valley Hi 15 1 29N22'24 98w38'21 6:34:33
Valley Junction 198 1 30N50'30 96w38'15 6:26:33
Valley Lodge 79 1 29N41 95w58 6:23:52
Valley Mills 18 1 31N39'33 97w28'19 6:29:53
Valley Ridge 220 1 32N35'14 97w14'29 6:28:58
Valley Spring 150 1 30N51'33 98w49'01 6:35:16
Valley View 46 1 29N46'21 98w16'31 6:33:06
Valley View 49 1 33N29'17 97w09'53 6:28:40
Valley View 62 1 29N06 97w17 6:29:08
Valley View 155 1 31N37'51 97w14'39 6:28:59
Valley View 168 1 32N29'38 100w46'32 6:43:06
Valley View 169 1 33N56'44 97w40'11 6:30:41
Valley View 200 1 31N45 99w57 6:39:48
Valley View 230 1 32N44 94w57 6:19:48
Valley View 243 1 33N52'23 98w45'46 6:35:03
Valley Wells 64 1 28N28'50 99w30'32 6:38:02
Val Verde 108 1 26N10'33 98w04'51 6:32:19
Val Verde 166 1 30N50'03 97w14'51 6:28:59
Van 234 1 32N31'29 95w38'13 6:22:33
Van Alstyne 91 1 33N25'17 96w34'37 6:26:18
Vance 193 1 29N48'56 100w00'48 6:40:03
Vancourt 226 1 31N20'34 100w10'36 6:40:42
Vandalia 194 1 33N40'18 95w00'56 6:20:04
Vandenburg 163 1 29N21 99w08 6:36:32
Vanderbilt 120 1 28N49'22 96w37'02 6:26:28
Vanderpool 10 1 29N44'42 99w33'17 6:38:13
Vandyke 47 1 31N58'20 98w33'38 6:34:15
Vanetia 145 1 31N14 96w16 6:25:04
Van Horn 55 1 31N02'23 104w49'49 6:59:19
Van Pelt 20 1 29N08'00 95w25'51 6:21:43
Van Raub 15 1 29N43'46 98w39'20 6:34:37
Van Vleck 116 1 29N01'03 95w53'21 6:23:33
Varisco 21 1 30N38'32 96w32'33 6:26:10
Vasco 60 1 33N24'54 95w29'42 6:21:59
Vashti 39 1 33N33'20 98w02'26 6:32:10
Vattmanville 137 1 27N19'55 97w45'07 6:31:00
Vaughan 109 1 31N54'52 97w10'24 6:28:42
Vealmoor 114 1 32N31'14 101w34'12 6:46:17
Veal Station 184 1 32N58 97w41 6:30:44
Vega 180 3 35N14'34 102w25'40 6:49:43
Velasco Heights 20 1 28N58'58 95w22'15 6:21:29
Vemo 155 1 31N33'00 97w05'05 6:28:20
Venable 203 1 31N27'50 94w05'22 6:16:21
Venadito 31 1 26N03'08 97w46'08 6:31:05
Venetia 145 1 31N08'48 96w15'52 6:25:03
Ventura 170 1 30N11'29 95w39'36 6:22:38
Venus 126 1 32N26'00 97w06'08 6:28:25
Vera 138 1 33N38'00 99w33'57 6:38:16
Vera Cruz 66 1 27N26'29 98w15'52 6:33:03
Verbena 85 1 33N16'29 101w11'43 6:44:47
Verde, Canada 247 1 29N11'30 98w16'31 6:33:06
Verdi 7 1 29N02'59 98w23'57 6:33:36
Verhalen 195 1 31N07'35 103w35'35 6:54:22
Verhelle 62 1 29N02'38 97w11'34 6:28:46
Veribest 226 1 31N28'35 100w15'33 6:41:02
Vernon 244 1 34N09'16 99w15'53 6:37:04
Verona 43 1 33N15'12 96w26'07 6:25:44
Vesrue 248 1 31N54'12 103w06'58 6:52:28
Vessey 194 1 33N43'15 94w58'00 6:19:52
Veterans Administration 14 1 31N06 97w21 6:29:24
Viboras 214 1 26N43'01 98w49'37 6:35:18
Vick 48 1 31N20'27 100w05'30 6:40:22
Vickery 57 1 32N54 96w44 6:26:56
Victor 72 1 32N12'09 98w29'58 6:34:00
Victor 101 1 29N55'37 95w12'39 6:20:51
Victoria 147 1 31N35'52 96w46'35 6:27:06
Victoria 235 1 28N48'18 97w00'12 6:28:01
Victory 158 1 32N47'53 94w34'07 6:18:16
Victory City 19 1 33N27'54 94w14'12 6:16:57
Victory Gardens 181 1 30N06 93w46 6:15:04
Vidauri 196 1 28N26'11 97w08'12 6:28:33
Vidor 181 1 30N07'53 94w00'55 6:16:04
Vienna 143 1 29N22'41 96w47'32 6:27:10
View 221 1 32N20'34 99w53'04 6:39:32
Vigo Park 219 3 34N39'09 101w29'44 6:45:59
Vilas 246 1 30N50'27 97w18'12 6:29:13
Villa 167 1 31N36'54 98w44'08 6:34:57
Villa Cavazos 31 1 26N01'04 97w36'29 6:30:26
Village 57 1 32N50 96w47 6:27:08
Village 165 1 32N00 102w05 6:48:20
Village Mills 100 1 30N29'37 94w23'50 6:17:35
Villa Nueva 31 1 25N57'02 97w33'21 6:30:13
Villareales 214 1 26N23 98w49 6:35:16
Villa Siesta Retirement Vill 227 1 30N22'20 97w40'15 6:30:41
Vincent 114 1 32N28'54 101w13'31 6:44:54
Vinegarone 233 1 29N56'56 100w45'38 6:43:03
Vineyard 119 1 33N10 97w59 6:31:56
Vinson 227 1 30N13'05 97w46'51 6:31:07
Vinton 71 2 31N57'04 106w36'07 7:06:24
Viola 178 1 27N50'31 97w31'24 6:30:06
Violet 178 1 27N47'00 97w35'42 6:30:23
Virginia Point 84 1 29N18'19 94w53'51 6:19:35
Vista 97 1 31N31'29 98w12'43 6:32:51
Vistula 113 1 31N06'16 95w38'12 6:22:33
Viterbo 123 1 29N57'20 94w02'34 6:16:10
Voca 154 1 31N00'39 99w11'03 6:36:44
Volente 227 1 30N26'01 97w54'12 6:31:37
Von Ormy 15 1 29N17'20 98w38'39 6:34:35
Voss 42 1 31N37'15 99w33'41 6:38:15
Votaw 100 1 30N26'07 94w40'23 6:18:42
Voth 123 1 30N10'30 94w12'06 6:16:48
Waco 155 1 31N32'57 97w08'47 6:28:35
Wadsworth 161 1 28N49'56 95w56'05 6:23:44
Waelder 89 1 29N42 97w18 6:29:12
Wagner 116 1 33N11'16 96w12'54 6:24:52
Wainwright 15 1 29N27 98w27 6:33:48
Waka 179 3 36N16'54 101w02'50 6:44:11
Wake 54 1 33N46'57 101w05'39 6:44:23
Wakefield 187 1 31N05'55 94w50'06 6:19:20
Waketon 61 1 33N03 97w03 6:28:12
Wake Village 19 1 33N25'36 94w06'22 6:16:25
Walburg 246 1 30N44'12 97w34'48 6:30:19
Walcott 59 3 34N55'50 102w48'53 6:51:16
Walda 187 1 30N52'20 94w51'44 6:19:27
Waldeck 75 1 30N03'48 96w47'33 6:27:10
Walden 123 1 30N02'06 94w08'58 6:16:36
Walden Woods 101 1 30N05'39 95w10'20 6:20:41
Waldon Place Windmill 2 1 32N20'02 102w27'20 6:49:49
Waldrip 154 1 31N26'33 99w25'22 6:37:41
Walhalla 75 1 30N01'23 96w45'33 6:27:02
Walker Crossing 154 1 31N26'04 99w21'43 6:37:27
Walker Place 22 1 30N12'30 103w09'04 6:52:36
Walkers Mill 102 1 32N35'21 94w33'11 6:18:13
Walkerton 246 1 30N31'58 97w50'06 6:31:20
Walker Village 14 1 31N08'09 97w43'27 6:30:54
Wall 226 1 31N22'26 100w18'26 6:41:14

Wallace 234 1 32N32'48 95W56'25 6:23:46
Wallace Chapel 230
1 33N00 94W58 6:19:52
Waller 237 1 30N03'23 95W55'36 6:23:42
Wallis 8 1 29N37'52 96W03'54 6:24:16
Wallisville 101
1 29N50'07 94W44'30 6:18:58
Walnut Forest 227
1 30N22'58 97W40'17 6:30:41
Walnut Grove 43
1 33N08 96W37 6:26:28
Walnut Grove 130
1 29N52'05 98W44'04 6:34:56
Walnut Grove 183
1 32N13'53 94W20'12 6:17:21
Walnut Grove 212
1 32N10'35 95W15'20 6:21:01
Walnut Ridge 139
1 33N43'45 95W22'08 6:21:29
Walnut Springs 18
1 32N03'27 97W44'57 6:31:00
Walnut Springs 70
1 32N31'19 96W33'17 6:26:13
Walston Springs 1
1 31N46 95W38 6:22:32
Walton 34 1 32N56'18 94W02'48 6:16:11
Walton 39 1 33N50'07 98W05'45 6:32:23
Walton 234 1 32N12 95W51 6:23:24
Waltonia 133 1 30N04'02 99W17'36 6:37:10
Wamba 19 1 33N30'21 94W07'43 6:16:31
Wampler 184 1 32N46'38 97W44'07 6:30:56
Waneta 113 1 31N34'04 95W21'00 6:21:24
Waples 111 1 32N29'01 97W43'12 6:30:53
Ward 1 1 31N54'25 95W48'16 6:23:13
Ward 70 1 32N27'51 97W01'38 6:28:07
Warda 75 1 30N03'18 96W54'49 6:27:39
Wardlaw 155 1 31N32'47 97W03'52 6:28:15
Ward Prairie 81
1 31N45'48 96W08'17 6:24:33
Wards Creek 19 1 33N21 94W31 6:18:04
Ward Spring 227
1 30N27'24 97W38'21 6:30:33
Ware 56 3 36N11'05 102W42'35 6:50:50
Waresville 232 1 29N36'17 99W31'19 6:38:05
Warfield 165 1 31N55'15 102W13'06 6:48:52
Waring 130 1 29N57'02 98W48'10 6:35:13
Warlock 158 1 32N50'21 94W37'26 6:18:30
Warners Landing Campgrounds 158
1 32N52'16 94W41'04 6:18:44
Warren 229 1 30N36'52 94W24'30 6:17:38
Warren City 92 1 32N33'17 94W53'45 6:19:35
Warren Springs 34
1 33N03'44 94W22'35 6:17:30
Warrenton 75 1 30N01'02 96W43'54 6:26:56
Warsaw 129 1 32N33'00 96W25'12 6:25:41
Warsaw Center 129
1 32N33'16 96W24'55 6:25:40
Warwick 22 1 30N12'11 103W06'25 6:52:26
Washburn 6 3 35N10'36 101W34'22 6:46:17
Washington 239 1 30N19'30 96W09'23 6:24:38
Waskom 102 1 32N28'43 94W03'34 6:16:14
Wasson 95 1 34N13'17 101W45'30 6:47:02
Wastella 177 1 32N30'37 100W38'57 6:42:36
Watauga 220 1 32N51'28 97W15'16 6:29:01
Waterloo 91 1 33N45 96W34 6:26:16
Waterloo 246 1 30N38'19 97W23'17 6:29:33
Waterman 210 1 31N48 94W11 6:16:44
Waters Bluff 212
1 32N30'08 95W07'08 6:20:29
Waters Park 227
1 30N25'04 97W42'18 6:30:49
Water Valley 226
1 31N40'03 100W43'00 6:42:52
Waterwood 204 1 30N44 95W19 6:21:16
Watkins 234 1 32N32'22 96W01'39 6:24:07
Watson 27 1 30N56'03 98W00'51 6:32:03
Watson 47 1 31N52'13 98W43'38 6:34:55
Watsonville 220
1 32N36'53 97W07'56 6:28:32
Watt 147 1 31N38'37 96W51'31 6:27:26
Watterson 11 1 29N59'20 97W23'15 6:29:33
Watts 28 1 29N45'24 97W34'01 6:30:16
Waukegan 170 1 30N18'35 95W20'21 6:21:21
Waverly 204 1 30N32 95W29 6:21:56
Waxahachie 70 1 32N23'11 96W50'53 6:27:24
Wayland 215 1 32N36'34 98W49'40 6:35:19
Wayside 6 3 34N47'34 101W32'48 6:46:11
Wayside 153 1 33N19 101W44 6:46:56
Wealthy 145 1 31N01'28 96W10'46 6:24:43
Weatherford 184
1 32N45'33 97W47'49 6:31:11
Weatherford Junction 126
1 32N21 97W23 6:29:32
Weaver 112 1 33N10'05 95W24'29 6:21:38
Webb 220 1 32N37'57 97W04'26 6:28:18
Webb 240 1 27N47'32 99W25'21 6:37:41
Webb Air Force Base 114
1 32N14 101W28 6:45:52
Webberville 227
1 30N13'51 97W30'59 6:30:04
Webb Village 114
1 32N13'10 101W29'51 6:45:59
Webbville 42 1 32N01'48 99W16'35 6:37:06
Webster 101 1 29N32'15 95W07'05 6:20:28
Webster 250 1 32N55'35 95W19'29 6:21:18
Weches 113 1 31N32'38 95W13'39 6:20:55
Wedgewood 220 1 32N40 97W22 6:29:28
Weedhaven 120 1 28N43'25 96W27'12 6:25:49
Weeks Settlement 176
1 31N05'08 93W50'17 6:15:21
Weeping Mary 37
1 31N35'48 95W09'34 6:20:38
Weesatche 88 1 28N50'49 97W26'52 6:29:47
Wehdem 8 1 30N04'16 96W23'15 6:25:33
Weiland 116 1 33N00'52 96W03'50 6:24:15
Weimar 45 1 29N42'10 96W46'49 6:27:07
Weinert 94 1 29N41'54 97W51'59 6:31:28
Weinert 104 1 33N19'21 99W40'20 6:38:41
Weir 112 1 33N18'20 95W35'05 6:22:20
Weir 246 1 30N40'25 97W35'04 6:30:20
Weirville 112 1 33N08 95W36 6:22:24
Welch 58 1 32N55'35 102W07'36 6:48:30
Welcome 8 1 29N58 96W30 6:26:00
Welcome Valley 72
1 32N12'02 98W09'00 6:32:36
Welder 89 1 29N41'35 97W17'56 6:29:12
Weldon 113 1 31N01'17 95W34'16 6:22:17
Welfare 130 1 29N48 98W45 6:35:00
Wellborn 21 1 30N32'06 96W18'05 6:25:12
Wellington 44 3 34N51'22 100W12'48 6:40:51
Wellman 223 1 33N02'54 102W25'39 6:49:43
Wells 37 1 31N29'18 94W56'23 6:19:46
Wells 153 1 32N58 101W50 6:47:20
Wells Creek 1 1 31N47'53 95W33'18 6:22:13
Wendt 75 1 29N54'22 96W53'59 6:27:36
Wentworth 234 1 32N34'23 95W48'20 6:23:13
Wesco 90 3 35N26'00 100W45'46 6:43:03
Weser 88 1 28N51'54 97W22'02 6:29:28
Weslaco 108 1 26N09'33 97W59'26 6:31:58
Weslaco Farm Labor Center 108
1 26N10 97W59 6:31:56
Wesley 239 1 30N04'12 96W30'06 6:26:00
Wesley Grove 236
1 30N37 95W53 6:23:32
West 155 1 31N48'08 97W05'29 6:28:22
West Austin 227
1 30N17 97W46 6:31:04
West Baytown 101
1 29N46 95W00 6:20:00
West Bluff 181 1 30N10'34 93W42'24 6:14:50
West Brazos 20 1 30N39 96W29 6:25:56
Westbrook 119 1 33N04'16 97W56'22 6:31:45
Westbrook 168 1 32N21'19 101W00'48 6:44:03
Westbrook 250 1 32N55'30 95W14'41 6:20:59
Westbury 123 1 30N06'07 94W18'34 6:17:14
West Carlisle 152
1 33N35 101W58 6:47:52
West Cliff 14 1 31N06'54 97W30'58 6:30:04
West Columbia 20
1 29N08'37 95W38'42 6:22:35
Westcott 204 1 30N24'46 95W02'52 6:20:11
West Crockett 53
1 30N47 101W39 6:46:36
West Delta 60 1 33N19'41 95W47'02 6:23:08
West End 8 1 29N58 96W28 6:25:52
West End 241 1 29N11 96W17 6:25:08
West End Place 152
1 33N34'32 101W56'59 6:47:48
Westfield 101 1 30N01'11 95W24'07 6:21:36
Westfield 241 1 29N11 96W17 6:25:08
Westfield Estates 101
1 29N52'29 95W21'14 6:21:25
Westgate 101 1 29N58 95W42 6:22:48
West Glaveston 84
1 29N18 94W50 6:19:20
Westhaven 46 1 29N51'56 98W16'39 6:33:07
Westheimer 101 1 29N44 95W32 6:22:08
Westhoff 62 1 29N11'41 97W28'15 6:29:53
Westlake 61 1 32N59'28 97W11'41 6:28:47
West Lake Hills 227
1 30N17'52 97W48'06 6:31:12
Westland 220 1 32N43'28 97W29'41 6:29:59
Westlawn 181 1 30N06 93W46 6:15:04
West Midway 225
1 33N08'14 95W05'41 6:20:23
West Mineola 250
1 32N40'17 95W31'08 6:22:05
Westminster 43 1 33N21'45 96W27'42 6:25:51
West Mountain 230
1 32N37 94W55 6:19:40
West New Hope 225
1 33N13'02 95W05'31 6:20:22
West Oakland 123
1 30N03'12 94W07'19 6:16:29
West Odessa 68 1 31N52 102W22 6:49:28
Weston 43 1 33N20'56 96W40'09 6:26:41
West Orange 181
1 30N04'55 93W45'29 6:15:02
Westover 12 1 33N29'50 99W01'03 6:36:04
Westover 68 1 31N52 102W22 6:49:28
Westover Hills 220
1 32N44'41 97W24'48 6:29:39
West Payne 241 1 29N11 96W17 6:25:08
Westphalia 73 1 31N07'08 97W06'54 6:28:28
West Point 75 1 29N56'37 97W02'12 6:28:09
West Point 153 1 33N10'00 102W02'58 6:48:12
West Port Arthur 123
1 29N51'03 93W58'37 6:15:54
West Saint Paul 205
1 28N06'04 97W38'14 6:30:33
West Side 123 1 30N06 94W09 6:16:36
West Sinton 205
1 28N01'44 97W40'22 6:30:41
West Sweden 154
1 31N11'28 99W26'37 6:37:46
West Tawakoni 116
1 32N53'37 96W01'45 6:24:07
West Tempe 187 1 30N45'26 95W02'27 6:20:10
West Temple 187
1 30N43 94W56 6:19:44
West Terrell 222
1 30N07 102W23 6:49:32
West Texarkana 19
1 33N26 94W04 6:16:16
West Texas 191 3 34N59 101W55 6:47:40
West University Place 101
1 29N43'04 95W26'01 6:21:44
West Vernon 244
1 34N09 99W18 6:37:12
Westview 155 1 31N32 97W11 6:28:44
Westville 228 1 31N04'20 95W11'19 6:20:45
Westway 59 3 34N49'26 102W32'45 6:50:11
Westway 71 2 31N55 106W36 7:06:24
Westwood Park 57
1 32N42'06 96W52'40 6:27:31
Westwood Park 101
1 29N40'04 95W26'34 6:21:46
Westwood Village 15
1 29N24'34 98W37'57 6:34:32
Westworth 220 1 32N45'26 97W24'38 6:29:39
Westworth Village 220
1 32N47 97W24 6:29:36
Wetmore 15 1 29N33'51 98W25'08 6:33:41
Wetsel 43 1 33N07'46 96W38'39 6:26:35
Whaley 19 1 33N27'49 94W20'06 6:17:20
Whaley Corner 79
1 29N26'45 95W40'26 6:22:42
Wharton 241 1 29N18'41 96W06'09 6:24:25
Whatley 19 1 33N29'23 94W02'49 6:16:11
Wheatland 99 3 34N18'40 99W53'49 6:39:35
Wheatland 220 1 32N36'57 97W32'22 6:30:09
Wheeler 242 3 35N26'43 100W16'14 6:41:05
Wheeler Springs 113
1 31N22'36 95W38'47 6:22:35
Wheelock 198 1 30N53'51 96W23'23 6:25:34
Whiskey Ford 123
1 30N04'17 94W26'26 6:17:46
Whispering Oaks 190
1 32N57 95W56 6:23:44
Whispering Pines 174
1 31N46'36 94W31'11 6:18:05
White City 203 1 31N15'03 94W12'11 6:16:49
White City 244 1 34N16'48 99W20'41 6:37:23
White Deer 33 3 35N26'07 101W10'21 6:44:41
Whiteface 40 1 33N36'00 102W36'48 6:50:27
Whiteflat 173 1 34N06 100W53 6:43:32
White Hall 14 1 31N13'09 97W25'46 6:29:43
Whitehall 93 1 30N18'08 95W58'24 6:23:54
White Hall 120 1 29N00'35 96W24'48 6:25:39
Whitehead 116 1 32N52'05 96W15'36 6:25:02
Whitehouse 212 1 32N13'36 95W13'31 6:20:54
Whiteland 154 1 31N09'51 99W30'20 6:38:01
White Mound 91 1 33N31'00 96W30'36 6:26:02
White Oak 92 1 32N31'40 94W51'40 6:19:27
White Oak 158 1 32N52'14 94W24'35 6:17:38
White Oak Junction 112
1 33N08'48 95W27'25 6:21:50
White Oaks 170 1 29N47 95W23 6:21:32
White Oak Springs 225
1 33N09'03 95W04'18 6:20:17
White Rock 57 1 32N52'31 96W40'49 6:26:43
Whiterock 91 1 33N33'43 96W28'15 6:25:53
White Rock 116 1 33N16'08 96W07'08 6:24:29
White Rock 194 1 33N39'27 94W55'26 6:19:42
White Rock 198 1 31N13'11 96W33'17 6:26:13
White Rock 203 1 31N33'25 94W02'04 6:16:08
Whitesboro 91 1 33N39'22 96W54'24 6:27:38
White Settlement 220
1 32N45'34 97W27'29 6:29:50
White Shed 74 1 33N37'57 96W09'55 6:24:40
Whites Ranch 36
1 29N47 94W23 6:17:32
Whitestar 173 1 34N14 100W59 6:43:56
White Stone 246
1 30N31'14 97W49'48 6:31:19
Whiteway 97 1 31N38'34 97W58'17 6:31:53
Whitewright 91 1 33N30'46 96W23'32 6:25:34
Whitharral 110 1 33N44'15 102W19'36 6:49:18
Whitman 239 1 30N10 96W24 6:25:36
Whitney 23 1 34N21'01 101W19'48 6:45:19
Whitney 109 1 31N57'06 97W19'16 6:29:17
Whiton 234 1 32N28'57 95W59'42 6:23:59
Whitsett 149 1 28N38'02 98W16'18 6:33:05
Whitson 50 1 31N20'01 97W26'25 6:29:46
Whitt 184 1 32N57'22 98W01'07 6:32:04
Whitton 234 1 32N33 95W52 6:23:28
Whon 42 1 31N29'25 99W18'21 6:37:13
Wichita Falls 243
1 33N54'49 98W29'35 6:33:58
Wichita Valley Farms 243
1 31N33 97W08 6:28:32
Wicker 21 1 30N32'18 96W18'38 6:25:15
Wickett 238 1 31N34'12 103W00'02 6:52:00
Wied 143 1 29N26'19 97W03'21 6:28:13
Wiedeville 239 1 30N13'09 96W20'24 6:25:22
Wieland 116 1 33N08 96W07 6:24:28
Wiergate 176 1 30N59'58 93W42'27 6:14:50
Wiggins 34 1 33N01 94W12 6:16:48
Wiggins 155 1 31N45'40 97W09'28 6:28:38
Wigginsville 170
1 30N15'29 95W20'13 6:21:21
Wilco 103 3 36N01'35 102W17'34 6:49:10
Wilcox 26 1 30N26'45 96W22'45 6:25:31
Wilderville 73 1 31N06'16 96W52'58 6:27:32
Wild Horse 55 1 31N03 104W50 6:59:20
Wild Hurst 113 1 31N31'24 95W01'05 6:20:04
Wildorado 180 3 35N12'34 102W12'00 6:48:48
Wild Peach 20 1 29N02 95W34 6:22:16
Wildwood 100 1 30N30 94W24 6:17:36
Wilford Hall U S A F Hosp 15
1 29N23 98W36 6:34:24
Wilhelm 33 3 35N31'42 101W35'19 6:46:21
Wilkins 230 1 32N33'27 95W00'32 6:20:02
Wilkinson 225 1 33N20'54 94W57'05 6:19:48
Willacy County Housing Auth 245
1 26N29 97W47 6:31:08
Willamar 245 1 26N27'19 97W37'07 6:30:28
William Beaumont General Hos 71
2 31N47 106W25 7:05:40
William Penn 239
1 30N18'54 96W16'55 6:25:08
William Rice 101
1 29N43 95W25 6:21:40
Williams 25 1 32N01'16 99W01'05 6:36:04
Williams 99 1 34N27'40 99W53'38 6:39:35
Williams 146 1 30N17'21 95W07'12 6:20:29
Williamsburg 139
1 33N40 95W31 6:22:04
Williamsburg 143
1 29N23'21 96W57'32 6:27:50
Williamson 227 1 30N13'33 97W49'20 6:31:17
William Spear Addition 229
1 32N20 95W18 6:21:12
Willis 170 1 30N25'29 95W28'47 6:21:55
Willman 11 1 29N55'58 97W15'36 6:29:02
Willow 101 1 30N06'06 95W32'16 6:22:09
Willow City 86 1 30N24'02 98W42'04 6:34:48
Willow Creek 198
1 31N17'10 96W26'10 6:25:45
Willow Grove 155
1 31N33'00 97W17'44 6:29:11
Willow Grove 210
1 31N58 94W03 6:16:12
Willow Oak 230 1 32N44 94W57 6:19:48
Willow Park 184
1 32N44 97W38 6:30:32
Willow Point 249
1 33N06'54 97W54'48 6:31:39

Place		Lat.	Long.	Time
Willow Springs 75	1	29N57'59	96w35'55	6:26:24
Willow Springs 190	1	32N48'59	95w45'02	6:23:00
Willow Springs 204	1	30N39'52	95w13'22	6:20:53
Willowview 99	1	34N21'30	99w42'18	6:38:49
Wills Point 234	1	32N42'33	96w00'29	6:24:02
Wilmer 57	1	32N35'20	96w41'06	6:26:44
Wilmeth 200	1	31N58'41	100w07'12	6:40:29
Wilsey 185	3	34N27'03	102w57'18	6:51:49
Wilson 47	1	31N55'53	98w16'00	6:33:04
Wilson 63	1	31N01'04	97w03'51	6:28:15
Wilson 129	1	32N40'57	96w17'30	6:25:10
Wilson 153	1	33N19'01	101w43'25	6:46:54
Wilson Place 134	1	30N24'10	100w05'09	6:40:21
Wimberley 105	1	29N59'50	98w05'54	6:32:24
Wimberly Place 180	3	35N20'26	102w40'56	6:50:44
Winchell 25	1	31N28'19	99w09'38	6:36:39
Winchester 75	1	30N00'33	97w00'49	6:28:03
Winchester 101	1	29N36'54	95w28'10	6:21:53
Windcrest 15	1	29N30'55	98w22'48	6:33:31
Windom 74	1	33N33'55	95w59'56	6:24:00
Windsor 155	1	31N31'19	97w20'30	6:29:22
Windthorst 5	1	33N34'34	98w26'11	6:33:45
Windy Hill 56	3	36N07'16	102w57'33	6:51:50
Winedale 75	1	30N05'13	96w38'26	6:26:34
Winfield 225	1	33N10'02	95w06'42	6:20:27
Winfree 36	1	29N52'46	94w49'12	6:19:17
Winfree 181	1	30N06	93w46	6:15:04
Wingate 200	1	32N02'38	100w06'35	6:40:26
Wink 248	1	31N45'04	103w09'34	6:52:38
Winkler 81	1	31N56'17	96w12'31	6:24:50
Winnie 101	1	29N49'12	94w23'02	6:17:32
Winningkoff 43	1	33N06'40	96w33'48	6:26:15
Winnsboro 250	1	32N57'26	95w17'24	6:21:10
Winona 212	1	32N29'22	95w10'01	6:20:40
Winscott 220	1	32N33'22	97w32'56	6:30:12
Winslow 109	1	31N59'45	97w07'26	6:28:30
Winterfield 112	1	33N04'28	95w21'53	6:21:28
Winter Haven 64	1	28N37'10	99w51'26	6:39:26
Winters 200	1	31N57'23	99w57'43	6:39:51
Wise 234	1	32N30'48	96w02'06	6:24:08
Witco 192	1	31N09'22	101w20'40	6:45:23
Withers 15	1	29N21'00	98w34'42	6:34:19
Witting 143	1	29N30'36	97w03'20	6:28:13
Wizard Wells 119	1	33N12'01	97w58'12	6:31:53
Woden 174	1	31N30'11	94w31'35	6:18:06
Wolf Creek 204	1	30N38'44	95w08'32	6:20:34
Wolfe City 116	1	33N22'14	96w04'07	6:24:16
Wolf Flat 96	1	34N24	100w54	6:43:36
Wolfforth 152	1	33N30'21	102w00'31	6:48:02
Wolters Village 182	1	32N49'26	98w03'59	6:32:16
Womack 18	1	31N50'13	97w29'45	6:29:59
Woodbine 49	1	33N36'38	97w00'55	6:28:04
Woodbranch 170	1	30N11	95w11	6:20:44
Woodburn Place 23	3	34N43'08	101w07'27	6:44:30
Woodbury 109	1	32N02'58	97w13'50	6:28:55
Woodcrest Acres 100	1	30N13'42	94w10'47	6:16:43
Woodlake 228	1	31N01'43	95w01'58	6:20:08
Woodlake Park 91	1	33N41'58	96w33'31	6:26:14
Woodland 14	1	31N07'52	97w29'21	6:29:57
Woodland 194	1	33N48'25	95w16'25	6:21:06
Woodland Heights 25	1	31N40'40	98w57'52	6:35:51
Woodland Hills 57	1	32N37'40	96w52'13	6:27:29
Woodland Hills 109	1	31N54'07	97w20'01	6:29:20
Woodlawn 3	1	31N21'57	94w46'59	6:19:08
Woodlawn 102	1	32N40'05	94w20'44	6:17:23
Woodley 102	1	32N34	94w25	6:17:40
Woodrow 109	1	32N08'53	97w18'59	6:29:16
Woodrow 152	1	33N26'48	101w50'37	6:47:22
Woods 183	1	31N57	94w15	6:17:00
Woodsboro 196	1	28N14'17	97w19'11	6:29:17
Woodson 146	1	30N04'20	94w40'27	6:18:42
Woodson 224	1	33N00'53	99w03'14	6:36:13
Woodsons 22	1	29N00'22	103w17'40	6:53:11
Wood Springs 212	1	32N28'29	95w24'17	6:21:37
Woodstock 19	1	33N33'29	94w27'46	6:17:51
Woodville 229	1	30N46'30	94w24'55	6:17:40
Woodward 142	1	28N32'00	99w19'14	6:37:17
Woodway 155	1	31N30'21	97w12'17	6:28:49
Woody Acres 170	1	29N47	95w23	6:21:32
Woosley 190	1	32N56	95w52	6:23:28
Worsham 195	1	31N21'46	103w31'47	6:54:07
Wortham 81	1	31N47'16	96w27'44	6:25:51
Worthing 143	1	29N24'47	97w00'53	6:28:04
Wright 95	1	34N15'07	101w49'42	6:47:19
Wright 184	1	32N51'02	97w43'59	6:30:56
Wright City 212	1	32N11'49	94w59'11	6:19:57
Wrightsboro 89	1	29N22'25	97w33'53	6:30:16
Wuthrich Hill 246	1	30N37'33	97w21'37	6:29:26
Wylie 43	1	33N00'54	96w32'19	6:26:09
Wylie 221	1	32N22'22	99w46'30	6:39:06
Yale 80	1	33N11	95w13	6:20:52
Yancey 116	1	33N08	96w07	6:24:28
Yancey 163	1	29N08'21	99w08'41	6:36:35
Yantis 250	1	32N55'49	95w34'29	6:22:18
Yarboro 93	1	30N20'12	95w57'19	6:23:49
Yard 1	1	31N50	95w50	6:23:20
Yarnall 33	3	35N12'38	101w32'17	6:46:09
Yarrelton 166	1	30N57'02	97w04'47	6:28:19
Yates 134	1	30N35'16	99w35'35	6:38:22
Yellow Mound 67	1	32N24	98w49	6:35:16
Yellowpine 202	1	31N15'33	93w49'28	6:15:18
Yescas 31	1	26N08	97w38	6:30:32
Yetes 109	1	31N57	97w19	6:29:16
Yoakum 62	1	29N17'15	97w09'06	6:28:36
Yokum 89	1	29N09'39	97w33'47	6:30:15
Yorktown 62	1	28N58'51	97w30'09	6:30:01
Youens 170	1	30N18'55	95w22'28	6:21:30
Yougeen 13	1	28N19'24	97w42'16	6:30:49
Young 81	1	31N50'31	96w04'47	6:24:19
Youngblood Place (reduced us 22	3	30N19'21	103w09'58	6:52:40
Youngsport 14	1	30N57'26	97w43'08	6:30:53
Yowell 60	1	33N20'43	95w51'36	6:23:26
Ysleta 71	2	31N41'54	106w19'28	7:05:18
Yturria 245	1	26N34'05	97w46'14	6:31:05
Yucote Acres 43	1	33N05'59	96w28'43	6:25:55
Zabcikville 14	1	31N02'42	97w09'59	6:28:40
Zacha Junction 57	1	32N51'53	96w40'08	6:26:41
Zapata 253	1	26N54'25	99w16'16	6:37:05
Zavalla 3	1	31N09'30	94w25'34	6:17:42
Zella 156	1	28N33'46	98w47'34	6:35:10
Zephyr 25	1	31N40'33	98w47'40	6:35:11
Ziler 114	1	32N16'25	101w24'16	6:45:37
Zion Grove 201	1	31N52'29	94w46'57	6:19:08
Zion Hill 121	1	30N50'07	93w58'17	6:15:53
Zionsville 239	1	30N10	96w24	6:25:36
Zionville 239	1	30N12'06	96w29'28	6:25:58
Zipp 94	1	29N33'34	98w00'58	6:32:04
Zipp City 57	1	32N46	96w37	6:26:28
Zipperlandville 73	1	31N04'07	97w03'18	6:28:13
Zipperlenville 73	1	31N04	96w58	6:27:52
Zita 191	3	35N07'53	101w51'14	6:47:25
Zorn 94	1	29N45'10	97w56'52	6:31:47
Zuehl 94	1	29N29'07	98w09'57	6:32:40
Zummo 123	1	30N02'26	94w04'07	6:16:16
Zunkerville 128	1	28N42'32	97w59'29	6:31:58
Zybach 106	3	35N35	100w17	6:41:08

TIME TABLES

UT # 1

Before 11/18/1883		LMT
11/18/1883	12:00	MST
3/31/1918	02:00	MWT
10/27/1918	02:00	MST
3/30/1919	02:00	MWT
10/26/1919	02:00	MST
2/09/1942	02:00	MWT
9/30/1945	02:00	MST
4/30/1967	02:00	US#1

....

UT # 2

Before 11/18/1883		LMT
11/18/1883	12:00	PST
3/31/1918	02:00	PWT
10/27/1918	02:00	PST
3/30/1919	02:00	PWT
10/26/1919	02:00	PST
2/09/1942	02:00	PWT
9/30/1945	02:00	PST
4/24/1966	02:00	PDT
10/30/1966	02:00	PST
4/30/1967	02:00	PDT
10/29/1967	02:00	PST
4/28/1968	02:00	PDT
10/27/1968	02:00	PST
4/27/1969	02:00	MDT
4/27/1969	02:00	US#1

COUNTIES

1 Beaver
2 Box Elder
3 Cache
4 Carbon
5 Daggett
6 Davis
7 Duchesne
8 Emery
9 Garfield
10 Grand
11 Iron
12 Juab
13 Kane
14 Millard
15 Morgan
16 Piute
17 Rich
18 Salt Lake
19 San Juan
20 Sanpete
21 Sevier
22 Summit
23 Tooele
24 Uintah
25 Utah
26 Wasatch
27 Washington
28 Wayne
29 Weber

Abraham 14 1 39N23'48 112w43'02 7:30:52
Adamsville 1 1 38N15'30 112w47'35 7:31:10
Agate 10 1 39N00'54 109w14'35 7:16:58
Alpine 25 1 40N27'12 111w46'38 7:27:07
Alta 18 1 40N35'20 111w38'14 7:26:33
Altamont 7 1 40N21'34 110w17'08 7:21:09
Alton 13 1 37N26'16 112w28'55 7:29:56
Altonah 7 1 40N24'05 110w17'35 7:21:10
Altus 22 1 40N45'09 111w37'03 7:26:28
Alunite 16 1 38N22'45 112w14'45 7:28:59
Amalga 3 1 41N51'40 111w53'42 7:27:35
American Fork 25
1 40N22'37 111w47'42 7:27:11
Anchorage 6 1 41N07 112w01 7:28:04
Anderson Junction 27
1 37N17'03 113w18'17 7:33:13
Aneth 19 1 37N12'58 109w11'11 7:16:45
Angels Grove 23
1 40N31'17 112w15'37 7:29:02
Angle 16 1 38N14'57 111w58'33 7:27:54
Annabella 21 1 38N42'33 112w03'33 7:28:14
Antimony 9 1 38N07'01 111w59'56 7:28:00
Aragonite 23 2 40N44'34 113w00'07 7:32:00
Arcadia 7 1 40N13'21 110w14'12 7:20:57
Arsenal 6 1 41N08'03 112w01'20 7:28:05
Arsenal Villa 29
1 41N09'35 112w02'00 7:28:08
Arthur 18 1 40N43'02 112w08'09 7:28:33
Aspen Grove 25 1 40N24'12 111w36'06 7:26:24
Atkinson 22 1 40N44'26 111w28'27 7:25:54
Atkinville 27 1 37N01'48 113w37'37 7:34:30
Atwood 18 1 40N37'58 111w53'51 7:27:35
Aurora 21 1 38N55'20 111w56'00 7:27:44
Austin 21 1 38N38 112w07 7:28:28
Avon 3 1 41N31'59 111w48'45 7:27:15
Avon 11 1 37N53'39 113w20'57 7:33:24
Axtell 20 1 39N03'19 111w49'16 7:27:17
Bacchus 18 1 40N39'47 112w05'43 7:28:23
Ballard Junction 3
1 41N47'07 111w59'10 7:27:57
Barnes 6 1 41N06'03 112w03'52 7:28:15
Barro 23 2 40N43'37 113w29'17 7:33:57
Barton 29 2 41N09'36 112w03'50 7:28:15
Bauer 23 1 40N28'19 112w21'41 7:29:27
Bear River 2 2 41N41 112w11 7:28:44
Bear River City 2
2 41N36'53 112w07'33 7:28:30
Bear Valley Junction 9
1 37N57'55 112w24'42 7:29:39
Beaver 1 1 38N16'37 112w38'25 7:30:34
Beaverdam 2 1 41N46 112w06 7:28:24
Becks 18 1 40N49'00 111w55'15 7:27:41
Beeton 2 1 41N42 112w05 7:28:20
Belknap 21 1 38N30'54 112w15'46 7:29:03
Belmont Heights 18
1 40N35 111w52 7:27:28
Benchland 2 1 41N46 112w05 7:28:20
Benjamin 25 1 40N05'54 111w43'50 7:26:55
Ben Lomond 29 1 41N16 111w58 7:27:52
Bennett 24 1 40N22'26 109w56'05 7:19:44
Bennion 18 1 40N38'19 111w56'17 7:27:45
Benson 3 1 41N47'15 111w55'46 7:27:43
Berry Junction 11
1 37N42'34 113w39'19 7:34:37
Beryl 11 1 37N53'45 113w39'38 7:34:39
Bicknell 28 1 38N20'27 111w32'36 7:26:10
Big Plain Junction 27
1 37N02'56 113w06'21 7:32:25
Big Water 13 1 37N04 111w37 7:26:28
Bingham 18 1 40N33 112w05 7:28:20
Bingham Canyon 18
1 40N32 112w09 7:28:36
Birdseye 25 1 39N55'28 111w32'56 7:26:12
Blair 23 2 40N44'17 113w58'38 7:35:55
Blanding 19 1 37N37'27 109w28'39 7:17:55
Bloom 14 1 38N56'01 112w48'29 7:31:14
Bloomington 27 1 37N02'48 113w36'19 7:34:25
Blueacre 1 1 38N29'07 113w07'52 7:32:31
Bluebell 7 1 40N21'34 110w13'00 7:20:52
Blue Creek 2 2 41N51'44 112w27'22 7:29:49
Bluff 19 1 37N17'04 109w33'04 7:18:12
Bluffdale 18 1 40N29'23 111w56'17 7:27:45
Bonanza 24 1 40N01'16 109w10'36 7:16:42
Boneta 7 1 40N21'35 110w20'27 7:21:22
Bone Valley 9 1 38N07'32 112w24'07 7:29:36
Bonnie 25 1 40N17 111w41 7:26:44
Borden 14 1 38N58'54 112w47'38 7:31:11
Bothwell 2 2 41N43'02 112w15'29 7:29:02
Boulder 9 1 37N55 111w25 7:25:40
Boulder Town 9 1 37N52'26 111w24'47 7:25:39
Bountiful 6 1 40N53'22 111w52'48 7:27:31
Bowery Haven 21
1 38N46 112w05 7:28:20
Bradford 2 2 41N37'48 112w08'20 7:28:33
Brendel 10 1 38N56'49 109w48'51 7:19:15
Bridgeland 7 1 40N09'47 110w14'01 7:20:56
Brigham City 2 1 41N30'37 112w00'53 7:28:04
Brighton 18 1 40N36'14 111w34'53 7:26:20
Brooklyn 21 1 38N41 112w09 7:28:36
Bruin Point 4 1 39N38'30 110w20'42 7:21:23
Bryce Canyon 9 1 37N37'42 112w10'01 7:28:40
Buena Vista 18 1 40N45'30 111w58'16 7:27:53
Bullion Falls 16
1 38N24'35 112w20'16 7:29:21
Bullionville 24
1 40N42'03 109w34'21 7:18:17
Bunker 25 1 40N18'30 111w43'58 7:26:56
Bunker Spur 25 1 40N17 111w41 7:26:44
Burbank 14 1 38N24 113w00 7:32:00
Burmester 23 2 40N41'28 112w27'05 7:29:48
Burrville 21 1 38N34'15 111w51'46 7:27:27
Burton 18 1 40N43 111w54 7:27:36
Bushnell 2 1 41N30 112w00 7:28:00
Butlerville 18 1 40N38 111w49 7:27:16
Cache Junction 3
1 41N50'08 112w00'07 7:28:00
Caineville 28 1 38N19'59 111w01'05 7:24:04
Callao 12 2 39N53'52 113w42'28 7:34:50
Camp Williams 18
1 40N34 111w57 7:27:48
Cannonville 9 1 37N34'01 112w03'11 7:28:13
Canyon Glen 25 1 40N19'49 111w37'05 7:26:28
Carbonville 4 1 39N37'12 110w50'01 7:23:20
Cardon 3 1 41N49'29 111w50'37 7:27:22
Caryhurst 25 1 40N18'28 111w39'14 7:26:37
Castilla 25 1 40N02'08 111w31'31 7:26:06
Castle Dale 8 1 39N12'44 111w01'08 7:24:05
Castle Gate 4 1 39N44 110w52 7:23:28
Castle Rock 22 1 41N06'42 111w12'09 7:24:49
Castleton 10 1 38N34 109w33 7:18:12
Cedar 8 1 39N23'38 110w27'15 7:21:49
Cedar Breaks Lodge 11
1 37N43 113w03 7:32:12
Cedar City 11 1 37N40'39 113w03'40 7:32:15
Cedar Creek 2 2 41N57'52 113w09'20 7:32:37
Cedar Fort (Cedar Valley PO) 25
1 40N19'38 112w06'13 7:28:25
Cedar Valley 25
1 40N20 112w06 7:28:24
Cedarview 7 1 40N21'37 110w02'32 7:20:10
Center Creek 26
1 40N28'41 111w21'23 7:25:26
Centerfield 20 1 39N07'31 111w49'06 7:27:16
Centerville 6 1 40N55'05 111w52'17 7:27:29
Central 21 1 38N42'14 112w05'53 7:28:24
Central 27 1 37N25'00 113w37'25 7:34:30
Champlin 12 1 39N39'04 112w18'11 7:29:13
Charleston 26 1 40N27'59 111w28'09 7:25:53
Chester 20 1 39N28'34 111w33'44 7:26:15
Christianburg 20
1 39N09 111w49 7:27:16
Christmas City 25
1 40N19'18 111w38'45 7:26:35
Circleville 16 1 38N10'18 112w16'11 7:29:05
Cisco 10 1 38N58'12 109w19'12 7:17:17
Clarkston 3 2 41N55'13 112w02'57 7:28:12
Clawson 8 1 39N07'59 111w05'47 7:24:23
Clay Hills Crossing 19
1 37N17'40 110w24'15 7:21:37
Clear Creek 2 2 42N00 113w17 7:33:08
Clear Creek 4 1 39N38'45 111w09'06 7:24:36
Clearfield 6 1 41N06'39 112w01'31 7:28:06
Clear Lake 14 1 39N07'06 112w44'12 7:30:57
Cleveland 8 1 39N20'56 110w51'03 7:23:24
Clifton 6 1 41N07 112w01 7:28:04
Clifton 23 2 40N06'16 113w48'59 7:35:16
Clinton 6 1 41N08'23 112w02'59 7:28:12
Clinton 25 1 40N23'13 111w56'06 7:27:44
Clive 23 2 40N42'31 113w07'00 7:32:28
Clover 23 1 40N20'13 112w27'38 7:29:51
Clyde 25 1 40N17 111w41 7:26:44
Coalville 22 1 40N55'04 111w23'55 7:25:36
College 3 1 41N43 111w49 7:27:16
College Ward 3 1 41N40'37 111w52'45 7:27:31
Collinston 2 1 41N46'29 112w05'39 7:28:23
Colton 25 1 39N51'09 111w00'44 7:24:03
Columbia 4 1 39N31'01 110w22'55 7:21:32
Columbia Junction 4
1 39N31'54 110w26'35 7:21:46
Como Springs 15
1 41N02'15 111w39'17 7:26:37
Cook Corner 1 1 38N17'42 113w02'48 7:32:11
Copperton 18 1 40N33'53 112w05'48 7:28:23
Corinne 2 2 41N33'04 112w06'34 7:28:26
Cornish 3 2 41N58'32 111w57'09 7:27:49
Cottonwood 10 1 39N03'52 109w10'51 7:16:43
Cottonwood 18 1 40N35 111w47 7:27:08
Cottonwood Heights 18
1 40N37'11 111w48'34 7:27:14
Cottonwood Meadows 18
1 40N40 111w50 7:27:20
Cove 3 1 41N57'49 111w48'19 7:27:13
Cove 21 1 38N35'41 112w14'55 7:29:00
Cove Fort 14 1 38N17 112w38 7:30:32
Cozydale 29 1 41N10'20 112w01'15 7:28:05
Cranmer 26 1 40N37'00 111w26'24 7:25:46
Crescent 18 1 40N33'05 111w53'25 7:27:34
Crescent Junction 10
1 38N56'35 109w49'00 7:19:16
Cropley 2 2 41N39'11 112w10'22 7:28:41
Crossroads 2 1 41N42'45 112w08'29 7:28:34
Croydon 15 1 41N04'07 111w30'47 7:26:03
Crystal Springs 2
1 41N39'37 112w05'12 7:28:21
Cunningham Hill 1
1 38N23'46 112w43'27 7:30:54
Curlew Junction 2
2 41N57'56 113w03'33 7:32:14
Curtis 25 1 40N16'31 111w41'39 7:26:47
Cushing 18 1 40N37 111w53 7:27:32
Dalton 18 1 40N33'40 112w03'35 7:28:14
Daniels 26 1 40N28'15 111w24'50 7:25:39
Defas Park 7 1 40N26 110w48 7:23:12
Defense Depot Ogden 29
1 41N13 111w58 7:27:52
Delle 23 2 40N45'36 112w46'36 7:31:06
Delta 14 1 39N21'08 112w34'35 7:30:18
Dennis 12 1 39N50'00 112w04'59 7:28:20
Deseret 14 2 39N17'13 112w39'07 7:30:36
Desert 8 1 39N05'17 110w19'05 7:21:16
Desert Mound 11
1 37N42'38 113w16'22 7:33:05
Devils Slide 15
1 41N03'49 111w32'33 7:26:10
Dewey 10 1 38N48'37 109w18'04 7:17:12
Deweyville (Dewey Station) 2
1 41N42'38 112w05'22 7:28:21
Diamond 12 1 39N52'54 112w05'48 7:28:23
Dividend 25 1 39N57'17 112w03'38 7:28:15
Dragerton 4 1 39N32'33 110w25'14 7:21:41
Dragon 24 1 39N47'09 109w04'22 7:16:17
Draper 18 1 40N31'29 111w51'47 7:27:27
Dry Fork 24 1 40N33'27 109w40'07 7:18:40
Duchesne 7 1 40N09'48 110w24'08 7:21:37
Ducket Crossing 19
1 37N44'37 110w16'45 7:21:07
Dugway 23 2 40N14 112w45 7:31:00
Dutch John 5 1 40N55'45 109w23'25 7:17:34
East Carbon 4 1 39N32'52 110w24'51 7:21:39
East Daggett 5 1 40N56 109w12 7:16:48
Eastland 19 1 37N48'13 109w08'00 7:16:32
East Layton 6 1 41N04'52 111w55'09 7:27:41
East Millcreek 18
1 40N42'00 111w48'35 7:27:14
East Wellington 4
1 39N33 110w44 7:22:56
Eastwood Hills 18
1 40N43 111w51 7:27:24
Echo 22 1 40N58'40 111w26'33 7:25:46
Eden 29 1 41N18'02 111w48'41 7:27:15
Edgemont 25 1 40N17'10 111w39'04 7:26:36
Eggnog 9 1 37N46'21 110w50'41 7:23:23
Eightmile Point 14
1 38N45'27 112w33'02 7:30:12
Elba 10 1 38N57'00 109w30'22 7:18:01
Elberta 25 1 39N57'10 111w57'20 7:27:49
Elgin 10 1 38N59'17 110w08'41 7:20:35
Elmo 8 1 39N23'23 110w48'52 7:23:15
Elsinore 21 1 38N40'58 112w08'51 7:28:35
Elwood 2 2 41N41'26 112w08'25 7:28:34
Emery 8 1 38N55'23 111w14'53 7:25:00
Emigration 18 1 40N43 111w47 7:27:08
Emory 22 1 41N02'56 111w18'13 7:25:13
Endot 18 1 40N35'17 111w54'09 7:27:37

Place		Latitude	Longitude	Time
Enoch 11	1	37N46'24	113w01'25	7:32:06
Enterprise 15	1	41N05'59	111w44'08	7:26:57
Enterprise 27	1	37N34'25	113w43'06	7:34:52
Ephraim 20	1	39N21'35	111w35'08	7:26:21
Erda 23	1	40N36'46	112w18'13	7:29:13
Escalante 9	1	37N46'13	111w36'05	7:26:24
Eskdale 14	2	39N06'26	113w57'06	7:35:48
Etna 2	2	41N40'18	113w57'13	7:35:49
Eureka 12	1	39N57'15	112w07'10	7:28:29
Evans 2	2	41N37'25	112w10'34	7:28:42
Evona 29	1	41N13'22	112w00'02	7:28:00
Fairbanks Crossing 24	1	39N43'47	109w43'56	7:18:56
Fairfield 25	1	40N15'44	112w05'32	7:28:22
Fairgrounds 18	1	40N49	111w56	7:27:44
Fairmont 29	1	41N14'27	111w54'07	7:27:36
Fairview 20	1	39N37'35	111w26'20	7:25:45
Farmington 6	1	40N58'50	111w53'12	7:27:33
Farr West 29	1	41N17'50	112w01'37	7:28:06
Faust 23	1	40N11'03	112w23'28	7:29:34
Fayette 20	1	39N13'31	111w51'21	7:27:25
Ferron 8	1	39N05'37	111w07'57	7:24:32
Ferron Mill 8	1	39N05'59	111w11'01	7:24:44
Fielding 2	2	41N48'53	112w06'55	7:28:28
Fillmore 14	1	38N58'08	112w19'22	7:29:17
Fish Lake 21	1	38N46	112w05	7:28:20
Five Points 29	1	41N15'34	111w58'10	7:27:53
Flowell 14	1	38N58'45	112w25'40	7:29:43
Floy 10	1	38N55'28	109w56'07	7:19:44
Flux 23	2	40N40'53	112w33'14	7:30:13
Foothill 18	1	40N44	111w50	7:27:20
Foothill Village 18	1	40N44'30	111w49'47	7:27:19
Fort Douglas 18	1	40N45'49	111w49'52	7:27:19
Fort Duchesne 24	1	40N17'17	109w51'14	7:19:25
Fort Johnson 11	1	37N46'45	113w01'53	7:32:08
Fountain Green 20	1	39N37'48	111w38'04	7:26:32
Francis 22	1	40N36'38	111w16'48	7:25:07
Freedom 20	1	39N32'33	111w38'55	7:26:36
Freeport Center 6	1	41N07	112w01	7:28:04
Fremont 28	1	38N27'27	111w37'08	7:26:29
Fremont Junction 21	1	38N45'21	111w22'51	7:25:31
Frisco 1	1	38N27'23	113w15'29	7:33:02
Fruita 28	1	38N17'08	111w14'46	7:24:59
Fruit Heights 6	1	41N01'56	111w54'05	7:27:36
Fruitland 7	1	40N12'46	110w50'20	7:23:21
Gandy 14	2	39N27'00	113w58'56	7:35:56
Garden City 17	1	41N56'49	111w23'34	7:25:34
Garfield 18	1	40N43'38	112w09'54	7:28:40
Garland 2	2	41N44'28	112w09'39	7:28:39
Garrison 14	2	38N56'04	114w01'56	7:36:08
Geneva 25	1	40N16'57	111w43'53	7:26:56
Genola 25	1	39N59'47	111w50'33	7:27:22
Georgetown 13	1	37N32'08	112w03'15	7:28:13
Gilluly 25	1	39N55'50	111w09'51	7:24:39
Glen Canyon 13	1	37N01	111w34	7:26:16
Glendale 13	1	37N19'04	112w35'47	7:30:23
Glenwood 21	1	38N45'48	111w59'22	7:27:57
Gold Hill 23	2	40N09'59	113w49'47	7:35:19
Gomex 25	1	40N04'28	111w34'42	7:26:19
Gooseberry 21	1	38N57	111w51	7:27:24
Gorder 29	1	41N12	111w58	7:27:52
Gorgosa 22	1	40N45'14	111w34'08	7:26:17
Goshen 25	1	39N57'11	111w54'00	7:27:36
Goshute 12	2	39N52'34	113w59'57	7:36:00
Grafton 27	1	37N10'02	113w04'45	7:32:19
Gramse 21	1	38N47'26	112w02'32	7:28:10
Granger 18	1	40N41'48	111w58'00	7:27:52
Granite 18	1	40N34'23	111w48'19	7:27:13
Granite Park 18	1	40N42	111w53	7:27:32
Grantsville 23	2	40N36'00	112w27'49	7:29:51
Gravel Crossing 19	1	37N42'26	110w14'21	7:20:57
Greendale 5	1	40N55	109w24	7:17:36
Greenfield Village 18	1	40N40	111w50	7:27:20
Green Lake 5	1	41N00	109w43	7:18:52
Green River 8	1	38N59'43	110w09'40	7:20:39
Greens Corner 3	1	41N38'49	111w54'39	7:27:39
Greenville 1	1	38N15'16	112w42'42	7:30:51
Greenville 3	1	41N45'59	111w50'51	7:27:23
Greenwich 16	1	38N25'52	111w55'20	7:27:41
Greenwood 14	1	39N07'21	112w21'07	7:29:24
Grouse Creek 2	2	41N42'34	113w52'57	7:35:32
Grouse Creek Junction 2	2	41N25'18	113w53'19	7:35:33
Grover 28	1	38N13'41	111w20'57	7:25:24
Gunlock 27	1	37N17'10	113w45'45	7:35:03
Gunnison 20	1	39N09'19	111w49'03	7:27:16
Gusher 24	1	40N18'07	109w49'04	7:19:16
Gypsum Mill 12	1	39N42'46	111w48'12	7:27:13
Hailstone 26	1	40N36'30	111w24'34	7:25:38
Halivah 11	1	37N42'38	113w10'27	7:32:42
Halls Crossing 19	1	37N27'25	110w42'44	7:22:51
Hamiltons Fort 11	1	37N37'10	113w09'00	7:32:36
Hamlin Valley 11	1	37N59'54	113w58'08	7:35:53
Hanksville 28	1	38N22'23	110w42'48	7:22:51
Hanna 7	1	40N24'15	110w45'52	7:23:03
Harding 14	1	39N17'21	112w27'48	7:29:51
Hardup 2	2	41N53'44	113w09'03	7:32:36
Hardy 25	1	40N20'19	111w44'17	7:26:57
Hardy Beet Spur 25	1	40N21	111w45	7:27:00
Harrisburg 27	1	37N12'21	113w23'37	7:33:34
Harrisburg Junction 27	1	37N09'43	113w25'51	7:33:43
Harrisville 29	1	41N16'53	111w59'15	7:27:57
Harrisville Heights 29	1	41N17'10	112w00'26	7:28:02
Hatch 9	1	37N38'59	112w26'01	7:29:44
Hatton 14	1	38N50'20	112w27'21	7:29:49
Hayden 24	1	40N25'58	109w58'21	7:19:53
Heber City 26	1	40N30'25	111w24'45	7:25:39
Heiner 4	1	39N42'29	110w51'56	7:23:28
Heist 11	1	37N51'11	113w50'52	7:35:23
Helper 4	1	39N41'03	110w51'14	7:23:25
Henefer 22	1	41N01'00	111w29'51	7:25:59
Henrieville 9	1	37N33'46	111w59'37	7:27:58
Hermitage 29	1	41N14'55	111w53'14	7:27:33
Herriman 18	1	40N30'51	112w01'56	7:28:08
Hiawatha 4	1	39N29'04	111w00'39	7:24:03
Hildale 27	1	37N01	112w58	7:31:52
Hill Air Force Base 6	1	41N14	111w57	7:27:48
Hill Creek 24	1	39N43	109w35	7:18:20
Hilldale 27	1	37N01	112w58	7:31:52
Hillsdale 9	1	37N43'09	112w22'53	7:29:32
Hillside 25	1	39N58'42	112w00'01	7:28:00
Hill Top 20	1	39N42'53	111w28'10	7:25:53
Hinckley 14	2	39N19'30	112w40'13	7:30:41
Hite 9	1	37N48'27	110w26'20	7:21:45
Hogup 2	2	41N15'33	113w07'24	7:32:30
Holden 14	1	39N05'56	112w16'12	7:29:05
Holladay 18	1	40N40'08	111w49'26	7:27:18
Holt 3	1	41N40'34	111w50'50	7:27:23
Homansville 25	1	39N58'30	112w05'00	7:28:20
Honeyville 2	1	41N38'19	112w04'43	7:28:19
Hooper 29	2	41N09'50	112w07'18	7:28:29
Howell 2	2	41N47'46	112w26'37	7:29:46
Hoytsville 22	1	40N52'28	111w22'47	7:25:31
Hunter 18	1	40N41'49	112w01'14	7:28:05
Huntington 8	1	39N19'36	110w57'50	7:23:51
Huntsville 29	1	41N15'39	111w46'09	7:27:05
Hurricane 27	1	37N10'31	113w17'21	7:33:09
Hyde Park 3	1	41N47'56	111w49'06	7:27:16
Hyrum 3	1	41N38'03	111w51'05	7:27:24
Ibapah 23	2	40N02'12	113w59'04	7:35:56
Ibex 14	1	38N52'57	113w26'28	7:33:46
Independence 24	1	40N14'53	109w56'04	7:19:44
Indianola 20	1	39N48'11	111w29'17	7:25:57
Indian Village 19	1	37N40'04	109w38'18	7:18:33
Ioka 7	1	40N15'31	110w06'47	7:20:27
Iron Basin 14	1	38N55'49	112w57'16	7:31:49
Iron Mountain 11	1	37N37'03	113w23'24	7:33:34
Iron Springs 11	1	37N44'59	113w14'02	7:32:56
Ironton 25	1	40N11'55	111w37'03	7:26:28
Ivins 27	1	37N10'07	113w40'43	7:34:43
Jensen 21	1	38N43'25	112w05'52	7:28:23
Jensen 24	1	40N22'11	109w20'03	7:17:20
Jericho 12	1	39N45'01	112w12'17	7:28:49
Jerusalem 20	1	39N33'50	111w39'25	7:26:38
Jordan 18	1	40N36	111w57	7:27:48
Jordanelle 26	1	40N35'40	111w25'36	7:25:42
Joseph 21	1	38N37'35	112w12'59	7:28:52
Joy 12	2	39N34'22	113w03'28	7:32:14
Juab 12	1	39N31'11	111w56'23	7:27:46
Junction 16	1	38N14'15	112w13'09	7:28:53
Kamas 22	1	40N38'35	111w16'48	7:25:07
Kanab 13	1	37N02'51	112w31'32	7:30:06
Kanarraville 11	1	37N32'20	113w11'00	7:32:44
Kanesville 29	2	41N11'26	112w04'59	7:28:20
Kanosh 14	1	38N48'05	112w26'12	7:29:45
Kanosh Indian Village 14	1	38N49'12	112w24'11	7:29:37
Kaysville 6	1	41N02'07	111w56'16	7:27:45
Kearns 18	1	40N39'36	111w59'44	7:27:59
Keetley 26	1	40N38'08	111w24'50	7:25:39
Keetley Junction 22	1	40N40'57	111w27'25	7:25:50
Keigley 25	1	40N00'20	111w48'31	7:27:14
Kelton 2	2	41N44'46	113w06'20	7:32:25
Kema 21	1	38N48'14	112w01'27	7:28:06
Kenilworth 4	1	39N41'18	110w48'18	7:23:13
Kimball Junction 22	1	40N43'38	111w32'36	7:26:10
Kingston 16	1	38N12'30	112w11'13	7:28:45
Kingsville Junction 29	2	41N09'38	112w04'58	7:28:20
Knight 12	1	39N56'36	112w11'43	7:28:47
Knightville 12	1	39N57'14	112w06'00	7:28:24
Knolls 23	2	40N43'23	113w17'20	7:33:09
Knudsen Corner 18	1	40N38	111w50	7:27:20
Knudsens Corner 18	1	40N38'17	111w48'41	7:27:15
Koosharem 21	1	38N30'37	111w52'50	7:27:31
Kyune 25	1	39N49'34	110w56'39	7:23:47
Lago 23	1	40N42'17	112w15'32	7:29:02
Laguna 25	1	39N59'31	112w01'51	7:28:07
Laho 1	1	38N15'55	113w06'54	7:32:28
Lake Point 23	1	40N40'51	112w15'44	7:29:03
Lake Point Junction 23	1	40N43'23	112w13'31	7:28:54
Lake Shore 25	1	40N07'19	111w43'47	7:26:55
Lakeside 2	2	41N13'21	112w51'53	7:31:28
Lakeside Resort 21	1	38N31	111w53	7:27:32
Laketown 17	1	41N49'32	111w19'18	7:25:17
Lakeview 25	1	40N15'29	111w42'42	7:26:51
Lakota 17	1	41N59'09	111w24'28	7:25:38
Lampo Junction 2	1	41N38'11	112w25'22	7:29:41
Lampton 18	1	40N33'32	111w54'02	7:27:36
Lant 25	1	39N57'45	111w54'53	7:27:40
Lapoint 24	1	40N24'14	109w47'34	7:19:10
Lark 18	1	40N31'30	112w05'44	7:28:23
La Sal 19	1	38N18'44	109w14'51	7:16:59
La Sal Junction 19	1	38N18'38	109w24'16	7:17:37
Latimer 11	1	38N06'01	113w18'54	7:33:16
Latuda 4	1	39N42'14	110w56'43	7:23:47
La Verkin 27	1	37N12'04	113w16'08	7:33:05
Lawrence 8	1	39N17'44	110w55'42	7:23:43
Layton 6	1	41N03'37	111w58'13	7:27:53
Laytona 6	1	41N05'21	111w58'23	7:27:54
Leamington 14	1	39N32'05	112w16'58	7:29:08
Leeds 27	1	37N14'19	113w21'30	7:33:26
Leeton 24	1	40N23'21	109w55'13	7:19:41
Lehi 25	1	40N23'30	111w51'00	7:27:24
Leland 25	1	40N05'56	111w41'22	7:26:45
Leota 24	1	40N11'20	109w39'07	7:18:36
Levan 12	1	39N33'31	111w51'40	7:27:27
Lewis 25	1	40N05'08	111w42'11	7:26:49
Lewiston 3	1	41N58'33	111w51'20	7:27:25
Liberty 29	1	41N20'01	111w51'46	7:27:27
Lincoln 23	1	40N33'54	112w15'21	7:29:01
Lincoln 25	1	40N16'44	111w41'40	7:26:47
Lindon 25	1	40N20'36	111w43'12	7:26:53
Little Bonanza 24	1	40N02'09	109w12'40	7:16:51
Little Mountain 29	1	41N14'40	112w15'14	7:29:01
Littleton 15	1	41N02'21	111w43'03	7:26:52
Loa 28	1	38N24'10	111w38'32	7:26:34
Lockerby 19	1	37N48'01	109w04'51	7:16:19
Lofgreen 23	1	40N01'27	112w18'35	7:29:14
Logan 3	1	41N44'08	111w50'01	7:27:20
Lone Tree Crossing 8	1	38N45'53	111w07'34	7:24:30
Long Valley Junction 13	1	37N29'17	112w30'38	7:30:03
Low 23	2	40N47'08	112w56'23	7:31:46
Lower Kimberly 16	1	38N29'25	112w23'24	7:29:34
Lucin 2	2	41N20'54	113w54'15	7:35:37
Lund 11	1	38N00'27	113w25'51	7:33:43
Lyman 28	1	38N23'49	111w35'20	7:26:21
Lynn 2	2	41N52'22	113w44'38	7:34:59
Lynndyl 14	1	39N31'09	112w22'30	7:29:30
Mack 14	1	39N32'01	112w18'46	7:29:15
Madsen 2	1	41N39'59	112w05'27	7:28:22
Maeser 24	1	40N28'38	109w35'10	7:18:21
Magna 18	1	40N42'33	112w06'03	7:28:24
Magna Mill 18	1	40N42'54	112w07'18	7:28:29
Malone 14	1	38N39'10	112w58'52	7:31:55
Mammoth 12	1	39N55'35	112w07'32	7:28:30
Mammoth Junction 12	1	39N56'13	112w08'52	7:28:35
Manderfield 1	1	38N21'34	112w38'17	7:30:33
Manila 5	1	40N59'17	109w43'19	7:18:53
Manti 20	1	39N16'06	111w38'10	7:26:33
Mantua 2	1	41N29'45	111w56'35	7:27:46
Maple Grove 14	1	39N00'54	112w05'32	7:28:22
Mapleton 25	1	40N07'49	111w34'40	7:26:19
Marion 22	1	40N40'39	111w16'49	7:25:07
Marriott 29	1	41N14'41	112w00'31	7:28:02
Marshall 23	2	40N36'09	112w23'34	7:29:34
Martin 4	1	39N42'07	110w52'03	7:23:28
Marysvale 16	1	38N26'58	112w13'46	7:28:55
Matlin 2	2	41N33'34	113w21'29	7:33:26
Mayfield 20	1	39N06'51	111w42'36	7:26:50
McCornick 14	1	39N12'56	112w24'27	7:29:38
McIntyre 12	1	39N50'05	112w10'06	7:28:40
Meadow 14	1	38N53'09	112w24'35	7:29:38
Meadowville 17	1	41N50'39	111w23'54	7:25:36
Mendon 3	1	41N42	111w59	7:27:56
Mercur 23	1	40N19'15	112w12'41	7:28:51
Mexican Hat 19	1	37N09'07	109w51'59	7:19:28
Middleton 27	1	37N07'15	113w32'24	7:34:10
Midlake 2	2	41N13'26	112w39'50	7:30:39
Midvale 18	1	40N36'40	111w53'57	7:27:36
Midway 26	1	40N30'44	111w28'25	7:25:54
Milburn 20	1	39N42'15	111w25'27	7:25:42
Milford 1	1	38N23'49	113w00'36	7:32:02
Millcreek 18	1	40N43	111w51	7:27:24
Mill Fork 25	1	39N57'50	111w18'26	7:25:14
Mills 12	1	39N28'58	112w01'38	7:28:07
Mills Junction 23	1	40N39'18	112w17'18	7:29:09
Millville 3	1	41N40'54	111w49'20	7:27:17
Milton 15	1	41N03'36	111w43'49	7:26:55
Minersville 1	1	38N12'51	112w55'22	7:31:41
Moab 10	1	38N34'24	109w32'57	7:18:12
Moark Junction 25	1	40N04'58	111w35'15	7:26:21
Modena 11	1	37N47'56	113w55'24	7:35:42
Mohrland 8	1	39N26'25	111w00'52	7:24:03
Molen 8	1	39N05'18	111w04'22	7:24:17
Mona 12	1	39N48'58	111w51'17	7:27:25
Monarch 7	1	40N25'02	110w06'17	7:20:25
Monroe 21	1	38N37'48	112w07'12	7:28:29
Montezuma Creek 19	1	37N16'22	109w20'14	7:17:21
Monticello 19	1	37N52'17	109w20'32	7:17:22
Monument Valley 19	1	37N09	109w52	7:19:28
Moore 8	1	38N58'00	111w09'10	7:24:37
Morgan 15	1	41N02'10	111w40'34	7:26:42
Moroni 20	1	39N31'30	111w35'23	7:26:22
Morton 3	2	41N56'21	111w56'50	7:27:47
Mosida 25	1	40N07'38	111w57'21	7:27:49
Motoqua 27	1	37N18'14	113w59'56	7:36:00
Mound City 26	1	40N31'31	111w29'28	7:25:58
Mountain Green 15	1	41N08'35	111w47'27	7:27:10
Mountain Home 7	1	40N24	110w23	7:21:32
Mount Aire 18	1	40N43'34	111w42'59	7:26:52
Mount Carmel 13	1	37N14'50	112w39'49	7:30:39
Mount Carmel Junction 13	1	37N13'27	112w40'47	7:30:43
Mount Emmons 7	1	40N20'52	110w16'28	7:21:06
Mount Olympus 18	1	40N41	111w48	7:27:12
Mount Pleasant 20	1	39N32'49	111w27'17	7:25:49
Mount Sterling 3	1	41N36'35	111w56'11	7:27:45
Murdock 1	1	38N30'13	112w59'00	7:31:56
Murray 18	1	40N40'01	111w53'14	7:27:33
Mutual Dell 25	1	40N26'47	111w38'36	7:26:34
Myton 7	1	40N11'40	110w03'40	7:20:15
Naples 24	1	40N25'37	109w29'55	7:18:00
Nash 18	1	40N27'17	111w55'17	7:27:41
Navajo 19	1	37N11	109w31	7:18:04
Neels 14	1	39N02'42	112w46'07	7:31:04
Neola 7	1	40N26'00	110w01'45	7:20:07
Nephi 12	1	39N42'37	111w50'08	7:27:21
Nerva 2	1	41N22'08	112w02'27	7:28:10
Newcastle 11	1	37N40'00	113w32'55	7:34:12
New Harmony 27	1	37N28'46	113w18'32	7:33:14

Newhouse 1 1 38N28'52 113w20'28 7:33:22
Newton 3 2 41N51'46 111w59'24 7:27:58
Nibley 3 1 41N40'28 111w49'56 7:27:20
Nibley 21 1 38N41'14 112w07'18 7:28:29
North Creek 1 1 38N20'14 112w34'38 7:30:19
North Davis 6 1 41N06 112w00 7:28:00
North Farmington Junction 6 1 41N00'44 111w54'44 7:27:39
North Logan 3 1 41N46'10 111w48'14 7:27:13
North Ogden 29 1 41N18'26 111w57'34 7:27:50
North Salt Lake 6 1 40N50'55 111w54'22 7:27:37
North View 11 1 37N39'27 112w50'01 7:31:20
Notom 28 1 38N14'00 111w07'04 7:24:28
Nunns 25 1 40N20'10 111w36'38 7:26:27
Oak City 14 1 39N22'30 112w20'05 7:29:20
Oak Creek 20 1 39N40'29 111w26'01 7:25:44
Oakley 22 1 40N42'53 111w18'00 7:25:12
Oasis 14 1 39N17'38 112w37'39 7:30:31
Ogden 29 1 41N13'23 111w58'23 7:27:54
Ogden Valley 29 1 41N18 111w44 7:26:56
Old Irontown 11 1 37N36'00 113w26'58 7:33:48
Old La Sal 19 1 38N19'53 109w08'55 7:16:36
Old Limber Pine 17 1 41N55'12 111w28'25 7:25:54
Olivers 18 1 40N29'04 111w55'21 7:27:41
Oljeto 19 1 37N02'10 110w19'03 7:21:16
Olmstead 25 1 40N19'00 111w39'13 7:26:37
Onaqui 23 1 40N13 112w23 7:29:32
Ophir 23 1 40N22'10 112w15'28 7:29:02
Orangeville 8 1 39N13'38 111w03'10 7:24:13
Orderville 13 1 37N16'33 112w38'13 7:30:33
Orem 25 1 40N17'49 111w41'38 7:26:47
Orem Station 25 1 40N18'35 111w42'15 7:26:49
Osiris 9 1 38N01'20 111w57'39 7:27:51
Ouray 24 1 40N05'21 109w40'36 7:18:42
Pallas 18 1 40N40 111w54 7:27:36
Palmyra 25 1 40N08'25 111w41'53 7:26:48
Panguitch 9 1 37N49'22 112w26'06 7:29:44
Paradise 3 1 41N34'08 111w50'14 7:27:21
Paragonah 11 1 37N53'09 112w46'28 7:31:06
Paria 13 1 37N14'54 111w56'54 7:27:48
Park City 22 1 40N38'46 111w29'50 7:25:59
Park Terrace 18 1 40N43 111w51 7:27:24
Park Valley 2 2 41N49'03 113w19'42 7:33:19
Parley 12 1 39N33'54 112w08'25 7:28:34
Parowan 11 1 37N50'32 112w49'38 7:31:19
Partoun 12 2 39N38'36 113w53'13 7:35:33
Patrick Place 25 1 40N05'09 111w25'11 7:25:41
Payson 25 1 40N02'40 111w43'53 7:26:56
Peerless 4 1 39N41'39 110w54'37 7:23:38
Pehrson 23 1 40N06'36 112w21'00 7:29:24
Penrose 2 1 41N39'03 112w18'03 7:29:12
Peoa 22 1 40N43'29 111w20'28 7:25:22
Perry 2 1 41N28 112w02 7:28:08
Petersboro 3 1 41N46'09 111w58'51 7:27:55
Peterson 15 1 41N07'05 111w46'01 7:27:04
Peterson 29 1 41N11'01 112w00'52 7:28:03
Phill 11 1 37N49'48 112w49'12 7:31:17
Pickleville 17 1 41N54'45 111w23'15 7:25:33
Pigeon 2 2 41N19'57 113w47'55 7:35:12
Pigeon Hollow Junction 20 1 39N25'18 111w33'30 7:26:14
Pine Cliff 22 1 40N55 111w24 7:25:36
Pinecrest 18 1 40N48'46 111w43'27 7:26:54
Pines 25 1 39N53'51 111w33'08 7:26:13
Pine Valley 27 1 37N23'28 113w30'48 7:34:03
Pinto 11 1 37N40 113w33 7:34:12
Pintura 27 1 37N20'27 113w16'24 7:33:06
Pioneer 18 1 40N46 111w53 7:27:32
Pittsburg 16 1 38N30'19 112w15'31 7:29:02
Plain City 29 2 41N17'53 112w05'07 7:28:20
Pleasant Green Acres 18 1 40N44 112w01 7:28:04
Pleasant Grove 25 1 40N21'51 111w44'16 7:26:57
Pleasant View 25 1 40N15'39 111w39'19 7:26:37
Pleasant View 29 1 41N19'06 111w59'29 7:27:58
Plymouth 2 2 41N52'32 112w08'36 7:28:34
Portage 2 2 41N58'33 112w14'19 7:28:57
Porterville 15 1 40N58'53 111w40'39 7:26:43
Prattsville 21 1 38N46'27 112w00'50 7:28:03
Price 4 1 39N35'58 110w48'36 7:23:14
Promontory 2 2 41N37'07 112w32'51 7:30:11
Promontory Point 2 2 41N13 112w25 7:29:40
Providence 3 1 41N42'23 111w48'59 7:27:16
Provo 25 1 40N14'02 111w39'28 7:26:38
Quigley Crossing 3 2 41N52'01 111w58'49 7:27:55
Rainbow 24 1 39N50'38 109w11'05 7:16:44
Randlett 24 1 40N13'58 109w48'25 7:19:14
Randolph 17 1 41N39'57 111w10'53 7:24:44
Read 14 1 38N34'21 112w59'03 7:31:56
Red Lake Village 19 1 37N11'50 109w19'23 7:17:18
Redmond 21 1 39N00'22 111w51'40 7:27:27
Red Point 12 1 39N25'42 112w02'05 7:28:08
Red Wash 24 1 40N11'55 109w18'31 7:17:14
Redwood 18 1 40N42'48 111w56'18 7:27:45
Relico 29 1 41N12'56 112w00'33 7:28:02
Richfield 21 1 38N46'21 112w05'00 7:28:20
Richmond 3 1 41N55'22 111w48'46 7:27:15
Richville 15 1 41N00'32 111w41'22 7:26:45
Rio 25 1 39N59'45 111w25'35 7:25:42
Riter 18 2 40N45'07 112w04'31 7:28:18
Riverdale 29 1 41N10'37 112w00'11 7:28:01
River Heights 3 1 41N43'18 111w49'14 7:27:17
Riverside 2 2 41N47'20 112w08'53 7:28:36
Riverton 18 1 40N31'19 111w56'18 7:27:45
Riverton Siding 18 1 40N31'36 111w54'14 7:27:37
Robbe 18 1 40N33'40 112w04'11 7:28:17
Rockville 27 1 37N09'40 113w02'15 7:32:09
Roosevelt 7 1 40N17'58 109w59'17 7:19:57
Roper 18 1 40N42'50 111w54'26 7:27:38
Rosedale 6 1 40N56'32 111w52'46 7:27:31
Rosette 2 2 41N49'07 113w24'44 7:33:39
Round Valley 17 1 41N49 111w19 7:25:16
Roy 29 1 41N09'42 112w01'32 7:28:06
Royal 4 1 39N44'46 110w52'46 7:23:31
Rozel 2 1 41N35'10 112w38'45 7:30:35
Rubys Inn 9 1 37N40 112w10 7:28:40
Sage Creek Junction 17 1 41N46'17 111w07'13 7:24:29
Sagers 10 1 38N57'52 109w35'56 7:18:24
Sahara Village 6 1 41N06'02 111w58'21 7:27:53
Saint George 27 1 37N06'15 113w35'00 7:34:20
Saint John 23 2 40N21'19 112w27'08 7:29:49
Salduro 23 2 40N44'06 113w51'20 7:35:25
Salem 25 1 40N03'11 111w40'22 7:26:41
Salina 21 1 38N57'28 111w51'33 7:27:26
Saline 2 2 41N12'51 112w28'19 7:29:53
Saltair 18 2 40N46'10 112w05'59 7:28:24
Salt Lake City 18 1 40N45'39 111w53'25 7:27:34
Samak 22 1 40N37'03 111w12'47 7:24:51
Sandy 18 1 40N35'30 111w53'00 7:27:32
Santa Clara 27 1 37N07'59 113w39'12 7:34:37
Santaquin 25 1 39N58'32 111w47'04 7:27:08
Santio Crossing 24 1 39N44'16 109w34'59 7:18:20
Saratoga Springs 25 1 40N20'57 111w54'14 7:27:37
Scipio 14 2 39N14'42 112w06'12 7:28:25
Scofield 4 1 39N43'27 111w09'36 7:24:38
Sego 10 1 39N01'59 109w42'09 7:18:49
Sevier 21 1 38N35'11 112w15'27 7:29:02
Sharp 12 1 39N37'25 111w53'20 7:27:33
Shauntie 1 1 38N20'28 113w09'57 7:32:40
Shem 27 1 37N11'30 113w46'05 7:35:04
Shenendoah City 1 1 38N20'58 113w08'48 7:32:35
Sherwood Park 18 1 40N35 111w52 7:27:28
Shivwits 27 1 37N10'52 113w45'24 7:35:02
Shunesburg 27 1 37N09'29 112w58'37 7:31:54
Sigurd 21 1 38N50'26 111w58'01 7:27:52
Silsbee 23 2 40N44'07 113w55'37 7:35:42
Silver City 12 1 39N54'36 112w07'45 7:28:31
Silver Creek Junction 22 1 40N43'53 111w29'50 7:25:59
Silver Fork 18 1 40N37'48 111w36'35 7:26:26
Silver Reef 27 1 37N15'10 113w22'01 7:33:28
Sixmile Point 14 1 38N46'18 112w31'11 7:30:05
Skull Valley Indian Res 23 1 40N22 112w45 7:31:00
Sky View 25 1 39N57'03 111w12'52 7:24:51
Slaterville 29 1 41N15'51 112w01'55 7:28:08
Smithfield 3 1 41N50'18 111w49'55 7:27:20
Smoot 25 1 40N15 111w40 7:26:40
Snow 25 1 40N17'23 111w41'41 7:26:47
Snowville 2 2 41N57'56 112w42'32 7:30:50
Snyder 18 1 40N31'55 112w04'48 7:28:19
Snyderville 22 1 40N41'40 111w32'35 7:26:10
Soldier Crossing 19 1 37N40'58 110w13'01 7:20:52
Soldier Summit 26 1 39N55'43 111w04'38 7:24:19
Solitude 10 1 38N57'33 110w01'08 7:20:05
Soma 12 1 39N35'09 112w09'40 7:28:39
South Cottonwood 18 1 40N38 111w50 7:27:20
South Davis 6 1 40N52 111w53 7:27:32
South Jordan 18 1 40N33'44 111w55'44 7:27:43
South Ogden 29 1 41N11'31 111w58'14 7:27:53
South Salt Lake 18 1 40N43'08 111w53'15 7:27:33
South Weber 6 1 41N07'57 111w55'46 7:27:43
Spanish Fork 25 1 40N06'54 111w39'15 7:26:37
Spearmint 20 1 39N06'42 111w48'11 7:27:13
Spring City 20 1 39N28'57 111w29'43 7:25:59
Springdale 27 1 37N11'20 113w00'00 7:32:00
Springdell 25 1 40N19'41 111w37'25 7:26:30
Spring Glen 4 1 39N39'34 110w51'10 7:23:25
Spring Lake 25 1 40N00'04 111w44'44 7:26:59
Springville 25 1 40N09'55 111w36'36 7:26:26
Spry 9 1 37N49 112w26 7:29:44
Squaw Crossing 24 1 39N58'08 109w40'07 7:18:40
Standardville 4 1 39N42'00 110w55'58 7:23:44
Standrod 2 2 41N59'38 113w25'06 7:33:40
Stansbury Park 23 1 40N32 112w18 7:29:12
Starr 12 1 39N52'06 111w51'16 7:27:25
Sterling 20 1 39N11'37 111w41'30 7:26:46
Stockton 23 1 40N27'10 112w21'36 7:29:26
Stoddard 15 1 41N04'01 111w42'38 7:26:51
Storrs 4 1 39N42'14 110w55'08 7:23:41
Strawberry Valley 26 1 40N04 111w04 7:24:16
Strong 14 1 39N26'05 112w28'09 7:29:53
Sugar House 18 1 40N43'33 111w51'52 7:27:27
Sugarville 14 1 39N27'55 112w38'55 7:30:36
Sulphurdale 1 1 38N33'37 112w34'52 7:30:19
Summit 11 1 37N48'04 112w56'08 7:31:45
Sundance 25 1 40N15 111w40 7:26:40
Sunnyside 4 1 39N33'05 110w23'14 7:21:33
Sunnyside Junction 4 1 39N31'32 110w34'20 7:22:17
Sunset 6 1 41N08'11 112w01'49 7:28:07
Sutherland 14 1 39N23'20 112w37'58 7:30:32
Sutro 25 1 40N05'31 111w35'47 7:26:23
Swan Creek 17 1 41N56 111w23 7:25:32
Syracuse 6 1 41N05'22 112w03'50 7:28:15
Tabiona 7 1 40N21'17 110w42'46 7:22:51
Taggarts 15 1 41N03'35 111w35'28 7:26:22
Talmage 7 1 40N20'24 110w25'36 7:21:42
Taylor 29 1 41N13'38 112w04'58 7:28:20
Taylorsville 18 1 40N40'04 111w56'17 7:27:45
Teasdale 28 1 38N17'10 111w28'36 7:25:54
Terminal 18 1 40N45'21 112w00'31 7:28:02
Terra 23 2 40N14 112w45 7:31:00
Thatcher 2 1 41N41'38 112w17'36 7:29:10
Thermo 1 1 38N12'52 113w10'15 7:32:41
Thistle 25 1 39N59'29 111w29'51 7:25:59
Thompson 10 1 38N58'16 109w42'47 7:18:51
Thompsonville 16 1 38N25'01 112w12'57 7:28:52
Three Creeks 1 1 38N17'48 112w25'09 7:29:41
Three Forks 9 1 37N59'29 110w29'40 7:21:59
Three Forks 25 1 40N05'04 111w21'17 7:25:25
Three Forks 26 1 39N58'29 110w57'23 7:23:50
Three Pines 10 1 39N25'10 109w23'59 7:17:36
Timpie 23 2 40N44'51 112w39'21 7:30:37
Tintic Junction 12 1 39N55'20 112w09'36 7:28:38
Tod Park 23 1 40N30 112w20 7:29:20
Tooele 23 1 40N31'51 112w17'51 7:29:11
Tooele Army Depot 23 1 40N32 112w18 7:29:12
Topliff 23 1 40N09'22 112w12'43 7:28:51
Toquerville 27 1 37N15'12 113w17'02 7:33:08
Torrey 28 1 38N17'56 111w25'06 7:25:40
Townsend 25 1 39N59'34 111w49'40 7:27:19
Tremonton 2 2 41N42'43 112w09'53 7:28:40
Trenton 3 2 41N55'04 111w56'30 7:27:46
Tresend 2 2 41N13'15 112w45'35 7:31:02
Tridell 24 1 40N27'13 109w50'57 7:19:24
Tropic 9 1 37N37'31 112w04'53 7:28:20
Trout Creek 12 2 39N41'22 113w49'40 7:35:19
Tucker 25 1 39N56'04 111w11'55 7:24:48
Uintah 29 1 41N08'39 111w55'21 7:27:41
Uintah Junction 29 1 41N08'23 111w54'51 7:27:39
Uisco 12 1 39N33'55 112w12'00 7:28:48
Union 18 1 40N37'14 111w52'17 7:27:29
Unitah and Ouray Indian Res 7 1 40N20 110w00 7:20:00
University 25 1 40N15 111w40 7:26:40
University Village 18 1 40N45'10 111w50'02 7:27:20
Upalco 7 1 40N16'41 110w13'03 7:20:52
Upper Kimberly 16 1 38N29'08 112w23'47 7:29:35
Upton 1 1 38N19'27 113w03'56 7:32:16
Upton 22 1 40N57'49 111w14'05 7:24:56
Utah Mine 4 1 39N41'37 111w09'15 7:24:37
Utahn 7 1 40N16'16 110w25'53 7:21:44
Utah State University 3 1 41N43 111w49 7:27:16
Utida 3 1 41N59'11 112w08'05 7:28:32
Uvada 11 1 37N43'04 114w02'39 7:36:11
Valencia 6 1 40N54'28 111w54'10 7:27:37
Val Verda 6 1 40N51'20 111w53'32 7:27:34
Van 14 2 39N13'50 112w40'04 7:30:40
Venice 21 1 38N48'01 112w00'20 7:28:01
Verdure 19 1 37N47'09 109w20'53 7:17:24
Vermillion 21 1 38N51'39 111w57'52 7:27:51
Vernal 24 1 40N27'20 109w31'41 7:18:07
Vernon 23 2 40N05'32 112w25'58 7:29:44
Veyo 27 1 37N20'17 113w41'32 7:34:46
Victor 8 1 39N24'05 110w42'53 7:22:52
Vineyard 25 1 40N17 111w41 7:26:44
Virgin 27 1 37N12'30 113w11'15 7:32:45
Vista 10 1 38N57'50 109w40'36 7:18:42
Vivian Park 25 1 40N21'18 111w34'24 7:26:18
Wahsatch 22 1 41N11'57 111w06'44 7:24:27
Wales 20 1 39N29'13 111w38'04 7:26:32
Wallsburg 26 1 40N23'16 111w25'18 7:25:41
Wanship 22 1 40N48'43 111w24'24 7:25:38
Warren 29 1 41N17'01 112w07'17 7:28:29
Wasatch Resort 18 1 40N34'13 111w45'37 7:27:02
Washakie 2 2 41N56'39 112w12'59 7:28:52
Washington 27 1 37N07'50 113w30'27 7:34:02
Washington Terrace 29 1 41N10'22 111w58'33 7:27:54
Watson 24 1 39N52'55 109w09'28 7:16:38
Wattis 4 1 39N31'49 111w00'59 7:24:04
Wattis Junction 4 1 39N32'03 110w59'34 7:23:58
Welby 18 1 40N35'17 111w59'26 7:27:58
Wellington 4 1 39N32'33 110w44'05 7:22:56
Wellsville 3 1 41N38'19 111w55'59 7:27:44
Wendover 23 2 40N44'14 114w02'12 7:36:09
West Bountiful 6 1 40N53'38 111w54'04 7:27:36
West Box Elder 2 2 41N41 113w32 7:34:08
West Daggett 5 1 40N58 109w43 7:18:52
West Ephraim 20 1 39N22'32 111w35'18 7:26:21
West Jordan 18 1 40N36'35 111w56'18 7:27:45
West Juab 12 2 39N43 113w06 7:32:24
West Kaysville 6 1 41N02'20 111w58'18 7:27:53
West Layton 6 1 41N03'37 111w59'53 7:28:00
West Mercur 23 1 40N18'53 112w16'39 7:29:07
West Ogden 29 1 41N13'23 111w59'26 7:27:58
West Point 6 1 41N07'06 112w05'00 7:28:20
West Portal 25 1 40N09'40 111w14'59 7:25:00
West Side 24 1 40N19 109w52 7:19:28
West Warren 29 1 41N15'01 112w09'06 7:28:36
Westwater 10 1 39N04'42 109w06'42 7:16:27
West Weber 29 1 41N14'56 112w04'39 7:28:19
Wheatgrass 11 1 37N58'19 112w47'34 7:31:10
Wheelon 2 1 41N49'45 112w03'19 7:28:13
Whipup 21 1 38N41'30 111w23'36 7:25:34
White Canyon 19 1 37N48'36 110w25'53 7:21:44
White City 18 1 40N34 111w52 7:27:28
White Horse Village 3 1 41N51'49 111w46'23 7:27:06
White Mesa Village 19 1 37N08'01 109w16'53 7:17:08
White Rock Curve Village 19 1 37N12'41 109w17'32 7:17:10
Whiterocks 24 1 40N28'05 109w55'48 7:19:43
Whites Crossing 15 1 40N56'59 111w39'25 7:26:38
Wicks 25 1 40N19'44 111w38'12 7:26:33
Widtsoe 9 1 37N49'56 111w59'41 7:27:59

Widtsoe Junction 9
1 37N49'52 112w00'07 7:28:00
Wildcat 4 1 39N39'03 110w55'06 7:23:40
Wildwood 25 1 40N21'55 111w33'24 7:26:14
Wildwood 29 1 41N15'17 111w52'09 7:27:29
Willard 2 1 41N24'33 112w02'07 7:28:08
Wilson 29 1 41N13'45 112w01'28 7:28:06
Wing 25 1 40N21'14 111w47'04 7:27:08
Winter Quarters 4
1 39N43'14 111w11'13 7:24:45
Wood Hill 4 1 39N36'40 110w48'42 7:23:15
Woodland 22 1 40N34'53 111w13'35 7:24:54
Woodrow 14 1 39N21 112w35 7:30:20
Woodruff 17 1 41N31'19 111w09'42 7:24:39
Woods Cross 6 1 40N52'18 111w53'29 7:27:34
Woodside 8 1 39N15'56 110w20'53 7:21:24
Yale Crossing 11
1 37N51'54 113w44'53 7:35:00
Yellow Banks 1 1 38N25'30 112w59'16 7:31:57
Yost 2 2 41N57'39 113w32'29 7:34:10
Zane 11 1 37N55'31 113w34'57 7:34:20
Zion Lodge 27 1 37N15'03 112w57'20 7:31:49
Zion National Park 27
1 37N11 113w00 7:32:00

TIME TABLES

VT # 1		
Before 11/18/1883		LMT
11/18/1883	12:00	EST
3/31/1918	02:00	EWT
10/27/1918	02:00	EST
3/30/1919	02:00	EWT
10/26/1919	02:00	EST
2/09/1942	02:00	EWT
9/30/1945	02:00	EST
4/24/1955	02:00	US#2

VT # 2		
Before 11/18/1883		LMT
11/18/1883	12:00	EST
3/31/1918	02:00	EWT
10/27/1918	02:00	EST
3/30/1919	02:00	EWT
10/26/1919	02:00	EST
4/24/1938	02:00	US#2

VT # 3		
Before 11/18/1883		LMT
11/18/1883	12:00	EST
3/31/1918	02:00	EWT
10/27/1918	02:00	EST
3/30/1919	02:00	EWT
10/26/1919	02:00	EST
4/30/1939	02:00	US#2

VT # 4		
Before 11/18/1883		LMT
11/18/1883	12:00	EST
3/31/1918	02:00	EWT
10/27/1918	02:00	EST
3/30/1919	02:00	EWT
10/26/1919	02:00	EST
4/28/1940	02:00	US#2

VT # 5		
Before 11/18/1883		LMT
11/18/1883	12:00	EST
3/31/1918	02:00	EWT
10/27/1918	02:00	EST
3/30/1919	02:00	EWT
10/26/1919	02:00	EST
4/27/1941	02:00	US#2

VT # 6		
Before 11/18/1883		LMT
11/18/1883	12:00	EST
3/31/1918	02:00	EWT
10/27/1918	02:00	EST
3/30/1919	02:00	EWT
10/26/1919	02:00	EST
2/09/1942	02:00	EWT
9/30/1945	02:00	EST
4/28/1946	02:00	US#2

VT # 7		
Before 11/18/1883		LMT
11/18/1883	12:00	EST
3/31/1918	02:00	EWT
10/27/1918	02:00	EST
3/30/1919	02:00	EWT
10/26/1919	02:00	EST
2/09/1942	02:00	EWT
9/30/1945	02:00	EST
4/27/1947	02:00	US#2

VT # 8		
Before 11/18/1883		LMT
11/18/1883	12:00	EST
3/31/1918	02:00	EWT
10/27/1918	02:00	EST
3/30/1919	02:00	EWT
10/26/1919	02:00	EST
2/09/1942	02:00	EWT
9/30/1945	02:00	EST
4/25/1948	02:00	US#2

VT # 9		
Before 11/18/1883		LMT
11/18/1883	12:00	EST
3/31/1918	02:00	EWT
10/27/1918	02:00	EST
3/30/1919	02:00	EWT
10/26/1919	02:00	EST
2/09/1942	02:00	EWT
9/30/1945	02:00	EST
4/24/1949	02:00	US#2

VT # 10		
Before 11/18/1883		LMT
11/18/1883	12:00	EST
3/31/1918	02:00	EWT
10/27/1918	02:00	EST
3/30/1919	02:00	EWT
10/26/1919	02:00	EST
2/09/1942	02:00	EWT
9/30/1945	02:00	EST
4/29/1951	02:00	US#2

VT # 11		
Before 11/18/1883		LMT
11/10/1883	12:00	EST
3/31/1918	02:00	EWT
10/27/1918	02:00	EST
3/30/1919	02:00	EWT
10/26/1919	02:00	EST
2/09/1942	02:00	EWT
9/30/1945	02:00	EST
4/27/1952	02:00	US#2

VT # 12		
Before 11/18/1883		LMT
11/18/1883	12:00	EST
3/31/1918	02:00	EWT
10/27/1918	02:00	EST
3/30/1919	02:00	EWT
10/26/1919	02:00	EST
4/27/1941	02:00	EDT
9/28/1941	02:00	EST
2/09/1942	02:00	EWT
9/30/1945	02:00	EST
4/24/1955	02:00	US#2

VT # 13		
Before 11/18/1883		LMT
11/18/1883	12:00	EST
3/31/1918	02:00	EWT
10/27/1918	02:00	EST
3/30/1919	02:00	EWT
10/26/1919	02:00	EST
4/28/1935	02:00	US#2

VT # 14		
Before 11/18/1883		LMT
11/18/1883	12:00	EST
3/31/1918	02:00	EWT
10/27/1918	02:00	EST
3/30/1919	02:00	EWT
10/26/1919	02:00	EST
2/09/1942	02:00	EWT
9/30/1945	02:00	EST
4/25/1948	02:00	EDT
9/26/1948	02:00	EST
4/24/1955	02:00	US#2

VT # 15		
Before 11/18/1883		LMT
11/18/1883	12:00	EST
3/31/1918	02:00	EWT
10/27/1918	02:00	EST
3/30/1919	02:00	EWT
10/26/1919	02:00	EST
4/26/1936	02:00	US#2

VT # 16		
Before 11/18/1883		LMT
11/18/1883	12:00	EST
3/31/1918	02:00	EWT
10/27/1918	02:00	EST
3/30/1919	02:00	EWT
10/26/1919	02:00	EST
4/26/1931	02:00	US#2

VT # 17		
Before 11/18/1883		LMT
11/18/1883	12:00	EST
3/31/1918	02:00	EWT
10/27/1918	02:00	EST
3/30/1919	02:00	EWT
10/26/1919	02:00	EST
4/28/1940	02:00	EDT
9/29/1940	02:00	EST
4/27/1941	02:00	EDT
9/28/1941	02:00	EST
2/09/1942	02:00	EWT
9/30/1945	02:00	EST
4/24/1955	02:00	US#2

VT # 18		
Before 11/18/1883		LMT
11/18/1883	12:00	EST
3/31/1918	02:00	EWT
10/27/1918	02:00	EST
3/30/1919	02:00	EWT
10/26/1919	02:00	EST
2/09/1942	02:00	EWT
9/30/1945	02:00	EST
4/24/1949	02:00	EDT
9/25/1949	02:00	EST
4/30/1950	02:00	EDT
9/24/1950	02:00	EST
4/24/1955	02:00	US#2

VT # 19		
Before 11/18/1883		LMT
11/18/1883	12:00	EST
3/31/1918	02:00	EWT
10/27/1918	02:00	EST
3/30/1919	02:00	EWT
10/26/1919	02:00	EST
4/30/1939	02:00	EDT
9/24/1939	02:00	EST
4/28/1940	02:00	EDT
9/29/1940	02:00	EST
4/27/1941	02:00	EDT
9/28/1941	02:00	EST
2/09/1942	02:00	EWT
9/30/1945	02:00	EST
4/24/1955	02:00	US#2

VT # 20		
Before 11/18/1883		LMT
11/18/1883	12:00	EST
3/31/1918	02:00	EWT
10/27/1918	02:00	EST
3/30/1919	02:00	EWT
10/26/1919	02:00	EST
2/09/1942	02:00	EWT
9/30/1945	02:00	EST
4/27/1947	02:00	EDT
9/28/1947	02:00	EST
4/25/1948	02:00	EDT
9/26/1948	02:00	EST
4/24/1949	02:00	EDT
9/25/1949	02:00	EST
4/24/1955	02:00	US#2

VT # 21		
Before 11/18/1883		LMT
11/18/1883	12:00	EST
3/31/1918	02:00	EWT
10/27/1918	02:00	EST
3/30/1919	02:00	EWT
10/26/1919	02:00	EST
4/24/1938	02:00	EDT
9/25/1938	02:00	EST
4/30/1939	02:00	EDT
9/24/1939	02:00	EST
4/28/1940	02:00	EDT
9/29/1940	02:00	EST
4/27/1941	02:00	EDT
9/28/1941	02:00	EST
2/09/1942	02:00	EWT
9/30/1945	02:00	EST
4/24/1955	02:00	US#2

VT # 22		
Before 11/18/1883		LMT
11/18/1883	12:00	EST
3/31/1918	02:00	EWT
10/27/1918	02:00	EST
3/30/1919	02:00	EWT
10/26/1919	02:00	EST
2/09/1942	02:00	EWT
9/30/1945	02:00	EST
4/27/1947	02:00	EDT
9/28/1947	02:00	EST
4/25/1948	02:00	EDT
9/26/1948	02:00	EST
4/24/1949	02:00	EDT
9/25/1949	02:00	EST
4/30/1950	02:00	EDT
9/24/1950	02:00	EST
4/24/1955	02:00	US#2

VT # 23		
Before 11/18/1883		LMT
11/18/1883	12:00	EST
3/31/1918	02:00	EWT
10/27/1918	02:00	EST
3/30/1919	02:00	EWT
10/26/1919	02:00	EST
4/30/1922	02:00	EDT
9/24/1922	02:00	EST
4/29/1923	02:00	EDT
9/30/1923	02:00	EST
4/27/1924	02:00	EDT
9/28/1924	02:00	EST
4/26/1925	02:00	EDT
9/27/1925	02:00	EST
4/25/1926	02:00	EDT
9/26/1926	02:00	EST
4/24/1927	02:00	EDT
9/25/1927	02:00	EST
4/29/1928	02:00	EDT
9/30/1928	02:00	EST
4/28/1929	02:00	EDT
9/29/1929	02:00	EST
4/27/1930	02:00	EDT
9/28/1930	02:00	EST
4/26/1931	02:00	EDT
9/27/1931	02:00	EST
4/24/1932	02:00	EDT
9/25/1932	02:00	EST
4/30/1933	02:00	EDT
10/01/1933	02:00	EST
4/28/1935	02:00	US#2

VT # 24		
Before 11/18/1883		LMT
11/18/1883	12:00	EST
3/31/1918	02:00	EWT
10/27/1918	02:00	EST
3/30/1919	02:00	EWT
10/26/1919	02:00	EST
4/28/1929	02:00	EDT
9/29/1929	02:00	EST
4/27/1930	02:00	EDT
9/28/1930	02:00	EST
4/26/1931	02:00	EDT
9/27/1931	02:00	EST
5/24/1936	02:00	EDT
9/27/1936	02:00	EST
4/25/1937	02:00	US#2

VT # 25		
Before 11/18/1883		LMT
11/18/1883	12:00	EST
3/31/1918	02:00	EWT
10/27/1918	02:00	EST
3/30/1919	02:00	EWT
10/26/1919	02:00	EST
4/24/1938	02:00	EDT
9/25/1938	02:00	EST
4/30/1939	02:00	EDT
9/24/1939	02:00	EST
4/28/1940	02:00	EDT
9/29/1940	02:00	EST
4/27/1941	02:00	EDT
9/28/1941	02:00	EST
2/09/1942	02:00	EWT
9/30/1945	02:00	EST
4/27/1947	02:00	US#2

VT # 26		
Before 11/18/1883		LMT
11/18/1883	12:00	EST
3/31/1918	02:00	EWT
10/27/1918	02:00	EST
3/30/1919	02:00	EWT
10/26/1919	02:00	EST
4/24/1938	02:00	EDT
9/25/1938	02:00	EST
4/30/1939	02:00	EDT
9/24/1939	02:00	EST
4/28/1940	02:00	EDT
9/29/1940	02:00	EST
4/27/1941	02:00	EDT
9/28/1941	02:00	EST
2/09/1942	02:00	EWT
9/30/1945	02:00	EST
4/25/1948	02:00	US#2

VT # 27		
Before 11/18/1883		LMT
11/18/1883	12:00	EST
3/31/1918	02:00	EWT
10/27/1918	02:00	EST
3/30/1919	02:00	EWT
10/26/1919	02:00	EST
4/25/1937	02:00	US#2

VT # 28		
Before 11/18/1883		LMT
11/18/1883	12:00	EST
3/31/1918	02:00	EWT
10/27/1918	02:00	EST
3/30/1919	02:00	EWT
10/26/1919	02:00	EST
4/24/1938	02:00	EDT
9/25/1938	02:00	EST
4/30/1939	02:00	EDT
9/24/1939	02:00	EST
4/28/1940	02:00	EDT
9/29/1940	02:00	EST
4/27/1941	02:00	EDT
9/28/1941	02:00	EST
2/09/1942	02:00	EWT
9/30/1945	02:00	EST
4/25/1948	02:00	EDT
9/26/1948	02:00	EST
4/24/1949	02:00	EDT
9/25/1949	02:00	EST
4/30/1950	02:00	EDT
9/24/1950	02:00	EST
4/24/1955	02:00	US#2

VT # 29		
Before 11/18/1883		LMT
11/18/1883	12:00	EST
3/31/1918	02:00	EWT
10/27/1918	02:00	EST
3/30/1919	02:00	EWT
10/26/1919	02:00	EST
4/29/1934	02:00	EDT
9/30/1934	02:00	EST
4/28/1935	02:00	EDT
9/29/1935	02:00	EST
4/26/1936	02:00	EDT
9/27/1936	02:00	EST
4/25/1937	02:00	EDT
9/26/1937	02:00	EST
4/24/1938	02:00	EDT
9/25/1938	02:00	EST
4/30/1939	02:00	EDT
9/24/1939	02:00	EST
4/28/1940	02:00	EDT
9/29/1940	02:00	EST
4/27/1941	02:00	EDT
9/28/1941	02:00	EST
2/09/1942	02:00	EWT
9/30/1945	02:00	EST
4/27/1947	02:00	EDT
9/28/1947	02:00	EST
4/29/1951	02:00	US#2

VT # 30		
Before 11/18/1883		LMT
11/18/1883	12:00	EST
3/31/1918	02:00	EWT
10/27/1918	02:00	EST
3/30/1919	02:00	EWT
10/26/1919	02:00	EST
4/30/1939	02:00	EDT
9/24/1939	02:00	EST
4/28/1940	02:00	EDT
9/29/1940	02:00	EST
4/27/1941	02:00	EDT
9/28/1941	02:00	EST
2/09/1942	02:00	EWT
9/30/1945	02:00	EST
4/27/1947	02:00	US#2

VT # 31		
Before 11/18/1883		LMT
11/18/1883	12:00	EST
3/31/1918	02:00	EWT
10/27/1918	02:00	EST
3/30/1919	02:00	EWT
10/26/1919	02:00	EST
4/24/1938	02:00	EDT
9/25/1938	02:00	EST
2/09/1942	02:00	EWT
9/30/1945	02:00	EST
4/24/1949	02:00	US#2

VT # 32		
Before 11/18/1883		LMT
11/18/1883	12:00	EST
3/31/1918	02:00	EWT
10/27/1918	02:00	EST
3/30/1919	02:00	EWT
10/26/1919	02:00	EST
4/30/1939	02:00	EDT
9/24/1939	02:00	EST
4/28/1940	02:00	EDT
9/29/1940	02:00	EST
4/27/1941	02:00	EDT
9/28/1941	02:00	EST
2/09/1942	02:00	EWT
9/30/1945	02:00	EST
4/29/1951	02:00	US#2

VT # 33		
Before 11/10/1883		LMT
11/18/1883	12:00	EST
3/31/1918	02:00	EWT
10/27/1918	02:00	EST
3/30/1919	02:00	EWT
10/26/1919	02:00	EST
4/28/1935	02:00	EDT
9/29/1935	02:00	EST
4/26/1936	02:00	EDT
9/27/1936	02:00	EST
4/24/1938	02:00	US#2

VT # 34		
Before 11/18/1883		LMT
11/18/1883	12:00	EST
3/31/1918	02:00	EWT
10/27/1918	02:00	EST
3/30/1919	02:00	EWT
10/26/1919	02:00	EST
4/30/1939	02:00	EDT
9/24/1939	02:00	EST
4/28/1940	02:00	EDT
9/29/1940	02:00	EST
4/27/1941	02:00	EDT
9/28/1941	02:00	EST
2/09/1942	02:00	EWT
9/30/1945	02:00	EST
4/27/1947	02:00	EDT
9/28/1947	02:00	EST
4/25/1948	02:00	EDT
9/26/1948	02:00	EST
4/24/1949	02:00	EDT
9/25/1949	02:00	EST
4/24/1955	02:00	US#2

VT # 35		
Before 11/18/1883		LMT
11/18/1883	12:00	EST
3/31/1918	02:00	EWT
10/27/1918	02:00	EST
3/30/1919	02:00	EWT
10/26/1919	02:00	EST
4/30/1939	02:00	EDT
9/24/1939	02:00	EST
4/28/1940	02:00	EDT
9/29/1940	02:00	EST
4/27/1941	02:00	EDT
9/28/1941	02:00	EST
2/09/1942	02:00	EWT
9/30/1945	02:00	EST
4/28/1946	02:00	EDT
9/29/1946	02:00	EST
4/25/1948	02:00	US#2

VT # 36		
Before 11/18/1883		LMT
11/18/1883	12:00	EST
3/31/1918	02:00	EWT
10/27/1918	02:00	EST
3/30/1919	02:00	EWT
10/26/1919	02:00	EST
4/25/1937	02:00	EDT
9/26/1937	02:00	EST
4/28/1940	02:00	US#2

VT # 37		
Before 11/18/1883		LMT
11/18/1883	12:00	EST
3/31/1918	02:00	EWT
10/27/1918	02:00	EST
3/30/1919	02:00	EWT
10/26/1919	02:00	EST
4/25/1937	02:00	EDT
9/26/1937	02:00	EST
4/24/1938	02:00	EDT
9/25/1938	02:00	EST
4/30/1939	02:00	EDT
9/24/1939	02:00	EST
4/28/1940	02:00	EDT
9/29/1940	02:00	EST
4/27/1941	02:00	EDT
9/28/1941	02:00	EST
2/09/1942	02:00	EWT
9/30/1945	02:00	EST
4/24/1955	02:00	US#2

VT # 38		
Before 11/18/1883		LMT
11/18/1883	12:00	EST
3/31/1918	02:00	EWT
10/27/1918	02:00	EST
3/30/1919	02:00	EWT
10/26/1919	02:00	EST
4/27/1941	02:00	EDT
9/28/1941	02:00	EST
2/09/1942	02:00	EWT
9/30/1945	02:00	EST
4/27/1947	02:00	US#2

VT # 39		
Before 11/18/1883		LMT
11/18/1883	12:00	EST
3/31/1918	02:00	EWT
10/27/1918	02:00	EST
3/30/1919	02:00	EWT
10/26/1919	02:00	EST
4/27/1941	02:00	EDT
9/28/1941	02:00	EST
2/09/1942	02:00	EWT
9/30/1945	02:00	EST
4/29/1951	02:00	US#2

VT # 40		
Before 11/18/1883		LMT
11/18/1883	12:00	EST
3/31/1918	02:00	EWT
10/27/1918	02:00	EST
3/30/1919	02:00	EWT
10/26/1919	02:00	EST
2/09/1942	02:00	EWT
9/30/1945	02:00	EST
4/24/1949	02:00	EDT
9/25/1949	02:00	EST
4/29/1951	02:00	US#2

VT # 41		
Before 11/18/1883		LMT
11/18/1883	12:00	EST
3/31/1918	02:00	EWT
10/27/1918	02:00	EST
3/30/1919	02:00	EWT
10/26/1919	02:00	EST
2/09/1942	02:00	EWT

TIME TABLES

9/30/1945	02:00	EST
4/24/1949	02:00	EDT
9/25/1949	02:00	EST
4/29/1951	02:00	EDT
9/30/1951	02:00	EST
4/26/1953	02:00	US#2

VT # 42

Before 11/18/1883		LMT
11/18/1883	12:00	EST
3/31/1918	02:00	EWT
10/27/1918	02:00	EST
3/30/1919	02:00	EWT
10/26/1919	02:00	EST
4/28/1940	02:00	EDT
9/29/1940	02:00	EST
5/18/1941	02:00	EDT
9/21/1941	02:00	EST
2/09/1942	02:00	EWT
9/30/1945	02:00	EST
4/24/1955	02:00	US#2

VT # 43

Before 11/18/1883		LMT
11/18/1883	12:00	EST
3/31/1918	02:00	EWT
10/27/1918	02:00	EST
3/30/1919	02:00	EWT
10/26/1919	02:00	EST
4/28/1940	02:00	EDT
9/29/1940	02:00	EST
5/01/1941	02:00	EDT
10/01/1941	02:00	EST
2/09/1942	02:00	EWT
9/30/1945	02:00	EST
4/25/1948	02:00	US#2

VT # 44

Before 11/18/1883		LMT
11/18/1883	12:00	EST
3/31/1918	02:00	EWT
10/27/1918	02:00	EST
3/30/1919	02:00	EWT
10/26/1919	02:00	EST
5/28/1939	02:00	EDT
9/10/1939	02:00	EST
5/26/1940	02:00	EDT
9/08/1940	02:00	EST
5/25/1941	02:00	EDT
9/14/1941	02:00	EST
2/09/1942	02:00	EWT
9/30/1945	02:00	EST
4/27/1952	02:00	EDT
9/28/1952	02:00	EST
4/24/1955	02:00	US#2

VT # 45

Before 11/18/1883		LMT
11/18/1883	12:00	EST
3/31/1918	02:00	EWT
10/27/1918	02:00	EST
3/30/1919	02:00	EWT
10/26/1919	02:00	EST
4/24/1938	02:00	EDT
9/25/1938	02:00	EST
4/30/1939	02:00	EDT
9/24/1939	02:00	EST
4/28/1940	02:00	EDT
9/29/1940	02:00	EST
4/27/1941	02:00	EDT
9/28/1941	02:00	EST
2/09/1942	02:00	EWT
9/30/1945	02:00	EST
4/28/1946	02:00	EDT
9/29/1946	02:00	EST
4/27/1947	02:00	EDT
9/28/1947	02:00	EST
4/25/1948	02:00	EDT
9/26/1948	02:00	EST
5/01/1949	02:00	EDT
9/25/1949	02:00	EST
4/25/1954	02:00	US#2

VT # 46

Before 11/18/1883		LMT
11/18/1883	12:00	EST
3/31/1918	02:00	EWT
10/27/1918	02:00	EST
3/30/1919	02:00	EWT
10/26/1919	02:00	EST
5/07/1939	02:00	EDT
9/24/1939	02:00	EST
5/05/1940	02:00	EDT
9/29/1940	02:00	EST
5/04/1941	02:00	EDT
9/28/1941	02:00	EST
2/09/1942	02:00	EWT
9/30/1945	02:00	EST
4/24/1955	02:00	US#2

VT # 47

Before 11/18/1883		LMT
11/18/1883	12:00	EST
3/31/1918	02:00	EWT
10/27/1918	02:00	EST
3/30/1919	02:00	EWT
10/26/1919	02:00	EST
5/01/1938	02:00	EDT
10/01/1938	02:00	EST
5/01/1939	02:00	EDT
10/01/1939	02:00	EST
5/01/1940	02:00	EDT
10/01/1940	02:00	EST
5/01/1941	02:00	EDT
10/01/1941	02:00	EST
2/09/1942	02:00	US#2

VT # 48

Before 11/18/1883		LMT
11/18/1883	12:00	EST
3/31/1918	02:00	EWT
10/27/1918	02:00	EST
3/30/1919	02:00	EWT
10/26/1919	02:00	EST
5/26/1939	02:00	EDT
9/03/1939	02:00	EST
5/26/1940	02:00	EDT
9/01/1940	02:00	EST
5/25/1941	02:00	EDT
9/07/1941	02:00	EST
2/09/1942	02:00	EWT
9/30/1945	02:00	EST
4/25/1948	02:00	EDT
9/26/1948	02:00	EST
4/24/1955	02:00	US#2

VT # 49

Before 11/18/1883		LMT
11/18/1883	12:00	EST
3/31/1918	02:00	EWT
10/27/1918	02:00	EST
3/30/1919	02:00	EWT
10/26/1919	02:00	EST
4/30/1939	02:00	EDT
9/24/1939	02:00	EST
5/01/1940	02:00	EDT
10/01/1940	02:00	EST
5/01/1941	02:00	EDT
10/01/1941	02:00	EST
2/09/1942	02:00	US#2

VT # 50

Before 11/18/1883		LMT
11/18/1883	12:00	EST
3/31/1918	02:00	EWT
10/27/1918	02:00	EST
3/30/1919	02:00	EWT
10/26/1919	02:00	EST
4/24/1938	02:00	EDT
10/29/1938	02:00	EST
4/30/1939	02:00	EDT
9/24/1939	02:00	EST
5/01/1940	02:00	EDT
10/01/1940	02:00	EST
5/01/1941	02:00	EDT
10/01/1941	02:00	EST
2/09/1942	02:00	EWT
9/30/1945	02:00	EST
4/29/1951	02:00	US#2

VT # 51

Before 11/18/1883		LMT
11/18/1883	12:00	EST
3/31/1918	02:00	EWT
10/27/1918	02:00	EST
3/30/1919	02:00	EWT
10/26/1919	02:00	EST
4/25/1937	02:00	EDT
9/26/1937	02:00	EST
5/29/1938	02:00	EDT
9/11/1938	02:00	EST
5/28/1939	02:00	EDT
9/10/1939	02:00	EST
5/26/1940	02:00	EDT
9/08/1940	02:00	EST
5/25/1941	02:00	EDT
9/14/1941	02:00	EST
2/09/1942	02:00	EWT
9/30/1945	02:00	EST
4/28/1946	02:00	US#2

VT # 52

Before 11/18/1883		LMT
11/18/1883	12:00	EST
3/31/1918	02:00	EWT
10/27/1918	02:00	EST
3/30/1919	02:00	EWT
10/26/1919	02:00	EST
4/28/1940	02:00	EDT
10/27/1940	02:00	EST
4/27/1941	02:00	EDT
10/26/1941	02:00	EST
2/09/1942	02:00	EWT
9/30/1945	02:00	EST
4/24/1955	02:00	US#2

VT # 53

Before 11/18/1883		LMT
11/18/1883	12:00	EST
3/31/1918	02:00	EWT
10/27/1918	02:00	EST
3/30/1919	02:00	EWT
10/26/1919	02:00	EST
4/28/1940	02:00	EDT
9/29/1940	02:00	EST
4/27/1941	02:00	EDT
9/28/1941	02:00	EST
2/09/1942	02:00	EWT
9/30/1945	02:00	EST
4/27/1947	02:00	US#2

VT # 54

Before 11/18/1883		LMT
11/18/1883	12:00	EST
3/31/1918	02:00	EWT
10/27/1918	02:00	EST
3/30/1919	02:00	EWT
10/26/1919	02:00	EST
2/09/1942	02:00	EWT
9/30/1945	02:00	EST
4/29/1951	02:00	EDT
9/30/1951	02:00	EST
4/24/1955	02:00	US#2

VT # 55

Before 11/18/1883		LMT
11/18/1883	12:00	EST
3/31/1918	02:00	EWT
10/27/1918	02:00	EST
3/30/1919	02:00	EWT
10/26/1919	02:00	EST
2/09/1942	02:00	EWT
9/30/1945	02:00	EST
4/29/1951	02:00	EDT
9/30/1951	02:00	EST
4/27/1952	02:00	EDT
9/28/1952	02:00	EST
4/26/1953	02:00	EDT
9/27/1953	02:00	EST
4/25/1954	02:00	EDT
9/26/1954	02:00	EST
4/24/1955	02:00	US#2

VT # 56

Before 11/18/1883		LMT
11/18/1883	12:00	EST
3/31/1918	02:00	EWT
10/27/1918	02:00	EST
3/30/1919	02:00	EWT
10/26/1919	02:00	EST
5/29/1938	02:00	EDT
9/25/1938	02:00	EST
4/30/1939	02:00	EDT
9/24/1939	02:00	EST
4/28/1940	02:00	EDT
9/29/1940	02:00	EST
4/27/1941	02:00	EDT
9/28/1941	02:00	EST
2/09/1942	02:00	EWT
9/30/1945	02:00	EST
4/27/1947	02:00	US#2

VT # 57

Before 11/18/1883		LMT
11/18/1883	12:00	EST
3/31/1918	02:00	EWT
10/27/1918	02:00	EST
3/30/1919	02:00	EWT
10/26/1919	02:00	EST
4/25/1937	02:00	EDT
9/26/1937	02:00	EST
4/30/1939	02:00	US#2

VT # 58

Before 11/18/1883		LMT
11/18/1883	12:00	EST
3/31/1918	02:00	EWT
10/27/1918	02:00	EST
3/30/1919	02:00	EWT
10/26/1919	02:00	EST
4/28/1935	02:00	EDT
9/29/1935	02:00	EST
4/26/1936	02:00	EDT
9/27/1936	02:00	EST
4/25/1937	02:00	EDT
9/26/1937	02:00	EST
4/24/1938	02:00	EDT
9/25/1938	02:00	EST
4/30/1939	02:00	EDT
9/24/1939	02:00	EST
4/28/1940	02:00	EDT
9/29/1940	02:00	EST
4/27/1941	02:00	EDT
9/28/1941	02:00	EST
2/09/1942	02:00	EWT
9/30/1945	02:00	EST
4/24/1955	02:00	US#2

VT # 59

Before 11/18/1883		LMT
11/18/1883	12:00	EST
3/31/1918	02:00	EWT
10/27/1918	02:00	EST
3/30/1919	02:00	EWT
10/26/1919	02:00	EST
4/24/1938	02:00	EDT
9/25/1938	02:00	EST
4/30/1939	02:00	EDT
9/24/1939	02:00	EST
2/09/1942	02:00	EWT
9/30/1945	02:00	EST
4/28/1946	02:00	US#2

VT # 60

Before 11/18/1883		LMT
11/18/1883	12:00	EST
3/31/1918	02:00	EWT
10/27/1918	02:00	EST
3/30/1919	02:00	EWT
10/26/1919	02:00	EST
4/30/1939	02:00	EDT
9/24/1939	02:00	EST
4/27/1941	02:00	EDT
9/28/1941	02:00	EST
2/09/1942	02:00	EWT
9/30/1945	02:00	EST
4/24/1955	02:00	US#2

VT # 61

Before 11/18/1883		LMT
11/18/1883	12:00	EST
3/31/1918	02:00	EWT
10/27/1918	02:00	EST
3/30/1919	02:00	EWT
10/26/1919	02:00	EST
5/08/1937	02:00	EDT
9/26/1937	02:00	EST
4/24/1938	02:00	US#2

VT # 62

Before 11/18/1883		LMT
11/18/1883	12:00	EST
3/31/1918	02:00	EWT
10/27/1918	02:00	EST
3/30/1919	02:00	EWT
10/26/1919	02:00	EST
4/25/1937	02:00	EDT
9/26/1937	02:00	EST
4/24/1938	02:00	EDT
9/25/1938	02:00	EST
4/30/1939	02:00	EDT
9/24/1939	02:00	EST
4/28/1940	02:00	EDT
9/29/1940	02:00	EST
4/27/1941	02:00	EDT
9/28/1941	02:00	EST
2/09/1942	02:00	EWT
9/30/1945	02:00	EST
4/27/1947	02:00	US#2

VT # 63

Before 11/18/1883		LMT
11/18/1883	12:00	EST
3/31/1918	02:00	EWT
10/27/1918	02:00	EST
3/30/1919	02:00	EWT
10/26/1919	02:00	EST
4/30/1939	02:00	EDT
9/24/1939	02:00	EST
4/27/1941	02:00	EDT
9/28/1941	02:00	EST
2/09/1942	02:00	EWT
9/30/1945	02:00	EST
4/27/1947	02:00	US#2

VT # 64

Before 11/18/1883		LMT
11/18/1883	12:00	EST
3/31/1918	02:00	EWT
10/27/1918	02:00	EST
3/30/1919	02:00	EWT
10/26/1919	02:00	EST
4/24/1938	02:00	EDT
9/25/1938	02:00	EST
4/30/1939	02:00	EDT
9/24/1939	02:00	EST
4/27/1941	02:00	EDT
9/28/1941	02:00	EST
2/09/1942	02:00	EWT
9/30/1945	02:00	EST
4/27/1947	02:00	US#2

VT # 65

Before 11/18/1883		LMT
11/18/1883	12:00	EST
3/31/1918	02:00	EWT
10/27/1918	02:00	EST
3/30/1919	02:00	EWT
10/26/1919	02:00	EST
4/25/1937	02:00	EDT
9/26/1937	02:00	EST
4/24/1938	02:00	EDT
9/25/1938	02:00	EST
4/30/1939	02:00	EDT
9/24/1939	02:00	EST
4/28/1940	02:00	EDT
9/29/1940	02:00	EST
4/27/1941	02:00	EDT
9/28/1941	02:00	EST
2/09/1942	02:00	EWT
9/30/1945	02:00	EST
4/28/1946	02:00	EDT
9/29/1946	02:00	EST
4/25/1948	02:00	US#2

VT # 66

Before 11/18/1883		LMT
11/18/1883	12:00	EST
3/31/1918	02:00	EWT
10/27/1918	02:00	EST
3/30/1919	02:00	EWT
10/26/1919	02:00	EST
4/24/1938	02:00	EDT
9/25/1938	02:00	EST
4/30/1939	02:00	EDT
9/24/1939	02:00	EST
4/28/1940	02:00	EDT
9/29/1940	02:00	EST
4/27/1941	02:00	EDT
9/28/1941	02:00	EST
2/09/1942	02:00	EWT
9/30/1945	02:00	EST
4/25/1948	02:00	EDT
9/26/1948	02:00	EST
4/24/1949	02:00	EDT
9/25/1949	02:00	EST
4/30/1950	02:00	EDT
9/24/1950	02:00	EST
4/29/1951	02:00	EDT
9/30/1951	02:00	EST
4/26/1953	02:00	US#2

VT # 67

Before 11/18/1883		LMT
11/18/1883	12:00	EST
3/31/1918	02:00	EWT
10/27/1918	02:00	EST
3/30/1919	02:00	EWT
10/26/1919	02:00	EST
2/09/1942	02:00	EWT
9/30/1945	02:00	EST
4/28/1946	02:00	EDT
9/29/1946	02:00	EST
4/25/1948	02:00	EDT
9/26/1948	02:00	EST
4/27/1952	02:00	US#2

COUNTIES

1 Addison
2 Bennington
3 Caledonia
4 Chittenden
5 Essex
6 Franklin
7 Grand Isle
8 Lamoille
9 Orange
10 Orleans
11 Rutland
12 Washington
13 Windham
14 Windsor

Abnaki 7	11	44N49	73w18	4:53:12
Adamant 12	1	44N19'45	72w30'12	4:50:01
Adams Landing 7	38	44N44'10	73w19'57	4:53:20
Addison 1	1	44N05'19	73w18'11	4:53:13
Albany 10	5	44N43'51	72w22'49	4:49:31
Albany Center 10	5	44N44'12	72w21'00	4:49:24
Alburg 7	31	44N58'30	73w18'02	4:53:12
Alburg Center 7	31	44N57'13	73w16'13	4:53:05
Alburg Springs 7	31	44N59	73w13	4:52:52
Alfrecha 11	24	43N33'51	72w58'23	4:51:54
Alpine Village 12	1	44N04'07	72w50'05	4:51:20
Ames Hill 13	1	42N51'17	72w41'17	4:50:45
Amsden 14	1	43N24'21	72w30'23	4:50:02
Andover 14	5	43N16'38	72w41'50	4:50:47
Arlington 2	27	43N04'29	73w09'16	4:52:37
Arnold Bay 1	66	44N10	73w15	4:53:00
Ascutney 14	6	43N24'25	72w24'27	4:49:38
Athens 13	1	43N08'01	72w34'06	4:50:16
Avalon Beach 11	1	43N38'24	73w13'32	4:52:54
Averill 5	1	44N59'53	71w42'39	4:46:51
Bailey Mills 14	1	43N30'19	72w34'13	4:50:17
Baileys Mills 14	10	43N17'52	72w36'19	4:50:25
Bakersfield 6	12	44N46'55	72w48'12	4:51:13
Baltimore 14	1	43N21'37	72w34'25	4:50:18
Barnard 14	1	43N43'43	72w37'10	4:50:29
Barnet 3	17	44N17'49	72w02'59	4:48:12
Barnumtown 1	63	44N12'29	73w09'50	4:52:39
Barnumville 2	62	43N11'23	73w01'18	4:52:05
Barre 12	27	44N11'49	72w30'09	4:50:01
Barton 10	17	44N44'53	72w10'36	4:48:42
Bartonsville 13	39	43N13'32	72w32'10	4:50:09
Basin Harbor 1	66	44N10	73w15	4:53:00
Bayside 4	15	44N30	73w11	4:52:44
Beanville 9	2	43N54'52	72w16'53	4:49:08
Beartown 2	62	43N11'23	73w07'48	4:52:31
Beaulieus Corner 6	1	44N56'48	73w00'58	4:52:04
Beebe Plain 10	37	45N00'19	72w08'28	4:48:34
Beecher Falls 5	26	45N00'29	71w30'30	4:46:02
Beldens 1	56	44N03'04	73w10'33	4:52:42

Bellows Falls 13 2 43N08'00 72W26'40 4:49:47
Belmont 11 1 43N24'56 72W49'22 4:51:17
Belvedere Junction 8 1 44N44'13 72W44'35 4:50:58
Belvidere 8 1 44N45'00 72W41'30 4:50:46
Belvidere Corners 8 1 44N45 72W41 4:50:44
Belvidere Junction 8 1 44N41 72W46 4:51:04
Bennington 2 23 42N52'41 73W11'50 4:52:47
Bennington College 2 23 42N53 73W12 4:52:48
Benson 11 1 43N42'25 73W18'42 4:53:15
Benson Landing 11 1 43N43'42 73W22'05 4:53:28
Berkshire 6 1 44N58'18 72W46'33 4:51:06
Berlin 12 12 44N12'36 72W34'35 4:50:18
Bethel 14 25 43N50'00 72W38'04 4:50:32
Bethel Gilead 14 2 43N55 72W40 4:50:40
Binghamville 6 1 44N40'30 72W55'26 4:51:42
Birdland 7 1 44N49 73W18 4:53:12
Birdport 1 1 43N59'06 73W18'47 4:53:15
Bliss Pond 12 1 44N20 72W31 4:50:04
Blissville 11 1 43N35'35 73W13'49 4:52:55
Bloomfield 5 12 44N45'14 71W37'58 4:46:32
Blossoms Corners 11 1 43N21 73W15 4:53:00
Bolton 4 1 44N22'22 72W52'52 4:51:31
Bolton Valley 4 49 44N24 73W00 4:52:00
Boltonville 9 1 44N10'15 72W06'01 4:48:24
Bomoseen 11 1 43N38'37 73W11'57 4:52:48
Bondville 2 1 43N09 72W53 4:51:32
Bordoville 6 1 44N50'36 72W49'09 4:51:17
Bouplon Corner 2 16 42N59'41 73W16'01 4:53:04
Bowlsville 11 1 43N26'52 72W51'09 4:51:25
Bowman Corners 4 27 44N34'25 73W03'27 4:52:14
Bradford 9 33 43N59'33 72W07'46 4:48:31
Bradford Center 9 33 44N00'47 72W10'16 4:48:41
Bragg 14 35 43N43'11 72W20'22 4:49:21
Braintree 9 12 43N58 72W43 4:50:52
Brandon 11 2 43N47'53 73W05'17 4:52:21
Brattleboro 13 13 42N51'03 72W33'30 4:50:14
Bread Loaf 1 56 43N57'12 72W59'35 4:51:58
Brewers Corner 11 17 43N37'09 72W52'38 4:51:31
Bridgewater 14 17 43N35'17 72W37'32 4:50:30
Bridgewater Center 14 1 43N36'59 72W39'35 4:50:38
Bridgewater Corners 14 1 43N35'18 72W39'23 4:50:38
Bridport 1 1 43N59 73W21 4:53:24
Brighton 5 1 44N48 71W52 4:47:28
Brimstone Corner 9 1 43N56'16 72W15'58 4:49:04
Brimstone Corners 11 1 43N21 73W11 4:52:44
Bristol 1 19 44N08'00 73W04'46 4:52:19
Brockways Mills 13 1 43N12'25 72W31'00 4:50:04
Brookfield 9 17 44N02'32 72W36'14 4:50:25
Brookfield Center 9 17 44N01'13 72W36'18 4:50:25
Brookline 13 12 43N01'54 72W36'07 4:50:24
Brookside 4 1 44N37 73W01 4:52:04
Brookside 13 1 42N57 72W46 4:51:04
Brooksville 1 56 44N03'56 73W10'24 4:52:42
Brownington Center 10 1 44N49'22 72W08'55 4:48:36
Brownington Village 10 1 44N49'51 72W10'20 4:48:41
Browns Corners 6 1 44N58'06 72W58'09 4:51:53
Browns Mill 5 12 44N41'08 71W38'06 4:46:32
Brownsville 14 1 43N28'07 72W28'17 4:49:53
Brunswick 5 1 44N44 71W40 4:46:40
Brunswick Springs 5 12 44N44'11 71W37'58 4:46:32
Buck Hollow 6 1 44N40 73W01 4:52:04
Buels Gore 4 1 44N13 72W57 4:51:48
Bullthroat 5 1 44N39'50 71W38'56 4:46:36
Burke 3 17 44N37 71W56 4:47:44
Burke Hollow 3 17 44N37'21 71W57'00 4:47:48
Burke Mountain 3 1 44N35 71W56 4:47:44
Burlington 4 15 44N28'33 73W12'45 4:52:51
Burnham Hill 12 1 44N30 72W22 4:49:28
Burnham Hollow 11 1 43N29'03 73W08'52 4:52:35
Butternut 11 1 43N22'31 73W12'10 4:52:49
Buttlers Corners 4 27 44N30'37 73W05'04 4:52:20
Button Bay 1 66 44N10 73W15 4:53:00
Cabot 12 42 44N24'05 72W18'46 4:49:15
Cadys Falls 8 1 44N34'41 72W36'44 4:50:27
Calais 12 1 44N22 72W27 4:49:48
Cambridge 8 1 44N38'41 72W52'36 4:51:30
Cambridge Junction 8 1 44N38'57 72W48'50 4:51:15
Cambridgeport 13 1 43N09'05 72W33'39 4:50:15
Campbell Corner 9 1 43N50'01 72W18'41 4:49:15
Camp Brook 14 1 43N51'01 72W41'37 4:50:46
Camp Grounds 6 1 44N54'32 72W53'02 4:51:32
Camp Maquam 6 51 44N54'10 73W09'58 4:52:40
Canaan 5 2 44N59'46 71W32'20 4:46:09
Castleton 11 26 43N36'38 73W10'49 4:52:43
Castleton Corners 11 1 43N36'30 73W12'30 4:52:50
Cavendish 14 3 43N22'55 72W36'31 4:50:26
Cavendish Center 14 1 43N24'36 72W36'22 4:50:25
Cedar Beach 4 1 44N17'30 73W18'12 4:53:13
Center Rutland 11 24 43N36'16 73W00'43 4:52:03
Centertown 14 1 43N39'39 72W22'54 4:49:32
Centerville 8 1 44N37'09 72W35'12 4:50:21
Centerville 14 1 43N40'35 72W23'13 4:49:33
Charleston 10 1 44N51 72W01 4:48:04
Charlotte 4 43 44N18'35 73W15'41 4:53:03
Chateauguay 14 1 43N39'37 72W41'43 4:50:47
Checkerberry 4 2 44N37'45 73W08'40 4:52:35
Chelsea 9 12 43N59'23 72W26'53 4:49:48
Chester 14 34 43N15'46 72W35'44 4:50:23
Chester Depot 14 10 43N16 72W35 4:50:20
Chimney Corner 4 2 44N35'17 73W10'00 4:52:40
Chimney Point 1 66 44N02'10 73W25'07 4:53:40
Chipman Lake 11 36 43N21 73W00 4:52:00
Chipmans Point 1 1 43N48 73W18 4:53:12
Chippenhook 11 27 43N31'06 73W00'52 4:52:03
Chiselville 2 27 43N04'16 73W08'06 4:52:32
Chittenden 11 1 43N42'28 72W56'55 4:51:48
Clarendon 11 24 43N30'58 72W58'13 4:51:53
Clarendon Springs 11 27 43N32'52 73W01'22 4:52:05
Cleveland Corners 8 1 44N35'37 72W33'47 4:50:15
Cloverdale 4 1 44N36'23 72W55'54 4:51:44
Colbyville 12 1 44N21'01 72W44'34 4:50:58
Colchester 4 15 44N32'38 73W08'54 4:52:36
Cold River 11 30 43N32'22 72W52'32 4:51:30
Cold Spring 11 1 43N40'17 73W24'26 4:53:38
Coleman Corner 1 7 44N15'31 73W13'20 4:52:53
Coles Corner 3 2 44N29'37 72W03'29 4:48:14
Concord 5 2 44N25'44 71W53'26 4:47:34
Concord Corner 5 1 44N24'05 71W51'43 4:47:27
Cookville (Corinth P O) 9 1 44N01'25 72W17'25 4:49:10
Copperfield 9 1 43N58 72W19 4:49:16
Copper Flat 9 1 43N50'06 72W20'04 4:49:20
Corinth 9 1 44N02 72W17 4:49:08
Corinth Corner 9 1 44N01'20 72W16'23 4:49:06
Corinth Corners 9 1 44N00'36 72W20'58 4:49:24
Cornwall 1 1 43N57'39 73W12'39 4:52:51
Coventry 10 1 44N51'56 72W15'55 4:49:04
Cozy Corner 4 2 44N37'25 73W07'06 4:52:28
Craftsbury 10 17 44N38'12 72W22'23 4:49:30
Craftsbury Common 10 1 44N39 72W23 4:49:32
Cream Hill 1 1 43N55'53 73W20'25 4:53:22
Crown Point 1 66 44N10 73W15 4:53:00
Crystal Beach 11 1 43N39'34 73W11'26 4:52:46
Cuttingsville 11 30 43N29'18 72W52'58 4:51:32
Damon Crossing 5 1 44N31'40 71W49'08 4:47:17
Danby 11 36 43N20'46 72W59'45 4:51:59
Danby Four Corners 11 36 43N21'17 73W02'50 4:52:11
Danville 3 19 44N24'40 72W08'23 4:48:34
Danville Center 3 19 44N25'12 72W07'15 4:48:29
Derby Center (Derby P O) 10 37 44N56'52 72W08'00 4:48:32
Derby Line 10 37 45N00'18 72W05'58 4:48:24
Deweys Mills 14 1 43N38'29 72W24'20 4:49:37
Dorset 2 57 43N15'17 73W05'57 4:52:24
Dothan 14 35 43N41'50 72W20'37 4:49:22
Dover 13 17 42N56'37 72W48'16 4:51:13
Dowdey Corner 9 1 43N53'29 72W37'39 4:50:31
Downers 14 1 43N24'01 72W30'53 4:50:04
Downingville 1 1 44N07'59 72W58'58 4:51:56
Dows 3 1 44N30 72W22 4:49:28
Dows Crossing 3 1 44N30'03 72W17'14 4:49:09
Dowsville 12 1 44N16'21 72W49'29 4:51:18
Dummerston 13 5 42N56 72W35 4:50:20
Dummerston Center 13 2 42N56'12 72W34'22 4:50:17
Duxbury 12 1 44N19'37 72W45'11 4:51:01
Eagle Point 10 1 44N56 72W13 4:48:52
East Albany 10 1 44N43'52 72W19'00 4:49:16
East Alburg 7 51 44N58'23 73W13'48 4:52:55
East Arlington 2 27 43N03'37 73W08'28 4:52:34
East Barnard 14 1 43N44'45 72W32'36 4:50:10
East Barnet Inwood Station 3 17 44N19'36 72W02'17 4:48:09
East Barre 12 27 44N09'29 72W27'03 4:49:48
East Berkshire 6 1 44N56'07 72W42'35 4:50:50
East Bethel 14 1 43N52'24 72W35'05 4:50:20
East Braintree 9 2 43N59'45 72W39'07 4:50:36
East Brighton 5 1 44N47'09 71W48'27 4:47:14
East Brookfield 9 2 44N01'39 72W34'19 4:50:17
East Burke 3 1 44N35'21 71W56'27 4:47:46
East Cabot 12 1 44N23'23 72W15'06 4:49:00
East Calais 12 1 44N21'59 72W25'49 4:49:43
East Cambridge 8 1 44N39 72W50 4:51:20
East Charleston 10 1 44N50'17 71W59'24 4:47:58
East Charlotte 4 1 44N19'11 73W11'21 4:52:45
East Clarendon 11 24 43N31'29 72W56'22 4:51:45
East Concord 5 6 44N25'29 71W45'15 4:47:01
East Corinth 9 1 44N03'50 72W13'22 4:48:53
East Craftsbury 10 1 44N38'33 72W20'37 4:49:22
East Dorset 2 57 43N14'23 73W00'35 4:52:02
East Dover 13 1 42N57'04 72W46'10 4:51:05
East Dummerston 13 2 42N55'56 72W33'13 4:50:13
East Elmore 8 1 44N33 72W27 4:49:48
East Enosburg 6 44 44N51'47 72W44'12 4:50:57
East Fairfield 6 1 44N47'04 72W51'32 4:51:26
East Fletcher 6 1 44N42'47 72W50'18 4:51:21
East Franklin 6 1 44N59'46 72W49'57 4:51:20
East Georgia 6 1 44N40'48 73W05'01 4:52:20
East Granville 1 64 44N01'01 72W45'36 4:51:02
East Greensboro 10 1 44N34'17 72W15'04 4:49:00
East Hardwick 3 1 44N31'18 72W18'33 4:49:14
East Haven 5 1 44N39'51 71W53'20 4:47:33
East Highgate 6 1 44N55'38 72W59'18 4:51:57
East Hubbardton 11 1 43N41'35 73W08'19 4:52:33
East Jamaica 13 1 43N04'26 72W44'07 4:50:56
East Johnson 8 1 44N38'24 72W39'43 4:50:39
East Kansas 2 27 43N03'28 73W07'08 4:52:29
East Lyndon 3 1 44N31'11 71W57'30 4:47:50
East Middlebury 1 1 43N58'24 73W06'24 4:52:26
East Monkton 1 1 44N12'32 73W06'54 4:52:28
East Montpelier 12 27 44N16'16 72W29'15 4:49:57
East Montpelier Center 12 27 44N17'01 72W31'33 4:50:06
East Orange 9 1 44N05'41 72W20'31 4:49:22
East Peacham 3 1 44N20'17 72W09'28 4:48:38
East Pittsford 11 24 43N40'16 72W56'36 4:51:46
East Poultney 11 1 43N31'35 73W12'18 4:52:49
East Putney 13 2 42N59'38 72W29'02 4:49:56
East Randolph 9 1 43N56'24 72W33'20 4:50:13
East Richford 10 1 45N00'40 72W35'11 4:50:21
East Roxbury 12 27 44N04'47 72W39'08 4:50:37
East Rupert 2 1 43N16'23 73W07'32 4:52:30
East Ryegate 3 1 44N12'18 72W03'42 4:48:15
East Saint Johnsbury 3 1 44N26'19 71W56'46 4:47:47
East Sheldon 6 1 44N53'56 72W52'28 4:51:30
East Shoreham (Shoreham Sta) 1 1 43N51'37 73W15'12 4:53:01
East Sutton Ridge 3 1 44N38 72W02 4:48:08
East Thetford 9 1 43N48'42 72W11'21 4:48:45
East Topsham 9 1 44N07'16 72W14'00 4:48:56
East Wallingford 11 2 43N26'58 72W52'35 4:51:30
East Warren 12 1 44N06'34 72W49'13 4:51:17
East Wells 11 12 43N25'18 73W08'30 4:52:34
Ecole Champlain 1 66 44N14'30 73W17'49 4:53:11
Eden 8 1 44N42'26 72W32'46 4:50:11
Eden Mills 8 1 44N42'25 72W32'46 4:50:11
Edgewater 12 1 44N19'25 72W20'05 4:49:20
Egypt 3 19 44N34'27 71W59'16 4:47:57
Egypt 6 1 44N47 72W52 4:51:28
Elmore 8 1 44N30 72W30 4:50:00
Ely 9 53 43N53 72W11 4:48:44
Emerson 14 1 43N50'27 72W47'51 4:51:11
English Mills 14 1 43N38'57 72W33'39 4:50:15
Enosburg Center 6 44 44N53'00 72W45'19 4:51:01
Enosburg Falls 6 44 44N54'25 72W48'25 4:51:14
Essex 4 27 44N30'43 73W03'36 4:52:14
Essex Junction 4 27 44N29'26 73W06'41 4:52:27
Ethan Allen Shopping Center 4 15 44N30 73W11 4:52:44
Evansville 10 1 44N48'11 72W07'51 4:48:31
Ewells Mills 3 17 44N21'36 72W10'19 4:48:41
Fairfax 6 17 44N39'55 73W00'33 4:52:02
Fairfax Falls 6 1 44N39'01 72W59'18 4:51:57
Fairfield 6 1 44N48'07 72W56'46 4:51:47
Fairground 6 1 44N53 72W57 4:51:48
Fair Haven 11 45 43N35'41 73W15'58 4:53:04
Fairlee 9 3 43N54'27 72W08'38 4:48:35
Farmingdale 1 1 43N57'53 73W08'08 4:52:33
Fays Corner 4 49 44N24'06 73W02'30 4:52:10
Fayston 12 1 44N13 72W51 4:51:24
Fayville 2 27 43N00'22 73W06'43 4:52:27
Felchville 14 1 43N27'23 72W32'18 4:50:09
Ferdinand 5 1 44N44 71W46 4:47:04
Fernville 1 1 43N51'39 73W04'06 4:52:16
Ferrisburg 1 7 44N12'20 73W14'48 4:52:59
Fieldsville 14 27 43N32'19 72W26'38 4:49:47
Fletcher 6 1 44N41'00 72W54'51 4:51:39
Florence 11 53 43N42'59 73W03'43 4:52:15
Folsom 3 1 44N35'03 71W58'51 4:47:55
Fonda 6 51 44N52'17 73W05'53 4:52:24
Forest Dale 11 1 43N49'40 73W03'15 4:52:13
Foxville 9 27 44N08'14 72W28'58 4:49:56
Franklin 6 1 44N58'55 72W55'00 4:51:40
Freedleyville 2 1 43N15'27 73W00'30 4:52:02
French Hollow 2 1 43N10'45 72W52'56 4:51:32
Gageville 13 1 43N08 72W27 4:49:48
Gallup Mills 5 1 44N34'30 71W47'05 4:47:08
Garfield 8 1 44N36'09 72W32'12 4:50:09
Gassetts 14 4 43N19'28 72W36'26 4:50:26
Gaysville 14 1 43N46'42 72W41'58 4:50:48
Gebbie Corner 10 12 44N37'55 72W17'07 4:49:08
Georgia Center 6 65 44N43'39 73W07'05 4:52:28
Georgia Plains 6 2 44N43'16 73W09'52 4:52:39
Gilberts Tannery 6 44 44N51'45 72W45'38 4:51:03
Gilman 5 58 44N24'44 71W43'22 4:46:53
Glover 10 1 44N42'16 72W12'51 4:48:51
Goodrich Corner 1 66 44N05'47 73W22'46 4:53:31
Goodrich Four Corners 14 35 43N45'18 72W16'47 4:49:07
Goose City 13 1 42N57'40 72W47'31 4:51:10
Goose Green 9 1 44N01 72W17 4:49:08
Gordon Landing 7 1 44N41'19 73W20'50 4:53:23
Gorhamtown 11 1 43N34'22 73W11'28 4:52:46
Goshen 1 1 43N50'58 73W01'21 4:52:05
Goshen 9 4 44N02'57 72W08'55 4:48:36

Goslants Mill 3 1 44N27'52 72w13'11 4:48:53
Goulds Mill 14 21 43N16'16 72w26'59 4:49:48
Grafton 13 17 43N10'18 72w36'24 4:50:26
Grahamville 14 61 43N25'11 72w42'26 4:50:50
Granby 5 1 44N34'14 71w45'33 4:47:02
Grand Isle 7 38 44N43'21 73w17'34 4:53:10
Grand Isle Station 7
1 44N42'02 73w19'47 4:53:19
Graniteville 12
27 44N09'04 72w29'36 4:49:58
Granville 1 12 43N59'05 72w50'48 4:51:23
Green Bay 3 1 44N18'17 72w12'10 4:48:49
Greenbush 14 1 43N25'01 72w31'06 4:50:04
Green Mountain 4
49 44N24 73w00 4:52:00
Green River 13 13 42N46'33 72w40'07 4:50:40
Greensboro 10 12 44N34'35 72w17'46 4:49:11
Greensboro Bend 10
1 44N32'56 72w15'55 4:49:04
Greens Corners 6
65 44N51'37 73w01'58 4:52:08
Groton 3 17 44N12'37 72w11'45 4:48:47
Grout 13 6 43N05 72w27 4:49:48
Grove 13 13 42N45'10 72w42'38 4:50:51
Guildhall 5 6 44N33'54 71w33'37 4:46:14
Guilford 13 17 42N49'04 72w34'37 4:50:18
Guilford Center 13
13 42N47'32 72w37'31 4:50:30
Halifax 13 1 42N46'11 72w44'45 4:50:59
Halls Lake 9 1 44N09 72w04 4:48:16
Hammondsville 14
1 43N29'25 72w33'13 4:50:13
Hancock 1 12 43N55'34 72w50'30 4:51:22
Hanksville 4 1 44N14'52 72w57'45 4:51:51
Hardscrabble 14
21 43N15'42 72w28'35 4:49:54
Hardwick 3 46 44N30'17 72w22'07 4:49:28
Hardwick Center 3
1 44N31'47 72w20'15 4:49:21
Hardwick Street 3
12 44N32'59 72w18'00 4:49:12
Harmonyville 13 1 43N02'18 72w39'47 4:50:39
Harrisville 13 13 42N48'56 72w44'34 4:50:58
Hartford 14 17 43N39'38 72w20'20 4:49:21
Hartland 14 59 43N32'26 72w23'58 4:49:36
Hartland Four Corners 14
59 43N32'47 72w25'30 4:49:42
Hartwellville 5 1 44N38'48 71w53'37 4:47:34
Harvey 3 1 44N23'00 72w08'38 4:48:35
Healdville 11 10 43N25'53 72w45'58 4:51:04
Heartwellville 2
1 42N49'47 72w59'17 4:51:57
Hectorville 10 1 44N50'18 72w36'32 4:50:26
Hewitts Corners 14
1 43N43'24 72w29'57 4:50:00
Highgate 6 60 44N58 73w02 4:52:08
Highgate Center 6
1 44N56'20 73w02'38 4:52:11
Highgate Falls 6
1 44N55'39 73w03'01 4:52:12
Highgate Springs 6
60 44N58'46 73w06'21 4:52:25
Hinesburg 4 17 44N19'45 73w06'40 4:52:27
Hinesburg 13 13 42N51 72w34 4:50:16
Holden 11 1 43N42 73w01 4:52:04
Holland 10 1 44N58'01 72w00'10 4:48:01
Hortonia 11 1 43N44'43 73w13'25 4:52:54
Hortonville 11 1 43N28'11 72w48'19 4:51:13
Hough Crossing 1
1 43N49'35 73w19'05 4:53:16
Houghtonville 13
1 43N11'50 72w38'47 4:50:35
Hubbard Corner 6
65 44N44'47 73w06'48 4:52:27
Hubbardton 11 1 43N42'26 73w11'05 4:52:44
Huntington 4 1 44N19'31 72w59'16 4:51:57
Huntington Center 4
1 44N17'49 72w58'05 4:51:52
Huntsville 6 1 44N41'59 72w59'04 4:51:56
Hutchins 10 1 44N51'34 72w36'37 4:50:26
Hyde Manor 11 1 43N47'00 73w12'11 4:52:49
Hyde Park 8 17 44N35'38 72w37'01 4:50:28
Hydeville 11 14 43N36'20 73w13'43 4:52:55
Indian Point 10 1 44N56 72w13 4:48:52
Inwood 3 1 44N18 72w03 4:48:12
Ira 11 1 43N32'04 73w03'45 4:52:15
Irasburg 10 12 44N48'12 72w16'48 4:49:07
Irasville 12 1 44N10'53 72w50'27 4:51:22
Island Pond 5 1 44N48'53 71w52'51 4:47:31
Isle la Motte 7 9 44N52'37 73w20'21 4:53:21
Ithiel Falls 8 1 44N38'57 72w43'30 4:50:54
Jackson Corner 9
52 44N05'14 72w31'03 4:50:04
Jacksonville 13 1 42N47'49 72w49'20 4:51:17
Jamaica 13 17 43N06'01 72w46'44 4:51:07
Jay 10 12 44N56'51 72w26'15 4:49:45
Jay Peak 10 1 45N00 72w24 4:49:36
Jeffersonville 8
19 44N38'38 72w49'47 4:51:19
Jenneville 14 27 43N32'04 72w29'23 4:49:58
Jericho 4 1 44N30'14 72w59'53 4:52:00
Jericho 14 35 43N42'10 72w22'25 4:49:30
Jericho Center 4
1 44N28'08 72w58'22 4:51:53
Jerusalem 1 1 44N10'11 72w58'15 4:51:53
Jerusalem 14 1 43N50'18 72w46'27 4:51:06
Joes Pond 3 1 44N25 72w12 4:48:48
Johnson 8 19 44N38'08 72w40'51 4:50:43
Jonesville 4 1 44N23'02 72w56'17 4:51:45
Kansas 2 27 43N03'28 73w07'53 4:52:32
Keeler Bay 7 1 44N39'35 73w19'12 4:53:17
Kendall 14 1 43N49 72w11 4:48:44
Kendricks Corner 14
1 43N20'44 72w31'18 4:50:05
Kents Corners 12
1 44N22'07 72w29'08 4:49:57
Killington 11 1 43N40 72w46 4:51:04
Kimball 10 1 44N45 72w11 4:48:44
Kirby 3 12 44N31 71w56 4:47:44
Kirby Corner 4 27 44N27'18 73w07'25 4:52:30
Lake Dunmore 1 1 43N54'32 73w05'15 4:52:21
Lake Elmore 8 1 44N32'33 72w31'33 4:50:06
Lake Fairlee 9 1 43N53 72w11 4:48:44
Lake Hortonia 11
1 43N36 73w16 4:53:04
Lake Morey 9 1 43N55 72w09 4:48:36
Lake Park 10 1 44N59'40 72w11'41 4:48:47
Lake Raponda 13 1 42N52 72w52 4:51:28
Lake Rescue 14 61 43N24 72w42 4:50:48
Lake Saint Catherine 11
1 43N31 73w14 4:52:56
Lakeside 3 1 44N15'06 72w15'46 4:49:03
Lakewood 6 51 44N55 73w07 4:52:28
Landgrove 2 1 43N16 72w51 4:51:24
Lanesboro 12 1 44N18'26 72w18'42 4:49:15
Lapham Bay 1 1 43N59 73w19 4:53:16
Larrabees Point 1
10 43N54 73w19 4:53:16
Leicester 1 41 43N52'00 73w06'30 4:52:26
Leicester Junction 1
41 43N51'21 73w09'03 4:52:36
Lemington 5 1 44N53 71w34 4:46:16
Lennington 5 1 44N51'29 71w33'05 4:46:12
Lewiston 14 6 43N42'14 72w18'02 4:49:12
Lilliesville 14 1 43N49'10 72w41'40 4:50:47
Lincoln 1 12 44N06'21 72w59'51 4:51:59
Lindsay Beach 10
37 44N58'15 72w11'21 4:48:45
Londonderry 13 21 43N13'35 72w48'25 4:51:14
Long Point 1 7 44N15 73w13 4:52:52
Lost Nation 5 1 44N41'49 71w50'39 4:47:23
Lowell 10 12 44N47'57 72w26'55 4:49:48
Lower Cabot 12 1 44N23'25 72w19'59 4:49:20
Lower Granville 1
1 43N58'06 72w50'36 4:51:22
Lower Narrows 3 1 44N25 72w12 4:48:48
Lower Plain 9 33 44N00 72w07 4:48:28
Lower Village 8 1 44N27'22 72w41'41 4:50:47
Lower Waterford 3
1 44N21'16 71w54'27 4:47:38
Lower Websterville 12
27 44N10'05 72w28'43 4:49:55
Ludlow 14 61 43N23'45 72w42'04 4:50:48
Lunenburg 5 19 44N27'47 71w40'57 4:46:44
Lyman 14 25 43N39 72w19 4:49:16
Lympus 14 1 43N49'20 72w43'10 4:50:53
Lyndon 3 1 44N30'51 72w00'41 4:48:03
Lyndon Center 3 1 44N32'14 72w00'48 4:48:03
Lyndonville 3 19 44N32'01 72w00'13 4:48:01
MacIntyre 2 27 43N01'26 73w04'18 4:52:17
Mackville 3 1 44N29'24 72w22'07 4:49:28
Madonna 8 1 44N39 72w50 4:51:20
Mad River Glen 12
1 44N11 72w50 4:51:20
Maidstone 5 6 44N38'55 71w34'21 4:46:17
Maidstone Lake 5
1 44N45 71w37 4:46:28
Mallets Bay 4 15 44N32'40 73w12'57 4:52:52
Manchester 2 62 43N09'49 73w04'22 4:52:17
Manchester Center 2
62 43N10'37 73w03'27 4:52:14
Manchester Depot 2
62 43N10'26 73w02'10 4:52:09
Maple Corners (Calais P O) 12
1 44N22'33 72w29'43 4:49:59
Maple Dell 14 1 43N18 72w29 4:49:56
Maquam 6 51 44N55'03 73w09'41 4:52:39
Marlboro 13 12 42N51'34 72w43'35 4:50:54
Marlboro College 13
1 42N52 72w43 4:50:52
Marshfield 12 1 44N21'03 72w21'16 4:49:25
Mary Meyer 13 1 43N03 72w40 4:50:40
McIndoe Falls (McIndoes Sta) 3
1 44N15'41 72w03'47 4:48:15
Mechanicsville 4
49 44N20'38 73w06'21 4:52:25
Medburyville 13 1 42N52'13 72w55'15 4:51:41
Melville 6 65 44N49 73w05 4:52:20
Melville Landing 6
12 44N45'41 73w09'57 4:52:40
Mendon 11 17 43N39'05 72w55'39 4:51:43
Merrill Corner 10
1 44N42'12 72w20'21 4:49:21
Michigan 11 1 43N47'22 72w53'07 4:51:32
Middlebury 1 56 44N00'55 73w10'04 4:52:40
Middlesex 12 4 44N17'34 72w40'47 4:50:43
Middletown 14 17 43N17'02 72w43'50 4:50:55
Middletown Springs 11
19 43N29'08 73w07'07 4:52:28
Mile Point 1 66 44N10 73w15 4:53:00
Miles Pond 5 6 44N26'50 71w47'49 4:47:11
Millbrook 14 1 43N43'28 72w27'24 4:49:50
Mill Village 5 19 44N29'51 71w39'37 4:46:38
Mill Village 9 1 43N57'38 72w17'58 4:49:12
Mill Village 10 1 44N39'58 72w22'33 4:49:30
Mill Village 12 1 44N20'29 72w44'54 4:51:00
Milton 4 2 44N38'23 73w06'39 4:52:27
Miltonboro 4 2 44N41'48 73w11'15 4:52:45
Missisquoi 6 1 45N00 72w40 4:50:40
Moccasin Mill 5 1 44N36'01 71w48'07 4:47:12
Monkton 1 1 44N14'15 73w08'40 4:52:35
Monkton Ridge 1 7 44N15'16 73w07'29 4:52:30
Montgomery 6 17 44N54'09 72w38'19 4:50:33
Montgomery Center 10
1 44N52'41 72w36'10 4:50:25
Montpelier 12 27 44N15'36 72w34'33 4:50:18
Montpelier Junction 12
12 44N15'25 72w36'30 4:50:26
Moretown 12 17 44N15'03 72w45'41 4:51:03
Morgan 10 12 44N54'49 72w00'53 4:48:04
Morgan Center 10
12 44N54'33 71w58'46 4:47:55
Morgan Corners 14
1 43N44'10 72w38'35 4:50:34
Morristown 8 17 44N33'26 72w37'27 4:50:30
Morrisville 8 1 44N33'42 72w35'56 4:50:24
Morses Line 6 1 45N00'44 72w58'43 4:51:55
Morses Mill 8 1 44N35'18 72w47'31 4:51:10
Morses Mills 3 2 44N22'48 72w05'33 4:48:22
Moscow 8 1 44N26'29 72w42'57 4:50:52
Mosquitoville 3 1 44N16'13 72w08'40 4:48:35
Mount Holly 11 40 43N27'08 72w49'31 4:51:18
Mount Pleasant 11
2 43N48'30 73w05'22 4:52:21
Mount Snow 13 1 42N56 72w50 4:51:20
Mount Tabor 11 1 43N22 72w56 4:51:44
Nashville 4 1 44N27'07 72w56'20 4:51:45
Nelsons Corner 14
17 43N24'37 72w29'24 4:49:58
Neshobe Beach 11
1 43N38'21 73w12'32 4:52:50
Nevesville (Walden P O) 3
1 44N27'00 72w13'23 4:48:54
Newark 3 1 44N42 71w55 4:47:40
Newark Hollow 3 1 44N41'59 71w55'46 4:47:43
New Boston 14 1 43N49'15 72w45'53 4:51:04
Newbury 9 4 44N04'45 72w03'32 4:48:14
Newbury Center 9
4 44N07'25 72w08'56 4:48:36
Newfane 13 17 42N59'08 72w39'23 4:50:38
New Haven 1 63 44N07'28 73w09'15 4:52:37
New Haven Junction 1
63 44N07'24 73w11'03 4:52:44
New Haven Mills 1
1 44N05'30 73w06'33 4:52:26
Newport 10 19 44N56'11 72w12'20 4:48:49
Newport Center 10
1 44N57'03 72w18'25 4:49:14
North Bennington 2
16 42N55'49 73w14'35 4:52:58
North Burlington 4
15 44N29 73w13 4:52:52
North Calais 12 1 44N23'24 72w26'49 4:49:47
North Cambridge 8
1 44N41'13 72w51'27 4:51:26
North Chester 14
34 43N16'22 72w35'23 4:50:22
North Chittenden 11
1 43N44'25 72w58'35 4:51:54
North Clarendon 11
24 43N34'00 72w57'57 4:51:52
North Concord 5 6 44N28'06 71w51'21 4:47:25
North Danville 3
2 44N27'32 72w05'40 4:48:23
North Derby 10 1 45N00'20 72w10'18 4:48:41
North Dorset 2 10 43N17'02 73w00'10 4:52:01
North Duxbury 12
1 44N21'30 72w49'46 4:51:19
North Enosburg 6
1 44N55'13 72w45'28 4:51:02
North Fairfax 6 1 44N45'38 73w03'45 4:52:15
North Fayston 12
1 44N14'31 72w50'19 4:51:21
North Ferrisburg 1
7 44N15'34 73w12'42 4:52:51
Northfield 12 27 44N09'04 72w39'25 4:50:38
Northfield Center 12
27 44N08'05 72w39'41 4:50:39
Northfield Falls 12
27 44N10'19 72w39'05 4:50:36
North Hartland (Evarts Sta) 14
18 43N35'34 72w21'08 4:49:25
North Hero 7 38 44N49'03 73w17'23 4:53:10
North Hyde Park 8
1 44N40'14 72w35'55 4:50:24
North Landgrove 2
1 43N15'35 72w50'57 4:51:24
North Montpelier 12
27 44N18'13 72w26'49 4:49:47
North Orwell 1 1 43N48 73w18 4:53:12
North Pawlet 11 1 43N22'58 73w12'16 4:52:49
North Peacham 3 1 44N25 72w12 4:48:48
North Pomfret 14
1 43N43'22 72w28'49 4:49:55
North Pownal 2 33 42N47'51 73w15'54 4:53:04
North Randolph 9
2 43N58'26 72w33'23 4:50:14
North Royalton 14
30 43N49'38 72w34'01 4:50:16
North Rupert 2 1 43N17'58 73w08'46 4:52:35
North Shaftsbury 2
62 43N08 73w04 4:52:16
North Sheldon 6 1 44N54'38 72w54'27 4:51:38
North Sherburne 11
1 43N42'37 72w49'40 4:51:19
North Shrewsbury 11
30 43N31'44 72w49'39 4:51:19
North Springfield 14
21 43N19'58 72w31'33 4:50:06
North Thetford 9
6 43N50'35 72w11'10 4:48:45
North Troy 10 17 44N59'40 72w24'01 4:49:36
North Tunbridge 9
1 43N54'53 72w28'44 4:49:55
North Underhill 4
1 44N35'07 72w55'58 4:51:44
North Vernon 13 4 42N46'56 72w31'27 4:50:06
North Westminster 13
1 43N07'08 72w27'20 4:49:49
North Williston 4
12 44N28'01 73w02'48 4:52:11
North Windham 13
1 43N13'03 72w44'25 4:50:58
North Wolcott 8 1 44N36'40 72w27'39 4:49:51
Norton 5 54 45N00'36 71w47'43 4:47:11
Norwich 14 35 43N42'55 72w18'30 4:49:14
Notown 14 1 43N41'42 72w43'07 4:50:52
Oakland 6 65 44N44'35 73w05'07 4:52:20
Oil City 9 1 43N52 72w23 4:49:32
Old Bennington 2
23 42N53'00 73w12'50 4:52:51
Old Church 14 2 43N55 72w40 4:50:40
Old City 9 1 43N52'49 72w22'06 4:49:28
Olympus 14 1 43N50 72w38 4:50:32
Orange 9 12 44N08'54 72w24'11 4:49:37
Orchard Lane 14 1 43N18 72w29 4:49:56
Orleans 10 19 44N48'42 72w12'13 4:48:49
Orwell 1 22 43N48'14 73w17'54 4:53:12
Packer Corner 13
13 42N44'20 72w38'37 4:50:34
Pages Corner 4 27 44N32'05 73w04'31 4:52:18
Palmer Corner 1 1 44N00'16 73w22'25 4:53:30
Panton 1 1 44N08'55 73w20'27 4:53:22
Paper Mill Village 2
16 42N54'42 73w14'10 4:52:57
Passumpsic 3 2 44N22'36 72w01'41 4:48:07
Pawlet 11 12 43N20'48 73w10'36 4:52:42
Peacham 3 17 44N19'44 72w10'10 4:48:41

Peacham Corner 3
1 44N20'24 72W16'08 4:49:05
Peach Four Corners 9
4 44N03'59 72W05'37 4:48:22
Pearl 7 1 44N41'15 73W19'38 4:53:19
Peaseville 14 1 43N16 72W36 4:50:24
Pedden Acres 14 1 43N18 72W29 4:49:56
Pekin 12 1 44N17 72W25 4:49:40
Perkinsville 14 1 43N22'25 72W30'51 4:50:03
Perry 3 1 44N41'46 72W05'12 4:48:21
Peru 2 17 43N13'47 72W53'54 4:51:36
Peth 9 2 43N58'12 72W40'06 4:50:40
Pierces Corner 11
24 43N32'28 72W57'16 4:51:49
Pikes Falls 13 1 43N05'49 72W51'20 4:51:25
Piper Crossing 1
1 43N58'08 73W09'55 4:52:40
Pittsfield 11 12 43N46'20 72W48'48 4:51:15
Pittsford 11 28 43N42'24 73W01'43 4:52:07
Plainfield 12 19 44N16'41 72W25'37 4:49:42
Pleasant Valley 8
1 44N35'33 72W51'47 4:51:27
Plymouth 14 12 43N32'09 72W43'19 4:50:53
Plymouth Kingdom 14
1 43N32 72W43 4:50:52
Plymouth Union 14
1 43N31'48 72W44'21 4:50:57
Podunk 13 1 43N00'31 72W51'33 4:51:26
Point of Pines 11
1 43N37'22 73W13'52 4:52:55
Pomfret 14 12 43N42'17 72W30'59 4:50:04
Pompanoosuc 14 1 43N45'20 72W13'53 4:48:56
Post Mills 9 1 43N53'08 72W15'40 4:49:03
Potash Bay 1 66 44N10 73W15 4:53:00
Potash Point 1 66 44N10 73W15 4:53:00
Pottersville 8 1 44N32'20 72W27'11 4:49:49
Poultney 11 47 43N31'01 73W14'12 4:52:57
Pownal 2 4 42N45'56 73W14'11 4:52:57
Pownal Center 2 4 42N47'47 73W13'25 4:52:54
Prindle Corners 4
1 44N18'05 73W09'44 4:52:39
Proctor 11 3 43N39'38 73W02'10 4:52:09
Proctorsville 14
2 43N22'56 72W38'20 4:50:33
Prospect Hill 11
24 43N39'25 72W58'27 4:51:54
Prosper 14 1 43N38 72W31 4:50:04
Putnamville 12 27 44N20'30 72W33'59 4:50:16
Putney 13 2 42N58'29 72W31'20 4:50:05
Quechee 14 1 43N38'46 72W25'08 4:49:41
Queen City Park 4
15 44N26'36 73W13'14 4:52:53
Ralston Corner 5
1 44N25'45 71W50'03 4:47:20
Ramsey Corner 3
17 44N34'14 72W06'40 4:48:27
Randolph 9 2 43N55'30 72W39'59 4:50:40
Randolph Center 9
1 43N56'27 72W36'29 4:50:26
Rawsonville 13 1 43N08'45 72W50'27 4:51:22
Reading 14 1 43N30 72W34 4:50:16
Readsboro 2 17 42N46'18 72W56'52 4:51:47
Readsboro Falls 2
1 42N48'12 72W58'31 4:51:54
Red Village 3 1 44N32 72W00 4:48:00
Reedville 14 1 43N15'43 72W39'30 4:50:38
Reid Hollow 13 13 42N48'37 72W43'09 4:50:53
Rhode Island Corner 4
49 44N21'40 73W04'28 4:52:18
Rices Mills 9 1 43N49'29 72W17'11 4:49:09
Richford 6 48 44N59'49 72W40'18 4:50:41
Richmond 4 49 44N24'19 72W59'36 4:51:58
Richville 1 1 43N52'26 73W16'20 4:53:05
Richville 2 62 43N09'21 73W03'08 4:52:13
Ricker Mills 3 1 44N14'19 72W14'23 4:48:58
Ripton 1 1 43N58'25 73W02'04 4:52:08
Riverside 4 1 44N31'13 72W56'53 4:51:48
Riverside 14 1 43N45'33 72W43'26 4:50:54
Riverton 12 12 44N12 72W38 4:50:32
Robinson 14 1 43N51'33 72W52'22 4:51:29
Rochester 14 19 43N52'28 72W48'30 4:51:14
Rockingham 13 32 43N11'15 72W29'22 4:49:57
Rock Landing 1 66 44N11'56 73W18'56 4:53:16
Rockville 1 1 44N14'44 73W03'53 4:52:16
Rocky Dale 1 1 44N07'45 73W02'58 4:52:12
Round Pond 9 1 44N11 72W09 4:48:36
Roxbury 12 64 44N05'39 72W44'00 4:50:56
Roxbury Flat 12
64 44N04 72W44 4:50:56
Royalton 14 30 43N48'57 72W32'46 4:50:11
Rupert 2 17 43N15'35 73W13'24 4:52:54
Russellville 11
30 43N29 72W53 4:51:32
Russtown 14 25 43N37'01 72W21'20 4:49:25
Rutland 11 24 43N36'38 72W58'23 4:51:54
Ryegate 3 1 44N12'30 72W06'15 4:48:25
Saint Albans 6 65 44N48'39 73W05'01 4:52:20
Saint Albans Bay 6
65 44N48'28 73W08'23 4:52:34
Saint Albans Hill 6
65 44N49 73W05 4:52:20
Saint George 4 1 44N23 73W08 4:52:32
Saint Johnsbury 3
2 44N25'09 72W00'56 4:48:04
Saint Johnsbury Center 3
2 44N27'24 72W00'58 4:48:04
Saint Rocks 6 65 44N51'03 72W56'41 4:51:47
Salisbury 1 11 43N53'47 73W06'01 4:52:24
Salisbury Station 1
1 43N55'05 73W09'41 4:52:39
Samsonville 6 1 44N55'25 72W43'59 4:50:56
Sanderson Corner 6
1 44N40'16 72W58'27 4:51:54
Sandgate 2 1 43N08'53 73W11'58 4:52:48
Satans Kingdom 1
1 43N52'35 73W03'53 4:52:16
Saxtons River 13
19 43N08'16 72W30'37 4:50:02
Scottsville 11 36 43N23'33 73W00'30 4:52:02
Searsburg 2 12 42N53'25 72W57'10 4:51:49
Shadow Lake 10 1 44N42 72W11 4:48:44
Shady Rill 12 27 44N20'39 72W35'23 4:50:22
Shaftsbury 2 29 43N00'31 73W11'30 4:52:46
Shaftsbury Center 2
29 42N58'57 73W12'25 4:52:50
Sharon 14 17 43N47'04 72W27'17 4:49:49
Shawville 6 1 44N55'11 72W57'58 4:51:52
Sheddsville 14 27 43N29'21 72W29'50 4:49:59
Sheffield 3 17 44N36'07 72W06'52 4:48:27
Sheffield Square 3
1 44N37'21 72W09'26 4:48:38
Shelburne 4 50 44N22'50 73W13'41 4:52:55
Shelburne Falls 4
50 44N22'14 73W12'57 4:52:52
Shelburne Road Section 4
15 44N27 73W12 4:52:48
Sheldon 6 17 44N52'54 72W56'36 4:51:46
Sheldon Junction 6
1 44N54'06 72W56'53 4:51:48
Sheldon Springs 6
1 44N54'22 72W58'41 4:51:55
Sherburne Center 11
1 43N39'33 72W46'28 4:51:06
Shipman Hill 4 15 44N31'37 73W12'25 4:52:50
Shoreham 1 10 43N53'37 73W18'59 4:53:16
Shrewsbury 11 17 43N30'32 72W52'02 4:51:28
Simmons Hill 5 1 44N51'37 71W35'19 4:46:21
Simonsville 14 1 43N15'28 72W42'59 4:50:52
Simpsonville 13 1 43N04'21 72W39'01 4:50:36
Skeels Corner 6 1 44N53'56 73W04'01 4:52:16
Smith Corner 3 1 44N28'00 72W16'18 4:49:05
Smith Four Corners 3
1 44N30 72W22 4:49:28
Smithville 14 61 43N23'17 72W40'06 4:50:40
Sodom 2 16 42N56'10 73W15'58 4:53:04
Somerset 13 1 42N57'01 72W59'13 4:51:57
South Albany 10 1 44N41'29 72W18'45 4:49:15
South Alburg 7 31 44N53'15 73W16'44 4:53:07
South Barre 12 27 44N10'37 72W30'22 4:50:01
South Burlington 4
15 44N28'01 73W10'17 4:52:41
South Cabot 12 1 44N22'03 72W16'34 4:49:06
South Cambridge 8
1 44N36'36 72W48'39 4:51:15
South Corinth 9
33 44N00'58 72W13'59 4:48:56
South Danville 3
1 44N22'38 72W07'18 4:48:29
South Dorset 2 57 43N13'21 73W04'26 4:52:18
South Duxbury 12
1 44N14'55 72W47'13 4:51:09
South End 11 36 43N19'02 72W59'35 4:51:58
South Franklin 6
1 44N54'41 72W52'00 4:51:28
South Hero 7 38 44N38'43 73W18'10 4:53:13
South Hinesburg 4
1 44N17'32 73W04'13 4:52:17
South Lincoln 1 1 44N04'17 72W58'23 4:51:54
South Londonderry 13
1 43N11'34 72W48'53 4:51:16
South Lunenburg 5
19 44N25'45 71W40'47 4:46:43
South Newbury 9 4 44N02'46 72W05'07 4:48:20
South Newfane 13
1 42N56'17 72W42'21 4:50:49
South Newport 10
1 44N52'49 72W20'10 4:49:21
South Northfield 12
27 44N06'55 72W39'17 4:50:37
South Peacham 3 1 44N18'53 72W09'59 4:48:40
South Pomfret 14
1 43N39'54 72W32'24 4:50:10
South Poultney 11
1 43N28'32 73W14'11 4:52:57
South Randolph 9
1 43N53'41 72W34'36 4:50:18
South Reading 14
1 43N28'27 72W35'23 4:50:22
South Richford 6
1 44N56'03 72W39'08 4:50:37
South Royalton 14
30 43N49'15 72W31'18 4:50:05
South Ryegate 3 1 44N11'18 72W08'29 4:48:34
South Shaftsbury 2
16 42N56'47 73W12'40 4:52:51
South Starksboro 1
1 44N09'45 73W00'51 4:52:03
South Strafford 9
1 43N50'07 72W22'00 4:49:28
South Tunbridge 9
1 43N51'19 72W30'12 4:50:01
South Vernon 13 4 42N43'37 72W27'54 4:49:52
South Vershire 9
1 43N55'20 72W19'02 4:49:16
South Walden 3 1 44N28'28 72W17'25 4:49:10
South Wallingford 11
25 43N24'46 72W59'35 4:51:58
South Wardsboro 13
1 43N00'41 72W47'02 4:51:08
South Washington 9
1 44N01'41 72W24'48 4:49:39
South Wheelock 3
1 44N32 72W00 4:48:00
South Windham 13
1 43N07'41 72W42'42 4:50:51
South Woodbury 12
1 44N24'54 72W25'19 4:49:41
South Woodstock 14
1 43N33'56 72W31'58 4:50:08
Spoonerville 14 1 43N18'43 72W32'49 4:50:11
Springfield 14 21 43N17'54 72W28'58 4:49:56
Stacy Crossroads 11
1 43N45'18 73W18'36 4:53:14
Stamford 2 17 42N45'22 73W04'06 4:52:16
Stannard 3 1 44N32'32 72W12'53 4:48:52
Starksboro 1 1 44N13'38 73W03'28 4:52:14
Starr Farm Beach 4
15 44N30'37 73W16'26 4:53:06
Stevens 5 6 44N35'53 71W33'40 4:46:15
Stevens Mills 10
1 44N59'43 72W36'52 4:50:27
Stevensville 4 1 44N30'18 72W52'01 4:51:28
Stockbridge 14 12 43N47'10 72W45'15 4:51:01
Stowe 8 19 44N27'55 72W41'06 4:50:44
Stowe Fork 8 1 44N30'08 72W45'24 4:51:02
Strafford 9 1 43N51'59 72W22'42 4:49:31
Stratton 13 1 43N02'34 72W54'41 4:51:39
Stratton Mountain 13
1 43N12 72W49 4:51:16
Stump Station 1 1 43N54 73W19 4:53:16
Sudbury 11 1 43N47'57 73W12'18 4:52:49
Summer Point 1 66 44N10 73W15 4:53:00
Summit 11 20 43N27 72W49 4:51:16
Sunderland 2 10 43N06'48 73W06'13 4:52:25
Sunmit 3 1 44N41'25 72W03'28 4:48:14
Sutton 3 17 44N37'59 72W01'34 4:48:06
Swanton 6 51 44N55'05 73W07'29 4:52:30
Swanton Junction 6
51 44N52'40 73W05'57 4:52:24
Tafts Corner 4 1 43N38 72W28 4:49:52
Taftsville 14 1 43N37'50 72W28'10 4:49:53
Talcville 14 1 43N51'31 72W48'21 4:51:13
Tarbellville 11 1 43N24'31 72W50'30 4:51:22
Taylor Bridge 3 1 44N29'03 72W17'35 4:49:10
Taylorville 3 1 44N30 72W22 4:49:28
Texas 5 1 44N25'04 71W49'30 4:47:18
The Bluffs 10 1 44N56 72W13 4:48:52
The Four Corners 10
1 44N35'39 72W13'47 4:48:55
The Island 14 1 43N15'16 72W47'43 4:51:11
Thetford 9 17 43N49'43 72W14'48 4:48:59
Thetford Hill 9 1 43N49'10 72W13'45 4:48:55
Thompsonburg 13 1 43N12'28 72W46'50 4:51:07
Thompson's Point 4
1 44N19 73W15 4:53:00
Tice 10 1 44N58'47 72W02'08 4:48:09
Tillotson Mill 10
1 44N46'55 72W31'05 4:50:04
Tinmouth 11 1 43N26'55 73W03'00 4:52:12
Tolman Corner 10
12 44N34'03 72W18'26 4:49:14
Topsham 9 12 44N08 72W15 4:49:00
Topsham Four Corners 9
1 44N05'56 72W13'30 4:48:54
Townshend 13 17 43N02'50 72W40'05 4:50:40
Trow Hill 12 27 44N12 72W30 4:50:00
Troy 10 1 44N54'05 72W24'07 4:49:36
Tunbridge 9 12 43N53'27 72W29'30 4:49:58
Tupper 11 1 43N48'26 72W47'07 4:51:08
Twin Orchards 4
15 44N26'14 73W12'38 4:52:51
Tyson 14 61 43N24 72W42 4:50:48
Una Bella 2 23 42N53 73W12 4:52:48
Underhill 4 1 44N31'33 72W56'44 4:51:47
Underhill Center 4
1 44N30'27 72W54'00 4:51:36
Union Village 9 1 43N47'19 72W15'21 4:49:01
Upper Graniteville 12
27 44N08'30 72W28'37 4:49:54
Upper Narrows 3 1 44N25 72W12 4:48:48
Vergennes 1 66 44N10'02 73W15'16 4:53:01
Vernon 13 4 42N45'43 72W30'50 4:50:03
Vershire 9 12 43N58'11 72W19'23 4:49:18
Vershire Center 9
12 43N57'10 72W20'17 4:49:21
Vershire Heights 9
1 43N59'15 72W22'10 4:49:29
Victory 5 1 44N30'34 71W50'47 4:47:23
Waitsfield 12 17 44N11'24 72W49'31 4:51:18
Waitsfield Common 12
1 44N11'24 72W47'53 4:51:12
Waits River 9 1 44N05'22 72W16'57 4:49:08
Walden 3 1 44N29 72W15 4:49:00
Walden Heights 3
1 44N27'08 72W15'27 4:49:02
Wallingford 11 25 43N28'18 72W58'40 4:51:55
Wallispond 5 1 45N00 71W32 4:46:08
Walnut Ledge 4 2 44N36'00 73W11'51 4:52:47
Waltham 1 1 44N08 73W14 4:52:56
Wardsboro 13 17 43N02'30 72W47'30 4:51:10
Wardsboro Center 13
17 43N02'10 72W48'30 4:51:14
Warren 12 17 44N06'43 72W51'23 4:51:26
Warrens Gore 5 1 44N55 71W52 4:47:28
Washington 9 17 44N06'20 72W25'59 4:49:44
Washington Heights 9
1 44N05'23 72W27'34 4:49:50
Waterbury 12 27 44N20'16 72W45'24 4:51:02
Waterbury Center 12
1 44N22'41 72W42'59 4:50:52
Waterford 3 1 44N23 71W57 4:47:48
Waterville 8 1 44N41'25 72W46'10 4:51:05
Weathersfield 14
17 43N23 72W28 4:49:52
Weathersfield Bow 14
1 43N21'14 72W24'28 4:49:38
Websterville 12
27 44N09'38 72W28'12 4:49:53
Wells 11 12 43N25'02 73W12'17 4:52:49
Wells River 9 6 44N09'15 72W02'51 4:48:11
Wenlock 5 1 44N46'35 71W45'13 4:47:01
West Addison 1 66 44N04'54 73W23'41 4:53:35
West Arlington 2
27 43N06'12 73W12'47 4:52:51
West Barnet 3 1 44N18'36 72W08'16 4:48:33
West Berkshire 6
1 44N59'21 72W48'51 4:51:15
West Berlin 12 12 44N12'00 72W38'00 4:50:32
West Bolton 4 1 44N26'44 72W53'54 4:51:36
West Braintree 9
12 43N58'20 72W44'50 4:50:59
West Branch 8 1 44N28'27 72W42'59 4:50:52
West Brattleboro 13
13 42N51'21 72W36'13 4:50:25
West Bridgewater 14
1 43N36'00 72W44'57 4:51:00
West Bridport 1 1 43N57'24 73W23'47 4:53:35
West Brookfield 9
2 44N01'15 72W40'21 4:50:41
West Burke 3 1 44N38'29 71W58'45 4:47:55
West Castleton 11
1 43N39'32 73W13'56 4:52:56
West Charleston 10
1 44N53'56 72W03'36 4:48:14
West Corinth 9 1 44N02'29 72W20'11 4:49:21
West Cornwall 1
56 43N56'37 73W14'06 4:52:56
West Danville 3 1 44N24'34 72W11'44 4:48:47
West Derby 10 1 44N56 72W13 4:48:52

West Dover 13 1 42N56'21 72W51'12 4:51:25
West Dummerston 13
1 42N55'35 72W36'57 4:50:28
West Enosburg 6
44 44N52'19 72W47'54 4:51:12
West Fairlee 9 12 43N54'33 72W15'49 4:49:03
West Fairlee Center 9
1 43N56'36 72W13'33 4:48:54
Westfield 10 1 44N53'22 72W25'44 4:49:43
West Fletcher 6 1 44N42'18 72W56'14 4:51:45
Westford 4 1 44N36'43 73W00'33 4:52:02
West Georgia 6 65 44N42'09 73W09'16 4:52:37
West Glover 10 1 44N43'42 72W13'28 4:48:54
West Groton 3 1 44N13'05 72W14'38 4:48:59
West Guilford 13
13 42N48'30 72W39'50 4:50:39
West Halifax 13 1 42N47'14 72W46'16 4:51:05
West Hartford 14
53 43N42'44 72W25'05 4:49:40
West Haven 11 1 43N39'05 73W20'52 4:53:23
West Hill 6 1 44N51'53 72W39'36 4:50:38
West Jamaica 13 1 43N04'06 72W51'07 4:51:24
West Lincoln 1 1 44N07'08 73W01'14 4:52:05
West Milton 4 2 44N37'50 73W10'20 4:52:41
Westminster 13 4 43N04'04 72W27'33 4:49:50
Westminster Station 13
6 43N05'08 72W26'23 4:49:46
Westminster West 13
4 43N03'50 72W32'28 4:50:10
Westmore 10 12 44N46'17 72W03'19 4:48:13
West Newbury 9 4 44N03'52 72W07'31 4:48:30
West Norwich 14
35 43N45'48 72W22'24 4:49:30
Weston 14 12 43N17'28 72W47'37 4:51:10
Weston Priory 14
1 43N17 72W48 4:51:12
West Pawlet 11 3 43N21'13 73W15'09 4:53:01
West Rupert 2 1 43N14'19 73W14'36 4:52:58
West Rutland 11 8 43N35'35 73W02'44 4:52:11
West Salisbury 1
1 43N55'22 73W09'06 4:52:36
West Sandgate 2 1 43N09'46 73W14'47 4:52:59
West Settlement 8
19 44N37'12 72W43'18 4:50:53
West Springfield 14
21 43N17'28 72W31'20 4:50:05
West Swanton 6 51 44N58'08 73W12'46 4:52:51
West Tinmouth 11
19 43N25'08 73W07'11 4:52:29
West Topsham 9 1 44N06'54 72W18'44 4:49:15
West Townshend 13
1 43N05'03 72W42'44 4:50:51
West View 4 2 44N37'32 73W08'13 4:52:33
West Wardsboro 13
1 43N01'46 72W51'11 4:51:25
West Waterford 3
2 44N21'27 71W57'22 4:47:49
West Windsor 14
12 43N29 72W29 4:49:56
West Woodstock 14
1 43N37'01 72W32'33 4:50:10
Weybridge 1 55 44N03'59 73W12'58 4:52:52
Weybridge Hill 1
56 44N02'18 73W12'49 4:52:51
Wheelock 3 1 44N35'17 72W05'20 4:48:21
White River Junction 14
25 43N38'56 72W19'11 4:49:17
Whites Corner 5 2 44N24'44 71W53'06 4:47:32
Whitesville 14 1 43N23'30 72W35'41 4:50:23
Whiting 1 67 43N51'50 73W12'03 4:52:48
Whitingham 13 17 42N47'21 72W53'08 4:51:33
Whitneyville 13
13 42N47'38 72W44'36 4:50:58
Wilder 14 35 43N40'22 72W18'33 4:49:14
Williamstown 9 52 44N07'18 72W32'31 4:50:10
Williamsville 13
1 42N56'48 72W40'46 4:50:43
Williamsville Station 13
17 42N56'49 72W38'31 4:50:34
Williston 4 12 44N26'15 73W04'07 4:52:16
Williston Road Section 4
15 44N28 73W10 4:52:40
Willow Point 1 66 44N01'21 73W24'02 4:53:36
Wilmington 13 19 42N52'06 72W52'19 4:51:29
Windham 13 12 43N10'45 72W43'35 4:50:54
Windsor 14 27 43N28'49 72W23'07 4:49:32
Winhall 2 17 43N10 72W56 4:51:44
Winooski 4 15 44N29'29 73W11'10 4:52:45
Winooski Park 4
15 44N30 73W11 4:52:44
Wolcott 8 1 44N32'47 72W27'32 4:49:50
Woodbury 12 12 44N26'27 72W25'01 4:49:40
Woodford 2 12 42N52'49 73W04'48 4:52:19
Woodford Hollow 2
23 42N53 73W12 4:52:48
Woodstock 14 21 43N37'27 72W31'08 4:50:05
Worcester 12 12 44N22'25 72W33'01 4:50:12
Wrightsville 12

TIME TABLES

VA # 1

Before 11/18/1883		LMT
11/18/1883	12:00	EST
3/31/1918	02:00	EWT
10/27/1918	02:00	EST
3/30/1919	02:00	EWT
10/26/1919	02:00	EST
2/09/1942	02:00	EWT
9/30/1945	02:00	EST
5/11/1947	02:00	EDT
9/28/1947	02:00	EST
5/02/1948	02:00	EDT
9/26/1948	02:00	EST
4/24/1949	02:00	EDT
9/25/1949	02:00	EST
5/04/1950	02:00	EDT
9/24/1950	02:00	EST
4/29/1951	02:00	EDT
9/30/1951	02:00	EST
4/27/1952	02:00	EDT
9/28/1952	02:00	EST
4/30/1953	02:00	EDT
9/27/1953	02:00	EST
4/25/1954	02:00	US#3

VA # 2

Before 11/18/1883		LMT
11/18/1883	12:00	EST
3/31/1918	02:00	EWT
10/27/1918	02:00	EST
3/30/1919	02:00	EWT
10/26/1919	02:00	EST
2/09/1942	02:00	EWT
9/30/1945	02:00	EST
5/05/1950	02:00	EDT
9/24/1950	02:00	EST
4/29/1951	02:00	EDT
9/30/1951	02:00	EST
4/27/1952	02:00	EDT
9/28/1952	02:00	EST
4/30/1953	02:00	EDT
9/27/1953	02:00	EST
4/25/1954	02:00	US#3

VA # 3

Before 11/18/1883		LMT
11/18/1883	12:00	EST
3/31/1918	02:00	EWT
10/27/1918	02:00	EST
3/30/1919	02:00	EWT
10/26/1919	02:00	EST
2/09/1942	02:00	EWT
9/30/1945	02:00	EST
5/02/1948	02:00	EDT
9/26/1948	02:00	EST
4/24/1949	02:00	EDT
9/25/1949	02:00	EST
6/28/1950	02:00	EDT
9/24/1950	02:00	EST
4/29/1951	02:00	EDT
9/30/1951	02:00	EST
4/27/1952	02:00	EDT
9/28/1952	02:00	EST
4/30/1953	02:00	EDT
9/27/1953	02:00	EST
4/25/1954	02:00	US#3

VA # 4

Before 11/18/1883		LMT
11/18/1883	12:00	EST
3/31/1918	02:00	EWT
10/27/1918	02:00	EST
3/30/1919	02:00	EWT
10/26/1919	02:00	EST
2/09/1942	02:00	EWT
9/30/1945	02:00	EST
5/31/1962	00:00	EDT
9/04/1962	00:00	EST
5/31/1963	00:00	EDT
9/03/1963	00:00	EST
6/01/1964	00:00	EDT
9/07/1964	00:00	EST
6/07/1965	00:00	EDT
9/06/1965	00:00	EST
4/24/1966	02:00	US#1

VA # 5

Before 11/18/1883		LMT
11/18/1883	12:00	EST
3/31/1918	02:00	EWT
10/27/1918	02:00	EST
3/30/1919	02:00	EWT
10/26/1919	02:00	EST
2/09/1942	02:00	EWT
9/30/1945	02:00	EST
4/28/1946	02:00	EDT
9/29/1946	02:00	EST
5/31/1962	00:00	EDT
9/04/1962	00:00	EST
5/31/1963	00:00	EDT
9/03/1963	00:00	EST
6/01/1964	00:00	EDT
9/07/1964	00:00	EST
6/07/1965	00:00	EDT
9/06/1965	00:00	EST
4/24/1966	02:00	US#1

VA # 6

Before 11/18/1883		LMT
11/18/1883	12:00	EST
3/31/1918	02:00	EWT
10/27/1918	02:00	EST
3/30/1919	02:00	EWT
10/26/1919	02:00	EST
2/09/1942	02:00	EWT
9/30/1945	02:00	EST
4/28/1946	02:00	EDT
9/30/1946	00:00	EST
4/25/1948	02:00	EDT
9/26/1948	02:00	EST
4/27/1952	02:00	EDT
9/28/1952	02:00	EST
5/31/1962	00:00	EDT
9/04/1962	00:00	EST
5/31/1963	00:00	EDT
9/03/1963	00:00	EST
6/01/1964	00:00	EDT
9/07/1964	00:00	EST
6/07/1965	00:00	EDT
9/06/1965	00:00	EST
4/24/1966	02:00	US#1

VA # 7

Before 11/18/1883		LMT
11/18/1883	12:00	EST
3/31/1918	02:00	EWT
10/27/1918	02:00	EST
3/30/1919	02:00	EWT
10/26/1919	02:00	EST
2/09/1942	02:00	EWT
9/30/1945	02:00	EST
4/28/1946	02:00	EDT
9/30/1946	02:00	EST
4/25/1948	02:00	US#5

VA # 8

Before 11/18/1883		LMT
11/18/1883	12:00	EST
3/31/1918	02:00	EWT
10/27/1918	02:00	EST
3/30/1919	02:00	EWT
10/26/1919	02:00	EST
2/09/1942	02:00	EWT
9/30/1945	02:00	EST
4/25/1948	02:00	US#5

VA # 9

Before 11/18/1883		LMT
11/18/1883	12:00	EST
3/31/1918	02:00	EWT
10/27/1918	02:00	EST
3/30/1919	02:00	EWT
10/26/1919	02:00	EST
2/09/1942	02:00	EWT
9/30/1945	02:00	EST
4/25/1948	02:00	EDT
9/26/1948	02:00	EST
4/24/1949	02:00	EDT
9/25/1949	02:00	EST
4/30/1950	02:00	EDT
9/24/1950	02:00	EST
4/29/1951	02:00	EDT
9/30/1951	02:00	EST
4/27/1952	02:00	EDT
9/28/1952	02:00	EST
4/30/1961	02:00	EDT
10/01/1961	02:00	EST
5/31/1962	00:00	EDT
9/04/1962	00:00	EST
5/31/1963	00:00	EDT
9/03/1963	00:00	EST
6/01/1964	00:00	EDT
9/07/1964	00:00	EST
6/07/1965	00:00	EDT
9/06/1965	00:00	EST
4/24/1966	02:00	US#1

VA # 10

Before 11/18/1883		LMT
11/18/1883	12:00	EST
3/31/1918	02:00	EWT
10/27/1918	02:00	EST
3/30/1919	02:00	EWT
10/26/1919	02:00	EST
2/09/1942	02:00	EWT
9/30/1945	02:00	EST
4/27/1952	02:00	US#5

VA # 11

Before 11/18/1883		LMT
11/18/1883	12:00	EST
3/31/1918	02:00	EWT
10/27/1918	02:00	EST
3/30/1919	02:00	EWT
10/26/1919	02:00	EST
2/09/1942	02:00	EWT
9/30/1945	02:00	EST
4/29/1956	02:00	US#5

VA # 12

Before 11/18/1883		LMT
11/18/1883	12:00	EST
3/31/1918	02:00	EWT
10/27/1918	02:00	EST
3/30/1919	02:00	EWT
10/26/1919	02:00	EST
2/09/1942	02:00	EWT
9/30/1945	02:00	EST
4/29/1956	02:00	EDT
9/30/1956	02:00	EST
4/30/1961	02:00	EDT
10/01/1961	02:00	EST
5/31/1962	00:00	EDT
9/04/1962	00:00	EST
5/31/1963	00:00	EDT
9/03/1963	00:00	EST
6/01/1964	00:00	EDT
9/07/1964	00:00	EST
6/07/1965	00:00	EDT
9/06/1965	00:00	EST
4/24/1966	02:00	US#1

VA # 13

Before 11/18/1883		LMT
11/18/1883	12:00	EST
3/31/1918	02:00	EWT
10/27/1918	02:00	EST
3/30/1919	02:00	EWT
10/26/1919	02:00	EST
2/09/1942	02:00	EWT
9/30/1945	02:00	EST
4/26/1959	02:00	EDT
10/25/1959	02:00	EST
4/30/1961	02:00	EDT
10/29/1961	02:00	EST
5/31/1962	00:00	EDT
9/04/1962	00:00	EST
5/31/1963	00:00	EDT
9/03/1963	00:00	EST
6/01/1964	00:00	EDT
9/07/1964	00:00	EST
6/07/1965	00:00	EDT
9/06/1965	00:00	EST
4/24/1966	02:00	US#1

VA # 14

Before 11/18/1883		LMT
11/18/1883	12:00	EST
3/31/1918	02:00	EWT
10/27/1918	02:00	EST
3/30/1919	02:00	EWT
10/26/1919	02:00	EST
2/09/1942	02:00	EWT
9/30/1945	02:00	EST
4/30/1961	02:00	EDT
10/29/1961	02:00	EST
5/31/1962	00:00	EDT
9/04/1962	00:00	EST
5/31/1963	00:00	EDT
9/03/1963	00:00	EST
6/01/1964	00:00	EDT
9/07/1964	00:00	EST
6/07/1965	00:00	EDT
9/06/1965	00:00	EST
4/24/1966	02:00	US#1

VA # 15

Before 11/18/1883		LMT
11/18/1883	12:00	EST
3/31/1918	02:00	EWT
10/27/1918	02:00	EST
3/30/1919	02:00	EWT
10/26/1919	02:00	EST
2/09/1942	02:00	EWT
9/30/1945	02:00	EST
5/31/1962	00:00	EDT
9/04/1962	00:00	EST
5/31/1963	00:00	EDT
9/03/1963	00:00	EST
4/30/1967	02:00	US#1

VA # 16

Before 11/18/1883		LMT
11/18/1883	12:00	EST
3/31/1918	02:00	EWT
10/27/1918	02:00	EST
3/30/1919	02:00	EWT
10/26/1919	02:00	EST
2/09/1942	02:00	EWT
9/30/1945	02:00	EST
5/03/1961	02:00	EDT
10/29/1961	02:00	EST
5/31/1962	00:00	EDT
9/04/1962	00:00	EST
5/31/1963	00:00	EDT
9/03/1963	00:00	EST
6/01/1964	00:00	EDT
9/07/1964	00:00	EST
6/07/1965	00:00	EDT
9/06/1965	00:00	EST
4/24/1966	02:00	US#1

VA # 17

Before 11/18/1883		LMT
11/18/1883	12:00	EST
3/31/1918	02:00	EWT
10/27/1918	02:00	EST
3/30/1919	02:00	EWT
10/26/1919	02:00	EST
2/09/1942	02:00	EWT
9/30/1945	02:00	EST
4/30/1961	00:00	EDT
10/01/1961	02:00	EST
5/31/1962	00:00	EDT
9/04/1962	00:00	EST
5/31/1963	00:00	EDT
9/03/1963	00:00	EST
6/01/1964	00:00	EDT
9/07/1964	00:00	EST
6/07/1965	00:00	EDT
9/06/1965	00:00	EST
4/24/1966	02:00	US#1

VA # 18

Before 11/18/1883		LMT
11/18/1883	12:00	EST
3/31/1918	02:00	EWT
10/27/1918	02:00	EST
3/30/1919	02:00	EWT
10/26/1919	02:00	EST
2/09/1942	02:00	EWT
9/30/1945	02:00	EST
5/23/1961	02:00	EDT
10/29/1961	02:00	EST
5/31/1962	00:00	EDT
9/04/1962	00:00	EST
5/31/1963	00:00	EDT
9/03/1963	00:00	EST
6/01/1964	00:00	EDT
9/07/1964	00:00	EST
6/07/1965	00:00	EDT
9/06/1965	00:00	EST
4/24/1966	02:00	US#1

VA # 19

Before 11/18/1883		LMT
11/18/1883	12:00	EST
3/31/1918	02:00	EWT
10/27/1918	02:00	EST
3/30/1919	02:00	EWT
10/26/1919	02:00	EST
2/09/1942	02:00	EWT
9/30/1945	02:00	EST
5/15/1961	00:00	EDT
10/29/1961	02:00	EST
5/31/1962	00:00	EDT
9/04/1962	00:00	EST
5/31/1963	00:00	EDT
9/03/1963	00:00	EST
6/01/1964	00:00	EDT
9/07/1964	00:00	EST
6/07/1965	00:00	EDT
9/06/1965	00:00	EST
4/24/1966	02:00	US#1

VA # 20

Before 11/18/1883		LMT
11/18/1883	12:00	EST
3/31/1918	02:00	EWT
10/27/1918	02:00	EST
3/30/1919	02:00	EWT
10/26/1919	02:00	EST
2/09/1942	02:00	EWT
9/30/1945	02:00	EST
4/30/1961	02:00	EDT
5/06/1961	02:00	EST
5/31/1962	00:00	EDT
9/04/1962	00:00	EST
5/31/1963	00:00	EDT
9/03/1963	00:00	EST
6/01/1964	00:00	EDT
9/07/1964	00:00	EST
6/07/1965	00:00	EDT
9/06/1965	00:00	EST
4/24/1966	02:00	US#1

VA # 21

Before 11/18/1883		LMT
11/18/1883	12:00	EST
3/31/1918	02:00	EWT
10/27/1918	02:00	EST
3/30/1919	02:00	EWT
10/26/1919	02:00	EST
2/09/1942	02:00	EWT
9/30/1945	02:00	EST
4/30/1961	02:00	EDT
9/04/1961	00:00	EST
5/31/1962	00:00	EDT
9/04/1962	00:00	EST
5/31/1963	00:00	EDT
9/03/1963	00:00	EST
6/01/1964	00:00	EDT
9/07/1964	00:00	EST
6/07/1965	00:00	EDT
9/06/1965	00:00	EST
4/24/1966	02:00	US#1

VA # 22

Before 11/18/1883		LMT
11/18/1883	12:00	EST
3/31/1918	02:00	EWT
10/27/1918	02:00	EST
3/30/1919	02:00	EWT
10/26/1919	02:00	EST
2/09/1942	02:00	EWT
9/30/1945	02:00	EST
4/30/1961	02:00	EDT
10/01/1961	02:00	EST
5/31/1962	00:00	EDT
9/04/1962	00:00	EST
5/31/1963	00:00	EDT
9/03/1963	00:00	EST
6/01/1964	00:00	EDT
9/07/1964	00:00	EST
6/07/1965	00:00	EDT
9/06/1965	00:00	EST
4/24/1966	02:00	US#1

VA # 23

Before 11/18/1883		LMT
11/18/1883	12:00	EST
3/31/1918	02:00	EWT
10/27/1918	02:00	EST
3/30/1919	02:00	EWT
10/26/1919	02:00	EST
2/09/1942	02:00	EWT
9/30/1945	02:00	EST
4/30/1961	02:00	EDT
10/15/1961	02:00	EST
5/31/1962	00:00	EDT
9/04/1962	00:00	EST
5/31/1963	00:00	EDT
9/03/1963	00:00	EST
6/01/1964	00:00	EDT
9/07/1964	00:00	EST
6/07/1965	00:00	EDT
9/06/1965	00:00	EST
4/24/1966	02:00	US#1

VA # 24

Before 11/18/1883		LMT
11/18/1883	12:00	EST
3/31/1918	02:00	EWT
10/27/1918	02:00	EST
3/30/1919	02:00	EWT
10/26/1919	02:00	EST
2/09/1942	02:00	EWT
9/30/1945	02:00	EST
4/29/1956	02:00	EDT
9/30/1956	02:00	EST
4/28/1957	02:00	EDT
9/29/1957	02:00	EST
4/27/1958	02:00	EDT
10/26/1958	02:00	EST
4/26/1959	02:00	EDT
10/25/1959	02:00	EST
4/24/1960	02:00	EDT
10/30/1960	02:00	EST
4/30/1961	02:00	EDT
10/01/1961	02:00	EST
4/29/1962	02:00	US#2

VA # 25

Before 11/18/1883		LMT
11/18/1883	12:00	EST
3/31/1918	02:00	EWT
10/27/1918	02:00	EST
3/30/1919	02:00	EWT
10/26/1919	02:00	EST
2/09/1942	02:00	EWT
9/30/1945	02:00	EST
4/28/1946	02:00	EDT
9/29/1946	02:00	EST
4/30/1967	02:00	US#1

VA # 26

Before 11/18/1883		LMT
11/18/1883	12:00	CST
3/31/1918	02:00	CWT
10/27/1918	02:00	CST
3/30/1919	02:00	CWT
10/26/1919	02:00	CST
2/09/1942	02:00	CWT
9/30/1945	02:00	CST
3/02/1946	02:00	EST
5/31/1962	00:00	EDT
9/04/1962	00:00	EST
5/31/1963	00:00	EDT
9/03/1963	00:00	EST
4/30/1967	02:00	US#1

COUNTIES

1 Accomack
2 Albemarle
3 Alleghany
4 Amelia
5 Amherst
6 Appomattox
7 Arlington
8 Augusta
9 Bath
10 Bedford
11 Bland
12 Botetourt
13 Brunswick
14 Buchanan
15 Buckingham
16 Campbell
17 Caroline
18 Carroll
19 Charles City
20 Charlotte
21 Chesterfield
22 Clarke
23 Craig
24 Culpeper
25 Cumberland
26 Dickenson
27 Dinwiddie
28 Essex
29 Fairfax
30 Fauquier
31 Floyd
32 Fluvanna
33 Franklin
34 Frederick
35 Giles
36 Gloucester
37 Goochland
38 Grayson
39 Greene
40 Greensville
41 Halifax
42 Hanover
43 Henrico
44 Henry
45 Highland
46 Isle of Wight
47 James City
48 King and Queen
49 King George
50 King William
51 Lancaster
52 Lee
53 Loudoun
54 Louisa
55 Lunenburg
56 Madison
57 Mathews
58 Mecklenburg
59 Middlesex
60 Montgomery
61 Nelson
62 New Kent
63 Northampton
64 Northumberland
65 Nottoway
66 Orange
67 Page
68 Patrick
69 Pittsylvania
70 Powhatan
71 Prince Edward
72 Prince George
73 Prince William
74 Pulaski
75 Rappahannock
76 Richmond
77 Roanoke
78 Rockbridge
79 Rockingham
80 Russell
81 Scott
82 Shenandoah
83 Smyth
84 Southampton
85 Spotsylvania
86 Stafford
87 Surry
88 Sussex
89 Tazewell
90 Warren
91 Washington
92 Westmoreland
93 Wise
94 Wythe
95 York
96 Alexandria
97 Bedford
98 Bristol
99 Buena Vista
100 Charlottesville
101 Chesapeake
102 Clifton Forge
103 Colonial Heights
104 Covington
105 Danville
106 Emporia
107 Fairfax
108 Falls Church
109 Franklin
110 Fredericksburg
111 Galax
112 Hampton
113 Harrisonburg
114 Hopewell
115 Lexington
116 Lynchburg
117 Manassas
118 Manassas Park
119 Martinsville
120 Newport News
121 Norfolk
122 Norton
123 Petersburg
124 Poquoson
125 Portsmouth
126 Radford
127 Richmond
128 Roanoke
129 Salem
130 South Boston
131 Staunton
132 Suffolk
133 Virginia Beach
134 Waynesboro
135 Williamsburg
136 Winchester

Aarons Creek 41 4 36N39'40 78W43'20 5:14:53
Abbot 23 4 37N25'45 80W08'23 5:20:34
Abbs Valley 89 4 37N14'38 81W27'09 5:25:49
Aberdeen Gardens 112 6 37N01'56 76W23'56 5:05:36
Abert 10 16 37N29'53 79W13'33 5:16:54
Abilene 20 4 37N08'29 78W32'40 5:14:11
Abingdon 91 15 36N42'35 81W58'39 5:27:55
Academy Park 125 6 36N48'20 76W21'04 5:05:24
Acca 127 17 37N34'42 77W28'13 5:09:53
Accomac 1 4 37N43'10 75W39'57 5:02:40
Accotink 29 3 38N42'30 77W09'35 5:08:38
Accotink Heights 29 1 38N50'07 77W12'47 5:08:51
Accotink Springs 29 3 38N45 77W12 5:08:48
Achash 56 4 38N19'55 78W09'56 5:12:40
Achilles 36 4 37N16'48 76W26'26 5:05:46
Achsah 56 4 38N20 78W10 5:12:40
Acorn 41 4 36N57'58 78W58'58 5:15:56
Acorn 92 19 38N01'09 76W38'58 5:06:36
Acors Corner 17 22 38N05'24 77W19'35 5:09:18
Acquinton 50 14 37N43 77W06 5:08:24
Acredale 133 6 36N47'49 76W10'29 5:04:42
Acree Acres 95 4 37N10'32 76W28'08 5:05:53
Ada 30 19 38N50'13 77W55'07 5:11:40
Adams Grove 84 4 36N41'35 77W23'08 5:09:33
Addington 93 15 36N58'36 82W37'17 5:30:29
Addison 27 22 37N11'51 77W30'10 5:10:01
Addison Heights 7 1 38N51'20 77W03'38 5:08:15
Aden 73 14 38N39'18 77W32'15 5:10:09
Adial 61 14 37N51'53 78W49'50 5:15:19
Adkins Store 19 14 37N27 77W02 5:08:08
Adner 36 4 37N29'55 76W38'01 5:06:32
Adria 89 4 37N10'07 81W32'46 5:26:11
Adsit 13 4 36N49'38 77W41'54 5:10:48
Advance Mills 2 14 38N10'59 78W26'20 5:13:45
Adwolf 83 15 36N47'21 81W34'56 5:26:20
Afton 61 14 38N01'56 78W50'22 5:15:21
Agnewville 73 13 38N40'09 77W17'10 5:09:09
Agricola 5 16 37N31'52 79W14'39 5:16:59
Ahoy Acres 101 6 36N48'03 76W23'51 5:05:35
Aiken Summit 44 4 36N35'42 79W42'18 5:18:49
Aily 26 15 37N05'13 82W17'08 5:29:09
Airlie 30 19 38N45'25 77W47'31 5:11:10
Airmont 53 14 39N05'05 77W47'14 5:11:09
Airpoint 77 4 37N10'16 80W06'52 5:20:27
Ajax 69 4 36N58'51 79W34'38 5:18:19
Alanthus 24 4 38N32'31 77W55'59 5:11:44
Alanton 133 6 36N52'57 76W01'20 5:04:05
Albano 66 14 38N12'26 78W18'16 5:13:13
Alban Woods 73 13 38N39 77W16 5:09:04
Alberene 2 14 37N53'11 78W37'00 5:14:28
Alberta 13 4 36N51'56 77W53'12 5:11:33
Albin 34 9 39N13'18 78W11'56 5:12:48
Alchie 41 4 36N53'32 79W01'00 5:16:04
Alcoma 15 4 37N32'55 78W35'33 5:14:22
Alcova Heights 7 1 38N51'52 77W05'51 5:08:23
Aldie 53 4 38N58'32 77W38'30 5:10:34
Alexander Corner 125 6 36N48'54 76W21'24 5:05:26
Alexanders Corner 42 14 37N35'12 77W13'24 5:08:54
Alexandria 96 1 38N48'17 77W02'50 5:08:11
Alfonso 51 4 37N48'31 76W30'30 5:06:02
Algoma 33 4 37N03'21 80W05'15 5:20:21
Algonquin Park 121 6 36N54'31 76W17'35 5:05:10
Algren 101 6 36N46'29 76W26'48 5:05:47
Alhambra 5 16 37N47'12 79W05'24 5:16:22
Alice Heights 21 22 37N27 77W28 5:09:52
Alleghany 3 4 37N44'50 80W14'26 5:20:58
Alleghany Springs 60 4 37N07'41 80W15'55 5:21:04
Allen 26 15 37N10 82W22 5:29:28
Allencrest 7 1 38N53'36 77W09'02 5:08:36
Allens Creek 61 14 37N32'48 78W52'08 5:15:29
Allen Shop Corner 48 4 37N42'20 76W50'42 5:07:23
Allenslevel 15 4 37N33'42 78W29'23 5:13:58
Allens Mill 71 4 37N16'49 78W33'09 5:14:13
Allentown 1 4 37N41'44 75W41'22 5:02:45
Alliance 87 4 37N08'17 76W47'02 5:07:08
Allison 94 4 36N55'50 80W50'11 5:23:21
Allison Gap 83 15 36N53'39 81W46'37 5:27:06
Allisonia 74 4 36N56'21 80W44'11 5:22:57
Allmondsville 36 4 37N23'36 76W39'04 5:06:36
Allnut 49 22 38N18'29 77W06'22 5:08:25
Allwington 30 19 38N44 77W44 5:10:56
Allwood 5 16 37N38'58 79W13'16 5:16:53
Alma 67 14 38N35'28 78W33'28 5:14:14
Almagro 105 4 36N34'14 79W23'19 5:17:33
Almira 93 15 37N08'31 82W37'20 5:30:29
Alonzaville 82 14 38N55'43 78W32'48 5:14:11
Alpha 15 4 37N34'58 78W25'03 5:13:40
Alpine 12 4 37N34'54 79W36'20 5:18:25
Alpine 29 1 38N49'54 77W11'11 5:08:45
Alpine 82 14 38N40'14 78W38'06 5:14:32
Alps 17 22 38N01 77W22 5:09:28
Alsop 85 22 38N12'25 77W38'59 5:10:36
Altavista 16 16 37N06'42 79W17'09 5:17:09
Alto 5 16 37N46'19 79W13'41 5:16:55
Alton 41 4 36N34'23 79W00'11 5:16:01
Alum Ridge 31 4 36N58 80W24 5:21:36
Alum Springs 74 4 37N09'35 80W48'17 5:23:13
Alum Wells 91 25 36N45'28 82W11'01 5:28:44
Alvarado 91 15 36N39'02 81W53'13 5:27:33
Ambar 49 22 38N19'30 77W10'42 5:08:43
Amburg 59 4 37N33'13 76W21'31 5:05:26
Amelia Court House 4 4 37N20'34 77W58'51 5:11:55
Americana Apartments 29 1 38N50 77W12 5:08:48
Amherst 5 16 37N35'06 79W03'06 5:16:12
Amherst 29 3 38N48 77W16 5:09:04
Amicus 39 14 38N15'20 78W28'49 5:13:55
Amissville 75 14 38N40'17 77W59'45 5:11:59
Ammon 4 4 37N12'40 77W46'06 5:11:04
Amonate 89 4 37N11'27 81W38'20 5:26:33
Ampt Hill 21 22 37N27'06 77W26'42 5:09:47
Amsterdam 12 4 37N25'38 79W54'23 5:19:38
Andersons Mill 69 4 36N52'55 79W32'22 5:18:09
Andersonville 15 4 37N28'02 78W34'09 5:14:17
Andover 93 26 36N55'25 82W47'48 5:31:11
Andrew Lewis Place 77 4 37N17 80W03 5:20:12
Angelico 84 4 36N43'01 77W14'13 5:08:57
Angelo 5 16 37N32'38 79W04'28 5:16:18
Angola 25 4 37N24'05 78W14'25 5:12:58
Ankum 13 4 36N36'12 77W52'52 5:11:31
Annalee Heights 29 3 38N51'35 77W10'51 5:08:43
Annandale 29 1 38N49'49 77W11'48 5:08:47
Annandale Acres 29 1 38N49'07 77W11'36 5:08:46
Annandale Gardens 29 1 38N50 77W12 5:08:48
Annandale Terrace 29 1 38N49'26 77W12'25 5:08:50
Annex 8 21 38N09'40 78W59'09 5:15:57
Ante 13 14 36N39'53 77W43'10 5:10:53
Antioch 32 4 37N50'47 78W25'15 5:13:41
Antioch 73 14 38N51'32 77W41'11 5:10:45
Antioch Fork 17 22 38N01'03 77W20'17 5:09:21
Antlers 58 4 36N40'14 78W19'14 5:13:17
Appalachia 93 26 36N54'24 82W46'55 5:31:08
Apple Grove 54 14 37N53'34 77W53'50 5:11:35
Appomattox 6 4 37N21'25 78W49'32 5:15:18
Aqua 78 14 37N53 79W17 5:17:08
Aquia 86 4 38N28'56 77W23'13 5:09:33
Aragona Acres 133 6 36N52 76W00 5:04:00
Aragona Village 133 6 36N51'55 76W08'46 5:04:35
Ararat 68 4 36N35'56 80W30'39 5:22:03
Arbor Estates 132 5 36N44 76W35 5:06:20
Arbor Hill 8 21 38N05'59 79W09'10 5:16:37
Arbuckle Landing 101 6 36N35'34 76W23'06 5:05:32
Arcadia 12 4 37N32'43 79W37'27 5:18:30
Arcadia 85 22 38N06'23 77W31'48 5:10:07
Arch Mills 12 4 37N32 79W41 5:18:44
Arco 90 14 38N51'36 78W10'30 5:12:42
Arcola 53 4 38N57'06 77W32'04 5:10:08
Arcturus 29 1 38N44'19 77W02'42 5:08:11
Ardmore 107 3 38N50'39 77W18'55 5:09:16
Areanum 15 4 37N26'51 78W30'36 5:14:02
Argyle Heights 86 4 38N17'13 77W25'57 5:09:44
Ark 36 4 37N26'18 76W34'34 5:06:18
Arkendale 86 4 38N26'18 77W20'34 5:09:22
Arkton 79 22 38N34'23 78W41'44 5:14:47
Arlandria 96 1 38N50'28 77W04'02 5:08:16
Arlington 7 1 38N53 77W07 5:08:28
Arlington 63 4 37N13'35 76W00'06 5:04:00
Arlington 114 14 37N17'00 77W17'43 5:09:11
Arlington Forest 7 1 38N52'07 77W06'48 5:08:27
Arlington Hall 7 1 38N52 77W06 5:08:24
Arlington Heights 7 1 38N52'10 77W05'33 5:08:22
Arlington Village 7 1 38N51'42 77W05'08 5:08:21
Arlingwood 7 1 38N55'39 77W07'20 5:08:29
Armel 34 9 39N04'45 78W08'38 5:12:35
Armistead Forest 125 6 36N52'22 76W24'42 5:05:39
Armstrong 9 4 38N06'43 79W31'18 5:18:05
Armstrong Gardens 112 6 37N00'29 76W21'34 5:05:26
Arna Valley 7 1 38N50'39 77W04'36 5:08:18
Arno 93 26 36N55'38 82W48'44 5:31:15
Arnolds Corner 49 22 38N16'34 77W12'15 5:08:49
Aroda 56 4 38N19'35 78W13'57 5:12:56
Arringdale 84 4 36N43'04 77W20'11 5:09:21
Arrington 61 14 37N41'02 78W54'05 5:15:36
Arritt 3 4 37N47 79W59 5:19:56
Arrowhead 2 14 37N58'45 78W35'40 5:14:23
Arrowhead 133 6 36N50'03 76W11'14 5:04:45
Arthur 60 4 37N10 80W15 5:21:00
Artrip 80 15 36N57'50 82W07'07 5:28:28
Arvonia 15 4 37N41'00 78W20'30 5:13:22
Asberrys 89 4 37N00'41 81W32'20 5:26:09
Ashburn 53 4 39N02'37 77W29'16 5:09:57
Ashburn Junction 53 4 39N04'15 77W28'48 5:09:55
Ashby 25 4 37N34'39 78W10'31 5:12:42
Ashby 90 14 39N00'39 78W08'08 5:12:33
Ashbys Corner 75 14 38N37'55 78W14'04 5:12:56
Ashcake 42 22 37N41'30 77W24'10 5:09:37
Ashland 42 22 37N45'32 77W28'49 5:09:55
Ashland Mill 42 22 37N48'23 77W28'24 5:09:54
Ashton Glen 73 2 38N47 77W28 5:09:52
Ashville 30 19 38N51'51 77W55'21 5:11:41
Ashwood 9 4 37N58'21 79W51'02 5:19:24
Aspen 20 4 37N02'27 78W49'37 5:15:18
Aspenwall 20 4 37N01'14 78W49'26 5:15:18
Assawoman 1 4 37N52 75W32 5:02:08
Athens 17 22 37N59'33 77W25'03 5:09:40
Athlone 79 22 38N32'09 78W42'23 5:14:50
Atkins 83 15 36N52'02 81W25'25 5:25:42
Atlantic 1 4 37N54'02 75W30'29 5:02:02
Atlantic Park 133 6 36N50'36 76W00'39 5:04:03
Atlee 42 22 37N39'27 77W24'26 5:09:38
Atoka 30 4 38N58'32 77W48'35 5:11:14
Attoway 83 15 36N48'48 81W28'03 5:25:52
Auburn 30 19 38N42'10 77W42'04 5:10:48

Augusta Springs 8 21 38N06'07 79w19'06 5:17:16
Aura Heights 29 1 38N51 77w09 5:08:36
Aurora Hills 7 1 38N51'05 77w03'52 5:08:15
Austinville 94 4 36N51'04 80w54'44 5:23:39
Avalon 64 18 37N54'24 76w25'27 5:05:42
Avalon 101 6 36N48'22 76w16'32 5:05:06
Avalon Hills 133 6 36N48'39 76w11'22 5:04:45
Avalon Terrace 133 6 36N48'58 76w11'34 5:04:46
Averett 58 4 36N34'29 78w39'06 5:14:36
Avon 61 14 37N59'59 78w49'36 5:15:18
Avon Forest 29 3 38N46'19 77w18'21 5:09:13
Axtell 15 4 37N42'04 78w36'06 5:14:24
Axton 44 4 36N39'34 79w42'44 5:18:51
Aylett 50 14 37N47'09 77w06'19 5:08:25
Aylett Mill 50 14 37N45'43 77w05'34 5:08:22
Aylor 56 4 38N26'05 78w18'08 5:13:13
Azalea Acres 121 7 36N53'29 76w13'01 5:04:52
Azalea Court 43 17 37N36 77w27 5:09:48
Bachelors Hall 69 4 36N36'11 79w31'53 5:18:08
Backbay 133 6 36N51 76w06 5:04:24
Backbone 3 4 37N46'23 80w09'20 5:20:37
Back Creek 34 4 39N10 78w17 5:13:08
Back Landing 124 4 37N06'44 76w20'57 5:05:24
Back River 112 4 37N03'37 76w20'19 5:05:21
Bacon 20 4 36N51 78w37 5:14:28
Bacons Fork 55 4 36N51'08 78w03'37 5:12:14
Bacova 9 4 38N03'14 79w50'38 5:19:23
Bacova Junction 9 4 38N00'37 79w52'29 5:19:30
Baden 26 15 37N08'04 82w31'57 5:30:08
Bagby 17 22 37N55'34 77w13'54 5:08:56
Bagdad 17 22 37N54'19 77w25'25 5:09:42
Bagleys Mills 55 4 36N50'24 78w11'24 5:12:46
Bailey 89 4 37N13'27 81w23'10 5:25:33
Baileys 36 4 37N23'11 76w27'45 5:05:51
Baileys Beach 46 4 37N05'01 76w39'51 5:06:39
Baileys Crossroads 29 1 38N51'01 77w07'48 5:08:31
Baileys Ford 34 9 39N20'01 78w11'59 5:12:48
Baileytown 132 5 36N48'17 76w30'41 5:06:03
Baird Landing 28 4 38N02'57 76w56'32 5:07:46
Bakers Crossing 132 5 36N40'19 76w40'17 5:06:41
Balcony Falls 78 14 37N37'40 79w27'22 5:17:49
Baldwin 12 4 37N44'23 79w51'03 5:19:24
Ballards Crossroads 46 4 36N43 76w50 5:07:20
Ballentine Place 121 6 36N52'09 76w15'10 5:05:01
Balls Ford 29 2 38N48'42 77w29'32 5:09:58
Balls Hills 29 1 38N56'28 77w11'40 5:08:47
Balls Mill 30 19 38N37'49 77w44'22 5:10:57
Ballston 7 1 38N52'48 77w06'51 5:08:27
Ballsville 70 14 37N29'54 78w04'02 5:12:16
Ballylynn Shores 133 6 36N49'52 76w13'17 5:04:53
Baltimore Corner 27 22 37N05'56 77w43'38 5:10:55
Balty 17 22 37N59'51 77w26'43 5:09:47
Banco 56 4 38N27'04 78w16'55 5:13:08
Bandy 89 4 37N08'34 81w42'04 5:26:48
Bane 35 4 37N16'02 80w42'46 5:22:51
Bangor 81 15 36N52'36 82w24'26 5:29:38
Banister 69 4 36N46'18 79w32'04 5:18:08
Banner 93 15 36N56'58 82w25'47 5:29:43
Banners Corner 80 15 36N52'18 82w18'01 5:29:12
Bannockburn Estates 29 3 38N51 77w15 5:09:00
Barbour 66 14 38N12 78w16 5:13:04
Barbours Creek 23 4 37N33'19 80w03'11 5:20:13
Barboursville 66 14 38N10'15 78w16'55 5:13:08
Barcroft 7 1 38N51'21 77w06'15 5:08:25
Barcroft Hills 29 1 38N50'26 77w10'14 5:08:41
Barcroft, Lake 29 1 38N50'52 77w09'22 5:08:37
Barcroft Woods 29 1 38N50'30 77w10'15 5:08:41
Barfoot 33 4 36N58'42 79w55'47 5:19:43
Barham 87 4 37N08'28 77w06'47 5:08:27
Barhamsville 62 14 37N27'16 76w50'26 5:07:22
Barker Crossroads 13 4 36N37'11 78w00'43 5:12:03
Barker Mill 91 15 36N42'02 82w19'11 5:29:17
Barkers Crossroads 29 3 38N45'30 77w12'59 5:08:52
Barkers Mill 42 22 37N33'38 77w15'29 5:09:02
Barlett 46 4 36N56'27 76w32'15 5:06:09
Barley 40 20 36N33'50 77w43'28 5:10:54
Barlows Corner 95 23 37N21'31 76w43'02 5:06:52
Barnes Junction 20 4 36N49'14 78w35'45 5:14:23
Barnesville 20 4 36N47 78w37 5:14:28
Barnett 80 15 36N55'25 82w00'04 5:28:00
Barnetts 19 14 37N22'01 77w09'29 5:08:38
Barren Ridge 8 21 38N09'45 78w57'01 5:15:48
Barren Springs 94 4 36N54'29 80w48'03 5:23:12
Barrets Corner 133 6 36N48'45 76w12'20 5:04:49
Barrett Acres 132 5 36N44 76w35 5:06:20
Barrett Corner 84 4 36N53'00 77w02'32 5:08:10
Barterbrook 8 21 38N04'00 79w01'38 5:16:07
Bartlett 46 4 36N57 76w34 5:06:16
Bartlick 26 15 37N14'49 82w19'29 5:29:18
Barton Crossroad 38 4 36N39'26 81w21'08 5:25:25
Bartonville 34 9 39N06'41 78w12'44 5:12:51
Barytes 91 25 36N37'19 82w09'27 5:28:38
Bascomb Church 80 15 37N00 81w59 5:27:56
Basham 60 4 37N02'10 80w20'34 5:21:22
Basic 134 22 38N04 78w54 5:15:36
Baskerville 58 4 36N41'20 78w16'30 5:13:06
Baskerville Mill 27 4 36N58'32 77w46'11 5:11:05
Bassett 44 4 36N45'33 79w59'26 5:19:58
Bassett Forks 44 4 36N44'27 79w56'04 5:19:44
Bastian 11 4 37N09'07 81w09'01 5:24:36
Basye 82 14 38N48'25 78w47'33 5:15:10
Batesville 2 14 37N59'44 78w43'21 5:14:53
Bath Alum 9 4 38N02'55 79w43'08 5:18:53
Batna 24 4 38N24'05 77w53'27 5:11:34
Batt 36 4 37N34'07 76w38'56 5:06:36
Battersea 123 22 37N13'29 77w25'21 5:09:41
Battery 28 14 37N57'56 77w01'27 5:08:06
Battery Park 43 17 37N36 77w29 5:09:56
Battery Park 46 4 36N59'47 76w34'28 5:06:18
Battle Creek 67 14 38N36'23 78w35'10 5:14:21
Battlefield Acres 43 22 37N40 77w30 5:10:00
Battlefield Farms 42 22 37N37 77w22 5:09:28
Battlefield Park 72 22 37N13 77w26 5:09:44
Battle Park 95 4 37N11'51 76w29'35 5:05:58
Battletown 22 4 39N08 77w55 5:11:40
Bavon 57 4 37N20'00 76w17'19 5:05:09
Bay 112 4 37N01 76w19 5:05:16
Bayberry Estates 49 12 38N20 77w03 5:08:12
Bay Colony 133 6 36N52'41 76w00'23 5:04:02
Bayford 63 4 37N28'40 75w55'59 5:03:44
Bay Island 133 6 36N54'32 76w02'57 5:04:12
Baylake Beach 133 6 36N54'40 76w06'29 5:04:26
Baylake Pines 133 6 36N54'31 76w06'56 5:04:28
Baylortown 17 22 38N05'59 77w19'28 5:09:18
Baynesville 92 19 38N08'52 76w52'58 5:07:32
Bayport 59 4 37N45'16 76w40'26 5:06:42
Bayside 1 4 37N44'52 75w43'04 5:02:52
Bayside 57 4 37N19'31 76w17'39 5:05:11
Bayside Park 73 13 38N38'16 77w14'40 5:08:59
Bayview 63 4 37N16'36 75w58'04 5:03:52
Bay View Beach 121 6 36N56'20 76w14'09 5:04:57
Bayville Park 133 6 36N54'08 76w07'27 5:04:30
Baywood 38 4 36N36'37 81w00'44 5:24:03
Beach 21 22 37N23 77w31 5:10:04
Beachland 87 4 37N05'07 76w48'58 5:07:16
Beacon Manor 29 1 38N46 77w04 5:08:16
Beaconsdale 120 6 37N03'51 76w28'23 5:05:54
Beales 84 4 36N47'50 77w02'04 5:08:08
Bealeton 30 19 38N34'18 77w45'51 5:11:03
Beamantown 93 26 36N52'05 82w45'47 5:31:03
Beamon 132 5 36N47'42 76w31'40 5:06:07
Bear Spring 35 4 37N14'51 80w38'02 5:22:32
Bearwallow 14 15 37N14'29 81w44'40 5:26:59
Beaties Mill 42 22 37N37'18 77w15'11 5:09:01
Beaufont Hills 21 17 37N30'41 77w30'30 5:10:02
Beaumont 70 14 37N39'55 77w54'30 5:11:38
Beaverdam 42 22 37N56'28 77w39'17 5:10:37
Beaverlett 57 4 37N24'22 76w18'33 5:05:14
Beaver Park 56 4 36N39'48 79w20'44 5:17:23
Beazley 28 14 37N57'53 77w04'13 5:08:17
Beazley Ford 71 4 37N21'31 78w33'18 5:14:13
Beckham 6 4 37N29'28 78w54'18 5:15:37
Bedford 82 14 38N49 78w34 5:14:16
Bedford 97 4 37N20'03 79w31'24 5:18:06
Bee 26 15 37N06'54 82w10'20 5:28:41
Beech Grove 61 14 37N52'32 78w56'21 5:15:45
Beech Grove 133 6 36N49 76w09 5:04:36
Beechmont 120 4 37N08'16 76w33'09 5:06:13
Beech Springs 52 26 36N40 83w07 5:32:28
Beechwood 58 4 36N37'02 78w12'50 5:12:51
Beechwood 72 22 37N17'01 77w10'59 5:08:44
Beechwood 120 4 37N07'55 76w33'41 5:06:15
Beechwood 133 6 36N53'55 76w08'11 5:04:33
Beechwood Hills 16 14 37N20'31 79w14'37 5:16:58
Beechwood Manor 72 22 37N17'36 77w12'23 5:08:50
Beechwood Park 43 22 37N32 77w19 5:09:16
Beelers Ford 82 14 39N03'35 78w20'52 5:13:23
Bel Air 29 3 38N51'47 77w10'37 5:08:42
Bel Air 86 4 38N20'08 77w26'04 5:09:44
Bel-Aire 121 6 36N55'10 76w13'56 5:04:56
Belair Springs 68 4 36N37'37 80w28'41 5:21:55
Beldor 79 14 38N21'00 78w36'27 5:14:26
Belfair Crossroads 73 2 38N34'45 77w25'41 5:09:43
Belfast 80 15 36N59'01 81w51'16 5:27:25
Belfast Mills 80 15 36N58'47 81w50'24 5:27:22
Belfield 40 20 36N43 77w33 5:10:12
Belinda 1 4 37N54'41 75w39'44 5:02:39
Bellair 2 14 38N02'21 78w31'52 5:14:07
Bell Air 86 4 38N23 77w27 5:09:48
Bellamy 36 4 37N23'52 76w34'22 5:06:17
Bellamy 81 26 36N39'39 82w40'33 5:30:42
Bellamytown 81 26 36N36'12 82w45'45 5:31:03
Bellany Manor 133 6 36N48'41 76w09'28 5:04:38
Bellbluff 21 22 37N27 77w28 5:09:52
Belleair 29 3 38N46'32 77w17'52 5:09:11
Bellefonte 65 4 37N07 77w57 5:11:48
Belle Forest 29 3 38N51 77w15 5:09:00
Belle Haven 1 4 37N33'15 75w49'15 5:03:17
Belle Haven 29 1 38N47'07 77w03'48 5:08:15
Belle Haven 133 6 36N51 76w07 5:04:28
Belle Meade 30 19 38N54'28 78w02'15 5:12:09
Belle Meadows 91 25 36N36 82w11 5:28:44
Belle View 29 1 38N46'21 77w03'28 5:08:14
Belleview 48 4 37N29'02 76w44'05 5:06:56
Belleville 132 6 36N51'54 76w26'10 5:05:45
Bellevue 10 4 37N21'35 79w22'20 5:17:29
Bellevue 127 17 37N36 77w27 5:09:48
Bellevue Forest 7 3 38N54'51 77w06'50 5:08:27
Bells Crossroad 85 22 38N09'29 77w49'27 5:11:18
Bells Crossroads 54 14 37N57'44 78w04'55 5:12:20
Bells Mill 101 6 36N43'24 76w16'21 5:05:05
Bell Spur 68 4 36N44 80w25 5:21:40
Bells Valley 78 14 38N01'39 79w26'56 5:17:48
Bellview Terrace 112 4 37N02'48 76w20'13 5:05:21
Bellvue 85 24 38N15'27 77w29'22 5:09:57
Bellwood 21 22 37N25'18 77w26'16 5:09:45
Bellwood Manor 21 22 37N23'59 77w25'12 5:09:41
Belmont 53 4 39N03'53 77w30'37 5:10:02
Belmont 60 4 37N09'46 80w26'50 5:21:47
Belmont 85 22 38N09'13 77w51'59 5:11:28
Belmont 100 14 38N02 78w29 5:13:56
Belmont Acres 21 22 37N27 77w28 5:09:52
Belmont Farms 60 4 37N08 80w24 5:21:36
Belmont Park 29 3 38N39'45 77w12'19 5:08:49
Belona 70 14 37N31'16 78w00'32 5:12:02
Belroi 36 4 37N23'14 76w35'18 5:06:21
Belspring 74 4 37N11'27 80w36'30 5:22:26
Belvedere 29 1 38N50'18 77w09'33 5:08:38
Belvedere 125 6 36N51'47 76w22'53 5:05:32
Belvedere Beach 49 22 38N20'06 77w16'17 5:09:05
Belvoir 30 19 38N51'34 77w49'14 5:11:17
Bena 36 4 37N16'15 76w27'21 5:05:49
Benbolt 89 4 37N07'40 81w29'38 5:25:59
Benbow 89 4 37N03'56 81w30'37 5:26:02
Benedict 52 26 36N50'35 83w01'48 5:32:07
Benefit 101 4 36N37'43 76w17'05 5:05:08
Benhams 91 25 36N40'43 82w13'06 5:28:52
Ben Hur 52 26 36N43'58 83w04'56 5:32:20
Bennett Corner 132 4 36N49'54 76w30'33 5:06:02
Bennett Creek 132 5 36N51'50 76w29'10 5:05:57
Bennett Harbor 132 5 36N50'59 76w30'05 5:06:00
Bennetts Mill 60 4 37N15'42 80w20'21 5:21:21
Bennett Springs 77 4 37N22'13 80w02'16 5:20:09
Bennington Mill 38 4 36N43'24 81w13'45 5:24:55
Benns Church 46 4 36N56'16 76w35'11 5:06:21
Bensley 21 22 37N27 77w28 5:09:52
Bensley Village 21 22 37N26'12 77w26'46 5:09:47
Bent Creek 6 4 37N32'05 78w49'38 5:15:19
Bent Mountain 77 4 37N08'28 80w07'10 5:20:29
Bentonville 90 14 38N49'54 78w19'00 5:13:16
Bentonville Landing 90 14 38N50'30 78w19'39 5:13:19
Berea 86 4 38N21'43 77w31'12 5:10:05
Bergton 79 22 38N45'56 78w56'57 5:15:48
Berkeley 2 14 38N04'44 78w29'12 5:13:57
Berkeley 19 22 37N19'05 77w10'47 5:08:43
Berkeley Hills 135 23 37N15'35 76w43'51 5:06:55
Berkley 121 6 36N49'54 76w17'03 5:05:08
Berkshire 7 1 38N53'52 77w09'06 5:08:36
Berlin 84 4 36N51'27 76w58'40 5:07:55
Berlin and Ivor 84 4 36N52 76w57 5:07:48
Bermuda 21 22 37N23 77w25 5:09:40
Bermuda Hundred 21 22 37N23 77w26 5:09:44
Bernietown 89 4 37N17'39 81w21'41 5:25:27
Berry Hill 69 4 36N33'11 79w36'48 5:18:27
Berrymans Corner 87 4 37N01'36 76w50'07 5:07:20
Berrys 22 4 39N02'19 77w59'49 5:11:59
Berrytown 79 14 38N22'06 78w39'26 5:14:38
Berryville 22 14 39N09'06 77w58'57 5:11:56
Bertha 94 4 36N54'08 80w49'43 5:23:19
Berthaville 49 22 38N20'00 77w07'34 5:08:30
Berton 35 4 37N15'17 80w36'50 5:22:27
Bertrand 51 4 37N40'08 76w31'04 5:06:04
Bess 3 4 37N47 79w59 5:19:56
Bessemer 12 4 37N39'00 79w49'07 5:19:16
Bestland 28 4 37N48'26 76w52'58 5:07:32
Bethany 94 4 36N50'37 80w52'50 5:23:31
Bethel 22 4 39N01'51 78w02'37 5:12:10
Bethel 30 19 38N45'58 77w48'58 5:11:16
Bethel 73 13 38N39'19 77w18'26 5:09:14
Bethel 90 14 38N56'34 78w15'33 5:13:02
Bethel 91 15 36N40'31 81w52'41 5:27:31
Bethel 95 4 37N07 76w26 5:05:44
Bethel Manor 95 4 37N07 76w31 5:06:04
Bethlehem Fork 28 22 38N00'50 77w05'23 5:08:22
Betz Landing 64 18 37N52'19 76w25'57 5:05:44
Beulah 21 22 37N25'28 77w28'15 5:09:53
Beulah 36 4 37N23'00 76w26'33 5:05:46
Beulah Church 28 14 37N55 76w52 5:07:28
Beulah Village 21 22 37N27 77w28 5:09:52
Beulahville 50 14 37N51'17 77w10'44 5:08:43

Beverley Hills 96 1 38N50'16 77w04'22 5:08:17
Beverley Mill 30 19 38N49'27 77w42'40 5:10:51
Beverly Forest 29 3 38N45'42 77w11'15 5:08:45
Beverly Heights 129 4 37N17'13 80w06'44 5:20:27
Beverly Hills 43 22 37N36 77w32 5:10:08
Beverly Hills 120 4 37N04'39 76w30'55 5:06:04
Beverly Manor 8 21 38N08 79w03 5:16:12
Beverly Manor 29 1 38N55 77w11 5:08:44
Beverlytown 5 16 37N39'07 79w18'13 5:17:13
Beverlyville 64 18 37N51'54 76w16'53 5:05:08
Big Bethel 112 6 37N05'23 76w25'26 5:05:42
Big Fork 58 4 36N40'17 78w12'47 5:12:51
Big Hill 91 15 36N38'58 81w38'15 5:26:33
Big Island 10 4 37N32'01 79w21'36 5:17:26
Big Laurel 93 15 37N00'45 82w37'19 5:30:29
Big Lick 77 4 37N19 79w51 5:19:24
Big Meadows 56 14 38N31'35 78w26'24 5:13:46
Big Otter Mill 10 4 37N23'25 79w30'18 5:18:01
Big River 8 21 37N59 79w30 5:18:00
Big Rock 14 15 37N21'30 82w11'15 5:28:45
Big Spring 67 14 38N43'30 78w25'25 5:13:42
Big Stone Gap 93 26 36N52'54 82w44'50 5:30:59
Big Vein 89 4 37N17'46 81w21'25 5:25:26
Biltmore 43 22 37N39'02 77w28'09 5:09:53
Binns Hall 19 14 37N20 77w04 5:08:16
Birch 41 4 36N42'53 79w10'02 5:16:40
Birch Creek 41 4 36N42 79w06 5:16:24
Birchett Estate 72 14 37N15'37 77w16'38 5:09:07
Birchleaf 26 15 37N10'38 82w16'20 5:29:05
Birch Town 1 4 37N55'13 75w22'08 5:01:29
Birchwood-Gardens 133 6 36N50'44 76w06'19 5:04:25
Birchwood Park 47 23 37N14'47 76w43'51 5:06:55
Birdneck Acres 133 6 36N52 76w00 5:04:00
Birdsnest 63 4 37N26'20 75w52'53 5:03:32
Birmingham 89 4 37N04'21 81w48'50 5:27:15
Biscoe 48 4 37N49'04 77w03'29 5:08:14
Bishop 89 4 37N12'31 81w33'30 5:26:14
Bishops Corner 55 4 36N55'24 78w05'23 5:12:22
Blackberry 44 4 36N43'00 80w02'20 5:20:09
Black Branch 58 4 36N49'31 78w29'50 5:13:59
Black Creek 62 14 37N32 77w10 5:08:40
Black Creek 84 4 36N46'17 76w55'31 5:07:42
Blackey 14 15 37N23'03 81w59'51 5:27:59
Blackford 80 15 36N59'45 81w56'35 5:27:46
Blacklick 94 4 36N56'35 81w15'25 5:25:02
Black Point Landing 1 4 37N54'34 75w23'01 5:01:32
Blackridge 58 4 36N38'42 78w03'26 5:12:14
Blacksburg 60 4 37N13'46 80w24'51 5:21:39
Blacksburg 78 14 37N49'07 79w19'10 5:17:17
Blacksburg 91 15 36N45'15 81w49'14 5:27:17
Blacksmith Corner 95 4 37N13'50 76w34'04 5:06:16
Blackstone 65 4 37N04'49 77w59'51 5:11:59
Black Walnut 41 4 36N38 78w55 5:15:40
Blackwater 52 26 36N37'38 83w03'03 5:32:12
Blackwater 57 4 37N25'36 76w24'00 5:05:36
Blackwater 133 6 36N36'21 76w05'13 5:04:21
Blackwater Bridge 133 6 36N51 76w06 5:04:24
Blackwells 64 18 37N51'15 76w21'27 5:05:26
Blackwells Chapel 91 15 36N46 81w52 5:27:28
Blackwood 93 15 36N55'30 82w41'35 5:30:46
Blades Corner 85 22 38N07'20 77w36'59 5:10:28
Blainesville 67 14 38N36'25 78w27'03 5:13:48
Blairs 56 4 36N40'47 79w22'24 5:17:30
Blairs 72 14 37N17'50 77w07'52 5:08:31
Blakes 57 4 37N29'57 76w22'04 5:05:28
Bland 11 4 37N06'07 81w06'59 5:24:28
Blandford 123 22 37N13'49 77w23'33 5:09:34
Blanton Crossing 42 22 37N45'38 77w23'04 5:09:32
Blantons 17 22 38N03'09 77w33'41 5:10:15
Bleak 30 19 38N31'17 77w40'55 5:10:44
Bledsoe Corner 66 14 38N19'41 77w54'24 5:11:38
Blendon 65 4 37N09 78w03 5:12:12
Blenheim 2 14 37N54'12 78w29'19 5:13:57
Blessing 94 4 36N56'08 81w12'19 5:24:49
Blevins Corner 55 4 36N58'50 78w26'13 5:13:45
Blevinstown 29 3 38N49'34 77w22'15 5:09:29
Bloom Crossing 73 2 38N45'51 77w26'35 5:09:46
Bloomer Spring 79 22 38N24'52 78w41'51 5:14:47
Bloomfield 53 4 39N03'12 77w49'15 5:11:17
Bloomingdale 43 17 37N36 77w29 5:09:56
Blowing Rock 26 15 37N13'35 82w25'51 5:29:43
Bloxom 1 4 37N49'46 75w37'25 5:02:30
Bloxoms Corner 112 4 37N03'34 76w18'02 5:05:12
Bluefield 89 4 37N15'09 81w16'17 5:25:05
Blue Grass 45 4 38N33'00 79w33'00 5:18:12
Blue Hole 79 22 38N30'20 79w02'56 5:16:12
Bluemont 53 4 39N06'40 77w50'03 5:11:20
Bluemont Junction 7 1 38N52'29 77w08'01 5:08:32
Bluemont Park 7 1 38N52'05 77w07'48 5:08:31
Blue Mountain 90 14 38N57'45 78w02'22 5:12:09
Blue Oaks 29 3 38N49'12 77w18'30 5:09:14
Blue Ridge 12 4 37N22'42 79w48'26 5:19:14
Blue Ridge Farms 116 14 37N24'57 79w13'11 5:16:53
Blue Ridge Mountains Estates 90 14 38N51'08 78w09'03 5:12:36
Blue Ridge Shores 54 14 38N06'18 78w01'30 5:12:06
Bluestone 58 4 36N43 78w32 5:14:08
Bluestone Landing 58 4 36N39'51 78w34'14 5:14:17
Bluff City 35 4 37N20'17 80w45'23 5:23:02
Blundon Corner 64 18 37N53'32 76w21'49 5:05:27
Boaz 46 4 36N44'48 76w45'43 5:07:03
Bobtown 1 4 37N39'03 75w47'37 5:03:10
Bocock 16 14 37N21'35 79w06'44 5:16:27
Body Camp 10 4 37N20 79w31 5:18:04
Boer 51 4 37N46'10 76w34'58 5:06:20
Bohannon 57 4 37N23'48 76w21'37 5:05:26
Boiling Spring 2 14 37N46'48 78w35'17 5:14:21
Boiling Spring 3 4 37N41'17 80w05'37 5:20:22
Boissevain 89 4 37N16'54 81w22'50 5:25:31
Bolar 9 4 38N13'02 79w40'36 5:18:42
Bolling Store 18 4 36N46 80w44 5:22:56
Bolton 80 15 36N48'17 82w11'52 5:28:47
Bon Air 7 1 38N52'23 77w07'37 5:08:30
Bon Air 21 22 37N31'29 77w33'29 5:10:14
Bondtown 93 15 36N57'02 82w28'15 5:29:53
Bonney Landing 133 6 36N41'11 76w02'39 5:04:11
Bonniemill Gardens 29 3 38N45 77w12 5:08:48
Bonny Blue 52 26 36N49 83w03 5:32:12
Bonsack 77 4 37N19'33 79w51'58 5:19:28
Boody 80 15 36N54'21 82w17'50 5:29:11
Booker 88 4 36N56'22 77w17'06 5:09:08
Boom Furnace 74 4 36N55'14 80w46'10 5:23:05
Boone 101 6 36N50'32 76w26'02 5:05:44
Boones Mill 33 4 37N07'00 79w57'20 5:19:49
Boonesville 2 14 38N14'10 78w35'53 5:14:24
Boonsboro 10 14 37N26'57 79w15'42 5:17:03
Booth Fork 87 4 36N58'45 76w56'50 5:07:47
Bordeaux 29 3 38N58 77w22 5:09:28
Borkey Store 42 22 37N37 77w22 5:09:28
Boscobel 37 4 37N35'56 77w43'54 5:10:56
Bosher 43 22 37N33'56 77w35'05 5:10:20
Boston 1 4 37N36'33 75w50'35 5:03:22
Boston 24 4 38N32'27 78w07'55 5:12:32
Boston 132 5 36N44 76w35 5:06:20
Boswells Store 86 4 38N25 77w24 5:09:36
Boswells Tavern 54 14 38N09 78w11 5:12:44
Botha 30 19 38N36'24 77w50'17 5:11:21
Boudar 43 17 37N37'37 77w29'57 5:10:00
Boudar Gardens 43 17 37N36 77w29 5:09:56
Boulder 81 26 36N40'28 82w44'36 5:30:58
Boulevard Estates 29 3 38N52'01 77w15'41 5:09:03
Boulevard Manor 133 6 36N50'52 76w10'04 5:04:40
Bowens Corner 13 4 36N34'01 77w49'17 5:11:17
Bowers Corner 13 4 36N38'10 77w57'40 5:11:51
Bowers Hill 101 6 36N47'12 76w24'47 5:05:39
Bowler 6 4 37N16'37 78w42'18 5:14:49
Bowlers Wharf 28 14 37N55 76w52 5:07:28
Bowling 52 26 36N40 83w07 5:32:28
Bowling Green 17 22 38N02'58 77w20'49 5:09:23
Bowmans 82 14 38N49 78w34 5:14:16
Bowmans Crossing 82 14 38N48'27 78w35'32 5:14:22
Boxley 35 4 37N16'08 80w57'15 5:23:49
Boxley Hills 77 4 37N19 79w55 5:19:40
Boxley Hills 120 6 37N06'06 76w31'30 5:06:06
Boxwood 44 4 36N38'20 79w42'52 5:18:51
Boyce 22 4 39N05'35 78w03'35 5:12:14
Boyds Mill 90 14 38N50'05 78w13'55 5:12:56
Boyd Tavern 2 14 38N02 78w40 5:14:40
Boydton 58 4 36N40'03 78w23'16 5:13:33
Boykins 84 4 36N34'59 77w12'01 5:08:48
Boys Home 3 4 37N47 79w59 5:19:56
Bracey 58 4 36N35'58 78w08'36 5:12:34
Braddock 96 1 38N49'15 77w04'06 5:08:16
Braddock Heights 96 1 38N49'50 77w04'39 5:08:19
Braddock Hills 29 1 38N50 77w12 5:08:48
Bradford Acres 133 6 36N53 76w08 5:04:32
Brad Lee 96 1 38N49'49 77w05'41 5:08:23
Bradley Acres 43 22 37N31'03 77w13'54 5:08:56
Bradley Forest 73 2 38N41'57 77w28'29 5:09:54
Bradshaw 77 4 37N17'59 80w13'28 5:20:54
Braehead Woods 110 24 38N16'49 77w28'48 5:09:55
Braggs Corner 24 14 38N28'23 77w57'11 5:11:49
Brambleton 121 6 36N50'53 76w16'17 5:05:05
Branchville 84 4 36N34'13 77w14'56 5:09:00
Brand 8 21 38N06'55 79w01'01 5:16:04
Brandon 72 22 37N15'21 76w59'56 5:08:00
Brandons Store 13 4 37N05 78w00 5:12:00
Brandon Village 7 1 38N52'32 77w06'58 5:08:28
Brandy Creek Estates 42 22 37N36'23 77w20'04 5:09:20
Brandy Station 24 4 38N30'06 77w53'38 5:11:35
Brandywine 17 22 38N06'54 77w10'51 5:08:43
Brays 28 14 37N53'44 76w52'25 5:07:30
Brays Landing 36 4 37N19'05 76w28'23 5:05:54
Break Reed Ford 44 4 36N34'16 79w45'54 5:19:04
Breaks 26 15 37N17'45 82w16'52 5:29:07
Brecon Ridge 29 3 38N51 77w15 5:09:00
Bremo Bluff 32 4 37N42'44 78w17'52 5:13:11
Bren Mar Park 29 1 38N47'55 77w09'20 5:08:37
Brents Landing 64 18 37N55'25 76w23'49 5:05:35
Brentsville 73 14 38N41'17 77w29'47 5:09:59
Brentwood 101 6 36N47'14 76w19'43 5:05:19
Briarcliff 77 4 37N23 79w49 5:19:16
Briarwood 91 25 36N36 82w11 5:28:44
Briarwood 125 6 36N51'57 76w22'48 5:05:31
Brickhouse Landing 50 14 37N34'00 76w55'55 5:07:44
Bridgeport 15 4 37N42'35 78w20'03 5:13:20
Bridges Creek Landing 92 19 38N12'05 76w56'00 5:07:44
Bridgetown 63 4 37N26'44 75w55'36 5:03:42
Bridgewater 79 22 38N22'55 78w58'37 5:15:54
Bridle Creek 38 4 36N37'08 81w14'37 5:24:58
Briery 71 4 37N05'29 78w27'29 5:13:50
Briery Branch 79 22 38N26'06 79w04'47 5:16:19
Briggs 22 14 39N06'28 78w00'51 5:12:03
Brighton Square 29 1 38N49 77w09 5:08:36
Brights 69 4 37N01'43 79w25'57 5:17:44
Brightwell Mill 5 14 37N27'30 79w02'51 5:16:11
Brightwood 67 4 38N25'17 78w11'38 5:12:47
Brilyn Park 29 1 38N53'55 77w10'29 5:08:42
Brink 41 20 36N37'04 77w38'05 5:10:32
Brinton 31 4 37N02 80w10 5:20:40
Bristersburg 30 19 38N35'00 77w36'51 5:10:27
Bristol 98 25 36N35'47 82w11'19 5:28:45
Bristow 29 1 38N48'43 77w12'51 5:08:51
Bristow 73 14 38N43'22 77w32'11 5:10:09
Britain 53 4 39N15'10 77w41'50 5:10:47
Britton Hills Farms 43 17 37N34 77w29 5:09:56
Broad Bay Colony 133 6 36N54'17 76w03'28 5:04:14
Broaddus 17 22 38N04'02 77w17'44 5:09:11
Broaddus 61 14 37N43 78w51 5:15:24
Broadford 83 15 36N55'38 81w40'22 5:26:41
Broadmoor 101 6 36N46'28 76w19'16 5:05:17
Broad Rock 127 17 37N29 77w29 5:09:56
Broad Run 73 14 38N59 77w29 5:09:56
Broad Run Farms 53 4 39N03'31 77w25'59 5:09:44
Broadwater 63 4 37N23'34 75w42'32 5:02:50
Broadway 79 22 38N36'47 78w47'57 5:15:12
Broadway Landing 1 4 37N42'44 75w49'52 5:03:19
Brockroad 85 22 38N16'28 77w40'46 5:10:43
Brodnax 13 4 36N42'23 78w01'54 5:12:08
Brokenburg 85 22 38N08'44 77w43'09 5:10:53
Broken Hill 30 19 38N45'04 77w42'30 5:10:50
Brooke 86 4 38N23 77w23 5:09:32
Brookes Corner 30 19 38N52'00 77w49'09 5:11:17
Brookeshire 48 4 37N31'38 76w46'46 5:07:07
Brookfield 29 3 38N54 77w26 5:09:44
Brookfield 86 4 38N18'40 77w25'59 5:09:44
Brookfield Park 121 6 36N55'53 76w13'59 5:04:56
Brookhaven 29 1 38N55'49 77w09'49 5:08:39
Brook Hill 29 1 38N48'41 77w12'18 5:08:49
Brook Hill 43 17 37N36'20 77w26'40 5:09:47
Brookland 43 22 37N38 77w29 5:09:56
Brookland Estates 29 3 38N47'17 77w07'53 5:08:32
Brookland Gardens 43 17 37N36 77w29 5:09:56
Brookley Acres 43 22 37N40 77w30 5:10:00
Brooklyn 41 4 36N40'22 79w09'30 5:16:38
Brookneal 16 16 37N03'00 78w56'40 5:15:47
Brook Vale 51 4 37N45'33 76w25'16 5:05:41
Brookville 96 1 38N49'16 77w07'07 5:08:28
Brookville 116 14 37N21'36 79w12'31 5:16:50
Brookwood 8 21 38N04'39 79w05'22 5:16:21
Brookwood 133 6 36N51 76w07 5:04:28
Brosville 69 4 36N37 79w37 5:18:28
Brown Field 73 14 38N31 77w18 5:09:12
Brown Grove 42 22 37N42'58 77w25'32 5:09:42
Brownsburg 78 14 37N55'42 79w19'10 5:17:17
Browns Corner 62 14 37N31'04 77w05'23 5:08:22
Browns Corner 64 4 37N49'23 76w25'08 5:05:41
Browns Cove 2 14 38N04 78w42 5:14:48
Browns Mill 29 3 38N57'03 77w17'04 5:09:08
Browns Store 18 4 36N44'03 80w48'02 5:23:12
Browns Store 55 4 36N58 78w06 5:12:24
Browns Store 64 18 37N49'44 76w25'45 5:05:43
Brownsville 2 14 38N03'06 78w41'58 5:14:48
Browntown 2 14 37N50'10 78w33'54 5:14:16
Browntown 5 16 37N37'40 79w10'19 5:16:41
Browntown 16 16 37N06'26 79w24'25 5:17:38
Browntown 90 14 38N48'39 78w14'02 5:12:56
Broyhill Crest 29 1 38N50'47 77w11'40 5:08:47
Broyhill Forest 7 3 38N54'55 77w07'22 5:08:29
Broyhill-Glen Gary Park 29 1 38N55'18 77w10'03 5:08:40
Broyhill-Langley Estates 29 1 38N56'57 77w11'08 5:08:45
Broyhill-McLean Estates 29 1 38N56'07 77w11'15 5:08:45
Broyhill Park 29 3 38N51'36 77w11'48 5:08:47
Bruce 101 6 36N50'04 76w23'58 5:05:36
Brucetown 34 4 39N15'16 78w04'01 5:12:16
Bruceville 71 4 37N05'30 78w22'45 5:13:31
Bruington 48 4 37N46'31 76w59'30 5:07:58

Bruno 81 26 36N38'15 82w25'20 5:29:41
Brunswick 13 4 36N38'51 77w52'15 5:11:29
Brush Harbor 60 4 37N11'03 80w17'28 5:21:10
Brush Tavern 16 14 37N19'44 79w14'47 5:16:59
Bruton 95 23 37N17 76w40 5:06:40
Brutus 69 4 37N00'39 79w16'10 5:17:05
Bryan Park 43 17 37N36 77w29 5:09:56
Bryant 61 14 37N48'03 78w57'24 5:15:50
Bryant Corner 64 18 37N52'59 76w27'33 5:05:50
Bryants Corner 40 20 36N35'18 77w24'57 5:09:40
Bryant Town 92 19 38N09'15 76w48'54 5:07:16
Bryn Mawr 29 1 38N55'51 77w10'40 5:08:43
Buchanan 12 4 37N31'38 79w40'48 5:18:43
Buck 18 4 36N48'16 80w55'50 5:23:43
Buckeye 42 22 37N41'14 77w19'00 5:09:16
Buckhall 73 2 38N43'54 77w25'53 5:09:44
Buckhorn 58 4 36N44 78w15 5:13:00
Buckingham 7 1 38N52'24 77w06'25 5:08:26
Buckingham 15 4 37N33'00 78w33'21 5:14:13
Buckingham 21 22 37N30'29 77w40'40 5:10:43
Buckingham Circle 2 14 38N01'46 78w31'51 5:14:07
Buckland 73 14 38N46'49 77w40'27 5:10:42
Bucknell Heights 29 1 38N45'53 77w04'40 5:08:19
Bucknell Manor 29 1 38N46'05 77w04'10 5:08:17
Buckner 54 14 37N57'43 77w46'23 5:11:06
Buckners Corner 75 14 38N37'18 78w14'08 5:12:57
Buckroe Beach 112 4 37N02'34 76w17'37 5:05:10
Buckroe Gardens 112 4 37N03'00 76w17'33 5:05:10
Buckton 90 14 38N57'19 78w15'15 5:13:01
Bucu 26 15 37N04'07 82w12'49 5:28:51
Buell 101 6 36N47'11 76w17'28 5:05:10
Buena 24 4 38N20'29 78w02'54 5:12:12
Buena Vista 99 14 37N44'03 79w21'15 5:17:25
Buffalo Bend 78 14 37N42'59 79w28'22 5:17:53
Buffalo Ford 91 25 36N44'51 82w11'10 5:28:45
Buffalo Forge 78 14 37N41'12 79w26'00 5:17:44
Buffalo Gap 8 21 38N11'13 79w14'23 5:16:58
Buffalo Hill 5 16 37N36'46 79w01'01 5:16:04
Buffalo Hills 7 1 38N52'10 77w09'21 5:08:37
Buffalo Junction 58 4 36N36'15 78w37'55 5:14:32
Buffalo Ridge 68 4 36N44'13 80w14'56 5:21:00
Buffalo Springs 58 4 36N38'45 78w39'43 5:14:39
Buffalo Springs 61 14 37N36'34 78w51'44 5:15:27
Bufford Crossroads 40 20 36N44'16 77w37'11 5:10:29
Buford 21 22 37N29 77w33 5:10:12
Buford 69 4 36N34'00 79w32'47 5:18:11
Bula 37 4 37N46'25 78w02'47 5:12:11
Bullbegger 1 4 37N57'28 75w36'53 5:02:28
Bullocks Corner 17 22 38N09'21 77w20'05 5:09:20
Bull Run 29 3 38N50 77w26 5:09:44
Bull Run Mountain Estates 73 14 38N54'13 77w39'43 5:10:39
Bulls Landing 63 4 37N10'39 75w56'26 5:03:46
Bumpass 54 14 37N57'48 77w44'15 5:10:57
Bundick 64 18 37N57'38 76w29'15 5:05:57
Bundy 52 26 36N49'47 82w55'52 5:31:43
Bungalow City 43 22 37N32 77w19 5:09:16
Bungletown 2 14 37N52'16 78w38'38 5:14:35
Bunker Hill 10 4 37N16'30 79w33'11 5:18:13
Bunker Hill 90 14 39N00'48 78w12'21 5:12:49
Burdette 84 4 36N46'06 76w53'55 5:07:36
Burgess 27 22 37N08'33 77w30'43 5:10:03
Burgess 64 18 37N52'59 76w20'53 5:05:24
Burgundy Farms 29 3 38N43 77w09 5:08:36
Burgundy Manor 29 1 38N47 77w05 5:08:20
Burgundy Village 29 3 38N47'55 77w05'16 5:08:21
Burkdale 120 6 37N06'08 76w32'18 5:06:09
Burke 29 3 38N47'36 77w16'19 5:09:05
Burke Heights 29 3 38N48 77w16 5:09:04
Burke Hills 29 3 38N48 77w16 5:09:04
Burkes Corner 95 23 37N21'09 76w43'56 5:06:56
Burkes Garden 89 4 37N05'53 81w20'28 5:25:22
Burkes Shop 17 22 38N07 77w25 5:09:40
Burkes Tavern 71 4 37N11'41 78w14'19 5:12:57
Burketown 8 21 38N18'10 78w56'05 5:15:44
Burkeville 65 4 37N11'15 78w12'06 5:12:48
Burks Fork 31 4 36N49 80w29 5:21:56
Burlington Mills 74 4 37N05'23 80w41'06 5:22:44
Burners Ford 67 14 38N48'02 78w22'02 5:13:28
Burning Knolls 34 9 39N09'39 78w06'15 5:12:25
Burnley 2 14 38N10'04 78w20'25 5:13:22
Burnley Town 9 4 37N17 81w23 5:25:32
Burnside Farms 42 22 37N37'34 77w23'39 5:09:35
Burnsville 9 4 38N10'40 79w38'52 5:18:35
Burnt Chimney 33 4 37N06'18 79w48'57 5:19:16
Burnt Factory 34 4 39N11'40 78w04'35 5:12:18
Burnt Store 58 4 36N42 78w06 5:12:24
Burnt Tree 56 4 38N17'54 78w10'45 5:12:43
Burr Hill 66 14 38N20'38 77w51'36 5:11:26
Burrowsville 72 22 37N12'52 77w04'34 5:08:18
Burruss Corner 17 22 37N53'35 77w24'59 5:09:40
Burson Place 91 25 36N39'57 82w10'40 5:28:43
Burtons 133 7 36N53'07 76w11'46 5:04:47
Burtons Corner 76 18 37N55'44 76w33'15 5:06:13
Burtons Ford 93 15 36N53'29 82w20'23 5:29:22
Burtons Shop 89 4 37N08 81w31 5:26:04
Burtonville 39 14 38N16'23 78w20'57 5:13:24
Burwell Bay 46 4 37N03'19 76w40'07 5:06:40
Bush Hill 29 3 38N43 77w09 5:08:36
Bush Hill Woods 29 3 38N47'20 77w07'23 5:08:30
Bush Mill 81 26 36N45'20 82w26'08 5:29:45
Bushy 59 4 37N34 76w26 5:05:44
Busthead 89 4 37N06'26 81w41'54 5:26:48
Bustleburg 78 14 37N53'31 79w21'53 5:17:28
Butlers Fork 17 22 37N57'15 77w14'04 5:08:56
Butterworth 27 22 37N03'04 77w37'38 5:10:31
Butts 91 15 36N43'56 82w02'12 5:28:09
Butts 101 6 36N44'36 76w13'27 5:04:54
Butts Corner 29 3 38N46'52 77w19'40 5:09:19
Butylo 28 4 37N46'15 76w41'18 5:06:45
Butzner Corner 86 22 38N15'20 77w21'28 5:09:26
Bybee 32 4 37N55'32 78w12'21 5:12:49
Byllesby 18 4 36N47'04 80w56'07 5:23:44
Byno 81 25 36N36 82w11 5:28:44
Bynum Store 58 4 36N48 78w28 5:13:52
Byrd 37 4 37N47 78w03 5:12:12
Byrd Mill 54 14 37N59'18 78w04'52 5:12:19
Byrdton 64 18 37N42'04 76w20'13 5:05:21
Cabin Point 87 4 37N10 76w58 5:07:52
Cadet 93 26 36N51'37 82w47'41 5:31:11
Cady 42 22 37N44'33 77w21'44 5:09:27
Caira 25 4 37N30 78w15 5:13:00
Caledonia 37 4 37N49'16 78w06'24 5:12:26
California 78 14 37N54'32 79w35'14 5:18:21
California Crossroads 87 4 37N06'31 76w46'28 5:07:06
Callaghan 3 4 37N48'43 80w04'28 5:20:18
Callahans Corner 58 4 36N42'41 78w17'03 5:13:08
Callahans Hills 69 4 36N36'15 79w31'08 5:18:05
Callands 69 4 36N49'12 79w35'13 5:18:21
Callao 64 18 37N58'09 76w33'36 5:06:14
Callaville 13 4 36N49'42 77w40'04 5:10:40
Callaway 33 4 37N00'41 80w02'59 5:20:12
Callison 9 4 37N58'43 79w54'42 5:19:39
Calno 50 14 37N48'47 77w18'06 5:09:12
Calvary 82 14 38N52'24 78w33'07 5:14:12
Calverton 30 19 38N37'55 77w40'15 5:10:41
Calvin 52 26 36N51'07 82w56'30 5:31:46
Cambria 60 4 37N08 80w24 5:21:36
Cambridge 21 22 37N31'49 77w34'48 5:10:19
Camden Heights 121 7 36N52'57 76w12'12 5:04:49
Camellia Shores 121 7 36N54'49 76w12'17 5:04:49
Camelot 29 1 38N50'23 77w13'55 5:08:56
Cameron 96 1 38N48'05 77w08'03 5:08:32
Cameron Hills 21 22 37N20'33 77w20'36 5:09:22
Cameron Valley 96 3 38N48'29 77w05'11 5:08:21
Cameron Villa Farms 29 3 38N46'49 77w08'16 5:08:33
Camm 15 4 37N38'45 78w35'36 5:14:22
Camp 83 15 36N47 81w25 5:25:40
Camp Appalachia 3 4 37N47 79w59 5:19:56
Camp Barrett 86 4 38N30 77w26 5:09:44
Campbell 2 14 38N01'54 78w18'09 5:13:13
Campbell Corner 15 4 37N39'34 78w17'06 5:13:08
Campbell Corner 17 22 37N51'33 77w24'15 5:09:37
Campbells Corner 17 22 37N55'33 77w20'39 5:09:23
Campbells Landing 133 6 36N36'24 75w59'29 5:03:58
Camp Corner 84 4 36N54'01 76w55'51 5:07:43
Campostella Heights 121 6 36N50'01 76w15'38 5:05:03
Camp Pickett 13 4 37N05 78w00 5:12:00
Camps Mill 132 5 36N44 76w35 5:06:20
Cana 18 4 36N35'22 80w40'19 5:22:41
Candlewax 80 15 37N01 81w59 5:27:56
Cannady 14 15 37N09'54 82w12'15 5:28:49
Cannon 29 1 38N47'39 77w05'52 5:08:23
Canova 73 2 38N40'37 77w26'32 5:09:46
Canterburg 34 4 39N06 78w13 5:12:52
Canterbury 43 22 37N36'06 77w36'10 5:10:25
Canterbury Hills 2 14 38N03'32 78w30'31 5:14:02
Canterbury Hills 47 23 37N15'43 76w44'36 5:06:58
Canterbury Woods 29 1 38N49'00 77w14'19 5:08:57
Canton 81 26 36N39'27 82w55'15 5:31:41
Cap 18 4 36N43 80w49 5:23:16
Capahosic 36 4 37N22'51 76w38'00 5:06:32
Cape Charles 63 4 37N16'04 76w01'04 5:04:04
Cape Henry Shores 133 6 36N52 76w00 5:04:00
Cape Junction 63 4 37N16'12 75w59'04 5:03:56
Cape Story By The Sea 133 6 36N54'36 76w03'28 5:04:14
Capeville 63 4 37N12'10 75w57'27 5:03:50
Capitol View 43 17 37N28'33 77w23'27 5:09:34
Capon Road 82 14 39N00 78w22 5:13:28
Capron 84 4 36N42'39 77w12'01 5:08:48
Captain 23 4 37N23'32 80w27'18 5:21:49
Carbo 80 15 36N55'42 82w11'40 5:28:47
Cardina Forest 29 3 38N46'59 77w14'10 5:08:57
Cardinal 57 4 37N25'13 76w22'55 5:05:32
Cardinal Estates 133 6 36N47'50 76w04'30 5:04:18
Cardinal Forest 29 3 38N49 77w14 5:08:56
Cardova 24 14 38N31'56 78w02'18 5:12:09
Cardwell 37 4 37N40'21 77w47'40 5:11:11
Cardwell Town 83 15 36N54'07 81w46'45 5:27:07
Caret 28 4 37N58'57 76w57'42 5:07:51
Carfax 93 15 36N53'26 82w22'40 5:29:31
Carlisle 44 4 36N39'42 79w47'13 5:19:09
Carloover 9 4 37N55'27 79w53'20 5:19:33
Carlson Store 51 4 37N55 76w28 5:05:52
Carlton Corner 48 4 37N43'48 76w49'59 5:07:20
Carmel 82 14 38N49'37 78w25'57 5:13:44
Carmines Landing 36 4 37N17'06 76w32'05 5:06:08
Carnot 11 4 37N02'30 81w05'47 5:24:23
Carolanne Farms 133 6 36N49'43 76w10'35 5:04:42
Carolina Junction 101 6 36N48'56 76w15'37 5:05:02
Caroline Pines 17 22 37N53'46 77w26'10 5:09:45
Carps Corner 62 14 37N31'25 77w00'33 5:08:02
Carriage Ford 73 14 38N38'33 77w35'17 5:10:21
Carriage Hill 29 3 38N55 77w14 5:08:56
Carriage Hill 120 4 37N07'09 76w32'13 5:06:09
Carrico Mill 81 26 36N43'16 82w32'09 5:30:09
Carrie 26 15 37N01'56 82w12'24 5:28:50
Carrollton 46 4 36N56'48 76w33'39 5:06:15
Carrol Mill 52 26 36N40'33 83w15'44 5:33:03
Carrsbrook 2 14 38N05'35 78w27'29 5:13:50
Carrsville 46 4 36N42'42 76w49'35 5:07:18
Carruthers Corner 49 22 38N16'07 77w05'56 5:08:24
Carsley 87 4 37N05'44 77w00'22 5:08:01
Carson 27 22 37N02'07 77w23'44 5:09:35
Carsonville 38 4 36N40'38 81w04'11 5:24:17
Carters Bridge 2 14 38N02 78w29 5:13:56
Carters Corner 17 22 38N02'59 77w17'17 5:09:09
Carters Mill 68 4 36N36'16 80w28'36 5:21:54
Carters Store 85 22 38N12 77w35 5:10:20
Cartersville 25 4 37N40'02 78w05'19 5:12:21
Carterton 80 15 36N54'48 82w13'16 5:28:53
Carthage 31 4 36N58'03 80w29'46 5:21:59
Carver Court 112 6 37N02'26 76w21'07 5:05:24
Carver Gardens 95 23 37N15'03 76w39'32 5:06:38
Carysbrook 32 4 37N48'44 78w14'34 5:12:58
Carys Corner 92 19 38N03'43 76w37'27 5:06:30
Casanova 30 19 38N39'27 77w43'02 5:10:52
Cascade 69 4 36N33'52 79w40'12 5:18:41
Casco 42 22 37N44'56 77w39'16 5:10:37
Cash 36 4 37N25 76w32 5:06:08
Cash Corner 2 14 38N05'17 78w16'35 5:13:06
Cash Corner 17 22 38N07'33 77w14'32 5:08:58
Cashs Corner 88 4 36N54'55 77w06'42 5:08:27
Cashville 1 4 37N42'07 75w48'31 5:03:14
Caski 61 4 37N32'22 78w49'49 5:15:19
Caskie 61 14 37N33 78w52 5:15:28
Castle Craig 16 16 37N14 79w17 5:17:08
Castle Heights 58 4 36N36'57 78w18'32 5:13:14
Castleton 75 14 38N36'21 78w06'25 5:12:26
Castlewood 80 15 36N53'24 82w16'47 5:29:07
Catalpa 24 14 38N30'38 77w59'17 5:11:57
Catawba 41 4 36N55'20 78w57'02 5:15:48
Catawba 77 4 37N22'57 80w06'35 5:20:26
Catharpin 73 14 38N51'15 77w34'20 5:10:17
Catherine Furnace 67 14 38N33'27 78w38'09 5:14:33
Catherton 117 2 38N47 77w28 5:09:52
Cathole Landing 132 4 36N33'30 76w53'32 5:07:34
Catlett 30 19 38N39'13 77w38'27 5:10:34
Cats Bridge 1 4 37N33'06 75w46'56 5:03:08
Cauthornville 48 4 37N52'52 77w03'56 5:08:16
Cavalcade 29 1 38N50 77w12 5:08:48
Cavalier Manor 125 6 36N47'59 76w21'49 5:05:27
Cavalier Park 133 6 36N52'25 75w59'19 5:03:57
Cave Mountain 78 14 37N37 79w30 5:18:00
Cave Spring 77 4 37N13'39 80w00'47 5:20:03
Cavetown 67 14 38N36'55 78w26'57 5:13:48
Caylor 52 26 36N37'50 83w29'40 5:33:59
Cedar Bluff 89 4 37N05'15 81w45'33 5:27:02
Cedar Bluff 91 15 36N38'08 81w51'36 5:27:26
Cedar Branch 83 15 36N53'24 81w44'47 5:26:59
Cedar Creek 9 4 38N02 79w51 5:19:24
Cedar Creek 34 4 39N02 78w17 5:13:08
Cedar Creek Battlefield 34 4 39N01'02 78w17'35 5:13:10
Cedar Creek Wayside 82 14 39N00'24 78w19'26 5:13:18
Cedar Crest 29 1 38N49'07 77w12'19 5:08:49
Cedar Forest 69 4 37N02'47 79w06'39 5:16:27
Cedar Fork 17 22 37N57'42 77w32'54 5:10:12
Cedar Green 8 21 38N09'03 79w07'44 5:16:31
Cedar Grove 34 9 39N16'05 78w11'22 5:12:45
Cedar Grove 41 4 36N37'04 78w59'24 5:15:58
Cedar Grove 58 4 36N44 78w07 5:12:28
Cedar Grove 63 4 37N10'22 75w57'56 5:03:52

Cedar Grove 78 14 37N52'57 79W23'02 5:17:32
Cedar Grove Acres 101
6 36N47'34 76W24'15 5:05:37
Cedar Hill 34 9 39N16'35 78W06'51 5:12:27
Cedar Hill 52 26 36N39'51 83W14'30 5:32:58
Cedar Hill 69 4 36N51'00 79W18'48 5:17:15
Cedar Landing 124
11 37N06'59 76W22'06 5:05:28
Cedar Lawn 43 17 37N32 77W24 5:09:36
Cedar Level 114
22 37N16'24 77W19'06 5:09:16
Cedar Mountain 24
4 38N24 78W02 5:12:08
Cedar Park 112 6 37N03'04 76W20'38 5:05:23
Cedar Point 37 4 37N41'30 77W54'35 5:11:38
Cedar Run 30 19 38N40 77W40 5:10:40
Cedar Springs 29
3 38N50 77W26 5:09:44
Cedar Springs 83
15 36N49'41 81W17'26 5:25:10
Cedar View 1 4 37N36'49 75W52'34 5:03:30
Cedarville 90 14 38N58'37 78W11'04 5:12:44
Cedarville 91 15 36N46 81W52 5:27:28
Cedon 17 22 38N03'40 77W31'08 5:10:05
Celt 39 14 38N18 78W26 5:13:44
Centenary 15 4 37N42'33 78W30'42 5:14:03
Center Cross 28 4 37N48'16 76W46'45 5:07:07
Center Star 27 22 37N11 77W38 5:10:32
Centerville 1 4 37N45'26 75W37'17 5:02:29
Centerville 8 21 38N20'18 79W00'21 5:16:01
Centerville 10 4 37N22'26 79W29'59 5:18:00
Centerville 37 4 37N40'15 77W41'16 5:10:45
Centerville 41 4 36N44'08 78W55'07 5:15:40
Centerville 47 23 37N19'00 76W47'22 5:07:09
Centerville 60 4 37N10'11 80W32'19 5:22:09
Central 7 1 38N53 77W07 5:08:28
Central 127 17 37N33 77W26 5:09:44
Central Garage 50
14 37N41 77W01 5:08:04
Central Gardens 43
17 37N33'25 77W24'18 5:09:37
Central Hill 46 4 36N54'38 76W44'27 5:06:58
Centralia 21 22 37N22'51 77W27'37 5:09:50
Central Point 17
22 37N59 77W08 5:08:32
Centre Heights 29
3 38N50'27 77W27'19 5:09:49
Centreville 29 1 38N50'20 77W25'40 5:09:43
Centreville Farms 29
1 38N50'37 77W24'55 5:09:40
Ceres 11 4 37N01'04 81W20'35 5:25:22
Chadswyck 101 6 36N49'04 76W24'35 5:05:38
Chalk Level 69 4 36N55'06 79W16'41 5:17:07
Chamberlain Village 73
14 38N31'44 77W17'42 5:09:11
Chamberlayne Farms 43
22 37N37'59 77W26'16 5:09:45
Chamberlayne Heights 43
22 37N37'38 77W25'57 5:09:44
Chamblissburg 10
4 37N15'15 79W42'26 5:18:50
Champlain 28 4 38N00'48 76W59'35 5:07:58
Chance 28 4 38N03'25 77W00'31 5:08:02
Chancellor 85 22 38N17'02 77W36'05 5:10:24
Chancellorsville 85
22 38N18'30 77W38'05 5:10:32
Chancetown 1 4 37N37'56 75W42'03 5:02:48
Chandler Crossing 17
22 37N53'45 77W27'52 5:09:51
Chandlers Forks 20
4 37N01'11 78W42'01 5:14:48
Chantilly 29 3 38N53'39 77W25'53 5:09:44
Chap 6 4 37N15'16 78W49'54 5:15:20
Chapel 22 14 39N06 78W01 5:12:04
Chapel Acres 29 3 38N44'29 77W14'44 5:08:59
Chapel Hill 96 3 38N49'09 77W05'17 5:08:21
Chapel Village 112
6 37N02'14 76W22'53 5:05:32
Chapin 8 21 38N08'55 79W16'39 5:17:07
Chapman Landing 82
14 38N50'43 78W31'45 5:14:07
Charity 68 4 36N49'11 80W13'07 5:20:52
Charlemont 10 4 37N28'01 79W24'19 5:17:37
Charles City 19
14 37N21 77W04 5:08:16
Charles Corner 95
23 37N15'00 76W37'10 5:06:29
Charleston Heights 95
23 37N16'16 76W40'16 5:06:41
Charlie Hope 13 4 36N42 78W02 5:12:08
Charlotte Court House 20
4 37N03'23 78W38'19 5:14:33
Charlottesville 100
14 38N01'45 78W28'37 5:13:54
Charlton 23 4 37N34'58 80W00'41 5:20:03
Chase City 58 4 36N47'57 78W27'31 5:13:50
Chase Crossing 1
4 37N45'45 75W40'04 5:02:40
Chatham 69 4 36N49'32 79W23'54 5:17:36
Chatham Heights 86
4 38N18'30 77W27'02 5:09:48
Chatham Hill 83
15 36N57'20 81W31'24 5:26:06
Chatmoss 44 4 36N39'24 79W48'45 5:19:15
Cheapside 63 4 37N12'04 75W59'04 5:03:56
Check 31 4 37N02 80W10 5:20:40
Chenaults Shop 17
22 37N59'07 77W17'06 5:09:08
Chericoke 50 14 37N38'05 77W06'46 5:08:27
Cheriton 63 4 37N17'22 75W58'18 5:03:53
Cherry Acres 112
6 37N02'27 76W20'37 5:05:22
Cherrydale 7 1 38N53'49 77W06'31 5:08:26
Cherry Grove 79
22 38N35'12 78W52'18 5:15:29
Cherry Grove 132
4 36N34'18 76W55'06 5:07:40
Cherry Hill 73 14 38N34'11 77W16'02 5:09:04
Cherrystone 63 4 37N18'22 76W00'07 5:04:00
Chesapeake 63 4 37N18'28 75W57'08 5:03:49
Chesapeake 101 6 36N49'08 76W16'31 5:05:06
Chesapeake Beach 64
18 37N50'27 76W15'02 5:05:00
Chesapeake Beach 133
6 36N54'55 76W07'14 5:04:29
Chesapeake Heights 112
4 37N02'07 76W18'14 5:05:13
Chesconessex 1 4 37N45'07 75W46'00 5:03:04
Chesopeian Colony 133
6 36N50'45 76W03'45 5:04:15
Chester 21 22 37N21'24 77W26'31 5:09:46
Chesterbrook 29 1 38N55'17 77W09'13 5:08:37
Chesterbrook Estates 29
1 38N55'41 77W07'59 5:08:32
Chesterbrook Gardens 29
1 38N54'58 77W10'16 5:08:41
Chesterbrook Mews 29
1 38N55 77W11 5:08:44
Chesterbrook Woods 29
1 38N55'33 77W08'22 5:08:33
Chester Estates 91
25 36N36 82W11 5:28:44
Chesterfield 21
22 37N22'37 77W30'22 5:10:01
Chester Gap 75 14 38N51'12 78W08'07 5:12:32
Chester Park 29 3 38N42 77W14 5:08:56
Chestnut Fork 10
4 37N12'15 79W29'47 5:17:59
Chestnut Grove 42
22 37N41'36 77W18'06 5:09:12
Chestnut Grove 51
18 37N49'20 76W26'23 5:05:46
Chestnut Grove Landing 62
14 37N32'40 76W56'23 5:07:46
Chestnut Hill 29
1 38N49'55 77W13'48 5:08:55
Chestnut Hill 49
22 38N17'57 77W06'40 5:08:27
Chestnut Hill Landing 76
4 37N59'39 76W48'16 5:07:13
Chestnut Knob 44
4 36N37'26 79W54'39 5:19:39
Chestnut Level 69
4 36N41 79W22 5:17:28
Chestnut Yard 18
4 36N43 80W49 5:23:16
Chevalle 73 2 38N47 77W28 5:09:52
Chewings Corner 85
22 38N03'02 77W39'44 5:10:39
Chickahominy 43
17 37N36'29 77W24'48 5:09:39
Chickahominy Haven 47
14 37N22'15 76W53'44 5:07:35
Chickahominy Shores 62
14 37N23'37 76W56'29 5:07:46
Childress 60 4 37N03'22 80W30'17 5:22:01
Childry 41 4 36N56 78W57 5:15:48
Chilesburg 17 22 37N59'58 77W35'34 5:10:22
Chilhowie 83 15 36N47'54 81W40'57 5:26:44
Chiltons 92 19 38N07'44 76W48'24 5:07:14
Chimney Corner 21
22 37N24'30 77W26'04 5:09:44
Chincoteague 1 4 37N55'59 75W22'45 5:01:31
Chinese Corner 133
6 36N50'44 76W09'22 5:04:37
Chinquapin Village 96
3 38N49'13 77W04'57 5:08:20
Chippokes 87 4 37N08'28 76W43'32 5:06:54
Chisford 92 19 38N08'34 76W48'01 5:07:12
Christ Church 51
4 37N40'54 76W25'24 5:05:42
Christensons Corner 47
23 37N23'16 76W42'32 5:06:50
Christian 8 21 38N10'56 79W13'40 5:16:55
Christianburg 60
4 37N07'47 80W24'33 5:21:38
Christiansburg 60
4 37N07'47 80W24'33 5:21:38
Christie 41 4 36N32'56 78W50'37 5:15:22
Christopher Fork 17
22 38N02'26 77W13'23 5:08:54
Chuckatuck 132 4 36N51'42 76W34'50 5:06:19
Chula 4 4 37N23'18 77W54'12 5:11:37
Church Hill 127
17 37N32'15 77W24'32 5:09:38
Churchill 29 3 38N54'04 77W10'05 5:08:40
Churchland 125 6 36N51'52 76W23'49 5:05:35
Church Road 27 22 37N11 77W38 5:10:32
Church View 59 4 37N40'39 76W40'43 5:06:43
Churchville 8 21 38N13'34 79W09'45 5:16:39
Cifax 10 4 37N24'39 79W24'28 5:17:38
Cismont 2 14 38N03'27 78W18'50 5:13:15
City Farm 16 14 37N19'32 79W11'23 5:16:46
City Gomingo 5 14 37N25'48 79W05'27 5:16:22
Civic Center 127
17 37N33 77W26 5:09:44
Claiborne 17 22 38N09'35 77W27'21 5:09:49
Clam 1 4 37N48'49 75W40'14 5:02:41
Clancie 48 4 37N34'49 76W41'36 5:06:46
Claraville 64 18 37N55'02 76W26'45 5:05:47
Claremont 7 1 38N50'35 77W06'18 5:08:25
Claremont 87 4 37N13'40 76W57'52 5:07:51
Claremont Manor 87
4 37N14'11 76W58'40 5:07:55
Clarendon 7 1 38N53'09 77W05'50 5:08:23
Claresville 40 20 36N37'21 77W27'04 5:09:48
Clarkes Gap 53 14 39N07 77W34 5:10:16
Clarks Corner 30
19 38N46'14 77W56'59 5:11:48
Clarks Crossing 29
3 38N55'16 77W17'09 5:09:09
Clarks Landing 87
4 37N10'00 76W50'46 5:07:23
Clarksville 58 4 36N37'26 78W33'26 5:14:14
Clarksville 91 15 36N47'55 81W45'55 5:27:04
Clarkton 41 4 36N58'59 78W54'22 5:15:37
Clary 82 14 39N01'31 78W21'54 5:13:28
Claudville 68 4 36N35'22 80W25'07 5:21:40
Clay 10 14 37N23'00 79W14'46 5:16:59
Clay Bank 36 4 37N20'51 76W36'28 5:06:26
Claybank Landing 47
23 37N15'54 76W51'36 5:07:26
Claypool Hill 89
4 37N03'45 81W45'07 5:27:00
Clays Corner 65 4 37N11'46 77W57'47 5:11:51
Clays Mill 41 4 36N49'35 78W52'06 5:15:28
Claytonville 22
14 39N05'29 78W01'19 5:12:05
Clayville 70 14 37N27'35 77W49'02 5:11:16
Clear Brook 34 4 39N15'23 78W05'47 5:12:23
Clearbrook 77 4 37N11'57 79W56'38 5:19:47
Clearfield 29 3 38N49 77W13 5:08:52
Clear Fork 11 4 37N12'43 81W11'15 5:24:45
Clearview Manor 29
1 38N55 77W11 5:08:44
Clearwater Park 3
4 37N50'13 79W59'10 5:19:57
Clell 14 15 37N08'16 81W58'04 5:27:52
Clementown Mills 4
4 37N26'27 78W05'26 5:12:22
Cleopus 132 4 36N35'34 76W49'49 5:07:19
Clermont Woods 29
3 38N47'50 77W06'39 5:08:27
Cleveland 80 15 36N56'37 82W09'07 5:28:36
Clifdale 3 4 37N47 79W59 5:19:56
Cliffield 89 4 37N05'52 81W39'25 5:26:38
Cliff Mills 30 19 38N43'15 77W54'31 5:11:38
Clifford 5 16 37N38'36 79W01'21 5:16:05
Cliffview 18 4 36N40'52 80W54'54 5:23:40
Clifton 29 1 38N46'48 77W23'13 5:09:33
Clifton 66 14 38N17'00 78W01'42 5:12:07
Clifton 80 15 37N01'46 81W49'50 5:27:19
Cliftondale 3 4 37N49 79W50 5:19:20
Cliftondale Park 3
4 37N49'24 79W47'56 5:19:12
Clifton Forge 102
4 37N48'58 79W49'29 5:19:18
Climax 69 4 36N53'13 79W29'22 5:17:57
Clinch 81 15 36N48'59 82W29'52 5:29:59
Clinchburg 91 15 36N49'55 81W48'53 5:27:16
Clinchco 26 15 37N09'40 82W21'36 5:29:26
Clinchfield 80 15 36N57'20 82W11'02 5:28:44
Clinchport 81 26 36N40'37 82W44'32 5:30:58
Cline 94 4 36N55'59 81W10'06 5:24:40
Clines Hacking 79
22 38N33'52 79W01'34 5:16:06
Clinton 25 4 37N32'33 78W07'33 5:12:30
Clintwood 26 15 37N09'00 82W27'22 5:29:49
Clito 38 4 36N43 80W59 5:23:56
Clito Mill 38 4 36N41'36 81W04'27 5:24:18
Cliveden 120 4 37N09'20 76W31'33 5:06:06
Clocks Corner 17
22 38N07 77W25 5:09:40
Clopton 36 4 37N20'44 76W32'24 5:06:10
Clover 41 4 36N49'57 78W44'01 5:14:56
Clover 96 3 38N48'42 77W04'45 5:08:19
Clover Creek 45 4 38N16'12 79W32'57 5:18:12
Cloverdale 12 4 37N21'54 79W54'21 5:19:37
Cloverdale 32 4 37N45'01 78W14'10 5:12:57
Cloverdale 101 6 36N49'16 76W15'58 5:05:04
Clover Hill 79 22 38N27'07 79W01'49 5:16:07
Cloverland 43 17 37N35'33 77W25'48 5:09:43
Cloverleaf Farm Estates 29
3 38N48'25 77W23'53 5:09:36
Cloyd 74 4 37N09 80W40 5:22:40
Club Court 43 17 37N36 77W27 5:09:48
Cluster Springs 41
4 36N37'15 78W55'19 5:15:41
Coalcreek 18 4 36N40 80W55 5:23:40
Coaldan 89 4 37N09'41 81W47'24 5:27:10
Coal Kiln Crossing 1
4 37N34'15 75W47'41 5:03:11
Coal Landing 86 4 38N26'45 77W23'12 5:09:33
Coal Mine 82 14 39N00 78W22 5:13:28
Coan 64 18 37N57'30 76W28'50 5:05:55
Coatesville 42 22 37N52'43 77W36'31 5:10:26
Cobbdale 107 3 38N51'54 77W18'54 5:09:16
Cobbs 63 4 37N16 76W00 5:04:00
Cobbs Corner 29 3 38N49'37 77W23'05 5:09:32
Cobbs Creek 57 4 37N30'20 76W23'50 5:05:35
Cobham 2 14 38N03'46 78W16'06 5:13:04
Cobham 87 4 37N07 76W47 5:07:08
Cobham Park 76 4 37N56'26 76W44'48 5:06:59
Cochran 13 4 36N50'35 77W54'19 5:11:37
Cody 41 4 36N58'39 79W05'55 5:16:24
Coeburn 93 15 36N56'38 82W27'51 5:29:51
Coffee 10 4 37N25'51 79W18'32 5:17:14
Coffey Corner 17
22 37N57'02 77W32'36 5:10:10
Cohasset 32 4 37N46'10 78W18'12 5:13:13
Cohoke 50 14 37N34'45 76W56'47 5:07:47
Coke 36 4 37N17 76W30 5:06:00
Colchester 29 3 38N40'07 77W14'04 5:08:56
Colchester Acres 29
3 38N48'48 77W22'23 5:09:30
Cold Harbor 42 22 37N37 77W15 5:09:00
Cold Harbor Farms 42
22 37N35'29 77W18'53 5:09:16
Cold Spring 8 21 37N59'40 79W08'05 5:16:32
Coldwater 48 4 37N39'15 76W44'05 5:06:56
Coleman Falls 10
4 37N30'05 79W18'14 5:17:13
Coleman Place 121
6 36N52'14 76W14'41 5:04:59
Colemans Mill 85
22 38N06'58 77W31'28 5:10:06
Colemans Mill Crossing 17
22 37N57'32 77W25'47 5:09:43
Coles 73 2 38N43 77W27 5:09:48
Coles Hill 69 4 36N52'32 79W18'03 5:17:12
Coles Point 92 19 38N08'37 76W38'09 5:06:33
Colier 94 4 36N49 81W11 5:24:44
Colleen 61 14 37N42'33 78W55'53 5:15:44
College 110 24 38N23 77W27 5:09:48
College Park 96 3 38N48'41 77W04'59 5:08:20
College Park 120
6 37N06'38 76W31'22 5:06:05
College Park 131
21 38N10'18 79W03'19 5:16:13
Colley 26 15 37N09'14 82W14'44 5:28:59
Collier 94 4 36N49'04 81W12'34 5:24:50
Collier Mill 52
26 36N42'53 83W01'49 5:32:07
Collierstown 78
14 37N47'08 79W35'22 5:18:21
Collingwood 29 1 38N43'54 77W02'43 5:08:11
Collins 17 22 38N07 77W25 5:09:40
Collins Crossing 17
22 38N06'03 77W23'57 5:09:36

Collinsville 34 4 39N19 78w18 5:13:12
Collinsville 44 4 36N42'54 79w54'56 5:19:40
Collinwood 80 15 36N44'20 82w19'29 5:29:18
Collosse 46 4 36N45'40 76w49'19 5:07:17
Cologne 48 4 37N31'50 76w41'29 5:06:46
Colonial Beach 92 19 38N15'16 76w57'50 5:07:51
Colonial Farms 29 3 38N45 77w08 5:08:32
Colonial Forest 42 22 37N40'58 77w21'18 5:09:25
Colonial Heights 98 25 36N38'00 82w07'14 5:28:29
Colonial Heights 103 22 37N14'38 77w24'38 5:09:39
Colonial Heights 121 6 36N55'29 76w14'47 5:04:59
Colonial Park 47 23 37N15'24 76w39'58 5:06:40
Colonial Place 121 6 36N53'05 76w17'29 5:05:10
Colonial Port Trailer Park 73 13 38N39 77w16 5:09:04
Colonial Village 7 8 38N53'35 77w05'11 5:08:21
Colony 5 14 37N24'51 79w07'05 5:16:28
Colony Acres 133 6 36N46'46 76w02'55 5:04:12
Colosse 46 4 36N43 76w50 5:07:20
Colthurst 2 14 38N03'59 78w31'30 5:14:06
Coltons Mill 10 4 37N27'43 79w27'48 5:17:51
Columbia 32 4 37N45'10 78w09'46 5:12:39
Columbia Forest 7 1 38N51'14 77w06'38 5:08:27
Columbia Furnace 82 14 38N52'34 78w37'33 5:14:30
Columbia Heights 7 1 38N51'27 77w07'17 5:08:29
Columbian Grove 55 4 36N52 78w12 5:12:48
Columbia Park 72 22 37N17 77w18 5:09:12
Columbia Pines 29 1 38N50'26 77w11'15 5:08:45
Colvin Run 29 3 39N00 77w15 5:09:00
Comans Well 88 4 36N46 77w17 5:09:08
Combat Village 73 2 38N35'58 77w27'13 5:09:49
Comers Rock 38 4 36N44'39 81w14'11 5:24:57
Comertown 67 14 38N29'54 78w35'16 5:14:21
Comet 46 4 36N59'05 76w44'39 5:06:59
Commodore Park 121 6 36N56'12 76w16'04 5:05:04
Community 29 3 38N45 77w06 5:08:24
Comorn 49 22 38N16'49 77w13'17 5:08:53
Compton 67 14 38N46'57 78w22'09 5:13:29
Comptons Corner 29 3 38N48'35 77w26'57 5:09:48
Conaway 14 15 37N21'08 82w12'43 5:28:51
Concord 13 4 36N57 77w47 5:11:08
Concord 16 16 37N20'33 78w58'31 5:15:54
Concord 86 4 38N28'23 77w32'41 5:10:11
Concord Heights 85 24 38N16'12 77w29'20 5:09:57
Concord Wharf 63 4 37N27 75w55 5:03:40
Conde 30 19 38N45'33 77w55'27 5:11:42
Confederate Heights 43 17 37N34 77w26 5:09:44
Confederate Ridge 110 24 38N16'45 77w29'13 5:09:57
Conicville 82 14 38N49'46 78w41'25 5:14:46
Conklin 53 4 38N53'47 77w31'01 5:10:04
Conners Grove 31 4 36N47'47 80w25'06 5:21:40
Conners Valley 94 4 37N00 80w45 5:23:00
Contra 48 4 37N45'38 76w50'38 5:07:23
Contreville 54 14 38N02'51 77w49'02 5:11:16
Coochevyville 1 4 37N38'51 75w51'09 5:03:25
Cook Landing 62 14 37N32'16 76w58'02 5:07:52
Cooks Corner 59 4 37N36'05 76w33'59 5:06:16
Cookstown 85 22 38N17'42 77w42'07 5:10:48
Cook Terrace Annex 95 4 37N12 76w27 5:05:48
Cooktown 29 3 38N59'12 77w23'01 5:09:32
Cool Spring 13 4 36N50'02 77w49'34 5:11:18
Coolspring 29 1 38N45 77w04 5:08:16
Coolwell 5 16 37N31'39 79w05'27 5:16:22
Cooper 59 4 37N36'38 76w31'08 5:06:05
Cooper Landing 64 18 37N52'17 76w25'08 5:05:41
Coopers Landing 64 18 37N51'41 76w23'04 5:05:32
Cootes Store 79 22 38N37 78w48 5:15:12
Copeland 9 4 37N53'17 79w41'59 5:18:48
Copenhavers 94 4 36N53'33 81w11'53 5:24:48
Cople 92 19 38N04 76w38 5:06:32
Copper Hill 31 4 37N04'54 80w08'04 5:20:32
Copper Valley 31 4 37N08 80w34 5:22:16
Corbin 17 22 38N11'58 77w23'21 5:09:33
Cordova 24 14 38N28 78w00 5:12:00
Corinth 18 4 36N47'19 80w52'47 5:23:31
Corinth 84 4 36N49'52 76w56'45 5:07:47
Corinth Fork 50 14 37N45'58 77w14'44 5:08:59
Corneals Store 42 22 37N37 77w22 5:09:28
Corner 80 15 36N57'11 82w02'14 5:28:09
Cornetts Store 38 4 36N42 81w26 5:25:44
Cornland 101 6 36N37'36 76w19'18 5:05:17
Corn Valley 80 15 36N53'59 81w56'06 5:27:44
Cornwall 78 14 37N48'16 79w19'08 5:17:17
Cornwell 73 2 38N41'20 77w26'30 5:09:46
Coronado 121 6 36N54'05 76w14'48 5:04:59
Cottage Green 85 24 38N15'51 77w29'14 5:09:57
Cotton Town 25 4 37N23'48 78w18'08 5:13:13
Coulson 18 4 36N43 80w49 5:23:16
Coulwood 80 15 36N59'36 82w03'16 5:28:13
Council 14 15 37N04'49 82w04'07 5:28:16
Countis Corner 91 25 36N36 82w11 5:28:44
Country Club Hills 7 3 38N54'50 77w07'52 5:08:31
Country Club Hills 107 3 38N51'27 77w17'38 5:09:11
Country Club Lake 73 14 38N36 77w19 5:09:16
Country Club Manor 7 3 38N54'49 77w08'17 5:08:33
Country Club View 29 3 38N49'12 77w18'58 5:09:16
Counts 26 15 36N59 82w17 5:29:08
County Line Cross Roads 20 4 37N08'27 78w31'44 5:14:07
Court House 7 1 38N53 77w06 5:08:24
Courthouse 88 4 36N55 77w18 5:09:12
Courthouse Landing 48 4 37N39'28 76w52'48 5:07:31
Courtland 84 4 36N42'58 77w04'06 5:08:16
Courtland Park 29 1 38N50'56 77w08'23 5:08:34
Courtney 43 22 37N40 77w30 5:10:00
Cove Colony 51 4 37N41'20 76w29'37 5:05:58
Cove Creek 89 4 37N10'41 81w17'37 5:25:10
Coverly 4 4 37N24'24 77w53'01 5:11:32
Covesville 2 14 37N53'24 78w42'18 5:14:49
Covingston Corner 17 22 37N51'35 77w22'43 5:09:31
Covington 104 4 37N47'36 79w59'39 5:19:59
Cowan 74 4 37N11'07 80w34'38 5:22:19
Cowan Mill 52 26 36N37'43 83w28'01 5:33:52
Cowart 64 18 37N59'43 76w28'20 5:05:53
Cowie Corner 40 20 36N46'27 77w34'19 5:10:17
Cox Corner 58 4 36N49'31 78w19'50 5:13:19
Cox Corner 86 4 38N17'55 77w21'35 5:09:26
Cox Landing 132 4 36N35'23 76w54'35 5:07:38
Cox Mill 38 4 36N37'52 80w53'59 5:23:36
Cox Mill 81 26 36N41'31 82w34'46 5:30:19
Coxs Chapel 38 4 36N35 81w20 5:25:20
Coyner Mountain Overlook 12 4 37N20'27 79w50'52 5:19:23
Crabbe Mill 64 18 37N53'15 76w27'02 5:05:48
Crab Orchard 93 15 36N55'37 82w25'56 5:29:44
Cracker Neck 93 26 36N50'48 82w42'33 5:30:50
Crackers Neck 81 15 36N46'50 82w25'51 5:29:43
Craddockville 1 4 37N34'54 75w52'09 5:03:29
Cradock 125 6 36N47'45 76w19'15 5:05:17
Craft Mill 81 26 36N42'31 82w39'06 5:30:36
Crafton 32 4 37N55'10 78w17'43 5:13:11
Craig 44 4 36N36'53 80w01'52 5:20:07
Craigs Mill 91 25 36N44'54 82w09'43 5:28:39
Craig Springs 23 4 37N29'05 80w17'32 5:21:10
Craigsville 8 21 38N04'43 79w23'00 5:17:32
Crandon 11 4 37N08'50 80w57'48 5:23:51
Crane 9 4 37N54'35 79w40'33 5:18:42
Cranes Corner 86 24 38N21'43 77w27'28 5:09:50
Cranes Nest 93 15 36N58'29 82w28'21 5:29:53
Craney Island Estates 42 22 37N38'53 77w24'39 5:09:39
Creeds 133 6 36N36'17 76w01'36 5:04:06
Creek Junction 91 15 36N38'50 81w40'42 5:26:43
Crescent Hill 114 14 37N17 77w18 5:09:12
Crescent Hills 7 1 38N54'17 77w08'46 5:08:35
Cresthill 30 19 38N46'03 78w00'31 5:12:02
Crestview 43 22 37N36'04 77w31'41 5:10:07
Crestwood 101 6 36N45'55 76w17'10 5:05:09
Crestwood Manor 29 1 38N49'31 77w11'24 5:08:46
Creswell 80 15 36N49'19 82w12'32 5:28:50
Crewe 65 4 37N10'23 78w07'25 5:12:30
Cricket Hill 57 4 37N28'59 76w18'36 5:05:14
Criders 79 22 38N45'05 79w00'16 5:16:01
Criglersville 56 4 38N27'28 78w18'05 5:13:12
Crimora 8 21 38N09'14 78w51'02 5:15:24
Cripple Creek 94 4 36N49'15 81w05'55 5:24:24
Crittenden 132 5 36N54'36 76w29'47 5:05:59
Critz 68 4 36N37'48 80w08'42 5:20:35
Croaker 47 23 37N23'48 76w45'13 5:07:01
Croaker Landing 47 23 37N25'38 76w43'32 5:06:54
Crockett 94 4 36N53'10 81w11'32 5:24:46
Crockett Springs 60 4 37N10 80w15 5:21:00
Crockett Town 1 4 37N40'49 75w48'44 5:03:15
Cromwell 30 19 38N32'17 77w34'07 5:10:16
Crooked Oak 18 4 36N43'12 80w36'29 5:22:26
Cropp 86 19 38N28'26 77w36'37 5:10:26
Crossbrook 93 26 36N55 82w48 5:31:12
Cross Creek Landing 87 4 37N10'34 76w49'38 5:07:19
Crosses Corner 42 22 37N43'36 77w21'59 5:09:28
Cross Junction 34 4 39N19'13 78w17'37 5:13:10
Cross Keys 79 22 38N21'33 78w50'32 5:15:22
Cross Keys 84 4 36N37'13 77w11'16 5:08:45
Crossroads 2 14 37N57'24 78w39'33 5:14:38
Crossroads 30 19 38N36'17 77w38'39 5:10:35
Crossroads 33 4 37N04'59 79w45'01 5:19:00
Crossroads 41 4 36N55'36 78w50'05 5:15:20
Cross Roads 82 14 38N45 78w39 5:14:36
Crossroads Mall Shopping Cen 128 4 37N19'01 79w57'36 5:19:50
Crossroads Store 78 14 37N49'28 79w19'44 5:17:19
Crosswinds 29 3 38N47 77w12 5:08:48
Crouch 48 4 37N45'44 76w53'51 5:07:35
Crowdertown 9 4 38N00'33 79w51'04 5:19:24
Crowells Corner 29 3 38N57'08 77w18'40 5:09:15
Crowgeys 94 4 36N57'43 81w06'16 5:24:25
Crows 3 4 37N43'10 80w12'10 5:20:49
Crozet 2 14 38N04'10 78w42'03 5:14:48
Crozier 37 4 37N38'12 77w47'51 5:11:11
Cruise 68 4 36N38 80w16 5:21:04
Crumps Mill 62 14 37N32'24 77w05'20 5:08:21
Crymes Store 55 4 36N59 78w14 5:12:56
Crystal Acres 133 6 36N52 76w00 5:04:00
Crystal Beach 1 4 37N43 75w44 5:02:56
Crystal Hill 41 4 36N51'20 78w54'33 5:15:38
Crystal Spring Knolls 7 1 38N54'12 77w06'19 5:08:25
Crystal Springs 29 3 38N50'28 77w23'03 5:09:32
Cuckoo 54 14 37N57'07 77w54'01 5:11:36
Cullen 20 4 37N07'03 78w38'58 5:14:36
Culls 63 4 37N16'41 75w57'24 5:03:50
Culmore 29 1 38N51'21 77w08'25 5:08:34
Culpeper 24 14 38N28'23 77w59'49 5:11:59
Cumberland 25 4 37N29'45 78w14'44 5:12:59
Cummings Heights 91 15 36N43'18 82w00'56 5:28:04
Cumnor 48 4 37N43'30 76w53'01 5:07:32
Cunningham 32 4 37N52'26 78w19'13 5:13:17
Curdsville 15 4 37N24'56 78w27'22 5:13:49
Curriomam Landing 92 19 38N09'15 76w45'42 5:07:03
Currituck Farms 43 22 37N30'33 77w13'58 5:08:56
Curtis 10 4 37N28'36 79w29'02 5:17:56
Cusco Willa 58 4 36N35'35 78w20'37 5:13:22
Cushmans Landing 63 4 37N10'32 75w56'29 5:03:46
Customhouse 121 6 36N54 76w16 5:05:04
Cutalong 54 14 38N07'16 78w03'10 5:12:13
Cypress 132 4 36N41 76w32 5:06:08
Cypress Bank Landing 19 14 37N24'17 76w58'00 5:07:52
Cypress Chapel 132 5 36N44 76w35 5:06:20
Cypress Manor 84 4 36N42'03 76w58'35 5:07:54
Cyrandall Valley 29 3 38N55 77w14 5:08:56
Dabneys 54 14 37N45'48 77w48'07 5:11:12
Daffan 86 24 38N21'24 77w24'30 5:09:38
Dahlgren 49 12 38N19'52 77w03'05 5:08:12
Dahlgren Junction 86 4 38N18'51 77w26'53 5:09:48
Dahlgrens Corner 48 4 37N42'32 76w55'30 5:07:42
Dahlia 40 20 36N34'11 77w32'21 5:10:09
Daingerfield Landing 28 4 38N01'13 76w55'48 5:07:43
Daisy 48 4 37N45'40 76w55'19 5:07:41
Dalbys 63 4 37N13'48 75w58'14 5:03:53
Dale 21 22 37N25 77w30 5:10:00
Dale City 73 14 38N38'13 77w18'41 5:09:15
Dalecrest 96 1 38N48'52 77w06'14 5:08:25
Dale Enterprise 79 22 38N27'16 78w56'23 5:15:46
Dale Ridge 93 15 37N00 82w28 5:29:52
Daleville 12 4 37N24'35 79w54'46 5:19:39
Dalhart 38 4 36N40 80w55 5:23:40
Daltons 17 22 38N08'07 77w25'11 5:09:41
Damascus 91 15 36N38'01 81w47'02 5:27:08
Dam Neck 133 6 36N47 75w58 5:03:52
Dam Neck Corner 133 6 36N47'10 75w59'58 5:04:00
Damon 2 14 37N49'22 78w39'34 5:14:38
Damtown 8 21 38N12'30 78w55'32 5:15:42
Dan 85 22 38N09'25 77w52'55 5:11:32
Danbury Forest 29 3 38N49 77w13 5:08:52
Dandy 95 4 37N12'43 76w25'48 5:05:43
Daniel 66 14 38N10'25 78w01'20 5:12:05
Daniel Boone 81 26 36N38 82w34 5:30:16
Daniel Corner 17 22 38N04'39 77w11'17 5:08:45
Daniels Mill 30 19 38N38'55 77w36'06 5:10:24
Danieltown 13 4 36N54'16 77w57'36 5:11:50
Danripple 41 4 36N37'47 79w01'27 5:16:06
Dante 80 15 36N58'42 82w17'52 5:29:11
Danton 66 14 38N10'59 77w54'56 5:11:40
Danville 105 4 36N35'09 79w23'43 5:17:35
Daphna 79 22 38N34'47 78w48'19 5:15:13
Darbyville 52 26 36N49'49 83w03'09 5:32:13
Dare 95 4 37N10'08 76w26'19 5:05:45
Darlington Heights 71 4 37N12'00 78w36'16 5:14:25
Darnell Town 52 26 36N51'32 82w54'11 5:31:37
Darvills 27 22 37N03'47 77w50'03 5:11:20
Darwin 26 15 37N06'01 82w29'28 5:29:58
Daugherty 1 4 37N41'22 75w39'59 5:02:40
Davenport 14 15 37N06'02 82w08'13 5:28:33
Davids Crossroads 73 14 38N33'40 77w32'07 5:10:08
Davis 78 14 37N55'07 79w15'50 5:17:03
Davis 82 14 39N01 78w23 5:13:32
Davis Corner 86 4 38N29'33 77w33'40 5:10:15
Davis Corner 133 6 36N51'15 76w10'37 5:04:42
Davis Landing 87 4 37N09'50 76w50'06 5:07:20
Davis Mill 10 4 37N12'15 79w34'58 5:18:20
Davis Wharf 1 4 37N33'10 75w52'42 5:03:31
Daw 80 15 37N03'09 81w51'26 5:27:26
Dawley Corners 133 6 36N41'13 76w00'02 5:04:00
Dawn 17 22 37N52 77w27 5:09:48
Dawsonville 39 4 38N15'55 78w18'55 5:13:16
Dayton 79 22 38N24'53 78w56'20 5:15:45
Deanes 132 6 36N50'22 76w27'46 5:05:51
Deanwood 29 3 39N01'46 77w18'19 5:09:13
Dearington 116 14 37N24'42 79w09'46 5:16:39
Deatonville 4 4 37N19'41 78w10'07 5:12:40
DeBree 121 6 36N52 76w17 5:05:08

DeBusk Mill 91 15 36N44'41 81W46'19 5:27:05
Decapolis 67 4 38N26'32 78W14'18 5:12:57
Decatur 78 14 37N52'35 79W20'09 5:17:21
Deel 14 15 37N14'10 82W05'18 5:28:21
Deep Bottom 43 22 37N24'24 77W18'35 5:09:14
Deep Creek 1 4 37N46'02 75W45'11 5:03:01
Deep Creek 101 6 36N44'32 76W20'34 5:05:22
Deep Creek 120 4 37N04'57 76W30'54 5:06:04
Deep Hole 1 4 37N56'14 75W21'13 5:01:25
Deep Landing 64 18 37N52'15 76W26'17 5:05:45
Deep Springs 52 26 36N47'00 82W52'01 5:31:28
Deerfield 8 21 38N11'47 79W24'25 5:17:38
Deerfield Estates 21 22 37N23'00 77W31'15 5:10:05
Deerock 61 14 37N50 78W44 5:14:56
Deer Park 73 2 38N47 77W28 5:09:52
Deer Park 120 4 37N04'32 76W28'42 5:05:55
De Haven 34 9 39N20'59 78W11'10 5:12:45
DeJarnette 17 22 37N59'57 77W19'16 5:09:17
De Kalb 81 26 36N45 82W35 5:30:20
Delaplane 30 19 38N54'54 77W55'14 5:11:41
Delaware 84 4 36N39'00 77W00'02 5:08:00
Delhart 38 4 36N34'53 80W59'07 5:23:56
Delila 41 4 36N35'03 79W08'26 5:16:34
Delk Crossroads 87 4 37N02'39 76W47'32 5:07:10
Delmar 91 15 36N38 81W47 5:27:08
Delos 17 22 38N05'47 77W16'20 5:09:05
Del Ray 96 1 38N49'16 77W03'47 5:08:15
Delta 96 1 38N48'43 77W05'47 5:08:23
Deltaville 59 4 37N33'17 76W20'14 5:05:21
Delton 74 4 37N00 80W45 5:23:00
Delvale 52 26 36N49'11 82W57'08 5:31:49
Denaro 4 4 37N14'42 77W59'04 5:11:56
Denbigh 120 4 37N07'40 76W32'23 5:06:10
Denby Park 121 6 36N54'55 76W15'45 5:05:03
Dendron 87 4 37N02'43 76W56'11 5:07:45
Denmark 78 14 37N52'02 79W32'59 5:18:12
Denniston 41 4 36N34'14 78W56'24 5:15:46
Dentons Corner 15 4 37N33'20 78W35'05 5:14:20
Derby 93 26 36N56'08 82W49'35 5:31:18
Derrings Mill 87 4 37N04'33 76W48'40 5:07:15
Desha 28 14 37N54'56 76W55'14 5:07:41
Deshazo Corner 48 4 37N44 76W55 5:07:40
Deskins 14 15 37N10'53 82W04'39 5:28:19
Detrick 82 14 38N50'43 78W24'54 5:13:40
Devon Park 29 1 38N54'50 77W11'09 5:08:45
Devonshire Gardens 29 3 38N52'15 77W11'16 5:08:45
Dewey 10 4 37N22 79W49 5:19:16
Dewey 93 15 37N04'49 82W39'32 5:30:38
DeWitt 27 22 37N02'19 77W38'37 5:10:34
Diamond Grove 13 4 36N42'31 77W56'14 5:11:45
Diamond Hill 10 4 37N11'30 79W41'16 5:18:45
Diamond Hill 16 16 37N12'03 79W02'43 5:16:11
Diamond Lake Estates 133 6 36N52'46 76W11'01 5:04:44
Diamond Springs 133 6 36N53 76W08 5:04:32
Diascund 47 14 37N23'39 76W52'15 5:07:29
Dickensdale 43 17 37N34 77W29 5:09:56
Dickensonville 80 15 36N50'30 82W13'31 5:28:54
Dickinson 33 4 36N55'13 79W42'26 5:18:50
Dickinsons Corner 49 22 38N12'37 77W04'06 5:08:16
Dickinson Store 85 22 37N58 77W46 5:11:04
Diggs 57 4 37N26'13 76W16'07 5:05:04
Dilbeck 82 14 38N53'45 78W22'10 5:13:29
Dillon 12 4 37N32'22 79W38'17 5:18:33
Dillons Fork 44 4 36N41'44 80W00'23 5:20:02
Dillons Mill 33 4 37N04'34 80W02'22 5:20:09
Dillwyn 15 4 37N32'34 78W27'27 5:13:50
Dinwiddie 27 22 37N04'40 77W35'13 5:10:21
Dinwiddie Gardens 27 22 37N13 77W26 5:09:44
Disputanta 72 22 37N07'27 77W13'34 5:08:54
Ditchley 64 18 37N43'59 76W19'29 5:05:18
Dixiana 93 15 37N01'38 82W40'11 5:30:41
Dixie 32 4 37N46'53 78W14'09 5:12:57
Dixie 57 4 37N30'02 76W24'53 5:05:40
Dixie Hill 29 3 38N51'06 77W21'45 5:09:27
Dixon Landing 48 4 37N35'00 76W47'31 5:07:10
Dobyns 68 4 36N38'17 80W20'13 5:21:21
Dockery 58 4 36N44 78W07 5:12:28
Dodds Corner 86 4 38N26'49 77W35'29 5:10:22
Dodds Store 5 16 37N35 79W03 5:16:12
Dodlyt 64 18 37N53'49 76W30'38 5:06:03
Dodson 68 4 36N49'58 80W06'30 5:20:26
Dodson Corner 58 4 36N44'02 78W25'48 5:13:43
Doe Hill 45 4 38N25'55 79W26'41 5:17:47
Doggetts Fork 17 22 37N53'55 77W21'08 5:09:25
Dogue 49 22 38N13'55 77W12'58 5:08:52
Dogwood Hill 131 21 38N08'28 79W04'35 5:16:18
Dogwood Knoll 42 22 37N37'03 77W19'58 5:09:20
Doles Crossroads 84 4 36N51'36 76W54'17 5:07:37
Dolphin 13 4 36N49'45 77W47'14 5:11:09
Dominion 52 26 36N48'39 83W04'17 5:32:17
Dominion Heights 7 1 38N53'34 77W06'29 5:08:26
Dominion Hills 7 1 38N52'33 77W08'29 5:08:34
Dona 52 26 36N35'39 82W59'28 5:31:58
Donaldsburg 78 14 37N50'37 79W18'32 5:17:14
Dongola 54 14 37N46'06 77W50'21 5:11:21
Donkey 93 15 37N08 82W36 5:30:24
Donna Lee Gardens 29 1 38N52'54 77W11'39 5:08:47
Donovans Corner 29 3 38N46'00 77W18'51 5:09:15
Dooley 93 15 36N55'50 82W39'16 5:30:37
Dooms 8 21 38N06'32 78W51'28 5:15:26
Doran 89 4 37N05'33 81W50'01 5:27:20
Dorcas 8 21 38N21 79W05 5:16:20
Dorchester 93 15 36N56'30 82W38'37 5:30:34
Dorchester Junction 93 15 36N55'41 82W39'15 5:30:37
Dorset 70 14 37N28'05 77W48'20 5:11:13
Dorset Woods 43 22 37N34'38 77W35'51 5:10:23
Dorter Mill 81 26 36N37'13 82W31'32 5:30:06
Dorton Fort 81 26 36N44'06 82W26'06 5:29:44
Dory 84 4 36N51'40 77W02'47 5:08:11
Doswell 42 22 37N51'36 77W27'52 5:09:51
Dot 52 26 36N46 83W02 5:32:08
Double Tollgate 22 4 39N03 78W06 5:12:24
Douglas Landing 101 6 36N38'14 76W22'24 5:05:30
Douglas Park 125 6 36N48'56 76W20'23 5:05:22
Douglass Park 7 1 38N50'59 77W05'36 5:08:22
Dover 7 1 38N54'24 77W06'22 5:08:25
Dover 37 4 37N39 77W43 5:10:52
Dover 53 14 38N58'35 77W40'29 5:10:42
Doveville 29 3 38N50'13 77W15'34 5:09:02
Dowden Terrace 29 1 38N50'14 77W07'42 5:08:31
Downings 76 4 37N50'40 76W37'24 5:06:30
Downings Corner 64 18 37N53'25 76W22'48 5:05:31
Doylesville 2 14 38N09'02 78W40'05 5:14:40
Doziers Corner 101 6 36N45'32 76W16'29 5:05:06
Dragonville 48 4 37N41'50 76W46'42 5:07:07
Drakes Branch 20 4 36N59'34 78W36'05 5:14:24
Drakes Corner 84 4 36N36'42 77W00'17 5:08:01
Dranesville 29 1 39N00'02 77W20'46 5:09:23
Draper 74 4 37N00'21 80W44'51 5:22:59
Drapersville 58 4 36N47'29 78W20'30 5:13:22
Drenn 18 4 36N37'10 80W46'42 5:23:07
Drewrys Bluff 21 22 37N25'35 77W27'29 5:09:50
Drewryville 84 4 36N42'56 77W18'24 5:09:14
Drill 80 15 37N01 81W59 5:27:56
Driver 132 4 36N49'23 76W30'10 5:06:01
Drouin Hill 43 22 37N35'00 77W36'41 5:10:27
Drowning Ford 91 15 36N39'05 81W50'28 5:27:22
Druid Hills 47 23 37N15'00 76W44'31 5:06:58
Drummonds Corner 112 11 37N05'36 76W23'34 5:05:34
Dry Branch 74 4 37N14'04 80W37'06 5:22:28
Dryburg 41 4 36N43'52 78W43'19 5:14:53
Dryden 52 26 36N46'39 82W56'30 5:31:46
Dry Fork 69 4 36N45'16 79W24'00 5:17:36
Dry Fork 83 15 36N44'00 81W37'14 5:26:29
Dry Fork 93 15 36N54'51 82W23'42 5:29:35
Dry Pond 68 4 36N35'00 80W20'41 5:21:23
Drytown 89 4 37N08'50 81W29'31 5:25:58
Duane 50 14 37N51'59 77W14'49 5:08:59
Duane Fork 50 14 37N52'27 77W13'51 5:08:55
Dublin 74 4 37N06'20 80W41'08 5:22:45
Dudie 30 19 38N44'42 77W53'04 5:11:32
Dudley 41 4 36N48'11 78W54'38 5:15:39
Duet 56 4 38N28'29 78W15'24 5:13:02
Duffield 81 26 36N43'08 82W47'46 5:31:11
Dugspur 18 4 36N49'04 80W36'36 5:22:26
Dugwell 33 4 37N02'24 79W57'33 5:19:50
Duke Gardens 96 1 38N48'38 77W05'59 5:08:24
Dumbarton 43 17 37N36'13 77W29'30 5:09:58
Dumfries 73 14 38N34'03 77W19'42 5:09:19
Dunavant 85 22 38N21'44 77W39'54 5:10:40
Dunbar 93 26 36N58'26 82W44'50 5:30:59
Dunbrooke 28 14 37N53'39 76W57'51 5:07:51
Duncan 31 4 36N54'43 80W29'24 5:21:58
Duncan Gap 93 15 37N01 82W35 5:30:20
Duncan Mill 81 26 36N45'47 82W38'51 5:30:35
Duncanville 91 15 36N49'24 81W59'19 5:27:57
Dundalow 132 5 36N44 76W35 5:06:20
Dundas 55 4 36N54'53 78W01'19 5:12:05
Dundee 10 4 37N06'56 79W30'43 5:18:03
Dundee 69 4 36N35'29 79W22'34 5:17:30
Dundee 77 4 37N14'27 79W52'55 5:19:32
Dunford Town 89 4 37N09 81W42 5:26:48
Dunford Village 89 4 37N10'27 81W37'49 5:26:31
Dungadin Heights 90 14 38N53'17 78W13'50 5:12:55
Dungannon 81 15 36N49'42 82W28'21 5:29:53
Dunlop 103 22 37N16'10 77W24'15 5:09:37
Dunn Loring 29 3 38N53'36 77W13'19 5:08:53
Dunn Loring Woods 29 3 38N52'56 77W14'20 5:08:57
Dunns Corner 58 4 36N44'46 78W16'28 5:13:06
Dunnsville 28 4 37N51'27 76W49'12 5:07:17
Durand 40 20 36N43'12 77W35'18 5:10:21
Durrett Town 61 14 37N58'59 78W48'30 5:15:14
Dutch Gap 21 22 37N21'35 77W24'56 5:09:40
Dutton 36 4 37N29'52 76W27'28 5:05:50
Duty 26 15 37N04'53 82W09'07 5:28:36
Dwale 26 15 37N11'28 82W24'20 5:29:37
Dwight 14 15 37N15'28 81W55'37 5:27:42
Dwight 46 4 36N51'11 76W48'45 5:07:15
Dwina 93 15 36N54'28 82W22'02 5:29:28
Dye 80 15 37N04'14 81W55'30 5:27:42
Dyke 39 14 38N15'13 78W32'24 5:14:10
Eads 7 1 38N51 77W05 5:08:20
Eagle Furnace 94 4 36N50'23 81W02'55 5:24:12
Eagle Rock 12 4 37N38'26 79W48'05 5:19:12
Earlehurst 3 4 37N40'09 80W14'04 5:20:56
Earls 4 4 37N13'48 77W53'36 5:11:34
Early 18 4 36N48'26 80W47'25 5:23:10
Earlysville 2 14 38N09'27 78W28'59 5:13:56
Earmans 79 22 38N27 78W52 5:15:28
East Brook 16 14 37N22'17 79W06'12 5:16:25
East Chesapeake 101 6 36N49 76W14 5:04:56
East End 127 17 37N33 77W24 5:09:36
Eastern 35 4 37N19 80W36 5:22:24
Eastern Park 133 6 36N51 76W07 5:04:28
Eastern View 42 22 37N37'35 77W08'40 5:08:35
East Falls Church 7 1 38N53'14 77W09'17 5:08:37
Eastham 2 14 38N04'18 78W24'43 5:13:39
East Hampton 112 4 37N02'14 76W19'55 5:05:20
East Highland Park 43 17 37N34'51 77W24'26 5:09:38
East Honaker 80 15 37N01 81W59 5:27:56
Eastland Creek Landing 58 4 36N36'04 78W22'10 5:13:29
East Leake 37 4 37N48'38 77W56'59 5:11:48
East Lexington 78 14 37N47'34 79W25'32 5:17:42
Eastmoreland 43 17 37N32 77W24 5:09:36
East Norton 122 15 36N59 82W38 5:30:32
East Norview 121 6 36N53'42 76W13'49 5:04:55
East Ocean View 121 6 36N55'53 76W12'22 5:04:49
Easton Place 121 6 36N50'30 76W11'32 5:04:46
Eastover 87 4 37N11'53 76W53'35 5:07:34
Eastover 132 5 36N44 76W35 5:06:20
Eastover Gardens 43 17 37N31'24 77W22'15 5:09:29
East Point 1 4 37N43'12 75W48'54 5:03:16
East Point 79 14 38N25'09 78W39'36 5:14:38
East Radford 126 4 37N08 80W34 5:22:16
East Stone Gap 93 26 36N52'00 82W44'33 5:30:58
East Suffolk Gardens 132 5 36N44 76W35 5:06:20
Eastville 63 4 37N21'09 75W56'46 5:03:47
Eastville Station 63 4 37N20'50 75W55'56 5:03:44
Eastwood 120 6 37N06'47 76W31'09 5:06:05
East Woodford 29 3 38N55 77W14 5:08:56
East Wytheville 94 4 37N00 81W05 5:24:20
Ebenezer 69 4 36N49'02 79W11'27 5:16:46
Ebony 13 4 36N34'43 77W59'28 5:11:58
Eclipse 132 5 36N55'01 76W29'20 5:05:57
Edds Mill 52 26 36N37'56 83W21'36 5:33:26
Edgar 17 14 37N51'11 77W17'49 5:09:11
Edge 16 16 37N10 79W05 5:16:20
Edgefield 125 6 36N53'23 76W23'29 5:05:34
Edgehill 36 4 37N24'46 76W31'09 5:06:05
Edgehill 49 22 38N15'53 77W08'38 5:08:35
Edgehill 84 4 36N42'54 76W56'28 5:07:46
Edgehill Park 27 22 37N13 77W26 5:09:44
Edgelea 29 3 38N48'46 77W24'02 5:09:36
Edgemont 104 4 37N45'42 79W59'23 5:19:58
Edgemont Park 91 15 36N43 81W58 5:27:52
Edgerton 13 4 36N46'44 77W46'40 5:11:07
Edgewater 121 6 36N53'41 76W18'29 5:05:14
Edgewood 72 22 37N13 77W17 5:09:08
Edgewood 101 6 36N44'12 76W13'59 5:04:56
Edgewood 120 4 37N04'23 76W30'38 5:06:03
Edgewood 128 4 37N17'31 80W01'01 5:20:04
Edinburg 82 14 38N49'15 78W33'58 5:14:16
Edmonds Corner 101 6 36N47'30 76W15'39 5:05:03
Ednam Forest 2 14 38N02'46 78W32'46 5:14:11
Ednas Mill 19 14 37N27'25 77W07'49 5:08:31
Edom 79 22 38N31'32 78W51'33 5:15:26
Edsall Park 29 3 38N48'24 77W10'35 5:08:42
Edwards Shop 24 4 38N31 77W51 5:11:24
Edwardsville 64 18 37N54'23 76W21'56 5:05:28
Effinger 78 14 37N45'46 79W33'02 5:18:12
Effna 11 4 37N03'31 81W14'38 5:24:59
Eggbornsville 24 4 38N34'50 78W03'33 5:12:14
Eggleston 35 4 37N17'14 80W37'08 5:22:29
Eheart 66 14 38N12'13 78W19'24 5:13:18
Elam 71 4 37N17'10 78W36'50 5:14:27
Elamsville 68 4 36N46'03 80W11'39 5:20:47
Elamtown 58 4 36N37'34 78W16'22 5:13:05
Elberon 87 4 37N04'27 76W53'02 5:07:32
Eldorada 24 4 38N33'21 78W03'31 5:12:14
Eldridge Corner 15 14 37N35'04 78W48'58 5:15:16
Eldridge Mill 15 4 37N36'35 78W27'40 5:13:51
Elephant Fork 132 5 36N45'33 76W35'14 5:06:21
Elevon 17 22 37N59'38 77W04'24 5:08:18
Elgin Corner 29 3 38N47'07 77W19'31 5:09:18
Elizabeth River Shores 133 6 36N49'43 76W12'41 5:04:51
Elizabeth River Terrace 133 6 36N51 76W09 5:04:36
Elk Creek 38 4 36N43'17 81W10'38 5:24:43
Elk Garden 80 15 36N54'32 81W58'49 5:27:55
Elk Hill 37 4 37N43'03 78W05'16 5:12:21
Elkhorn 41 4 36N51'52 79W06'36 5:16:26
Elkins 29 1 38N55 77W11 5:08:44
Elko 43 22 37N28'22 77W12'42 5:08:51
Elk Run 30 19 38N33'18 77W40'16 5:10:41
Elkton 79 14 38N24'28 78W37'26 5:14:30
Elkwood 24 4 38N30'42 77W51'22 5:11:25
Ellendale 83 15 36N54'59 81W34'12 5:26:17
Ellendale Ford 83 15 36N55'04 81W34'53 5:26:20
Ellerson 42 22 37N37'04 77W23'52 5:09:35
Ellerson Mill 42 22 37N35'42 77W21'29 5:09:26
Ellett 60 4 37N11'29 80W22'01 5:21:28

Elletts Crossing 42 22 37N47'54 77w28'11 5:09:53
Ellis Fork 87 4 37N00'11 76w54'03 5:07:36
Elliston 60 4 37N12'59 80w13'58 5:20:56
Ellisville 54 14 38N05'50 77w59'41 5:11:59
Elly 56 4 38N20'17 78w12'27 5:12:50
Elma 61 14 37N45'13 78w47'43 5:15:11
Elmhurst 121 6 36N53'00 76w13'50 5:04:55
Elmington 36 4 37N25'28 76w27'21 5:05:49
Elmo 41 4 36N40'35 79w07'21 5:16:29
Elmont 42 22 37N42'40 77w29'34 5:09:58
Elmwood Estates 29 1 38N56'35 77w12'01 5:08:48
El Nido 29 1 38N55'05 77w10'00 5:08:40
Elon 5 16 37N31'03 79w11'43 5:16:47
Elsing Green 50 14 37N36'09 77w03'04 5:08:12
Elsom 48 4 37N34'17 76w45'16 5:07:01
Eltham 62 14 37N31'25 76w49'35 5:07:18
Elvan 53 4 39N16'38 77w40'10 5:10:41
Elwood 132 4 36N40'34 76w49'27 5:07:18
Elysian Woods 73 13 38N39 77w16 5:09:04
Emmerton 76 4 37N53'57 76w40'48 5:06:43
Emory 91 15 36N46'22 81w50'11 5:27:21
Emporia 40 20 36N41'09 77w32'34 5:10:10
Endicott 33 4 36N53'15 80w09'00 5:20:36
Enfield 50 14 37N44'43 77w13'08 5:08:53
Engleside 29 3 38N45 77w08 5:08:32
Enon 37 4 37N45'49 78w00'38 5:12:03
Enon 86 4 38N23 77w27 5:09:48
Enonville 15 4 37N29'59 78w31'25 5:14:06
Eona 18 4 36N43'35 80w46'03 5:23:04
Eppes Fork 58 4 36N33'10 78w21'43 5:13:27
Epworth 50 14 37N47'27 77w12'44 5:08:51
Erica 92 19 38N07'06 76w40'45 5:06:43
Ervinton 26 15 37N03 82w20 5:29:20
Esmont 2 14 37N49'52 78w36'27 5:14:26
Esnon 58 4 36N45'20 78w28'20 5:13:53
Esserville 93 15 36N57'19 82w36'40 5:30:27
Essex Meadows 101 6 36N45'40 76w14'48 5:04:59
Essex Mill 28 4 37N51 76w49 5:07:16
Estabrook 121 6 36N52'46 76w14'49 5:04:59
Estabrook Park 121 6 36N52'22 76w14'27 5:04:58
Estaline 8 21 38N03'47 79w21'26 5:17:26
Estes 75 14 38N37'10 78w03'41 5:12:15
Estillville 81 26 36N38 82w37 5:30:28
Ethel 76 4 37N59'46 76w46'52 5:07:07
Etlan 56 4 38N31'31 78w15'46 5:13:03
Etna Mills 50 14 37N45'56 77w15'58 5:09:04
Etta 17 22 38N08'34 77w10'25 5:08:42
Etter 94 4 36N54 81w16 5:25:04
Ettrick 21 22 37N14'24 77w25'49 5:09:43
Eubank Corner 17 22 38N08'15 77w18'40 5:09:15
Eubanks 53 14 39N09'30 77w46'12 5:11:05
Euclid 133 6 36N51 76w09 5:04:36
Euclid Place 133 6 36N51 76w09 5:04:36
Euclid Terrace 133 6 36N51'08 76w09'44 5:04:39
Eureka 20 4 37N02'47 78w33'11 5:14:13
Eureka Mills 20 4 37N02 78w29 5:13:56
Eureka Park 133 6 36N50'23 76w03'40 5:04:15
Eustaces Corner 30 19 38N37'03 77w42'04 5:10:48
Everets 132 5 36N50'21 76w37'33 5:06:30
Evergreen 6 4 37N19'06 78w45'58 5:15:04
Evergreen Hills 91 25 36N39'11 82w04'33 5:28:18
Evergreen Mills 53 14 39N01'03 77w34'31 5:10:18
Evergreen Shores 95 4 37N11'14 76w25'01 5:05:40
Everona 66 14 38N18'17 77w58'03 5:11:52
Evington 16 16 37N14'01 79w17'23 5:17:10
Evol 16 16 37N10 79w05 5:16:20
Ewell 47 23 37N19'44 76w44'33 5:06:58
Ewing 52 26 36N38'12 83w25'54 5:33:44
Exeter 93 26 36N52'33 82w51'15 5:31:25
Exmore 63 4 37N31'54 75w49'24 5:03:18
Ezell 13 4 36N41'39 77w51'21 5:11:25
Faber 61 14 37N49'54 78w44'16 5:14:57
Factory Hill 132 4 36N33'41 76w51'31 5:07:26
Fagg 60 4 37N11'46 80w19'24 5:21:18
Fairchester 107 3 38N51'24 77w19'21 5:09:17
Fairfax 107 3 38N50'46 77w18'24 5:09:14
Fairfax Acres 29 3 38N52'18 77w19'07 5:09:16
Fairfax Circle 107 3 38N51 77w15 5:09:00
Fairfax Farms 29 3 38N52'09 77w21'03 5:09:24
Fairfax Forest 29 3 38N51'40 77w15'07 5:09:00
Fairfax Heights 107 3 38N51 77w15 5:09:00
Fairfax Hills 29 1 38N50'03 77w13'25 5:08:54
Fairfax Park 29 3 38N46'39 77w14'27 5:08:58
Fairfax Station 29 3 38N48'03 77w19'33 5:09:18
Fairfax Villa 29 3 38N51 77w15 5:09:00
Fairfax Woods 107 3 38N51'38 77w18'51 5:09:15
Fairfield 28 4 37N51 76w49 5:07:16
Fairfield 78 14 37N52'45 79w17'23 5:17:10
Fairfield Landing 59 4 37N32'22 76w28'35 5:05:54
Fair Haven 29 1 38N47'06 77w04'29 5:08:18
Fair Hill 29 3 38N51 77w15 5:09:00
Fair Hill 43 22 37N23'43 77w19'48 5:09:19
Fairland 29 1 38N48'55 77w09'56 5:08:40
Fairlawn 74 4 37N08'54 80w34'43 5:22:19
Fairlawn 104 4 37N46'34 79w58'56 5:19:56
Fairlawn Estates 121 6 36N51'28 76w11'59 5:04:48
Fairlee 29 3 38N52'25 77w16'18 5:09:05
Fair Meadows 133 6 36N51'02 76w10'31 5:04:42
Fairmount Park 121 6 36N52'42 76w15'20 5:05:01
Fair Oaks 43 22 37N31'50 77w18'59 5:09:16
Fair Oaks 107 3 38N50'27 77w17'24 5:09:10
Fairplay 76 4 37N50'14 76w37'11 5:06:29
Fairport 64 18 37N50'00 76w17'26 5:05:10
Fair Vernon 29 3 38N46'06 77w11'23 5:08:46
Fairview 28 14 37N53'53 76w48'47 5:07:15
Fairview 29 3 38N58'40 77w15'27 5:09:02
Fairview 58 4 36N48'55 78w28'01 5:13:52
Fairview 60 4 37N04 80w27 5:21:48
Fairview 63 4 37N15'59 75w58'09 5:03:53
Fairview 67 14 38N39'15 78w25'46 5:13:43
Fairview 81 26 36N38'04 82w54'09 5:31:37
Fairview 94 15 36N51'24 81w16'35 5:25:06
Fairview Beach 49 22 38N19'48 77w14'51 5:08:59
Fairview Farms 112 6 37N02'51 76w21'06 5:05:24
Fairview Heights 3 4 37N49'00 79w48'46 5:19:15
Fairview Heights 116 14 37N23'16 79w08'45 5:16:35
Fairview Manor 101 6 36N49 76w14 5:04:56
Fairwood 38 4 36N41'59 81w29'06 5:25:56
Fairwood Acres 29 3 38N46'53 77w19'12 5:09:17
Falconerville 5 16 37N35 79w03 5:16:12
Falling Creek 21 22 37N27 77w28 5:09:52
Falling Creek Farms 21 22 37N26'35 77w34'09 5:10:17
Falling Spring 3 4 37N53'11 79w58'47 5:19:55
Falls Church 108 1 38N53 77w10 5:08:40
Falls Hill 29 3 38N53'31 77w12'04 5:08:48
Falls Mills 89 4 37N16'35 81w18'31 5:25:14
Fallville 38 4 36N44'44 81w06'12 5:24:25
Falmouth 86 24 38N19'26 77w28'07 5:09:52
False Cape Landing 133 6 36N35'39 75w53'17 5:03:33
Fancy Gap 18 4 36N39'57 80w41'33 5:22:46
Fancy Hill 5 16 37N40'04 79w07'37 5:16:30
Fancy Hill 78 14 37N40'39 79w30'02 5:18:00
Farley Park Corner 59 4 37N38'33 76w40'35 5:06:42
Farmers 17 22 38N07 77w25 5:09:40
Farmers Fork 28 4 38N03'40 77w06'23 5:08:26
Farmers Fork 76 4 38N02'16 76w47'43 5:07:11
Farmers Shop Corner 42 22 37N38'31 77w11'44 5:08:47
Farmers Store 94 4 36N55'47 80w56'28 5:23:46
Farmingdale 72 22 37N17 77w18 5:09:12
Farmington 2 14 38N03'04 78w32'40 5:14:11
Farmington 43 22 37N36 77w32 5:10:08
Farmville 71 4 37N18'07 78w23'32 5:13:34
Farnham 76 4 37N53'07 76w37'31 5:06:30
Farrington 42 22 37N43'56 77w35'03 5:10:20
Farrs Corner 29 3 38N44'32 77w20'28 5:09:22
Faulconerville 5 16 37N31'56 79w06'02 5:16:24
Fauquier Springs 30 19 38N44 77w44 5:10:56
Favonia 94 4 36N58'24 81w11'03 5:24:44
Fawcett Gap 34 9 39N11 78w10 5:12:40
Fayette Park 43 17 37N35'46 77w25'21 5:09:41
Fears Corner 20 4 37N02'45 78w42'59 5:14:52
Featherstone 73 13 38N38'06 77w15'51 5:09:03
Featherstone Fork 17 22 38N12'06 77w19'46 5:09:19
Featherstone Shores 73 13 38N37'47 77w14'57 5:09:00
Featherstone Terrace 73 13 38N39 77w16 5:09:04
Federal Reserve 127 17 37N32 77w28 5:09:52
Felgates Crossing 95 4 37N15'31 76w34'39 5:06:19
Fentress 101 6 36N42'07 76w11'50 5:04:47
Fentress 133 6 36N53'34 76w08'14 5:04:33
Fenwick Park 29 3 38N52'08 77w12'10 5:08:49
Fergusonville 65 4 37N13'03 78w04'15 5:12:17
Ferncliff 54 14 37N55'59 78w06'37 5:12:26
Ferndale Gardens 27 22 37N13 77w26 5:09:44
Ferndale Park 27 22 37N13'17 77w28'29 5:09:54
Ferrell 49 22 38N16 77w11 5:08:44
Ferrol 8 21 38N06'31 79w17'08 5:17:09
Ferrum 33 4 36N55'22 80w00'49 5:20:03
Ferry Farms 86 4 38N17'35 77w26'16 5:09:45
Fieldale 44 4 36N42'00 79w56'20 5:19:45
Fields Crossroads 40 20 36N49'54 77w32'58 5:10:12
Fieldstown 4 4 37N23'07 77w56'51 5:11:47
Fife 37 4 37N44'57 78w03'44 5:12:15
Fifty Seven Mile Siding 88 4 37N02 77w07 5:08:28
Figsboro 44 4 36N47'11 79w51'32 5:19:26
File 17 22 38N03 77w21 5:09:24
Fincastle 12 4 37N29'57 79w52'39 5:19:31
Finchley 58 4 36N39'08 78w29'33 5:13:58
Fine Creek Mills 70 14 37N35'52 77w49'10 5:11:17
Fines Corner 86 4 38N19'19 77w22'08 5:09:29
Finneywood 58 4 36N52'31 78w28'50 5:13:55
First Colony 47 23 37N14'18 76w48'10 5:07:13
First Ford 35 4 37N15'59 80w57'48 5:23:51
Fishers Hill 82 14 38N59 78w24 5:13:36
Fishersville 8 21 38N05'56 78w58'10 5:15:53
Fish Hole Landing 47 14 37N24'10 76w54'12 5:07:37
Fitchetts 57 4 37N27'32 76w17'25 5:05:10
Fitzhugh 13 4 36N39'56 77w45'52 5:11:03
Five Forks 5 16 37N31'05 79w07'16 5:16:29
Five Forks 10 4 37N16'54 79w31'04 5:18:04
Five Forks 18 4 36N45'49 80w48'02 5:23:12
Five Forks 21 22 37N24'26 77w34'02 5:10:16
Five Forks 27 22 37N08'21 77w37'23 5:10:30
Five Forks 29 3 38N46'36 77w16'34 5:09:06
Five Forks 41 4 36N43'06 78w51'37 5:15:26
Five Forks 47 23 37N15'11 76w45'57 5:07:04
Five Forks 55 4 36N53'29 78w27'50 5:13:51
Five Forks 56 4 38N17'56 78w08'08 5:12:33
Five Forks 61 14 37N34'45 78w51'32 5:15:26
Five Forks 68 4 36N35'03 80w16'43 5:21:07
Five Forks 71 4 37N14'17 78w34'38 5:14:19
Five Forks 75 14 38N39'00 78w10'07 5:12:40
Five Forks 114 14 37N16'48 77w17'43 5:09:11
Fivemile Fork 85 22 38N17'24 77w33'13 5:10:13
Five Oaks 89 4 37N08'58 81w29'20 5:25:57
Flagpond 81 26 36N38 83w03 5:32:12
Flag Pond Landing 1 4 37N56'08 75w39'24 5:02:38
Flat Gap 93 15 37N04'27 82w42'11 5:30:49
Flat Iron 92 19 38N08'52 76w55'17 5:07:41
Flat Ridge 38 4 36N41'49 81w20'45 5:25:23
Flat Rock 70 14 37N31'21 77w49'25 5:11:18
Flat Rock 81 26 36N36'37 82w50'31 5:31:22
Flat Run 66 14 38N21'53 77w46'00 5:11:04
Flat Spur 26 15 36N59 82w17 5:29:08
Flat Top 26 15 37N01'44 82w23'51 5:29:35
Flatwood 94 4 36N51'11 80w53'15 5:23:33
Flatwoods 12 4 37N32'42 79w52'47 5:19:31
Flatwoods 93 15 36N53'26 82w25'44 5:29:43
Fleeburg 67 14 38N28'22 78w35'42 5:14:23
Fleenors 91 25 36N36 82w11 5:28:44
Fleenor Spring 91 25 36N40'55 82w08'17 5:28:33
Fleenortown 52 26 36N42'19 83w07'50 5:32:31
Fleet 91 15 36N47'30 81w44'29 5:26:58
Fleet 121 6 36N56 76w19 5:05:16
Fleeton 64 18 37N48'54 76w16'53 5:05:08
Flemingtown 26 15 37N10'31 82w25'31 5:29:42
Fletcher 39 14 38N23'34 78w26'01 5:13:44
Fletcher Ford 52 26 36N36'11 83w17'39 5:33:11
Fletcher Mill 75 14 38N38'50 78w12'24 5:12:50
Fletcherville 30 19 38N45'04 77w48'55 5:11:16
Flint Hill 10 4 37N15'28 79w38'15 5:18:33
Flint Hill 29 3 38N55 77w14 5:08:56
Flint Hill 69 4 36N47'43 79w29'40 5:17:59
Flint Hill 75 14 38N45'46 78w06'01 5:12:24
Flood 6 4 37N17'32 78w44'02 5:14:56
Flood 45 4 38N20 79w29 5:17:56
Flordon 2 14 38N03'21 78w33'24 5:14:14
Floris 29 3 38N56'13 77w24'47 5:09:39
Floyd 31 4 36N54'40 80w19'13 5:21:17
Folly 64 18 37N52'46 76w19'41 5:05:19
Folly Creek Landing 1 4 37N41'38 75w37'56 5:02:32
Folly Mills 8 21 38N05'54 79w05'56 5:16:24
Foneswood 76 4 38N06'17 76w54'05 5:07:36
Fontaine 44 4 36N38'41 79w51'36 5:19:26
Ford 27 22 37N09 77w44 5:10:56
Fordham 112 4 37N02'15 76w18'52 5:05:15
Ford Park 101 6 36N49 76w14 5:04:56
Fordsville 56 4 38N24'05 78w06'59 5:12:28
Fordwick 8 21 38N04'24 79w22'27 5:17:30
Forest 10 4 37N21'49 79w17'24 5:17:10
Forest Hill 116 14 37N24'57 79w12'14 5:16:49
Forest Hill 127 17 37N28 77w28 5:09:52
Forest Hill Park 135 23 37N16'53 76w41'20 5:06:45
Forest Hills 133 6 36N53'11 76w03'50 5:04:15
Forest Lake Hills 42 22 37N42'11 77w24'25 5:09:38
Forest Lodge Acres 43 22 37N40 77w30 5:10:00
Forestville 29 3 39N00 77w15 5:09:00
Forestville 82 14 38N42'54 78w43'21 5:14:53
Fork 90 14 38N55 78w16 5:13:04
Fork Ridge 89 4 37N08'02 81w53'00 5:27:32
Fork Shop 48 4 37N37 76w47 5:07:08
Forks of Buffalo 5 16 37N40'46 79w13'20 5:16:53
Forksville 58 4 36N45'08 78w02'47 5:12:11
Fork Union 32 4 37N45'47 78w15'45 5:13:03
Formosa 20 4 36N52'52 78w39'21 5:14:37
Forrest Landing 64 4 37N56'28 76w29'04 5:05:56
Fort Alexander 43 17 37N27'09 77w22'31 5:09:30
Fort Barnard 7 1 38N50'53 77w05'32 5:08:22
Fort Barnard Heights 7 1 38N50'47 77w05'23 5:08:22
Fort Belvoir 29 8 38N43 77w09 5:08:36
Fort Blackmore 81 26 36N46'28 82w35'13 5:30:21
Fort Brady 43 22 37N23'29 77w21'43 5:09:27
Fort C F Smith 7 8 38N54'03 77w05'26 5:08:22
Fort Chiswell 94 4 36N56'49 80w56'30 5:23:46
Fort Christanna 13 4 36N42'48 77w52'15 5:11:29
Fort Darling 21 22 37N25'16 77w25'35 5:09:42
Fort Davis 72 22 37N11'33 77w22'33 5:09:30
Fort Defiance 8 21 38N14'25 78w58'20 5:15:53
Fort Ellsworth 96 1 38N48'27 77w04'13 5:08:17
Fort Emory 27 11 37N09'23 77w26'32 5:09:46
Fortener Addition 83 15 36N50 81w31 5:26:04
Fort Ethan Allen 7 3 38N55'28 77w07'25 5:08:30

Fort Eustis 120 10 37N09 76w35 5:06:20
Fort Farnsworth 29 1 38N47'19 77w04'25 5:08:18
Fort Fisher 27 11 37N10'30 77w27'15 5:09:49
Fort Gilmer 43 17 37N26'51 77w22'53 5:09:32
Fort Gregg 43 17 37N26'36 77w22'51 5:09:31
Fort Harrison 43 17 37N25'40 77w22'24 5:09:30
Fort Hill 43 22 37N35 77w31 5:10:04
Fort Hill 116 14 37N23'10 79w11'00 5:16:44
Fort Hoke 43 22 37N25'02 77w23'09 5:09:33
Fort Hunt 29 3 38N43 77w04 5:08:16
Fort Johnson 43 17 37N26'15 77w22'49 5:09:31
Fort Lee 27 11 37N12'00 77w26'09 5:09:45
Fort Lee 43 22 37N29'44 77w20'08 5:09:21
Fort Lewis 9 4 38N07'37 79w37'12 5:18:29
Fort Lewis Terrace 129 4 37N17 80w03 5:20:12
Fort Lyon 29 3 38N47'38 77w04'40 5:08:19
Fort Lyons Heights 29 1 38N47 77w05 5:08:20
Fort Marcy 29 1 38N56'08 77w07'35 5:08:30
Fort McLean 86 4 38N23'27 77w20'37 5:09:22
Fort Milroy 136 9 39N11'46 78w10'35 5:12:42
Fort Mitchell 55 4 36N55'05 78w29'11 5:13:57
Fort Monroe 112 7 37N00'11 76w18'28 5:05:14
Fort Myer 7 8 38N53 77w04 5:08:16
Fort Myer Heights 7 8 38N53'31 77w04'47 5:08:19
Fort Nonsense 57 4 37N27'54 76w26'43 5:05:47
Fort Norfolk 121 7 36N51'29 76w18'33 5:05:14
Fort Nottoway 88 4 36N53'08 77w25'27 5:09:42
Fort Powhatan 72 22 37N16'15 77w04'49 5:08:19
Fort Story 133 6 36N55 76w01 5:04:04
Fort Strong 7 8 38N53'49 77w05'17 5:08:21
Fort Urmston 27 11 37N10'20 77w26'26 5:09:46
Fort Wadsworth 27 11 37N09'58 77w25'03 5:09:40
Fort Ward Heights 96 1 38N50'09 77w06'30 5:08:26
Fort Welch 27 11 37N10'24 77w27'32 5:09:50
Fort Wheaton 27 11 37N10'04 77w26'58 5:09:48
Fort Willard 29 1 38N46'58 77w03'59 5:08:16
Fort Wool 112 7 36N59'11 76w18'02 5:05:12
Fort Worth 96 1 38N48'53 77w05'56 5:08:24
Foster 57 4 37N27'10 76w23'07 5:05:32
Foster Fork 30 19 38N46'29 77w45'13 5:11:01
Fosters Falls 94 4 36N53'00 80w51'09 5:23:25
Fosters Landing 67 14 38N46'12 78w25'22 5:13:41
Foundation Park 101 6 36N48'55 76w14'56 5:05:00
Four Corners 29 3 38N55'49 77w16'17 5:09:05
Four Forks 61 14 37N34'55 78w50'41 5:15:23
Fourmile Fork 86 24 38N15'19 77w29'53 5:10:00
Foursquare 46 4 36N57'51 76w41'32 5:06:46
Fourway 75 14 38N44'59 78w16'06 5:13:04
Fourway (Burkes Garden Sdng) 89 4 37N07'58 81w29'37 5:25:58
Foust Ford 81 26 36N38'10 82w29'23 5:29:58
Fox 38 4 36N36'33 81w17'37 5:25:10
Fox Corner 112 6 37N02'31 76w25'40 5:05:43
Fox Hall Park 121 6 36N52'19 76w13'17 5:04:53
Fox Hill 112 4 37N04'51 76w17'45 5:05:11
Foxlee 53 4 39N00 77w24 5:09:36
Fox Mill Estates 29 3 38N58 77w22 5:09:28
Foxwells 51 14 37N37'45 76w18'41 5:05:15
Fractionville 91 15 36N42'34 82w00'13 5:28:01
Fraleytown 81 26 36N42'16 82w49'22 5:31:17
Francisco 15 4 37N26 78w34 5:14:16
Franconia 29 3 38N46'55 77w08'48 5:08:35
Franklin 109 4 36N40'39 76w55'22 5:07:41
Franklin City 1 4 38N00'28 75w23'02 5:01:32
Franklin Forest 29 1 38N54'33 77w09'38 5:08:39
Franklin Heights 33 4 37N00 79w53 5:19:32
Franklin Junction 132 5 36N36'48 76w38'44 5:06:35
Franklin Park 29 1 38N54'36 77w09'13 5:08:37
Franks Mill 8 21 38N13'19 79w06'26 5:16:26
Franktown 63 4 37N28'43 75w52'45 5:03:31
Frederick Hall 54 14 37N59 77w49 5:11:16
Frederick Heights 34 9 39N10'19 78w07'42 5:12:31
Fredericksburg 78 14 37N53'34 79w26'17 5:17:45
Fredericksburg 110 24 38N18'11 77w27'39 5:09:51
Freeling 26 15 37N10'27 82w29'10 5:29:57
Freeman 13 4 36N45'17 77w41'37 5:10:46
Freemont 18 4 36N46 80w44 5:22:56
Freeport 36 4 37N32'22 76w30'27 5:06:02
Free Shade Corner 59 4 37N33'37 76w27'02 5:05:48
Free Union 2 14 38N09'17 78w33'53 5:14:16
Fremac 133 6 36N52 76w00 5:04:00
Fremont 26 15 37N07'32 82w23'07 5:29:32
French Hay 42 22 37N41'13 77w27'44 5:09:51
Freyco 34 4 39N14'28 78w05'53 5:12:24
Friendship 91 15 36N43'48 81w44'30 5:26:58
Fries 38 4 36N42'58 80w58'44 5:23:55
Fries Junction 18 4 36N45'43 80w57'20 5:23:49
Fringer 12 4 37N32 79w41 5:18:44
Frisco 81 26 36N35'38 82w37'57 5:30:32
Fritters Corner 86 4 38N22'41 77w21'24 5:09:26
Frog Level 89 4 37N05'59 81w33'49 5:26:15
Frogtown 22 4 39N03'58 77w56'02 5:11:44
Front Royal 90 14 38N55'05 78w11'41 5:12:47
Front Royal Junction 90 14 38N55'52 78w11'08 5:12:45
Frytown 30 19 38N42'26 77w45'57 5:11:04
Fugates Hill 80 15 36N44'57 82w18'18 5:29:13
Fugua Farms 21 22 37N27 77w28 5:09:52
Fulkerson 81 26 36N39'45 82w26'05 5:29:44
Fulks Run 79 22 38N39'36 78w54'23 5:15:38
Furnace 67 14 38N26'48 78w33'28 5:14:14
Furnace Hill 83 15 36N49'25 81w29'27 5:25:58
Furnace Mountain 53 14 39N15'34 77w32'41 5:10:11
Gainesboro 34 4 39N16'42 78w15'34 5:13:02
Gaines Mill 42 22 37N35'15 77w18'06 5:09:12
Gaines Mill Estates 42 22 37N37 77w22 5:09:28
Gainesville 73 14 38N47'44 77w36'51 5:10:27
Gala 12 4 37N41'19 79w48'34 5:19:14
Galax 111 4 36N39'40 80w55'27 5:23:42
Galena 94 4 36N52'52 80w53'36 5:23:34
Gallops Corner 133 6 36N47'59 76w07'47 5:04:31
Galts Mill 5 14 37N26'52 79w00'46 5:16:03
Galveston 69 4 36N55'11 79w23'01 5:17:32
Gapstore 89 4 37N05 81w46 5:27:04
Garden 14 15 37N13 81w53 5:27:32
Garden City 7 1 38N54'00 77w08'08 5:08:33
Garden City 128 4 37N13'54 79w55'43 5:19:43
Garden Wood Park 133 6 36N53'47 76w10'27 5:04:42
Gardner 80 15 37N01'50 81w56'09 5:27:45
Gardner Mills 18 4 36N44'19 80w45'11 5:23:01
Gardners Crossroads 54 14 37N53'40 77w50'52 5:11:23
Garfield Estates 73 13 38N36'20 77w17'52 5:09:11
Gargatha 1 4 37N48'00 75w35'54 5:02:24
Garland Heights 21 22 37N27 77w28 5:09:52
Garners Mill 40 20 36N33'21 77w40'15 5:10:41
Garnett Crossing 42 22 37N50'54 77w26'37 5:09:46
Garrisonville 86 4 38N28'57 77w25'37 5:09:42
Garrisonville Estates 86 4 38N28'22 77w28'29 5:09:54
Gary 55 4 36N51'54 78w12'02 5:12:48
Garysville 72 22 37N14'59 77w09'29 5:08:38
Gasburg 13 4 36N34'00 77w53'45 5:11:35
Gate City 81 26 36N38'16 82w34'52 5:30:19
Gatewood 85 22 38N04'55 77w40'09 5:10:41
Gatewood Park 133 7 36N50'01 76w02'52 5:04:11
Gaylord 22 4 39N11'15 77w55'51 5:11:43
Gaynor Heights 44 4 36N40 79w52 5:19:28
Gayton 43 22 37N36'35 77w36'42 5:10:27
Geer 39 14 38N17'53 78w29'56 5:14:00
Geneva Park 101 6 36N46'51 76w20'11 5:05:21
Genito 70 14 37N27'43 77w51'34 5:11:26
Genoa 79 22 38N38'25 78w55'05 5:15:40
Georges Fork 26 15 37N08'56 82w29'11 5:29:57
Georges Mill 53 4 39N17'16 77w39'47 5:10:39
Georges Tavern 37 4 37N44'08 78w03'15 5:12:13
Georgetown 64 4 37N49'54 76w26'48 5:05:47
Georgetown 82 14 38N44'13 78w40'04 5:14:40
Georgetown South 117 2 38N44'36 77w28'32 5:09:54
Georgetown Village 73 13 38N35'29 77w17'56 5:09:12
George Washington 86 4 38N17 77w23 5:09:32
George Washington 96 1 38N50 77w04 5:08:16
George Washington Park 133 6 36N51 76w07 5:04:28
Gera 49 22 38N14'02 77w10'48 5:08:43
Germans Corner 76 4 38N00'08 76w51'20 5:07:25
Germantown 30 19 38N36'49 77w44'31 5:10:58
Gertie 101 4 36N41 76w16 5:05:04
Gether 17 22 37N54'58 77w12'27 5:08:50
Getz 82 14 38N45 78w39 5:14:36
Getz Corner 82 14 38N44'35 78w45'46 5:15:03
Ghent 121 6 36N51'45 76w18'04 5:05:12
Gholsonville 13 4 36N38'51 77w53'44 5:11:35
Gibeon 64 18 37N58'20 76w37'12 5:06:29
Gibson Mill 52 26 36N36'22 83w34'34 5:34:18
Gibson Station 52 26 36N36'15 83w35'51 5:34:23
Gidsville 5 16 37N41'38 79w06'29 5:16:26
Giesley Mill 91 15 36N46'46 81w52'54 5:27:32
Gilbert 2 14 38N08'45 78w22'27 5:13:30
Gilbert Gardens 43 17 37N31'09 77w22'14 5:09:29
Gilbert Mill 68 4 36N35'06 80w14'42 5:20:59
Gilberts Corner 53 4 38N58'08 77w37'22 5:10:29
Giles 4 4 37N21 77w58 5:11:52
Gillespie 10 4 37N12'50 79w25'57 5:17:44
Gillespie 89 4 37N05'30 81w40'15 5:26:41
Gilley 93 15 37N05'57 82w40'30 5:30:42
Gilliamsville 15 4 37N40'03 78w15'37 5:13:02
Gillick Corner 64 18 37N53'32 76w30'05 5:06:00
Gills 4 4 37N18 78w06 5:12:24
Gills Corner 55 4 36N51'38 78w02'07 5:12:08
Gilman 42 22 37N46'42 77w34'51 5:10:19
Gilmerton 101 6 36N46'15 76w18'44 5:05:15
Gilmore Mills 78 14 37N36'31 79w32'30 5:18:10
Ginter Park 127 17 37N35'15 77w27'21 5:09:49
Gladehill 33 4 36N59'22 79w45'47 5:19:03
Gladesboro 18 4 36N41'09 80w36'36 5:22:26
Glade Spring 91 15 36N47'28 81w46'17 5:27:05
Gladeville 93 15 37N01 82w36 5:30:24
Gladstone 61 14 37N32'48 78w50'59 5:15:24
Gladys 16 16 37N09'47 79w04'26 5:16:18
Glamorgan 93 15 36N59'55 82w35'40 5:30:23
Glasgow 78 14 37N38'02 79w27'02 5:17:48
Glass 36 4 37N17 76w30 5:06:00
Glasses Store 52 26 36N40 83w07 5:32:28
Glebe Mills 12 4 37N25'31 79w55'57 5:19:44
Gleedsville 53 14 39N02'57 77w36'18 5:10:25
Glen Alden 29 3 38N50'50 77w21'32 5:09:26
Glen Allen 43 22 37N39'57 77w30'24 5:10:02
Glenbrook Hills 43 22 37N34'49 77w33'47 5:10:15
Glencarlyn 7 1 38N51'42 77w07'46 5:08:31
Glendale 29 3 38N58'11 77w14'58 5:09:00
Glendale 43 22 37N26'44 77w14'00 5:08:56
Glendale 120 4 37N04'14 76w29'36 5:05:58
Glendie 86 4 38N23'59 77w32'07 5:10:08
Glendower 2 14 37N50'14 78w32'38 5:14:11
Glen Echo 76 17 37N33 77w24 5:09:36
Glen Echo 90 14 38N51'00 78w13'29 5:12:54
Glenford 91 15 36N47'24 81w55'47 5:27:43
Glen Forest 29 1 38N51'18 77w08'01 5:08:32
Glen Gary 29 1 38N55 77w11 5:08:44
Glenita 81 26 36N41 82w45 5:31:00
Glenland 69 16 36N59'58 79w13'06 5:16:52
Glen Lyn 35 4 37N22'05 80w51'52 5:23:27
Glenmore 15 4 37N40'17 78w35'25 5:14:22
Glenns 36 4 37N33'56 76w36'47 5:06:27
Glen Oaks 29 3 38N48 77w16 5:09:04
Glenora 85 22 38N05'19 77w47'40 5:11:11
Glenrochie 91 15 36N43 81w58 5:27:52
Glen Rock 121 6 36N51'01 76w11'56 5:04:48
Glen Roy Estates 36 4 37N24'16 76w29'02 5:05:56
Glenvar 77 4 37N16'26 80w08'03 5:20:32
Glen Wilton 12 4 37N45'10 79w49'09 5:19:17
Glenwood 69 4 36N35'19 79w21'59 5:17:28
Glenwood Farms 43 17 37N34'35 77w23'08 5:09:33
Glenwood Park 121 6 36N55'43 76w18'47 5:05:15
Glimpses Corner 42 22 37N37'48 77w09'19 5:08:37
Globe 50 14 37N48'44 77w12'00 5:08:48
Gloucester 36 4 37N24'49 76w31'33 5:06:06
Gloucester Point 36 4 37N15'14 76w29'50 5:05:59
Gloversville 132 4 36N51'38 76w34'07 5:06:16
Goad Heights 77 4 37N23 79w49 5:19:16
Goblintown 68 4 36N38 80w16 5:21:04
Goby 49 22 38N18'49 77w16'28 5:09:06
Gogginsville 33 4 37N02'25 79w55'34 5:19:42
Golansville 17 22 37N58'50 77w30'04 5:10:00
Goldbond 35 4 37N22'48 80w40'00 5:22:40
Gold Dale 66 14 38N16'01 77w48'22 5:11:13
Gold Hill 15 4 37N37'24 78w22'14 5:13:29
Goldmans Corner 17 22 38N06'48 77w12'21 5:08:49
Goldvein 30 19 38N26'56 77w39'20 5:10:37
Gonyon 64 18 37N54'13 76w20'20 5:05:21
Goochland 37 4 37N41'03 77w53'08 5:11:33
Goodall 42 22 37N46'57 77w38'14 5:10:33
Goode 10 4 37N21'31 79w23'31 5:17:34
Goode Crossing 70 14 37N25'16 77w51'30 5:11:26
Good Luck 51 18 37N44'37 76w21'46 5:05:27
Goodrich Fork 87 4 37N00'01 76w55'04 5:07:40
Goods Mills 79 22 38N23 78w48 5:15:12
Goodview 10 4 37N12'51 79w43'31 5:18:54
Goodwin Neck Estates 95 4 37N12'30 76w25'24 5:05:42
Goodwins Ferry 35 4 37N18 80w30 5:22:00
Goose Pimple Junction 91 25 36N35'48 82w06'13 5:28:25
Gordon 66 14 38N16 77w48 5:11:12
Gordon Corner 58 4 36N43'23 78w16'51 5:13:07
Gordon Crossing 61 14 37N44'24 78w49'02 5:15:16
Gordonsville 66 14 38N08'14 78w11'17 5:12:45
Gore 34 4 39N15'50 78w19'56 5:13:20
Gose Mill 89 4 37N07'30 81w21'22 5:25:25
Goshen 78 14 37N59'13 79w29'53 5:18:00
Goshen Cross Road 42 22 37N52'20 77w38'21 5:10:33
Gosport 125 6 36N48'37 76w19'24 5:05:18
Gossan Junction 18 4 36N40 80w55 5:23:40
Gouldin 42 22 37N46'20 77w42'05 5:10:48
Government 94 4 36N57 81w05 5:24:20
Grady 69 4 36N47'13 79w38'15 5:18:33
Grafton 59 4 37N33'32 76w28'14 5:05:53
Grafton 95 4 37N09'55 76w28'08 5:05:53
Grafton Village 86 4 38N19'24 77w26'32 5:09:46
Grahams Forge 94 4 36N56'23 80w53'06 5:23:32
Grandin Road 128 4 37N15 79w59 5:19:56
Grand View 112 4 37N04'40 76w16'33 5:05:06
Grandy Park 121 6 36N50'34 76w14'54 5:05:00
Grangeville 1 4 37N39 75w44 5:02:56
Granite 21 17 37N31'58 77w30'27 5:10:02
Granite Springs 85 22 38N11'18 77w51'17 5:11:25
Grant 38 4 36N39'44 81w24'15 5:25:37
Grant's Field 27 22 37N13 77w26 5:09:44
Granville 19 14 37N22'55 77w14'30 5:08:58
Grapefield 11 4 37N08'58 81w14'32 5:24:58
Grassfield 101 6 36N43'04 76w19'23 5:05:18

Grassland 66 14 38N15'49 77w59'11 5:11:57
Grass Ridge 29 1 38N55 77w11 5:08:44
Grassy Creek 44 4 36N38'34 79w55'17 5:19:41
Grassy Creek 80 15 36N46'51 82w20'18 5:29:21
Gratton 89 4 37N08'05 81w24'51 5:25:39
Gravel Hill 15 4 37N35'02 78w22'30 5:13:30
Gravel Hill 21 17 37N32'11 77w30'54 5:10:04
Gravel Lick 80 15 36N57'03 82w13'51 5:28:55
Gravel Ridge 16 16 37N10 79w05 5:16:20
Gravel Springs 34 4 39N04'30 78w26'26 5:13:46
Graves Corner 49 22 38N15'24 77w16'53 5:09:08
Graves Landing 19 14 37N23'06 76w56'14 5:07:45
Graves Mill 56 4 38N25'21 78w22'04 5:13:28
Graves Store 10 4 37N10 79w28 5:17:52
Gray 88 4 36N47'48 77w20'38 5:09:23
Grays 81 15 36N48'00 82w30'09 5:30:01
Grays Corner 15 4 37N39'00 78w37'56 5:14:32
Grays Corner 92 19 38N01'25 76w36'45 5:06:27
Grays Ford 81 15 36N48'13 82w30'17 5:30:01
Grays Hill Village 29 3 38N42 77w09 5:08:36
Grays Landing 87 4 37N10'13 76w49'32 5:07:18
Grayson 18 4 36N46'03 80w56'56 5:23:48
Graysontown 60 4 37N02'18 80w33'41 5:22:15
Graysville 1 4 37N42'48 75w40'45 5:02:43
Great Bridge 101 6 36N42'49 76w14'21 5:04:57
Great Falls 29 3 38N59'53 77w17'19 5:09:09
Great Neck Estates 133 6 36N52'54 76w03'01 5:04:12
Great Neck Manor 133 6 36N52'56 76w02'32 5:04:10
Green Acres 101 6 36N50'32 76w24'11 5:05:37
Green Acres 107 3 38N50'23 77w18'14 5:09:13
Greenbackville 1 4 38N00'41 75w23'26 5:01:34
Green Bay 42 14 37N57'54 77w41'42 5:10:47
Green Bay 71 4 37N08'01 78w18'54 5:13:16
Greenbriar 29 3 38N51 77w15 5:09:00
Greenbriar 125 6 36N50'59 76w20'49 5:05:23
Greenbush 1 4 37N44'27 75w40'53 5:02:44
Green Cove 91 15 36N37'03 81w38'36 5:26:34
Greendale 43 17 37N36'50 77w29'49 5:09:59
Greendale 91 15 36N44'50 82w03'04 5:28:12
Greendale Manor 43 17 37N34 77w29 5:09:56
Greenes Corner 54 14 37N58'33 77w43'13 5:10:53
Greenfield 61 14 37N55'39 78w50'18 5:15:21
Greenfield 69 4 36N56'17 79w16'58 5:17:08
Greenfield 85 22 38N14'53 77w25'17 5:09:41
Greenfield 91 15 36N43'53 81w50'28 5:27:22
Greenfield Farms 125 6 36N51'35 76w22'54 5:05:32
Green Hill 16 16 37N03'42 79w04'22 5:16:17
Green Hill Farms 121 6 36N53'43 76w15'09 5:05:01
Greenlee 78 14 37N36'52 79w29'59 5:18:00
Green Meadow Point 101 6 36N50'25 76w24'37 5:05:38
Green Mount 79 22 38N31'10 78w53'28 5:15:34
Green Plain 40 20 36N41'48 77w27'08 5:09:49
Green Pond 69 4 36N52'52 79w30'33 5:18:02
Greens Corner 24 14 38N28'14 77w56'33 5:11:46
Green Spring 34 9 39N18'15 78w10'11 5:12:41
Green Spring 54 14 38N05 78w09 5:12:36
Green Spring 91 15 36N38'05 81w59'45 5:27:59
Green Springs 54 14 38N05'09 78w06'43 5:12:27
Green Springs 91 15 36N43 81w58 5:27:52
Greensprings 95 23 37N17'17 76w42'54 5:06:52
Greentown 13 4 36N41'15 77w46'46 5:11:07
Green Valley 9 4 38N04'49 79w35'58 5:18:24
Green Valley 91 25 36N36 82w11 5:28:44
Greenville 8 21 38N00'12 79w09'22 5:16:37
Greenville 30 19 38N43'04 77w39'46 5:10:39
Greenway 19 14 37N20'27 77w04'55 5:08:20
Greenway 22 4 39N03 78w05 5:12:20
Greenway 29 3 38N58 77w14 5:08:56
Greenway 61 14 37N35'03 78w50'02 5:15:20
Greenway Court 22 4 39N02'46 78w07'08 5:12:29
Greenway Downs 29 3 38N52'37 77w11'01 5:08:44
Greenway Hills 107 3 38N51'17 77w17'22 5:09:09
Greenway Wharf 36 4 37N18 76w25 5:05:40
Greenwich 73 14 38N44'57 77w38'54 5:10:36
Greenwich 133 6 36N50'30 76w11'13 5:04:45
Greenwood 2 14 38N03'20 78w46'15 5:15:05
Greenwood 9 4 37N57'14 79w58'00 5:19:52
Greenwood 43 22 37N39'45 77w28'06 5:09:52
Greenwood 79 14 38N26'21 78w39'21 5:14:37
Greenwood 121 6 36N52'57 76w14'12 5:04:57
Greenwood Farms 112 6 37N01'46 76w24'51 5:05:39
Greenwood Heights 34 9 39N09'54 78w07'04 5:12:28
Gregory Corner 58 4 36N48'01 78w21'53 5:13:28
Gressitt 48 4 37N29'14 76w42'29 5:06:50
Greta 1 4 37N55'04 75w31'39 5:02:07
Gretna 69 4 36N57'13 79w21'33 5:17:26
Greyledge 12 4 37N34'20 79w40'00 5:18:40
Greys Corner 92 19 38N02 76w35 5:06:20
Griffinsburg 24 14 38N31'19 78w05'55 5:12:24
Griffins Landing 51 4 37N45'05 76w31'21 5:06:05
Griffith 3 4 37N51'57 79w43'37 5:18:54
Griffiths Corner 92 19 38N02 76w35 5:06:20
Grimes 34 9 39N16'41 78w07'35 5:12:30
Grimes Landing 50 14 37N39'20 77w06'31 5:08:26
Grimsleyville 14 15 37N10'05 81w54'11 5:27:37
Grimstead 57 4 37N30'01 76w18'06 5:05:12
Grindall Creek 21 22 37N27 77w28 5:09:52
Grinels 59 4 37N34'11 76w21'31 5:05:26
Grit 69 16 37N04'34 79w14'53 5:17:00
Grizzard 88 4 36N43'35 77w26'16 5:09:45
Groseclose 83 15 36N53'22 81w20'50 5:25:23
Groseclose Store 11 4 36N59'07 81w23'44 5:25:35
Grotons 1 4 37N55'34 75w38'38 5:02:35
Groton Town 1 4 37N51'59 75w35'14 5:02:21
Grottoes 79 22 38N16'02 78w49'34 5:15:18
Grove 47 23 37N13'47 76w37'38 5:06:31
Grove Hill 67 14 38N31'43 78w36'45 5:14:27
Grove Hill Landing 67 14 38N31'38 78w35'39 5:14:23
Groveland 133 6 36N51 76w07 5:04:28
Grove Park 125 6 36N49'32 76w21'22 5:05:25
Groveton 29 1 38N46'02 77w05'06 5:08:20
Groveton 73 14 38N48'45 77w32'55 5:10:12
Groveton Gardens 29 1 38N47 77w05 5:08:20
Groveton Heights 29 1 38N46'13 77w05'38 5:08:23
Grubb 94 4 36N54'41 81w09'28 5:24:38
Grubbs Store 54 14 38N02 78w00 5:12:00
Grundy 14 15 37N16'40 82w05'57 5:28:24
Guildfield Corner 84 4 36N53'56 76w54'44 5:07:39
Guilford 1 4 37N49'29 75w39'07 5:02:36
Guilford 29 3 38N46'56 77w07'40 5:08:31
Guilford 87 4 37N09 76w59 5:07:56
Guinea 17 22 38N08'37 77w26'17 5:09:45
Guinea Mills 25 4 37N26'13 78w19'55 5:13:20
Gullysville 61 14 37N51'47 78w52'05 5:15:28
Gulvey 49 22 38N14'34 77w05'42 5:08:23
Gum 84 4 36N38'06 77w04'58 5:08:20
Gum Fork 36 4 37N22'00 76w34'15 5:06:17
Gum Spring 54 14 37N46'32 77w53'49 5:11:35
Gum Springs 29 3 38N44'25 77w04'57 5:08:20
Gum Tree 42 22 37N49'09 77w28'28 5:09:54
Gunn Hall Manor 133 6 36N46'37 76w00'17 5:04:01
Gunston Heights 29 3 38N40'26 77w12'43 5:08:51
Gunston Manor 29 3 38N38'52 77w08'38 5:08:35
Gunton Park 94 4 36N58 80w57 5:23:48
Gwaltney Corner 87 4 37N06'42 77w01'27 5:08:06
Gwathmey 42 22 37N44'02 77w29'23 5:09:58
Gwynn 57 4 37N30'15 76w17'20 5:05:09
Gwynn Island Landing 57 4 37N29'30 76w18'35 5:05:14
Hackleys Crossroad 75 19 38N43'39 78w01'53 5:12:08
Hacksneck 1 4 37N38'35 75w52'15 5:03:29
Haddonfield 93 15 37N09'10 82w36'15 5:30:25
Haden 12 4 37N42'59 79w50'03 5:19:20
Hadensville 37 4 37N49'31 78w00'00 5:12:00
Hadlock 63 4 37N31'03 75w50'02 5:03:20
Hagan 52 26 36N42'15 83w17'12 5:33:09
Hague 92 19 38N04'20 76w39'05 5:06:36
Hale Creek 14 15 37N15'40 81w56'34 5:27:46
Halenhurst 107 3 38N50'29 77w17'49 5:09:11
Hales Bottom 89 4 37N15'56 81w17'45 5:25:11
Haleys Corner 17 22 37N50'53 77w22'10 5:09:29
Halfway 30 19 38N54'5? 77w44'42 5:10:59
Halifax 41 4 36N45'57 78w55'43 5:15:43
Hall Addition 83 15 36N50 81w31 5:26:04
Hall Ford 52 26 36N38'12 83w13'48 5:32:55
Halliahurst Park 77 4 37N23 79w49 5:19:16
Hallieford 57 4 37N29'37 76w20'26 5:05:22
Hallowing Point River Estate 29 3 38N38'15 77w08'39 5:08:35
Hallsboro 21 22 37N29'18 77w43'32 5:10:54
Halls Hill 7 1 38N53'51 77w07'44 5:08:31
Hallwood 1 4 37N52'39 75w35'22 5:02:21
Hallwood 112 4 37N03'48 76w17'53 5:05:12
Hamburg 67 14 38N39'29 78w30'53 5:14:04
Hamburg 82 14 38N48'18 78w38'16 5:14:33
Hamilton 25 14 37N39'32 78w07'31 5:12:30
Hamilton 27 22 37N01'45 77w36'20 5:10:25
Hamilton 53 14 39N08'03 77w39'46 5:10:39
Hamilton Crossing 85 22 38N14'36 77w26'04 5:09:44
Hamiltontown 93 15 36N59 82w38 5:30:32
Hamlin 80 15 36N55'41 82w16'43 5:29:07
Hamlins Corner 64 4 37N56'29 76w27'40 5:05:51
Hammock Landing 1 4 37N54'13 75w41'00 5:02:44
Hampden 71 4 37N11 78w28 5:13:52
Hampden Sydney 71 4 37N14'32 78w27'36 5:13:50
Hampstead 49 22 38N20'00 77w08'31 5:08:34
Hampstead 62 14 37N36'21 77w07'48 5:08:31
Hampton 112 6 37N01'47 76w20'44 5:05:23
Hampton Institute 112 6 37N01 76w21 5:05:24
Hampton Roads 121 6 36N56 76w19 5:05:16
Hams Ford 85 22 38N07'20 77w33'06 5:10:12
Hanckel 91 15 36N50'58 81w48'21 5:27:13
Handsom 84 4 36N38'32 77w01'51 5:08:07
Haneytown 39 14 38N17'25 78w32'08 5:14:09
Hanging Rock 77 4 37N19'41 80w02'25 5:20:10
Hanover 42 22 37N45'59 77w22'14 5:09:29
Hanover Farms 42 22 37N35'00 77w17'48 5:09:11
Hanover Heights 120 4 37N08'32 76w31'39 5:06:07
Hanover Hills 42 22 37N42'04 77w23'53 5:09:36
Hanovertown 42 22 37N41'50 77w14'49 5:08:59
Hansonville 80 15 36N49'26 82w08'47 5:28:35
Happy Creek 90 14 38N55'47 78w08'56 5:12:36
Harborton 1 4 37N39'42 75w49'51 5:03:19
Harbor View 29 3 38N40'15 77w13'31 5:08:54
Harcum 36 4 37N31'06 76w30'20 5:06:01
Hard Corner 17 22 38N00'23 77w17'17 5:09:09
Hardesty 90 14 38N55 78w12 5:12:48
Hardings 64 18 37N44'55 76w19'48 5:05:19
Hardins Corner 64 18 37N49'07 76w23'48 5:05:35
Hardscrabble 45 4 38N33'41 79w34'24 5:18:18
Hardware 32 4 37N44'34 78w24'21 5:13:37
Hardwood 81 15 36N50 82w28 5:29:52
Hardy 10 4 37N13'54 79w48'39 5:19:15
Hardy 46 4 36N58 76w43 5:06:52
Hardyville 59 4 37N33'24 76w22'20 5:05:29
Hare Valley 63 4 37N29'42 75w51'34 5:03:26
Harfield 59 4 37N33'04 76w26'47 5:05:47
Hargraves 29 1 38N47 77w07 5:08:28
Harless 60 4 37N08 80w24 5:21:36
Harman 14 15 37N17'35 82w12'08 5:28:49
Harman 89 4 37N09'35 81w42'27 5:26:50
Harman Junction 14 15 37N18'36 82w09'45 5:28:39
Harmony 41 4 36N33'32 78w57'56 5:15:52
Harmony 82 14 38N52'24 78w35'51 5:14:23
Harmony Village 59 4 37N34'53 76w29'16 5:05:57
Harper 93 26 36N52'41 82w46'45 5:31:07
Harpersville 120 4 37N05'44 76w27'17 5:05:49
Harrell Corner 30 19 38N52'39 78w03'52 5:12:15
Harrell Siding 132 5 36N44 76w35 5:06:20
Harrells Mill 88 4 36N46'29 77w23'30 5:09:34
Harrington 3 4 37N50'38 79w58'32 5:19:54
Harrisburg 20 4 37N01'35 78w44'53 5:15:00
Harris Grove 95 4 37N11'39 76w28'56 5:05:56
Harrisonburg 113 22 38N26'58 78w52'09 5:15:29
Harrisons Landing 19 22 37N18'48 77w10'48 5:08:43
Harriston 8 21 38N16 78w49 5:15:16
Harrisville 82 14 38N57'03 78w27'43 5:13:51
Harrowgate 21 22 37N23 77w26 5:09:44
Harryhogan 64 18 37N58 76w34 5:06:16
Harryhogan Point 64 18 38N00'25 76w32'40 5:06:11
Hart Corner 17 22 37N50'58 77w25'20 5:09:41
Hartfield 59 4 37N33 76w27 5:05:48
Hartford 81 26 36N37'57 82w28'47 5:29:55
Harts Shop 54 14 38N01 77w54 5:11:36
Hartwood 86 4 38N24'08 77w33'56 5:10:16
Harvey 52 26 36N47'03 82w49'04 5:31:16
Harveys 64 18 37N44'40 76w20'22 5:05:21
Harwoods Mill 95 4 37N08'17 76w27'02 5:05:48
Haskell 91 25 36N38'52 82w11'33 5:28:46
Hassen Heights 91 25 36N36 82w11 5:28:44
Hatcher 25 4 37N33'42 78w17'58 5:13:12
Hatchers 70 14 37N34'49 78w03'06 5:12:12
Hat Creek 16 16 37N07'07 78w54'15 5:15:37
Hatton 2 14 37N45'33 78w30'47 5:14:03
Hattontown 29 3 38N56'42 77w23'36 5:09:34
Havelock 76 4 38N01'14 76w50'20 5:07:21
Haven Heights 133 6 36N48'46 76w10'34 5:04:42
Haw Branch 4 4 37N24'37 78w01'15 5:12:05
Hawk 25 4 37N24'35 78w21'23 5:13:26
Hawkins Mill 80 15 36N48'29 82w10'39 5:28:43
Hawkinstown 82 14 38N46'21 78w36'48 5:14:27
Hawlin 75 14 38N35'44 78w12'30 5:12:50
Hawthorne 75 14 38N35 78w14 5:12:56
Hawthorne 93 15 36N56'29 82w36'03 5:30:24
Hawtree Landing 95 23 37N18'10 76w39'37 5:06:38
Haycock 31 4 36N52'22 80w16'14 5:21:05
Hayes 36 4 37N16'41 76w30'15 5:06:01
Hayfield 29 3 38N45'06 77w08'10 5:08:33
Hayfield 34 4 39N14'03 78w17'24 5:13:10
Hayfield Farms 29 3 38N43 77w09 5:08:36
Haymakertown 12 4 37N27'58 79w58'15 5:19:53
Haymarket 73 14 38N48'43 77w38'12 5:10:33
Haynesville 76 4 37N57'00 76w39'46 5:06:39
Hay Run 33 4 36N59'31 79w56'48 5:19:47
Haysi 26 15 37N12'19 82w17'39 5:29:11
Hayter 91 15 36N44'08 81w55'12 5:27:41
Haytokah 65 4 37N11 78w11 5:12:44
Haywood 56 4 38N27'12 78w15'09 5:13:01
Haywood Landing 48 4 37N27'56 76w39'31 5:06:38
Hazel 80 15 36N59'26 82w15'14 5:29:01
Hazel Grove 85 22 38N18'10 77w39'13 5:10:37
Hazel Heights 91 25 36N36 82w11 5:28:44
Hazel Hill 110 24 38N17'48 77w27'31 5:09:50
Hazel River 24 4 38N35 77w59 5:11:56
Head Waters 45 4 38N19 79w25 5:17:40
Healing Springs 9 4 37N57'39 79w51'46 5:19:27
Health Science 127 17 37N33 77w26 5:09:44
Healys 59 4 37N34'22 76w30'43 5:06:03
Heards 2 14 37N55'12 78w45'14 5:15:01
Heaths Store 42 22 37N44'08 77w27'05 5:09:48
Heathsville 64 18 37N55'03 76w28'21 5:05:53
Hebron 8 21 38N08'30 79w09'20 5:16:37
Hebron 18 4 36N44'26 80w54'27 5:23:38
Hebron 27 22 37N08'39 77w48'20 5:11:13

Heckler Village 43
17 37N32'13 77W22'09 5:09:29
Heflin 86 4 38N29'18 77W34'42 5:10:19
Height 14 15 37N16'50 81W48'51 5:27:15
Heights 123 22 37N12'40 77W24'27 5:09:38
Helm 33 4 37N04'46 79W56'52 5:19:47
Helmet 48 4 37N54'59 77W06'19 5:08:25
Hematite 3 4 37N44'23 80W10'35 5:20:42
Hemlock 31 4 37N10 80W15 5:21:00
Henderson 91 15 36N52'27 81W51'24 5:27:26
Hendersons Store 61
14 37N44'35 78W59'56 5:16:00
Hendricks Store 10
4 37N11 79W37 5:18:28
Henegartown 52 26 36N40'39 83W18'01 5:33:12
Henley 94 4 36N51'07 81W06'47 5:24:27
Henley Fork 28 4 37N53'08 76W53'56 5:07:36
Henleys Fork 48 4 37N45'20 76W59'27 5:07:58
Henleys Store 5
16 37N35 79W03 5:16:12
Henrico 58 4 36N35'33 78W36'59 5:14:28
Henry 33 4 36N49'45 79W59'31 5:19:58
Henry 88 4 36N47'48 77W23'35 5:09:34
Henry Clay Heights 42
22 37N40'26 77W23'22 5:09:33
Henry Crossroads 88
4 36N50 77W28 5:09:52
Henry Fork 33 4 36N57'58 79W52'14 5:19:29
Henrys Mill 69 4 36N46'29 79W09'50 5:16:39
Henrytown 83 15 36N53'01 81W47'15 5:27:09
Hepners 82 14 38N45'42 78W48'13 5:15:13
Herald 26 15 36N59'16 82W24'08 5:29:37
Herberts Corner 101
6 36N43'39 76W18'09 5:05:13
Hereford 89 4 37N15'25 81W19'35 5:25:18
Heritage Square 29
1 38N50 77W12 5:08:48
Heritage Village 29
1 38N50 77W12 5:08:48
Herman 20 4 36N56 78W40 5:14:40
Hermitage 8 21 38N08'29 78W54'52 5:15:39
Hermitage Court 43
17 37N36 77W29 5:09:56
Hermitage Farms 43
17 37N36 77W29 5:09:56
Hermitage Park 43
17 37N36 77W29 5:09:56
Hermosa 41 4 36N56'24 79W07'18 5:16:29
Herndon 29 1 38N58'10 77W23'11 5:09:33
Herndon Heights 29
3 38N58'47 77W23'56 5:09:36
Herndon Junction 29
3 39N00'51 77W22'16 5:09:29
Hessian Hills 2
14 38N03'48 78W30'10 5:14:01
Hewlett 42 22 37N55'20 77W34'36 5:10:18
Hickman 33 4 37N01'26 79W59'01 5:19:56
Hickory 101 6 36N37'55 76W12'30 5:04:50
Hickory Flat 18 4 36N41'53 80W55'54 5:23:44
Hickory Fork 17
22 38N03'24 77W13'40 5:08:55
Hickory Grove 41
4 36N55'36 79W05'47 5:16:23
Hickory Grove 73
14 38N54'00 77W37'41 5:10:31
Hickory Haven 37
4 37N39'54 77W40'32 5:10:42
Hickory Hill 2 14 38N02 78W29 5:13:56
Hickory Junction 80
15 37N01'44 81W58'04 5:27:52
Hickory Run 13 4 36N57'54 77W50'57 5:11:24
Hickory Sign Post 47
23 37N17 76W43 5:06:52
Hicksford 40 20 36N35 77W38 5:10:32
Hicks Mill 13 4 36N40'56 77W56'13 5:11:45
Hicks Mill 17 22 38N05'38 77W15'30 5:09:02
Hicksville 11 4 37N11'35 81W08'06 5:24:32
Hiddenbrook 29 3 38N58 77W22 5:09:28
Hiddenwood 120 4 37N03'54 76W30'19 5:06:01
Higgins Crossroads 18
4 36N39'04 80W48'53 5:23:16
Highgate 87 4 37N07'38 76W44'37 5:06:58
High Hill 41 4 36N38'09 78W44'58 5:15:00
Highland 74 4 37N09'53 80W40'44 5:22:43
Highland-Biltmore 125
6 36N48'40 76W20'13 5:05:21
Highland Gardens 43
17 37N34 77W26 5:09:44
Highland Homes 86
4 38N19'46 77W26'31 5:09:46
Highland Landing 64
18 37N44'58 76W20'45 5:05:23
Highland Park 73
2 38N47 77W28 5:09:52
Highland Park 114
14 37N17'40 77W17'53 5:09:12
Highland Park 127
17 37N34'22 77W25'54 5:09:44
Highlands 7 8 38N53'53 77W05'00 5:08:20
Highland Springs 43
22 37N32'45 77W19'41 5:09:19
High Meadows 91
25 36N36 82W11 5:28:44
High Point 114 14 37N17 77W18 5:09:12
High Rock 41 4 36N46'46 79W05'50 5:16:23
High Rock 94 4 36N46 80W44 5:22:56
High Rocks Mill 94
4 36N52'52 80W46'23 5:23:06
Hightown 45 4 38N25'52 79W37'55 5:18:32
Hightown 79 22 38N31'35 78W48'15 5:15:13
High View Manor 34
4 39N09'43 78W19'17 5:13:17
Highview Park 7 1 38N53'37 77W07'40 5:08:31
High Woods 1 4 37N45'37 75W39'22 5:02:37
Hilander Park 91
25 36N39'18 82W04'56 5:28:20
Hiland Park 112 4 37N02'38 76W20'14 5:05:21
Hilda 88 4 36N49'13 77W19'46 5:09:19
Hill 81 26 36N38 82W34 5:30:16
Hillbrook 29 1 38N49'34 77W11'09 5:08:45
Hillbrook Forest 29
1 38N50 77W12 5:08:48
Hillcrest 25 4 37N28'57 78W16'28 5:13:06
Hill Crest 34 9 39N11'24 78W13'09 5:12:53
Hillcrest Estates 73
2 38N43'24 77W26'24 5:09:46
Hill Grove 69 16 37N03'28 79W15'24 5:17:02
Hill Landing 133
6 36N39'23 75W58'53 5:03:56
Hillsboro 53 14 39N11'53 77W43'23 5:10:54
Hills Corner 133
6 36N45'06 76W00'38 5:04:03
Hillsdale 132 5 36N44 76W35 5:06:20
Hillsman Corner 16
14 37N18'38 79W14'15 5:16:57
Hillsville 18 4 36N45'45 80W44'06 5:22:56
Hill Top 119 4 36N40 79W52 5:19:28
Hilltop 133 6 36N52 76W00 5:04:00
Hilltown 38 4 36N43'49 80W58'58 5:23:56
Hillwood 108 3 38N52'35 77W10'04 5:08:40
Hiltons 81 26 36N39'16 82W28'02 5:29:52
Hilton Village 120
6 37N01'53 76W27'53 5:05:52
Hinesville 69 4 36N42'06 79W34'24 5:18:18
Hinnom 92 19 38N06'37 76W44'14 5:06:57
Hinton 79 22 38N27'57 78W58'21 5:15:53
Hipes 12 4 37N39'14 79W54'59 5:19:40
Hitesburg 41 4 36N36'36 78W43'34 5:14:54
Hiwassee 74 4 36N58'07 80W42'50 5:22:51
Hixburg 6 4 37N19'43 78W38'50 5:14:35
Hoadly 73 14 38N40'49 77W21'34 5:09:26
Hobbs Ford 91 26 36N42'34 82W17'20 5:29:09
Hobson 132 5 36N53'41 76W30'44 5:06:03
Hockett 52 26 36N43'49 83W11'09 5:32:45
Hockley 36 4 37N23'43 76W27'39 5:05:51
Hockley 48 4 37N30'33 76W43'54 5:06:56
Hockman 89 4 37N15 81W17 5:25:08
Hodges 16 16 37N07'18 79W09'34 5:16:38
Hodges Ferry 101
6 36N49'20 76W24'20 5:05:37
Hodges Manor 125
6 36N48'59 76W22'59 5:05:32
Hodgesville 33 4 37N00 79W53 5:19:32
Hogans Hill 92 19 37N59'37 76W39'32 5:06:38
Hoges Chapel 35 4 37N19'17 80W35'56 5:22:24
Holcomb Rock 10
14 37N26 79W11 5:16:44
Holdcroft 19 14 37N21'55 76W56'07 5:07:44
Holiday Hills 21
22 37N32'43 77W34'56 5:10:20
Holiday Point 132
5 36N44 76W35 5:06:20
Holiday Point Estates 132
5 36N52'02 76W29'48 5:05:59
Holladay 85 22 38N07'13 77W52'09 5:11:29
Holland 132 4 36N40'52 76W46'50 5:07:07
Holliday 42 22 37N56'03 77W36'29 5:10:26
Hollinbrook Park 29
3 38N45 77W06 5:08:24
Hollindale 29 3 38N45'03 77W03'49 5:08:15
Hollin Hall 29 3 38N45'26 77W03'59 5:08:16
Hollins 77 4 37N20'28 79W56'36 5:19:46
Hollins College 77
4 37N21 79W57 5:19:48
Hollinswood 29 3 38N55 77W14 5:08:56
Holloday 85 14 38N01 77W54 5:11:36
Holly Brook 11 4 37N11'18 80W57'03 5:23:48
Hollybrook 47 23 37N14'38 76W44'44 5:06:59
Holly Corner 86 4 38N21'48 77W33'59 5:10:16
Holly Forest 29 3 38N48 77W20 5:09:20
Holly Forks 62 14 37N28'05 76W47'02 5:07:08
Holly Glen Estates 43
22 37N40'12 77W27'33 5:09:50
Holly Grove 54 14 37N47'44 77W48'53 5:11:16
Holly Hills 70 22 37N30'20 77W45'23 5:11:02
Holly Hills 95 4 37N10'31 76W27'19 5:05:49
Holly Homes 112 4 37N02'58 76W18'59 5:05:16
Holly Landing 19
14 37N25'46 77W01'43 5:08:07
Hollymead 2 14 38N07'01 78W26'31 5:13:46
Holly Park 29 3 38N50'10 77W17'06 5:09:08
Holly Park Estates 29
3 38N50'22 77W17'05 5:09:08
Holly Point 46 4 37N04'31 76W40'05 5:06:40
Hollyridge 86 4 38N23 77W27 5:09:48
Hollys Mill 69 4 36N46'57 79W35'44 5:18:23
Hollywood 6 4 37N23'25 78W42'57 5:14:52
Hollywood 69 4 36N50'01 79W29'47 5:17:59
Hollywood 133 6 36N51'38 76W10'50 5:04:43
Holman 79 22 38N38 78W46 5:15:04
Holmes Run Acres 29
3 38N51'10 77W12'33 5:08:50
Holmes Run Heights 29
1 38N50'53 77W12'45 5:08:51
Holmes Run Park 29
3 38N50'56 77W10'28 5:08:42
Holmhead 32 4 37N46'24 78W12'33 5:12:50
Holston 91 15 36N46'38 82W04'59 5:28:20
Holston Mill 83
15 36N46'09 81W35'36 5:26:22
Holts Corner 42
22 37N33'36 77W14'59 5:09:00
Holts Crossing 16
16 37N04'27 78W58'53 5:15:56
Holy Neck 132 4 36N41 76W43 5:06:52
Home Creek 14 15 37N21'01 82W04'15 5:28:17
Home Crest 29 3 38N52 77W13 5:08:52
Homeland 24 14 38N36'35 78W01'57 5:12:08
Homestead 133 6 36N48'38 76W10'57 5:04:44
Homeville 88 4 36N56'55 77W10'18 5:08:41
Homewood 29 3 38N47'39 77W14'49 5:08:59
Homewood 87 23 37N11'30 76W40'56 5:06:44
Honaker 80 15 37N00'58 81W58'28 5:27:54
Honaker Junction 80
15 37N01 81W59 5:27:56
Honey Branch 93
15 36N58 82W18 5:29:12
Honeycamp 26 15 37N09 82W27 5:29:48
Honeyville 67 14 38N34'43 78W33'45 5:14:15
Honeyville 79 22 38N40'15 78W48'22 5:15:13
Hood 56 4 38N21'17 78W22'59 5:13:32
Hooes 49 12 38N21'26 77W04'02 5:08:16
Hooks Mill 3 4 37N42'52 79W54'46 5:19:39
Hoopes Landing 120
4 37N07'23 76W34'05 5:06:16
Hopeful 54 14 37N58 77W46 5:11:04
Hopeton 1 4 37N48'26 75W38'16 5:02:33
Hopewell 30 14 38N52'23 77W43'11 5:10:53
Hopewell 69 4 36N44'48 79W27'51 5:17:51
Hopewell 114 14 37N18'15 77W17'15 5:09:09
Hopkins 1 4 37N47'28 75W42'17 5:02:49
Hopkins Mill 33 4 36N56'23 79W46'03 5:19:04
Hopkins Spring 79
22 38N24'27 78W43'34 5:14:54
Hop Yard Landing 49
22 38N14'39 77W13'34 5:08:54
Horizon Hills 91
25 36N36 82W11 5:28:44
Horners 92 19 38N06'43 76W56'50 5:07:47
Hornets Nest 36 4 37N30'11 76W31'28 5:06:06
Hornsbyville 95 4 37N11'47 76W28'07 5:05:52
Horntown 1 4 37N58'10 75W27'51 5:01:51
Horntown Landing 1
4 37N57'55 75W26'08 5:01:45
Horse Gap 93 15 37N08 82W36 5:30:24
Horse Head 64 18 37N53'31 76W25'09 5:05:41
Horse Landing 50
14 37N42'21 76W59'38 5:07:59
Horse Pasture 44
4 36N37'42 79W57'04 5:19:48
Horsepen 89 4 37N13'41 81W31'12 5:26:05
Horsepen Cove 89
4 37N12'49 81W30'29 5:26:02
Horseshoe 42 22 37N39'48 77W08'56 5:08:36
Horseshoe Bend 83
15 36N46'39 81W34'25 5:26:18
Horsey 1 4 37N55'31 75W33'32 5:02:14
Horton Summit (Post Office) 81
26 36N43'35 82W46'02 5:31:04
Hotchkiss 9 4 38N00'05 79W34'52 5:18:19
Hotchkiss Field 127
17 37N34'11 77W25'26 5:09:42
Hot Springs 9 4 37N59'58 79W49'55 5:19:20
Houchins 60 4 37N09'06 80W21'36 5:21:26
Houstons Corner 17
22 37N56'33 77W31'55 5:10:08
Howards Corner 17
22 38N05'39 77W17'28 5:09:10
Howardsville 2 14 37N44'04 78W38'51 5:14:35
Howardsville 53 4 39N02'16 77W50'20 5:11:21
Howell Mills 12 4 37N30'03 79W54'42 5:19:39
Howells Mill 88 4 36N53'20 77W19'50 5:09:19
Howellsville 90
14 38N58'29 78W04'46 5:12:19
Howertons 28 4 37N49'52 76W53'25 5:07:34
Howland 64 18 37N52'15 76W27'20 5:05:49
Hubbard Junction 80
15 37N01 81W59 5:27:56
Hubbard Springs 52
26 36N43'22 83W13'14 5:32:53
Huddle 94 4 36N50'55 81W02'11 5:24:09
Huddleston 10 4 37N09'24 79W28'29 5:17:54
Hudgins 57 4 37N28'15 76W19'34 5:05:18
Hudson Crossroads 82
14 38N47'44 78W43'31 5:14:54
Huffman 23 4 37N20'52 80W24'07 5:21:36
Huff Store 18 4 36N49 80W37 5:22:28
Huffville 31 4 37N03'44 80W17'08 5:21:09
Hughesville 53 14 39N05'59 77W39'30 5:10:38
Hugo 84 4 36N32'57 77W17'44 5:09:11
Huguenot 70 14 37N31 77W47 5:11:08
Hulls Chapel 86 4 38N23 77W27 5:09:48
Hume 30 19 38N49'55 77W59'59 5:12:00
Hume 96 1 38N49'52 77W03'34 5:08:14
Hunter 29 3 38N43'20 77W03'55 5:08:16
Hunterdale 84 4 36N42'05 76W57'41 5:07:51
Hunter Estates 29
3 38N43'59 77W10'30 5:08:42
Hunters 32 4 37N56'26 78W14'45 5:12:59
Hunters Valley 29
3 38N55 77W14 5:08:56
Huntersville 121
6 36N51'44 76W16'36 5:05:06
Hunting Creek 29
1 38N47 77W05 5:08:20
Hunting Ridge 29
1 38N55 77W11 5:08:44
Huntington 29 1 38N47'32 77W04'16 5:08:17
Huntington 43 22 37N36 77W32 5:10:08
Huntington 120 6 37N00'38 76W26'47 5:05:47
Huntington 133 6 36N49'55 76W10'11 5:04:41
Huntly 75 14 38N49'35 78W06'45 5:12:27
Hunton 43 22 37N41'18 77W30'00 5:10:00
Hunts Village 29
3 38N50'00 77W15'38 5:09:03
Hupp 79 22 38N38 78W46 5:15:04
Hurley 14 15 37N25'13 82W01'12 5:28:05
Hurleyville 30 19 38N38'34 77W45'49 5:11:03
Hurricane 14 15 37N08 82W03 5:28:12
Hurricane 93 15 37N00'14 82W32'09 5:30:09
Hurt 69 16 37N05'33 79W17'48 5:17:11
Hurtsville 6 4 37N21'55 78W36'58 5:14:28
Huske 88 4 36N53'51 77W25'08 5:09:41
Hustle 28 4 38N02'33 77W04'11 5:08:17
Hutton Heights 43
22 37N40 77W30 5:10:00
Hyacinth 64 18 37N59'26 76W35'26 5:06:22
Hybla Valley 29 1 38N44'51 77W05'00 5:08:20
Hybla Valley Farms 29
3 38N45 77W06 5:08:24
Hyco 41 4 36N36'43 78W51'05 5:15:24
Hydraulic 2 14 38N05'40 78W29'10 5:13:57
Hylas 42 22 37N42'35 77W38'12 5:10:33
Hylton Park 21 22 37N29'38 77W35'52 5:10:23
Iberis 51 4 37N43'07 76W27'23 5:05:50
Ida 67 14 38N35'20 78W25'27 5:13:42
Idlewilde 104 4 37N45'11 79W59'02 5:19:56
Idylwood 29 3 38N53'42 77W12'43 5:08:51
Igo 49 22 38N23 77W27 5:09:48
Ilda 29 3 38N50'17 77W15'06 5:09:00
Imboden 93 26 36N53'12 82W48'17 5:31:13
Independence 38 4 36N37'20 81W09'04 5:24:36
Independent Hill 73
2 38N38'09 77W26'17 5:09:45
Index 49 22 38N12 77W05 5:08:20
Indian 89 4 37N05 81W46 5:27:04
Indian Field 76 4 37N56'54 76W43'01 5:06:52
Indian Gap 14 15 37N14 82W06 5:28:24
Indian Neck 48 4 37N54'07 77W02'01 5:08:08

Indian River 101 6 36N49 76w14 5:04:56
Indian River Estates 133 6 36N51 76w09 5:04:36
Indian River Park 101 6 36N48'36 76w13'19 5:04:53
Indian Rock 12 4 37N32 79w41 5:18:44
Indian Run Park 29 1 38N48'45 77w09'26 5:08:38
Indian Springs 29 1 38N49 77w09 5:08:36
Indian Town 66 14 38N22'08 77w47'56 5:11:12
Indian Valley 31 4 36N54'31 80w33'08 5:22:13
Indigo Terrace 47 23 37N16'23 76w44'43 5:06:59
Indika 46 4 36N49'13 76w41'02 5:06:44
Inez 54 14 37N58 77w46 5:11:04
Ingham 67 14 38N31'44 78w34'42 5:14:19
Ingles 74 4 37N02 80w39 5:22:36
Ingleside 29 1 38N55 77w11 5:08:44
Ingleside 121 6 36N50'55 76w14'11 5:04:57
Inglewood 79 14 38N23'25 78w39'54 5:14:40
Ingram 41 4 36N44'39 79w09'31 5:16:38
Inlet 24 14 38N28 78w00 5:12:00
Inlet 133 6 36N52 76w00 5:04:00
Inman 93 26 36N54'37 82w48'10 5:31:13
Ino 48 4 37N45'44 76w47'53 5:07:12
Interior 35 4 37N23 80w40 5:22:40
Intervale 3 4 37N49'11 79w59'10 5:19:57
Ira 14 15 37N25 82w07 5:28:28
Iraville 28 4 38N05'19 77w04'21 5:08:17
Irby 65 4 37N01'53 78w02'34 5:12:10
Irisburg 44 4 36N37'14 79w45'31 5:19:02
Irish Creek 78 14 37N50'51 79w11'29 5:16:46
Iriswood 44 4 36N40 79w47 5:19:08
Irondale 93 26 36N50'36 82w45'39 5:31:03
Iron Gate 3 4 37N47'51 79w47'29 5:19:10
Irongate 73 2 38N47 77w28 5:09:52
Iron Hill Springs 3 4 37N40'09 80w12'32 5:20:50
Ironto 60 4 37N13'07 80w16'42 5:21:07
Irving 10 4 37N21'31 79w40'15 5:18:41
Irvington 51 14 37N39'41 76w25'10 5:05:41
Irwin 37 4 37N41'38 77w55'24 5:11:42
Isaac 84 4 36N41'39 76w57'57 5:07:52
Island Creek 18 4 36N46 80w44 5:22:56
Island Farm 28 14 37N54'27 76w49'31 5:07:18
Island Ford 79 14 38N21'06 78w41'20 5:14:45
Isle of Wight 46 4 36N54'27 76w42'29 5:06:50
Islington Landing 76 4 37N54'34 76w46'40 5:07:07
Isom 26 15 37N11'13 82w27'43 5:29:51
Itata 87 4 37N02'56 76w47'09 5:07:09
Ivakota 29 3 38N47'28 77w24'27 5:09:38
Ivandale 53 14 39N08'42 77w40'13 5:10:41
Ivandale 76 4 37N51'06 76w40'07 5:06:40
Ivanhoe 94 4 36N50'24 80w58'01 5:23:52
Ivor 84 4 36N54'14 76w54'00 5:07:36
Ivy 2 14 38N03'23 78w35'49 5:14:23
Ivyview 41 4 36N45 79w06 5:16:24
Jack 27 22 37N11'47 77w30'34 5:10:02
Jacks Fork 28 14 37N55'07 76w52'45 5:07:31
Jackson 54 14 37N52'20 77w49'19 5:11:17
Jackson Creek 59 4 37N33 76w20 5:05:20
Jackson Heights 116 14 37N23'28 79w08'02 5:16:32
Jackson Hills 29 3 39N00 77w15 5:09:00
Jackson River 3 4 37N47 79w52 5:19:28
Jacksons Ferry 94 4 36N51 80w55 5:23:40
Jaffa 105 4 36N35 79w23 5:17:32
Jahile 80 15 37N02'14 82w09'41 5:28:39
Jamaica 59 4 37N42'54 76w41'40 5:06:47
James Crossroads 63 4 37N21'50 75w56'26 5:03:46
James River 15 4 37N36 78w41 5:14:44
James River Estates 37 17 37N34'38 77w39'45 5:10:39
James River Junction 40 4 36N42'13 77w28'23 5:09:54
James Store 36 4 37N28 76w28 5:05:52
James Terrace 47 23 37N15'43 76w40'17 5:06:41
Jamestown 47 14 37N12'29 76w46'28 5:07:06
Jamestown Farms 47 23 37N15'31 76w44'54 5:07:00
Jamesville 63 4 37N30'54 75w55'51 5:03:43
Janey 14 15 37N13'19 82w01'50 5:28:07
Jarman Gap 2 14 38N04 78w42 5:14:48
Jarratt 40 4 36N48'51 77w28'07 5:09:52
Jasper 51 26 36N46'05 82w49'23 5:31:18
Java 69 4 36N50'09 79w13'41 5:16:55
Jayne Mill 81 26 36N38'19 82w33'52 5:30:15
Jefferson 29 3 38N52 77w13 5:08:52
Jefferson 70 14 37N36'48 77w54'18 5:11:37
Jefferson 91 15 36N50 81w53 5:27:32
Jefferson Apartments 29 3 38N52 77w13 5:08:52
Jefferson Manor 29 1 38N47'23 77w04'48 5:08:19
Jefferson Mews 29 3 38N58 77w22 5:09:28
Jefferson Park 72 22 37N15'50 77w19'21 5:09:17
Jefferson Park 96 1 38N49'39 77w04'24 5:08:18
Jeffersonton 24 4 38N38'13 77w54'55 5:11:40
Jefferson Village 29 3 38N52'14 77w10'47 5:08:43
Jeffersonville 89 4 37N09 81w34 5:26:16
Jeffress 58 4 36N39'13 78w32'14 5:14:09
Jenkins Bridge 1 4 37N55 75w37 5:02:28
Jenkins Ford 3 4 37N56'17 79w57'02 5:19:48
Jenkins Landing 28 4 37N58'49 76w55'35 5:07:42
Jennings 65 4 37N11 78w07 5:12:28
Jennings Ford 81 26 36N39'27 82w42'42 5:30:51
Jennings Gap 8 21 38N14 79w10 5:16:40
Jennings Mission 81 26 36N38 82w34 5:30:16
Jennings Ordinary 65 4 37N13'31 78w08'45 5:12:35
Jennings Store 81 26 36N41 82w45 5:31:00
Jericho 18 4 36N43 80w49 5:23:16
Jericho 132 5 36N44 76w34 5:06:16
Jermantown 29 3 38N51'25 77w19'57 5:09:20
Jerome 82 14 38N51'45 78w43'44 5:14:55
Jersey 49 22 38N12'41 77w08'23 5:08:34
Jerusalem 84 4 36N46 77w00 5:08:00
Jessees Mill 80 15 36N54'51 82w10'03 5:28:40
Jessup Farm Acres 21 22 37N27'10 77w30'28 5:10:02
Jessup Farms 21 22 37N27 77w28 5:09:52
Jester Gardens 101 6 36N49'17 76w25'09 5:05:41
Jetersville 4 4 37N17'39 78w05'40 5:12:23
Jett 94 4 36N53'42 80w47'03 5:23:08
Jett Ford 81 26 36N40'26 82w21'58 5:29:28
Jewell Hollow 67 14 38N40 78w27 5:13:48
Jewell Ridge 89 4 37N11'05 81w47'19 5:27:09
Jewell Valley 14 15 37N14'50 81w48'06 5:27:12
Johnson 81 26 36N44 82w26 5:29:44
Johnson Corner 1 4 37N55'20 75w32'59 5:02:12
Johnson Corner 58 4 36N46'02 78w15'34 5:13:02
Johnson Corner 84 4 36N58'31 76w51'37 5:07:26
Johnson Creek 68 4 36N36 80w31 5:22:04
Johnsons Corner 29 3 38N50 77w26 5:09:44
Johnsons Corner 49 22 38N16'36 77w19'52 5:09:19
Johnsons Landing 72 22 37N13'53 77w04'17 5:08:17
Johnsons Springs 37 4 37N41'53 77w42'41 5:10:51
Johnsontown 63 4 37N25'31 75w54'52 5:03:39
Johnston 82 14 38N52 78w26 5:13:44
Joliffs 101 6 36N50 76w25 5:05:40
Jolivue 8 21 38N06'35 79w04'24 5:16:18
Jollett 67 14 38N27'50 78w31'27 5:14:06
Jolliff 101 6 36N48'38 76w26'09 5:05:45
Jones 85 22 38N10'12 77w48'34 5:11:14
Jonesboro 13 4 37N05 78w00 5:12:00
Jonesboro 61 14 37N47'00 78w58'43 5:15:55
Jones Corner 17 22 38N01'36 77w11'29 5:08:46
Jones Corner 29 1 38N55 77w11 5:08:44
Jones Corner 42 22 37N51'54 77w41'33 5:10:46
Jones Creek 119 4 36N42'21 79w52'37 5:19:30
Jones Landing 50 14 37N46'45 77w04'48 5:08:19
Jones Landing 76 4 38N01'32 76w54'21 5:07:37
Jones Mill 69 4 36N45'49 79w27'56 5:17:52
Jones Store 20 4 36N47 78w37 5:14:28
Jonestown 78 14 37N53'21 79w16'03 5:17:04
Jonesville 52 26 36N41'20 83w06'40 5:32:27
Jonesville Camp Ground 52 26 36N40'54 83w08'38 5:32:35
Joplin 73 14 38N33'39 77w23'07 5:09:32
Joppa Mill 10 4 37N15'59 79w35'17 5:18:21
Jordan Mines 3 4 37N39'40 80w06'58 5:20:28
Jordan Springs 34 4 39N12'55 78w05'03 5:12:20
Josephine 93 15 36N55'41 82w39'57 5:30:40
Joshua Falls 5 14 37N25'30 79w02'41 5:16:11
Joyce Heights 107 3 38N50'46 77w19'21 5:09:17
Joyceville 13 4 36N34'10 78w02'12 5:12:09
Joyner 84 4 36N46'45 77w15'07 5:09:00
Justisville 1 4 37N47'45 75w41'11 5:02:45
Ka 81 15 36N50 82w28 5:29:52
Kamp Washington 107 3 38N51 77w15 5:09:00
Kanodes Mill 60 4 37N14'17 80w28'25 5:21:54
Karo 90 14 38N52'19 78w15'08 5:13:01
Karo Landing 90 14 38N52'14 78w15'15 5:13:01
Kasey 10 4 37N04'40 79w34'58 5:18:20
Kathmoor 29 3 38N46'58 77w08'32 5:08:34
Katrine 15 4 37N35'05 78w34'42 5:14:19
Kayan 64 18 37N53'27 76w16'13 5:05:05
Kayoulah 74 4 36N54'59 80w46'27 5:23:06
Keats 58 4 36N32'38 78w17'49 5:13:11
Kecoughtan 112 6 37N00'51 76w20'48 5:05:23
Keeling 56 4 36N43'12 79w17'19 5:17:09
Keene 2 14 37N51'54 78w33'20 5:14:13
Keene Homes 29 1 38N45 77w04 5:08:16
Keene Mill Heights 29 3 38N46'23 77w15'35 5:09:02
Keene Mill Manor 29 3 38N47'02 77w13'21 5:08:53
Keen Mountain 14 15 37N12'08 81w59'11 5:27:57
Keever 16 16 37N10 79w05 5:16:20
Keezletown 79 22 38N24'54 78w48'08 5:15:13
Kegleys 94 4 36N58'54 81w08'31 5:24:34
Keith 50 14 37N50'28 77w15'24 5:09:02
Keller 1 4 37N37'09 75w45'51 5:03:03
Kelley View 93 26 36N58 82w47 5:31:08
Kells Corner 55 4 36N52'42 78w24'29 5:13:38
Kelly 16 14 37N23'09 79w03'47 5:16:15
Kellys Ford 24 4 38N28'38 77w46'49 5:11:07
Kelly View 93 26 36N55'28 82w44'40 5:30:59
Kelsa 14 15 37N26'26 82w04'08 5:28:17
Kelso Mill 10 4 37N23'47 79w33'23 5:18:14
Kemmerer Gem No 2 52 26 36N49 83w03 5:32:12
Kemp Corner 17 22 37N55'46 77w22'24 5:09:30
Kemps Place 43 17 37N32 77w24 5:09:36
Kempsville 133 6 36N49'36 76w09'38 5:04:39
Kempsville Colony 133 6 36N49'05 76w09'34 5:04:38
Kempsville Gardens 133 6 36N49'32 76w09'22 5:04:37
Kempsville Heights 133 6 36N50'03 76w09'27 5:04:38
Kenady 26 15 37N05 82w27 5:29:48
Kenbridge 55 4 36N57'43 78w07'31 5:12:30
Kendall Grove 63 4 37N22'04 75w55'17 5:03:41
Kenmore 29 3 38N57'16 77w16'10 5:09:05
Kennard 76 4 37N54'56 76w44'53 5:07:00
Kennelworth 123 22 37N12'56 77w26'12 5:09:45
Kent 94 4 36N57'07 81w01'08 5:24:05
Kent Gardens 29 1 38N54'42 77w10'23 5:08:42
Kent Junction 93 26 36N55'14 82w43'42 5:30:55
Kentland Farms 29 3 38N58 77w22 5:09:28
Kents Store 32 4 37N52'45 78w07'45 5:12:31
Kentuck 56 4 36N39'35 79w17'55 5:17:12
Kentucky Farms 95 4 37N08'44 76w29'37 5:05:58
Kenwood 29 1 38N50'19 77w11'40 5:08:47
Kenwood 42 22 37N42'32 77w29'58 5:10:00
Kenwood 114 14 37N16'50 77w18'56 5:09:16
Kenyon 132 5 36N44'00 76w39'19 5:06:37
Keokee 52 26 36N51'32 82w54'11 5:31:37
Kerfoot 30 19 38N57'37 77w54'09 5:11:37
Kermit 81 26 36N37'31 82w43'14 5:30:53
Kerns 81 26 36N45'26 82w37'05 5:30:28
Kern Springs 82 14 38N55'38 78w35'42 5:14:23
Kernstown 136 9 39N08'42 78w11'22 5:12:45
Kerrs Creek 78 22 37N51'14 79w29'44 5:17:59
Kessler Mill 129 4 37N18'46 80w02'01 5:20:08
Kesterson Mill 52 26 36N37'38 83w29'40 5:33:59
Keswick 2 14 38N01'21 78w21'34 5:13:26
Ketron 91 25 36N38'34 82w17'22 5:29:09
Ketrontown 81 26 36N36'07 82w29'12 5:29:57
Keysville 20 4 37N02'25 78w29'01 5:13:56
Key West 2 14 38N03'26 78w26'28 5:13:46
Keywood 91 15 36N49'29 81w47'27 5:27:10
Kibler 68 4 36N37'51 80w27'11 5:21:49
Kidds Fork 17 22 37N56'33 77w18'03 5:09:12
Kidds Store 32 4 37N48'12 78w21'43 5:13:27
Kidville 8 21 38N06'39 78w56'38 5:15:47
Kiels Gardens 29 3 38N50'56 77w20'36 5:09:22
Kilby 132 5 36N43'55 76w37'46 5:06:31
Kilby Shores 132 5 36N44 76w35 5:06:20
Kildare Annex 43 17 37N34 77w29 5:09:56
Kilmarnock 51 14 37N42'37 76w22'48 5:05:31
Kilmarnock Wharf 51 14 37N43 76w23 5:05:32
Kimages 19 14 37N21'09 77w11'41 5:08:47
Kimball 67 14 38N41'13 78w24'10 5:13:37
Kimballton 35 4 37N21'58 80w40'39 5:22:43
Kimberling 11 4 37N09'42 81w02'10 5:24:09
Kincaid 3 4 37N57'02 79w56'21 5:19:45
Kincer Mill 52 26 36N38'04 83w06'22 5:32:25
Kinderhook 56 14 38N22'11 78w25'42 5:13:43
Kindrick 94 4 36N57 81w05 5:24:20
King and Queen 48 4 37N40 76w53 5:07:32
King and Queen Court House 48 4 37N40'11 76w52'40 5:07:31
King George 49 22 38N16'05 77w11'05 5:08:44
Kingman 125 6 36N52'14 76w22'13 5:05:29
Kingsberry 40 20 36N42'33 77w34'03 5:10:16
Kingsbury Manor 8 21 38N05'15 78w56'34 5:15:46
Kings Corner 47 14 37N24'02 76w52'26 5:07:30
Kings Crossing 82 14 38N46'09 78w29'56 5:14:00
Kings Crossroads 20 4 36N49'26 78w36'28 5:14:26
Kings Crossroads 73 14 38N39'59 77w35'02 5:10:20
Kingsdale 84 4 36N37'59 76w54'04 5:07:36
Kings Eddy 90 14 38N53'20 78w14'39 5:12:59
Kings Fork 132 5 36N46'48 76w37'30 5:06:30
Kings Grant 133 6 36N51'20 76w05'02 5:04:20
Kings Hill 43 17 37N32 77w24 5:09:36
Kingsland 21 22 37N27 77w28 5:09:52
Kings Manor 29 1 38N55 77w11 5:08:44
Kings Park 29 3 38N48'22 77w14'37 5:08:58
Kings Point 47 23 37N17 76w43 5:06:52
Kings Store 31 4 37N05 80w08 5:20:32
Kingston 16 16 37N12'29 79w12'07 5:16:48
Kingstown 77 4 37N19'58 79w59'54 5:20:00
Kingsville 71 4 37N14'45 78w26'39 5:13:47
Kingswood 47 23 37N14'54 76w44'26 5:06:58
Kingswood 61 14 37N41'12 78w56'48 5:15:47
Kingswood Court 42 22 37N41'02 77w25'47 5:09:43
Kingtown 98 25 36N36'08 82w10'03 5:28:40
King William 50 14 37N41'14 77w00'50 5:08:03
Kino 28 14 37N54'16 76w56'30 5:07:46
Kinsale 92 19 38N01'46 76w34'52 5:06:19
Kiptopeke 63 4 37N08'16 75w58'01 5:03:52
Kiptopeke Beach 63 4 37N16 76w00 5:04:00
Kire 35 4 37N26'24 80w31'09 5:22:05
Kirkside 29 3 38N45 77w06 5:08:24
Klines Mill 34 4 39N02'49 78w14'27 5:12:58
Klocks Corner 17 22 38N07 77w25 5:09:40
Klotz 35 4 37N20'32 80w40'33 5:22:42
Knightly 8 21 38N14'00 78w55'41 5:15:43
Knob Hill 133 6 36N48'52 76w12'39 5:04:51
Knox 14 15 37N24 82w03 5:28:12
Koehler 44 4 36N41'23 79w54'33 5:19:38
Konnarock 91 15 36N39'57 81w38'18 5:26:33

Kopp 73 2 38N35'24 77w26'46 5:09:47
Korea 24 14 38N37'53 78w00'47 5:12:03
Kremlin 92 19 38N01'46 76w41'30 5:06:46
Kress 13 4 36N55'49 77w48'38 5:11:15
Kyles Mills 12 4 37N32'57 79w49'59 5:19:20
Laban 57 4 37N24'01 76w17'02 5:05:08
Laburnum Manor 43 17 37N34 77w26 5:09:44
Lacey Forest 7 1 38N52'58 77w07'46 5:08:31
Lacey Landing 50 14 37N36'46 77w05'24 5:08:22
Lacey Spring 79 22 38N32'28 78w46'00 5:15:04
Lackey 95 4 37N13'51 76w33'11 5:06:13
La Crosse 58 4 36N42'00 78w06'00 5:12:24
Ladd 8 21 38N03'21 78w57'13 5:15:49
Ladysmith 17 22 38N01'03 77w30'56 5:10:04
Lafayette 60 4 37N14'10 80w12'42 5:20:51
Lafayette Annex 121 6 36N52'39 76w15'50 5:05:03
Lafayette Boulevard 121 6 36N53 76w16 5:05:04
Lafayette Shores 121 6 36N53'04 76w15'57 5:05:04
Lagrange 24 4 38N26'29 77w51'12 5:11:25
Lahore 66 14 38N11'55 77w58'11 5:11:53
Lake 64 18 37N58'27 76w28'12 5:05:53
Lake 86 4 38N23 77w27 5:09:48
Lake Barcroft 29 1 38N51 77w09 5:08:36
Lake Crystal Farms 21 22 37N28'27 77w35'11 5:10:21
Lake Hills 29 3 38N42 77w14 5:08:56
Lake Jackson 73 2 38N42'09 77w27'18 5:09:49
Lakeland 121 7 36N53'59 76w13'18 5:04:53
Lake Ridge 73 13 38N39 77w16 5:09:04
Lakes 10 4 37N11 79w30 5:18:00
Lake Shores 133 6 36N54'10 76w09'05 5:04:36
Lakeside 43 22 37N36'27 77w28'38 5:09:55
Lakeside 129 4 37N17 80w03 5:20:12
Lakeside Hills 43 17 37N36 77w29 5:09:56
Lakeside Homes 95 4 37N08'36 76w26'59 5:05:48
Lakeside Village 25 4 37N39'48 78w10'43 5:12:43
Lake Smith 133 6 36N53'27 76w10'05 5:04:40
Lakesmith Terrace 133 6 36N53 76w08 5:04:32
Lake Terrace 121 6 36N51'41 76w11'57 5:04:48
Lakeview 103 22 37N16'10 77w25'32 5:09:42
Lakeview Heights 61 14 37N44'34 78w52'10 5:15:29
Lakeview Park 133 6 36N53'22 76w09'03 5:04:36
Lakeview Shores 133 6 36N53'18 76w08'30 5:04:34
Lakeville Estates 133 6 36N49'07 76w12'12 5:04:49
Lakewood 29 1 38N50'29 77w09'02 5:08:36
Lakewood 47 23 37N14'14 76w45'04 5:07:00
Lakewood 69 4 36N34'50 79w18'19 5:17:13
Lakewood 121 6 36N53'27 76w16'11 5:05:05
Lakewood Estates 29 3 38N44'34 77w21'12 5:09:25
Lakota 24 4 38N34'58 77w52'42 5:11:31
Lamberts Point 121 6 36N52'51 76w18'29 5:05:14
Lambs 88 4 36N59'29 77w15'24 5:09:02
Lambsburg 18 4 36N35'07 80w45'41 5:23:03
Lambs Creek 49 22 38N15'49 77w16'10 5:09:05
Lanahan 33 4 36N55 80w01 5:20:04
Lancaster 51 4 37N46'11 76w28'00 5:05:52
Landmark Square 73 2 38N47 77w28 5:09:52
Land of Promise 133 6 36N51 76w06 5:04:24
Land O'Pines 21 22 37N25'51 77w31'45 5:10:07
Landtown 133 6 36N46'44 76w05'08 5:04:21
Lanes Corner 42 22 37N44'40 77w32'33 5:10:10
Lanes Corner 85 22 38N09'34 77w44'11 5:10:57
Lanes Ford 61 14 37N45'12 78w59'11 5:15:57
Lanesville 50 14 37N36'52 76w58'44 5:07:55
Laneview 28 4 37N45'31 76w43'30 5:06:54
Lanexa 62 14 37N25'25 76w54'05 5:07:36
Langhorne Acres 29 3 38N51 77w15 5:09:00
Langley 29 3 38N56'47 77w09'33 5:08:38
Langley Air Force Base 112 11 37N05 76w21 5:05:24
Langley Forest 29 1 38N57'21 77w10'43 5:08:43
Langley Ridge 29 1 38N55 77w11 5:08:44
Langley View 112 11 37N04'35 76w20'05 5:05:20
Laniers Mill 69 4 36N39'54 79w27'38 5:17:51
Lankford Corner 51 4 37N46'49 76w24'05 5:05:36
Lano 81 26 36N47'47 82w35'48 5:30:23
Lansdale 121 7 36N52'37 76w12'47 5:04:51
Lantz Mills 82 14 38N49 78w34 5:14:16
Laprades Mill 33 4 36N54'49 79w38'07 5:18:32
Lara 76 18 37N51'10 76w31'04 5:06:04
Larchmont 7 1 38N53'11 77w07'41 5:08:31
Larchmont 121 6 36N53'52 76w18'11 5:05:13
Lark 89 4 37N06 81w48 5:27:12
Lark Downs 133 6 36N51 76w09 5:04:36
Larkspur 133 6 36N49'12 76w08'16 5:04:33
Larrymore Acres 121 6 36N55'34 76w12'56 5:04:52
Larrymore Lawns 121 6 36N54'41 76w13'43 5:04:55
Larwood Acres 91 25 36N36 82w11 5:28:44
Laswell 94 4 36N53'39 80w54'33 5:23:38
Latanes 92 19 38N10'36 76w57'48 5:07:51
Lauraville 17 22 37N57'37 77w11'44 5:08:47
Laurel 43 22 37N38'34 77w30'33 5:10:02
Laurel 80 15 37N02'50 81w59'13 5:27:57
Laurel 93 26 36N55'00 82w49'53 5:31:20
Laurel Branch 31 4 36N54'51 80w23'35 5:21:34
Laureldale 91 15 36N37'25 81w45'44 5:27:03
Laurel Dell 43 17 37N36 77w29 5:09:56
Laurel Fork 18 4 36N43'03 80w31'08 5:22:05
Laurel Grove 29 3 37N16 76w00 5:04:00
Laurel Grove 69 4 36N40'43 79w12'48 5:16:51
Laurel Grove 93 15 36N58'47 82w39'10 5:30:37
Laurel Grove Estates 42 22 37N39'32 77w23'26 5:09:34
Laurel Heights 43 17 37N36 77w29 5:09:56
Laurel Hill 8 21 38N11'27 78w57'44 5:15:51
Laurel Hill 82 14 39N03 78w22 5:13:28
Laurel Manor 133 6 36N51'17 76w01'09 5:04:05
Laurel Mills 75 14 38N38'53 78w05'22 5:12:21
Laurel Park 43 17 37N38'35 77w29'59 5:10:00
Laurel Springs Crossroads 87 4 37N07'20 77w07'57 5:08:32
Lavender 60 4 37N10 80w15 5:21:00
Lawford 15 4 37N36'59 78w16'38 5:13:07
Lawndale Farms 43 17 37N31'17 77w21'40 5:09:27
Lawrenceville 13 4 36N45'27 77w50'50 5:11:23
Lawrenceville Hills 13 4 36N44'37 77w51'32 5:11:26
Lawson 46 4 37N00'40 76w37'51 5:06:31
Lawson Forest 133 6 36N52'28 76w10'39 5:04:43
Lawsons Store 58 4 36N48 78w28 5:13:52
Lawthorne Mill 61 14 37N49'39 78w47'16 5:15:09
Lawyers 16 14 37N17'59 79w12'43 5:16:51
Layman 79 22 38N27 78w52 5:15:28
Layton 28 19 38N05'15 76w59'28 5:07:58
Lazy Oak Corner 87 4 37N07'06 76w53'44 5:07:35
LC Page 121 6 36N55 76w13 5:04:52
Lead Mines 94 4 36N52 80w54 5:23:36
Leaksville 67 14 38N37'35 78w31'35 5:14:06
Leaksville Junction 69 4 36N32'31 79w39'35 5:18:38
Leatherwood 44 4 36N44'27 79w44'48 5:18:59
Leavells 85 24 38N14'41 77w31'32 5:10:06
Lebanon 80 15 36N54'03 82w04'49 5:28:19
Lebanon Church 82 14 39N03 78w22 5:13:28
Lecato 1 4 37N56'20 75w33'01 5:02:12
Leck 26 15 37N02'17 82w24'03 5:29:36
Leda 41 4 36N54'15 79w05'11 5:16:21
Lee 37 4 37N36'41 77w49'00 5:11:16
Lee Boulevard Heights 29 1 38N51'59 77w08'41 5:08:35
Lee Dale Shores 64 18 37N50'29 76w20'39 5:05:23
Leedstown 92 19 38N06'41 76w59'56 5:08:00
Lee Forest 29 3 38N50'03 77w15'10 5:09:01
Lee Hall 120 4 37N11'30 76w34'19 5:06:17
Lee Heights 7 1 38N54'07 77w07'03 5:08:28
Lee Hill 85 24 38N15 77w28 5:09:52
Lee-Hi Village 29 3 38N50'33 77w21'06 5:09:24
Leeland 86 24 38N20'59 77w26'02 5:09:44
Lee Manor 29 3 38N51 77w15 5:09:00
Leemaster 14 15 37N11'12 82w07'51 5:28:31
Lee Meadows 29 3 38N50'12 77w15'56 5:09:04
Lee Mont 1 4 37N46'43 75w40'53 5:02:44
Lee Park 43 22 37N33 77w22 5:09:28
Leesburg 53 14 39N06'56 77w33'50 5:10:15
Lees Corner 29 3 38N54'15 77w25'02 5:09:40
Lees Mill 46 4 36N40'57 76w53'45 5:07:35
Lees Mill 72 22 37N06'32 77w19'29 5:09:18
Leesville 16 16 37N07'09 79w23'07 5:17:32
Lee Town 14 15 37N17 82w06 5:28:24
Leetown 34 4 39N13'37 78w04'40 5:12:19
Leewood 29 3 38N48'28 77w11'20 5:08:45
Legato 29 3 38N50'52 77w21'58 5:09:28
Leigh Mill 29 3 39N00 77w15 5:09:00
Leighs 29 1 39N01'56 77w20'29 5:09:22
Leithtown 53 14 39N00'48 77w45'33 5:11:02
Lenah 53 4 38N57'10 77w34'50 5:10:19
Lennig 41 4 36N54'03 78w54'37 5:15:38
Lenox 121 6 36N56'34 76w15'18 5:05:01
Lent 17 22 38N07'04 77w14'35 5:08:58
Leon 67 4 38N26'15 78w08'19 5:12:33
Leona Mines 52 26 36N49 83w03 5:32:12
Leonard 91 25 36N41'53 82w14'43 5:28:59
Leonardo Store 52 26 36N38 83w26 5:33:44
Lerty 92 19 38N08'31 76w52'04 5:07:28
Leslie 77 4 37N13'15 79w53'36 5:19:34
Lester Manor 50 14 37N41 77w01 5:08:04
LeSueur 15 4 37N40'58 78w21'16 5:13:25
Level Run 69 16 37N02'23 79w11'58 5:16:48
Levi 53 4 38N59 77w39 5:10:36
Levisa 14 15 37N21 82w12 5:28:48
Levy 85 22 38N02'08 77w42'29 5:10:50
Lewinsville 29 1 38N55'44 77w11'53 5:08:48
Lewinsville Heights 29 1 38N55'17 77w11'25 5:08:46
Lewisetta 64 18 37N59'52 76w27'47 5:05:51
Lewis Gardens 43 22 37N30'48 77w20'20 5:09:21
Lewis Park 29 3 38N49'15 77w22'36 5:09:30
Lewis Store 32 4 37N48 78w29 5:13:56
Lewiston 55 4 36N59 78w16 5:13:04
Lewiston 85 22 38N04'07 77w44'33 5:10:58
Lewistown 42 22 37N43'04 77w27'16 5:09:49
Lewisville 22 14 39N11'52 77w57'00 5:11:48
Lexington 115 14 37N47'02 79w26'35 5:17:46
Liberia Woods 117 2 38N47 77w28 5:09:52
Liberty 17 22 38N08'36 77w21'13 5:09:25
Liberty 41 4 36N53'04 78w58'30 5:15:54
Liberty 45 4 38N17'20 79w27'35 5:17:50
Liberty 89 4 37N03'24 81w39'15 5:26:37
Liberty Fork 17 22 38N02'48 77w10'34 5:08:42
Liberty Hill 18 4 36N49'51 80w41'51 5:22:47
Liberty Mills 66 14 38N13'51 78w13'12 5:12:53
Lick Fork 26 15 37N00 82w28 5:29:52
Lickinghole 37 4 37N43 77w55 5:11:40
Lick Run 12 4 37N38 79w48 5:19:12
Lick Skillet 83 15 36N53'39 81w47'29 5:27:10
Lifestyle 29 3 38N58 77w22 5:09:28
Liggans Corner 42 22 37N37'18 77w13'33 5:08:54
Lightfoot 47 14 37N20'26 76w45'17 5:07:01
Lignite 12 4 37N37'38 79w59'55 5:20:00
Lignum 24 4 38N24'57 77w49'37 5:11:18
Lilian 64 18 37N51'42 76w18'00 5:05:12
Lilly 79 22 38N27'59 79w00'51 5:16:03
Lima 105 4 36N35 79w23 5:17:32
Lime Hill 91 25 36N38'56 82w14'51 5:28:59
Limeton 90 14 38N51'16 78w16'37 5:13:06
Limstrong 73 2 38N42'57 77w27'54 5:09:52
Lincoln 53 14 39N06'55 77w41'43 5:10:47
Lincolnia 29 1 38N49'06 77w08'37 5:08:34
Lincolnia Heights 29 1 38N49'46 77w08'57 5:08:36
Lincolnia Park 29 1 38N48'56 77w08'43 5:08:35
Lincoln Park 29 3 38N49'41 77w21'39 5:09:27
Lincoln Park 121 6 36N54'54 76w14'47 5:04:59
Lindell 91 15 36N48'16 81w54'03 5:27:36
Linden 90 14 38N54'32 78w04'33 5:12:18
Linden 93 26 36N54'55 82w49'16 5:31:17
Lindenwood 77 4 37N23 79w49 5:19:16
Lindsay 2 14 38N05'17 78w14'48 5:12:59
Linkhorn 133 6 36N51'41 76w01'26 5:04:06
Linkhorn Estates 133 6 36N51'54 76w01'07 5:04:04
Linkhorn Park 133 6 36N52'01 75w59'36 5:03:58
Linkhorn Shores 133 6 36N52'37 76w01'00 5:04:04
Linlier 133 6 36N51'03 76w01'00 5:04:04
Linville 79 22 38N31'13 78w50'16 5:15:21
Lipps 93 15 37N00'15 82w39'05 5:30:36
Lipscomb 8 21 38N01'09 78w58'44 5:15:55
Lithia 12 4 37N28'41 79w45'06 5:19:00
Little Baltimore 8 21 38N11'01 79w22'58 5:17:32
Little Creek 133 6 36N53 76w08 5:04:32
Little Duck 81 15 36N44'39 82w20'55 5:29:24
Little Falls 86 4 38N16'22 77w25'15 5:09:41
Little Ferry Landing 49 22 38N17'29 77w03'18 5:08:13
Little Haven 133 6 36N51'48 76w04'37 5:04:18
Little Johnsontown 63 4 37N26'00 75w51'22 5:03:25
Little Mill 88 4 36N52'21 77w29'28 5:09:58
Little Montgomery 60 4 37N01'24 80w32'50 5:22:11
Little Neck Village 133 6 36N51 76w07 5:04:28
Little Plymouth 48 4 37N37'38 76w47'35 5:07:10
Little River 31 4 36N58 80w15 5:21:00
Little River Crossing 42 22 37N49'15 77w25'34 5:09:42
Little River Hills 107 3 38N50'51 77w17'26 5:09:10
Little River Pines 29 3 38N51 77w15 5:09:00
Little Run Estates 29 3 38N49'24 77w16'24 5:09:06
Little Salisbury 63 4 37N19'14 75w56'07 5:03:44
Little Texas 84 4 36N36'07 77w20'23 5:09:22
Littleton 88 4 36N54'09 77w08'58 5:08:36
Little Town 89 4 37N06'50 81w21'08 5:25:25
Little Vienna Estates 29 3 38N55 77w14 5:08:56
Littlevine 18 4 36N46 80w44 5:22:56
Litwalton 51 4 37N48'03 76w34'12 5:06:17
Litz 91 15 36N48'42 81w47'32 5:27:10
Lively 51 4 37N46'39 76w30'50 5:06:03
Livingston 85 22 38N10 77w47 5:11:08
Lloyd Place 132 5 36N43 76w34 5:06:16
Lloyds 28 4 38N00'03 77w00'55 5:08:04
Locher 78 14 37N38 79w27 5:17:48
Lochhaven 121 6 36N54'52 76w18'40 5:05:15
Loch Laird 99 14 37N44 79w21 5:17:24
Loch Leven 55 4 36N51 78w04 5:12:16
Loch Lomond 73 2 38N47 77w28 5:09:52
Lockes Landing 22 14 39N06'08 77w57'53 5:11:52
Lockett 71 4 37N16 78w17 5:13:08
Lockhart Flats 26 15 37N08'57 82w25'50 5:29:43
Locklies 59 4 37N35'40 76w26'24 5:05:46
Locks Corner 17 22 38N09'49 77w23'40 5:09:35
Locust Creek 54 14 37N52'00 77w47'07 5:11:08
Locust Dale 56 4 38N20'10 78w07'38 5:12:31
Locust Grove 31 4 37N03 80w10 5:20:40
Locust Grove 48 4 37N43'24 77w00'29 5:08:02
Locust Grove 66 14 38N18 77w49 5:11:16
Locust Hill 59 4 37N35'57 76w30'41 5:06:03
Locust Hill 94 4 36N57'30 80w54'55 5:23:40
Locust Mount 1 4 37N36'37 75w42'00 5:02:48
Locustville 1 4 37N39'13 75w40'43 5:02:43
Lodebar 61 14 37N54'13 78w50'57 5:15:24
Lodge 64 18 37N59'31 76w32'36 5:06:10
Lodi 91 15 36N42'53 81w46'39 5:27:07
Lodore 4 4 37N26'21 78w01'22 5:12:05
Lofton 8 21 37N57'18 79w09'53 5:16:40
Logan 85 22 38N13'03 77w45'41 5:11:03
Log Landing 48 4 37N40'33 76w54'18 5:07:37

Lois 30 19 38N31'30 77w43'36 5:10:54
Loisdale 29 3 38N45 77w12 5:08:48
Loisdale Estates 29 3 38N45'42 77w10'51 5:08:43
Lomax 81 26 36N46 82w35 5:30:20
Lombardy Grove 58 4 36N41'03 78w12'23 5:12:50
London Bridge 133 6 36N50'30 76w03'00 5:04:12
London Towne 29 3 38N50 77w26 5:09:44
Lone Ash 94 4 36N55'09 80w49'41 5:23:19
Lone Fountain 8 21 38N14'48 79w11'01 5:16:44
Lone Gum 10 4 37N10 79w28 5:17:52
Lone Oak 42 22 37N48'55 77w39'35 5:10:38
Lone Oak Mill 72 22 37N11'34 77w06'36 5:08:26
Lone Star 12 4 37N27'43 79w59'36 5:19:58
Longbottom 14 15 37N16'54 82w05'08 5:28:21
Long Branch 17 22 38N11'15 77w23'37 5:09:34
Long Branch 26 15 36N59 82w17 5:29:08
Long Branch 29 3 38N49 77w15 5:09:00
Longdale 3 4 37N50'00 79w46'33 5:19:06
Longdale 43 22 37N39'29 77w28'12 5:09:53
Longdale Furnace 3 4 37N48'36 79w41'01 5:18:44
Longfork 8 21 38N23 78w59 5:15:56
Long Island 16 16 37N04'42 79w05'40 5:16:23
Longist Forks 28 4 37N53'27 76w54'25 5:07:38
Long Marsh 22 14 39N11 78w01 5:12:04
Long Mountain 16 16 37N19 79w03 5:16:12
Long Ridge 101 6 36N37'49 76w09'48 5:04:39
Longshoal 18 4 36N56 80w44 5:22:56
Longshop 60 4 37N08 80w24 5:21:36
Long Spur 11 4 37N06 80w41 5:22:44
Longview 46 4 36N53'20 76w36'25 5:06:26
Longview 73 2 38N43'33 77w28'15 5:09:53
Longwood Acres 21 22 37N27'00 77w33'11 5:10:13
Looney 23 4 37N28'16 80w09'46 5:20:39
Looney's Creek 14 15 37N17 82w06 5:28:24
Lord Fairfax Estates 107 3 38N51'19 77w18'14 5:09:13
Loretto 28 4 38N04'34 77w03'03 5:08:12
Lorfax Heights 29 3 38N43'15 77w15'21 5:09:01
Lorne 17 22 37N51'44 77w21'17 5:09:25
Lorraine 43 22 37N34'04 77w37'13 5:10:29
Lorton 29 3 38N42'15 77w13'41 5:08:55
Lorton Valley 29 3 38N42 77w14 5:08:56
Lost Corner 22 9 39N05'34 78w05'59 5:12:24
Lottsburg 64 18 37N57'39 76w31'09 5:06:05
Loudoun Heights 53 4 39N18'47 77w43'05 5:10:52
Louisa 54 14 38N01'30 78w00'16 5:12:01
Love 8 14 37N53'07 79w00'37 5:16:02
Loves Mill 55 4 36N54'21 78w17'03 5:13:08
Loves Mill 91 15 36N44'50 81w41'15 5:26:45
Loves Shop 41 4 36N46 78w56 5:15:44
Lovettsville 53 4 39N16'21 77w38'13 5:10:33
Loving Fork 17 22 38N05'47 77w21'12 5:09:25
Lovingston 61 14 37N45'35 78w52'16 5:15:29
Lower Brandon 72 22 37N10 76w58 5:07:52
Lower Elk Creek 38 4 36N42'50 81w09'34 5:24:38
Lower Exeter 93 26 36N52'48 82w49'49 5:31:19
Lowery Hills 91 25 36N36 82w11 5:28:44
Lowesville 61 16 37N43'08 79w03'54 5:16:16
Low Gap 38 4 36N34'01 80w53'56 5:23:36
Lowland 91 15 36N46'21 81w59'00 5:27:56
Low Moor 3 4 37N47'19 79w53'02 5:19:32
Lowry 10 4 37N21'02 79w25'52 5:17:43
Loxley Gardens 101 6 36N46'31 76w20'03 5:05:20
Loxley Place 125 6 36N47'55 76w20'16 5:05:21
Lucas Gap 67 14 38N32'02 78w29'47 5:13:59
Luck 69 4 36N50 79w14 5:16:56
Lucketts 53 14 39N12'56 77w32'05 5:10:08
Lucks 69 4 36N48'47 79w13'09 5:16:53
Lucky Hill 30 19 38N32 77w49 5:11:16
Lumberton 88 4 36N52'53 77w12'39 5:08:51
Lummis 132 5 36N41'42 76w42'05 5:06:48
Lunenburg 55 4 36N57'39 78w15'57 5:13:04
Lunt 96 1 38N48'01 77w08'23 5:08:34
Luray 67 14 38N39'55 78w27'35 5:13:50
Lurich 35 4 37N22'51 80w50'28 5:23:22
Lusters Gate 60 4 37N14 80w25 5:21:40
Luttrellville 76 18 37N56'42 76w35'04 5:06:20
Luttrels Corner 64 18 37N56'01 76w24'26 5:05:38
Lydia 39 14 38N19'49 78w29'28 5:13:58
Lyells 76 4 37N59'49 76w43'45 5:06:55
Lyman Park 73 14 38N31 77w18 5:09:12
Lynchburg 116 14 37N24'49 79w08'33 5:16:34
Lynch Station 16 16 37N08'46 79w18'04 5:17:12
Lyndhurst 8 21 38N01'45 78w56'43 5:15:47
Lynhams 64 18 37N43'06 76w20'35 5:05:22
Lynhaven 96 1 38N50'00 77w03'27 5:08:14
Lynndale Estates 133 6 36N51 76w07 5:04:28
Lynn Grove 43 17 37N35'13 77w24'08 5:09:37
Lynnhaven 112 6 37N02'53 76w24'35 5:05:38
Lynnhaven 133 6 36N50'15 76w04'08 5:04:17
Lynnhaven Acres 133 6 36N51'13 76w04'09 5:04:17
Lynnhaven Colony 133 6 36N54'27 76w04'15 5:04:17
Lynn Haven Hills 77 4 37N23 79w49 5:19:16
Lynnhaven Shores 133 6 36N54'38 76w04'55 5:04:20
Lynn Shores 133 6 36N51'16 76w06'48 5:04:27
Lynn Spring 80 15 37N06'16 81w56'02 5:27:44
Lynnwood 79 22 38N18'36 78w46'19 5:15:05
Lynnwood 133 6 36N52'24 76w05'32 5:04:22
Lynobrook 29 3 38N47'18 77w10'59 5:08:44
Lynwood 73 13 38N39 77w16 5:09:04
Lyon Park 7 8 38N52'50 77w05'26 5:08:22
Lyons 93 15 37N00'49 82w28'04 5:29:52
Lyon Village 7 1 38N53'41 77w05'43 5:08:23
Mabe 81 26 36N41 82w45 5:31:00
Mabelton 42 14 37N50'27 77w44'33 5:10:58
Mabry Mill 31 4 36N45'00 80w24'18 5:21:37
Macanie 82 14 38N46'33 78w45'28 5:15:02
Macedonia 1 4 37N49'33 75w36'18 5:02:25
Mace Springs 81 26 36N39 82w28 5:29:52
Machipongo 63 4 37N24'21 75w54'07 5:03:36
Machodoc 92 19 38N04'49 76w41'49 5:06:47
Mackall Hill 29 1 38N55 77w11 5:08:44
Mack Creek Village 74 4 36N59'07 80w41'25 5:22:46
Macon 70 14 37N31'18 77w57'44 5:11:51
Macons Corner 133 6 36N48'00 76w00'16 5:04:01
Madison 56 4 38N22'49 78w15'28 5:13:02
Madison College 113 22 38N27 78w52 5:15:28
Madison Heights 5 14 37N25'51 79w07'24 5:16:30
Madison Manor 7 1 38N52'49 77w08'51 5:08:35
Madison Mills 56 4 38N16'51 78w08'28 5:12:34
Madison Run 66 14 38N11'48 78w07'50 5:12:31
Madisonville 20 4 37N11'17 78w41'25 5:14:46
Madrid 8 21 38N08'22 78w52'51 5:15:31
Madrillon Farms 29 3 38N54'29 77w13'49 5:08:55
Maggie 23 4 37N25'24 80w22'56 5:21:32
Magnet 46 4 36N58'52 76w42'04 5:06:48
Magnolia 132 5 36N44'45 76w32'27 5:06:10
Magnolia Gardens 132 5 36N44 76w35 5:06:20
Magotha 63 4 37N10'48 75w56'57 5:03:48
Magruder 95 23 37N17 76w43 5:06:52
Maidens 37 4 37N40'08 77w52'56 5:11:32
Maiden Spring 89 4 37N01'41 81w40'57 5:26:44
Major 10 4 37N33'28 79w22'13 5:17:29
Major 38 4 36N35 81w20 5:25:20
Makemie Park 1 4 37N54 75w33 5:02:12
Makleys Corner 29 3 38N45'31 77w20'26 5:09:22
Malbrook 29 1 38N50'52 77w10'04 5:08:40
Malcolm 91 25 36N36 82w11 5:28:44
Malibu 133 6 36N50'48 76w05'44 5:04:23
Mallow 3 4 37N46'15 79w58'22 5:19:53
Malmaison 69 4 36N41 79w22 5:17:28
Mammoth Oak 120 4 37N05'00 76w30'16 5:06:01
Manakin 117 4 37N36'05 77w42'09 5:10:49
Manakin Farms 37 4 37N36'14 77w42'51 5:10:51
Manassas 73 2 38N45'03 77w28'32 5:09:54
Manassas Park 118 2 38N47'02 77w28'12 5:09:53
Manbur 43 17 37N32'04 77w20'33 5:09:22
Manchester 21 22 37N28 77w30 5:10:00
Maness 52 26 36N46'56 83w03'28 5:32:14
Mangohick 50 14 37N48'36 77w16'23 5:09:06
Mannboro 4 4 37N15'05 77w49'25 5:11:18
Mann Ford 81 26 36N38 82w34 5:30:16
Manning 132 5 36N42'18 76w38'55 5:06:36
Mannoni 60 4 37N08 80w24 5:21:36
Manquin 50 14 37N42'36 77w09'11 5:08:37
Manry 84 4 36N53'30 77w02'06 5:08:08
Mantapike 48 4 37N41'47 76w55'16 5:07:41
Manteo 15 14 37N40'36 78w39'49 5:14:39
Mantua 29 3 38N51'13 77w15'35 5:09:02
Mantua Hills 29 3 38N51'16 77w16'00 5:09:04
Manville 81 26 36N38 82w34 5:30:16
Maple Grove 78 14 37N48'24 79w36'07 5:18:24
Maple Grove 92 19 38N15'06 77w01'54 5:08:08
Maple Grove 120 6 37N06'22 76w31'28 5:06:06
Maple Grove Estates 29 3 38N47'03 77w08'45 5:08:35
Maple Hills 107 3 38N50'18 77w18'01 5:09:12
Maple Terrace 29 3 38N51 77w15 5:09:00
Maple Terrace 133 6 36N52 76w00 5:04:00
Mapleton 133 6 36N48'00 76w05'09 5:04:21
Maplewood 4 4 37N18'58 78w02'56 5:12:12
Mappsburg 1 4 37N34'39 75w45'50 5:03:03
Mappsville 1 4 37N50'45 75w34'01 5:02:16
Marble Valley 8 21 38N08'07 79w25'32 5:17:42
Marcem 81 26 36N37'49 82w36'31 5:30:26
Marengo 58 4 36N38'18 78w07'11 5:12:29
Marford 132 5 36N44 76w35 5:06:20
Margo 85 22 38N09'38 77w43'28 5:10:54
Marion 83 15 36N50'05 81w30'54 5:26:04
Marion Hill 43 17 37N32 77w24 5:09:36
Marionville 63 4 37N27'09 75w51'18 5:03:25
Markham 30 19 38N54'14 78w00'08 5:12:01
Markham 69 4 36N52'45 79w14'31 5:16:58
Marksville 67 14 38N34'30 78w28'47 5:13:55
Marlan Forest 29 1 38N46 77w04 5:08:16
Marlbank 95 4 37N12'31 76w28'56 5:05:56
Marlboro 21 22 37N29 77w29 5:09:56
Marlboro 34 4 39N04'53 78w19'21 5:13:17
Marlbrook 78 14 37N51'43 79w15'12 5:17:01
Marlin Forest 29 1 38N45'39 77w03'20 5:08:13
Marlo Heights 29 1 38N51'29 77w10'09 5:08:41
Marmora 27 22 37N11 77w38 5:10:32
Marrowbone Heights 44 4 36N33 79w51 5:19:24
Marshall 30 19 38N51'53 77w51'29 5:11:26
Marshall Farms 29 3 38N50 77w26 5:09:44
Marshall Heights 36 4 37N16'06 76w29'50 5:05:59
Marshalls Beach 64 18 37N57'02 76w21'21 5:05:25
Marshalltown 23 4 37N32'17 80w03'36 5:20:14
Martha Gap 26 15 37N12 82w18 5:29:12
Martin Ford 91 15 36N41'27 82w18'51 5:29:15
Martins Corner 17 22 38N05'16 77w12'28 5:08:50
Martins Corner 65 4 37N06'50 78w08'13 5:12:33
Martins Siding 63 4 37N23'24 75w54'36 5:03:38
Martins Store 5 14 37N25 79w08 5:16:32
Martins Store 41 4 36N56 78w57 5:15:48
Martins Store 61 14 38N02 78w50 5:15:20
Martinsville 119 4 36N41'29 79w52'22 5:19:29
Marumsco Acres 73 13 38N38'35 77w15'35 5:09:02
Marumsco Hills 73 13 38N38'37 77w16'31 5:09:06
Marumsco Village 73 13 38N39'41 77w15'29 5:09:02
Marumsco Woods 73 13 38N37'19 77w15'39 5:09:03
Marvin 14 15 37N10'56 81w56'47 5:27:47
Marye 85 22 38N04'48 77w35'03 5:10:20
Maryes Heights 110 24 38N17'56 77w28'37 5:09:54
Mary Gray 8 21 38N07'52 79w03'10 5:16:13
Mary Lee Park 29 3 38N45 77w08 5:08:32
Marysville 16 16 37N06'32 79w07'21 5:16:29
Maryton 17 22 38N14'16 77w20'16 5:09:21
Maryus 36 4 37N16'46 76w24'11 5:05:37
Mascot 48 4 37N37'37 76w42'27 5:06:50
Mason 29 1 38N52 77w10 5:08:40
Mason 88 4 36N45'34 77w23'08 5:09:33
Mason Cove 77 4 37N22'15 80w04'03 5:20:16
Mason Creek 129 4 37N17 80w03 5:20:12
Masons Corner 4 4 37N25'58 77w53'35 5:11:34
Masonville 29 1 38N50'46 77w12'11 5:08:49
Massanetta Springs 79 22 38N24'01 78w50'04 5:15:20
Massaponax 85 22 38N11'36 77w30'33 5:10:02
Massie 74 4 37N07 80w47 5:23:08
Massies Corner 75 14 38N43'25 78w06'54 5:12:28
Massies Mill 61 14 37N46'37 79w00'05 5:16:00
Mastins Corner 85 22 38N11'23 77w46'31 5:11:06
Mathews 57 4 37N26'13 76w19'13 5:05:17
Matney 14 15 37N18'50 81w58'47 5:27:55
Matoaca 21 22 37N13'49 77w28'40 5:09:55
Mattaponi 48 4 37N32'05 76w46'23 5:07:06
Mattoax 4 14 37N25'37 77w52'22 5:11:29
Mauck 67 14 38N35 78w30 5:14:00
Maurertown 82 14 38N55'47 78w27'50 5:13:51
Mauzy 79 22 38N33'51 78w44'33 5:14:58
Mavisdale 14 15 37N11'54 82w00'29 5:28:02
Max 18 4 36N40 80w55 5:23:40
Max Creek 74 4 36N58 80w43 5:22:52
Maxie 14 15 37N18'04 82w10'28 5:28:42
Max Meadows 94 4 36N58'13 80w56'59 5:23:48
Maxwell 89 4 37N06'18 81w37'23 5:26:30
Maxwell Garden 120 4 37N05'28 76w30'48 5:06:03
Mayberry 68 4 36N44 80w25 5:21:40
Maybrook 35 4 37N18'11 80w32'22 5:22:09
Mayfair Place 43 17 37N34'16 77w23'15 5:09:33
Mayfield 43 17 37N34 77w29 5:09:56
Mayfield 110 4 38N17'08 77w27'22 5:09:49
Mayfield Farms 42 22 37N37'22 77w22'57 5:09:32
Mayflower 5 16 37N35 79w03 5:16:12
Mayflower 52 26 36N49'47 83w04'51 5:32:19
Mayland 79 22 38N35'18 78w46'17 5:15:05
Maynards Crossroads 46 4 36N44'31 76w52'34 5:07:30
Mayo 41 4 36N34'19 78w53'01 5:15:32
Mayo 44 4 36N37 80w00 5:20:00
Mayo River 68 4 36N38 80w09 5:20:36
Maysville 15 4 37N33 78w33 5:14:12
Maytown 93 15 36N56'16 82w27'44 5:29:51
McAdam 74 4 37N01'49 80w43'30 5:22:54
McBryant Corner 17 22 37N55'53 77w24'09 5:09:37
McCall Gap 91 15 36N48'40 81w45'56 5:27:04
McCarthys Corner 86 4 38N18'33 77w23'52 5:09:35
McChesney Heights 98 25 36N36'51 82w09'31 5:28:38
McClung 9 4 38N03'11 79w41'35 5:18:46
McClung Mill 78 14 37N56'07 79w20'37 5:17:22
McClure 26 15 37N06'09 82w22'35 5:29:30
McConnell 81 26 36N43'52 82w28'49 5:29:55
McConnell Mill 81 26 36N41'47 82w26'58 5:29:48
McCorkle 81 26 36N39 82w28 5:29:52
McCowan Spring 9 4 38N06'12 79w34'31 5:18:18
McCoy 60 4 37N13'01 80w35'53 5:22:24
McCoys Ford 90 14 38N52'13 78w17'08 5:13:09
McCready 83 15 36N54'12 81w44'11 5:26:57
McCullough 2 14 37N45'25 78w36'56 5:14:28
McDonalds Mill 60 4 37N18'00 80w16'33 5:21:06
McDonald's Small Farms 43 22 37N40 77w30 5:10:00
McDowell 45 4 38N20'08 79w29'27 5:17:58
McDuff 17 22 37N57'20 77w27'40 5:09:51
McFadden Ford 91 26 36N42'41 82w16'39 5:29:07
McGaheysville 79 22 38N22'16 78w43'57 5:14:56
McHenry 85 22 38N10'19 77w42'23 5:10:50
McKendree 41 4 36N46 78w56 5:15:44
McKenney 27 22 36N59'12 77w43'24 5:10:54
McKinley 8 21 38N02'33 79w17'57 5:17:12

McKnights Mill 38 4 36N36'32 80W54'10 5:23:37
McLean 29 1 38N56'03 77W10'40 5:08:43
McLean Estates 29 1 38N55 77W11 5:08:44
McLean Hamlet 29 1 38N56'23 77W13'09 5:08:53
McLean Manor 29 1 38N55'37 77W10'44 5:08:43
McMullen 39 14 38N20'54 78W27'29 5:13:50
McMullin 83 15 36N48'51 81W34'42 5:26:19
McNeals Corner 51 4 37N47'30 76W28'31 5:05:54
McRae 25 4 37N27'40 78W16'58 5:13:08
Meade 28 14 37N52'40 76W57'50 5:07:51
Meade 93 15 37N07'47 82W33'41 5:30:15
Meador 10 4 37N12'01 79W39'24 5:18:38
Meadowbrook 21 22 37N27 77W28 5:09:52
Meadowbrook 121 6 36N54'48 76W18'14 5:05:13
Meadowbrook Forest 121 6 36N54'24 76W13'35 5:04:54
Meadowcreek 38 4 36N40 80W55 5:23:40
Meadowcrest 91 25 36N36 82W11 5:28:44
Meadowdale 45 4 38N22'34 79W39'55 5:18:40
Meadowfield 68 4 36N35'45 80W26'38 5:21:47
Meadow Mills 34 4 39N01'23 78W18'22 5:13:13
Meadowood 43 17 37N36 77W27 5:09:48
Meadows of Dan 68 4 36N44 80W25 5:21:40
Meadows of Newgate 29 3 38N50 77W26 5:09:44
Meadow View 21 22 37N27 77W28 5:09:52
Meadowview 91 15 36N45'37 81W51'47 5:27:27
Meadowville 21 22 37N22'14 77W19'22 5:09:17
Meadowville 30 19 38N47'53 77W48'56 5:11:16
Meadville 41 4 36N50'04 79W01'56 5:16:08
Mears Corner 133 6 36N46'49 76W11'31 5:04:46
Mears Station 1 4 37N51'22 75W36'21 5:02:25
Mearsville 1 4 37N51'33 75W37'27 5:02:30
Mechanicsburg 11 4 37N08'53 80W56'29 5:23:46
Mechanicsville 42 22 37N36'31 77W22'25 5:09:30
Mechanicsville 53 14 39N13'11 77W44'41 5:10:59
Mechanicsville 78 14 37N42'47 79W24'22 5:17:37
Mechanicsville 79 22 38N40'04 78W47'17 5:15:09
Mechums River 2 14 38N02 78W29 5:13:56
Media Park 43 17 37N32 77W24 5:09:36
Medley 77 4 37N18'56 80W00'19 5:20:01
Meems 82 14 38N43'31 78W39'43 5:14:39
Meetze 30 19 38N40'57 77W45'34 5:11:02
Meherrin 55 4 37N06'11 78W22'01 5:13:28
Melfa 1 4 37N38'57 75W44'30 5:02:58
Melrose 16 16 37N02'58 79W03'19 5:16:13
Melrose 79 22 38N29'50 78W48'13 5:15:13
Melrose 128 4 37N18 79W59 5:19:56
Melrose Gardens 73 14 38N33 77W19 5:09:16
Melrose Landing 48 4 37N38'14 76W51'19 5:07:25
Melton 54 14 38N06'39 78W08'37 5:12:34
Memorial Heights 29 1 38N46'07 77W04'45 5:08:19
Menchville 120 6 37N05'14 76W31'42 5:06:07
Mendota 91 26 36N42'39 82W18'06 5:29:12
Menokin Landing 76 4 38N00'04 76W48'28 5:07:14
Mentow 10 4 37N11'33 79W25'38 5:17:43
Mercer 53 14 39N01 77W45 5:11:00
Merchant 13 4 36N40'41 77W57'08 5:11:49
Meredithville 13 4 36N48'24 77W57'25 5:11:50
Meridan Park 29 1 38N53 77W13 5:08:52
Merrifield 29 1 38N52'27 77W13'38 5:08:55
Merrifield 125 6 36N52'45 76W22'58 5:05:32
Merrimac 24 4 38N27'09 78W04'44 5:12:19
Merrimac 60 4 37N11'22 80W25'33 5:21:42
Merrimack Park 121 6 36N56'24 76W16'23 5:05:06
Merrimac Mines 60 4 37N08 80W24 5:21:36
Merrimac Shores 112 6 37N00'28 76W21'01 5:05:24
Merritt Hills 130 4 36N43 78W54 5:15:36
Merry Oaks 29 3 38N55 77W14 5:08:56
Merry Point 51 4 37N44'01 76W28'58 5:05:56
Merry Point Estates 120 4 37N03'49 76W31'10 5:06:05
Messongo 1 4 37N54'52 75W38'23 5:02:34
Meter 92 19 38N07'31 76W38'01 5:06:32
Metompkin 1 4 37N46'09 75W36'11 5:02:25
Mew 80 15 36N51'33 82W20'35 5:29:22
Mica 17 22 38N08'26 77W21'21 5:09:25
Michaelwood 133 6 36N52'13 76W06'02 5:04:24
Michaux 70 14 37N38'55 77W54'08 5:11:37
Middlebrook 8 21 38N03'04 79W12'51 5:16:51
Middleburg 53 14 38N58'07 77W44'09 5:10:57
Middleridge 29 3 38N51 77W15 5:09:00
Middle River 8 21 38N12 78W53 5:15:32
Middlesex 1 4 37N35'04 75W48'36 5:03:14
Middleton 43 17 37N36 77W29 5:09:56
Middleton 133 6 36N53'09 76W10'48 5:04:43
Middleton Gardens 129 4 37N17 80W03 5:20:12
Middletons Corner 64 18 37N56'43 76W26'44 5:05:47
Middletown 34 4 39N01'39 78W16'51 5:13:07
Middletown 63 4 37N29'02 75W52'04 5:03:28
Middletowne Farms 95 23 37N16'04 76W40'52 5:06:43
Midland 30 19 38N35'58 77W43'29 5:10:54
Midlothian 21 22 37N30'21 77W38'58 5:10:36
Mid-Town 125 6 36N50 76W20 5:05:20
Midvale 78 14 37N50'09 79W17'13 5:17:09
Midway 2 14 38N01'39 78W42'24 5:14:50
Midway 9 4 37N59'03 79W50'19 5:19:21
Midway 41 4 36N47'53 78W46'43 5:15:07
Midway 50 14 37N45'20 77W07'36 5:08:30
Midway 58 4 36N40'17 78W15'31 5:13:02
Midway Island 86 4 38N29'55 77W22'09 5:09:29
Midway Mills 61 14 37N39'57 78W43'21 5:14:53
Mike 16 16 37N21 78W59 5:15:56
Mila 64 18 37N50'32 76W19'40 5:05:19
Milan 121 6 36N53 76W18 5:05:12
Mildred Crossing 54 14 38N02'31 78W02'45 5:12:11
Miles 57 4 37N25 76W22 5:05:28
Milestone 51 4 37N46'05 76W26'48 5:05:47
Milford 17 22 38N01'23 77W22'25 5:09:30
Milford Landing 57 4 37N29'44 76W17'27 5:05:10
Milk Landing 132 4 36N36'40 76W54'25 5:07:38
Millboro 38 4 37N58'30 79W36'11 5:18:25
Millboro Springs 9 4 37N59 79W36 5:18:24
Mill Creek 33 4 36N50'08 80W01'16 5:20:05
Mill Creek 38 4 36N37'03 81W27'43 5:25:51
Mill Creek Landing 84 4 36N35'00 76W58'51 5:07:55
Mill Creek Park 29 1 38N50'13 77W13'33 5:08:54
Milldale 90 14 39N00'07 78W05'54 5:12:24
Millenbeck 51 4 37N40'11 76W29'20 5:05:57
Miller Landing 36 4 37N28'13 76W39'14 5:06:37
Miller Park 116 14 37N24 79W10 5:16:40
Miller School 2 14 38N02 78W29 5:13:56
Millers Tavern 28 4 37N49'41 76W56'43 5:07:47
Mill Farms 95 4 37N07'58 76W27'25 5:05:50
Mill Gap 45 4 38N19'18 79W42'15 5:18:49
Millington 2 14 38N07'24 78W36'45 5:14:27
Mill Run Acres 29 3 39N00 77W15 5:09:00
Millstone 41 4 36N52'36 79W00'56 5:16:04
Milltown 53 4 39N14'07 77W37'34 5:10:30
Millville 101 6 36N44'50 76W18'24 5:05:14
Millwood 22 4 39N04'10 78W02'17 5:12:09
Milteer Acres 132 5 36N44 76W35 5:06:20
Milton 2 14 38N00'18 78W24'10 5:13:37
Milton 19 22 37N18'26 77W01'29 5:08:06
Minebank Ford 34 14 39N02'28 78W19'58 5:13:20
Mineral 54 14 38N00'38 77W54'32 5:11:38
Miners Store 52 26 36N40 83W07 5:32:28
Mine Run 66 14 38N15'26 77W50'16 5:11:21
Minnieville 73 13 38N38'09 77W21'09 5:09:25
Minor 48 14 37N50'21 76W58'59 5:07:56
Mint Spring 8 21 38N04'28 79W06'04 5:16:24
Miona 1 4 37N58'19 75W34'39 5:02:19
Miskimon 64 4 37N50'16 76W28'35 5:05:54
Mission Home 39 14 38N17 78W37 5:14:28
Mitchell Crossroads 18 4 36N51'44 80W43'05 5:22:52
Mitchell Mill 16 16 37N09'23 79W07'09 5:16:29
Mitchells 24 4 38N22'37 78W01'43 5:12:07
Mitchells Mill 40 20 36N35'43 77W34'18 5:10:17
Mitchells Store 17 22 37N52 77W27 5:09:48
Mitchelltown 9 4 38N00'46 79W48'42 5:19:15
Mobjack 57 4 37N22'30 76W20'52 5:05:23
Moccasin Gap 81 26 36N38 82W33 5:30:12
Mock Mill 91 15 36N43'00 81W49'54 5:27:20
Modern 112 6 37N01 76W25 5:05:40
Modest Town 1 4 37N48'46 75W33'55 5:02:16
Moffats Creek 8 21 38N03 79W13 5:16:52
Moffett 41 4 36N37'51 78W45'14 5:15:01
Mogarts Beach 46 4 37N01'55 76W36'04 5:06:24
Mollusk 51 4 37N43'48 76W32'18 5:06:09
Monarch 52 26 36N50'07 83W01'52 5:32:07
Monaskon 51 4 37N44'15 76W33'57 5:06:16
Moncure Corner 17 22 37N57'02 77W28'04 5:09:52
Monday 31 4 36N44 80W25 5:21:40
Moneta 10 4 37N10'52 79W37'03 5:18:28
Money Point 101 6 36N50 76W16 5:05:04
Moneys Corner 29 3 38N55'28 77W22'21 5:09:29
Mongle Spring 91 15 36N47'06 82W02'45 5:28:11
Monitor 5 16 37N37'02 79W05'01 5:16:20
Monroe 5 16 37N30'07 79W07'41 5:16:31
Monroe Corner 17 22 38N09'19 77W15'56 5:09:04
Monroe Gardens 112 6 37N02'44 76W20'42 5:05:23
Monroe Hall 92 19 38N14'23 76W59'33 5:07:58
Monrovia 66 14 38N09'18 77W59'57 5:12:00
Montague 28 4 37N46'05 76W44'16 5:06:57
Montague 49 22 38N14'40 77W11'16 5:08:45
Montague Landing 50 14 37N37'06 77W05'22 5:08:21
Montebello 61 14 37N51'49 79W08'17 5:16:33
Monterey 45 4 38N24'44 79W34'51 5:18:19
Montevideo 79 22 38N21'52 78W46'11 5:15:05
Montevue 2 14 38N02 78W29 5:13:56
Montezuma 79 22 38N24'33 78W59'18 5:15:57
Montezuma Gardens 43 17 37N33 77W24 5:09:36
Montford 66 14 38N14'26 78W10'05 5:12:40
Montgomery 60 4 37N09'23 80W19'09 5:21:17
Monticello 2 14 38N02 78W29 5:13:56
Monticello Forest 29 3 38N47'07 77W11'26 5:08:46
Monticello Park 96 1 38N49'56 77W04'09 5:08:17
Monticello Village 121 6 36N55'16 76W15'46 5:05:03
Monticello Woods 29 3 38N47'14 77W10'14 5:08:41
Montpelier 19 14 37N22'35 77W09'35 5:08:38
Montpelier 42 22 37N49'16 77W41'05 5:10:44
Montpelier Station 66 14 38N14 78W11 5:12:44
Montrose 43 17 37N32 77W24 5:09:36
Montrose Heights 127 17 37N31'10 77W23'33 5:09:34
Montrose Terrace 43 17 37N32 77W24 5:09:36
Montross 92 19 38N05'42 76W49'40 5:07:19
Montvale 10 4 37N23'04 79W43'53 5:18:56
Montvue 2 14 38N04'14 78W30'49 5:14:03
Monumental Mills 24 4 38N35'59 78W00'22 5:12:01
Monument Heights 43 22 37N35 77W31 5:10:04
Moodys Corner 42 22 37N52'13 77W42'44 5:10:51
Moon 57 4 37N26'36 76W17'35 5:05:10
Moon Corner 76 18 37N52'06 76W32'53 5:06:12
Moonlight 40 20 36N43'48 77W30'34 5:10:02
Moonlight 46 4 37N02'01 76W43'21 5:06:53
Mooreland 43 22 37N34'08 77W35'56 5:10:24
Mooreland Farms 43 22 37N34'24 77W35'27 5:10:22
Moores 124 4 37N07'36 76W24'37 5:05:38
Moores Corner 55 4 37N00'10 78W20'01 5:13:20
Moores Corner 86 4 38N27'03 77W29'20 5:09:57
Moores Mill 76 4 37N55'06 76W39'32 5:06:38
Moores Store 82 14 38N41 78W41 5:14:44
Mooretown 9 4 38N06'15 79W54'05 5:19:36
Mooring 87 4 37N05'41 76W51'50 5:07:27
Moran 71 4 37N13'45 78W15'35 5:13:02
Moratico 51 4 37N47'21 76W37'46 5:06:31
Morefield 80 15 36N54'49 82W18'08 5:29:13
Morgan Ford 90 14 38N57'30 78W07'18 5:12:29
Morgan Landing 62 14 37N32'12 76W56'35 5:07:46
Morgantown 30 19 38N50'44 77W52'45 5:11:31
Morgarts Beach 46 4 36N59 76W38 5:06:32
Morningside Hills 91 15 36N43'36 81W56'33 5:27:46
Morning Star 67 14 38N38'46 78W21'58 5:13:28
Morrisdale 21 22 37N23 77W26 5:09:44
Morrison 120 6 37N03'19 76W27'47 5:05:51
Morrison Farms 43 22 37N32 77W19 5:09:16
Morrisonville 53 4 39N13'23 77W40'07 5:10:40
Morrisville 30 19 38N30'06 77W42'01 5:10:48
Morven 4 4 37N25'05 78W04'33 5:12:18
Mosby 29 3 38N52 77W13 5:08:52
Mosby Woods 29 3 38N51'59 77W17'50 5:09:11
Moscow 8 21 38N19'01 79W05'21 5:16:21
Moseley 70 14 37N28'30 77W46'45 5:11:07
Moss Crest 29 3 38N55 77W14 5:08:56
Mossingford 20 4 36N57'50 78W38'33 5:14:34
Moss Neck 17 22 38N13'14 77W17'58 5:09:12
Moss Run 3 4 37N47'18 80W06'07 5:20:24
Mossy Creek 8 21 38N23 78W59 5:15:56
Motley 69 16 37N04'10 79W20'29 5:17:22
Motleys Mill 69 4 36N49'19 79W18'41 5:17:15
Motorun 57 4 37N20'14 76W18'03 5:05:12
Mountain Falls 34 9 39N07'02 78W23'45 5:13:35
Mountain Gap 53 14 39N07 77W34 5:10:16
Mountain Grove 9 4 38N05'55 79W53'13 5:19:33
Mountain Hill 69 4 36N33'24 79W19'08 5:17:17
Mountain Lake 35 4 37N21'19 80W32'17 5:22:09
Mountain View 35 4 37N17'21 80W39'22 5:22:37
Mountain View 49 22 38N23 77W27 5:09:48
Mountain View 74 4 37N05'17 80W37'14 5:22:29
Mountain View 78 14 37N54'04 79W17'01 5:17:08
Mountain View 91 15 36N43 81W58 5:27:52
Mount Airy 19 14 37N21'04 76W55'06 5:07:40
Mount Airy 69 4 36N56'34 79W11'33 5:16:46
Mount Airy 82 14 38N43'11 78W37'45 5:14:31
Mount Alto 2 14 37N50 78W36 5:14:24
Mount Blanco 21 22 37N23 77W26 5:09:44
Mount Carmel 41 4 36N35 79W04 5:16:16
Mount Carmel 83 15 36N51'12 81W28'42 5:25:55
Mountcastle 62 14 37N27'12 77W05'39 5:08:23
Mount Clifton 82 14 38N45'41 78W42'42 5:14:51
Mount Clinton 79 22 38N29'10 78W57'36 5:15:50
Mount Crawford 79 22 38N21'25 78W56'28 5:15:46
Mount Cross 69 4 36N38'20 79W29'17 5:17:57
Mount Daniel 29 1 38N53'51 77W10'58 5:08:44
Mount Elliott Springs 8 21 38N07'36 79W17'01 5:17:08
Mountfair 2 14 38N10'11 78W40'28 5:14:42
Mount Garland 54 14 37N56'08 77W48'44 5:11:15
Mount Gilead 53 14 39N06 77W43 5:10:52
Mount Hebron Park 29 1 38N47'30 77W09'04 5:08:36
Mount Hermon 69 4 36N40'42 79W25'21 5:17:41
Mount Heron 14 15 37N11'16 82W00'17 5:28:01
Mount Holly 92 19 38N05'28 76W43'06 5:06:52
Mount Ida 96 1 38N49'48 77W03'58 5:08:16
Mount Jackson 82 14 38N44'45 78W38'33 5:14:34

Mount Landing 28
14 37N56'24 76w55'18 5:07:41
Mount Laurel 41 4 36N52'31 78w47'16 5:15:09
Mount Meridian 8
21 38N16 78w49 5:15:16
Mount Nebo 1 4 37N40'28 75w48'12 5:03:13
Mount Nebo 21 22 37N30'38 77w34'47 5:10:19
Mount Olive 64 18 37N47'37 76w21'58 5:05:28
Mount Olive 82 14 38N58'40 78w27'27 5:13:50
Mount Olivet 74 4 37N02'40 80w48'37 5:23:14
Mount Pisgah 8 21 38N15'12 79w00'11 5:16:01
Mount Pleasant 5
16 37N35 79w03 5:16:12
Mount Pleasant 29
1 38N49'58 77w09'46 5:08:39
Mount Pleasant 34
4 39N10'19 78w17'43 5:13:11
Mount Pleasant 85
22 38N06'54 77w38'40 5:10:35
Mount Pleasant 87
4 37N12'16 76w49'31 5:07:18
Mount Pleasant 101
6 36N42'36 76w08'10 5:04:33
Mount Pleasant Estates 86
4 38N20'11 77w27'15 5:09:49
Mount Rush 15 4 37N32'15 78w36'53 5:14:28
Mount Sidney 8 21 38N15'26 78w57'35 5:15:50
Mount Solon 8 21 38N20'41 79w05'07 5:16:20
Mount Tabor 60 4 37N15'59 80w24'01 5:21:36
Mount Torry Furnace 8
21 37N56'43 78w57'51 5:15:51
Mount Union 12 4 37N27'06 79w58'13 5:19:53
Mount Vernon 29 3 38N42'28 77w05'11 5:08:21
Mount Vernon Cedars 29
3 38N45 77w08 5:08:32
Mount Vernon Forest 29
3 38N45 77w08 5:08:32
Mount Vernon Grove 29
3 38N45 77w08 5:08:32
Mount Vernon Hills 29
3 38N45 77w08 5:08:32
Mount Vernon Manor 29
3 38N43'08 77w06'37 5:08:26
Mount Vernon Park 29
3 38N45 77w08 5:08:32
Mount Vernon Square Apartmen 29
3 38N45 77w06 5:08:24
Mount Vernon Terrace 29
3 38N45 77w08 5:08:32
Mount Vernon Valley 29
3 38N45 77w08 5:08:32
Mount Vernon Woods 29
3 38N44'25 77w06'18 5:08:25
Mountville 53 14 39N01'31 77w42'44 5:10:51
Mount Vinco 15 4 37N35'32 78w36'06 5:14:24
Mount Williams 34
9 39N09'07 78w19'59 5:13:20
Mount Zephyr 29 3 38N45 77w08 5:08:32
Mount Zion 16 16 37N12'56 79w02'24 5:16:10
Mouth of Laurel 89
4 37N07'01 81w42'43 5:26:51
Mouth of Wilson 38
4 36N35'22 81w20'12 5:25:21
Muddy Cross 46 4 36N55'21 76w36'02 5:06:24
Mud Fork 89 4 37N13'07 81w27'31 5:25:50
Mulberry Hill 20
4 36N54'23 78w41'59 5:14:48
Mulch 76 4 37N54'12 76w34'16 5:06:17
Mumpower 91 25 36N36 82w11 5:28:44
Munden 133 6 36N34'40 76w02'10 5:04:09
Mundy Point 64 18 37N58 76w34 5:06:16
Munson Hill 29 1 38N51'35 77w08'45 5:08:35
Murat 78 14 37N44'45 79w31'34 5:18:06
Murdens Corner 133
6 36N47'14 76w03'09 5:04:13
Murdocks 65 4 37N01'37 78w03'37 5:12:14
Murpheyville 94 4 36N53'31 81w17'20 5:25:09
Murphy 14 15 37N07'35 82w10'28 5:28:42
Murrayfield 91 15 36N43'26 81w41'25 5:26:46
Museville 69 4 36N54'44 79w35'30 5:18:22
Musket Hills 73 2 38N47 77w28 5:09:52
Mustoe 45 4 38N19'25 79w38'26 5:18:34
Mustoe 49 22 38N18'31 77w16'48 5:09:07
Mutt 65 4 37N11'23 78w10'20 5:12:41
Mutton Hunk 1 4 37N47'02 75w36'00 5:02:24
Myrtle 132 5 36N46'22 76w41'32 5:06:46
Nace 12 4 37N26'22 79w49'27 5:19:18
Naff 33 4 37N08'53 80w00'45 5:20:03
Nahor 32 4 37N54'31 78w20'54 5:13:24
Nain 34 9 39N14'21 78w12'00 5:12:48
Namozine 4 4 37N11 77w38 5:10:32
Nance 19 14 37N27'40 77w07'40 5:08:31
Nancy 26 15 37N07'48 82w16'41 5:29:07
Nancy Wrights Corner 17
22 38N05'25 77w30'46 5:10:03
Nandua 1 4 37N37'27 75w51'01 5:03:24
Nansemond 132 5 36N46'01 76w31'52 5:06:07
Nansemond Shores 132
5 36N51'52 76w29'54 5:06:00
Naola 5 16 37N33'18 79w18'43 5:17:15
Naptha 13 4 36N49'44 77w50'28 5:11:22
Narrows 35 4 37N19'53 80w48'41 5:23:15
Naruna 16 16 37N06'21 79w00'10 5:16:01
Nash 61 14 37N51'27 79w02'47 5:16:11
Nash Corner 1 4 37N56'46 75w32'24 5:02:10
Nash Ford 80 15 36N58'12 82w04'32 5:28:18
Nash Mill 52 26 36N54'07 83w35'00 5:34:20
Nashs Store 52 26 36N38 83w26 5:33:44
Nash Town 92 19 38N10'34 77w00'14 5:08:01
Nasons 66 14 38N15'18 78w01'37 5:12:06
Nassawadox 63 4 37N28'29 75w51'31 5:03:26
Natal 69 4 36N59'12 79w16'03 5:17:04
Nathalie 41 4 36N56'05 78w56'51 5:15:47
National Airport 7
1 38N55 77w01 5:08:04
National Heights 43
17 37N32 77w24 5:09:36
Natural Bridge 78
14 37N37'48 79w32'36 5:18:10
Natural Bridge Station 78
14 37N37'15 79w30'22 5:18:01
Natural Tunnel 81
26 36N42'00 82w45'00 5:31:00

Natural Well 3 4 38N00 79w50 5:19:20
Naulakla 17 22 38N04'58 77w10'52 5:08:43
Naval Air Station 121
7 36N56 76w19 5:05:16
Naval Amphibious Base 133
7 36N52 76w11 5:04:44
Naval Hospital 125
7 36N51 76w18 5:05:12
Naval Weapons Station 95
11 37N12 76w27 5:05:48
Navy 29 8 38N53'23 77w22'42 5:09:31
Navy Annex 7 8 38N52 77w06 5:08:24
Navy Yard 125 7 36N49 76w18 5:05:12
Naxera 36 4 37N20'26 76w26'51 5:05:47
Naylors Beach 76
14 37N58'39 76w51'48 5:07:27
Neabsco 73 14 38N39 77w20 5:09:20
Neals Corner 41 4 36N53'20 78w47'49 5:15:11
Nealy Ridge 26 15 37N07'16 82w20'28 5:29:22
Nebo 83 15 36N56'30 81w26'31 5:25:46
Needmore 93 15 36N57'28 82w37'58 5:30:32
Needwood 17 22 37N52 77w27 5:09:48
Neenah 92 19 38N02'54 76w43'15 5:06:53
Neersville 53 4 39N15'40 77w43'34 5:10:54
Neff 91 15 36N42'37 81w51'46 5:27:27
Negro Foot 42 22 37N46 77w22 5:09:28
Nellysford 61 14 37N53'25 78w52'21 5:15:29
Nelson 58 4 36N34 78w42 5:14:48
Nelson Estates 43
17 37N32 77w24 5:09:36
Nelsonia 1 4 37N49'11 75w35'15 5:02:21
Nelson Park 95 23 37N16'01 76w40'15 5:06:41
Neslon 58 4 36N33'44 78w42'18 5:14:49
Nesting 59 4 37N44'02 76w38'56 5:06:36
Nethers 56 4 38N34'13 78w16'41 5:13:07
Nettleridge 68 4 36N35'09 80w08'23 5:20:34
New Alexandria 29
1 38N46'35 77w03'25 5:08:14
New Baltimore 30
19 38N46'02 77w43'43 5:10:55
Newbern 74 4 37N04'24 80w41'27 5:22:46
New Bohemia 72 22 37N11'01 77w19'14 5:09:17
New Canton 15 4 37N42'18 78w17'59 5:13:12
New Castle 23 4 37N30'00 80w06'40 5:20:27
New Church 1 4 37N58'44 75w31'53 5:02:08
New Cold Harbor 42
22 37N34'58 77w17'29 5:09:10
Newcomb Hall 100
14 38N02 78w29 5:13:56
New Copley Hill 2
14 38N02 78w29 5:13:56
New Design 105 4 36N38'01 79w23'52 5:17:35
New Ellett 60 4 37N11'58 80w21'49 5:21:27
New Garden 80 15 37N03 81w58 5:27:52
New Glasgow 5 16 37N37'45 78w58'45 5:15:55
New Hampden 45 4 38N29'34 79w33'49 5:18:15
New Hope 8 21 38N11'52 78w54'22 5:15:37
New Hope 19 14 37N20'28 77w03'42 5:08:15
New Hope 29 1 38N50'52 77w14'03 5:08:56
Newington 29 3 38N44'18 77w11'07 5:08:44
Newington Station 29
3 38N47 77w12 5:08:48
Newington Woods 29
3 38N47 77w12 5:08:48
New Kent 62 14 37N31'03 76w58'45 5:07:55
Newland 76 4 38N02'59 76w52'19 5:07:29
New Light 133 6 36N48'03 76w10'57 5:04:44
New London 16 16 37N18'06 79w16'50 5:17:07
New London 17 22 38N08'19 77w19'05 5:09:16
Newman 42 22 37N37'38 77w17'55 5:09:12
New Market 82 14 38N38'52 78w40'18 5:14:41
Newmarket 120 6 37N01'08 76w25'47 5:05:43
New Mount Cross 69
4 36N38'52 79w29'56 5:18:00
New Point 57 4 37N20'44 76w16'41 5:05:07
Newport 8 21 38N00'03 79w18'04 5:17:12
Newport 35 4 37N17'39 80w29'44 5:21:59
Newport 46 4 36N56 76w36 5:06:24
Newport 67 14 38N34'43 78w35'48 5:14:23
Newport News 120
6 36N58'43 76w25'42 5:05:43
New Post 85 22 38N13'58 77w24'23 5:09:38
New Quarry 83 15 36N53 81w46 5:27:04
New River 74 4 37N08'00 80w35'30 5:22:22
News Ferry 41 4 36N43 78w54 5:15:36
Newsoms 84 4 36N37'28 77w07'30 5:08:30
New Store 15 4 37N18 78w24 5:13:36
Newton Woods 29 3 38N43'50 77w05'52 5:08:23
Newtown 2 14 38N02'45 78w47'15 5:15:09
Newtown 39 14 38N14'15 78w20'15 5:13:21
Newtown 48 4 37N54'48 77w07'45 5:08:31
Newtown 51 4 37N47'20 76w29'05 5:05:56
Newtown 52 26 36N50'29 82w54'04 5:31:36
Newtown 78 14 37N46'28 79w28'08 5:17:53
Newtown 79 14 38N24'55 78w35'54 5:14:24
Newtown 125 6 36N49'29 76w18'14 5:05:13
New Upton 36 4 37N25 76w32 5:06:08
Newville 72 22 37N11'06 77w08'51 5:08:35
Newville 88 4 37N00'46 77w10'36 5:08:42
Niagara 77 4 37N15'18 79w52'22 5:19:29
Nicelytown 3 4 37N50'29 79w44'55 5:19:00
Nicewood 120 4 37N06'32 76w32'03 5:06:08
Nicholas 32 14 37N45'57 78w28'03 5:13:52
Nickelsville 81
26 36N45'10 82w24'53 5:29:40
Niday 11 4 37N15'17 81w01'45 5:24:07
Nieswanders Fort 34
4 39N02'48 78w17'48 5:13:11
Nightingale Trailer Park 29
3 38N45 77w06 5:08:24
Nimmo 133 6 36N45'35 76w01'00 5:04:04
Nimrod Hall 9 4 37N59 79w36 5:18:24
Ninde 49 12 38N16'16 77w03'23 5:08:14
Nineveh 90 14 39N00'57 78w09'55 5:12:40
Noble Furnace 94
4 36N48'33 81w05'49 5:24:23
Noel 42 22 37N54'16 77w32'40 5:10:11
Nohead Bottom 59
4 37N35'35 76w29'59 5:06:00
Nokesville 73 14 38N41'55 77w34'48 5:10:19
Nokomis 64 4 37N56'39 76w28'49 5:05:55
Nomini 92 19 38N05'54 76w44'17 5:06:57

Nomini Grove 92
19 38N02'06 76w44'55 5:07:00
Nora 26 15 37N04'15 82w20'51 5:29:23
Norcross 35 4 37N21'01 80w42'01 5:22:48
Norcum Park 125 7 36N49'53 76w20'03 5:05:20
Nordick 91 15 36N42 82w18 5:29:12
Norfolk 121 6 36N50'48 76w17'08 5:05:09
Norfolk Highlands 101
6 36N48'56 76w13'56 5:04:56
Norge 47 14 37N22'07 76w46'15 5:07:05
Norland 26 15 37N09'51 82w31'28 5:30:06
Norman 24 14 38N30'45 78w03'55 5:12:16
North 7 1 38N54 77w08 5:08:32
North 57 4 37N27 76w25 5:05:40
Northampton 112 6 37N02'42 76w25'27 5:05:42
North Anna 42 22 37N53'27 77w31'04 5:10:04
North Bassett 44
4 36N46'09 80w00'00 5:20:00
North Bristol 98
25 36N36 82w11 5:28:44
North Camellia Acres 121
7 36N55'19 76w12'10 5:04:49
Northeast 33 4 37N05 79w48 5:19:12
North Emporia 106
20 36N41 77w32 5:10:08
North Fairlington 7
1 38N50'11 77w05'51 5:08:23
Northfields 2 14 38N04'46 78w27'32 5:13:50
North Fork 53 14 39N03'43 77w41'51 5:10:47
North Fork 83 15 36N55 81w38 5:26:32
North Gap 11 4 37N15'23 81w06'58 5:24:28
North Garden 2 14 37N56'26 78w38'13 5:14:33
North Grundy 14
15 37N19 82w03 5:28:12
North Halifax 41
16 37N01'36 78w57'25 5:15:50
North Holston 83
15 36N54'39 81w42'58 5:26:52
North Jerico 132
5 36N44 76w35 5:06:20
North Landing 133
6 36N43'06 76w06'00 5:04:24
North Linkhorn Park 133
6 36N52'48 76w00'03 5:04:00
North Mountain 8
21 38N09'35 79w16'13 5:17:05
North Mount Vernon 29
1 38N43'14 77w03'29 5:08:14
North Pine Ridge 29
3 38N51 77w15 5:09:00
North Pulaski 74
4 37N05 80w46 5:23:04
North Rolleston 121
6 36N50'35 76w12'10 5:04:49
North Run Hills 43
17 37N36 77w29 5:09:56
Northside 121 6 36N55'58 76w15'14 5:05:01
Northside 127 17 37N34 77w26 5:09:44
North Springfield 29
3 38N48'15 77w12'18 5:08:49
North Stanton 41
4 36N57'58 79w04'59 5:16:20
North Tazewell 89
4 37N07'58 81w31'38 5:26:07
North View 58 4 36N46'50 78w14'40 5:12:59
North Virginia Beach 133
6 36N54'14 75w59'34 5:03:58
North Weems 51 14 37N39'40 76w26'25 5:05:46
North Wellville 65
4 37N09'01 77w55'02 5:11:40
Northwest 33 4 37N04 79w59 5:19:56
Northwest 101 4 36N33'41 76w12'05 5:04:48
North Woodley 29
1 38N53 77w13 5:08:52
Norton 122 15 36N56'00 82w37'45 5:30:31
Nortonsville 2 14 38N14'14 78w32'54 5:14:12
Norvella Heights 121
6 36N53'26 76w13'35 5:04:54
Norvello 58 4 36N37'41 78w19'43 5:13:19
Norview 121 6 36N53'18 76w14'45 5:04:59
Norwood 10 4 37N22'56 79w21'29 5:17:26
Norwood 61 14 37N38'35 78w48'33 5:15:14
Nottingham 21 17 37N33'19 77w32'57 5:10:12
Nottingham 81 26 36N38'07 82w30'54 5:30:04
Nottoway 65 4 37N08 78w05 5:12:20
Novelty 33 4 36N59 79w38 5:18:32
Novum 67 4 38N29'01 78w11'23 5:12:46
Nuckols 15 4 37N35'38 78w19'18 5:13:17
Nurney 132 5 36N38'32 76w36'51 5:06:27
Nurneysville 132
5 36N39'21 76w38'16 5:06:33
Nutbush 55 4 37N02'41 78w16'36 5:13:06
Nuttall 36 4 37N25'57 76w28'50 5:05:55
Nuttsville 51 4 37N47'36 76w33'04 5:06:12
Oak 62 14 37N24 76w55 5:07:40
Oak Corner 17 22 37N59'49 77w19'00 5:09:16
Oakcrest 7 1 38N50'43 77w03'31 5:08:14
Oakdale 78 14 37N44'10 79w35'49 5:18:23
Oakdale Farms 121
6 36N55'19 76w15'26 5:05:02
Oak Forest 25 4 37N30 78w15 5:13:00
Oak Forest 42 22 37N40'31 77w21'07 5:09:24
Oak Grove 18 4 36N46'56 80w54'10 5:23:37
Oak Grove 53 4 38N59'02 77w24'15 5:09:37
Oak Grove 60 4 37N06'48 80w22'00 5:21:28
Oak Grove 64 18 37N50 76w26 5:05:44
Oak Grove 91 25 36N38'40 82w10'49 5:28:43
Oak Grove 92 19 38N10'54 76w59'50 5:07:59
Oak Grove 101 6 36N43'57 76w14'25 5:04:58
Oak Grove 132 4 36N39'37 76w50'42 5:07:23
Oak Hall 1 4 37N56 75w33 5:02:12
Oak Hill 2 14 38N00'18 78w31'24 5:14:06
Oak Hill 8 22 38N03'03 78w55'27 5:15:42
Oak Hill 38 4 36N35'56 81w20'17 5:25:21
Oak Hill 43 17 37N33'46 77w23'58 5:09:36
Oak Hill 67 14 38N44'04 78w24'47 5:13:39
Oak Hill 69 4 36N33'16 79w35'49 5:18:23
Oak Hill Corner 87
4 37N09'33 77w04'11 5:08:17
Oakhurst 72 22 37N13 77w26 5:09:44
Oakland 43 17 37N29'49 77w24'20 5:09:37
Oakland 54 14 38N05'18 78w02'45 5:12:11
Oakland 132 4 36N51'05 76w35'24 5:06:22

Oakland Park 63 4 37N30'38 75w49'18 5:03:17
Oaklette 101 6 36N49'36 76w14'19 5:04:57
Oak Level 41 4 36N46 78w56 5:15:44
Oak Level 44 4 36N48'55 79w56'09 5:19:45
Oakley 28 4 37N46'29 76w45'19 5:07:01
Oakley 77 4 37N17 80w03 5:20:12
Oakley Landing 76 4 37N47'55 76w39'10 5:06:37
Oak Park 29 3 38N48'09 77w05'22 5:08:21
Oakpark 56 4 38N22'00 78w09'37 5:12:38
Oak Ridge 29 3 38N55 77w14 5:08:56
Oak Ridge 69 4 36N34'53 79w32'46 5:18:11
Oakridge 132 5 36N44 76w35 5:06:20
Oakridge Estates 73 2 38N47 77w28 5:09:52
Oakridge Estates 132 5 36N44 76w35 5:06:20
Oak Row 76 4 38N03'36 76w52'56 5:07:32
Oak Shade 30 19 38N34'53 77w47'21 5:11:09
Oakton 29 3 38N52'51 77w18'04 5:09:12
Oaktree 53 4 39N00 77w24 5:09:36
Oaktree 95 23 37N20'00 76w42'18 5:06:49
Oak Valley 29 3 38N55 77w14 5:08:56
Oak Valley Estates 29 3 38N55 77w14 5:08:56
Oak View 43 17 37N36 77w29 5:09:56
Oakville 6 4 37N25'54 78w51'23 5:15:26
Oakwood 7 1 38N53'50 77w09'46 5:08:39
Oakwood 14 15 37N12'48 82w00'23 5:28:02
Oakwood 29 3 38N43'07 77w05'45 5:08:23
Oakwood 79 22 38N31'07 78w43'05 5:14:52
Oakwood Forest 3 4 37N47'52 80w00'30 5:20:02
Oatlands 53 14 39N07 77w34 5:10:16
Occoquan 73 13 38N41'01 77w15'38 5:09:03
Occupacia 28 4 38N02'25 77w01'04 5:08:04
Oceana 133 6 36N50'31 76w00'48 5:04:03
Oceana Gardens 133 6 36N48 76w01 5:04:04
Oceanair 121 6 36N56'12 76w14'44 5:04:59
Oceana Naval Air Station 133 7 36N49 76w02 5:04:08
Ocean Park 133 6 36N54'33 76w06'06 5:04:24
Ocean View 121 6 36N56'59 76w14'48 5:04:59
Ocoonita 52 26 36N44'00 83w08'15 5:32:33
Ocran 51 14 37N39'37 76w20'58 5:05:24
Odricks Corner 29 1 38N56'19 77w13'54 5:08:56
Office Hall 49 22 38N14'20 77w09'02 5:08:36
Offutt Village 108 1 38N53'35 77w11'12 5:08:45
Ogburn 58 4 36N47'48 78w13'34 5:12:54
Oilville 37 4 37N42'14 77w47'08 5:11:09
Olaf 77 4 37N17 80w03 5:20:12
Old 38 4 36N37 80w57 5:23:48
Old Bandana 42 22 37N53'29 77w39'56 5:10:40
Old Church 42 22 37N38'40 77w13'17 5:08:53
Old Cold Harbor 42 22 37N35'27 77w16'15 5:09:05
Old Courthouse 29 3 38N54'50 77w14'17 5:08:57
Old Creek Estates 29 3 38N51 77w15 5:09:00
Old Dominion 2 14 37N49'39 78w39'59 5:14:40
Old Dominion Gardens 29 1 38N56'38 77w11'30 5:08:46
Olde Forge 29 3 38N51 77w15 5:09:00
Olde Towne 96 1 38N49 77w05 5:08:20
Oldewood 29 3 38N54 77w13 5:08:52
Oldfield 133 6 36N52 76w00 5:04:00
Old Glade Spring 91 15 36N46'09 81w46'51 5:27:07
Old Gun 21 22 37N32'04 77w35'33 5:10:22
Old Hall Landing 48 14 37N48'06 77w05'33 5:08:22
Oldhams 92 19 38N00'09 76w40'09 5:06:41
Oldhouse Landing 19 14 37N25'11 77w01'31 5:08:06
Old Liberty 44 4 36N39'18 79w49'26 5:19:18
Old Mill 10 4 37N23'27 79w30'15 5:18:01
Old Orchard 120 6 37N06'26 76w32'43 5:06:11
Old Somerset 66 14 38N13'25 78w13'13 5:12:53
Old Tavern 30 19 38N49'53 77w48'44 5:11:15
Oldtown 38 4 36N39'18 80w57'31 5:23:50
Old Trap 85 22 38N08'17 77w32'45 5:10:11
Old Trower 1 4 37N35'30 75w42'21 5:02:49
Old Well 20 4 37N05 78w45 5:15:00
Olean 35 4 37N23'26 80w39'35 5:22:38
Olinger 52 26 36N49'02 82w51'53 5:31:28
Olive 17 22 38N13'10 77w26'29 5:09:46
Olive 125 6 36N49 76w21 5:05:24
Oliver 42 22 37N51'29 77w31'59 5:10:08
Oliver Estates 29 3 39N00 77w15 5:09:00
Oliver Landing 36 4 37N18'36 76w33'22 5:06:13
Olivers Corner 85 22 38N12'21 77w39'22 5:10:37
Olney Corner 17 22 38N14'04 77w19'36 5:09:18
Omaha 26 15 37N05'51 82w26'05 5:29:44
Omega 41 4 36N40'18 78w48'25 5:15:14
Onan 61 14 37N59'17 78w49'28 5:15:18
Onancock 1 4 37N42'42 75w44'58 5:03:00
O'Neal 56 4 38N20'46 78w16'04 5:13:04
Onemo 57 4 37N23'44 76w16'23 5:05:06
Onley 1 4 37N41'27 75w42'59 5:02:52
Ontario 20 4 36N59'18 78w29'11 5:13:57
Opal 30 19 38N37'15 77w48'01 5:11:12
Opequon 34 4 39N09'26 78w14'49 5:12:59
Ophelia 64 18 37N54'36 76w17'02 5:05:08
Opie 58 4 36N46'07 78w10'59 5:12:44
Oral Oaks 55 4 36N54'54 78w11'46 5:12:47
Oranda 82 14 39N01'39 78w20'01 5:13:20
Orange 66 14 38N14'43 78w06'40 5:12:27
Orange Hunt 29 3 38N45 77w12 5:08:48
Orapax Farms 62 14 37N32'01 77w12'21 5:08:49
Orbit 46 4 36N49 76w45 5:07:00
Orchid 54 14 37N49'44 77w53'44 5:11:35
Ordinary 36 4 37N18'55 76w30'49 5:06:03
Ordsburg 13 4 36N57'01 77w52'32 5:11:30
Ore Bank 15 4 37N41 78w20 5:13:20
Oregon Acres 125 6 36N49'00 76w21'27 5:05:26
Oreton 93 26 36N48'56 82w46'54 5:31:08
Orgainville 58 4 36N43'03 78w35'06 5:14:20
Oriana 120 4 37N08'01 76w31'31 5:06:06
Oriskany 12 4 37N36'59 79w59'02 5:19:56
Orkney Springs 82 14 38N47'43 78w48'53 5:15:16
Orlando 132 5 36N44 76w35 5:06:20
Orlean 30 19 38N44'59 77w57'44 5:11:51
Orleans Village 29 1 38N49 77w09 5:08:36
Oronoco 5 16 37N44'14 79w15'14 5:17:01
Osaka 93 26 36N56'49 82w48'39 5:31:15
Osbornes Chapel 52 26 36N38 83w03 5:32:12
Osborn Landing 62 14 37N24'49 76w58'08 5:07:53
Osborn Rock 93 15 36N53'46 82w35'05 5:30:20
Osborns Gap 26 15 37N09 82w27 5:29:48
Osborns Store 89 4 36N58 81w38 5:26:32
Osbos 10 4 37N27 79w31 5:18:04
Osceola 91 15 36N40'23 81w51'46 5:27:27
Osso 49 22 38N18'35 77w13'51 5:08:55
Otey 60 4 37N10 80w15 5:21:00
Othma 37 4 37N46'21 77w58'48 5:11:55
Otter Hill 10 4 37N15'28 79w26'53 5:17:48
Otter River 16 16 37N09 79w18 5:17:12
Otterville 10 4 37N25'51 79w29'10 5:17:57
Ottobine 79 22 38N25'53 79w02'23 5:16:10
Ottoman 51 4 37N42'06 76w31'13 5:06:05
Overall 90 14 38N48'22 78w20'52 5:13:23
Overlee Knolls 7 1 38N53'22 77w08'53 5:08:36
Overton 2 14 37N57'26 78w28'04 5:13:52
Owen Corner 81 26 36N38'33 82w29'40 5:29:59
Owens 12 4 37N37'06 79w49'19 5:19:17
Owens 49 22 38N20'19 77w05'12 5:08:21
Owens 88 4 36N51'13 77w25'29 5:09:42
Owens Landing 63 4 37N16'56 76w00'39 5:04:03
Owensville 2 14 38N06'04 78w34'31 5:14:18
Owenton 48 4 37N53'01 77w06'02 5:08:24
Oxford 21 22 37N32'21 77w32'53 5:10:12
Oxford Ford 52 26 36N39'43 83w06'04 5:32:24
Oxford Furnace 16 14 37N22'32 79w02'29 5:16:10
Ox Hill 29 3 38N54 77w26 5:09:44
Ox Place 81 26 36N50'22 82w39'54 5:30:40
Oyster 63 4 37N17'11 75w55'22 5:03:41
Oyster Point 120 6 37N06'19 76w30'28 5:06:02
Ozeana 28 4 37N49'30 76w48'06 5:07:12
Paces 41 4 36N38'43 79w05'56 5:16:24
Paeonian Springs 53 14 39N08'57 77w37'10 5:10:29
Page 14 15 37N10'47 81w59'44 5:27:59
Page 17 22 38N07 77w25 5:09:40
Page Hollow 83 15 36N53'07 81w40'52 5:26:43
Paige 17 22 38N04'21 77w25'09 5:09:41
Paineville 4 4 37N23'14 78w07'14 5:12:29
Paint Bank 23 4 37N34'08 80w15'44 5:21:03
Painter 1 4 37N35'07 75w47'07 5:03:08
Paint Lick 89 4 37N05 81w43 5:26:52
Palls 50 14 37N41 77w01 5:08:04
Palmer 51 14 37N37'25 76w21'06 5:05:24
Palmer Crossroads 58 4 36N34'20 78w12'15 5:12:49
Palmers Crossroads 30 19 38N42'44 77w55'43 5:11:43
Palmer Springs 58 4 36N33'38 78w14'22 5:12:57
Palmetto 68 4 36N33'18 80w13'01 5:20:52
Palmyra 32 4 37N51'39 78w15'49 5:13:03
Palmyra 132 5 36N45'35 76w35'28 5:06:22
Palo Alto 45 4 38N25'24 79w22'14 5:17:29
Palos 79 22 38N34'22 78w57'56 5:15:52
Pamlico 121 6 36N56'37 76w15'49 5:05:03
Pampa 36 4 37N31'33 76w35'35 5:06:22
Pampatike Landing 50 14 37N40'02 77w08'12 5:08:33
Pamplin City 6 4 37N15'48 78w40'58 5:14:44
Panier 85 22 38N10'51 77w45'50 5:11:03
Pannill Fork 44 4 36N42'32 80w00'48 5:20:03
Panorama 75 14 38N39'33 78w19'18 5:13:17
Panoramic Hills 29 1 38N50 77w12 5:08:48
Pardee 93 26 37N00'24 82w45'06 5:31:00
Paris 30 19 39N00'16 77w57'06 5:11:48
Park 83 15 36N51 81w34 5:26:16
Park 134 22 38N04 78w54 5:15:36
Parker 85 22 38N16'30 77w45'27 5:11:02
Parker Field 127 17 37N34'18 77w27'52 5:09:51
Parker Landing 1 4 37N48'13 75w40'39 5:02:43
Parkfairfax 96 1 38N50'13 77w04'47 5:08:19
Parkglen 7 1 38N51'21 77w07'00 5:08:28
Parkins Mills 34 9 39N06'25 78w09'26 5:12:38
Parklawn 29 1 38N50'02 77w08'56 5:08:36
Park Lee Place 21 22 37N27 77w28 5:09:52
Park Manor 125 6 36N49'30 76w23'09 5:05:33
Park Place 121 6 36N52'17 76w17'18 5:05:09
Parksley 1 4 37N46'55 75w39'14 5:02:37
Parks Mill 91 15 36N38'37 81w57'34 5:27:50
Park View 79 22 38N27'58 78w52'51 5:15:31
Parkview 125 6 36N50'26 76w18'38 5:05:15
Parkview Hills 29 1 38N57'37 77w10'48 5:08:43
Parkway Estates 95 23 37N16'51 76w40'21 5:06:41
Parkwood 29 1 38N51 77w09 5:08:36
Parkwood Estates 91 25 36N36 82w11 5:28:44
Parnassus 8 21 38N17'41 79w07'06 5:16:28
Parr 12 4 37N39'35 79w54'35 5:19:38
Parrish Court 104 4 37N45'32 79w59'16 5:19:57
Parrott 74 4 37N12'18 80w36'57 5:22:28
Parsonage 80 15 36N50'09 82w14'51 5:28:59
Partlow 85 22 38N02'19 77w38'21 5:10:33
Partridge Landing 48 4 37N27'39 76w40'29 5:06:42
Passapatanzy 49 22 38N17'50 77w18'52 5:09:15
Passing 17 22 38N03 77w21 5:09:24
Pastoria 1 4 37N44'59 75w37'50 5:02:31
Pastures 8 21 38N11 79w15 5:17:00
Patersons Corner 17 22 37N56'09 77w27'49 5:09:51
Patna 45 4 38N14'01 79w31'27 5:18:06
Patrick Henry 16 16 37N07 79w00 5:16:00
Patrick Henry Heights 42 22 37N41'03 77w23'10 5:09:33
Patrick Springs 68 4 36N38'30 80w11'43 5:20:47
Patterson 14 15 37N15'52 81w58'34 5:27:54
Patterson 94 4 36N53'26 80w47'07 5:23:08
Pattersons Store 62 14 37N32 77w10 5:08:40
Pattonsville 81 26 36N41'58 82w51'05 5:31:24
Pat Town 63 4 37N17'54 75w57'01 5:03:48
Pauls Crossroads 28 4 37N51'54 76w54'38 5:07:39
Payne 32 4 37N45'09 78w26'33 5:13:46
Payne 44 4 36N42'53 79w56'15 5:19:45
Paynes Corner 86 4 38N22'54 77w32'35 5:10:10
Paynes Mill 15 4 37N44'31 78w27'42 5:13:51
Paynes Mill 32 4 37N57'21 78w17'16 5:13:09
Paynesville 14 15 37N19'54 81w53'27 5:27:34
Paytes 85 22 38N13'38 77w49'59 5:11:20
Peach Bottom 38 4 36N35'20 81w04'01 5:24:16
Peacock 29 3 38N58'25 77w15'13 5:09:01
Peakland 116 14 37N26'40 79w12'20 5:16:49
Peaks 10 4 37N27 79w31 5:18:04
Peaks 42 22 37N43'23 77w23'21 5:09:33
Peaksville 10 4 37N24'32 79w32'44 5:18:11
Peales Crossroads 79 22 38N23'33 78w48'38 5:15:15
Peapatch 14 15 37N17'02 81w47'19 5:27:09
Pearch 10 14 37N30'16 79w16'44 5:17:07
Pearisburg 35 4 37N19'35 80w44'07 5:22:56
Pearly 14 15 37N16'27 82w08'37 5:28:34
Pearsons Corner 42 22 37N40'35 77w22'51 5:09:31
Peary 57 4 37N22'19 76w16'47 5:05:07
Peatross 17 22 37N55'02 77w23'07 5:09:32
Pecan Gardens 133 6 36N49'05 76w05'46 5:04:23
Pedlar 5 16 37N37 79w15 5:17:00
Pedlar Mills 5 16 37N33'35 79w15'06 5:17:00
Pedro 28 4 38N06 77w08 5:08:32
Peeds 92 4 38N06'02 76w55'22 5:07:41
Pemberton 37 4 37N40'28 78w05'06 5:12:20
Pembroke 35 4 37N19'10 80w38'21 5:22:33
Pembroke Manor 133 6 36N51'07 76w08'11 5:04:33
Pen Daw 29 1 38N46'53 77w04'45 5:08:19
Pender 29 3 38N52'14 77w22'09 5:09:29
Penderbrook 29 3 38N52'22 77w21'51 5:09:27
Penderlan 29 3 38N51'21 77w22'14 5:09:29
Penderwood 29 3 38N52'51 77w22'11 5:09:29
Pendletons 54 14 37N59'41 77w53'54 5:11:36
Penhook 33 4 36N58'56 79w37'42 5:18:31
Penicks Mill 10 4 37N23'17 79w36'53 5:18:28
Penlan 15 4 37N39'49 78w22'03 5:13:28
Penn Acres 21 22 37N29'34 77w33'06 5:10:12
Penn Daw Terrace 29 1 38N46 77w04 5:08:16
Penn Daw Village 29 1 38N47'09 77w04'55 5:08:20
Penneys Crossroad 85 22 38N06'11 77w41'32 5:10:46
Pennington Gap 52 26 36N45'30 83w01'38 5:32:07
Penn Laird 79 22 38N23'08 78w48'10 5:15:13
Penn Lee 52 26 36N47'23 83w03'24 5:32:14
Pennsand 81 26 36N38 82w34 5:30:16
Penns Store 68 4 36N37 80w00 5:20:00
Pennstown 121 6 36N52'33 76w14'00 5:04:56
Penny Corner 17 22 38N04'44 77w14'13 5:08:57
Pennyville 1 4 37N37'03 75w49'59 5:03:20
Penola 17 22 37N57'26 77w22'16 5:09:29
Pentagon 7 1 38N52 77w06 5:08:24
Penvir 35 4 37N17'45 80w52'41 5:23:31
Peola Mills 75 4 38N32'50 78w14'47 5:12:59
Pepper 60 4 37N09'49 80w32'56 5:22:12
Pera 5 16 37N37'03 79w17'30 5:17:10
Perkins Park 116 14 37N23'00 79w09'21 5:16:37
Perkins Point 9 4 37N57'42 79w58'07 5:19:52
Perkinsville 37 14 37N44'40 77w49'25 5:11:18
Perrin 36 4 37N16'12 76w25'28 5:05:42
Perrows 16 16 37N06'26 79w11'45 5:16:47
Perrowville 10 4 37N25'03 79w21'03 5:17:24
Perryville 83 15 36N53 81w46 5:27:04
Persimmon Point 1 4 37N50'44 75w32'40 5:02:11
Perth 41 4 37N00'59 78w59'43 5:15:59
Petersburg 123 22 37N13'40 77w24'08 5:09:37
Peters Creek 68 4 36N35'32 80w19'01 5:21:16
Peterson 81 26 36N43'42 82w47'51 5:31:11
Petsworth 36 4 37N29 76w37 5:06:28
Pettys Corner 58 4 36N46'21 78w15'27 5:13:02
Petunia 94 4 36N56'32 81w07'18 5:24:29
Peyton 8 21 38N08'04 79w02'36 5:16:10
Peytonsburg 69 4 36N49'26 79w10'04 5:16:40
Phenix 20 4 37N04'47 78w44'53 5:15:00
Philadelphia 132 5 36N44 76w35 5:06:20
Philbeck Crossroads 58 4 36N46'10 78w33'33 5:14:14
Phillip 91 25 36N40'55 82w16'41 5:29:07
Phillis 58 4 36N36'21 78w19'31 5:13:18
Philomont 53 4 39N03'22 77w44'26 5:10:58
Philpott 44 4 36N47'25 80w00'23 5:20:02

Phipps 93 15 37N09'49 82w34'37 5:30:18
Phlegar 35 4 37N15'57 80w58'44 5:23:55
Phoebus 112 4 37N01'17 76w19'06 5:05:16
Piankatank Shores 59 4 37N32'44 76w29'45 5:05:59
Piankitank 57 4 37N29 76w20 5:05:20
Pickadat Corner 21 22 37N17'07 77w24'42 5:09:39
Pickaway 69 4 36N46'42 79w11'08 5:16:45
Pickerel 69 4 36N58'35 79w24'42 5:17:39
Pickwick 29 3 38N48 77w20 5:09:20
Pico 12 4 37N29'53 79w41'42 5:18:47
Piedmont 8 21 38N12'50 78w53'58 5:15:36
Piedmont 60 4 37N06'00 80w13'09 5:20:53
Piedmont 61 14 37N36'39 78w55'19 5:15:41
Piedmont 75 14 38N40 78w14 5:12:56
Piedmont Mill 33 4 37N05'37 79w51'17 5:19:25
Pierce Mill 94 4 36N51'12 80w59'17 5:23:57
Pierces Corner 51 4 37N46 76w28 5:05:52
Pierces Shop 66 14 38N13 78w06 5:12:24
Piggen 1 4 37N35'41 75w43'15 5:02:53
Pigg River 69 4 36N59 79w28 5:17:52
Pike City 18 4 36N43'52 80w28'59 5:21:56
Pilgrams Knob 14 15 37N15 81w55 5:27:40
Pilkinton 70 14 37N25'48 77w50'30 5:11:22
Pilot 60 4 37N03'07 80w21'50 5:21:27
Pimmit Hills 29 3 38N54'46 77w12'04 5:08:48
Pine 74 4 37N00 80w45 5:23:00
Pineaire 132 5 36N44 76w35 5:06:20
Pine Chapel Village 112 6 37N02'07 76w22'24 5:05:30
Pine Creek 18 4 36N50 80w42 5:22:48
Pinecrest 29 1 38N49'38 77w09'25 5:08:38
Pinecrest Heights 29 1 38N50 77w12 5:08:48
Pinedale 43 22 37N36 77w32 5:10:08
Pine Grove 67 14 38N32'09 78w28'43 5:13:55
Pine Grove 91 15 36N43'21 82w16'05 5:29:04
Pine Grove Court 112 6 37N03'25 76w20'36 5:05:22
Pine Grove Terrace 112 4 37N03'06 76w20'20 5:05:21
Pine Hill 42 22 37N38'54 77w19'21 5:09:17
Pinehurst 125 6 36N50'44 76w22'23 5:05:30
Pine Ridge 29 3 38N51'39 77w14'32 5:08:58
Pinero 36 4 37N29'32 76w32'25 5:06:10
Pine Spring 29 3 38N52'02 77w12'22 5:08:49
Pine Springs 29 3 38N52 77w13 5:08:52
Pinetia 101 6 36N49 76w14 5:04:56
Pine Top 59 4 37N34 76w25 5:05:40
Pine Tree 59 4 37N39'08 76w36'33 5:06:26
Pine Tree 70 14 37N39 78w05 5:12:20
Pinetta 36 4 37N24'55 76w38'19 5:06:33
Pinetta 101 6 36N46'27 76w14'18 5:04:57
Pine View 30 19 38N26'52 77w41'41 5:10:47
Pineville 79 22 38N20'37 78w47'37 5:15:10
Pinewood Gardens 133 6 36N50'29 76w04'21 5:04:17
Pinewood Lawns 29 3 38N45 77w08 5:08:32
Pinewood Park 73 2 38N47 77w28 5:09:52
Pinewood South 29 3 38N45 77w08 5:08:32
Piney Court 96 1 38N49'27 77w06'16 5:08:25
Piney Grove 41 4 36N47'23 78w50'19 5:15:21
Piney Grove 76 4 38N01'36 76w47'12 5:07:09
Piney Grove 88 4 36N59'21 77w02'30 5:08:10
Piney Point Estates 95 4 37N08'53 76w26'08 5:05:45
Piney River 61 14 37N42'18 79w01'24 5:16:06
Piney Run 29 3 38N43 77w09 5:08:36
Pipers Gap 18 4 36N38'39 80w50'32 5:23:22
Pisgah 89 4 37N07'15 81w34'25 5:26:18
Pitmans Corner 51 4 37N40'31 76w24'53 5:05:40
Pittmantown 132 4 36N34'05 76w49'09 5:07:17
Pittston 69 4 36N37 79w12 5:16:48
Pittsville 69 4 36N58'54 79w27'44 5:17:51
Pizarro 31 4 36N56'16 80w13'14 5:20:53
Plains 79 22 38N38 78w49 5:15:16
Plains Mill 79 14 38N38'48 78w43'10 5:14:53
Plain View 48 4 37N29'45 76w40'05 5:06:40
Plain View 70 14 37N32'17 77w53'19 5:11:33
Plantation Heights 95 23 37N17'31 76w42'41 5:06:51
Plantersville 55 4 36N55'33 78w26'31 5:13:46
Plasterco 91 15 36N51'38 81w47'27 5:27:10
Plato 41 4 36N47'47 79w02'55 5:16:12
Pleasant Gap 69 4 36N42'10 79w26'44 5:17:47
Pleasant Grove 44 4 36N41'12 80w00'08 5:20:01
Pleasant Grove 55 4 37N00'02 78w22'17 5:13:29
Pleasant Grove 58 4 36N45'54 78w10'45 5:12:43
Pleasant Grove 69 4 36N32'40 79w23'40 5:17:35
Pleasant Hill 79 22 38N27 78w52 5:15:28
Pleasant Hill 89 4 37N11'12 81w44'48 5:26:59
Pleasant Hill 132 5 36N43 76w35 5:06:20
Pleasant Manor 112 6 37N01'01 76w22'01 5:05:28
Pleasant Point 87 14 37N10'31 76w46'51 5:07:07
Pleasant Ridge 29 1 38N50'40 77w12'36 5:08:50
Pleasant Ridge 133 6 36N52 76w00 5:04:00
Pleasant Shade 40 20 36N45'04 77w38'50 5:10:35
Pleasant Valley 15 4 37N28'04 78w28'14 5:13:53
Pleasant Valley 53 4 38N54'43 77w28'34 5:09:54
Pleasant Valley 79 22 38N23'05 78w53'51 5:15:35
Pleasant View 5 16 37N36'22 79w14'39 5:16:59
Plum Creek 91 15 36N48'40 81w44'29 5:26:58
Plum Point 62 14 37N30'59 76w48'50 5:07:15
Plum Tree 54 14 38N00'45 77w46'20 5:11:05
Plunkettsville 131 21 38N09'04 79w05'39 5:16:23
Plymouth 55 4 37N00'01 78w09'53 5:12:40
Plymouth Park 101 6 36N49'10 76w15'06 5:05:00
Poages Mill 77 4 37N11'53 80w03'24 5:20:14
Pocahontas 89 4 37N18'13 81w20'23 5:25:22
Pocahontas 123 22 37N14'14 77w24'02 5:09:36
Pocahontas Village 133 6 36N50'16 76w08'35 5:04:34
Pocket 52 26 36N46'53 83w02'34 5:32:10
Pocoshock 127 17 37N29 77w33 5:10:12
Poetown 14 15 37N16'58 82w06'31 5:28:26
Poff 31 4 36N56'16 80w18'48 5:21:15
Pohick 29 3 38N42'36 77w11'49 5:08:47
Pohick Estates 29 3 38N43'02 77w12'11 5:08:49
Pohick Hills 29 3 38N45'03 77w13'35 5:08:54
Pohick River Pines 29 3 38N42 77w14 5:08:56
Poindexter 54 14 38N00'05 78w08'42 5:12:35
Poindexters 42 22 37N41'28 77w26'23 5:09:46
Point Eastern 17 22 37N55 77w29 5:09:56
Pointers Landing 50 14 37N45'04 77w05'17 5:08:21
Point of View 133 6 36N51 76w09 5:04:36
Point of Woods 73 2 38N47 77w28 5:09:52
Point O'Woods 133 6 36N50'46 76w02'42 5:04:11
Point Pleasant 11 4 37N07'27 81w01'01 5:24:04
Pole Green 42 22 37N38'13 77w20'13 5:09:21
Pollard 4 4 37N18 78w06 5:12:24
Pollards Corner 50 14 37N47'23 77w11'06 5:08:44
Pondtown 80 15 36N55'38 82w05'54 5:28:24
Pons 46 4 37N00'01 76w47'31 5:07:10
Poole 27 22 37N11 77w38 5:10:32
Poolesville 87 4 37N05'33 76w43'28 5:06:54
Poorhouse Corner 17 22 38N01'42 77w16'15 5:09:05
Pope 84 4 36N43'10 77w10'02 5:08:40
Popes Creek Landing 92 19 38N11'29 76w54'16 5:07:37
Poplar 17 22 38N00'51 77w24'44 5:09:39
Poplar Camp 94 4 36N53 80w51 5:23:24
Poplar Cove 1 4 37N43 75w44 5:02:56
Poplar Flats 61 14 37N44'50 78w55'32 5:15:42
Poplar Forest 10 14 37N20'54 79w15'53 5:17:04
Poplar Grove 62 14 37N35'06 77w02'19 5:08:09
Poplar Halls 121 6 36N51'04 76w13'01 5:04:52
Poplar Heights 29 1 38N53'14 77w11'47 5:08:47
Poplar Hill 29 1 38N50 77w12 5:08:48
Poplar Hill 35 4 37N13'03 80w44'21 5:22:57
Poplar Inn 17 22 38N01 77w22 5:09:28
Poplar Landing 50 14 37N45'53 77w04'57 5:08:20
Poquoson 124 4 37N07'20 76w20'46 5:05:23
Poquoson Shores 124 4 37N09'15 76w24'22 5:05:37
Porta Bello 95 23 37N18'04 76w38'51 5:06:35
Port Conway 49 22 38N10'38 77w11'11 5:08:45
Port Dumfries 73 14 38N33 77w19 5:09:16
Porters 2 14 37N49'30 78w35'57 5:14:24
Porters 85 22 38N11'37 77w47'30 5:11:10
Porters Crossroads 94 4 36N51'52 80w58'57 5:23:56
Port Haywood 57 4 37N23'09 76w19'03 5:05:16
Portlock 101 6 36N47'06 76w16'40 5:05:07
Port Norfolk 125 6 36N50'54 76w20'08 5:05:21
Port Republic 79 22 38N17'46 78w48'39 5:15:15
Port Richmond 50 14 37N33'06 76w48'40 5:07:15
Port Royal 17 22 38N10'18 77w11'29 5:08:46
Port Royal Cross Roads 17 22 38N09'48 77w12'00 5:08:48
Portsmouth 125 6 36N50'07 76w17'55 5:05:12
Portsmouth Heights 125 6 36N49'15 76w22'09 5:05:29
Possum Trot 45 4 38N28'12 79w31'57 5:18:08
Post Oak 85 22 38N09'58 77w39'49 5:10:39
Potato Creek 38 4 36N35 81w20 5:25:20
Poteet Ford 52 26 36N39'56 83w05'06 5:32:20
Potomac 49 22 38N19 77w08 5:08:32
Potomac 96 1 38N49 77w04 5:08:16
Potomac Beach 92 19 38N16'13 76w59'10 5:07:57
Potomac Hills 29 1 38N55'49 77w09'13 5:08:37
Potomac Mills 92 19 38N09'46 76w56'33 5:07:46
Potomac Run 86 4 38N23 77w27 5:09:48
Potters Flats 26 15 37N19 82w21 5:29:24
Pottomoi 42 22 37N40'35 77w23'59 5:09:36
Potts Creek 3 4 37N37'13 80w11'16 5:20:45
Poulson 1 4 37N52'33 75w38'39 5:02:35
Pound 93 15 37N07'25 82w36'05 5:30:24
Pounding Mill 89 4 37N04'31 81w42'32 5:26:50
Powan 48 4 37N46'56 76w56'35 5:07:46
Powcan 48 4 37N47 77w00 5:08:00
Powell 81 26 36N39 82w51 5:31:24
Powell Corner 2 14 37N53'27 78w35'56 5:14:24
Powells Corner 133 6 36N48'47 76w05'53 5:04:24
Powells Crossroads 133 6 36N49'56 76w08'27 5:04:34
Powells Store 10 4 37N32 79w22 5:17:28
Powell Store 2 14 37N50 78w36 5:14:24
Powellton 13 4 36N40'00 77w47'33 5:11:10
Powers Ford 81 26 36N41'04 82w51'36 5:31:26
Powhatan 70 14 37N32'31 77w55'09 5:11:41
Powhatan Place 124 4 37N07'56 76w24'19 5:05:37
Prater 14 15 37N12'47 82w11'49 5:28:47
Pratts 56 4 38N20'51 78w16'13 5:13:05
Premier 89 4 37N07 81w52 5:27:28
Prentiss Park 125 6 36N49'22 76w19'01 5:05:16
Presque Isle 21 14 37N21'20 77w16'07 5:09:04
Preston 44 4 36N39'29 79w58'48 5:19:55
Preston Hills 91 25 36N38'37 82w05'56 5:28:24
Preston King 7 1 38N53 77w08 5:08:32
Pribble 57 4 37N23'46 76w22'33 5:05:30
Price Hill 91 15 36N45'37 81w45'23 5:27:02
Price Mill 13 4 36N48'46 77w55'20 5:11:41
Prices Fork 60 4 37N12'35 80w29'25 5:21:58
Prices Store 5 14 37N25 79w08 5:16:32
Prilliman 33 4 36N52'26 80w00'28 5:20:02
Prim 49 12 38N14'55 77w04'13 5:08:17
Prince George 72 22 37N13'13 77w17'18 5:09:09
Princess Anne 133 6 36N45'05 76w03'12 5:04:13
Princess Anne Hills 133 6 36N52 76w00 5:04:00
Princess Anne Plaza 133 6 36N49'54 76w05'24 5:04:22
Proffit 2 14 38N06'31 78w25'28 5:13:42
Proffits Store 32 4 37N48 78w29 5:13:56
Progress 33 4 36N55'04 79w40'32 5:18:42
Prospect 71 4 37N18'10 78w33'34 5:14:14
Prospectdale 35 4 37N16'41 80w44'36 5:22:58
Prospect Hill 29 1 38N55 77w11 5:08:44
Providence 38 4 36N41'58 81w01'00 5:24:04
Providence 41 4 36N56'14 78w49'11 5:15:17
Providence Church 132 5 36N47'02 76w38'00 5:06:32
Providence Forge 62 14 37N26'30 77w02'38 5:08:11
Providence Junction 101 6 36N47'00 76w15'30 5:05:02
Providence Park 43 17 37N34 77w26 5:09:44
Providence Terrace 101 6 36N50 76w16 5:05:04
Provost 70 14 37N36'20 77w58'59 5:11:56
Public Fork 20 4 36N49'40 78w38'47 5:14:35
Public Landing 133 6 36N34'08 75w59'38 5:03:59
Pughs 52 26 36N45'04 82w59'30 5:31:58
Pughsville 132 6 36N50'52 76w26'37 5:05:46
Pulaski 74 4 37N02'52 80w46'48 5:23:07
Pullens 69 4 36N56'05 79w29'56 5:18:00
Pullers Corner 17 22 38N09'26 77w20'33 5:09:22
Pulleys Crossroads 84 4 36N52'15 76w57'51 5:07:51
Pullontown 81 25 36N37'20 82w18'48 5:29:15
Pumpkin Center 11 4 37N13'39 81w00'31 5:24:02
Pungo 133 6 36N43'24 76w01'05 5:04:04
Pungoteague 1 4 37N37'49 75w48'50 5:03:15
Purcell 52 26 36N47'46 82w59'42 5:31:59
Purcell 80 15 36N55'50 82w08'07 5:28:32
Purcellville 53 14 39N08'12 77w42'54 5:10:52
Purchase 81 26 36N41 82w45 5:31:00
Purdy 40 20 36N49'20 77w35'18 5:10:21
Purkins Corner 49 22 38N15'26 77w09'56 5:08:40
Puryear Corner 58 4 36N36'47 78w35'20 5:14:21
Putnam 80 15 37N01'19 81w57'56 5:27:52
Putneys Mill 62 14 37N36'19 77w05'36 5:08:22
Pyletown 22 4 39N06'20 78w02'36 5:12:10
Quail 54 14 37N55'47 78w02'01 5:12:08
Quail Oaks 21 22 37N27 77w28 5:09:52
Quantico 73 11 38N31'20 77w17'38 5:09:11
Quantico Station 73 11 38N31 77w18 5:09:12
Quarry 83 15 36N53 81w46 5:27:04
Quebec 83 15 36N45'34 81w30'11 5:26:01
Queens Lake 95 23 37N17'25 76w39'29 5:06:38
Queenstown 51 4 37N40'49 76w29'16 5:05:57
Quicksburg 82 14 38N41'35 78w40'45 5:14:43
Quicks Mill 8 21 38N12'44 79w01'46 5:16:07
Quinby 1 4 37N33'13 75w44'03 5:02:56
Quinque 39 14 38N15'00 78w23'53 5:13:36
Quinton 62 14 37N32'01 77w07'17 5:08:29
Quoit 31 4 36N44 80w25 5:21:40
Rabat 41 4 36N58'37 78w56'56 5:15:48
Raccoon Ford 24 14 38N21'47 77w56'30 5:11:46
Rackettown 94 4 36N51'48 80w49'45 5:23:19
Racume 13 4 36N44'53 77w43'20 5:10:53
Radford 10 4 37N08'17 79w37'05 5:18:28
Radford 126 4 37N07'54 80w34'36 5:22:18
Radford College 126 4 37N08 80w34 5:22:16
Radiant 56 4 38N18'48 78w12'27 5:12:50
Radium 40 20 36N43'54 77w37'43 5:10:31
Radnor Heights 7 1 38N53'20 77w04'24 5:08:18
Ragged Point Beach 92 19 38N08'55 76w37'00 5:06:28
Raines Corner 17 22 38N11'35 77w20'00 5:09:20
Raines Tavern 25 4 37N22'00 78w22'30 5:13:30

Rainswood 64 18 37N55'01 76w32'56 5:06:12
Raketown 18 4 36N49'12 80w57'34 5:23:50
Ralco 55 4 36N58 78w07 5:12:28
Raleigh Heights 101 6 36N50 76w16 5:05:04
Raleigh Place 101 6 36N48'30 76w24'26 5:05:38
Raleigh Terrace 112 6 37N00'15 76w22'05 5:05:28
Ramey Fork 76 4 38N01'46 76w51'45 5:07:27
Ramoth 86 4 38N25'19 77w28'11 5:09:53
Ramsey 93 15 36N56'24 82w35'42 5:30:23
Ramsey Flats 26 15 37N12'17 82w27'06 5:29:48
Randolph 20 4 36N53'36 78w41'52 5:14:47
Randolph 25 4 37N22 78w22 5:13:28
Randolph Corner 53 4 39N01'44 77w49'44 5:11:19
Random Hills 29 3 38N51'28 77w20'41 5:09:23
Range Corner 17 22 38N04'19 77w18'46 5:09:15
Rangeley 44 4 36N41'46 79w57'46 5:19:51
Ransons 15 4 37N38'12 78w30'42 5:14:03
Raphine 78 14 37N56'14 79w13'59 5:16:56
Rapidan 24 4 38N18'45 78w03'58 5:12:16
Rappahannock Academy 17 22 38N11 77w17 5:09:08
Rapps Mill 78 14 37N40'13 79w38'03 5:18:32
Raven 89 4 37N05'13 81w51'19 5:27:25
Ravensworth 29 3 38N48'14 77w13'15 5:08:53
Ravensworth Farms 29 3 38N49 77w13 5:08:52
Ravensworth Grove 29 1 38N49'04 77w12'53 5:08:52
Ravensworth Park 29 1 38N48'43 77w12'51 5:08:51
Ravenwood 29 1 38N51'42 77w09'11 5:08:37
Ravenwood 73 2 38N43'17 77w23'35 5:09:34
Rawhide 52 26 36N51'20 82w54'40 5:31:39
Rawley Springs 79 22 38N30'19 79w03'24 5:16:14
Rawlings 13 4 36N56'54 77w46'45 5:11:07
Ray 69 4 36N56'10 79w18'40 5:17:15
Raymondale 29 3 38N52 77w13 5:08:52
Raymonds Fork 17 22 38N04'36 77w19'31 5:09:18
Raynor 46 4 36N56'53 76w46'59 5:07:08
Rayo 85 22 38N12 77w35 5:10:20
Rayon Terrace 104 4 37N45'54 79w59'47 5:19:59
Readus 82 14 38N51'21 78w35'28 5:14:22
Reams 27 22 37N06'02 77w24'24 5:09:38
Reavistown 38 4 36N38'24 80w58'01 5:23:52
Reba 10 4 37N24'45 79w38'14 5:18:33
Rectortown 30 19 38N55'16 77w51'42 5:11:27
Red Apple Orchard 61 14 37N42'14 78w46'45 5:15:07
Redart 57 4 37N28'12 76w18'07 5:05:12
Red Ash 89 4 37N06'48 81w52'16 5:27:29
Red Bank 41 4 36N35'42 78w45'14 5:15:01
Red Bank 63 4 37N26'40 75w50'32 5:03:22
Red Bank Landing 36 4 37N27'39 76w39'42 5:06:39
Redeye 69 4 36N54'18 79w20'35 5:17:54
Red Fox Forest 29 1 38N48'46 77w15'21 5:09:01
Red Hill 1 4 37N35'33 75w45'08 5:03:01
Red Hill 2 14 37N57 78w38 5:14:32
Red Hill 18 4 36N44'46 80w38'56 5:22:36
Red Hill 94 4 36N55'15 80w50'52 5:23:23
Red Hill Village 120 4 37N07'39 76w30'42 5:06:03
Red House 20 4 37N11 78w49 5:15:16
Rediviva 75 14 38N41'05 78w12'08 5:12:49
Red Lane 70 14 37N32'48 77w50'59 5:11:24
Redlawn 58 4 36N37'55 78w14'33 5:12:58
Red Mills 8 21 38N09 78w51 5:15:24
Red Mills 78 14 37N38'23 79w33'39 5:18:15
Red Oak 13 4 36N54 77w52 5:11:28
Red Oak 20 4 36N47 78w37 5:14:28
Red Oak Hollow 69 4 36N43'35 79w11'46 5:16:47
Red Top 132 5 36N47'10 76w35'16 5:06:21
Red Valley 33 4 37N08'06 79w51'42 5:19:27
Redwood 33 4 37N01'11 79w48'44 5:19:15
Reed Creek 44 4 36N46 79w56 5:19:44
Reed Creek 52 26 36N52 82w54 5:31:36
Reed Junction 74 4 36N55'53 80w45'08 5:23:01
Reeds 25 4 37N20'16 78w24'15 5:13:37
Reedtown 63 4 37N22'47 75w54'55 5:03:40
Reedtown 133 6 36N52'40 76w07'56 5:04:32
Reedville 64 18 37N50'31 76w16'34 5:05:06
Reedy Church 17 22 37N53 77w22 5:09:28
Reedy Mill 17 22 37N54'23 77w18'05 5:09:12
Reekes Mill 55 4 36N49'21 78w16'59 5:13:08
Reesedale 60 4 37N13'45 80w17'57 5:21:12
Reese Shop 20 4 36N54 78w42 5:14:48
Reflection Place 29 3 38N58 77w22 5:09:28
Refuge 34 4 39N06 78w13 5:12:52
Regent 59 4 37N35'17 76w26'31 5:05:46
Regina 51 4 37N48'14 76w25'04 5:05:40
Rehoboth 55 4 36N55'11 78w21'18 5:13:25
Rehoboth Church 51 14 37N43 76w23 5:05:32
Reids Ferry 132 5 36N44 76w35 5:06:20
Reids Grove 29 1 38N55 77w11 5:08:44
Reliance 90 14 39N00'23 78w15'02 5:13:00
Relief 34 9 39N11 78w10 5:12:40
Remington 30 19 38N32'01 77w48'31 5:11:14
Remlik 59 4 37N39'41 76w37'09 5:06:29
Remo 64 18 37N48'57 76w21'11 5:05:25
Renan 69 4 36N58'29 79w11'39 5:16:47
Repass 80 15 36N59'20 81w48'20 5:27:13
Repton Mills 56 4 38N19'21 78w15'20 5:13:01
Republican Grove 41 4 36N56'42 79w02'39 5:16:11
Rescue 46 4 36N59'45 76w33'39 5:06:15
Reservoir Hill 104 4 37N47 79w59 5:19:56
Rest 34 4 39N17'25 78w04'59 5:12:20
Reston 29 3 38N58'07 77w20'29 5:09:22
Retreat 33 4 37N00 79w53 5:19:32
Return 17 22 38N10 77w12 5:08:48
Retz 57 4 37N25'44 76w21'14 5:05:25
Reusens 116 14 37N27'29 79w11'18 5:16:45
Reva 24 4 38N29'38 78w08'01 5:12:32
Revercombs Corner 75 4 38N33'09 78w14'12 5:12:57
Revis 59 4 37N40'14 76w39'20 5:06:37
Rexburg 28 14 37N56'11 76w59'14 5:07:57
Reynolds Corner 64 18 37N54'42 76w32'48 5:06:11
Reynolds Mill 68 4 36N38'11 80w07'43 5:20:31
Reynolds Store 34 4 39N19 78w18 5:13:12
Rhoadesville 66 14 38N16'24 77w55'43 5:11:43
Rhodes 46 4 36N49 76w45 5:07:00
Rhoton Mill 81 26 36N42'56 82w39'38 5:30:39
Ribbon 54 14 38N02'48 77w57'23 5:11:50
Rice 71 4 37N16'30 78w17'30 5:13:10
Riceville 69 4 36N53'28 79w10'09 5:16:41
Richardson 18 4 36N49'27 80w46'52 5:23:07
Richardsville 24 4 38N24'00 77w43'45 5:10:55
Rich Creek 35 4 37N22'56 80w49'22 5:23:17
Richfield 77 4 37N16 80w02 5:20:08
Richland Hills 116 14 37N21'54 79w13'29 5:16:54
Richlands 89 4 37N05'35 81w47'38 5:27:11
Richmond 127 17 37N33'13 77w27'38 5:09:51
Richmond Beach 28 14 37N54'53 76w50'17 5:07:21
Richmond Heights 43 17 37N27'49 77w23'54 5:09:36
Rich Neck 76 19 37N58'30 76w39'38 5:06:39
Rich Neck Heights 135 23 37N15'24 76w43'53 5:06:56
Rich Patch 3 4 37N43'36 79w55'10 5:19:41
Rich Patch Mines 3 4 37N45'19 79w55'00 5:19:40
Richtown 51 4 37N45'17 76w27'38 5:05:51
Rich Valley 83 15 36N53 81w46 5:27:04
Rickahock 48 4 37N42'38 76w58'20 5:07:53
Ridge 43 22 37N36 77w32 5:10:08
Ridgecrest 29 3 38N53 77w18 5:09:12
Ridgedale 83 15 36N56'26 81w34'26 5:26:18
Ridgelea Estates 29 3 38N51 77w15 5:09:00
Ridge Manor 29 3 38N51 77w15 5:09:00
Ridgeview 29 3 38N47'20 77w06'18 5:08:25
Ridgeway 41 4 36N48'24 79w08'39 5:16:35
Ridgeway 44 4 36N34'36 79w51'31 5:19:26
Ridgeway 69 4 36N59'21 79w28'58 5:17:56
Ridings Mill 34 4 39N01'46 78w14'30 5:12:58
Riggs 81 26 36N41 82w45 5:31:00
Rileyville 67 14 38N45'54 78w23'18 5:13:33
Riner 60 4 37N03'59 80w26'27 5:21:46
Ringgold 69 4 36N36'29 79w17'44 5:17:11
Rinkerton 82 14 38N45'21 78w40'11 5:14:41
Ripplemead 35 4 37N20'13 80w41'11 5:22:45
Rip Rap 41 4 36N33 78w47 5:15:08
Rivanna 2 14 38N07'29 78w27'40 5:13:51
River Bend Estates 73 13 38N39'26 77w14'38 5:08:59
Rivercrest 7 3 38N55'19 77w07'10 5:08:29
Riverdale 41 4 36N41'14 78w54'01 5:15:36
Riverdale 84 4 36N33'04 76w57'36 5:07:50
Riverdale 101 6 36N48'50 76w15'07 5:05:00
Riverdale 112 6 37N02'55 76w22'17 5:05:29
Riverdale 128 4 37N15'18 79w54'51 5:19:39
River Forest Shores 121 6 36N50'04 76w12'09 5:04:49
Riverhead 8 21 38N01 79w09 5:16:36
Riverhill 18 4 36N45'24 80w56'03 5:23:44
River Jack 89 4 37N07'48 81w33'03 5:26:12
Rivermont 8 21 38N00'31 79w01'39 5:16:07
Rivermont 21 22 37N19'06 77w18'44 5:09:15
Rivermont 104 4 37N48'27 79w59'19 5:19:57
Rivermont 116 14 37N25'43 79w09'15 5:16:37
River Oaks 29 1 38N57'27 77w11'00 5:08:44
River Oaks 121 6 36N52'08 76w13'08 5:04:53
River Park 125 6 36N50'39 76w20'45 5:05:23
River Road Hills 43 22 37N34'33 77w33'13 5:10:13
Riverside 38 4 36N40'23 81w01'14 5:24:05
Riverside 77 4 37N14'46 80w10'31 5:20:42
Riverside 78 14 37N47'22 79w20'26 5:17:22
Riverside 83 15 36N55'25 81w37'33 5:26:30
Riverside 90 14 38N54'05 78w12'50 5:12:51
Riverside 120 4 37N02'52 76w29'53 5:06:00
Riverside Estates 29 3 38N43'49 77w05'14 5:08:21
Riverside Gardens 29 1 38N43'33 77w03'52 5:08:15
Riverside Park Homes 101 6 36N49 76w14 5:04:56
Rivers Mill 84 4 36N45'04 77w18'41 5:09:15
River Terrace 112 6 37N03'44 76w20'42 5:05:23
Riverton 90 14 38N56'47 78w11'59 5:12:48
Riverton Junction 90 14 38N56'30 78w11'22 5:12:45
Riverview 93 15 36N56'07 82w28'55 5:29:56
Riverview 121 6 36N52'57 76w16'44 5:05:07
Riverview Marina Apartments 73 13 38N39 77w16 5:09:04
Riverville 5 16 37N31'30 78w53'49 5:15:35
Riverwood 7 1 38N54'19 77w06'10 5:08:25
Rives 72 22 37N11 77w21 5:09:24
Rixey 17 22 38N04'44 77w22'57 5:09:32
Rixeyville 24 4 38N34'47 77w58'45 5:11:55
Rixlew 73 2 38N45'39 77w30'22 5:10:01
Roaches Corner 19 14 37N23'27 77w03'11 5:08:13
Roane 48 4 37N26'53 76w42'20 5:06:49
Roanes 36 4 37N22'09 76w30'24 5:06:02
Roanoke 128 4 37N16'15 79w56'30 5:19:46
Roaring Fork 93 26 36N58'09 82w44'04 5:30:56
Roaring Park 93 26 36N58 82w47 5:31:08
Roaring Run 12 4 37N32 79w41 5:18:44
Robbin Dale Farms 43 22 37N33 77w22 5:09:28
Robbins Chapel 52 26 36N52 82w54 5:31:36
Robbins Corner 133 6 36N53'41 76w08'38 5:04:35
Roberson 93 15 37N06 82w36 5:30:24
Roberts 47 14 37N13 76w38 5:06:32
Roberts Mill 83 15 36N46'27 81w26'20 5:25:45
Robertson 56 4 38N27 78w14 5:12:56
Robertsons 10 4 37N20 79w31 5:18:04
Robeys Mill 29 3 38N48'53 77w21'59 5:09:28
Robinhood Forest 133 6 36N51'53 76w03'49 5:04:15
Robin Park 43 22 37N32 77w19 5:09:16
Robinson 74 4 37N03 80w50 5:23:20
Robinwood 43 17 37N30'45 77w21'19 5:09:25
Robious 21 22 37N31'19 77w36'45 5:10:27
Robley 76 4 37N50'48 76w34'50 5:06:19
Robnel 117 2 38N47 77w28 5:09:52
Rochambeau Village 95 4 37N12'49 76w34'40 5:06:19
Rochelle 56 4 38N17'25 78w16'22 5:13:05
Rockaway 32 4 37N51'05 78w15'51 5:13:03
Rockbridge Baths 78 14 37N54 79w24 5:17:36
Rock Castle 37 4 37N41 77w53 5:11:32
Rockdell 80 15 36N53'26 81w57'14 5:27:49
Rock Enon Springs 34 4 39N12'43 78w23'12 5:13:33
Rockfish 61 14 37N48'04 78w45'21 5:15:01
Rock Hill 53 4 39N03'57 77w49'43 5:11:19
Rock Hill 86 4 38N27 77w28 5:09:52
Rockhouse 89 4 37N02'18 81w41'01 5:26:44
Rockland 90 14 38N59'22 78w08'29 5:12:34
Rockland Village 29 3 38N54 77w26 5:09:44
Rock Lick 14 15 37N20 82w10 5:28:40
Rock Mills 75 14 38N39'18 78w07'47 5:12:31
Rock Springs 21 22 37N27 77w28 5:09:52
Rock Springs 29 1 38N51 77w09 5:08:36
Rocktown 91 25 36N42'44 82w08'25 5:28:34
Rockville 41 22 37N43'33 77w40'43 5:10:43
Rocky Bar 79 14 38N20'37 78w42'07 5:14:48
Rocky Gap 11 4 37N14'32 81w06'27 5:24:26
Rocky Mount 33 4 36N59'51 79w53'32 5:19:34
Rocky Point 12 4 37N34'46 79w36'43 5:18:27
Rocky Run 27 22 37N04'32 77w41'05 5:10:44
Rocky Station 52 26 36N46 83w01 5:32:04
Roda 93 26 36N58'04 82w49'59 5:31:20
Rodden 41 4 36N49'55 79w04'42 5:16:19
Rodophil 4 4 37N22'07 78w09'31 5:12:38
Roebuck 91 15 36N46'26 82w06'48 5:28:27
Roetown 91 15 36N38'35 81w49'39 5:27:19
Rogers 60 4 37N05'30 80w23'25 5:21:34
Rogers Corner 58 4 36N43'12 78w25'05 5:13:40
Rohoic 27 22 37N12 77w27 5:09:48
Roland Park 121 6 36N53'47 76w15'47 5:05:03
Rolands Mill 19 14 37N19'47 77w10'54 5:08:44
Rolling Brook 73 13 38N39 77w16 5:09:04
Rolling Hill 20 4 37N11 78w49 5:15:16
Rolling Hills 29 3 38N45 77w08 5:08:32
Rolling Valley 29 3 38N45 77w12 5:08:48
Rollins Fork 49 22 38N11'05 77w03'45 5:08:15
Roman 8 21 38N16'57 79w00'55 5:16:04
Romancoke 50 14 37N34'24 76w51'03 5:07:24
Rondo 69 4 36N49'42 79w31'55 5:18:08
Ronk 35 4 37N24'21 80w38'25 5:22:34
Roosevelt Gardens 121 6 36N55'19 76w12'47 5:04:51
Roosevelt Park 43 17 37N33 77w24 5:09:36
Rosa 41 4 36N51'09 79w00'06 5:16:00
Roseann 14 15 37N21'21 82w03'04 5:28:12
Rose Bower 6 4 37N21 78w50 5:15:20
Rosedale 80 15 36N57'33 81w55'53 5:27:44
Rose Hill 29 3 38N47 77w07 5:08:28
Rose Hill 52 26 36N40'18 83w22'03 5:33:28
Rose Hill 75 14 38N42'59 78w07'32 5:12:30
Rose Hill Farms 29 1 38N46'39 77w06'48 5:08:27
Roseland 61 14 37N44'51 78w58'34 5:15:54
Rosemont 29 1 38N55'25 77w10'55 5:08:44
Rosemont 121 6 36N54'04 76w13'58 5:04:56
Roses Mill 61 14 37N42'05 78w59'48 5:15:59
Rosespout 50 14 37N45'20 77w05'27 5:08:22
Roseville 86 4 38N27'54 77w30'15 5:10:01
Roslyn Hills 43 22 37N34'34 77w33'58 5:10:16
Rosney 15 4 37N30'33 78w25'32 5:13:42
Rosslyn 7 1 38N53'48 77w04'22 5:08:17
Roth 14 15 37N14'41 81w58'23 5:27:54
Rough Creek 20 4 37N07'12 78w45'30 5:15:02
Round Bottom 11 4 37N15'16 81w03'21 5:24:13
Round Hill 34 9 39N11'31 78w13'56 5:12:56
Round Hill 53 14 39N07'57 77w46'08 5:11:05
Round Hill 75 14 38N33'35 78w09'30 5:12:38
Roundstone 93 26 36N53'24 82w42'45 5:30:51
Round Top 93 15 37N01 82w35 5:30:20
Roundtree 29 3 38N52 77w13 5:08:52
Rourkes Gap 89 4 37N07'40 81w37'24 5:26:30
Rowanta 27 22 37N02 77w24 5:09:36
Rowanty 27 22 37N05 77w33 5:10:12
Rowe 14 15 37N08'10 82w01'58 5:28:08
Rowe Crossroads 94 4 36N50'57 81w09'36 5:24:38
Rowes Landing 64 4 37N56'10 76w28'57 5:05:56
Roxbury 19 14 37N27'53 77w08'28 5:08:34
Royal City 14 15 37N15'35 82w06'03 5:28:24
Royal Court 29 1 38N50 77w12 5:08:48
Royal Oak 83 15 36N49 81w31 5:26:04
Ruark 59 4 37N32'39 76w20'32 5:05:22

Rubermont 55 4 37N03'45 78W12'23 5:12:50
Ruby 86 4 38N30'15 77W30'57 5:10:04
Ruckersville 39 14 38N13'59 78W22'10 5:13:29
Rudee Heights 133 6 36N49'37 75W58'37 5:03:54
Rue 1 4 37N47'14 75W36'23 5:02:26
Ruff 57 4 37N24'36 76W18'46 5:05:15
Ruffin 2 14 37N47 78W42 5:14:48
Rugby 2 14 38N00'49 78W19'41 5:13:19
Rugby 38 4 36N36'38 81W27'03 5:25:48
Rumford 50 14 37N43'29 77W05'23 5:08:22
Runnymede 87 4 37N02'04 76W51'06 5:07:24
Rural Retreat 94 4 36N53'37 81W16'34 5:25:06
Rush Corner 91 25 36N41'45 82W11'30 5:28:46
Rushmere 46 4 37N04'00 76W40'36 5:06:42
Rushmere Shores 46 4 37N05'44 76W39'34 5:06:38
Rushville 79 22 38N25'54 78W58'46 5:15:55
Russell 80 15 37N01 81W59 5:27:56
Russell 132 5 36N41'08 76W35'17 5:06:21
Russell Corner 58 4 36N46'40 78W15'01 5:13:00
Russell Creek 93 15 36N58 82W18 5:29:12
Rustburg 16 16 37N16'36 79W06'04 5:16:24
Rust Hollow 91 15 36N41'53 82W03'52 5:28:15
Rustic 19 14 37N17'29 76W56'02 5:07:44
Ruth 56 4 38N23'39 78W18'51 5:13:15
Rutherford 29 3 38N49'44 77W15'38 5:09:03
Ruther Glen 17 22 37N55'43 77W27'22 5:09:49
Ruthland 43 17 37N36 77W29 5:09:56
Ruthville 19 14 37N22'02 77W02'29 5:08:10
Ryan 53 4 39N00'54 77W29'36 5:09:58
Rye Cove 81 26 36N43'31 82W41'47 5:30:47
Ryefield Landing 48 4 37N35'19 76W47'38 5:07:11
Rye Valley 83 15 36N45 81W32 5:26:08
Ryland Corner 17 22 38N02'19 77W31'03 5:10:04
Sabot 37 4 37N36'47 77W44'50 5:10:59
Saddlers Crossroads 84 4 36N54'17 76W56'52 5:07:47
Sadler Heights 132 5 36N45'54 76W35'29 5:06:22
Sago 33 4 36N53'19 79W38'29 5:18:34
Saint Brides 101 4 36N36'23 76W11'52 5:04:47
Saint Charles 52 26 36N48'06 83W03'27 5:32:14
Saint Clair 89 4 37N14'17 81W19'10 5:25:17
Saint Clair Bottom 83 15 36N48 81W41 5:26:44
Saint Davids Church 82 14 38N48 78W27 5:13:48
Saint Elmo 96 1 38N49'52 77W03'22 5:08:13
Saint Josephs Villa 43 22 37N37'53 77W27'42 5:09:51
Saint Joy 15 4 37N32'19 78W38'50 5:14:35
Saint Just 66 14 38N16 77W58 5:11:52
Saint Louis 53 4 39N00'05 77W47'35 5:11:10
Saint Luke 82 14 38N54'12 78W34'51 5:14:19
Saint Paul 93 15 36N54'19 82W18'40 5:29:15
Saint Peters 62 14 37N31 77W04 5:08:16
Saint Stephens 30 19 38N39 77W39 5:10:36
Saint Stephens Church 48 4 37N48 77W03 5:08:12
Salem 24 14 38N31'02 78W04'45 5:12:19
Salem 67 14 38N38'39 78W32'53 5:14:12
Salem 129 4 37N17'36 80W03'18 5:20:13
Salem 133 6 36N47'22 76W07'30 5:04:30
Sales Corner 17 22 38N10'58 77W18'16 5:09:13
Salisbury 12 4 37N36'27 79W46'57 5:19:08
Salisbury 21 22 37N29 77W34 5:10:16
Salona Village 29 1 38N56'21 77W10'08 5:08:41
Salt Creek 5 16 37N30'24 79W13'17 5:16:53
Saltpetre 12 4 37N38 79W48 5:19:12
Saltville 83 15 36N52'53 81W45'44 5:27:03
Saluda 59 4 37N36'21 76W35'43 5:06:23
Saluda Landing 59 4 37N37'20 76W34'54 5:06:20
Salvia 48 4 37N56'57 77W07'59 5:08:32
Sam 89 4 37N14'23 81W20'28 5:25:22
Samos 59 4 37N42'02 76W38'18 5:06:33
Sampson 8 21 38N10'26 78W50'52 5:15:23
Samuel Miller 2 14 37N59 78W43 5:14:52
Samuels Corner 17 22 38N10'20 77W15'28 5:09:02
Sanburne Park 43 22 37N31'15 77W20'15 5:09:21
Sandbridge Beach 133 6 36N44'45 75W56'40 5:03:47
Sandidges 5 16 37N39'50 79W08'24 5:16:34
Sand Lick 26 15 37N09 82W17 5:29:08
Sandston 43 22 37N31'24 77W18'58 5:09:16
Sandybottom 19 14 37N24'47 77W02'41 5:08:11
Sandy Bottom 79 14 38N21'03 78W34'39 5:14:19
Sandy Bottom 132 4 36N52'18 76W32'42 5:06:11
Sandy Fork 58 4 36N36'53 78W36'34 5:14:26
Sandy Hook 37 4 37N45'09 77W54'46 5:11:39
Sandy Landing 132 4 36N34'43 76W54'34 5:07:38
Sandy Level 69 4 36N34 79W44 5:18:56
Sandy Point 64 18 37N49'12 76W18'29 5:05:14
Sandy Point 92 19 38N03'38 76W32'01 5:06:08
Sandy River 69 4 36N43'23 79W39'06 5:18:36
Sanford 1 4 37N55'30 75W39'53 5:02:40
Sangerville 8 21 38N23'19 79W05'01 5:16:20
Sanville 44 4 36N43'11 80W03'34 5:20:14
Sapony 27 22 36N58 77W37 5:10:28
Sarah 57 4 37N23'19 76W16'56 5:05:08
Saratoga 22 4 39N04'59 78W03'35 5:12:14
Saratoga 29 3 38N47 77W12 5:08:48
Saratoga Place 132 5 36N43 76W36 5:06:24
Sardis 5 16 37N37'17 79W06'47 5:16:27
Sassafras 36 4 37N24'24 76W36'25 5:06:26
Saumsville 82 14 38N56'08 78W29'58 5:14:00
Saunders 127 17 37N33 77W27 5:09:48
Saunders 132 5 36N38'24 76W34'33 5:06:18
Savage Crossing 132 5 36N44 76W35 5:06:20
Savage Town 1 4 37N33'07 75W48'06 5:03:12
Savageville 1 4 37N40'51 75W45'26 5:03:02
Savedge 87 4 37N08'01 77W01'10 5:08:05
Sawmill Corner 47 23 37N14'24 76W36'02 5:06:24
Saxe 20 4 36N55'47 78W39'49 5:14:39
Saxis 1 4 37N55'26 75W43'20 5:02:53
Sayersville 89 4 37N10'58 81W37'05 5:26:28
Scaggs Ford 31 4 37N00'16 80W27'41 5:21:51
Scarboroughs Neck 1 4 37N32 75W52 5:03:28
Scenic Park 91 25 36N36 82W11 5:28:44
Schenck Estates 95 23 37N19'54 76W42'44 5:06:51
Schley 36 4 37N23'22 76W27'19 5:05:49
Schneider Crossroads 29 4 38N52'53 77W29'09 5:09:57
Scholfield 71 4 37N06'10 78W19'30 5:13:18
Schoolfield 105 4 36N33'49 79W25'39 5:17:43
Schuyler 61 14 37N47'32 78W41'55 5:14:48
Scotchtown 42 22 37N50'39 77W35'13 5:10:21
Scotland 87 14 37N11'01 76W47'12 5:07:09
Scotland Landing 50 14 37N41'19 76W58'03 5:07:52
Scott 30 19 38N55 77W48 5:11:12
Scott Addition 91 15 36N43'13 81W56'30 5:27:46
Scott Ford 91 15 36N46'05 82W06'42 5:28:27
Scottie Farms 43 22 37N32 77W19 5:09:16
Scottsburg 41 4 36N45'26 78W47'24 5:15:10
Scotts Corner 76 4 37N53'00 76W36'24 5:06:26
Scotts Crossroad 58 4 36N48'56 78W24'16 5:13:37
Scotts Fork 4 4 37N19'05 77W53'26 5:11:34
Scottsville 2 14 37N47'55 78W29'45 5:13:59
Scottswood 84 4 36N42'16 76W58'58 5:07:56
Scrabble 75 14 38N34'55 78W09'35 5:12:38
Screamersville 21 22 37N19'46 77W19'53 5:09:20
Scruggs 33 4 37N04'47 79W39'43 5:18:39
Scuffleburg 30 19 38N56'31 77W57'15 5:11:49
Scuffletown 66 14 38N15'31 78W17'55 5:13:12
Seaboard 89 4 37N08'25 81W46'57 5:27:08
Seacock Corner 84 4 36N51'27 76W55'32 5:07:42
Seaford 95 4 37N11'53 76W26'00 5:05:44
Seaford Shores 95 4 37N11'33 76W25'19 5:05:41
Sealston 49 22 38N15'41 77W19'56 5:09:20
Sea Pines 133 6 36N52 76W00 5:04:00
Seatack 133 6 36N50'29 75W59'48 5:03:59
Seaview 63 4 37N15'42 75W56'46 5:03:47
Seawright Spring 8 21 38N15 78W58 5:15:52
Sebrell 84 4 36N47'01 77W07'40 5:08:31
Sedalia 10 4 37N29'15 79W26'26 5:17:46
Seddon 11 4 37N07 81W07 5:24:28
Sedgefield 120 6 37N02'38 76W27'35 5:05:50
Sedgefield Manor 43 17 37N36 77W29 5:09:56
Sedley 84 4 36N46'33 76W59'04 5:07:56
Selden 36 4 37N21'22 76W28'10 5:05:53
Selma 3 4 37N48'23 79W50'54 5:19:24
Selma 131 21 38N09'44 79W04'31 5:16:18
Selton 26 15 36N59 82W17 5:29:08
Seminary 52 26 36N48'38 82W50'01 5:31:20
Seminary Valley 96 1 38N49'06 77W07'04 5:08:28
Seneca 16 16 37N05'35 79W07'35 5:16:30
Seng Camp 14 15 37N11 81W48 5:27:12
Senora 51 4 37N40'35 76W31'17 5:06:05
Septa 46 4 37N00'30 76W41'55 5:06:48
Seven Corners 7 1 38N52'19 77W09'20 5:08:37
Seven Fountains 82 14 38N51'40 78W23'59 5:13:36
Seven Mile Ford 83 15 36N48'37 81W37'47 5:26:31
Seven Pines 43 22 37N31'13 77W18'11 5:09:13
Seven Pines Villa 43 22 37N33 77W22 5:09:28
Severn 36 4 37N17'39 76W24'57 5:05:40
Severn Manor 36 4 37N18'25 76W28'16 5:05:53
Sewells Gardens 121 6 36N53'47 76W14'44 5:04:59
Shacklefords 48 4 37N33'05 76W43'57 5:06:56
Shacklefords Fork 48 4 37N32'38 76W42'14 5:06:49
Shad Landing 1 4 37N56'22 75W40'17 5:02:41
Shadow 57 4 37N20'57 76W17'49 5:05:11
Shadowlawn Heights 133 6 36N52 76W00 5:04:00
Shadow Valley 91 25 36N36 82W11 5:28:44
Shadwell 2 14 38N00'46 78W23'45 5:13:35
Shady Grove 10 4 37N19'11 79W43'17 5:18:53
Shady Grove 39 14 38N15'37 78W35'34 5:14:22
Shady Grove 41 4 36N35'52 78W50'39 5:15:23
Shady Grove 91 15 36N43'25 81W58'11 5:27:53
Shady Grove Corner 85 22 38N13'18 77W42'41 5:10:51
Shady Lane 61 14 37N42'52 79W01'22 5:16:05
Shady Oak 29 3 39N00 77W15 5:09:00
Shadyside 63 4 37N23'52 75W54'45 5:03:39
Shakerag 9 4 38N03'20 79W48'00 5:19:12
Shakesville 91 25 36N36'34 82W08'21 5:28:33
Shaklefords Fork 48 4 37N33 76W44 5:06:56
Shanghai 48 4 37N36'29 76W46'44 5:07:07
Shannandale 89 4 37N12'52 81W21'44 5:25:27
Shannon Hill 37 4 37N52'54 78W02'19 5:12:09
Shannon Hills 44 4 36N33 79W51 5:19:24
Sharon 11 4 37N02 81W19 5:25:16
Sharon 69 4 36N39'30 79W31'50 5:18:07
Sharon Springs 11 4 37N02'58 81W17'11 5:25:09
Sharps 76 4 37N49'26 76W42'04 5:06:48
Shavertown 82 14 38N39'49 78W37'35 5:14:30
Shawnee 34 9 39N09 78W09 5:12:36
Shawnee Land 34 9 39N11'29 78W20'45 5:13:23
Shawsville 60 4 37N10'06 80W15'20 5:21:01
Shawver Mill 89 4 37N09'12 81W21'14 5:25:25
Shea Terrace 125 6 36N50'31 76W19'31 5:05:18
Sheep Point 92 19 38N12'18 76W58'13 5:07:53
Sheep Town 18 4 36N49'26 80W54'53 5:23:40
Sheffield Court 21 22 37N31'52 77W33'55 5:10:16
Shelby 56 4 38N19'16 78W18'30 5:13:14
Shelfar 54 14 37N48'38 77W52'04 5:11:28
Shelleys 81 25 36N38'13 82W20'18 5:29:21
Shelors Mill 31 4 36N52'32 80W22'25 5:21:30
Shelton 133 6 36N53 76W08 5:04:32
Shenandoah 67 14 38N29'06 78W37'31 5:14:30
Shenandoah 114 14 37N17 77W18 5:09:12
Shenandoah Caverns 82 14 38N41 78W41 5:14:44
Shenandoah Farms 90 14 38N58'54 78W04'33 5:12:18
Shenandoah Hills 34 9 39N11'05 78W07'07 5:12:28
Shenandoah Iron Works 67 14 38N32 78W35 5:14:20
Shenandoah Place 43 22 37N35 77W31 5:10:04
Shenandoah Shores 90 14 38N57'37 78W08'36 5:12:34
Shepherd Hill 52 26 36N50'35 82W56'40 5:31:47
Shepherds Store 32 4 37N47 78W10 5:12:40
Sheppards 15 4 37N23'26 78W29'08 5:13:57
Sheppards Mill 68 4 36N32'39 80W05'49 5:20:23
Sheps End 63 4 37N26'05 75W52'07 5:03:28
Sherando 8 21 37N58'52 78W57'15 5:15:49
Sherry Park 133 6 36N49'14 76W13'04 5:04:52
Sherwill 16 16 37N16'56 78W57'36 5:15:50
Sherwood 29 1 38N53 77W13 5:08:52
Sherwood Farms 2 14 38N00'53 78W32'26 5:14:10
Sherwood Forest 8 21 38N09 79W05 5:16:20
Sherwood Forest 19 14 37N20'02 77W01'13 5:08:05
Sherwood Forest 130 4 36N43 78W54 5:15:36
Sherwood Hall 29 3 38N45 77W06 5:08:24
Sherwood Hills 103 22 37N16'31 77W25'14 5:09:41
Sherwood Park 112 6 37N03'28 76W20'57 5:05:24
Sheva 69 4 36N51'57 79W20'06 5:17:20
Shields 1 4 37N34'12 75W51'14 5:03:25
Shields 71 4 37N16'00 78W38'52 5:14:35
Shifflet Corner 56 4 38N18'31 78W16'24 5:13:06
Shiloh 49 22 38N13'17 77W06'41 5:08:27
Shiloh 74 4 37N01'29 80W42'52 5:22:51
Shiloh 84 4 36N36'34 77W12'00 5:08:48
Shiloh 86 4 38N30'13 77W30'24 5:10:02
Shiloh 94 4 36N48'04 81W05'01 5:24:20
Shilsons Corner 95 4 37N15'06 76W33'22 5:06:13
Shiny Rock 58 4 36N33'11 78W35'51 5:14:23
Shipman 61 14 37N43'25 78W50'22 5:15:21
Ships Corner 133 6 36N47'31 76W04'49 5:04:19
Shipyard Landing 47 14 37N20'30 76W52'20 5:07:29
Shirley 19 14 37N20'30 77W15'39 5:09:03
Shirley Acres 29 3 38N42 77W14 5:08:56
Shirley Duke 96 1 38N48'55 77W06'34 5:08:26
Shirley Gate Park 29 3 38N50'36 77W20'22 5:09:21
Shirley Springs 29 3 38N45 77W12 5:08:48
Shirlington 7 1 38N50'30 77W05'19 5:08:21
Shockeysville 34 9 39N23'09 78W14'39 5:12:59
Shockoe 69 4 36N48'31 79W15'51 5:17:03
Shooters Hill 96 1 38N48'38 77W04'16 5:08:17
Shore Park 120 4 37N06'36 76W33'11 5:06:13
Shores 32 4 37N51 78W16 5:13:04
Shorewood 101 6 36N50'00 76W24'38 5:05:39
Short Lane 36 4 37N25 76W32 5:06:08
Short Pump 43 22 37N39'01 77W36'46 5:10:27
Shorts Creek 18 4 36N50'19 80W50'46 5:23:23
Shorts Store 92 19 38N04 76W39 5:06:36
Shortsville 91 15 36N46'20 81W54'28 5:27:38
Shortt Gap 14 15 37N09'26 81W52'23 5:27:30
Shoulders Hill 132 6 36N49'09 76W28'09 5:05:53
Shreveport Park 43 22 37N32 77W19 5:09:16
Shrevewood 29 3 38N54 77W13 5:08:52
Shumansville 17 22 37N56'56 77W16'46 5:09:07
Shumate 35 4 37N18'53 80W50'54 5:23:24
Shupe 94 4 36N59'00 81W09'42 5:24:39
Siddon 58 4 36N34'17 78W40'48 5:14:43
Sideburn 29 3 38N48'00 77W18'33 5:09:14
Side Landing 76 4 37N59'22 76W49'09 5:07:17
Sigma 52 26 36N49'48 82W56'12 5:31:45
Sigma 133 6 36N43'54 75W59'11 5:03:57
Signboard 17 22 37N53'58 77W24'46 5:09:39
Signpine 36 4 37N26'37 76W38'43 5:06:35
Sign Post 1 4 37N59'47 75W27'40 5:01:51
Sign Rock 41 4 36N49'43 79W06'40 5:16:27
Silcott Spring 53 14 39N06'06 77W44'32 5:10:58
Siler 34 9 39N21'02 78W14'21 5:12:57
Silica 81 15 36N41'25 82W20'56 5:29:24

Siloam 94 4 36N54'38 80W57'59 5:23:52
Silva 1 4 37N59 75W32 5:02:08
Silver Beach 63 4 37N29'07 75W57'39 5:03:51
Silver Hill 30 19 38N28'58 77W41'47 5:10:47
Silver Springs 29 3 38N47'02 77W07'46 5:08:31
Silverwood 101 6 36N51'18 76W24'00 5:05:36
Simeon 2 14 37N59'29 78W26'40 5:13:47
Simmerman 94 4 36N48'59 81W08'26 5:24:34
Simmonsville 23 4 37N23'03 80W21'43 5:21:27
Simons Corner 76 4 37N51'07 76W41'12 5:06:45
Simonsdale 125 6 36N49'25 76W22'41 5:05:31
Simonson 76 4 37N48'24 76W38'02 5:06:32
Simpkins 63 4 37N19'27 75W56'38 5:03:47
Simpkins Corner 42 22 37N35'25 77W19'03 5:09:16
Simpkinstown 74 4 37N00'46 80W34'14 5:22:17
Simplicity 55 4 37N04'47 78W25'28 5:13:42
Simpsons 31 4 37N02'16 80W12'17 5:20:49
Sinai 41 4 36N44'20 78W56'13 5:15:45
Sinclair Farms 112 6 37N03'11 76W21'09 5:05:25
Singer 77 4 37N17 80W03 5:20:12
Singerly 76 4 38N04'49 76W53'48 5:07:35
Singers Glen 79 22 38N33'09 78W54'49 5:15:39
Sinking Creek 23 4 37N25'08 80W15'55 5:21:04
Sinnickson 1 4 37N59'10 75W25'47 5:01:43
Sirons Mill 45 4 38N23'51 79W28'24 5:17:54
Sissons Corner 64 18 37N56'14 76W26'45 5:05:47
Six Mile 16 14 37N23'35 79W03'37 5:16:14
Skeetertown 132 5 36N39'37 76W34'48 5:06:19
Skeetrock 26 15 37N13'19 82W24'50 5:29:39
Skeggs 14 15 37N10'02 82W00'53 5:28:04
Skidmore Corner 86 4 38N28'05 77W31'18 5:10:05
Skimino 95 23 37N20'49 76W42'18 5:06:49
Skimino Farms 95 23 37N21'20 76W41'22 5:06:45
Skinkers Corner 17 22 38N12'23 77W17'03 5:09:08
Skinquarter 21 14 37N23'49 77W46'54 5:11:08
Skippers 40 20 36N36'42 77W32'49 5:10:11
Skipwith 58 4 36N41'39 78W29'28 5:13:58
Skipwith Farms 43 22 37N36 77W32 5:10:08
Skipwith Farms 135 23 37N17'54 76W43'53 5:06:56
Skipworth Farms 135 23 37N17 76W43 5:06:52
Skyland 67 14 38N35'37 78W22'56 5:13:32
Skyland Estates 90 14 38N55'23 78W04'57 5:12:20
Skymont 131 21 38N10'11 79W04'31 5:16:18
Sky View Park 29 3 38N45 77W08 5:08:32
Slabtown 51 4 37N40'33 76W29'49 5:05:59
Slabtown 80 15 36N54'19 82W05'24 5:28:22
Slabtown 81 26 36N39'00 82W33'02 5:30:12
Slabtown 83 4 36N45'28 81W28'14 5:25:53
Slash 64 19 37N58'31 76W37'43 5:06:31
Slate 14 15 37N18'20 81W56'57 5:27:48
Slate Hill 15 4 37N37'55 78W23'14 5:13:33
Slate Mills 75 14 38N31'53 78W10'59 5:12:44
Slate River 15 4 37N41 78W30 5:14:00
Slaterville 62 14 37N29'56 76W56'33 5:07:46
Slates Corner 40 20 36N41 77W32 5:10:08
Sleep Hollow Manor 29 1 38N51'57 77W09'21 5:08:37
Sleepy Hole 132 4 36N48 76W31 5:06:04
Sleepy Hollow 29 3 38N52'02 77W09'54 5:08:40
Sleepy Hollow Estates 29 1 38N51'12 77W09'57 5:08:40
Sleepy Hollow Estates 43 22 37N36 77W32 5:10:08
Sleepy Hollow Manor 29 1 38N52 77W12 5:08:48
Sleepy Hollow Run 29 1 38N50 77W12 5:08:48
Sleepy Hollow Woods 29 1 38N50'27 77W10'50 5:08:43
Sliders 15 4 37N27'25 78W41'06 5:14:44
Sloantown 81 26 36N38'47 82W47'08 5:31:09
Smedley 75 14 38N41'54 78W13'01 5:12:52
Smiley 52 26 36N41'33 83W17'15 5:33:09
Smith Beach 63 4 37N21'46 75W59'28 5:03:58
Smithfield 46 4 36N58'56 76W37'53 5:06:32
Smithfield 80 15 36N56'11 81W58'00 5:27:52
Smith Hill 92 19 38N10'25 77W01'00 5:08:04
Smith Lake Terrace 133 6 36N52'55 76W08'18 5:04:33
Smith Landing 92 19 38N10'04 76W55'30 5:07:42
Smith Mount Landing 92 19 38N05'10 76W57'24 5:07:50
Smith River 68 4 36N46 80W13 5:20:52
Smiths Crossroads 58 4 36N39'35 78W11'06 5:12:44
Smiths Crossroads 70 14 37N33'58 78W00'44 5:12:03
Smiths Mill 85 22 38N10'19 77W31'09 5:10:05
Smithville 1 4 37N40'01 75W50'38 5:03:23
Smoky 13 4 36N46 77W51 5:11:24
Smoots 17 22 38N01'00 77W16'43 5:09:07
Smoots Landing 76 4 38N02'12 76W54'34 5:07:38
Smothers 69 4 36N54'16 79W22'57 5:17:32
Snake Creek 18 4 36N46 80W44 5:22:56
Snapp 91 15 36N48 81W46 5:27:04
Sneads Corner 55 4 36N54'26 78W08'59 5:12:36
Sneads Spring 65 4 37N06'30 78W06'34 5:12:26
Snell 85 22 38N08'52 77W36'06 5:10:24
Snodgrass Ford 52 26 36N37'12 83W15'05 5:33:00
Snowden 5 16 37N36'06 79W23'48 5:17:35
Snowden 29 1 38N43'49 77W03'06 5:08:12
Snowflake 81 26 36N41'23 82W29'24 5:29:58
Snow Hill 48 4 37N32'23 76W45'01 5:07:00
Snowville 74 4 37N01'57 80W33'41 5:22:15
Snyder 8 21 38N08'35 79W08'30 5:16:34
Soapstone 69 4 36N40'21 79W38'44 5:18:35
Soles 57 4 37N29'34 76W26'14 5:05:45
Solitude 12 4 37N33'49 79W36'24 5:18:26
Solomons Store 43 22 37N38'22 77W27'35 5:09:50
Solsburg 79 14 38N24'11 78W39'12 5:14:37
Somers 51 4 37N47'17 76W34'00 5:06:16
Somerset 66 14 38N12'27 78W13'06 5:12:52
Somerset Beach 49 22 38N20'28 77W11'00 5:08:44
Somerton 132 4 36N34'05 76W45'06 5:07:00
Somerville 30 19 38N31'18 77W36'35 5:10:26
Sonans 69 4 36N53'09 79W19'03 5:17:16
Sorocco 132 5 36N44 76W35 5:06:20
Sorrell 17 22 37N57'15 77W11'46 5:08:47
Soudan 58 4 36N33'46 78W31'15 5:14:05
South 7 1 38N52 77W06 5:08:24
Southampton 112 6 37N02 76W21 5:05:24
South Anna 42 22 37N48'12 77W25'21 5:09:41
South Anna 54 14 37N51'32 77W54'20 5:11:37
South Boston 130 4 36N41'55 78W54'06 5:15:36
South Chesconessex 1 4 37N44'35 75W46'44 5:03:07
South Clinchfield 80 15 36N57'45 82W10'34 5:28:42
Southeast 33 4 36N55 79W45 5:19:00
Southern Pine 27 22 37N13 77W26 5:09:44
Southern Points 133 6 36N51'43 76W03'20 5:04:13
South Fairlington 7 1 38N49'57 77W05'24 5:08:22
South Fairview 101 6 36N49'30 76W14'40 5:04:59
South Gap 11 4 37N13'00 81W05'18 5:24:21
South Garden 2 14 37N57 78W38 5:14:32
South Grundy 14 15 37N16 82W05 5:28:20
South Hill 58 4 36N43'35 78W07'45 5:12:31
South Hill 101 6 36N50 76W16 5:05:04
South Jackson 82 14 38N44'17 78W38'34 5:14:34
Southland Acres 116 14 37N21'14 79W11'19 5:16:45
South Martinsville 119 4 36N40 79W52 5:19:28
South Norfolk 101 6 36N50 76W16 5:05:04
Southport 73 13 38N39 77W16 5:09:04
South Quay 132 4 36N37'20 76W53'20 5:07:33
Southridge 29 1 38N55'07 77W11'01 5:08:44
South River 78 14 37N46'28 79W23'18 5:17:33
South Roanoke 128 4 37N14 79W57 5:19:48
South Salem 129 4 37N17 80W03 5:20:12
Southside 6 4 37N18 78W51 5:15:24
Southside 127 17 37N29 77W29 5:09:56
South Suffolk 132 5 36N44 76W35 5:06:20
Southwest 33 4 36N56 80W01 5:20:04
South Woodley 29 3 38N52 77W13 5:08:52
Sowego 30 19 38N35'56 77W34'36 5:10:18
Sowers 31 4 37N00'12 80W22'46 5:21:31
Spainville 65 4 37N11'19 77W54'59 5:11:40
Spanish Grove 58 4 36N47'44 78W32'08 5:14:09
Sparkling Springs 79 22 38N33'05 78W57'07 5:15:48
Sparta 17 22 37N59'30 77W13'50 5:08:55
Spec 12 4 37N27'16 79W46'18 5:19:05
Speedwell 94 4 36N48'49 81W10'19 5:24:41
Spencer 44 4 36N37'11 80W00'27 5:20:02
Sperryville 75 14 38N39'25 78W13'35 5:12:54
Spillmans Landing 86 4 38N20'42 77W21'05 5:09:24
Spitler 67 14 38N40 78W27 5:13:48
Spivey Ford 81 26 36N39'34 82W42'12 5:30:49
Spivey Mill 81 26 36N39'46 82W39'24 5:30:38
Spivey Store 81 26 36N38 82W34 5:30:16
Splashdam 26 15 37N12 82W18 5:29:12
Spotswood 66 14 38N14 78W07 5:12:28
Spotsylvania 85 22 38N12'03 77W35'22 5:10:21
Spottswood 8 21 37N57'18 79W12'50 5:16:51
Spout Spring 6 4 37N20'59 78W54'34 5:15:38
Spratleys Mill 87 4 37N04'38 76W55'30 5:07:42
Spring Bank 29 1 38N46'55 77W04'33 5:08:18
Springbrook Forest 29 3 38N51 77W15 5:09:00
Spring City 80 15 36N55'06 82W06'28 5:28:26
Spring Creek 79 22 38N24'03 79W02'04 5:16:08
Springdale 35 4 37N12'58 80W42'42 5:22:51
Springdale 43 17 37N35'06 77W23'49 5:09:35
Springdale 91 25 36N36 82W11 5:28:44
Springfield 29 3 38N47'21 77W11'15 5:08:45
Springfield 67 14 38N42'16 78W26'47 5:13:47
Springfield 78 14 37N37'38 79W35'15 5:18:21
Springfield Estates 29 3 38N47'00 77W10'30 5:08:42
Springfield Forest 29 3 38N46'25 77W09'51 5:08:39
Springfield Woods 29 3 38N45 77W12 5:08:48
Spring Garden 69 4 36N46'49 79W18'18 5:17:13
Spring Garden 98 25 36N36'38 82W10'58 5:28:44
Spring Grove 87 4 37N09'56 76W58'25 5:07:54
Springhaven Estates 29 1 38N55 77W11 5:08:44
Spring Hill 8 21 38N15'22 79W03'10 5:16:13
Spring Hill 29 1 38N55 77W11 5:08:44
Spring Meadows 42 22 37N36'51 77W20'58 5:09:24
Spring Mills 16 4 37N14'42 78W55'10 5:15:41
Springvale 29 3 38N46'26 77W11'41 5:08:47
Spring Valley 38 4 36N44'17 81W03'58 5:24:16
Spring Valley 86 24 38N19'52 77W27'39 5:09:51
Springville 89 4 37N11'47 81W24'11 5:25:37
Springwood 12 4 37N32'56 79W44'42 5:18:59
Sprouses Corner 15 4 37N31'45 78W29'32 5:13:58
Stacher Ford 91 26 36N41'36 82W17'47 5:29:11
Stacy 14 15 37N19'15 81W59'47 5:27:59
Stafford 86 4 38N25'19 77W24'31 5:09:38
Staffordshire 21 22 37N32'06 77W35'09 5:10:21
Staffordsville 35 4 37N14'29 80W43'01 5:22:52
Stage Bridge 61 14 37N43 78W51 5:15:24
Stage Junction 32 4 37N47'27 78W09'13 5:12:37
Staley Crossroads 94 4 36N54'35 81W16'25 5:25:06
Stampers 59 4 37N32'23 76W25'58 5:05:44
Stanards Mill 85 22 38N08'52 77W30'57 5:10:04
Stanardsville 39 14 38N17'50 78W26'25 5:13:46
Stanley 67 14 38N34'31 78W30'10 5:14:01
Stanleytown 44 4 36N44'39 79W57'47 5:19:51
Stanleytown 81 26 36N46'15 82W41'22 5:30:45
Staples Mill 43 17 37N36 77W29 5:09:56
Stapleton 5 14 37N28'08 78W58'44 5:15:55
Star Fort 34 9 39N12'22 78W09'52 5:12:39
Starkey 129 4 37N12'02 79W59'56 5:20:00
Starlings Crossroads 44 4 36N33'28 79W43'37 5:18:54
Starnes 81 26 36N44'05 82W37'25 5:30:30
Star Tannery 34 4 39N05 78W26 5:13:44
Statesville 84 4 36N32'45 77W04'19 5:08:17
Station Hills 29 3 38N48'02 77W20'39 5:09:23
Staunton 131 21 38N08'58 79W04'19 5:16:17
Staunton Park 131 21 38N09'50 79W05'34 5:16:22
Staunton River 69 4 37N02 79W16 5:17:04
Stave Landing 92 19 38N14'42 76W58'59 5:07:56
Stearnes 32 4 37N42'01 78W14'21 5:12:57
Steeleburg 89 4 37N05 81W46 5:27:04
Steeles Tavern 8 21 37N55'32 79W12'10 5:16:49
Steelmans Landing 63 4 37N10'55 75W56'26 5:03:46
Steinman 26 15 37N10'43 82W20'30 5:29:22
Stella 68 4 36N37'50 80W05'06 5:20:20
Stemphleytown 79 22 38N24'39 78W57'34 5:15:50
Stephens 93 15 36N59'31 82W36'09 5:30:25
Stephens City 34 4 39N05'00 78W13'06 5:12:52
Stephens Fort 34 4 39N04'41 78W19'33 5:13:18
Stephenson 34 4 39N14 78W07 5:12:28
Sterling 53 4 39N00'22 77W25'44 5:09:43
Sterling Park 53 4 39N00'13 77W24'03 5:09:36
Sterling Point 125 6 36N50'32 76W22'58 5:05:32
Stevensburg 24 4 38N26'35 77W54'00 5:11:36
Stevens Creek 38 4 36N43'43 80W59'57 5:24:00
Stevensville 48 4 37N43'40 76W55'12 5:07:41
Stewardsburg 78 14 37N45'04 79W22'27 5:17:30
Stewart 127 17 37N34 77W29 5:09:56
Stewartsburg 78 14 37N44 79W21 5:17:24
Stewarts Landing 63 4 37N30'31 75W54'16 5:03:37
Stewartsville 10 4 37N16'14 79W47'34 5:19:10
Stickleys 29 1 38N47 77W07 5:08:28
Stickleyville 52 26 36N42'25 82W54'26 5:31:38
Stingray Point 59 4 37N33'31 76W18'20 5:05:13
Stith 41 4 36N50 78W44 5:14:56
Stockton 44 4 36N40 79W43 5:18:52
Stoddert 15 4 37N21'01 78W17'43 5:13:11
Stoke 53 14 38N58'31 77W40'00 5:10:40
Stokesland 69 4 36N32'58 79W27'39 5:17:51
Stokesville 8 21 38N21'09 79W08'57 5:16:36
Stone Bridge 22 4 39N03 78W06 5:12:24
Stone Bruise 80 15 36N52'52 82W04'27 5:28:18
Stone Creek 52 26 36N46'35 83W03'25 5:32:14
Stonega 93 26 36N57'11 82W47'29 5:31:10
Stonehouse 47 14 37N24 76W48 5:07:12
Stone Mill 91 15 36N41'53 81W59'30 5:27:58
Stone Mountain 10 4 37N20 79W31 5:18:04
Stones Corner 86 4 38N19'41 77W23'27 5:09:34
Stones Mill 55 4 36N49'40 78W03'31 5:12:14
Stones Mill 94 4 36N56'07 81W04'24 5:24:18
Stone Springs 113 22 38N27 78W52 5:15:28
Stones Store 44 4 36N44'39 80W04'38 5:20:19
Stonewall 6 4 37N24'37 78W57'38 5:15:51
Stonewall Acres 73 2 38N46'20 77W29'22 5:09:57
Stonewall Manor 29 3 38N53'32 77W14'07 5:08:56
Stonewall Mills 6 4 37N26'53 78W54'58 5:15:40
Stoney Brook Estates 120 4 37N08'55 76W33'20 5:06:13
Stony 81 15 36N50 82W28 5:29:52

Stony Battery 83 15 36N44'41 81w33'55 5:26:16
Stony Creek 88 4 36N56'52 77w24'04 5:09:36
Stony Man 67 14 38N37'50 78w26'05 5:13:44
Stony Mill 69 4 36N38'22 79w32'39 5:18:11
Stony Point 2 14 38N06'46 78w22'18 5:13:29
Stony Point Mills 25 4 37N30 78w15 5:13:00
Stony Ridge 89 4 37N11'18 81w32'02 5:26:08
Storck 86 4 38N25'09 77w36'50 5:10:27
Stormont 59 4 37N35'49 76w34'07 5:06:16
Story 84 4 36N43 77w04 5:08:16
Stott 46 4 36N49 76w45 5:07:00
Stotts Crossroads 46 4 36N55'34 76w46'14 5:07:05
Stovall 41 4 36N59'48 79w02'48 5:16:11
Stover 8 21 38N16'19 79w08'50 5:16:35
Straightstone 69 4 37N00'57 79w08'59 5:16:36
Strangeway Landing 76 14 37N59'26 76w50'45 5:07:23
Strasburg 82 14 38N59'19 78w21'32 5:13:26
Strasburg Junction 82 14 38N59'49 78w22'42 5:13:31
Stratford 29 1 38N45 77w04 5:08:16
Stratford 92 19 38N09 76w51 5:07:24
Stratford Hall 92 19 38N09'05 76w50'05 5:07:20
Stratford Hills 7 3 38N54'31 77w08'27 5:08:34
Stratford Hills 21 17 37N33'06 77w32'11 5:10:09
Stratford Landing 29 1 38N43'18 77w04'28 5:08:18
Stratford Mill 92 19 38N09'44 76w49'54 5:07:20
Stratford On The Potomac 29 3 38N42'50 77w04'02 5:08:16
Stratford Village 43 17 37N34 77w26 5:09:44
Strathmeade Springs 29 1 38N51'13 77w14'01 5:08:56
Strathmore 32 4 37N42 78w18 5:13:12
Strathouse 32 4 37N43'25 78w19'56 5:13:20
Stratton 26 15 37N05'16 82w21'38 5:29:27
Stribling Springs 8 21 38N18'31 79w10'29 5:16:42
Stringtown 22 14 39N11'17 77w58'42 5:11:55
Stringtown 81 26 36N46'24 82w26'42 5:29:47
Stringtown 94 4 36N58'37 81w02'02 5:24:08
Strom 12 4 37N41'30 79w53'25 5:19:34
Stroupes Store 94 4 36N57 81w05 5:24:20
Stuart 68 4 36N38'27 80w15'57 5:21:04
Stuart Corner 17 22 38N08'58 77w19'00 5:09:16
Stuarts Draft 8 21 38N01'48 79w02'02 5:16:08
Stubbs 85 22 38N09'01 77w49'44 5:11:19
Studley 42 22 37N40'32 77w17'28 5:09:10
Stukeley Hall Farms 43 17 37N36 77w27 5:09:48
Stultz Mill 79 22 38N30'50 78w56'55 5:15:48
Stumptown 53 14 39N12'30 77w33'06 5:10:12
Stumptown 63 4 37N20'25 75w56'49 5:03:47
Sturgeon 13 4 36N50 77w45 5:11:00
Sturgeonville 13 4 36N54'02 77w48'38 5:11:15
Subletts 70 4 37N35'08 77w44'58 5:11:00
Suburban Acres 121 6 36N54'23 76w15'52 5:05:03
Suburban Apartments 43 17 37N34 77w29 5:09:56
Success 90 14 38N59'50 78w09'03 5:12:36
Sudley 73 2 38N47 77w28 5:09:52
Sudley Springs 73 14 38N50'28 77w32'17 5:10:09
Suffolk 132 5 36N43'41 76w35'02 5:06:20
Sugar Grove 60 4 37N06'06 80w19'44 5:21:19
Sugar Grove 83 15 36N46'32 81w24'45 5:25:39
Sugar Hill 16 16 37N04'30 78w55'01 5:15:40
Sugarland Run 53 4 39N00 77w24 5:09:36
Sugar Loaf 77 4 37N15 80w01 5:20:04
Suiter 11 4 37N07'11 81w12'49 5:24:51
Sulgrave Manor 29 3 38N43'01 77w06'04 5:08:24
Sully Plantation 29 3 38N54'27 77w25'51 5:09:43
Sulphur Springs 18 4 36N46 80w53 5:23:32
Sulphur Springs 52 26 36N43'32 83w04'51 5:32:19
Sulphur Springs 81 15 36N50 82w28 5:29:52
Sumerduck 30 19 38N27'36 77w43'42 5:10:55
Summerdean 8 21 38N04'30 79w15'23 5:17:02
Summit 85 22 38N23 77w27 5:09:48
Summit 94 15 36N53'32 81w18'03 5:25:12
Sun (Midway) 80 15 36N56'30 82w17'09 5:29:09
Sunbeam 84 4 36N35'15 77w01'41 5:08:07
Sunbright 81 26 36N43'48 82w45'41 5:31:03
Sunlight 85 22 38N12 77w35 5:10:20
Sunnybank 64 18 37N53'10 76w16'03 5:05:04
Sunnybrook Estates 73 2 38N46'19 77w29'32 5:09:58
Sunny Point 80 15 36N49'12 82w22'34 5:29:30
Sunny Ridge 29 3 38N43 77w09 5:08:36
Sunny Side 15 4 37N38'05 78w25'40 5:13:43
Sunnyside 18 4 36N43'48 80w42'30 5:22:50
Sunny Side 25 4 37N28'45 78w09'34 5:12:38
Sunnyside 34 9 39N12'22 78w10'22 5:12:41
Sunnyview 29 3 38N44'01 77w05'16 5:08:21
Sunray 101 6 36N46'50 76w24'41 5:05:39
Sunset Heights 43 17 37N32 77w24 5:09:36
Sunset Hills 29 3 38N57'17 77w21'00 5:09:24
Sunset Manor 29 1 38N50'40 77w07'41 5:08:31
Sunset Village 129 4 37N17'58 80w01'18 5:20:05
Supply 28 4 38N06 77w08 5:08:32
Surber 12 4 37N37'52 79w56'35 5:19:46
Surprise Hill 64 18 37N52'12 76w18'51 5:05:15
Surrey Square 29 3 38N51 77w15 5:09:00
Surry 87 4 37N08'16 76w50'08 5:07:21
Susan 57 4 37N21'57 76w18'50 5:05:15
Sussex 88 4 36N54'54 77w16'46 5:09:07
Sussex 121 6 36N55'01 76w17'11 5:05:09
Sussex At Hampton 112 6 37N00'20 76w21'11 5:05:25
Sutherland 27 22 37N11'45 77w33'36 5:10:14
Sutherland 93 15 36N58'29 82w38'09 5:30:33
Sutherland 94 4 36N57'27 81w09'41 5:24:39
Sutherlin 41 4 36N37'29 79w11'50 5:16:47
Sutton Place 29 3 38N51 77w15 5:09:00
Swannanoa 8 14 38N01'42 78w52'14 5:15:29
Swans Corner 17 22 37N56'48 77w25'59 5:09:44
Swansons Mill 69 4 36N47'27 79w38'54 5:18:36
Swansonville 69 4 36N44'11 79w34'45 5:18:19
Sweet Briar 5 16 37N33'10 79w04'00 5:16:16
Sweet Briar Park 43 22 37N37'13 77w31'55 5:10:08
Sweet Chalybeate 3 4 37N38'41 80w14'17 5:20:57
Sweet Hall 50 14 37N33 76w48 5:07:12
Sweet Hall Landing 50 14 37N34'09 76w54'18 5:07:37
Swift Creek 103 22 37N23 77w28 5:09:52
Swift Run 79 14 38N22'06 78w34'52 5:14:19
Swimley 22 14 39N14'34 78w00'28 5:12:02
Swinks Mill 29 1 38N57'29 77w12'18 5:08:49
Switch Back 9 4 38N00'46 79w50'35 5:19:22
Swoope 8 21 38N09'29 79w12'24 5:16:50
Swords Creek 80 15 37N02'10 81w55'05 5:27:40
Sycamore 69 4 37N01'27 79w21'31 5:17:26
Sycamore Crossroads 46 4 36N59'06 76w50'02 5:07:20
Sycamore Landing 47 23 37N26'26 76w44'44 5:06:59
Sycolin 53 4 39N03'49 77w33'07 5:10:12
Sydnorsville 33 4 36N53'31 79w51'56 5:19:28
Sylvania Heights 85 22 38N16'26 77w26'42 5:09:47
Sylvatus 18 4 36N51'30 80w45'50 5:23:03
Syria 56 4 38N29'16 78w19'35 5:13:18
Syringa 59 4 37N34'44 76w27'25 5:05:50
Tabb 95 4 37N07'23 76w27'28 5:05:50
Taber 16 16 37N04'23 79w12'12 5:16:49
Tabernacle 57 4 37N25'23 76w17'48 5:05:11
Tabors 89 4 37N15'26 81w22'42 5:25:31
Tabscott 37 4 37N51'41 78w03'52 5:12:15
Tacketts Mill 86 4 38N30'22 77w33'51 5:10:15
Tacoma 93 15 36N56'16 82w32'03 5:30:08
Taft 51 14 37N37'58 76w23'30 5:05:34
Taggart 15 4 37N43'22 78w25'18 5:13:41
Talbot Park 121 6 36N54'13 76w16'47 5:05:07
Tallent Town 76 4 38N00'47 76w46'11 5:07:05
Tall Oaks 29 1 38N50 77w12 5:08:48
Tallysville 62 14 37N31'28 77w04'32 5:08:18
Tamworth 25 4 37N38'53 78w04'52 5:12:19
Tandy 26 15 37N12'36 82w23'14 5:29:33
Tangier 50 4 37N49'34 75w59'31 5:03:58
Tanglewood 101 6 36N49'58 76w13'58 5:04:56
Tankards Beach 63 4 37N20'49 76w00'08 5:04:01
Tanners 56 4 38N18'15 78w09'10 5:12:37
Tannersville 89 4 36N58'24 81w37'32 5:26:30
Tanyard Landing 36 4 37N27'17 76w40'02 5:06:40
Tappahannock 28 14 37N55'31 76w51'34 5:07:26
Tapscott 2 14 37N47'14 78w34'38 5:14:19
Tara 7 1 38N53'25 77w08'07 6:08:32
Taro 20 4 37N08'10 78w38'27 5:14:34
Tarpon 26 15 37N11'09 82w21'05 5:29:24
Tarrallton 121 6 36N55'14 76w13'13 5:04:53
Tarters Store 94 4 36N57 81w05 5:24:20
Tasley 1 4 37N42'37 75w42'03 5:02:48
Tasso 93 15 37N01 82w35 5:30:20
Tatum 66 14 38N12'40 77w53'44 5:11:35
Tauxemont 29 1 38N45 77w04 5:08:16
Taylor 33 4 37N05'55 79w54'18 5:19:37
Taylors Corner 17 22 38N07'58 77w17'39 5:09:11
Taylors Corner 72 22 37N13'45 77w02'26 5:08:10
Taylors Store 33 4 37N04 79w53 5:19:32
Taylorstown 53 14 39N15'15 77w34'30 5:10:18
Taylors Valley 91 15 36N37'40 81w42'39 5:26:51
Taylorsville 42 22 37N49'37 77w27'34 5:09:50
Taylorwood Estates 101 6 36N50'10 76w25'30 5:05:42
Tazewell 89 4 37N06'53 81w31'11 5:26:05
TB Crossroads 63 4 37N30'41 75w50'37 5:03:22
Teas 83 15 36N47 81w25 5:25:40
Telegraph Spring 53 14 39N06'18 77w42'31 5:10:50
Teman 42 22 37N56'13 77w37'44 5:10:31
Temperance 5 16 37N40 79w03 5:16:12
Temperanceville 1 4 37N53'34 75w32'51 5:02:11
Temple Hill 80 15 36N52'43 82w16'33 5:29:06
Templeman 92 19 38N04'14 76w46'31 5:07:06
Templeton 72 22 37N04'56 77w21'19 5:09:25
Tenso 26 15 37N09'27 82w19'52 5:29:19
Tenth Legion 79 22 38N34'38 78w43'54 5:14:56
Terrell Store 42 22 37N55'24 77w39'34 5:10:38
Terrys Fork 31 4 37N02'45 80w15'53 5:21:04
Terryville 20 4 37N01'47 78w52'56 5:15:32
Tetotum 49 22 38N16'33 77w02'44 5:08:11
Tettington 19 4 37N14'29 76w56'49 5:07:47
Thalia 133 6 36N50'36 76w07'16 5:04:29
Thalia Gardens 133 6 36N51'12 76w07'01 5:04:28
Thalia Manor 133 6 36N50'55 76w06'57 5:04:28
Thalia Shores 133 6 36N51'17 76w06'27 5:04:26
Thalia Village 133 6 36N50'29 76w07'16 5:04:29
Thaxton 10 4 37N21'10 79w37'00 5:18:28
The Cedars 83 15 36N50 81w31 5:26:04
The Cross Roads 80 15 36N50'34 82w09'26 5:28:38
The English Hills 29 3 38N48 77w20 5:09:20
The Hollow 68 4 36N36 80w31 5:22:04
The Islands 1 4 37N56 75w22 5:01:28
The Knolls 73 13 38N39 77w16 5:09:04
Thelma 54 14 38N02'44 78w14'32 5:12:58
The Manors 73 13 38N39 77w16 5:09:04
The Meadows 2 14 38N02 78w29 5:13:56
The Oaks 1 4 37N53'38 75w30'40 5:02:03
Theological Seminary 96 1 38N49 77w07 5:08:28
The Plains 30 19 38N51'43 77w46'27 5:11:06
The Ridge 58 4 36N40'59 78w20'44 5:13:23
Thessalia 35 4 37N15'08 80w47'12 5:23:09
Theta 16 16 37N10 79w05 5:16:20
The Timbers 29 3 38N45 77w12 5:08:48
The Villas 73 13 38N39 77w16 5:09:04
Thomas 14 15 37N20'42 82w10'05 5:28:40
Thomas Bridge 83 15 36N50 81w31 5:26:04
Thomas Corner 121 6 36N51'20 76w12'34 5:04:50
Thomason Park 73 14 38N32'24 77w19'50 5:09:19
Thomas Terrace 16 14 37N22'26 79w00'51 5:16:03
Thomastown 9 4 38N00'29 79w50'27 5:19:22
Thompson Ford 81 26 36N45'08 82w22'55 5:29:32
Thompson Landing 132 5 36N46'24 76w33'27 5:06:14
Thompsons 41 4 36N46'00 79w07'02 5:16:28
Thompson Valley 89 4 37N04'42 81w32'52 5:26:11
Thornburg 85 22 38N08'00 77w31'19 5:10:05
Thorncliff 37 4 37N38'49 77w50'32 5:11:22
Thornhill 66 14 38N09'15 77w58'06 5:11:52
Thoroughfare 73 14 38N50 77w43 5:10:52
Thoroughgood 133 6 36N53'30 76w07'46 5:04:31
Three Chopt 43 22 37N37 77w32 5:10:08
Three Forks 16 16 37N14'33 79w03'04 5:16:12
Three Forks 81 26 36N48'45 82w39'30 5:30:38
Threemile Corner 54 14 37N55'49 77w51'59 5:11:28
Three Springs 91 25 36N37'07 82w14'38 5:28:59
Three Square 37 4 37N39'54 77w59'42 5:11:59
Threeway 92 19 37N59'33 76w41'58 5:06:48
Tibbstown 66 14 38N11'01 78w15'23 5:13:02
Tibitha 64 18 37N50'18 76w15'45 5:05:03
Ticktown 1 4 37N43'12 75w41'34 5:02:46
Tidemill 36 4 37N16'04 76w29'00 5:05:56
Tidewater 76 4 37N51'18 76w41'56 5:06:48
Tidwells 92 19 38N07'16 76w38'42 5:06:35
Tignor 17 22 37N58'33 77w06'28 5:08:26
Timberlake 16 16 37N19'14 79w15'28 5:17:02
Timberly Heights 72 22 37N13 77w17 5:09:08
Timber Ridge 78 14 37N51'19 79w21'55 5:17:28
Timber Ridge 79 21 38N19'56 78w51'54 5:15:28
Timberville 79 22 38N38'20 78w46'27 5:15:06
Timothy Park 29 3 38N45 77w08 5:08:32
Tindall 31 4 37N00'14 80w20'17 5:21:21
Tinkertown 9 4 37N56'27 79w52'34 5:19:30
Tiny 26 15 37N06'20 82w14'23 5:28:58
Tinytown 74 4 36N58'55 80w41'48 5:22:47
Tipers 64 18 37N50'41 76w22'18 5:05:29
Tiptop 89 4 37N12'39 81w26'03 5:25:44
Tito 81 26 36N45'29 82w48'52 5:31:15
Tivis 26 15 37N14'48 82w22'21 5:29:29
Toano 47 14 37N22'47 76w48'16 5:07:13
Tobaccoville 70 14 37N28'56 78w05'46 5:12:23
Todds Tavern 85 22 38N14'53 77w40'08 5:10:41
Toga 15 4 37N29'38 78w38'01 5:14:32
Tola 20 4 37N05 78w45 5:15:00
Tomahawk 69 4 36N50 79w24 5:17:36
Toms Bottom 26 15 37N12 82w18 5:29:12
Toms Brook 82 14 38N56'47 78w26'22 5:13:45
Toms Creek 93 15 36N58'00 82w27'17 5:29:49
Tookland 14 15 37N15'01 82w06'31 5:28:26
Topnot 82 14 39N00 78w22 5:13:28
Topping 59 4 37N35'17 76w28'29 5:05:54
Toshes 69 4 36N58'09 79w29'11 5:17:57
Totaro 13 4 36N44'50 77w41'45 5:10:47
Totten 90 14 38N55 78w12 5:12:48
Totuskey 76 18 37N56'38 76w37'03 5:06:28
Towell Ford 52 26 36N38'02 83w10'31 5:32:42
Town and Country Estates 29 3 38N55 77w14 5:08:56
Town Point Landing 67 4 37N24'55 76w20'13 5:05:21
Townsend 63 4 37N11'04 75w57'31 5:03:50
Trammel 26 15 37N00'52 82w17'38 5:29:11
Transco Village 69 4 36N49'53 79w20'05 5:17:20
Trantwood Shores 133 6 36N52'09 76w03'07 5:04:12
Trapp 53 4 39N03'29 77w51'57 5:11:28
Travis Mill 17 22 38N08'54 77w19'37 5:09:18
Tree Brooke 29 3 38N53 77w18 5:09:12
Treherneville 63 4 37N25'37 75w53'26 5:03:34
Tremont Gardens 29 3 38N52'22 77w12'07 5:08:48

Trenholm 25 14 37N35'41 78w03'44 5:12:15
Trent Mill 25 4 37N30 78w15 5:13:00
Trenton Mills 25 4 37N37'45 78w13'43 5:12:55
Trevilians 54 14 38N03'05 78w04'23 5:12:18
Triangle 73 14 38N32'48 77w20'13 5:09:21
Trigg 35 4 37N14'44 80w40'49 5:22:43
Trimble 45 4 38N18'16 79w37'09 5:18:29
Trimbles Mill 8 21 38N08'07 79w13'08 5:16:53
Trimmers Crossing 66 14 38N17'20 78w05'17 5:12:21
Trinity 12 4 37N27'21 79w53'24 5:19:34
Triplet 13 4 36N36'37 77w45'58 5:11:04
Trone 34 4 39N16 78w20 5:13:20
Trout Dale 38 4 36N42'07 81w26'26 5:25:46
Troutville 12 4 37N25'05 79w52'30 5:19:30
Trower 1 4 36N21 75w44'32 5:02:58
Troy 32 4 37N57'03 78w14'48 5:12:59
True Blue 66 14 38N21'21 77w55'36 5:11:42
Truhart 48 4 37N38'55 76w50'24 5:07:22
Truxillo 4 4 37N22'15 78w02'31 5:12:10
Tryme 67 4 38N27'13 78w10'19 5:12:41
Tuckahoe 43 22 37N35'24 77w33'24 5:10:14
Tuckahoe Park 43 22 37N36 77w32 5:10:08
Tuckahoe Village 43 22 37N35'52 77w37'26 5:10:30
Tucker Hill 92 19 38N03'59 76w35'40 5:06:23
Tuck Fork 50 14 37N49'39 77w15'20 5:09:01
Tuggle 71 4 37N18'21 78w29'20 5:13:57
Tulip 34 4 39N06 78w13 5:12:52
Tumbez 80 15 36N46'05 82w15'57 5:29:04
Tumbling Creek 91 15 36N52'27 81w50'46 5:27:23
Tunis 79 22 38N42'10 78w52'03 5:15:28
Tunnels Mill 1 4 37N57'59 75w34'52 5:02:19
Tunstall 62 14 37N35'46 77w06'10 5:08:25
Tunstall 69 4 36N37 79w29 5:17:56
Turbeville 41 4 36N37'23 79w02'23 5:16:10
Turkey Fork 38 4 36N43 81w11 5:24:44
Turkey Fork 69 4 36N48'58 79w38'01 5:18:32
Turleytown 79 22 38N36'50 78w52'17 5:15:29
Turnbull 30 19 38N40'03 77w51'38 5:11:27
Turners Crossroads 40 20 36N33'01 77w35'12 5:10:21
Turners Siding 52 26 36N49'04 83w02'56 5:32:12
Turner Store 13 4 36N48 77w57 5:11:48
Turpin 50 14 37N45'40 77w08'50 5:08:35
Tuxamount 29 1 38N45 77w04 5:08:16
Twin Pines 125 6 36N52'44 76w23'32 5:05:34
Twin Poplars 61 14 37N51'38 78w48'15 5:15:13
Twin Springs 81 26 36N46'29 82w27'52 5:29:51
Twymans Mill 56 4 38N19'04 78w10'18 5:12:41
Tye River 61 14 37N39'09 78w56'54 5:15:48
Tyler Gardens 108 3 38N52'56 77w10'38 5:08:43
Tyler Park 29 3 38N52'21 77w11'44 5:08:47
Tylers 42 22 37N57'21 77w42'05 5:10:48
Tylerton 86 4 38N16'54 77w26'05 5:09:44
Tyro 61 14 37N49'17 79w00'18 5:16:01
Tysons Corner 29 3 38N55'07 77w13'53 5:08:56
Tysons Green 29 3 38N55'18 77w14'59 5:09:00
Union 10 4 37N19'37 79w40'04 5:18:40
Union 31 4 36N48'37 80w26'31 5:21:46
Union Hall 33 4 37N00 79w41 5:18:44
Union Hill 5 16 37N33'29 79w01'13 5:16:05
Union Hill 15 4 37N32'16 78w19'46 5:13:19
Union Level 58 4 36N42'58 78w14'07 5:12:56
Union Mills 32 4 37N56'21 78w18'03 5:13:12
Uniontown 29 3 38N49'15 77w27'07 5:09:48
Unionville 66 14 38N15'35 77w58'07 5:11:52
Unison 53 14 39N02'06 77w47'27 5:11:10
Unity 84 4 36N48'45 76w53'24 5:07:34
University Gardens Apartment 100 14 38N02 78w29 5:13:56
University Heights 43 22 37N36 77w32 5:10:08
University of Richmond 127 17 37N32 77w28 5:09:52
University of Virginia 100 14 38N02 78w29 5:13:56
Uno 56 4 38N15'32 78w13'52 5:12:55
Unthanks 52 26 36N40 83w07 5:32:28
Upper Brandon 72 22 37N17'19 77w01'38 5:08:07
Upper Mount Landing 28 14 37N56'50 76w56'20 5:07:45
Upper Pocosin 39 14 38N24'03 78w28'56 5:13:56
Upperville 30 19 38N59'38 77w53'06 5:11:32
Upper Zion 17 22 38N03'55 77w14'36 5:08:58
Upright 28 4 37N48'35 76w50'17 5:07:21
Upshaw 50 14 37N47'38 77w08'50 5:08:35
Upton Hill 7 1 38N52'27 77w08'48 5:08:35
Urbanna 59 4 37N38'15 76w34'29 5:06:18
Vadens Mill 69 4 36N54'46 79w22'17 5:17:29
Vails Mill 91 15 36N38'24 81w48'40 5:27:15
Valaho 81 15 36N50 82w28 5:29:52
Vale 29 3 38N53'27 77w20'55 5:09:24
Valentine Hills 43 17 37N36 77w29 5:09:56
Valentines 13 4 36N35'18 77w49'49 5:11:19
Valley 12 4 37N23 79w53 5:19:32
Valley Brook 29 3 38N50'59 77w11'08 5:08:45
Valley Creek 81 15 36N45 82w25 5:29:40
Valley Mill 23 4 37N22'45 80w20'53 5:21:24
Valley Mills 8 21 38N10 79w12 5:16:48
Valley Ridge 3 4 37N47 79w59 5:19:56
Valley Springs 9 4 37N57 79w51 5:19:24
Valley Stream 101 6 36N49 76w14 5:04:56
Valley View 3 4 37N54'08 79w54'06 5:19:36
Valley View 29 1 38N45'54 77w05'21 5:08:21
Valleyview Corner 17 22 38N12'20 77w18'28 5:09:14
Valleywood 73 13 38N39 77w16 5:09:04
Van 52 26 36N36'49 83w09'20 5:32:37
Van Buren Furnace 82 14 38N58'34 78w33'23 5:14:14
Vance 69 4 36N39'58 79w33'31 5:18:14
Vanderpool 45 4 38N22'10 79w37'32 5:18:30
Vandola 69 4 36N34'40 79w30'42 5:18:03
Vandyke 14 15 37N08'31 81w55'22 5:27:41
Vanlear 8 21 38N01 79w02 5:16:08
Vannoy Acres 29 3 38N49'50 77w22'22 5:09:29
Vannoy Park 29 3 38N48'42 77w22'57 5:09:32
Vansant 14 15 37N13'56 82w05'57 5:28:24
Varina 43 22 37N30 77w20 5:09:20
Varina Grove 43 17 37N26'35 77w20'56 5:09:24
Varsity Park 96 1 38N49'25 77w06'45 5:08:27
Vashti 33 4 36N51'48 79w38'23 5:18:34
Vaucluse 34 4 39N03'29 78w14'50 5:12:59
Vaughn 67 14 38N43'07 78w23'52 5:13:35
Vawter Corner 54 14 38N07'44 78w00'52 5:12:03
Vawters Shore 54 14 38N02 78w00 5:12:00
Velma 48 4 37N38'49 76w42'58 5:06:52
Venia 14 15 37N05'28 82w03'00 5:28:12
Venter 50 14 37N45'44 77w08'08 5:08:33
Ventosa 121 6 36N50'46 76w13'49 5:04:55
Vera 6 4 37N24'48 78w45'50 5:15:03
Verbena 67 14 38N27'55 78w36'59 5:14:28
Verdi 81 26 36N41 82w45 5:31:00
Verdiersville 66 14 38N16'18 77w54'10 5:11:37
Verdon 42 22 37N52'41 77w30'21 5:10:01
Vernon Hill 41 4 36N45'23 79w06'11 5:16:25
Vernon Mills 30 19 38N48'11 77w57'23 5:11:50
Vernon Square 29 3 38N42'21 77w06'13 5:08:25
Verona 8 21 38N12'07 79w00'31 5:16:02
Vertain Park 29 3 38N51 77w15 5:09:00
Vesta 68 4 36N43'00 80w21'29 5:21:26
Vests Store 70 14 37N29 77w55 5:11:40
Vesuvius 78 14 37N54'22 79w11'51 5:16:47
Veterans Administration Hosp 127 17 37N33 77w26 5:09:44
Vicco 93 15 36N57'37 82w25'28 5:29:42
Vicey 14 15 37N12'25 82w13'43 5:28:55
Vicker 60 4 37N09'49 80w29'17 5:21:57
Vicker Heights 60 4 37N09'54 80w28'40 5:21:55
Vicksville 84 4 36N48'48 77w01'21 5:08:05
Victoria 55 4 36N59'41 78w13'39 5:12:55
Victoria Hills 21 22 37N23 77w26 5:09:44
Victory Park 125 6 36N47'35 76w21'07 5:05:24
Vienna 29 3 38N54'04 77w15'56 5:09:04
Vienna Woods 29 3 38N53'16 77w14'52 5:08:59
Viers 26 15 37N10'19 82w14'11 5:28:57
Viewtown 75 14 38N38'21 78w02'23 5:12:10
Village 76 18 37N56'56 76w36'16 5:06:25
Villa Heights 44 4 36N40 79w52 5:19:28
Villa Loring 29 3 38N55 77w14 5:08:56
Villamay 29 1 38N45'30 77w03'16 5:08:13
Villamont 10 4 37N23'43 79w46'35 5:19:06
Villboro 17 22 38N08'06 77w23'23 5:09:34
Vincent Corner 20 4 37N08'31 78w42'13 5:14:49
Vine 133 6 36N34'17 76w04'37 5:04:18
Vinita 37 17 37N34'55 77w40'58 5:10:44
Vint Hill Farms 30 19 38N44 77w44 5:10:56
Vint Hill Farms Station 30 19 38N45 77w41 5:10:44
Vinton 77 4 37N16'51 79w53'50 5:19:35
Virgilina 41 4 36N32'36 78w46'31 5:15:06
Virginia Beach 133 6 36N51'10 75w58'42 5:03:55
Virginia City 93 15 36N55'06 82w20'42 5:29:23
Virginia Estates 29 3 38N42 77w14 5:08:56
Virginia Forest 108 3 38N53'00 77w11'23 5:08:46
Virginia Gardens 121 6 36N54'45 76w17'10 5:05:09
Virginia Heights 7 1 38N51'03 77w07'00 5:08:28
Virginia Heights 43 17 37N31'12 77w20'47 5:09:23
Virginia Heights 98 25 36N37'06 82w10'06 5:28:40
Virginia Highlands 7 1 38N51'30 77w03'54 5:08:16
Virginia Hills 29 3 38N46'43 77w05'59 5:08:24
Virginia Hills 91 25 36N36 82w11 5:28:44
Virginia Mineral Springs 23 4 37N31'39 80w03'59 5:20:16
Virginia Union University 127 17 37N33 77w27 5:09:48
Virginia Village Apartments 29 1 38N49 77w09 5:08:36
Vir-Mar Beach 64 18 37N55'45 76w18'22 5:05:13
Virso 71 4 37N05'37 78w24'22 5:13:37
Virts Corner 53 14 39N05'11 77w35'17 5:10:21
Viscose City 90 14 38N54'58 78w12'20 5:12:49
Vista 16 16 37N09 79w17 5:17:08
Vista Acres 116 14 37N20'52 79w11'33 5:16:46
Volens 41 4 36N56'06 79w00'45 5:16:03
Volney 38 4 36N37'30 81w23'18 5:25:33
Vontay 42 22 37N45'27 77w45'02 5:11:00
Vulcan 66 14 38N12'53 77w55'22 5:11:41
Wabun 77 4 37N14'56 80w08'30 5:20:34
Wachapreague 1 4 37N36'15 75w41'24 5:02:46
Wades Mill 78 14 37N56'56 79w17'11 5:17:09
Wadesville 22 14 39N14'33 78w02'21 5:12:09
Waidsboro 33 4 36N56'55 79w57'36 5:19:50
Wake 59 4 37N34'05 76w25'46 5:05:43
Wakefield 87 4 37N13'21 76w56'30 5:07:46
Wakefield 88 4 36N58'05 76w59'24 5:07:58
Wakefield 96 1 38N48'41 77w06'27 5:08:26
Wakefield 100 14 38N04'09 78w28'24 5:13:54
Wakefield Chapel 29 1 38N50 77w12 5:08:48
Wakefield Chapel Woods 29 1 38N50 77w12 5:08:48
Wakefield Corner 92 19 38N10'19 76w56'58 5:07:48
Wakefield Forest 29 1 38N50'07 77w14'22 5:08:57
Wakefield Manor 75 14 38N48'59 78w06'27 5:12:26
Wake Forest 60 4 37N13'17 80w34'20 5:22:17
Wakema 50 4 37N39'10 76w53'53 5:07:36
Wakemans Grove 82 14 38N50'47 78w37'05 5:14:28
Wakenva 26 15 37N02'30 82w18'48 5:29:15
Walden 120 4 37N06'44 76w31'48 5:06:07
Waldon Woods 29 3 38N43'36 77w05'10 5:08:21
Waldrop 54 14 38N04'25 78w12'07 5:12:48
Walhaven 29 3 38N43 77w09 5:08:36
Walker Chapel 7 3 38N55'17 77w07'47 5:08:31
Walkerford 5 16 37N33 78w52 5:15:28
Walkers 27 22 37N09'29 77w42'23 5:10:50
Walkers 62 14 37N24'55 76w56'25 5:07:46
Walkers Corner 64 18 37N54'42 76w32'48 5:06:11
Walkers Creek 78 14 37N55 79w22 5:17:28
Walkers Ford 5 16 37N30'09 78w56'09 5:15:45
Walkers Store 64 18 37N51 76w17 5:05:08
Walker Store 58 4 36N48 78w28 5:13:52
Walkerton 48 4 37N43'34 77w01'23 5:08:06
Wallace 91 15 36N39'10 82w07'41 5:28:31
Wallaces Store 20 4 37N00 78w36 5:14:24
Wallaceton 101 6 36N36'52 76w22'45 5:05:31
Wallers Corner 17 22 38N04'47 77w32'27 5:10:10
Walmsley 64 18 37N56'28 76w32'08 5:06:09
Walnut Grove 91 15 36N42'25 82w15'04 5:29:00
Walnut Hill 123 22 37N12'01 77w23'32 5:09:34
Walnut Hills 135 23 37N15'43 76w43'42 5:06:55
Walnut Point 64 18 37N55 76w28 5:05:52
Walter Heights 29 1 38N55 77w11 5:08:44
Walters 46 4 36N46'20 76w50'59 5:07:24
Walters Woods 29 1 38N51'05 77w09'46 5:08:39
Walthall 21 22 37N18'48 77w24'29 5:09:38
Walthall Mill 21 22 37N19'10 77w22'16 5:09:29
Walton 20 4 37N04 78w32 5:14:08
Walton 60 4 37N09'12 80w30'50 5:22:03
Walton Furnace 94 4 36N53'01 80w56'05 5:23:44
Waltons Store 10 4 37N10 79w28 5:17:52
Wan 36 4 37N25'28 76w30'21 5:06:01
Wangle Junction 31 4 36N58'39 80w28'03 5:21:52
Waples Mill 29 3 38N52'26 77w20'14 5:09:21
Ward 14 15 37N29 82w04 5:28:16
Wardell 89 4 37N01'52 81w47'41 5:27:11
Wards Corner 121 6 36N54'53 76w16'23 5:05:06
Wards Mill 18 4 36N40 80w55 5:23:40
Wardtown 63 4 37N32'05 75w52'38 5:03:31
Ware 36 4 37N26 76w30 5:06:00
Ware Neck 36 4 37N24'09 76w27'32 5:05:50
Wares Crossroads 54 14 38N04'46 77w52'49 5:11:31
Wares Wharf 28 4 37N52'25 76w47'02 5:07:08
Warfield 13 4 36N53'44 77w49'34 5:11:18
Warminster 61 14 37N41'14 78w41'53 5:14:48
Warm Springs 9 4 38N02'46 79w47'27 5:19:10
Warner 59 4 37N38'18 76w38'45 5:06:35
Warren 2 14 37N45'57 78w33'29 5:14:14
Warren Mill 47 14 37N22'22 76w50'28 5:07:22
Warren Park 90 14 38N56'18 78w11'39 5:12:47
Warrenton 30 19 38N42'48 77w47'44 5:11:11
Warren Woods 29 3 38N50'35 77w19'43 5:09:19
Warsaw 76 4 37N57'31 76w45'30 5:07:02
Warwick 120 6 37N02 76w27 5:05:48
Warwick Corner 84 4 36N54'55 76w50'13 5:07:21
Warwick Lawns 120 6 37N07'20 76w31'28 5:06:06
Warwick Village 96 1 38N50'03 77w03'53 5:08:16
Washington 75 14 38N42'48 78w09'35 5:12:38
Washington City 130 4 36N43 78w54 5:15:36
Washington Corner 17 22 38N07'18 77w24'18 5:09:37
Washington Forest 96 1 38N50'16 77w07'02 5:08:28
Washington Gardens 112 4 37N02'35 76w18'55 5:05:16
Washington Park 40 20 36N41 77w32 5:10:08
Washington Park 121 6 36N54'31 76w14'44 5:04:59
Watauga 91 15 36N40'41 81w56'00 5:27:44
Waterfall 73 14 38N51'44 77w40'19 5:10:41
Waterfence Landing 48 4 37N35'32 76w47'57 5:07:12
Waterford 53 4 39N11'12 77w36'37 5:10:26
Waterlick 90 14 38N57'58 78w17'10 5:13:09
Waterloo 22 4 39N04'58 78w05'00 5:12:20
Waterloo 30 19 38N41'45 77w54'23 5:11:38
Water View 59 4 37N43'28 76w36'50 5:06:27
Waterview 125 6 36N50'13 76w21'19 5:05:25
Watkins Corner 13 4 36N42'02 77w56'33 5:11:46

Watkins Corner 84 4 36N40'01 76W58'59 5:07:56
Watson 53 14 38N59'36 77W35'46 5:10:23
Watts 2 14 38N08'07 78W23'34 5:13:34
Wattsboro 55 4 36N52'59 78W15'49 5:13:03
Wattsville 1 4 37N56'02 75W30'00 5:02:00
Waugh 10 4 37N31'01 79W20'41 5:17:23
Waverly 88 4 37N02'09 77W05'44 5:08:23
Waverly Village 85 24 38N17'18 77W31'08 5:10:05
Waxpool 53 4 39N00'50 77W31'27 5:10:06
Wayland 21 22 37N32'20 77W34'35 5:10:18
Wayland 81 26 36N38 82W34 5:30:16
Waylands Mill 24 4 38N24'25 78W06'06 5:12:24
Wayne 8 21 38N06 78W54 5:15:36
Waynesboro 134 22 38N04'06 78W53'23 5:15:34
Waynewood 29 1 38N43'34 77W02'57 5:08:12
Wayside 19 14 37N22'20 77W11'42 5:08:47
Wayside Manor 121 6 36N50'23 76W12'04 5:04:48
Weal 69 4 36N49'29 79W27'28 5:17:50
Weaversville 30 19 38N38'13 77W37'45 5:10:31
Webbs Mill 13 4 36N44'10 77W41'43 5:10:47
Webbs Mill 23 4 37N23'59 80W12'31 5:20:50
Webbtown 22 14 39N08'29 77W56'30 5:11:46
Weber City 32 4 37N45'18 78W17'03 5:13:08
Weber City 81 26 36N37'22 82W33'44 5:30:15
Webster 12 4 37N21'05 79W49'37 5:19:18
Wedgewood 43 22 37N37'00 77W34'05 5:10:16
Weedons Fork 49 22 38N13'52 77W07'15 5:08:29
Weedonville 49 22 38N17'54 77W09'32 5:08:38
Weems 51 4 37N39'17 76W26'39 5:05:47
Weir Creek 62 14 37N29 76W50 5:07:20
Weirwood 63 4 37N27'25 75W52'12 5:03:29
Welchs 17 22 38N05'26 77W29'09 5:09:57
Welcome 49 22 38N11'48 77W08'10 5:08:33
Weldon 74 4 37N05'16 80W48'20 5:23:13
Welfleet 73 3 38N43 77W09 5:08:36
Weller 14 15 37N19'47 82W10'35 5:28:42
Wellesley 53 14 39N07 77W34 5:10:16
Wellford 76 4 37N53'08 76W45'58 5:07:04
Wellington 29 1 38N44'44 77W03'20 5:08:13
Wellington 73 2 38N47'24 77W33'39 5:10:15
Wellington Heights 29 1 38N45'01 77W03'17 5:08:13
Welltown 34 4 39N15'12 78W08'04 5:12:32
Wellville 65 4 37N07'38 77W55'16 5:11:41
West Arlington 7 1 38N53'38 77W10'07 5:08:40
West Augusta 8 21 38N16'12 79W18'29 5:17:14
West Bassett 44 4 36N45'52 80W01'24 5:20:06
West Bottom 32 4 37N43'01 78W15'40 5:13:03
Westbourne 43 17 37N34 77W29 5:09:56
Westbriar 43 22 37N37'23 77W33'46 5:10:15
West Chesapeake 101 6 36N50 76W16 5:05:04
Westchester 21 22 37N32'05 77W34'41 5:10:19
Westchester 29 3 38N51 77W15 5:09:00
Westdale 43 22 37N36 77W32 5:10:08
West Dante 26 15 36N58'44 82W19'18 5:29:17
West End 36 4 37N26'15 76W41'58 5:06:48
West End 131 21 38N08'45 79W04'39 5:16:19
West End Manor 43 22 37N36 77W32 5:10:08
Western 35 4 37N20 80W50 5:23:20
Western 123 22 37N13 77W26 5:09:44
West Falls Church 108 1 38N53'27 77W11'05 5:08:44
Westfield 98 25 36N36 82W11 5:28:44
West Fork 69 4 36N37'28 79W37'52 5:18:31
West Fredericksburg 110 24 38N23 77W27 5:09:48
West Galax 111 4 36N39'05 80W55'51 5:23:43
West Gate of Lomond 73 2 38N47'08 77W29'33 5:09:58
West Ghent 121 6 36N52'15 76W18'19 5:05:13
Westgrove 29 1 38N45'54 77W03'26 5:08:14
Westham 43 22 37N35'20 77W32'25 5:10:10
Westhampton 29 3 38N54 77W13 5:08:52
Westhampton 43 17 37N35'11 77W30'54 5:10:04
West Hampton 112 6 37N01'33 76W22'13 5:05:29
Westhaven 125 6 36N49'54 76W21'34 5:05:26
Westhaven Park 125 6 36N49'34 76W20'36 5:05:22
West Hope 88 4 36N55'15 77W18'43 5:09:15
West Hopewell 114 14 37N17 77W18 5:09:12
West Irvington 51 14 37N39'33 76W25'51 5:05:43
Westland 51 14 37N37'01 76W17'35 5:05:10
West Landing 101 6 36N39'13 76W22'08 5:05:29
West Landing 133 6 36N41'31 76W04'02 5:04:16
West Langley 29 1 38N56'46 77W11'55 5:08:48
Westlawn 29 3 38N51'56 77W10'50 5:08:43
West Leigh 2 14 38N04'05 78W34'42 5:14:19
West Lewinsville Heights 29 1 38N55 77W11 5:08:44
West Lexington 78 14 37N47 79W26 5:17:44
West Lynchburg 116 14 37N24'11 79W10'42 5:16:43
West McLean 29 1 38N55 77W11 5:08:44
Westmont 7 1 38N51'45 77W05'32 5:08:22
Westmoreland 2 14 38N05'11 78W27'17 5:13:49
Westmoreland 92 19 38N03'51 76W33'33 5:06:14
Westmoreland Heights 29 3 38N54 77W13 5:08:52
Westmoreland Park 29 1 38N53 77W13 5:08:52
West Munden 101 6 36N48'25 76W15'24 5:05:02
West Norfolk 125 6 36N51'50 76W20'59 5:05:24
Westover 7 1 38N53'13 77W08'23 5:08:34
Westover 19 14 37N18'42 77W09'01 5:08:36
Westover 101 6 36N46'30 76W16'11 5:05:05
Westover Heights 21 17 37N31'13 77W31'21 5:10:05
Westover Hills 8 21 38N05'10 78W56'38 5:15:47
Westover Hills 40 20 36N41 77W32 5:10:08
Westover Hills 105 4 36N36'01 79W28'05 5:17:52
Westover Hills 127 17 37N31'33 77W29'30 5:09:58
West Petersburg 27 22 37N13 77W26 5:09:44
West Piney 94 4 36N53'03 81W00'35 5:24:02
West Point 50 14 37N31'53 76W47'48 5:07:11
West Raven 80 4 37N05'03 81W51'45 5:27:27
West Springfield 29 3 38N46'21 77W13'17 5:08:53
Wests Store 41 4 36N56 78W57 5:15:48
West View 8 21 38N10'07 79W10'21 5:16:41
West View 37 4 37N38'44 78W00'30 5:12:02
Westview Hills 29 3 38N46'35 77W12'55 5:08:52
Westville 57 4 37N23 76W20 5:05:20
Westwood 3 4 37N47 79W59 5:19:56
Westwood 42 14 37N36'05 77W10'40 5:08:43
Westwood Estates 91 15 36N43 81W58 5:27:52
Westwood Park 29 1 38N53'03 77W12'02 5:08:48
Westwood Place 3 4 37N48'02 80W01'00 5:20:04
West Wytheville 94 4 36N59 81W08 5:24:32
Weyanoke 19 22 37N17'29 77W03'57 5:08:16
Weyanoke 29 1 38N49'09 77W09'23 5:08:38
Weyers Cave 8 21 38N17'18 78W54'48 5:15:39
Whaley 132 4 36N35'29 76W40'12 5:06:41
Whaleyville 132 4 36N35'17 76W41'06 5:06:44
Wheatfield 82 14 39N04'24 78W22'21 5:13:29
Wheatland 53 14 39N11'27 77W40'33 5:10:42
Wheeler 52 26 36N37'19 83W33'19 5:34:13
Whitacre 34 4 39N19'56 78W19'39 5:13:19
Whitebank 50 14 37N43'11 77W02'07 5:08:08
White Chapel 51 4 37N44 76W32 5:06:08
White City 40 20 36N41 77W32 5:10:08
White Cliffs 63 4 37N21'56 75W59'20 5:03:57
White Ford 81 15 36N41'01 82W19'56 5:29:20
White Gate 35 4 37N20 80W44 5:22:56
White Hall 2 14 38N07'04 78W39'42 5:14:39
White Hall 34 9 39N17'28 78W08'54 5:12:36
Whitehall 48 4 37N44'01 77W02'35 5:08:10
White Hill 8 21 38N02'36 79W03'47 5:16:15
White House 58 4 36N34 78W42 5:14:48
Whitehouse Landing 67 14 38N38'46 78W32'06 5:14:08
Whitehurst Landing 133 6 36N49'25 76W11'16 5:04:45
White Landing 50 14 37N35'10 76W59'05 5:07:56
White Marsh 36 4 37N20'32 76W31'18 5:06:05
White Mill 91 15 36N46'06 81W59'16 5:27:57
White Oak 41 4 36N48'22 79W01'22 5:16:05
White Oak 86 4 38N18'02 77W22'32 5:09:30
White Oak Landing 50 14 37N41'29 76W58'15 5:07:53
White Oaks 29 1 38N45'42 77W04'11 5:08:17
White Oak Swamp 43 22 37N30'22 77W17'20 5:09:09
White Pine Lodge 35 4 37N23'25 80W33'01 5:22:12
White Plains 13 4 36N38'39 77W57'31 5:11:50
White Post 22 4 39N03'25 78W06'14 5:12:25
White Rock 61 14 37N53'25 79W03'39 5:16:15
White Rock Hill 116 14 37N24'11 79W08'23 5:16:34
Whites Corner 49 22 38N15'06 77W11'27 5:08:46
White Shoals 52 26 36N39 83W14 5:32:56
White Shop 50 14 37N41 77W01 5:08:04
White Stone 51 14 37N38'54 76W23'22 5:05:33
White Stone Beach 51 14 37N37'49 76W23'28 5:05:34
Whitesville 1 4 37N46'56 75W39'48 5:02:39
Whitesville 41 4 36N54'18 78W53'15 5:15:33
Whitethorne 60 4 37N11'59 80W33'53 5:22:16
Whitetop 38 4 36N36'05 81W37'33 5:26:30
Whiteville 25 4 37N36'08 78W10'04 5:12:40
Whitewood 14 15 37N14'08 81W51'26 5:27:26
Whitfield 69 4 36N32'49 79W28'22 5:17:53
Whitley 46 4 36N53'07 76W45'35 5:07:02
Whitlock 54 14 38N03'58 78W14'41 5:12:59
Whitmell 69 4 36N42'08 79W31'26 5:18:06
Whittles 69 4 36N53'11 79W23'17 5:17:33
Wicker Corner 42 22 37N34'40 77W13'58 5:08:56
Wickford 29 3 38N43 77W09 5:08:36
Wickham Crossing 42 22 37N46'42 77W24'25 5:09:38
Wickliffe 22 4 39N09'58 77W53'33 5:11:34
Wicomico 36 4 37N17'27 76W30'35 5:06:02
Wicomico 64 18 37N47 76W22 5:05:28
Wicomico Church 64 18 37N48'54 76W22'41 5:05:31
Wida 8 21 38N01'05 79W05'37 5:16:22
Widewater 86 4 38N27'53 77W19'32 5:09:18
Widewater Beach 86 4 38N24'54 77W20'00 5:09:20
Wightman 58 4 36N47'24 78W18'11 5:13:13
Wilberts Corner 92 19 37N58'48 76W38'24 5:06:34
Wilburdale 29 1 38N48'57 77W11'28 5:08:46
Wilburn 55 4 36N50'59 78W16'18 5:13:05
Wilda 8 21 38N01 79W02 5:16:08
Wildcat Corner 86 4 38N16'49 77W22'41 5:09:31
Wilde Acres 34 9 39N08'49 78W24'00 5:13:36
Wilder 80 15 36N57 82W09 5:28:36
Wilderness 66 14 38N20 77W44 5:10:56
Wilderness Corner 85 22 38N19'16 77W42'04 5:10:48
Wildwood 29 3 38N42 77W14 5:08:56
Wildwood 32 4 37N54'11 78W15'26 5:13:02
Wildwood 43 17 37N36 77W27 5:09:48
Wiley 29 3 38N40'21 77W12'24 5:08:50
Wilkerson Landing 132 5 36N52'19 76W31'06 5:06:04
Wilkins Beach 63 4 37N21'16 75W59'44 5:03:59
Wilkinsons Store 27 22 37N11 77W38 5:10:32
Wilkinson Terrace 21 22 37N27'30 77W30'27 5:10:02
Will 49 22 38N16 77W11 5:08:44
Willard Park 121 6 36N53'06 76W15'23 5:05:02
Williams 57 4 37N24'04 76W19'41 5:05:19
Williamsburg 135 23 37N16'14 76W42'28 5:06:50
Williamsburg Manor 29 1 38N45 77W04 5:08:16
Williamsburg Village 7 1 38N54'18 77W09'19 5:08:37
Williams Corner 64 18 37N53'18 76W28'01 5:05:52
Williams Court 125 6 36N47'55 76W19'44 5:05:19
Williams Mill 81 26 36N40'37 82W33'07 5:30:12
Williams Mills 55 4 37N02 78W29 5:13:56
Williamson Road 128 4 37N19 79W55 5:19:40
Williamsville 9 4 38N11'41 79W34'16 5:18:17
Williamsville 82 14 38N43'16 78W40'34 5:14:42
Willis 31 4 36N51'28 80W28'52 5:21:55
Willis 80 15 36N52'06 82W06'51 5:28:27
Willis Store 52 26 36N40 83W07 5:32:28
Willisville 53 4 39N00'26 77W50'04 5:11:20
Willis Wharf 63 4 37N30'56 75W48'25 5:03:14
Willoughby Beach 121 6 36N58'01 76W17'17 5:05:09
Willoughby Terrace 121 6 36N56'59 76W15'49 5:05:03
Willow 5 16 37N41'25 79W14'29 5:16:58
Willowbrook 54 14 37N50'06 77W48'57 5:11:16
Willowbrook 132 5 36N45'06 76W34'25 5:06:18
Willow Grove 63 4 37N16 76W00 5:04:00
Willow Grove 82 14 38N50'37 78W32'09 5:14:09
Willow Hill 72 22 37N15'18 77W03'29 5:08:14
Willow Lakes 101 6 36N47'37 76W26'42 5:05:47
Willow Landing 86 4 38N25'49 77W22'04 5:09:28
Willow Lawn 43 17 37N34 77W29 5:09:56
Willow Run 29 1 38N49'20 77W10'28 5:08:42
Willow Springs 29 3 38N50'23 77W24'18 5:09:37
Willow Springs 80 15 36N46'38 82W14'20 5:28:57
Willow Tree 52 26 36N38 83W26 5:33:44
Willow Woods 29 1 38N49'23 77W15'21 5:09:01
Wills Corner 46 4 36N52'50 76W34'56 5:06:20
Willston 29 1 38N52 77W12 5:08:48
Wilmington 32 4 37N50'57 78W12'06 5:12:48
Wilroy 132 5 36N47'11 76W32'02 5:06:08
Wilson 91 15 36N38 82W07 5:28:28
Wilson 94 4 36N55'54 81W13'36 5:24:54
Wilson Creek 38 4 36N39 81W23 5:25:32
Wilson Grove 74 4 37N04 80W47 5:23:08
Wilson Hill 52 26 36N38'25 83W16'58 5:33:08
Wilsons 27 22 37N08'21 77W51'58 5:11:28
Wilsons Corner 4 4 37N17'26 77W52'36 5:11:30
Wilson Springs 78 14 37N55'14 79W26'09 5:17:45
Wilton 59 4 37N32'58 76W24'27 5:05:38
Wilton Woods 29 3 38N47'19 77W05'42 5:08:23
Winchester 136 9 39N11'08 78W09'49 5:12:39
Windcliff 43 17 37N36 77W29 5:09:56
Windmill Point 51 14 37N39 76W23 5:05:32
Windsor 46 4 36N48'30 76W44'40 5:06:59
Windsordale 43 22 37N36 77W32 5:10:08
Windsor Estates 29 3 38N45'45 77W09'47 5:08:39
Windsor Farms 127 17 37N33'19 77W29'55 5:10:00
Windsor Great Park 120 4 37N08'50 76W30'54 5:06:04
Windsor Place 43 17 37N32'17 77W22'28 5:09:30
Windsor Shades 62 14 37N27 77W02 5:08:08
Windsor Terrace 112 6 37N02'25 76W22'22 5:05:29
Windsor Woods 133 6 36N49'46 76W06'03 5:04:24
Windy Hill Estates 42 22 37N36'33 77W23'13 5:09:33
Winegar Mill 81 26 36N36'07 82W36'17 5:30:25
Winesap 5 16 37N29'08 79W08'51 5:16:35
Winfall 16 16 37N13'27 79W05'41 5:16:23
Winfields Mill 27 4 36N56'52 77W29'45 5:09:59
Wingina 61 14 37N38'23 78W43'27 5:14:54
Wininger 81 26 36N36'27 82W40'45 5:30:43
Winnie 65 4 37N04'23 78W07'57 5:12:32
Winningham 65 4 37N11 78W08 5:12:32
Winns Landing 19 14 37N24'50 77W00'14 5:08:01
Winona 121 6 36N52'48 76W16'06 5:05:04
Winslow Hills 29 3 38N47'37 77W07'14 5:08:29
Winston 24 14 38N24'36 78W00'35 5:12:02
Winston Terrace 47 23 37N15'12 76W44'17 5:06:57
Wintergreen 61 14 37N53'05 78W53'59 5:15:36
Winterham 4 4 37N22'03 77W55'54 5:11:44
Winterpock 21 22 37N20'45 77W43'11 5:10:53
Winterville 1 4 37N50'18 75W38'32 5:02:34
Wirtz 33 4 37N04'35 79W53'23 5:19:34

Wise 93 15 36N58'33 82w34'33 5:30:18
Wishart 1 4 37N53'02 75w29'41 5:01:59
Wisharts Point 1 4 37N54 75w30 5:02:00
Wistar Farms 43 17 37N36 77w29 5:09:56
Witch Duck 133 6 36N51 76w09 5:04:36
Witch Duck Point 133 6 36N53 76w08 5:04:32
Withams 1 4 37N56'44 75w34'39 5:02:19
Withers 91 25 36N43'34 82w06'17 5:28:25
Witt 69 4 36N40'50 79w24'00 5:17:36
Wittens Fort 89 4 37N07'04 81w34'20 5:26:17
Wittens Mills 89 4 37N09'55 81w28'44 5:25:55
Wolf Glade 18 4 36N41'52 80w52'51 5:23:31
Wolford 14 15 37N21'52 81w59'29 5:27:58
Wolfsnare Plantation 133 6 36N51'31 76w02'39 5:04:11
Wolftown 56 4 38N21'20 78w20'52 5:13:23
Wolf Trap 41 4 36N42'48 78w49'44 5:15:19
Womacks 20 4 37N04'24 78w41'47 5:14:47
Wood 81 26 36N46 82w35 5:30:20
Woodberry Forest 56 4 38N18 78w08 5:12:32
Woodbridge 73 13 38N39'29 77w15'00 5:09:00
Woodbrook 2 14 38N05'09 78w27'59 5:13:52
Woodburn 53 14 39N05'24 77w37'10 5:10:29
Woodburn Heights 29 1 38N50 77w12 5:08:48
Woodford 17 22 38N06'47 77w24'33 5:09:38
Woodford Corner 10 4 37N10'44 79w25'47 5:17:43
Woodhaven 133 6 36N48'27 76w11'58 5:04:48
Woodhaven Shores 62 14 37N29'30 77w07'44 5:08:31
Woodhouse Corner 133 6 36N45'52 76w00'54 5:04:04
Woodland Acres 7 1 38N54'45 77w08'44 5:08:35
Woodland Hills 91 15 36N43 81w58 5:27:52
Woodland Park 29 3 38N43'17 77w05'12 5:08:21
Woodland Park 67 14 38N40'28 78w27'35 5:13:50
Woodland Park 90 14 38N55'02 78w10'48 5:12:43
Woodlawn 18 4 36N43'20 80w49'23 5:23:18
Woodlawn 42 22 37N37'18 77w14'00 5:08:56
Woodlawn 103 22 37N16'03 77w25'02 5:09:40
Woodlawn Manor 29 3 38N42'40 77w07'09 5:08:29
Woodlawn Mansion 29 3 38N42 77w09 5:08:36
Woodlawn Park 29 3 38N45 77w08 5:08:32
Woodlawn Terrace 29 3 38N45 77w08 5:08:32
Woodlawn Terrace 43 22 37N33 77w22 5:09:28
Woodlee 131 21 38N09'58 79w03'29 5:16:14
Woodley 29 3 38N51'50 77w11'40 5:08:47
Woodley Hills 29 3 38N43'26 77w06'08 5:08:25
Woodley North 29 3 38N52'09 77w11'28 5:08:46
Woodman Terrace 43 17 37N38'48 77w29'28 5:09:58
Woodmont 7 1 38N54'02 77w05'43 5:08:23
Woodmont 21 22 37N31'53 77w35'10 5:10:21
Woodridge 2 14 37N53'49 78w26'11 5:13:45
Woodrow Wilson 8 21 38N06 78w58 5:15:52
Woodrum 8 21 38N09 79w05 5:16:20
Woods Corner 15 4 37N34'52 78w38'57 5:14:36
Woods Crossroads 36 4 37N28'40 76w37'01 5:06:28
Woodside Estates 29 1 38N55 77w11 5:08:44
Woods Mill 61 14 37N50'41 78w49'21 5:15:17
Woods of Ilda 29 3 38N49'41 77w15'23 5:09:02
Woodson 5 16 37N45'04 79w04'05 5:16:16
Woodstock 59 4 37N32'26 76w29'10 5:05:57
Woodstock 82 14 38N52'54 78w30'22 5:14:01
Woodvale 21 22 37N21'00 77w20'37 5:09:22
Woodville 75 14 38N36'24 78w10'32 5:12:42
Woodway 52 26 36N43'54 82w59'32 5:31:58
Woolsey 73 14 38N52'11 77w38'09 5:10:33
Woolwine 68 4 36N47'23 80w16'39 5:21:07
Worlds 69 4 36N51'08 79w35'28 5:18:22
Worrell 84 4 36N43'32 77w12'59 5:08:52
Worsham 71 4 37N13'48 78w26'36 5:13:46
Worshams 70 14 37N29 77w55 5:11:40
Wren 20 4 37N07'07 78w51'00 5:15:24
Wright 77 4 37N09'55 79w58'26 5:19:54
Wright 121 6 36N55 76w17 5:05:08
Wrights Corner 17 22 38N02'18 77w26'52 5:09:47
Wrights Corner 62 14 37N29'57 77w08'18 5:08:33
Wrights Fork 17 22 37N57'16 77w18'40 5:09:15
Wrights Shop 5 14 37N26'35 79w05'21 5:16:21
Wrightsville 17 22 38N01'42 77w19'54 5:09:20
Wright Woods 29 3 38N42 77w09 5:08:36
Wurno 74 4 37N04'17 80w43'25 5:22:54
Wyche 13 4 36N37'33 77w47'44 5:11:11
Wylliesburg 20 4 36N51'19 78w35'26 5:14:22
Wyndale 91 15 36N40'50 82w04'43 5:28:19
Wythe 112 6 37N00'11 76w22'41 5:05:31
Wytheville 94 4 36N56'54 81w05'06 5:24:20
Yacht Haven 29 3 38N42'07 77w06'46 5:08:27
Yacht Haven Estates 29 3 38N45 77w08 5:08:32
Yadkin 101 6 36N45'48 76w21'44 5:05:27
Yale 88 4 36N50'44 77w17'16 5:09:09
Yancey Mills 2 14 38N02'48 78w43'32 5:14:54
Yanceyville 54 14 37N56'17 77w58'57 5:11:56
Yankeetown 79 22 38N41'05 78w56'53 5:15:48
Yards 89 4 37N17 81w19 5:25:16
Yates Ford 29 3 38N45'47 77w24'47 5:09:39
Yellow Branch 16 16 37N15'21 79w11'04 5:16:44
Yellow Springs 91 15 36N46 81w52 5:27:28
Yellow Sulphur 60 4 37N10'17 80w23'49 5:21:35
Yellow Sulphur Springs 60 4 37N10'42 80w23'51 5:21:35
Yellow Tavern 43 22 37N38'05 77w27'33 5:09:50
Yokum Station 52 26 36N50 82w53 5:31:32
York Haven Anchorage 95 4 37N08'39 76w23'01 5:05:32
York Manor 43 22 37N32 77w19 5:09:16
Yorkshire 73 2 38N47'35 77w26'53 5:09:48
Yorkshire Acres 73 2 38N47'01 77w26'27 5:09:46
Yorkshire Park 73 2 38N47'35 77w27'55 5:09:52
York Terrace 95 23 37N15'46 76w39'42 5:06:39
Yorktown 95 4 37N14'19 76w30'36 5:06:02
Yost 9 4 38N03'08 79w32'26 5:18:10
Youbedamn Landing 86 22 38N23'21 77w18'56 5:09:16
Young Corner 17 22 38N08'05 77w21'47 5:09:27
Youngers Store 41 4 36N46 78w56 5:15:44
Yuma 81 26 36N36'54 82w36'45 5:30:27
Zacata 92 19 38N07'12 76w46'57 5:07:08
Zack 78 14 37N59'34 79w21'40 5:17:27
Zanoni 36 4 37N23'19 76w29'16 5:05:57
Zenda 79 22 38N30'19 78w46'09 5:15:05
Zenobia 91 15 36N45'05 82w12'27 5:28:50
Zepp 82 14 39N00'24 78w29'53 5:14:00
Zeus 67 4 38N24'10 78w13'19 5:12:53
Ziegler Ford 33 4 36N57'04 79w42'15 5:18:49
Zion 40 20 36N32 77w28 5:09:52
Zion 54 14 37N59'53 78w14'03 5:12:56
Zion Crossroads 54 14 37N58'15 78w13'12 5:12:53
Ziontown 43 22 37N35'16 77w33'40 5:10:15
Zirkle 79 22 38N29'38 78w51'18 5:15:25
Zulla 30 19 38N55'22 77w47'07 5:11:08
Zuni 46 4 36N51'57 76w49'52 5:07:19

TIME TABLES

WA # 1

Before 11/18/1883		LMT
11/18/1883	12:00	PST
3/31/1918	02:00	PWT
10/27/1918	02:00	PST
3/30/1919	02:00	PWT
10/26/1919	02:00	PST
2/09/1942	02:00	PWT
9/30/1945	02:00	PST
4/30/1961	02:00	PDT
9/24/1961	02:00	PST
4/29/1962	02:00	PDT
9/30/1962	02:00	PST
4/28/1963	02:00	US#2

WA # 2

Before 11/18/1883		LMT
11/18/1883	12:00	PST
3/31/1918	02:00	PWT
10/27/1918	02:00	PST
3/30/1919	02:00	PWT
10/26/1919	02:00	PST
2/09/1942	02:00	PWT
9/30/1945	02:00	PST
5/02/1950	02:00	PDT
9/24/1950	02:00	PST
4/30/1961	02:00	PDT
9/24/1961	02:00	PST
4/29/1962	02:00	PDT
9/30/1962	02:00	PST
4/28/1963	02:00	US#2

WA # 3

Before 11/18/1883		LMT
11/18/1883	12:00	PST
3/31/1918	02:00	PWT
10/27/1918	02:00	PST
3/30/1919	02:00	PWT
10/26/1919	02:00	PST
2/09/1942	02:00	PWT
9/30/1945	02:00	PST
4/30/1950	02:00	PDT
9/24/1950	02:00	PST
4/30/1961	02:00	PDT
9/24/1961	02:00	PST
4/29/1962	02:00	PDT
9/30/1962	02:00	PST
4/28/1963	02:00	US#2

WA # 4

Before 11/18/1883		LMT
11/18/1883	12:00	PST
3/31/1918	02:00	PWT
10/27/1918	02:00	PST
3/30/1919	02:00	PWT
10/26/1919	02:00	PST
2/09/1942	02:00	PWT
9/30/1945	02:00	PST
6/01/1949	00:01	PDT
9/01/1949	00:01	PST
4/29/1951	02:00	PDT
9/30/1951	02:00	PST
6/01/1952	02:00	PDT
9/28/1952	02:00	PST
4/30/1961	02:00	PDT
9/24/1961	02:00	PST
4/29/1962	02:00	PDT
9/30/1962	02:00	PST
4/28/1963	02:00	US#2

WA # 5

Before 11/18/1883		LMT
11/18/1883	12:00	PST
3/31/1918	02:00	PWT
10/27/1918	02:00	PST
3/30/1919	02:00	PWT
10/26/1919	02:00	PST
2/09/1942	02:00	PWT
9/30/1945	02:00	PST
6/01/1949	00:01	PDT
9/01/1949	00:01	PST
6/02/1950	02:00	PDT
9/07/1950	02:00	PST
4/30/1961	02:00	PDT
9/24/1961	02:00	PST
4/29/1962	02:00	PDT
9/30/1962	02:00	PST
4/28/1963	02:00	US#2

WA # 6

Before 11/18/1883		LMT
11/18/1883	12:00	PST
3/31/1918	02:00	PWT
10/27/1918	02:00	PST
3/30/1919	02:00	PWT
10/26/1919	02:00	PST
2/09/1942	02:00	PWT
9/30/1945	02:00	PST
6/01/1949	00:01	PDT
8/31/1949	00:01	PST
4/30/1950	02:00	PDT
9/24/1950	02:00	PST
4/30/1961	02:00	PDT
9/24/1961	02:00	PST
4/29/1962	02:00	PDT
9/30/1962	02:00	PST
4/28/1963	02:00	US#2

WA # 7

Before 11/18/1883		LMT
11/18/1883	12:00	PST
3/31/1918	02:00	PWT
10/27/1918	02:00	PST
3/30/1919	02:00	PWT
10/26/1919	02:00	PST
2/09/1942	02:00	PWT
9/30/1945	02:00	PST
6/01/1949	00:01	PDT
9/01/1949	00:01	PST
4/30/1961	02:00	PDT
9/24/1961	02:00	PST
4/29/1962	02:00	PDT
9/30/1962	02:00	PST
4/28/1963	02:00	US#2

WA # 8

Before 11/18/1883		LMT
11/18/1883	12:00	PST
3/31/1918	02:00	PWT
10/27/1918	02:00	PST
3/30/1919	02:00	PWT
10/26/1919	02:00	PST
5/07/1933	02:00	PDT
8/27/1933	02:00	PST
2/09/1942	02:00	PWT
9/30/1945	02:00	PST
6/03/1948	00:01	PDT
9/25/1948	00:01	PST
6/01/1949	02:00	PDT
9/25/1949	02:00	PST
4/30/1950	02:00	PDT
9/24/1950	02:00	PST
4/29/1951	02:00	PDT
9/30/1951	02:00	PST
4/30/1961	02:00	PDT
9/24/1961	02:00	PST
4/29/1962	02:00	PDT
9/30/1962	02:00	PST
4/28/1963	02:00	US#2

WA # 9

Before 11/18/1883		LMT
11/18/1883	12:00	PST
3/31/1918	02:00	PWT
10/27/1918	02:00	PST
3/30/1919	02:00	PWT
10/26/1919	02:00	PST
2/09/1942	02:00	PWT
9/30/1945	02:00	PST
6/01/1949	00:01	PDT
9/25/1949	00:01	PST
5/02/1950	02:00	PDT
9/24/1950	02:00	PST
4/29/1951	02:00	PDT
9/30/1951	02:00	PST
6/01/1952	02:00	PDT
9/28/1952	02:00	PST
4/30/1961	02:00	PDT
9/24/1961	02:00	PST
4/29/1962	02:00	PDT
9/30/1962	02:00	PST
4/28/1963	02:00	US#2

WA # 10

Before 11/18/1883		LMT
11/18/1883	12:00	PST
3/31/1918	02:00	PWT
10/27/1918	02:00	PST
3/30/1919	02:00	PWT
10/26/1919	02:00	PST
2/09/1942	02:00	PWT
9/30/1945	02:00	PST
4/27/1952	02:00	PDT
9/28/1952	02:00	PST
4/30/1961	02:00	PDT
9/24/1961	02:00	PST
4/29/1962	02:00	PDT
9/30/1962	02:00	PST
4/28/1963	02:00	US#2

WA # 11

Before 11/18/1883		LMT
11/18/1883	12:00	PST
3/31/1918	02:00	PWT
10/27/1918	02:00	PST
3/30/1919	02:00	PWT
10/26/1919	02:00	PST
5/07/1933	02:00	PDT
8/27/1933	02:00	PST
2/09/1942	02:00	PWT
9/30/1945	02:00	PST
6/01/1948	00:01	PDT
8/31/1948	00:01	PST
6/01/1949	00:01	PDT
9/01/1949	00:01	PST
4/30/1950	02:00	PDT
9/24/1950	02:00	PST
4/30/1961	02:00	PDT
9/24/1961	02:00	PST
4/29/1962	02:00	PDT
9/30/1962	02:00	PST
4/28/1963	02:00	US#2

WA # 12

Before 11/18/1883		LMT
11/18/1883	12:00	PST
3/31/1918	02:00	PWT
10/27/1918	02:00	PST
3/30/1919	02:00	PWT
10/26/1919	02:00	PST
2/09/1942	02:00	PWT
9/30/1945	02:00	PST
6/01/1949	00:01	PDT
9/30/1949	00:01	PST
4/30/1950	02:00	PDT
9/24/1950	02:00	PST
4/29/1951	02:00	PDT
9/30/1951	02:00	PST
6/01/1952	02:00	PDT
9/28/1952	02:00	PST
4/30/1961	02:00	PDT
9/24/1961	02:00	PST
4/29/1962	02:00	PDT
9/30/1962	02:00	PST
4/28/1963	02:00	US#2

WA # 13

Before 11/18/1883		LMT
11/18/1883	12:00	PST
3/31/1918	02:00	PWT
10/27/1918	02:00	PST
3/30/1919	02:00	PWT
10/26/1919	02:00	PST
2/09/1942	02:00	PWT
9/30/1945	02:00	PST
6/01/1948	00:01	PDT
9/25/1948	00:01	PST
6/01/1949	00:01	PDT
9/30/1949	00:01	PST
4/30/1950	02:00	PDT
9/24/1950	02:00	PST
4/29/1951	02:00	PDT
9/30/1951	02:00	PST
4/27/1952	02:00	PDT
9/28/1952	02:00	PST
4/30/1961	02:00	PDT
9/24/1961	02:00	PST
4/29/1962	02:00	PDT
9/30/1962	02:00	PST
4/28/1963	02:00	US#2

WA # 14

Before 11/18/1883		LMT
11/18/1883	12:00	PST
3/31/1918	02:00	PWT
10/27/1918	02:00	PST
3/30/1919	02:00	PWT
10/26/1919	02:00	PST
2/09/1942	02:00	PWT
9/30/1945	02:00	PST
6/14/1948	00:01	PDT
9/25/1948	00:01	PST
4/30/1961	02:00	PDT
9/24/1961	02:00	PST
4/29/1962	02:00	PDT
9/30/1962	02:00	PST
4/28/1963	02:00	US#2

WA # 15

Before 11/18/1883		LMT
11/18/1883	12:00	PST
3/31/1918	02:00	PWT
10/27/1918	02:00	PST
3/30/1919	02:00	PWT
10/26/1919	02:00	PST
2/09/1942	02:00	PWT
9/30/1945	02:00	PST
4/24/1949	00:01	PDT
9/01/1949	00:01	PST
4/30/1950	02:00	PDT
9/24/1950	02:00	PST
4/27/1952	02:00	PDT
9/28/1952	02:00	PST
4/30/1961	02:00	PDT
9/24/1961	02:00	PST
4/29/1962	02:00	PDT
9/30/1962	02:00	PST
4/28/1963	02:00	US#2

WA # 16

Before 11/18/1883		LMT
11/18/1883	12:00	PST
3/31/1918	02:00	PWT
10/27/1918	02:00	PST
3/30/1919	02:00	PWT
10/26/1919	02:00	PST
2/09/1942	02:00	PWT
9/30/1945	02:00	PST
6/01/1949	02:00	PDT
9/30/1949	02:00	PST
4/30/1950	02:00	PDT
9/03/1950	02:00	PST
4/30/1961	02:00	PDT
9/24/1961	02:00	PST
4/29/1962	02:00	PDT
9/30/1962	02:00	PST
4/28/1963	02:00	US#2

WA # 17

Before 11/18/1883		LMT
11/18/1883	12:00	PST
3/31/1918	02:00	PWT
10/27/1918	02:00	PST
3/30/1919	02:00	PWT
10/26/1919	02:00	PST
5/10/1933	02:00	PDT
8/31/1933	02:00	PST
2/09/1942	02:00	PWT
9/30/1945	02:00	PST
6/01/1948	00:01	PDT
9/25/1948	00:01	PST
6/01/1949	00:01	PDT
9/01/1949	00:01	PST
6/02/1950	02:00	PDT
9/07/1950	02:00	PST
4/29/1951	02:00	PDT
9/30/1951	02:00	PST
4/30/1961	02:00	PDT
9/24/1961	02:00	PST
4/29/1962	02:00	PDT
9/30/1962	02:00	PST
4/28/1963	02:00	US#2

WA # 18

Before 11/18/1883		LMT
11/18/1883	12:00	PST
3/31/1918	02:00	PWT
10/27/1918	02:00	PST
3/30/1919	02:00	PWT
10/26/1919	02:00	PST
2/09/1942	02:00	PWT
9/30/1945	02:00	PST
6/01/1948	00:01	PDT
9/25/1948	00:01	PST
6/01/1949	00:01	PDT
9/01/1949	00:01	PST
6/02/1950	02:00	PDT
9/07/1950	02:00	PST
4/30/1961	02:00	PDT
9/24/1961	02:00	PST
4/29/1962	02:00	PDT
9/30/1962	02:00	PST
4/28/1963	02:00	US#2

WA # 19

Before 11/18/1883		LMT
11/18/1883	12:00	PST
3/31/1918	02:00	PWT
10/27/1918	02:00	PST
3/30/1919	02:00	PWT
10/26/1919	02:00	PST
2/09/1942	02:00	PWT
9/30/1945	02:00	PST
6/01/1948	00:01	PDT
9/25/1948	00:01	PST
4/30/1961	02:00	PDT
9/24/1961	02:00	PST
4/29/1962	02:00	PDT
9/30/1962	02:00	PST
4/28/1963	02:00	US#2

WA # 20

Before 11/18/1883		LMT
11/18/1883	12:00	PST
3/31/1918	02:00	PWT
10/27/1918	02:00	PST
3/30/1919	02:00	PWT
10/26/1919	02:00	PST
2/09/1942	02:00	PWT
9/30/1945	02:00	PST
6/01/1952	02:00	PDT
9/28/1952	02:00	PST
4/30/1961	02:00	PDT
9/24/1961	02:00	PST
4/29/1962	02:00	PDT
9/30/1962	02:00	PST
4/28/1963	02:00	US#2

WA # 21

Before 11/18/1883		LMT
11/18/1883	12:00	PST
3/31/1918	02:00	PWT
10/27/1918	02:00	PST
3/30/1919	02:00	PWT
10/26/1919	02:00	PST
2/09/1942	02:00	PWT
9/30/1945	02:00	PST
6/06/1948	00:01	PDT
9/25/1948	00:01	PST
4/30/1961	02:00	PDT
9/24/1961	02:00	PST
4/29/1962	02:00	PDT
9/30/1962	02:00	PST
4/28/1963	02:00	US#2

WA # 22

Before 11/18/1883		LMT
11/18/1883	12:00	PST
3/31/1918	02:00	PWT
10/27/1918	02:00	PST
3/30/1919	02:00	PWT
10/26/1919	02:00	PST
2/09/1942	02:00	PWT
9/30/1945	02:00	PST
6/03/1948	00:01	PDT
9/25/1948	00:01	PST
5/01/1952	02:00	PDT
9/28/1952	02:00	PST
4/30/1961	02:00	PDT
9/24/1961	02:00	PST
4/29/1962	02:00	PDT
9/30/1962	02:00	PST
4/28/1963	02:00	US#2

WA # 23

Before 11/18/1883		LMT
11/18/1883	12:00	PST
3/31/1918	02:00	PWT
10/27/1918	02:00	PST
3/30/1919	02:00	PWT
10/26/1919	02:00	PST
2/09/1942	02:00	PWT
9/30/1945	02:00	PST
6/01/1949	00:01	PDT
9/01/1949	00:01	PST
4/30/1950	02:00	PDT
9/24/1950	02:00	PST
4/29/1951	02:00	PDT
9/30/1951	02:00	PST
6/01/1952	02:00	PDT
9/01/1952	02:00	PST
4/30/1961	02:00	PDT
9/24/1961	02:00	PST
4/29/1962	02:00	PDT
9/30/1962	02:00	PST
4/28/1963	02:00	US#2

WA # 24

Before 11/18/1883		LMT
11/18/1883	12:00	PST
3/31/1918	02:00	PWT
10/27/1918	02:00	PST
3/30/1919	02:00	PWT
10/26/1919	02:00	PST
5/07/1933	02:00	PDT
8/27/1933	02:00	PST
2/09/1942	02:00	PWT
9/30/1945	02:00	PST
6/01/1948	00:01	PDT
9/25/1948	00:01	PST
6/01/1949	00:01	PDT
9/30/1949	00:01	PST
4/30/1950	02:00	PDT
9/24/1950	02:00	PST
6/01/1952	02:00	PDT
9/28/1952	02:00	PST
4/30/1961	02:00	PDT
9/24/1961	02:00	PST
4/29/1962	02:00	PDT
9/30/1962	02:00	PST
4/28/1963	02:00	US#2

WA # 25

Before 11/18/1883		LMT
11/18/1883	12:00	PST
3/31/1918	02:00	PWT
10/27/1918	02:00	PST
3/30/1919	02:00	PWT
10/26/1919	02:00	PST
2/09/1942	02:00	PWT
9/30/1945	02:00	PST
6/01/1949	00:01	PDT
9/30/1949	00:01	PST
5/02/1950	02:00	PDT
9/24/1950	02:00	PST
4/30/1961	02:00	PDT
9/24/1961	02:00	PST
4/29/1962	02:00	PDT
9/30/1962	02:00	PST
4/28/1963	02:00	US#2

WA # 26

Before 11/18/1883		LMT
11/18/1883	12:00	PST
3/31/1918	02:00	PWT
10/27/1918	02:00	PST
3/30/1919	02:00	PWT
10/26/1919	02:00	PST
2/09/1942	02:00	PWT
9/30/1945	02:00	PST
6/03/1948	00:01	PDT
9/25/1948	00:01	PST
6/01/1949	00:01	PDT
9/30/1949	00:01	PST
4/30/1950	02:00	PDT
9/24/1950	02:00	PST
4/29/1951	02:00	PDT
9/30/1951	02:00	PST
4/30/1961	02:00	PDT
9/24/1961	02:00	PST
4/29/1962	02:00	PDT
9/30/1962	02:00	PST
4/28/1963	02:00	US#2

WA # 27

Before 11/18/1883		LMT
11/18/1883	12:00	PST
3/31/1918	02:00	PWT
10/27/1918	02:00	PST
3/30/1919	02:00	PWT
10/26/1919	02:00	PST
2/09/1942	02:00	PWT
9/30/1945	02:00	PST
6/01/1949	00:01	PDT
9/01/1949	00:01	PST
4/30/1950	02:00	PDT
9/24/1950	02:00	PST
4/29/1951	02:00	PDT
9/30/1951	02:00	PST
6/01/1952	02:00	PDT
9/28/1952	02:00	PST
4/30/1961	02:00	PDT
9/24/1961	02:00	PST
4/29/1962	02:00	PDT
9/30/1962	02:00	PST
4/28/1963	02:00	US#2

WA # 28

Before 11/18/1883		LMT
11/18/1883	12:00	PST
3/31/1918	02:00	PWT
10/27/1918	02:00	PST
3/30/1919	02:00	PWT
10/26/1919	02:00	PST
2/09/1942	02:00	PWT
9/30/1945	02:00	PST
4/24/1949	00:01	PDT
9/01/1949	00:01	PST
4/30/1950	02:00	PDT
9/24/1950	02:00	PST
4/29/1951	02:00	PDT
9/30/1951	02:00	PST
4/27/1952	02:00	PDT
9/28/1952	02:00	PST
4/30/1961	02:00	PDT
9/24/1961	02:00	PST
4/29/1962	02:00	PDT
9/30/1962	02:00	PST
4/28/1963	02:00	US#2

WA # 29

Before 11/18/1883		LMT
11/18/1883	12:00	PST
3/31/1918	02:00	PWT
10/27/1918	02:00	PST
3/30/1919	02:00	PWT
10/26/1919	02:00	PST
2/09/1942	02:00	PWT
9/30/1945	02:00	PST
6/20/1948	00:01	PDT
9/25/1948	00:01	PST
4/30/1961	02:00	PDT
9/24/1961	02:00	PST
4/29/1962	02:00	PDT
9/30/1962	02:00	PST
4/28/1963	02:00	US#2

WA # 30

Before 11/18/1883		LMT
11/18/1883	12:00	PST
3/31/1918	02:00	PWT
10/27/1918	02:00	PST
3/30/1919	02:00	PWT
10/26/1919	02:00	PST
2/09/1942	02:00	PWT
9/30/1945	02:00	PST
6/01/1948	00:01	PDT
9/25/1948	00:01	PST
4/30/1950	02:00	PDT
9/24/1950	02:00	PST

TIME TABLES

4/29/1951 02:00 PDT
9/30/1951 02:00 PST
6/01/1952 02:00 PDT
9/28/1952 02:00 PST
4/30/1961 02:00 PDT
9/24/1961 02:00 PST
4/29/1962 02:00 PDT
9/30/1962 02:00 PST
4/28/1963 02:00 US#2

WA # 31
Before 11/18/1883 LMT
11/18/1883 12:00 PST
3/31/1918 02:00 PWT
10/27/1918 02:00 PST
3/30/1919 02:00 PWT
10/26/1919 02:00 PST
2/09/1942 02:00 PWT
9/30/1945 02:00 PST
6/01/1949 00:01 PDT
9/30/1949 00:01 PST
4/30/1961 02:00 PDT
9/24/1961 02:00 PST
4/29/1962 02:00 PDT
9/30/1962 02:00 PST
4/28/1963 02:00 US#2

WA # 32
Before 11/18/1883 LMT
11/18/1883 12:00 PST
3/31/1918 02:00 PWT
10/27/1918 02:00 PST
3/30/1919 02:00 PWT
10/26/1919 02:00 PST
2/09/1942 02:00 PWT
9/30/1945 02:00 PST
6/01/1948 00:01 PDT
9/25/1948 00:01 PST
4/24/1949 00:01 PDT
9/11/1949 00:01 PST
4/30/1950 02:00 PDT
9/24/1950 02:00 PST
4/29/1951 02:00 PDT
9/30/1951 02:00 PST
4/27/1952 02:00 PDT
9/28/1952 02:00 PST
4/30/1961 02:00 PDT
9/24/1961 02:00 PST
4/29/1962 02:00 PDT
9/30/1962 02:00 PST
4/28/1963 02:00 US#2

WA # 33
Before 11/18/1883 LMT
11/18/1883 12:00 PST
3/31/1918 02:00 PWT
10/27/1918 02:00 PST
3/30/1919 02:00 PWT
10/26/1919 02:00 PST
2/09/1942 02:00 PWT
9/30/1945 02:00 PST
6/03/1948 00:01 PDT
9/25/1948 00:01 PST
6/01/1949 00:01 PDT
8/31/1949 00:01 PST
4/30/1950 02:00 PDT
9/24/1950 02:00 PST
4/30/1961 02:00 PDT
9/24/1961 02:00 PST
4/29/1962 02:00 PDT
9/30/1962 02:00 PST
4/28/1963 02:00 US#2

WA # 34
Before 11/18/1883 LMT
11/18/1883 12:00 PST
3/31/1918 02:00 PWT
10/27/1918 02:00 PST
3/30/1919 02:00 PWT
10/26/1919 02:00 PST
2/09/1942 02:00 PWT
9/30/1945 02:00 PST
6/01/1949 00:01 PDT
8/31/1949 00:01 PST
4/30/1950 02:00 PDT
9/24/1950 02:00 PST
6/01/1952 02:00 PDT
9/28/1952 02:00 PST
4/30/1961 02:00 PDT
9/24/1961 02:00 PST
4/29/1962 02:00 PDT
9/30/1962 02:00 PST
4/28/1963 02:00 US#2

WA # 35
Before 11/18/1883 LMT
11/18/1883 12:00 PST
3/31/1918 02:00 PWT
10/27/1918 02:00 PST
3/30/1919 02:00 PWT
10/26/1919 02:00 PST
2/09/1942 02:00 PWT
9/30/1945 02:00 PST
6/13/1950 02:00 PDT
9/07/1950 02:00 PST
4/30/1961 02:00 PDT
9/24/1961 02:00 PST
4/29/1962 02:00 PDT
9/30/1962 02:00 PST
4/28/1963 02:00 US#2

WA # 36
Before 11/18/1883 LMT
11/18/1883 12:00 PST
3/31/1918 02:00 PWT
10/27/1918 02:00 PST
3/30/1919 02:00 PWT
10/26/1919 02:00 PST
5/14/1933 02:00 PDT
8/27/1933 02:00 PST
2/09/1942 02:00 PWT
9/30/1945 02:00 PST
6/01/1948 00:01 PDT
9/25/1948 00:01 PST
6/01/1949 00:01 PDT
9/01/1949 00:01 PST
5/01/1950 02:00 PDT
9/24/1950 02:00 PST
4/29/1951 02:00 PDT
9/30/1951 02:00 PST
6/01/1952 02:00 PDT
9/28/1952 02:00 PST
4/30/1961 02:00 PDT
9/24/1961 02:00 PST
4/29/1962 02:00 PDT
9/30/1962 02:00 PST
4/28/1963 02:00 US#2

WA # 37
Before 11/18/1883 LMT
11/18/1883 12:00 PST
3/31/1918 02:00 PWT
10/27/1918 02:00 PST
3/30/1919 02:00 PWT
10/26/1919 02:00 PST
2/09/1942 02:00 PWT
9/30/1945 02:00 PST
6/01/1948 00:01 PDT
9/25/1948 00:01 PST
6/01/1949 00:01 PDT
9/30/1949 00:01 PST
5/02/1950 02:00 PDT
9/24/1950 02:00 PST
4/30/1961 02:00 PDT
9/24/1961 02:00 PST
4/29/1962 02:00 PDT
9/30/1962 02:00 PST
4/28/1963 02:00 US#2

WA # 38
Before 11/18/1883 LMT
11/18/1883 12:00 PST
3/31/1918 02:00 PWT
10/27/1918 02:00 PST
3/30/1919 02:00 PWT
10/26/1919 02:00 PST
2/09/1942 02:00 PWT
9/30/1945 02:00 PST
6/01/1949 00:01 PDT
9/30/1949 00:01 PST
4/30/1950 02:00 PDT
9/24/1950 02:00 PST
4/29/1951 02:00 PDT
9/30/1951 02:00 PST
4/30/1961 02:00 PDT
9/24/1961 02:00 PST
4/29/1962 02:00 PDT
9/30/1962 02:00 PST
4/28/1963 02:00 US#2

WA # 39
Before 11/18/1883 LMT
11/18/1883 12:00 PST
3/31/1918 02:00 PWT
10/27/1918 02:00 PST
3/30/1919 02:00 PWT
10/26/1919 02:00 PST
2/09/1942 02:00 PWT
9/30/1945 02:00 PST
6/03/1948 00:01 PDT
9/25/1948 00:01 PST
5/30/1949 00:01 PDT
9/01/1949 00:01 PST
4/29/1951 02:00 PDT
9/30/1951 02:00 PST
6/01/1952 02:00 PDT
9/28/1952 02:00 PST
4/30/1961 02:00 PDT
9/24/1961 02:00 PST
4/29/1962 02:00 PDT
9/30/1962 02:00 PST
4/28/1963 02:00 US#2

WA # 40
Before 11/18/1883 LMT
11/18/1883 12:00 PST
3/31/1918 02:00 PWT
10/27/1918 02:00 PST
3/30/1919 02:00 PWT
10/26/1919 02:00 PST
2/09/1942 02:00 PWT
9/30/1945 02:00 PST
6/01/1949 00:01 PDT
9/30/1949 00:01 PST
4/30/1950 02:00 PDT
9/24/1950 02:00 PST
4/29/1951 02:00 PDT
9/30/1951 02:00 PST
5/05/1952 02:00 PDT
10/05/1952 02:00 PST
4/30/1961 02:00 PDT
9/24/1961 02:00 PST
4/29/1962 02:00 PDT
9/30/1962 02:00 PST
4/28/1963 02:00 US#2

WA # 41
Before 11/18/1883 LMT
11/18/1883 12:00 PST
3/31/1918 02:00 PWT
10/27/1918 02:00 PST
3/30/1919 02:00 PWT
10/26/1919 02:00 PST
2/09/1942 02:00 PWT
9/30/1945 02:00 PST
4/24/1949 02:00 PDT
9/25/1949 02:00 PST
5/02/1950 02:00 PDT
9/24/1950 02:00 PST
6/10/1951 02:00 PDT
9/02/1951 02:00 PST
4/29/1956 02:00 PDT
9/29/1956 02:00 PST
4/30/1961 02:00 PDT
9/24/1961 02:00 PST
4/29/1962 02:00 PDT
9/30/1962 02:00 PST
4/28/1963 02:00 US#2

WA # 42
Before 11/18/1883 LMT
11/18/1883 12:00 PST
3/31/1918 02:00 PWT
10/27/1918 02:00 PST
3/30/1919 02:00 PWT
10/26/1919 02:00 PST
2/09/1942 02:00 PWT
9/30/1945 02:00 PST
4/24/1949 00:01 PDT
9/01/1949 00:01 PST
4/27/1952 02:00 PDT
9/28/1952 02:00 PST
4/30/1961 02:00 PDT
9/24/1961 02:00 PST
4/29/1962 02:00 PDT
9/30/1962 02:00 PST
4/28/1963 02:00 US#2

WA # 43
Before 11/18/1883 LMT
11/18/1883 12:00 PST
3/31/1918 02:00 PWT
10/27/1918 02:00 PST
3/30/1919 02:00 PWT
10/26/1919 02:00 PST
2/09/1942 02:00 PWT
9/30/1945 02:00 PST
4/24/1949 00:01 PDT
9/01/1949 00:01 PST
4/30/1961 02:00 PDT
9/24/1961 02:00 PST
4/29/1962 02:00 PDT
9/30/1962 02:00 PST
4/28/1963 02:00 US#2

WA # 44
Before 11/18/1883 LMT
11/18/1883 12:00 PST
3/31/1918 02:00 PWT
10/27/1918 02:00 PST
3/30/1919 02:00 PWT
10/26/1919 02:00 PST
5/07/1933 02:00 PDT
8/27/1933 02:00 PST
2/09/1942 02:00 PWT
9/30/1945 02:00 PST
6/01/1948 00:01 PDT
9/25/1948 00:01 PST
6/01/1949 00:01 PDT
9/30/1949 00:01 PST
4/30/1950 02:00 PDT
9/24/1950 02:00 PST
4/29/1951 02:00 PDT
9/30/1951 02:00 PST
6/01/1952 02:00 PDT
9/28/1952 02:00 PST
4/30/1961 02:00 PDT
9/24/1961 02:00 PST
4/29/1962 02:00 PDT
9/30/1962 02:00 PST
4/28/1963 02:00 US#2

WA # 45
Before 11/18/1883 LMT
11/18/1883 12:00 PST
3/31/1918 02:00 PWT
10/27/1918 02:00 PST
3/30/1919 02:00 PWT
10/26/1919 02:00 PST
2/09/1942 02:00 PWT
9/30/1945 02:00 PST
6/01/1948 00:01 PDT
9/25/1948 00:01 PST
4/30/1950 02:00 PDT
9/24/1950 02:00 PST
4/29/1951 02:00 PDT
9/30/1951 02:00 PST
4/30/1961 02:00 PDT
9/24/1961 02:00 PST
4/29/1962 02:00 PDT
9/30/1962 02:00 PST
4/28/1963 02:00 US#2

WA # 46
Before 11/18/1883 LMT
11/18/1883 12:00 PST
3/31/1918 02:00 PWT
10/27/1918 02:00 PST
3/30/1919 02:00 PWT
10/26/1919 02:00 PST
2/09/1942 02:00 PWT
9/30/1945 02:00 PST
6/01/1948 00:01 PDT
9/25/1948 00:01 PST
5/01/1950 02:00 PDT
9/25/1950 02:00 PST
4/30/1961 02:00 PDT
9/24/1961 02:00 PST
4/29/1962 02:00 PDT
9/30/1962 02:00 PST
4/28/1963 02:00 US#2

WA # 47
Before 11/18/1883 LMT
11/18/1883 12:00 PST
3/31/1918 02:00 PWT
10/27/1918 02:00 PST
3/30/1919 02:00 PWT
10/26/1919 02:00 PST
2/09/1942 02:00 PWT
9/30/1945 02:00 PST
6/06/1948 00:01 PDT
9/25/1948 00:01 PST
4/29/1951 02:00 PDT
9/30/1951 02:00 PST
6/01/1952 02:00 PDT
9/28/1952 02:00 PST
4/30/1961 02:00 PDT
9/24/1961 02:00 PST
4/29/1962 02:00 PDT
9/30/1962 02:00 PST
4/28/1963 02:00 US#2

WA # 48
Before 11/18/1883 LMT
11/18/1883 12:00 PST
3/31/1918 02:00 PWT
10/27/1918 02:00 PST
3/30/1919 02:00 PWT
10/26/1919 02:00 PST
5/07/1933 02:00 PDT
8/27/1933 02:00 PST
2/09/1942 02:00 PWT
9/30/1945 02:00 PST
4/30/1961 02:00 PDT
9/24/1961 02:00 PST
4/29/1962 02:00 PDT
9/30/1962 02:00 PST
4/28/1963 02:00 US#2

WA # 49
Before 11/18/1883 LMT
11/18/1883 12:00 PST
3/31/1918 02:00 PWT
10/27/1918 02:00 PST
3/30/1919 02:00 PWT
10/26/1919 02:00 PST
5/07/1933 02:00 PDT
8/27/1933 02:00 PST
2/09/1942 02:00 PWT
9/30/1945 02:00 PST
6/01/1948 00:01 PDT
9/25/1948 00:01 PST
6/01/1949 00:01 PDT
9/01/1949 00:01 PST
4/30/1950 02:00 PDT
9/24/1950 02:00 PST
4/29/1951 02:00 PDT
9/30/1951 02:00 PST
5/17/1952 02:00 PDT
9/28/1952 02:00 PST
4/30/1961 02:00 PDT
9/24/1961 02:00 PST
4/29/1962 02:00 PDT
9/30/1962 02:00 PST
4/28/1963 02:00 US#2

WA # 50
Before 11/18/1883 LMT
11/18/1883 12:00 PST
3/31/1918 02:00 PWT
10/27/1918 02:00 PST
3/30/1919 02:00 PWT
10/26/1919 02:00 PST
2/09/1942 02:00 PWT
9/30/1945 02:00 PST
6/01/1949 00:01 PDT
9/30/1949 00:01 PST
4/30/1950 02:00 PDT
9/24/1950 02:00 PST
4/27/1952 02:00 PDT
9/28/1952 02:00 PST
4/30/1961 02:00 PDT
9/24/1961 02:00 PST
4/29/1962 02:00 PDT
9/30/1962 02:00 PST
4/28/1963 02:00 US#2

WA # 51
Before 11/18/1883 LMT
11/18/1883 12:00 PST
3/31/1918 02:00 PWT
10/27/1918 02:00 PST
3/30/1919 02:00 PWT
10/26/1919 02:00 PST
5/07/1933 02:00 PDT
8/27/1933 02:00 PST
2/09/1942 02:00 PWT
9/30/1945 02:00 PST
6/01/1948 00:01 PDT
9/25/1948 00:01 PST
4/24/1949 00:01 PDT
9/11/1949 00:01 PST
5/01/1950 02:00 PDT
9/24/1950 02:00 PST
4/29/1951 02:00 PDT
9/30/1951 02:00 PST
4/27/1952 02:00 PDT
9/28/1952 02:00 PST
4/30/1961 02:00 PDT
9/24/1961 02:00 PST
4/29/1962 02:00 PDT
9/30/1962 02:00 PST
4/28/1963 02:00 US#2

WA # 52
Before 11/18/1883 LMT
11/18/1883 12:00 PST
3/31/1918 02:00 PWT
10/27/1918 02:00 PST
3/30/1919 02:00 PWT
10/26/1919 02:00 PST
5/07/1933 02:00 PDT
8/27/1933 02:00 PST
2/09/1942 02:00 PWT
9/30/1945 02:00 PST
6/03/1948 00:01 PDT
9/25/1948 00:01 PST
4/30/1961 02:00 PDT
9/24/1961 02:00 PST
4/29/1962 02:00 PDT
9/30/1962 02:00 PST
4/28/1963 02:00 US#2

WA # 53
Before 11/18/1883 LMT
11/18/1883 12:00 PST
3/31/1918 02:00 PWT
10/27/1918 02:00 PST
3/30/1919 02:00 PWT
10/26/1919 02:00 PST
2/09/1942 02:00 PWT
9/30/1945 02:00 PST
4/24/1949 00:01 PDT
9/01/1949 00:01 PST
4/30/1950 02:00 PDT
9/24/1950 02:00 PST
4/29/1951 02:00 PDT
9/30/1951 02:00 PST
4/30/1961 02:00 PDT
9/24/1961 02:00 PST
4/29/1962 02:00 PDT
9/30/1962 02:00 PST
4/28/1963 02:00 US#2

COUNTIES

1 Adams
2 Asotin
3 Benton
4 Chelan
5 Clallam
6 Clark
7 Columbia
8 Cowlitz
9 Douglas
10 Ferry
11 Franklin
12 Garfield
13 Grant
14 Grays Harbor
15 Island
16 Jefferson
17 King
18 Kitsap
19 Kittitas
20 Klickitat
21 Lewis
22 Lincoln
23 Mason
24 Okanogan
25 Pacific
26 Pend Oreille
27 Pierce
28 San Juan
29 Skagit
30 Skamania
31 Snohomish
32 Spokane
33 Stevens
34 Thurston
35 Wahkiakum
36 Walla Walla
37 Whatcom
38 Whitman
39 Yakima

Aberdeen 14 8 46n58'32 123w48'52 8:15:15
Aberdeen Gardens 14 1 46n58 123w45 8:15:00
Aberdeen Junction 14 1 46n58'44 123w45'42 8:15:03
Academy 32 1 47n26 117w23 7:49:32
Acme 37 1 48n43'02 122w12'14 8:08:49
Adco 13 1 47n23 119w29 7:57:56
Addy 33 1 48n21'22 117w50'11 7:51:21

Adelaide 17 9 47N19'52 122W21'33 8:09:26
Adelma Beach 16
31 48N07 122W47 8:11:08
Adkins 36 1 46N15'13 118W42'06 7:54:48
Adna 21 5 46N37'45 123W03'36 8:12:14
Adrian 13 1 47N23'28 119W54'59 7:59:40
Aeneas 24 1 48N32'51 118W58'39 7:55:55
Agate 23 1 47N12'49 123W00'40 8:12:03
Agate Beach 5 2 48N08 123W44 8:14:56
Agate Point 18 1 47N42'51 122W33'07 8:10:12
Agnew 5 2 48N06'21 123W14'50 8:12:59
Ahtanum 39 1 46N33'35 120W37'15 8:02:29
Ainsworth Junction 11
1 46N12'35 119W02'12 7:56:09
Airway Heights 32
1 47N38'41 117W35'32 7:50:22
Ajlune 21 1 46N30'56 122W26'01 8:09:44
Aladdin 33 1 48N43'43 117W40'13 7:50:41
Albion 38 1 46N47'28 117W14'58 7:49:00
Alder 27 6 46N48'02 122W17'20 8:09:09
Alderdale 20 1 45N50'06 119W55'11 7:59:41
Alder Grove 14 1 46N59 123W36 8:14:24
Alderton 27 6 47N10'11 122W13'41 8:08:55
Alderwood Manor 31
1 47N49'20 122W16'51 8:09:07
Alexander Beach 29
1 48N28'31 122W39'32 8:10:38
Alfafa 39 1 46N19'50 120W14'16 8:00:57
Alger 29 1 48N37'12 122W20'24 8:09:22
Algona 17 9 47N16'45 122W15'03 8:09:00
Allen 29 1 48N31 122W21 8:09:24
Allentown 17 4 47N29'40 122W16'30 8:09:06
Allison 27 6 47N08'26 122W23'40 8:09:35
Allyn 23 1 47N23'09 122W49'35 8:11:18
Almira 22 1 47N42'40 118W56'23 7:55:46
Almota 38 1 46N42'11 117W28'06 7:49:52
Aloha 14 1 47N12'04 124W10'00 8:16:40
Alpental 17 4 47N32 121W49 8:07:16
Alpha 21 5 46N36'42 122W36'15 8:10:25
Alstown 9 1 47N33'40 119W59'38 7:59:59
Alta Vista 21 7 46N29'59 122W22'16 8:09:29
Alto 7 1 46N23'11 118W06'38 7:52:27
Altoona 35 1 46N16'01 123W39'18 8:14:37
Amanda Park 14 1 47N27'48 123W53'05 8:15:32
Amber 32 1 47N21'07 117W42'38 7:50:51
Amboy 6 1 45N54'37 122W26'43 8:09:47
American Lake 27
6 47N09 122W33 8:10:12
American Lake Garden Tract 27
6 47N07'21 122W32'03 8:10:08
Ames Lake 17 4 47N39 122W09 8:08:36
Anacortes 29 1 48N30'46 122W36'41 8:10:27
Anacortes Crossing 37
1 48N47'00 120W49'43 8:03:19
Anatone 2 1 46N08'06 117W07'53 7:48:32
Anderson Island 27
6 47N11 122W42 8:10:48
Andron 31 1 48N15'46 121W36'18 8:06:25
Anglin 24 1 48N39'25 119W17'17 7:57:09
Ankeny 1 1 46N51'00 118W09'13 7:52:37
Annapolis 18 1 47N32'52 122W37'10 8:10:29
Appledale 9 1 47N21'16 119W58'24 7:59:54
Appleton 20 1 45N48'43 121W16'12 8:05:05
Appleyard 4 1 47N23'52 120W18'07 8:01:12
Apricot 39 1 46N14'12 119W51'23 7:59:26
Arbor Heights 17
4 47N31'03 122W22'32 8:09:30
Arcadia 23 1 47N11'53 122W56'18 8:11:45
Arden 33 1 48N27'37 117W52'31 7:51:30
Ardenvoir 4 1 47N44'15 120W22'04 8:01:28
Argyle 28 1 48N30'53 123W01'06 8:12:04
Ariel 8 3 45N57'25 122W34'11 8:10:17
Arletta 27 6 47N17'25 122W39'59 8:10:40
Arlington 31 1 48N11'56 122W07'26 8:08:30
Arlington Heights 31
1 48N12'08 122W03'39 8:08:15
Arlington Junction 31
1 48N12'22 122W07'40 8:08:31
Armar 31 24 48N04 122W10 8:08:40
Armstrong 38 1 46N45'37 117W13'28 7:48:54
Arnada Park Annex 6
51 45N39 122W40 8:10:40
Arrowhead 17 4 47N43 122W13 8:08:52
Arrowhead 27 6 47N09 122W33 8:10:12
Arroyo Heights 17
4 47N30'23 122W22'49 8:09:31
Artic 14 1 46N53'21 123W42'48 8:14:51
Artondale 27 49 47N17'59 122W23'70 8:09:37
Arzina 33 1 48N26'31 118W06'47 7:52:27
Ash 36 1 46N15'12 118W50'32 7:55:22
Ashby 1 1 47N09'08 118W04'00 7:52:16
Ashford 27 6 46N45'31 122W01'47 8:08:07
Ashue 39 1 46N24'16 120W27'30 8:01:50
Asotin 2 1 46N20'22 117W02'50 7:48:11
Attalia 36 1 46N06'29 118W55'08 7:55:41
Atwood 13 1 47N06'02 119W07'23 7:56:30
Auburn 17 9 47N18'27 122W13'38 8:08:55
Audrey 3 1 46N37'39 119W36'51 7:58:27
Ault Field 15 2 48N20 122W39 8:10:36
Austin 15 2 47N59'30 122W32'19 8:10:09
Austin 32 1 47N41'06 117W09'49 7:48:39
Avon 29 1 48N26'33 122W22'38 8:09:31
Avondale 17 4 47N42'12 122W05'30 8:08:22
Ayer 36 1 46N34'48 118W23'03 7:53:32
Azwell 4 1 47N56'14 119W52'31 7:59:30
Babb 32 1 47N27'30 117W39'24 7:50:38
Babcock 36 1 46N19'33 118W35'32 7:54:22
Baby Island Heights 15
2 48N05'47 122W31'13 8:10:05
Bacon 13 1 47N30'03 119W19'45 7:57:19
Badger 3 1 46N12'01 119W21'30 7:57:26
Bagdad Junction 22
1 47N52'26 118W56'11 7:55:45
Bagley Junction 17
4 47N23'37 121W50'42 8:07:23
Baileysburg 7 1 46N17'57 117W57'06 7:51:48
Baird 9 1 47N37 119W17 7:57:08
Baker Heights 29
1 48N26'08 122W15'06 8:09:00
Baker-Langdon 36
48 46N01'29 118W19'25 7:53:18
Bakerview 37 11 48N45 122W29 8:09:56
Balch 14 35 46N48'53 123W14'31 8:12:58
Balder 38 1 47N10'58 117W24'16 7:49:37
Balford 37 1 48N56'05 122W08'57 8:08:36
Ballard 17 44 47N40'34 122W23'10 8:09:33
Ballow 23 1 47N14'26 122W51'57 8:11:28
Bandera 17 4 47N23'13 121W31'57 8:06:08
Bangor 18 1 47N43'16 122W44'41 8:10:59
Banner 18 1 47N29'20 122W32'30 8:10:10
Barberton 6 51 45N41'36 122W35'52 8:10:23
Barco 31 1 48N16'50 121W40'17 8:06:41
Barham 13 1 47N05'03 119W00'43 7:56:03
Baring 17 4 47N46'24 121W29'03 8:05:56
Barker 24 1 48N34'39 119W28'51 7:57:55
Barneston 17 4 47N23'16 121W51'36 8:07:26
Barron 37 1 48N45'12 120W42'55 8:02:52
Barstow 10 1 48N46'38 118W08'30 7:52:34
Basin City 11 1 46N35'39 119W09'04 7:56:36
Bassett Junction 13
1 47N02'33 119W05'17 7:56:21
Bates 20 1 45N42'18 120W25'32 8:01:42
Battle Ground 6
10 45N46'52 122W31'56 8:10:08
Battle Point 18
1 47N39'27 122W35'01 8:10:20
Batum 1 1 47N14'01 118W48'33 7:55:14
Bay Center 25 1 46N37'54 123W57'13 8:15:49
Bay Center Junction 25
1 46N35'57 123W55'01 8:15:40
Bay City 14 1 46N51'53 124W03'29 8:16:14
Bayne 17 4 47N17'43 121W54'30 8:07:38
Bayne Junction 17
4 47N18'04 121W54'27 8:07:38
Bayshore 23 1 47N14'47 123W02'42 8:12:11
Bay View 15 2 48N00'28 122W27'36 8:09:50
Bayview 27 6 47N16'47 122W36'16 8:10:25
Bay View 29 1 48N29'02 122W28'35 8:09:54
Beachcrest 34 36 47N06'30 122W44'51 8:10:59
Beach Haven 28 1 48N41'32 122W56'58 8:11:48
Beacon Hill 8 32 46N10'31 122W55'15 8:11:41
Beacon Hill 17
44 47N34'40 122W18'31 8:09:14
Bear 33 1 48N42'39 118W02'35 7:52:10
Beatrice 1 1 46N52'55 118W45'57 7:55:04
Beaux Arts 17 4 47N35'02 122W11'40 8:08:47
Beaver 5 2 48N03'27 124W20'46 8:17:23
Beaver Valley 16
1 47N55'34 122W43'44 8:10:55
Beckett Point 16
31 48N07 122W47 8:11:08
Bedal 31 1 48N05'56 121W23'41 8:05:35
Bedford 25 39 46N39'41 123W28'00 8:13:52
Beebe 9 1 47N50'21 119W56'59 7:59:48
Bees Mill 16 1 47N45'45 122W51'17 8:11:25
Belfair 18 1 47N30'09 122W46'34 8:11:06
Bellevue 17 4 47N36'38 122W11'58 8:08:48
Bellingham 37 11 48N45'35 122W29'13 8:09:57
Bells Beach 15 2 48N04'37 122W28'04 8:09:52
Belmont 38 1 47N05'17 117W09'41 7:48:39
Belmore 34 36 46N59'15 122W57'40 8:11:51
Belvedere 24 1 48N03'00 118W59'02 7:55:56
Bench Drive 14 1 46N58 123W45 8:15:00
Benge 1 1 46N54'34 118W06'05 7:52:24
Bennett Hill 37
11 48N45 122W29 8:09:56
Benroy 27 9 47N14'34 122W14'42 8:08:59
Benton City 3 1 46N15'48 119W29'12 7:57:57
Berne 4 1 47N46'12 120W58'47 8:03:55
Berrian 3 1 45N56'16 119W09'03 7:56:36
Berrydale 17 4 47N20 122W08 8:08:32
Berryman 36 1 46N13'23 118W23'15 7:53:33
Berry Patch 21 7 46N28'01 121W31'35 8:06:06
Bethel 18 1 47N29'39 122W37'48 8:10:31
Bettie 3 1 46N40'35 119W31'38 7:58:07
Beverly 13 1 46N50'13 119W55'55 7:59:44
Beverly Beach 15
2 48N03'40 122W30'41 8:10:03
Beverly Junction 19
1 46N49'53 119W56'55 7:59:48
Beverly Park 31
24 47N58 122W14 8:08:56
B & G 31 24 47N58 122W14 8:08:56
Bickleton 20 1 45N59'53 120W17'58 8:01:12
Big Lake 29 1 48N24'11 122W14'24 8:08:58
Bingen 20 1 45N42'54 121W27'48 8:05:51
Bingville 33 1 48N23'06 117W37'44 7:50:31
Birch 17 4 47N13'29 121W58'05 8:07:52
Birch Bay 37 1 48N55'05 122W44'36 8:10:58
Birch Bay Circle Grange 37
1 48N56'02 122W44'48 8:10:59
Birchfield 39 1 46N34'38 120W26'00 8:01:44
Birdsview 29 1 48N31'21 121W52'27 8:07:30
Bitter Lake 17 4 47N44 122W21 8:09:24
Black Diamond 17
4 47N18'32 122W00'07 8:08:00
Black Lake 33 1 48N33 117W54 7:51:36
Black River 17 4 47N29'30 122W15'11 8:09:01
Black River Junction 17
40 47N29 122W12 8:08:48
Blacks Corner 39
1 46N16'22 119W55'30 7:59:42
Blaine 37 1 48N59'38 122W44'45 8:10:59
Blakely Island 28
1 48N30 122W37 8:10:28
Blakeslee Junction 21
5 46N44'07 122W58'23 8:11:54
Blanchard 29 1 48N35'37 122W24'55 8:09:40
Blewett 4 1 47N25'24 120W39'29 8:02:38
Blockhouse 20 1 45N50'23 120W56'11 8:03:45
Blue Canyon 37 1 48N40'57 122W16'34 8:09:06
Bluecreek 33 1 48N19'08 117W49'12 7:51:17
Bluelight 20 1 46N02'29 120W10'34 8:00:42
Blueslide 26 1 48N33'23 117W20'41 7:49:23
Bluestem 22 1 47N31'30 118W07'32 7:52:30
Blurock Landing 6
51 45N40'01 122W45'27 8:11:02
Blyn 5 2 48N01'21 123W00'17 8:12:01
Bodie 24 1 48N49'58 118W53'44 7:55:35
Bogachiel 5 2 47N57 124W23 8:17:32
Boise 27 1 47N10'50 122W00'52 8:08:03
Boistfort 21 5 46N32'07 123W07'57 8:12:32
Bolles 36 1 46N16'42 118W13'17 7:52:53
Bonneville Spur 37
11 48N45 122W29 8:09:56
Bonney Lake 27 6 47N10'38 122W11'07 8:08:44
Bonspur 9 1 47N18'19 120W02'11 8:00:09
Bordeaux 34 7 46N53'42 123W04'44 8:12:19
Bossburg 33 1 48N45'09 118W02'27 7:52:10
Boston Harbor 34
36 47N08'19 122W53'59 8:11:36
Bothell 17 12 47N45'36 122W12'16 8:08:49
Bow 29 1 48N33'43 122W23'49 8:09:35
Boyds 10 1 48N42'50 118W07'54 7:52:32
Boylston 19 1 46N54'50 120W14'00 8:00:56
Brace 39 19 46N37'40 120W34'34 8:02:18
Brady 14 1 46N59'46 123W30'38 8:14:03
Breakers 25 1 46N22'16 124W02'58 8:16:12
Breidablick 18 1 47N48'08 122W38'53 8:10:36
Bremer 21 7 46N34'43 122W24'50 8:09:39
Bremerton 18 13 47N34'03 122W37'53 8:10:32
Bremerton Junction 18
1 47N31'53 122W43'58 8:10:56
Brennan 37 1 48N49'21 122W33'40 8:10:15
Brewster 24 14 48N05'46 119W46'46 7:59:07
Bridgeport 9 1 48N00'30 119W40'12 7:58:41
Bridle Trail 17
4 47N41 122W12 8:08:48
Brier 31 1 47N47'05 122W16'23 8:09:06
Briercrest 17 44 47N44'02 122W17'12 8:09:09
Brighton 17 44 47N32'47 122W16'28 8:09:06
Brinnon 16 1 47N40'46 122W53'49 8:11:35
Bristol 19 1 47N08'41 120W47'48 8:03:11
Broadmoor 17 44 47N38'01 122W17'18 8:09:09
Broadway 17 44 47N38'03 122W19'27 8:09:18
Bromart 31 1 47N53'59 122W05'52 8:08:23
Brookdale 27 6 47N08'31 122W22'55 8:09:32
Brookfield 35 1 46N15'54 123W33'34 8:14:14
Brooklyn 25 1 46N46'35 123W30'31 8:14:02
Browns Point 27
49 47N18'02 122W26'24 8:09:46
Brownstown 39 1 46N24'16 120W36'21 8:02:25
Brownsville 18 1 47N39'21 122W36'55 8:10:28
Bruce 1 1 46N50'23 119W03'04 7:56:12
Bruceport 25 1 46N40'46 123W53'56 8:15:36
Brush Prairie 6
1 45N43'59 122W32'43 8:10:11
Bryant 31 1 48N14'21 122W09'24 8:08:38
Bryn Mawr 17 40 47N30'13 122W13'54 8:08:56
Buckeye 32 1 47N50'33 117W22'24 7:49:30
Buckhorn 28 1 48N42'24 122W52'05 8:11:28
Buckley 27 6 47N09'48 122W01'32 8:08:06
Bucoda 34 7 46N47'57 122W52'07 8:11:28
Buena 39 1 46N25'44 120W18'44 8:01:15
Buena Vista 15 2 48N14 122W21 8:09:24
Buenna 17 9 47N19'53 122W20'36 8:09:22
Bumping Crossing Campground 39
1 46N52'46 121W16'56 8:05:08
Bunker 21 5 46N38'40 123W06'55 8:12:28
Bunker Hill 8 32 46N12'09 123W08'15 8:12:33
Burbank 36 1 46N12'00 119W00'43 7:56:03
Burbank Heights 36
1 46N12'39 119W00'24 7:56:02
Burien 17 4 47N28'14 122W20'44 8:09:23
Burley 18 1 47N25'05 122W37'47 8:10:31
Burlington 29 1 48N28'33 122W19'27 8:09:18
Burnett 27 6 47N07'46 122W02'52 8:08:11
Buroker 36 1 46N07'02 118W13'02 7:52:52
Burr 36 1 46N27'44 118W37'45 7:54:31
Burrows 14 1 47N03'24 124W02'09 8:16:09
Burt 25 1 46N39'59 123W27'33 8:13:50
Burton 17 4 47N23'21 122W27'34 8:09:50
Busby 38 1 46N41'33 117W08'58 7:48:36
Bush Point 15 2 48N02 122W36 8:10:24
Byron 39 1 46N11'17 119W52'24 7:59:30
B Z Corner 20 1 45N51'01 121W30'28 8:06:02
Cabin Creek 19 1 47N14'30 121W13'48 8:04:55
Cactus 11 1 46N36'36 118W55'54 7:55:44
Calhounville 36
1 46N00'04 118W26'03 7:53:44
Calispell 26 1 48N20'38 117W17'58 7:49:12
Cama Beach 15 2 48N14 122W21 8:09:24
Camano 15 2 48N10'27 122W31'37 8:10:06
Camas 6 15 45N35'14 122W23'54 8:09:36
Camden 26 1 48N02'51 117W14'20 7:48:57
Camelot 17 9 47N19 122W14 8:08:56
Camp Diana 15 2 48N06'22 122W25'47 8:09:43
Camp Discovery 16
1 47N48'41 122W47'33 8:11:10
Camp Orkila 28 1 48N42'05 122W56'26 8:11:46
Camp Union 18 1 47N35 122W40 8:10:40
Campus 37 11 48N45 122W29 8:09:56
Canby 22 1 47N29'56 118W01'23 7:52:06
Canyon Park 31
12 47N47'28 122W11'29 8:08:46
Capitol Hill 17
44 47N37'25 122W19'06 8:09:16
Caples Landing 8
3 45N54'19 122W48'06 8:11:12
Capsante 29 1 48N30 122W37 8:10:28
Carbonado 27 6 47N04'48 122W03'01 8:08:12
Carlisle 14 1 47N09'18 124W05'50 8:16:23
Carlisle East 14
1 47N08'32 124W05'57 8:16:24
Carlisle West 14
1 47N09'09 124W06'24 8:16:26
Carlmar 1 1 47N03'09 118W07'45 7:52:31
Carlsborg 5 2 48N05'27 123W10'15 8:12:41
Carlson 21 7 46N42'01 122W11'54 8:08:48
Carlson Landing 35
1 46N15'54 123W37'57 8:14:32
Carlton 24 1 48N14'54 120W06'54 8:00:28
Carlyle 17 4 47N43 122W13 8:08:52
Carnation 17 4 47N38'53 121W54'46 8:07:39
Carriage Hill 18
1 46N31 122W09 8:08:36
Carrolls 8 3 46N04'18 122W51'40 8:11:27
Carrs Corner 33
1 48N11'20 117W52'45 7:51:31
Carson 30 1 45N43'32 121W49'05 8:07:16
Cascade Junction 27
6 47N08'14 122W04'36 8:08:18
Cascade Vista 17
40 47N29 122W12 8:08:48
Cashmere 4 1 47N31'21 120W28'07 8:01:52
Cashup 38 1 47N03'38 117W22'43 7:49:31
Castle Rock 8 16 46N16'31 122W54'23 8:11:38
Cathcart 31 1 47N50'53 122W05'53 8:08:24
Cathlamet 35 1 46N12'12 123W22'55 8:13:32

Cavalero Corner 31
1 47N58'42 122w08'01 8:08:32
Cavelero Beach 15
2 48N14 122w21 8:09:24
Cedar Crossing 37
1 48N44'49 120w49'01 8:03:16
Cedardale 29 1 48N21'34 122w19'21 8:09:17
Cedar Falls 17 4 47N25'32 121w46'32 8:07:06
Cedar Grove 17 4 47N26'09 122w03'39 8:08:15
Cedarhome 31 1 48N14 122w21 8:09:24
Cedarhurst 17 1 47N28'56 122w28'41 8:09:55
Cedar Mountain 17
40 47N26'54 122w04'19 8:08:17
Cedar Valley 31
1 47N48'50 122w18'08 8:09:13
Cedarview 27 6 47N13 122w15 8:09:00
Cedarville 14 1 46N51'31 123w16'52 8:13:07
Cedarville 37 1 48N50'25 122w17'40 8:09:11
Cedonia 33 1 48N09'14 118w10'05 7:52:40
Center 16 1 47N49 122w53 8:11:32
Centerville 20 1 45N45'12 120w54'13 8:03:37
Central Ferry 38
1 46N37'36 117w49'03 7:51:16
Centralia 21 17 46N42'59 122w57'11 8:11:49
Central Park 14
1 46N58'25 123w41'28 8:14:46
Central Valley 18
1 47N39'48 122w38'55 8:10:36
Ceres 21 5 46N36'29 123w09'08 8:12:37
Chaffee 3 1 46N15'37 119w36'20 7:58:25
Chain Hill 34 50 46N52'50 122w50'40 8:11:23
Chambers 38 1 46N38'35 117w11'01 7:48:44
Chard 12 1 46N32'17 117w51'21 7:51:25
Charleston 18 1 47N33'41 122w39'30 8:10:38
Charter Oak 6 1 45N49'28 122w33'25 8:10:14
Chattaroy 32 1 47N53'23 117w21'24 7:49:26
Chautauqua 17 4 47N25'24 122w25'54 8:09:44
Chehalis 21 18 46N39'44 122w57'46 8:11:51
Chehalis Indian Reservation 14
1 46N49 123w12 8:12:48
Chelan 4 1 47N50'28 120w00'55 8:00:04
Chelan Falls 4 1 47N48'06 119w59'05 7:59:56
Chelatchie 6 1 45N55'41 122w22'42 8:09:31
Chelsea Park 17
4 47N26 122w21 8:09:24
Cheney 32 1 47N29'15 117w34'29 7:50:18
Chenois Creek 14
1 46N59 123w53 8:15:32
Chenowith 30 1 45N44 121w32 8:06:08
Cherokee 24 1 48N27'03 119w27'55 7:57:52
Cherokee Bay Park 17
4 47N21'38 122w02'57 8:08:12
Cherry Crest 17
4 47N35 122w10 8:08:40
Cherry Gardens 17
4 47N45 121w59 8:07:56
Cherry Grove 6 1 45N47'43 122w34'40 8:10:19
Chesaw 24 1 48N56'46 119w03'01 7:56:12
Chester 32 1 47N37'05 117w14'58 7:49:00
Cheviot 19 1 46N53'53 120w10'12 8:00:41
Chew 36 1 46N36'07 118w19'00 7:53:16
Chewack Campground 24
1 48N40'39 120w07'43 8:00:31
Chewelah 33 1 48N16'35 117w42'52 7:50:51
Chico 18 1 47N36'42 122w42'33 8:10:50
Chillowist 24 1 48N18'15 119w38'09 7:58:33
Chimacum 16 1 48N00'40 122w46'03 8:11:04
Chinook 25 1 46N16'23 123w56'39 8:15:47
Chiwaukum 4 1 47N41'26 120w44'05 8:02:56
Chopaka 24 1 48N59'58 119w43'25 7:58:54
Christopher 17 9 47N20'03 122w13'51 8:08:55
Chuckanut 37 11 48N39'57 122w28'57 8:09:56
Chuckanut Junction 29
1 48N29'10 122w20'04 8:09:20
Chuckanut Village 37
11 48N42'04 122w29'33 8:09:58
Chumstick 4 1 47N41'18 120w38'17 8:02:33
Cicero 31 1 48N16'08 122w00'33 8:08:02
Cinebar 21 7 46N36'16 122w31'50 8:10:07
Cispus 21 7 46N29'33 122w07'16 8:08:29
Clallam Bay 5 2 48N15'17 124w15'30 8:17:02
Claquato 21 5 46N38'37 123w00'58 8:12:04
Claremont 31 24 47N58 122w14 8:08:56
Clarkston 2 1 46N24'59 117w02'39 7:48:11
Clarkston Heights 2
1 46N23'47 117w04'53 7:48:20
Clavton 33 1 47N59'49 117w33'26 7:50:14
Clay City 27 6 46N55'33 122w15'17 8:09:01
Clayton 33 1 48N00 117w33 7:50:12
Clearbrook 37 1 48N58'44 122w19'16 8:09:17
Clear Lake 29 1 48N27'52 122w13'58 8:08:56
Clearview 31 1 47N50'02 122w07'29 8:08:30
Clearwater 16 1 47N34'40 124w17'36 8:17:10
Cle Elum 19 1 47N11'44 120w56'17 8:03:45
Cleveland 20 1 45N58'15 120w21'07 8:01:24
Cliffdell 19 1 46N56'47 121w04'04 8:04:16
Climax 36 1 46N14'49 118w27'58 7:53:52
Cline 33 1 48N03'44 117w45'02 7:51:00
Clinton 15 2 47N58'43 122w21'16 8:09:25
Clinton Park 27
6 47N10'05 122w31'38 8:10:07
Clipper 37 1 48N45'37 122w12'03 8:08:48
Cloverdale 8 3 46N01 122w51 8:11:24
Cloverland 2 1 46N15'02 117w14'58 7:49:00
Clover Park 27 6 47N09'38 122w31'10 8:10:05
Clyde 36 1 46N24'41 118w26'46 7:53:47
Clyde Hill 17 4 47N37'55 122w13'00 8:08:52
Coal Creek 8 32 46N12'01 123w00'56 8:12:04
Coal Creek 17 4 47N33 122w04 8:08:16
Coalfield 17 4 47N30'10 122w07'14 8:08:29
Coey 32 48 47N29'53 117w06'40 7:48:27
Cohassett 14 1 46N52'22 124w06'19 8:16:25
Cohassett Beach 14
1 46N53 124w07 8:16:28
Cokedale 29 1 48N31'20 122w10'15 8:08:41
Colbert 32 1 47N49'36 117w20'27 7:49:22
Colby 18 1 47N31'58 122w32'40 8:10:11
Colchester 18 1 47N32'43 122w32'25 8:10:10
Coles Corner 4 1 47N45'23 120w44'17 8:02:57
Colfax 38 1 46N52'49 117w21'48 7:49:27
College Place 36
1 46N02'58 118w23'14 7:53:33
Colton 12 1 46N34'05 117w07'39 7:48:31

Columbia 17 44 47N33'51 122w16'27 8:09:06
Columbia 37 1 48N58'02 122w09'42 8:08:39
Columbia Beach 15
2 47N58'14 122w21'00 8:09:24
Columbia Heights 8
32 46N09'52 122w56'25 8:11:46
Columbia Valley Gardens 8
32 46N09'28 122w58'25 8:11:54
Colville 33 1 48N32'48 117w54'16 7:51:37
Colville Indian Agency 24
1 48N10 118w58 7:55:52
Colville Indian Reservation 10
1 48N10 118w58 7:55:52
Colvos 17 1 47N28'35 122w29'22 8:09:57
Comar 37 1 48N43'55 122w12'08 8:08:49
Conconully 24 1 48N33'27 119w44'55 7:59:00
Concora 17 4 47N24 122w17 8:09:08
Concrete 29 1 48N32'22 121w44'42 8:06:59
Conifer View 17
4 47N43 122w13 8:08:52
Connell 11 1 46N39'49 118w51'36 7:55:26
Conway 29 1 48N20'26 122w20'30 8:09:22
Cook 30 1 45N43 121w28 8:05:52
Copalis Beach 14
1 47N06'46 124w10'21 8:16:41
Copalis Crossing 14
1 47N06'29 124w04'05 8:16:16
Coppei 36 1 46N13'19 118w07'26 7:52:30
Cordell 24 1 48N52'00 119w24'39 7:57:39
Corfu 13 1 46N48'55 119w27'15 7:57:49
Corkindale 29 1 48N30'32 121w28'21 8:05:53
Cornell 15 2 48N07'20 122w25'29 8:09:42
Cornwall 37 11 48N45 122w29 8:09:56
Cosmopolis 14 1 46N57'20 123w46'21 8:15:05
Cottage Lake 17
4 47N45 122w09 8:08:36
Cottonwood Beach 37
1 48N56'24 122w45'21 8:11:01
Cougar 8 3 46N03'06 122w17'54 8:09:12
Cougar Valley 39
1 47N01'11 121w21'25 8:05:26
Coulee City 13 1 47N36'41 119w17'28 7:57:10
Coulee Dam 24 19 47N57'56 118w58'30 7:55:54
Country Homes 32
48 47N44'55 117w24'12 7:49:37
Coupeville 15 2 48N13'12 122w41'06 8:10:44
Covada 10 1 48N13'14 118w12'28 7:52:50
Cove 17 1 47N27'08 122w30'24 8:10:02
Coveland 15 2 48N13'59 122w44'04 8:10:56
Covello 7 1 46N23'00 117w49'55 7:51:20
Coville 5 2 48N07'37 123w37'41 8:14:31
Covington 17 4 47N20'54 122w06'49 8:08:27
Cowiche 39 1 46N40'12 120w42'40 8:02:51
Cowley 17 4 47N29'55 122w27'49 8:09:51
Cowlitz 21 5 46N27'32 122w50'29 8:11:22
Coyle 16 1 47N41'53 122w48'15 8:11:13
Cozy Nook 33 1 48N19'27 117w42'17 7:50:49
Crabtree 38 1 47N02'03 117w11'24 7:48:46
Craige 2 1 46N08 117w08 7:48:32
Crane 5 2 48N06'25 123w19'11 8:13:17
Crater 13 1 47N14'45 119w56'51 7:59:47
Crawford 6 1 45N48'11 122w29'01 8:09:56
Creosote 18 1 47N36'52 122w30'10 8:10:01
Crescent 5 2 48N05'41 123w48'21 8:15:13
Crescent Beach 5
2 48N08 123w44 8:14:56
Crescent Valley 27
6 47N20 122w35 8:10:20
Creston 22 1 47N45'31 118w31'07 7:54:04
Creswell Heights 6
1 45N41'24 122w20'07 8:09:20
Crewport 39 1 46N20 120w11 8:00:44
Crocker 27 6 47N06 122w12 8:08:48
Croker 27 6 47N05'34 122w09'20 8:08:37
Cromwell 27 6 47N16'28 122w37'16 8:10:29
Crosby 18 1 47N34'56 122w51'53 8:11:28
Croskey 22 1 47N18'27 117w50'27 7:51:22
Crown Hill 17 44 47N41'41 122w22'27 8:09:30
Crown Point Vista 9
19 47N58'17 118w59'09 7:55:57
Cruzatt 30 1 45N35'29 122w09'06 8:08:36
Crystal Mountain 27
6 47N12 121w59 8:07:56
Crystal Springs 18
1 47N36'13 122w34'26 8:10:18
Cumberland 17 4 47N16'59 121w55'33 8:07:42
Cunningham 1 1 46N49'20 118w48'19 7:55:13
Curlew 10 1 48N53'08 118w35'54 7:54:24
Curry 11 1 46N39'01 118w49'35 7:55:18
Curtis 21 5 46N35'14 123w06'32 8:12:26
Cushman Dam 23 1 47N24 123w09 8:12:36
Cusick 26 1 48N20'15 117w17'46 7:49:11
Custer 27 6 47N10'36 122w31'35 8:10:06
Custer 37 1 48N55'03 122w38'12 8:10:33
Dabob 16 1 47N50'50 122w48'11 8:11:13
Dahlia 35 1 46N15'41 123w36'47 8:14:27
Daisy 33 1 48N21'41 118w09'32 7:52:38
Dalkena 26 1 48N15 117w14 7:48:56
Dallesport 20 1 45N37'03 121w10'42 8:04:43
Danville 10 1 48N59'33 118w30'25 7:54:02
Darknell 32 1 47N25'41 117w09'53 7:48:40
Darlington 31 24 47N57'14 122w16'08 8:09:05
Darrington 31 1 48N15'20 121w36'01 8:06:24
Dartford 32 48 47N47'05 117w24'57 7:49:40
Dash Point 27 49 47N19'09 122w25'31 8:09:42
Davenport 22 1 47N39'15 118w08'56 7:52:36
Davin 11 1 46N36'31 118w19'24 7:53:18
Davis 25 1 46N39'43 123w25'27 8:13:42
Davis Terrace 8
3 46N08'05 122w53'43 8:11:35
Day Creek 29 1 48N29'54 122w03'55 8:08:16
Day Island 27 6 47N14 122w32 8:10:08
Dayton 7 1 46N19'26 117w58'17 7:51:53
Dayton 23 1 47N13'37 123w13'26 8:12:54
Decatur 28 1 48N30'02 122w49'06 8:11:16
Deckerville 23 1 47N13'39 123w28'25 8:13:54
Deep Creek 32 1 47N38'35 117w42'40 7:50:51
Deep River 35 1 46N20'55 123w41'02 8:14:44
Deer Harbor 28 1 48N37 123w00 8:12:00
Deer Lake 33 1 48N04 117w38 7:50:32
Deer Park 32 1 47N57'16 117w28'33 7:49:54
Deer Valley 26 1 48N10'54 117w17'59 7:49:12
Delaney 7 1 46N30'39 117w58'15 7:51:53

Delano Heights 13
1 47N56'01 119w01'01 7:56:04
Delkena 26 1 48N14'51 117w14'15 7:48:57
Dellesta Park 37
11 48N45 122w29 8:09:56
Delphi 34 7 46N58'45 123w01'03 8:12:04
Delridge 17 4 47N33'08 122w22'11 8:09:29
Delta Junction 31
24 48N00'48 122w11'15 8:08:45
Deming 37 1 48N49'33 122w12'53 8:08:52
Denison 32 1 47N54'35 117w26'15 7:49:45
Denny Creek 17 4 47N24'47 121w26'28 8:05:46
Denny Park 17 4 47N41 122w12 8:08:48
Des Moines 17 4 47N24'07 122w19'23 8:09:18
Dewatto 23 1 47N27'09 123w04'13 8:12:17
Dewey 29 1 48N25'31 122w36'26 8:10:26
Dewey 37 11 48N47'36 122w25'42 8:09:43
Dexter By The Sea 25
1 46N43'17 124w00'45 8:16:03
Diablo 37 1 48N42'49 121w08'24 8:04:34
Diamond 38 1 46N55'05 117w29'15 7:49:57
Diamond City 26
1 48N37'00 117w17'20 7:49:09
Diamond Lake 26
1 48N07'19 117w11'53 7:48:48
Dieringer 27 6 47N14'27 122w13'26 8:08:54
Dilworth 17 4 47N27'56 122w26'02 8:09:44
Dines Point 15 2 48N06 122w34 8:10:16
Disautel 24 1 48N21'38 119w14'10 7:56:57
Discovery Bay 16
31 48N07 122w47 8:11:08
Discovery Junction 16
31 47N59'38 122w52'24 8:11:30
Dishman 32 1 47N39'25 117w16'56 7:49:08
Disque 5 2 48N08'21 123w46'09 8:15:05
Divine Place 33
1 48N46'15 117w37'30 7:50:30
Dixie 36 1 46N08'25 118w09'15 7:52:37
Dockton 17 4 47N22'19 122w27'29 8:09:50
Dodge 12 1 46N31'30 117w49'15 7:51:17
Doe Bay 28 1 48N38'29 122w46'47 8:11:07
Dole 6 1 45N47'00 122w20'12 8:09:21
Dollar Corner 6
1 45N46'49 122w35'56 8:10:24
Donahue 38 1 47N12'39 117w21'16 7:49:25
Donald 39 1 46N28'36 120w23'44 8:01:35
Doran 37 1 48N40'43 122w11'40 8:08:47
Doris 19 1 46N52'04 120w00'31 8:00:02
Dot 20 1 45N52'00 120w20'39 8:01:23
Doty 21 7 46N38'05 123w16'35 8:13:06
Douglas 9 1 47N37'17 120w00'13 8:00:01
Downing 9 44 47N38 122w20 8:09:20
Downs 22 1 47N22'18 118w23'46 7:53:35
Draper Spring 20
1 46N01 121w17 8:05:08
Driftwood Shores 15
2 48N11'33 122w28'19 8:09:53
Dryad 21 5 46N38'13 123w15'00 8:13:00
Dryden 4 1 47N32'29 120w33'35 8:02:14
Dry Falls Junction 13
1 47N37'35 119w19'52 7:57:19
Duckabush 16 1 47N39'08 122w55'51 8:11:43
Dulwich 10 1 48N50'51 118w11'47 7:52:47
Dumas 7 1 46N17'14 118w03'37 7:52:14
Duncan 32 1 47N30'17 117w20'38 7:49:23
Dungeness 5 2 48N08'49 123w07'19 8:12:29
Dunlap 17 4 47N31'54 122w16'06 8:09:04
Dupont 27 6 47N05'49 122w37'48 8:10:31
Durham 17 4 47N20'18 121w53'23 8:07:34
Dusty 38 1 46N48'37 117w39'03 7:50:36
Dutch Settlement 19
1 47N15'14 120w27'24 8:01:50
Duvall 17 4 47N44'33 121w59'04 8:07:56
Duwamish 17 4 47N24 122w17 8:09:08
Dyer 9 1 47N58'41 119w46'13 7:59:05
Dynamite 32 1 47N29'46 117w27'00 7:49:48
Eagle Cliff 35 1 46N10'16 123w13'59 8:12:56
Eagledale 18 1 47N36'52 122w30'51 8:10:03
Eaglemount 16 1 47N58'12 122w50'54 8:11:24
Earl 22 1 47N33'07 118w22'42 7:53:31
Earlington 17 40 47N29 122w12 8:08:48
Earlmont 17 4 47N41'37 122w08'57 8:08:36
Earlmount 17 4 47N39 122w09 8:08:36
East Aberdeen 14
8 46N58'41 123w48'03 8:15:12
East Auburn 17 9 47N19 122w14 8:08:56
East Bremerton 18
1 47N35'53 122w37'42 8:10:31
East Cheney 32 1 47N25'52 117w30'32 7:50:02
East Coulee Dam 24
1 47N58 118w59 7:55:56
East Cromwell 27
6 47N16'27 122w36'11 8:10:25
East Crossing Camp 5
2 47N57'55 123w06'17 8:12:25
East Farms 32 1 47N42'27 117w03'05 7:48:12
Eastgate 17 4 47N34'01 122w09'26 8:08:38
Eastgate 36 1 46N04 118w20 7:53:20
East Hill 17 30 47N24 122w15 8:09:00
East Hoquiam 14
26 46N58'31 123w51'51 8:15:27
East Kittitas 19
1 46N58'28 120w21'48 8:01:27
Eastman 36 1 46N08'05 118w08'21 7:52:33
East Olympia 34
36 46N58'04 122w50'04 8:11:20
Easton 19 1 47N14'14 121w10'40 8:04:43
East Port Orchard 18
1 47N31'25 122w37'23 8:10:30
East Quilcene 16
1 47N49'37 122w51'03 8:11:24
East Redmond 17
4 47N39 122w09 8:08:36
East Selah 39 19 46N39'53 120w29'12 8:01:57
Eastsound 28 1 48N41'49 122w54'15 8:11:37
East Spokane 32
48 47N39'13 117w18'51 7:49:15
East Stanwood 31
1 48N14'39 122w20'44 8:09:23
East Union 17 44 47N37 122w18 8:09:12
Eastward 27 10 47N08'44 122w37'19 8:10:29
East Wenatchee 9
1 47N24'57 120w17'31 8:01:10

East Wenatchee Bench 9 1 47N26 120w18 8:01:12
East White Bluffs 3 1 46N40'25 119w27'36 7:57:50
Eatonville 27 6 46N52'03 122w15'55 8:09:04
Eatonville Junction 27 6 46N52'47 122w15'40 8:09:03
Ebeys Landing 15 2 48N11'31 122w42'24 8:10:50
Echo 33 1 48N38'53 117w55'54 7:51:44
Echo Lake 17 4 47N44 122w21 8:09:24
Eden 35 1 46N17'55 123w39'04 8:14:36
Eden 38 1 47N02'05 117w09'13 7:48:37
Edgecomb 31 1 48N09'07 122w08'22 8:08:33
Edgemont 19 1 46N55'30 120w27'35 8:01:50
Edgemont 27 6 47N14 122w17 8:09:08
Edgemoor 37 11 48N45 122w29 8:09:56
Edgewater 31 24 47N57'10 122w16'46 8:09:07
Edgewater Park 17 44 47N38'31 122w16'40 8:09:07
Edgewood 27 6 47N15'01 122w17'33 8:09:10
Edison 29 1 48N33'45 122w26'33 8:09:46
Edison Station 29 1 48N33'57 122w25'15 8:09:41
Edmonds 31 20 47N48'39 122w22'34 8:09:30
Edna 3 1 46N35'23 119w24'48 7:57:39
Edwall 22 1 47N30'17 117w57'00 7:51:48
Edwards 11 1 46N32'59 119w00'13 7:56:01
Eglon 18 2 47N51'46 122w30'48 8:10:03
Elanor 22 1 47N36'15 117w53'20 7:51:33
Elbe 27 6 46N45'54 122w11'33 8:08:46
Elberton 38 1 46N58'53 117w13'13 7:48:53
Eldon 23 1 47N32'44 123w02'41 8:12:11
Electric City 13 1 47N55'57 119w02'13 7:56:09
Electron 27 6 46N59'34 122w11'35 8:08:46
Elgin 27 6 47N20 122w35 8:10:20
Elk 32 1 48N00'59 117w16'32 7:49:06
Elkcoal 17 4 47N22 121w52 8:07:28
Elk Creek 25 1 46N39'54 123w26'45 8:13:47
Elk Plain 27 6 47N03'12 122w23'47 8:09:35
Ellensburg 19 21 46N59'48 120w32'48 8:02:11
Elliot 17 40 47N27'57 122w08'19 8:08:33
Ellisford 24 1 48N47'19 119w23'58 7:57:36
Ellisport 17 4 47N25'14 122w26'03 8:09:44
Ellisville 17 4 47N31'21 121w45'25 8:07:02
Ellsworth 6 1 45N36'15 122w33'47 8:10:15
Elma 14 22 47N00'13 123w24'27 8:13:38
Elmer City 24 1 47N59'53 118w57'12 7:55:49
Eltopia 11 1 46N27'32 119w00'58 7:56:04
Elwha 5 2 48N03'39 123w35'35 8:14:22
Elwood 36 1 46N22'56 118w30'51 7:54:03
Emden 1 1 47N06'17 118w07'18 7:52:29
Emerald 39 1 46N18'10 120w04'49 8:00:19
Emerald Hills 17 4 47N35 122w10 8:08:40
Endicott 38 1 46N55'33 117w40'55 7:50:44
Enetai 18 1 47N35'06 122w35'51 8:10:23
English Boom 31 2 48N15'47 122w26'17 8:09:45
Ennis 36 1 46N14'15 118w22'05 7:53:28
Enterprise 24 1 48N43'57 119w35'40 7:58:23
Enterprise 33 1 48N04 118w12 7:52:48
Entiat 4 1 47N40'34 120w12'26 8:00:50
Entiat Lake 9 1 47N45 120w05 8:00:20
Enumclaw 17 23 47N12'16 121w59'25 8:07:58
Enumclaw Plateau 17 4 47N16 122w00 8:08:00
Ephrata 13 1 47N19'04 119w33'09 7:58:13
Erlands Point 18 1 47N36'00 122w41'30 8:10:46
Ernies Grove 17 4 47N32'07 121w44'39 8:06:59
Eschbach 39 1 46N40'11 120w37'48 8:02:31
Espanola 32 1 47N36'12 117w44'26 7:50:58
Essex 34 7 46N48'15 123w00'19 8:12:01
Estes 11 1 46N38'02 118w39'07 7:54:36
Estes 38 1 46N44 117w00 7:48:00
Ethel 3 1 46N34'50 119w35'49 7:58:23
Ethel 21 5 46N31'56 122w44'21 8:10:57
Etna 6 1 45N56'18 122w35'50 8:10:23
Eufaula 8 32 46N11'45 123w02'48 8:12:11
Eufaula Heights 8 32 46N12'58 123w03'06 8:12:12
Eureka 36 1 46N18'12 118w36'56 7:54:28
Eureka 37 11 48N45'47 122w27'02 8:09:48
Evaline 21 5 46N32'23 122w56'13 8:11:45
Evans 33 1 48N42'49 118w01'27 7:52:06
Evansville 17 4 47N28'53 122w19'54 8:09:20
Everett 31 24 47N58'45 122w12'03 8:08:48
Evergreen 6 1 45N39 122w35 8:10:20
Everson 37 1 48N55'13 122w20'29 8:09:22
Ewan 38 1 47N07'01 117w44'02 7:50:56
Ewartsville 38 1 46N42'12 117w18'05 7:49:12
Factoria 17 4 47N34'56 122w09'57 8:08:40
Fairbanks 38 1 47N13'28 117w12'51 7:48:51
Fairchild 32 1 47N38'03 117w40'03 7:50:40
Fairchild Air Force Base 32 1 47N38 117w38 7:50:32
Fairfax 27 6 47N00'38 122w00'54 8:08:04
Fairfield 32 1 47N23'07 117w10'14 7:48:41
Fair Harbor 23 1 47N20'32 122w49'51 8:11:19
Fairholm 5 2 48N04'06 123w54'53 8:15:40
Fairmont 16 1 47N59'35 122w51'53 8:11:28
Fairmont 31 24 47N54'08 122w15'11 8:09:01
Fairview 18 1 47N37'18 122w40'02 8:10:40
Fairview 33 1 48N21'45 117w43'14 7:50:53
Fairview 39 19 46N35 120w20 8:01:52
Fall City 17 4 47N33'03 121w53'11 8:07:33
Fallon 38 1 46N50'05 117w06'53 7:48:28
Fargher Lake 6 1 45N53'19 122w30'47 8:10:03
Farmer 9 1 47N36'46 119w48'39 7:59:15
Farmington 38 1 47N05'22 117w02'35 7:48:10
Farrington 11 1 46N32'23 118w34'39 7:54:19
Farron 39 1 46N24'17 120w31'13 8:02:05
Fauntleroy 17 4 47N31'24 122w23'30 8:09:34
Federal 17 44 47N36 122w20 8:09:20
Federal Reservation 3 1 46N30 119w33 7:58:12
Federal Way 17 4 47N19'21 122w18'41 8:09:15
Felida 6 51 45N42'35 122w42'22 8:10:49
Ferlton 17 4 47N40'10 122w11'48 8:08:47
Ferncliff 18 1 47N38'34 122w30'33 8:10:02
Ferndale 37 1 48N50'48 122w35'23 8:10:22
Fern Heath 17 4 47N23'47 122w24'35 8:09:38
Fern Hill 27 49 47N10'52 122w25'56 8:09:44
Fern Prairie 6 1 45N38'12 122w23'51 8:09:35
Fernwood 18 1 47N30'24 122w39'06 8:10:36
Fife 27 6 47N14'22 122w21'21 8:09:25
Fife Heights 27 6 47N15'33 122w20'40 8:09:23
Finley 3 1 46N09'15 119w01'58 7:56:08
Finn Hall 8 3 45N54 122w45 8:11:00
Fircrest 27 49 47N14'23 122w30'53 8:10:04
Firdale 25 39 46N37'27 123w34'16 8:14:17
Firloch 17 4 47N42'12 122w10'24 8:08:42
Firwood 27 6 47N12 122w20 8:09:20
Fisher 6 1 45N35'24 122w30'09 8:10:01
Fish Town 29 21 48N21'51 122w28'09 8:09:53
Fishtrap 22 1 47N23'19 117w49'47 7:51:19
Five Corners 11 1 46N30'08 118w51'55 7:55:28
Five Corners 17 4 47N27'35 122w19'58 8:09:20
Five Corners 34 7 46N55'59 122w35'18 8:10:21
Five Points 36 1 46N04'49 118w06'39 7:52:27
Flaig 38 1 47N09'38 117w15'57 7:49:04
Fletcher Bay 18 1 47N38'27 122w34'33 8:10:18
Flint 39 1 46N26'47 120w20'39 8:01:23
Florence 31 1 48N13'15 122w19'50 8:09:19
Fobes Hill 31 1 47N56'57 122w07'07 8:08:28
Foothill 32 48 47N42 117w22 7:49:28
Forbes 23 1 47N06'38 123w07'47 8:12:31
Ford 33 1 47N55 117w49 7:51:16
Fordair 13 1 47N38'10 119w16'06 7:57:04
Fords Prairie 21 5 46N44'07 122w59'16 8:11:57
Forest 21 5 46N40 122w58 8:11:52
Forest Beach 23 1 47N22'58 122w56'43 8:11:47
Forest Beach 27 6 47N17'39 122w41'14 8:10:45
Forest City 18 1 47N32 122w38 8:10:32
Forest Glade 31 1 47N58'54 121w58'19 8:07:53
Forest Hills Addition 32 48 47N43 117w25 7:49:40
Forest Park 17 4 47N45 122w17 8:09:08
Forks 5 25 47N57'02 124w23'03 8:17:32
Fort Canby 25 1 46N17'01 124w03'10 8:16:13
Fort Lawton 17 4 47N40 122w25 8:09:40
Fort Lewis 27 6 47N06 122w35 8:10:20
Fort Nisqually 27 49 47N18'11 122w31'37 8:10:06
Fort Rains 30 1 45N39'10 121w55'02 8:07:40
Fortson 31 1 48N16'07 121w43'34 8:06:54
Fort Spokane 22 1 47N54'17 118w18'29 7:53:14
Foster 17 4 47N28'54 122w16'28 8:09:06
Four Corners 16 31 48N02'58 122w49'05 8:11:16
Four Corners 18 1 47N49'02 122w38'34 8:10:34
Four Corners 34 7 46N57 122w36 8:10:24
Four Lakes 32 1 47N33'41 117w35'35 7:50:22
Fourth Plain 6 51 45N38 122w37 8:10:28
Fox Island 27 6 47N16 122w38 8:10:32
Foy 17 4 47N44'03 122w20'38 8:09:23
Fragaria 18 1 47N27'51 122w31'48 8:10:07
Frances 25 1 46N32'33 123w30'13 8:14:01
Frankfort 25 1 46N16'50 123w45'17 8:15:01
Frederickson 27 6 47N05'47 122w21'27 8:09:26
Fredonia 29 1 48N26'47 122w26'34 8:09:46
Freedom 32 1 47N22'35 117w22'54 7:49:32
Freeland 15 2 48N00'35 122w31'29 8:10:06
Freeman 32 1 47N31'06 117w11'41 7:48:47
Fremont 17 44 47N39'35 122w21'21 8:09:25
Friday Harbor 28 1 48N32'04 123w00'57 8:12:04
Frischknecht 11 1 46N42'29 118w56'17 7:55:45
Frisken Wye 23 1 47N14'04 123w28'53 8:13:56
Frontier 33 1 49N00'00 117w49'48 7:51:19
Fruitland 33 1 48N04'16 118w11'52 7:52:47
Fruitvale 39 19 46N37'05 120w33'07 8:02:12
Fryelands 31 1 47N52'18 122w00'28 8:08:02
Fuller 14 1 46N58'27 123w28'11 8:13:53
Furport 26 1 48N14'31 117w10'30 7:48:42
Galena (Site) 31 1 47N53'33 121w26'32 8:05:46
Gales Addition 5 2 48N06 123w24 8:13:36
Galvin 21 5 46N44'33 123w01'33 8:12:06
Garcia 17 4 47N25'26 121w37'16 8:06:29
Gardena 36 1 46N01'09 118w40'25 7:54:42
Garden City 14 1 47N03'16 123w18'07 8:13:12
Gardenville 27 49 47N16 122w24 8:09:36
Gardiner 16 1 48N03'00 122w54'52 8:11:39
Garfield 38 1 47N00'29 117w08'24 7:48:34
Garland 32 48 47N41 117w25 7:49:40
Garrett 36 1 46N03'08 118w24'06 7:53:36
Gate 34 7 46N51 123w08 8:12:32
Geib 32 1 47N26'04 117w39'34 7:50:38
Geiger Field 32 1 47N38 117w30 7:50:00
Geiger Heights 32 1 47N35'34 117w29'23 7:49:58
Geneva 37 11 48N44'45 122w24'02 8:09:36
Geneva Junction 3 41 46N27'57 119w19'28 7:57:18
George 13 1 47N04'45 119w51'17 7:59:25
Georgetown 17 4 47N33'07 122w19'40 8:09:19
Getchell 31 1 48N04'20 122w05'45 8:08:23
Gibbon 3 1 46N14'10 119w39'38 7:58:39
Gibraltar 29 1 48N25'51 122w34'53 8:10:20
Gibson Creek 14 1 46N50 123w14 8:12:56
Gifford 33 1 48N18'23 118w08'43 7:52:35
Gig Harbor 27 34 47N19'46 122w34'44 8:10:19
Gig Harbor Peninsula 27 6 47N19 122w37 8:10:28
Gilbert 24 1 48N27'25 120w33'33 8:02:14
Gilberton 18 1 47N38'21 122w36'13 8:10:25
Gillian 36 1 46N07'39 118w10'39 7:52:43
Gilmer 20 1 45N52'17 121w27'51 8:05:51
Gilmore Corners 8 3 46N19 122w44 8:10:56
Ginger 3 1 46N40'51 119w30'17 7:58:01
Givens Corner 39 1 46N15'04 119w59'53 8:00:00
Glacier 37 1 48N53'25 121w56'40 8:07:47
Glacier View 27 6 46N49'09 121w57'06 8:07:48
Glade 11 1 46N20'10 119w06'36 7:56:26
Gleed 39 1 46N39'30 120w36'44 8:02:27
Glen Acres 17 4 47N28'33 122w26'43 8:09:47
Glen Cove 16 31 48N05'31 122w48'17 8:11:13
Glencove 27 6 47N20'46 122w44'09 8:10:57
Glendale 15 1 47N56'23 122w21'26 8:09:26
Glenoma 21 7 46N30'53 122w09'32 8:08:38
Glenrose 32 1 47N37'41 117w20'01 7:49:20
Glenwood 18 1 47N25'31 122w41'17 8:10:45
Glenwood 20 1 46N01'08 121w17'22 8:05:09
Glenwood 38 1 46N55'40 117w16'44 7:49:07
Globe 25 1 46N33'19 123w32'06 8:14:08
Gloyd 13 1 47N15'54 119w16'43 7:57:07
Gold Bar 31 1 47N51'25 121w41'45 8:06:47
Goldendale 20 1 45N49'15 120w49'14 8:03:17
Goldendale Observatory 20 1 45N50 120w49 8:03:16
Goldfield Mill 33 1 48N46'27 117w39'58 7:50:40
Goldstake 10 1 48N55'14 118w12'36 7:52:50
Good Hope 6 1 45N45'56 122w37'09 8:10:29
Goodnoe 20 1 45N42'58 120w30'46 8:02:03
Goodnoe Hills 20 1 45N45'05 120w28'45 8:01:55
Gooseneck 20 1 45N43'00 121w01'45 8:04:07
Goose Prairie 39 1 46N53'43 121w15'57 8:05:04
Gordon 38 1 46N45'49 118w01'18 7:52:05
Gorst 18 1 47N31'32 122w42'13 8:10:49
Goshen 37 1 48N51'17 122w20'23 8:09:22
Gould City 12 1 46N35'18 117w34'37 7:50:18
Govan 22 1 47N44'20 118w49'19 7:55:17
Grace 31 1 47N46'40 122w08'58 8:08:36
Graham 27 6 47N03'11 122w17'35 8:09:10
Graham Point 23 1 47N14'52 122w56'12 8:11:45
Grahams 26 1 48N05'32 117w10'17 7:48:41
Grahams Landing 2 1 46N13'14 116w57'32 7:47:50
Grand Coulee 13 1 47N56'30 119w00'08 7:56:01
Grand Mound 34 7 46N47'17 123w00'36 8:12:02
Grandview 39 1 46N15'04 119w54'02 7:59:36
Granger 39 1 46N20'32 120w11'10 8:00:45
Granite Falls 31 1 48N05'03 121w58'03 8:07:52
Grant 23 1 47N15'20 122w55'40 8:11:43
Grant Road Addition 9 1 47N26 120w19 8:01:16
Granville Grange 31 1 48N05 121w58 8:07:52
Grapeview 23 1 47N19'55 122w50'02 8:11:20
Grassmere 29 1 48N32'25 121w46'44 8:07:07
Gravelles 22 1 47N37'16 117w59'53 7:52:00
Gravelly Lake 27 6 47N10 122w32 8:10:08
Gray Gables 14 1 47N00'49 124w00'29 8:16:02
Grayland 14 1 46N48'37 124w05'31 8:16:22
Grays Harbor City 14 1 46N59'07 123w57'36 8:15:50
Grays Landing 32 1 48N01'09 117w21'57 7:49:28
Grays River 35 1 46N21'23 123w36'29 8:14:26
Greenacres 32 1 47N40'05 117w09'47 7:48:39
Greenbank 15 2 48N05'54 122w34'18 8:10:17
Green Bluff 32 48 47N49'39 117w16'14 7:49:05
Green Lake 17 44 47N41'14 122w19'55 8:09:20
Green Mountain 6 1 45N54 122w45 8:11:00
Green River 17 4 47N17'20 122w05'17 8:08:21
Greens Landing 4 1 47N55'51 120w11'27 8:00:46
Greenwater 27 4 47N09'22 121w38'57 8:06:36
Greenwood 14 1 46N58 123w45 8:15:00
Greenwood 17 44 47N42'00 122w21'15 8:09:25
Greenwood 33 1 48N34'57 118w02'55 7:52:12
Greenwood 37 1 48N54'51 122w26'26 8:09:46
Grinnell 38 1 46N57'44 117w04'04 7:48:16
Grisdale 14 1 47N21'26 123w36'40 8:14:27
Gromore 39 19 46N35'19 120w41'49 8:02:47
Grotto 17 4 47N44'11 121w25'20 8:05:41
Guemes 29 1 48N31'49 122w37'25 8:10:30
Guerrier 21 5 46N40 122w58 8:11:52
Guler 20 1 45N59'59 121w32'22 8:06:09
Hadley 36 1 46N10'37 118w22'54 7:53:32
Hadlock 16 1 48N01'55 122w45'25 8:11:02
Halford 31 4 47N47'19 121w30'11 8:06:01
Haller Lake 17 44 47N43'25 122w20'17 8:09:21
Halterman 31 1 48N16'10 121w52'57 8:07:32
Hamann Corner 32 1 47N49'50 117w25'27 7:49:42
Hamilton 29 1 48N31'18 121w59'17 8:07:57
Hamilton Junction 29 1 40N31'36 122w00'20 8:08:01
Hampton 37 1 48N56'32 122w20'27 8:09:22
Hanford 3 1 46N35'02 119w23'12 7:57:33
Hanson 13 1 47N43'43 119w00'25 7:56:02
Hansville 18 1 47N55'08 122w33'11 8:10:13
Happy Valley 5 25 48N02'58 123w05'43 8:12:23
Happy Valley 37 11 48N42'53 122w27'59 8:09:52
Harbert 36 1 46N05'17 118w14'28 7:52:58
Harbor Center 15 2 48N01 122w32 8:10:08
Harbor Heights 17 4 47N22'12 122w29'12 8:09:57

Harder 11 1 46N39'43 118w29'16 7:53:57
Harman Heights 17
4 47N28'34 121w47'36 8:07:10
Harmony 21 5 46N33'30 122w28'57 8:09:56
Harmony Falls Landing 30
1 46N15'57 122w08'30 8:08:34
Harper 18 1 47N31'15 122w31'06 8:10:04
Harpole 38 1 46N55'42 117w24'56 7:49:40
Harrah 39 1 46N24'16 120w32'35 8:02:10
Harrington 22 1 47N28'52 118w15'12 7:53:01
Harsha 36 1 46N17'20 118w29'10 7:53:57
Harstine 23 1 47N13 123w06 8:12:24
Harter 10 1 48N37'56 118w07'09 7:52:29
Hartford 31 1 48N01 122w04 8:08:16
Hartland 20 1 45N42 121w17 8:05:08
Hartline 13 1 47N41'26 119w06'26 7:56:26
Hartstene 23 1 47N16'36 122w53'09 8:11:33
Harvey 36 1 46N23'30 118w28'04 7:53:52
Harwood 39 19 46N34'57 120w39'18 8:02:37
Hatch 36 1 46N16'30 118w40'04 7:54:40
Hatton 1 1 46N46'34 118w49'31 7:55:18
Havillah 24 1 48N49'41 119w12'11 7:56:49
Hay 38 1 46N40'44 117w54'53 7:51:40
Hayes 6 3 45N55'54 122w40'34 8:10:42
Hayes Park 32 48 47N42 117w22 7:49:28
Hayford 32 1 47N36'23 117w33'46 7:50:15
Hazel 31 1 48N16'39 121w48'28 8:07:14
Hazel Dell 6 51 45N40'18 122w39'42 8:10:39
Hazelwood 17 40 47N33'04 122w11'25 8:08:46
Hazelwood 32 48 47N39 117w27 7:49:48
Headquarters 8 3 46N14'54 122w47'27 8:11:10
Heather 25 1 46N46'18 124w04'47 8:16:19
Hedges 3 1 46N10'34 119w01'58 7:56:08
Heisson 6 1 45N49'30 122w29'24 8:09:58
Helen 3 1 46N37'37 119w36'16 7:58:25
Hells Crossing Campground 39
1 46N57'54 121w15'55 8:05:04
Helsing Junction 34
7 46N48'22 123w07'15 8:12:29
Herrington Place 8
3 46N13'53 122w25'58 8:09:44
Herron 27 6 47N16'28 122w48'40 8:11:15
Herron Island 27
6 47N15 122w46 8:11:04
Highland 2 1 46N24 117w03 7:48:12
Highland 6 1 45N54'35 122w37'03 8:10:28
Highland 31 1 48N01 122w04 8:08:16
Highland 32 1 47N41'39 117w31'46 7:50:07
Highland Heights 14
1 47N13'02 124w12'06 8:16:48
Highland Park 8
3 46N09 122w54 8:11:36
Highland Park 17
44 47N31'43 122w21'05 8:09:24
Highlands 17 40 47N29 122w12 8:08:48
High Point 17 4 47N32'09 122w22'30 8:09:30
High Rock 31 1 47N48'47 121w58'53 8:07:56
Hilda 25 7 46N38'13 123w22'06 8:13:28
Hillcrest 1 1 47N00'39 118w16'53 7:53:08
Hillgrove 14 1 47N04'00 123w16'00 8:13:04
Hillhurst 27 6 47N05'13 122w30'21 8:10:01
Hillsdale 27 49 47N11'57 122w25'55 8:09:44
Hillside 27 6 47N06'16 122w34'39 8:10:19
Hilltop 17 4 47N33'17 122w08'27 8:08:34
Hillyard 32 48 47N42'03 117w21'55 7:49:28
Hintzville 18 1 47N33'51 122w53'25 8:11:34
Hite 32 1 47N39'51 117w46'40 7:51:07
Hite Center 18 1 47N36'07 122w51'46 8:11:27
Hobart 17 4 47N25'19 121w58'18 8:07:53
Hockinson 6 1 45N44'17 122w29'09 8:09:57
Hoh Indian Reservation 16
1 47N44 124w25 8:17:40
Hoko 5 2 48N16 124w18 8:17:12
Holcomb 25 39 46N34'20 123w36'58 8:14:28
Holden 4 1 48N12'03 120w46'28 8:03:06
Holden Village 4
1 47N50 120w01 8:00:04
Holly 18 1 47N33'28 122w58'38 8:11:55
Holly Park 17 44 47N32'31 122w17'26 8:09:10
Hollywood 17 4 47N43'52 122w07'41 8:08:31
Hollywood Beach 4
1 47N55'40 120w12'41 8:00:51
Holman 25 1 46N19'36 124w03'13 8:16:13
Holmes 19 21 46N57'30 120w31'44 8:02:07
Holtzinger 39 1 46N40'40 120w43'10 8:02:53
Homan 6 51 45N42'02 122w34'54 8:10:20
Home 27 6 47N16'37 122w45'56 8:11:04
Home Acres 31 24 47N58 122w14 8:08:56
Home Valley 30 1 45N41'54 121w46'31 8:07:06
Hood 30 1 45N43'30 121w33'25 8:06:14
Hoodsport 23 1 47N24'22 123w08'17 8:12:33
Hoogdal 29 1 48N33'30 122w15'29 8:09:02
Hooper 1 1 46N46'30 118w08'51 7:52:35
Hooper Junction 1
1 46N45'05 118w09'48 7:52:39
Hope 27 6 47N14'17 122w36'04 8:10:24
Hoquiam 14 26 46N58'52 123w53'17 8:15:33
Horizon View 17
4 47N35 122w10 8:08:40
Horlick 19 1 47N07'49 120w47'01 8:03:08
Horseshoe Lake 18
1 47N32 122w38 8:10:32
Houghton 17 4 47N39'40 122w12'17 8:08:49
Houser 12 1 46N30'07 117w46'31 7:51:06
Howard 9 1 47N53'53 119w49'25 7:59:18
Howards Corner 29
1 48N27'17 122w34'54 8:10:20
Humorist 36 1 46N11'37 118w55'33 7:55:42
Humphrey 17 4 47N14'05 121w42'45 8:06:51
Humptulips 14 1 47N13'59 123w57'29 8:15:50
Hunters 33 1 48N07'01 118w12'03 7:52:48
Huntley 38 1 47N07'07 117w32'23 7:50:10
Hunts Point 17 4 47N38'37 122w13'44 8:08:55
Huntsville 7 1 46N17'14 118w06'22 7:52:25
Husum 20 1 45N47'58 121w29'09 8:05:57
Hutton Settlement 32
1 47N42'05 117w15'54 7:49:04
Hyak 19 4 47N23'35 121w23'30 8:05:34
Hyland 31 1 48N01'38 122w01'46 8:08:07
Illahee 14 1 46N59 123w53 8:15:32
Illahee 18 1 47N36'47 122w35'44 8:10:23
Illia 12 1 46N40'34 117w30'12 7:50:01
Illwaco 25 1 46N18'33 124w02'31 8:16:10
Ilwaco 25 1 46N19 124w03 8:16:12
Image 6 1 45N39 122w35 8:10:20
Impach 10 1 48N17'18 118w14'08 7:52:57
Inchelium 10 1 48N17'49 118w11'44 7:52:47
Independence 34
7 46N47'57 123w09'14 8:12:37
Index 31 1 47N49'15 121w33'14 8:06:13
Indian Beach 15
2 48N09'48 122w31'12 8:10:05
Indianola 18 1 47N44'50 122w31'28 8:10:06
Indian Village 29
1 48N34'23 122w38'58 8:10:36
Inglesea 17 4 47N29'09 122w21'19 8:09:25
Inglewood 17 4 47N37'21 122w04'01 8:08:16
Interbay 17 44 47N38'29 122w23'41 8:09:35
Intercity 31 24 47N54'54 122w14'02 8:08:56
Interlaken 27 6 47N09'21 122w32'26 8:10:10
International 17
44 47N38 122w20 8:09:20
Ione 26 1 48N44'28 117w24'58 7:49:40
Irby 22 1 47N21'34 118w51'00 7:55:24
Ireland 6 1 45N39'34 122w22'16 8:09:29
Irondale 16 31 48N02'32 122w46'17 8:11:05
Iron Springs 14
1 47N09'35 124w11'14 8:16:45
Irwin 32 1 47N41'34 117w14'37 7:48:58
Island Center 18
1 47N38 122w31 8:10:04
Island Lake 18 1 47N44 122w38 8:10:32
Island View 3 1 46N14'22 119w13'20 7:56:53
Issaquah 17 27 47N31'49 122w01'53 8:08:08
Issaquah Plateau 17
4 47N33 122w01 8:08:04
Iverson 5 2 48N01'14 124w23'07 8:17:32
Jackson 7 1 46N32'04 117w54'43 7:51:39
Jamestown 5 2 48N07'42 123w05'09 8:12:21
Jamieson Park 32
48 47N39 117w27 7:49:48
Jamison Corner 31
1 47N56'08 122w00'39 8:08:03
Janis 24 1 48N38'51 119w27'51 7:57:51
Jantz 1 1 47N13'48 118w38'29 7:54:34
Jared 26 1 48N28'09 117w18'52 7:49:15
Jericho 13 1 46N50'05 119w47'25 7:59:10
Jerita 38 1 46N44'35 117w53'09 7:51:33
Jerry 2 1 46N19'28 117w06'27 7:48:26
Jims Corner 27 6 46N59'42 122w17'36 8:09:10
Johnson 38 1 46N37'54 117w08'13 7:48:33
Johnson Landing 27
6 47N11'03 122w41'21 8:10:45
Johnsons Corner 27
6 46N58'50 122w21'23 8:09:26
Jordan 31 1 48N08'53 122w02'10 8:08:09
Joso 11 1 46N36'42 118w13'03 7:52:52
Jovita 17 6 47N15'40 122w16'50 8:09:07
Joyce 5 2 48N08'12 123w43'58 8:14:56
Juanita 17 4 47N42'12 122w12'21 8:08:49
Junction 17 4 47N36'50 121w48'04 8:07:12
Junction City 14
1 46N58'16 123w46'20 8:15:05
Juniper Beach 15
2 48N13'52 122w24'21 8:09:37
Juno 38 1 47N06'54 117w34'26 7:50:18
Kahlotus 11 1 46N38'36 118w33'21 7:54:13
Kalaloch 16 1 47N36'17 124w22'16 8:17:29
Kalama 8 28 46N00'31 122w50'36 8:11:22
Kalber 21 5 46N35 123w07 8:12:28
Kamilche 23 1 47N07'50 123w05'48 8:12:23
Kanaskat 17 4 47N19'14 121w53'33 8:07:34
Kanaskat Junction 17
4 47N19'56 121w53'26 8:07:34
Kangley 17 4 47N21'43 121w52'44 8:07:31
Kapowsin 27 6 46N59'09 122w13'28 8:08:54
Karamin 10 1 48N46'24 118w38'53 7:54:36
Keller 10 1 48N04'44 118w41'02 7:54:44
Kellogg Marsh 31
1 48N12 122w07 8:08:28
Kellys Korner 34
36 46N59'06 122w46'01 8:11:04
Kelso 8 28 46N08'49 122w54'26 8:11:38
Kendall 37 1 48N55'02 122w08'05 8:08:32
Kenmore 17 4 47N45'27 122w14'34 8:08:58
Kennard Corner 31
1 47N49'13 122w12'23 8:08:50
Kennewick 3 29 46N12'41 119w08'10 7:56:33
Kennydale 17 40 47N31'15 122w12'20 8:08:49
Kenova 38 1 47N12'25 117w33'07 7:50:12
Kenroy 9 1 47N26 120w19 8:01:16
Kent 17 30 47N22'52 122w14'01 8:08:56
Kerriston 17 4 47N27'18 121w51'23 8:07:26
Ketron 27 10 47N09'16 122w37'01 8:10:28
Kettle Falls 33
1 48N36'39 118w03'17 7:52:13
Kewa 10 1 48N12'04 118w16'39 7:53:07
Key Center 27 6 47N20 122w35 8:10:20
Keymes Beach 16
31 48N02'58 122w49'40 8:11:19
Keyport 18 1 47N42'08 122w37'11 8:10:29
Keystone 1 1 47N14'27 118w09'01 7:52:36
Keystone Ferry Landing 15
2 48N09'34 122w40'12 8:10:41
Kibler 36 1 46N05'17 118w13'10 7:52:53
Kickerville 37 1 48N53'07 122w42'10 8:10:49
Kid Valley 8 3 46N22'23 122w37'05 8:10:28
Kiesling 32 48 47N38 117w24 7:49:36
King Corner 6 1 45N47'41 122w35'55 8:10:24
King Hill 5 2 48N02'18 123w16'25 8:13:06
Kingsgate 17 4 47N41 122w12 8:08:48
Kingston 18 1 47N47'56 122w29'49 8:09:59
Kiona 3 1 46N14'59 119w28'35 7:57:54
Kirby 12 1 46N30'48 117w23'23 7:49:34
Kirkland 17 27 47N40'54 122w12'27 8:08:50
Kitsap Lake 18 1 47N34'59 122w42'26 8:10:50
Kittitas 19 1 46N59'00 120w24'57 8:01:40
Kitts Corner 17
4 47N17'50 122w18'43 8:09:15
Kitzmiller 38 1 46N45'30 117w10'00 7:48:40
Klaber 21 5 46N33'43 123w07'36 8:12:30
Klahanie 17 4 47N25'53 122w26'07 8:09:44
Klickitat 20 1 45N49'02 121w09'05 8:04:36
Klickitat Heights 20
1 45N46'58 121w19'20 8:05:17
Klickitat Springs 20
1 45N49'16 121w06'58 8:04:28
Klipsan Beach 25
1 46N28'00 124w03'06 8:16:12
Knab 21 5 46N26 122w51 8:11:24
Knapp 6 1 45N44'17 122w43'53 8:10:56
Knapp Landing 6
1 45N44'22 122w45'15 8:11:01
Knappton 25 1 46N16'36 123w48'49 8:15:15
Koontzville 24 1 48N00'57 118w56'46 7:55:47
Kooskooskie 36 1 46N00'37 118w07'09 7:52:29
Kopiah 21 5 46N42'22 122w48'24 8:11:14
Koren 1 1 46N47'43 119w00'55 7:56:04
Kosmos 21 7 46N29'53 122w11'12 8:08:45
Krain 17 4 47N14'35 121w59'17 8:07:57
Krupp 13 1 47N25 118w59 7:55:56
Kruse 31 24 48N06'00 122w10'26 8:08:42
Kruse Junction 31
1 48N06'15 122w10'43 8:08:43
K Street 27 49 47N15 122w29 8:09:56
Kummer 17 4 47N17'13 122w01'12 8:08:05
Lacamas 21 5 46N33'40 122w39'02 8:10:36
La Center 6 10 45N51'45 122w40'09 8:10:41
Lacey 34 36 47N02'04 122w49'19 8:11:17
La Conner 29 21 48N23'33 122w29'37 8:09:58
La Crosse 38 1 46N48'51 117w52'51 7:51:31
Ladow 38 1 46N59'09 117w05'04 7:48:20
Lagoon Point 15
2 48N06 122w34 8:10:16
LaGrande 27 6 46N50'04 122w19'03 8:09:16
Laing 13 1 47N06'56 119w02'21 7:56:09
Lairds 38 1 46N54'50 117w05'11 7:48:21
Lake Alice 17 4 47N34 121w53 8:07:32
Lakebay 27 6 47N15'26 122w45'26 8:11:02
Lake City 17 44 47N43'04 122w16'57 8:09:08
Lake City 27 6 47N08'56 122w33'00 8:10:12
Lake Crescent 5
2 48N06 123w24 8:13:36
Lakedale 19 1 47N15'15 121w03'22 8:04:13
Lake Dolloff 17
9 47N19 122w14 8:08:56
Lake Forest 17 4 47N44'55 122w17'00 8:09:08
Lake Forest Park 17
4 47N45'25 122w16'47 8:09:07
Lake Heights 17
4 47N33'33 122w10'58 8:08:44
Lake Hills 17 4 47N36'49 122w07'13 8:08:29
Lake Joy 17 4 47N39 121w55 8:07:40
Lakeland Village 32
1 47N33'04 117w42'14 7:50:49
Lake Leota 17 4 47N45 122w09 8:08:36
Lake Louise 27 6 47N09 122w33 8:10:12
Lake Retreat 17
4 47N21 121w59 8:07:56
Lake Ridge 17 4 47N30'24 122w14'36 8:08:58
Lakes 27 6 47N10 122w32 8:10:08
Lake Sawyer 17
30 47N24 122w15 8:09:00
Lake Shore 6 51 45N40 122w37 8:10:28
Lakeside 4 1 47N50'08 120w02'57 8:00:12
Lake Stevens 31
1 48N01 122w04 8:08:16
Lakeview 27 6 47N09'34 122w29'49 8:09:59
Lakeview Park 13
1 47N22'36 119w30'24 7:58:02
Lake Washington 17
4 47N44 122w13 8:08:52
Lake Wilderness 17
4 47N25 122w03 8:08:12
Lakewood 31 1 48N09'08 122w12'22 8:08:49
Lakewood Center 27
6 47N10'19 122w31'02 8:10:04
Lakota 17 4 47N19'59 122w22'16 8:09:29
Lamar 36 1 46N17'24 118w30'26 7:54:02
Lamberts Corner 34
36 47N00'13 122w57'52 8:11:51
Lamoine 9 1 47N43'44 119w53'50 7:59:35
Lamona 22 1 47N21'34 118w28'53 7:53:56
Lamont 38 1 47N12'06 117w54'15 7:51:37
Lancaster 38 1 47N01'52 117w39'48 7:50:39
Landsburg 17 4 47N22'30 121w58'14 8:07:53
Langdon 36 48 46N01'38 118w20'17 7:53:21
Langley 15 2 48N02'25 122w24'18 8:09:37
Lankner 14 1 46N54'50 123w19'15 8:13:17
La Push 5 2 47N54'32 124w38'07 8:18:32
Larchmont 27 49 47N10'12 122w25'57 8:09:44
Larimers Corner 31
1 47N53'31 122w08'36 8:08:34
Larson Mill 37
11 48N45'21 122w24'49 8:09:39
Latah 32 1 47N16'54 117w09'16 7:48:37
Lauer 1 1 47N13'32 118w43'41 7:54:55
Laurel 20 1 45N56'39 121w22'44 8:05:31
Laurel 37 11 48N51'19 122w29'19 8:09:57
Laurel Heights 31
24 47N58 122w14 8:08:56
Laurelhurst 17
44 47N39'49 122w16'33 8:09:06
Laurier 10 1 48N59'56 118w13'23 7:52:54
Lavilla 17 44 47N41'50 122w16'26 8:09:06
Lavista 38 1 47N08'35 117w42'18 7:50:49
Lawrence 37 1 48N51'28 122w17'32 8:09:10
Laws Corner 20 1 45N45'14 121w25'28 8:05:42
Leadpoint 33 1 48N54'34 117w35'11 7:50:21
Leahy 9 1 47N55'09 119w23'16 7:57:33
Leary 29 1 48N30'43 122w29'04 8:09:56
Leavenworth 4 1 47N35'47 120w39'37 8:02:38
Lebam 25 1 46N33'33 123w32'52 8:14:11
Lee 36 1 46N21'19 118w33'18 7:54:13
LeGrow 36 1 46N10'24 118w49'51 7:55:19
Leland 16 1 47N53'31 122w53'07 8:11:32
Lemolo 17 4 47N17'18 121w48'05 8:07:12
Lemolo 18 1 47N42'43 122w37'16 8:10:29
Leon 38 1 46N31'55 117w02'18 7:48:09
Lester 17 4 47N12'34 121w29'34 8:05:58
Levering 19 1 46N46'49 119w57'24 7:59:50
Levey 36 1 46N16'33 118w50'37 7:55:22
Lexington 8 3 46N11'15 122w54'15 8:11:37
Liberty 19 1 47N15'14 120w39'51 8:02:39
Liberty 39 1 46N21'21 120w08'42 8:00:35
Liberty Lake 32
1 47N38'54 117w05'29 7:48:22
Lichty 39 1 46N17'34 119w57'07 7:59:48

Lilliwaup 23 1 47N27'49 123w06'47 8:12:27
Limestone Junction 37 1 48N57'24 122w09'21 8:08:37
Lincoln 18 1 47N44'39 122w37'10 8:10:29
Lincoln 22 1 47N49'44 118w24'50 7:53:39
Lind 1 1 46N58'20 118w36'51 7:54:27
Lindberg 21 7 46N33 122w22 8:09:28
Lisabuela 17 4 47N24'27 122w30'59 8:10:04
Littell 21 5 46N38'13 123w02'03 8:12:08
Little Boston 18 1 47N51'09 122w34'08 8:10:17
Little Elkhorn 6 1 45N42'27 122w24'54 8:09:40
Little Falls 22 1 47N49'49 117w54'43 7:51:39
Little Hoquiam 23 1 47N19'19 122w57'33 8:11:50
Little Oklahoma 5 2 48N02'38 123w18'19 8:13:13
Littlerock 34 7 46N54'07 123w01'00 8:12:04
Lochsloy 31 1 48N03'06 122w01'51 8:08:07
Locke 26 1 48N25'36 117w19'00 7:49:16
Lofall 18 1 47N48'44 122w39'25 8:10:38
Lona Beach 15 2 48N12'16 122w26'43 8:09:47
Lone Pine 24 1 47N58'57 118w57'43 7:55:51
Lone Pine 38 1 47N13'22 117w08'57 7:48:36
Long 7 1 46N17'30 118w01'32 7:52:06
Long Beach 25 1 46N21'09 124w03'11 8:16:13
Longbranch 27 6 47N12'33 122w45'20 8:11:01
Long Lake 18 1 47N32 122w38 8:10:32
Long Lake 22 1 47N50'10 117w50'52 7:51:23
Longmire 27 6 46N45'00 121w48'41 8:07:15
Longview 8 32 46N08'18 122w56'13 8:11:45
Longview Junction 8 3 46N06'17 122w53'13 8:11:33
Loomis 24 1 48N49'16 119w37'56 7:58:32
Loon Lake 33 1 48N03'42 117w37'54 7:50:32
Lopez 28 1 48N31'26 122w54'48 8:11:39
Lost Creek 26 1 48N36'34 117w21'45 7:49:27
Loveland 27 6 47N03'51 122w24'28 8:09:38
Lowden 36 1 46N03'23 118w35'05 7:54:20
Lowell 31 24 47N57'21 122w11'45 8:08:47
Lower Elwha 5 2 48N08'40 123w33'05 8:14:12
Lower Peninsula 27 6 47N14 122w43 8:10:52
Lower Snoqualmie Valley 17 4 47N43 122w04 8:08:16
Low Gap 13 1 46N59'10 119w47'26 7:59:10
Lowman Beach Park 17 4 47N32'27 122w23'41 8:09:35
Loyal Heights 17 44 47N41'20 122w23'30 8:09:34
Lucerne 4 1 48N12'09 120w35'24 8:02:22
Lucia 6 1 45N50'18 122w26'00 8:09:44
Lummi Indian Reservation 37 1 48N47 122w38 8:10:32
Lummi Island 37 1 48N43'29 122w41'06 8:10:44
Lyle 20 1 45N41'46 121w17'06 8:05:08
Lyman 29 1 48N31'38 122w03'38 8:08:15
Lynden 37 1 48N56'48 122w27'03 8:09:48
Lynnwood 31 20 47N49'16 122w18'50 8:09:15
Lynwood 32 1 47N49 122w19 8:09:16
Lynwood Center 18 1 47N36'17 122w32'46 8:10:11
Lyons 32 1 47N40'50 117w34'31 7:50:18
Mabana 15 2 48N05'41 122w24'50 8:09:39
Mabton 39 1 46N12'54 119w59'44 7:59:59
MacCall 1 1 47N03'39 118w00'48 7:52:03
Machias 31 1 47N58'54 122w02'41 8:08:11
Mack 1 1 46N54'19 118w11'04 7:52:44
Madigan General Hospital 27 49 47N14 122w28 8:09:52
Madison Park 17 44 47N38'06 122w16'42 8:09:07
Madrona 17 44 47N36'30 122w17'39 8:09:11
Madrona Beach 15 2 48N13'03 122w31'58 8:10:08
Madson 38 1 46N49'19 117w05'34 7:48:22
Mae 13 1 47N07'03 119w23'40 7:57:35
Magallon 36 1 46N35'23 118w28'27 7:53:54
Magnolia 17 44 47N39 122w24 8:09:36
Magnolia Beach 17 4 47N23 122w29 8:09:56
Magnolia Bluff 17 44 47N39'09 122w24'00 8:09:36
Magnolia Heights 27 6 47N15'55 122w35'39 8:10:23
Makah Indian Reservation 5 2 48N22 124w37 8:18:28
Malaga 4 1 47N22'21 120w12'00 8:00:48
Malden 38 1 47N13'44 117w28'18 7:49:53
Malo 10 1 48N48'06 118w36'21 7:54:25
Malone 14 1 46N58 123w20 8:13:20
Malott 24 1 48N16'58 119w42'20 7:58:49
Maltby 31 4 47N48'19 122w06'43 8:08:27
Manchester 18 1 47N33'22 122w32'37 8:10:10
Manette 18 1 47N35 122w40 8:10:40
Manito 32 48 47N30'28 117w07'53 7:48:32
Manito Club Estates 32 48 47N38 117w24 7:49:36
Manitou 27 49 47N11'51 122w29'30 8:09:58
Manitou Beach 18 1 47N39'21 122w30'34 8:10:02
Manning 38 1 46N55'56 117w24'24 7:49:38
Manor 6 1 45N47 122w32 8:10:08
Mansfield 9 1 47N48'42 119w38'08 7:58:33
Mansford 29 1 48N18'27 121w31'18 8:06:05
Manson 4 1 47N53'06 120w09'26 8:00:38
Manzanita 17 4 47N21'03 122w28'20 8:09:53
Manzanita 18 1 47N40'35 122w33'30 8:10:14
Maple Beach 18 1 47N38 122w51 8:11:24
Maple Beach 37 1 49N00'03 123w02'10 8:12:09
Maple Falls 37 1 48N55'28 122w04'33 8:08:18
Maple Grove 5 2 48N04'53 123w42'14 8:14:49
Mapleleaf 17 44 47N41'39 122w19'18 8:09:17
Maple Valley 17 4 47N24'24 122w02'15 8:08:09
Maplewood 17 40 47N28'06 122w09'42 8:08:39
Maplewood 27 6 47N24'07 122w33'21 8:10:13
Marble 33 1 48N50'57 117w54'02 7:51:36
Marblemount 29 1 48N31'40 121w26'54 8:05:48
Marcellus 1 1 47N14'01 118w24'15 7:53:37
Marcus 33 1 48N39'48 118w04'02 7:52:16
Marengo 1 1 47N01'33 118w11'15 7:52:45
Marengo 7 1 46N26'27 117w44'52 7:50:59
Marietta 37 1 48N47'14 122w34'45 8:10:19
Marine Drive 18 1 47N35'20 122w40'26 8:10:42
Marketown 15 2 48N19'34 122w40'06 8:10:40
Markham 14 1 46N54'20 123w59'47 8:15:59
Marlin (Krupp) 13 1 47N24'27 118w59'02 7:55:56
Marmac 23 1 47N06'42 123w08'37 8:12:34
Marshall 32 1 47N34 117w30 7:50:00
Martin 19 4 47N16'51 121w19'00 8:05:16
Martindale 11 1 46N14'35 118w57'43 7:55:51
Maryhill 20 1 45N41'14 120w48'45 8:03:15
Marys Corner 21 5 46N32'50 122w49'17 8:11:17
Marysville 31 24 48N03'07 122w10'33 8:08:42
Mason 32 1 47N23'01 117w44'43 7:50:59
Mason City 24 1 47N58 119w02 7:56:08
Mathews Corner 11 1 46N27'36 119w11'36 7:56:46
Matlock 23 1 47N14'17 123w24'24 8:13:38
Matneys Spur 10 1 48N36 118w03 7:52:12
Mats Mats (Port Ludlow P O) 16 1 47N56'31 122w41'11 8:10:45
Mattawa 13 1 46N44'17 119w54'06 7:59:36
Matthew 36 1 46N33'28 118w32'07 7:54:08
Maud 33 1 48N19'52 118w04'42 7:52:19
Maury 17 9 47N23'20 122w22'44 8:09:31
Maxwelton 15 2 47N56'15 122w26'35 8:09:46
May Creek 17 40 47N31'53 122w11'57 8:08:48
Mayfield 21 5 46N30'32 122w34'05 8:10:16
May Junction 3 1 46N32'48 119w23'26 7:57:34
Maynard 16 1 47N59'52 122w52'57 8:11:32
Maytown 34 36 47N02 122w51 8:11:24
Mayview 12 1 46N37'52 117w27'53 7:49:52
Maywood 17 4 47N13'49 121w38'02 8:06:32
Mazama 24 1 48N35'32 120w24'10 8:01:37
McAdam 11 1 46N41'49 118w25'16 7:53:41
McCall 36 1 46N17'31 118w15'39 7:53:03
McChord 27 10 47N08 122w29 8:09:56
McChord Air Force Base 27 10 47N07 122w35 8:10:20
McCleary 14 1 47N03'12 123w15'51 8:13:03
McCleary Junction 14 1 47N04'06 123w16'16 8:13:05
McCormick 21 7 46N33'14 123w19'29 8:13:18
McCoy 38 1 47N11'09 117w18'31 7:49:14
McCredie 20 1 45N49'15 119w59'48 7:59:59
McDonald 13 1 47N04'17 119w12'52 7:56:51
McDonald 21 5 46N40 122w58 8:11:52
McGowan 25 1 46N14'47 123w54'22 8:15:37
McKay 7 1 46N20'15 118w08'13 7:52:33
McKees Beach 31 1 48N07'39 122w21'44 8:09:27
McKenna 27 6 46N56'06 122w33'19 8:10:13
McLoughlin 6 1 45N36'39 122w35'59 8:10:24
McLoughlin Heights 6 1 45N37'27 122w35'59 8:10:24
McMicken Heights 17 4 47N24 122w17 8:09:08
McMillin 27 6 47N08'24 122w14'07 8:08:56
McMurray 29 1 48N18'59 122w14'03 8:08:56
McVan 17 4 47N27'05 122w17'16 8:09:09
Mead 32 1 47N46'03 117w21'14 7:49:25
Meadow Brook 17 4 47N32 121w49 8:07:16
Meadowdale 18 1 47N37'42 122w37'39 8:10:31
Meadowdale 31 1 47N51'11 122w19'56 8:09:20
Meadow Glade 6 1 45N45'31 122w33'33 8:10:14
Medical Lake 32 1 47N34'23 117w40'52 7:50:43
Medina 17 4 47N37'16 122w13'35 8:08:54
Medina Heights 17 4 47N35 122w10 8:08:40
Meeker 27 6 47N11'11 122w16'34 8:09:06
Megler 25 1 46N15'04 123w51'23 8:15:26
Melbourne 14 1 46N56'44 123w37'29 8:14:30
Melone 14 1 46N57'41 123w19'45 8:13:19
Menlo 25 1 46N37'18 123w38'45 8:14:35
Menlo Park 27 6 47N14 122w32 8:10:08
Menoken 7 1 46N17'58 118w09'39 7:52:39
Mercer Island 17 4 47N34'15 122w13'15 8:08:53
Mercer Island Town 17 44 47N35'04 122w14'30 8:08:58
Meredith 17 9 47N20'48 122w14'05 8:08:56
Meridan Heights 17 30 47N24 122w15 8:09:00
Meridian 17 44 47N40'11 122w19'45 8:09:19
Meridian Heights 17 4 47N22'21 122w07'17 8:08:29
Merritt 4 1 47N46'52 120w50'31 8:03:22
Mesa 11 1 46N34'35 119w00'20 7:56:01
Meskill 21 5 46N38'18 123w10'11 8:12:41
Metaline 26 1 48N51'02 117w23'23 7:49:34
Metaline Falls 26 1 48N51'50 117w22'17 7:49:29
Meteor 10 1 48N15'59 118w17'02 7:53:08
Methow 24 1 48N07'49 120w00'09 8:00:01
Metreco 27 6 47N07 122w35 8:10:20
Metum 17 44 47N41'31 122w24'10 8:09:37
Miami Beach 18 1 47N38 122w51 8:11:24
Mica 32 1 47N33'22 117w12'40 7:48:51
Michigan Hill 34 7 46N46'41 123w05'57 8:12:24
Middle Nemah 25 1 46N29'02 123w53'09 8:15:33
Midlakes 17 4 47N36'58 122w10'53 8:08:44
Midland 27 49 47N10'02 122w24'13 8:09:37
Midland Acres 6 1 45N35 122w24 8:09:36
Midvale 39 1 46N17'04 120w00'48 8:00:03
Midvale Corner 15 2 47N59'34 122w24'59 8:09:40
Midway 5 2 48N23'26 124w40'21 8:18:41
Midway 17 30 47N23'12 122w17'08 8:09:09
Midway 27 6 47N18'18 122w35'18 8:10:21
Milan 32 1 47N58'01 117w19'50 7:49:19
Milco 8 3 46N09 122w54 8:11:36
Miles 22 1 47N54'39 118w17'29 7:53:10
Mileta 17 4 47N23'22 122w25'33 8:09:42
Mill A 30 1 45N45'25 121w38'57 8:06:36
Millburn 21 5 46N37'50 123w05'46 8:12:23
Miller River 17 4 47N43'12 121w23'50 8:05:35
Milltown 29 1 48N18'31 122w20'48 8:09:23
Millwood 32 1 47N40'53 117w16'54 7:49:08
Milton 27 4 47N14'54 122w18'42 8:09:15
Mima 34 7 46N51'56 123w03'55 8:12:16
Mineral 21 7 46N43'02 122w10'47 8:08:43
Minkler 29 1 48N31'17 122w06'39 8:08:27
Minnehaha 6 51 45N39'33 122w38'51 8:10:35
Minnick 36 1 46N09'55 118w07'47 7:52:31
Minter 27 6 47N21'44 122w41'11 8:10:45
Mirror Lake 17 9 47N19 122w14 8:08:56
Mirror Lake 37 1 48N39'39 122w12'38 8:08:51
Mission Beach 31 24 48N02'56 122w16'18 8:09:05
Mitchell 13 1 47N11'12 119w13'20 7:56:53
Moab (Newman Lake P O) 32 1 47N43'28 117w04'00 7:48:16
Mobase 27 6 47N06 122w35 8:10:20
Mock 32 1 47N23'50 117w38'57 7:50:36
Mock City 27 7 46N59'00 122w35'15 8:10:21
Mockonema 38 1 46N52'39 117w26'27 7:49:46
Moclips 14 1 47N14'11 124w12'42 8:16:51
Moffetts Hot Springs 30 1 45N39'19 121w57'24 8:07:50
Mohler 22 1 47N24'18 118w19'41 7:53:19
Mohrweis 23 1 47N18'42 123w14'00 8:12:56
Mojonnier 36 1 46N01'37 118w25'26 7:53:42
Mold 9 1 47N44'35 119w20'27 7:57:22
Molson 24 1 48N58'52 119w11'58 7:56:48
Mondovi 22 1 47N40'53 118w00'55 7:52:04
Monitor 4 1 47N29'13 120w25'01 8:01:40
Monohan 17 4 47N34'48 122w04'24 8:08:18
Monroe 31 1 47N51'20 121w58'11 8:07:53
Monroe Junction 31 1 47N51'23 121w57'40 8:07:51
Monse 24 1 48N08'29 119w40'36 7:58:42
Monta Vista 27 6 47N10'52 122w28'57 8:09:56
Montborne 29 1 48N22'53 122w13'14 8:08:53
Monte Cristo 31 1 47N59'09 121w23'34 8:05:34
Montesano 14 33 46N58'53 123w36'05 8:14:24
Moody 1 1 47N13'22 118w54'56 7:55:40
Moona 20 1 45N47'09 120w06'16 8:00:25
Moore 4 1 48N14'07 120w36'53 8:02:28
Moores Corner 25 1 46N20'46 124w02'24 8:16:10
Moorlands 17 4 47N43 122w13 8:08:52
Mora 5 2 47N55'17 124w37'00 8:18:28
Moran Prairie 32 48 47N38 117w24 7:49:36
Morgan Acres 32 48 47N42 117w22 7:49:28
Morganville 17 4 47N18'45 122w01'11 8:08:05
Morningside 17 44 47N42'05 122w18'38 8:09:15
Morton 21 7 46N33'31 122w16'26 8:09:06
Moses 38 1 46N25'46 117w12'35 7:48:50
Moses Lake 13 1 47N07'49 119w16'37 7:57:06
Moses Lake North 13 1 47N09 119w18 7:57:12
Mossyrock 21 7 46N31'47 122w29'02 8:09:56
Mountain Home Park 7 1 46N14'14 117w53'33 7:51:34
Mountain Top 7 1 46N14'31 117w45'48 7:51:03
Mountain View 2 1 46N02'31 117w20'19 7:49:21
Mountain View 37 1 48N50'54 122w40'12 8:10:41
Mountain View Beach 15 2 48N14 122w21 8:09:24
Mount Baker 17 44 47N34'43 122w17'18 8:09:09
Mount Brook 20 1 45N44 121w29 8:05:56
Mount Hope 32 1 47N26'58 117w12'57 7:48:52
Mountlake Terrace 31 1 47N47'18 122w18'27 8:09:14
Mount Pleasant 5 2 48N06 123w24 8:13:36
Mount Pleasant 6 1 45N33'48 122w14'53 8:09:00
Mount Rainier 27 6 47N01 121w57 8:07:48
Mount Spokane 32 1 47N47 117w08 7:48:32
Mount Vernon 29 3 48N25'17 122w19'58 8:09:20
Mount View 17 44 47N29'41 122w20'55 8:09:24
Mowich Illahee 24 1 48N23'51 119w48'46 7:59:15
Moxee City 39 1 46N33'14 120w22'55 8:01:32
Muckleshoot Indian Res 17 1 47N15 122w07 8:08:28
Mukilteo 31 1 47N56'41 122w18'12 8:09:13
Murdock 20 1 45N39'16 121w11'14 8:04:45
Murnen 21 7 46N37'45 123w19'18 8:13:17
Murphys Corner 31 24 47N52'42 122w12'20 8:08:49
Mushroom Corner 34 36 47N02'49 122w45'49 8:11:03
Myers 11 1 46N43'18 118w45'39 7:55:03
Naches 39 1 46N43'52 120w41'54 8:02:48
Naco 17 4 47N16'38 121w55'43 8:07:43
Nagrom 17 4 47N13'31 121w36'08 8:06:25
Nahcotta 25 1 46N29'55 124w01'56 8:16:08
Nalpee 25 39 46N33'30 123w36'40 8:14:27
Nancy 3 1 46N39'53 119w34'07 7:58:16
Napavine 21 5 46N34'29 122w54'25 8:11:38
Naselle 25 1 46N21'56 123w48'34 8:15:14
Nason Creek 4 1 47N45'59 120w47'43 8:03:11
Nass 39 1 46N20'20 120w08'42 8:00:35
National 27 6 46N45'24 122w03'17 8:08:13
Naval Depot Junction 18 1 47N35'48 122w42'37 8:10:50
Navy Yard City 18 1 47N33'13 122w39'48 8:10:39
Naylor 13 1 47N15'46 119w36'45 7:58:27
Neah Bay 5 2 48N22'06 124w37'25 8:18:30
Neilton 14 1 47N24'47 123w52'45 8:15:31
Nelson 19 1 47N11'38 121w03'07 8:04:12

Nelsons Corner 31
1 47N55'19 122w17'57 8:09:12
Nemah 25 1 46N30'44 123w53'05 8:15:32
Nemah Junction 25
1 46N31'14 123w53'04 8:15:32
Nemo 22 1 47N20'35 118w35'40 7:54:23
Neptune Beach 37
1 48N48'58 122w42'23 8:10:50
Nesika 21 7 46N28'27 122w17'17 8:09:09
Nespelem 24 1 48N10'02 118w58'25 7:55:54
Newaukum 17 1 47N15'27 122w06'02 8:08:24
Newaukum 21 5 46N37'42 122w57'59 8:11:52
Newcastle 17 40 47N32'21 122w09'16 8:08:37
Newhalem 37 1 48N40'26 121w14'46 8:04:59
New Kamilche 23
1 47N06'43 123w05'04 8:12:20
New London 14 1 47N03'27 123w55'33 8:15:42
Newman Lake 32 1 47N44 117w04 7:48:16
Newport 17 4 47N34'17 122w10'46 8:08:43
Newport 26 1 48N11'00 117w02'31 7:48:10
Newport Hills 17
4 47N32'28 122w10'31 8:08:42
Newport Shores 17
4 47N34'15 122w11'28 8:08:46
New Reliance 27
6 46N48'37 122w15'54 8:09:04
Newton 14 1 47N04'53 124w03'15 8:16:13
Nighthawk 24 1 48N58'00 119w38'27 7:58:34
Nile 39 1 46N49'15 120w56'18 8:03:45
Nilles Corner 9
1 48N00'20 119w24'25 7:57:38
Nine Mile Falls 32
1 47N47 117w33 7:50:12
Nisqually 34 6 47N03'24 122w42'00 8:10:48
Nisqually Indian Reservation 27
1 47N00 122w41 8:10:44
Nisqually Vista 27
6 46N47'13 121w44'47 8:06:59
Nisson 14 1 46N59 123w53 8:15:32
Noble 17 4 47N22'46 122w00'21 8:08:01
Nooksack 37 1 48N55'40 122w19'13 8:09:17
Nooksack Salmon Hatchery 37
1 48N53'50 122w08'28 8:08:34
Noon 37 11 48N48'15 122w23'50 8:09:35
Nordland 16 1 48N03'04 122w41'23 8:10:46
Norman 31 1 48N12'31 122w15'56 8:09:04
Normandy Park 17
4 47N26'11 122w20'22 8:09:21
North Avon 29 1 48N25 122w19 8:09:16
North Bend 17 4 47N29'45 121w47'08 8:07:09
North Bonneville 30
1 45N38'15 121w58'30 8:07:54
North Cedarville 37
1 48N50'37 122w17'13 8:09:09
North Central 32
48 47N42 117w26 7:49:44
North City 17 4 47N45'21 122w18'44 8:09:15
North Cove 25 1 46N42 123w59 8:15:56
Northeast Tacoma 27
6 47N16'52 122w22'08 8:09:29
North Fort Lewis 27
6 47N06 122w35 8:10:20
Northgate 17 44 47N43 122w18 8:09:12
North Highline 17
44 47N30 122w20 8:09:20
North Lake 17 9 47N19 122w14 8:08:56
North Lynnwood 31
1 47N50 122w17 8:09:08
North McNary 3 1 45N56'34 119w18'27 7:57:14
North Nemah 25 1 46N30'50 123w51'45 8:15:27
North Olympia 34
36 47N06'10 122w52'53 8:11:32
North Park 17 44 47N42'24 122w20'55 8:09:24
North Pine 32 1 47N16'55 117w21'50 7:49:27
Northport 33 1 48N54'58 117w46'50 7:51:07
North Prosser 39
1 46N13'56 119w46'02 7:59:04
North Puyallup 27
6 47N12'25 122w16'52 8:09:07
Northrup 17 4 47N37'59 122w11'03 8:08:44
Northwood 37 1 48N57'52 122w24'22 8:09:37
Norwood Village 17
4 47N35'21 122w10'09 8:08:41
Novara 1 1 46N52'33 119w09'09 7:56:37
Novelty 17 4 47N42'33 121w59'00 8:07:56
Nulls Crossing 21
5 46N42'23 122w51'40 8:11:27
Oakbrook 27 6 47N09 122w33 8:10:12
Oakesdale 38 1 47N07'42 117w14'30 7:48:58
Oak Harbor 15 2 48N17'36 122w38'31 8:10:34
Oakland 23 1 47N13'38 123w03'54 8:12:16
Oakland 27 49 47N13'53 122w29'17 8:09:57
Oak Park 6 1 45N34'56 122w23'14 8:09:33
Oak Point 8 32 46N11'28 123w11'15 8:12:45
Oakville 14 35 46N50'26 123w13'52 8:12:55
Obrien 17 30 47N24'45 122w14'09 8:08:57
Ocean City 14 1 47N04'16 124w09'53 8:16:40
Ocean Grove 14 1 47N10'56 124w11'42 8:16:47
Ocean Park 25 1 46N29'30 124w02'56 8:16:12
Ocean Shores 14
1 46N57'47 124w09'50 8:16:39
Ocean Shores Estates 14
1 46N59 123w53 8:15:32
Oceanside 25 1 46N24'31 124w03'04 8:16:12
Ocosta 14 1 46N53'20 124w02'14 8:16:09
Odair 13 1 47N36'40 119w16'00 7:57:04
Odessa 22 1 47N20'00 118w41'23 7:54:46
Offutt Lake 34
36 46N54'38 122w49'28 8:11:18
Ohop 27 6 46N56'45 122w11'22 8:08:45
Oil City 16 1 47N45'02 124w25'27 8:17:42
Okanogan 24 14 48N21'41 119w34'56 7:58:20
Olalla 18 1 47N25'46 122w32'40 8:10:11
Old Royal 5 2 48N10'46 124w27'26 8:17:50
Olds 4 1 47N27'49 120w19'39 8:01:19
Old Tacoma 27 49 47N16'34 122w28'05 8:09:52
Old Toroda 24 1 48N46'40 118w54'37 7:55:38
Old Town 5 2 48N09'02 123w09'00 8:12:36
Old Wauconda 24
1 48N42'45 118w57'13 7:55:49
Old Willapa 25
39 46N41 123w44 8:14:56
Olema 24 1 48N17'09 119w48'11 7:59:13
Olequa 8 7 46N22'27 122w56'19 8:11:45
Olga 28 1 48N37'11 122w50'03 8:11:20
Ollalla Valley 18
1 47N26 122w33 8:10:12
Olympia 17 4 47N35 122w10 8:08:40
Olympia 34 36 47N02'17 122w53'58 8:11:36
Olympic Hot Springs 5
2 47N58'35 123w41'13 8:14:45
Olympic View 18
1 47N41'39 122w44'21 8:10:57
Omak 24 14 48N24'40 119w31'35 7:58:06
Omans 22 1 47N36'08 118w04'37 7:52:18
Onalaska 21 5 46N34'31 122w43'01 8:10:52
Oneida 35 1 46N18'52 123w40'39 8:14:43
Onion Creek 33 1 48N33 117w54 7:51:36
Onslow 14 1 47N10'14 124w06'47 8:16:27
Opportunity 32 1 47N39'27 117w14'20 7:48:57
Orcas 28 1 48N35'53 122w56'36 8:11:46
Orchard Avenue 32
48 47N40'54 117w18'10 7:49:13
Orchard Heights 18
1 47N31'50 122w35'52 8:10:23
Orchard Park 32
48 47N40'32 117w19'27 7:49:18
Orchard Prairie 32
48 47N42 117w22 7:49:28
Orchards 6 1 45N40'00 122w33'35 8:10:14
Orient 10 1 48N51'58 118w12'06 7:52:48
Orillia 17 30 47N26'29 122w14'40 8:08:59
Orin 33 1 48N29'28 117w54'32 7:51:38
Orondo 9 1 47N37'34 120w13'27 8:00:54
Oroville 24 1 48N56'21 119w26'04 7:57:44
Orting 27 6 47N05'53 122w12'11 8:08:49
Osborn Corner 31
1 47N52'40 122w09'53 8:08:40
Osborne Corner 9
1 48N02'56 119w14'01 7:56:56
Osceola 17 4 47N11'43 122w02'10 8:08:09
Oskams Corner 17
4 47N43'56 122w11'33 8:08:46
Oso 31 1 48N16'15 121w55'42 8:07:43
Ostrander 8 7 46N11'34 122w53'27 8:11:34
Othello 1 1 46N49'34 119w10'27 7:56:42
Otis Orchards 32
1 47N42'02 117w06'19 7:48:25
Outlook 39 1 46N19'53 120w05'24 8:00:22
Overlake 17 4 47N35 122w09 8:08:36
Overlook 18 1 47N32 122w38 8:10:32
Ovington 5 2 48N03'54 123w51'32 8:15:26
Oyhat 14 1 46N59 123w53 8:15:32
Oyhut 14 1 47N01'03 124w09'38 8:16:39
Oysterville 25 1 46N32'57 124w01'37 8:16:06
Ozette 5 2 48N09'18 124w39'57 8:18:40
Pacific 17 9 47N15'53 122w14'56 8:09:00
Pacific Beach 14
1 47N12'33 124w12'07 8:16:48
Packard 1 1 47N12'54 118w29'35 7:53:58
Packwood 21 7 46N36'24 121w40'10 8:06:41
Paddock 36 1 46N15'37 118w27'48 7:53:51
Page 36 1 46N19'46 118w44'29 7:54:58
Paha 1 1 47N01'24 118w29'17 7:53:57
Palisades 9 1 47N25 119w54 7:59:36
Palmer 17 4 47N18'52 121w53'28 8:07:34
Palmer Junction 17
4 47N18'44 121w53'20 8:07:33
Palm Lake 1 1 47N13'05 118w00'49 7:52:03
Palouse 38 1 46N54'37 117w04'29 7:48:18
Palouse Falls 38
1 46N43 118w12 7:52:48
Pampa 38 1 46N46'39 117w57'11 7:51:49
Panakanic 20 1 45N53'52 121w19'15 8:05:17
Pandora 38 1 47N14'27 117w16'20 7:49:05
Paradise 6 1 45N54 122w45 8:11:00
Paradise 27 6 46N47'11 121w44'03 8:06:56
Paradise Inn 27
6 46N47 121w44 8:06:56
Park 37 1 48N30 122w14 8:08:56
Parker 39 1 46N30'04 120w27'51 8:01:51
Parker Landing Light 6
1 45N34'43 122w22'54 8:09:32
Park Junction 27
6 46N45'39 122w08'22 8:08:33
Parkland 27 49 47N09'20 122w25'58 8:09:44
Park Rapids 33 1 48N31'35 117w38'17 7:50:33
Parkwater 32 48 47N40'35 117w19'51 7:49:19
Parkwood 18 1 47N32 122w38 8:10:32
Parrott Crossing 39
1 46N04'45 121w15'53 8:05:04
Parvin 38 1 46N50'54 117w16'56 7:49:08
Pasadena Park 32
1 47N41'49 117w16'54 7:49:08
Pasco 11 29 46N13'43 119w05'58 7:56:24
Pasco West 11 1 46N14 119w09 7:56:36
Pataha 16 1 46N33'37 118w10'52 7:52:43
Pataha City 12 1 46N28'24 117w32'08 7:50:09
Pateros 24 1 48N03'04 119w54'08 7:59:37
Paterson 3 1 45N56'14 119w36'06 7:58:24
Patit 7 1 46N20'09 117w51'30 7:51:26
Paxton 1 1 47N03'03 118w00'13 7:52:01
Peach Acres 27 6 47N12'05 122w32'28 8:10:10
Pearcot 9 1 47N26 120w19 8:01:16
Pearl 3 1 46N35'04 119w33'55 7:58:16
Pearson 18 1 47N42'44 122w38'35 8:10:34
Pearson Eddy 31
4 47N47'34 121w59'48 8:07:59
Pebble Beach 15
2 48N04'00 122w23'10 8:09:33
Pedigo 36 1 46N04'42 118w26'21 7:53:45
Pe Ell 21 7 46N34'14 123w17'46 8:13:11
Penawawa 38 1 46N42'18 117w41'16 7:50:45
Pend Oreille Village 26
1 48N52'06 117w21'53 7:49:28
Penn Cove Park 15
2 48N14'24 122w40'19 8:10:41
Penrith 26 1 48N09'08 117w05'54 7:48:24
Peola 12 1 46N18'33 117w28'55 7:49:56
Peone 32 48 47N48'08 117w13'41 7:48:55
Perrinville 31 1 47N49'44 122w20'25 8:09:22
Perry 11 1 46N35'45 118w13'40 7:52:55
Peshastin 4 1 47N34'15 120w36'10 8:02:25
Peterson Corner 34
7 46N49'26 123w06'57 8:12:28
Peyton 38 1 46N37'42 117w47'57 7:51:12
Phinney 17 44 47N40'21 122w21'34 8:09:26
Pickard 36 1 46N25'33 118w25'31 7:53:42
Picnic Point 27
6 47N20 122w35 8:10:20
Piedmont 5 2 48N05'38 123w47'25 8:15:10
Pierce 3 1 46N38'06 119w27'04 7:57:48
Pifer 1 1 47N15'19 118w05'02 7:52:20
Pigeon Springs 8
3 46N03'12 122w37'22 8:10:29
Pillar Rock 35 1 46N20 123w38 8:14:32
Pine City 38 1 47N12'09 117w31'24 7:50:06
Pinecliff 39 1 46N53'58 121w00'43 8:04:03
Pinecroft 32 48 47N40 117w20 7:49:20
Pine Grove 6 1 45N54'09 122w39'29 8:10:38
Pinehurst 31 24 47N56'10 122w12'16 8:08:49
Pine Lake 17 4 47N33 122w04 8:08:16
Pines 17 40 47N32'45 122w11'21 8:08:45
Ping 12 1 46N39'51 117w40'04 7:50:40
Pinkney City 33
1 48N34'35 117w52'37 7:51:30
Pioneer 27 6 47N12'12 122w34'49 8:10:19
Pitt 20 1 45N47'45 121w11'59 8:04:48
Pizarro 1 1 46N57'00 118w26'42 7:53:47
Plain 4 1 47N46 120w39 8:02:36
Plaza 32 1 47N19'13 117w22'58 7:49:32
Pleasant Beach 18
1 47N38 122w31 8:10:04
Pleasant Hill 8
7 46N13'32 122w53'34 8:11:34
Pleasant Hill 17
4 47N36'56 121w54'30 8:07:38
Pleasant Prairie 32
48 47N42 117w22 7:49:28
Pleasant Valley 6
51 45N40 122w37 8:10:28
Pleasant Valley 20
1 45N50'05 120w35'26 8:02:22
Pleasant Valley 37
1 48N51'51 120w37'28 8:02:30
Plumb 34 7 46N56 122w51 8:11:24
Pluvius 25 1 46N32'54 123w24'28 8:13:38
Plymouth 3 1 45N56'05 119w20'57 7:57:24
Pocahontas Bay 32
1 48N01'44 117w22'22 7:49:29
Point Ellice 25
1 46N16 123w57 8:15:48
Point Roberts 37
1 48N59'08 123w04'36 8:12:18
Point White 18 1 47N35'32 122w33'53 8:10:16
Pollard 10 1 48N43'41 118w39'56 7:54:40
Pomeroy 12 1 46N28'30 117w36'06 7:50:24
Pomona 39 19 46N41'26 120w29'10 8:01:57
Pomona Heights 39
19 46N39'27 120w28'53 8:01:56
Ponder 27 6 47N10 122w32 8:10:08
Ponderosa Estates 27
6 47N13 122w15 8:09:00
Ponders Corner 27
6 47N08'29 122w31'30 8:10:06
Pontius Park 31
1 47N43 122w13 8:08:52
Portage 17 4 47N24 122w26 8:09:44
Port Angeles 5
37 48N07'06 123w25'46 8:13:43
Port Blakely 18
1 47N35'51 122w30'32 8:10:02
Port Discovery 16
31 48N00'56 122w51'38 8:11:27
Porter 14 1 46N56'21 123w18'34 8:13:14
Port Gamble 18 1 47N51'16 122w34'57 8:10:20
Port Gamble Indian Res 18
1 47N51 122w34 8:10:16
Port Kelley 36 1 46N01'32 118w56'13 7:55:45
Port Ludlow 16 1 47N55'32 122w40'56 8:10:44
Port Madison 18
1 47N42'10 122w31'23 8:10:06
Port Madison Indian Res 18
1 47N45 122w30 8:10:00
Port of Kennewick 3
29 46N12'47 119w06'05 7:56:24
Port Orchard 18
1 47N32'26 122w38'06 8:10:32
Port Stanley 28
1 48N32'26 122w52'14 8:11:29
Port Townsend 16
31 48N07'02 122w45'33 8:11:02
Port Williams 5
25 48N05'49 123w02'40 8:12:11
Possession 15 1 47N55'04 122w22'30 8:09:30
Potlatch 23 1 47N22'35 123w08'53 8:12:36
Poulsbo 18 1 47N44'10 122w38'43 8:10:35
Powell 33 1 48N42'19 118w01'11 7:52:05
Powers 7 1 46N32'17 118w09'05 7:52:36
Prairie 29 1 48N36'10 122w14'00 8:08:56
Prairie Center 15
2 48N12'29 122w41'06 8:10:44
Prairie Ridge 27
6 47N13 122w15 8:09:00
Preachers Slough 14
1 46N59 123w36 8:14:24
Prescott 36 1 46N17'59 118w18'50 7:53:15
Preston 17 4 47N31'26 121w55'33 8:07:42
Prevost 28 1 48N41'03 123w12'36 8:12:50
Prindle 30 1 45N35'08 122w09'18 8:08:37
Proctor 27 49 47N17 122w30 8:10:00
Proebstel 6 1 45N40'08 122w28'50 8:09:55
Prosser 3 1 46N12'25 119w46'04 7:59:04
Providence 1 1 46N54'44 118w44'01 7:54:56
Puget 34 6 47N08'48 122w47'33 8:11:10
Puget Island 35
1 46N13 123w23 8:13:32
Pullman 38 1 46N43'53 117w10'43 7:48:43
Pullman Junction 38
1 46N42'51 117w09'36 7:48:38
Purdy 27 6 47N23'21 122w37'27 8:10:30
Purrington 38 1 46N39'49 117w45'54 7:51:04
Puyallup 27 38 47N11'28 122w17'22 8:09:09
Puyallup River Junction 27
6 47N00'23 122w11'31 8:08:46
Pysht 5 2 48N11'55 124w06'54 8:16:28
Queen Anne 17 44 47N38'10 122w21'54 8:09:28
Queensborough 31
1 47N43 122w13 8:08:52

Queensgate 17 4 47N43 122w13 8:08:52
Queets 16 1 47N32'23 124w19'52 8:17:19
Quendall 17 40 47N29 122w12 8:08:48
Quilcene 16 1 47N49'21 122w52'28 8:11:30
Quillayute Indian Res 5
1 47N54 124w38 8:18:32
Quinault 14 1 47N28'02 123w50'39 8:15:23
Quinault Indian Reservation 14
1 47N21 124w17 8:17:08
Quincy 13 1 47N14'04 119w51'05 7:59:24
Raeco 17 4 47N23'00 122w24'24 8:09:38
Ragnar 17 4 47N26'28 121w42'24 8:06:50
Rahms 32 1 47N19'11 117w10'31 7:48:42
Rainier 34 7 46N53'18 122w41'14 8:10:45
Rainier Beach 17
4 47N31'01 122w15'25 8:09:02
Rainier Valley 17
44 47N33'20 122w17'19 8:09:09
Ralston 1 1 46N59'02 118w20'30 7:53:22
Ramapo 5 2 48N07'18 123w40'54 8:14:44
Randle 21 7 46N32'07 121w57'21 8:07:49
Raugust 13 1 47N09 119w18 7:57:12
Ravenna 17 44 47N40'33 122w17'47 8:09:11
Ravensdale 17 4 47N21'09 121w58'57 8:07:56
Raymond 25 39 46N41'12 123w43'54 8:14:56
Rayville 14 1 47N40'40 123w18'58 8:13:16
R Corner 5 2 48N05'39 123w16'25 8:13:06
Reardan 22 1 47N40'11 117w52'36 7:51:30
Redd 36 1 46N20'50 118w45'25 7:55:02
Redmond 17 27 47N40'27 122w07'13 8:08:29
Redondo 17 4 47N20'55 122w19'20 8:09:17
Rees Corner 31 1 47N52'41 122w06'32 8:08:26
Reese 36 1 46N04'19 118w46'49 7:55:07
Regal 19 1 46N59'25 120w27'57 8:01:52
Reiman 1 1 47N13'30 118w40'51 7:54:43
Reiter 31 1 47N50'29 121w37'47 8:06:31
Reliance 27 6 46N46'22 122w15'53 8:09:04
Relief 7 1 46N27'12 118w05'05 7:52:20
Renslow 19 1 46N57'26 120w18'18 8:01:13
Renton 17 40 47N28'59 122w12'57 8:08:52
Republic 10 1 48N38'54 118w44'12 7:54:57
Retsil 18 1 47N33 122w36 8:10:24
Revere 38 1 47N04'53 117w55'45 7:51:43
Rexville 29 1 48N21'56 122w25'28 8:09:42
Rhodesia Beach 25
1 46N36'50 123w57'21 8:15:49
Rhododendron Park 27
6 47N13 122w15 8:09:00
Rice 33 1 48N25'44 118w10'09 7:52:41
Richardson 28 1 48N27'06 122w53'51 8:11:35
Richland 3 41 46N17'09 119w17'00 7:57:08
Richland Junction 3
1 46N13'57 119w13'34 7:56:54
Richmond Beach 17
20 47N46'11 122w23'20 8:09:33
Richmond Highlands 17
4 47N45'41 122w20'42 8:09:23
Ridgecrest 17 4 47N45 122w17 8:09:08
Ridgefield 6 42 45N48'55 122w44'29 8:10:58
Ridpath 38 1 46N35'20 117w53'52 7:51:35
Riffe 21 7 46N30'51 122w22'09 8:09:29
Rifton 36 1 46N36'03 118w20'24 7:53:22
Rimrock 39 1 46N39'52 121w07'26 8:04:30
Ringo 38 1 46N52'18 117w03'39 7:48:15
Ringold 11 1 46N35 119w00 7:56:00
Riparia 38 1 46N34'43 118w05'09 7:52:21
Risbeck 38 1 46N51'50 117w18'46 7:49:15
Ritell 13 1 47N02'08 119w05'06 7:56:20
Ritzville 1 1 47N07'39 118w22'44 7:53:31
Riverside 24 1 48N30'09 119w30'19 7:58:01
Riverside 31 1 48N06'51 122w00'03 8:08:00
Riverton 17 4 47N29'04 122w17'36 8:09:10
Riverton Heights 17
4 47N28'09 122w18'01 8:09:12
Roanoke 17 4 47N35'41 122w14'30 8:08:58
Robe 31 1 48N05'51 121w48'44 8:07:15
Robinson 36 1 46N17'57 118w17'34 7:53:10
Robinson 38 1 47N06'26 117w13'26 7:48:54
Robinswood 17 4 47N35 122w10 8:08:40
Roche Harbor 28
1 48N36'36 123w08'51 8:12:35
Rochester 34 7 46N49'19 123w05'42 8:12:23
Rockaway Beach 15
2 48N12'20 122w32'07 8:10:08
Rock Creek Crossing Campgrou 4
1 47N58'12 120w47'20 8:03:09
Rockdale 17 4 47N23'33 121w27'11 8:05:49
Rockford 32 1 47N27'08 117w07'47 7:48:31
Rock Island 9 1 47N22'38 120w08'34 8:00:34
Rocklyn 22 1 47N37'47 118w16'07 7:53:04
Rockport 29 1 48N29'09 121w35'47 8:06:23
Rockwell 1 1 47N08'51 118w00'34 7:52:02
Rocky Butte 9 1 48N06 119w47 7:59:08
Rocky Point 8 3 46N10'19 122w54'27 8:11:38
Rocky Point 15 2 48N14 122w21 8:09:24
Rocky Point 18 1 47N35'35 122w40'02 8:10:40
Rocky Ridge 27 6 47N01'12 122w22'04 8:09:28
Rodena Beach 15
2 48N13'09 122w37'47 8:10:31
Rodna 32 1 47N17'44 117w47'56 7:51:12
Rogersburg 2 1 46N04'42 116w58'43 7:47:55
Rollingbay 18 1 47N39'53 122w30'32 8:10:02
Ronald 17 4 47N44'57 122w20'19 8:09:21
Ronald 19 1 47N14'07 121w01'20 8:04:05
Ronan 7 1 46N21'50 117w55'17 7:51:41
Rony 14 1 46N56'38 123w21'03 8:13:24
Roosevelt 20 1 45N44'35 120w12'53 8:00:52
Roosevelt 31 1 47N53'33 122w00'40 8:08:03
Rosalia 38 1 47N14'10 117w22'08 7:49:29
Rosario 28 1 48N38'56 122w52'29 8:11:30
Rosario Beach 29
1 48N25'11 122w39'47 8:10:39
Rosburg 35 1 46N19'52 123w38'14 8:14:33
Rosedale 27 6 47N19'54 122w39'04 8:10:36
Rose Hill 17 4 47N41 122w12 8:08:48
Rosehilla 17 4 47N20'45 122w27'59 8:09:52
Rose Springs 12
1 46N16'31 117w33'12 7:50:13
Rosewood 32 48 47N43 117w25 7:49:40
Roslyn 19 1 47N13'25 120w59'31 8:03:58
Rowan 31 1 48N16'27 121w51'05 8:07:24
Roxboro 1 1 46N57'09 118w51'12 7:55:25
Roy 27 6 47N00'16 122w32'19 8:10:09
Royal City 13 1 46N54'04 119w37'46 7:58:31
Roza 19 1 46N47'02 120w27'12 8:01:49
Ruby 3 1 46N22'34 119w16'56 7:57:08
Ruby 24 1 48N29'53 119w43'29 7:58:54
Ruby 26 1 48N31'20 117w17'53 7:49:12
Ruff 13 1 47N10'11 118w59'50 7:55:59
Rulo 36 1 46N10'28 118w30'05 7:54:00
Rupple 39 1 46N24'16 120w37'48 8:02:31
Russell 36 1 46N08'02 118w20'42 7:53:23
Russell Landing 6
1 45N36'22 122w34'58 8:10:20
Ruston 27 6 47N17'58 122w30'25 8:10:02
Ruth 3 1 46N38'41 119w27'21 7:57:49
Ruth 21 5 46N36'26 123w07'07 8:12:28
Ruxby 36 1 46N34'31 118w29'23 7:53:58
Ryan 33 1 48N48'51 117w57'58 7:51:52
Ryderwood 8 43 46N22'36 123w02'33 8:12:10
Rye 6 51 45N40'31 122w37'44 8:10:31
Rye 19 1 46N52'09 120w07'00 8:00:28
Sagehill 11 1 46N35 119w00 7:56:00
Sagemoor 11 1 46N23'56 119w03'38 7:56:15
Saginaw 14 1 46N58'21 123w23'08 8:13:33
Saint Andrews 9
1 47N41'59 119w25'31 7:57:42
Saint Clair 34 1 47N01'27 122w43'23 8:10:54
Saint Helens 8 3 46N20'40 122w31'39 8:10:07
Saint John 38 1 47N05'30 117w34'51 7:50:19
Saint Marys Hot Springs 30
1 45N43'40 121w47'44 8:07:11
Saint Urban 21 5 46N31'05 122w53'07 8:11:32
Salishan 27 6 47N13'03 122w24'22 8:09:37
Salkum 21 7 46N31'56 122w37'29 8:10:30
Salmon Creek 6
51 45N42'39 122w38'52 8:10:35
Samish 29 1 48N36'40 122w26'04 8:09:44
Samish Island 29
1 48N34'34 122w32'23 8:10:10
Sammamish 17 4 47N38'31 122w04'45 8:08:19
Sampson 14 1 47N02'31 124w09'50 8:16:39
San de Fuca 15 2 48N14'07 122w43'19 8:10:53
Sandy Hook Park 18
1 47N44 122w38 8:10:32
Sandy Shores 17
4 47N22 122w28 8:09:52
Sapolil 36 1 46N07'14 118w14'12 7:52:57
Sappho 5 2 48N04'13 124w16'41 8:17:07
Sara 6 1 45N45'06 122w42'43 8:10:51
Saratoga 15 2 48N04'25 122w27'54 8:09:52
Saratoga Shores 15
2 48N08'12 122w30'37 8:10:02
Satsop 14 1 47N00'12 123w28'56 8:13:56
Satus 39 1 46N16'13 120w08'57 8:00:36
Sawyer 39 1 46N27'24 120w21'37 8:01:26
Saxby 32 1 47N29'25 117w02'50 7:48:11
Saxon 37 1 48N41'16 122w11'15 8:08:45
Scammon Landing 19
1 47N02'23 120w01'21 8:00:05
Scandia 18 1 47N43 122w39 8:10:36
Scenic 17 4 47N43 121w09 8:04:36
Schawana 13 1 46N50 119w56 7:59:44
Schlomer 11 1 46N41'51 118w55'19 7:55:41
Schneiders Prairie 34
36 47N02 122w51 8:11:24
Schoonover 1 1 47N13'54 118w34'49 7:54:19
Schrag 1 1 47N04'24 118w51'11 7:55:25
Schwana 13 1 46N49'27 119w55'29 7:59:42
Schwarder 39 1 46N33 120w32 8:02:08
Scopa 17 40 47N29 122w12 8:08:48
Scotia 26 1 48N06'23 117w09'11 7:48:37
Scott 36 1 46N30'27 118w36'17 7:54:25
Scotton Corner 6
10 45N46'00 122w32'09 8:10:09
Scribner 32 1 47N33'21 117w30'01 7:50:00
Sea Acre 28 1 48N39'09 122w45'20 8:11:01
Seabeck 18 1 47N38'23 122w49'38 8:11:19
Seabold 18 1 47N42'03 122w33'22 8:10:13
Sea First 17 44 47N36 122w20 8:09:20
Seahurst 17 4 47N28'10 122w21'39 8:09:27
Seal Rock 16 1 47N42'50 122w53'04 8:11:32
Seatons Grove 24
1 48N01'26 118w57'00 7:55:48
Seattle 17 44 47N36'23 122w19'51 8:09:19
Seattle Heights 31
20 47N48'38 122w19'22 8:09:17
Seaview 25 1 46N20'05 124w03'12 8:16:13
Sedro-Woolley 29
1 48N30'14 122w14'10 8:08:57
Sekiu 5 2 48N15'45 124w18'00 8:17:12
Selah 39 19 46N39'15 120w31'44 8:02:07
Selleck 17 4 47N22'33 121w52'02 8:07:28
Seltice 38 1 47N09'20 117w05'10 7:48:21
Seola Beach 17
44 47N29'37 122w22'00 8:09:28
Sequim 5 25 48N04'47 123w06'02 8:12:24
Servia 1 1 46N55'23 118w45'13 7:55:01
Seven Mile 32 1 47N44'32 117w30'37 7:50:02
Shadow 5 2 48N08'50 123w51'23 8:15:26
Shano 1 1 46N45'48 118w59'15 7:55:57
Sharon 32 48 47N38 117w24 7:49:36
Sharpes Corner 29
1 48N27'50 122w34'51 8:10:19
Shaw Island 28 1 48N35'04 122w55'40 8:11:43
Shawnee 17 4 47N23'04 122w28'46 8:09:55
Shawnee 38 1 46N49'27 117w16'13 7:49:05
Sheffler 36 1 46N24'32 118w38'05 7:54:32
Shelton 24 45 47N12'56 123w05'46 8:12:23
Sheridan Beach 17
4 47N45 122w17 8:09:08
Sheridan Park 18
1 47N35'06 122w38'05 8:10:32
Sherman 22 1 47N49'39 118w36'14 7:54:25
Sherwood Forest 17
4 47N35 122w10 8:08:40
Shine 16 1 47N52 122w39 8:10:36
Shoalwater Indian Res 25
1 46N42 124w01 8:16:04
Shore Acres 17 6 47N21'18 122w26'49 8:09:47
Shoreline 17 4 47N45 122w20 8:09:20
Shorewood Beach 27
6 47N16 122w38 8:10:32
Shoultes 31 1 48N05 122w10 8:08:40
Shreck 38 1 46N41'51 117w53'11 7:51:33
Shrine Beach 4 1 47N55'14 120w12'34 8:00:50
Sieler 13 1 47N04'04 119w10'33 7:56:42
Sifton 6 1 45N40'22 122w31'48 8:10:07
Sightly 8 3 46N18'00 122w42'26 8:10:50
Silcott 2 1 46N24'55 117w11'48 7:48:47
Silvana 31 1 48N12'09 122w15'09 8:09:01
Silvana Terraces 31
1 48N12'10 122w16'56 8:09:08
Silver Beach 37
11 48N46'01 122w24'48 8:09:39
Silver Brook 21
7 46N32'18 121w54'25 8:07:38
Silver Creek 21
5 46N31'32 122w35'21 8:10:21
Silverdale 18 1 47N38'41 122w41'37 8:10:46
Silverlake 8 3 46N17'51 122w48'34 8:11:14
Silver Lake 31
24 47N58 122w14 8:08:56
Silverton 31 1 48N04'43 121w33'57 8:06:16
Simenson 1 1 46N52'59 119w04'05 7:56:16
Similk Beach 29
1 48N26'53 122w34'36 8:10:18
Sims Corner 9 1 47N48'56 119w21'39 7:57:27
Sine 14 1 47N01'54 123w15'48 8:13:03
Sisco 31 1 48N07'40 122w08'09 8:08:33
Sisco Heights 31
1 48N06'56 122w05'45 8:08:23
Sixprong 20 1 45N51'27 120w01'57 8:00:08
Sixth Avenue 27
49 47N16 122w29 8:09:56
Skagit City 29 3 48N23'01 122w21'42 8:09:27
Skamania 30 1 45N37'03 122w02'26 8:08:10
Skamokawa 35 1 46N16'14 123w27'21 8:13:49
Skokomish Indian Reservation 23
1 47N20 123w09 8:12:36
Skookumchuck 34
36 46N54'20 122w46'11 8:11:05
Skykomish 17 4 47N42'34 121w21'32 8:05:26
Skyway 17 4 47N30 122w15 8:09:00
Slater 36 1 46N11'12 118w48'21 7:55:13
Sleepy Hollow 35
1 46N16'25 123w27'04 8:13:48
Smith Place 16 1 47N39'31 123w55'48 8:15:43
Smithville 20 1 45N38'56 121w09'46 8:04:39
Smokey Point 31
1 48N09'09 122w10'53 8:08:44
Smyrna 13 1 46N50'22 119w39'40 7:58:39
Snake River 11 1 46N23 118w41 7:54:44
Snee-oosh-Beach 29
1 48N23 122w29 8:09:56
Snohomish 31 46 47N54'47 122w05'49 8:08:23
Snoose Junction 17
4 47N23'33 121w49'03 8:07:16
Snoqualmie 17 4 47N31'44 121w49'27 8:07:18
Snoqualmie Falls 17
4 47N32'24 121w48'31 8:07:14
Snoqualmie National Forest 17
4 47N29 121w31 8:06:04
Snoqualmie Pass 17
4 47N32 121w49 8:07:16
Snoquera 27 4 47N02'17 121w33'50 8:06:15
Snowden 20 1 45N49'57 121w21'09 8:05:25
Snug Harbor 5 2 48N04'31 123w42'06 8:14:48
Snyders Corner 17
4 47N40'00 122w09'44 8:08:39
Soap Lake 13 1 47N23'22 119w29'22 7:57:57
Sokulk 38 1 47N04'27 117w12'38 7:48:51
Sol Duc Hot Springs 5
2 48N06 123w24 8:13:36
South Aberdeen 14
1 46N58'08 123w48'05 8:15:12
South Aberdeen Junction 14
1 46N58 123w45 8:15:00
South Arbor 14 1 46N55'16 123w58'50 8:15:55
South Bay 34 36 47N04'50 122w50'41 8:11:23
South Beach 18 1 47N34'30 122w30'24 8:10:02
South Beach 37 1 48N58'39 123w02'57 8:12:12
South Bellingham 37
11 48N43'09 122w29'19 8:09:57
South Bend 25 47 46N40 123w48 8:15:12
South Benton 3 1 46N01 119w28 7:57:52
South Broadway 39
1 46N34 120w31 8:02:04
South Cheney 32
1 47N27'57 117w34'31 7:50:18
South Cle Elum 19
1 47N11'09 120w56'52 8:03:47
South Colby 18 1 47N31'20 122w32'10 8:10:09
South Elma 14 1 46N58'53 123w24'44 8:13:39
Southern Heights 17
4 47N29'45 122w18'29 8:09:14
Southgate 27 6 47N10 122w32 8:10:08
South Highlands 3
29 46N11'37 119w08'11 7:56:33
South Highline 17
4 47N26 122w19 8:09:16
South Montesano 14
1 46N57'28 123w36'15 8:14:25
South Park 17 4 47N31'36 122w18'48 8:09:15
South Prairie 27
6 47N08'22 122w05'49 8:08:23
South Seattle 17
4 47N33'42 122w18'42 8:09:15
South Snohomish 31
1 47N53'57 122w06'28 8:08:26
South Tacoma 27
49 47N12'22 122w28'56 8:09:56
South Union 34 7 46N56'36 122w54'22 8:11:37
Southworth 18 1 47N30'44 122w30'02 8:10:00
Spanaway 27 6 47N06'15 122w26'00 8:09:44
Spangle 32 1 47N25'39 117w22'45 7:49:31
Spear 32 48 47N40 117w21 7:49:24
Spee-Bi-Dah 31 1 48N05'30 122w19'19 8:09:17
Sperry 11 1 46N42'00 118w24'32 7:53:38
Spirit 33 1 48N49'47 117w38'58 7:50:36
Spirit Lake 30 1 46N16 122w09 8:08:36
Spokane 32 48 47N39'32 117w25'30 7:49:42
Spokane Indian Reservation 33
1 47N53 117w59 7:51:56
Sprague 22 1 47N18'01 117w58'28 7:51:54
Spring Beach 17
4 47N20'58 122w31'33 8:10:06
Springdale 33 1 48N03'27 117w44'25 7:50:58
Spring Glen 17 4 47N33'41 121w51'37 8:07:26

Spring Valley 32
1 47N16'29 117W17'01 7:49:08
Squaxon Island Indian Res 23
1 47N12 122W54 8:11:36
Stabler 30 1 45N48'30 121W54'23 8:07:38
Staley 38 1 46N40'11 117W08'51 7:48:35
Stampede 17 4 47N15'47 121W22'55 8:05:28
Standard 37 1 48N44'43 122W12'02 8:08:48
Stanwood 31 1 48N14'29 122W22'10 8:09:29
Starbuck 7 1 46N31'11 118W07'40 7:52:31
Star Lake 17 4 47N21'29 122W17'25 8:09:10
Starr 24 1 47N59'43 119W52'42 7:59:31
Startup 31 1 47N52'05 121W44'21 8:06:57
State Camp 35 1 46N15 123W19 8:13:16
Stateline 36 1 46N00'04 118W24'48 7:53:39
Stayman 4 1 47N45'57 120W05'19 8:00:21
Stehekin 4 1 48N18'34 120W39'19 8:02:37
Steilacoom 27 6 47N10'12 122W36'05 8:10:24
Stella 8 32 46N11'27 123W07'07 8:12:28
Stentz Spring 12
1 46N13'41 117W34'41 7:50:19
Steptoe 38 1 47N00'22 117W21'18 7:49:25
Sterling 29 1 48N29'32 122W16'46 8:09:07
Stevens Lake 31
1 48N00'55 122W03'45 8:08:15
Stevenson 30 20 45N42 121W53 8:07:32
Stiebels Corner 18
1 47N44 122W33 8:10:12
Stillwater 17 4 47N40'59 121W55'08 8:07:41
Stimson 23 1 47N05'26 123W13'50 8:12:55
Stimson Crossing 31
1 48N07'23 122W10'55 8:08:44
Stonehenge Replica 20
1 45N42 120W49 8:03:16
Straight Point 20
1 45N41'51 121W23'41 8:05:35
Strandell 37 1 48N54'44 122W21'25 8:09:26
Stratford 13 1 47N25'38 119W25'14 7:57:41
Striebels Corner 18
1 47N48'18 122W34'01 8:10:16
Stringtown 25 1 46N18'23 123W58'39 8:15:55
Stuart 17 4 47N41'19 121W56'50 8:07:47
Stuck 17 9 47N16'58 122W13'39 8:08:55
Sudbury 36 48 46N05'39 118W28'35 7:53:54
Sulphur 11 1 46N38'15 118W43'29 7:54:54
Sultan 31 1 47N51'46 121W48'55 8:07:16
Sumach 39 19 46N36 120W29 8:01:56
Sumas 37 1 49N00'00 122W15'49 8:09:03
Summerhurst 17 6 47N20'50 122W27'06 8:09:48
Summit 27 4 47N22 122W01 8:08:04
Summit Park 29 1 48N30 122W37 8:10:28
Sumner 27 6 47N12'12 122W14'21 8:08:57
Sunbeach 23 6 47N25'25 122W53'39 8:11:35
Sundale 20 1 45N43'12 120W19'00 8:01:16
Sundins Beach 15
2 48N14 122W21 8:09:24
Sunlight Beach 15
2 47N59'28 122W28'45 8:09:55
Sunnybank 4 1 47N51'36 120W08'57 8:00:36
Sunny Bay 27 6 47N20 122W35 8:10:20
Sunnydale 17 4 47N27'48 122W19'57 8:09:20
Sunnydale 34 7 46N50'02 122W55'54 8:11:44
Sunny Shore Acres 15
2 48N06'32 122W24'20 8:09:37
Sunny Shores 31
1 48N06'31 122W20'42 8:09:23
Sunnyside 31 24 47N58 122W14 8:08:56
Sunnyside 37 11 48N43'53 122W18'51 8:09:15
Sunnyside 39 1 46N19'26 120W00'27 8:00:02
Sunnyslope 4 1 47N28'23 120W20'08 8:01:21
Sunnyslope 18 1 47N30'17 122W43'40 8:10:55
Sunrise 27 6 46N54'54 121W38'28 8:06:34
Sunrise Beach 27
6 47N21 122W34 8:10:16
Sunrise Point 15
2 48N14 122W21 8:09:24
Sunset 29 1 48N32'43 122W24'16 8:09:37
Sunset 38 1 47N07'15 117W29'04 7:49:56
Sunset Beach 14
1 47N13'34 124W12'28 8:16:50
Sunset Beach 15
2 48N14 122W21 8:09:24
Sunset Beach 23
6 47N24'30 122W53'03 8:11:32
Sunset Beach 27
6 47N13'06 122W34'17 8:10:17
Sunset Hill 17
44 47N40'33 122W23'50 8:09:35
Sunshine 38 1 46N43'11 117W05'42 7:48:23
Sun Village 17 4 47N43 122W13 8:08:52
Supplee 9 1 47N39'07 119W52'54 7:59:32
Suquamish 18 1 47N43'53 122W33'04 8:10:12
Surprise Valley 27
6 46N55'50 122W13'54 8:08:56
Susie 3 1 46N35'32 119W37'20 7:58:29
Sutico 25 39 46N37'59 123W31'28 8:14:06
Sutton 38 1 46N54'10 117W50'35 7:51:22
Svensens Landing 35
1 46N19'12 123W42'24 8:14:50
Swale 20 1 45N45'31 121W04'16 8:04:17
Swansonville 16
1 47N56'14 122W41'57 8:10:48
Swantown 15 2 48N18'19 122W42'42 8:10:51
Swan Trail 31 24 47N58 122W14 8:08:56
Swede Heaven 31
1 48N17'04 121W43'37 8:06:54
Swede Hill 27 6 47N21'12 122W37'04 8:10:28
Swem 25 1 46N39'36 123W24'12 8:13:37
Swift 38 1 46N40'31 117W35'53 7:50:24
Swinomish Indian Reservation 29
1 48N25 122W32 8:10:08
Swofford 21 1 46N30'19 122W23'14 8:09:33
Sylvan 27 6 47N16 122W38 8:10:32
Synarep 24 1 48N31'16 119W19'47 7:57:19
Tacoma 27 49 47N15'11 122W26'35 8:09:46
Tacoma Junction 27
6 47N14'27 122W23'36 8:09:34
Tahlequah 17 4 47N19'58 122W30'22 8:10:01
Taholah 14 1 47N20'51 124W17'31 8:17:10
Tahuya 23 1 47N22'17 123W03'16 8:12:13
Tampico 39 19 46N32'07 120W51'58 8:03:28
Tanglewild 34 36 47N02 122W51 8:11:24
Tanner 17 4 47N28'32 121W44'42 8:06:59
Tanwax 27 6 47N00'13 122W14'32 8:08:58
Tasker 39 1 46N41'45 120W44'34 8:02:58
Tavnton 1 1 46N48'11 119W20'40 7:57:23
T Bridge Corner 32
1 47N58'30 117W28'42 7:49:55
Teanaway 19 1 47N10'30 120W51'23 8:03:26
Tekoa 38 1 47N13'24 117W04'16 7:48:17
Telford 22 1 47N41'40 118W24'22 7:53:37
Telma 4 1 47N50'36 120W48'52 8:03:15
Tenino 34 50 46N51'25 122W51'06 8:11:24
Terminal Annex 32
48 47N42 117W25 7:49:40
Terrace Heights 39
1 46N36'23 120W26'19 8:01:45
Terrys Corner 15
2 48N14'41 122W27'17 8:09:49
Teske 1 1 47N04'27 118W09'06 7:52:36
Thatcher 28 1 48N33'18 122W49'03 8:11:16
Thavis 1 1 46N57'28 118W13'08 7:52:53
The Highlands 17
4 47N44'38 122W22'06 8:09:28
Thera 38 1 46N56'10 117W33'13 7:50:13
Thiel 36 48 46N08'25 118W29'26 7:53:58
Thomas 17 30 47N21'14 122W13'40 8:08:55
Thompson Place 34
36 47N03'20 122W46'56 8:11:08
Thornton 38 1 47N07'15 117W23'19 7:49:33
Thornwood 29 1 48N35'01 122W13'45 8:08:55
Thorp 19 1 47N04'05 120W40'12 8:02:41
Thrall 19 1 46N55'50 120W30'36 8:02:02
Thrashers Corner 31
1 47N48'33 122W12'24 8:08:50
Three Lakes 31 1 47N57 122W01 8:08:04
Thrift 27 6 47N03'10 122W15'04 8:09:00
Tieton 39 1 46N42'08 120W45'15 8:03:01
Tietonview Grange 39
19 46N35'36 120W42'27 8:02:50
Tiflis 13 1 47N04'10 119W03'27 7:56:14
Tiger 26 1 48N42 117W24 7:49:36
Tillicum 27 6 47N07'25 122W33'21 8:10:13
Tillicum Beach 15
2 48N14 122W21 8:09:24
Times Square 17
44 47N37 122W20 8:09:20
Tire Junction 30
1 46N05'53 121W43'14 8:06:53
Titlow 27 6 47N14'48 122W33'06 8:10:12
Tokeland 25 1 46N42'24 123W58'50 8:15:55
Tokio 1 1 47N12'35 118W16'07 7:53:04
Tokul 17 4 47N33'44 121W49'23 8:07:18
Toledo 21 5 46N26'24 122W50'44 8:11:23
Tompkins 36 1 46N27'38 118W22'08 7:53:29
Tonasket 24 1 48N42'19 119W26'18 7:57:45
Tono 34 7 46N46'34 122W49'22 8:11:17
Toppenish 39 1 46N22'39 120W18'27 8:01:14
Torboy 10 1 48N40'48 118W39'42 7:54:39
Toroda 10 1 48N56'35 118W45'39 7:55:03
Touchet 36 1 46N02'24 118W40'16 7:54:41
Touhey 9 1 47N45'15 119W42'38 7:58:51
Toutle 8 3 46N19'41 122W41'25 8:10:46
Towal 20 1 45N45'05 120W36'10 8:02:25
Town and Country 32
48 47N43 117W25 7:49:40
Tracy 36 1 46N05'00 118W11'16 7:52:45
Tracyton 10 1 47N36'33 122W39'14 8:10:37
Trafton 31 1 48N14'14 122W03'26 8:08:14
Trend 17 4 47N41 122W12 8:08:48
Trentwood 32 1 47N41'48 117W12'35 7:48:50
Tri-Cities 11 1 46N14 119W06 7:56:24
Trinidad 13 1 47N13'48 119W59'58 8:00:00
Trinity 4 1 48N04'29 120W51'05 8:03:24
Triton 23 1 47N36'18 122W59'19 8:11:57
Trout Lake 20 1 45N59'51 121W31'37 8:06:06
Trude 17 4 47N23'23 121W55'28 8:07:42
Trunbull 32 1 47N26 117W33 7:50:12
Tucannon 7 1 46N29'21 117W57'33 7:51:50
Tukey 16 31 48N03'15 122W50'30 8:11:22
Tukwila 17 4 47N28'27 122W15'35 8:09:02
Tulalip 31 1 48N04'07 122W17'26 8:09:10
Tulalip Indian Reservation 31
1 48N05 122W15 8:09:00
Tulalip Shores 31
24 48N04 122W10 8:08:40
Tulare Beach 31
1 48N06'07 122W20'31 8:09:22
Tulips 14 1 47N04'20 124W02'21 8:16:09
Tulker 31 1 48N16'54 121W45'51 8:07:03
Tumtum 33 1 47N53'30 117W40'55 7:50:44
Tumwater 34 36 47N00'27 122W54'29 8:11:38
Turk 33 1 48N03'15 118W06'44 7:52:27
Turner 7 1 46N24'45 117W51'13 7:51:25
Turner Corner 31
1 47N48'17 122W08'32 8:08:34
Tweedie 26 1 48N05'09 117W02'41 7:48:11
Twin 5 2 48N09'54 123W57'10 8:15:49
Twisp 24 1 48N21'49 120W07'16 8:00:29
Two Rivers 36 1 46N08'27 118W56'29 7:55:46
Tyee 5 2 48N04 124W21 8:17:24
Tyee Beach 15 2 48N05'34 122W23'04 8:09:32
Tyler 32 1 47N26'10 117W46'57 7:51:08
Umtanum 19 1 46N51'54 120W28'43 8:01:55
Uncas 16 1 47N59'16 122W52'54 8:11:32
Underwood 30 1 45N43'47 121W31'30 8:06:06
Underwood Heights 30
1 45N44'09 121W31'34 8:06:06
Union 6 1 45N42'29 122W33'02 8:10:12
Union 23 1 47N21'19 123W05'59 8:12:24
Union Center 38
1 46N44'36 117W19'51 7:49:19
Union Gap 39 1 46N33'27 120W28'26 8:01:54
Union Mill 34 36 47N01'58 122W46'24 8:11:06
Uniontown 38 1 46N32'22 117W05'12 7:48:21
University 17 44 47N40'00 122W18'31 8:09:14
University of Washington 17
44 47N40 122W19 8:09:16
University Place 27
6 47N14'09 122W32'57 8:10:12
Upper Fairfax 27
6 47N00'21 121W59'57 8:08:00
Upper Mill 17 4 47N11'37 121W55'33 8:07:42
Upper Preston 17
4 47N30'19 121W54'23 8:07:38
Upper Salmon Junction 25
1 46N21'16 123W44'03 8:14:56
Upper Snoqualmie Valley 17
4 47N32 121W49 8:07:16
Urban 29 1 48N37'05 122W41'27 8:10:46
Usk 26 1 48N18'50 117W16'43 7:49:07
Utsalady 31 2 48N15'07 122W28'33 8:09:54
Vader 21 7 46N24'10 122W57'33 8:11:50
Vail 34 7 46N50'43 122W39'18 8:10:37
Valhalla 17 4 47N43 122W13 8:08:52
Valley 33 1 48N10'31 117W43'25 7:50:54
Valleyford 32 1 47N31'55 117W14'17 7:48:57
Valley Grove 36
1 46N09'09 118W20'52 7:53:23
Van Buren 37 1 48N55 122W21 8:09:24
Vancouver 6 51 45N38'20 122W39'37 8:10:38
Vancouver Junction 6
51 45N40'39 122W41'27 8:10:46
Vanderpool Crossing 24
1 48N39'35 120W19'51 8:01:19
Van Horn 29 1 48N31'00 121W42'15 8:06:49
Vantage 19 1 46N56'44 119W59'10 7:59:57
Van Wyck 37 11 48N48'14 122W25'10 8:09:41
Van Zandt 37 1 48N47'21 122W11'26 8:08:46
Varna 7 1 46N17'23 118W04'52 7:52:19
Vashon 17 4 47N26'51 122W27'31 8:09:50
Vashon Center 17
4 47N27 122W28 8:09:52
Vashon Heights 17
4 47N30'21 122W27'51 8:09:51
Vashon Island 17
4 47N26 122W28 8:09:52
Vaughn 27 6 47N20'40 122W45'43 8:11:03
Veazey 17 9 47N14'51 121W57'08 8:07:49
Velox 32 1 47N41'45 117W10'57 7:48:44
Velvet 33 1 48N59'10 117W49'33 7:51:18
Venersborg 6 1 45N46'26 122W25'24 8:09:42
Venice 18 1 47N40'02 122W34'43 8:10:19
Venner 39 1 46N24'18 120W30'03 8:02:00
Vera 32 1 47N39'20 117W11'11 7:48:45
Veradale 32 1 47N39'25 117W11'43 7:48:47
Verlot 31 1 48N05'26 121W46'34 8:07:06
Vesta 14 1 46N50'00 123W35'15 8:14:21
Veterans Administration Hosp 6
51 45N38 122W37 8:10:28
Veterans Administration Hosp 36
48 46N04 118W22 7:53:28
Victor 23 1 47N22'40 122W48'53 8:11:16
Victor 37 11 48N50'00 122W26'31 8:09:46
View 6 1 45N52 122W40 8:10:40
View Park 18 1 47N32 122W38 8:10:32
View Ridge 17 44 47N40'47 122W16'22 8:09:05
Villa Beach 27 6 47N11 122W42 8:10:48
Villard Junction 36
1 46N10'43 118W59'29 7:55:58
Vinland 18 1 47N46'24 122W41'46 8:10:47
Virden 19 1 47N12'11 120W42'29 8:02:50
Virginia 18 1 47N42'27 122W38'10 8:10:33
Vision Acres 8 3 46N05'15 122W51'58 8:11:28
Vista 3 1 46N12'46 119W12'32 7:56:50
Voltage 9 1 47N20'54 120W05'43 8:00:23
Voss Resort 27 6 46N58'26 122W13'57 8:08:56
Wabash 17 4 47N14'35 122W03'23 8:08:14
Wacota 11 1 46N39'29 118W29'32 7:53:50
Wagner 31 1 47N52'45 121W56'07 8:07:44
Wagnersburg 4 1 47N36'05 120W14'27 8:00:58
Wahkiacus 20 1 45N49'33 121W05'50 8:04:23
Wahl 37 1 48N50'11 122W21'47 8:09:27
Wahluke 3 1 46N42'35 119W32'28 7:58:10
Waitsburg 36 1 46N16'14 118W09'08 7:52:37
Wakefield 24 1 48N12'09 119W42'33 7:58:50
Waldron 28 1 48N41'16 123W02'08 8:12:09
Walker 36 1 46N25'50 118W37'49 7:54:31
Walkers Landing 23
1 47N16'58 122W55'27 8:11:42
Walla Walla 36
48 46N03'53 118W20'31 7:53:22
Wallicut 25 1 46N18 124W02 8:16:08
Wallingford 17
44 47N39'21 122W19'35 8:09:18
Wallner 32 1 47N15'54 117W03'34 7:48:14
Wallula 36 1 46N05'08 118W54'15 7:55:37
Wallula Junction 36
1 46N03'31 118W54'31 7:55:38
Walnut Grove 6 1 45N40'05 122W35'52 8:10:23
Walters 38 1 47N02'29 117W06'19 7:48:25
Walville 21 7 46N33'11 123W21'14 8:13:25
Wanapum Village 13
1 46N51'41 119W56'46 7:59:47
Wapato 39 1 46N26'52 120W25'09 8:01:41
Ward 33 1 48N36'16 118W01'20 7:52:05
Warden 13 1 46N58'04 119W02'19 7:56:09
Warm Beach 31 1 48N10'15 122W21'48 8:09:27
Warner 38 1 47N09'12 117W08'11 7:48:33
Warnick 37 1 48N54'08 121W59'17 8:07:57
Warren 27 6 47N16'56 122W39'04 8:10:36
Warrenville 18 1 47N39'38 122W46'10 8:11:05
Warwick 20 1 45N43'19 120W59'51 8:03:59
Washington Harbor 5
25 48N04'45 123W02'38 8:12:11
Washougal 6 10 45N34'58 122W21'08 8:09:25
Washtucna 1 1 46N45'24 118W18'34 7:53:14
Waterman 18 1 47N34'25 122W34'46 8:10:19
Waterman Point 18
1 47N35'05 122W34'07 8:10:16
Waterville 9 1 47N38'50 120W04'12 8:00:17
Wauconda 24 1 48N43'33 119W00'45 7:56:03
Waukon 22 1 47N32'23 117W50'32 7:51:22
Wauna 27 6 47N22'45 122W38'29 8:10:34
Waunch Prairie 21
5 46N44 122W59 8:11:56
Wautauga Beach 18
1 47N35'11 122W32'49 8:10:11
Waverly 32 1 47N20'34 117W13'37 7:48:54
Wawawai 38 1 46N38 117W23 7:49:32
Wayne 17 4 47N44'53 122W12'34 8:08:50
Weber 1 1 47N05'03 118W56'16 7:55:45
Wedgewood 17 44 47N41'13 122W17'40 8:09:11
Wedgwood 17 44 47N41 122W18 8:09:12
Wegoe 27 6 47N06 122W35 8:10:20
Weikel 39 19 46N37'58 120W39'58 8:02:40
Weikswood 14 1 46N53'43 123W27'09 8:13:49
Weir Park 6 1 45N35 122W24 8:09:36

Welcome 37 1 48N49 122W13 8:08:52
Welland 36 1 46N13'40 118W44'44 7:54:59
Wellpinit 33 1 47N53'17 117W59'13 7:51:57
Wenas 39 1 46N52'22 120W46'22 8:03:05
Wenatchee 4 52 47N25'25 120W18'33 8:01:14
Wenatchee Heights 4 1 47N21'36 120W17'10 8:01:09
Wenatchee Suburban 4 1 47N26 120W20 8:01:20
West Beach 28 1 48N41'15 122W57'23 8:11:50
West Blakely 18 1 47N35'54 122W32'18 8:10:09
West Clarkston 2 1 46N24 117W03 7:48:12
West Coulee 9 1 47N58 118W59 7:55:56
West Duwamish 17 4 47N30'26 122W17'23 8:09:10
Western Junction 34 36 46N54'33 122W47'28 8:11:10
Westfair 17 9 47N19 122W14 8:08:56
West Fairfield 32 1 47N22'15 117W13'13 7:48:53
West Fork 10 1 48N27'28 118W44'57 7:55:00
Westhaven 14 1 46N54'31 124W06'43 8:16:27
West Highlands 3 1 46N12'49 119W10'48 7:56:43
West Kelso 8 3 46N08'46 122W55'18 8:11:41
Westlake 13 1 47N06'15 119W20'08 7:57:21
West Park 18 1 47N33'48 122W40'38 8:10:43
Westport 14 1 46N53'25 124W06'10 8:16:25
West Richland 3 41 46N18'16 119W21'37 7:57:26
West Seattle 17 44 47N34'16 122W23'07 8:09:32
West Side 39 19 46N36 120W32 8:02:08
West Sound 28 1 48N37'53 122W57'18 8:11:49
West Spokane 32 48 47N39'38 117W26'28 7:49:46
West Warden 13 1 46N58'03 119W03'38 7:56:15
West Wenatchee 4 1 47N27 120W20 8:01:20
Westwood 18 1 47N37'09 122W34'28 8:10:18
Weyerhauser 27 6 46N52 122W16 8:09:04
Wheeler 13 1 47N07'51 119W10'15 7:56:41
Wheeler Corner 22 1 47N33'03 117W58'17 7:51:53
Whelan 38 1 46N47'03 117W06'56 7:48:28
Whetstone 7 1 46N23'36 117W53'45 7:51:35
Whidbey Island Naval Air Sta 15 2 48N19 122W39 8:10:36
Whiskey Bend 5 2 47N58'07 123W34'54 8:14:20
Whitcomb 3 1 45N51'56 119W47'01 7:59:08
White 17 4 47N42'28 122W05'15 8:08:21
White Bluffs 3 1 46N40'00 119W29'01 7:57:56
White Center 17 4 47N31'03 122W21'13 8:09:25
White Horse 31 1 48N16'08 121W42'18 8:06:49
White Pass 39 1 46N44 120W42 8:02:48
Whites 14 1 47N00 123W24 8:13:36
White Salmon 20 1 45N43'40 121W29'07 8:05:56
White Swan 39 1 46N22'59 120W43'48 8:02:55
Whitlow 38 1 46N43'17 117W08'57 7:48:36
Whitman Nat Hist Site 36 48 46N02 118W28 7:53:52
Whitmarsh Junction 29 1 48N27'57 122W32'08 8:10:09
Whitney 29 21 48N26'53 122W28'13 8:09:53
Whitstran 3 1 46N14'08 119W42'16 7:58:49
Whittier 19 4 47N17'24 121W18'59 8:05:16
Whittier Heights 17 44 47N41'28 122W22'17 8:09:29
Wickersham 37 1 48N39'19 122W12'42 8:08:51
Wilbur 22 1 47N45'32 118W42'16 7:54:49
Wilburton 17 4 47N36'12 122W10'47 8:08:43
Wilcox 38 1 46N48'36 117W29'22 7:49:57
Wildcat Lake 18 1 47N36'17 122W45'56 8:11:04
Wilderness Village 17 4 47N25 122W03 8:08:12
Wild Goose 7 1 46N35'11 117W55'03 7:51:40
Wildwood 18 1 47N27'51 122W40'26 8:10:42
Wildwood 21 5 46N35 123W07 8:12:28
Wiley 39 19 46N36 120W29 8:01:56
Wiley City 39 19 46N33'06 120W38'53 8:02:36
Wilkeson 27 6 47N06'20 122W02'40 8:08:11
Willa 3 1 46N34'45 119W31'05 7:58:04
Willada 38 1 47N05 117W35 7:50:20
Willapa 25 39 46N40'30 123W39'54 8:14:40
Willard 30 1 45N46'52 121W37'47 8:06:31
Willard 38 1 47N14'25 117W02'19 7:48:09
Willow Grove 8 32 46N09 122W56 8:11:44
Willows 17 4 47N42'13 122W09'04 8:08:36
Willy Dick Crossing 39 1 46N17'39 120W53'59 8:03:36
Wilma 38 1 46N41 117W09 7:48:36
Wilson 21 5 46N27'11 122W33'13 8:10:13
Wilson Creek 13 1 47N25'24 119W07'11 7:56:29
Winchester 13 1 47N14'57 119W43'07 7:58:52
Windust 11 1 46N32'10 118W34'28 7:54:18
Windy Arm 5 2 47N59'28 123W35'58 8:14:24
Winesap 4 1 47N45'35 120W11'56 8:00:48
Winlock 21 5 46N29'29 122W56'12 8:11:45
Winona 38 1 46N56'45 117W47'58 7:51:12
Winslow 18 19 47N37'29 122W31'12 8:10:05
Winston 21 7 46N29'09 122W31'15 8:10:05
Wintermutes Corner 31 1 47N50'59 122W12'59 8:08:52
Winthrop 24 1 48N28'41 120W11'06 8:00:44
Winton 4 1 47N44'08 120W44'24 8:02:58
Wishkah 14 1 46N58 123W45 8:15:00
Wishram 20 1 45N39'27 120W57'56 8:03:52
Wishram Heights 20 1 45N39'49 120W58'22 8:03:53
Withrow 9 1 47N42'18 119W48'27 7:59:14
Wollochet 27 6 47N16'08 122W34'58 8:10:20
Woodinville 17 4 47N45'16 122W09'44 8:08:39
Woodland 8 53 45N54'17 122W44'34 8:10:58
Woodland 31 1 48N14 122W21 8:09:24
Woodland Beach 15 2 48N14 122W21 8:09:24
Woodland Park 8 3 45N59'26 122W28'28 8:09:54
Woodlawn 14 1 47N00'03 123W52'47 8:15:31
Woodmans 16 31 48N00'57 122W49'55 8:11:20
Woodmont Beach 17 4 47N21'42 122W18'39 8:09:15
Woodruff Mill 20 1 45N51'27 121W08'54 8:04:36
Woodway 31 20 47N47'47 122W22'54 8:09:32
Wycoff 18 1 47N35 122W40 8:10:40
Wye Lake 18 1 47N32 122W38 8:10:32
Wymer 19 1 46N49'34 120W27'31 8:01:50
Yacht Haven 28 1 48N35'07 123W10'01 8:12:40
Yacolt 6 1 45N51'58 122W24'18 8:09:37
Yakima 39 19 46N36'08 120W30'17 8:02:01
Yakima Indian Reservation 39 1 46N23 120W30 8:02:00
Yale 8 3 45N59'44 122W22'44 8:09:31
Yardley 32 48 47N40'02 117W19'57 7:49:20
Yarrow Point 17 4 47N38'47 122W12'58 8:08:52
Yellepit 3 1 46N03'40 118W57'01 7:55:48
Yelm 34 7 46N56'32 122W36'17 8:10:25
Yeomalt 18 1 47N38'05 122W29'34 8:09:58
Yesler Terrace 17 44 47N36'04 122W18'53 8:09:16
Yethonat 39 1 46N24'17 120W23'43 8:01:35
Yokeko Point 29 1 48N24'50 122W37'00 8:10:28
Yoman Ferry 27 6 47N11 122W42 8:10:48
York 17 4 47N42'33 122W09'09 8:08:37
Zangar Junction 36 1 46N04'28 118W50'19 7:55:21
Zenith 17 4 47N23'12 122W19'19 8:09:17
Zillah 39 1 46N24'08 120W15'39 8:01:03
Zumwalt 12 1 46N27'40 117W41'02 7:50:44

TIME TABLES

WV # 1

Before	7/01/1887	LMT
7/01/1887	12:00	EST
3/31/1918	02:00	EWT
10/27/1918	02:00	EST
3/30/1919	02:00	EWT
10/26/1919	02:00	EST
2/09/1942	02:00	EWT
9/30/1945	02:00	EST
4/28/1963	02:00	EDT
9/29/1963	02:00	EST
4/26/1964	02:00	EDT
9/27/1964	02:00	EST
4/25/1965	02:00	EDT
9/26/1965	02:00	EST
4/24/1966	02:00	US#1

WV # 2

Before	7/01/1887	LMT
7/01/1887	12:00	EST
3/31/1918	02:00	EWT
10/27/1918	02:00	EST
3/30/1919	02:00	EWT
10/26/1919	02:00	EST
2/09/1942	02:00	EWT
9/30/1945	02:00	EST
4/28/1963	02:00	US#2

WV # 3

Before	7/01/1887	LMT
7/01/1887	12:00	EST
3/31/1918	02:00	EWT
10/27/1918	02:00	EST
3/30/1919	02:00	EWT
10/26/1919	02:00	EST
2/09/1942	02:00	EWT
9/30/1945	02:00	EST
4/30/1950	02:00	EDT
9/24/1950	02:00	EST
4/29/1951	02:00	EDT
9/30/1951	02:00	EST
4/27/1952	02:00	EDT
9/28/1952	02:00	EST
4/26/1953	02:00	EDT
9/27/1953	02:00	EST
4/25/1954	02:00	EDT
9/26/1954	02:00	EST
4/24/1955	02:00	EDT
9/25/1955	02:00	EST
4/29/1956	02:00	EDT
9/30/1956	02:00	EST
4/28/1957	02:00	EDT
10/27/1957	02:00	EST
4/27/1958	02:00	EDT
10/26/1958	02:00	EST
4/26/1959	02:00	EDT
10/25/1959	02:00	EST
4/24/1960	02:00	EDT
10/30/1960	02:00	EST
4/30/1961	02:00	EDT
10/29/1961	02:00	EST
4/29/1962	02:00	EDT
9/30/1962	02:00	EST
4/28/1963	02:00	US#2

WV # 4

Before	7/01/1887	LMT
7/01/1887	12:00	EST
3/31/1918	02:00	EWT
10/27/1918	02:00	EST
3/30/1919	02:00	EWT
10/26/1919	02:00	EST
2/09/1942	02:00	EWT
9/30/1945	02:00	EST
4/29/1951	02:00	EDT
9/30/1951	02:00	EST
4/27/1952	02:00	EDT
9/28/1952	02:00	EST
4/26/1953	02:00	EDT
9/27/1953	02:00	EST
4/25/1954	02:00	EDT
9/26/1954	02:00	EST
4/24/1955	02:00	EDT
9/25/1955	02:00	EST
4/29/1956	02:00	EDT
9/30/1956	02:00	EST
4/28/1957	02:00	EDT
10/27/1957	02:00	EST
4/27/1958	02:00	EDT
10/26/1958	02:00	EST
4/26/1959	02:00	EDT
10/25/1959	02:00	EST
4/24/1960	02:00	EDT
10/30/1960	02:00	EST
4/30/1961	02:00	EDT
10/29/1961	02:00	EST
4/29/1962	02:00	EDT
9/30/1962	02:00	EST
4/28/1963	02:00	US#2

WV # 5

Before	7/01/1887	LMT
7/01/1887	12:00	EST
3/31/1918	02:00	EWT
10/27/1918	02:00	EST
3/30/1919	02:00	EWT
10/26/1919	02:00	EST
2/09/1942	02:00	EWT
9/30/1945	02:00	EST
4/27/1952	02:00	EDT
9/28/1952	02:00	EST
4/26/1953	02:00	EDT
9/27/1953	02:00	EST
4/25/1954	02:00	EDT
9/26/1954	02:00	EST
4/24/1955	02:00	EDT
9/25/1955	02:00	EST
4/29/1956	02:00	EDT
9/30/1956	02:00	EST
4/28/1957	02:00	EDT
9/29/1957	02:00	EST
4/27/1958	02:00	EDT
9/28/1958	02:00	EST
4/26/1959	02:00	EDT
9/27/1959	02:00	EST
4/24/1960	02:00	EDT
9/25/1960	02:00	EST
4/30/1961	02:00	EDT
9/24/1961	02:00	EST
4/29/1962	02:00	EDT
9/30/1962	02:00	EST
4/28/1963	02:00	EDT
9/29/1963	02:00	EST
4/26/1964	02:00	EDT
9/27/1964	02:00	EST
4/25/1965	02:00	EDT
9/26/1965	02:00	EST
4/24/1966	02:00	US#1

WV # 6

Before	7/01/1887	LMT
7/01/1887	12:00	EST
3/31/1918	02:00	EWT
10/27/1918	02:00	EST
3/30/1919	02:00	EWT
10/26/1919	02:00	EST
2/09/1942	02:00	EWT
9/30/1945	02:00	EST
4/27/1952	02:00	EDT
9/28/1952	02:00	EST
4/26/1953	02:00	EDT
9/27/1953	02:00	EST
4/25/1954	02:00	EDT
9/26/1954	02:00	EST
4/24/1955	02:00	EDT
9/25/1955	02:00	EST
4/29/1956	02:00	EDT
9/30/1956	02:00	EST
4/28/1957	02:00	EDT
9/29/1957	02:00	EST
4/27/1958	02:00	US#2

WV # 7

Before	7/01/1887	LMT
7/01/1887	12:00	EST
3/31/1918	02:00	EWT
10/27/1918	02:00	EST
3/30/1919	02:00	EWT
10/26/1919	02:00	EST
2/09/1942	02:00	EWT
9/30/1945	02:00	EST
4/27/1952	02:00	EDT
9/28/1952	02:00	EST
4/28/1963	02:00	US#2

WV # 8

Before	7/01/1887	LMT
7/01/1887	12:00	EST
3/31/1918	02:00	EWT
10/27/1918	02:00	EST
3/30/1919	02:00	EWT
10/26/1919	02:00	EST
2/09/1942	02:00	EWT
9/30/1945	02:00	EST
4/26/1953	02:00	EDT
9/27/1953	02:00	EST
4/25/1954	02:00	EDT
9/26/1954	02:00	EST
4/24/1955	02:00	EDT
9/25/1955	02:00	EST
4/29/1956	02:00	EDT
9/30/1956	02:00	EST
4/28/1957	02:00	EDT
10/27/1957	02:00	EST
4/27/1958	02:00	US#2

WV # 9

Before	7/01/1887	LMT
7/01/1887	12:00	EST
3/31/1918	02:00	EWT
10/27/1918	02:00	EST
3/30/1919	02:00	EWT
10/26/1919	02:00	EST
2/09/1942	02:00	EWT
9/30/1945	02:00	EST
4/26/1953	02:00	EDT
9/27/1953	02:00	EST
4/25/1954	02:00	EDT
9/26/1954	02:00	EST
4/24/1955	02:00	EDT
9/25/1955	02:00	EST
4/29/1956	02:00	EDT
9/30/1956	02:00	EST
4/28/1957	02:00	EDT
9/29/1957	02:00	EST
4/27/1958	02:00	EDT
9/28/1958	02:00	EST
4/26/1959	02:00	EDT
9/27/1959	02:00	EST
4/24/1960	02:00	US#2

WV # 10

Before	7/01/1887	LMT
7/01/1887	12:00	EST
3/31/1918	02:00	EWT
10/27/1918	02:00	EST
3/30/1919	02:00	EWT
10/26/1919	02:00	EST
2/09/1942	02:00	EWT
9/30/1945	02:00	EST
4/25/1954	02:00	EDT
9/26/1954	02:00	EST
4/24/1955	02:00	EDT
9/25/1955	02:00	EST
4/29/1956	02:00	EDT
9/30/1956	02:00	EST
4/28/1957	02:00	EDT
9/29/1957	02:00	EST
4/27/1958	02:00	EDT
9/28/1958	02:00	EST
4/26/1959	02:00	EDT
9/27/1959	02:00	EST
4/24/1960	02:00	EDT
9/25/1960	02:00	EST
4/30/1961	02:00	EDT
9/24/1961	02:00	EST
4/29/1962	02:00	EDT
9/30/1962	02:00	EST
4/28/1963	02:00	EDT
9/29/1963	02:00	EST
4/26/1964	02:00	EDT
9/27/1964	02:00	EST
4/25/1965	02:00	EDT
9/26/1965	02:00	EST
4/24/1966	02:00	US#1

WV # 11

Before	7/01/1887	LMT
7/01/1887	12:00	EST
3/31/1918	02:00	EWT
10/27/1918	02:00	EST
3/30/1919	02:00	EWT
10/26/1919	02:00	EST
2/09/1942	02:00	EWT
9/30/1945	02:00	EST
4/25/1954	02:00	EDT
9/26/1954	02:00	EST
4/24/1955	02:00	EDT
9/25/1955	02:00	EST
4/29/1956	02:00	EDT
9/30/1956	02:00	EST
4/28/1957	02:00	EDT
9/29/1957	02:00	EST
4/27/1958	02:00	EDT
9/28/1958	02:00	EST
4/26/1959	02:00	EDT
9/27/1959	02:00	EST
4/24/1960	02:00	EDT
9/25/1960	02:00	EST
4/30/1961	02:00	EDT
9/24/1961	02:00	EST
4/29/1962	02:00	US#2

WV # 12

Before	7/01/1887	LMT
7/01/1887	12:00	EST
3/31/1918	02:00	EWT
10/27/1918	02:00	EST
3/30/1919	02:00	EWT
10/26/1919	02:00	EST
2/09/1942	02:00	EWT
9/30/1945	02:00	EST
4/28/1957	02:00	EDT
9/29/1957	02:00	EST
4/27/1958	02:00	EDT
9/28/1958	02:00	EST
4/26/1959	02:00	EDT
9/27/1959	02:00	EST
4/24/1960	02:00	EDT
9/25/1960	02:00	EST
4/30/1961	02:00	EDT
9/24/1961	02:00	EST
4/29/1962	02:00	US#2

WV # 13

Before	7/01/1887	LMT
7/01/1887	12:00	EST
3/31/1918	02:00	EWT
10/27/1918	02:00	EST
3/30/1919	02:00	EWT
10/26/1919	02:00	EST
2/09/1942	02:00	EWT
9/30/1945	02:00	EST
4/24/1955	02:00	EDT
9/25/1955	02:00	EST
4/29/1956	02:00	EDT
9/30/1956	02:00	EST
4/28/1957	02:00	EDT
10/27/1957	02:00	EST
4/27/1958	02:00	US#2

WV # 14

Before	7/01/1887	LMT
7/01/1887	12:00	EST
3/31/1918	02:00	EWT
10/27/1918	02:00	EST
3/30/1919	02:00	EWT
10/26/1919	02:00	EST
2/09/1942	02:00	EWT
9/30/1945	02:00	EST
4/29/1956	02:00	EDT
9/30/1956	02:00	EST
4/28/1957	02:00	EDT
9/29/1957	02:00	EST
4/27/1958	02:00	EDT
9/28/1958	02:00	EST
4/26/1959	02:00	EDT
9/27/1959	02:00	EST
4/24/1960	02:00	EDT
9/25/1960	02:00	EST
4/30/1961	02:00	EDT
9/24/1961	02:00	EST
4/29/1962	02:00	EDT
9/30/1962	02:00	EST
4/28/1963	02:00	EDT
9/29/1963	02:00	EST
4/26/1964	02:00	EDT
9/27/1964	02:00	EST
4/25/1965	02:00	EDT
9/26/1965	02:00	EST
4/24/1966	02:00	US#1

WV # 15

Before	7/01/1887	LMT
7/01/1887	12:00	EST
3/31/1918	02:00	EWT
10/27/1918	02:00	EST
3/30/1919	02:00	EWT
10/26/1919	02:00	EST
2/09/1942	02:00	EWT
9/30/1945	02:00	EST
4/29/1956	02:00	EDT
9/30/1956	02:00	EST
4/28/1957	02:00	EDT
10/27/1957	02:00	EST
4/27/1958	02:00	US#2

WV # 16

Before	7/01/1887	LMT
7/01/1887	12:00	EST
3/31/1918	02:00	EWT
10/27/1918	02:00	EST
3/30/1919	02:00	EWT
10/26/1919	02:00	EST
2/09/1942	02:00	EWT
9/30/1945	02:00	EST
4/29/1956	02:00	EDT
9/30/1956	02:00	EST
4/28/1957	02:00	EDT
9/29/1957	02:00	EST
4/27/1958	02:00	EDT
9/28/1958	02:00	EST
4/26/1959	02:00	EDT
9/27/1959	02:00	EST
4/24/1960	02:00	US#2

WV # 17

Before	7/01/1887	LMT
7/01/1887	12:00	EST
3/31/1918	02:00	EWT
10/27/1918	02:00	EST
3/30/1919	02:00	EWT
10/26/1919	02:00	EST
2/09/1942	02:00	EWT
9/30/1945	02:00	EST
4/28/1957	02:00	EDT
9/29/1957	02:00	EST
4/27/1958	02:00	EDT
9/28/1958	02:00	EST
4/26/1959	02:00	EDT
9/27/1959	02:00	EST
4/24/1960	02:00	EDT
9/25/1960	02:00	EST
4/30/1961	02:00	EDT
9/24/1961	02:00	EST
4/29/1962	02:00	EDT
9/30/1962	02:00	EST
4/28/1963	02:00	EDT
9/29/1963	02:00	EST
4/26/1964	02:00	EDT
9/27/1964	02:00	EST
4/25/1965	02:00	EDT
9/26/1965	02:00	EST
4/24/1966	02:00	US#1

WV # 18

Before	7/01/1887	LMT
7/01/1887	12:00	EST
3/31/1918	02:00	EWT
10/27/1918	02:00	EST
3/30/1919	02:00	EWT
10/26/1919	02:00	EST
2/09/1942	02:00	EWT
9/30/1945	02:00	EST
4/28/1957	02:00	EDT
9/29/1957	02:00	EST
4/28/1963	02:00	EDT
9/29/1963	02:00	EST
4/26/1964	02:00	EDT
9/27/1964	02:00	EST
4/25/1965	02:00	EDT
9/26/1965	02:00	EST
4/24/1966	02:00	US#1

WV # 19

Before	7/01/1887	LMT
7/01/1887	12:00	EST
3/31/1918	02:00	EWT
10/27/1918	02:00	EST
3/30/1919	02:00	EWT
10/26/1919	02:00	EST
2/09/1942	02:00	EWT
9/30/1945	02:00	EST
4/29/1962	02:00	US#2

WV # 20

Before	7/01/1887	LMT
7/01/1887	12:00	EST
3/31/1918	02:00	EWT
10/27/1918	02:00	EST
3/30/1919	02:00	EWT
10/26/1919	02:00	EST
2/09/1942	02:00	EWT
9/30/1945	02:00	EST
5/06/1962	02:00	EDT
9/03/1962	02:00	EST
4/28/1963	02:00	EDT
9/29/1963	02:00	EST
4/26/1964	02:00	EDT
9/27/1964	02:00	EST
4/25/1965	02:00	EDT
9/26/1965	02:00	EST
4/24/1966	02:00	US#1

WV # 21

Before	7/01/1887	LMT
7/01/1887	12:00	EST
3/31/1918	02:00	EWT
10/27/1918	02:00	EST
3/30/1919	02:00	EWT
10/26/1919	02:00	EST
2/09/1942	02:00	EWT
9/30/1945	02:00	EST
4/30/1950	02:00	EDT
10/29/1950	02:00	EST
4/29/1951	02:00	EDT
9/30/1951	02:00	EST
4/27/1952	02:00	EDT
9/28/1952	02:00	EST
4/26/1953	02:00	EDT
9/27/1953	02:00	EST
4/25/1954	02:00	EDT
9/26/1954	02:00	EST
4/24/1955	02:00	EDT
9/25/1955	02:00	EST
4/29/1956	02:00	EDT
9/30/1956	02:00	EST
4/28/1957	02:00	EDT
10/27/1957	02:00	EST
4/27/1958	02:00	US#2

WV # 22

Before	7/01/1887	LMT
7/01/1887	12:00	EST
3/31/1918	02:00	EWT
10/27/1918	02:00	EST
3/30/1919	02:00	EWT
10/26/1919	02:00	EST
4/25/1937	00:01	EDT
9/05/1937	00:01	EST
2/09/1942	02:00	EWT
9/30/1945	02:00	EST
4/29/1956	02:00	EDT
9/30/1956	02:00	EST
4/28/1957	02:00	EDT
9/29/1957	02:00	EST
4/27/1958	02:00	EDT
9/28/1958	02:00	EST
4/26/1959	02:00	EDT
9/27/1959	02:00	EST
4/24/1960	02:00	EDT
9/25/1960	02:00	EST
4/30/1961	02:00	EDT
9/24/1961	02:00	EST
4/29/1962	02:00	EDT
9/30/1962	02:00	EST
4/28/1963	02:00	EDT
9/29/1963	02:00	EST
4/26/1964	02:00	EDT
9/27/1964	02:00	EST
4/25/1965	02:00	EDT
9/26/1965	02:00	EST
4/24/1966	02:00	US#1

WV # 23

Before	7/01/1887	LMT
7/01/1887	12:00	EST
3/31/1918	02:00	EWT
10/27/1918	02:00	EST
3/30/1919	02:00	EWT
10/26/1919	02:00	EST
2/09/1942	02:00	EWT
9/30/1945	02:00	EST
4/25/1948	02:00	EDT
9/26/1948	02:00	EST
4/24/1949	02:00	EDT
9/25/1949	02:00	EST
5/27/1950	02:00	EDT
9/01/1950	02:00	EST
4/29/1951	02:00	EDT
9/30/1951	02:00	EST
4/27/1952	02:00	EDT
9/28/1952	02:00	EST
4/26/1953	02:00	EDT
9/27/1953	02:00	EST
4/25/1954	02:00	EDT
9/26/1954	02:00	EST
4/24/1955	02:00	EDT
9/25/1955	02:00	EST
4/29/1956	02:00	EDT
9/30/1956	02:00	EST
4/28/1957	02:00	EDT
9/29/1957	02:00	EST
4/27/1958	02:00	EDT
9/28/1958	02:00	EST
4/26/1959	02:00	EDT
9/27/1959	02:00	EST
4/24/1960	02:00	EDT
9/25/1960	02:00	EST
4/30/1961	02:00	EDT
9/24/1961	02:00	EST
4/29/1962	02:00	US#2

WV # 24

Before	7/01/1887	LMT
7/01/1887	12:00	EST
3/31/1918	02:00	EWT
10/27/1918	02:00	EST
3/30/1919	02:00	EWT
10/26/1919	02:00	EST
2/09/1942	02:00	EWT
9/30/1945	02:00	EST
4/27/1947	02:00	EDT
9/28/1947	02:00	EST
4/25/1948	02:00	EDT
9/26/1948	02:00	EST
4/24/1949	02:00	EDT
9/25/1949	02:00	EST
4/29/1956	02:00	EDT
9/30/1956	02:00	EST
4/28/1957	02:00	EDT
9/29/1957	02:00	EST
4/27/1958	02:00	EDT
9/28/1958	02:00	EST
4/26/1959	02:00	EDT
9/27/1959	02:00	EST
4/24/1960	02:00	EDT
9/25/1960	02:00	EST
4/30/1961	02:00	EDT
9/24/1961	02:00	EST
4/29/1962	02:00	EDT
9/30/1962	02:00	EST
4/28/1963	02:00	EDT
9/29/1963	02:00	EST
4/26/1964	02:00	EDT
9/27/1964	02:00	EST
4/25/1965	02:00	EDT
9/26/1965	02:00	EST
4/24/1966	02:00	US#1

TIME TABLES

WV # 25		
Before 7/01/1887		LMT
7/01/1887	12:00	EST
3/31/1918	02:00	EWT
10/27/1918	02:00	EST
3/30/1919	02:00	EWT
10/26/1919	02:00	EST
2/09/1942	02:00	EWT
9/30/1945	02:00	EST
4/28/1946	02:00	EDT
9/29/1946	02:00	EST
4/24/1949	02:00	EDT
9/25/1949	02:00	EST
4/30/1950	02:00	EDT
9/24/1950	02:00	EST
4/29/1956	02:00	EDT
9/30/1956	02:00	EST
4/28/1957	02:00	EDT
9/29/1957	02:00	EST
4/27/1958	02:00	EDT
9/28/1958	02:00	EST
4/26/1959	02:00	EDT
9/27/1959	02:00	EST
4/24/1960	02:00	EDT
9/25/1960	02:00	EST
4/30/1961	02:00	EDT
9/24/1961	02:00	EST
4/29/1962	02:00	EDT
9/30/1962	02:00	EST
4/28/1963	02:00	EDT
9/29/1963	02:00	EST
4/26/1964	02:00	EDT
9/27/1964	02:00	EST
4/25/1965	02:00	EDT
9/26/1965	02:00	EST
4/24/1966	02:00	US#1

WV # 26		
Before 7/01/1887		LMT
7/01/1887	12:00	EST
3/31/1918	02:00	EWT
10/27/1918	02:00	EST
3/30/1919	02:00	EWT
10/26/1919	02:00	EST
2/09/1942	02:00	EWT
9/30/1945	02:00	EST
4/28/1946	02:00	EDT
9/29/1946	02:00	EST
4/28/1957	02:00	EDT
9/29/1957	02:00	EST
4/27/1958	02:00	EDT
9/28/1958	02:00	EST
4/26/1959	02:00	EDT
9/27/1959	02:00	EST
4/24/1960	02:00	EDT
9/25/1960	02:00	EST
4/30/1961	02:00	EDT
9/24/1961	02:00	EST
4/29/1962	02:00	EDT
9/30/1962	02:00	EST
4/28/1963	02:00	EDT
9/29/1963	02:00	EST
4/26/1964	02:00	EDT
9/27/1964	02:00	EST
4/25/1965	02:00	EDT
9/26/1965	02:00	EST
4/24/1966	02:00	US#1

WV # 27		
Before 7/01/1887		LMT
7/01/1887	12:00	EST
3/31/1918	02:00	EWT
10/27/1918	02:00	EST
3/30/1919	02:00	EWT
10/26/1919	02:00	EST
2/09/1942	02:00	EWT
9/30/1945	02:00	EST
4/25/1948	02:00	EDT
9/26/1948	02:00	EST
4/24/1949	02:00	EDT
9/25/1949	02:00	EST
4/30/1950	02:00	EDT
9/24/1950	02:00	EST
4/29/1951	02:00	EDT
9/30/1951	02:00	EST
4/27/1952	02:00	EDT
9/28/1952	02:00	EST
4/26/1953	02:00	EDT
9/27/1953	02:00	EST
4/25/1954	02:00	EDT
9/26/1954	02:00	EST
4/24/1955	02:00	EDT
9/25/1955	02:00	EST
4/29/1956	02:00	EDT
9/30/1956	02:00	EST
4/27/1958	02:00	EDT
10/26/1958	02:00	EST
4/26/1959	02:00	EDT
9/27/1959	02:00	EST
4/24/1960	02:00	EDT
9/25/1960	02:00	EST
4/23/1961	02:00	EDT
9/24/1961	02:00	EST
4/29/1962	02:00	US#2

WV # 28		
Before 7/01/1887		LMT
7/01/1887	12:00	EST
3/31/1918	02:00	EWT
10/27/1918	02:00	EST
3/30/1919	02:00	EWT
10/26/1919	02:00	EST
4/27/1941	02:00	EDT
10/28/1941	02:00	EST
2/09/1942	02:00	EWT
9/30/1945	02:00	EST
4/28/1946	02:00	EDT
9/29/1946	02:00	EST
4/27/1947	02:00	EDT
9/28/1947	02:00	EST
4/25/1948	02:00	EDT
9/26/1948	02:00	EST
4/24/1949	02:00	EDT
9/25/1949	02:00	EST
4/30/1950	02:00	EDT
9/24/1950	02:00	EST
4/28/1957	02:00	EDT
9/29/1957	02:00	EST
4/27/1958	02:00	EDT
9/28/1958	02:00	EST
4/26/1959	02:00	EDT
9/27/1959	02:00	EST
4/24/1960	02:00	EDT
9/25/1960	02:00	EST
4/30/1961	02:00	EDT
9/24/1961	02:00	EST
4/29/1962	02:00	EDT
9/30/1962	02:00	EST
4/28/1963	02:00	EDT
9/29/1963	02:00	EST
4/26/1964	02:00	EDT
9/27/1964	02:00	EST
4/25/1965	02:00	EDT
9/26/1965	02:00	EST
4/24/1966	02:00	US#1

WV # 29		
Before 7/01/1887		LMT
7/01/1887	12:00	EST
3/31/1918	02:00	EWT
10/27/1918	02:00	EST
3/30/1919	02:00	EWT
10/26/1919	02:00	EST
4/27/1941	02:00	EDT
10/28/1941	02:00	EST
2/09/1942	02:00	EWT
9/30/1945	02:00	EST
4/28/1957	02:00	EDT
9/29/1957	02:00	EST
4/27/1958	02:00	EDT
9/28/1958	02:00	EST
4/26/1959	02:00	EDT
9/27/1959	02:00	EST
4/24/1960	02:00	EDT
9/25/1960	02:00	EST
4/30/1961	02:00	EDT
9/24/1961	02:00	EST
4/29/1962	02:00	US#2

WV # 30		
Before 7/01/1887		LMT
7/01/1887	12:00	EST
3/31/1918	02:00	EWT
10/27/1918	02:00	EST
3/30/1919	02:00	EWT
10/26/1919	02:00	EST
2/09/1942	02:00	EWT
9/30/1945	02:00	EST
4/24/1949	02:00	EDT
9/25/1949	02:00	EST
4/28/1963	02:00	US#2

WV # 31		
Before 7/01/1887		LMT
7/01/1887	12:00	EST
3/31/1918	02:00	EWT
10/27/1918	02:00	EST
3/30/1919	02:00	EWT
10/26/1919	02:00	EST
2/09/1942	02:00	EWT
9/30/1945	02:00	EST
4/28/1946	02:00	EDT
9/29/1946	02:00	EST
4/26/1953	02:00	EDT
9/27/1953	02:00	EST
4/25/1954	02:00	EDT
9/26/1954	02:00	EST
4/24/1955	02:00	EDT
9/25/1955	02:00	EST
4/29/1956	02:00	EDT
9/30/1956	02:00	EST
4/28/1957	02:00	EDT
9/29/1957	02:00	EST
4/27/1958	02:00	EDT
9/28/1958	02:00	EST
4/26/1959	02:00	EDT
9/27/1959	02:00	EST
4/24/1960	02:00	EDT
9/25/1960	02:00	EST
4/30/1961	02:00	EDT
9/24/1961	02:00	EST
4/29/1962	02:00	US#2

WV # 32		
Before 7/01/1887		LMT
7/01/1887	12:00	EST
3/31/1918	02:00	EWT
10/27/1918	02:00	EST
3/30/1919	02:00	EWT
10/26/1919	02:00	EST
4/28/1941	02:00	EDT
10/28/1941	02:00	EST
2/09/1942	02:00	EWT
9/30/1945	02:00	EST
4/25/1948	02:00	EDT
9/26/1948	02:00	EST
4/24/1949	02:00	EDT
9/25/1949	02:00	EST
4/30/1950	02:00	EDT
9/24/1950	02:00	EST
4/29/1951	02:00	EDT
9/30/1951	02:00	EST
4/27/1952	02:00	EDT
9/28/1952	02:00	EST
4/26/1953	02:00	EDT
9/27/1953	02:00	EST
4/25/1954	02:00	EDT
9/26/1954	02:00	EST
4/24/1955	02:00	EDT
9/25/1955	02:00	EST
4/29/1956	02:00	EDT
9/30/1956	02:00	EST
4/28/1957	02:00	EDT
9/29/1957	02:00	EST
4/27/1958	02:00	EDT
9/28/1958	02:00	EST
4/26/1959	02:00	EDT
9/27/1959	02:00	EST
4/24/1960	02:00	EDT
10/30/1960	02:00	EST
4/30/1961	02:00	EDT
10/29/1961	02:00	EST
4/29/1962	02:00	EDT
10/28/1962	02:00	EST
4/28/1963	02:00	EDT
10/27/1963	02:00	EST
4/26/1964	02:00	EDT
10/25/1964	02:00	EST
4/25/1965	02:00	EDT
10/24/1965	02:00	EST
4/24/1966	02:00	US#1

WV # 33		
Before 7/01/1887		LMT
7/01/1887	12:00	EST
3/31/1918	02:00	EWT
10/27/1918	02:00	EST
3/30/1919	02:00	EWT
10/26/1919	02:00	EST
4/27/1941	02:00	EDT
10/28/1941	02:00	EST
2/09/1942	02:00	EWT
9/30/1945	02:00	EST
4/25/1948	02:00	EDT
9/26/1948	02:00	EST
4/24/1949	02:00	EDT
9/25/1949	02:00	EST
4/30/1950	02:00	EDT
9/24/1950	02:00	EST
4/29/1951	02:00	EDT
9/30/1951	02:00	EST
4/27/1952	02:00	EDT
9/28/1952	02:00	EST
4/26/1953	02:00	EDT
9/27/1953	02:00	EST
4/25/1954	02:00	EDT
9/26/1954	02:00	EST
4/24/1955	02:00	EDT
9/25/1955	02:00	EST
4/29/1956	02:00	EDT
9/30/1956	02:00	EST
4/28/1957	02:00	EDT
9/29/1957	02:00	EST
4/27/1958	02:00	EDT
9/28/1958	02:00	EST
4/26/1959	02:00	EDT
9/27/1959	02:00	EST
4/24/1960	02:00	US#2

WV # 34		
Before 3/31/1887		LMT
3/31/1887	12:00	EST
3/31/1918	02:00	EWT
10/27/1918	02:00	EST
3/30/1919	02:00	EWT
10/26/1919	02:00	EST
4/26/1937	02:00	EDT
10/27/1937	02:00	EST
4/27/1941	02:00	EDT
10/28/1941	02:00	EST
2/09/1942	02:00	EWT
9/30/1945	02:00	EST
4/28/1946	02:00	EDT
9/29/1946	02:00	EST
4/27/1947	02:00	EDT
9/28/1947	02:00	EST
4/25/1948	02:00	EDT
9/26/1948	02:00	EST
4/24/1949	02:00	EDT
9/25/1949	02:00	EST
4/30/1950	02:00	EDT
9/24/1950	02:00	EST
4/29/1951	02:00	EDT
9/30/1951	02:00	EST
4/27/1952	02:00	EDT
9/28/1952	02:00	EST
4/26/1953	02:00	EDT
9/27/1953	02:00	EST
4/25/1954	02:00	EDT
9/26/1954	02:00	EST
4/24/1955	02:00	EDT
9/25/1955	02:00	EST
4/29/1956	02:00	EDT
9/30/1956	02:00	EST
4/28/1957	02:00	EDT
9/29/1957	02:00	EST
4/27/1958	02:00	US#2

WV # 35		
Before 7/01/1887		LMT
7/01/1887	12:00	EST
3/31/1918	02:00	EWT
10/27/1918	02:00	EST
3/30/1919	02:00	EWT
10/26/1919	02:00	EST
4/27/1941	02:00	EDT
9/28/1941	02:00	EST
2/09/1942	02:00	EWT
9/30/1945	02:00	EST
4/29/1956	02:00	EDT
9/30/1956	02:00	EST
4/28/1957	02:00	EDT
9/29/1957	02:00	EST
4/27/1958	02:00	EDT
9/28/1958	02:00	EST
4/26/1959	02:00	EDT
9/27/1959	02:00	EST
4/24/1960	02:00	EDT
9/25/1960	02:00	EST
4/30/1961	02:00	EDT
9/24/1961	02:00	EST
4/29/1962	02:00	EDT
9/30/1962	02:00	EST
4/28/1963	02:00	EDT
9/29/1963	02:00	EST
4/26/1964	02:00	EDT
9/27/1964	02:00	EST
4/25/1965	02:00	EDT
9/26/1965	02:00	EST
4/24/1966	02:00	US#1

COUNTIES

1 Barbour
2 Berkeley
3 Boone
4 Braxton
5 Brooke
6 Cabell
7 Calhoun
8 Clay
9 Doddridge
10 Fayette
11 Gilmer
12 Grant
13 Greenbrier
14 Hampshire
15 Hancock
16 Hardy
17 Harrison
18 Jackson
19 Jefferson
20 Kanawha
21 Lewis
22 Lincoln
23 Logan
24 McDowell
25 Marion
26 Marshall
27 Mason
28 Mercer
29 Mineral
30 Mingo
31 Monongalia
32 Monroe
33 Morgan
34 Nicholas
35 Ohio
36 Pendelton
37 Pleasants
38 Pocahontas
39 Preston
40 Putnam
41 Raleigh
42 Randolph
43 Ritchie
44 Roane
45 Summers
46 Taylor
47 Tucker
48 Tyler
49 Upshur
50 Wayne
51 Webster
52 Wetzel
53 Wirt
54 Wood
55 Wyoming

Aarrons Fork 20	1	38N26	81w29	5:25:56
Abbott 49	1	38N55'18	80w19'18	5:21:17
Aberdeen 21	1	39N03'30	80w18'58	5:21:16
Abney 41	1	37N41'18	81w12'15	5:24:49
Abraham 41	1	37N47'26	80w57'19	5:23:49
Accoville 23	1	37N46'07	81w50'14	5:27:21
Acme 20	1	38N02'12	81w27'21	5:25:49
Acup 20	1	38N21'43	81w20'32	5:25:22
Ada 28	20	37N17'41	81w08'49	5:24:35
Adaland 1	1	39N12'31	80w04'37	5:20:18
Adaline 26	21	39N45'55	80w38'48	5:22:35
Adam 7	1	38N49'48	81w10'19	5:24:41
Adams 3	1	38N10'12	81w51'09	5:27:25
Adamston 17	24	39N17'26	80w21'29	5:21:26
Adamsville 17	1	39N23'43	80w14'41	5:20:59
Addison 51	1	38N29	80w25	5:21:40
Adkin 24	1	37N21	81w30	5:26:00
Adlai 37	1	39N20'16	81w03'48	5:24:15
Adolph 42	1	38N44'40	80w02'45	5:20:11
Adonis 48	2	39N30'20	80w59'13	5:23:57
Adrian 49	1	38N54'19	80w16'33	5:21:06
Advent 18	1	38N36'37	81w33'32	5:26:14
Affinity 41	1	37N42'46	81w13'34	5:24:54
Afton 39	12	39N32'09	79w32'20	5:18:09
Aggregate 42	35	38N56'10	79w55'08	5:19:41
Airport Village 20	22	38N22'00	81w34'55	5:26:20
Ajax 30	1	37N48'09	82w18'17	5:29:13
Albright 39	12	39N29'38	79w38'35	5:18:34
Alderson 13	1	37N43'33	80w38'32	5:22:34
Aldridge 19	23	39N18'04	77w55'22	5:11:41
Alexander 49	1	38N46'58	80w13'22	5:20:53
Algoma 24	1	37N25'08	81w25'34	5:25:42
Alice 11	1	38N59'51	80w48'58	5:23:16
Alkires Mills 21	1	38N58'42	80w27'06	5:21:48
Alkol 22	1	38N09'46	81w55'30	5:27:42
Allen 33	11	39N38	78w10	5:12:40
Allendale 26	34	40N01'07	80w42'13	5:22:49
Allen Ford 17	14	39N13'17	80w22'35	5:21:30
Allen Junction 55	1	37N35'21	81w21'03	5:25:24
Allensville 2	2	39N34'59	77w59'36	5:11:58
Allentown 44	1	38N45'53	81w30'46	5:26:03
Alley Grove 26	4	39N57'39	80w31'35	5:22:06
Alliance 17	1	39N27'23	80w28'52	5:21:55
Allied 17	1	39N23'21	80w16'31	5:21:06
Allingdale 34	1	38N21'26	80w36'42	5:22:27
Allister 52	2	39N36'05	80w41'39	5:22:47
Alloy 10	14	38N08'15	81w16'28	5:25:06
Alma 48	2	39N26	80w49	5:23:16
Almoris 34	1	38N17	80w51	5:23:24
Alpena 42	1	38N54'35	79w39'05	5:18:36
Alpha 17	14	39N13	80w21	5:21:24
Alpoca 55	1	37N32'37	81w23'21	5:25:33
Alta 10	1	38N12'26	81w10'39	5:24:43
Alta 13	1	37N52'10	80w32'35	5:22:10
Altizer 7	1	38N49'38	81w08'53	5:24:36
Alton 49	1	38N49'09	80w12'51	5:20:51
Alum Bridge 21	1	39N02'21	80w39'19	5:22:37
Alum Creek 20	1	38N17'12	81w48'19	5:27:13
Alvon 13	14	37N54'18	80w12'52	5:20:51
Alvord 44	1	38N48'27	81w20'57	5:26:24
Alvy 48	2	39N27	80w42	5:22:48
Amandaville 20	18	38N23'50	81w51'22	5:27:25
Amblersburg 39	12	39N23'11	79w37'46	5:18:31
Amboy 39	12	39N20'54	79w34'07	5:18:16
Ambrosia 27	1	38N48'20	82w03'10	5:28:13
Ameagle 41	1	37N56'59	81w25'08	5:25:41
Amelia 20	1	38N17'21	81w17'46	5:25:11
Ames 10	18	38N05'10	81w05'10	5:24:21
Ames Heights 10	18	38N05'07	81w04'33	5:24:18
Amherstdale 23	1	37N47'07	81w48'34	5:27:14
Amigo 41	1	37N35'47	81w19'16	5:25:17

Amma 44	1	38N34'07	81w15'57	5:25:04
Anawalt 24	1	37N20'09	81w26'12	5:25:45
Andersonville 26	21	39N46'48	80w31'19	5:22:05
Andrew 3	1	38N06'00	81w43'03	5:26:52
Angerona 18	1	38N49'50	81w48'16	5:27:13
Anjean 13	1	38N01'12	80w38'00	5:22:32
Anmoore 17	24	39N15'24	80w17'33	5:21:10
Annamoriah 7	1	38N56'26	81w13'38	5:24:55
Ansted 10	1	38N08'10	81w05'59	5:24:24
Anthem 52	2	39N38'48	80w31'43	5:22:07
Anthony 13	1	37N53'45	80w19'56	5:21:20
Anthony Creek 13	1	37N56	80w12	5:20:48
Antioch 9	1	39N18	80w47	5:23:08
Antioch 29	2	39N19'25	79w01'04	5:16:04
Antioch 44	1	38N47'09	81w30'18	5:26:01
Antler 24	1	37N27'12	81w37'26	5:26:30
Aplin 18	1	38N46	81w33	5:26:12
Apple Farm 7	1	38N48	81w04	5:24:16
Apple Grove 24	1	37N26'15	81w48'18	5:27:13
Apple Grove 27	1	38N39'54	82w10'09	5:28:41
Aracoma 23	1	37N51'32	81w59'32	5:27:58
Arborland Acres 20	18	38N23	81w49	5:27:16
Arbovale 38	1	38N26'07	79w49'04	5:19:16
Arbuckle 27	1	38N42'46	81w56'54	5:27:48
Arbutus Park 17	24	39N15'59	80w19'26	5:21:18
Archer 52	2	39N30'38	80w35'43	5:22:23
Archer Heights 5	32	40N21'39	80w36'01	5:22:24
Arcola 51	1	38N28'00	80w31'10	5:22:05
Ardel 50	1	38N16'14	82w27'20	5:29:49
Arden 1	1	39N12'37	79w59'36	5:19:58
Arden 2	27	39N24'56	78w02'37	5:12:10
Argonne 23	1	37N51	82w03	5:28:12
Argyle 23	1	37N49'32	81w52'37	5:27:30
Arista 28	1	37N28'21	81w15'39	5:25:03
Arkansas 16	1	39N04'28	78w43'46	5:14:55
Arlee 27	1	38N43'57	82w05'41	5:28:23
Arlington 17	24	39N18'30	80w20'49	5:21:23
Arlington 49	1	38N48'00	80w20'36	5:21:22
Armilda 50	1	38N11'01	82w24'06	5:29:36
Arnett 4	1	38N48'33	80w43'18	5:22:53
Arnett 41	1	37N50'00	81w25'49	5:25:43
Arnettsville 31	28	39N35'08	80w05'33	5:20:22
Arnold 5	32	40N17'55	80w34'49	5:22:19
Arnold 21	1	38N54'49	80w30'12	5:22:01
Arnold Ford 14	1	39N13'41	78w27'29	5:13:50
Arnold Hill 42	35	38N53'00	79w51'50	5:19:27
Arnoldsburg 7	1	38N47'20	81w07'40	5:24:31
Arroyo 15	9	40N30	80w37	5:22:28
Arthur 12	1	39N04'02	79w06'44	5:16:27
Arthurdale 39	12	39N29'42	79w48'55	5:19:16
Artie 41	1	37N55'57	81w21'35	5:25:26
Arvilla 37	1	39N26'07	81w04'16	5:24:17
Arvondale 42	1	38N41'40	80w16'00	5:21:04
Asbury 13	1	37N49'11	80w33'34	5:22:14
Asbury Church 16	1	39N02	78w45	5:15:00
Asco 24	1	37N30'07	81w37'34	5:26:30
Ashford 3	1	38N10'45	81w42'40	5:26:51
Ashland 24	1	37N24'30	81w21'10	5:25:25
Ashley 9	1	39N24'16	80w40'34	5:22:42
Ashton 27	1	38N37'27	82w09'53	5:28:40
Aspinall 21	14	38N55'34	80w36'16	5:22:25
Assurance 32	1	37N29'44	80w40'23	5:22:42
Astor 46	1	39N14'25	80w08'29	5:20:34
Astor Junction 46	1	39N16	80w08	5:20:32
Atenville 22	1	38N02'53	82w08'35	5:28:34
Athens 28	1	37N25'20	81w00'59	5:24:04
Atlas 49	1	38N58'39	80w16'48	5:21:07
Atwell 24	1	37N20'57	81w45'46	5:27:03
Atwood 48	2	39N30'41	80w44'33	5:22:58
Auburn 43	1	39N05'44	80w51'23	5:23:26
Audra 1	1	39N02'31	80w04'01	5:20:16
Augusta 14	1	39N17'43	78w38'17	5:14:33
Augusta 28	1	37N22	81w05	5:24:20
Aurora 39	12	39N19'27	79w33'17	5:18:13
Austen 39	12	39N23'17	79w48'04	5:19:12
Auto 13	1	37N58	80w19	5:21:16
Auvil 47	1	39N10'40	79w43'26	5:18:54
Auville 24	1	37N28	81w49	5:27:16
Avis 45	14	37N39'59	80w53'17	5:23:33
Avoca 8	1	38N27'11	81w03'03	5:24:12
Avon 9	1	39N11'43	80w38'57	5:22:36
Avondale 9	1	39N17'52	80w44'41	5:22:59
Avondale 24	1	37N24'45	81w47'04	5:27:08
Ayers 7	1	38N58'41	81w05'55	5:24:24
Babcock 10	1	38N04'57	80w53'19	5:23:33
Baber 23	1	38N00'30	82w02'45	5:28:11
Bablin 21	1	38N45'54	80w26'13	5:21:45
Bachman 10	1	38N05'58	81w07'20	5:24:29
Backus 10	1	37N51'15	80w58'30	5:23:54
Baden 27	1	38N47'54	81w53'15	5:27:33
Baileysville 55	1	37N35'21	81w40'46	5:26:43
Baisden 23	1	37N49'12	82w01'44	5:28:07
Baisden 30	1	37N35'02	81w54'19	5:27:37
Baker 16	1	39N02'30	78w44'42	5:14:59
Baker Heights 2	27	39N25'24	77w55'32	5:11:42
Baker Park 20	18	38N23	81w49	5:27:16
Baker Ridge 31	28	39N40'26	79w56'53	5:19:48
Bakers Run 4	1	38N38'06	80w35'35	5:22:22
Bakerton 19	3	39N21'46	77w45'48	5:11:03
Bald Knob 3	1	37N52'15	81w38'09	5:26:33
Baldwin 11	1	38N58'22	80w45'17	5:23:01
Ballard 32	1	37N28'29	80w46'46	5:23:07
Ballengee 32	1	37N37'01	80w44'18	5:22:57
Balls Gap 6	1	38N26	82w08	5:28:32
Bamboo 34	1	38N09	80w44	5:22:56
Banco 23	1	38N00'09	82w00'31	5:28:02
Bancroft 40	1	38N30'34	81w50'24	5:27:22
Bandmill Junction 23	1	37N50'25	81w57'18	5:27:49
Bandytown 3	1	37N56'26	81w38'24	5:26:34
Bane 52	2	39N30'16	80w35'16	5:22:21
Banks 49	1	38N48	80w19	5:21:16
Bannen 26	21	39N43'42	80w35'13	5:22:21
Barboursville 6	1	38N24'34	82w17'41	5:29:11
Bardane 19	2	39N21'46	77w51'56	5:11:28
Bargers Springs 45	1	37N36'51	80w45'29	5:23:02
Barker 1	1	39N03	79w56	5:19:44
Barker 52	2	39N34'46	80w39'38	5:22:39
Barkers Ridge 55	1	37N31	81w21	5:25:24
Barksdale 45	14	37N42'27	80w53'12	5:23:33
Barn 28	1	37N35	81w06	5:24:24
Barnabus 23	1	37N44'38	82w00'34	5:28:02
Barnes Mill 14	1	39N21'04	78w38'12	5:14:33
Barnet Run 51	1	38N30	80w46	5:23:04
Barnettown 45	1	37N41'51	80w40'38	5:22:43
Barnum 29	6	39N26'30	79w06'53	5:16:28
Barrackville 25	17	39N30'13	80w10'01	5:20:40
Barren Creek 20	1	38N28'49	81w17'00	5:25:08
Barrett 3	1	37N53'14	81w40'13	5:26:41
Barrs 44	1	38N49'23	81w22'51	5:25:31
Barry Mine 46	1	39N16	80w08	5:20:32
Bartley 24	1	37N20'26	81w44'16	5:26:57
Bartow 38	14	38N32'28	79w47'04	5:19:08
Basin 55	1	37N30	81w20	5:25:20
Basnettville 25	17	39N35'10	80w14'09	5:20:57
Basore 16	1	38N51'49	78w49'50	5:15:19
Bass 16	1	38N56'54	79w00'09	5:16:01
Bath 33	11	39N37	78w14	5:12:56
Battelle 31	17	39N41	80w20	5:21:20
Baughman Settlement 16	1	39N00'41	78w44'20	5:14:57
Baxter 2	2	39N33'27	78w04'40	5:12:19
Baxter 25	17	39N32'38	80w08'33	5:20:34
Bayard 12	1	39N16'22	79w21'53	5:17:28
Bays Heights 10	1	37N59'59	81w09'58	5:24:40
Bealls Mills 21	1	38N58'06	80w36'41	5:22:27
Bean Settlement 16	1	39N06'54	78w49'34	5:15:18
Beans Mill 49	1	38N49'55	80w12'03	5:20:48
Bear Creek 4	1	38N40	80w46	5:23:04
Beard 38	1	38N04'36	80w13'39	5:20:55
Beard Heights 38	1	38N12'26	80w06'27	5:20:26
Beards Fork 10	14	38N03'49	81w13'39	5:24:55
Bear Mountain 1	1	39N13'02	80w10'01	5:20:40
Bear Mountain Mine 1	1	39N13	80w09	5:20:36
Bearsville 48	2	39N24'27	80w54'50	5:23:39
Beartown 24	1	37N23'10	81w48'42	5:27:15
Beason 43	1	39N17	80w58	5:23:52
Beatrice 43	1	39N05'02	81w08'24	5:24:34
Beatysville 18	1	39N08	81w44	5:26:56
Beauty 10	1	38N02'41	81w00'59	5:24:04
Beaver 34	1	38N19'42	80w39'56	5:22:40
Beaver 41	18	37N44'51	81w08'33	5:24:34
Beaverdam 53	1	38N54'46	81w20'17	5:25:21
Beaver Pond 28	20	37N18	81w12	5:24:48
Bebee 52	12	39N39'06	80w43'22	5:22:53
Becco 23	1	37N47'00	81w48'52	5:27:15
Beckley 41	18	37N46'41	81w11'18	5:24:45
Beckley Junction 41	18	37N45'50	81w11'46	5:24:47
Beckwith 10	1	38N05'52	81w09'13	5:24:37
Bedington 2	27	39N31'20	77w54'21	5:11:37
Beebe 23	1	37N49'36	82w03'45	5:28:15
Beech 7	1	38N45'45	81w10'21	5:24:41
Beech Bottom 5	33	40N13'35	80w39'06	5:22:36
Beech Creek 30	1	37N37	82w04	5:28:16
Beech Glen 34	1	38N13'38	81w09'20	5:24:37
Beech Grove 43	1	39N19'23	81w00'17	5:24:01
Beech Hill 27	1	38N45'53	82w00'10	5:28:01
Beechwood 12	1	39N12'00	79w28'06	5:17:52
Beechwood 31	28	39N39	79w58	5:19:52
Beechwood 54	1	39N17'20	81w32'46	5:26:11
Beechwood 55	1	37N34'54	81w21'22	5:25:25
Beelick Knob 10	1	37N52'27	80w52'03	5:23:28
Beeson 28	1	37N28'15	81w11'39	5:24:47
Behler 31	17	39N38'45	80w08'24	5:20:34
Belfont 4	1	38N42'13	80w51'47	5:23:27
Belgium 46	1	39N19'25	80w06'59	5:20:28
Belgrove 18	1	38N42'33	81w34'38	5:26:19
Belington 1	1	39N01'30	79w56'09	5:19:45
Bellburn 13	1	38N02'30	80w44'00	5:22:56
Belle 20	1	38N13'55	81w32'16	5:26:09
Bellepoint 45	14	37N38'57	80w52'55	5:23:32
Belleville 54	1	39N07'27	81w44'08	5:26:57
Bellmeade 27	1	38N52'50	82w07'39	5:28:31
Bells Ford 7	1	38N55'46	81w09'17	5:24:37
Bellton 26	21	39N45'23	80w33'20	5:22:13
Bellview 25	17	39N29'58	80w08'00	5:20:32
Bellwood 10	1	37N55'18	80w49'49	5:23:19
Belmont 37	1	39N22'46	81w15'31	5:25:02
Belo 30	1	37N46'27	82w14'16	5:28:57
Belva 34	1	38N13'52	81w11'32	5:24:46
Bemis 42	1	38N48'43	79w44'21	5:18:57
Benbush 47	1	39N09'31	79w31'16	5:18:05
Ben Dale 21	1	39N00'56	80w28'39	5:21:55
Bennett 21	1	38N53'28	80w33'56	5:22:16
Benson 17	1	39N09'43	80w33'07	5:22:12
Bens Run 48	2	39N27'57	81w06'31	5:24:26
Bentons Ferry 25	17	39N26'16	80w10'04	5:20:40
Bentree 8	1	38N17'01	81w11'28	5:24:46
Benwood 26	13	40N01'05	80w44'04	5:22:56
Benwood Junction 26	13	40N00'20	80w44'04	5:22:56
Berea 43	1	39N08'11	80w56'02	5:23:44
Bergoo 51	1	38N29'11	80w18'03	5:21:12
Berkeley 2	27	39N30'11	77w55'39	5:11:43
Berkeley Place 2	27	39N27'02	77w57'37	5:11:50
Berkeley Springs 33	11	39N37'37	78w13'39	5:12:55
Berlin 21	1	39N03'09	80w21'19	5:21:25
Bernardstown 51	1	38N30'28	80w20'41	5:21:23
Bernie 22	1	38N14	81w59	5:27:56
Berryburg 1	1	39N12'00	80w05'05	5:20:20
Berryburg Junction 1	1	39N11'15	80w01'54	5:20:08
Berryburg Mine No 1 1	1	39N16	80w08	5:20:32
Berry Siding 4	1	38N43	80w39	5:22:36
Berryville 33	11	39N36'56	78w13'48	5:12:55
Bert 48	2	39N27'03	80w57'32	5:23:50
Bertha 45	14	37N34'21	80w52'16	5:23:29
Bertha Hill 31	28	39N39'52	79w59'33	5:19:58
Berwind 24	1	37N16'07	81w40'01	5:26:40
Beryl 29	6	39N28'20	79w03'50	5:16:15
Besoco 41	1	37N37'39	81w14'28	5:24:58
Bessemer 2	27	39N30'52	77w55'48	5:11:43
Bethany 5	9	40N12'20	80w33'25	5:22:14
Bethel 36	1	38N41	79w11	5:16:44
Bethel Place 54	1	39N16	81w40	5:26:40
Bethesada 50	1	38N13	82w27	5:29:48
Bethesda 50	1	38N11'22	82w25'22	5:29:41
Bethlehem 17	1	39N23'31	80w16'51	5:21:07
Bethlehem 35	34	40N02'38	80w41'27	5:22:46
Betty Zane 35	34	40N08'36	80w39'45	5:22:39
Beulah 42	1	38N45'04	79w45'29	5:19:02
Beury 10	18	37N57'34	81w02'27	5:24:10
Beurytown 45	1	37N49'38	80w54'19	5:23:37
Beverly 42	1	38N50'26	79w52'32	5:19:30
Beverly Hills 6	5	38N24'23	82w24'19	5:29:37
Beverly Hills 25	17	39N28'47	80w10'08	5:20:41
Bias 30	1	37N44'28	82w11'42	5:28:47
Bickmore 8	1	38N22'53	81w06'44	5:24:27
Big Battle 9	1	39N17	80w34	5:22:16
Bigbend 7	1	38N57'49	81w09'43	5:24:39
Big Branch 55	1	37N35'15	81w46'20	5:27:05
Big Chimney 20	14	38N24'20	81w32'09	5:26:09
Big Creek 23	1	38N00'15	82w02'25	5:28:10
Big Four 24	1	37N24'53	81w31'15	5:26:05
Big Isaac 9	1	39N12'00	80w32'20	5:22:09
Big Moses 48	2	39N25'53	80w47'04	5:23:08
Big Mountain 20	1	38N13	81w26	5:25:44
Big Otter 8	1	38N36	81w03	5:24:12
Big Run 25	17	39N28'15	80w22'39	5:21:31
Big Run 26	21	39N47'52	80w33'26	5:22:14
Big Run 51	1	38N35'59	80w28'20	5:21:53
Big Run 52	2	39N35'04	80w34'40	5:22:19
Big Sandy 20	1	38N30	81w22	5:25:28
Big Sandy 24	1	37N27'51	81w41'54	5:26:48
Bigson 3	1	37N59'29	81w43'25	5:26:54
Big Springs 7	1	38N59'07	81w04'20	5:24:17
Big Stick 41	1	37N41'40	81w15'14	5:25:01
Big Sycamore 8	1	38N22	81w10	5:24:40
Billings 44	1	38N51'26	81w24'14	5:25:37
Bim 3	1	37N55'18	81w41'22	5:26:45
Bingamon 25	17	39N27'50	80w20'22	5:21:21
Bingham 13	1	38N02'01	80w47'38	5:23:11
Birch 4	1	38N38	80w54	5:23:36
Birch River 34	1	38N29'55	80w45'19	5:23:01
Birchton 41	18	37N55'58	81w32'30	5:26:10
Birds Creek 39	12	39N26'09	79w48'27	5:19:14
Bishop 24	1	37N12'30	81w33'37	5:26:14
Bismarck 12	1	39N13'04	79w14'00	5:16:56
Bison 4	1	38N39'19	80w44'31	5:22:58
Blackberry City 30	1	37N36'41	82w10'00	5:28:40
Black Betsy 40	1	38N29'59	81w50'08	5:27:21
Black Bottom 23	1	37N50'46	82w00'14	5:28:01
Blackburn 11	14	38N55'23	80w40'31	5:22:42
Blackeagle 55	1	37N34'22	81w21'46	5:25:27
Black Fork 47	1	39N05	79w40	5:18:40
Blackhawk 20	22	38N20'01	81w35'13	5:26:21
Blacksville 31	17	39N43'12	80w12'44	5:20:51
Black Wolf 24	1	37N20'10	81w29'11	5:25:57
Blaine 29	2	39N23'09	79w10'48	5:16:43
Blair 19	2	39N17'42	77w47'46	5:11:11
Blair 23	1	37N52'42	81w49'41	5:27:19
Blairton 2	27	39N27'09	77w55'14	5:11:41
Blakeley 20	1	38N17'46	81w18'14	5:25:13
Blaker Mills 13	1	37N45'42	80w36'27	5:22:26
Blandville 9	1	39N15'24	80w42'39	5:22:51
Blaser 39	19	39N23'12	79w43'04	5:18:52
Blennerhassett 54	1	39N15'49	81w37'46	5:26:31
Blocton 30	1	37N47'48	82w20'32	5:29:22
Bloomery 14	1	39N23'13	78w22'24	5:13:30
Bloomery 19	23	39N15'17	77w49'10	5:11:17
Bloomingrose 3	1	38N08'33	81w38'00	5:26:32
Blount 20	1	38N19'16	81w25'36	5:25:42
Blue 48	2	39N26'51	80w49'32	5:23:18
Blue Bend 13	14	37N55'18	80w16'08	5:21:05
Blue Creek 20	1	38N27'02	81w27'27	5:25:50
Bluefield 28	20	37N16'11	81w13'21	5:24:53
Blue Jay 6 41	1	37N40'58	81w06'49	5:24:27
Blue Pennant 3	18	37N58'15	81w33'35	5:26:14
Blue Ridge Acres 19	3	39N17'10	77w46'23	5:11:06
Blue Rock 42	1	38N43'29	80w05'28	5:20:22
Blues Beach 14	1	39N25'33	78w42'56	5:14:52
Blue Spring 42	1	38N32'12	80w06'45	5:20:27
Bluestone 28	20	37N18'43	81w19'05	5:25:16
Blue Sulphur 6	1	38N24'55	82w14'54	5:29:00
Blue Sulphur 13	1	37N49	80w39	5:22:36
Blue Sulphur Springs 13	1	37N49'30	80w38'11	5:22:33
Blueville 46	14	39N20'46	80w00'13	5:20:01
Bluewell 28	20	37N18'45	81w15'36	5:25:02
Blundon 20	1	38N32'24	81w31'15	5:26:05
Board 27	1	38N54	81w56	5:27:44
Boaz 54	1	39N21'41	81w30'08	5:26:01
Bob White 3	1	37N57'15	81w43'07	5:26:52
Boggs 51	1	38N28'07	80w37'31	5:22:30
Bois 51	1	38N43'31	80w26'06	5:21:44
Bolair 51	1	38N26'15	80w26'39	5:21:47
Bolivar 19	3	39N19'24	77w45'11	5:11:01
Bolt 41	1	37N45'44	81w24'45	5:25:39
Bomont 8	1	38N26'59	81w13'57	5:24:56
Bonnie 4	1	38N46'10	80w41'36	5:22:46
Bonnivale 54	1	39N10'27	81w30'20	5:26:01
Booher 48	2	39N26'38	80w46'17	5:23:05
Boomer 10	14	38N09'02	81w17'15	5:25:09
Boonesborough 10	14	38N07'46	81w12'59	5:24:52
Booth 31	17	39N35'49	80w00'56	5:20:04
Booths Creek 46	1	39N22	80w08	5:20:32
Boothsville 25	17	39N23'41	80w11'43	5:20:47
Booton 50	1	38N16'14	82w22'54	5:29:32
Borderland 30	1	37N42'50	82w18'33	5:29:14
Boreman 54	14	39N17'15	81w28'36	5:25:54
Borgman 39	19	39N26'45	79w44'40	5:18:59
Borland 37	1	39N17'52	81w16'58	5:25:08
Bottom Creek 24	1	37N25'12	81w29'44	5:25:59

Boulder (Rangoon P O) 1
1 39N04'07 80W06'13 5:20:25
Bowan Ridge 6 5 38N24 82W26 5:29:44
Bowden 42 1 38N54'31 79W42'36 5:18:50
Bowen 50 1 38N18'22 82W20'36 5:29:22
Bower 4 14 38N51'30 80W43'12 5:22:53
Bowers Hill 44 1 38N47'34 81W18'29 5:25:14
Bowes 13 14 37N50'28 80W22'28 5:21:30
Bowlby 31 28 39N42'41 80W01'01 5:20:04
Bowles 22 1 38N19'25 82W03'25 5:28:14
Boyd 49 1 38N50 80W21 5:21:24
Boyer 38 1 38N29'20 79W48'03 5:19:12
Bozoo 32 1 37N27'46 80W49'21 5:23:17
Brabant 50 1 38N06'55 82W19'03 5:29:16
Braden (Lima Post Office) 48
2 39N26'25 80W44'39 5:22:59
Bradley 3 1 38N09'30 81W43'03 5:26:52
Bradley 41 1 37N51'55 81W11'39 5:24:47
Bradshaw 23 1 37N48'06 82W01'55 5:28:08
Bradshaw 24 1 37N21'06 81W47'56 5:27:12
Brady Gate 42 1 38N32'51 80W04'39 5:20:19
Bradyville 22 1 38N08'47 82W11'02 5:28:44
Braeholm 23 1 37N46'30 81W49'18 5:27:17
Bragg 41 1 37N46'56 80W59'26 5:23:58
Brake 16 1 38N53'22 79W02'11 5:16:09
Bramwell 28 1 37N19'30 81W18'43 5:25:15
Branchland 22 1 38N13'15 82W12'14 5:28:49
Brandonville 39
12 39N39'57 79W37'15 5:18:29
Brandywine 36 1 38N37'29 79W14'42 5:16:59
Brantville 13 1 37N54'14 80W26'04 5:21:44
Braucher 38 14 38N35'55 79W49'15 5:19:17
Braxton 4 1 38N47'22 80W43'46 5:22:55
Bream 20 1 38N24'12 81W31'45 5:26:07
Breece 3 1 38N08'13 81W53'47 5:27:35
Breeden 30 1 37N55'31 82W15'58 5:29:04
Brenton 55 1 37N35'45 81W38'10 5:26:33
Bretz 39 12 39N32'32 79W48'03 5:19:12
Bretz 47 1 39N05'43 79W39'51 5:18:39
Brewer Hill 31 28 39N39'13 79W59'23 5:19:58
Brewsterdale 24 1 37N14'57 81W33'06 5:26:12
Briarwood Estates 54
14 39N17 81W32 5:26:08
Brick Church 50 1 38N07 82W36 5:30:24
Bridgeport 17 1 39N17'11 80W15'23 5:21:02
Bridgeport Hill 17
1 39N17 80W15 5:21:00
Bridgeway 48 2 39N29'12 80W54'26 5:23:38
Brighton 27 1 38N47'59 82W02'26 5:28:10
Brink 52 17 39N32'53 80W29'35 5:21:58
Briscoe 54 14 39N20'58 81W31'59 5:26:08
Bristol 17 1 39N17'16 80W31'27 5:22:06
Broaddus 1 1 39N09 80W03 5:20:12
Broadmoor 54 1 39N16 81W40 5:26:40
Broad Oaks 17 24 39N16'25 80W19'43 5:21:19
Brohard 53 1 39N02'11 81W10'35 5:24:42
Brookhaven 31 28 39N36'42 79W54'17 5:19:37
Brooklin 45 14 37N40'23 80W53'51 5:23:35
Brooklyn 10 18 37N59'27 81W02'56 5:24:12
Brooklyn 52 29 39N38'07 80W51'49 5:23:27
Brooks 45 14 37N43'27 80W53'12 5:23:33
Brookside 39 12 39N19'33 79W31'36 5:18:06
Brounland 20 22 38N14'31 81W46'05 5:27:04
Brown 17 1 39N23'15 80W27'40 5:21:51
Browning 45 14 37N39'08 80W51'30 5:23:26
Brownlow 46 14 39N21'05 79W59'49 5:19:59
Brownsburg 38 1 38N16'04 80W04'32 5:20:18
Browns Chapel 31
28 39N29'52 79W54'56 5:19:40
Browns Corner 19
2 39N19'38 77W53'48 5:11:35
Browns Creek 24 1 37N27 81W34 5:26:16
Browns Mill 39 12 39N28'46 79W49'42 5:19:19
Brownsville 10 1 38N11'18 81W11'37 5:24:46
Brownsville 21 1 39N00'08 80W28'34 5:21:54
Brownton 1 1 39N13'12 80W09'01 5:20:36
Bruce 34 1 38N09'47 80W46'37 5:23:06
Bruceton Mills 39
12 39N39'31 79W38'29 5:18:34
Bruno 23 1 37N41'26 81W52'09 5:27:29
Brush Camp Low Place 42
1 38N26'59 80W09'58 5:20:40
Brush Fork 28 20 37N16'51 81W15'22 5:25:01
Brushton (Costa Post Office) 3
1 38N09'58 81W42'33 5:26:50
Brushy Run 36 1 38N50'15 79W14'52 5:16:59
Brydon 46 1 39N16'48 80W03'54 5:20:16
Bryson 41 1 37N44 81W18 5:25:12
Bubbling Spring 14
1 39N15'15 78W27'30 5:13:50
Buck 45 14 37N36'06 80W49'27 5:23:18
Buckeye 38 1 38N11'09 80W08'05 5:20:32
Buckhannon 49 1 38N59'38 80W13'56 5:20:56
Bud 55 1 37N32'15 81W22'46 5:25:31
Buffalo 40 1 38N37'03 81W58'55 5:27:56
Buffalo Creek 50
14 38N21'20 82W30'34 5:30:02
Buff Lick 20 1 38N13 81W26 5:25:44
Bula 31 17 39N42'11 80W15'27 5:21:02
Bulger 22 1 38N08'00 81W58'53 5:27:56
Bull 50 1 37N54 82W27 5:29:48
Bull Run 39 12 39N35'02 79W46'13 5:19:05
Bulltown 4 1 38N47'19 80W34'00 5:22:16
Bunker Hill 2 2 39N20'00 78W03'17 5:12:13
Bunker Hill 20 14 38N21 81W44 5:26:56
Bunners Ridge 25
17 39N28 80W10 5:20:40
Burchfield 52 2 39N35'12 80W32'28 5:22:10
Burdette 13 1 38N03'47 80W47'59 5:23:12
Burk 39 12 39N31'35 79W48'53 5:19:16
Burl 34 1 38N16'31 80W55'35 5:23:42
Burlington 29 2 39N20'15 78W55'06 5:15:40
Burner 38 14 38N37'01 79W48'26 5:19:14
Burning Springs 20
14 38N15 81W33 5:26:12
Burning Springs 53
1 38N58'52 81W18'51 5:25:15
Burnsides 38 1 38N06'30 80W12'31 5:20:50
Burnsville 4 14 38N51'22 80W39'18 5:22:37
Burnt Factory 33
11 39N39'21 78W12'32 5:12:50
Burnt House 43 1 39N02'47 80W59'15 5:23:57
Burnwell 20 1 38N03'09 81W22'32 5:25:30
Burton 52 2 39N39'50 80W25'51 5:21:43
Butchersville 21
1 39N03 80W28 5:21:52
Cabell 41 18 37N47'19 81W13'54 5:24:56
Cabin Creek 20 1 38N11'45 81W28'40 5:25:55
Cabin Run 29 2 39N26 78W54 5:15:36
Cabins 12 1 38N59'56 79W12'20 5:16:49
Cabot 3 1 38N02'11 81W36'55 5:26:28
Cabot Station 7 1 38N55'46 81W06'41 5:24:27
Cacapon 33 2 39N33 78W22 5:13:28
Caddell 39 12 39N27'47 79W39'02 5:18:36
Cairo 43 1 39N12'31 81W09'27 5:24:38
Calcutta 37 1 39N21'02 81W11'41 5:24:47
Caldwell 13 1 37N46'50 80W23'39 5:21:35
Calhoun 1 1 39N05'28 79W59'09 5:19:57
Calis 26 21 39N56'21 80W33'04 5:22:12
Callaway 41 1 37N54 81W10 5:24:40
Calvert 20 18 38N23 81W49 5:27:16
Calvin 34 1 38N20'12 80W42'53 5:22:52
Cambria 17 1 39N22'02 80W21'37 5:21:26
Cambria 34 1 38N15'55 81W11'59 5:24:48
Camden 21 1 39N03'16 80W34'00 5:22:16
Camden On Gauley 51
1 38N22'00 80W35'45 5:22:23
Cameo 3 1 38N06'41 81W55'53 5:27:44
Cameron 26 21 39N49'37 80W34'00 5:22:16
Camp 9 1 39N23 80W49 5:23:16
Campbells 33 19 39N37'05 78W24'43 5:13:39
Campbelltown 38 1 38N14'30 80W05'27 5:20:22
Camp Creek 28 1 37N30 81W06 5:24:24
Camp Ground 39 19 39N24'50 79W44'00 5:18:56
Campus 55 1 37N44 81W41 5:26:44
Canaan 49 1 38N44'40 80W17'45 5:21:11
Canaan Crossing 42
1 38N58'29 79W27'50 5:17:51
Canaan Heights 47
1 39N05'53 79W25'51 5:17:43
Canaan Valley 47
1 39N08 79W28 5:17:52
Canebrake 24 1 37N14'51 81W38'28 5:26:34
Cane Fork 20 1 38N05 81W27 5:25:48
Canfield 4 1 38N35'39 80W45'15 5:23:01
Canfield 42 35 38N54'58 79W48'58 5:19:16
Cannelton 10 1 38N11'39 81W17'46 5:25:11
Canterbury 30 1 37N49'17 82W15'25 5:29:02
Canton 9 1 39N21'47 80W44'08 5:22:57
Cantwell 43 1 39N07'57 81W07'53 5:24:32
Canvas 34 1 38N16'06 80W46'28 5:23:06
Canyon 31 28 39N40'35 79W53'30 5:19:34
Capehart 27 1 38N42'47 81W52'52 5:27:31
Capels 24 1 37N27'16 81W36'06 5:26:24
Caperton 10 1 38N01'16 81W01'36 5:24:06
Capitol 20 22 38N21 81W37 5:26:28
Capon Bridge 14 1 39N17'53 78W26'11 5:13:45
Capon Lake 14 1 39N09'21 78W32'17 5:14:09
Capon Springs 14
1 39N08'10 78W29'05 5:13:56
Captina 26 4 39N49'08 80W48'48 5:23:15
Carbide 52 2 39N32'22 80W40'01 5:22:40
Carbon 20 1 38N01'10 81W24'23 5:25:38
Carbondale 10 1 38N11'10 81W17'58 5:25:12
Caress 4 1 38N42'16 80W32'58 5:22:12
Caretta 24 1 37N20'08 81W40'23 5:26:42
Carew 45 1 37N30'53 80W53'15 5:23:33
Carl 34 1 38N06'38 80W41'05 5:22:44
Carlisle 10 1 37N57'40 81W10'50 5:24:43
Carl Lee Ray 54 1 39N16 81W40 5:26:40
Carlos 24 1 37N23'45 81W48'06 5:27:12
Carmel 39 12 39N19'50 79W33'17 5:18:13
Carolina 25 17 39N28'49 80W16'25 5:21:06
Carroll 22 1 38N17 82W06 5:28:24
Carrollton 1 1 39N05'25 80W05'14 5:20:21
Carswell 24 1 37N26'22 81W30'32 5:26:02
Carter 49 1 38N50'40 80W16'57 5:21:08
Carters Ford 19 2 39N15'52 78W02'00 5:12:08
Cascade 39 12 39N33'48 79W48'53 5:19:16
Cashmere 32 1 37N26'59 80W46'48 5:23:07
Cass 38 1 38N23'48 79W54'54 5:19:40
Cassity 42 1 38N49'34 80W02'06 5:20:08
Cassville 31 17 39N39'56 80W03'50 5:20:15
Catawba 25 17 39N31'37 80W04'41 5:20:19
Cave 36 1 38N39 79W20 5:17:20
Cazy 3 1 37N56'32 81W42'36 5:26:50
Cedar 30 1 37N33'18 82W06'14 5:28:25
Cedar 41 18 37N44'13 81W12'45 5:24:51
Cedar Grove 20 1 38N13'16 81W25'41 5:25:43
Cedar Grove 54 14 39N13'40 81W30'24 5:26:02
Cedarville 11 1 38N50'32 80W49'10 5:23:17
Centennial 32 1 37N34'57 80W19'46 5:21:19
Center Branch 17
24 39N14'50 80W18'55 5:21:16
Center Hill 53 1 39N04 81W24 5:25:36
Center Point 9 1 39N23'30 80W38'08 5:22:33
Centerville 48 2 39N25'55 80W50'25 5:23:22
Centerville 50 1 38N15'41 82W31'47 5:30:07
Central 9 1 39N17 80W51 5:23:24
Central 54 14 39N20'44 81W31'23 5:26:06
Centralia 4 1 38N37'23 80W34'05 5:22:16
Central Station 9
1 39N17'38 80W49'33 5:23:18
Century 1 1 39N05'59 80W11'20 5:20:45
Century Junction 1
1 39N04'27 80W07'02 5:20:28
Century No 2 1 1 39N05 80W08 5:20:32
Ceredo 50 16 38N23'47 82W33'32 5:30:14
Ceres 28 20 37N18'28 81W08'53 5:24:36
Chaffee 29 2 39N24'23 79W09'45 5:16:39
Cham 23 1 37N50 81W52 5:27:28
Chambers 23 1 37N49'16 81W52'49 5:27:31
Champwood 29 2 39N26'36 78W49'10 5:15:17
Chapel 4 1 38N44'51 80W48'18 5:23:13
Chapman 4 14 38N51'15 80W32'39 5:22:11
Chapman 51 1 38N32'42 80W27'39 5:21:51
Chapman Addition 5
33 40N17 80W37 5:22:28
Chapmanville 23 1 37N58'25 82W01'03 5:28:04
Charles 19 23 39N18 77W51 5:11:24
Charleston 20 22 38N20'59 81W37'58 5:26:32
Charles Town 19
23 39N17'20 77W51'36 5:11:26
Charlton Heights 10
1 38N07'25 81W14'03 5:24:56
Charmco 13 1 38N00'08 80W44'14 5:22:57
Chatham Hill 25
17 39N30'44 80W14'13 5:20:57
Chattaroy 30 1 37N42'12 82W16'52 5:29:07
Chauncey 23 1 37N45'58 81W59'16 5:27:57
Cheat Junction 42
1 38N47'41 79W45'17 5:19:01
Cheat Neck 39 28 39N41'06 79W50'03 5:19:20
Chelyan 20 1 38N11'43 81W29'28 5:25:58
Cherokee 20 1 38N04 81W27 5:25:48
Cherokee 24 1 37N24'25 81W20'13 5:25:21
Cherry 53 1 39N00'21 81W20'27 5:25:22
Cherry Falls 51 1 38N27'56 80W23'39 5:21:35
Cherry Grove 36 1 38N38'26 79W31'23 5:18:06
Cherry Run 33 10 39N37'39 78W02'03 5:12:08
Chesapeake 20 1 38N13'24 81W32'11 5:26:09
Chesapeake 25 17 39N30'25 80W09'08 5:20:37
Chester 15 9 40N36'47 80W33'47 5:22:15
Chesterville 54 1 39N09'20 81W29'54 5:26:00
Chestnut Heights 5
33 40N17 80W37 5:22:28
Chestnut Hill 15
32 40N24'52 80W33'02 5:22:12
Chestnut Knob 10
1 37N55'26 80W58'31 5:23:54
Chestnut Knob 28
1 37N24'21 80W54'23 5:23:38
Chestnut Ridge 31
28 39N38'57 79W56'31 5:19:46
Chiefton 17 24 39N17'46 80W25'16 5:21:41
Chiefton 25 17 39N26'37 80W15'29 5:21:02
Childs 52 2 39N36'09 80W46'43 5:23:07
Chimney Corner 10
1 38N08'20 81W08'50 5:24:35
Chloe 7 1 38N41'33 81W05'12 5:24:21
Christian 23 1 37N41'31 81W51'22 5:27:25
Church 52 2 39N40 80W27 5:21:48
Churchville 21 1 39N05'50 80W35'30 5:22:22
Cicerone 44 1 38N37'11 81W30'32 5:26:02
Cinco 20 22 38N20'13 81W27'59 5:25:52
Cinderella 30 1 37N41'03 82W14'12 5:28:57
Circle View 41 18 37N47'48 81W15'03 5:25:00
Circleville 36 1 38N40'15 79W29'29 5:17:58
Cirtsville 41 18 37N52'53 81W15'58 5:25:04
Cisco 43 1 39N07'43 81W17'05 5:25:08
Claremont 10 1 37N55'05 81W03'04 5:24:12
Clarence 44 1 38N46'32 81W28'53 5:25:56
Clark 17 14 39N16 80W22 5:21:28
Clark 24 1 37N25 81W26 5:25:44
Clarksburg 17 14 39N16'50 80W20'41 5:21:23
Claude 39 12 39N17'23 79W54'35 5:19:38
Clawson 38 1 38N16'06 80W01'49 5:20:07
Clay 8 1 38N27'37 81W05'07 5:24:20
Clay Junction 8 1 38N28'29 81W04'40 5:24:19
Claypool 23 1 37N43'59 81W48'53 5:27:16
Claypool 45 1 37N49'58 80W52'15 5:23:29
Claysville 29 2 39N20'56 79W03'24 5:16:14
Clayton 45 1 37N43'24 80W43'45 5:22:55
Clearco 13 1 38N05'36 80W34'10 5:22:17
Clear Creek 41 1 37N54'58 81W20'40 5:25:23
Clear Fork 55 1 37N37'51 81W40'59 5:26:44
Clear Fork Junction 24
1 37N26'56 81W44'24 5:26:58
Clearview 35 6 40N08'28 80W41'18 5:22:45
Clem 4 1 38N38'03 80W54'52 5:23:39
Clemtown 1 1 39N13'57 79W58'39 5:19:55
Clendenenville 13
1 37N52'44 80W24'44 5:21:39
Clendenin 20 1 38N29'19 81W20'54 5:25:24
Cleveland 51 1 38N43'37 80W23'33 5:21:34
Clifftop 10 1 38N00'15 80W56'39 5:23:47
Clifftop 41 1 37N46'17 81W07'19 5:24:29
Clifton 27 1 39N00'08 82W02'30 5:28:10
Clifton Ford 51 1 38N35'55 80W29'20 5:21:57
Clifton Mills 39
12 39N41'49 79W37'05 5:18:28
Clifty 10 1 38N08'44 80W57'44 5:23:51
Clinton 3 1 37N52'57 81W39'06 5:26:36
Clinton 31 17 39N33 79W58 5:19:52
Clinton 35 6 40N07'26 80W37'35 5:22:30
Clinton Furnace 31
28 39N30'57 79W58'00 5:19:52
Clintonville 13 1 37N53'38 80W35'57 5:22:24
Clio 44 1 38N34'52 81W18'05 5:25:12
Clips Mill 19 23 39N15'05 77W50'24 5:11:22
Clothier 3 1 37N56'48 81W48'38 5:27:15
Clouston 26 21 39N50'52 80W33'20 5:22:13
Clover 6 1 38N35'00 82W13'40 5:28:55
Clover 44 1 38N43'23 81W17'23 5:25:10
Clover 47 1 39N09 79W46 5:19:04
Cloverdale 32 1 37N27'00 80W48'56 5:23:16
Clover Lick 38 1 38N19'51 79W58'16 5:19:53
Cluster 37 1 39N19'24 81W19'33 5:25:18
Clyde 20 22 38N22 81W38 5:26:32
Clyde 52 2 39N38 80W41 5:22:44
Coal 17 14 39N18 80W22 5:21:28
Coalburg 20 1 38N12'27 81W27'34 5:25:50
Coal City 41 1 37N40'44 81W12'38 5:24:51
Coaldale 28 1 37N21'47 81W20'04 5:25:20
Coalfield 10 1 38N00'16 81W21'02 5:25:24
Coal Fork 20 1 38N19'03 81W31'16 5:26:05
Coal Mountain 55
1 37N40'10 81W43'43 5:26:55
Coalridge 20 1 38N22'21 81W23'36 5:25:34
Coalton 42 1 38N53'47 79W58'05 5:19:52
Coal Valley 23 1 37N56'29 81W48'59 5:27:16
Coalwood 24 1 37N23'14 81W39'10 5:26:37
Cobb 13 1 38N05'08 80W35'18 5:22:21
Coburn 52 2 39N35'34 80W30'13 5:22:01
Coco 20 1 38N24'11 81W25'10 5:25:41
Coe 34 1 38N19'38 80W33'17 5:22:13
Cofoco 20 1 38N06 81W27 5:25:48
Cokeleys 43 1 39N09'37 81W06'35 5:24:26
Coketon 47 1 39N08'24 79W30'44 5:18:03
Coketown 5 32 40N20'44 80W36'21 5:22:25
Colcord 41 1 37N56'39 81W26'14 5:25:45
Cold Stream 14 1 39N20'22 78W26'32 5:13:46
Coldwater 9 1 39N10'06 80W38'01 5:22:32
Colebank 39 1 39N14'38 79W50'33 5:19:22
Coleman 50 1 38N09'44 82W28'30 5:29:54
Colfax 25 17 39N26'05 80W07'55 5:20:32
Colliers 5 32 40N22'01 80W32'29 5:22:10
Collinsdale 10 1 38N02'09 81W21'49 5:25:27

Collins Settlement 21
1 38N52 80w28 5:21:52
Cologne 27 1 38N47 81w56 5:27:44
Colored Hill 28 1 37N22 81w07 5:24:28
Columbia 10 14 38N07'22 81w18'40 5:25:15
Combs Addition 23
1 37N43'50 81w48'01 5:27:12
Comfort 3 1 38N07'49 81w36'57 5:26:28
Conaway 48 2 39N30'27 80w46'12 5:23:05
Concho 10 1 37N58'01 81w05'17 5:24:21
Concord 39 12 39N24'53 79w49'05 5:19:16
Condit 25 17 39N34'33 80w20'37 5:21:22
Confidence 40 1 38N34'21 81w49'44 5:27:19
Congo 15 9 40N36'30 80w38'10 5:22:33
Conings 11 1 39N04'47 80w46'01 5:23:04
Consol No 9 25 17 39N32'23 80w15'19 5:21:01
Cool Ridge 41 1 37N39'29 81w05'45 5:24:23
Cool Springs 54 1 39N09'45 81w28'31 5:25:54
Coopers 28 1 37N19'20 81w19'36 5:25:18
Coopertown 3 1 38N04'41 81w35'24 5:26:22
Copen 4 1 38N50'15 80w43'47 5:22:55
Copley 21 1 38N58'10 80w38'52 5:22:35
Copper 27 1 38N51 81w59 5:27:56
Cora 23 1 37N50'03 82w01'36 5:28:06
Corder Crossing 1
1 39N11'37 80w03'13 5:20:13
Cordova 13 1 38N03'49 80w25'20 5:21:41
Core 31 17 39N40'48 80w06'27 5:20:26
Corinne 55 1 37N34'22 81w21'24 5:25:26
Corinth 39 12 39N25'18 79w29'31 5:17:58
Corley 1 1 39N04'51 79w59'14 5:19:57
Corley 4 1 38N44'12 80w35'59 5:22:24
Corliss 10 1 38N02'03 80w52'13 5:23:29
Cornstalk 13 1 37N56'46 80w31'47 5:22:07
Cornwallis 43 1 39N13'38 81w07'07 5:24:28
Corrinne 55 1 37N35 81w21 5:25:24
Cortland 47 1 39N04'01 79w25'40 5:17:43
Corton 20 1 38N29'22 81w16'32 5:25:06
Costa 3 1 38N10 81w43 5:26:52
Cottageville 18 1 38N51'56 81w49'25 5:27:18
Cottle 34 1 38N20'47 80w37'36 5:22:30
Cotton 44 1 38N32'41 81w21'00 5:25:24
Cotton Hill 10 1 38N06'48 81w08'42 5:24:35
Cottontown 52 2 39N39'25 80w25'28 5:21:42
Couch 27 1 38N47'19 82w03'32 5:28:14
Countsville 44 1 38N41'36 81w26'27 5:25:46
Courtright 17 1 39N17'12 80w16'38 5:21:07
Cove 15 32 40N24 80w35 5:22:20
Cove Gap 50 1 38N05'44 82w15'16 5:29:01
Covel 55 1 37N29'27 81w19'22 5:25:17
Cowen 51 1 38N24'34 80w33'29 5:22:14
Cox Landing 6 1 38N28'24 82w18'03 5:29:12
Coxs Mills 11 1 39N02'40 80w49'37 5:23:18
Cox Town 21 1 39N01'40 80w28'31 5:21:54
Crab Orchard 41
18 37N44'26 81w13'51 5:24:55
Craddock 49 1 38N43'21 80w15'59 5:21:04
Crag 13 1 37N58 80w46 5:23:04
Craig 13 1 37N54'30 80w44'59 5:23:00
Craigmoor 17 14 39N11'36 80w16'46 5:21:07
Craigsville 34 1 38N19'50 80w39'12 5:22:37
Cranberry 41 18 37N49'18 81w11'43 5:24:47
Craneco 23 1 37N47'48 81w43'56 5:26:56
Cranesville 39 12 39N33'11 79w29'42 5:17:59
Crany 55 1 37N44'24 81w32'10 5:26:09
Crave Creek 26 21 39N51 80w36 5:22:24
Crawford 21 1 38N52'19 80w26'13 5:21:45
Crawley 13 1 37N56'05 80w39'08 5:22:37
Creamery 32 1 37N38'32 80w40'41 5:22:43
Crede 20 22 38N22 81w38 5:26:32
Creed 20 22 38N23'46 81w33'46 5:26:15
Creekvale 14 1 39N25'49 78w33'05 5:14:12
Creels 54 1 39N11'48 81w30'02 5:26:00
Cremo 7 1 38N53'05 81w12'37 5:24:50
Cresap 26 4 39N50'36 80w49'01 5:23:16
Crescent 10 1 38N10'25 81w18'32 5:25:14
Cressmont 8 1 38N27'23 80w58'41 5:23:55
Creston 53 1 38N56'49 81w16'16 5:25:05
Crichton 13 1 38N03'22 80w42'59 5:22:52
Crickmer 10 1 37N53'30 80w54'23 5:23:38
Crimson Springs 32
1 37N31'04 80w28'55 5:21:56
Crites 23 1 37N47'54 81w45'44 5:27:03
Crockett 50 1 38N13'53 82w22'40 5:29:31
Crook 3 1 37N56 81w41 5:26:44
Crooked Creek 23
1 37N52'55 81w58'53 5:27:56
Crosby 8 1 38N19'15 81w12'34 5:24:50
Cross Creek 5 8 40N19 80w34 5:22:16
Cross Lanes 20 18 38N25'13 81w47'27 5:27:10
Crossroads 31 17 39N39'33 80w18'08 5:21:13
Crossroads 45 1 37N42'40 80w48'49 5:23:15
Crosstown 29 2 39N21'22 79w10'37 5:16:42
Crow 41 18 37N45'33 81w04'37 5:24:18
Crown 23 1 37N45'30 81w50'39 5:27:23
Crown 31 28 39N34'59 80w06'10 5:20:25
Crown City 6 1 38N34'50 82w16'42 5:29:07
Crown Hill 20 1 38N12'00 81w24'50 5:25:39
Crow Summit 18 1 38N57 81w46 5:27:04
Crum 50 1 37N54'20 82w26'46 5:29:47
Crumpler 24 1 37N25'29 81w20'31 5:25:22
Crumps Bottom 45
1 37N30'30 80w50'41 5:23:23
Crystal 28 1 37N22 81w13 5:24:52
Crystal Block 23
1 37N42'28 81w59'19 5:27:57
Crystal Lake 9 1 39N18 80w47 5:23:08
Crystal Springs 42
35 38N56'27 79w52'39 5:19:31
Crystal Springs 54
1 39N16 81w40 5:26:40
Cuba 18 1 38N59'28 81w40'09 5:26:41
Cubana 42 1 38N49'23 80w05'57 5:20:24
Cub City 55 1 37N36'38 81w47'57 5:27:12
Cucumber 24 1 37N16'40 81w37'37 5:26:30
Culloden 6 1 38N25'12 82w03'20 5:28:13
Cumberland Heights 28
20 37N15'35 81w11'37 5:24:46
Cunard 10 1 37N59'55 81w02'23 5:24:10
Cunningham 16 1 39N05'46 78w56'39 5:15:47
Curry 40 1 38N23 82w00 5:28:00
Curtin 34 1 38N17'07 80w38'12 5:22:33
Curtin 51 1 38N28'28 80w21'46 5:21:27
Curtis 44 1 38N48 81w28 5:25:52
Curtisville 25 17 39N31'15 80w26'21 5:21:45
Cusicks Crossing 52
2 39N40'23 80w27'06 5:21:48
Custer Addition 17
24 39N15'36 80w21'39 5:21:27
Cutlips 4 1 38N47'19 80w45'16 5:23:01
Cuzzart 39 12 39N35'37 79w33'54 5:18:16
Cuzzie 22 1 38N07'25 82w13'17 5:28:53
Cyclone 55 1 37N43'58 81w41'20 5:26:45
Cyrus 50 14 38N18'19 82w34'22 5:30:17
Czar 42 1 38N43'48 80w11'14 5:20:45
Dabney 23 1 37N48'43 81w55'43 5:27:43
Dahmer 36 1 38N34'10 79w19'36 5:17:18
Dailey 42 1 38N47'55 79w53'47 5:19:35
Daisy 23 1 38N00'31 82w03'14 5:28:13
Dakota 25 17 39N30'49 80w08'08 5:20:33
Dale 48 2 39N27'28 80w39'02 5:22:36
Dallas 26 4 40N00'58 80w31'38 5:22:07
Dallison 54 1 39N14'55 81w23'06 5:25:32
Dameron 41 1 37N49'31 81w22'10 5:25:29
Dan 24 1 37N21 81w48 5:27:12
Danese 10 1 37N55'50 80w54'12 5:23:37
Daniels 41 1 37N44'35 81w07'23 5:24:30
Dans Run 29 2 39N32'46 78w41'30 5:14:46
Danstown 18 1 38N46'15 81w47'37 5:27:09
Danville 3 18 38N04'51 81w50'03 5:27:20
Darkesville 2 2 39N22'16 78w01'41 5:12:07
Dartmont 3 1 38N11'29 81w43'21 5:26:53
Dartmoor 42 1 38N59'43 79w56'11 5:19:45
Davenport 48 31 39N34 81w00 5:24:00
Davin 23 1 37N43'54 81w49'46 5:27:19
Davis 23 1 37N49'36 82w05'05 5:28:20
Davis 47 1 39N07'43 79w27'54 5:17:52
Davis Creek 20 1 38N20'14 81w42'14 5:26:49
Davis Ford 14 1 39N11'47 78w30'03 5:14:00
Davisville 54 1 39N12'04 81w29'55 5:26:00
Davy 24 1 37N28'42 81w39'13 5:26:37
Dawes 20 1 38N08'34 81w27'08 5:25:49
Dawmont 17 14 39N19'03 80w20'33 5:21:22
Dawson 13 1 37N51'22 80w42'40 5:22:51
Daybrook 31 17 39N39'59 80w12'48 5:20:51
Daysville 49 1 38N57'38 80w09'40 5:20:39
Dayton 39 12 39N18'46 79w35'15 5:18:21
Dean 52 2 39N38'58 80w35'25 5:22:22
Deanville 21 1 39N03'17 80w27'54 5:21:52
Deanville 49 1 38N59'23 80w12'24 5:20:50
Decota 20 1 38N01'04 81w25'15 5:25:41
Deep Valley 25 17 39N31'19 80w23'18 5:21:33
Deep Valley 48 2 39N20'19 80w50'38 5:23:23
Deepwater 10 14 38N07'36 81w15'50 5:25:03
Deepwell 34 1 38N14'03 80w45'24 5:23:02
Deer Creek 38 1 38N23'11 79w55'31 5:19:42
Deer Run 36 1 38N43'12 79w13'51 5:16:55
Deerwalk 54 1 39N15'14 81w19'41 5:25:19
Dehue 23 1 37N48'22 81w54'22 5:27:37
De Kalb 11 1 38N56'33 80w55'56 5:23:44
Delbarton 30 1 37N42'38 82w11'03 5:28:44
Dellslow 31 17 39N36'25 79w53'32 5:19:34
Delmar 31 17 39N36'16 80w00'27 5:20:02
DeLong 37 1 39N24'05 81w09'46 5:24:39
Delorme (Edgarton P O) 30
1 37N34'09 82w08'32 5:28:34
Delphi 34 1 38N23'17 80w40'13 5:22:41
Delray 14 1 39N11'40 78w36'16 5:14:25
Dempsey 10 18 38N03'14 81w09'46 5:24:39
Denmar 38 1 38N05'10 80w13'21 5:20:53
Dennis 13 1 37N55'50 80w42'42 5:22:51
Dent 1 19 39N17'39 79w52'39 5:19:31
Denver 26 21 39N50 80w34 5:22:16
Denver 39 19 39N22'56 79w46'14 5:19:05
Denver Heights 26
21 39N43'56 80w32'42 5:22:11
Depue 44 1 38N50'17 81w23'50 5:25:35
Derryhale 10 1 37N54'48 81w09'51 5:24:39
Despard 17 24 39N17'19 80w18'22 5:21:13
Dessie 4 1 38N39'14 80w54'54 5:23:40
Devon 30 1 37N32'14 82w03'46 5:28:15
Dewitt 10 1 37N55'53 81w07'36 5:24:30
Diamond 20 14 38N12'53 81w31'00 5:26:04
Diamond 23 1 37N49'30 82w04'54 5:28:20
Diana 51 1 38N34'25 80w27'24 5:21:50
Dickinson (Quincy P O) 20
1 38N12'13 81w30'10 5:26:01
Dickson 13 1 37N46'09 80w20'47 5:21:23
Dickson 50 14 38N17'53 82w26'50 5:29:47
Dille 8 1 38N29'20 80w49'33 5:23:18
Dilleys Mill 38 1 38N16'08 79w57'46 5:19:51
Dillon 41 1 37N46'13 80w57'03 5:23:48
Dimmock 10 1 37N57'52 81w04'11 5:24:17
Dingess 30 1 37N52'20 82w10'30 5:28:42
Dingy 4 1 38N39'06 80w56'49 5:23:47
Dink 8 1 38N34'07 81w03'35 5:24:14
Divide 10 1 38N04'00 80w57'59 5:23:52
Dixie 34 1 38N15'03 81w11'36 5:24:46
Doak 9 1 39N19'13 80w38'01 5:22:32
Doane 50 1 37N59'15 82w22'24 5:29:30
Dobbin 12 1 39N14'19 79w24'52 5:17:39
Dobra 23 1 37N56'04 81w49'28 5:27:18
Dock 20 18 38N23 81w49 5:27:16
Doddtown 44 1 38N34'28 81w25'12 5:25:41
Dodrill 7 1 38N51'46 81w02'05 5:24:08
Dodson Junction 3
1 38N07'59 81w54'33 5:27:38
Doe Gully 33 2 39N36'27 78w23'24 5:13:34
Dog Patch 23 1 37N49'10 81w59'56 5:28:00
Dogway 51 1 38N14'27 80w22'22 5:21:29
Dola 17 1 39N22'35 80w25'19 5:21:41
Don 23 1 37N44'31 81w56'21 5:27:45
Donald 34 1 38N15'56 80w42'34 5:22:50
Donaldson 14 1 39N29'51 78w39'17 5:14:37
Donaldson 51 1 38N23'14 80w30'43 5:22:03
Donlan 11 1 38N57'31 80w40'38 5:22:43
Donwood 20 1 38N09'44 81w19'56 5:25:20
Doortown 51 1 38N29'02 80w25'21 5:21:41
Dorcas 12 1 38N56'20 79w06'23 5:16:26
Dorfee 8 1 38N26'37 81w10'30 5:24:42
Dority 39 12 39N30'04 79w33'17 5:18:13
Dorothy 41 18 37N57'18 81w26'59 5:25:48
Dorr 32 1 37N37'10 80w28'27 5:21:54
Dothan 10 1 37N58'02 81w13'20 5:24:53
Dott 28 1 37N29 81w15 5:25:00
Douglas 7 1 38N40'20 81w03'29 5:24:14
Douglas 47 1 39N07'37 79w31'15 5:18:05
Douglas Grove 2
27 39N25'08 77w57'28 5:11:50
Doyle 54 1 39N16'58 81w22'34 5:25:30
Drennen 34 1 38N16'14 80w59'54 5:24:00
Drews Creek 41 1 37N52 81w29 5:25:56
Drift Run 18 1 38N56'25 81w38'04 5:26:32
Droop 38 1 38N04'37 80w17'07 5:21:08
Droop Mountain 13
1 38N01'30 80w15'24 5:21:02
Dry Branch 20 1 38N10'48 81w28'01 5:25:52
Dry Creek 41 1 37N51'35 81w27'50 5:25:51
Dryfork 42 1 38N58'07 79w30'11 5:18:01
Dry Hill 41 18 37N48'54 81w13'12 5:24:53
Dry Run 36 1 38N36'46 79w31'30 5:18:06
Dubree 10 1 38N03 81w00 5:24:00
Duck 8 1 38N35'00 80w56'13 5:23:45
Duckworth 9 1 39N16'38 80w52'35 5:23:30
Dudeon 18 1 38N41 81w40 5:26:40
Dudley Gap 6 1 38N30'10 82w08'40 5:28:35
Duffields 19 2 39N21'45 77w49'40 5:11:19
Duffy 21 1 38N47'27 80w26'41 5:21:47
Duhring 28 1 37N20'51 81w15'50 5:25:03
Dukes 44 1 38N53'47 81w27'07 5:25:48
Dulaney 52 2 39N38'05 80w37'47 5:22:31
Dunbar 20 14 38N21'38 81w44'15 5:26:57
Dunbar Village 20
14 38N23 81w45 5:27:00
Duncan 18 1 38N54'10 81w34'25 5:26:18
Dundon 8 1 38N27'35 81w04'08 5:24:17
Dungriff 20 22 38N14'25 81w42'51 5:26:51
Dunloup 10 1 37N54'17 81w09'17 5:24:37
Dunlow 50 1 38N01'23 82w25'54 5:29:44
Dunmore 38 1 38N21'34 79w52'52 5:19:31
Dunns 28 1 37N32'35 81w03'12 5:24:13
Duo 13 1 38N04'16 80w35'52 5:22:23
Dupont Circle 54
1 39N16 81w40 5:26:40
Dupont City 20 14 38N16'10 81w33'56 5:26:16
Durbin 38 14 38N32'44 79w49'31 5:19:18
Durgon 16 1 38N59'35 79w02'45 5:16:11
Dutch 4 1 38N48'18 80w37'06 5:22:28
Dutchman 43 1 39N03'38 81w09'55 5:24:40
Dutch Ridge 20 1 38N29 81w21 5:25:24
Duval 22 1 38N13 81w56 5:27:44
Dyer 51 1 38N22'52 80w28'30 5:21:54
Eads Mill 28 1 37N28'47 81w04'27 5:24:18
Eagle 10 1 38N09'30 81w18'17 5:25:13
Eagle 17 1 39N23 80w22 5:21:28
Eakle 8 1 38N26'49 80w55'38 5:23:43
Earling 23 1 37N45'59 81w54'56 5:27:40
Earnshaw 52 2 39N37'21 80w28'04 5:21:52
Easly 3 1 38N09'08 81w44'00 5:26:56
East Bank 20 1 38N13'05 81w26'35 5:25:46
East Beckley 41
18 37N46'09 81w10'20 5:24:41
East Dailey 42 1 38N46'49 79w53'28 5:19:34
Eastgulf 41 1 37N37'46 81w17'42 5:25:11
East Kermit 30 1 37N48'49 82w24'03 5:29:36
East Kingston 10
1 37N58'42 81w17'41 5:25:11
East Lynn 50 1 38N10'04 82w22'41 5:29:31
East Nitro 20 18 38N23'59 81w50'11 5:27:21
East Oak Hill 10
1 37N59'37 81w07'57 5:24:32
Easton 31 28 39N39'09 79w54'47 5:19:39
East Pea Ridge 6
5 38N25'05 82w18'34 5:29:14
East River 28 1 37N22 81w03 5:24:12
East Salem 17 1 39N17'20 80w32'11 5:22:09
East Side 20 22 38N21'15 81w38'27 5:26:34
Eastside 25 17 39N28 80w10 5:20:40
East Steubenville 5
32 40N21'24 80w35'58 5:22:24
East View 17 24 39N16'09 80w18'45 5:21:15
East Williamson 30
1 37N39'44 82w15'48 5:29:03
Eaton 54 1 39N11'46 81w18'50 5:25:15
Eby 46 12 39N19'08 79w53'58 5:19:36
Eccles 41 1 37N46'59 81w15'58 5:25:04
Echo 50 1 38N10'40 82w28'55 5:29:56
Eckman 24 1 37N24'16 81w27'52 5:25:51
Eden 3 1 38N07'55 81w37'47 5:26:31
Eden 35 34 40N04'01 80w38'19 5:22:33
Eden 49 1 38N44'37 80w19'41 5:21:19
Edgarton 30 1 37N34 82w09 5:28:36
Edgemont 25 17 39N28'12 80w10'14 5:20:41
Edgewood 17 24 39N18'12 80w21'14 5:21:25
Edgewood 20 22 38N22'48 81w38'38 5:26:35
Edgewood 35 34 40N04'43 80w41'03 5:22:44
Edgewood Acres 20
22 38N22'52 81w37'53 5:26:32
Edison 28 20 37N18'13 81w09'20 5:24:37
Edith 55 1 37N40'36 81w36'27 5:26:26
Edmond 10 1 38N03'44 81w01'39 5:24:07
Edna 31 28 39N34'30 80w03'15 5:20:13
Edray 38 1 38N16'28 80w05'30 5:20:22
Edwight 41 1 37N53'04 81w31'57 5:26:08
Effie 50 1 38N05'40 82w30'30 5:30:02
Effler 24 1 37N20'43 81w26'47 5:25:47
Egeria 28 1 37N32'21 81w12'01 5:24:48
Eggleton 40 1 38N17'35 82w01'15 5:28:05
Eglon 39 12 39N18'05 79w31'10 5:18:05
Egypt 19 2 39N21'07 77w56'52 5:11:47
Elana 44 1 38N37'06 81w06'31 5:24:26
Elbert 24 1 37N20'07 81w32'22 5:26:09
Eldora 25 17 39N25'02 80w12'16 5:20:49
Eleanor 40 1 38N32'15 81w55'57 5:27:44
Elgood 28 1 37N23'58 80w55'53 5:23:44
Eli 54 1 39N11'36 81w38'55 5:26:36
Elizabeth 53 1 39N03'48 81w23'43 5:25:35
Elk 20 22 38N21'39 81w39'56 5:26:40
Elk 47 1 39N01'18 79w32'17 5:18:09
Elk City 1 1 39N08'32 80w06'30 5:20:26
Elk Forest 20 22 38N23'22 81w35'36 5:26:22
Elk Garden 29 2 39N23'00 79w09'16 5:16:37
Elk Hills (Mink Shoals) 20
22 38N24'00 81w34'25 5:26:18
Elkhorn 24 1 37N23'08 81w24'40 5:25:39
Elkhurst 8 1 38N26'51 81w09'22 5:24:37
Elkins 42 35 38N55'33 79w50'49 5:19:23
Elkins Junction 42
35 38N54'51 79w51'54 5:19:28

Elkridge 10 14 38N04'49 81W20'03 5:25:20
Elkridge 24 1 37N25 81W26 5:25:44
Elk River Junction 42 1 38N47'30 79W45'41 5:19:03
Elk Run Junction 3 18 37N59'31 81W32'35 5:26:10
Elkview 20 1 38N26'34 81W28'50 5:25:55
Elkwater 42 1 38N38'11 80W00'56 5:20:04
Ella 26 4 39N43 80W49 5:23:16
Ellamore 49 1 38N55'27 80W05'26 5:20:22
Ellenboro 43 1 39N15'52 81W03'23 5:24:14
Elliber Spring 29 2 39N14 78W56 5:15:44
Ellis 11 1 38N56'16 80W43'00 5:22:52
Ellison 45 1 37N35'02 80W59'31 5:23:58
Ellison Ridge 45 1 37N34'38 81W02'26 5:24:10
Ellsworth 48 2 39N31 80W52 5:23:28
Elm Grove 35 34 40N02'44 80W39'06 5:22:36
Elmhurst 32 1 37N38'01 80W37'47 5:22:31
Elmira 4 1 38N39'05 80W59'28 5:23:58
Elmore 55 1 37N34'00 81W24'20 5:25:37
Elm Terrace 35 34 40N01'57 80W39'51 5:22:39
Elmwood 27 1 38N41'44 81W51'11 5:27:25
Elmwood 50 1 38N12'31 82W26'15 5:29:45
Elmwood Heights 54 1 39N24 81W27 5:25:48
Eloise 50 1 38N01 82W26 5:29:44
Elton 45 1 37N49'42 80W48'12 5:23:13
Elverton 10 1 38N01'40 81W02'05 5:24:08
Emerson 41 18 37N56'27 81W29'52 5:25:59
Emma 40 1 38N38'13 81W42'51 5:26:51
Emmart 21 1 38N52'59 80W28'26 5:21:54
Emmett 23 1 37N40'57 81W49'38 5:27:19
Emmons 20 1 38N12'16 81W45'12 5:27:01
Emoryville 29 2 39N21'12 79W10'14 5:16:41
Endicott 52 2 39N40'41 80W35'02 5:22:20
Engle 19 3 39N20'39 77W46'53 5:11:08
English 24 1 37N20'16 81W42'55 5:26:52
Ennis 24 1 37N22'33 81W23'35 5:25:34
Enoch 8 1 38N25'28 80W56'05 5:23:44
Enon 34 1 38N18'34 80W53'49 5:23:35
Enterprise 17 1 39N25'15 80W16'41 5:21:07
Enterprise 53 1 39N00'25 81W22'11 5:25:29
Entry 36 1 38N38'23 79W20'55 5:17:24
Epperly 41 1 37N40'20 81W14'32 5:24:58
Erbacon 51 1 38N31'08 80W35'21 5:22:21
Erie 17 14 39N20'24 80W19'37 5:21:18
Erin 24 1 37N26'29 81W41'34 5:26:46
Erwin 39 12 39N17'47 79W38'19 5:18:33
Eskdale 20 1 38N05'28 81W26'38 5:25:47
Estar 18 1 38N53'53 81W50'30 5:27:22
Esty 13 1 38N00'54 80W22'59 5:21:32
Etam 39 12 39N17'07 79W43'42 5:18:55
Ethel 23 1 37N51'59 81W54'45 5:27:39
Etowah 20 22 38N22'34 81W36'04 5:26:24
Euclid 7 1 38N43'59 81W02'41 5:24:11
Eunice 41 18 37N56'47 81W32'37 5:26:10
Eureka 37 1 39N22'21 81W16'52 5:25:07
Eva 43 1 39N01'59 81W01'42 5:24:07
Evans 18 1 38N49'13 81W46'47 5:27:07
Evansdale 31 28 39N38'57 79W57'52 5:19:51
Evansville 39 12 39N19'59 79W52'08 5:19:29
Evenwood 42 1 38N53'44 79W38'55 5:18:36
Everett 48 2 39N29'17 81W02'05 5:24:08
Everettville 31 17 39N33'49 80W03'48 5:20:15
Evergreen 49 1 38N51'15 80W15'30 5:21:02
Evergreen Hills 18 1 38N51'54 81W50'49 5:27:23
Everson 25 17 39N26'58 80W14'32 5:20:58
Excelsior 24 1 37N18'34 81W41'39 5:26:47
Excelsior 49 1 38N57'20 80W08'22 5:20:33
Excelsior 51 1 38N27'18 80W28'22 5:21:53
Exchange 4 1 38N46 80W44 5:22:56
Extra 40 1 38N37'02 81W51'06 5:27:24
Factory 33 11 39N38 78W14 5:12:56
Fairbanks 4 1 38N43'36 80W40'57 5:22:44
Fairdale 41 1 37N46'53 81W21'48 5:25:27
Fairfax 12 1 39N11'20 79W28'37 5:17:54
Fairlea 13 14 37N46'50 80W27'26 5:21:50
Fairmont 25 25 39N29'06 80W08'34 5:20:34
Fairmor 31 28 39N37'55 79W59'12 5:19:57
Fairplain 18 1 38N45'09 81W41'10 5:26:45
Fairview 25 17 39N35'33 80W14'52 5:20:59
Fairview 26 4 39N44'23 80W47'27 5:23:10
Fairview 27 1 38N58'44 82W00'25 5:28:02
Fairview 30 1 37N40'40 82W18'10 5:29:13
Fairview 42 1 38N41'43 80W13'56 5:20:56
Fairview 52 2 39N32'23 80W33'00 5:22:12
Fallen Timber 52 2 39N30 80W34 5:22:16
Falling Rock 20 1 38N28'08 81W24'07 5:25:36
Falling Spring 13 1 37N59'30 80W21'15 5:21:25
Falling Waters 2 2 39N33'33 77W53'28 5:11:34
Falls 10 1 38N11 81W13 5:24:52
Falls 12 1 39N10'30 79W07'09 5:16:29
Falls Mill 4 1 38N46'25 80W33'00 5:22:12
Falls Mills 48 2 39N26'27 81W00'30 5:24:02
Falls View 10 14 38N07'34 81W14'47 5:24:59
Fame 36 1 38N44'31 79W09'44 5:16:39
Fanco 23 1 37N46'36 81W49'07 5:27:16
Fanny 55 1 37N33'49 81W37'46 5:26:31
Fanrock 55 1 37N34'01 81W39'08 5:26:37
Far 52 2 39N34 80W44 5:22:56
Faraday 24 1 37N12'23 81W38'15 5:26:33
Farley 45 1 37N32'09 80W55'27 5:23:42
Farmdale 13 1 37N54'17 80W42'40 5:22:51
Farmington 25 17 39N30'46 80W14'57 5:21:00
Farnum 17 14 39N19'20 80W19'37 5:21:18
Faulkner 42 1 38N54'34 79W43'36 5:18:54
Fayette 10 18 38N03'48 81W04'25 5:24:18
Fayette Heights 10 1 38N01'27 81W06'55 5:24:28
Fayetteville 10 18 38N03'10 81W06'15 5:24:25
Federal 28 20 37N16 81W14 5:24:56
Federal 37 1 39N24 81W12 5:24:48
Federal Mine 25 17 39N33 80W11 5:20:44
Fellowsville 39 12 39N19'50 79W49'29 5:19:18
Fenwick 34 14 38N13'43 80W34'57 5:22:20
Ferguson 50 1 38N04'32 82W26'00 5:29:44
Ferrell 20 18 38N21'10 81W50'01 5:27:20
Ferrellsburg 22 1 38N01'30 82W06'20 5:28:25
Festus 25 17 39N28'14 80W17'15 5:21:09
Fetterman 46 12 39N20'58 80W02'18 5:20:09
Fieldcrest 31 28 39N39'30 79W55'51 5:19:43
Filbert 24 1 37N19'05 81W32'39 5:26:11
Files Crossroad 2 27 39N27'24 77W54'15 5:11:37
Finch 43 1 39N18'44 81W04'53 5:24:20
Finegan Ford 1 1 38N59'02 80W03'10 5:20:13
Fink 21 1 39N06'36 80W38'56 5:22:36
Finley 20 1 38N17 81W48 5:27:12
Finster 21 14 38N56'17 80W34'47 5:22:19
Fireco 41 1 37N38'41 81W11'54 5:24:48
Fisher 16 1 39N03'05 79W00'13 5:16:01
Fishers Crossing 51 1 38N38'57 80W28'58 5:21:56
Fitzpatrick 41 18 37N44'38 81W11'12 5:24:45
Five Block 23 1 37N53'42 81W49'27 5:27:18
Five Forks 7 1 38N58'09 81W03'39 5:24:15
Five Forks 39 12 39N43'15 79W32'54 5:18:12
Five Forks 43 1 39N10'35 80W58'43 5:23:55
Five Forks 49 1 39N00'22 80W06'00 5:20:24
Fivemile 20 1 38N20'43 81W28'43 5:25:55
Fivemile 27 1 38N45'03 82W04'54 5:28:20
Flaggy Meadow 31 17 39N34'17 80W02'04 5:20:08
Flatrock 27 1 38N50'55 82W01'00 5:28:04
Flats 16 1 39N14 78W56 5:15:44
Flats 41 1 37N52 81W29 5:25:56
Flat Top 28 1 37N35'22 81W06'25 5:24:26
Flat Top Lake 41 1 37N37 81W07 5:24:28
Flatwoods 4 1 38N43'23 80W39'00 5:22:36
Flatwoods 18 1 38N52'47 81W46'47 5:27:07
Fleming 50 1 38N05'16 82W28'16 5:29:53
Flemington 46 1 39N15'59 80W07'56 5:20:32
Fletcher 18 1 38N39'13 81W34'31 5:26:18
Flinderation 17 1 39N17'52 80W30'45 5:22:03
Flinn 54 1 39N04'30 81W41'28 5:26:46
Flint 9 1 39N20'02 80W39'48 5:22:39
Flint 42 1 38N51'13 79W43'49 5:18:55
Flint Town 44 1 38N44'57 81W29'52 5:25:59
Flipping 28 1 37N20'40 81W15'58 5:25:04
Floe 8 1 38N38'38 81W00'45 5:24:03
Flower 4 1 38N49'53 80W46'24 5:23:06
Foch 3 18 38N02'24 81W47'35 5:27:10
Fola 8 1 38N21'27 81W06'14 5:24:25
Follansbee 5 8 40N19'39 80W35'46 5:22:23
Folsom 52 2 39N28'14 80W31'14 5:22:05
Fonzo 43 1 39N04'23 81W03'06 5:24:12
Forest Hill 45 1 37N34'12 80W47'23 5:23:10
Forest Hills 20 14 38N21'06 81W40'05 5:26:40
Forest Hills 35 34 40N05'14 80W41'55 5:22:48
Forge Hill 29 6 39N27'01 78W57'18 5:15:49
Fork Junction 22 1 38N09'26 81W53'50 5:27:35
Fork Lick 51 1 38N28 80W22 5:21:28
Forksburg 25 17 39N28 80W10 5:20:40
Forks of Cacapon 14 19 39N32 78W28 5:13:52
Forks of Coal 20 1 38N16'36 81W48'01 5:27:12
Forks of Hurricane 50 1 38N07 82W36 5:30:24
Forman 12 1 39N08'24 79W04'31 5:16:18
Fort Ashby 29 2 39N30'11 78W46'08 5:15:05
Fort Branch 23 1 37N50'57 81W56'38 5:27:47
Fort Gay 50 1 38N06'58 82W35'45 5:30:23
Fort Grand 31 17 39N34'31 80W05'08 5:20:21
Fort Henry Mall 35 34 40N04 80W42 5:22:48
Fort Hill 20 22 38N21'10 81W39'14 5:26:37
Fort Martin 31 28 39N41 79W59 5:19:56
Fort Neal 54 14 39N17 81W32 5:26:08
Fort Run 16 1 39N04'00 78W55'22 5:15:41
Fort Seybert 36 1 38N41'38 79W11'33 5:16:46
Fort Spring 13 14 37N44'42 80W32'22 5:22:09
Foster 3 18 38N05'50 81W46'48 5:27:07
Fosterville 3 1 38N05'31 81W36'15 5:26:25
Four Mile 52 2 39N35'13 80W37'09 5:22:29
Four States 25 17 39N28'47 80W18'36 5:21:14
Fowlerston 5 33 40N16'47 80W33'20 5:22:13
Frame 20 1 38N30'15 81W28'34 5:25:54
Frametown 4 1 38N38'16 80W51'31 5:23:26
Francis 17 17 39N24'29 80W14'42 5:20:59
Francis 41 1 37N36 81W18 5:25:12
Frank 38 14 38N32'54 79W48'21 5:19:13
Frankford 13 1 37N55'30 80W23'05 5:21:32
Frankfort 29 2 39N34 78W47 5:15:08
Franklin 5 33 40N16'28 80W32'33 5:22:10
Franklin 26 4 39N47'35 80W49'29 5:23:18
Franklin 36 1 38N38'34 79W19'53 5:17:20
Franklintown 19 2 39N12'17 77W56'04 5:11:44
Frazier 13 14 37N44'28 80W33'47 5:22:15
Fraziers Bottom 40 1 38N34'13 81W59'27 5:27:58
Freed 7 1 39N00'39 81W08'17 5:24:33
Freeman 28 1 37N19'48 81W18'29 5:25:14
Freeman 49 1 38N55'04 80W19'43 5:21:19
Freemansburg 21 1 39N05'20 80W31'45 5:22:07
Freemans Creek 21 1 39N05 80W34 5:22:16
Freeport 39 12 39N23'41 79W30'29 5:18:02
Freeport 53 1 39N08'34 81W20'16 5:25:21
Freeze Fork 23 1 37N51'40 81W54'09 5:27:37
Frenchburg 14 1 39N18'55 78W39'39 5:14:39
French Creek 49 1 38N53'08 80W17'51 5:21:11
Frenchton 49 1 38N52'22 80W21'24 5:21:26
Frew 48 2 39N28'02 80W50'11 5:23:21
Friars Hill 13 1 38N00'51 80W26'22 5:21:45
Friendly 48 2 39N30'57 81W03'34 5:24:14
Friendly View 41 1 37N51'26 81W27'32 5:25:50
Frogtown 23 1 37N49'41 82W04'04 5:28:16
Frost 38 1 38N16'14 79W52'51 5:19:31
Frozen Camp 18 1 38N54 81W32 5:26:08
Fry 22 1 38N00'54 82W05'00 5:28:20
Fulton 35 34 40N04'38 80W42'43 5:22:51
Gage 42 1 38N58'13 79W57'39 5:19:51
Gaines 49 1 38N46'49 80W19'13 5:21:17
Gale 49 1 38N54'16 80W06'13 5:20:25
Gallagher 20 1 38N10'23 81W24'07 5:25:36
Gallipolis 27 1 38N47'26 82W12'02 5:28:48
Gallipolis Ferry 27 1 38N46'14 82W11'56 5:28:48
Galloway 1 1 39N13'54 80W07'20 5:20:29
Galloway Junction 1 1 39N13 80W09 5:20:36
Galmish 52 2 39N33'53 80W42'19 5:22:49
Gamoca 10 1 38N11'36 81W11'07 5:24:44
Gandeeville 44 1 38N42'18 81W24'38 5:25:39
Gandy 42 1 38N49'37 79W34'12 5:18:17
Ganotown 2 2 39N24'14 78W08'59 5:12:36
Gap Mills 32 1 37N33'44 80W24'30 5:21:38
Gap of the Ridge 28 20 37N16 81W14 5:24:56
Garden Village 25 17 39N29'03 80W10'01 5:20:40
Gardner 13 1 37N55'23 80W20'55 5:21:24
Gardner 28 1 37N25'25 81W04'28 5:24:18
Gardner Junction 28 1 37N23'45 81W05'09 5:24:21
Garfield 18 1 38N57'17 81W32'41 5:26:11
Garland 24 1 37N24'02 81W47'05 5:27:08
Garretts Bend 22 1 38N18'14 81W54'54 5:27:40
Garrison 3 18 37N59'46 81W30'25 5:26:02
Garten 10 18 38N02'04 81W04'37 5:24:18
Garwood 55 1 37N28'55 81W19'17 5:25:17
Gary 24 1 37N21'49 81W33'01 5:26:12
Gassaway 4 1 38N40'23 80W46'30 5:23:06
Gaston 21 1 39N00'31 80W23'42 5:21:35
Gaston Junction 25 17 39N28'07 80W08'50 5:20:35
Gates 32 1 37N33'56 80W29'24 5:21:58
Gatewood 10 18 38N00'38 81W03'40 5:24:15
Gatzmer 47 1 39N11'06 79W23'01 5:17:32
Gauley 10 1 38N08'57 81W10'46 5:24:43
Gauley Bridge 10 1 38N10'06 81W11'42 5:24:47
Gauley Mills 51 1 38N21'41 80W35'01 5:22:20
Gawthrop 49 1 38N59 80W13 5:20:52
Gay 18 1 38N46'14 81W33'12 5:26:13
Gaymont 10 1 38N06'53 81W05'48 5:24:23
Geary 44 1 38N35 81W14 5:24:56
Gem 4 14 38N50 80W40 5:22:40
Genoa 50 1 38N07'19 82W27'36 5:29:50
Georges Run 48 2 39N18 80W47 5:23:08
Georgetown 2 2 39N34'26 77W57'46 5:11:51
Georgetown 21 1 38N57'38 80W23'05 5:21:32
Georgetown 26 21 39N44'23 80W31'26 5:22:06
Georgetown 31 28 39N35'41 80W05'23 5:20:22
Gerrardstown 2 2 39N22'13 78W05'45 5:12:23
Gerstell 29 2 39N29'00 78W55'59 5:15:44
Ghent 41 1 37N37'01 81W06'54 5:24:28
Giatto 28 1 37N25'03 81W15'22 5:25:01
Gilbert 30 1 37N36'51 81W52'00 5:27:28
Gilboa 34 1 38N18'12 80W56'12 5:23:45
Giles 20 1 38N08'03 81W26'51 5:25:47
Gilkerson 50 1 38N12'30 82W19'26 5:29:18
Gill 22 1 38N05'16 82W07'17 5:28:29
Gillespie 4 1 38N39'49 80W37'05 5:22:28
Gilliam 24 1 37N25'26 81W24'55 5:25:40
Gillman Bottom 23 1 37N43'43 81W47'39 5:27:11
Gillooly 21 14 38N58'39 80W34'13 5:22:17
Gilman 42 35 38N58'23 79W50'24 5:19:22
Gilmer 11 14 38N52'45 80W43'01 5:22:52
Gip 4 1 38N40'40 80W59'39 5:23:59
Girard 50 1 38N10'04 82W18'56 5:29:16
Girta 43 1 39N05'06 81W15'38 5:25:03
Given 18 1 38N44'03 81W44'01 5:26:56
Glace 32 1 37N40'37 80W20'37 5:21:22
Glade 10 1 37N49'56 81W00'04 5:24:00
Glade Farms 39 12 39N42'20 79W31'28 5:18:06
Glade Springs 41 1 37N45 81W07 5:24:28
Gladesville 39 12 39N28'01 79W52'38 5:19:31
Glade View 51 1 38N24'22 80W31'44 5:22:07
Gladwin 47 1 39N00'25 79W32'42 5:18:11
Glady 42 1 38N47'54 79W43'11 5:18:53
Glady Creek 25 17 39N28 80W10 5:20:40
Glasgow 20 1 38N12'55 81W25'29 5:25:42
Glen 8 1 38N23'39 81W14'34 5:24:58
Glen Alum 30 1 37N35'05 81W59'35 5:27:58
Glen Alum Junction 30 1 37N32'34 81W59'44 5:27:59
Glencoe 10 1 38N02 81W16 5:25:04
Glendale 26 34 39N56'57 80W45'16 5:23:01
Glendale 43 1 39N17'06 81W09'20 5:24:37
Glendale Heights 26 34 39N57'38 80W44'45 5:22:59
Glen Daniel 41 1 37N46'44 81W20'14 5:25:21
Glendon 4 1 38N35'28 80W53'20 5:23:33
Glen Easton 26 4 39N50'00 80W38'54 5:22:36
Glen Elk 17 24 39N17'06 80W20'20 5:21:21
Glen Falls 17 24 39N18'28 80W19'32 5:21:18
Glen Ferris 10 14 38N09'11 81W12'54 5:24:52
Glen Fork 55 1 37N41'45 81W31'45 5:26:07
Glengary 2 2 39N23'02 78W09'21 5:12:37
Glenhayes 50 1 38N00'51 82W31'17 5:30:05
Glen Hedrick 41 18 37N45 81W08 5:24:32
Glen Jean 10 1 37N55'35 81W09'01 5:24:36
Glenmore 42 35 38N53'53 79W50'25 5:19:22
Glen Morgan 41 18 37N45'21 81W09'31 5:24:38
Glenray 45 1 37N43'46 80W40'11 5:22:41
Glen Rogers 55 1 37N42'55 81W25'05 5:25:40
Glen View 41 18 37N44'29 81W15'28 5:25:02
Glenville 11 1 38N56'03 80W50'16 5:23:21
Glen White 41 1 37N43'49 81W16'48 5:25:07
Glenwood 27 1 38N36'30 82W11'12 5:28:45
Glenwood 28 1 37N20'09 81W08'58 5:24:36
Glenwood 35 34 40N04'34 80W42'10 5:22:49
Glenwood Park 28 20 37N16 81W14 5:24:56
Glover 55 1 37N35'11 81W35'26 5:26:22
Glover Gap 25 17 39N35 80W22 5:21:28
Godby 23 1 37N58 82W01 5:28:04

Godby Heights 23
1 37N56'13 82W00'33 5:28:02
Godfrey 28 1 37N21'54 81W15'39 5:25:03
Goffs 43 1 39N05'24 81W02'05 5:24:08
Golden 13 1 38N00'39 80W18'19 5:21:13
Golden 26 4 39N58'57 80W32'13 5:22:09
Goldtown 18 1 38N36'42 81W39'11 5:26:37
Good 14 1 39N21'27 78W21'41 5:13:27
Goodhope 17 1 39N10'53 80W26'22 5:21:45
Goodman 30 1 37N41'23 82W17'53 5:29:12
Goodwill 28 1 37N21'15 81W17'23 5:25:10
Goodwin 49 1 38N55'40 80W09'38 5:20:39
Goose Nest 2 2 39N26'45 78W04'36 5:12:18
Gordon 3 1 37N59'13 81W41'44 5:26:47
Gore 14 1 39N23 78W35 5:14:20
Gore 17 24 39N18'52 80W21'08 5:21:25
Gormania 12 1 39N17'34 79W20'41 5:17:23
Gormley 49 1 38N58'20 80W05'21 5:20:21
Goshen 49 1 38N42'44 80W18'24 5:21:14
Gould 8 1 38N31'49 81W02'32 5:24:10
Gould 49 1 38N54'03 80W15'20 5:21:01
Grace 14 1 39N25'50 78W42'49 5:14:51
Grace 44 1 38N53'09 81W21'11 5:25:25
Grafton 46 14 39N20'27 80W01'09 5:20:05
Graham 27 1 38N58 81W58 5:27:52
Graham Heights 25
17 39N28'32 80W06'22 5:20:25
Grand Central Mall 54
14 39N17 81W32 5:26:08
Grandview 41 18 37N49'30 81W04'08 5:24:17
Grangeville 25 17 39N27'22 80W24'23 5:21:38
Grantsville 7 1 38N55'24 81W05'46 5:24:23
Grant Town 25 17 39N33'29 80W10'55 5:20:44
Granville 31 28 39N38'45 79W59'15 5:19:57
Grape Island 37 1 39N25'17 81W10'55 5:24:44
Grapevine 24 1 37N23 81W49 5:27:16
Grassy Falls 34 1 38N10'21 80W41'16 5:22:45
Grassy Meadows 13
1 37N49'36 80W43'16 5:22:53
Grave Creek 26 21 39N52'18 80W43'24 5:22:54
Graydon 10 1 38N35'13 81W03'23 5:24:14
Graysville 26 4 39N49'00 80W47'41 5:23:11
Great Cacapon 33
11 39N37'12 78W17'34 5:13:10
Green 52 2 39N34 80W45 5:23:00
Green Bank 38 1 38N25'12 79W49'54 5:19:20
Green Bottom 6 1 38N33'08 82W17'02 5:29:08
Greenbrier Junction 42
1 38N46'48 79W45'56 5:19:04
Greencastle 20 1 38N03'48 81W22'23 5:25:30
Greencastle 53 1 39N07'52 81W22'46 5:25:31
Greendale 34 1 38N17'44 81W09'13 5:24:37
Green Hill 52 12 39N38'18 80W46'31 5:23:06
Greenland 12 1 39N11'31 79W09'12 5:16:37
Greenland 54 1 39N16 81W40 5:26:40
Green Ridge 33 19 39N35'13 78W26'21 5:13:45
Green Run 37 1 39N22'51 81W13'18 5:24:53
Greensburg 2 27 39N29'03 77W53'03 5:11:32
Green Spring 14 1 39N31'54 78W37'00 5:14:28
Greenstown 10 1 37N57'39 81W08'51 5:24:35
Green Sulphur Springs 45
1 37N48'28 80W48'59 5:23:16
Green Valley 28
20 37N18'40 81W08'22 5:24:33
Green Valley 34 1 38N05'58 80W41'56 5:22:48
Greenview 3 18 37N59'39 81W48'57 5:27:16
Greenville (Hunt P O) 23
1 37N43'15 81W52'19 5:27:29
Greenville 32 1 37N32'36 80W40'58 5:22:44
Greenwood 3 1 37N51'19 81W37'51 5:26:31
Greenwood 9 1 39N16'29 80W53'27 5:23:34
Greer 27 1 38N49'10 82W01'49 5:28:07
Greer 31 28 39N34'19 79W50'57 5:19:24
Greggsville 35 34 40N05'21 80W41'17 5:22:45
Gregory 4 1 38N44'37 80W31'40 5:22:07
Greyeagle 30 1 37N50'58 82W25'01 5:29:40
Griffithsville 22
1 38N14'19 81W59'22 5:27:57
Grimms Landing 27
1 38N40'39 81W56'56 5:27:48
Grippe 3 22 38N11'56 81W44'11 5:26:57
Grove 9 1 39N08'49 80W46'19 5:23:05
Groves 8 1 38N33'22 80W57'43 5:23:51
Grubbs Corner 2
27 39N24'48 77W58'25 5:11:54
Guardian 51 1 38N38'10 80W28'00 5:21:52
Gum Spring 31 28 39N31'06 79W54'38 5:19:39
Gunville 27 1 38N46'29 81W52'22 5:27:29
Guseman 39 12 39N30'59 79W48'33 5:19:14
Guthrie 20 22 38N24'22 81W39'42 5:26:39
Guyan 55 1 37N38'25 81W46'30 5:27:06
Guyandotte 6 14 38N25'37 82W23'07 5:29:32
Guyan Estates 6 1 38N25 82W17 5:29:08
Guyan Terrace 23
1 37N54'59 81W58'26 5:27:54
Gwinn 6 1 38N33'39 82W12'52 5:28:51
Gypsy 17 1 39N22'07 80W19'05 5:21:16
Hackers Creek 21
1 39N04 80W24 5:21:36
Hacker Valley 51
1 38N39'09 80W23'02 5:21:32
Hagans 31 17 39N37'13 80W07'47 5:20:31
Hager 22 1 38N12'52 82W05'13 5:28:21
Hainesville 2 27 39N31'35 77W55'11 5:11:41
Hales Gap 28 20 37N16 81W14 5:24:56
Half Way 13 14 37N43'53 80W35'25 5:22:22
Hall 1 1 38N59 80W13 5:20:52
Hallburg 8 1 38N37'19 80W59'50 5:23:59
Halleck 31 28 39N28'45 79W56'22 5:19:45
Halltown 19 2 39N18'50 77W47'53 5:11:12
Hallwood 27 1 38N58'21 82W04'53 5:28:20
Halo 51 1 38N27'00 80W32'13 5:22:09
Hambleton 47 1 39N04'55 79W38'44 5:18:35
Hamilton 10 1 38N01'17 81W15'48 5:25:03
Hamilton 34 1 38N25 80W46 5:23:04
Hamlin 22 1 38N16'43 82W06'11 5:28:25
Hammond 25 17 39N24'21 80W06'05 5:20:24
Hampden 30 1 37N38'22 81W56'56 5:27:48
Hampshire 29 6 39N28'19 79W04'38 5:16:19
Hampton (Ivanhoe P O) 49
1 38N56'17 80W14'24 5:20:58
Hancock 33 19 39N41'34 78W10'40 5:12:43
Handley 20 1 38N11'13 81W21'56 5:25:28
Hanna 54 1 39N10'06 81W23'43 5:25:35
Hannahdale 43 1 39N13'19 81W01'34 5:24:06
Hannahsville 47 1 39N14'29 79W42'42 5:18:51
Hannan 27 1 38N35 82W07 5:28:28
Hanover 55 1 37N34'22 81W47'59 5:27:12
Hansford 20 1 38N12'14 81W23'45 5:25:35
Hansrote 33 19 39N34'36 78W24'58 5:13:40
Hany 50 1 38N01 82W26 5:29:44
Hardee 30 1 37N47 82W15 5:29:00
Harding 42 1 38N56'53 79W57'34 5:19:50
Hardman 11 1 38N54'56 80W56'44 5:23:47
Hardman 46 12 39N23'25 79W53'42 5:19:35
Hardy 28 1 37N18'37 81W01'40 5:24:07
Harewood 10 14 38N09'26 81W17'30 5:25:10
Harewood 19 23 39N18'08 77W54'59 5:11:40
Harlem Heights 10
1 38N00'20 81W07'21 5:24:29
Harley 44 1 38N37'54 81W18'51 5:25:15
Harlin 9 1 39N17'58 80W41'01 5:22:44
Harman 42 1 38N55'20 79W31'31 5:18:06
Harmco 55 1 37N35 81W23 5:25:32
Harmony 44 1 38N41'10 81W28'45 5:25:55
Harmony Grove 31
28 39N36'25 79W59'25 5:19:58
Harper 36 1 38N31'10 79W28'18 5:17:53
Harper 41 1 37N47'55 81W15'42 5:25:03
Harper 44 1 38N41 81W29 5:25:56
Harper Heights 41
18 37N48'11 81W14'42 5:24:59
Harpers Ferry 19
3 39N19'31 77W44'21 5:10:57
Harpertown 42 35 38N56'21 79W50'20 5:19:21
Harriet 34 1 38N20'30 80W59'45 5:23:59
Harris 54 1 39N09 81W43 5:26:52
Harris Ferry 54 1 39N12 81W42 5:26:48
Harrison 8 1 38N30'46 80W57'13 5:23:49
Harrison 29 2 39N22'38 79W12'14 5:16:49
Harrisville 43 1 39N12'34 81W03'07 5:24:12
Harter 38 1 38N16'51 80W00'46 5:20:03
Harters Hill 25
17 39N27 80W15 5:21:00
Hartford 27 1 39N00'14 81W59'21 5:27:57
Hartland 8 1 38N25'55 81W06'46 5:24:27
Hartley 43 1 39N08'22 81W07'06 5:24:28
Hartmansville 29
2 39N19'19 79W09'19 5:16:37
Harts 22 1 38N01'52 82W07'46 5:28:31
Harts Creek 22 1 38N02 82W07 5:28:28
Hartzel 52 2 39N26'37 80W31'27 5:22:06
Harvey 10 1 37N55'57 81W08'21 5:24:33
Harvey 30 1 37N54 82W13 5:28:52
Harveytown 6 5 38N23'55 82W28'08 5:29:53
Hastings 52 2 39N33'04 80W40'25 5:22:42
Hatcher 28 1 37N21'57 80W58'42 5:23:55
Hatcher 55 1 37N41'45 81W37'11 5:26:29
Hatfield 30 1 37N43'39 82W18'58 5:29:16
Hatfield Bottom 30
1 37N37 82W10 5:28:40
Hathaway 7 1 38N51'28 81W05'00 5:24:20
Hattie 7 1 38N53'59 81W00'46 5:24:03
Havaco 24 1 37N24'36 81W34'39 5:26:19
Hawks Nest 10 1 38N06'57 81W07'02 5:24:28
Haywood 17 1 39N22'52 80W20'10 5:21:21
Hazel 52 17 39N32'51 80W30'43 5:22:03
Hazelgreen 43 1 39N04'56 80W59'14 5:23:57
Hazelton 39 12 39N39'13 79W31'51 5:18:07
Hazelwood 42 1 38N51'41 79W51'36 5:19:26
Headsville 29 2 39N23'33 78W51'22 5:15:25
Heaters 4 1 38N45'42 80W38'30 5:22:34
Heatherfield 19
30 39N26'11 77W49'54 5:11:20
Heavener Grove 49
1 38N58'46 80W10'37 5:20:42
Hebron 37 1 39N21'36 81W01'06 5:24:04
Hedgesville 2 2 39N33'12 77W59'43 5:11:59
Hedgeview 23 1 37N50'53 82W02'00 5:28:08
Heights 27 1 38N51'49 82W08'00 5:28:32
Heizer 40 1 38N32'09 81W46'07 5:27:04
Helen 41 1 37N38'05 81W18'51 5:25:15
Helens Run 25 17 39N27'39 80W15'08 5:21:01
Helvetia 42 1 38N42'21 80W12'05 5:20:48
Hemlock 10 1 37N52'25 80W58'29 5:23:54
Hemlock 18 1 38N53'42 81W44'29 5:26:58
Hemlock 49 1 38N47'02 80W08'26 5:20:34
Hemlock Hollow 10
1 37N52 80W59 5:23:56
Hemphill 24 1 37N26'41 81W35'44 5:26:23
Henderson 27 1 38N50'01 82W08'18 5:28:33
Hendricks 47 1 39N04'30 79W37'52 5:18:31
Henlawson 23 1 37N54'08 81W59'18 5:27:57
Henning 13 1 37N53'46 80W21'36 5:21:26
Henrietta 7 1 38N54'29 81W02'42 5:24:11
Henry 8 1 38N29 81W06 5:24:24
Henry 12 1 39N13'23 79W25'17 5:17:41
Hensley 24 1 37N28'26 81W42'00 5:26:48
Hensley Heights 23
1 37N43'45 81W52'47 5:27:31
Hepzibah 17 14 39N19'57 80W20'08 5:21:21
Hepzibah 46 1 39N21'00 80W10'09 5:20:41
Hereford 18 1 38N49'11 81W37'03 5:26:28
Herndon 55 1 37N30'19 81W20'26 5:25:22
Herndon Heights 55
1 37N30'12 81W21'32 5:25:26
Hernshaw 20 1 38N13'30 81W36'09 5:26:25
Herold 4 1 38N34'02 80W48'36 5:23:14
Herring 39 12 39N32'33 79W44'18 5:18:57
Hettie 4 1 38N46'18 80W29'22 5:21:57
Hetzel 23 1 37N51'39 81W52'40 5:27:31
Hewett 3 1 37N57'44 81W51'08 5:27:25
Hewlet 50 1 38N10'03 82W37'37 5:30:30
Hiawatha 28 1 37N26'24 81W14'39 5:24:59
Hickman Run 25 17 39N28 80W10 5:20:40
Hickory 27 1 38N52 82W08 5:28:32
Hickory Grove 13
1 37N50'02 80W40'34 5:22:42
Hico 10 1 38N07'02 81W00'21 5:24:01
Hicumbottom 20 22 38N21 81W38 5:26:32
Higginsville 14 1 39N25'05 78W34'48 5:14:19
Highland 25 17 39N26'07 80W15'14 5:21:01
Highland 43 1 39N18'13 81W03'07 5:24:12
Highland Lake Terrace 54
1 39N16 81W40 5:26:40
Highland Park 42
35 38N56'45 79W51'13 5:19:25
Highlawn 20 18 38N22'35 81W48'34 5:27:14
Highlawns 25 17 39N32 80W07 5:20:28
High View 14 1 39N13'50 78W24'31 5:13:38
Hildebrand 31 28 39N35'26 79W59'52 5:19:59
Hillcrest 25 17 39N29'27 80W09'22 5:20:37
Hilldale 45 14 37N38'16 80W47'15 5:23:09
Hillsboro 38 1 38N08'07 80W12'48 5:20:51
Hills Crossing 18
1 38N56'30 81W48'52 5:27:15
Hillsdale 20 22 38N22'05 81W37'02 5:26:28
Hillsdale 32 1 37N37'07 80W29'24 5:21:58
Hilltop 10 1 37N56'34 81W09'04 5:24:36
Hill Top 45 1 37N27'55 80W54'31 5:23:38
Hillview 6 5 38N25 82W23 5:29:32
Hillview 25 17 39N26'21 80W10'45 5:20:43
Hillview Terrace 26
21 39N51 80W36 5:22:24
Hilton Village 10
1 38N00'54 80W54'06 5:23:36
Hinch 30 1 37N36'39 82W00'53 5:28:04
Hines 13 1 37N59'00 80W43'06 5:22:52
Hinkleville 49 1 38N55'36 80W15'45 5:21:03
Hinton 45 14 37N40'26 80W53'22 5:23:33
Hiorra 39 12 39N23'32 79W49'08 5:19:17
Hiram 39 14 39N17'35 79W55'57 5:19:44
Hite 25 17 39N32 80W07 5:20:28
Hitop 20 1 38N17'03 81W17'38 5:25:11
Hix 45 1 37N43'48 80W49'11 5:23:17
Hoard 31 28 39N42'17 79W55'57 5:19:44
Hodam 51 1 38N37'13 80W22'58 5:21:32
Hodges 6 5 38N21'45 82W25'44 5:29:43
Hodgesville 49 1 39N03'57 80W11'40 5:20:47
Hogsett 27 1 38N41'33 82W10'34 5:28:42
Hokes Mill 13 14 37N41'59 80W31'35 5:22:06
Holbrook 43 1 39N09'08 80W51'22 5:23:25
Holcomb 34 14 38N15'22 80W36'04 5:22:24
Holden 23 1 37N49'27 82W03'35 5:28:14
Holidays Cove 15
32 40N24'02 80W35'24 5:22:22
Holly 4 1 38N40'13 80W32'53 5:22:12
Holly 20 1 38N03'42 81W26'38 5:25:47
Hollygrove 20 1 38N11'25 81W23'46 5:25:35
Holly Grove 49 1 38N48'07 80W17'23 5:21:10
Holly Hill Church 16
1 39N02 78W45 5:15:00
Hollyhurst 20 22 38N14'05 81W46'31 5:27:06
Hollywood 32 1 37N36'44 80W26'39 5:21:47
Holton 33 10 39N36'08 78W04'12 5:12:17
Homeland 21 1 39N07 80W25 5:21:40
Hometown 40 1 38N31'58 81W51'41 5:27:27
Homewood 21 1 39N01'13 80W28'36 5:21:54
Hominy Falls 34 1 38N08'43 80W43'08 5:22:53
Hoodsville 25 17 39N34'23 80W09'16 5:20:37
Hoohoo 41 1 37N44'34 81W18'36 5:25:14
Hookersville 34 1 38N22'12 80W49'20 5:23:17
Hooks Mills 14 1 39N14'31 78W27'50 5:13:51
Hooverson Heights 5
32 40N19'29 80W34'40 5:22:19
Hoover Town 49 1 38N52'50 80W18'28 5:21:14
Hopemont 39 12 39N26'14 79W31'03 5:18:04
Hopeville 12 1 38N58'02 79W17'13 5:17:09
Hopewell 1 1 39N12'01 80W03'11 5:20:13
Hopewell 10 1 38N07'35 81W04'25 5:24:18
Hopewell 25 17 39N28'16 80W05'43 5:20:23
Hopkins Fork 3 1 38N04'59 81W38'29 5:26:34
Hopper 13 1 37N49'16 80W21'55 5:21:28
Horner 21 1 39N00'02 80W22'58 5:21:32
Horrock 13 1 38N01'34 80W17'41 5:21:11
Horse Creek Junction 3
1 38N09'52 81W51'29 5:27:26
Horseneck 37 1 39N19'17 81W16'51 5:25:07
Horsepen 24 1 37N14 81W31 5:26:04
Horse Shoe Run 39
12 39N16'15 79W30'52 5:18:03
Horton 42 1 38N48'26 79W32'34 5:18:10
Hosterman 38 14 38N28'23 79W51'43 5:19:27
Hotchkiss 41 1 37N40'26 81W22'06 5:25:28
Hotcoal 41 1 37N41'46 81W14'53 5:25:00
Hoult 25 17 39N30'45 80W07'39 5:20:31
Hovatter 47 1 39N14'06 79W45'19 5:19:01
Howard 26 21 39N43'52 80W38'34 5:22:34
Howells Mill 6 1 38N26'30 82W13'11 5:28:53
Howesville 39 19 39N26'21 79W45'22 5:19:01
Hoy 14 1 39N19'04 78W33'08 5:14:13
Hoyt 52 2 39N36'46 80W38'13 5:22:33
Hubball 22 1 38N11'56 82W11'17 5:28:45
Hubbardstown 50 1 38N11'38 82W35'55 5:30:24
Hudson 39 12 39N35'56 79W42'05 5:18:48
Huff Creek 55 1 37N33 81W48 5:27:12
Huff Junction 23
1 37N43'46 81W52'04 5:27:28
Hughart 13 1 37N54'07 80W33'05 5:22:12
Hughes 17 1 39N21 80W19 5:21:16
Hugheston 20 1 38N12'34 81W22'22 5:25:29
Hugo 40 1 38N35'01 81W51'27 5:27:26
Hull 24 1 37N28 81W49 5:27:16
Humphrey 54 1 39N08'33 81W43'54 5:26:56
Hundred 52 7 39N41'01 80W27'33 5:21:50
Hunt 23 1 37N45 81W53 5:27:32
Huntersville 38 1 38N11'19 80W00'59 5:20:04
Hunting Ground 36
1 38N38 79W31 5:18:04
Huntington 6 5 38N25'09 82W26'43 5:29:47
Hur 7 1 38N52'24 81W10'11 5:24:41
Hurricane 40 1 38N26'57 82W01'13 5:28:05
Hurst 21 1 39N04'23 80W41'57 5:22:48
Hutchinson 23 1 37N49'00 81W54'30 5:27:38
Hutchinson 25 17 39N26'26 80W16'27 5:21:06
Huttonsville 42 1 38N42'46 79W58'45 5:19:55
Hyers 4 14 38N51'49 80W41'58 5:22:48
Iaeger 24 1 37N27'52 81W48'50 5:27:15
Idamay 25 17 39N29'49 80W15'26 5:21:02
Ikes Fork 55 1 37N31'19 81W48'16 5:27:13
Imperial 49 1 38N51'45 80W12'16 5:20:49
Imperial Junction 20
1 38N03 81W23 5:25:32
Independence 8 1 38N18'45 81W10'36 5:24:42
Independence 18 1 38N54'25 81W40'31 5:26:42
Independence 39
12 39N23'35 79W52'19 5:19:29
Indian 20 18 38N23 81W49 5:27:16

Indian Meadows 6 1 38N26 82w13 5:28:52
Indian Mills 45 1 37N31'42 80w49'02 5:23:16
Indore 8 1 38N21'10 81w08'49 5:24:35
Industrial 9 24 39N16'41 80w34'54 5:22:20
Industrial 17 24 39N16'12 80w19'13 5:21:17
Industry 7 1 39N00 81w12 5:24:48
Inez 6 1 38N21'26 82w14'20 5:28:57
Ingleside 28 1 37N18'53 81w03'09 5:24:13
Ingo 21 1 38N46'09 80w24'37 5:21:38
Ingram Branch 10 1 38N01'04 81w14'21 5:24:57
Inkerman 16 1 39N08'17 78w46'08 5:15:05
Institute 20 14 38N23'01 81w45'56 5:27:04
Intermont 14 1 39N08'46 78w32'50 5:14:11
Inwood 2 2 39N21'28 78w02'25 5:12:10
Ireland 21 1 38N48'56 80w27'43 5:21:51
Irene 22 1 38N11'33 81w50'51 5:27:23
Irish Corner 13 14 37N43 80w28 5:21:52
Irish Hill 2 27 39N27'31 77w57'27 5:11:50
Irona 39 12 39N26'56 79w42'59 5:18:52
Irontown 46 12 39N22'45 79w54'55 5:19:40
Iroquois 55 1 37N34'52 81w20'27 5:25:22
Isaban 24 1 37N31'48 81w53'18 5:27:33
Island Branch 20 1 38N34'27 81w31'55 5:26:08
Island Creek 23 1 37N47 82w01 5:28:04
Isom 23 1 37N56'37 81w52'14 5:27:29
Israel 39 19 39N24 79w45 5:19:00
Itmann 55 1 37N34'24 81w25'06 5:25:40
Iuka 48 2 39N30'54 80w47'25 5:23:10
Ivanhoe 49 1 38N56 80w14 5:20:56
Ivy 49 1 38N56'24 80w11'05 5:20:44
Ivydale 8 1 38N32'08 81w02'06 5:24:08
Ivydale 20 1 38N18'36 81w42'17 5:26:49
Jacksonburg 52 2 39N31'56 80w38'31 5:22:34
Jackson Flats 24 1 37N19'54 81w52'46 5:27:31
Jackson Mill 21 1 39N05'46 80w28'34 5:21:54
Jacksonville 21 1 38N53'27 80w29'32 5:21:58
Jacobs Fork 24 1 37N13'40 81w35'35 5:26:22
Jacox 38 1 38N05'20 80w18'28 5:21:14
Jakes Run 31 17 39N39'29 80w10'17 5:20:41
Jamestown 19 2 39N14'29 77w59'04 5:11:56
Jamison Mine No 9 25 17 39N31 80w15 5:21:00
Jane Lew 21 1 39N06'35 80w24'25 5:21:38
Janie 3 18 37N58'56 81w32'19 5:26:09
Jarretts Ford 20 1 38N25'53 81w29'10 5:25:57
Jarrods Valley 41 18 37N58'30 81w31'45 5:26:07
Jarvisville 17 1 39N14'00 80w29'15 5:21:57
Jawood 41 1 37N36 81w19 5:25:16
Jayenn 25 17 39N28 80w10 5:20:40
Jed 24 1 37N24'15 81w34'29 5:26:18
Jefferson Village 19 2 39N19'34 77w53'13 5:11:33
Jeffrey 3 1 37N58'17 81w49'18 5:27:17
Jenkinjones 24 1 37N17'37 81w25'34 5:25:42
Jenks 22 1 38N11'55 82w06'11 5:28:25
Jenky 10 1 38N07 81w00 5:24:00
Jenningston 47 1 38N59'17 79w31'51 5:18:07
Jenny Gap 41 1 37N44 81w18 5:25:12
Jere 31 17 39N40'01 80w02'08 5:20:09
Jerome 33 19 39N35'04 78w27'25 5:13:50
Jerrys Run 54 1 39N04'01 81w39'29 5:26:38
Jerryville 51 1 38N25'32 80w18'41 5:21:15
Jesse 55 1 37N40'05 81w34'24 5:26:18
Jessop 39 19 39N25'06 79w45'28 5:19:02
Jetsville 34 14 38N10'08 80w36'04 5:22:24
Jewell 21 1 38N51'47 80w24'05 5:21:36
Jimtown 17 1 39N23'55 80w24'13 5:21:37
Jimtown 33 11 39N38'13 78w13'04 5:12:52
Jimtown 42 1 38N55'06 80w00'04 5:20:00
Job 42 1 38N51'51 79w33'26 5:18:14
Jockeycamp Run 9 1 39N18 80w47 5:23:08
Jodie 10 1 38N13'49 81w08'53 5:24:36
Joe Branch 55 1 37N34'08 81w27'17 5:25:49
Joes Creek 3 1 38N05'36 81w33'26 5:26:14
Joetown 25 17 39N27'47 80w24'28 5:21:38
Johnnycake 24 1 37N28'56 81w49'02 5:27:16
Johns 3 1 38N08'55 81w42'06 5:26:48
Johnson 14 1 39N16'32 78w49'33 5:15:18
Johnson Crossroads 32 1 37N37'03 80w38'03 5:22:32
Johnsons Mill 33 11 39N34'09 78w11'59 5:12:48
Johnsontown 2 2 39N34'42 78w02'23 5:12:10
Johnsontown 19 2 39N20'20 77w53'14 5:11:33
Johnstown 17 1 39N07'24 80w16'46 5:21:07
Johnstown 24 1 37N13'37 81w35'56 5:26:24
Joker 7 1 38N54'21 81w10'11 5:24:41
Jolo 24 1 37N19'45 81w48'54 5:27:16
Jonben 41 1 37N39'22 81w11'32 5:24:46
Jones 1 1 39N03'30 79w59'28 5:19:58
Jones Crossing 18 1 38N53'55 81w37'43 5:26:31
Jones Springs 2 2 39N29'29 78w05'44 5:12:23
Joplin 20 14 38N20'35 81w40'50 5:26:43
Joppa 4 1 38N46'43 80w29'18 5:21:57
Jordan 25 17 39N32'55 80w04'53 5:20:20
Jordan Run 12 1 39N01'50 79w15'16 5:17:01
Josephine 41 1 37N37'12 81w13'26 5:24:54
Josephs Mills 48 2 39N26 80w49 5:23:16
Joy 9 1 39N13'58 80w52'44 5:23:31
Judson 45 1 37N42'39 80w46'35 5:23:06
Judy Gap 36 1 38N45 79w26 5:17:44
Julia 13 1 38N01'28 80w18'15 5:21:13
Julian 3 1 38N09'26 81w51'21 5:27:25
Jumbo 51 1 38N33'45 80w23'17 5:21:33
Jumping Branch 45 1 37N39'27 80w58'36 5:23:54
Junction 14 1 39N18'47 78w51'47 5:15:27
Junior 42 1 38N58'43 79w56'59 5:19:48
Justice 30 1 37N35'19 81w50'08 5:27:21
Justice Addition 23 1 37N53'33 81w59'35 5:27:58
Kabletown 19 23 39N12'59 77w51'26 5:11:26
Kalamazoo 1 1 39N08'29 79w54'58 5:19:40
Kale 28 1 37N23'03 81w11'08 5:24:45
Kanawha 54 1 39N11'56 81w27'37 5:25:50
Kanawha City 20 22 38N19'17 81w34'56 5:26:20
Kanawha Drive 11 1 38N57'13 80w53'59 5:23:36
Kanawha Estates 20 22 38N18'00 81w33'55 5:26:16
Kanawha Falls 10 1 38N08'33 81w12'24 5:24:50
Kanawha Head 49 1 38N46'22 80w20'48 5:21:23
Kanawha Station 54 1 39N12 81w30 5:26:00
Kanes Creek 39 12 39N30'32 79w45'10 5:19:01
Kanetown 39 19 39N21'59 79w45'52 5:19:03
Kasson 1 1 39N13'29 79w52'32 5:19:30
Katy 25 17 39N30'39 80w13'28 5:20:54
Katy Lick 17 24 39N19'03 80w25'25 5:21:42
Kausooth 26 21 39N45'16 80w35'45 5:22:23
Kayford 20 1 38N00'56 81w27'08 5:25:49
Kaymoor 10 1 38N03'00 81w03'18 5:24:13
Kaymoor No 1 10 18 38N02'30 81w04'26 5:24:18
Kearneysville 19 2 39N23'17 77w53'09 5:11:33
Kedron 49 1 38N53'45 80w07'40 5:20:31
Keeler Glade 39 12 39N37'47 79w28'41 5:17:55
Keenan 32 1 37N35'07 80w29'08 5:21:57
Keeneys Creek 10 1 38N02'14 81w01'47 5:24:07
Kegley 28 1 37N23'49 81w07'55 5:24:32
Keister 13 14 37N51'46 80w20'35 5:21:22
Keith 3 1 38N02'34 81w34'26 5:26:18
Kelly 23 1 37N50'55 81w48'22 5:27:13
Kelly Hill 20 1 38N28'59 81w21'49 5:25:27
Kellysville 28 1 37N20'41 80w55'41 5:23:43
Kempton Junction 12 1 39N12'55 79w26'47 5:17:47
Kendalia 20 1 38N20'11 81w18'48 5:25:15
Kenna 18 1 38N40'35 81w39'37 5:26:38
Kennison 38 1 38N06'27 80w11'10 5:20:45
Kenova 50 14 38N23'56 82w34'42 5:30:19
Kent 26 4 39N45'59 80w51'41 5:23:27
Kentuck 18 1 38N39'20 81w35'26 5:26:22
Kentucky 34 1 38N13 80w41 5:22:44
Kera Landing 18 1 38N53 81w51 5:27:24
Kerens 42 1 39N00'45 79w48'50 5:19:15
Kermit 30 1 37N50'37 82w24'34 5:29:38
Keslers Cross Lanes 34 1 38N14'07 80w56'09 5:23:45
Kesling Mill 49 1 39N00'19 80w08'33 5:20:34
Kessel 16 1 39N04'29 79w02'12 5:16:09
Kessler 13 1 37N59'06 80w40'09 5:22:41
Ketterman 36 1 38N52'41 79w15'16 5:17:01
Kettle 44 1 38N34'29 81w29'24 5:25:58
Key 36 1 38N45 79w26 5:17:44
Keyrock 55 1 37N37'49 81w31'04 5:26:04
Keyser 29 6 39N26'27 78w58'27 5:15:54
Keystone 24 1 37N24'53 81w27'04 5:25:48
Keystone 25 17 39N34'05 80w12'14 5:20:49
Kiahsville 50 1 38N05'29 82w19'39 5:29:19
Kidwell 48 2 39N32'03 80w53'29 5:23:34
Kieffer 13 1 37N56'24 80w36'35 5:22:26
Killarm 25 1 39N25'21 80w14'30 5:20:58
Killarney 41 1 37N37'41 81w16'38 5:25:07
Kilsyth 10 1 37N53'25 81w10'57 5:24:44
Kimball 24 1 37N25'32 81w30'25 5:26:02
Kimberly 10 14 38N08'08 81w18'10 5:25:13
Kimberly 31 17 39N41'37 80w17'23 5:21:10
Kincaid 10 1 38N02'26 81w16'13 5:25:05
Kincheloe 17 1 39N08'59 80w30'11 5:22:01
Kinder 22 1 38N10 82w11 5:28:44
King 52 2 39N30'04 80w40'54 5:22:44
Kingmont 25 17 39N26'49 80w10'34 5:20:42
Kingston 10 1 37N58'25 81w18'17 5:25:13
Kingstown 52 2 39N34'46 80w35'32 5:22:22
Kingsville 42 1 38N56'01 80w02'04 5:20:08
Kingwood 39 12 39N28'18 79w41'01 5:18:44
Kirby 14 1 39N10'58 78w43'35 5:14:54
Kirbyton 3 1 38N05'55 81w36'48 5:26:27
Kirk 30 1 37N53'39 82w14'36 5:28:58
Kirkwood 34 1 38N21'02 80w48'07 5:23:12
Kirt 1 1 39N06'58 79w52'28 5:19:30
Kistler 23 1 37N45'22 81w51'37 5:27:26
Kitchen 23 1 37N58'53 82w02'04 5:28:08
Kitsonville 21 1 39N01'57 80w28'26 5:21:54
Kline 36 1 38N46'44 79w13'32 5:16:54
Kline Gap 12 1 39N04'20 79w11'34 5:16:46
Klondike 31 17 39N38'04 80w17'15 5:21:09
KM Junction 10 1 38N09'44 81w11'39 5:24:47
Knapp 38 1 38N14'02 80w03'04 5:20:12
Knawl 4 1 38N49'36 80w31'46 5:22:07
Knob Fork 52 2 39N38'55 80w32'49 5:22:11
Knobs 32 1 37N36'41 80w35'18 5:22:21
Knollwood 20 22 38N22 81w38 5:26:32
Knottsville 46 12 39N18'40 79w57'55 5:19:52
Knoxville 26 21 39N53'15 80w38'01 5:22:32
Kodol 52 2 39N37'22 80w32'27 5:22:10
Kohlsaat 3 1 37N56'30 81w42'17 5:26:49
Kopperston 55 1 37N44'54 81w34'11 5:26:17
Kovan 51 1 38N32'22 80w22'40 5:21:31
Krollitz 24 1 37N28'18 81w51'38 5:27:27
Kyle 6 5 38N24 82w29 5:29:56
Kyle 24 1 37N24'29 81w25'33 5:25:42
Lacoma 55 1 37N44'36 81w40'47 5:26:43
Lafayette 37 1 39N22 81w03 5:24:12
LaFrank 34 14 38N13'07 80w33'33 5:22:14
Lahmansville 12 1 39N07'41 79w04'54 5:16:20
Laing 20 1 38N02'11 81w25'42 5:25:43
Lake 23 1 37N55'47 81w54'02 5:27:36
Lake Floyd 17 1 39N17'10 80w30'27 5:22:02
Lake Ridge 17 1 39N16'47 80w12'52 5:20:51
Lake Ron 54 1 39N16 81w40 5:26:40
Lake Washington 40 1 38N26 82w01 5:28:04
Lakin 27 1 38N57'31 82w05'14 5:28:21
Lamar 28 1 37N27'14 81w18'18 5:25:13
Lamberton 43 1 39N16'15 81w02'49 5:24:11
Lanark 41 18 37N49'39 81w08'47 5:24:35
Landes 12 1 38N53'48 79w11'53 5:16:48
Landgraff 24 1 37N24'42 81w28'26 5:25:54
Landisburg 10 1 37N58'37 80w56'25 5:23:46
Lando Mines 30 1 37N42'18 82w08'47 5:28:35
Landville 23 1 37N42'44 81w52'03 5:27:28
Laneville 47 1 38N58'26 79w25'03 5:17:40
Lanham 40 1 38N28'37 81w44'20 5:26:57
Lansing 10 18 38N04'24 81w03'57 5:24:16
Lanta 3 1 37N59'32 81w44'13 5:26:57
Lantz 1 1 38N56 80w06 5:20:24
Largent 14 11 39N28'40 78w22'57 5:13:32
Larkmead 54 14 39N14'54 81w35'32 5:26:22
Lashmeet 28 1 37N25'15 81w11'58 5:24:48
Latonia 11 1 38N56'01 80w59'00 5:23:56
Latrobe 23 1 37N47'26 81w46'08 5:27:05
Lattimer 44 1 38N50'31 81w30'54 5:26:04
Lauchport 54 14 39N15'12 81w34'14 5:26:17
Lauckport 54 14 39N17 81w32 5:26:08
Laura Lee Mine 17 1 39N21'46 80w21'45 5:21:27
Laurel Branch 32 1 37N31'50 80w21'00 5:21:24
Laurel Court 4 1 38N40 80w43 5:22:52
Laurel Creek 10 1 37N51'26 80w59'38 5:23:59
Laurel Dale 29 2 39N18'30 79w05'32 5:16:22
Laurel Fork 4 1 38N41'21 80w40'30 5:22:42
Laurel Hill 22 1 38N08 82w12 5:28:48
Laurel Iron Works 31 28 39N39 79w58 5:19:52
Laurel Point 31 28 39N37'09 80w00'30 5:20:02
Laurel Run 39 12 39N39'04 79w43'22 5:18:53
Lavalette 50 14 38N19'22 82w26'49 5:29:47
Lavern 28 1 37N25'54 80w52'28 5:23:30
Lawford 43 1 39N04'07 80w56'11 5:23:45
Lawn 13 1 37N50'23 80w45'11 5:23:01
Lawrenceville 15 9 40N37'03 80w32'38 5:22:11
Lawton 10 1 37N52 80w59 5:23:56
Layland 10 1 37N53'21 80w58'17 5:23:53
Layland Heights 10 1 37N54'26 80w57'36 5:23:50
Layopolis 11 1 38N55 80w45 5:23:00
Layville 3 1 38N07'36 81w56'03 5:27:44
Leachtown 54 1 39N08'31 81w26'36 5:25:46
Lead Mine 47 1 39N11'40 79w35'06 5:18:20
Leadsville 42 35 38N56'36 79w51'18 5:19:25
League 43 1 39N17'32 81w05'55 5:24:24
Leander 10 1 38N11'28 81w00'30 5:24:02
Leatherbark 7 1 38N47'18 81w11'49 5:24:47
Leatherwood 30 1 37N37'25 81w48'39 5:27:15
Leckie 24 1 37N20'42 81w25'05 5:25:40
Lee 10 1 37N52'58 81w09'23 5:24:38
Lee Bell 42 1 38N40'58 80w00'21 5:20:01
Lee Creek 54 1 39N09'11 81w44'23 5:26:58
Leet 22 1 38N04'07 82w04'34 5:28:18
Leetown 19 2 39N20'54 77w56'02 5:11:44
Leevale 41 18 37N57'58 81w31'31 5:26:06
Leewood 20 1 38N04'03 81w27'00 5:25:48
Left Hand 44 1 38N37 81w15 5:25:00
Lego 41 1 37N38'02 81w14'20 5:24:57
Lehew 14 1 39N11'57 78w26'18 5:13:45
Leivasy 34 1 38N09'40 80w41'28 5:22:46
Lennyville 15 9 40N36'05 80w37'52 5:22:31
Lenore 30 1 37N47'56 82w17'13 5:29:09
Lenox 39 12 39N34'00 79w35'26 5:18:22
Leon 27 1 38N45'02 81w57'39 5:27:51
Leonard 13 1 38N04'58 80w24'13 5:21:37
Leopold 9 1 39N07'31 80w44'27 5:22:58
Lerona 28 1 37N29'58 80w58'45 5:23:55
LeRoy 18 1 38N54'21 81w32'43 5:26:11
Lesage 6 1 38N30'23 82w17'55 5:29:12
Leslie 13 1 38N02'40 80w43'23 5:22:54
Lesmalinston 46 12 39N20'20 79w58'12 5:19:53
Lester 41 1 37N44'05 81w17'59 5:25:12
Letart 27 1 38N53'41 81w56'01 5:27:44
Letch 4 1 38N48'03 80w29'48 5:21:59
Letherbark 7 1 38N47 81w08 5:24:32
Letter Gap 11 1 38N53 80w55 5:23:40
Levels 14 1 39N29'04 78w33'14 5:14:13
Lewis 27 1 38N51 82w05 5:28:20
Lewisburg 13 14 37N48'06 80w26'45 5:21:47
Lex 24 1 37N22'13 81w48'02 5:27:12
Liberty 17 24 39N17'20 80w22'45 5:21:31
Liberty 40 1 38N36'18 81w43'48 5:26:55
Liberty Hill 7 1 38N47'25 81w10'06 5:24:40
Lick Creek 45 1 37N29'04 80w54'42 5:23:39
Lick Fork 10 18 38N03 81w06 5:24:24
Licking 47 1 39N13 79w44 5:18:56
Lico 20 22 38N14'29 81w44'21 5:26:57
Lightburn 21 1 39N07'33 80w27'05 5:21:48
Lila 24 1 37N19'18 81w26'28 5:25:46
Lile 13 1 38N07'37 80w37'12 5:22:29
Lillybrook 41 1 37N38'41 81w13'14 5:24:53
Lillydale 32 1 37N33'24 80w36'38 5:22:27
Lillydale 55 1 37N40'34 81w39'48 5:26:39
Lilly Grove 28 1 37N22'18 81w04'15 5:24:17
Lillyhaven 55 1 37N41'13 81w39'33 5:26:38
Lilly Park 13 1 37N57'01 80w47'55 5:23:12
Lima 48 2 39N26 80w45 5:23:00
Limestone 26 21 39N56'09 80w38'45 5:22:35
Limestone 29 6 39N25'39 78w57'32 5:15:50
Limestone Hill 53 1 39N04 81w24 5:25:36
Lincoln 55 1 37N35'10 81w44'45 5:26:59
Linden 44 1 38N43'11 81w12'40 5:24:51
Lindsey 30 1 37N32'21 82w01'46 5:28:07
Lindside 32 1 37N27'13 80w40'12 5:22:41
Lindytown 3 1 37N54'35 81w36'09 5:26:25
Lineburg 33 11 39N38'17 78w20'49 5:13:23
Link 48 2 39N29'04 80w44'51 5:22:59
Linn 11 1 39N00'29 80w43'09 5:22:53
Lintz Addition 23 1 37N50'54 82w01'19 5:28:05
Linwood 38 1 38N25'15 80w02'39 5:20:11
Little 48 2 39N28'29 80w59'50 5:23:59
Little Birch 4 1 38N34'44 80w42'25 5:22:50
Little Cacapon 14 1 39N30'56 78w29'40 5:13:59
Little Falls 31 17 39N33'24 80w00'00 5:20:00
Little Georgetown 2 2 39N35'06 77w57'05 5:11:48
Little Italy 8 1 38N31'21 81w02'01 5:24:08
Little Italy 42 1 38N47'39 79w32'58 5:18:12

Little Laurel Creek 34
14 38N14 80w32 5:22:08
Little Levels 38
1 38N08 80w14 5:20:56
Little Otter 4 1 38N41'10 80w45'50 5:23:03
Little Pittsburg 48
2 39N23'45 80w44'38 5:22:59
Littlesburg 28 20 37N19'24 81w12'55 5:24:52
Littleton 52 2 39N41'52 80w31'02 5:22:04
Litwar 24 1 37N28'53 81w50'19 5:27:21
Lively 10 1 37N56'25 81w15'27 5:25:02
Liverpool 44 1 38N53'41 81w31'51 5:26:07
Livingston 20 1 38N09'27 81w24'25 5:25:38
Lizemores 8 1 38N20'02 81w10'31 5:24:42
Lloydsville 4 1 38N44'22 80w42'13 5:22:49
Lobata 30 1 37N38'55 82w11'21 5:28:45
Lobelia 38 1 38N08'01 80w17'41 5:21:11
Lochgelly 10 18 38N00'38 81w08'43 5:24:35
Lockbridge 45 1 37N49'39 80w50'43 5:23:23
Locke 48 2 39N27'17 80w55'20 5:23:41
Lockhart 18 1 38N57'54 81w36'55 5:26:28
Lockney 11 1 38N51'22 80w58'02 5:23:52
Lockwood 34 1 38N15'34 81w02'06 5:24:08
Locust 38 1 38N04'03 80w14'20 5:20:57
Loda 42 1 38N48'04 80w04'56 5:20:20
Lodgeville 17 1 39N17'15 80w17'02 5:21:08
Logan 23 1 37N50'55 81w59'37 5:27:58
Logan Heights 23
1 37N50'13 82w01'34 5:28:06
Logansport 25 17 39N31'09 80w24'50 5:21:39
Lomax 24 1 37N19'07 81w42'29 5:26:50
London 20 1 38N11'40 81w22'08 5:25:29
Lone Cedar 18 1 39N05'05 81w45'10 5:27:01
Lone Oak 26 21 39N54'01 80w36'04 5:22:24
Lonetree 48 2 39N31'42 80w49'06 5:23:16
Longacre 10 14 38N10'03 81w18'13 5:25:13
Long Branch 10 1 37N55'22 81w16'33 5:25:06
Long Branch 55 1 37N37'04 81w45'52 5:27:03
Longdale 27 1 38N55'34 81w54'47 5:27:39
Longpole 24 1 37N30'45 81w51'49 5:27:27
Long Reach 48 2 39N29'03 81w05'34 5:24:22
Long Run 9 1 39N16'13 80w39'10 5:22:37
Long Run 17 1 39N25'41 80w17'50 5:21:11
Longview 1 1 39N05'02 80w08'21 5:20:33
Lookout 10 1 38N03'55 80w58'07 5:23:52
Loom 14 1 39N18 78w38 5:14:32
Loom Cemetery 14
1 39N16'43 78w30'42 5:14:03
Looneyville 44 1 38N39'52 81w18'12 5:25:13
Loop 18 1 38N34'24 81w38'09 5:26:33
Loopemount 13 14 37N50'36 80w21'00 5:21:24
Lorado 23 1 37N47'44 81w42'54 5:26:52
Lorentz 49 1 39N00'39 80w18'09 5:21:13
Lorton Lick 28 20 37N19'47 81w14'34 5:24:58
Lory 3 18 38N05 81w50 5:27:20
Lost City 16 1 38N55'47 78w50'04 5:15:20
Lost Creek 17 1 39N09'40 80w21'08 5:21:25
Lost River 16 1 38N55 78w51 5:15:24
Loudendale 20 22 38N18'14 81w39'11 5:26:37
Loudenville 26 21 39N50'07 80w35'59 5:22:24
Loudon 20 22 38N18 81w40 5:26:40
Loudon Heights 20
22 38N19'48 81w37'50 5:26:31
Louise 5 33 40N18'14 80w33'56 5:22:16
Louther 18 1 38N47'48 81w32'59 5:26:12
Lovada 7 1 38N57'47 81w04'24 5:24:18
Loveridge 13 1 38N04'58 80w22'26 5:21:30
Lovern 28 1 37N26'03 80w52'32 5:23:30
Lowdell 54 1 39N03'35 81w36'41 5:26:27
Lowell 45 1 37N39'16 80w43'45 5:22:55
Lower Belle 20 14 38N15'10 81w33'52 5:26:15
Lower Falls 20 18 38N23 81w49 5:27:16
Low Gap 3 18 38N01'53 81w50'09 5:27:21
Low Gap 43 1 39N12'40 81w07'59 5:24:32
Lowney 30 1 37N56'13 82w16'31 5:29:06
Lowsville 31 17 39N33'46 80w03'12 5:20:13
Lubeck 54 1 39N14'07 81w37'53 5:26:32
Lucas 10 1 38N11'31 81w02'22 5:24:09
Lucerne 11 1 38N59'55 80w52'49 5:23:31
Lucile 53 1 38N56'43 81w23'10 5:25:33
Lucretia 46 14 39N19'46 80w00'05 5:20:00
Lumberport 17 1 39N22'26 80w20'55 5:21:24
Lundale 23 1 37N48'04 81w44'40 5:26:59
Lyburn 23 1 37N48'07 81w55'53 5:27:44
Lydia 8 1 38N39'16 81w02'04 5:24:08
Lynco 55 1 37N41'53 81w40'38 5:26:43
Lynn 30 1 37N36'09 82w09'19 5:28:37
Lynn Camp 26 4 39N46'12 80w42'27 5:22:50
Lynwinn 41 1 37N40'51 81w13'39 5:24:55
Lyon 39 12 39N25 79w51 5:19:24
Lyonsville 34 1 38N15'33 81w03'28 5:24:14
Maben 55 1 37N38'19 81w23'39 5:25:35
Mabie 42 1 38N52'35 79w59'00 5:19:56
Mabscott 41 18 37N46'15 81w12'31 5:24:50
MacArthur 41 18 37N45'30 81w12'46 5:24:51
MacCorkle 22 1 38N15 81w53 5:27:32
Macdale 31 17 39N43'09 80w14'00 5:20:56
MacDonald 10 1 38N07'02 81w07'17 5:24:29
MacDunn 10 14 38N05 81w19 5:25:16
Mace 38 1 38N27'22 80w01'51 5:20:07
Macfarlan 43 1 39N04'40 81w11'56 5:24:48
Macksville 36 1 38N48'02 79w23'59 5:17:36
Macomber 39 12 39N19'08 79w41'22 5:18:45
Madam Creek 45 14 37N40 80w53 5:23:32
Madeline 41 1 37N34'49 81w18'16 5:25:13
Madison 3 18 38N04'01 81w49'10 5:27:17
Madison Run 39 12 39N19 79w33 5:18:12
Maggie 27 1 38N56'44 82w05'19 5:28:21
Magnolia 33 19 39N33'42 78w25'38 5:13:43
Magnolia 49 1 38N53 80w18 5:21:12
Mahan 10 1 38N01'22 81w21'19 5:25:25
Maher 30 1 37N46'09 82w19'39 5:29:19
Mahone 43 1 39N06'33 81w04'29 5:24:18
Maidsville 31 28 39N41'18 79w58'49 5:19:55
Maitland 24 1 37N25'43 81w33'06 5:26:12
Majorsville 26 4 39N57'56 80w31'12 5:22:05
Maken 17 1 39N17'06 80w29'04 5:21:56
Malcom Spring Heights 6
1 38N26 82w08 5:28:32
Malden 20 14 38N18'02 81w33'26 5:26:14
Mallory 23 1 37N43'50 81w50'17 5:27:21
Mammoth 20 1 38N15'48 81w22'20 5:25:29
Man 23 1 37N44'23 81w52'40 5:27:31

Mand 52 2 39N37'10 80w44'31 5:22:58
Mandeville 45 1 37N29'44 80w49'22 5:23:17
M and K Junction 39
12 39N21 79w41 5:18:44
Manheim 39 12 39N21'37 79w41'28 5:18:46
Manila 3 1 37N59'12 81w56'35 5:27:46
Manleys Church 25
17 39N28 80w10 5:20:40
Mannings 19 3 39N14'43 77w46'52 5:11:07
Mannington 25 26 39N31'51 80w20'37 5:21:22
Manown 39 12 39N29'34 79w44'43 5:18:59
Mansfield 1 1 39N09'00 80w03'14 5:20:13
Manus 23 1 37N51 82w03 5:28:12
Maple 31 17 39N42'33 80w21'31 5:21:26
Maple Acre 28 20 37N19'27 81w08'19 5:24:33
Mapledale 13 14 37N50'06 80w15'29 5:21:02
Maple Fork 41 1 37N52'16 81w13'51 5:24:55
Maple Lake 17 1 39N17'43 80w12'26 5:20:50
Maple Meadow 41 1 37N44'28 81w20'41 5:25:23
Maple Point 25 17 39N30 80w10 5:20:40
Maple View 28 20 37N17'54 81w09'44 5:24:39
Maplewood 10 1 37N55'35 80w56'00 5:23:44
Marcus 51 1 38N25 80w33 5:22:12
Marfork 41 18 37N56'39 81w30'40 5:26:03
Marfrance 13 1 38N03'20 80w41'29 5:22:46
Margaret 17 1 39N27'30 80w26'37 5:21:46
Marianna 55 1 37N36'01 81w36'41 5:26:27
Marie 45 1 37N35'01 80w45'42 5:23:03
Marie Heights 54
14 39N17 81w32 5:26:08
Marine 24 1 37N27'46 81w37'51 5:26:31
Marion 52 12 39N40'32 80w46'18 5:23:05
Market 9 1 39N12'18 80w42'12 5:22:49
Markwood 29 2 39N20 78w55 5:15:40
Marlaing Addition 20
18 38N23 81w49 5:27:16
Marland Heights 15
32 40N23'54 80w36'20 5:22:25
Marlinton 38 1 38N13'24 80w05'41 5:20:23
Marlowe 2 2 39N35'18 77w51'35 5:11:26
Marmet 20 14 38N14'43 81w34'02 5:26:16
Marne 8 1 38N28'22 81w11'51 5:24:47
Marnie 3 1 37N57'19 81w39'24 5:26:38
Marpleton 4 1 38N40'39 80w30'14 5:22:01
Marquess 39 19 39N17'54 79w51'04 5:19:24
Marrtown 54 14 39N15'32 81w34'56 5:26:20
Marshall 18 1 38N49'29 81w32'10 5:26:09
Marshall Terrace 5
33 40N15'26 80w36'13 5:22:25
Marshall University 6
5 38N25 82w25 5:29:40
Marsh Fork 41 1 37N52 81w28 5:25:52
Marshville 17 1 39N19'17 80w27'52 5:21:51
Martha 6 1 38N22'36 82w17'13 5:29:09
Marthatown 3 1 37N56'04 81w41'52 5:26:47
Martin 12 1 39N13'27 79w05'21 5:16:21
Marting 10 1 38N12'07 81w15'11 5:25:01
Martinsburg 2 27 39N27'22 77w57'51 5:11:51
Marvel 10 1 38N10'26 81w04'33 5:24:18
Marybill 34 1 38N16'07 80w40'57 5:22:44
Maryland Junction 29
2 39N37'57 78w47'05 5:15:08
Marytown 24 1 37N28'11 81w40'47 5:26:43
Mason 27 1 39N01'18 82w01'45 5:28:07
Masontown 39 12 39N33'08 79w47'53 5:19:12
Masonville 12 1 38N55'07 79w05'02 5:16:20
Masseyville 41 1 37N50'17 81w27'06 5:25:48
Matewan 30 1 37N37'19 82w09'48 5:28:39
Matheny 54 1 39N16 81w40 5:26:40
Matheny 55 1 37N39'53 81w36'02 5:26:24
Mathias 16 1 38N52'40 78w51'59 5:15:28
Matoaka 28 1 37N25'12 81w14'36 5:24:58
Maud 52 12 39N39 80w51 5:23:24
Mavis 4 1 38N38 80w52 5:23:28
Maxine 3 1 38N07'57 81w37'20 5:26:29
Maxwell 37 1 39N20'37 81w07'33 5:24:30
Maxwell Acres 26
21 39N51 80w36 5:22:24
Maxwelton 13 1 37N51'58 80w24'36 5:21:38
May 38 14 38N39'12 79w48'09 5:19:13
Maybeury 24 1 37N22'15 81w22'00 5:25:28
Maynor 41 18 37N51'57 81w16'05 5:25:04
Maysel 8 1 38N29'09 81w06'46 5:24:27
Maysville 12 1 39N06'54 79w09'54 5:16:40
Maywood 10 1 37N58'18 80w48'55 5:23:16
McAlpin 17 1 39N20'37 80w14'14 5:20:57
McAlpin 41 1 37N41'30 81w16'41 5:25:07
McCauley 16 1 39N02'32 78w42'44 5:14:51
McClain 18 1 38N59'41 81w32'12 5:26:09
McClellan 25 17 39N33'13 80w17'07 5:21:08
McCloud 30 1 37N52 82w10 5:28:40
McComas 6 1 38N20 82w15 5:29:00
McComas 28 1 37N23'24 81w17'30 5:25:10
McConnell 23 1 37N49'32 81w58'01 5:27:52
McCorkle 22 1 38N12'57 81w50'10 5:27:21
McCreery 41 1 37N50'56 81w05'33 5:24:22
McCuetown 49 1 38N56'59 80w19'55 5:21:20
Mccurdyville 31
17 39N36'44 80w10'22 5:20:41
McDowell 24 1 37N24'10 81w22'50 5:25:31
McDunn 10 1 38N03'25 81w18'33 5:25:14
McElroy 48 2 39N26 80w45 5:23:00
McGee 46 14 39N21'39 80w07'40 5:20:31
McGlone 32 1 37N31'15 80w29'30 5:21:58
McGraws 55 1 37N40'15 81w27'48 5:25:51
McGuire Park 21 1 39N01'24 80w24'58 5:21:40
McIntire 17 14 39N20 80w20 5:21:20
McKeefrey 26 21 39N53'36 80w47'23 5:23:10
McKendree 10 1 37N53'16 81w03'49 5:24:15
McKim 48 1 39N22'48 80w57'39 5:23:51
McKinleyville 5
33 40N14'37 80w35'47 5:22:23
McMechen 26 15 39N59'17 80w43'54 5:22:56
McNeill 16 1 39N08'24 78w54'49 5:15:39
McNutt 4 1 38N41'42 80w40'10 5:22:41
McRoss 13 1 37N59'19 80w44'55 5:23:00
McVey 41 1 37N42'46 81w12'19 5:24:49
McWhorter 17 1 39N07'38 80w22'59 5:21:32
Mead 41 1 37N37'28 81w15'39 5:25:03
Meadland 46 1 39N19'18 80w09'30 5:20:38
Meador 30 1 37N37'08 82w03'45 5:28:15
Meadow Bluff 13 1 37N54'13 80w39'06 5:22:36

Meadow Bridge 10
1 37N51'32 80w51'16 5:23:25
Meadowbrook 17 1 39N21'06 80w19'08 5:21:17
Meadowbrook 20 22 38N22'52 81w33'43 5:26:15
Meadowbrook 27 1 38N52'20 82w07'01 5:28:28
Meadow Creek 45 1 37N48'36 80w55'24 5:23:42
Meadowdale 18 1 38N53'51 81w36'02 5:26:24
Meadowdale 25 17 39N29'44 80w05'36 5:20:22
Meadow Fork 10 1 37N55'59 81w06'16 5:24:25
Meadowville 1 1 39N07'05 79w54'35 5:19:38
Meadville 48 2 39N24'31 81w00'11 5:24:01
Mechanicsburg 14
1 39N20'07 78w48'38 5:15:15
Mechanicstown 19
23 39N15'38 77w49'47 5:11:19
Mechlenberg Heights 19
30 39N26'00 77w49'48 5:11:19
Medina 18 1 38N59'56 81w37'43 5:26:31
Medley 12 1 39N10'34 79w03'29 5:16:14
Medo 10 1 38N03'19 80w55'38 5:23:43
Meeker 48 2 39N27'58 80w47'17 5:23:09
Meighen 26 4 39N47'04 80w43'09 5:22:53
Meldah 54 1 39N13'35 81w41'15 5:26:45
Melissa 6 1 38N22'48 82w20'05 5:29:20
Mellin 43 1 39N07'21 81w10'16 5:24:41
Mellville 23 1 37N50'29 81w56'42 5:27:47
Melrose 28 1 37N23'12 81w03'16 5:24:13
Melrose 54 1 39N16 81w40 5:26:40
Melville 23 1 37N51 81w58 5:27:52
Mercers Bottom 27
1 38N38'41 82w09'45 5:28:39
Meredith Springs 25
17 39N28 80w10 5:20:40
Meriden 1 1 39N09'51 80w01'26 5:20:06
Merrimac 30 1 37N38'07 82w12'58 5:28:52
Metalton 41 1 37N46'00 81w17'23 5:25:10
Metz 25 17 39N34'49 80w22'12 5:21:29
Meyerstown 19 23 39N12'21 77w51'49 5:11:27
Miami 20 1 38N09'08 81w26'53 5:25:48
Micajah 28 1 37N27'59 81w19'34 5:25:18
Micco 23 1 37N46'58 81w59'25 5:27:58
Middlebourne 48 2 39N29'32 80w54'14 5:23:37
Middle Fork 1 1 39N03'43 80w02'49 5:20:11
Middle Fork 20 1 38N21'30 81w19'22 5:25:17
Middle Grave Creek 26
21 39N51 80w36 5:22:24
Middle Point 9 1 39N12'21 80w44'49 5:22:59
Middle Run 4 1 38N35'38 80w48'36 5:23:14
Middletown 34 14 38N14 80w32 5:22:08
Middleway 19 2 39N18'12 77w58'59 5:11:56
Midkiff 22 1 38N10'34 82w10'44 5:28:43
Midland 42 35 38N53'08 79w50'53 5:19:24
Midvale 49 1 38N56'14 80w05'24 5:20:22
Midway 1 1 39N01 79w56 5:19:44
Midway 10 1 38N00'10 81w08'54 5:24:36
Midway 28 20 37N15'57 81w15'34 5:25:02
Midway 40 1 38N33'36 81w57'52 5:27:51
Midway 41 1 37N43'10 81w14'14 5:24:57
Mifflin 23 1 37N56'28 81w49'20 5:27:17
Milam 16 1 38N48'50 79w05'58 5:16:24
Milam 55 1 37N40'53 81w28'23 5:25:54
Milburn 10 1 37N59'54 81w20'20 5:25:21
Mile Branch 24 1 37N25 81w47 5:27:08
Miles 36 1 38N45'21 79w07'38 5:16:31
Miletus 9 1 39N13'50 80w35'20 5:22:21
Millard 44 1 38N48 81w21 5:25:24
Millbrook 14 1 39N12'59 78w32'51 5:14:11
Mill Creek 42 1 38N43'53 79w58'13 5:19:53
Mill Creek Road 13
1 37N59 80w43 5:22:52
Millen 14 1 39N31'06 78w37'49 5:14:31
Millersport 6 1 38N32'09 82w17'30 5:29:10
Millersville 25
17 39N27'40 80w08'54 5:20:36
Millertown 46 14 39N17'59 79w57'33 5:19:50
Millesons Mill 14
1 39N26'25 78w40'28 5:14:42
Milliken 20 14 38N24'06 81w32'46 5:26:11
Mill Point 38 1 38N09'29 80w10'52 5:20:43
Mill Run 36 1 38N48 79w16 5:17:04
Millsboro 26 21 39N43'56 80w40'00 5:22:40
Millstone 7 1 38N48'05 81w05'47 5:24:23
Millstone 30 1 37N42 82w11 5:28:44
Milltown 3 1 38N02'41 81w37'03 5:26:28
Millville 19 2 39N17'38 77w47'10 5:11:09
Millwood 18 1 38N52'55 81w51'43 5:27:27
Milo 7 1 38N43'20 81w08'38 5:24:35
Milroy 4 1 38N43'37 80w30'03 5:22:00
Milroy 12 1 38N58 79w10 5:16:40
Milton 6 1 38N26'04 82w07'57 5:28:32
Minden 10 1 37N58'33 81w07'11 5:24:29
Mineral City 23 1 37N44'01 81w49'26 5:27:18
Mineral Springs 50
1 38N07'23 82w34'57 5:30:20
Mineralwells 54 1 39N11'25 81w31'56 5:26:08
Minerva 22 1 38N09'45 82w14'15 5:28:57
Mingo 42 1 38N29'55 80w03'16 5:20:13
Mink Shoals 20 22 38N22 81w38 5:26:32
Minnehaha Springs 38
1 38N09'47 79w58'52 5:19:55
Minnie 52 12 39N35'23 80w48'37 5:23:14
Minnora 7 1 38N42'34 81w05'54 5:24:24
Miracle Run 31 17 39N40'38 80w16'05 5:21:04
Missouri Branch 50
1 37N59'54 82w24'23 5:29:38
Mitchell 36 1 38N32'32 79w20'30 5:17:22
Mitchell Branch 30
1 37N39 82w08 5:28:32
Mitchell Heights 23
1 37N54'26 81w59'00 5:27:56
Moats 1 1 39N12'37 79w56'00 5:19:44
Moatstown 36 1 38N32'17 79w23'42 5:17:35
Moatsville 1 1 39N13 79w56 5:19:44
Mobley 52 2 39N33'25 80w32'56 5:22:12
Modoc 13 1 38N01'27 80w20'43 5:21:23
Mohegan 24 1 37N27'11 81w37'51 5:26:31
Mohrtown 27 1 38N44'15 82w07'33 5:28:30
Moler Crossroads 19
3 39N23'45 77w45'55 5:11:04
Molers 19 30 39N26 77w48 5:11:12
Monarch 20 1 38N12'54 81w27'26 5:25:50
Monaville 23 1 37N48'43 81w59'42 5:27:59
Monclo 23 1 37N54'30 81w50'19 5:27:21

Monitor 23 1 37N49'58 82w00'06 5:28:00
Monitor 32 1 37N39'21 80w29'26 5:21:58
Monkeytown 36 1 38N45 79w26 5:17:44
Monongah 25 17 39N27'45 80w13'06 5:20:52
Monson 24 1 37N15'54 81w28'59 5:25:56
Montana (Montana Mines P O) 25
17 39N31'24 80w06'35 5:20:26
Montana Mines 25
17 39N32 80w07 5:20:28
Montcalm 28 1 37N21'14 81w15'10 5:25:01
Montcoal 41 18 37N54'50 81w32'09 5:26:09
Montecarlo 55 1 37N30'58 81w21'43 5:25:27
Monterville 42 1 38N33'32 80w06'19 5:20:25
Montgomery 20 17 38N10'49 81w19'43 5:25:19
Montgomery Heights 10
1 38N07'47 81w16'22 5:25:05
Montpelier 17 24 39N16'51 80w19'31 5:21:18
Montrose 42 1 39N04'06 79w48'38 5:19:15
Moore 44 1 38N52'57 81w24'28 5:25:38
Moore 47 1 39N05'03 79w43'05 5:18:52
Moorefield 16 1 39N03'44 78w58'11 5:15:53
Mooresville 31 17 39N41'24 80w08'54 5:20:36
Morgan 18 1 39N01'34 81w45'48 5:27:03
Morgan 31 28 39N37 79w55 5:19:40
Morgan Grove 19
30 39N25'23 77w49'14 5:11:17
Morgan Heights 31
28 39N38'03 79w59'06 5:19:56
Morgansville 9 1 39N16'53 80w41'48 5:22:47
Morgantown 31 28 39N37'46 79w57'22 5:19:49
Morning Star 44 1 38N48 81w21 5:25:24
Morrall Mine 1 1 39N09 80w03 5:20:12
Morris 34 1 38N30'21 80w48'10 5:23:13
Morristown 53 1 39N02'49 81w29'34 5:25:58
Morrisvale 3 1 38N08'09 81w54'45 5:27:39
Moscow 15 9 40N32'44 80w37'57 5:22:32
Moss 11 1 38N52'15 80w48'18 5:23:13
Mossy 10 1 37N58'34 81w16'55 5:25:08
Mound 20 14 38N23 81w45 5:27:00
Moundsville 26 4 39N55'13 80w44'36 5:22:58
Mountain 43 1 39N21'43 80w54'38 5:23:39
Mountain Cove 10
1 38N07'43 81w02'59 5:24:12
Mountaindale 39
12 39N40 79w38 5:18:32
Mountain Mission 19
3 39N14'45 77w47'38 5:11:11
Mountain View 39
19 39N24 79w45 5:19:00
Mount Alto 18 1 38N51'52 81w52'42 5:27:31
Mount Carbon 10
14 38N08'16 81w17'09 5:25:09
Mount Clare 17 14 39N13 80w21 5:21:24
Mount de Chantal 35
34 40N04'12 80w41'19 5:22:45
Mount Echo 26 6 40N06'08 80w31'47 5:22:07
Mount Gay 23 1 37N50'29 82w00'32 5:28:02
Mount Harmony 25
17 39N30'35 80w04'41 5:20:19
Mount Home 8 1 38N32 81w02 5:24:08
Mount Hope 3 1 38N06'18 81w31'06 5:26:04
Mount Hope 10 18 37N53'43 81w09'52 5:24:39
Mount Hope 44 1 38N36'46 81w26'44 5:25:47
Mount Liberty 1 1 39N04'45 80w01'19 5:20:05
Mount Lookout 34
1 38N10'00 80w54'43 5:23:39
Mount Moriah 18 1 38N47'11 81w45'57 5:27:04
Mount Nebo 34 1 38N12'00 80w51'05 5:23:24
Mount Olive 10 1 38N14'16 81w14'01 5:24:56
Mount Olive 27 1 38N31'28 82w04'07 5:28:16
Mount Olive 28 1 37N24'43 81w11'41 5:24:47
Mount Olive 44 1 38N48 81w21 5:25:24
Mount Olivet 26
34 40N01'09 80w41'43 5:22:47
Mount Olivet 39
12 39N20'19 79w37'14 5:18:29
Mount Pisgah 12 2 39N17'23 79w10'18 5:16:41
Mount Pleasant 19
2 39N15'31 77w56'55 5:11:48
Mount Storm 12 1 39N16'38 79w14'28 5:16:58
Mount Tabor 17 1 39N25'00 80w25'54 5:21:44
Mount Tabor 41 18 37N47'54 81w13'58 5:24:56
Mount Tabor Church 20
18 38N21'03 81w48'49 5:27:15
Mount Tell 18 1 38N37'27 81w37'01 5:26:28
Mount Vernon 39
12 39N31'32 79w49'48 5:19:19
Mount Vernon 40 1 38N26 82w01 5:28:04
Mountview 41 1 37N38'31 81w03'56 5:24:16
Mount Welcome 44
1 38N36'03 81w23'24 5:25:34
Mount Zion 7 1 38N51'44 81w07'23 5:24:30
Mount Zion 47 1 39N10 79w42 5:18:48
Mouth of Seneca 36
1 38N50 79w23 5:17:32
Moyers 36 1 38N30'57 79w21'45 5:17:27
Mozart 26 34 40N01'56 80w42'54 5:22:52
Mozer 36 1 38N48'09 79w12'33 5:16:50
Mud 22 1 38N08 82w01 5:28:04
Muddlety 34 1 38N22'02 80w49'40 5:23:19
Mudfork 7 1 38N38'21 81w04'31 5:24:18
Mudfork 23 1 37N51 82w03 5:28:12
Mullens 55 1 37N34'59 81w22'50 5:25:31
Mullensville 55 1 37N34'38 81w33'32 5:26:14
Munday 53 1 39N00'19 81w12'23 5:24:50
Murphy 1 1 39N03'27 80w08'29 5:20:34
Murphy 43 1 39N05 81w06 5:24:24
Murphytown 54 1 39N14'02 81w26'37 5:25:46
Murray 18 1 38N53'44 81w38'25 5:26:34
Murraysville 18 1 39N04'39 81w48'24 5:27:14
Muses Bottom 18 1 39N05 81w48 5:27:12
Musick 30 1 37N39'18 82w04'30 5:28:18
Mustang Acres 54
14 39N17 81w32 5:26:08
Myerstown 19 23 39N17 77w52 5:11:28
Myra 22 1 38N13'17 82w06'46 5:28:27
Myrtle 3 1 38N09 81w40 5:26:40
Myrtle 30 1 37N46'04 82w11'29 5:28:46
Nabob 20 1 38N01 81w25 5:25:40
Nallen 10 1 38N06'38 80w52'38 5:23:31
Nancy Run 44 1 38N49'05 81w21'06 5:25:24
Naoma 41 1 37N52'03 81w29'15 5:25:57
Napier 4 1 38N47'27 80w35'20 5:22:21
Narrows Run 51 1 38N38 80w28 5:21:52
National 31 28 39N35'02 80w02'16 5:20:09
Natrium 26 4 39N44'53 80w51'06 5:23:24
Naugatuck 30 1 37N47'23 82w20'57 5:29:24
Naval Ordnance Plant 20
14 38N21 81w42 5:26:48
Neal 50 14 38N21'24 82w35'35 5:30:22
Neals Run 14 1 39N29'00 78w29'48 5:13:59
Nebo 8 1 38N38'04 81w02'34 5:24:10
Nebo 49 1 38N59'18 80w05'05 5:20:20
Needmore 16 1 39N03'02 78w47'13 5:15:09
Neffs 29 2 39N25'03 79w09'19 5:16:37
Neibert 23 1 37N47'17 81w56'31 5:27:46
Nelco 30 1 37N41 82w16 5:29:04
Nellis 3 1 38N09'03 81w44'34 5:26:58
Nelson 3 1 38N04'08 81w37'22 5:26:29
Nemours 28 1 37N18'05 81w18'16 5:25:13
Neola 13 1 37N57'57 80w07'49 5:20:31
Neponset 45 1 37N28'06 80w50'47 5:23:23
Neptune 18 1 39N04'31 81w46'48 5:27:07
Nestlow 50 1 38N10'32 82w17'01 5:29:08
Nestorville 1 1 39N10'47 79w54'34 5:19:38
Nethkin 29 2 39N23'24 79w08'02 5:16:32
Nettie 34 1 38N13'06 80w41'10 5:22:45
Neville 41 18 37N47 81w11 5:24:44
New 41 1 37N47 80w57 5:23:48
Newark 53 1 39N07'08 81w23'52 5:25:35
Newberne 11 1 39N02'38 80w53'35 5:23:34
Newburg 39 12 39N23'18 79w51'11 5:19:25
New Creek 29 2 39N22'30 79w01'37 5:16:06
New Cumberland 15
9 40N29'48 80w36'25 5:22:26
Newdale 52 12 39N40'20 80w42'39 5:22:51
Newell 15 9 40N37'06 80w36'16 5:22:25
New England 54 1 39N12'25 81w42'32 5:26:50
New England Heights 54
1 39N16 81w40 5:26:40
New Era 18 1 38N54'34 81w39'50 5:26:39
Newfound 55 1 37N36'26 81w28'36 5:25:54
Newhall 24 1 37N15'49 81w37'08 5:26:29
New Hamlin 22 1 38N16'44 82w06'52 5:28:27
New Haven 27 1 38N59'11 81w58'25 5:27:54
New Hill 31 17 39N40'06 80w04'18 5:20:17
New Hope 28 1 37N20'20 81w10'00 5:24:40
New Hope 33 11 39N35'48 78w10'27 5:12:42
New Interest 42 1 39N03 79w49 5:19:16
Newlandsville 37
1 39N16'54 81w15'34 5:25:02
Newlon 49 1 38N45 80w14 5:20:56
Newlonton 42 1 38N44'40 80w14'09 5:20:57
Newlyn 10 1 37N56'39 81w05'08 5:24:21
New Manchester 15
9 40N31'53 80w34'49 5:22:19
New Martinsville 52
29 39N38'40 80w51'28 5:23:26
New Milton 9 1 39N13'48 80w40'58 5:22:44
Newport 54 14 39N15'30 81w33'41 5:26:15
New Richmond 55 1 37N34'12 81w29'20 5:25:57
New Thacker 30 1 37N36 82w08 5:28:32
Newton 44 1 38N35'29 81w10'44 5:24:43
Newtown 10 1 37N59'44 81w09'16 5:24:37
Newtown 30 1 37N37'40 82w05'09 5:28:21
Newtown Mall 35
34 40N04 80w42 5:22:48
Newville 4 1 38N40'43 80w35'27 5:22:22
Next 48 31 39N34 81w00 5:24:00
Nickells Mill 32
1 37N41'25 80w30'19 5:22:01
Nicolette 54 14 39N12'37 81w30'48 5:26:03
Nicut 7 1 38N42'47 81w01'20 5:24:05
Nida 38 14 38N27'43 79w52'37 5:19:30
Nile 34 1 38N18'16 80w44'07 5:22:56
Nimitz 45 1 37N38'46 80w57'37 5:23:50
Nina 9 1 39N14'26 80w38'10 5:22:33
Nipetown 2 27 39N31'53 77w55'39 5:11:43
Nitro 20 18 38N24'53 81w50'39 5:27:23
Nitro Park Addition 20
18 38N25 81w50 5:27:20
Nobe 7 1 38N59'11 81w02'04 5:24:08
Nolan 30 1 37N44'23 82w19'53 5:29:20
Nollville 2 27 39N27'45 78w01'13 5:12:05
Normantown 11 1 38N51'06 80w56'12 5:23:45
North Bend 13 14 38N13'47 80w26'36 5:21:46
North Berkeley 33
11 39N37'51 78w13'17 5:12:53
North Caldwell 13
1 37N47'04 80w24'06 5:21:36
North Charleston 20
14 38N22'27 81w41'04 5:26:44
North Fairmont 25
17 39N28 80w10 5:20:40
Northfork 24 1 37N25'15 81w26'25 5:25:46
North Hill 18 1 38N49 81w42 5:26:48
North Matewan 30
1 37N37'35 82w08'54 5:28:36
North Mitchell Heights 23
1 37N55'16 81w58'29 5:27:54
North Mountain 2
2 39N33'48 77w58'50 5:11:55
North Page 10 14 38N04'15 81w15'40 5:25:03
North Parkersburg 54
14 39N17'16 81w31'59 5:26:08
North Ravenswood 18
1 38N57 81w46 5:27:04
North River Mills 14
1 39N20'11 78w30'12 5:14:01
North Spring 55 1 37N34'05 81w49'32 5:27:18
North View 17 24 39N17'43 80w21'04 5:21:24
Norton 42 1 38N55'54 79w57'57 5:19:52
Norway 25 17 39N28'14 80w11'12 5:20:45
Norwood 25 17 39N29'37 80w06'33 5:20:26
Nottingham 38 14 38N31'05 79w50'36 5:19:22
Nuckolls 20 1 38N05'33 81w23'29 5:25:34
Numan 9 1 39N17 80w34 5:22:16
Nuriva 55 1 37N35'51 81w22'54 5:25:32
Nuttall 10 1 38N05 80w59 5:23:56
Nutter Farm 43 1 39N14'27 81w13'30 5:24:54
Nutter Fort 17 24 39N15'48 80w19'12 5:21:17
Nutterville 13 1 38N05'15 80w48'51 5:23:15
Nuzums 18 1 38N54'57 81w42'25 5:26:50
Nye 40 1 38N20'09 82w02'13 5:28:09
Oak Acres 54 1 39N16 81w40 5:26:40
Oakdale 17 1 39N26'57 80w23'46 5:21:35
Oak Flat 36 1 38N39'34 79w12'47 5:16:51
Oak Grove 28 1 37N23'14 81w03'49 5:24:15
Oak Grove 36 1 38N37'33 79w21'18 5:17:25
Oak Hill 7 1 38N55'20 81w01'07 5:24:04
Oak Hill 10 17 37N58'20 81w08'56 5:24:36
Oak Hill 12 1 39N08'12 79w09'09 5:16:37
Oak Hill 18 1 38N47'29 81w42'36 5:26:50
Oak Hill Junction 10
1 37N58'56 81w10'28 5:24:42
Oakland 33 2 39N28'52 78w15'07 5:13:00
Oakmont 29 2 39N22'00 79w11'19 5:16:45
Oakmont 35 34 40N03'44 80w40'36 5:22:42
Oak Ridge 10 18 38N04'30 81w06'35 5:24:26
Oakton 8 1 38N29'16 81w02'51 5:24:11
Oakvale 28 1 37N20'03 80w57'46 5:23:51
Oakview Heights 50
14 38N24 82w35 5:30:20
Oakwood 20 14 38N20'32 81w39'50 5:26:39
Oakwood Estates 54
14 39N17 81w32 5:26:08
O'Brion 8 1 38N34'31 80w57'43 5:23:51
Oceana 55 1 37N41'31 81w37'27 5:26:30
Odaville 18 1 38N55'57 81w38'27 5:26:34
Odd 41 1 37N35'36 81w11'39 5:24:47
Odell 20 1 38N23'25 81w21'56 5:25:28
Odell Town 34 1 38N11'52 80w42'49 5:22:51
Odessa 8 1 38N25'43 81w14'17 5:24:57
Ogden 54 1 39N18'06 81w24'08 5:25:37
Ohley 20 1 38N06'25 81w26'57 5:25:48
Oka 7 1 38N39'22 81w08'12 5:24:33
Okonoko 14 1 39N31'23 78w31'32 5:14:06
Olcott 20 22 38N14'04 81w43'28 5:26:54
Old Arthur 12 1 39N04 79w07 5:16:28
Old Fields 16 1 39N08'05 78w57'00 5:15:48
Old Gauley 10 1 38N09'22 81w11'31 5:24:46
Olive 17 1 39N20'52 80w27'32 5:21:50
Olive 38 14 38N33'49 79w49'13 5:19:17
Omar 23 1 37N45'20 81w59'59 5:28:00
Omps 33 11 39N38 78w14 5:12:56
Ona 6 1 38N25'29 82w12'48 5:28:51
Onego 36 1 38N50'52 79w25'20 5:17:41
O'Neill 17 24 39N17'35 80w24'41 5:21:39
Oney Gap 28 1 37N22 81w05 5:24:20
Onoto 38 1 38N16'16 80w06'25 5:20:26
Opal 34 1 38N23'12 80w45'59 5:23:04
Opekiska 31 17 39N33'26 80w03'21 5:20:13
Opequon 2 27 39N29 77w55 5:11:40
Oral Lake 17 1 39N16'31 80w12'57 5:20:52
Orchard 32 1 37N29 80w47 5:23:08
Oreide 46 17 39N21'40 80w12'00 5:20:48
Organ Cave 13 14 37N42'46 80w26'29 5:21:46
Orgas 3 1 38N03'30 81w34'21 5:26:17
Orient Hill 13 1 38N01'41 80w43'34 5:22:54
Orlando 4 14 38N52'16 80w35'38 5:22:23
Orleans Cross Roads 33
2 39N37'28 78w22'46 5:13:31
Orma 7 1 38N44'53 81w06'00 5:24:24
Orndoff 51 1 38N32'15 80w25'28 5:21:42
Orr 39 12 39N33'12 79w31'43 5:18:07
Orr 42 1 38N56'23 80w03'14 5:20:13
Ortin Heights 40
18 38N26'51 81w49'05 5:27:16
Orton 11 1 38N50'06 80w55'43 5:23:43
Orville 23 1 37N48'51 81w53'32 5:27:34
Osage 31 17 39N39'31 80w00'28 5:20:02
Osborne 20 1 38N29'57 81w20'55 5:25:24
Osbornes Mill 44
1 38N32'39 81w18'29 5:25:14
Oscar 13 1 38N03'31 80w22'04 5:21:28
Osceola 42 1 38N42'50 79w38'01 5:18:32
Osgood 31 17 39N34'00 80w04'38 5:20:19
Ossia 8 1 38N35'20 81w01'37 5:24:06
O'Toole 24 1 37N20 81w26 5:25:44
Otsego 55 1 37N36'45 81w22'32 5:25:30
Ottawa 3 1 37N57'31 81w49'00 5:27:16
Otto 44 1 38N45'08 81w13'16 5:24:53
Ovapa 8 1 38N31'17 81w08'56 5:24:36
Overfield 1 1 39N10'09 80w12'16 5:20:49
Overhill 49 1 38N57'43 80w09'06 5:20:36
Owens Crossing 6
1 38N21'05 82w16'24 5:29:06
Owings 17 1 39N22'46 80w15'33 5:21:02
Oxbow 43 1 39N05'38 81w12'42 5:24:51
Oxford 9 1 39N12'20 80w51'54 5:23:28
Packs Branch 10 1 37N54'19 81w14'05 5:24:56
Packsville 41 18 37N57'07 81w31'42 5:26:07
Pad 44 1 38N38 81w24 5:25:36
Paden City 48 31 39N36'10 80w56'13 5:23:45
Page 10 14 38N03'10 81w16'12 5:25:05
Pageton 24 1 37N20'57 81w27'56 5:25:52
Paint Creek Junction 20
1 38N13 81w25 5:25:40
Palace Valley 49
1 38N45'19 80w09'27 5:20:38
Palermo 22 1 38N10'10 82w03'31 5:28:14
Palestine 13 1 37N43'56 80w37'46 5:22:31
Palestine 53 1 39N01'48 81w24'25 5:25:38
Palmer 4 1 38N39'27 80w35'22 5:22:21
Pancake 14 1 39N15'29 78w50'03 5:15:20
Pansy 12 1 38N54'45 79w11'10 5:16:45
Panther 24 1 37N29'00 81w53'46 5:27:35
Paradise 40 1 38N35'05 81w48'00 5:27:12
Parchment Valley 18
1 38N46'19 81w44'14 5:26:57
Parcoal 51 1 38N27'33 80w22'25 5:21:30
Pardee 23 1 37N48'21 81w42'06 5:26:48
Park Addition 5
33 40N17 80w37 5:22:28
Parkersburg 54 14 39N16'00 81w33'42 5:26:15
Parkview 35 34 40N03'07 80w39'41 5:22:39
Park View 46 14 39N19'03 80w01'42 5:20:07
Parkway Terrace 20
18 38N22'54 81w48'09 5:27:13
Par Metta Crest 54
1 39N20 81w22 5:25:28
Parsley 30 1 37N50'59 82w12'01 5:28:48
Parsley Bottom 30
1 37N47'28 82w16'01 5:29:04
Parsons 47 1 39N05'47 79w40'52 5:18:43
Patterson Creek 29
2 39N34'00 78w44'00 5:14:56
Patton 32 14 37N41'31 80w29'16 5:21:57
Paw Paw 25 17 39N32'55 80w09'12 5:20:37

Paw Paw 33 19 39N31'55 78W27'31 5:13:50
Pax 10 1 37N54'35 81W15'52 5:25:03
Paxton 8 1 38N29'53 81W10'05 5:24:40
Paynesville 24 1 37N19'53 81W53'30 5:27:34
Peabody 52 12 39N42'09 80W44'38 5:22:59
Peach Creek 23 1 37N52'28 81W59'06 5:27:56
Peanut 25 17 39N32 80W20 5:21:20
Peapatch 24 1 37N17'03 81W47'23 5:27:10
Pear 41 1 37N47 80W57 5:23:48
Pecks Mill 23 1 37N55'41 81W58'52 5:27:55
Pecks Run 49 1 39N03'09 80W10'45 5:20:43
Pedlar 31 17 39N39'59 80W07'17 5:20:29
Pedro 32 1 37N39'46 80W18'53 5:21:16
Peeltree 1 1 39N07'46 80W12'39 5:20:51
Peewee 53 1 38N57'45 81W29'30 5:25:58
Pemberton 41 1 37N43'04 81W13'09 5:24:53
Pembroke 4 1 38N43'29 80W44'26 5:22:58
Pence Springs 45 1 37N40'41 80W43'31 5:22:54
Peniel 44 1 38N49'38 81W28'04 5:25:52
Pennsboro 43 1 39N17'06 80W58'07 5:23:52
Pentacre 20 1 38N23'25 81W24'13 5:25:37
Pentress 31 17 39N42'37 80W09'38 5:20:39
Peora 17 1 39N25'17 80W20'42 5:21:23
Pepper 1 1 39N11'19 80W09'24 5:20:38
Perkins 11 1 38N47'04 80W55'34 5:23:42
Perry 16 1 38N58'17 78W40'31 5:14:42
Persinger 34 1 38N19'19 80W45'08 5:23:01
Peru 16 1 38N50'27 79W04'28 5:16:18
Petersburg 12 1 38N59'33 79W07'27 5:16:30
Peters Junction 34 1 38N13'28 81W02'55 5:24:12
Peterson 21 1 38N53'34 80W32'23 5:22:10
Peterstown 32 1 37N23'50 80W47'58 5:23:12
Petroleum 43 1 39N11'27 81W16'07 5:25:04
Pettit Heights 5 33 40N13'46 80W38'02 5:22:32
Pettry 28 1 37N26'10 80W57'51 5:23:51
Pettry Bottom 41 1 37N52'23 81W30'06 5:26:00
Pettus 41 18 37N57'23 81W32'16 5:26:09
Pettyville 54 14 39N12'43 81W32'36 5:26:10
Pew Hill 43 1 39N10'56 81W08'39 5:24:35
Peytona 3 1 38N08'29 81W41'05 5:26:44
Pharoah 50 1 38N15 82W36 5:30:24
Phico 23 1 37N57'02 82W00'51 5:28:03
Philippi 1 1 39N09'08 80W02'26 5:20:10
Philoah 40 1 38N36 81W44 5:26:56
Piatt 20 14 38N15 81W33 5:26:12
Pickaway 32 1 37N38'18 80W30'23 5:22:02
Pickens 42 1 38N39'18 80W12'43 5:20:51
Pickle Street 21 1 39N02 80W40 5:22:40
Pickshin 41 1 37N38'30 81W13'42 5:24:55
Pie 30 1 37N39'12 82W01'33 5:28:06
Piedmont 28 1 37N27'02 81W15'50 5:25:03
Piedmont 29 11 39N28'49 79W02'53 5:16:12
Pierce 47 1 39N10'25 79W30'38 5:18:03
Piercys Mill 13 1 37N50'37 80W34'26 5:22:18
Pierpont 31 28 39N39'14 79W53'23 5:19:34
Pierpont 55 1 37N37'41 81W23'29 5:25:34
Pigeon 44 1 38N32'12 81W12'31 5:24:50
Pike 43 1 39N17'00 81W04'54 5:24:20
Pike Hill 27 1 38N58'35 82W02'42 5:28:11
Pikeside 2 27 39N25'03 77W59'22 5:11:57
Pinch 20 1 38N24'31 81W28'55 5:25:56
Pine Bluff 17 1 39N25'05 80W19'39 5:21:19
Pine Creek 23 1 37N45'06 82W05'33 5:28:22
Pine Grove 10 1 38N04'51 81W02'45 5:24:11
Pine Grove 20 18 38N25 81W50 5:27:20
Pine Grove 25 17 39N30'00 80W11'47 5:20:47
Pine Grove 52 2 39N33'57 80W40'45 5:22:43
Pineknob 41 1 37N50'35 81W28'54 5:25:56
Pineville 55 1 37N34'59 81W32'14 5:26:09
Piney 52 2 39N30'57 80W41'41 5:22:47
Piney View 41 1 37N50'10 81W08'06 5:24:32
Pink 7 1 38N47'07 81W13'13 5:24:53
Pinoak 28 1 37N26'44 81W12'29 5:24:50
Pioneer Rocks 31 28 39N36'34 79W53'11 5:19:33
Pipestem 45 1 37N32'40 80W57'37 5:23:50
Pisgah 39 12 39N38'41 79W45'25 5:19:02
Pittman 10 1 37N57'20 80W55'16 5:23:41
Pleasant Creek 1 1 39N09 80W03 5:20:12
Pleasantdale 14 1 39N17'39 78W35'11 5:14:21
Pleasantdale 39 12 39N30'08 79W41'03 5:18:44
Pleasant Hill 7 1 38N57'13 81W03'39 5:24:15
Pleasant Hill 18 1 38N52'39 81W44'14 5:26:57
Pleasant Hill 54 1 39N11'13 81W35'30 5:26:22
Pleasant Home 54 1 39N08 81W44 5:26:56
Pleasant Run 47 1 39N02'39 79W43'25 5:18:54
Pleasants 37 1 39N19'26 81W10'50 5:24:43
Pleasant Valley 25 17 39N27'19 80W08'31 5:20:34
Pleasant Valley 26 21 39N55'00 80W37'35 5:22:30
Pleasant View 18 1 38N55'21 81W47'18 5:27:09
Pleasant View 22 1 38N14'58 82W11'26 5:28:46
Pleasant View 25 17 39N32'56 80W07'15 5:20:29
Pleasant View 54 14 39N12'35 81W34'43 5:26:19
Pleasure Valley 1 1 39N06'19 79W50'40 5:19:23
Pliny 40 1 38N37'13 81W59'15 5:27:57
Plum Orchard 18 1 38N42'19 81W37'37 5:26:30
Plum Run 48 1 39N22'29 80W59'59 5:24:00
Pluto 41 14 37N42'37 80W59'33 5:23:58
Plymouth 40 1 38N30'57 81W50'42 5:27:23
Poca 40 1 38N28'20 81W48'52 5:27:15
Pocatalico 20 1 38N29'25 81W38'51 5:26:35
Poe 34 1 38N15'07 80W57'58 5:23:52
Pohick 54 1 39N22'40 81W28'54 5:25:56
Point Lick Junction 20 22 38N21 81W38 5:26:32
Point Mills 26 6 40N04'57 80W34'52 5:22:19
Point Pleasant 27 1 38N50'40 82W08'14 5:28:33
Points 14 1 39N26'24 78W36'38 5:14:27
Polard 48 2 39N31'18 80W50'54 5:23:24
Polemic 4 1 38N40 80W43 5:22:52
Poling 51 1 38N41'20 80W26'10 5:21:45
Polk 18 1 39N03'04 81W47'47 5:27:11
Polk Gap 55 1 37N40'36 81W25'22 5:25:41
Pondco 3 1 37N53'53 81W40'19 5:26:41
Pond Creek 54 1 39N05'39 81W44'36 5:26:58
Pond Fork 20 1 38N19'33 81W18'39 5:25:15
Pond Gap 20 1 38N16'41 81W16'44 5:25:07
Pond Junction 3 18 38N04 81W49 5:27:16
Pool 34 1 38N09'49 80W51'52 5:23:27
Port Amherst 20 22 38N18'35 81W33'25 5:26:14
Porter 8 1 38N29'00 81W15'22 5:25:01
Porters Falls 52 2 39N34'47 80W46'35 5:23:06
Portersville 22 1 38N20'07 82W07'50 5:28:31
Porterwood 47 1 39N04'11 79W41'54 5:18:48
Portland 39 12 39N27 79W35 5:18:20
Porto Rico 9 1 39N10'55 80W45'47 5:23:03
Posey 41 1 37N48'13 81W25'58 5:25:44
Potomac 35 6 40N09'10 80W31'46 5:22:07
Potomac Manor 29 2 39N23 79W12 5:16:48
Potomac Park 2 2 39N34 77W54 5:11:36
Powell 25 17 39N24'19 80W07'28 5:20:30
Powell Creek 3 18 38N00'48 81W49'32 5:27:18
Powellton 10 14 38N05'56 81W19'27 5:25:18
Power 5 33 40N12'40 80W39'34 5:22:38
Powhatan 24 1 37N24'02 81W25'14 5:25:41
Prairietown 6 1 38N20'48 82W10'31 5:28:42
Pratt 20 1 38N12'36 81W23'03 5:25:32
Premier 24 1 37N25'20 81W38'38 5:26:35
Prenter 3 1 38N00'52 81W37'38 5:26:31
Preston 39 12 39N26'06 79W41'09 5:18:45
Prestonia 51 1 38N34'44 80W35'03 5:22:20
Price 22 1 38N08'38 82W07'37 5:28:30
Price 31 17 39N42'29 80W07'43 5:20:31
Price Hill 3 18 38N02'36 81W48'26 5:27:14
Price Hill 31 17 39N36'15 79W59'48 5:19:59
Price Hill 41 1 37N52'56 81W11'23 5:24:46
Price Hill Junction 10 1 37N54 81W10 5:24:40
Pricetown 21 1 39N02'57 80W31'30 5:22:06
Pricetown 52 2 39N30'27 80W30'42 5:22:03
Prichard 50 1 38N14'24 82W35'55 5:30:24
Priestley 22 1 38N15'37 81W50'13 5:27:21
Prince 10 1 37N51'32 81W03'14 5:24:13
Princeton 28 1 37N21'58 81W06'10 5:24:25
Princewick 41 1 37N39'36 81W13'05 5:24:52
Procious 8 1 38N29'44 81W12'28 5:24:50
Proctor 52 2 39N42'42 80W49'26 5:23:18
Propstburg 36 1 38N36'03 79W15'34 5:17:02
Prospect Valley 17 1 39N24'01 80W20'32 5:21:22
Prosperity 41 18 37N50'11 81W12'07 5:24:48
Providence 18 1 38N48'30 81W50'30 5:27:22
Prudence 10 1 37N56'12 81W08'02 5:24:32
Prunty 43 1 39N06'26 81W00'20 5:24:01
Pruntytown 46 14 39N20'02 80W04'37 5:20:18
Pugh 51 1 38N39'29 80W23'57 5:21:36
Pullman 43 1 39N11'14 80W57'00 5:23:48
Pumpkintown 42 1 38N53'34 80W01'28 5:20:06
Purdy 7 1 38N56'38 81W08'06 5:24:32
Purgitsville 14 1 39N14'21 78W55'17 5:15:41
Puritan 30 1 37N41 82W10 5:28:40
Pursglove 31 17 39N40'03 80W01'35 5:20:06
Pursley 48 31 39N32'12 80W57'23 5:23:50
Putney 20 1 38N17'47 81W22'23 5:25:30
Quaker 50 1 38N03'08 82W25'40 5:29:43
Quarrier 20 1 38N03'01 81W25'57 5:25:44
Queens 49 1 38N51'25 80W08'13 5:20:33
Queen Shoals 8 1 38N28'16 81W17'00 5:25:08
Quick 20 1 38N22'21 81W24'08 5:25:37
Quiet Dell 17 14 39N13'09 80W17'38 5:21:11
Quincy 20 14 38N15 81W33 5:26:12
Quinland 3 18 38N01'00 81W46'13 5:27:05
Quinnimont 10 1 37N51'16 81W02'41 5:24:11
Quinwood 13 1 38N03'27 80W42'25 5:22:50
Rabbit Hill 5 32 40N17'31 80W36'06 5:22:24
Rachel 25 17 39N31'06 80W18'14 5:21:13
Racine 3 1 38N08'31 81W39'38 5:26:39
Racket 11 1 39N02'39 80W56'14 5:23:45
Racy 43 1 39N08'19 81W14'17 5:24:57
Rada 14 1 39N16'26 78W54'49 5:15:39
Radcliff 25 17 39N31'24 80W05'14 5:20:21
Radnor 50 1 38N04'46 82W27'24 5:29:50
Ragland 30 1 37N42'09 82W07'39 5:28:31
Ragtown 31 17 39N38'54 80W15'55 5:21:04
Rainelle 13 1 37N58'07 80W46'02 5:23:04
Raines Corner 32 1 37N31'07 80W37'03 5:22:28
Raintown 38 1 38N09 80W11 5:20:44
Raleigh 41 18 37N45'24 81W10'28 5:24:42
Ralph 51 1 38N28'38 80W22'08 5:21:29
Ramage 3 1 37N59'03 81W49'32 5:27:18
Ramp 45 1 37N45'01 80W49'23 5:23:18
Ramsey 10 1 38N10'11 81W01'51 5:24:07
Rand 20 14 38N16'57 81W33'45 5:26:15
Randall 31 28 39N39'36 79W59'39 5:19:59
Ranger 22 1 38N07'14 82W11'08 5:28:45
Rangoon 1 1 39N04 80W06 5:20:24
Ranson 19 23 39N17'42 77W51'39 5:11:27
Raven 34 1 38N17 80W51 5:23:24
Ravencliff 55 1 37N41'53 81W28'53 5:25:56
Raven Rock 37 1 39N26'22 81W09'03 5:24:36
Raven Rocks 14 1 39N26'40 78W40'48 5:14:43
Ravenseye 10 1 38N00'14 80W53'46 5:23:35
Ravenswood 18 1 38N56'53 81W45'40 5:27:03
Rawl 30 1 37N38'59 82W13'11 5:28:53
Rayburn 27 1 38N52'22 82W01'36 5:28:06
Raymond City 40 1 38N28'56 81W49'07 5:27:16
Raysal 24 1 37N20'35 81W46'57 5:27:08
Raywood 38 1 38N22'06 79W56'03 5:19:44
Read 42 35 38N57'11 79W50'35 5:19:22
Reader 52 2 39N34'08 80W43'59 5:22:56
Ream 24 1 37N20'59 81W33'00 5:26:12
Reamer (Sybial P O) 20 1 38N28'33 81W22'16 5:25:29
Redbird 41 1 37N47'22 81W26'25 5:25:46
Red Campbell 23 1 37N51'16 81W55'58 5:27:44
Red Creek 47 1 39N00 79W30 5:18:00
Redhill 54 14 39N17 81W32 5:26:08
Red House 40 1 38N32'21 81W53'49 5:27:35
Red Jacket 30 1 37N38'54 82W08'25 5:28:34
Red Knob 44 1 38N43'29 81W30'47 5:26:03
Redmond 27 1 38N48'15 82W08'03 5:28:32
Red Rock 49 1 39N00'43 80W16'35 5:21:06
Redrock Crossing 33 19 39N41'23 78W09'07 5:12:36
Red Run 47 1 39N05 79W38 5:18:32
Red Spring 10 1 37N52'07 80W54'59 5:23:40
Redstar 10 1 37N56'07 81W08'48 5:24:35
Red Sulphur 32 1 37N27 80W45 5:23:00
Red Sulphur Springs 32 1 37N29 80W47 5:23:08
Red Warrior 20 1 38N03'17 81W27'29 5:25:50
Red Warrior Junction 20 1 38N04 81W27 5:25:48
Redwing 22 1 38N10'39 82W14'05 5:28:56
Reedson 19 2 39N21'09 77W48'06 5:11:12
Reedsville 39 12 39N30'38 79W47'55 5:19:12
Reedy 44 1 38N53'58 81W25'30 5:25:42
Reedyville 44 1 38N48'37 81W26'28 5:25:46
Reeses Mill 29 2 39N25'50 78W51'18 5:15:25
Reger 49 1 38N58'55 80W11'28 5:20:46
Renick 13 1 38N00 80W22 5:21:28
Renicks Valley 13 1 38N03'16 80W18'12 5:21:13
Reno 39 12 39N20 79W46 5:19:04
Rensford 20 22 38N18'50 81W28'52 5:25:55
Replete 51 1 38N42'02 80W27'51 5:21:51
Republic 20 1 38N00'33 81W23'34 5:25:34
Reston 3 18 38N04 81W49 5:27:16
Revere 11 1 38N58'29 80W59'58 5:24:00
Reynolds 20 22 38N20 81W38 5:26:32
Reynoldsville 17 1 39N17'18 80W26'06 5:21:44
Rhoda 7 1 38N58'47 81W07'20 5:24:29
Rhodell 41 1 37N36'31 81W18'21 5:25:13
Richard 31 28 39N36'24 79W54'24 5:19:38
Richardson 7 1 38N51'55 81W14'12 5:24:57
Richland 13 14 37N48 80W27 5:21:48
Richland 35 6 40N08 80W40 5:22:40
Richlands 13 14 37N51'58 80W29'00 5:21:56
Richmond 41 1 37N45 80W59 5:23:56
Richwood 34 14 38N13'29 80W32'00 5:22:08
Rider 17 1 39N10'21 80W22'15 5:21:29
Ridersville 33 11 39N37'26 78W11'27 5:12:46
Ridgedale 14 1 39N24'41 78W44'06 5:14:56
Ridgedale 31 28 39N32'49 79W56'09 5:19:45
Ridge Farms 25 17 39N33'52 80W06'51 5:20:27
Ridgeley 29 2 39N38'29 78W46'29 5:15:06
Ridgeview 3 1 38N08'18 81W45'35 5:27:02
Ridgeview 23 1 37N50'36 82W00'59 5:28:04
Ridgeville 29 2 39N20'54 78W59'27 5:15:58
Ridgeway 2 2 39N17'50 78W04'19 5:12:17
Riffe 45 1 37N40'36 80W41'11 5:22:45
Riffle 4 1 38N45 80W44 5:22:56
Rift 24 1 37N17'05 81W40'19 5:26:41
Rig 16 1 39N02'20 79W02'45 5:16:11
Riley 41 18 37N49 81W10 5:24:40
Rimel 38 1 38N07'24 79W57'06 5:19:48
Rinehart 17 1 39N25'26 80W31'00 5:22:04
Ringold 31 28 39N33'48 79W56'36 5:19:46
Rio 14 1 39N08'18 78W40'13 5:14:41
Ripley 18 1 38N49'07 81W42'39 5:26:51
Ripley Landing 18 1 38N53'27 81W50'46 5:27:23
Ripling Waters 18 1 38N35 81W36 5:26:24
Rippon 19 2 39N13'06 77W54'20 5:11:37
Rita 23 1 37N46'13 81W55'56 5:27:44
Ritchie 35 34 40N03 80W43 5:22:52
Ritters 14 1 39N25'25 78W43'30 5:14:54
Riverbend 20 18 38N23 81W49 5:27:16
Riverlake Estates 20 18 38N23 81W49 5:27:16
Riverlawn 20 18 38N23 81W49 5:27:16
Riverside 19 23 39N10'24 77W51'23 5:11:26
Riverside 20 1 38N12'25 81W24'20 5:25:37
Riverside 31 28 39N38'16 79W58'36 5:19:54
Riverside 43 1 39N10'22 81W10'37 5:24:42
Riverside 54 14 39N16'42 81W33'30 5:26:14
Riverton 36 1 38N44'38 79W26'10 5:17:45
Riverview 20 22 38N20'05 81W35'48 5:26:23
Rivesville 25 17 39N31'47 80W07'01 5:20:28
Roach 6 1 38N25 82W17 5:29:08
Roanoke 21 1 38N55'54 80W29'35 5:21:58
Roaring Creek 42 1 38N54 79W59 5:19:56
Roberts 9 1 39N22'42 80W40'07 5:22:40
Robertsburg 40 1 38N39'19 81W57'05 5:27:48
Robey 17 1 39N21'45 80W22'35 5:21:30
Robinette 23 1 37N47'06 81W47'38 5:27:11
Robinson 27 1 38N54 82W04 5:28:16
Robson 10 14 38N06'06 81W14'38 5:24:59
Rock 28 1 37N22'04 81W13'20 5:24:53
Rock Camp 32 1 37N29'53 80W36'25 5:22:26
Rock Castle 18 1 38N43 81W47 5:27:08
Rock Cave 49 1 38N50'12 80W20'34 5:21:22
Rock Cliff 13 1 37N57'49 80W37'27 5:22:30
Rock Creek 3 18 38N06'11 81W50'46 5:27:23
Rock Creek 41 1 37N51'02 81W27'07 5:25:48
Rockdale 5 32 40N18'17 80W34'49 5:22:19
Rockford 17 1 39N08'11 80W19'57 5:21:20
Rock Forge 31 28 39N36'18 79W55'03 5:19:40
Rock Gap 33 2 39N32 78W15 5:13:00
Rock Lake 25 17 39N28 80W10 5:20:40
Rock Lake Village 20 14 38N20'50 81W44'28 5:26:58
Rockland 13 14 37N43'46 80W30'47 5:22:03
Rockland 16 1 38N56'39 78W41'34 5:14:46
Rocklick 3 1 37N50'46 81W37'44 5:26:31
Rocklick 10 1 37N58'52 81W06'09 5:24:25
Rocklick 26 21 39N52'23 80W31'38 5:22:07
Rock Oak 16 1 39N08'54 78W44'10 5:14:57
Rockport 52 2 39N42'27 80W34'53 5:22:20
Rockport 54 1 39N04'27 81W33'12 5:26:13
Rockridge 24 1 37N22'36 81W49'37 5:27:18
Rock Run 9 1 39N18 80W47 5:23:08
Rocksdale 7 1 38N50'41 81W13'06 5:24:52

Rockton 4 1 38N37'10 80W51'23 5:23:26
Rock View 55 1 37N37'04 81W32'21 5:26:09
Rockville 22 1 38N09'58 82W10'38 5:28:43
Rockville 39 12 39N37'17 79W42'18 5:18:49
Rocky Ford 49 1 38N57'17 80W17'16 5:21:09
Rocky Fork 20 22 38N27'19 81W43'22 5:26:53
Rodemer 39 12 39N24'56 79W35'36 5:18:22
Roderfield 24 1 37N27'01 81W42'21 5:26:49
Rohr 39 12 39N35'14 79W49'02 5:19:16
Rohrbough 21 1 38N58'55 80W29'36 5:21:58
Rolfe 24 1 37N25'04 81W24'05 5:25:36
Rollins 27 1 38N48'19 81W57'01 5:27:48
Rollins Branch 55
1 37N43'22 81W35'47 5:26:23
Rollyson 4 1 38N47'00 80W38'28 5:22:34
Romance 18 1 38N35'50 81W35'56 5:26:24
Romines Mills 17
1 39N10'11 80W15'52 5:21:03
Romney 14 1 39N20'31 78W45'25 5:15:02
Romont 10 1 38N10'53 81W06'15 5:24:25
Ronceverte 13 14 37N44'59 80W27'47 5:21:51
Ronda 20 1 38N10'04 81W26'51 5:25:47
Roneys Point 26 6 40N03'52 80W36'23 5:22:26
Rorer 13 1 38N01'30 80W16'38 5:21:07
Rosbys Rock 26 21 39N50'29 80W42'44 5:22:51
Rosebud 17 1 39N22'03 80W24'45 5:21:39
Roseby Rock 26 21 39N51 80W36 5:22:24
Rosedale 4 1 38N44'21 80W56'35 5:23:46
Rosedale 10 1 37N59'57 81W08'26 5:24:34
Rosedale 31 28 39N41'12 79W57'55 5:19:52
Rosemont 2 27 39N27'47 77W58'46 5:11:55
Rosemont 46 1 39N16'07 80W09'47 5:20:39
Roseville Addition 20
5 38N25 82W27 5:29:48
Ross 52 2 39N29'49 80W41'58 5:22:48
Rossmore 23 1 37N48'33 81W58'53 5:27:56
Rough Run 12 1 38N53'43 79W07'12 5:16:29
Round Bottom 52 2 39N41'59 80W26'09 5:21:45
Round Knob 40 1 38N37 81W59 5:27:56
Rouzer 8 1 38N27'58 81W11'32 5:24:46
Rover 53 1 39N00'52 81W25'38 5:25:43
Rowlesburg 39 12 39N20'54 79W40'16 5:18:41
Roxalana 20 14 38N23 81W45 5:27:00
Roxalana 44 1 38N41'35 81W15'44 5:25:03
Roxalia 32 1 37N36'08 80W21'00 5:21:24
Royal 41 18 37N51'10 81W04'05 5:24:16
Ruddle 36 1 38N42'45 79W18'31 5:17:14
Rumble 3 1 38N11'00 81W41'58 5:26:48
Rum Junction 23 1 37N48'57 81W56'08 5:27:45
Runa 34 1 38N08'34 80W51'05 5:23:24
Rupert 13 1 37N57'47 80W41'23 5:22:46
Ruraldale 49 1 39N04'01 80W13'55 5:20:56
Rush Creek 44 1 38N48 81W21 5:25:24
Rushville 44 1 38N42'02 81W20'21 5:25:21
Rusk 43 1 39N09'18 81W15'15 5:25:01
Russelldale 29 2 39N17'33 78W55'49 5:15:43
Russellville 10 1 38N04'35 80W53'33 5:23:34
Russett 7 1 38N52'23 81W03'24 5:24:14
Ruth 20 22 38N18'37 81W43'42 5:26:55
Ruthbelle 39 12 39N30'27 79W38'36 5:18:34
Ruthdale 20 22 38N19'11 81W43'23 5:26:54
Rutherford 43 1 39N09'02 81W10'15 5:24:41
Rutledge 20 14 38N21'51 81W32'26 5:26:10
Ryan 44 1 38N38'33 81W28'23 5:25:54
Ryanville 17 1 39N18'52 80W13'17 5:20:53
Rymer 25 17 39N32'27 80W26'25 5:21:46
Sabine 55 1 37N40'43 81W30'06 5:26:00
Sabraton 31 28 39N37'46 79W55'43 5:19:43
Sago 49 1 38N54'51 80W13'49 5:20:55
Saint Albans 20
18 38N23'08 81W50'11 5:27:21
Saint Clara 9 1 39N07'19 80W41'15 5:22:45
Saint Cloud 31 17 39N42'07 80W24'04 5:21:36
Saint George 47 1 39N10'00 79W42'09 5:18:49
Saint Joe 39 12 39N29'19 79W37'57 5:18:32
Saint Joseph 26 4 39N43'49 80W42'48 5:22:51
Saint Leo 31 17 39N38'34 80W21'40 5:21:27
Saint Marys 37 1 39N23'30 81W12'19 5:24:49
Salem 10 1 37N59'21 81W06'56 5:24:28
Salem 17 1 39N16'58 80W33'33 5:22:14
Salt Hill 18 1 38N46'39 81W41'07 5:26:44
Salt Lick 4 1 38N48 80W35 5:22:20
Saltlick Bridge 4
1 38N46 80W38 5:22:32
Saltpetre 50 1 38N04'55 82W32'51 5:30:11
Salt Rock 6 1 38N19'23 82W13'16 5:28:53
Salt Sulphur Springs 32
1 37N34'13 80W33'30 5:22:14
Saltwell 17 1 39N21'50 80W16'17 5:21:05
Sam Black Church 13
1 37N54 80W36 5:22:24
Sand Creek 22 1 38N07 82W11 5:28:44
Sanderson 20 1 38N21'52 81W22'06 5:25:28
Sand Fork 8 1 38N28'02 81W00'22 5:24:01
Sand Fork 11 1 38N54'50 80W45'00 5:23:00
Sand Hill 26 4 39N59'15 80W35'07 5:22:20
Sandhill 43 1 39N15'12 81W15'52 5:25:03
Sand Hill 54 1 39N22'15 81W29'25 5:25:58
Sandlick 28 20 37N20'21 81W13'13 5:24:53
Sand Lick Junction 46
1 39N16 80W05 5:20:20
Sand Ridge 7 1 38N48'06 81W04'01 5:24:16
Sand Run 49 1 38N55'23 80W07'28 5:20:30
Sandstone 45 1 37N46'15 80W53'30 5:23:34
Sandusky 48 2 39N33'20 80W51'33 5:23:26
Sandy 20 14 38N24'33 81W30'40 5:26:03
Sandy 31 17 39N38'07 80W11'42 5:20:47
Sandy Huff 24 1 37N28'41 81W46'31 5:27:06
Sandy River 24 1 37N26 81W50 5:27:20
Sandy Summit 44 1 38N53'57 81W30'28 5:26:02
Sandyville 18 1 38N54'21 81W39'39 5:26:39
Sanford 25 17 39N31'10 80W07'38 5:20:31
Sanger 10 1 37N57'23 81W06'47 5:24:27
Sanoma 53 1 38N57'52 81W19'29 5:25:18
Santiago 46 17 39N22'11 80W12'06 5:20:48
Santown 27 1 38N49'14 82W00'43 5:28:03
Sarah 6 1 38N19'48 82W15'28 5:29:02
Sarah Ann 23 1 37N42'40 81W59'15 5:27:57
Sardis 17 1 39N20'15 80W25'05 5:21:40
Sarton 32 1 37N34'57 80W38'25 5:22:34
Sassafras 27 1 38N56'03 82W00'47 5:28:03
Sattes 20 18 38N23'29 81W49'07 5:27:16
Saulsbury 54 1 39N07'21 81W32'37 5:26:10
Saulsville 55 1 37N38'34 81W27'25 5:25:50
Saunders 23 1 37N47'59 81W40'21 5:26:41
Saxman 34 14 38N12'35 80W35'50 5:22:23
Saxon 41 1 37N47'53 81W24'54 5:25:40
Scarbro 10 1 37N57'11 81W09'57 5:24:40
Scarlet 30 1 37N46'33 82W08'50 5:28:35
Scary 40 18 38N26'14 81W51'19 5:27:25
Schell 29 2 39N20'31 79W15'26 5:17:02
Scherr 12 1 39N11'35 79W10'13 5:16:41
Schrader 20 1 38N24'54 81W24'55 5:25:41
Schultz 37 1 39N19'12 81W14'25 5:24:58
Scotch Hill 39 12 39N22'27 79W51'58 5:19:28
Scott 4 1 38N38 80W52 5:23:28
Scott Depot 40 1 38N26'30 81W55'01 5:27:40
Scott Run 5 32 40N17'59 80W31'57 5:22:08
Scotts 42 1 38N58 79W30 5:18:00
Scrabble 2 30 39N29'01 77W49'58 5:11:20
Seaman 44 1 38N54'12 81W27'38 5:25:51
Secoal 3 18 37N58'46 81W48'30 5:27:14
Secondcreek 32 1 37N39'55 80W27'15 5:21:49
Sector 14 1 39N13'41 78W51'22 5:15:25
Sedalia 9 1 39N21'35 80W34'44 5:22:19
Sedan 14 1 39N14'06 78W34'25 5:14:18
Seebert 38 1 38N07'44 80W10'40 5:20:43
Selbyville 49 1 38N45'14 80W14'12 5:20:57
Sell 39 12 39N15'54 79W35'13 5:18:21
Selwyn 30 1 37N51'31 82W22'43 5:29:31
Seminole 17 1 39N22'43 80W19'17 5:21:17
Seminole 45 1 37N33'18 80W50'31 5:23:22
Seneca Rocks 36 1 38N50'05 79W22'35 5:17:30
Seng Creek 3 18 37N59 81W32 5:26:08
Servia 4 1 38N37'13 80W57'27 5:23:50
Seth 3 1 38N06'29 81W37'24 5:26:30
Seven Pines 25 17 39N34'00 80W26'31 5:21:46
Sewell 10 1 37N59'50 81W01'16 5:24:05
Sewell Mountain 10
1 37N58 80W55 5:23:40
Seymour 29 2 39N35'33 78W49'02 5:15:16
Seymourville 12 1 39N03'25 79W06'33 5:16:26
Shady Brook 21 1 39N03'02 80W28'09 5:21:53
Shady Grove 33 11 39N38'15 78W09'05 5:12:36
Shadyside 4 1 38N39'04 80W49'00 5:23:16
Shady Spring 41 1 37N42 81W06 5:24:24
Shafer 47 1 39N13'09 79W34'05 5:18:16
Shahan 49 1 38N45'43 80W10'05 5:20:40
Shamrock 23 1 37N50'26 82W01'11 5:28:05
Shanghai 2 2 39N26'29 78W07'57 5:12:32
Shanks 14 1 39N18'51 78W41'17 5:14:45
Shannondale 19 3 39N13'01 77W48'28 5:11:14
Sharlow 3 1 38N07'57 81W38'04 5:26:32
Sharon 20 1 38N09'34 81W26'50 5:25:47
Sharon Heights 30
1 37N38'16 81W56'14 5:27:45
Sharples 23 1 37N55'13 81W49'46 5:27:19
Shatto 18 1 38N47'24 81W39'18 5:26:37
Shaw 29 2 39N24'58 79W07'51 5:16:31
Shawver 10 1 37N53'12 80W45'57 5:23:04
Shawvers Crossing 13
1 37N57'12 80W39'30 5:22:38
Shegon 23 1 37N51'20 82W04'09 5:28:17
Shelton 8 1 38N25'53 81W11'43 5:24:47
Shenandoah Junction 19
2 39N21'31 77W50'36 5:11:22
Shepherdstown 19
30 39N25'48 77W48'16 5:11:13
Sheridan 22 1 38N14'25 82W11'55 5:28:48
Sherman 18 1 38N59'30 81W45'43 5:27:03
Sherrard 26 34 39N59'14 80W40'34 5:22:42
Sherwood 9 1 39N16'46 80W48'40 5:22:43
Shiloh 41 1 37N47'58 81W23'34 5:25:34
Shiloh 48 2 39N27'22 81W00'42 5:24:03
Shinnston 17 1 39N23'44 80W18'01 5:21:12
Shirley 48 2 39N23'53 80W45'55 5:23:04
Shively 23 1 37N57'57 82W07'06 5:28:28
Shoals 50 14 38N19'37 82W28'31 5:29:54
Shock 11 1 38N46'42 80W58'00 5:23:52
Short Creek 5 9 40N11'08 80W40'29 5:22:42
Short Creek Valley 5
34 40N04 80W42 5:22:48
Short Gap 29 6 39N32'37 78W48'41 5:15:15
Short Line Junction 17
24 39N16 80W19 5:21:16
Shrewsbury 20 1 38N12'22 81W28'18 5:25:53
Shriver 31 17 39N40 80W03 5:20:12
Shryock 13 1 37N57'17 80W09'02 5:20:36
Sias 22 1 38N11'05 82W05'15 5:28:21
Sidney 50 1 38N09'25 82W28'22 5:29:53
Sidneyville 18 1 38N51'29 81W43'58 5:26:56
Sigman 40 1 38N34'54 81W53'07 5:27:02
Silica 42 1 38N41'14 80W14'25 5:20:58
Silver Grove 19 3 39N17'58 77W45'07 5:11:00
Silver Hill 52 12 39N39 80W51 5:23:24
Silver Lake 39 12 39N15'15 79W29'53 5:18:00
Silverton 18 1 38N55'34 81W43'21 5:26:53
Simmons 28 1 37N19'41 81W18'07 5:25:12
Simoda 36 1 38N43'37 79W29'00 5:17:56
Simon 55 1 37N36'43 81W43'59 5:26:56
Simpson 46 1 39N16'00 80W05'37 5:20:22
Sims 13 1 37N56'36 80W48'07 5:23:12
Sincerity 52 2 39N35'57 80W32'21 5:22:09
Sinclair 39 12 39N16'05 79W49'15 5:19:17
Sinks Grove 32 1 37N39'51 80W32'28 5:22:10
Sir Johns Run 33
11 39N38'53 78W14'06 5:12:56
Sissonville 20 1 38N31'41 81W37'52 5:26:31
Sistersville 48
31 39N33'51 80W59'46 5:23:59
Sitlington 38 1 38N21'30 79W55'31 5:19:42
Six 24 1 37N22'08 81W38'17 5:26:33
Six Hill 43 1 39N11'39 81W07'58 5:24:32
Six Mile 3 18 38N05 81W50 5:27:20
Skeetersville 19
2 39N21'51 77W48'57 5:11:16
Skelt 51 1 38N33'19 80W19'20 5:21:17
Skelton 41 18 37N48'38 81W11'15 5:24:45
Skidmore 18 1 38N45'38 81W38'46 5:26:35
Skidmore Crossing 51
1 38N28'48 80W26'33 5:21:46
Skin Creek 21 1 38N58 80W23 5:21:32
Skull Run 18 1 39N00'30 81W45'34 5:27:02
Skygusty 24 1 37N19'26 81W28'35 5:25:54
Skyline 29 2 39N19'25 79W07'46 5:16:31
Slab 43 1 39N07'44 80W58'36 5:23:54
Slab Fork 41 1 37N41'13 81W19'54 5:25:20
Slabtown 30 1 37N37'44 81W52'12 5:27:29
Slagle 23 1 37N49'10 81W50'27 5:27:22
Slanesville 14 1 39N22'23 78W31'23 5:14:06
Slate 54 1 39N08'09 81W26'46 5:25:47
Slaty Fork 38 1 38N25'05 80W07'48 5:20:31
Sleepy Creek 33
10 39N40'01 78W04'58 5:12:20
Smithburg 9 1 39N17'21 80W44'04 5:22:56
Smith Crossing 42
1 39N03'15 79W49'04 5:19:16
Smith Crossroads 33
2 39N34'04 78W13'39 5:12:55
Smithers 10 1 38N10'52 81W18'26 5:25:14
Smithfield 19 2 39N23 77W53 5:11:32
Smithfield 52 2 39N29'58 80W33'43 5:22:15
Smithtown 31 28 39N31'46 80W02'30 5:20:10
Smithville 25 17 39N33'11 80W07'11 5:20:29
Smithville 43 1 39N04'26 81W05'40 5:24:23
Smoke Hole 36 1 38N48 79W17 5:17:08
Smokeless 28 1 37N25'57 81W15'05 5:25:00
Smoot 13 1 37N52'43 80W39'33 5:22:38
Snider 39 12 39N27'36 79W42'01 5:18:48
Snowden 22 1 38N11'51 81W56'15 5:27:45
Snowflake 13 14 37N44'48 80W33'17 5:22:13
Snow Hill 20 22 38N19'29 81W34'18 5:26:17
Snow Hill 34 1 38N08'07 80W46'54 5:23:08
Sod 22 1 38N14'39 81W52'35 5:27:30
Sodom 23 1 37N54'59 81W50'00 5:27:20
Somerville 54 1 39N16 81W40 5:26:40
Sophia 41 1 37N42'27 81W15'03 5:25:00
South Bluefield 28
20 37N15'28 81W13'06 5:24:52
South Caperton 10
1 38N01'05 81W01'38 5:24:07
South Charleston 20
14 38N22'06 81W41'59 5:26:48
South Fayette 10
18 38N03'55 81W04'51 5:24:19
South Fork 16 1 38N59 79W01 5:16:04
South Grafton 46
14 39N20'13 80W01'14 5:20:05
South Hills 20 22 38N20'30 81W38'38 5:26:35
South Hills 31 28 39N37'10 79W56'24 5:19:46
South Madison 3
18 38N03'13 81W48'21 5:27:13
South Malden 20
22 38N17'32 81W34'05 5:26:16
South Nuttall 10
1 38N02'48 81W02'15 5:24:09
South Park 20 22 38N18'49 81W36'11 5:26:25
South Park 21 1 39N06'24 80W23'39 5:21:35
South Parkersburg 54
14 39N14'12 81W32'33 5:26:10
South Ruffner 20
22 38N19'57 81W37'08 5:26:29
Southside 27 1 38N43'00 81W58'08 5:27:53
South Side Junction 10
1 37N58 81W05 5:24:20
Southwest 9 1 39N10 80W50 5:23:20
South Worthington 25
17 39N26'50 80W16'11 5:21:05
Sovereign 23 1 37N51'42 81W49'35 5:27:18
Spangler 20 1 38N18'02 81W17'18 5:25:09
Spangler 42 1 38N36'22 80W01'26 5:20:06
Spanishburg 28 1 37N26'45 81W07'13 5:24:29
Spaulding 30 1 37N52'42 82W21'18 5:29:25
Spears 22 1 38N10 82W11 5:28:44
Speed 44 1 38N44'01 81W22'40 5:25:31
Speedway 28 1 37N27'23 81W00'38 5:24:03
Spelter 17 1 39N20'42 80W19'05 5:21:16
Spencer 44 1 38N48'07 81W21'04 5:25:24
Spice 38 1 38N03'03 80W14'06 5:20:56
Sprague 41 18 37N47'35 81W11'03 5:24:44
Sprattsville 30 1 37N36'00 81W52'22 5:27:29
Spread 8 1 38N29'45 81W04'15 5:24:17
Sprigg 30 1 37N37'43 82W11'51 5:28:47
Spring Creek 13 1 37N57'14 80W20'57 5:21:24
Spring Creek 53 1 38N57 81W20 5:25:20
Spring Dale 10 1 37N52'47 80W48'13 5:23:13
Springdale 35 34 40N03'45 80W39'13 5:22:37
Springfield 14 1 39N27'02 78W41'38 5:14:47
Spring Fork 20 22 38N21 81W38 5:26:32
Spring Gap 14 1 39N22 78W31 5:14:04
Spring Hill 17 24 39N16 80W19 5:21:16
Spring Hill 20 14 38N21'16 81W43'53 5:26:56
Spring Hill Chapel 17
14 39N14'40 80W22'06 5:21:28
Spring Mills 2 2 39N33'30 77W57'15 5:11:49
Spring Run 37 1 39N25'57 81W10'03 5:24:40
Springton 28 1 37N27'21 81W14'40 5:24:59
Spring Valley 50
5 38N24 82W26 5:29:44
Sproul 20 1 38N15'04 81W47'44 5:27:11
Spruce 38 1 38N27'24 79W57'22 5:19:49
Spruce Valley 23
1 37N53'05 81W49'29 5:27:18
Spurgeon 11 1 39N06'03 80W46'50 5:23:07
Spurlockville 22
1 38N07'34 82W01'16 5:28:05
Squire 24 1 37N14'18 81W36'36 5:26:26
Stafford 30 1 37N36 81W54 5:27:36
Stanaford 41 18 37N48'57 81W09'09 5:24:37
Standard 20 1 38N08'10 81W24'03 5:25:36
Stanley 43 1 39N18'31 80W53'32 5:23:34
Star 42 1 38N42'56 80W07'59 5:20:32
Star City 31 28 39N39'30 79W59'12 5:19:57
Stark 3 1 37N54'43 81W44'39 5:26:59
Staten 7 1 38N52'13 81W02'57 5:24:12
Statler Run 31 17 39N36 80W15 5:21:00
Statts Mills 18 1 38N44'15 81W37'21 5:26:29
Stealey 17 24 39N16'45 80W21'35 5:21:26
Steele 54 1 39N05 81W35 5:26:20
Steeles 55 1 37N32'20 81W46'32 5:27:06
Steelton 52 12 39N41'04 80W51'27 5:23:26
Steep Gut Hollow 30
1 37N45 82W19 5:29:16
Stephenson 55 1 37N34'49 81W19'35 5:25:18
Steptown 50 1 37N51'47 82W25'00 5:29:40
Stevensburg 39 12 39N18'03 79W47'45 5:19:11
Stewart 54 14 39N14'33 81W30'58 5:26:04
Stewartstown 31
28 39N42'15 79W54'03 5:19:36

Stickney 41 1 37N54'05 81W31'40 5:26:07
Stillman 49 1 38N50 80W21 5:21:24
Stillwell 38 1 38N12'30 80W05'55 5:20:24
Stiltner 50 1 38N07'55 82W22'50 5:29:31
Stinson 7 1 38N39'23 81W04'29 5:24:18
Stirrat 23 1 37N43'35 82W00'09 5:28:01
Stohrs Crossroads 33 11 39N38'00 78W08'50 5:12:35
Stollings 23 1 37N50'15 81W57'53 5:27:52
Stone Branch 23 1 37N59'34 82W02'31 5:28:10
Stonecoal 50 1 37N53'00 82W25'04 5:29:40
Stonecoal Junction 41 1 37N36'11 81W18'49 5:25:15
Stoneville 55 1 37N33'36 81W39'05 5:26:36
Stonewall 20 22 38N22 81W38 5:26:32
Stonewall 50 1 38N08 82W21 5:29:24
Stonewood 17 24 39N15'03 80W18'45 5:21:15
Stony Bottom 38 1 38N21'51 79W57'45 5:19:51
Stony River 12 1 39N17 79W14 5:16:56
Stotesbury 41 1 37N40'54 81W17'20 5:25:09
Stotlers Crossroads 33 2 39N30'48 78W13'27 5:12:54
Stouts Mills 11 1 38N53'42 80W43'50 5:22:55
Stover 41 1 37N48'51 81W21'15 5:25:25
Stowe 23 1 37N48'22 81W45'32 5:27:02
Straight Fork 49 1 38N52 80W26 5:21:44
Strange Creek 4 1 38N33'47 80W53'53 5:23:36
Streby 12 1 39N04'49 79W14'23 5:16:58
Streeter 45 1 37N37'38 81W01'05 5:24:04
Stringtown 1 1 39N01'43 79W54'32 5:19:38
Stringtown 25 17 39N28'55 80W21'09 5:21:25
Stringtown 44 1 38N40'06 81W20'22 5:25:21
Stringtown (Alvy P O) 48 2 39N26'43 80W41'54 5:22:48
Strouds 51 1 38N23'16 80W37'00 5:22:28
Stumptown 11 1 38N50'56 80W59'39 5:23:59
Sturgisson 31 28 39N39 79W58 5:19:52
Sturms Mill 25 17 39N27'08 80W19'26 5:21:18
Suck Creek 45 1 37N36'28 80W59'14 5:23:57
Sue 13 1 37N57'23 80W12'35 5:20:50
Sugar Camp 9 1 39N14 80W41 5:22:44
Sugar Grove 36 1 38N30'40 79W19'19 5:17:17
Sugar Tree 22 1 38N14 81W59 5:27:56
Sugar Valley 37 1 39N25'10 81W05'14 5:24:21
Sugar Valley 39 12 39N36'40 79W38'25 5:18:34
Sullivan 41 1 37N42'13 81W11'40 5:24:47
Sullivan 42 35 38N54'26 79W52'12 5:19:29
Sully 42 1 38N57'25 79W34'23 5:18:18
Sulphur City 29 2 39N21'11 79W08'16 5:16:33
Sulphur Springs 23 1 37N49'51 82W06'11 5:28:25
Sumerco 22 1 38N13'52 81W54'42 5:27:39
Summerlee 10 1 38N00'10 81W09'37 5:24:38
Summers 9 1 39N09'27 80W49'44 5:23:19
Summersville 34 1 38N16'52 80W51'10 5:23:25
Summit 22 1 38N13'11 81W54'25 5:27:38
Summit 54 14 39N21'16 81W30'43 5:26:03
Summit Park 17 24 39N16'54 80W18'38 5:21:15
Summit Point 19 2 39N14'58 77W57'32 5:11:50
Sun 10 1 37N55'09 81W10'12 5:24:41
Sunbeam 23 1 37N50'48 81W56'43 5:27:47
Suncrest 31 28 39N39'18 79W58'29 5:19:54
Suncrest 42 1 38N41'17 80W15'13 5:21:01
Sundial 41 1 37N52'34 81W30'53 5:26:04
Sunflower 44 1 38N54'18 81W28'42 5:25:55
Sun Hill 55 1 37N37'25 81W42'12 5:26:49
Sunlight 13 1 37N59'13 80W27'42 5:21:51
Sunrise 54 14 39N16'14 81W30'14 5:26:01
Sunset Acres 21 1 39N02'49 80W29'48 5:21:59
Sunset Beach 39 28 39N40'46 79W51'24 5:19:26
Sunset Court 23 1 37N57'38 82W01'19 5:28:05
Sunshine 25 17 39N32 80W20 5:21:20
Sun Valley 15 32 40N26'40 80W34'06 5:22:16
Sun Valley 17 24 39N16'38 80W26'15 5:21:45
Sun Valley 20 18 38N23 81W49 5:27:16
Superior 24 1 37N25'16 81W32'33 5:26:10
Superior Bottom 23 1 37N44'56 81W59'58 5:28:00
Surbaugh 10 1 38N00'52 80W47'44 5:23:11
Surosa 30 1 37N38'29 82W10'31 5:28:42
Surveyor 41 1 37N45'57 81W19'05 5:25:16
Sutton 4 1 38N39'52 80W42'36 5:22:50
Swamp Run 49 1 38N59 80W13 5:20:52
Swandale 8 1 38N28'14 80W57'35 5:23:50
Swann 6 1 38N31'23 82W09'32 5:28:38
Swan Pond 2 27 39N28'09 77W52'39 5:11:31
Sweeneyburg 41 18 37N50'11 81W15'29 5:25:02
Sweetland 22 1 38N15'34 82W02'32 5:28:10
Sweet Run 50 14 38N22'01 82W34'49 5:30:19
Sweet Springs 32 1 37N37'42 80W14'30 5:20:58
Swiss 34 1 38N13'59 81W07'41 5:24:31
Switchback 24 1 37N22'16 81W23'09 5:25:33
Switzer 23 1 37N47'35 81W59'16 5:27:57
Sycamore 7 1 38N50'07 81W05'44 5:24:23
Sycamore 16 1 39N09'10 78W54'52 5:15:39
Sycamore 17 1 39N17 80W28 5:21:52
Sycamore 23 1 37N49'40 82W04'17 5:28:17
Sycamore Junction 30 1 37N41 82W16 5:29:04
Sydnor Addition 30 1 37N35'44 82W08'13 5:28:33
Sylvester 3 18 38N00'37 81W33'28 5:26:14
Tablerock 41 18 37N45 81W08 5:24:32
Tablers 2 2 39N22 78W03 5:12:12
Tablers Station 2 27 39N23'55 78W00'40 5:12:03
Tacy 1 1 39N09'43 79W56'32 5:19:46
Tad 20 1 38N20'00 81W29'40 5:25:59
Tague 4 1 38N42'06 80W54'56 5:23:40
Talbott 1 1 38N58'37 80W00'49 5:20:03
Talcott 45 1 37N39'05 80W45'16 5:23:01
Tallmans 54 1 39N14'45 81W41'09 5:26:45
Tallmansville 49 1 38N54'48 80W10'49 5:20:43
Tallyho 54 1 39N16'51 81W26'23 5:25:46
Tamcliff 30 1 37N38'18 81W52'36 5:27:30
Tams 41 1 37N39'53 81W18'28 5:25:14
Tango 22 1 38N15'08 81W55'35 5:27:42
Tanner 11 1 38N58'53 80W56'59 5:23:48
Tannery 16 1 39N03'05 78W57'27 5:15:50
Taplin 23 1 37N45'30 81W53'45 5:27:35
Tappan 46 14 39N22'34 80W09'30 5:20:38
Tarico Heights 2 2 39N19'35 78W00'15 5:12:01
Tariff 44 1 38N41 81W12 5:24:48
Tate 4 1 38N36'57 80W54'40 5:23:39
Tavennersville 54 14 39N15'08 81W33'02 5:26:12
Taylor 16 1 39N02'49 78W58'48 5:15:55
Taylorville 30 1 37N39'51 82W09'24 5:28:38
Teaberry 13 14 37N46'14 80W26'26 5:21:46
Teays 40 1 38N26'30 81W57'11 5:27:49
Teays Valley 40 1 38N29 82W00 5:28:00
Tekram 30 1 37N42 82W11 5:28:44
Tempa 45 1 37N43'30 80W45'18 5:23:01
Tenmile 17 1 39N18 80W31 5:22:04
Tenmile 49 1 38N52'26 80W11'23 5:20:46
Tennerton 49 1 38N57'48 80W13'27 5:20:54
Tera Rosa 54 1 39N16 81W40 5:26:40
Terra Alta 39 12 39N26'44 79W32'48 5:18:11
Terry 41 1 37N51'39 81W05'57 5:24:24
Terry Junction 41 1 37N50'59 81W05'00 5:24:20
Tesla 4 1 38N36'07 80W42'13 5:22:49
Teter 49 1 39N03'42 80W09'28 5:20:38
Teterton 36 1 38N49'59 79W24'20 5:17:37
Thacker 30 1 37N35'40 82W07'54 5:28:32
Thacker Mines 30 1 37N36'13 82W05'49 5:28:23
Thayer 10 1 37N54'04 81W01'52 5:24:07
The Flats 31 28 39N39'08 79W57'50 5:19:51
The Mileground 31 28 39N38'33 79W55'51 5:19:43
The Y 18 1 38N53'47 81W40'12 5:26:41
Thoburn 25 17 39N27'47 80W13'44 5:20:55
Thomas 47 1 39N08'56 79W29'54 5:18:00
Thompson Town 23 1 37N50'55 82W01'36 5:28:06
Thornhill 28 1 37N23 81W17 5:25:08
Thornton 46 12 39N20'44 79W56'32 5:19:46
Thornwood 38 14 38N33'30 79W44'14 5:18:57
Thorny Creek 38 1 38N15'10 80W02'14 5:20:09
Thorpe 24 1 37N22'07 81W31'00 5:26:04
Three Churches 14 1 39N24'03 78W39'16 5:14:37
Threefork Bridge 39 12 39N26'25 79W50'59 5:19:24
Three Mile 20 1 38N25'49 81W25'47 5:25:43
Thurmond 10 1 37N57'41 81W04'57 5:24:20
Thursday 43 1 39N04 81W05 5:24:20
Tichenal 17 1 39N11'24 80W28'36 5:21:54
Tidewater 24 1 37N26 81W30 5:26:00
Tigheville 42 1 38N58'47 79W55'12 5:19:41
Tilden 41 1 37N43'44 81W10'37 5:24:42
Timber Ridge 33 2 39N28 78W16 5:13:04
Tioga 34 1 38N25'13 80W39'23 5:22:38
Tipton 34 1 38N15'32 80W59'21 5:23:57
Tolleys 41 1 37N45'21 81W18'42 5:25:15
Toll Gate 43 1 39N16'21 80W54'55 5:23:40
Tomahawk 2 2 39N31'49 78W02'50 5:12:11
Toney 22 1 38N00'39 82W04'23 5:28:18
Toney Fork 55 1 37N42'46 81W35'52 5:26:23
Tophet 45 1 37N32 80W58 5:23:52
Topins Grove 18 1 39N03'05 81W42'26 5:26:50
Tornado 20 18 38N20 81W51 5:27:24
Tourison 10 18 38N03 81W06 5:24:24
Town 41 18 37N48 81W13 5:24:52
Town Hill 12 1 39N00'09 79W07'54 5:16:32
Trace 30 1 37N53'14 82W11'49 5:28:47
Trace Fork 20 22 38N21 81W38 5:26:32
Trace Junction 23 1 37N49'31 82W03'00 5:28:12
Trainer 13 1 38N02'23 80W01'55 5:20:08
Tralee 55 1 37N33'26 81W24'03 5:25:36
Trap Hill 41 1 37N46'58 81W20'37 5:25:22
Triadelphia 35 6 40N03'09 80W37'43 5:22:31
Tribble 27 1 38N41'15 81W50'17 5:27:21
Triplett 8 1 38N28'35 81W02'10 5:24:09
Triplett 44 1 38N50'22 81W17'54 5:25:12
Tripp 50 1 37N55'30 82W28'47 5:29:55
Tristan 44 1 38N48'09 81W13'38 5:24:55
Triune 31 28 39N29'47 79W58'31 5:19:54
Trout 13 1 38N01'00 80W25'05 5:21:40
Troy 11 1 39N01'11 80W45'48 5:23:03
Troy Town 23 1 37N51'25 82W04'38 5:28:19
Trubada 11 1 38N56 80W50 5:23:20
True 45 1 37N34'50 80W56'11 5:23:45
Truebada 11 1 38N55'48 80W46'40 5:23:07
Tuckahoe 13 14 37N45'08 80W16'25 5:21:06
Tucker 53 1 39N03 81W31 5:26:04
Tug River 30 1 37N42 82W15 5:29:00
Tunnelton 39 19 39N23'30 79W44'55 5:19:00
Turkey 55 1 37N38'25 81W34'42 5:26:19
Turkey Gap 28 1 37N29 81W15 5:25:00
Turkey Knob 10 1 37N53'56 81W09'11 5:24:37
Turner 20 1 38N28'53 81W18'41 5:25:15
Turner Douglass 39 12 39N22'30 79W29'40 5:17:59
Turnertown 21 1 39N04'28 80W27'55 5:21:52
Turtle Creek 3 18 38N01'47 81W52'23 5:27:30
Twiggs 37 1 39N23'51 81W01'55 5:24:08
Twilight 3 1 37N55'38 81W37'25 5:26:30
Twilight 26 6 40N02'10 80W35'37 5:22:22
Twin Branch 24 1 37N28'29 81W40'07 5:26:40
Twistville 4 1 38N38 80W52 5:23:28
Two Lick 17 1 39N07 80W25 5:21:40
Twomile 20 22 38N22'01 81W36'25 5:26:26
Two Run 53 1 39N02 81W24 5:25:36
Tygart 54 14 39N13 81W33 5:26:12
Tygart Junction 1 1 39N05'54 80W04'31 5:20:18
Tyler 48 2 39N25'59 80W49'37 5:23:18
Tyler Heights 20 22 38N25'52 81W45'14 5:27:01
Tyler Mountain 20 14 38N23'33 81W43'16 5:26:53
Tyrone 39 28 39N38'22 79W51'32 5:19:26
Tyson Store 44 1 38N48 81W21 5:25:24
Uffington 31 28 39N35'11 79W58'35 5:19:54
Uler 44 1 38N37'04 81W08'36 5:24:34
Ulvilla 19 2 39N22 77W51 5:11:24
Uneeda 3 18 38N02'08 81W46'51 5:27:07
Unger 33 2 39N26'12 78W15'15 5:13:01
Union 32 1 37N35'29 80W32'38 5:22:11
Union Addition 20 1 38N11 81W21 5:25:24
Union City 24 1 37N25'50 81W47'48 5:27:11
Union Corner 2 2 39N23'55 78W05'09 5:12:21
Union Mills 37 1 39N23'28 81W08'07 5:24:32
Union Ridge 6 1 38N35 82W11 5:28:44
Uniontown 52 2 39N38'01 80W33'30 5:22:14
United 20 1 37N59'26 81W25'36 5:25:42
Uno 55 1 37N37'43 81W44'14 5:26:57
Unus 13 1 37N56'27 80W26'40 5:21:47
Upland 24 1 37N23'33 81W25'18 5:25:41
Upland 27 1 38N34'07 82W04'23 5:28:18
Upper Addis Run 43 1 39N13 81W03 5:24:12
Upper Falls (Tornado P O) 20 18 38N20'34 81W50'40 5:27:23
Upper Flats 27 1 38N55'31 81W59'32 5:27:58
Upperglade 51 1 38N24'33 80W30'25 5:22:02
Upper Leatherwood 8 1 38N26'07 81W06'14 5:24:25
Upper Mingo 42 1 38N30 80W03 5:20:12
Upper Tract 36 1 38N47'14 79W16'58 5:17:08
Upper Whitman 23 1 37N47'35 82W03'11 5:28:13
Upton 25 17 39N32'30 80W13'42 5:20:55
Upton Creek 20 18 38N23 81W49 5:27:16
Ury 41 1 37N39'13 81W18'55 5:25:16
Utica 18 1 39N02'43 81W39'32 5:26:38
Uvilla 19 2 39N22'08 77W48'02 5:11:12
Vadis 21 1 39N02'32 80W42'09 5:22:49
Vago 13 1 37N52'58 80W22'21 5:21:29
Vainville 2 27 39N28 77W58 5:11:52
Vale 13 1 37N52'49 80W43'19 5:22:53
Valley Bend 1 1 39N03'42 79W58'18 5:19:53
Valley Camp 26 6 40N03'52 80W36'28 5:22:26
Valley Chapel 21 1 39N07 80W30 5:22:00
Valley Falls 25 17 39N23'22 80W05'16 5:20:21
Valley Fork 8 1 38N31'30 81W07'05 5:24:28
Valley Furnace 1 1 39N11'42 79W52'37 5:19:30
Valley Grove 26 6 40N05'15 80W34'14 5:22:17
Valley Head 42 1 38N32'42 80W02'10 5:20:09
Valley Heights 45 1 37N41'32 80W42'58 5:22:52
Valley Mills 54 1 39N19'04 81W26'36 5:25:46
Valley Point 39 12 39N34'48 79W38'13 5:18:33
Vallscreek 24 1 37N13'55 81W38'43 5:26:35
Van 3 1 37N58'16 81W42'40 5:26:51
Van Camp 52 12 39N35'14 80W53'41 5:23:35
Vance 14 1 39N22'41 78W44'20 5:14:57
Van Clevesville 2 27 39N25'44 77W54'19 5:11:37
Vandalia 20 14 38N21'23 81W39'51 5:26:39
Vandalia 21 1 38N55'37 80W24'14 5:21:37
Vandalia 44 1 38N45'34 81W26'40 5:25:47
Vanderlip 14 1 39N21 78W45 5:15:00
Vanetta 10 1 38N10'31 81W11'38 5:24:47
Van Junction 3 1 37N58 81W43 5:26:52
Vannoys Mill 1 1 39N07'50 79W57'31 5:19:50
Vanville 2 27 39N22'47 77W58'48 5:11:55
Van Voorhis 31 28 39N40'58 79W57'19 5:19:49
Varner 18 1 38N54'26 81W42'15 5:26:49
Varney 30 1 37N40'09 82W07'20 5:28:29
Varneytown 8 1 38N29'14 81W08'49 5:24:35
Vaucluse 37 1 39N23'05 81W13'54 5:24:56
Vaughan 34 1 38N16'42 81W08'41 5:24:35
Vegan 49 1 38N57'50 80W06'50 5:20:27
Venus 24 1 37N21'43 81W32'13 5:26:09
Verdunville 23 1 37N50'40 82W03'19 5:28:13
Verner 30 1 37N39'48 81W51'02 5:27:24
Vernon 4 1 38N42'40 80W29'40 5:21:59
Vernon 52 12 39N39'26 80W48'23 5:23:14
Veto 52 29 39N36'42 80W50'33 5:23:22
Vicars 44 1 38N39'23 81W30'06 5:26:00
Victor 10 1 38N07'57 81W04'36 5:24:18
Victor 20 1 38N25'24 81W25'35 5:25:42
Victoria 39 12 39N25'04 79W53'22 5:19:33
Vienna 54 1 39N19'37 81W32'55 5:26:12
Viola 25 17 39N30'47 80W06'03 5:20:24
Viola 26 21 39N57'54 80W35'24 5:22:22
Violet 38 1 38N09'25 80W08'32 5:20:34
Virginia Heights 20 18 38N23'09 81W51'06 5:27:24
Virginville 5 32 40N17'34 80W31'26 5:22:06
Viropa 17 1 39N24'41 80W16'56 5:21:08
Vivian 24 1 37N25'05 81W29'15 5:25:57
Volcano 54 1 39N11 81W23 5:25:32
Volga 1 1 39N04'42 80W08'08 5:20:33
Vulcan 30 1 37N33'08 82W07'34 5:28:30
Wade 34 1 38N32'16 80W49'15 5:23:17
Wade 52 2 39N42'28 80W33'43 5:22:15
Wadestown 31 17 39N40'31 80W20'18 5:21:21
Wadeville 54 1 39N09'02 81W38'09 5:26:33
Waggener 27 1 38N59 82W02 5:28:08
Wagoner 29 2 39N32'17 78W40'21 5:14:41
Wahoo 25 17 39N27'18 80W13'37 5:20:54
Wainville 51 1 38N29'29 80W34'23 5:22:18
Waiteville 32 1 37N28'25 80W25'20 5:21:41
Waldeck 21 1 39N02'52 80W30'34 5:22:02
Walgrove 20 1 38N27'50 81W26'14 5:25:45
Walker 54 1 39N10'45 81W23'03 5:25:32
Walker Lanes 54 1 39N16 81W40 5:26:40
Walkersville 21 1 38N52'10 80W27'25 5:21:50
Wallace 17 1 39N24'34 80W29'24 5:21:58
Wallace Heights 20 22 38N22 81W40 5:26:40
Wallback 44 1 38N33'56 81W07'50 5:24:31
Walnut 7 1 38N41'20 81W03'28 5:24:14
Walnut 38 1 38N25'23 80W04'27 5:20:18
Walnut Bottom 16 1 39N06'21 79W00'59 5:16:04
Walnut Grove 44 1 38N44'06 81W18'10 5:25:13
Walnut Hill 23 1 37N49'25 82W01'46 5:28:07
Walnut Valley Acres 20 22 38N22 81W40 5:26:40
Walton 44 1 38N38'20 81W24'08 5:25:37
Wana 31 17 39N42'13 80W17'55 5:21:12
Wanda 23 1 37N51'31 81W55'41 5:27:43

Waneta 51 1 38N32'55 80w14'36 5:20:58
Wanless 38 1 38N26'14 79w54'26 5:19:38
Wapocomo 14 1 39N23'42 78w44'06 5:14:56
War 24 1 37N18'04 81w41'28 5:26:46
Ward 20 1 38N14'47 81w23'18 5:25:33
Warden 41 18 37N48'28 81w09'40 5:24:39
Wardensville 16 1 39N04'30 78w35'53 5:14:24
War Eagle 30 1 37N31'42 81w56'39 5:27:47
Warfield 8 1 38N23'12 81w11'02 5:24:44
Warnocks 29 6 39N27'43 79w05'52 5:16:23
Warren 49 1 39N04 80w13 5:20:52
Warriormine 24 1 37N17'34 81w41'50 5:26:47
Warwick 38 1 38N16'56 80w03'51 5:20:15
Warwood 35 34 40N07'00 80w42'00 5:22:48
Washburn 43 1 39N08'32 81w02'49 5:24:11
Washington 54 1 39N15'40 81w40'19 5:26:41
Washington Gardens 54 1 39N16 81w40 5:26:40
Washington Heights 3 18 38N02'08 81w49'54 5:27:20
Washington Lake 54 1 39N16 81w40 5:26:40
Wasp 37 1 39N25'48 81w02'39 5:24:11
Waterloo 27 1 38N43'51 81w56'05 5:27:44
Watoga 38 1 38N08'44 80w09'05 5:20:36
Watson 25 17 39N27'49 80w09'37 5:20:38
Wattsville 8 1 38N29'45 80w51'40 5:23:27
Waverly 54 1 39N20'17 81w22'47 5:25:31
Wayne 50 1 38N13'17 82w26'33 5:29:46
Wayside 32 1 37N35'31 80w41'20 5:22:45
Weaver 42 1 38N58'09 79w55'52 5:19:43
Webb 50 1 37N58'11 82w28'57 5:29:56
Weberwood 20 14 38N20'56 81w40'15 5:26:41
Webster 46 14 39N17'48 80w02'44 5:20:11
Webster Springs 51 1 38N28'45 80w24'49 5:21:39
Weese 42 1 38N53'05 79w42'38 5:18:51
Weese 51 1 38N28'55 80w33'22 5:22:13
Weircrest 15 32 40N26'26 80w35'58 5:22:24
Weirton 15 32 40N25'08 80w35'23 5:22:22
Weirton Heights 15 32 40N24'30 80w32'22 5:22:09
Weirton Junction 5 32 40N23'20 80w35'39 5:22:23
Weirwood 10 1 37N53'41 81w16'14 5:25:05
Welch 24 1 37N25'58 81w35'05 5:26:20
Welch Glade 51 1 38N23'50 80w33'51 5:22:15
Wellford 20 1 38N31'50 81w20'24 5:25:22
Wellington Heights 1 1 39N08'30 80w04'02 5:20:16
Wellsburg 5 33 40N16'19 80w36'35 5:22:26
Welton 12 1 39N00'06 79w05'07 5:16:20
Wendel 46 1 39N17'47 80w06'20 5:20:25
Wenonah 28 1 37N27'55 81w14'45 5:24:59
Werner 1 1 39N01'04 80w00'38 5:20:03
Werth 34 1 38N21'18 80w45'15 5:23:01
West 52 2 39N40'42 80w40'12 5:22:41
Westchester 25 17 39N28'21 80w10'56 5:20:44
West Columbia 27 1 38N58'59 82w03'49 5:28:15
West Dunbar 20 14 38N23 81w45 5:27:00
West End 25 17 39N28'07 80w09'22 5:20:37
West End 39 19 39N23'25 79w46'16 5:19:05
Westerly 10 1 37N59'32 81w19'15 5:25:17
West Gilbert 30 1 37N37 81w52 5:27:28
West Grafton 46 14 39N20'13 80w01'32 5:20:06
West Hamlin 22 1 38N17'08 82w11'45 5:28:47
West Huntington 6 5 38N24'38 82w29'02 5:29:56
West Junction 3 1 37N58'27 81w43'00 5:26:52
West Liberty 35 6 40N10'11 80w35'38 5:22:23
West Logan 23 1 37N52'00 81w59'12 5:27:57
West Milford 17 1 39N12'03 80w24'16 5:21:37
West Montgomery 20 17 38N10'43 81w20'06 5:25:20
Westmoreland 50 5 38N24'02 82w30'44 5:30:03
Weston 21 1 39N02'18 80w28'03 5:21:52
Westover 31 28 39N38'04 79w58'12 5:19:53
West Pea Ridge 6 5 38N24'33 82w20'38 5:29:23
West Raleigh 41 18 37N46 81w11 5:24:44
West Sabraton 31 28 39N37'00 79w55'42 5:19:43
West Side 20 22 38N21'56 81w39'07 5:26:36
West Union 9 1 39N17'47 80w46'38 5:23:07

West Van Vooris 31 28 39N41'07 79w57'04 5:19:48
West Virginia Central Juncti 29 6 39N28'17 79w03'41 5:16:15
West Williamson 30 1 37N40'33 82w17'32 5:29:10
Wevaco 20 1 38N00'07 81w25'30 5:25:42
Weyanoke 28 1 37N24'55 81w15'40 5:25:03
Wharncliffe 30 1 37N33'19 81w57'57 5:27:52
Wharton 3 1 37N54'12 81w40'39 5:26:43
Wheat 52 2 39N37'35 80w35'42 5:22:23
Wheatland 19 2 39N14'10 77w54'01 5:11:36
Wheeler 51 1 38N41'11 80w24'10 5:21:37
Wheeling 35 34 40N03'50 80w43'16 5:22:53
Wheeling Island 35 34 40N04 80w42 5:22:48
Whetstone 8 1 38N30'06 81w03'21 5:24:13
Whipple 10 1 37N57'42 81w09'58 5:24:40
Whipple Junction 10 1 37N57'23 81w09'58 5:24:40
Whirlwind 23 1 38N02 82w07 5:28:28
Whitby 41 1 37N39'58 81w11'04 5:24:44
White Chapel 20 1 38N30'12 81w38'46 5:26:35
Whitehall 25 17 39N25'16 80w10'58 5:20:44
White Oak 41 1 37N41'34 81w04'23 5:24:18
Whiteoak Grove 13 1 38N00'05 80w20'01 5:21:20
White Oak Junction 10 1 37N55'13 81w09'31 5:24:38
White Oak Springs 39 12 39N29'13 79w30'03 5:18:00
White Pine 7 1 38N56'48 81w01'46 5:24:07
White Rock 25 17 39N28 80w10 5:20:40
Whites Addition 23 1 37N50'13 82w00'19 5:28:01
Whites Creek 50 1 38N15 82w36 5:30:24
White Sulphur Springs 13 14 37N47'47 80w17'52 5:21:11
Whitesville 3 18 37N58'29 81w31'45 5:26:07
Whitman 23 1 37N48'48 82w01'29 5:28:06
Whitman Junction 23 1 37N49'53 82w01'57 5:28:08
Whitmer 42 1 38N48'46 79w32'57 5:18:12
Whittaker 20 1 38N04'39 81w22'49 5:25:31
Whyte 42 35 38N59'20 79w49'54 5:19:20
Wick 48 2 39N24'47 80w58'27 5:23:54
Wickham 14 1 39N12'44 78w52'07 5:15:28
Wickham 41 18 37N46'56 81w13'01 5:24:52
Widen 8 1 38N27'58 80w51'27 5:23:26
Wiggins 45 14 37N39'33 80w50'17 5:23:21
Wihiteoak 43 1 39N11 80w57 5:23:48
Wikel 32 1 37N30'43 80w38'52 5:22:35
Wilbur 23 1 37N46 81w55 5:27:40
Wilbur 48 2 39N22'35 80w49'29 5:23:18
Wilcoe 24 1 37N22'52 81w33'51 5:26:15
Wildcat 21 1 38N45'12 80w26'18 5:21:45
Wildell 38 1 38N42'40 79w46'51 5:19:07
Wilderness 34 1 38N10 80w50 5:23:20
Wilding 18 1 38N56'53 81w41'11 5:26:45
Wild Meadow 13 14 37N51'50 80w14'18 5:20:57
Wiley 37 1 39N19'49 81w07'32 5:24:30
Wiley Ford 29 2 39N36'52 78w46'31 5:15:06
Wileyville 52 2 39N37'50 80w40'25 5:22:42
Wilkinson 23 1 37N49'40 81w59'52 5:27:59
Willard 17 1 39N23'02 80w16'17 5:21:05
William 47 1 39N10'19 79w29'34 5:17:58
Williams 54 1 39N24'02 81w26'54 5:25:48
Williamsburg 13 1 37N58'12 80w29'33 5:21:58
Williams Mountain 3 1 38N01'33 81w40'10 5:26:41
Williamson 30 1 37N40'27 82w16'39 5:29:07
Williamsport 12 1 39N12'05 79w01'42 5:16:07
Williamstown 54 1 39N24 81w27 5:25:48
Willibet 41 1 37N37'05 81w11'47 5:24:47
Willis Branch 10 1 37N53'37 81w15'46 5:25:03
Willow Bend 32 1 37N32 80w32 5:22:08
Willowdale 18 1 39N01'40 81w41'22 5:26:45
Willow Island 37 1 39N21'30 81w18'30 5:25:14
Willowton 28 1 37N20'56 80w53'11 5:23:33
Wills 20 1 38N27'26 81w29'50 5:25:59
Wilmore 24 1 37N27'31 81w45'09 5:27:01
Wilsie 4 1 38N41'08 80w53'10 5:23:33
Wilson 6 5 38N25'34 82w19'49 5:29:19
Wilson 12 1 39N15'15 79w23'53 5:17:36
Wilson 20 22 38N23'07 81w35'37 5:26:22

Wilsonburg 17 14 39N17'33 80w23'47 5:21:35
Wilsondale 50 1 37N57'13 82w19'40 5:29:19
Wilsonia 12 1 39N12'22 79w26'59 5:17:48
Wilsontown 49 1 38N49'16 80w20'20 5:21:21
Winding Gulf 41 1 37N40'41 81w14'24 5:24:58
Windom 55 1 37N35'55 81w34'14 5:26:17
Windsor Heights 5 9 40N11'28 80w39'56 5:22:40
Windy 53 1 39N01'41 81w31'42 5:26:07
Winebrenners Crossroad 2 27 39N25'41 77w53'45 5:11:35
Winfield 25 17 39N28'49 80w04'55 5:20:20
Winfield 40 1 38N31'59 81w53'37 5:27:34
Wingrove 10 1 37N56'21 81w09'48 5:24:39
Winifrede 20 1 38N11'29 81w33'25 5:26:14
Winifrede Junction 20 1 38N12'30 81w31'14 5:26:05
Winona 10 1 38N02'47 80w59'33 5:23:58
Winslow 50 1 38N18'24 82w18'28 5:29:14
Winter 40 1 38N30'34 81w44'51 5:26:59
Wiseburg 18 1 38N58'48 81w35'05 5:26:20
Witcher 20 14 38N13'31 81w30'58 5:26:04
Withers 11 1 38N53'59 80w57'53 5:23:52
Wolfcreek 32 1 37N39'55 80w37'27 5:22:30
Wolfe 28 1 37N18'26 81w19'44 5:25:19
Wolf Pen 55 1 37N32 81w36 5:26:24
Wolf Run 26 21 39N54'26 80w33'56 5:22:16
Wolf Summit 17 1 39N16'51 80w27'40 5:21:51
Womelsdorf 42 1 38N54 79w58 5:19:52
Woodbine 34 1 38N17'55 80w36'53 5:22:28
Woodcliff Acres 54 1 39N16 81w40 5:26:40
Woodland 26 4 39N43 80w49 5:23:16
Woodland Park 25 17 39N28 80w10 5:20:40
Woodland Park 54 14 39N17'25 81w30'44 5:26:03
Woodlands 26 4 39N48'24 80w49'02 5:23:16
Woodman 13 1 37N54'43 80w18'56 5:21:16
Woodmont 33 11 39N37'42 78w18'40 5:13:15
Woodpeck 41 1 37N41'36 81w11'47 5:24:47
Woodrow 38 1 38N16'52 80w09'31 5:20:38
Woodruff 26 21 39N46'18 80w32'17 5:22:09
Woodsdale 35 34 40N04'38 80w41'37 5:22:46
Woodville 22 1 38N09'41 81w53'32 5:27:34
Woodzell 51 1 38N31'22 80w18'53 5:21:16
Woosley 55 1 37N31'13 81w35'19 5:26:21
Worley 31 17 39N42'26 80w08'55 5:20:36
Worth 24 1 37N24'53 81w23'24 5:25:34
Worthington 25 17 39N27'09 80w15'38 5:21:03
Wright 41 1 37N49'40 81w06'07 5:24:24
Wriston 10 18 38N00'47 81w12'13 5:24:49
Wyatt 17 1 39N26'06 80w21'13 5:21:25
Wyco 55 1 37N35'56 81w20'35 5:25:22
Wylo 23 1 37N40'35 81w50'50 5:27:23
Wymer 21 1 38N51'33 80w25'20 5:21:41
Wymer 42 1 38N53'36 79w37'08 5:18:29
Wyndal 10 1 38N12'52 81w10'56 5:24:44
Wyoma 27 1 38N45'48 82w07'44 5:28:31
Wyoming 55 1 37N34'56 81w36'07 5:26:24
Wyoming City (Mohawk P O) 24 1 37N30'35 81w55'43 5:27:43
Yards 28 1 37N17'32 81w18'37 5:25:14
Yates 6 1 38N26 82w13 5:28:52
Yates Crossing 6 1 38N26'29 82w11'24 5:28:46
Yawkey 22 1 38N13'30 81w57'54 5:27:52
Yellow Spring 14 1 39N10'56 78w30'35 5:14:02
Yerba 24 1 37N29'34 81w37'27 5:26:30
Yokum 49 1 38N58'30 80w03'46 5:20:15
Yolyn 23 1 37N49'45 81w51'41 5:27:27
York 27 1 38N54'21 82w07'32 5:28:30
Young 18 1 38N38'20 81w40'37 5:26:42
Youngs Bottom 20 1 38N27'44 81w25'36 5:25:42
Youngstown 10 1 38N05'31 81w08'39 5:24:35
Yukon 24 1 37N19'09 81w41'47 5:26:47
Zackville 53 1 38N58'27 81w28'13 5:25:53
Zela 34 1 38N17'09 80w57'00 5:23:48
Zenith 32 1 37N30'14 80w31'54 5:22:08
Zevely 39 12 39N28 79w41 5:18:44
Zigler 36 1 38N36'51 79w24'01 5:17:36
Zinnia 9 1 39N13'38 80w36'14 5:22:25
Zion 49 1 38N53 80w18 5:21:12
Zona 44 1 38N43'19 81w27'21 5:25:49

TIME TABLES

WI # 1

Date	Time	Zone
Before 11/18/1883		LMT
11/18/1883	12:00	CST
3/31/1918	02:00	CWT
10/27/1918	02:00	CST
3/30/1919	02:00	CWT
10/26/1919	02:00	CST
2/09/1942	02:00	CWT
9/30/1945	02:00	CST
4/28/1957	02:00	CDT
9/29/1957	02:00	CST
4/27/1958	02:00	CDT
9/28/1958	02:00	CST
4/26/1959	02:00	CDT
9/27/1959	02:00	CST
4/24/1960	02:00	CDT
9/25/1960	02:00	CST
4/30/1961	02:00	CDT
9/24/1961	02:00	CST
4/29/1962	02:00	CDT
9/30/1962	02:00	CST
4/28/1963	02:00	CDT
9/29/1963	02:00	CST
4/26/1964	02:00	CDT
9/27/1964	02:00	CST
4/25/1965	02:00	CDT
10/31/1965	02:00	CST
4/24/1966	02:00	US#1

WI # 2

Date	Time	Zone
Before 11/18/1883		LMT
11/18/1883	12:00	CST
3/31/1918	02:00	CWT
10/27/1918	02:00	CST
3/30/1919	02:00	CWT
10/26/1919	02:00	CST
4/24/1921	02:00	CDT
10/30/1921	02:00	CST
2/09/1942	02:00	CWT
9/30/1945	02:00	CST
4/28/1957	02:00	CDT
9/29/1957	02:00	CST
4/27/1958	02:00	CDT
9/28/1958	02:00	CST
4/26/1959	02:00	CDT
9/27/1959	02:00	CST
4/24/1960	02:00	CDT
9/25/1960	02:00	CST
4/30/1961	02:00	CDT
9/24/1961	02:00	CST
4/29/1962	02:00	CDT
9/30/1962	02:00	CST
4/28/1963	02:00	CDT
9/29/1963	02:00	CST
4/26/1964	02:00	CDT
9/27/1964	02:00	CST
4/25/1965	02:00	CDT
10/31/1965	02:00	CST
4/24/1966	02:00	US#1

WI # 3

Date	Time	Zone
Before 11/18/1883		LMT
11/18/1883	12:00	CST
3/31/1918	02:00	CWT
10/27/1918	02:00	CST
3/30/1919	02:00	CWT
10/26/1919	02:00	CST
4/30/1922	02:00	CDT
10/24/1922	02:00	CST
4/29/1923	02:00	CDT
9/30/1923	02:00	CST
2/09/1942	02:00	CWT
9/30/1945	02:00	CST
4/28/1957	02:00	CDT
9/29/1957	02:00	CST
4/27/1958	02:00	CDT
9/28/1958	02:00	CST
4/26/1959	02:00	CDT
9/27/1959	02:00	CST
4/24/1960	02:00	CDT
9/25/1960	02:00	CST
4/30/1961	02:00	CDT
9/24/1961	02:00	CST
4/29/1962	02:00	CDT
9/30/1962	02:00	CST
4/28/1963	02:00	CDT
9/29/1963	02:00	CST
4/26/1964	02:00	CDT
9/27/1964	02:00	CST
4/25/1965	02:00	CDT
10/31/1965	02:00	CST
4/24/1966	02:00	US#1

WI # 4

Date	Time	Zone
Before 11/18/1883		LMT
11/18/1883	12:00	CST
3/31/1918	02:00	CWT
10/27/1918	02:00	CST
3/30/1919	02:00	CWT
10/26/1919	02:00	CST
4/24/1921	02:00	CDT
10/30/1921	02:00	CST
4/30/1922	02:00	CDT
10/24/1922	02:00	CST
4/29/1923	02:00	CDT
9/30/1923	02:00	CST
2/09/1942	02:00	CWT
9/30/1945	02:00	CST
4/28/1957	02:00	CDT
9/29/1957	02:00	CST
4/27/1958	02:00	CDT
9/28/1958	02:00	CST
4/26/1959	02:00	CDT
9/27/1959	02:00	CST
4/24/1960	02:00	CDT
9/25/1960	02:00	CST
4/30/1961	02:00	CDT
9/24/1961	02:00	CST
4/29/1962	02:00	CDT
9/30/1962	02:00	CST
4/28/1963	02:00	CDT
9/29/1963	02:00	CST
4/26/1964	02:00	CDT
9/27/1964	02:00	CST
4/25/1965	02:00	CDT
10/31/1965	02:00	CST
4/24/1966	02:00	US#1

WI # 5

Date	Time	Zone
Before 11/18/1883		LMT
11/18/1883	12:00	CST
3/31/1918	02:00	CWT
10/27/1918	02:00	CST
3/30/1919	02:00	CWT
10/26/1919	02:00	CST
4/24/1921	02:00	CDT
10/30/1921	02:00	CST
4/30/1922	02:00	CDT
10/24/1922	02:00	CST
4/29/1923	02:00	CDT
5/11/1923	02:00	CST
2/09/1942	02:00	CWT
9/30/1945	02:00	CST
4/28/1957	02:00	CDT
9/29/1957	02:00	CST
4/27/1958	02:00	CDT
9/28/1958	02:00	CST
4/26/1959	02:00	CDT
9/27/1959	02:00	CST
4/24/1960	02:00	CDT
9/25/1960	02:00	CST
4/30/1961	02:00	CDT
9/24/1961	02:00	CST
4/29/1962	02:00	CDT
9/30/1962	02:00	CST
4/28/1963	02:00	CDT
9/29/1963	02:00	CST
4/26/1964	02:00	CDT
9/27/1964	02:00	CST
4/25/1965	02:00	CDT
10/31/1965	02:00	CST
4/24/1966	02:00	US#1

WI # 6

Date	Time	Zone
Before 11/18/1883		LMT
11/18/1883	12:00	CST
3/31/1918	02:00	CWT
10/27/1918	02:00	CST
3/30/1919	02:00	CWT
10/26/1919	02:00	CST
2/09/1942	02:00	CWT
9/30/1945	02:00	CST
4/24/1955	02:00	CDT
9/25/1955	02:00	CST
4/29/1956	02:00	CDT
9/30/1956	02:00	CST
4/28/1957	02:00	CDT
9/29/1957	02:00	CST
4/27/1958	02:00	CDT
9/28/1958	02:00	CST
4/26/1959	02:00	CDT
9/27/1959	02:00	CST
4/24/1960	02:00	CDT
9/25/1960	02:00	CST
4/30/1961	02:00	CDT
9/24/1961	02:00	CST
4/29/1962	02:00	CDT
9/30/1962	02:00	CST
4/28/1963	02:00	CDT
9/29/1963	02:00	CST
4/26/1964	02:00	CDT
9/27/1964	02:00	CST
4/25/1965	02:00	CDT
10/31/1965	02:00	CST
4/24/1966	02:00	US#1

COUNTIES

1 Adams
2 Ashland
3 Barron
4 Bayfield
5 Brown
6 Buffalo
7 Burnett
8 Calumet
9 Chippewa
10 Clark
11 Columbia
12 Crawford
13 Dane
14 Dodge
15 Door
16 Douglas
17 Dunn
18 Eau Claire
19 Florence
20 Fond du Lac
21 Forest
22 Grant
23 Green
24 Green Lake
25 Iowa
26 Iron
27 Jackson
28 Jefferson
29 Juneau
30 Kenosha
31 Kewaunee
32 La Crosse
33 Lafayette
34 Langlade
35 Lincoln
36 Manitowoc
37 Marathon
38 Marinette
39 Marquette
40 Menominee
41 Milwaukee
42 Monroe
43 Oconto
44 Oneida
45 Outagamie
46 Ozaukee
47 Pepin
48 Pierce
49 Polk
50 Portage
51 Price
52 Racine
53 Richland
54 Rock
55 Rusk
56 St Croix
57 Sauk
58 Sawyer
59 Shawano
60 Sheboygan
61 Taylor
62 Trempealeau
63 Vernon
64 Vilas
65 Walworth
66 Washburn
67 Washington
68 Waukesha
69 Waupaca
70 Waushara
71 Winnebago
72 Wood

Place		Lat	Long	Time
Abbotsford 10	1	44N56'47	90W18'57	6:01:16
Abells Corners 65	1	42N43'34	88W32'33	5:54:10
Abrams 43	1	44N46'45	88W03'35	5:52:14
Ackerville 67	1	43N18'36	88W15'29	5:53:02
Ackley 34	1	45N10	89W15	5:57:00
Ada 60	1	43N52'37	87W53'44	5:51:35
Adams 1	1	43N57'22	89W49'05	5:59:16
Adams 65	1	42N48'02	88W31'58	5:54:08
Adams Beach 59	1	44N41'10	88W40'05	5:54:40
Addison 67	1	43N25'22	88W22'28	5:53:30
Adell 60	1	43N37'09	87W57'07	5:51:48
Adella Beach 71	1	44N08'32	88W27'42	5:53:51
Adrian 42	1	43N56	90W35	6:02:20
Advance 59	1	44N47'16	88W19'56	5:53:20
Afton 54	1	42N36'14	89W04'16	5:56:17
Agenda 2	1	46N03	90W22	6:01:28
Ahnapee 31	1	44N38	87W28	5:49:52
Ainsworth 34	1	45N23	88W59	5:55:56
Akan 53	1	43N20	90W35	6:02:20
Alaska 31	1	44N32'26	87W30'04	5:50:00
Alban 50	1	44N37'40	89W17'05	5:57:08
Albany 23	1	42N42'28	89W26'13	5:57:45
Albertville 9	1	44N57'36	91W36'01	6:06:24
Albion 13	1	42N52'46	89W04'11	5:56:17
Alden 49	1	45N15	92W31	6:10:04
Alderley 14	1	43N13'03	88W26'59	5:53:48
Algoma 31	1	44N36'32	87W25'57	5:49:44
Allen 18	1	44N39'41	91W22'00	6:05:28
Allen Grove 65	1	42N34'49	88W45'45	5:55:03
Allenton 67	1	43N25'14	88W20'27	5:53:22
Allenville 71	1	44N07'59	88W37'08	5:54:29
Allouez 5	1	44N28'39	88W00'58	5:52:04
Allouez 16	1	46N41'19	92W01'28	6:08:06
Alma 6	1	44N19'12	91W54'53	6:07:40
Alma Center 27	1	44N26'14	90W54'40	6:03:39
Almena 3	1	45N25'01	92W01'58	6:08:08
Almon 59	1	44N54	89W03	5:56:12
Almond 50	1	44N15'32	89W24'25	5:57:38
Alpha 7	1	45N46'21	92W34'46	6:10:19
Altdorf 72	1	44N29	89W58	5:59:52
Alto 20	1	43N40'36	88W47'42	5:55:11
Altoona 18	1	44N48'17	91W26'35	6:05:46
Alverno 36	1	44N05'06	87W44'23	5:50:58
Alvin 21	1	45N59'06	88W49'45	5:55:19
Amberg 38	1	45N30'11	87W59'37	5:51:58
Ambridge 16	1	46N38'12	92W04'13	6:08:17
Amery 49	1	45N18'25	92W21'43	6:09:27
Amherst 50	1	44N27'03	89W17'05	5:57:08
Amherst Junction 50	1	44N28'08	89W18'45	5:57:15
Amnicon 16	1	46N36	91W52	6:07:28
Amnicon Falls 16	1	46N36'14	91W53'23	6:07:34
Anacker 39	1	43N37'32	89W26'37	5:57:46
Anderson 54	1	42N43'01	89W01'00	5:56:04
Angelica 59	1	44N40'26	88W18'49	5:53:15
Angelo 42	1	43N58'15	90W46'40	6:03:07
Angus 3	1	45N38'52	91W36'06	6:06:24
Aniwa 59	1	45N00'31	89W12'51	5:56:51
Annaton 22	1	42N54'41	90W32'15	6:02:09
Anson 9	1	44N58'51	91W17'12	6:05:09
Anston 5	1	44N37'02	88W09'37	5:52:38
Anthony 18	1	44N34	91W41	6:06:44
Antigo 34	1	45N08'25	89W09'08	5:56:37
Anton 16	1	46N37'09	92W14'07	6:08:56
Apollonia 55	1	45N27'00	91W18'05	6:05:12
Apple Creek 45	1	44N19'32	88W22'28	5:53:30
Apple River 49	1	45N25	92W21	6:09:24
Appleton 45	1	44N15'43	88W24'55	5:53:40
Arbor Vitae 64	1	45N55'14	89W39'48	5:58:39
Arcade 20	1	43N51'31	88W52'15	5:55:29
Arcadia 62	1	44N15'10	91W30'05	6:06:00
Arena 25	1	43N09'56	89W54'46	5:59:39
Argonne 21	1	45N39'35	88W52'45	5:55:31
Argyle 33	1	42N42'04	89W52'01	5:59:28
Arkansaw 47	1	44N38'02	92W01'52	6:08:07
Arkdale 1	1	44N01'38	89W53'16	5:59:33
Arland 3	1	45N20'18	92W01'22	6:08:05
Arlington 11	1	43N20'17	89W22'49	5:57:31
Armenia 29	1	44N10	90W01	6:00:04
Armstrong 20	1	43N42'37	88W11'41	5:52:47
Armstrong 43	1	45N10	88W26	5:53:44
Armstrong Creek 21	1	45N39'30	88W26'46	5:53:47
Arnold 9	1	45N14'56	91W00'15	6:04:01
Arnott 50	1	44N27'26	89W26'48	5:57:47
Arpin 72	1	44N32'26	90W02'06	6:00:08
Artesia Beach 20	1	43N56'05	88W18'54	5:53:16
Arthur 9	1	45N04	91W09	6:04:36
Arthur 22	1	42N50'48	90W26'47	6:01:47
Ashford 20	1	43N35'13	88W22'14	5:53:29
Ashippun 14	1	43N12'43	88W30'58	5:54:04
Ashland 2	1	46N35'33	90W53'01	6:03:32
Ashland Junction 4	1	46N34'26	90W58'16	6:03:53
Ashley 37	1	44N41'34	89W36'29	5:58:26
Ash Ridge 53	1	43N30	90W40	6:02:40
Ashton 13	1	43N08'26	89W32'29	5:58:10
Ashton Corners 13	1	43N08'25	89W31'14	5:58:05
Ashwaubenon 5	1	44N28	88W05	5:52:20
Askeaton 5	1	44N16'12	88W06'39	5:52:27
Astico 14	1	43N19'59	88W56'23	5:55:46
Athelstane 38	1	45N25'26	88W05'43	5:52:23
Athens 37	1	45N01'59	90W04'26	6:00:18
Atkins 21	1	45N39'55	89W01'23	5:56:06
Atlanta 55	1	45N31	91W20	6:05:20
Atlas 49	1	45N38'08	92W35'26	6:10:22
Attica 23	1	42N46'12	89W28'50	5:57:55
Atwater 14	1	43N33'39	88W44'04	5:54:56
Atwood 10	1	44N53'10	90W28'54	6:01:56
Aubrey 53	1	43N18'53	90W17'36	6:01:10
Auburndale 72	1	44N37'37	90W00'27	6:00:02
Augusta 18	1	44N40'49	91W07'11	6:04:29
Aurora 19	1	45N47'08	88W06'03	5:52:24
Aurora 67	1	43N25'39	88W18'06	5:53:12
Auroraville 70	1	44N03'07	88W59'33	5:55:58
Avalanche 63	1	43N36'08	90W46'49	6:03:07
Avalon 54	1	42N37'58	88W52'03	5:55:28
Avoca 25	1	43N10'55	90W19'28	6:01:18
Avon 33	1	42N40'04	90W07'34	6:00:30
Avon 54	1	42N32'36	89W19'53	5:57:20
Aztalan 28	1	43N04'22	88W51'44	5:55:27
Babcock 72	1	44N18'06	90W06'40	6:00:27
Bad River Indian Reservation 2	1	46N35	90W42	6:02:48
Bagley 22	1	42N54'20	91W06'04	6:04:24
Bagley Junction 38	1	45N08'18	87W45'04	5:51:00
Baileys Harbor 15	1	45N03'54	87W07'27	5:48:30
Bakerville 72	1	44N37'38	90W13'05	6:00:52
Baldwin 56	1	44N58'00	92W22'27	6:09:30
Ballou 2	1	46N19'03	90W35'04	6:02:20
Balsam Lake 49	1	45N27'08	92W27'16	6:09:49
Bancroft 50	1	44N18'35	89W30'49	5:58:03
Bangor 32	1	43N53'35	90W59'25	6:03:58
Banner 20	1	43N46'23	88W12'34	5:52:50
Bannerman 70	1	43N59'48	89W13'30	5:56:54
Baraboo 57	1	43N28'16	89W44'39	5:58:59
Bardwell 65	1	42N35'13	88W45'02	5:55:00
Bark Point 4	1	46N53'15	91W11'00	6:04:44
Barksdale 4	1	46N37'17	90W55'55	6:03:44
Barnes 4	1	46N20	91W29	6:05:56
Barneveld 25	1	43N00'56	89W53'43	5:59:35
Barnum 12	1	43N13'08	90W50'22	6:03:21
Barre 32	1	43N50	91W05	6:04:20
Barre Mills 32	1	43N50'29	91W06'50	6:04:27
Barron 3	1	45N24'05	91W50'56	6:07:24
Barronett 3	1	45N38'13	91W59'34	6:07:58
Barron Junction 3	1	45N24	91W51	6:07:24
Barry Corner 47	1	44N31'05	92W10'46	6:08:43
Bartelme 59	1	44N54	88W55	5:55:40
Barton 67	1	43N26'37	88W10'50	5:52:43
Basco 13	1	42N54'43	89W30'53	5:58:04
Bashaw 7	1	45N46	91W58	6:07:52
Bass Bay 68	1	42N55	88W07	5:52:28
Bassett 30	1	42N32'26	88W13'40	5:52:55
Basswood 53	1	43N15'45	90W29'57	6:02:00
Batavia 60	1	43N35'40	88W03'03	5:52:12
Bateman 9	1	44N55'52	91W16'04	6:05:04
Bavaria 34	1	45N18'51	89W21'50	5:57:27
Bay City 48	1	44N35'08	92W27'01	6:09:48
Bayfield 4	1	46N48'39	90W49'05	6:03:16
Bay Mills 35	1	45N28	89W44	5:58:56

Bay Settlement 5 1 44N33'11 87W53'26 5:51:34
Bayside 41 1 43N10'50 87W54'02 5:51:36
Bayview 4 1 46N44 90W59 6:03:56
Bay View 31 1 44N37'58 87W44'39 5:50:59
Bay View 41 1 42N59 87W54 5:51:36
Beachs Corners 62 1 44N12'05 91W14'14 6:04:57
Bear Bluff 27 1 44N13 90W21 6:01:24
Bear Creek 45 1 44N31'53 88W43'35 5:54:54
Bear Lake 55 1 45N36 91W50 6:07:20
Bear Trap 2 1 46N35 90W53 6:03:32
Bear Valley 53 1 43N18'29 90W11'42 6:00:47
Beaumont 52 1 42N44'32 88W06'37 5:52:26
Beaver 38 1 45N08'15 88W01'04 5:52:04
Beaver Brook 66 1 45N45'12 91W50'20 6:07:21
Beaver Dam 14 1 43N27'28 88W50'14 5:55:21
Beaver Dam Junction 14 1 43N27 88W51 5:55:24
Beaver Edge 14 1 43N27 88W51 5:55:24
Beebe 16 1 46N24'26 91W50'21 6:07:21
Beecher 38 1 45N35'18 87W59'41 5:51:59
Beecher Lake 38 1 45N34'09 87W59'51 5:51:59
Beechwood 60 1 43N35'34 88W07'13 5:52:29
Beetown 22 1 42N47'42 90W53'07 6:03:32
Belcrest 54 1 42N32'29 89W05'46 5:56:23
Beldenville 48 1 44N46'26 92W30'27 6:10:02
Belgium 46 1 43N29'59 87W51'01 5:51:24
Bell 4 1 46N50 91W06 6:04:24
Bell Center 12 1 43N17'30 90W49'36 6:03:18
Belle Fountain 11 1 43N36'52 89W15'48 5:57:03
Belle Plaine 59 1 44N42'55 88W39'58 5:54:40
Belleville 13 1 42N51'35 89W32'17 5:58:09
Bellevue 5 1 44N26'39 87W55'12 5:51:41
Bell Heights 45 1 44N16'50 88W24'57 5:53:40
Bellinger 61 1 45N04'31 90W48'00 6:03:12
Bellwood 16 1 46N34'19 91W38'15 6:06:33
Belmont 33 1 42N44'10 90W20'03 6:01:20
Beloit 54 1 42N30'30 89W01'54 5:56:08
Belt Line Junction 26 1 46N27 90W12 6:00:48
Belton 41 1 43N01 88W00 5:52:00
Belvidere 6 1 44N16 91W51 6:07:24
Benderville 5 1 44N36'41 87W51'18 5:51:25
Bennett 16 1 46N26'55 91W51'12 6:07:25
Benoit 4 1 46N30'07 91W04'36 6:04:18
Benson 7 1 45N43'02 92W51'20 6:11:25
Benton 33 1 42N34'11 90W22'50 6:01:31
Bergen 54 1 42N29'38 88W51'55 5:55:28
Bergen Beach 20 1 43N51'38 88W22'15 5:53:29
Berlin 24 1 43N58'05 88W56'36 5:55:46
Bern 37 1 45N03 90W08 6:00:32
Berry 13 1 43N10 89W40 5:58:40
Bethel 72 1 44N32'26 90W05'23 6:00:22
Bethesda 68 1 42N59'16 88W19'06 5:53:16
Bevent 37 1 44N46'14 89W23'22 5:57:33
Big Bend 68 1 42N52'53 88W12'24 5:52:50
Big Falls 69 1 44N36'56 89W00'58 5:56:04
Big Flats 1 1 44N06'43 89W48'28 5:59:14
Big Fork Prairie 65 6 42N29'43 88W35'58 5:54:24
Bigpatch 22 1 42N40'00 90W28'34 6:01:54
Big Spring 1 1 43N40'10 89W38'37 5:58:34
Billings Park 16 1 46N43'06 92W07'27 6:08:30
Binghamton 45 1 44N25'37 88W28'26 5:53:54
Birch 2 1 46N32'18 90W34'31 6:02:18
Birch 35 1 45N20 89W36 5:58:24
Birch Creek 9 1 45N14 91W14 6:04:56
Birchwood 31 1 44N27'29 87W34'17 5:50:17
Birchwood 66 1 45N39'59 91W33'21 6:06:13
Birnam Wood 59 1 44N56'00 89W12'34 5:56:50
Biron 72 1 44N25'26 89W46'49 5:59:07
Black Brook 49 1 45N15 92W21 6:09:24
Black Creek 45 1 44N28'39 88W27'02 5:53:48
Black Creek Junction 45 1 44N28 88W27 5:53:48
Black Earth 13 1 43N08'14 89W44'48 5:58:59
Black Hawk 57 1 43N16'09 89W55'38 5:59:43
Blackhawk Island 28 1 42N53'54 88W53'32 5:55:34
Black River 16 1 46N33'44 92W08'50 6:08:35
Black River 60 1 43N44 87W46 5:51:04
Black River Falls 27 1 44N17'41 90W51'05 6:03:24
Blackwell 21 1 45N30'51 88W36'45 5:54:27
Blackwell Junction 21 1 45N31'54 88W39'15 5:54:37
Black Wolf 71 1 43N56'16 88W31'25 5:54:06
Black Wolf Point 71 1 43N55'39 88W28'17 5:53:53
Blaine 7 1 46N07 92W10 6:08:40
Blaine 50 1 44N18'33 89W18'56 5:57:16
Blair 62 1 44N17'40 91W14'06 6:04:56
Blanchard 33 1 42N48 89W54 5:59:36
Blanchardville 33 1 42N48'37 89W51'43 5:59:27
Blenker (Sherry Station) 72 1 44N36'48 89W54'54 5:59:40
Bloom City 53 1 43N29'40 90W27'53 6:01:52
Bloomer 9 1 45N06'01 91W29'19 6:05:57
Bloomingdale 63 1 43N38'35 90W46'39 6:03:07
Bloomington 22 1 42N53'07 90W55'24 6:03:42
Bloomville 35 1 45N17'36 89W31'39 5:58:07
Blueberry 16 1 46N34'49 91W40'07 6:06:40
Blue Mounds 13 1 43N01'03 89W49'56 5:59:20
Blue River 22 1 43N11'18 90W34'00 6:02:16
Bluff Siding 6 1 44N04'17 91W37'04 6:06:28
Bluffview 57 1 43N22'16 89W46'23 5:59:06
Boardman 56 1 45N03'56 92W35'59 6:10:24
Boaz 53 1 43N19'53 90W31'33 6:02:06
Bohners Lake 52 1 42N38 88W17 5:53:08
Bohri 6 1 44N07 91W41 6:06:44
Bolt 31 1 44N20'31 87W42'19 5:50:49
Boltonville 67 1 43N31'38 88W06'02 5:52:24
Bonduel 59 1 44N44'25 88W26'41 5:53:47
Bone Lake 49 1 45N35 92W21 6:09:24
Bonita 43 1 45N07'11 88W27'31 5:53:50
Bonneval 21 1 45N39'02 88W32'19 5:54:09
Borea 16 1 46N35'08 92W10'56 6:08:44
Borth 70 1 44N05'28 88W53'45 5:55:35
Boscobel 12 1 43N08'04 90W42'19 6:02:49
Bosstown 53 1 43N23'25 90W36'36 6:02:26
Boulder Junction 64 1 46N06'48 89W38'40 5:58:35
Bovina 45 1 44N28 88W33 5:54:12
Bowers 65 1 42N41'29 88W26'40 5:53:47
Bowler 59 1 44N51'47 88W58'55 5:55:56
Boyceville 17 1 45N02'37 92W02'27 6:08:10
Boyd 9 1 44N57'07 91W02'05 6:04:08
Boydtown 12 1 43N06'38 90W48'13 6:03:13
Boylston 16 1 46N35'51 92W07'43 6:08:31
Boylston Junction 16 1 46N36'51 92W07'10 6:08:29
Brackett 18 1 44N42'05 91W21'03 6:05:24
Bradford 54 1 42N38 88W50 5:55:20
Bradley 35 1 45N32'22 89W45'18 5:59:01
Bradley 37 1 44N48'04 90W00'53 6:00:04
Bradley 41 1 43N09 87W59 5:51:56
Branch 36 1 44N08'45 87W45'40 5:51:03
Brandon 20 1 43N44'07 88W46'52 5:55:07
Branstad 7 1 45N44'15 92W40'58 6:10:44
Brant 8 1 44N04'24 88W12'13 5:52:49
Brantwood 51 1 45N33'46 90W06'54 6:00:28
Brazeau 43 1 45N06 88W13 5:52:52
Breed 43 1 45N04'23 88W25'27 5:53:42
Briarton 59 1 44N36'12 88W25'35 5:53:42
Brickson Park 13 1 43N02 89W17 5:57:08
Bridge Creek 18 1 44N40 91W06 6:04:24
Bridgeport 12 1 43N00'33 91W03'28 6:04:14
Briggsville 39 1 43N39'18 89W35'07 5:58:20
Brigham 25 1 43N00 89W53 5:59:32
Brighton 30 1 42N37'45 88W05'59 5:52:24
Brighton Beach 71 1 44N12'12 88W25'14 5:53:41
Brill 3 1 45N36'10 91W40'19 6:06:41
Brillion 8 1 44N10'38 88W03'51 5:52:15
Bristol 30 1 42N33'32 88W02'57 5:52:12
Bristow 63 1 43N33 90W53 6:03:32
British Hollow 22 1 42N42'21 90W41'12 6:02:45
Brockville 36 1 44N09 87W49 5:51:16
Brockway 27 1 44N17 90W48 6:03:12
Brodhead 23 1 42N37'06 89W22'34 5:57:30
Brodtville 22 1 42N57'09 91W02'47 6:04:11
Brokaw 37 1 45N01'38 89W39'11 5:58:37
Brookfield 68 1 43N03'38 88W06'23 5:52:26
Brooklyn 23 1 42N51'13 89W22'13 5:57:29
Brooks 1 1 43N49'31 89W38'40 5:58:35
Brookside 1 1 43N51'40 89W49'00 5:59:16
Brookside 43 1 44N48'17 87W59'52 5:51:59
Brookville 56 1 44N57 92W18 6:09:12
Brookwood 13 1 43N04 89W27 5:57:48
Brothertown 8 1 43N58'05 88W18'32 5:53:14
Brown Deer 41 1 43N09'48 87W57'52 5:51:51
Browning 61 1 45N09 90W13 6:00:52
Browns Lake 52 1 42N41 88W14 5:52:56
Brownsville 14 1 43N36'59 88W29'26 5:53:58
Browntown 23 1 42N34'40 89W47'39 5:59:11
Brownville 9 1 45N01'53 90W56'01 6:03:44
Bruce 55 1 45N27'25 91W16'23 6:05:06
Bruemmerville 31 1 44N36'24 87W28'12 5:49:53
Brule 16 1 46N33'11 91W34'35 6:06:18
Brunet 9 1 45N10 91W09 6:04:36
Brunswick 18 1 44N43 91W35 6:06:20
Brushville 70 1 44N10'12 88W59'45 5:55:59
Brussels 15 1 44N44'10 87W37'15 5:50:29
Bryant 34 1 45N12'29 89W01'26 5:56:06
Buchanan 45 1 44N15 88W18 5:53:12
Buckbee 69 1 44N38'56 88W50'06 5:55:20
Buck Creek 53 1 43N25'14 90W21'41 6:01:27
Buckhorn Corner 14 1 43N30'30 88W48'21 5:55:13
Buckman 5 1 44N24'52 87W47'07 5:51:08
Bud 63 1 43N33'30 90W59'16 6:03:57
Budd 63 1 43N33 90W53 6:03:32
Budsin 39 1 43N55'10 89W18'43 5:57:15
Buena Park 52 1 42N47'34 88W13'15 5:52:53
Buena Vista 68 1 43N03'56 88W21'06 5:53:24
Buffalo 6 1 44N13'50 91W51'51 6:07:27
Buffalo Shore Estates 39 1 43N44'27 89W28'15 5:57:53
Bundy 35 1 45N29'59 89W26'01 5:57:44
Bunker Hill 53 1 43N29'45 90W15'25 6:01:02
Bunyan 49 1 45N28'34 92W22'01 6:09:28
Burke 13 1 43N08'09 89W16'34 5:57:06
Burkhardt 56 1 45N01'18 92W40'01 6:10:40
Burlington 52 1 42N40'41 88W16'34 5:53:06
Burnett 14 1 43N30'17 88W42'25 5:54:50
Burns 32 1 43N56'42 90W58'33 6:03:54
Burnside 62 1 44N25 91W28 6:05:52
Burr Oak 32 1 44N03'26 91W03'16 6:04:13
Burton 22 1 42N43'04 90W49'02 6:03:16
Busseyville 28 1 42N53'55 88W59'16 5:55:57
Butler 68 1 43N06'21 88W04'10 5:52:17
Butman Corners 62 1 44N04'41 91W17'30 6:05:10
Butte des Morts 71 1 44N05'58 88W39'14 5:54:37
Butternut 2 1 46N00'47 90W29'25 6:01:58
Byrds Creek 53 1 43N13'12 90W32'54 6:02:12
Byron 20 1 43N39'08 88W27'03 5:53:48
Cable 4 1 46N12'29 91W17'31 6:05:10
Caddy Vista 52 1 42N50 87W57 5:51:48
Cadiz 23 1 42N33 89W48 5:59:12
Cadott 9 1 44N56'53 91W09'02 6:04:36
Cady 56 1 44N54 92W12 6:08:48
Cainville 54 1 42N42'35 89W15'07 5:57:00
Calamine 33 1 42N44'33 90W09'43 6:00:39
Calamus 14 1 43N24 88W57 5:55:48
Caldwell 52 1 42N50'07 88W16'35 5:53:06
Caledonia 52 1 42N48'28 87W55'27 5:51:42
Calhoun 68 1 43N00'48 88W07'37 5:52:30
Callon 37 1 44N53'52 89W30'17 5:58:01
Calumet 20 1 43N56 88W15 5:53:00
Calumet Harbor 20 1 43N54'47 88W19'56 5:53:20
Calumetville 20 1 43N56'10 88W18'12 5:53:13
Calvary 20 1 43N50'48 88W14'38 5:52:59
Calvert 32 1 43N45'15 91W12'18 6:04:49
Cambria 11 1 43N32'32 89W06'26 5:56:26
Cambridge 28 1 43N00'13 89W00'59 5:56:04
Cameron 3 1 45N24'31 91W44'38 6:06:59
Campbell 32 1 43N51 91W16 6:05:04
Campbellsport 20 1 43N35'52 88W16'44 5:53:07
Camp Douglas 29 1 43N55'21 90W16'17 6:01:05
Campia 3 1 45N32'15 91W39'56 6:06:40
Camp Lake 30 1 42N32'05 88W08'37 5:52:34
Camp Leonard 13 1 43N02 89W17 5:57:08
Camp McCoy 42 1 43N56 90W49 6:03:16
Camp Whitcomb 68 1 43N10'17 88W19'37 5:53:18
Canton 3 1 45N25'41 91W39'35 6:06:38
Carcajou 28 1 42N53'23 88W57'43 5:55:51
Carey 26 1 46N19 90W13 6:00:52
Carlsville 15 1 44N57'06 87W20'12 5:49:21
Carlton 31 1 44N22 87W36 5:50:24
Carnegie 16 1 46N38'00 92W11'33 6:08:46
Carnot 15 1 44N42'18 87W25'07 5:49:40
Carol Beach 30 1 42N30'44 87W48'33 5:51:14
Carol Beach Estates 30 1 42N35 87W51 5:51:24
Caroline 59 1 44N43'15 88W53'29 5:55:34
Carrollville 41 1 42N52'48 87W51'17 5:51:25
Carson 50 1 44N34 89W47 5:59:08
Carter 21 1 45N23'27 88W37'40 5:54:31
Carter 26 1 46N13'44 90W07'49 6:00:31
Cary 72 1 44N28 90W16 6:01:04
Caryville 17 1 44N45'05 91W40'28 6:06:42
Cascade 60 1 43N39'30 88W00'25 5:52:02
Casco 31 1 44N33'28 87W37'05 5:50:28
Casco Junction 31 1 44N31'50 87W39'02 5:50:36
Casey 66 1 45N56 91W58 6:07:52
Cashton 42 1 43N44'31 90W46'45 6:03:07
Casimir 50 1 44N34'12 89W36'27 5:58:26
Cassel 37 1 44N56 89W54 5:59:36
Cassell 25 1 43N12'24 89W52'30 5:59:30
Cassian 44 1 45N41 89W40 5:58:40
Cassville 22 1 42N42'52 90W59'26 6:03:58
Castle Rock 22 1 43N05 90W29 6:01:56
Caswell 21 1 45N40 88W39 5:54:36
Cataract 42 1 44N05'16 90W50'32 6:03:22
Catawba 51 1 45N32'11 90W31'47 6:02:07
Cato 36 1 44N08'34 87W51'40 5:51:27
Cavour 21 1 45N39'08 88W37'46 5:54:31
Cayuga 2 1 46N14'40 90W40'56 6:02:44
Cazenovia 53 1 43N31'23 90W11'46 6:00:47
Cecil 59 1 44N48'36 88W27'08 5:53:49
Cedar 26 1 46N30'26 90W29'53 6:02:00
Cedarburg 46 1 43N17'48 87W59'15 5:51:57
Cedar Creek 67 1 43N20'23 88W13'22 5:52:53
Cedar Falls 17 1 44N56'09 91W53'02 6:07:32
Cedar Grove 60 1 43N34'11 87W49'24 5:51:18
Cedar Lake 3 1 45N36 91W36 6:06:24
Cedar Lake 67 1 43N21'14 88W17'33 5:53:10
Cedar Park 52 1 42N41'20 88W13'50 5:52:55
Cedar Rapids 55 1 45N35 90W51 6:03:24
Cedarville 38 1 45N27'13 87W58'58 5:51:56
Center House 24 1 43N42 88W59 5:55:56
Center Lake Woods 30 1 42N31 88W07 5:52:28
Center Valley 45 1 44N24'08 88W27'35 5:53:50
Centerville 22 1 43N01'01 90W25'42 6:01:43
Centerville 36 1 43N57 87W46 5:51:04
Centerville 56 1 44N52'01 92W24'48 6:09:39
Centerville 62 1 44N04'12 91W27'04 6:05:48
Centuria 49 1 45N27'05 92W33'14 6:10:13
Chaffey 16 1 46N30 92W17 6:09:08
Chambers Island 15 1 45N08 87W15 5:49:00
Champion 5 1 44N35'21 87W47'39 5:51:11
Chapel Ridge 5 1 44N31'54 87W54'16 5:51:37
Chapel Ridge Heights 5 1 44N30 88W01 5:52:04
Chapultepee 62 1 44N13'23 91W16'52 6:05:07
Charlesburg 8 1 43N58'11 88W10'12 5:52:41
Charlestown 8 1 44N01 88W05 5:52:20
Charlie Bluff 54 1 42N50'25 88W58'41 5:55:55
Charme 12 1 43N10'04 91W08'16 6:04:33
Chase 43 1 44N43'05 88W09'24 5:52:38
Chaseburg 63 1 43N39'28 91W05'47 6:04:23
Chelsea 61 1 45N17'25 90W18'26 6:01:14
Chenequa 68 1 43N06'42 88W23'32 5:53:34
Cherneyville 31 1 44N25'44 87W44'05 5:50:56
Cherokee 37 1 44N54'08 90W13'04 6:00:52
Chester 14 1 43N36 88W43 5:54:52
Chetek 3 1 45N18'51 91W39'03 6:06:36
Chicago 30 3 42N35'10 87W49'29 5:51:18
Chicago Corners 45 1 44N27'32 88W15'03 5:53:00
Chicago Junction 66 1 45N48'12 91W53'11 6:07:33
Chicog 66 1 46N02 91W58 6:07:52
Chili 10 1 44N37'37 90W21'23 6:01:26
Chilton 8 1 44N01'44 88W09'46 5:52:39
Chimney Rock 62 1 44N30 91W28 6:05:52
Chippewa 2 1 46N02 90W42 6:02:48
Chippewa Falls 9 1 44N56'13 91W23'34 6:05:34
Chittamo 66 1 46N07'41 91W42'59 6:06:52
Chiwaukee 30 1 42N35 87W51 5:51:24
Choate 34 1 45N22'41 88W49'20 5:55:17
Christie 10 1 44N38'50 90W35'47 6:02:23
Christilla Heights 54 1 42N31'44 89W04'22 5:56:17
Cicero 45 1 44N34'25 88W23'14 5:53:33
City Point 27 1 44N21'08 90W19'17 6:01:17
Clam Falls 49 1 45N41'19 92W17'36 6:09:10
Clam Lake 2 1 46N09'50 90W54'08 6:03:37
Clark 10 1 45N01'45 90W39'32 6:02:38
Clarks Mills 36 1 44N05'24 87W51'51 5:51:27
Clarks Point 71 1 44N09'03 88W42'37 5:54:50
Clarno 23 1 42N31'07 89W38'52 5:58:35
Claybanks 15 1 44N44 87W22 5:49:28
Clayton 12 1 43N24 90W47 6:03:08
Clayton 49 1 45N19'53 92W10'16 6:08:41
Claywood 43 1 44N53 88W17 5:53:08
Clear Creek 18 1 44N39 91W21 6:05:24
Clearfield 29 1 43N56 90W08 6:00:32
Clear Lake 49 1 45N15'07 92W16'16 6:09:05
Clearwater Lake 44 1 45N51'13 89W11'17 5:56:45

Place		Lat	Long	Time
Cleghorn 18	1	44N41'01	91W25'36	6:05:42
Cleveland 36	1	43N54'54	87W44'50	5:50:59
Clifford 35	1	45N33'19	90W02'35	6:00:10
Clifton 42	1	43N52'45	90W21'24	6:01:26
Clinton 54	1	42N33'28	88W51'54	5:55:28
Clintonville 69	1	44N37'14	88W45'44	5:55:03
Clover 4	1	46N48	91W14	6:04:56
Clover 36	1	44N02'17	87W42'06	5:50:48
Cloverdale 29	1	44N01'30	90W10'44	6:00:43
Cloverland 16	1	46N40'37	91W40'44	6:06:43
Clyde 25	1	43N07'10	90W12'41	6:00:51
Clyde 31	1	44N30'58	87W34'58	5:50:20
Clyman 14	1	43N18'41	88W43'12	5:54:53
Clyman Junction 14	1	43N19'31	88W43'04	5:54:52
Cobb 25	1	42N58'03	90W19'46	6:01:19
Cobban 9	1	45N06'11	91W12'22	6:04:49
Cobb Town 69	1	44N22'32	89W12'55	5:56:52
Cochrane 6	1	44N13'39	91W50'06	6:07:20
Coddington 50	1	44N22'13	89W32'53	5:58:12
Colburn 9	1	45N02'25	91W02'41	6:04:11
Colby 10	1	44N54'36	90W18'56	6:01:16
Cold Spring 28	1	42N53'27	88W46'27	5:55:06
Cold Springs 32	1	43N50'52	91W12'45	6:04:51
Coleman 38	1	45N03'54	88W02'03	5:52:08
Colfax 17	1	44N59'51	91W43'37	6:06:54
Colgate 68	1	43N11'35	88W12'24	5:52:50
Collins 36	1	44N05'08	87W58'58	5:51:56
Coloma 70	1	44N02'08	89W31'17	5:58:05
Coloma Corners 70	1	44N02	89W31	5:58:04
Columbia 10	1	44N30'59	90W43'11	6:02:53
Columbus 11	1	43N20'17	89W00'55	5:56:04
Combined Locks 45	1	44N15'57	88W18'51	5:53:15
Comfort 17	1	44N46'30	92W02'07	6:08:08
Comfort, Point 71	1	43N56'01	88W28'26	5:53:54
Commonwealth 19	1	45N54'49	88W14'24	5:52:58
Como 65	1	42N36'44	88W28'56	5:53:56
Como, Lake 65	1	42N35'25	88W30'07	5:54:00
Comstock 3	1	45N28'40	92W04'30	6:08:18
Concord 28	1	43N04'10	88W35'55	5:54:24
Connorsville 17	1	45N08'10	92W05'41	6:08:23
Conover 64	1	46N03'17	89W15'28	5:57:02
Conrath 55	1	45N23'10	91W02'17	6:04:09
Cooks Valley 9	1	45N04	91W36	6:06:24
Cooksville 54	1	42N50'07	89W14'26	5:56:58
Coomer 7	1	45N44'51	92W15'25	6:09:02
Coon 63	1	43N41	90W58	6:03:52
Coon Rock 25	1	43N09'03	89W59'22	5:59:57
Coon Valley 63	1	43N42'08	91W00'47	6:04:03
Cooperstown 36	1	44N18'46	87W46'28	5:51:06
Coppens Corner 5	1	44N27'30	87W47'08	5:51:09
Coral City 62	1	44N22'46	91W16'38	6:05:07
Corinth 37	1	45N00'10	90W08'21	6:00:33
Cormier 5	1	44N33'46	88W04'41	5:52:19
Cornelia 22	1	42N41'22	90W34'39	6:02:19
Cornell 9	1	45N10'02	91W08'57	6:04:36
Corning 35	1	45N13	89W59	5:59:56
Cornucopia 4	1	46N51'14	91W06'06	6:04:24
Cottage Grove 13	1	43N04'34	89W11'58	5:56:48
Couderay 58	1	45N47'44	91W18'24	6:05:14
Council Bay 32	1	44N03'27	91W17'01	6:05:08
County Line 43	1	44N59'25	87W51'09	5:51:25
County Line 48	1	44N51	92W14	6:08:56
Courtland 11	1	43N30	89W04	5:56:16
Cox 9	1	45N10	90W48	6:03:12
Cozy Corner 16	1	46N09'53	92W14'16	6:08:57
Cranberry Lake 51	1	45N38'25	90W20'50	6:01:23
Cranberry Marsh 60	1	43N34'18	88W05'08	5:52:21
Crandon 21	1	45N34'19	88W54'10	5:55:37
Cranmoor 72	1	44N18'53	90W01'58	6:00:08
Crawford Crossing 57	1	43N27'16	89W43'45	5:58:55
Cream 6	1	44N18'58	91W46'18	6:07:05
Crescent 9	1	45N04'04	91W08'48	6:04:35
Crescent 44	1	45N36	89W29	5:57:56
Crescent Corner 44	1	45N34'12	89W29'21	5:57:57
Crescent Park 13	1	43N02	89W17	5:57:08
Crestview 52	1	42N49'01	87W48'36	5:51:14
Crestview 54	1	42N32'30	89W01'52	5:56:07
Crivitz 38	1	45N13'57	88W00'27	5:52:02
Cross 6	1	44N11	91W39	6:06:36
Cross Plains 13	1	43N06'52	89W39'20	5:58:37
Crystal 66	1	45N51	91W43	6:06:52
Crystal Lake Corners 69	1	44N21	89W05	5:56:20
Cuba City 22	1	42N36'20	90W25'47	6:01:43
Cudahy 41	1	42N57'35	87W51'41	5:51:27
Cullen 43	1	44N57'42	87W51'11	5:51:25
Cumberland 3	1	45N31'56	92W01'09	6:08:05
Curran 27	1	44N22	91W06	6:04:24
Curran 31	1	44N21'22	87W44'44	5:50:59
Curtiss 10	1	44N57'19	90W26'04	6:01:44
Cushing 49	1	45N34'14	92W39'03	6:10:36
Custer 50	1	44N30'38	89W25'34	5:57:42
Cutler 29	1	44N01'33	90W14'12	6:00:57
Cutter 16	1	46N37'59	91W57'31	6:07:50
Cylon 56	1	45N07'20	92W21'10	6:09:25
Czechville 6	1	44N11'14	91W46'24	6:07:06
Dacada 60	1	43N32'36	87W54'31	5:51:38
Dairyland 16	1	46N12'58	92W09'19	6:08:37
Dakota 70	1	43N59'25	89W21'23	5:57:26
Dale 45	1	44N16'23	88W40'42	5:54:43
Daleyville 13	1	42N54'54	89W48'53	5:59:16
Dallas 3	1	45N15'33	91W48'53	6:07:16
Dalton 24	1	43N39'25	89W12'23	5:56:50
Danbury 7	1	46N00'24	92W22'16	6:09:29
Dancy 37	1	44N41'16	89W42'47	5:58:51
Dane 13	1	43N15'02	89W30'05	5:58:00
Daniels 7	1	45N46	92W28	6:09:52
Danville 14	1	43N19'10	88W57'20	5:55:49
Darboy 8	1	44N14'36	88W19'26	5:53:18
Darien 65	1	42N36'06	88W42'27	5:54:50
Darlington 33	1	42N40'59	90W07'03	6:00:28
Davis Corners 1	1	43N38	89W47	5:59:08
Day 37	1	44N50	90W02	6:00:08
Dayton 23	1	42N49'37	89W30'47	5:58:03
Deansville 13	1	43N10'54	89W06'12	5:56:25
Decatur 23	1	42N38	89W26	5:57:44
Decker 46	1	43N28'14	87W51'45	5:51:27
Decker Corner 46	1	43N21'05	88W02'42	5:52:11
Decorah Beach 71	1	43N55'22	88W28'30	5:53:54
Decorah Prairie 62	1	44N06	91W21	6:05:24
Dedham 16	1	46N32'32	92W11'52	6:08:47
Deerbrook 34	1	45N14'01	89W09'20	5:56:37
Deerfield 13	1	43N03'07	89W04'32	5:56:18
Deer Park 56	1	45N11'17	92W23'07	6:09:32
DeForest 13	1	43N14'52	89W20'37	5:57:22
Dekorra 11	1	43N27'27	89W28'03	5:57:52
Delafield 68	1	43N03'39	88W24'13	5:53:37
Delavan 65	1	42N37'59	88W38'37	5:54:34
Delavan Lake 65	1	42N35'03	88W37'57	5:54:32
Dell 63	1	43N39	90W51	6:03:24
Dellona 57	1	43N36	89W54	5:59:36
Dell Prairie 1	1	43N42	89W45	5:59:00
Dellwood 1	1	43N59'03	89W56'19	5:59:45
Dellwood 57	1	43N33'48	89W50'26	5:59:22
Delmar 9	1	45N00	91W00	6:04:00
Delta 4	1	46N28'22	91W16'12	6:05:05
Delton 57	1	43N35	89W47	5:59:08
Denmark 5	1	44N20'52	87W49'38	5:51:19
Denoon 68	1	42N55	88W07	5:52:28
Denzer 57	1	43N20'39	89W53'12	5:59:33
De Pere 5	1	44N26'56	88W03'37	5:52:14
Deronda 49	1	45N18'13	92W25'41	6:09:43
DeSoto 12	1	43N25'23	91W11'56	6:04:48
Devils Corner 47	1	44N30'39	92W08'06	6:08:32
Devils Lake 57	1	43N28	89W45	5:59:00
Dewey 16	1	46N34'10	92W14'41	6:08:59
Dewhurst 10	1	44N28	90W44	6:02:56
Dexter 20	1	43N50'33	88W29'16	5:53:57
Dexter 72	1	44N23	90W07	6:00:28
Dexterville 72	1	44N22'35	90W06'38	6:00:27
Dheinsville 67	1	43N15'00	88W08'34	5:52:34
Diamond Bluff 48	1	44N39'02	92W37'44	6:10:31
Diamond Grove 22	1	42N47'33	90W55'10	6:03:41
Dickeyville 22	1	42N37'38	90W35'31	6:02:22
Diefenbach Corners 67	1	43N21'13	88W15'38	5:53:03
Dilly 63	1	43N38'32	90W26'24	6:01:46
Disco 27	1	44N15'44	91W00'32	6:04:02
Dobie 3	1	45N33'07	91W41'00	6:06:44
Dobie 16	1	46N31'36	91W48'16	6:07:13
Dodge 62	1	44N07'56	91W33'07	6:06:12
Dodges Corners 68	1	42N52	88W20	5:53:20
Dodgeville 25	1	42N57'37	90W07'48	6:00:31
Doering 35	1	45N14'07	89W27'29	5:57:50
Donald 61	1	45N15'09	90W53'49	6:03:35
Door Creek 13	1	43N01'51	89W13'59	5:56:48
Dorchester 10	1	45N00'11	90W20'08	6:01:21
Dorns Faro Springs Beach 8	1	44N07'21	88W19'09	5:53:17
Dorns Twilight Beach 8	1	44N02'22	88W19'14	5:53:17
Doty 43	1	45N13	88W36	5:54:24
Dotyville 20	1	43N45'08	88W15'39	5:53:03
Douglas 39	1	43N41	89W33	5:58:12
Dousman 68	1	43N00'51	88W28'21	5:53:53
Dover 51	1	45N40'18	90W11'15	6:00:45
Dovre 3	1	45N15	91W37	6:06:28
Downing 17	1	45N02'47	92W07'55	6:08:32
Downsville 17	1	44N46'29	91W55'55	6:07:44
Doyle 3	1	45N31	91W36	6:06:24
Doylestown 11	1	43N25'40	89W09'00	5:56:36
Drammen 18	1	44N38	91W35	6:06:20
Draper 58	1	45N53'11	90W49'51	6:03:19
Dresser 49	1	45N21'22	92W38'00	6:10:32
Druecker 46	1	43N26'24	87W52'16	5:51:29
Drummond 4	1	46N20'13	91W15'28	6:05:02
Drywood 9	1	45N02'54	91W10'05	6:04:40
Duck Creek 5	1	44N33'43	88W04'09	5:52:17
Dudley 35	1	45N20'08	89W27'55	5:57:52
Dunbar 38	1	45N39'03	88W10'17	5:52:41
Dunbarton 33	1	42N33'42	90W07'59	6:00:32
Dundas 8	1	44N14'03	88W11'54	5:52:48
Dundee 20	1	43N39'19	88W09'52	5:52:39
Dunkirk 13	1	42N52'53	89W12'35	5:56:50
Dunnville 17	1	44N43'07	91W54'19	6:07:37
Duplainville 68	1	43N04'26	88W11'53	5:52:48
Dupont 69	1	44N38	88W55	5:55:40
Durand 47	1	44N37'35	91W57'56	6:07:52
Durham 68	1	42N51'59	88W04'14	5:52:17
Durham Hill 68	1	42N53	88W00	5:52:00
Durwards Glen 11	1	43N26'19	89W35'29	5:58:22
Duvall 31	1	44N39'40	87W42'48	5:50:51
Duveneck 36	1	44N01'01	87W42'42	5:50:51
Dyckesville 5	1	44N38'36	87W45'40	5:51:03
Eadsville 10	1	45N00'35	90W51'40	6:03:27
Eagle 68	1	42N52'46	88W28'27	5:53:54
Eagle Corners 53	1	43N12	90W26	6:01:44
Eagle Lake 52	1	42N41	88W07	5:52:28
Eagle Lake Manor 52	1	42N41'54	88W08'06	5:52:32
Eagle Point 9	1	45N01'54	91W23'45	6:05:35
Eagle River 64	1	45N55'02	89W14'39	5:56:59
Eagleton 9	1	45N03'37	91W21'05	6:05:33
Eagleville 68	1	42N51'17	88W25'58	5:53:44
Earl 66	1	45N54'38	91W35'37	6:07:02
East Bristol 13	1	43N16'06	89W09'09	5:56:37
East Delavan 65	1	42N36'32	88W33'38	5:54:15
East Ellsworth 48	1	44N44'03	92W28'04	6:09:52
East End 16	1	46N42'32	92W03'33	6:08:14
Easter Rock 12	1	43N09'04	90W43'15	6:02:53
East Farmington 49	1	45N15'11	92W41'50	6:10:47
East Friesland 11	1	43N32	89W00	5:56:00
East Krok 31	1	44N25'44	87W36'08	5:50:25
Eastman 12	1	43N09'59	91W01'03	6:04:04
Eastmar 72	1	44N33	89W58	5:59:52
Easton 1	1	43N50'17	89W48'24	5:59:14
East Side 13	1	43N08	89W22	5:57:28
East Troy 65	1	42N47'07	88W24'18	5:53:37
East Waupun 14	1	43N37'27	88W41'26	5:54:46
Eastwin 36	1	44N09	87W35	5:50:20
East Winona 6	1	44N02'52	91W35'42	6:06:23
Eau Claire 18	1	44N48'41	91W29'54	6:06:00
Eau Galle 17	1	44N41'32	92W00'41	6:08:03
Ebenezer 28	1	43N08'18	88W44'16	5:54:57
Eckers Lakeland 8	1	44N00'12	88W19'22	5:53:17
Eden 20	1	43N41'37	88W21'39	5:53:27
Edgar 37	1	44N55'38	89W57'48	5:59:51
Edgerton 54	1	42N50'07	89W04'03	5:56:16
Edgewater 58	1	45N44'32	91W28'30	6:05:54
Edgewater Beach 5	1	44N37'25	87W49'47	5:51:19
Edgewood 68	1	43N03'45	88W18'06	5:53:12
Edithton Beach 30	1	42N35	87W51	5:51:24
Edmund 25	1	42N58'03	90W15'52	6:01:03
Edson 9	1	44N55'48	91W02'05	6:04:08
Edwards 60	1	43N55	87W45	5:51:00
Edwards Park 13	1	43N02	89W17	5:57:08
Egg Harbor 15	1	45N02'47	87W17'49	5:49:11
Eidsvold 10	1	44N57'51	90W51'59	6:03:28
Eight Corners 72	1	44N28'04	89W55'31	5:59:42
Eileen 4	1	46N33	90W59	6:03:56
Eisenstein 51	1	45N57	90W18	6:01:12
Eland 59	1	44N52'14	89W12'54	5:56:52
Elba 14	1	43N19	88W57	5:55:48
Elcho 34	1	45N26'09	89W11'00	5:56:44
Elderon 37	1	44N47'02	89W14'41	5:56:59
Eldorado 20	1	43N49'29	88W37'18	5:54:29
Eleva 62	1	44N34'33	91W28'12	6:05:53
Elk 51	1	45N41	90W30	6:02:00
Elk Creek 62	1	44N25'37	91W23'58	6:05:36
Elk Grove 33	1	42N40'18	90W23'27	6:01:34
Elkhart Lake 60	1	43N50'00	88W01'48	5:52:04
Elkhorn 65	1	42N40'22	88W32'40	5:54:11
Elk Mound 17	1	44N52'23	91W41'27	6:06:46
Ella 47	1	44N32	92W03	6:08:12
Ellenboro 22	1	42N47'00	90W36'49	6:02:27
Ellington 45	1	44N22	88W33	5:54:12
Ellis 50	1	44N34'31	89W26'47	5:57:47
Ellison Bay 15	1	45N15'17	87W04'17	5:48:17
Ellisville 31	1	44N27'28	87W41'03	5:50:44
Ellsworth 48	1	44N43'56	92W29'14	6:09:57
Elm Grove 68	1	43N02'35	88W04'44	5:52:19
Elmhurst 34	1	45N03'30	89W11'03	5:56:44
Elm Island 52	1	42N46	88W13	5:52:52
Elmo 22	1	42N38'34	90W26'09	6:01:45
Elmore 20	1	43N34'30	88W18'10	5:53:13
Elm Tree Corners 5	1	44N33'17	88W05'53	5:52:24
Elmwood 48	1	44N46'52	92W08'45	6:08:35
Elmwood Park 52	1	42N41	87W50	5:51:20
Elo 71	1	43N56'18	88W42'22	5:54:49
El Paso 48	1	44N46'11	92W20'38	6:09:23
Elroy 29	1	43N44'27	90W16'20	6:01:05
Elton 34	1	45N10'06	88W53'11	5:55:33
Elvers 13	1	43N04'11	89W47'52	5:59:11
Embarrass 69	1	44N39'56	88W42'26	5:54:50
Emerald 56	1	45N04'59	92W15'29	6:09:02
Emerald Grove 54	1	42N39'22	88W52'50	5:55:31
Emery 51	1	45N43	90W07	6:00:28
Empire 20	1	43N45	88W21	5:53:24
Endeavor 39	1	43N42'57	89W27'58	5:57:52
Engle 11	1	43N37'28	89W07'40	5:56:31
Enterprise 44	1	45N29'50	89W15'30	5:57:02
Ephraim 15	1	45N09'23	87W10'05	5:48:40
Erdman 60	1	43N47'24	87W45'34	5:51:02
Erin 56	1	45N07	92W32	6:10:08
Erin 67	1	43N14	88W22	5:53:28
Erin Corner 56	1	45N04'46	92W26'13	6:09:45
Erin Prairie 56	1	45N05	92W27	6:09:48
Esadore Lake 61	1	45N08	90W21	6:01:24
Esdaile 48	1	44N37'15	92W26'19	6:09:45
Esofea 63	1	43N37'52	90W57'47	6:03:51
Estella 9	1	45N09	91W07	6:04:28
Etna 33	1	42N33'57	90W19'39	6:01:19
Ettrick 62	1	44N10'06	91W16'08	6:05:05
Eureka 49	1	45N31	92W37	6:10:28
Eureka 71	1	44N00'16	88W50'30	5:55:22
Eureka Center 49	1	45N30'46	92W39'05	6:10:36
Euren 31	1	44N37'06	87W36'08	5:50:25
Evansville 54	1	42N46'49	89W17'57	5:57:12
Evergreen Park 60	1	43N44	87W46	5:51:04
Excelsior 53	1	43N15'06	90W37'41	6:02:31
Excelsior 57	1	43N31	89W53	5:59:32
Exeland 58	1	45N40'05	91W14'38	6:04:59
Exeter 23	1	42N47'26	89W34'59	5:58:20
Exile 48	1	44N41'57	92W09'56	6:08:40
Fairbanks 59	1	44N43	89W02	5:56:08
Fairburn 24	1	43N58'16	89W02'14	5:56:09
Fairchild 18	1	44N36'01	90W57'46	6:03:51
Fairfield 57	1	43N32	89W40	5:58:40
Fairfield 65	1	42N37'59	88W46'35	5:55:06
Fair Play 22	1	42N32'08	90W33'38	6:02:15
Fairview 6	1	44N25	92W00	6:08:00
Fairview 12	1	43N22'05	90W56'34	6:03:46
Fairview 41	1	43N00	88W00	5:52:00
Fairview Beach 71	1	44N05'06	88W30'41	5:54:03
Fairwater 20	1	43N44'38	88W52'01	5:55:28
Fall City 17	1	44N52	91W42	6:06:48
Fall Creek 18	1	44N45'49	91W16'37	6:05:06
Fall Hall Glen 27	1	44N11'47	90W50'23	6:03:22
Fall River 11	1	43N23'04	89W02'42	5:56:11
Falls City 17	1	44N47'50	91W46'07	6:07:04
Falun 7	1	45N46'19	92W31'39	6:10:07
Fancher 50	1	44N27'47	89W23'08	5:57:33
Fargo 63	1	43N27'21	90W57'26	6:03:50
Farmersville 14	1	43N33'30	88W31'53	5:54:08
Farmhill 48	1	44N47	92W09	6:08:36
Farmington 28	1	43N04'34	88W40'19	5:54:41

Fayette 33 1 42n45'15 90w02'07 6:00:08
Fence 19 1 45n44'40 88w25'27 5:53:42
Fennimore 22 1 42n59'01 90w39'19 6:02:37
Fenwood 37 1 44n51'58 90w00'55 6:00:04
Fern 19 1 45n50'10 88w23'09 5:53:33
Ferron Park 7 1 45n50 91w53 6:07:32
Ferryville 12 1 43n21'02 91w06'07 6:04:24
Fifield 51 1 45n52'47 90w25'19 6:01:41
Fillmore 67 1 43n29'54 88w03'38 5:52:15
Finley 29 1 44n12'48 90w08'10 6:00:33
Fish Creek 15 1 45n07'40 87w14'49 5:48:59
Fishermans Landing 26 1 46n05'31 90w10'12 6:00:41
Fisherville 36 1 44n14'26 87w40'48 5:50:43
Fisk 71 1 43n57'21 88w40'41 5:54:43
Fitchburg 13 1 42n57'39 89w28'11 5:57:53
Fitzgerald 71 1 43n58'56 88w37'16 5:54:29
Five Corners 45 1 44n24'53 88w22'27 5:53:30
Five Corners 46 1 43n17 87w58 5:51:52
Five Corners 59 1 44n48'40 89w02'33 5:56:10
Five Points 13 1 43n00'58 89w31'59 5:58:08
Five Points 22 1 42n48'52 90w48'27 6:03:14
Five Points 53 1 43n19'11 90w35'43 6:02:23
Flambeau 55 1 45n13 91w07 6:04:28
Flintville 5 1 44n38'48 88w07'04 5:52:28
Flora Fountain 22 1 42n49'55 90w50'23 6:03:22
Florence 19 1 45n55'20 88w15'06 5:53:00
Folsom 63 1 43n26'18 90w50'18 6:03:21
Fond du Lac 20 2 43n46'23 88w26'49 5:53:47
Fontana 65 1 42n33'05 88w34'30 5:54:18
Fontenoy 5 1 44n22'16 87w47'10 5:51:09
Footville 54 1 42n40'15 89w12'32 5:56:50
Ford 61 1 45n10 90w44 6:02:56
Forest 56 1 45n08'12 92w15'34 6:09:02
Forest Glen Beach 24 1 43n49'01 88w55'56 5:55:44
Forest Junction 8 1 44n12'45 88w08'39 5:52:35
Forestville 15 1 44n41'24 87w28'45 5:49:55
Fort Atkinson 28 1 42n55'44 88w50'13 5:55:21
Fort Winnebago 11 1 43n37 89w26 5:57:44
Forward 13 1 42n53'49 89w45'22 5:59:01
Foster 18 1 44n38'35 91w18'42 6:05:15
Foster Junction 2 1 46n18'49 90w42'14 6:02:49
Fountain 29 1 43n51 90w14 6:00:56
Fountain City 6 1 44n07'55 91w43'07 6:06:52
Fountain Prairie 11 1 43n25 89w04 5:56:16
Fountain Valley 70 1 44n05'27 88w59'10 5:55:57
Four Corners 7 1 45n40'17 92w35'26 6:10:22
Four Corners 34 1 45n10'06 88w50'41 5:55:23
Foxboro 16 1 46n29'55 92w17'16 6:09:09
Fox Creek 49 1 45n29'01 92w20'43 6:09:23
Foxhollow 54 1 42n30'50 88w54'28 5:55:38
Fox Lake 14 1 43n33'56 88w54'23 5:55:38
Fox Lake Junction 14 1 43n31'52 88w54'09 5:55:37
Fox Point 41 1 43n09'27 87w54'06 5:51:36
Fox River 30 1 42n33'25 88w11'04 5:52:44
Francis Creek 36 1 44n11'58 87w43'17 5:50:53
Franklin 27 1 44n12'46 91w07'25 6:04:30
Franklin 41 1 42n53'19 88w02'18 5:52:09
Franklin 60 1 43n50'08 87w54'05 5:51:36
Franksville 52 1 42n45'36 87w54'48 5:51:39
Franzen 37 1 44n49 89w18 5:57:12
Frazer 59 1 44n40 88w15 5:53:00
Frazer Corners 59 1 44n40'28 88w21'44 5:53:27
Frederic 49 1 45n39'33 92w28'01 6:09:52
Fred John 41 1 43n07 88w01 5:52:04
Fredonia 46 1 43n28'14 87w57'02 5:51:48
Freedom 45 1 44n23'11 88w17'19 5:53:09
Freeman 12 1 43n22 91w04 6:04:16
Freeman 34 1 45n20'59 88w49'44 5:55:19
Freistadt 46 1 43n14'10 88w02'33 5:52:10
Fremont 69 1 44n15'35 88w51'53 5:55:28
French Island 32 1 43n49 91w14 6:04:56
Frenchville 62 1 44n08'59 91w19'22 6:05:17
Friendship 1 1 43n58'14 89w49'00 5:59:16
Friesland 11 1 43n35'19 89w04'02 5:56:16
Frog Creek 66 1 46n07 91w42 6:06:48
Frostville 43 1 45n00'19 88w19'30 5:53:18
Fulton 54 1 42n48'29 89w07'39 5:56:31
Fussville 68 1 43n09'06 88w04'40 5:52:19
Gagen 44 1 45n39'45 89w08'17 5:56:33
Gale 62 1 44n07 91w19 6:05:16
Galesville 62 1 44n04'54 91w20'56 6:05:24
Galloway 37 1 44n42'46 89w15'51 5:57:03
Garden Valley 27 1 44n28 90w59 6:03:56
Garden Village 54 1 42n33'17 89w01'45 5:56:07
Gardner 15 1 44n48 87w35 5:50:20
Garfield 50 1 44n33'43 89w17'39 5:57:11
Garnet 20 1 43n56'08 88w15'46 5:53:03
Gaslyn 7 1 45n53 92w22 6:09:28
Gays Mills 12 1 43n19'03 90w50'41 6:03:23
Genesee 68 1 42n57'10 88w21'32 5:53:26
Genesee Depot 68 1 42n58'00 88w22'16 5:53:29
Geneva 65 1 42n37 88w29 5:53:56
Geneva, Lake 65 1 42n35'30 88w26'00 5:53:44
Genevesta 65 1 42n36 88w28 5:53:52
Genoa 63 1 43n34'36 91w13'27 6:04:54
Genoa City 65 1 42n29'54 88w19'47 5:53:19
Georgetown 22 1 42n37'27 90w29'04 6:01:56
Germania 26 1 46n26'18 90w13'28 6:00:54
Germania 39 1 43n53'26 89w15'25 5:57:02
Germantown 53 1 43n31'33 90w13'17 6:00:53
Germantown 67 1 43n13'43 88w06'37 5:52:26
Gibbsville 60 1 43n39'08 87w49'36 5:51:18
Gibraltar 15 1 45n07 87w14 5:48:56
Gibson 36 1 44n17 87w43 5:50:52
Gile 26 1 46n25'42 90w13'30 6:00:54
Gillett 43 1 44n53'24 88w18'26 5:53:14
Gillingham 53 1 43n25'35 90w26'42 6:01:47
Gills Landing 69 1 44n18'10 88w53'00 5:55:32
Gills Rock 15 1 45n17'24 87w01'18 5:48:05
Gilman 61 1 45n10'00 90w48'27 6:03:14
Gilmanton 6 1 44n28'15 91w40'33 6:06:42
Gingles 2 1 46n32 90w51 6:03:24
Girard Jct Lookout Tower 38 1 45n29'49 88w12'12 5:52:49
Gladstone Beach 20 1 43n51'56 88w22'08 5:53:29
Glandon 37 1 45n05'20 89w25'37 5:57:42
Glasgow 62 1 44n11 91w16 6:05:04
Gleason 35 1 45n18'32 89w29'47 5:57:59
Glenbeulah 60 1 43n47'50 88w02'50 5:52:11
Glencoe 6 1 44n17 91w35 6:06:20
Glendale 41 1 43n08'07 87w56'08 5:51:45
Glendale 42 1 43n46'56 90w20'44 6:01:23
Glen Flora 55 1 45n29'45 90w53'38 6:03:35
Glen Haven 22 1 42n49'35 91w04'15 6:04:17
Glenmore 5 1 44n23'09 87w55'38 5:51:43
Glenn Oaks Beach 28 1 42n52'53 88w59'55 5:56:00
Glen Oak 39 1 43n44'39 89w21'41 5:57:27
Glenwood City 56 1 45n03'31 92w10'20 6:08:41
Glidden 2 1 46n08'06 90w34'42 6:02:19
Globe 10 1 44n39'16 90w39'33 6:02:38
Glover 56 1 44n54'47 92w40'49 6:10:43
Goerkes Corner 68 1 43n02'11 88w09'58 5:52:40
Goetz 9 1 44n59 91w08 6:04:32
Goldenthal 67 1 43n14'10 88w09'43 5:52:39
Goll 38 1 45n16'49 87w45'03 5:51:00
Goodman 38 1 45n37'53 88w21'12 5:53:25
Goodnow 44 1 45n41'50 89w40'18 5:58:41
Goodrich 61 1 45n08'58 90w05'08 6:00:21
Gooseville 60 1 43n35'14 88w01'16 5:52:05
Gordon 16 1 46n14'49 91w47'54 6:07:12
Gotham 53 1 43n13'24 90w17'29 6:01:10
Grafton 46 1 43n19'11 87w57'12 5:51:49
Graham Corners 20 1 43n43'57 88w10'30 5:52:42
Grand Avenue Park 54 1 42n31 89w03 5:56:12
Grand Chute 45 1 44n17 88w25 5:53:40
Grand Crossing 32 1 43n50'43 91w13'46 6:04:55
Grand Marsh 1 1 43n53'13 89w42'22 5:58:49
Grand Rapids 72 1 44n23 89w46 5:59:04
Grand View 4 1 46n22'03 91w06'29 6:04:26
Grange Hall 48 1 44n33 92w19 6:09:16
Granite Heights (Heights Sta 37 1 45n03'36 89w38'22 5:58:33
Granton 10 1 44n35'20 90w27'40 6:01:51
Grantsburg 7 1 45n46'35 92w40'57 6:10:44
Granville 41 1 43n10'39 88w02'38 5:52:11
Gratiot 33 1 42n34'44 90w01'21 6:00:05
Gravesville 8 1 44n02'11 88w08'46 5:52:35
Graytown 3 1 45n11'58 92w07'37 6:08:30
Green Bay 5 1 44n31'09 88w01'11 5:52:05
Greenbush 60 1 43n46'36 88w05'02 5:52:20
Greendale 41 1 42n56'26 87w59'45 5:51:59
Greenfield 41 1 42n57'41 88w00'45 5:52:03
Green Grove 10 1 44n54 90w29 6:01:56
Green Lake 24 1 43n50'39 88w57'36 5:55:50
Green Lake Terrace 24 1 43n46'57 89w03'52 5:56:15
Greenleaf 5 1 44n18'48 88w05'46 5:52:23
Greenridge Park 13 1 43n02 89w17 5:57:08
Greenstreet 36 1 44n17 87w49 5:51:16
Green Valley 59 1 44n47'44 88w16'13 5:53:05
Greenville 45 1 44n18'01 88w32'11 5:54:09
Greenwood 10 1 44n46'13 90w35'57 6:02:24
Greenwood 63 1 43n33'50 90w25'06 6:01:40
Gregorville 31 1 44n37'06 87w32'47 5:50:11
Grellton 28 1 43n08'06 88w47'18 5:55:09
Gresham 59 1 44n51'11 88w47'17 5:55:09
Grimms 36 1 44n08'46 87w54'06 5:51:36
Grow 55 1 45n26 90w58 6:03:52
Guenther 37 1 44n49 89w33 5:58:12
Gull Lake 66 1 46n01 91w43 6:06:52
Gurney 26 1 46n28'22 90w30'29 6:02:02
Guthrie 68 1 43n01 88w12 5:52:48
Hackett 51 1 45n36 90w19 6:01:16
Haevers Corners 5 1 44n30'46 87w58'40 5:51:55
Hager City 48 1 44n36'06 92w32'17 6:10:09
Halder 37 1 44n47'57 89w52'14 5:59:29
Hale 62 1 44n27'57 91w15'44 6:05:03
Hale Corner 18 1 44n39'42 91w16'35 6:05:06
Hales Corners 41 1 42n56'15 88w02'55 5:52:12
Hallie 9 1 44n52'58 91w25'57 6:05:44
Halsey 37 1 45n03 90w01 6:00:04
Hamburg 38 1 45n05'26 89w53'06 5:59:32
Hamilton 20 1 43n41'51 88w27'31 5:53:50
Hamilton 32 1 43n55 91w05 6:04:20
Hamilton 46 1 43n17'03 87w58'18 5:51:53
Hammel 61 1 45n10 90w29 6:01:56
Hammond 56 1 44n58'44 92w26'08 6:09:45
Hampden 11 1 43n20 89w11 5:56:44
Hamples Corner 45 1 44n21'06 88w28'31 5:53:54
Hampton 41 1 43n07 88w00 5:52:00
Hancock 70 1 44n08'01 89w31'23 5:58:06
Hanerville 13 1 42n52'32 89w09'41 5:56:39
Haney 12 1 43n15 90w51 6:03:24
Hannibal 61 1 45n15'09 90w47'20 6:03:09
Hanover 54 1 42n38'19 89w09'43 5:56:39
Hansen 72 1 44n28 90w00 6:00:00
Happy Corners 22 1 42n36 90w26 6:01:44
Harbor 41 1 43n01 87w56 5:51:44
Harbor Springs 71 1 44n03'51 88w41'08 5:54:45
Harding 35 1 45n17 89w52 5:59:28
Harmony 38 1 45n05'57 87w49'11 5:51:17
Harmony Corners 38 1 45n06 87w37 5:50:28
Harmony Grove 11 1 43n22'18 89w33'03 5:58:12
Harris 39 1 43n52 89w25 5:57:40
Harrison 8 1 44n08'03 88w17'30 5:53:10
Harrison 35 1 45n28'39 89w30'24 5:58:02
Harrisville 39 1 43n52'40 89w24'19 5:57:37
Harshaw 44 1 45n39'56 89w39'19 5:58:37
Hartford 67 1 43n19'04 88w22'44 5:53:31
Hartland 68 1 43n06'18 88w20'31 5:53:22
Hatch Landing 55 1 45n20'19 91w19'29 6:05:18
Hatchville 17 1 44n51'29 92w08'10 6:08:33
Hatfield 27 1 44n24'53 90w43'50 6:02:55
Hatley 37 1 44n53'15 89w20'19 5:57:21
Hauer 58 1 45n48'10 91w27'36 6:05:50
Haugen 3 1 45n36'32 91w46'29 6:07:06
Haven 60 1 43n51 87w45 5:51:00
Hawkins 55 1 45n30'54 90w43'11 6:02:53
Hawkins Corner 47 1 44n31'05 92w09'55 6:08:40
Hawthorne 16 1 46n30'11 91w51'38 6:07:27
Hay Creek 18 1 44n37'20 91w04'29 6:04:18
Hayen 60 1 43n50'57 87w44'45 5:50:59
Hayes 43 1 44n59'59 88w25'22 5:53:41
Hay River 17 1 45n05 91w57 6:07:48
Hay Stack Corner 58 1 45n38'55 90w52'32 6:03:30
Hayton 8 1 44n01'21 88w06'58 5:52:28
Hayward 58 1 46n00'47 91w29'04 6:05:56
Hazel Green 22 1 42n31'58 90w26'04 6:01:44
Hazelhurst 44 1 45n48'28 89w43'30 5:58:54
Heafford Junction 35 1 45n32'50 89w42'55 5:58:52
Heart Prairie 65 1 42n45'56 88w38'31 5:54:34
Heath Mills 28 1 42n59'02 88w34'27 5:54:18
Hebel 5 1 44n21 87w50 5:51:20
Hebron 28 1 42n55'31 88w41'33 5:54:46
Heffron 70 1 44n14'37 89w18'22 5:57:13
Hegg 62 1 44n12'33 91w11'32 6:04:46
Helena 25 1 43n10'17 90w01'20 6:00:05
Helenville 28 1 43n00'43 88w41'58 5:54:48
Helvetia 69 1 44n33 89w03 5:56:12
Hematite 19 1 45n54'33 88w12'34 5:52:50
Hemlock 10 1 44n49'25 90w36'42 6:02:27
Hendren 10 1 44n43 90w44 6:02:56
Henrietta 53 1 43n30 90w23 6:01:32
Henrysville 5 1 44n26'38 87w47'09 5:51:09
Herbster 4 1 46n49'57 91w15'39 6:05:03
Herman Center 14 1 43n24'50 88w27'36 5:53:50
Hermans Landing 58 1 45n56'03 91w11'15 6:04:45
Herold 6 1 44n18'20 91w50'31 6:07:22
Herrington 32 4 43n46'42 91w13'09 6:04:53
Hersey 56 1 44n57'46 92w12'41 6:08:51
Hertel 7 1 45n48'31 92w10'30 6:08:42
Hewett 10 1 44n33 90w44 6:02:56
Hewitt 37 1 45n03 89w25 5:57:40
Hewitt 72 1 44n38'42 90w06'00 6:00:24
Hickory Corners 43 1 45n00'17 88w15'14 5:53:01
Hickory Grove 22 1 43n06'22 90w35'57 6:02:24
Hickory Grove 36 1 44n17'54 87w52'03 5:51:28
High Bridge 2 1 46n23'20 90w44'10 6:02:57
High Cliff 8 1 44n13 88w25 5:53:40
Highland 25 1 43n02'48 90w22'47 6:01:31
Highland Beach 8 1 44n11'12 88w18'57 5:53:16
Highland Park 20 1 43n53'39 88w20'51 5:53:23
Highland Shore 71 1 44n03'03 88w37'50 5:54:31
Hika 36 1 43n55 87w45 5:51:00
Hilbert 8 1 44n08'25 88w09'50 5:52:39
Hilbert Junction 8 1 44n08'46 88w09'34 5:52:38
Hilburn 65 1 42n47'18 88w21'18 5:53:25
Hiles 21 1 45n42'14 88w58'38 5:55:55
Hill 51 1 45n26 90w13 6:00:52
Hillcrest 16 1 46n30'11 91w53'53 6:07:36
Hilldale 13 1 43n07 89w27 5:57:48
Hill Point 57 1 43n25'28 90w06'45 6:00:27
Hillsboro 63 1 43n39'08 90w20'38 6:01:23
Hillsdale 3 1 45n18'57 91w51'34 6:07:26
Hillside 13 1 42n56'05 89w02'34 5:56:10
Hilltop 41 1 43n03 87w56 5:51:44
Hines 16 1 46n32'35 91w54'29 6:07:38
Hingham 60 1 43n38'20 87w54'51 5:51:39
Hintz 43 1 44n54'57 88w24'36 5:53:38
Hixon 10 1 44n59 90w37 6:02:28
Hixton 27 1 44n23'09 91w00'51 6:04:03
Hoard 10 1 44n59 90w30 6:02:00
Hobart 5 1 44n30 88w10 5:52:40
Hochheim 14 1 43n27'25 88w28'09 5:53:53
Hofa Park 59 1 44n37'49 88w19'58 5:53:20
Hoffman Corners 42 1 43n47 90w22 6:01:28
Hogarty 37 1 45n01'47 89w18'20 5:57:13
Holcombe 9 1 45n13'28 91w07'02 6:04:28
Holiday Heights 32 1 43n51'55 91w12'03 6:04:48
Holiday Hills 54 1 42n32'53 89w01'49 5:56:07
Holland 5 1 44n14'55 88w10'18 5:52:41
Hollandale 25 1 42n52'33 89w56'10 5:59:45
Hollister 34 1 45n14'53 88w47'29 5:55:10
Holmen 32 1 43n57'48 91w15'22 6:05:01
Holt 37 1 44n43'03 89w19'31 5:57:18
Holton 37 1 45n00 90w15 6:01:00
Holts Landing 2 1 46n00'36 90w22'17 6:01:29
Holway 61 1 45n05 90w29 6:01:56
Holy Cross 46 1 43n28'13 87w53'44 5:51:35
Homestead 19 1 45n47 88w15 5:53:00
Honey Creek 57 1 43n19 89w55 5:59:40
Honey Creek 65 1 42n44'54 88w18'28 5:53:14
Honey Lake 52 1 42n42'57 88w18'21 5:53:13
Hoopers Mill 28 1 43n05'48 88w52'53 5:55:32
Hope 13 1 43n03'06 89w14'46 5:56:59
Hopokoekau Beach 20 1 43n49'20 88w23'16 5:53:33
Horicon 14 1 43n27'05 88w37'52 5:54:31
Horns Corner 46 1 43n20'29 88w01'26 5:52:06
Horse Creek 49 1 45n15'27 92w34'59 6:10:20

Horseman 3 1 45N29'40 91W33'34 6:06:14
Hortonia 45 1 44N21 88W40 5:54:40
Hortonville 45 1 44N20'05 88W38'17 5:54:33
Houghton 4 1 46N41 90W54 6:03:36
Houlton 56 1 45N03'38 92W47'28 6:11:10
How 43 1 44N59 88W25 5:53:40
Howard 5 1 44N32'37 88W05'17 5:52:21
Howard 9 1 44N57'02 91W32'15 6:06:09
Howards Grove 60 1 43N50'02 87W49'12 5:51:17
Hoyt 26 1 46N24'38 90W17'58 6:01:12
Hubbellton 28 1 43N11'37 88W52'55 5:55:32
Hub City 53 1 43N28'16 90W21'22 6:01:25
Hubertus 67 1 43N14'12 88W13'16 5:52:53
Hudson 56 1 44N58'29 92W45'24 6:11:02
Hughes 4 1 46N32 91W29 6:05:56
Hughey 61 1 45N14'55 90W42'00 6:02:48
Hullsburg 14 1 43N23'03 88W27'38 5:53:51
Hulls Crossing 60 1 43N48'57 88W06'41 5:52:27
Humbird 10 1 44N31'45 90W53'21 6:03:33
Humboldt 5 1 44N30'07 87W49'33 5:51:18
Hunter 58 1 45N55 91W13 6:04:52
Hunting 59 1 44N41'00 88W58'17 5:55:53
Huntington 56 1 45N11'31 92W33'31 6:10:14
Hurley 26 1 46N26'59 90W11'11 6:00:45
Huron 9 1 45N07'10 90W58'57 6:03:56
Hurricane 22 1 42N47'05 90W46'16 6:03:05
Husher 52 1 42N48'51 87W53'40 5:51:35
Hushsford 14 1 43N20'46 88W36'02 5:54:24
Hustisford 14 1 43N21 88W36 5:54:24
Hustler 29 1 43N52'48 90W16'18 6:01:05
Hutchins 59 1 44N59 89W02 5:56:08
Hyde 25 1 43N04'24 89W58'54 5:59:56
Idlewild 15 1 44N53'18 87W25'38 5:49:43
Iduna 62 1 44N11'55 91W18'45 6:05:15
Imalone 55 1 45N33'08 91W13'38 6:04:55
Independence 62 1 44N21'25 91W25'13 6:05:41
Indian Creek 49 1 45N42'19 92W12'26 6:08:50
Indianford 54 1 42N48'15 89W05'28 5:56:22
Indian Shores 71 1 44N08'21 88W42'06 5:54:48
Ingersoll 37 1 44N52 89W12 5:56:48
Ingram 55 1 45N30'18 90W48'44 6:03:15
Inlet 65 1 42N37'38 88W35'06 5:54:20
Ino 4 1 46N31'51 91W10'43 6:04:43
Institute 15 1 44N53'36 87W17'13 5:49:09
Interwald 61 1 45N13'26 90W06'59 6:00:28
Iola 69 1 44N30'29 89W07'50 5:56:31
Ipswich 33 1 42N42'27 90W24'37 6:01:38
Irma 35 1 45N21'05 89W39'59 5:58:40
Iron Belt 26 1 46N24'02 90W19'27 6:01:18
Iron Ridge 14 1 43N23'59 88W31'57 5:54:08
Iron River 4 1 46N33'52 91W24'29 6:05:38
Ironton 57 1 43N32'46 90W08'28 6:00:34
Irvine 9 1 44N55'32 91W25'11 6:05:41
Irving 27 1 44N11 90W58 6:03:52
Irvington 17 1 44N50'10 91W57'16 6:07:49
Isaar 45 1 44N34'18 88W17'04 5:53:08
Isabelle 48 1 44N35 92W25 6:09:40
Island Beach 71 1 44N05'28 88W30'10 5:54:01
Island Lake 55 1 45N19'08 91W22'08 6:05:29
Island Park 71 1 44N01'22 88W48'08 5:55:13
Itasca 16 1 46N40'29 92W00'23 6:08:02
Ithaca 53 1 43N20'27 90W16'54 6:01:08
Ives 52 1 42N46'12 87W48'19 5:51:13
Ives Grove 52 1 42N43'45 87W57'58 5:51:52
Ixonia 28 1 43N08'38 88W35'50 5:54:23
Jackson 67 1 43N19'26 88W10'00 5:52:40
Jacksonport 15 1 44N58'43 87W11'08 5:48:45
Jacobs 2 1 46N07 90W35 6:02:20
Jamestown 22 1 42N35'16 90W32'54 6:02:12
Janesville 54 1 42N40'58 89W01'07 5:56:04
Jefferson 28 1 43N00'20 88W48'26 5:55:14
Jefferson Junction 28 1 43N02'13 88W47'24 5:55:10
Jeffris 35 1 45N30'07 89W25'49 5:57:43
Jenkinsville 33 1 42N38'05 90W22'11 6:01:29
Jennings 44 1 45N30'27 89W04'19 5:56:17
Jericho 8 1 43N58'12 88W15'59 5:53:04
Jericho 68 1 42N52'42 88W25'22 5:53:41
Jersey City 35 1 45N29'07 89W44'40 5:58:59
Jewett 56 1 45N07'03 92W26'10 6:09:45
Jim Falls 9 1 45N02'43 91W16'22 6:05:05
Jimtown 53 1 43N21'12 90W38'18 6:02:33
Joel 49 1 45N21'38 92W14'04 6:08:56
Johannesburg 56 1 45N09'55 92W35'38 6:10:23
Johnsburg 20 1 43N52'38 88W17'23 5:53:10
Johnson 37 1 45N00 90W08 6:00:32
Johnson Creek 28 1 43N04'34 88W46'27 5:55:06
Johnsonville 60 1 43N47'54 87W54'34 5:51:38
Johnstown 54 1 42N42'00 88W48'22 5:55:13
Johnstown Center 54 1 42N41'45 88W50'22 5:55:21
Jonesdale 25 1 42N53'56 90W00'48 6:00:03
Jordan 23 1 42N39 89W46 5:59:04
Jordan 50 1 44N34'29 89W30'18 5:58:01
Juda 23 1 42N35'23 89W30'21 5:58:01
Jump River 61 1 45N21'11 90W48'04 6:03:12
Junction 10 1 45N00'35 90W54'08 6:03:37
Junction City 50 1 44N35'27 89W46'02 5:59:04
Juneau 14 1 43N24'20 88W42'18 5:54:49
Juneau 41 1 43N03 87W54 5:51:36
Kaiser 51 1 45N56 90W27 6:01:48
Kalinke 37 1 45N01'50 89W23'49 5:57:35
Kansasville 52 1 42N40'57 88W06'37 5:52:26
Karlsborg 7 1 45N53 92W22 6:09:28
Kaukauna 45 1 44N16'41 88W16'19 5:53:05
Keene 50 1 44N22'01 89W28'27 5:57:54
Keenville 71 1 44N03'41 88W31'31 5:54:06
Kegonsa 13 1 42N58'38 89W12'01 5:56:48
Kekoskee 14 1 43N31'48 88W33'39 5:54:15
Kelley Brook 43 1 44N58 88W03 5:52:12
Kellner 50 1 44N21'32 89W43'29 5:58:54
Kellners Corners 36 1 44N07'34 87W42'34 5:50:50
Kellnersville 36 1 44N13'33 87W48'08 5:51:13
Kelly 4 1 46N27 90W59 6:03:56
Kelly 29 1 43N58'00 90W05'59 6:00:24
Kelly 37 1 44N54'48 89W33'45 5:58:15
Kelly Brook 43 1 44N57'37 88W12'57 5:52:52
Kempster 34 1 45N17'23 89W10'00 5:56:40
Kendall 42 1 43N47'32 90W22'06 6:01:28
Kennan 51 1 45N31'53 90W35'13 6:02:21
Kennedy 51 1 45N54'37 90W39'26 6:02:38
Kenosha 30 3 42N35'05 87W49'16 5:51:17
Keowns 67 1 43N22'07 88W08'10 5:52:33
Keshena 40 1 44N53'02 88W38'01 5:54:32
Keshena Falls 40 1 44N53'36 88W39'14 5:54:37
Kewaskum 67 1 43N31'15 88W13'44 5:52:55
Kewaunee 31 1 44N27'30 87W30'11 5:50:01
Keyeser 11 1 43N17'48 89W15'21 5:57:01
Keyesville 53 1 43N26 90W07 6:00:28
Keyser 11 1 43N15 89W21 5:57:24
Keystone 4 1 46N31 91W09 6:04:36
Keystone 9 1 45N10 91W09 6:04:36
Keysville 53 1 43N20'23 90W13'07 6:00:52
Kickapoo 63 1 43N28 90W45 6:03:00
Kickapoo Center 63 1 43N30 90W40 6:02:40
Kiel 36 1 43N54'45 88W02'08 5:52:09
Kieler 22 1 42N34'53 90W36'09 6:02:25
Kilbournville 52 1 42N48'28 87W57'08 5:51:49
Kildare 29 1 43N44 89W54 5:59:36
Kimball 26 1 46N28'55 90W18'21 6:01:13
Kimberly 45 1 44N16'20 88W20'20 5:53:21
King 35 1 45N31 89W36 5:58:24
King 69 1 44N20'15 89W08'30 5:56:34
Kingsbridge 36 1 44N12'41 87W40'52 5:50:43
Kingston 24 1 43N41'44 89W07'39 5:56:31
Kinnickinnic 56 1 44N54 92W33 6:10:12
Kirby 42 1 44N05'26 90W32'21 6:02:09
Kirchhayn 67 1 43N17'39 88W05'42 5:52:23
Klevenville 13 1 43N01'28 89W40'04 5:58:40
Klondike 30 1 42N35'24 88W07'10 5:52:29
Klondike 43 1 45N04'05 88W09'35 5:52:38
Kloten 8 1 44N02'07 88W15'57 5:53:04
Knapp 17 1 44N57'19 92W04'31 6:08:18
Kneeland 52 1 42N49'36 88W00'30 5:52:02
Knellsville 46 1 43N24'51 87W52'15 5:51:29
Knight 26 1 46N17 90W21 6:01:24
Knowles 14 1 43N34'22 88W30'15 5:54:01
Knowlton 37 1 44N42'59 89W40'57 5:58:44
Knox 51 1 45N32 90W06 6:00:24
Knox Mills 51 1 45N34 90W07 6:00:28
Kodan 31 1 44N39'40 87W29'52 5:49:59
Koehler Ford 10 1 44N44'18 90W53'41 6:03:35
Koepenick 34 1 45N20'12 89W10'00 5:56:40
Kohlberg 15 1 44N43'09 87W32'56 5:50:12
Kohler 46 1 43N29'47 88W01'24 5:52:06
Kohler 60 1 44N44'21 87W46'54 5:51:08
Kohlsville 67 1 43N28'16 88W19'19 5:53:17
Kolb 5 1 44N25'22 87W57'47 5:51:51
Komensky 27 1 44N22 90W38 6:02:32
Koro 71 1 43N58'05 88W50'40 5:55:23
Koshkonong 28 1 42N50'46 88W55'09 5:55:41
Koshkonong Manor 28 1 42N54'05 88W57'36 5:55:50
Koshkonong Mounds 28 1 42N52'27 88W54'43 5:55:39
Kossuth 36 1 44N12 87W44 5:50:56
Krakow 59 1 44N45'42 88W15'05 5:53:00
Kremlin 38 1 45N39'03 87W50'41 5:51:23
Kroghville 28 1 43N03'42 89W00'29 5:56:02
Krok 31 1 44N25'44 87W37'59 5:50:32
Kronenwetter 37 1 44N53 89W38 5:58:32
Kruger 7 1 45N53 92W22 6:09:28
Kunesh 5 1 44N36'56 88W11'25 5:52:46
Lac Courte Oreilles Indian R 58 1 45N53 91W21 6:05:24
Lac du Flambeau 64 1 45N58'11 89W53'31 5:59:34
Lac du Flambeau Indian Res 26 1 45N58 89W53 5:59:32
Lac La Belle 68 1 43N08'39 88W31'50 5:54:07
La Crosse 32 4 43N48'05 91W14'22 6:04:57
Ladoga 20 1 43N43'12 88W40'27 5:54:42
Ladysmith 55 1 45N27'47 91W06'14 6:04:25
LaFarge 63 1 43N34'29 90W38'25 6:02:34
La Follette 7 1 45N46 92W13 6:08:52
La Grange 65 1 42N47'59 88W36'08 5:54:25
Lake Beulah 65 1 42N49'17 88W19'15 5:53:17
Lake Butte des Morts 71 1 44N02 88W36 5:54:24
Lake Church 46 1 43N29'59 87W49'14 5:51:17
Lake Como Beach 65 1 42N36 88W28 5:53:52
Lake Delton 57 1 43N36'04 89W47'37 5:59:10
Lake Eau Claire 18 1 44N41 91W07 6:04:28
Lake Emily 50 1 44N28 89W17 5:57:08
Lakefield 46 1 43N17'42 87W55'32 5:51:42
Lake Five 68 1 43N11'33 88W16'15 5:53:05
Lake Geneva 65 1 42N36 88W26 5:53:44
Lake George 30 1 42N34 88W03 5:52:12
Lake George 44 1 45N38 89W25 5:57:40
Lake Hallie 9 1 44N52'33 91W26'26 6:05:46
Lake Holcombe 9 1 45N15 91W06 6:04:24
Lake Keesus 68 1 43N07 88W23 5:53:32
Lakeland 3 1 45N36 91W58 6:07:52
Lakeland College 60 1 43N44 87W46 5:51:04
Lake Lawn 65 1 42N37'33 88W35'39 5:54:23
Lake Michigan Estates 30 1 42N35 87W51 5:51:24
Lake Mills 28 1 43N04'53 88W54'42 5:55:39
Lake Nebagamon 16 1 46N30'54 91W41'59 6:06:48
Lakeport 47 1 44N26'55 92W10'47 6:08:43
Lakeshore 60 1 43N44 87W46 5:51:04
Lakeside 16 1 46N39 91W49 6:07:16
Lake Tomahawk 44 1 45N48'51 89W35'37 5:58:22
Laketown 49 1 45N35 92W35 6:10:20
Lakeview 13 1 42N58'31 89W22'19 5:57:29
Lake View 60 1 43N44 87W46 5:51:04
Lake Wazeecha 72 1 44N23 89W46 5:59:04
Lake Windsor 13 1 43N12'15 89W20'52 5:57:23
Lake Wissota 9 1 44N55'35 91W18'03 6:05:12
Lakewood 43 1 45N18'03 88W31'24 5:54:06
Lamar 49 1 45N25'33 92W34'12 6:10:17
Lamartine 20 1 43N44'00 88W34'07 5:54:16
Lamont 33 1 42N42'17 89W59'07 5:59:56
Lampson 66 1 45N58'59 91W48'58 6:07:16
Lanark 50 1 44N23 89W14 5:56:56
Lancaster 22 1 42N50'51 90W42'38 6:02:51
Lancaster Junction 22 1 42N58'37 90W36'50 6:02:27
Land o' Lakes 64 1 46N10 89W13 5:56:52
Landstad 59 1 44N39'38 88W26'37 5:53:46
Laney 59 1 44N38'40 88W17'21 5:53:09
Langes Corners 5 1 44N23'08 87W51'39 5:51:27
Langlade 34 1 45N11'24 88W43'56 5:54:56
Lannon 68 1 43N08'46 88W09'58 5:52:40
Laona 21 1 45N33'53 88W40'26 5:54:42
Laona Junction 21 1 45N39'22 88W41'38 5:54:47
Lapham Junction 27 1 44N17'51 90W28'41 6:01:55
La Pointe 2 1 46N46'45 90W47'11 6:03:09
La Prairie 54 1 42N38 88W56 5:55:44
Lark 5 1 44N18'51 87W56'59 5:51:48
Larrabee 36 1 44N16'05 87W42'54 5:50:52
Larrabee 69 1 44N39 88W49 5:55:16
Larsen 71 1 44N11'30 88W37'26 5:54:30
Larsons Beach 13 1 43N02 89W17 5:57:08
LaRue 57 1 43N26'10 89W53'22 5:59:33
Lasleys Point 71 1 44N07'37 88W42'23 5:54:50
Latto 25 1 42N58 90W08 6:00:32
Lauderdale 65 1 42N45'55 88W33'20 5:54:13
Laudolff Beach 20 1 43N52'40 88W21'26 5:53:26
La Valle 57 1 43N34'56 90W07'41 6:00:31
LaVerne Dilweg 5 1 44N31 88W03 5:52:12
Lawrence 39 1 43N53'01 89W32'40 5:58:11
Lawton 48 1 44N46'33 92W24'56 6:09:40
Layton Park 41 1 43N00 87W56 5:51:44
Lead Mine 33 1 42N34'15 90W20'43 6:01:23
Lebanon 14 1 43N15'19 88W37'36 5:54:30
Leeds 11 1 43N18'38 89W19'28 5:57:18
Leeds Center 11 1 43N20 89W23 5:57:32
Leef 7 1 45N53 92W22 6:09:28
Leeman 45 1 44N34'27 88W33'23 5:54:14
Lehigh 3 1 45N26'28 91W33'03 6:06:12
Leipsig 14 1 43N24'03 88W51'51 5:55:27
Leland 57 1 43N20'08 89W56'51 5:59:47
Lemington 58 1 45N45'33 91W21'10 6:05:25
Lemonweir 29 1 43N47'04 90W01'01 6:00:04
Lena 43 1 44N57'04 88W02'48 5:52:11
Lennox 44 1 45N30'43 89W04'18 5:56:17
Lenroot 58 1 46N07 91W26 6:05:44
Lenroot Landing 58 1 46N06'23 91W27'18 6:05:49
Leola 1 1 44N13 89W39 5:58:36
Leon 42 1 43N52'39 90W49'48 6:03:19
Leonards 4 1 46N10'11 91W19'16 6:05:17
Leonards Point 71 1 44N02'48 88W37'21 5:54:29
Leopolis 59 1 44N46'05 88W50'41 5:55:23
LeRoy 14 1 43N34'25 88W33'38 5:54:15
Leslie 33 1 42N46'14 90W21'59 6:01:28
Lessor 59 1 44N37 88W25 5:53:40
Levis 27 1 44N18'28 90W48'43 6:03:15
Lewis 49 1 45N42'39 92W24'08 6:09:37
Lewiston 11 1 43N34'50 89W38'08 5:58:33
Leyden 54 1 42N43'51 89W07'44 5:56:31
Liberty 63 1 43N30'59 90W44'02 6:02:56
Liberty Corners 30 1 42N31'15 88W05'57 5:52:24
Liberty Grove 15 1 45N13 87W03 5:48:12
Liberty Pole 63 1 43N29'24 90W54'31 6:03:38
Liddell 9 1 44N55 91W23 6:05:32
Lilly Lake 30 1 42N40 88W16 5:53:04
Lily 34 1 45N18'25 88W51'14 5:55:25
Lima Center 54 1 42N47'22 88W49'38 5:55:19
Lime Ridge 57 1 43N28'04 90W09'17 6:00:37
Lincoln 31 1 44N37'05 87W38'31 5:50:34
Lind 7 1 45N44'24 92W47'43 6:11:11
Lind 69 1 44N17 89W03 5:56:12
Lind Center 69 1 44N21 89W05 5:56:20
Linden 25 1 42N55'04 90W16'24 6:01:06
Linden Beach 20 1 43N51'15 88W22'24 5:53:30
Lindina 29 1 43N45'36 90W08'49 6:00:35
Lindsey 72 1 44N33'21 90W18'00 6:01:12
Lindwerm 41 1 43N07 87W57 5:51:48
Linn 65 1 42N33 88W29 5:53:56
Linton 65 1 42N32'04 88W30'06 5:54:00
Linwood 50 1 44N29 89W40 5:58:40
Little Black 61 1 45N06'22 90W19'46 6:01:19
Little Chicago 37 1 45N02'50 89W50'39 5:59:23
Little Chute 45 1 44N16'48 88W19'06 5:53:16
Little Eau Claire 37 1 44N47'11 89W26'51 5:57:47
Little Falls 42 1 44N05 90W51 6:03:24
Little Falls 49 1 45N16'26 92W25'07 6:09:40
Little Grant 22 1 42N54 90W50 6:03:20
Little Hope 69 1 44N19'06 89W06'32 5:56:26
Little Kohler 46 1 43N28 87W57 5:51:48
Little Norway 13 1 43N01'37 89W47'22 5:59:09
Little Point 71 1 43N55'08 88W28'07 5:53:52
Little Prairie 65 1 42N50'20 88W32'20 5:54:09
Little Rapids 5 1 44N22'49 88W07'38 5:52:31
Little Rice 44 1 45N39 89W51 5:59:24
Little River 43 1 44N58 87W53 5:51:32
Little Rose 37 1 44N48'03 90W10'13 6:00:41
Little Sturgeon 15 1 44N50'20 87W33'45 5:50:15
Little Suamico 43 1 44N43'03 88W00'33 5:52:02
Little Waupon 50 1 44N35'38 89W23'40 5:57:35
Little Wolf 69 1 44N28 88W56 5:55:44
Livingston 22 1 42N54'00 90W25'51 6:01:43

Loddes Mill 57 1 43N15'50 89w48'02 5:59:12
Lodi 11 1 43N18'50 89w31'35 5:58:06
Loganville 57 1 43N26'25 90w02'09 6:00:09
Lohrville 70 1 44N02'14 89w07'01 5:56:28
Lombard 10 1 44N57'33 90w44'21 6:02:57
Lomira 14 1 43N35'29 88w26'37 5:53:46
London 13 1 43N02'52 89w00'46 5:56:03
Lone Rock 29 1 43N56'38 90w12'50 6:00:51
Lone Rock 53 1 43N11'00 90w11'52 6:00:47
Long Lake 19 1 45N50'34 88w40'04 5:54:40
Longwood 10 1 44N53'13 90w35'53 6:02:24
Lookout 6 1 44N27'30 91w34'45 6:06:19
Loomis 38 1 45N11'33 87w53'57 5:51:36
Loraine 49 1 45N33 92w13 6:08:52
Loreta 57 1 43N20'44 90w06'26 6:00:26
Loretta 58 1 45N53'08 90w51'10 6:03:25
Lostcreek 48 1 44N44 92w29 6:09:56
Lost Lake 14 1 43N27'32 88w59'20 5:55:57
Louisburg 22 1 42N34'45 90w33'20 6:02:13
Louis Corners 36 1 43N56'07 87w57'07 5:51:48
Lowell 14 1 43N20'25 88w49'01 5:55:16
Lower Nemahbin Lake 68 1 43N06 88w29 5:53:56
Lowville 11 1 43N22'57 89w19'37 5:57:18
Loyal 10 1 44N44'13 90w29'45 6:01:59
Loyd 53 1 43N25'23 90w14'34 6:00:58
Lublin 61 1 45N04'38 90w43'28 6:02:54
Lucas 17 1 44N54 92w04 6:08:16
Luck 49 1 45N34'34 92w28'57 6:09:56
Luco 20 1 43N48'05 88w25'09 5:53:41
Ludington 18 1 44N49'45 91w07'38 6:04:31
Lufkin 18 1 44N45'04 91w36'38 6:06:27
Luger 51 1 45N37 90w21 6:01:24
Lugerville 51 1 45N46'32 90w30'22 6:02:01
Lund 48 1 44N32'23 92w12'21 6:08:49
Lunds 59 1 44N41'58 88w32'43 5:54:11
Luxemburg 31 1 44N32'19 87w42'14 5:50:49
Lykens 49 1 45N25'28 92w28'08 6:09:53
Lymantown 51 1 45N56'03 90w27'09 6:01:49
Lyndhurst 59 1 44N50'31 88w48'45 5:55:15
Lyndon Dale 14 1 43N34'38 88w55'50 5:55:43
Lyndon Station 29 1 43N42'44 89w53'58 5:59:36
Lynn 10 1 44N34'57 90w24'35 6:01:38
Lynne 44 1 45N40 89w59 5:59:56
Lynxville 12 1 43N14'47 91w03'22 6:04:13
Lyons 65 1 42N39'04 88w21'30 5:53:26
Mackford 24 1 43N41 88w56 5:55:44
Mackville 45 1 44N20'37 88w24'54 5:53:40
Madge 66 1 45N44'25 91w43'25 6:06:54
Madison 13 1 43N04'23 89w24'04 5:57:36
Madsen 36 1 44N04'52 87w49'19 5:51:17
Magenta 18 1 44N48 91w29 6:05:56
Magnolia 54 1 42N42'57 89w17'19 5:57:09
Maiden Rock 48 1 44N33'39 92w18'34 6:09:14
Mallwood 54 1 42N50 89w04 5:56:16
Malone 20 1 43N51'37 88w16'53 5:53:08
Malvern 44 1 45N36'28 89w17'06 5:57:08
Manawa 69 1 44N27'52 88w55'11 5:55:41
Manchester 24 1 43N41'26 89w02'54 5:56:12
Manitowish 26 1 46N07'59 90w00'48 6:00:03
Manitowish Waters 64 1 46N08'06 89w53'15 5:59:33
Manitowoc 36 1 44N05'19 87w39'27 5:50:38
Manitowoc Rapids 36 1 44N05'57 87w42'03 5:50:48
Mann 37 1 44N42'01 90w13'01 6:00:52
Manning 63 1 43N27 90w46 6:03:04
Manor Heights 60 1 42N54 91w06 6:04:24
Maple 16 1 46N35'23 91w43'14 6:06:53
Maple Bluff 13 1 43N07'06 89w22'46 5:57:31
Maple Creek 45 1 44N28 88w41 5:54:44
Mapledale 60 1 43N44 87w46 5:51:04
Maple Grove 32 1 43N44'58 91w11'55 6:04:48
Maple Grove 36 1 44N11'22 87w55'25 5:51:42
Maple Heights 8 1 43N57'23 88w19'03 5:53:16
Maple Hill 9 1 45N01'01 90w59'01 6:03:56
Maplehurst 61 1 45N04 90w37 6:02:28
Maple Plain 3 1 45N36 92w06 6:08:24
Mapleton 68 1 43N10'44 88w27'36 5:53:50
Maple Valley 43 1 44N59 88w18 5:53:12
Maplewood 15 1 44N44'51 87w28'45 5:49:55
Marathon (Marathon City) 37 1 44N55'45 89w50'25 5:59:22
Marblehead 20 1 43N42'15 88w23'01 5:53:32
Marcellon 11 1 43N34'07 89w15'56 5:57:04
March Rapids 37 1 44N50'40 90w09'00 6:00:36
Marcy 68 1 43N06'27 88w07'58 5:52:32
Marengo 2 1 46N25'21 90w49'00 6:03:16
Maribel 36 1 44N16'35 87w48'26 5:51:14
Marietta 12 1 43N10 90w47 6:03:08
Marinette 38 1 45N06'00 87w37'50 5:50:31
Marion 69 1 44N40'15 88w53'21 5:55:33
Markesan 24 1 43N42'26 88w59'24 5:55:58
Markton 34 1 45N07'19 88w39'53 5:54:40
Marlands 64 1 45N57'22 89w48'58 5:59:16
Marquette 24 1 43N44'51 89w08'19 5:56:33
Marshall 13 1 43N10'06 89w04'00 5:56:16
Marshfield 72 1 44N40'08 90w10'18 6:00:41
Marshland 6 1 44N04'25 91w33'17 6:06:13
Martell 48 1 44N49'47 92w23'51 6:09:35
Martinsville 13 1 43N10'49 89w35'24 5:58:22
Martintown 23 1 42N30'30 89w48'02 5:59:12
Marxville 13 1 43N11'28 89w39'35 5:58:38
Marytown 20 1 43N54'49 88w12'08 5:52:49
Mason 4 1 46N26'07 91w03'35 6:04:14
Mather 29 1 44N08'34 90w18'31 6:01:14
Matteson 69 1 44N38 88w41 5:54:44
Mattoon 59 1 45N00'15 89w02'31 5:56:10
Mauston 29 1 43N47'50 90w04'38 6:00:19
Maxville 6 1 44N31'54 92w00'31 6:08:02
May Corner 38 1 45N02'57 87w51'02 5:51:24
Mayfair 41 1 43N03 88w02 5:52:08
Mayfield 67 1 43N19'45 88w11'48 5:52:47
Mayville 14 1 43N29'39 88w32'41 5:54:11
Mazomanie 13 1 43N10'36 89w47'41 5:59:11
McAllister 38 1 45N19'38 87w43'16 5:50:53
McCartney 22 1 42N41'00 90w51'03 6:03:24
McCord 35 1 45N33'19 89w53'58 5:59:36
McFarland 13 1 43N00'45 89w17'23 5:57:10
McKinley 49 1 45N34'17 92w10'35 6:08:42
McMillan 37 1 44N49 90w07 6:00:28
McNaughton 44 1 45N43'57 89w32'39 5:58:11
Mead 10 1 44N49 90w44 6:02:56
Meadowbrook 58 1 45N41 91w07 6:04:28
Meadow Valley 29 1 44N12'55 90w13'16 6:00:53
Mecan 39 1 43N47'46 89w12'54 5:56:52
Medary 32 1 43N51'19 91w12'34 6:04:50
Medford 61 1 45N08'19 90w20'24 6:01:22
Medina 45 1 44N16'22 88w38'16 5:54:33
Medina Junction 71 1 44N13'59 88w37'18 5:54:29
Meehan 50 1 44N26'10 89w38'50 5:58:35
Meeker 67 1 43N13'18 88w10'23 5:52:42
Meekers Grove 33 1 42N38'44 90w22'10 6:01:29
Meeme 36 1 43N55'14 87w49'53 5:51:20
Meenon 7 1 45N52 92w20 6:09:20
Meggers 8 1 43N58'20 88w02'29 5:52:10
Mellen 2 1 46N19'32 90w39'39 6:02:39
Melnik 36 1 44N14'51 87w44'45 5:50:59
Melrose 27 1 44N07'50 90w59'53 6:04:00
Melrose Park 71 1 44N01'58 88w35'41 5:54:23
Melvina 42 1 43N48'20 90w46'19 6:03:05
Menasha 71 1 44N12'08 88w26'47 5:53:47
Menasha Junction 71 1 44N13 88w25 5:53:40
Menchalville 36 1 44N13'33 87w52'56 5:51:32
Menekaunee 38 1 45N06 87w37 5:50:28
Menominee 41 1 45N01 88w42 5:54:48
Menomonee Falls 68 1 43N10'44 88w07'02 5:52:28
Menomonie 17 1 44N52'32 91w55'09 6:07:41
Menomonie Junction 17 1 44N54'51 91w55'29 6:07:42
Mentor 10 1 44N33 90w52 6:03:28
Mequon 46 1 43N14'11 87w59'04 5:51:56
Mercer 26 1 46N09'56 90w03'45 6:00:15
Meridean 17 1 44N44'17 91w47'27 6:07:10
Merrill 35 1 45N10'50 89w41'00 5:58:44
Merrillan 27 1 44N27'04 90w50'28 6:03:22
Merrimac 57 1 43N22'24 89w37'24 5:58:30
Merton 68 1 43N08'48 88w18'24 5:53:14
Meteor 58 1 45N41'22 91w21'53 6:05:28
Metomen 20 1 43N46 88w49 5:55:16
Metz 71 1 44N12'49 88w53'11 5:55:33
Mid-city 41 1 43N03 87w58 5:51:52
Middle Inlet 38 1 45N17'30 87w59'32 5:51:58
Middle Ridge 32 1 43N48'03 90w56'48 6:03:47
Middleton 13 1 43N05'50 89w30'15 5:58:01
Middleton Junction 13 1 43N03'37 89w31'40 5:58:07
Midway 5 1 44N30 88w01 5:52:04
Midway 32 1 43N55'45 91w15'28 6:05:02
Midway 65 1 42N47'32 88w18'30 5:53:14
Mifflin 25 1 42N52'16 90w21'14 6:01:25
Mikana 3 1 45N35'31 91w36'04 6:06:24
Mikesville 71 1 44N01 88w33 5:54:12
Milan 37 1 44N58'52 90w10'46 6:00:43
Milford 28 1 43N06'03 88w50'48 5:55:23
Milladore 72 1 44N36'15 89w51'17 5:59:25
Millard 65 1 42N44'04 88w37'17 5:54:29
Mill Center 5 1 44N35'17 88w09'38 5:52:39
Mill Creek Community 50 1 44N32'25 89w40'39 5:58:43
Millersville 60 1 43N44 87w46 5:51:04
Millhome 36 1 43N53'42 87w57'44 5:51:51
Mills Center 5 1 44N30 88w01 5:52:04
Millston 27 1 44N11'35 90w38'51 6:02:35
Milltown 49 1 45N31'34 92w30'30 6:10:02
Millville 22 1 43N02'00 90w55'48 6:03:43
Milton 54 1 42N46'32 88w56'38 5:55:47
Milton Junction 54 1 42N46'57 88w57'46 5:55:51
Milwaukee 41 5 43N02'20 87w54'23 5:51:38
Minawa Beach 20 1 43N50'47 88w22'53 5:53:32
Mindoro 32 1 44N01'16 91w06'06 6:04:24
Mineral Point 23 1 42N42'43 89w28'00 5:57:52
Mineral Point 25 1 42N51'36 90w10'47 6:00:43
Minersville 2 1 46N24'25 90w47'50 6:03:11
Minnesota Junction 14 1 43N27'09 88w41'49 5:54:47
Minocqua 44 1 45N52'17 89w42'39 5:58:51
Minong 66 1 46N05'58 91w49'29 6:07:18
Misha Mokwa 6 1 44N29'50 92w00'37 6:08:02
Mishicot 36 1 44N14'21 87w38'28 5:50:34
Mitchell 60 1 43N40 88w06 5:52:24
Mitterhofer 61 1 44N57 90w48 6:03:12
Modena 6 1 44N27'27 91w47'47 6:07:11
Moeville 48 1 44N41'19 92w31'38 6:10:07
Mole Lake 21 1 45N28'47 88w58'59 5:55:56
Mole Lake Indian Reservation 21 1 45N29 88w59 5:55:56
Molitor 61 1 45N14 90w30 6:02:00
Monches 68 1 43N11'28 88w20'37 5:53:22
Mondovi 6 1 44N34'04 91w40'15 6:06:41
Monico 44 1 45N34'35 89w09'18 5:56:37
Monona 13 1 43N03'44 89w20'02 5:57:20
Monroe 23 1 42N36'04 89w38'18 5:58:33
Monroe Center 1 1 44N06'43 89w56'22 5:59:45
Montana 6 1 44N20'29 91w39'53 6:06:40
Montello 39 1 43N47'29 89w19'11 5:57:17
Monterey 68 1 43N10'16 88w29'58 5:54:00
Montfort 22 1 42N58'18 90w25'59 6:01:44
Montgomeryville 12 1 43N21'23 90w44'23 6:02:58
Monticello 23 1 42N44'44 89w35'41 5:58:23
Montpelier 31 1 44N27 87w42 5:50:48
Montreal 26 1 46N25'41 90w14'45 6:00:59
Montrose 13 1 42N52'58 89w34'38 5:58:19
Moon 37 1 44N46'18 89w47'16 5:59:09
Moon Valley 57 1 43N22'13 89w40'21 5:58:41
Moose Junction 16 1 46N17'15 92w09'17 6:08:37
Moquah 4 1 46N34'14 91w04'59 6:04:20
Morgan 43 1 44N47'38 88w11'24 5:52:46
Morgan 59 1 44N53'06 88w49'28 5:55:18
Morris 59 1 44N49 89w02 5:56:08
Morrison 5 1 44N17'57 87w59'20 5:51:57
Morrisonville 13 1 43N16'38 89w21'34 5:57:26
Morris Park 13 1 43N02 89w17 5:57:08
Morse 2 1 46N13'20 90w37'39 6:02:31
Morton Corner 48 1 44N47'26 92w28'19 6:09:53
Moscow 25 1 42N50'00 89w51'18 5:59:25
Mosel 60 1 43N48'20 87w44'25 5:50:58
Mosinee 37 1 44N47'35 89w42'11 5:58:49
Mosinee Spur 16 1 46N15 91w48 6:07:12
Mosling 43 1 44N52'08 88w22'10 5:53:29
Moundville 39 1 43N41 89w27 5:57:48
Mountain 43 1 45N11'05 88w28'25 5:53:54
Mount Calvary 20 1 43N49'35 88w14'46 5:52:59
Mount Hope 22 1 42N58'02 90w51'32 6:03:26
Mount Hope Corners 18 1 44N44'04 91w34'07 6:06:16
Mount Horeb 13 1 43N00'31 89w44'18 5:58:57
Mount Ida 22 1 42N58'19 90w45'39 6:03:03
Mount Morris 70 1 44N06'52 89w11'26 5:56:46
Mount Sterling 12 1 43N18'55 90w55'43 6:03:43
Mount Tabor 63 1 43N42'02 90w27'15 6:01:49
Mount Vernon 13 1 42N56'49 89w39'21 5:58:37
Mount View 37 1 44N57'06 89w43'36 5:58:54
Mount Zion 12 1 43N15'24 90w44'01 6:02:56
Mukwa 69 1 44N22 88w48 5:55:12
Mukwonago 68 1 42N52'00 88w20'00 5:53:20
Murat 61 1 45N11'22 90w26'44 6:01:47
Murphy Corner 45 1 44N23'11 88w20'05 5:53:20
Murrays Landing 26 1 46N04'55 90w04'47 6:00:19
Murry 55 1 45N36'02 91w12'02 6:04:48
Muscoda 22 1 43N11'06 90w26'35 6:01:46
Muskeg 4 1 46N34'14 91w29'26 6:05:58
Muskego 68 1 42N54'21 88w08'20 5:52:33
Myra 67 1 43N24'57 88w05'44 5:52:23
Nabob 67 1 43N25'13 88w16'15 5:53:05
Namekagon 4 1 46N12'46 91w02'43 6:04:11
Namur 15 1 44N44'05 87w40'12 5:50:41
Naples 6 1 44N33 91w35 6:06:20
Nasbro 14 1 43N35'41 88w30'17 5:54:01
Nasewaupee 15 1 44N49 87w27 5:49:48
Nash 4 1 46N35 90w53 6:03:32
Nashotah 68 1 43N05'52 88w24'08 5:53:37
Nashville 21 1 45N31'22 89w01'29 5:56:06
Nasonville 72 1 44N35'56 90w15'30 6:01:02
Naugart 37 1 45N04'34 89w47'18 5:59:09
Navarino 59 1 44N36'40 88w29'13 5:53:58
Necedah 29 1 44N01'34 90w04'26 6:00:18
Neda 14 1 43N25'17 88w32'15 5:54:09
Neenah 71 1 44N11'09 88w27'45 5:53:51
Neillsville 10 1 44N33'36 90w35'46 6:02:23
Neith 60 1 43N48 88w01 5:52:04
Nekimi 71 1 43N57 88w36 5:54:24
Nekoosa 72 1 44N18'45 89w54'15 5:59:37
Nekoosa Junction 72 1 44N20'16 89w53'21 5:59:33
Nelma 21 1 46N01'11 88w49'04 5:55:16
Nelson 6 1 44N25'13 92w00'29 6:08:02
Nelsonville 50 1 44N29'42 89w18'35 5:57:14
Nenno 67 1 43N26'46 88w23'29 5:53:34
Neopit 40 1 44N58'51 88w49'51 5:55:19
Neosho 14 1 43N18'37 88w31'05 5:54:04
Nepeuskun 71 1 43N57 88w51 5:55:24
Neptune 53 1 43N22'23 90w16'02 6:01:04
Nerike 48 1 44N33'02 92w09'56 6:08:40
Neshkoro 39 1 43N57'57 89w13'03 5:56:52
Neuern 31 1 44N32 87w42 5:50:48
Neva 34 1 45N14'22 89w06'47 5:56:27
Neva Corners 34 1 45N13'12 89w08'40 5:56:35
Nevins 10 1 44N29'47 90w21'54 6:01:28
Newald 21 1 45N44'19 88w42'19 5:54:49
New Amsterdam 32 1 43N58'58 91w18'59 6:05:16
Newark 54 1 42N32'32 89w13'39 5:56:55
New Auburn 9 1 45N12'15 91w33'29 6:06:14
New Berlin 68 1 42N58'35 88w06'30 5:52:26
Newbold 44 1 45N41'53 89w30'36 5:58:02
Newburg 67 1 43N25'54 88w02'47 5:52:11
Newburg Corners 32 1 43N53 90w59 6:03:56
New Centerville 56 1 44N58 92w23 6:09:32
New Chester 1 1 43N52 89w39 5:58:36
New Denmark 5 1 44N23 87w49 5:51:16
New Diggings 33 1 42N32'07 90w20'07 6:01:20
New Fane 20 1 43N33'18 88w11'09 5:52:45
New Franken 5 1 44N31'51 87w49'33 5:51:18
New Glarus 23 1 42N48'52 89w38'06 5:58:32
New Holstein 8 1 43N57'00 88w05'03 5:52:20
New Hope 50 1 44N30'13 89w15'49 5:57:03
New Johannesburg 56 1 45N07 92w32 6:10:08
New Lisbon 29 1 43N52'45 90w09'55 6:00:40
New London 69 1 44N23'34 88w44'23 5:54:58
New Lyme 42 1 44N07 90w45 6:03:00
New Miner 29 1 44N10'11 90w02'10 6:00:09
New Munster 30 1 42N34'46 88w13'40 5:52:55
New Paris 60 1 43N43'59 87w58'19 5:51:53
Newport 11 1 43N37 89w42 5:58:48
New Post 58 1 45N53'45 91w11'09 6:04:45
New Prospect 20 1 43N36'57 88w10'43 5:52:43
New Richmond 56 1 45N07'23 92w32'11 6:10:09
New Rome 1 1 44N13'10 89w52'51 5:59:31
Newry 63 1 43N42'42 90w49'02 6:03:16
Newton 36 1 43N59'38 87w43'35 5:50:54
Newton 63 1 43N35'23 91w03'46 6:04:15
Newtonburg 36 1 44N03'06 87w45'42 5:51:03
Newville 54 1 42N49'44 89w01'17 5:56:05
Niagara 38 1 45N46'17 87w59'41 5:51:59
Nichols 45 1 44N33'47 88w27'48 5:53:51
Nichols Shore Acres 71 1 44N05'50 88w38'23 5:54:34
Nippersink Manor 65 1 42N30 88w19 5:53:16
Nobleton 66 1 45N40'45 91w42'09 6:06:49
Nokomis 44 1 45N36 89w44 5:58:56
Nora 13 1 43N01'51 89w09'00 5:56:36
Nordheim 71 1 44N01 88w33 5:54:12
Norma 9 1 44N57'06 91w22'10 6:05:29
Norman 31 1 44N22'15 87w36'12 5:50:25
Norrie 37 1 44N53'08 89w15'15 5:57:01

Norske 69 1 44N39'09 89w12'30 5:56:50
North Andover 22 1 42N48'56 90w57'57 6:03:52
North Bay 15 1 45N08'46 87w04'58 5:48:20
North Bay 52 1 42N45'53 87w46'47 5:51:07
North Beloit 54 1 42N31 89w03 5:56:12
North Bend 27 1 44N05'29 91w07'00 6:04:28
North Branch 27 1 44N26'51 90w59'56 6:04:00
North Bristol 13 1 43N16'00 89w12'44 5:56:51
North Cape 52 1 42N46'43 88w04'15 5:52:17
North Clayton 12 1 43N22'51 90w42'34 6:02:50
North Creek 62 1 44N16'15 91w25'55 6:05:44
Northeim 36 1 43N59'39 87w41'55 5:50:48
Northfield 27 1 44N27'33 91w05'58 6:04:24
North Fond du Lac 20 1 43N48'41 88w29'00 5:53:56
North Freedom 57 1 43N27'35 89w52'06 5:59:28
North Grimms 36 1 44N09'12 87w54'08 5:51:37
North Hudson 56 1 44N59'35 92w45'24 6:11:02
North La Crosse 32 1 43N50'47 91w14'53 6:05:00
North Lake 68 1 43N09'22 88w22'14 5:53:29
North Lancaster 22 1 42N54 90w43 6:02:52
Northland 69 1 44N35'42 89w12'28 5:56:50
North Leeds 11 1 43N19'55 89w19'31 5:57:18
Northline 56 1 44N59'21 92w42'54 6:10:52
North Lowell 14 1 43N22'13 88w47'46 5:55:11
North Menomonie 17 1 44N53'52 91w55'54 6:07:44
North Park 52 1 42N48 87w49 5:51:16
Northport 15 1 45N17'31 86w58'48 5:47:55
Northport 69 1 44N24'35 88w47'38 5:55:11
North Prairie 68 1 42N56'04 88w24'19 5:53:37
North Readfield 69 1 44N17'12 88w46'10 5:55:05
North Red Wing 48 1 44N34'38 92w32'51 6:10:11
North Shore 28 1 42N54'40 88w55'13 5:55:41
Northside 32 1 43N49 91w14 6:04:56
North Star 50 1 44N37'03 89w25'21 5:57:41
North Tomah 42 1 43N59 90w30 6:02:00
Northwoods Beach 58 1 45N54'51 91w24'12 6:05:37
North York 2 1 46N23'34 90w46'39 6:03:07
Norton 17 1 45N00'59 91w50'03 6:07:20
Norwalk 42 1 43N49'50 90w37'17 6:02:29
Norway 52 1 42N49 88w09 5:52:36
Norway Grove 13 1 43N14'55 89w24'09 5:57:37
Norway Ridge 42 1 44N07'29 90w19'45 6:01:19
Norwood 34 1 45N05 89w02 5:56:08
Nuern 31 1 44N30'07 87w43'29 5:50:54
Nutterville 37 1 45N00'14 89w31'38 5:58:07
Nye 49 1 45N18'52 92w34'49 6:10:19
Oak Center 20 1 43N39'39 88w36'00 5:54:24
Oak Creek 41 1 42N53'09 87w51'47 5:51:27
Oakdale 42 1 43N57'35 90w22'54 6:01:32
Oakfield 20 1 43N41'10 88w32'47 5:54:11
Oak Grove 14 1 43N23'10 88w44'44 5:54:59
Oak Hall 13 1 42N57'02 89w26'13 5:57:45
Oak Hill 28 1 42N56'09 88w35'12 5:54:21
Oak Knoll 68 1 42N52'07 88w20'16 5:53:21
Oakland 7 1 45N56'15 92w22'07 6:09:28
Oakland 28 1 42N58'36 88w57'20 5:55:49
Oakley 23 1 42N31'37 89w28'04 5:57:52
Oak Orchard 43 1 44N46'53 87w55'33 5:51:42
Oakridge 30 1 42N31 88w07 5:52:28
Oakridge 48 1 44N35'18 92w23'43 6:09:35
Oakwood 41 1 42N51'29 87w55'28 5:51:42
Oakwood 71 1 44N02'47 88w36'10 5:54:25
Oasis 70 1 44N12 89w24 5:57:36
Oconomowoc 68 1 43N06'42 88w29'57 5:54:00
Oconomowoc Lake 68 1 43N06'16 88w27'33 5:53:50
Oconto 43 1 44N53'14 87w51'52 5:51:27
Oconto Falls 43 1 44N52'26 88w08'34 5:52:34
Odanah 2 1 46N36'30 90w41'48 6:02:47
Ogdensburg 69 1 44N27'07 89w01'54 5:56:08
Ogema 51 1 45N26'37 90w17'53 6:01:12
Oil City 42 1 43N45'02 90w35'12 6:02:21
Ojibwa 58 1 45N47'53 91w07'00 6:04:28
Okauchee 68 1 43N06'49 88w26'09 5:53:45
Okee 11 1 43N21'28 89w34'48 5:58:19
Old Albertville 9 1 44N56'12 91w36'00 6:06:24
Old Ashippun 14 1 43N13'29 88w31'11 5:54:05
Old Lebanon 14 1 43N13'34 88w37'49 5:54:31
Oliver 16 1 46N39'27 92w11'42 6:08:47
Olivet 48 1 44N47'11 92w15'25 6:09:02
Oma 26 1 46N17 90w02 6:00:08
Omro 71 1 44N02'22 88w44'39 5:54:59
Onalaska 32 1 43N53'04 91w14'06 6:04:56
Oneida 5 1 44N29'55 88w10'58 5:52:44
Oneida Indian Reservation 5 1 44N30 88w11 5:52:44
Ono 48 1 44N39'20 92w15'22 6:09:01
Ontario 63 1 43N43'33 90w35'29 6:02:22
Oostburg 60 1 43N37'22 87w47'40 5:51:11
Orange 29 1 43N56 90w15 6:01:00
Orange Mill 29 1 43N54'06 90w13'56 6:00:56
Orchard Grove 67 1 43N29'54 88w08'27 5:52:34
Oregon 13 1 42N55'34 89w23'04 5:57:32
Orfordville 54 1 42N37'39 89w15'11 5:57:01
Orienta 4 1 46N45 91w28 6:05:52
Orihula 71 1 44N12'33 88w49'58 5:55:20
Orion 53 1 43N12'11 90w25'40 6:01:43
Ormsby 34 1 45N15'22 89w15'09 5:57:01
Orva 26 1 46N27'07 90w13'53 6:00:56
Osborn 45 1 44N27 88w21 5:53:24
Osceola 49 1 45N19'14 92w42'17 6:10:49
Oshkosh 71 1 44N01'29 88w32'33 5:54:10
Osman 36 1 43N58'07 87w49'15 5:51:17
Osseo 62 1 44N34'20 91w13'38 6:04:55
Ostrander 69 1 44N23'34 88w50'16 5:55:21
Otis 35 1 45N16'08 89w41'36 5:58:46
Otsego 11 1 43N24'08 89w09'58 5:56:40
Ottawa 68 1 42N58'34 88w26'59 5:53:48
Ottman Corners 48 1 44N42'12 92w31'01 6:10:04
Oulu 4 1 46N37'59 91w31'54 6:06:08
Ourtown 60 1 43N41'50 87w49'16 5:51:17
Owen 10 1 44N57 90w33 6:02:12
Oxbo 58 1 45N51'46 90w42'15 6:02:49
Oxford 39 1 43N46'53 89w34'21 5:58:17
Pacific 11 1 43N30 89w24 5:57:36
Packard 38 1 45N21'17 87w41'39 5:50:47
Packwaukee 39 1 43N45'48 89w27'30 5:57:50
Paddock Lake 30 1 42N34'39 88w06'18 5:52:25
Padus 21 1 45N29'35 88w39'51 5:54:39
Palmyra 28 1 42N52'40 88w35'10 5:54:21
Paoli 13 1 42N55'46 89w31'25 5:58:06
Pardeeville 11 1 43N32'16 89w18'00 5:57:12
Parfreyville 69 1 44N18'46 89w07'52 5:56:31
Paris 30 1 42N38'01 88w03'05 5:52:12
Park Falls 51 1 45N56'04 90w26'29 6:01:46
Parkland 16 1 46N38'52 91w59'51 6:07:59
Parklawn 41 1 43N05 87w58 5:51:52
Park Mills 38 1 45N06 87w37 5:50:28
Park Ridge 50 1 44N31'10 89w32'45 5:58:11
Parrish 34 1 45N25'11 89w24'09 5:57:37
Patch Grove 22 1 42N56'25 90w58'19 6:03:53
Patzau 16 1 46N29'29 92w13'14 6:08:53
Paukotuk 71 1 43N58'05 88w31'15 5:54:05
Pearson 34 1 45N21'51 89w00'59 5:56:04
Peck 34 1 45N15 89w14 5:56:56
Pecks Station 65 1 42N41 88w33 5:54:12
Peebles 20 1 43N48'59 88w22'35 5:53:30
Peeksville 2 1 46N05'53 90w31'48 6:02:07
Pelican Lake 44 1 45N29'58 89w10'00 5:56:40
Pella 59 1 44N44'33 88w48'12 5:55:13
Pell Lake 65 1 42N32'17 88w21'03 5:53:24
Pembine 38 1 45N38'07 87w59'27 5:51:58
Pence 26 1 46N24'55 90w16'17 6:01:05
Peninsula Center 15 1 45N04 87w07 5:48:28
Pennington 51 1 45N31'55 90w23'32 6:01:34
Pensaukee 43 1 44N49'23 87w54'47 5:51:39
Pepin 47 1 44N26'28 92w08'52 6:08:35
Peplin 37 1 44N47'10 89w37'08 5:58:29
Perida 7 1 45N53 92w22 6:09:28
Perkinstown 61 1 45N12'15 90w36'53 6:02:28
Perry 13 1 42N54 89w49 5:59:16
Perry Go Place 54 1 42N33 89w02 5:56:08
Pershing 61 1 45N15 90w51 6:03:24
Peru 50 1 44N34 89w15 5:57:00
Peshtigo 38 1 45N03'16 87w44'57 5:51:00
Petersburg 12 1 43N16'20 90w50'15 6:03:21
Petes Landing 2 1 46N02'59 90w19'38 6:01:19
Pewaukee 68 1 43N04'50 88w15'40 5:53:03
Pewaukee West 68 1 43N04'29 88w19'51 5:53:19
Peyton 16 1 46N39'01 92w01'16 6:08:05
Phantom Lake 68 1 42N52 88w20 5:53:20
Pheasant Branch 13 1 43N06'15 89w29'02 5:57:56
Phelps 64 1 46N03'52 89w05'15 5:56:21
Phillips 51 1 45N41'48 90w24'01 6:01:36
Phipps 58 1 46N03'46 91w24'48 6:05:39
Phlox 34 1 45N03'04 89w00'51 5:56:03
Piacenza 71 1 44N08'47 88w42'26 5:54:50
Pickerel 34 1 45N21'34 88w54'39 5:55:39
Pickett 71 1 43N54'41 88w43'47 5:54:55
Piehl 44 1 45N41 89w07 5:56:28
Pierce 31 1 44N32 87w30 5:50:00
Pierceville 13 1 43N08'09 89w09'11 5:56:37
Pigeon 62 1 44N26 91w13 6:04:52
Pigeon Falls 62 1 44N25'35 91w12'37 6:04:50
Pike Lake 67 1 43N18'50 88w20'31 5:53:22
Pike River 4 1 46N27'36 91w14'23 6:04:58
Pikeville 30 1 42N29'46 88w01'28 5:52:06
Pilsen 31 1 44N26'37 87w43'30 5:50:54
Pine Bluff 13 1 43N03'39 89w39'20 5:58:37
Pine Creek 62 1 44N08'04 91w31'36 6:06:06
Pine Grove 5 1 44N24'59 87w59'19 5:51:33
Pine Grove 9 1 44N53'59 91w37'49 6:06:31
Pine Grove 50 1 44N18 89w33 5:58:12
Pinehill 27 1 44N17 90w51 6:03:24
Pinehurst 9 1 44N51'30 91w27'45 6:05:51
Pine Knob 25 1 42N48 89w51 5:59:24
Pine Lake 26 1 46N15'22 90w08'26 6:00:34
Pine Lake 44 1 45N42 89w23 5:57:32
Pine River 35 1 45N08'03 89w37'19 5:58:29
Pine River 70 1 44N09'08 89w04'37 5:56:18
Pine Valley 10 1 44N33 90w37 6:02:28
Pipe 20 1 43N54'51 88w18'45 5:53:15
Pipersville 28 1 43N08'32 88w39'00 5:54:36
Pittsfield 5 1 44N35'58 88w14'42 5:52:59
Pittsville 72 1 44N26'21 90w07'28 6:00:30
Plain 57 1 43N16'44 90w02'37 6:00:10
Plainfield 70 1 44N12'50 89w29'32 5:57:58
Plainville 1 1 43N42'32 89w48'45 5:59:15
Plat 67 1 43N12'28 88w16'51 5:53:07
Platteville 22 1 42N44'03 90w28'42 6:01:55
Pleasant Prairie 30 1 42N33'11 87w56'00 5:51:44
Pleasant Ridge 25 1 43N03'17 90w04'24 6:00:18
Pleasant Valley 63 1 43N43'16 91w10'24 6:04:42
Pleasant View 27 1 44N17 90w51 6:03:24
Pleasantville 62 1 44N27'13 91w18'17 6:05:13
Plover 50 1 44N27'23 89w32'38 5:58:11
Plugtown 12 1 43N13'21 90w44'54 6:03:00
Plum City 48 1 44N37'45 92w11'32 6:08:46
Plum Lake 64 1 46N02 89w31 5:58:04
Plummer Point 71 1 44N05'15 88w37'45 5:54:31
Plymouth 60 1 43N44'55 87w58'37 5:51:54
Pokegama 16 1 46N38'49 92w08'46 6:08:35
Poland 5 1 44N26'37 87w49'34 5:51:18
Polar 34 1 45N10'07 88w59'24 5:55:58
Polifka Corners 36 1 44N09 87w49 5:51:16
Polk 67 1 43N20 88w15 5:53:00
Polley 61 1 45N08'28 90w48'25 6:03:14
Polonia 50 1 44N34'12 89w24'47 5:57:39
Poniatowski 37 1 44N59'42 89w59'36 5:59:58
Poplar 16 1 46N35'02 91w47'56 6:07:12
Popple Lake 9 1 44N55 91w23 6:05:32
Popple River 21 1 45N47'29 88w41'06 5:54:44
Porcupine 47 1 44N35'02 92w05'44 6:08:23
Portage 11 1 43N32'21 89w27'45 5:57:51
Port Andrew 53 1 43N12'26 90w34'02 6:02:16
Port Arthur 55 1 45N25'45 91w09'43 6:04:39
Port Edwards 72 1 44N21'03 89w51'55 5:59:28
Porter 54 1 42N48 89w11 5:56:44
Porterfield 38 1 45N09'16 87w47'40 5:51:11
Porters 54 1 42N31'43 88w57'33 5:55:50
Port Junction 46 1 43N23 87w53 5:51:32
Portland 28 1 43N11'56 88w58'29 5:55:54
Portland 42 1 43N46'08 90w51'29 6:03:26
Port Washington 46 1 43N23'14 87w52'32 5:51:30
Port Wing 4 1 46N46'29 91w23'11 6:05:33
Poskin 3 1 45N24'33 91w57'41 6:07:51
Post Lake 34 1 45N26'27 89w04'49 5:56:19
Postville 23 1 42N47'57 89w45'10 5:59:01
Potawatomi Indian Res 21 1 45N26 88w30 5:54:00
Potosi 22 1 42N41'22 90w42'43 6:02:51
Potter 8 1 44N07'14 88w05'57 5:52:24
Potter Lake 65 1 42N48 88w24 5:53:36
Potts Corners 63 1 43N35 90w38 6:02:32
Pound 38 1 45N05'39 88w02'02 5:52:08
Powell 26 1 46N05'19 89w57'30 5:59:50
Powers Lake 30 1 42N33'13 88w17'40 5:53:11
Poygan 71 1 44N06 88w49 5:55:16
Poynette 11 1 43N23'25 89w24'10 5:57:37
Poy Sippi 70 1 44N08'14 88w59'43 5:55:59
Praag 6 1 44N22'41 91w45'02 6:07:00
Prairie Corners 22 1 42N32'09 90w32'00 6:02:08
Prairie du Chien 12 1 43N03'06 91w08'28 6:04:34
Prairie du Sac 57 1 43N17'13 89w43'26 5:58:54
Prairie Farm 3 1 45N14'14 91w58'53 6:07:56
Prairie Lake 3 1 45N21 91w43 6:06:52
Pratt 4 1 46N20 91w05 6:04:20
Pratt Junction 44 1 45N28'57 89w09'52 5:56:39
Pray 27 1 44N22'24 90w29'50 6:01:59
Preble 5 1 44N29'51 87w58'11 5:51:53
Prentice 51 1 45N32'46 90w17'11 6:01:09
Prescott 48 1 44N44'56 92w48'07 6:11:12
Presque Isle 64 1 46N14'50 89w43'45 5:58:55
Preston 22 1 42N58'30 90w32'49 6:02:11
Price 27 1 44N34'54 91w03'16 6:04:13
Price 34 1 45N15 88w59 5:55:56
Primrose 13 1 42N54'05 89w39'44 5:58:39
Princeton 24 1 43N51'03 89w07'18 5:56:29
Prospect 68 1 42N56'40 88w09'32 5:52:38
Pucketville 48 1 44N34'10 92w32'21 6:10:09
Pukwana Beach 20 1 43N55'40 88w19'01 5:53:16
Pulaski 5 1 44N40'20 88w14'33 5:52:58
Pulcifer 59 1 44N50'39 88w21'36 5:53:26
Purdy 63 1 43N31'01 91w02'53 6:04:12
Pureair 4 1 46N47'25 90w50'50 6:03:23
Quarry 36 1 44N09 87w57 5:51:48
Queenstown 61 1 45N21'07 90w17'17 6:01:09
Quincy 1 1 43N54 89w55 5:59:40
Quinney 8 1 44N00'52 88w18'26 5:53:14
Racine 52 1 42N43'34 87w46'58 5:51:08
Radisson 58 1 45N46'08 91w13'16 6:04:53
Radspur 4 1 46N10'43 91w19'00 6:05:16
Rainbow Beach 71 1 44N09'24 88w26'42 5:53:47
Randall 7 1 45N41'45 92w50'06 6:11:20
Randall 30 1 42N32 88w15 5:53:00
Randolph 11 1 43N32'21 89w00'24 5:56:02
Random Lake 60 1 43N33'08 87w57'42 5:51:51
Range 49 1 45N23'44 92w17'04 6:09:08
Rangeline 37 1 44N44'37 89w57'50 5:59:51
Rankin 31 1 44N35'46 87w30'12 5:50:01
Rantoul 8 1 44N06 88w06 5:52:24
Rantz 44 1 45N49'54 89w43'46 5:58:55
Rawson 41 1 42N55 87w54 5:51:36
Raymond 52 1 42N48'03 88w00'45 5:52:03
Raymore 42 1 43N59'51 90w37'09 6:02:29
Readfield 69 1 44N16'21 88w46'11 5:55:05
Readstown 63 1 43N26'58 90w45'33 6:03:02
Red Banks 5 1 44N36'40 87w51'47 5:51:27
Red Banks 69 1 44N16'37 88w51'31 5:55:26
Red Cedar 17 1 44N41'21 91w53'03 6:07:32
Red Cliff 4 1 46N51'20 90w47'16 6:03:09
Red Cliff Indian Reservation 4 1 46N51 90w47 6:03:08
Redgranite 70 1 44N02'31 89w05'54 5:56:24
Red Mound 63 1 43N28'21 91w08'41 6:04:35
Red River 31 1 44N38 87w43 5:50:52
Red River 59 1 44N49'30 88w42'16 5:54:49
Red Rock 33 1 42N38'33 90w02'51 6:00:11
Red Springs 59 1 44N53 88w48 5:55:12
Redville 61 1 44N57 90w36 6:02:24
Reedsburg 57 1 43N31'57 90w00'09 6:00:01
Reedsville 36 1 44N09'13 87w57'24 5:51:50
Reeseville 14 1 43N18'18 88w50'41 5:55:23
Reeve 3 1 45N14'19 92w07'33 6:08:30
Regina 59 1 44N53'41 89w01'18 5:56:05
Reid 37 1 44N53 89w25 5:57:40
Reifs Mills 36 1 44N10'56 87w47'57 5:51:12
Reighmoor 71 1 44N03'27 88w40'25 5:54:42
Remington 72 1 44N18 90w11 6:00:44
Renet Lake 30 1 42N29'53 88w04'54 5:52:20
Requa 27 1 44N35'12 91w08'41 6:04:35
Reseburg 10 1 44N54'55 90w45'36 6:03:02
Reserve 58 1 45N52'53 91w23'11 6:05:33
Retreat 63 1 43N26'44 91w04'50 6:04:19
Rewey 25 1 42N50'34 90w23'43 6:01:35
Rhine 60 1 43N51'46 87w57'24 5:51:50
Rhinelander 44 1 45N38'12 89w24'43 5:57:39
Rib Falls 37 1 44N58'16 89w54'13 5:59:37
Rib Lake 61 1 45N19'03 90w12'30 6:00:50
Rib Mountain 37 1 44N56 89w41 5:58:44
Rice Lake 3 1 45N30'22 91w44'17 6:06:57
Richardson 49 1 45N19'09 92w11'59 6:08:48

Place		Lat	Long	Time
Richfield 67	1	43N15'22	88W11'38	5:52:47
Richford 70	1	44N01'25	89W26'07	5:57:44
Richland Center 53	1	43N20'05	90W23'12	6:01:33
Richmond 65	1	42N42'53	88W44'57	5:55:00
Richwood 14	1	43N14'29	88W46'59	5:55:08
Ricker Bay 71	1	44N07'52	88W28'14	5:53:53
Ridgeland 17	1	45N12'13	91W53'43	6:07:35
Ridgetop 19	1	45N55'47	88W16'12	5:53:05
Ridgeville 42	1	43N52	90W36	6:02:24
Ridgeway 25	1	43N00'08	89W59'25	5:59:58
Rief's Mills 36	1	44N09	87W49	5:51:16
Rietbrock 37	1	44N59	90W01	6:00:04
Riley 13	1	43N01'24	89W37'21	5:58:29
Ring 71	1	43N54'33	88W38'25	5:54:34
Ringle 37	1	44N53'28	89W25'32	5:57:42
Rio 11	1	43N26'52	89W14'23	5:56:58
Rio Creek 31	1	44N35'21	87W32'28	5:50:10
Riplinger 10	1	44N49'30	90W24'11	6:01:37
Ripon 20	1	43N50'32	88W50'09	5:55:21
Rising Sun 12	1	43N25'05	90W57'29	6:03:50
River Falls 48	1	44N51'41	92W37'25	6:10:30
River Hills 41	1	43N10'27	87W55'27	5:51:42
Rivermoor 71	1	44N04'22	88W41'10	5:54:45
Riverside 7	1	46N04'35	92W14'51	6:08:59
Riverside 33	1	42N35'38	90W01'21	6:00:05
Riverview 16	1	46N40'35	92W11'06	6:08:44
Riverview 43	1	45N15	88W27	5:53:48
Roaringcreek 27	1	44N17	90W51	6:03:24
Roberts 56	1	44N59'02	92W33'21	6:10:13
Robinson 65	1	42N36	88W28	5:53:52
Rochester 52	1	42N44'29	88W13'27	5:52:54
Rockaway Beach 8	1	44N05'52	88W19'37	5:53:18
Rockaway Beach 71	1	44N02'47	88W30'35	5:54:02
Rockbridge 53	1	43N26'54	90W21'50	6:01:27
Rock Creek 17	1	44N43	91W43	6:06:52
Rockdale 13	1	42N58'19	89W01'51	5:56:07
Rock Elm 48	1	44N44'12	92W12'59	6:08:52
Rock Falls 17	1	44N43'07	91W41'23	6:06:46
Rock Falls 35	1	45N20	89W44	5:58:56
Rockfield 67	1	43N15'27	88W07'34	5:52:30
Rockland 32	1	43N54'23	90W55'09	6:03:41
Rockmont 16	1	46N35'09	91W54'31	6:07:38
Rock Springs 57	1	43N29'33	89W55'08	5:59:41
Rockton 63	1	43N38'28	90W36'06	6:02:24
Rockville 22	1	42N43'38	90W40'55	6:02:44
Rockville 36	1	43N55'12	87W59'52	5:51:59
Rockwood 36	1	44N10'05	87W42'20	5:50:49
Rocky Corners 37	1	44N42'51	89W36'28	5:58:26
Rocky Run 50	1	44N32'40	89W38'25	5:58:34
Rodell 18	1	44N43'12	91W11'17	6:04:45
Rogersville 20	1	43N44'57	88W37'56	5:54:32
Rolling 34	1	45N05	89W09	5:56:36
Rolling Ground 12	1	43N19'46	90W44'25	6:02:58
Rolling Prairie 14	1	43N27'33	88W44'03	5:54:56
Romance 63	1	43N33'08	91W08'41	6:04:35
Rome 1	1	44N12	89W46	5:59:04
Rome 28	1	42N58'49	88W37'52	5:54:31
Roosevelt 44	1	45N40'19	89W18'53	5:57:16
Roosevelt 59	1	44N51	88W47	5:55:08
Rose 70	1	44N12	89W18	5:57:12
Rosecrans 36	1	44N16'36	87W49'37	5:51:18
Rosedale 42	1	44N04'30	90W54'49	6:03:39
Rose Lawn 59	1	44N36'05	88W19'30	5:53:18
Rosemere 36	1	44N06	87W41	5:50:44
Rosendale 20	1	43N48'28	88W40'29	5:54:42
Rosendale Center 20	1	43N51'06	88W43'13	5:54:53
Rosewood 52	1	42N40'33	88W10'07	5:52:40
Rosholt 50	1	44N37'40	89W18'31	5:57:14
Rosiere 15	1	44N40'32	87W36'43	5:50:27
Ross 21	1	45N44	88W44	5:54:56
Ross 63	1	43N32'28	90W45'11	6:03:01
Ross Crossing 23	1	42N49'45	89W33'08	5:58:13
Rostok 31	1	44N30'06	87W30'05	5:50:00
Rothschild 37	1	44N53'14	89W37'12	5:58:29
Round Lake 58	1	46N02	91W14	6:04:56
Rouse 26	1	46N21'23	90W27'56	6:01:52
Rowleys Bay 15	1	45N13'11	87W02'07	5:48:08
Roxbury 13	1	43N14'58	89W40'31	5:58:42
Royalton 69	1	44N24'46	88W51'46	5:55:27
Rozellville 37	1	44N44'36	90W01'28	6:00:06
Rube 36	1	44N03'06	87W48'05	5:51:12
Rubicon 14	1	43N20'25	88W27'27	5:53:50
Ruby 9	1	45N10'38	90W59'17	6:03:57
Rubys Corner 38	1	45N10'44	87W44'23	5:50:58
Rudolph 72	1	44N29'46	89W48'27	5:59:14
Rugby Junction 67	1	43N17'31	88W13'07	5:52:52
Rural 69	1	44N18'47	89W09'11	5:56:37
Rushford 71	1	44N01	88W50	5:55:20
Rush Lake 71	1	43N55'26	88W50'21	5:55:21
Rush Lake Junction 71	1	43N51	88W50	5:55:20
Rush River 56	1	44N54	92W25	6:09:40
Rusk 17	1	44N54'28	91W50'02	6:07:20
Russell 62	1	44N23	91W26	6:05:44
Rutland 13	1	42N52'44	89W21'00	5:57:24
Rutledge 22	1	42N33'17	90W38'01	6:02:32
Ryans Corner 31	1	44N30'48	87W36'28	5:50:26
Sabin 53	1	43N25'49	90W34'07	6:02:16
Saint Anna 8	1	43N53'36	88W07'17	5:52:29
Saint Anthony 67	1	43N26'33	88W20'30	5:53:22
Saint Catherines Bay 8	1	44N05'00	88W19'28	5:53:18
Saint Cloud 20	1	43N49'22	88W10'01	5:52:40
Saint Croix Falls 49	1	45N24'36	92W38'22	6:10:33
Saint Croix Indian Res 66	1	45N31	92W16	6:09:04
Saint Francis 41	1	42N58'03	87W52'39	5:51:31
Saint George 60	1	43N42	87W49	5:51:16
Saint Germain 64	1	45N54'06	89W29'14	5:57:57
Saint John 8	1	44N10'08	88W12'14	5:52:49
Saint Joseph 20	1	43N50	88W10	5:52:40
Saint Joseph 32	1	43N47'08	91W02'30	6:04:10
Saint Joseph 56	1	45N03	92W43	6:10:52
Saint Kilian 20	1	43N32'35	88W21'41	5:53:27
Saint Lawrence 67	1	43N22'11	88W19'58	5:53:20
Saint Lawrence 69	1	44N27	89W03	5:56:12
Saint Marie 24	1	43N54	89W05	5:56:20
Saint Martins 41	1	42N54'08	88W03'23	5:52:14
Saint Marys 42	1	43N47'53	90W41'14	6:02:45
Saint Michaels 67	1	43N30'48	88W09'38	5:52:39
Saint Nazianz 36	1	44N00'29	87W55'20	5:51:41
Saint Peter 20	1	43N50'11	88W20'29	5:53:22
Saint Rose 22	1	42N37'26	90W26'04	6:01:44
Saint Wendel 36	1	43N55	87W45	5:51:00
Salem 30	1	42N33'17	88W06'39	5:52:27
Salem 48	1	44N37'23	92W21'26	6:09:26
Salem Oaks 30	1	42N33'31	88W05'32	5:52:22
Salmo 4	1	46N46'53	90W51'54	6:03:28
Salter 67	1	43N25	88W11	5:52:44
Salvatorian Center 8	1	43N57	88W06	5:52:24
Sampson 9	1	45N14	91W21	6:05:24
Sampson 43	1	44N45'54	88W11'10	5:52:45
Sanborn 2	1	46N25'59	90W54'31	6:03:38
Sand Bay 4	1	46N56'45	90W53'27	6:03:34
Sand Creek 17	1	45N10'01	91W41'10	6:06:45
Sand Lake 49	1	45N22'06	92W33'30	6:10:14
Sand Prairie 53	1	43N12'19	90W36'41	6:02:27
Sandrock 26	1	46N18'49	90W08'42	6:00:35
Sandstone Bluff 24	1	43N49'02	88W58'01	5:55:52
Sandusky 57	1	43N23'43	90W09'07	6:00:36
Sandy Hook 22	1	42N32'36	90W36'36	6:02:26
Saratoga 72	1	44N18	89W49	5:59:16
Sarona 66	1	45N42'40	91W48'23	6:07:14
Sauk City 57	1	43N16'15	89W43'19	5:58:53
Saukville 46	1	43N22'54	87W56'26	5:51:46
Saunders 16	1	46N38'19	92W06'32	6:08:26
Sauntry 16	1	46N22'28	91W49'21	6:07:17
Saxeville 70	1	44N10'34	89W06'52	5:56:27
Saxon 26	1	46N29'36	90W24'51	6:01:39
Saylesville 14	1	43N18'01	88W26'21	5:53:45
Saylesville 68	1	42N56'58	88W19'13	5:53:17
Sayner 64	1	45N59'10	89W31'57	5:58:08
Scandinavia 69	1	44N27'42	89W08'57	5:56:36
Scarboro 31	1	44N32	87W42	5:50:48
Schleswig 36	1	43N57	87W59	5:51:56
Schley 35	1	45N15	89W30	5:58:00
Schmidt Corner 69	1	44N36'11	89W07'21	5:56:29
Schnappsville 37	1	44N58'24	90W01'30	6:00:06
Schneyville 23	1	42N31'01	89W38'22	5:58:33
Schoepke 44	1	45N31	89W09	5:56:36
Schofield 37	1	44N54'35	89W36'16	5:58:25
School Hill 36	1	43N57'00	87W53'38	5:51:35
Schultz 23	1	42N41'24	89W36'09	5:58:25
Scotts Junction 42	1	43N57'53	90W40'09	6:02:41
Sechlerville 27	1	44N22'22	91W01'51	6:04:07
Sedgwick 2	1	46N28'01	90W36'19	6:02:25
Seeleys 58	1	46N07'16	91W21'40	6:05:27
Seif 10	1	44N38	90W44	6:02:56
Seminary Springs 13	1	43N06'31	89W14'55	5:57:00
Seneca 12	1	43N15'54	90W57'30	6:03:50
Sevastopol 15	1	44N54	87W20	5:49:20
Seven Mile Creek 29	1	43N41	90W01	6:00:04
Sextonville 53	1	43N16'42	90W17'27	6:01:10
Seymour 45	1	44N30'54	88W19'49	5:53:19
Shady Dell 22	1	42N57'32	90W47'28	6:03:10
Shamrock 27	1	44N10'27	90W48'16	6:03:13
Shanagolden 2	1	46N07'03	90W38'09	6:02:33
Shangri La Point 71	1	44N03'59	88W36'27	5:54:26
Shantytown 37	1	44N41'16	89W25'26	5:57:42
Sharon 65	1	42N30'09	88W43'44	5:54:55
Shawano 59	1	44N46'56	88W36'32	5:54:26
Shawano North Beach 59	1	44N47	88W36	5:54:24
Shaw Landing 69	1	44N21'59	88W48'33	5:55:14
Shawtown 18	1	44N47'42	91W32'13	6:06:09
Sheboygan 60	1	43N45'03	87W42'52	5:50:51
Sheboygan Falls 60	1	43N43'45	87W48'38	5:51:15
Shelby 32	1	43N46'09	91W09'39	6:04:39
Sheldon 55	1	45N18'38	90W57'21	6:03:49
Shell Lake 66	1	45N44'22	91W55'31	6:07:42
Shennington 42	1	44N01'33	90W19'03	6:01:16
Shepley 59	1	44N51'44	89W06'10	5:56:25
Sheppard 27	1	44N15'39	90W46'50	6:03:07
Sheridan 69	1	44N23'45	89W11'53	5:56:48
Sherry 72	1	44N35'03	89W54'56	5:59:40
Sherry Junction 34	1	45N13'09	88W59'16	5:55:57
Sherwood 8	1	44N10'25	88W15'35	5:53:02
Sherwood 10	1	44N28'03	90W21'20	6:01:25
Shiocton 45	1	44N26'41	88W34'44	5:54:19
Shirley 5	1	44N21'25	87W56'51	5:51:47
Shoemaker Point 15	1	44N43'14	87W43'14	5:50:53
Shopiere 54	1	42N34'21	88W56'18	5:55:45
Shoreview 30	1	42N31	88W07	5:52:28
Shorewood 41	1	43N05'21	87W53'15	5:51:33
Shorewood Hills 13	1	43N04'39	89W26'44	5:57:47
Shortville 10	1	44N29'42	90W30'59	6:02:04
Shoto 36	1	44N10'31	87W38'57	5:50:36
Shullsburg 33	1	42N34'24	90W13'51	6:00:55
Sidney 10	1	44N33'10	90W38'19	6:02:33
Silica 20	1	43N51'01	88W20'30	5:53:22
Silver Cliff 38	1	45N26	88W21	5:53:24
Silver Creek 60	1	43N33'25	88W01'30	5:52:06
Silver Lake 30	1	42N32'46	88W09'56	5:52:40
Silver Lake 70	1	44N03'19	89W13'34	5:56:54
Sinsinawa 22	1	42N31'25	90W32'21	6:02:09
Sioux 4	1	46N44'14	90W52'48	6:03:31
Sioux Creek 3	1	45N15	91W43	6:06:52
Siren 7	1	45N47'09	92W22'51	6:09:31
Sister Bay 15	1	45N11'14	87W07'15	5:48:29
Skanawan 35	1	45N26	89W37	5:58:28
Slab City 59	1	44N43'13	88W26'44	5:53:47
Slabtown 28	1	42N58'01	88W38'06	5:54:32
Slades Corners 30	1	42N34'55	88W17'38	5:53:11
Slag Pile 56	1	44N57	92W18	6:09:12
Slateford 33	1	42N47'08	90W11'36	6:00:46
Slinger 67	1	43N20'01	88W17'10	5:53:09
Slovan 31	1	44N31'51	87W34'59	5:50:20
Smelser 22	1	42N38	90W29	6:01:56
Smith Landing 48	1	44N41'21	92W41'30	6:10:46
Snell 37	1	45N03'31	89W17'06	5:57:08
Snells 71	1	44N08'30	88W29'26	5:53:58
Sniderville 5	1	44N21'06	88W11'28	5:52:46
Snows Corner 48	1	44N40'26	92W29'48	6:09:59
Sobieski 43	1	44N43'15	88W04'19	5:52:17
Sobieski Corners 43	1	44N43'16	88W03'08	5:52:13
Soldiers Grove 12	1	43N23'43	90W46'27	6:03:06
Solon Springs 16	1	46N21'12	91W49'20	6:07:17
Somers 30	1	42N38'25	87W54'37	5:51:38
Somerset 56	1	45N07'28	92W40'24	6:10:42
Somo 35	1	45N31	89W59	5:59:56
Sono Junction 56	1	44N59'22	92W40'43	6:10:43
Soperton 21	1	45N26'18	88W38'10	5:54:33
South Beaver Dam 14	1	43N26'27	88W53'10	5:55:33
South Byron 20	1	43N38'20	88W29'11	5:53:57
South Chase 43	1	44N41'24	88W09'04	5:52:36
South Chippewa 9	1	44N55	91W23	6:05:32
South Fork 55	1	45N35	90W45	6:03:00
South Itasca 16	1	46N39'42	92W00'18	6:08:01
South Janesville 54	1	42N41	89W01	5:56:04
South Kenosha 30	1	42N32'25	87W50'03	5:51:20
South Lancaster 22	1	42N49	90W43	6:02:52
South Luxemburg 31	1	44N32	87W42	5:50:48
South Milwaukee 41	1	42N54'38	87W51'38	5:51:27
South Necedah 29	1	44N02	90W04	6:00:16
South Oshkosh 71	1	44N01	88W33	5:54:12
South Randolph 14	1	43N30'40	88W59'56	5:56:00
South Range 16	1	46N36'29	91W59'00	6:07:56
South Superior 16	1	46N40'10	92W05'42	6:08:23
South Wayne 33	1	42N34'08	89W52'47	5:59:31
South Wisconsin Rapids 72	1	44N25	89W48	5:59:12
Sparta 42	1	43N56'39	90W48'46	6:03:15
Spaulding 27	1	44N21'21	90W24'56	6:01:40
Speck Oaks 27	1	44N18'01	90W34'14	6:02:17
Spencer 37	1	44N45'28	90W17'48	6:01:11
Spider Lake 58	1	46N07	91W11	6:04:44
Spirit 51	1	45N27'15	90W06'51	6:00:27
Spirit Falls 35	1	45N27'11	89W58'50	5:59:55
Split Rock 59	1	44N42'18	89W01'33	5:56:06
Spokeville 10	1	44N42'45	90W26'03	6:01:44
Spooner 66	1	45N49'21	91W53'21	6:07:33
Sprague 29	1	44N08'52	90W07'53	6:00:32
Spread Eagle 19	1	45N52'55	88W08'23	5:52:34
Spring Bank Park 42	1	44N00'24	90W37'15	6:02:29
Spring Bluff 1	1	44N02	89W31	5:58:04
Springbrook 66	1	45N56'55	91W41'17	6:06:45
Springdale 13	1	43N00	89W41	5:58:44
Springfield 65	1	42N38'30	88W24'43	5:53:39
Springfield Corners 13	1	43N11'31	89W33'59	5:58:16
Spring Green 57	1	43N10'31	90W04'04	6:00:16
Spring Grove 23	1	42N33	89W26	5:57:44
Spring Grove 24	1	43N48'54	88W56'29	5:55:46
Spring Lake 48	1	44N48	92W14	6:08:56
Spring Lake 70	1	44N01'24	89W09'31	5:56:38
Spring Prairie 65	1	42N41'29	88W24'15	5:53:37
Springstead 26	1	46N01'31	90W08'12	6:00:33
Springstead Landing 26	1	46N04'25	90W10'26	6:00:42
Spring Valley 36	1	43N56'20	87W50'22	5:51:21
Spring Valley 48	1	44N50'43	92W14'19	6:08:57
Springville 1	1	43N47	89W47	5:59:08
Springville 63	1	43N35'01	90W56'23	6:03:46
Springwater 70	1	44N11	89W11	5:56:44
Spruce 43	1	44N57'09	88W09'53	5:52:40
Stadium 5	1	44N30	88W04	5:52:16
Stanberry 66	1	46N00'26	91W37'34	6:06:30
Stanbery 66	1	45N57	91W41	6:06:44
Standart 25	1	42N58	90W08	6:00:32
Stanfold 3	1	45N31	91W51	6:07:24
Stangelville 31	1	44N24'01	87W41'04	5:50:44
Stanley 9	1	44N57'36	90W56'13	6:03:45
Stanton 56	1	45N10'23	92W28'01	6:09:52
Stark 36	1	44N21	87W50	5:51:20
Stark 63	1	43N36	90W58	6:02:32
Starks 44	1	45N39'47	89W13'18	5:56:53
Star Lake 64	1	46N02'18	89W28'20	5:57:53
Star Prairie 56	1	45N11'49	92W31'50	6:10:07
Star Valley 12	1	43N24	90W47	6:03:08
State Line 30	1	42N29'40	87W49'15	5:51:17
Stearns 23	1	42N39'23	89W36'26	5:58:26
Stebbinsville 54	1	42N50'40	89W10'23	5:56:42
Steinthal 36	1	43N58'57	88W00'08	5:52:01
Stella 44	1	45N41	89W14	5:56:56
Stephenson 38	1	45N16	88W06	5:52:24
Stephensville 45	1	44N22'24	88W35'03	5:54:20

Stetsonville 61 1 45N04'37 90W18'54 6:01:16
Stettin (historical) 37 1 44N58'23 89W48'27 5:59:14
Steuben 12 1 43N10'52 90W51'31 6:03:26
Stevens Hill 15 1 44N50'25 87W22'10 5:49:29
Stevens Point 50 1 44N31'25 89W34'28 5:58:18
Stevenstown 32 1 44N02'11 91W10'17 6:04:41
Stiles 43 1 44N51'40 88W02'54 5:52:12
Stiles Junction 43 1 44N53'00 88W02'48 5:52:11
Stinnett 66 1 46N01 91W37 6:06:28
Stitzer 22 1 42N55'36 90W37'23 6:02:30
Stockbridge 8 1 44N04'18 88W17'56 5:53:12
Stockbridge-Munsee Indian Re 59 1 44N54 88W50 5:55:20
Stockholm 47 1 44N29'00 92W15'43 6:09:03
Stockton 50 1 44N30'41 89W28'01 5:57:52
Stoddard 63 1 43N39'43 91W13'06 6:04:52
Stone 13 1 42N52'29 89W18'36 5:57:14
Stonebank 68 1 43N08'33 88W24'38 5:53:39
Stone Lake 58 1 45N50'44 91W32'25 6:06:10
Stony Beach 71 1 43N59'17 88W31'40 5:54:07
Stoughton 13 1 42N55'01 89W13'04 5:56:52
Strader 18 1 44N41 91W07 6:04:28
Stratford 37 1 44N48'04 90W04'45 6:00:19
Strawbridge 33 1 42N31'58 90W22'43 6:01:31
Strickland 55 1 45N26'12 91W31'16 6:06:05
Strongs Prairie 1 1 44N03'41 89W58'33 5:59:54
Strum 62 1 44N32'59 91W23'33 6:05:34
Stubbs 55 1 45N26 91W21 6:05:24
Sturgeon Bay 15 1 44N50'03 87W22'37 5:49:30
Sturtevant 52 1 42N41'53 87W53'40 5:51:35
Suamico 5 1 44N37'55 88W02'21 5:52:09
Sugar Bush 5 1 44N30'06 87W47'08 5:51:09
Sugar Bush 45 1 44N28'54 88W44'09 5:54:57
Sugar Camp 44 1 45N47'40 89W18'50 5:57:15
Sugar Creek 65 1 42N43 88W35 5:54:20
Sugar Grove 63 1 43N25'33 90W41'01 6:02:44
Sugar Island 14 1 43N13'33 88W34'47 5:54:19
Sullivan 28 1 43N00'46 88W35'17 5:54:21
Sullivan 32 1 43N53 91W14 6:04:56
Summit 42 1 43N50 90W37 6:02:28
Summit Corners 68 1 43N04'36 88W28'12 5:53:53
Summit Lake 34 1 45N22'40 89W11'41 5:56:47
Sumner 3 1 45N23'11 91W39'08 6:06:37
Sumpter 57 1 43N21 89W46 5:59:04
Sunnyside 16 1 46N36'15 92W03'23 6:08:14
Sun Prairie 13 1 43N11'01 89W12'49 5:56:51
Sunrise Bay 71 1 44N09'49 88W26'19 5:53:45
Sunset 37 1 45N00'12 89W29'31 5:57:58
Sunset Beach 8 1 44N03'51 88W19'35 5:53:18
Sunset Beach 14 1 43N30'06 88W51'56 5:55:28
Sunset Point 71 1 44N03'20 88W35'15 5:54:21
Superior 16 1 46N43'15 92W06'14 6:08:25
Superior Village 16 1 46N39'25 92W06'15 6:08:25
Suring 43 1 44N59'57 88W22'19 5:53:29
Sussex 68 1 43N08'02 88W13'19 5:52:53
Sutherland 4 1 46N26'15 91W10'35 6:04:42
Sweetheart City 38 1 45N18'33 87W58'34 5:51:54
Swiss 7 1 46N01 92W17 6:09:08
Sylvan 53 1 43N25'21 90W37'41 6:02:31
Sylvania 52 1 42N41'55 87W57'30 5:51:50
Sylvan Mounds 28 1 42N59'57 88W58'42 5:55:55
Sylvester 23 1 42N39 89W32 5:58:08
Symco 69 1 44N30'48 88W54'14 5:55:37
Tabor 52 1 42N48'56 87W50'06 5:51:20
Taegesville 37 1 45N02'48 89W43'35 5:58:54
Taft 61 1 45N05 90W51 6:03:24
Tainter 17 1 45N00 91W51 6:07:24
Tamarack 62 1 44N10'30 91W26'52 6:05:47
Tannery 35 1 45N28 89W44 5:58:56
Tarrant 47 1 44N35'48 91W50'35 6:07:22
Taus 36 1 44N11'21 87W51'43 5:51:27
Tavera 53 1 43N17'03 90W38'44 6:02:35
Taycheedah 20 1 43N48'32 88W23'42 5:53:35
Taylor 27 1 44N19'16 91W07'11 6:04:29
Teegarden 17 1 44N53 91W56 6:07:44
Tell 6 1 44N22'50 91W51'58 6:07:28
Templeton 68 1 43N08 88W13 5:52:52
Tennyson 22 1 42N41'24 90W41'06 6:02:44
Terrill 70 1 44N03 89W07 5:56:28
Tess Corners 68 1 42N55'20 88W05'58 5:52:24
Teutonia 41 1 43N04 87W56 5:51:44
Texas 37 1 45N03 89W35 5:58:20
Theresa 14 1 43N31'02 88W27'04 5:53:48
Theresa Station 14 1 43N31'36 88W25'40 5:53:43
Thiel's Corner 67 1 43N17 87W58 5:51:52
Thiensville 46 1 43N14'15 87W58'43 5:51:55
Thirty Daems 31 1 44N36'11 87W41'35 5:50:46
Thompson 67 1 43N15'31 88W22'14 5:53:29
Thompsonville 52 1 42N46'43 87W57'10 5:51:49
Thornapple 55 1 45N24'35 91W13'10 6:04:53
Thornton 59 1 44N47'48 88W41'28 5:54:46
Thorp 10 1 44N57'40 90W47'59 6:03:12
Three Lakes 44 1 45N47'54 89W09'46 5:56:39
Tibbets 65 1 42N44'05 88W34'53 5:54:20
Tichigan 52 1 42N49'44 88W11'51 5:52:47
Tiffany 17 1 45N05 92W05 6:08:20
Tiffany 54 1 42N34'57 88W55'37 5:55:42
Tigerton 59 1 44N44'27 89W03'47 5:56:15
Tilden 9 1 45N00'24 91W26'15 6:05:45
Tilleda 59 1 44N48'56 88W54'40 5:55:39
Timberland 7 1 45N40'34 92W06'21 6:08:25
Tioga 10 1 44N41'03 90W47'35 6:03:10
Tipler 19 1 45N55'30 88W38'05 5:54:32
Tisch Mills 36 1 44N19'38 87W37'25 5:50:30
Tobin 30 1 42N30'27 87W50'26 5:51:22
Token Creek 13 1 43N11'40 89W17'37 5:57:10
Tomah 42 1 43N58'43 90W30'14 6:02:01
Tomahawk 35 1 45N28'16 89W43'47 5:58:55
Tonet 31 1 44N35'21 87W44'01 5:50:56
Tony 55 1 45N28'59 90W59'33 6:03:58
Topside 4 1 46N33'33 91W19'21 6:05:17
Torun 50 1 44N36'49 89W30'34 5:58:02
Towerville 12 1 43N24'27 90W53'21 6:03:33
Townsend 43 1 45N19'41 88W35'22 5:54:21
Trade Lake 7 1 45N41'23 92W35'34 6:10:22
Trade River 7 1 45N38'54 92W40'21 6:10:41
Trego 66 1 45N53'59 91W49'15 6:07:17
Tremble 5 1 44N38'17 88W04'10 5:52:17
Trempealeau 62 1 44N00'20 91W26'31 6:05:46
Trenton 48 1 44N36'14 92W33'53 6:10:16
Trevino 6 1 44N25'43 92W04'04 6:08:16
Trevor 30 1 42N30'45 88W07'15 5:52:29
Tri City 41 1 42N54 87W56 5:51:44
Trimbelle 48 1 44N43'54 92W34'47 6:10:19
Tripoli 35 1 45N33'19 89W59'38 5:59:59
Tripp 4 1 46N38 91W22 6:05:28
Trippville 63 1 43N42'33 90W24'15 6:01:37
Trout Run 27 1 44N17 90W51 6:03:24
Troy 65 1 42N46'44 88W26'41 5:53:47
Troy Center 65 1 42N48'35 88W27'54 5:53:52
True 55 1 45N31 90W53 6:03:32
Truesdell 30 1 42N34'00 87W54'04 5:51:36
Truman 33 1 42N43'10 90W13'47 6:00:55
Tuleta Hills 24 1 43N48'31 88W58'52 5:55:55
Tunnel City 42 1 44N00'26 90W33'56 6:02:16
Tunnelville 53 1 43N33'11 90W39'30 6:02:38
Turtle 54 1 42N33 88W57 5:55:48
Turtle Lake 3 1 45N23'40 92W08'32 6:08:34
Tuscobia 3 1 45N34'01 91W45'29 6:07:02
Tustin 70 1 44N09'46 88W53'32 5:55:34
Twelve Corners 45 1 44N24'06 88W26'05 5:53:44
Twin Bluffs 53 1 43N16'26 90W18'46 6:01:15
Twin Grove 23 1 42N31'53 89W32'35 5:58:10
Twin Lakes 30 1 42N31'52 88W14'53 5:53:00
Twin Town 3 1 45N21'36 92W01'56 6:08:08
Two Creeks 36 1 44N18'08 87W33'47 5:50:15
Two Rivers 36 1 44N09'14 87W34'09 5:50:17
Tyler Forks 26 1 46N20'09 90W31'39 6:02:07
Tyran 19 1 45N56'56 88W18'19 5:53:13
Ubet 49 1 45N21'14 92W31'45 6:10:07
Ulao 46 1 43N19'14 87W54'59 5:51:40
Underhill 43 1 44N52'31 88W23'04 5:53:32
Union 22 1 42N49'49 90W31'34 6:02:06
Union 54 1 42N49'28 89W18'06 5:57:12
Union Center 29 1 43N41'07 90W16'00 6:01:04
Union Church 52 1 42N50'37 88W04'09 5:52:17
Union Grove 52 1 42N41'17 88W03'05 5:52:12
Union Mills 25 1 42N58 90W08 6:00:32
Unity 10 1 44N51'06 90W18'59 6:01:16
University 13 1 43N06 89W24 5:57:36
Upham 34 1 45N20 89W11 5:56:44
Upper French Creek 62 1 44N13'03 91W19'29 6:05:18
Upson 26 1 46N22'09 90W24'24 6:01:38
Urne 6 1 44N29'55 91W53'32 6:07:34
Utica 13 1 42N57'56 89W07'19 5:56:29
Utica 68 1 43N01'20 88W29'05 5:53:56
Utley 24 1 43N43'39 88W54'22 5:55:37
Utowana Beach 8 1 44N12'18 88W21'49 5:53:27
Valders 36 1 44N03'58 87W53'03 5:51:32
Valley 63 1 43N38'30 90W32'30 6:02:10
Valley Junction 42 1 44N03'12 90W24'44 6:01:39
Valmy 15 1 44N54'29 87W15'47 5:49:03
Valton 57 1 43N34'23 90W16'27 6:01:06
Van Buskirk 26 1 46N23'14 90W08'36 6:00:34
Vance Creek 3 1 45N14 92W07 6:08:28
Vandenbroek 45 1 44N18 88W19 5:53:16
Van Dyne 20 1 43N53'15 88W30'15 5:54:01
Vaudreuil 27 1 44N18'23 90W48'35 6:03:14
Veedum 72 1 44N24'35 90W10'24 6:00:42
Veefkind 10 1 44N41'30 90W22'24 6:01:30
Vermont 13 1 43N04 89W48 5:59:12
Vernon 68 1 42N54'13 88W15'08 5:53:01
Verona 13 1 42N59'27 89W31'59 5:58:08
Vesper 72 1 44N28'56 89W57'50 5:59:51
Veterans Administration Hosp 13 1 43N07 89W27 5:57:48
Victory 63 1 43N29'08 91W12'45 6:04:51
Victory Center 67 1 43N12'25 88W04'57 5:52:20
Victory Heights 54 1 42N32'34 89W05'26 5:56:22
Vienna 13 1 43N15 89W25 5:57:40
Vignes 15 1 44N43'34 87W22'39 5:49:31
Viking 48 1 44N51'42 92W21'32 6:09:26
Vilas 13 1 43N05'23 89W14'05 5:56:56
Vilas 34 1 45N15 89W21 5:57:24
Villard 41 1 43N07 87W57 5:51:48
Vinland 71 1 44N08 88W34 5:54:16
Vinnie Ha Ha 28 1 42N52'50 88W54'17 5:55:37
Viola 53 1 43N30'22 90W40'05 6:02:40
Viroqua 63 1 43N33'25 90W53'19 6:03:33
Wabeno 21 1 45N26'19 88W39'37 5:54:38
Wagner 38 1 45N18'08 87W44'08 5:50:57
Waino 16 1 46N38'23 91W34'24 6:06:18
Waldo 60 1 43N40'29 87W56'55 5:51:48
Waldwick 25 1 42N49'32 90W02'23 6:00:10
Wales 68 1 43N00'16 88W22'36 5:53:30
Walhain 31 1 44N32'43 87W45'15 5:51:01
Walsh 38 1 45N10'46 87W45'45 5:51:03
Walworth 65 6 42N31'52 88W35'58 5:54:24
Wandawega 65 1 42N41 88W33 5:54:12
Wanderoos 49 1 45N18'31 92W29'39 6:09:59
Warner 10 1 44N48 90W37 6:02:28
Warrens 42 1 44N07'52 90W29'59 6:02:00
Warrentown 48 1 44N34'33 92W21'30 6:09:26
Wascott 16 1 46N10'21 91W47'53 6:07:12
Washburn 4 1 46N40'24 90W53'41 6:03:35
Washington 15 1 45N23'41 86W55'53 5:47:44
Washington Island 15 1 45N21'24 86W55'50 5:47:43
Waterbury 27 1 44N23'07 90W35'54 6:02:24
Waterford 52 1 42N45'47 88W12'51 5:52:51
Waterford Woods 52 1 42N46 88W13 5:52:52
Waterloo 28 1 43N11'02 88W59'18 5:55:57
Watertown 28 1 43N11'41 88W43'44 5:54:55
Waterville 47 1 44N38 92W04 6:08:16
Waterville 68 1 43N01'12 88W26'17 5:53:45
Watterstown 22 1 43N09 90W36 6:02:24
Waubeek 47 1 44N39 91W59 6:07:56
Waubeesee 52 1 42N46 88W13 5:52:52
Waubeka 46 1 43N28'30 87W59'25 5:51:58
Waucousta 20 1 43N39'09 88W15'37 5:53:02
Waukau 71 1 43N59'21 88W46'18 5:55:05
Waukechon 59 1 44N43 88W32 5:54:08
Waukesha 68 1 43N00'42 88W13'53 5:52:56
Waumandee 6 1 44N18'11 91W42'20 6:06:49
Waunakee 13 1 43N11'31 89W27'20 5:57:49
Waupaca 69 1 44N21'29 89W05'09 5:56:21
Waupun 20 1 43N38'00 88W43'46 5:54:55
Wausau 37 1 44N57'33 89W37'48 5:58:31
Wausau Junction 37 1 44N56'28 89W36'31 5:58:26
Wausaukee 38 1 45N22'15 87W57'08 5:51:49
Wausau West 37 1 44N57 89W39 5:58:36
Wautoma 70 1 44N04'29 89W17'16 5:57:09
Wauwatosa 41 1 43N02'58 88W00'27 5:52:02
Wauzeka 12 1 43N05'07 90W52'59 6:03:32
Waverly 48 1 44N43'43 92W15'24 6:09:02
Waverly Beach 71 1 44N12'37 88W24'16 5:53:37
Waxdale 52 1 42N41'53 87W52'40 5:51:31
Wayne 67 1 43N30'51 88W19'17 5:53:17
Wayside 5 1 44N15'19 87W57'09 5:51:49
Webb Lake 7 1 46N00'34 92W07'57 6:08:32
Webster 5 1 44N30 88W01 5:52:04
Webster 7 1 45N52'39 92W22'02 6:09:28
Weedens 60 1 43N41'16 87W46'19 5:51:05
Wein 37 1 44N54'07 90W01'28 6:00:06
Weirgor 58 1 45N41'24 91W16'04 6:05:04
Welling Beach 20 1 43N52'14 88W21'50 5:53:27
Wellington 42 1 43N46 90W30 6:02:00
Wells 36 1 44N05'44 88W02'36 5:52:10
Wells 42 1 43N51 90W44 6:02:56
Wentworth 16 1 46N36'00 91W50'09 6:07:21
Wequiock 5 1 44N34'03 87W52'52 5:51:31
Werley 22 1 43N01'10 90W45'55 6:03:04
Wescott 59 1 44N49 88W33 5:54:12
West Allis 41 1 43N01'00 88W00'25 5:52:02
West Almond 50 1 44N17'10 89W27'39 5:57:51
West Bancroft 50 1 44N18'17 89W31'51 5:58:07
West Baraboo 57 1 43N28'28 89W46'13 5:59:05
West Bend 67 1 43N25'31 88W11'00 5:52:44
West Bloomfield 70 1 44N13'15 88W58'18 5:55:53
Westboro 61 1 45N21'19 90W17'45 6:01:11
Westby 63 1 43N39'25 90W51'15 6:03:25
Westchester 68 1 43N04 88W05 5:52:20
West Denmark 49 1 45N34'12 92W30'34 6:10:02
West De Pere 5 1 44N26'44 88W04'31 5:52:18
Western 41 1 43N04 87W58 5:51:52
Westfield 39 1 43N53'01 89W29'36 5:57:58
West Granville 41 1 43N08'26 88W02'42 5:52:11
West Jacksonport 15 1 45N03 87W18 5:49:12
West Kewaunee 31 1 44N27 87W35 5:50:20
West Kraft 35 1 45N26'47 89W44'57 5:59:00
West La Crosse 32 1 43N50'44 91W15'44 6:05:03
West Lima 53 1 43N32'47 90W31'49 6:02:07
West Marshland 7 1 45N53 92W37 6:10:28
West Milwaukee 41 1 43N00'45 87W58'21 5:51:53
Weston 17 1 44N48'45 92W04'17 6:08:17
Weston 37 1 44N56 89W36 5:58:24
West Plainfield 70 1 44N13 89W29 5:57:56
West Point 11 1 43N20 89W39 5:58:36
Westport 13 1 43N10 89W26 5:57:44
Westport 53 1 43N12'18 90W38'28 6:02:34
West Prairie 62 1 44N03'51 91W30'56 6:06:04
West Prairie 63 1 43N28'00 91W01'21 6:04:05
West Racine 52 1 42N44 87W50 5:51:20
Westrap 72 1 44N25 89W48 5:59:12
West Rosendale 20 1 43N49'21 88W43'30 5:54:54
West Salem 32 1 43N53'57 91W04'52 6:04:19
West Sussex 68 1 43N08 88W13 5:52:52
West Sweden 49 1 45N42'21 92W29'48 6:09:59
Weurtsburg 37 1 45N01 90W04 6:00:16
Weyauwega 69 1 44N19'17 88W56'01 5:55:44
Weyerhaeuser 55 1 45N25'26 91W24'42 6:05:39
Wheatland 30 1 42N35'38 88W12'30 5:52:50
Wheaton 9 1 44N54 91W32 6:06:08
Wheeler 17 1 45N02'40 91W54'31 6:07:38
Whispering Pines 45 1 44N16'49 88W23'03 5:53:32
Whitcomb 59 1 44N47'00 89W07'07 5:56:28
White City 63 1 43N37'07 90W27'11 6:01:49
White Creek 1 1 43N49'33 89W51'17 5:59:25
Whitefish Bay 15 1 44N55 87W13 5:48:52
Whitefish Bay 41 1 43N06'48 87W54'00 5:51:36
Whitehall 62 1 44N22'03 91W18'59 6:05:16
White Lake 34 1 45N09'26 88W45'52 5:55:03
Whitelaw 36 1 44N08'41 87W49'17 5:51:17
White Oak 33 1 42N31'06 90W16'37 6:01:06
White Oak Springs 33 1 42N31 90W16 6:01:04
White River 2 1 46N32'09 90W51'02 6:03:24
White River Village 65 1 42N36 88W28 5:53:52
Whitestown 63 1 43N41 90W35 6:02:20
Whitewater 65 1 42N50'01 88W43'56 5:54:56
Whiting 50 1 44N29'37 89W33'31 5:58:14
Whittlesey 61 1 45N13'23 90W19'43 6:01:19
Wickware 3 1 45N21'05 91W47'10 6:07:09
Wien 37 1 44N56 90W01 6:00:04
Wilcox 38 1 44N59'52 87W50'07 5:51:20
Wild Rose 53 1 43N17'13 90W34'54 6:02:20
Wild Rose 70 1 44N10'43 89W14'56 5:57:00
Wildwood 56 1 44N53'31 92W17'57 6:09:12
Wilkinson 55 1 45N31 91W28 6:05:52
Willard 10 1 44N44'06 90W43'09 6:02:53
Williams Bay 65 1 42N34'41 88W32'27 5:54:10
Williamstown 14 1 43N30 88W36 5:54:24
Willow 53 1 43N25 90W14 6:00:56
Willow Creek 67 1 43N12'26 88W09'30 5:52:38

Place		Latitude	Longitude	Time
Willow Springs 33	1	42N45	90w09	6:00:36
Willow Springs 68	1	43N08'20	88w11'03	5:52:44
Wills 4	1	46N32'21	91w32'21	6:06:09
Wilmoore Heights 20	1	43N53'19	88w48'30	5:55:14
Wilmot 30	1	42N30'46	88w10'55	5:52:44
Wilson 9	1	44N49'41	91w01'21	6:04:05
Wilson 56	1	44N57'13	92w10'24	6:08:42
Wilton 42	1	43N48'49	90w31'40	6:02:07
Winchester 64	1	46N13'19	89w53'52	5:59:35
Winchester 71	1	44N11'55	88w39'53	5:54:40
Wind Lake 52	1	42N49'46	88w09'31	5:52:38
Wind Point 52	1	42N47'04	87w45'58	5:51:04
Windsor 13	1	43N13'06	89w20'29	5:57:22
Winfield 57	1	43N37	90w01	6:00:04
Wingville 22	1	42N59	90w29	6:01:56
Winnebago 71	1	44N04'33	88w31'30	5:54:06
Winnebago Heights 20	1	43N54'01	88w20'33	5:53:22
Winnebago Indian Reservation 27	1	44N16	90w41	6:02:44
Winnebago Mission 27	1	44N20'46	90w45'17	6:03:01
Winnebago Park 20	1	43N53'07	88w21'09	5:53:25
Winneboujou 16	1	46N31'03	91w36'03	6:06:24
Winneconne 71	1	44N06'39	88w42'45	5:54:51
Winter 58	1	45N49'11	91w00'42	6:04:03
Wiota 33	1	42N38'12	89w57'09	5:59:49
Wiscona 41	1	43N07	87w57	5:51:48
Wisconsin Dells 11	1	43N37'39	89w46'15	5:59:05
Wisconsin Junction 21	1	45N39'22	88w54'40	5:55:39
Wisconsin Rapids 72	1	44N23'01	89w49'02	5:59:16
Wiswell 5	1	44N30	88w01	5:52:04
Withee 10	1	44N57'23	90w35'51	6:02:23
Wittenberg 59	1	44N49'38	89w10'10	5:56:41
Witwen 57	1	43N17'07	89w53'14	5:59:33
Wolf Creek 49	1	45N33'22	92w43'21	6:10:53
Wolf Lake 20	1	43N50	88w10	5:52:40
Wonewoc 29	1	43N39'10	90w13'24	6:00:54
Wood 41	1	43N07	88w01	5:52:04
Wood 72	1	44N28	90w08	6:00:32
Woodboro 44	1	45N36'27	89w33'15	5:58:13
Wooddale 58	1	45N41'06	91w27'39	6:05:51
Woodford 33	1	42N38'55	89w51'45	5:59:27
Woodhull 20	1	43N46'39	88w34'23	5:54:18
Woodhull Station 20	1	43N59	88w56	5:55:44
Woodland 14	1	43N22'13	88w31'07	5:54:04
Woodland 57	1	43N37	90w15	6:01:00
Woodland Corner 7	1	46N08'36	92w14'18	6:08:57
Woodlawn 21	1	45N25'56	88w49'17	5:55:17
Woodman 22	1	43N05'24	90w48'04	6:03:12
Woodmohr 9	1	45N05	91w28	6:05:52
Wood River 7	1	45N46	92w35	6:10:20
Woodruff 44	1	45N53'47	89w41'56	5:58:48
Woodstock 53	1	43N28'21	90w25'38	6:01:43
Woodville 56	1	44N57'11	92w17'28	6:09:10
Woodworth 30	1	42N33'29	88w00'04	5:52:00
Worcester 51	1	45N36'13	90w17'31	6:01:10
Worden 10	1	44N54	90w52	6:03:28
Wrightstown 5	1	44N19'33	88w09'46	5:52:39
Wrightsville 27	1	44N26	90w54	6:03:36
Wuertsburg 37	1	44N57'37	90w05'56	6:00:24
Wyalusing 22	1	42N56'38	91w08'29	6:04:34
Wyeville 42	1	44N01'42	90w23'04	6:01:32
Wyocena 11	1	43N29'45	89w18'30	5:57:14
Wyoming 25	1	43N07'34	90w06'42	6:00:27
Yarnell 58	1	45N43'37	91w25'09	6:05:41
Yellow Lake 7	1	45N56	92w23	6:09:32
Yellowstone 33	1	42N47'54	89w58'13	5:59:53
York 27	1	44N27'00	91w08'42	6:04:35
York Center 13	1	43N14'21	89w04'13	5:56:17
Yorkville 52	1	42N44'31	88w01'36	5:52:06
Young America 67	1	43N27'06	88w11'09	5:52:45
Yuba 53	1	43N32'20	90w25'47	6:01:43
Zachow 59	1	44N43'56	88w21'49	5:53:27
Zander 36	1	44N18'47	87w42'19	5:50:49
Zenda 65	6	42N30'43	88w28'54	5:53:56
Zion 71	1	43N59'49	88w39'43	5:54:39
Zittau 71	1	44N13'00	88w47'10	5:55:09
Zoar 40	1	45N00'54	88w53'56	5:55:36

TIME TABLES

Before 11/18/1883		LMT
11/18/1883	12:00	MST
3/31/1918	02:00	MWT
10/27/1918	02:00	MST
3/30/1919	02:00	MWT
10/26/1919	02:00	MST
2/09/1942	02:00	MWT
9/30/1945	02:00	MST
4/30/1967	02:00	US#1

COUNTIES

1 Albany	7 Fremont	13 Natrona	19 Sweetwater
2 Big Horn	8 Goshen	14 Niobrara	20 Teton
3 Campbell	9 Hot Springs	15 Park	21 Uinta
4 Carbon	10 Johnson	16 Platte	22 Washakie
5 Converse	11 Laramie	17 Sheridan	23 Weston
6 Crook	12 Lincoln	18 Sublette	

Acme 17	44N54'38	106w59'04	7:07:56
Adon 3	44N31'06	105w13'57	7:00:56
Afton 12	42N43'30	110w55'52	7:23:43
Air Base Acres 13	42N52'56	106w26'26	7:05:46
Airport 11	41N08	104w49	6:59:16
Aladdin 6	44N38'24	104w10'59	6:56:44
Albany 1	41N11'03	106w07'53	7:04:32
Alberta 5	42N51'20	105w36'12	7:02:25
Albin 11	41N25'04	104w05'52	6:56:23
Alcova 13	42N33'08	106w42'57	7:06:52
Alcova Po 13	42N33'36	106w43'22	7:06:53
Allendale 13	42N48'53	106w18'36	7:05:14
Almy 21	41N19'54	111w00'14	7:24:01
Alpine 12	43N10'31	111w02'02	7:24:08
Alpine Junction 12	43N10'21	111w01'04	7:24:04
Alta 20	43N45'14	111w02'10	7:24:09
Altamont 21	41N11'32	110w47'20	7:23:09
Altus 11	41N28'28	105w13'08	7:00:53
Altvan 11	41N07'23	104w41'58	6:58:48
Alva 6	44N41'41	104w26'27	6:57:46
Ammon 5	42N37'35	105w07'47	7:00:31
Antelope 21	41N25'16	110w31'46	7:22:07
Arapahoe 7	42N57'44	108w29'21	7:13:57
Archer 11	41N09'28	104w39'56	6:58:40
Arcola 11	41N06'03	104w27'24	6:57:50
Arlington 4	41N35'41	106w12'28	7:04:50
Arminto 13	43N10'44	107w15'25	7:09:02
Arnold Place 5	42N28'04	105w37'45	7:02:31
Arrow Head Lodge 17	44N48	106w57	7:07:48
Arvada 17	44N39'13	106w07'50	7:04:31
Aspen 21	41N12'21	110w45'04	7:23:00
Athol 11	41N00'46	104w49'40	6:59:19
Atlantic City 7	42N29'48	108w43'48	7:14:55
Auburn 12	42N47'32	111w00'09	7:24:01
Ayers 19	41N58'46	105w00'09	7:00:01
Badger Basin 15	44N55'33	109w04'21	7:16:17
Badwater 13	43N19'22	107w25'37	7:09:42
Bagan 21	41N16'17	110w39'25	7:22:38
Baggs 4	41N02'09	107w39'25	7:10:38
Bain Place 7	43N30'05	109w27'56	7:17:52
Bairoil 19	42N14'40	107w33'32	7:10:14
Banner 10	44N36'05	106w51'53	7:07:28
Bannock Ford 15	44N53'37	110w22'34	7:21:30
Barnes 8	42N10'45	104w26'23	6:57:46
Barnum 10	43N39'51	106w54'32	7:07:38
Basin 2	44N22'48	108w02'18	7:12:09
Battle 4	41N09'21	106w58'54	7:07:56
Baxter 19	41N36'53	109w06'12	7:16:25
Bear Lodge 17	44N52	107w16	7:09:04
Beartown 21	41N09'24	110w50'50	7:23:23
Beaver Creek 20	43N41'14	110w44'05	7:22:56
Beck Place 13	43N08'17	106w42'42	7:06:51
Beckton 17	44N44'55	107w07'45	7:08:31
Beckwith 12	41N54'42	110w57'59	7:23:52
Bedford 12	42N53'58	110w55'57	7:23:44
Bennett Place 1	42N17'29	105w48'49	7:03:15
Bentley 23	44N07'25	104w40'28	6:58:42
Beulah 6	44N32'40	104w05'19	6:56:21
Big Horn 17	44N41'00	106w59'30	7:07:58
Big Horn Central 2	44N32	108w11	7:12:44
Big Piney 18	42N32'18	110w06'49	7:20:27
Big Sandy 18	42N45	109w43	7:18:52
Bill 5	43N14	105w16	7:01:04
Binford 1	42N20'00	105w20'33	7:01:22
Birkner Hill 5	43N06'50	105w42'50	7:02:51
Bishop 13	42N57'27	106w26'58	7:05:48
Bitter Creek 19	41N33'04	108w33'17	7:14:13
Black Buttes 19	41N32'52	108w41'46	7:14:47
Blairtown 19	41N34'24	109w13'48	7:16:55
Blazon Junction 12	41N41'06	110w33'07	7:22:12
Blue Hill 13	43N18'15	106w40'20	7:06:41
Bona 5	42N36'31	105w06'05	7:00:24
Bondurant 18	43N12'11	110w24'29	7:21:38
Bonneville 7	43N16'08	108w04'22	7:12:17
Bordeaux 19	41N56'10	104w50'39	6:59:23
Border Junction 12	42N12'48	111w02'30	7:24:10
Borie 11	41N05'26	104w59'42	6:59:59
Bosler 1	41N34'34	105w41'41	7:02:47
Bosler Junction 1	41N33'10	105w40'51	7:02:43
Boulder 18	42N44'54	109w43'01	7:18:52
Boxelder 5	42N36'52	105w51'34	7:03:26
Boysen 7	43N26'30	108w10'21	7:12:41
Breakneck Hill 5	42N29'46	105w58'11	7:03:53
Breniman Place 4	41N24'17	106w36'03	7:06:24
Bridger 21	41N22'53	110w35'38	7:22:23
Bridger Valley 21	41N15	110w21	7:21:24
Brinton 16	41N43'06	104w53'59	6:59:36
Bronx 18	42N59'34	110w06'54	7:20:28
Brookhurst 13	42N51'27	106w14'09	7:04:57
Browns Landing 1	41N13'41	105w24'07	7:01:36
Bryan 19	41N34'14	109w40'53	7:18:44
Buckboard Crossing 19	41N14'49	109w35'01	7:18:20
Buckhorn 23	44N08'58	104w05'43	6:56:23
Bucknum 13	43N01'15	106w37'32	7:06:30
Buck Place 5	42N34'30	105w55'13	7:03:41
Buckskin Crossing 18	42N33'23	109w21'45	7:17:27
Buffalo 10	44N20'54	106w41'54	7:06:48
Buffalo Ford 15	44N55'30	110w22'38	7:21:31
Buford 1	41N07'19	105w18'15	7:01:13
Burgess Junction 17	44N46'12	107w31'09	7:10:05
Burlington 2	44N26'50	108w25'54	7:13:44
Burns 11	41N11'34	104w21'31	6:57:26
Burntfork 19	41N01'45	110w00'13	7:20:01
Burris 7	43N21'51	109w16'27	7:17:06
Byrnes Crossing 21	41N16'55	110w38'16	7:22:33
Byron 2	44N47'47	108w30'21	7:14:01
Cadoma 13	42N57'43	106w27'14	7:05:49
Calpet 18	42N17'02	110w15'30	7:21:02
Cambria 23	43N56'21	104w12'25	6:56:50
Camel Hump 13	43N18'21	106w34'06	7:06:16
Canyon Village 15	44N44'02	110w29'21	7:21:57
Carbon 4	41N50'55	106w22'35	7:05:30
Carey 5	42N51'34	105w40'15	7:02:41
Careyhurst 5	42N50'57	105w40'27	7:02:42
Caribou Camp 10	44N21	106w42	7:06:48
Carlas Corner 14	43N23'54	104w18'17	6:57:13
Carlile 6	44N29'13	104w48'03	6:59:12
Carlile Junction 6	44N30'08	104w41'16	6:58:45
Carlson 12	41N51'18	110w58'17	7:23:53
Carpenter 11	41N02'44	104w21'58	6:57:28
Carter 21	41N26'16	110w25'40	7:21:43
Carter Cedars 21	41N31'05	110w30'47	7:22:03
Casper 13	42N52'00	106w18'45	7:05:15
Cassa 16	42N24'58	104w56'58	6:59:48
Centennial 1	41N17'54	106w08'28	7:04:34
Chamberlain Place 5	42N34'45	105w42'34	7:02:50
Chatham 22	44N01	107w57	7:11:48
Cherokee 19	41N43'13	107w37'59	7:10:32
Cheyenne 11	41N08'00	104w49'00	6:59:16
Cheyenne West 11	41N12	105w02	7:00:08
Childers Place 13	42N35'40	106w49'14	7:07:17
Chugwater 16	41N45'24	104w49'16	6:59:17
Church Butte 21	41N33	110w11	7:20:44
Clareton 23	43N42'02	104w41'31	6:58:46
Clark 15	44N53'58	109w09'01	7:16:36
Clay 23	43N59	104w25	6:57:40
Clay Spur 23	44N01	104w28	6:57:52
Clayton 5	42N51'14	105w45'04	7:03:00
Clearmont 17	44N38'25	106w22'49	7:05:31
Clifton 23	43N38'27	104w05'38	6:56:23
Cody 15	44N31'35	109w03'21	7:16:13
Cokeville 12	42N04'57	110w57'16	7:23:49
Collins 1	41N06'36	106w09'45	7:04:39
Collins Place 7	43N31'44	109w05'27	7:16:22
Colloid 23	44N06'37	104w39'23	6:58:38
Colony 6	44N55'31	104w11'55	6:56:48
Colores 1	41N09'16	105w31'18	7:02:05
Colter 22	43N57'23	108w00'48	7:12:03
Colter Bay 20	43N29	110w46	7:23:04
Colter Bay Village 20	43N54'17	110w38'24	7:22:34
Como 4	41N54'34	106w22'28	7:05:30
Cooper Lake 1	41N37'58	105w46'08	7:03:05
Copperton 4	41N08'35	107w07'17	7:08:29
Cora 18	42N56'23	109w58'44	7:19:55
Cottier 8	42N01'20	104w15'47	6:57:03
Cow Hollow 13	42N51'13	106w06'23	7:04:26
Cowley 2	44N53'00	108w28'08	7:13:53
Coyote Springs 4	41N46'59	106w46'12	7:07:05
C R A Camp 13	43N25	106w16	7:05:04
Crane 16	42N19'03	104w43'26	6:58:54
Creston 19	41N42'14	107w45'22	7:11:01
Creston Junction 19	41N43'37	107w43'36	7:10:54
Crimson Dawn 13	42N44'01	106w16'44	7:05:07
Croton 3	44N31'27	105w57'11	7:03:49
Crowheart 7	43N18'35	109w11'36	7:16:46
Curtis 16	42N05'23	104w56'58	6:59:48
Dad 4	41N19'34	107w45'28	7:11:02
Dakoming 23	43N35'51	104w04'20	6:56:17
Dale Creek 1	41N04'59	105w23'27	7:01:34
Dana 4	41N50'11	106w42'13	7:06:49
Daniel 18	42N51'52	110w04'13	7:20:17
Daniel Junction 18	42N53'24	110w04'05	7:20:16
Davis 4	41N23'11	106w45'04	7:07:00
Days 4	41N21'33	106w44'00	7:06:56
Dayton 17	44N52'31	107w15'42	7:09:03
Dead Man Crossing 5	42N41'40	105w40'58	7:02:44
Deadmans Corner 5	42N38'15	105w04'05	7:00:16
Dead Woman Crossing 10	43N32'13	106w19'20	7:05:17
Deaver 2	44N53'19	108w35'50	7:14:23
Deerwood 1	41N14'12	106w07'52	7:04:31
Delfelder 7	43N04'10	108w20'41	7:13:23
Devils Den 15	44N53'32	110w23'13	7:21:33
Devils Tower 6	44N35	104w42	6:58:48
Devils Washtub 16	42N10'07	105w12'13	7:00:49
Diamond 16	41N39'55	104w59'51	6:59:59
Diamondville 12	41N46'46	110w32'16	7:22:09
Dickie 9	44N01	107w57	7:11:48
Dillon 4	41N10'36	107w05'30	7:08:22
Dines 19	41N43'34	109w10'19	7:16:41
Dixon 4	41N02'00	107w32'06	7:10:08
Dornick 9	43N29'06	108w09'56	7:12:40
Dorr Place 4	42N14'32	107w18'42	7:09:15
Douglas 5	42N45'35	105w22'54	7:01:32
Downer Addition 17	44N48	106w57	7:07:48
Dry Creek 15	44N18'49	108w56'15	7:15:45
Dubois 7	43N32'01	109w37'47	7:18:31
Dumbell 15	44N06'08	108w59'16	7:15:57
Duncan 7	43N32	109w38	7:18:32
Duncan Homestead 9	43N37'12	108w32'09	7:14:09
Duncan Place 8	42N14'55	104w05'51	6:56:23
DuNoir 7	43N33'57	109w48'54	7:19:16
Durham 11	41N12'20	104w35'43	6:58:23
Durkee 22	44N07'50	107w54'46	7:11:39
Duroc 8	41N45'23	104w14'25	6:56:58
Dwyer 16	42N14'32	104w57'20	6:59:49
Dwyer Junction 16	42N14'05	104w59'40	6:59:59
Eadsville 13	42N43'55	106w21'12	7:05:25
Eastman Place 7	43N37'54	109w31'14	7:18:05
East Thermopolis 9	43N38'47	108w11'51	7:12:47
Eccles 22	44N08'18	107w54'58	7:11:38
Echeta 3	44N27'29	105w52'33	7:03:30
Eden 19	42N03'03	109w26'11	7:17:45
Edgerton 13	43N24'47	106w14'56	7:05:00
Edson 4	41N48'45	106w47'22	7:07:09
Egbert 11	41N10'11	104w15'23	6:57:02
Elk 20	43N47	110w33	7:22:12
Elk Basin 15	44N59'26	108w51'48	7:15:27
Elkhorn Creek 16	42N34'39	105w04'02	7:00:16
Elkhorn Junction 18	42N25'56	109w14'27	7:16:58
Elkhurst 21	41N29'31	110w20'59	7:21:24
Elk Mountain 4	41N41'15	106w24'46	7:05:39
Elkol 12	41N43'26	110w36'42	7:22:27
Elmo 4	41N52'44	106w32'08	7:06:09
Embar 9	43N42'50	108w40'23	7:14:42
Emblem 2	44N30'21	108w23'28	7:13:34
Emigrant Hill 16	42N20'37	104w45'39	6:59:03
Encampment 4	41N12'34	106w47'21	7:07:09
Erramouspe Place 7	42N25'04	108w48'17	7:15:13
Ervay 13	42N50	106w23	7:05:32
Esterbrook 5	42N24'42	105w21'37	7:01:26
Ethete 7	43N02	108w47	7:15:08
Ethete Saint Michael Mission 7	43N01'30	108w46'19	7:15:05
Etna 12	43N02'00	111w00'37	7:24:02
Evanston 21	41N16'06	110w57'45	7:23:51
Evansville 13	42N51'36	106w16'04	7:05:04
Fairview 12	42N41'19	110w58'54	7:23:56
Fairview 23	43N48'01	104w39'29	6:58:38
Farrall 6	44N35'02	104w15'25	6:57:02
Farson 19	42N06'38	109w26'25	7:17:46
Farthing (Iron Mountain P O) 11	41N32'47	105w12'53	7:00:52
Federal 11	41N16	105w07	7:00:28
Fenton 15	44N23'53	108w34'26	7:14:18
Ferguson Corner 19	41N57'43	105w07'32	7:00:30
Ferris 4	42N11'42	107w10'49	7:08:43
Fetterman 5	42N50'21	105w33'02	7:02:12
Firehole Canyon 19	41N21'05	109w26'28	7:17:46
Fish Cut 19	41N32'52	109w30'22	7:18:01
Fisher 5	42N41'49	105w06'01	7:00:24
Fish Hatchery 4	41N27	106w48	7:07:12
Fishing Bridge 20	44N30	110w30	7:22:00
Five Mile Creek 7	43N26	108w54	7:15:36
Flattop 16	42N40	104w45	6:59:00
Fletcher 5	42N51'43	105w42'16	7:02:49
Flitners Corner 2	44N31'50	107w51'43	7:11:27
Fonda 8	41N50'27	104w18'12	6:57:13
Fontenelle 12	41N59'06	110w03'30	7:20:14
Fort Bridger 21	41N19'00	110w23'01	7:21:32
Fort LaClede 19	41N24'55	108w23'19	7:13:33

Fort Laramie 8	42N12'46	104w31'00	6:58:04
Fort Sanders 1	41N16'16	105w35'53	7:02:24
Fort Steele 4	41N46'41	106w56'45	7:07:47
Fort Washakie 7	43N00'23	108w52'54	7:15:32
Fossil 12	41N48'58	110w43'24	7:22:54
Fossil Forest 15	44N51'38	110w14'02	7:20:56
Foster 5	42N40'23	105w18'27	7:01:14
Four Corners 23	44N05	104w08	6:56:32
Fox Farm 11	41N07	104w47	6:59:08
Foxpark 1	41N04'46	106w09'07	7:04:36
Francis E Warren A F B 11	41N08	104w49	6:59:16
Frannie 2	44N58'09	108w37'15	7:14:29
Freedom 12	42N58'54	111w02'33	7:24:10
Fremont Crossing 18	43N05'31	109w39'37	7:18:38
French George Crossing 7	42N31'05	108w29'36	7:13:58
French Vee 22	43N43'08	107w14'07	7:08:56
Frewen 19	41N39'19	108w03'44	7:12:15
Frontier 12	41N48'51	110w32'11	7:22:09
Fry 13	42N52'03	106w07'58	7:04:32
Garland 15	44N46'47	108w39'35	7:14:38
Garrett 1	42N06'48	105w36'34	7:02:26
Gas Camp 01 13	43N25	106w16	7:05:04
Gas Hills 7	43N02	108w23	7:13:32
Gebo 9	43N47'27	108w13'47	7:12:55
Gibbs Place 7	43N16'37	107w50'09	7:11:21
Gibson 16	42N01'07	104w57'25	6:59:50
Gilespie Place 7	42N26'59	108w30'29	7:14:02
Gillette 3	44N17'28	105w30'06	7:02:00
Gleason 11	41N00'40	104w52'31	6:59:30
Glencoe Junction 12	41N43'53	110w33'34	7:22:14
Glendo 16	42N30'10	105w01'32	7:00:06
Glenrock 5	42N51'41	105w52'18	7:03:29
Goodland 8	41N52'21	104w18'18	6:57:13
Goose Egg 13	42N45'45	106w29'10	7:05:57
Goshen Hole 8	41N49	104w21	6:57:24
Gramm 1	41N02'18	106w07'43	7:04:31
Grand Teton Natl Park 20	43N50	110w40	7:22:40
Granger 19	41N35'37	109w58'05	7:19:52
Granger Junction 19	41N32'47	109w54'48	7:19:39
Granite 11	41N06'00	105w09'28	7:00:38
Granite Canon 11	41N06	105w09	7:00:36
Grants Village 20	44N30	110w30	7:22:00
Grass Creek 9	43N56	108w39	7:14:36
Greene Place 13	42N42'06	106w27'57	7:05:52
Greenhough Place 19	41N04'26	109w14'39	7:16:59
Green River 19	41N31'43	109w27'56	7:17:52
Greybull 2	44N29'21	108w03'20	7:12:13
Gros Ventre Junction 20	43N34'27	110w43'57	7:22:56
Grover 12	42N47'30	110w56'09	7:23:45
Grovont 20	43N38	110w37	7:22:28
Guernsey 16	42N16'11	104w44'28	6:58:58
Hadsell 4	41N46'41	107w22'39	7:09:31
Hadsell Place 19	41N45'09	107w54'49	7:11:39
Halfway 18	42N48'31	110w20'17	7:21:21
Hallville 19	41N36'37	108w44'14	7:14:57
Hamilton Dome 9	43N46	108w35	7:14:20
Hampton 21	41N32'10	110w18'29	7:21:14
Hamsfork 12	41N48	110w32	7:22:08
Hanna 4	41N52'12	106w33'41	7:06:15
Hanna Junction 4	41N51'15	106w32'51	7:06:11
Harmony 1	41N10'18	105w51'46	7:03:27
Harold Place 23	43N54'38	105w04'26	7:00:18
Harper 1	41N42'34	105w53'17	7:03:33
Harriman 11	41N00'19	105w14'57	7:01:00
Hartville 16	42N19'39	104w43'29	6:58:54
Hat Creek 14	42N56'22	104w22'09	6:57:29
Hatton 1	41N18'18	105w58'58	7:03:56
Hawkeye 15	44N08'37	109w37'23	7:18:30
Hawk Springs 8	41N47'10	104w15'51	6:57:03
Hayward Place 12	41N35'54	110w45'56	7:23:04
Hazelton 10	44N05'48	106w58'06	7:07:62
Heart Mountain 15	44N45	108w45	7:15:00
Hecla 11	41N09'27	105w10'22	7:00:41
Heldt 8	42N00'03	104w20'22	6:57:21
Hells Half Acre 13	42N58	107w02	7:08:08
Henry Place 7	43N22'37	107w33'40	7:10:15
Hermosa 1	41N05'00	105w29'13	7:01:57
Hewitt Place 2	44N14'42	108w30'58	7:14:04
Hightower 16	42N02'54	105w02'19	7:00:09
Hiland 13	43N06'55	107w20'54	7:09:24
Hilight 3	43N49'29	105w21'38	7:01:27
Hilliard 21	41N08'16	110w48'40	7:23:15
Hillsdale 11	41N12'46	104w28'37	6:57:54
Hilltop 13	42N50	106w23	7:05:32
Himes 2	44N42'52	108w10'54	7:12:44
Hirsig 1	41N11'29	105w18'04	7:01:12
Hoback 20	43N16'55	110w46'59	7:23:08
Hoback Junction 20	43N19'21	110w43'47	7:22:55
Holdup Hollow 5	43N05'39	105w42'48	7:02:51
Holland Place 7	43N34'14	108w50'32	7:15:22
Holly 8	41N56'03	104w12'43	6:56:51
Horse Creek 11	41N24'54	105w10'54	7:00:44
Horse Creek Siding 11	41N25'22	105w11'43	7:00:47
Horseshoe Bend 21	41N11'53	110w43'04	7:22:52
Howell 1	41N25'04	105w36'53	7:02:28
Hudson 7	42N54'22	108w34'58	7:14:20
Hulett 6	44N40'58	104w36'04	6:58:24
Huntley 8	41N55'58	104w08'44	6:56:35
Hyattville 2	44N14'45	107w36'08	7:10:25
Illco 13	43N00'21	106w29'59	7:06:00
Iron Mountain 11	41N33	105w13	7:00:52
Irvine 5	42N39'54	105w18'18	7:01:13
Ishawooa 15	44N31	109w04	7:16:16
Islay 11	41N19'04	105w08'06	7:00:32
Ivans Grove 4	41N35'16	106w30'14	7:06:01
Jack Pine 20	43N19'34	110w26'00	7:21:44
Jackson 20	43N28'48	110w45'42	7:23:03
Jackson Hole 20	43N32	110w44	7:22:56
Jackson Lake Junction 20	43N51'56	110w34'14	7:22:17
James Town 19	41N33'19	109w30'58	7:18:04
Jay Em 8	42N27'41	104w22'09	6:57:29
Jays Roost 4	41N10'03	106w19'50	7:05:19
Jeffrey City 7	42N29'41	107w49'36	7:11:18
Jelm 1	41N03'28	106w00'46	7:04:03
Jenny Lake 20	43N40	110w43	7:22:52
Jerome 23	44N02'54	104w31'46	6:58:07
Jimmys Place 4	42N17'11	107w11'56	7:08:48
Johnson Place 7	43N26'12	107w35'21	7:10:21
J O Junction 19	41N32'07	108w23'27	7:13:34
Kamms Corner 15	44N43'32	108w55'55	7:15:44
Kanda 19	41N32'34	109w20'27	7:17:22
Kane 2	44N50'37	108w12'08	7:12:49
Kara 6	44N11'38	104w50'42	6:59:23
Kaycee 10	43N42'37	106w38'18	7:06:33
Kearny 10	44N31'55	106w48'56	7:07:16
Keeline 14	42N45'25	104w45'22	6:59:01
Kelly 20	43N37'23	110w37'22	7:22:29
Kemmerer 12	41N47'33	110w32'13	7:22:09
Kemmerer West 12	42N01	110w53	7:23:32
Kendall 18	42N56	109w59	7:19:56
Kendrick 17	44N43'15	106w12'05	7:04:48
Keystone 1	41N10'05	106w15'29	7:05:02
Kinnear 7	43N09'07	108w40'37	7:14:42
Kirby 9	43N48'16	108w10'51	7:12:43
Kirtley 14	42N49'51	104w07'20	6:56:29
Kirwin 15	43N52'35	109w17'50	7:17:11
Kleenburn 17	44N54'13	107w00'43	7:08:03
Kortes Dam 4	42N12	106w52	7:07:28
Kotey Place 7	42N43'29	108w36'12	7:14:25
La Barge 12	42N15'43	110w11'38	7:20:47
LaGrange 8	42N01'46	105w45'45	7:03:03
Laird 7	43N03'15	108w21'36	7:13:26
Lake 20	44N30	110w30	7:22:00
Lake Creek Resort 1	41N19	105w35	7:02:20
Lake Hotel 20	44N32'59	110w24'01	7:21:36
Lake Junction 20	44N34'06	110w23'12	7:21:33
Lambert 11	41N37'15	105w07'18	7:00:29
Lamont 4	42N13'14	107w28'35	7:09:54
Lance Creek 14	43N01'57	104w38'29	6:58:34
Lander 7	42N49'59	108w43'48	7:14:55
Laprele 5	42N45	105w23	7:01:32
Laramie 1	41N18'41	105w35'26	7:02:22
Laramie West 1	41N17	105w51	7:03:24
Lariat 3	44N34'03	106w00'23	7:04:02
Larsen Place 4	42N12'39	107w13'04	7:08:52
Last Crossing Ford No 9 7	42N22'32	108w43'09	7:14:53
Latham 19	41N41'47	107w49'36	7:11:18
Leahy Place 5	42N30'27	105w56'35	7:03:46
Leckie 18	42N34'15	109w16'42	7:17:07
Leefe 12	41N48'42	111w01'25	7:24:06
Leiter 17	44N43'05	106w16'07	7:05:04
Leo 4	42N15'01	106w48'10	7:07:13
Linch 10	43N36'23	106w11'44	7:04:47
Lindbergh 11	41N18'42	104w06'33	6:56:26
Linden 6	44N19'14	104w35'45	6:58:23
Lingle 8	42N08'11	104w20'42	6:57:23
Linstead Place 10	43N34'57	106w31'20	7:06:05
Little America 19	41N32'37	109w51'30	7:19:26
Little Medicine 1	42N23'04	105w58'39	7:03:55
Lockett 5	42N51'49	106w00'24	7:04:02
Logan Place 19	41N14'37	109w13'42	7:16:55
Lonetree 21	41N03'16	110w09'12	7:20:37
Lone Tree Crossing 15	44N26'53	108w42'12	7:14:49
Lookout 1	41N39'57	105w48'06	7:03:12
Lost Cabin 7	43N17'11	107w37'55	7:10:32
Lost Springs 5	42N45'56	104w55'29	6:59:42
Lovell 2	44N50'15	108w23'20	7:13:33
Lower Shell Creek Crossing 19	41N02'31	108w25'59	7:13:44
Lucerne 9	43N44'06	108w10'33	7:12:42
Lucky MacCamp 7	43N02	108w23	7:13:32
Lusk 14	42N45'45	104w27'06	6:57:48
Lyman 21	41N19'39	110w17'32	7:21:10
Lysite 7	43N16'05	107w41'23	7:10:46
Macy Place 5	42N46'52	105w45'43	7:03:03
Madden 7	43N12'20	107w31'10	7:10:05
Madison Junction 20	44N38'45	110w51'34	7:23:26
Mammoth 15	44N58'36	110w42'03	7:22:48
Manderson 2	44N16'10	107w57'48	7:11:51
Mantua 15	44N50'22	108w40'40	7:14:43
Manville 14	42N46'45	104w37'02	6:58:28
Marbleton 18	42N33'13	110w06'31	7:20:26
Marse 12	42N09'01	110w59'09	7:23:57
Marshall 1	42N18'07	105w51'00	7:03:24
Marvin Place 4	42N13'16	107w11'29	7:08:46
Mayoworth 10	43N49'55	106w47'29	7:07:10
McCargar Place 4	42N12'04	107w07'55	7:08:32
McFadden 4	41N39'16	106w07'48	7:04:31
McKinley 5	42N37'56	105w08'18	7:00:33
McKinnon 19	41N01'40	109w56'07	7:19:44
McKinnon Junction 19	41N19'01	109w39'02	7:18:36
Meadowdale 16	42N33'09	104w41'42	6:58:47
Meads 4	41N41'31	106w45'55	7:07:04
Medicine Bow 4	41N53'44	106w12'15	7:04:49
Meeteetse 15	44N09'26	108w52'15	7:15:29
Meridan PO 11	41N31'15	104w20'28	6:57:22
Meriden 11	41N32'37	104w19'07	6:57:16
Merino 13	43N12'24	106w35'51	7:06:23
Merna 18	42N56'47	110w20'24	7:21:22
Mers Hill 8	41N52'51	104w37'01	6:58:28
Mexican Place 7	43N26'57	108w25'49	7:13:43
Midvale 7	43N12'54	108w26'40	7:13:47
Midway 4	41N36'35	106w49'27	7:07:18
Midway 11	41N24'08	104w27'41	6:57:51
Midwest 13	43N24'41	106w16'46	7:05:07
Midwest Heights 13	42N51'15	106w21'40	7:05:27
Mihel Place 4	42N13'57	106w57'46	7:07:51
Milford 7	42N52'35	108w47'01	7:15:08
Millbrook 1	41N19'15	105w55'11	7:03:41
Millburne 21	41N15'30	110w24'43	7:21:39
Miller 1	41N18'34	105w52'08	7:03:29
Millersville 21	41N23'24	110w12'28	7:20:50
Mills 13	42N50'26	106w21'55	7:05:28
Mills Place 13	42N43'49	106w29'20	7:05:57
Milo 4	41N37'15	106w25'10	7:05:41
Miners Delight 7	42N31'59	108w40'48	7:14:43
Minnesela 9	43N35'09	108w12'59	7:12:52
Minturn 3	44N17'15	105w22'21	7:01:29
Mona 6	44N48'36	104w22'51	6:57:31
Monarch 17	44N54'11	107w02'04	7:08:08
Monell 19	41N35'26	108w29'00	7:13:56
Moneta 7	43N09'42	107w43'27	7:10:54
Moorcroft 6	44N15'48	104w56'59	6:59:48
Moose 20	43N39'21	110w43'03	7:22:52
Moose Junction 20	43N39'03	110w42'26	7:22:50
Moran 20	43N50'30	110w30'25	7:22:02
Moran Junction 20	43N50'24	110w30'34	7:22:02
Morgan 4	41N29'12	106w08'28	7:04:34
Morrisey 23	43N31'05	104w22'59	6:57:32
Morton 5	42N49'00	105w26'07	7:01:44
Morton 7	43N12'02	108w46'26	7:15:06
Moskee 6	44N16'18	104w10'42	6:56:43
Mountain Home 1	41N00'29	106w10'19	7:04:41
Mountain View 13	42N51'13	106w23'17	7:05:33
Mountain View 21	41N16'08	110w20'21	7:21:21
Moxa 12	41N40'04	110w04'12	7:20:17
Moyer 12	41N48'15	110w34'59	7:22:20
Muddy Gap 4	42N21'06	107w27'24	7:09:50
Muddy Gap Junction 4	42N21'53	107w26'25	7:09:46
Mule Creek 14	43N22'44	104w13'18	6:56:53
Murke 11	41N25'29	105w12'53	7:00:52
Muthart Place 16	42N22'46	104w41'25	6:58:46
Myersville 7	42N33'48	108w06'20	7:12:25
Natrona 13	43N01'47	106w48'31	7:07:14
Natwick 19	41N57'39	105w03'22	7:00:13
Neble 7	43N06'36	108w15'41	7:13:03
Newcastle 23	43N51'17	104w12'16	6:56:49
New Fork 18	42N42'06	109w42'52	7:18:51
New Haven 6	44N44'39	104w50'39	6:59:23
New Jelm 1	41N04'55	106w00'34	7:04:02
Nickelson Place 9	43N32'10	108w03'11	7:12:13
Niobrara West 14	43N00	104w38	6:58:32
Node 14	42N43'09	104w17'53	6:57:12
Norris Junction 15	44N44'01	110w41'40	7:22:47
North Baxter 19	41N38'30	109w06'52	7:16:27
North Jenny Lake Junction 20	43N48'07	110w40'50	7:22:43
Nutria 12	41N46	110w10	7:20:40
O'Donnell 15	44N44'15	108w47'58	7:15:12
O'Donnell Spur 15	44N45	108w45	7:15:00
Oil Springs 4	41N59'28	106w16'01	7:05:04
Old Bennett Place 4	42N16'54	106w09'56	7:04:40
Old Brooks Place 4	41N41'10	106w20'27	7:05:22
Old Faithful 20	44N30	110w30	7:22:00
Old Frazier Place 4	41N33'18	106w56'22	7:07:45
Old Haymaker Place 4	41N31'56	106w52'59	7:07:32
Old Johnson Place 4	41N34'33	106w57'29	7:07:50
Old Kamp Place 1	42N25'04	106w02'50	7:04:11
Old Kelly Place 5	43N13'03	105w03'10	7:00:13
Old McKeal Place 4	41N35'19	106w57'32	7:07:50
Old Pennock Place 4	41N31'47	106w44'04	7:06:56
Old Percy 4	41N47'55	106w30'33	7:06:02
Old Potters Place 13	43N05'50	106w49'02	7:07:16
Old Tobin Place 13	42N37'05	106w04'28	7:04:18
Opal 12	41N46'09	110w19'31	7:21:18
Orchard Valley 11	41N05'50	104w48'52	6:59:15
Orin 5	42N39'12	105w11'31	7:00:46
Orin Junction 5	42N39'21	105w11'00	7:00:44
Oriva 3	44N19'01	105w40'18	7:02:41
Orpha 5	42N51'17	105w30'11	7:02:01
Osage 23	43N58'51	104w25'17	6:57:41
Osborne Place 13	43N05'57	107w25'13	7:09:41
Oshoto 6	44N35'15	104w56'14	6:59:45
Osmond 12	42N44	110w56	7:23:44
Osmond Community 12	42N40'59	110w55'53	7:23:44
Otto 2	44N24'12	108w16'25	7:13:06
Otto 11	41N05'27	105w04'28	7:00:18
Overland 4	41N37'13	106w48'24	7:07:14
Owens 23	43N42'58	104w08'03	6:56:32
Pahaska 15	44N31	109w04	7:16:16
Paradise 4	42N05'27	106w26'56	7:05:48
Paradise Valley 13	42N49'03	106w23'52	7:05:35
Parkerton 5	42N51'04	105w58'21	7:03:53
Parkman 17	44N57'25	107w19'55	7:09:20
Pavillion 7	43N14'41	108w41'22	7:14:45
Pearson 13	42N51'29	106w08'52	7:04:35
Pedro 23	43N54'18	104w20'25	6:57:22
Peru 19	41N32'59	109w35'06	7:18:20
Petes Place 19	41N00'10	109w01'27	7:16:06
Petrie 13	43N01'54	106w44'23	7:06:58
Piedmont 21	41N12'58	110w37'36	7:22:30
Pine Bluffs 11	41N10'55	104w04'07	6:56:16
Pinedale 18	42N52'00	109w51'37	7:19:26
Pixley 12	42N00'09	110w56'51	7:23:47
Pleasantdale 3	44N04'34	105w43'08	7:02:53
Point of Rocks 1	42N20'32	105w16'38	7:01:07
Point of Rocks 4	42N13'31	106w23'46	7:05:35
Point of Rocks 19	41N40'49	108w47'06	7:15:08
Powder River 13	43N01'56	106w59'12	7:07:57
Powell 15	44N45'14	108w45'24	7:15:02
Prairie Center 8	42N04	104w11	6:56:44
Price Place 13	42N43'36	106w25'49	7:05:43
Quealy 19	41N32'18	109w13'19	7:16:53
Raderville 13	42N54'20	107w22'41	7:09:31

Ragan 21 41N16 110w40 7:22:40
Rairden 2 44N11'31 107w54'14 7:11:37
Ralston 15 44N42'58 108w51'50 7:15:27
Rambler 4 41N09'31 107w00'22 7:08:01
Ranchester 17 44N54'32 107w09'46 7:08:39
Rawhide Creek 8 42N24 104w21 6:57:24
Rawlins 4 41N47'28 107w14'17 7:08:57
Raymond 12 42N05 110w57 7:23:48
Recluse 3 44N44'28 105w42'27 7:02:50
Redbird 14 43N14'33 104w17'08 6:57:09
Red Buttes 1 41N10'57 105w35'39 7:02:23
Red Buttes Village 13 42N48'29 106w25'17 7:05:41
Red Desert 19 41N39'13 108w07'16 7:12:29
Red Lane 9 43N40'43 108w12'19 7:12:49
Reed Place 1 42N16'05 105w43'30 7:02:54
Reeves Corner 2 44N31'17 107w51'51 7:11:27
Reliance 19 41N40'09 109w11'47 7:16:47
Rendezvous 19 41N03'11 109w57'08 7:19:49
Reno Junction 3 43N45'56 105w28'32 7:01:54
Richardson Acres 13 42N53'55 106w20'32 7:05:22
Riddle 15 44N31 109w04 7:16:16
Riner 19 41N44'07 107w33'00 7:10:12
Riovista 19 41N33'08 109w30'44 7:18:03
Riverside 4 41N13'03 106w46'42 7:07:07
Riverton 7 43N01'30 108w22'46 7:13:31
Riverview 14 43N25'15 104w11'41 6:56:47
Riview 19 41N33'03 109w31'32 7:18:06
Robbers Roost Stage Station 14 43N25'29 104w13'13 6:56:53
Robertson 21 41N11'07 110w24'45 7:21:39
Robinson 19 41N37'38 108w19'42 7:13:19
Robinson Place 11 41N30'38 104w30'15 6:58:01
Rock Creek 1 41N50'30 105w51'56 7:03:28
Rockeagle 8 42N00'10 104w34'52 6:58:19
Rock River 1 41N44'29 105w58'27 7:03:54
Rock Springs 19 41N35'15 109w12'08 7:16:49
Rocky Crossing 12 41N36'46 110w07'27 7:20:30
Rocky Crossing 19 42N06'17 108w19'46 7:13:19
Rocky Ford 15 44N50'46 109w35'13 7:18:21
Rockypoint 3 44N54'26 105w05'42 7:00:23
Rogers Place 5 42N33'12 105w35'01 7:02:20
Ross 5 43N26'46 105w53'10 7:03:33
Rozet 3 44N16'41 105w12'20 7:00:49
Rudefeha 4 41N11'20 107w04'13 7:08:17
Ryan Park 4 41N19'17 106w30'30 7:06:02
Ryegrass Junction 18 42N50'18 110w18'08 7:21:13
Saddlestring 10 44N27 106w54 7:07:36
Sage 12 41N48'49 110w57'27 7:23:50
Saint Stephens 7 42N59'02 108w24'57 7:13:40
Sales Place 2 44N11'24 108w32'08 7:14:09
Salt Creek 13 43N20'56 106w19'31 7:05:18
Salt Wells 19 41N39'17 108w59'07 7:15:56
Sampo 4 41N54'07 106w29'31 7:05:58
Sand Creek Crossing 6 44N24'50 104w05'44 6:56:23
Sand Draw 7 42N45'38 108w10'51 7:12:43
Saratoga 4 41N27'18 106w48'21 7:07:13
Savageton 3 43N51'57 105w47'13 7:03:09
Savery 4 41N01'30 107w26'57 7:09:48
Seely 6 44N48'28 104w37'12 6:58:29
Seminoe Dam 4 42N09'24 106w54'48 7:07:39
Shawnee 5 42N44'52 105w00'33 7:00:02
Shell 2 44N32'08 107w46'45 7:11:07
Shellback 11 41N10'38 105w01'48 7:00:07
Sheridan 17 44N47'50 106w57'20 7:07:49
Sheridan Gardens 17 44N48 106w57 7:07:48
Sheridan West 17 44N52 107w11 7:08:44
Sherman 1 41N05'52 105w21'01 7:01:24
Shiprock 19 41N40'45 108w50'10 7:15:21
Shirley 4 42N11'20 106w28'53 7:05:56
Shoshoni 7 43N14'09 108w06'35 7:12:26
Sibylee 16 42N04'53 104w56'59 6:59:48
Siddons 7 43N16'39 108w07'27 7:12:30
Silver Crown 11 41N10'28 105w02'10 7:00:09
Silver Tip 8 41N54'53 104w15'58 6:57:04
Simmerson Place 7 43N40'50 109w34'58 7:18:20
Sinclair 4 41N46'30 107w06'45 7:08:27
Skull Creek 23 44N06'33 104w22'00 6:57:28
Slater 16 41N52'23 104w49'10 6:59:17
Smoot 12 42N37'14 110w54'49 7:23:39
Snyder Place 7 43N25'09 107w33'26 7:10:14
Soda Butte 15 44N52'40 110w09'09 7:20:37
Soda Well 3 44N38 105w20 7:01:20
Sodium 13 43N02'04 106w50'45 7:07:23
South Baxter 19 41N22'05 109w07'16 7:16:29
South Jenny Lake Junction 20 43N44'58 110w43'21 7:22:53
South Landing 20 43N49'18 110w37'22 7:22:29
South Laramie 1 41N19 105w35 7:02:20
South Pass City 7 42N28'06 108w47'57 7:15:12
South Superior 19 41N45'43 108w57'58 7:15:52
South Torrington 8 42N02'59 104w10'44 6:56:43
Sowders Place 4 41N23'01 106w34'03 7:06:16
Speer 11 41N03'16 104w53'48 6:59:35
Spence 2 44N38'01 108w07'54 7:12:32
Spencer 23 43N47'28 104w09'40 6:56:39
Spotted Horse 3 44N42'30 105w50'04 7:03:20
Spring Valley 21 41N15'08 110w41'05 7:22:44
Squaw Hollow 19 41N09'49 109w33'35 7:18:14
Squaw Place 1 42N22'12 105w42'12 7:02:49
Stansbury 19 41N42'10 109w11'14 7:16:45
Stansbury Junction 19 41N41'24 109w13'44 7:16:55
Star Valley 12 42N49 110w58 7:23:52
Stinson Hill 5 42N42'19 105w35'08 7:02:21
Story 17 44N34'29 106w53'10 7:07:33
Stroner 6 44N46 105w03 7:00:12
Strouds 13 42N51'18 106w14'27 7:04:58
Stucco 2 44N35'12 108w07'40 7:12:31
Sullivan 13 42N53'03 106w24'22 7:05:37
Sundance 6 44N24'23 104w22'31 6:57:30
Sunrise 16 42N19'49 104w42'18 6:58:49
Sunrise Hill 16 42N20'21 104w41'37 6:58:46
Sunshine 15 44N01'39 108w59'25 7:15:58
Sunside 13 42N50 106w23 7:05:32
Superior 19 41N46'10 108w58'33 7:15:54
Sussex 10 43N41'54 106w17'40 7:05:11
Sussex Unit (Continental Ca 10 43N36'28 106w12'05 7:04:48
Swaim Place 13 43N20'53 107w22'32 7:09:30
Sweetwater 7 42N34 107w54 7:11:36
Sweetwater Crossing 7 42N32'30 108w10'44 7:12:43
Sweetwater Station 7 42N32'32 108w10'59 7:12:44
Table Rock 19 41N36'51 108w23'14 7:13:33
Tahaska Tepee 15 44N30'11 109w57'44 7:19:51
Taylor 3 43N25 106w16 7:05:04
Teckla 3 43N33'30 105w20'58 7:01:24
Tenmile 4 41N21'10 106w32'04 7:06:08
Ten Sleep 22 44N02'03 107w27'02 7:09:48
Teton Village 20 43N35'17 110w49'38 7:23:19
Thayer Junction 19 41N41'13 108w54'38 7:15:39
Thayne 12 42N55'15 111w00'05 7:24:00
The Old Bob Place 4 41N38'39 106w55'52 7:07:43
Thermopolis 9 43N38'46 108w12'41 7:12:51
Thermopolis West 9 43N45 108w24 7:13:36
Thorndale Acres 13 42N49'11 106w18'45 7:05:15
Thornton 23 44N09'46 104w44'34 6:58:58
Three Forks 4 42N21'45 107w26'39 7:09:47
Three Forks 21 41N23'51 110w58'46 7:23:55
Three River Junction 20 44N17'21 110w53'32 7:23:34
Thumb 20 44N30 110w30 7:22:00
Tie Siding 1 41N04'49 105w30'25 7:02:02
Tipton 19 41N37'40 108w15'46 7:13:03
Toltec 1 42N18'25 105w39'10 7:02:37
Torrington 8 42N03'54 104w10'52 6:56:43
Tower Junction 15 44N54'59 110w24'58 7:21:40
Tracy 11 41N08'54 104w09'28 6:56:38
Trelona 8 41N46'22 104w25'57 6:57:44
Tremain 11 41N33'08 104w06'30 6:56:26
Tullis 4 41N13'43 107w17'54 7:09:12
Turnercrest 3 43N33'46 105w40'07 7:02:40
Turnerville 12 42N54 110w56 7:23:44
Twin Groves 4 41N21'33 107w09'51 7:08:39
Ucross 10 44N33'39 106w32'22 7:06:09
Ulm 17 44N39'06 106w35'19 7:06:21
Underwood Crossing 5 43N29'46 104w56'39 6:59:47
University 1 41N19 105w35 7:02:20
Upton 23 44N05'59 104w37'39 6:58:31
Urie 21 41N18'58 110w20'08 7:21:21
Uva 16 42N07'55 104w55'09 6:59:41
Valley 15 44N11 109w36 7:18:24
Valley Station 4 41N39'23 106w05'37 7:04:22
Van Tassell 14 42N39'46 104w05'16 6:56:21
Vedauwoo Glen 1 41N09'41 105w22'25 7:01:30
Verne 21 41N35 110w05 7:20:20
Verona 17 44N44'24 106w40'08 7:06:41
Verse 5 43N25'10 105w24'15 7:01:37
Veteran 8 41N57'52 104w22'48 6:57:31
Viola 12 42N15'58 110w22'40 7:21:31
Vocation 15 44N39'48 108w56'34 7:15:46
Wakeley 17 44N49'41 106w53'24 7:07:34
Walcott 4 41N45'40 106w50'40 7:07:23
Walcott Junction 4 41N44'58 106w50'12 7:07:21
Waltman 13 43N03'48 107w11'43 7:08:47
Wamsutter 19 41N40'23 107w58'43 7:11:55
Wapiti 15 44N28'07 109w26'13 7:17:45
Warren 11 41N09 104w52 6:59:28
Washington Place 19 42N01'52 109w21'44 7:17:27
Weaver Homestead 8 41N34'45 104w35'09 6:58:21
Welch 5 42N51'36 105w42'56 7:02:52
Wendover 16 42N19'39 104w52'23 6:59:30
Wester Hills 11 41N08 104w49 6:59:16
West Lance Creek 14 43N02'44 104w41'33 6:58:46
West Laramie 1 41N18'32 105w37'12 7:02:29
Weston 3 44N38'13 105w20'08 7:01:21
West Poison Spider 13 42N50 106w23 7:05:32
West Thumb 20 44N24'56 110w34'29 7:22:18
Westvaco 19 41N37'22 109w48'35 7:19:14
Westvaco Section 19 41N37'18 109w51'33 7:19:26
Wheatland 16 42N03'16 104w57'08 6:59:49
Whipple Hollow 5 43N05'51 105w35'53 7:02:24
Whiting 16 42N00'44 104w57'36 6:59:50
Whitman 14 42N53'16 104w06'52 6:56:27
Widdowfield 4 41N37'14 106w24'50 7:05:39
Wilcox 1 41N47'33 105w59'00 7:03:56
Wildcat 3 44N36'06 105w40'31 7:02:42
Wiley 15 44N23'48 108w57'52 7:15:51
Wilkinson Place 11 41N30'01 104w33'03 6:58:12
Williams Mill 22 44N02'09 107w16'54 7:09:08
Willow Addition 12 41N47'57 110w32'02 7:22:08
Willow Creek 7 43N17'06 109w08'29 7:16:34
Willow Springs 6 44N18'42 104w08'18 6:56:33
Willwood 15 44N45 108w45 7:15:00
Wilson 16 42N03 104w57 6:59:48
Wilson 20 43N30'03 110w52'28 7:23:30
Winchester 22 43N52 108w10 7:12:40
Wind River 7 42N59'11 108w53'01 7:15:32
Wind River Indian Res 7 43N20 108w45 7:15:00
Winter Crossing 13 42N42'34 106w33'47 7:06:15
Winton 19 41N44'50 109w10'00 7:16:40
Winton Junction 19 41N42'46 109w14'17 7:16:57
Wolf 17 44N46 107w14 7:08:56
Woodedge 4 41N31'03 106w08'42 7:04:35
Woods Landing 1 41N06'38 106w00'46 7:04:03
Worland 22 44N01'01 107w57'17 7:11:49
Wyarno 17 44N48'48 106w46'24 7:07:06
Wycross 8 41N40'50 104w11'22 6:56:45
Wyocolo 1 41N00'16 106w10'19 7:04:41
Wyodak 3 44N17'29 105w22'45 7:01:31
Wyoming 1 41N28'39 105w38'10 7:02:33
Wyopo 7 42N51'20 108w41'19 7:14:45
XH Crossing 5 42N44'44 105w06'30 7:00:26
Yanceys 15 44N55'51 110w26'08 7:21:45
Yellowstone Natl Park 44N30 110w30 7:22:00
Yoder 8 41N55'01 104w17'43 6:57:11

NOTES

NOTES

NOTES

NOTES

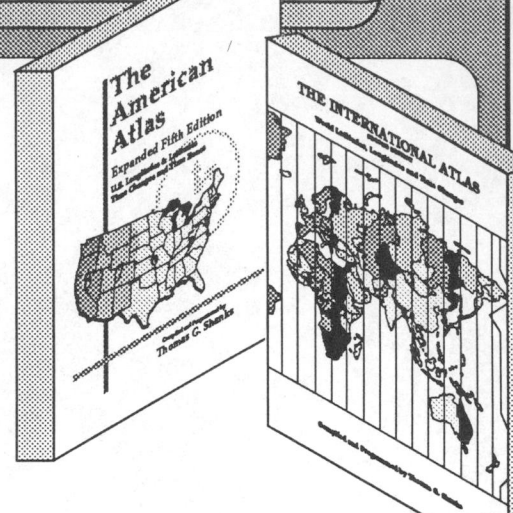

State Alpha Code Table

AL	Alabama	LA	Louisiana	OK	Oklahoma
AK	Alaska	ME	Maine	OR	Oregon
AZ	Arizona	MD	Maryland	PA	Pennsylvania
AR	Arkansas	MA	Massachusetts	PR	Puerto Rico
CA	California	MI	Michigan	RI	Rhode Island
CO	Colorado	MN	Minnesota	SC	South Carolina
CT	Connecticut	MS	Mississippi	SD	South Dakota
DE	Delaware	MO	Missouri	TN	Tennessee
DC	District of Columbia	MT	Montana	TX	Texas
FL	Florida	NE	Nebraska	UT	Utah
GA	Georgia	NV	Nevada	VT	Vermont
HI	Hawaii	NH	New Hampshire	VA	Virginia
ID	Idaho	NJ	New Jersey	WA	Washington
IL	Illinois	NM	New Mexico	WV	West Virginia
IN	Indiana	NY	New York	WI	Wisconsin
IA	Iowa	NC	North Carolina	WY	Wyoming
KS	Kansas	ND	North Dakota		
KY	Kentucky	OH	Ohio		

Time Zones and Abbreviations

Abbr.	Name	Standard Meridian	Hours from Greenwich Mean Time Standard	Daylight (War)
A	Atlantic	60°	4:00	3:00
E	Eastern	75°	5:00	4:00
C	Central	90°	6:00	5:00
M	Mountain	105°	7:00	6:00
P	Pacific	120°	8:00	7:00
Y	Yukon	135°	9:00	8:00
AH	Alaska-Hawaii	150°	10:00	9:00
H	Hawaiian	157°30′	10:30	9:30
B	Bering	165°	11:00	10:00

Abbr.	Time Type
S	Standard
D	Daylight
W	War